GROSSWÖRTERBUCH DEUTSCH ▸ ENGLISCH ENGLISCH ▸ DEUTSCH

GERMAN ▸ ENGLISH ENGLISH ▸ GERMAN DICTIONARY

COLLINS GERMAN ▸ ENGLISH ENGLISH ▸ GERMAN DICTIONARY

Unabridged

by

Peter Terrell

Veronika Schnorr Wendy V.A. Morris

Roland Breitsprecher

THIRD EDITION

HarperCollins*Publishers*

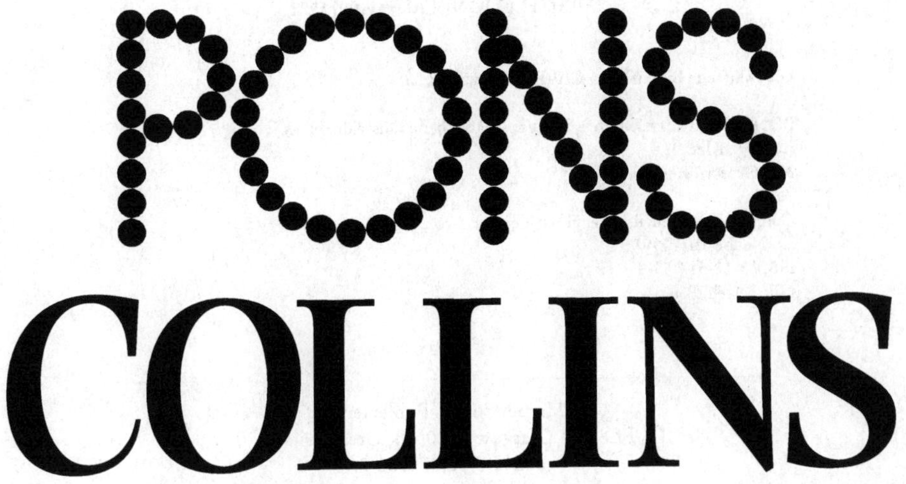

COLLINS

Großwörterbuch

DEUTSCH ▸ ENGLISCH
ENGLISCH ▸ DEUTSCH

von
Peter Terrell
Veronika Schnorr Wendy V. A. Morris
Roland Breitsprecher

NEUBEARBEITUNG 1997

Ernst Klett Verlag
Stuttgart · München · Düsseldorf · Leipzig

THIRD EDITION/3. AUFLAGE 1997

Die Deutsche Bibliothek - CIP-Einheitsaufnahme

PONS-Grosswörterbuch. - Stuttgart ; München ; Düsseldorf ;
Leipzig : Klett.
NE: Grosswörterbuch

Collins deutsch-englisch, englisch-deutsch / von Peter Terrell
... - Neubearb. - 1997
ISBN 3-12-517153-9
NE: Terrell, Peter

HarperCollins Publishers
PO Box, Glasgow G4 0NB, Great Britain
ISBN 0-00-470580-7
with thumb index 0-00-470581-5

---

10 East 53rd Street, New York
New York 10022
ISBN 0-06-270199-1

First HarperCollins edition published 1993

Library of Congress Cataloging-in-Publication Data:

HarperCollins German dictionary unabridged / by Peter Terrell ... [et al.] .— 3rd ed.
p. cm.
ISBN 0-06-270199-1
1. German language—Dictionaries—English. 2. English language—Dictionaries—German . I. Terrell, Peter.
PF3640.H28 1997
433'.21—dc21 96-46435

---

97 98 99 00 01 CIBM 10 9 8 7 6 5 4 3 2 1

Lizenzausgabe für Ernst Klett Verlag GmbH,
Stuttgart 1991

---

3. Auflage 1997
Ernst Klett Verlag GmbH, Stuttgart
ISBN 3-12-517153-9
(mit Daumenregister) ISBN 3-12-517154-7

Typeset by Morton Word Processing Ltd, Scarborough
Printed and bound in Great Britain by Caledonian International Book Manufacturing Ltd, Glasgow, G64

SECOND AND THIRD EDITIONS ZWEITE UND DRITTE AUFLAGE

SENIOR EDITORS LEITENDE REDAKTEURE

Peter Terrell
Horst Kopleck
Helga Holtkamp John Whitlam

PUBLISHING STAFF VERLAGSANGESTELLTE

Lorna Sinclair Vivian Marr
Diana Feri Stephen Clarke
Joyce Littlejohn Diane Robinson Christine Bahr

CONTRIBUTIONS FROM MITARBEIT

Veronika Schnorr
Michael Finn Tim Connell
Roland Breitsprecher

FIRST EDITION ERSTE AUSGABE

SENIOR EDITORS LEITENDE REDAKTEURE

Peter Terrell
Veronika Schnorr Wendy V. A. Morris
Roland Breitsprecher

EDITORS REDAKTEURE

Dr Kathryn Rooney Ingrid Schumacher Dr Lorna A. Sinclair
Dorothee Ziegler Ulrike Seeberger Petra Schlupp

COMPILERS MITARBEITER

Dr Christine R. Barker
Alexa H. Barnes
Michael Clark
Francis J. Flaherty
Susanne Flatauer
Ian Graham
Barbara Hellmann
Birgit Kahl
Christian Kay
Angelika Moeller
Günter Ohnemus
Dr John Pheby
Irmgard Rieder
Hanns Schumacher
Olaf Thyen
Karin Wiese
Renate Zenker-Callum

COLLINS STAFF VERLAGSANGESTELLTE

Richard Thomas
Anne Dickinson Irene Lakhani
Susan Dunsmore Valerie McNulty Alice Truten
Elspeth Anderson

CONTENTS

INHALT

PREFACE

A dictionary is like a map, and like a map it can portray its subject in varying ways, with varying degrees of detail and of observation. This dictionary is a map of the German and English languages and of the correspondences between the two. It has taken the most important and pervasive areas of language - the language of everyday communication, of newspapers, radio, television, the language of business, politics, the language of technology as it spreads into the layman's vocabulary, the language of literature and the arts - and has drawn a detailed picture. But where, as is the case with language (and in particular with the documented correlation of two languages) the terrain to be mapped is endless, subject to change and everything in it capable of being viewed from a multiplicity of angles, a wealth of details can easily become an inextricable maze. Detail needs clarity. And clarity has been made the principal criterion by reference to which the entries in this dictionary have been built up. Detail is never shown out of context, out of relation to the whole picture. Separate areas of meaning are clearly marked off, levels and types of language are pinpointed, dangers signalled, safe paths of idiomatic modes of expression are indicated. This dictionary is presented in the hope that the observations and distinctions that the editors have made in finding their way through two languages will enable the user to find his way too. And it is hoped too that the use of this book will be a source not only of understanding but also of pleasure.

PMT
Lexus
Glasgow

VORWORT

Ein Wörterbuch ist wie eine Landkarte, und wie eine Landkarte kann es seinen Gegenstand auf verschiedene Weise, nach verschiedenen Graden der Genauigkeit und Detailliertheit, abbilden. Dieses Wörterbuch ist eine Landkarte der deutschen und der englischen Sprache und deren Beziehung zueinander. Es beschäftigt sich mit den wichtigsten Bereichen der Sprache, die von größter allgemeiner Bedeutung sind, der Sprache, wie sie uns im täglichen Umgang miteinander, in Presse, Rundfunk und Fernsehen, im Geschäftsleben und in der Politik begegnet, mit der Sprache der Technik, soweit der Laie sie in seinen Wortschatz aufgenommen hat, mit der Sprache von Literatur und Kunst - und versucht, sie in ihren Einzelaspekten abzubilden. Wo aber, wie in der Sprache, und ganz besonders in der documentarischen Gegenüberstellung zweier Sprachen, das Feld unendlich, Wandel permanent und Betrachtung aus den verschiedensten Blickwinkeln möglich ist, kann aus einer Fülle von Einzelheiten leicht ein Labyrinth werden. Zum Detail muß Klarheit treten, und Klarheit ist das grundlegende Kriterium für den Artikelaufbau in diesem Wörterbuch. Kein Detail ohne Kontext, in beziehungsloser Isolation. Bedeutungsunterschiede sind klar bezeichnet, Schattierungen beschrieben, Sprachebenen und -formen deutlich herausgehoben. Wo nötig, werden Gefahrensignale gesetzt, während Anwendungsbeispiele den Weg zum sichern idiomatischen Ausdruck weisen. Wir legen dieses Wörterbuch in der Hoffnung vor, daß die Beobachtungen und Unterschiedungen, die die Verfasser bei ihrem Versuch gemacht haben, sich einen Weg durch zwei Sprachen zu bahnen, es dem Benutzer ermöglichen, sich seinerseits zurechtzufinden. Wir hoffen außerdem, daß die Benutzung dieses Wörterbuchs nicht nur die Verständigung erleichtert, sondern auch Spaß macht.

INTRODUCTION

This dictionary aims to provide the user with a detailed, accurate and thoroughly up-to-date source of reference for the study and use of the English and German languages. It is the conviction of the editors that the fundamental conception of this dictionary is such that it can justifiably claim to furnish the user not simply with a new and more modern reference book but with one that has such a significant difference in approach as to make it stand apart from existing German-English dictionaries. The character of this dictionary can best be described by an account of three aspects: scope; method; and treatment of entries.

Scope

The main emphasis of this dictionary is placed firmly on the contemporary English and German languages, with particular attention paid to the language of everyday communication. The total number of headwords and illustrative phrases is greater than 280,000. And a brief look through a selection of these headwords and phrases will readily show that the fullness of the coverage is not attained by the inclusion of rare or marginal words or expressions. In fact, on the contrary, a conscious effort has been made throughout all stages of the compilation of this dictionary to avoid the deadwood, the defunct term.

Nor is the fullness attained simply by the inclusion of neologisms, although, of course, new words do figure largely in the text of this dictionary, along with newly coined idioms.

The fullness derives quite simply from an in-depth treatment of the ordinary English and German languages. There is an underlying central core of English and of German, the nuts and bolts of the languages, that often does not find expression in other bilingual (or indeed monolingual) dictionaries and that this dictionary has made its main concern. A huge range of quite ordinary words and expressions, the essential elements of communication (often quite complex to translate) are treated here in depth.

This, however, is not to say that older or more technical language does not figure at all in this dictionary. It most certainly does. If one were to define the range of the dictionary's wordlist in a slogan as 'the vocabulary of the educated layman' then where technical and old expressions have a place in this vocabulary they will have a place in the dictionary. Thus for example the language of computer technology and of microcomputers is recorded in this book along with the more traditional technical areas.

The geographical spread of language is not neglected either. A wide coverage of American English is given. Swiss, Austrian and former East German usages are treated. And regionalisms from within the main body of British English and German are covered.

Although the German Democratic Republic or East Germany has now ceased to exist, vocabulary items specific to this former state continue to exist. The dictionary label (DDR) has, therefore, been deliberately retained to indicate this.

In short then the aim of this dictionary as far as scope is concerned is to provide a range of words that will be genuinely useful in the modern world.

German Spelling Reform

Words which have been affected by the Spelling Reform are marked on the German-English side of the dictionary with the ⚠ symbol. The new spelling forms are listed alphabetically in the supplement (pp 1754-1769) with their corresponding old spelling form given alongside. The supplement also gives explanations on the extent of the Spelling Reform and the ways words are affected by it (pp 1749-1753).

Method

It has been axiomatic throughout the compilation of this dictionary that English text was to be written only by lexicographers whose mother tongue was English and that German text was to be written by lexicographers of German mother tongue. This is the guarantee of authenticity of idiom both as regards source language and target language.

English and German lexicographers have worked together as a team, and at every stage of the compilation period there has been discussion between English-speaker and German-speaker. The whole text, that is, compiled by lexicographers writing solely in their own native language, is vetted bilingually. This is the surest way to achieve the most accurate slotting-together of the two languages.

Treatment of entries

The distinguishing characteristic of the treatment of entries in this dictionary is the systematic use of indicators and collocators (see p xiii) to identify and mark out varying areas of meaning and usage so that translations are only given with specific reference to the context or type of context in which they are valid. The user is not confronted by an undifferentiated barrage of possible but different translations; rather he is given context-specific translations. This applies both to translations where different meanings of a source language word have to be distinguished as well as to words where usage varies with context as, for example, in the combination (collocation) of nouns with an adjective.

The phrases which form a main part of this dictionary can be divided into two broad types. First there are the fixed expressions of the German and English languages: the proverbs, sayings and indeed the clichés. Secondly there are the phrases which serve to show the structural correspondence between the two languages, how, for example, a particular general translation, which is a noun, might have to be re-expressed as a verbal construction in a particular context if idiomaticity (and even, at times, intelligibility) is to be preserved.

To complete this detailed presentation of entries a sophisticated system of style labels is used to give the user information on the appropriateness of any particular translation or on the status of any headword he might look up from the point of view of register. The user, that is, is told, warned, if a word is informal, poetic, formal, old, dated, euphemistic etc. He is told if a word if likely to give offence, cause amusement, sound pompous, quaint, donnish or disgusting.

Further information on the structure of entries is given in the pages that follow. But, of course, the text itself is its own best exponent.

EINLEITUNG

Dieses Wörterbuch will dem Benutzer zum Studium und Gebrauch der deutschen und englischen Sprache ein ausführliches und zuverlässiges Nachschlagewerk an die Hand geben, das gründlich durchdacht und auf dem neuesten Stand ist. Die Verfasser sind der Überzeugung, daß das Wörterbuch in seiner Grundkonzeption so angelegt ist, daß es mit Recht den Anspruch erheben kann, dem Benutzer ein Nachschlagewerk zu bieten, das nicht einfach neuer und zeitgemäßer als andere ist. Es unterscheidet sich darüber hinaus schon in seinem Ansatz so beträchtlich von vorliegenden deutsch-englischen Wörterbüchern, daß ihm eine Sonderstellung zukommt. Die Eigenart dieses Wörterbuches läßt sich am besten durch die Darstellung folgender drei Aspekte beschreiben: Inhalt und Umfang; Methodik; Artikelaufbau.

Inhalt und Umfang

Bei diesem Wörterbuch liegt das Schwergewicht eindeutig auf der englischen und deutschen Gegenwartssprache, wobei der Sprache des Alltags besondere Aufmerksamkeit gilt. Die Gesamtzahl der Stichwörter, Zusammensetzungen und Anwendungsbeispiele ist höher als 280.000. Schon ein kurzer Blick auf eine Auswahl von Stichwörtern und Wendungen zeigt deutlich, daß der Grund für diese Vollständigkeit nicht in der Aufnahme von seltenen Wörtern oder Redewendungen an der Peripherie der Sprache zu suchen ist. Ganz im Gegenteil ist in allen Arbeitsphasen bewußt Wert darauf gelegt worden, Abgelebtes und Ausgestorbenes aus diesem Wörterbuch zu verbannen. Auch ist die Vollständigkeit nicht einfach auf die Aufnahme von Neologismen zurückzuführen, obwohl freilich neue Wörter ebenso wie neugeprägte Redensarten einen breiten Raum in diesem Buch einnehmen.

Die Vollständigkeit beruht ganz einfach auf der Gründlichkeit und Ausführlichkeit, mit der die deutsche und englische Alltagssprache behandelt werden. Diesen eigentlichen Kern, den Baustoff der deutschen und englischen Sprache, der in anderen zweisprachigen (oder sogar einsprachigen) Wörterbüchern oft keinen Ausdruck findet, hat dieses Wörterbuch zu seinem Hauptanliegen gemacht. Es behandelt ein enormes Spektrum ganz gewöhnlicher Wörter und Redewendungen, die unentbehrlichen - oft recht schwierig zu übersetzenden – Elemente der sprachlichen Kommunikation, in aller Gründlichkeit. Damit soll jedoch nicht gesagt sein, daß älteres oder sondersprachliches Wortgut schlechthin in diesem Wörterbuch unberücksichtigt bleibt. Ganz im Gegenteil. Wenn man den Umfang des Wörterverzeichnisses schlagwortartig als den "Wortschatz des gebildeten Laien" beschreibt, heißt das gleichzeitig, daß ältere und sondersprachliche Ausdrücke, die in diesen Wortschatz eingegangen sind, auch in das Wörterbuch aufgenommen wurden. So ist zum Beispiel die Sprache der Computertechnik und der Mikrocomputer ebenso wie die der traditionelleren Fachgebiete dokumentiert.

Auch die Verbreitung beider Sprachen in geographischer Hinsicht wird nicht vernachlässigt. Amerikanisches Englisch ist weitgehend berücksichtigt worden, und außer dem Sprachgebrauch in der Bundesrepublik Deutschland und der ehemaligen Deutschen Demokratischen Republik wird dem in Österreich und der Schweiz gesprochenen Deutsch ausführlich Rechnung getragen. Das gleiche gilt für den regionalen Sprachgebrauch in Deutschland und Großbritannien.

Obgleich die Deutsche Demokratische Republik nicht mehr existiert, ist das mit der früheren DDR assoziierte Vokabular weiterhin Bestandteil der Sprache. Daher wurde die Bereichsangabe (DDR) mit Absicht beibehalten.

Kurzgefaßt läßt sich also sagen, daß dieses Wörterbuch nach Inhalt und Umfang das Ziel verfolgt, ein Spektrum von Wörtern anzubieten, die von echtem Nutzen in der heutigen Zeit sind.

Deutsche Rechtschreibreform

Alle von der Rechtschreibreform betroffenen Wörter, die im deutsch-englischen Teil des Wörterbuchs als Stichwörter erscheinen, sind mit dem Symbol ⚠ gekennzeichnet. Die neuen Schreibungen werden im Anhang (S. 1754-1769) in Form einer alphabetischen Liste gegeben, in der jeweils die alte der neuen Schreibweise gegenübergestellt wird. Erläuterungen zu Art und Umfang der deutschen Rechtschreibreform sind ebenfalls im Anhang (S. 1749-1753) enthalten.

Methodik

Für die Verfasser dieses Wörterbuches ist es von Anfang an eine Selbstverständlichkeit gewesen, daß der deutsche Text ausschließlich von Lexikographen mit Deutsch als Muttersprache und der englische Text ausschließlich von Lexikographen mit Englisch als Muttersprache verfaßt werden mußte. Damit ist die idiomatische Authentizität sowohl in der Ausgangssprache als auch in der Zielsprache gewährleistet.

Deutsche und englische Lexikographen haben im Team gearbeitet, und während der Redaktionsarbeit haben in allen Arbeitsphasen Diskussionen zwischen deutschen und englischen Muttersprachlern stattgefunden. Das heißt, daß der gesamte Text von Redakteuren ausschließlich in ihrer eigenen Sprache verfaßt wurde und aus zweisprachiger Sicht geprüft worden ist. Dies ist die sicherste und zuverlässigste Methode, beide Sprachen miteinander zu verzahnen.

Artikelaufbau

Der Artikelaufbau in diesem Wörterbuch zeichnet sich vor allem durch die systematische Verwendung von Indikatoren und Kollokatoren (siehe Seite xiii) aus, die verschiedene Bedeutungs- und Anwendungsbereiche bezeichnen, so daß die angegebenen Übersetzungen sich immer auf den Kontext oder Kontextbereich beziehen, für den sie gelten. Der Benutzer wird nicht mit zwar möglichen, aber dennoch unterschiedlichen beziehungslosen Übersetzungen bombardiert. Statt dessen werden ihm kontextspezifische Übersetzungen geboten. Dies gilt sowohl für Übersetzungen, wo die unterschiedlichen Bedeutungen eines Wortes in der Ausgangssprache zu zeigen sind, als auch für Wörter, deren Gebrauch sich nach dem Kontext richtet, was z.B. bei der Verbindung (Kollokation) von Substantiv und Adjektiv der Fall ist.

Die Phraseologie bildet einen der wichtigsten Teile des Wörterbuchs und läßt sich grob in zwei Bereiche gliedern. Da sind zunächst die festen Wendungen im Deutschen und Englischen: die Sprichwörter, Redensarten und auch die Klischees; dann die Anwendungsbeispiele, mit denen die strukturelle Entsprechung beider Sprachen illustriert werden soll. So wird z.B. gezeigt, wie eine bestimmte allgemeine Übersetzung, sagen wir ein Substantiv, unter Umständen in einem bestimmten Kontext in eine Verbkonstruktion verwandelt werden muß, um die idiomatische Korrektheit – gelegentlich sogar die Verständlichkeit – zu wahren.

Zur Vervollständigung dieses detaillierten Artikelaufbaus wird ein hochentwickeltes System von Stilangaben verwendet, damit der Benutzer erkennt, ob eine bestimmte Übersetzung angemessen ist oder welchen Stellenwert ein Stichwort, das er nachschlagen möchte, aus stilistischer Sicht hat. Es wird dem Benutzer mitgeteilt, ja er wird gewarnt, wenn ein Wort umgangssprachlich, dichterisch, förmlich, veraltet, altmodisch, verhüllend o.ä. ist, und es wird ihm gesagt, ob ein Ausdruck möglicherweise Anstoß erregt, Heiterkeit hervorruft, schwülstig, betulich, professoral oder abstoßend klingt. Weitere Erläuterungen zum Artikelaufbau werden auf den folgenden Seiten gegeben. Jedoch ist der Text selbst sein bester Interpret.

Using the Dictionary

Hinweise zur Benutzung des Wörterbuchs

Layout and order

1.1 Alphabetical order is followed throughout. If two variant spellings are not alphabetically adjacent each is treated as a separate headword and there is a cross-reference to the form treated in depth. Where a letter occurs in brackets in a headword, this letter is counted for the alphabetical order, eg **Beamte(r)** will be found in the place of **Beamter, vierte(r, s)** in the place of **vierter.**

1.2 Abbreviations, acronyms and **proper nouns** will be found in their alphabetical place in the word list.

1.3 Superior numbers are used to differentiate between words spelt the same way.

Aufbau und Anordnung der Einträge

1.1 Die alphabetische Anordnung der Einträge ist durchweg gewahrt. Wo zwei verschiedene Schreibweisen alphabetisch nicht unmittelbar benachbart sind, wird jede als eigenes Stichwort behandelt. Es erfolgt ein Querverweis zu der ausführlich dargestellten Variante. In Klammern stehende Buchstaben in einem Stichwort unterliegen ebenfalls der Alphabetisierung, so findet man z.B. **Beamte(r)** an der Stelle von **Beamter, vierte(r, s)** unter **vierter.**

1.2 Abkürzungen, Akronyme und **Eigennamen** sind in alphabetischer Ordnung im Wörterverzeichnis zu finden.

1.3 Hochgestellte Ziffern werden verwendet, um zwischen Wörtern gleicher Schreibung zu unterscheiden.

rowing^1, rowing^2; durchsetzen^1, durchsetzen^2.

1.4 Nouns which are always used in the plural are entered in the plural form.

1.4 Substantive, die stets im Plural verwendet werden, sind in der Pluralform angegeben.

trousers *npl,* **Ferien** *pl.*

1.5 Compounds will be found in their alphabetical place in the word list. The term "compound" is taken to cover not only those written in one word or hyphenated (eg **Bettwäsche, large-scale**) but also attributive uses of English nouns (eg **defence mechanism**) and other set word combinations (eg **long jump**) which function in a similar way. Where possible a general translation has been given for the first element.

1.5 Zusammengesetzte Wörter stehen an ihrer Stelle im Alphabet. Der Begriff „zusammengesetzte Wörter" bezeichnet nicht nur zusammengeschriebene oder durch Bindestrich verbundene Komposita (z.B. **Bettwäsche, largescale**) sondern auch die attributive Verwendung englischer Substantive (z.B. **defence mechanism**) und andere feste Verbindungen (z.B. **long jump**), die eine ähnliche Funktion haben. Wo immer möglich, ist für das erste Element eine allgemeine Übersetzung angegeben.

Silber- *in cpds* silver.

From this the user can derive the translation for compounds not given in the word list. In the case of German compounds of the form **Brennessel, schnellebig** where the spelling changes if the word is split at the end of a line, this change is indicated.

Daraus kann der Benutzer die Übersetzung hier nicht angegebener Zusammensetzungen erschließen. Bei deutschen Komposita des Typs **Brennessel, schnellebig,** bei denen sich die Schreibweise bei Silbentrennung ändert, ist die getrennte Schreibweise angegeben.

Brennessel *f getrennt:* **Brenn-nessel**

In a compound block the split form is given in its alphabetical place with a cross-reference to the standard form.

Where alphabetical order permits, compounds are run on in blocks with the first element printed in a large boldface type at the beginning of each block, the second in a slightly smaller typeface for easy identification. Illustrative phrases appear in a different typeface so that they can easily be distinguished from compounds.

In einem Block von Komponista ist die getrennte Form an der entsprechenden Stelle in der alphabetischen Reihenfolge aufgeführt und auf die einfache Form verwiesen.

Wo die alphabetische Ordnung es gestattet, werden die Zusammensetzungen in Blöcken angeordnet, wobei der erste Bestandteil am Anfang jedes Blocks fett und der zweite halbfett erscheinen. Für Wendungen wird eine andere Schrift verwendet, um dem Benutzer die schnelle Identifizierung von Wendungen und zusammengesetzten Wörtern zu erleichtern.

gum: **~-tree** *n* Gummibaum *m;* **to be up a ~-tree** (*Brit inf*) aufgeschmissen sein (*inf*).

1.6 Phrasal verbs (marked ◆) will be found immediately after the main headword entry.

1.7 Idioms and set phrases will normally be found under the first meaningful element or the first word in the phrase which remains constant despite minor variations in the phrase itself. Thus, 'to breast the tape' is included under **breast** whereas 'to lend sb a hand' is treated under **'hand'** because it is equally possible to say 'to give sb a hand'.

1.6 *Phrasal verbs* (feste Verb-Partikel-Verbindungen im Englischen, durch ◆ bezeichnet) folgen unmittelbar auf das Hauptstichwort.

1.7 Redensarten und feste Wendungen sind im allgemeinen unter dem ersten bedeutungstragenden Element oder dem ersten Wort der Wendung, das trotz leichter Abwandlungen in der Wendung selbst unverändert bleibt, zu finden. So ist 'to breast the tape' unter '**breast**' aufgenommen, 'to lend sb a hand' dagegen wird unter '**hand**'

Certain very common English and German verbs such as 'be, get, have, make, put, bringen, haben, geben, machen, tun', which form the basis of a great many phrases e.g. 'to make sense', 'to make a mistake', 'etw in Ordnung bringen', 'etw in Gang bringen' have been considered as having a diminished meaning and in such cases the set phrase will be found under the most significant element in the phrase.

abgehandelt, weil es ebenfalls möglich ist, 'to give sb a hand' zu sagen.

Bei als Funktionsverben gebrauchte Verben wie 'be, get, have, make, put, bringen, haben, geben, machen, tun' werden die meisten festen Wendungen, wie z.B. 'to make sense', 'to make a mistake', 'etw in Ordnung bringen', 'etw in Gang bringen', unter dem bedeutungstragenden Bestandteil der Wendung behandelt.

Explanatory material

General explanatory notes or 'signposts' in the dictionary are printed *in italics* and take the following forms:

2.1 Indicators in brackets ( ):

2.1.1 synonyms and partial definitions

Erklärende Zusätze

Allgemeine erklärende Zusätze im Wörterbuch sind *kursiv* gedruckt und erscheinen in folgender Form:

2.1 Indikatoren, in Klammern stehend ( ):

2.1.1 Synonyme und Teildefinitionen

gefühlvoll *adj* (**a**) *(empfindsam)* sensitive; *(ausdrucksvoll)* expressive. (**b**) *(liebevoll)* loving.

2.1.2 within verb entries, typical subjects of the headword

2.1.2 in Verb-Einträgen typische Substantiv-Ergänzungen

peel 3 *vi (wallpaper)* sich lösen; *(paint)* abblättern; *(skin, person)* sich schälen *or* pellen *(inf)*.

2.1.3 within noun entries, typical noun complements of the headword

2.1.3 typische Substantiv-Ergänzungen des Stichworts in Substantiv-Einträgen

Schar[1] *f* **-, -en** crowd, throng *(liter)*; *(von Vögeln)* flock; *(von Insekten, Heuschrecken etc)* swarm.

2.2 Collocators or typical complements, not in brackets:

2.2 Kollokatoren oder typische Ergänzungen, ohne Klammern stehend:

2.2.1 in transitive verb entries, typical objects of the headword

2.2.1 typische Objekte des Stichworts bei transitiven Verb-Einträgen

dent 2 *vt hat, car, wing* einbeulen, verbeulen; *wood, table* eine Delle machen in *(+acc)*; *(inf) pride* anknacksen *(inf)*.

2.2.2 in adjective entries, typical nouns modified by the headword

2.2.2 typische, durch das Stichwort näher bestimmte Substantive in Adjektiv-Einträgen

neu *adj* new; *Seite, Kräfte, Hoffnung, Truppen auch* fresh; (*kürzlich entstanden auch*) recent; *Wäsche, Socken* clean; *Wein* young.

2.2.3 in adverb entries, typical verbs or adjectives modified by the headword

2.2.3 typische, durch das Stichwort näher bestimmte Verben oder Adjektive bei Adverb-Einträgen

vaguely *adv* vage; *remember also* dunkel; *speak also* unbestimmt; *understand* ungefähr, in etwa.

2.3 Field labels are used:

2.3.1 to differentiate various meanings of the headword

2.3 Sachbereichsangaben werden verwendet:

2.3.1 um die verschiedenen Bedeutungen des Stichworts zu unterscheiden

Jungfrau *f* virgin; *(Astron, Astrol)* Virgo.

2.3.2 when the meaning in the source language is clear but may be ambiguous in the target language

2.3.2 wenn die Bedeutung in der Ausgangssprache klar ist, jedoch in der Zielsprache mehrdeutig sein könnte

Virgo *n (Astrol)* Jungfrau *f*.

A list of the field labels used in this dictionary is given inside the front and back covers.

2.4 Style labels are used to mark all words and phrases which are not neutral in style level or which are no longer current in the language. This labelling is given for both source and target languages and serves primarily as an aid to the non-native speaker.

When a style label is given at the beginning of an entry or category it covers all meanings and phrases in that entry or category.

Eine Liste dieser Sachbereichsangaben befindet sich auf den Umschlag-Innenseiten.

2.4 Stilangaben werden verwendet zur Kennzeichnung aller Wörter und Wendungen, die keiner neutralen Stilebene oder nicht mehr dem modernen Sprachgebrauch angehören. Die Angaben erfolgen sowohl in der Ausgangs- als auch in der Zielsprache und sollen in erster Linie dem Nicht-Muttersprachler helfen.

Stilangaben zu Beginn eines Eintrages oder einer Kategorie beziehen sich auf alle Bedeutungen und Wendungen innerhalb dieses Eintrages oder dieser Kategorie.

(*inf*) denotes colloquial language typically used in an informal conversational context or a chatty letter, but which would be inappropriate in more formal speech or writing.

(*sl*) indicates that the word or phrase is highly informal and is only appropriate in very restricted contexts, for example among members of a particular age group. When combined with a field label eg (*Mil sl*), (*Sch sl*) it denotes that the expression belongs to the jargon of that group.

(*vulg*) denotes words generally regarded as taboo which are likely to cause offence.

(*geh*) denotes an elevated style of spoken or written German such as might be used by an educated speaker choosing his words with care.

(*form*) denotes formal language such as that used on official forms, for official communications and in formal speeches.

(*spec*) indicates that the expression is a technical term restricted to the vocabulary of specialists.

(*dated*) indicates that the word or phrase, while still occasionally being used especially by older speakers, now sounds somewhat old-fashioned.

(*old*) denotes language no longer in current use but which the user will find in reading.

(*obs*) denotes obsolete words which the user will normally only find in classical literature.

(*liter*) denotes language of a literary style level. It should not be confused with the field label (*Liter*) which indicates that the expression belongs to the field of literary studies, or with the abbreviation (*lit*) which indicates the literal as opposed to the figurative meaning of a word.

Style labels used in this dictionary are given inside the front and back covers.

2.5 ***also, auch*** used after explanatory material denotes that the translation(s) following it can be used in addition to the first translation given in the respective entry, category or phrase.

(*inf*) bezeichnet umgangssprächlichen Gebrauch, wie er für eine formlose Unterhaltung oder einen zwanglosen Brief typisch ist, in förmlicherer Rede oder förmlicherem Schriftverkehr jedoch unangebracht wäre.

(*sl*) soll anzeigen, daß das Wort oder die Wendung äußerst salopp ist und nur unter ganz bestimmten Umständen, z.B. unter Mitgliedern einer besonderen Altersgruppe, verwendet wird. In Verbindung mit einer Sachbereichsangabe, z.B. (*Mil sl*), (*Sch sl*), wird auf die Zugehörigkeit des Ausdrucks zum Jargon dieser Gruppe hingewiesen.

(*vulg*) bezeichnet Wörter, die allgemein als tabu gelten und an denen vielfach Anstoß genommen wird.

(*geh*) bezeichnet einen gehobenen Stil sowohl im gesprochenen wie geschriebenen Deutsch, wie er von gebildeten, sich gewählt ausdrückenden Sprechern verwendet werden kann.

(*form*) bezeichnet förmlichen Sprachgebrauch, wie er uns auf Formularen, im amtlichen Schriftverkehr oder in förmlichen Ansprachen begegnet.

(*spec*) gibt an, daß es sich um einen Fachausdruck handelt, der ausschließlich dem Wortschatz von Fachleuten angehört.

(*dated*) weist darauf hin, daß das Wort bzw. die Wendung heute recht altmodisch klingt, obwohl sie besonders von älteren Sprechern noch gelegentlich benutzt werden.

(*old*) bezeichnet nicht mehr geläufiges Wortgut, das dem Benutzer jedoch noch beim Lesen begegnet.

(*obs*) bezeichnet veraltete Wörter, die der Benutzer im allgemeinen nur in der klassischen Literatur antreffen wird.

(*liter*) bezeichnet literarischen Sprachgebrauch. Es sollte nicht mit der Sachbereichsangabe (*Liter*) verwechselt werden, die angibt, daß der betreffende Ausdruck dem Gebiet der Literaturwissenschaften angehört, und ebensowenig mit der Abkürzung (*lit*), die die wörtliche im Gegensatz zur übertragenen Bedeutung eines Wortes bezeichnet.

In diesem Wörterbuch verwendete Stilangaben und ihre Bedeutungen befinden sich auf den Umschlag-Innenseiten.

2.5 ***also, auch*** nach erklärenden Zusätzen gibt an, daß die folgende(n) Übersetzung(en) zusätzlich zu der ersten Übersetzung, die in dem Eintrag oder der Kategorie angegeben ist, benutzt werden kann/können.

Grammatical Information

Gender

3.1 All German **nouns** are marked for gender in both sections of the dictionary.

3.2 Where two or more German nouns of the same gender are given consecutively as interchangeable translations, the gender is given only after the last translation in the series.

Grammatische Angaben

Geschlecht

3.1 Alle deutschen **Substantive** sind in beiden Teilen des Wörterbuchs mit der Geschlechtsangabe versehen.

3.2 Wo zwei oder mehr deutsche Substantive gleichen Geschlechts als austauschbare Übersetzungen hintereinander stehen, wird das Geschlecht nur nach der letzten Übersetzung in der Folge angegeben.

computer *n* Computer, Rechner *m*.

3.3 Where a German translation consists of an adjective plus a noun, the adjective is given in the indefinite form which shows gender and therefore no gender is given for the noun.

3.3 Wenn eine deutsche Übersetzung aus einem Adjektiv und einem Substantiv besteht, wird das Adjektiv in der unbestimmten Form angegeben, die das Geschlecht erkennen läßt. Für das Substantiv erfolgt daher keine Geschlechtsangabe.

große Pause; zweites Frühstück.

3.4 Nouns listed in the form **Reisende(r)** *mf decl as adj* can be either masculine or feminine and take the same endings as adjectives.

3.4 Substantive nach dem Muster **Reisende(r)** *mf decl as adj* können sowohl männlich wie weiblich sein und haben die gleichen Deklinationsendungen wie Adjektive.

m **der Reisende, ein Reisender, die Reisenden** *pl*
f **die Reisende, eine Reisende, die Reisenden** *pl*

3.5 Nouns listed in the form **Beamte(r)** *m decl as adj* take the same endings as adjectives.

3.5 Substantive nach dem Muster **Beamte(r)** *m decl as adj* haben die gleichen Deklinationsendungen wie Adjektive.

der Beamte, ein Beamter, die Beamten *pl*

3.6 **Adjectives** listed in the form **letzte(r, s)** do not exist in an undeclined form and are only used attributively.

3.6 **Adjektive** nach dem Muster **letzte(r, s)** haben keine unflektierte Form und werden nur attributiv verwendet.

der letzte Mann, ein letzter Mann
die letzte Frau, eine letzte Frau
das letzte Kind, ein letztes Kind

3.7 Nouns listed in the form **Schüler(in** *f*) *m* are only used in the bracketed form in the feminine.

3.7 Substantive nach dem Muster **Schüler(in** *f*) *m* werden nur im Femininum in der eingeklammerten Form benutzt.

der/ein Schüler
die/eine Schülerin

3.8 The **feminine forms** are shown, where relevant, for all German noun headwords; unless otherwise indicated, the English translation will be the same as for the masculine form.

Where the feminine form is separated alphabetically from the masculine form but has the same translation, it is given as a separate headword with a cross-reference to the masculine form.

Where the feminine form requires a different translation in English it is given as a separate headword.

Where there is no distinction between the translations given for the masculine and feminine forms and yet the context calls for a distinction, the user should prefix the translation with "male/female *or* woman *or* lady ..."

3.8 Für alle deutschen Substantive, die ein natürliches Geschlecht haben, wird die **weibliche** neben der **männlichen Form** angegeben. Wenn nicht anders angegeben, lautet die englische Form für beide gleich.

Wo die weibliche Form in der alphabetischen Reihenfolge nicht unmittelbar auf die männliche folgt, aber die gleiche Übersetzung hat, wird sie als eigenes Stichwort angegeben, wobei ein Querverweis auf die männliche Form erfolgt.

Wenn die weibliche Form im Englischen eine andere Übersetzung hat, wird sie als eigenes Stichwort angegeben.

Wo die für die männliche und die für die weibliche Form angegebene Übersetzung dieselbe ist, im entsprechenden Zusammenhang aber betont werden soll, daß es sich um einen Mann bzw. eine Frau handelt, sollte der Benutzer der Übersetzung „male/female *or* woman *or* lady" voranstellen.

Lehrer(in) = male teacher/female *or* **woman** *or* **lady teacher**

Nouns

For German compound nouns the feminine forms have only been given where the English calls for a different translation.

4.1 Nouns marked *no pl* are not normally used in the plural or with an indefinite article or with numerals.

no pl is used:

(a) to give warning to the non-native speaker who might otherwise use the word wrongly;
(b) as an indicator to distinguish the uncountable meanings of a headword in the source language.

4.2 Nouns marked *no art* are not normally used with either a definite or an indefinite article except when followed by a relative clause.

4.3 The **genitive and plural endings** are given for all German noun headwords except for those with certain regular noun endings. A complete list of these is given on page xxi.

The genitive and plural endings of German compound nouns are only given where the final element does not exist as a headword in its own right.

Substantive

Die weiblichen Formen der deutschen zusammengesetzten Substantive sind nur angegeben, wenn im Englischen eine eigene Übersetzung erforderlich ist.

4.1 Substantive mit der Angabe *no pl* werden im allgemeinen nicht im Plural, mit dem unbestimmten Artikel oder mit Zahlwörtern verwendet.

no pl dient:

(a) als Warnung an den Nicht-Muttersprachler, der das Wort sonst falsch benutzen könnte;
(b) zur Unterscheidung der unzählbaren und zählbaren Bedeutungen in der Ausgangssprache.

4.2 Mit *no art* bezeichnete Substantive stehen im allgemeinen weder mit dem unbestimmten noch mit dem bestimmten Artikel, außer wenn ein Relativsatz von ihnen abhängig ist.

4.3 Bei allen deutschen Substantiv-Stichwörtern sind **Genitivendung und Plural** angegeben, mit Ausnahme bestimmter regelmäßiger Endungen. Diese sind in einer vollständigen Liste auf Seite xxi erfaßt.

Die Genitivendung und der Plural sind ist bei zusammengesetzten Substantiven nur dann angegeben, wenn das letzte Element der Zusammensetzung nicht als Einzelwort vorkommt.

4.4 Irregular plural forms of English nouns are given on the English-German side.

4.4.1 Most English nouns take *-s* in the plural.

bed -s, site -s, key -s, roof -s

4.4.2 Nouns ending in *-s, -z, -x, -sh, -ch* take *-es*

gas -es, box -es, patch -es

4.4.3 Nouns ending in *-y* preceded by a consonant change the *-y* to *ie* and add *-s* in the plural, except in the case of proper nouns.

lady — ladies, berry — berries
Henry — two Henrys

Nouns ending in *-quy* also change the *-y* to *- ie* and add *-s* in the plural, except in the case of proper nouns.

soliloquy — soliloquies

Adjectives and adverbs

5.1 As a general rule, adjective translations consisting of more than one word should be used postnominally or adverbially, but not before the noun.

ordnungsgemäß *adj* according to *or* in accordance with the rules, proper

5.2 On the German-English side of the dictionary adverbs have only been treated as separate grammatical entries distinct from adjective entries:
(a) when their use is purely adverbial

höchst, wohl, sehr

(b) when the adverbial use is as common as the adjectival use

schön

(c) when the English translation of the adverbial use cannot be derived from the adjectival translations by the rules of adverb formation

gut, schnell

Where no separate entry is given for the adverbial use of a German adjective, the user should form the English adverb from the translations given according to the rules given on page xx.

5.3 On the English-German side of the dictionary adverbs have been accorded the status of headwords in their own right.

In cases where an adverb is cross-referred to its related adjective, the German translations given under the adjective apply to the adverb too.

moodily *adv see* **moody.**
moody *adj* launisch, launenhaft; (*bad-tempered*) schlechtgelaunt *attr,* schlecht gelaunt *pred; look, answer* verdrossen, übellaunig.

In cases where the adverb and its related adjective occur consecutively in the alphabetical order and where the same translations apply to both, the entries have been conflated.

4.4 Unregelmäßige Pluralformen englischer Substantive sind im englisch-deutschen Teil angegeben.

4.4.1 Die meisten englischen Substantive bilden den Plural durch Anhängen von *-s*.

4.4.2 Substantive, die auf *-s, -z, -x, -sh, -ch* enden, erhalten die Endung *-es*.

4.4.3 Substantive, die auf Konsonant + *-y* enden, verwandeln im Plural das auslautende *-y* in *-ie*, auf das die Pluralendung *-s* folgt. Ausnahmen bilden Eigennamen.

Auf *-quy* auslautende Substantive verwandeln bei der Pluralbildung ihr *-y* ebenfalls in *-ie*, worauf *-s* folgt.

Adjektive und Adverbien

5.1 Grundsätzlich sollten Übersetzungen von Adjektiven, die aus mehreren Wörtern bestehen, nur nachgestellt oder adverbial gebraucht und nicht dem Substantiv vorangestellt werden.

5.2 Im deutsch-englischen Teil des Wörterbuchs sind Adverbien als selbständige grammatische Einträge von Adjektiven nur dann unterschieden worden:
(a) wenn es sich um echte Adverbien handelt

(b) wenn der adverbiale Gebrauch genauso häufig ist wie der adjektivische

(c) wenn die englische Übersetzung eines adverbial verwendeten Adjektivs nicht mit Hilfe der Regeln erschlossen werden kann, nach denen im Englischen Adverbien aus Adjektiven gebildet werden

Wo für den adverbialen Gebrauch eines deutschen Adjektivs kein gesonderter Eintrag vorliegt, ist es dem Benutzer selbst überlassen, aus den angegebenen Übersetzungen die englischen Adverbien nach den auf Seite xx angeführten Regeln zu bilden.

5.3 Im englisch-deutschen Teil des Wörterbuchs sind die Adverbien als selbständige Stichwörter aufgeführt.

In Fällen, wo ein Adverb auf sein Adjektiv-Äquivalent verweisen wird, gelten die für das Adjektiv angegebenen Übersetzungen auch für das Adverb.

In Fällen, wo Adjektiv und dazugehöriges Adverb in der alphabetischen Anordnung aufeinanderfolgen und wo die gleichen Übersetzungen für beide gelten, sind die Einträge zusammengefaßt worden.

maladroit *adj*, **~ly** *adv* ungeschickt.

Verbs

6.1 All German verbs which form the past participle without *ge-* are marked with an asterisk in the text.

Verben

6.1 Alle Verben im Deutschen, die das 2. Partizip ohne *ge-* bilden, sind in Text durch Sternchen gekennzeichnet.

umarmen* *vt insep ptp* **umarmt**
manövrieren* *vti ptp* **manövriert**

6.2 All German verbs beginning with a prefix which can be separable are marked *sep* or *insep* as appropriate.

6.2 Alle deutschen Verben, die mit einer trennbaren Vorsilbe beginnen, werden durch *sep* oder *insep* (= trennbar/untrennbar) bezeichnet.

überrieseln *vt insep* **ein Schauer überrieselte ihn**
umschmeißen *vt sep* **das schmeißt alle meine Pläne um**

Verbs beginning with the prefixes *be-, er-, ver-, zer-* are always inseparable.

Verben mit den Vorsilben *be-, er-, ver-, zer-* sind immer untrennbar.

6.3 All German verbs which form their perfect, pluperfect and future perfect tenses with "sein" as the auxiliary are marked *aux sein.*

6.3 Alle deutschen Verben, die die zusammengesetzten Zeiten mit dem Hilfsverb „sein" bilden, sind durch *aux sein* gekennzeichnet.

gehen *pret* **ging**, *ptp* **gegangen** *aux sein* **er ist gegangen** he went.

Where the auxiliary is not stated, "haben" is used.

Erfolgt keine Angabe, ist „haben" zu verwenden.

6.4 German **irregular verbs** composed of prefix and verb are marked *irreg,* and the forms can be found under the simple verb. For example, the irregular forms of "eingehen" will be found under "gehen".

6.4 Zusammengesetzte **unregelmäßige** Verben im Deutschen sind durch *irreg* bezeichnet, ihre Stammformen sind beim Simplex angegeben. So sind beispielsweise die Stammformen von „eingehen" unter „gehen" zu finden.

6.5 If the present or past participle of a verb occurs simply as an adjective it is treated as a separate headword in its alphabetical place.

6.5 Wenn 1. oder 2. Partizip eines Verbs den Status eines Adjektivs haben, werden sie als eigenständige Stichwörter in alphabetischer Reihenfolge aufgeführt.

gereift *adj (fig)* mature.
struggling *adj artist etc* am Hungertuch nagend.

Phrasal verbs

7.1 Phrasal verbs are covered in separate entries marked ◆ following the main headword.

Phrasal verbs

7.1 *Phrasal verbs* (feste Verb-Partikel-Verbindungen) sind in eigenen Einträgen abgehandelt. Sie sind durch ◆ gekennzeichnet und folgen dem Stichworteintrag für das Verb.

7.2 Verb + adverb and verb + preposition combinations have been treated as phrasal verbs:
(a) where either the meaning or the translation is not simply derivable from the individual constituents;
(b) for clarity in the case of the longer verb entries.

7.2 Die Zusammensetzungen Verb + Adverb und Verb + Präposition werden als *phrasal verbs* abgehandelt:
(a) wo entweder die Bedeutung oder die Übersetzung sich nicht aus den Einzelbestandteilen ergibt;
(b) aus Gründen der Übersichtlichkeit bei längeren Verbeinträgen.

Where a combination consists simply of a verb plus an adverb or preposition of direction it will frequently be covered under the main headword.

Bei einfachen Kombinationen von Verb + Adverb oder Präposition der Richtung ist unter dem Haupteintrag zu suchen.

dash ... **3** *vi* (**a**) *(rush)* ... **to ~ away/back/up** fort-/zurück-/hinaufstürzen

7.3 Irregular preterites and past participles are only given in phrasal verb entries in the rare cases where they differ from those given in the main entry.

7.3 Unregelmässige Formen des Präteritums und des 2. Partizips werden in Einträgen, die *phrasal verbs* behandeln, nur in den seltenen Fällen angegeben, wo sie von den im Haupteintrag angegebenen abweichen.

7.4 Phrasal verbs are treated in four grammatical categories:

7.4 *Phrasal verbs* werden unter vier grammatischen Kategorien abgehandelt:

7.4.1 *vi* (intransitive verb)

7.4.1 *vi* (intransitives Verb)

◆ **grow apart** *vi (fig)* sich auseinanderentwickeln.

7.4.2 *vi +prep obj*
This indicates that the verbal element is intransitive but that the particle requires an object.

7.4.2 *vi +prep obj*
Hiermit soll gezeigt werden, daß das Verbelement intransitiv ist, daß aber die Partikel ein Objekt erfordert.

◆ **hold with** *vi +prep obj (inf)* **I don't ~ ~ that** ich bin gegen so was *(inf)*.

7.4.3 *vt*
This indicates that the verbal element is transitive. In most cases the object can be placed either before or after the particle; these cases are marked *sep*.

7.4.3 *vt*
Dies gibt an, daß das Verbelement transitiv ist. In den meisten Fällen kann das Objekt vor oder hinter der Partikel stehen; diese Fälle sind mit *sep* bezeichnet.

◆ **hand in** *vt sep* abgeben; *forms, thesis also, resignation* einreichen.

In some cases the object must precede the particle; these cases are marked *always separate*.

In einigen Fällen muß das Objekt der Partikel vorangehen; solche Fälle sind durch *always separate* bezeichnet.

◆**get over with** *vt always separate* hinter sich *(acc)* bringen.
let's ~ it ~ (~) bringen wir's hinter uns.

Occasionally the object must come after the particle, these cases are marked *insep*.

Gelegentlich muß das Objekt der Partikel nachgestellt werden; solche Fälle sind durch *insep* bezeichnet.

◆**put forth** *vt insep (liter) buds, shoots* hervorbringen.

7.4.4 *vt +prep obj*
This indicates that both the verbal element and the particle require an object.

7.4.4 *vt +prep obj*
Hiermit wird gezeigt, daß *sowohl* das Verbelement als auch die Partikel ein Objekt verlangen.

◆**take upon** *vt +prep obj* **he took that job ~ himself** er hat das völlig ungebeten getan.

In cases where a prepositional object is optional its translation is covered under *vi* or *vt*.

In Fällen, wo ein Präpositionalobjekt, möglich, aber nicht nötig ist, findet man die entsprechende Übersetzung unter *vi* oder *vt*.

◆**get off** *vi (from bus, train etc)* aussteigen *(prep obj* aus*)*;
(from bicycle, horse) absteigen *(prep obj* von*)*.
◆**go down** *vi* hinuntergehen *(prep obj acc)*.

For example:

Zum Beispiel:

he got off er stieg aus/ab
he got off the bus er stieg aus dem Bus aus
he got off his bicycle er stieg von seinem Fahrrad ab
she went down sie ging hinunter
she went down the street sie ging die Straße hinunter

Cross references

8.1 Cross-references are used in the following instances:

8.1.1 to refer the user to the most common term or to the spelling variant treated in depth;

8.1.2 to refer the user to the headword where a particular construction or idiom has been treated;

8.1.3 to avoid the repetition of indicating material where one word has been treated in depth and derivatives of that word have corresponding semantic divisions;

8.1.4 to refer the user from an English adverb to the related adjective in cases where the general translations given there also apply to the adverb;

8.1.5 to draw the user's attention to the full treatment of such words as numerals, languages, days of the week and months of the year under certain key words.

Querverweise

8.1 Querverweise sind in folgenden Fällen verwendet worden:

8.1.1 um den Benutzer auf den gebräuchlichsten Ausdruck oder auf die geläufigste Schreibweise zu verweisen, wo die ausführliche Darstellung des Stichworts zu finden ist;

8.1.2 um den Benutzer auf das Stichwort zu verweisen, wo eine bestimmte Konstruktion oder Wendung abgehandelt wird;

8.1.3 um die Wiederholung erklärender Zusätze zu vermeiden, wenn ein Wort bereits ausführlich behandelt worden ist und seine Ableitungen semantisch analog gegliedert sind;

8.1.4 um den Benutzer von einem englischen Adverb auf das entsprechende Adjektiv zu verweisen, wo die dort angegebenen allgemeinen Übersetzungen auch für das Adverb gelten;

8.1.5 um die Aufmerksamkeit des Benutzers auf die ausführliche Behandlung solcher Wortklassen wie Zahlwörter, Sprachbezeichnungen, Wochentage und Monate unter bestimmten Schlüsselwörtern zu lenken.

9 Punctuation and Symbols

between translations indicates that the translations are interchangeable; between alternative phrases to be translated indicates that the phrases have the same meaning.

9 Satzzeichen und Symbole

zwischen Übersetzungen zeigt an, daß die Übersetzungen gleichwertig sind; zwischen Wendungen in der Ausgangssprache zeigt an, daß die Wendungen die gleiche Bedeutung haben.

between translations indicates a difference in meaning which is clarified by explanatory material unless: (a) the distinction has already been made within the same entry; (b) in the case of some compounds the distinction is made under the simple form; (c) the distinction is self-evident.	;	zwischen Übersetzungen zeigt einen Bedeutungsunterschied an, der durch erklärende Zusätze erläutert ist, außer: (a) wenn die Unterscheidung innerhalb desselben Eintrags schon gemacht worden ist; (b) bei Komposita, wo die Unterscheidung schon unter dem Simplex getroffen wurde (c) wenn die Unterscheidung offensichtlich ist.
between a headword and a phrase indicates that the headword is normally only used in that phrase.	:	zwischen Stichwort und Wendung gibt an, daß das Stichwort im allgemeinen nur in der aufgeführten Wendung vorkommt.
between translations indicates parallel structure but different meanings, e.g. **to feel good/bad**. (a) in a source language phrase it will normally be paralleled in the translation; where this is not the case, the translation covers both meanings (b) in a target language phrase where it is not paralleled by an oblique in the source language the distinction will either be made clear earlier in the entry or will be self-evident (c) in compounds it may be used to reflect a distinction made under the simple form.	/	zwischen Übersetzungen zeigt an, daß es sich um analoge Strukturen, aber verschiedene Übersetzungen handelt, z.B. **to feel good/bad**. (a) der Schrägstrich in einer ausgangssprachlichen Wendung wird im allgemeinen seine Entsprechung in der Übersetzung finden; wo das nicht der Fall ist, gilt die Übersetzung für beide Bedeutungen; (b) hat ein Schrägstrich in der Zielsprache kein Äquivalent in der Ausgangssprache, geht die getroffene Unterscheidung entweder aus in dem Eintrag bereits Gesagtem hervor, oder sie ist offensichtlich; (c) bei Zusammensetzungen kann der Schrägstrich verwendet werden, um an eine für das Simplex getroffene Unterscheidung anzuknüpfen.
is used within an entry to represent the headword whenever it occurs in an unchanged form. In German headwords of the form **Reisende(r)** *mf decl as adj*, and **höchste(r, s)** *adj* it only replaces the element outside the brackets. In blocks of German compounds it represents the first element exactly as given at the beginning of the block. If it is given there with a capital, any subsequent occurence in a compound or phrase where it requires a small letter is clearly shown eg **Wochen-**: ...; **w~lang** *adj, adv* ...	~	wird innerhalb von Einträgen verwendet, um das unveränderte Stichwort zu ersetzen. Bei deutschen Stichwörtern des Typs **Reisende(r)** *mf decl as adj* und **höchste(r, s)** *adj* ersetzt der Strich den außerhalb der Klammer stehenden Teil des Wortes. In deutschen Komposita-Blöcken ersetzt der Strich das erste Element der Zusammensetzung genau, wie es am Anfang des Blocks erscheint. Soll von Großschreibung auf Kleinschreibung übergegangen werden, ist dies angegeben, z.B. **Wochen-**: ...; **w~lang** *adv, adv* ...
separates two speakers.	—	unterscheidet zwischen zwei Sprechern.
indicates that the translation is approximate or the cultural equivalent of the term and may not have exactly the same sense; in the case of institutions, they are those of the country indicated and obviously not the same.	≃	weist darauf hin, daß die Übersetzung eine Entsprechung ist oder auf Grund kultureller Unterschiede nicht genau die gleiche Bedeutung hat. Bei Institutionen werden die des jeweiligen Landes angegeben, die natürlich nicht identisch sind.
after a German verb indicates that the past participle is formed without *ge-*.	*	nach einem deutschen Verb gibt an, daß das 2. Partizip ohne *ge-* gebildet wird.
is used to separate parts of a word or phrase which are semantically interchangeable.	*or*	wird verwendet, um Bestandteile einer Wendung zu unterscheiden, die semantisch austauschbar sind.
used after indicating material denotes that the translation(s) following it can be used in addition to the first translation(s) given in the respective entry, category or phrase.	*also, auch*	nach erklärenden Zusätzen gibt an, daß die folgende(n) Übersetzung(en), zusätzlich zu der ersten Übersetzung oder Folge von austauschbaren Übersetzungen, die in dem Eintrag oder der Kategorie angegeben sind, benutzt werden kann/können.
in a source language phrase indicate that the word is stressed.	***bold italics Halbfette kursiv***	in ausgangssprachlichen Wendungen bezeichnet betonte Wörter oder Silben.
in the translation of a phrase indicate that the word is stressed.	*italics Kursivdruck*	in der Übersetzung einer Wendung gibt an, daß das Wort betont ist.

Adjectives and Adverbs

Declension of German adjectives

Adjectives ending in *-abel, -ibel, -el* drop the *-e-* when declined.

miserable	**ein miserabler Stil** **eine miserable Handschrift** **ein miserables Leben**
heikel	**ein heikler Fall** **eine heikle Frage** **ein heikles Problem**

Adjectives ending in *-er, -en* usually keep the *-e-* when declined, except:

1 in language of an elevated style level

finster	**seine finstren Züge**

2 in adjectives of foreign origin

makaber	**eine makabre Geschichte**
integer	**ein integrer Beamter**

Adjectives ending in *-auer, -euer* usually drop the *-e-* when declined.

teuer	**ein teures Geschenk**
sauer	**saure Gurken**

German adverbs

German adverbs are in most cases identical in form to the adjective, so except where there is a particular problem of translation the adverbial usage does not receive separate treatment in this dictionary.

Comparison of German adjectives and adverbs

Irregular comparative and superlative forms are given in the text, including those of adjectives and adverbs with the vowels *a, o, u* which take an umlaut:

hoch *adj comp* **höher**, *superl* **höchste(r, s)** *or (adv)* **am höchsten**

Where no forms are given in the text, the comparative and superlative are formed according to the following rules:

1 Both adjectives and adverbs add *-er* for the comparative before the declensional endings:

schön — schöner
eine schöne Frau — eine schönere Frau

2 Most adjectives add *-ste(r, s)* for the superlative:

schön — schönste(r, s)
ein schöner Tag — der schönste Tag

3 Most adverbs form the superlative according to the following pattern:

schön — am schönsten
schnell — am schnellsten

4 Adjectives and adverbs of one syllable or with the stress on the final syllable add *-e* before the superlative ending:

(i)	always if they end in *-s, -ß, -st, -tz, -x, -z*
(ii)	usually if they end in *-d, -t, -sch*
spitz	*adj* **spitzeste(r, s)** *adv* **am spitzesten**
gerecht	*adj* **gerechteste(r, s)** *adv* **am gerechtesten**

The same applies if they are used with a prefix or in compounds, regardless of where the stress falls:

unsanft	*adj* **unsanfteste(r, s)** *adv* **am unsanftesten**

Adjektive und Adverbien

Adverbialbildung im Englischen

1 Die meisten Adjektive bilden das Adverb durch Anhängen von *-ly*:

strange -ly, odd -ly, beautiful -ly

2 Adjektive, die auf Konsonant *+y* enden, wandeln das auslautende *-y* in *-i* um und erhalten dann die Endung *-ly*:

happy — happily
merry — merrily

3 Adjektive, die auf *-ic* enden, bilden normalerweise das Adverb durch Anhängen vom *-ally*:

scenic -ally
linguistic -ally

Steigerung der englischen Adjektive und Adverbien

Adjektive und Adverbien, deren Komparativ und Superlativ im allgemeinen durch Flexionsendungen gebildet werden, sind im Text durch (*+er*) bezeichnet, z.B.

young *adj (+er)*

Komparativ und Superlativ aller nicht durch (*+er*) bezeichneten Adjektive und Adverbien sind mit *more* und *most* zu bilden. Das gilt auch für alle auf *-ly* endenden Adverbien, z.B.

grateful — more grateful — most grateful
fully — more fully — most fully

Unregelmäßige Formen des Komparativs und Superlativs sind im Text angegeben, z.B.

bad *adj comp* **worse**, *superl* **worst**
well *adv comp* **better**, *superl* **best**

Die flektierten Formen des Komparativs und Superlativs werden nach folgenden Regeln gebildet:

1 Die meisten Adjektive und Adverbien fügen *-er* zur Bildung des Komparativs und *-est* zur Bildung des Superlativs an:

small — smaller — smallest

2 Bei auf Konsonant *+y* endenden Adjektiven und Adverbien wird das auslautende *-y* in *-i* umgewandelt, bevor die Endung *-er* bzw. *-est* angefügt wird:

happy — happier — happiest

3 Mehrsilbige Adjektive auf *-ey* wandeln diese Endsilbe in *-ier, -iest* um:

homey — homier — homiest

4 Bei Adjektiven und Adverbien, die auf stummes *-e* enden, entfällt dieser Auslaut:

brave — braver — bravest

5 Bei Adjektiven und Adverbien, die auf *-ee* enden, entfällt das zweite *-e*:

free — freer — freest

6 Adjektive und Adverbien, die auf einen Konsonanten nach einfachem betontem Vokal enden, verdoppeln den Konsonanten im Auslaut:

sad — sadder — saddest

Nach Doppelvokal wird der auslautende Konsonant nicht verdoppelt:

loud — louder — loudest

Regular German Noun Endings

The Genitive of Proper Names

The genitive of the proper names of people, cities, countries etc takes two forms. 1. When used with an article the word remains unchanged, e.g. **des Aristoteles, der Bertha, des schönen Berlin**. 2. When used without an article an 's' is added to the noun, e.g. **die Straßen Berlins, Marias Auto, Olafs Hut**. When the noun ends in *s, ß, tz, x* or *z* an apostrophe is added, e.g. **Aristoteles' Schriften, die Straßen Calais'**.
In most cases in this dictionary the genitive form given for the proper names of people is that which is correct for use with an article. For the proper names of countries and cities the form for use without an article is given.

nom		gen	pl
-ade	*f*	-ade	-aden
-ant	*m (wk)*	-anten	-anten
-anz	*f*	-anz	-anzen
-ar	*m*	-ars	-are
-är	*m*	-ärs	-äre
-at	*nt*	-at(e)s	-ate
-atte	*f*	-atte	-atten
-chen	*nt*	-chens	-chen
-ei	*f*	-ei	-eien
-elle	*f*	-elle	-ellen
-ent	*m (wk)*	-enten	-enten
-enz	*f*	-enz	-enzen
-esse	*f*	-esse	-essen
-ette	*f*	-ette	-etten
-eur	*m*	-eurs	-eure
-eurin	*f*	-eurin	-eurinnen
-euse	*f*	-euse	-eusen
-graph	*m (wk)*	-graphen	-graphen
-heit	*f*	-heit	-heiten
-ie	*f*	-ie	-ien
-ik	*f*	-ik	-iken
-in	*f*	-in	-innen
-ine	*f*	-ine	-inen
-ion	*f*	-ion	-ionen
-ist	*m (wk)*	-isten	-isten
-ium	*nt*	-iums	-ien
-ius	*m*	-ius	-iusse
-ive	*f*	-ive	-iven
-ivum	*nt*	-ivums	-iva
-keit	*f*	-keit	-keiten
-lein	*nt*	-leins	-lein
-ling	*m*	-lings	-linge
-ment	*nt*	-ments	-mente
-mus	*m*	-mus	-men
-nis	*f*	-nis	-nisse
-nis	*nt*	-nisses	-nisse
-nom	*m (wk)*	-nomen	-nomen
-oge	*m (wk)*	-ogen	-ogen
-or	*m*	-ors	-oren
-rich	*m*	-richs	-riche
-schaft	*f*	-schaft	-schaften
-sel	*nt*	-sels	-sel
-tät	*f*	-tät	-täten
-tiv	*nt, m*	-tivs	-tive
-tum	*nt*	-tums	-tümer
-ung	*f*	-ung	-ungen
-ur	*f*	-ur	-uren

General rules for forming the genitive

Genitive endings are formed

for masculine and neuter nouns by adding **-s** or **-es**

der Mann: *(gen)* **des Mann(e)s**
das Rad: *(gen)* **des Rad(e)s**

for feminine nouns: no change

die Frau: *(gen)* **der Frau·**

Masculine or neuter nouns ending in **-s, -ß, -x** and **-z** always take the full form of **-es** for the genitive

das Glas: *(gen)* **des Glases**
das Maß: *(gen)* **des Maßes**
der Komplex: *(gen)* **des Komplexes**
der Geiz: *(gen)* **des Geizes**

Masculine or neuter nouns ending in **-sch** or **-st** normally take the full form of **-es**, as do those ending in a double consonant

der Wunsch: *(gen)* **des Wunsches**
der Gast: *(gen)* **des Gastes**
das Feld: *(gen)* **des Feldes**
der Kampf: *(gen)* **des Kampfes**

Masculine or neuter nouns ending in **-en, -em, -el, -er** and **-ling** always take the short form of **-s**

der Regen: *(gen)* **des Regens**
der Atem: *(gen)* **des Atems**
der Mantel: *(gen)* **des Mantels**
der Sänger: *(gen)* **des Sängers**
der Flüchtling: *(gen)* **des Flüchtlings**

Masculine or neuter nouns ending in **-ß** preceded by a short vowel will change the **ß** to **ss**

der Fluß: *(gen)* **des Flusses**

If the genitive is not formed according to these patterns it will be shown in the entry after the gender and before the plural ending

Herz *nt* **-ens, en**
Klerus *m* -, *no pl*

Plural endings

We have not shown plural endings where the regular patterns shown on page xxi apply. All other plural endings are shown in the entry after the gender and the genitive ending (where given). If only one ending is given this will be the plural, unless otherwise indicated.

Weak nouns

Weak nouns (marked as *wk*) have the same **-en** ending in the accusative, genitive and dative cases in both singular and plural forms

der Mensch: *(acc)* **den Menschen**
(gen) **des Menschen**
(dat) **dem Menschen**

The Pronunciation of German

German pronunciation is largely regular, and a knowledge of the basic patterns is assumed.
A full list of IPA symbols used is given on page xxv.

Stress

1. The stress and the length of the stressed vowel are shown for every German headword.
2. The stressed vowel is usually marked in the headword, either with a dot if it is a short vowel:

sofọrt, Mạtte

or a dash if it is a long vowel or diphthong:

hochmütig, kaufen

Glottal Stop

1. A glottal stop *(Knacklaut)* occurs at the beginning of any word starting with a vowel.
2. A glottal stop always occurs in compounds between the first and second elements when the second element begins with a vowel.
3. When a glottal stop occurs elsewhere it is marked by a hairline before the vowel:

Be|ạmte(r)

Vowel length

1. When phonetics are given for the headword a long vowel is indicated in the transcription by the length mark after it:

Chemie [çe'miː]

2. Where no phonetics are given a short stressed vowel is marked with a dot in the headword:

Mụtter

and a long stressed vowel is marked with a dash:

Vater

3. Unstressed vowels are usually short; if not, phonetics are given for that vowel:

Ạlmosen [-oː-]

Diphthongs and double vowels

1. Where phonetics are not given, vowel combinations which represent a stressed diphthong or a stressed long vowel are marked with an unbroken dash in the headword:

beiderlei, Haar, sieben

2. **ie**

Stressed **ie** pronounced [iː] is marked by an unbroken dash:

sieben

When the plural ending **-n** is added, the pronunciation changes to [-iːən]:

Allegorie, *pl* **Allegorien** [-iːən]

When **ie** occurs in an unstressed syllable the pronunciation of that syllable is given:

Hortẹnsie [-iə]

3. **ee** is pronounced [eː]

When the plural ending **-n** is added the change in pronunciation is shown:

Allee *f* **-n** [-eːən]

Consonants

Where a consonant is capable of more than one pronunciation the following rules have been assumed:

1. **v**

(i) **v** is generally pronounced [f]:

Vater ['faːtɐ]

Where this is not the case phonetics are given:

Sklave ['sklaːvə]

(ii) Words ending in **-iv** are pronounced [iːf] when undeclined, but when an ending is added the pronunciation changes to [iːv]:

aktiv [ak'tiːf]
aktive (as in **der aktive Sportler**) [ak'tiːvə]

2. **ng**

(i) **ng** is generally pronounced [ŋ]:

Finger ['fɪŋɐ]

Where this is not the case phonetics are given:

Angora [aŋ'goːra]

(ii) In compound words where the first element ends in **-n** and the second element begins with **g-** the two sounds are pronounced individually:

Eingang ['aingaŋ]
ungeheuer ['ʊngəhɔyɐ]

3. **tion** is always pronounced [-tsioːn] at the end of a word and [-tsion-] in the middle of a word:

Nation [na'tsioːn]
national [natsio'naːl]

4. **st, sp**

(i) Where **st** or **sp** occurs in the middle or at the end of a word the pronunciation is [st], [sp]:

Fest [fɛst], **Wespe** ['vɛspə]

(ii) At the beginning of a word or at the beginning of the second element of a compound word the standard pronunciation is [ʃt], [ʃp]:

Stand [ʃtant], **sperren** ['ʃpɛrən]
Abstand ['ap-ʃtant], **absperren** ['ap-ʃpɛrən]

5. **ch**

(i) **ch** is pronounced [ç] after *ä-, e-, i-, ö-, ü-, y-, ai-, ei-, äu, eu-* and after consonants:

ich [ɪç], **Milch** [mɪlç]

(ii) **ch** is pronounced [x] after *a-, o-, u-, au-*:

doch [dɔx], **Bauch** [baux]

Phonetics are given for all words beginning with **ch**.

6. **ig** is pronounced [ɪç] at the end of a word:

König ['køːniç]

When an ending beginning with a vowel is added, it is pronounced [ig]:

Könige ['køːnɪgə]

7. **h** is pronounced [h]:

(i) at the beginning of a word

(ii) between vowels in interjections:

oho [o'hoː]

(iii) in words such as **Ahorn** ['aːhɔrn] and **Uhu** ['uːhu].

It is mute in the middle and at the end of non-foreign words:

leihen ['laiən], **weh** [veː]

Where **h** is pronounced in words of foreign origin, this is shown in the text.

8. **th** is pronounced [t].
9. **qu** is pronounced [kv].
10. **z** is pronounced [ts].

Phonetics are given where these rules do not apply and for foreign words which do not follow the German pronunciation patterns.
Where more than one pronunciation is possible this is also shown.
Partial phonetics are given where only part of a word presents a pronunciation difficulty.
Where the pronunciation of a compound or derivative can be deduced from the simplex no phonetics are given.

Ausspracheangaben zum Englischen

Die Zeichen der im Text verwendeten Lautschrift entsprechen denen der *International Phonetic Association.* Die angegebene Aussprache basiert auf dem weltweit als maßgebend anerkannten „English Pronouncing Dictionary“ von Daniel Jones (vierzehnte Auflage, ausführlich überarbeitet und herausgegeben von A. C. Gimson).

Die Lautschrift gibt die Aussprache für das in Südengland gesprochene britische Englisch (Received Pronunciation) an, das in der gesamten Englisch sprechenden Welt akzeptiert und verstanden wird. Nordamerikanische Formen werden angegeben, wenn die Aussprache des betreffenden Wortes im amerikanischen Englisch erheblich abweicht (z.B. **lever**), nicht aber, wenn die Abweichung nur im „Akzent“ besteht, wenn also Verständigungsschwierigkeiten nicht zu befürchten sind.

Jedes Stichwort im englischen Teil ist mit der Lautschrift versehen. Ausnahmen dazu bilden folgende Fälle:

1. zusammengesetzte Stichwörter (*Komposita*), die getrennt geschrieben werden (z.B. **buffet car**, **buffalo grass**). Die Aussprache der einzelnen Teile ist unter dem entsprechenden Stichwort angegeben.

2. *phrasal verbs* (z.B. **bring back**, **bring down**, **bring round**), wo ebenfalls die Einzelbestandteile an anderer Stelle behandelt sind.

3. gleichlautende Stichwörter mit hochgestellten Ziffern (z.B. **bore²**, **bore³**, **bore⁴**), wo die Aussprache nur einmal beim ersten Eintrag in der Reihe (d.h. bei **bore¹**) angeführt ist.

4. wenn ein Stichwort auf eine andere Schreibweise verwiesen wird, die Aussprache aber gleich lautet (z.B. **checkered** ... *see* **chequered**). In diesem Falle wird die Aussprache nur unter dem Wort, auf das verwiesen wird (**chequered**) angegeben.

Sonstiges

1. Die Aussprache von Abkürzungen, die als Kurzwörter (*Akronyme*) gebraucht werden, ist angegeben (z.B. **NATO** ['neɪtəʊ], **ASLEF** ['æzlef]). Wenn jeder Buchstabe einzeln ausgesprochen wird (z.B. **MOT**, **RIP**) erfolgt keine Ausspracheangabe.

2. Endungen in **-less** und **-ness** sind in der Lautschrift als [-lɪs] bzw. [-nɪs] wiedergegeben. Die Aussprache [-ləs] bzw. [nəs] ist ebenso gebräuchlich.

3. Stammformen unregelmäßiger Verben: Präteritum und 1. Partizip sind gesondert an der entsprechenden Stelle in der alphabetischen Reihenfolge angeführt und dort mit der Lautschrift versehen. Die Ausspracheangabe wird bei der Grundform des Verbs nicht wiederholt. So findet man z.B. die phonetische Umschrift für **bought**, **sold** usw. unter diesen Einträgen, nicht aber unter **buy**, **sell** usw.

Acknowledgements
The editors would like to express their thanks to Mr Peter P. Hasler and Dr Kurt-Michael Pätzold for their help in the initial stages of the work on the first edition of this book.

Die Redaktion möchte Herrn Peter P. Hasler und Herrn Dr. Kurt-Michael Pätzold für ihre Mithilfe während der Anfangsstadien der Arbeit an der ersten Auflage dieses Buches ihren Dank aussprechen.

Phonetic Symbols

Zeichen der Lautschrift

Phonetic transcriptions in square brackets are given for all headwords in the English-German section, apart from compounds and from words spelt the same way and with the same pronunciation. In the German-English section, phonetics are only given where the pronunciation is not in accordance with the rules listed on page xxiii.

Die Lautschrift wird für alle Hauptstichwörter im englisch-deutschen Teil angegeben, außer dann, wenn Wörter in Schreibweise und Aussprache genau übereinstimmen. Im deutsch-englischen Teil wird die Lautschrift nur dann angegeben, wenn die Aussprache von den auf Seite xxiii gegebenen Regeln abweicht.

Vowels/Vokale

m*a*tt	[a]	
F*ah*ne	[aː]	
Vat*er*	[ɐ]	
	[ɑː]	c*al*m, p*ar*t
	[æ]	s*a*t
Ch*an*son	[ã]	
Ch*an*ce	[ɑ̃]	
	[ɑ̃ː]	double *en*t*en*dre
*E*tage	[e]	*e*gg
S*ee*le, M*eh*l	[eː]	
W*ä*sche, B*e*tt	[ɛ]	
z*äh*len	[ɛː]	
T*ein*t	[ɛ̃ː]	
mach*e*	[ə]	*a*bove
	[ɜː]	b*ur*n, *ear*n
K*i*ste	[ɪ]	p*i*t, awfull*y*
V*i*tamin	[i]	
Z*ie*l	[iː]	p*ea*t
*O*ase	[o]	
*o*ben	[oː]	
F*on*due	[õ]	
Chans*on*	[õː]	
M*o*st	[ɔ]	
	[ɒ]	c*o*t
	[ɔː]	b*or*n, j*aw*
*ö*konomisch	[ø]	
bl*ö*d	[øː]	
G*ö*tter	[œ]	
Parf*um*	[œ̃ː]	
	[ʌ]	h*u*t
z*u*letzt	[u]	
M*u*t	[uː]	p*oo*l
M*u*tter	[ʊ]	p*u*t
T*y*p	[y]	
K*ü*bel	[yː]	
S*ü*nde	[ʏ]	

Diphthongs/Diphthonge

w*ei*t	[ai]	
	[aɪ]	b*uy*, d*ie*, m*y*
H*au*s	[au]	
	[aʊ]	h*ou*se, n*ow*
	[eɪ]	p*ay*, m*a*te
	[ɛə]	p*ai*r, m*a*re
	[əʊ]	n*o*, b*oa*t
	[ɪə]	m*e*re, sh*ea*r
H*eu*, H*äu*ser	[ɔy]	
	[ɔɪ]	b*oy*, c*oi*n
	[ʊə]	t*ou*r, p*oo*r

Consonants/Konsonanten

*B*all	[b]	*b*all
mi*ch*	[ç]	
	[tʃ]	*ch*ild
*f*ern	[f]	*f*ield
*g*ern	[g]	*g*ood
*H*and	[h]	*h*and
*j*a, Mill*i*on	[j]	*y*et, mill*i*on
	[dʒ]	*j*ust
*K*ind	[k]	*k*ind, *c*atch
*l*inks, Pu*l*t	[l]	*l*eft, *l*itt*l*e
*m*att	[m]	*m*at
*N*est	[n]	*n*est
la*ng*	[ŋ]	lo*ng*
*P*aar	[p]	*p*ut
*r*ennen	[r]	*r*un
fa*s*t, fa*ss*en	[s]	*s*it
*Ch*ef, *S*tein, *Sch*lag	[ʃ]	*sh*all
*T*afel	[t]	*t*ab
	[θ]	*th*ing
	[ð]	*th*is
*w*er	[v]	*v*ery
	[w]	*w*et
Lo*ch*	[x]	lo*ch*
fi*x*	[ks]	bo*x*
*s*ingen	[z]	pod*s*, *z*ip
*Z*ahn	[ts]	
*g*enieren	[ʒ]	mea*s*ure

Other signs/Andere Zeichen

|	glottal stop/Knacklaut
[ʳ]	[r] pronounced before a vowel/vor Vokal ausgesprochenes [r]
[ˈ]	main stress/Hauptton
[ˌ]	secondary stress/Nebenton

NB: Vowels and consonants which are frequently elided (not spoken) are given in *italics:*

Vokale und Konsonanten, die häufig elidiert (nicht ausgesprochen) werden, sind *kursiv* dargestellt:

convention [kə*n*ˈvenʃən]
attempt [əˈtem*p*t]

WÖRTERBUCH DEUTSCH~ENGLISCH

GERMAN~ENGLISH DICTIONARY

A, a [aː] *nt* -, - *or (inf)* -s, -s A, a ◆ **das A und (das) O** *(fig)* the essential thing(s), the be-all and end-all; *(eines Wissensgebietes)* the basics *pl*; **von A bis Z** *(fig inf)* from beginning to end, from A to Z; **sie/ihr alle, von A bis Z** them/you, the whole lot of them/you; **wer A sagt, muß auch B sagen** *(prov)* in for a penny, in for a pound *(prov)*; *(moralisch)* if you start something, you should see it through.

à [a] *prep (esp Comm)* at.

Ä, ä [ɛː] *nt* -, - *or (inf)* -s, -s Ae, ae, A/a umlaut.

Aa [aˈ|a] *nt* -, *no pl (baby-talk)* ~ **machen** to do big jobs *(baby-talk) or* number two *(baby-talk)*.

AA[1] [aːˈ|aː] *nt* -s, *no pl abbr of* **Auswärtiges Amt** FO *(Brit)*.

AA[2] [aːˈ|aː] *m* -s, -s *abbr of* **Anonyme Alkoholiker** AA.

Aal *m* -(e)s, -e eel ◆ **sich (drehen und) winden wie ein ~** *(aus Verlegenheit)* to wriggle like an eel; *(aus Unaufrichtigkeit)* to try and wriggle out of it; **glatt wie ein ~** *(fig)* (as) slippery as an eel.

aalen *vr (inf)* to stretch out ◆ **sich in der Sonne ~** to bask in the sun.

Aal-: a~glatt *adj (pej)* slippery (as an eel), slick; **er verstand es meisterhaft, sich a~glatt herauszureden** he very slickly *or* smoothly managed to talk himself out of it; **~suppe** *f* eel soup.

a.a.O. *abbr of* **am angegebenen** *or* **angeführten Ort** loc cit.

Aar *m* -(e)s, -e *(obs liter)* eagle, lord of the skies *(liter)*.

Aargau *m* -s **der ~** the Aargau.

Aas *nt* -es, -e **(a)** *(Tierleiche)* carrion, rotting carcass. **(b)** *pl* **Äser** *(inf: Luder)* bugger *(sl)*, sod *(sl)*, devil *(inf)* ◆ **kein ~** not a single bloody person *(inf)*.

aasen *vi (inf)* to be wasteful ◆ **mit etw ~** to waste sth; *mit Geld, Gütern auch* to squander sth, to be extravagant *or* wasteful with sth; *mit Gesundheit* to ruin sth.

Aas-: ~fresser *m* scavenger, carrion-eater; **~geier** *m (lit, fig)* vulture.

aasig [1] *adj attr* abominable, horrible, disgusting. **2** *adv (inf: sehr)* horribly, abominably *(inf)*.

Aaskäfer *m* burying *or* sexton beetle.

ab [ap] [1] *adv* off, away; *(Theat)* exit *sing*, exeunt *pl* ◆ **die nächste Straße rechts ~** the next street (off) to *or* on the right; **~ Zoologischer Garten** from Zoological Gardens; **~ Hamburg** after Hamburg; **München ~ 12[20] Uhr** *(Rail)* leaving Munich 12.20; **~ wann?** from when?, as of when?; **~ nach Hause** go *or* off you go home; **~ ins Bett mit euch!** off to bed with you *or* you go; **Mütze/Helm ~!** caps/hats off; **Tell ~** exit Tell; **N und M ~** *(Theat)* exeunt N and M; **~ durch die Mitte** *(inf)* beat it! *(inf)*, hop it! *(inf)*; **kommt jetzt, ~ durch die Mitte!** come on, let's beat *or* hop it! *(inf)*; **~ und zu** *or (N Ger)* **an** from time to time, now and again, now and then; *siehe* **von**.

[2] *prep +dat* **(a)** *(räumlich)* from; *(zeitlich)* from, as of, as from ◆ **Kinder ~ 14 Jahren** children from (the age of) 14 up; **alle ~ Gehaltsstufe 4** everybody from grade 4 up; **Soldaten ~ Gefreitem** soldiers from private up; **~ Werk** *(Comm)* ex works; **~ sofort** as of now/then. **(b)** *(Sw: in Zeitangaben)* past; **Viertel ~ 7** a quarter past 7.

Abakus *m* -, - abacus.

ab|änderbar, ab|änderlich *(old) adj* amendable.

ab|ändern *vt sep* to alter *(in +acc* to); *(überarbeiten auch)* to revise; *Gesetzentwurf* to amend *(in +acc* to); *Strafe, Urteil* to revise *(in +acc* to).

Ab|änderung *f siehe vt* alteration *(gen* to); revision; amendment ◆ **in ~** *(Parl, Jur)* in amendment.

Ab|änderungs-: ~antrag *m (Parl)* proposed amendment; **einen ~antrag einbringen** to submit an amendment; **~vorschlag** *m* proposed amendment; **einen ~vorschlag machen** to propose an amendment.

ab|arbeiten *sep* [1] *vt* **(a)** *Schuld* to work off; *Überfahrt* to work; *(hinter sich bringen) Vertragszeit* to work. **(b)** *(Comput) Programme* to run; *Befehle* to execute.

[2] *vr* to slave (away), to work like a slave; *siehe* **abgearbeitet**.

Ab|art *f* variety *(auch Biol)*; *(Variation)* variation *(gen* on).

ab|artig *adj* [1] (a) abnormal, deviant, unnatural. **(b)** *(widersinnig)* perverse.

[2] *adv (inf)* **das tut ~ weh** that hurts like hell *(inf)*.

Ab|artigkeit *f* abnormality, deviancy.

Abbau *m* -(e)s, *no pl* **(a)** *(Förderung) (über Tage)* quarrying; *(unter Tage)* mining.

(b) *(lit, fig: Demontage)* dismantling.

(c) *(Chem)* decomposition; *(im Körper auch)* breakdown; *(fig: Verfall)* decline; *(der Persönlichkeit)* disintegration.

(d) *(Verringerung) (von Personal, Produktion etc)* reduction *(gen* in, of), cutback *(gen* in); *(von überflüssigen Vorräten)* gradual elimination *(gen* of); *(von Preisen)* cut *(gen* in), reduction *(gen* in, of); *(von Privilegien)* reduction *(gen* of), stripping away *(gen* of); *(von Vorurteilen)* gradual collapse *(gen* of) ◆ **der ~ von Beamtenstellen** the reduction in the number of civil service posts.

abbaubar *adj (Chem)* degradable ◆ **schwer ~e Chemikalien** chemicals that are difficult to break down; **biologisch ~** biodegradable.

abbauen *sep* [1] *vt* **(a)** *(fördern) (über Tage)* to quarry; *(unter Tage)* to mine.

(b) *(demontieren) Gerüst, System* to dismantle; *Maschine auch* to strip down; *Gerüst auch* to take down; *Kulissen* to take down, to strike; *Zelt* to strike; *Lager* to break, to strike ◆ **ein System allmählich ~** to phase out a system.

(c) *(Chem)* to break down, to decompose.

(d) *(verringern) Produktion, Personal, Bürokratie* to cut back, to reduce, to cut down on; *Preise* to reduce, to cut back; *Arbeitsplätze, -kräfte* to reduce the number of; *Privilegien* to cut back, to strip away.

[2] *vi (inf) (Sportler etc)* to go downhill; *(erlahmen)* to flag, to wilt; *(abschalten)* to switch off.

Abbauprodukt *nt (Chem)* by-product.

abbeißen *sep irreg* [1] *vt* to bite off ◆ **eine Zigarre ~** to bite the end off a cigar; **sich** *(dat)* **die Zunge ~** to bite one's tongue off.

[2] *vi* to take a bite ◆ **nun beiß doch mal richtig ab!** now bite it off properly!

abbeizen *vt sep* to strip.

Abbeizmittel *nt* paint stripper.

abbekommen* *vt sep irreg* **(a)** to get ◆ **etwas ~** to get some (of it); *(beschädigt werden)* to get damaged; *(verletzt werden)* to get hurt; *(Prügel ~)* to catch *or* cop it *(inf)*; **das Auto/er hat dabei ganz schön was ~** *(inf)* the car/he really copped it *(inf)*; **nichts ~** not to get any (of it); *(nicht beschädigt werden)* not to get damaged; *(nicht verletzt werden)* to come off unscathed; **sein(en) Teil ~** *(lit, fig)* to get one's fair share.

(b) *(abmachen können)* to get off *(von etw* sth).

abberufen* *vt sep irreg Diplomaten, Minister* to recall ◆ **(von Gott) ~ werden** *(euph)* to be called to one's maker.

Abberufung *f* recall; *(euph: Tod)* departure from this life.

abbestellen* *vt sep* to cancel; *jdn auch* to tell not to call *or* come; *Telefon* to have disconnected.

Abbestellung *f siehe vt* cancellation; disconnection.

abbetteln *vt sep* **jdm etw ~** to scrounge sth off *or* from sb *(inf)*.

abbezahlen* *sep* [1] *vt Raten, Auto etc* to pay off.

[2] *vi (auf Raten)* to pay in instalments; *(Raten ~)* to pay sth off.

abbiegen *sep irreg* [1] *vt* **(a)** to bend; *(abbrechen)* to bend off.

(b) *(inf: verhindern) Frage, Thema* to head off, to avoid; *Frage* to deflect ◆ **das Gespräch ~** to change the subject; **zum Glück konnte ich das ~** luckily I managed to stop that; **diesen Vorschlag hat die Gewerkschaft abgebogen** the union put a stop to this proposal.

[2] *vi aux sein* to turn off *(in +acc* into); *(bei Gabelungen auch)* to fork off; *(Straße)* to bend ◆ **nach rechts ~** to turn (off to the) right; to fork right; to bend (to the) right.

Abbiegerspur *f (Mot)* filter lane.

Abbild *nt (Nachahmung, Kopie)* copy, reproduction; *(Spiegelbild)* reflection; *(Wiedergabe)* picture, portrayal, representation; *(von Mensch)* image, likeness ◆ **er ist das genaue ~ seines Vaters** he's the spitting image of his father.

abbilden *vt sep (lit, fig)* to depict, to portray, to show; *Verhältnisse etc auch* to reflect; *(wiedergeben)* to reproduce ◆ **auf der Titelseite ist ein Teddybär abgebildet** there's a picture of a teddy bear on the front page; **auf dem Foto ist eine Schulklasse abgebildet** there's a school class (shown) in the photo.

Abbildung *f* **(a)** *(das Abbilden)* depiction, portrayal; *(Wiedergabe)* reproduction. **(b)** *(Illustration)* illustration; *(Schaubild)* diagram ◆ **siehe ~ S.12** see the illustration on p12; **das Buch ist mit zahlreichen ~en versehen** the book is copiously illustrated *or* has numerous illustrations.

abbinden *sep irreg* [1] *vt* **(a)** to undo, to untie ◆ **sich** *(dat)* **die Schürze ~** to take off one's apron. **(b)** *(Med) Arm, Bein etc* to ligature. **(c)** *(Cook)* to bind.

[2] *vi (Beton, Mörtel)* to set; *(Cook)* to bind.

Abbitte *f* apology ◆ **(bei jdm wegen etw) ~ tun** *or* **leisten** to make *or* offer one's apologies *or* to apologize (to sb for sth).

abbitten *vt sep irreg (liter)* **jdm etw ~** to beg sb's pardon for sth, to make *or*

⚠: for details of spelling reform, see supplement

offer one's apologies to sb for sth.

abblasen *sep irreg* [1] *vt* **(a)** *Staub, Schmutz* to blow off (*von etw* sth); *Tisch, Buch* to blow the dust *etc* off, to blow clean; *Gas* to release, to let off ◆ **eine Hauswand mit Sandstrahl ~** to sandblast a house wall. **(b)** (*Tech*) *Hochofen* to let burn down. **(c)** (*inf*) *Veranstaltung, Feier, Streik* to call off.
[2] *vi* (*Tech: Hochofen*) to burn down.

abblättern *vi sep aux sein* (*Putz, Farbe*) to flake *or* peel (off).

abbleiben *vi sep irreg aux sein* (*N Ger inf*) to get to (*inf*) ◆ **wo ist er abgeblieben?** where has he got to?; **irgendwo muß er/es abgeblieben sein** he/it must be somewhere.

abblendbar *adj Rückspiegel* anti-dazzle.

Abblende *f* (*Film*) fade(-out).

abblenden *sep* [1] *vt Lampe* to shade, to screen; (*Aut*) *Scheinwerfer* to dip (*Brit*), to dim (*US*).
[2] *vi* (*Phot*) to stop down; (*Film*) to fade out; (*Aut*) to dip (*Brit*) *or* dim one's headlights ◆ **dann wurde abgeblendet** the scene (was) faded out.

Abblendlicht *nt* (*Aut*) dipped (*Brit*) *or* dimmed (*US*) headlights *pl* ◆ **mit ~ fahren** to drive on dipped *or* dimmed headlights.

abblitzen *vi sep aux sein* (*inf*) to be sent packing (*bei* by) (*inf*) ◆ **jdn ~ lassen** to send sb packing (*inf*), to send sb off with a flea in his/her ear (*inf*).

abblocken *sep* [1] *vt* (*Sport, fig*) to block; *Gegner* to stall.
[2] *vi* to stall.

abblühen *vi sep aux sein* (*rare*) *siehe* **verblühen.**

Abbrand *m* **(a)** (*Verbrennen*) combustion. **(b)** (*Kernenergie*) burn-up.

abbrausen *sep* [1] *vt* to give a shower; *Körperteil* to wash under the shower ◆ **sich ~** to have *or* take a shower, to shower.
[2] *vi aux sein* (*inf*) to roar off *or* away.

abbrechen *sep irreg* [1] *vt* **(a)** to break off; *Zweig, Ast auch* to snap off; *Bleistift* to break, to snap ◆ **etw von etw ~** to break sth off sth; **(nun) brich dir (mal) keine Verzierung(en)** (*inf*) *or* **keinen** (*sl*) **ab!** don't make such a palaver (*inf*) *or* song and dance (*inf*); **sich** (*dat*) **einen ~** (*sl*) (*Umstände machen*) to make heavy weather of it (*inf*); (*sich sehr anstrengen*) to go to a lot of bother, to bust one's arse (*vulg*).
(b) (*abbauen*) *Zelt* to strike; *Lager auch* to break; (*niederreißen*) to demolish; *Gebäude* to demolish, to pull *or* tear down; *siehe* **Zelt.**
(c) (*beenden*) to break off; *Raumflug, Experiment,* (*Comput*) *Operation* to abort; *Veranstaltung* to stop; *Streik* to call off; *Schwangerschaft* to terminate; *siehe* **abgebrochen.**
[2] *vi* **(a)** *aux sein* to break off; (*Ast, Zweig auch*) to snap off; (*Bleistift, Fingernagel*) to break.
(b) (*aufhören*) to break off, to stop.

Abbrecher(in *f*) *m* **-s, -** (*Student*) drop-out.

abbremsen *sep* [1] *vt Motor* to brake; (*fig*) to curb ◆ **auf 30 ~** to brake down to 30.
[2] *vi siehe* **bremsen.**

abbrennen *sep irreg* [1] *vt Wiesen* to burn off *or* away the stubble in; *Böschung* to burn off *or* away the scrub on; *Gehöft, Dorf* to burn down; *Feuerwerk, Rakete* to let off; *Kerze etc* to burn; (*wegbrennen*) *Lack* to burn off; (*Tech: abbeizen*) to pickle, to scour; *Stahl* to blaze off ◆ **ein Feuerwerk ~** to have fireworks *or* a firework display.
[2] *vi aux sein* to burn down ◆ **unser Gehöft ist/wir sind abgebrannt** our farm was/we were burnt down; **dreimal umgezogen ist einmal abgebrannt** (*prov*) by the time you've moved house three times, you've lost as much as if the place had been burnt out; *siehe* **abgebrannt.**

Abbreviatur [abrevia'tuːɐ] *f* (*Typ, Mus*) abbreviation.

abbringen *vt sep irreg* **(a) jdn davon ~, etw zu tun** to stop sb doing sth; (*abraten auch*) to persuade sb not to do sth, to dissuade sb from doing sth; **jdn von etw ~** to make sb change his/her mind about sth; **ich lasse mich von meiner Meinung nicht ~** you won't get me to change my mind, nothing will make me change my mind; **jdn vom Thema ~** to get sb off the subject; **jdn/einen Hund von der Spur ~** to throw *or* put sb/a dog off the scent; **jdn/etw vom Kurs ~** to throw *or* put sb/sth off course.
(b) (*inf: esp S Ger*) *Deckel etc* to get off.

abbröckeln *vi sep aux sein* to crumble away; (*fig*) to fall off (*auch St Ex*), to drop off ◆ **die Aktienkurse sind am A~** the share prices are falling (off); **die Familie/der Ruf der Firma ist am A~** the family/firm's reputation is gradually declining.

Abbruch *m, no pl* **(a)** (*das Niederreißen*) demolition; (*von Gebäuden auch*) pulling down ◆ **auf ~ verkaufen** to sell for demolition; **auf ~ stehen** to be scheduled *or* due for demolition, to be condemned.
(b) (*Beendigung*) (*von Schwangerschaft*) termination; (*von Beziehungen, Verhandlungen, Reise*) breaking off; (*von Raumflug etc*) abortion, aborting; (*von Veranstaltung*) stopping ◆ **einem Land mit ~ der diplomatischen Beziehungen drohen** to threaten to break off diplomatic relations with a country; **es kam zum ~ des Kampfes** the fight had to be stopped.
(c) (*Schaden*) harm, damage ◆ **einer Sache** (*dat*) **~ tun** to harm *or* damage sth, to do (some) harm *or* damage to sth; **das tut der Liebe keinen ~** it doesn't harm their/our relationship; **das tut unseren Interessen ~** that is detrimental to our interests.

Abbruch-: ~arbeiten *pl* demolition work; **~firma** *f* demolition firm; **~liste** *f siehe* **Abrißliste; a~reif** *adj* only fit for demolition; (*zum ~ freigegeben*) condemned.

abbrühen *vt sep* to scald; *Mandeln* to blanch; *siehe* **abgebrüht.**

abbrummen *sep* [1] *vt* (*inf*) *Zeit* to do (*inf*) ◆ **eine Strafe ~** to do time (*inf*).
[2] *vi aux sein* (*inf*) to roar off *or* away.

abbuchen *vt sep* (*im Einzelfall*) to debit (*von* to, against); (*durch Dauerauftrag*) to pay by standing order (*von* from); (*fig: abschreiben*) to write off ◆ **für das A~ erhebt die Bank Gebühren** the bank makes a charge for each debit/for a standing order.

Abbuchung *f siehe vt* debit; (payment by) standing order; writing off ◆ **etw durch ~ erledigen** to settle sth by standing order.

abbummeln *vt sep* (*inf*) *Stunden* to take off ◆ **Überstunden ~** to take time off for overtime done.

abbürsten *vt sep* **(a)** *Staub* to brush off (*von etw* sth); *Kleid, Mantel, Jacke* to brush (down); *Schuhe* to brush. **(b)** (*inf: heruntermachen*) **jdn ~** to give sb the brush-off, to brush sb aside.

abbusseln *vt sep* (*Aus inf*) *siehe* **abküssen.**

abbüßen *vt sep Strafe* to serve.

Abbüßung *f* serving ◆ **nach ~ der Strafe** after serving *or* having served the sentence.

Abc [abe'tseː, aːbeː'tseː] *nt* **-, -** (*lit, fig*) ABC ◆ **Wörter/Namen nach dem ~ ordnen** to arrange words/names in alphabetical order *or* alphabetically.

ABC- *in cpds* (*Mil*) atomic, biological and chemical, Abc.

abchecken ['aptʃɛkn] *vt sep* to check; (*abhaken*) to check off (*US*), to tick off (*Brit*).

Abc-Schütze *m* (*hum*) school-beginner ◆ **dies Bild zeigt mich als ~n** this picture shows me when I was starting school.

Abdachung *f* **(a)** (*Geog*) declivity, downward slope. **(b)** (*Build*) camber, cambering.

abdämmen *vt sep Fluß* to dam (up); (*fig*) to curb, to check.

Abdampf *m* exhaust steam.

abdampfen *sep* [1] *vi aux sein* **(a)** (*Speisen*) to dry off. **(b)** (*Chem: verdunsten*) to evaporate. **(c)** (*Zug*) to steam off; (*fig inf: losgehen, -fahren*) to hit the trail (*inf*) *or* road (*inf*), to push off (*inf*).
[2] *vt* (*Chem: verdunsten lassen*) to evaporate.

abdämpfen *vt sep siehe* **dämpfen.**

abdanken *sep* [1] *vi* to resign; (*König etc*) to abdicate.
[2] *vt* (*old*) *siehe* **abgedankt.**

Abdankung *f* **(a)** (*Thronverzicht*) abdication; (*Rücktritt*) resignation ◆ **jdn zur ~ zwingen** to force sb to abdicate/resign. **(b)** (*Dienstentlassung*) retirement. **(c)** (*Sw: Trauerfeier*) funeral service.

abdecken *vt sep* **(a)** (*herunternehmen*) *Bettdecke* to turn back *or* down.
(b) (*freilegen*) *Tisch* to clear; *Bett* to turn down; *Haus* to tear the roof off.
(c) (*old: Fell abziehen*) *Tierkadaver* to flay, to skin.
(d) (*zudecken*) *Grab, Loch* to cover (over); (*verdecken auch*) to hide.
(e) (*schützen, ausgleichen, einschließen*) to cover; (*Ftbl auch*) to mark.
(f) (*fig*) *Bereich, Thema* to cover.

Abdecker(in *f*) *m* **-s, -** knacker.

Abdeckerei *f* knacker's yard.

Abdeckung *f* **(a)** cover. **(b)** *no pl* (*Vorgang*) covering.

abdichten *vt sep* (*isolieren*) to insulate; (*verschließen*) *Loch, Leck, Rohr* to seal (up); *Ritzen* to fill, to stop up ◆ **gegen Luft/Wasser ~** to make airtight/watertight; **gegen Feuchtigkeit/Zugluft ~** to damp-proof/(make) draught-proof; **gegen Lärm/Geräusch/Schall ~** to soundproof.

Abdichtung *f* (*Isolierung*) insulation; (*das Isolieren auch*) insulating; (*Verschluß, Dichtung*) seal; (*das Verschließen*) sealing; (*von Ritzen*) filling, stopping up ◆ **~ gegen Zugluft/Feuchtigkeit/Wasser** draughtproofing/damp-proofing /waterproofing; **~ gegen Lärm/Geräusch/Schall** soundproofing.

abdienen *vt sep* (*old: abarbeiten*) to work off; (*Mil: ableisten*) to serve.

Abdikation *f* (*old*) abdication.

abdingbar *adj* (*Jur*) capable of alteration subject to mutual agreement.

abdingen, *pret* **dingte ab,** *ptp* **abgedungen** *vt sep* (*rare*) **jdm etw ~** *Zugeständnis* to strike a deal with sb for sth; **diese Rechte lassen wir uns nicht ~** we shall not cede these rights.

abdizieren* *vi insep* (*old*) *siehe* **abdanken.**

abdorren *vi sep aux sein* (*Zweig*) to dry up, to wither.

abdrängen *vt sep* to push away (*von* from) *or* out of the way (*von* of); (*fig*) *Bettler etc* to shake off ◆ **einen Spieler vom Ball ~** to push *or* barge a player off the ball; **vom Winde abgedrängt werden** to be blown off course (by the wind).

abdrehen *sep* [1] *vt* **(a)** *Gas, Wasser, Hahn* to turn off; *Licht, Radio auch* to switch off.
(b) *Film* to shoot, to film.
(c) *Hals* to wring ◆ **er drehte dem Huhn/der Blume den Kopf ab** he wrung the chicken's neck/he twisted the head off the flower; **jdm den Hals** *or* **die Gurgel ~** to wring sb's neck (*inf*); (*sl: ruinieren*) to strangle sb, to bankrupt sb.
[2] *vi aux sein or haben* (*Richtung ändern*) to change course; (*zur Seite auch*) to veer off *or* away ◆ **nach Osten ~** to turn east.

abdreschen *vt sep siehe* **abgedroschen.**

Abdrift *f* **-, -en** (*Naut, Aviat*) drift.

abdriften *vi sep aux sein* (*Naut, Aviat, fig*) to drift off.

abdrosseln *vt sep Motor* to throttle back *or* (*gänzlich auch*) down; (*fig*) *Produktion* to cut back, to cut down on.

Abdrosselung, △**Abdroßlung** *f* throttling back/down; (*fig*) cutback (*gen* in).

Abdruck[1] *m* **-(e)s, Abdrücke** imprint, impression; (*Stempel~*) stamp; (*von Schlüssel*) impression, mould; (*Finger~, Fuß~*) print; (*Gebiß~*) mould, cast, impression; (*Gesteins~*) imprint, impression, cast ◆ **einen ~ abnehmen** *or* **machen** (*inf*) to take *or* make an impression.

Abdruck[2] *m* **-(e)s, -e** (*das Nachdrucken*) reprinting; (*das Kopieren*) copying;

(*Kopie*) copy; (*Nachdruck*) reprint ◆ **der ~ dieses Romans wurde verboten** it was forbidden to reprint this novel; **ich habe den ~ des Interviews im SPIEGEL gelesen** I read the text *or* printed version of the interview in Spiegel; **dieser Roman erschien auch als ~ in ...** this novel was also printed in ...

abdrucken *vt sep* to print ◆ **wieder ~** to reprint.

abdrücken *sep* [1] *vt* **(a)** *Gewehr* to fire.
(b) (*inf*) *jdn* to squeeze, to hug.
(c) (*nachbilden*) to make an impression of.
(d) *Vene* to constrict ◆ **jdm fast die Finger/Hand ~** to almost squeeze sb's fingers/hand off; **jdm die Luft ~** (*inf*) (*lit*) to squeeze all the breath out of sb; (*fig*) to force sb into bankruptcy, to squeeze the lifeblood out of sb.
[2] *vi* to pull *or* squeeze the trigger.
[3] *vr* to leave an imprint *or* impression ◆ **sich (durch etw) ~** to show through (sth).

abducken *vi sep* (*Boxen*) to duck.

abdunkeln *vt sep Lampe* to dim; *Zimmer auch* to darken; *Farbe* to darken, to make darker.

abduschen *vt sep siehe* **abbrausen 1.**

ab|ebben *vi sep aux sein* to die *or* fade away; (*Zorn, Lärm auch*) to abate.

⚠**abend** *adv* **heute/gestern/morgen/Mittwoch ~** this/yesterday/tomorrow/ Wednesday evening, tonight/last/tomorrow/Wednesday night.

-abend *m* **der Mittwoch~** Wednesday evening *or* night.

Abend *m* **-s, -e (a)** evening ◆ **am ~** in the evening; (*jeden ~*) in the evening(s); **am ~ des 4. April** on the evening *or* night of April 4th; **die Vorstellung wird zweimal pro ~ gegeben** there are two performances every night *or* evening; **jeden ~** every evening *or* night; **gegen ~** towards (the) evening; **~ für** *or* **um** (*geh*) ~ every evening *or* night, night after night; **am nächsten** *or* **den nächsten ~** the next evening; **eines ~s** one evening; **den ganzen ~ über** the whole evening; **es wird ~** it's getting late, evening is drawing on; **es wurde ~** evening came; **jdm guten ~ sagen** to say good evening to sb, to bid sb good evening (*form*); **guten ~** good evening; **'n ~** [na:mt] (*inf*) evening (*inf*); **der ~ kommt** (*geh*) *or* **naht** (*liter*) evening is drawing nigh (*liter*) *or* on; **des ~s** (*geh*) in the evening(s), of an evening; **du kannst mich am ~ besuchen!** (*euph inf*) you can take a running jump (*inf*); **zu ~ essen** to have supper *or* dinner; **je später der ~, desto schöner** *or* **netter die Gäste** (*prov*) the best guests always come late; **es ist noch nicht aller Tage ~** it's early days still *or* yet; **man soll den Tag nicht vor dem ~ loben** (*Prov*) don't count your chickens before they're hatched (*Prov*).
(b) (*Vor~*) eve ◆ **am ~ vor der Schlacht** on the eve of the battle.
(c) (*liter: Ende*) close ◆ **am ~ des Lebens** in the twilight *or* evening of one's life (*liter*), in one's twilight years (*liter*); **am ~ des Jahrhunderts** towards the close of the century.

Abend- *in cpds* evening; **~andacht** *f* evening service; **~anzug** *m* dinner jacket *or* suit, DJ (*inf*), tuxedo (*US*); **im ~anzug erscheinen** to come in a dinner jacket/dinner jackets *etc*; **~blatt** *nt* evening (news)paper; **~brot** *nt* supper, tea (*Scot, N Engl*); **~brot essen** to have (one's) supper/tea; **~dämmerung** *f* dusk, twilight.

abendelang *adj attr* night after *or* upon night, evening after *or* upon evening ◆ **unsere ~en Diskussionen** our discussions night after *or* upon night.

Abend-: ~essen *nt* supper, evening meal, dinner; **mit dem ~essen auf jdn warten** to wait with supper *or* dinner *or* one's evening meal for sb; **~friede(n)** *m* (*liter*) still *or* quiet of the evening; **a~füllend** *adj* taking up the whole evening; *Film, Stück* full-length; **a~füllend sein** to take up *or* fill the whole evening; **~gesellschaft** *f* soirée; **~gymnasium** *nt* night school (*where one can study for the Abitur*); **~kasse** *f* (*Theat*) box office; **~kleid** *nt* evening dress *or* gown; **~kurs(us)** *m* evening course, evening classes *pl* (*für* in); **~land** *nt, no pl* (*geh*) West, western world, Occident (*liter*); **das christliche ~land** the Christian West; **a~ländisch** (*geh*) [1] *adj* western, occidental (*liter*); [2] *adv* in a western way *or* fashion.

abendlich *adj no pred* evening *attr* ◆ **~ stattfindende Veranstaltungen** evening events, events taking place in the evening; **die ~e Stille** the quiet *or* still of evening; **die ~e Kühle** the cool of the evening; **es war schon um drei Uhr ~ kühl** at three it was already as cool as (in the) evening.

Abendmahl *nt* **(a)** (*Eccl*) Communion, Lord's Supper ◆ **das ~ nehmen** *or* **empfangen** to take *or* receive Communion, to communicate (*form*); **das ~ spenden** *or* **reichen** *or* **erteilen** to administer (Holy) Communion, to communicate (*form*); **zum ~ gehen** to go to (Holy) Communion.
(b) das (Letzte) ~ the Last Supper.

Abendmahls-: ~gottesdienst *m* (Holy) Communion, Communion service; **~wein** *m* Communion wine.

Abend-: ~mahlzeit *f* evening meal; **~programm** *nt* (*Rad, TV*) evening('s) programmes *pl*; **damit ist unser heutiges ~programm beendet** and that ends our programmes for this evening; **~rot** *nt*, **~röte** *f* (*liter*) sunset; **die Felder lagen im ~rot** the fields lay bathed in the glow of the sunset *or* the light of the setting sun.

abends *adv* in the evening; (*jeden Abend*) in the evening(s) ◆ **spät ~** late in the evening; **~ um neun** at nine in the evening.

Abend-: ~schule *f* night school; **~schüler** *m* night-school student; **~stern** *m* evening star; **~stille** *f* still *or* quiet of the evening; **~stunde** *f* evening (hour); **zu dieser späten ~stunde** at this late hour of the evening; **die frühen/schönen ~stunden** the early hours of the evening/the beautiful evening hours; **sich bis in die ~stunden hinziehen** to go on (late) into the evening; **~vorstellung** *f* evening performance; (*Film auch*) evening showing; **~zeit** *f* **zur ~zeit** in the evening; **~zeitung** *f* evening paper.

Abenteuer *nt* **-s, -** adventure; (*Liebes~ auch*) affair ◆ **ein militärisches/ politisches/verbrecherisches ~** a military/political/criminal venture; **auf ~ ausgehen/aussein** to go out in search of adventure/to be looking for adventure; **die ~ des Geistes** (*liter*) intellectual adventure.

Abenteuer- *in cpds* adventure; **~ferien** *pl siehe* **~urlaub**.

abenteuerlich *adj* **(a)** adventurous; (*erlebnishungrig auch*) adventuresome.
(b) (*phantastisch*) bizarre; *Gestalten, Verkleidung auch* eccentric; *Erzählung auch* fantastic.

Abenteuerlichkeit *f siehe adj* adventurousness; bizarreness; eccentricity; (*Unwahrscheinlichkeit*) improbability, unlikeliness.

Abenteuer-: ~lust *f* thirst for adventure; **von der ~lust gepackt werden** to be seized with a thirst for adventure; **~roman** *m* adventure story; **~spielplatz** *m* adventure playground; **~urlaub** *m* adventure holiday.

Abenteurer *m* **-s, -** adventurer (*auch pej*).

Abenteurer- *in cpds siehe* **Abenteuer-**.

Abenteu(r)erin *f* adventuress.

Abenteurernatur *f* adventurous person, adventurer.

aber [1] *conj* **(a)** but ◆ **~ dennoch** *or* **trotzdem** but still; **es regnete, ~ dennoch haben wir uns köstlich amüsiert** it was raining, but we still had a great time *or* but we had a great time though *or* all the same; **schönes Wetter heute, was? — ja, ~ etwas kalt** nice weather, eh? — yes, a bit cold though *or* yes but it's a bit cold; **..., ~ ich wünschte, sie hätte es mir gesagt** (al)though *or* but I wished she had told me; **komm doch mit! — ~ ich habe keine Zeit** *or* **ich habe ~ keine Zeit!** come with us! — but I haven't got the time!; **da er ~ nicht wußte ...** but since he didn't know ..., since, however, he didn't know ..., however, since he didn't know ...; **oder ~** or else.
(b) (*zur Verstärkung*) **~ ja!** oh, yes!; (*sicher*) but of course; **~ selbstverständlich** *or* **gewiß (doch)!** but of course; **~ nein!** oh, no!; (*selbstverständlich nicht*) of course not!; **~ Renate!** but Renate!; **~, ~!** now, now!, tut, tut!, come, come!; **~ ich kann nichts dafür!** but I can't help it!; **~ das wollte ich doch gar nicht!** but I didn't want that!; **das ist ~ schrecklich!** but that's awful!; **das mach' ich ~ nicht!** I will *not* do that!; **dann ist er ~ wütend geworden** then he really got mad, (God), did he get mad!; **das ist ~ heiß/schön!** that's really hot/ nice; **du hast ~ einen schönen Ball** you've got a nice ball, haven't you?; **bist du ~ braun!** aren't you brown!; **das geht ~ zu weit!** that's just *or* really going too far!; **schreib das noch mal ab, ~ sauber!** write it out again, and make it tidy!
[2] *adv* (*liter*) **~ und ~mals** again and again, time and again; **tausend und ~ tausend** *or* (*Aus*) **~tausend** thousands and *or* upon thousands.

Aber *nt* **-s, -** *or* (*inf*) **-s** but ◆ **kein ~!** no buts (about it); **die Sache hat ein ~** there's just one problem *or* snag.

Aberglaube(n) *m* superstition; (*fig auch*) myth ◆ **zum ~n neigen** to be superstitious.

abergläubisch *adj* superstitious ◆ **er hängt ~ an .../er fürchtet sich ~ vor ...** he has a superstitious attachment to .../fear of ...

ab|erkennen* *vt sep or* (*rare*) *insep irreg* **jdm etw ~** to deprive *or* strip sb of sth; **jdm den Sieg ~** (*Sport*) to disallow sb's victory.

Ab|erkennung *f* deprivation, stripping; (*von Sieg*) disallowing.

aber-: ~malig *adj attr* repeated; **~mals** *adv* once again *or* more.

ab|ernten *vti sep* to harvest.

Ab|erration *f* (*Astron*) aberration.

Aber-: a~tausend *num* (*esp Aus*) thousands upon thousands of; **~tausende** *pl* (*esp Aus*) thousands upon thousands *pl*.

Aberwitz *m* (*liter*) *siehe* **Wahnwitz**.

aberwitzig *adj* (*liter*) *siehe* **wahnwitzig**.

ab|essen *sep irreg* [1] *vt* **(a)** (*herunteressen*) to eat ◆ **sie aß nur die Erdbeeren von der Torte ab** she just ate the strawberries off the tart. **(b)** (*leer essen*) to eat *or* finish up; *Teller* to finish.
[2] *vi* to eat up.

Abessinien [-iən] *nt* **-s** Abyssinia.

Abessinier(in *f*) [-iɐ, -iərɪn] *m* **-s, -** Abyssinian.

abessinisch *adj* Abyssinian.

Abf. *abbr of* **Abfahrt** departure, dep.

abfackeln *vt Gas* to burn off.

abfahrbereit *adj siehe* **abfahrtbereit**.

abfahren *sep irreg aux sein* [1] *vi* **(a)** to leave, to depart (*form*); (*Schiff auch*) to sail; (*Ski: zu Tal fahren*) to ski down ◆ **~!** (*Rail*) *order given to a train driver to pull out;* **der Zug fährt um 8^{00} in** *or* **von Bremen ab** the train leaves Bremen *or* departs from Bremen at 8 o'clock; **der Zug fährt in Kürze ab** the train will be leaving *or* will depart shortly; **der Zug ist abgefahren** (*lit*) the train has left *or* gone; (*fig*) we've/you've *etc* missed the boat; **wir müssen schon um 7^{00} ~** we must set off *or* leave *or* start (out) at 7 o'clock.
(b) (*inf: abgewiesen werden*) **jdn ~ lassen** to tell sb to push off (*inf*) *or* get lost (*inf*); **er ist bei ihr abgefahren** she told him to push off (*inf*) *or* get lost (*inf*).
(c) (*sl*) **auf jdn/etw ~** to go for sb/sth (*inf*), to be into sb/sth (*inf*); **sie fährt voll auf ihn ab** she's into him in a big way (*inf*).
[2] *vt* **(a)** *Güter* to take away, to remove, to cart off (*inf*).
(b) *Körperteil* to cut off, to sever; *Stück von Mauer etc* to knock off ◆ **der Trecker hat ihm ein Bein abgefahren** the tractor cut off *or* severed his leg.
(c) *aux sein or haben Strecke* (*bereisen*) to cover, to do (*inf*); (*überprüfen, ausprobieren*) to go over ◆ **er hat ganz Belgien abgefahren** he travelled *or* went all over Belgium; **wir mußten die ganze Strecke noch einmal ~, um ... zu suchen** we had to go over the whole stretch again to look for ...
(d) (*abnutzen*) *Schienen, Skier* to wear out; *Reifen auch* to wear down; (*benutzen*) *Fahrkarte* to use; (*ausnutzen*) *Zeitkarte, Fahrkarte* to get one's

⚠: for details of spelling reform, see supplement

money's worth for ◆ **abgefahrene Reifen/Schienen** worn tyres/rails; **das Geld fährst du doch allemal ab** you'll certainly get your money's worth.
(e) (*Film, TV: beginnen*) *Kamera* to roll; *Film* to start ◆ **bitte ~!** roll 'em!
[3] *vr* (*Reifen etc*) to wear out *or* down.

Abfahrt *f* **(a)** (*von Zug, Bus etc*) departure ◆ **bis zur ~ sind es noch fünf Minuten** there's still five minutes before the train/bus leaves *or* goes; **Vorsicht bei der ~ des Zuges!** stand clear, the train is about to leave! **(b)** (*Ski*) (*Talfahrt*) descent; (*~sstrecke*) (ski-)run. **(c)** (*inf: Autobahn~*) exit ◆ **die ~ Gießen** the Gießen exit, the exit for Gießen.

abfahrtbereit *adj* ready to leave.

Abfahrts-: ~lauf *m* (*Ski*) downhill; **~zeit** *f* departure time.

Abfall *m* **-s, Abfälle (a)** *no pl* (*Müll*) refuse; (*Haus~*) rubbish (*Brit*), garbage (*US*); (*Straßen~*) litter ◆ **in den ~ kommen** to be thrown away *or* out, to go into the dustbin *or* trashcan (*US*); **(Fleisch-/Stoff)abfälle** scraps (of meat/ material).
(b) (*Rückstand*) waste *no pl*.
(c) *no pl* (*Lossagung*) break (*von* with); (*von Partei*) breaking away (*von* from) ◆ **seit ihrem ~ von der Kirche/Partei ...** since they broke with *or* since their break with the Church/since they broke away from the party; **seit dem ~ der Niederlande von Spanien** since the Netherlands broke with Spain.
(d) *no pl* (*Rückgang*) drop (*gen* in), fall (*gen* in), falling off; (*Verschlechterung auch*) deterioration.

Abfall-: ~beseitigung *f* refuse *or* garbage (*US*) disposal; **~eimer** *m* rubbish bin, waste bin, garbage *or* trashcan (*US*); (*auf öffentlichen Plätzen*) litter bin (*Brit*), trashcan (*US*).

abfallen *vi sep irreg aux sein* **(a)** (*herunterfallen*) to fall *or* drop off; (*Blätter, Blüten etc*) to fall ◆ **von etw ~** to fall *or* drop off (from) sth.
(b) (*sich senken: Gelände*) to fall *or* drop away; (*sich vermindern: Druck, Temperatur*) to fall, to drop ◆ **der Weg talwärts verläuft sacht ~d** the path down to the valley slopes gently *or* falls gently away.
(c) (*fig: übrigbleiben*) to be left (over) ◆ **das, was in der Küche abfällt** the kitchen leftovers; **der Stoff, der beim Schneidern abfällt** the leftover scraps of material.
(d) (*schlechter werden*) to fall *or* drop off, to go downhill; (*Sport: zurückbleiben*) to drop back ◆ **gegen etw ~** to compare badly with sth.
(e) (*fig: sich lösen*) to melt away ◆ **alle Unsicherheit/Furcht fiel von ihm ab** all his uncertainty/fear left him, all his uncertainty/fear melted away (from him) *or* dissolved.
(f) (*von einer Partei*) to break (*von* with), to drop out (*von* of); (*Fraktion*) to break away (*von* from) ◆ **vom Glauben ~** to break with *or* leave the faith.
(g) (*inf: herausspringen*) **wieviel fällt bei dem Geschäft für mich ab?** how much do I get out of the deal?; **es fällt immer ziemlich viel Trinkgeld ab** you/they *etc* always get quite a lot of tips (out of it).

Abfall-: ~erzeugnis *nt siehe* **~produkt; ~grube** *f* rubbish pit; **~haufen** *m* rubbish *or* refuse dump *or* tip.

abfällig *adj Bemerkung, Kritik* disparaging, derisive; *Lächeln* derisive; *Urteil* adverse ◆ **über jdn ~ reden/sprechen** to be disparaging of *or* about sb, to speak disparagingly of *or* about sb; **darüber wurde ~ geurteilt** a very dim view was taken of this; **über jdn ~ urteilen** to be disparaging about sb; **etw ~ beurteilen** to be disparaging about sth.

Abfall-: ~produkt *nt* waste-product; (*von Forschung*) by-product, spin-off; **~schacht** *m* waste *or* (*US*) garbage disposal chute; **~tourismus** *m* international trade in (hazardous) waste; **~verwertung** *f* waste utilization.

abfälschen *vti sep* (*Sport*) to deflect.

abfangen *vt sep irreg* **(a)** *Flugzeug, Funkspruch, Brief, Ball* to intercept; *Menschen auch* to catch (*inf*); *Schlag* to block; (*inf: anlocken*) *Kunden* to catch (*inf*), to lure *or* draw away.
(b) (*abstützen*) *Gebäude* to prop up, to support.
(c) (*bremsen*) *Fahrzeug* to bring under control; *Flugzeug auch* to pull out; *Aufprall* to absorb; *Trend* to check.

Abfangjäger *m* (*Mil*) interceptor.

abfärben *vi sep* **(a)** (*Wäsche*) to run ◆ **paß auf, die Wand färbt ab!** be careful, the paint comes off the wall; **das rote Handtuch hat auf die weißen Tischdecken abgefärbt** the colour has come out of the red towel onto the white tablecloths. **(b)** (*fig*) **auf jdn ~** to rub off on sb.

abfassen *vt sep* **(a)** (*verfassen*) to write; *Erstentwurf* to draft. **(b)** (*inf: abtasten*) to touch up (*inf*).

Abfassung *f siehe vt* (*a*) writing; drafting.

abfaulen *vi sep aux sein* to rot away *or* off.

abfedern *sep* [1] *vt Sprung, Stoß* to cushion.
[2] *vi* to absorb the shock; (*Sport*) (*beim Abspringen*) to push off; (*beim Aufkommen*) to bend at the knees ◆ **er ist** *or* **hat schlecht abgefedert** he landed stiffly.

abfegen *vt sep Schmutz* to sweep away *or* off; *Balkon, Hof* to sweep ◆ **den Schnee vom Dach ~** to sweep the snow off the roof.

abfeiern *vt sep* (*inf*) **Überstunden ~** to take time off in lieu (of overtime).

abfeilen *vt sep* to file off *or* (*glättend*) down.

abferkeln *vi sep* to have a litter.

abfertigen *sep* [1] *vt* **(a)** (*versandfertig machen*) *Pakete, Waren* to prepare *or* make ready *or* get ready for dispatch, to process (*form*); *Gepäck* to check (in); (*be- und entladen*) *Flugzeug* to service, to make ready for take-off; *Schiff* to make ready to sail ◆ **die Schauerleute fertigen keine Schiffe aus Chile mehr ab** the dockers won't handle any more ships from Chile.
(b) (*bedienen*) *Kunden, Antragsteller* to attend to, to deal with; (*inf: Sport*) *Gegner* to deal with ◆ **jdn kurz** *or* **schroff ~** (*inf*) to snub sb; **ich lasse mich doch nicht mit 10 Mark ~** I'm not going to be fobbed off with 10 marks.
[2] *vti* (*kontrollieren*) *Waren, Reisende* to clear ◆ **beim Zoll/an der Grenze abgefertigt werden** to be cleared by customs/at the border; **die Zöllner fertigten (die Reisenden) sehr zügig ab** the customs officers dealt with the travellers very quickly; **die Zollbeamten hatten den Zug fast abgefertigt, als ...** the customs officials had almost finished checking the train when ...

Abfertigung *f* **(a)** *siehe vt* **(a)** making ready for dispatch, processing (*form*); checking; servicing, making ready for take-off; making ready to sail.
(b) (*Bedienung*) (*von Kunden*) service; (*von Antragstellern*) dealing with; (*fig: Abweisung*) rebuff, snub ◆ **die geschickte ~ des Gegners** (*Sport*) the skilful way of dealing with his opponent.
(c) (*von Waren, Reisenden*) clearance ◆ **die ~ an der Grenze** customs clearance; **zollamtliche ~** customs clearance.
(d) (*~sstelle*) (*für Waren*) dispatch office; (*im Flughafen*) check-in.

Abfertigungshalle *f* (*Aviat*) terminal building.

Abfertigungsschalter *m* dispatch counter; (*von Zollamt*) customs clearance; (*im Flughafen*) check-in desk.

abfeuern *vt sep* to fire; (*Ftbl inf*) to let fire with.

abfinden *sep irreg* [1] *vt* to pay off; *Gläubiger auch* to settle with; (*entschädigen*) to compensate ◆ **er wurde von der Versicherung mit 20.000 DM abgefunden** he was paid 20,000 DM (in) compensation by the insurance company; **einen Fürst/König mit einer Apanage ~** to endow a prince/king with an appanage; **jdn mit leeren Versprechungen ~** to fob sb off with empty promises.
[2] *vr* **sich mit jdm/etw ~** to come to terms with sb/sth; **sich mit jdm/etw nicht ~ können** to be unable to accept sb/sth *or* to come to terms with sb/ sth; **er konnte sich nie damit ~, daß ...** he could never accept the fact that ...; **sich mit jdm/etw schwer ~** to find it hard to accept sb/sth; **mit allem kann ich mich ~, aber nicht ...** I can put up with most things, but not ...

Abfindung *f* **(a)** (*von Gläubigern*) paying off; (*Entschädigung*) compensation; (*bei Entlassung*) severance pay; (*wegen Rationalisierung*) redundancy payment. **(b)** *siehe* **Abfindungssumme.**

Abfindungssumme *f* payment, (sum in) settlement; (*Entschädigung*) compensation *no pl*, indemnity ◆ **eine/keine ~ für einen Unfall bekommen** to receive a sum in compensation *or* an indemnity/no compensation *or* no indemnity for an accident.

abfischen *vt sep* to fish dry.

abflachen *sep* [1] *vt* to level (off), to flatten (out).
[2] *vr* (*Land*) to flatten out, to grow *or* get flatter; (*fig: sinken*) to drop *or* fall (off).
[3] *vi aux sein* (*fig: sinken*) to drop *or* fall (off), to decline.

Abflachung *f* flattening out; (*fig*) dropping off, falling off.

abflauen *vi sep aux sein* **(a)** (*Wind*) to drop, to die away *or* down, to abate ◆ **nach (dem) A~ des Windes** when the wind had dropped *or* died down *or* abated.
(b) (*fig*) (*Empörung, Erregung*) to fade, to die away; (*Interesse auch*) to flag, to wane; (*Börsenkurse*) to fall, to drop; (*Geschäfte*) to fall *or* drop off.

abfliegen *sep irreg* [1] *vi aux sein* (*Aviat*) to take off (*nach* for); (*Zugvögel*) to migrate, to fly off *or* away; (*inf: sich lösen*) to fly off ◆ **sie sind gestern nach München/von Hamburg abgeflogen** they flew to Munich/from Hamburg yesterday.
[2] *vt Gelände* to fly over; *Verwundete* to fly out (*aus* of).

abfließen *vi sep irreg aux sein* (*wegfließen*) to drain *or* run *or* flow away; (*durch ein Leck*) to leak away ◆ **ins Ausland ~** (*Geld*) to flow out of the country; **der Ausguß/die Wanne fließt nicht/schlecht ab** the water isn't running *or* draining out of the sink/bath (at all)/very well.

Abflug *m* take-off; (*von Zugvögeln*) migration; (*inf: ~stelle*) departure point ◆ **~ Glasgow 8⁰⁰** departure Glasgow 8.00 a.m.

Abflug-: a~bereit *adj* ready for take-off; **~hafen** *m* departure airport; **~halle** *f* departure lounge; **~schalter** *m* check-in desk.

⚠ **Abfluß** *m* **(a)** (*Abfließen*) draining away; (*durch ein Leck*) leaking away; (*fig: von Geld*) draining away ◆ **den ~ des Wassers verhindern** to prevent the water (from) draining *or* running *or* flowing away; **durch die Verstopfung kam kein ~ zustande** because of the blockage the water couldn't drain away; **dem ~ von Kapital ins Ausland Schranken setzen** to impose limits on the (out)flow of capital out of the country.
(b) (*~stelle*) drain; (*von Teich etc*) outlet; (*~rohr*) drainpipe; (*von sanitären Anlagen auch*) wastepipe.

⚠ **Abfluß-: ~graben** *m* drainage ditch; **~hahn** *m* tap, drain-cock; **~rinne** *f* gutter; **~rohr** *nt* outlet; (*im Gebäude*) waste pipe; (*außen am Gebäude*) drainpipe; (*unterirdisch*) drain, sewer.

abfohlen *vi sep* (*Zool*) to foal.

Abfolge *f* (*geh*) sequence, succession.

abfordern *vt sep* **jdm etw ~** to demand sth from sb; **jdm den Ausweis ~** to ask to see sb's papers.

abfotografieren* *vt sep* to photograph.

Abfrage *f* (*Comput*) query ◆ **eine ~ eingeben** to key in a query.

abfragen *vt sep* **(a)** (*Comput*) *Information* to call up; *Datenbank* to query, to interrogate. **(b)** (*esp Sch*) **jdn** *or* **jdm etw ~** to question sb on sth; (*Lehrer*) to test sb orally on sth; **eine Lektion ~** to give an oral test on a lesson.

abfressen *vt sep irreg Blätter* to eat; *Gras auch* to crop; *Metall, Schicht* to eat away, to corrode ◆ **das Aas bis auf die Knochen ~** to strip the carcass to the bones; **die Giraffe frißt die Blätter von den Bäumen ab** the giraffe strips the leaves off the trees.

abfretten *vr sep* (*Aus inf*) to struggle along.

⚠: Informationen zur Rechtschreibreform im Anhang

abfrieren *sep irreg* [1] *vi aux sein* to get frostbitten ◆ **ihm sind die Füße abgefroren** his feet got frostbite; **abgefroren sein** (*Körperteil*) to be frostbitten.
[2] *vr* **sich** (*dat*) **etw ~** to get frostbite in sth; **sich** (*dat*) **einen ~** (*sl*) to freeze to death (*inf*).

abfrottieren* *vt sep* to towel down *or* dry.

Abfuhr *f* **-, -en** (**a**) *no pl* (*Abtransport*) removal. (**b**) (*inf: Zurückweisung*) snub, rebuff ◆ **jdm eine ~ erteilen** to snub *or* rebuff sb, to give sb a snub *or* rebuff; (*Sport*) to thrash sb (*inf*), to give sb a thrashing (*inf*); **sich** (*dat*) **eine ~ holen** to meet with a snub *or* a rebuff, to be snubbed; **sich** (*dat*) **(gegen jdn) eine ~ holen** (*Sport*) to be given a thrashing *or* be thrashed (by sb) (*inf*).

abführen *sep* [1] *vt* (**a**) (*wegführen*) to lead *or* take away; (*ableiten*) *Gase etc* to draw off ◆ **~!** away with him/her *etc*, take him/her *etc* away!; **das führt uns vom Thema ab** that will take us away *or* divert us from our subject.
(**b**) (*abgeben*) *Betrag* to pay (*an +acc* to) ◆ **Stuhl(gang) ~** to evacuate *or* move one's bowels, to have a bowel movement.
[2] *vi* (**a**) (*wegführen*) **der Weg führt hier (von der Straße) ab** the path leaves the road here; **das würde vom Thema ~** that would take us off the subject.
(**b**) (*den Darm anregen*) to have a laxative effect.
(**c**) (*Stuhlgang haben*) to move *or* evacuate one's bowels, to have a bowel movement.

abführend *adj* laxative *no adv*, aperient *no adv* (*form*) ◆ **~ wirken** to have a laxative effect.

Abführ- *in cpds* laxative; **~mittel** *nt* laxative, aperient (*form*).

Abführung *f* closing quotation marks *pl*.

Abfüll-: ~anlage *f* bottling plant; **~betrieb** *m* bottling factory.

abfüllen *vt sep* (**a**) (*abziehen*) *Wein etc* to draw off (*in +acc* into); (*in Flaschen*) to bottle; *Flasche* to fill ◆ **Wein in Flaschen ~** to bottle wine. (**b**) **jdn ~** (*inf*) to get sb pickled (*inf*) *or* sloshed (*inf*).

abfüttern[1] *vt sep Vieh, (hum) Menschen* to feed.

abfüttern[2] *vt sep* (*Sew*) to line.

Abfütterung *f* feeding *no pl*; (*hum Mahlzeit*) meal (*inf*).

Abgabe *f* (**a**) *no pl* (*Abliefern*) handing *or* giving in; (*von Gepäck auch*) depositing; (*Übergabe: von Brief etc*) delivery, handing over ◆ **zur ~ von etw aufgefordert werden** to be told to hand sth in.
(**b**) *no pl* (*Verkauf*) sale ◆ **~ (von Prospekten) kostenlos** leaflets given away free.
(**c**) *no pl* (*von Wärme etc*) giving off, emission.
(**d**) *no pl* (*von Schuß, Salve*) firing ◆ **nach ~ von vier Schüssen** after firing four shots.
(**e**) *no pl* (*von Erklärung, Urteil, Meinungsäußerung etc*) giving; (*von Gutachten*) submission, submitting; (*von Stimme*) casting.
(**f**) (*Sport*) (*Abspiel*) pass ◆ **nach ~ von zwei Punkten** ... after conceding two points.
(**g**) (*Steuer*) tax; (*auf Tabak etc auch*) duty; (*soziale ~*) contribution.

Abgabe(n)-: a~frei *adj, adv* tax-free, exempt from tax; **~ordnung** *f* (*Jur*) tax law; **a~pflichtig** *adj* liable to taxation.

Abgabetermin *m* closing date; (*für Dissertation etc*) submission date.

Abgang *m* (**a**) *no pl* (*Absendung*) dispatch ◆ **vor ~ der Post** before the post goes.
(**b**) *no pl* (*Abfahrt*) departure.
(**c**) *no pl* (*Ausscheiden*) (*aus einem Amt*) leaving, departure; (*Schul~*) leaving ◆ **seit seinem ~ vom Gymnasium** since he left the grammar school.
(**d**) *no pl* (*Theat, fig*) exit ◆ **sich** (*dat*) **einen guten/glänzenden ~ verschaffen** to make a grand exit.
(**e**) (*Sport*) dismount ◆ **einen guten/schwierigen ~ turnen** to do a good/difficult dismount from the apparatus.
(**f**) (*Med: Ausscheidung*) passing; (*von Eiter*) discharging; (*Fehlgeburt*) miscarriage, abortion (*form*); (*Fötus*) aborted foetus.
(**g**) (*Person*) (*Schul~*) leaver; (*Med Mil sl*) death.
(**h**) (*sl: Ejakulation*) ejaculation.
(**i**) (*Comm*) waste; (*Aus: Fehlbetrag*) missing amount.

Abgänger(in *f*) *m* **-s, -** (*Sch*) (school) leaver.

abgängig *adj* (*Aus Admin*) missing (*aus* from) ◆ **ein A~er** a missing person.

Abgängigkeits|anzeige *f* (*Aus Admin*) *notification to the authorities that a person is missing* ◆ **~ erstatten** to report a person missing.

Abgangs-: ~prüfung *f* leaving examination; **~zeugnis** *nt* leaving certificate.

Abgas *nt* exhaust *no pl*, exhaust fumes *pl*, waste gas (*esp Tech*) ◆ **Luftverschmutzung durch ~e** exhaust gas pollution.

Abgas-: a~arm *adj Fahrzeug* low-pollution; **das Auto ist a~arm** the car has a low level of exhaust emissions; **a~frei** *adj Motor, Fahrzeug* exhaust-free; **a~frei verbrennen** to burn without producing exhaust; **a~freie Produktionsverfahren** production methods which produce no waste gases; **~norm** *f* exhaust emission standard; **~reinigung** *f* (*Aut*) purification of exhaust gases; **~rückführung** *f* (*Aut*) exhaust gas recirculation, EGR; **~sonderuntersuchung** *f* (*Aut*) *compulsory annual test of a car's emission levels*; **~wolke** *f* cloud of exhaust.

abgaunern *vt sep* (*inf*) **jdm etw ~** to con *or* trick sb out of sth (*inf*).

ABGB ['a:be:ge:'be:] *nt* **-** (*Aus*) *abbr of* **Allgemeines Bürgerliches Gesetzbuch.**

abge|arbeitet *adj* (*verbraucht*) workworn; (*erschöpft*) worn out, exhausted.

abgeben *sep irreg* [1] *vt* (**a**) (*abliefern*) to hand *or* give in; (*hinterlassen*) to leave; *Gepäck, Koffer* to leave, to deposit; (*übergeben*) to hand over, to deliver.
(**b**) (*weggeben*) to give away; (*verkaufen*) to sell; (*an einen anderen Inhaber*) to hand over ◆ **Kinderwagen preisgünstig abzugeben** pram for sale at (a) bargain price.
(**c**) (*verschenken*) to give away ◆ **jdm etw ~** to give sth to sb; **jdm etw von seinem Kuchen ~** to give sb some of one's cake.
(**d**) (*überlassen*) *Auftrag* to hand *or* pass on (*an +acc* to); (*abtreten*) *Posten* to relinquish, to hand over (*an +acc* to).
(**e**) (*Sport*) *Punkte, Rang* to concede; (*abspielen*) to pass.
(**f**) (*ausströmen*) *Wärme, Sauerstoff* to give off, to emit.
(**g**) (*abfeuern*) *Schuß, Salve* to fire.
(**h**) (*äußern*) *Erklärung* to give; *Gutachten* to submit; *Meinungsäußerung auch* to express; *Stimmen* to cast.
(**i**) (*darstellen*) *Rahmen, Hintergrund,* (*liefern*) *Stoff, Material etc* to give, to provide, to furnish ◆ **den Vermittler ~** (*inf*) to act as mediator.
(**j**) (*verkörpern*) to make ◆ **er würde einen guten Schauspieler ~** he would make a good actor.
[2] *vr* **sich mit jdm/etw ~** (*sich beschäftigen*) to bother *or* concern oneself with sb/sth; (*sich einlassen*) to associate with sb/sth.
[3] *vi* (*Sport*) to pass.

abgebrannt *adj pred* (*inf*) broke (*inf*) ◆ **völlig ~ sein** to be flat *or* stony broke (*inf*).

abgebrochen *adj* (*nicht beendet*) *Studium* uncompleted; *Worte* disjointed ◆ **mit einem ~en Studium kommt man nicht sehr weit** you don't get very far if you haven't finished university *or* your university course; **er ist ~er Mediziner** (*inf*) he broke off his medical studies.

abgebrüht *adj* (*inf*) (*skrupellos*) hard-boiled (*inf*), hardened; (*frech*) cool.

abgedankt *adj Offizier, Dienstbote* discharged.

abgedreht *adj* (*Aus inf*) hardened, tough.

abgedroschen *adj* (*inf*) hackneyed, well-worn; *Witz auch* corny (*inf*) ◆ **eine ~e Phrase/Redensart** a cliché/a hackneyed saying.

abgefeimt *adj* cunning, wily.

Abgefeimtheit *f* cunning, wiliness.

abgegriffen *adj Buch* (well-)worn; (*fig*) *Klischees, Phrasen etc* well-worn, hackneyed.

abgehackt *adj* clipped ◆ **~ sprechen** to clip one's words, to speak in a clipped manner.

abgehalftert *adj* haggard ◆ **ein ~er Politiker** a political has-been.

abgehangen *adj* **(gut) ~** well-hung.

abgehärmt *adj* careworn.

abgehärtet *adj* tough, hardy; (*fig*) hardened ◆ **gegen Erkältungen ~ sein** to be immune to colds.

abgehen *sep irreg aux sein* [1] *vi* (**a**) (*abfahren*) to leave, to depart (*nach* for); (*Schiff auch*) to sail (*nach* for) ◆ **der Zug ging in** *or* **von Frankfurt ab** the train left from Frankfurt; **der Zug ging in** *or* **von Frankfurt pünktlich ab** the train left Frankfurt on time.
(**b**) (*Sport: abspringen*) to jump down ◆ **er ging gekonnt mit einem Doppelsalto vom Barren ab** he did a skilful double somersault down from *or* off the bars.
(**c**) (*Theat: abtreten*) to exit, to make one's exit ◆ **Othello geht ab** exit Othello.
(**d**) (*ausscheiden*) (*von der Schule, old: aus einem Amt*) to leave ◆ **von der Schule ~** to leave school; **mit dem Tode** *or* **mit Tod ~** (*old form*) to die in office.
(**e**) (*Med sl: sterben*) to die.
(**f**) (*sich lösen*) to come off; (*herausgehen: Farbe etc auch*) to come out ◆ **an meiner Jacke ist ein Knopf abgegangen** a button has come off my jacket.
(**g**) (*abgesondert werden*) to pass out; (*Eiter etc*) to be discharged; (*Fötus*) to be aborted ◆ **dem Kranken ging viel Blut ab** the invalid lost a lot of blood; **ihm ist einer abgegangen** (*vulg*) he shot *or* came off (*vulg*).
(**h**) (*losgehen: Schuß*) to be fired, to be loosed off.
(**i**) (*abgesandt werden*) to be sent *or* dispatched; (*Funkspruch*) to be sent ◆ **etw ~ lassen** to send *or* dispatch sth.
(**j**) (*inf: fehlen*) **jdm geht Verständnis/Taktgefühl ab** sb lacks understanding/tact.
(**k**) (*abgezogen werden*) (*vom Preis*) to be taken off; (*von Verdienst auch*) to be deducted; (*vom Gewicht*) to come off ◆ **(von etw) ~** (*von Preis*) to be taken off (sth); (*von Verdienst auch*) to be deducted (from sth); (*von Gewicht*) to be taken off (sth); **davon gehen 5% ab** 5% is taken off that.
(**l**) (*abzweigen*) to branch off; (*bei Gabelung auch*) to fork off.
(**m**) (*abweichen*) **von einem Plan/einer Forderung ~** to give up *or* drop a plan/demand; **von seiner Meinung ~** to change *or* alter one's opinion; **von einem Thema ~** to digress (from a subject); **davon kann ich nicht ~** I must insist on that; (*bei Versprechungen etc*) I can't go back on that.
(**n**) (*verlaufen*) to go ◆ **gut/glatt/friedlich ~** to go well/smoothly/peacefully; **es ging nicht ohne Streit ab** there was an argument.
(**o**) (*sl*) **das geht gut ab** that's really great; **da geht aber was ab** things are really happening; **gestern ging es gar nicht ab** it was really boring yesterday.
[2] *vt* (**a**) (*entlanggehen*) to go or walk along; (*hin und zurück*) to walk *or* go up and down; (*Mil*) *Gebäudekomplex, Gelände* to patrol; (*inspizieren*) to inspect.
(**b**) (*messen*) to pace out.
(**c**) (*Sch inf: verweisen*) **abgegangen werden** to be thrown *or* chucked (*inf*) out.

abgehend *adj Post* outgoing; *Zug, Schiff* departing ◆ **die morgen ~e Post** the post which will go out tomorrow.

abgehetzt *adj* out of breath.

abgekämpft *adj* exhausted, shattered (*inf*), worn-out.

abgeklärt *adj* serene, tranquil.

Abgeklärtheit *f* serenity, tranquillity.

abgelagert *adj Wein* mature; *Holz, Tabak* seasoned.

abgelebt *adj* **(a)** (*verbraucht*) decrepit. **(b)** (*altmodisch*) *Tradition, Vorstellung* antiquated.

abgelegen *adj* (*entfernt*) *Dorf, Land* remote; (*einsam*) isolated.

Abgelegenheit *f siehe adj* remoteness; isolation.

abgeleiert *adj* (*pej*) *Melodie etc* banal, trite; *Redensart etc auch* hackneyed; *Schallplatte* worn out, crackly.

abgelten *vt sep irreg Ansprüche* to satisfy; *Verlust* to make up, to compensate for; *Schuld* to wipe out ♦ **sein Urlaub wurde durch Bezahlung abgegolten** he was given payment in lieu of holiday.

abgemacht [1] *interj* OK, that's settled; (*bei Kauf*) it's a deal, done.
[2] *adj* **eine ~e Sache** a fix (*inf*); **das war doch schon vorher eine ~e Sache** it was all fixed up *or* arranged beforehand.

abgemagert *adj* (*sehr dünn*) thin; (*ausgemergelt*) emaciated ♦ **er war bis zum Skelett ~** he was nothing but skin and bones, he was a walking skeleton.

abgemergelt *adj* emaciated.

abgemessen *adj Schritt, Takt, Worte* measured, deliberate ♦ **~ gehen/sprechen** to walk with measured steps/speak in measured tones.

abgeneigt *adj* averse *pred* (*dat* to) ♦ **ich wäre gar nicht ~** (*inf*) actually I wouldn't mind; **der allem Neuen ~e Direktor** the headmaster, who objected to anything new; **jdm ~ sein** to dislike sb.

abgenutzt *adj* worn, shabby; *Bürste, Besen* worn-out; *Reifen* worn-down; (*fig*) *Klischees, Phrasen* hackneyed, well-worn.

Abge|ordneten-: ~bank *f* bench; **~haus** *nt* parliament; (*in West-Berlin*) House of Representatives.

Abge|ordnete(r) *mf decl as adj* (elected) representative; (*von Nationalversammlung*) member of parliament ♦ **Herr ~r/Frau ~!** sir/madam.

abgereichert *adj Uran* depleted.

abgerissen *adj* **(a)** (*zerlumpt*) *Kleidung, Eindruck* ragged, tattered. **(b)** (*unzusammenhängend*) *Worte, Gedanken* disjointed, incoherent.

Abgesandte(r) *mf decl as adj* envoy.

Abgesang *m* (*Poet*) abgesang, *concluding section of the final strophe of the minnesang;* (*fig liter*) swan song, farewell.

abgeschabt *adj* (*abgewetzt*) *Kleider* threadbare.

abgeschieden *adj* **(a)** (*geh: einsam*) secluded ♦ **~ leben/wohnen** to live a secluded life/in seclusion. **(b)** (*liter: tot*) departed ♦ **der A~e/die A~en** the departed.

Abgeschiedenheit *f* seclusion.

abgeschlafft *adj* (*inf*) whacked (*inf*) ♦ **~e Typen** lazy bums (*inf*).

abgeschlagen *adj* **(a)** (*erschöpft*) washed out (*inf*), shattered (*inf*). **(b)** (*zurück*) behind; (*besiegt*) defeated ♦ **weit ~ liegen** to be way behind; **er landete ~ auf dem 8. Platz** he finished up way down in 8th place.

Abgeschlagenheit *f* (feeling of) exhaustion.

abgeschlossen [1] *ptp of* **abschließen.**
[2] *adj* (*einsam*) isolated; (*attr: geschlossen*) *Wohnung* self-contained; *Grundstück, Hof* enclosed ♦ **~ leben** to live in isolation.

Abgeschlossenheit *f* isolation.

abgeschmackt *adj* fatuous; *Witz auch* corny; *Preis* outrageous.

Abgeschmacktheit *f* (*geh*) fatuousness; (*von Witz auch*) corniness; (*Bemerkung*) platitude ♦ **alberne Witze und ähnliche ~en** stupid jokes and similar corny things.

abgesehen [1] *ptp of* **absehen** ♦ **es auf jdn ~ haben** to have it in for sb (*inf*); **es auf jdn/etw ~ haben** (*interessiert sein*) to have one's eye on sb/sth; **du hast es nur darauf ~, mich zu ärgern** you're only trying to annoy me.
[2] *adv*: **~ von jdm/etw** apart from sb/sth; **~ davon, daß ...** apart from the fact that ...

abgesondert *adj* isolated.

abgespannt *adj* weary, tired.

Abgespanntheit *f, no pl* weariness, tiredness.

abgespielt *adj Schallplatte* worn.

abgestanden *adj Luft, Wasser* stale; *Bier, Limonade etc* flat; (*fig*) *Witz, Redensart* hackneyed.

abgestorben *adj Glieder* numb; *Pflanze, Ast, Gewebe* dead ♦ **von der Kälte war mein Arm wie ~** my arm was numb with cold.

abgestraft *adj* (*Aus*) *siehe* **vorbestraft.**

abgestumpft *adj* (*gefühllos*) *Person* insensitive; *Gefühle, Gewissen* dulled, blunted ♦ **sie war in ihren Gefühlen so ~, daß ...** her feelings had been dulled *or* blunted so much that ...

Abgestumpftheit *f siehe adj* insensitivity; dullness, bluntedness.

abgetakelt *adj* (*pej inf*) worn out, shagged out (*sl*).

abgetan *adj pred* finished *or* done with ♦ **damit ist die Sache ~** that settles the matter, that's the matter done with; **damit ist es (noch) nicht ~** that's not the end of the matter.

abgetragen *adj* worn ♦ **~e Kleider** old clothes.

abgewinnen *vt sep irreg* **(a)** (*lit*) **jdm etw ~** to win sth from sb.
(b) (*fig*) **jdm Achtung ~** to win respect from sb *or* sb's respect; **jdm ein Lächeln ~** to persuade sb to smile; **dem Meer Land ~** to reclaim land from the sea; **jdm/einer Sache keinen Reiz ~ können** to be unable to see anything attractive in sb/sth; **einer Sache** (*dat*) **Geschmack ~** to acquire a taste for sth.

abgewirtschaftet *adj* (*pej*) rotten; *Firma auch* run-down ♦ **einen total ~en Eindruck machen** to be on its last legs.

abgewogen [1] *ptp of* **abwägen.**
[2] *adj Urteil, Worte* balanced.

Abgewogenheit *f* balance.

abgewöhnen *vt sep* **jdm etw ~** *Gewohnheiten, schlechte Manieren* to cure sb of sth; *das Rauchen, Trinken* to get sb to give up *or* stop sth; **sich** (*dat*) **etw/das Trinken ~** to give sth up/give up *or* stop drinking; **noch eins/einen zum A~** (*hum*) one last one; (*von Alkohol auch*) one for the road; **das/die ist ja zum A~** (*sl*) that/she is enough to put anyone off.

abgewrackt *adj* (*pej*) rotten; (*abgetakelt*) *Mensch* washed-up.

abgezehrt *adj* emaciated.

abgießen *vt sep irreg* **(a)** *Flüssigkeit* to pour off *or* away; *Kartoffeln, Gemüse* to strain ♦ **du mußt den Eimer etwas ~** you must pour some of the water *etc* out of the bucket; **gieß dir/ich gieße dir einen Schluck ab** help yourself to/I'll give you a drop; **er goß einen Schluck in mein Glas ab** he poured a drop into my glass. **(b)** (*Art, Metal*) to cast.

Abglanz *m* reflection (*auch fig*) ♦ **nur ein schwacher** *or* **matter ~** (*fig*) a pale reflection.

Abgleich *m* **-s,** *no pl* (*von Dateien, Einträgen*) comparison.

abgleichen *vt sep irreg* **(a)** (*Build*) to level out. **(b)** (*Elec*) to tune; (*fig*) *Termine, Vorgehensweise* to coordinate; *Dateien, Einträge* to compare.

abgleiten *vi sep irreg aux sein* (*geh*) **(a)** (*abrutschen*) to slip; (*Gedanken*) to wander; (*Fin: Kurs*) to drop, to fall ♦ **von etw ~** to slip off sth; **in Nebensächlichkeiten ~** to wander off *or* go off into side issues; **in Anarchie ~** to descend into anarchy; **er gleitet in Gedanken immer ab** his thoughts always wander; **von der rechten Bahn** *or* **dem rechten Weg ~** to wander *or* stray from the straight and narrow.
(b) (*fig: abprallen*) **an/von jdm ~** to bounce off sb.

abglitschen *vi sep aux sein* (*inf*) to slip ♦ **er glitschte mit den Händen ab** his hands slipped.

Abgott *m*, **Abgöttin** *f* idol ♦ **Abgöttern dienen** to worship false gods; **jdn zum ~ machen** to idolize sb.

abgöttisch *adj* idolatrous ♦ **~e Liebe** blind adoration; **jdn ~ lieben** to idolize sb; (*Eltern, Ehepartner auch*) to dote on sb; **jdn ~ verehren** to idolize sb, to worship sb (like a god).

abgraben *vt sep irreg Erdreich* to dig away ♦ **jdm das Wasser ~** (*fig inf*) to take the bread from sb's mouth, to take away sb's livelihood.

abgrasen *vt sep Feld* to graze; (*fig inf*) *Ort, Geschäfte* to scour, to comb; *Gebiet, Thema* to do to death (*inf*).

abgrätschen *vi sep aux sein* (*Sport*) to straddle off.

abgreifen *sep irreg* [1] *vt* **(a)** *Strecke, Entfernung* to measure off. **(b)** *Buch, Heft* to wear; *siehe* **abgegriffen. (c)** *siehe* **abtasten.**
[2] *vr* to wear *or* become worn.

abgrenzen *sep* [1] *vt Grundstück, Gelände* to fence off; (*fig*) *Rechte, Pflichten, Einflußbereich, Befugnisse, Begriff* to delimit (*gegen, von* from) ♦ **etw durch einen Zaun/ein Seil/eine Mauer/Hecke ~** to fence/rope/wall/hedge sth off; **diese Begriffe lassen sich nur schwer (gegeneinander) ~** it is hard to distinguish (between) these two concepts.
[2] *vr* to dis(as)sociate oneself (*gegen* from).

Abgrenzung *f* **(a)** *no pl siehe vt* fencing/roping/walling/hedging off; (*fig*) delimitation; distinguishing. **(b)** *siehe vr* dis(as)sociation (*gegen* from). **Politik der ~** politics of separation. **(c)** (*Umzäunung, Zaun*) fencing *no pl.*

Abgrund *m* precipice; (*Schlucht, fig*) abyss, chasm ♦ **sich am Rande eines ~es befinden** (*fig*) to be on the brink (of disaster); **diese Politik bedeutet ein Wandeln am Rande des ~es** this policy is an exercise in brinkmanship; **in einen ~ von Verrat/Gemeinheit blicken** (*fig*) to stare into a bottomless pit of treason/baseness; **die menschlichen Abgründe, der ~ der menschlichen Seele** the blackest depths of the human soul.

⚠ **abgrundhäßlich** *adj* loathsome, incredibly hideous.

abgründig *adj Humor, Ironie* cryptic.

abgrundtief *adj Haß, Verachtung* profound.

abgucken *vti sep* to copy ♦ **jdm etw ~** to copy sth from sb; **bei jdm (etw) ~** (*Sch*) to copy (sth) from *or* off (*inf*) sb; **ich guck' dir nichts ab!** (*inf*) don't worry, I've seen it all before.

Abgunst *f* **-,** *no pl* (*old*) *siehe* **Mißgunst.**

⚠ **Abguß** *m* **(a)** (*Art, Metal*) (*Vorgang*) casting; (*Form*) cast. **(b)** (*dial: Ausguß*) sink.

abhaben *vt sep irreg* (*inf*) **(a)** (*abgenommen haben*) *Brille, Hut* to have off; (*abgemacht haben*) to have got off; (*abgerissen haben*) to have off. **(b)** (*abbekommen*) to have ♦ **willst du ein Stück/etwas (davon) ~?** do you want a bit/some (of it)?

abhacken *vt sep* to chop off, to hack off; *siehe* **Rübe, abgehackt.**

abhaken *vt sep* **(a)** (*abnehmen*) to unhook. **(b)** (*markieren*) to tick *or* (*esp US*) check off; (*fig*) to cross off.

abhalftern *vt sep Pferd* to take the halter off; *siehe* **abgehalftert.**

Abhalfterung *f* (*fig inf*) *siehe vt* getting rid of; ousting.

abhalten *vt sep irreg* **(a)** (*fernhalten*) *Kälte, Hitze* to keep off; *Mücken, Fliegen auch* to keep off *or* away; (*draußen halten*) to keep out.
(b) (*hindern*) to stop, to prevent ♦ **jdn von etw/vom Trinken/von der Arbeit ~** to keep sb from sth/drinking/working; **jdn davon ~, etw zu tun** to stop sb doing sth, to prevent sb from doing sth; **laß dich nicht ~!** don't let me/us *etc* stop you.
(c) ein Kind auf der Toilette/Straße ~ to hold a child over the toilet/on the street (*while it goes to the toilet*).
(d) (*veranstalten*) *Versammlung, Wahlen, Gottesdienst* to hold.

Abhaltung *f, no pl* (*Durchführung*) holding ♦ **nach ~ der Wahlen** after the elections (were held).

abhandeln *vt sep* **(a)** *Thema* to treat, to deal with.
(b) (*abkaufen*) **jdm etw ~** to do *or* strike a deal with sb for sth; **sie wollte sich** (*dat*) **das Armband nicht ~ lassen** she didn't want to let her bracelet go.

(c) (*vom Preis* ~) **jdm 8 Mark/etwas** ~ to beat sb down 8 marks/a bit, to get sb to knock 8 marks/a bit off (the price); **er ließ sich von seinen Bedingungen nichts** ~ he wouldn't give up any of his conditions.
abhanden *adv* ~ **kommen** to get lost; **jdm ist etw** ~ **gekommen** sb has lost sth.
Abhandenkommen *nt* **-s,** *no pl* loss.
Abhandlung *f* **(a)** treatise, discourse (*über +acc* (up)on) ◆ **~en** (*einer Akademie etc*) transactions. **(b)** (*das Abhandeln*) treatment.
Abhang *m* slope, incline.
abhängen *sep* 1 *vt* **(a)** (*herunternehmen*) *Bild* to take down; (*abkuppeln*) *Schlafwagen, Kurswagen* to uncouple; *Wohnwagen, Anhänger* to unhitch.
(b) (*inf: hinter sich lassen*) *jdn* to shake off (*inf*).
2 *vi* **(a)** *irreg* (*Fleisch etc*) to hang; *siehe* **abgehangen.**
(b) *irreg aux haben or* (*S Ger, Aus*) *sein* **von etw** ~ to depend (up)on sth, to be dependent (up)on sth; **das hängt ganz davon ab** it all depends; **davon hängt viel/zuviel ab** a lot/too much depends on it; **von jdm (finanziell)** ~ to be (financially) dependent on sb.
(c) (*inf: Telefon auflegen*) to hang up (*inf*).
abhängig *adj* **(a)** (*bedingt durch*) dependent (*auch Math*); *Satz auch* subordinate; *Rede* indirect; *Kasus* oblique ◆ **von etw** ~ **sein** (*Gram*) to be governed by sth.
(b) (*angewiesen auf, euph: süchtig*) dependent (*von* on) ◆ **gegenseitig** *or* **voneinander** ~ **sein** to be dependent on each other *or* mutually dependent *or* interdependent.
Abhängige(r) *mf decl as adj* dependent, dependant; *siehe* **Unzucht.**
-abhängige(r) *mf decl as adj* (*-süchtiger*) addict; *siehe* **Drogen-, Lohn-** *etc.*
Abhängigkeit *f* **(a)** *no pl* (*Bedingtheit*) dependency *no pl* (*von* on); (*Gram: von Sätzen*) subordination (*von* to). **(b)** (*Angewiesensein, euph: Sucht*) dependence (*von* on) ◆ **gegenseitige** ~ mutual dependence, interdependence.
Abhängigkeitsverhältnis *nt* dependent relationship; (*gegenseitig*) interdependence ◆ **in einem** ~ **mit jdm stehen** to be dependent on sb.
abhärmen *vr sep* to pine away (*um* for); *siehe* **abgehärmt.**
abhärten *sep* 1 *vt* to toughen up.
2 *vi* **... das härtet (gegen Erkältung) ab ...** that toughens you up (and stops you catching cold).
3 *vr* to toughen oneself up ◆ **sich gegen etw** ~ to toughen oneself against sth; (*fig*) to harden oneself to sth; *siehe* **abgehärtet.**
Abhärtung *f siehe vb* toughening up; hardening.
abhaspeln *vt sep Garn, Wolle* to unwind; (*fig*) *Rede, Gedicht* to reel *or* rattle off.
abhauen *sep* 1 *ptp* **abgehauen** *vi aux sein* (*inf*) to clear out; (*verschwinden auch*) to push off; (*aus einem Land auch*) to get away ◆ **hau ab!** beat it (*inf*), get lost (*inf*).
2 *vt* **(a)** *pret* **hieb** *or* (*inf*) **haute ab,** *ptp* **abgehauen** *Kopf* to chop *or* cut off; *Baum auch* to chop *or* cut down.
(b) *pret* **haute ab,** *ptp* **abgehauen** (*wegschlagen*) *Verputz, Schicht* to knock off.
abhäuten *vt sep siehe* **häuten.**
abheben *sep irreg* 1 *vti* **(a)** (*anheben*) to lift (up), to raise; (*abnehmen*) to take off; *Telefonhörer* to pick up, to lift (up); *Telefon* to answer; (*beim Stricken*) *Masche* to slip ◆ **laß es doch klingeln, du brauchst nicht abzuheben** let it ring, you don't have to answer (it).
(b) *vt only* (*Cards*) to take, to pick up.
(c) *Geld* to withdraw ◆ **du kannst nicht dauernd (Geld)** ~**!** you can't keep on withdrawing money *or* drawing money out; **wenn Sie** ~ **wollen ...** if you wish to make a withdrawal.
2 *vi* **(a)** (*Flugzeug*) to take off; (*Rakete*) to lift off.
(b) auf etw (*acc*) ~ (*form, Jur*) to emphasize sth.
(c) (*Cards*) (*vor Spielbeginn etc*) to cut; (*Karte nehmen*) to take a card.
3 *vr* **sich von jdm/etw** *or* **gegen jdn/etw** ~ to stand out from/against sb/sth; **nur um sich von anderen** *or* **gegen andere abzuheben** just to be different (from other people), just to make oneself stand out; **sich wohltuend gegen etw** ~ to make a pleasant contrast *or* to contrast pleasantly with sth.
abheften *vt sep* **(a)** *Rechnungen, Schriftverkehr* to file away. **(b)** (*Sew*) to tack, to baste.
abheilen *vi sep aux sein* to heal (up).
abhelfen *vi sep irreg +dat* to remedy; *einem Fehler auch* to rectify, to correct ◆ **dem ist leicht abzuhelfen** that can be *or* is easily remedied *etc.*
abhetzen *sep* 1 *vt Tiere* to exhaust, to tire out ◆ **hetz' mich nicht so ab!** (*inf*) stop hustling me like that! (*inf*).
2 *vr* to wear *or* tire oneself out; *siehe* **abgehetzt.**
abheuern *sep* (*Naut*) 1 *vi* to be paid off.
2 *vt* to pay off.
Abhilfe *f* **-,** *no pl* remedy, cure ◆ ~ **schaffen** to take remedial action; **in einer Angelegenheit** ~ **schaffen** to remedy a matter.
abhin *adv* (*Sw*) **vom 18.9.90** ~ from 18.9.90 onwards.
Abhitze *f siehe* **Abwärme.**
abhobeln *vt sep Holz* to plane down ◆ **wir müssen noch 2 cm** ~ we need to plane another 2 cms off.
abhold *adj +dat* (*old liter*) **jdm/einer Sache** ~ **sein** to be averse *or* ill-disposed to(wards) sb/averse to sth; **jdm/einer Sache nicht** ~ **sein** (*iro*) not to be averse to sb/sth.
abholen *vt sep* to collect (*bei* from); *Bestelltes auch* to call for (*bei* at); *Fundsache* to claim (*bei* from); *jdn* to call for; (*mit dem Wagen auch*) to pick up; (*euph: verhaften*) to take away ◆ **jdn am Bahnhof/Flughafen** ~ to collect sb from *or* meet sb at the station/airport; (*mit dem Wagen auch*) to pick sb up from the station/airport; **ich hole dich heute abend ab** I'll call for you *or* pick you up this evening; **er kam und wollte mich zu einem Spaziergang** ~ he called and asked me to go for a walk; **etw** ~ **lassen** to have sth collected; **„Geldbörse gefunden, abzuholen bei ..."** "purse found, claim from ..."
Abholer *m* **-s,** - (*Comm*) ~ **sein** *to collect one's post from the post office/parcels from the station etc.*
Abholung *f* collection ◆ **zur** ~ **bereit** ready for *or* awaiting collection.
abholzen *vt sep Wald* to clear, to deforest; *Baumreihe* to fell, to cut down.
Abholzung *f siehe vt* clearing, deforesting; felling, cutting down.
Abhör-: ~aktion *f* bugging operation; **~anlage** *f* bugging system.
abhorchen *sep* 1 *vt* to sound, to listen to; *Patienten auch* to auscultate (*form*); *Boden* to put one's ear to.
2 *vi* to auscultate (*form*).
Abhör|einrichtung *f* bugging device; (*System*) bugging system.
abhören *vt sep* **(a)** (*auch vi: überwachen*) *Gespräch* to bug; (*mithören*) to listen in on; *Telefon* to tap ◆ **abgehört werden** (*inf*) to be bugged; **der Geheimdienst darf (Telefone)** ~ the Secret Service are allowed to tap telephones.
(b) (*zuhören*) *Sender, Schallplatte etc* to listen to.
(c) (*Med*) to sound, to listen to ◆ **jdm das Herz** ~ to listen to *or* sound sb's heart.
(d) (*Sch: abfragen*) **einen** *or* **einem Schüler etw** ~ to test a pupil orally on sth; **einen** *or* **einem Schüler ein Gedicht** ~ to hear a pupil recite a poem.
Abhör-: ~gerät *nt* bugging device; **a~sicher** *adj* bugproof.
abhungern *vr sep* **er mußte sich** (*dat*) **sein Studium** ~ he had to starve himself to pay for his studies, he had to starve his way through college *etc*; **sich** (*dat*) **Gewicht/10 Kilo** ~ to lose weight/10 kilos by going on a starvation diet; **abgehungerte Gestalten** emaciated figures.
abhusten *vi sep* to have a good cough.
abi (*Aus inf*) = **hinab.**
Abi *nt* **-s, -s** (*Sch inf*) *abbr of* **Abitur.**
ab|irren *vi sep aux sein* (*geh*) to lose one's way; (*fig: abschweifen*) (*Gedanken*) to wander ◆ **vom Weg(e)** ~ to wander off the path, to stray from the path; **vom rechten Weg** ~ (*fig*) to stray *or* wander *or* err from the straight and narrow.
Ab|irrung *f* (*geh*) **(a)** (*Verirrung*) lapse, aberration. **(b)** (*Astron*) aberration.
Abitur *nt* **-s,** (*rare*) **-e** *school-leaving exam and university entrance qualification,* ≃ A-levels *pl* (*Brit*), Highers *pl* (*Scot*) ◆ **(sein** *or* **das)** ~ **machen** to do *or* take (one's) school-leaving exam *or* A-levels *or* Highers; **sein** *or* **das** ~ **ablegen** (*form*) to obtain one's school-leaving exam *or* A-levels *or* Highers, ≃ to graduate from high school (*US*).
Abiturfeier *f* school-leaver's party, graduation ball (*US*).
Abiturient(in *f*) *m person who is doing/has done the Abitur.*
Abitur-: ~klasse *f final year class at school who will take the Abitur,* ≃ sixth form (*Brit*), senior grade (*US*); **~zeugnis** *nt* certificate of having passed the Abitur, ≃ A-level (*Brit*) *or* Highers (*Scot*) certificate.
abjagen *sep* 1 *vt* **(a)** *siehe* **abhetzen 1. (b) jdm etw** ~ to get sth off sb.
2 *vr* (*inf*) to wear oneself out.
Abk. *abbr of* **Abkürzung** abbreviation, abbr.
abkalben *vi sep* (*Agr*) to calve.
abkämmen *vt sep* (*fig*) to comb, to scour.
abkämpfen *sep* 1 *vt* (*geh*) **jdm etw** ~ to wring sth out of sb.
2 *vr* to fight hard; *siehe* **abgekämpft.**
abkanzeln *vt sep* (*inf*) **jdn** ~ to give sb a dressing-down.
Abkanz(e)lung *f* dressing-down.
abkapseln *vr sep* (*lit*) to become encapsulated; (*fig*) to shut *or* cut oneself off, to isolate oneself.
Abkaps(e)lung *f* (*lit*) encapsulation; (*fig*) isolation.
abkarren *vt sep* to cart away; (*fig*) *Menschen* to cart off.
abkarten *vt sep* to rig (*inf*), to fix ◆ **die Sache war von vornherein abgekartet** the whole thing was a put-up job (*inf*).
abkassieren* *vti sep* (*inf*) to cash up (*inf*) ◆ **jdn** *or* **bei jdm** ~ to get sb to pay; **darf ich mal (bei Ihnen)** ~**?** could I ask you to pay now?
abkauen *vt sep Fingernägel* to bite; *Bleistift* to chew.
abkaufen *vt sep* **jdm etw** ~ to buy sth from *or* off (*inf*) sb; (*inf: glauben*) to buy sth (*inf*); **diese Geschichte kauft uns keiner ab!** nobody will buy that story (*inf*).
Abkehr *f* **-,** *no pl* turning away (*von* from); (*von Glauben, von der Welt etc*) renunciation (*von* of); (*von der Familie*) estrangement (*von* from) ◆ **die** ~ **vom Materialismus** turning away from *or* rejecting materialism.
abkehren[1] *vt sep* (*abfegen*) *Schmutz* to sweep away *or* off; *Hof, Dach* to sweep.
abkehren[2] *sep* 1 *vt* (*geh*) (*abwenden*) *Blick, Gesicht* to avert, to turn away ◆ **sie mußte den Blick (davon)** ~ she had to look away (from it).
2 *vr* (*fig*) to turn away (*von* from); (*von Gott etc auch*) to renounce; (*von einer Politik*) to give up ◆ **die von uns abgekehrte Seite des Mondes** the side of the moon away from us, the far side of the moon.
abkippen *sep* 1 *vt* (*abladen*) *Abfälle, Baustoffe* to tip; (*herunterklappen*) to let down.
2 *vi aux sein* to tilt; (*Flugzeug*) to nosedive.
abklappern *vt sep* (*inf*) *Läden, Gegend, Straße* to scour, to comb (*nach* for); *Kunden, Museen* to do (*inf*).
abklären *sep* 1 *vt* **(a)** (*sich setzen lassen*) *Flüssigkeit* to clarify. **(b)** (*klarstellen*) *Angelegenheit* to clear up, to clarify.
2 *vr* **(a)** (*sich setzen*) to clarify. **(b)** (*sich beruhigen*) to calm down; *siehe* **abgeklärt.**
Abklärung *f* **(a)** (*von Flüssigkeit*) clarification, clarifying. **(b)** (*von*

➤ SPRACHE AKTIV: **abhängen: 2b** → 33.3, 52.4

Angelegenheit) clearing up.

Abklatsch *m* **-(e)s, -e** (*Art*) cast, casting; (*fig pej*) poor imitation *or* copy.

abklatschen *sep* [1] *vt* **er klatschte sie ab** he got to dance with her during the excuse-me; **es wird abgeklatscht** it's an excuse-me.
[2] *vi* **beim A~** during the excuse-me.

Abklatscher *m* **-s, -** (*Ftbl sl*) rebound.

abklemmen *vt sep Nabelschnur, Leitung, Adern* to clamp ◆ **er hat sich** (*dat*) **in der Maschine den Finger abgeklemmt** he lost his finger in the machine.

abklingen *vi sep irreg aux sein* **(a)** (*leiser werden*) to die *or* fade away. **(b)** (*nachlassen*) to wear off, to abate; (*Erregung, Fieber auch*) to subside.

abklopfen *sep* [1] *vt* **(a)** (*herunterklopfen*) to knock off; (*klopfend säubern*) to brush down; *Staub etc* to brush off; *Teppich, Polstermöbel* to beat ◆ **er klopfte die Asche von der Zigarre ab** he tapped *or* knocked the ash off his cigar; **sich** (*dat*) **die Schuhe ~** to knock the mud *etc* off one's shoes; **den Staub nicht abbürsten, sondern ~** do not brush the dust off, pat it off.
(b) (*beklopfen*) to tap; (*Med*) to sound, to percuss (*spec*).
(c) (*fig inf: untersuchen*) to look into ◆ **etw auf etw** (*acc*) **~** to trace sth (back) to sth.
[2] *vi* (*Mus*) **der Dirigent klopfte ab** the conductor stopped the orchestra (*by rapping his baton*).

abknabbern *vt sep* (*inf*) to nibble off; *Knochen* to gnaw at.

abknallen *vt sep* (*sl*) to shoot down (*inf*).

abknappen, abknapsen *vt sep* (*inf*) **sich** (*dat*) **etw ~** to scrape together sth; **sich** (*dat*) **jeden Pfennig ~ müssen** to have to scrimp and save; **er hat mir 20 Mark abgeknapst** he got 20 marks off me.

abkneifen *vt sep irreg* to nip off; (*mit Zange auch*) to clip off.

abknicken *sep* [1] *vt* (*abbrechen*) to break *or* snap off; (*einknicken*) to break.
[2] *vi aux sein* (*abzweigen*) to fork *or* branch off ◆ **~de Vorfahrt** traffic turning left/right has priority; **in den Knien ~** to bend at the knees.

abknipsen *vt sep* (*inf*) to snip off; *Film* to finish.

abknöpfen *vt sep* **(a)** (*abnehmen*) to unbutton. **(b)** (*inf: ablisten*) **jdm etw ~** to get sth off sb; **jdm Geld ~** to get money out of sb.

abknutschen *vt sep* (*inf*) to canoodle with (*inf*) ◆ **sich ~** to canoodle (*inf*).

abkochen *sep* [1] *vt* (*gar kochen*) to boil; (*durch Kochen keimfrei machen*) to sterilize (by boiling); *Milch auch* to scald ◆ **jdn ~** (*sl*) to rook *or* fleece sb (*inf*).
[2] *vi* to cook a meal in the open air, to have a cookout (*US*).

abkommandieren* *vt sep* (*Mil*) (*zu anderer Einheit*) to post; (*zu bestimmtem Dienst*) to detail (*zu* for) ◆ **jdn ins Ausland ~** to post sb abroad.

Abkomme *m* **-n, -n** (*liter*) *siehe* **Nachkomme.**

abkommen *vi sep irreg aux sein* **(a)** (*Sport: wegkommen*) to get away ◆ **schlecht/gut ~** (*wegkommen*) to get away to *or* to make a bad/good start.
(b) (*beim Schießen*) to aim ◆ **wie ist sie abgekommen?** how well did she shoot?, how was her shot?
(c) von etw ~ (*abweichen*) to leave sth; (*abirren*) to wander off sth, to stray from sth; **vom Kurs ~** to deviate from *or* leave one's course; **(vom Thema) ~** to get off the subject, to digress; **vom rechten Weg ~** (*fig*) to stray *or* wander from the straight and narrow.
(d) (*aufgeben*) **von etw ~** to drop sth, to give sth up; (*von Angewohnheit*) to give sth up; (*von Idee, Plan*) to abandon *or* drop sth; **von einer Meinung ~** to revise one's opinion, to change one's mind; **von diesem alten Brauch kommt man immer mehr ab** this old custom is dying out more and more.

Abkommen *nt* **-s, -** agreement (*auch Pol*).

Abkommenschaft *f* (*liter*) *siehe* **Nachkommenschaft.**

abkömmlich *adj* available ◆ **nicht ~ sein** to be unavailable.

Abkömmling *m* **(a)** (*Nachkomme*) descendant; (*fig*) adherent. **~e** *pl* (*Jur*) issue *no pl* ◆ **er war (der) ~ einer Bankiersfamilie** he came from a banking family. **(b)** (*Chem*) derivative.

abkönnen *vt sep irreg* (*sl*) **(a)** (*trinken*) **der kann ganz schön was ab** he can knock it back (*inf*) *or* put it away (*inf*); **er kann nicht viel ab** he can't take much (drink). **(b)** (*mögen*) **das kann ich überhaupt nicht ab** I can't stand *or* abide it.

abkoppeln [1] *vt sep* (*Rail*) to uncouple; *Pferd* to untie; *Degen, Pistole* to unbuckle, to take off; *Raumfähre* to undock; *Anhänger* to unhitch.
[2] *vr sep* (*inf: sich lösen*) to sever one's ties (*von* with).

Abkopplung *f siehe vt* uncoupling; untying; unbuckling, taking off; undocking; unhitching.

abkratzen *sep* [1] *vt Schmutz etc* to scratch off; (*mit einem Werkzeug*) to scrape off; *Wand, Gegenstand* to scratch; to scrape ◆ **die Schuhe ~** to scrape the mud/snow *etc* off one's shoes.
[2] *vi aux sein* (*sl: sterben*) to kick the bucket (*sl*), to croak (*sl*).

Abkratzer *m* **-s, -** shoe scraper.

abkriegen *vt sep* (*inf*) *siehe* **abbekommen.**

abkucken *vti siehe* **abgucken.**

abkühlen *sep* [1] *vt* to cool; *Speise auch* to cool down; (*fig*) *Freundschaft, Zuneigung* to cool; *Zorn, Leidenschaft* to cool, to calm.
[2] *vi aux sein* to cool down; (*fig: Freundschaft etc*) to cool off; (*Begeisterung*) to cool.
[3] *vr* to cool down *or* off; (*Wetter*) to become cool(er); (*fig*) to cool; (*Beziehungen auch*) to become cool(er).

Abkühlung *f* cooling.

Abkunft *f* **-,** *no pl* (*liter*) descent, origin; (*Nationalität auch*) extraction ◆ **französischer ~ sein** to be of French descent *etc.*

abkupfern *vt sep* (*inf*) to crib (*inf*), to copy.

abkuppeln *vt sep siehe* **abkoppeln.**

abkürzen *sep* [1] *vt* **(a)** (*abschneiden*) **den Weg ~** to take a short cut.
(b) (*verkürzen*) to cut short; *Verfahren* to shorten; *Aufenthalt, Urlaub auch* to curtail.
(c) (*verkürzt schreiben*) *Namen* to abbreviate ◆ **Millimeter wird mm abgekürzt** millimetres is abbreviated as mm, mm is the abbreviation for millimetres.
[2] *vi* **(a)** (*abschneiden*) to take a short cut; (*Weg*) to be a short cut.
(b) (*verkürzt schreiben*) to abbreviate, to use abbreviations.

Abkürzung *f* **(a)** (*Weg*) short cut ◆ **durch die ~ haben wir eine Stunde gespart** we've saved an hour by taking the short cut, taking the short cut has saved us an hour.
(b) (*von Aufenthalt*) curtailment, cutting short; (*von Verfahren*) shortening; (*von Vortrag*) shortening, cutting short ◆ **gibt es keine ~ dieses Verfahrens?** isn't there any way of shortening this process?
(c) (*von Wort*) abbreviation.

Abkürzungsverzeichnis *nt* list of abbreviations.

abküssen *vt sep* to smother with kisses ◆ **sie küßten sich stundenlang ab** they kissed away for hours.

abladen *vti sep irreg Last, Wagen* to unload; *Schutt* to dump; (*esp Comm*) *Passagiere, Ware* to off-load; (*fig inf*) *Kummer, Ärger auch* to vent (*bei jdm* on sb); *Verantwortung* to off-load, to shove (*inf*) (*auf +acc* onto) ◆ **seine Kinder/Arbeit auf jdn ~** (*fig inf*) to unload *or* dump (*inf*) one's children/work on sb; **sie lud ihren ganzen Kummer bei ihrem Mann ab** (*inf*) she unburdened herself *or* all her worries to her husband.

Abladeplatz *m* unloading area; (*für Schrott, Müll etc*) dump, dumping ground.

Ablage *f* **-, -n** **(a)** (*Gestell*) place to keep/put sth ◆ **wir brauchen eine ~ für die Akten** we need somewhere for our files *or* where we can keep our files; **der Tisch dient als ~ für ihre Bücher** her books are kept on the table; **etw als ~ benutzen** (*für Akten, Bücher etc*) to use sth for storage; **sie haben das Bett als ~ benutzt** they put everything on the bed; **gibt es hier irgendeine ~ für Taschen und Schirme?** is there anywhere here where bags and umbrellas can be left *or* for bags and umbrellas?
(b) (*Aktenordnung*) filing.
(c) (*Sw*) *siehe* **Annahmestelle, Zweigstelle.**

Ablagekorb *m* filing tray.

ablagern *sep* [1] *vt* **(a)** (*anhäufen*) to deposit.
(b) (*deponieren*) to leave, to store.
[2] *vi aux sein or haben* (*ausreifen*) to mature; (*Holz auch*) to season ◆ **~ lassen** to allow to mature; *Holz auch* to (allow to) season; *siehe* **abgelagert.**
[3] *vr* to be deposited ◆ **in einem Wasserkessel lagert sich Kalk ab** a chalk deposit forms *or* builds up in a kettle.

Ablagerung *f* (*Vorgang*) depositing, deposition; (*von Wein*) maturing, maturation; (*von Holz*) maturing, seasoning; (*abgelagerter Stoff*) deposit.

ablandig *adj* (*Naut*) *Wind* offshore.

⚠ **Ablaß** *m* **-sses, Ablässe** **(a)** (*Eccl*) indulgence. **(b)** *no pl* (*das Ablassen*) letting out; (*von Dampf*) letting off; (*Entleerung*) drainage, draining. **(c)** (*Vorrichtung*) outlet.

⚠ **Ablaßbrief** *m* (*Eccl*) letter of indulgence.

ablassen *sep irreg* [1] *vt* **(a)** (*herauslaufen lassen*) *Wasser, Luft* to let out; *Motoröl auch* to drain off; *Dampf* to let off; (*Zug, Kessel*) to give *or* let off ◆ **die Luft aus den Reifen ~** to let the air out of the tyres, to let the tyres down.
(b) (*leerlaufen lassen*) *Teich, Schwimmbecken* to drain, to empty.
(c) *Brieftaube* to let off; *Zug* to start.
(d) (*verkaufen, geben*) **jdm etw ~** to let sb have sth.
(e) (*ermäßigen*) to knock off (*inf*) ◆ **er hat mir 20 Mark (vom Preis) abgelassen** he knocked 20 marks off (the price) for me (*inf*), he reduced the price by 20 marks for me.
(f) (*inf: nicht befestigen, anziehen*) to leave off.
[2] *vi* (*liter*) **(a)** (*mit etw aufhören*) to desist ◆ **von einem Vorhaben** *etc* **~** to abandon a plan *etc*.
(b) (*jdn in Ruhe lassen*) **von jdm ~** to leave sb alone.

⚠ **Ablaß-: ~handel** *m* (*Eccl*) selling of indulgences; **~ventil** *nt* outlet valve.

Ablativ *m* ablative (case).

ablatschen *sep* (*sl*) [1] *vt Schuhe* to wear out ◆ **abgelatscht** (*fig*) worn-out, down at heel.
[2] *vi aux sein* to wander off (*inf*), to push off (*inf*).

Ablauf *m* **(a)** (*Abfluß*) drain; (*~stelle*) outlet; (*~rohr*) drain(pipe); (*im Haus*) wastepipe; (*Rinne*) drainage channel.
(b) (*Ablaufen*) draining *or* running away.
(c) (*Verlauf*) course; (*von Empfang, Staatsbesuch*) order of events (*gen* in); (*von Verbrechen*) sequence of events (*gen* in); (*von Handlung im Buch etc*) development ◆ **er sprach mit uns den ~ der Prüfung durch** he took us through the exam; **er hat den ~ des Unglücks geschildert** he described the way the accident happened; **der ~ der Ereignisse vollzog sich wie geplant** the course of events was as planned; **nach ~ der Vorstellung ...** after the performance (was over) ...; **es gab keinerlei Störungen im ~ des Programms** the programme went off without any disturbances.
(d) (*von Frist etc*) expiry ◆ **nach ~ der Frist** after the deadline had passed *or* expired.
(e) (*von Zeitraum*) passing ◆ **nach ~ von 4 Stunden** after 4 hours (have/had passed *or* gone by); **nach ~ des Jahres/dieser Zeit** at the end of the year/this time.

Ablaufbrett *nt* (*an Spüle*) draining board.

ablaufen *sep irreg* [1] *vt* **(a)** (*abnützen*) *Schuhsohlen, Schuhe* to wear out; *Absätze* to wear down ◆ **sich** (*dat*) **die Beine** *or* **Hacken** *or* **Absätze** *or* **Schuhsohlen nach etw ~** (*inf*) to walk one's legs off looking for sth; *siehe* **Horn.**

⚠: Informationen zur Rechtschreibreform im Anhang

(b) *aux sein or haben (entlanglaufen) Strecke* to go *or* walk over; *(hin und zurück)* to go *or* walk up and down; *Stadt, Straßen, Geschäfte* to comb, to scour (round).

[2] *vi aux sein* **(a)** *(abfließen: Flüssigkeit)* to drain *or* run away *or* off; *(sich leeren: Behälter)* to drain (off), to empty (itself); *(trocken werden: Geschirr)* to dry off ◆ **aus der Badewanne ~** to run *or* drain out of the bath; **bei ~dem Wasser** *(Naut)* with an outgoing tide; **an ihm läuft alles ab** *(fig)* he just shrugs everything off; **jede Kritik läuft an ihm ab** *(fig)* with him criticism is just like water off a duck's back.

(b) *(vonstatten gehen)* to go off ◆ **wie ist das bei der Prüfung abgelaufen?** how did the exam go (off)?; **zuerst sah es sehr gefährlich aus, aber dann ist die Sache doch glimpflich abgelaufen** at first things looked pretty dangerous but it was all right in the end.

(c) *(sich abwickeln: Seil, Kabel)* to wind out, to unwind; *(sich abspulen: Film, Tonband)* to run; *(Schallplatte)* to play ◆ **eine Platte/einen Film/Tonband ~ lassen** to play a record/to run *or* show a film/to run *or* play a tape; **ein Programm ~ lassen** *(Comput)* to run a program; **abgelaufen sein** *(Film etc)* to have finished, to have come to an end.

(d) *(ungültig werden: Paß, Visum etc)* to expire, to run out; *(enden: Frist, Vertrag etc auch)* to run out, to be up ◆ **die Frist ist abgelaufen** the period has run out *or* is up.

(e) *(vergehen: Zeitraum)* to pass, to go by.

(f) *(Sport: starten)* to start.

ạblauschen *vt sep (geh)* to learn *(dat* from) ◆ **dem Leben abgelauscht** *(fig liter)* taken *or* culled *(liter)* from life.

Ạblaut *m (Gram)* ablaut.

ạblauten *vi sep (Gram)* to undergo ablaut, to change by ablaut.

ạbleben *sep (old)* [1] *vi aux sein* to pass away, to decease *(form)*.

[2] *vt Zeit* to live out; *siehe* **abgelebt**.

Ạbleben *nt -s, no pl (form)* demise *(form)*, decease *(form)*.

ạblecken *vt sep* to lick; *Teller, Löffel, Finger* to lick (clean); *Blut, Marmelade* to lick off ◆ **sich** *(dat)* **etw von der Hand ~** to lick sth off one's hand.

ạbledern *vt sep Fenster, Auto* to leather (off), to polish with a leather.

ạblegen *sep* [1] *vt* **(a)** *(niederlegen)* to put down; *Last, Waffen auch* to lay down; *(Zool) Eier* to lay.

(b) *(abheften) Schriftwechsel* to file (away); *(Comput) Daten* to store.

(c) *(ausziehen) Hut, Mantel, Kleider* to take off, to remove *(form)*.

(d) *(nicht mehr tragen) Anzug, Kleid* to discard, to cast off; *Trauerkleidung, Ehering* to take off; *Orden, Auszeichnungen* to renounce ◆ **abgelegte Kleider** cast-off *or* discarded clothes.

(e) *(aufgeben) Mißtrauen, Scheu, Stolz* to lose, to shed, to cast off *(liter)*; *schlechte Gewohnheit* to give up, to get rid of; *kindische Angewohnheit* to put aside; *Namen* to give up.

(f) *(ableisten, machen) Schwur, Eid* to swear; *Gelübde auch* to make; *Zeugnis* to give; *Bekenntnis, Beichte, Geständnis* to make; *Prüfung* to take, to sit; *(erfolgreich)* to pass.

(g) *(Cards)* to discard, to throw down.

[2] *vi* **(a)** *(abfahren) (Schiff)* to cast off; *(Space auch)* to separate.

(b) *(Schriftwechsel ~)* to file.

(c) *(Garderobe ~)* to take one's things off ◆ **wenn Sie ~ möchten** ... if you would like to take your things *or* hats and coats off ...

(d) *(Cards)* to discard.

[3] *vt impers (geh: absehen)* **es auf etw** *(acc)* **~** to be out for sth.

Ạbleger *m -s, - (Bot)* layer; *(fig: Zweigunternehmen)* branch, subsidiary; *(iro: Sohn)* son, offspring *no pl* ◆ **durch ~** by layering.

ạblehnen *vt sep* **(a)** *auch vi (zurückweisen, nein sagen)* to decline, to refuse; *Antrag, Angebot, Vorschlag, Bewerber, Stelle* to turn down, to reject; *(Parl) Gesetzentwurf* to throw out ◆ **eine ~de Antwort** a negative answer; **ein ~der Bescheid** a rejection; **es ~, etw zu tun** to decline *or* refuse to do sth; **dankend ~** to decline with thanks. **(b)** *(mißbilligen)* to disapprove of. **jede Form von Gewalt ~** to be against any form of violence.

Ạblehnung *f* **(a)** *(Zurückweisung)* refusal; *(von Antrag, Bewerber etc)* rejection ◆ **niemand hatte mit seiner ~ gerechnet** nobody had expected him to refuse/reject it *or* turn it down; **auf ~ stoßen** to be refused/rejected, to meet with a refusal/a rejection.

(b) *(Mißbilligung)* disapproval ◆ **auf ~ stoßen** to meet with disapproval.

ạbleiern *vt sep Melodie* to churn out; *(inf) Gedicht etc* to reel off; *siehe* **abgeleiert**.

ạbleisten *vt sep (form) Zeit* to complete.

ạbleitbar *adj* **(a)** *(herleitbar)* derivable, deducible; *Wort* derivable *(aus* from). **(b)** *siehe vt (b)* able to be diverted/drawn off *or* out/conducted.

ạbleiten *sep* [1] *vt* **(a)** *(herleiten)* to derive; *(logisch folgern auch)* to deduce *(aus* from); *(Math) Gleichung* to differentiate.

(b) *(umleiten) Bach, Fluß* to divert; *(herausleiten) Rauch, Dampf, Flüssigkeit* to draw off *or* out; *(ablenken) Blitz* to conduct.

[2] *vr (sich herleiten)* to be derived *(aus* from); *(logisch folgen auch)* to be deduced *(aus* from).

Ạbleitung *f* **(a)** *siehe vt* derivation; deduction; differentiation; diversion; drawing off *or* out; conduction. **(b)** *(Wort, Math)* derivative.

Ạbleitungssilbe *f* derivative affix.

ạblenken *sep* [1] *vt* **(a)** *(ab-, wegleiten)* to deflect *(auch Phys)*, to turn aside *or* away; *Wellen, Licht* to refract; *Schlag* to parry; *Katastrophe* to avert.

(b) *(zerstreuen)* to distract ◆ **er ließ sich durch nichts ~** he wouldn't let anything distract him; **wir mußten die Kinder ~** we had to find something to take the children's minds off things; **jdn von seinem Schmerz/seinen Sorgen ~** to make sb forget his pain/worries, to take sb's mind off his pain/worries.

(c) *(abbringen)* to divert; *Verdacht* to avert ◆ **jdn von der Arbeit ~** to distract sb from his work.

[2] *vi* **(a)** *(ausweichen)* **(vom Thema) ~** to change the subject; *(bei einem Gespräch auch)* to turn the conversation.

(b) *(zerstreuen)* to create a distraction ◆ **sie geht jede Woche ins Kino, das lenkt ab** she goes to the cinema every week, which takes her mind off things.

[3] *vr* to take one's mind off things.

Ạblenkung *f* **(a)** *(Ab-, Wegleitung)* deflection *(auch Phys)*; *(von Wellen, Licht)* refraction.

(b) *(Zerstreuung)* diversion, distraction ◆ **~ brauchen** to need something to take one's mind off things; **sich** *(dat)* **~ verschaffen** to provide oneself with a distraction *or* with something to take one's mind off things.

(c) *(Störung)* distraction.

(d) *(von Plan, jds Interesse)* diversion; *(von Verdacht)* aversion, averting.

(e) *(von Thema)* changing of the subject.

Ạblenkungsmanöver *nt* diversionary tactic; *(um vom Thema, Problem abzulenken auch)* red herring.

ạblesbar *adj Rede, Meßgerät* readable ◆ **die Erregung war von seinem Gesicht noch deutlich ~** excitement was still written all over his face; **daraus ist ohne weiteres ~, daß** ... it can be clearly seen from this that ...

ạblesen *vt sep irreg* **(a)** *(auch vi: vom Blatt)* to read ◆ **er muß (alles/seine Rede) ~** he has to read everything/his speech (from notes *etc*); **(jdm) etw von den Lippen ~** to lip-read sth (that sb says).

(b) *(auch vi: registrieren) Meßgeräte, Barometer, Strom* to read; *Barometerstand* to take ◆ **nächste Woche wird abgelesen** the meter(s) will be read next week.

(c) *(herausfinden, erkennen, folgern)* to see ◆ **jdm etw vom Gesicht/von der Stirn ~** to see *or* tell sth from sb's face, to read sth in sb's face; **das konnte man ihr vom Gesicht ~** it was written all over her face; **aus der Reaktion der Presse war die Stimmung im Volke deutlich abzulesen** the mood of the people could be clearly gauged *or* read from the press reaction; **jdm jeden Wunsch an** *or* **von den Augen ~** to anticipate sb's every wish.

(d) *(wegnehmen) Beeren, Raupen etc* to pick off *(von etw* sth); *(leer machen) Acker, Strauch etc* to pick clean.

Ạbleser(in *f)* *m* meter-reader, meter-man.

ạbleuchten *vt sep* to light up, to illuminate.

ạbleugnen *sep* [1] *vt Schuld, Tat* to deny; *Verantwortung auch* to disclaim; *Glauben* to renounce.

[2] *vi* **er hat weiter abgeleugnet** he continued to deny it.

Ạbleugnung *f* denial; *(von Glauben)* renunciation.

ạblichten *vt sep (form)* to photocopy; *(fotografieren)* to photograph.

Ạblichtung *f (form) siehe vt* photocopy; photograph; *(Vorgang)* photocopying; photographing.

ạbliefern *vt sep (bei einer Person)* to hand over *(bei* to); *Examensarbeit auch* to hand in; *(bei einer Dienststelle)* to hand in *(bei* to); *(liefern)* to deliver *(bei* to); *(inf) Kinder, Freundin* to deposit *(inf)*; *(nach Hause bringen)* to bring/take home.

Ạblieferung *f siehe vt* handing-over *no pl*; handing-in *no pl*; delivery.

ạbliegen *vi sep irreg* **(a)** *(entfernt sein)* to be at a distance; *(fig)* to be removed ◆ **das Haus liegt weit ab** the house is a long way off *or* away *or* is quite a distance away; **das liegt sehr weit ab von unserem Thema** that is very far removed from *or* is a long way from the topic we are dealing with; *siehe* **abgelegen**.

(b) *(S Ger: lagern) (Obst)* to ripen; *(Fleisch)* to hang.

ạblisten *vt sep* **jdm etw ~** to trick sb out of sth; **jdm die Erlaubnis ~, etw zu tun** to trick sb into giving one permission to do sth.

ạblocken *vt sep* **jdm etw ~** to get sth out of sb; **diese Äußerung lockte ihm nur ein müdes Lächeln ab** this statement only drew a tired smile from him *or* got a tired smile out of him; **er lockte seiner Geige süße Töne ab** he coaxed sweet sounds from his violin.

ạblösbar *adj* **(a)** *(abtrennbar)* removable, detachable ◆ **die Etiketten sind nur schwer ~** the labels are difficult to remove. **(b)** *(ersetzbar)* replaceable. **(c)** *(tilgbar)* redeemable.

ạblöschen *vt sep* **(a)** *(mit dem Löschblatt)* to blot. **(b)** *Tafel* to wipe, to clean. **(c)** *(Cook)* to add water to.

Ạblöse *f -, -n* **(a)** *(Abstand)* key money. **(b)** *(Ablösungssumme)* transfer fee.

ạblösen *sep* [1] *vt* **(a)** *(abmachen)* to take off, to remove; *Etikett, Briefmarke etc auch* to detach; *Pflaster etc auch* to peel off.

(b) *(Fin) (kapitalisieren) Rente* to get paid in a lump sum; *(auszahlen)* to pay (off) in a lump sum; *(tilgen) Schuld, Hypothek* to pay off, to redeem.

(c) *(ersetzen) Wache* to relieve; *Kollegen auch* to take over from ◆ **drei Minister wurden abgelöst** *(euph)* three ministers were relieved of their duties.

(d) *(fig: an Stelle treten von)* to take the place of; *(Methode, System)* to supersede ◆ **Regen hat jetzt das schöne Wetter abgelöst** the fine weather has now given way to rain.

[2] *vr* **(a)** *(abgehen)* to come off; *(Lack etc auch)* to peel off; *(Netzhaut)* to become detached.

(b) *(auch* **einander ~***)* to take turns; *(Fahrer, Kollegen auch, Wachen)* to relieve each other ◆ **wir lösen uns alle drei Stunden beim Babysitten ab** we each do three-hour shifts of babysitting, we take turns at babysitting, doing three hours each.

(c) *(auch* **einander ~***: alternieren)* to alternate ◆ **bei ihr lösen sich Fröhlichkeit und Trauer ständig ab** she constantly alternates between being happy and being miserable.

➤ SPRACHE AKTIV: **ablehnen: a** → 35.5, 38.3, 39.1, 39.3, 41

Ạblösesumme *f (Sport)* transfer fee.
Ạblösung *f* **(a)** *(Fin) (von Rente)* lump payment; *(von Hypothek, Schuld)* paying off, redemption.
(b) *(Wachwechsel)* relieving; *(Wache)* relief; *(Entlassung)* replacement ◆ **wann findet die ~ der Wache statt?** when will the guard be relieved?; **er kam als ~** he came as a replacement; **bei dieser Arbeit braucht man alle zwei Stunden eine ~** you need relieving every two hours in this work.
(c) *(das Ablösen)* removal, detachment; *(von Pflaster etc auch)* peeling off; *(das Sichablösen)* separation; *(von Lack etc)* peeling off; *(von Netzhaut)* detachment.
Ạblösungssumme *f (Sport)* transfer fee.
ạblotsen, ạbluchsen *vt sep (inf)* **jdm etw ~** to get *or* wangle *(inf)* sth out of sb.
Ạbluft *f -, no pl (Tech)* used air.
ạblutschen *vt sep* to lick ◆ **das Blut/den Honig (von etw) ~** to lick the blood/honey off (sth); **sich** *(dat)* **die Finger ~** to lick one's fingers (clean); **jdm einen ~** *(vulg)* to suck sb off *(vulg)*, to give sb a blow-job *(sl)*.
ABM [aːbeː'|ɛm] *abbr of* **(a) Antiballistic Missile** ABM. **(b) Arbeitsbeschaffungsmaßnahme.**
ạbmachen *vt sep (inf)* **(a)** *(entfernen)* to take off; *Schnur, Kette etc auch* to undo; *(herunternehmen)* to take down ◆ **er machte dem Hund die Leine ab** he took the dog's lead off.
(b) *(vereinbaren) Termin, Erkennungszeichen* to agree (on) ◆ **wir haben abgemacht, daß wir das tun werden** we've agreed to do it, we've agreed on doing it; **es ist noch nichts abgemacht worden** nothing's been agreed (on) yet; *siehe* **abgemacht.**
(c) *(besprechen)* to sort out, to settle ◆ **etw mit sich allein ~** to sort sth out for oneself, to come to terms with sth oneself.
(d) *(ableisten) Zeit* to do.
Ạbmachung *f* agreement.
ạbmagern *vi sep aux sein* to get thinner, to lose weight ◆ **sehr ~** to lose a lot of weight; *siehe* **abgemagert.**
Ạbmagerung *f, no pl (Auszehrung)* emaciation; *(Gewichtsverlust)* slimming.
Ạbmagerungskur *f* diet ◆ **eine ~ machen** to be on a diet, to be dieting; *(anfangen)* to go on a diet, to diet.
ạbmähen *vt sep* to mow.
ạbmahnen *vt sep (form)* to caution.
Ạbmahnschreiben *nt siehe* **Abmahnungsschreiben.**
Ạbmahnung *f (form)* caution.
Ạbmahnungsschreiben *nt (form)* formal letter of caution.
ạbmalen *vt sep (abzeichnen)* to paint.
ạbmarkten *vt sep* **davon lassen wir uns** *(dat)* **nichts ~** we will cede nothing on this point; **er ließ sich** *(dat)* **seine Rechte nicht ~** he would not bargain away his rights.
Ạbmarsch *m* departure; *(von Soldaten auch)* march-off; *(von Demonstranten etc auch)* moving off ◆ **ich sah dem ~ der Bergsteiger/Wanderer zu** I watched the climbers setting out *or* off; **zum ~ antreten** *(Mil)* to fall in (ready) for the march-off.
ạbmarschbereit *adj* ready to set out *or* off *or* move off; *(Mil)* ready to move off *or* march.
ạbmarschieren* *vi sep aux sein* to set out *or* off, to move off; *(Mil)* to march *or* move off.
Ạbmelde-: ~bestätigung *f document confirming that one has cancelled one's registration with the local authorities;* **~formular** *nt form to be filled in when one cancels one's registration with the local authorities.*
ạbmelden *sep* [1] *vt* **(a)** *Zeitungen etc* to cancel; *Telefon* to have disconnected; *(bei Verein) jdn* to cancel the membership of ◆ **sein Auto ~** to take one's car off the road; **seinen Fernsehapparat ~** to cancel one's television licence; **ein Kind von einer Schule ~** to take a child away from *or* remove a child from a school; **seine Familie polizeilich ~** to inform *or* notify the police that one's family is moving away.
(b) *(inf)* **abgemeldet sein** *(Sport)* to be outplayed/outboxed/outdriven *etc*; **jd/etw ist bei jdm abgemeldet** sb has lost interest in sb/sth; **er/sie ist bei mir abgemeldet** I don't want anything to do with him/her.
[2] *vr* to ask for permission to be absent; *(vor Abreise)* to say one is leaving, to announce one's departure; *(im Hotel)* to check out ◆ **sich bei jdm ~** to tell sb that one is leaving; **sich polizeilich** *or* **bei der Polizei ~** to inform *or* notify the police that one is moving away, to cancel one's registration with the police; **sich bei einem Verein ~** to cancel one's membership of a club.
Ạbmeldung *f (von Zeitungen etc)* cancellation; *(von Telefon)* disconnection; *(beim Einwohnermeldeamt)* cancellation of one's registration; *(inf: Formular) form to be filled in so that one's registration with the local authorities is cancelled* ◆ **seit der ~ meines Autos** since I took my car off the road; **die ~ meines Fernsehapparats** the cancellation of my television licence; **die ~ eines Kindes von einer Schule** the removal of a child from a school; **nach seiner ~ bei dem Verein** after he had cancelled his membership of the club.
ạbmergeln *vr sep* to slave away; *siehe* **abgemergelt.**
ạbmessen *vt sep irreg* **(a)** *(ausmessen)* to measure; *(genaue Maße feststellen von)* to measure up; *(fig) Worte* to weigh; *(abschätzen) Verlust, Schaden* to measure ◆ **er maß seine Schritte genau ab** *(fig)* he walked with great deliberation *or* very deliberately *or* with measured tread *(liter)*; *siehe* **abgemessen.**
(b) *(abteilen)* to measure off.
Ạbmessung *f usu pl* measurement; *(Ausmaß)* dimension.
ạbmildern *vt sep Geschmack* to tone down; *Äußerung auch* to moderate; *Aufprall* to cushion, to soften; *Schock* to lessen.

ạbmontieren* *vt sep Räder, Teile* to take off *(von etw* sth); *Maschine* to dismantle.
ABM-Stelle [aːbeː'|ɛm-] *f* temporary post (through job creation scheme).
ạbmühen *vr sep* to struggle (away) ◆ **sich mit jdm/etw ~** to struggle *or* slave away with sb/sth.
ạbmurksen *vt sep (dated sl) jdn* to bump off *(sl)*, to do in *(inf)*; *(schlachten)* to kill; *Motor* to stall.
ạbmustern *sep (Naut)* [1] *vt Besatzung* to pay off.
[2] *vi* to sign off, to leave the ship.
ABM-Vertrag [aːbeː'|ɛm-] *m (Pol)* ABM treaty.
ạbnabeln *sep* [1] *vt* **ein Kind ~** to cut a baby's umbilical cord.
[2] *vr* to cut oneself loose, to make the break ◆ **sich vom Elternhaus ~** to leave the parental home, to leave the nest *(inf)*; **abgenabelt vom Chef** independent of the boss.
ạbnagen *vt sep* to gnaw off; *Knochen* to gnaw ◆ **Fleisch vom Knochen ~** to gnaw meat off a bone.
ạbnähen *vt sep* to take in.
Ạbnäher *m -s, -* dart.
Ạbnahme *f -, -n* **(a)** *(Wegnahme)* removal; *(Herunternahme)* taking down; *(Amputation)* amputation ◆ **die ~ vom Kreuz(e)** the Descent from the Cross, the Deposition *(form)*.
(b) *(Verringerung)* decrease *(gen* in); *(bei Anzahl, Menge auch)* drop *(gen* in); *(von Niveau auch)* decline *(gen* in); *(von Kräften, Energie)* decline *(gen* in); *(von Interesse, Nachfrage)* falling off, decline; *(von Aufmerksamkeit)* falling off, flagging, waning; *(Verlust)* loss.
(c) *(von Prüfung)* holding; *(von Neubau, Fahrzeug etc)* inspection; *(von TÜV)* carrying out; *(von Eid)* administering ◆ **die ~ der Parade** the taking of the parade, the review of the troops; **die ~ der Prüfung kann erst erfolgen, wenn ...** the exam can only be held if ...
(d) *(Comm)* purchase ◆ **bei ~ von 50 Exemplaren** if you/we *etc* purchase *or* take 50 copies; **keine/gute ~ finden** to find no market, not to sell/to sell well.
ạbnehmbar *adj* removable, detachable.
ạbnehmen *sep irreg* [1] *vt* **(a)** *(herunternehmen)* to take off, to remove; *Hörer* to lift, to pick up; *Obst* to pick; *(lüften) Hut* to raise; *Vorhang, Bild, Wäsche* to take down; *Maschen* to decrease; *(abrasieren) Bart* to take *or* shave off; *(amputieren)* to amputate; *(Cards) Karte* to take from the pile ◆ **das Telefon ~** to answer the telephone.
(b) *(an sich nehmen)* **jdm etw ~** to take sth from sb, to relieve sb of sth *(form)*; *(fig) Arbeit, Sorgen* to take sth off sb's shoulders, to relieve sb of sth; **darf ich Ihnen den Mantel/die Tasche ~?** can I take your coat/bag?; **kann ich dir etwas ~?** *(tragen)* can I take something for you?; *(helfen)* can I do anything for you?; **jdm die Beichte ~** to hear confession from sb; **jdm einen Eid ~** to administer an oath to sb; **jdm ein Versprechen ~** to make sb promise something; **jdm einen Weg ~** to save sb a journey; **jdm eine Besorgung ~** to do some shopping for sb.
(c) *(wegnehmen)* to take away *(jdm* from sb); *(rauben, abgewinnen)* to take *(jdm* off sb); *(inf: abverlangen)* to take *(jdm* off sb) ◆ **diese Schweine haben mir alles abgenommen** the bastards have taken everything (I had).
(d) *(begutachten) Gebäude, Wohnung, Auto* to inspect; *(abhalten) Prüfung* to hold; *TÜV* to carry out.
(e) *(abkaufen)* to take *(dat* off), to buy *(dat* from, off).
(f) *Fingerabdrücke* to take; *Totenmaske* to make *(dat* of).
(g) *(fig inf: glauben)* to buy *(inf)* ◆ **dieses Märchen nimmt dir keiner ab!** *(inf)* nobody'll buy that tale!
[2] *vi* **(a)** *(sich verringern)* to decrease; *(Vorräte auch)* to go down, to diminish; *(zahlenmäßig, mengenmäßig auch)* to drop; *(Unfälle, Diebstähle etc)* to decrease (in number); *(Niveau)* to go down, to decline; *(Kräfte, Energie)* to fail, to decline; *(Fieber)* to lessen, to go down; *(Interesse, Nachfrage)* to fall off, to decline; *(Aufmerksamkeit)* to fall off, to flag, to wane; *(Mond)* to wane; *(Tage)* to grow *or* get shorter; *(beim Stricken)* to decrease ◆ **(an Gewicht) ~** to lose weight; **in letzter Zeit hast du im Gesicht abgenommen** your face has got thinner recently.
(b) *(Hörer, Telefon ~)* to answer.
Ạbnehmer *m -s, - (Comm)* buyer, purchaser, customer ◆ **keine/viele/wenige ~ finden** not to sell/to sell well/badly.
Ạbnehmerkreis *m* buyers *pl*, customers *pl*, market.
Ạbneigung *f* dislike *(gegen* of); *(Widerstreben)* aversion *(gegen* to).
abnọrm, ạbnormal *adj* abnormal.
Abnormität *f* abnorm(al)ity; *(Monstrum auch)* freak.
ạbnötigen *vt sep (geh)* **jdm etw ~** to wring *or* force sth from sb; **jdm Bewunderung ~** to win *or* gain sb's admiration; **jdm Respekt ~** to gain sb's respect.
ạbnutzen, ạbnützen *sep* [1] *vt* to wear out ◆ **dieser Begriff ist schon sehr abgenutzt worden** this idea is pretty well-worn *or* has become hackneyed; *siehe* **abgenutzt.**
[2] *vr* to wear out, to get worn out.
Ạbnutzung, Ạbnützung *f* wear (and tear) ◆ **die jahrelange ~ der Reifen** the years of wear (and tear) on the tyres; **die normale ~ ist im Mietpreis berücksichtigt** general wear and tear is included in the rent.
Ạbnutzungserscheinung *f* sign of wear (and tear).
Ạbo *nt -s, -s (inf) abbr of* **Abonnement.**
Ạbo-Kündigung *f (inf)* cancellation of subscription.
Abonnement [abɔnə'mãː] *nt -s, -s or -e* **(a)** *(Zeitungs~)* subscription ◆ **eine Zeitung im ~ beziehen** to subscribe to a newspaper, to have a subscription

for a newspaper.
(b) (*Theater~*) season ticket, subscription ◆ **ein ~ im Theater haben** to have a season ticket *or* subscription for the theatre *or* a theatre season ticket.
Abonnementfernsehen, Abonnenten-Fernsehen *nt* subscription television, pay TV.
Abonnent(in *f*) *m* (*Zeitungs~*) subscriber; (*Theater~*) season-ticket holder.
abonnieren* [1] *vt Zeitung* to subscribe to, to have a subscription for; *Konzertreihe, Theater* to have a season ticket *or* subscription for.
[2] *vi* **auf eine Zeitung abonniert sein** to subscribe to *or* to have a subscription for a newspaper; **auf eine Konzertreihe abonniert sein** to have a season ticket *or* subscription for a concert series.
Abo-pegel *f* (*inf*) level of subscriptions.
ab|ordnen *vt sep* to delegate ◆ **jdn zu einer Versammlung ~** to send sb as a delegate to a meeting.
Ab|ordnung *f* delegation; (*Delegation auch*) deputation.
Abort¹ *m* **-s, -e** (*dated*) lavatory, toilet.
Abort² *m* **-s, -e, Ab|ortus** *m* **-, -** (*spec*) (*Fehlgeburt*) miscarriage, abortion (*form*); (*Abtreibung*) abortion.
Abo-Werbung *f* (*inf*) subscription promotion.
abpacken *vt sep* to pack ◆ **ein abgepacktes Brot** a wrapped loaf.
abpassen *vt sep* **(a)** (*abwarten*) *Gelegenheit, Zeitpunkt* to wait for; (*ergreifen*) to seize ◆ **den richtigen Augenblick** *or* **Zeitpunkt ~** (*abwarten*) to bide one's time, to wait for the right time; (*ergreifen*) to move at the right time; **ich habe den Zeitpunkt nicht richtig abgepaßt** I mistimed it; **etw gut ~** to manage *or* arrange sth well; (*zeitlich auch*) to time sth well.
(b) (*auf jdn warten*) to catch; (*jdm auflauern*) to waylay.
abpausen *vt sep* to trace, to make a tracing of.
abperlen *vi sep aux sein* to drip off (*von etw* sth); (*Tautropfen*) to fall.
abpfeifen *sep irreg* (*Sport*) [1] *vi* (*Schiedsrichter*) to blow one's whistle.
[2] *vt* **das Spiel/die erste Halbzeit ~** to blow the whistle for the end of the game/for half-time.
Abpfiff *m* (*Sport*) final whistle ◆ **~ zur Halbzeit** half-time whistle, whistle for half-time.
abpflücken *vt sep* to pick.
abplacken (*inf*), **abplagen** *vr sep* to struggle (away) ◆ **sich sein ganzes Leben lang (mit etw) ~** to slave away one's whole life (at sth).
abplatten *vt sep* to flatten (out).
abplatzen *vi sep aux sein* (*Lack, Ölfarbe*) to flake *or* crack off; (*Knopf*) to fly *or* burst off ◆ **drei Knöpfe platzten ihm ab** three of his buttons flew off.
abprägen *vr sep* (*Muster*) to leave an imprint *or* mark.
Abprall *m* (*von Ball*) rebound; (*von Geschoß, Kugel*) ricochet (*von* off).
abprallen *vi sep aux sein* (*Ball*) to bounce off; (*Kugel*) to ricochet (off) ◆ **von** *or* **an etw** (*dat*) **~** to bounce/ricochet off sth; **an jdm ~** (*fig*) to make no impression on sb; (*Beleidigungen*) to bounce off sb.
Abpraller *m* **-s, -** (*Sport*) rebound ◆ **er hat den ~ eingeköpft** he headed it in on the rebound.
abpressen *vt sep* **jdm etw ~** to wring sth from sb; *Geld* to extort sth from sb; **die Angst preßte ihm den Atem/das Herz ab** he could scarcely breathe for fear/fear ate into his heart.
abprotzen *sep* [1] *vti* (*Mil*) *Geschütz* to unlimber.
[2] *vi* (*Mil sl*) to crap (*sl*), to have a crap (*sl*).
abpumpen *vt sep Teich, Schwimmbecken* to pump dry, to pump the water out of; *Wasser, Öl* to pump off; *Muttermilch* to express.
abputzen *sep* [1] *vt* to clean; *Schmutz* to clean off *or* up ◆ **sich** (*dat*) **die Nase/den Mund/die Hände/den Hintern ~** to wipe one's nose/mouth/hands/to wipe *or* clean one's bottom; **putz dir die Schuhe ab, bevor du ins Haus kommst** wipe your feet before you come into the house.
[2] *vr* (*S Ger, Aus, Sw*) to clean oneself.
abquälen *sep* [1] *vr* to struggle (away).
[2] *vt* **sich** (*dat*) **ein Lächeln ~** to force (out) a smile; **sich** (*dat*) **eine Erklärung/Antwort ~** to finally manage to produce an explanation/answer; **er quält sich immer noch mit seiner Doktorarbeit ab** he's still struggling with *or* sweating away over (*inf*) his PhD.
abqualifizieren* *vt sep* to dismiss, to write off.
abquetschen *vt sep* to crush ◆ **sich** (*dat*) **den Arm ~** to get one's arm crushed; **sich** (*dat*) **ein paar Tränen ~** to force *or* squeeze out a couple of tears; **sich** (*dat*) **ein Gedicht/eine Rede ~** to deliver oneself of a poem/speech (*iro*).
abrackern *vr sep* (*inf*) to struggle ◆ **sich für jdn ~** to slave away for sb; **warum sollen wir uns hier ~?** why should we break our backs here? (*inf*); **sich im Garten ~** to sweat away in the garden (*inf*).
Abraham *m* **-s** Abraham ◆ **in ~s Schoß** in the bosom of Abraham; **sicher wie in ~s Schoß** safe and secure.
abrahmen *vt sep Milch* to skim.
Abrakadabra *nt* **-s,** *no pl* (*Zauberwort*) abracadabra.
abrasieren* *vt sep* to shave off; (*inf*) *Gebäude* to flatten, to raze to the ground.
➤ **abraten** *vti sep irreg* **jdm (von) etw ~** to advise sb against sth; **jdm davon ~, etw zu tun** to warn *or* advise sb against doing sth.
Abraum *m* (*Min*) overburden, overlay shelf.
abräumen *vti sep* **(a)** to clear up *or* away ◆ **den Tisch ~** to clear the table. **(b)** (*Min*) to clear.
Abraumhalde *f* (*Min*) slag heap.
abrauschen *vi sep aux sein* (*inf*) to roar away *or* off; (*Aufmerksamkeit erregend*) to sweep away; (*aus Zimmer*) to sweep out.

abreagieren* *sep* [1] *vt Spannung, Wut* to work off, to get rid of, to abreact (*Psych*) ◆ **seinen Ärger an anderen ~** to take it out on others.
[2] *vr* to work it off ◆ **er war ganz wütend, aber jetzt hat er sich abreagiert** he was furious, but he's simmered down *or* cooled down now; **sich an der Katze ~** to take it out on the cat.
abrechnen *sep* [1] *vi* **(a)** (*Kasse machen*) to cash up ◆ **der Kellner wollte ~** the waiter was wanting us/them to pay our/their bill (*Brit*) *or* check (*US*); **darf ich ~?** would you like to settle your bill *or* check now?
(b) mit jdm ~ to settle up with sb; (*fig*) to settle (the score with) sb, to get even with sb.
[2] *vt* **(a)** (*abziehen*) to deduct, to take off; (*berücksichtigen*) to allow for, to make allowance(s) for.
(b) die Kasse ~ to cash up.
Abrechnung *f* **(a)** (*Aufstellung*) statement (*über +acc* for); (*Rechnung*) bill, invoice; (*Bilanz*) balancing, reckoning up; (*das Kassemachen*) cashing up; (*fig: Rache*) revenge ◆ **wieviel mußten Sie ausgeben? — ich bin gerade dabei, die ~ zu machen** *or* **ich bin gerade bei der ~** how much did you have to spend? — I'm just working it out now; **bei der ~ der Konten** when the accounts are/were being balanced; **er muß noch die ganzen ~en machen** he still has to do all the accounts *or* the bookwork; **der Tag der ~** (*fig*) the day of reckoning.
(b) (*Abzug*) deduction ◆ **nach ~ von** after the deduction of; **in ~ bringen** *or* **stellen** (*form*) to deduct; **folgende Beträge kommen in ~** (*form*) the following sums are to be deducted.
Abrechnungs-: ~termin *m* accounting date; **~verfahren** *nt* clearing procedure; **~verkehr** *m* clearing business.
Abrede *f* (*form*) agreement ◆ **etw in ~ stellen** to deny *or* dispute sth.
abregen *vr sep* (*inf*) to calm *or* cool *or* simmer down ◆ **reg dich ab!** relax!, cool it! (*inf*).
abreiben *vt sep irreg Schmutz, Rost* to clean *or* rub off; (*säubern*) *Fenster, Schuhe* to wipe; (*trocknen*) to rub down, to give a rub-down; (*Cook*) to grate.
Abreibung *f* (*Med*) rub-down; (*inf: Prügel*) hiding, beating, thrashing.
abreichern *vt sep siehe* **abgereichert**.
Abreise *f* departure (*nach* for) ◆ **bei der/meiner ~** when I left/leave, on my departure.
abreisen *vi sep aux sein* to leave (*nach* for) ◆ **wann reisen Sie ab?** when will you be leaving?
abreißen *sep irreg* [1] *vt* **(a)** (*abtrennen*) to tear *or* rip off; *Tapete, Blätter auch* to strip off; *Pflanzen* to tear out ◆ **er hat sich** (*dat*) **den Knopf abgerissen** he's torn his button off; **er wird dir nicht (gleich) den Kopf ~** (*inf*) he won't bite your head off (*inf*); *siehe* **abgerissen**.
(b) (*niederreißen*) *Gebäude* to pull down, to demolish ◆ **das A~ von Gebäuden** the demolition of buildings.
(c) (*sl: absitzen*) *Haftstrafe* to do.
[2] *vi aux sein* (*sich lösen*) to tear *or* come off; (*Schnürsenkel*) to break (off); (*fig: unterbrochen werden*) to break off ◆ **das reißt nicht ab** (*fig*) there is no end to it; **den Kontakt** *etc* **nicht ~ lassen** to stay in touch.
Abreißkalender *m* tear-off calendar.
abreiten *sep irreg* [1] *vi aux sein* to ride off *or* away.
[2] *vt* **(a)** *aux sein or haben* (*inspizieren*) *Front* to ride along; (*hin und zurück*) to ride up and down; *Strecke* to ride over; *Gelände* to patrol (on horseback). **(b)** (*Naut*) *Sturm* to ride out.
abrennen *sep irreg* (*inf*) [1] *vt* **(a)** *aux sein or haben Stadt, Geschäfte* to scour (round), to run round (*nach* looking for). **(b) sich** (*dat*) **die Hacken** *or* **Beine (nach etw) ~** to run one's legs off (looking for sth).
[2] *vr* to run oneself off one's feet.
abrichten *vt sep* **(a)** (*dressieren*) *Tier, Menschen* to train ◆ **der Hund ist nur auf Einbrecher abgerichtet** the dog is trained to go only for burglars; **darauf abgerichtet sein, etw zu tun** to be trained to do sth. **(b)** (*Tech*) *Werkstück, Brett* to true off *or* up.
Abrichter *m* **-s, -** trainer.
Abrichtung *f siehe vt* **(a)** training. **(b)** truing.
abriegeln *vt sep* (*verschließen*) *Tür* to bolt; (*absperren*) *Straße, Gebiet* to seal *or* cordon *or* block off.
Abrieg(e)lung *f siehe vt* bolting; sealing *or* cordoning *or* blocking off.
abringen *vt sep irreg* **jdm etw ~** to wring *or* force sth from *or* out of sb, to wrest sth from sb (*liter*); **sich** (*dat*) **ein Lächeln ~** to force a smile; **sich** (*dat*) **eine Entscheidung/ein paar Worte ~** to force oneself into (making) a decision/to manage to produce a few words; **dem Meer Land ~** (*liter*) to wrest land away from the sea (*liter*).
⚠ **Abriß** *m* **(a)** (*Abbruch*) demolition. **(b)** (*Übersicht*) outline, summary. **(c)** (*von Eintrittskarte etc*) tear-off part.
⚠ **Abriß-: ~arbeiten** *pl* demolition work; **~birne** *f* wrecking ball; **~liste** *f* (*inf*) demolition list; **auf der ~liste stehen** to be condemned; **a~reif** *adj* only fit for demolition; (*zum Abriß freigegeben*) condemned.
abrollen *sep* [1] *vt Papier, Stoff* to unroll; *Film, Bindfaden* to unwind, to unreel; *Kabel, Tau* to uncoil, to unwind.
[2] *vi aux sein* **(a)** (*Papier, Stoff*) to unroll, to come unrolled; (*Film, Bindfaden*) to unwind, to come unwound; (*Kabel, Tau*) to uncoil, to come uncoiled.
(b) (*Sport*) to roll.
(c) (*abfahren*) (*Züge, Waggons*) to roll off *or* away; (*Flugzeug*) to taxi off.
(d) (*inf*) (*vonstatten gehen*) (*Programm*) to run; (*Veranstaltung*) to go off; (*Ereignisse*) to unfold ◆ **etw rollt vor jds Augen ab** sth unfolds *or* unfurls before sb's (very) eyes; **mein ganzes Leben rollte noch einmal vor meinen Augen ab** my whole life passed before me again.
[3] *vr* (*Papier, Stoff*) to unroll itself, to come unrolled; (*Film, Bindfaden*) to un-

⚠: for details of spelling reform, see supplement

➤ SPRACHE AKTIV: **abraten** → 29.2

wind itself, to come unwound; (*Kabel, Tau*) to uncoil itself, to come uncoiled.

abrücken *sep* [1] *vt* (*wegschieben*) to move away ◆ **etw von der Wand ~** to move sth away from *or* out from the wall.
[2] *vi aux sein* **(a)** (*wegrücken*) to move away; (*fig: sich distanzieren*) to dissociate oneself (*von* from). **(b)** (*abmarschieren*) to move out.

Abruf *m* **(a) sich auf ~ bereit halten** to be ready to be called (for); **Ihr Wagen steht jederzeit auf ~ bereit** your car will be ready at any time; **auf ~ zur Verfügung stehen** to be available on call.
(b) (*Comm*) **etw auf ~ bestellen/kaufen** to order/buy sth (to be delivered) on call.
(c) (*Comput*) retrieval ◆ **auf ~ bereit** readily retrievable; **der Computer hat diese Daten auf ~ bereit** this data is readily retrievable *or* can readily be called up from the computer.

Abruf-: a~bar *adj* **(a)** (*Comput*) *Daten* retrievable; **(b)** (*Fin*) ready on call; **(c)** (*fig*) accessible; **~barkeit** *f* retrievability; accessibility; **a~bereit** *adj* **(a)** *Mensch* ready to be called (for); (*einsatzbereit*) ready (and waiting); (*abholbereit*) ready to be called for; **(b)** (*Comm, Fin*) ready on call.

abrufen *vt sep irreg* **(a)** (*wegrufen*) to call away ◆ **jdn aus dem Leben ~** (*euph*) to gather sb to his fathers (*euph*). **(b)** (*Comm*) to request delivery of; (*Fin: abheben*) to withdraw; *staatliche Zuschüsse* to call. **(c)** *Daten, Informationen* to call up, to retrieve.

abrunden *vt sep* (*lit, fig*) to round off ◆ **eine Zahl nach unten ~** to round a number down; **wir haben die Summe abgerundet** we made it a round sum, we rounded it up/down; **DM 13,12, also abgerundet DM 13,10** 13 marks 12, so call it 13 marks 10; **die abgerundete, endgültige Form einer Sonate/eines Gedichts** the final polished *or* rounded form of a sonata/poem.

Abrundung *f* (*lit, fig*) rounding off ◆ **zur ~ von etw** to round sth off.

abrupfen *vt sep Gras, Blumen* to rip *or* pull out; *Laub* to strip off; *Blätter* to pull *or* strip off.

abrupt *adj* abrupt.

Abruptheit *f* abruptness.

abrüsten *sep* [1] *vi* **(a)** (*Mil, Pol*) to disarm. **(b)** (*Build*) to take down *or* remove the scaffolding.
[2] *vt* **(a)** (*Mil, Pol*) to disarm. **(b)** *Gebäude* to take down *or* remove the scaffolding from *or* on.

Abrüstung *f, no pl* **(a)** (*Mil, Pol*) disarmament. **(b)** (*Build*) removal of the scaffolding.

Abrüstungs-: ~abkommen *nt* disarmament treaty; **~gespräche** *pl* disarmament talks *pl*; **~konferenz** *f* disarmament conference.

abrutschen *vi sep aux sein* (*abgleiten*) to slip; (*nach unten*) to slip down; (*Wagen*) to skid; (*Aviat*) to sideslip; (*fig*) (*Mannschaft, Schüler*) to drop (down) (*auf +acc* to); (*Leistungen*) to drop off, to go downhill; (*moralisch*) to let oneself go, to go downhill.

ABS [a:be:'|ɛs] *nt -, no pl* (*Aut*) *abbr of* **Antiblockiersystem** ABS.

Abs. *abbr of* **Absatz; Absender.**

absäbeln *vt sep* (*inf*) to hack *or* chop off.

absacken *vi sep aux sein* (*sinken*) to sink; (*Boden, Gebäude auch*) to subside; (*Flugzeug, Blutdruck*) to drop, to fall; (*fig inf: nachlassen*) to fall *or* drop off; (*Schüler*) to go down; (*verkommen*) to go to pot (*inf*) ◆ **sie ist in ihren Leistungen sehr abgesackt** her performance has dropped off a lot.

Absage *f -, -n* refusal; (*auf Einladung auch*) negative reply ◆ **das ist eine ~ an die Demokratie** that's a denial of democracy; **jdm/einer Sache eine ~ erteilen** to reject sb/sth.

absagen *sep* [1] *vt* (*rückgängig machen*) *Veranstaltung, Besuch* to cancel, to call off; (*ablehnen*) *Einladung* to decline, to turn down, to refuse ◆ **er hat seine Teilnahme abgesagt** he decided against taking part.
[2] *vi* to cry off ◆ **jdm ~** to tell sb that one can't come; **wenn ich ihn einlade, sagt er jedesmal ab** whenever I invite him he says no.

absägen *vt sep* **(a)** (*abtrennen*) to saw off. **(b)** (*fig inf*) to chuck *or* sling out (*inf*); *Minister, Beamten* to oust; *Schüler* to make fail.

Absahne *f -, no pl* (*inf*) bonanza.

absahnen *sep* [1] *vt Milch* to skim; (*fig inf*) *Geld* to rake in; (*sich verschaffen*) to cream off; *das Beste* to take ◆ **den Markt ~** to take the cream, to take the pick of the bunch.
[2] *vi* to skim milk; (*fig inf*) to take the best; (*in bezug auf Menschen auch*) to take the cream; (*in bezug auf Geld*) to clean up (*inf*).

absatteln *vti sep* to unsaddle.

Absatz *m -es, Absätze* **(a)** (*Abschnitt*) paragraph; (*Typ*) indention; (*Jur*) section ◆ **einen ~ machen** to start a new paragraph/to indent.
(b) (*Treppen~*) half-landing; (*Mauer~*) overhang; (*herausragend*) ledge.
(c) (*Schuh~*) heel ◆ **spitze Absätze** stilettos, stiletto heels; **sich auf dem ~ (her)umdrehen, auf dem ~ kehrtmachen** to turn on one's heel.
(d) (*Verkauf*) sales *pl* ◆ **um den/unseren ~ zu steigern** to increase sales/our sales; **~ finden** *or* **haben** to sell; **guten/begeisterten** *or* **starken** *or* **reißenden ~ finden** to sell well/like hot cakes.

Absatz-: ~chance *f* sales potential *no pl*; **a~fähig** *adj* marketable, saleable; **~flaute** *f* slump in sales *or* in the market; **~forschung** *f* sales research; **~gebiet** *nt* sales area; **~genossenschaft** *f* marketing cooperative; **~krise** *f* sales crisis; **~land** *nt* customer, buyer; **~markt** *m* market; **~planung** *f* sales planning; **~schwierigkeiten** *pl* sales problems *pl*; **auf ~schwierigkeiten stoßen** to meet with sales resistance; **~steigerung** *f* increase in sales, sales increase; **~strategie** *f* sales strategy; **a~weise** *adj* in paragraphs.

absaufen *vi sep irreg aux sein* (*sl: ertrinken*) to drown; (*inf: Motor, Min: Grube*) to flood; (*sl: Schiff etc*) to go down.

absaugen *vt sep Flüssigkeit, Gas, Staub* to suck out *or* off; (*mit Staubsauger*) to hoover (*Brit* ®) *or* vacuum up; *Teppich, Sofa* to hoover ®, to vacuum.

ABS- [a:be:'|ɛs-]: **~-Bremse** *f* ABS brakes *pl*; **~-Bremssystem** *nt* ABS braking system.

abschaben *vt sep* to scrape off; (*säubern*) to scrape (clean); *Stoff* to wear thin; *siehe* **abgeschabt.**

abschaffen *sep* [1] *vt* **(a)** (*außer Kraft setzen*) to abolish, to do away with. **(b)** (*nicht länger halten*) to get rid of; *Auto etc auch* to give up.
[2] *vr* (*S Ger inf: sich abarbeiten*) to slave away (*inf*), to work like a slave.

Abschaffung *f siehe vt* **(a)** abolition. **(b)** getting rid of; giving up.

abschälen *sep* [1] *vt Haut, Rinde* to peel off; *Baumstamm* to strip ◆ **die Rinde eines Baumes ~** to strip *or* peel the bark off a tree.
[2] *vr* to peel off.

abschalten *sep* [1] *vt* to switch off; *Kontakt* to break.
[2] *vi* (*fig*) to unwind.
[3] *vr* to switch itself off.

Abschaltung *f* switching off; (*von Kontakt*) breaking.

abschatten, abschattieren* *vt sep* (*lit*) to shade; (*fig*) to give a slight nuance to.

Abschattung, Abschattierung *f* (*lit*) shading; (*fig*) nuance.

abschätzen *vt sep* to estimate, to assess; *Menschen, Fähigkeiten* to assess, to appraise ◆ **seine Lage ~** to take stock of *or* assess one's position; **ein ~der Blick** an appraising look; **jdn mit einer ~den Miene betrachten** to look at sb appraisingly.

abschätzig [1] *adj* disparaging; *Bemerkung auch* derogatory.
[2] *adv* disparagingly ◆ **sich ~ über jdn äußern** to make disparaging *or* derogatory remarks about sb.

Abschaum *m, no pl* scum ◆ **der ~ der Menschheit** *or* **der menschlichen Gesellschaft** the scum of the earth.

abscheiden *sep irreg* [1] *vt* **(a)** (*ausscheiden*) to give off, to produce; (*Biol auch*) to secrete; (*Chem*) to precipitate.
(b) (*rare: absondern, trennen*) to separate off; *siehe* **abgeschieden.**
[2] *vr* (*Flüssigkeit etc*) to be given off *or* produced; (*Biol auch*) to be secreted; (*Chem*) to be precipitated.
[3] *vi aux sein* (*euph liter: sterben*) to depart this life (*liter*), to pass away ◆ **sein A~** his passing; *siehe* **abgeschieden.**

abscheren *vt sep Haare, Wolle* to shear off; *Bart* to shave off; *Kopf, Kinn* to shave; *Schafe* to shear.

Abscheu *m -(e)s, no pl or f -, no pl* repugnance, repulsion, abhorrence (*vor +dat* at) ◆ **vor jdm/etw ~ haben** *or* **empfinden** to loathe *or* detest *or* abhor sb/sth; **~ in jdm erregen** to repulse sb.

abscheuern *sep* [1] *vt* **(a)** (*reinigen*) *Fußboden, Wand* to scrub (down); *Schmutz* to scrub off. **(b)** (*abschürfen*) *Haut* to rub *or* scrape off. **(c)** (*abwetzen*) *Kleidung, Stoff* to rub *or* wear thin; *Ellbogen* to wear out *or* through ◆ **ein abgescheuerter Kragen** a worn collar.
[2] *vr* (*Stoff*) to wear thin; (*Tierfell*) to get rubbed *or* scraped off.

abscheu|erregend *adj* repulsive, loathsome, abhorrent.

abscheulich *adj* abominable, atrocious, loathsome; *Verbrechen auch* heinous; *Anblick auch* repulsive; (*inf*) awful, terrible (*inf*) ◆ **wie ~!** how ghastly *or* awful *or* terrible!; **es ist ~ kalt** it's hideously cold.

Abscheulichkeit *f* (*Untat*) atrocity, abomination; (*no pl: Widerwärtigkeit*) loathsomeness, atrociousness; (*von Verbrechen auch*) heinousness; (*von Geschmack, Anblick*) repulsiveness.

abschicken *vt sep* to send; *Paket, Brief* to send off, to dispatch; (*mit der Post auch*) to post, to mail (*esp US*).

Abschiebehaft *f* (*Jur*) remand pending deportation ◆ **jdn in ~ nehmen** to put sb on remand pending deportation.

abschieben *sep irreg* [1] *vt* **(a)** (*wegschieben*) *Schrank etc* to push out *or* away (*von* from); (*fig*) *Verantwortung, Schuld* to push *or* shift (*auf +acc* onto) ◆ **er versucht immer, die Verantwortung auf andere abzuschieben** he always tries to pass the buck.
(b) (*ausweisen*) *Ausländer, Häftling* to deport.
(c) (*inf: loswerden*) to get rid of ◆ **jdn in eine andere Abteilung ~** to shunt sb off to another department.
[2] *vi aux sein* (*sl*) to push *or* clear off (*inf*) ◆ **schieb ab!** shove off! (*inf*).

Abschiebung *f, no pl* (*Ausweisung*) deportation.

Abschied *m -(e)s,* (*rare*) *-e* **(a)** (*Trennung*) farewell, parting ◆ **von jdm/etw ~ nehmen** to say goodbye to sb/sth, to take one's leave of sb/sth; **ein Kuß zum ~** a farewell *or* goodbye kiss; **zum ~ überreichte er ihr einen Blumenstrauß** on parting, he presented her with a bunch of flowers; **ein trauriger ~** a sad farewell; **es war für beide ein schwerer ~** parting was hard for both of them; **ich hasse ~e** I hate farewells *or* goodbyes; **es war ein ~ für immer** *or* **fürs Leben** it was goodbye for ever; **beim ~ meinte er, ...** as he was leaving he said ...; **beim ~ auf Bahnhöfen ...** saying goodbye at stations ...; **der ~ von der Heimat fiel ihm schwer** it was hard for him to say goodbye to the land of his birth; **ihr ~ von der Bühne/vom Film** her farewell from the stage/from films; (*letzte Vorstellung*) her farewell performance; **ihre Heirat bedeutete für sie den ~ von der Kindheit** her marriage marked the end of her childhood; **der ~ von der Vergangenheit** breaking *or* the break with the past.
(b) (*Rücktritt*) (*von Beamten*) resignation; (*von Offizieren*) discharge ◆ **seinen ~ nehmen** *or* **einreichen** to tender *or* hand in one's resignation/to apply for a discharge; **seinen ~ erhalten** *or* **bekommen** to be dismissed/discharged.

Abschieds- *in cpds* farewell; **~besuch** *m* farewell *or* goodbye visit; **~brief** *m* letter of farewell, farewell letter; **~feier** *f* farewell *or* going-away *or* leaving party; **~geschenk** *nt* (*für Kollegen etc*) leaving present; (*für Freund*) going-away present; **~gesuch** *nt* (*Pol*) letter of resignation; **sein ~gesuch einreichen** to tender one's resignation; **~gruß** *m* farewell; (*Wort zum Abschied*) word of farewell; ⚠**~kuß** *m* farewell *or* parting *or* goodbye kiss; **~rede** *f* farewell speech, valedictory (speech) (*form*); **~schmerz** *m* pain of parting; **~stimmung** *f* mood of parting *or* farewell; **~stunde** *f* time *or* hour of parting, time to say goodbye; **~szene** *f* farewell scene; **~träne** *f* tear at parting.

abschießen *sep irreg* 1 *vt* **(a)** (*losschießen*) *Geschoß, Gewehr, Kanone* to fire; *Pfeil* to shoot (off), to loose off; *Rakete* to launch; (*auf ein Ziel*) to fire; (*fig*) *Blick* to shoot; *Fragen, Befehle, Bemerkung* to fire (*auf +acc* at).
(b) (*außer Gefecht setzen*) *Flugzeug, Pilot* to shoot down; *Panzer* to knock out; (*wegschießen*) *Bein etc* to shoot off.
(c) (*totschießen*) *Wild* to shoot; (*sl: Menschen*) to shoot down; *siehe* **Vogel.**
(d) (*fig inf: abschieben*) to get rid of.
2 *vi* (*Sport*) to kick off.

abschilfern *vi sep aux sein* to peel off.

abschinden *vr sep irreg* (*inf*) to knacker oneself (*sl*); (*schwer arbeiten*) to work one's fingers to the bone ◆ **sich mit Gartenarbeit/einem schweren Koffer ~** to knacker oneself gardening/carrying a heavy suitcase.

Abschirmdienst *m* (*Mil*) counter-espionage service.

abschirmen *sep* 1 *vt* to shield; (*schützen auch*) to protect; (*vor Licht auch*) to screen; *Lampe* to cover ◆ **jdn vor etw** (*dat*) **~** to shield *or* protect sb from sth; **etw gegen die Sonne ~** to screen *or* shield sth from the sun.
2 *vr* to shield oneself (*gegen* from); (*sich schützen*) to protect oneself (*gegen* from *or* against); (*sich isolieren*) to isolate oneself, to cut oneself off (*gegen* from).

Abschirmung *f, no pl* **(a)** *siehe vt* shielding; protection; screening; covering. **(b)** (*fig*) (*Selbstschutz, Pol*) protection; (*Isolierung*) isolation.

abschirren *vt sep* to unharness; *Ochsen* to unyoke.

abschlachten *vt sep* to slaughter; *Menschen auch* to butcher.

Abschlachtung *f siehe vt* slaughter; butchering *no pl.*

abschlaffen *sep* (*inf*) 1 *vi aux sein* to flag.
2 *vt* to whack (*inf*).

Abschlag *m* **(a)** (*Preisnachlaß*) reduction; (*Abzug*) deduction. **(b)** (*Zahlung*) part payment (*auf +acc* of). **(c)** (*Ftbl*) kick-out, punt; (*Hockey*) bully(-off); (*Golf*) tee-off; (*~fläche*) tee. **(d)** (*Abholzung*) felling.

▼ **abschlagen** *irreg* 1 *vt* **(a)** (*mit Hammer etc*) to knock off; (*mit Schwert etc*) to cut off; (*mit Beil*) to cut *or* chop off; *Baum, Wald* to cut *or* chop down; (*herunterschlagen*) to knock down.
(b) *Gerüst etc* to take down.
▼ **(c)** (*ablehnen*) to refuse; *Einladung, Bitte auch, Antrag* to turn down ◆ **jdm etw ~** to refuse sb sth; **sie/er kann niemandem etwas ~** she/he can never refuse anybody anything.
(d) (*zurückschlagen*) *Angriff, Feind* to beat *or* drive off, to repulse; *Konkurrenten* to wipe out; *siehe* **abgeschlagen.**
(e) *auch vi* (*Ftbl*) to punt; (*Hockey*) to bully off; (*Golf*) to tee off.
(f) sein Wasser ~ (*dated inf*) to relieve oneself.
2 *vr* (*Dampf etc*) to condense.

abschlägig *adj* negative ◆ **jdn/etw ~ bescheiden** (*form*) to reject sb/sth, to turn sb/sth down.

Abschlag(s)zahlung *f* part payment.

abschlecken *vt sep* (*S Ger, Aus*) *siehe* **ablecken.**

abschleifen *sep irreg* 1 *vt Kanten, Ecken, Unebenheiten* to grind down; *Rost* to polish off; *Messer* to grind; *Holzboden* to sand (down).
2 *vr* to get worn off, to wear down; (*fig*) (*Angewohnheit etc*) to wear off; (*Mensch*) to have the rough edges taken off ◆ **das schleift sich (noch) ab** (*fig*) that'll wear off.

Abschleppdienst *m* breakdown service, (vehicle) recovery service.

abschleppen *sep* 1 *vt* **(a)** (*wegziehen*) to drag *or* haul off *or* away; *Fahrzeug, Schiff* to tow, to take in tow; (*Behörde*) to tow away.
(b) (*inf*) *Menschen* to drag along; (*sich aneignen*) to get one's hands on (*inf*); (*aufgabeln*) to pick up (*inf*).
2 *vr* **sich mit etw ~** (*inf*) to struggle with sth.

Abschlepp-: ~fahrzeug *nt* breakdown *or* recovery vehicle; **~kosten** *pl* recovery costs *pl*; **~öse** *f* tow loop; **~seil** *nt* towrope; **~stange** *f* tow-bar.

abschließbar *adj* lockable.

abschließen *sep irreg* 1 *vt* **(a)** (*zuschließen*) to lock; *Auto, Raum, Schrank* to lock (up) ◆ **etw luftdicht ~** to put an airtight seal on sth.
(b) (*beenden*) *Sitzung, Vortrag etc* to conclude, to bring to a close; (*mit Verzierung*) to finish off; *Kursus* to complete ◆ **sein Studium ~** to take one's degree, to graduate; **mit abgeschlossenem Studium** with a degree.
(c) (*vereinbaren*) *Geschäft* to conclude, to transact; *Versicherung* to take out; *Wette* to place ◆ **einen Vertrag ~** (*Pol*) to conclude a treaty; (*Jur, Comm*) to conclude a contract.
(d) (*Comm: abrechnen*) *Bücher* to balance; *Konto auch* to settle; *Geschäftsjahr* to close; *Inventur* to complete; *Rechnung* to make up.
2 *vr* (*sich isolieren*) to cut oneself off, to shut oneself away ◆ **sich von der Außenwelt ~** to cut *or* shut oneself off from the outside world; *siehe* **abgeschlossen.**
3 *vi* **(a)** (*zuschließen*) to lock up ◆ **sieh mal nach, ob auch abgeschlossen ist** will you see if everything's locked?
(b) (*enden*) to close, to come to a close, to conclude; (*mit Verzierung*) to be finished off.
(c) (*Comm*) (*Vertrag schließen*) to conclude the deal; (*Endabrechnung machen*) to do the books.
(d) (*Schluß machen*) to finish, to end ◆ **mit allem/dem Leben ~** to finish with everything/life; **mit der Vergangenheit ~** to break with the past.

abschließend 1 *adj* concluding.
2 *adv* in conclusion, finally.

⚠**Abschluß** *m* **(a)** (*Beendigung*) end; (*inf: ~prüfung*) final examination; (*Univ*) degree ◆ **zum ~ von etw** at the close or end of sth; **zum ~ möchte ich ...** finally *or* to conclude I would like ...; **seinen ~ finden** (*geh*), **zum ~ kommen** to come to an end; **etw zum ~ bringen** to finish sth; **ein Wort zum ~** a final word; **kurz vor dem ~ stehen** to be in the final stages; **sie hat die Universität ohne ~ verlassen** she left the university without taking her degree; *siehe* **krönen.**
(b) *no pl* (*Vereinbarung*) conclusion; (*von Wette*) placing; (*von Versicherung*) taking out ◆ **bei ~ des Vertrages** on completion of the contract.
(c) (*Comm: Geschäft*) business deal ◆ **zum ~ kommen** to make a deal.
(d) *no pl* (*Comm: der Bücher*) balancing; (*von Konto*) settlement; (*von Geschäftsjahr*) close; (*von Inventur*) completion.
(e) (*Rand, abschließender Teil*) border.

⚠**Abschluß-: ~ball** *m* (*von Tanzkurs*) final ball; **~feier** *f* (*Sch*) speech *or* prize-giving day; **~klasse** *f* (*Sch*) final class *or* year; **~kommuniqué** *nt* final communiqué; **~prüfung** *f* **(a)** (*Sch*) final examination; (*Univ auch*) finals *pl*; **(b)** (*Comm*) audit; **~rechnung** *f* final account; **~zeugnis** *nt* (*Sch*) leaving certificate, diploma (*US*).

abschmälzen, abschmalzen (*Aus*) *vt sep* to gratinate.

abschmatzen *vt sep* (*inf*) to slobber over (*inf*).

abschmecken *sep* 1 *vt* (*kosten*) to taste, to sample; (*würzen*) to season.
2 *vi* (*kosten*) to taste; (*nachwürzen*) to add some seasoning.

abschmeicheln *vt sep* **jdm etw ~** to wheedle *or* coax sth out of sb.

abschmelzen *vti sep irreg* (*vi: aux sein*) to melt (away); (*Tech*) to melt down.

abschmettern *vt sep* (*inf*) (*Sport*) to smash; (*fig inf: zurückweisen*) to throw out ◆ **mit seinem Antrag wurde er abgeschmettert** his application was thrown *or* flung out; **er wurde abgeschmettert** he was shot down (*inf*).

abschmieren *sep* 1 *vt* **(a)** (*Tech*) *Auto* to grease, to lubricate. **(b)** (*inf: abschreiben*) to crib (*inf*).
2 *vi aux sein* (*Aviat*) to go down.

Abschmierpresse *f* grease gun.

abschminken *vt sep* **(a)** *Gesicht, Haut* to remove the make-up from ◆ **sich ~** to take off *or* remove one's make-up. **(b)** (*sl: aufgeben*) **sich** (*dat*) **etw ~** to get sth out of one's head.

abschmirgeln *vt sep* to sand down.

Abschn. *abbr of* **Abschnitt** para.

abschnacken *vt sep* (*N Ger inf*) **jdm etw ~** to wheedle *or* coax sth out of sb.

abschnallen *sep* 1 *vt* to unfasten, to undo.
2 *vr* to unfasten one's seat belt.
3 *vi* (*sl*) **(a)** (*nicht mehr folgen können*) to give up. **(b)** (*fassungslos sein*) to be staggered (*inf*) ◆ **wenn man sich das überlegt, schnallt man ab** it's staggering if you think about it; **da schnallste ab!** it's unbelievable!

abschneiden *sep irreg* 1 *vt* (*lit, fig*) to cut off; *Flucht, Ausweg auch* to block off; *Blumen, Scheibe* to cut (off); *Zigarre* to cut the end off; *Fingernägel, Haar* to cut; *Rock, Kleid* to cut the seam off ◆ **jdm die Rede/das Wort ~** to cut sb short; *siehe* **Scheibe.**
2 *vi* **bei etw gut/schlecht ~** (*inf*) to come off well/badly in sth.

abschnippeln *vt sep* (*inf*) **etw von etw ~** to cut a bit off sth; (*mit Schere auch*) to snip sth off sth.

Abschnitt *m* **(a)** section; (*Math*) segment; (*Mil*) sector, zone; (*Geschichts~, Zeit~*) period. **(b)** (*Kontroll~*) (*von Scheck etc*) counterfoil; (*von Karte*) section; (*von Papier*) slip.

abschnitt(s)weise *adv* in sections ◆ **der Lehrer nahm das Buch ~ durch** the teacher went through the book section by section.

abschnüren *vt sep* to cut off (*von* from); (*Med*) *Glied* to put a tourniquet on ◆ **jdm das Blut ~** to cut off sb's circulation; **jdm die Luft ~** (*lit*) to stop sb breathing; (*fig*) to bankrupt *or* ruin sb; **die Angst schnürte ihr das Herz ab** (*liter*) she was paralyzed by fear.

abschöpfen *vt sep* to skim off; (*fig*) *Dank, Ruhm* to reap; *Kaufkraft* to absorb; (*für sich gewinnen*) to cream off ◆ **den Rahm** *or* **das Fett ~** (*fig*) to cream off the best part; **den Gewinn ~** to siphon off the profits.

Abschöpfung *f* (*Fin: von Kaufkraft*) absorption ◆ **sparen Sie durch ~** save by automatic transfer.

abschotten *vt sep* (*Naut*) to separate with a bulkhead, to bulk head off ◆ **sich gegen etw ~** (*fig*) to cut oneself off from sth; **etw ~** to shield *or* screen sth.

abschrägen *vt sep* to slope; *Holz, Brett* to bevel ◆ **ein abgeschrägtes Dach** a sloping roof; **er schrägte das Brett an den Kanten ab** he bevelled the edges of the board.

Abschrägung *f* slope; (*von Brett*) bevel.

abschrauben *vt sep* to unscrew.

abschrecken *sep* 1 *vt* **(a)** (*fernhalten*) to deter, to put off; (*verjagen: Hund, Vogelscheuche*) to scare off ◆ **jdn von etw ~** to deter sb from sth, to put sb off sth; **ich lasse mich dadurch nicht ~** that won't deter me, I won't be deterred by that. **(b)** (*abkühlen*) *Stahl* to quench; (*Cook*) to rinse with cold water.
2 *vi* (*Strafe*) to act as a deterrent.

abschreckend *adj* **(a)** (*warnend*) deterrent ◆ **ein ~es Beispiel** a warning; **eine ~e Wirkung haben, ~ wirken** to act as a deterrent. **(b)** (*abstoßend*) *Häßlichkeit* repulsive.

Abschreckung *f* **(a)** (*das Fernhalten, Mil*) deterrence; (*das Verjagen*) scaring off; (*~smittel*) deterrent. **(b)** (*Abkühlung*) (*von Stahl*) quenching; (*Cook*) rinsing with cold water.

Abschreckungs-: ~maßnahme *f* deterrent; **~mittel** *nt* deterrent; **~theorie** *f* (*Jur*) theory of deterrence; **~waffe** *f* deterrent weapon.

abschreiben *sep irreg* [1] *vt* **(a)** (*kopieren*) to copy out; (*Sch: abgucken*) to copy, to crib (*inf*); (*plagiieren*) to copy (*bei, von* from).
(b) (*schreibend abnutzen*) to use up; *siehe* **Finger.**
(c) (*Comm: absetzen, abziehen*) to deduct.
(d) (*verloren geben*) to write off ♦ **er ist bei mir abgeschrieben** I'm through *or* finished with him.
[2] *vi* **(a)** (*Sch*) to copy, to crib (*inf*).
(b) jdm ~ to write to sb to tell him that one cannot come *etc.*
[3] *vr* (*Bleistift, Farbband*) to get used up; (*Kugelschreiber, Filzstift auch*) to run out.

Abschreiber *m* (*pej*) plagiarist; (*Sch*) cribber.

Abschreibung *f* (*Steuer~*) tax write-off; (*Comm*) deduction; (*Wertverminderung*) depreciation.

Abschreibungsprojekt *nt* tax avoidance scheme.

abschreiten *vt sep irreg* **(a)** (*entlanggehen*) to walk along; (*hin und zurück*) to walk up and down; *Gelände* to patrol; (*inspizieren*) *Front* to inspect. **(b)** (*messen*) to pace out.

Abschrift *f* copy.

abschrubben *vt sep* (*inf*) *Schmutz* to scrub off *or* away; *Rücken, Kleid, Fußboden* to scrub (down) ♦ **schrubbt euch richtig ab!** give yourselves a good scrub!

abschuften *vr sep* (*inf*) to slog one's guts out (*inf*).

abschuppen *sep* [1] *vt Fisch* to scale.
[2] *vr* to flake off.

abschürfen *vt sep* to graze.

Abschürfung *f* (*Wunde*) graze.

⚠ **Abschuß** *m* **(a)** (*das Abfeuern*) firing, shooting; (*von Pfeil auch*) loosing off; (*von Rakete*) launch(ing); (*auf ein Ziel*) firing.
(b) (*das Außer-Gefecht-Setzen*) shooting down; (*von Panzer*) knocking out ♦ **die Luftwaffe erzielte zwölf Abschüsse** the airforce shot *or* brought down twelve planes.
(c) (*von Wild*) shooting ♦ **Fasanen sind jetzt zum ~ freigegeben** pheasant-shooting is now permitted; **die Zahl der Abschüsse** the number of kills; **durch ~ des Ministers** (*fig inf*) by getting rid of the minister.
(d) (*Sport*) (goal) kick.

⚠ **Abschußbasis** *f* launching base.

abschüssig *adj* sloping ♦ **eine sehr ~e Straße** a steep road, a steeply sloping road.

Abschüssigkeit *f* slope.

⚠ **Abschuß-: ~liste** *f* (*inf*) **er steht auf der ~liste** his days are numbered; **jdn auf die ~liste setzen** to put sb on the hit list (*inf*); **auf jds ~liste stehen** to be on sb's hit list (*inf*); **~rampe** *f* launching pad.

abschütteln *vt sep Staub, Schnee* to shake off; *Decke, Tuch* to shake (out); (*fig*) *lästige Menschen, Verfolger* to shake off, to lose (*inf*); *Gedanken, Ärger etc* to get rid of ♦ **das Joch der Knechtschaft ~** to throw off the yoke of slavery.

abschütten *vt sep Flüssigkeit, Mehl, Sand etc* to pour off; (*Cook*) *Flüssigkeit* to drain off; *Kartoffeln etc* to drain; *Eimer* to empty.

abschwächen *sep* [1] *vt* to weaken; *Behauptung, Formulierung, Foto* to tone down; *Schock, Aufprall* to lessen; *Wirkung, Einfluß auch* to lessen; *Stoß, Eindruck* to soften.
[2] *vr* to drop *or* fall off, to diminish; (*Lärm*) to decrease; (*Met: Hoch, Tief*) to disperse; (*Preisauftrieb, Andrang*) to ease off; (*St Ex: Kurse*) to weaken.

Abschwächung *f siehe vb* weakening; toning down; lessening; softening; decrease; dispersal; easing off; reduction.

abschwatzen, abschwätzen (*S Ger*) *vt sep* (*inf*) **jdm etw ~** to talk sb into giving one sth; **das habe ich mir von meinem Bruder ~ lassen** I let my brother talk me into giving it to him.

abschweifen *vi sep aux sein* (*lit, fig*) to stray, to wander (off *or* away); (*Redner auch*) to digress ♦ **er schweifte vom Thema ab** he deviated from the subject.

Abschweifung *f siehe vi* digression; deviation.

abschwellen *vi sep irreg aux sein* (*Entzündung, Fluß*) to go down; (*Lärm*) to die *or* fade *or* ebb away ♦ **der geschwollene Fuß ist wieder abgeschwollen** the swelling in his foot has gone down.

abschwemmen *vt sep* to wash away.

abschwenken *sep* [1] *vi aux sein* to turn away; (*Kamera*) to swing round, to pan ♦ **(von der Straße) ~** to turn off (the road); **er ist nach links abgeschwenkt** (*lit*) he turned off to the left; (*fig*) he swung (over) to the left; **(nach rechts) ~** (*Mil*) to wheel (right); **er schwenkte zur Medizin ab** he changed over to medicine.
[2] *vt Kartoffeln, Gemüse* to drain (off).

abschwimmen *sep irreg* [1] *vi aux sein* (*losschwimmen*) to swim off *or* away.
[2] *vt* **(a)** *aux sein or haben Strecke* to swim; *Gewässer* to swim along. **(b)** (*verlieren*) **(sich** *dat***) überflüssige Pfunde ~** to swim off those extra pounds.

abschwindeln *vt sep* **jdm etw ~** to swindle sb out of sth.

abschwingen *vi sep irreg* (*Ski*) to do a downhill turn.

abschwirren *vi sep aux sein* to whirr off; (*fig inf: weggehen*) to buzz off (*inf*) ♦ **die Vögel schwirrten plötzlich ab** with a flutter of wings the birds suddenly flew off.

abschwitzen *vt sep* to sweat off ♦ **sich** (*dat*) **einen ~** (*sl*) to sweat like mad (*inf*) *or* crazy (*inf*).

abschwören *sep irreg* [1] *vi* (*old, liter*) to renounce (*dat* sth) ♦ **dem Glauben/Teufel ~** to renounce one's faith/the devil; **seinen Ketzereien ~** to recant one's heresies; **dem Alkohol ~** (*inf*) to give up drinking.
[2] *vt* (*old: ableugnen*) *Schuld, Mittäterschaft* to deny, to repudiate; *Glauben* to renounce.

Abschwung *m* (*Sport*) dismount; (*Ski*) downhill turn; (*Comm*) downward trend, recession.

absegeln *sep* [1] *vi* **(a)** *aux sein* (*lossegeln*) to sail off *or* away, to set sail; (*inf: weggehen*) to sail off ♦ **der Schoner segelte von Bremen ab** the schooner sailed from Bremen *or* set sail from Bremen. **(b)** (*Sport: die Saison beenden*) to have one's last sail.
[2] *vt Strecke* to sail; *Küste* to sail along.

absegnen *vt sep* (*inf*) *Vorschlag, Plan* to give one's blessing to ♦ **von jdm abgesegnet sein** to have sb's blessing.

absehbar *adj* foreseeable ♦ **in ~er/auf ~e Zeit** in/for the foreseeable future; **das Ende seines Studiums ist noch nicht ~** the end of his studies is not yet in sight; **die Folgen sind noch gar nicht ~** there's no telling what the consequences will be.

absehen *sep irreg* [1] *vt* **(a)** (*abgucken*) **(bei) jdm etw ~** to pick sth up from sb; (*abschreiben*) to copy sth from sb.
(b) (*voraussehen*) to foresee ♦ **es ist noch gar nicht abzusehen, wie lange die Arbeit dauern wird** there's no telling yet how long the work will last; **es ist ganz klar abzusehen, daß** ... it's easy to see that ...; **das Ende läßt sich noch nicht ~** the end is not yet in sight; *siehe* **abgesehen 1.**
[2] *vi* **von etw ~** (*verzichten*) to refrain from sth; (*nicht berücksichtigen*) to disregard sth, to leave sth out of account *or* consideration; **davon ~, etw zu tun** to dispense with *or* to refrain from doing sth; *siehe* **abgesehen 2.**

abseifen *vt sep* to soap down; *Gegenstand auch* to wash down ♦ **jdm den Rücken ~** to soap sb's back.

abseilen *sep* [1] *vt* to let *or* lower down on a rope.
[2] *vr* to let *or* lower oneself down on a rope; (*Bergsteiger*) to abseil (down); (*fig inf*) to skedaddle (*inf*).

⚠ **absein** *vi sep irreg aux sein* (*inf*) **(a)** (*weg sein*) to be off ♦ **die Farbe/der Knopf ist ab** the paint/button has come off. **(b)** (*erschöpft sein*) to be knackered (*sl*) *or* shattered (*inf*). **(c)** (*abgelegen sein*) to be far away.

abseitig *adj* (*geh: abseits liegend*) remote.

abseits [1] *adv* to one side; (*abgelegen*) out of the way, remote; (*Sport*) offside ♦ **~ liegen** to be out of the way *or* remote; **~ vom Wege** off the beaten track; **~ von der Straße** away from the road; **~ stehen** (*fig*) to be on the outside; (*Sport*) to be offside; **nicht ~** (*Sport*) onside, not offside; **~ bleiben, sich ~ halten** (*fig*) to hold *or* keep to oneself.
[2] *prep +gen* away from ♦ **~ des Weges** off the beaten track.

Abseits *nt -, -* (*Sport*) offside ♦ **im ~ stehen** to be offside; **ein Leben im ~ führen, im ~ leben** (*fig*) to live in the shadows; **ins politische ~ geraten** to end up on the political scrapheap.

Abseits-: ~falle *f* (*Ftbl*) offside trap; **~position** *f* offside position; **~regel** *f* (*Sport*) offside rule; **~stellung** *f siehe* **~position**; **~tor** *nt* offside goal.

absenden *vt sep* to send; *Brief, Paket* to send off, to dispatch; (*mit der Post auch*) to post, to mail (*esp US*).

Absender(in *f***)** *m* **-s, -** sender; (*Adresse*) (sender's) address.

Absenderkennung *f* sender's reference.

absengen *vt sep* to singe off.

absenken *sep* [1] *vt* **(a)** (*Build*) *Grundwasserstand* to lower; *Fundamente* to sink.
(b) (*Agr*) *Weinstöcke etc* to layer.
[2] *vr* to subside ♦ **das Gelände senkt sich zum Seeufer ab** the terrain slopes down towards the shore.

Absenker *m* **-s, -** (*Hort*) *siehe* **Ableger.**

absentieren* *vr sep* (*old, hum*) to absent oneself.

Absenz *f* (*old, Sch: Aus, Sw*) absence.

abservieren* *sep* [1] *vi* to clear the table.
[2] *vt* **(a)** *Geschirr, Tisch* to clear. **(b)** (*inf: entlassen, kaltstellen*) **jdn ~** to push sb out, to get rid of sb. **(c)** (*sl: umbringen*) to do in (*inf*). **(d)** (*Sport sl: besiegen*) to thrash (*inf*).

absetzbar *adj Ware* saleable; *Betrag* deductible.

absetzen *sep* [1] *vt* **(a)** (*abnehmen*) *Hut, Brille* to take off, to remove; (*hinstellen*) *Gepäck, Glas* to set *or* put down; *Geigenbogen, Feder* to lift; *Gewehr* to unshoulder.
(b) (*aussteigen lassen*) *Mitfahrer, Fahrgast* to set down, to drop; *Fallschirmjäger* to drop ♦ **wo kann ich dich ~?** where can I drop you?
(c) (*Naut*) to push off.
(d) *Theaterstück, Oper* to take off; *Fußballspiel, Turnier, Versammlung, Termin* to cancel ♦ **etw vom Spielplan ~** to take sth off the programme.
(e) (*entlassen*) to dismiss; *Minister, Vorsitzenden auch* to remove from office; *König, Kaiser* to depose.
(f) (*entwöhnen*) *Jungtier* to wean; (*Med*) *Medikament, Tabletten* to come off, to stop taking; *Behandlung* to break off, to discontinue; (*Mil*) *Ration etc* to stop ♦ **die Tabletten mußten abgesetzt werden** I/she *etc* had to stop taking the tablets *or* come off the tablets.
(g) (*Comm: verkaufen*) *Waren* to sell ♦ **sich gut ~ lassen** to sell well.
(h) (*abziehen*) *Betrag, Summe* to deduct ♦ **das kann man ~** that is tax-deductible.
(i) (*ablagern*) *Geröll* to deposit.
(j) (*Sew*) to trim.
(k) (*kontrastieren*) to contrast ♦ **etw gegen etw ~** to set sth off against sth.
(l) (*Typ*) *Manuskript* to (type)set, to compose ♦ **(eine Zeile) ~** to start a new line.
[2] *vr* **(a)** (*Chem, Geol*) to be deposited; (*Feuchtigkeit, Staub etc*) to collect.

(b) (*inf: weggehen*) to get *or* clear out (*aus* of) (*inf*); (*Sport: Abstand vergrößern*) to pull ahead ◆ **sich nach Brasilien ~** to clear off to Brazil.
(c) **sich gegen jdn/etw ~** to stand out against sb/sth; **sich vorteilhaft gegen jdn/etw ~** to contrast favourably with sb/sth; **das macht er, nur um sich gegen die anderen abzusetzen** he only does that to be different from the others *or* to make himself stand out from the crowd.
[3] *vi* to put one's glass down ◆ **er trank das Glas aus, ohne abzusetzen** he emptied his glass in one.
Absetzung *f* (a) (*Entlassung*) (*von Beamten*) dismissal; (*von Minister, Vorsitzendem auch*) removal from office; (*von König*) deposing, deposition.
(b) (*Fin: Abschreibung*) deduction.
(c) (*von Theaterstück etc*) withdrawal; (*von Fußballspiel, Termin etc*) cancellation.
(d) (*von Jungtier*) weaning; (*Med*) discontinuation.
absichern *sep* [1] *vt* to safeguard; (*garantieren*) to cover; *Bauplatz, Gefahrenstelle* to make safe; *Dach* to support; (*Comput*) *Daten* to store; (*schützen*) to protect ◆ **jdn über die Landesliste ~** (*Pol*) ≃ to give sb a safe seat.
[2] *vr* (*sich schützen*) to protect oneself; (*sich versichern*) to cover oneself.
➤ **Absicht** *f* **-, -en** (*Vorsatz*) intention; (*Zweck*) purpose; (*Jur*) intent ◆ **in der besten ~** with the best of intentions; **in der ~, etw zu tun** with the idea *or* object of doing sth, with a view to doing sth, with the intention of doing sth; **die ~ haben, etw zu tun** to intend to do sth; **eine ~ mit etw verfolgen** to have something in mind with sth; **ernste ~en haben** (*inf*) to have serious intentions; **das war nicht meine ~!** I didn't intend that; **das war doch keine ~!** (*inf*) it wasn't deliberate *or* intentional; **etw mit/ohne ~ tun** to do/not to do sth on purpose *or* deliberately.
➤ **absichtlich** *adj* deliberate, intentional ◆ **etw ~ tun** to do sth on purpose *or* deliberately *or* intentionally.
Absichts-: ~erklärung *f* declaration of intent; **a~los** *adj* unintentional; **~satz** *m* (*Gram*) *siehe* **Finalsatz**; **a~voll** *adj siehe* **absichtlich**.
absiedeln *vt sep* (a) (*Admin*) *Bürger* to resettle. (b) (*Med*) *Tochtergeschwulst* to form.
Absiedlung *f* (a) (*Admin*) resettlement. (b) (*Med*) metastasis.
absingen *vt sep irreg* (a) (*vom Blatt*) to sight-read. (b) (*bis zu Ende*) to sing (right) through ◆ **unter A~ der Nationalhymne/Internationale** with the singing of the national anthem/Internationale.
absinken *vi sep irreg aux sein* (*Schiff*) to sink; (*Boden auch*) to subside; (*Temperatur, Wasserspiegel, Kurs*) to fall, to go down; (*Interesse, Leistungen*) to fall *or* drop off; (*fig: moralisch ~*) to go downhill.
Absinth *m* **-(e)s, -e** absinth.
absitzen *sep irreg* [1] *vt* (a) (*verbringen*) *Zeit* to sit out; (*verbüßen*) *Strafe* to serve.
(b) (*abnutzen*) *Hose etc* to wear thin (at the seat); *Sessel, Polster* to wear (thin).
[2] *vi aux sein* **(vom Pferd) ~** to dismount (from a horse); **abgesessen!** dismount!
[3] *vr* (*Hose etc*) to wear thin (at the seat); (*Sessel, Polster*) to wear (thin).
absolut *adj* (*alle Bedeutungen*) absolute; (*völlig auch*) complete, total ◆ **~ nicht/nichts** absolutely not/nothing; **das ist ~ unmöglich** that's quite *or* absolutely impossible; **~ genommen** *or* **betrachtet** considered in the absolute.
Absolute(s) *nt decl as adj* (*Philos*) Absolute, absolute.
Absolutheit *f, no pl* absoluteness.
Absolutheits|anspruch *m* claim to absolute right ◆ **einen ~ vertreten** to claim absoluteness.
Absolution *f* (*Eccl*) absolution ◆ **jdm die ~ erteilen** to grant *or* give sb absolution.
Absolutismus *m, no pl* absolutism.
absolutistisch *adj* absolutist.
Absolvent(in *f*) [apzɔl'vɛnt(ɪn)] *m* (*Univ*) graduate ◆ **die ~en eines Lehrgangs** the students who have completed a course.
absolvieren* [apzɔl'viːrən] *vt insep* (a) (*Eccl*) to absolve. (b) (*durchlaufen*) *Studium, Probezeit* to complete; *Schule* to finish, to graduate from (*US*); *Prüfung* to pass ◆ **er hat die technische Fachschule absolviert** he completed a course at technical college. (c) (*ableisten*) to complete.
Absolvierung *f siehe vt* (*b, c*) completion; finishing; graduation (*gen* from); passing.
absonderlich *adj* peculiar, strange.
Absonderlichkeit *f* (a) *no pl* strangeness. (b) (*Eigenart*) peculiarity.
absondern *sep* [1] *vt* (a) (*trennen*) to separate; (*isolieren*) to isolate. (b) (*ausscheiden*) to secrete.
[2] *vr* (a) (*Mensch*) to cut oneself off ◆ **sie sondert sich immer sehr ab** she always keeps herself very much to herself; *siehe auch* **abgesondert**. (b) (*ausgeschieden werden*) to be secreted.
Absonderung *f* (a) *siehe vt* separation; isolation; secretion. (b) *siehe vr* segregation; secretion. (c) (*abgeschiedener Stoff*) secretion.
Absorber [ap'zɔrbɐ] *m* **-s, -** (*Tech*) absorber.
absorbieren* *vt insep* (*lit, fig*) to absorb.
Absorption *f* absorption.
abspalten *vtr sep* to split off; (*Chem*) to separate (off).
Abspann *m* **-s, -e** (*TV, Film*) final credits *pl*.
abspannen *sep* [1] *vt* (a) (*ausspannen*) *Pferd, Wagen* to unhitch; *Ochsen* to unyoke. (b) (*Build*) to anchor.
[2] *vi* (a) to unhitch (the) horses *etc*; (*Ochsen ~*) to unyoke (the) oxen. (b) (*fig: entspannen*) to relax; *siehe auch* **abgespannt**.
Abspannung *f* (a) (*Erschöpfung*) *siehe* **Abgespanntheit**. (b) (*Build*) anchoring; (*Spannseil*) anchor (cable).
absparen *vt sep* **sich** (*dat*) **Geld von etw ~** to save money from sth; **sich** (*dat*) **ein Auto vom Lohn ~** to save up for a car from one's wages; **sich** (*dat*) **etw vom** *or* **am Munde** *or* **am eigenen Leib ~** to scrimp and save for sth.
abspecken *sep* (*inf*) [1] *vt* to shed; (*fig: verkleinern*) to slim down, to trim.
[2] *vi* to lose weight.
abspeichern *vt sep Daten* to store (away).
abspeisen *vt sep* (a) (*inf: beköstigen*) to feed. (b) (*fig: abfertigen*) **jdn mit etw ~** to fob sb off with sth.
abspenstig *adj* **jdm jdn/etw ~ machen** to lure sb/sth away from sb; **jdm die Freundin ~ machen** to pinch sb's girlfriend (*inf*); **jdm seine Kunden ~ machen** to lure *or* draw sb's customers away from him.
absperren *sep* [1] *vt* (a) (*versperren*) to block *or* close off. (b) (*abdrehen*) *Wasser, Strom, Gas etc* to turn *or* shut off. (c) (*S Ger: zuschließen*) to lock.
[2] *vi* to lock up.
Absperr-: ~gitter *nt* barrier; **~kette** *f* chain.
Absperrung *f* (a) (*Abriegelung*) blocking *or* closing off. (b) (*Sperre*) barrier; (*Kordon*) cordon.
Abspiel *nt* (*das Abspielen*) passing; (*Schuß*) pass.
abspielen *sep* [1] *vt* (a) *Schallplatte, Tonband* to play (through); *Nationalhymne* to play; (*vom Blatt*) *Musik* to sight-read; *siehe auch* **abgespielt**. (b) (*Sport*) *Ball* to pass; (*beim Billard*) to play.
[2] *vr* (*sich ereignen*) to happen; (*stattfinden*) to take place ◆ **wie mein Leben sich abspielt** what my life is like; **da spielt sich (bei mir) nichts ab!** (*inf*) nothing doing! (*inf*).
absplittern *sep* [1] *vti* (*vi: aux sein*) to chip off; *Holz auch* to splinter off.
[2] *vr* to split *or* splinter off.
Absplitterung *f siehe vb* chipping off; splintering off; splitting off.
Absprache *f* arrangement ◆ **eine ~ treffen** to make *or* come to an arrangement; **ohne vorherige ~** without prior consultation.
absprachegemäß *adv* as arranged.
absprechen *sep irreg* [1] *vt* (a) **jdm etw ~** (*verweigern*) *Recht* to deny *or* refuse sb sth; (*in Abrede stellen*) *Begabung* to deny *or* dispute sb's sth.
(b) (*verabreden*) *Termin* to arrange ◆ **die Zeugen hatten ihre Aussagen vorher abgesprochen** the witnesses had agreed on what to say in advance.
[2] *vr* **sich mit jdm ~** to make an arrangement with sb; **die beiden hatten sich vorher abgesprochen** they had agreed on what to do/say *etc* in advance; **ich werde mich mit ihr ~** I'll arrange *or* fix things with her.
abspreizen *vt sep* to extend; (*Build*) to brace.
abspringen *vi sep irreg aux sein* (a) (*herunterspringen*) to jump down (*von* from); (*herausspringen*) to jump out (*von* of); (*Aviat*) to jump (*von* from); (*bei Gefahr*) to bale out; (*Sport*) to dismount; (*losspringen*) to take off ◆ **A~ während der Fahrt verboten!** passengers are forbidden to alight while the vehicle/train *etc* is in motion; **mit dem rechten Bein ~** to take off on the right leg.
(b) (*sich lösen*) to come off; (*Farbe, Lack auch*) to flake *or* peel off; (*abprallen*) to bounce off (*von etw* sth).
(c) (*fig inf: sich zurückziehen*) to get out; (*von Partei, Kurs etc*) to back out ◆ **von etw ~** to get *or* back out of sth.
abspritzen *sep* [1] *vt* (a) **etw/jdn/sich ~** to spray sth/sb/oneself down; *Schmutz* to spray off (*von etw* sth); (*Cook*) to sprinkle. (b) (*NS euph sl: töten*) to give a lethal injection to.
[2] *vi* (a) *aux sein* to spray off. (b) *aux haben* (*vulg: ejakulieren*) to spunk (*vulg*).
Absprung *m* jump (*auch Aviat*), leap; (*Sport*) take-off; (*Abgang*) dismount ◆ **den ~ schaffen** (*fig*) to make the break (*inf*), to make it (*inf*); **er hat den ~ gewagt** (*fig*) he took the jump; **den ~ (ins Berufsleben) verpassen** (*fig*) to miss the boat *or* bus.
abspulen *vt sep Kabel, Garn* to unwind; (*inf*) (*filmen*) to shoot; (*vorführen*) to show; (*fig*) to reel off.
abspülen *sep* [1] *vt Hände, Geschirr* to rinse; *Fett etc* to rinse off.
[2] *vi* to wash up, to do the washing up.
abstammen *vi sep no ptp* to be descended (*von* from); (*Ling*) to be derived (*von* from).
Abstammung *f* descent; (*Abkunft auch*) origin, extraction; (*Ling*) origin, derivation ◆ **ehelicher/unehelicher ~** (*Jur*) of legitimate/illegitimate birth; **französischer ~** of French extraction *or* descent.
Abstammungs-: ~lehre, ~theorie *f* theory of evolution.
Abstand *m* (a) (*Zwischenraum*) distance; (*kürzerer ~*) gap, space; (*Zeit~*) interval; (*Punkte~*) gap; (*fig*) (*Distanz*) distance; (*Unterschied*) difference ◆ **mit ~** by far, far and away; **~ von etw gewinnen** (*fig*) to distance oneself from sth; **in regelmäßigen Abständen/Abständen von 10 Minuten** at regular/10 minute intervals; **~ halten** to keep one's distance; **mit großem ~ führen/gewinnen** to lead/win by a wide margin.
(b) (*form: Verzicht*) **von etw ~ nehmen** to dispense with sth; **davon ~ nehmen, etw zu tun** to refrain from doing sth, to forbear to do sth (*old, form*).
(c) (*Abfindung*) indemnity.
Abstandssumme *f* (*form*) indemnity.
abstatten *vt sep* (*form*) **jdm einen Besuch ~** to pay sb a visit; **jdm seinen Dank ~** to give thanks to sb.
abstauben *vti sep* (a) *Möbel etc* to dust. (b) (*inf*) (*wegnehmen*) to pick up; (*schnorren*) to cadge (*von, bei, dat* off, from) ◆ **er will immer nur ~** he's always on the scrounge. (c) (*Ftbl inf*) **(ein Tor** *or* **den Ball) ~** to put the ball into the

net, to tuck the ball away.

Abstauber *m* **-s, -** (*Ftbl inf*) **(a)** (*auch* **~tor**) easy goal. **(b)** (*Spieler*) goal-hanger (*inf*).

abstechen *sep irreg* 1 *vt* **(a) ein Tier ~** to cut an animal's throat. **(b)** (*abtrennen*) *Torf* to cut; *Rasen* to trim (the edges of). **(c)** (*ablaufen lassen*) *Hochofen, Metall* to tap; *Gewässer* to drain; *Wein* to rack.
2 *vi* **gegen jdn/etw ~, von jdm/etw ~** to stand out against sb/sth.

Abstecher *m* **-s, -** (*Ausflug*) excursion, trip; (*Umweg*) detour; (*fig*) sortie.

abstecken *vt sep* **(a)** *Gelände, Grenze, Trasse* to mark out; (*mit Pflöcken auch*) to peg *or* stake out; (*fig*) *Verhandlungsposition, Programm* to work out. **(b)** *Kleid, Naht* to pin.

abstehen *sep irreg* 1 *vi* (*entfernt stehen*) to stand away; (*nicht anliegen*) to stick out ◆ **~de Ohren** ears that stick out; *siehe* **abgestanden.**
2 *vt* (*inf*) **sich** (*dat*) **die Beine ~** to stand for hours and hours.

absteifen *vt sep* (*Build*) to shore up.

Absteige *f* **-, -n** (*inf*) dosshouse (*inf*), flophouse (*US inf*); cheap hotel.

absteigen *vi sep irreg aux sein* **(a)** (*heruntersteigen*) to get off (*von etw* sth); (*vom Pferd, Rad auch*) to dismount ◆ **von einem Pferd/Rad** *etc* ~ to dismount, to get off a horse/bicycle *etc*; **Radfahrer ~!** no cycling, cycling prohibited.
(b) (*abwärts gehen*) to make one's way down; (*Bergsteiger auch*) to climb down ◆ **in ~der** *or* **der ~den Linie** in the line of descent; **auf dem ~den Ast sein, sich auf dem ~den Ast befinden** (*inf*) to be going downhill, to be on the decline.
(c) (*einkehren*) to stay; (*im Hotel auch*) to put up (*in +dat* at).
(d) (*Sport: Mannschaft*) to go down, to be relegated ◆ **aus der ersten Liga ~** to be relegated from the first division.

Absteigequartier *nt siehe* **Absteige.**

Absteiger *m* **-s, -** (*Sport*) relegated team; team facing relegation ◆ **gesellschaftlicher ~** (*fig*) someone who has come down in the world.

Abstellbahnhof *m* railway yard.

abstellen *sep* 1 *vt* **(a)** (*hinstellen*) to put down.
(b) (*unterbringen*) to put; (*Aut: parken auch*) to park.
(c) (*abrücken, entfernt stellen*) to put away from ◆ **das Klavier von der Wand ~** to leave the piano out from *or* away from the wall.
(d) (*abkommandieren*) to order off, to detail; *Offizier auch* to second; (*fig: abordnen*) to assign; (*Sport*) *Spieler* to release.
(e) (*ausrichten auf*) **etw auf jdn/etw ~** to gear sth to sb/sth.
(f) (*abdrehen*) to turn off; *Geräte, Licht auch* to switch off; (*Zufuhr unterbrechen*) *Gas, Strom* to cut off; *Telefon* to disconnect ◆ **den Haupthahn für das Gas ~** to turn the gas off at the mains.
(g) (*sich abgewöhnen*) to give up, to stop.
(h) (*unterbinden*) *Mangel, Unsitte etc* to bring to an end ◆ **das läßt sich nicht/läßt sich ~** nothing/something can be done about that; **läßt sich das nicht ~?** couldn't that be changed?
2 *vi* **auf etw** (*acc*) **~** to be geared to sth; (*etw berücksichtigen*) to take sth into account.

Abstell-: ~gleis *nt* siding; **jdn aufs ~gleis schieben** (*fig*) to push *or* cast sb aside; **auf dem ~gleis sein** *or* **stehen** (*fig*) to have been pushed *or* cast aside; **~kammer** *f* boxroom; **~raum** *m* storeroom.

abstempeln *vt sep* to stamp; *Post* to postmark; (*fig*) to stamp, to brand (*zu, als* as).

Abstemp(e)lung *f siehe vt* stamping; postmarking; branding.

absteppen *vt sep* to stitch, to sew; *Wattiertes, Daunendecke* to quilt; *Kragen etc* to topstitch.

absterben *vi sep irreg aux sein* (*eingehen, Med*) to die; (*gefühllos werden: Glieder*) to go *or* grow numb; (*fig*) (*Gefühle*) to die; (*Sitten*) to die out ◆ **mir sind die Zehen abgestorben** my toes have gone *or* grown numb; *siehe* **abgestorben.**

Abstich *m* **-(e)s, -e** (*von Wein*) racking; (*von Metall, Hochofen*) tapping; (*Öffnung des Hochofens*) taphole.

Abstieg *m* **-(e)s, -e** (*das Absteigen*) way down, descent; (*Weg*) descent; (*Niedergang*) decline; (*Sport*) relegation ◆ **einen alten Pfad als ~ benutzen** to come down (on) an old path; **vom ~ bedroht** (*Sport*) threatened by relegation, in danger of being relegated.

abstillen *sep* 1 *vt Kind* to wean, to stop breastfeeding.
2 *vi* to stop breastfeeding.

abstimmen *sep* 1 *vi* to take a vote ◆ **über etw** (*acc*) **~** to vote *or* take a vote on sth; **über etw** (*acc*) **~ lassen** to put sth to the vote; **geheim ~** to have a secret ballot.
2 *vt* (*harmonisieren*) *Instrumente* to tune (*auf +acc* to); *Radio* to tune (in) (*auf +acc* to); (*in Einklang bringen*) *Farben, Kleidung* to match (*auf +acc* with); *Termine* to coordinate (*auf +acc* with); (*anpassen*) to suit (*auf +acc* to); (*Comm*) *Bücher* to balance ◆ **gut auf etw** (*acc*)**/aufeinander abgestimmt sein** (*Instrumente*) to be in tune with sth/with each other; (*Farben, Speisen etc*) to go well with sth/with each other *or* together; (*Termine*) to fit in well with sth/with each other; (*einander angepaßt sein*) to be well-suited to sth/(to each other); **etw miteinander ~** (*vereinbaren*) to settle sth amongst ourselves/themselves *etc.*
3 *vr* **sich ~ (mit jdm/miteinander)** to come to an agreement (with sb/amongst ourselves/themselves *etc*).

Abstimmung *f* **(a)** (*Stimmabgabe*) vote; (*geheime ~*) ballot; (*das Abstimmen*) voting ◆ **zur ~ kommen** *or* **schreiten** (*form*) to come to the vote; **eine ~ durchführen** *or* **vornehmen** to take a vote/to hold a ballot; **zur ~ bringen** (*form*) to put to the vote. **(b)** *siehe vt* tuning; matching; coordination; suiting; balancing. **(c)** (*Vereinbarung*) agreement.

Abstimmungs-: a~berechtigt *adj siehe* **stimmberechtigt**; **~ergebnis** *nt* result of the vote; **~niederlage** *f* **eine ~niederlage erleiden** to be defeated in a/the vote; **~sieg** *m* **einen ~sieg erringen** to win a/the vote.

abstinent *adj* teetotal; (*geschlechtlich*) abstinent, continent, not indulging in sex ◆ **~ leben** to live a life of abstinence.

Abstinenz *f, no pl* teetotalism, abstinence; (*geschlechtlich*) abstinence.

Abstinenz-: ~erscheinung *f* (*Med*) withdrawal symptom; **~gebot** *nt* (*Eccl*) requirement of abstinence.

Abstinenzler(in *f*) *m* **-s, -** teetotaller.

Abstinenztag *m* (*Eccl*) day of abstinence.

abstoppen *sep* 1 *vt* **(a)** *Auto, Maschine, Verkehr* to stop, to bring to a standstill *or* halt; (*drosseln*) to halt. **(b)** (*Sport*) *Ball* to stop; (*mit Stoppuhr*) to time ◆ **jds Zeit ~** to time sb.
2 *vi* to stop, to come to a halt.

Abstoß *m* **(a)** (*Ftbl*) goal kick; (*nach Fangen des Balls*) clearance. **(b) der ~ vom Ufer war so kräftig, daß ...** the boat was pushed away *or* out from the shore so forcefully that ...

abstoßen *sep irreg* 1 *vt* **(a)** (*wegstoßen*) *Boot* to push off *or* away *or* out; (*abschlagen*) *Ecken* to knock off; *Möbel* to batter; (*abschaben*) *Ärmel* to wear thin ◆ **sich** (*dat*) **die Ecken und Kanten ~** (*fig*) to have the rough edges knocked off one; *siehe* **Horn.**
(b) (*zurückstoßen*) to repel; (*Comm*) *Ware, Aktien* to get rid of, to sell off; (*Med*) *Organ* to reject; (*fig: anwidern*) to repulse, to repel ◆ **dieser Stoff stößt Wasser ab** this material is water-repellent.
(c) (*Ftbl*) **den Ball ~** to take the goal kick; (*nach Fangen*) to clear (the ball).
2 *vr* **(a)** (*abgeschlagen werden*) to get broken; (*Möbel*) to get battered.
(b) (*esp Sport: Mensch*) to push oneself off ◆ **sich mit den Füßen vom Boden ~** to push oneself off.
3 *vi* **(a)** *aux sein or haben* (*weggestoßen werden*) to push off.
(b) (*anwidern*) to be repulsive ◆ **sich von etw abgestoßen fühlen** to be repelled by sth, to find sth repulsive.
(c) (*Ftbl*) to take a goal kick; (*nach Fangen*) to clear (the ball).

abstoßend *adj Aussehen, Äußeres* repulsive ◆ **sein Wesen hat etwas A~es** there's something repulsive about him.

Abstoßung *f* (*Phys*) repulsion.

Abstoßungsreaktion *f* (*Med*) rejection.

abstottern *vt sep* (*inf*) to pay off.

abstrafen *vt sep siehe* **bestrafen.**

abstrahieren* [apstra'hi:rən] *vti insep* to abstract (*aus* from).

abstrahlen *vt sep* **(a)** *Wärme, Energie, Programm etc* to emit. **(b)** *Fassade* (*mit Sandstrahlgebläse*) to sandblast.

abstrakt [ap'strakt] *adj* abstract ◆ **etw zu ~ ausdrücken** to express sth too abstractly *or* too much in the abstract.

Abstraktheit [-st-] *f* abstractness.

Abstraktion [-st-] *f* abstraction.

Abstraktionsvermögen [-st-] *nt* ability to abstract.

Abstraktum [-st-] *nt* **-s, Abstrakta** (*Begriff*) abstract (concept); (*Ling: Substantiv*) abstract noun.

abstrampeln *vr sep* (*inf*) to kick the bedclothes off; (*fig*) to sweat (away) (*inf*), to flog one's guts out (*sl*).

abstreichen *sep irreg* 1 *vt* **(a)** (*wegstreichen*) to wipe off *or* away; *Asche* to knock *or* tap off; (*säubern*) to wipe ◆ **den Hals/die Zunge ~** (*Med*) to take a throat/tongue swab.
(b) (*abziehen*) *Betrag* to knock off, to deduct; (*fig*) to discount ◆ **davon kann/muß man die Hälfte ~** (*fig*) you have to take it with a pinch of salt.
(c) (*Hunt*) *Feld* to beat; (*Mil*) *Gebiet, Himmel* to sweep.
2 *vi aux sein* (*Hunt*) to fly off *or* away.

abstreifen *vt sep* **(a)** (*abtreten*) *Schuhe, Füße* to wipe; *Schmutz* to wipe off. **(b)** (*abziehen*) *Kleidung, Schmuck* to take off, to remove, to slip off; (*entfernen*) *Haut* to cast, to shed; (*fig*) *Gewohnheit, Fehler* to get rid of.

abstreiten *vt sep irreg* (*streitig machen*) to dispute; (*leugnen*) to deny ◆ **das kann man ihm nicht ~** you can't deny it.

Abstrich *m* **(a)** (*Kürzung*) cutback ◆ **~e machen** to cut back (*an +dat* on), to make cuts (*an +dat* in); (*weniger erwarten etc*) to lower one's sights.
(b) (*Med*) swab; (*Gebärmutter~*) smear ◆ **einen ~ machen** to take a swab/smear.
(c) (*Mus, beim Schreiben*) downstroke ◆ **zu dicke ~e machen** to make one's downstrokes too thick.

abströmen *vi sep aux sein* to flow away *or* off; (*Wasser auch*) to run away *or* off; (*Menschenmassen*) to stream out.

abstrus [ap'stru:s] *adj* (*geh*) abstruse.

abstufen *sep* 1 *vt Gelände* to terrace; *Haare* to layer; *Farben* to shade; *Gehälter, Steuern, Preise* to grade.
2 *vr* to be terraced ◆ **der Weinberg stuft sich zum Fluß hin ab** the vineyard goes down in terraces to the river.

Abstufung *f siehe vt* terracing; layering; (*Nuancierung*) shading; (*Nuance*) shade; (*Staffelung*) grading; (*Stufe*) grade.

abstumpfen *sep* 1 *vt* **(a)** (*lit rare*) *Ecken, Kanten* to blunt; *Messer, Schneide auch* to take the edge off, to dull.
(b) *Menschen* to dull; *Sinne auch* to deaden; *Gerechtigkeitssinn, Gewissen, Urteilsvermögen auch* to blunt; *siehe* **abgestumpft.**
2 *vi aux sein* (*fig: Geschmack etc*) to become dulled ◆ **wenn man ewig dasselbe machen muß, stumpft man nach und nach ab** always having to do the same thing dulls the mind; **er ist als Kritiker abgestumpft** his critical sensibilities have become blunted; **gegen etw ~** to become inured to sth.

Abstumpfung *f siehe vt* **(b)** dulling; deadening; blunting.

Absturz *m siehe vi* crash; fall ◆ **ein Flugzeug zum ~ bringen** to bring a plane

down.
abstürzen *vi sep aux sein* **(a)** (*Flugzeug*) to crash; (*Bergsteiger*) to fall. **(b)** (*schroff abfallen*) to fall *or* drop away. **(c)** (*inf: hereinfallen*) to back a loser. **(d)** (*sl: betrunken werden*) to go on a bender (*inf*).
Absturzstelle *f* location of a/the crash; (*beim Bergsteigen*) location of a/the fall ♦ **die Rettungsarbeiten an der ~** the rescue work at the scene of the crash.
abstützen *sep* [1] *vt* to support (*auch fig*), to prop up; *Haus, Mauer auch* to shore up.
[2] *vr* to support oneself, to prop oneself up; (*bei Bewegung*) to support oneself.
absuchen *vt sep* **(a)** to search; *Gegend auch* to comb, to scour; *Himmel, Horizont* to scan; (*Scheinwerfer*) to sweep ♦ **wir haben den ganzen Garten abgesucht** we searched all over the garden.
(b) (*suchend absammeln*) *Raupen etc* to pick off; *Strauch etc* to pick clean.
Absud ['apzu:t] *m* **-(e)s, -e** (*old*) decoction.
absurd *adj* absurd, preposterous ♦ **~es Drama** *or* **Theater** theatre of the absurd; **das A~e** the absurd.
Absurdität *f* absurdity (*auch Philos*), preposterousness.
⚠**Abszeß** *m* **-sses, -sse** abscess.
Abszisse *f* **-, -n** abscissa.
Abt *m* **-(e)s, ⸚e** abbot.
Abt. *abbr of* **Abteilung** dept.
abtakeln *vt sep Schiff* to unrig; (*außer Dienst stellen*) to lay up; *siehe* **abgetakelt**.
Abtak(e)lung *f siehe vt* unrigging; laying up.
abtasten *vt sep* to feel; (*Med auch*) to palpate; (*Elec*) to scan; (*bei Durchsuchung*) to frisk (*auf +acc* for); (*fig: erproben*) *jdn* to sound out, to suss out (*sl*); (*Sport*) to get the measure of, to size up, to suss out (*sl*).
Abtastung *f* (*Elec, TV*) scanning.
abtauchen *vi sep aux sein* **(a)** (*U-Boot*) to dive. **(b)** (*inf*) to go underground.
abtauen *sep* [1] *vt* to thaw out; *Kühlschrank* to defrost.
[2] *vi aux sein* to thaw ♦ **der Schnee ist vom Dach abgetaut** the snow has thawed off the roof.
Abtausch *m* **-(e)s, -e** (*Chess, Sw: Tausch*) exchange.
abtauschen *vt sep* (*Chess, Sw: tauschen*) to exchange.
Abtei *f* abbey.
Abteikirche *f* abbey (church).
Abteil *nt* **-(e)s, -e** compartment ♦ **~ erster Klasse** first-class compartment; **~ für Mutter und Kind** *compartment reserved for mothers with young children*; **~ für Raucher/Nichtraucher** smoker/non-smoker, no smoking compartment.
abteilen *vt sep* **(a)** (*einteilen*) to divide up ♦ **fünf Stücke ~** to cut off five pieces. **(b)** (*abtrennen*) to divide off; (*mit Wand auch*) to partition off.
Abteilung[1] *f, no pl siehe vt* dividing up; cutting off; dividing off; partitioning off.
Abteilung[2] *f* **(a)** (*in Firma, Kaufhaus, Hochschule*) department; (*in Krankenhaus, Jur*) section; (*Mil*) unit, section. **(b)** (*old: Abschnitt*) section.
Abteilungsleiter *m* head of department; (*in Kaufhaus*) department manager.
abtelefonieren* *vi sep* to telephone *or* ring *or* call to say one can't make it *or* come.
abteufen *vt sep Schacht* to sink.
abtippen *vt sep* (*inf*) to type out.
Äbtissin *f* abbess.
abtönen *vt sep Farbe* to tone down ♦ **zwei Farben gegeneinander ~** to tone two colours in with each other.
Abtönung *f* (*von Farbe*) toning down; (*Farbton*) tone, shade.
abtöten *vt sep* (*lit, fig*) to destroy, to kill (off); *Nerv* to deaden; *sinnliche Begierde* to mortify ♦ **in mir ist jedes Gefühl abgetötet** I am dead to all feeling.
Abtötung *f siehe vt* destruction, killing (off); deadening; mortification.
Abtrag *m* **-(e)s,** *no pl* (*old*) harm ♦ **einer Sache** (*dat*) **~ tun** to harm sth.
abtragen *vt sep irreg* **(a)** (*auch vi: abräumen*) *Geschirr, Speisen* to clear away.
(b) (*einebnen*) *Boden, Gelände* to level down.
(c) (*abbauen*) *Gebäude, Mauer* to dismantle, to take down; (*Fluß*) *Ufer* to erode, to wear away.
(d) (*abbezahlen*) *Schulden* to pay off.
(e) (*abnutzen*) *Kleider, Schuhe* to wear out; *siehe* **abgetragen**.
abträgig (*Sw*), **abträglich** *adj* detrimental, harmful, injurious; *Bemerkung, Kritik etc* adverse, unfavourable.
Abträglichkeit *f* harmfulness, injuriousness; (*von Bemerkung etc*) adverseness.
Abtragung *f* **(a)** (*Geol*) erosion. **(b)** (*Abbau*) dismantling, taking down. **(c)** (*Tilgung*) paying off.
Abtransport *m* transportation; (*aus Katastrophengebiet*) evacuation ♦ **beim ~ der Gefangenen** when the prisoners were being taken away *or* transported.
abtransportieren* *vt sep Waren* to transport; *Personen auch* to take off *or* away; (*aus Katastrophengebiet*) to evacuate.
abtreiben *sep irreg* [1] *vt* **(a) vom Kurs ~** *Flugzeug* to send *or* drive off course; *Boot auch, Schwimmer* to carry off course.
(b) (*zu Tal treiben*) *Vieh* to bring down.
(c) *Kind, Leibesfrucht* to abort ♦ **sie hat das Kind abgetrieben** *or* **~ lassen** she had an abortion.
(d) (*Aus, S Ger: Cook*) to whisk.
[2] *vi* **(a)** *aux sein* **(vom Kurs) ~** (*Flugzeug*) to be sent *or* driven off course; (*Boot auch, Schwimmer*) to be carried off course.
(b) (*Abort vornehmen*) to carry out an abortion; (*generell*) to carry out *or* do abortions; (*Abort vornehmen lassen*) to have an abortion.
Abtreibung *f* abortion ♦ **eine ~ vornehmen lassen/vornehmen** to have/carry out an abortion.
Abtreibungs-: ~gegner *m* anti-abortionist; ⚠**~paragraph** *m* abortion laws *pl*; **~pille** *f* abortion pill; **~versuch** *m* attempt at an abortion; **einen ~versuch vornehmen** to try to give oneself an abortion, to attempt an abortion.
abtrennbar *adj* (*lostrennbar*) detachable; *Knöpfe, Besatz etc auch* removable; (*abteilbar*) separable; *Verfahren* severable (*form*).
abtrennen *vt sep* **(a)** (*lostrennen*) to detach; *Knöpfe, Besatz etc* to remove, to take off; (*abschneiden*) to cut off; *Bein, Finger etc* (*durch Unfall*) to sever, to cut off ♦ **„hier ~"** "detach here".
(b) (*abteilen*) to separate off; (*räumlich auch*) to divide off; (*mit Zwischenwand etc auch*) to partition off ♦ **diese Zeit läßt sich nicht einfach von der Geschichte des Landes ~** this period cannot simply be set aside from the history of the country.
Abtrennung *f siehe vt* (*b*) separation; division; partitioning.
abtretbar *adj* (*Jur*) *Ansprüche* transferable, cedable (*form*).
abtreten *sep irreg* [1] *vt* **(a)** *Teppich* to wear; (*völlig*) to wear out; *Schnee, Schmutz* to stamp off ♦ **sich** (*dat*) **die Füße** *or* **Schuhe ~** to wipe one's feet.
(b) (*überlassen*) (*jdm or an jdn* to sb) to hand over; *Gebiet, Land auch* to cede (*form*); *Rechte, Ansprüche* to transfer, to cede (*form*); *Haus, Geldsumme* to transfer, to assign (*form*).
[2] *vr* (*Teppich etc*) to wear, to get worn; (*völlig*) to wear out.
[3] *vi aux sein* (*Theat*) to go off (stage), to make one's exit; (*Mil*) to dismiss; (*inf: zurücktreten*) (*Politiker*) to step down (*inf*), to resign; (*Monarch*) to abdicate, to step down (*inf*); (*euph: sterben*) to make one's last exit ♦ **~!** (*Mil*) dismiss!; **aus dem Leben ~** (*euph*) to quit this life.
Abtreter *m* **-s, -** (*Fuß~*) doormat.
Abtretung *f* (*an +acc* to) transfer; (*von Rechten, Ansprüchen auch, von Gebiet*) ceding, cession (*form*); (*von Haus, Geldsumme auch*) assignment (*form*) ♦ **durch ~ aller Ansprüche an seinen Teilhaber** by transferring all rights to his partner.
Abtrieb *m* **-(e)s, -e (a)** (*Vieh~*) **im Herbst beginnt der ~ des Viehs von den Bergweiden** in autumn they start to bring the cattle down from the mountain pastures. **(b)** (*Tech*) output. **(c)** (*Aus*) mixture.
Abtrift *f* **-, -en** *siehe* **Abdrift**.
abtrinken *vt sep irreg* to drink ♦ **einen Schluck ~** to have *or* take a sip.
Abtritt *m* **(a)** (*Theat*) exit; (*Rücktritt*) (*von Minister*) resignation; (*von Monarch*) abdication. **(b)** (*old: Klosett*) privy (*old*).
Abtrockentuch *nt* tea *or* dish (*US*) towel.
abtrocknen *sep* [1] *vt* to dry (off); *Geschirr* to dry, to wipe.
[2] *vi* to dry up, to do the drying-up.
abtropfen *vi sep aux sein* to drip; (*Geschirr*) to drain ♦ **etw ~ lassen** *Wäsche etc* to let sth drip; *Salat* to drain sth; *Geschirr* to let sth drain.
abtrotzen *vt sep* **jdm etw ~** (*geh*) to wring sth out of sb.
abtrünnig *adj* renegade, apostate (*form, esp Eccl*); (*rebellisch*) rebel; (*treulos auch*) disloyal ♦ **jdm/einer Gruppe** *etc* **~ werden** to desert sb/a group; (*sich erheben gegen*) to rebel against sb/a group; **er ist dem Glauben ~ geworden** he has left *or* deserted the faith, he has apostatized (*form*).
Abtrünnigkeit *f* apostasy (*form*); (*Treulosigkeit auch*) disloyalty; (*rebellische Gesinnung*) rebelliousness ♦ **die ~ einer der Mitverschwörer** the desertion *or* apostasy (*form*) of one of the plotters.
abtun *vt sep irreg* **(a)** (*fig: beiseite schieben*) to dismiss ♦ **etw mit einem Achselzucken/einem Lachen ~** to shrug/laugh sth off; **etw kurz ~** to brush sth aside; *siehe* **abgetan**.
(b) (*dial: ablegen*) to take off.
abtupfen *vt sep Tränen, Blut* to dab away; *Gesicht, Mundwinkel* to dab; *Wunde* to swab, to dab.
ab|urteilen *vt sep* to pass sentence *or* judgement on; (*fig: verdammen*) to condemn ♦ **Verbrecher, die noch nicht abgeurteilt worden sind** criminals upon whom sentence has not yet been passed.
Ab|urteilung *f* sentencing; (*fig*) condemnation ♦ **bei der ~ des Täters** when sentence was/is being passed on the accused.
Abverkauf *m* (*Aus*) sale.
abverlangen* *vt sep siehe* **abfordern**.
abwägen *vt sep irreg* to weigh up; *Worte* to weigh ♦ **er wog beide Möglichkeiten gegeneinander ab** he weighed up the two possibilities; *siehe* **abgewogen**.
Abwägung *f* weighing up; (*von Worten*) weighing.
Abwahl *f* voting out ♦ **es kam zur ~ des gesamten Vorstands** the whole committee was voted out.
abwählbar *adj* **der Präsident ist nicht ~** the president cannot be voted out (of office).
abwählen *vt sep* to vote out (of office); (*Sch*) *Fach* to give up.
abwälzen *vt sep Schuld, Verantwortung* to shift (*auf +acc* onto); *Arbeit* to unload (*auf +acc* onto); *Kosten* to pass on (*auf +acc* to) ♦ **die Schuld von sich ~** to shift the blame onto somebody else.
abwandelbar *adj siehe vt* adaptable; modifiable.
abwandeln *vt sep Melodie* to adapt; *Thema auch* to modify.
Abwand(e)lung *f siehe* **Abwandlung**.
abwandern *vi sep aux sein* to move (away) (*aus* from); (*Bevölkerung: zu einem anderen Ort auch*) to migrate (*aus* from); (*Kapital*) to be transferred (*aus* out of); (*inf: aus einer Veranstaltung etc*) to wander away *or* off (*inf*) ♦ **viele Spieler/**

⚠: for details of spelling reform, see supplement

Abonnenten *etc* **wandern ab** a lot of players/subscribers *etc* are transferring.
Abwanderung *f siehe vi* moving away; migration; transference.
Abwanderungsverlust *m (Sociol)* population drain.
Abwandlung *f* adaptation, variation; *(von Thema etc auch)* modification.
Abwärme *f* waste heat.
Abwart(in *f*) *m (Sw)* concierge, janitor/janitress.
abwarten *sep* [1] *vt* to wait for ◆ **das Gewitter ~** to wait till the storm is over, to wait the storm out; **er kann es nicht mehr ~** he can't wait any longer; **das bleibt abzuwarten** that remains to be seen.
[2] *vi* to wait ◆ **warten Sie ab!** just wait a bit!; **~ und Tee trinken** *(inf)* to wait and see; **im Moment können wir gar nichts tun, wir müssen ~** we can't do anything at the moment, we'll have to bide our time; **eine ~de Haltung einnehmen** to play a waiting game, to adopt a policy of wait-and-see.
abwärts *adv* down; *(nach unten auch)* downwards ◆ **den Fluß/Berg ~** down the river/mountain; **„~!"** *(im Fahrstuhl)* "going down!"; **vom Abteilungsleiter ~** from the head of department down(wards).
Abwärts-: ~entwicklung *f* downwards *or* downhill trend; **~fahrt** *f* journey down.
⚠ **abwärtsgehen** *vi impers sep aux sein (fig)* **mit ihm/dem Land geht es abwärts** he/the country is going downhill.
abwärtskompatibel *adj (Comput)* downward compatible.
Abwärtstrend *m* downwards *or* downhill trend.
Abwasch[1] *m* **-s,** *no pl* washing-up *(Brit)*, dirty dishes *pl* ◆ **den ~ machen** to do the washing-up, to wash up *(Brit)*, to wash the dishes *(US)*; **... dann kannst du das auch machen, das ist (dann) ein ~** *(inf)* ... then you could do that as well and kill two birds with one stone *(prov)*.
Abwasch[2] *f* **-, -en** *(Aus)* sink.
abwaschbar *adj Tapete* washable.
Abwaschbecken *nt* sink.
abwaschen *sep irreg* [1] *vt Gesicht* to wash; *Geschirr* to wash (up); *Farbe, Schmutz* to wash off; *Pferd, Auto* to wash down; *(fig liter) Schande, Schmach* to wipe out ◆ **den Schmutz (vom Gesicht) ~** to wash the dirt off (one's face).
[2] *vi* to wash up, to do the washing-up.
Abwasch-: ~lappen *m* dishcloth, washing-up cloth; **~wasser** *nt* washing-up water, dishwater; *(fig inf)* dishwater *(inf)*.
Abwasser *nt* sewage *no pl* ◆ **industrielle Abwässer** industrial effluents *pl or* waste *sing*.
Abwasser-: ~aufbereitung *f* reprocessing of sewage/effluents; **~kanal** *m* sewer; **~reinigung** *f* purification of sewage/effluents.
abwechseln *vir sep* to alternate ◆ **sich** *or* **einander ~** to alter- nate; *(Menschen auch)* to take turns; **sich mit jdm ~** to take turns with sb; **(sich) miteinander ~** to alternate (with each other *or* one another); to take turns; **Regen und Schnee wechselten (sich) miteinander ab** first it rained and then it snowed; **ihre Launen wechseln oft blitzschnell miteinander ab** her moods often change *or* vary from one minute to the next.
abwechselnd *adv* alternately ◆ **wir haben ~ Klavier gespielt** we took turns playing the piano; **er war ~ fröhlich und traurig** he alternated between being happy and sad, he was by turns happy and sad.
Abwechs(e)lung *f* change; *(Zerstreuung)* diversion ◆ **eine angenehme/schöne ~** a pleasant/nice change; **zur ~** for a change; **für ~ sorgen** to provide entertainment; **dort ist reichlich für ~ gesorgt** there's quite a variety of things going on there; **hier haben wir wenig ~** there's not much variety in life here; **da gibt es mehr ~** there's more going on there.
abwechslungs-: ~halber *adv* for a change, to make a change; **~los** *adj* monotonous; **~reich** *adj* varied.
Abweg ['apveːk] *m (fig)* mistake, error ◆ **jdn auf ~e führen** to mislead sb, to lead sb astray *(auch moralisch)*; **auf ~e geraten** *or* **kommen** to go astray; *(moralisch auch)* to stray from the straight and narrow.
abwegig ['apveːgɪç] *adj (geh)* erroneous; *(bizarr)* eccentric, off-beat; *Verdacht* unfounded, groundless.
Abwegigkeit *f (geh) siehe adj* erroneousness; eccentricity, off-beat nature; groundlessness.
Abwehr *f, no pl* **(a)** *(Biol, Psych, Med)* defence *(gen* against); *(Schutz)* protection *(gen* against) ◆ **Mechanismen der ~** defence mechanisms; **der ~ von etw dienen** to provide *or* give protection against sth.
(b) *(Zurückweisung)* repulse; *(Abweisung)* rejection; *(Spionage~)* counter-intelligence (service) ◆ **die ~ des Feindes** the repulsing *or* repelling of the enemy; **bei der ~ sein** to be with *or* in counter-intelligence; **auf ~ stoßen** to be repulsed, to meet with a repulse.
(c) *(Sport)* defence; *(~aktion)* piece of defence (work); *(abgewehrter Ball)* clearance; *(gefangen auch)* save ◆ **er ist besser in der ~** he's better in *or* at defence.
Abwehr-: a~bereit *adj (Mil)* ready for defence; **~bereitschaft** *f* defence readiness; **~dienst** *m* counter-intelligence service.
abwehren *sep* [1] *vt* **(a)** *Gegner* to fend *or* ward off; *Angriff, Feind auch* to repulse, to repel; *Ball* to clear; *Schlag* to parry, to ward off ◆ **hervorragend, wie der Torwart den Ball abwehrte** that was a really good save the goalkeeper made there.
(b) *(fernhalten)* to keep away; *Krankheitserreger* to protect against; *Gefahr, üble Folgen* to avert.
(c) *(abweisen) Anschuldigung* to dismiss ◆ **eine ~de Geste** a dismissive wave of the hand.
[2] *vi* **(a)** *(Sport)* to clear; *(Torwart auch)* to make a save ◆ **mit dem Kopf ~** to head clear; **zur Ecke ~** to clear a corner.
(b) *(ablehnen)* to refuse ◆ **nein, wehrte sie ab** no, she said in refusal.

Abwehr-: ~handlung *f* defence reaction; **~kampf** *m (Mil, Sport)* defence; **ein ~kampf** a defensive action; **~kräfte** *pl (Physiol)* (the body's) defences; **~mechanismus** *m (Psych)* defence mechanism; **~reaktion** *f (Psych)* defence reaction; **~spieler** *m* defender.
abweichen[1] *vi sep irreg aux sein (sich entfernen)* to deviate; *(sich unterscheiden)* to differ; *(zwei Theorien, Auffassungen etc)* to differ, to diverge ◆ **vom Kurs ~** to deviate *or* depart from one's course; **vom Thema ~** to digress, to go off the point; **vom rechten Weg ~** *(fig)* to wander *or* err from the straight and narrow; **ich weiche erheblich von seiner Meinung ab** I hold quite a different view from him; **~des Verhalten** *(Psych, Sociol)* deviant behaviour.
abweichen[2] *vti sep Briefmarke etc* to soak off.
Abweichler(in *f*) *m* **-s, -** deviant.
abweichlerisch *adj (Pol)* deviant.
Abweichlertum *nt (Pol)* deviancy.
Abweichung *f siehe* **abweichen**[1] deviation; difference; divergence; *(von Magnetnadel)* declination ◆ **~ von der Wahrheit** departure from the truth; **~ von der Parteilinie** failure to toe the party line, deviation from the party line; **zulässige ~** *(Tech)* tolerance; *(zeitlich, zahlenmäßig)* allowance.
abweiden *vt sep (rare) Wiese* to graze.
abweisen *vt sep irreg* to turn down, to reject; *(weg schicken)* to turn away; *Bitte auch* to refuse; *(Jur) Klage* to dismiss ◆ **er läßt sich nicht ~** he won't take no for an answer.
abweisend *adj Ton, Blick* cold, chilly.
Abweisung *f siehe vt* rejection; turning away; refusal; dismissal.
abwendbar *adj* avoidable.
abwenden *sep reg or irreg* [1] *vt* **(a)** *(zur Seite wenden)* to turn away; *Blick* to avert; *Kopf* to turn ◆ **er wandte das Gesicht ab** he looked away. **(b)** *(verhindern) Unheil, Folgen* to avert.
[2] *vr* to turn away.
abwerben *vt sep irreg* to woo away *(dat* from).
Abwerbung *f* wooing away.
abwerfen *sep irreg* [1] *vt* to throw off; *Reiter* to throw; *Bomben, Flugblätter etc* to drop; *Ballast* to jettison; *Geweih* to shed, to cast; *Blätter, Nadeln* to shed; *(Cards)* to discard, to throw away; *(Comm) Gewinn* to yield, to return, to show; *Zinsen* to bear, to yield; *(fig liter) Joch, Fesseln* to cast *or* throw off.
[2] *vti (Sport) (Ftbl) Ball* to throw out; *Speer etc* to throw; *Latte* to knock off *or* down.
abwerten *vt sep* **(a)** *auch vi Währung* to devalue. **(b)** *(fig) Ideale* to debase, to cheapen ◆ **diese Tugend ist heute vollkommen abgewertet** this virtue is no longer valued today; **er muß immer alles ~** he always has to run everything down.
abwertend *adj* pejorative.
Abwertung *f siehe vt* **(a)** *(von Währung)* devaluation ◆ **eine ~ vornehmen** to devalue (the currency). **(b)** *(fig)* debasement, cheapening. **solche Ideale erfahren eine immer stärkere ~** such ideals are valued less and less *or* are constantly losing their value.
abwesend *adj* absent; *(von Hause auch)* away *pred*; *(iro: zerstreut auch)* far away; *Blick* absent-minded ◆ **die A~en** the absentees.
Abwesenheit *f* absence; *(fig: Geistes~)* abstraction ◆ **in ~** *(Jur)* in absence; **durch ~ glänzen** *(iro)* to be conspicuous by one's absence.
Abwetter *pl (Min)* used air.
abwetzen *sep* [1] *vt (abschaben)* to wear smooth.
[2] *vi aux sein (inf)* to hare off *(inf)*, to bolt *(inf)*.
abwichsen *vt sep*: **sich/jdm einen ~** *(vulg)* to jerk *or* wank off *(sl)*/jerk sb off *(sl)*.
abwickeln *sep* [1] *vt* **(a)** *(abspulen)* to unwind; *Verband auch* to take off, to remove.
(b) *(fig: erledigen)* to deal with; *ein Geschäft* to complete, to conclude; *Kontrolle* to carry out; *Veranstaltung* to run; *(Comm: liquidieren)* to wind up ◆ **die Versammlung wurde in aller Ruhe abgewickelt** the meeting went off peacefully.
[2] *vr* to unwind; *(vonstatten gehen)* to go *or* pass off.
Abwicklung *f siehe vt* **(a)** unwinding; taking off, removal. **(b)** completion, conclusion; carrying out; running; winding up ◆ **die Polizei sorgte für eine reibungslose ~ der Veranstaltung** the police made sure that the event went *or* passed off smoothly.
abwiegeln *sep* [1] *vt* to appease; *wütende Menge etc auch* to calm down.
[2] *vi* to calm things down ◆ **das A~** appeasement.
abwiegen *vt sep irreg* to weigh out.
Abwiegler(in *f*) *m* **-s, -** appeaser, conciliator.
abwimmeln *vt sep (inf) jdn* to get rid of *(inf)*; *Auftrag* to get out of *(inf)* ◆ **die Sekretärin hat mich abgewimmelt** his secretary turned me away; **laß dich nicht ~** don't let them get rid of you.
Abwind *m (Aviat)* downwash; *(Met)* down current.
abwinkeln *vt sep Arm* to bend ◆ **mit abgewinkelten Armen** *(in den Hüften)* with arms akimbo.
abwinken *sep* [1] *vi (inf) (abwehrend)* to wave it/him *etc* aside; *(resignierend)* to groan; *(fig: ablehnen)* to say no ◆ **als er merkte, wovon ich reden wollte, winkte er gleich ab** when he realised what I wanted to talk about he immediately put me off *or* stopped me; **der Chef winkt bei so einem Vorschlag bestimmt gleich ab** the boss is bound to say no to *or* turn down a suggestion like that; **wenn Bonn abwinkt ...** if the (German) government turns us/them *etc* down *or* says no ...; *siehe* **müde**.
[2] *vti (bei Zug)* to give the "go" signal ◆ **ein Rennen ~** to wave the chequered flag; *(nach Unfall etc)* to stop the race; **einen Rennfahrer ~** to wave

a driver down.

abwirtschaften *vi sep (inf)* to go downhill ♦ **abgewirtschaftet haben** to have reached rock bottom; *siehe* **abgewirtschaftet.**

abwischen *vt sep Staub, Schmutz etc* to wipe off *or* away; *Hände, Nase etc* to wipe; *Augen, Tränen* to dry ♦ **er wischte sich** *(dat)* **den Schweiß/die Stirn ab** he mopped (the sweat from) his brow.

abwohnen *vt sep* **(a)** *Möbel* to wear out; *Haus, Zimmer* to make shabby. **(b)** *Baukostenzuschuß* to pay off with the rent ♦ **die Miete voll ~** to stay for the time for which rent has been paid.

abwracken *vt sep Schiff, Auto, technische Anlage* to break (up); *siehe* **abgewrackt.**

Abwurf *m* throwing off; *(von Reiter)* throw; *(von Bomben etc)* dropping; *(von Ballast)* jettisoning; *(von Geweih)* casting; *(Comm: von Zinsen, Gewinn)* yield; *(Sport) (der Latte)* knocking down *or* off; *(des Speers etc)* throwing ♦ **ein ~ vom Tor** a goal-throw, a throw-out.

abwürgen *vt sep (inf)* to scotch; *Motor* to stall ♦ **etw von vornherein ~** to nip sth in the bud.

abzahlen *vt sep* to pay off.

abzählen *sep* [1] *vt* to count ♦ **er zählte zwanzig Hundertmarkscheine ab** he counted out twenty hundred-mark notes; **das läßt sich an den (zehn** *or* **fünf) Fingern ~** *(fig)* that's plain to see, any fool can see that *(inf)*; **bitte das Fahrgeld abgezählt bereithalten** please tender exact *or* correct fare *(form)*.
[2] *vi* to number off.

Abzählreim, Abzählvers *m* counting-out rhyme *(such as "eeny meeny miney mo", for choosing a person)*.

Abzahlung *f* **(a)** *(Rückzahlung)* repayment, paying off. **(b)** *(Ratenzahlung)* hire purchase *(Brit)*, HP *(Brit)*, instalment plan *(US)*; *(Rate)* (re)payment, instalment ♦ **etw auf ~ kaufen** to buy sth on HP *(Brit) or* on hire purchase *(Brit) or* on the instalment plan *(US)*.

Abzahlungsgeschäft *nt* hire purchase *(Brit)*, HP *(Brit)*, instalment plan *(US)*.

abzapfen *vt sep* to draw off ♦ **jdm Blut ~** *(inf)* to take blood from sb; **jdm Geld ~** to get some money out of sb.

abzäumen *vt sep Pferd etc* to unbridle.

abzäunen *vt sep* to fence off.

Abzäunung *f* fencing.

abzehren *sep* [1] *vt (liter)* to emaciate; *siehe* **abgezehrt.**
[2] *vr* to waste *or* pine away.

Abzehrung *f* emaciation.

Abzeichen *nt* badge; *(Mil)* insignia *pl*; *(Orden, Auszeichnung)* decoration.

abzeichnen *sep* [1] *vt* **(a)** to draw. **(b)** *(signieren)* to initial.
[2] *vr* to stand out; *(Unterwäsche)* to show; *(fig) (deutlich werden)* to emerge, to become apparent; *(drohend bevorstehen)* to loom (on the horizon).

abzgl. *abbr of* **abzüglich.**

Abziehbild *nt* transfer.

abziehen *sep irreg* [1] *vt* **(a)** to skin; *Fell, Haut* to remove, to take off; *grüne Bohnen* to string.
(b) *Bett* to strip; *Bettzeug* to strip off.
(c) *(Sw: ausziehen) Mantel, Schürze, Ring etc* to take off; *Hut* to raise.
(d) *Schlüssel* to take out, to remove; *Abzugshahn* to press, to squeeze; *Pistole* to fire.
(e) *(zurückziehen) Truppen, Kapital* to withdraw; *(subtrahieren) Zahlen* to take away, to subtract; *Steuern* to deduct ♦ **DM 20 vom Preis ~** to take DM 20 off the price; **man hatte mir zuviel abgezogen** they'd deducted *or* taken off too much, I'd had too much deducted.
(f) *(abfüllen) Wein* to bottle ♦ **Wein auf Flaschen ~** to bottle wine.
(g) *(Typ: vervielfältigen)* to run off; *Korrekturfahnen auch* to pull; *(Phot) Bilder* to make prints of, to print ♦ **etw zwanzigmal ~** to run off twenty copies of sth.
(h) *(schleifen)* to sharpen; *Rasiermesser auch* to strop; *Parkett* to sand (down).
(i) *(Cook) Suppe, Sauce* to thicken ♦ **die Suppe mit einem Ei ~** to beat an egg into the soup.
(j) *(sl) Fest, Veranstaltung* to put on; *siehe* **Nummer, Schau.**
[2] *vi* **(a)** *aux sein (sich verflüchtigen) (Rauch, Dampf)* to escape, to go away; *(Sturmtief etc)* to move away.
(b) *aux sein (Soldaten)* to pull out *(aus* of), to withdraw *(aus* from); *(inf: weggehen)* to go off *or* away ♦ **zieh ab!** *(inf)* clear off! *(inf)*, beat it! *(inf)*.
(c) *(abdrücken)* to pull *or* squeeze the trigger, to fire.

Abzieher(in *f***)** *m* **-s, -** *(Typ)* proof puller.

Abziehpresse *f* proof press.

abzielen *vi sep* **auf etw** *(acc)* **~** *(Mensch)* to aim at sth; *(in Rede)* to get at sth; *(Bemerkung, Maßnahme etc)* to be aimed *or* directed at sth; **ich merkte sofort, worauf sie mit dieser Anspielung abzielte** I saw immediately what she was driving *or* getting at with that allusion.

abzinsen *vt insep (Fin)* to discount ♦ **abgezinste Sparbriefe** savings certificates sold at discounted interest.

Abzinsung *f (Fin)* discounting.

abzirkeln *vt sep (rare: mit Zirkel abmessen)* to measure (off) with compasses; *(fig: vorausplanen)* to calculate very carefully; *Worte, Bewegungen* to measure.

abzocken *vt sep (inf)* **jdn ~** to rip sb off *(inf)*; **hier wird man nur abgezockt** they just rip you off here *(inf)*.

abzotteln *vi sep aux sein (inf)* to toddle off *(inf)*.

Abzug ['aptsu:k] *m* **(a)** *no pl (Weggang)* departure; *(Met: von Tief)* moving away; *(Wegnahme: von Truppen, Kapital etc)* withdrawal ♦ **jdm freien ~ gewähren** to give *or* grant sb a safe conduct.
(b) *(usu pl: vom Lohn etc)* deduction; *(Rabatt)* discount ♦ **ohne ~** *(Comm)* net terms only; **er verdient ohne Abzüge ...** before deductions *or* stoppages he earns ...; **etw in ~ bringen** *(form)* to deduct sth.
(c) *(Typ)* copy; *(Korrekturfahne)* proof; *(Phot)* print.
(d) *(Öffnung für Rauch, Gas)* flue ♦ **es muß für hinreichenden ~ gesorgt werden** there must be sufficient means for the gas/smoke to escape *or* to be drawn off.
(e) *(am Gewehr)* trigger.

abzüglich *prep +gen (Comm)* minus, less.

Abzugs-: a~fähig *adj (Fin)* (tax-)deductible; **a~frei** *adj* tax-free; **~haube** *f* extractor hood; **~rohr** *nt* flue (pipe).

abzupfen *vt sep* to pull *or* pluck off *(von etw* sth); *(S Ger: pflücken)* to pick.

abzwacken *vt sep (dial)* **(a)** *(abkneifen)* to pinch off. **(b)** *siehe* **abknapsen.**

abzwecken *vi sep* **auf etw** *(acc)* **~** to be aimed at sth.

Abzweig *m (form)* junction ♦ **der ~ nach Saarbrücken** the turn-off to *or* for Saarbrücken.

Abzweigdose *f* junction box.

abzweigen *sep* [1] *vi aux sein* to branch off.
[2] *vt (inf)* to set *or* put on one side.

Abzweigung *f* junction, turn-off; *(Nebenstrecke)* turn-off; *(Gabelung)* fork; *(Rail: Nebenlinie)* branch line; *(Elec)* junction.

abzwicken *vt sep* to pinch *or* nip off.

abzwingen *vt sep irreg* **jdm Respekt** *etc* **~** to gain sb's respect *etc*; **er zwang sich** *(dat)* **ein Lächeln ab** he forced a smile.

abzwitschern *vi sep aux sein (inf)* to go off, to take oneself off.

Accessoires [aksɛ'soa:ɐ(s)] *pl* accessories *pl*.

Acetat [atse'ta:t] *nt* **-s, -e** acetate.

Aceton [atse'to:n] *nt* **-s, -e** acetone.

Acetylen [atsety'le:n] *nt* **-s,** *no pl* acetylene.

Acetylen(sauerstoff)brenner *m* oxyacetylene burner.

ach [ax] [1] *interj* oh; *(poet auch)* O; *(bedauernd auch)* alas *(old, liter)* ♦ **~ nein!** oh no!; *(überrascht)* no!, really!; *(ablehnend)* no, no!; **~ nein, ausgerechnet der!** well, well, him of all people; **~ so!** I see!, aha!; *(ja richtig)* of course!; **~ was** *or* **wo!** of course not; **~ was** *or* **wo, das ist doch nicht so schlimm!** come on now, it's not that bad; **~ was** *or* **wo, das ist nicht nötig!** no, no that's not necessary; **~ wirklich?** oh really?, do you/does he *etc* really?; **~ je!** oh dear!, oh dear(ie) me!
[2] *adv (geh)* **~ so schnell/schön** *etc* oh so quickly/lovely *etc*.

Ach *nt*: **mit ~ und Krach** *(inf)* by the skin of one's teeth *(inf)*; **eine Prüfung mit ~ und Krach bestehen** to scrape through an exam (by the skin of one's teeth); **ich habe die Behandlung überstanden, aber nur mit ~ und Weh** I had the treatment but I screamed blue murder *(inf)*.

Achäer(in *f***)** [a'xɛ:ɐ, -ɛ:ərɪn] *m* **-s, -** *(Hist)* Achaean.

Achat *m* **-(e)s, -e** agate.

achaten *adj attr* agate.

Achill(es) *m* Achilles.

Achillesferse *f* Achilles heel.

Ach-Laut *m* voiceless velar fricative *(the sound "ch" in the Scottish "loch")*.

Achs-: ~abstand *m* wheelbase; **~bruch** *m siehe* **Achsenbruch; ~druck** *m* axle weight.

Achse ['aksə] *f* **-, -n** **(a)** axis ♦ **die ~ (Rom-Berlin)** *(Hist)* the (Rome-Berlin) Axis. **(b)** *(Tech)* axle; *(Propeller~)* shaft ♦ **auf (der) ~ sein** *(inf)* to be out (and about); *(Kraftfahrer, Vertreter etc)* to be on the road.

Achsel ['aksl] *f* **-, -n** **(a)** shoulder ♦ **die ~n** *or* **mit den ~n zucken** to shrug (one's shoulders). **(b)** *(~höhle)* armpit.

Achsel-: ~griff *m* underarm grip; **~haare** *pl* **die ~haare** underarm hair, the hair under one's arms; **~höhle** *f* armpit; **~klappe** *f*, **~stück** *nt siehe* **Schulterklappe; ~zucken** *nt* shrug; **mit einem ~zucken** with a shrug (of one's shoulders); **a~zuckend** *adj* shrugging; **er stand a~zuckend da** he stood there shrugging his shoulders.

Achsen-: ~bruch *m* broken axle; **~kreuz** *nt siehe* **Koordinatenkreuz; ~mächte** *pl (Hist)* Axis powers *pl*.

Achs-: ~lager *nt* axle bearing; **~last** *f siehe* **~druck; ~schenkel** *m* stub axle, steering knuckle *(US)*; **~stand** *m* wheelbase; **~welle** *f* axle shaft.

acht *num* eight ♦ **für** *or* **auf ~ Tage** for a week; **in ~ Tagen** in a week *or* a week's time; **heute/morgen in ~ Tagen** a week today/tomorrow, today/tomorrow week; **heute vor ~ Tagen war ich ...** a week ago today I was ...; **vor ~ Tagen werden sie wohl nicht fertig sein** they won't be ready for a week at least; *siehe auch* **vier.**

Acht[1] *f* **-, -en** eight; *(bei Fahrrad)* buckled wheel; *(beim Eislaufen etc)* figure (of) eight; *siehe auch* **Vier.**

Acht[2] *f*: **sich in a~ nehmen** to be careful, to take care, to watch *or* look out; **etw außer a~ lassen** to leave sth out of consideration, to disregard sth; **etw außer aller ~ lassen** *(geh)* to pay no attention *or* heed whatsoever to sth, not to heed sth; *siehe* **achtgeben.**

Acht[3] *f* **-,** *no pl (Hist)* outlawry, proscription ♦ **jdn in ~ und Bann tun** to outlaw *or* proscribe sb; *(Eccl)* to place sb under the ban; *(fig)* to ostracize sb.

achtbar *adj (geh) Gesinnung, Eltern* worthy.

Achtbarkeit *f* worthiness.

Acht|eck *nt* octagon.

acht|eckig *adj* octagonal, eight-sided.

achtel *adj* eighth; *siehe auch* **viertel.**

Achtel *nt* **-s, -** eighth; *siehe auch* **Viertel[1] (a).**

Achtel-: ~finale *nt round before the quarter-final*, 2nd/3rd *etc* round; **ein Platz im ~finale** a place in the last sixteen; **~note** *f* quaver *or* eighth note

⚠: for details of spelling reform, see supplement

(*US*); ~**pause** *f* quaver *or* eighth note (*US*) rest.

▼ **achten** [1] *vt* **(a)** (*schätzen*) to respect, to think highly of, to hold in high regard ◆ **geachtete Leute** respected people.
(b) (*respektieren*) *Gesetze, Bräuche, jds Gesinnung* to respect.
(c) (*geh: betrachten*) to regard ◆ **etw (für) gering ~** to have scant regard for sth.
▼ [2] *vi* **auf etw** (*acc*) **~** to pay attention to sth; **auf die Kinder ~** to keep an eye on the children; **darauf ~, daß** ... to be careful *or* to see *or* to take care that ...

ächten *vt* (*Hist*) to outlaw, to proscribe; (*fig*) to ostracize.

achtens *adv* eighthly, in the eighth place.

achtenswert *adj Person* worthy; *Bemühungen, Handlung auch* commendable.

achte(r, s) *adj* eighth; *siehe auch* **vierte(r, s)**.

Achte(r) *mf decl as adj* eighth; *siehe auch* **Vierte(r)**.

Achter *m* **-s, -** (*Rudern*) eight; (*Eislauf etc*) figure (of) eight; *siehe auch* **Vierer**.

Achter-: **a~aus** *adv* (*Naut*) astern; **~bahn** *f* big dipper (*Brit*), roller coaster (*US*), switchback; **~deck** *nt* (*Naut*) afterdeck; **a~lastig** *adj* (*Naut*) *Schiff* stern-heavy.

achtern *adv* aft, astern ◆ **nach ~ gehen/abdrehen** to go aft/to turn astern; **von ~** from astern.

Acht-: **a~fach** [1] *adj* eightfold; **in a~facher Ausfertigung** with seven copies; *siehe auch* **vierfach**; [2] *adv* eightfold, eight times; **~füßer** *m* **-s, -** (*Zool*) octopod.

achtgeben *vi sep irreg* to take care, to be careful (*auf +acc* of); (*aufmerksam sein*) to pay attention (*auf +acc* to) ◆ **auf jdn/etw ~** (*beaufsichtigen*) to keep an eye on *or* to look after sb/sth; **wenn man im Straßenverkehr nur einen Augenblick nicht achtgibt**, ... if your attention wanders for just a second in traffic ...; **„O Mensch, gib acht!"** "O man, take heed".

achthaben *vi sep irreg* (*geh*) *siehe* **achtgeben**.

Acht-: **a~hundert** *num* eight hundred; *siehe auch* **vierhundert**; **~kampf** *m* gymnastic competition with eight events; **a~kantig** *adj* (*lit*) eight-sided; **a~kantig rausfliegen** (*sl*) to be flung out on one's ear (*inf*) *or* arse over tit (*sl*).

achtlos *adj* careless, thoughtless ◆ **er hat meinen Aufsatz nur ~ durchgeblättert** he just casually leafed through my essay; **viele gehen ~ daran vorbei** many people just pass by without noticing them.

Achtlosigkeit *f* carelessness, thoughtlessness.

achtmal *adv* eight times.

achtsam *adj* (*geh*) attentive; (*sorgfältig*) careful ◆ **mit etw ~ umgehen** to be careful with sth.

Achtsamkeit *f* attentiveness; (*Sorgfalt*) care.

Acht-: **~stundentag** *m* eight hour day; **a~tägig** *adj* lasting a week, week-long; **mit a~tägiger Verspätung** a week late; **der a~tägige Streik ist** ... the week-old *or* week-long strike is ...; **a~täglich** *adj* weekly; **a~tausend** *num* eight thousand; **ein ~tausender** *a mountain eight thousand metres in height*; *siehe auch* **viertausend**.

Achtung *f, no pl* **(a)** ~! watch *or* look out!; (*Mil: Befehl*) attention!; ~, ~! (your) attention please!; **„~ Hochspannung!"** "danger, high voltage"; **„~ Lebensgefahr!"** "danger"; **„~ Stufe!"** "mind the step"; **~, fertig, los!** ready, steady *or* get set, go!
(b) (*Wertschätzung*) respect (*vor +dat* for) ◆ **die ~ vor sich selbst** one's self-respect *or* self-esteem; **bei aller ~ vor jdm/etw** with all due respect to sb/sth; **in hoher ~ bei jdm stehen** to be held in high esteem *or* be highly esteemed by sb; **jdm ~ einflößen** to command *or* gain sb's respect; **sich** (*dat*) **~ verschaffen** to make oneself respected, to gain respect for oneself; **jdm die nötige ~ entgegenbringen** to give sb the respect due to him/her *etc*; **alle ~!** good for you/him *etc*!

Ächtung *f, no pl* (*Hist, des Krieges etc*) proscription, outlawing; (*fig: gesellschaftlich*) ostracism.

⚠ **achtunggebietend** *adj* (*geh*) awe-inspiring.

Achtungs-: **~applaus** *m* polite applause; **~erfolg** *m* succès d'estime; **a~voll** *adj* (*rare*) respectful.

achtzehn *num* eighteen; *siehe auch* **vierzehn**.

achtzig *num* eighty ◆ **auf ~ sein** (*inf*) to be livid, to be hopping mad (*inf*); **da war er gleich auf ~** (*inf*) then he got livid; *siehe auch* **vierzig**.

Achtziger(in *f*) *m* **-s, -** (*Mensch*) eighty-year-old, octogenarian; *siehe auch* **Vierziger**.

ächzen *vi* to groan (*vor +dat* with); (*Brücke, Baum etc auch*) to creak ◆ **~ und stöhnen** to moan and groan.

Ächzer *m* **-s, -** groan.

Acker *m* **-s, ⸚** **(a)** (*Feld*) field ◆ **den ~/die ⸚ bestellen** to till the soil/plough the fields; **einen ~ bebauen** *or* **bewirtschaften** to work the land. **(b)** (*old: Feldmaß*) ≃ acre.

Acker-: **~bau** *m* **-s,** *no pl* agriculture, farming; **~bau betreiben** to farm the land; **~bau und Viehzucht** farming; **~bauer** *m* husbandman (*old, liter*), farmer; ⚠**a~bautreibend** *adj attr* farming; **~bürger** *m* (*Hist*) *townsman who farms a smallholding*; **~fläche** *f* area of arable land; **~furche** *f* furrow; **~gaul** *m* (*pej*) farm horse, old nag (*pej*); *siehe* **Rennpferd**; **~gerät** *nt* farm *or* agricultural implement; **~krume** *f* topsoil; **~land** *nt* arable land; **~mann** *m siehe* **Ackersmann**.

ackern [1] *vi* **(a)** (*inf*) to slog away (*inf*). **(b)** (*old*) to till the soil.
[2] *vt* (*old: pflügen*) to till.

Acker-: **~salat** *m* (*SGer*) lamb's lettuce; **~scholle** *f* (*liter*) soil.

Ackersmann *m* (*old, liter*) husbandman (*old, liter*).

Acker-: **~walze** *f* (land) roller; **~winde** *f* (*Bot*) field bindweed.

a conto *adv* (*Comm*) on account.

Acryl *nt* **-s** acrylic.

Acryl- *in cpds* acrylic; **~farbe** *f* acrylic paint; **~glas** *nt* acrylic glass; **~platte** *f* acrylic tile.

Action ['ækʃən] *f* **-,** *no pl* action.

Actionfilm *m* (*inf*) action film.

A.D. *abbr of* **Anno Domini** AD.

a.D. [aː'deː] *abbr of* **außer Dienst** ret(d).

Adabei ['aːdabai] *m* **-s, -s** (*Aus inf*) limelighter (*inf*).

ad absurdum *adv* **~ führen** to make a nonsense of; *Argument etc* to reduce to absurdity *or* absurdum.

ADAC [aːdeː|aː'tseː] *abbr of* **Allgemeiner Deutscher Automobil-Club** ≃ AA (*Brit*), RAC (*Brit*), AAA (*US*).

ad acta *adv*: **etw ~ legen** (*fig*) to consider sth finished; *Frage, Problem* to consider sth closed.

Adam *m* **-s** Adam ◆ **seit ~s Zeiten** (*inf*) since the year dot (*inf*); **das stammt noch von ~ und Eva** (*inf*) it's out of the ark (*inf*); **bei ~ und Eva anfangen** (*inf*) to start right from scratch (*inf*) *or* from square one (*inf*); *siehe* **Riese**[1].

Adams-: **~apfel** *m* (*inf*) Adam's apple; **~kostüm** *nt* (*inf*) birthday suit; **im ~kostüm** in one's birthday suit, as nature made one.

Adap(ta)tion *f* adaptation.

Adapter *m* **-s, -** adapter, adaptor.

Adapterkarte *f* (*Comput*) adapter card.

adaptieren* *vt* **(a)** to adapt. **(b)** (*Aus: herrichten*) to fix up.

Adaptierung, Adaption *f siehe* **Adap(ta)tion**.

adaptiv *adj* adaptive.

adäquat *adj* (*geh*) *Bemühung, Belohnung, Übersetzung* adequate; *Stellung, Verhalten* suitable; *Kritik* valid ◆ **einer Sache** (*dat*) **~ sein** to be adequate to sth.

Adäquatheit *f* (*geh*) *siehe adj* adequacy; suitability; validity.

addieren* [1] *vt* to add (up).
[2] *vi* to add.

Addiermaschine *f* adding machine.

Addis Abeba *nt* **- -s** Addis Ababa.

Addition *f* addition; (*fig*) agglomeration.

Additionsmaschine *f* adding machine.

Additiv *nt* **-s, -e** additive.

ade *interj* (*old, S Ger*) farewell (*old, liter*), adieu (*old, liter*) ◆ **jdm ~ sagen** to bid sb farewell; **einer Sache** (*dat*) **~ sagen** to say farewell to sth.

Adebar *m* **-s, -e** (*N Ger*) stork.

Adel *m* **-s,** *no pl* **(a)** (*Adelsgeschlecht, -stand*) nobility; (*Brit auch*) peerage; (*hoher auch*) aristocracy ◆ **von ~ sein** to be a member of the nobility, to be of noble birth; **eine Familie von ~** an aristocratic family; **er stammt aus altem ~** he comes from an old aristocratic family; **der niedere ~** the lesser nobility, the gentry; **der hohe ~** the higher nobility, the aristocracy; **das ist verarmter ~** they are impoverished nobility; **~ verpflichtet** noblesse oblige.
(b) (*~stitel*) title; (*des hohen Adels auch*) peerage ◆ **erblicher/persönlicher ~** hereditary/non-hereditary title; hereditary/life peerage.
(c) (*liter: edle Gesinnung*) nobility ◆ **~ der Seele/des Herzens/des Geistes** nobility of the soul/of the heart/of mind.

adelig *adj siehe* **adlig**.

Adelige(r) *mf decl as adj siehe* **Adlige(r)**.

adeln [1] *vt* to bestow a peerage on, to make a (life) peer (*Brit*), to ennoble; (*den Titel „Sir" verleihen*) to knight; (*niedrigen Adel verleihen*) to bestow a title on; (*fig liter: auszeichnen*) to ennoble.
[2] *vi* **etw adelt** (*geh*) sth ennobles the soul.

Adels-: **~bezeichnung** *f* title; **~brief** *m* patent of nobility; **~prädikat** *nt* mark of nobility (*in a name*); **~stand** *m* nobility; (*Brit auch*) peerage; (*hoher auch*) aristocracy; **in den ~stand erheben** *siehe* **adeln**; **~stolz** *m* pride in one's noble birth; **~titel** *m* title.

Adelung *f siehe vt* raising to the peerage; ennoblement; knighting; bestowing a title (*gen* on).

Adept(in *f*) *m* **-en, -en** (*old: der Geheimwissenschaften*) initiate; (*iro geh*) disciple.

Ader *f* **-, -n** (*Bot, Geol*) vein; (*Physiol*) blood vessel; (*Elec: Leitungsdraht*) core; (*fig: Veranlagung*) bent ◆ **das spricht seine künstlerische/musikalische ~ an** that appeals to the artist/musician in him; **eine/keine ~ für etw haben** to have feeling/no feeling for sth; **eine poetische/musikalische ~ haben** to have a feeling for poetry/music, to be of *or* have a poetic/musical bent; **sich** (*dat*) **die ~n öffnen** (*geh*) to slash one's wrists; **jdn zur ~ lassen** (*old, fig inf*) to bleed sb.

Äderchen *nt dim of* **Ader**.

⚠ **Aderlaß** *m* **-lasses, -lässe** (*old Med*) blood-letting (*auch fig*), bleeding ◆ **bei jdm einen ~ machen** to bleed sb; **die Abwanderung der Akademiker ist ein ~, den sich das Land nicht länger leisten kann** the country can no longer afford the bleeding of its resources through the exodus of its academics.

ädern *vt siehe* **geädert**.

Äderung *f* veining.

Adhäsion *f* (*Phys*) adhesion.

Adhäsions-: **~kraft** *f* adhesive power, power of adhesion; ⚠**~verschluß** *m* adhesive seal.

ad hoc *adv* (*geh*) ad hoc ◆ **~ ~ wurde ein Komitee gebildet** an ad hoc committee was set up.

Ad-hoc- *in cpds* ad hoc; **~-Maßnahme** *f* ad hoc measure.

adieu [adi'øː] *interj* (*old, dial*) adieu (*obs*), farewell (*old*) ◆ **jdm ~ sagen** to bid sb farewell (*old*), to say farewell *or* adieu to sb.

Adjektiv *nt* adjective.

adjektivisch *adj* adjectival.
Adjektivum *nt* **-s, Adjektiva** *siehe* **Adjektiv.**
Adjunkt *m* **-en, -en** *(Aus, Sw)* junior civil servant.
adjustieren* *vt* **(a)** *(Tech) Werkstück* to adjust; *Meßgerät* to set. **(b)** *(Aus)* to issue with uniforms/a uniform.
Adjustierung *f* **(a)** *siehe vt* adjustment; setting; issue of uniforms. **(b)** uniform.
Adjutant *m* adjutant; *(von General)* aide(-de-camp).
Adlatus *m* **-, Adlaten** *or* **Adlati** *(old, iro)* assistant.
Adler *m* **-s, -** eagle.
Adler-: ~auge *nt (fig)* eagle eye; **~augen haben** to have eyes like a hawk, to be eagle-eyed; **~blick** *m (fig)* eagle eye; **~farn** *m* bracken; **~horst** *m* (eagle's) eyrie; **~nase** *f* aquiline nose.
adlig *adj (lit, fig)* noble ♦ **~ sein** to be of noble birth.
Adlige(r) *mf decl as adj* member of the nobility, nobleman/-woman; *(Brit auch)* peer/peeress; *(hoher auch)* aristocrat.
Administration *f* administration.
administrativ *adj* administrative.
Administrator(in *f***)** [-'to:rɪn] *m* administrator.
administrieren* *vi (geh: verwalten)* to administrate.
Admiral *m* **-s, -e** *or* **Admiräle (a)** admiral. **(b)** *(Zool)* red admiral.
Admiralität *f* **(a)** *(die Admirale)* admirals *pl.* **(b)** *(Marineleitung)* admiralty.
Admiralsrang *m* rank of admiral.
Adoleszenz *f (form)* adolescence.
Adonis *m* **-, -se** *(geh)* Adonis.
Adonisröschen *nt* pheasant's-eye.
adoptieren* *vt* to adopt.
Adoption *f* adoption.
Adoptiv-: ~eltern *pl* adoptive parents *pl*; **~kind** *nt* adopted child.
Adr. *abbr of* **Adresse.**
Adrenalin *nt* **-s,** *no pl* adrenalin.
Adrenalin-: ~spiegel *m, no pl* adrenalin level; **~stoß** *m* surge of adrenalin.
Adressant *m (geh)* sender; *(Comm auch)* consignor *(form)*.
Adressat *m* **-en, -en** *(geh)* addressee; *(Comm auch)* consignee *(form)* ♦ **~en** *(fig)* target group.
Adressatengruppe *f* target group.
⚠ **Adreßbuch** *nt* directory; *(privat)* address book.
Adresse *f* **-, -n (a)** *(Anschrift, Comput)* address ♦ **eine Warnung an jds ~** *(acc)* **richten** *(fig)* to address a warning to sb; **dieser Vorwurf geht an Ihre eigene ~** this reproach is directed at *or* addressed to you (personally); **sich an die richtige ~ wenden** *(inf)* to go/come to the right place *or* person/people; **an die falsche** *or* **verkehrte ~ kommen** *or* **geraten** *(all inf)* to go/come to the wrong person *(inf)*; **an der falschen ~ sein** *(inf)* to have gone/come to the wrong person, to be knocking at the wrong door *(inf)*.
(b) *(form: Botschaft)* address.
Adressen-: ~aufkleber *m* address label; **~verwaltung** *f (Comput)* address filing system.
adressieren* *vt* to address *(an +acc* to).
Adressiermaschine *f* addressograph.
adrett *adj (dated)* neat.
Adria *f* **-** Adriatic (Sea).
Adriatisches Meer *nt (form)* Adriatic Sea.
Adstringens [at'strɪŋgens] *nt* **-, -genzien** astringent.
Advantage [ad'va:ntɪdʒ] *m* **-s, -s** *(Sport)* advantage.
Advent [at'vɛnt] *m* **-s, -e** Advent ♦ **im ~** in Advent; **erster/vierter ~** first/fourth Sunday in Advent.
Adventist [-vɛn-] *m (Rel)* (Second) Adventist.
Advents-: ~kalender *m* Advent calendar; **~kranz** *m* Advent wreath; **~sonntag** *m* Sunday in Advent; **~zeit** *f* (season of) Advent.
Adverb [at'vɛrp] *nt* **-s, -ien** adverb.
adverbial *adj* adverbial.
Adverbial-: ~bestimmung *f* adverbial qualification; **mit ~bestimmung** qualified adverbially; **~satz** *m* adverbial clause.
adversativ [atvɛrza'ti:f] *adj (Gram)* adversative.
Adversativsatz *m* adversative clause.
Advocatus diaboli *m* **- -, Advocati -** *(geh)* devil's advocate.
Advokat [atvo'ka:t] *m* **-en, -en** *(old Jur, fig)* advocate; *(Aus, Sw, auch pej)* lawyer.
Advokatur [-vo-] *f* **(a)** legal profession. **(b)** *(Büro)* lawyer's office.
Advokaturbüro *nt (Sw)*, **Advokaturskanzlei** *f (Aus)* lawyer's office.
Aero- [aero] *in cpds* aero.
Aerobic [ae'rɔbɪk] *nt* **-(s),** *no pl* aerobics *sing.*
Aero-: ~dynamik *f* aerodynamics; **a~dynamisch** *adj* aerodynamic; **~gramm** *nt* air-letter, aerogramme; **~nautik** *f* aeronautics *sing;* **a~nautisch** *adj* aeronautic(al); **~sol** *nt* **-s, -e** aerosol.
Affäre *f* **-, -n (a)** *(Angelegenheit)* affair, business *no pl*; *(Liebesabenteuer)* affair ♦ **in eine ~ verwickelt sein** to be mixed up *or* involved in an affair; **sich aus der ~ ziehen** *(inf)* to get (oneself) out of it *(inf)*. **(b)** *(Zwischenfall)* incident, episode.
Äffchen *nt dim of* **Affe.**
Affe *m* **-n, -n (a)** monkey; *(Menschen~)* ape ♦ **der Mensch stammt vom ~n ab** man is descended from the apes; **der nackte ~** the naked ape; **klettern wie ein ~** to climb like a monkey; **du bist wohl vom wilden ~n gebissen!** *(sl)* you must be out of your tiny mind! *(inf) or* off your rocker! *(sl)*; *siehe* **lausen, Schleifstein.**
(b) *(sl: Kerl)* clown *(inf)*, berk *(Brit sl)*, twit *(Brit sl)* ♦ **ein eingebildeter ~** a conceited ass *(inf)*; **du (alter) ~!** *(sl)* you (great) berk *or* twit *(sl)*.
(c) *(Mil inf)* knapsack.
Affekt *m* **-(e)s, -e** emotion, affect *(form)* ♦ **ein im ~ begangenes Verbrechen** a crime committed under the effect of emotion *or* in the heat of the moment; **im ~ handeln** to act in the heat of the moment.
Affekt-: a~geladen *adj (geh)* impassioned, passionate; **~handlung** *f* act committed under the influence of emotion.
affektiert *adj (pej)* affected ♦ **sich ~ benehmen** to be affected, to behave affectedly.
Affektiertheit *f* affectation, affectedness.
affektiv *adj (Psych)* affective.
Affektstau *m (Psych)* emotional block.
Affen-: ~arsch *m (sl)* berk *(Brit sl)*, stupid bum *(sl)*; **a~artig** *adj* like a monkey; *(menschen~artig)* apelike; **a~artig klettern** to climb like a monkey; **mit a~artiger Geschwindigkeit** *(inf)* like greased lightning *(inf)*, like *or* in a flash *(inf)*; **~brotbaum** *m* monkey-bread (tree), baobab; **a~geil** *adj (sl)* wicked *(sl)*, right on *(sl)*; **~geschwindigkeit** *f (inf) siehe* **~tempo**; **~haus** *nt* ape house; **~hitze** *f (inf)* sweltering heat *(inf)*; **gestern war eine ~hitze** yesterday was a scorcher *(inf) or* it was sweltering *(inf)*; **~jäckchen** *nt*, **~jacke** *f (Mil inf)* monkey jacket; **~käfig** *m* monkey's/ape's cage; **~liebe** *f* blind adoration *(zu* of); **~mensch** *m (inf)* ape-man; **~pinscher** *m* griffon (terrier); **~schande** *f (inf)* crying shame *(inf)*; **~schaukel** *f (inf) (Mil)* fourragère; *(usu pl: Frisur)* looped plait; **~spektakel** *nt (inf)* hullabaloo *(inf)*, uproar; **~tanz** *m (inf) siehe* **~theater**; **~tempo** *nt (inf)* breakneck speed *(inf)*; **in** *or* **mit einem ~tempo** at breakneck speed *(inf)*; *(laufen auch)* like the clappers *(sl)*; **~theater** *nt (inf)* to-do *(inf)*, carry-on *(inf)*, fuss; **ein ~theater aufführen** to make a fuss; **~weibchen** *nt* female monkey/ape; **~zahn** *m (sl) siehe* **~tempo.**
affig *adj (inf) (eitel)* stuck-up *(inf)*, conceited; *(geziert)* affected; *(lächerlich)* ridiculous, ludicrous ♦ **sich ~ anstellen** *or* **haben** to be stuck-up *(inf)*/affected/ridiculous *or* ludicrous.
Affigkeit *f (inf) (Geziertheit)* affectedness; *(Lächerlichkeit)* ridiculousness, ludicrousness.
Äffin *f* female monkey/ape.
Affinität *f* affinity.
Affirmation *f (geh)* affirmation.
affirmativ *adj (geh)* affirmative.
Affix *nt* **-es, -e** *(Ling)* affix.
Affrikata *f* **-, Affrikaten** *(Ling)* affricate.
Affront [a'frõ:] *m* **-s, -s** *(geh)* affront, insult *(gegen* to).
Afghane *m* **-n, -n, Afghanin** *f* Afghan.
afghanisch *adj* Afghan ♦ **~er Windhund** Afghan (hound).
Afghanistan *nt* **-s** Afghanistan.
Afrika *nt* **-s** Africa.
Afrikaans *nt* **-** Afrikaans.
Afrikaner(in *f***)** *m* **-s, -** African.
afrikanisch *adj* African.
Afrikanistik *f* African studies *pl.*
Afro-: ~amerikaner *m* Afro-American; **~asiat** *m* Afro-Asian; **a~asiatisch** *adj* Afro-Asian; **~-Look** *m* **-s** Afro-look.
After *m* **-s, -** *(form)* anus.
After-shave, After Shave ['a:ftɐʃeɪv] *nt* **-(s), -s** aftershave.
AG [a:'ge:] *f* **-, -s** *abbr of* **Aktiengesellschaft** plc *(Brit)*, corp., inc. *(US)*.
Ägäis [ɛ'gɛ:ɪs] *f* **-** Aegean (Sea).
ägäisch [ɛ'gɛ:ɪʃ] *adj* Aegean ♦ **Ä~es Meer** Aegean Sea.
Agave [a'ga:və] *f* **-, -n** agave.
Agende *f* **-, -n** *(Eccl)* liturgy.
Agens *nt* **-, Agenzien** [a'gɛntsɪen] *(Philos, Med, Ling)* agent.
Agent *m* agent; *(Spion)* secret *or* foreign agent.
Agenten-: ~führer *m* spymaster; **~netz** *nt* spy network; **~ring** *m* spy ring; **~tätigkeit** *f* espionage; **ihre ~tätigkeit** her activity as a secret *or* foreign agent.
Agentin *f* secret *or* foreign agent.
Agent provocateur [a'ʒã:provoka'tø:ɐ] *m* **- -, -s -s** agent provocateur.
Agentur *f* agency.
Agenturbericht *m* (news) agency report.
Agglomerat *nt (Tech, Geol)* agglomerate; *(fig geh auch)* agglomeration, conglomeration.
Agglutination *f (Ling)* agglutination.
agglutinieren* *vi (Ling)* to agglutinate ♦ **~d** agglutinative; *Sprache auch* agglutinating.
Aggregat *nt (Geol)* aggregate; *(Tech)* unit, set of machines.
Aggregatzustand *m* state ♦ **die drei Aggregatzustände** the three states of matter.
Aggression *f* aggression *(gegen* towards) ♦ **~en gegen jdn empfinden** to feel aggressive *or* aggression towards sb.
Aggressions-: a~geladen *adj* charged with aggression; **a~lüstern** *adj (pej)* belligerent, bellicose; **~trieb** *m (Psych)* aggressive impulse.
aggressiv *adj* aggressive.
Aggressivität *f* aggression, aggressiveness.
Aggressor *m* aggressor.
Ägide *f* **-,** *no pl (liter)*: **unter jds ~** *(dat) (Schutz)* under the aegis of sb; *(Schirmherrschaft auch)* under sb's patronage.
agieren* *vi* to operate, to act; *(Theat)* to act ♦ **als jd ~** *(Theat)* to act *or* play

⚠: for details of spelling reform, see supplement

the part of sb.

agil *adj (körperlich)* agile, nimble ◆ **(geistig)** ~ sharp, nimble-minded, mentally agile.

Agilität *f siehe adj* agility, nimbleness; sharpness, nimble-mindedness.

Agio ['a:dʒo] *nt* **-, Agien** ['a:dʒən] *(Fin) (von Wertpapier)* premium; *(von Geldsorte)* agio.

Agiopapiere *pl (Fin)* securities redeemable at a premium.

Agitation *f (Pol)* agitation ◆ **~ treiben** to agitate.

Agitator(in *f***)** [-'to:rɪn] *m (Pol)* agitator.

agitatorisch *adj (Pol)* agitative; *Rede* inflammatory, agitating *attr* ◆ **~ argumentieren** to argue in an inflammatory style.

agitieren* *vi* to agitate.

Agitprop *f* **-**, *no pl* agitprop.

Agnostiker(in *f***)** *m* **-s, -** agnostic.

agnostisch *adj* agnostic.

Agnostizismus *m* agnosticism.

Agonie *f (lit, fig geh)* throes *pl* of death, death pangs *pl* ◆ **in (der) ~ liegen** to be in the throes of death.

Agrar- *in cpds* agrarian; **~gesellschaft** *f* agrarian society.

Agrarier [-iɐ] *m* **-s, -** landowner; *(hum, pej)* country squire.

agrarisch *adj* agrarian.

Agrar-: ~land *nt* agrarian country; **~markt** *m* agricultural commodities market; **~politik** *f* agricultural policy; **~zoll** *m* import tariff *(on produce)*.

Agrément [agre'mã:] *nt* **-s, -s** *(Pol)* agrément.

Agrikultur *f (form)* agriculture.

Agrikulturchemie, Agrochemie *f* agricultural chemistry.

Agronom(in *f***)** *m (DDR)* agronomist.

Agronomie *f (DDR)* agronomy.

Agrotechnik *f (DDR)* agricultural technology.

Ägypten *nt* **-s** Egypt.

Ägypter(in *f***)** *m* **-s, -** Egyptian.

ägyptisch *adj* Egyptian ◆ **~e Finsternis** *(liter)* Stygian darkness *(liter)*.

Ägyptologie *f* Egyptology.

ah [a:] *interj (genießerisch)* ooh, ah, mmm; *(überrascht, bewundernd, verstehend)* ah, oh.

Ah *nt* **-s, -s** oh, ah.

äh [ɛ:] *interj (beim Sprechen)* er, um; *(Ausdruck des Ekels)* ugh.

aha *interj* aha; *(verstehend auch)* I see.

Aha-Erlebnis *nt* sudden insight, aha-experience *(Psych)*.

Ahle *f* **-, -n** awl; *(Typ)* bodkin.

Ahn *m* **-(e)s** *or* **-en, -en** *(geh)* ancestor, for(e)father *(liter)*; *(fig)* for(e)bear *(liter)*.

ahnden *vt (liter) Freveltat, Verbrechen* to avenge; *(form) Übertretung, Verstoß* to punish.

Ahndung *f siehe vt* avengement; punishment.

Ahne[1] *m* **-n, -n** *(liter) siehe* **Ahn.**

Ahne[2] *f* **-, -n** *(geh) (weiblicher Vorfahr)* ancestress; *(fig)* for(e)bear *(liter)*.

ähneln *vi +dat* to be like, to be similar to, to resemble ◆ **sich** *or* **einander** *(geh)* ~ to be alike, to be similar, to resemble one another; **in diesem Punkt ähnelt sie sehr ihrem Vater** she's very like her father *or* very similar to her father *or* she greatly resembles her father in this respect; **diese Erklärung ähnelt seiner früheren Aussage überhaupt nicht mehr** this explanation bears no resemblance whatsoever to his earlier statement; **die beiden Systeme ~ einander nicht sehr/~ sich wenig** the two systems are not very similar *or* alike/ have little in common.

ahnen [1] *vt (voraussehen)* to foresee, to know; *Gefahr, Tod etc* to have a presentiment *or* premonition *or* foreboding of; *(vermuten)* to suspect; *(erraten)* to guess ◆ **das kann ich doch nicht ~!** I couldn't be expected to know that!; **nichts Böses ~** to have no sense of foreboding, to be unsuspecting; **nichts Böses ~d** unsuspectingly; **da sitzt man friedlich an seinem Schreibtisch, nichts Böses ~d ...** *(hum)* there I was sitting peacefully at my desk minding my own business ... *(hum)*; **ohne zu ~, daß ...** without dreaming *or* suspecting (for one minute) that ...; **ohne es zu ~** without suspecting, without having the slightest idea; **davon habe ich nichts geahnt** I didn't have the slightest inkling of it, I didn't suspect it for one moment; **so etwas habe ich doch geahnt** I did suspect something like that; **(ach), du ahnst es nicht!** *(inf)* would you believe it! *(inf)*; **du ahnst es nicht, wen ich gestern getroffen habe!** you'll never guess *or* believe who I met yesterday!; **die Umrisse waren/der Nußgeschmack war nur zu ~** the contours could only be guessed at/there was only the merest hint *or* suspicion of a nutty flavour.

[2] *vi (geh)* **mir ahnt etwas Schreckliches** I have a dreadful foreboding; **mir ahnt nichts Gutes** I have a premonition that all is not well.

Ahnen-: ~bild *nt* ancestral portrait; *(auch* **~figur)** ancestral figure; **~forschung** *f* genealogy; **~galerie** *f* ancestral portrait gallery; **~kult** *m* ancestor worship *or* cult; ⚠**~paß** *m (im Dritten Reich)* proof of ancestry, pedigree; **~reihe** *f* ancestral line; **~tafel** *f* genealogical tree *or* table, genealogy, pedigree; **~verehrung** *f* ancestor worship.

Ahn-: ~frau *f (liter)* ancestress; *(Stammutter)* progenitrix *(form, liter)*; **~herr** *m (liter)* ancestor; *(Stammvater)* progenitor *(form, liter)*.

▼ **ähnlich** [1] *adj* similar *(+dat* to) ◆ **ein dem Rokoko ~er Stil** a style similar to rococo, a similar style to rococo; **das dem Vater ~e Kind** the child that resembles his father *or* that is like his father; **~ wie er/sie** like him/her; **~ wie damals/vor 10 Jahren** as then/10 years ago; **sie sind sich ~** they are similar *or* alike; **ein ~ aussehender Gegenstand** a similar-looking object; **eine ~ komplizierte Sachlage** a similarly complicated state of affairs; **ich denke ~** my thinking is similar, I think likewise; **jdm ~ sehen** to be like sb, to resemble sb; **das sieht ihm (ganz) ~!** *(inf)* that's just like him!, that's him all over! *(inf)*; **(etwas) Ä~es** something similar, something like it/that.

[2] *prep +dat* similar to, like.

Ähnlichkeit *f (mit* to) *(Vergleichbarkeit)* similarity; *(ähnliches Aussehen)* similarity, resemblance ◆ **mit jdm/etw ~ haben** to resemble sb/sth, to be like sb/sth.

Ahnung *f* **(a)** *(Vorgefühl)* hunch, presentiment; *(düster)* foreboding, premonition.

(b) *(Vorstellung, Wissen)* idea; *(Vermutung)* suspicion, hunch ◆ **keine ~!** *(inf)* no idea! *(inf)*, I haven't a clue! *(inf)*; **er hat keine blasse** *or* **nicht die geringste ~** he hasn't a clue *or* the foggiest, he hasn't the faintest idea *(all inf)*; **ich hatte keine ~, daß ...** I had no idea that ...; **hast du eine ~, wo er sein könnte?** have you any *or* an idea where he could be?; **hast du eine ~!** *(iro inf)* a (fat) lot you know (about it)! *(inf)*, that's what *you* know (about it)!

Ahnungs-: a~los [1] *adj (nichts ahnend)* unsuspecting; *(unwissend)* clueless *(inf)*; [2] *adv* unsuspectingly, innocently; **~losigkeit** *f (Unwissenheit)* cluelessness *(inf)*, ignorance; **er bewies seine völlige ~losigkeit darüber, daß ...** he showed how totally unsuspecting he was of the fact that ...; **a~voll** *adj (geh)* full of presentiment *or (Böses ahnend)* foreboding.

ahoi [a'hɔy] *interj (Naut)* **Schiff ~!** ship ahoy!

Ahorn *m* **-s, -e** maple.

Ahornblatt *nt* maple leaf.

Ähre *f* **-, -n** *(Getreide~)* ear; *(allgemeiner, Gras~)* head ◆ **~n lesen** to glean (corn).

Ähren-: ~kranz *m* garland of corn; **~lese** *f* gleaning; **~leser** *m* gleaner.

AHV [a:ha:'fau] *(Sw) abbr of* **Alters- und Hinderungsversicherung** age and disability insurance.

Aide-mémoire ['ɛ:tme'moa:ɐ] *nt* **-, -** aide-mémoire.

Aids [eɪdz] *no art* **-**, *no pl* Aids.

Aids- *in cpds* Aids; **~-Erreger** *m* Aids virus; **~-Hilfe** *f* Aids support; **~-infiziert** *adj* infected with Aids; **~-Infizierte(r)** *mf decl as adj* person infected with Aids; **~-krank** *adj* suffering from Aids; **~-Kranke(r)** *mf* Aids sufferer; **~-Test** *m* Aids test.

Air [ɛ:ɐ] *nt* **-(s), -s** *(geh)* air, aura.

Air- [ɛ:ɐ-]: **~bag** [-bɛ:g] *m* **-s, -s** *(Aut)* airbag; **~bus** ['ɛ:ɐbʊs] *m (Aviat)* airbus; **~surfing** *nt* **-s** air surfing.

ais, Ais ['a:ɪs] *nt* **-, -** A sharp.

Aischylos ['aɪsçylɔs] *m* **-** Aeschylus.

Ajatollah *m* **-(s), -s** ayatollah.

Akademie *f* academy; *(Fachschule)* college, school.

Akademiker(in *f***)** *m* **-s, -** person with a university education; *(Student)* (university) student; *(Hochschulabsolvent)* (university) graduate; *(Universitätslehrkraft)* academic; *(rare: Akademiemitglied)* academician.

akademisch *adj (lit, fig)* academic ◆ **die ~e Jugend** (the) students *pl*; **das ~e Proletariat** (the) jobless graduates *pl*; **das ~e Viertel** *(Univ) the quarter of an hour allowed between the announced start of a lecture etc and the actual start*; **~ gebildet sein** to have (had) a university education, to be a graduate.

Akademisierung *f* **die ~ des öffentlichen Dienstes** turning the Civil Service into a graduate profession.

Akanthus *m* **-, -, Akanthusblatt** *nt* acanthus (leaf).

Akazie [-iə] *f* acacia.

Akelei *f* aquilegia, columbine.

Akklamation *f (form)* acclaim, acclamation ◆ **Wahl per** *or* **durch ~** election by acclamation.

akklamieren* *(form, Aus)* [1] *vi* to applaud *(jdm* sb).

[2] *vt Schauspieler, Szene* to acclaim, to applaud; *(wählen)* to elect by acclamation.

Akklimatisation *f (form)* acclimatization.

akklimatisieren* [1] *vr (lit, fig) (in +dat* to) to become acclimatized, to acclimatize oneself/itself.

[2] *vt* to acclimatize.

Akklimatisierung *f* acclimatization.

Akkolade *f* **(a)** *(Typ)* brace; *(Mus)* accolade. **(b)** *(Hist)* accolade.

Akkord *m* **-(e)s, -e (a)** *(Mus)* chord. **(b)** *(Stücklohn)* piece rate ◆ **im** *or* **in** *or* **auf ~ arbeiten** to do piecework. **(c)** *(Jur)* settlement.

Akkord-: ~arbeit *f* piecework; **~arbeiter** *m* piece-worker.

Akkordeon [-eɔn] *nt* **-s, -s** accordion.

Akkordeonist(in *f***), Akkordeonspieler(in** *f***)** *m* accordionist.

Akkord-: ~lohn *m* piece wages *pl*, piece rate; **~satz** *m* piece rate; **~zuschlag** *m* piece rate bonus.

akkreditieren* *vt* **(a)** *(Pol)* to accredit *(bei* to, at).

(b) *(Fin)* **jdn ~** to give sb credit facilities; **akkreditiert sein** to have credit facilities; **jdn für einen Betrag ~** to credit an amount to sb *or* sb's account, to credit sb *or* sb's account with an amount.

Akkreditierung *f* **(a)** *(Pol)* accrediting, accreditation *(bei* to, at). **(b)** *(Fin)* provision of credit facilities *(gen* to); *(von Betrag)* crediting.

Akkreditiv *nt* **(a)** *(Pol)* credentials *pl.* **(b)** *(Fin)* letter of credit ◆ **jdm ein ~ eröffnen** to open a credit in favour of sb.

Akku ['aku] *m* **-s, -s** *(inf) abbr of* **Akkumulator** accumulator.

Akkumulation *f* accumulation.

Akkumulator *m* accumulator.

akkumulieren* *vtir* to accumulate.

akkurat [1] *adj* precise; *(sorgfältig auch)* meticulous.

[2] *adv* precisely, exactly; *(tatsächlich)* naturally, of course.

Akkuratesse *f, no pl (dated) siehe adj* precision; meticulousness.
Akkusativ *m* accusative ◆ **im ~ stehen** to be in the accusative.
Akkusativ|objekt *nt* accusative object.
Akne *f* **-, -n** acne.
Akoluth, Akolyth *m* **-en, -en** *(Eccl)* acolyte.
Akontozahlung *f* payment on account.
akquirieren* [akvi'ri:rən] **1** *vt* **(a)** *Spenden* to collect ◆ **Inserate/Kunden ~** to sell advertising space/to canvass for customers. **(b)** *(old: erwerben)* to acquire.
2 *vi (Comm)* to canvass for custom.
Akquisiteur(in *f***)** [akvizi'tø:ɐ, -tø:rɪn] *m* agent, canvasser.
Akquisition [akvizitsi'o:n] *f (old)* acquisition; *(Comm)* (customer) canvassing.
Akribie *f, no pl (geh)* meticulousness, (meticulous) precision.
akribisch *adj (geh)* meticulous, precise.
Akrobat(in *f***)** *m* **-en, -en** acrobat.
Akrobatik *f, no pl* acrobatics *pl*; *(Geschicklichkeit)* acrobatic abilities *pl or* skill.
akrobatisch *adj* acrobatic.
Akronym *nt* **-s, -e** acronym.
Akt[1] *m* **-(e)s, -e (a)** *(Tat)* act; *(Zeremonie)* ceremony, ceremonial act. **(b)** *(Theat, Zirkus~)* act. **(c)** *(Art: ~bild)* nude. **(d)** *(Geschlechts~)* sexual act, coitus *no art (form)*.
Akt[2] *m* **-(e)s, -en** *(Aus) siehe* **Akte.**
Akt-: ~aufnahme *f* nude (photograph); **~bild** *nt* nude (picture *or* portrait).
Akte *f* **-, -n** file, record ◆ **die ~ Schmidt** the Schmidt file; **das kommt in die ~n** this goes on file *or* record; **etw zu den ~n legen** to file sth away, to put sth on file; *(fig) Fall etc* to drop.
Akten-: ~berg *m (inf)* mountain of files *or* records *(inf)*; **~deckel** *m* folder; **~einsicht** *f (form)* inspection of records *or* files; **~koffer** *m* attaché case, executive case; **a~kundig** *adj* on record; **a~kundig werden** to be put on record; **~mappe** *f* **(a)** *(Tasche)* briefcase, portfolio; **(b)** *(Umschlag)* folder, file; **~notiz** *f* memo(randum); **~ordner** *m* file; **~schrank** *m* filing cabinet; **~tasche** *f siehe* **~mappe (a)**; **~vermerk** *m* memo(randum); **~zeichen** *nt* reference.
Akteur(in *f***)** [ak'tø:ɐ, tø:rɪn] *m (geh)* participant, protagonist.
Akt-: ~foto *nt* nude (photograph); **~fotografie** *f* nude photography; *(Bild)* nude photograph.
Aktie ['aktsiə] *f* share; *(~nschein)* share certificate ◆ **in ~n anlegen** to invest in (stocks and) shares; **die ~n fallen/steigen** share prices are falling/rising; **die ~n stehen gut** share prices are looking good, shares are buoyant; *(fig)* things *or* the prospects are looking good; **wie stehen die ~n?** *(hum inf)* how are things?; *(wie sind die Aussichten)* what are the prospects?
Aktien-: ~besitz *m* shareholdings *pl*, shares *pl* held; **~besitzer** *m* shareholder, stockholder *(esp US)*; **~börse** *f* stock exchange; **~gesellschaft** *f* joint-stock company; **~index** *m (Fin)* share index; **~kapital** *nt* share capital; *(von Gesellschaft auch)* (capital) stock; **~kurs** *m* share price; **~markt** *m* stock market.
Aktinium *nt, no pl (abbr* **Ac***)* actinium.
Aktion *f (Handlung)* action *(auch Mil)*; *(Kampagne)* campaign; *(Werbe~)* promotion; *(geplantes Unternehmen, Einsatz)* operation *(auch Mil)*; *(Art)* action painting ◆ **in ~** in action; **sie muß ständig in ~ sein** she always has to be active *or* on the go *(inf)*; **in ~ treten** to go into action.
Aktionär(in *f***)** *m* shareholder, stockholder *(esp US)*.
Aktionärsversammlung *f* shareholders' meeting.
Aktionismus *m, no pl (Pol)* actionism.
aktionistisch *adj (Pol)* actionist(ic).
Aktions-: ~art *f (Gram)* aspect; ⚠**~ausschuß** *m* action committee; **~einheit** *f (Pol)* unity in action, working unity; **a~fähig** *adj* capable of action; **~komitee** *nt* action committee; **~preis** *m (Werbung)* special-offer price; **~radius** *m (Aviat, Naut)* range, radius; *(fig: Wirkungsbereich)* scope (for action); **a~unfähig** *adj* incapable of action.
aktiv *adj* active; *(Econ) Bilanz* positive, favourable; *(Mil) Soldat etc* on active service ◆ **sich ~ an etw** *(dat)* **beteiligen** to take an active part in sth; **~ dienen** *(Mil)* to be on active duty *or* service; **~ sein** *(Univ)* to be a full member of a/the students' association; *siehe* **Wahlrecht.**
Aktiv[1] *nt (Gram)* active.
Aktiv[2] *nt* **-s, -s** *or* **-e** *(esp DDR)* work team.
Aktiva *pl* assets *pl* ◆ **~ und Passiva** assets and liabilities.
Aktive *f* **-n, -n** *(sl)* fag *(esp Brit sl)*, butt *(US sl)*.
Aktive(r) *mf decl as adj (Sport)* active participant; *(Univ)* full member (of a/the students' association).
Aktivgeschäft *nt (Fin)* lending business.
aktivieren* [akti'vi:rən] *vt (Sci)* to activate; *(fig) Arbeit, Kampagne* to step up; *Mitarbeiter* to get moving; *(Comm)* to enter on the assets side.
aktivisch *adj (Gram)* active.
Aktivismus *m, no pl* activism.
Aktivist(in *f***)** *m* activist.
Aktivität *f* activity.
Aktiv-: ~posten *m (lit, fig)* asset; **~saldo** *m* credit balance; **~seite** *f* assets side; **~vermögen** *nt* realizable assets *pl*; **~zinsen** *pl* interest receivable *sing*.
Akt-: ~malerei *f* nude painting; **~modell** *nt* nude model.
Aktrice [ak'tri:sə] *f* **-, -n** *(dated)* actress.
Aktstudie *f* nude study.
aktualisieren* *vt* to make topical; *Datei, Nachschlagewerk* to update.
Aktualisierung *f* updating.
Aktualität *f* relevance (to the present *or* current situation), topicality. **~en** *pl (geh: neueste Ereignisse)* current events.
Aktuar *m* **(a)** *(old) siehe* **Gerichtsschreiber. (b)** *(Sw) siehe* **Schriftführer.**
aktuell *adj* relevant (to the current situation); *Frage auch* topical; *Buch, Film auch* of topical interest; *Thema* topical; *(gegenwärtig) Problem, Theorie, Thema* current; *(Fashion: modern) Mode* latest *attr*, current; *Stil auch* the (latest or current) fashion *pred*, fashionable; *(Econ) Bedarf, Kaufkraft* actual ◆ **von ~em Interesse** *or* **~er Bedeutung** of topical interest/of relevance to the present situation; **dieses Problem ist nicht mehr ~** this is no longer a (current) problem; **das Buch ist wieder ~ geworden** the book has become relevant again *or* has regained topicality; **eine ~e Sendung** *(Rad, TV)* a current-affairs programme.
Aktzeichnung *f* nude (drawing), drawing of a nude.
Akupressur *f, no pl* acupressure.
Akupunkteur [-'tø:ɐ] *m* acupuncturist.
akupunktieren* **1** *vt* to acupuncture.
2 *vi* to perform acupuncture.
Akupunktur *f* acupuncture.
Akustik *f, no pl (von Gebäude etc)* acoustics *pl*; *(Phys: Lehre)* acoustics *sing.*
Akustikkoppler *m* **-s, -** *(Comput)* acoustic coupler.
akustisch *adj* acoustic ◆ **ich habe dich rein ~ nicht verstanden** I simply didn't catch what you said (properly).
akut *adj (Med, fig)* acute; *Frage auch* pressing, urgent.
Akut *m* **-(e)s, -e** acute (accent).
AKW [a:ka:'ve:] *nt* **-s, -s** *abbr of* **Atomkraftwerk.**
Akzent *m* **-(e)s, -e** *(Zeichen, Aussprache)* accent; *(Betonung auch)* stress; *(fig auch)* emphasis, stress ◆ **den ~ auf etw** *(acc)* **legen** *(lit)* to stress sth, to put the stress *or* accent on sth; *(fig auch)* to emphasize sth; **dieses Jahr liegen die (modischen) ~e bei ...** this year the accent *or* emphasis is on ...; **~e setzen** *(fig)* *(Wichtiges hervorheben)* to bring out *or* emphasize the main points *or* features; *(Hinweise geben)* to give the main points; **dieses Jahr hat neue ~e gesetzt** this year has seen the introduction of new trends.
Akzent-: ~buchstabe *m* accented letter; **a~frei** *adj* without any *or* an accent.
akzentuieren* *vt* to articulate, to enunciate; *(betonen)* to stress; *(fig: hervorheben)* to accentuate.
Akzentverschiebung *f (Ling)* stress shift; *(fig)* shift of emphasis.
Akzept *nt* **-(e)s, -e** *(Comm)* acceptance.
akzeptabel *adj* acceptable.
Akzeptanz *f* **-,** *no pl (Comm)* acceptance ◆ **unsere Produkte haben keine ~ auf dem deutschen Markt** our products have not been accepted by the German market; **um die ~ unserer Produkte zu erhöhen** to make our products more acceptable.
akzeptierbar *adj* acceptable.
▼ **akzeptieren*** *vt* to accept.
Akzeptierung *f* acceptance.
Akzidens *nt* **-, Akzidenzien** [-iən] *(Philos)* accident; *(Mus)* accidental.
akzident(i)ell [-'tɛl, -tsi'ɛl] *adj* accidental.
Akzidenz *f (Typ)* job ◆ **~en** job printing.
Akzidenz-: ~druck *m* job printing; **~druckerei** *f* jobbing printer's.
AL [a:'|ɛl] *f* **-, -s** *abbr of* **Alternative Liste.**
à la [a la] *adv* à la.
alaaf *interj (dial)* **Kölle ~!** up Cologne! *(used in carnival procession)*.
Alabaster *m* **-s, - (a)** alabaster. **(b)** *(dial: Murmel)* marble.
Alarm *m* **-(e)s, -e** *(Warnung)* alarm; *(Flieger~)* air-raid warning; *(Zustand)* alert ◆ **bei ~** following an alarm/air-raid warning; *(während ~)* during an alert; **~!** fire!/air-raid! *etc*; **~ schlagen** to give *or* raise *or* sound the alarm.
Alarm-: ~anlage *f* alarm system; **a~bereit** *adj* on the alert; *Feuerwehr, Polizei auch* standing by; **sich a~bereit halten** to be on the alert/standing by; **~bereitschaft** *f siehe adj* alert; stand-by; **in ~bereitschaft sein** *or* **stehen** to be on the alert/standing by; **in ~bereitschaft versetzen** to put on the alert, to alert; **~glocke** *f* alarm bell.
alarmieren* *vt Polizei etc* to alert; *(fig: beunruhigen)* to alarm ◆ **~d** *(fig)* alarming; **aufs höchste alarmiert** *(fig)* highly alarmed.
Alarm-: ~ruf, ~schrei *m* warning cry; **~signal** *nt* alarm signal; **~stufe** *f* alert stage; **~übung** *f* practice exercise *or* drill; **~vorrichtung** *f* alarm; **~zustand** *m* alert; **im ~zustand sein** to be on the alert.
Alaska *nt* **-s** Alaska.
Alaun *m* **-s, -e** alum.
Alaun-: ~stein, ~stift *m* styptic pencil.
Alb[1] *m* **-(e)s, -en** *(Myth)* elf.
Alb[2] *f* **-,** *no pl (Geog)* mountain region.
Albaner(in *f***)** *m* **-s, -** Albanian.
Albanien [-iən] *nt* **-s** Albania.
albanisch *adj* Albanian.
Albatros *m* **-, -se** albatross.
Albdruck *m siehe* **Alpdruck.**
Albe *f* **-, -n** *(Eccl)* alb.
Alben *pl of* **Alb**[1]**, Albe, Album.**
Alberei *f* silliness; *(das Spaßmachen)* fooling about *or* around; *(Tat)* silly prank; *(Bemerkung)* inanity.
albern **1** *adj* silly, stupid, foolish; *(inf: lächerlich)* stupid, silly, ridiculous ◆ **sich ~ benehmen** to act silly; *(Quatsch machen)* to fool about *or* around; **~es Zeug** (silly) nonsense.

2 *vi* to fool about *or* around ◆ **ich weiß, ich bin unwiderstehlich, alberte er** I know I'm irresistible he said jokingly.
Albernheit *f* **(a)** *no pl* (*albernes Wesen*) silliness, foolishness; (*Lächerlichkeit*) ridiculousness. **(b)** (*Tat*) silly prank; (*Bemerkung*) inanity.
Albinismus *m, no pl* albinism, albinoism.
Albino *m* **-s, -s** albino.
Albion ['albiɔn] *nt* **-s** (*liter*) Albion (*poet*).
Albtraum *m siehe* **Alptraum.**
Album *nt* **-s, Alben** album.
Albumin *nt* **-s, -e** albumen.
Alchemie (*esp Aus*), **Alchimie** *f* alchemy.
Alchemist(in *f*) (*esp Aus*), **Alchimist (in** *f*) *m* alchemist.
alchemistisch (*esp Aus*), **alchimistisch** *adj* alchemic(al).
al dente *adj* al dente.
Alemanne *m* **-n, -n, Alemannin** *f* Alemannic.
alemannisch *adj* Alemannic.
alert *adj* (*geh*) vivacious, lively.
Aleuten *pl* (*Geog*) **die ~** the Aleutians.
Alexandria *f,* **Alexandrien** [-iən] *nt* Alexandria.
Alexandriner *m* **-s,** - (*Poet*) alexandrine.
Alexandrit *m* **-s, -e** alexandrite.
Alge *f* **-, -n** alga.
Algebra *f* **-,** *no pl* algebra.
algebraisch *adj* algebraic(al).
Algerien [-iən] *nt* **-s** Algeria.
Algerier(in *f*) [-iɐ, -iərɪn] *m* **-s,** - Algerian.
algerisch *adj* Algerian.
Algier ['alʒiːɐ] *nt* **-s** Algiers.
Algol *nt* **-(s),** *no pl* Algol.
algorithmisch *adj* algorithmic.
Algorithmus *m* algorithm.
alias *adv* alias, also *or* otherwise known as.
Alibi *nt* **-s, -s** (*Jur, fig*) alibi.
Alibi- *in cpds* alibi; **~beweis** *m* evidence to support one's alibi; **~frau** *f* token woman; **~funktion** *f* (*fig*) **~funktion haben** to be used as an alibi.
Alimente *pl* maintenance *sing.*
alimentieren* *vt* (*geh*) to maintain, to support.
Alk¹ *m* **-(e)s, -en** (*Orn*) auk.
Alk² *m* **-(e)s** *no pl* (*sl: Alkohol*) booze (*inf*).
Alkali *nt* **-s, Alkalien** [-iən] alkali ◆ **mit ~ düngen** to fertilize with an alkali.
alkalisch *adj* alkaline.
Alkaloid *nt* **-(e)s, -e** alkaloid.
Alki, Alkie *m* **-s, -s** (*sl*) alky (*sl*), alkie (*sl*).
Alkohol ['alkohoːl, alko'hoːl] *m* **-s, -e** alcohol; (*alkoholische Getränke auch*) drink ◆ **seinen Kummer im ~ ertränken** to drown one's sorrows; **unter ~ stehen** to be under the influence (of alcohol *or* drink).
Alkohol-: a~arm *adj* low in alcohol (content); **~ausschank** *m* sale of alcohol(ic drinks); ⚠**~einfluß** *m,* **~einwirkung** *f* influence of alcohol *or* drink; **unter ~einfluß** under the influence of alcohol *or* drink; **~fahne** *f* (*inf*) smell of alcohol; **eine ~fahne haben** to smell of alcohol *or* drink; **a~frei** *adj* non-alcoholic; *Getränk auch* soft; *Gegend, Stadt* dry; **ein a~freier Tag** a day without drink *or* alcohol; **~gegner** *m* opponent of alcohol; (*selbst abstinent*) teetotaller; (*Befürworter des ~verbots*) prohibitionist; **~gehalt** *m* alcohol(ic) content; ⚠**~genuß** *m* consumption of alcohol; **a~haltig** *adj* alcoholic, containing alcohol.
Alkoholika *pl* alcoholic drinks *pl,* liquor *sing.*
Alkoholiker(in *f*) *m* **-s,** - alcoholic.
alkoholisch *adj* alcoholic.
alkoholisieren* *vt Wein* to fortify ◆ **jdn ~** (*hum*) to get sb drunk.
alkoholisiert *adj* (*betrunken*) inebriated ◆ **in ~em Zustand** in a state of inebriation.
Alkoholismus *m* alcoholism.
Alkohol-: ~konsum *m* consumption of alcohol; **~kontrolle** *f* drink-driving check; ⚠**~mißbrauch** *m* alcohol abuse; **~pegel** (*hum*), **~spiegel** *m* **jds ~pegel** *or* **~spiegel** the level of alcohol in sb's blood; **~steuer** *f* duty *or* tax on alcohol; **a~süchtig** *adj* addicted to alcohol, suffering from alcoholism; **~sünder** *m* (*inf*) drunk(en) driver; **~test** *m* breath test; **~verbot** *nt* ban on alcohol; **der Arzt hat ihm ~verbot verordnet** the doctor told him not to touch alcohol; **~vergiftung** *f* alcohol(ic) poisoning.
Alkoven [al'koːvn, 'alkoːvn] *m* **-s,** - alcove.
all *indef pron* **~ das/mein** ... *etc* all the/my *etc*; *siehe* **alle(r, s).**
All *nt* **-s,** *no pl* (*Sci, Space*) space *no art*; (*außerhalb unseres Sternsystems*) outer space; (*liter, geh*) universe ◆ **Spaziergang im ~** space walk, walk in space; **das weite ~** the immense universe.
all-: ~abendlich 1 *adj* (which takes place) every evening; **der ~abendliche Spaziergang** the regular evening walk; 2 *adv* every evening; **~bekannt** *adj* known to all *or* everybody, universally known; **~dem** *pron siehe* **alledem; ~dieweil** (*old, hum*) 1 *adv* (*währenddessen*) all the while; 2 *conj* (*weil*) because.
➤ **alle** 1 *pron siehe* **alle(r, s).**
➤ 2 *adv* (*inf*) all gone ◆ **die Milch ist ~** the milk's all gone, there's no milk left; **etw/jdn ~ machen** (*inf*) to finish sth/sb off; **ich bin ganz ~** I'm all in; **~ werden** to be finished; (*Vorräte auch*) to run out.
alledem *pron* **bei/trotz** *etc* **~** with/in spite of *etc* all that; **von ~ stimmt kein Wort** there's no truth in any of that *or* it; **zu ~** moreover.
Allee *f* **-, -n** [-eːən] avenue.
Allegorie *f* allegory.
Allegorik *f* allegory ◆ **in der griechischen ~** in Greek allegory.
allegorisch *adj* allegorical.
Allegretto *nt* **-s, -s** *or* **Allegretti** allegretto.
Allegro *nt* **-s, -s** *or* **Allegri** allegro.
allein 1 *adj pred* (*esp inf auch* **alleine**) alone; *Gegenstand, Wort auch* by itself, on its own; (*ohne Gesellschaft, Begleitung, Hilfe auch*) by oneself, on one's own; (*einsam*) lonely, lonesome ◆ **für sich ~** by oneself, on one's own, alone; **sie waren endlich ~** they were alone (together) *or* on their own at last; **von ~** by oneself/itself; **ich tue es schon von ~e** I'll do that in any case; **das weiß ich von ~(e)** you don't have to tell me (that); **ganz ~** (*einsam*) quite *or* all alone; (*ohne Begleitung, Hilfe*) all by oneself, all on one's own; **jdm ganz ~ gehören** to belong to sb alone, to belong completely to sb; **auf sich** (*acc*) **~ angewiesen sein** to be left to cope on one's own, to be left to one's own devices.
2 *adv* (*nur*) alone ◆ **das ist ~ seine Verantwortung** that is his responsibility alone, that is exclusively or solely his responsibility; **nicht ~, ... sondern auch** not only ... but also; **~ schon der Gedanke, (schon) der Gedanke ~ ...** the very *or* mere thought ..., the thought alone ...; **das Porto ~ kostet** ... the postage alone costs ..., just the postage is ...
3 *conj* (*old: jedoch*) however, but.
Allein-: ~erbe *m* sole *or* only heir; ⚠**a~erziehend** *adj Mutter, Vater* single, unmarried; ⚠**~erziehende(r)** *mf decl as adj* single parent; **~flug** *m* solo flight; **im ~flug** solo; **~gang** *m* (*inf*) (*Sport*) solo run; (*von Bergsteiger*) solo climb; (*fig: Tat*) solo effort; **etw im ~gang machen** (*fig*) to do sth on one's own; **die Möglichkeit eines ~gangs** the possibility of going it alone; **~heit** *f* (*Philos*) (universal) unity *or* oneness; **~herrschaft** *f* autocratic rule, absolute dictatorship; (*fig*) monopoly; **~herrscher** *m* autocrat, absolute dictator; **der ~herrscher in der Familie sein** (*fig*) to reign supreme in the family.
alleinig *adj attr* sole, only; (*Aus, S Ger*) (*alleinstehend*) single; (*ohne Begleitung*) unaccompanied.
Allein-: ~sein *nt* being on one's own *no def art,* solitude; (*Einsamkeit*) loneliness; ⚠**a~seligmachend** *adj* **die a~seligmachende Kirche** the only true church; **er betrachtet seine Lehre als die a~seligmachende** he considers his doctrine to be the only true one; ⚠**a~stehend** *adj* living on one's own, living alone; ⚠**~stehende(r)** *mf decl as adj* single person; **~unterhalter** *m* solo entertainer; **~untermiete** *f* (*Aus*) subletting (*where main tenant lives elsewhere*); **in ~untermiete wohnen** ≃ to live in a furnished flat; **~verkauf** *m* sole *or* exclusive right of sale (*+gen, von* for); **~vertreter** *m* (*Comm*) sole agent.
Alleinvertretung *f* (*Comm*) sole agency; (*Pol*) sole representation.
Alleinvertretungsanspruch *m* (*Pol*) claim to sole representation.
Alleinvertrieb *m* sole *or* exclusive marketing *or* distribution rights *pl.*
alleluja *interj siehe* **halleluja.**
allemal *adv* every *or* each time; (*ohne Schwierigkeit*) without any problem *or* trouble ◆ **was er kann, kann ich noch ~** anything he can do I can do too; **~!** no problem *or* trouble! (*inf*); **ein für ~** once and for all.
allenfalls *adv* (*nötigenfalls*) if need be, should the need arise; (*höchstens*) at most, at the outside; (*bestenfalls*) at best ◆ **es waren ~ 40 Leute da** there were at most 40 people there, there were 40 people there at the outside; **das schaffen wir ~ in 3 Stunden/bis übermorgen** we'll do it in 3 hours/by the day after tomorrow at best.
allenthalben *adv* (*liter*) everywhere, on all sides.
alle(r, s) 1 *indef pron* **(a)** *attr* all; (*bestimmte Menge, Anzahl*) all the; (*auf eine Person bezüglich: all sein*) *Geld, Liebe, Freunde, Erfahrungen* all one's ◆ **~ Kinder unter 10 Jahren** all children under 10; **~ Kinder dieser Stadt** all the children in this town; **die Eltern fuhren mit ~n Kindern weg** the parents went off with all their children; **~s Brot wird gebacken** all bread is baked; **im Geschäft war ~s Brot ausverkauft** all the bread in the shop was sold out; **~ meine Kinder** all (of) my children; **wir haben ~n Haß vergessen** we have forgotten all (our *or* the) hatred; **~ Anwesenden/Beteiligten/Betroffenen** all those present/taking part/affected; **~s erforderliche Material** all the required material; **mit ~m Nachdruck** with every emphasis; **trotz ~r Mühe** in spite of every effort; **ohne ~n Grund** without any reason, with no reason at all; **mit ~r Deutlichkeit** quite distinctly; **ohne ~n Zweifel** without any doubt; *siehe auch* **all.**
(b) (*substantivisch*) **~s** *sing* everything; (*inf: alle Menschen*) everybody, everyone; **~s, was** ... all *or* everything that/everybody *or* everyone who ...; **das ~s** all that; **~s Schöne** everything beautiful, all that is beautiful; **„~s für das Baby/den Heimwerker"** "everything for baby/the handyman"; **(ich wünsche Dir) ~s Gute** (I wish you) all the best; **~s und jedes** anything and everything; **in ~m** (*in jeder Beziehung*) in everything; **~s in ~m** all in all; **trotz ~m** in spite of everything; **über ~s** above all else; (*mehr als alles andere*) more than anything else; **vor ~m** above all; **du bist mein ein und (mein) ~s** you are everything to me, you are my everything *or* all; **das ist ~s, das wäre ~s** that's all, that's it (*inf*); **das ist ~s andere als** ... that's anything but ...; **er ist ~s, nur kein Kaufmann** he's anything but a salesman; **das ist mir ~s gleich** it's all the same to me; **was soll das ~s?** what's all this supposed to mean!; **~s schon mal dagewesen!** (*inf*) it's all been done before!; **es hat ~s keinen Sinn mehr** nothing makes sense any more, it has all become meaningless; **was habt ihr ~s gemacht?** what did you get up to?; **wer war ~s da?** who was there?; **was er (nicht) ~s weiß/kann!** the things he knows/can do!; **was es**

nicht ~s gibt! well (now) I've seen everything!, well I never (*inf*).
(c) (*substantivisch*) ~ *pl* all; (*alle Menschen auch*) everybody, everyone ◆ **sie sind ~ alt** they're all old; **die haben mir ~ nicht gefallen** I didn't like any of them; **ich habe (sie) ~ verschenkt** I've given them all *or* all of them away; **~ beide/drei** both of them/all three of them; **~ drei/diejenigen, die ...** all three/(those) who ...; **diese ~** all (of) these; **der Kampf ~r gegen ~** the free-for-all; **~ für einen und einer für ~** all for one and one for all; **sie kamen ~** they all came, all of them came; **sie haben ~ kein Geld mehr** none of them has any money left; **redet nicht ~ auf einmal!** don't all talk at once!
(d) (*mit Zeit-, Maßangaben*) *usu pl* every ◆ **~ fünf Minuten/fünf Meter/halbe Stunde** every five minutes/five metres/half-hour; **~ Jahre wieder** year after year.
[2] *adv siehe* **alle.**

aller- *in cpds mit superl* (*zur Verstärkung*) by far ◆ **das ~größte/die ~hübscheste** by far the biggest/prettiest, the biggest/prettiest by far.

aller|aller- *in cpds mit superl* (*inf: zur Verstärkung*) far and away ◆ **das ~größte/die ~hübscheste** far and away the biggest/prettiest.

aller-: ~art *adj attr inv* (*dated*) all sorts *or* kinds of; **~beste(r, s)** *adj* very best, best of all, best ... of all; (*exquisit*) *Waren, Qualität* very best; **ich wünsche Dir das A~beste** (I wish you) all the best; **der/die/das A~beste** the very best/the best of all; **es ist das ~beste** *or* **am ~besten, zu .../wenn ...** the best thing would be to .../if ...; **~dings** *adv* **(a)** (*einschränkend*) though, mind you; **ich komme mit, ich muß ~dings erst zur Bank** I'm coming but I must go to the bank first though, I'm coming though I must go to the bank first; **das ist ~dings wahr, aber ...** that may be true, but ..., (al)though that's true ...; **(b)** (*bekräftigend*) certainly; **~dings!** (most) certainly!; **~erste(r, s)** *adj* very first; **~frühestens** *adv* at the very earliest.

Allergen *nt* **-s, -e** (*Med*) allergen.

Allergie *f* (*Med*) allergy; (*fig*) aversion (*gegen* to) ◆ **eine ~ gegen etw haben** to be allergic to sth (*auch fig hum*); (*fig auch*) to have an aversion to sth.

Allergiker(in *f*) *m* **-s, -** person suffering from an allergy.

allergisch *adj* (*Med, fig*) allergic (*gegen* to) ◆ **auf etw** (*acc*) **~ reagieren** to have an allergic reaction to sth.

Allergologe *m*, **Allergologin** *f* allergist.

Aller-: a~hand *adj inv* (*substantivisch*) (*allerlei*) all kinds of things; (*ziemlich viel*) rather a lot; (*attributiv*) all kinds or sorts of; rather a lot of; **das ist a~hand!** (*zustimmend*) that's quite something!, not bad at all! (*inf*); **das ist ja** *or* **doch a~hand!** (*empört*) that's too much!, that's the limit!; **~heiligen** *nt* **-s** All Saints' Day, All Hallows (Day); **~heiligste(s)** *nt decl as adj* (*Rel*) inner sanctum; (*jüdisch, fig*) Holy of Holies; (*katholisch*) Blessed Sacrament; **a~höchste(r, s)** *adj Berg etc* highest of all, highest ... of all, very highest; *Betrag, Belastung, Geschwindigkeit* maximum; *Funktionäre* highest, top *attr*; *Instanz, Kreise* very highest; **es wird a~höchste Zeit, daß ...** it's really high time that ...; **a~höchstens** *adv* at the very most; **a~lei** *adj inv* (*substantivisch*) all sorts *or* kinds of things; (*attributiv*) all sorts *or* kinds of; **~lei** *nt* **-s,** *no pl* (*Durcheinander*) farrago, pot pourri, welter; **Leipziger ~lei** (*Cook*) Leipzig mixed vegetables *pl*; **a~letzte(r, s)** *adj* very last; (*a~neueste*) very latest; (*inf: unmöglich*) most awful *attr* (*inf*); **in a~letzter Zeit** very recently; **der/die/das ~letzte** the very last (person)/thing; **der/das ist (ja) das ~letzte** (*inf*) he's/it's the absolute end! (*inf*); **a~liebst** *adj* (*old: reizend*) enchanting, delightful; **a~liebste(r, s)** *adj* (*Lieblings-*) most favourite *attr*; **sie ist mir die ~liebste** she's my absolute favourite; **es wäre mir das a~liebste** *or* **am a~liebsten, wenn ...** I would much prefer it if ...; **am a~liebsten geh' ich ins Kino** I like going to the cinema most *or* best of all; **~liebste(r)** *mf decl as adj* (*old, hum*) beloved, love of one's life; (*Frau auch*) ladylove; **a~meiste(r, s)** *adj* most of all, most ... of all; (*weitaus beste*) by far the most; **am a~meisten** most of all; **die ~meisten** the vast majority; **a~nächste(r, s)** *adj* (*in Folge*) very next; (*räumlich*) nearest of all; *Verwandte* very closest; *Route* very shortest; **in a~nächster Nähe** right nearby, right close by; **in a~nächster Zeit** *or* **Zukunft** in the very near future; **a~neu(e)ste(r, s)** *adj* very latest; **a~orten, a~orts** *adv* (*old*) everywhere; **~seelen** *nt* **-s** All Souls' Day; **a~seits** *adv* on all sides, on every side; **guten Abend a~seits!** good evening everybody *or* everyone *or* all; **vielen Dank a~seits** thank you all *or* everybody *or* everyone; **a~spätestens** *adv* at the very latest.

Allerwelts- *in cpds* (*Durchschnitts-*) common; (*nichtssagend*) commonplace; **~kerl** *m* Jack of all trades.

Aller-: a~wenigstens *adv* at the very least; **a~wenigste(r, s)** *adj* least of all, least ... of all; (*pl*) fewest of all, fewest ... of all; (*äußerst wenig*) very little; (*pl*) very few; (*geringste*) *Mühe* least possible; **die a~wenigsten Menschen wissen das** very (very) few people know that; **das ist noch das ~wenigste!** that's the very least of it; **das ist doch das ~wenigste, was man erwarten könnte** but that's the very least one could expect; **er hat von uns allen das a~wenigste** *or* **am a~wenigsten Geld** he has the least money of any of us; **sie hat von uns allen die a~wenigsten** *or* **am a~wenigsten Sorgen** she has the fewest worries of any of us; **das am a~wenigsten!** least of all that!; **~werteste(r)** *m decl as adj* (*hum*) posterior (*hum*).

alles *indef pron siehe* **alle(r, s) (b).**

allesamt *adv* all (of them/us *etc*), to a man ◆ **ihr seid ~ Betrüger!** you're all cheats!, you're cheats, all *or* the lot of you!

Alles-: ~fresser *m* omnivore; **~kleber** *m* all-purpose adhesive *or* glue; **~wisser** *m* **-s, -** (*iro*) know-all (*inf*), know-it-all (*US inf*).

allewege *adv* (*old*) everywhere.

allezeit *adv* (*liter*) *siehe* **allzeit.**

All-: a~fällig *adv* (*Aus, Sw*) where applicable; (*eventuell*) possibly; **~gegenwart** *f* omnipresence, ubiquity; **a~gegenwärtig** *adj* omnipresent, ubiquitous.

allgemein [1] *adj* general; *Ablehnung, Zustimmung auch* common; *Feiertag* public; *Regelungen, Wahlrecht* universal; *Wehrpflicht* compulsory; (*öffentlich auch*) public ◆ **im ~en** in general, generally; **im ~en Interesse** in the common interest; in the public interest; **von ~em Interesse** of general interest; **~e Redensarten** (*idiomatische Ausdrücke*) set expressions; (*Phrasen*) commonplaces; **auf ~en Wunsch** by popular *or* general request; **die ~e Meinung** the general opinion, the generally held opinion; public opinion; **das ~e Wohl** the common good; (the) public welfare, the public good; **die Diskussion darüber wurde ~** a general discussion developed; **wir sind ganz ~ geblieben** (*inf*) we stayed on a general level; **das A~e und das Besondere** the general and the particular.
[2] *adv* (*überall, bei allen, von allen*) generally; (*ausnahmslos von allen*) universally; (*generell auch*) in the main, for the most part; (*nicht spezifisch*) in general terms ◆ **seine Thesen sind so ~ abgefaßt, daß ...** his theses are worded in such general terms that ...; **du kannst doch nicht so ~ behaupten, daß ...** you can't make such a generalization and say that ..., you can't generalize like that and say that ...; **es ist ~ bekannt** it's common knowledge; **es ist ~ üblich, etw zu tun** it's the general rule that we/they *etc* do sth, it's commonly *or* generally the practice to do sth; **~ verbreitet** widespread; **~ zugänglich** open to all, open to the general public.

Allgemein-: ~befinden *nt* general condition, general state of being; ⚠**a~bildend** *adj* providing (a) general *or* all-round education; *Studium auch* with general educational value; **~bildung** *f* general *or* all-round education; ⚠**a~gültig** *adj attr* general, universal, universally *or* generally applicable *or* valid; **~gültigkeit** *f* universal *or* general validity, universality; **~gut** *nt* (*fig*) common property; **~heit** *f* **(a)** (*no pl: Öffentlichkeit*) general public, public at large; (*alle*) everyone, everybody; **(b)** (*no pl: Unbestimmtheit*), (*Unspezifisches*) generality; **~medizin** *f* general medicine; **Arzt für ~medizin** general practitioner, GP; **~platz** *m* (*pej*) commonplace, platitude; ⚠**a~verbindlich** *adj attr* generally binding; ⚠**a~verständlich** *adj no pred* generally intelligible, intelligible to all; **~wissen** *nt* general knowledge; **~wohl** *nt* public good *or* welfare.

All-: ~gewalt *f* (*liter*) omnipotence; **a~gewaltig** *adj* omnipotent, all-powerful; **~heilmittel** *nt* universal remedy, cure-all, panacea (*esp fig*); **a~hier** *adv* (*obs, liter*) here.

Allianz *f* **(a)** alliance. **(b)** (*NATO*) Alliance.

Allianzpartner *m* partner in the alliance; (*bei NATO*) partner in NATO, NATO partner.

Alligator *m* alligator.

alliieren* *vr* (*geh*) to form an alliance ◆ **sich mit jdm ~** to ally (oneself) with sb.

alliiert *adj attr* allied; (*im 2. Weltkrieg*) Allied.

Alliierte(r) *mf decl as adj* ally ◆ **die ~n** (*im 2. Weltkrieg*) the Allies.

Alliteration *f* (*Poet*) alliteration.

alliterierend *adj* (*Poet*) alliterative.

allj. *abbr of* **alljährlich.**

All-: a~jährlich [1] *adj* annual, yearly; [2] *adv* annually, yearly, every year; **~macht** *f* (*esp von Gott*) omnipotence; (*von Konzern etc*) all-pervading power; **a~mächtig** *adj* all-powerful, omnipotent; *Gott auch* almighty; **~mächtige(r)** *m decl as adj* (*Gott*) **der ~mächtige** Almighty God, God (the) Almighty, the Almighty; **~mächtiger!** good Lord!, heavens above!

allmählich [1] *adj attr* gradual.
[2] *adv* gradually; (*schrittweise auch*) bit by bit, step by step; (*inf: endlich*) at last ◆ **es wird ~ Zeit** (*inf*) it's about time; **~ verstand er, daß ...** it gradually dawned on him that ..., he realized gradually that ...; **ich werde (ganz) ~ müde** (*inf*) I'm beginning to get tired; **wir sollten ~ gehen** (*inf*) shall we think about going?

Allmende *f* **-, -n** common land.

All-: a~monatlich [1] *adj* monthly; [2] *adv* every month, monthly; **a~morgendlich** [1] *adj* which takes place every morning; **die a~morgendliche Eile** the regular morning rush; [2] *adv* every morning; **~mutter** *f* (*liter*) Mother of all; **die ~mutter Natur** Mother Nature; **a~nächtlich** [1] *adj* nightly; [2] *adv* nightly, every night.

Allopathie *f* allopathy.

Allophon *nt* (*Ling*) allophone.

Allotria *nt* **-(s),** *no pl* (*inf*) (*Unfug*) monkey business (*inf*) *no indef art*; (*ausgelassen, freudig*) skylarking (*inf*) *no indef art*, fooling around *or* about (*inf*) *no indef art*; (*Lärm*) racket (*inf*), din ◆ **~ treiben** (*inf*) to lark about (*inf*), to fool around *or* about (*inf*).

Allrad|antrieb *m* all-wheel drive.

Allround- ['ɔːl'raʊnd] *in cpds* all-round.

allseitig *adj* (*allgemein*) general; (*ausnahmslos*) universal; (*vielseitig*) all-round *attr* ◆ **~ begabt sein** to have all-round talents, to be an all-rounder; **jdn ~ ausbilden** to provide sb with a general *or* an all-round education; **zur ~en Zufriedenheit** to the satisfaction of all *or* everyone.

allseits *adv* (*überall*) everywhere, on all sides; (*in jeder Beziehung*) in every respect.

Allstrom-: ~empfänger *m* (*Rad*) all-mains *or* AC-DC receiver; **~gerät** *nt* (*Rad*) all-mains *or* AC-DC appliance.

Alltag *m* **(a)** (*Werktag*) weekday ◆ **am ~, an ~en** on weekdays; **Kleidung, die man am ~ trägt** clothes for everyday wear; **mitten im ~** in the middle of the week. **(b)** (*fig*) everyday life. **der ~ der Ehe** the mundane side of married life.

alltäglich *adj* **(a)** (*tagtäglich*) daily. **(b)** (*üblich*) everyday *attr*, ordinary, mundane (*pej*); *Gesicht, Mensch* ordinary; *Bemerkung* commonplace ◆ **es ist ganz ~** it's nothing unusual *or* out of the ordinary; **das ist nichts A~es, daß/wenn ...** it doesn't happen every day that ..., it's not every day that ...; **was ich suche, ist nicht das A~e** I'm looking for something a bit out of the ordinary.

Alltäglichkeit *f* **(a)** *no pl siehe adj (b)* ordinariness; commonplaceness. **(b)** (*Gemeinplatz*) commonplace.

alltags *adv* on weekdays ◆ **etw ~ tragen** to wear sth for every day.

Alltags- *in cpds* everyday; **~ehe** *f* mundane marriage; **~leben** *nt* everyday life; **danach begann wieder das ~leben** after that life got back to normal again; **~mensch** *m* ordinary person; **~rhythmus** *m* daily rhythm; **~trott** *m* (*inf*) daily round, treadmill of everyday life.

all|über|all *adv* (*old, poet*) everywhere.

all|umfassend *adj* all-embracing, global.

Allüren *pl* behaviour; (*geziertes Verhalten*) affectations *pl*; (*eines Stars etc*) airs and graces *pl*.

Alluvium [a'lu:viʊm] *nt* **-s,** *no pl* diluvial *or* holocene epoch.

All-: a~wissend *adj* omniscient; **(Gott,) der ~wissende** God the Omniscient; **ich bin nicht a~wissend!** I don't know everything!, I'm not omniscient!; **~wissenheit** *f* omniscience; **a~wöchentlich** [1] *adj* weekly; [2] *adv* every week; **a~zeit** *adv* (*geh*) always; **a~zeit bereit!** be prepared!

allzu *adv* all too; (*+neg*) too ◆ **~ viele Fehler** far too many mistakes; **nur ~** only *or* all too.

⚠ **allzu-: ~früh** *adv* far too early; (*+neg*) too early; **~gern** *adv mögen* only too much; (*bereitwillig*) only too willingly; (*+neg*) all that much/willingly, too much/willingly; **etw (nur) ~gern/nicht ~gern machen** to like doing sth only too much/not like doing sth all that much *or* too much *or* overmuch; **er ißt Muscheln nur ~gern** he's only too fond of mussels; **~sehr** *adv* too much; *mögen* all too much; (*+neg*) too much, all that much, overmuch; *sich freuen, erfreut sein* only too; (*+neg*) too; *versuchen* too hard; *sich ärgern, enttäuscht sein* too; **... — nicht ~sehr ... —** not too much *or* all that much; **sie war ~sehr/nicht ~sehr in ihn verliebt** she was too much/wasn't too in love with him; **~viel** *adv* too much; **~viel ist ungesund** (*Prov*) you can have too much of a good thing (*prov*).

Allzweck- *in cpds* general purpose; **~halle** *f* multi-purpose hall.

Alm *f* **-, -en** alpine pasture.

Alm|abtrieb *m driving cattle down from the alpine pastures.*

Alma mater *f* **- -,** *no pl* alma mater.

Almanach *m* **-s, -e** almanac.

Alm-: ~auftrieb *m driving cattle up to the alpine pastures*; **~hütte** *f* alpine hut.

Almosen [-o:-] *nt* **-s, - (a)** (*geh: Spende*) alms *pl* (*old*). ~ *pl* (*fig*) charity. **(b)** (*geringer Lohn*) pittance.

Almrausch *m,* **Almrose** *f siehe* **Alpenrose.**

Aloe ['a:loe] *f* **-, -n** aloe.

alogisch *adj* (*geh*) illogical.

Alp[1] *f* **-, -en** *siehe* **Alm.**

⚠ **Alp**[2] *m* **-(e)s, -e** (*old: Nachtmahr*) *demon believed to cause nightmares*; (*fig geh: Bedrückung*) nightmare ◆ **ihn drückte der ~** (*old*) he had a nightmare; **jdm wie ein ~ auf der Brust liegen** (*fig geh*), **wie ein ~ auf jdm lasten** (*fig geh*) to lie *or* weigh heavily (up)on sb.

Alpaka *nt* **-s, -s (a)** (*Lamaart*) alpaca. **(b)** *no pl* (*auch* **~wolle**) alpaca (wool). **(c)** *no pl* (*Neusilber*) German *or* nickel silver.

⚠ **Alpdruck** *m* (*lit, fig*) nightmare ◆ **wie ein ~ auf jdm lasten** to weigh sb down, to oppress sb.

Alpen *pl* Alps *pl*.

Alpen- *in cpds* alpine; **~dollar** *m* (*hum*) Austrian schilling; **~glühen** *nt* **-s, -** alpenglow; **~jäger** *m* (*Mil*) mountain infantryman; *pl* mountain troops *pl* *or* infantry; **~kette** *f* alpine chain; **~land** *nt* alpine country; **a~ländisch** *adj* alpine; ⚠**~paß** *m* alpine pass; **~republik** *f* (*hum*) **die ~republiken** Austria and Switzerland; **~rose** *f* Alpine rose *or* rhododendron; **~rot** *nt* **-s,** *no pl* red snow; **~veilchen** *nt* cyclamen; **~vorland** *nt* foothills *pl* of the Alps.

alph. *abbr of* **alphabetisch.**

Alpha *nt* **-(s), -s** alpha.

Alphabet[1] *nt* **-(e)s, -e** alphabet ◆ **nach dem ~** alphabetically, in alphabetical order; **das ~ lernen/aufsagen** to learn/say the *or* one's alphabet.

Alphabet[2] *m* **-en, -en** literate person.

alphabetisch *adj* alphabetical ◆ **~ geordnet** arranged in alphabetical order *or* alphabetically.

alphabetisieren* *vt* to make literate.

Alphabetisierung *f* **ein Programm zur ~ Indiens** a programme against illiteracy in India; **die ~ Kubas ist abgeschlossen** the population of Cuba is now largely literate.

Alpha-: ⚠**a~numerisch** *adj* alphanumeric; **~strahlen** *pl* alpha rays *pl*; **~teilchen** *nt* alpha particle.

Alp-: ~horn *nt* alp(en)horn; **~hütte** *f siehe* **Almhütte.**

alpin *adj* alpine.

Alpinist(in *f***)** *m* alpinist.

Alpinistik *f* alpinism.

Älpler(in *f***)** *m* **-s, -** inhabitant of the Alps.

älplerisch *adj* Tyrolean *no adv*.

⚠ **Alp-: ~traum** *m* (*lit, fig*) nightmare; **a~traumartig** *adj* nightmarish.

Alraun *m* **-(e)s, -e, Alraune** *f* **-, -n** mandrake.

als [1] *conj* **(a)** (*nach comp*) than ◆ **ich kam später ~ er** I came later than he (did) *or* him; **Hans ist größer ~** *or* **~ wie** (*strictly incorrect*) **sein Bruder** Hans is taller than his brother; **mehr ~ arbeiten kann ich nicht** I can't do more than work.

(b) (*bei Vergleichen*) **so ... ~ ...** as ... as ...; **soviel/soweit ~ möglich** as much/far as possible; **~ wie** as; **nichts/niemand/nirgend anders ~** nothing/nobody/nowhere but; **eher** *or* **lieber ... ~** rather ... than; **ich würde eher sterben ~ das zu tun** I would rather die than do that *or* die rather than do that; **anders sein ~** to be different from; **das machen wir anders ~ ihr** we do it differently to you; **alles andere ~** anything but.

(c) (*in Modalsätzen*) as if *or* though ◆ **es sieht aus, ~ würde es bald schneien** it looks as if *or* though it will snow soon; **sie sah aus, ~ ob** *or* **wenn sie schliefe** she looked as if *or* though she were asleep; **~ ob ich das nicht wüßte!** as if I didn't know!; *siehe auch* **ob.**

(d) (*in Aufzählung*) **~ (da sind): ...** that is to say, ..., to wit, ... (*old, form*).

(e) (*in Konsekutivsätzen*) **sie ist zu alt, ~ daß sie das noch verstehen könnte** she is too old to understand that; **die Zeit war zu knapp, ~ daß wir ...**the time was too short for us to ...; **das ist um so trauriger, ~ es nicht das erste Mal war** that's all the sadder in that it wasn't the first time.

(f) (*in Temporalsätzen*) when; (*gleichzeitig*) as ◆ **gleich, ~** as soon as; **damals, ~** (in the days) when; **gerade, ~** just as.

(g) (*in der Eigenschaft*) as ◆ **~ Beweis** as proof; **~ Antwort/Warnung** as an answer/a warning; **sich ~ wahr/falsch erweisen** to prove to be true/false; **~ Held/Revolutionär** as a hero/revolutionary; **~ Kind/Mädchen** *etc* as a child/girl *etc*; **~ Rentner will er ein Buch schreiben** when he retires he is going to write a book; *siehe* **sowohl, insofern, insoweit.**

[2] *adv* (*dial inf*) (*immer*) **etw ~ (nochmal) tun** to keep on (and on) doing sth; **gehen Sie ~ geradeaus** keep going straight ahead.

als-: ~bald *adv* (*old, liter*) directly, straightway (*old*); **~baldig** *adj* (*form*) immediate; **„zum ~baldigen Verbrauch bestimmt"** "do not keep", "for immediate use only"; **~dann** *adv* **(a)** (*old liter: dann*) then; **(b)** (*dial*) well then, well ... then.

also [1] *conj* **(a)** (*folglich*) so, therefore ◆ **er war Künstler, ein hochsensibler Mensch ~** he was an artist, (and) therefore a highly sensitive person.

(b) (*old: so, folgendermaßen*) thus.

[2] *adv* so; (*nach Unterbrechung anknüpfend*) well; (*zusammenfassend, erklärend*) that is ◆ **~ doch** so ... after all; **du machst es ~?** so you'll do it then?; **~ wie ich schon sagte** well (then), as I said before.

[3] *interj* (*verwundert, entrüstet, auffordernd*) well; (*drohend*) just ◆ **~, daß du dich ordentlich benimmst!** (you) just see that you behave yourself!; **~ doch!** so he/they *etc* did!; **na ~!** there you are!, you see?; **~, ich hab's doch gewußt!** I knew it!; **~ nein!** (oh) no!; **~ nein, daß sie sich das gefallen läßt** my God, she can't put up with that!; **~ gut** *or* **schön** well all right then; **~ dann!** right then!; **~ so was/so eine Frechheit!** well (I never)/what a cheek!

Alster(wasser) *nt* (*N Ger*) shandy (*Brit*), beer and lemonade.

alt *adj, comp* **¨er,** *superl* **¨este(r, s)** *or adv* **am ¨esten (a)** old; (*betagt*) *Mensch auch* aged (*liter*); (*sehr ~*) *Mythos, Sage, Aberglaube auch, Griechen, Geschichte* ancient; *Sprachen* classical ◆ **das ~e Rom** ancient Rome; **das A~e Testament** the Old Testament; **die A~ Welt** the Old World; **der ~e Herr** (*inf: Vater*) the *or* one's old man (*inf*); **die ~e Dame** (*inf: Mutter*) the old lady (*inf*); **~er Junge** *or* **Freund** old boy (*dated*) *or* fellow (*dated*); **~ und jung** (everybody) old and young; **ein drei Jahre ~es Kind** a three-year-old child, a child of three years of age; **wie ~ bist du?** how old are you?; **etw ~ kaufen** to buy sth second-hand; **man ist so ~, wie man sich fühlt** you're only as old as you feel (*prov*); **ich werde heute nicht ~ (werden)** (*inf*) I won't last long today/tonight *etc* (*inf*); **hier werde ich nicht ~** (*inf*) this isn't my scene (*inf*); **aus ~ mach neu** (*Prov inf*) make do and mend (*Prov*); *siehe* **Eisen, Hase, Haus.**

(b) (*dieselbe, gewohnt*) same old ◆ **sie ist ganz die ~e (Ingrid)** she's the same old Ingrid, she hasn't changed a bit; **jetzt ist sie wieder ganz die ~e lustige Veronika** she's the old happy Veronika again; **wir bleiben die ~en, auch wenn sich alle andern verändern** we stay the same even when everybody else changes; **er ist nicht mehr der ~e** he's not what he was *or* the man he was; **es ist nicht mehr das ~e Glasgow** it's not the (same old) Glasgow I/we *etc* knew; **alles bleibt beim ~en** everything stays as it was; **alles beim ~en lassen** to leave everything as it was.

(c) (*lange bestehend*) old ◆ **~e Liebe rostet nicht** (*Prov*) true love never dies (*prov*); **in ~er Freundschaft, dein ...** yours as ever ...

(d) ~ aussehen (*sl: dumm dastehen*) to look stupid.

Alt[1] *m* **-s, -e** (*Mus*) alto; (*von Frau auch*) contralto; (*Gesamtheit der Stimmen*) altos *pl*; contraltos *pl*.

Alt[2] *nt* **-s, -** *siehe* **Altbier.**

Altan *m* **-(e)s, -e** balcony.

alt-: ~angesehen *adj Familie* old and respected; *Firma* old-established; **~angesessen, ~ansässig** *adj* old-established.

Altar *m* **-s, Altäre** altar ◆ **eine Frau zum ~ führen** to lead a woman to the altar.

Altar- *in cpds* altar; **~bild** *nt* altarpiece, reredos; **~gemälde** *nt* altarpiece; **~gerät** *nt* altar furniture; **~raum** *m* chancel.

Alt-: a~backen *adj* **(a)** stale; **(b)** (*fig*) *Mensch* old-fashioned; *Kleidung, Ansichten auch* outdated, out of date; **~batterie** *f* used battery; **~bau** *m* old building; **~bauwohnung** *f* flat in an old building; **a~bekannt** *adj* well-known; **a~bewährt** *adj Mittel, Methode etc* well-tried; *Sitte, Tradition, Freundschaft etc* long-standing *usu attr*, of long standing; **~bier** *nt top-fermented German dark beer*; **~bundeskanzler** *m* former German/Austrian Chancellor; **~bürger** *m* senior citizen; **a~christlich** *adj* early Christian; **a~deutsch** *adj* old German; *Möbel, Stil* German Renaissance.

Alte *siehe* **Alte(r), Alte(s).**

Alt-: a~ehrwürdig *adj* venerable; *Bräuche* time-honoured; **a~eingeführt** *adj* introduced long ago; **a~eingesessen** *adj siehe* **a~angesessen**; **~eisen** *nt* scrap metal; **a~englisch** *adj* Old English; **~englisch(e)** *nt* Old English, Anglo-Saxon.

Alten-: ~heim *nt siehe* **Altersheim**; **~herrschaft** *f* gerontocracy; **~hilfe** *f* old people's welfare; **~pfleger** *m* old people's nurse; **~tagesstätte** *f* old people's day centre; **~teil** *nt cottage or part of a farm reserved for the farmer when he hands the estate over to his son*; **sich aufs ~teil setzen** *or* **zurückziehen** (*fig*) to retire *or* withdraw from public life.

Alte(r) *mf decl as adj* (*alter Mann, inf: Ehemann, Vater*) old man; (*alte Frau, inf: Ehefrau, Mutter*) old woman; (*inf: Vorgesetzter*) boss ◆ **die ~n** (*Eltern*) the folk(s) *pl* (*inf*); (*Tiereltern*) the parents *pl*; (*ältere Generation*) the old people *pl or* folk *pl*; (*aus klassischer Zeit*) the ancients *pl*; **wie die ~n sungen, so zwitschern auch die Jungen** (*prov*) like father like son (*prov*); **komischer ~r** (*Theat*) comic old man.

Alter *nt* **-s, -** age; (*letzter Lebensabschnitt, hohes ~*) old age ◆ **im ~** in one's old age; **im ~ wird man weiser** one grows wiser with age; **in deinem ~** at your age; **er ist in deinem ~** he's your age; **im ~ von 18 Jahren** at the age of 18; **von mittlerem ~** middle-aged; **er hat keinen Respekt vor dem ~** he has no respect for his elders; **~ schützt vor Torheit nicht** (*Prov*) there's no fool like an old fool (*prov*).

älter *adj* **(a)** *comp of* **alt** older; *Bruder, Tochter etc auch* elder ◆ **werden Frauen ~ als Männer?** do women live longer than men? **(b)** *attr* (*nicht ganz jung*) elderly ◆ **die ~en Herrschaften** the older members of the party.

Alterchen *nt* (*inf*) Grandad (*inf*).

Ältere(r) *mf decl as adj* **(a)** (*älterer Mensch*) older man/woman *etc* ◆ **die ~n** the older ones. **(b)** (*bei Namen*) Elder ◆ **Holbein der ~** Holbein the Elder.

alt|erfahren *adj* experienced, of long experience.

altern [1] *vi aux sein or* (*rare*) *haben* to age; (*Mensch auch*) to get older; (*Wein*) to mature ◆ **vorzeitig ~** to grow old before one's time; **~d** ageing.
[2] *vt* to age; *Wein* to mature; *Metall* to age-harden.

alternativ *adj* (*geh*) alternative ◆ **~ leben** to live an alternative lifestyle; **A~e Liste** (*Pol*) *electoral pact of alternative political groupings*.

Alternativ- *in cpds* alternative.

Alternative *f* alternative (*etw zu tun* of doing sth).

Alternative(r) *mf decl as adj* person with alternative views ◆ **die ~n** those who favour the alternative society.

alternieren* *vi* to alternate.

alternierend *adj* alternate; *Strom, Verse* alternating; *Fieber* intermittent.

alt|erprobt *adj* well-tried.

alters *adv* (*geh*) **von** *or* **seit ~ (her)** from time immemorial; **vor ~** in olden days *or* times, in days of yore (*old, liter*).

Alters-: ~abstand *m* age difference; **~asyl** *nt* (*Sw*) *siehe* **~heim**; **a~bedingt** *adj* related to a particular age; related to *or* caused by old age; **~beschwerden** *pl* complaints *pl* of old age, geriatric complaints *pl*; **~erscheinung** *f* sign of old age; **~fleck** *m* age mark, blotch; **~forschung** *f* gerontology; **~fürsorge** *f* care of the elderly; **~genosse** *m* contemporary; (*Kind*) child of the same age; (*Psych, Sociol*) peer; **wir sind ja ~genossen** we are the same age; **~gliederung** *f* age structure; **~grenze** *f* age limit; (*Rentenalter*) retirement age; **flexible ~grenze** flexible retirement age; **~gründe** *pl* **aus ~gründen** for reasons of age; **~gruppe** *f* age-group; **a~halber** *adv* because of *or* on account of one's age; **~heim** *nt* old people's home; **~klasse** *f* (*Sport*) age-group; **~krankheit** *f* geriatric illness; **~präsident** *m* president by seniority; **⚠~prozeß** *m* ageing process, senescence (*spec*); **~pyramide** *f* age pyramid *or* diagram; **~rente** *f* old age pension; **~ruhegeld** *nt* retirement benefit; **a~schwach** *adj Mensch* old and infirm; *Tier* old and weak; *Auto, Möbel* decrepit; **~schwäche** *f siehe adj* infirmity; weakness; decrepitude; **a~sichtig** *adj* presbyopic (*form*); **~sitz** *m* **sein ~sitz war München** he spent his retirement in Munich; **~soziologie** *f* sociology of old age; **~sport** *m* sport for the elderly; **~starrsinn** *m* senile stubbornness; **~stufe** *f* age-group; (*Lebensabschnitt*) age, stage in life; **~versicherung** *f* retirement insurance; **~versorgung** *f* provision for (one's) old age; **~werk** *nt* later works *pl*; **~zulage** *f* increment for age.

Altertum *nt, no pl* antiquity *no art* ◆ **das deutsche ~** early German history.

Altertümelei *f* antiquarianism.

altertümeln *vi* to antiquarianize.

Altertümer *pl* antiquities *pl*.

altertümlich *adj* (*aus dem Altertum*) ancient; (*veraltet*) antiquated.

Altertümlichkeit *f siehe adj* ancientness; antiquated nature.

Altertums-: ~forscher *m* archeologist; **~forschung** *f* archeology, archeological research; **~kunde** *f* archeology; **~wert** *m* **das hat schon ~wert** (*hum*) it has antique value (*hum*).

Alterung *f* **(a)** *siehe* **altern 1** ageing; maturation. **(b)** *siehe* **altern 2** ageing; maturation; age-hardening.

Alte(s) *nt decl as adj* **das ~** (*das Gewohnte, Traditionelle*) the old; (*alte Dinge*) old things *pl*; **er hängt sehr am ~n** he clings to the past; **das ~ und das Neue** the old and the new, old and new; **sie hat Freude an allem ~n** she gets a lot of pleasure from anything old.

Ältestenrat *m* council of elders; (*BRD Pol*) parliamentary advisory committee, ≃ think-tank (*Brit*).

Älteste(r, s) *mf decl as adj* oldest; (*Sohn, Tochter auch*) eldest; (*Eccl*) elder.

älteste(r, s) *adj superl of* **alt** oldest; *Bruder etc auch* eldest ◆ **der ~ Junge** (*Skat*) the jack of clubs.

Alt-: ~flöte *f* treble recorder; (*Querflöte*) bass *or* alto flute; **a~fränkisch** *adj* quaint; *Stadt etc auch* olde-worlde (*inf*); **~französisch(e)** *nt* Old French; **~gerät** *nt* old appliance; **~glas** *nt no pl* waste glass; **~glasbehälter** *m* bottle bank; **~glascontainer** *m* bottle bank; **~gold** *nt* old gold; (*Goldart*) artificially darkened gold; **a~griechisch** *adj* ancient Greek; (*Ling*) classical Greek; **~griechisch(e)** *nt* classical Greek; **a~hergebracht, a~herkömmlich** *adj* (*old*) traditional; **~herrenfußball** *m* veterans' football; **~herrenmannschaft** *f* (*Sport*) *team of players over thirty*; **a~hochdeutsch** *adj*, **~hochdeutsch(e)** *nt* Old High German.

Altist(in *f*) *m* (*Mus*) alto.

Altjahrs(s)-: ~abend *m* (*dial*) New Year's Eve, Hogmanay (*esp Scot*); **~tag** *m* (*dial*) New Year's Eve, Hogmanay (*esp Scot*).

Alt-: a~jüngferlich *adj* old-maidish, spinsterish; **~kanzler** *m* former chancellor; **~katholik** *m*, **a~katholisch** *adj* Old Catholic; **~kleiderhändler** *m* second-hand clothes dealer; **~kleidersammlung** *f* collection of old clothes; **a~klug** *adj* precocious; **~lage** *f* (*Mus*) alto range; **~last** *f* (*Ökologie*) dangerous waste from the past.

ältlich *adj* oldish.

Alt-: ~material *nt* scrap; **~meister** *m* doyen; (*Sport*) ex-champion; **~metall** *nt* scrap metal; **a~modisch** *adj* old-fashioned; (*rückständig*) outmoded; **~neubau** *m* prewar building; **~papier** *nt* wastepaper; **~papiersammlung** *f* wastepaper collection; **~partie** *f* (*Mus*) alto part; **~philologe** *m* classical philologist; **~philologie** *f* classical philology; **a~philologisch** *adj Abteilung* of classical philology; *Bücher, Artikel* on classical philology; **a~renommiert** *adj* old-established; **a~rosa** *adj* old rose.

Altruismus *m, no pl* (*geh*) altruism.

Altruist(in *f*) *m* (*geh*) altruist.

altruistisch *adj* (*geh*) altruistic.

Alt-: a~sächsisch *adj* old Saxon; **~sängerin** *f* contralto (singer); **~schlüssel** *m* (*Mus*) alto clef; **~schnee** *m* old snow; **~sein** *nt* being old *no art*; **~silber** *nt* old silver; (*Silberart*) artificially darkened silver; **~sprachler(in** *f*) *m* **-s, -** classicist; (*Sprachwissenschaftler*) classical philologist; **a~sprachlich** *adj Zweig, Abteilung* classics *attr*; **a~sprachliches Gymnasium** grammar school (*Brit*), *school teaching classical languages*; **~stadt** *f* old (part of a/the) town; **die Ulmer ~stadt** the old part of Ulm; **~stadtsanierung** *f* renovation of the old part of a/the town; **~steinzeit** *f* Palaeolithic Age, Old Stone Age; **a~steinzeitlich** *adj* Palaeolithic; **~stimme** *f* (*Mus*) alto; (*von Frau auch*) contralto, contralto voice; (*Partie*) alto/contralto part; **~stoff** *m usu pl* waste material ◆ **~e sammeln** to collect (recyclable) waste; **gefährliche ~e** dangerous waste; **~-Taste** *f* (*Comput*) Alt key; **a~testamentarisch, a~testamentlich** *adj* Old Testament *attr*; **a~überkommen, a~überliefert** *adj* traditional; **a~väterisch, a~väterlich** *adj Bräuche, Geister* ancestral; (*altmodisch*) old-fashioned *no adv*; *Erscheinung etc* patriarchal; **~wähler** *m* hardened voter; **~waren** *pl* second-hand goods *pl*; **~warenhändler** *m* second-hand dealer.

Altweiber-: ~geschwätz *nt* old woman's talk; **~sommer** *m* **(a)** (*Nachsommer*) Indian summer; **(b)** (*Spinnfäden*) gossamer.

Alu *nt* **-s,** *no pl siehe* **Aluminium.**

Alufolie *f* tin *or* kitchen *or* aluminium foil.

Aluminium *nt* **-s,** *no pl* (*abbr* **Al**) aluminium (*Brit*), aluminum (*US*).

Aluminium-: ~folie *f* tin *or* aluminium foil; **~(staub)lunge** *f* (*Med*) aluminosis (*form*).

Alveolar [alveo'laːɐ] *m* (*Phon*) alveolar (sound).

Alzheimer-Krankheit *f* Alzheimer's disease.

am *prep* **(a)** *contr of* **an dem.**

(b) (*zur Bildung des Superlativs*) **er war ~ tapfersten** he was (the) bravest; **sie hat es ~ schönsten gemalt** she painted it (the) most beautifully; **~ besten machen wir das morgen** we'd do best to do it tomorrow, the best thing would be for us to do it tomorrow; **~ seltsamsten war ...** the strangest thing was ...

(c) (*als Zeitangabe*) on ◆ **~ letzten Sonntag** last Sunday; **~ 8. Mai** on the eighth of May, on May (the *Brit*) eighth; (*geschrieben*) on May 8th; **~ Morgen/Abend** in the morning/evening; **~ Tag darauf/zuvor** (on) the following/previous day.

(d) (*als Ortsangabe*) on the; (*bei Gebirgen*) at the foot of the; *siehe auch* **an 1 (a).**

(e) (*inf: als Verlaufsform*) **ich war gerade ~ Weggehen** I was just leaving.

(f) (*Aus: auf dem*) on the.

(g) (*Comm*) **~ Lager** in stock.

(h) *in Verbindung mit n siehe auch dort* **du bist ~ Zug** it's your turn; **~ Ball sein/bleiben** to be/keep on the ball.

Amalgam *nt* **-s, -e** amalgam.

amalgamieren* *vtr* (*lit, fig*) to amalgamate.

Amaryllis *f* **-, Amaryllen** amaryllis.

Amateur [-'tøːɐ] *m* amateur.

Amateur- *in cpds* amateur; **~funker** *m* radio amateur *or* ham (*inf*); **a~haft** *adj* amateurish.

Amazonas *m* **-** Amazon.

Amazone *f* **-, -n (a)** (*Myth*) Amazon; (*fig*) amazon. **(b)** (*Sport*) woman show-jumper.

Amber *m* **-s, -(n)** ambergris.

Ambiente *nt* **-,** *no pl* (*geh*) ambience.

Ambition *f* (*geh*) ambition ◆ **~en auf etw** (*acc*) **haben** to have ambitions of getting sth.

ambivalent [-va'lɛnt] *adj* ambivalent.

Ambivalenz [-va'lɛnts] *f* ambivalence.
⚠ **Amboß** *m* **-sses, -sse** anvil; (*Anat auch*) incus.
Ambra *f* **-, Ambren** *siehe* **Amber.**
Ambrosia *f* **-,** *no pl* ambrosia.
ambulant *adj* **(a)** (*Med*) *Versorgung, Behandlung* out-patient *attr* ◆ **~e Patienten** out-patients; **~ behandelt werden** (*Patient*) to receive out-patient treatment; (*Fall*) to be treated in the out-patient department. **(b)** (*wandernd*) itinerant.
Ambulanz *f* **(a)** (*Klinikstation*) out-patient department, out-patients *sing* (*inf*). **(b)** (*~wagen*) ambulance.
Ambulanz-: ~hubschrauber *m* ambulance helicopter; **~wagen** *m* ambulance.
Ameise *f* **-, -n** ant.
Ameisen-: ~bär *m* anteater; (*größer*) ant-bear, great anteater; **a~haft** *adj* ant-like; *Getriebe etc* beaver-like; **~haufen** *m* anthill; **~säure** *f* formic acid; **~staat** *m* ant colony.
amen *interj* amen; *siehe* **ja.**
Amen *nt* **-s, -** amen ◆ **sein ~ zu etw geben** to give one's blessing to sth; **das ist so sicher wie das ~ in der Kirche** (*inf*) you can bet your bottom dollar on that (*inf*).
Americium [-tsiʊm] *nt, no pl* (*abbr* **Am**) americium.
Amerikaner(in *f*) *m* **-s, - (a)** American. **(b)** (*Gebäck*) *flat iced cake.*
amerikanisch *adj* American.
amerikanisieren* *vt* to Americanize.
Amerikanisierung *f* Americanization.
Amerikanismus *m* Americanism.
Amerikanist(in *f*) *m* specialist in American studies.
Amerikanistik *f* American studies *pl.*
Amethyst *m* **-s, -e** amethyst.
Ami *m* **-s, -s** (*inf*) Yank (*inf*); (*sl: Soldat*) GI (*inf*).
Aminosäure *f* amino acid.
Ammann *m* (*Sw*) **(a)** mayor. **(b)** (*Jur*) local magistrate.
Amme *f* **-, -n** (*old*) foster-mother; (*Nährmutter*) wet nurse.
Ammenmärchen *nt* fairy tale *or* story.
Ammer *f* **-, -n** (*Orn*) bunting.
Ammoniak *nt* **-s,** *no pl* ammonia.
Ammonit *m* **-en, -en** (*Archeol*) ammonite.
Ammonshorn *nt* **(a)** (*Anat*) hippocampus major (*spec*). **(b)** (*Archeol*) ammonite.
Amnesie *f* (*Med*) amnesia.
Amnestie *f* amnesty.
amnestieren* *vt* to grant an amnesty to.
Amöbe *f* **-, -n** (*Biol*) amoeba.
Amöbenruhr *f* (*Med*) amoebic dysentery.
Amok ['a:mɔk, a'mɔk] *m*: **~ laufen** to run amok *or* amuck; **~ fahren** to drive like a madman *or* lunatic.
Amok-: ~fahrer *m* mad *or* lunatic driver; **~fahrt** *f* mad *or* crazy ride; **~lauf** *m* **einen ~lauf aufführen** to run amok *or* amuck; **~läufer** *m* madman; **~schütze** *m* crazed gunman.
Amor *m* **-** Cupid.
amoralisch *adj* **(a)** (*unmoralisch*) immoral. **(b)** (*wertfrei*) amoral.
Amoralität *f* immorality.
Amorette *f* little cupid, amoretto.
amorph *adj* (*geh*) amorphous.
Amortisation *f* amortization.
Amortisationsdauer *f* length of amortization period.
amortisieren* 1 *vt* (*Econ*) **eine Investition ~** to ensure that an investment pays for itself.
2 *vr* to pay for itself.
Amouren [a'mu:rən] *pl* (*old, hum*) amours *pl* (*old, hum*).
amourös [amu'rø:s] *adj* (*geh*) amorous.
Ampel *f* **-, -n (a)** (*Verkehrs~*) (traffic) lights *pl* ◆ **er hat eine ~ umgefahren** he knocked a traffic light over; **halte an der nächsten ~** stop at the next (set of) (traffic) lights. **(b)** (*geh*) (*Hängelampe*) hanging lamp; (*Hängeblumentopf*) hanging flowerpot.
Ampel-: ~anlage *f* (set of) traffic lights; **~koalition** *f* (*Pol*) *coalition formed by SPD, FDP and Green Party;* **~kreuzung** *f* (*inf*) junction controlled by traffic lights; **~phase** *f* traffic light sequence; **die langen ~phasen an dieser Kreuzung** the length of time the lights take to change at this junction.
Ampere [am'pe:ɐ, am'pɛ:ɐ] *nt* **-(s), -** amp, ampere (*form*).
Ampere-: ~meter *nt* ammeter; **~sekunde** *f* ampere-second; **~stunde** *f* ampere-hour.
Ampfer *m* **-s, -** (*Bot*) dock; (*Sauer~*) sorrel.
Amphetamin *nt* **-s, -e** amphetamine.
Amphibie [-iə] *f* (*Zool*) amphibian.
Amphibienfahrzeug *nt* amphibious vehicle.
amphibisch *adj* amphibious.
Amphitheater *nt* amphitheatre.
Amphora *f* **-, Amphoren** amphora.
Amplitude *f* **-, -n** (*Phys*) amplitude.
Ampulle *f* **-, -n (a)** (*Behälter*) ampoule. **(b)** (*Anat*) ampulla.
Amputation *f* amputation.
amputieren* *vt* to amputate ◆ **jdm den Arm ~** to amputate sb's arm; **amputiert werden** (*Mensch*) to have an amputation.
Amputierte(r) *mf decl as adj* amputee, person who has had a limb amputated.
Amsel *f* **-, -n** blackbird.
Amsterdam *nt* **-s** Amsterdam.
Amsterdamer *adj attr* Amsterdam.
Amsterdamer(in *f*) *m* native of Amsterdam; (*Einwohner*) inhabitant of Amsterdam.
Amt *nt* **-(e)s, ¨er (a)** (*Stellung*) office; (*Posten*) post ◆ **im ~ sein** to be in *or* hold office; **jdn aus einem ~ entfernen** to remove sb from office; **in ~ und Würden** in an exalted position; **von ~s wegen** (*aufgrund von jds Beruf*) because of one's job; **kraft seines ~es** (*geh*) by virtue of one's office.
(b) (*Aufgabe*) duty, task ◆ **seines ~es walten** (*geh*) to carry out *or* discharge (*form*) one's duties.
(c) (*Behörde*) (*Friedhofs~, Fürsorge~, Sozial~ etc*) cemeteries/welfare department *etc*/department of social security; (*Einwohnermelde~, Paß~, Finanz~*) registration/passport/tax office; (*Stadtverwaltung*) council offices *pl*; (*Oberschul~*) secondary school authority ◆ **zum zuständigen ~ gehen** to go to the relevant authority; **die ¨er der Stadt** the town authorities; **von ~s wegen** (*auf behördliche Anordnung hin*) officially.
(d) (*Telefon~*) operator; (*Zentrale*) exchange ◆ **geben Sie mir bitte ein ~** could you give me a line, please?
Ämter-: ~jagd *f* position-hunting; **~kauf** *m* buying one's way into office; **~patronage** *f* autocratic distribution of offices.
amtieren* *vi* **(a)** (*Amt innehaben*) to be in office ◆ **~d** incumbent; **der ~de Bürgermeister/Weltmeister** the (present) mayor/the reigning world champion; **als Minister/Lehrer/Bürgermeister ~** to hold the post of minister/to have a position as a teacher/to hold the office of mayor. **(b)** (*Amt vorübergehend wahrnehmen*) to act. **er amtiert als Bürgermeister** he is acting mayor. **(c)** (*fungieren*) **als ... ~** to act as ...
amtl. *abbr of* **amtlich.**
amtlich *adj* official; (*wichtig*) *Miene, Gebaren* officious; (*inf: sicher*) certain ◆ **~es Kennzeichen** registration (number), license number (*US*).
amtlicherseits *adv* officially.
Amtlichkeit *f* officialdom *no pl.*
Amtmann *m, pl* **-männer** *or* **-leute, Amtmännin** *f* **(a)** (*Admin*) senior civil servant. **(b)** (*Jur*) local magistrate.
Amts-: ~adel *m* (*Hist*) *non-hereditary nobility who were created peers because of their office*; **~anmaßung** *f* unauthorized assumption of authority; (*Ausübung eines Amtes*) fraudulent exercise of a public office; **~antritt** *m* assumption of office/one's post; **~anwalt** *m prosecuting counsel in relatively minor cases*; **~apparat** *m* official machinery; **~arzt** *m* medical officer; **a~ärztlich** *adj Zeugnis* from the medical officer; *Untersuchung* by the medical officer; **a~ärztlich untersucht werden** to have an official medical examination; **~befugnis** *f*, **~bereich** *m* area of competence; **~bezirk** *m* area of jurisdiction; **~blatt** *nt* gazette; **~bote** *m* official messenger; **~bruder** *m* (*Eccl*) fellow clergyman; **~dauer** *f* term of office; **~deutsch(e)** *nt* officialese; **~diener** *m* clerk; (*Bote*) messenger; **~eid** *m* oath of office; **den ~eid ablegen** to be sworn in, to take the oath of office; **~einführung, ~einsetzung** *f* instalment, inauguration; **~enthebung, ~entsetzung** (*Sw, Aus*) *f* dismissal *or* removal from office; **~erschleichung** *f* obtaining office by devious means; **~geheimnis** *nt* **(a)** (*geheime Sache*) official secret; **(b)** (*Schweigepflicht*) official secrecy; **~gericht** *nt* ≃ county (*Brit*) *or* district (*US*) court; **~gerichtsrat** *m* ≃ county (*Brit*) *or* district (*US*) court judge; **~geschäfte** *pl* official duties *pl*; **~gewalt** *f* authority; **a~handeln** *vi insep* (*Aus*) to take official action, to act officially; **~handlung** *f* official duty; **seine erste ~handlung bestand darin, ...** the first thing he did in office was ...; **~hilfe** *f* cooperation between authorities; **~kanzlei** *f* (*Aus*) office; **~kette** *f* chain of office; **~kleidung** *f* robes *pl* of office; **~kollege** *m*, **~kollegin** *f* opposite number; **~leitung** *f* (*Telec*) exchange line; **~miene** *f* official air; **seine ~miene aufsetzen** to get *or* go all official (*inf*); ⚠**~mißbrauch** *m* abuse of one's position; **~niederlegung** *f* resignation; **~periode** *f* term of office; **~person** *f* official; **~pflicht** *f* official duty; **~richter** *m* ≃ county (*Brit*) *or* district (*US*) court judge; **~schimmel** *m* (*hum*) officialdom; **den ~schimmel reiten** to do everything by the book; **der ~schimmel wiehert** officialdom rears its ugly head; **~sprache** *f* official language; **~stube** *f* (*dated*) office; **~stunden** *pl* hours *pl* open to the public; **~tracht** *f* robes *pl* of office; (*Eccl*) vestments *pl*; **~träger** *m* office bearer; **~übergabe** *f* handing-over of office; **~übernahme** *f* assumption of office/a post; **~vergehen** *nt* malfeasance (*form*); **~vermittlung** *f* (*Telec*) connection by the operator; **~verwalter, ~verweser** (*old*) *m* deputy; **~vormund** *m* (*Jur*) public guardian; **~vormundschaft** *f* (*Jur*) public guardianship; **~vorstand, ~vorsteher** *m* head *or* chief of a/the department *etc*; **~weg** *m* official channels *pl*; **den ~weg beschreiten** to go through the official channels; **~zeichen** *nt* (*Telec*) dialling tone (*Brit*), dial tone (*US*); **~zeit** *f* period of office; **~zimmer** *nt* office.
Amulett *nt* **-(e)s, -e** amulet, charm, talisman.
amüsant *adj* amusing; *Film, Geschichte auch* funny ◆ **~ plaudern** to talk in an amusing way.
Amüsement [amyzə'mã:] *nt* **-s, -s** (*geh*) amusement, entertainment.
Amüsierbetrieb *m* (*inf*) nightclub; (*Spielhalle etc*) amusement arcade ◆ **der ~ in Las Vegas** the pleasure industry in Las Vegas.
amüsieren* 1 *vt* to amuse ◆ **was amüsiert dich denn so?** what do you find so amusing *or* funny?; **lassen Sie sich ein bißchen ~** have some fun; **amüsiert zuschauen** to look on amused *or* with amusement.
2 *vr* (*sich vergnügen*) to enjoy oneself, to have a good time, to have fun ◆ **sich mit etw ~** to amuse oneself with sth; (*iro*) to keep oneself amused

with sth; **sich über etw** *(acc)* ~ to find sth funny; *(über etw lachen)* to laugh at sth; *(unfreundlich)* to make fun of sth; **sich darüber ~, daß ...** to find it funny that ...; **sich mit jdm ~** to have a good time with sb; **amüsiert euch gut** have fun, enjoy yourselves.

Amüsier-: ~lokal *nt* nightclub; **~viertel** *nt* nightclub district.

amusisch *adj* unartistic.

an [1] *prep +dat* **(a)** *(räumlich: wo?)* at; *(~ etw dran)* on ◆ **am Haus/Bahnhof** at the house/station; **~ dieser Schule** at this school; **~ der Wand stehen** to stand by the wall; **am Fenster sitzen** to sit at *or* by the window; **am Tatort** at the scene of the crime; **~ der Tür/Wand** on the door/wall; **~ der Donau/ Autobahn/am Ufer/am Rhein** by *or (direkt ~ gelegen)* on the Danube/ motorway/bank/Rhine; **Frankfurt ~ der Oder** Frankfurt on (the) Oder; **~ etw hängen** *(lit)* to hang from *or* on sth; **zu nahe ~ etw stehen** to be too near to sth; **etw ~ etw festmachen** to fasten sth to sth; **jdn ~ der Hand nehmen** to take sb by the hand; **oben am Berg** up the mountain; **unten am Fluß** down by the river; **sie wohnen Tür ~ Tür** they live next door to one another, they are next-door neighbours; **Haus ~ Haus/Laden ~ Laden** one house/shop after the other; **~ etw vorbeigehen** to go past sth, to pass sth; *siehe* **am, Bord, Land** *etc.*
(b) *(zeitlich)* on ◆ **~ diesem Abend** (on) that evening; **am Tag zuvor** the day before, the previous day; **~ dem Abend, als ich ...** the evening I ...; **~ Ostern/Weihnachten** *(dial)* at Easter/Christmas; *siehe* **am.**
(c) *(fig) siehe auch Substantive, Adjektive, Verben* **jung ~ Jahren sein** to be young in years; **fünf ~ der Zahl** five in number; **jdn ~ etw erkennen** to recognize sb by sth; **der Mangel/das Angebot ~ Waren** the lack/choice of goods; **~ etw arbeiten/schreiben/kauen** to be working on/writing/chewing sth; **~ etw sterben/leiden** to die of/suffer from sth; **was haben Sie ~ Weinen da?** what wines do you have?; **unübertroffen ~ Qualität** unsurpassed in quality; **~ etw schuld sein** to be to blame for sth; **~ der ganzen Sache ist nichts** there is nothing in it; **es ~ der Leber** *etc* **haben** *(inf)* to have trouble with one's liver *etc*, to have liver *etc* trouble; **was findet sie ~ dem Mann?** what does she see in that man?; **es ist ~ dem** *(es stimmt)* that's right; **sie hat etwas ~ sich, das ...** there is something about her that ...; **es ist ~ ihm, etwas zu tun** *(geh)* it's up to him to do something.
[2] *prep +acc* **(a)** *(räumlich: wohin?)* to; *(gegen)* on, against ◆ **etw ~ die Wand/ Tafel schreiben** to write sth on the wall/blackboard; **die Zweige reichten (bis) ~ den Boden/mein Fenster** the branches reached down to the ground/up to my window; **etw ~ etw hängen** to hang sth on sth; **er ging ~s Fenster** he went (over) to the window; **A~ den Vorsitzenden ...** *(bei Anschrift)* The Chairman ...; **~s Telefon gehen** to answer the phone; *siehe* **bis, Bord, Land.**
(b) *(zeitlich: woran?)* **~ die Zukunft/Vergangenheit denken** to think of the future/past; **bis ~ mein Lebensende** to the end of my days.
(c) *(fig) siehe auch Substantive, Adjektive, Verben* **~ die Arbeit gehen** to get down to work; **~ jdn/etw glauben** to believe in sb/sth; **ich habe eine Bitte/ Frage ~ Sie** I have a request to make of you/question to ask you; **~ (und für) sich** actually; **eine ~ (und für) sich gute Idee** actually quite a good idea, as such quite a good idea; **wie war es? — ~ (und für) sich ganz schön** how was it? — on the whole it was quite nice; *siehe* **ab.**
[3] *adv* **(a)** *(ungefähr)* about ◆ **~ (die) hundert** about a hundred.
(b) *(Ankunftszeit)* **Frankfurt ~: 18.30** *(Rail)* arriving Frankfurt 18.30.
(c) von diesem Ort ~ from here onwards; **von diesem Tag/heute ~** from this day on(wards)/from today onwards.
(d) *(inf: angeschaltet, angezogen)* on ◆ **Licht ~!** lights on!; **ohne etwas ~** with nothing on, without anything on; *siehe* **ansein.**

Anabaptismus *m* anabaptism.

Anabaptist(in *f***)** *m* anabaptist.

anabol *adj* anabolic ◆ **~e Steroide** anabolic steroids.

Anabolikum *nt* **-s, -bolika** anabolic steroid.

Anachronismus [-kr-] *m (geh)* anachronism.

anachronistisch [-kr-] *adj (geh)* anachronistic.

anaerob [an|ae'ro:p] *adj attr* anaerobic.

Anagramm *nt (Liter)* anagram.

Anakoluth *nt* **-s, -e** anacoluthon.

Anakonda *f* **-, -s** anaconda.

anakreontisch *adj* anacreontic.

anal *adj (Psych, Anat)* anal.

Anal-: ~erotik *f* anal eroticism; **~öffnung** *f (form)* anal orifice *(form)*.

analog *adj* **(a)** analogous *(+dat, zu* to). **(b)** *(Telec, Comput etc)* analogue *(Brit)*, analog *(US, esp Comput)*.

Analogie *f* analogy.

Analogie-: ~bildung *f (Ling)* analogy; **⚠~schluß** *m (Philos, Jur)* argument by analogy.

analogisch *adj* analogous.

Analog-: ~rechner *m* analog computer; **~uhr** *f* analogue clock.

Analphabet(in *f***)** *m* **-en, -en** **(a)** illiterate (person). **(b)** *(pej: Unwissender)* ignoramus, dunce.

Analphabetentum *nt*, **Analphabetismus** *m* illiteracy.

analphabetisch *adj* illiterate.

Analverkehr *m* anal intercourse.

Analyse *f* **-, -n** analysis *(auch Psych)*.

analysieren* *vt* to analyze.

Analysis *f* **-,** *no pl (Math)* analysis.

Analytiker(in *f***)** *m* **-s, -** analyst; *(analytisch Denkender)* analytical thinker.

analytisch *adj* analytical.

Anämie *f* anaemia.

anämisch *adj* anaemic.

Anamnese *f* **-, -n** case history.

Ananas *f* **-, -** *or* **-se** pineapple.

Anapäst *m* **-(e)s, -e** *(Poet)* anap(a)est.

Anarchie *f* anarchy.

anarchisch *adj* anarchic ◆ **~ leben** to live an anarchic life.

Anarchismus *m* anarchism.

Anarchist(in *f***)** *m* anarchist.

anarchistisch *adj* anarchistic; *(den Anarchismus vertretend auch)* anarchist *attr.*

Anarcho *m* **-s, -s** *(pej)* anarchist.

Anarcho- *in cpds* anarcho-.

Anästhesie *f* ana(e)sthesia.

anästhesieren* *vt* to an(a)esthetize.

Anästhesist(in *f***)** *m* an(a)esthetist *(Brit)*, anesthesiologist *(US)*.

Anästhetikum *nt* **-s, Anästhetika** an(a)esthetic.

anästhetisch *adj* an(a)esthetic; *(unempfindlich auch)* an(a)esthetized.

Anatolien [-iən] *nt* **-s** Anatolia.

Anatolier(in *f***)** [-iɐ, -iərɪn] *m* **-s, -** Anatolian.

anatolisch *adj* Anatolian.

Anatom(in *f***)** *m* **-en, -en** anatomist.

Anatomie *f* **(a)** *(Wissenschaft, Körperbau)* anatomy. **(b)** *(Institut)* anatomical institute.

Anatomiesaal *m* anatomical *or* anatomy lecture theatre.

anatomisch *adj* anatomical.

anbacken *sep* [1] *vt (Cook)* to start baking.
[2] *vi aux sein* **(a)** *(kurz gebacken werden)* to bake for a short time. **(b)** *(sich festsetzen)* to bake on *(an +dat* -to); *(dial: Lehm, Schnee etc)* to stick *(an +dat* to).

anbahnen *sep* [1] *vt* to initiate.
[2] *vr (sich andeuten)* to be in the offing; *(Unangenehmes)* to be looming; *(Möglichkeiten, Zukunft etc)* to be opening up ◆ **zwischen den beiden bahnt sich etwas an** *(Liebesverhältnis)* there is something going on between those two.

Anbahnung *f* initiation *(von, gen* of).

anbandeln *(S Ger, Aus)*, **anbändeln** *vi sep* **(a)** *(Bekanntschaft schließen)* to take up *(mit* with). **(b)** *(Streit anfangen)* to start an argument *(mit* with).

Anbau[1] *m* **-(e)s,** *no pl* **(a)** *(Anpflanzung)* cultivation, growing. **(b)** *(von Gebäuden)* building ◆ **den ~ einer Garage planen** to plan to build on a garage.

Anbau[2] *m* **-(e)s, -ten** *(Nebengebäude)* extension; *(freistehend)* annexe; *(Stallungen etc)* outhouse, outbuilding.

anbauen *sep* [1] *vt* **(a)** to cultivate, to grow; *(anpflanzen)* to plant; *(säen)* to sow. **(b)** *(Build)* to add, to build on ◆ **etw ans Haus ~** to build sth onto the house.
[2] *vi* to build an extension ◆ **Möbel zum A~** unit furniture.

Anbau-: a~fähig *adj* **(a)** *Boden* cultivable; *Gemüse* growable; **(b)** *(Build)* extendible; **~fläche** *f* (area of) cultivable land; *(bebaute Ackerfläche)* area under cultivation; **~gebiet** *nt* cultivable area; **ein gutes ~gebiet für etw** a good area for cultivating sth; **~grenze** *f* limit of cultivation; **~möbel** *pl* unit furniture; **~plan** *m (DDR)* plan for land cultivation; **~schrank** *m* cupboard unit; **~technik** *f*, **~verfahren** *nt (Agr)* growing methods *pl.*

anbefehlen* *vt sep irreg (liter)* **(a)** *(befehlen)* to urge *(jdm etw* sth on sb). **(b)** *(anvertrauen)* to commend *(jdm etw* sth to sb).

Anbeginn *m (geh)* beginning ◆ **von ~ (an)** from the (very) beginning; **seit ~ der Welt** since the world began.

anbehalten* *vt sep irreg* to keep on.

anbei *adv (form)* enclosed ◆ **~ schicken wir Ihnen ...** please find enclosed ...

anbeißen *sep irreg* [1] *vi (Fisch)* to bite; *(fig)* to take the bait.
[2] *vt Apfel etc* to bite into ◆ **ein angebissener Apfel** a half-eaten apple; **sie sieht zum A~ aus** *(inf)* she looks nice enough to eat.

anbekommen* *vt sep irreg (inf)* to (manage to) get on; *Feuer* to (manage to) get going.

anbelangen* *vt sep* to concern ◆ **was das/mich anbelangt ...** as far as that is/I am concerned ...

anbellen *vt sep* to bark at.

anbequemen* *vr sep (geh)* **sich einer Sache** *(dat)* **~** to adapt (oneself) to sth.

anberaumen* *vt sep or (rare) insep (form)* to arrange, to fix; *Termin, Tag auch* to set; *Treffen auch* to call.

Anberaumung *f siehe vt* arrangement, fixing; setting; calling.

anbeten *vt sep* to worship; *Menschen auch* to adore; *siehe* **Angebetete(r).**

Anbeter *m* **-s, -** *(Verehrer)* admirer.

▼ **Anbetracht** *m*: **in ~** *(+gen)* in consideration *or* view of; **in ~ dessen, daß ...** in consideration *or* view of the fact that ...

anbetreffen* *vt sep irreg siehe* **anbelangen.**

anbetteln *vt sep* **jdn ~** to beg from sb; **jdn um etw ~** to beg sth from sb.

Anbetung *f siehe vt* worship; adoration.

anbetungswürdig *adj* admirable; *Schönheit* adorable.

anbezahlen* *vt sep siehe* **anzahlen.**

anbiedern *vr sep (pej)* **sich (bei jdm) ~** to try to get pally (with sb).

Anbiederung *f siehe vr* currying favour *(gen* with); chatting-up.

Anbiederungsversuch *m* attempt to curry favour with sb/chat sb up.

▼ **anbieten** *sep irreg* [1] *vt* to offer *(jdm etw* sb sth); *(Comm) Waren* to offer for sale; *seinen Rücktritt* to tender ◆ **haben wir etwas zum A~ da?** have we any-

⚠: for details of spelling reform, see supplement

➤ SPRACHE AKTIV: **Anbetracht** → 44.1 **anbieten: 1** → 30

thing to offer our guests?; **jdm das Du ~** *to suggest sb uses the familiar form of address.*

[2] *vr* **(a)** *(Mensch)* **sich (als etw) ~** to offer one's services (as sth); *(Ftbl)* to be in position; **sich für die Arbeit ~, sich ~, die Arbeit zu tun** to offer to do the work; **sich zur Unzucht ~** to solicit; **der Ort bietet sich für die Konferenz an** that is the obvious place for the conference; **das Fahrrad bietet sich geradezu zum Mitnehmen an** that bicycle is just asking to be taken.

(b) *(in Betracht kommen: Gelegenheit)* to present itself ◆ **das bietet sich als Lösung an** that would provide a solution; **es bieten sich mehrere Lösungsmöglichkeiten an** there are several possible solutions, several possible solutions present themselves; **es bietet sich an, das Museum zu besuchen** the thing to do would be to visit the museum.

Ạnbieter *m* **-s, -** supplier.

ạnbinden *sep irreg* [1] *vt (an +acc or dat to)* **(a)** to tie (up); *Pferd auch* to tether; *Boot auch* to moor ◆ **jdn ~** *(fig)* to tie sb down. **(b)** *(verbinden)* to connect; *(verketten)* to link; *siehe* **angebunden.**

[2] *vi siehe* **anbändeln.**

Ạnbindung *f (Verbindung)* connection; *(Verkettung)* linkage.

ạnblaffen *vt sep (inf) (lit, fig)* to bark at.

ạnblasen *vt sep irreg* **(a)** *(blasen gegen)* to blow at; *(anfachen)* to blow on ◆ **jdn mit Rauch ~** to blow smoke at sb. **(b)** *(Mus) Instrument* to blow; *Ton* to sound. **(c)** *(durch Blassignal ankündigen)* **die Jagd ~** to sound the horn for the start of the hunt.

ạnblecken *vt sep (lit, fig)* to bare one's teeth at.

ạnblenden *vt sep* to flash at; *(fig: kurz erwähnen)* to touch on.

Ạnblick *m* sight ◆ **beim ersten ~** at first sight; **beim ~ des Hundes** when he *etc* saw the dog; **in den ~ von etw versunken sein** to be absorbed in looking at sth; **in dem Hut bist du ein ~ für die Götter** you really look a sight in that hat.

ạnblicken *vt sep* to look at ◆ **jdn lange/feindselig ~** to gaze/glare at sb.

ạnblinken *vt sep* **jdn ~** *(Fahrer, Fahrzeug)* to flash (at) sb; *(Lampe)* to flash in sb's eyes; *(Gold)* to shine before sb's very eyes.

ạnblinzeln *vt sep* **(a)** *(blinzelnd ansehen)* to squint at. **(b)** *(zublinzeln)* to wink at.

ạnbohren *vt sep* **(a)** *(teilweise durchbohren)* to bore into; *(mit Bohrmaschine auch)* to drill into. **(b)** *(zugänglich machen) Quellen etc* to open up (by boring/drilling).

ạnborgen *vt sep (dated)* **jdn (um etw) ~** to borrow (sth) from sb.

Anbot ['anbo:t] *nt* **-(e)s, -e** *(Aus) siehe* **Angebot.**

ạnbranden *vi sep aux sein* to surge.

ạnbraten *vt sep irreg* to brown; *Steak etc* to sear ◆ **etw zu scharf ~** to brown sth too much.

ạnbrauchen *vt sep* to start using ◆ **eine angebrauchte Schachtel/Flasche** an opened box/bottle; **das ist schon angebraucht** that has already been used/worn/opened.

ạnbräunen *vt sep (Cook)* to brown (lightly).

ạnbrausen *vi sep aux sein* to roar up ◆ **angebraust kommen** to come roaring up.

ạnbrechen *sep irreg* [1] *vt* **(a)** *Packung, Flasche etc* to open; *Vorrat* to broach; *Ersparnisse, Geldsumme, Geldschein* to break into; *siehe* **angebrochen.**

(b) *(teilweise brechen) Brett, Gefäß, Knochen etc* to crack ◆ **angebrochen sein** to be cracked.

[2] *vi aux sein (Epoche etc)* to dawn; *(Tag auch)* to break; *(Nacht)* to fall; *(Jahreszeit)* to begin; *(Winter)* to close in.

ạnbremsen *vti sep* **(den Wagen) ~** to brake, to apply the brakes.

ạnbrennen *sep irreg* [1] *vi aux sein* to start burning, to catch fire; *(Holz, Kohle etc)* to catch light; *(Essen)* to burn, to get burnt; *(Stoff)* to scorch, to get scorched ◆ **mir ist das Essen angebrannt** I burnt the food, I let the food get burnt; **der Torwart ließ nichts ~** *(Sport sl)* the goalkeeper didn't let a single goal in; *siehe* **angebrannt.**

[2] *vt* to light.

ạnbringen *vt sep irreg* **(a)** *(hierherbringen)* to bring (with one); *(nach Hause)* to bring home (with one).

(b) *(befestigen)* to fix, to fasten *(an +dat* (on)to); *(aufstellen, aufhängen)* to put up; *Telefon, Feuermelder etc* to put in, to install; *Stiel an Besen* to put on; *Beschläge, Hufeisen* to mount; *Komma* to insert.

(c) *(äußern) Bemerkung, Bitte, Gesuch, Beschwerde* to make *(bei* to); *Kenntnisse, Wissen* to display; *Argument* to use ◆ **er konnte seine Kritik/seinen Antrag nicht mehr ~** he couldn't get his criticism/motion in; *siehe* **angebracht.**

(d) *(inf: loswerden) Ware* to get rid of *(inf).*

(e) *(inf) siehe* **anbekommen.**

Ạnbringung *f siehe vt (b)* fixing, fastening; putting up; putting in, installing; putting on; mounting; insertion.

Ạnbruch *m, no pl* **(a)** *(geh: Anfang)* beginning; *(von Zeitalter, Epoche)* dawn(ing) ◆ **bei ~ des Tages/Morgens** at daybreak, at break of day; **bei ~ der Nacht/Dunkelheit** at nightfall. **(b)** *(Min)* seam. **(c)** *(Hunt)* rotting game. **(d)** *(Forest)* decayed *or* rotten wood.

ạnbrüllen *sep* [1] *vt (Löwe etc)* to roar at; *(Kuh, Stier)* to bellow at; *(inf: Mensch)* to shout *or* bellow at.

[2] *vi* **gegen etw ~** to shout above (the noise of) sth.

ạnbrummen *sep* [1] *vt* to growl at; *(fig)* to grumble at.

[2] *vi aux sein* **angebrummt kommen** to come roaring along *or (auf einen zu)* up.

ạnbrüten *vt sep* to begin to sit on.

Anchorman ['ɛŋkəmɛn] *m* **-s, -men** *(TV)* anchorman.

Anchovis [an'çoːvɪs, an'ʃoːvɪs] *f* **-, -** *siehe* **Anschovis.**

Ạndacht *f* **-, -en** **(a)** *no pl (das Beten)* (silent) prayer *or* worship ◆ **~ halten** to be at one's devotions; **in tiefer ~ versunken sein** to be sunk in deep devotion.

(b) *(Gottesdienst)* prayers *pl.*

(c) *(Versenkung)* rapt interest; *(Ehrfurcht)* reverence ◆ **in tiefe(r) ~ versunken sein** to be completely absorbed; **er trank den Wein mit ~** *(hum)* he drank the wine reverently; **etw voller ~ tun** to do sth reverently.

ạndächtig *adj* **(a)** *(im Gebet)* in prayer ◆ **die ~en Gläubigen** the worshippers at their devotions *or* prayers. **(b)** *(versunken)* rapt; *(ehrfürchtig)* reverent.

Ạndachts-: **~bild** *nt* devotional picture; **a~voll** *adj siehe* **andächtig (b).**

Andalusien [-iən] *nt* **-s** Andalusia.

Andalusier(in *f)* [-iɐ, -iərɪn] *m* **-s, -** Andalusian.

ạndampfen *vi sep aux sein (inf)* **angedampft kommen** *(lit, fig)* to steam *or* come steaming along *or (auf einen zu)* up; *(Mensch)* to charge *or* come charging along *or (auf einen zu)* up.

ạndauen *vt sep* to begin to digest ◆ **angedaute Speisen** partially digested food.

Ạndauer *f, no pl* **bei langer ~ des Fiebers** if the fever continues for a long time.

ạndauern *vi sep* to continue; *(anhalten)* to last ◆ **das dauert noch an** that is still going on *or* is continuing; **der Regen dauert noch an** the rain hasn't stopped; **das schöne Wetter wird nicht ~** the fine weather won't last.

ạndauernd *adj (ständig)* continuous; *(anhaltend)* continual ◆ **die bis in den frühen Morgen ~en Verhandlungen** the negotiations which went on *or* continued till early morning; **wenn du mich ~ unterbrichst** ... if you keep on interrupting me ...

Ạnden *pl* Andes *pl.*

Ạndenken *nt* **-s,** *no pl* **(a)** memory ◆ **das ~ von etw feiern** to commemorate sth; **jdn in freundlichem ~ behalten** to have fond memories of sb; **zum ~ an jdn/etw** *(an Verstorbenen etc)* in memory *or* remembrance of sb/sth; *(an Freunde/Urlaub etc)* to remind you/us *etc* of sb/sth. **(b)** *(Reise~)* souvenir *(an +acc* of); *(Erinnerungsstück)* memento, keepsake *(an +acc* from).

ạnderbar *adj* alterable, changeable ◆ **eine nicht mehr ~e Entscheidung** a decision which can no longer be changed; **der Entwurf ist jederzeit ~** the draft can be altered *or* changed at any time.

Ạnderbarkeit *f* alterability, changeability.

ạnder(e)n-: **~falls** *adv* otherwise; **~orts** *adv (geh)* elsewhere; **~tags** *adv (geh)* (on) the next *or* following day; **~teils** *adv (geh) siehe* **and(e)rerseits.**

ạndere(r, s) *indef pron* [1] *(adjektivisch)* **(a)** different; *(weiterer)* other ◆ **ein ~r Mann/~s Auto/eine ~ Frau** a different man/car/woman; *(ein weiterer etc)* another man/car/woman; **jede ~ Frau hätte** ... any other woman would have ...; **haben Sie noch ~ Fragen?** do you have any more questions?; **ich habe eine ~ Auffassung als sie** my view is different from hers, I take a different view from her; **das machen wir ein ~s Mal** we'll do that another time; **das ~ Geschlecht** the other sex; **er ist ein ~r Mensch geworden** he is a changed *or* different man; **~ Länder, ~ Sitten** different countries have different customs.

(b) *(folgend)* next, following ◆ **am ~n Tag, ~n Tags** *(liter)* (on) the next *or* following day.

[2] *(substantivisch)* **(a)** *(Ding)* **ein ~r** a different one; *(noch einer)* another one; **etwas ~s** something *or (jedes, in Fragen)* anything else; **alle ~n** all the others; **er hat noch drei ~** he has three others *or (von demselben)* more; **ja, das ist etwas ~s** yes, that's a different matter; **das ist etwas ganz ~s** that's something quite different; **hast du etwas ~s gedacht?** did you think otherwise?; **ich muß mir etwas ~s anziehen** I must put on something else *or* different; **einen Tag um den ~n/ein Mal ums ~** every single day/time; **ich habe ~s gehört** I heard differently; **nichts ~s** nothing else; **nichts ~s als** ... nothing but ...; **es blieb mir nichts ~s übrig, als selbst hinzugehen** I had no alternative but to go myself; **und vieles ~ mehr** and much more besides; **alles ~ als zufrieden** anything but pleased, far from pleased; **bist du müde? — nein, alles ~ als das** are you tired? — no, far from it *or* anything but; **unter ~m** among other things; **und ~s mehr** and more besides; **es kam eins zum ~n** one thing led to another; ... **man kann doch eines tun, ohne das ~ zu lassen** ... but you can have the best of both worlds; **sie hat sich eines ~n besonnen** she changed her mind; **von einem Tag zum ~n** overnight; **von etwas ~m sprechen** to change the subject; **eines besser als das ~** each one better than the next.

(b) *(Person)* **ein ~r/eine ~** a different person; *(noch einer)* another person; **jeder ~/kein ~r** anyone/no-one else; **es war kein ~r als** ... it was none other than ...; **niemand ~s** no-one else; **das haben mir ~ auch schon gesagt** other people *or* others have told me that too; **die ~n** the others; **alle ~n** all the others, everyone else; **jemand ~s** *or* **~r** *(S Ger)* somebody *or (jeder, in Fragen)* anybody else; **wer ~s?** who else?; **wir/ihr ~n** the rest of us/you; **sie hat einen ~n** she has someone else; **der eine oder der ~ von unseren Kollegen** one or other of our colleagues; **es gibt immer den einen oder den ~n, der faulenzt** there is always someone who is lazy; **der eine ..., der ~** ... this person ..., that person...; **einer nach dem ~n** one after the other; **eine schöner als die ~** each one more beautiful than the next; **der eine kommt, der ~ geht** as one person comes another goes; *(man geht ein und aus)* people are coming and going; **das kannst du ~n erzählen!** *(inf)* who are you kidding! *(inf).*

▼ **ạnd(e)rerseits** *adv* on the other hand.

ạnderlei *adj inv (geh)* other.

ạndermal *adv:* **ein ~** some other time.

ạndern [1] *vt* to change, to alter; *Meinung, Richtung* to change; *Kleidungsstück*

to alter ◆ **das ändert die Sache** that changes things, that puts a different complexion on things; **ich kann es nicht ~** I can't do anything about it; **das ist nicht zu ~, das läßt sich nicht (mehr) ~** nothing can be done about it; **das ändert nichts an der Tatsache, daß ...** that doesn't alter the fact that ...
[2] *vr* **(a)** to change, to alter; (*Meinung, Richtung*) to change ◆ **hier ändert sich das Wetter oft** the weather here is very changeable; **es hat sich nichts/viel geändert** nothing/a lot has changed.
(b) (*Mensch*) to change; (*sich bessern*) to change for the better ◆ **wenn sich das nicht ändert ...** if things don't improve ...

andern- *in cpds siehe* **ander(e)n-**.

anders *adv* **(a)** (*sonst*) else ◆ **jemand/niemand ~** somebody *or* anybody/nobody else; **wer/wo ~?** who/where else?; **irgendwo ~** somewhere else; **wie ~ hätte ich es machen sollen?** how else should I have done it?
(b) (*verschieden, besser, schöner*) differently; (*andersartig*) *sein, aussehen, klingen, schmecken* different (*als* to) ◆ **~ als jd denken/reagieren/aussehen** to think/react differently/look different from sb; **~ als jd** (*geh: im Gegensatz zu*) unlike sb; **es** *or* **die Sache verhält sich ganz ~** things *or* matters are quite different; **~ geartet sein als jd** to be different from *or* to sb; **~ ausgedrückt** to put it another way, in other words; **das machen wir so und nicht ~** we'll do it this way and no other; **das hat sie nicht ~ erwartet** she expected nothing else; **wie nicht ~ zu erwarten** as was to be expected; **sie ist ~ geworden** she has changed; **wie könnte es ~ sein?** how could it be otherwise?; **es geht nicht ~** there's no other way; **ich kann nicht ~** (*kann es nicht lassen*) I can't help it; (*muß leider*) I have no choice; **es sich** (*dat*) **~ überlegen** to change one's mind; **da wird mir ganz ~** I start to feel funny *or* (*übel auch*) peculiar; **ich kann auch ~** (*inf*) you'd/he'd *etc* better watch it (*inf*); **das klingt schon ~** (*inf*) now that's more like it.
(c) (*inf: anderenfalls*) otherwise, or else.

Anders-: a~artig *adj, no comp* different; **~artigkeit** *f* (*des Lebens*) different quality; **jdn wegen seiner ~artigkeit nicht verstehen** not to understand sb because he/she is different; ⚠**a~denkend** *adj attr* dissident, dissenting; ⚠**~denkende(r)** *mf decl as adj* dissident, dissenter; **die Freiheit des ~denkenden** the freedom to dissent.

anderseits *adv siehe* **and(e)rerseits**.

Anders-: a~farbig *adj* of a different colour; ⚠**a~geartet** *adj siehe* **a~artig**; **a~geschlechtlich** *adj* of the other *or* opposite sex; ⚠**a~gesinnt** *adj* of a different opinion; **a~gesinnt sein** to have a different opinion, to disagree (*in +dat* on); **~gesinnte(r)** *mf decl as adj* person of a different opinion; ⚠**a~gläubig** *adj* of a different faith *or* religion *or* creed; **a~gläubig sein** to be of *or* have a different faith *etc*; **~gläubige(r)** *mf decl as adj* person of a different faith *or* religion *or* creed; **a~(he)rum** [1] *adv* the other way round; **a~(he)rum gehen** to go the other way round; **dreh die Schraube mal a~(he)rum** turn the screw the other way; [2] *adj* (*sl: homosexuell*) **a~(he)rum sein** to be bent (*inf*); ⚠**a~lautend** *adj attr* (*form*) contrary; **a~lautende Berichte** contrary reports, reports to the contrary; **a~rum** (*inf*) *adv, adj siehe* **a~(he)rum**; **a~sprachig** *adj Literatur* foreign(-language); **die a~sprachige Minderheit** the minority who speak a different language; **a~wie** *adv* (*inf*) (*auf andere Weise*) some other way; (*unterschiedlich*) differently; **a~wo** *adv* elsewhere; **das gibt es nicht a~wo** you don't get that anywhere else; **a~woher** *adv* from elsewhere; **a~wohin** *adv* elsewhere; **ich gehe nicht gerne a~wohin** I don't like going anywhere else.

anderthalb *num* one and a half ◆ **~ Pfund Kaffee** a pound and a half of coffee; **~ Stunden** an hour and a half; **das Kind ist ~ Jahre alt** the child is eighteen months old *or* one and a half.

anderthalb-: ~fach *adj* one and a half times; **nimm die ~fache Menge/das A~fache** use half as much again; *siehe auch* **vierfach**; **~mal** *adv* one and a half times; **~mal soviel/so viele** half as much/many again.

Änderung *f* change, alteration (*an +dat, gen* in, to); (*in jdm*) change (*in +dat* in); (*an Kleidungsstück, Gebäude*) alteration (*an +dat* to); (*der Gesellschaft, der Politik etc*) change (*gen* in).

Änderungs-: ~antrag *m* (*Parl*) amendment; **~schneider** *m* tailor (who does alterations); **~vorschlag** *m* suggested change *or* alteration; **einen ~vorschlag machen** to suggest a change *or* an alteration; **~wunsch** *m* wish to make changes *or* alterations; **haben Sie ~wünsche?** are there any changes *or* alterations you would like made?

ander-: ~wärtig *adj attr* (*geh*) *siehe* **~weitig 1**; **~wärts** *adv* elsewhere, somewhere else; **~weit** *adv* (*geh*) *siehe* **~weitig 2**; **~weitig** [1] *adj attr* (*andere, weitere*) other; **~weitige Ölvorkommen** (*an anderer Stelle*) other oil strikes, oil strikes elsewhere; [2] *adv* (*anders*) otherwise; (*an anderer Stelle*) elsewhere; **~weitig vergeben/besetzt werden** to be given to/filled by someone else; **etw ~weitig verwenden** to use sth for a different purpose.

andeuten *sep* [1] *vt* (*zu verstehen geben*) to hint, to intimate (*jdm etw* sth to sb); (*kurz erwähnen*) *Problem* to mention briefly; (*Art, Mus*) to suggest; (*erkennen lassen*) to indicate ◆ **der Wald war nur mit ein paar Strichen angedeutet** a few strokes gave a suggestion of the wood.
[2] *vr* to be indicated; (*Melodie etc*) to be suggested; (*Gewitter*) to be in the offing.

Andeutung *f* (*Anspielung, Anzeichen*) hint; (*flüchtiger Hinweis*) short *or* brief mention; (*Art, Mus*) suggestion *no pl*; (*Spur*) sign, trace; (*Anflug eines Lächelns etc auch*) faint suggestion ◆ **eine ~ machen** to hint (*über +acc* at), to drop a hint (*über +acc* about); **versteckte ~en machen** to drop veiled hints; **eine Besserung zeichnet sich in ~en ab** there are vague signs of an improvement.

andeutungsweise [1] *adv* (*als Anspielung, Anzeichen*) by way of a hint; (*als flüchtiger Hinweis*) in passing ◆ **jdm ~ zu verstehen geben, daß ...** to hint to sb that ...; **man kann die Mauern noch ~ erkennen** you can still see traces of the walls.
[2] *adj attr* (*rare*) faint.

andichten *vt sep* **(a) jdm etw ~** (*inf*) to impute sth to sb; *Fähigkeiten* to credit sb with sth; **alles kann man ihm ~, aber ...** you can say what you like about him but ... **(b) jdn ~** to write a poem/poems to sb; **jdn in Sonetten ~** to write sonnets to sb.

andicken *vt sep Suppe, Soße* to thicken.

andienen *sep* (*pej*) [1] *vt* **jdm etw ~** to press sth on sb; **man diente ihm einen hohen Posten im Ausland an, um ihn loszuwerden** they tried to get rid of him by palming him off with a high position abroad.
[2] *vr* **sich jdm ~** to offer sb one's services (*als* as).

Andienungsstraße *f* (*Mot*) service road.

andiskutieren* *vt sep* to discuss briefly, to touch on.

andocken *vti sep* (*Space*) to dock.

andonnern *sep* (*inf*) [1] *vi aux sein* (*usu* **angedonnert kommen**) to come thundering *or* roaring along.
[2] *vt jdn* to shout *or* bellow at.

Andorra *nt* Andorra.

Andorraner(in *f*) *m* Andorran.

andorranisch *adj* Andorran.

Andrang *m* **-(e)s,** *no pl* **(a)** (*Zustrom, Gedränge*) crowd, crush ◆ **es herrschte großer ~** there was a great crowd *or* crush. **(b)** (*von Blut*) rush; (*von Wassermassen*) onrush.

andrängen *vi sep aux sein* to push forward; (*Menschenmenge auch*) to surge forward; (*Wassermassen*) to surge ◆ **die ~de Menschenmenge** the surging crowd.

Andreas *m* **-** Andrew.

Andreaskreuz *nt* diagonal cross; (*Rel*) St Andrew's cross.

andrehen *vt sep* **(a)** (*anstellen*) to turn on. **(b)** (*festdrehen*) to screw on; *Schraube* to screw in. **(c) jdm etw ~** (*inf*) to palm sth off on sb.

andren- *in cpds siehe* **ander(e)n-**.

andre(r, s) *adj siehe* **andere(r, s)**.

andrerseits *adv siehe* **and(e)rerseits**.

andringen *vi sep irreg aux sein* (*geh*) (*Menschen etc*) to push forward, to press (*gegen* towards); (*Wasser*) to press, to push (*gegen* against).

Androgen *nt* **-s, -e** androgen.

androgyn *adj* androgynous.

Androgyn *m* **-s, -e** androgyne.

Androgynität *f* **-,** *no pl* androgyny.

androhen *vt sep* to threaten (*jdm etw* sb with sth).

Androhung *f* threat ◆ **unter ~ der** *or* **von Gewalt** with the threat of violence; **unter der ~, etw zu tun** with the threat of doing sth; **unter ~** (*Jur*) under penalty (*von, gen* of).

Android(e) *m* **-en, -en** android.

Andruck *m* **(a)** (*Typ*) proof. **(b)** *no pl* (*Space*) g-force, gravitational force.

andrucken *sep* (*Typ*) [1] *vt* to pull a proof of.
[2] *vi* to pull proofs; (*mit dem Druck beginnen*) to start *or* begin printing.

andrücken *vt sep* **(a)** *Pflaster* to press on (*an +acc* to) ◆ **als ich kräftiger andrückte** when I pressed *or* pushed harder. **(b)** (*beschädigen*) *Obst etc* to bruise. **(c)** (*durch Druck einschalten*) *Licht etc* to switch on (by pressing a button).

Andruckexemplar *nt* (*Typ*) proof copy.

andudeln *vr sep* **sich** (*dat*) **einen ~** (*sl*) to get merry *or* tipsy (*inf*).

andünsten *vti sep* (*Cook*) to braise lightly; (*beginnen zu dünsten*) to start braising.

Äneas *m* **-** Aeneas.

an|ecken *vi sep aux sein* (*inf*) **(bei jdm/allen) ~** to rub sb/everyone up the wrong way; **mit seinen** *or* **wegen seiner Bemerkungen ist er schon oft angeeckt** his remarks have often rubbed people up the wrong way.

an|eifern *vt sep* (*S Ger, Aus*) *siehe* **anspornen**.

an|eignen *vr sep* **sich** (*dat*) **etw ~** (*etw erwerben*) to acquire sth; (*etw wegnehmen*) to appropriate sth; (*sich mit etw vertraut machen*) to learn sth; (*sich etw angewöhnen*) to pick sth up.

An|eignung *f siehe vr* acquisition; appropriation; learning; picking up ◆ **widerrechtliche ~** (*Jur*) misappropriation.

an|einander *adv* **(a)** (*gegenseitig, an sich*) **~ denken** to think of each other; **sich ~ gewöhnen** to get used to each other; **sich ~ halten** to hold on to each other; **sich ~ stoßen** (*lit*) to knock into each other; **Freude ~ haben** to enjoy each other's company.
(b) (*mit Richtungsangabe*) **~ vorüber-/vorbeigehen** to go past each other; **~ vorbeireden** to talk *or* be at cross-purposes.
(c) (*einer am anderen, zusammen*) *befestigen* together ◆ **die Häuser stehen zu dicht ~** the houses are built too close together.

an|einander- *in cpds* together; ⚠**~bauen** *vt sep* to build together; **die Häuser waren ganz dicht ~gebaut** the houses were built very close together; ⚠**~fügen** *sep* [1] *vt* to put together; [2] *vr* to join together; ⚠**~geraten*** *vi sep irreg aux sein* to come to blows (*mit* with); (*streiten*) to have words (*mit* with); ⚠**~grenzen** *vi sep* to border on each other; **in Istanbul grenzen Orient und Okzident ~** in Istanbul East and West meet; **~**⚠**halten** *vt sep irreg* to hold against each other; **~**⚠**hängen** *sep irreg* [1] *vi* **(a)** (*zusammenhängen*) to be linked (together); **(b)** (*fig: Menschen*) to be attached to each other; [2] *vt* to link together; **~**⚠**kleben** *sep* [1] *vt* to stick together; [2] *vi* to be stuck together; (*inf: unzertrennlich sein*) to be glued together (*inf*); ⚠**~koppeln** *vt sep* to couple; *Raumschiffe* to link up; ⚠**~lehnen** *vr sep* to lean on *or* against each other; ⚠**~liegen** *vi sep irreg* to be adjacent (to each other), to be next to each other; ⚠**~prallen** *vi sep aux sein* to collide; (*fig*) to clash; ⚠**~reihen** *sep* [1] *vt* to string together; [2] *vr* to be strung together; (*zeitlich: Tage etc*) to run together; **A~reihung** *f* stringing together; ⚠**~schmieden** *vt sep siehe* **zusammenschmieden**; ⚠**~schmiegen** *vr sep* to snuggle up; ⚠**~setzen** *vt sep* to put together; ⚠**~stellen** *vt sep* to put together; ⚠**~stoßen** *sep irreg* [1] *vt* to bang together; [2] *vi aux sein* to collide; (*Fahrzeuge, Köpfe auch, Menschen*) to bump into each other; (*~grenzen*) to meet.

Aneis [ɛ'ne:ɪs] *f* - Aeneid.

Anekdötchen *nt* (*hum*) little story *or* anecdote.

Anekdote *f* -, -n anecdote.

anekdotenhaft *adj* anecdotal.

anekdotisch *adj* (*Liter*) anecdotic ◆ **sein Vortrag war ~ aufgelockert** his lecture was lightened by anecdotes.

an|ekeln *vt sep* **(a)** (*anwidern*) to disgust, to nauseate ◆ **die beiden ekeln sich nur noch an** they just find each other nauseating *or* make each other sick.
(b) (*inf: beleidigen*) to be offensive to ◆ **..., ekelte er mich an** ..., he spat at me.

Anemone *f* -, -n anemone.

an|empfehlen* *vt sep or insep irreg* (*geh*) to recommend.

an|empfunden *adj* (*geh*) artificial, spurious, false ◆ **nicht echt, sondern nur ~** not genuine.

An|erbe *m* (*old*) *siehe* **Hoferbe**.

An|erbieten *nt* -s, - (*geh*) offer.

an|erbieten* *vr sep or insep irreg* (*geh*) to offer one's services ◆ **sich ~, etw zu tun** to offer to do sth.

an|erkannt [1] *ptp of* **anerkennen**.
[2] *adj* recognized; *Tatsache auch* established; *Werk* standard; *Bedeutung* accepted; *Experte* acknowledged.

an|erkanntermaßen *adv* **diese Mannschaft ist ~ besser** it is generally recognized *or* accepted *or* acknowledged that this team is better, this team is generally recognized *etc* to be better.

an|erkennen* *vt sep or insep irreg Staat, König, Rekord* to recognize; *Forderung auch, Rechnung* to accept; *Vaterschaft* to accept, to acknowledge; (*würdigen*) *Leistung, Bemühung* to appreciate; *Meinung* to respect; (*loben*) to praise ◆ **..., das muß man ~** (*zugeben*) admittedly, ..., ... you can't argue with that; (*würdigen*) ... one has to appreciate that; **als gleichwertiger Partner anerkannt sein** to be accepted as an equal partner; **ihr ~der Blick** her appreciative look.

an|erkennenswert *adj* commendable.

An|erkenntnis *nt* (*Jur*) acknowledgement.

An|erkennung *f siehe vt* recognition; acceptance; acknowledgement; appreciation; respect; praise.

An|erkennungsschreiben *nt* letter of appreciation *or* commendation.

an|erziehen* *vt insep irreg*: **jdm etw ~** (*Kindern*) to instil sth into sb; (*neuen Angestellten etc auch*) to drum sth into sb; **sich** (*dat*) **etw ~** to train oneself to do sth.

an|erzogen *adj* acquired ◆ **das ist alles ~** she *etc* has just been trained to be like that.

Anf. *abbr of* **Anfang**.

anfachen *vt sep* (*geh*) **(a)** *Glut, Feuer* to fan. **(b)** (*fig*) to arouse; *Leidenschaft auch* to inflame, to fan the flames of; *Haß auch* to inspire.

anfahren *sep irreg* [1] *vi aux sein* **(a)** (*losfahren*) to start (up) ◆ **angefahren kommen** (*herbeifahren*) (*Wagen, Fahrer*) to drive up; (*Zug*) to pull up; (*ankommen*) to arrive; **beim A~** when starting (up); **das A~ am Berg üben** to practise a hill start.
(b) (*inf*) **laß mal noch eine Runde ~** let's have another round.
[2] *vt* **(a)** (*liefern*) *Kohlen, Kartoffeln* to deliver.
(b) (*inf: spendieren*) to lay on.
(c) (*ansteuern*) *Ort* to stop *or* call at; *Hafen auch* to put in at; (*Aut*) *Kurve* to approach ◆ **die Insel wird zweimal wöchentlich von der Fähre angefahren** the ferry calls twice a week at the island.
(d) (*anstoßen*) *Passanten, Baum etc* to run into, to hit; (*fig: ausschelten*) to shout at.

Anfahrt *f* (*~sweg, ~szeit*) journey; (*Zufahrt*) approach; (*Einfahrt*) drive ◆ **„nur ~ zum Krankenhaus"** "access to hospital only".

Anfall *m* **(a)** attack; (*Wut~, epileptischer*) fit ◆ **einen ~ haben/bekommen** (*lit*) to have an attack *or* fit; (*fig inf*) to have *or* throw a fit (*inf*); **da könnte man Anfälle kriegen** (*inf*) it's enough to send *or* drive you round the bend (*inf*); **in einem ~ von** (*fig*) in a fit of.
(b) (*Ertrag, Nebenprodukte*) yield (*an +dat* of); (*von Zinsen auch*) accrual.
(c) (*von Reparaturen, Kosten*) amount (*an +dat* of); (*form: Anhäufung*) accumulation ◆ **bei ~ von Reparaturen** if repairs are necessary.

anfallen *sep irreg* [1] *vt* **(a)** (*überfallen*) to attack; (*Sittenstrolch etc*) to assault.
(b) (*liter*) **Heimweh/Sehnsucht fiel ihn an** he was assailed by homesickness/ filled with longing.
[2] *vi aux sein* (*sich ergeben*) to arise; (*Zinsen*) to accrue; (*Nebenprodukte*) to be obtained; (*sich anhäufen*) to accumulate ◆ **die ~den Kosten/Reparaturen/ Probleme** the costs/repairs/problems incurred; **die ~de Arbeit** the work which comes up.

anfällig *adj* (*nicht widerstandsfähig*) delicate; *Motor, Maschine* temperamental ◆ **gegen** *or* **für etw/eine Krankheit ~ sein** to be susceptible to sth/prone to an illness.

Anfälligkeit *f siehe adj* delicateness; temperamental nature; susceptibility; proneness.

Anfang *m* -(e)s, **Anfänge** (*Beginn*) beginning, start; (*erster Teil*) beginning; (*Ursprung*) beginnings *pl*, origin ◆ **zu** *or* **am ~** to start with; (*anfänglich*) at first; **gleich zu ~ darauf hinweisen, daß ...** to mention right at the beginning *or* outset that ...; **am ~ schuf Gott Himmel und Erde** in the beginning God created the heaven(s) and the earth; **im ~ war das Wort** (*Bibl*) in the beginning was the Word; **~ Fünfzig** in one's early fifties; **~ Juni/1978** *etc* at the beginning of June/1978 *etc*; **von ~ an** (right) from the beginning *or* start; **von ~ bis Ende** from start to finish; **den ~ machen** to start *or* begin; (*den ersten Schritt tun*) to make the first move; **einen neuen ~ machen** to make a new start; (*im Leben*) to turn over a new leaf; **ein ~ ist gemacht** it's a start; **seinen ~ nehmen** (*geh*) to commence; **aller ~ ist schwer** (*Prov*) the first step is always the most difficult; **aus kleinen/bescheidenen Anfängen** from small/ humble beginnings; **der ~ vom Ende** the beginning of the end.

anfangen *sep irreg* [1] *vt* **(a)** (*beginnen*) *Arbeit, Brief, Gespräch,* (*inf: anbrauchen*) *neue Tube etc* to start, to begin; *Streit, Verhältnis, Fabrik* to start.
(b) (*anstellen, machen*) to do ◆ **das mußt du anders ~** you'll have to go about it differently; **was soll ich damit ~?** what am I supposed to do with that?; (*was nützt mir das?*) what's the use of that?; **damit kann ich nichts ~** (*nützt mir nichts*) that's no good to me; (*verstehe ich nicht*) it doesn't mean a thing to me; **nichts mit sich/jdm anzufangen wissen** not to know what to do with oneself/sb; **mit dir ist heute (aber) gar nichts anzufangen!** you're no fun at all today!
[2] *vi* to begin, to start ◆ **wer fängt an?** who's going to start *or* begin?; **fang (du) an!** (you) begin *or* start!; **ich habe schon angefangen** I've already started; **du hast angefangen!** you started!; (*bei Streit*) you started it!; **es fing zu regnen an** *or* **an zu regnen** it started raining *or* to rain; **das fängt ja schön** *or* **heiter an!** (*iro*) that's a good start!; **jetzt fängt das Leben erst an** life is only just beginning; **fang nicht wieder davon** *or* **damit an!** don't start all that again!, don't bring all that up again!; **mit etw ~** to start sth; **klein/unten ~** to start small/at the bottom; **er hat als kleiner Handwerker angefangen** he started out as a small-time tradesman; **bei einer Firma ~** to start with a firm *or* working for a firm.

Anfänger(in *f*) *m* -s, - beginner; (*Neuling*) novice; (*Aut*) learner; (*inf: Nichtskönner*) amateur (*pej*) ◆ **du ~!** (*inf*) you amateur; **sie ist keine ~in mehr** (*hum*) she's certainly no beginner.

Anfänger-: **~kurs(us)** *m* beginners' course; **~übung** *f* (*Univ*) introductory course.

anfänglich [1] *adj attr* initial.
[2] *adv* at first, initially.

anfangs [1] *adv* at first, initially ◆ **wie ich schon ~ erwähnte** as I mentioned at the beginning; **gleich ~ auf etw** (*acc*) **hinweisen** to mention sth right at the beginning *or* outset.
[2] *prep +gen* **~ der zwanziger Jahre/des Monats** in the early twenties/at the beginning of the month.

Anfangs- *in cpds* initial; **~buchstabe** *m* first letter; **kleine/große ~buchstaben** small/large *or* capital initials; **~gehalt** *nt* initial *or* starting salary; **~geschwindigkeit** *f* starting speed; (*esp Phys*) initial velocity; **~gründe** *pl* rudiments *pl*, elements *pl*; **~kapital** *nt* starting capital; **~kurs** *m* (*Fin*) opening price; **~silbe** *f* first *or* initial syllable; **~stadium** *nt* initial stage; **im ~stadium dieser Krankheit/dieses Projekts** in the initial stages of this illness/project; **meine Versuche sind schon im ~stadium steckengeblieben** my attempts never really got off the ground; **~unterricht** *m* first lessons *pl*; **~zeit** *f* starting time.

anfassen *sep* [1] *vt* **(a)** (*berühren*) to touch ◆ **faß mal meinen Kopf an** just feel my head.
(b) (*bei der Hand nehmen*) **jdn ~** to take sb's hand *or* sb by the hand; **sich** *or* **einander** (*geh*) **~** to take each other by the hand; **faßt euch an!** hold hands!; **angefaßt gehen** to walk holding hands.
(c) (*fig*) (*anpacken*) *Problem* to tackle, to go about; (*behandeln*) *Menschen* to treat.
(d) (*geh: befallen*) to seize.
[2] *vi* **(a)** (*berühren*) to feel ◆ **nicht ~!** don't touch!
(b) (*mithelfen*) **mit ~, (mit) ~ helfen** to give a hand.
(c) (*fig*) **zum A~** (*Mensch, Sache*) accessible; (*Mensch auch*) approachable; **Politik zum A~** grassroots politics.
[3] *vr* (*sich anfühlen*) to feel ◆ **es faßt sich weich an** it feels *or* is soft (to the touch).

anfauchen *vt sep* (*Katze*) to spit at; (*fig inf*) to snap at.

anfaulen *vi sep aux sein* to begin to go bad; (*Holz*) to start rotting ◆ **angefault** half-rotten.

anfechtbar *adj* contestable.

Anfechtbarkeit *f* contestability ◆ **wegen der ~ seiner Argumentation** because his argument is/was contestable.

anfechten *vt sep irreg* **(a)** (*nicht anerkennen*) to contest; *Meinung, Aussage auch* to challenge; *Urteil, Entscheidung* to appeal against; *Vertrag* to dispute; *Ehe* to contest the validity of. **(b)** (*beunruhigen*) to trouble; (*in Versuchung bringen*) to tempt, to lead into temptation ◆ **das ficht mich gar nicht an** that doesn't concern me in the slightest. **(c)** (*obs: einfallen, überkommen*) **was ficht/focht dich an, das zu tun?** what possessed you to do that?

Anfechtung *f* **(a)** *siehe vt* (*a*) contesting; challenging; appeal (*gen* against); disputing; (*von Ehe*) action for nullification *or* annulment. **(b)** (*Versuchung*) temptation; (*Selbstzweifel*) doubt.

Anfechtungsklage *f* (*Jur*) (*zu Ehescheidung*) action for nullification *or* annulment; (*zu Testament*) action to set aside a/the will; (*zu Patent*) opposition proceedings.

anfegen *vi sep aux sein* (*inf*) **angefegt kommen** to come belting along *or* (*auf* *einen zu)* up *(inf)*.

anfeinden *vt sep* to treat with hostility.

Anfeindung *f* hostility ◆ **trotz aller ~en** although he had aroused so much animosity.

anfertigen *vt sep* to make; *Arznei* to make up; *Schriftstück* to draw up; *Hausaufgaben, Protokoll* to do ◆ **jdm etw ~** to make sth for sb; **sich** *(dat)* **einen Anzug** *etc* **~ lassen** to have a suit *etc* made.

Anfertigung *f siehe vt* making; making up; doing ◆ **die ~ dieser Übersetzung/der Arznei hat eine halbe Stunde gedauert** it took half an hour to do the translation/to make up the prescription.

Anfertigungskosten *pl* production costs *pl* ◆ **die ~ eines Smokings** the cost of making a dinner jacket/having a dinner jacket made.

anfeuchten *vt sep* to moisten; *Schwamm, Lippen auch* to wet; *Bügelwäsche auch* to damp.

anfeuern *vt sep Ofen* to light; *(Ind)* to fire; *(fig: ermutigen)* to spur on.

Anfeuerung *f (fig)* spurring on.

Anfeuerungsruf *m* cheer; *(esp Pol)* chant; *(Anfeuerungswort)* shout of encouragement.

anfinden *vr sep irreg* to be found, to turn up (again).

anfixen *vt sep (sl)* **jdn ~** to give sb his/her first fix *(sl)*; *(abhängig machen)* to get sb hooked (on drugs) *(sl)*.

anflegeln *vt sep (inf)* to speak rudely to ◆ **ich lasse mich doch nicht von dir ~!** I'm not prepared to have you swearing at me!

anflehen *vt sep* to beseech, to implore *(um* for) ◆ **ich flehe dich an, tu das nicht!** I beg you, don't!

anfletschen *vt sep* to bare one's teeth at.

anfliegen *sep irreg* [1] *vi aux sein (auch* **angeflogen kommen**) *(Flugzeug)* to come in to land; *(Vogel, Geschoß, fig geh: Pferd, Fuhrwerk, Reiter)* to come flying up.
[2] *vt* **(a)** *(Flugzeug) Flughafen, Piste, (Mil) Stellung* to approach; *(landen)* to land *(in/auf* in/on) ◆ **diese Fluggesellschaft fliegt Bali an** this airline flies to Bali *or* operates a service to Bali. **(b)** *(geh: befallen)* to overcome.

anflitzen *vi sep aux sein (inf) (usu* **angeflitzt kommen**) to come racing along *or (auf einen zu)* up *(inf)*.

Anflug *m* **(a)** *(Flugweg)* flight; *(das Heranfliegen)* approach ◆ **wir befinden uns im ~ auf Paris** we are now approaching Paris. **(b)** *(Spur)* trace; *(fig: Hauch auch)* hint.

Anflug-: ~weg *m* landing path; **~zeit** *f (Zeitraum)* descent; *(Zeitpunkt)* time of starting a/the descent.

anflunkern *vt sep (inf)* to tell fibs/a fib to.

anfordern *vt sep* to request, to ask for.

Anforderung *f* **(a)** *no pl (das Anfordern)* request *(gen, von* for) ◆ **bei der ~ von Ersatzteilen** when requesting spare parts.
(b) *(Anspruch)* requirement; *(Belastung)* demand ◆ **große ~en an jdn/etw stellen** to make great demands on sb/sth; **hohe/zu hohe ~en stellen** to demand a lot/too much *(an +acc* of); **den ~en im Beruf/in der Schule gewachsen sein** to be able to meet the demands of one's job/of school.
(c) ~en *pl (Niveau)* standards *pl*.

Anforderungsprofil *nt (für Personen)* job description; *(für Software etc)* product profile.

▼ **Anfrage** *f (auch Comput)* inquiry; *(Parl)* question ◆ **kleine ~** *Parliamentary question dealt with in writing;* **große ~** *Parliamentary question dealt with at a meeting of the Lower House.*

anfragen *vi sep* to inquire *(bei jdm* of sb), to ask *(bei jdm* sb) ◆ **um Erlaubnis/Genehmigung ~** to ask for permission/approval.

anfressen *vt sep irreg* **(a)** *(Maus)* to nibble at; *(Vogel)* to peck (at) ◆ **sich** *(dat)* **einen Bauch~** *(sl)* to get a paunch through overeating. **(b)** *(zersetzen)* to eat away, to erode.

anfreunden *vr sep* to make *or* become friends ◆ **sich mit etw ~** *(fig)* to get to like sth; *mit Pop-Musik etc* to acquire a taste for sth.

anfrieren *sep irreg* [1] *vi aux sein (leicht gefrieren)* to start to freeze; *(Pflanze)* to get a touch of frost; *(haften bleiben)* to freeze on *(an +acc* -to); *(fig: Mensch)* to freeze stiff.
[2] *vr* **ich habe mir die Hände angefroren** my hands are frozen.

anfügen *vt sep* to add.

Anfügung *f* addition; *(zu einem Buch)* addendum.

anfühlen *sep* [1] *vt* to feel.
[2] *vr* to feel ◆ **sich glatt/weich** *etc* **~** to feel smooth/soft *etc*, to be smooth/soft *etc* to the touch.

Anfuhr *f* **-, -en** transport(ation).

anführbar *adj* quotable.

anführen *vt sep* **(a)** *(vorangehen, befehligen)* to lead.
(b) *(zitieren)* to quote, to cite; *Tatsachen, Beispiel, Einzelheiten auch* to give; *Umstand* to cite, to refer to; *Grund, Beweis* to give, to offer; *(benennen) jdn* to name, to cite.
(c) *(Typ)* to indicate *or* mark with (opening) quotation marks *or* inverted commas.
(d) jdn ~ *(inf)* to have sb on *(inf)*, to take sb for a ride *(inf)*; **der läßt sich leicht ~** he's easily taken in *or* had on *(inf)*.

Anführer *m (Führer)* leader; *(pej: Anstifter)* ringleader.

Anführung *f* **(a)** *(das Vorangehen)* leadership; *(Befehligung auch)* command ◆ **unter ~ von ...** under the leadership of ..., led by ... **(b)** *(das Anführen) siehe vt (b)* quotation, citation; giving; citing, referring to; giving, offering; naming; citing; *(Zitat)* quotation ◆ **die ~ von Zitaten/Einzelheiten** giving quotations/details.

Anführungs-: ~strich *m*, **~zeichen** *nt* quotation *or* quote mark, inverted comma; **in ~strichen** *or* **~zeichen** in inverted commas, in quotation marks, in quotes; **~striche** *or* **~zeichen unten/oben** quote/unquote; **das habe ich in ~zeichen gesagt** I was saying that in inverted commas.

anfüllen *vt sep* to fill (up) ◆ **mit etw angefüllt sein** to be full of sth, to be filled with sth.

anfunkeln *vt sep* to flash at.

anfuttern *vr sep (inf)* **sich** *(dat)* **einen Bauch~** to acquire *or* develop a paunch.

Angabe ['anga:-] *f* **-, -n** **(a)** *usu pl (Aussage)* statement; *(Anweisung)* instruction; *(Zahl, Detail)* detail ◆ **~n über etw** *(acc)* **machen** to give details about sth; **laut ~n** *(+gen)* according to; **nach Ihren eigenen ~n** by your own account; **nach ~n des Zeugen** according to (the testimony of) the witness; **~n zur Person** *(form)* personal details *or* particulars.
(b) *(Nennung)* giving ◆ **wir bitten um ~ der Einzelheiten/Preise** please give *or* quote details/prices; **er ist ohne ~ seiner neuen Adresse verzogen** he moved without informing anyone of *or* telling anyone his new address; **ohne ~ von Gründen** without giving any reasons; **vergessen Sie nicht die ~ des Datums auf dem Brief** don't forget to give *or* put the date on the letter.
(c) *no pl (inf: Prahlerei)* showing-off; *(Reden auch)* bragging, boasting.
(d) *(Sport: Aufschlag)* service, serve ◆ **wer hat ~?** whose service *or* serve is it?, whose turn is it to serve?

angaffen ['anga-] *vt sep (pej)* to gape at.

angähnen ['angɛ:-] *vt sep* to yawn at.

angaloppieren* ['anga-] *vi sep aux sein* to gallop up ◆ **angaloppiert kommen** to come galloping up.

angängig ['angɛ-] *adj (form)* feasible; *(erlaubt auch)* permissible.

angeben ['ange:-] *sep irreg* [1] *vt* **(a)** *(nennen)* to give; *(als Zeugen)* to name, to cite; *(schriftlich)* to indicate; *(erklären)* to explain; *(beim Zoll)* to declare; *(anzeigen) Preis, Temperatur etc* to indicate; *(aussagen)* to state; *(behaupten)* to maintain.
(b) *(bestimmen) Tempo, Kurs* to set; *(Mus) Tempo, Note* to give ◆ **den Takt ~** *(klopfen)* to beat time; *siehe* **Ton**[2].
(c) *(dated: anzeigen)* to report *(bei* to).
[2] *vi* **(a)** *(prahlen)* to show off, to pose *(inf)*; *(durch Reden auch)* to boast, to brag *(mit* about).
(b) *(Tennis etc)* to serve.
(c) *(Cards)* to deal.

Angeber(in *f***)** ['ange:-] *m* **-s, -** *(Prahler)* show-off, poser *(inf)*; *(durch Reden auch)* boaster.

Angeberei [ange:-] *f (inf)* **(a)** *no pl (Prahlerei)* showing-off, posing *(inf) (mit* about); *(verbal auch)* boasting, bragging *(mit* about). **(b)** *usu pl (Äußerung)* boast.

angeberisch ['ange:-] *adj Reden* boastful; *Aussehen, Benehmen, Tonfall* pretentious, posy *(inf)*.

Angebertum ['ange:-] *nt, no pl (in äußerer Erscheinung)* ostentation; *(durch Reden)* boastfulness; *(in Benehmen)* pretension.

Angebetete(r) ['angə-] *mf decl as adj (hum, geh) (verehrter Mensch)* idol; *(Geliebte(r))* beloved.

Angebinde ['angə-] *nt* **-s, -** *(dated geh)* gift, present.

angeblich ['ange:-] [1] *adj attr* so-called, alleged.
[2] *adv* supposedly, allegedly ◆ **er ist ~ Musiker** he says he's a musician.

angeboren ['angə-] *adj* innate, inherent; *(Med, fig inf)* congenital *(bei* to) ◆ **an seine Faulheit mußt du dich gewöhnen, die ist ~** *(inf)* you'll have to get used to his laziness, he was born that way.

▼ **Angebot** ['angə-] *nt* **(a)** *(Anerbieten, angebotener Preis)* offer; *(bei Auktion)* bid; *(Comm: Offerte auch)* tender *(über +acc, für* for); *(Kostenvoranschlag auch)* quote ◆ **im ~** *(preisgünstig)* on special offer. **(b)** *no pl (Comm, Fin)* supply *(an +dat, von* of); *(inf: Sonder~)* special offer ◆ **~ und Nachfrage** supply and demand.

Angebots- ['angə-]: **~lücke** *f* gap in the market; **~preis** *m* asking price; **~überhang** *m* surplus, supply.

angebracht ['angə-] [1] *ptp of* **anbringen**.
[2] *adj* appropriate; *(sinnvoll)* reasonable ◆ **schlecht ~** uncalled-for.

angebrannt ['angə-] [1] *ptp of* **anbrennen**.
[2] *adj* burnt ◆ **~ riechen/schmecken** to smell/taste burnt; **es riecht hier so ~** there's a smell of burning here.

angebrochen ['angə-] *adj Packung, Flasche* open(ed) ◆ **wieviel ist von den ~en hundert Mark übrig?** how much is left from the 100 marks we'd started using?; **ein ~er Abend/Nachmittag/Urlaub** *(hum)* the rest of an evening/afternoon/a holiday; **das Parken kostet für jede ~e Stunde eine Mark** parking costs one mark for every hour or part of an hour.

angebunden ['angə-] *adj (beschäftigt)* tied (down) ◆ **kurz ~ sein** *(inf)* to be abrupt *or* curt *or* brusque.

angedeihen* ['angə-] *vt sep irreg* **jdm etw ~ lassen** *(geh)* to provide sb with sth.

Angedenken ['angə-] *nt* **-s,** *no pl (geh)* remembrance ◆ **mein Großvater seligen ~s** my late lamented grandfather.

angeduselt ['angə-] *adj (inf)* tipsy, merry *(inf)*.

ange|ekelt ['angə-] *adj* disgusted.

angeführt ['angə-] *adj siehe* **angegeben**.

angegangen ['angə-] *adj (inf)* **~ sein** to have gone off; **~e Lebensmittel** food which has gone off.

angegeben ['angə-] *adj* **am ~en Ort** loco citato.

angegilbt ['angə-] *adj* yellowed.

angegossen ['angə-] *adj* **wie ~ sitzen** *or* **passen** to fit like a glove.

angegraut ['angə-] *adj* grey; *Schläfen, Haar auch* greying.

➤ SPRACHE AKTIV: **Anfrage** → 47.1 **Angebot** → 46.6

angegriffen ['angə-] [1] *ptp of* **angreifen.**
[2] *adj Gesundheit* weakened; *Mensch, Aussehen* frail; (*erschöpft*) exhausted; (*nervlich*) strained ◆ **sie ist nervlich/gesundheitlich immer noch ~** her nerves are still strained/health is still weakened.
angehalten ['angə-] *adj* **~ sein, etw zu tun/unterlassen** to be required *or* obliged to do/refrain from doing sth; **zu Pünktlichkeit ~ sein** to be required to be punctual.
angehaucht ['angə-] *adj* **links/rechts ~ sein** to have *or* show left-/right-wing tendencies *or* leanings.
angeheiratet ['angə-] *adj* related by marriage ◆ **ein ~er Cousin** a cousin by marriage.
angeheitert ['angə-] *adj* (*inf*) merry (*inf*), tipsy.
angehen ['ange:-] *sep irreg* [1] *vi aux sein* **(a)** (*inf: beginnen*) (*Schule, Theater etc*) to start; (*Feuer*) to start burning, to catch; (*Radio*) to come on; (*Licht*) to come *or* go on.
(b) (*entgegentreten*) **gegen jdn ~** to fight sb, to tackle sb; **gegen etw ~** to fight sth; *gegen Flammen, Hochwasser* to fight sth back, to combat sth; *gegen Mißstände, Zustände* to take measures against sth; **dagegen muß man ~** something must be done about it.
(c) *siehe* **angegangen.**
[2] *vt* **(a)** *aux haben or* (*S Ger*) *sein* (*anpacken*) *Aufgabe, Schwierigkeiten, Hindernis* to tackle; *Gegner auch* to attack; *Kurve* to take.
(b) *aux haben or* (*S Ger*) *sein* (*bitten*) to ask (*jdn um etw* sb for sth).
(c) *aux sein* (*in bezug auf Personen*), *aux haben* (*in bezug auf Sachen*) (*betreffen*) to concern ◆ **was mich angeht** for my part; **was geht das ihn an?** (*inf*) what's that got to do with him?; **das geht ihn gar nichts** *or* **einen Dreck** *or* **einen feuchten Staub an** (*inf*) that's none of his business, that's got nothing *or* damn all (*inf*) to do with him.
[3] *vi impers aux sein* **das geht nicht/keinesfalls an** that won't do, that's not on, that's quite out of the question.
angehend ['ange:-] *adj Musiker, Künstler* budding; *Lehrer, Ehemann, Vater* prospective ◆ **mit 16 ist sie jetzt schon eine ~e junge Dame** at 16 she's rapidly becoming *or* is almost a young lady; **er ist ein ~er Sechziger** he's approaching sixty.
angehören* ['angə-] *vi sep +dat* to belong to; (*einer Partei, einer Familie auch*) to be a member of ◆ **jdm/einander ~** (*liter*) to belong to sb/one another *or* each other.
angehörig ['angə-] *adj* belonging (*dat* to) ◆ **keiner Partei ~e Bürger** citizens who do not belong to any party.
Angehörige(r) ['angə-] *mf decl as adj* **(a)** (*Mitglied*) member. **(b)** (*Familien~*) relative, relation ◆ **der nächste ~** the next of kin.
Angeklagte(r) ['angə-] *mf decl as adj* accused, defendant.
angeknackst ['angə-] *adj* (*inf*) *Mensch* (*seelisch*) uptight (*inf*); *Selbstvertrauen, Selbstbewußtsein* weakened ◆ **er/seine Gesundheit ist ~** he is in bad shape *or* a bad way; **sie ist noch immer etwas ~** she still hasn't got over it yet.
angekränkelt ['angə-] *adj* (*geh*) sickly, frail, ailing ◆ **vom Geist ~** afflicted by *or* suffering from overintellectualizing.
angekratzt ['angə-] *adj* (*inf*) seedy (*inf*), the worse for wear.
Angel *f* **-, -n (a)** (*Tür~, Fenster~*) hinge ◆ **etw aus den ~n heben** (*lit*) to lift sth off its hinges; (*fig*) to revolutionize sth completely; **die Welt aus den ~n heben** (*fig*) to turn the world upside down. **(b)** (*Fischfanggerät*) (fishing) rod and line, fishing pole (*US*); (*zum Schwimmenlernen*) swimming harness ◆ **die ~ auswerfen** to cast (the line); **jdm an die ~ gehen** (*fig*) to fall for *or* swallow sb's line.
angelegen ['angə-] *adj* **sich** (*dat*) **etw ~ sein lassen** (*form*) to concern oneself with sth.
Angelegenheit ['angə-] *f* matter; (*politisch, persönlich*) affair; (*Aufgabe*) concern ◆ **das ist meine/nicht meine ~** that's my/not my concern *or* business; **sich um seine eigenen ~en kümmern** to mind one's own business; **in einer dienstlichen ~** on official business; **in eigener ~** on a private *or* personal matter.
angelegentlich ['angə-] *adj* (*geh*) *Bitte, Frage* pressing, insistent; (*dringend*) pressing, urgent; *Bemühung* enthusiastic; *Empfehlung* warm, eager ◆ **sich ~ über jdn erkundigen** to ask particularly about sb.
angelegt ['angə-] *adj* calculated (*auf +acc* for).
angelernt ['angə-] *adj Arbeiter* semi-skilled ◆ **der Lohn für A~e** the wage for semi-skilled workers.
Angel-: ~gerät *nt* fishing tackle *no pl*; **~haken** *m* fish-hook; **~leine** *f* fishing line.
angeln [1] *vi* **(a)** to angle, to fish ◆ **~ gehen** to go angling *or* fishing; **nach etw** *or* **auf etw** (*acc*) (*form*) **~** (*lit*) to fish for sth; **nach Komplimenten/Lob** *etc* **~** to fish *or* angle for compliments/praise.
(b) (*zu greifen versuchen, hervorziehen*) to fish ◆ **nach etw ~** to fish (around) for sth.
[2] *vt Fisch* to fish for; (*fangen*) to catch ◆ **sich** (*dat*) **einen Mann ~** (*inf*) to catch (oneself) a man; **den werde ich mir ~** (*inf: vornehmen*) I'll give him a piece of my mind.
Angeln *pl* (*Hist*) Angles *pl.*
angeloben* ['angə-] *vt sep* **(a)** (*liter*) **jdm etw ~** to swear sth to sb. **(b)** (*Aus: vereidigen*) to swear in.
Angel-: ~punkt *m* crucial *or* central point; (*Frage*) key *or* central issue; **~rute** *f* fishing rod.
Angelsachse *m decl as adj* Anglo-Saxon.
angelsächsisch *adj* Anglo-Saxon.
Angel-: ~schein *m* fishing permit; **~schnur** *f* fishing line; **~sport** *m* angling, fishing; **a~weit** *adv siehe* **sperrangelweit.**
angemessen ['angə-] *adj* (*passend, entsprechend*) appropriate (*dat* to, for); (*adäquat*) adequate (*dat* for); *Preis* reasonable, fair ◆ **eine der Leistung ~e Bezahlung** payment commensurate with performance.
Angemessenheit ['angə-] *f siehe adj* appropriateness; adequacy; fairness, reasonableness.
angenehm ['angə-] *adj* pleasant, agreeable ◆ **das wäre mir sehr ~** I should be very *or* most grateful, I should greatly appreciate it; **es ist mir gar nicht ~, wenn ich früh aufstehen muß/daß er mich besuchen will** I don't like getting up early/the idea of him wanting to visit me; **ist es Ihnen so ~?** is that all right for you?, is it all right like that for you?; **wenn Ihnen das ~er ist** if you prefer; **~e Ruhe/Reise!** *etc* have a good *or* pleasant rest/journey *etc*; **(sehr) ~!** (*form*) delighted (to meet you); **das A~e mit dem Nützlichen verbinden** to combine business with pleasure.
▼ **angenommen** ['angə-] [1] *adj* assumed; *Name auch, Kind* adopted.
[2] *conj* assuming.
⚠ **angepaßt** ['angə-] *adj* conformist.
⚠ **Angepaßtheit** ['angə-] *f* conformism.
Anger *m* **-s, - ** (*dial*) **(a)** (*Dorf~*) village green; (*old: Wiese*) pasture, meadow. **(b)** (*Schind~*) knacker's yard.
Angerdorf *nt* village built around a village green.
angeregt ['angə-] *adj* lively, animated ◆ **~ diskutieren** to have a lively *or* an animated discussion.
Angeregtheit ['angə-] *f* liveliness, animation.
angereichert ['angə-] [1] *ptp of* **anreichern.**
[2] *adj Uran* enriched.
angesäuselt ['angə-] *adj* (*inf*) tipsy, merry (*inf*).
angeschissen ['angə-] *adj* (*sl*) buggered (*sl*) ◆ **~ sein** to be buggered (*sl*) *or* in dead shtuck (*sl*).
angeschlagen ['angə-] *adj* (*inf*) *Mensch, Aussehen, Nerven* shattered (*inf*); *Gesundheit* poor (*inf*); (*betrunken*) sloshed (*inf*) ◆ **von etw ~ sein** to be shattered by sth (*inf*).
angeschlossen ['angə-] *adj* affiliated (*dat* to *or* (*US*) with), associated (*dat* with).
angeschmiert ['angə-] *adj pred* (*inf*) in trouble, in dead shtuck (*sl*) ◆ **mit dem/der Waschmaschine bist du ganz schön ~** he/the washing machine is not all he/it is cracked up to be (*inf*); **der/die A~e sein** to have been had (*inf*).
angeschmutzt ['angə-] *adj* soiled; (*Comm*) shop-soiled.
angeschossen ['angə-] *adj* (*inf*) **wie ein A~er** like a scalded cat (*inf*); **wie ~** like a chicken with no head (*inf*).
angeschrieben ['angə-] *adj* (*inf*) **bei jdm gut/schlecht ~ sein** to be in sb's good/bad books, to be well in/not very well in with sb (*inf*).
Angeschuldigte(r) ['angə-] *mf decl as adj* suspect.
angesehen ['angə-] [1] *ptp of* **ansehen.**
[2] *adj* respected.
angesessen ['angə-] *adj siehe* **eingesessen.**
Angesicht ['angə-] *nt* **-(e)s, -er** *or* (*Aus*) **-e** (*geh*) face, countenance (*liter*) ◆ **von ~ zu ~** face to face; **jdn von ~ sehen** to see sb face to face; **jdn von ~ kennen** to know sb by sight; **im ~** *+gen* (*fig*) in the face of.
angesichts ['angə-] *prep +gen* in the face of; (*im Hinblick auf*) in view of ◆ **~ des Todes** in the face of death; **~ des Sternenhimmels kommt sich der Mensch winzig und nichtig vor** in contrast to the starry sky man seems minute and insignificant.
angesoffen ['angə-] *adj* (*sl*) pissed (*sl*), sloshed (*inf*) ◆ **~** *or* **in ~em Zustand Auto fahren** to drive (a car) (when) sloshed (*inf*).
angespannt ['angə-] *adj* **(a)** (*angestrengt*) *Nerven* tense, strained; *Aufmerksamkeit* close, keen ◆ **aufs höchste ~ sein** to be very *or* highly tense; **~ zuhören** to listen attentively *or* closely. **(b)** (*bedrohlich*) *politische Lage* tense, strained; (*Comm*) *Markt, Lage* tight, overstretched.
Angest. *abbr of* **Angestellte(r).**
angestammt ['angə-] *adj* (*überkommen*) traditional; (*ererbt*) *Rechte* hereditary, ancestral; *Besitz* inherited.
angestellt ['angə-] *adj pred* **~ sein** to be an employee *or* on the staff (*bei* of); **er ist bei Collins ~** he works for Collins; **fest ~ sein** to be on the permanent staff; **ich bin nicht beamtet, sondern nur ~** I don't have permanent tenure in my job.
Angestellte(r) ['angə-] *mf decl as adj* (salaried) employee; (*Büro~*) office-worker, white-collar worker; (*Behörden~*) public employee (without tenure).
Angestellten- ['angə-]: **~gewerkschaft** *f* white-collar union; **~verhältnis** *nt* employment (without permanent tenure); **im ~verhältnis** in non-tenured employment; **~versicherung** *f* (salaried) employees' insurance.
angestochen ['angə-] *adj* (*inf*) **wie ~** like a stuck pig (*inf*).
angestrengt ['angə-] *adj Gesicht* strained; *Arbeiten, Denken* hard ◆ **~ diskutieren** to have an intense discussion.
angetan ['angətan] [1] *ptp of* **antun.**
[2] *adj pred* **(a) von jdm/etw ~ sein** to be taken with sb/sth; **es jdm ~ haben** to have made quite an impression on sb; **das Mädchen hat es ihm ~** he has fallen for that girl.
(b) danach *or* **dazu ~ sein, etw zu tun** (*geh*) to be suitable for doing sth; (*Wesen, Atmosphäre, Benehmen etc*) to be apt *or* calculated to do sth.
Angetraute(r) ['angə-] *mf decl as adj* (*hum*) spouse, better half (*hum*).
angetrunken ['angə-] *adj Mensch, Zustand* inebriated, intoxicated.

➤ SPRACHE AKTIV: angenommen → 28.1

angewandt ['angə-] *adj attr Wissenschaft etc* applied.

angewiesen ['angə-] *adj* **auf jdn/etw ~ sein** to have to rely on sb/sth, to be dependent on sb/sth; **auf sich selbst ~ sein** to have to fend for oneself; (*Kind*) to be left to one's own devices; **in dieser Arbeit war er auf sich selbst und sein eigenes Wissen ~** in this work he had to rely on himself and his own knowledge; **darauf bin ich nicht ~** I can get along without it, I don't need it; **ich bin selbst auf jede Mark ~** I need every mark myself.

angewöhnen* ['angə-] *vt sep* **jdm etw ~** to get sb used to sth, to accustom sb to sth; **sich** (*dat*) **etw ~ /es sich** (*dat*) **~, etw zu tun** to get into the habit of sth/of doing sth.

Angewohnheit ['angə-] *f* habit.

angezecht ['angə-] *adj* (*inf*) tight (*inf*), pickled (*inf*).

angezeigt ['angə-] *adj* (*form*) advisable; (*angebracht*) appropriate.

angezogen ['angə-] *adj* dressed ◆ **dieser Mantel sieht ~er aus** this coat looks dressier *or* more dressy.

angiften ['angɪ-] *vt sep* (*pej inf*) to snap at, to let fly at.

Angina [aŋ'gi:na] *f* **-, Anginen** (*Med*) angina ◆ **~ pectoris** angina (pectoris).

angleichen ['angl-] *sep irreg* [1] *vt* to bring into line, to align (*dat, an +acc* with).
[2] *vr* (*gegenseitig: Kulturen, Geschlechter, Methoden*) to grow closer together ◆ **sich jdm/einer Sache ~** (*einseitig*) to become like sb/sth; **die beiden haben sich (aneinander) angeglichen** the two of them have become more alike.

Angleichung *f* **(a)** *siehe vt* alignment (*an +acc* with). **(b)** *siehe vr* **die zunehmende ~ der Kulturen** the increasing similarity between the cultures; **die ~ Deutschlands an Amerika** Germany's growing similarity with America.

Angler(in *f*) *m* **-s, -** angler.

angliedern ['angl-] *vt sep* (*Verein, Partei*) to affiliate (*dat, an +acc* to *or* (*US*) with); *Land* to annexe (*dat, an +acc* to).

Angliederung *f siehe vt* affiliation; annexation.

anglikanisch [aŋgli-] *adj* Anglican ◆ **die A~e Kirche** the Anglican Church, the Church of England.

Anglikanismus [aŋgli-] *m* anglicanism.

anglisieren* [aŋgli-] *vt* to anglicize.

Anglisierung [aŋgli-] *f* anglicizing.

Anglist(in *f*) [aŋ'glɪ-] *m* English specialist, Anglicist; (*Student*) student of English; (*Professor etc*) lecturer in/professor of English.

Anglistik [aŋ'glɪ-] *f* English (language and literature).

Anglizismus [aŋgli-] *m* anglicism.

Anglo- [-ŋg-] *in cpds* Anglo; **~-Amerikaner** *m* Anglo-Saxon, member of the English-speaking world; **~amerikaner** *m* Anglo-American; **a~phil** *adj* anglophil(e); **a~phob** *adj* anglophobe, anglophobic.

anglotzen ['angl-] *vt sep* (*inf*) to gawp *or* gape at (*inf*).

anglühen ['angl-] *vt sep* (*lit*) to heat red-hot; (*fig*) to glow at.

Angola [aŋ'go:la] *nt* **-s** Angola.

Angolaner(in *f*) [aŋgo-] *m*, **-s, -** Angolan.

angolanisch [aŋgo-] *adj* Angolan.

Angora- [aŋ'go:ra] *in cpds* Angora; **~kaninchen** *nt* Angora rabbit; **~katze** *f* Angora cat; **~wolle** *f* Angora (wool).

Angostura [aŋgɔ-] *m* **-s, -s** Angostura (bitters *pl*).

angreifbar ['angr-] *adj Behauptung, Politiker* open to attack.

angreifen ['angr-] *sep irreg* [1] *vt* **(a)** (*überfallen, Sport, kritisieren*) to attack.
(b) (*schwächen*) *Organismus, Organ, Nerven* to weaken; *Gesundheit, Pflanzen* to affect; (*ermüden, anstrengen*) to strain; (*schädlich sein für, zersetzen*) *Lack, Farbe* to attack ◆ **seine Krankheit hat ihn sehr angegriffen** his illness weakened him greatly; **das hat ihn sehr angegriffen** that affected him greatly; *siehe* **angegriffen.**
(c) (*anbrechen*) *Vorräte, Geld* to break into, to draw on.
(d) (*dial: anfassen*) to touch; (*fig: unternehmen, anpacken*) to attack, to tackle.
[2] *vi* **(a)** (*Mil, Sport, fig*) to attack.
(b) (*geh: ansetzen*) to proceed *or* start (*an +dat* from).
(c) (*dial: anfassen*) to touch.
[3] *vr* (*dial: sich anfühlen*) to feel.

Angreifer(in *f*) ['angr-] *m* **-s, -** attacker (*auch Sport, fig*).

angrenzen ['angr-] *vi sep* **an etw** (*acc*) **~** to border on sth, to adjoin sth.

angrenzend *adj attr* adjacent (*an +acc* to), adjoining (*an etw* (*acc*) sth).

Angriff ['angr-] *m* (*Mil, Sport, fig*) attack (*gegen, auf +acc* on); (*Luft~*) (air) raid ◆ **~ ist die beste Verteidigung** (*prov*) attack is the best means of defence; **zum ~ übergehen** to go over to the attack, to take the offensive; **zum ~ blasen** (*Mil, fig*) to sound the charge; **etw in ~ nehmen** to tackle sth.

angriffig ['angr-] *adj* (*Sw*) aggressive.

Angriffs-: ~fläche *f* target; **jdm/einer Sache eine ~fläche bieten** (*lit, fig*) to provide sb/sth with a target; **eine ~fläche bieten** to present a target; **~krieg** *m* war of aggression; **~lust** *f* aggressiveness, aggression; **a~lustig** *adj* aggressive; **~punkt** *m* target; **~spiel** *nt* (*Sport*) aggressive *or* attacking game; **~spieler** *m* (*Sport*) attacking player; (*Ftbl*) forward; **~taktik** *f* attacking tactics *pl*; **~waffe** *f* offensive weapon.

angrinsen ['angr-] *vt sep* to grin at.

Angst *f* **-, ¨e** (*innere Unruhe, Psych*) anxiety (*um* about); (*Sorge*) worry (*um* about); (*Befürchtung*) fear (*um* for, *vor +dat* of); (*stärker: Furcht, Grauen*) fear, dread (*vor +dat* of); (*Existenz~*) angst ◆ **~ haben** to be afraid *or* scared; **~ vor Spinnen/vorm Fliegen haben** to be afraid *or* scared of spiders/flying; **~ um jdn/etw haben** to be anxious *or* worried about sb/sth; **~ bekommen** *or* **kriegen** to get *or* become afraid *or* scared; (*erschrecken*) to take fright; **aus ~, etw zu tun** for fear of doing sth; **keine ~!** don't be afraid; **keine ~, ich sage es ihm schon** don't you worry, I'll tell him; **jdm ~ einflößen** *or* **einjagen** to frighten sb; **in tausend ¨en schweben** to be terribly worried *or* anxious.

angst *adj pred* afraid ◆ **ihr wurde ~ (und bange)** she became worried *or* anxious; **das machte ihm ~ (und bange)** that worried him *or* made him anxious; **mir ist um deine Gesundheit ~** I'm worried about your health.

Angst-: a~erfüllt *adj* frightened; **~gefühl** *nt* feeling of anxiety; **~gegner** *m* (*Sport*) formidable opponent; **~hase** *m* (*inf*) scaredy-cat (*inf*).

ängstigen [1] *vt* to frighten; (*unruhig machen*) to worry.
[2] *vr* to be afraid; (*sich sorgen*) to worry ◆ **sich vor etw** (*dat*) **~** to be afraid of sth; **sich wegen etw ~** to worry about sth.

Angst-: ~kauf *m* panic buying *no pl*; **~laut** *m* alarm cry.

ängstlich *adj* **(a)** (*verängstigt*) anxious, apprehensive; (*schüchtern*) timid, timorous. **(b)** (*übertrieben genau*) particular, scrupulous, fastidious ◆ **~ darauf bedacht sein, etw zu tun** to be at pains to do sth; **ein ~ gehütetes Geheimnis** a closely guarded secret.

Ängstlichkeit *f siehe adj* **(a)** anxiety, apprehension; timidity, timorousness. **(b)** particularity, scrupulousness, fastidiousness.

Angst-: ~lust *f* (*Psych*) *enjoyment and excitement combined with fear*; **~mache** *f* (*inf*) scaremongering *no pl*; **~macher** *m* (*inf*) scaremonger; **~neurose** *f* anxiety neurosis; **~neurotiker** *m* neurotic; **~parole** *f* (*inf*) scaremongering *no pl*; **~parolen verbreiten** to spread alarm, to scaremonger; **~psychose** *f* anxiety psychosis; **~schrei** *m* cry of fear; **~schweiß** *m* cold sweat; **mir brach der ~schweiß aus** I broke out in a cold sweat; **~traum** *m* nightmare; **a~verzerrt** *adj* petrified, terror-struck; **a~voll** *adj* apprehensive, fearful; **~zustand** *m* state of panic; **~zustände bekommen** to get into a state of panic.

angucken ['angʊ-] *vt sep* to look at.

angurten ['angʊ-] *vt sep siehe* **anschnallen.**

anhaben *vt sep irreg* **(a)** (*angezogen haben*) to have on, to wear.
(b) (*zuleide tun*) to do harm ◆ **jdm etwas ~ wollen** to want to harm sb; **die Kälte kann mir nichts ~** the cold doesn't worry *or* bother me.
(c) (*am Zeuge flicken*) **Sie können/die Polizei kann mir nichts ~!** (*inf*) you/the police can't touch me.

anhaften *vi sep* **(a)** (*lit*) to stick (*an +dat* to), to cling (*an +dat* to) ◆ **~de Farbreste** bits of paint left sticking on. **(b)** (*fig*) *+dat* to stick to, to stay with; (*zugehören: Risiko etc*) to be attached to.

Anhalt *m* **-(e)s,** (*rare*) **-e** (*Hinweis*) clue (*für* about); (*für Verdacht*) grounds *pl* (*für* for); (*Hilfe*) hint, indication (*für* of, about).

anhalten *sep irreg* [1] *vi* **(a)** (*stehenbleiben*) to stop ◆ **mit dem Sprechen ~** to stop talking.
(b) (*fortdauern*) to last.
(c) (*werben*) **(bei jdm) um ein Mädchen** *or* **um die Hand eines Mädchens ~** to ask (sb) for a girl's hand in marriage.
[2] *vt* **(a)** (*stoppen*) to stop; *siehe* **Atem, Luft.**
(b) (*anlegen*) *Lineal* to use ◆ **sie hielt mir/sich das Kleid an** she held the dress up against me/herself.
(c) (*anleiten*) to urge, to encourage; *siehe* **angehalten.**

anhaltend *adj* continuous, incessant.

Anhalter(in *f*) *m* **-s, -** hitch-hiker, hitcher (*inf*) ◆ **per ~ fahren** to hitch-hike, to hitch (*inf*).

Anhaltspunkt *m* (*Vermutung*) clue (*für* about); (*für Verdacht*) grounds *pl* ◆ **ich habe keinerlei ~e** I haven't a clue (*inf*), I have no idea.

anhand, an Hand *prep +gen siehe* **Hand.**

Anhang *m* **-(e)s, Anhänge (a)** (*Nachtrag*) appendix; (*von Testament*) codicil. **(b)** *no pl* (*Gefolgschaft*) following; (*Angehörige*) family ◆ **Witwe, 62, ohne ~** widow, 62, no family; **mit etw ~/keinen ~ gewinnen** to gain support *or* a following/no support *or* no following.

anhängen *sep* [1] *vt* **(a)** (*ankuppeln*) to attach (*an +acc* to); (*Rail auch*) to couple on (*an +acc* -to); *Anhänger* to hitch up (*an +acc* to); (*fig: anfügen*) to add (*dat, an +acc* to).
(b) (*inf*) **jdm etw ~** (*verkaufen*) to palm sth off on sb; (*andrehen*) to foist sth on sb; *Krankheit* to pass sth on to sb; (*nachsagen, anlasten*) to blame sb for sth, to blame sth on sb; *schlechten Ruf, Spitznamen* to give sb sth; *Verdacht, Schuld* to pin sth on sb; **ich weiß nicht, warum er mir unbedingt etwas ~ will** I don't know why he always wants to give me a bad name.
[2] *vr* (*lit*) to hang on (*dat, an +acc* to); (*fig*) to tag along (*dat, an +acc* with); (*jdm hinterherfahren*) to follow (*dat, an +acc* sth).
[3] *vi irreg* (*fig*) **(a)** (*anhaften*) **jdm ~** to stay with sb; (*schlechter Ruf, Gefängnisstrafe auch*) to stick with sb.
(b) (*sich zugehörig fühlen*) *+dat* to adhere to, to subscribe to.

Anhänger *m* **-s, - (a)** supporter; (*von Sportart auch*) fan; (*von Partei auch*) follower; (*von Verein*) member. **(b)** (*Wagen*) trailer; (*Straßenbahn~*) second car ◆ **die Straßenbahn hatte zwei ~** the tram had two extra cars. **(c)** (*Schmuckstück*) pendant. **(d)** (*Koffer~ etc*) tag, label.

Anhängerin *f siehe* **Anhänger (a).**

Anhänger-: ~schaft *f siehe* **Anhänger (a)** supporters *pl*; fans *pl*; following, followers *pl*; membership, members *pl*; **~zahl** *f siehe* **Anhänger (a)** number of supporters/fans/followers/members.

Anhänge-: ~schild *nt* tag, label; **~vorrichtung** *f* coupling device; (*an Auto etc*) tow bar.

anhängig *adj* (*Jur*) sub judice; *Zivilverfahren* pending ◆ **etw ~ machen** to start legal proceedings over sth.

anhänglich *adj Kind, Freundin* clinging; *Haustier* devoted ◆ **mein Sohn/Hund ist sehr ~** my son/dog hardly leaves my side.

Anhänglichkeit *f siehe adj* tendency to cling to one; devotion.

Anhängsel *nt* **(a)** (*Überflüssiges, Mensch*) appendage (*an +dat* to); (*von Gruppe, Partei*) hanger-on ◆ **das ist ein ~ am Wort** that is added onto the word.
(b) (*Schildchen*) tag; (*rare: Schmuckstück*) pendant; (*an Armband*) charm; (*an Uhrenkette*) fob ◆ **die ~ am Weihnachtsbaum** the things hanging on the Christmas tree.
(c) (*Zusatz*) addition; (*Nachtrag*) appendix.
Anhauch *m* (*geh*) aura; (*in Stimme*) trace, tinge.
anhauchen *vt sep* to breathe on; *siehe* **angehaucht.**
anhauen *vt sep* **(a)** (*auch irreg*) *Baum* to cut a notch in. **(b)** (*sl: ansprechen*) to accost (*um* for) ◆ **jdn um etw ~** to be on the scrounge for sth from sb (*inf*); *um Geld auch* to touch sb for sth (*inf*).
anhäufen *sep* [1] *vt* to accumulate, to amass; *Vorräte, Geld* to hoard.
[2] *vr* to pile up, to accumulate; (*Zinsen*) to accumulate, to accrue.
Anhäufung *f siehe vt* accumulation, amassing; hoarding.
anheben¹ *sep irreg* [1] *vt* **(a)** (*hochheben*) to lift (up); *Glas* to raise. **(b)** (*erhöhen*) to raise.
[2] *vi* to lift.
anheben² *pret* **hob** *or* (*obs*) **hub an,** *ptp* **angehoben** *vi sep irreg* (*old*) to commence, to begin ◆ **zu singen ~** to begin singing; ..., **hub er an** (*obs*) ..., quoth he (*old*).
Anhebung *f* increase (*gen, von* in); (*das Anheben auch*) raising (*gen, von* of); (*Betrag, Größe auch*) rise (*gen, von* in) ◆ **eine ~ der Gehälter um 15%** an increase *or* a rise of 15% in salaries.
anheften *vt sep* (*an +acc or dat* to) to fasten (on), to attach ◆ **jdm einen Orden ~** to pin a medal on sb; **etw mit Reißzwecken/Heftklammern/Büroklammern/Stichen ~** to pin/staple/paperclip/tack sth on (*an +acc or dat* to).
anheilen *vi sep aux sein* to heal (up); (*Knochen*) to set, to mend.
anheimelnd *adj* (*geh*) homely; *Klänge* familiar.
anheim-: **~fallen** *vi sep irreg aux sein +dat* (*liter*) to pass *or* fall to; *einer Krankheit* to fall prey to; *einem Betrug* to fall victim to; **der Vergessenheit ~fallen** to sink into oblivion; **~geben** *vt sep irreg +dat* (*liter*) to commit *or* entrust to; **etw den Flammen ~geben** to commit sth to the flames; **etw der Entscheidung eines anderen ~geben** to entrust the decision about sth to somebody else; **~stellen** *vt sep +dat* (*geh*) **jdm etw ~stellen** to leave sth to sb's discretion.
anheiraten *vt sep siehe* **angeheiratet.**
anheischig *adv* **sich ~ machen, etw tun zu können** (*form*) to assert that one can do sth; **niemand kann sich ~ machen zu behaupten, alles zu wissen** no-one can claim to know *or* allege that they know everything.
anheizen *vt sep* **(a)** *Ofen* to light. **(b)** (*fig inf*) (*ankurbeln*) *Wirtschaft, Wachstum* to stimulate; (*verschlimmern*) *Krise* to aggravate.
anherrschen *vt sep* to bark at.
anhetzen *vi sep aux sein* **angehetzt kommen** to come rushing along *or* (*auf einen zu*) up.
anheuern *vti sep* (*Naut, fig*) to sign on *or* up.
Anhieb *m*: **auf (den ersten) ~** (*inf*) straight *or* right away, straight off (*inf*), first go (*inf*); **das kann ich nicht auf ~ sagen** I can't say offhand.
Anhimmelei *f* (*inf*) adulation, idolization; (*schwärmerische Blicke*) adoring gaze.
anhimmeln *vt sep* (*inf*) to idolize, to worship; (*schwärmerisch ansehen*) to gaze adoringly at.
Anhöhe *f* hill.
anhören *sep* [1] *vt* **(a)** (*Gehör schenken*) to hear; *Schallplatten, Konzert* to listen to ◆ **jdn ganz ~** to hear sb out.
(b) (*zufällig mithören*) to overhear ◆ **ich kann das nicht mehr mit ~** I can't listen to that any longer.
(c) (*anmerken*) **man konnte ihr/ihrer Stimme die Verzweiflung ~** one could hear the despair in her voice; **das hört man ihm aber nicht an!** you can't tell that from his accent *or* from hearing him speak; **man hört ihm sofort den Ausländer an** you can hear at once that he's a foreigner.
[2] *vr* **(a) sich** (*dat*) **etw ~** to listen to sth; **das höre ich mir nicht mehr länger mit an** I'm not going to listen to that any longer; **können Sie sich mal einen Moment ~, was ich zu sagen habe?** can you just listen for a moment to what I have to say?
(b) (*klingen*) to sound ◆ **das hört sich ja gut an** (*inf*) that sounds good.
Anhörtermin *m* date for a hearing.
Anhörung *f* hearing.
Anhörungsverfahren *nt* hearing.
anhupen *vt sep* to hoot at, to sound one's horn at.
anhusten *vt sep* to cough at; *jdn* to cough in sb's face.
Änigma *nt* **-s, -ta** *or* **Änigmen** (*liter*) enigma.
Anilin *nt* **-s,** *no pl* aniline.
Anilinfarbe *f siehe* **Teerfarben.**
Anima *f* **-, -s** (*Psych*) anima.
animalisch *adj* animal; (*pej auch*) bestial, brutish.
Animateur(in *f***)** [-'tøːɐ, -'tøːrɪn] *m* host/hostess.
Animation *f* (*Film*) animation.
Animationsfilm *m* (animated) cartoon (film).
Animator, Animatorin *mf* (*Film*) animator.
Animierdame *f* nightclub *or* bar hostess.
animieren* *vt* **(a)** (*anregen*) to encourage ◆ **jdn zu einem Streich ~** to put sb up to a trick; **sich animiert fühlen, etw zu tun** to feel prompted to do sth; **durch das schöne Wetter animiert** encouraged *or* prompted by the good weather. **(b)** (*Film*) to animate.
animierend *adj* (*geh*) stimulating.
Animier-: **~lokal** *nt* hostess bar, clipjoint (*pej*); **~mädchen** *nt siehe* **Animierdame.**
Animo *nt* **-s,** *no pl* (*Aus*) **(a)** (*Vorliebe*) liking. **(b)** (*Schwung*) **mit ~ mitmachen** to join in with gusto.
Animosität *f* (*geh*) (*gegen* towards) (*Feindseligkeit*) animosity, hostility; (*Abneigung*) hostility; (*Äußerung*) hostile remark.
Animus *m* **-,** *no pl* **(a)** (*Psych*) animus. **(b)** (*inf*) hunch (*inf*), feeling.
Anion ['an|ioːn] *nt* **-s, -en** (*Chem*) anion.
Anis [a'niːs, (*S Ger, Aus*) 'aːnɪs] *m* **-(es), -e** (*Gewürz*) aniseed; (*Schnaps*) aniseed brandy; (*Pflanze*) anise.
Anisett *m* **-s, -s, Anislikör** *m* anisette, aniseed liqueur.
Ank. *abbr of* **Ankunft** arr.
ankämpfen *vi sep* **gegen etw ~** *gegen die Elemente, Strömung* to battle with sth; *gegen Gefühle, Neigungen, Versuchungen, Müdigkeit* to fight sth; *gegen Inflation, Mißbrauch, Korruption, Ideen* to fight (against) sth; **gegen jdn ~** to fight (against) sb, to (do) battle with sb; **gegen die Tränen ~** to fight back one's tears.
ankarren *vt sep* (*inf*) to cart along.
Ankauf *m* purchase, purchasing ◆ **durch den ~ einer Sache** (*gen*) through the purchase of sth, by purchasing sth; **An- und Verkauf von ...** we buy and sell ...; **An- und Verkaufs-Geschäft** ≃ second-hand shop.
ankaufen *sep* [1] *vti* to purchase, to buy.
[2] *vr* **sich (an einem Ort) ~** to buy oneself a place (somewhere).
Ankäufer *m* purchaser, buyer.
Ankaufsrecht *nt* (*Jur*) option, right of purchase.
ankeifen *vt sep* (*inf*) to scream *or* holler (*inf*) at.
Anker *m* **-s, -** (*Naut, Archit, fig*) anchor; (*Elec*) armature; (*von Uhr*) anchor ◆ **~ werfen** to drop anchor; **vor ~ gehen** to drop anchor; (*fig*) (*hum: heiraten*) to settle down (*bei* with); (*inf: Rast machen*) to stop over; **sich vor ~ legen** to drop anchor; **vor ~ liegen** *or* **treiben** to lie *or* ride *or* be at anchor; **ein Schiff vor ~ legen** to bring a ship to anchor; **den/die ~ hieven** *or* **lichten** to weigh anchor.
Anker-: **~boje** *f* anchor buoy; **~grund** *m* anchorage; **~kette** *f* anchor cable; **~klüse** *f* (*Naut*) hawsehole; **~mann** *m, pl* **-männer** (*TV*) anchorman.
ankern *vi* (*Anker werfen*) to anchor; (*vor Anker liegen*) to be anchored.
Anker-: **~platz** *m* anchorage; **~tau** *nt* anchor hawser *or* rope; **~winde** *f* capstan.
anketten *vt sep* to chain up (*an +acc or dat* to) ◆ **angekettet sein** (*fig*) to be tied up.
ankeuchen *vi sep aux sein* (*inf*) **angekeucht kommen** to come panting along *or* (*auf einen zu*) up.
ankieken *vt sep* (*N Ger inf*) *siehe* **angucken.**
ankitten *vt sep* to stick on (with putty) (*an +acc* -to).
ankläffen *vt sep* (*pej*) to bark at; (*kleiner Hund*) to yap at.
Anklage *f* **(a)** (*Jur*) charge; (*~vertretung*) prosecution ◆ **gegen jdn ~ erheben** to bring *or* prefer charges against sb; **jdn unter ~ stellen** to charge sb (*wegen* with); **(wegen etw) unter ~ stehen** to have been charged (with sth); **als Vertreter der ~ fragte Herr Stein ...** acting for the prosecution Mr Stein asked ..., Mr Stein, prosecuting *or* for the prosecution, asked ...
(b) (*fig*) (*Verurteilung*) condemnation (*gegen, gen* of); (*Beschuldigung*) accusation; (*Anprangerung*) indictment (*an +acc* of) ◆ **ihr Blick war voller ~** her eyes were full of reproach.
Anklage-: **~bank** *f* dock; **auf der ~bank (sitzen)** (*lit, fig*) (to be) in the dock; **jdn auf die ~bank bringen** to put sb in the dock; **~behörde** *f* prosecution; **~erhebung** *f* preferral of charges.
anklagen *sep* [1] *vt* **(a)** (*Jur*) to charge, to accuse ◆ **jdn einer Sache** (*gen*) *or* **wegen etw ~** to charge sb with sth, to accuse sb of sth. **(b)** (*fig*) (*verurteilen*) to condemn; (*Buch, Rede*) to be a condemnation of; (*anprangern*) to be an indictment of ◆ **jdn einer Sache** (*gen*) **~** (*beschuldigen*) to accuse sb of sth; **jdn ~, etw getan zu haben** to accuse sb of having done sth.
[2] *vi* to cry out in protest *or* accusation; (*Buch, Bilder etc*) to cry out in condemnation.
anklagend *adj* *Ton* accusing, accusatory; *Blick* reproachful; *Buch, Bild etc* that cries out in condemnation.
Anklagepunkt *m* charge.
Ankläger *m* **-s, -** (*Jur*) prosecutor.
anklägerisch *adj siehe* **anklagend.**
Anklage-: **~schrift** *f* indictment; **~vertreter** *m* (public) prosecutor, counsel for the prosecution.
anklammern *sep* [1] *vt* (*mit Büroklammer*) to clip (*an +acc or dat* (on)to); (*mit Heftmaschine*) to staple (*an +acc or dat* on(to), to); *Wäsche* to peg (*an +acc or dat* on).
[2] *vr* **sich an etw** (*acc or dat*) **~** to cling (on)to sth, to hang onto sth.
Anklang *m* **(a)** *no pl* (*Beifall*) approval ◆ **~ (bei jdm) finden** to meet with (sb's) approval, to be well received (by sb); **großen/wenig/keinen ~ finden** to be very well/poorly/badly received.
(b) (*Reminiszenz*) **die Anklänge an Mozart sind unverkennbar** the echoes of Mozart are unmistakable; **ich konnte in seinem Buch einen deutlichen ~ an Thomas Mann erkennen** I found his book (to be) distinctly reminiscent of Thomas Mann; **Anklänge an etw** (*acc*) **enthalten** to be reminiscent of sth.
anklatschen *sep* (*inf*) [1] *vt* *Plakat etc* to slap *or* bung up (*inf*).
[2] *vi aux sein* **seine Kleider/Haare klatschen an** *or* **sind angeklatscht** his clothes are clinging to him/his hair is plastered down.
ankleben *sep* [1] *vt* to stick up (*an +acc or dat* on).

[2] *vi aux sein* to stick.
ankleckern *vi sep aux sein (inf)* **angekleckert kommen** to come drifting along *or (auf einen zu)* up; *(nach und nach eintreffen)* to come in dribs and drabs *(inf)*.
Ankleidekabine *f* changing cubicle.
ankleiden *vtr sep (geh)* to dress.
Ankleidepuppe *f siehe* **Schaufensterpuppe.**
Ankleider(in *f*) *m* **-s, -** *(Theat)* dresser.
Ankleideraum *m*, **Ankleidezimmer** *nt* dressing-room; *(im Schwimmbad, Geschäft)* changing room.
anklicken *vti (Comput)* to click on.
anklingeln *vti sep (inf)* to ring *or* phone (up) *(Brit)*, to call (up) *(US)* ◆ **jdn** *or* **bei jdm ~** to give sb a ring *or* a buzz *(inf) (Brit)*, to ring *or* phone sb (up) *(Brit)*, to call sb (up) *(US)*.
anklingen *vi sep aux sein (erinnern)* to be reminiscent *(an +acc* of); *(angeschnitten werden)* to be touched (up)on; *(spürbar werden)* to be discernible ◆ **in diesem Lied klingt etwas von Sehnsucht an** there is a suggestion *or* hint *or* note of longing (discernible) in this song.
anklopfen *vi sep* to knock *(an +acc or dat* at, on) ◆ **bei jdm wegen etw ~** *(fig inf)* to go/come knocking at sb's door for sth.
anknabbern *vt sep (inf) (annagen)* to gnaw *or* nibble (at); *(fig) Ersparnisse etc* to gnaw away at, to nibble away ◆ **zum A~ (aussehen)** *(fig)* (to look) good enough to eat.
anknacksen *vt sep (inf)* **(a)** *Knochen* to crack; *Fuß, Gelenk etc* to crack a bone in. **(b)** *(fig) Gesundheit* to affect; *Stolz* to injure, to deal a blow to ◆ **sein Selbstvertrauen/Stolz wurde dadurch angeknackst** that was a blow to his self-confidence/pride; *siehe* **angeknackst.**
anknattern *vi sep aux sein (inf)* **angeknattert kommen** to come roaring along *or (auf einen zu)* up.
anknipsen *vt sep* to switch *or* put on; *Schalter* to flick.
anknöpfen *vt sep* to button on *(an +acc or dat* -to).
anknoten *vt sep* to tie on *(an +acc or dat* -to).
anknüpfen *sep* [1] *vt* to tie on *(an +acc or dat* -to); *Beziehungen* to establish; *Verhältnis* to form, to start up; *Gespräch* to start up, to enter into.
[2] *vi* **an etw** *(acc)* **~** to take sth up.
Anknüpfung *f (fig) siehe vt* establishing; forming; starting up ◆ **in ~ an etw** *(acc)* following on from sth.
Anknüpfungspunkt *m* link.
anknurren *vt sep (lit, fig)* to growl at.
ankohlen *vt sep* **(a)** *Holz* to char. **(b)** *(inf: belügen)* to have on *(inf)*.
ankommen *sep irreg aux sein* [1] *vi* **(a)** to arrive; *(Brief, Paket auch)* to come; *(Zug, Bus etc auch)* to get in, to arrive ◆ **bist du gut angekommen?** did you arrive safely *or* get there all right?; **bei etw angekommen sein** to have reached sth, to have got to sth; **wir sind schon beim Dessert angekommen** we've already reached the dessert stage; **das Kind soll in 6 Wochen ~** the baby is due (to arrive) in 6 weeks.
(b) *(Anklang, Resonanz finden) (bei* with) to go down well; *(Mode, Neuerungen)* to catch on ◆ **dieser Witz kam gut an** the joke went down very well; **mit deinem dummen Gerede kommst du bei ihm nicht an!** you won't get anywhere with him with your stupid talk!; **ein Lehrer, der bei seinen Schülern ausgezeichnet ankommt** a teacher who is a great success *or* who hits it off marvellously with his pupils.
(c) *(inf) (auftreten, erscheinen)* to come along; *(wiederholt erwähnen)* to come up *(mit* with) ◆ **jdm mit etw ~** to come to sb with sth; **komm mir nachher nicht an, und verlange, daß ich ...** don't come running to me afterwards wanting me to ...; **komm mir nur nicht wieder damit an, daß du Astronaut werden willst** don't start up again with this business about (your) wanting to be an astronaut.
(d) *(sich durchsetzen)* **gegen etw ~** *gegen Gewohnheit, Sucht etc* to be able to fight sth; **gegen diese Konkurrenz kommen wir nicht an** we can't fight this competition; **er ist zu stark, ich komme gegen ihn nicht an** he's too strong, I'm no match for him.
[2] *vi impers* **(a)** *(wichtig sein)* **es kommt auf etw** *(acc)* **an** sth matters; **darauf kommt es (uns) an** that is what matters (to us); **es kommt darauf an, daß wir ...** what matters is that we ...; **auf eine halbe Stunde kommt es jetzt nicht mehr an** it doesn't matter about the odd half-hour, an extra half-hour is neither here nor there *(inf)*; **darauf soll es mir nicht ~** that's not the problem.
(b) *(abhängig sein)* to depend *(auf +acc* on) ◆ **es kommt darauf an** it (all) depends; **es käme auf einen Versuch an** we'd have to give it a try; **es kommt (ganz) darauf an, in welcher Laune er ist** it (all) depends (on) what mood he's in.
(c) *(inf)* **es darauf ~ lassen** to take a chance, to chance it; **laß es nicht drauf ~!** don't push your luck! *(inf)*; **lassen wir's darauf ~** let's chance it; **er ließ es in der Prüfung darauf ~** he took a chance in the exam; **er ließ es auf einen Streit/einen Versuch ~** he was prepared to argue about it/to give it a try; **laß es doch nicht deswegen auf einen Prozeß ~** for goodness sake don't let it get as far as the courts.
[3] *vt (sein, erscheinen)* **etw kommt jdn schwer/hart an** sth is difficult/hard for sb; **das Rauchen aufzugeben, kommt ihn sauer an** he's finding it difficult to give up smoking.
Ankömmling *m* (new) arrival.
ankoppeln *vt sep* to hitch up *(an +acc* to) *or* on *(an +acc* -to); *(Rail)* to couple up *(an +acc* to) *or* on *(an +acc* -to); *(Space)* to link up *(an +acc* with, to).
ankotzen *vt sep (sl)* **(a)** *(lit)* to be sick over, to puke (up) over *(sl)*. **(b)** *(anwidern)* to make sick *(inf)*.

ankrallen *vr sep* to clutch *(an +dat* at).
ankratzen *sep* [1] *vt* to scratch; *(fig) jds Ruf etc* to damage; *siehe* **angekratzt.**
[2] *vr (fig inf)* **sich bei jdm ~** to suck up to sb *(inf)*.
ankrausen *vt sep (Sew)* to gather.
ankreiden *vt sep* **(a)** *(obs: Schulden aufschreiben)* to chalk up. **(b)** *(fig)* **jdm etw (dick** *or* **übel) ~** to hold sth against sb; **jdm sein Benehmen als Frechheit/Schwäche ~** to regard sb's behaviour as an impertinence/as weakness.
Ankreis *m (Math)* escribed circle.
ankreuzen *vt sep* **(a)** to mark with a cross, to put a cross beside. **(b)** *aux sein or haben (Naut)* **gegen den Wind ~** to sail against *or* into the wind.
ankünden *vtr sep (old) siehe* **ankündigen.**
ankündigen *sep* [1] *vt* **(a)** *(ansagen, anmelden)* to announce; *(auf Plakat, in Zeitung etc)* to advertize ◆ **heute kam endlich der angekündigte Brief** today the letter I/we had been expecting arrived; **er besucht uns nie, ohne sich (nicht) vorher anzukündigen** he never visits us without letting us know in advance *or* without giving us advance notice.
(b) *(auf etw hindeuten)* to be a sign of.
[2] *vr (fig)* to be heralded *(durch* by) ◆ **der Frühling kündigt sich an** spring is in the air; **diese Krankheit kündigt sich durch ... an** this illness is preceded by ...
Ankündigung *f* announcement; *(vorherige Benachrichtigung)* advance notice ◆ **Preisänderungen nur nach vorheriger ~** price changes will be announced in advance, advance notice will be given of price changes.
Ankunft *f* **-, Ankünfte** arrival ◆ **bei** *or* **nach ~** on arrival.
Ankunfts-: ~halle *f* arrivals lounge; **~ort** *m* place of arrival; **~tafel** *f* arrivals (indicator) board; **~zeit** *f* time of arrival.
ankuppeln *vt sep siehe* **ankoppeln.**
ankurbeln *vt sep Maschine* to wind up; *(Aut)* to crank; *(fig) Wirtschaft, Konjunktur* to boost, to reflate.
Ankurbelung *f (fig)* reflation.
ankuscheln *vr sep* **sich bei jdm** *or* **an jdn ~** to snuggle up to sb.
Anl. *abbr of* **Anlage** encl.
anlabern *vt sep (sl) siehe* **anquatschen.**
anlächeln *vt sep* to smile at; *(fig: Schicksal, Glück etc)* to smile (up)on ◆ **jdn ~** to smile at sb, to give sb a smile; **der Kuchen lächelte mich förmlich an** *(hum)* the cake sat there just asking to be eaten.
anlachen *vt sep* to smile at; *(fig: Himmel, Sonne)* to smile (up)on ◆ **sich** *(dat)* **jdn ~** *(inf)* to pick sb up *(inf)*.
➤ **Anlage** *f* **-, -n (a)** *(Fabrik~)* plant.
(b) *(Grün~, Park~)* (public) park; *(um ein Gebäude herum)* grounds *pl*.
(c) *(Einrichtung) (Mil, Elec)* installation(s); *(sanitäre ~n)* bathroom *or* sanitary *(form)* installations *pl*; *(Sport~ etc)* facilities *pl*.
(d) *(inf: Stereo~)* (stereo) system *or* equipment; *(EDV-~)* system.
(e) *(Plan, Grundidee)* conception; *(eines Dramas etc)* structure.
(f) *(Veranlagung) usu pl* aptitude, gift, talent *(zu* for); *(Neigung)* predisposition, tendency *(zu* to).
(g) *(das Anlegen) (von Park)* laying out; *(von Stausee etc)* construction, building ◆ **die ~ einer Kartei veranlassen** to start a file; **die Stadt hat die ~ von weiteren Grünflächen beschlossen** the town has decided to provide more parks.
(h) *(Kapital~)* investment.
➤ **(i)** *(Beilage zu einem Schreiben)* enclosure ◆ **als ~** *or* **in der ~ erhalten Sie ...** please find enclosed ...
anlagebedingt *adj* inherent ◆ **Krampfadern sind ~** some people have an inherent tendency *or* a predisposition to varicose veins.
Anlage-: ~berater *m* investment advisor; **~kapital** *nt* investment capital; **~papier** *nt* long-term investment bond.
anlagern *sep* [1] *vt* to take up.
[2] *vr (Chem)* to be taken up *(an +acc* by).
Anlagevermögen *nt* fixed assets *pl*.
anlanden *sep* [1] *vi* **(a)** *aux sein (Naut)* to land. **(b)** *aux sein or haben (Geol)* to accrete.
[2] *vt* to land.
anlangen *sep* [1] *vi aux sein (an einem Ort)* to arrive ◆ **in der Stadt/am Gipfel angelangt sein** to have reached the town/summit, to have arrived in *or* at the town/at the summit.
[2] *vt* **(a)** *(betreffen)* to concern. **(b)** *(S Ger: anfassen)* to touch.
⚠ ➤ **Anlaß** *m* **-sses, Anlässe (a)** *(Veranlassung)* (immediate) cause *(zu* for) ◆ **zum ~ von etw werden** to bring sth about, to trigger sth off; **das war zwar nicht der Grund, aber der ~** that wasn't the real reason but that's what finally brought it about *or* triggered it off; **welchen ~ hatte er, das zu tun?** what prompted him to do that?; **er hat keinen ~ zur Freude** he has no cause *or* reason *or* grounds for rejoicing; **es besteht kein ~ ...** there is no reason ...; **das ist kein ~ zu feiern** that doesn't call for a celebration; **etw zum ~ nehmen, zu ...** to use sth as an opportunity to ...; **beim geringsten/bei jedem ~** for the slightest reason/at every opportunity; **jdm ~ zu Beschwerden geben, jdm ~ geben, sich zu beschweren** to give sb reason *or* cause *or* grounds for complaint *or* for complaining.
(b) *(Gelegenheit)* occasion ◆ **aus ~** *(+gen)* on the occasion of; **aus gegebenem ~** in view of the occasion; **aus diesem ~** on this occasion; **dem ~ entsprechend** as befits the occasion, as is befitting to the occasion.
(c) *(Sw: Lustbarkeit)* social.
anlassen *sep irreg* [1] *vt* **(a)** *(in Gang setzen) Motor, Wagen* to start (up).
(b) *(inf) Schuhe, Mantel* to keep on; *Wasserhahn, Motor* to leave running *or* on; *Licht, Radio* to leave on; *Kerze* to leave burning; *Feuer* to leave in *or* burn-

ing.
[2] *vr* **sich gut/schlecht ~** to get off to a good/bad start; (*Lehrling, Student, Geschäft etc auch*) to make a good/bad start *or* beginning; **das Wetter läßt sich gut an** the weather looks promising; **wie läßt er sich in der Sache denn an?** what sort of start has he made on it?

Anlasser *m* **-s, -** (*Aut*) starter.

anläßlich ⚠ *prep +gen* on the occasion of.

anlasten *vt sep* **(a) jdm etw ~** to blame sb for sth, to lay the blame for sth on sb; **jdm die Schuld für etw ~** to lay the blame for sth at sb's door *or* on sb; **jdm etw als Schwäche ~** to regard *or* see sth as a weakness on sb's part. **(b)** (*dated*) *Kosten* to charge (*jdm* to sb).

anlatschen *vi sep aux sein* (*usu* **angelatscht kommen**) (*inf*) to come slouching along *or* (*auf einen zu*) up.

Anlauf *m* **-(e)s, Anläufe (a)** (*Sport*) run-up; (*Ski*) approach run; (*Mil: Ansturm*) onset, attack ◆ **mit/ohne ~** with a run-up/from standing; **Sprung mit/ohne ~** running/standing jump; **~ nehmen** to take a run-up; **~ zu etw nehmen** (*fig*) to pluck up courage to do sth.
(b) (*fig: Versuch*) attempt, try ◆ **beim ersten/zweiten ~** at the first/second attempt, first/second go (*Brit inf*); **noch einen ~ nehmen** *or* **machen** to have another go (*Brit inf*) *or* try, to make another attempt.
(c) (*Beginn*) start.

anlaufen *sep irreg* [1] *vi aux sein* **(a)** (*beginnen*) to begin, to start; (*Saison auch, Film*) to open; (*Motor*) to start.
(b) (*usu* **angelaufen kommen**) to come running along *or* (*auf einen zu*) up.
(c) (*sich ansammeln*) to mount up (*auf +acc* to); (*Zinsen auch*) to accrue; (*dial: auch* **dick ~**) to swell (up).
(d) (*beschlagen*) (*Brille, Spiegel etc*) to steam *or* mist up; (*Metall*) to tarnish ◆ **rot/blau ~** to turn *or* go red/blue.
(e) (*Sport*) (*zu laufen beginnen*) to start off; (*Anlauf nehmen*) to take a run-up.
(f) gegen etw ~ (*fig*) to stand up to sth; **er kann kaum gegen so einen starken Wind ~** he can hardly walk against such a strong wind.
[2] *vt* **(a)** (*Naut*) *Hafen etc* to put into, to call at.
(b) (*Sport*) *Rennen* to start off; *Strecke* to run.

Anlauf-: ~stelle *f* shelter, refuge; **~zeit** *f* (*Aut*) warming-up time *or* period; (*fig*) time to get going *or* started; (*Film, Theat*) (time of the) first few performances; **ein paar Wochen ~zeit** a few weeks to get going *or* started.

Anlaut *m* (*Phon*) initial sound ◆ **im ~ stehen** to be in initial position.

anlauten *vi sep* to begin.

anläuten *vt sep* **(a)** *Spiel, Pause* to ring the bell for ◆ **eben wird die Pause angeläutet** there goes *or* there's the bell for break. **(b)** *auch vi* (*dial: anrufen*) **jdn** *or* **bei jdm ~** to ring sb (up), to phone *or* call sb.

anlautend *adj attr* initial.

anlecken *vt sep* to lick.

Anlegebrücke *f* landing stage, jetty.

anlegen *sep* [1] *vt* **(a)** *Leiter* to put up (*an +acc* against); *Brett, Karte, Dominostein* to lay (down) (*an +acc* next to, beside); *Holz, Kohle* to put *or* lay on; *Lineal* to position, to set ◆ **das Gewehr ~** to raise the gun to one's shoulder; **das Gewehr auf jdn/etw ~** to aim the gun at sb/sth; **den Säugling ~** to put the baby to one's breast; **strengere Maßstäbe ~** to impose *or* lay down stricter standards (*bei* in).
(b) (*geh: anziehen*) to don (*form*).
(c) (*anbringen*) **jdm etw ~** to put sth on sb; **jdm/einer Sache Zügel ~** to take sb in hand/to contain *or* control sth.
(d) *Kartei, Akte* to start; *Vorräte* to lay in; *Garten, Gelände, Aufsatz, Bericht, Schaubild* to lay out; *Liste, Plan, Statistiken* to draw up; *Roman, Drama* to structure.
(e) (*investieren*) *Geld, Kapital* to invest; (*ausgeben*) to spend (*für* on).
(f) es darauf ~, daß ... to be determined that ...; **du legst es wohl auf einen Streit mit mir an** you're determined to have a fight with me, aren't you?
(g) *siehe* **angelegt.**
[2] *vi* **(a)** (*Naut*) to berth, to dock.
(b) (*Cards*) to lay down cards/a card (*bei jdm* on sb's hand).
(c) (*Gewehr* **~**) to aim (*auf +acc* at).
[3] *vr* **sich mit jdm ~** to pick an argument *or* quarrel *or* fight with sb.

Anlegeplatz *m* berth.

Anleger(in *f*) *m* **-s, -** (*Fin*) investor.

Anlege-: ~steg *m* jetty, landing stage; **~stelle** *f* mooring.

anlehnen *sep* [1] *vt* to lean *or* rest (*an +acc* against); *Tür, Fenster* to leave ajar *or* slightly open ◆ **angelehnt sein** (*Tür, Fenster*) to be ajar *or* slightly open.
[2] *vr* (*lit*) to lean (*an +acc* against) ◆ **sich an etw** (*acc*) **~** (*fig*) to follow sth.

Anlehnung *f* **(a)** (*Stütze*) support (*an +acc* of); (*Anschluß*) dependence (*an +acc* on) ◆ **~ an jdn suchen** to seek sb's support. **(b)** (*Imitation*) following (*an jdn/etw* sb/sth) ◆ **in ~ an jdn/etw** following sb/sth.

Anlehnungs-: ~bedürfnis *nt* need of loving care; **a~bedürftig** *adj* needing loving care.

anleiern *vt sep* (*inf: in die Wege leiten*) to get going.

Anleihe *f* **-, -n, Anleihen** *nt* **-s, -** (*Sw*) **(a)** (*Fin*) (*Geldaufnahme*) loan; (*Wertpapier*) bond ◆ **eine ~ aufnehmen** to take out a loan; **bei jdm eine ~ machen** to borrow (money) from sb. **(b)** (*von geistigem Eigentum*) borrowing ◆ **bei jdm eine ~ machen** (*hum inf*) to borrow from sb.

anleimen *vt sep* to stick on (*an +acc or dat* -to) ◆ **jdn ~** (*inf*) (*foppen*) to pull sb's leg; (*betrügen*) to do sb (*inf*).

anleinen *vt sep* (*festmachen*) to tie up; (*fig*) to keep tied to one's apron-strings ◆ **den Hund ~** to put the dog's lead on, to put the dog on the lead; **den Hund an etw** (*acc or dat*) **~** to tie the dog to sth.

anleiten *vt sep* **(a)** (*unterweisen*) to show, to teach, to instruct ◆ **jdn bei einer Arbeit ~** to teach sb a job, to show sb how to do a job. **(b)** (*erziehen*) **jdn zu etw ~** to teach sb sth; **jdn zu selbständigem Denken ~** to teach sb to think for himself/herself.

Anleitung *f* (*Erklärung, Hilfe*) instructions *pl* ◆ **unter der ~ seines Vaters** under his father's guidance *or* direction.

Anlernberuf *m* semi-skilled job.

anlernen *vt sep* **(a)** (*ausbilden*) to train; *siehe* **angelernt. (b)** (*oberflächlich lernen*) **sich** (*dat*) **etw ~** to learn sth up; **angelerntes Wissen** superficially acquired knowledge.

Anlernling *m* trainee.

anlesen *vt sep irreg* **(a)** *Buch, Aufsatz* to begin *or* start reading ◆ **das angelesene Buch** the book I have/she has started reading. **(b)** (*aneignen*) **sich** (*dat*) **etw ~** to learn sth by reading; **angelesenes Wissen** knowledge which comes straight out of books.

anleuchten *vt sep* **jdn ~** to shine a light/lamp *etc* at sb; **jdn mit etw ~** to shine sth at sb.

anliefern *vt sep* to deliver.

Anlieferung *f* delivery.

Anliegen *nt* **-s, - (a)** (*Bitte*) request. **(b)** (*wichtige Angelegenheit*) matter of concern.

anliegen *sep irreg* [1] *vi* **(a)** (*anstehen, vorliegen*) to be on. **(b)** (*Kleidung*) to fit closely *or* tightly (*an etw (dat)* sth); (*Haar*) to lie flat (*an +dat* against, on). **(c)** (*Naut*) **an den richtigen Kurs ~** to be (headed) on the right course.
[2] *vt* (*Naut*) (*zusteuern*) to be headed for; *Kurs* to be (headed) on.

anliegend *adj* **(a)** *Ohren* flat ◆ **(eng) ~** *Kleidung* tight- *or* close-fitting. **(b)** (*in Briefen*) enclosed. **(c)** *Grundstück* adjacent.

Anlieger *m* **-s, -** neighbour; (*Anwohner*) (local) resident ◆ **die ~ der Nordsee** the countries bordering (on) the North Sea; **~ frei, frei für ~** no thoroughfare — residents only.

Anlieger-: ~staat *m* **die ~staaten des Schwarzen Meers** the countries bordering (on) the Black Sea; **~verkehr** *m* (local) residents' vehicles; **„~verkehr frei"** "residents only".

anlinsen *vt sep* (*inf*) to take a sly look at ◆ **jdn aus den Augenwinkeln ~** to look at sb out of the corner of one's eye.

anlocken *vt sep Touristen* to attract; *Vögel, Tiere auch* to lure.

Anlockung *f* attraction.

anlöten *vt sep* to solder on (*an +acc or dat* -to).

anlügen *vt sep irreg* to lie *or* tell lies to.

anluven *vt sep* (*Naut*) to luff.

Anm. *abbr of* **Anmerkung.**

Anmache *f* **-,** *no pl* (*sl*) pick-up (*inf*); (*Belästigung*) harassment.

anmachen *vt sep* **(a)** (*inf: befestigen*) to put up (*an +acc or dat* on).
(b) (*zubereiten*) to mix; *Salat* to dress.
(c) (*anstellen*) *Radio, Licht, Heizung etc* to put *or* turn on; *Feuer* to light.
(d) (*sl: ansprechen*) to chat up (*inf*); (*belästigen*) to harass ◆ **mach mich nicht an** leave me alone.
(e) (*sl: begeistern*) to drive wild; (*sexuell*) to turn on (*inf*) ◆ **das Publikum ~** to get the audience going (*inf*); **der Typ macht mich total an** that guy really turns me on (*inf*).
(f) (*sl: kritisieren*) to slam (*inf*).

anmahnen *vt sep* to send a reminder about.

anmalen *sep* [1] *vt* **(a)** (*bemalen*) *Wand, Gegenstand* to paint; (*ausmalen*) to colour in.
(b) (*anzeichnen*) to paint (*an +acc* on).
(c) (*schminken*) **sich** (*dat*) **die Lippen/Lider** *etc* **~** to paint one's lips/eyelids *etc*; **sich** (*dat*) **einen Schnurrbart/Sommersprossen ~** to paint a moustache/freckles on one's face *or* on oneself.
[2] *vr* (*pej: schminken*) to paint one's face *or* oneself.

Anmarsch *m, no pl* (*Weg*) walk (there); (*Mil*) advance ◆ **im ~ sein** to be advancing (*auf +acc* on); (*hum inf*) to be on the way.

anmarschieren* *vi sep aux sein* (*Mil*) to advance ◆ **anmarschiert kommen** to come marching along *or* (*auf einen zu*) up.

Anmarschweg *m* walk.

anmaßen *vr sep* **sich** (*dat*) **etw ~** *Befugnis, Recht* to claim sth (for oneself); *Kritik* to take sth upon oneself; *Titel, Macht, Autorität* to assume sth; **sich** (*dat*) **ein Urteil/eine Meinung über etw** (*acc*) **~** to presume to pass judgement on/have an opinion about sth; **sich** (*dat*) **~, etw zu tun** to presume to do sth.

anmaßend *adj* presumptuous.

Anmaßung *f* presumption, presumptuousness ◆ **mit seinen ständigen ~en machte er sich viele Feinde** he made a lot of enemies with his presumptuous behaviour; **es ist eine ~ zu meinen, ...** it is presumptuous to maintain that ...

anmeckern *vt sep* (*inf*) to keep on at (*inf*).

Anmelde-: ~formular *nt* application form; **~frist** *f* registration period; **~gebühr** *f* registration fee.

anmelden *sep* [1] *vt* **(a)** (*ankündigen*) *Besuch* to announce ◆ **einen Freund bei jdm ~** to let sb know that a friend is coming to visit.
(b) (*bei Schule, Kurs etc*) to enrol (*bei* at, *zu* for).
(c) (*eintragen lassen*) *Patent* to apply for; *neuen Wohnsitz, Auto, Untermieter* to register (*bei* at); *Fernseher* to get a licence for ◆ **Konkurs ~** to declare oneself bankrupt.
(d) (*vormerken lassen*) to make an appointment for.
(e) (*Telec*) **ein Gespräch nach Deutschland ~** to book a call to Germany.
(f) (*geltend machen*) *Recht, Ansprüche,* (*zu Steuerzwecken*) to declare; *Bedenken,*

Zweifel, Protest to register; *Wünsche, Bedürfnisse* to make known ◆ **ich melde starke Bedenken an** I have serious doubts about that, I'm rather doubtful *or* dubious about that.

[2] *vr* **(a)** (*ankündigen*) (*Besucher*) to announce one's arrival; (*im Hotel*) to book (in); (*fig*) (*Baby*) to be on the way; (*Probleme, Zweifel etc*) to appear on the horizon ◆ **sich bei jdm ~** to tell sb one is coming.

(b) (*an Schule, zu Kurs etc*) to enrol (oneself) (*an +dat* at, *zu* for) ◆ **sich polizeilich ~** to register with the police.

(c) (*sich einen Termin geben lassen*) to make an appointment ◆ **sich beim Arzt** *etc* **~** to make an appointment at the doctor's *etc or* with the doctor *etc*.

Anmelde-: ~pflicht *f siehe adj* compulsory licensing/registration/notification; **a~pflichtig** *adj* **a~pflichtig sein** (*Fernsehgerät, Hund*) to have to be licensed; (*Auto, Untermieter, Ausländer*) to have to be registered; (*Einfuhr, Waffenbesitz etc*) to be notifiable; **~schein** *m* registration form.

Anmeldung *f* **(a)** *siehe vt* announcement; declaration; registration; making known (*von etw* sth); enrolment; application (*von, gen* for); licensing; making an appointment (*gen* for); (*Konkurs~*) bankruptcy petition ◆ **die ~ eines Gespräches** booking a call; **die erneute ~ seines Protestes** his renewed protest ...

(b) (*Ankündigung*) announcement of one's arrival; (*im Hotel*) booking; (*an Schule, zu Kurs etc*) enrolment (*an +dat* at, *zu* for); (*bei Polizei*) registration; (*beim Arzt etc*) making an appointment ◆ **nur nach vorheriger ~** by appointment only.

(c) (*Anmelderaum*) reception.

anmerken *vt sep* (*sagen*) to say; (*anstreichen*) to mark; (*als Fußnote*) to note ◆ **sich** (*dat*) **etw ~** to make a note of sth, to note sth down; **jdm seine Verlegenheit** *etc* **~** to notice sb's embarrassment *etc or* that sb is embarrassed *etc*; **sich** (*dat*) **etw ~ lassen** to let sth show; **man merkt ihm nicht an, daß ...** you wouldn't know *or* can't tell that ...

Anmerkung *f* (*Erläuterung*) note; (*Fußnote*) (foot)note; (*iro: Kommentar*) remark, comment.

anmessen *vt sep irreg* **(a) jdm etw ~** (*geh*) to measure sb for sth. **(b)** (*Phot*) *Objekt* to take a reading off *or* from.

anmieten *vt sep* to rent; *Auto etc auch* to hire.

anmit *adv* (*Sw*) herewith.

anmontieren* *vt sep* to fix on (*an +acc or dat* -to).

anmustern *vti* (*Naut*) to sign on.

Anmut *f* **-**, *no pl* grace; (*Grazie auch*) gracefulness; (*Schönheit*) beauty, loveliness; (*von Landschaft, Gegenständen*) charm, beauty.

anmuten *sep* [1] *vt* (*geh*) to appear, to seem (*jdn* to sb) ◆ **jdn seltsam ~** to appear *or* seem odd to sb; **es mutete ihn wie ein Traum an** it seemed like a dream to him.

[2] *vi* **es mutet sonderbar an** it is *or* seems curious; **eine eigenartig ~de Geschichte** a story that strikes one as odd.

anmutig *adj* (*geh*) (*geschmeidig, behende*) *Bewegung* graceful; (*hübsch anzusehen*) lovely, charming.

anmut(s)- (*geh*): **~los** *adj* graceless, lacking grace; (*nicht hübsch*) lacking charm; **~voll** *adj Lächeln* lovely, charming; (*geschmeidig, behende*) graceful.

annageln *vt sep* to nail on (*an +acc or dat* -to) ◆ **er stand wie angenagelt da** he stood there rooted to the spot.

annagen *vt sep* to gnaw (at); (*fig*) *Ersparnisse etc* to gnaw away at, to nibble away.

annähen *vt sep* to sew on (*an +acc or dat* -to); *Saum* to sew up.

annähern *sep* [1] *vt* to bring closer (*dat, an +acc* to); (*in größere Übereinstimmung bringen auch*) to bring more into line (*dat, an +acc* with) ◆ **zwei Länder/Standpunkte soweit als möglich ~** to bring two nations as close (to each other)/two points of view as much into line (with each other) as possible.

[2] *vr* **(a)** (*lit, fig: sich nähern*) to approach (*einer Sache* (*dat*) sth).

(b) (*sich angleichen, näherkommen*) to come closer (*dat, an +acc* to).

annähernd [1] *adj* (*ungefähr*) approximate, rough.

[2] *adv* (*etwa*) roughly; (*fast*) almost ◆ **können Sie mir den Betrag ~ nennen?** can you give me an approximate *or* a rough idea of the amount?; **nicht ~** not nearly, nothing like; **nur ~ soviel** only about this/that much; **nicht ~ soviel** not nearly as much, nothing like as much.

Annäherung *f* (*lit: Näherkommen, fig: Angleichung*) approach (*an +acc* towards); (*von Standpunkten*) convergence (*dat, an +acc* with) ◆ **eine ~ an die Wirklichkeit** an approximation of reality; **die ~ zwischen Ost und West** the rapprochement of East and West; **die ~ von zwei Menschen** when two people come close (together); **die ~ an den Partner** coming closer to one's partner.

Annäherungs-: ~politik *f* policy of rapprochement; **~versuch** *m* overtures *pl*; *siehe* **plump**; **a~weise** *adv* approximately; **~wert** *m siehe* **Näherungswert**.

▼ **Annahme** *f* **-, -n (a)** (*Vermutung, Voraussetzung*) assumption ◆ **in der ~, daß ...** on the assumption that ...; **gehe ich recht in der ~, daß ...?** am I right in assuming *or* in the assumption that ...?; **der ~ sein, daß ...** to assume that ...; **von einer ~ ausgehen** to work on *or* from an assumption.

(b) *siehe* **annehmen** *vt* (*a-e, g*) acceptance; taking; taking on; taking up; approval; passing; adoption; picking up; acquisition; assuming ◆ **~ an Kindes Statt** (child) adoption.

(c) *siehe* **Annahmestelle**.

Annahme-: ~frist *f* **~frist bis zum 17. Juli** closing date 17th July; **die ~frist einhalten** to meet the deadline for applications/bets *etc*; **die ~frist für die Bewerbung ist schon vorbei** applications can no longer be accepted; ⚠**~schluß** *m* closing date; **~stelle** *f* (*für Pakete, Telegramme*) counter; (*für Wetten, Lotto, Toto etc*) place where bets *etc* are accepted; (*für Reparaturen*) reception; (*für Material*) delivery point; **die ~stelle für das Altmaterial ist ...** please bring your jumble to ..., jumble will be taken at ...; **~verweigerung** *f* refusal; **bei ~verweigerung** when delivery *or* when a parcel/letter *etc* is refused.

Annalen *pl* annals *pl* ◆ **in die ~ eingehen** (*fig*) to go down in the annals *or* in history.

annehmbar [1] *adj* acceptable; (*nicht schlecht*) reasonable, not bad ◆ **sein altes Auto hat noch einen ~en Preis erzielt** he didn't get a bad price *or* he got a reasonable price for his old car.

[2] *adv* reasonably well.

Annehmbarkeit *f* acceptability.

▼ **annehmen** *sep irreg* [1] *vt* **(a)** (*entgegennehmen, akzeptieren*) to accept; *Geld auch, Nahrung, einen Rat, Telegramm, Gespräch, Telefonat, Lottoschein, Reparaturen* to take; *Arbeit, Auftrag, Wette auch* to take on; *Herausforderung, Angebot auch* to take up; *siehe* **Wahl, Vernunft**.

(b) (*billigen*) to approve; *Gesetz* to pass; *Resolution* to adopt; *Antrag* to accept.

(c) (*sich aneignen*) to adopt; *Gewohnheit etc auch* to pick up; *Staatsangehörigkeit auch* to take on; *Akzent, Tonfall* to acquire, to take on; *Gestalt, Namen* to assume, to take on ◆ **ein angenommener Name** an assumed name.

(d) (*zulassen*) *Patienten, Bewerber* to accept, to take on.

(e) (*adoptieren*) to adopt ◆ **jdn an Kindes Statt ~** to adopt sb.

(f) (*aufnehmen*) *Farbe* to take ◆ **dieser Stoff/das Gefieder nimmt kein Wasser an** this material is/the feathers are water-repellent.

(g) (*Sport*) to take.

(h) (*vermuten*) to presume, to assume ◆ **von jdm etw ~** (*erwarten*) to expect sth of sb; (*glauben*) to believe sth of sb; **er ist nicht so dumm, wie man es von ihm ~ könnte** he's not as stupid as you might think *or* suppose.

▼ **(i)** (*voraussetzen*) to assume ◆ **wir wollen ~, daß ...** let us assume that ...; **etw als gegeben** *or* **Tatsache ~** to take sth as read *or* for granted; **das kann man wohl ~** you can take that as read; *siehe* **angenommen**.

[2] *vr* **sich jds/einer Sache ~** to look after a person/to see to *or* look after a matter.

Annehmlichkeit *f* (*Bequemlichkeit*) convenience; (*Vorteil*) advantage. **~en** *pl* comforts *pl*.

annektieren* *vt* to annex.

Annektierung *f siehe* **Annexion**.

Annex *m* **-es, -e** (*Archit*) annex(e); (*Jur*) annex, appendix.

Annexion *f* annexation.

anniesen *vt sep* to sneeze over *or* on.

annieten *vt sep* to rivet on (*an +acc or dat* -to).

Anno, anno (*Aus*) *adv* in (the year) ◆ **der härteste Winter seit ~ zwölf** the coldest winter since 1912; **ein harter Winter, wie ~ 81** a cold winter, like the winter of '81; **von ~ dazumal** *or* **dunnemals** *or* **Tobak** (*all inf*) from the year dot (*inf*); **das war im Deutschland von ~ dazumal so üblich** that was the custom in Germany in olden days; **ein Überbleibsel von ~ dazumal** *or* **dunnemals** *or* **Tobak** (*all inf*) a hangover from the olden days; **~ dazumal** *or* **dunnemals war alles viel billiger** in those days everything was much cheaper.

Anno Domini *adv* in the year of Our Lord.

Annonce [a'nõ:sə] *f* **-, -n** advertisement, advert (*Brit inf*), ad (*inf*).

Annoncenteil *m* classified (advertisement) section.

annoncieren* [anõ'si:rən] [1] *vi* to advertise.

[2] *vt* to advertise; (*geh: ankündigen*) *Veröffentlichung, Heirat etc* to announce.

annullieren* *vt* (*Jur*) to annul.

Annullierung *f* annulment.

Anode *f* **-, -n** anode.

an|öden *vt sep* (*inf*) (*langweilen*) to bore stiff (*inf*) *or* to tears (*inf*).

anomal *adj* (*regelwidrig*) unusual, abnormal; (*nicht normal*) strange, odd.

Anomalie *f* anomaly; (*Med: Mißbildung*) abnormality.

anonym *adj* anonymous ◆ **A~e Alkoholiker** Alcoholics Anonymous.

anonymisieren* *vt* (*Admin*) *Daten, Fragebögen* to make anonymous.

Anonymisierung *f* (*Admin*) **die ~ der Daten ist erforderlich** data must be made anonymous.

Anonymität *f* anonymity ◆ **er wollte die ~ wahren** he wanted to preserve his anonymity.

Anonymus *m* **-, Anonymi** *or* **Anonymen** anonym (*rare*), anonymous artist/author *etc*.

Anorak *m* **-s, -s** anorak.

an|ordnen *vt sep* **(a)** (*befehlen, festsetzen*) to order. **(b)** (*nach Plan ordnen, aufstellen*) to arrange; (*systematisch*) to order.

An|ordnung *f* **(a)** (*Befehl*) order ◆ **laut (polizeilicher) ~** by order (of the police); **auf ~ des Arztes** on doctor's orders; **~en treffen** to give orders.

(b) (*Aufstellung*) arrangement; (*systematische ~*) order; (*Formation*) formation ◆ **in welcher ~ wollen Sie die Tische für die Konferenz?** how do you want the tables arranged for the conference?

Anorexie *f* **-**, *no pl* anorexia (nervosa).

an|organisch *adj* **(a)** (*Chem*) inorganic. **(b)** (*rare*) haphazard; *Wachstum* random *attr* ◆ **die Stadt ist ~ gewachsen** the town has grown in a haphazard way.

anormal *adj* (*inf*) *siehe* **anomal**.

anpacken *sep* (*inf*) [1] *vt* **(a)** (*anfassen*) to take hold of, to grab; (*angreifen: Hund*) to grab. **(b)** (*handhaben, beginnen*) to tackle, to set about. **(c)** (*umgehen mit*) *jdn* to treat.

[2] *vi* (*helfen*) (*auch* **mit ~**) to lend a hand.

➤ SPRACHE AKTIV: **Annahme: a** → 39.1, 42.2 **annehmen: 1a** → 27.3, 29.2, 46.6, 52.1 **1i** → 53.1, 53.2, 53.6

anpappen *sep (inf)* [1] *vt* to stick on (*an +dat* -to).
[2] *vi aux sein* to stick (*an +dat* to).
anpassen *sep* [1] *vt* (a) *Kleidung* to fit (*dat* on); *Bauelemente* to fit (*dat* to). (b) (*abstimmen*) **etw einer Sache** (*dat*) ~ to suit sth to sth. (c) (*angleichen*) **etw einer Sache** (*dat*) ~ to bring sth into line with sth.
[2] *vr* to adapt (oneself) (*dat* to); (*gesellschaftlich*) to conform ◆ **gesellschaftlich angepaßt** conformist; **Kinder passen sich leichter an als Erwachsene** children adapt (themselves) more easily *or* are more adaptable than adults; **wir mußten uns (ihren Wünschen) ~** we had to fit in with their wishes *or* them; *siehe* **angepaßt.**
Anpassung *f* (*an +acc* to) adaptation; (*von Gehalt etc*) adjustment; (*an Gesellschaft, Normen etc*) conformity.
Anpassungs-: a~fähig *adj* adaptable; **~fähigkeit** *f* adaptability; **~mechanismus** *m* (*Sociol*) adaptation mechanism; **~schwierigkeiten** *pl* difficulties *pl* in adapting; **~vermögen** *nt* (*Sociol*) adaptability.
anpeilen *vt sep* (*ansteuern*) to steer *or* head for; (*mit Radar, Funk etc*) to take a bearing on ◆ **etw ~** (*fig inf*) to set *or* have one's sights on sth; **jdn ~** (*inf*) to eye sb.
anpeitschen *vt sep* to push (hard) ◆ **von der Menge angepeitscht** driven *or* pushed on by the crowd.
Anpeitscher *m* **-s, -** slavedriver, slavemaster; (*fig*) rabble-rouser.
anpesen *vi sep aux sein* (*inf*) (*usu* **angepest kommen**) to come belting along *or* (*auf einen zu*) up (*inf*).
anpfeifen *sep irreg* [1] *vi* (*Sport*) to blow the whistle.
[2] *vt* (a) (*Sport*) **das Spiel ~** to start the game (by blowing one's whistle). (b) (*inf*) to bawl out (*inf*).
Anpfiff *m* (a) (*Sport*) (starting) whistle; (*Spielbeginn*) kick-off. (b) (*inf*) bawling out (*inf*).
anpflanzen *vt sep* (*bepflanzen*) to plant; (*anbauen*) to grow.
Anpflanzung *f* (a) *siehe vt* planting; growing. (b) (*Fläche*) cultivated area. **eine ~ anlegen** to lay out an area for cultivation.
anpflaumen *vt sep* (*inf*) to poke fun at.
anpflocken *vt sep* to tie up; *Tier auch* to tether.
anpinkeln *vt sep* (*inf*) to pee on (*inf*); (*fig: kritisieren*) to put down.
anpinnen *vt sep* (*N Ger inf*) to pin up (*an +acc or dat* on).
anpinseln *vt sep* to paint; *Parolen etc* to paint (up).
anpirschen *sep* [1] *vt* to stalk.
[2] *vr* to creep up (*an +acc* on).
anpissen *vt sep* (*sl*) to piss on (*sl*).
Anpöbelei *f* (*inf*) rudeness *no pl.*
anpöbeln *vt sep* (*inf*) to be rude to.
anpochen *vi sep* to knock (*an +acc* on, at) ◆ **bei jdm ~, ob ...** (*inf*) to sound sb out (as to) whether ...
Anprall *m* impact ◆ **beim ~ gegen** on impact with.
anprallen *vi sep aux sein* to crash (*an or gegen jdn/etw* into sb/against sth).
anprangern *vt sep* to denounce ◆ **jdn als Betrüger/etw als Korruption ~** to denounce sb as a fraud/sth as corrupt.
Anprangerung *f* denunciation.
anpreisen *vt sep irreg* to extol (*jdm etw* sth to sb) ◆ **sich (als etw) ~** to sell oneself as sth.
anpreschen *vi sep aux sein* (*usu* **angeprescht kommen**) to come hurrying along *or* (*auf einen zu*) up.
anpressen *vt sep* to press on (*an +acc* -to) ◆ **das Ohr an die Tür ~** to press *or* put one's ear to the door.
Anprobe *f* (a) fitting. (b) (*Raum*) (*im Kaufhaus*) changing room; (*beim Schneider*) fitting room.
anprobieren* *sep* [1] *vt* to try on ◆ **jdm etw ~** (*inf*) to try sth on sb.
[2] *vi* (*beim Schneider*) to have a fitting ◆ **kann ich mal ~?** can I try this/it *etc* on?; **ich muß noch ~** I'll have to try it on.
anpumpen *vt sep* (*inf*) to borrow from ◆ **jdn um 50 Mark ~** to touch sb for 50 marks (*inf*), to borrow 50 marks from sb.
anpusten *vt sep* (*inf*) to blow at; *Feuer* to blow on.
anquasseln *vt sep* (*inf*) to speak to.
anquatschen *vt sep* (*inf*) to speak to; *Mädchen* to chat up (*inf*).
Anrainer *m* **-s, -** (a) neighbour ◆ **die ~ der Nordsee** the countries bordering (on) the North Sea. (b) (*esp Aus*) *siehe* **Anlieger.**
anranzen *vt sep* (*inf*) to bawl out (*inf*).
Anranzer *m* **-s, -** (*inf*) bawling-out (*inf*).
anrasen *vi sep aux sein* (*usu* **angerast kommen**) to come tearing *or* rushing along *or* (*auf einen zu*) up.
➤ **anraten** *vt sep irreg* **jdm etw ~** to recommend sth to sb; **auf A~ des Arztes** *etc* on the doctor's *etc* advice *or* recommendation.
anrattern *vi sep aux sein* (*usu* **angerattert kommen**) to come clattering *or* rattling along *or* (*auf einen zu*) up.
anrauchen *vt sep Zigarre etc* to light (up) ◆ **eine angerauchte Zigarette** a partly *or* half-smoked cigarette.
anräuchern *vt sep* to smoke lightly.
⚠ **anrauhen** *vt sep* to roughen; *Stimme* to make hoarse ◆ **angerauht sein** to be rough.
anraunzen *vt sep* (*inf*) to tell *or* tick off (*inf*).
Anraunzer *m* **-s, -** (*inf*) telling *or* ticking off (*inf*).
anrauschen *vi sep aux sein* (*usu* **angerauscht kommen**) to come rushing *or* hurrying along *or* (*auf einen zu*) up.
anrechenbar *adj* countable ◆ **auf etw** (*acc*) **~ sein** to count towards sth.
anrechnen *vt sep* (a) (*in Rechnung stellen*) to charge for (*jdm* sb) ◆ **das wird Ihnen später angerechnet** you'll be charged for that later, that will be charged to you later.
(b) (*gutschreiben*) to count, to take into account (*jdm* for sb) ◆ **das alte Auto rechnen wir (Ihnen) mit DM 500 an** we'll allow (you) DM 500 for the old car; **den alten Fernseher ~** to allow something on the old television.
(c) (*bewerten*) **dem Schüler wird die schlechte Arbeit nicht angerechnet** the pupil's bad piece of work is not being taken into account; **jdm etw hoch ~** to think highly of sb for sth; **jdm etw als Fehler ~** (*Lehrer*) to count sth as a mistake (for sb); (*fig*) to consider sth as a fault on sb's part; **ich rechne es ihm als Verdienst an, daß ...** I think it is greatly to his credit that ..., I think it says a lot for him that ...; **ich rechne es mir zur Ehre an** (*form*) I consider it an honour, I consider myself honoured.
Anrechnung *f* allowance; (*fig: Berücksichtigung*) counting, taking into account (*auf +acc* towards) ◆ **jdm etw in ~ bringen** *or* **stellen** (*form*) to charge sb for sth.
anrechnungsfähig *adj siehe* **anrechenbar.**
Anrecht *nt* (a) (*Anspruch*) right, entitlement (*auf +acc* to) ◆ **ein ~ auf etw** (*acc*) **haben** *or* **besitzen** *auf Respekt, Ruhe etc* to be entitled to sth; *auf Geld, Land etc auch* to have a right to sth; **sein ~ (auf etw) geltend machen** to enforce one's right (to sth).
(b) (*Abonnement*) subscription.
Anrede *f* form of address; (*Brief~ auch*) salutation (*form*).
Anredefall, Anredekasus *m* (*Gram*) vocative (case).
anreden *sep* [1] *vt* to address ◆ **jdn mit „du" ~** to address sb as "du", to use the "du" form (of address) to sb; **jdn mit seinem Titel ~** to address sb by his title.
[2] *vi* **gegen jdn/etw ~** to argue against sb/to make oneself heard against sth.
anregen *vt sep* (a) (*ermuntern*) to prompt (*zu* to) ◆ **jdn zum Denken ~** to make sb think.
(b) (*geh: vorschlagen*) *Verbesserung* to propose, to suggest.
(c) (*beleben*) to stimulate; *Appetit auch* to whet, to sharpen ◆ **Kaffee** *etc* **regt an** coffee *etc* is a stimulant *or* has a stimulating effect; *siehe* **angeregt.**
(d) (*Phys*) to activate.
anregend *adj* stimulating ◆ **ein ~es Mittel** a stimulant; **die Verdauung/den Kreislauf ~e Mittel** stimulants to the digestion/circulation.
Anregung *f* (a) (*Antrieb, Impuls*) stimulus ◆ **jdm eine ~ zum Denken geben** to make sb think. (b) (*Vorschlag*) idea ◆ **auf ~ von** *or +gen* at *or* on the suggestion of. (c) (*Belebung*) stimulation.
Anregungsmittel *nt* stimulant.
anreichen *vt sep* to pass, to hand.
anreichern *sep* [1] *vt* (*gehaltvoller machen*) to enrich; (*vergrößern*) *Sammlung* to enlarge, to increase ◆ **das Gemisch mit Sauerstoff ~** (*zufügen*) to add oxygen to the mixture; **angereichert werden** (*Chem: gespeichert werden*) to be accumulated; **mit Rauch angereicherte Luft** smoky air; *siehe* **angereichert.**
[2] *vr* (*Chem*) to accumulate.
Anreicherung *f* (*Bereicherung*) enrichment; (*Vergrößerung*) enlargement; (*Speicherung*) accumulation.
anreihen *sep* [1] *vt* (a) (*einer Reihe anfügen*) to add (*an +acc* to). (b) (*anheften*) to tack on; *Saum* to tack (up).
[2] *vr* to follow (*einer Sache* (*dat*) sth) ◆ **reihen Sie sich bitte hinten an!** join the end of the queue, please.
Anreise *f* (a) (*Anfahrt*) journey there/here ◆ **die ~ zu diesem abgelegenen Ort ist sehr mühsam** it is very difficult to get to this remote place. (b) (*Ankunft*) arrival ◆ **Tag der ~ war Sonntag** the day of arrival was Sunday.
anreisen *vi sep aux sein* (a) (*ein Ziel anfahren*) to make a/the journey *or* trip (there/here) ◆ **über welche Strecke wollen Sie ~?** which route do you want to take (there/here)? (b) (*eintreffen*) (*auch* **angereist kommen**) to come.
anreißen *vt sep irreg* (a) (*einreißen*) to tear, to rip. (b) (*inf: anbrechen*) to start, to open. (c) *Außenbordmotor etc* to start (up). (d) (*Tech*) to mark (out). (e) (*kurz zur Sprache bringen*) to touch on. (f) (*pej inf*) *Kunden* to draw, to attract. (g) *Streichholz* to strike.
Anreißer *m* **-s, -** (*pej inf*) (*Kundenfänger*) tout; (*Gegenstand*) bait.
anreißerisch *adj* (*pej inf*) attention-grabbing *attr.*
Anreißschablone *f* (*Tech*) template.
anreiten *sep irreg* [1] *vi aux sein* (*usu* **angeritten kommen**) to come riding along *or* (*auf einen zu*) up.
[2] *vt* (a) *Ziel etc* to ride towards. (b) **gegen etw ~** (*Mil*) to charge sth. (c) *Pferd* to break in.
Anreiz *m* incentive ◆ **ein ~ zum Lernen** *etc* an incentive to learn *etc or* for learning *etc*; **jdm den ~ nehmen, etw zu tun** to take away sb's incentive for doing sth.
anreizen *sep* [1] *vt* (a) (*anspornen*) to encourage ◆ **jdn zum Kauf/zu großen Leistungen ~** to encourage sb to buy/to perform great feats. (b) (*erregen*) to stimulate, to excite.
[2] *vi* to act as an incentive (*zu* to) ◆ **dazu ~, daß jd etw tut** to act as an incentive for sb to do sth.
anrempeln *vt sep* (a) (*anstoßen*) to bump into; (*absichtlich*) *Menschen* to jostle. (b) (*fig: beschimpfen*) to insult.
anrennen *vi sep irreg aux sein* (a) **gegen etw ~** *gegen Wind etc* to run against sth; (*Mil*) to storm sth; (*Sport*) to attack sth; (*sich stoßen*) to run into sth; (*fig: bekämpfen*) to fight against sth. (b) **angerannt kommen** (*inf*) to come running.
Anrichte *f* **-, -n** (a) (*Schrank*) dresser; (*Büfett*) sideboard. (b) (*Raum*) pantry.
anrichten *vt sep* (a) (*zubereiten*) *Speisen* to prepare; (*servieren*) to serve; *Salat* to

➤ SPRACHE AKTIV: anraten → 29.2

dress ◆ **es ist angerichtet** (*form*) dinner *etc* is served (*form*). **(b)** (*fig: verursachen*) *Schaden, Unheil* to cause, to bring about ◆ **etwas ~** (*inf: anstellen*) to get up to something (*inf*); **da hast du aber etwas angerichtet!** (*inf*) (*verursachen*) you've started something there all right; (*anstellen*) you've really made a mess there.

anriechen *vt sep irreg* to sniff at ◆ **jdm/einer Sache etw ~** to be able to tell sth by smelling sb/sth; **ich rieche dir doch an, daß du geraucht hast** I can smell that you've been smoking.

⚠ **Anriß** *m* (*Tech*) scribing, marking.

Anritt *m* (*old*) approach (on horseback) (*auf +acc* towards); (*Angriff*) charge (*gegen* on, against).

anritzen *vt sep* to slit (slightly).

anrollen *sep* [1] *vi aux sein* (*zu rollen beginnen*) to start to roll; (*heranrollen*) to roll up; (*Aviat*) to taxi ◆ **gegen etw/jdn ~** (*fig: in feindlicher Absicht*) to move against sth/sb; **angerollt kommen** to roll along *or* (*auf einen zu*) up.
[2] *vt* to roll; (*heranrollen*) to roll up.

anrosten *vi sep aux sein* to get (a bit) rusty.

anrösten *vt sep* to brown lightly.

anrotzen *vt sep* (*vulg*) to gob at (*sl*) ◆ **jdn ~** (*fig: beschimpfen*) to give sb a bollocking (*sl*).

anrüchig *adj* **(a)** (*von üblem Ruf*) of ill repute; (*berüchtigt*) *Lokal etc* notorious. **(b)** (*anstößig*) offensive; (*unanständig*) indecent.

Anrüchigkeit *f siehe adj* ill repute; notoriety; offensiveness; indecency.

anrücken *sep* [1] *vi aux sein* **(a)** (*Truppen*) to advance; (*Polizei etc*) to move in; (*hum: Essen, Besuch*) to turn up ◆ **die Verwandten kamen angerückt** the relations turned up. **(b)** (*weiter heranrücken*) to move up *or* closer.
[2] *vt* to move up ◆ **etw an etw** (*acc*) **~** to push sth against sth.

Anruf *m* call; (*Mil: eines Wachtpostens*) challenge ◆ **etw auf ~ tun** to do sth when called; **ohne ~ schießen** to shoot without warning.

➤ **Anrufbe|antworter** *m* **-s, -** (telephone) answering machine, answerphone.

➤ **anrufen** *sep irreg* [1] *vt* **(a)** to shout to; (*Telec*) to ring, to phone, to call; (*Mil: Posten*) to challenge ◆ **darf ich dich ~?** can I give you a ring?, can I call you? **(b)** (*fig: appellieren an*) (*um* for) to appeal to; *Gott* to call on.
➤ [2] *vi* (*inf: telefonieren*) to phone, to make a (phone) call/phone calls ◆ **bei jdm ~** to phone sb; **kann man hier bei Ihnen ~?** can I make a (phone) call from here?; **kann man Sie** *or* **bei Ihnen ~?** are you on the phone?; **ins Ausland/nach Amerika ~** to phone abroad/America.

Anrufer(in *f*) *m* caller.

Anrufung *f* (*Gottes, der Heiligen etc*) invocation; (*Jur*) appeal (*gen* to) ◆ **nach ~ des Gerichts** after an appeal to the court.

anrühren *vt sep* **(a)** (*berühren, sich befassen mit*) to touch; (*fig*) *Thema* to touch upon ◆ **er rührt kein Fleisch/keinen Alkohol an** he doesn't touch meat/alcohol. **(b)** (*fig liter: rühren*) to move, to touch. **(c)** (*mischen*) *Farben* to mix; *Sauce* to blend; (*verrühren*) to stir.

anrührend *adj* touching.

anrußen *vt sep* to blacken.

ans *contr of* **an das** ◆ **sich ~ Arbeiten machen** *or* **begeben** to set to work; **wenn es ~ Sterben geht** when it comes to dying.

ansäen *vt sep* to sow.

Ansage *f* **-, -n** announcement; (*Diktat*) dictation; (*Cards*) bid ◆ **er übernimmt bei diesem Programm die ~** he is doing the announcements for this programme; **einen Brief nach ~ schreiben** to take a letter down (on dictation); **er hat die ~** (*Cards*) it's his bid.

ansagen *sep* [1] *vt* **(a)** to announce ◆ **jdm den Kampf ~** to declare war on sb; *siehe* **Bankrott**.
(b) (*diktieren*) to dictate.
(c) (*Cards*) (*Bridge*) to bid; (*Skat*) to declare.
(d) (*inf*) **angesagt sein** (*modisch sein*) to be in; (*erforderlich sein*) to be called for; (*auf dem Programm stehen*) to be the order of the day; **Spannung ist angesagt** we are in for a bit of excitement.
[2] *vr* (*Besuch ankündigen*) to say that one is coming; (*Termin vereinbaren*) to make an appointment; (*Zeit, Frühling*) to announce oneself (*liter*).
[3] *vi* **(a)** (*old, liter*) **sag an, Fremdling ...** pray tell, stranger (*old, liter*) ...
(b) sie sagt im Radio an she's an announcer on the radio.

ansägen *vt sep* to saw into.

Ansager(in *f*) *m* **-s, -** (*Radio etc*) announcer; (*im Kabarett*) compère.

ansammeln *sep* [1] *vt* **(a)** (*anhäufen*) to accumulate; *Reichtümer* to amass; *Vorräte* to build up; *Zinsen* to build up, to accrue (*form*).
(b) (*zusammenkommen lassen*) to gather together; *Truppen* to concentrate.
[2] *vr* **(a)** (*sich versammeln*) to gather, to collect.
(b) (*aufspeichern, aufhäufen*) to accumulate; (*Staub, Wasser auch, Fragen*) to collect; (*Druck, Stau, fig: Wut*) to build up; (*Zinsen*) to build up, to accrue (*form*).

Ansammlung *f* **(a)** (*Anhäufung*) accumulation; (*Sammlung*) collection; (*von Druck, Stau, Wut*) build-up; (*Haufen*) pile. **(b)** (*Auflauf*) gathering, crowd; (*von Truppen*) concentration.

ansässig *adj* (*form*) resident ◆ **sich in London ~ machen** to settle *or* take up residence (*form*) in London; **alle in diesem Ort A~en** all local residents.

Ansatz *m* **(a)** (*von Hals, Arm, Henkel etc*) base; (*an Stirn*) hairline; (*Haarwurzeln*) roots *pl*.
(b) (*Tech*) (*Zusatzstück*) attachment; (*zur Verlängerung*) extension; (*Naht*) join.
(c) (*das Ansetzen: von Rost, Kalk etc*) formation, deposition; (*Schicht*) coating, layer.
(d) (*erstes Anzeichen, Beginn*) first sign(s *pl*), beginning(s *pl*); (*Versuch*) attempt (*zu etw* at sth); (*Ausgangspunkt*) starting-point ◆ **den ~ zu etw zeigen** to show the first signs *or* the beginnings of sth; **einen neuen ~ zu etw machen** to make a fresh attempt at sth; **Ansätze zeigen, etw zu tun** to show signs of doing sth; **sie zeigte Ansätze von Senilität** she showed signs of senility; **die ersten Ansätze** the initial stages; **im ~** basically.
(e) (*esp Philos, Liter etc*) approach.
(f) (*Sport: Anlauf*) run-up; (*zum Sprung*) take-off.
(g) (*Math*) formulation.
(h) (*Mus*) intonation; (*Lippenstellung*) embouchure.
(i) (*Econ form*) estimate; (*Fonds für Sonderzwecke*) appropriation ◆ **außer ~ bleiben** to be excluded, to be left out of account; **etw für etw in ~ bringen** to appropriate sth for sth.

Ansatz-: ~punkt *m* starting-point; **~stück** *nt* (*Tech*) attachment; (*zur Verlängerung*) extension.

ansäuern *sep* [1] *vt* to make sour; *Brotteig* to leaven; (*Chem*) to acidify.
[2] *vi aux sein* to start to go sour.

ansaufen *vr sep irreg* (*sl*) **sich** (*dat*) **einen (Rausch) ~** to get plastered *or* sloshed (*sl*); **sich** (*dat*) **einen Bauch ~** to get a beer-belly; *siehe* **angesoffen, antrinken**.

ansaugen *sep* [1] *vt* to suck *or* draw in; (*anfangen zu saugen*) to start to suck.
[2] *vr* to attach itself (*by suction*).

ansäuseln *vr sep* **sich** (*dat*) **einen ~** (*hum*) to have a tipple (*inf*); *siehe* **angesäuselt**.

anschaffen *sep* [1] *vt* (**sich** *dat*) **etw ~** to get oneself sth; (*kaufen*) to buy sth; **sich** (*dat*) **Kinder ~** (*inf*) to have children.
[2] *vi* **(a)** (*Aus, S Ger*) to give orders ◆ **jdm ~** to order sb about, to give sb orders.
(b) (*sl: durch Prostitution*) **~ gehen** to be on the game (*inf*); **für jdn ~ gehen** to go on the game for sb (*inf*).

Anschaffung *f* **(a)** *no pl* acquisition; (*das Kaufen auch*) buying ◆ **ich habe mich zur ~ eines Autos entschlossen** I have decided to get *or* buy a new car.
(b) (*angeschaffter Gegenstand*) acquisition; (*gekaufter Gegenstand auch*) purchase, buy ◆ **~en machen** to acquire things; (*kaufen*) to make purchases.

Anschaffungs-: ~kosten *pl* cost *sing* of purchase; **~kredit** *m* (personal) loan; **~preis** *m* purchase price; **~wert** *m* value at the time of purchase.

anschalten *vt sep* to switch on.

anschauen *vt sep* (*esp dial*) to look at; (*prüfend*) to examine ◆ **sich** (*dat*) **etw ~** to have a look at sth; **(da) schau einer an!** (*inf*) well I never!

anschaulich *adj* clear; (*lebendig, bildhaft*) vivid; *Beschreibung* graphic; *Beispiel* concrete ◆ **etw ~ machen** to illustrate sth; **den Unterricht sehr ~ machen** to make teaching come alive.

Anschaulichkeit *f siehe adj* clearness; vividness; graphicness; concreteness.

Anschauung *f* (*Ansicht, Auffassung*) view; (*Meinung*) opinion; (*Vorstellung*) idea, notion; (*innere Versenkung*) contemplation; (*~svermögen*) ability to visualize things ◆ **nach neuerer ~** according to the current way of thinking; **in ~** *+gen* (*geh*) in view of; **aus eigener ~** from one's own experience.

Anschauungs-: ~material *nt* illustrative material, visual aids *pl*; **~unterricht** *m* visual instruction; **~vermögen** *nt* ability to visualize things; **~weise** *f* (*geh*) view.

Anschein *m* appearance; (*Eindruck*) impression ◆ **allem ~ nach** to all appearances, apparently; **den ~ erwecken, als ...** to give the impression that ...; **sich** (*dat*) **den ~ geben, als ob man informiert sei** to pretend to be informed; **es hat den ~, als ob ...** it appears that *or* seems as if ...

anscheinen *vt sep irreg* to shine (up)on.

anscheinend *adj* apparent.

anscheißen *vt sep irreg* (*fig sl*) **(a)** (*betrügen*) **jdn ~** to do the dirty on sb (*sl*); **da hast du dich aber ~ lassen** you were really done there; *siehe* **angeschissen**. **(b)** (*beschimpfen*) **jdn ~** to give sb a bollocking (*sl*).

anschesen *vi sep aux sein* **angeschest kommen** (*N Ger inf*) to come tearing (*inf*) along *or* (*auf einen zu*) up.

anschicken *vr sep* **sich ~, etw zu tun** (*geh*) (*sich bereit machen*) to get ready *or* prepare to do sth; (*im Begriff sein, etw zu tun*) to be on the point of doing sth, to be about to do sth.

anschieben *vt sep irreg* *Fahrzeug* to push ◆ **können Sie mich mal ~?** can you give me a push?

anschießen *sep irreg* [1] *vt* **(a)** (*verletzen*) to shoot (and wound); *Vogel* (*in Flügel*) to wing; *siehe* **angeschossen**.
(b) *Gewehr* to test-fire.
(c) (*Sport*) *Rennen* to start.
(d) *Tor* to shoot at; *Latte, Pfosten, Spieler* to hit.
(e) (*inf: kritisieren*) to hit out at (*inf*).
[2] *vi aux sein* (*inf*) (*heranrasen*) to shoot up ◆ **angeschossen kommen** to come shooting along *or* (*auf einen zu*) up.

anschimmeln *vi sep aux sein* to (start to) go mouldy.

anschirren *vt sep* to harness.

⚠ **Anschiß** *m* **-sses, -sse** (*sl*) bollocking (*sl*).

Anschlag *m* **(a)** (*Plakat*) poster, bill, placard; (*Bekanntmachung*) notice ◆ **einen ~ machen** to put up a poster/notice.
(b) (*Überfall*) attack (*auf +acc* on); (*Attentat*) attempt on sb's life; (*Verschwörung*) plot (*auf +acc* against) ◆ **einen ~ auf jdn verüben** to make an attempt on sb's life; **einem ~ zum Opfer fallen** to be assassinated.
(c) (*Kosten~*) estimate ◆ **etw in ~ bringen** (*form*) to take sth into account; **eine Summe in ~ bringen** (*form*) to calculate an amount.
(d) (*Aufprall*) impact; (*von Wellen auch*) beating.

(e) (*Sport*) (*beim Schwimmen*) touch; (*beim Versteckspiel*) home.
(f) (*von Klavier(spieler), Schreibmaschine*) touch ◆ **200 Anschläge in der Minute** ≃ 40 words per minute.
(g) (*in Strickanleitung*) **~ von 20 Maschen** cast on 20 stitches.
(h) (*von Hund*) bark.
(i) (*bei Hebel, Knopf etc*) stop ◆ **etw bis zum ~ durchdrücken/drehen** to push sth right down/to turn sth as far as it will go.
(j) (*Mil*) aiming *or* firing position ◆ **ein Gewehr im ~ haben** to have a rifle at the ready.

Anschlagbrett *nt* notice-board (*Brit*), bulletin board (*US*).

anschlagen *sep irreg* [1] *vt* **(a)** (*befestigen*) to fix on (*an+acc* -to); (*mit Nägeln*) to nail on (*an +acc* -to); (*aushängen*) *Plakat* to put up, to post (*an +acc* on).
(b) *Stunde, Taste, Akkord* to strike; (*anstimmen*) *Melodie* to strike up; *Gelächter* to burst into; (*Mus*) to play ◆ **eine schnellere Gangart ~** (*fig*) to strike up a faster pace, to speed up; **ein anderes Thema/einen anderen Ton ~** (*fig*) to change the subject/one's tune; **einen weinerlichen/frechen Ton ~** to adopt a tearful tone/cheeky attitude.
(c) (*beschädigen, verletzen*) *Geschirr* to chip ◆ **sich** (*dat*) **den Kopf** *etc* **~** to knock one's head *etc*; *siehe* **angeschlagen.**
(d) (*Sport*) *Ball* to hit ◆ **den Ball seitlich ~** to chip the ball.
(e) (*Aus: anzapfen*) *Faß* to tap.
(f) (*vormarkieren*) *Baum* to mark (for felling).
(g) *Gewehr* to aim, to level (*auf +acc* at).
(h) (*aufnehmen*) *Maschen* to cast on.
(i) (*Naut*) to fasten; *Segel, Tau* to bend.
(j) (*geh*) *Kosten etc* to estimate.
[2] *vi* **(a)** (*Welle*) to beat (*an +acc* against) ◆ **mit etw gegen/an etw** (*acc*) **~** to strike *or* knock sth against/on sth.
(b) (*Sport*) (*Tennis etc*) to serve; (*beim Schwimmen*) to touch.
(c) (*Glocke*) to ring.
(d) (*Taste betätigen*) to strike the keys.
(e) (*Laut geben*) (*Hund*) to give a bark; (*Vogel*) to give a screech.
(f) (*wirken: Arznei etc*) to work, to take effect.
(g) (*inf: dick machen*) **bei jdm ~** to make sb put on weight.

Anschlag-: a~frei *adj Drucker* non-impact; **~säule** *f* advertising pillar; **~zettel** *m* notice.

anschleichen *sep irreg* [1] *vi aux sein* to creep along *or* (*auf einen zu*) up ◆ **angeschlichen kommen** (*inf*) to come creeping along/up.
[2] *vr* **sich an jdn/etw ~** to creep up on sb/sth; (*sich anpirschen*) to stalk sth.

anschleifen *vt sep* **(a)** *irreg Schere* to grind, to sharpen. **(b)** (*inf: herbeischleppen*) to drag along ◆ **was schleifst du denn da für einen Plunder an?** what's that junk you're carting up? (*inf*).

anschlendern *vi sep aux sein* to stroll *or* saunter along *or* (*auf einen zu*) up.

anschleppen *vt sep* **(a)** *Auto* to tow-start. **(b)** (*inf*) (*unerwünscht mitbringen*) to bring along; (*nach Hause*) to bring home; *Freund etc auch* to drag along (*inf*); (*mühsam herbeibringen*) to drag along (*inf*); (*hum: hervorholen, anbieten*) to bring out.

➤ **anschließen** *sep irreg* [1] *vt* **(a)** (*an +acc* to) to lock; (*mit Schnappschloß*) to padlock; (*anketten*) to chain (up).
(b) (*an +acc* to) (*Tech, Elec, Telec etc: verbinden*) to connect; (*in Steckdose*) to plug in.
(c) (*fig: hinzufügen*) to add; *siehe* **angeschlossen.**
➤ [2] *vr* **sich jdm** *or* **an jdn ~** (*folgen*) to follow sb; (*zugesellen*) to join sb; (*beipflichten*) to side with sb; **sich einer Sache** (*dat*) *or* **an etw** (*acc*) **~** (*folgen*) to follow sth; (*beitreten, sich beteiligen*) to join sth; (*beipflichten*) to endorse sth; (*angrenzen*) to adjoin sth; **dem Vortrag** *or* **an den Vortrag schloß sich ein Film an** the lecture was followed by a film.
[3] *vi* **an etw** (*acc*) **~** to follow sth.

anschließend [1] *adv* afterwards.
[2] *adj* following; *Ereignis, Diskussion auch* ensuing ◆ **Essen mit ~em Tanz** dinner with a dance afterwards.

⚠ **Anschluß** *m* **(a)** (*Verbindung*) connection; (*Beitritt*) entry (*an +acc* into); (*an*
➤ *Klub*) joining (*an +acc* of); (*Hist euph*) Anschluss ◆ **~ haben nach** (*Rail*) to have a connection to; **den ~ verpassen** (*Rail etc*) to miss one's connection; (*fig*) to miss the boat *or* bus; (*alte Jungfer*) to be left on the shelf; **ihm gelang der ~ an die Spitze** (*Sport*) he managed to catch up with the leaders.
➤ **(b)** (*Telec, Comput*) connection; (*Anlage*) telephone (connection); (*weiterer Apparat*) extension; (*Wasser~*) supply point; (*für Waschmaschine*) point ◆ **elektrischer ~** power point; **einen ~ beantragen** to apply for a telephone to be connected; **~ bekommen** to get through; **der ~ ist besetzt** the line is engaged *or* busy (*esp US*); **kein ~ unter dieser Nummer** number unobtainable.
(c) **im ~ an** (*+acc*) (*nach*) subsequent to, following; (*mit Bezug auf*) in connection with, further to; (*in Anlehnung an*) following, after.
(d) (*fig*) (*Kontakt*) contact (*an +acc* with); (*Bekanntschaft*) friendship, companionship; (*Aufnahme*) integration ◆ **~ finden** to make friends (*an +acc* with); **er sucht ~** he wants to make friends.

⚠ **Anschluß-: ~dose** *f* **(a)** (*Elec*) junction box; (*Steckdose*) socket; **(b)** (*Telec*) connection box; **a~fertig** *adj* fully wired; **~finanzierung** *f* follow-up financing; **~flug** *m* connecting flight; **~nummer** *f* extension; **~rohr** *nt* connecting pipe; **~schnur** *f* extension lead; **~stelle** *f* (*Mot*) junction; **~zug** *m* (*Rail*) connecting train, connection.

anschmachten *vt sep* **jdn ~** to gaze lovingly at sb.

anschmeißen *vt sep irreg* (*sl*) (*in Gang setzen*) to turn on.

anschmieden *vt sep* to forge on (*an +acc* -to); (*anketten*) to chain (*an +acc* to); (*fig inf: fesseln*) to rivet (*an +acc* to).

anschmiegen *sep* [1] *vt* to nestle (*an +acc* against).
[2] *vr* **sich an jdn/etw ~** (*Kind, Hund*) to snuggle *or* nestle up to *or* against sb/sth; (*Kleidung*) to cling to sb/sth; (*geh: Dorf an Berg etc*) to nestle against sth.

anschmiegsam *adj Wesen* affectionate; *Material* smooth.

anschmieren *sep* [1] *vt* **(a)** (*bemalen*) to smear.
(b) **jdn/sich mit etw ~** (*inf*) (*beschmutzen*) to get sth all over sb/oneself; (*pej: schminken*) to smear sth over sb's/one's lips/face *etc.*
(c) (*inf*) (*betrügen*) to con (*inf*), to take for a ride (*inf*); (*Streiche spielen*) to play tricks on; *siehe* **angeschmiert.**
[2] *vr* **sich bei jdm ~** (*inf*) to make up to sb (*inf*), to be all over sb (*inf*).

anschmoren *vt sep* (*Cook*) to braise lightly.

anschnallen *sep* [1] *vt* **(a)** *Rucksack* to strap on; *Skier* to clip on.
(b) *Person, Kind* to strap up; (*in etw*) to strap in; (*Aviat, Aut*) to fasten sb's seat belt.
[2] *vr* (*Aviat, Aut*) to fasten one's seat belt ◆ **bitte ~!** fasten your seat belts, please!; **hast du dich** *or* **bist du angeschnallt?** have you fastened your seat belt?, are you strapped in?

Anschnallpflicht *f* obligatory wearing of seat belts ◆ **für Kinder besteht ~** children must wear seat belts.

anschnauben *sep* [1] *vt* to snort at; (*fig inf: anschnauzen*) to bawl out (*inf*).
[2] *vi aux sein* (*usu:* **angeschnaubt kommen**) (*inf*) to come along huffing and puffing.

anschnaufen *vi sep aux sein:* **angeschnauft kommen** to come panting along *or* (*auf einen zu*) up.

anschnauzen *vt sep* (*inf*) to yell at.

Anschnauzer *m* **-s, -** (*inf*) **sich** (*dat*) **einen ~ holen, einen ~ kriegen** to get yelled at (*inf*).

anschneiden *vt sep irreg* **(a)** *Brot etc* to (start to) cut. **(b)** (*fig*) *Frage, Thema* to touch on. **(c)** (*Aut*) *Kurve,* (*Sport*) *Ball* to cut. **(d)** (*Archeol*) to come across.

Anschnitt *m* (*Schnittfläche*) cut part; (*erstes Stück*) first slice; (*Ende*) cut end.

anschnorren *vt sep* (*pej inf*) to (try to) tap (*inf*) ◆ **jdn um etw ~** to cadge sth from sb, to tap sb for sth (*inf*).

Anschovis [an'ʃo:vɪs] *f* **-, -** anchovy.

anschrauben *vt sep* to screw on (*an +acc* -to); (*festschrauben*) to screw tight *or* up.

anschreiben *sep irreg* [1] *vt* **(a)** (*aufschreiben*) to write up (*an +acc* on) ◆ **etw mit Kreide ~** to chalk sth up; **angeschrieben stehen** to be written up; *siehe* **angeschrieben.**
(b) (*inf: in Rechnung stellen*) to chalk up (*inf*).
(c) *Behörde, Versandhaus etc* to write to ◆ **es antworteten nur 20% der Angeschriebenen** only 20% of the people written to replied.
[2] *vi* (*inf*) **unser Kaufmann schreibt nicht an** our grocer doesn't give anything on tick (*inf*); **sie läßt immer ~** she always buys on tick (*inf*).

anschreien *vt sep irreg* to shout *or* yell at.

Anschrift *f* address ◆ **ein Brief ohne ~** an unaddressed letter.

anschuldigen *vt sep* to accuse (*gen* of).

Anschuldigung *f* accusation.

anschüren *vt sep* to stoke up; (*fig*) *Streit* to stir up, to kindle.

anschwärmen *sep* [1] *vt* (*inf: verehren*) to idolize, to have a crush on (*inf*).
[2] *vi aux sein* (*auch* **angeschwärmt kommen**) to come in swarms.

anschwärzen *vt sep* **(a)** (*lit*) to blacken; (*beschmutzen*) to get dirty. **(b)** (*fig inf*) **jdn ~** to blacken sb's name (*bei* with); (*denunzieren*) to run sb down (*bei* to).

anschweben *vi sep aux sein* **(a)** (*Aviat*) to come in to land. **(b)** (*fig*) **sie kam angeschwebt** she came floating along *or* (*auf einen zu*) up.

anschweigen *vt sep irreg* to say nothing to; (*demonstrativ*) to refuse to speak to ◆ **sich gegenseitig ~** to say nothing to each other.

anschweißen *vt sep* **(a)** to weld on (*an +acc* -to). **(b)** (*Hunt*) to wound, to draw blood from.

anschwellen *vi sep irreg aux sein* to swell (up); (*Wasser auch, Lärm*) to rise ◆ **dick angeschwollen** very swollen.

anschwemmen *sep* [1] *vt* to wash up *or* ashore ◆ **angeschwemmtes Land** alluvial land.
[2] *vi aux sein* to be washed up *or* ashore.

Anschwemmung *f* (*in Fluß, Hafen*) silting up.

anschwimmen *sep irreg* [1] *vt Ziel* to swim towards.
[2] *vi* **(a)** *aux sein* **angeschwommen kommen** (*Schwimmer, Wasservogel*) to come swimming along *or* (*auf einen zu*) up; (*Leiche, Brett*) to come drifting along *or* (*auf einen zu*) up; (*Flasche*) to come floating along *or* (*auf einen zu*) up. **(b)** *aux sein* **gegen etw ~** to swim against sth.

anschwindeln *vt sep* (*inf*) **jdn ~** to tell sb fibs (*inf*).

anschwirren *vi sep aux sein* (*usu* **angeschwirrt kommen**) to come swarming along *or* (*auf einen zu*) up; (*Insekt auch*) to come buzzing along *or* (*auf einen zu*) up.

ansegeln *sep* [1] *vt* (*zusegeln auf*) to sail for *or* towards, to make for; (*anlegen in*) *Hafen* to put into.
[2] *vi aux sein* **angesegelt kommen** (*inf, fig*) to come sailing along *or* (*auf einen zu*) up.

ansehen *vt sep irreg* **(a)** (*betrachten*) to look at ◆ **er sah mich ganz verwundert/groß/böse an** he looked at me with great surprise/stared at me/gave me an angry look; **hübsch/schrecklich** *etc* **anzusehen** pretty/terrible *etc* to look at; **jdn nicht mehr ~** (*fig inf*) not to want to know sb any more; **sieh mal einer an!** (*inf*) well, I never! (*inf*).
(b) (*fig*) to regard, to look upon (*als, für* as) ◆ **ich sehe es als meine Pflicht an** I

consider it to be my duty; **sie sieht ihn nicht für voll an** she doesn't take him seriously; *siehe* **angesehen.**

(c) (sich *dat*) **etw ~** (*besichtigen*) to (have a) look at sth; *Fernsehsendung* to watch sth; *Film, Stück, Sportveranstaltung* to see sth; **sich** (*dat*) **jdn/etw gründlich ~** (*lit, fig*) to take a close look at sb/sth; **sich** (*dat*) **die Welt ~** to see something of the world.

(d) das sieht man ihm an/nicht an he looks it/doesn't look it; **das sieht man ihm an der Gesichtsfarbe an** you can tell (that) by the colour of his face; **man kann ihm die Strapazen der letzten Woche ~** he's showing the strain of the last week; **man sieht ihm sein Alter nicht an** he doesn't look his age; **jdm etw (an den Augen** *or* **an der Nasenspitze** *hum*) **~** to tell *or* guess sth by looking at sb; **jeder konnte ihm sein Glück ~** everyone could see that he was happy.

(e) etw (mit) ~ to watch sth, to see sth happening; **das kann man doch nicht mit ~** you can't stand by and watch that; **ich kann das nicht länger mit ~** I can't stand it any more; **das habe ich (mir) lange genug (mit) angesehen!** I've had enough of that!

Ansehen *nt* **-s,** *no pl* **(a)** (*Aussehen*) appearance ♦ **ein anderes ~ gewinnen** to take on a different appearance *or* (*fig*) aspect; **jdn vom ~ kennen** to know sb by sight.

(b) (*guter Ruf*) (good) reputation, standing; (*Prestige*) prestige ♦ **jdn zu ~ bringen** to bring sb standing *or* a good reputation; **großes ~ genießen** to enjoy a good reputation, to have a lot of standing; **zu ~ kommen** to acquire standing *or* a good reputation; **(bei jdm) in hohem ~ stehen** to be held in high regard *or* esteem (by sb); **an ~ verlieren** to lose credit *or* standing.

(c) (*Jur*) **ohne ~ der Person** without respect of person.

ansehnlich *adj* (*beträchtlich*) considerable; *Leistung* impressive; (*dated: gut aussehend, stattlich*) handsome ♦ **ein ~es Sümmchen/~er Bauch** (*hum*) a pretty *or* tidy little sum/quite a stomach.

Ansehung *f*: **in ~** *+gen* (*form*) in view of.

anseilen *vt sep* **jdn/sich ~** to rope sb/oneself up; **etw ~ und herunterlassen** to fasten sth with a rope and let it down.

⚠ **ansein** *vi sep irreg aux sein* (*Zusammenschreibung nur bei infin und ptp*) (*inf*) to be on.

ansengen *vti sep* (*vi: aux sein*) to singe ♦ **es riecht angesengt** there's a smell of singeing.

ansetzen *sep* [1] *vt* **(a)** (*anfügen*) to attach (*an +acc* to), to add (*an +acc* to), to put on (*an +acc* -to); (*annähen*) to sew on.

(b) (*in Ausgangsstellung bringen*) to place in position ♦ **eine Leiter an etw** (*acc*) **~** to put a ladder up against sth; **den Bleistift/die Feder ~** to put pencil/pen to paper; **die Flöte/Trompete** *etc* **~** to raise the flute/trumpet to one's mouth; **das Glas ~** to raise the glass to one's lips; **an welcher Stelle muß man den Wagenheber ~?** where should the jack be put *or* placed?

(c) (*mit, auf +acc* at) (*festlegen*) *Kosten, Termin* to fix; (*veranschlagen*) *Kosten, Zeitspanne* to estimate, to calculate.

(d) (*Sport*) *Spurt, Absprung* to start.

(e) (*einsetzen*) **jdn auf jdn/etw ~** to put sb on(to) sb/sth; **Hunde (auf jdn/jds Spur) ~** to put dogs on sb/sb's trail.

(f) (*entstehen lassen*) *Blätter etc* to put out; *Frucht* to form, to produce ♦ **Fett ~** to put on weight; **Rost ~** to get rusty.

(g) (*Cook*) (*vorbereiten*) to prepare; *Bowle* to start; (*auf den Herd setzen*) to put on.

(h) (*Math*) to formulate.

[2] *vr* (*Rost*) to form; (*Kalk etc*) to be deposited; (*Gekochtes*) to stick.

[3] *vi* **(a)** (*beginnen*) to start, to begin ♦ **mit der Arbeit ~** to start *or* begin work; **zur Landung ~** (*Aviat*) to come in to land; **zum Trinken/Sprechen ~** to start to drink/speak; **er setzte immer wieder an, aber ...** he kept opening his mouth to say something but ...; **zum Sprung/Spurt ~** to prepare *or* get ready to jump/to start one's spurt.

(b) (*hervorkommen*) (*Knospen*) to come forth; (*Früchte*) to set; (*Bäume*) to sprout.

(c) (*Cook: sich festsetzen*) to stick.

➤ **Ansicht** *f* **-, -en (a)** view ♦ **~ von hinten/vorn** rear/front view; **~ von oben/unten** view from above/below, top/bottom view (*Tech*).

(b) (*das Betrachten, Prüfen*) inspection ♦ **bei ~ (von unten** *etc*) on inspection (from below *etc*); **zur ~** (*Comm*) for (your/our *etc*) inspection; **jdm Waren zur ~ schicken** (*Comm*) to send sb goods on approval.

➤ **(c)** (*Meinung*) opinion, view ♦ **nach ~** *+gen* in the opinion of; **meiner ~ nach** in my opinion *or* view; **ich bin der ~, daß ...** I am of the opinion that ...; **anderer/der gleichen ~ sein** to be of a different/the same opinion, to disagree/agree; **über etw** (*acc*) **anderer ~ sein** to take a different view of sth, to have a different opinion about sth; **ich bin ganz Ihrer ~** I entirely agree with you; **die ~en sind geteilt** *or* **verschieden** opinions differ, opinion is divided.

ansichtig *adj* **jds/einer Sache ~ werden** (*dated, geh*) to set eyes on sb/sth.

Ansichts-: ~(post)karte *f* picture postcard; **~sache** *f* **das ist ~sache** that is a matter of opinion; **~sendung** *f* article(s *pl*) sent on approval; **jdm eine ~sendung schicken** to send sb articles/an article on approval.

ansiedeln *sep* [1] *vt* to settle; *Tierart* to introduce; *Vogelkolonie, Industrie* to establish ♦ **dieser Begriff ist in der Literaturkritik angesiedelt** this term belongs to the field of literary criticism.

[2] *vr* to settle; (*Industrie etc*) to get established; (*Bakterien etc*) to establish themselves.

Ansiedler *m* settler.

Ansiedlung *f* **(a)** settlement. **(b)** (*das Ansiedeln*) settling; (*Kolonisierung von Tieren*) colonization; (*von Betrieben*) establishing.

Ansinnen *nt* (*dated, geh*) (*Gedanke*) notion, idea; (*Vorschlag*) suggestion ♦ **ein seltsames ~ an jdn stellen** to make an unreasonable suggestion to sb.

Ansitz *m* (*Hunt*) raised hide; (*Aus*) residence ♦ **„~ Claudia"** "Claudia House".

ansonsten *adv* (*im anderen Fall, inf: im übrigen*) otherwise ♦ **~ gibt's nichts Neues** (*inf*) there's nothing new apart from that; **~ hast du nichts auszusetzen?** (*iro*) have you any more complaints?

anspannen *sep* [1] *vt* **(a)** (*straffer spannen*) to tauten, to tighten; *Muskeln* to tense.

(b) (*anstrengen*) to strain, to tax; *Geduld, Mittel auch* to stretch ♦ **jdn zu sehr ~** to overtax sb; **alle seine Kräfte ~** to strain every nerve, to exert all one's energy; *siehe* **angespannt.**

(c) *Wagen* to hitch up; *Pferd auch* to harness; *Ochsen auch* to yoke up (*zu* for) ♦ **jdn (zu einer Arbeit) ~** (*inf*) to get sb to do a job.

[2] *vi* (*Pferde/Wagen ~*) to hitch up ♦ **~ lassen** to get a/the carriage ready; **es ist angespannt!** the carriage is ready.

Anspannung *f* (*fig*) strain; (*körperliche Anstrengung auch*) effort ♦ **unter ~ aller Kräfte** by exerting all one's energies.

anspazieren* *vi sep aux sein* (*usu* **anspaziert kommen**) to come strolling along *or* (*auf einen zu*) up.

anspeien *vt sep irreg* to spit at.

Anspiel *nt* (*Sport*) start of play; (*Cards*) lead; (*Chess*) first move.

anspielen *sep* [1] *vt* **(a)** (*Sport*) to play the ball *etc* to; *Spieler* to pass to.

(b) (*Mus*) *Stück* to play part of; *Instrument* to try out (for the first time).

[2] *vi* **(a)** (*Spiel beginnen*) to start; (*Ftbl*) to kick off; (*Cards*) to lead, to open; (*Chess*) to open.

(b) auf jdn/etw ~ to allude to sb/sth; **worauf wollen Sie ~?** what are you driving at?, what are you insinuating?; **spielst du damit auf mich an?** are you getting at me?

Anspielung *f* allusion (*auf +acc* to); (*böse*) insinuation, innuendo (*auf +acc* regarding).

anspinnen *sep irreg* [1] *vt Faden* to join; (*fig*) *Verhältnis, Thema* to develop, to enter into.

[2] *vr* (*fig*) to develop, to start up ♦ **da spinnt sich doch etwas an!** (*inf*) something is going on there!

anspitzen *vt sep* **(a)** *Bleistift etc* to sharpen. **(b)** (*inf: antreiben*) to have a go at ♦ **jdn ~, daß er etw tut** to have a go at sb to do sth.

Ansporn *m* **-(e)s,** *no pl* incentive ♦ **ihm fehlt der innere ~** he has no motivation.

anspornen *vt sep Pferd* to spur (on); (*fig auch*) to encourage (*zu* to); *Mannschaft* to cheer on ♦ **Kinder zum Lernen ~** to encourage children to learn.

Ansprache *f* **(a)** (*Rede*) address, speech ♦ **eine ~ halten** to hold an address, to make a speech. **(b)** (*Beachtung*) attention.

ansprechbar *adj* (*bereit, jdn anzuhören*) open to conversation; (*gut gelaunt*) amenable; *Patient* responsive ♦ **er ist beschäftigt/wütend und zur Zeit nicht ~** he's so busy/angry that you can't talk to him just now; **auf etw** (*acc*) **~ sein** to respond to sth.

ansprechen *sep irreg* [1] *vt* **(a)** (*anreden*) to speak to; (*die Sprache an jdn richten, mit Titel, Vornamen etc*) to address; (*belästigend*) to accost ♦ **jdn auf etw** (*acc*)/**um etw ~** to ask *or* approach sb about/for sth; **es kommt darauf an, wie man die Leute anspricht** it depends on how you talk to people; **damit sind Sie alle angesprochen** this is directed at all of you.

(b) (*gefallen*) to appeal to; (*Eindruck machen auf*) to make an impression on.

(c) (*fig geh*) **etw als ... ~** (*ansehen*) to declare sth to be ...; (*beschreiben*) to describe sth as ...

(d) (*erwähnen*) to mention.

[2] *vi* **(a)** (*auf +acc* to) (*reagieren*) (*Patient, Gaspedal etc*) to respond; (*Meßgerät auch*) to react ♦ **diese Tabletten sprechen bei ihr nicht an** these tablets don't have any effect on her; **leicht ~de Bremsen** very responsive brakes.

(b) (*Anklang finden*) to go down well, to meet with a good response.

ansprechend *adj* (*reizvoll*) *Äußeres, Verpackung etc* attractive, appealing; (*angenehm*) *Umgebung etc* pleasant.

Ansprech-: ~partner *m* (*form*) contact; **~zeit** *f* (*Aut, Tech*) response *or* operating time.

anspringen *sep irreg* [1] *vt* **(a)** (*anfallen*) to jump; (*Raubtier*) to pounce (up)on; (*Hund: hochspringen*) to jump up at.

(b) (*Sport*) *Gerät, Latte* to jump at; *Rolle, Überschlag* to dive into.

[2] *vi aux sein* **(a) angesprungen kommen** to come bounding along *or* (*auf einen zu*) up; **auf etw** (*acc*) **~** (*fig inf*) to jump at sth (*inf*); **gegen etw ~** to jump against sth.

(b) (*Sport*) to jump.

(c) (*Motor*) to start.

anspritzen *sep* [1] *vt* (*bespritzen*) to splash; (*mit Spritzpistole, -düse etc*) to spray.

[2] *vi aux sein* **angespritzt kommen** (*inf*) to come tearing (*inf*) along *or* (*auf einen zu*) up.

➤ **Anspruch** *m* **-(e)s, Ansprüche (a)** (*esp Jur*) claim; (*Recht*) right (*auf +acc* to) ♦ **~ auf Schadenersatz erheben/haben** to make a claim for damages/to be entitled to damages; **~ auf etw** (*acc*) **haben** to be entitled to sth, to have a right to sth.

(b) (*Anforderung*) demand; (*Standard*) standard, requirement ♦ **an jdn dauernd Ansprüche stellen** to make constant demands on sb; **große** *or* **hohe Ansprüche stellen** to be very demanding; (*hohes Niveau verlangen*) to demand high standards; **den erforderlichen Ansprüchen gerecht werden** to meet the necessary requirements.

(c) (*Behauptung*) claim, pretension ◆ **diese Theorie erhebt keinen ~ auf Unwiderlegbarkeit** this theory does not claim to be irrefutable, this theory lays no claim to irrefutability.

(d) etw in ~ nehmen *Recht* to claim sth; *jds Hilfe, Dienste* to enlist sth; *Möglichkeiten, Kantine etc* to take advantage of sth; *Zeit, Aufmerksamkeit, Kräfte* to take up sth; **jdn völlig in ~ nehmen** to take up all of sb's time; (*jds Aufmerksamkeit, Gedanken*) to engross *or* preoccupy sb completely; **sehr in ~ genommen** very busy/preoccupied; **darf ich Ihre Aufmerksamkeit in ~ nehmen?** may I have your attention?

Anspruchsdenken *nt* high (material) expectations *pl*.

anspruchslos *adj* (*ohne große Ansprüche*) unpretentious; (*bescheiden*) modest, unassuming; (*schlicht*) plain, simple; (*geistig nicht hochstehend*) lowbrow; *Roman etc* light; (*minderwertig*) *Produkte* downmarket; (*wenig Pflege, Geschick etc erfordernd*) undemanding.

Anspruchslosigkeit *f siehe adj* unpretentiousness; modesty, unassuming nature; plainness, simplicity; lowbrow character; lightness; undemanding nature.

anspruchsvoll *adj* (*viel verlangend*) demanding; (*übertrieben ~*) hard to please, fastidious; (*wählerisch*) discriminating; (*kritisch*) critical; (*hohe Ansprüche stellend*) *Stil, Buch* ambitious; *Geschmack, Musik* highbrow; (*kultiviert*) sophisticated; (*hochwertig*) high-quality, superior, upmarket ◆ **eine Zeitung/der Füllhalter für A~e** a newspaper for the discriminating reader/ the pen for people with discrimination.

anspucken *vt sep* to spit at *or* on.

anspülen *vt sep* to wash up *or* ashore.

anstacheln *vt sep* to spur (on); (*antreiben*) to drive *or* goad on.

Anstalt *f* **-, -en (a)** institution (*auch euph*); (*Institut*) institute ◆ **eine ~ öffentlichen Rechts** a public institution.

(b) ~en *pl* (*Maßnahmen*) measures *pl*; (*Vorbereitungen*) preparations *pl* ◆ **für** *or* **zu etw ~en treffen** to take measures/make preparations for sth; **~en/keine ~en machen, etw zu tun** to make a/no move to do sth.

Anstalts-: ~arzt *m* resident physician; **~geistliche(r)** *m* resident chaplain; **~kleidung** *f* institutional clothing; (*in Gefängnis*) prison clothing; **~zögling** *m* (*in Erziehungsanstalt*) child from an institution; (*in Internat*) boarding-school pupil; (*in Fürsorgeheim*) child from a home.

Anstand[1] *m* **(a)** *no pl* (*Schicklichkeit*) decency, propriety; (*Manieren*) (good) manners *pl* ◆ **keinen ~ haben** to have no sense of decency/no manners; **den ~ verletzen** to offend against decency; **das kann man mit ~/nicht mit ~ tun** it's quite in order to do that/you can't in all decency do that; **sich mit ~ zurückziehen** to withdraw with good grace.

(b) (*geh: Einwand*) **ohne ~** without demur (*form*) *or* hesitation; **~/keinen ~ an etw** (*dat*) **nehmen** to object/not to object to sth, to demur/not to demur at sth (*form*); **keinen ~ nehmen, etw zu tun** not to hesitate to do sth.

(c) (*esp S Ger: Ärger*) trouble *no pl*.

Anstand[2] *m* (*Hunt*) raised hide ◆ **auf den ~ gehen** to sit on the raised hide.

anständig **1** *adj* decent; *Witz auch* clean; (*ehrbar*) respectable; (*inf: beträchtlich*) sizeable, large ◆ **das war nicht ~ von ihm** that was pretty bad of him; **bleib ~!** behave yourself!; **eine ~e Tracht Prügel** (*inf*) a good hiding.

2 *adv* decently ◆ **sich ~ benehmen** to behave oneself; **sich ~ hinsetzen** to sit properly; **jdn ~ bezahlen** (*inf*) to pay sb well; **~ essen/ausschlafen** (*inf*) to have a decent meal/sleep; **es regnet ganz ~** (*inf*) it's raining pretty hard; **sie hat sich ~ gestoßen** (*inf*) she really took a knock (*inf*).

anständigerweise *adv* out of decency ◆ **du könntest ihm die zerbrochene Vase ~ bezahlen** you could in all decency pay him for the broken vase.

Anständigkeit *f* decency; (*Ehrbarkeit*) respectability.

Anstands-: ~besuch *m* formal call; (*aus Pflichtgefühl*) duty visit; **~dame** *f* chaperon(e); **~formen** *pl* manners *pl*; **a~halber** *adv* out of politeness; **~happen** *m* (*inf*) **einen ~happen übriglassen** to leave something for manners; **a~los** *adv* without difficulty; **~unterricht** *m* lessons *pl* in deportment; **~wauwau** *m* (*hum inf*) chaperon(e); **den ~wauwau spielen** to play gooseberry.

anstänkern *vt sep* (*sl*) **jdn ~** to lay into sb (*sl*).

anstarren *vt sep* to stare at.

anstatt **1** *prep +gen* instead of.

2 *conj* **~ zu arbeiten** instead of working; **~, daß er das tut, ...** instead of doing that ...

anstauben *vi sep aux sein* to become *or* get dusty.

anstauen *sep* **1** *vt Wasser* to dam up; *Gefühle* to bottle up.

2 *vr* to accumulate; (*Blut in Adern etc*) to congest; (*fig auch: Gefühle*) to build up ◆ **angestaute Wut** pent-up rage.

anstaunen *vt sep* to gaze *or* stare at in wonder, to marvel at; (*bewundern*) to admire ◆ **was staunst du mich so an?** what are you staring at me like that for?

Anstauung *f* (*von Wasser*) accumulation; (*von Blut*) congestion; (*fig: von Gefühlen*) build-up.

anstechen *vt sep irreg* to make a hole in, to pierce; *Kartoffeln, Fleisch* to prick; *Reifen* to puncture; *Blase* to lance, to pierce; *Faß* to tap, to broach; (*Archeol*) to open up; *siehe* **angestochen**.

anstecken *sep* **1** *vt* **(a)** (*befestigen*) to pin on; *Ring* to put *or* slip on.

(b) (*anzünden*) to light; (*in Brand stecken*) to set fire to, to set alight.

(c) (*Med, fig*) to infect ◆ **ich will dich nicht ~** I don't want to give it to you.

2 *vr* **sich (mit etw) ~** to catch sth (*bei* from).

3 *vi* (*Med, fig*) to be infectious *or* catching; (*durch Berührung, fig*) to be contagious.

ansteckend *adj* (*Med, fig*) infectious, catching *pred* (*inf*); (*durch Berührung, fig*) contagious.

Anstecker *m* **-s, -** (*inf: Button*) badge; (*Schmuck*) small brooch.

Anstecknadel *f* pin, badge.

Ansteckung *f* (*Med*) infection; (*durch Berührung*) contagion.

Ansteckungs-: ~gefahr *f* risk of infection; **~herd** *m* centre of infection.

anstehen *vi sep irreg aux haben or* (*S Ger etc*) *sein* **(a)** (*in Schlange*) to queue (up) (*Brit*), to stand in line (*nach* for).

(b) (*auf Erledigung warten*) to be due to be dealt with; (*Verhandlungspunkt*) to be on the agenda ◆ **~de Probleme** problems facing us/them *etc*; **etw ~ lassen** to put off *or* delay *or* defer sth; **eine Schuld ~ lassen** to put off paying a debt, to defer payment of a debt (*form*).

(c) (*Jur: Termin etc*) to be fixed *or* set (*für* for).

(d) (*geh: zögern*) **nicht ~, etw zu tun** not to hesitate to do sth.

(e) (*geh: geziemen*) **jdm ~** to become *or* befit sb (*form, old*); **das steht ihm schlecht an** that ill becomes *or* befits him.

(f) (*Geol*) to be exposed, to crop out (*Geol*) ◆ **~des Gestein** outcrop.

ansteigen *vi sep irreg aux sein* to rise; (*Weg auch, Mensch*) to ascend; (*Temperatur, Preis, Zahl auch*) to go up, to increase.

anstelle *prep +gen* instead of, in place of.

anstellen *sep* **1** *vt* **(a)** to place; (*anlehnen*) to lean (*an +acc* against).

(b) (*dazustellen*) to add (*an +acc* to).

(c) (*beschäftigen*) to employ, to take on ◆ **jdn zu etw ~** (*inf*) to get sb to do sth; *siehe* **angestellt**.

(d) (*anmachen, andrehen*) to turn on; (*in Gang setzen auch*) to start.

(e) *Betrachtung, Vermutung etc* to make; *Vergleich auch* to draw; *Verhör, Experiment* to conduct ◆ **(neue) Überlegungen ~ (, wie ...)** to (re)consider (how ...).

(f) (*machen, unternehmen*) to do; (*fertigbringen*) to manage ◆ **ich weiß nicht, wie ich es ~ soll** *or* **kann** I don't know how to do *or* manage it.

(g) (*inf: Unfug treiben*) to get up to, to do ◆ **etwas ~** to get up to mischief; **was hast du da wieder angestellt!** what have you done now?, what have you been up to now?

2 *vr* **(a)** (*Schlange stehen*) to queue (up) (*Brit*), to stand in line.

(b) (*inf: sich verhalten*) to act, to behave ◆ **sich dumm/ungeschickt ~** to act stupid/clumsily, to be stupid/clumsy; **sich geschickt ~** to go about sth well.

(c) (*inf: sich zieren*) to make a fuss, to act up (*inf*) ◆ **stell dich nicht so an!** don't make such a fuss!; (*sich dumm ~*) don't act so stupid!

Anstellerei *f* (*inf*) **(a)** (*Ziererei*) fuss ◆ **laß diese ~!** don't make such a fuss! **(b)** (*Schlangestehen*) (*Brit*) queueing (*Brit*), standing in line.

anstellig *adj* (*dated*) able, clever.

Anstellung *f* employment; (*Stelle*) position, employment.

Anstellungsverhältnis *nt* contractual relationship between employer and employee; (*Vertrag*) contract ◆ **im** *or* **mit ~** under *or* with a contract (of employment); **im ~ sein** to have a contract, to be under contract.

ansteuern *vt sep* to make *or* steer *or* head (*auch hum*) for; (*lit, fig*) *Kurs* to head on, to follow; (*fig*) *Thema* to steer onwards.

Anstich *m* (*von Faß*) tapping, broaching; (*erstes Glas*) first draught; (*erster Spatenstich*) digging the first sod; (*Archeol*) opening.

anstiefeln *vi sep aux sein* **angestiefelt kommen** (*inf*) to come marching along *or* (*auf einen zu*) up.

Anstieg *m* **-(e)s, -e (a)** (*Aufstieg*) climb, ascent; (*Weg*) ascent. **(b)** (*von Straße*) incline; (*von Temperatur, Kosten, Preisen etc*) rise, increase (*+gen* in).

anstieren *vt sep* (*pej*) to stare at.

anstiften *vt sep* (*anzetteln*) to instigate; (*verursachen*) to bring about, to cause ◆ **jdn zu etw ~** to incite sb to (do) sth, to put sb up to sth (*inf*); **jdn zu einem Verbrechen ~** to incite sb to commit a crime.

Anstifter(in *f*) *m* instigator (*+gen, zu* of); (*Anführer*) ringleader.

Anstiftung *f* (*von Mensch*) incitement (*zu* to); (*von Tat*) instigation.

anstimmen *sep* **1** *vt* **(a)** (*singen*) to begin singing; (*Chorleiter*) *Grundton* to give; (*spielen*) to start playing; (*Kapelle*) to strike up, to start playing.

(b) (*fig*) **ein Geheul/Geschrei/Proteste** *etc* **~** to start whining/crying/ protesting *etc*; **ein Gelächter ~** to burst out laughing.

2 *vi* to give the key-note.

anstinken *sep irreg* (*fig inf*) **1** *vt* **das stinkt mich an** I'm sick of that.

2 *vi* **dagegen/gegen ihn kannst du nicht ~** you can't do anything about it/ him.

anstolzieren* *vi sep aux sein* **anstolziert kommen** to come strutting *or* swaggering along *or* (*auf einen zu*) up; (*Pfau etc*) to come strutting along/up.

Anstoß *m* **(a) den (ersten) ~ zu etw geben** to initiate sth, to get sth going; **den ~ zu weiteren Forschungen geben** to give the impetus to *or* to stimulate further research; **jdm den ~ geben, etw zu tun** to give sb the inducement *or* to induce sb to do sth; **der ~ zu diesem Plan/der ~ ging von ihr aus** she originally got this plan/things going; **den ~ zu etw bekommen, den ~ bekommen, etw zu tun** to be prompted *or* encouraged to do sth; **es bedurfte eines neuen ~es** new impetus *or* a new impulse was needed.

(b) (*Sport*) kick-off; (*Hockey*) bully-off.

(c) (*Ärgernis*) annoyance (*für* to) ◆ **~ erregen** to cause offence (*bei* to); **ein Stein des ~es** (*umstrittene Sache*) a bone of contention; **die ungenaue Formulierung des Vertrags war ein ständiger Stein des ~es** the inexact formulation of the contract was a constant obstacle *or* stumbling block; **das ist mir ein Stein des ~es** *or* **ein Stein des ~es für mich** that really annoys me.

(d) (*Hindernis*) difficulty ◆ **ohne jeden ~** without a hitch *or* any difficulty.

anstoßen *sep irreg* **1** *vi* **(a)** *aux sein* **(an etw** *acc*) **~** to bump into sth; **paß auf, daß du nicht anstößt** take care that you don't bump into anything; **mit dem**

Kopf an etw (*acc*) ~ to bump *or* knock one's head on sth; **mit der Zunge** ~ to lisp.
(b) **(mit den Gläsern)** ~ to touch *or* clink glasses; **auf jdn/etw** ~ to drink to sb/sth.
(c) (*Sport*) to kick off; (*Hockey*) to bully off.
(d) *aux sein* (*Anstoß erregen*) to cause offence ◆ **bei jdm** ~ to offend sb.
(e) (*angrenzen*) **an etw** (*acc*) ~ to adjoin sth; (*Land auch*) to border on sth.
[2] *vt jdn* to knock (into); (*mit dem Fuß*) to kick; (*in Bewegung setzen*) to give a push; *Kugel, Ball* to hit ◆ **sich** (*dat*) **den Kopf/Fuß** *etc* ~ to bang *or* knock one's head/foot.

anstoßend *adj siehe* **angrenzend.**

anstößig *adj* offensive; *Kleidung* indecent.

Anstößigkeit *f siehe adj* offensiveness; indecency.

anstrahlen *vt sep* to floodlight; (*im Theater*) to spotlight; (*strahlend ansehen*) to beam at ◆ **das Gebäude wird rot/von Scheinwerfern angestrahlt** the building is lit with a red light/is floodlit; **sie strahlte/ihre Augen strahlten mich an** she beamed at me.

anstreben *vt sep* to strive for.

anstrebenswert *adj* worth striving for.

anstreichen *vt sep irreg* (a) (*mit Farbe etc*) to paint. (b) (*markieren*) to mark ◆ **(jdm) etw als Fehler** ~ to mark sth wrong (for sb); **er hat das/nichts angestrichen** he marked it wrong/didn't mark anything wrong. (c) (*Mus*) *Saite* to bow. (d) (*streichen*) *Zündholz* to strike, to light.

Anstreicher(in *f*) *m* **-s, -** (house) painter.

anstrengen *sep* [1] *vt* (a) to strain; *Muskel, Geist* to exert; (*strapazieren*) *jdn* to tire out; *esp Patienten* to fatigue ◆ **das viele Lesen strengt meine Augen/mich an** all this reading is *or* puts a strain on my eyes/is a strain (for me); **alle Kräfte** ~ to use all one's strength *or* (*geistig*) faculties; **sein Gedächtnis** ~ to rack one's brains; **streng doch mal deinen Verstand ein bißchen an** think hard; *siehe* **angestrengt.**
(b) (*Jur*) **eine Klage** ~ to initiate *or* institute proceedings (*gegen* against).
[2] *vr* to make an effort; (*körperlich auch*) to exert oneself ◆ **sich mehr/sehr** ~ to make more of an effort/a big effort; **sich übermäßig** ~ to make too much of an effort; to overexert oneself; **sich ~, etw zu tun** to make an effort *or* try hard to do sth; **unsere Gastgeberin hatte sich sehr angestrengt** our hostess had gone to *or* taken a lot of trouble.

anstrengend *adj* (*körperlich*) strenuous; (*geistig*) demanding, taxing; *Zeit* taxing, exhausting; (*erschöpfend*) exhausting, tiring ◆ **das ist ~ für die Augen** it's a strain on the eyes.

Anstrengung *f* effort; (*Strapaze*) strain ◆ **große ~en machen** to make every effort; **~en machen, etw zu tun** to make an effort to do sth; **mit äußerster/letzter** ~ with very great/one last effort.

Anstrich *m* (a) (*das Anmalen, Tünchen*) painting; (*Farbüberzug*) paint; (*fig*) (*Anflug*) touch; (*von Wissenschaftlichkeit etc*) veneer; (*Anschein*) air ◆ **ein zweiter** ~ a second coat of paint.
(b) (*Mus*) first touch.
(c) (*beim Schreiben*) upstroke.

anstricken *vt sep* to knit on (*an +acc* -to); *Strumpf* to knit a piece onto.

anströmen *vi sep aux sein* (*Menschenmassen*) to stream along; (*Wasser*) to flow in ◆ **angeströmt kommen** to come streaming *or* rushing along *or* (*auf einen zu*) up; **~de Kaltluft** a stream of cold air.

anstückeln, anstücken *vt sep Stück* to attach (*an +acc* to) ◆ **etw (an etw** *acc*) ~ to add sth (onto sth).

Ansturm *m* onslaught; (*Andrang*) (*auf Kaufhaus etc*) rush; (*auf Bank*) run; (*Menschenmenge*) crowd.

anstürmen *vi sep aux sein* **gegen etw** ~ (*Mil*) to attack *or* storm sth; (*Wellen, Wind*) to pound sth; (*fig: ankämpfen*) to attack sth; **angestürmt kommen** to come storming along *or* (*auf einen zu*) up.

anstürzen *vi sep aux sein* **angestürzt kommen** to charge along *or* (*auf einen zu*) up.

ansuchen *vi sep* (*dated, Aus*) **bei jdm um etw** ~ (*bitten um*) to ask sb for sth; (*beantragen*) to apply to sb for sth.

Ansuchen *nt* **-s, -** (*dated, Aus*) request; (*Gesuch*) application ◆ **auf jds** ~ (*acc*) at sb's request.

Antagonismus *m* antagonism.

Antagonist(in *f*) *m* antagonist.

antagonistisch *adj* antagonistic.

antanzen *vi sep aux sein* (a) (*fig inf*) to turn *or* show up (*inf*) ◆ **er kommt jeden Tag angetanzt** (*inf*) he turns up here every day. (b) (*lit*) to come dancing along.

Antarktika *f* **-,** *no pl* Antarctica.

Antarktis *f* **-,** *no pl* Antarctic.

antarktisch *adj* antarctic.

antasten *vt sep* (a) (*verletzen*) *Ehre, Würde* to offend; *Rechte* to infringe, to encroach upon; (*anbrechen*) *Vorräte, Ersparnisse etc* to break into. (b) (*berühren*) to touch; (*fig*) *Thema, Frage* to touch on, to mention.

antauen *vti sep* (*vi: aux sein*) to begin to defrost.

antäuschen *vi sep* to feint; (*Ftbl etc auch*) to dummy; (*Tennis*) to disguise one's shot ◆ **links** ~ to feint/dummy to the left.

Anteil *m* **-(e)s, -e** (a) share; (*von Erbe auch*) portion; (*Fin*) share, interest ◆ **er hat bei dem Unternehmen ~e von 30%** he has a 30% interest *or* share in the company.
(b) (*Beteiligung*) ~ **an etw** (*dat*) **haben** (*beitragen*) to contribute to sth, to make a contribution to sth; (*teilnehmen*) to take part in sth; **an dieser Sache will ich keinen ~ haben** I want no part in this.
(c) (*Teilnahme: an Leid etc*) sympathy (*an +dat* with) ◆ **an etw** (*dat*) ~ **nehmen** *an Leid etc* to be deeply sympathetic over sth; *an Freude etc* to share in sth; **sie nahmen alle an dem Tod seiner Frau/an seinem Leid** ~ they all felt deeply for him when his wife died/felt for him in his sorrow.
(d) (*Interesse*) interest (*an +dat* in), concern (*an +dat* about) ◆ **regen ~ an etw** (*dat*) **nehmen/zeigen** *or* **bekunden** (*geh*) to take/show a lively interest in sth.

anteilig, anteilmäßig *adj* proportionate, proportional.

Anteilnahme *f* **-,** *no pl* (a) (*Beileid*) sympathy (*an +dat* with) ◆ **mit ~ zuhören** to listen sympathetically. (b) (*Beteiligung*) participation (*an +dat* in).

antelefonieren* *vti sep* (*inf*) to phone ◆ **bei jdm** ~ to phone sb up.

Antenne *f* **-, -n** (*Rad*) aerial; (*Zool*) feeler, antenna ◆ **eine/keine ~ für etw haben** (*fig inf*) to have a/no feeling for sth.

Anthologie *f* anthology.

Anthrazit *m* **-s,** (*rare*) **-e** anthracite.

anthrazit(farben, -farbig) *adj* charcoal-grey, charcoal.

Anthropologe *m*, **Anthropologin** *f* anthropologist.

Anthropologie *f* anthropology.

anthropologisch *adj* anthropological.

anthropomorph *adj* anthropomorphous.

Anthroposoph(in *f*) *m* **-en, -en** anthroposophist.

Anthroposophie *f* anthroposophy.

anthroposophisch *adj* anthroposophic.

anthropozentrisch *adj* anthropocentric.

Anti- *pref* anti; **~alkoholiker** *m* teetota(l)ler; **~amerikanismus** *m* **-,** *no pl* anti-Americanism; **a~autoritär** *adj* antiauthoritarian; **~babypille, ~-Baby-Pille** *f* (*inf*) contraceptive pill; **a~bakteriell** *adj* antibacterial; **~beschlagtuch** *nt* (*Aut*) anti-mist cloth; **~biotikum** *nt* **-s, ~biotika** antibiotic; **~blockier(brems)system** *nt* (*Aut*) anti-lock braking system; **~christ** *m* (a) **-(s)** Antichrist; (b) **-en, -en** opponent of Christianity, antichristian; **a~christlich** *adj* antichristian; **a~demokratisch** *adj* antidemocratic; **~depressivum** *nt* **-s, ~depressiva** antidepressant; **~faschismus** *m* antifascism; **~faschist** *m* antifascist; **a~faschistisch** *adj* antifascist.

Antigen *nt* **-s, -e** (*Med, Biol*) antigen.

antigern *vi sep aux sein siehe* **tigern.**

Anti-: ~held *m* antihero; **~heldin** *f* antiheroine; **~histamin** *nt* **-s, -e** antihistamine.

antik *adj* (a) (*Hist*) ancient ◆ **der ~e Mensch** man in the ancient world. (b) (*Comm, inf*) antique.

Antike *f* **-, -n** (a) *no pl* antiquity ◆ **die Kunst der** ~ the art of the ancient world. (b) (*Kunstwerk*) antiquity.

Anti-: ~kernkraftbewegung *f* anti-nuclear movement; **a~klerikal** *adj* anticlerical; **~klerikalismus** *m* anticlericalism; **~klopfmittel** *nt* (*Tech*) antiknock (mixture); **~kommunismus** *m* anticommunism; **~kommunist** *m* anticommunist; **a~kommunistisch** *adj* anticommunist; **~körper** *m* (*Med*) antibody.

Antilope *f* **-, -n** antelope.

Anti-: ~militarismus *m* antimilitarism; **~militarist** *m* antimilitarist; **a~militaristisch** *adj* antimilitaristic.

Antimon *nt* **-s,** *no pl* (*abbr* **Sb**) antimony.

Anti-: a~monarchisch *adj* antimonarchist; **~pathie** *f* antipathy (*gegen* to); **~pode** *m* **-n, -n** antipodean; **die Engländer sind die ~poden Australiens** the English live on the opposite side of the world from Australia.

antippen *vt sep* to tap; *Pedal, Bremse* to touch; (*fig*) *Thema* to touch on ◆ **jdn** ~ to tab sb on the shoulder/arm *etc*; **bei jdm ~, (ob ...)** (*inf*) to sound sb out (as to whether ...).

Antiqua *f* **-,** *no pl* (*Typ*) roman (type).

Antiquar(in *f*) *m* antiquarian *or* (*von moderneren Büchern*) second-hand bookseller.

Antiquariat *nt* (*Laden*) antiquarian *or* (*modernerer Bücher*) second-hand bookshop; (*Abteilung*) antiquarian/second-hand department; (*Handel*) antiquarian/second-hand book trade ◆ **modernes** ~ remainder bookshop/department.

antiquarisch *adj* antiquarian; (*von moderneren Büchern*) second-hand ◆ **ein Buch ~ kaufen** to buy a book second-hand.

antiquiert *adj* (*pej*) antiquated.

Antiquität *f usu pl* antique.

Antiquitäten-: ~geschäft *nt* antique shop; **~handel** *m* antique business *or* trade; **~händler** *m* antique dealer; **~laden** *m* antique shop; **~sammler** *m* antique collector.

Anti-: ~(raketen)rakete *f* anti(-missile)-missile; **~-Satelliten-Waffe** *f* anti-satellite weapon; **~semit** *m* antisemite; **a~semitisch** *adj* antisemitic; **~semitismus** *m* antisemitism; **a~septisch** *adj* antiseptic.

Antistatik- *in cpds* antistatic.

Anti-: a~statisch *adj* antistatic; **~teilchen** *nt* (*Phys*) antiparticle.

Antiterror- *in cpds* antiterrorist.

Anti-: ~these *f* antithesis; **a~thetisch** *adj* antithetical; **~transpirant** *nt* **-s, -e** *or* **-s** (*form*) antiperspirant.

Anti-Viren-Software *f* (*Comput*) anti-virus software.

Antizipation *f* (*geh*) anticipation *no pl.*

antizipieren* *vt insep* to anticipate.

antizyklisch *adj* anticyclical.

Antlitz *nt* **-es, -e** (*poet*) countenance (*liter*), face.

antoben *vi sep* (a) **gegen jdn/etw** ~ to rail at sb/sth. (b) **angetobt kommen** to come storming along *or* (*auf einen zu*) up.

Antonym *nt* **-s, -e** antonym.

antörnen *vt sep siehe* **anturnen**[2].

antraben *vi sep aux sein* to start trotting, to go into a trot ◆ **angetrabt kommen** to come trotting along *or* (*auf einen zu*) up.

Antrag *m* **-(e)s, Anträge (a)** (*auf +acc* for) application; (*Gesuch auch*) request; (*Formular*) application form ◆ **einen ~ auf etw** (*acc*) **stellen** to make an application for sth; **auf ~** *+gen* at the request of.
(b) (*Jur*) petition; (*Forderung bei Gericht*) claim ◆ **einen ~ auf etw** (*acc*) **stellen** to file a petition/claim for sth.
(c) (*Parl*) motion ◆ **einen ~ auf etw** (*acc*) **stellen** to propose a motion for sth.
(d) (*dated: Angebot*) proposal ◆ **jdm unzüchtige Anträge machen** to make improper suggestions to sb.

antragen *vt sep irreg* (*geh*) to offer (*jdm etw* sb sth).

Antragsformular *nt* application form.

Antragsteller(in *f***)** *m* **-s, -** claimant; (*für Kredit etc*) applicant.

antrainieren* *vt sep* **jdm/sich schnelle Reaktion/Tricks/gute Manieren ~** to train sb/oneself to have fast reactions/to do tricks/to be well-mannered.

antrauen *vt sep* (*old*) **jdn jdm ~** to marry sb to sb; **mein angetrauter Ehemann** my lawful wedded husband.

antreffen *vt sep irreg* to find; *Situation auch* to meet; (*zufällig auch*) to come across ◆ **er ist schwer anzutreffen** it's difficult to catch him in; **ich habe ihn in guter Laune angetroffen** I found him in a good mood.

antreiben *sep irreg* **1** *vt* **(a)** (*vorwärtstreiben*) *Tiere, Gefangene, Kolonne* to drive; (*fig*) to urge; (*veranlassen: Neugier, Liebe, Wunsch etc*) to drive on ◆ **jdn zur Eile/Arbeit ~** to urge sb to hurry up/to work; **jdn zu größerer Leistung ~** to urge sb to achieve more; **ich lasse mich nicht ~** I won't be pushed.
(b) (*bewegen*) *Rad, Fahrzeug etc* to drive; (*mit Motor auch*) to power.
(c) (*anschwemmen*) to wash up *or* (*an Strand auch*) ashore ◆ **etw ans Ufer ~** to wash sth (up) on to the bank.
2 *vi aux sein* to wash up *or* (*an Strand auch*) ashore.

Antreiber *m* (*pej*) slave-driver (*pej*).

antreten *sep irreg* **1** *vt* **(a)** *Reise, Strafe* to begin; *Stellung* to take up; *Amt* to take up, to assume; *Erbe, Erbschaft* to come into ◆ **den Beweis ~** to offer proof; **den Beweis ~, daß ...** to prove that ...; **seine Lehrzeit ~** to start one's apprenticeship; **seine Amtszeit ~** to take office; **die Regierung ~** to come to power.
(b) *Motorrad* to kickstart.
(c) (*festtreten*) *Erde* to press *or* tread down firmly.
2 *vi aux sein* **(a)** (*sich aufstellen*) to line up; (*Mil*) to fall in.
(b) (*erscheinen*) to assemble; (*bei einer Stellung*) to start; (*zum Dienst*) to report.
(c) (*zum Wettkampf*) to compete; (*spurten*) to put on a spurt; (*Radfahrer*) to sprint.

Antrieb *m* **(a)** impetus *no pl*; (*innerer*) drive ◆ **jdm ~/neuen ~ geben, etw zu tun** to give sb the/a new impetus to do sth; **aus eigenem ~** on one's own initiative, off one's own bat (*inf*).
(b) (*Triebkraft*) drive ◆ **Auto mit elektrischem ~** electrically driven *or* powered car; **welchen ~ hat das Auto?** how is the car driven *or* powered?

Antriebs-: ~achse *f* (*Aut*) propeller shaft; **a~arm** *adj siehe* **a~schwach**; **~kraft** *f* (*Tech*) power; **~rad** *nt* drive wheel; **a~schwach** *adj* (*Psych*) lacking in drive; **a~stark** *adj* (*Psych*) full of drive; **~welle** *f* driveshaft, half-shaft.

antrinken *vt sep irreg* (*inf*) to start drinking ◆ **sie hat ihren Kaffee nur angetrunken** she only drank some of her coffee; **sich** (*dat*) **einen** *or* **einen Rausch/Schwips ~** to get (oneself) drunk/tipsy; **sich** (*dat*) **Mut ~** to give oneself Dutch courage; **eine angetrunkene Flasche** an opened bottle; *siehe* **angetrunken**.

Antritt *m* **-(e)s,** *no pl* **(a)** (*Beginn*) beginning, commencement (*form*) ◆ **bei ~ der Reise** when beginning one's journey; **nach ~ der Stellung/des Amtes/der Erbschaft/der Regierung** after taking up the post/taking up *or* assuming office/coming into the inheritance/coming to power. **(b)** (*Sport: Spurt*) acceleration *no indef art*.

Antritts-: ~rede *f* inaugural speech; (*Parl*) maiden speech; **~vorlesung** *f* inaugural lecture.

antrocknen *vi sep aux sein* to dry on (*an, in +dat* -to); (*trocken werden*) to begin *or* start to dry.

antuckern *vi sep aux sein* (*inf*) (*usu* **angetuckert kommen**) to chug along *or* (*auf einen zu*) up.

antun *vt sep irreg* **(a)** (*erweisen*) **jdm etw ~** to do sth for sb; **jdm etwas Gutes ~** to do sb a good turn; **tun Sie mir die Ehre an, und speisen Sie mit mir** (*geh*) do me the honour of dining with me.
(b) (*zufügen*) **jdm etw ~** to do sth to sb; **das könnte ich ihr nicht ~** I couldn't do that to her; **sich** (*dat*) **ein Leid ~** to injure oneself; **sich** (*dat*) **etwas ~** (*euph*) to do away with oneself; **jdm Schaden/Unrecht ~** to do sb an injury/injustice; **tu mir keine Schande an!** don't bring shame upon me; **tun Sie sich** (*dat*) **keinen Zwang an!** (*inf*) don't stand on ceremony; **darf ich rauchen? — tu dir keinen Zwang an!** may I smoke? — feel free *or* please yourself.
(c) (*Sympathie erregen*) **es jdm ~** to appeal to sb; *siehe* **angetan**.
(d) (*Aus*) **sich** (*dat*) **etwas ~** (*sich aufregen*) to get excited *or* het-up (*inf*); (*sich Mühe geben*) to take a lot of trouble.
(e) *Kleid etc* to put on; *siehe* **angetan**.

anturnen[1] *vi sep* (*Sport*) *to open the season with a gymnastic event*.

anturnen[2] ['antœrnən] *sep* (*sl*) **1** *vt* (*Drogen, Musik*) to turn on (*sl*).
2 *vi* to turn you on (*sl*).
3 *vr* to turn oneself on (*sl*) ◆ **sich angeturnt haben** to be turned on (*sl*); **sich** (*dat*) **einen ~** to get stoned (*sl*).

Antw. *abbr of* **Antwort**.

▼ **Antwort** *f* **-, -en (a)** answer, reply; (*Lösung, bei Examen, auf Fragebogen*) answer ◆ **sie gab mir keine ~** she didn't reply (to me) *or* answer (me); **sie gab mir keine ~ auf die Frage** she didn't reply to *or* answer my question; **das ist doch keine ~** that's no answer; **in ~ auf etw** (*acc*) (*form*) in reply to sth; **um umgehende ~ wird gebeten** please reply by return; **um ~ wird gebeten** (*auf Einladungen*) RSVP; **keine ~ ist auch eine ~** (*Prov*) your silence is answer enough; *siehe* **Rede**.
(b) (*Reaktion*) response ◆ **als ~ auf etw** (*acc*) in response to sth.

Antwortbrief *m* reply, answer.

▼ **antworten** *vi* **(a)** to answer, to reply ◆ **jdm ~** to answer sb, to reply to sb; **auf etw** (*acc*) **~** to answer sth, to reply to sth; **was soll ich ihm ~?** what answer should I give him?, what should I tell him?; **jdm auf eine Frage ~** to reply to *or* answer sb's question; **mit Ja/Nein ~** to answer yes/no *or* in the affirmative/negative.
(b) (*reagieren*) to respond (*auf +acc* to, *mit* with).

Antwort-: ~karte *f* reply card; **~schein** *m* (international) reply coupon; **~schreiben** *nt* reply, answer.

anvertrauen* *sep* **1** *vt* **(a)** (*übergeben, anheimstellen*) **jdm etw ~** to entrust sth to sb *or* sb with sth.
(b) (*vertraulich erzählen*) **jdm etw ~** to confide sth to sb; **etw seinem Tagebuch ~** to confide sth to one's diary.
2 *vr* **sich jdm ~** (*sich mitteilen*) to confide in sb; (*sich in jds Schutz begeben*) to entrust oneself to sb; **sich jds Führung** (*dat*)**/Schutz** (*dat*) **~** to entrust oneself to sb's leadership/protection.

anverwandt *adj* (*geh*) related.

Anverwandte(r) *mf decl as adj* (*geh*) relative, relation.

anvisieren* ['anvi-] *vt sep* (*lit*) to sight; (*fig*) to set one's sights on; *Entwicklung, Zukunft etc* to envisage.

anwachsen *vi sep irreg aux sein* **(a)** (*festwachsen*) to grow on; (*Haut*) to take; (*Nagel*) to grow; (*Pflanze etc*) to take root ◆ **auf etw** (*dat*) **~** to grow onto sth; **bei ihr sind die Ohrläppchen angewachsen** her ear lobes are attached to the side of her head. **(b)** (*zunehmen*) (*auf +acc* to) to increase; (*Lärm auch*) to grow.

Anwachsen *nt siehe vi* **(a)** growing on; taking; growing; taking root. **(b)** increase; growth ◆ **im ~ (begriffen) sein** to be on the increase, to be growing.

anwackeln *vi sep aux sein* (*usu* **angewackelt kommen**) to come waddling along *or* (*auf einen zu*) up; (*fig inf*) to come wandering up.

anwählen *vt sep* to dial; *jdn* to call.

Anwalt *m* **-(e)s, Anwälte, Anwältin** *f* **(a)** *siehe* **Rechtsanwalt. (b)** (*fig: Fürsprecher*) advocate; (*der Armen etc auch*) champion.

Anwaltsbüro *nt* **(a)** lawyer's office; **(b)** (*Firma*) firm of lawyers *or* solicitors (*Brit*).

Anwaltschaft *f* **(a)** (*Vertretung*) **eine ~ übernehmen** to take over a case; **die ~ für jdn übernehmen** to accept sb's brief, to take over sb's case. **(b)** (*Gesamtheit der Anwälte*) solicitors *pl*, legal profession.

Anwalts-: ~gebühr *f* lawyer's fees *pl*; **~kammer** *f professional association of lawyers*, ≃ Law Society (*Brit*); **~kosten** *pl* legal expenses *pl*; **~praxis** *f* legal practice; (*Räume*) lawyer's office; **~zwang** *m obligation to be represented in court*.

anwalzen *vi sep aux sein* (*usu* **angewalzt kommen**) to come rolling along *or* (*auf einen zu*) up.

anwandeln *vt sep* (*geh*) to come over ◆ **jdn wandelt die Lust an, etw zu tun** sb feels the desire to do sth.

Anwandlung *f* (*von Furcht etc*) feeling; (*Laune*) mood; (*Drang*) impulse ◆ **aus einer ~ heraus** on (an) impulse; **in einer ~ von Freigebigkeit** *etc* in a fit of generosity *etc*; **dann bekam er wieder seine ~en** (*inf*) then he had one of his fits again.

anwärmen *vt sep* to warm up.

Anwärter(in *f***)** *m* (*Kandidat*) candidate (*auf +acc* for); (*Sport*) contender (*auf +acc* for); (*Thron~*) heir (*auf +acc* to) ◆ **der ~ auf den Thron** the pretender *or* (*Thronerbe*) heir to the throne.

Anwartschaft *f, no pl* candidature; (*Sport*) contention ◆ **seine ~ auf die Titel anmelden** to say one is in contention for the title; **~ auf den Thron** claim to the throne.

Anwartschaftszeit *f* (*Admin*) *minimum period between registering as unemployed and receiving unemployment benefit*, waiting days *pl*.

anwatscheln *vi sep aux sein* (*inf*) (*usu* **angewatschelt kommen**) to come waddling along *or* (*auf einen zu*) up.

anwehen *sep* **1** *vt* *Sand* to blow; *Schnee* to drift; *jdn* (*fig geh: Gefühl*) to come over ◆ **warme Luft wehte ihn/sein Gesicht an** warm air blew over him/his face.
2 *vi aux sein* to drift.

anweisen *vt sep irreg* **(a)** (*anleiten*) *Schüler, Lehrling etc* to instruct; (*beauftragen, befehlen auch*) to order. **(b)** (*zuweisen*) (*jdm etw* sb sth) to allocate; *Zimmer auch* to give ◆ **jdm einen Platz ~** to show sb to a seat. **(c)** *Geld* to transfer. **(d)** *siehe* **angewiesen**.

Anweisung *f* **(a)** (*Fin*) payment; (*auf Konto etc*) transfer; (*Formular*) payment slip; (*Post~*) postal order.
(b) (*Anordnung*) instruction, order ◆ **eine ~ befolgen** to follow an instruction, to obey an order; **~ haben, etw zu tun** to have instructions to do sth; **auf ~ der Schulbehörde** on the instructions of *or* on instruction from the school authorities.
(c) (*Zuweisung*) allocation.
(d) (*Anleitung*) instructions *pl*; (*Gebrauchs~ auch*) set of instructions.

anwendbar *adj Theorie, Regel* applicable (*auf +acc* to) ◆ **die Methode ist auch hier ~** the method can also be applied *or* used here; **das ist in der Praxis**

nicht ~ that is not practicable.

Anwendbarkeit *f* applicability (*auf +acc* to).

anwenden *vt sep auch irreg* **(a)** (*gebrauchen*) *Methode, Mittel, Technik, Gewalt* to use (*auf +acc* on); *Sorgfalt, Mühe* to take (*auf +acc* over) ◆ **etw gut** *or* **nützlich ~** to make good use of sth.
(b) *Theorie, Prinzipien, Regel* to apply (*auf + acc* to); *Erfahrung, Einfluß* to use, to bring to bear (*auf +acc* on) ◆ **sich auf etw** (*acc*) **~ lassen** to be applicable to sth; *siehe* **angewandt.**

Anwender(in *f*) *m* **-s, -** (*Comput*) user.

Anwender-: (*Comput*) **~programm** *nt* user *or* application program; **~software** *f* user *or* applications software.

Anwendung *f siehe vt* **(a)** use (*auf +acc* on); application; taking ◆ **etw in ~** (*acc*) *or* **zur ~ bringen** (*form*) to use/apply sth; **zur ~ gelangen** *or* **kommen, ~ finden** (*all form*) to be used/applied. **(b)** application (*auf +acc* to); using, bringing to bear (*auf +acc* on).

Anwendungs-: **~bereich** *m*, **~gebiet** *nt* area of application; **~möglichkeit** *f* possible application; **~vorschrift** *f* instructions *pl* for use.

anwerben *vt sep irreg* to recruit (*für* to); (*Mil auch*) to enlist (*für* in) ◆ **sich ~ lassen** to enlist.

Anwerbung *f siehe vt* recruitment; enlistment.

anwerfen *sep irreg* [1] *vt* **(a)** *Wand* to roughcast ◆ **Kalk** *etc* **an eine Wand ~** to roughcast a wall (with lime *etc*). **(b)** (*Tech*) to start up; *Propeller* to swing; (*inf*) *Gerät* to switch on.
[2] *vi* (*Sport*) to take the first throw.

Anwesen *nt* **-s, -** (*geh*) estate.

anwesend *adj* present ◆ **die nicht ~en Mitglieder** the members who are not present; **~ sein** to be present (*bei, auf +dat* at); **ich war nicht ganz ~** (*hum inf*) my thoughts were elsewhere, I was thinking of something else.

Anwesende(r) *mf decl as adj* person present ◆ **die ~n** those present; **jeder ~/alle ~n** everyone/all those present.

Anwesenheit *f* presence ◆ **in ~** *+gen or* **von** in the presence of.

Anwesenheits-: **~liste** *f* attendance list; **~pflicht** *f* obligation to attend.

anwidern *vt sep* **jdn ~** (*Essen, Anblick*) to make sb feel sick; **es/er widert mich an** I can't stand *or* I detest it/him; *siehe* **angewidert.**

anwinkeln *vt sep* to bend.

Anwohner(in *f*) *m* **-s, -** resident ◆ **die ~ des Rheins** the people who live on the Rhine.

Anwohnerschaft *f, no pl* residents *pl.*

Anwurf *m* **(a)** (*Sport*) first throw. **(b)** (*dated Build*) roughcast.

anwurzeln *vi sep aux sein* to take root ◆ **wie angewurzelt dastehen/stehenbleiben** to stand rooted to the spot.

Anzahl *f, no pl* number ◆ **die Parteien waren in ungleicher ~ vertreten** the parties were not represented in equal numbers; **eine ganze ~** quite a number.

anzahlen *vt sep Ware* to pay a deposit on, to make a down payment on ◆ **einen Betrag/100 DM ~** to pay an amount/100 DM as a deposit.

anzählen *vt sep* (*Sport*) **jdn ~** to start giving sb the count.

Anzahlung *f* deposit, down payment (*für, auf +acc* on); (*erste Rate*) first instalment ◆ **eine ~ machen** *or* **leisten** (*form*) to pay a deposit.

anzapfen *vt sep Faß* to broach; *Fluß* to breach; *Baum, Telefon* to tap; *elektrische Leitung* to tap ◆ **jdn (um Geld) ~** (*inf*) to touch sb (for money); **jdn ~** (*inf*) (*ausfragen*) to pump sb; (*Telec*) to tap sb's phone.

Anzeichen *nt* sign; (*Med auch*) symptom ◆ **alle ~ deuten darauf hin, daß ...** all the signs are that ...; **wenn nicht alle ~ trügen** if all the signs are to be believed.

anzeichnen *vt sep* to mark; (*zeichnen*) to draw (*an +acc* on).

▼ **Anzeige** *f* **(a)** (*bei Behörde*) report (*wegen* of); (*bei Gericht*) legal proceedings *pl* ◆ **wegen einer Sache (eine) ~ bei der Polizei erstatten** *or* **machen** to report sth to the police; **wegen einer Sache (eine) ~ bei Gericht erstatten** *or* **machen** to institute legal proceedings over sth; **jdn/etw zur ~ bringen** (*form*) (*bei Polizei*) to report sb/sth to the police; (*bei Gericht*) to take sb/bring sth to court.
▼ **(b)** (*Bekanntgabe*) (*Karte, Brief*) announcement; (*in Zeitung auch*) notice; (*Inserat, Reklame*) advertisement.
(c) (*das Anzeigen: von Temperatur, Geschwindigkeit etc*) indication; (*Instrument*) indicator; (*Meßwerte*) reading; (*auf Informationstafel*) information ◆ **auf die ~ des Spielstands warten** to wait for the score to be shown *or* indicated.
(d) (*Tafel, Comput*) display.

▼ **anzeigen** *sep* [1] *vt* **(a)** **jdn ~** (*bei der Polizei*) to report sb (to the police); (*bei Gericht*) to institute legal proceedings against sb; **sich selbst ~** to give oneself up.
▼ **(b)** (*bekanntgeben*) *Heirat, Verlobung etc* to announce; (*ausschreiben auch, Reklame machen für*) to advertise.
(c) (*mitteilen*) to announce; *Richtung* to indicate ◆ **jdm etw ~** (*durch Zeichen*) to signal sth to sb.
(d) (*angeben*) *Spielstand, Temperatur, Zeit, Wetterlage, Geschwindigkeit* to show, to indicate; *Datum* to show; (*fig: deuten auf*) to indicate, to show.
(e) (*Comput*) to display.
(f) *siehe* **angezeigt.**
[2] *vi* (*Zeiger, Kompaßnadel etc*) to register.

Anzeigen-: **~blatt** *nt* advertiser, freesheet; **~kampagne** *f* advertising campaign; **~preise** *pl* advertising rates *pl*; **~teil** *m* advertisement section; **~werbung** *f* newspaper and magazine advertising.

Anzeigepflicht *f, no pl obligation to notify or report an event, illness etc* ◆ **der ~ unterliegen** (*form*) (*Krankheit*) to be notifiable.

anzeigepflichtig *adj* notifiable.

Anzeiger *m* **(a)** (*bei Polizei*) *person reporting offence etc to the police.* **(b)** (*Tech*) indicator. **(c)** (*Zeitung*) advertiser, gazette.

Anzeigerin *f siehe* **Anzeiger (a).**

Anzeigetafel *f* indicator board; (*Sport*) scoreboard.

anzetteln *vt sep* to instigate; *Unsinn* to cause.

anziehen *sep irreg* [1] *vt* **(a)** *Kleidung* to put on ◆ **sich** (*dat*) **etw ~** to put sth on; (*fig inf*) to take sth personally; *siehe* **angezogen.**
(b) (*straffen*) to pull (tight); *Bremse* (*betätigen*) to apply, to put on; (*härter einstellen*) to adjust; *Zügel* to pull; *Saite, Schraube* to tighten; (*dial*) *Tür* to pull to.
(c) (*an den Körper ziehen*) to draw up.
(d) (*lit*) *Geruch, Feuchtigkeit* to absorb; (*Magnet, fig*) to attract; *Besucher* to attract, to draw ◆ **sich von etw angezogen fühlen** to feel attracted to *or* drawn by sth.
(e) (*obs: zitieren*) to quote, to cite.
[2] *vi* **(a)** (*sich in Bewegung setzen*) (*Pferde*) to start pulling *or* moving; (*Zug, Auto*) to start moving; (*beschleunigen*) to accelerate.
(b) (*Chess etc*) to make the first move.
(c) (*Fin: Preise, Aktien*) to rise.
(d) *aux sein* (*heranziehen*) to approach ◆ **aus vielen Ländern angezogen kommen** to come from far and near.
[3] *vr* **(a)** (*sich kleiden*) to get dressed.
(b) (*fig*) (*Menschen*) to be attracted to each other; (*Gegensätze*) to attract.

anziehend *adj* (*ansprechend*) attractive; (*sympathisch*) pleasant.

Anziehung *f* attraction ◆ **die Stadt hat eine große ~ für sie** she is very attracted to the town.

Anziehungskraft *f* (*Phys*) force of attraction; (*fig*) attraction, appeal ◆ **eine große ~ auf jdn ausüben** to attract sb strongly.

anzischen *sep* [1] *vt* (*lit, fig inf*) to hiss at.
[2] *vi aux sein* **angezischt kommen** to come whizzing along *or* (*auf einen zu*) up.

anzockeln *vi sep aux sein* (*usu* **angezockelt kommen**) (*inf*) to dawdle along *or* (*auf einen zu*) up; (*Pferd*) to plod along/up.

Anzug *m* **-(e)s, Anzüge** **(a)** (*Herren~*) suit ◆ **aus dem ~ kippen** (*inf*) to be bowled over (*inf*) *or* flabbergasted (*inf*); (*ohnmächtig werden*) to pass out; *siehe* **hauen.**
(b) (*Sw: Bezug*) cover.
(c) (*das Heranrücken*) approach ◆ **im ~ sein** to be coming; (*Mil*) to be advancing; (*fig*) (*Gewitter, Gefahr*) to be in the offing; (*Krankheit*) to be coming on.
(d) (*Chess etc*) opening move ◆ **Weiß ist als erster im ~** white has first move.
(e) (*von Auto etc*) acceleration.

anzüglich *adj* lewd, suggestive ◆ **~ werden** to get personal; **er ist mir gegenüber immer so ~** he always makes lewd *etc* remarks to me.

Anzüglichkeit *f* lewdness, suggestiveness ◆ **~en** personal *or* lewd *or* suggestive remarks.

Anzugskraft *f*, **Anzugsvermögen** *nt* acceleration.

anzünden *vt sep Feuer* to light ◆ **das Haus** *etc* **~** to set fire to the house *etc*, to set the house *etc* on fire.

Anzünder *m* lighter.

anzweifeln *vt sep* to question, to doubt.

anzwinkern *vt sep* to wink at.

anzwitschern *sep* (*inf*) [1] *vr* **sich** (*dat*) **einen ~** to get tipsy.
[2] *vi aux sein* (*usu* **angezwitschert kommen**) to come strolling along *or* (*auf einen zu*) up.

AOK [aː|oː'kaː] *f* **-, -s** *abbr of* **Allgemeine Ortskrankenkasse.**

Äolsharfe ['ɛːɔls-] *f* aeolian harp.

Äon [ɛ'oːn, 'ɛːɔn] *m* **-s, -en** *usu pl* (*geh*) (a)eon.

Aorta *f* **-, Aorten** aorta.

Apanage [-'naːʒə] *f* **-, -n** appanage (*obs*), (large) allowance (*auch fig*).

apart [1] *adj* distinctive, unusual; *Mensch, Aussehen, Kleidungsstück auch* striking.
[2] *adv* (*old*) separately, individually.

Apartheid [a'paːɐthait] *f* **-,** *no pl* apartheid.

Apartheidpolitik *f* policy of apartheid, apartheid policy.

Apartment [a'partmənt] *nt* **-s, -s** flat (*Brit*), apartment (*esp US*).

Apartment-: **~haus** *nt* block of flats (*Brit*), apartment house (*esp US*), condominium (*US*), condo (*US inf*); **~wohnung** *f siehe* **Apartment.**

Apathie *f* apathy; (*von Patienten*) listlessness.

apathisch *adj* apathetic; *Patient* listless.

aper *adj* (*Sw, Aus, S Ger*) snowless.

Aperçu [apɛr'syː] *nt* **-s, -s** (*geh*) witty remark, bon mot.

Aperitif *m* **-s, -s** *or* **-e** aperitif.

apern *vi* (*Sw, Aus, S Ger*) **es apert/die Hänge ~** the snow/the snow on the slopes is going.

Apex *m* **-, Apizes** **(a)** (*Astron*) apex. **(b)** (*Phon*) (*Längezeichen*) length mark; (*Akzentzeichen*) stress mark.

Apfel *m* **-s, ¨** apple ◆ **in den sauren ~ beißen** (*fig inf*) to bite the bullet, to swallow the bitter pill; **etw für einen ~ (und ein Ei) kaufen** (*inf*) to buy sth dirt cheap (*inf*) *or* for a song (*inf*); **der ~ fällt nicht weit vom Stamm** (*Prov*) it's in the blood, an apple doesn't fall far from the tree (*US*); like father like son (*prov*).

Apfel- *in cpds* apple; **~baum** *m* apple tree; **~blüte** *f* **(a)** apple blossom; **(b)** (*das Blühen*) blossoming of the apple trees; **zur Zeit der ~blüte geboren** born when the apple trees were in blossom.

➤ SPRACHE AKTIV: **Anzeige: b** → 46.1 **anzeigen: 1b** → 51.1

Äpfelchen *nt dim of* **Apfel.**

Apfel-: ~griebs *m* **-(es), -e** apple core; **~klare(r)** *m* clear apple schnapps; **~kompott** *nt* stewed apple, apple purée; **~kuchen** *m* apple cake; **~most** *m* apple juice; **~mus** *nt* apple purée *or (als Beilage)* sauce; **jdn zu ~mus hauen** *(inf)* to beat sb to a pulp; **~saft** *m* apple juice; **~säure** *f* malic acid; **~schimmel** *m* dapple-grey (horse).

Apfelsine *f* **(a)** orange. **(b)** *(Baum)* orange tree.

Apfel-: ~strudel *m* apfelstrudel; **~tasche** *f* apple turnover; **~wein** *m* cider; **~wickler** *m* **-s, -** *(Zool)* codlin moth.

Aphasie *f (Psych)* aphasia.

Aphorismus *m* aphorism.

aphoristisch *adj* aphoristic.

Aphrodisiakum *nt* **-s, Aphrodisiaka** aphrodisiac.

Apo, APO ['a:po] *f* **-,** *no pl abbr of* **außerparlamentarische Opposition.**

apodiktisch *adj* apod(e)ictic.

Apokalypse *f* **-, -n** apocalypse.

apokalyptisch *adj* apocalyptic ◆ **die A~en Reiter** the Four Horsemen of the Apocalypse.

apolitisch *adj* non-political, apolitical.

Apoll *m* **-s,** *(rare)* **-s (a)** *(Myth) siehe* **Apollo. (b)** *(fig geh: schöner Mann)* **er ist nicht gerade ein ~** he doesn't exactly look like a Greek god.

apollinisch *adj (geh)* apollonian.

Apollo *m* **-s** Apollo.

Apologet(in *f***)** *m* **-en, -en** *(geh)* apologist.

Apologetik *f (geh)* **(a)** *siehe* **Apologie. (b)** *(Theol)* apologetics.

Apologie *f* apologia.

Aporie *f (geh)* aporia *(rare)*, problem.

Apostel *m* **-s, -** apostle.

Apostel-: ~brief *m* epistle; **~geschichte** *f* Acts of the Apostles *pl.*

aposteriorisch *adj (Philos)* a posteriori.

apostolisch *adj* apostolic ◆ **der A~e Stuhl** the Holy See; **das A~e Glaubensbekenntnis** the Apostles' Creed.

Apostroph *m* **-s, -e** apostrophe.

apostrophieren* *vt* **(a)** *(Gram)* to apostrophize. **(b)** *(bezeichnen)* **jdn als etw** *(acc)* **~** to call sb sth, to refer to sb as sth.

Apotheke *f* **-, -n (a)** dispensing chemist's *(Brit)*, pharmacy. **(b)** *(Haus~)* medicine chest *or* cupboard; *(Reise~, Auto~)* first-aid box.

apothekenpflichtig *adj* available only at a chemist's shop *(Brit) or* pharmacy.

Apotheker(in *f***)** *m* **-s, -** pharmacist, (dispensing) chemist *(Brit).*

Apotheker-: ~gewicht *nt* apothecaries' weight; **~waage** *f* (set of) precision scales.

Apotheose *f* **-, -n** apotheosis.

Appalachen *pl (Geog)* Appalachian Mountains *pl*, Appalachians *pl.*

▼ **Apparat** *m* **-(e)s, -e (a)** apparatus *no pl*, appliance; *(kleineres, technisches, mechanisches Gerät auch)* gadget; *(Röntgen~ etc)* machine.
(b) *(Radio)* radio; *(Fernseher)* set; *(Rasier~)* razor; *(Foto~)* camera.
▼ **(c)** *(Telefon)* (tele)phone; *(Anschluß)* extension ◆ **am ~** on the phone; *(als Antwort)* speaking; **wer war am ~?** who did you speak to?; **jdn am ~ verlangen** to ask to speak to sb; **bleiben Sie am ~!** hold the line.
(d) *(sl) (nicht bestimmter Gegenstand)* thing; *(großer Gegenstand)* whopper *(inf).*
(e) *(Personen und Hilfsmittel)* set-up; *(Verwaltungs~, Partei~)* machinery, apparatus; *(technischer etc)* equipment, apparatus.
(f) *(Zusammenstellung von Büchern) collection of books to be used in conjunction with a particular course.*
(g) *(Liter)* **(text)kritischer ~** critical apparatus.

Apparate-: ~bau *m* instrument-making, machine-making; **~medizin** *f (pej)* high-tech medicine.

apparativ *adj* **~e Einrichtungen** (technical) appliances *or* equipment; **~e Neuerungen** new ideas in technical equipment; **~e Untersuchung/~er Versuch** examination/experiment using technical equipment; **~e Lernhilfen** technical teaching aids.

Apparatschik *m* **-s, -s** *(pej)* apparatchik.

Apparatur *f* **(a)** equipment *no pl*, apparatus *no pl* ◆ **~en/eine ~** pieces/a piece of equipment. **(b)** *(fig Pol)* machinery, apparatus.

Apparillo *m* **-s, -s** *(hum inf)* contraption.

Appartement [apartə'mã:] *nt* **-s, -s (a)** *siehe* **Apartment. (b)** *(Zimmerflucht)* suite.

Appel *m (N Ger: Apfel)* apple ◆ **für 'n ~ und 'n Ei** *(inf)* for peanuts *(inf).*

Appell *m* **-s, -e (a)** *(Aufruf)* appeal *(an +acc* to, *zu* for) ◆ **einen ~ an jdn richten** to (make an) appeal to sb. **(b)** *(Mil)* roll call ◆ **zum ~ antreten** to line up for roll call.

Appellation *f (Jur: obs, Sw)* appeal.

Appellativ, Apellativum [-'ti:vum] *nt* **-s, Appellativa** [-'ti:va] *(Ling)* appellative.

appellieren* *vi* to appeal *(an + acc* to).

Appendix *m* **-, Appendizes** appendix; *(fig: Anhängsel)* appendage.

Appenzell *nt* **-s** Appenzell.

Appetit *m* **-(e)s,** *no pl (lit, fig)* appetite ◆ **~ auf etw** *(acc)* **haben** *(lit, fig)* to feel like sth; **das kann man mit ~ essen** that's something you can really enjoy *or* tuck into; **guten ~!** enjoy your meal; **jdm den ~ verderben** to spoil sb's appetite; *(inf: Witz etc)* to make sb feel sick; **jdm den ~ an etw** *(dat)* **verderben** *(fig)* to put sb off sth; **der ~ kommt beim** *or* **mit dem Essen** *(prov)* appetite grows with the eating *(prov).*

Appetit-: a~anregend *adj Speise etc* appetizing; **a~anregendes Mittel** appetite stimulant; **~bissen, ~happen** *m* canapé; **a~hemmend** *adj* appetite suppressant; **a~hemmendes Mittel** appetite suppressant; **~hemmer** *m* **-s, -** appetite suppressant; **a~lich** *adj (lecker)* appetizing; *(verlockend aussehend, riechend)* tempting; *(hygienisch)* hygienic, savoury, *(fig) Mädchen* attractive; **a~lich verpackt** hygienically packed; **a~los** *adj* without any appetite; **a~los sein** to have lost one's appetite; **~losigkeit** *f* lack of appetite; **~zügler** *m* **-s, -** appetite suppressant.

Appetizer ['apətaizɐ] *m* **-s, -s** *(Pharm)* appetite stimulant.

applaudieren* *vti* to applaud ◆ **jdm/einer Sache ~** to applaud sb/sth.

Applaus *m* **-es,** *no pl* applause.

applikabel *adj (geh)* applicable.

Applikation *f* **(a)** *(geh, Med) (Anwendung)* application; *(von Heilmethode)* administering. **(b)** *(Sew)* appliqué.

applizieren* *vt* **(a)** *(geh: anwenden)* to apply; *(Med) Heilmethode* to administer. **(b)** *(Sew: aufbügeln)* to apply; *(aufnähen auch)* to appliqué.

apport *interj (Hunt)* fetch.

Apport *m* **-s, -e (a)** *(Hunt)* retrieving, fetching. **(b)** *(Parapsychologie)* apport.

apportieren* *vti* to retrieve, to fetch.

Apportierhund *m* retriever.

Apposition *f* apposition.

appretieren* *vt (Tex)* to starch; *(imprägnieren)* to waterproof; *Holz* to dress, to finish; *Paper* to glaze.

Appretur *f* **(a)** *(Mittel)* finish; *(Tex)* starch; *(Wasserundurchlässigkeit)* waterproofing; *(für Papier auch)* glaze. **(b)** *siehe* **appretieren** starching; waterproofing; dressing, finishing; glazing.

Approbation *f (von Arzt, Apotheker)* certificate *(enabling a doctor etc to practise)* ◆ **einem Arzt die ~ entziehen** to take away a doctor's licence to practise, to strike a doctor off (the register) *(Brit).*

approbieren* *vt (old: genehmigen)* to approve.

approbiert *adj Arzt, Apotheker* registered, certified.

Approximation *f (Math)* approximation, approximate value.

Après-Ski [aprɛ'ʃi:] *nt* **-, -s** après-ski; *(Kleidung)* après-ski clothes.

Aprikose *f* **-, -n** apricot ◆ **Wangen wie ~n** soft rosy cheeks.

Aprikosen-: ~likör *m* apricot brandy; **~marmelade** *f* apricot jam.

April *m* **-s,** *no pl* April ◆ **~, ~!** April fool!; **jdn in den ~ schicken** to make an April fool of sb; *siehe* **März.**

April-: ~scherz *m* April fool's trick; **das ist doch wohl ein ~scherz** *(fig)* you/they *etc* must be joking; **~wetter** *nt* April weather.

a priori *adv (Philos, geh)* a priori.

apriorisch *adj (Philos)* a priori.

apropos [apro'po:] *adv* by the way, that reminds me ◆ **~ Afrika** talking about Africa.

Apside *f* **-, -n** *(Astron)* apsis.

Apsis *f* **-, Apsiden (a)** *(Archit)* apse. **(b)** *(von Zelt)* bell.

Aquädukt *nt* **-(e)s, -e** aqueduct.

Aqua-: ~marin *nt* **-s, -e** aquamarine; **a~marinblau** *adj* aquamarine; **~naut(in** *f***)** *m* **-en, -en** aquanaut; **~planing** *nt* **-s,** *no pl (Aut)* aquaplaning.

Aquarell *nt* **-s, -e** watercolour (painting) ◆ **~ malen** to paint in watercolours.

Aquarell-: ~farbe *f* watercolour; **~maler** *m* watercolourist; **~malerei** *f* **(a)** *(Bild)* watercolour (painting); **(b)** *(Vorgang)* painting in watercolours, watercolour painting.

Aquarien- [-iən] *in cpds* aquarium.

Aquarium *nt* aquarium.

Aquatinta *f* **-, Aquatinten** aquatint.

Äquator *m* **-s,** *no pl* equator.

äquatorial *adj* equatorial.

Äquatortaufe *f (Naut)* crossing-the-line ceremony.

Aquavit [akva'vi:t] *m* **-s, -e** aquavit.

Äquilibrist(in *f***)** *m* juggler; *(Seiltänzer)* tight-rope walker.

Äquinoktium *nt* equinox.

Aquitanien [-iən] *nt* **-s** Aquitaine.

Äquivalent [-va'lɛnt] *nt* **-s, -e** equivalent; *(Ausgleich)* compensation.

äquivalent [-va'lɛnt] *adj* equivalent.

Äquivalenz [-va'lɛnts] *f* equivalence.

Ar *nt or m* **-s, -e** *(Measure)* are (100 m^2).

Ära *f* **-, Ären** era ◆ **die ~ Adenauer** the Adenauer era.

Araber [*auch* 'a:-] *m* **-s, -** *(auch Pferd)*, **Araberin** *f* Arab.

Arabeske *f* **-, -n** arabesque; *(Verzierung)* flourish.

Arabien [-iən] *nt* **-s** Arabia.

arabisch *adj* Arab; *Ziffer, Sprache, Schrift etc* Arabic ◆ **die A~e Halbinsel** *(Geog)* the Arabian Peninsula, Arabia.

Arabisch(e) *nt* Arabic; *siehe auch* **Deutsch(e).**

Arabistik *f, no pl* Arabic studies *pl.*

Aragón, Aragonien [-iən] *nt* **-s** Aragon.

aragonisch *adj* Aragonese.

Aralsee *m* Aral Sea, Lake Aral.

aramäisch *adj* Aramaic.

Arbeit *f* **(a)** *(Tätigkeit, Phys, Sport)* work; *(das Arbeiten auch)* working; *(Pol, Econ, Lohn für ~)* labour ◆ **~ und Kapital** capital and labour; **Tag der ~** Labour Day; **die ~en an der Autobahn** the work on the motorway; **es kann mit den ~en begonnen werden** work can begin; **bei der ~ mit Kindern** when working with children; **viel ~ machen** to be a lot of work *(jdm* for sb); **das ist/kostet viel ~** it's a lot of work *or* a big job; **an** *or* **bei der ~ sein** to be working; **sich**

an die ~ machen, an die ~ gehen to get down to work, to start working; **an die ~!** to work!; **jdm bei der ~ zusehen** to watch sb working; **etw ist in ~** work on sth has started *or* is in progress; **Ihr Bier ist in ~** (*inf*) your beer is on its way; **etw in ~ haben** to be working on sth; **etw in ~ nehmen** to undertake to do *or* (*manuelle Arbeit*) make sth; **etw in ~ geben** to have sth done/made; **jdm etw in ~ geben** to get sb to do/make sth; **die ~ läuft dir nicht davon** (*hum*) the work will still be there when you get back; **erst die ~, dann das Vergnügen** (*prov*) business before pleasure (*prov*); **~ schändet nicht** (*Prov*) work is no disgrace.
(b) *no pl* (*Ausführung*) work ◆ **ganze** *or* **gründliche ~ leisten** (*lit, fig iro*) to do a good job.
(c) *no pl* (*Mühe*) trouble, bother ◆ **jdm ~ machen** to put sb to trouble; **machen Sie sich keine ~!** don't go to any trouble *or* bother; **das war vielleicht eine ~!** what hard work *or* what a job that was!; **die ~ zahlt sich aus** it's worth the trouble *or* effort.
(d) (*Berufstätigkeit, inf: Arbeitsplatz, -stelle, -zeit*) work *no indef art*; (*Arbeitsverhältnis auch*) employment; (*Position*) job ◆ **eine ~ als etw** work *or* a job as sth; **(eine) ~ suchen/finden** to look for/find work *or* a job; **einer (geregelten) ~ nachgehen** to have a (steady) job; **ohne ~ sein** to be out of work *or* unemployed; **zur** *or* **auf** (*inf*) **~ gehen/von der ~ kommen** to go to/come back from work.
(e) (*Aufgabe*) job ◆ **seine ~ besteht darin, zu ...** his job is to ...
(f) (*Produkt*) work; (*handwerkliche*) piece of work; (*Prüfungs~*) (examination) paper; (*wissenschaftliche*) paper; (*Buch*) work.
(g) (*Sch*) test ◆ **~en korrigieren** to mark test papers; **eine ~ schreiben/schreiben lassen** to do/set a test.

▼ **arbeiten** [1] *vi* **(a)** to work (*an +dat* on); (*sich anstrengen auch*) to labour (*old, liter*), to toil (*liter*) ◆ **der Sänger hat viel an sich** (*dat*) **gearbeitet** the singer has worked hard *or* has done a lot of work; **~ wie ein Pferd/Wilder** (*inf*) to work like a Trojan *or* horse/like mad (*inf*); **die Zeit arbeitet für/gegen uns** we have time on our side, time is on our side/against us; **er arbeitet für zwei** (*inf*) he does the work of two *or* enough work for two; **er arbeitet über Schiller** he's working on Schiller; **er arbeitet mit Wasserfarben** he works in *or* uses watercolours.
(b) (*funktionieren*) (*Organ*) to function, to work; (*Maschine, Anlage etc auch*) to operate ◆ **die Anlage arbeitet automatisch** the plant is automatic; **die Anlage arbeitet elektrisch/mit Kohle** the plant runs *or* operates on electricity/coal.
▼ **(c)** (*berufstätig sein*) to work ◆ **seine Frau arbeitet auch** his wife works *or* is working *or* goes out to work too; **für eine/bei einer Firma/Zeitung ~** to work for a firm/newspaper; **die ~de Bevölkerung/Jugend** the working population/youth.
(d) (*in Bewegung sein*) to work; (*Most etc auch*) to ferment; (*Holz*) to warp ◆ **in meinem Magen arbeitet es** my stomach's rumbling; **in seinem Kopf arbeitet es** his mind is at work; **in ihm begann es zu ~** he started to react, it began to work on him.
[2] *vr* **(a) sich krank/müde/krüpplig ~** to make oneself ill/tire oneself out with work/to work oneself silly (*inf*); **sich zu Tode ~** to work oneself to death; **sich** (*dat*) **die Hände wund ~** to work one's fingers to the bone.
(b) (*sich fortbewegen*) to work oneself (*in +acc* into, *durch* through, *zu* to) ◆ **sich in die Höhe** *or* **nach oben/an die Spitze ~** (*fig*) to work one's way up/(up) to the top.
(c) *impers* **es arbeitet sich gut/schlecht** you can/can't work well; **es arbeitet sich hier auch nicht besser** it's no better working here either; **mit ihr arbeitet es sich angenehm** it's nice working with her.
[3] *vt* **(a)** (*herstellen*) to make; (*aus Ton etc auch*) to work, to fashion.
(b) (*tun*) to do ◆ **was arbeitest du dort?** what are you doing there?; (*beruflich*) what do you do there?; **ich habe heute noch nichts gearbeitet** I haven't done anything *or* any work today; **du kannst auch ruhig mal was ~!** (*inf*) it wouldn't hurt you to do something *or* a bit of work either!

Arbeiter *m* **-s, -** worker; (*im Gegensatz zum Angestellten*) blue-collar worker; (*auf Bau, Bauernhof*) labourer; (*bei Straßenbau, im Haus*) workman ◆ **der 22-jährige ~ Horst Kuhn** the 22-year-old factory worker/labourer/workman Horst Kuhn; **die ~** (*Proletariat, Arbeitskräfte*) the workers; **~ und Arbeiterinnen** male and female workers; **er ist ein guter/langsamer ~** he is a good/slow worker.

Arbeiter-: ~ameise *f* worker (ant); **~aufstand** *m* workers' revolt; **~bewegung** *f* labour movement; **~biene** *f* worker (bee); **~demonstration** *f* workers' demonstration; **~denkmal** *nt* **(a)** (*lit*) monument erected to the labouring *or* working classes; **(b)** (*hum*) statue/monument to inactivity (*hum*); **~dichter** *m* poet of the working class; **~familie** *f* working-class family; **a~feindlich** *adj* anti-working-class; **a~freundlich** *adj* pro-working-class; **~führer** *m* (*Pol*) leader of the working classes; **~gewerkschaft** *f* blue-collar (trade) union, labor union (*US*).

Arbeiterin *f* **(a)** *siehe* **Arbeiter. (b)** (*Zool*) worker.

Arbeiter-: ~jugend *f* young workers *pl*; **~kampfgruß** *m* clenched-fist salute; **~kampflied** *nt* socialist workers' song; **~kind** *nt* child from a working-class family *or* background; **~klasse** *f* working class(es *pl*); **~kneipe** *f* workers' pub; **~lied** *nt* workers' song; **~massen** *pl* working masses *pl*; **~milieu** *nt* working-class environment; **im ~milieu** in a working-class environment; **~organisation** *f* association of workers, labour organization; **~partei** *f* workers' party; **~priester** *m* worker-priest; **~rat** *m* workers' council; **~schaft** *f* work force; **~schriftsteller** *m* working-class writer; **~selbstverwaltung** *f* workers' control; **~siedlung** *f* workers' housing estate; **~sohn** *m* son of a working-class family; **~stadt** *f* working-class town; **~student(in** *f*) *m* (*DDR*) *mature student who was previously a factory worker*; **~-und-Bauern-Fakultät** *f* (*DDR*) *university department responsible for preparing young factory and agricultural workers for university*; **~-und-Bauern-Staat** *m* (*DDR*) workers' and peasants' state; **~-und-Soldaten-Rat** *m* workers' and soldiers' council; **~unruhen** *pl* worker unrest, unrest among the workers; **~viertel** *nt* working-class area; **~wohlfahrt** *f* workers' welfare association; **~zeitung** *f* paper of the labour movement.

Arbeitgeber(in *f*) *m* employer.

Arbeitgeber-: ~anteil *m* employer's contribution; **~seite** *f* employers' side; **~verband** *m* employers' federation.

Arbeitnehmer(in *f*) *m* employee.

Arbeitnehmer-: ~anteil *m* employee's contribution; **~schaft** *f* employees *pl*; **~seite** *f* employees' side.

Arbeits|ablauf *m* work routine; (*von Fabrik*) production *no art*.

arbeitsam *adj* industrious, hard-working.

Arbeits|ameise *f* worker (ant).

Arbeitsamkeit *f* industriousness.

Arbeits-: ~amt *nt* employment exchange, job centre (*Brit*); **~anfall** *m* workload; **~anleitung** *f* instructions *pl*; **~antritt** *m* commencement of work (*form*); **beim ~antritt** when starting work; **~anzug** *m* working suit; **~atmosphäre** *f* work(ing) atmosphere, work climate; **~auffassung** *f* attitude to work; **~aufwand** *m* expenditure of energy; (*Ind*) labour; **mit geringem/großem ~aufwand** with little/a lot of work; ⚠**a~aufwendig** *adj* energy-consuming; (*Ind*) labour-intensive; **a~aufwendig/nicht sehr a~aufwendig sein** to involve a lot of/not much work/labour; **~ausfall** *m* loss of working hours; ⚠**~ausschuß** *m* working party; **~bedingungen** *pl* working conditions *pl*; **~beginn** *m* start of work; **bei ~beginn** when one starts work; **~belastung** *f* workload; **~bereich** *m* **(a)** (*~gebiet*) field of work; (*Aufgabenbereich*) area of work; **das gehört nicht in meinen ~bereich** that's not my job; **(b)** (*Umkreis*) field of operations; (*von Kran etc*) operating radius; **~bericht** *m* work report; **~beschaffung** *f* **(a)** (*Arbeitsplatzbeschaffung*) job creation; **(b)** (*Auftragsbeschaffung*) getting *or* bringing work in *no art*; **~beschaffungsmaßnahme** *f* (*Admin*) job creation scheme; **~bescheinigung** *f* certificate of employment; **~besuch** *m* working visit; **~biene** *f* worker (bee); (*fig*) busy bee; **~blatt** *nt* (*Comput*) worksheet, spreadsheet; **~dienst** *m* (*NS*) labour service; **~direktor** *m* personnel manager; **~disziplin** *f* discipline at work *no art*; **~eifer** *m* enthusiasm for one's work; **~einheit** *f* **(a)** (*DDR*) work unit; **(b)** (*Phys*) system of units; **~einkommen** *nt* earned income; **~einstellung** *f* **(a)** *siehe* **~auffassung**; **(b)** (*~niederlegung*) walkout; **die Belegschaft reagierte mit ~einstellung** the work force reacted by downing tools *or* walking out; **~emigrant** *m* immigrant worker; **~ende** *nt siehe* **~schluß**; **~erlaubnis** *f* (*Recht*) permission to work; (*Bescheinigung*) work permit; **~erleichterung** *f* **das bedeutet eine große ~erleichterung** that makes the work much easier; **~essen** *nt* (*esp Pol*) working lunch/dinner; **~ethos** *nt* work ethic; **~exemplar** *nt* desk copy; **a~fähig** *adj Person* able to work; (*gesund*) fit for *or* to work; *Regierung etc* viable; **~fähigkeit** *f siehe adj* ability to work; fitness for work; viability; **~feld** *nt* (*geh*) field of work; **~fieber** *nt* work mania; **~fläche** *f* work surface, worktop; **~freude** *f* willingness to work; **~friede(n)** *m* peaceful labour relations *pl, no art*; **~gang** *m* **(a)** (*Abschnitt*) operation; **(b)** *siehe* **~ablauf**; **~gebiet** *nt* field of work; **~gemeinschaft** *f* team; (*Sch, Univ*) study-group; (*in Namen*) association; **~genehmigung** *f siehe* **~erlaubnis**; **~gerät** *nt* **(a)** tool; **(b)** *no pl* tools *pl*, equipment *no pl*; **~gericht** *nt* industrial tribunal (*Brit*), labor court (*US*); **~gruppe** *f* team; **~haltung** *f* attitude to work; **~haus** *nt* (*old*) workhouse; **~hilfe** *f* aid; **~hypothese** *f* working hypothesis; **~inspektion** *f* (*Aus, Sw*) factory supervision; **a~intensiv** *adj* labour-intensive; **~kampf** *m* industrial action; **~kampfmaßnahmen** *pl* industrial action *sing*; **~kleidung** *f* working clothes *pl*; **~klima** *nt* work climate, work(ing) atmosphere; **~kollege** *m* (*bei Angestellten etc*) colleague; (*bei Arbeitern*) workmate; **~kollektiv** *nt* (*DDR*) team; **~konflikt** *m* industrial dispute; **~kosten** *pl* labour costs *pl*.

Arbeitskraft *f* **(a)** *no pl* capacity for work ◆ **die menschliche ~ ersetzen** to replace human labour; **seine ~ verkaufen** to sell one's labour; **(b)** (*Arbeiter*) worker.

Arbeitskräfte *pl* work force.

Arbeitskräfte-: ~mangel *m* labour shortage; **~überhang** *m* labour surplus.

Arbeits-: ~kreis *m siehe* **~gemeinschaft**; **~lager** *nt* labour *or* work camp; **~lärm** *m* industrial noise; **~last** *f* burden of work; **~leben** *nt* working life; **~leistung** *f* (*quantitativ*) output, performance; (*qualitativ*) performance; **~lohn** *m* wages *pl*, earnings *pl*.

arbeitslos *adj* **(a)** unemployed, out of work. **(b)** *Einkommen* unearned.

Arbeitslosen-: ~geld *nt* earnings-related benefit; **~heer** *nt* army of unemployed; **~hilfe** *f* unemployment benefit; **~quote** *f* rate of unemployment; **~unterstützung** *f* (*dated*) unemployment benefit, dole money (*Brit inf*); **~versicherung** *f* **(a)** ≃ National Insurance (*Brit*), social insurance (*US*); **(b)** (*Amt*) ≃ Department of Health and Social Security (*Brit*), social insurance office (*US*); **~zahlen** *pl*, **~ziffer** *f* unemployment figures *pl*.

Arbeitslose(r) *mf decl as adj* unemployed person/man/woman *etc* ◆ **die ~n** the unemployed; **die Zahl der ~n** the number of unemployed *or* of people out of work.

Arbeitslosigkeit *f* unemployment.

Arbeits-: ~lust *f* enthusiasm for work; **~mangel** *m* lack of work; **~markt** *m* labour market; **a~mäßig** *adj* with respect to work; **~material** *nt* material for one's work; (*Sch*) teaching aids *pl*; **~medizin** *f* industrial medicine; **~mensch** *m* (hard) worker; **~merkmale** *pl* job characteristics *pl*; **~methode** *f* method of working; **~minister** *m* Employment Secretary (*Brit*), Labor Secretary (*US*); **~mittel** *nt siehe* **~material**; **~möglichkeit** *f* possibility of getting a job; **~moral** *f siehe* **~ethos**; **~nachweis** *m* **(a)** employment agency; (*amtlich*) employment exchange; **(b)** (*Bescheinigung*) certificate of employment; **~niederlegung** *f* walkout; **~norm** *f* **(a)** average work rate; **(b)** (*DDR*) time per unit of production; **~organisation** *f* organization of the/one's work; **~ort** *m* place of work; **~papier** *nt* working paper; **~papiere** *pl* cards, employment papers (*form*) *pl*.

arbeitsparend *adj* labour-saving.

Arbeits-: ~pause *f* break; **~pensum** *nt* quota of work; **~pferd** *nt* (*lit*) workhorse; (*fig*) slogger (*inf*), hard worker; **~pflicht** *f* requirement to work; **~plan** *m* work schedule; (*in Fabrik*) production schedule; **~platte** *f* worktop.

Arbeitsplatz *m* **(a)** (*~stätte*) place of work, workplace ◆ **am ~** at work; (*in Büro auch*) in the office; (*in Fabrik auch*) on the shop floor; **Demokratie am ~** industrial democracy.

(b) (*in Fabrik*) work station; (*in Büro*) workspace ◆ **die Bibliothek hat 75 Arbeitsplätze** the library has room for 75 people to work *or* has working space for 75 people.

(c) (*Stelle*) job ◆ **freie Arbeitsplätze** vacancies.

Arbeitsplatz-: ~abbau *m* job cuts *pl*; **~beschreibung** *f* job description; **~computer** *m* personal computer; **~garantie** *f* guaranteed job; **eine ~garantie aussprechen** to offer guaranteed employment *or* a job guarantee; **~rechner** *m* (*Comput*) workstation; **~sicherung** *f* safeguarding of jobs; **~teilung** *f* job sharing; **~wechsel** *m* change of jobs *or* employment (*form*).

Arbeits-: ~probe *f* sample of one's work; **~produktivität** *f* productivity per man-hour worked; ⚠**~prozeß** *m* work process; **~psychologie** *f* industrial psychology; **~raum** *m* workroom; (*für geistige Arbeit*) study; **~recht** *nt* industrial law; **a~rechtlich** *adj Streitfall, Angelegenheit* concerning industrial law; *Literatur* on industrial law; **a~reich** *adj* full of *or* filled with work, busy; **~reserven** *pl* labour reserves *pl*; **~rhythmus** *m* work rhythm; **~richter** *m* judge in an industrial tribunal; **~ruhe** *f* (*kurze Zeit*) break from work; **gestern herrschte ~ruhe** the factories and offices were closed yesterday; **~sachen** *pl* (*inf*) working clothes *pl or* things *pl* (*inf*); **a~scheu** *adj* workshy; ⚠**~schluß** *m* end of work; **~schluß ist um 17⁰⁰** work finishes at 5 p.m.; **nach ~schluß** after work.

Arbeitsschutz *m* maintenance of industrial health and safety standards.

Arbeitsschutz-: ~bestimmung *f* health and safety regulation; **~gesetzgebung** *f* legislation concerning health and safety at work; **~vorschriften** *pl* health and safety regulations *pl*.

Arbeits-: ~sitzung *f* working session; **~sklave** *m* (*fig*) slave to one's job; **~sklaven** *pl* slave labour *sing*; **~soziologie** *f* industrial sociology; **a~sparend** *adj siehe* **arbeitsparend**; **~speicher** *m* (*Comput*) main memory; **~stab** *m* planning staff; **~stätte** *f* place of work; **Goethes ~stätte** the place where Goethe worked; **~stelle** *f* **(a)** place of work; **(b)** (*Stellung*) job; **(c)** (*Abteilung*) section; **~stil** *m* workstyle, style of working; **~stimmung** *f* **in der richtigen ~stimmung sein** to be in the (right) mood for work; **~studie** *f* time and motion study; **~stunde** *f* man-hour; **~stunden werden extra berechnet** labour will be charged separately; **~suche** *f* search for work *or* employment *or* a job; **auf ~suche sein** to be looking for a job *or* be job-hunting; **~tag** *m* working day; **ein harter ~tag** a hard day; **~tagung** *f* conference, symposium; **~takt** *m* (*Tech*) **(a)** (*von Motor*) power stroke; **(b)** (*bei Fließbandarbeit*) time for an/the operation, phase time; **~tätigkeit** *f* work; **~team** *nt* team; **~technik** *f* technique of working; **a~teilig** [1] *adj* based on the division of labour; [2] *adv* on the principle of the division of labour; **~teilung** *f* division of labour; **~tempo** *f* rate of work; **~therapie** *f* work therapy; **~tier** *nt* **(a)** (*lit*) working animal; **(b)** (*fig*) glutton for work; (*Geistesarbeiter auch*) workaholic (*inf*); **~tisch** *m* work-table; (*für geistige Arbeit*) desk; (*für handwerkliche Arbeit*) workbench; **~titel** *m* provisional *or* draft title; **~überlastung** *f* (*von Mensch*) overworking; (*von Maschine*) overloading; **wegen ~überlastung ist es uns nicht möglich, ...** pressure of work makes it impossible for us to ...

Arbeit-: ~suche *f siehe* **Arbeitssuche**; ⚠**a~suchend** *adj attr* looking for work *or* a job, seeking employment; ⚠**~suchende(r)** *mf decl as adj* person *etc* looking for a job.

Arbeits-: a~unfähig *adj* unable to work; (*krank*) unfit for *or* to work; *Regierung etc* non-viable; **~unfähigkeit** *f siehe adj* inability to work; unfitness for work; non-viability; **dauernde ~unfähigkeit** permanent disability; **~unfähigkeitsbescheinigung** *f* certificate of unfitness for work; **~unfall** *m* industrial accident, accident at work; **~unlust** *f* disinclination to work; **~unterlage** *f* work paper; (*Buch etc*) source for one's work; **a~unwillig** *adj* reluctant *or* unwilling to work; **~urlaub** *m* working holiday; (*Mil*) *leave from the forces to carry on one's usual employment*; **~verdienst** *m* earned income; **~vereinfachung** *f* simplification of the/one's work; **~verfahren** *nt* process; **~verhältnis** *nt* employee-employer relationship; **ein ~verhältnis eingehen** to enter employment; **~verhältnisse** *pl* working conditions *pl*; **~verlust** *m* loss of working hours; **~vermittlung** *f* **(a)** (*Vorgang*) arranging employment; **(b)** (*Amt*) employment exchange; (*privat*) employment agency; **~vertrag** *m* contract of employment; **~verweigerung** *f* refusal to work; **~vorbereitung** *f* **(a)** preparation for the/one's work; **(b)** (*Ind*) production planning; **~vorgang** *m* work process; **~vorhaben** *nt* project; **~vorlage** *f* sketch/plan/model to work from; **~weise** *f* (*Praxis*) way *or* method of working, working method; (*von Maschine*) mode of operation; **die ~weise dieser Maschine** the way this machine works; **~welt** *f* working world; **die industrielle ~welt** the world of industry; **a~willig** *adj* willing to work; **~willige(r)** *mf decl as adj* person willing to work; **~wissenschaft** *f* industrial science, manpower studies *sing* (*US*); **~woche** *f* working week; **~wut** *f* work mania; **ihn hat die ~wut gepackt** he's turned into a workaholic; **a~wütig** *adj* work-happy (*inf*).

Arbeitszeit *f* **(a)** working hours *pl* ◆ **während der ~** in *or* during working hours. **(b)** (*benötigte Zeit*) **die ~ für etw** the time spent on sth; (*in Fabrik*) the production time for sth; **er ließ sich die ~ bezahlen** he wanted to be paid for his time.

Arbeitszeit-: ~ordnung *f* working-time regulations *pl*; **~verkürzung** *f* reduction in working hours.

Arbeits-: ~zeug *nt* (*inf*) **(a)** *siehe* **~kleidung**; **(b)** (*Werkzeug*) tools *pl*; **~zeugnis** *nt* reference from one's employer; **~zimmer** *nt* study; **~zwang** *m* requirement to work.

Arbitrage [-a:ʒə] *f* -, **-n** (*St Ex*) arbitrage *no art*; (*~geschäft*) arbitrage business.

arbiträr *adj* (*geh*) arbitrary.

Arboretum *nt* **-s, Arboreten** arboretum.

Archaikum, Archäikum *nt* (*Geol*) arch(a)ean period.

archaisch *adj* archaic.

Archaismus *m* archaism.

Archäologe *m*, **Archäologin** *f* archaeologist.

Archäologie *f* archaeology.

archäologisch *adj* archaeological.

Arche *f* -, **-n die ~ Noah** Noah's Ark.

Archetyp *m* **-s, -en** archetype.

archetypisch *adj* archetypal.

Archetypus *m siehe* **Archetyp**.

Archimedes *m* - Archimedes.

archimedisch *adj* Archimedean ◆ **~es Axiom** (*Math*) Archimedes' theorem; **~e Schraube** (*Tech*) Archimedes' screw.

Archipel *m* **-s, -e** archipelago.

Architekt(in *f*) *m* **-en, -en** (*lit, fig*) architect.

Architekten-: ~büro *nt* architect's office; **~kollektiv** *nt* team of architects.

Architektonik *f* architecture; (*geh: Aufbau von Kunstwerk*) structure, architectonics *sing* (*form*).

architektonisch *adj siehe n* architectural; structural, architectonic (*form*).

Architektur *f* architecture (*auch Comput*); (*Bau*) piece of architecture.

Architrav [-a:f] *m* **-s, -e** [-a:və] architrave.

Archiv *nt* archives *pl*.

Archivalien [-'va:liən] *pl* records *pl*.

Archivar(in *f*) [-'va:ɐ, -'va:rɪn] *m* archivist.

Archiv-: ~bild *nt* library photo, photo from the archives; **~exemplar** *nt* file copy.

archivieren* [-'vi:rən] *vt* to archive.

Archivmaterial *nt* records *pl*.

Arcus *m siehe* **Arkus**.

ARD ['a:|ɛr'de:] *f* -, *no pl abbr of* **Arbeitsgemeinschaft der Rundfunkanstalten Deutschlands.**

Are *f* -, **-n** (*Sw*) *siehe* **Ar**.

Areal *nt* **-s, -e** area.

areligiös *adj* areligious.

Ären *pl of* **Ära**.

Arena *f* -, **Arenen** (*lit, fig*) arena; (*Zirkus~, Stierkampf~*) ring.

Areopag *m* **-s,** *no pl* (*Hist*) Areopagus.

arg [1] *adj, comp* **⸚er**, *superl* **⸚ste(r, s)** (*esp S Ger*) **(a)** (*old: böse*) evil, wicked ◆ **~ denken** to think evil thoughts.

(b) (*schlimm*) bad; *Wetter auch, Gestank, Katastrophe, Verlust, Blamage, Verlegenheit, Schicksal* terrible; *Enttäuschung, Feind* bitter; *Säufer, Raucher* confirmed, inveterate ◆ **sein ⸚ster Feind** his worst enemy; **etw noch ⸚er machen** to make sth worse; **das Ä~ste befürchten** to fear the worst; **ich habe an nichts A~es gedacht** I didn't think anything of it; **etw liegt im ~en** sth is at sixes and sevens; **das ist mir ~** (*dial*) I'm very sorry about that.

(c) *attr* (*stark, groß*) terrible; (*dial*) *Freude, Liebenswürdigkeit etc* tremendous.

[2] *adv, comp* **⸚er**, *superl* **am ⸚sten** (*schlimm*) badly; (*dial inf: sehr*) terribly (*inf*) ◆ **es geht ihr ~ schlecht** (*inf*) she's in a really bad way; **er hat sich ~ vertan** (*inf*) he's made a bad mistake; **sie ist ~ verliebt** (*inf*) she is very much *or* terribly in love; **es zu ~ treiben** to go too far, to take things too far.

Arg *nt* **-s,** *no pl* (*old*) malice.

Arge *m* **-n,** *no pl* (*old*) **der ~** Satan, the devil.

Argentinien [-iən] *nt* **-s** Argentina, the Argentine.

Argentinier(in *f*) [-iɐ, iərɪn] *m* **-s, -** Argentine, Argentinian.

argentinisch *adj* Argentine, Argentinian.

ärger *comp of* **arg**.

Ärger *m* **-s,** *no pl* **(a)** annoyance; (*stärker*) anger ◆ **wenn ihn der ~ packt** when he gets annoyed/angry; **~ über etw** (*acc*) **empfinden** to feel annoyed about sth; **zu jds ~** *or* **jdm zum ~** to sb's annoyance.

(b) (*Unannehmlichkeiten, Streitigkeiten*) trouble; (*ärgerliche Erlebnisse auch*) bother; (*Sorgen*) worry ◆ **jdm ~ machen** *or* **bereiten** to cause sb a lot of trouble *or* bother; **der tägliche ~ im Büro** the hassle (*inf*) in the office every day; **~ bekommen** *or* **kriegen** (*inf*) to get into trouble; **~ mit jdm haben** to be having trouble with sb; **mach keinen ~!** (*inf*) don't make *or* cause any trouble!, cool it (*sl*); **mach mir keinen ~** (*inf*) don't make any trouble for me;

so ein ~! (*inf*) how annoying!, what a nuisance!; **es gibt ~** (*inf*) there'll be trouble.

ärgerlich *adj* **(a)** (*verärgert*) annoyed, cross ◆ **~ über** *or* **auf jdn/über etw** (*acc*) **sein** to be annoyed *or* cross with sb/about sth, to be angry *or* infuriated with *or* mad (*inf*) at sb/about sth.
(b) (*unangenehm*) annoying; (*stärker*) maddening, infuriating ◆ **eine ~e Tatsache** an unpleasant fact.

Ärgerlichkeit *f* **(a)** *no pl* (*Verärgertsein*) annoyance, crossness ◆ **die ~ seines Tons** the annoyance in *or* crossness of his voice. **(b)** (*Unerquicklichkeit, ärgerlicher Vorfall*) nuisance, annoyance.

ärgern [1] *vt* **(a)** to annoy, to irritate; (*stärker*) to make angry ◆ **jdn krank/zu Tode ~** to drive sb mad; **sich krank/zu Tode ~** to drive oneself to distraction; **über so etwas könnte ich mich krank/zu Tode ~** that sort of thing drives me mad; **das ärgert einen doch!** but it's so annoying!
(b) (*necken*) to torment.
[2] *vr* (*ärgerlich sein/werden*) to be/get annoyed; (*stärker*) to be/get angry *or* infuriated (*über jdn/etw* with sb/about sth) ◆ **du darfst dich darüber nicht so ~** you shouldn't let it annoy you so much; **nicht ~, nur wundern!** (*inf*) that's life.

Ärgernis *nt* **(a)** *no pl* (*Anstoß*) offence, outrage ◆ **~ erregen** to cause offence; **~ an etw** (*dat*) **nehmen** (*old*) to be offended by sth; **bei jdm ~ erregen** to offend sb; **wegen Erregung öffentlichen ~ses angeklagt werden** to be charged with offending public decency.
(b) (*etwas Anstößiges*) outrage; (*etwas Ärgerliches*) terrible nuisance ◆ **es ist ein ~ für sie, wenn ...** it annoys her (terribly) when ...; **um ~se zu vermeiden** to avoid upsetting anybody.
(c) (*Ärgerlichkeit, Unannehmlichkeit*) trouble.

Arglist *f* **-,** *no pl* (*Hinterlist*) cunning, guile, craftiness; (*Boshaftigkeit*) malice; (*Jur*) fraud.

arglistig *adj* cunning, crafty; (*böswillig*) malicious ◆ **~e Täuschung** fraud.

Arglistigkeit *f siehe adj* cunning, craftiness; maliciousness.

arglos *adj* innocent; (*ohne Täuschungsabsicht*) guileless.

Arglosigkeit *f siehe adj* innocence; guilelessness.

Argon *nt* **-s,** *no pl* (*abbr* **Ar**) argon.

Argonaut *m* **-en, -en** (*Myth*) Argonaut.

Argot [ar'goː] *m or nt* **-s, -s** argot.

ärgste(r, s) *superl of* **arg.**

➤ **Argument** *nt* argument ◆ **das ist kein ~** that's no argument; (*wäre unsinnig*) that's no way to go about things; (*keine Entschuldigung*) that's no excuse.

Argumentation *f* **(a)** argument; (*Darlegung*) argumentation *no pl.* **(b)** (*Sch: Aufsatz*) critical analysis.

Argumentationshilfe *f* (*form*) advice on how to present one's case.

argumentativ (*geh*), **argumentatorisch** (*rare*) *adj* **~ ist er sehr schwach** his argumentation is weak; **~e Werbung betreiben** to use persuasive advertising; **etw ~ erreichen/bekämpfen** to achieve sth by (force of) argument/to fight sth with arguments.

argumentieren* *vi* to argue ◆ **mit etw ~** to use sth as an argument.

Argus *m* **-, -se** Argus.

Argusauge *nt* (*geh*) Argus eye ◆ **mit ~n** Argus-eyed.

Argwohn *m* **-s,** *no pl* suspicion ◆ **jds ~ erregen/zerstreuen** to arouse/allay sb's suspicions; **~ gegen jdn hegen/schöpfen** (*geh*) to have/form doubts about sb, to be/become suspicious of sb; **mit** *or* **voller ~** suspiciously.

argwöhnen *vt insep* (*geh*) to suspect.

argwöhnisch *adj* suspicious.

arid *adj* (*Geog*) arid.

Aridität *f* (*Geog*) aridity.

Arie [-iə] *f* (*Mus*) aria.

Arier(in *f*) [-iɐ, -iərɪn] **-s, -** Aryan.

⚠ **Arierparagraph** *m* (*NS*) *law precluding non-Aryans from becoming public servants.*

Aries ['aːriɛs] *m* (*Astron*) Aries.

arisch *adj* **(a)** (*Ling*) Indo-European, Indo-Germanic. **(b)** (*NS*) Aryan.

arisieren* *vt* (*NS sl*) to Aryanize.

Aristokrat(in *f*) *m* **-en, -en** aristocrat.

Aristokratie *f* aristocracy.

aristokratisch *adj* aristocratic.

Aristoteles *m* **-** Aristotle.

Aristoteliker(in *f*) *m* **-s, -** Aristotelian.

aristotelisch *adj* Aristotelian.

Arithmetik *f* **-,** *no pl* arithmetic.

Arithmetiker(in *f*) *m* **-s, -** arithmetician.

arithmetisch *adj* arithmetic(al).

Arkade *f* (*Bogen*) arch(way). **~n** *pl* (*Bogengang*) arcade.

Arkadien [-iən] *nt* Arcadia.

arkadisch *adj* (*geh*) Arcadian.

Arktis *f* **-,** *no pl* Arctic.

arktisch *adj* arctic.

Arkus *m* **-, -** (*Math*) arc.

arm *adj, comp* **¨er,** *superl* **¨ste(r, s)** *or adv* **am ¨sten** (*lit, fig*) poor; (*gering*) *Vegetation, Wachstum* sparse ◆ **~ und reich** rich and poor; **die A~en** the poor *pl*; **du ißt mich noch mal ~!** (*inf*) you'll eat me out of house and home!; **du machst mich noch mal ~** (*inf*) you'll ruin me yet; **~ an etw** (*dat*) **sein** to be somewhat lacking in sth; **der Boden ist ~ an Nährstoffen** the soil is poor in nutrients; **~ an Vitaminen** low in vitamins; **um jdn/etw ¨er werden/sein** to lose/have lost sb/sth; **um 55 Mark ¨er sein** to be 55 marks worse off *or* poorer; **ach, du/Sie A~er!** (*iro*) you poor thing!, poor you!; **ich A~er!** (*poet*) woe is me! (*poet*); **~e Seelen** (*Rel*) holy souls; **~ dran sein** (*inf*) to have a hard time of it; **~es Schwein** (*inf*) poor so-and-so (*inf*); **~er Irrer** (*sl*) mad fool (*inf*); (*bedauernswert*) poor fool.

-arm *adj suf* lacking in.

Arm *m* **-(e)s, -e (a)** (*Anat, Tech, fig*) arm; (*Fluß~ auch, Baum~*) branch; (*Waage~*) beam; (*Ärmel*) sleeve ◆ **~ in ~** arm in arm; **über/unter den ~** over/under one's arm; **die ~e voll haben** to have one's arms full; **jds ~ nehmen** to take sb's arm *or* sb by the arm; **jdm den ~ bieten** (*geh*) *or* **reichen** to offer sb one's arm; **jdn im ~** *or* **in den ~en halten** to hold sb in one's arms; **jdn am ~ führen** to lead sb by the arm; **jdn in die ~e nehmen** to take sb in one's arms; **jdn in die ~e schließen** to take *or* clasp sb in an embrace; **sich in den ~en liegen** to lie in each other's arms; **jdm/sich in die ~e fallen** *or* **sinken** to fall into sb's/each other's arms; **sich aus jds ~en lösen** (*geh*) to free oneself from sb's embrace; **jdn auf den ~ nehmen** to take sb onto one's arm; (*fig inf*) to pull sb's leg (*inf*); **jdm unter die ~e greifen** (*fig*) to help sb out; **jdm in die ~e laufen** (*fig inf*) to run *or* bump (*inf*) into sb; **jdn mit offenen ~en empfangen** (*fig*) to welcome sb with open arms; **jdm in den ~ fallen** (*fig*) to put a spoke in sb's wheel, to spike sb's guns; **sich jdm/einer Sache in die ~e werfen** (*fig*) to throw oneself at sb/into sth; **jdn jdm/einer Sache in die ~e treiben** (*fig*) to drive sb into sb's arms/to sth; **jdn am steifen ~ verhungern lassen** (*lit hum*) to get sb in an armlock; (*fig*) to put the screws on sb (*inf*); **der ~ des Gesetzes** the long arm of the law; **der ~ der Gerechtigkeit** (*fig*) justice; **einen langen/den längeren ~ haben** (*fig*) to have a lot of/more pull (*inf*) *or* influence; **jds verlängerter ~** an extension of sb.
(b) (*euph hum*) *siehe* **Arsch.**

Armada *f* **-, -s** *or* **Armaden** (*lit, fig*) armada.

Armageddon *nt* **-(s)** Armageddon.

Arm- *in cpds* arm; **a~amputiert** *adj* with an arm amputated; **a~amputiert sein** to have had an arm amputated; **~arbeit** *f* (*Boxen*) fist work.

Armatur *f, usu pl* (*Tech*) (*Hahn, Leitung etc*) fitting; (*Instrument*) instrument.

Armaturen-: ~beleuchtung *f* (*Aut*) dash light; **~brett** *nt* instrument panel; (*Aut*) dashboard.

Arm-: ~band *nt* bracelet; (*von Uhr*) (watch)strap; **~banduhr** *f* wristwatch; **~beuge** *f* **(a)** inside of one's elbow; **(b)** (*Sport*) arm bend; **~binde** *f* armband; (*Med*) sling; **~bruch** *m* (*Med*) broken *or* fractured arm; **~brust** *f* crossbow.

Ärmchen *nt dim of* **Arm.**

armdick *adj* as thick as one's arm.

Armee *f* **-, -n** [-eːən] (*Mil, fig*) army; (*Gesamtheit der Streitkräfte*) (armed) forces *pl* ◆ **bei der ~** in the army/forces.

Armee- *in cpds* army; **~befehl** *m* army order.

Ärmel *m* **-s, -** sleeve ◆ **sich** (*dat*) **die ~ hoch-** *or* **aufkrempeln** (*lit, fig*) to roll up one's sleeves; **etw aus dem ~ schütteln** to produce sth just like that.

Ärmel|aufschlag *m* cuff.

Ärmeleute-: ~essen *nt* poor man's food; **~geruch** *m* smell of poverty.

Ärmelhalter *m* sleeve band.

-ärm(e)lig *adj suf* -sleeved.

Ärmelkanal *m* (English) Channel.

ärmellos *adj* sleeveless.

Armenhaus *nt* (*old*) poorhouse.

Armenien [-iən] *nt* Armenia.

Armenier(in *f*) [-iɐ, -iərɪn] *m* Armenian.

armenisch *adj* Armenian.

Armen-: ~kasse *f* (*Hist*) poor box; **~recht** *nt* (*Jur*) legal aid.

Armensünder- *in cpds* (*Aus*) *siehe* **Armsünder-.**

Armenviertel *nt* poor district *or* quarter.

ärmer *comp of* **arm.**

Armeslänge *f* arm's length ◆ **um zwei ~n** by two arms' length.

Armesünder *m* **Armensünders, Armensünder** (*obs*) condemned man.

Armesünder- *in cpds siehe* **Armsünder-.**

Arm-: ~flor *m* black armband; **~gelenk** *nt* elbow joint; **~hebel** *m* (*Sport*) arm lever.

armieren* *vt* **(a)** (*old Mil*) to arm. **(b)** (*Tech*) *Kabel* to sheathe; *Beton* to reinforce.

-armig *adj suf* -armed.

Arm-: a~lang *adj* arm-length; **~länge** *f* arm length; **~lehne** *f* armrest; (*von Stuhl etc auch*) arm; **~leuchter** *m* **(a)** chandelier; **(b)** (*pej inf: Mensch*) twit (*Brit inf*), fool, twirp (*inf*).

ärmlich *adj* (*lit, fig*) poor; *Kleidung, Wohnung* shabby; *Essen* meagre; *Verhältnisse* humble ◆ **einen ~en Eindruck machen** to look poor/shabby; **aus ~en Verhältnissen** from a poor family.

Ärmlichkeit *f siehe adj* poorness; shabbiness; meagreness; humbleness.

-ärmlig *adj suf siehe* **-ärm(e)lig.**

Ärmling *m* oversleeve.

Arm-: ~loch *nt* **(a)** armhole; **(b)** (*euph: Arschloch*) bum (*sl*); **~muskel** *m* biceps; **~polster** *nt* **(a)** (*an Kleidung*) shoulder padding; **(b)** (*~lehne*) padded armrest; **~prothese** *f* artificial arm; **~reif(en)** *m* bangle; **~schlüssel** *m* (*Sport*) armlock, hammerlock (*US*); **~schutz** *m* (*Sport*) arm guard.

armselig *adj* (*dürftig*) miserable; (*mitleiderregend*) pathetic, pitiful, piteous; *Feigling etc* pathetic, miserable, wretched; *Summe, Ausrede* paltry ◆ **für ~e zwei Mark** for a paltry two marks, for two paltry marks.

Armseligkeit *f siehe adj* miserableness; pitifulness, piteousness; wretchedness.

Armsessel, Armstuhl (*old*) *m* armchair.

ärmste(r, s) *superl of* **arm.**

Arm-: ~stummel *(inf)*, **~stumpf** *m* stump of one's arm; **~stütze** *f* armrest.

Armsünder-: ~bank *f*, **~bänkchen** *nt (hum) (beim Essen) small table at which children sit; (bei Prüfung, Quiz etc)* hot seat; **dasitzen wie auf dem ~bänkchen** to be sitting there looking as though the world were about to end; **~glocke** *f knell tolled during an execution*; **~miene** *f (hum)* hangdog expression.

Armut *f -, no pl (lit, fig)* poverty ◆ **charakterliche ~** lack of character; **geistige ~** intellectual poverty; *(von Mensch)* lack of intellect.

-armut *f in cpds* lack of.

Armuts-: ~grenze *f, no pl* poverty line; **~zeugnis** *nt (fig)* **jdm/sich (selbst) ein ~zeugnis ausstellen** to show *or* prove sb's/one's (own) shortcomings; **das ist ein ~zeugnis für ihn** that shows him up.

⚠**Armvoll** *m -, -* armful ◆ **zwei ~ Holz** two armfuls of wood.

Arnika *f -, -s* arnica.

Arom *nt -s, -e (poet)* fragrance, scent.

Aroma *nt -s,* **Aromen** *or* **-s** *or (dated)* **-ta** **(a)** *(Geruch)* aroma. **(b)** *(Geschmack)* flavour, taste. **(c)** *no pl* flavouring.

Aromatherapie *f (Med)* aromatherapy.

aromatisch *adj* **(a)** *(wohlriechend)* aromatic. **(b)** *(wohlschmeckend)* savoury.

aromatisieren* *vt* to give aroma to ◆ **aromatisiert** aromatic; **zu stark aromatisiert sein** to have too strong an aroma.

Aronsstab *m* arum.

Arrak *m -s, -s or* **-e** arrack.

Arrangement [arãʒə'mã:] *nt -s, -s (alle Bedeutungen)* arrangement.

Arrangeur(in *f)* [arã'ʒø:ɐ, -ʒø:rɪn] *m (geh)* organizer; *(Mus)* arranger ◆ **er war der ~ dieses Abkommens** he arranged this agreement.

arrangieren* [arã'ʒi:rən] **1** *vti (alle Bedeutungen)* to arrange *(jdm* for sb).
2 *vr* **sich mit jdm ~** to come to an arrangement with sb; **sich mit etw ~** to come to terms with sth.

Arrest *m -(e)s, -s* **(a)** *(Sch, Mil, Jur: Jugend~)* detention ◆ **seine Eltern bestraften ihn mit ~** his parents punished him by not letting him go out *or* by keeping him in.
(b) *(Econ, Jur) (auch* **persönlicher ~***)* attachment; *(auch* **dinglicher ~***)* distress *(form)*, distraint ◆ **~ in jds Vermögen** distress upon sb's property.

Arrestant [-st-] *m (dated Jur)* detainee.

Arrest-: ~lokal *nt (dated)* detention room; *(Mil)* guardroom; **~zelle** *f* detention cell.

arretieren* *vt* **(a)** *(dated) jdn* to take into custody. **(b)** *(Tech)* to lock (in place).

Arretierung *f* **(a)** *siehe vt* taking into custody; locking. **(b)** *(Vorrichtung)* locking mechanism.

Arrhythmie *f (Med)* arrhythmia.

arrivieren* [-'vi:-] *vi aux sein* to make it *(inf)*, to become a success ◆ **zu etw ~** to rise to become sth.

arriviert [-'vi:ɐt] *adj* successful; *(pej)* upstart ◆ **er ist jetzt ~** he has arrived, he has made it *(inf)*.

Arrivierte(r) *mf decl as adj* arrivé; *(pej)* parvenu.

arrogant *adj* arrogant.

Arroganz *f -, no pl* arrogance.

arrondieren* *vt (geh)* **(a)** *Grenze* to realign, to adjust; *Grundstück* to realign *or* adjust the boundaries of. **(b)** *Kanten etc* to round off.

Arsch *m -(e)s, ⸗e* **(a)** *(vulg)* arse *(vulg)*, ass *(sl)*, bum *(sl)*, fanny *(US sl)*, butt *(US sl)* ◆ **jdm** *or* **jdn in den ~ treten** to give sb a kick up the arse *(vulg) or* ass *(sl)*; **auf den ~ fallen** *(fig: scheitern)* to fall flat on one's face; **den ~ voll kriegen** to get a bloody good hiding *(sl)*; **leck mich am ~!** *(laß mich in Ruhe)* get stuffed! *(inf)*, fuck off! *(vulg)*; *(verdammt noch mal)* bugger! *(sl)*, fuck it! *(vulg)*; *(überrascht)* bugger me! *(sl)*, fuck me! *(vulg)*; **er kann mich (mal) am ~ lecken** he can get stuffed *(inf) or* fuck off *(vulg)*; **jdm in den ~ kriechen** to lick sb's arse *(vulg) or* ass *(sl)*; **du hast wohl den ~ offen!** *(sl)* you're out of your tiny mind *(inf)*; **~ mit Ohren** *(sl)* silly bugger *(sl)*; **am ~ der Welt** *(sl)* in the back of beyond; **im** *or* **am ~ sein/in den ~ gehen** *(sl)* to be/get fucked up *(vulg)*; **jdn am ~ kriegen** *(sl)* to get sb by the short and curlies *(inf)*; **den ~ zukneifen** *(sl)* to snuff it *(inf)*; **jdm den ~ aufreißen** *(esp Mil)* to work the shit out of sb *(sl)*; **ihm geht der ~ mit Grundeis** *(sl)* he's got the shits *(sl)*, he's shit-scared *(sl)*; **Schütze ~** *(Mil)* simple private; **sich auf den** *or* **seinen ~ setzen** *(lit)* to park one's arse *(vulg) or* fanny *(US sl)*; *(fig sl) (sich Mühe geben)* to get one's arse in gear *(vulg)*, to get one's finger out *(sl)*; *(aus Überraschung)* to be knocked out *(sl)*.
(b) *(sl: Mensch)* bastard, bugger, sod *(all sl)*; *(Dummkopf)* stupid bastard *etc (sl)*.

Arsch-: ~backe *f (vulg)* buttock, cheek; **~ficker** *m* **(a)** *(lit vulg)* bum-fucker *(vulg)*; **(b)** *(fig sl)* slimy bastard *(sl)*; **~geige** *f (sl) siehe* **Arsch (b)**; **~kriecher** *m (sl)* ass-kisser *(sl)*; **~kriecherei** *f (sl)* ass-kissing *(sl)*; **~lecker** *m -s, - (sl)* ass-kisser *(sl)*.

ärschlings *adv (old)* backwards, arse first *(vulg)*.

Arsch-: ~loch *nt (vulg)* **(a)** *(lit)* arse-hole *(vulg)*, ass-hole *(sl)*; **(b)** *siehe* **Arsch (b)**; **~tritt** *m (sl)* kick up the arse *(vulg) or* behind *(inf)*; **~-und-Titten-Presse** *f (sl)* tit-and-bum press *(inf)*.

Arsen *nt -s, no pl (abbr* **As***)* arsenic.

Arsenal *nt -s, -e (lit, fig)* arsenal.

arsenhaltig *adj* arsenic.

Arsenik *nt -s, no pl* arsenic, arsenic trioxide *(form)*.

Art. *abbr of* **Artikel.**

Art *f -, -en* **(a)** kind, sort, type; *(von Pflanze, Insekt etc auch)* variety ◆ **diese ~ Leute/Buch** people/books like that, that kind *or* sort of person/book; **jede ~ (von) Buch/Terror** any kind *etc* of book/terrorism, a book of any kind *etc*/ terrorism in any form; **alle möglichen ~en von Büchern, Bücher aller ~** all kinds *or* sorts of books, books of all kinds *or* sorts; **einzig in seiner ~ sein** to be the only one of its kind, to be unique; **aus der ~ schlagen** not to take after anyone in the family.
(b) *(Biol)* species.
(c) *(Methode)* way ◆ **auf die ~** in that way *or* manner; **auf die ~ geht es am schnellsten** that is the quickest way; **auf merkwürdige/grausame** *etc* **~** in a strange/cruel *etc* way; **die einfachste ~, etw zu tun** the simplest way to do sth *or* of doing sth; **auf diese ~ und Weise** in this way.
(d) *(Wesen)* nature; *(übliche Verhaltensweise)* way ◆ **es entspricht nicht meiner ~** it's not my nature; **das ist eigentlich nicht seine ~** it's not like him; **von lebhafter ~ sein** to have a lively nature; to have a lively way (with one).
(e) *(Stil)* style ◆ **Schnitzel nach ~ des Hauses** schnitzel à la maison.
(f) *(Benehmen)* behaviour ◆ **das ist doch keine ~!** that's no way to behave!; **was ist das (denn) für eine ~?** what sort of a way to behave is that?; **ist das vielleicht** *or* **etwa eine ~!** that's no way to behave!

Art-: ~angabe *f (Gram)* adverb of manner; *(Adverbialbestimmung)* adverbial phrase of manner; **~bildung** *f* speciation *(form)*.

Artefakt *nt -(e)s, -e (geh)* artefact.

art|eigen *adj* characteristic (of the species).

arten *vi aux sein (geh)* **nach jdm ~** to take after sb; *siehe auch* **geartet.**

Arten-: a~reich *adj* with a large number of species; **diese Tierklasse ist sehr a~reich** this class of animal contains a large number of species; **~reichtum** *m (Biol)* large number of species; **~schutz** *m* protection of species; **~schwund** *m* extinction of species; **~sterben** *nt* extinction of species; **~tod** *m* extinction as a species ◆ **vom ~tod bedroht sein** to be threatened with extinction as a species; **den ~tod sterben** to die out as a species.

Art-: a~erhaltend *adj* survival *attr*; **das wirkte sich a~erhaltend aus** that contributed to the survival of the species; **~erhaltung** *f* survival of the species.

Arterie [-iə] *f* artery.

arteriell *adj* arterial.

Arterienverkalkung [-iən-] *f (inf)* hardening of the arteries ◆ **~ haben** *(fig)* to be senile.

Arteriosklerose *f* arteriosclerosis.

artesisch *adj* **~er Brunnen** artesian well.

Art-: a~fremd *adj* foreign; **~genosse** *m* animal/plant of the same species; *(Mensch)* person of the same type; **a~gerecht** *adj Tierhaltung* appropriate to the species; **a~gleich** *adj* of the same species; *Mensch* of the same type.

Arthritis *f -,* **Arthritiden** arthritis.

arthritisch *adj* arthritic.

Arthrose *f -, -n* arthrosis.

artifiziell *adj (geh)* artificial.

artig *adj* **(a)** *Kind, Hund etc* good, well-behaved *no adv* ◆ **sei schön ~** be a good boy/dog! *etc*, be good! **(b)** *(old: galant)* courteous, civil. **(c)** *(old: anmutig)* charming.

-artig *adj suf* -like.

Artigkeit *f* **(a)** *siehe adj (Wohlerzogenheit)* good behaviour; courtesy, courteousness, civility; charm. **(b)** *(old) (Kompliment)* compliment; *(höfliche Bemerkung)* pleasantry ◆ **jdm einige ~en sagen** to pay sb compliments/make a few civil remarks to sb.

-artigkeit *f in cpds* -like quality.

Artikel *m -s, - (alle Bedeutungen)* article; *(Lexikon~ auch)* entry; *(Comm auch)* item.

-artikel *pl in cpds (Ausrüstungen)* equipment; *(Kleidung)* wear.

Artikulation *f* articulation; *(deutliche Aussprache auch)* enunciation; *(Mus)* phrasing.

Artikulations-: a~fähig *adj* articulate; *(Phon)* able to articulate; **~fähigkeit** *f siehe adj* articulateness; ability to articulate; **~organe** *pl* organs of speech *pl*; **~vermögen** *nt siehe* **~fähigkeit.**

artikulatorisch *adj (Phon)* articulatory.

artikulieren* **1** *vti* to articulate; *(deutlich aussprechen auch)* to enunciate; *(Mus)* to phrase ◆ **sich artikuliert ausdrücken** to be articulate.
2 *vr (fig geh)* to express oneself.

Artikulierung *f siehe vb* articulation; enunciation; phrasing; expression.

Artillerie *f* artillery.

Artillerie- *in cpds* artillery; ⚠**~beschuß** *m* artillery fire.

Artillerist *m* artilleryman.

Artischocke *f -, -n* (globe) artichoke.

Artischockenboden *m, usu pl* artichoke heart.

Artist(in *f) m* **(a)** (circus/variety) artiste *or* performer. **(b)** *(obs, geh: Meister)* artist *(gen* at). **(c)** *(inf: Mensch)* joker *(inf)*.

Artistenfakultät *f (Hist)* Faculty of Arts.

Artistik *f* artistry; *(Zirkus-, Varietékunst)* circus/variety performing.

Artistin *f siehe* **Artist.**

artistisch *adj* **(a)** **sein ~es Können** his ability as a performer; **eine ~e Glanzleistung/~ einmalige Leistung** a miraculous/unique feat of circus *etc* artistry; **eine ~e Sensation** a sensational performance. **(b)** *(geschickt)* masterly *no adv*. **(c)** *(formalkünstlerisch)* artistic.

Artothek *f -, -en* picture (lending) library.

Artur *m -s* Arthur.

Artus *m - (Hist, Myth)* (King) Arthur.

Art-: a~verschieden *adj* of different species; **a~verwandt** *adj* generically

⚠: Informationen zur Rechtschreibreform im Anhang

related; **~wort** *nt* (*Gram*) adjective.
Arznei *f* (*lit, fig*) medicine ◆ **das war für ihn eine bittere/heilsame ~** (*fig*) that was a painful/useful lesson for him.
Arznei-: ~buch *nt* pharmacopoeia; **~fläschchen** *nt* medicine bottle; **~kunde, ~lehre** *f* pharmacology.
Arzneimittel *nt* drug.
Arzneimittel-: ~forschung *f* pharmacological research; **~gesetz** *nt* law governing the manufacture and prescription of drugs; **~hersteller** *m* drug manufacturer *or* company; **~lehre** *f* pharmacology; ⚠**~mißbrauch** *m* drug abuse; **~versorgung** *f* provision of drugs (*gen* to).
Arznei-: ~pflanze *f* medicinal plant; **~schränkchen** *nt* medicine cupboard.
Arzt *m* **-es, ¨-e** doctor, physician (*old, form*), medical practitioner (*form*); (*Fach~*) specialist; (*Chirurg*) surgeon ◆ **praktischer ~** general practitioner, GP *abbr*.
Arztberuf *m* medical profession.
Ärzte-: ~besteck *nt* set of surgical instruments; **~kammer** *f* ≃ General Medical Council (*Brit*), State Medical Board of Registration (*US*); **~kollegium** *nt*, **~kommission** *f* medical advisory board; **~mangel** *m* shortage of doctors; **~schaft** *f* medical profession; **~vertreter** *m* pharmaceutical consultant.
Arzt-: ~frau *f* doctor's wife; **~helferin, ~hilfe** *f siehe* **Sprechstundenhilfe.**
Ärztin *f* woman doctor; *siehe auch* **Arzt.**
ärztlich *adj* medical ◆ **er ließ sich ~ behandeln** he went to a doctor for treatment, he got medical treatment; **~ empfohlen** recommended by the medical profession.
Arzt-: ~praxis *f* doctor's practice; **~rechnung** *f* doctor's bill; **~wahl** *f* choice of doctor.
As[1] *nt* **-ses, -se** (*lit, fig*) ace ◆ **alle vier ~se** (*lit*) all the aces.
As[2] *nt* (*Mus*) A flat.
Asbest *nt* **-(e)s,** *no pl* asbestos.
Asbest- *in cpds* asbestos; **~beton** *m* asbestos cement.
Asbestose *f* **-, -n** asbestosis.
Asbestplatte *f* (*für Topf*) asbestos mat; (*für Bügeleisen*) asbestos stand.
⚠**Aschantinuß** *f* (*Aus*) *siehe* **Erdnuß.**
Asch-: ~becher *m siehe* **Aschenbecher**; **a~blond** *adj* ash-blonde.
Asche *f* **-** ash(es *pl*); (*von Zigarette, Vulkan*) ash; (*fig*) (*sterbliche Überreste*) ashes *pl*; (*Trümmer*) ruins *pl*; (*nach Feuer*) ashes *pl* ◆ **zu ~ werden** to turn to dust; **sich** (*dat*) **~ aufs Haupt streuen** (*fig geh*) to wear sackcloth and ashes.
Asch|eimer *m* (*dial*) ash can (*esp US*) *or* bin.
Aschen-: ~bahn *f* cinder track; **~becher** *m* ashtray; **~brödel** *nt* **-s, -** (*Liter, fig*) Cinderella, Cinders (*inf*); **~brödeldasein** *nt* Cinderella existence; **~eimer** *m siehe* **Ascheimer**; **~kasten** *m* ash pan; **~puttel** *nt* **-s, -** *siehe* **~brödel**; **~regen** *m* shower of ash.
Ascher *m* **-s, -** (*inf*) ashtray.
Aschermittwoch *m* Ash Wednesday.
Asch-: a~fahl *adj* ashen; **a~farben, a~farbig** *adj* ash-coloured; **a~grau** *adj* ash-grey; **~kasten** *m* ash pan.
Aschram *m* **-s, -s** *siehe* **Ashram.**
ASCII- ['aski:-] (*Comput*): **~-Code** *m* ASCII code; **~-Datei** *f* ASCII file.
Ascorbinsäure [askɔr'bi:n-] *f* ascorbic acid.
A-Seite *f* (*von Schallplatte*) A-side.
Asen *pl* (*Myth*) Aesir *pl*.
äsen (*Hunt*) [1] *vir* to graze, to browse.
[2] *vt* to graze on.
aseptisch *adj* aseptic.
Äser[1] *pl of* **Aas.**
Äser[2] *m* **-s, -** (*Hunt*) mouth.
asexuell *adj* asexual.
Ashram *m* **-s, -s** ashram.
Asiat(in *f*) *m* **-en, -en** Asian.
Asiatika *pl* Orientalia *pl*.
asiatisch *adj* Asian, Asiatic ◆ **~e Grippe** Asian *or* Asiatic (*US*) flu.
Asien [-iən] *nt* **-s** Asia.
Askese *f* **-,** *no pl* asceticism.
Asket *m* **-en, -en** ascetic.
asketisch *adj* ascetic.
Askorbinsäure *f* ascorbic acid.
Äskulap-: ~schlange *f* snake of Aesculapius; **~stab** *m* staff of Aesculapius.
Äsop *m* **-s** Aesop.
äsopisch *adj* Aesopic ◆ **eine Ä~e Fabel** one of Aesop's Fables.
asozial *adj* antisocial.
Asoziale(r) *mf decl as adj* (*pej*) antisocial man/woman *etc*. **~** *pl* antisocial elements.
Asozialität *f* antisocialness.
➤ **Aspekt** *m* **-(e)s, -e** aspect ◆ **unter diesem ~ betrachtet** looking at it from this aspect *or* this point of view; **einen neuen ~ bekommen** to take on a different complexion.
Asphalt *m* **-(e)s, -e** asphalt.
Asphalt-: ~beton *m* asphalt; **~decke** *f* asphalt surface.
asphaltieren* *vt* to asphalt, to tarmac.
asphaltiert *adj* asphalt.
Asphaltstraße *f* asphalt road.
Aspik *m or* (*Aus*) *nt* **-s, -e** aspic.
Aspirant(in *f*) *m* (**a**) (*geh*) candidate (*für, auf +acc* for). (**b**) (*DDR Univ*) research assistant.
Aspirantur *f* (*esp DDR*) research assistantship.
Aspirata *f* **-, Aspiraten** (*Phon*) aspirate.
Aspiration *f* (**a**) *usu pl* (*geh*) aspiration ◆ **~en auf etw** (*acc*) *or* **nach etw haben** to have aspirations towards sth, to aspire to sth. (**b**) (*Phon*) aspiration.
aspirieren* [1] *vi* (*geh*) to aspire (*auf +acc* to); (*Aus*) to apply (*auf +acc* for).
[2] *vt* (*Phon*) to aspirate.
⚠**aß** *pret of* **essen.**
Aß *nt* (*Aus*) *siehe* **As**[1].
Assekuranz *f* (*old*) assurance; (*Gesellschaft*) assurance company.
Assel *f* **-, -n** isopod (*spec*); (*Roll~, Keller~, Land~ auch*) woodlouse.
Assembler *m* **-s, -** (*Comput*) assembler.
Assemblersprache *f* (*Comput*) assembly language.
Asservat [-'va:t] *nt* (court) exhibit.
Asservaten-: ~kammer *f*, **~raum** *m room where court exhibits are kept.*
Assessor(in *f*) *m graduate civil servant who has completed his/her traineeship.*
Assimilation *f* assimilation; (*Anpassung*) adjustment (*an +acc* to).
assimilatorisch *adj* assimilatory, assimilative.
assimilieren* [1] *vti* to assimilate.
[2] *vr* to become assimilated ◆ **sich an etw** (*acc*) **~** (*Mensch*) to adjust to sth.
Assistent(in *f*) [-st-] *m* assistant.
Assistenz [-st-] *f* assistance ◆ **unter ~ von ...** with the assistance of ...
Assistenz-: ~arzt *m* houseman (*Brit*), intern (*US*); **~professor** *m* assistant professor.
assistieren* [-st-] *vi* to assist (*jdm* sb).
Assonanz *f* (*Poet*) assonance.
Assoziation *f* association.
Assoziations-: ~freiheit *f siehe* **Vereinigungsfreiheit**; **~kette** *f* chain of associations.
assoziativ *adj* (*Psych, geh*) associative.
assoziieren* (*geh*) [1] *vt* **mit Grün assoziiere ich Ruhe** I associate green with peace; **die Musik assoziierte bei mir Unangenehmes** the music suggested something unpleasant to me.
[2] *vi* to make associations ◆ **frei ~** to make free associations.
[3] *vr* (**a**) (*Vorstellungen etc*) to have associations (*in +dat, bei* for) ◆ **beim Anblick des Hauses ~ sich in** *or* **bei mir Kindheitserinnerungen** when I see the house I think of my childhood.
(**b**) (*an-, zusammenschließen*) **sich mit jdm ~** to join with sb; **sich an jdn/etw ~** to become associated to sb/sth.
assoziiert *adj* associated.
Assuan(stau)damm *m* Aswan (High) Dam.
Assyrer(in *f*) *m* **-s, -** Assyrian.
Assyrien [-iən] *nt* **-s** Assyria.
Assyrier(in *f*) [-iɐ, -iərın] *m* **-s, -** *siehe* **Assyrer(in).**
assyrisch *adj* Assyrian.
Ast *m* **-(e)s, ¨-e** (**a**) branch, bough; (*fig: von Nerv*) branch ◆ **sich in ¨-e teilen** to branch; **den ~ absägen, auf dem man sitzt** (*fig*) to dig one's own grave; **einen ~ durchsägen** (*hum*) to snore like a grampus (*inf*), to saw wood (*US inf*); *siehe* **absteigen (b).**
(**b**) (*im Holz*) knot.
(**c**) (*inf*) (*Rücken*) back; (*Buckel*) hump(back), hunchback ◆ **sich** (*dat*) **einen ~ lachen** (*inf*) to double up (with laughter).
AStA ['asta] *m* **-s, Asten** (*Univ*) *abbr of* **Allgemeiner Studentenausschuß.**
Astat, Astatin *nt, no pl* (*abbr* **At**) astatine.
Ästchen *nt dim of* **Ast.**
asten (*inf*) [1] *vi* (**a**) (*sich anstrengen*) to slog (*inf*). (**b**) (*büffeln*) to swot. (**c**) *aux sein* (*sich fortbewegen*) to drag oneself.
[2] *vt* to hump (*inf*), to lug (*Brit inf*).
Aster *f* **-, -n** aster, Michaelmas daisy.
Astgabel *f* fork (in a branch) ◆ **eine ~** the fork of a branch.
Astheniker(in *f*) *m* **-s, -** asthenic.
Ästhet(in *f*) *m* **-en, -en** aesthete.
Ästhetik *f* (**a**) (*Wissenschaft*) aesthetics *sing*. (**b**) (*Schönheit*) aesthetics *pl*. (**c**) (*Schönheitssinn*) aesthetic sense.
Ästhetiker(in *f*) *m* **-s, -** aesthetician.
Ästhetin *f siehe* **Ästhet.**
ästhetisch *adj* aesthetic.
ästhetisieren* (*usu pej, geh*) [1] *vt* to aestheticize.
[2] *vi* to talk about aesthetics.
Ästhetizismus *m* (*pej geh*) aestheticism.
Ästhetizist(in *f*) *m* aestheticist.
Asthma *nt* **-s,** *no pl* asthma.
Asthmatiker(in *f*) *m* **-s, -** asthmatic.
asthmatisch *adj* asthmatic.
astig *adj Holz* knotty, gnarled.
Astloch *nt* knothole.
astral *adj* astral.
Astral-: ~körper, ~leib *m* (*Philos*) astral body; (*iro inf*) beautiful *or* heavenly body.
astrein *adj* (**a**) *Holz, Brett* free of knots. (**b**) (*fig inf: moralisch einwandfrei*) straight (*inf*), above board, on the level (*inf*). (**c**) (*fig inf: echt*) genuine. (**d**) (*sl: prima*) fantastic.
Astro-: ~loge *m*, **~login** *f* astrologer; **~logie** *f* astrology; **a~logisch** *adj* astrological; **~naut(in** *f*) *m* **-en, -en** astronaut; **~nautik** *f* astronautics *sing*; **a~nautisch** *adj* astronautic(al); **~nom(in** *f*) *m* astronomer; **~nomie**

f astronomy; **a~nomisch** *adj (lit)* astronomical; *(fig auch)* astronomic; **a~nomische Navigation** astronavigation.
astrophisch *adj (Poet)* not divided into strophes.
Astro-: ~physik *f* astrophysics *sing*; **a~physikalisch** *adj* astrophysical; **~physiker(in** *f*) *m* astrophysicist.
Astwerk *nt* branches *pl*.
ASU ['asu] *f* -, *no pl abbr of* **Abgassonderuntersuchung**.
Äsung *f (Hunt)* grazing.
ASW [aːǀɛsˈveː] *no art* -, *no pl abbr of* **außersinnliche Wahrnehmung** ESP.
Asyl *nt* **-s, -e (a)** *(Schutz)* sanctuary *no art (liter)*; *(politisches ~)* (political) asylum *no art* ◆ **jdm ~ gewähren** to grant sb sanctuary *(liter)*/(political) asylum; **um ~ bitten** *or* **nachsuchen** *(form)* to ask *or* apply *(form)* for (political) asylum.
(b) *(old: Heim)* home, asylum.
Asylant(in *f*) *m* person seeking political asylum, asylum-seeker.
Asylantenwohnheim *nt* home for people seeking political asylum.
Asyl-: ~antrag *m* application for political asylum; **a~berechtigt** *adj* entitled to political asylum; **~bewerber(in** *f*) *m* applicant for political asylum; **~recht** *nt (Pol)* right of (political) asylum; ⚠**~suchende(r)** *mf decl as adj* person seeking (political) asylum; **~verfahren** *nt court hearing to determine a person's right to political asylum*; **~werber(in** *f*) *m (Aus) siehe* **Asylsuchende(r)**.
Asymmetrie *f* lack of symmetry, asymmetry.
asymmetrisch *adj* asymmetric(al); *(fig) Gespräch* one-sided.
Asymptote *f* **-, -n** asymptote.
asymptotisch *adj* asymptotic.
asynchron [-kroːn] *adj* asynchronous *(form, Comput)*, out of synchronism.
asyndetisch *adj (Ling)* paratactic(al).
Asyndeton *nt* **-s, Asyndeta** *(Ling)* parataxis.
Aszendent *m* **(a)** *(Astrol)* ascendant. **(b)** *(Vorfahr)* ancestor, ascendant *(form)*.
aszendieren* *vi* **(a)** *aux sein (Astron)* to be in the ascendant. **(b)** *aux sein or haben (obs)* to be promoted *(zu* to).
Aszese *f* -, *no pl siehe* **Askese**.
at ['aːˈteː] *abbr of* **Atmosphäre** *(Phys)*.
A.T. *abbr of* **Altes Testament** OT.
ata *adv (baby-talk)* **~ (~) gehen** to go walkies *(baby-talk)*.
ataktisch *adj* unco-ordinated.
Atavismus [-vɪs-] *m* atavism.
atavistisch [-vɪs-] *adj* atavistic.
Atelier [-ˈlieː] *nt* **-s, -s** studio ◆ **das Filmprojekt ging letzte Woche ins ~** shooting (on the film) started last week.
Atelier-: ~aufnahme *f* **(a)** *(Produkt)* studio shot; **(b)** *usu pl (Vorgang)* studio work *no pl*; **~fenster** *nt* studio window; **~fest** *nt* studio party; **~wohnung** *f* studio apartment.
Atem *m* **-s,** *no pl* **(a)** *(das Atmen)* breathing ◆ **den ~ anhalten** *(lit, fig)* to hold one's breath; **mit angehaltenem ~** *(lit)* holding one's breath; *(fig)* with bated breath; **einen kurzen ~ haben** to be short-winded; **wieder zu ~ kommen** to get one's breath back; **einen langen/den längeren ~ haben** *(fig)* to have a lot of/more staying power; **jdn in ~ halten** to keep sb in suspense *or* on tenterhooks; **das verschlug mir den ~** that took my breath away; *siehe* **ausgehen**.
(b) *(lit, fig: ~luft)* breath ◆ **~ holen** *or* **schöpfen** *(lit)* to take *or* draw a breath; *(fig)* to get one's breath back.
(c) *(fig geh: Augenblick)* **in einem/im selben ~** in one/the same breath.
Atem-: ~beklemmung *f* difficulty in breathing; **a~beraubend** *adj* breathtaking; **~beschwerden** *pl* trouble in breathing; **~gerät** *nt* breathing apparatus; *(Med)* respirator; **~geräusch** *nt* respiratory sounds *pl*; **~gymnastik** *f* breathing exercises *pl*; **~holen** *nt* **-s,** *no pl* breathing; **man kommt nicht mehr zum ~holen** *(fig)* you hardly have time to breathe; **zum ~holen auftauchen** to come up for air; **~lähmung** *f* respiratory paralysis; **a~los** *adj (lit, fig)* breathless; **~luft** *f* **unsere ~luft** the air we breathe; **~maske** *f* breathing mask; **~not** *f* difficulty in breathing; **~pause** *f (fig)* breathing time *no art*, breathing space; **eine ~pause einlegen/brauchen** to take/need a breather; **~schutzgerät** *nt* breathing apparatus; **~schutzmaske** *f*; *siehe* **Atemmaske**; **~technik** *f* breathing technique; **~übung** *f (Med)* breathing exercise; **~wege** *pl (Anat)* respiratory tracts *pl*; **~wegserkrankung** *f* respiratory disease; **~zentrum** *nt (Anat)* respiratory centre; **~zug** *m* breath; **in einem/im selben ~zug** *(fig)* in one/the same breath.
Atheismus *m* atheism.
Atheist(in *f*) *m* atheist.
atheistisch *adj* atheist(ic).
Athen *nt* **-s** Athens.
Athener *adj* Athenian.
Athener(in *f*) *m* **-s, -** Athenian.
athenisch *adj* Athenian.
Äther *m* **-s,** *no pl* **(a)** ether. **(b)** *(poet)* (a)ether *(poet)*; *(Rad)* air ◆ **etw in den ~ schicken** to put sth on the air; **über den ~** over the air.
ätherisch *adj (Liter, Chem)* ethereal.
ätherisieren* *vt* to etherize.
Äther-: ~krieg *m (Press sl)* radio propaganda war; **~narkose** *f* etherization; **~wellen** *pl (Rad)* radio waves *pl*.
Äthiopien [ɛˈtioːpiən] *nt* **-s** Ethiopia, Abyssinia.
Äthiopier(in *f*) [-piɐ, -iərɪn] *m* **-s, -** Ethiopian, Abyssinian.
Athlet(in *f*) *m* **-en, -en** athlete.
Athletik *f* -, *no pl* athletics *sing*.
Athletiker(in *f*) *m* **-s, -** athletic type.
athletisch *adj* athletic.
Äthylalkohol *m* ethyl alcohol.
Äthyläther *m* ethyl ether.
Atlant *m* atlas.
Atlanten *pl of* **Atlas**[1].
Atlantik *m* **-s** Atlantic.
Atlantikwall *m (Mil Hist)* Atlantic Wall.
atlantisch *adj* Atlantic ◆ **ein ~es Hoch** a high-pressure area over/from the Atlantic; **der A~e Ozean** the Atlantic Ocean.
Atlas[1] *m* - *or* **-ses, Atlanten** *or* **-se** atlas.
Atlas[2] *m* -, *no pl (Myth)* Atlas.
Atlas[3] *m* **-ses, -se** *(Seiden~)* satin; *(Baumwolle)* sateen.
Atlas[4] *m* - *(Geog)* Atlas Mountains *pl*.
Atlasseide *f* satin.
atmen [1] *vt (lit, fig geh)* to breathe.
[2] *vi* to breathe, to respire *(form)* ◆ **frei ~** *(fig)* to breathe freely.
Atmosphäre *f* **-, -n** *(Phys, fig)* atmosphere.
Atmosphären-: ~druck *m* atmospheric pressure; **~überdruck** *m* **(a)** atmospheric excess pressure; **(b)** *(Maßeinheit)* atmosphere (of pressure) above atmospheric pressure.
atmosphärisch *adj* atmospheric ◆ **~e Störungen** atmospherics *pl*.
Atmung *f* -, *no pl* breathing; *(Eccl, Med)* respiration.
Atmungs-: ~apparat *m siehe* **Atemgerät**; **~organe** *pl* respiratory organs *pl*; **~zentrum** *nt siehe* **Atemzentrum**.
Atoll *nt* **-s, -e** atoll.
Atom *nt* **-s, -e** atom.
Atom- *in cpds* atomic; *siehe auch* **Kern-**; **~abfall** *m* nuclear *or* radioactive *or* atomic waste; **~angriff** *m* nuclear attack; **~anlage** *f* atomic plant; **~antrieb** *m* nuclear *or* atomic propulsion; **ein U-Boot mit ~antrieb** a nuclear-powered submarine.
atomar *adj* atomic, nuclear; *Struktur* atomic; *Drohung* nuclear.
Atom-: ~basis *f* nuclear base; **~behörde** *f* Atomic Energy Authority *(Brit) or* Commission *(US)*; **a~betrieben** *adj* nuclear-powered; **~bombe** *f* atomic *or* atom bomb; **~bombenexplosion** *f* atomic *or* nuclear explosion; **a~bombensicher** *adj* atomic *or* nuclear blast-proof; **~bombenversuch** *m* atomic *or* nuclear test; **~bomber** *m* nuclear bomber; **~bunker** *m* atomic *or* nuclear blast-proof bunker; **~busen** *m (dated inf)* big bust *or* boobs *pl (inf)*; **~energie** *f siehe* **Kernenergie**; **~explosion** *f* atomic *or* nuclear explosion; **~forscher** *m* nuclear scientist; **~forschung** *f* atomic *or* nuclear research; **~forschungszentrum** *nt* atomic *or* nuclear research centre; **~gemeinde** *f* pro-nuclear lobby; **a~getrieben** *adj* nuclear-powered; **~gewicht** *nt* atomic weight; **~industrie** *f* nuclear industry.
atomisch *adj (Sw) siehe* **atomar**.
atomisieren* *vt* to atomize; *(fig)* to smash to pieces *or* smithereens.
Atomismus *m* atomism.
Atom-: ~kern *m* atomic nucleus; **~klub** *m (Press sl)* nuclear club; **~kraft** *f* atomic *or* nuclear power *or* energy; **~kraftwerk** *nt* atomic *or* nuclear power station; **~krieg** *m* atomic *or* nuclear war; **~macht** *f* nuclear power; **~meiler** *m siehe* **Kernreaktor**; **~modell** *nt* model of the atom; **~müll** *m* atomic *or* nuclear *or* radioactive waste; **~physik** *f* atomic *or* nuclear physics *sing*; **~physiker** *m* nuclear physicist; **~pilz** *m* mushroom cloud; **~rakete** *f* nuclear-powered rocket; *(Waffe)* nuclear missile; **~reaktor** *m* atomic *or* nuclear reactor; **~rüstung** *f* nuclear armament; **~schwelle** *f* nuclear threshold; **~spaltung** *f* nuclear fission; **die erste ~spaltung** the first splitting of the atom; **~sperrvertrag** *m siehe* **~waffensperrvertrag**; **~sprengkopf** *m* atomic *or* nuclear warhead; **~staat** *m* nuclear power; **~stopp** *m* nuclear ban; **~strahlung** *f* nuclear radiation; **~streitmacht** *f* nuclear capability; **~strom** *m (inf)* electricity generated by nuclear power; **~technik** *f* nuclear technology, nucleonics *sing*.
Atomtest *m* nuclear test.
Atomtest-: ~stopp *m* **-s,** *no pl* nuclear test ban; **~stoppabkommen** *nt* nuclear test ban treaty.
Atom-: ~tod *m (Press sl)* nuclear death; **~triebwerk** *nt* nuclear engine; **~-U-Boot** *nt* nuclear submarine; **~uhr** *f* atomic clock; **~versuch** *m* nuclear test; **~versuchsstopp** *m* nuclear test ban.
Atomwaffe *f* nuclear *or* atomic weapon.
Atomwaffen-: a~frei *adj* nuclear-free; **~sperrvertrag** *m* nuclear *or* atomic weapons non-proliferation treaty; **~test, ~versuch** *m* nuclear test.
Atom-: ~wissenschaft *f* nuclear *or* atomic science; **~wissenschaftler** *m* nuclear *or* atomic scientist; **~zeit** *f* nuclear time; **~zeitalter** *nt* atomic *or* nuclear age; **~zerfall** *m* atomic disintegration *or* decay; **~zertrümmerung** *f* splitting of the atom.
atonal *adj* atonal.
Atonalität *f* atonality.
atoxisch *adj (form)* non-toxic.
Atrium *nt (Archit, Anat)* atrium.
Atriumhaus *nt* house built around an atrium *or* open court.
Atrophie *f (Med)* atrophy.
atrophisch *adj* atrophied.
ätsch *interj (inf)* ha-ha.
Attaché [ataˈʃeː] *m* **-s, -s** attaché.
Attacke *f* **-, -n** *(Angriff)* attack; *(Mil Hist)* (cavalry) charge ◆ **eine ~ gegen jdn/**

etw reiten (*lit*) to charge sb/sth; (*fig*) to attack sb/sth.

attackieren* *vt* (*angreifen*) to attack; (*Mil Hist*) to charge.

Attentat [-taːt] *nt* -(e)s, -e assassination; (*~sversuch*) assassination attempt ◆ ein ~ auf jdn verüben to assassinate sb; to make an attempt on sb's life; ich habe ein ~ auf dich vor (*hum*) listen, I've got a great idea.

Attentäter(in *f*) *m* -s, - assassin; (*bei gescheitertem Versuch*) would-be assassin.

Attest *nt* -(e)s, -e certificate.

attestieren* *vt* (*form*) to certify ◆ jdm seine Dienstuntauglichkeit *etc* ~ to certify sb as unfit for duty *etc*.

Attika *nt* -s (*Geog*) Attica.

attisch *adj* Attic.

Attitüde *f* -, -n (*geh*) (a) attitude. (b) (*Geste*) gesture.

Attraktion *f* attraction.

attraktiv *adj* attractive.

Attraktivität *f* attractiveness.

Attrappe *f* -, -n dummy; (*fig: Schein*) sham ◆ die ~ eines ... a dummy ...; bei ihr ist alles ~ everything about her is false.

Attribut *nt* -(e)s, -e (*geh, Gram*) attribute.

Attributsatz *m* (*Gram*) relative clause.

atü [aːˈtyː] *abbr of* Atmosphärenüberdruck.

Atü *nt* -s, - atmospheric excess pressure.

atypisch *adj* (*geh*) atypical.

atzen *vt* (*Hunt*) to feed.

ätzen *vti* (a) to etch. (b) (*Säure*) to corrode. (c) (*Med*) to cauterize.

ätzend *adj* (a) (*lit*) *Säure* corrosive; (*Med*) caustic. (b) *Geruch* pungent; *Rauch* choking; *Spott* caustic. (c) (*sl*) (*furchtbar*) lousy (*inf*); (*toll*) magic (*sl*) ◆ echt ~ (*toll*) pure magic (*sl*); der Typ ist echt ~ that guy really grates on you.

Ätz-: ~mittel *nt* (*Chem*) corrosive; (*Med*) cautery, caustic; **~natron** *nt* caustic soda; **~stift** *m* (*Med*) cautery; (*bei Friseur*) styptic pencil.

Atzung *f* (*Hunt, hum*) (*Vorgang*) feeding; (*Futter*) food, fodder ◆ wann gibt es ~? (*hum*) when is it feeding time?

Ätzung *f, no pl siehe vti* etching; corrosion; cauterization, cautery.

Au *f* -, -en (*S Ger, Aus*) *siehe* Aue.

au *interj* (a) ow, ouch ◆ ~, das war knapp! oh *or* God, that was close! (b) (*Ausdruck der Begeisterung*) oh.

aua *interj* ow, ouch.

aubergine [obɛrˈʒiːnə] *adj pred*, **auberginefarben** *adj* aubergine.

Aubergine [obɛrˈʒiːnə] *f* aubergine, eggplant.

auch *adv* (a) (*zusätzlich, gleichfalls*) also, too, as well ◆ die Engländer müssen ~ zugeben, daß ... the English must admit too *or* as well *or* must also admit that ...; ~ die Engländer müssen ... the English too must ...; das kann ich ~ I can do that too *or* as well; das ist ~ möglich that's possible too *or* as well, that's also possible; ja, das ~ yes, that too; ~ gut that's OK too; du ~? you too?, you as well?; ~ nicht not ... either; das ist ~ nicht richtig that's not right either; er kommt — ich ~ he's coming — so am I *or* me too; ich will eins — ich ~ I want one — so do I *or* me too; er kommt nicht — ich ~ nicht he's not coming — nor *or* neither am I *or* I'm not either *or* me neither; nicht nur ..., sondern ~ not only ... but also ..., not only ... but ... too *or* as well; ~ das noch! that's all I needed!
(b) (*tatsächlich*) too, as well ◆ und das tue/meine ich ~ and I'll do it/I mean it too *or* as well; wenn sie sagt, sie geht, dann geht sie ~ if she says she's going then she'll go; Frechheit! — ja, das ist es ~ what a cheek! — you can say that again; du siehst müde aus — das bin ich ~ you look tired — (so) I am; das ist er ja ~ (and so) he is; so ist es ~ (so) it is.
(c) (*sogar*) even ◆ ~ wenn du Vorfahrt hast even if you (do) have right of way; ohne ~ nur zu fragen without even asking.
(d) (*emph*) den Teufel ~! damn it (all)!; zum Donnerwetter ~! blast it!; so ein Dummkopf ~! what an absolute blockhead!; so was Ärgerliches aber ~! it's really too annoying!; wozu ~? what on earth *or* whatever for?
(e) (*~ immer*) wie dem ~ sei be that as it may; was er ~ sagen mag whatever he might say; und mag er ~ noch so klug sein, wenn er ~ noch so klug ist however clever he may be; so schnell er ~ laufen mag however fast he runs *or* may run, no matter how fast he runs; *siehe* immer.

Audienz *f* (*bei Papst, König etc*) audience.

Audienzsaal *m* audience chamber.

Audimax *nt* -, *no pl* (*Univ sl*) main lecture hall.

audiovisuell *adj* audiovisual.

auditiv *adj* auditory.

Auditorium *nt* (a) (*Hörsaal*) lecture hall ◆ ~ maximum (*Univ*) main lecture hall. (b) (*geh: Zuhörerschaft*) audience.

Aue *f* -, -n (a) (*dial, poet*) meadow, pasture, lea (*poet*), mead (*poet*). (b) (*dial: Insel*) island.

Auerbachsprung *m* (*Sport*) backward *or* reverse somersault.

Auerhahn *m* -(e)s, **Auerhähne** *or* (*Hunt*) -en capercaillie.

Auerhenne *f*, **Auerhuhn** *nt* capercaillie (hen).

Auer|ochse *m* aurochs.

Auf *nt inv*: das ~ und Ab *or* Nieder the up and down; (*fig*) the ups and downs; das ~ und Ab des Kolbens the up(ward) and down(ward) movement of the piston.

auf [1] *prep siehe auch Substantive, Verben etc* (a) +*dat* on; (*esp Schriftsprache auch*) upon ◆ ~ (der Insel) Skye on the island of Skye; ~ den Orkneyinseln on *or* in the Orkney Islands; ~ See at sea; ~ meinem Zimmer in my room; ~ der Bank/Post/dem Rathaus at the bank/post office/town hall; mein Geld ist ~ der Bank my money is in the bank; ~ der Straße on *or* in the street.
(b) ~ der Geige spielen to play the violin; etw ~ der Geige spielen to play sth on the violin; ~ einem Ohr taub/einem Auge kurzsichtig sein to be deaf in one ear/short-sighted in one eye; das hat nichts ~ sich (*inf*) it does not mean anything; was hat es damit ~ sich? what does it mean?; die Tachonadel steht ~ 105 the speedometer is at *or* on 105; ~ der Fahrt/dem Weg *etc* on the journey/way *etc*; Greenwich liegt ~ 0 Grad Greenwich lies at 0 degrees.
(c) +*acc* on, onto ◆ etw ~ etw heben to lift sth onto sth; etw ~ etw stellen to put sth on(to) *or* on top of sth; sich ~ etw setzen/legen to sit/lie (down) on sth; sich ~ die Straße setzen to sit down on *or* in the road; das Wrack ist ~ den Meeresgrund gesunken the wreck sank to the bottom of the sea; jdm ~ den Rücken klopfen to slap sb on the back; er fiel ~ den Rücken he fell on(to) his back; etw ~ einen Zettel schreiben to write sth on a piece of paper; er ist ~ die Orkneyinseln gefahren he has gone to the Orkney Islands; er segelt ~ das Meer hinaus he is sailing out to sea; man konnte nicht weiter als ~ 10 m herankommen you couldn't get any nearer than 10 m; geh mal ~ die Seite go to the side; Geld ~ die Bank bringen to take money to the bank; (*einzahlen*) to put money in the bank; ~ sein Zimmer/die Post/die Polizei *etc* gehen to go to one's room/the post office/the police *etc*; ~s Gymnasium gehen to go to (the) grammar school; die Uhr ~ 10 stellen to put *or* set the clock to 10; Heiligabend fällt ~ einen Dienstag Christmas Eve falls on a Tuesday; die Sitzung ~ morgen legen/verschieben to arrange the meeting for tomorrow/to postpone the meeting until tomorrow; ~ eine Party/ein Bankett *etc* gehen to go to a party/banquet *etc*; ~ ihn! at him!, get him!
(d) +*acc* ~ 10 km/drei Tage for 10 km/three days; ~ eine Tasse Kaffee/eine Zigarette(nlänge) for a cup of coffee/a smoke.
(e) +*acc* (*Häufung*) Niederlage ~ Niederlage defeat after *or* upon defeat; Beleidigung ~ Beleidigung insult upon insult; einer ~ den anderen one after another.
(f) +*acc* (*im Hinblick auf*) for ◆ ein Manuskript ~ Fehler prüfen to check a manuscript for errors.
(g) +*acc* (*als Reaktion, auch*: auf ... hin) at ◆ ~ seinen Vorschlag (hin) at his suggestion; ~ meinen Brief hin because of *or* on account of my letter; ~ seine Bitte (hin) at *or* upon his request.
(h) (*sl: in einer bestimmten Art*) ~ die Elegante/Ehrliche *etc* elegantly/honestly *etc*; ~ die Billige on the cheap; komm mir bloß nicht ~ die wehleidige Tour! just don't try the sad approach with me.
(i) (*sonstige Anwendungen*) es geht ~ Weihnachten zu Christmas is approaching; er kam ~ mich zu und sagte ... he came up to me and said ...; während er ~ mich zukam as he was coming towards me; die Nacht (von Montag) ~ Dienstag Monday night; das Bier geht ~ mich (*inf*) the beer's on me; ~ wen geht das Bier? (*inf*) who's paying for the beer?; ~ das *or* ~s schändlichste/liebenswürdigste *etc* (*geh*) most shamefully/kindly *etc*; ~ einen Polizisten kommen 1.000 Bürger there is one policeman for *or* to every 1,000 citizens; ~ jeden kamen zwei Flaschen Bier there were two bottles of beer (for) each; ~ den Millimeter/die Sekunde genau precise to the *or* to within one millimetre/second; ~ unseren lieben Onkel Egon/ein glückliches Gelingen *etc* here's to dear Uncle Egon/a great success; ~ deine Gesundheit (your very) good health; ~ morgen/bald till tomorrow/soon; zwanzig ~ sieben (*dial*) twenty to seven; die Dauer ~ ein Jahr reduzieren to reduce the duration to one year; ein Brett ~ einen Meter absägen to saw a plank down to one metre.
[2] *adv* (a) (*offen*) open ◆ Mund/Fenster ~! open your mouth/the window.
(b) (*hinauf*) up ◆ ~ und ab *or* nieder (*geh*) up and down.
(c) (*sonstige Anwendungen*) Helm/Brille ~! helmets/glasses on; ich war die halbe Nacht ~ I've been up half the night; nachmittags Unterricht, und dann noch soviel ~! (*inf*) school in the afternoon, and all that homework too!; Handschuhe an, Wollmütze ~, so wird er sich nicht erkälten with his gloves and woollen hat on he won't catch cold; ~ nach Chicago! let's go to Chicago; ~ geht's! let's go!; ~ und davon up and away, off; ~, an die Arbeit! come on, let's get on with it; Sprung ~! marsch, marsch! (*Mil*) jump to it!, at the double!; *siehe* aufsein.
[3] *conj* (*old, liter*) ~ daß that (*old, liter*); ~ daß wir niemals vergessen mögen lest we should ever forget, that we might never forget.

auf|addieren* *vtr sep* to add up.

auf|arbeiten *vt sep* (a) (*erneuern*) to refurbish, to do up; *Möbel etc auch* to recondition. (b) (*auswerten*) *Literatur etc* to incorporate critically; *Vergangenheit* to reappraise. (c) (*erledigen*) *Korrespondenz, Liegengebliebenes* to catch up with *or* on, to clear. (d) (*Phys*) *Brennelemente* to reprocess.

Auf|arbeitung *f siehe vt* refurbishing; reconditioning; critical incorporation; reappraisal; catching up; reprocessing ◆ die ~ des Liegengebliebenen dauerte einige Zeit it took some time to catch up with *or* clear the backlog.

auf|atmen *vi sep* (*lit, fig*) to breathe *or* heave a sigh of relief ◆ ein A~ a sigh of relief.

aufbacken *vt sep* to warm *or* crisp up.

aufbahren *vt sep Sarg* to lay on the bier; *Leiche* to lay out ◆ einen Toten feierlich ~ to put a person's body to lie in state.

Aufbahrung *f* laying out; (*feierlich*) lying in state.

Aufbau *m* (a) *no pl* (*das Aufbauen*) construction, building; (*von neuem Staat*) building; (*das Wiederaufbauen*) reconstruction ◆ der wirtschaftliche ~ the building up of the economy. (b) *pl* -ten (*Aufgebautes, Aufgesetztes*) top; (*von Auto, LKW*) coachwork *no pl*, body. (c) *no pl* (*Struktur*) structure.

Aufbau|arbeit *f* construction (work); (*Wiederaufbau*) reconstruction (work).

aufbauen *sep* [1] *vt* (a) (*errichten*) to put up; *zusammensetzbare Möbel, Lautsprecheranlage auch* to fix up; (*hinstellen*) *Ausstellungsstücke, kaltes Buffet, Brettspiel*

etc to set *or* lay out; (*inf*) *Posten, Ordnungspersonal etc* to post; (*zusammenbauen*) *Motor, elektrische Schaltung etc* to put together, to assemble.
(b) (*daraufbauen*) *Stockwerk* to add (on), to build on; *Karosserie* to mount.
(c) (*fig: gestalten*) *Organisation, Land, Armee, Geschäft, Angriff, Druck, Spannung, Verbindung, Eiweiß* to build up; *Zerstörtes* to rebuild; *Theorie, Plan, System* to construct ◆ **sich** (*dat*) **eine (neue) Existenz** *or* **ein Leben ~** to build (up) a new life for oneself.
(d) (*fig: fördern, weiterentwickeln*) *Gesundheit, Kraft* to build up; *Star, Politiker auch* to promote; *Beziehung* to build ◆ **jdn/etw zu etw ~** to build sb/sth up into sth.
(e) (*fig: gründen*) **etw auf etw** (*dat or acc*) **~** to base *or* found sth on sth.
(f) (*strukturieren, konstruieren*) to construct; *Maschine auch* to build; *Aufsatz, Rede, Organisation auch, Komposition* to structure.
[2] *vi* **(a)** (*sich gründen*) to be based *or* founded (*auf +dat or acc* on).
(b) wir wollen ~ und nicht zerstören we want to build and not destroy.
[3] *vr* **(a)** (*inf: sich postieren*) to take up position ◆ **sie bauten sich in einer Reihe auf** they formed (themselves) up into a line; **er baute sich vor dem Feldwebel/Lehrer auf und ...** he stood up in front of the sergeant/teacher and ...; **sich vor jdm drohend ~** to plant oneself in front of sb (*inf*).
(b) (*sich bilden: Wolken, Hochdruckgebiet*) to build up.
(c) (*bestehen aus*) **sich aus etw ~** to be built up *or* composed of sth.
(d) (*sich gründen*) **sich auf etw** (*dat or acc*) **~** to be based *or* founded on sth.

Aufbaukurs *m* continuation course.

aufbäumen *vr sep* (*Tier*) to rear ◆ **sich gegen jdn/etw ~** (*fig*) to rebel *or* revolt against sb/sth; **sich vor Schmerz ~** to writhe with pain.

Aufbauprinzip *nt* structural principle ◆ **die Motoren sind alle nach demselben ~ konstruiert** the engines are all constructed on the same principle.

aufbauschen *sep* [1] *vt* to blow out; *Segel auch* to (make) billow out, to belly out; (*fig*) to blow up, to exaggerate.
[2] *vr* to blow out; (*Segel auch*) to billow (out), to belly (out); (*fig*) to blow up (*zu* into).

Aufbau-: ~studium *nt* (*Univ*) course of further study; **~stufe** *f* (*Sch*) *school class leading to university entrance*, ≃ sixth form (*Brit*).

Aufbauten *pl* (*Naut*) superstructure.

aufbegehren* *vi sep* (*geh*) to rebel, to revolt (*gegen* against).

aufbehalten* *vt sep irreg Hut, Brille etc* to keep on; *Tür, Schrank etc* to leave *or* keep open; *Knopf* to leave *or* keep undone.

aufbeißen *vt sep irreg Verpackung etc* to bite open; *Nuß etc* to crack with one's teeth ◆ **sich** (*dat*) **die Lippe ~** to bite one's lip (and make it bleed).

aufbekommen* *vt sep irreg* (*inf*) **(a)** (*öffnen*) to get open. **(b)** *Aufgabe* to get as homework ◆ **habt ihr keine Hausarbeiten ~?** didn't you get any homework? **(c)** *Essen* to (manage to) eat up ◆ **ich habe nur die halbe Portion ~** I could only manage (to eat) half a portion.

aufbereiten* *vt sep* to process; *Erze, Kohlen* to prepare, to dress; *Trinkwasser auch* to purify; *Daten* to edit; *Text etc* to work up ◆ **etw literarisch/dramaturgisch ~** to turn sth into literature/to adapt sth for the theatre.

Aufbereitung *f siehe vt* processing; preparation, dressing; purification; editing; working up; adaptation.

Aufbereitungs|anlage *f* processing plant.

aufbessern *vt sep* to improve; *Gehalt etc auch* to increase.

Aufbesserung, ⚠Aufbeßrung *f siehe vt* improvement; increase.

aufbewahren* *vt sep* to keep; *Lebensmittel auch* to store; (*behalten*) *alte Zeitungen etc auch* to save; *Wertsachen etc* to look after ◆ **ein Dokument gut/Medikamente kühl ~** to keep a document in a safe place/medicines in a cool place; **jds Dokumente ~** to be looking after sb's documents, to have sb's documents in one's keeping; **kann ich hier mein Gepäck ~ lassen?** can I leave my luggage here?

Aufbewahrung *f* **(a)** *siehe vt* keeping; storage; saving ◆ **jdm etw zur ~ übergeben** to give sth to sb for safekeeping, to put sth in(to) sb's safekeeping; **einen Koffer in ~ geben** to deposit a suitcase (at the left-luggage).
(b) (*Stelle*) left-luggage (office) (*Brit*), check room (*US*).

Aufbewahrungs|ort *m place where sth is kept*, home (*inf*) ◆ **etw an einen sicheren ~ bringen** to put sth in a safe place; **das ist kein geeigneter ~ für Medikamente** that is not the right place to keep medicines.

Aufbewahrungsschein *m* left-luggage receipt *or* ticket (*Brit*), check room ticket (*US*).

aufbiegen *sep irreg* [1] *vt* to bend open.
[2] *vr* (*Ring etc*) to bend open; (*sich hochbiegen: Zweig etc*) to bend itself upright.

aufbieten *vt sep irreg* **(a)** *Menschen, Mittel* to muster; *Kräfte, Fähigkeiten auch* to summon (up); *Militär, Polizei* to call in; (*old*) *Soldaten* to levy (*old*). **(b)** *Brautpaar* to call the banns of. **(c)** (*bei Auktionen*) to put up.

Aufbietung *f siehe vt (a)* mustering; summoning (up); calling in; levy ◆ **unter** *or* **bei ~ aller Kräfte ...** summoning (up) all his/her *etc* strength ...

aufbinden *vt sep irreg* **(a)** (*öffnen*) *Schuh etc* to undo, to untie.
(b) (*hochbinden*) *Haare* to put up *or* tie; *Pflanzen, Zweige etc* to tie (up) straight.
(c) (*befestigen*) to tie on ◆ **etw auf etw** (*acc*) **~** to tie sth on(to) sth.
(d) laß dir doch so etwas nicht ~ (*fig*) don't fall for that; **jdm eine Lüge ~** to take sb in, to tell sb a lie.
(e) (*Typ*) *Buch* to bind.

aufblähen *sep* [1] *vt* to blow out; *Segel auch* to fill, to billow out, to belly out; (*Med*) to distend, to swell; (*fig*) to inflate.
[2] *vr* to blow out; (*Segel auch*) to billow *or* belly out; (*Med*) to become distended *or* swollen; (*fig pej*) to puff oneself up.

Aufblähung *f* (*Med*) distension.

aufblasbar *adj* inflatable.

aufblasen *sep irreg* [1] *vt* **(a)** to blow up; *Reifen etc auch* to inflate; *Backen* to puff out, to blow out. **(b)** (*hochblasen*) to blow up.
[2] *vr* (*fig pej*) to puff oneself up; *siehe* **aufgeblasen.**

aufbleiben *vi sep irreg aux sein* **(a)** to stay up ◆ **wegen jdm ~** to wait *or* stay up for sb. **(b)** (*geöffnet bleiben*) to stay open.

Aufblende *f* (*Film*) fade-in.

aufblenden *sep* [1] *vi* (*Phot*) to open up the lens, to increase the aperture; (*Film*) to fade in; (*Aut*) to turn the headlights on full (beam) ◆ **er fährt aufgeblendet** he drives on full beam.
[2] *vt* (*Aut*) *Scheinwerfer* to turn on full (beam); (*Film*) *Einstellung* to fade in.

aufblicken *vi sep* to look up ◆ **zu jdm/etw ~** (*lit, fig*) to look up to sb/sth.

aufblinken *vi sep* (*lit, fig*) to flash; (*Aut inf: kurz aufblenden*) to flash (one's headlights).

aufblitzen *vi sep* **(a)** to flash. **(b)** *aux sein* (*fig*) (*Emotion, Haß etc*) to flare up; (*Gedanke, Erinnerung*) to flash through one's mind.

aufblühen *vi sep aux sein* **(a)** (*Knospe*) to blossom (out); (*Blume auch*) to bloom. **(b)** (*fig*) (*Mensch*) to blossom out; (*Wissenschaft, Kultur auch*) to (begin to) flourish; (*Gesicht*) to take on a rosy bloom.

aufbocken *vt sep Auto* to jack up; *Motorrad* to put on its stand.

aufbohren *vt sep* to bore *or* drill a hole in; *Zahn auch* to drill.

aufbranden *vi sep aux sein* (*geh*) to surge; (*fig: Beifall*) to burst forth ◆ **Beifall brandete immer wieder auf** there was wave upon wave of applause.

aufbraten *vt sep irreg Essen* to warm up; (*in der Pfanne auch*) to fry up.

aufbrauchen *sep* [1] *vt* to use up ◆ **seine Geduld ist aufgebraucht** his patience is exhausted.
[2] *vr* (*sich verbrauchen*) to get used up; (*Reifen: sich abnutzen*) to get worn out, to wear out.

aufbrausen *vi sep aux sein* **(a)** (*Brandung etc*) to surge; (*Brausetablette, Brause etc*) to fizz up; (*fig: Beifall, Jubel*) to break out, to burst forth. **(b)** (*fig: Mensch*) to flare up, to fly off the handle (*inf*).

aufbrausend *adj Temperament* irascible; *Mensch auch* quick-tempered, liable to flare up.

aufbrechen *sep irreg* [1] *vt* to break *or* force open; *Deckel* to prise off; *Tresor auch, Auto* to break into; *Boden, Asphalt, Oberfläche* to break up; (*geh*) *Brief* to break open; (*fig*) *System, soziale Struktur etc* to break down.
[2] *vi aux sein* **(a)** (*sich öffnen*) (*Straßenbelag etc*) to break up; (*Knospen*) to (burst) open; (*Wunde*) to open.
(b) (*fig: Konflikte, Haß etc*) to break out.
(c) (*sich auf den Weg machen*) to start *or* set out *or* off.

aufbrennen *sep irreg* [1] *vt* **(a) einem Tier ein Zeichen ~** to brand an animal; **jdm eins ~** (*inf*) (*schlagen*) to wallop *or* clout sb (one) (*inf*); (*anschießen*) to shoot sb, to put a slug into sb (*sl*).
(b) (*verbrennen*) *Kerze, Kohlen etc* to burn up.
[2] *vi aux sein* (*lit, fig*) (*Baum etc*) to go up in flames; (*Kerze*) to burn out; (*Feuer, Leidenschaft*) to flare up.

aufbringen *vt sep irreg* **(a)** (*beschaffen*) to find; *Geld auch* to raise; *Kraft, Mut, Energie auch* to summon up.
(b) (*erzürnen*) to make angry, to irritate ◆ **jdn gegen jdn/etw ~** to set sb against sb/sth; *siehe* **aufgebracht.**
(c) (*ins Leben rufen*) to start; *Gerücht auch* to set going, to put about.
(d) (*Naut*) *Schiff* to seize; (*in Hafen zwingen*) to bring in.
(e) (*auftragen*) *Farbe etc* to put on, to apply ◆ **etw auf etw** (*acc*) **~** to put sth on sth, to apply sth to sth.
(f) (*dial: aufbekommen*) *Tür etc* to get open.

Aufbruch *m* **(a)** *no pl* (*Abreise, das Losgehen*) departure ◆ **das Zeichen zum ~ geben** to give the signal to set out *or* off; **der ~ ins 21. Jahrhundert** the emergence into the 21st century; **eine Zeit des ~s** a time of new departures.
(b) (*aufgebrochene Stelle*) crack.

Aufbruchs-: a~bereit *adj* ready to set off *or* go *or* depart; **~signal** *nt* signal to set off; **hast du das ~signal gehört?** did you hear the off?; **~stimmung** *f* **hier herrscht schon ~stimmung** (*bei Party etc*) it's all breaking up; (*in Gastwirtschaft*) they're packing up; **es herrschte allgemeine ~stimmung (unter den Gästen)** the party was breaking up; **bist du schon in ~stimmung?** are you wanting *or* ready to go already?

aufbrühen *vt sep* to brew up.

aufbrüllen *vi sep* to shout *or* yell out; (*Tier*) to bellow.

aufbrummen *sep* [1] *vt* (*inf*) **jdm etw ~** to give sb sth; **jdm die Kosten ~** to land sb with the costs (*inf*).
[2] *vi* **(a)** to roar out. **(b)** *aux sein* (*Aut inf*) to bang *or* prang (*inf*) (*auf +acc* into); (*Naut sl*) to run aground, to hit the bottom.

aufbügeln *vt sep* **(a)** *Kleidungsstück* to iron out; (*fig inf*) to vamp up (*inf*). **(b)** *Flicken, Bild etc* to iron on ◆ **Flicken zum A~** iron-on patches.

aufbumsen *vi sep* (*inf*) *aux sein* to bang ◆ **etw auf etw** (*dat*) **~ lassen** to plump *or* plonk (*inf*) sth down on sth; **mit dem Hinterkopf ~** to bump *or* bang the back of one's head.

aufbürden *vt sep* (*geh*) **jdm etw ~** (*lit*) to load sth onto sb; (*fig*) to encumber sb with sth; **jdm die Schuld für etw ~** to put the blame for sth on sb.

aufbürsten *vt sep* **etw ~** to give sth a brush, to brush sth up.

aufdämmern *vi sep aux sein* (*geh*) (*Morgen, Tag*) to dawn, to break; (*fig: Verdacht*) to arise ◆ **der Gedanke/die Einsicht dämmerte in ihm auf** the idea/realization dawned on him.

⚠**auf daß** *conj siehe* **auf 3.**

⚠: Informationen zur Rechtschreibreform im Anhang

aufdecken *sep* [1] *vt* **(a)** *jdn* to uncover; *Bett(decke)* to turn down; *Gefäß* to open; *Spielkarten* to show.
(b) *(fig) Wahrheit, Verschwörung, Zusammenhänge* to discover, to uncover; *Verbrechen auch* to expose; *Schwäche* to lay bare; *Geheimnis, Rätsel* to solve; *wahren Charakter* to disclose, to lay bare, to expose.
(c) *(auf den Eßtisch stellen)* to put on the table ◆ **das Geschirr ~** to lay *(Brit) or* set the table.
[2] *vi* to lay *(Brit) or* set the table.

Aufdeckung *f siehe vt (b)* uncovering; exposing, exposure; laying bare; solving; disclosing, disclosure.

aufdonnern *vr sep (pej inf)* to tart oneself up *(pej inf)*, to get dolled up *(inf) or* tarted up *(pej inf)*; *siehe* **aufgedonnert**.

aufdrängen *sep* [1] *vt* **jdm etw ~** to impose *or* force *or* push sth on sb.
[2] *vr* to impose ◆ **sich jdm ~** *(Mensch)* to impose oneself *or* one's company on sb; *(fig: Erinnerung)* to come involuntarily to sb's mind; **dieser Gedanke/Verdacht drängte sich mir auf** I couldn't help thinking/suspecting that.

aufdrehen *sep* [1] *vt* **(a)** *Wasserhahn, Wasser etc* to turn on; *Ventil* to open; *Schraubverschluß* to unscrew; *Schraube* to loosen, to unscrew; *Radio etc* to turn up; *(Aus: einschalten) Licht, Radio etc* to turn *or* switch on.
(b) *(inf: aufziehen) Uhr, Federtrieb etc* to wind up.
(c) *(aufrollen) Haar* to put in rollers; *Schnurrbart* to turn *or* twist up.
[2] *vi (inf) (beschleunigen)* to put one's foot down hard, to open up; *(fig)* to get going, to start going like the clappers *(Brit inf)*; *(fig: ausgelassen werden)* to get going, to let it all hang out *(sl)*; *siehe* **aufgedreht**.

aufdringen *vtr sep irreg siehe* **aufdrängen**.

aufdringlich *adj Benehmen, Tapete* obtrusive; *Geruch, Parfüm* powerful; *Farbe auch* loud, insistent; *Mensch* insistent, pushing, pushy *(inf)*, importunate *(liter)* ◆ **die ~e Art meines Mitreisenden** the way my fellow-passenger forced himself *or* his company upon me; **dieser ~e Kerl kam einfach auf mich zu** this chap just forced himself *or* his company on me; **beim Tanzen wurde er ~** when we/they were dancing he kept trying to get fresh *(inf)*.

Aufdringlichkeit *f siehe adj* obtrusiveness; powerfulness; loudness, insistence; pushiness, importunateness *(liter)*; *(aufdringliche Art)* pushy way *or* nature ◆ **die ~ meiner Nachbarin** the way my neighbour forces herself *or* her company on you.

aufdröseln *vt sep (lit, fig)* to unravel; *Strickarbeit* to undo.

Aufdruck *m* **(a)** *(Aufgedrucktes)* imprint; *(auf Briefmarke)* overprint. **(b)** *(Phys)* upward pressure.

aufdrucken *vt sep* **etw auf etw** *(acc)* **~** to print sth on sth; **Postwertstempel auf Briefe ~** to stamp letters.

aufdrücken *sep* [1] *vt* **(a) etw (auf etw** *acc*) **~** to press sth on (sth); **den Bleistift nicht so fest ~!** don't press (on) your pencil so hard.
(b) *(aufdrucken)* **etw auf etw** *(acc)* **~** to stamp sth on sth; **ein Siegel auf einen Brief ~** to impress a seal on a letter; **jdm einen ~** *(inf)* to give sb a kiss *or* a quick peck *(inf)*; *siehe* **Stempel**.
(c) *(öffnen) Tür etc* to push open; *Ventil auch* to force open; *Pickel etc* to squeeze.
(d) *(inf: durch Knopfdruck öffnen) Tür* to open *(by pressing the button)* ◆ **er drückte die Tür auf** he pressed *or* pushed the button and the door opened.
[2] *vi* **(a)** to press.
(b) *(inf: die Tür elektrisch öffnen)* to open the door *(by pressing a button)*.
[3] *vr* leave an impression *(auf +acc* on).

auf|einander *adv* **(a)** on (top of) each other *or* one another. **(b) sich ~ verlassen können** to be able to rely on each other *or* one another; **~ zufahren** to drive towards each other.

auf|einander-: ⚠**~beißen** *vt sep irreg Zähne* to clench, to bite together; ⚠**~drücken** *vt sep* to press together; ⚠**~fahren** *vi sep irreg aux sein* to drive *or* crash into each other; **A~folge** *f, no pl* sequence; *(zeitlich auch)* succession; **in schneller A~folge** in quick succession; ⚠**~folgen** *vi sep aux sein* to follow each other *or* one another, to come after each other *or* one another; **die beiden Söhne/Termine folgten unmittelbar ~** the two sons/appointments followed *or* came one immediately after the other, one son/appointment came immediately after the other; ⚠**~folgend** *adj* successive; **drei schnell ~folgende Tore** three goals in quick succession; ⚠**~hängen** *sep* [1] *vi irreg* **(a)** *(inf: Leute)* to hang around together *(inf)*; **die beiden Autos hängen zu nah ~** the two cars are sticking too close (together); **in einer kleinen Wohnung hängt man immer zu eng ~** in a small flat you're always too much on top of each other *(inf)*; **(b)** *(übereinanderhängen)* to hang one over the other; [2] *vt* to hang on top of each other; ⚠**~hetzen** *vt sep* to set on *or* at each other; ⚠**~hocken** *vi sep (inf) siehe* **~hängen 1 (a)**; ⚠**~knallen** *sep (inf)* [1] *vi aux sein (lit, fig)* to collide; [2] *vt* to bang together; ⚠**~legen** *sep* [1] *vt* to lay on top of each other, to lay one on top of the other; [2] *vr* to lie on top of each other; ⚠**~liegen** *vi sep irreg aux sein or haben* to lie on top of each other; ⚠**~passen** *vi sep* to fit on top of each other; ⚠**~prallen** *vi sep aux sein (Autos etc)* to collide; *(Truppen etc, Meinungen)* to clash; ⚠**~pressen** *vt sep* to press together; ⚠**~rasen** *vi sep aux sein* to hurtle into each other; ⚠**~schichten** *vt sep* to put in layers one on top of the other; ⚠**~schlagen** *sep irreg* [1] *vi aux sein* to knock *or* strike against each other; [2] *vt* to knock *or* strike together; ⚠**~setzen** *sep* [1] *vt* to put on top of each other; [2] *vr (Gegenstände)* to be placed one on top of the other *or* on top of each other; *(Bienen etc)* to settle on each other; ⚠**~sitzen** *vi sep irreg aux sein or haben* **(a)** *(Gegenstände)* to lie on top of each other; **(b)** *(inf)* **die Autos sitzen zu dicht ~** the cars are too close together; **(c)** *(inf: Menschen)* to sit on top of each other *(inf)*; *(eng wohnen)* to live on top of each other *(inf)*; ⚠**~stellen** *sep* [1] *vt* to put *or* place on top of each other; [2] *vr* to get on top of each other; ⚠**~stoßen** *vi sep irreg aux sein* to bump into each other, to collide; *(fig: Meinungen, Farben)* to clash; ⚠**~treffen** *vi sep irreg aux sein (Mannschaften, Gruppen etc)* to meet; *(Meinungen)* to clash, to come into conflict; *(Kugeln, Gegenstände etc)* to hit each other; ⚠**~türmen** *vt sep* to pile on top of each other.

Auf|enthalt *m* **-(e)s, -e (a)** *(das Sich-Aufhalten)* stay; *(das Wohnen)* residence ◆ **der ~ im Aktionsbereich des Krans ist verboten** do not stand within the radius of the crane, keep well clear of the crane.
(b) *(Aufenthaltszeit)* stay, sojourn *(liter)*.
(c) *(esp Rail)* stop; *(bei Anschluß)* wait ◆ **der Zug hat 20 Minuten ~** the train stops for 20 minutes; **wie lange haben wir ~?** how long do we stop for *or* do we have to wait?
(d) *(geh: Verzögerung)* delay, wait.
(e) *(geh: Aufenthaltsort)* abode *(form)*, domicile, place of residence ◆ **~ nehmen** to take up residence.

Auf|enthalter(in *f*) *m* **-s, -** *(Sw)* foreign resident, resident alien *(form)*.

Auf|enthalts-: ~berechtigung *f* right of residence; **~bewilligung** *f siehe* **~erlaubnis**; **~dauer** *f* length *or* duration of stay; **~erlaubnis, ~genehmigung** *f* residence permit; **~ort** *m* whereabouts *sing or pl*; *(Jur)* abode, residence; **man weiß nicht, was sein augenblicklicher ~ort ist** his present whereabouts is *or* are not known; **~raum** *m* day room; *(in Betrieb)* recreation room; *(auf Flughafen)* lounge; **~verbot** *nt* **jdm ~verbot erteilen** to ban sb from staying (in a country *etc*); **er hat ~verbot** he is not allowed to stay (in the country *etc*), he is banned.

auf|erlegen* *vt sep or insep (geh)* to impose *(jdm etw* sth on sb); *Strafe auch* to inflict.

Auf|erstandene(r) *m decl as adj (Rel)* risen Christ.

auf|erstehen* *vi sep or insep irreg aux sein* to rise from the dead, to rise again *(esp Rel)* ◆ **Christus ist auferstanden** Christ is (a)risen.

Auf|erstehung *f* resurrection ◆ **(fröhliche) ~ feiern** *(hum)* to have been resurrected.

Auf|erstehungsfest *nt (geh)* Feast of the Resurrection.

auf|erwecken* *vt sep or insep (geh)* to raise from the dead; *(fig)* to reawaken.

Auf|erweckung *f* raising from the dead.

auf|essen *sep irreg* [1] *vt* to eat up.
[2] *vi* to eat (everything) up.

auffächern *sep* [1] *vt* to fan out; *(fig)* to arrange *or* order neatly.
[2] *vr* to fan out.

auffädeln *vt sep* to thread *or* string (together).

auffahren *sep irreg* [1] *vi aux sein* **(a)** *(aufprallen)* **auf jdn/etw ~** to run *or* drive into sb/sth; **auf eine Sandbank ~** to run onto *or* run aground on a sandbank.
(b) *(näher heranfahren)* to drive up, to move up ◆ **zu dicht ~** to drive too close behind (the car in front); **mein Hintermann fährt dauernd so dicht auf** the car behind me is right on my tail all the time.
(c) *(nach oben fahren) (Bergleute)* to go up; *(Rel)* to ascend.
(d) *(hinauffahren)* **auf etw** *(acc)* **~** to drive onto sth; *(auf Autobahn)* to enter sth.
(e) *(aufschrecken)* to start ◆ **aus dem Schlaf ~** to awake with a start.
(f) *(aufbrausen)* to flare up, to fly into a rage.
[2] *vt* **(a)** *(herbeischaffen) Truppen etc* to bring up; *Sand, Erde, Torf etc* to put down; *(inf) Getränke etc* to serve up; *Speisen, Argumente* to dish *(inf) or* serve up ◆ **laß mal eine Runde ~** *(inf)* how about buying us a round? *(inf)*.
(b) *(aufwühlen)* to churn *or* dig up.

auffahrend *adj Temperament* irascible, hasty; *Mensch auch* quick-tempered.

Auffahrt *f* **(a)** *(das Hinauffahren)* climb, ascent. **(b)** *(Zufahrt)* approach (road); *(bei Haus etc)* drive; *(Rampe)* ramp. **(c)** *(von Fahrzeugen)* driving up. **(d)** *(Sw) siehe* **Himmelfahrt**.

Auffahr|unfall *m (von zwei Autos)* collision; *(von mehreren Autos)* pile-up.

auffallen *sep irreg* [1] *vi aux sein* **(a)** *(sich abheben)* to stand out; *(unangenehm ~)* to attract attention; *(sich hervortun)* to be remarkable *(durch* for) ◆ **er fällt durch seine roten Haare auf** his red hair makes him stand out; **er ist schon früher als unzuverlässig/Extremist aufgefallen** it has been noticed before that he is unreliable/an extremist; **angenehm/unangenehm ~** to make a good/bad impression; **man soll möglichst nicht ~** you should try to be as inconspicuous as possible, you should keep a low profile, you should try to avoid being noticed; **nur nicht ~!** just don't be conspicuous, just don't make yourself noticed.
(b) *(bemerkt werden)* **jdm fällt etw auf** sb notices sth, sth strikes sb; **so etwas fällt doch sofort/nicht auf** that will be noticed immediately/that will never be noticed; **der Fehler fällt nicht besonders auf** the mistake is not all that noticeable *or* does not show all that much; **fällt es/der Fleck auf?** does it/the stain show?, is it/the stain noticeable?; **das muß dir doch aufgefallen sein!** surely you must have noticed (it).
(c) *(auftreffen: Regen, Licht etc)* **auf etw** *(acc)* **~** to fall onto sth, to strike sth; **er fiel mit dem Knie (auf einen Stein) auf** he fell and hurt his knee (on a stone).
[2] *vr (rare)* **sich** *(dat)* **etw ~** to fall and hurt sth, to fall on sth.

auffallend *adj* conspicuous, noticeable; *Schönheit, Ähnlichkeit, Farbe, Kleider* striking ◆ **das A~ste an ihr sind die roten Haare** her most striking feature *or* the most striking thing about her is her red hair; **er ist ~ intelligent** he is strikingly *or* remarkably intelligent; **stimmt ~!** *(hum)* too true!, how right you are!

auffällig *adj* conspicuous; *Farbe, Kleidung* loud ◆ **er hat sich ~ genau erkundigt** he made a point of inquiring precisely; **er hat ~ wenig mit ihr geredet** it

⚠: for details of spelling reform, see supplement

was conspicuous how little he talked with her; **~er geht's nicht mehr** they/he *etc* couldn't make it more obvious *or* conspicuous if they/he *etc* tried.

auffalten *vtr sep* to unfold; (*Fallschirm*) to open; (*Geol*) to fold upward.

Auffangbecken *nt* collecting tank; (*fig*) gathering place; (*für Flüchtlinge*) focal point.

auffangen *vt sep irreg* **(a)** *Ball, Gesprächsfetzen* to catch; *Wagen, Flugzeug* to get *or* bring under control; *Flugzeug* to pull out; (*Telec*) *Nachricht* to pick up ◆ **jds Blick ~** to catch sb's eye.
(b) (*abfangen*) *Aufprall etc* to cushion, to absorb; *Faustschlag* to block; (*fig*) *Preissteigerung etc* to offset, to counterbalance.
(c) (*sammeln*) *Regenwasser etc* to collect, to catch; (*fig*) *Flüchtlinge etc* to assemble.

Auffang-: ~gesellschaft *f* (*Fin*) rescue company; **~lager** *nt* reception camp *or* centre.

auffassen *sep* [1] *vt* **(a)** to interpret, to understand ◆ **etw als etw** (*acc*) **~** to take sth as sth; **die Planeten als Götter ~** to conceive of the planets as gods; **das Herz als (eine Art) Pumpe ~** to think *or* conceive of the heart as a (kind of) pump; **etw falsch/richtig ~** to take sth the wrong way/in the right way.
(b) (*geistig aufnehmen*) to take in, to grasp.
[2] *vi* to understand.

Auffassung *f* **(a)** (*Meinung, Verständnis*) opinion, view; (*Begriff*) conception, view ◆ **nach meiner ~** in my opinion, to my mind; **nach christlicher ~** according to Christian belief. **(b)** (*Auffassungsgabe*) perception.

Auffassungs-: a~fähig *adj* intelligent; **~fähigkeit, ~gabe** *f* intelligence, grasp; **er hat eine große ~fähigkeit** *or* **~gabe** he has tremendous mental grasp; **~kraft** *f* intellectual *or* mental powers *pl*; **~sache** *f* (*inf*) question of interpretation; (*Ansichtssache*) matter of opinion; **~vermögen** *nt siehe* **~fähigkeit**; **~weise** *f* interpretation; **es hängt von der ~weise ab** it depends (on) how you interpret it.

auffegen *sep* [1] *vt* to sweep up.
[2] *vi siehe* **fegen.**

auffi *adv* (*Aus*) *siehe* **herauf, hinauf.**

auffindbar *adj* **es ist nicht/ist ~** it isn't/is to be found, it can't/can be found.

auffinden *vt sep irreg* to find, to discover.

auffischen *vt sep* **(a)** to fish up; (*inf*) *Schiffbrüchige* to fish out. **(b)** (*fig inf*) to find; *Menschen auch* to dig up (*inf*).

aufflackern *vi sep aux sein* (*lit, fig*) to flare up.

aufflammen *vi sep aux sein* (*lit, fig: Feuer, Unruhen etc*) to flare up ◆ **in seinen Augen flammte Empörung auf** his eyes flashed in indignation.

auffliegen *vi sep irreg aux sein* **(a)** (*hochfliegen*) to fly up.
(b) (*sich öffnen*) to fly open.
(c) (*fig inf: jäh enden*) (*Konferenz etc*) to break up; (*Rauschgiftring, Verbrecher etc*) to be busted (*inf*) ◆ **einen Schmugglerring/eine Konferenz ~ lassen** to bust a ring of smugglers/to bust up (*inf*) *or* break up a meeting.

auffordern *vt sep* **(a)** to ask ◆ **wir fordern Sie auf, ...** you are required to ...
(b) (*bitten*) to ask, to invite; (*zum Wettkampf etc*) to challenge. **(c)** (*zum Tanz bitten*) to ask to dance.

auffordernd *adj* inviting.

Aufforderung *f* request; (*nachdrücklicher*) demand; (*Einladung*) invitation; (*Jur*) incitement ◆ **eine ~ zum Tanz** (*fig*) a challenge.

Aufforderungs-: ~charakter *m* (*Psych*) stimulative nature; **den ~charakter einer Äußerung nachweisen** (*Jur*) to prove that a statement constitutes incitement; **~satz** *m* (*Gram*) (*Hauptsatz*) imperative sentence, command (sentence); (*Teilsatz*) imperative clause.

aufforsten *sep* [1] *vt Gebiet* to reafforest; *Wald* to retimber, to restock.
[2] *vi* **man ist dabei, aufzuforsten** they are doing some reafforesting/retimbering.

Aufforstung *f siehe vt* reafforestation; retimbering, restocking.

auffressen *sep irreg* [1] *vt* (*lit, fig*) to eat up ◆ **ich könnte dich ~** (*inf*) I could eat you; **er wird dich deswegen nicht gleich ~** (*inf*) he's not going to eat you (*inf*).
[2] *vi* (*Tier*) to eat all its food up; (*inf: aufessen*) to finish eating.

auffrischen *sep* [1] *vt* to freshen (up); *Anstrich, Farbe auch* to brighten up; *Möbel etc* to renovate, to refurbish; (*ergänzen*) *Vorräte* to replenish; (*fig*) *Erinnerungen* to refresh; *Kenntnisse* to polish up; *Sprachkenntnisse* to brush up; *persönliche Beziehungen* to renew; *Impfung* to boost.
[2] *vi aux sein or haben* (*Wind*) to freshen.
[3] *vi impers aux sein* to get fresher *or* cooler.

Auffrischung *f siehe vt* freshening (up); brightening up; renovation, refurbishment; replenishment; refreshing; polishing up; brushing up; renewal; boosting.

Auffrischungs|impfung *f* booster ◆ **eine ~ vornehmen lassen** to have a booster.

aufführbar *adj* (*Mus*) performable; (*Theat auch*) stageable ◆ **Faust II ist praktisch gar nicht ~** it is practically impossible to perform *or* stage Faust II.

aufführen *sep* [1] *vt* **(a)** to put on; *Drama, Oper auch* to stage, to perform; *Musikwerk, Komponist* to perform ◆ **ein Theater ~** (*fig*) to make a scene; **sie führte einen wahren Freudentanz auf** she danced with joy.
(b) (*auflisten*) to list; (*nennen*) *Zeugen, Beispiel* to cite; *Beispiel* to give, to quote, to cite ◆ **einzeln ~** to itemize.
[2] *vr* to behave ◆ **sich wie ein Betrunkener ~** to act like a drunkard; **wie er sich wieder aufgeführt hat!** what a performance!

Aufführung *f* **(a)** *siehe vt (a)* putting on; staging, performance ◆ **etw zur ~ bringen** (*form*) to perform sth; **zur ~ kommen** *or* **gelangen** (*form*) to be performed. **(b)** (*Auflistung*) listing; (*Liste*) list ◆ **einzelne ~** itemization.

Aufführungs-: ~recht *nt* performing rights *pl*; **a~reif** *adj* ready to be performed.

auffüllen *vt sep* **(a)** (*vollständig füllen*) to fill up; (*nachfüllen*) to top up; *Mulde etc auch* to fill in.
(b) (*ergänzen*) *Flüssigkeit* to dilute; *Vorräte* to replenish; *Öl* to top up ◆ **Benzin ~** to tank up, to fill up with petrol (*Brit*) *or* gas (*US*).
(c) *auch vi Suppe, Essen* to serve. (*Glas ~*) can I top you up?

auffuttern *vt sep* (*inf*) to eat up, to polish off.

Aufgabe *f* **(a)** (*Arbeit, Pflicht*) job, task ◆ **es ist deine ~, ...** it is your job *or* task *or* responsibility to ...; **es ist nicht ~ der Regierung, ...** it is not the job *or* task *or* responsibility of the government to ...; **sich** (*dat*) **etw zur ~ machen** to make sth one's job *or* business.
(b) (*Zweck, Funktion*) purpose, job.
(c) (*esp Sch*) (*Problem*) question; (*Math auch*) problem; (*zur Übung*) exercise; (*usu pl: Haus~*) homework *no pl*.
(d) (*Abgabe, Übergabe*) (*von Koffer, Gepäck*) registering, registration; (*Aviat*) checking(-in); (*von Brief, Postsendung*) handing in; (*von Anzeige*) placing *no pl*, insertion.
(e) (*Verzicht auf weiteren Kampf, weitere Anstrengungen*) (*Sport*) retirement; (*Mil etc*) surrender ◆ **er hat das Spiel durch ~ verloren** he lost the game by retiring; **die Polizei forderte die Geiselnehmer zur ~ auf** the police appealed to the kidnappers to give themselves up *or* to surrender.
(f) (*von Gewohnheit, Geschäft*) giving up; (*von Plänen, Forderungen auch*) dropping; (*von Hoffnung, Studium*) abandoning, abandonment ◆ **unter ~ all ihrer Habe ...** abandoning all their property; **er riet ihm zur ~ seines Studiums** he advised him to give up *or* abandon *or* drop his studies.
(g) (*das Verlorengeben*) giving up for lost.
(h) (*Volleyball, Tennis etc*) service, serve.

aufgabeln *vt sep Heu, Mist etc* to fork up; (*fig inf*) *jdn* to pick up (*inf*) ◆ **wo hat er denn die aufgegabelt?** (*inf*) where did he dig her up?

Aufgaben-: ~bereich *m*, **~gebiet** *nt* area of responsibility; **~heft** *nt* (*Sch*) homework book; **~kreis** *m* (*geh*) *siehe* **~bereich**; **~sammlung** *f* set of exercises *or* problems; maths (*Brit*) *or* math (*US*) question book; **~stellung** *f* **(a)** (*Formulierung*) formulation; **(b)** (*Aufgabe*) type of problem; **~verteilung** *f* allocation of responsibilities *or* tasks.

Aufgabe-: ~ort *m* place where a letter *etc* was posted; **~stempel** *m* postmark.

Aufgang *m* **(a)** (*von Sonne, Mond*) rising; (*von Stern auch*) ascent; (*fig: von Stern*) appearance, emergence. **(b)** (*Treppen~*) stairs *pl*, staircase ◆ **im ~** on the stairs *or* staircase. **(c)** (*Aufstieg*) ascent. **(d)** (*Sport*) opening, beginning, start.

Aufgangspunkt *m* (*Astron*) **der ~ eines Sterns** the point at which a star rises.

▼ aufgeben *sep irreg* [1] *vt* **(a)** *Hausaufgaben* to give, to set; *schwierige Frage, Problem* to pose (*jdm* for sb) ◆ **jdm viel/nichts ~** (*Sch*) to give *or* set sb a lot of/no homework.
▼ (b) (*übergeben, abgeben*) *Koffer, Gepäck* to register; *Luftgepäck* to check in; *Brief* to post; *Anzeige* to put in, to place; *Bestellung* to place.
(c) *Kampf, Hoffnung, Arbeitsstelle, Freund etc* to give up ◆ **gib's auf!** why don't you give up?
(d) (*verloren geben*) *Patienten* to give up; (*fig*) *Sohn, Schüler* to give up (with *or* on).
(e) (*inf*) *Essen* to serve ◆ **jdm etw ~** to give sb sth.
[2] *vi* **(a)** (*sich geschlagen geben*) to give up *or* in.
(b) (*inf: bei Tisch*) to serve (*jdm* sb) ◆ **kann ich dir noch mal ~?** can I give you some more?

aufgeblasen *adj* (*fig*) puffed-up, self-important.

Aufgeblasenheit *f* (*fig*) self-importance.

Aufgebot *nt* **(a)** (*Jur*) public notice.
(b) (*zur Eheschließung*) notice of intended marriage; (*Eccl*) banns *pl* ◆ **das ~ bestellen** to give notice of one's intended marriage; (*Eccl*) to put up the banns; **das ~ veröffentlichen** to publish the announcement of one's intended marriage; (*Eccl*) to call the banns.
(c) (*Ansammlung*) (*von Menschen*) contingent, (*von Material etc*) array.
(d) (*Aufbietung*) **unter** *or* **mit dem ~ aller Kräfte ...** summoning all his strength ...

aufgebracht *adj* outraged, incensed.

aufgedonnert *adj* (*pej inf*) tarted up (*pej inf*).

aufgedreht *adj* (*inf*) in high spirits.

aufgedunsen *adj* swollen, bloated; *Gesicht auch* puffy.

aufgehen *vi sep irreg aux sein* **(a)** (*Sonne, Mond, Sterne*) to come up, to rise; (*Tag*) to break, to dawn.
(b) (*sich öffnen*) to open; (*Theat: Vorhang*) to go up; (*Knopf, Knoten etc*) to come undone.
(c) (*aufkeimen, Med: Pocken*) to come up.
(d) (*Cook*) to rise; (*Hefeteig auch*) to prove.
(e) (*klarwerden*) **jdm geht etw auf** sb realizes sth, sth dawns on sb, sth becomes apparent to sb.
(f) (*Math*) (*Rechnung etc*) to work out, to come out; (*fig*) to come off, to work (out) ◆ **wenn man 20 durch 6 teilt, geht das nicht auf** 20 divided by 6 doesn't go; **im Kriminalroman muß alles sauber ~** in a detective story everything has to work out *or* be resolved neatly.
(g) (*seine Erfüllung finden*) **in etw** (*dat*) **~** to be wrapped up in sth, to be taken up with sth; **er geht ganz in der Familie auf** his whole life revolves around his family.

(h) *(sich auflösen)* **in Flammen** *etc* **~** to go up in flames *etc*; **in der Masse ~** to disappear *or* merge into the crowd.
(i) *(Hunt: Jagdzeit)* to begin.

aufgehoben *adj* **(bei jdm) gut/schlecht ~ sein** to be/not to be in good keeping *or* hands (with sb).

aufgeilen *vt sep (sl)* **jdn ~** to get sb worked up *(inf)* ♦ **er geilt sich an diesen Fotos auf** he gets off on these photos *(sl)*.

aufgeklärt *adj* **(a)** enlightened *(auch Philos)* ♦ **der ~e Absolutismus** *(Hist)* Benevolent Despotism. **(b)** *(sexualkundlich)* **~ sein** to know the facts of life.

Aufgeklärtheit *f* enlightenment; *(sexualkundlich)* knowledge of the facts of life.

aufgeknöpft *adj (inf)* chatty *(inf)*.

aufgekratzt *adj (inf)* in high spirits, full of beans *(inf)*, boisterous.

Aufgekratztheit *f, no pl* high spirits *pl*, boisterousness.

Aufgeld *nt (dial: Zuschlag)* extra charge; *(old: Anzahlung)* deposit, earnest (money) *(old)*.

aufgelegt *adj* **gut/schlecht** *etc* **~** in a good/bad *etc* mood; **(dazu) ~ sein, etw zu tun** to feel like doing sth; **zum Musikhören ~ sein** to be in the mood for *or* to feel like listening to music.

aufgelöst *adj* **(a)** *(außer sich)* beside oneself *(vor +dat* with), distraught; *(bestürzt)* upset ♦ **in Tränen ~** in tears. **(b)** *(erschöpft)* exhausted, drained, shattered *(inf)*.

aufgeräumt *adj (geh)* blithe, light-hearted.

aufgeregt *adj (erregt)* excited; *(sexuell auch)* aroused; *(nervös)* nervous; *(durcheinander)* flustered.

Aufgeregtheit *f, no pl siehe adj* excitement; arousal; nervousness; flustered state.

aufgeschlossen *adj (nicht engstirnig)* open-minded *(für, gegenüber* about, as regards); *(empfänglich)* receptive, open *(für, gegenüber* to) ♦ **ich bin Vorschlägen gegenüber** *or* **für Vorschläge jederzeit ~** I'm always open to suggestion(s); **einer Sache** *(dat)* **~ gegenüberstehen** to be open-minded about *or* as regards sth.

Aufgeschlossenheit *f, no pl siehe adj* open-mindedness; receptiveness, openness.

aufgeschmissen *adj pred (inf)* in a fix *(inf)*, stuck *(inf)*.

aufgeschossen *adj* **(hoch** *or* **lang) ~** who/that has shot up; **ein lang ~er Junge** a tall lanky lad.

aufgeschwemmt *adj* bloated, swollen; *Mensch* bloated.

aufgetakelt *adj (pej)* dressed up to the nines *(inf)*.

aufgeweckt *adj* bright, quick, sharp.

Aufgewecktheit *f* intelligence, quickness, sharpness.

aufgewühlt *adj (geh)* agitated, in a turmoil *pred*; *Gefühle auch* turbulent; *Wasser, Meer* churning, turbulent ♦ **völlig ~** *(fig)* in a complete turmoil.

aufgießen *vt sep irreg* **(a) etw (auf etw** *acc* **) ~** to pour sth on (sth); **das angebräunte Mehl mit Brühe ~** to pour stock on(to) the browned flour. **(b)** *Kaffee* to make; *Tee auch* to brew.

aufglänzen *vi sep aux sein (lit, fig)* to light up; *(Mond, Sonne, Sterne)* to come out; *(Strahlen reflektierend)* to (begin to) gleam.

aufgliedern *sep* [1] *vt (in +acc* into) to split up, to (sub)divide; *(analysieren auch)* to break down, to analyse; *(in Kategorien auch)* to categorize, to break down.
[2] *vr (in +acc* into) to (sub)divide, to break down.

Aufgliederung *f siehe vt* division; breakdown, analysis; categorization, breakdown.

aufglimmen *vi sep irreg aux sein* to light up, to begin to glow; *(fig)* to glimmer.

aufglühen *vi sep aux sein or haben* to light up, to begin to glow; *(fig) (Gesicht)* to light up, to glow; *(Haß, Neid)* to (begin to) gleam; *(Leidenschaft, Liebe)* to awaken.

aufgraben *vt sep irreg* to dig up.

aufgrätschen *vi sep aux sein or haben (Sport)* **auf etw** *(acc)* **~** to straddle sth.

aufgreifen *vt sep irreg* **(a)** *(festnehmen)* to pick up, to apprehend *(form)*. **(b)** *(weiterverfolgen) Thema, Gedanken* to take up, to pick up; *(fortsetzen) Gespräch* to continue, to take up again.

➤ **aufgrund** *prep +gen*, **auf Grund** *siehe* **Grund**.

aufgucken *vi sep (inf)* to look up *(von* from).

⚠ **Aufguß** *m* brew, infusion *(auch Sci)*; *(fig pej)* rehash.

⚠ **Aufgußbeutel** *m* sachet (containing coffee/herbs *etc*) for brewing; *(Teebeutel)* tea bag.

aufhaben *sep irreg* [1] *vt* **(a)** *Hut, Brille* to have on, to wear ♦ **sie hat ihre Brille nicht aufgehabt** she didn't have her glasses on, she wasn't wearing her glasses.
(b) *Tür, Augen, Laden, Jacke* to have open.
(c) *(Sch: als Hausaufgabe)* **etw ~** to have sth (to do); **ich habe heute viel auf** I've got a lot of homework today.
(d) *(inf: aufgemacht haben)* to have got *or* gotten *(US)* open.
(e) *(inf: aufgegessen haben)* to have eaten up.
[2] *vi (Laden etc)* to be open.

aufhacken *vt sep Straße* to break up; *(Vogel)* to break *or* peck open.

aufhalsen *vt sep (inf)* **jdm/sich etw ~** to saddle *or* land sb/oneself with sth *(inf)*, to land sth on sb/oneself *(inf)*; **sich** *(dat)* **etw ~ lassen** to get oneself saddled *or* landed with sth *(inf)*.

aufhalten *sep irreg* [1] *vt* **(a)** *(zum Halten bringen) Fahrzeug, Entwicklung* to stop, to halt; *Vormarsch auch, Inflation etc* to check, to arrest; *(verlangsamen)* to hold up, to delay; *(abhalten, stören) (bei* from) to hold back, to keep back ♦ **ich will dich nicht länger ~** I don't want to keep *or* hold you back any longer.
(b) *(inf: offenhalten)* to keep open ♦ **die Hand ~** to hold one's hand out.
[2] *vr* **(a)** *(an einem Ort bleiben)* to stay.
(b) *(sich verzögern)* to stay on, to linger; *(bei der Arbeit etc)* to take a long time *(bei* over).
(c) *(sich befassen)* **sich bei etw ~** to dwell on sth, to linger over sth; **sich mit jdm/etw ~** to spend time dealing with sb/sth.
(d) *(sich entrüsten)* **sich über etw** *(acc)* **~** to rail against sth.

aufhängen *sep* [1] *vt* **(a)** to hang up; *(Aut) Rad* to suspend.
(b) *(töten)* to hang *(an +dat* from).
(c) *(inf)* **jdm etw ~** *(aufschwatzen)* to palm sth off on sb; *(glauben machen)* to talk sb into believing sth; *(aufbürden)* to land *or* saddle sb with sth *(inf)*.
(d) etw an einer Frage/einem Thema ~ *(fig: entwickeln)* to use a question/theme as a peg to hang sth on.
[2] *vr (sich töten)* to hang oneself *(an +dat* from); *(hum: seine Kleider ~)* to hang one's things up.

Aufhänger *m* tag, loop ♦ **ein ~ (für etw)** *(fig inf)* a peg to hang sth on *(fig)*.

Aufhängung *f (Tech)* suspension.

aufharken *vt sep* to rake up.

aufhauen *sep* [1] *vt reg or (geh) irreg (öffnen)* to knock open, to hew open *(liter)*; *Eis* to open up, to hew open *(liter)* ♦ **sich** *(dat)* **den Kopf** *etc* **~** to gash one's head *etc* open.
[2] *vi aux sein (inf: auftreffen)* **mit dem Kopf** *etc* **auf etw** *(acc or dat)* **~** to bash *(inf)* *or* bump one's head *etc* against *or* on sth.

aufhäufen *sep* [1] *vt* to pile up, to accumulate; *(fig auch)* to amass.
[2] *vr* to accumulate, to pile up.

aufhebbar *adj* revocable, voidable *(form)*.

aufheben *sep irreg* [1] *vt* **(a)** *(vom Boden)* to pick up; *größeren Gegenstand auch* to lift up; *(in die Höhe heben)* to raise, to lift (up); *Deckel* to lift off.
(b) *(nicht wegwerfen)* to keep ♦ **jdm etw ~** to put sth aside for sb, to keep sth (back) for sb; *siehe* **aufgehoben**.
(c) *(ungültig machen)* to abolish, to do away with; *Gesetz auch* to repeal, to rescind; *Vertrag* to cancel, to annul, to revoke; *Parlament* to dissolve; *Urteil* to reverse, to quash; *Verlobung* to break off ♦ **dieses Gesetz hebt das andere auf** this law supersedes the other.
(d) *(beenden) Blockade, Belagerung* to raise, to lift; *Beschränkung* to remove, to lift; *Sitzung* to close; *siehe* **Tafel**.
(e) *(ausgleichen)* to offset, to make up for; *Widerspruch* to resolve; *Schwerkraft* to neutralize, to cancel out.
(f) *(obs: festnehmen)* to capture, to seize.
[2] *vr* **(a)** *(old: aufstehen)* to rise *(old, form)*.
(b) *(sich ausgleichen)* to cancel each other out, to offset each other; *(Math)* to cancel (each other) out.

Aufheben *nt* **-s,** *no pl* fuss ♦ **viel ~(s) (von etw) machen** to make a lot of fuss (about *or* over sth); **viel ~(s) von jdm machen** to make a lot of fuss about sb; **ohne (jedes) ~/ohne viel** *or* **großes ~** without any/much *or* a big fuss.

Aufhebung *f* **(a)** *siehe vt (c)* abolition; repeal, rescinding; cancellation, annulment, revocation; dissolving; reversal, quashing; breaking off.
(b) *siehe vt (d)* raising, lifting; removal; closing.
(c) *(von Widerspruch)* resolving, resolution; *(von Schwerkraft)* neutralization, cancelling out.
(d) *(obs: Festnahme)* capture, seizure.

aufheitern *sep* [1] *vt jdn* to cheer up; *Rede, Leben* to brighten up *(jdm* for sb).
[2] *vr (Himmel)* to clear, to brighten (up); *(Wetter)* to clear up, to brighten up.

aufheiternd *adj (Met)* becoming brighter, brightening up.

Aufheiterung *f siehe vt* cheering up; brightening up; *(Met)* brighter period ♦ **zunehmende ~** gradually brightening up.

aufheizen *sep* [1] *vt* to heat (up); *(fig) Zuhörer* to inflame, to stir up ♦ **die Stimmung ~** to whip *or* stir up feelings.
[2] *vr* to heat up; *(fig)* to hot up *(inf)*, to intensify, to build up.

aufhelfen *vi sep irreg (lit: beim Aufstehen)* to help up *(jdm* sb) ♦ **einer Sache** *(dat)* **~** *(aufbessern)* to help sth (to) improve; *(stärker)* to help strengthen sth.

aufhellen *sep* [1] *vt* to brighten (up); *Haare* to lighten; *(fig: klären)* to throw *or* shed light upon.
[2] *vr (Himmel, Wetter, fig: Miene)* to brighten (up); *(fig: Sinn)* to become clear.

Aufheller *m* **-s, -** *(in Reinigungsmitteln)* colour-brightener; *(für Haare)* lightener.

Aufhellung *f siehe vb* brightening; lightening; clarification ♦ **es kam zu zeitweisen ~en** from time to time the weather brightened up.

aufhetzen *vt sep* to stir up, to incite ♦ **jdn gegen jdn/etw ~** to stir up sb's animosity against sb/sth; **jdn zu etw ~** to incite sb to (do) sth.

Aufhetzerei *f (inf)* agitation; *(esp durch Reden)* rabble-rousing.

aufhetzerisch *adj* inflammatory, rabble-rousing.

Aufhetzung *f* incitement, agitation.

aufheulen *vi sep* to give a howl *(vor* of), to howl *(vor* with); *(Sirene)* to (start to) wail; *(Motor, Menge)* to (give a) roar; *(weinen)* to start to howl.

aufhocken *vi sep aux sein or haben* **(a)** *(Sport)* to crouch-jump *(auf +acc* on to).
(b) *(dial)* **auf etw** *(acc)* **~** to sit on sth.

aufholen *sep* [1] *vt* **(a)** *Zeit, Verspätung, Vorsprung* to make up; *Lernstoff* to catch up on; *Strecke* to make up, to catch up ♦ **Versäumtes ~** to make up for lost time.
(b) *(Naut)* to haul up, to raise.
[2] *vi (Wanderer, Mannschaft, Schüler, Arbeiter)* to catch up; *(Läufer, Rennfahrer etc auch)* to make up ground; *(Zug)* to make up time; *(Versäumtes ~)* to make

up for lost time.

aufhorchen *vi sep* to prick up one's ears, to sit up (and take notice) ♦ **das ließ ~** that made people sit up (and take notice).

aufhören *vi sep* to stop; (*bei Stellung*) to finish; (*Musik, Lärm, Straße auch, Freundschaft, Korrespondenz*) to (come to an) end ♦ **nicht ~/~, etw zu tun** to keep on/stop doing sth; **hör doch endlich auf!** (will you) stop it!; **mit etw ~** to stop sth; **da hört sich doch alles auf!** (*inf*) that's the (absolute) limit!; **da hört bei ihm der Spaß auf** (*inf*) he's not amused by that.

aufhüpfen *vi sep aux sein* (*Mensch*) to jump *or* leap up; (*Vogel*) to hop; (*Ball etc*) to bounce ♦ **vor Angst/Freude ~** to jump with fear/joy.

aufjagen *vt sep* (*lit*) to disturb; (*fig*) to chase away.

aufjauchzen *vi sep* to shout (out) (*vor* with).

aufjaulen *vi sep* to give a howl (*vor* of), to howl (*vor* with).

aufjubeln *vi sep* to shout (out) with joy, to cheer.

aufjuchzen *vi sep* to whoop with joy, to give a whoop of joy.

Aufkauf *m* buying up.

aufkaufen *vt sep* to buy up.

Aufkäufer *m* buyer.

aufkehren *vti sep* (*esp S Ger*) *siehe* **auffegen.**

aufkeimen *vi sep aux sein* to germinate, to sprout; (*fig*) (*Hoffnung, Liebe, Sympathie*) to bud, to burgeon (*liter*); (*Zweifel*) to (begin to) take root ♦ **~d** (*fig*) budding, burgeoning (*liter*), nascent (*liter*); *Zweifel* growing, nascent (*liter*).

aufklaffen *vi sep aux sein or haben* to gape; (*Abgrund auch*) to yawn ♦ **~d** (*lit, fig*) gaping.

aufklappbar *adj Fenster, Tafel* hinged; *Truhe* which opens up; *Klappe* which lets down; *Verdeck* which folds back, fold-back.

aufklappen *sep* [1] *vt* to open up; *Klappe* to let down; *Verdeck* to fold back; *Messer* to unclasp; *Fenster, Buch* to open; (*hochschlagen*) *Kragen* to turn up.
[2] *vi aux sein* to open.

aufklaren *sep* (*Met*) [1] *vi impers* to clear (up), to brighten (up) (*auch fig*).
[2] *vi* (*Wetter*) to clear *or* brighten (up); (*Himmel*) to clear, to brighten (up).

aufklären *sep* [1] *vt* **(a)** *Mißverständnis, Irrtum* to clear up, to resolve; *Verbrechen, Rätsel auch* to solve; *Ereignis, Vorgang* to throw *or* shed light upon, to elucidate.
(b) *jdn* to enlighten ♦ **Kinder ~** (*sexualkundlich*) to explain the facts of life to children, to tell children the facts of life; (*in der Schule*) to give children sex education; **jdn über etw** (*acc*) **~** to inform sb about sth; **klär mich mal auf, wie ...** (*inf*) (can you) enlighten me as to how ...; *siehe* **aufgeklärt.**
(c) (*Mil*) to reconnoitre.
[2] *vr* (*Irrtum, Geheimnis etc*) to resolve itself, to be cleared up; (*Himmel*) to clear, to brighten (up); (*fig: Miene, Gesicht*) to brighten (up).

Aufklärer *m* **-s, -** **(a)** (*Philos*) philosopher of the Enlightenment. **(b)** (*Mil*) reconnaissance plane; (*klein*) scout (plane).

aufklärerisch *adj* (*Philos*) (of the) Enlightenment; (*freigeistig*) progressive, striving to enlighten the people; (*erzieherisch, unterrichtend*) informative; (*Pol*) educational.

Aufklärung *f* **(a)** (*Philos*) **die ~** the Enlightenment.
(b) *siehe vt (a)* clearing up, resolution; solution; elucidation.
(c) (*Information*) enlightenment; (*von offizieller Stelle*) informing (*über +acc* about); (*Pol*) instruction.
(d) (sexuelle) ~ (*in Schulen*) sex education; **die ~ von Kindern** explaining the facts of life to children.
(e) (*Mil*) reconnaissance.

Aufklärungs-: ~arbeit *f* instructional *or* educational work; **~broschüre** *f* informative pamphlet; (*sexualkundlich*) sex education pamphlet; **~buch** *nt* sex education book; **~film** *m* sex education film; **~flugzeug** *nt* reconnaissance plane; (*klein*) scout (plane); **~kampagne** *f* information campaign; **~literatur** *f* informative literature; (*Pol*) educational literature; (*sexualkundlich*) sex education literature; (*Philos*) literature of the Enlightenment; **~material** *nt* informational material; **~pflicht** *f* (*Jur*) *judge's duty to ensure that all the relevant facts of a case are clearly presented*; (*Med*) *duty to inform the patient of the possible dangers of an operation/a course of treatment etc*; **~quote** *f* (*in Kriminalstatistik*) success rate (in solving cases), percentage of cases solved; **~satellit** *m* spy satellite; **~schiff** *nt* (*Mil*) reconnaissance ship; **~schrift** *f* information pamphlet; (*Pol*) educational pamphlet; (*sexualkundlich*) sex education pamphlet; **~zeit** *f*, **~zeitalter** *nt* Age of Enlightenment; **~ziel** *nt* (*Mil*) reconnaissance object, object of reconnaissance.

aufklatschen *vi sep aux sein* (*auf +acc* on) to land with a smack; (*auf Wasser auch*) to land with a splash.

aufklauben *vt sep* (*dial*) (*lit, fig*) to pick up.

aufkleben *vt sep* (*auf +acc* -to) to stick on; (*mit Leim, Klebstoff auch*) to glue on; (*mit Kleister*) to paste on; *Briefmarke auch* to affix (*form*) (*auf +acc* to), to put on.

Aufkleber *m* sticker.

aufklingen *vi sep irreg aux sein* to ring out; (*fig*) to echo.

aufklopfen *sep* [1] *vt* (*öffnen*) to crack open; (*aufschütteln*) *Kissen* to fluff up.
[2] *vi* to (give a) knock (*auf +acc* on).

aufknacken *vt sep Nüsse etc* to crack (open); (*inf*) *Tresor* to break into, to break open, to crack (*inf*); *Auto* to break into.

aufknallen *sep* (*inf*) [1] *vt* **(a)** (*öffnen*) to bang (open).
(b) (*als Strafe*) to give.
[2] *vi aux sein* (*Auto*) to crash; (*Gegenstand, Mensch*) to crash down ♦ **auf etw** (*acc*) **~** (*gegen etw knallen*) to crash into sth; (*auf etw fallen*) to crash (down) onto sth; **mit dem Kopf (auf etw** *acc*) **~** to bang *or* hit one's head on sth.

aufknöpfen *vt sep* (*öffnen*) to unbutton, to undo ♦ **etw auf etw** (*acc*) **~** to button sth to sth; *siehe* **aufgeknöpft.**

aufknoten *vt sep* to untie, to undo.

aufknüpfen *sep* [1] *vt* **(a)** (*aufhängen*) to hang (*an +dat* from), to string up (*inf*) (*an +dat* on).
(b) (*aufknoten*) to untie, to undo.
[2] *vr* to hang oneself (*an +dat* from).

aufkochen *sep* [1] *vt* **(a)** (*zum Kochen bringen*) to bring to the boil. **(b)** (*erneut kochen lassen*) to boil up again.
[2] *vi* **(a)** *aux sein* to come to the boil; (*fig*) to begin to boil *or* seethe ♦ **etw ~ lassen** to bring sth to the boil; **das Pulver in die aufkochende Milch schütten** sprinkle the powder in the milk as it comes to the boil. **(b)** (*Aus*) to prepare a fine spread.

aufkommen *vi sep irreg aux sein* **(a)** (*lit, fig: entstehen*) to arise; (*Nebel*) to come down; (*Wind*) to spring *or* get up; (*auftreten: Mode etc auch*) to appear (on the scene) ♦ **etw ~ lassen** (*fig*) *Zweifel, Kritik* to give rise to sth; *üble Stimmung* to allow to develop.
(b) ~ für (*Kosten tragen*) to bear the costs of, to pay for; (*Verantwortung tragen*) to carry the responsibility for, to be responsible for; (*Haftung tragen*) to be liable for; **für die Kinder ~** (*finanziell*) to pay for the children's upkeep; **für die Kosten ~** to bear *or* defray (*form*) the costs; **für den Schaden ~** to make good the damage, to pay for the damage.
(c) gegen jdn/etw ~ to prevail against sb/sth; **gegen jdn nicht ~ können** to be no match for sb.
(d) er läßt niemanden neben sich (*dat*) **~** he won't allow anyone to rival him.
(e) (*aufsetzen, auftreffen*) to land (*auf +dat* on).
(f) (*dated*) (*sich erheben*) to rise, to get up; (*sich erholen*) to recover.
(g) (*Naut: herankommen*) to come up; (*Sport: Rückstand aufholen*) (*bei Match*) to come back; (*bei Wettlauf, -rennen*) to catch up, to make up ground.
(h) (*dial: Schwindel, Diebstahl etc*) to come out, to be discovered.

Aufkommen *nt* **-s, - (a)** *no pl* (*das Auftreten*) appearance; (*von Methode, Mode etc auch*) advent, emergence ♦ **~ frischer Winde gegen Abend** fresh winds will get up towards evening.
(b) (*Fin*) (*Summe, Menge*) amount; (*von Steuern*) revenue (*aus, +gen* from).
(c) (*DDR: Plansoll*) target.
(d) *no pl* (*von Flugzeug*) landing ♦ **beim ~** on touchdown.

aufkorken *vt sep* to uncork.

aufkratzen *sep* [1] *vt* (*zerkratzen*) to scratch; (*öffnen*) *Wunde* to scratch open; (*hum: rauh machen*) *Kehle* to make rough *or* raw; (*fig inf: aufheitern*) to liven up; *siehe* **aufgekratzt.**
[2] *vr* to scratch oneself sore.

aufkreischen *vi sep* (*Mensch*) to (give a) scream *or* shriek; (*Bremsen, Maschine*) to (give a) screech.

aufkrempeln *vt sep* **(jdm/sich) die Ärmel/Hose ~** to roll up sb's/one's sleeves/trousers.

aufkreuzen *vi sep* **(a)** *aux sein* (*inf: erscheinen*) to turn *or* show up (*inf*). **(b)** *aux sein or haben* **gegen den Wind ~** (*Naut*) to tack.

aufkriegen *vt sep* (*inf*) *siehe* **aufbekommen.**

aufkünden (*geh*), **aufkündigen** *vt sep Vertrag etc* to revoke, to terminate ♦ **jdm den Dienst ~** to hand in one's notice to sb, to give notice to sb that one is leaving (one's employment); **jdm die Freundschaft ~** (*geh*) to terminate one's friendship with sb; **jdm den Gehorsam ~** to refuse obedience to sb.

Aufkündigung *f* termination, revocation; (*von Freundschaft*) termination.

Aufl. *abbr of* **Auflage.**

auflachen *vi sep* to (give a) laugh; (*schallend*) to burst out laughing.

aufladbar *adj* chargeable; (*neu ~*) rechargeable.

aufladen *sep irreg* [1] *vt* **(a) etw (auf etw** *acc*) **~** to load sth on(to) sth; **jdm/sich etw ~** to load sb/oneself down with sth, to burden sb/oneself with sth; (*fig*) to saddle sb/oneself with sth.
(b) (*elektrisch*) to charge; (*neu ~*) to recharge ♦ **emotional aufgeladen** (*fig*) emotionally charged.
(c) (*Aut*) *Motor* to supercharge, to boost.
[2] *vr* (*Batterie etc*) to be charged; (*neu*) to be recharged; (*elektrisch/elektrostatisch geladen werden*) to become charged.

Aufladung *f* (*Elec*) (*das Aufladen*) charging; (*Ladung*) charge.

Auflage *f* **(a)** (*Ausgabe*) edition; (*Druck*) impression; (*~höhe*) number of copies; (*von Zeitung*) circulation ♦ **das Buch/die Zeitung hat hohe ~n erreicht** a large number of copies of this book have been published/this paper has attained a large circulation.
(b) (*Econ: Fertigungsmenge*) production.
(c) (*Bedingung*) condition ♦ **jdm etw zur ~ machen** to impose sth on sb as a condition; **jdm zur ~ machen, etw zu tun** to make it a condition for sb to do sth, to impose a condition on sb that he do sth; **er bekam die Genehmigung nur mit der ~, das zu tun** he obtained permission only on condition that he do that; **die ~ haben, etw zu tun** to be obliged to do sth.
(d) (*Stütze*) support, rest.
(e) (*Überzug*) plating *no pl*, coating; (*Polsterung*) pad, padding *no pl* ♦ **eine ~ aus Silber** silver plating *or* coating.
(f) (*DDR: Plansoll*) target.

Auflage-: ~fläche *f* supporting surface; **~(n)höhe** *f* (*von Buch*) number of copies published; (*von Zeitung*) circulation; **das Buch/die Zeitung hatte eine ~höhe von 12.000** 12,000 copies of the book were published/the paper had a circulation of 12,000; **a~(n)schwach** *adj* low-circulation *attr*; **a~(n)stark** *adj* high-circulation *attr*; **~(n)ziffer** *f* circulation (figures *pl*); (*von Buch*) number of copies published; **~punkt** *m* point of support.

auflandig *adj* (*Naut*) landward, coastward; *Wind auch* onshore *attr*.

auflassen *vt sep irreg* **(a)** (*inf*) (*offenlassen*) to leave open; (*aufbehalten*) *Hut* to keep *or* leave on ◆ **das Kind länger ~** to let the child stay up (longer).
(b) (*schließen*) (*Min*) *Grube*, (*Aus, S Ger*) *Betrieb* to close *or* shut down ◆ **eine aufgelassene Grube** a closed-down *or* an abandoned mine.
(c) (*Jur*) *Grundstück* to convey (*form*), to transfer, to make over (*form*).

Auflassung *f* **(a)** (*Min, Aus, S Ger: von Geschäft*) closing down, shut-down. **(b)** (*Jur*) conveyancing (*form*), conveyance (*form*), transference.

auflasten *vt sep siehe* **aufbürden**.

auflauern *vi sep +dat* to lie in wait for; (*und angreifen, ansprechen*) to waylay.

Auflauf *m* **(a)** (*Menschen~*) crowd. **(b)** (*Cook*) (baked) pudding (*sweet or savoury*).

auflaufen *vi sep irreg aux sein* **(a)** (*auf Grund laufen: Schiff*) to run aground (*auf +acc or dat* on); (*fig*) to run into trouble ◆ **jdn ~ lassen** to drop sb in it (*inf*).
(b) (*aufprallen*) **auf jdn/etw ~** to run into sb/sth, to collide with sb/sth; **jdn ~ lassen** (*Ftbl*) to bodycheck sb.
(c) (*sich ansammeln*) to accumulate, to mount up.
(d) (*Wasser: ansteigen*) to rise ◆ **~des Wasser** flood tide, rising tide.
(e) (*dial: anschwellen*) to swell (up).

Auflaufform *f* (*Cook*) ovenproof dish.

aufleben *vi sep aux sein* to revive; (*munter, lebendig werden*) to liven up, to come to life again; (*neuen Lebensmut bekommen*) to find a new lease of life ◆ **Erinnerungen wieder ~ lassen** to revive memories.

auflecken *vt sep* to lick up.

▼ **auflegen** *sep* [1] *vt* **(a)** to put on; *Gedeck* to lay; *Kompresse auch* to apply; *Hörer* to put down, to replace ◆ **jdm die Hand ~** (*Rel*) to lay hands on sb.
(b) (*herausgeben*) *Buch* to bring out, to publish, to print ◆ **ein Buch neu ~** to reprint a book; (*neu bearbeitet*) to bring out a new edition of a book.
(c) (*zur Einsichtnahme*) to display, to put up.
(d) (*Econ*) *Serie* to launch.
(e) (*Fin*) *Aktien* to issue, to float.
(f) (*Naut*) *Schiff* to lay up.
(g) *siehe* **aufgelegt 2**.
[2] *vi* **(a)** (*Telefonhörer ~*) to hang up, to ring off (*Brit*).
(b) (*Feuerholz etc ~*) to put on more firewood/coal *etc*.
[3] *vr* (*rare*) **sich** (*dat*) **Entbehrungen** *etc* **~** to impose sacrifices *etc* on oneself, to suffer self-imposed privations *etc*.

auflehnen *sep* [1] *vr* **sich gegen jdn/etw ~** to revolt *or* rebel against sb/sth.
[2] *vt* (*dial*) **den Arm ~** to lean on one's arm; **die Arme auf etw** (*acc or dat*) **~** to lean one's arms on sth.

Auflehnung *f* revolt, rebellion.

aufleimen *vt sep* to glue on (*auf +acc* -to).

auflesen *vt sep irreg* (*lit, fig inf*) to pick up ◆ **jdn/etw von der Straße ~** to pick sb/sth up off the street.

aufleuchten *vi sep aux sein or haben* (*lit, fig*) to light up.

auflichten *sep* [1] *vt* **(a)** *Wald, Gebüsch* to thin out. **(b)** (*aufhellen*) *Bild, Raum* to brighten up; (*fig*) *Hintergründe, Geheimnis* to clear up, to get to the bottom of.
[2] *vr* (*Himmel*) to clear; (*fig: Hintergründe*) to be cleared up, to become clear.

Auflichtung *f siehe vb* thinning out; brightening up; clearing up; clearing.

Auflieferer *m* (*form*) sender; (*von Fracht*) consignor.

aufliefern *vt sep* (*form*) to dispatch; *Fracht* to consign (for delivery).

Auflieferung *f siehe vt* (*form*) dispatch; consignment (for delivery).

aufliegen *sep irreg* [1] *vi* **(a)** to lie *or* rest on top; (*Schallplatte*) to be on the turntable; (*Hörer*) to be on; (*Tischdecke*) to be on (the table) ◆ **auf etw** (*dat*) **~** to lie *or* rest/be on sth.
(b) (*ausliegen*) (*zur Ansicht*) to be displayed; (*zur Benutzung*) to be available.
(c) (*erschienen sein: Buch*) to be published.
(d) (*Naut*) to be laid up.
[2] *vr* (*inf*) (*Patient*) to get bedsores ◆ **sich** (*dat*) **den Rücken** *etc* **~** to get bedsores on one's back.

auflisten *vt sep* to list.

Auflistung *f* (*auch Comput*) listing; (*Liste*) list.

auflockern *sep* [1] *vt* **(a)** *Boden* to break up, to loosen (up).
(b) **die Muskeln ~** to loosen up (one's muscles); (*durch Bewegung auch*) to limber up.
(c) (*abwechslungsreicher machen*) *Unterricht, Stoff, Vortrag* to make less monotonous, to give relief to (*durch* with); (*weniger streng machen*) to make less severe; *Frisur, Muster* to soften, to make less severe.
(d) (*entspannen, zwangloser machen*) to make more relaxed; *Verhältnis, Atmosphäre auch* to ease ◆ **in aufgelockerter Stimmung** in a relaxed mood.
[2] *vr* **(a)** (*Sport*) to limber *or* loosen up.
(b) (*Bewölkung*) to break up, to disperse.

Auflockerung *f* **(a)** (*von Boden*) breaking up, loosening (up); (*von Muskeln*) loosening up ◆ **... trägt zur ~ des Stoffes/des strengen Musters bei ...** helps to make the material less monotonous/the pattern less severe; **ihm gelang die ~ einer gespannten Atmosphäre** he succeeded in easing a tense atmosphere.
(b) *siehe vr* limbering *or* loosening up; breaking up, dispersal, dispersing.

auflodern *vi sep aux sein* (*Flammen*) to flare up; (*in Flammen aufgehen*) to go up in flames; (*lodernd brennen*) to blaze; (*fig: Kämpfe, Haß, Leidenschaft*) to flare up.

auflösbar *adj* soluble; *Gleichung auch* solvable; *Ehe* dissolvable; *Verlobung* that can be broken off; *Vertrag* revocable, able to be cancelled.

auflösen *sep* [1] *vt* **(a)** (*in Flüssigkeit*) to dissolve; (*in Bestandteile zerlegen, Phot*) to resolve (*in +acc* into); (*Math*) *Klammern* to eliminate; *Gleichung* to (re)solve; (*Mus*) *Vorzeichen* to cancel; *Dissonanz* to resolve (*in +acc* into); *siehe* **aufgelöst 2**.
(b) (*aufklären*) *Widerspruch, Mißverständnis* to clear up, to resolve; *Rätsel auch* to solve.
(c) (*zerstreuen*) *Wolken, Versammlung* to disperse, to break up.
(d) (*aufheben*) to dissolve (*auch Parl*); *Einheit, Gruppe* to disband; *Firma* to wind up; *Verlobung* to break off; *Vertrag* to cancel; *Konto* to close; *Haushalt* to break up.
(e) (*geh*) *Haar* to let down; *geflochtenes Haar* to let loose; *Knoten* to undo ◆ **mit aufgelösten Haaren** with one's hair loose.
[2] *vr* **(a)** (*in Flüssigkeit*) to dissolve; (*sich zersetzen: Zellen, Reich, Ordnung*) to disintegrate; (*Zweifel, Probleme*) to disappear ◆ **all ihre Probleme haben sich in nichts aufgelöst** all her problems have dissolved into thin air *or* have disappeared.
(b) (*sich zerstreuen*) to disperse; (*Wolken auch*) to break up; (*Nebel auch*) to lift.
(c) (*auseinandergehen*) (*Verband*) to disband; (*Firma*) to cease trading; (*sich formell ~: esp Parl*) to dissolve.
(d) (*sich aufklären*) (*Mißverständnis, Problem*) to resolve itself, to be resolved; (*Rätsel auch*) to be solved.
(e) **sich in etw** (*acc*) **~** (*verwandeln*) to turn into sth; (*undeutlich werden*) to dissolve into sth.
(f) (*geh: Schleife, Haar*) to become undone.
(g) (*Phot*) to be resolved.

Auflösung *f siehe vt* (*a-d*) **(a)** dissolving; resolution; elimination; (re)solving; cancellation.
(b) clearing up, resolving; solving.
(c) dispersal.
(d) dissolving; disbanding; winding up; breaking off; cancellation; closing; breaking up.
(e) *siehe vr* dissolving; disintegration; disappearance; dispersal; disbandment; dissolution; resolution; solution (*gen, von* to).
(f) (*Verstörtheit*) distraction.

Auflösungs-: ~erscheinung *f* sign of breaking up; **~zeichen** *nt* (*Mus*) natural.

aufmachen *sep* [1] *vt* **(a)** (*öffnen*) to open; (*lösen, aufknöpfen, aufschnallen*) to undo; *Haar* to loosen; (*inf: operieren*) to open up (*inf*), to cut open (*inf*).
(b) (*eröffnen, gründen*) *Geschäft, Unternehmen* to open (up).
(c) (*gestalten*) *Buch, Zeitung* to make *or* get up; (*zurechtmachen*) *jdn* to dress, to get up (*pej*); (*in Presse*) *Ereignis, Prozeß etc* to feature ◆ **der Prozeß wurde groß aufgemacht** the trial was given a big spread *or* was played up (in the press).
(d) (*dial: anbringen*) *Plakat, Vorhänge* to put up, to hang (up).
[2] *vi* (*Tür öffnen*) to open up, to open the door; (*Geschäft (er)öffnen*) to open (up).
[3] *vr* **(a)** (*sich zurechtmachen*) to get oneself up.
(b) (*sich anschicken*) to get ready, to make preparations; (*aufbrechen*) to set out, to start (out) ◆ **sich zu einem Spaziergang ~** to set out on a walk.
(c) (*liter: Wind*) to rise (*liter*), to get up.

Aufmacher *m* (*Press*) lead.

Aufmachung *f* **(a)** (*Kleidung*) turn-out, rig-out (*inf*) ◆ **in großer ~ erscheinen** to turn up in full dress.
(b) (*Gestaltung*) presentation, style; (*von Buch*) presentation, make-up; (*von Seite, Zeitschrift*) layout ◆ **der Artikel erschien in großer ~** the article was given a big spread *or* was featured prominently.
(c) (*Press: Artikel etc auf Titelseite*) lead feature.

aufmalen *vt sep* to paint on (*auf etw* (*acc*) sth); (*inf*) to scrawl (*auf +acc* on).

Aufmarsch *m* **(a)** (*Mil*) (*das Aufmarschieren*) marching up; (*in Stellung, Kampflinie*) deployment; (*Parade*) marchpast. **(b)** (*Sw*) attendance.

Aufmarschgebiet *nt* deployment zone.

aufmarschieren* *vi sep aux sein* (*heranmarschieren*) to march up; (*Mil: in Stellung gehen*) to deploy; (*vorbeimarschieren*) to march past ◆ **~ lassen** (*Mil: an Kampflinie etc*) to deploy; (*fig hum*) to have march up/past.

Aufmaß *nt* (*Build*) dimension.

aufmeißeln *vt sep* (*Med*) to trephine.

aufmerken *vi sep* (*aufhorchen*) to sit up and take notice; (*geh: achtgeben*) to pay heed *or* attention (*auf +acc* to).

aufmerksam *adj* **(a)** *Zuhörer, Beobachter, Schüler* attentive; *Blicke auch, Augen* keen; (*scharf beobachtend*) observant ◆ **jdn auf etw** (*acc*) **~ machen** to draw sb's attention to sth; **jdn darauf ~ machen, daß ...** to draw sb's attention to the fact that ...; **auf etw** (*acc*) **~werden** to become aware of sth; **~ werden** to sit up and take notice.
(b) (*zuvorkommend*) attentive ◆ **(das ist) sehr ~ von Ihnen** (that's) most kind of you.

Aufmerksamkeit *f* **(a)** *no pl* attention, attentiveness ◆ **das ist meiner ~ entgangen** I failed to notice that, that slipped my notice *or* escaped my attention.
(b) *no pl* (*Zuvorkommenheit*) attentiveness.
(c) (*Geschenk*) token (gift) ◆ **(nur) eine kleine ~** (just) a little something *or* gift; **kleine ~en** little gifts.

aufmischen *vt sep* (*inf*) (*provozieren*) to stir up; (*agitieren*) to shake up.

➤ SPRACHE AKTIV: **auflegen: 1a** → 27.3, 27.6

aufmöbeln *vt sep (inf) Gegenstand* to do up *(inf)*; *Kenntnisse* to polish up *(inf)*; *jdn (beleben)* to buck up *(inf)*, to pep up *(inf)*; *(aufmuntern)* to buck up *(inf)*, to cheer up.

aufmontieren* *vt sep* to mount, to fit (on) ◆ **etw auf etw** *(acc)* ~ to mount sth on sth, to fit sth on *or* to sth.

aufmotzen *sep (inf)* 1 *vt* to zap up *(inf)*; *Theaterstück auch* to revamp.
2 *vi* to get cheeky *(esp Brit) or* fresh *(esp US)*.

aufmucken, aufmucksen *vi sep (inf)* to protest *(gegen* at, against).

aufmuntern *vt sep (aufheitern)* to cheer up; *(beleben)* to liven up, to ginger up *(inf)*; *(ermutigen)* to encourage ◆ **jdn zu etw** ~ to encourage sb to do sth; **ein ~des Lächeln** an encouraging smile.

Aufmunterung *f siehe vt* cheering up; livening up, gingering up *(inf)*; encouragement.

aufmüpfig *adj (inf)* rebellious.

Aufmüpfigkeit *f (inf)* rebelliousness.

aufnageln *vt sep* to nail on *(auf +acc* -to).

aufnähen *vt sep* to sew on *(auf +acc* -to).

Aufnahme *f -, -n* **(a)** *(Empfang, fig: Reaktion)* reception; *(Empfangsraum)* reception (area) ◆ **bei jdm freundliche ~ finden** *(lit, fig)* to meet with a warm reception from sb; **jdm eine freundliche ~ bereiten** to give sb a warm reception; **die ~ in ein Krankenhaus** admission (in)to hospital; **wie war die ~ beim Publikum?** how did the audience receive it *or* react?
(b) *(in Verein, Orden etc)* admission *(in +acc* to); *(Aufgenommener)* recruit.
(c) *no pl (lit, fig: Absorption)* absorption; *(Nahrungs~)* taking, ingestion *(form)*.
(d) *no pl (Einbeziehung)* inclusion, incorporation; *(in Liste, Bibliographie)* inclusion.
(e) *no pl (von Geldern, Kapital, Hypothek)* raising.
(f) *no pl (Aufzeichnung: von Protokoll, Diktat)* taking down; *(von Personalien)* taking (down); *(von Telegramm)* taking ◆ **die ~ eines Unfalls** taking down details of an accident.
(g) *no pl (Beginn) (von Gespräch etc)* start, commencement; *(von Tätigkeit auch)* taking up; *(von Beziehung, Verbindung auch)* establishment.
(h) *no pl (das Fotografieren)* taking, photographing; *(das Filmen)* filming, shooting ◆ **Achtung, ~!** action!
(i) *(Fotografie)* photo(graph), shot *(inf)*; *(Schnappschuß, Amateur~)* snap *(inf)* ◆ **eine ~ machen** to take a photo(graph) *etc*.
(j) *(auf Tonband)* recording.

Aufnahme-: ~antrag *m* application for membership *or* admission; **~bedingung** *f* condition of admission; **a~bereit** *adj Boden* ready for planting; *Kamera* ready to shoot; *(fig)* receptive, open *(für* to); **~bereitschaft** *f (fig)* receptiveness, receptivity; **a~fähig** *adj* **(a) für etw a~fähig sein** to be able to take sth in; **ich bin nicht mehr a~fähig** I can't take anything else in; **(b)** *Markt* active; **~fähigkeit** *f* ability to take things in; **~gebühr** *f* enrolment fee; *(in Verein)* admission fee; **~gerät** *nt (Film)* (film) camera; *(Tonband~)* recorder; **~lager** *nt* reception camp; **~land** *nt* host country *(für* to); **~leiter** *m (Film)* production manager; *(Rad, TV)* producer; **~prüfung** *f* entrance examination; **~stopp** *m (für Flüchtlinge etc)* ban on immigration; **~studio** *nt* (film/recording) studio; **~vermögen** *nt* **(a)** *(~fähigkeit)* receptiveness, receptivity *(für* to); **(b)** *(Fassungsvermögen)* capacity; **~wagen** *m (Rad)* recording van; **a~würdig** *adj (für Verein)* worthy of admittance; *(für Wörterbuch etc)* worth including.

Aufnahmsprüfung *f (Aus) siehe* **Aufnahmeprüfung.**

aufnehmen *vt sep irreg* **(a)** *(vom Boden)* to pick up; *(heben)* to lift up.
(b) *(lit: empfangen, fig: reagieren auf)* to receive.
(c) *(unterbringen)* to take (in); *(fassen)* to take, to hold; *Arbeitskräfte, Einwanderer* to absorb.
(d) *(in Verein, Orden etc)* to admit *(in +acc* to); *(Schule auch, Aus: anstellen)* to take on.
(e) *(absorbieren)* to absorb, to take up; *(im Körper ~)* to take; *(fig: eindringen lassen) Eindrücke* to take in; *(begreifen auch)* to grasp ◆ **etw in sich** *(dat)* ~ to take sth in; **er nimmt (alles) schnell auf** he takes things in *or* grasps things quickly, he's quick on the uptake.
(f) *(mit einbeziehen)* to include, to incorporate; *(in Liste, Bibliographie)* to include; *(fig: aufgreifen)* to take up.
(g) *(esp Ftbl) Ball* to take, to receive.
(h) *(dial) (aufwischen)* to wipe up; *(mit Stück Brot auch)* to mop *or* soak up.
(i) *(beginnen)* to begin, to commence; *Verbindung, Beziehung* to establish; *Tätigkeit, Studium auch* to take up ◆ **den Kampf ~** to commence battle; *(fig auch)* to take up the struggle; **Kontakt** *or* **Fühlung mit jdm ~** to contact sb.
(j) *Kapital, Summe, Gelder, Hypothek* to raise; *Kredit auch* to get.
(k) *(niederschreiben) Protokoll, Diktat* to take down; *Personalien* to take (down); *Telegramm* to take.
(l) *(fotografieren)* to take (a photograph *or* picture of), to photograph; *(filmen)* to film, to shoot *(inf)*.
(m) *(auf Tonband)* to record, to tape.
(n) *(beim Stricken) Maschen* to increase, to make.
(o) es mit jdm/etw ~ können to be a match for sb/sth, to be able to match sb/sth; **es mit jdm/etw nicht ~ können** to be no match for sb/sth; **an Naivität kann es keiner mit ihm ~** where naïveté is concerned there's no-one to beat him.

aufnehmenswert *adj siehe* **aufnahmewürdig.**

Aufnehmer *m (dial)* **(a)** *(N. Ger: Scheuertuch)* cloth. **(b)** *(dial: Müllschaufel)* shovel.

äufnen *vt (Sw) Geld etc* to accumulate.

aufnesteln *vt sep (inf) Knoten, Schnur* to undo; *Bluse, Haken auch* to unfasten.

aufnotieren* *vt sep* **(sich** *dat)* **etw ~** to note sth down, to make a note of sth.

aufnötigen *vt sep* **jdm etw ~** *Geld, Essen* to force *or* press sth on sb; *Entscheidung, Meinung* to force *or* impose sth on sb; **die Lage nötigt (uns) Vorsicht auf** the situation requires *or* demands that we be cautious *or* requires caution (on our part).

auf|oktroyieren* *vt sep* **jdm etw ~** *(geh)* to impose *or* force sth on sb.

auf|opfern *sep* 1 *vr* to sacrifice oneself.
2 *vt* to sacrifice, to give up.

auf|opfernd *adj Mensch* self-sacrificing; *Liebe, Tätigkeit, Arbeit* devoted ◆ **ein ~es Leben** a life of self-sacrifice.

Auf|opferung *f* **(a)** *(Aufgabe)* sacrifice ◆ **durch ~ einer Sache** *(gen)* by sacrificing sth; **unter ~ einer Sache** *(gen)* at the cost of sth. **(b)** *(Selbst~)* self-sacrifice ◆ **mit ~** with devotion.

Auf|opferungs-: a~bereit *adj* self-sacrificing; **~bereitschaft** *f* self-sacrifice; **a~voll** *adj* self-sacrificing.

aufpacken *vt sep* **jdm/einem Tier etw ~** to load sth onto sb/an animal, to load sb/an animal with sth; **jdm etw ~** *(fig)* to burden *or* saddle *(inf)* sb with sth; **er packte sich** *(dat)* **den Rucksack auf** he put on his rucksack.

aufpäppeln *vt sep (inf) (mit Nahrung)* to feed up; *(durch Pflege)* to nurse back to health.

▼ **aufpassen** *vi sep* **(a)** *(beaufsichtigen)* **auf jdn/etw ~** to watch sb/sth, to keep an eye on sb/sth; *(hüten)* to look after *or* to mind sb/sth; *(Aufsicht führen)* to supervise sb/sth; *(bei Examen)* to invigilate sb.
▼ **(b)** *(aufmerksam sein, achtgeben)* to pay attention ◆ **paß auf!, aufgepaßt!** look, watch; *(sei aufmerksam)* pay attention; *(Vorsicht)* watch out, mind (out).

Aufpasser(in *f) m* **-s, -** *(pej: Aufseher, Spitzel)* spy *(pej)*, watchdog *(inf)*; *(für VIP etc)* minder; *(Beobachter)* supervisor; *(bei Examen)* invigilator; *(Wächter)* guard.

aufpeitschen *vt sep Meer, Wellen* to whip up; *(fig) Sinne* to inflame, to fire; *Menschen* to inflame, to work up; *(stärker)* to whip up into a frenzy ◆ **eine ~de Rede** a rabble-rousing *(pej) or* inflammatory speech.

aufpeppen *vt sep (inf)* to jazz up *(inf)*.

aufpflanzen *sep* 1 *vt* to plant; *(Mil) Bajonett* to fix.
2 *vr* **sich vor jdm ~** to plant oneself in front of sb.

aufpflügen *vt sep* to plough up ◆ **das Meer ~** *(liter: Schiff)* to plough through the sea.

aufpfropfen *vt sep (lit)* to graft on *(+dat* -to); *(fig)* to superimpose *(+dat* on).

aufpicken *vt sep* **(a)** to peck up; *(fig)* to glean, to pick up. **(b)** *(öffnen)* to peck open.

aufpinseln *vt sep (inf) (hinschreiben)* to scrawl *(auf +acc* on); *(auftragen) Lack* to slap on *(inf) (auf etw (acc)* sth).

aufplatzen *vi sep aux sein* to burst open; *(Wunde)* to open up, to rupture; *(Knopf)* to pop open.

aufplustern *sep* 1 *vt Federn* to ruffle up; *(fig) Vorfall, Ereignis* to blow up, to exaggerate.
2 *vr (Vogel)* to ruffle (up) its feathers, to puff itself up; *(Mensch)* to puff oneself up.

aufpolieren* *vt sep (lit, fig)* to polish up.

aufprägen *vt sep* to emboss, to stamp ◆ **einen Stempel auf etw** *(acc)* **~** to emboss sth with a stamp; **jdm/einer Sache seinen/einen gewissen Stempel ~** *(fig)* to leave one's/its mark on sb/sth.

Aufprall *m* **-(e)s,** *(rare)* **-e** impact.

aufprallen *vi sep aux sein* **auf etw** *(acc)* ~ to strike *or* hit sth; *(Fahrzeug auch)* to collide with sth, to run into sth.

Aufpreis *m* extra *or* additional charge ◆ **gegen ~** for an extra *or* additional charge.

aufpressen *vt sep* to press on *(auf +acc* -to); *(öffnen)* to press open.

aufprobieren* *vt sep* to try (on).

aufpulvern *vt sep (inf)* to pep *or* buck up *(inf)*; *Moral* to lift, to boost.

aufpumpen *sep* 1 *vt Reifen, Ballon* to pump up, to inflate; *Fahrrad* to pump up *or* inflate the tyres of.
2 *vr (Vogel, fig: sich aufspielen)* to puff oneself up; *(fig: wütend werden)* to work oneself up *(inf)*.

aufpusten *vt (inf) siehe* **aufblasen.**

aufputschen *sep* 1 *vt* **(a)** *(aufwiegeln)* to rouse; *Gefühle, öffentliche Meinung auch* to whip *or* stir up *(gegen* against) ◆ **jdn zu etw ~** to incite sb to do sth.
(b) *(durch Reizmittel)* to stimulate ◆ **~de Mittel** stimulants.
2 *vr* to pep oneself up *(inf)*, to dope oneself *(Sport inf)*.

Aufputschmittel *nt* stimulant.

Aufputz *m* get-up *(inf)*, rig-out *(inf)*; *(festlich geschmückt)* finery *(iro)*, attire *(iro)*.

aufputzen *vt sep* **(a)** *(schmücken) Haus, Buch etc* to decorate; *(schön machen) jdn* to dress up, to deck out; *(fig: aufpolieren) Gegenstand* to do up; *Image* to polish *or* brush up; *Zahlen* to dress up. **(b)** *(dial: aufwischen) Boden* to clean (up); *Flüssigkeit* to mop *or* wipe up.

aufquellen *vi sep irreg aux sein* **(a)** *(anschwellen)* to swell (up) ◆ **aufgequollen** swollen; *Gesicht auch* puffy, bloated; *Mensch* bloated(-looking); **etw ~ lassen** to soak sth (to allow it to swell up). **(b)** *(geh: aufsteigen) (Rauch)* to rise; *(Flüssigkeit auch, fig: Gefühle auch)* to well *or* spring up.

aufraffen *sep* 1 *vr* to pull oneself up; *(vom Boden auch)* to pick oneself up ◆ **sich ~, etw zu tun, sich zu etw ~** *(inf)* to rouse oneself to do sth.
2 *vt Rock, Papiere, Eigentum* to gather up; *(schnell aufheben)* to snatch up.

aufragen *vi sep aux sein or haben (in die Höhe ~)* to rise; *(sehr hoch, groß auch)* to tower (up) (*über +dat* above, over) ◆ **die hoch ~den Türme** the soaring towers; **die hoch ~den Fabrikkamine/Tannen** the towering factory chimneys/fir trees.

aufrappeln *vr sep (inf)* **(a)** *siehe* **aufraffen 1. (b)** *(wieder zu Kräften kommen)* to recover, to get over it ◆ **er hat sich nach seiner Krankheit endlich wieder aufgerappelt** he at last recovered from *or* got over his illness.

aufrauchen *vt sep (zu Ende rauchen)* to finish (smoking); *(aufbrauchen)* to smoke, to get through.

⚠ **aufrauhen** *vt sep* to roughen (up); *(Tex) Stoff* to nap; *Haut, Hände* to roughen, to make rough.

aufräumen *sep* 1 *vt* to tidy *or* clear up; *(wegräumen auch)* to clear *or* put away.
2 *vi* **(a) mit etw ~** to do away with sth.
(b) *(pej: dezimieren)* **unter der Bevölkerung (gründlich) ~** *(Seuche etc)* to decimate the population, to wreak havoc among the population; *(Tyrann etc)* to slaughter the population wholesale.
(c) *siehe* **aufgeräumt 2.**

Aufräumungs|arbeiten *pl* clear(ing)-up operations *pl*.

aufrechnen *vt sep* **(a) jdm etw ~** to charge sth to sb *or* to sb's account; *(fig: vorwerfen)* to throw sth in sb's face. **(b) etw gegen etw ~** to set sth off *or* offset sth against sth.

aufrecht *adj (lit, fig)* upright; *Körperhaltung, Gangart auch* erect ◆ **~ gehen/stehen** to walk/stand upright *or* erect; **~ sitzen** to sit up(right); **etw ~ hinstellen** to place sth upright *or* in an upright position.

aufrecht|erhalten* *vt sep irreg* to maintain; *Kontakt, Bräuche auch* to keep up; *Behauptung auch* to stick to; *Entschluß, Glauben auch* to keep *or* adhere to, to uphold; *Verein* to keep going; *(moralisch stützen) jdn* to keep going, to sustain.

Aufrecht|erhaltung *f siehe vt* maintenance, maintaining; keeping up; sticking *(gen* to); adherence *(gen* to), upholding; keeping going.

aufrecken *sep* 1 *vt* to stretch up; *Hals* to crane.
2 *vr* to stretch up.

aufreden *vt sep siehe* **aufschwatzen.**

aufregen *sep* 1 *vt (ärgerlich machen)* to irritate, to annoy; *(nervös machen)* to make nervous *or* edgy *(inf)*; *(beunruhigen)* to agitate, to disturb; *(bestürzen)* to upset; *(erregen)* to excite ◆ **du regst mich auf!** you're getting on my nerves; **er regt mich auf** he drives me mad *(inf)*.
2 *vr* to get worked up *(inf) or* excited *(über +acc* about); *siehe* **aufgeregt.**

aufregend *adj* exciting.

Aufregung *f* excitement *no pl*; *(Beunruhigung)* agitation *no pl* ◆ **nur keine ~!** don't get excited, don't get worked up *(inf) or* in a state *(inf)*!; **die Nachricht hat das ganze Land in ~ versetzt** the news caused a great stir throughout the country; **jdn in ~ versetzen** to put sb in a flurry, to get sb in a state *(inf)*; **alles war in heller ~** everything was in utter confusion, there was complete bedlam.

aufreiben *sep irreg* 1 *vt* **(a)** *(wundreiben) Haut etc* to chafe, to rub sore ◆ **sich** *(dat)* **die Hände/Haut ~** to chafe one's hands/oneself, to rub one's hands/oneself sore.
(b) *(fig: zermürben)* to wear down *or* out.
(c) *(Mil: völlig vernichten)* to wipe out, to annihilate.
2 *vr (durch Sorgen etc)* to wear oneself out; *(durch Arbeit auch)* to work oneself into the ground.

aufreibend *adj (fig)* wearing, trying; *(stärker)* stressful ◆ **nervlich ~** stressful.

aufreihen *sep* 1 *vt (in Linie)* to line up, to put in a line/lines *or* a row/rows; *Perlen* to string; *(fig) (aufzählen)* to list, to enumerate.
2 *vr* to line up, to get in a line/lines *or* a row/rows.

aufreißen[1] *sep irreg* 1 *vt* **(a)** *(durch Reißen öffnen, aufbrechen)* to tear *or* rip open; *Straße* to tear *or* rip up.
(b) *Tür, Fenster* to fling open; *Augen, Mund* to open wide.
(c) *(beschädigen) Kleidung* to tear, to rip; *Haut* to gash (open).
(d) *(Sport inf) Deckung, Abwehr* to open up.
(e) *(in großen Zügen darstellen) Thema* to outline.
(f) *(sl) Mädchen* to pick up *(inf)*; *(sich verschaffen) Job, Angebot* to land (oneself) *(inf)*, to get.
2 *vi aux sein (Naht)* to split, to burst; *(Hose)* to tear, to rip; *(Wunde)* to tear open; *(Wolkendecke)* to break up.

aufreißen[2] *vt sep irreg (Tech)* to draw the/an elevation of.

aufreizen *vt sep* **(a)** *(herausfordern)* to provoke; *(aufwiegeln)* to incite. **(b)** *(erregen)* to excite; *(stärker)* to inflame.

aufreizend *adj* provocative.

aufribbeln *vt sep (inf)* to unpick.

Aufrichte *f* **-, -n** *(Sw) siehe* **Richtfest.**

aufrichten *sep* 1 *vt* **(a)** *(in aufrechte Lage bringen) Gegenstand* to put *or* set upright; *jdn* to help up; *Oberkörper* to raise (up), to straighten (up).
(b) *(aufstellen)* to erect, to put up; *(fig)* to set up.
(c) *(fig: moralisch)* to put new heart into, to give fresh heart to, to lift.
2 *vr (gerade stehen)* to stand up (straight); *(gerade sitzen)* to sit up (straight); *(aus gebückter Haltung)* to straighten up; *(fig: moralisch)* to pick oneself up, to get back on one's feet ◆ **sich im Bett ~** to sit up in bed; **sich an jdm ~** *(fig)* to find new strength in sb, to take heart from sb.

aufrichtig *adj* sincere *(zu, gegen* towards); *(ehrlich auch)* honest.

Aufrichtigkeit *f siehe adj* sincerity; honesty.

aufriegeln *vt sep* to unbolt.

⚠ **Aufriß** *m* **(a)** *(Tech)* elevation ◆ **etw im ~ zeichnen** to draw the side/front elevation of sth. **(b)** *(fig: Abriß)* outline, sketch.

⚠ **Aufrißzeichnung** *f (Tech, Archit)* elevation.

aufritzen *vt sep (öffnen)* to slit open; *(verletzen)* to cut (open).

aufrollen *sep* 1 *vt* **(a)** *(zusammenrollen) Teppich, Ärmel* to roll up; *Kabel* to coil *or* wind up; *(auf Rolle)* to wind up.
(b) *(entrollen)* to unroll; *Fahne* to unfurl; *Kabel* to uncoil, to unwind; *(von Rolle)* to unwind, to reel off.
(c) *(fig) Problem* to go into ◆ **einen Fall/Prozeß wieder ~** to reopen a case/trial.
2 *vr (sich zusammenrollen)* to roll up.

aufrücken *vi sep aux sein* **(a)** *(weiterrücken, aufschließen)* to move up *or* along. **(b)** *(befördert werden)* to move up, to be promoted; *(Schüler)* to move *or* go up ◆ **zum Geschäftsleiter ~** to be promoted to manager.

Aufruf *m* **(a)** appeal *(an +acc* to). **(b)** *(von Namen)* **seinen ~ abwarten** to wait for one's name to be called, to wait to be called; **nach ~** on being called, when called; **letzter ~ für Flug LH 1615** last call for flight LH 1615. **(c)** *(Datenverarbeitung)* call. **(d)** *(Fin: von Banknoten)* calling in.

aufrufen *sep irreg* 1 *vt* **(a)** *Namen* to call; *Wartenden* to call (the name of) ◆ **Sie werden aufgerufen** your name *or* you will be called; **einen Schüler ~** to ask a pupil (to answer) a question.
(b) *(auffordern)* **jdn zu etw ~** *(zu Mithilfe, Unterstützung etc)* to appeal to *or* call upon sb for sth; **jdn ~, etw zu tun** to appeal to *or* call upon sb to do sth; **Arbeiter zu einer Demonstration/zum Streik ~** to call upon workers to attend a demonstration/to strike.
(c) *(Jur) Zeugen* to summon; *Erben* to give notice to.
(d) *(Comput)* to call up.
(e) *(Fin: einziehen) Banknoten* to call in.
2 *vi* **zum Widerstand/Streik** *etc* **~** to call for resistance/a strike *etc*, to call upon people to resist/strike *etc*.

Aufruhr *m* **-(e)s, -e (a)** *(Auflehnung)* revolt, rebellion, uprising. **(b)** *(Bewegtheit, fig: Erregung)* tumult, turmoil; *(in Stadt, Publikum auch)* pandemonium *(gen* in) ◆ **ihr innerlicher ~** the tumult *or* turmoil within her; **in ~ sein** to be in a tumult *or* turmoil; *(Gefühle, Stadt auch)* to be in a tumult; **in ~ geraten** to be in a turmoil; **jdn in ~ versetzen** to throw sb into a turmoil.

aufrühren *vt sep* to stir up; *(fig auch) Gefühle* to rouse ◆ **alte Geschichten wieder ~** to rake *or* stir up old stories.

Aufrührer(in *f***)** *m* **-s, -** rabble-rouser.

aufrührerisch *adj* **(a)** *(aufwiegelnd) Rede, Pamphlet* rabble-rousing, inflammatory. **(b)** *attr (in Aufruhr)* rebellious; *(meuternd)* mutinous.

aufrunden *vt sep Betrag, Zahl etc* to round up *(auf +acc* to).

aufrüsten *vti sep* to arm ◆ **ein Land atomar ~** to give a country nuclear arms; **wieder ~** to rearm.

Aufrüstung *f* arming ◆ **atomare ~** acquiring nuclear armaments.

aufrütteln *vt sep* to rouse *(aus* from); *(aus Lethargie etc auch)* to shake up *(aus* out of) ◆ **jdn/jds Gewissen ~** to stir sb/sb's conscience; **jdn zum Handeln ~** to rouse sb to action.

Aufrütt(e)lung *f (fig) (das Aufrütteln)* rousing; *(aus Lethargie etc auch)* shaking up; *(Zustand)* excitement.

aufs *contr of* **auf das.**

aufsagen *vt sep* **(a)** *Gedicht etc* to recite, to say. **(b)** *(geh: für beendet erklären)* **jdm die Freundschaft ~** to break off one's friendship with sb; **jdm den Dienst/Gehorsam ~** to refuse to serve/obey sb.

aufsammeln *vt sep (lit, fig)* to pick up.

aufsässig *adj* rebellious; *esp Kind auch* recalcitrant, obstreperous.

Aufsässigkeit *f siehe adj* rebelliousness; recalcitrance, obstreperousness.

aufsatteln *vt sep* **(a)** *Pferd* to saddle (up). **(b)** *(Tech) Anhänger* to hitch (up), to couple (on) *(an +acc* to).

Aufsatz *m* **(a)** *(Abhandlung)* essay; *(Schul~ auch)* composition. **(b)** *(oberer Teil)* top *or* upper part; *(zur Verzierung)* bit on top; *(von Kamera etc)* attachment ◆ **ein Schrank mit abnehmbarem ~** a cupboard with a removable top part *or* section. **(c)** *(Mil: von Geschütz)* (gun) sight.

Aufsatz-: ~heft *nt* essay *or* composition book; **~sammlung** *f* collection of essays; **~thema** *nt* essay subject.

aufsaugen *vt sep irreg Flüssigkeit* to soak up; *(Sonne auch)* to absorb; *(fig)* to absorb ◆ **etw mit dem Staubsauger ~** to vacuum sth up; **etw in sich** *(dat)* **~** *(Mensch)* to absorb sth, to soak sth in.

aufschauen *vi sep (dial) siehe* **aufblicken.**

aufschaufeln *vt sep* **(a)** *(aufhäufen)* to pile up. **(b)** *(aufgraben)* to dig up.

aufschaukeln *vr sep (fig inf: Haß, Emotionen)* to build up.

aufschäumen *sep* 1 *vi aux sein (Meer)* to foam; *(Getränke)* to foam *or* froth up ◆ **vor Zorn ~** to boil with anger.
2 *vt Kunststoff* to foam.

aufscheinen *vi sep irreg aux sein* **(a)** *(geh: aufleuchten)* to light up; *(Licht)* to appear; *(fig liter)* to shine out. **(b)** *(Aus: erscheinen)* to appear.

aufscheuchen *vt sep* to startle; *(inf) Öffentlichkeit* to startle, to shock ◆ **jdn aus etw ~** to jolt sb out of sth; **jdn von seiner Arbeit/Lektüre ~** to disturb sb when he is working/reading.

aufscheuern *sep* 1 *vt Fuß etc* to rub sore; *Haut* to chafe.
2 *vr* to rub oneself sore ◆ **sich** *(dat)* **die Hände/Füße ~** to take the skin off one's hands/feet.

aufschichten *vt sep* to stack, to pile up; *Stapel* to build up.

Aufschichtung *f siehe vt* stacking, piling up; building.

aufschieben *vt sep irreg Fenster, Tür* to slide open; *Riegel* to push *or* slide back; *(fig: verschieben)* to put off ◆ **aufgeschoben ist nicht aufgehoben** *(prov)* putting something off does not mean it's solved.

aufschießen *sep irreg* 1 *vi aux sein* **(a)** *(Saat, Jugendlicher)* to shoot up;

⚠: for details of spelling reform, see supplement

(*Flammen, Fontäne etc auch*) to leap up ◆ **wie Pilze ~** (*Hochhäuser etc*) to mushroom; *siehe* **aufgeschossen. (b)** (*emporschnellen, hochfahren*) to shoot *or* leap up.
[2] *vt* (*Naut*) *Tau* to coil.

aufschimmern *vi sep aux sein or haben* (*geh*) to flash ◆ **in etw** (*dat*) **~** (*fig*) to illuminate sth.

Aufschlag *m* **(a)** (*das Aufschlagen*) impact; (*Geräusch*) crash.
(b) (*Tennis etc*) service, serve ◆ **wer hat ~?** whose service *or* serve (is it)?; **sie hat ~** she's serving, it's her service *or* serve.
(c) (*Preis~*) surcharge, extra charge.
(d) (*Ärmel~*) cuff; (*Hosen~*) turn-up (*Brit*), cuff (*US*); (*Mantel~ etc*) lapel.

Aufschlag- *in cpds* (*Sport*) service; **~ball** *m* (*Tennis*) service, serve.

aufschlagen *sep irreg* [1] *vi* **(a)** *aux sein* (*auftreffen*) **auf etw** (*dat*) **~** to hit sth; **das Flugzeug schlug in einem Waldstück auf** the plane crashed into a wood; **mit dem Kopf** *etc* **auf etw** (*acc or dat*) **~** to hit one's head *etc* on sth; **dumpf ~** to thud (*auf +acc* onto); **sie fühlte, wie ihr Kopf hart aufschlug** she felt the hard crack on her head.
(b) *aux sein* (*sich öffnen*) to open.
(c) *aux sein* (*Flammen*) to leap *or* blaze up (*aus* out of).
(d) *aux haben or* (*rare*) *sein* (*Waren, Preise*) to rise, to go up (*um* by).
(e) (*Tennis etc*) to serve ◆ **du mußt ~** it's your service *or* serve.
[2] *vt* **(a)** (*durch Schlagen öffnen*) to crack; *Nuß* to crack (open); *Eis* to crack a hole in ◆ **jdm/sich den Kopf/die Augenbraue ~** to crack *or* cut open sb's/one's head/cut open sb's/one's eyebrow.
(b) (*aufklappen*) to open; (*zurückschlagen*) *Bett, Bettdecke* to turn back; (*hochschlagen*) *Kragen etc* to turn up; *Schleier* to lift up, to raise ◆ **schlagt Seite 111 auf** open your books at page 111.
(c) *Augen* to open.
(d) (*aufbauen*) *Bett, Liegestuhl* to put up; *Zelt auch* to pitch; (*Nacht)lager* to set up, to pitch ◆ **er hat seinen Wohnsitz in Wien/einem alten Bauernhaus aufgeschlagen** he has taken up residence in Vienna/an old farmhouse.
(e) (*Comm*) *Preise* to put up, to raise ◆ **10% auf etw** (*acc*) **~** to put 10% on sth.

Aufschläger *m* (*Tennis etc*) server.

Aufschlag-: ~fehler *m* service fault; **~spiel** *nt* service game; **~zünder** *m* (*Mil*) percussion fuse.

aufschlecken *vt sep* (*S Ger*) *siehe* **auflecken.**

aufschließen *sep irreg* [1] *vt* **(a)** (*öffnen*) to unlock; (*geh: erklären*) to elucidate (*jdm* to sb) ◆ **jdm die Tür** *etc* **~** to unlock the door *etc* for sb.
(b) (*geh: offenbaren*) **jdm sein Herz/Innerstes ~** to open one's heart to sb/tell sb one's innermost thoughts.
(c) (*Chem, Biol*) to break down.
(d) *Rohstoffvorkommen, Bauland* to develop.
[2] *vr* (*geh*) **sich leicht ~** to find it easy to be open *or* frank; **sich jdm ~** to be open *or* frank with sb; *siehe* **aufgeschlossen.**
[3] *vi* **(a)** (*öffnen*) **(jdm) ~** to unlock the door (for sb).
(b) (*heranrücken*) to close up; (*Sport*) to catch up (*zu* with).

aufschlitzen *vt sep* to rip (open); (*mit Messer auch*) to slit (open); *Gesicht* to slash; *Bauch* to slash open.

aufschluchzen *vi sep* (*geh*) to sob convulsively.

⚠**Aufschluß** *m* **(a)** (*Aufklärung*) information *no pl* ◆ **(jdm) ~ über etw** (*acc*) **geben** to give (sb) information about sth; **~ über etw** (*acc*) **verlangen** to demand an explanation of sth. **(b)** (*Chem, Biol*) breaking down. **(c)** (*Min: Erschließung*) development.

aufschlüsseln *vt sep* to break down (*nach* into); (*klassifizieren*) to classify (*nach* according to).

Aufschlüsselung, ⚠**Aufschlüßlung** (*rare*) *f siehe vt* breakdown; classification.

⚠**aufschlußreich** *adj* informative, instructive.

aufschmeißen *vt sep irreg* **(a)** (*Aus inf*) *jdn* to send up (*inf*). **(b)** *siehe* **aufgeschmissen.**

aufschmieren *vt sep* (*inf*) to spread on; *Farbe* to smear on.

aufschnallen *vt sep* **(a)** (*befestigen*) to buckle *or* strap on (*auf etw* (*acc*) (-to) sth). **(b)** (*losschnallen*) to unbuckle, to unstrap.

aufschnappen *sep* [1] *vt* to catch; (*inf*) *Wort etc* to pick up.
[2] *vi aux sein* to snap *or* spring open.

aufschneiden *sep irreg* [1] *vt* **(a)** to cut open; (*tranchieren*) *Braten* to carve; *Buch* to cut; (*Med*) *Geschwür* to lance; *siehe* **Pulsader. (b)** (*in Scheiben schneiden*) to slice.
[2] *vi* (*inf: prahlen*) to brag, to boast.

Aufschneider *m* (*inf*) braggart, boaster.

Aufschneiderei *f* (*inf*) bragging *no pl*, boasting *no pl*.

aufschneiderisch *adj* (*inf*) boastful.

aufschnellen *vi sep aux sein* **(a)** (*hochschnellen*) to leap *or* jump up; (*Schlange*) to rear up. **(b)** (*rare: sich plötzlich öffnen*) to fly *or* spring open.

Aufschnitt *m, no pl* (assorted) sliced cold meat *or* (*rare: Käse*) cheese ◆ **kalter ~** (assorted) sliced cold meat, cold cuts (*US*).

aufschnüren *vt sep* **(a)** (*lösen*) to untie, to undo; *Schuh auch* to unlace. **(b)** (*rare: befestigen*) to tie on (*auf +acc* -to).

aufschrammen *vt sep siehe* **aufschürfen.**

aufschrauben *vt sep* **(a)** *Schraube etc* to unscrew; *Flasche etc* to take the top off. **(b)** (*festschrauben*) to screw on (*auf +acc* -to).

aufschrecken *sep pret* **schreckte auf,** *ptp* **aufgeschreckt** [1] *vt* to startle; (*aus Gleichgültigkeit*) to rouse (*aus* from), to jolt (*aus* out of) ◆ **jdn aus dem Schlaf ~** to rouse sb from sleep.
[2] *vi pret auch* **schrak auf** *aux sein* to start (up), to be startled ◆ **aus dem Schlaf ~** to wake up with a start; **aus seinen Gedanken ~** to start.

Aufschrei *m* yell; (*schriller ~*) scream, shriek ◆ **ein ~ der Empörung/Entrüstung** (*fig*) an outcry.

aufschreiben *vt sep irreg* **(a)** (*niederschreiben*) **etw ~** to write *or* note sth down.
(b) (*notieren*) **sich** (*dat*) **etw ~** to make a note of sth.
(c) (*als Schulden anschreiben*) to put on the slate (*inf*), to chalk up (*inf*).
(d) (*inf: verordnen*) to prescribe.
(e) (*inf: polizeilich ~*) **jdn ~** to take sb's particulars; **das Auto ~** to take the car's number.

aufschreien *vi sep irreg* to yell out; (*schrill*) to scream *or* shriek out.

Aufschrift *f* (*Beschriftung*) inscription; (*Etikett*) label ◆ **eine Flasche mit der ~ „Vorsicht Gift" versehen** to label a bottle "Danger — Poison".

Aufschub *m* (*Verzögerung*) delay; (*Vertagung*) postponement ◆ **die Sache duldet** *or* **leidet** (*old*) **keinen ~** (*geh*) the matter brooks no delay (*liter*); **jdm ~ gewähren** (*Zahlungs~*) to give sb an extension of the payment deadline, to allow sb grace.

aufschürfen *vt sep* **sich** (*dat*) **die Haut/das Knie ~** to graze *or* scrape oneself/one's knee.

aufschütteln *vt sep Kissen etc* to shake *or* plump up.

aufschütten *vt sep* **(a)** *Flüssigkeit* to pour on ◆ **Wasser auf etw** (*acc*) **~** to pour water on *or* over sth; **Kaffee ~** to make coffee. **(b)** (*nachfüllen*) *Kohle* to put on (the fire). **(c)** *Stroh, Steine* to spread; *Damm, Deich* to throw up; *Straße* to raise. **(d)** (*Geol*) to deposit.

Aufschüttung *f* **(a)** (*Damm*) bank of earth. **(b)** (*Geol*) deposit.

aufschwatzen, aufschwätzen (*dial*) *vt sep* (*inf*) **jdm etw ~** to talk sb into taking sth; **sie hat ihr ihren Sohn aufgeschwatzt** she talked her into marrying her son.

aufschweißen *vt sep* to cut open (with an oxyacetylene torch).

aufschwellen *sep* [1] *vi irreg aux sein* to swell (up).
[2] *vt reg* to swell; (*fig*) *Satz, Buch* to pad out (*inf*).

aufschwemmen *vti sep* **(jdn) ~** to make sb bloated; **jds Gesicht ~** to make sb's face bloated *or* puffy; *siehe* **aufgeschwemmt.**

aufschwingen *vr sep irreg* to swing oneself up; (*Vogel*) to soar (up); (*fig: Gedanken*) to rise to higher realms ◆ **sich zu etw ~** (*sich aufraffen*) to bring oneself to do sth; (*sich aufwerfen*) to set oneself up to be sth; (*sich hocharbeiten*) to work one's way up to be(come) sth; (*hum: etw kaufen*) to bring oneself to get sth.

Aufschwung *m* **(a)** (*Antrieb*) lift; (*der Phantasie*) upswing; (*der Seele*) uplift; (*der Wirtschaft etc*) upturn, upswing (*gen* in) ◆ **das gab ihr (einen) neuen ~** that gave her a lift. **(b)** (*Turnen*) swing-up.

aufsehen *vi sep irreg siehe* **aufblicken.**

Aufsehen *nt* **-s,** *no pl* sensation ◆ **großes ~ erregen** to cause a sensation *or* stir; **um etw viel ~ machen** to make a lot of fuss about sth; **ohne großes ~** without any to-do (*inf*) *or* fuss; **ich möchte jedes ~ vermeiden** I want to avoid any fuss; **bitte kein ~, meine Herren** no fuss please, gentlemen.

⚠**aufsehen|erregend** *adj* sensational.

Aufseher(in *f*) *m* (*allgemein*) supervisor; (*bei Prüfung*) invigilator; (*Sklaven~*) overseer; (*Gefängnis~*) warder (*Brit*), guard (*US*); (*Park~, Museums~ etc*) attendant.

⚠**aufsein** *vi sep irreg aux sein* (*Zusammenschreibung nur bei infin und ptp*) **(a)** (*aufgestanden sein*) to be up. **(b)** (*geöffnet sein*) to be open.

aufsetzen *sep* [1] *vt* **(a)** (*auf etw setzen*) *Brille, Topf, Essen etc* to put on; *Kegel* to set up; *Knöpfe, Flicken etc* to put on; *Steine* to lay; *Tonarm* to lower; *Fuß* to put on the ground *or* down; (*fig*) *Lächeln, Miene etc* to put on ◆ **ich kann den Fuß nicht richtig ~** I can't put any weight on my foot; **sich** (*dat*) **den Hut ~** to put on one's hat; *siehe* **Dämpfer, Horn** *etc.*
(b) *Flugzeug* to land, to bring down; *Boot* to pull up, to beach; (*unabsichtlich*) to ground, to run aground.
(c) (*aufrichten*) *Kranken etc* to sit up.
(d) (*verfassen*) to draft; (*ein Konzept machen für auch*) to make a draft of.
[2] *vr* to sit up.
[3] *vi* (*Flugzeug*) to touch down, to land; (*Tonarm*) to come down.

Aufsetzer *m* **-s, -** (*Sport*) bouncing ball.

aufseufzen *vi sep* **(tief/laut) ~** to heave a (deep/loud) sigh.

Aufsicht *f* **-, -en (a)** *no pl* (*Überwachung*) supervision (*über +acc* of); (*Obhut*) charge ◆ **unter jds ~** (*dat*) under the supervision of sb; in the charge of sb; **unter polizeilicher/ärztlicher ~** under police/medical supervision; **~ über jdn/etw führen** to be in charge of sb/sth; **bei einer Prüfung ~ führen** to invigilate an exam; **im Pausenhof ~ führen** to be on duty during break; **jdn ohne ~ lassen** to leave sb unsupervised *or* without supervision; **der Kranke darf niemals ohne ~ sein** the patient must be kept under constant supervision; **jdm obliegt die ~ über etw** (*acc*) (*form*) sb is in charge of *or* responsible for sth.
(b) (*~führender*) person in charge; (*Aufseher*) supervisor ◆ **die ~ fragen** (*~sschalter*) to ask at the office.
(c) (*Math: Draufsicht*) top view.

⚠**Aufsicht-: a~führend** *adj attr Behörde* supervisory; *Beamter* supervising; **~führende(r)** *mf decl as adj siehe* **Aufsicht (b).**

Aufsichts-: ~beamte(r) *m* (*in Museum, Zoo etc*) attendant; **~behörde** *f* supervisory authority *or* body; **~personal** *nt* supervisory staff; **~pflicht** *f* (*Jur*) *legal responsibility to care for sb esp children*; **die elterliche ~pflicht, die ~pflicht der Eltern** (legal) parental responsibility; **~rat** *m* (supervisory) board; (*Mitglied*) member of the board; **im ~rat einer Firma sitzen** to be *or* sit

on the board of a firm; **~ratsvorsitzende(r)** *m* chairman of the board.
aufsitzen *vi sep irreg* **(a)** (*aufgerichtet sitzen, aufbleiben*) to sit up.
(b) *aux sein* (*auf Reittier*) to mount; (*auf Fahrzeug*) to get on ◆ **aufs Pferd ~** to mount the horse; **aufgesessen!** (*Mil*) mount!
(c) (*ruhen auf*) to sit on (*auf etw* (*dat*) sth).
(d) (*Naut*) to run aground (*auf+dat* on).
(e) *aux sein* (*inf: hereinfallen*) **jdm/einer Sache ~** to be taken in by sb/sth.
(f) *aux sein* (*inf*) **jdn ~ lassen** (*im Stich lassen*) to leave sb in the lurch, to let sb down; (*Verabredung nicht einhalten*) to stand sb up (*inf*).
aufspalten *vtr sep* to split; (*fig auch*) to split up ◆ **eine Klasse in drei Gruppen ~** to split up *or* divide up a class into three groups.
Aufspaltung *f* splitting; (*fig auch*) splitting-up ◆ **seit der ~ der Partei** since the party split up.
aufspannen *vt sep* **(a)** *Netz, Sprungtuch* to stretch *or* spread out; *Schirm* to put up, to open. **(b)** (*aufziehen*) *Leinwand* to stretch (*auf +acc* onto); *Saite* to put on (*auf etw* (*acc*) sth).
aufsparen *vt sep* to save (up), to keep ◆ **sich** (*dat*) **eine Bemerkung ~** to save *or* keep a remark.
aufspeichern *vt sep* to store (up); *Energie auch* to accumulate; (*fig*) *Zorn etc* to build up.
Aufspeicherung *f* storage; (*von Energie auch*) accumulation.
aufsperren *vt sep* **(a)** (*S Ger, Aus: aufschließen*) *Tür etc* to unlock. **(b)** (*aufreißen*) *Tür, Schnabel* to open wide ◆ **die Ohren ~** to prick up one's ears.
aufspielen *sep* [1] *vi* (*dated*) to play; (*anfangen*) to strike up ◆ **die Mannschaft spielte glänzend auf** the team began playing brilliantly.
[2] *vr* (*inf*) **(a)** (*sich wichtig tun*) to give oneself airs. **(b)** (*sich ausgeben als*) **sich als etw ~** to set oneself up as sth; **sich als Boß ~** to play the boss.
aufspießen *vt sep* to spear; (*durchbohren*) to run through; (*mit Hörnern*) to gore; *Schmetterlinge* to pin; *Fleisch* (*mit Spieß*) to skewer; (*mit Gabel*) to prong ◆ **sie schien mich mit Blicken ~ zu wollen** she looked daggers at me.
aufsplittern *sep* [1] *vti* (*vi: aux sein*) (*Holz*) to splinter; (*Gruppe*) to split (up).
[2] *vr* (*Gruppe etc*) to split (up).
aufsprengen *vt sep* to force open; (*mit Sprengstoff*) to blow open.
aufsprießen *vi sep irreg aux sein* (*geh*) to burst forth, to sprout.
aufspringen *vi sep irreg aux sein* **(a)** (*hochspringen*) to jump *or* leap to one's feet *or* up ◆ **auf etw** (*acc*) **~** to jump onto sth.
(b) (*auftreffen*) to bounce; (*Ski*) to land.
(c) (*sich öffnen*) (*Tür*) to burst *or* fly open; (*platzen*) to burst; (*Rinde, Lack*) to crack; (*Haut, Lippen etc*) to crack, to chap; (*liter: Knospen*) to burst open.
aufspritzen *sep* [1] *vt* **etw (auf etw** *acc*) **~** to spray sth on (sth).
[2] *vi aux sein* to spurt (up).
aufsprudeln *vi sep aux sein* to bubble up.
aufsprühen *sep* [1] *vt* **etw (auf etw** *acc*) **~** to spray sth on (sth).
[2] *vi aux sein* to spray up.
Aufsprung *m* (*Sport*) landing; (*von Ball*) bounce.
aufspulen *vt sep* to wind on a spool; *Angelschnur, Garn auch* to wind on a reel.
aufspülen *vt sep* **(a)** (*anspülen*) *Sand, Schlick etc* to wash up. **(b)** (*aufwirbeln*) *Sand, Schlamm etc* to whirl up.
aufspüren *vt sep* (*lit, fig*) to track down.
aufstacheln *vt sep siehe* **anstacheln** ◆ **jdn ~, etw zu tun** (*aufwiegeln*) to goad *or* urge sb on to do sth *or* into doing sth.
aufstampfen *vi sep* to stamp ◆ **mit dem Fuß ~** to stamp one's foot.
Aufstand *m* rebellion, revolt ◆ **im ~** in rebellion *or* revolt; **den ~ proben** (*fig*) to flex one's muscles.
aufständisch *adj* rebellious, insurgent.
Aufständische(r) *mf decl as adj* rebel, insurgent.
aufstapeln *vt sep* to stack *or* pile up.
aufstauen *sep* [1] *vt Wasser* to dam ◆ **etw in sich** (*dat*) **~** (*fig*) to bottle sth up inside (oneself).
[2] *vr* to accumulate, to collect; (*fig: Ärger*) to be/become bottled up.
aufstechen *vt sep irreg* to puncture; (*Med*) to lance; (*dial: aufdecken*) to bring into the open.
aufstecken *sep* [1] *vt* **(a)** (*auf etw stecken*) to put on (*auf +acc* -to); *Fahne, Gardinen* to put up (*auf +acc* on) ◆ **sich/jdm einen Ring ~** to put on a ring/put a ring on sb's finger; **Kerzen auf einen Leuchter/den Baum ~** to put candles in a candlestick/on the tree.
(b) (*mit Nadeln*) to pin up; *Haar auch* to put up.
(c) (*inf: aufgeben*) to pack in (*inf*).
[2] *vi* (*inf: aufgeben*) to pack it in (*inf*); (*bei Rennen etc auch*) to retire.
aufstehen *vi sep irreg aux sein* **(a)** (*sich erheben*) to get *or* stand up; (*morgens aus dem Bett*) to get up; (*fig: Persönlichkeit*) to arise ◆ **aus dem Sessel/Bett ~** to get up out of the chair/to get out of bed; **vor jdm/für jdn ~** to stand up for sb; **~ dürfen** (*Kranker*) to be allowed (to get) up; **er steht nicht mehr** *or* **wieder auf** (*fig inf*) he's a goner (*inf*); **da mußt du früher** *or* **eher ~!** (*fig inf*) you'll have to do better than that!
(b) (*inf: offen sein*) to be open.
(c) (*sich auflehnen*) to rise (in arms).
(d) *aux haben* (*auf dem Boden etc stehen*) to stand (*auf +dat* on) ◆ **der Tisch steht nur mit drei Beinen/nicht richtig auf** the table is only standing on three legs/is not standing firmly.
aufsteigen *vi sep irreg aux sein* **(a)** (*auf Berg, Leiter*) to climb (up); (*Vogel, Drachen*) to soar (up); (*Flugzeug*) to climb; (*Stern, Sonne, Nebel*) to rise; (*Gewitter, Wolken*) to gather; (*Gefühl*) to rise; (*geh: aufragen*) to tower, to rise up; (*drohend*) to loom ◆ **zum Gipfel ~** to climb (up) to the summit; **einen Ballon ~ lassen** to release a balloon; **in einem Ballon ~** to go up in a balloon; **an die Oberfläche ~** to rise to the surface; **~de Linie** ascending line; **in jdm ~** (*Haß, Verdacht, Erinnerung etc*) to well up in sb.
(b) (*auf Fahrrad etc*) to get on (*auf etw* (*acc*) (-to) sth); (*auf Pferd auch*) to mount (*auf etw* (*acc*) sth).
(c) (*fig: im Rang etc*) to rise (*zu* to); (*beruflich auch*) to be promoted; (*Sport*) to go up, to be promoted (*in +acc* to) ◆ **zum Abteilungsleiter ~** to rise to be head of department; **das ~de Bürgertum** the rising middle classes.
Aufsteiger *m* **(a)** (*Sport*) league climber; (*in höhere Liga*) promoted team. **(b)** (*auch* **~in** *f*) **(sozialer) ~** social climber.
aufstellen *sep* [1] *vt* **(a)** (*aufrichten, aufbauen*) to put up (*auf +dat* on); *etw Liegendes* to stand up; *Zelt auch* to pitch; *Schild, Mast, Denkmal auch* to erect; *Kegel* to set up; *Verkehrsampel auch* to install; *Maschine* to put in, to install; *Falle* to set; (*Mil*) to deploy; (*postieren*) *Wachposten* to post, to station; *Wagen* to line up; (*hochstellen*) *Kragen etc* to put up; (*aufrichten*) *Ohren, Stacheln* to prick up.
(b) *Essen etc* (*auf Herd*) to put on.
(c) (*fig: zusammenstellen*) *Truppe* to raise; (*Sport*) *Spieler* to select, to pick; *Mannschaft* to draw up.
(d) (*benennen*) *Kandidaten* to nominate; (*erzielen*) *Rekord* to set (up).
(e) *Forderung, Behauptung, Vermutung* to put forward; *System* to establish; *Programm, Satzungen, Rechnung* to draw up; *Liste auch* to make.
[2] *vr* **(a)** (*sich postieren*) to stand; (*hintereinander*) to line up; (*Soldaten*) to fall into line ◆ **sich im Karree/Kreis** *etc* **~** to form a square/circle *etc*.
(b) (*Ohren etc*) to prick up.
Aufstellung *f* **(a)** *no pl* (*das Aufstellen*) putting up; (*von Zelt*) pitching; (*von Schild, Mast, Denkmal auch*) erection; (*von Verkehrsampel*) installation; (*von Maschine*) putting in, installation; (*von Falle*) setting; (*Mil*) deployment; (*von Wachposten*) posting, stationing; (*von Wagen*) lining up ◆ **~ nehmen** (*Mil*) to take up position.
(b) *no pl* (*das Aufstellen*) (*von Truppen*) raising; (*von Spielern*) selecting, picking; (*von Mannschaft*) drawing up; (*Mannschaft*) line-up (*inf*), team.
(c) *siehe vt* (*d*) nominating; setting.
(d) *no pl siehe vt* (*e*) putting forward; establishing; drawing up.
(e) (*Liste*) list; (*Tabelle*) table; (*Inventar*) inventory.
aufstemmen *vt sep* to force *or* prise open (with a chisel *etc*); (*mit der Schulter*) to force open.
aufstempeln *vt sep* to stamp on ◆ **etw auf etw** (*acc*) **~** to stamp sth on sth; **jdm ein Etikett ~** (*fig*) to put a label on sb.
aufsteppen *vt sep* to sew *or* stitch on (*auf etw* (*acc*) (-to) sth).
aufstieben *vi sep irreg aux sein* to fly up.
Aufstieg *m* **-(e)s, -e (a)** *no pl* (*auf Berg*) climb, ascent; (*von Flugzeug, Rakete*) climb; (*von Ballon*) ascent.
(b) (*fig*) (*Aufschwung*) rise; (*beruflich, politisch, sozial*) advancement; (*Sport: von Mannschaft*) climb, rise; (*in höhere Liga*) promotion (*in +acc* to) ◆ **den ~ zu etw/ins Management schaffen** to rise to (become) sth/to work one's way up into the management.
(c) (*Weg*) way up (*auf etw* (*acc*) sth), ascent (*auf +acc* of).
Aufstiegs-: ~chance, ~möglichkeit *f* prospect of promotion; **~runde** *f* (*Sport*) round deciding promotion; **~spiel** *nt* (*Sport*) match deciding promotion.
aufstöbern *vt sep Wild* to start, to flush; *Rebhühner etc auch* to put up; (*fig: stören*) to disturb; (*inf: entdecken*) to run to earth.
aufstocken *sep* [1] *vt* **(a)** *Haus* to build another storey onto. **(b)** *Kapital, Kredit, Armee* to increase (*um* by); *Vorräte* to build *or* stock up.
[2] *vi* to build another storey.
aufstöhnen *vi sep* to groan loudly, to give a loud groan ◆ **erleichtert ~** to give a loud sigh of relief.
aufstören *vt sep* to disturb; *Wild* to start ◆ **jdn aus dem** *or* **im Schlaf ~** to disturb sb while he is sleeping.
aufstoßen *sep irreg* [1] *vt* **(a)** (*öffnen*) to push open; (*mit dem Fuß*) to kick open.
(b) (*rare*) **etw auf etw** (*acc*) **~** to strike sth on sth, to hit sth against sth; **er stieß den Stock (auf den Boden) auf** he tapped his stick on the ground.
[2] *vi* **(a)** *aux sein* **auf etw** (*acc*) **~** to hit (on *or* against) sth; **ich bin mit dem Ellbogen auf die Bordsteinkante aufgestoßen** I hit my elbow on *or* against the kerb.
(b) *aux haben* (*rülpsen*) to burp.
(c) *aux sein or haben* (*Speisen*) to repeat ◆ **Radieschen stoßen mir auf** radishes repeat on me; **das könnte dir noch sauer** *or* **übel ~** (*fig inf*) you might have to pay for that; **das ist mir sauer aufgestoßen** (*fig inf*) it left a nasty taste in my mouth.
(d) *aux sein* (*fig: auffallen*) to strike (*jdm* sb).
[3] *vr* to graze oneself ◆ **sich** (*dat*) **das Knie ~** to graze one's knee.
Aufstoßen *nt* **-s,** *no pl* burping, flatulence (*form*).
aufstreben *vi sep aux sein* (*geh: aufragen*) to soar, to tower ◆ **hoch ~de Türme/Berge** high soaring towers/mountains.
aufstrebend *adj* (*fig*) *Land, Volk* striving for progress, aspiring; *Stadt* up-and-coming, striving; *junger Mann* ambitious; *Bürgertum* rising.
aufstreichen *vt sep irreg* to put on (*auf etw* (*acc*) sth); *Butter etc* to spread (*auf +acc* on).
aufstreuen *vt sep* to sprinkle on ◆ **etw auf etw** (*acc*) **~** to sprinkle sth on(to) *or* over sth; **Splitt/Salz auf die Straßen ~** to grit/salt the roads.
Aufstrich *m* **-(e)s, -e (a)** (*auf Brot*) spread ◆ **was möchten Sie als ~?** what would you like on your bread/toast *etc*? **(b)** (*Mus*) up-bow. **(c)** (*beim*

Schreiben) upstroke.

aufstülpen *vt sep* **(a)** (*draufstülpen*) to put on ◆ **etw auf etw** (*acc*) ~ to put sth on sth; **sich** (*dat*) **den Hut** ~ to put *or* pull on one's hat.
(b) (*umstülpen*) *Ärmel, Kragen etc* to turn up ◆ **die Lippen** ~ (*schmollend*) to pout.

aufstützen *sep* [1] *vt Kranken etc* to prop up; *Ellbogen, Arme* to rest (*auf +acc or dat* on) ◆ **den Kopf** ~ to rest one's head on one's hand.
[2] *vr* to support oneself; (*im Bett, beim Essen*) to prop oneself up ◆ **sich auf die** *or* **der Hand** ~ to support oneself with one's hand.

aufsuchen *vt sep* **(a)** *Bekannten* to call on; *Arzt, Ort, Toilette* to go to ◆ **das Bett** ~ (*geh*) to retire to bed. **(b)** (*aufsammeln*) to pick up; (*auf Landkarte, in Buch*) to find.

aufsummen, aufsummieren* *vtr sep* to add up.

auftafeln *vti sep* to serve (up).

auftakeln *vt sep* (*Naut*) to rig up ◆ **sich** ~ (*pej inf*) to tart oneself up (*inf*); *siehe* **aufgetakelt.**

Auftakt *m* **(a)** (*Beginn*) start; (*Vorbereitung*) prelude ◆ **den** ~ **von** *or* **zu etw bilden** to mark the beginning *or* start of sth/to form a prelude to sth. **(b)** (*Mus*) upbeat; (*Poet*) arsis (*form*).

auftanken *vti sep* to fill up; (*Aviat*) to refuel; *500 Liter* to refuel with, to take on; *10 Liter* to put in ◆ **Benzin** ~ to fill up with petrol (*Brit*) *or* gas (*US*).

auftauchen *vi sep aux sein* **(a)** (*aus dem Wasser*) to surface; (*Taucher etc auch*) to come up.
(b) (*fig*) (*sichtbar werden*) to appear; (*aus Nebel etc auch*) to emerge; (*Zweifel, Problem*) to arise.
(c) (*gefunden werden, sich zeigen, kommen*) to turn up.

auftauen *sep* [1] *vi aux sein* to thaw; (*fig auch*) to unbend.
[2] *vt Eis* to thaw; *Tiefkühlkost, Wasserleitung* to thaw (out).

aufteilen *vt sep* **(a)** (*aufgliedern*) to divide *or* split up (*in +acc* into). **(b)** (*verteilen*) to share out (*an +acc* between).

Aufteilung *f siehe vt* division; sharing out.

auftippen *vi sep aux sein* to bounce.

auftischen *vt sep* to serve up; (*fig inf*) to come up with ◆ **jdm etw** ~ (*lit*) to give sb sth, to serve sb (with) sth; **jdm Lügen** *etc* ~ (*inf*) to give sb a lot of lies *etc.*

Auftrag *m* **-(e)s, Aufträge (a)** *no pl* (*Anweisung*) orders *pl*, instructions *pl*; (*zugeteilte Arbeit*) job, task; (*Jur*) brief ◆ **jdm den ~ geben, etw zu tun** to give sb the job of doing sth, to instruct sb to do sth; **einen ~ ausführen** to carry out an order; **ich habe den ~, Ihnen mitzuteilen ...** I have been instructed to tell you ...; **in jds** ~ (*dat*) (*für jdn*) on sb's behalf; (*auf jds Anweisung*) on sb's instructions; **die Oper wurde im ~ des Königs komponiert** the opera was commissioned by the king; **im** ~ *or* **i.A.: G. W. Kurz** pp G. W. Kurz.
(b) (*Comm*) order (*über +acc* for); (*bei Künstlern, Freischaffenden etc*) commission (*über +acc* for) ◆ **etw in ~ geben** to order/commission sth (*bei* from); **im ~ und auf Rechnung von** by order and for account of.
(c) *no pl* (*geh: Mission, Aufgabe*) task.
(d) (*von Farbe etc*) application.

auftragen *sep irreg* [1] *vt* **(a)** (*servieren*) to serve ◆ **es ist aufgetragen!** (*geh*) lunch/dinner *etc* is served!
(b) *Farbe, Salbe, Schminke* to apply, to put on ◆ **etw auf etw** (*acc*) ~ to apply sth to sth, to put sth on sth.
(c) **jdm etw** ~ (*form*) to instruct sb to do sth; **er hat mir Grüße an Sie aufgetragen** he has asked me to give you his regards.
(d) *Kleider* to wear out.
[2] *vi* **(a)** (*Kleider*) to make sb look fat ◆ **die Jacke trägt auf** the jacket is not very flattering to your/her figure.
(b) (*übertreiben*) **dick** *or* **stark** ~ (*inf*) to lay it on thick (*inf*) *or* with a trowel (*inf*).

Auftrag-: ~geber(in *f*) *m* client; (*von Firma, Freischaffenden*) customer; **~nehmer(in** *f*) *m* (*Comm*) firm accepting the order; (*Build*) contractor.

Auftrags-: ~bestätigung *f* confirmation of order; **a~gemäß** *adj, adv* as instructed; (*Comm*) as per order; **~lage** *f* order situation, situation concerning orders; **~polster** *nt* **wir haben ein dickes ~polster** our order books are well-filled; **~rückgang** *m* drop in orders; **~walze** *f* (*Typ*) inking roller.

auftreffen *vi sep irreg aux sein* **auf etw** (*dat or acc*) ~ to hit *or* strike sth; (*Rakete*) to land on sth; **er traf mit dem Kopf auf der Kante auf** he hit his head on the edge; **~de Strahlen** incident rays.

auftreiben *sep irreg* [1] *vt* **(a)** (*geh: hochtreiben*) *Staub etc* to raise.
(b) *Teig* to make rise; *Leib* to distend, to bloat.
(c) (*inf: ausfindig machen*) to find, to get hold of (*inf*).
(d) *Vieh* (*zum Verkauf*) to drive to market; (*auf die Alm*) to drive up to the (Alpine) pastures.
[2] *vi aux sein* (*Teig*) to rise; (*Bauch etc*) to become distended *or* bloated ◆ **sein aufgetriebener Bauch** his swollen *or* distended stomach.

auftrennen *vt sep* to undo.

auftreten *sep irreg* [1] *vi aux sein* **(a)** (*lit*) to tread ◆ **der Fuß tut so weh, daß ich (mit ihm) nicht mehr ~ kann** my foot hurts so much that I can't walk on it *or* put my weight on it.
(b) (*erscheinen*) to appear ◆ **als Zeuge/Kläger** ~ to appear as a witness/as plaintiff; **zum ersten Mal (im Theater)** ~ to make one's début *or* first (stage) appearance; **er tritt zum ersten Mal in Köln auf** he is appearing in Cologne for the first time; **gegen jdn/etw** ~ to stand up *or* speak out against sb/sth; **geschlossen** ~ to put up a united front.
(c) (*fig: eintreten*) to occur; (*Schwierigkeiten etc*) to arise.
(d) (*sich benehmen*) to behave ◆ **bescheiden/arrogant** ~ to have a modest/arrogant manner; **vorsichtig** ~ to tread warily.
(e) (*handeln*) to act ◆ **als Vermittler/Friedensstifter** *etc* ~ to act as intermediary/peacemaker *etc.*
[2] *vt Tür etc* to kick open.

Auftreten *nt* **-s,** *no pl* **(a)** (*Erscheinen*) appearance. **(b)** (*Benehmen*) manner. **(c)** (*Vorkommen*) occurrence ◆ **bei ~ von Schwellungen ...** in case swelling occurs ..., in the event of swelling ...

Auftrieb *m, no pl* **(a)** (*Phys*) buoyancy (force); (*Aviat*) lift.
(b) (*fig: Aufschwung*) impetus; (*Preis~*) upward trend (*gen* in); (*Ermunterung*) lift ◆ **das wird ihm ~ geben** that will give him a lift.
(c) *no pl* (*des Alpenviehs*) **der ~ findet Anfang Mai statt** the cattle are driven up to the (Alpine) pastures at the beginning of May.
(d) *no pl* (*von Marktvieh*) **der ~ an Vieh/Kälbern** the number of cattle/calves (at the market).

Auftriebskraft *f* buoyancy force; (*Aviat*) lift.

Auftritt *m* **(a)** (*Erscheinen*) entrance ◆ **ich habe meinen ~ erst im zweiten Akt** I don't go *or* come on until the second act. **(b)** (*Theat: Szene*) scene. **(c)** (*Streit*) row.

Auftrittsverbot *nt* stage ban ◆ ~ **bekommen/haben** to be banned from making a public appearance; ~ **über jdn verhängen** (*inf*) to ban sb from appearing.

auftrumpfen *vi sep* to be full of oneself (*inf*); (*sich schadenfroh äußern*) to crow; (*seine Leistungsstärke zeigen*) to show how good one is ◆ **~d sagte er ...** ..., he crowed.

auftun *sep irreg* [1] *vt* **(a)** (*dated: öffnen*) to open ◆ **tu den Mund auf, wenn du was willst** say when you want something.
(b) (*dial: eröffnen*) to open (up); *Verein* to start.
(c) (*inf: servieren*) **jdm/sich etw** ~ to put sth on sb's/one's plate, to help sb/oneself to sth.
(d) (*inf: ausfindig machen*) to find.
(e) (*dial: aufsetzen*) to put on.
[2] *vr* **(a)** (*sich öffnen*) to open (up).
(b) (*dial: eröffnet werden*) to open (up); (*Verein*) to start.

auftürmen *sep* [1] *vt* to pile *or* stack up; (*Geol*) to build up (in layers).
[2] *vr* (*Gebirge etc*) to tower *or* loom up; (*Schwierigkeiten*) to pile *or* mount up ◆ **hoch aufgetürmte Felsen** towering cliffs.

aufwachen *vi sep aux sein* (*lit, fig*) to wake up ◆ **aus seiner Lethargie/einer Narkose** ~ to snap out of one's lethargy/to come out of an anaesthetic.

aufwachsen *vi sep irreg aux sein* to grow up.

aufwallen *vi sep aux sein* to bubble up; (*Cook*) to boil up; (*Leidenschaft etc*) to surge up ◆ **die Soße einmal ~ lassen** bring the sauce to the boil; **seine ~de Wut/Leidenschaft** his seething rage/the passion surging up in him.

Aufwallung *f* (*fig*) (*von Leidenschaft*) surge; (*Wut*) outburst, fit (of rage).

Aufwand *m* **-(e)s,** *no pl* **(a)** (*von Geld*) expenditure (*an +dat* of) ◆ **das erfordert einen ~ von 10 Millionen Mark** that will cost *or* take 10 million marks; **das erfordert einen großen ~ an Zeit/Energie/Geld** that requires a lot of time/energy/money; **der ~ war umsonst, das war ein unnützer ~** that was a waste of money/time/energy *etc*; **der dazu nötige ~ an Konzentration/Zeit** the concentration/time needed.
(b) (*Luxus, Prunk*) extravagance ◆ **(großen) ~ treiben** to be (very) extravagant; **was da für ~ getrieben wurde!** the extravagance!

Aufwands|entschädigung *f* expense allowance.

aufwärmen *sep* [1] *vt* to heat *or* warm up; (*inf: wieder erwähnen*) to bring up, to drag up (*inf*).
[2] *vr* to warm oneself up; (*Sport*) to warm *or* limber up.

Aufwartefrau *f* char(woman).

aufwarten *vi sep* **(a)** (*geh: bedienen*) to serve (*jdm* sb) ◆ **(bei Tisch)** ~ to wait at table; **uns wurde mit Sekt aufgewartet** we were served champagne.
(b) (*zu bieten haben*) **mit etw** ~ to offer sth; **er hat viel Geld, damit kann ich nicht** ~ he's very rich, I can't compete with that.
(c) (*dated: besuchen*) **jdm** ~ to wait on sb (*old*), to visit sb.

aufwärts *adv* up, upward(s); (*bergauf*) uphill ◆ **die Ecken haben sich ~ gebogen** the corners have curled up; **den Fluß** ~ upstream; **von einer Million** ~ from a million up(wards); **vom Feldwebel** ~ from sergeant up; *siehe* **aufwärtsgehen.**

Aufwärts-: ~bewegung *f* upward movement; (*Tech*) upstroke; **~entwicklung** *f* upward trend (*gen* in); ⚠**a~gehen** *vi impers sep irreg aux sein* **mit dem Staat/der Firma geht es a~** things are looking up *or* getting better *or* improving for the country/firm; **mit ihm geht es a~** (*finanziell, beruflich*) things are looking up for him; (*in der Schule, gesundheitlich*) he's doing *or* getting better; **mit seinen Leistungen geht es a~** he's doing better; **~haken** *m* (*Boxen*) uppercut; **a~kompatibel** *adj* (*Comput*) upward compatible; **~trend** *m* upward trend.

Aufwartung *f* **(a)** *no pl* (*dated: Bedienung*) waiting at table; (*Reinemachen*) cleaning. **(b)** (*geh: Besuch*) **jdm seine ~ machen** to wait (up)on sb (*old*), to visit sb. **(c)** (*dial: Aufwartefrau etc*) char(woman).

Aufwasch *m* **-(e)s,** *no pl* (*dial*) *siehe* **Abwasch[1].**

aufwaschen *vt sep irreg* (*dial*) *siehe* **abwaschen.**

aufwecken *vt sep* to wake (up), to waken; (*fig*) to rouse; *siehe* **aufgeweckt.**

aufwehen *sep* [1] *vt* **(a)** (*in die Höhe wehen*) to blow up; (*auftürmen*) to pile up ◆ **der Wind hat Dünen aufgeweht** the wind has blown the sand into dunes.
(b) (*öffnen*) to blow open.
[2] *vi aux sein* to blow up.

aufweichen *sep* [1] *vt* to make soft; *Weg, Boden* to make sodden; *Brot* to soak; (*durch Wärme*) to soften; (*fig: lockern*) to weaken; *Doktrin, Gesetz* to water

down; *Gegner* to soften up.
[2] *vi aux sein* to become *or* get soft; (*Weg, Boden*) to become *or* get sodden; (*fig: sich lockern*) to be weakened; (*Doktrin*) to become *or* get watered down.

aufweisen *vt sep irreg* to show ◆ **die Leiche wies keinerlei Verletzungen auf** the body showed no signs of injury; **das Buch weist einige Fehler auf** the book contains some mistakes *or* has some mistakes in it; **etw aufzuweisen haben** to have sth to show for oneself; **man muß schon einiges an Veröffentlichungen aufzuweisen haben** you have to have something to show in the way of publications.

aufwenden *vt sep irreg* to use; *Zeit, Energie* to expend; *Mühe* to take; *Geld* to spend ◆ **viel Mühe/Zeit ~, etw zu tun** to take a lot of trouble/spend a lot of time doing sth; **das wäre unnütz aufgewandte Zeit/Energie** that would be a waste of time/energy.

⚠ **aufwendig** *adj* costly; (*üppig*) lavish.

Aufwendung *f* **(a)** *no pl siehe vt* using; expenditure; taking; spending ◆ **unter ~ von ...** by using/expending/taking/spending ... **(b)** **~en** *pl* expenditure.

➤ **aufwerfen** *sep irreg* [1] *vt* **(a)** (*nach oben werfen*) to throw up; (*aufhäufen*) to pile up; *Damm etc* to build (up).
(b) *Kopf* to toss; *Lippen* to purse ◆ **ein aufgeworfener Mund** pursed lips.
(c) *Tür* to throw open.
➤ **(d)** (*zur Sprache bringen*) *Frage, Probleme* to raise, to bring up.
[2] *vr* **sich zu etw ~** to set oneself up as sth; **sich zum Richter ~** to set oneself up as judge.

aufwerten *vt sep* **(a)** (*auch vi*) *Währung* to revalue. **(b)** (*fig*) to increase the value of; *Menschen, Ideal auch* to enhance the status of.

Aufwertung *f* (*von Währung*) revaluation; (*fig*) increase in value ◆ **das kommt einer ~ des Terrorismus gleich** that is tantamount to enhancing the status of terrorism.

aufwickeln *vt sep* **(a)** (*aufrollen*) to roll up; (*inf*) *Haar* to put in curlers.
(b) (*lösen*) to untie; *Windeln, Verband* to take off.

auf Wiedersehen, auf Wiederschauen (*geh, S Ger, Aus, Sw*) *interj* goodbye.

Aufwiegelei *f siehe* **Aufwiegelung.**

aufwiegeln *vt sep* to stir up ◆ **jdn zum Streik/Widerstand ~** to incite sb to strike/resist.

Aufwiegelung *f* incitement.

aufwiegen *vt sep irreg* (*fig*) to offset ◆ **das ist nicht mit Geld aufzuwiegen** that can't be measured in terms of money.

Aufwiegler(in *f*) *m* **-s, -** agitator; (*Anstifter*) instigator.

aufwieglerisch *adj* seditious; *Rede, Artikel auch* inflammatory.

Aufwind *m* (*Aviat*) upcurrent; (*Met*) upwind ◆ **guter ~** good upcurrents *pl*; **(durch etw) neuen ~ bekommen** (*fig*) to get new impetus (from sth); **einer Sache** (*dat*) **~ geben** (*fig*) to give sth impetus; **sich im ~ fühlen** to feel one is on the way up *or* in the ascendant.

aufwirbeln *sep* [1] *vi aux sein* (*Staub, Schnee*) to swirl *or* whirl up.
[2] *vt* to swirl *or* whirl up; *Staub auch* to raise ◆ **(viel) Staub ~** (*fig*) to cause a (big) stir.

aufwischen *sep* [1] *vt Wasser etc* to wipe *or* mop up; *Fußboden* to wipe ◆ **die Küche (feucht) ~** to wash the kitchen floor; **das Bier vom Boden ~** to mop the beer up off the floor.
[2] *vi* to wipe the floor(s) ◆ **feucht ~** to wash the floor(s).

aufwogen *vi sep aux sein* (*liter*) to heave.

aufwühlen *vt sep* **(a)** (*lit*) *Erde, Meer* to churn (up). **(b)** (*geh*) to stir; (*schmerzhaft*) to churn up; *Leidenschaften* to rouse ◆ **das hat seine Seele zutiefst aufgewühlt** that stirred him to the depths of his soul; **~d** stirring; *siehe* **aufgewühlt.**

aufzahlen *vt sep* (*S Ger, Aus*) **100 Schilling/einen Zuschlag ~** to pay an additional 100 schillings/a surcharge (on top).

aufzählen *vt sep* (*aufsagen*) to list; *Gründe, Namen etc auch* to give (*jdm* sb); (*aufführen auch*) to enumerate; *Geld* to count out (*jdm* for sb) ◆ **er hat mir alle meine Fehler aufgezählt** he told me all my faults, he enumerated all my faults to me.

Aufzahlung *f* (*S Ger, Aus*) additional charge.

Aufzählung *f* list; (*von Gründen, Fehlern etc auch*) enumeration.

aufzäumen *vt sep* to bridle ◆ **etw verkehrt ~** to go about sth the wrong way.

aufzehren *sep* [1] *vt* to exhaust; (*fig*) to sap.
[2] *vr* to burn oneself out.

Aufzehrung *f* exhaustion; (*fig*) sapping.

aufzeichnen *vt sep* **(a)** *Plan etc* to draw, to sketch. **(b)** (*notieren, Rad, TV*) to record.

Aufzeichnung *f* **(a)** (*Zeichnung*) sketch. **(b)** *usu pl* (*Notiz*) note; (*Niederschrift auch*) record. **(c)** (*Magnetband~, Film~*) recording.

aufzeigen *sep* [1] *vt* to show; (*nachweisen auch*) to demonstrate.
[2] *vi* (*dated Sch: sich melden*) to put one's hand up.

aufziehen *sep irreg* [1] *vt* **(a)** (*hochziehen*) to pull *or* draw up; *schweren Gegenstand auch* to haul up; (*mit Flaschenzug etc*) to hoist up; *Schlagbaum, Zugbrücke* to raise; *Flagge, Segel* to hoist; *Jalousien* to let up; (*Med*) *Spritze* to fill; *Flüssigkeit* to draw up.
(b) (*öffnen*) *Reißverschluß* to undo; *Schleife etc auch* to untie; *Schublade* to (pull) open; *Flasche* to uncork; *Gardinen* to draw (back).
(c) (*aufspannen*) *Foto etc* to mount; *Leinwand, Stickerei* to stretch; *Landkarte etc* to pull up; *Saite, Reifen* to fit, to put on ◆ **Saiten/neue Saiten auf ein Instrument ~** to string/restring an instrument; *siehe* **Saite.**
(d) (*spannen*) *Feder, Uhr etc* to wind up.
(e) (*großziehen*) to raise; *Kind auch* to bring up; *Tier auch* to rear.
(f) (*inf*) (*veranstalten*) to set up; *Fest* to arrange; (*gründen*) *Unternehmen* to start up.
(g) (*verspotten*) **jdn ~** (*inf*) to make fun of sb, to tease sb (*mit* about).
[2] *vi aux sein* (*dunkle Wolke*) to come up; (*Gewitter, Wolken auch*) to gather; (*aufmarschieren*) to march up ◆ **die Wache zog vor der Kaserne auf** the soldiers mounted guard in front of the barracks.
[3] *vr* to wind ◆ **sich von selbst ~** to be self-winding.

Aufzinsung *f* (*Fin*) accumulation.

Aufzucht *f* **(a)** *no pl* (*das Großziehen*) rearing, raising. **(b)** (*Nachwuchs*) young family.

Aufzug *m* **(a)** (*Fahrstuhl*) lift (*Brit*), elevator (*US*); (*Güter~ auch*) hoist.
(b) (*Phot*) wind-on.
(c) (*Marsch*) parade; (*Festzug auch*) procession ◆ **der ~ der Wache** the mounting of the guard.
(d) (*von Gewitter etc*) gathering.
(e) (*Turnen*) pull-up.
(f) (*Theat*) act.
(g) *no pl* (*pej inf: Kleidung*) get-up (*inf*).

Aufzug- *in cpds* lift (*Brit*), elevator (*US*); **~führer** *m* lift *or* elevator operator.

aufzwicken *vr sep* (*Aus inf*) **sich** (*dat*) **jdn ~** to chat sb up (*inf*).

aufzwingen *sep irreg* [1] *vt* **jdm etw/seinen Willen ~** to force sth on sb/impose one's will on sb.
[2] *vr* to force itself on one ◆ **sich jdm ~** to force itself on sb; (*Gedanke*) to strike sb forcibly; **das zwingt sich einem doch förmlich auf** the conclusion is unavoidable.

Aug|apfel *m* eyeball ◆ **jdn/etw wie seinen ~ hüten** to cherish sb/sth like life itself.

Auge *nt* **-s, -n** **(a)** (*Sehorgan*) eye ◆ **gute/schlechte ~n haben** to have good/bad eyesight *or* eyes; **die ~n aufmachen** *or* **aufsperren** (*inf*) *or* **auftun** (*inf*) to open one's eyes; **mit den ~n zwinkern/blinzeln** to wink/blink; **jdm in die ~n sehen** to look sb in the eye(s); **jdn mit** *or* **aus großen ~n ansehen** to look at sb wide-eyed; **etw mit eigenen ~n gesehen haben** to have seen sth with one's own eyes; **die ~n schließen** (*lit*) to close one's eyes; (*euph*) to fall asleep; **mit bloßem** *or* **nacktem ~** with the naked eye; **~n rechts/links!** (*Mil*) eyes right/left!; **mit verbundenen ~n** (*lit, fig*) blindfold; **etw im ~ haben** (*lit*) to have sth in one's eye; (*fig*) to have one's eye on sth; **ein sicheres ~ für etw haben** to have a good eye for sth; **da muß man seine ~n überall** *or* **hinten und vorn** (*inf*) **haben** you need eyes in the back of your head; **ich kann doch meine ~n nicht überall haben** I can't look everywhere at once; **ich hab' doch hinten keine ~n!** I don't have eyes in the back of my head; **haben Sie keine ~n im Kopf?** (*inf*) haven't you got any eyes in your head?, use your eyes!; **große ~n machen** to be wide-eyed; **jdm schöne** *or* **verliebte ~n machen** to make eyes at sb; **ich konnte kaum aus den ~n sehen** *or* **gucken** I could hardly see straight; **die ~n offen haben** *or* **offenhalten** to keep one's eyes open *or* skinned (*inf*) *or* peeled (*inf*); **wenn du mir noch einmal unter die ~n kommst, ...** if you let me see you *or* catch sight of you again ...; **geh mir aus den ~n!** get out of my sight!; **komm mir nicht unter die ~n!** keep out of my sight!; **jdn/etw mit den ~n verschlingen** to devour sb/sth with one's eyes; **er guckte** *or* **schaute** (*inf*) **sich** (*dat*) **die ~n aus dem Kopf** (*inf*) his eyes were popping out of his head (*inf*) *or* coming out on stalks (*inf*); **dem fallen bald die ~n raus** (*sl*) his eyes will pop out of his head in a minute (*inf*); **unter jds ~n** (*dat*) (*fig*) before sb's very eyes; **vor aller ~n** in front of everybody; **jdn/etw mit anderen ~n (an)sehen** to see sb/sth in a different light; **etwas fürs ~ sein** to be a delight to the eyes, to be a treat to look at; **nur fürs ~** good to look at but not much else (*inf*); **die ~n sind größer als der Magen** *or* **Bauch** (*inf*) his *etc* eyes are bigger than his *etc* stomach; **aus den ~n, aus dem Sinn** (*Prov*) out of sight, out of mind (*Prov*); **das ~ des Gesetzes** the law; **sich** (*dat*) **die ~n ausweinen** *or* **aus dem Kopf weinen** (*inf*) to cry one's eyes out; **soweit das ~ reicht** *or* **blicken kann** as far as the eye can see; **er hatte nur ~n für sie** he only had eyes for her; **ich habe kein ~ zugetan** I didn't sleep a wink; **da blieb kein ~ trocken** (*hum*) there wasn't a dry eye in the place; **ein ~ auf jdn/etw haben** (*aufpassen*) to keep an eye on sb/sth; **ein ~ auf jdn/etw (geworfen) haben** to have one's eye on sb/sth; **jdm etw aufs ~ drücken** (*inf*) to force *or* impose sth on sb; **die ~n vor etw** (*dat*) **verschließen** to close one's eyes to sth; **ein ~/beide ~n zudrücken** (*inf*) to turn a blind eye; **er läßt kein ~ von ihr** he can't let her out of his sight for two minutes together; **jdn im ~ behalten** (*beobachten*) to keep an eye on sb; (*vormerken*) to keep *or* bear sb in mind; **etw im ~ behalten** to keep *or* bear sth in mind; **sein Ziel im ~ behalten** to keep one's goal in mind; **sie ließen ihn nicht aus den ~n** they didn't let him out of their sight; **jdn/etw aus den ~n verlieren** to lose sight of sb/sth; (*fig*) to lose touch with sb/sth; **ins ~ stechen** (*fig*) to catch the eye; **das springt** *or* **fällt einem gleich ins ~** it hits you right in the face; **jdm etw vor ~n führen** (*fig*) to make sb aware of sth; **etw steht** *or* **schwebt jdm vor ~n** sb has sth in mind; **etw ins ~ fassen** to contemplate sth; **etw noch genau** *or* **lebhaft vor ~n haben** to remember sth clearly *or* vividly; **das muß man sich** (*dat*) **mal vor ~n führen!** just imagine it!; **es führt sich offenbar niemand richtig vor ~n, ...** obviously nobody is really aware ...; **jdm die ~n öffnen** (*fig*) to open sb's eyes; **ein ~ riskieren** (*hum*) to have a peep (*inf*); **das kann leicht ins ~ gehen** (*fig inf*) it might easily go wrong; **in den ~n der Leute/Öffentlichkeit** in the eyes of most people/the public; **in meinen ~n** in my opinion *or* view; **mit offenen ~n schlafen** (*fig*) to daydream; **ganz ~ und Ohr sein** to be all ears; **mit einem lachenden und einem weinenden ~** with mixed feelings; **~ in ~** face to face; **~ um ~, Zahn um Zahn** (*Bibl*) an eye for an eye and a tooth for a tooth; **vor meinem geistigen** *or* **inneren ~** in my mind's eye; **etw/den Tod**

vor ~n sehen to face sth/death; **dem Tod ins ~ sehen** to look death in the face.
(b) (*Knospenansatz*) (*bei Kartoffel*) eye; (*bei Zweig*) axil.
(c) (*Punkt, Tupfen*) eye; (*Fett~*) globule of fat; (*Punkt bei Spielen*) point ◆ **wieviel ~n hat der König?** how much is *or* how many points is the king worth?
(d) (*Rad*) **magisches ~** magic eye.
(e) (*von Hurrikan*) eye.

äugen *vi* to look.

Augen-: ~abstand *m* interocular distance (*form*), distance between the eyes; **~arzt** *m* eye specialist, ophthalmologist; **a~ärztlich** *adj attr Gutachten etc* ophthalmological; *Behandlung* eye *attr*, ophthalmic; **~aufschlag** *m* look; **~auswischerei** *f, no pl* (*fig inf*) *siehe* **~wischerei**; **~bad** *nt* eyebath; **ein ~bad nehmen** to bathe one's eye(s); **~bank** *f* eyebank; **~binde** *f* eye bandage; (*~klappe*) eye patch.

Augenblick *m* moment ◆ **alle ~e** constantly, all the time; **jeden ~** any time *or* minute *or* moment; **einen ~, bitte** one moment please!; **~ mal!** (*inf*) just a minute *or* second *or* sec! (*inf*); **im ~** at the moment; **im letzten/richtigen** *etc* **~** at the last/right *etc* moment; **im ersten ~** for a moment; **im nächsten ~** the (very) next moment; **er ist gerade im ~ gegangen** he just left this very moment; **es geschah in einem ~** it happened in an instant; **er zögerte keinen ~** he didn't hesitate for a moment.

augenblicklich [1] *adj* **(a)** (*sofortig*) immediate. **(b)** (*gegenwärtig*) present, current ◆ **die ~e Lage** the present *or* current situation, the situation at the moment. **(c)** (*vorübergehend*) temporary; (*einen Augenblick dauernd*) momentary.
[2] *adv* **(a)** (*sofort*) at once, immediately, instantly. **(b)** (*zur Zeit*) at the moment, presently.

augenblicks *adv* at once, immediately, instantly.

Augenblicks-: ~erfolg *m* short-lived success; **~idee** *f* idea thought up on the spur of the moment; **~sache** *f* quick job; **das ist nur eine ~sache** it'll just take a moment; **das war eine ~sache** it was over in a flash.

Augen-: ~blinzeln *nt* **~s,** *no pl* wink; **~braue** *f* eyebrow; **~brauenstift** *m* eyebrow pencil; **~deckel** *m siehe* **~lid**; **~entzündung** *f* inflammation of the eyes; **a~fällig** *adj* conspicuous; (*offensichtlich*) obvious; **~farbe** *f* colour of eyes; **Menschen mit einer dunklen ~farbe** people with dark eyes; **~fehler** *m* eye defect; **~flimmern** *nt* **-s,** *no pl* flickering before the eyes; **a~freundlich** *adj Bildschirm* easy on the eyes; **~glas** *nt* (*dated*) monocle; **~gläser** *pl* (*esp Aus*) glasses *pl*, spectacles *pl*; **~gymnastik** *f* eye exercises *pl*; **~heilkunde** *f* ophthalmology; **~höhe** *f* **in ~höhe** at eye level; **~höhle** *f* eye socket, orbit (*form*); **~klappe** *f* **(a)** eye patch; **(b)** (*für Pferde*) blinker, blinder (*US*); **~klinik** *f* eye clinic *or* hospital; **~krankheit** *f* eye disease; **~leiden** *nt* eye complaint; **~licht** *nt, no pl* (eye)sight; **~lid** *nt* eyelid; **~maß** *nt* eye; (*für Entfernungen*) eye for distance(s); (*fig*) perceptiveness; **nach ~maß** by eye; **~maß haben** (*lit*) to have a good eye (for distance(s)); (*fig*) to be able to assess *or* gauge things *or* situations; **ein gutes/schlechtes ~maß haben** to have a good eye/no eye (for distance(s)); **ein ~maß für etw haben** (*fig*) to have an eye for sth; **~mensch** *m* (*inf*) visual(ly oriented) person; **~merk** *nt* **-s,** *no pl* (*Aufmerksamkeit*) attention; **jds/sein ~merk auf etw** (*acc*) **lenken** *or* **richten** to direct sb's/one's attention to sth; **einer Sache** (*dat*) **sein ~merk zuwenden** to turn one's attention to a matter; **~nerv** *m* optic nerve; **~operation** *f* eye operation; **~optiker** *m* optician; **~paar** *nt* pair of eyes; **~prothese** *f* artificial eye; **~ränder** *pl* rims of the/one's eyes; **er hatte rote ~ränder, seine ~ränder waren gerötet** the rims of his eyes were red; **~ringe** *pl* rings round *or* under the/one's eyes; **~salbe** *f* eye ointment; **~schatten** *pl* shadows *pl* under *or* round the/one's eyes; **~schein** *m* **-(e)s,** *no pl* **(a)** (*Anschein*) appearance; **dem ~schein nach** by all appearances, to judge by appearances; **der ~schein trügt** appearances are deceptive; **nach dem ~schein urteilen** to judge by appearances; **(b) jdn/etw in ~schein nehmen** to look closely at sb/sth, to have a close look at sb/sth; **a~scheinlich** *adj* obvious, evident; **die beiden sind a~scheinlich zerstritten** the two have obviously *or* clearly had a quarrel; **~schmaus** *m* (*hum*) feast for the eyes; **~spiegel** *m* ophthalmoscope; **~spiegelung** *f* ophthalmoscopy; **~stern** *m* **(a)** (*Liter: Pupille*) pupil, orb (*poet*); **(b)** (*dated: Liebstes*) apple of one's eye, darling; **~tropfen** *pl* eyedrops *pl*; **~weide** *f* feast *or* treat for the eyes; **nicht gerade eine ~weide** (*iro*) a bit of an eyesore; **~wimper** *f* eyelash; **~winkel** *m* corner of the/one's eye; **~wischerei** *f* (*fig*) eyewash; **~zahl** *f* (*Cards etc*) number of points; **~zahn** *m* eyetooth; **~zeuge** *m* eyewitness (*bei* to); **ich war ~zeuge dieses Unfalls** *or* **bei diesem Unfall** I was an eyewitness to this accident; **~zeugenbericht** *m* eyewitness account; **~zwinkern** *nt* **-s,** *no pl* winking; **a~zwinkernd** *adj* winking *attr*; (*fig*) sly; **er grinste mich a~zwinkernd an** he grinned at me, winking; **jdm etw a~zwinkernd zu verstehen geben** to give sb to understand sth with a wink.

Augiasstall *m* (*fig geh*) dunghill, Augean stables *pl* (*liter*).

-äugig *adj suf* -eyed.

Augur *m* **-s** *or* **-en, -en** (*Hist, fig geh*) augur.

Augurenlächeln *nt* (*pej geh*) knowing smile.

August[1] *m* **-(e)s, -e** August; *siehe* **März**.

August[2] *m* **-s** Augustus ◆ **der dumme ~** (*inf*) the clown; **den dummen ~ spielen** to play *or* act the clown *or* fool.

August|apfel *m* Laxton.

Augustfeier *f* (*Sw*) August public holiday.

Augustiner(mönch) *m* **-s, -** Augustinian (monk).

Auktion *f* auction.

Auktionator(in *f*) [-'to:rın] *m* auctioneer.

Auktionshaus *nt* auction house *or* company, auctioneers *pl*.

Aula *f* **-, Aulen** (*Sch, Univ etc*) (assembly) hall; (*Atrium*) atrium.

Au-pair- [o'pɛ:r]: **~-Mädchen** *nt* au-pair (girl); **als ~-Mädchen arbeiten** to work (as an) au-pair; **~-Stelle** *f* au-pair job.

Aura *f* **-,** *no pl* (*Med, geh*) aura.

Aureole *f* **-, -n** (*Art*) aureole, halo; (*Met*) corona, aureole; (*fig rare*) aura.

Aurikel *f* **-, -n** (*Bot*) auricula.

Aurora *f* **-s** (*Myth, liter*) Aurora.

aus [1] *prep +dat* **(a)** (*räumlich*) from; (*aus dem Inneren von*) out of ◆ **~ dem Fenster/der Tür** out of the window/door; **~ unserer Mitte** from our midst; **~ der Flasche trinken** to drink from *or* out of the bottle; **jdm ~ einer Verlegenheit helfen** to help sb out of a difficulty.
(b) (*Herkunft, Quelle bezeichnend*) from ◆ **~ dem Deutschen** from (the) German; **~ ganz Frankreich** from all over France; **~ guter Familie** from *or* of a good family; **ein Wort ~ dem Zusammenhang herausgreifen** to take a word out of (its) context.
(c) (*auf Ursache deutend*) out of ◆ **~ Haß/Gehorsam/Mitleid** out of hatred/obedience/sympathy; **~ Erfahrung** from experience; **~ Furcht vor/Liebe zu** for fear/love of; **~ dem Grunde, daß** ... for the reason that ...; **~ einer Laune heraus** on (an) impulse; **~ Spaß** for fun, for a laugh (*inf*); **~ Unachtsamkeit** due to carelessness; **~ Versehen** by mistake; **~ sich heraus** of one's own accord, off one's own bat (*inf*); **ein Mord ~ Berechnung** a calculated murder; **ein Mord** *or* **ein Verbrechen ~ Leidenschaft** a crime of passion.
(d) (*zeitlich*) from ◆ **~ dem Barock** from the Baroque period.
(e) (*beschaffen ~*) (made out) of ◆ **ein Herz ~ Stein** a heart of stone.
(f) (*Herstellungsart*) out of, from; (*fig: Ausgangspunkt*) out of ◆ **kann man ~ diesem Stoff noch etwas machen?** can something still be made out of *or* from this material?; **einen Soldaten/Pfarrer ~ jdm machen** to make a soldier/minister (out) of sb; **einen anständigen Menschen ~ jdm machen** to make sb into a decent person; **was ist ~ ihm/dieser Sache geworden?** what has become of him/this?; **~ der Sache ist nichts geworden** nothing came of it; **~ ihm wird einmal ein guter Arzt** he'll make a good doctor one day; **~ mir ist nichts geworden** I never got anywhere (in life).
(g) ~ dem Gleichgewicht out of balance; (*Mensch, Gegenstand*) off balance; **~ der Mode** out of fashion.
(h) (*Aus: in*) in ◆ **eine Prüfung ~ Geschichte** an examination in *or* on history.
(i) (*Typ*) **gesetzt ~** ... set in ...
[2] *adv siehe auch* **aussein (a)** (*Sport*) out; (*Ftbl, Rugby auch*) out of play, in touch.
(b) (*inf: vorbei, zu Ende*) over ◆ **~ jetzt!** that's enough!, that'll do now! (*inf*); **~ und vorbei** over and done with.
(c) (*gelöscht*) out; (*an Geräten*) off ◆ **Licht ~!** lights out!
(d) (*in Verbindung mit von*) **vom Fenster ~** from the window; **von München ~** from Munich; **von sich** (*dat*) **~** off one's own bat (*inf*), of one's own accord; **von ihm ~** as far as he's concerned; **ok, von mir ~** OK, if you like; *no pl siehe* **ein**.

Aus *nt* **-, - (a)** *no pl* (*Ftbl, Rugby*) touch *no art* ◆ **ins ~ gehen** to go out of play; (*seitlich*) to go into touch; **ins politische ~ geraten** to end up on the political scrapheap. **(b)** *no pl* (*Ausscheiden*) exit (*für* of). **(c)** (*Ende*) end ◆ **das ~ für die Firma ist unabwendbar** the company is doomed to close down.

aus|arbeiten *sep* [1] *vt* to work out; (*errichten, entwerfen auch*) *System, Gedankengebäude* to elaborate, to draw up; (*vorbereiten*) to prepare; (*formulieren auch*) to formulate, to compose.
[2] *vr* to work until one is fit to drop; (*Sport*) to have a work-out.

Aus|arbeitung *f siehe vt* working out; elaboration, drawing up; preparation; formulation, composition.

aus|arten *vi sep aux sein* **(a)** (*Party etc*) to get out of control ◆ **~ in** (*+acc*) *or* **zu** to degenerate into.
(b) (*ungezogen etc werden*) to get out of hand, to become unruly; (*pöbelhaft, ordinär etc werden*) to misbehave; to use bad language.

aus|atmen *vti sep* to breathe out, to exhale.

ausbacken *vt sep irreg* **(a)** (*in Fett backen*) to fry. **(b)** (*zu Ende backen*) to bake (for) long enough; (*durchbacken*) to bake (right) through.

ausbaden *vt sep* (*inf*) to carry the can for (*inf*), to pay for ◆ **ich muß jetzt alles ~** I have to carry the can (*inf*).

ausbaggern *vt sep Graben* to excavate; *Fahrrinne, Schlamm* to dredge (out).

ausbalancieren* *sep* (*lit, fig*) [1] *vt* to balance (out).
[2] *vr* to balance (each other out).

ausbaldowern* *vt sep* (*inf*) to scout *or* nose out (*inf*) ◆ **~, ob** ... to scout *or* nose around to find out whether ... (*inf*).

Ausball *m* (*Sport*) **bei ~** when the ball goes out of play.

Ausbau *m* **-(e)s, -ten (a)** *siehe vt* removal; extension (*zu* into); reinforcement; conversion (*zu* (in)to); fitting out; building up, cultivation; elaboration; consolidation, strengthening. **(b)** (*am Haus*) extension. **(c)** (*Einzelgehöft*) (small) farmstead (*separated from main settlement*).

ausbauen *vt sep* **(a)** (*herausmontieren*) to remove (*aus* from).
(b) (*lit, fig: erweitern, vergrößern*) to extend (*zu* into); *Befestigungsanlagen* to reinforce; (*umbauen*) to convert (*zu* (in)to); (*innen ~*) to fit out; *Beziehungen, Freundschaft* to build up, to cultivate; *Plan* to elaborate; (*festigen*) *Position, Vorsprung* to consolidate, to strengthen; *siehe* **ausgebaut**.

ausbaufähig *adj Position* with good prospects; *Geschäft, Produktion, Markt, Computer* expandable; *Beziehungen* that can be built up; *Machtstellung* that can be consolidated *or* strengthened; (*inf*) *Schüler, Mitarbeiter* promising.

ausbedingen *vr sep irreg* **sich** (*dat*) **etw ~** to insist on sth, to make sth a condition; **sich** (*dat*) **~, daß** ... to stipulate that ..., to make it a condition that

...; **ich bin dazu bereit, aber ich bedinge mir aus, ...** I'm prepared to do it but (only) on condition that ...; **sich** (*dat*) **das Recht ~, etw zu tun** to reserve the right to do sth.

ausbeißen *vr sep irreg* **sich** (*dat*) **einen Zahn ~** to break *or* lose a tooth (*when biting into sth*); **sich** (*dat*) **an etw** (*dat*) **die Zähne ~** (*fig*) to have a tough time of it with sth.

ausbekommen* *vt sep irreg* (*inf*) to get off.

ausbessern *vt sep* to repair; *Gegenstand, Wäsche etc auch* to mend; *Roststelle etc* to remove; *Gemälde etc* to restore; *Fehler* to correct.

Ausbesserung *f siehe vt* repair; mending; removal; restoration; correction.

Ausbesserungs-: ~arbeiten *pl* repair work *sing*; **a~bedürftig** *adj* in need of repair *etc*; **~werk** *nt* (*Rail*) repair shop.

ausbetonieren* *vt sep* to concrete.

ausbeulen *sep* [1] *vt* (**a**) *Kleidung* to make baggy; *Hut* to make floppy; *siehe* **ausgebeult.** (**b**) (*Beule entfernen*) to remove a dent/dents in; (*Tech: durch Hämmern*) to beat out.
[2] *vr* (*Hose*) to go baggy; (*Hut*) to go floppy.

Ausbeulung *f* (*Tech: das Ausbeulen*) beating (out).

Ausbeute *f* (*Gewinn*) profit, gain; (*Ertrag einer Grube etc*) yield (*an +dat* in); (*fig*) result(s); (*Einnahmen*) proceeds *pl* ♦ **die ~ an verwertbaren Erkenntnissen war gering** the useful results (gleaned) were minimal.

ausbeuten *vt sep* (*lit, fig*) to exploit; (*Min*) *eine Grube auch* to work; (*Agr*) *Boden* to overwork, to deplete.

Ausbeuter(in *f*) *m* **-s, -** exploiter ♦ **~ und Ausgebeutete** the exploiters and the exploited.

Ausbeuterei *f* (*pej*) exploitation.

Ausbeutergesellschaft *f* society based on exploitation.

ausbeuterisch *adj* exploitative (*form*); *Firma* which exploits ♦ **die Arbeiter ~ zu Überstunden antreiben** to exploit the workers by forcing them to work overtime.

Ausbeutung *f siehe vt* exploitation; working; overworking, depletion.

ausbezahlen* *vt sep Geld* to pay out; *Arbeitnehmer* to pay off; (*abfinden*) *Erben etc* to buy out, to pay off ♦ **in bar ausbezahlt** paid in cash; **wieviel kriegst du pro Woche ausbezahlt?** what is your weekly take-home pay?

Ausbezahlung *f* payment; (*von Erben etc*) buying out, paying off.

ausbieten *vt sep irreg* to put on offer, to offer (for sale) ♦ **ausgeboten werden** to be on offer; (*bei Versteigerung auch*) to be up for auction.

ausbilden *sep* [1] *vt* (**a**) (*beruflich, Sport, Mil*) to train; (*unterrichten auch*) to instruct; (*akademisch*) to educate ♦ **sich in etw** (*dat*)/**als** *or* **zu etw ~ lassen** (*esp Arbeiter, Lehrling*) to train in sth/as sth; (*studieren*) to study sth/to study to be sth; (*Qualifikation erwerben*) to qualify in sth/as sth; **sich am Klavier** *etc* **~ lassen** to have piano *etc* tuition; **jdn als Sänger ~ lassen** to have sb trained as a singer; **ein ausgebildeter Übersetzer** a trained/qualified translator.
(**b**) *Fähigkeiten* to develop, to cultivate; (*Mus*) *Stimme* to train.
(**c**) (*formen*) to form; (*gestalten*) to shape; (*entwickeln*) to develop ♦ **etw oval ~** to give sth an oval shape; (*Designer etc*) to design sth with an oval shape.
[2] *vr* (**a**) (*sich entwickeln*) to develop; (*sich bilden*) to form.
(**b**) (*sich schulen*) **sich in etw** (*dat*) **~** (*esp Arbeiter, Lehrling*) to train in sth; (*studieren*) to study sth; (*Qualifikation erwerben*) to qualify in sth.

Ausbilder(in *f*) *m* **-s, -** instructor/instructress.

Ausbildner *m* **-s, -** (*Aus Mil*) instructor.

Ausbildung *f siehe vt* training; instruction; education; development, cultivation; formation; shaping/shape ♦ **er ist noch in der ~** he's still a trainee; he hasn't finished his education.

Ausbildungs-: ~beihilfe *f* (*für Schüler*) (education) grant; (*für Lehrling*) training allowance; **~beruf** *m* occupation that requires training; **~betrieb** *m company that takes on trainees*; **~förderung** *f* promotion of training/education; (*Stipendium*) grant; **~gang** *m* training; **~jahr** *nt* year of training; **~kompanie** *f* training unit (*for weapons training*); **~kurs(us)**, **~lehrgang** *m* training course; **~methode** *f* training method, method of training; **~munition** *f* blank ammunition (*used in training*); **~offizier** *m* training officer; **~ordnung** *f* training regulations *pl*; **~platz** *m* place to train; (*Stelle*) training vacancy; **~stand** *m* level of training; **~stätte** *f* place of training; **~versicherung** *f* education insurance; **~vertrag** *m* articles *pl* of apprenticeship; **~zeit** *f* period of training; **nach zweijähriger ~zeit** after a two-year period of training *or* training period; **~ziel** *nt* aims *pl* of education; **die ~ziele der Schule** the aims of school education *or* education at school.

ausbitten *vr sep irreg* **sich** (*dat*) **(von jdm) etw ~** (*geh*) to ask (sb) for sth, to request sth (from sb) (*form*); **das möchte ich mir (auch) ausgebeten haben!** I should think so too!; **ich bitte mir Ruhe aus!** I must *or* will have silence!

ausblasen *vt sep irreg* to blow out; *Hochofen* to shut down, to extinguish; *Ei* to blow.

ausbleiben *vi sep irreg aux sein* (*fortbleiben*) to stay out; (*nicht erscheinen: Gäste, Schüler, Schneefall*) to fail to appear; (*nicht eintreten: Erwartung, Befürchtung*) to fail to materialize; (*überfällig sein*) to be overdue; (*aufhören: Puls, Atmung etc*) to stop ♦ **die Strafe/ein Krieg wird nicht ~** punishment/a war is inevitable; **das blieb nicht lange aus** that wasn't long in coming; **es konnte nicht ~, daß ...** it was inevitable that ...; **bei manchen Patienten bleiben diese Symptome aus** in some patients these symptoms are absent *or* do not appear.

Ausbleiben *nt* **-s,** *no pl* (*Fehlen*) absence; (*Nichterscheinen*) non-appearance ♦ **bei ~ von ...** in the absence of ...; **bei ~ der Periode** if your period doesn't come.

ausbleichen *vti sep irreg aux sein* to fade, to bleach.

ausblenden *sep* [1] *vti* (*TV etc*) to fade out; (*plötzlich*) to cut out.
[2] *vr* **sich (aus einer Übertragung) ~** to leave a transmission.

Ausblendung *f siehe vt* fade-out; cutting-out, cut.

Ausblick *m* (**a**) view (*auf +acc* of), outlook (*auf +acc* over, onto) ♦ **ein Zimmer mit ~ auf die Straße/aufs Meer** a room overlooking the street/with a view of the sea *or* overlooking the sea.
(**b**) (*fig*) prospect, outlook (*auf +acc, in +acc* for) ♦ **einen ~ auf etw** (*acc*) **geben** to give the prospects for sth.

ausblicken *vi sep* (*geh*) **nach jdm ~** to look for sb.

ausbluten *sep* [1] *vi* (**a**) *aux sein* (*verbluten*) to bleed to death; (*fig*) to be bled white ♦ **ein Schwein ~ lassen** to bleed a pig dry. (**b**) (*Wunde*) to stop bleeding.
[2] *vt* (*fig*) to bleed white.

ausbohren *vt sep* to bore; (*mit Bohrgerät, Med*) to drill; (*herausbohren*) to bore/drill out.

ausbomben *vt sep* to bomb out ♦ **die Ausgebombten** people who have been bombed out (of their homes).

ausbooten *sep* [1] *vt* (**a**) (*inf*) *jdn* to kick *or* boot out (*inf*). (**b**) (*Naut*) to disembark (*in boats*); (*abladen*) to unload.
[2] *vi* (*Naut*) to disembark (*in boats*).

ausborgen *vt sep* (*inf*) **sich** (*dat*) **etw (von jdm) ~** to borrow sth (from sb); **jdm etw ~** to lend sb sth, to lend sth (out) to sb.

ausbraten *sep irreg* [1] *vt* (**a**) (*zu Ende braten*) to roast/fry (for) long enough; (*durchbraten*) to roast/fry (right) through. (**b**) (*auslassen*) *Speck* to fry the fat out of.
[2] *vi aux sein* (*Fett*) to run out (*aus* of) ♦ **ausgebratenes Fett** melted bacon *etc* fat.

ausbrechen *sep irreg* [1] *vt* (**a**) (*herausbrechen*) *Steine* to break off (*aus* from); *Mauer* to break up; *Tür, Fenster* to put in ♦ **sich** (*dat*) **einen Zahn ~** to break off a tooth.
(**b**) (*erbrechen*) to bring up, to vomit (up).
[2] *vi aux sein* (**a**) (*lit, fig: sich befreien*) to break out (*aus* of) (*auch Mil*), to escape (*aus* from); (*herausbrechen*) to break *or* come away.
(**b**) (*Richtung ändern: Pferd, Wagen*) to swerve; (*Auto auch*) to career out of control.
(**c**) (*Krieg, Seuche, Feuer, Schweiß etc*) to break out; (*Jubel, Zorn etc*) to erupt, to explode; (*Vulkan*) to erupt ♦ **in Gelächter/Tränen** *or* **Weinen ~** to burst into laughter/tears, to burst out laughing/crying; **in Jubel ~** to erupt with jubilation; **in den Ruf: „ ...“ ~** to burst out with the cry: “...”; **in Schweiß ~** to break out in a sweat; **bei dir ist wohl der Wohlstand ausgebrochen** (*fig inf*) have you struck it rich?

Ausbrecher(in *f*) *m* **-s, -** (**a**) (*inf*) (*Gefangener*) escaped prisoner, escapee; (*notorischer ~*) jail-breaker (*inf*); (*Tier*) escaped animal, runaway. (**b**) (*Pferd*) horse that swerves round jumps.

ausbreiten *sep* [1] *vt Landkarte, Handtuch* to spread (out); *Flügel, Äste* to spread (out), to extend; *Arme* to stretch out, to extend; (*ausstellen, fig: zeigen*) to display; *Licht, Wärme* to spread ♦ **einen Plan/sein Leben** *etc* **vor jdm ~** to unfold a plan to sb/to lay one's whole life before sb.
[2] *vr* (**a**) (*sich verbreiten*) to spread.
(**b**) (*sich erstrecken*) to extend, to stretch (out), to spread out.
(**c**) (*inf: sich breitmachen*) to spread oneself out.
(**d**) **sich über etw** (*acc*) **~** (*fig*) to dwell on sth; **sich in Einzelheiten ~** to go into great detail; **darüber will ich mich jetzt nicht ~** I'd rather not go into that now.

Ausbreitung *f* (*das Sichausbreiten*) spread; (*das Ausbreiten*) spreading.

Ausbreitungsdrang *m* expansionist drive.

ausbrennen *sep irreg* [1] *vi aux sein* (**a**) (*zu Ende brennen*) to burn out; (*Vulkan*) to become extinct. (**b**) (*völlig verbrennen*) to be burnt out, to be gutted ♦ **er ist ausgebrannt** (*fig*) he's burnt out.
[2] *vt* to burn out; (*Sonne: ausdörren*) to scorch; (*Med*) to cauterize.

ausbringen *vt sep irreg* (**a**) *Trinkspruch* to propose. (**b**) (*Naut*) *Boot, Anker* to lower. (**c**) (*Typ*) *Zeile* to space out.

Ausbruch *m* (**a**) (*aus* from) (*aus Gefängnis*) break-out (*auch Mil*), escape (*auch fig*). (**b**) (*Beginn*) outbreak; (*von Vulkan*) eruption ♦ **zum ~ kommen** to break out. (**c**) (*fig*) (*Gefühls~, Zorn~*) outburst; (*stärker*) eruption, explosion ♦ **zum ~ kommen** to erupt, to explode.

Ausbruchs-: ~herd *m* (*Geol*) focus (*of an earthquake*); **~versuch** *m* (*aus* from) attempted break-out (*auch Mil*) *or* escape, break-out *or* escape attempt; (*fig*) attempt at escape.

ausbrüten *vt sep* to hatch; (*esp in Brutkasten*) to incubate; (*fig inf*) *Plan etc* to cook up (*inf*), to hatch (up).

ausbuchen *vt sep siehe* **ausgebucht.**

ausbüchsen *vi sep* (*N Ger: ausreißen*) to break out, to run away.

ausbuchten *sep* [1] *vt Ufer* to hollow out; *Straße* to make a curve in the side of; *Wand* to round out.
[2] *vr* to bulge *or* curve out.

Ausbuchtung *f* bulge; (*von Strand*) (small) cove.

ausbuddeln *vt sep* (*inf*) to dig up (*auch fig inf*).

ausbügeln *vt sep* to iron out; (*inf*) *Fehler, Verlust, Mängel* to make good; *Mißverständnis, Angelegenheit* to iron out (*inf*).

ausbuhen *vt sep* (*inf*) to boo.

Ausbund *m* **-(e)s,** *no pl* (*von Tugend, Schönheit*) paragon, model, epitome ♦ **ein ~ von Tugend** a paragon *or* model of virtue, the epitome of virtue; **er ist ein ~ an** *or* **von Gemeinheit/Frechheit** he is baseness/cheek itself *or* personified.

ausbürgern *vt sep* **jdn ~** to expatriate sb.

Ausbürgerung *f* expatriation.
ausbürsten *vt sep* to brush out (*aus* of); *Anzug* to brush.
ausbüxen *vi sep aux sein* (*hum inf*) to run off, to scarper (*sl*) ◆ **jdm ~** to run away from sb.
Ausdauer *f -, no pl* staying power, stamina; (*im Ertragen*) endurance; (*Beharrlichkeit*) perseverance, persistence, tenacity; (*Hartnäckigkeit*) persistence ◆ **beim Lernen/Lesen keine ~ haben** to have no staying power when it comes to learning/reading.
ausdauernd *adj* **(a)** (*Mensch*) with staying power, with stamina; (*im Ertragen*) with endurance; (*beharrlich*) persevering, tenacious; (*hartnäckig*) persistent; *Bemühungen, Anstrengungen* untiring ◆ **~ lernen** to apply oneself to learning. **(b)** (*Bot: Pflanze*) perennial.
Ausdauertraining *nt* stamina training.
ausdehnbar *adj* expandable; (*dehnbar*) *Gummi etc* elastic; (*fig*) extendable (*auf +acc* to), extensible.
ausdehnen *sep* [1] *vt* **(a)** (*vergrößern*) to expand; (*dehnen*) to stretch, to extend; (*länger machen*) to elongate, to stretch.
(b) (*fig*) to extend; (*zeitlich auch*) to prolong (*auf +acc* to).
[2] *vr* **(a)** (*größer werden*) to expand; (*durch Dehnen*) to stretch; (*sich erstrecken*) to extend, to stretch (*bis* as far as) ◆ **die Seuche/der Krieg dehnte sich über das ganze Land aus** the epidemic/the war spread over the whole country.
(b) (*fig*) to extend (*über +acc* over, *bis* as far as, to); (*zeitlich*) to go on (*bis* until), to extend (*bis* until); *siehe* **ausgedehnt.**
Ausdehnung *f* **(a)** (*das Ausdehnen*) *siehe vt* expansion; stretching, extension; elongation; extension; prolongation. **(b)** (*Umfang*) expanse; (*Math: von Raum*) extension ◆ **eine ~ von 10.000 km² haben** to cover an area of 10,000 sq km.
Ausdehnungs-: a~fähig *adj* (*esp Phys*) capable of expansion, expansile, expansible; **~fähigkeit** *f* ability to expand; **~vermögen** *nt* (*esp Phys*) capacity to expand, expansibility.
ausdenken *vt sep irreg* **sich** (*dat*) **etw ~** (*erfinden*) to think sth up; *Idee, Plan auch* to devise sth; (*in Einzelheiten*) to think sth out, to devise sth; *Wunsch* to think of sth; *Entschuldigung auch* to contrive sth; *Überraschung* to plan sth; *Geschichte auch* to make sth up; (*sich vorstellen*) to imagine sth; (*durchdenken*) to think sth through; **eine ausgedachte Geschichte** a made-up story; **das ist nicht auszudenken** (*unvorstellbar*) it's inconceivable; (*zu schrecklich etc*) it doesn't bear thinking about; **da mußt du dir schon etwas anderes ~!** (*inf*) you'll have to think of something better than that!
ausdeuten *vt sep* to interpret; *Äußerung, Wort auch* to construe ◆ **falsch ~** to misinterpret; to misconstrue.
ausdeutschen *vt sep* (*Aus inf*) **jdm etw ~** to explain sth to sb in words of one syllable *or* ≃ in plain English.
Ausdeutung *f* interpretation.
ausdienen *vi sep* **ausgedient haben** (*Mil old*) to have finished one's military service; (*im Ruhestand sein*) to have been discharged; (*fig inf*) to have had its day; (*Kugelschreiber etc*) to be used up *or* finished; *siehe* **ausgedient.**
ausdiskutieren* *sep* [1] *vt Thema* to discuss fully.
[2] *vi* (*zu Ende diskutieren*) to finish discussing *or* talking.
ausdorren *vi sep aux sein siehe* **ausdörren 2.**
ausdörren *sep* [1] *vt* to dry up; *Kehle* to parch; *Pflanzen* to shrivel.
[2] *vi aux sein* to dry up; (*Boden auch*) to become parched; (*Pflanze auch*) to shrivel up; *siehe* **ausgedörrt.**
ausdrehen *vt sep* (*ausschalten*) to turn *or* switch off; *Licht auch* to turn out; (*rare: herausdrehen*) *Glühbirne etc* to unscrew; (*Tech*) *Bohrloch* to drill, to bore; *Gelenk* to dislocate.
ausdreschen *sep irreg* [1] *vt* to thresh (fully).
[2] *vi* (*das Dreschen beenden*) to finish (the) threshing.
Ausdruck[1] *m* **-(e)s, Ausdrücke (a)** *no pl* (*Gesichts~*) expression ◆ **der ~ ihrer Gesichter** the expression(s) on their faces.
(b) *no pl* **als ~ meiner Dankbarkeit** as an expression of my gratitude; **mit dem ~ des Bedauerns** (*form*) expressing regret, with an expression of regret; **ohne jeden ~ singen/spielen** to sing/play without any expression; **etw zum ~ bringen, einer Sache** (*dat*) **~ geben** *or* **verleihen** (*form*) to express sth, to give expression to sth; **in seinen Worten/seinem Verhalten kam Mitleid zum ~** his words expressed/behaviour showed his sympathy.
(c) (*Wort*) expression; (*Math, Fach~ auch*) term ◆ **das ist gar kein ~!** that's not the word for it; **sich im ~ vergreifen** to use the wrong word.
Ausdruck[2] *m* **-(e)s, -e** (*von Computer etc*) print-out; (*Typ*) end of printing.
ausdrucken *sep* [1] *vt* **(a)** (*Typ*) (*fertig drucken*) to finish printing; (*ungekürzt drucken*) to print in full *or* out ◆ **ausgedruckte Exemplare** fully printed copies. **(b)** (*Telec, Comput*) to print out.
[2] *vi* (*Buchstaben etc*) to come out.
ausdrücken *sep* [1] *vt* **(a)** to press out, to squeeze out; *Pickel* to squeeze; (*ausmachen*) to put out; *Zigarette* to stub out ◆ **den Saft einer Zitrone ~** to press *or* squeeze juice out of a lemon, to squeeze a lemon.
(b) (*zum Ausdruck bringen*) to express (*jdm* to sb); (*Verhalten, Gesicht auch*) *Trauer etc* to reveal ◆ **um es anders/gelinde auszudrücken** to put it another way/mildly; **anders ausgedrückt** in other words; **einfach ausgedrückt** put simply, in simple terms, in words of one syllable.
[2] *vr* (*Mensch*) to express oneself; (*Emotion*) to be expressed *or* revealed ◆ **in ihrem Gesicht/Verhalten drückte sich Verzweiflung aus** her face/behaviour showed her despair; **er kann sich gewandt ~** he is very articulate.
ausdrücklich [1] *adj attr Wunsch, Genehmigung* express.
[2] *adv* expressly, explicitly; (*besonders*) particularly ◆ **etw ~ betonen** to emphasize sth particularly *or* specifically.
Ausdrücklichkeit *f*: **in aller ~** expressly, explicitly.
Ausdrucks-: ~bedürfnis *nt* need to express oneself; **a~fähig** *adj* expressive; (*gewandt*) articulate; **~fähigkeit** *f siehe adj* expressiveness; articulateness; **~form** *f* form of expression; **~kraft** *f, no pl* expressiveness; (*von Schriftsteller*) articulateness, word-power; **a~leer** *adj* expressionless; **~leere** *f* expressionlessness; **a~los** *adj* inexpressive; *Gesicht, Blick auch* expressionless; **~losigkeit** *f siehe adj* inexpressiveness; expressionlessness; **~mittel** *nt* means of expression; **~möglichkeit** *f* mode of expression; **a~schwach** *adj* inexpressive; **a~stark** *adj* expressive; **~tanz** *m* free dance; **a~voll** *adj* expressive; **~weise** *f* way of expressing oneself, mode of expression; **was ist denn das für eine ~weise!** what sort of language is that to use!
ausdünnen *sep* [1] *vt* **(a)** *Pflanzen, Haare* to thin out. **(b)** *Verkehr, Kapital* to reduce.
[2] *vr* (*Kursus*) to thin out.
ausdünsten *sep* [1] *vt Geruch* to give off; (*Med, Bot auch*) to transpire.
[2] *vi* (*Dunst/Geruch absondern*) to give off vapour/a smell; (*Bot, Med*) to transpire.
Ausdünstung *f* **(a)** (*das Ausdünsten*) evaporation; (*von Körper, Pflanze*) transpiration. **(b)** (*Dampf*) vapour; (*Geruch*) fume, smell; (*von Tier*) scent; (*von Mensch*) smell; (*fig*) emanation.
aus|einander *adv* **(a)** (*voneinander entfernt, getrennt*) apart ◆ **weit ~** far apart; *Augen, Beine etc* wide apart; *Zähne* widely spaced; *Meinungen* very different; **die Ereignisse liegen (um) zwei Tage ~** the events are separated by two days *or* are two days apart; **etw ~ schreiben** to write sth as two words; **zwei Kinder ~ setzen** to separate two children; **sich ~ setzen** to sit apart; **die beiden sind (im Alter) ein Jahr ~** there is a year between the two of them; **~ sein** (*inf: Paar*) to have broken *or* split up; **die Verlobung ist ~** (*inf*) the engagement is off.
(b) (*jedes aus dem anderen*) from one another ◆ **diese Begriffe kann man nur ~ erklären** one can only explain these concepts in relation to one another.
⚠**aus|einander-: ~bekommen*** *vt sep irreg* to be able to get apart; **~biegen** *vt sep irreg* to bend apart; **~brechen** *sep irreg* [1] *vt* to break in two; [2] *vi aux sein* (*lit, fig*) to break up; **~breiten** *vt sep siehe* **~falten; ~bringen** *vt sep irreg* (*inf*) to manage *or* be able to get apart (*auch fig*); **~dividieren*** *vt sep* to divide ◆ **eine Gruppe ~dividieren** to create divisions within a group; **~driften** *vi sep* to drift apart; **~entwickeln*** *vr sep* to grow apart (from each other); (*Partner*) to drift apart; **~fallen** *vi sep irreg aux sein* **(a)** (*zerfallen*) to fall apart; (*fig auch*) to collapse; **(b)** (*fig: sich gliedern*) to divide up (*in +acc* into); **~falten** *vt sep* to unfold; **~fliegen** *vi sep irreg aux sein* to fly apart; (*nach allen Seiten*) to fly in all directions; **~fließen** *vi sep irreg aux sein* (*nach allen Seiten*) to flow in all directions; (*zerfließen*) to melt; (*Farben*) to run; **~gehen** *vi sep irreg aux sein* **(a)** (*lit, fig: sich trennen*) (*Menschen, Vorhang*) to part, to separate; (*Menge*) to disperse; (*Versammlung, Ehe etc*) to break up; (*auseinanderfallen: Schrank etc*) to fall apart; **(b)** (*sich verzweigen: Weg etc*) to divide, to branch, to fork; (*zwei Wege*) to diverge; (*fig: Ansichten etc*) to diverge, to differ; **(c)** (*inf: dick werden*) to get fat; *siehe* **Hefeteig; ~halten** *vt sep irreg* to keep apart; (*unterscheiden*) *Begriffe* to distinguish between; *esp Zwillinge etc* to tell apart; **~jagen** *vt sep* to scatter; **~kennen** *vt sep irreg* (*inf*) to tell apart; **~klaffen** *vi sep aux sein* to gape open; (*fig: Meinungen*) to be far apart, to diverge (wildly); **~klamüsern*** *vt sep* (*dial, hum*) to sort out; **jdm etw ~klamüsern** to spell sth out for sb; **~klauben** *vt sep* (*esp S Ger, Aus, Sw*) to sort out; **~kriegen** *vt sep* (*inf*) *siehe* **~bekommen; ~laufen** *vi sep irreg aux sein* **(a)** (*zerlaufen*) to melt; (*Farbe*) to run; (*sich ausbreiten*) to spread; **(b)** (*inf: sich trennen*) to break up; (*Menge*) to disperse; (*sich ~entwickeln*) to go their separate ways; **(c)** (*Wege*) to divide, to fork, to diverge; **~leben** *vr sep* to drift apart (*mit* from); **~machen** *vt sep* (*inf*) **(a)** (*~nehmen*) to take apart; **(b)** (*~falten*) to unfold; **(c)** (*spreizen*) *Arme, Beine* to spread (apart), to open; **~nehmen** *vt sep irreg* to take apart; *Maschine etc auch* to dismantle; (*kritisch*) to tear apart *or* to pieces; **~pflücken** *vt sep siehe* **zerpflücken; ~reißen** *vt sep irreg* to tear *or* rip apart; (*fig*) *Familie* to tear apart; **~schlagen** *vt sep irreg* (*zerschlagen*) to hack apart; (*öffnen*) *Mantel, Vorhang* to fling open; **~schrauben** *vt sep* to unscrew; **~setzen** *sep* [1] *vt* (*fig*) (*jdm* to sb) to explain; (*schriftlich auch*) to set out; [2] *vr* **sich mit etw ~setzen** (*sich befassen*) to have a good look at sth; **sich kritisch mit etw ~setzen** to have a critical look at sth; **sich damit ~setzen, was/weshalb ...** to tackle the problem of what/why ...; **sich mit jdm ~setzen** to talk *or* (*sich streiten*) to argue with sb; **sich mit jdm gerichtlich ~setzen** to take sb to court.
Aus|einandersetzung *f* **(a)** (*Diskussion*) discussion, debate (*über +acc* about, on); (*Streit*) argument; (*feindlicher Zusammenstoß*) clash (*wegen* over). **(b)** (*das Befassen*) examination (*mit* of); (*kritisch*) analysis (*mit* of).
⚠**aus|einander-: ~spreizen** *vt sep* to open, to spread apart; **~sprengen** *sep* [1] *vt* **(a)** (*sprengen*) to blow up; (*zerbersten lassen*) to burst (apart); **(b)** (*~jagen*) to scatter; *Demonstranten auch* to disperse; [2] *vi aux sein* to scatter; **~springen** *vi sep irreg aux sein* to shatter; **~stieben** *vi sep irreg aux sein* to scatter; **~streben** *vi sep aux sein* (*lit*) to splay; (*fig: Meinungen, Tendenzen*) to diverge; **~treiben** *sep irreg* [1] *vt* (*trennen*) to drive apart; (*~jagen*) to scatter; *Demonstranten* to disperse; [2] *vi aux sein* to drift apart; **~ziehen** *sep irreg* [1] *vt* **(a)** (*dehnen*) to stretch; **(b)** (*trennen*) to pull apart; *Gardinen auch* to pull open; [2] *vi aux sein* (*gemeinsame Wohnung aufgeben*) to separate (and live apart); [3] *vr* to spread out; (*Kolonne auch*) to string out.
aus|erkiesen* *vt sep irreg* (*liter*) (*Gott*) to ordain (*liter*) ◆ **zu etw auserkoren (worden) sein** to be chosen *or* selected for sth.
aus|erkoren *adj* (*liter*) chosen, selected ◆ **jds A~e(r)** (*hum*) sb's intended (*inf*).

⚠: Informationen zur Rechtschreibreform im Anhang

aus|erlesen [1] *adj (ausgesucht)* select; *Speisen, Weine auch* choice *attr.*
[2] *ptp* **zu etw ~ (worden) sein** to be chosen *or* selected for sth.
[3] *adv (verstärkend)* particularly, especially.
aus|ersehen* *vt sep irreg (geh)* to choose; *(für Amt auch)* to designate *(zu* as) ◆ **dazu ~ sein, etw zu tun** to be chosen to do sth.
aus|erwählen* *vt sep (geh)* to choose ◆ **das auserwählte Volk** the Chosen People.
Aus|erwählte(r) *mf decl as adj (geh)* chosen one ◆ **die ~n** the elect, the chosen (ones); **seine ~/ihr ~r** *(hum)* his/her intended *(inf)*.
aus|essen *sep irreg* [1] *vt Speise* to eat up, to finish (eating); *Schüssel* to empty, to clear; *Pampelmuse* to eat.
[2] *vi* to finish eating.
ausfädeln *vr sep* **sich ~ aus** *(Aut)* to slip out of *or* from.
ausfahrbar *adj* extensible, extendable; *Antenne, Fahrgestell* retractable.
ausfahren *sep irreg* [1] *vt* **(a)** *jdn (im Kinderwagen/Rollstuhl)* to take for a walk (in the pushchair *(Brit)* or stroller *(US)*/wheelchair); *(im Auto)* to take for a drive *or* ride.
(b) *(ausliefern) Waren* to deliver.
(c) *(abnutzen) Weg* to rut, to wear out ◆ **sich in ausgefahrenen Bahnen bewegen** *(fig)* to keep to well-trodden paths.
(d) *(Aut) Kurve* to (drive) round; *(mit aux sein) Rennstrecke* to drive round.
(e) *(austragen) Rennen* to hold.
(f) **ein Auto** *etc* **(voll) ~** to drive a car *etc* flat out.
(g) *(Tech)* to extend; *Fahrgestell etc auch* to lower.
[2] *vi aux sein* **(a)** *(spazierenfahren)* to go for a ride *or (im Auto auch)* drive ◆ **mit dem Baby ~** to take the baby out in the pushchair *(Brit) or* stroller *(US)*.
(b) *(abfahren) (Zug)* to pull out *(aus* of), to leave; *(Schiff)* to put to sea, to sail ◆ **aus dem Hafen ~** to sail out of the harbour, to leave harbour.
(c) *(Min: aus dem Schacht)* to come up.
(d) *(Straße verlassen)* to turn off, to leave a road/motorway.
(e) *(Tech: Fahrgestell, Gangway)* to come out.
(f) *(eine heftige Bewegung machen)* to gesture ◆ **mit ~den Bewegungen** with expansive gestures.
(g) *(böser Geist)* to come out *(aus* of).
Ausfahrer *m (Aus, S Ger)* delivery man.
Ausfahrt *f* **(a)** *no pl (Abfahrt)* departure; *(Min: aus Schacht)* ascent *(aus* from) ◆ **der Zug hat keine ~** the train has not been cleared for departure. **(b)** *(Spazierfahrt)* drive, ride. **eine ~ machen** to go for a drive *or* ride. **(c)** *(Ausgang, Autobahn~)* exit ◆ **~ Gütersloh** Gütersloh exit, exit for Gütersloh; **„~ freihalten"** "keep clear".
Ausfahrt(s)-: ~schild *nt* exit sign; **~signal** *nt (Rail)* departure signal; **~straße** *f* exit road.
Ausfall *m* **(a)** *no pl (das Herausfallen)* loss.
(b) *(Verlust, Fehlbetrag, Mil)* loss; *(das Versagen) (Tech, Med)* failure; *(von Motor)* breakdown; *(Produktionsstörung)* stoppage ◆ **bei ~ des Stroms ...** in case of a power failure.
(c) *no pl (von Sitzung, Unterricht etc)* cancellation ◆ **wir hatten einen hohen ~ an Schulstunden** a lot of school lessons were cancelled.
(d) *no pl (das Ausscheiden)* dropping out; *(im Rennen)* retirement; *(Abwesenheit)* absence.
(e) *(Ling)* dropping, omission.
(f) *(Mil: Ausbruch)* sortie, sally.
(g) *(Sport) (Fechten)* thrust, lunge; *(Gewichtheben)* jerk.
(h) *(fig: Angriff)* attack.
Ausfallbürgschaft *f (Econ)* fine, penalty.
ausfallen *vi sep irreg aux sein* **(a)** *(herausfallen)* to fall out; *(Chem)* to be precipitated; *(Ling)* to be dropped *or* omitted ◆ **mir fallen die Haare aus** my hair is falling out.
(b) *(nicht stattfinden)* to be cancelled ◆ **etw ~ lassen** to cancel sth; **die Schule/die erste Stunde fällt morgen aus** there's no school/first lesson tomorrow.
(c) *(nicht funktionieren)* to fail; *(Motor)* to break down.
(d) *(wegfallen: Verdienst)* to be lost.
(e) *(ausscheiden)* to drop out; *(während Rennen auch)* to retire; *(fernbleiben)* to be absent.
(f) **gut/schlecht** *etc* **~** to turn out well/badly *etc*; **die Rede ist zu lang ausgefallen** the speech was too long *or* turned out to be too long; **die Bluse fällt zu eng aus** the blouse is too tight.
(g) *(Mil)* to fall, to be lost *(bei* in); *(old: einen Ausfall machen)* to make a sortie.
(h) *(Fechten)* to thrust, to lunge.
(i) *siehe* **ausgefallen.**
ausfällen *vt sep (Chem)* to precipitate.
ausfallend, ausfällig *adj* abusive.
Ausfallstraße *f* arterial road.
Ausfall(s)winkel *m (Phys)* angle of reflection.
Ausfallzeit *f (Insur) time which counts towards pension although no payments were made.*
ausfasern *vi sep aux sein or haben* to fray, to become frayed.
ausfechten *vt sep irreg (fig)* to fight (out).
ausfegen *vt sep Schmutz* to sweep up; *Zimmer* to sweep out.
ausfeilen *vt sep* to file (out); *(glätten)* to file down; *(fig)* to polish; *siehe* **ausgefeilt.**
ausfertigen *vt sep (form)* **(a)** *Dokument* to draw up; *Rechnung, Lieferschein* to make out; *Paß* to issue. **(b)** *(unterzeichnen)* to sign.
Ausfertigung *f (form)* **(a)** *no pl siehe vt* drawing up; making out; issuing; signing. **(b)** *(Abschrift)* copy ◆ **die erste ~** the top copy; **in doppelter/dreifacher ~** in duplicate/triplicate; **Zeugnisse in vierfacher** *etc* **~** four *etc* copies of references.
Ausfertigungsdatum *nt (von Paß, Urkunde)* date of issue.
ausfindig *adj:* **~ machen** to find, to discover; *(Aufenthaltsort feststellen)* to locate, to trace.
ausfischen *vt sep Karpfen etc* to catch; *Teich* to fish dry *or* out.
ausflennen *vir sep (inf) siehe* **ausheulen.**
ausfliegen *sep irreg* [1] *vi aux sein (wegfliegen)* to fly away *or* off; *(aus Gebiet etc)* to fly out *(aus* of); *(flügge werden)* to leave the nest; *(fig inf: weggehen)* to go out ◆ **ausgeflogen sein** *(fig inf)* to be out, to have gone out; **der Vogel ist ausgeflogen** *(fig inf)* the bird has *or* is flown.
[2] *vt (Aviat)* **(a)** *Verwundete etc* to evacuate (by air), to fly out *(aus* from).
(b) *Flugzeug* to fly full out.
ausfliesen *vt sep* to tile.
ausfließen *vi sep irreg aux sein (herausfließen)* to flow out *(aus* of); *(auslaufen: Öl etc, Faß)* to leak *(aus* out of); *(Eiter etc)* to be discharged.
ausflippen *vi sep aux sein (sl)* to freak out *(sl)*; *siehe* **ausgeflippt.**
ausflocken *vti sep (Chem)* to precipitate.
Ausflucht *f -,* **Ausflüchte** excuse; *(geh: Flucht)* escape *(in +acc* into) ◆ **Ausflüchte machen** to make excuses; **keine Ausflüchte!** (I want) no excuses!
Ausflug *m* **(a)** trip, outing; *(esp mit Reisebüro)* excursion; *(Betriebs~, Schul~)* outing; *(Wanderung)* walk, hike; *(fig)* excursion ◆ **einen ~ machen** to go on *or* for a trip *etc*; **einen ~ in die Politik machen** to make an excursion into politics.
(b) *(von Vögeln etc)* flight; *(von Bienen)* swarming.
(c) *(am Bienenstock)* hive exit.
Ausflügler(in *f)* *m* **-s, -** tripper ◆ **Fahrkarte für ~** excursion ticket.
Ausflugschneise *f (Aviat)* take-off path.
Ausflugs-: ~dampfer *m* pleasure steamer; **~fahrt** *f* pleasure trip, excursion; **~lokal** *nt* tourist café; *(am Meer)* seaside café; **~ort** *m* place to go for an outing; **~verkehr** *m (an Feiertagen)* holiday traffic; *(am Wochenende)* weekend holiday traffic; **~ziel** *nt* destination (of one's outing).
⚠**Ausfluß** *m* **(a)** *(das Herausfließen)* outflow; *(das Auslaufen)* leaking. **(b)** *(~stelle)* outlet. **(c)** *(Med)* discharge. **(d)** *(fig geh)* product, result.
ausfolgen *vt sep (Aus form)* to hand over *(jdm* to sb).
ausformen *sep* [1] *vt* to mo(u)ld, to shape *(zu* into); *Manuskript etc* to polish, to refine.
[2] *vr* to take shape, to be formed.
ausformulieren* *vt sep* to formulate; *Rede* to tidy up.
Ausformulierung *f siehe vt* formulation; tidying up.
Ausformung *f* **(a)** *siehe vt* mo(u)lding, shaping; polishing, refining. **(b)** *(Form)* shape, form.
ausforschen *vt sep* **(a)** *Sache* to find out; *(erforschen)* to investigate. **(b)** *(Aus) Täter* to apprehend.
Ausforschung *f siehe vt* **(a)** finding out; investigating. **(b)** questioning. **(c)** apprehension.
ausfragen *vt sep* to question, to quiz *(inf) (nach* about); *(strenger)* to interrogate ◆ **so fragt man die Leute aus** *(inf)* that would be telling *(inf)*.
ausfransen *sep* [1] *vir (vi: aux sein)* to fray, to become frayed.
[2] *vt* to fray.
ausfratscheln *vt sep (Aus inf)* to quiz *(inf)*.
ausfressen *vt sep irreg* **(a)** *siehe* **auffressen. (b)** *(ausspülen: Wasser, Fluß)* to erode, to eat away. **(c)** *(inf: anstellen)* **etwas ~** to do something wrong; **was hat er denn wieder ausgefressen?** what's he (gone and) done now? *(inf)*.
Ausfuhr *f -,* **-en (a)** *no pl (das Ausführen)* export; *(~handel)* exports *pl.* **(b)** **~en** *pl (~güter)* exports *pl.*
Ausfuhr|artikel *m* export.
ausführbar *adj* **(a)** *Plan* feasible, practicable, workable ◆ **schwer ~** difficult to carry out. **(b)** *(Comm)* exportable.
Ausführbarkeit *f* feasibility, practicability.
Ausfuhr- *in cpds siehe auch* **Export-** export; **~bestimmungen** *pl* export regulations *pl.*
ausführen *vt sep* **(a)** *(zu Spaziergang, ins Theater etc)* to take out; *Hund* to take for a walk; *(hum) Kleid* to parade.
(b) *(durchführen)* to carry out; *Aufgabe, (Med) Operation auch* to perform; *Auftrag, Plan, Befehl, Bewegung, (Mil) Operation auch* to execute; *Anweisung auch, Gesetz* to implement; *Bauarbeiten* to undertake; *(Sport) Freistoß etc* to take ◆ **die ~de Gewalt** *(Pol)* the executive.
(c) *(gestalten) Plan, Entwurf, Bild etc* to execute.
(d) *(erklären)* to explain; *(darlegen)* to set out; *(argumentierend)* to argue; *(sagen)* to say.
(e) *(Comm) Waren* to export.
Ausführende(r) *mf decl as adj* **(a)** *(Spieler)* performer. **(b)** *(Handelnder)* executive.
Ausfuhr-: ~güter *pl* export goods *pl*, exports *pl*; **~hafen** *m* port of exportation; **~handel** *m* export trade; **~land** *nt* **(a)** *(Land, das ausführt)* exporting country; **ein ~land für Jute** a jute-exporting country; **(b)** *(Land, in das ausgeführt wird)* export market.
ausführlich ['ausfy:ɐlɪç, *(Aus)* aus'fy:ɐlɪç] [1] *adj* detailed; *Informationen, Gespräche, Katalog auch* full.
[2] *adv* in detail, in full ◆ **sehr ~** in great detail; **~er** in more *or* greater detail.
Ausführlichkeit *f siehe adj* detail; fullness ◆ **in aller ~** in (great) detail, in full.
Ausfuhr-: ~prämie *f* export premium; **~sperre** *f* export ban *or* embargo;

⚠**~überschuß** *m* export surplus.

Ausführung *f* **(a)** *no pl siehe vt (b)* carrying out; performance; execution; implementation; undertaking; taking ◆ **zur ~ gelangen** *or* **kommen** to be carried out.
(b) *siehe vt (c)* execution.
(c) *(Erklärung)* explanation; *(von Thema etc)* exposition; *(Bemerkung)* remark; *(usu pl: Bericht)* report.
(d) *(von Waren)* design; *(Tech: äußere ~)* finish; *(Qualität)* quality; *(Modell)* model.

Ausfuhr-: ~volumen *nt* volume of exports; **~waren** *pl* exports *pl*, export goods *pl*; **~zoll** *m* export duty.

ausfüllen *vt sep* to fill; *Loch* to fill (up *or* out); *Ritze* to fill in; *Platz* to take up; *Formular* to fill in *(Brit) or* out; *Posten* to fill ◆ **jdn (voll** *or* **ganz) ~** *(befriedigen)* to give sb (complete) fulfilment, to satisfy sb (completely); *(Zeit in Anspruch nehmen)* to take (all) sb's time; **er füllt den Posten nicht/gut aus** he is not fitted/well-fitted for the post; **der Gedanke an dich füllt mich ganz aus** the thought of you occupies my every minute; **seine Zeit mit etw ~** to pass one's time doing sth, to fill up one's time with sth; **ein ausgefülltes Leben** a full life.

ausfüttern *vt sep (Sew)* to line.

Ausgabe *f* **-, -n (a)** *no pl (Austeilung) (von Proviant, Decken etc)* distribution, giving out; *(von Befehl, Fahrkarten, Dokumenten etc)* issuing; *(von Essen)* serving; *(Ausdruck)* print-out.
(b) *(Schalter)* issuing counter; *(in Bibliothek)* issue desk; *(in Kantine)* serving counter; *(Stelle, Büro)* issuing office.
(c) *(von Buch, Zeitung, Sendung)* edition; *(von Zeitschrift auch, Aktien)* issue.
(d) *(Ausführung)* version; *(inf: Abklatsch auch)* edition.
(e) *(Geldaufwand)* expense, expenditure *no pl.* **~n** *pl (Geldverbrauch)* expenditure *sing (für* on); *(Kosten)* expenses *pl*, costs *pl.*
(f) *(Datenverarbeitung)* print-out.

Ausgabe-: ~daten *pl (Comput)* output data; **~gerät** *nt (Comput)* output device; **~kurs** *m (Fin)* rate of issue.

Ausgabe(n)-: ~beleg *m* receipt for expenditure; **~buch** *nt* cashbook.

Ausgaben-: ~politik *f* expenditure policy; **~seite** *f* expenditure column.

Ausgabe-: ~schalter *m* issuing counter; *(in Bibliothek etc)* issue desk; **~termin** *m* date of issue.

Ausgang *m* **(a)** *(Erlaubnis zum Ausgehen)* permission to go out; *(Mil)* pass ◆ **~ haben** to have the day off *or (am Abend)* the evening off; *(Mil)* to have a pass; **bis 10 Uhr ~ haben** to be allowed out/to have a pass till 10 o'clock.
(b) *(Spaziergang)* walk *(under supervision)*.
(c) *(Auslaß, Weg nach draußen)* exit, way out *(gen, von* from); *(Dorf~)* end; *(von Wald)* edge; *(Med: von Organ)* opening *(gen* out of); *(Aviat)* gate.
(d) *no pl (Ende)* end; *(von Epoche auch)* close; *(von Roman, Film auch)* ending; *(Ergebnis)* outcome, result ◆ **ein Unfall mit tödlichem ~** a fatal accident; **ein Ausflug mit tragischem ~** an excursion with a tragic outcome.
(e) *no pl (Ausgangspunkt)* starting point, point of departure; *(Anfang)* beginning ◆ **von hier nahm diese weltweite Bewegung ihren ~** this was where this worldwide movement started.
(f) *no pl (Abschicken von Post)* mailing, sending off.
(g) Ausgänge *pl (Post)* outgoing mail *sing*; *(Waren)* outgoing goods *pl.*

ausgangs *prep +gen (auch adv* **~ von)** at the end of; *(der Schlußkurve etc)* coming out of ◆ **eine Frau ~ der Siebziger** a woman in her late seventies.

Ausgangs-: ~basis *f* starting point, basis; **~frage** *f* initial question; **~lage** *f siehe* **~position; ~material** *nt* source material; **~position** *f* initial *or* starting position; **~punkt** *m* starting point; *(von Reise auch)* point of departure; **~sperre** *f* ban on going out; *(esp bei Belagerungszustand)* curfew; *(für Soldaten)* confinement to barracks; **~sperre haben** *(Soldat)* to be confined to barracks; *(Schüler)* to be banned from going out, to be gated *(Brit inf)*; **~sprache** *f* source language; **~stellung** *f (Sport)* starting position; *(Mil)* initial position; **~tür** *f* exit (door); **~verbot** *nt siehe* **~sperre; ~zeile** *f (Typ)* club-line, widow; **~zustand** *m* initial *or* original condition *or (Lage)* position; *(Pol auch)* status quo.

ausgebaut *adj Schul-, Verkehrssystem etc* fully developed ◆ **gut/nicht gut ~** well/badly planned.

ausgeben *sep irreg* [1] *vt* **(a)** *(austeilen) Proviant, Decken etc* to distribute, to give out; *(aushändigen) Dokumente, Fahrkarten, Aktien etc* to issue; *Befehl* to issue, to give; *Essen* to serve; *(Cards)* to deal; *(ausdrucken) Text* to print out.
(b) *Geld* to spend *(für* on) ◆ **eine Runde ~** to stand a round *(inf)*; **ich gebe heute abend einen aus** *(inf)* it's my treat this evening; **unser Chef hat einen ausgegeben** our boss treated us; **darf ich dir einen/einen Whisky ~?** may I buy you a drink/a whisky?; **er gibt nicht gern einen aus** he doesn't like buying people drinks.
(c) jdn/etw als *or* **für jdn/etw ~** to pass sb/sth off as sb/sth; **sich als jd/etw ~** to pose as sb/sth, to pass oneself off as sb/sth.
[2] *vr* to exhaust oneself; *(sein Geld ganz ~)* to spend all one's money.

ausgebeult *adj Kleidung* baggy; *Hut* battered.

Ausgebeutete(r) *mf decl as adj* **die ~n** the exploited *pl.*

ausgebrannt *adj (lit, fig inf)* burnt out; *(Gebäude auch)* gutted; *(Brennstab)* spent ◆ **geistig ~** mentally exhausted.

ausgebucht *adj Reise etc, (inf) Person* booked up.

ausgebufft *adj (sl)* **(a)** *(erledigt)* washed-up *(inf)*; *(erschöpft)* knackered *(sl)*. **(b)** *(trickreich)* shrewd, fly *(sl)*.

Ausgeburt *f (pej) (der Phantasie etc)* monstrous product *or* invention; *(Geschöpf, Kreatur, Institution)* monster ◆ **eine ~ der Hölle** a fiend from hell, a fiendish monster; **sie ist eine ~ von Eitelkeit und Dummheit** she is a monstrous combination of vanity and stupidity.

ausgedehnt *adj Gummiband* (over-)stretched; *(breit, groß, fig: weitreichend)* extensive; *(zeitlich)* lengthy, extended; *Spaziergang* long, extended.

ausgedient *adj* **(a)** *(dated)* **ein ~er Soldat** a veteran, an ex-serviceman. **(b)** *(inf: unbrauchbar) Auto, Maschine* clapped-out *(inf)* ◆ **meine ~en Sachen/Bücher** *etc* the things/books *etc* I don't have any further use for.

ausgedörrt *adj* dried up; *Boden, Kehle* parched; *Pflanzen* shrivelled; *Land, Gebiet* arid; *(fig) Hirn* ossified, dull ◆ **mein Hirn ist völlig ~** *(fig)* I can't think straight any more.

ausgefallen *adj (ungewöhnlich)* unusual; *(übertrieben)* extravagant; *Mensch* eccentric; *(überspannt)* odd, weird.

Ausgefallenheit *f siehe adj* unusualness; extravagance; eccentricity; oddness, weirdness.

ausgefeilt *adj (fig)* polished; *Schrift* stylized.

Ausgefeiltheit *f* polish; *(von Schrift)* stylized character.

ausgeflippt *adj (sl)* freaky *(sl)*, freaked-out *(sl)*, flipped-out *(sl)*; *(aus der Gesellschaft)* drop-out *(inf)* ◆ **er ist ein richtig ~er Typ** he's really freaky *(sl) or* freaked out *(sl)*/a real drop-out *(inf)*.

Ausgeflippte(r) *mf decl as adj (sl)* freak *(sl)*; *(aus der Gesellschaft)* drop-out *(inf)*.

ausgefuchst *adj (inf)* clever; *(listig)* crafty *(inf)*; *Kartenspieler* cunning.

ausgeglichen *adj* balanced; *Spiel, Klima* even; *Torverhältnis* equal; *(gleichbleibend)* consistent.

Ausgeglichenheit *f siehe adj* balance; evenness; consistency ◆ **ihre ~** her balanced nature *or* character.

ausgegoren *adj Most* fully fermented; *(fig inf) Pläne* worked out ◆ **wenig ~** half-baked *(inf)*.

ausgehen *sep irreg aux sein* [1] *vi* **(a)** *(weggehen, zum Vergnügen)* to go out; *(spazierengehen auch)* to go (out) for a walk ◆ **er geht selten aus** he doesn't go out much; **wir gehen heute abend ganz groß aus** we're going out for a big celebration tonight.
(b) *(ausfallen: Haare, Federn, Zähne)* to fall out; *(Farbe)* to run; *(dial: Stoff)* to fade ◆ **ihm gehen die Haare/Zähne aus** his hair is falling out/he is losing his teeth.
(c) *(seinen Ausgang nehmen)* to start *(von* at); *(herrühren: Idee, Anregung etc)* to come *(von* from) ◆ **von dem Platz gehen vier Straßen aus** four streets lead off (from) the square; **etw geht von jdm/etw aus** *(wird ausgestrahlt)* sb/sth radiates sth; **von der Rede des Ministers ging eine große Wirkung aus** the minister's speech had a great effect.
(d) *(abgeschickt werden: Post)* to be sent off ◆ **die ~de Post** the outgoing mail.
(e) *(zugrunde legen)* to start out *(von* from) ◆ **gehen wir einmal davon aus, daß ...** let us assume that ..., let us start from the assumption that ...; **wovon gehst du bei dieser Behauptung aus?** on what are you basing your statement?; **davon kann man nicht ~** you can't go by that.
(f) auf etw *(acc)* **~** to be intent on sth; **auf Gewinn ~** to be intent on making a profit; **auf Eroberungen ~** *(hum inf)* to be out to make a few conquests.
(g) *(einen bestimmten Ausgang haben: esp Sport)* to end; *(ausfallen)* to turn out ◆ **gut/schlecht ~** to turn out well/badly; *(Film etc)* to end happily/unhappily; *(Abend, Spiel)* to end well/badly.
(h) *(Ling: enden)* to end.
(i) straffrei *or* **straflos ~** to receive no punishment; to get off scot-free *(inf)*; **leer ~** *(inf)* to come away empty-handed.
(j) *(zu Ende sein: Vorräte etc)* to run out; *(dial: Vorstellung, Schule etc)* to finish ◆ **mir ging die Geduld/das Geld aus** I lost (my) patience/ran out of money; **ihm ist die Luft** *or* **die Puste** *or* **der Atem ausgegangen** *(inf) (lit)* he ran out of breath/puff *(inf)*; *(fig)* he ran out of steam *(inf)*; *(finanziell)* he ran out of funds.
(k) *(aufhören zu brennen)* to go out.
(l) *(inf: sich ausziehen lassen)* to come off ◆ **die nassen Sachen gehen so schwer aus** these wet things are so hard to take off.
[2] *vr (Aus)* **es geht sich aus** it works out all right; *(Vorräte, Geld etc)* there is enough.

ausgehend *adj attr* **im ~en Mittelalter** towards the end of the Middle Ages; **das ~e 20. Jahrhundert** the end *or* close of the 20th century.

Ausgeh|erlaubnis *f* permission to go out; *(Mil)* pass.

ausgehungert *adj* starved; *(abgezehrt) Mensch etc* emaciated ◆ **wie ~e Wölfe** like starving wolves; **nach etw ~ sein** *(fig)* to be starved of sth.

Ausgeh-: ~uniform *f* walking-out uniform; **~verbot** *nt* **jdm ~verbot erteilen** to forbid sb to go out; *(Mil)* to confine sb to barracks; **~verbot haben/bekommen** to be forbidden to go out; *(Mil)* to be confined to barracks.

ausgeklügelt *adj (inf) System* cleverly thought-out; *(genial)* ingenious.

ausgekocht *adj (pej inf) (durchtrieben)* cunning ◆ **er ist ein ~er Bursche** he's a thoroughly bad character.

ausgelassen *adj (heiter)* lively; *Stimmung* happy; *(wild) Kinder* boisterous; *Stimmung, Party* mad.

Ausgelassenheit *f siehe adj* liveliness; happiness; boisterousness; madness.

ausgelastet *adj Mensch* fully occupied; *Maschine, Anlage* working to capacity ◆ **mit dem Job ist er nicht (voll) ~** he is not fully stretched in that job; **mit den vier Kindern ist sie voll ~** her four children keep her fully occupied, she has her hands full with her four children; **unsere Kapazitäten sind voll ~** we're working at full capacity.

ausgelatscht *adj (inf) Schuhe* worn ◆ **meine Schuhe sind völlig ~** my shoes have gone completely out of shape.

ausgeleiert *adj Gummiband, Gewinde, Feder* worn; *Hosen, Pullover* baggy;

Redensart hackneyed.

ausgelernt *adj (inf)* qualified.

ausgelesen *adj (fig geh) Ware* select, choice.

Ausgeliefertsein *nt* subjection (*an +acc* to) ◆ **unser ~ an die Gesellschaft** the fact that we are at the mercy of society.

ausgemacht *adj* **(a)** (*abgemacht*) agreed ◆ **es ist eine ~e Sache, daß ...** it is agreed that ... **(b)** *attr (inf: vollkommen)* complete, utter.

ausgemergelt *adj Körper, Gesicht* emaciated, gaunt.

ausgenommen *conj* except, apart from ◆ **niemand/alle, ~ du, niemand/alle, du** *or* **dich ~** no-one/everyone except (for) you *or* apart from *or* save yourself; **täglich ~ sonntags** daily except for *or* excluding Sundays; **Anwesende ~** present company excepted; **~ wenn/daß ...** except when/that ...

ausgepicht *adj (inf) (raffiniert) Mensch, Plan* cunning; *(verfeinert) Geschmack* refined.

ausgepowert [-paʊɐt] *adj (inf)* washed out *(inf)*, done in *(inf)*.

ausgeprägt *adj Gesicht* distinctive; *Eigenschaft* distinct; *Charakter, Interesse* marked, pronounced ◆ **ein (stark) ~er Sinn für alles Schöne** a well-developed sense for everything beautiful.

ausgepumpt *adj (inf)* whacked *(inf)*.

ausgerechnet *adv* ~ **du/er** *etc* you/he *etc* of all people; **~ mir muß das passieren** why does it have to happen to me (of all people)?; **~ heute/gestern** today/yesterday of all days; **muß das ~ heute sein?** does it have to be today (of all days)?; **~ jetzt kommt er** he would have to come just now; **~ dann kam er** he would have to come just at that moment; **~, als wir spazierengehen wollten, ...** just when we wanted to go for a walk ...

ausgeruht *adj* (well) rested.

ausgeschamt *adj (dial) siehe* **unverschämt.**

▼ **ausgeschlossen** *adj pred (unmöglich)* impossible; *(nicht in Frage kommend)* out of the question ◆ **es ist nicht ~, daß ...** it's just possible that ...; **diese Möglichkeit ist nicht ~** it's not impossible; **jeder Irrtum ist ~** there is no possibility of a mistake.

ausgeschnitten *adj Bluse, Kleid* low-cut ◆ **sie geht heute tief ~** *(inf)* she's wearing a very low-cut dress/blouse *etc* today; **ein weit** *or* **tief ~es Kleid** a dress with a plunging neckline.

ausgeschrieben *adj Schrift* bold.

ausgespielt *adj* **~ haben** to be finished; **er hat bei mir ~** *(inf)* he's had it as far as I am concerned *(inf)*, I'm finished *or* through with him.

ausgesprochen [1] *adj (besonders) Schönheit, Qualität, Vorliebe* definite; *(ausgeprägt) Trinkernase etc auch* pronounced; *Begabung* particular; *Ähnlichkeit auch* marked; *Geiz, Großzügigkeit* extreme; *(groß) Pech, Freundlichkeit, Hilfsbereitschaft etc* real ◆ **eine ~e Frohnatur** a very sunny person; **~es Pech haben** to have really bad luck, to be really unlucky.

[2] *adv* really; *schön, begabt, groß, hilfsbereit etc auch* extremely; *geizig, frech etc auch* terribly.

ausgesprochenermaßen *adv siehe* **ausgesprochen 2.**

ausgestalten* *vt sep (künstlerisch, musikalisch)* to arrange; *(planend gestalten)* to organize; *(dekorieren, einrichten)* to decorate; *(ausbauen) Theorie, Begriff, Methode* to build up ◆ **Bücher künstlerisch ~** to do the art work for books.

Ausgestaltung *f* **(a)** *siehe vt* arranging; organizing; decorating; building up. **(b)** *(Gestalt, Form)* form.

ausgestellt *adj Rock etc* flared.

ausgestorben *adj Tierart* extinct; *(fig)* deserted ◆ **der Park war wie ~** the park was deserted.

Ausgestoßene(r) *mf decl as adj* outcast.

ausgesucht [1] *adj* **(a)** *(besonders groß)* extreme, exceptional.

(b) *(erlesen) Wein* choice, select; *Gesellschaft* select; *Worte* well-chosen.

[2] *adv (überaus, sehr)* extremely, exceptionally.

ausgetreten *adj Schuhe* well-worn; *Pfad auch* well-trodden; *Stufe* worn down ◆ **~e Wege gehen** *(fig)* to tread a beaten track.

ausgewachsen *adj* fully-grown; *(inf) Blödsinn* utter, complete; *Skandal* huge.

ausgewählt *adj* select; *Satz etc* well-chosen; *Werke* selected.

Ausgewanderte(r) *mf decl as adj* emigrant.

Ausgewiesene(r) *mf decl as adj* expellee.

ausgewogen *adj* balanced; *Maß* equal ◆ **ein ~es Kräfteverhältnis** a balance of powers.

Ausgewogenheit *f* balance.

ausgezeichnet *adj* excellent ◆ **sie kann ~ schwimmen/tanzen** she is an excellent swimmer/dancer; **es geht mir ~** I'm feeling marvellous.

ausgiebig [1] *adj Mahlzeit etc* substantial, large; *Mittagsschlaf* long; *Gebrauch* extensive ◆ **~en Gebrauch von etw machen** to make full *or* good use of sth.

[2] *adv* **~ frühstücken** to have a substantial breakfast; **~ schlafen/schwimmen** to have a good (long) sleep/swim; **~ einkaufen** to buy a lot of things; **etw ~ gebrauchen** to use sth extensively.

ausgießen *vt sep irreg* **(a)** *(aus einem Behälter)* to pour out; *(weggießen)* to pour away; *Behälter* to empty; *(verschütten)* to spill; *(über jdn/etw gießen)* to pour *(über +acc* over) ◆ **seinen Spott/Hohn über jdn ~** *(geh)* to pour scorn on/to mock sb.

(b) *(füllen) Gußform* to fill; *Ritzen, Fugen* to fill in.

Ausgleich *m* **-(e)s,** *(rare)* **-e** **(a)** *(Gleichgewicht)* balance; *(von Konto)* balancing; *(von Schulden)* settling; *(von Verlust, Fehler, Mangel)* compensation; *(von Abweichung, Unterschieden)* balancing out; *(von Meinungsverschiedenheiten, Konflikten)* evening out ◆ **zum/als ~ für etw** in order to compensate for sth; **er treibt zum ~ Sport** he does sport for exercise; **Tennisspielen ist für mich ein guter ~** I like playing tennis, it gives me a change; **ein Ingenieur, der zum ~ ins Theater geht** an engineer who goes to the theatre to get a change; **wenn er ins Ausland geht, bekommt sie zum ~ ein Auto** when he goes abroad, she gets a car to even things out; **dieses Jahr fährt er zum ~ ans Meer** this year he's going to the seaside for a change; **zum ~ Ihres Kontos** to balance your account.

(b) *no pl (Ballspiele)* equalizer; *(Tennis)* deuce.

ausgleichen *sep irreg* [1] *vt Ungleichheit, Unterschiede* to even out; *Unebenheit* to level out; *Konto* to balance; *Schulden* to settle; *Verlust, Fehler* to make good; *Verlust, Mangel* to compensate for; *Meinungsverschiedenheiten, Konflikte* to reconcile ◆ **etw durch etw ~** to compensate for sth with sth/by doing sth; **~de Gerechtigkeit** poetic justice.

[2] *vi* **(a)** *(Sport)* to equalize ◆ **zum 1:1 ~** to equalize the score at 1 all.

(b) *(vermitteln)* to act as a mediator ◆ **~des Wesen** conciliatory manner.

[3] *vr* to balance out; *(Einnahmen und Ausgaben)* to balance ◆ **das gleicht sich wieder aus** it balances itself out; **das gleicht sich dadurch aus, daß ...** it's balanced out by the fact that ...

Ausgleichs-: ~getriebe *nt (Tech)* differential gear; **~gymnastik** *f* exercises *pl*; **~sport** *m* keep-fit activity; **als ~sport** to keep fit; **~treffer** *m* equalizer, equalizing goal; **~zahlung** *f* compensation.

ausgleiten *vi sep irreg aux sein* **(a)** *(ausrutschen)* to slip *(auf +dat* on) ◆ **es ist ihm ausgeglitten** it slipped from his hands *or* grasp. **(b)** *(Boot, Skifahrer)* to coast in.

ausgliedern *vt sep* to exclude.

ausglitschen *vi sep aux sein siehe* **ausgleiten (a).**

ausglühen *sep* [1] *vt* **(a)** *Metall* to anneal; *(Med)* to sterilize *(by heating)*. **(b)** *(ausdörren) Land* to scorch.

[2] *vi aux sein* to burn out.

ausgraben *vt sep irreg* to dig up; *Grube, Loch* to dig out; *Altertümer auch* to excavate; *(fig)* to dig up; *(hervorholen)* to dig out; *alte Geschichten* to bring up.

Ausgrabung *f (das Ausgraben)* excavation; *(Ort)* excavation site; *(Fund)* (archaeological) find.

ausgräten *vt sep siehe* **entgräten.**

ausgreifen *vi sep irreg (Pferd)* to lengthen its stride; *(beim Gehen)* to stride out; *(fig: Redner)* to go far afield ◆ **weit ~d** *Schritte* long, lengthy; *Bewegung* striding.

ausgrenzen *vt sep* to exclude.

Ausgrenzung *f* exclusion.

ausgründen *vt sep (Econ)* to establish.

Ausguck *m* **-(e)s, -e** lookout ◆ **~ halten** to keep a lookout.

ausgucken *sep (inf)* [1] *vi* **(a)** *(Ausschau halten)* to look out *(nach* for). **(b)** *(auskundschaften)* to have a look.

[2] *vr* **sich** *(dat)* **die Augen nach jdm ~** to look everywhere for sb.

[3] *vt (aussuchen, entdecken)* **sich jdn ~** to set one's sights on sb, to pick sb out.

⚠ **Ausguß** *m* **(a)** *(Becken)* sink; *(Abfluß)* drain; *(dial: ausgegossene Flüssigkeit)* waste (water *etc*); *(Tülle)* spout. **(b)** *(Tech)* tap hole.

aushaben *sep irreg (inf)* [1] *vt (fertig sein mit) Buch, Essen etc* to have finished; *(ausgezogen haben)* to have taken off.

[2] *vi (Arbeit, Schule etc beendet haben)* to finish.

aushacken *vt sep* **(a)** *Unkraut* to hoe; *Rüben etc* to hoe out. **(b)** *(Vogel) Augen* to peck out; *Federn* to tear out; *siehe* **Krähe.**

aushaken *sep* [1] *vt Fensterladen, Kette* to unhook; *Reißverschluß* to undo.

[2] *vi (inf)* **es hat bei ihm ausgehakt** *(nicht begreifen)* he gave up *(inf)*; *(wild werden)* something in him snapped *(inf)*.

[3] *vr (Reißverschluß)* to come undone.

aushalten *sep irreg* [1] *vt* **(a)** *(ertragen können)* to bear, to stand, to endure; *(standhalten) Gewicht etc* to bear; *Druck* to stand, to withstand; *jds Blick* to return ◆ **den Vergleich mit etw ~** to bear comparison with sth; **es läßt sich ~** it's bearable; **hier läßt es sich ~** this is not a bad place; **das ist nicht auszuhalten** *or* **zum A~** it's unbearable; **ich halte es vor Hitze/zu Hause nicht mehr aus** I can't stand the heat/being at home any longer; **er hält es in keiner Stellung lange aus** he never stays in one job for long; **wie kann man es bei der Firma bloß ~?** how can anyone stand working for that firm?; **es bis zum Ende ~** *(auf Party etc)* to stay until the end; **hältst du's noch bis zur nächsten Tankstelle aus?** *(inf)* can you hold out till the next garage?; **er hält viel/nicht viel aus** he can take a lot/can't take much; **ein Stoff, der viel ~ muß** a material which has to take a lot of wear (and tear).

(b) *Ton* to hold.

(c) *(inf: unterhalten)* to keep ◆ **sich von jdm ~ lassen** to be kept by sb.

[2] *vi* **(a)** *(durchhalten)* to hold out ◆ **hältst du noch aus?** can you hold out (any longer)?

(b) auf einem Ton ~ to hold a note.

aushämmern *vt sep Beule* to hammer out; *Gefäß* to beat out.

aushandeln *vt sep Vertrag, Lösung* to negotiate; *bessere Bedingungen, höhere Löhne* to negotiate for; *(erfolgreich)* to negotiate.

aushändigen *vt sep* **jdm etw/einen Preis ~** to hand sth over to sb/give sb a prize; **wann können Sie mir die Ware ~?** when can you deliver (the goods)?

Aushändigung *f* handing over; *(von Gütern etc)* delivery ◆ **nach ~ seiner Papiere** after his papers had been handed over to him; **die ~ der Preise nimmt der Direktor vor** the headmaster will be giving out the prizes.

Aushang *m* **-(e)s, Aushänge** *(Bekanntmachung)* notice, announcement; *(das Aushängen)* posting ◆ **etw durch ~ bekanntgeben** to put up a notice about sth; **etw im ~ lesen** to read a notice of *or* about sth.

Aushängekasten *m* (glass-fronted) noticeboard.

aushängen *sep* [1] *vt* **(a)** *(bekanntmachen) Nachricht etc* to put up; *Plakat auch* to post; *(inf: ausstellen)* to show.

(b) *(herausheben) Tür* to unhinge; *Haken* to unhook.
[2] *vi irreg (Anzeige, Aufgebot)* to have been put up; *(inf: Brautleute)* to have the banns up ◆ **am schwarzen Brett ~** to be on the noticeboard.
[3] *vr (sich glätten: Falten, Locken)* to drop out ◆ **das Kleid wird sich ~** the creases will drop *or* hang out of the dress.
Aushänger *m (von Buch)* folded section.
Aushängeschild *nt (lit: Reklametafel)* sign; *(fig: Reklame)* advertisement.
ausharren *vi sep (geh)* to wait ◆ **auf seinem Posten ~** to stand by one's post.
aushauchen *vt sep (geh) Luft, Atem, Rauch* to exhale; *(fig) Worte, Seufzer* to breathe; *(ausströmen) Geruch, Dünste* to emit ◆ **sein Leben ~** to breathe one's last.
aushauen *vt sep irreg* **(a)** *Loch, Stufen* to cut out; *Weg, Durchgang* to hew out; *Statue* to carve out. **(b)** *(roden) Wald, Weinberg* to clear; *(einzelne Bäume fällen)* to cut down; *(Zweige entfernen)* to prune.
aushäusig *adj (außer Haus)* outside the home; *(unterwegs)* away from home ◆ **du warst doch letzte Woche wieder ~?** you were out gallivanting again last week, weren't you?
aushebeln *vt sep (form)* to annul, to cancel.
ausheben *vt sep irreg* **(a)** *Tür etc* to take off its hinges ◆ **sich** *(dat)* **die Schulter ~** *(dial inf)* to put out one's shoulder *(inf)*.
(b) *Erde* to dig out; *Graben, Grab* to dig; *Baum* to dig up.
(c) *Vogelnest* to rob; *Vogeleier, Vogeljunge* to steal; *(fig) Diebesnest* to raid; *Bande* to make a raid on; *(Aus: leeren) Briefkasten* to empty.
(d) *(old) Truppen* to levy *(old)*.
Aushebung *f (old: von Truppen)* levying.
aushecken *vt sep (inf) Plan* to cook up *(inf)*, to hatch ◆ **neue Streiche ~** to think up new tricks; **sich** *(dat)* **etw ~** to think sth up.
ausheilen *sep* [1] *vt Krankheit* to cure; *Organ, Wunde* to heal.
[2] *vi aux sein (Krankheit, Patient)* to be cured; *(Organ, Wunde)* to heal.
[3] *vr* to recover.
Ausheilung *f siehe vt* curing; healing ◆ **nach völliger ~ der Krankheit/Wunde** after a complete recovery from the illness/after the wound is completely healed.
aushelfen *vi sep irreg* to help out *(jdm* sb).
ausheulen *sep (inf)* [1] *vi (aufhören)* to stop crying; *(Sirene)* to stop sounding.
[2] *vr* to have a good cry ◆ **sich bei jdm ~** to have a good cry on sb's shoulder.
Aushilfe *f* **(a)** help, aid; *(Notbehelf)* temporary *or* makeshift substitute ◆ **jdn zur ~ haben** to have sb to help out; **Stenotypistin zur ~ gesucht** shorthand typist wanted for temporary work.
(b) *(Mensch)* temporary worker; *(esp im Büro auch)* temp *(inf)* ◆ **als ~ arbeiten** to help out; *(im Büro auch)* to temp *(inf)*.
Aushilfs-: ~kraft *f* temporary worker; *(esp im Büro auch)* temp *(inf)*; **~lehrer** *m* supply teacher; **~personal** *nt* temporary staff; **a~weise** *adv* on a temporary basis; *(vorübergehend)* temporarily; **sie kocht ab und zu a~weise** she sometimes cooks to help out.
aushöhlen *vt sep* to hollow out; *Ufer, Steilküste* to erode; *(fig) (untergraben)* to undermine; *(erschöpfen)* to weaken.
Aushöhlung *f* **(a)** *(ausgehöhlte Stelle)* hollow. **(b)** *no pl siehe vt* hollowing out; erosion; undermining; weakening.
ausholen *vi sep* **(a)** *(zum Schlag)* to raise one's hand/arm *etc*; *(zum Wurf)* to reach back; *(mit Schläger, Boxer)* to take a swing ◆ **weit ~** *(zum Schlag, beim Tennis)* to take a big swing; *(zum Wurf)* to reach back a long way; *(fig: Redner)* to go far afield; **bei einer Erzählung weit ~** to go a long way back in a story; **mit dem Arm/der Hand zum Wurf/Schlag ~** to raise one's arm/hand ready to throw/strike; **zum Gegenschlag ~** *(lit, fig)* to prepare for a counter-attack.
(b) *(ausgreifen)* to stride out ◆ **er ging mit weit ~den Schritten** he walked with long strides.
ausholzen *vt sep* **(a)** *(lichten)* to thin (out). **(b)** *(abholzen) Schneise* to clear.
aushorchen *vt sep (inf) jdn* to sound out.
aushülsen *vt sep Erbsen* to shell, to pod.
aushungern *vt sep* to starve out; *siehe* **ausgehungert**.
aushusten *sep* [1] *vt* to cough up.
[2] *vi (zu Ende husten)* to finish coughing; *(Schleim ~)* to cough up phlegm/blood.
[3] *vr* to finish coughing ◆ **er hustete sich aus, bis ...** he coughed and coughed until ...
aus|ixen *vt sep (inf)* to cross *or* ex out.
ausjammern *vr sep* to have a good moan.
ausjäten *vt sep Blumenbeet* to weed ◆ **im Garten Unkraut ~** to weed the garden.
auskämmen *vt sep* **(a)** *(entfernen) Staub, Haare* to comb out. **(b)** *(frisieren)* to comb out. **(c)** *(fig) (heraussuchen)* to weed out; *(durchsuchen)* to comb.
auskauen *vti sep* to finish chewing.
auskegeln *sep* [1] *vt* **den Pokal ~** to bowl for the cup.
[2] *vi* to finish bowling.
auskehren *sep* [1] *vt Schmutz* to sweep away; *Zimmer* to sweep out.
[2] *vi* to do the sweeping.
auskeilen *vi sep* **(a)** *(ausschlagen)* to kick out. **(b)** *(keilförmig auslaufen)* to taper off.
auskeimen *vi sep aux sein (Getreide)* to germinate; *(Kartoffeln)* to sprout.
auskennen *vr sep irreg (an einem Ort)* to know one's way around; *(auf einem Gebiet)* to know a lot *(auf or in +dat* about) ◆ **sich in der Stadt ~** to know one's way around the town; **sich bei Männern/Frauen (gut) ~** to know (a lot) about men/women; **man kennt sich bei ihm nie aus** you never know where you are with him.
auskernen *vt sep Obst* to stone.
auskippen *vt sep (inf)* to empty (out); *Flüssigkeit* to pour out.
ausklammern *vt sep Problem* to leave aside, to ignore; *(Math) Zahl* to put outside the brackets.
ausklamüsern* *vt sep (inf)* to work out.
Ausklang *m (geh)* conclusion, end; *(esp Mus)* finale ◆ **zum ~ des Abends ...** to conclude the evening ...
ausklappbar *adj* folding ◆ **dieser Tisch/diese Fußstütze ist ~** this table can be opened out/this footrest can be pulled out.
ausklappen *vt sep* to open out; *Fußstütze etc* to pull out.
auskleiden *sep* [1] *vt* **(a)** *(geh: entkleiden)* to undress. **(b)** *(beziehen)* to line.
[2] *vr (geh)* to get undressed.
Auskleidung *f* lining.
ausklingen *vi sep irreg* **(a)** *(Glocken)* to finish ringing.
(b) *aux sein (Lied)* to finish; *(Abend, Feier etc)* to end *(in +dat* with) ◆ **die Verhandlungen klangen in die hoffnungsvolle Note aus, daß ...** the negotiations ended on the hopeful note that ...; **das ~de Jahrhundert** *(geh)* the close of the century.
ausklinken *sep* [1] *vt* to release.
[2] *vi* to release; *(sl: durchdrehen)* to flip one's lid *(inf)*, to blow one's top *(inf)*.
[3] *vr* to release (itself); *(sl: sich absetzen)* to split *(sl)*.
ausklopfen *vt sep Teppich* to beat; *Pfeife* to knock out; *Kleider* to beat the dust out of ◆ **jdn ~** *(inf)* to spank sb *or* give sb a spanking.
Ausklopfer *m* carpet beater.
ausklügeln *vt sep* to work out; *siehe* **ausgeklügelt**.
auskneifen *vi sep irreg aux sein (inf)* to run away *(dat, von* from).
ausknipsen *vt sep (inf) Licht, Lampe* to turn out *or* off, to switch out *or* off.
ausknobeln *vt sep* **(a)** *(inf) Plan* to figure *(inf) or* work out. **(b)** *(durch Knobeln entscheiden)* ≃ to toss for.
ausknocken [-nɔkn] *vt sep (Boxen, fig)* to knock out.
ausknöpfbar *adj Futter* detachable.
auskochen *vt sep* **(a)** *(Cook) Knochen* to boil; *(dial: Fett, Speck)* to melt. **(b)** *Wäsche* to boil; *(Med) Instrumente* to sterilize *(in boiling water)*; *(fig inf: sich ausdenken)* to cook up *(inf)*; *siehe* **ausgekocht**.
auskommen *vi sep irreg aux sein* **(a)** *(genügend haben, zurechtkommen)* to get by *(mit* on), to manage *(mit* on, with) ◆ **das Auto kommt mit sieben Litern aus** the car only needs seven litres; **ohne jdn/etw ~** to manage *or* do without sb/sth.
(b) mit jdm (gut) ~ to get on *or* along well with sb; **mit ihm ist nicht auszukommen** he's impossible to get on *or* along with.
Auskommen *nt* **-s,** *no pl (Einkommen)* livelihood ◆ **sein ~ haben/finden** to get by; **mit ihr ist kein ~** she's impossible to get on with.
auskömmlich *adj Gehalt* adequate; *Verhältnisse* comfortable ◆ **~ leben** to live comfortably.
auskosten *vt sep* **(a)** *(genießen)* to make the most of; *Leben* to enjoy to the full. **(b)** *(geh: erleiden)* **etw ~ müssen** *(geh)* to have to suffer sth.
auskotzen *sep (sl)* [1] *vt* to throw up *(inf)*; *(fig) Wissen* to spew out *(inf)*.
[2] *vr* to throw up *(inf)*; *(fig: sich aussprechen)* to have a bloody good moan *(sl)*.
auskramen *vt sep (inf)* **(a)** to dig out, to unearth; *(fig) alte Geschichten etc* to bring up; *Schulkenntnisse* to dig up. **(b)** *(leeren)* to turn out.
auskratzen *sep vt* to scrape out; *(Med) Gebärmutter* to scrape; *Patientin* to give a scrape ◆ **jdm die Augen ~** to scratch sb's eyes out.
Auskratzung *f (Med)* scrape.
auskriechen *vi sep irreg aux sein* to hatch out.
auskriegen *vt sep (inf) Buch* to finish; *Flasche etc* to empty.
Auskristallisation *f* crystallization.
auskristallisieren* *sep vtir (vi: aux sein)* to crystallize.
Auskuck *m* **-(e)s, -e** *(N Ger) siehe* **Ausguck**.
auskucken *vti sep (N Ger) siehe* **ausgucken**.
auskugeln *vr sep* **sich** *(dat)* **den Arm/die Schulter ~** to dislocate one's arm/shoulder.
auskühlen *sep* [1] *vt Speise* to cool; *Ofen etc* to cool down; *Körper, Menschen* to chill through.
[2] *vi aux sein (abkühlen)* to cool down; *(Körper, Menschen)* to chill through ◆ **etw ~ lassen** to leave sth to cool.
Auskühlung *f* cooling; *(von Mensch)* loss of body heat.
auskundschaften *sep* [1] *vt Weg, Lage* to find out; *Versteck* to spy out; *Geheimnis* to ferret out; *(esp Mil)* to reconnoitre, to scout.
[2] *vi* to find out ◆ **jdn zum A~ vorschicken** to send sb ahead to reconnoitre.
▼ **Auskunft** *f* **-, Auskünfte** **(a)** *(Mitteilung)* information *no pl (über +acc* about) ◆ **nähere ~** more information, further details; **jdm eine ~ erteilen** *or* **geben** to give sb some information; **wo bekomme ich ~?** where can I get some information?; **eine ~** *or* **Auskünfte einholen** *or* **einziehen** to make (some) enquiries *(über +acc* about).
▼ **(b)** *(Schalter)* information office/desk; *(am Bahnhof auch)* enquiry office/desk; *(Telefon~)* information *no art*; *(Fernsprech~)* directory enquiries *no art*.
(c) *(inf: Auskunftsperson)* information man/woman *(inf)*.
Auskunftei *f* credit enquiry agency.
Auskunfts-: ~beamte(r) *m* information officer; *(am Bahnhof)* information clerk; **~dienst** *m* information service; **~person** *f* informer; *(Beamter)* information clerk; **~pflicht** *f (Jur)* obligation to give information; **die Bank hat gegenüber dem Finanzamt ~pflicht** the bank has a duty *or* is obliged to inform the inland revenue; **die ~pflicht des Arbeitgebers gegenüber der**

➤ SPRACHE AKTIV: **Auskunft: b** → 27.1

Polizei the employer's duty to inform the police; **a~pflichtig** *adj (Jur)* required to give information; **~schalter** *m* information desk; *(am Bahnhof)* enquiry desk; **~stelle** *f* information office.

auskuppeln *vi sep* to disengage the clutch.

auskurieren* *sep (inf)* [1] *vt* to cure; *Krankheit auch* to get rid of *(inf)*.
[2] *vr* to get better.

auslachen *sep* [1] *vt jdn* to laugh at ◆ **laß dich nicht ~** don't make a fool of yourself.
[2] *vr* to have a good laugh.
[3] *vi* to stop laughing.

ausladen *sep irreg* [1] *vt* **(a)** *Ware, Ladung* to unload; *(Naut auch)* to discharge. **(b)** *(inf)* **jdn ~** to tell sb not to come, to uninvite sb *(hum)*.
[2] *vi (Äste)* to spread; *(Dach, Balkon)* to protrude, to jut out; *(Gelände)* to extend.

ausladend *adj Kinn etc* protruding; *Dach* overhanging, projecting; *Gebärden, Bewegung* sweeping.

Auslage *f* **(a)** *(von Waren)* display; *(Schaufenster)* (shop) window; *(Schaukasten)* showcase. **(b)** *(Sport)* basic stance; *(Fechten)* on guard position. **(c)** *usu pl* expense ◆ **seine ~n für Verpflegung** his outlay for food.

auslagern *vt sep* to evacuate; *(aus dem Lager bringen)* to take out of store.

Auslagerung *f siehe vt* evacuation; taking out of store.

Ausland *nt* **-(e)s,** *no pl* foreign countries *pl*; *(fig: die Ausländer)* foreigners *pl* ◆ **ins/im ~** abroad; **aus dem** *or* **vom ~** from abroad; **wie hat das ~ darauf reagiert?** what was the reaction abroad?; **Handel mit dem ~** foreign trade, trade with other countries; **das feindliche/nichtkapitalistische ~** enemy/non-capitalist countries.

Ausländer(in *f***)** *m* **-s, -** foreigner; *(Admin, Jur)* alien.

Ausländerbeauftragte(r) *mf* official looking after foreign immigrants.

ausländerfeindlich *adj* hostile to foreigners, xenophobic.

Ausländerfeindlichkeit *f* hostility to foreigners, xenophobia.

Ausländerwahlrecht *nt* **allgemeines/kommunales ~** aliens' right to vote in general/local elections.

ausländisch *adj* **(a)** *attr* foreign; *Erzeugnisse, Freunde etc auch* from abroad; *(Bot)* exotic. **(b)** *(fig: fremdländisch)* exotic.

Auslands- *in cpds* foreign; **~anleihe** *f* foreign loan; **~aufenthalt** *m* stay abroad; **~beziehungen** *pl* foreign relations *pl*; **~brief** *m* letter going/from abroad, overseas letter *(Brit)*; **~deutsche(r)** *mf* expatriate German, German national (living abroad); **~geschäft** *nt* foreign business *or* trade; **~gespräch** *nt* international call; **~investition** *f* foreign investment; **~korrespondent** *m* foreign correspondent; **~krankenschein** *m (Med)* certificate of entitlement to benefits in kind *(during a stay abroad)*; **~reise** *f* journey *or* trip abroad; **~schulden** *pl* foreign exchange debts; **~schule** *f* British/German *etc* school (abroad); **die ~schulen in Brüssel** the foreign schools in Brussels; **~schutzbrief** *m* international travel cover; *(Dokument)* certificate of entitlement for international travel cover; **~vertretung** *f* agency abroad; *(von Firma)* foreign branch.

auslassen *sep irreg* [1] *vt* **(a)** *(weglassen, aussparen, übergehen)* to leave *or* miss out; *(versäumen) Chance, Gelegenheit* to miss ◆ **er läßt kein Geschäft aus** he doesn't miss a chance to make a deal.
(b) *(abreagieren)* to vent *(an +dat* on) ◆ **seine Gefühle ~** to vent one's feelings, to let off steam *(inf)*.
(c) *Butter, Fett* to melt; *Speck auch* to render (down).
(d) *Kleider etc* to let out; *Saum* to let down.
(e) *(inf) Radio, Motor, Ofen etc* to leave off; *Licht auch* to leave out; *(nicht anziehen) Kleidung* to leave off.
(f) *Hund* to let out.
(g) *(Aus) (los-, freilassen)* to let go; *(in Ruhe lassen)* to leave alone.
(h) *siehe* **ausgelassen.**
[2] *vr* to talk *(über +acc* about) ◆ **sich über jdn/etw ~** *(pej)* to go on about sb/sth *(pej)*; **er hat sich nicht näher darüber ausgelassen** he didn't say any more about it.
[3] *vi (Aus: loslassen)* to let go.
(b) *(versagen)* to fail.

Auslassung *f* **(a)** *(Weglassen)* omission. **(b) ~en** *pl (pej: Äußerungen)* remarks *pl*.

Auslassungs-: ~punkte *pl* suspension points *pl*, ellipsis *sing*; **~zeichen** *nt* apostrophe.

auslasten *vt sep* **(a)** *Fahrzeug* to make full use of; *Maschine auch* to use to capacity. **(b)** *jdn* to occupy fully; *siehe* **ausgelastet.**

Auslastung *f (von Maschine)* full *or* capacity utilization.

auslatschen *vt sep (inf)* to wear out of shape ◆ **latsch deine Schuhe nicht so aus** don't walk on your shoes like that; *siehe* **ausgelatscht.**

Auslauf *m* **-(e)s, Ausläufe** **(a)** *no pl (Bewegungsfreiheit)* exercise; *(für Kinder)* room to run about.
(b) *(Gelände)* run.
(c) *(Sport) (Leichtathletik)* slowing down; *(Ski: Strecke)* out-run.
(d) *no pl (das Auslaufen)* discharge; *(das Lecken)* leakage.
(e) *(Stelle)* outlet.

auslaufen *sep irreg* [1] *vi aux sein* **(a)** *(Flüssigkeit)* to run out *(aus* of); *(Behälter)* to empty; *(undicht sein)* to leak; *(Wasserbett, Blase, Auge)* to drain; *(Eiter)* to drain, to discharge.
(b) *(Naut: Schiff, Besatzung)* to sail.
(c) *(nicht fortgeführt werden: Modell, Serie)* to be discontinued; *(ausgehen: Vorräte, Lager)* to run out ◆ **etw ~ lassen** *Produkt etc* to phase sth out.
(d) *(aufhören: Straße, Vertrag etc)* to run out.
(e) *(ein bestimmtes Ende nehmen)* to turn out.
(f) *(zum Stillstand kommen) (Motor, Förderband)* to come to a stop; *(Sport) (Läufer)* to ease off, to slow down; *(Skifahrer)* to coast to a stop.
(g) *(übergehen in)* to run; *(fig: Streit etc)* to turn *(in +acc* into) ◆ **die Berge laufen in die Ebene/spitz aus** the mountains run into the plain/come to a point; **in eine Bucht ~** to open out into a bay.
(h) *(Farbe, Stoff)* to run.
[2] *vr* to have some exercise ◆ **sich ~ können** *(Kinder)* to have room to run about.

Ausläufer *m* **(a)** *(Bot)* runner. **(b)** *(Met) (von Hoch)* ridge; *(von Tief)* trough. **(c)** *(Vorberge)* foothill *usu pl*. **(d)** *(von Stadt)* suburb. **(e)** *(Sw: Bote)* delivery boy/man.

auslaufsicher *adj* leakproof.

auslaugen *vt sep (lit) Boden* to exhaust; *(Regen)* to wash the goodness out of; *Haut* to dry out; *(fig)* to exhaust, to wear out.

Auslaut *m (Ling)* final position.

auslauten *vi sep* to end *(auf +dat* in) ◆ **~der Konsonant** final consonant.

ausläuten *sep* [1] *vt* to ring out; *Gottesdienst* to ring out the end of; *(old) Nachricht* to ring out, to proclaim.
[2] *vi* to finish *or* cease ringing.

ausleben *sep* [1] *vr (Mensch)* to live it up; *(Phantasie etc)* to run free.
[2] *vt (geh)* to realize.

auslecken *vt sep* to lick out.

ausleeren *vt sep Flüssigkeit* to pour out, to empty; *Gefäß* to empty; *(austrinken auch)* to drain.

auslegen *sep* [1] *vt* **(a)** *(ausbreiten)* to lay out; *Waren etc auch* to display; *Köder* to put down; *Reusen* to drop; *Kabel, Minen* to lay; *Saatgut* to sow; *Kartoffeln* to plant.
(b) *(bedecken)* to cover; *(auskleiden)* to line; *(mit Einlegearbeit)* to inlay ◆ **den Boden/das Zimmer (mit Teppichen) ~** to carpet the floor/room; **das Gebiet mit Minen ~** to lay mines in *or* to mine the area.
(c) *(erklären)* to explain; *(deuten)* to interpret ◆ **etw richtig/falsch ~** to interpret sth correctly/wrongly *or* misinterpret sth; **jds Scherz/Tat übel ~** to take sb's joke/action badly.
(d) *Geld* to lend *(jdm etw* sb sth) ◆ **sie hat die 5 Mark für mich ausgelegt** she paid the 5 marks for me.
(e) *(Tech)* to design *(auf +acc, für* for) ◆ **straff ausgelegt sein** *(Federung)* to be tightly set.
[2] *vi (dial inf: dicklich werden)* to put (it) on a bit *(inf)*.
[3] *vr (Fechten)* to adopt the on guard position.

Ausleger *m* **-s, -** **(a)** *(von Kran etc)* jib, boom. **(b)** *(an Ruderboot)* rowlock; *(Kufe gegen Kentern)* outrigger. **(c)** *(Deuter)* interpreter.

Auslegung *f (Deutung)* interpretation; *(Erklärung)* explanation *(zu* of) ◆ **falsche ~** misinterpretation.

Auslegungs-: ~frage *f* question *or* matter of interpretation; **~methode** *f* method of interpretation; **~sache** *f* matter of interpretation.

ausleiden *vi sep irreg* **sie hat ausgelitten** her suffering is at an end.

ausleiern *sep* [1] *vt (inf)* **etw ~** *Gummiband, Gewinde, Feder* to wear sth out; *Hosen, Pullover* to make sth go baggy.
[2] *vi aux sein* to wear out; *(Pullover)* to go baggy; *siehe* **ausgeleiert.**

Ausleih-: ~bibliothek, ~ bücherei *f* lending library.

Ausleihe *f (das Ausleihen)* lending; *(Schalter)* issue desk ◆ **eine ~ ist nicht möglich** it is not possible to lend out anything.

ausleihen *vt sep irreg (verleihen)* to lend *(jdm, an jdn* to sb); *(von jdm leihen)* to borrow ◆ **sich** *(dat)* **etw ~** to borrow sth *(bei, von* from).

auslernen *vi sep (Lehrling)* to finish one's apprenticeship; *(inf: Schüler, Student etc)* to finish school/college *etc* ◆ **man lernt nie aus** *(prov)* you live and learn *(prov)*; *siehe* **ausgelernt.**

Auslese *f* **-, -n** **(a)** *no pl (Auswahl)* selection; *(Liter: verschiedener Autoren)* anthology ◆ **natürliche ~** natural selection; **eine ~ treffen** *or* **vornehmen** to make a selection. **(b) die ~** the élite. **(c)** *(Wein) high-quality wine made from selected grapes*.

auslesen *vt sep irreg* **(a)** *(auswählen)* to select; *(aussondern) Schlechtes* to pick out; *Erbsen, Linsen etc* to pick over; *siehe* **ausgelesen.**
(b) *(auch vi) (inf) Buch etc* to finish reading ◆ **hast du bald ausgelesen?** will you finish (reading) it soon?; **er legte das ausgelesene Buch beiseite** he put away the book he had finished reading.

Auslese-: ⚠~prozeß *m* selection process; **~verfahren** *nt* selection procedure.

ausleuchten *vt sep* to illuminate; *(fig)* to throw light on.

Ausleuchtung *f* **-,** *no pl* illumination.

auslichten *vt sep* to thin out.

ausliefern *vt sep* **(a)** *Waren* to deliver.
(b) *jdn* to hand over *(an +acc* to); *(an anderen Staat)* to extradite *(an +acc* to); *(fig: preisgeben)* to leave *(jdm* in the hands of) ◆ **sich der Polizei/Justiz ~** to give oneself up *or* surrender oneself to the police/to justice; **jdm/einer Sache ausgeliefert sein** to be at sb's mercy/the mercy of sth.

Auslieferung *f siehe vt* **(a)** delivery. **(b)** handing over; *(von Gefangenen)* extradition.

Auslieferungs-: ~antrag *m (Jur)* application for extradition; **~lager** *nt (Comm)* distribution centre; **~vertrag** *m (Jur)* extradition treaty.

ausliegen *vi sep irreg (Waren)* to be displayed; *(Zeitschriften, Liste etc)* to be available (to the public); *(Schlinge, Netz etc)* to be down.

Auslinie *f (Sport) (Ftbl)* touchline; *(bei Tennis, Hockey etc)* sideline ◆ **die ~n** *(Tennis)* the tramlines *pl*.

⚠: for details of spelling reform, see supplement

ausloben vt sep (form) (als Belohnung aussetzen) Geldbetrag to offer as a reward; (als Preis aussetzen) to offer as a prize.

Auslobung f siehe vt offer of a reward/prize; (Belohnung) reward.

auslöffeln vt sep Suppe etc to eat up completely; Teller to empty ◆ **etw ~ müssen** (inf) to have to take the consequences (of sth); **~ müssen, was man sich eingebrockt hat** (inf) to have to take the consequences.

auslöschen vt sep (a) Feuer to put out, to extinguish; Kerze auch to snuff out; (geh) Licht to extinguish.
(b) (auswischen) Spuren to obliterate; (mit Schwamm etc) to wipe out; Schrift to erase (an +dat from); Erinnerung, Schmach to blot out ◆ **ein Menschenleben ~** (geh) to destroy or blot out a human life.

auslosen vt sep to draw lots for; Preis, Gewinner to draw ◆ **es wurde ausgelost, wer beginnt** lots were drawn to see who would start.

auslösen vt sep (a) Mechanismus, Alarm, Reaktion to set or trigger off, to trigger; Kameraverschluß, Bombe to release; (fig) Wirkung to produce; Begeisterung, Mitgefühl, Überraschung to arouse; Aufstand, Beifall to trigger off.
(b) (dated: einlösen) Gefangene to release; (durch Geld) to ransom; Wechsel, Pfand to redeem.
(c) (dial) Knochen etc to take out.

Auslöser m -s, - (a) trigger; (für Bombe) release button; (Phot) shutter release. (b) (Anlaß) cause ◆ **der ~ für etw sein** to trigger sth off. (c) (Psych) trigger mechanism.

Auslosung f draw.

Auslösung f (a) siehe vt (a) setting or triggering off, triggering; release, releasing; producing; arousing; triggering off. (b) (von Gefangenen) release; (von Wechsel, Pfand) redemption; (Lösegeld) ransom. (c) (dial) taking out. (d) (Entschädigung) travel allowance.

ausloten vt sep (Naut) Fahrrinne to sound the depth of; Tiefe to sound; (Tech) Mauer to plumb; (fig geh) to plumb; jds Wesen, Charakter to plumb the depths of ◆ **die Sache muß ich doch mal ~** (fig inf) I'll have to try to get to the bottom of the matter or to fathom it out.

auslüften sep [1] vti to air ◆ **lüfte dein Gehirn ein bißchen aus** (inf) get your thoughts or ideas straightened out.
[2] vr (inf) to get some fresh air.

auslutschen vt sep (inf) Orange, Zitrone etc to suck; Saft to suck out; (fig) to suck dry ◆ **ausgelutscht** (Thema, Streit) stale.

▼ **ausmachen** vt sep (a) Feuer, Kerze, Zigarette to put out; elektrisches Licht auch, Radio, Gas to turn off.
(b) (ermitteln, sichten) to make out; (ausfindig machen) to locate; (feststellen) to determine ◆ **es läßt sich nicht mehr ~, warum ...** it can no longer be determined why ...
(c) (vereinbaren) to agree; Streitigkeiten to settle ◆ **einen Termin ~** to agree (on) a time; **wir müssen nur noch ~, wann wir uns treffen** we only have to arrange when we should meet; **etw mit sich selbst ~ (müssen)** to (have to) sort sth out for oneself; siehe **ausgemacht.**
(d) (bewirken, darstellen) (to go) to make up ◆ **alles, was das Leben ausmacht** everything that is a part of life; **all der Luxus, der ein angenehmes Leben ausmacht** all the luxuries which go to make up a pleasant life; **ihm fehlt alles, was einen Musiker ausmacht** he has none of the qualities which go to make up a musician; **die Farben machen den Reiz an diesem Bild aus** the colours make this picture attractive.
(e) (betragen) Summe to come to; Unterschied auch to make; (zeitlich) to make up.
(f) (bedeuten) **viel/wenig** or **nicht viel ~** to make a big/not much difference; **das macht nichts aus** that doesn't matter; (ist egal auch) that doesn't make any difference.
▼ (g) (stören) to matter (jdm to) ◆ **macht es Ihnen etwas aus, wenn ...?** would you mind if ...?; **es macht mir nichts aus, den Platz zu wechseln** I don't mind changing places.
(h) (dial) Kartoffeln, Rüben to dig up.

ausmahlen vt sep to grind (down).

ausmalen vt sep **sich** (dat) **etw/sein Leben ~** to imagine sth/picture one's life.

ausmanövrieren* vt sep to outmanoeuvre.

ausmären vr sep (dial inf) (langsam arbeiten) to dawdle (inf); (viel erzählen) to rattle on (über +acc about) (inf) ◆ **mär dich endlich aus!** stop dawdling!

Ausmarsch m departure.

ausmarschieren* vi sep aux sein to march out.

Ausmaß nt (Größe: von Gegenstand, Fläche) size; (Umfang: von Katastrophe) extent; (Grad) degree, extent; (meiner Liebe etc) extent; (Größenordnung: von Änderungen, Verlust etc) scale. **~e** pl proportions pl ◆ **ein Verlust in diesem ~** a loss on this scale; **das Feuer war nur von geringem ~** the fire was only on a small scale.

ausmergeln vt sep Gesicht, Körper etc to emaciate; Boden to exhaust; siehe **ausgemergelt.**

ausmerzen vt sep (ausrotten) Ungeziefer, Unkraut to eradicate; (aussondern) schwache Tiere to cull; (fig) schwache Teilnehmer to sort or weed out; Fehler, Mißstände to eradicate; Erinnerungen to obliterate.

ausmessen vt sep irreg Raum, Fläche etc to measure (out) ◆ **das Zimmer ~** (fig) to pace up and down the room.

Ausmessung f (a) siehe vt measuring (out). (b) (Maße) dimensions pl.

ausmisten sep [1] vt Stall to muck out; (fig inf) Schrank etc to tidy out; Zimmer to clean out.
[2] vi (lit) to muck out; (fig) to have a clean-out.

ausmontieren* vt sep to take out.

ausmustern vt sep Maschine, Fahrzeug etc to take out of service; (Mil: entlassen) to invalid out.

Ausnahme f -, -n exception ◆ **mit ~ von ihm** or **seiner** (geh) with the exception of him, except (for) him; **ohne ~** without exception; **~n bestätigen die Regel** (prov), **keine Regel ohne ~** (prov) the exception proves the rule (prov).

Ausnahme-: ~bestimmung f special regulation; **~erscheinung** f exception; **~fall** m exception, exceptional case; **~genehmigung** f special (case) authorization; **~situation** f special or exceptional situation; **~stellung** f special position; **~zustand** m (Pol) state of emergency; **den ~zustand verhängen** to declare a state of emergency.

ausnahmslos [1] adv without exception.
[2] adj Bewilligung, Zustimmung unanimous ◆ **das ~e Erscheinen der ganzen Belegschaft** the appearance of all the staff without exception.

ausnahmsweise adv **darf ich das machen? — ~** may I do that? — just this once; **wenn er ~ auch mal einen Fehler macht** when he makes a mistake too just for once; **sie hat es mir ~ einmal erlaubt** she let me do it once as a special exception; **er darf heute ~ früher von der Arbeit weggehen** as an exception he may leave work earlier today.

ausnehmen sep irreg [1] vt (a) (fig) Verbrecherbande, Diebesnest etc to raid; (Mil) Stellung to take out ◆ **das Nest ~** to remove the eggs from the nest.
(b) Fisch, Kaninchen to gut, to dress; Geflügel to draw; Hammel, Rind etc to dress; Eingeweide, Herz etc to take out, to remove.
(c) (ausschließen) jdn to make an exception of; (befreien) to exempt ◆ **ich nehme keinen aus** I'll make no exceptions; siehe **ausgenommen.**
(d) (inf) jdn to fleece; (beim Kartenspiel) to clean out.
(e) (Aus: erkennen) to make out.
[2] vr (geh: wirken) **sich schön** or **gut/schlecht ~** to look good/bad.

ausnehmend adj (geh) exceptional ◆ **das gefällt mir ~ gut** I like that very much indeed.

ausnüchtern vtir sep to sober up.

Ausnüchterung f sobering up.

Ausnüchterungszelle f drying-out cell.

ausnutzen, ausnützen (esp S Ger, Aus) vt sep to use, to make use of; (ausbeuten) to exploit; Gelegenheit to make the most of; jds Gutmütigkeit, Leichtgläubigkeit etc to take advantage of.

Ausnutzung, Ausnützung (esp S Ger, Aus) f use; (Ausbeutung) exploitation.

auspacken sep [1] vti Koffer to unpack; Geschenk to unwrap.
[2] vi (inf: alles sagen) to talk (inf); (seine Meinung sagen) to speak one's mind.

auspeitschen vt sep to whip.

auspellen sep (inf) [1] vt to peel; Nuß, Erbsen to shell.
[2] vr to strip off.

Auspendler(in f) m commuter.

auspennen vir sep (inf) to have a (good) kip (inf).

auspfeifen vt sep irreg to boo or hiss at; Stück, Schauspieler to boo off the stage.

auspflanzen vt sep (Hort) to plant out.

Auspizium nt, usu pl (geh) auspice.

ausplappern vt sep (inf) to blurt out (inf).

ausplaudern sep [1] vt to let out.
[2] vr (dial) to have a good chat.

ausplündern vt sep Dorf etc to plunder, to pillage; Kasse, Laden, (hum) Speisekammer etc to raid; jdn to plunder (inf), to clean out (inf).

auspolstern vt sep Mantel etc to pad (out); Kiste etc to line, to pad ◆ **sie ist gut ausgepolstert** (fig hum) she's well-padded (hum).

ausposaunen* vt sep (inf) to broadcast (inf).

auspowern [-po:vɐn] vt sep to impoverish; (ausbeuten) Massen, Boden to exploit; siehe **ausgepowert.**

Auspowerung f siehe vt impoverishment; exploitation.

ausprägen sep [1] vt Münzen etc to mint ◆ **Metall zu Münzen ~** to stamp coins out of metal.
[2] vr (Begabung, Charaktereigenschaft etc) to reveal or show itself ◆ **die Erziehung prägt sich im Charakter/Verhalten aus** one's upbringing shapes or stamps one's character/behaviour or leaves its stamp on one's character/behaviour; siehe **ausgeprägt.**

Ausprägung f (a) no pl (von Charakter) shaping, moulding. (b) no pl (das Ausgeprägtsein) markedness ◆ **in einer derart starken ~ ist mir diese Krankheit noch nicht untergekommen** I have never come across this illness to such a marked degree. (c) (Ausdruck) expression.

auspreisen vt sep Waren to price.

auspressen vt sep (a) (herauspressen) Saft, Schwamm etc to squeeze out; Zitrone etc to squeeze. (b) (fig: ausbeuten) to squeeze dry, to bleed white. (c) (fig: ausfragen) to press ◆ **jdn wie eine Zitrone ~** to squeeze sb like a lemon (for information).

ausprobieren* vt sep to try out; Auto auch to test-drive.

Auspuff m -(e)s, -e exhaust.

Auspuff-: ~gase pl exhaust fumes pl; **~rohr** nt exhaust pipe; **~topf** m silencer (Brit), muffler (US).

auspumpen vt sep (a) to pump out. (b) (inf: erschöpfen) to drain; siehe **ausgepumpt.**

auspunkten vt sep (Boxen) to outpoint, to beat on points.

auspusten vt sep (inf) to blow out ◆ **die Luft kräftig ~** to blow out hard; **jdm das Lebenslicht ~** to snuff out sb's life.

ausputzen sep [1] vt (a) (esp S Ger, Aus: reinigen) to clean out; Kleider to clean; Flecken to get out. (b) (Ftbl) Ball to clear. (c) (dial: ausnutzen) to use.

➤ SPRACHE AKTIV: **ausmachen: g** → 28.1, 31, 34.5

[2] *vi* (*Ftbl*) to clear (the ball); (*Ausputzer sein*) to act as *or* be the sweeper.
Ausputzer *m* **-s, -** (*Ftbl*) sweeper.
ausquartieren* *vt sep* ti move out; (*Mil*) to billet out.
Ausquartierung *f* moving out; (*Mil*) billeting out.
ausquatschen *sep* (*sl*) [1] *vt* to blurt out (*inf*).
[2] *vr* to have a heart-to-heart (*bei jdm* with sb), to get a load off one's chest.
[3] *vi* to finish.
ausquetschen *vt sep Saft etc* to squeeze out; *Zitrone etc* to squeeze; (*inf: ausfragen*) (*Polizei etc*) to grill (*inf*); (*aus Neugier*) to pump (*inf*).
ausradieren* *vt sep* to rub out, to erase; (*fig: vernichten*) to wipe out ◆ **etw aus dem Gedächtnis ~** to erase sth from one's mind *or* memory.
ausrangieren* *vt sep Kleider* to throw out; *Maschine, Auto* to scrap ◆ **ein altes ausrangiertes Auto** an old disused car.
ausrasieren* *vt sep* to shave; *Koteletten* to trim ◆ **jdm/sich die Haare im Nacken ~** to shave sb's/one's neck.
ausrasten *sep* [1] *vi aux sein* **(a)** (*Tech*) to come out. **(b)** (*hum inf: zornig werden*) to blow one's top (*inf*), to do one's nut (*inf*).
[2] *vr* (*Aus, S Ger: ausruhen*) to have a rest.
[3] *vi impers* (*inf*) **es rastet bei jdm aus** something snaps in sb (*inf*).
ausrauben *vt sep* to rob.
ausräubern *vt sep* (*auch hum*) to plunder, to raid ◆ **jdn ~** to clean sb out (*inf*).
ausrauchen *sep* [1] *vt Zigarette etc* to finish (smoking).
[2] *vi* **(a)** (*zu Ende rauchen*) to finish smoking. **(b)** *aux sein* (*Aus*) (*verdunsten*) to evaporate; (*Geschmack verlieren*) to lose its taste.
ausräuchern *vt sep Zimmer* to fumigate; *Tiere,* (*fig*) *Schlupfwinkel, Bande* to smoke out.
ausraufen *vt sep* to tear *or* pull out ◆ **ich könnte mir die Haare ~** I could kick myself.
ausräumen *vt sep* to clear out; *Möbel auch*to move out; *Magen, Darm* to purge; (*fig*) *Mißverständnisse, Konflikt* to clear up; *Vorurteile, Bedenken* to dispel; (*inf: ausrauben*) to clean out (*inf*).
ausrechnen *vt sep* to work out; (*ermitteln*) *Gewicht, Länge etc* to calculate ◆ **sich** (*dat*) **etw ~ können** (*fig*) to be able to work sth out (for oneself); **sich** (*dat*) **große Chancen/einen Vorteil ~** to reckon *or* fancy that one has a good chance/an advantage; *siehe* **ausgerechnet.**
Ausrechnung *f siehe vt* working out; calculation.
ausrecken *vt sep* to stretch (out) ◆ **sich** (*dat*) **den Hals ~** to crane one's neck.
Ausrede *f* excuse.
ausreden *sep* [1] *vi* to finish speaking ◆ **er hat mich gar nicht erst ~ lassen** he didn't even let me finish (speaking).
[2] *vt* **jdm etw ~** to talk sb out of sth.
[3] *vr* (*esp Aus*) (*sich aussprechen*) to have a heart-to-heart; (*Ausflüchte machen*) to make excuses ◆ **er versucht sich immer auf irgendwas auszureden** he is always trying to make some excuse.
ausregnen *vir impers sep* to stop raining.
ausreiben *vt sep irreg Fleck etc* to rub out; *Topf etc* to scour; *Gläser* to wipe out ◆ **sich** (*dat*) **die Augen ~** to rub one's eyes.
ausreichen *vi sep* to be sufficient *or* enough ◆ **die Zeit reicht nicht aus** there is not sufficient time; **mit etw ~** (*dial*) to manage on sth.
ausreichend [1] *adj* sufficient, enough; (*Sch*) satisfactory.
[2] *adv* sufficiently.
ausreifen *vi sep aux sein* to ripen; (*fig auch*) to mature.
Ausreise *f* **bei der ~** on leaving the country; (*Grenzübertritt*) on crossing the border; **jdm die ~ verweigern** to prohibit sb from leaving the country.
Ausreise-: ~antrag *m* application for an exit visa; **~erlaubnis, ~genehmigung** *f* exit permit.
ausreisen *vi sep aux sein* to leave (the country) ◆ **ins Ausland/nach Frankreich ~** to go abroad/to France.
Ausreise-: ~sperre *f* ban on leaving the country; **~visum** *nt* exit visa; **~willige(r)** *mf decl as adj* prospective emigrant.
ausreißen *sep irreg* [1] *vt Haare, Blatt* to tear out; *Unkraut, Blumen, Zahn* to pull out ◆ **einem Käfer die Flügel/Beine ~** to pull a beetle's wings/legs off; **er hat sich** (*dat*) **kein Bein ausgerissen** (*inf*) he didn't exactly overstrain himself *or* bust a gut (*sl*); **ich könnte Bäume ~** (*inf*) I feel full of beans; *siehe* **Fliege.**
[2] *vi aux sein* **(a)** (*sich lösen*) (*Ärmel etc*) to come away; (*Knopf, Griff*) to come off; (*einreißen*) (*Naht*) to come out; (*Knopfloch*) to tear.
(b) (+*dat* from) (*inf: davonlaufen*) to run away; (*Sport*) to break away.
Ausreißer(in *f*) *m* **-s, -** (*inf*) runaway; (*Mil*) stray bullet; (*Sport*) runner/cyclist who breaks away.
ausreiten *sep irreg* [1] *vi aux sein* to ride out, to go riding *or* for a ride.
[2] *vt Pferd* to take out, to exercise ◆ **ein Pferd voll ~** to ride a horse to its limit.
ausreizen *vt sep Karten* to bid up to strength; *Kontrahenten* to outbid; (*fig: ausschöpfen*) to drain, to use up, to exhaust.
ausrenken *vt sep* to dislocate ◆ **sich/jdm den Arm ~** to dislocate one's/sb's arm; **sich** (*dat*) **(fast) den Hals ~** (*inf*) to crane one's neck.
▼ **ausrichten** *sep* [1] *vt* **(a)** (*aufstellen*) to line up, to get *or* bring into line; *Arbeitsstück etc auch, Gewehre* to align ◆ **jdn/etw auf etw** (*acc*) **~** (*einstellen*) to orientate sb/sth to sth, to align sb/sth with sth; (*abstellen*) to gear sb/sth to sth.
(b) (*veranstalten*) to organize; *Hochzeit, Fest* to arrange.
(c) (*erreichen*) to achieve ◆ **ich konnte bei ihr nichts ~** I couldn't get anywhere with her.
▼ **(d)** (*übermitteln*) to tell; *Nachricht* to pass on ◆ **jdm ~, daß ...** to tell sb (that) ...; **jdm etwas ~** to give sb a message; **kann ich etwas ~?** can I give him/her *etc* a message?; **bitte richten Sie ihm einen Gruß aus** please give him my regards.
(e) (*Aus: schlechtmachen*) to run down.
[2] *vr* to line up in a straight row; (*Mil*) to dress ranks ◆ **sich nach dem Nebenmann/Vordermann/Hintermann ~** to line up (exactly) with the person next to/in front of/behind one; **ausgerichtet in einer Reihe stehen** to stand next to one another in a straight line; **sich an etw** (*dat*) **~** (*fig*) to orientate oneself to sth.
Ausrichtung *f siehe vt* **(a)** lining up; alignment. **(b)** organization; arrangement. **(c)** (*fig*) (*auf Ideologie etc*) orientation (*auf* +*acc* towards), alignment (*auf* +*acc* with); (*auf Bedürfnisse etc*) gearing (*auf* +*acc* to); (*an einer Ideologie*) orientation (*an* +*dat* to).
ausringen *vt sep irreg* (*dial*) *siehe* **auswringen.**
Ausritt *m* ride (out); (*das Ausreiten*) riding out.
ausrollen *sep* [1] *vt Teig, Teppich* to roll out; *Kabel auch* to run *or* pay out.
[2] *vi aux sein* (*Flugzeug*) to taxi to a standstill *or* stop; (*Fahrzeug*) to coast to a stop.
ausrotten *vt sep* to wipe out; *Wanzen etc* to destroy; *Tiere, Volk auch* to exterminate; *Religion, Ideen auch* to stamp out, to eradicate.
Ausrottung *f siehe vt* wiping out; destruction; extermination; stamping out, eradication.
ausrücken *sep* [1] *vi aux sein* **(a)** (*Mil*) to move *or* set out; (*Polizei, Feuerwehr*) to turn out.
(b) (*inf: ausreißen*) to make off; (*von zu Hause*) to run away; (*aus Gefängnis*) to run away, to get out.
[2] *vt* **(a)** (*Tech*) to disengage, to release.
(b) (*Typ*) *Zeilen etc* to reverse-indent (*spec*), to move out.
Ausruf *m* **(a)** (*Ruf*) cry, shout. **(b)** (*Bekanntmachung*) proclamation ◆ **etw durch ~ bekanntmachen** to proclaim sth.
ausrufen *vt sep irreg* to exclaim; *Schlagzeilen* to cry out; *Waren* to cry; (*auf Auktion*) to start; (*verkünden*) to call out; *Haltestellen, Streik* to call ◆ **die Stunden ~** (*Hist*) to call the hours; **jdn zum** *or* **als König ~** to proclaim sb king; **jdn** *or* **jds Namen ~ (lassen)** (*über Lautsprecher etc*) to put out a call for sb; (*im Hotel*) to page sb.
Ausrufer *m* **-s, -** (*Hist*) (town) crier; (*von Waren*) crier.
Ausrufe-: ~satz *m* exclamation; **~wort** *nt* exclamation, interjection; **~zeichen** *nt* exclamation mark.
Ausrufung *f* proclamation ◆ **die ~ eines Streiks** a strike call.
Ausrufungszeichen *nt siehe* **Ausrufezeichen.**
ausruhen *vtir sep* to rest; (*Mensch auch*) to take *or* have a rest ◆ **meine Augen müssen (sich) ein wenig ~** I shall have to rest my eyes a little; **seine Augen ~ (lassen)** to rest one's eyes; *siehe* **ausgeruht, Lorbeer.**
ausrupfen *vt sep* to pull out; *Federn auch* to pluck out.
ausrüsten *vt sep* (*lit, fig*) to equip; *Fahrzeug, Schiff* to fit out; *Tuch* to treat ◆ **ein Fahrzeug mit etw ~** to fit a car with sth.
Ausrüstung *f* **(a)** *no pl siehe vt* equipping; fitting-out; treating. **(b)** (*~gegenstände*) equipment; (*esp Kleidung*) outfit.
Ausrüstungs-: ~gegenstand *m*, **~stück** *nt* piece of equipment.
ausrutschen *vi sep aux sein* to slip; (*Fahrzeug*) to skid; (*fig inf*) (*sich schlecht benehmen*) to drop a clanger (*inf*); (*straffällig werden*) to get into trouble ◆ **das Messer/die Hand ist mir ausgerutscht** my knife/my hand slipped.
Ausrutscher *m* **-s, -** (*inf*) (*lit, fig*) slip; (*schlechte Leistung auch*) slip-up.
Aussaat *f* **(a)** *no pl* (*das Säen*) sowing. **(b)** (*Saat*) seed.
aussäen *vt sep* (*lit, fig*) to sow.
Aussage *f* **-, -n** statement; (*Behauptung*) opinion; (*Bericht*) report; (*Jur*) (*eines Beschuldigten, Angeklagten*) statement; (*Zeugen~*) evidence *no pl*, testimony; (*fig: von Roman etc*) message ◆ **eine eidliche/schriftliche ~** a sworn/written statement; **hier steht ~ gegen ~** it's one person's word against another's; **der Angeklagte/Zeuge verweigerte die ~** the accused refused to make a statement/the witness refused to give evidence *or* testify; **eine ~ machen** to make a statement; to give evidence; **nach ~ seines Chefs** according to his boss.
Aussage-: ~kraft *f* meaningfulness; **a~kräftig** *adj* meaningful.
aussagen *sep* [1] *vt* to say (*über* +*acc* about); (*behaupten*) to state; (*unter Eid*) to testify ◆ **was will der Roman ~?** what message does this novel try to convey?; **etw über jdn ~** (*Jur*) to give sth in evidence about sb.
[2] *vi* (*Jur*) (*Zeuge*) to give evidence; (*Angeklagter, schriftlich*) to make a statement; (*unter Eid auch*) to testify ◆ **eidlich** *or* **unter Eid ~** to give evidence under oath; **für/gegen jdn ~** to give evidence *or* to testify for/against sb; **schriftlich ~** to make a written statement.
aussägen *vt sep* to saw out.
Aussage-: ~satz *m* statement; **a~stark** *adj* powerful; **~verweigerung** *f* (*Jur*) refusal to give evidence *or* to testify; **ein Recht auf ~verweigerung haben** to have a right to refuse to give evidence *or* to testify.
Aussatz *m* **-es,** *no pl* (*Med*) leprosy; (*fig*) pestilence.
aussätzig *adj* (*Med*) leprous.
Aussätzige(r) *mf decl as adj* (*lit, fig*) leper.
aussaufen *sep irreg* [1] *vt* (*Tier*) *Wasser* to drink up; *Napf* to empty; (*sl: Mensch*) *Flüssigkeit* to swill down (*inf*); *Glas etc* to empty ◆ **wer hat mein Glas/meinen Whisky ausgesoffen?** (*sl*) who's drunk my drink/whisky?
[2] *vi* (*sl*) **sauf endlich aus!** come on, get that down you!
aussaugen *vt sep Saft etc* to suck out; *Frucht* to suck (dry); *Wunde* to suck the poison out of; (*leersaugen*) *Glasglocke etc* to evacuate; (*fig: ausbeuten*) to drain dry ◆ **jdn bis aufs Blut** *or* **Mark ~** to bleed sb white.

ausschaben *vt sep* to scrape out; (*Med auch*) to curette.
Ausschabung *f* (*Med*) curettage, scrape.
ausschachten *vt sep* to dig, to excavate; *Erde* to dig up; *Brunnen* to sink.
Ausschachtung *f* **(a)** *no pl siehe vt* digging, excavation; digging up; sinking. **(b)** (*Grube etc*) excavation.
Ausschachtungs|arbeiten *pl* excavation work.
ausschalen *vt sep* (*Build*) *siehe* **verschalen.**
ausschälen *vt sep* to remove, to cut out; *Nüsse, Hülsenfrüchte* to shell.
Ausschaltautomatik *f* auto *or* automatic stop.
ausschalten *vt sep* **(a)** (*abstellen*) to switch off, to turn off ◆ **sich (automatisch)** ~to switch *or* turn (itself) off (automatically). **(b)** (*fig*) to eliminate.
Ausschaltung *f siehe vt* **(a)** switching off, turning off. **(b)** elimination.
Ausschank *m* **-(e)s, Ausschänke, Ausschänke** *f* (*Aus*) **(a)** (*Schankraum*) bar, pub (*Brit*); (*Schanktisch*) bar, counter.
(b) (*no pl: Getränkeausgabe*) serving of drinks ◆ **„~ von 9⁰⁰ bis 14⁰⁰"** "open from 9.00 to 14.00"; **~ über die Straße** off-sales *pl*; **„kein ~ an Jugendliche unter 16 Jahren"** "drinks not sold to persons under the age of 16".
Ausschank|erlaubnis *f* licence (*Brit*), license (*US*).
Ausschau *f, no pl*: **~ halten** (*nach* for) to look out, to be on the *or* keep a look-out.
ausschauen *vi sep* **(a)** (*geh*) (*nach* for) to look out, to be on the *or* keep a look-out. **(b)** (*dial*) *siehe* **aussehen. wie schaut's aus?** (*inf*) how's things? (*inf*).
ausschaufeln *vt sep Grube, Grab* to dig; *Erde* to dig out; *Leiche* to dig up.
ausschäumen *vt sep* (*Tech*) to foam.
Ausscheid *m* **-(e)s, -e** (*DDR*) *siehe* **Ausscheidungskampf.**
ausscheiden *sep irreg* [1] *vt* (*aussondern*) to take out; *esp Menschen* to remove; (*Physiol*) to excrete.
[2] *vi aux sein* **(a)** (*aus einem Amt*) to retire (*aus* from); (*aus Club, Firma*) to leave (*aus etw* sth); (*Sport*) to be eliminated; (*in Wettkampf*) to drop out ◆ **wer unfair kämpft, muß ~** whoever cheats will be disqualified.
(b) (*nicht in Betracht kommen: Plan, Möglichkeit etc*) to be ruled out ◆ **das/er scheidet aus** that/he has to be ruled out.
Ausscheidung *f* **(a)** *no pl* (*das Aussondern*) removal; (*Physiol*) excretion. **(b)** (*Med*) **~en** *pl* excretions *pl.* **(c)** (*Sport*) elimination; (*Vorkampf*) qualifying contest.
Ausscheidungs- *in cpds* (*Physiol*) excretory; (*Sport*) qualifying; **~kampf** *m* (*Sport*) qualifying contest; (*Leichtathletik, Schwimmen*) heat; **~organ** *nt* excretory organ; **~produkt** *nt* excretory product; **~spiel** *nt* qualifying match *or* game.
ausscheißen *vr sep irreg* (*vulg*) to have a good shit (*vulg*).
ausschelten *vt sep irreg* (*geh*) to scold.
ausschenken *vti sep* to pour (out); (*am Ausschank*) to serve.
ausscheren *vi sep aux sein* (*aus Kolonne*) (*Soldat*) to break rank; (*Fahrzeug, Schiff*) to leave the line *or* convoy; (*Flugzeug*) to break formation, to peel off; (*zum Überholen*) to pull out; (*ausschwenken, von gerader Linie abweichen*) to swing out; (*fig*) to step out of line ◆ **aus der Parteilinie ~** to deviate from the party line.
ausschicken *vt sep* to send out.
ausschießen *sep irreg* [1] *vt* **(a)** to shoot out ◆ **jdm ein Auge ~** to shoot out sb's eye. **(b)** (*in Wettbewerb*) to shoot for. **(c)** (*old: aussondern*) to reject, to throw out. **(d)** (*Typ*) to impose.
[2] *vi aux sein* **(a)** (*Pflanzen*) to shoot up. **(b)** (*S Ger, Aus: verbleichen*) to fade.
ausschiffen *sep* [1] *vt* to disembark; *Ladung, Waren* to unload, to discharge.
[2] *vr* to disembark.
Ausschiffung *f siehe vb* disembarkation; unloading, discharging.
ausschildern *vt sep* to signpost.
ausschimpfen *vt sep* to tell off.
ausschirren *vt sep Pferd* to unharness; *Ochsen* to unyoke.
ausschl. *abbr of* **ausschließlich** excl.
ausschlachten *vt sep* **(a)** to gut, to dress. **(b)** (*fig*) *Fahrzeuge, Maschinen etc* to cannibalize. **(c)** (*fig inf: ausnutzen*) *Skandal, Ereignis* to exploit; *Buch, Werk etc* to get everything out of.
ausschlafen *sep irreg* [1] *vt Rausch etc* to sleep off.
[2] *vir* to have a good sleep.
Ausschlag *m* **(a)** (*Med*) rash ◆ **(einen) ~ bekommen** to come out in a rash. **(b)** (*von Zeiger etc*) swing; (*von Kompaßnadel*) deflection. **(c)** (*fig*) decisive factor ◆ **den ~ geben** (*fig*) to be the decisive factor; **die Stimme des Vorsitzenden gibt den ~** the chairman has the casting vote.
ausschlagen *sep irreg* [1] *vt* **(a)** (*herausschlagen*) to knock out; (*dial: ausschütteln*) *Staubtuch etc* to shake out ◆ **jdm die Zähne ~** to knock sb's teeth out.
(b) *Feuer* to beat out.
(c) (*breit schlagen*) *Metall* to beat out.
(d) (*auskleiden*) to line.
(e) (*ablehnen*) to turn down; *Erbschaft* to waive ◆ **jdm etw ~** to refuse sb sth.
[2] *vi* **(a)** *aux sein or haben* (*Baum, Strauch*) to come out, to start to bud, to burgeon (out) (*liter*).
(b) (*los-, zuschlagen*) to hit *or* lash out; (*mit Füßen*) to kick (out); (*Pferd*) to kick.
(c) *aux sein or haben* (*Zeiger etc*) to swing; (*Kompaßnadel*) to be deflected; (*Wünschelrute etc*) to dip.
(d) ausgeschlagen haben (*Turmuhr*) to have finished striking; (*liter: Herz*) to have beat its last (*liter*).
(e) *aux sein* **günstig/nachteilig ~** to turn out well *or* favourably/badly; **zum Guten ~** to turn out all right.
ausschlaggebend *adj* decisive; *Stimme auch* deciding ◆ **~ sein** to be the decisive factor; **das ist von ~er Bedeutung** that is of prime importance.
ausschlecken *vt sep* (*S Ger*) *siehe* **auslecken.**
ausschleifen *vt sep irreg* (*Tech*) to grind out.
➤ **ausschließen** *vt sep irreg* **(a)** (*aussperren*) to lock out.
➤ **(b)** (*ausnehmen*) to exclude; (*aus Gemeinschaft*) to expel; (*vorübergehend*) to suspend; (*Sport*) to disqualify; (*Typ*) to justify; *Panne, Fehler, Möglichkeit etc* to rule out ◆ **das eine schließt das andere nicht aus** the one does not exclude the other; **ich will nicht ~, daß er ein Dieb ist, aber ...** I don't want to rule out the possibility that he's a thief but ...; **die Öffentlichkeit ~** (*Jur*) to exclude the public; *siehe* **ausgeschlossen.**
ausschließlich [1] *adj attr* exclusive; *Rechte auch* sole.
[2] *adv* exclusively.
[3] *prep +gen* exclusive of, excluding.
Ausschließlichkeit *f* exclusiveness.
Ausschließlichkeits|anspruch *m* claim to sole rights.
Ausschließung *f siehe* **Ausschluß.**
ausschlüpfen *vi sep aux sein* to slip out; (*aus Ei, Puppe*) to hatch out.
⚠ **Ausschluß** *m siehe* **ausschließen (b)** exclusion; expulsion; suspension; disqualification; (*Typ*) spacing material ◆ **mit ~ von** (*dated*) with the exception of; **unter ~ der Öffentlichkeit stattfinden** to be closed to the public; *siehe* **Rechtsweg.**
ausschmücken *vt sep* to decorate; (*fig*) *Erzählung* to embroider, to embellish ◆ **~de Details** embellishments.
Ausschmückung *f siehe vt* decorating, decoration; embroidery, embellishment.
ausschnauben *vr sep* to blow one's nose.
Ausschneidebogen *m* cut-out sheet.
ausschneiden *vt sep irreg* **(a)** (*herausschneiden*) to cut out; *Zweige etc* to cut away; *siehe* **ausgeschnitten. (b)** *Baum etc* to prune.
Ausschnitt *m* **(a)** (*Zeitungs~*) cutting, clipping.
(b) (*Math*) sector.
(c) (*Kleid~*) neck ◆ **ein tiefer ~** a low neckline; **er versuchte, ihr in den ~ zu schauen** he was trying to look down her dress.
(d) (*fig: Teil*) part; (*aus einem Bild*) detail; (*aus einem Roman*) excerpt, extract; (*aus einem Film*) clip ◆ **ich kenne das Buch/den Film nur in ~en** I only know parts of the book/film.
ausschnittweise *adj* partial; *Veröffentlichung* in extracts ◆ **bei ~m Lesen** by reading sections.
ausschnitzen *vt sep* to carve out.
ausschnüffeln *vt sep* (*inf*) to ferret *or* nose out (*inf*).
ausschöpfen *vt sep* **(a)** (*herausschöpfen*) *Wasser etc* to ladle out (*aus* of); (*aus Boot*) to bale out (*aus* of). **(b)** (*leeren*) to empty; *Faß etc auch* to drain; *Boot* to bale out; (*fig*) to exhaust ◆ **die Kompetenzen voll ~** to do everything within one's power.
ausschreiben *vt sep irreg* **(a)** to write out; (*ungekürzt schreiben*) to write (out) in full; *siehe* **ausgeschrieben.**
(b) (*ausstellen*) *Rechnung etc* to make out; *Formular* to fill in (*Brit*) *or* out.
(c) (*bekanntmachen*) to announce; *Versammlung, Wahlen* to call; *Projekt* to invite tenders for; *Stellen* to advertise; *Steuern* to impose.
Ausschreibung *f siehe vt* **(a)** *no pl* (*rare: ungekürzte Schreibung*) writing out. **(b)** making out; filling in (*Brit*) *or* out. **(c)** announcement; calling; invitation of tenders (*gen* for); advertising; imposition.
ausschreien *sep irreg* [1] *vt* **(a)** *siehe* **ausrufen. (b)** (*ausbuhen*) to shout down.
[2] *vr* **(a)** (*inf: zu Ende schreien*) to finish shouting. **(b) sich** (*dat*) **die Kehle/Lunge ~** (*inf*) to shout one's head off (*inf*).
[3] *vi* to finish shouting.
ausschreiten *sep irreg* [1] *vi aux sein* (*geh*) to stride out, to step out.
[2] *vt* to pace.
Ausschreitung *f usu pl* (*Aufruhr*) riot, rioting *no pl*; (*dated: Ausschweifung*) excess.
ausschulen *sep* [1] *vt* **ausgeschult werden** to leave school.
[2] *vi aux sein* (*Aus*) to leave school.
⚠ **Ausschuß** *m* **(a)** *no pl* (*Comm*) rejects *pl*; (*fig inf*) trash. **(b)** (*Komitee*) committee. **(c)** (*eines Geschosses*) exit point; (*Wunde*) exit wound.
⚠ **Ausschuß-: ~mitglied** *nt* committee member; **~öffnung** *f* point of exit, exit point/wound; **~sitzung** *f* committee meeting; **~ware** *f* (*Comm*) rejects *pl.*
ausschütteln *vt sep* to shake out.
ausschütten *sep* [1] *vt* **(a)** (*auskippen*) to tip out; *Eimer, Glas, Füllhorn* to empty ◆ **jdm sein Herz ~** (*fig*) to pour out one's heart to sb; *siehe* **Kind. (b)** (*verschütten*) to spill. **(c)** (*Fin*) *Dividende etc* to distribute.
[2] *vr* **sich (vor Lachen) ~** (*inf*) to split one's sides laughing.
Ausschüttung *f* **(a)** (*Fin*) distribution; (*Dividende*) dividend. **(b)** (*Phys*) fall-out.
ausschwärmen *vi sep aux sein* (*Bienen, Menschen*) to swarm out; (*Mil*) to fan out.
ausschwefeln *vt sep* to sulphur, to fumigate (with sulphur);
ausschweifen *sep* [1] *vi aux sein* (*Redner*) to digress; (*Phantasie*) to run riot; (*in Lebensweise*) to lead a dissipated life.
[2] *vt Möbelstück* to curve.
ausschweifend *adj Leben* dissipated; *Phantasie* wild.
Ausschweifung *f* (*Maßlosigkeit*) excess; (*in Lebensweise*) dissipation.
ausschweigen *vr sep irreg* to remain silent (*über +acc, zu* about) ◆ **sich eisern**

➤ SPRACHE AKTIV: **ausschließen: b** → 43.3, 53.4

~ to maintain a stony silence.

ausschwemmen *vt sep* to wash out; *Giftstoffe* to flush out (*aus* of); (*aushöhlen*) to hollow out.

Ausschwemmung *f* **(a)** *no pl siehe vt* washing out; flushing out; hollowing out. **(b)** (*Stelle*) hollow.

ausschwenken *sep* [1] *vt* **(a)** (*ausspülen*) to rinse out. **(b)** *Kran* to swing out.
[2] *vi aux sein* **(a)** (*Mil*) to wheel ◆ **nach links/rechts ~** to wheel left/right. **(b)** (*Kran, Boot*) to swing out.

ausschwitzen *sep* [1] *vt* to sweat out; (*Wände*) to sweat.
[2] *vi aux sein* to sweat.

aussegnen *vt sep* (*Eccl*) *Toten* to give the last blessing to.

aussehen *vi sep irreg* **(a)** to look ◆ **gut ~** to look good; (*hübsch*) to be good looking; (*gesund*) to look well; **gesund/elend ~** to look healthy/wretched; **zum Fürchten ~** to look frightening; **es sieht nach Regen aus** it looks like rain *or* as if it's going to rain; **wie jd/etw ~** to look like sb/sth; **weißt du, wie ein Gnu aussieht?** do you know what a gnu looks like?; **wie sieht's aus?** (*inf: wie steht's*) how's things? (*inf*); **wie siehst du denn (bloß) aus?** what *do* you look like!, just look at you!; **ich habe (vielleicht) ausgesehen!** you should have seen me!; **er sieht nach nichts aus** he doesn't look anything special; **es soll nach etwas ~** it's got to look good; **es sieht danach** *or* **so aus, als ob ...** it looks as if ...; **ihr seht mir danach aus** (*iro*) I bet!; **seh' ich so** *or* **danach aus?** (*inf*) what do you take me for?; **so siehst du (gerade) aus!** (*inf*) that's what you think!; **er sieht ganz so** *or* **danach aus** he looks it; **es sieht nicht gut mit ihm aus** things don't look good for him; **bei mir sieht es gut aus** I'm doing fine.
(b) (*geh: Ausschau halten*) to look out (*nach* for).

Aussehen *nt* **-s,** *no pl* appearance ◆ **dem ~ nach** to go by appearances, by the looks of it; **etw dem ~ nach beurteilen** to judge sth by appearances.

⚠ **aussein** *sep irreg aux sein* (*Zusammenschreibung nur bei infin und ptp*) [1] *vi* (*inf*) **(a)** (*zu Ende sein*) (*Schule*) to be out, to have finished; (*Krieg, Stück*) to have ended; (*nicht ansein*) (*Feuer, Ofen*) to be out; (*Radio, Fernseher etc*) to be off; (*Sport*) (*außerhalb sein: Ball*) to be out (of play); (*ausgeschieden sein: Spieler*) to be out.
(b) **auf etw** (*acc*) **~** to be (only) after sth *or* interested in sth *or* out for sth; **auf jdn ~** to be after sb (*inf*); **nur auf Männer/auf eins ~** to be interested only in men/one thing; **ich war gestern abend (mit ihr) aus** I went out (with her) last night.
[2] *vi impers* **es ist aus (und vorbei) zwischen uns** it's (all) over between us; **es ist aus mit ihm** he is finished, he has had it (*inf*); **es ist aus (und vorbei) mit dem bequemen Leben** the life of leisure is (all) over; **daraus ist nichts geworden, damit ist es aus** nothing came of it, it's finished *or* all over.

außen *adv* **(a) die Tasse ist ~ bemalt** the cup is painted on the outside; **~ an der Windschutzscheibe** on the outside of the windscreen; **von ~ sieht es gut aus** outwardly *or* on the outside it looks good; **er läuft ~** he's running on the outside; **er spielt ~** he's playing on the wing; **das Fenster geht nach ~ auf** the window opens outwards; **nach ~ hin** (*fig*) outwardly. **(b) ~ vor sein** to be left out; **etw ~ vor lassen** (*etw ausschließen*) to leave sth out, to exclude sth. **(c)** (*Aus*) *siehe* **draußen.**

Außen[1] *m* **-, -** (*Sport*) wing ◆ **~ spielen** to play on the wing.

Außen[2] *nt* **-,** *no pl* outside.

Außen-: ~abmessung *f* external dimensions *pl*; **~ansicht** *f* exterior, view of the outside; **~antenne** *f* outdoor aerial; **~arbeiten** *pl* work on the exterior; **~aufnahme** *f* outdoor shot, exterior; **~bahn** *f* outside lane; **~beleuchtung** *f* exterior lighting; **~bezirk** *m* outlying district; **~border** *m* (*inf*) outboard; **~bordmotor** *m* outboard motor; **a~bords** *adv* (*Naut*) outboard; **~deich** *m* outside dyke.

aussenden *vt sep irreg* to send out.

Außendienst *m* external duty ◆ **im ~ sein** to work outside the office; **~ machen** *or* **haben** to work outside the office.

Außendienstmitarbeiter *m* sales representative.

Außen-: ~fläche *f* outside, outside *or* exterior surface; (*Flächeninhalt*) external surface area; **~hafen** *m* outer harbour; (*Hafenstadt*) port.

Außenhandel *m* foreign trade.

Außenhandels-: ~beziehungen *pl* foreign trade relations *pl*; **~bilanz** *f* balance of trade; **~politik** *f* foreign trade policy.

Außen-: ~haut *f* outer skin; **~kurve** *f* outside bend; **~linie** *f* (*Sport*) boundary (line); **~minister** *m* foreign minister, foreign secretary (*Brit*), secretary of state (*US*); **~ministerium** *nt* foreign ministry, foreign office (*Brit*), state department (*US*); **~netz** *nt* (*Ftbl*) side netting; **~politik** *f* (*Gebiet*) foreign politics *sing*; (*bestimmte*) foreign policy/policies; **~politiker** *m* foreign affairs politician; **a~politisch** *adj Debatte etc* foreign policy *attr; Fehler* as regards foreign affairs; *Berichterstattung* of foreign affairs; *Schulung, Erfahrung* in foreign affairs; *Sprecher* on foreign affairs; **a~politische Angelegenheiten** foreign affairs; **a~politisch gesehen, aus a~politischer Sicht** from the point of view of foreign affairs; **ein Experte auf a~politischem Gebiet** an expert on foreign affairs; **a~politisch sinnvoll sein** to be sensible foreign policy; **~seite** *f* outside; **die vordere ~seite des Hauses** the front exterior of the house.

Außenseiter(in *f*) *m* **-s, -** (*Sport, fig*) outsider.

Außenseiter-: ~rolle *f* role as an outsider; **eine ~rolle spielen** to play the role of an outsider; **~tum** *nt, no pl* being an outsider; **das ~tum als literarisches Thema** the outsider as a literary theme.

Außen-: ~spiegel *m* (*Aut*) outside mirror; **~stände** *pl* (*esp Comm*) outstanding debts *pl*, arrears *pl*; **wir haben noch 2.000 Mark ~stände** we still have *or* there are still 2,000 marks outstanding; **~stehende(r)** *mf decl as adj* outsider; **~stelle** *f* branch; **~stürmer** *m* (*Ftbl*) wing; **~tasche** *f* outside pocket; **~temperatur** *f* outside temperature; (*außerhalb Gebäude*) outdoor temperature; **wir haben 20° ~temperatur ~temperatur** the temperature outdoors is 20°; **~toilette** *f* outside toilet; (*auf dem Flur*) shared toilet; **~treppe** *f* outside staircase; **~wand** *f* outer wall; **~welt** *f* outside world; **~winkel** *m* (*Math*) exterior angle; **~wirtschaft** *f* foreign trade; **~zoll** *m* external tariff.

außer [1] *prep +dat or* (*rare*) *gen* **(a)** (*räumlich*) out of ◆ **~ Sicht/Gefecht/Kurs** *etc* out of sight/action/circulation *etc*; **~ sich** (*acc*) **geraten** to go wild; **~ sich** (*dat*) **sein** to be beside oneself; **~ Haus** *or* **Hauses sein/essen** to be/eat out; **~ Atem** out of breath; *siehe* **Acht**[2]**, Betrieb, Land** *etc.*
(b) (*ausgenommen*) except (for); (*abgesehen von*) apart from, aside from (*esp US*) ◆ **~ ihm habe ich keine Verwandten mehr** I have no relatives left apart from him *or* but him.
(c) (*zusätzlich zu*) in addition to.
[2] *conj* except ◆ **~ daß** ... except that ...; **~ wenn** ... except when...; **~ sonntags** except Sundays.

Außer-: ~achtlassen *nt*, **~achtlassung** *f* disregard; **unter ~achtlassung der Regeln** in total disregard of *or* with total disregard for the rules; **a~amtlich** *adj* unofficial; **a~betrieblich** *adj Veranstaltung, Regelung* private; *Tätigkeiten* outside; **sie treffen sich auch a~betrieblich** they also meet outside work.

außerdem *adv* besides; (*dazu*) in addition, as well; (*überdies*) anyway ◆ **ich kann ihn nicht leiden, (und) ~ lügt er immer** I can't stand him and besides *or* anyway he always tells lies; **er ist Professor und ~ noch Gutachter** he's a professor and a consultant besides *or* as well.

außerdienstlich *adj* (*nicht dienstlich*) *Telefonat, Angelegenheit* private; (*außerhalb der Arbeitszeit*) social ◆ **ich bin heute ~ unterwegs** I'm not on business today.

außer|ehelich [1] *adj* extramarital; *Kind* illegitimate.
[2] *adv* outside marriage ◆ **das Kind war ~ gezeugt worden** the child had been conceived out of wedlock.

äußere(r, s) *adj* (*außerhalb gelegen, Geog*) outer; *Durchmesser, Verletzung,* (*außenpolitisch*) external; *Schein, Eindruck* outward.

Äußere(s) *nt decl as adj* exterior; (*fig: Aussehen auch*) outward appearance ◆ **das ~ täuscht oft** appearances are often deceptive; **Minister des ~n** *siehe* **Außenminister.**

Außer-: a~europäisch *adj attr* non-European; *Raum* outside Europe; **a~fahrplanmäßig** *adj* non-scheduled; **a~gerichtlich** *adj* out of court; **a~gesetzlich** *adj* extralegal; (*gesetzbrecherisch*) illegal; **a~gewöhnlich** [1] *adj* unusual, out of the ordinary; (*sehr groß auch*) remarkable; **~gewöhnliches leisten** to do some remarkable things; [2] *adv* (*sehr*) extremely.

außerhalb [1] *prep +gen* outside ◆ **~ der Stadt** outside the town, out of town; **~ der Dienststunden** outside *or* out of office hours; **~ der Legalität** outside the law.
[2] *adv* (*außen*) outside; (*~ der Stadt*) out of town ◆ **~ wohnen/arbeiten** to live/work out of town; **nach ~** outside/out of town; **von ~** from outside/out of town; **~ stehen** (*fig*) to be on the outside.

Außer-: a~irdisch *adj* extraterrestrial; **a~kirchlich** *adj* non-ecclesiastic(al); *Trauung* civil; **~kraftsetzung** *f* repeal; **~kurssetzung** *f* (*von Währung*) withdrawal (from circulation); (*fig*) rejection.

äußerlich *adj* **(a)** external. **(b)** (*fig*) (*oberflächlich*) superficial; (*scheinbar*) outward; (*esp Philos*) *Wahrnehmung* external ◆ **„nur ~!", „nur zur ~en Anwendung!"** for external use only; **rein ~ betrachtet** on the face of it; **einer Sache** (*dat*) **~ sein** (*geh*) to be extrinsic to sth.

Äußerlichkeit *f* **(a)** (*fig*) triviality; (*Oberflächlichkeit*) superficiality; (*Formalität*) formality. **(b)** (*lit*) external characteristic ◆ **~en** (outward) appearances.

äußerln *vti infin only* (*Aus*) **einen Hund ~ (führen)** to take a dog for a walk.

➤ **äußern** [1] *vt* (*sagen*) to say; *Wunsch etc* to express; *Worte* to utter; *Kritik* to voice ◆ **seine Meinung ~** to give one's opinion *or* views.
➤ [2] *vr* (*Mensch*) to speak; (*Krankheit, Symptom*) to show *or* manifest itself ◆ **sich dahin gehend ~, daß** ... to make a comment to the effect that ...; **ich will mich dazu nicht ~** I don't want to say anything about that.

Außer-: a~ordentlich [1] *adj* extraordinary; (*ungewöhnlich auch*) exceptional; (*bemerkenswert auch*) remarkable, exceptional; *Professor* associate; **~ordentliches leisten** to achieve some remarkable things; [2] *adv* (*sehr*) exceptionally, extremely, extraordinarily; **a~orts** *adv* (*Sw, Aus*) out of town; **a~parlamentarisch** *adj* extraparliamentary; **a~planmäßig** *adj Besuch, Treffen* unscheduled; *Mahlzeit* additional; *Ausgaben* non-budgetary; **a~schulisch** *adj Aktivitäten, Interessen* extracurricular; **~sinnlich** *adj* **~sinnliche Wahrnehmung** extrasensory perception.

äußerst [1] *adv* extremely, exceedingly.
[2] *adj siehe* **~e(r, s).**

⚠ **außerstande** *adv* (*unfähig*) incapable; (*nicht in der Lage*) unable ◆ **~ sein, etw zu tun** to be incapable of doing sth; to be unable to do sth.

äußerstenfalls *adv* at most.

äußerste(r, s) *adj, superl of* **äußere(r, s)** (*räumlich*) furthest; *Planet, Schicht* outermost; *Norden etc* extreme; (*zeitlich*) latest possible; (*fig*) utmost, extreme ◆ **der ~ Preis** the last price; **mein ~s Angebot** my final offer; **im ~n Falle** if the worst comes to the worst; **mit ~r Kraft** with all one's strength; **von ~r Dringlichkeit/Wichtigkeit** of (the) utmost urgency/importance.

Äußerste(s) *nt decl as adj* **bis zum ~n gehen** to go to extremes; **er geht bis zum ~n** he would go to any extreme; **er hat sein ~s gegeben** he gave his all; **das ~ wagen** to risk everything; **ich bin auf das ~ gefaßt** I'm prepared for

➤ SPRACHE AKTIV: **äußern: 2→33.3**

the worst.

außer-: ~tariflich *adj Regelung* non-union; *Zuschlag* supplementary to agreed union rates; **~tariflich bezahlt werden** to be paid non-union rates; **~tourlich** [-'tu:r-] *adj (Aus, S Ger)* additional; **ein ~tourlicher Bus** a special; **und ich mache ~tourlich noch Überstunden** and I do overtime as well *or* on top.

Äußerung *f (Bemerkung)* remark, comment; *(Ling, Behauptung)* statement; *(Zeichen)* expression ◆ **Tränen als ~ der Trauer** tears as an expression of mourning.

Äußerungsform *f* manifestation.

aussetzen *sep* [1] *vt* **(a)** *Kind, Haustier* to abandon; *Wild, Fische* to release; *Pflanzen* to plant out; *(Naut) Passagiere* to maroon; *Boot* to lower.
(b) *(preisgeben)* **jdn/etw einer Sache** *(dat)* **~** to expose sb/sth to sth; **jdm/einer Sache ausgesetzt sein** *(ausgeliefert)* to be at the mercy of sb/sth; **jdn dem Gelächter ~** to expose sb to ridicule.
(c) *(festsetzen) Belohnung, Preis* to offer; *(in Testament)* to bequeath, to leave ◆ **auf jds Kopf** *(acc)* **1000 Dollar ~** to put 1,000 dollars on sb's head.
(d) *(unterbrechen)* to interrupt; *Debatte, Prozeß* to adjourn; *Zahlung* to break off.
(e) *(vertagen) Strafvollstreckung, Verfahren* to suspend; *Urteilsverkündung* to defer ◆ **eine Strafe zur Bewährung ~** to give a suspended sentence.
(f) an jdm/etw etwas auszusetzen haben to find fault with sb/sth; **daran ist nichts auszusetzen** there is nothing wrong with it; **daran habe ich nur eines auszusetzen** I've only one objection to make to that; **was haben Sie daran auszusetzen?** what don't you like about it?
(g) *Billardkugel* to place.
(h) *(Eccl)* to expose.
[2] *vi (aufhören)* to stop; *(Mensch auch)* to break off; *(bei Spiel)* to sit out; *(Herz)* to stop (beating); *(Motor auch)* to fail; *(versagen)* to give out ◆ **mit etw ~** to stop sth; **mit der Pille/Behandlung ~** to stop taking the pill/to interrupt the treatment; **zwei Wochen mit der Arbeit ~** to interrupt one's work for two weeks; **ich setze besser mal aus** I'd better have a break; *(bei Spiel)* I'd better sit this one out; **einen Tag ~** to take a day off; **ohne auszusetzen** without a break.

Aussetzung *f* **(a)** *siehe vt (a)* abandonment; releasing; planting out; marooning; lowering.
(b) *siehe vt (c)* offer; bequest ◆ **durch ~ einer Belohnung** by offering a reward, by the offer of a reward.
(c) *siehe vt (d)* interruption; adjournment; breaking off.
(d) *(Jur) siehe vt (e)* suspension; deferment ◆ **die ~ der Strafe zur Bewährung war in diesem Falle nicht möglich** it was impossible to give a suspended sentence in this case.
(e) *(Eccl: des Allerheiligsten)* exposition.

Aussicht *f* **(a)** *(Blick)* view *(auf +acc* of) ◆ **ein Zimmer mit ~ auf den Park** a room overlooking the park; **jdm die ~ nehmen/verbauen** to block *or* obstruct sb's view.
(b) *(fig)* prospect *(auf +acc* of) ◆ **die ~, daß etw geschieht** the chances of sth happening; **gute ~en haben** to have good prospects; **unser Plan hat große ~en auf Erfolg** our plan has every prospect *or* chance of succeeding; **keine** *or* **nicht die geringste ~** no *or* not the slightest prospect *or* chance; **etw in ~ haben** to have good prospects of sth; **jdn/etw in ~ nehmen** *(form)* to take sb/sth into consideration; **jdm etw in ~ stellen** to promise sb sth; **in ~ stehen** to be expected; **das sind ja schöne ~en!** *(iro inf)* what a prospect!

Aussichts-: a~los *adj* hopeless; *(zwecklos)* pointless; *(völlig hoffnungslos)* desperate; **eine a~lose Sache** a lost cause; **~punkt** *m* vantage point; **a~reich** *adj* promising; *Stellung* with good prospects; **~turm** *m* observation *or* lookout tower; **a~voll** *adj siehe* **a~reich**; **~wagen** *m (Rail)* observation car.

aussieben *vt sep (lit, fig)* to sift out; *(Rad) Störungen* to filter out.

aussiedeln *vt sep* to resettle; *(evakuieren)* to evacuate.

Aussiedler *m (Auswanderer)* emigrant; *(Evakuierter)* evacuee.

Aussiedlung *f* resettlement; *(Evakuierung)* evacuation.

aussitzen *vt sep irreg Problem* to sit out.

aussöhnen *sep* [1] *vt* **jdn mit jdm/etw ~** to reconcile sb with sb/to sth; **jdn ~** to appease sb.
[2] *vr* **sich mit jdm/etw ~** to become reconciled with sb/to sth; **wir haben uns wieder ausgesöhnt** we have made it up again.
[3] *vi* **mit etw ~** to compensate for sth.

Aussöhnung *f* reconciliation *(mit jdm* with sb, *mit etw* to sth).

aussondern *vt sep* **(a)** to select; *Schlechtes* to pick out; *(euph) Menschen auch* to single out ◆ **die ausgesonderte Ware wird billig abgegeben** the reject goods are sold cheaply. **(b)** *(Physiol) siehe* **absondern**.

Aussonderung *f siehe vt* **(a)** selection; picking out; singling out. **(b)** *siehe* **Absonderung**.

aussorgen *vi sep*: **ausgesorgt haben** to have no more money worries, to be set up for life.

aussortieren* *vt sep* to sort out.

ausspähen *sep* [1] *vi* **nach jdm/etw ~** to look out for sb/sth.
[2] *vt* to spy out; *(Mil)* to reconnoitre.

ausspannen *sep* [1] *vt* **(a)** *Tuch, Netz* to spread out; *Schnur, Leine* to put up.
(b) *(ausschirren)* to unharness, to unhitch; *Ochsen* to unyoke; *(aus Schreibmaschine) Bogen* to take out.
(c) *(fig inf)* **jdm etw ~** to do sb out of sth *(inf)*; **jdm die Freundin** *etc* **~** to pinch sb's girlfriend *etc (inf)*.
[2] *vi* **(a)** *(sich erholen)* to have a break.
(b) *(Pferde ~)* to unharness the horses; *(Ochsen ~)* to unyoke the oxen.

Ausspannung *f, no pl (fig)* relaxation ◆ **zur ~** for relaxation.

aussparen *vt sep Fläche* to leave blank; *(fig)* to omit.

Aussparung *f (Lücke)* gap; *(unbeschriebene Stelle)* blank space.

ausspeien *sep irreg* [1] *vt (ausspucken)* to spit out; *(erbrechen)* to bring up, to disgorge *(form)*; *(fig: herausschleudern)* to spew out *or* forth.
[2] *vi* to spit out ◆ **das A~** spitting.

aussperren *vt sep* to lock out.

Aussperrung *f (Ind)* lockout ◆ **mit ~ drohen** to threaten (the workers with) a lockout; **die ~ sollte illegal sein** lockouts should be made illegal.

ausspielen *sep* [1] *vt* **(a)** *Karte* to play; *(am Spielanfang)* to lead with ◆ **seinen letzten/einen Trumpf ~** *(lit, fig)* to play one's last card/a *or* one's last trump card.
(b) *Rolle, Szene* to act out ◆ **er hat (seine Rolle) ausgespielt** *(fig)* he's finished *or* through *(inf)*, he's played out *(fig)*.
(c) *(zu Ende spielen)* to finish playing.
(d) *(fig: einsetzen) Überlegenheit etc* to display.
(e) *(fig)* **jdn/etw gegen jdn/etw ~** to play sb/sth off against sb/sth.
(f) *(Sport) Pokal, Meisterschaft* to play for; *Gegner* to outplay.
(g) *Gewinne* to give as a prize/as prizes.
[2] *vi* **(a)** *(Cards)* to play a card; *(als erster)* to lead ◆ **wer spielt aus?** whose lead is it?, who has the lead?
(b) *(zu Ende spielen)* to finish playing; *siehe* **ausgespielt**.

Ausspielung *f (im Lotto)* pay-out.

ausspinnen *vt sep irreg* to spin out; *(sich ausdenken)* to think up.

ausspionieren* *vt sep Pläne etc* to spy out; *Person* to spy (up)on.

ausspotten *vt sep (S Ger, Sw, Aus) siehe* **verspotten**.

Aussprache *f* **(a)** pronunciation; *(Art des Artikulierens auch)* articulation; *(Akzent)* accent. **(b)** *(Meinungsaustausch)* discussion; *(Gespräch auch)* talk ◆ **es kam zu einer offenen ~ zwischen den beiden** they talked things out; **eine ~ herbeiführen** to bring things out into the open.

Aussprache-: ~angabe, ~bezeichnung *f (Ling)* phonetic transcription; **~wörterbuch** *nt* dictionary of pronunciation, pronouncing dictionary.

aussprechbar *adj* pronounceable ◆ **leicht/schwer/nicht ~** easy/difficult to pronounce/unpronounceable.

aussprechen *sep irreg* [1] *vt Wörter, Urteil etc* to pronounce; *Scheidung* to grant; *(zu Ende sprechen) Satz* to finish; *(äußern)* to express *(jdm* to sb); *Verdächtigung* to voice; *Warnung* to give, to deliver ◆ **jdm ein Lob ~** to give sb a word of praise; **der Regierung sein Vertrauen ~** to pass a vote of confidence in the government.
[2] *vr* **(a)** *(Partner)* to talk things out; *(sein Herz ausschütten, seine Meinung sagen)* to say what's on one's mind ◆ **sich mit jdm (über etw** *acc***) ~** to have a talk with sb (about sth); *(jdm sein Herz ausschütten)* to have a heart-to-heart with sb (about sth); **sich für/gegen etw ~** to declare *or* pronounce oneself in favour of/against sth, to come out in favour of/against sth; **sich lobend über jdn/etw ~** to speak highly of sb/sth.
(b) *(Wort)* to be pronounced ◆ **dieses Wort spricht sich leicht/schwer aus** this word is easy/difficult to pronounce.
[3] *vi (zu Ende sprechen)* to finish (speaking); *siehe* **ausgesprochen**.

aussprengen *vt sep (mit Sprengstoff)* to blast out.

ausspringen *sep irreg* [1] *vi aux sein (Feder, Kette)* to jump out.
[2] *vt (Ski)* **eine Schanze voll ~** to jump the maximum length on a ski-jump.

ausspritzen *vt sep* **(a)** *Flüssigkeit* to squirt out; *(sprühend)* to spray out; *(fig) Gift* to pour out. **(b)** *Bottich* to flush (out); *(Med) Zahn etc* to rinse out; *Ohr* to syringe. **(c)** *Feuer* to put out.

Ausspruch *m* remark; *(geflügeltes Wort)* saying.

ausspucken *sep* [1] *vt* to spit out; *(fig) Produkte* to pour *or* spew out; *(hum inf) Geld* to cough up *(inf)*; *Gelerntes* to regurgitate.
[2] *vi* to spit ◆ **vor jdm ~** to spit at sb's feet; *(fig)* to spit upon sb.

ausspülen *vt sep* to rinse (out); *(kräftiger)* to flush (out); *(Med, Geol)* to wash out ◆ **sich** *(dat)* **den Mund ~** to rinse one's mouth (out).

Ausspülung *f (Med)* irrigation; *(Geol)* erosion.

ausstaffieren* *vt sep (inf)* to equip, to fit out; *jdn* to rig *or* kit out; *(herausputzen)* to dress up ◆ **sein Roman ist mit sämtlichen Klischees ausstaffiert** his novel is peppered with all the clichés.

Ausstaffierung *f (inf)* equipment, fittings *pl*; *(Kleidung)* rig(-out) *(inf)*, outfit.

Ausstand *m* **(a)** *(Streik)* strike, industrial action ◆ **im ~ sein** to be on strike; **in den ~ treten** to (go on) strike, to take industrial action. **(b)** *usu pl (Comm)* outstanding debt. **(c) seinen ~ geben** to hold a leaving party.

ausständig *adj (esp Aus)* outstanding.

ausstanzen *vt sep Metallteil* to stamp out; *Loch* to punch (out).

ausstatten *vt sep* to equip; *(versorgen)* to provide, to furnish; *(mit Rechten)* to vest *(esp Jur)*; *(möblieren)* to furnish; *Buch* to produce ◆ **mit Humor/Intelligenz** *etc* **ausgestattet sein** to be endowed with humour/intelligence *etc*; **ein Zimmer neu ~** to refurbish a room.

Ausstattung *f* **(a)** *siehe vt* equipping; provision; vesting; furnishing; production. **(b)** *(Ausrüstung)* equipment; *(Tech auch)* fittings *pl*; *(Kapital)* provisions *pl*; *(von Zimmer etc)* furnishings *pl*; *(Theat)* décor and costumes; *(Mitgift)* dowry; *(von Buch)* presentation.

Ausstattungs-: ~film *m* spectacular (film); **~stück** *nt* **(a)** *(Theat)* spectacular (show); **(b)** *(Möbelstück)* piece of furniture.

ausstechen *vt sep irreg* **(a)** *Pflanzen, Unkraut* to dig up; *Torf, Plätzchen* to cut out; *Apfel* to core; *Graben* to dig (out).
(b) *Augen (esp als Strafe)* to gouge out, to put out.
(c) *(fig) jdn (verdrängen)* to push out; *(übertreffen)* to outdo ◆ **jdn bei einem**

Mädchen/beim Chef ~ to take sb's place in a girl's affections/push sb out of favour with the boss.

Ausstech-: ~form *f*, **~ förmchen** *nt (Cook)* cutter.

ausstehen *sep irreg* [1] *vt (ertragen)* to endure; *(erdulden auch)* to put up with; *Sorge, Angst* to go through, to suffer ◆ **ich kann ihn/so etwas nicht ~** I can't bear *or* stand him/anything like that; **jetzt ist es ausgestanden** now it's all over; **mit jdm viel auszustehen haben** to have to go through a lot with sb *or* put up with a lot from sb.
[2] *vi* **(a)** to be due; *(Antwort)* to be still to come; *(Buch)* to be still to appear; *(Entscheidung)* to be still to be taken; *(Lösung)* to be still to be found; *(noch zu erwarten sein)* to be still expected.
(b) *(Schulden)* to be owing ◆ **Geld ~ haben** to have money owing; **~de Forderungen** outstanding demands.

aussteigen *vi sep irreg aux sein* **(a)** to get out *(aus* of); *(aus Bus, Zug etc auch)* to get off *(aus etw* sth), to alight *(aus* from) *(form)*; *(Aviat sl)* to bale *or* bail out *(aus* of); *(fig: aus Gesellschaft)* to opt out ◆ **alles ~!** everybody out!; *(von Schaffner)* all change!; **das A~ während der Fahrt ist verboten** do not alight while train *etc* is in motion.
(b) *(Sport: aufgeben)* to give up, to retire *(aus* from); *(bei Wettrennen auch)* to drop out *(aus* of) ◆ **einen Gegenspieler ~ lassen** *(esp Ftbl)* to outplay an opponent.
(c) *(inf: aus Geschäft etc)* to get out *(aus* of).

Aussteiger(in *f*) *m* **-s, -** *(aus Gesellschaft)* person who opts out, dropout *(esp pej)*.

ausstellen *sep* [1] *vt* **(a)** *(zur Schau stellen)* to display; *(auf Messe, in Museum etc)* to exhibit.
(b) *(ausschreiben)* to make out *(jdm* to sb), to write (out) *(jdm* sb); *(behördlich ausgeben)* to issue *(jdm etw* sb with sth, sth to sb) ◆ **einen Scheck auf jdn ~** to make out a cheque to sb, to make a cheque payable to sb; **eine Rechnung über DM 100 ~** to make out a bill for DM 100.
(c) *(ausschalten) Gerät* to turn *or* switch off; *siehe* **ausgestellt.**
[2] *vi* to exhibit.

Aussteller(in *f*) *m* **-s, - (a)** *(auf Messe)* exhibitor. **(b)** *(von Dokument)* issuer; *(von Scheck)* drawer.

Ausstellfenster *nt (Aut)* quarterlight.

Ausstellung *f* **(a)** *(Kunst~, Messe)* exhibition; *(Blumen~, Hunde~ etc)* show. **(b)** *no pl (von Scheck, Rezept, Rechnung etc)* making out; *(behördlich)* issuing.

Ausstellungs-: ~datum *nt* date of issue; **~fläche** *f* exhibition area; **~gelände** *nt* exhibition site *or* area; **~halle** *f* exhibition hall; **~katalog** *m* exhibition catalogue; **~stand** *m* exhibition stand; **~stück** *nt (in Ausstellung)* exhibit; *(in Schaufenster etc)* display item; **~tag** *m* day of issue.

Aussterbe|etat *m (hum)* **auf dem ~ stehen** *or* **sein** to be being phased out; **etw auf den ~ setzen** to phase sth out.

Aussterben *nt* **-s,** *no pl* extinction ◆ **im ~ begriffen** dying out, becoming extinct; **vom ~ bedroht sein** to be threatened by extinction.

aussterben *vi sep irreg aux sein* to die out; *(esp Spezies, Geschlecht auch)* to become extinct ◆ **die Dummen sterben nie aus** there's one born every minute; *siehe* **ausgestorben.**

Aussteuer *f* **-, -n** dowry.

aussteuern *vt sep* **(a)** *Tochter* to provide with a dowry. **(b)** *(Insur)* to disqualify.

Aussteuerung *f (Insur)* disqualification.

Aussteuerungsautomatik *f* automatic tuning.

Aussteuerversicherung *f* endowment insurance *(for one's daughter's wedding etc)*.

Ausstieg *m* **-(e)s, -e (a)** *no pl (das Aussteigen)* climbing out *(aus* of); *(aus Bus, Zug etc)* getting out or off, alighting *(aus* from) *(form)*; *(fig) (aus Gesellschaft)* opting out *(aus* of) ◆ **der ~ aus der Kernenergie** abandoning nuclear energy; **der ~ aus einer Organisation** withdrawal from an organization. **(b)** *(Ausgang)* exit. **(c)** *(auch* **~luke)** escape hatch.

ausstopfen *vt sep Kissen etc, Tiere* to stuff; *Ritzen* to fill ◆ **sich** *(dat)* **den Bauch ~** to pad one's stomach.

Ausstoß *m* **(a)** *(esp Phys, Tech: das Ausstoßen)* expulsion, ejection, discharge; *(von Torpedo, Geschoß)* firing. **(b)** *(Ausschluß von Verein etc)* expulsion. **(c)** *(Produktion)* output, production.

ausstoßen *vt sep irreg* **(a)** *(herausstoßen)* to eject, to discharge; *Atem, Plazenta* to expel; *Gas etc* to give off, to emit; *(Naut) Torpedo* to fire; *(herstellen) Teile, Stückzahl* to put *or* turn out, to produce.
(b) sich *(dat)* **ein Auge/einen Zahn ~** to lose an eye/a tooth; **jdm ein Auge/einen Zahn ~** to put sb's eye out/to knock sb's tooth out.
(c) *(ausschließen) (aus Verein, Armee etc)* to expel *(aus* from); *(verbannen)* to banish *(aus* from) ◆ **jdn aus der Gesellschaft ~** to banish sb *or* cast sb out from society; *siehe* **Ausgestoßene(r).**
(d) *(äußern)* to utter; *Schrei* to give; *Seufzer* to heave.
(e) *(Ling) Laut* to drop.

Ausstoßrohr *nt (Naut)* torpedo tube.

Ausstoßung *f* **-,** *no pl* **(a)** *(aus* from) *(Ausschließung)* expulsion; *(aus der Gesellschaft)* banishment; *(aus einer Gemeinschaft auch)* exclusion. **(b)** *(Ling: eines Lautes)* dropping.

ausstrahlen *sep* [1] *vt* to radiate *(auch fig)*; *esp Licht, Wärme auch* to give off; *(Rad, TV)* to transmit, to broadcast.
[2] *vi aux sein* to radiate; *(esp Licht, Wärme auch)* to be given off; *(Schmerz)* to extend, to spread *(bis in +acc* as far as) ◆ **seine Freude strahlte auf die Zuhörer aus** his joy was communicated to the listeners.

Ausstrahlung *f* radiation; *(Rad, TV)* transmission, broadcast(ing); *(fig: von Ort)* aura; *(von Mensch)* charisma.

ausstrecken *sep* [1] *vt* to extend *(nach* towards); *Fühler auch* to put out; *Hand auch, Beine etc* to stretch out; *Zunge* to stick out *(nach* at) ◆ **mit ausgestreckten Armen** with arms extended.
[2] *vr* to stretch (oneself) out.

ausstreichen *vt sep irreg* **(a)** *Geschriebenes* to cross *or* strike out, to delete; *(fig)* to obliterate ◆ **jds Namen auf einer Liste ~** to cross *or* strike sb's name off a list, to delete sb's name from a list.
(b) *(glätten) Falten* to smooth out.
(c) *(breit streichen) Teig* to spread out.
(d) *Backform (mit Fett)* to grease.
(e) *(ausfüllen) Risse* to fill, to smooth over.

ausstreuen *vt sep* to scatter, to spread; *(fig) Gerücht* to spread, to put about ◆ **etw mit etw ~** to cover sth with sth.

Ausstrich *m* **-s, -e** *(Med)* smear.

ausströmen *sep* [1] *vi aux sein* **(a)** *(herausfließen)* to stream *or* pour out *(aus* of); *(entweichen)* to escape *(aus* from).
(b) *(ausstrahlen)* **die Hitze, die vom Ofen ausströmt** the heat which is radiated from the stove; **etw strömt von jdm/etw aus** *(fig)* sb/sth radiates sth.
[2] *vt Duft, Gas* to give off; *(ausstrahlen) Wärme, Ruhe etc* to radiate.

ausstudieren* *vi sep (inf)* to finish studying.

aussuchen *vt sep* **(a)** *(auswählen)* to choose; *(esp iro)* to pick ◆ **such dir was aus!** choose *or* pick what you want, take your pick; *siehe* **ausgesucht. (b)** *(old: durchsuchen)* to search.

austäfeln *vt sep* to panel.

austapezieren* *vt sep* to paper.

austarieren* *vt sep* **(a)** *(ins Gleichgewicht bringen)* to balance; *(fig auch)* to equalize, to share out equally. **(b)** *(Aus: Leergewicht feststellen)* to determine the tare weight of.

Austausch *m* exchange; *(von Gedanken etc auch)* interchange; *(Ersatz)* replacement; *(Sport)* substitution ◆ **im ~ für** *or* **gegen** in exchange for.

austauschbar *adj* exchangeable; *(untereinander ~)* interchangeable; *(ersetzbar)* replaceable.

austauschen *vt sep (lit, fig)* to exchange *(gegen* for); *(untereinander ~)* to interchange; *(ersetzen)* to replace *(gegen* with) ◆ **er ist wie ausgetauscht** *(fig)* he's (become) a different person, he's completely changed.

Austausch-: ~lehrer *m* exchange teacher; **~motor** *m* replacement engine; **~schüler** *m* exchange student *or* pupil; **~student** *m* exchange student; **a~weise** *adv* as part of an exchange; *(bei Studenten etc)* on an exchange basis.

austeilen *vt sep* to distribute *(unter +dat, an +acc* among); *(aushändigen auch)* to hand out *(unter +dat, an +acc* to); *Spielkarten* to deal (out); *Essen* to serve; *Sakrament* to administer, to dispense; *Befehle* to give, to issue; *Prügel* to hand out, to administer.

Austeilung *f* distribution; *(Aushändigung auch)* handing out; *(von Essen etc)* serving; *(von Sakrament)* administration, dispensation.

Auster *f* **-, -n** oyster.

Austern-: ~bank *f* oyster bed *or* bank; **~fischer** *m (Orn)* oyster catcher; **~park** *m* oyster farm *or* park; **~pilz** *m* Chinese mushroom; **~schale** *f* oyster shell; **~zucht** *f* oyster farm; *(~züchtung)* oyster farming.

austilgen *vt sep* to eradicate *(auch fig)*; *Schädlinge auch, Menschen* to exterminate; *Erinnerung* to obliterate.

Austilgung *f siehe vt* eradication; extermination; obliteration.

austoben *sep* [1] *vt* to work off *(an +dat* on).
[2] *vr* **(a)** *(Mensch)* to let off steam; *(sich müde machen)* to tire oneself out; *(ein wildes Leben führen)* to have one's fling ◆ **ein Garten, wo sich die Kinder ~ können** a garden where the children can romp about; **hat sie sich jetzt ausgetobt?** has she cooled down now?
(b) *(abebben: Leidenschaft, Sturm, Fieber etc)* to die down.

austollen *vr sep (umherspringen etc)* to have a good romp; *(Energie loswerden)* to let off steam; *(sich amüsieren)* to let one's hair down.

Austrag *m* **-(e)s,** *no pl* settlement, resolution; *(Sport: von Wettkampf)* holding ◆ **zum ~ kommen/gelangen** to be up for settlement/to be settled *or* decided.

austragen *sep irreg* [1] *vt* **(a)** *Problem, Frage* to deal with; *Duell, Wettkampf etc* to hold ◆ **einen Streit mit jdm ~** to have it out with sb.
(b) *Waren, Post etc* to deliver.
(c) ein Kind ~ to carry a child (through) to the full term; *(nicht abtreiben)* to have a child.
(d) *(abmelden)* to sign out; *(löschen) Zahlen, Daten* to take out; *(aus Liste, bei Buchung) jdn* to cancel sb's name.
[2] *vr* to sign out.

Austräger(in *f*) *m* delivery man/boy *etc*; *(von Zeitungen)* newspaper man/boy *etc* ◆ **wir suchen Studenten als ~** we are looking for students to deliver newspapers.

Austragung *f (Sport)* holding.

Austragungs|ort *m (Sport)* venue.

austrainiert *adj (Sport)* well-prepared.

Australide(r) *mf decl as adj* Australoid.

Australien [-iən] *nt* **-s** Australia ◆ **~ und Ozeanien** Australasia.

Australier(in *f*) [-iɐ, -iərɪn] *m* **-s, -** Australian.

australisch *adj* Australian ◆ **A~er Bund** the Commonwealth of Australia.

Australneger *m (dated) siehe* **Australide.**

austräumen *vt sep* to finish dreaming ◆ **sein Traum von Reichtümern ist ausgeträumt** *(fig)* his dream of riches is over.

austreiben *sep irreg* 1 *vt* **(a)** *Vieh* to drive *or* turn out.
(b) *(vertreiben)* to drive out; *Teufel etc auch* to exorcise, to cast out *(esp old, liter)* ◆ ..., **daß es mir den Schweiß austrieb** ... until the sweat was pouring off me; **jdm etw ~** to cure sb of sth; *(esp durch Schläge)* to knock sth out of sb.
(c) *(Typ) Zeilen* to space out.
(d) *(rare: hervorbringen) Blüten, Knospen* to put forth.
2 *vi (sprießen)* to sprout.

Austreibung *f* expulsion; *(von Teufel etc)* exorcism, driving out, casting out *(esp old, liter)*.

austreten *sep irreg* 1 *vi aux sein* **(a)** *(herauskommen)* to come out *(aus* of); *(Blut etc auch)* to issue *(aus* from); *(entweichen: Gas etc)* to escape *(aus* from, through).
(b) *(Med: bei Bruch)* to protrude.
(c) *(inf: zur Toilette gehen)* to go to the loo *or* john *(US) (inf)*; *(Sch)* to be excused *(euph)*.
(d) *(ausscheiden)* to leave *(aus etw* sth); *(formell)* to resign *(aus* from); *(aus politischer Gemeinschaft)* to withdraw *(aus* from).
(e) *(Hunt)* to come out (into the open) ◆ **aus der Deckung ~** to break cover.
2 *vt Spur, Feuer etc* to tread out; *Schuhe* to wear out (of shape); *siehe* **ausgetreten.**

austricksen *vt sep (inf: Sport, fig)* to trick.

austrinken *vti sep irreg* to finish ◆ **trink (deine Milch) aus!** drink (your milk) up.

Austritt *m* **(a)** *no pl (das Heraustreten) (von Flüssigkeit)* outflow; *(das Entweichen)* escape; *(von Kugel)* exit; *(esp von Eiter)* discharge; *(von Blut)* issue; *(Med: von Bruch)* protrusion.
(b) *(das Ausscheiden)* leaving *no art (aus etw* sth); *(formell)* resignation *(aus* from); *(aus politischer Gemeinschaft)* withdrawal *(aus* from) ◆ **die ~e aus der Kirche häufen sich** there are more and more people leaving the church.

Austritts|erklärung *f* (notice of) resignation.

Austro- *in cpds* Austro-.

austrocknen *sep* 1 *vi aux sein* to dry out; *(Fluß etc)* to dry up; *(Kehle)* to become parched.
2 *vt* to dry out; *Fluß etc* to dry up; *Kehle* to make parched; *(trockenlegen) Sumpf auch* to drain.

austrommeln *vt sep (Hist)* to announce on the drum; *(fig)* to shout from the rooftops.

austrompeten* *vt sep siehe* **ausposaunen.**

austüfteln *vt sep (inf)* to work out; *(ersinnen)* to think up.

aus|üben *vt sep* **(a)** *Beruf, Kunst* to practise; *Gewerbe auch* to carry on; *Aufgabe, Funktion, Amt* to perform; *(innehaben) Amt* to hold ◆ **eine Praxis ~** to have a practice, to be in practice.
(b) *Druck, Einfluß* to exert *(auf +acc* on); *Macht, Recht* to exercise; *Wirkung* to have *(auf +acc* on) ◆ **einen Reiz auf jdn ~** to have *or* hold an attraction for sb.

aus|übend *adj Arzt, Rechtsanwalt, Künstler* practising; *Gewalt* executive.

Aus|übung *f siehe vt* **(a)** practice; performance; holding ◆ **die ~ einer Praxis** having a practice; **in ~ seines Dienstes/seiner Pflicht** *(form)* in the execution of his duty; **in ~ seines Berufs** *(form)* in pursuance of one's profession *(form)*.
(b) exertion; exercise.

aus|ufern *vi sep aux sein (lit rare: Fluß)* to burst *or* break its banks; *(fig)* to get out of hand; *(Konflikt etc)* to escalate *(zu* into).

Ausverkauf *m* (clearance) sale; *(wegen Geschäftsaufgabe)* closing-down sale; *(fig: Verrat)* sell-out ◆ **etw im ~ kaufen** to buy sth at the sale(s).

ausverkaufen* *vt sep* to sell off, to clear.

ausverkauft *adj* sold out ◆ **vor ~em Haus spielen** to play to a full house.

ausverschämt *adj (dial) siehe* **unverschämt.**

auswachsen *sep irreg* 1 *vi aux sein* **(a) das ist (ja) zum A~** *(inf)* it's enough to drive you mad *or* round the bend *(inf)*; **zum A~ langweilig** *(inf)* incredibly boring; *siehe* **ausgewachsen.**
(b) *(Getreide)* to sprout.
(c) *(Narbe)* to grow over; *(Mißbildung auch)* to right itself.
2 *vt (rare) Kleider* to grow out of, to outgrow.
3 *vr* **(a)** *(verschwinden)* to disappear; *(Narbe auch)* to grow over; *(sich verbessern)* to right itself.
(b) sich zu etw ~ *(fig: Streit etc)* to turn into sth.

Auswahl *f* -, *no pl* selection *(an +dat* of); *(Angebot auch)* range; *(Wahl)* choice; *(die Besten)* pick; *(Vielfalt)* variety; *(Sport)* representative team ◆ **ohne ~** indiscriminately; **viel/eine reiche ~** a large/wide selection *or* range; **hier gibt es keine ~** there is no choice; **viele Sachen zur ~ haben** to have many things to choose from; **drei Bewerber stehen zur ~** there are three applicants to choose from, there is a choice of three applicants; **jdm drei Sachen zur ~ vorlegen** to offer sb a choice of three things; **eine ~ treffen** *(eines auswählen)* to make a choice; *(einige auswählen)* to make a selection.

Auswahl-: ~antwort *f* answer (to a/the multiple choice question); **~band** *m* selection.

auswählen *vt sep* to select, to choose *(unter +dat* from among) ◆ **sich** *(dat)* **etw ~** to select *or* choose sth (for oneself); *siehe* **ausgewählt.**

Auswahl-: ~mannschaft *f* representative team; **~möglichkeit** *f* choice; **~prinzip** *nt* selection principle, criterion; **~sendung** *f* (selection of) samples; **~spieler** *m* representative player.

auswalzen *vt sep* **(a)** *Metall* to roll out. **(b)** *(fig)* to go to town on; *Thema auch* to drag out.

Auswanderer *m* emigrant.

Auswanderer-: ~schiff *nt* emigrant ship; **~visum** *nt* emigration visa.

Auswanderin *f* emigrant.

auswandern *vi sep aux sein* to emigrate *(nach, in +acc* to); *(Volk)* to migrate.

Auswanderung *f* emigration; *(Massen~)* migration.

auswärtig *adj attr* **(a)** *(nicht ansässig)* non-local; *Schüler, Mitglied* from out of town. **(b)** *(Pol)* foreign ◆ **der ~e Dienst** the foreign service; **das A~e Amt** the Foreign Office *(Brit)*, the State Department *(US)*; **der Minister des A~en** *(form)* the Foreign Minister *(Brit)*, the Secretary of State *(US)*.

auswärts *adv* **(a)** *(nach außen)* outwards. **(b)** *(außerhalb des Hauses)* away from home; *(außerhalb der Stadt)* out of town; *(Sport)* away ◆ **von ~ anrufen** to call long distance ◆ **~ essen** to eat out; **~ sprechen** *(hum inf)* to speak foreign *(hum inf)*.

Auswärtsspiel *nt (Sport)* away (game).

auswaschen *sep irreg* 1 *vt* to wash out; *(spülen)* to rinse (out); *(Geol auch)* to erode.
2 *vr (Farbe)* to wash out.

auswechselbar *adj* (ex)changeable; *(untereinander ~)* interchangeable; *(ersetzbar)* replaceable.

auswechseln *sep* 1 *vt* to change; *(esp gegenseitig)* to exchange; *(ersetzen)* to replace; *(Sport)* to substitute *(gegen* for) ◆ **er ist wie ausgewechselt** *(fig)* he's a changed *or* different person.
2 *vi (Sport)* to bring on a substitute, to make a substitution.

Auswechselspieler *m* substitute.

Auswechs(e)lung *f* exchange; *(Ersatz)* replacement; *(Sport)* substitution.

Ausweg *m* way out; *(fig: Lösung auch)* solution ◆ **der letzte ~** a last resort; **er sieht keinen anderen ~, als ... zu** he can see no other way out but to ...; **sich** *(dat)* **einen ~ offenlassen** *or* **offenhalten** to leave oneself an escape route *or* a way out.

Ausweg-: a~los *adj (fig)* hopeless; **~losigkeit** *f (fig)* hopelessness.

ausweichen *vi sep irreg aux sein* **(a)** *(Hindernis, Gefahr umgehen)* to get out of the way *(+dat* of); *(Platz machen)* to make way *(+dat* for) ◆ **nach rechts ~** to get out of the way/to make way by going to the right.
(b) *(zu entgehen versuchen) (lit)* to get out of the way; *(fig)* to evade the point/issue *etc* ◆ **einer Sache** *(dat)* **~** *(lit)* to avoid sth; *(fig)* to evade *or* dodge *(inf)* sth; **jdm/einer Begegnung ~** to avoid sb/a meeting; **dem Feind ~** to avoid (contact with) the enemy; **eine ~de Antwort** an evasive answer.
(c) auf etw *(acc)* **~** *(fig)* to switch to sth.

Ausweich-: ~flughafen *m* alternative airport; **~gleis** *nt (Rail)* siding; **~lager** *nt* reserve depot *or* store; **~manöver** *nt* evasive action *or* manoeuvre; **~möglichkeit** *f (fig)* alternative; *(lit)* possibility of getting out of the way; **~stelle** *f (auf Straßen)* passing place.

ausweiden *vt sep (Hunt)* to break up; *Opfertier etc* to disembowel.

ausweinen *sep* 1 *vr* to have a (good) cry; *(zu Ende weinen)* to finish crying ◆ **sich bei jdm ~** to have a cry on sb's shoulder; **sich** *(dat)* **die Augen ~** to cry one's eyes *or* heart out *(nach* over).
2 *vi* to finish crying.
3 *vt* **seinen Kummer** *etc* **~** to weep *(bei jdm* on sb's shoulder).

Ausweis *m* **-es, -e (a)** *(Mitglieds~/Leser~/Studenten~ etc)* (membership/library/student) card; *(Personal~)* identity card; *(Berechtigungsnachweis)* pass ◆ **~, bitte** your papers please.
(b) *(Beleg)* proof; *(von Identität)* proof of identity, identification ◆ **nach ~** *+gen (form)* according to.
(c) *(Bank~)* bank return.
(d) *(dated Aus Sch: Zeugnis)* report.

ausweisen *sep irreg* 1 *vt* **(a)** *(aus dem Lande)* to expel, to deport; *siehe* **Ausgewiesene(r).**
(b) *(Identität nachweisen)* to identify.
(c) *(zeigen)* to reveal.
2 *vr* **(a)** to identify oneself ◆ **können Sie sich ~?** do you have any means of identification?
(b) sich als etw ~ *(sich erweisen)* to prove oneself to be sth.

Ausweis-: ~karte *f siehe* **Ausweis (a)**; **~kontrolle** *f* identity check; **~papiere** *pl* identity papers *pl*; **~pflicht** *f* obligation to carry an identity card.

Ausweisung *f* expulsion, deportation.

Ausweisungsbefehl *m* expulsion *or* deportation order.

ausweiten *sep* 1 *vt* to widen; *esp Dehnbares* to stretch; *(fig)* to expand *(zu* into).
2 *vr* to widen; *(esp Dehnbares)* to stretch; *(fig) (Thema, Bewegung)* to expand *(zu* into); *(sich verbreiten)* to spread.

Ausweitung *f* widening; *(Ausdehnung)* stretching; *(fig)* expansion; *(von Konflikt etc auch)* widening; *(Verbreitung)* spreading.

auswendig *adv* by heart, from memory ◆ **etw ~ können/lernen** to know/learn sth (off) by heart; **das kann ich schon ~** *(fig inf)* I know it backwards *(inf) or* by heart; **ein Musikstück ~ spielen** to play a piece (of music) from memory; *siehe* **inwendig.**

Auswendiglernen *nt* **-s,** *no pl (von Geschichtszahlen, Fakten)* learning by heart, memorizing ◆ **ein Gedicht zum ~** a poem to learn by heart.

auswerfen *vt sep irreg* **(a)** *Anker, Netz, Leine* to cast.
(b) *(hinausschleudern) Lava, Asche* to throw out, to eject; *Geschoßhülsen* to eject.
(c) *(ausspucken) Schleim, Blut* to cough up.
(d) *(herausschaufeln)* to shovel out; *Graben* to dig out.
(e) *(verteilen) Dividende* to pay out; *(zuteilen) Mittel, Summen* to allocate.
(f) *(Comm) Posten* to set out.
(g) *(produzieren)* to produce, to put *or* turn out.

(h) *Fenster* to break, to smash.
(i) **jdm ein Auge ~** to put out sb's eye.
auswerten *vt sep* (a) (*bewerten*) to evaluate; (*analysieren*) to analyse. (b) (*nutzbar machen*) to utilize.
Auswertung *f siehe vt* (a) evaluation; analysis. (b) utilization.
auswetzen *vt sep* to grind out.
auswickeln *vt sep Paket, Bonbon etc* to unwrap ♦ **ein Kind ~** to take a child out of its blankets *etc*; (*Hist: Windeln entfernen*) to unswaddle a child.
auswiegen *vt sep irreg* to weigh (out); *siehe* **ausgewogen.**
auswirken *vr sep* to have an effect (*auf +acc* on) ♦ **sich günstig/negativ ~** to have a favourable/negative effect; **sich in etw** (*dat*) **~** to result in sth; **sich zu jds Vorteil ~** to work *or* turn out to sb's advantage.
Auswirkung *f* (*Folge*) consequence; (*Wirkung*) effect; (*Rückwirkung*) repercussion.
auswischen *vt sep* to wipe out; *Glas etc, Wunde* to wipe clean; *Schrift etc* to rub *or* wipe out ♦ **sich** (*dat*) **die Augen ~** to rub *or* wipe one's eyes; **jdm eins ~** (*inf*) to get one over on sb (*inf*); (*aus Rache*) to get one's own back on sb.
auswringen *vt sep irreg* to wring out.
Auswuchs *m* (a) (out)growth; (*Med, Bot auch*) excrescence (*form*); (*Mißbildung*) deformity. (b) (*fig*) (*Erzeugnis*) product; (*Mißstand, Übersteigerung*) excess.
auswuchten *vt sep Räder* to balance.
Auswurf *m, no pl* (a) (*von Lava etc*) ejection, eruption; (*ausgeworfene Lava etc auch*) ejecta *pl* (*Geol*).
(b) (*Med*) sputum ♦ **~/blutigen ~ haben** to bring up phlegm/be coughing up blood.
(c) (*pej: Abschaum*) scum; (*Schund*) trashy product ♦ **der ~ der Menschheit** the dregs *pl or* scum of humanity.
auswürfeln *sep* [1] *vi* to throw dice; (*das Glück entscheiden lassen*) to draw lots.
[2] *vt* to (throw) dice for.
auswüten *vir sep:* **(sich) ausgewütet haben** to have calmed down; (*Sturm*) to have abated.
auszacken *vt sep* to serrate.
auszahlen *sep* [1] *vt Geld etc* to pay out; *Arbeiter, Gläubiger* to pay off; *Kompagnon* to buy out ♦ **er bekommt DM 400 die Woche ausgezahlt** his net pay is DM 400 a week.
[2] *vr* (*sich lohnen*) to pay (off).
auszählen *sep* [1] *vt Stimmen* to count (up); (*durch Zählen wählen*) *Person* to choose *or* select (by counting); (*Boxen*) to count out.
[2] *vi* (*bei Kinderspielen*) to count out.
Auszählreim *m siehe* **Abzählreim.**
Auszahlung *f siehe vt* paying out; paying off; buying out ♦ **zur ~ kommen** (*form*) *or* **gelangen** (*form*) to be paid out.
Auszählung *f* (*von Stimmen etc*) counting (up), count.
Auszahlungs-: ~anweisung *f* order to pay; **~stelle** *f* payments office.
Auszählvers *m siehe* **Abzählvers.**
auszahnen *vt sep* (*Tech*) to tooth.
auszanken *vi sep* (*zu Ende zanken*) to finish quarrelling.
auszehren *vt sep* to drain, to exhaust; *Land* to drain ♦ **~de Krankheit** wasting disease.
Auszehrung *f* (a) (*Kräfteverfall*) emaciation ♦ **unter personeller ~ leiden** (*fig*) to be short-staffed. (b) (*obs Med*) consumption (*old*).
auszeichnen *sep* [1] *vt* (a) (*mit Zeichen versehen*) to mark; *Waren* to label; (*Typ*) *Manuskript* to mark up; *Überschrift* to display ♦ **etw mit einem Preis(schild) ~** to price sth.
(b) (*ehren*) to honour ♦ **jdn mit einem Orden ~** to decorate sb (with a medal); **jdn mit einem Preis/Titel ~** to award a prize/title to sb.
(c) (*hervorheben*) to distinguish (from all others); (*kennzeichnen*) to be a feature of.
[2] *vr* to stand out (*durch* due to), to distinguish oneself (*durch* by) (*auch iro*) ♦ **dieser Wagen zeichnet sich durch gute Straßenlage aus** one of the remarkable features of this car is its good road-holding, what makes this car stand out is its good road-holding; *siehe* **ausgezeichnet.**
Auszeichnung *f* (a) (*no pl: das Auszeichnen*) (*von Baum etc*) marking; (*von Waren*) labelling; (*mit Preisschild*) pricing; (*Typ: von Manuskript*) mark up.
(b) (*no pl: das Ehren*) honouring; (*mit Orden*) decoration ♦ **jds/seine ~ mit einem Preis** *etc* the awarding of a prize *etc* to sb/his being awarded a prize *etc*.
(c) (*Markierung*) marking (*+gen, an +dat* on); (*an Ware*) ticket; (*Typ: auf Manuskript*) mark up.
(d) (*Ehrung*) honour, distinction; (*Orden*) decoration; (*Preis*) award, prize ♦ **mit ~ bestehen** to pass with distinction.
Auszeit *f* (*Sport*) time out.
ausziehbar *adj* extendible, extensible; *Antenne* telescopic ♦ **ein ~er Tisch** a pull-out table.
ausziehen *sep irreg* [1] *vt* (a) (*herausziehen*) to pull out; (*verlängern auch*) to extend; *Metall* (*zu Draht*) to draw out (*zu* into).
(b) *Kleider* to take off, to remove; *jdn* to undress ♦ **jdm die Jacke** *etc* **~** to take off sb's jacket *etc*; **sich** (*dat*) **etw ~** to take off sth; **die Uniform ~** (*fig*) to retire from the services; **das zieht einem ja die Schuhe** *or* **Socken** *or* **Stiefel aus!** (*sl*) it's enough to make you cringe!
(c) (*dated rare*) (*exzerpieren*) to excerpt, to extract; (*zusammenfassen*) to summarize.
(d) *Wirkstoffe* (*aus Kräutern*) to extract; *Kräuter* to make an extract from.
(e) (*ausbleichen*) *Farbe* to bleach (out), to take out.
(f) (*nachzeichnen*) *Linie* to trace (*mit Tusche* in ink).

[2] *vr* (*sich entkleiden*) to undress, to take off one's clothes.
[3] *vi aux sein* (*aufbrechen, abreisen*) to set out; (*demonstrativ*) to walk out; (*aus einer Wohnung*) to move (*aus* out of) ♦ **auf Abenteuer/Raub ~** to set off *or* out in search of adventure/to rob and steal; **zur Jagd ~** to set off for the hunt; **zum Kampf ~** to set off to battle.
Auszieh-: ~feder *f* drawing pen; **~leiter** *f* extension ladder; **~platte** *f* (*von Tisch*) leaf; **~tisch** *m* extending *or* pull-out table; **~tusche** *f* drawing ink.
auszischen *vt sep* (*Theat*) to hiss (off).
Auszubildende(r) *mf decl as adj* trainee.
Auszug *m* (a) (*das Weggehen*) departure; (*demonstrativ*) walk-out; (*zeremoniell*) procession; (*aus der Wohnung*) move ♦ **der ~ der Kinder Israel** (*Bibl*) the Exodus (of the Children of Israel).
(b) (*Ausschnitt, Exzerpt*) excerpt; (*aus Buch auch*) extract; (*Zusammenfassung*) abstract, summary; (*Konto~*) statement; (*Chem*) extract; (*Mus*) arrangement ♦ **etw in Auszügen drucken** to print extracts of sth.
(c) (*ausziehbarer Teil*) extension.
Auszugs-: ~mehl *nt* super-fine flour; **a~weise** *adv* in extracts *or* excerpts; (*gekürzt*) in an/the abridged version; **a~weise aus etw lesen** to read extracts from sth.
autark *adj* self-sufficient (*auch fig*), autarkical (*Econ*).
Autarkie *f* self-sufficiency (*auch fig*), autarky (*Econ*).
authentisch *adj* authentic; (*Mus*) *Kadenz* perfect.
Authentizität *f* authenticity.
Autismus *m* autism.
autistisch *adj* autistic.
Auto *nt* **-s, -s** car, automobile (*esp US, dated*) ♦ **~ fahren** (*selbst*) to drive (a car); (*als Mitfahrer*) to go by car; **mit dem ~ fahren** to go by car; **er guckt wie ein ~** (*inf*) his eyes are popping out of his head (*inf*).
Auto-: ~apotheke *f* first-aid kit (for the car); **~atlas** *m* road atlas.
Autobahn *f* motorway (*Brit*), expressway (*US*).
Autobahn- *in cpds* motorway *etc*; **~ausfahrt** *f* motorway *etc* exit; **~dreieck** *nt* motorway *etc* merging point; **~gebühr** *f* toll; **~kreuz** *nt* motorway *etc* intersection; **~rasthof** *m*, **~raststätte** *f* motorway *etc* service area *or* services *pl*; **~ring** *m* motorway ring road; **~zubringer** *m* motorway *etc* approach road *or* feeder.
Auto-: ≂batterie *f* car battery; ⚠**~biograph** *m* autobiographer; ⚠**~biographie** *f* autobiography; ⚠**a~biographisch** *adj* autobiographical; **≂bombe** *f* car bomb.
Autobus *m* bus; (*Reiseomnibus*) coach (*Brit*), bus ♦ **einstöckiger/zweistöckiger ~** single-decker/double-decker (bus).
Auto-: ≂camping *nt* driving and camping; **≂car** *m* **-s, -s** (*Sw*) coach (*Brit*), bus; **a~chthon** [autɔx'to:n] *adj* (*geh*) autochthonous (*form*); **≂-Cross** *nt* **-**, *no pl* autocross; **~dafé** *nt* **-s, -s** (*geh*) auto-da-fé; **~didakt(in f)** *m* **-en, -en** autodidact (*form*), self-educated person; **~didaktentum** *nt* autodidacticism (*form*); **a~didaktisch** *adj* autodidactic (*form*), self taught *no adv*; **sich a~didaktisch bilden** to educate oneself; **≂dieb** *m* car thief; **≂diebstahl** *m* car theft; **~drom** *nt* **-s, -e** (a) motor-racing circuit; (b) (*Aus*) dodgems *pl*; **≂droschke** *f* (*dated*) taxi-cab; **≂elektrik** *f* (car) electrics *pl*; **~erotik** *f* auto-eroticism; **≂fähre** *f* car ferry; **≂fahren** *nt* driving (a car); (*als Mitfahrer*) driving in a car; **≂fahrer** *m* (car) driver; **≂fahrergruß** *m* (*iro inf*) **jdm den ~fahrergruß bieten** ≃ to give sb a V (*Brit*) *or* the finger (*US*) sign; **≂fahrt** *f* drive; **≂falle** *f* (*bei Überfällen*) road trap; (*Radarkontrolle*) speed *or* radar trap; **≂focuskamera** *f* auto-focus camera; **≂friedhof** *m* (*inf*) car dump; **≂gas** *nt* liquefied petroleum gas.
autogen *adj* autogenous ♦ **~es Training** (*Psych*) relaxation through self-hypnosis.
Autogenschweißen *nt* autogenous welding.
Autogramm *nt* **-s, -e** autograph.
Autogramm-: ~jäger *m* autograph hunter; **~stunde** *f* autograph(ing) session.
Auto-: ⚠**~graph** *nt* **-s, -en** autograph; **~hypnose** *f* autohypnosis; **≂industrie** *f* car industry; **≂karte** *f* road map; **≂kino** *nt* drive-in cinema (*Brit*) *or* movie theater (*US*); **≂knacker** *m* (*inf*) car burglar; **≂kolonne** *f* line of cars; **~krat** *m* **-en, -en** autocrat; **~kratie** *f* autocracy; **a~kratisch** *adj* autocratic; **≂kunde** *m* customer with a car; **≂lenker** *m* (*Sw*) (car) driver; **≂marder** *m* (*sl*) *siehe* **~knacker**; **≂marke** *f* make (of car).
Automat *m* **-en, -en** (*auch fig: Mensch*) machine; (*Verkaufs~*) vending machine; (*Roboter*) automaton, robot; (*Musik~*) jukebox; (*Spiel~*) slot-machine; (*Rechen~*) calculator; (*rare: Telefon~*) pay-phone; (*Elec: selbsttätige Sicherung*) cut-out.
Automaten-: ~buffet *nt* (*esp Aus*) automat; **~knacker** *m* (*inf*) vandal (*who breaks into vending machines*); **~restaurant** *nt siehe* **~buffet**; **~straße** *f* vending machines *pl*.
Automatic, Automatik[1] *m* **-s, -s** (*Aut*) automatic.
Automatik[2] *f* automatic mechanism (*auch fig*); (*Gesamtanlage*) automatic system; (*Rad*) automatic frequency control, AFC; (*Aut*) automatic transmission.
Automatik-: ~gurt *nt* inertia(-reel) seat belt; **~schaltung** *f* automatic transmission; **~wagen** *m* automatic.
Automation *f* automation.
automatisch *adj* automatic.
automatisieren* *vt* to automate.
Automatisierung *f* automation.
Automatismus *m* automatism.
Auto-: ~mechaniker *m* car *or* motor mechanic; **~minute** *f* minute by car,

minute's drive.

Automobil *nt* **-s, -e** (*dated, geh*) motor-car, automobile (*esp US, dated*).

Automobil-: ~ausstellung *f* motor show; (*ständige ~ausstellung*) car exhibition; **~bau** *m* **-s,** *no pl* car *or* automobile (*US*) manufacture; **~club** *m* automobile association.

Automobilist *m* (*Sw, geh*) (car) driver.

Automobil-: ~klub *m siehe* **~club; ~salon** *m* motor show.

Auto-: ≈modell *nt* (car) model; (*Miniaturauto*) model car; **a~nom** *adj* autonomous (*auch fig*); *Nervensystem* autonomic; **~nome(r)** *mf decl as adj* (*Pol*) independent; **~nomie** *f* autonomy (*auch fig*); **~nomist** *m* autonomist; **≈nummer** *f* (car) number; **≈öl** *nt* motor oil; **~pilot** *m* (*Aviat*) autopilot; **vom ~piloten gesteuert werden** to be on autopilot.

Autopsie *f* (*Med*) autopsy.

Autor *m* [au'to:rən] author.

Auto-: ~radio *nt* car radio; **~reifen** *m* car tyre; **~reisezug** *m* ≃ motorail train; **mit dem ~reisezug fahren** to go by motorail.

Autorenkollektiv *nt* team of authors.

Auto-: ~rennbahn *f* motor-racing circuit; **~rennen** *nt* (motor) race; (*Rennsport*) motor racing; **~rennsport** *m* motor racing.

Autorenregister *nt* index of authors.

Autoreparaturwerkstatt *f* garage, car repair shop.

Autoreverse-Funktion [-re'vɛrs-] *f* autoreverse (function).

Autorin *f* authoress.

Autorisation *f* (*geh*) authorization.

autorisieren* *vt* to authorize.

autoritär *adj* authoritarian.

Autorität *f* (*alle Bedeutungen*) authority.

autoritativ *adj* (*geh*) authoritative.

Autoritäts-: a~gläubig *adj* trusting in authority; **~gläubigkeit** *f* trust in authority; **a~hörig** *adj* slavishly following authority; **a~hörig sein** to be a slave to authority.

Autor-: ~korrektur *f* (*Korrekturfahne*) author's proof; (*Änderung*) author's correction; **~schaft** *f* authorship.

Auto-: ≈schalter *m* drive-in counter; **≈schlange** *f* queue (*Brit*) *or* line of cars; **≈schlosser** *m* panel beater; **≈schlosserei** *f* body shop; **≈skooter** *m* dodgem *or* bumper car; **≈spengler** *m* (*S Ger, Aus, Sw*) *siehe* **~schlosser; ≈spenglerei** *f* (*S Ger, Aus, Sw*) *siehe* **~schlosserei; ≈sport** *m* motor sport; **≈stellplatz** *m* (car) parking space; **≈stop(p)** *m* (*esp S Ger*) hitch-hiking, hitching; **~stop(p) machen, per ~stop(p) fahren** to hitch(-hike); **≈straße** *f* main road, highway (*esp US*); **≈strich** *m* (*inf*) *prostitution to car-drivers*; (*Gegend*) kerb-crawling area (*inf*); **≈stunde** *f* hour's drive; **~suggestion** *f* autosuggestion; **≈telefon** *nt* car phone; **~typie** *f* autotypy; **≈unfall** *m* car accident; **≈verkehr** *m* motor traffic; **≈verleih** *m*, **≈vermietung** *f* car hire *or* rental; (*Firma*) car hire *or* rental firm; **≈versicherung** *f* car *or* motor insurance; **≈werkstatt** *f* garage, car repair shop (*US*); **≈wrack** *nt* (car) wreck, wrecked car; **~zoom** *nt* (*Phot*) automatic zoom (lens); **≈zubehör** *nt* car *or* motor accessories *pl*; **≈zug** *m siehe* **~reisezug.**

autsch *interj* (*inf*) ouch, ow.

auweh, auwei(a) *interj* oh dear.

Avance [a'vã:sə] *f* **-, -n jdm ~n machen** (*geh*) to make approaches to sb.

avancieren* [avã'si:rən] *vi aux sein* (*dated, geh*) to advance (*zu* to).

Avant- [avã]: **~garde** *f* (*geh*) (*Art*) avant-garde; (*Pol*) vanguard; **~gardismus** *m* avant-gardism; **~gardist** *m* member of the avant-garde, avant-gardist; **a~gardistisch** *adj* avant-garde.

AvD [a:fau'de:] *abbr of* **Automobilclub von Deutschland.**

Ave-Maria ['a:vema'ri:a] *nt* **-(s), -(s)** Ave Maria; (*Gebet auch*) Hail Mary.

Avers [a'vɛrs] *m* **-es, -e** face, obverse.

Aversion [avɛr'zio:n] *f* aversion (*gegen* to).

Aviarium [a'via:rium] *nt* aviary.

Avis [a'vi:] *m or nt* **-, -, Avis** [a'vi:s] *m or nt* **-es, -e** (*Comm*) advice (*Comm*); (*schriftlich*) advice-note.

avisieren* [avi'zi:rən] *vt* to send notification of, to advise of.

Aviso [a'vi:zo] *nt* **-s, -s** (*Aus*) *siehe* **Avis.**

Avitaminose [avɪtami'no:zə] *f* **-, -n** (*Med*) avitaminosis.

Avocado, Avocato [avo'ka:do, -to] *f* **-, -s** avocado.

Axel *m* **-s, -** (*Sport*) axel.

axial *adj* axial.

Axiallager *nt* (*Tech*) axial *or* thrust bearing.

Axiom *nt* **-s, -e** axiom.

Axiomatik *f*, *no pl* axiomatics *sing.*

axiomatisch *adj* axiomatic.

Axt *f* **-, ¨-e** axe (*Brit*), ax (*US*) ◆ **sich wie eine** *or* **die ~ im Wald benehmen** (*fig inf*) to behave like a peasant *or* boor; **die ~ im Haus erspart den Zimmermann** (*Prov*) self-help is the best help; **die ~ an etw/an die Wurzel einer Sache legen** (*fig*) to tear up the very roots of sth.

Axthieb *m* blow of the/an axe.

Ayatollah *m* **-s, -s** ayatollah.

Azalee, Azalie [-iə] *f* **-, -n** (*Bot*) azalea.

Azetat *nt* acetate.

Azetatseide *f* acetate silk.

Azeton *nt* **-s,** *no pl* (*Chem*) *siehe* **Aceton.**

Azetylen *nt* **-s,** *no pl* (*Chem*) *siehe* **Acetylen.**

Azimut *nt* **-s, -e** (*Astron*) azimuth.

Azoren *pl* (*Geog*) Azores *pl.*

Azteke *m* **-n, -n** Aztec.

Aztekenreich *nt* Aztec empire.

Aztekin *f* Aztec.

aztekisch *adj* Aztec.

Azubi [a:'tsu:bi:] *m* **-s, -s** *abbr of* **Auszubildende(r).**

Azur *m* **-s,** *no pl* (*poet*) azure sky; (*Farbe*) azure.

azurblau, azurn (*poet*) *adj* azure(-blue).

azyklisch *adj* acyclic.

B

B, b [beː] *nt* -, - B, b; (*Mus*) (*Ton*) B flat; (*Versetzungszeichen*) flat ◆ **B-dur/b-Moll** (the key of) B flat major/minor.
Baas *m* **-es, -e** (*Naut*) boss.
babbeln *vi* (*inf*) to babble; (*Schwätzer auch*) to chatter.
Babel *nt* **-s** (*Bibl*) Babel; (*fig*) (*Sünden~*) sink of iniquity; (*von Sprachen*) melting pot.
Baby ['beːbi] *nt* **-s, -s** baby.
Baby- *in cpds* baby; **~ausstattung** *f* layette; **~doll** *nt* **-(s), -s** baby-dolls *pl*, baby-doll pyjamas *pl*; **~korb** *m* bassinet.
Babylon ['baːbylɔn] *nt* **-s** Babylon.
babylonisch *adj* Babylonian ◆ **eine ~e Sprachverwirrung** a Babel of languages; **der B~e Turm** the Tower of Babel; **die B~e Gefangenschaft** Babylonian captivity.
Baby-: ~nahrung *f* baby food; **b~sitten** *vi insep* to babysit; **~sitter(in *f*)** *m* **-s, -** babysitter; **~speck** *m* (*inf*) puppy fat; **~strich** *m* child prostitution *no art*; (*Gegend*) pick-up place for child prostitutes; **~tragetasche** *f* carry-cot; **~waage** *f* scales *pl* for weighing babies; **~wippe** *f* bouncing cradle.
Baccara *nt* **-s,** *no pl* (*Cards*) *siehe* **Bakkarat.**
Bacchanal [baxa'naːl] *nt* **-s, -ien** [-liən] **(a)** (*in der Antike*) Bacchanalia. **(b)** *pl* **-e** (*geh*) bacchanal, drunken orgy.
Bacchant(in *f*) [ba'xant(ɪn)] *m* bacchant.
bacchantisch [ba'xantɪʃ] *adj* bacchanalian.
bacchisch ['baxɪʃ] *adj* (*Myth*) Bacchic.
Bacchus ['baxʊs] *m* - (*Myth*) Bacchus ◆ **dem ~ huldigen** (*geh*) to imbibe (*form*).
Bach *m* **-(e)s, ¨-e** stream (*auch fig*), brook; (*Naut, Aviat sl: Gewässer*) drink (*inf*).
bach|ab *adv* (*Sw*) downstream ◆ **etw ~ schicken** (*fig inf*) to throw sth away; **~ gehen** (*fig inf*) to go up the creek (*inf*) *or* spout (*inf*).
Bachblütentherapie *f* (*Med*) Bach flower remedies *pl*.
Bache *f* **-, -n** (wild) sow.
Bächelchen *nt dim of* **Bach.**
Bachforelle *f* brown trout.
Bächlein *nt dim of* **Bach** (small) stream, brooklet ◆ **ein ~ machen** (*baby-talk*) to do a wee-wee (*baby-talk*).
Bachstelze *f* **-, -n** wagtail.
back *adv* (*Naut*) back.
Back *f* **-, -en** (*Naut*) **(a)** (*Deck*) forecastle, fo'c'sle. **(b)** (*Schüssel*) dixie, mess-tin, mess kit (*US*); (*Tafel*) mess table; (*Besatzung*) mess.
Backblech *nt* baking tray.
Backbord *nt* **-(e)s,** *no pl* (*Naut*) port (side) ◆ **von ~ nach Steuerbord** from port to starboard; **über ~** over the port side.
backbord(s) *adv* (*Naut*) on the port side ◆ **(nach) ~** to port.
Bäckchen *nt* (little) cheek.
Backe *f* **-, -n (a)** (*Wange*) cheek ◆ **mit vollen ~n kauen** to chew *or* eat with bulging cheeks; (*mit Genuß*) to eat heartily; **au ~!** (*dated inf*) oh dear! **(b)** (*inf: Hinter~*) buttock, cheek. **(c)** (*von Schraubstock*) jaw; (*Brems~*) (*bei Auto*) shoe; (*bei Fahrrad*) block; (*von Skibindung*) toe-piece; (*von Gewehr*) cheek-piece.
backen[1] *pret* **backte** *or* (*old*) **buk**, *ptp* **gebacken** [1] *vt* to bake; *Brot, Kuchen auch* to make; (*braten*) *Fisch, Eier etc* to fry; (*dial: dörren*) *Obst* to dry ◆ **frisch/knusprig gebackenes Brot** fresh crusty bread; **wir ~ alles selbst** we do all our own baking; **gebackener Fisch** fried fish; (*im Ofen*) baked fish.
[2] *vi* (*Brot, Kuchen*) to bake; (*dial: braten*) to fry; (*dial: dörren*) to dry ◆ **der Kuchen muß noch 20 Minuten ~** the cake will have to be in the oven *or* will take another 20 minutes; **sie bäckt gern** she enjoys baking.
backen[2] (*dial inf*) [1] *vi* (*kleben: Schnee etc*) to stick (*an +dat* to), to cake (*an +dat* on, onto).
[2] *vt* **etw an etw** (*acc*) **~** to stick sth onto sth.
Backen-: ~bart *m* sideboards *pl*, sideburns *pl*, (side) whiskers *pl*; **~bremse** *f* (*bei Auto*) shoe brake; (*bei Fahrrad*) block brake; **~knochen** *m* cheekbone; **~tasche** *f* (*Zool*) cheek pouch; **~zahn** *m* molar.
Bäcker *m* **-s, -** baker ◆ **~ lernen** to learn the baker's trade, to be an apprentice baker; **~ werden** to be *or* become a baker; **beim ~** at the baker's; **zum ~ gehen** to go to the baker's.
Back|erbsen *pl small round noodles eaten in soup.*
Bäckerei *f* **(a)** (*Bäckerladen*) baker's (shop); (*Backstube*) bakery. **(b)** (*Gewerbe*) bakery, baking trade. **(c)** (*Aus*) (*Gebäck*) pastries *pl*; (*Kekse*) biscuits *pl*.

Bäcker-: ~geselle *m* (journeyman) baker; **~junge** *m* baker's boy; (*Lehrling*) baker's apprentice; **~laden** *m* baker's (shop); **~meister** *m* master baker.
Bäckersfrau *f* baker's wife.
Backfeige *f* (*dial*) *siehe* **Ohrfeige.**
Back-: b~fertig *adj* oven-ready; **~fett** *nt* cooking fat; **~fisch** *m* **(a)** fried fish; **(b)** (*dated*) teenager, teenage girl; **~form** *f* baking tin; (*für Kuchen auch*) cake tin.
Background ['bɛkgraunt] *m* **-s, -s** background.
Back-: ~hähnchen, ~hendl (*S Ger, Aus*), **~huhn, ~hühnchen** *nt* roast chicken; **~mulde** *f siehe* **~trog**; **~obst** *nt* dried fruit; **~ofen** *m* oven; **es ist heiß wie in einem ~ofen** it's like an oven; **~pfeife** *f* (*dial*) slap on *or* round (*inf*) the face; **~pflaume** *f* prune; **~pulver** *nt* baking powder; **~rohr** *nt* (*Aus*), **~röhre** *f* oven.
Backspacetaste ['bɛkspeɪs-] *f* (*Comput*) backspace key.
Backstein *m* brick.
Backstein-: ~bau *m* brick building; **~gotik** *f Gothic architecture built in brick.*
Back-: ~stube *f* bakery; **~trog** *m* kneading *or* dough trough, dough tray, hutch.
Backup ['bɛkʌp-] *nt* **-s, -s** (*Comput*) backup.
Backup-Programm *nt* (*Comput*) backup program.
Back-: ~vorschrift *f* baking instructions *pl*; **~waren** *pl* bread, cakes and pastries *pl*; **~werk** *nt* (*old*) cakes and pastries *pl*; **~zeit** *f* baking time.
Bad *nt* **-(e)s, ¨-er (a)** (*Wannen~, Badewanne, Phot*) bath; (*das Baden*) bathing ◆ **ein ~ nehmen** to have *or* take a bath; **(sich** *dat*) **ein ~ einlaufen lassen** to run (oneself) a bath; **jdm ¨-er verschreiben** (*Med*) to prescribe sb a course of (therapeutic) baths; **~ in der Menge** (*fig*) walkabout; **ein ~ in der Menge nehmen** to go (on a) walkabout.
(b) (*im Meer etc*) bathe, swim; (*das Baden*) bathing, swimming.
(c) (*Badezimmer*) bathroom ◆ **Zimmer mit ~** room with (private) bath.
(d) (*Schwimm~*) (swimming) pool *or* bath(s) ◆ **die städtischen ¨-er** the public baths.
(e) (*Heil~*) spa; (*See~*) (seaside) resort.
Bade-: ~anstalt *f* (public) swimming baths *pl*; **~anzug** *m* swimsuit, bathing suit (*US*); **~arzt** *m* spa doctor; **~gast** *m* **(a)** (*im Kurort*) spa visitor; **(b)** (*im Schwimmbad*) bather, swimmer; **~gelegenheit** *f* **gibt es dort eine ~gelegenheit?** can one swim *or* bathe there?; **~(hand)tuch** *nt* bath towel; **~haube** *f* (*dated*) *siehe* **~kappe**; **~hose** *f* (swimming *or* bathing) trunks *pl*; **eine ~hose** a pair of (swimming *or* bathing) trunks; **~kabine** *f* changing cubicle; **~kappe** *f* swimming cap *or* hat, bathing cap; **~kostüm** *nt* (*geh*) swimming *or* bathing costume; **~laken** *nt* bath sheet; **~mantel** *m* beach robe; (*Morgenmantel*) bathrobe, dressing gown (*Brit*); **~matte** *f* bathmat; **~meister** *m* (*im Schwimmbad*) (pool) attendant; (*am Strand*) lifeguard; **~mütze** *f siehe* **~kappe.**
baden [1] *vi* **(a)** to have a bath, to bath ◆ **hast du schon gebadet?** have you had your bath already?; **warm/kalt ~** to have a hot/cold bath.
(b) (*im Meer, Schwimmbad etc*) to swim, to bathe ◆ **sie hat im Meer gebadet** she swam *or* bathed *or* had a swim in the sea; **die B~den** the bathers; **~ gehen** to go swimming *or* (*einmal*) for a swim.
(c) (*inf*) **~ gehen** to come a cropper (*inf*); **wenn das passiert, gehe ich ~** I'll be for it if that happens (*inf*).
[2] *vt* **(a)** *Kind etc* to bath ◆ **er ist als Kind zu heiß gebadet worden** (*hum*) he was dropped on the head as a child (*hum*); **in Schweiß gebadet** bathed in sweat.
(b) *Augen, Wunde etc* to bathe.
[3] *vr* to bathe, to have a bath.
Baden *nt* **-s** (*Geog*) Baden.
Badener(in *f*), Badenser(in *f*) (*inf*) *m* **-s, -** person *or* man/woman from Baden ◆ **er ist ~** he comes from Baden.
Badenixe *f* (*hum*) bathing beauty *or* belle.
Baden-Württemberg *nt* **-s** Baden-Württemberg.
Bade-: ~ofen *m* boiler; **~ort** *m* (*Kurort*) spa; (*Seebad*) (seaside) resort; **~platz** *m* place for bathing.
Bader *m* **-s, -** (*old*) barber (*old*); (*dial: Arzt*) village quack (*hum*).
Bäderbehandlung *f medical treatment using therapeutic baths.*
Badereise *f* (*dated*) trip to a spa.

⚠: for details of spelling reform, see supplement

Bäder-: ~kunde *f* balneology; **~kur** *f siehe* **~behandlung.**
Bade-: ~sachen *pl siehe* **~zeug**; **~saison** *f* swimming season; (*in Kurort*) spa season; **~salz** *nt* bath salts *pl*; **~schaum** *m* bubble bath; **~schuh** *m* bathing shoe; **~schwamm** *m* sponge; **~strand** *m* (bathing) beach; **~stube** *f* (*N Ger*) bathroom; **~tuch** *nt siehe* **~(hand)tuch**; **~verbot** *nt* ban on bathing; **~wanne** *f* bath(tub); **~wasser** *nt* bath water; **~wetter** *nt* weather warm enough for bathing *or* swimming; **~zeit** *f* bathing *or* swimming season; **~zeug** *nt* swimming gear, swimming *or* bathing things *pl*; **~zimmer** *nt* bathroom; **~zusatz** *m* bath salts, bubble bath *etc.*
badisch *adj* Baden *attr*; *Wein etc auch* from Baden; *Dialekt auch* of Baden; *Landschaft auch* around Baden ◆ **das Dorf ist ~** *or* **im B~en** the village is in Baden.
Badminton ['bɛtmɪntən] *nt* **-,** *no pl* badminton.
baff *adj pred* (*inf*) **~ sein** to be flabbergasted.
Bafög ['ba:føk] *nt* **-,** *no pl abbr of* **Bundesausbildungsförderungsgesetz**; **er kriegt ~** he gets a grant.
Bagage [ba'ga:ʒə] *f* **-,** *no pl* **(a)** (*old, Sw, inf: Gepäck*) luggage, baggage.
(b) (*dated inf*) (*Gesindel*) crowd, crew (*inf*), gang (*inf*); (*Familie*) pack (*inf*) ◆ **die ganze ~** the whole bloody lot (*sl*).
Bagatell *f* **-, -en** (*Aus inf*) *siehe* **Bagatelle.**
Bagatelldelikt *nt* petty *or* minor offence.
Bagatelle *f* trifle, bagatelle; (*Mus*) bagatelle.
bagatellisieren* [1] *vt* to trivialize, to minimize.
[2] *vi* to trivialize.
Bagatell-: ~sache *f* (*Jur*) petty *or* minor case; **~schaden** *m* minor *or* superficial damage.
Bagdad ['bakdat, bak'da:t] *nt* **-s** Baghdad.
Bagger *m* **-s, -** excavator; (*für Schlamm*) dredger.
Baggerführer *m* driver of an/the excavator/dredger.
baggern *vti Graben* to excavate, to dig; *Fahrrinne* to dredge.
Bagger-: ~schaufel *f* excavator shovel; **~see** *m artificial lake in gravel pit etc.*
Baguette [ba'gɛt] *nt* **-s, -s** baguette.
bah, bäh *interj* **(a)** (*aus Schadenfreude*) hee-hee (*inf*); (*vor Ekel*) ugh. **(b) ~ machen** (*baby-talk: Schaf*) to baa, to go baa.
Bahama|inseln *pl*, **Bahamas** *pl* Bahamas *pl.*
Bählamm *nt* (*baby-talk*) baa-lamb (*baby-talk*).
Bahn *f* **-, -en (a)** (*Weg*) path, track; (*von Fluß*) course; (*fig*) path; (*Fahr~*) carriageway ◆ **~ frei!** make way!, (get) out of the way!; **jdm/einer Sache die ~ ebnen/frei machen** (*fig*) to pave/clear the way for sb/sth; **die ~ ist frei** (*fig*) the way is clear; **sich** (*dat*) **~ brechen** (*lit*) to force one's way; (*fig*) to make headway; (*Mensch*) to forge ahead; **einer Sache** (*dat*) **~ brechen** to blaze the trail for sth; **sich auf neuen ~en bewegen** to break new *or* fresh ground; **in gewohnten ~en verlaufen** (*fig*) to go on in the same old way, to continue as before; **von der rechten ~ abkommen** (*geh*) to stray from the straight and narrow; **jdn auf die rechte ~ bringen** (*fig*) to put sb on the straight and narrow; **etw in die richtige ~** *or* **die richtigen ~en lenken** (*fig*) to channel sth properly; **jdn aus der ~ werfen** *or* **schleudern** to throw sb off the track; (*fig*) to shatter sb; *siehe* **schief.**
(b) (*Eisen~*) railway, railroad (*US*); (*Straßen~*) tram, streetcar (*US*); (*Zug*) (*der Eisen~, U-~*) train; (*der Straßen~*) tram, streetcar (*US*); (*~hof*) station; (*Verkehrsnetz, Verwaltung*) railway *usu pl*, railroad (*US*) ◆ **mit der** *or* **per ~** by train *or* rail/tram; **frei ~** (*Comm*) carriage free to station of destination; **er ist** *or* **arbeitet bei der ~** he's with the railways *or* railroad (*US*), he works for *or* on the railways.
(c) (*Sport*) track; (*für Pferderennen auch*) course; (*in Schwimmbecken*) pool; (*Kegel~*) (bowling) alley; (*für einzelne Teilnehmer*) lane; (*Schlitten~, Bob~*) run.
(d) (*Astron*) orbit, path; (*Raketen~, Geschoß~*) (flight) path, trajectory.
(e) (*Stoff~, Tapeten~*) length, strip.
(f) (*Tech: von Werkzeug*) face.
Bahn-: b~amtlich *adj Tarife etc* official railway *or* railroad (*US*) *attr*; ⚠**~anschluß** *m* railway *or* railroad (*US*) connection *or* link; **~anschluß haben** to be connected *or* linked to the railway *or* railroad (*US*) (system); **~arbeiter** *m* railwayman, railroader (*US*); **~beamte(r)** *m* railway *or* railroad (*US*) official; **~betriebswerk** *nt* railway *or* railroad (*US*) depot; **b~brechend** *adj* pioneering; **~brechendes leisten** to pioneer new developments; **b~brechend sein/wirken** to be pioneering; (*Erfinder etc*) to be a pioneer; **~brecher(in** *f*) *m* pioneer; **~bus** *m bus run by railway company*; **~Card** ® *f* **-, -s** railcard.
Bähnchen *nt dim of* **Bahn.**
Bahndamm *m* (railway) embankment.
bahnen *vt Pfad* to clear; *Flußbett* to carve *or* channel out ◆ **jdm/einer Sache den/einen Weg ~** to clear the/a way for sb/sth; (*fig*) to pave *or* prepare the way for sb/sth; **sich** (*dat*) **einen Weg ~** to fight one's way.
bahnenweise *adv* in lengths *or* strips.
Bahner *m* **-s, -** (*inf*) railwayman (*Brit*), railroad employee (*US*).
Bahn-: ~fahrt *f* rail journey; **~fracht** *f* rail freight; **b~frei** *adj* (*Comm*) carriage free to station of destination; **~gelände** *nt* railway *or* railroad (*US*) area; **~gleis** *nt* railway *or* railroad (*US*) line; (*von Straßen~*) tram *or* streetcar (*US*) line.
Bahnhof *m* (railway *or* railroad (*US*)/bus/tram *or* streetcar *US*) station; (*dated: Straßen~*) tram *or* streetcar (*US*) depot ◆ **am** *or* **auf dem ~** at the station; **~ Schöneberg** Schöneberg station; **ich verstehe nur ~** (*hum inf*) it's as clear as mud (to me) (*inf*), it's all Greek to me (*inf*); **er wurde mit großem ~ empfangen** he was given the red carpet treatment, they rolled the red carpet out for him; **es wurde auf einen großen ~ verzichtet** they didn't bother with the red carpet treatment.
Bahnhof- (*esp S Ger, Aus, Sw*), **Bahnhofs-** *in cpds* station; **~buffet** *nt* (*esp Aus, Sw*) station buffet; **~gaststätte** *f* station restaurant; **~halle** *f* (station) concourse; **in der ~halle** in the station; **~mission** *f charitable organisation for helping needy rail travellers*, traveller's aid; **~platz** *m* station square; **~uhr** *f* station clock; **~vorplatz** *m* station forecourt; **sich auf dem ~vorplatz versammeln** to meet in front of the station; **~vorstand** (*Aus, Sw*), **~vorsteher** *m* stationmaster; **~wirtschaft** *f* station bar; (*~restaurant*) station restaurant.
Bahn-: ~körper *m* track; **b~lagernd** *adj* (*Comm*) to be collected from the station.
Bähnler *m* **-s, -** (*Sw*) railwayman (*Brit*), railroad employee (*US*).
Bahn-: ~linie *f* (railway *or* railroad *US*) line *or* track; **~meisterei** *f* railway *or* railroad (*US*) board; **~netz** *nt* rail(way) *or* railroad (*US*) network; **~polizei** *f* railway *or* railroad (*US*) police; **~schranke** *f*, **~schranken** *m* (*Aus*) level *or* grade (*US*) crossing barrier *or* gate; **~steig** *m* platform; **~steigkarte** *f* platform ticket; **~strecke** *f* railway *or* railroad (*US*) route *or* line; **~transport** *m* rail transport; (*Güter*) consignment sent by rail; **~überführung** *f* railway *or* railroad (*US*) footbridge; **~übergang** *m* level *or* grade (*US*) crossing; **beschrankter/unbeschrankter ~übergang** level crossing with gates/ unguarded level crossing; **~unterführung** *f* railway *or* railroad (*US*) underpass; **~wärter** *m* (*an ~übergängen*) gatekeeper, (level crossing) attendant; (*Streckenwärter*) platelayer, trackman (*US*).
Bahre *f* **-, -n** (*Kranken~*) stretcher; (*Toten~*) bier.
Bahrein *nt* **-s** Bahrain.
Bahrtuch *nt* pall.
Bai *f* **-, en** bay.
bairisch *adj* (*Hist, Ling*) Bavarian.
Baiser [bɛ'ze:] *nt* **-s, -s** meringue.
Baisse ['bɛ:s(ə)] *f* **-, -n** (*St Ex*) fall; (*plötzliche*) slump ◆ **auf (die) ~ spekulieren** to bear.
Baissespekulant *m*, **Baissier** [bɛ'sie:] *m* **-s, -s** bear.
Bajadere *f* **-, -n** bayadere.
Bajazzo *m* **-s, -s** clown.
Bajonett *nt* **-(e)s, -e** bayonet; *siehe* **fällen.**
Bajonett-: ~fassung *f* (*Elec*) bayonet fitting; ⚠**~verschluß** *m* (*Elec*) bayonet socket.
Bajuware *m* **-n, -n, Bajuwarin** *f* (*old, hum*) Bavarian.
bajuwarisch *adj* (*old, hum*) Bavarian.
Bake *f* **-, -n** (*Naut*) marker buoy; (*Aviat*) beacon; (*Verkehrszeichen*) distance warning signal; (*vor Bahnübergang, an Autobahn auch*) countdown marker; (*Surv*) marker pole.
Bakelit ® *nt* **-(e)s,** *no pl* Bakelite ®.
Bakkarat ['bakara(t)] *nt* **-s,** *no pl* (*Cards*) baccarat.
Bakken *m* **-(s), -** (*Ski*) ski-jump.
Bakschisch *nt* **-s, -e** *or* **-s** baksheesh; (*Bestechungsgeld*) bribe, backhander (*inf*) ◆ **~ geben** to give baksheesh/a bribe *or* backhander.
Bakterie [-riə] *f* **-, -n** *usu pl* germ, bacterium (*spec*) ◆ **~n** germs *pl*, bacteria *pl.*
bakteriell *adj* bacterial, bacteria *attr* ◆ **~ verursacht** caused by germs *or* bacteria.
Bakterien- *in cpds* bacteria; **~kultur** *f* bacteria culture; **~träger** *m* carrier; **~züchtung** *f* growing *or* culturing of bacteria.
Bakteriologe *m*, **Bakteriologin** *f* bacteriologist.
Bakteriologie *f* bacteriology.
bakteriologisch *adj Forschung, Test* bacteriological; *Krieg* biological.
Bakterium *nt* (*form*) *siehe* **Bakterie.**
bakterizid *adj* germicidal, bactericidal.
Bakterizid *nt* **-s, -e** germicide, bactericide.
Balalaika *f* **-, -s** *or* **Balalaiken** balalaika.
Balance [ba'lã:s(ə)] *f* **-, -n** balance, equilibrium ◆ **die ~ halten/verlieren** to keep/lose one's balance.
Balance|akt [ba'lã:s(ə)-] *m* (*lit*) balancing *or* tightrope *or* high-wire act; (*fig*) balancing act.
balancieren* [balã'si:rən] [1] *vi aux sein* to balance; (*fig*) to achieve a balance (*zwischen +dat* between) ◆ **über etw** (*acc*) **~** to balance one's way across sth.
[2] *vt* to balance.
Balancierstange *f* (balancing) pole.
balbieren* *vt* (*inf*): **jdn über den Löffel ~** to pull the wool over sb's eyes, to lead sb by the nose (*inf*).
bald [1] *adv, comp* **eher** *or* **¨er** (*old, dial*), *superl* **am ehesten (a)** (*schnell, in Kürze*) soon ◆ **er kommt ~** he'll be coming soon; **~ ist Weihnachten/Winter** it will soon be Christmas/winter; **~ darauf** soon afterwards, a little later; **(all)zu ~** (all) too soon; **so ~ wie** *or* **als möglich, möglichst ~** as soon as possible; **das gibt es so ~ nicht noch einmal** you won't find one of those again in a hurry; (*besonderes Ereignis*) that won't happen again in a hurry; **wirst du wohl ~ ruhig sein?** will you just be quiet!; **wird's ~?** get a move on; **bis ~!** see you soon.
(b) (*fast*) almost, nearly ◆ **das ist ~ nicht mehr schön** that is really beyond a joke.
[2] *conj* (*geh*) **~ ..., ~ ...** one moment ..., the next ..., now ..., now ...; **~ hier, ~ da** now here, now there; **~ so, ~ so** now this way, now that.
Baldachin [-xi:n] *m* **-s, -e** canopy, baldachin; (*Archit*) baldachin, baldaquin.
Bälde *f*: **in ~** in the near future.

⚠: Informationen zur Rechtschreibreform im Anhang

baldig *adj attr, no comp* quick, speedy; *Antwort, Wiedersehen* early ◆ **wir hoffen auf Ihr ~es Kommen** we hope you will come soon; **auf ~es Wiedersehen!** (hope to) see you soon!
baldigst *adv superl of* **baldig** *(form)* as soon as possible, without delay.
baldmöglichst *adv* as soon as possible.
baldowern* *vti (inf) siehe* **ausbaldowern.**
Baldrian *m* **-s, -e** valerian.
Baldriantropfen *pl* valerian (drops *pl*).
Baldur *m* **-s** *(Myth)* Balder.
Balearen *pl* **die ~** the Balearic Islands *pl.*
Balg[1] *m* **-(e)s, ¨e (a)** *(Tierhaut)* pelt, skin; *(von Vogel)* skin; *(inf: Bauch)* belly *(inf)*; *(einer Puppe)* body ◆ **einem Tier den ~ abziehen** to skin an animal; **sich** *(dat)* **den ~ vollschlagen** *or* **vollstopfen** *(inf)* to stuff oneself *(inf)*; **ich habe eine Wut im ~** *(inf)* I'm mad or livid; *siehe* **rücken.**
(b) *(Blase~, Phot, Rail)* bellows *pl* ◆ **die ¨e treten** to work the bellows.
Balg[2] *m or nt* **-(e)s, ¨er** *(pej inf: Kind)* brat *(pej inf)*.
Balgen *m* **-s, -** *(Phot)* bellows *pl.*
balgen *vr* to scrap *(um* over).
Balgerei *f* scrap, tussle ◆ **hört jetzt auf mit der ~!** stop scrapping!
Balkan *m* **-s (a)** *(~halbinsel, ~länder)* **der ~** the Balkans *pl*; **auf dem ~** in the Balkans; **dort herrschen Zustände wie auf dem ~** *(fig inf)* things are in a terrible state there. **(b)** *(~gebirge)* Balkan Mountains *pl.*
Balkanhalb|insel *f* Balkan Peninsula.
balkanisch *adj* Balkan.
balkanisieren* *vt* to Balkanize.
Balkanisierung *f* Balkanization.
Balkanländer *pl* Balkan States.
Bälkchen *nt dim of* **Balken.**
Balken *m* **-s, - (a)** *(Holz~, Schwebe~)* beam; *(Stütz~)* prop, shore; *(Quer~)* joist, crossbeam; *(Sport: bei Hürdenlauf)* rail ◆ **der ~ im eigenen Auge** *(Bibl)* the beam in one's own eye; **lügen, daß sich die ~ biegen** *(inf)* to lie through one's teeth, to tell a pack of lies; **Wasser hat keine ~** *(Prov)* not everyone can walk on water.
(b) *(Strich)* bar; *(Her auch)* fess(e); *(Uniformstreifen)* stripe.
(c) *(an Waage)* beam.
Balken-: ~brücke *f* girder bridge; **~decke** *f* ceiling with wooden beams; **~diagramm** *nt* bar chart; **~holz** *nt* (piece of) (squared) timber; *(~gerüst)* timbers *pl*, beams *pl*; **~konstruktion** *f* timber-frame construction; **~überschrift** *f (Press)* banner headline; **~waage** *f* (beam) balance; **~werk** *nt* timbering, timbers *pl*, beams *pl.*
Balkon [bal'kɔŋ, bal'koːn] *m* **-s, -s** *or* **-e** balcony; *(Theat)* (dress) circle ◆ **~ sitzen** *(Theat)* to have seats in the (dress) circle.
Balkon-: ~möbel *pl* garden furniture *sing*; **~pflanze** *f* balcony plant; **~tür** *f* French window(s); **~zimmer** *nt* room with a balcony.
Ball[1] *m* **-(e)s, ¨e** ball ◆ **~ spielen** to play (with a) ball; **am ~ sein** *(lit)* to have the ball, to be in possession of the ball; **immer am ~ sein** *(fig)* to be on the ball; **am ~ bleiben** *(lit)* to keep (possession of) the ball; *(fig: auf dem neuesten Stand bleiben)* to stay on the ball; **bei jdm am ~ bleiben** *(fig)* to keep in with sb; **er bemüht sich, bei ihr am ~ zu bleiben** he is trying to keep in the running with her; **hart am ~ bleiben** to stick at it; **jdm den ~ zuspielen** *(lit)* to pass (the ball) to sb; **jdm/sich gegenseitig die ¨e zuspielen** *or* **zuwerfen** *(fig)* to feed sb/each other lines; **einen ~ machen** *(Billard)* to pocket a ball; **der glutrote ~ der Sonne** *(poet)* the sun's fiery orb *(poet)*.
Ball[2] *m* **-(e)s, ¨e** *(Tanzfest)* ball ◆ **auf dem ~** at the ball.
balla-balla *adj pred (dated inf)* mad, crazy, nuts *(inf)*.
Ballade *f* ballad.
balladenhaft, balladesk [1] *adj* balladic, ballad-like.
[2] *adv* in a balladic *or* ballad-like way *or* manner.
Balladensänger *m* balladeer, ballad-singer.
Ballast [*or* -'-] *m* **-(e)s,** *(rare)* **-e** *(Naut, Aviat)* ballast; *(fig)* burden, encumbrance; *(in Büchern)* padding ◆ **~ abwerfen** *or* **über Bord werfen** *(lit)* to discharge *or* shed ballast; *(fig)* to get rid of a burden *or* an encumbrance; **mit ~ beladen** *or* **beschweren** to ballast, to load with ballast; **jdn/etw als ~ empfinden** to find sb/sth (to be) a burden *or* an encumbrance.
Ballaststoffe *pl (Med)* roughage *sing.*
Bällchen *nt dim of* **Ball**[1].
Ballen *m* **-s, - (a)** bale; *(Kaffee~)* sack ◆ **in ~ verpacken** to bale. **(b)** *(Anat: an Daumen, Zehen)* ball; *(an Pfote)* pad. **(c)** *(Med: am Fußknochen)* bunion.
ballen [1] *vt Faust* to clench; *Papier* to crumple (into a ball); *Lehm etc* to press (into a ball); *siehe* **geballt, Faust.**
[2] *vr (Menschenmenge)* to crowd; *(Wolken)* to gather, to build up; *(Verkehr)* to build up; *(Faust)* to clench.
ballenweise *adv* in bales.
Ballerei *f (inf)* shoot-out *(inf)*, shoot-up *(inf)*.
Ballerina[1] *f* **-, Ballerinen** ballerina, ballet dancer.
Ballerina[2] *m* **-s, -s** *(Schuh)* pump.
Ballermann *m* **-s, Ballermänner** *(sl)* iron *(sl)*, gun.
ballern [1] *vi (inf)* to shoot, to fire; *(Schuß)* to ring out ◆ **gegen die Tür ~** to hammer on the door.
[2] *vt Stein etc* to hurl; *Tür etc* to slam ◆ **jdm eine ~** *(sl)* to sock sb one *(inf)*.
Ballett *nt* **-(e)s, -e** ballet ◆ **beim ~ sein** *(inf)* to be (a dancer) with the ballet, to be a ballet dancer; **zum ~ gehen** to become a ballet dancer.
⚠ **Ballettänzer(in** *f) m getrennt:* **Ballett-tänzer** ballet dancer.
Balletteuse [-'tøːzə] *f (usu pej)* ballet dancer.
Ballett- *in cpds* ballet; **~meister** *m* ballet master, maître de ballet; **~ratte** *f* *(inf)* ballet pupil; **~röckchen** *nt* tutu; **~tänzer** *m siehe* **Ballettänzer;** **~truppe** *f* ballet (company).
Ball-: b~förmig *adj* ball-shaped, round; **~führung** *f (Sport)* ball control; **~gefühl** *nt (Sport)* feel for the ball.
Ballistik *f, no pl* ballistics *sing.*
ballistisch *adj* ballistic.
Ball-: ~junge *m (Tennis)* ball boy; **~kleid** *nt* ball dress *or* gown; **~königin** *f* belle of the ball; **~künstler** *m (Ftbl)* artist with the ball; **~ mädchen** *nt (Tennis)* ball girl.
Ballon [ba'lɔŋ, ba'loːn] *m* **-s, -s** *or* **-e (a)** balloon. **(b)** *(Chem)* carboy, demijohn. **(c)** *(sl: Kopf)* nut *(inf)* ◆ **einen roten ~ kriegen** to go bright red.
Ballon- [ba'loːn-]: **~dilatation** *f* **-, -en** *(Med)* balloon dilatation; **~mütze** *f* baker's boy cap; **~reifen** *m* balloon tyre.
Ball-: ~saal *m* ballroom; **~schani** *m* **-s, -** *(Aus inf) siehe* **~junge; ~schuh** *m* evening *or* dancing shoe; **~spiel** *nt* ball game; **~spielen** *nt* **-s,** *no pl* playing ball; „**~spielen verboten**" "no ball games"; **~technik** *f (Sport)* technique with the ball; **~treter** *m* **-s, -** *(inf)* footballer.
Ballung *f* concentration; *(von Truppen auch)* massing.
Ballungs-: ~gebiet *nt,* **~raum** *m* conurbation; **~zentrum** *nt* centre *(of population, industry etc)*.
Ballwechsel *m (Sport)* rally.
Balneologie *f* balneology.
Bal paradox *m* **- -, -s -** *ball at which women ask men to dance.*
Bal paré *m* **- -, -s -s** grand ball.
Balsaholz *nt* balsa wood.
Balsam *m* **-s, -e** balsam, balm *(liter)*; *(fig)* balm ◆ **~ in jds Wunden** *(acc)* **träufeln** *(liter)* to pour balm on sb's wounds; **die Zeit ist ein heilender ~** *(liter)* time is a great healer.
balsamieren* *vt siehe* **einbalsamieren.**
balsamisch *adj (liter)* **(a)** *(duftend)* balmy *(liter)*, fragrant. **(b)** *(lindernd)* soothing.
Balte *m* **-n, -n, Baltin** *f* person *or* man/woman from the Baltic ◆ **er ist ~** he comes from the Baltic.
Baltikum *nt* **-s das ~** the Baltic States *pl.*
baltisch *adj* Baltic *attr.*
Balustrade *f* balustrade.
Balz *f* **-, -en (a)** *(Paarungsspiel)* courtship display. **(b)** *(Paarungszeit)* mating season.
balzen *vi* to perform the courtship display; *(pej: Sänger)* to croon.
Balz-: ~ruf *m* mating call *or* cry; **~zeit** *f siehe* **Balz (b).**
Bambi[1] *nt* **-s, -s** *(inf: Rehkitz)* bambi.
Bambi[2] *m* **-s, -s** Bambi *(West German film award)*.
Bambule *f* **-, -n** *(sl)* ructions *pl* ◆ **~ machen** to go on the rampage.
Bambus *m* **-ses** *or* **-, -se** bamboo.
Bambus-: *in cpds* bamboo; **~rohr** *nt* bamboo cane; **~sprossen** *pl* bamboo shoots *pl*; **~stab** *m (Sport)* bamboo (vaulting) pole; **~vorhang** *m (Pol)* bamboo curtain.
Bammel *m* **-s,** *no pl (inf)* **(einen) ~ vor jdm/etw haben** to be nervous *or (stärker)* scared of sb/sth.
bammeln *vi (inf)* to swing, to dangle *(an +dat, von* from).
banal *adj* banal, trite.
banalisieren* *vt* to trivialize.
Banalität *f* **(a)** *no pl* banality, triteness. **(b)** *usu pl (Äußerung)* platitude ◆ **~en äußern** to utter platitudes.
Banane *f* **-, -n** banana.
Bananen-: ~dampfer *m* banana boat; **~republik** *f (Pol pej)* banana republic; **~schale** *f* banana skin; **~stecker** *m* jack plug.
Banause *m* **-n, -n** *(pej)* peasant *(inf)*; *(Kultur~ auch)* philistine.
Banausen-: b~haft *adj* philistine; **~tum** *nt, no pl (pej)* philistinism.
band *pret of* **binden.**
Band[1] *nt* **-(e)s, ¨er (a)** *(Seiden~ etc)* ribbon; *(Isolier~, Maß~, Ziel~)* tape; *(Haar~, Hut~)* band; *(Schürzen~)* string; *(Tech: zur Verpackung)* (metal) band; *(Faß~)* hoop; *(Art: Ornament)* band ◆ **das Blaue ~** the Blue Riband; **das silberne ~ des Nils** *(liter)* the silver ribbon of the Nile.
(b) *(Ton~)* (recording) tape ◆ **etw auf ~ aufnehmen** to tape *or* (tape-)record sth; **etw auf ~ sprechen/diktieren** to record sth on tape/dictate sth onto tape.
(c) *(Fließ~)* conveyor belt; *(als Einrichtung)* production line; *(Montage~)* assembly line; *(in Autowerk)* track *(inf)* ◆ **am ~ arbeiten** *or* **stehen** to work on the production line *etc*; **vom ~ laufen** to come off the conveyor belt *etc*; **ein neues Auto auf ~ legen** *(Ind inf)* to put a new car into production; **am laufenden ~** *(fig)* non-stop, continuously; **es gab Ärger am laufenden ~** there was non-stop *or* continuous trouble; **etw am laufenden ~ tun** to keep on doing sth.
(d) *(Rad)* wavelength, frequency band ◆ **auf dem 44m-~ senden** to broadcast on the 44m band.
(e) *(Anat) usu pl* ligament.
(f) *(Baubeschlag)* hinge.
Band[2] *nt* **-(e)s, -e** *(liter)* **(a) das ~ der Freundschaft/Liebe** *etc* the bonds *or* ties of friendship/love *etc*; **familiäre ~e** family ties; **mit jdm freundschaftliche ~e anknüpfen** to become *or* make friends with sb; **zarte ~e knüpfen sich an** Cupid is at work; **zarte ~e knüpfen** to start a romance.
(b) ~e *pl (Fesseln)* bonds *pl*, fetters *pl*; *(fig auch)* shackles *pl* ◆ **jdn in ~e schlagen** to clap *or* put sb in irons.
Band[3] *m* **-(e)s, ¨e** *(Buch~)* volume ◆ **ein gewaltiger ~** a mighty tome; **dar-**

⚠: for details of spelling reform, see supplement

über könnte man ⁼e schreiben/erzählen you could write volumes *or* a book about that; mit etw ⁼e füllen to write volumes about sth; das spricht ⁼e that speaks volumes.

Band[4] [bɛnt] *f* -, -s (*Mus*) band; (*Beat~ auch*) group.

Bandage [-'da:ʒə] *f* -, -n bandage ◆ mit harten ~n kämpfen (*fig inf*) to fight with no holds barred.

bandagieren* [-'ʒi:rən] *vt* to bandage (up).

Band-: ~**aufnahme** *f* tape-recording; ~**aufnahmegerät** *nt* tape-recorder; ~**breite** *f* (a) (*Rad*) waveband, frequency range; (b) (*fig*) range; (c) (*Fin*) (range of) fluctuation *or* variation.

Bändchen *nt dim of* **Band**[1] **(a), Band**[3].

Bande[1] *f* -, -n gang; (*Schmuggler~*) band; (*inf: Gruppe*) bunch (*inf*), crew (*inf*).

Bande[2] *f* -, -n (*Sport*) (*von Eisbahn*) barrier; (*von Reitbahn auch*) fence; (*Billard*) cushion; (*von Kegelbahn*) edge ◆ die Kugel an die ~ spielen to play the ball off the cushion/edge.

Band|eisen *nt* metal hoop.

Bändel *m or nt* -s, - (*dial*) ribbon; (*Schnürsenkel*) shoelace ◆ jdn am ~ haben *or* führen (*dated inf*) to be able to twist sb round one's little finger (*inf*).

Banden-: ~**bekämpfung** *f* (*Mil sl*) guerilla warfare; ~**chef** *m* (*inf*) gang-leader; ~**diebstahl** *m* (*Jur*) gang robbery; ~**führer** *m siehe* ~**chef**; ~**krieg** *m* gang war; ~**werbung** *f* pitch-perimeter advertising.

Banderole *f* -, -n tax *or* revenue seal.

Bänder- (*Med*): ⚠ ~**riß** *m* torn ligament; ~**zerrung** *f* pulled ligament.

Band-: ~**filter** *m or nt* (*Rad*) band-pass filter; ~**förderer** *m* conveyor belt.

-bändig *adj suf* -volume ◆ eine drei~e Ausgabe a three-volume edition, an edition in three volumes.

bändigen *vt* (*zähmen*) to tame; *Brand* to bring under control; (*niederhalten*) *Menschen, Tobenden etc* to (bring under) control, to subdue; (*zügeln*) *Leidenschaften etc* to (bring under) control, to master; *Wut* to control; *Naturgewalten* to harness; *Kinder* to (bring under) control ◆ du mußt lernen, dich zu ~ you must learn to control yourself.

Bändiger(in *f***)** *m* -s, - (animal) tamer.

Bändigung *m, no pl siehe vt* taming; controlling, subduing; mastering; harnessing; taming.

Bandit *m* -en, -en bandit, brigand; (*fig pej*) brigand ◆ einarmiger ~ one-armed bandit.

Banditen-: ~**tum,** ~**(un)wesen** *nt* banditry.

Bandkeramik *f* (*Archeol*) ribbon ware, band ceramics *pl*.

Bändl *nt* -s, - *siehe* **Bändel**.

Bandlaufwerk *nt* (*Comput*) tape streamer.

Bandleader ['bɛntli:dɐ] *m* -s, - band leader.

Band-: ~**maß** *nt* tape measure; ~**nudeln** *pl* ribbon noodles *pl*.

Bandoneon, Bandonion *nt* -s, -s bandoneon, bandonion.

Band-: ~**säge** *f* band-saw; ~**salat** *m* (*inf*) dann bekommen Sie ~salat then your tape gets tangled up *or* gets into a tangle; ~**scheibe** *f* (*Anat*) (intervertebral) disc; er hat's an *or* mit der ~scheibe (*inf*) he has slipped a disc *or* has a slipped disc; ~**scheibenschaden,** ~**scheibenvorfall** *m* slipped disc; ~**stahl** *m* strip *or* band steel; ~**werk** *nt* (*Art*) *siehe* **Flechtwerk**; ~**wurm** *m* tapeworm; ein ~wurm von einem Satz (*hum*) an endless *or* never-ending sentence; ~**wurmsatz** *m* (*inf*) long *or* lengthy sentence.

Bangbüx *f* -, -en (*N Ger inf*) scaredy-cat (*inf*).

bang(e) *adj, comp* -er *or* ⁼er, *superl* -ste(r, s) *or* ⁼ste(r, s) (a) *attr* (*ängstlich*) scared, frightened; (*vor jdm auch*) afraid ◆ mir ist ~e vor ihm/der Prüfung I'm scared *or* frightened *or* afraid of him/scared *or* frightened of the exam; das wird schon klappen, da ist mir gar nicht ~(e) it will be all right, I am quite sure of it; jdm ~e machen to scare *or* frighten sb; ~e machen gilt nicht (*inf*) you can't scare me, you won't put the wind up me (*inf*); *siehe* **angst**.

(b) (*geh: beklommen*) uneasy; *Augenblicke, Stunden auch* anxious, worried (*um* about) ◆ es wurde ihr ~ ums Herz her heart sank, she got a sinking feeling; ihr wurde ~ und ⁼er she became more and more afraid; eine ~e Ahnung a sense of foreboding.

(c) (*S Ger*) ihr war ~ nach dem Kinde she longed *or* yearned (*liter*) for the child *or* to be with the child.

Bange *f* -, *no pl* (*esp N Ger*) ~ haben to be scared *or* frightened (*vor +dat* of); nur keine ~! (*inf*) don't worry *or* be afraid.

Bange-: ~**machen** *nt* scaremongering; ~machen gilt nicht (*inf*) you can't scare me, you won't put the wind up me (*inf*); ~**macher** *m* scaremonger.

bangen (*geh*) [1] *vi* (a) (*Angst haben*) to be afraid (*vor +dat* of) ◆ es bangt mir, mir bangt vor ihm I'm afraid *or* frightened of him, I fear him.

(b) (*sich sorgen*) to worry, to be worried (*um* about) ◆ um jds Leben ~ to fear for sb's life.

(c) (*dial, liter*) nach jdm/etw ~ to long *or* yearn (*liter*) for sb/sth.

[2] *vr* to be worried *or* anxious (*um* about).

Bangigkeit *f* (*Furcht*) nervousness; (*Sorge*) anxiety; (*Beklemmung*) apprehension.

Bangladesch *nt* -s Bangladesh.

bänglich *adj* (*geh*) nervous.

Banjo ['banjo, 'bɛndʒo, 'bandʒo] *nt* -s, -s banjo.

Bank[1] *f* -, ⁼e (a) bench; (*mit Lehne auch*) seat; (*Schul~, an langem Tisch auch*) form; (*Kirchen~*) pew; (*Parlaments~*) bench; (*Anklage~*) dock ◆ auf *or* in der ersten/letzten ~ on the front/back bench *etc*; er predigte vor leeren ⁼en he preached to an empty church; die Debatte fand vor leeren ⁼en statt the debate took place in an empty house; (alle) durch die ~ (*inf*) every single *or* last one, the whole lot (of them) (*inf*); etw auf die lange ~ schieben (*inf*) to put sth off.

(b) (*Arbeitstisch*) (work) bench; (*Dreh~*) lathe.

(c) (*Sand~*) sandbank, sandbar; (*Nebel~, Wolken~*) bank; (*Austern~*) bed; (*Korallen~*) reef; (*Geol*) layer, bed.

(d) (*Wrestling*) crouch (position).

Bank[2] *f* -, -en (a) (*Comm*) bank ◆ Geld auf der ~ liegen haben to have money in the bank; bei der ~ at the bank; ein Konto bei einer ~ eröffnen to open an account with a bank; bei der ~ arbeiten *or* sein (*inf*) to work for the bank, to be with the bank.

(b) (*bei Glücksspielen*) bank ◆ (die) ~ halten (*inf*) to hold *or* be the bank, to be banker; die ~ sprengen to break the bank.

Bank-: ~**angestellte(r)** *mf*, ~**beamte(r)** *m* (*dated*) bank employee; ~**anweisung** *f* banker's order; ~**automat** *m* cash dispenser.

Bänkchen *nt dim of* **Bank**[1] **(a)**.

Bank-: ~**direktor** *m* director of a/the bank; ~**einbruch** *m* bank raid; ~**einlage** *f* (*Comm*) bank deposit.

Bänkel-: ~**lied** *nt* street ballad; ~**sang** *m* ballad; ~**sänger** *m* ballad-singer, minstrel.

Bankenviertel *nt* banking area.

Banker *m* -s, - (*inf*) banker.

Bankert *m* -s, -e (*old pej*) bastard.

Bankett[1] *nt* -(e)s, -e, **Bankette** *f* (a) (*an Straßen*) verge (*Brit*), shoulder (*US*); (*an Autobahnen*) (hard) shoulder ◆ „~e nicht befahrbar", „weiche ~e" "soft verges (*Brit*) *or* shoulder (*US*)". (b) (*Build*) footing.

Bankett[2] *nt* -(e)s, -e (*Festessen*) banquet.

Bank-: ~**fach** *nt* (a) (*Beruf*) banking, banking profession; im ~fach in banking *or* the banking profession; (b) (*Schließfach*) safe-deposit box; ~**filiale** *f* branch of a bank; ~**gebäude** *nt* bank; ~**gebühr** *f* bank charge; ~**geheimnis** *nt* confidentiality in banking; ~**geschäft** *nt* (a) banking transaction; (b) *no pl* (*~wesen*) banking world; ~**guthaben** *nt* bank balance; ~**halter** *m* (*bei Glücksspielen*) bank, banker; ~**haus** *nt* ~haus Grün & Co Grün & Co., Bankers.

Bankier [-'kie:] *m* -s, -s banker.

Bank-: ~**kauffrau** *f*, ~**kaufmann** *m* (qualified) bank clerk; ~**konto** *nt* bank account; ~**kredit** *m* bank loan; ~**leitzahl** *f* bank code number, bank sorting code; ~**nachbar** *m* (*Sch*) sie ist mein ~nachbar I sit next to her (at school); ~**note** *f* banknote, bill (*US*); ~**raub** *m* bank robbery; ~**räuber** *m* bank robber.

bankrott *adj* bankrupt; *Mensch, Politik* discredited; *Kultur* debased; (*moralisch*) bankrupt ◆ ~ gehen *or* machen to go *or* become bankrupt; jdn ~ machen to make sb (go) bankrupt, to bankrupt sb; er ist politisch/innerlich ~ he is a politically discredited/a broken man.

Bankrott *m* -(e)s, -e bankruptcy; (*fig*) breakdown, collapse; (*moralisch*) bankruptcy ◆ ~ machen to become *or* go bankrupt; den ~ anmelden *or* ansagen *or* erklären to declare oneself bankrupt.

Bankrott|erklärung *f* declaration of bankruptcy; (*fig*) sell-out (*inf*).

Bankrotteur(in *f***)** [-'tø:ɐ, -'tø:rɪn] *m* (*lit, fig*) bankrupt; (*fig*) moral bankrupt.

Bank-: ~**scheck** *m* cheque; ~**überfall** *m* bank raid; ~**überweisung** *f* bank transfer; **b**~**üblich** *adj* es ist b~üblich it is normal banking practice; ~**verbindung** *f* banking arrangements *pl*; geben Sie bitte Ihre ~verbindung an please give your account details; ~**verkehr** *m* bank transactions *pl*; ~**wesen** *nt* das ~wesen banking.

Bann *m* -(e)s, -e (a) *no pl* (*geh: magische Gewalt*) spell ◆ im ~ eines Menschen/einer Sache stehen *or* sein to be under sb's spell/the spell of sth; jdn in seinen ~ schlagen to captivate sb; sie zog *or* zwang ihn in ihren ~ she cast her spell over him.

(b) (*Hist: Kirchen~*) excommunication ◆ jdn in den ~ tun, jdn mit dem ~ belegen, den ~ über jdn aussprechen to excommunicate sb; jdn vom ~ lösen to absolve sb.

Bannbrief *m*, **Bannbulle** *f* (*Hist*) letter of excommunication.

bannen *vt* (a) (*geh: bezaubern*) to bewitch, to captivate, to entrance ◆ (wie) gebannt fascinated, in fascination; (*stärker*) spellbound; jdn/etw auf die Platte (*inf*)/die Leinwand ~ (*geh*) to capture sb/sth on film/canvas. (b) (*vertreiben*) *böse Geister, Teufel* to exorcize; (*abwenden*) *Gefahr* to avert, to ward off. (c) (*Hist*) to excommunicate.

Banner *nt* -s, - (*geh*) banner; (*fig auch*) flag ◆ das ~ des Sozialismus hochhalten to wave the banner *or* fly the flag of socialism.

Bannerträger *m* (*geh*) standard-bearer; (*fig*) vanguard *no pl*.

Bannfluch *m* excommunication.

bannig *adv* (*N Ger inf*) terribly, really; (*mit adj auch*) ever so (*inf*) ◆ das hat ~ Spaß gemacht that was great fun.

Bann-: ~**kreis** *m* (*fig*) in jds ~kreis (*dat*) stehen to be under sb's influence; ~**meile** *f* inviolable precincts *pl* (*of city, Parliament etc*); ~**spruch** *m* excommunication; ~**strahl** *m* (*liter*) *siehe* ~**fluch**; ~**wald** *m* (*Aus, Sw*) *forest for protection against avalanches etc*; ~**wart** *m* (*Sw*) forester.

Bantam-: ~**gewicht** *nt* bantamweight; ~**gewichtler** *m* -s, - bantamweight; ~**(huhn)** *nt* bantam.

Bantu *m* -(s), -(s) Bantu.

Bantu-: ~**frau** *f* Bantu woman; ~**neger** *m* Bantu; ~**sprache** *f* Bantu language.

Baptist(in *f***)** *m* Baptist.

Baptisterium *nt* (*Eccl*) baptistry; (*Taufbecken*) font.

bar *adj, no comp* (a) cash ◆ ~es Geld cash; (in) ~ bezahlen to pay (in) cash; ~ auf die Hand cash on the nail; (Verkauf) nur gegen ~ cash (sales) only; etw für ~e Münze nehmen (*fig*) to take sth at face value.

(b) *attr (rein) Zufall* pure; *Unsinn auch* utter, absolute.
(c) *pred +gen (liter)* devoid of, utterly *or* completely without ♦ **~ aller Hoffnung, aller Hoffnung ~** devoid of hope, completely *or* utterly without hope.
(d) *(liter: bloß)* bare ♦ **~en Hauptes** bareheaded.

Bar[1] *f* **-, -s (a)** *(Nachtlokal)* nightclub, bar. **(b)** *(Theke)* bar.

Bar[2] *nt* **-s, -s** *(Met)* bar.

Bär *m* **-en, -en (a)** bear ♦ **stark wie ein ~** *(inf)* (as) strong as an ox *or* a horse; **der Große/Kleine ~** *(Astron)* the Great/Little Bear, Ursa Major/Minor; **jdm einen ~en aufbinden** *(inf)* to have sb on *(inf)*; *siehe* **schlafen**.
(b) *(Tech) (Schlag~)* hammer; *(Ramm~)* rammer.

Baraber *m* **-s, -** *(Aus inf)* labourer; *(Straßenarbeiter)* navvy *(inf)*.

barabern* *vi (Aus inf)* to labour.

Baracke *f* **-, -n** hut, shack.

Baracken-: ~lager *nt*, **~siedlung** *f* camp (made of huts); *(für Flüchtlinge)* refugee camp.

Barbar(in *f*) *m* **-en, -en (a)** *(pej)* barbarian; *(Rohling auch)* brute. **(b)** *(Hist)* Barbarian.

Barbarei *f (pej)* **(a)** *(Unmenschlichkeit)* barbarity. **(b)** *(no pl: Kulturlosigkeit)* barbarism.

barbarisch *adj* **(a)** *(pej) (unmenschlich) Grausamkeit, Folter, Sitten* barbarous, savage, brutal; *(ungebildet) Benehmen, Mensch* barbaric, uncivilized. **(b)** *(Hist) Volk, Stamm* barbarian.

Barbarismus *m (Liter)* barbarism.

Barbe *f* **-, -n** *(Zool)* barbel.

Barbecue ['bɑːbɪkjuː] *nt* **-(s), -s** barbecue.

bärbeißig *adj (inf) Gesicht, Miene, Mensch* grouchy *(inf)*, grumpy; *Antwort etc auch* gruff.

Bar-: ~bestand *m (Comm)* cash; *(Buchführung)* cash in hand; **~betrag** *m* cash sum *or* amount.

Barbie *f* **-, -s** Barbie.

Barbie-Puppe *f* Barbie doll.

Barbier *m* **-s, -e** *(old, hum)* barber.

barbieren* *vt (old, hum)* **jdn ~** to shave sb; *(Bart beschneiden)* to trim sb's beard; *(die Haare schneiden)* to cut sb's hair; **sich** *(dat)* **~ lassen** to go to the barber's; *siehe* **balbieren**.

Barbiturat *nt* barbiturate.

Barbitursäure *f* barbituric acid.

barbrüstig, barbusig *adj* topless.

Bardame *f* barmaid; *(euph: Prostituierte)* hostess *(euph)*.

Barde *m* **-n, -n** *(Liter)* bard; *(iro)* minstrel.

Bären-: ~dienst *m* **jdm/einer Sache einen ~dienst erweisen** to do sb/sth a bad turn *or* a disservice; **~dreck** *m (S Ger, Aus, Sw: inf)* liquorice; **~fang** *m (Likör)* ≃ mead; **~führer** *m* bear trainer; *(hum)* (tourist) guide; **~hatz** *f siehe* **~jagd**; **~haut** *f*: **auf der ~haut liegen, sich auf die ~haut legen** *(dated)* to laze *or* loaf about; **~hunger** *m (inf)* **einen ~hunger haben** to be famished *(inf) or* ravenous *(inf)*; **~jagd** *f* bear hunt/hunting; **~kräfte** *pl* the strength *sing* of an ox; **~mütze** *f* bearskin, busby; **~natur** *f* **eine ~natur haben** *(inf)* to be (physically) tough; **b~stark** *adj* **(a)** strapping, strong as an ox; **(b)** *(inf)* terrific; **ein b~starkes Buch** an amazing book; **~zwinger** *m* bear cage.

Barett *nt* **-(e)s, -e** *or* **-s** cap; *(für Geistliche, Richter etc)* biretta; *(Univ)* mortarboard; *(Baskenmütze)* beret.

barfuß *adj pred* barefoot(ed) ♦ **~ gehen** to go/walk barefoot(ed); **ich bin ~** I've got nothing on my feet, I am barefoot(ed).

barfüßig *adj* barefooted.

barg *pret of* **bergen**.

Bar-: ~geld *nt* cash; **b~geldlos** [1] *adj* cashless, without cash; **b~geldloser Zahlungsverkehr** payment by money transfer; [2] *adv* without using cash; **b~haupt** *adj pred (liter)*, **b~häuptig** *adj (geh)* bareheaded; **~hocker** *m* (bar) stool.

bärig *adj (Aus inf)* tremendous, fantastic.

Bärin *f* (she-)bear.

Bariton [-tɔn] *m* **-s, -e** [-toːnə] baritone.

Barium *nt, no pl (abbr* **Ba***)* barium.

Bark *f* **-, -en** *(Naut)* barque.

Barkarole *f* **-, -n** *(Mus)* barcarol(l)e.

Barkasse *f* **-, -n** launch; *(Beiboot auch)* longboat.

Barkauf *m* cash purchase ♦ **~ ist billiger** it is cheaper to pay (in) cash.

Barke *f* **-, -n** *(Naut)* skiff; *(liter)* barque *(liter)*.

Barkeeper ['baːɐkiːpɐ] *m* **-s, -** barman, bartender.

Barkredit *m* cash loan.

Bärlapp *m* **-s, -e** *(Bot)* lycopod(ium).

Barmann *m* barman.

barmen [1] *vi (dial)* to moan, to grumble *(über +acc* about).
[2] *vt (liter)* **er barmt mich** I feel pity for him.

barmherzig *adj (liter, Rel)* merciful; *(mitfühlend)* compassionate ♦ **~er Himmel!** *(old, dial)* good heavens above!; **der ~e Samariter** *(lit, fig)* the good Samaritan; **B~e Schwestern** Sisters of Charity.

Barmherzigkeit *f (liter, Rel)* mercy, mercifulness; *(Mitgefühl)* compassion ♦ **~ (an jdm) üben** to show mercy (to sb)/compassion (towards sb); **Herr, übe ~ an mir!** Lord, have mercy on me!; *siehe* **Gnade**.

Barmittel *pl* cash (reserves *pl*).

Barmixer *m* barman.

barock *adj* baroque; *(fig) (überladen auch, verschnörkelt)* ornate; *Sprache* florid; *(seltsam) Einfälle* bizarre, eccentric ♦ **sie hat eine sehr ~e Figur** *(hum)* she has a very ample figure.

Barock *nt or m* **-(s),** *no pl* baroque ♦ **das Zeitalter des ~** the baroque age.

Barock- *in cpds* baroque; **~zeit** *f* baroque period.

Barometer *nt* **-s, -** *(lit, fig)* barometer ♦ **das ~ steht auf Sturm** the barometer is on stormy; *(fig)* things look stormy.

Barometerstand *m* barometer reading.

barometrisch *adj attr* barometric.

Baron *m* **-s, -e (a)** baron ♦ **~ (von) Schnapf** Baron *or* Lord Schnapf; **Herr ~** my lord. **(b)** *(fig: Industrie~ etc)* baron, magnate.

⚠**Baroneß** *f* **-, -ssen** *(dated)*, **Baronesse** *f* daughter of a baron ♦ **Fräulein ~** my lady.

Baronin *f* baroness ♦ **Frau ~** my lady.

Barras *m* **-,** *no pl (sl)* army ♦ **beim ~** in the army; **zum ~ gehen** to join up *(inf)*; **er muß nächstes Jahr zum ~** he's got to do his military service *or* he'll be drafted next year.

Barrel ['bɛrəl] *nt* **-s, -s** *or* **-** barrel.

Barren *m* **-s, - (a)** *(Metall~)* bar; *(esp Gold~)* ingot. **(b)** *(Sport)* parallel bars *pl*. **(c)** *(S Ger, Aus: Futtertrog)* trough.

Barrengold *nt* gold bullion.

Barriere *f* **-, -n** *(lit, fig)* barrier.

Barrikade *f* barricade ♦ **auf die ~n gehen** *(lit, fig)* to go to the barricades.

Barrikaden-: ~kampf *m* street battle; *(das Kämpfen)* street fighting *no pl*; **~stürmer** *m (fig)* revolutionary.

barrikadieren* *vt siehe* **verbarrikadieren**.

Barsch *m* **-(e)s, -e** perch.

barsch *adj* brusque, curt; *Befehl auch* peremptory ♦ **jdm eine ~e Abfuhr erteilen** to give sb short shrift; **jdn ~ anfahren** to snap at sb.

Barschaft *f, no pl* cash ♦ **meine ganze ~ bestand aus 10 Mark** all I had on me was 10 marks.

Barscheck *m* open *or* uncrossed cheque.

Barschheit *f siehe adj* brusqueness, curtness; peremptoriness.

Barsoi *m* **-s, -s** borzoi.

Barsortiment *nt* book wholesaler's.

barst *pret of* **bersten**.

Bart *m* **-(e)s, ¨e (a)** *(von Mensch, Ziege, Vogel, Getreide)* beard; *(von Katze, Maus, Robbe etc)* whiskers *pl* ♦ **sich** *(dat)* **einen ~ wachsen** *or* **stehen lassen** to grow a beard; **ein drei Tage alter ~** three days' growth (on one's chin).
(b) *(fig inf)* **(sich** *dat***) etwas in den ~ murmeln** *or* **brumme(l)n** to murmur *or* mutter sth in one's boots *or* beard *(inf)*; **jdm um den ~ gehen, jdm Honig um den ~ streichen** *or* **schmieren** to butter sb up *(inf)*, to soft-soap sb *(inf)*; **der Witz hat einen ~** that's a real oldie *(inf) or* an old chestnut; **der ~ ist ab** that's that!, that's the end of it *or* that.
(c) *(Schlüssel~)* bit.

Bartbinde *f device for keeping a moustache in shape.*

Bärtchen *nt (Kinn~)* (small) beard; *(Oberlippen~)* toothbrush moustache; *(Menjou~)* pencil moustache.

Barteln *pl siehe* **Bartfäden**.

Bartenwal *m* whalebone *or* baleen whale.

Bart-: ~fäden *pl (Zool)* barbels *pl*; **~flechte** *f* **(a)** *(Med)* sycosis, barber's itch; **(b)** *(Bot)* beard lichen *or* moss; **~haar** *nt* facial hair; *(Bart auch)* beard.

Bartholomäus *m* **-** Bartholomew.

Bartholomäusnacht *f (Hist)* Massacre of St. Bartholomew.

bärtig *adj* bearded.

Bart-: b~los *adj* beardless; *(glattrasiert)* clean-shaven; *Jüngling auch* smooth-faced; **~nelke** *f* sweet william; **~stoppel** *f* piece of stubble; **~stoppeln** *pl* stubble *sing*; **~tasse** *f* moustache cup; **~tracht** *f* beard/moustache style; **~wisch** *m* **-(e)s, -e** *(S Ger, Aus)* hand brush; **~wuchs** *m* beard; *(esp weiblicher)* facial hair *no indef art*; **er hat starken ~wuchs** he has a strong *or* heavy growth of beard; **~zotteln** *pl* wispy beard *sing*.

Bar-: ~verkauf *m* cash sales *pl*; **ein ~verkauf** a cash sale; **~vermögen** *nt* cash *or* liquid assets *pl*; **~zahlung** *f* payment by *or* in cash; **(Verkauf) nur gegen ~zahlung** cash (sales) only; **bei ~zahlung 3% Skonto** 3% discount for cash.

Basalt *m* **-(e)s, -e** basalt.

basalten, basaltig *adj* basaltic.

Basar *m* **-s, -e (a)** *(orientalischer Markt)* bazaar ♦ **auf dem ~** in the bazaar. **(b)** *(Wohltätigkeits~)* bazaar. **(c)** *(DDR: Einkaufszentrum)* department store.

Bäschen ['bɛːsçən] *nt dim of* **Base**[1].

Base[1] *f* **-, -n** *(old, dial)* cousin; *(Tante)* aunt.

Base[2] *f* **-, -n** *(Chem)* base.

Baseball ['beːsboːl] *m* **-s,** *no pl* baseball.

Baseballschläger *m* baseball bat.

Basedow [-do] *m* **-s,** *no pl (inf)*, **Basedowsche Krankheit** *f* (exophthalmic) goitre.

Basel *nt* **-s** Basle, Basel.

Baseler *adj attr siehe* **Basler**.

Basen *pl of* **Basis, Base**.

basieren* [1] *vi (auf +dat* on) to be based, to rest.
[2] *vt* to base *(auf +acc or (rare) dat* on).

Basilika *f* **-, Basiliken** basilica.

Basilikum *nt* **-s,** *no pl* basil.

Basilisk *m* **-en, -en** basilisk.

Basiliskenblick *m (liter)* baleful glare.

Basis *f* **-, Basen** basis; *(Archit, Mil, Math)* base ♦ **auf breiter ~** on a broad basis; **auf einer festen** *or* **soliden ~ ruhen** to be firmly established; **sich auf gleicher ~ treffen** to meet on an equal footing *or* on equal terms; **~ und Überbau**

⚠: for details of spelling reform, see supplement

(*Pol, Sociol*) foundation and superstructure; **die ~** (*inf*) the grass roots (level); (*die Leute*) (those at the) grass roots.

Basis-: ~arbeit *f* (*Pol*) groundwork; **~camp** *nt* base camp.

basisch *adj* (*Chem*) basic.

Basis-: ~demokratie *f* grass-roots democracy; **b~demokratisch** *adj* grass-roots; **~gruppe** *f* action group.

Baske *m* **-n, -n, Baskin** *f* Basque.

Basken-: ~land *nt* Basque region; **~mütze** *f* beret.

Basketball *m* **-s,** *no pl* basketball.

baskisch *adj* Basque.

Baskisch(e) *nt decl as adj* Basque; *siehe* **Deutsch(e).**

Basler *adj attr* Basle *attr.*

Basler(in *f*) *m* **-s, -** native of Basle; (*Einwohner*) inhabitant of Basle.

Basrelief ['barelief] *nt* (*Archit, Art*) bas-relief.

⚠ **Baß** *m* **-sses, ¨-sse (a)** (*Stimme, Sänger*) bass ♦ **hoher/tiefer** *or* **schwarzer ~** basso cantante/profundo; **einen hohen/tiefen ~ haben** to be a basso cantante/profundo. **(b)** (*Instrument*) double bass; (*im Jazz auch*) bass. **(c)** (*~partie*) bass (part).

⚠ **baß** *adv* (*old, hum*): **~ erstaunt** much *or* uncommonly (*old*) amazed.

⚠ **Baßbariton** *m* bass baritone.

Bassetthorn *nt* basset horn.

⚠ **Baßgeige** *f* (*inf*) (double) bass.

Bassin [ba'sɛ̃:] *nt* **-s, -s** (*Schwimm~*) pool; (*Garten~*) pond.

Bassist(in *f*) *m* **(a)** (*Sänger*) bass (singer). **(b)** (*im Orchester etc*) (double) bass player ♦ **~ sein** to be a (double) bass player, to play the (double) bass.

⚠ **Baß-: ~klarinette** *f* bass clarinet; **~partie** *f* bass part; **~sänger** *m* bass (singer); **~schlüssel** *m* bass clef; **~stimme** *f* bass (voice); (*Partie*) bass (part).

Bast *m* **-(e)s,** (*rare*) **-e (a)** (*zum Binden, Flechten*) raffia; (*Bot*) bast, phloem. **(b)** (*an Geweih*) velvet.

basta *interj* **(und damit) ~!** (and) that's that.

Bastard *m* **-(e)s, -e (a)** (*Hist: uneheliches Kind*) bastard. **(b)** (*Biol: Kreuzung*) (*Pflanze*) hybrid; (*Tier*) cross-breed, cross; (*Mensch*) half-caste, half-breed.

bastardieren* *vt Pflanzen* to hybridize; *Tiere, Arten* to cross.

Bastardschrift *f* (*Typ*) bastard type.

Bastei *f* bastion.

Bastel|arbeit *f* piece of handcraft; (*das Basteln*) (doing) handcraft *or* handicrafts ♦ **etw in langer ~ bauen** to spend a long time making *or* building sth; **sich viel mit ~en beschäftigen** to do a lot of handcraft *or* handicrafts.

Bastelei *f* (*inf*) handcraft; (*Stümperei*) botched job (*inf*).

basteln [1] *vi* **(a)** (*als Hobby*) to make things with one's hands; (*Handwerksarbeiten herstellen auch*) to do handcraft *or* handicrafts ♦ **sie kann gut ~** she is good with her hands.
(b) an etw (*dat*) **~** to make sth, to work on sth; (*an Modellflugzeug etc*) to build *or* make sth; (*an etw herumbasteln*) to mess around *or* tinker with sth.
[2] *vt* to make; *Geräte etc auch* to build.

Basteln *nt* **-s,** *no pl* handicraft, handicrafts *pl.*

Bastelraum *m* workroom.

Bastfaser *f* bast fibre.

Bastille [bas'ti:jə, -tɪljə] *f* - (*Hist*) **der Sturm auf die ~** the storming of the Bastille.

Bastion *f* bastion, ramparts *pl*; (*fig*) bastion, bulwark.

Bastler(in *f*) *m* **-s, -** (*von Modellen etc*) modeller; (*von Möbeln etc*) do-it-yourselfer ♦ **ein guter ~ sein** to be good *or* clever with one's hands, to be good at making things.

Bastonade *f* bastinado.

Bastseide *f* wild silk, shantung (silk).

BAT ['be:|a:'te:] *abbr of* **Bundesangestelltentarif.**

bat *pret of* **bitten.**

Bataille [ba'ta:jə] *f* **-, -n** (*old*) battle.

Bataillon [batal'jo:n] *nt* **-s, -e** (*Mil, fig*) battalion.

Bataillons-: ~führer, ~kommandeur *m* battalion commander.

Batate *f* **-, -n** sweet potato, yam (*esp US*), batata.

Batik *f* **-, -en** *or m* **-s, -en** batik.

batiken [1] *vi* to do batik.
[2] *vt* to decorate with batik ♦ **eine gebatikte Bluse** a batik blouse.

Batist *m* **-(e)s, -e** batiste, cambric.

Batterie *f* (*Elec, Mil, Lege~*) battery; (*Misch~ etc*) regulator; (*Reihe von Flaschen auch*) row.

Batterie-: ~betrieb *m* **das Radio ist für ~betrieb eingerichtet** the radio takes batteries *or* can be battery-powered; **b~betrieben** *adj* battery-powered; **~gerät** *nt* battery-powered radio *etc*; **~zündung** *f* battery ignition (system).

Batzen *m* **-s, - (a)** (*dated: Klumpen*) clod, lump. **(b)** (*obs: Münze*) batz (*silver coin*) ♦ **ein (schöner) ~ Geld** (*inf*) a tidy sum (*inf*), a pretty penny (*inf*).

Bau *m* **(a) -(e)s,** *no pl* (*das Bauen*) building, construction ♦ **im** *or* **in ~** under construction; **sich im ~ befinden** to be under construction; **der ~ des Hauses dauerte ein Jahr** it took a year to build the house; **mit dem ~ beginnen, an den ~ gehen** to begin building *or* construction; **den ~ beenden, mit dem ~ fertig sein** to finish building, to complete construction.
(b) -(e)s, *no pl* (*Auf~*) structure; (*von Satz, Maschine, Apparat auch*) construction ♦ **von kräftigem/schwächlichem ~ sein** (*Körper~*) to be powerfully/slenderly built, to have a powerful/slender build *or* physique.
(c) -s, *no pl* (*~stelle*) building site ♦ **auf dem ~ arbeiten, beim ~ sein** to be a building worker, to work on a building site; **vom ~ sein** (*fig inf*) to know the ropes (*inf*).
(d) -(e)s, -ten (*Gebäude*) building; (*~werk*) construction ♦ **~ten** (*Film*) sets.
(e) -(e)s, -e (*Erdhöhle*) burrow, hole; (*Biber~*) lodge; (*Fuchs~*) den; (*Dachs~*) set(t) ♦ **heute gehe ich nicht aus dem ~** (*inf*) I'm not sticking my nose out of doors today (*inf*); **zu ~ gehen** (*Hunt*) to go to earth.
(f) -(e)s, -e (*Min*) workings *pl* ♦ **im ~ sein** to be down the pit *or* mine.
(g) -(e)s, *no pl* (*Mil sl*) guardhouse ♦ **4 Tage ~** 4 days in the guardhouse.

Bau-: ~abnahme *f* building inspection; **~abschnitt** *m* stage *or* phase of construction; **~amt** *nt* planning department and building control office; **~arbeiten** *pl* building *or* construction work *sing*; (*Straßen~*) roadworks *pl*; **~arbeiter** *m* building *or* construction worker, building labourer; **~art** *f* construction, design; (*Stil*) style; **~aufsicht** *f* supervision of building *or* construction; **die ~aufsicht liegt bei der Stadtverwaltung** the town council is supervising the construction; **~ausführung** *f* construction, building; **~ausführung Firma Meyer** builders *or* constructors Meyer and Co; **~behörde** *f* planning department and building control office; **~block** *m, pl* **-s** block; **~bude** *f* building workers' hut.

Bauch *m* **-(e)s, Bäuche (a)** (*von Mensch*) stomach, tummy (*inf*); (*Anat*) abdomen; (*von Tier*) stomach, belly; (*Fett~*) paunch, potbelly (*inf*) ♦ **ihm tat der ~ weh** he had stomach-ache *or* tummy-ache (*inf*); **sich** (*dat*) **den ~ vollschlagen** (*sl*) to stuff oneself (*inf*); **ein voller ~ studiert nicht gern** (*Prov*) you can't study on a full stomach; **sich** (*dat*) **(vor Lachen) den ~ halten** (*inf*) to split one's sides (laughing) (*inf*); **einen dicken ~ haben** (*sl: schwanger sein*) to have a bun in the oven (*inf*); **vor jdm auf dem ~ rutschen** (*inf*) *or* **kriechen** (*inf*) to grovel *or* kowtow to sb (*inf*), to lick sb's boots (*inf*); **mit etw auf den ~ fallen** (*inf*) to come a cropper with sth (*inf*); *siehe* **Wut, Loch, Bein** *etc.*
(b) (*Wölbung, Hohlraum*) belly; (*Innerstes: von Schiff auch, von Erde*) bowels *pl.*

Bauch-: ~ansatz *m* beginning(s) of a paunch; **~binde** *f* **(a)** (*für Frack*) cummerbund; (*Med*) abdominal bandage *or* support; **(b)** (*um Zigarre, Buch*) band; **~decke** *f* abdominal wall; **~fell** *nt* **(a)** (*Anat*) peritoneum; **(b)** (*Fell am Bauch*) stomach *or* belly fur; **~fell|entzündung** *f* peritonitis; **~fleck** *m* (*Aus inf*) *siehe* **~klatscher; ~flosse** *f* ventral fin; **~gegend** *f* abdominal region; **~grimmen** *nt* **-s,** *no pl* (*inf*) stomach- *or* tummy- (*inf*) ache; **~höhle** *f* abdominal cavity, abdomen; **~höhlenschwangerschaft** *f* ectopic pregnancy.

bauchig *adj Gefäß* bulbous.

Bauch-: ~klatscher *m* **-s, -** (*inf*) belly-flop (*inf*); **~laden** *m* sales tray; **~landung** *f* (*inf*) (*Aviat*) belly landing; (*bei Sprung ins Wasser*) belly-flop; **mit dem neuen Stück/mit der neuen Firma haben wir eine ~landung gemacht** (*fig*) the new play/the new company was a flop.

Bäuchlein *nt* tummy (*inf*); (*hum: Fett~*) bit of a stomach *or* tummy (*inf*).

bäuchlings *adv* on one's front, face down.

Bauch-: ~muskel *m* stomach *or* abdominal muscle; **~nabel** *m* navel, belly-button (*inf*); **b~pinseln** *vt* (*inf*) *siehe* **gebauchpinselt; b~reden** *vi sep infin, ptp only* to ventriloquize; **~redner** *m* ventriloquist; **~schmerzen** *pl* stomach- *or* tummy- (*inf*) ache; ⚠ **~schuß** *m* shot in the stomach; (*Verletzung*) stomach wound; **einen ~schuß abbekommen** to be shot in the stomach; **~speck** *m* (*Cook*) belly of pork; (*hum*) spare tyre (*inf*); **~speicheldrüse** *f* pancreas; **~tanz** *m* belly-dance/dancing; **b~tanzen** *vi sep infin, ptp only* to belly-dance; **~tänzerin** *f* belly-dancer.

Bauchung *f* bulge.

Bauch-: ~wand *f* stomach *or* abdominal wall; **~weh** *nt siehe* **~schmerzen; ~welle** *f* (*Sport*) circle on the beam.

Baudenkmal *nt* historical monument.

Baud-Rate *f* (*Comput*) baud rate.

Bau|element *nt* component part.

bauen [1] *vt* **(a)** to build, to construct; (*anfertigen auch*) to make; *Satz* to construct; *Höhle* to dig, to make ♦ **sich** (*dat*) **ein Haus/Nest ~** to build oneself a house/make *or* build oneself a nest (*auch fig*); **seine Hoffnung auf jdn/etw ~** to build one's hopes on sb/sth; **die Betten ~** (*esp Mil*) to make the beds; *siehe* **gebaut.**
(b) (*inf: verursachen*) *Unfall* to cause ♦ **da hast du Mist** (*inf*) *or* **Scheiße** (*sl*) **gebaut** you really messed (*inf*) *or* cocked (*Brit sl*) that up; **bleib ruhig, bau keine Scheiße** (*sl*) cool it, don't make trouble (*inf*).
(c) (*inf: machen, ablegen*) *Prüfung etc* to pass ♦ **den Führerschein ~** to pass one's driving test; **seinen Doktor ~** to get one's doctorate.
(d) (*rare: an~*) *Kartoffeln etc* to grow; (*liter: bestellen*) *Acker* to cultivate.
[2] *vi* **(a)** to build ♦ **wir haben neu/auf Sylt gebaut** we built a new house/a house on Sylt; **nächstes Jahr wollen wir ~** we're going to build *or* start building next year; **an etw** (*dat*) **~** to be working on sth, to be building sth (*auch fig*); **hier wird viel gebaut** there is a lot of building *or* development going on round here; **hoch ~** to build high-rise buildings.
(b) (*vertrauen*) to rely, to count (*auf +acc* on).

Bau|entwurf *m* building plans *pl.*

Bauer[1] *m* **-n** *or* (*rare*) **-s, -n (a)** (*Landwirt*) farmer; (*als Vertreter einer Klasse*) peasant; (*pej: ungehobelter Mensch*) (country) bumpkin, yokel ♦ **die dümmsten ~n haben die größten** *or* **dicksten Kartoffeln** (*prov inf*) fortune favours fools (*prov*); **was der ~ nicht kennt, das frißt er nicht** (*prov inf*) you can't change the habits of a lifetime.
(b) (*Chess*) pawn; (*Cards*) jack, knave.
(c) (*vulg: Samenerguß*) **ein kalter ~** a wet dream.

Bauer[2] *nt or* (*rare*) *m* **-s, -** (bird-)cage.

Bäuerchen *nt* **(a)** *dim of* **Bauer**[1]. **(b)** (*baby-talk*) burp. **(ein) ~ machen** to (do a) burp.

⚠: Informationen zur Rechtschreibreform im Anhang

Bäuerin *f* **(a)** (*Frau des Bauern*) farmer's wife. **(b)** (*Landwirtin*) farmer; (*als Vertreterin einer Klasse*) peasant (woman).
bäuerisch *adj siehe* **bäurisch.**
Bäuerlein *nt* (*liter, hum*) farmer.
bäuerlich *adj* rural; (*ländlich*) *Fest, Bräuche, Sitten* rustic, country *attr* ◆ **~e Klein- und Großbetriebe** small and large farms.
Bauern-: ~aufstand *m* peasants' revolt *or* uprising; **~brot** *nt* coarse rye bread; **~dorf** *nt* farming *or* country village; **~fang** *m*: **auf ~fang ausgehen** (*inf*) to play con tricks; **~fänger** *m* (*inf*) con-man (*inf*), swindler; **~fängerei** *f* (*inf*) con (*inf*), swindle; **~frau** *f siehe* **Bauersfrau; ~frühstück** *nt* bacon and potato omelette; **~gut** *nt* farm(stead); **~haus** *nt* farmhouse; **~hochzeit** *f* country wedding; **~hof** *m* farm; **~junge** *m* country lad; **~kalender** *m* country almanac; **~kriege** *pl* (*Hist*) Peasant War(s); **~legen** *nt* **-s,** *no pl* (*Hist, Pol pej*) expropriation of peasants' land; **~mädchen** *nt* country girl *or* lass (*inf*); **~magd** *f* farmer's maid; **~opfer** *nt* (*fig*) (*Mensch*) fall guy; (*Sache*) necessary sacrifice; **~partei** *f* country party; **~regel** *f* country saying; **~schädel** *m* (large) head; (*pej*) thick skull (*inf*); **~schaft** *f, no pl* farming community; (*ärmlich*) peasantry; **~schläue** *f* native *or* low cunning, craftiness, shrewdness; **~stand** *m* farming community, farmers *pl*; **~stube** *f* farmhouse parlour; (*in Gasthaus*) ploughman's bar; **~theater** *nt* rural folk theatre; **~tölpel** *m* (*pej*) country bumpkin, yokel; **~tum** *nt, no pl* (*~stand*) farming community, farmers *pl*; **er ist stolz auf sein ~tum** he is proud of coming from farming stock; **~verband** *m* farmers' organization.
Bauers-: ~frau *f* farmer's wife; **~leute** *pl* farm(ing) folk, farmers *pl*; **~mann** *m* (*old, liter*) farmer.
Bau-: ~erwartungsland *nt* (*Admin*) development area; **~fach** *nt* construction industry; **b~fällig** *adj* dilapidated; *Decke, Gewölbe* unsound, unsafe; **~fälligkeit** *f* dilapidation; **wegen ~fälligkeit gesperrt** closed because building unsafe; **~firma** *f* building contractor *or* firm; **~flucht** *f* line; **~form** *f* form *or* shape (of a building); **~gelände** *nt* land for building; (*~stelle*) building site; **~geld** *nt* building capital; **~genehmigung** *f* planning and building permission; **~genossenschaft** *f* housing association; **~gerüst** *nt* scaffolding; **~geschäft** *nt* building firm; **~gesellschaft** *f* property company; **~gewerbe** *nt* building and construction trade; **~glied** *nt* (*Archit*) part of a building; **~grube** *f* excavation; **~grundstück** *nt* plot of land for building; **~handwerk** *nt* building trade; **~handwerker** *m* (trained) building worker; **~haus** *nt* (*Archit, Art*) Bauhaus; **~herr** *m* client (*for whom sth is being built*); **seitdem er ~herr ist ...** since he has been having a house built ...; **der ~herr ist die Stadt** the clients are the town authorities; **~herr: Ministerium des Innern** under construction for Ministry of the Interior; **~herrenmodell** *nt scheme by which tax relief is obtained on investment in building projects*; **~holz** *nt* building timber; **~hütte** *f* **(a)** *siehe* **~bude; (b)** (*Hist, Archit*) church masons' guild; **~industrie** *f* building and construction industry; **~ingenieur** *m* civil engineer.
Bauj. *abbr of* **Baujahr.**
Bau-: ~jahr *nt* year of construction; (*von Gebäude auch*) year of building; (*von Auto*) year of manufacture; **VW ~jahr 90** VW 1990 model, 1990 VW; **welches ~jahr?** what year?; **~kasten** *m* building *or* construction kit; (*mit Holzklötzen*) box of bricks; (*Chemie~*) set; **~kastensystem** *nt* (*Tech*) modular *or* unit construction system; **~klotz** *m* (building) brick *or* block; **~klötze(r) staunen** (*inf*) to gape (in astonishment); **~klötzchen** *nt* (building) block; **~kolonne** *f* gang of building workers *or* (*bei Straßenbau*) navvies; **~kosten** *pl* building *or* construction costs *pl*; ⚠**~kostenzuschuß** *m* building subsidy *or* grant; **~kunst** *f* (*geh*) architecture; **~land** *nt* building land; (*für Stadtplanung*) development area; **einen Acker als ~land verkaufen** to sell a field for building; **~leiter** *m* (building) site manager; **~leitung** *f* **(a)** (*Aufsicht*) (building) site supervision; (*Büro*) site office; **(b)** (*die ~leiter*) (building) site supervisory staff; **b~lich** *adj* structural; **in gutem/schlechtem b~lichem Zustand** structurally sound/unsound; **~löwe** *m* building speculator; **~lücke** *f* empty site.
Baum *m* **-(e)s, Bäume** tree ◆ **auf dem ~** in the tree; **der ~ der Erkenntnis** (*Bibl*) the tree of knowledge; **er ist stark wie ein ~** he's as strong as a horse; **zwischen ~ und Borke stecken** *or* **stehen** to be in two minds; **die Bäume wachsen nicht in den Himmel** (*prov*) all good things come to an end; **einen alten ~** *or* **alte Bäume soll man nicht verpflanzen** (*prov*) you can't teach an old dog new tricks (*prov*); *siehe* **ausreißen, Wald.**
Bau-: ~markt *m* property market; (*Geschäft*) builder's yard; (*für Heimwerker*) DIY superstore; **~maschine** *f* piece of building machinery; **~maschinen** *pl* building machinery *or* plant *sing*; **~material** *nt* building material.
Baum-: ~bestand *m* tree population *no pl*, stock of trees; **~blüte** *f* blossom.
Bäumchen *nt* small tree; (*junger Baum auch*) sapling ◆ **~, wechsle dich spielen** to play tag; (*hum: Partnertausch*) to swap partners.
Baumeister *m* **(a)** master builder; (*Bauunternehmer*) building contractor; (*Architekt*) architect. **(b)** (*Erbauer*) builder.
baumeln *vi* to dangle (*an +dat* from) ◆ **die Haarsträhnen baumelten ihm ins Gesicht** the strands of hair hung in his face; **jdn ~ lassen** (*sl*) to let sb swing (*inf*).
Baum-: ~farn *m* tree fern; **~frevel** *m* (*form*) malicious damage to trees; **~grenze** *f* tree *or* timber line; **~gruppe** *f* coppice, cluster of trees; **b~hoch** *adj* tree-high; **~krone** *f* treetop; **b~lang** *adj* **ein b~langer Kerl** (*inf*) a beanpole (*inf*); **~läufer** *m* tree creeper; **b~los** *adj* treeless; **b~reich** *adj* wooded; **~riese** *m* (*liter*) giant tree; **~rinde** *f* tree bark; **~schere** *f* (tree) pruning shears *pl*, secateurs *pl*; **~schule** *f* tree nursery; **~stamm** *m* tree-trunk; **b~stark** *adj Arme* massive; *Mann* beefy (*inf*), hefty; **~steppe** *f* scrub; **~sterben** *nt* tree death; **~struktur** *f* (*Comput*) tree structure; **~strunk, ~stumpf** *m* tree stump; **~wipfel** *m* treetop.
Baumwoll- *in cpds* cotton.
Baumwolle *f* cotton ◆ **ein Hemd aus ~** a cotton shirt.
baumwollen *adj attr* cotton.
Baumwuchs *m* tree growth.
Bau-: ~ordnung *f* building regulations *pl*; **~plan** *m* building plan *or* (*Vorhaben auch*) project; **~planung** *f* planning (of a building); **~plastik** *f* architectural sculpture; **~platz** *m* site (for building); **~polizei** *f* building control department; **~preis** *m* building price; **~rat** *m* head of the planning department and building control office; **~recht** *nt* planning and building laws and regulations; **b~reif** *adj Grundstück* available for building; **~reihe** *f* **-, -n** (*von Auto*) model range; (*von Flugzeug, Computer*) series.
bäurisch *adj* (*pej*) boorish, rough.
Bau-: ~ruine *f* (*inf*) unfinished building; **~sachverständige(r)** *mf decl as adj* quantity surveyor; **~satz** *m* kit.
Bausch *m* **-es, Bäusche** *or* **-e (a)** (*Watte~*) ball; (*Med auch*) swab. **(b)** (*Krause*) (*an Vorhang*) pleat; (*an Kleid*) bustle; (*an Ärmel*) puff. **(c) in ~ und Bogen** lock, stock and barrel.
Bauschaffende(r) *mf decl as adj* (*DDR*) *person working in the construction industry.*
Bäuschchen *nt dim of* **Bausch.**
bauschen [1] *vr* **(a)** (*sich aufblähen*) to billow (out). **(b)** (*Kleidungsstück*) to puff out; (*ungewollt*) to bunch (up).
[2] *vt* **(a)** *Segel, Vorhänge* to fill, to swell. **(b)** (*raffen*) to gather ◆ **gebauschte Ärmel** puffed sleeves.
[3] *vi* (*Kleidungsstück*) to bunch (up), to become bunched.
Bauschen *m* **-s, -** (*S Ger, Aus*) *siehe* **Bausch (a).**
bauschig *adj* **(a)** (*gebläht*) billowing. **(b)** *Rock, Vorhänge* full.
Bau-: ~schlosser *m* fitter on a building site; **~schutt** *m* building rubble; **~schuttmulde** *f* skip.
bausparen *vi sep usu infin* to save with a building society (*Brit*) *or* building and loan association (*US*).
Bausparer *m* saver with a building society (*Brit*) *or* building and loan association (*US*).
Bauspar-: ~kasse *f* building society (*Brit*), building and loan association (*US*); **~vertrag** *m* savings contract with a building society (*Brit*) *or* building and loan association (*US*).
Bau-: ~stahl *m* mild *or* structured steel; **~stein** *m* stone (for building); (*Spielzeug*) brick; (*elektronischer ~stein*) chip; (*fig: Bestandteil*) building block; (*Tech*) module; **~stelle** *f* building *or* construction site; (*bei Straßenbau*) roadworks *pl*; (*bei Gleisbau*) railway construction site; **„Achtung, ~stelle!"** "danger, men at work"; **„Betreten der ~stelle verboten"** "unauthorized entry prohibited", "trespassers will be prosecuted"; **die Strecke ist wegen einer ~stelle gesperrt** the road/line is closed because of roadworks/(railway) construction work; **~stellenverkehr** *m* heavy traffic (from a building site); **„Achtung, ~stellenverkehr!"** "heavy plant crossing"; **~stil** *m* architectural style; **~stoff** *m siehe* **~material; ~stopp** *m* **einen ~stopp verordnen** to impose a halt on building (projects); **~substanz** *f* fabric, structure; **die ~substanz ist gut** the house is structurally sound; **~summe** *f* total building cost; **~tätigkeit** *f* building; **eine rege ~tätigkeit** a lot of building; **~techniker** *m* site engineer; **b~technisch** *adj* structural; **eine b~technische Glanzleistung** a superb feat of structural engineering; **~teil** *m* prefabricated part (of a building).
Bauten *pl of* **Bau (d).**
Bau-: ~tischler *m* joiner; **~träger** *m* builder, building contractor; **~unternehmen** *nt* **(a)** (*Firma*) building contractor; **(b)** *siehe* **~vorhaben; ~unternehmer** *m* building contractor, builder; **~volumen** *nt* volume of building; **~vorhaben** *nt* building project *or* scheme; **~weise** *f* type *or* method of construction; (*Stil*) style; **in konventioneller ~weise** built in the conventional way/style; **offene/geschlossene ~weise** detached/terraced houses; **~werk** *nt* construction; (*Gebäude auch*) edifice, building; **~wesen** *nt* building and construction industry; **ein Ausdruck aus dem ~wesen** a building term; **~wich** *m* **-(e)s, -e** (*Archit*) space between two neighbouring buildings; **~wirtschaft** *f* building and construction industry.
Bauxit *m* **-s, -e** bauxite.
bauz *interj* wham, crash, bang ◆ **~ machen** (*baby-talk*) to go (crash bang) wallop.
Bau-: ~zaun *m* hoarding, fence; **~zeichnung** *f* building plan *usu pl*; **~zeit** *f* time taken for building *or* construction; **die ~zeit betrug drei Jahre** it took three years to build.
b.a.w. *abbr of* **bis auf weiteres** until further notice.
Bayer(in *f*) ['baiɐ, -ərɪn] *m* **-n, -n** Bavarian.
bay(e)risch ['bai(ə)rɪʃ] *adj* Bavarian ◆ **der B~e Wald** the Bavarian Forest.
Bay(e)risch(e) ['bai(ə)rɪʃ(ə)] *nt decl as adj* Bavarian (dialect).
Bayern ['baiɐn] *nt* **-s** Bavaria.
Bazar *m* **-s, -e** *siehe* **Basar.**
Bazi *m* **-, -** (*Aus inf*) blighter, scoundrel.
Bazille *f* **-, -n** (*incorrect*) *siehe* **Bazillus.**
Bazillen-: ~furcht *f* germ phobia; **~träger** *m* carrier.
Bazillus *m* **-, Bazillen (a)** bacillus, microbe; (*Krankheitserreger auch*) germ. **(b)** (*fig*) cancer, growth.
Bazooka [ba'zu:ka] *f* **-, -s** bazooka.
Bd. *abbr of* **Band.**
BDA [be:de:'|a:] *f abbr of* **Bundesvereinigung der Arbeitgeberverbände** ≃ CBI

⚠: for details of spelling reform, see supplement

(*Brit*); **Bund deutscher Architekten.**
Bde *abbr of* **Bände.**
BDI ['beːdeː'|iː] *m* **-,** *no pl abbr of* **Bundesverband der Deutschen Industrie** ≃ CBI (*Brit*).
BDM ['beːdeː'|ɛm] *m* **-,** *no pl* (*NS*) *abbr of* **Bund Deutscher Mädel.**
▼ **be|absichtigen*** *vti* to intend ◆ **eine Reise/Steuererhöhung ~** (*form*) to intend to go on a journey/to increase taxes; **das hatte ich nicht beabsichtigt** I didn't mean it *or* intend that to happen; **das war beabsichtigt** that was deliberate *or* intentional; **die beabsichtigte Wirkung** the desired *or* intended effect.
be|achten* *vt* **(a)** (*befolgen*) to heed; *Ratschlag auch* to follow; *Vorschrift, Verbot, Verkehrszeichen* to observe, to comply with; *Regel* to observe, to follow; *Gebrauchsanweisung* to follow ◆ **etw besser ~** to pay more attention to sth; *siehe* **Vorfahrt.**
(b) (*berücksichtigen*) to take into consideration *or* account ◆ **es ist zu ~, daß** ... it should be taken into consideration *or* account that ...
(c) (*Aufmerksamkeit schenken*) *jdn* to notice, to pay attention to; (*bei* (*Bild*)*erklärungen, Reiseführung etc*) to observe ◆ **jdn nicht ~** to ignore sb, to take no notice of sb; **von der Öffentlichkeit kaum beachtet** scarcely noticed by the public; **das Ereignis wurde in der Öffentlichkeit kaum/stark beachtet** the incident aroused little/considerable public attention; **„bitte Stufe ~!"** "mind the step".
be|achtenswert *adj* noteworthy, remarkable.
be|achtlich [1] *adj* **(a)** (*beträchtlich*) considerable; *Verbesserung, Zu- or Abnahme auch* marked; *Erfolg* notable; *Talent auch* remarkable, notable.
(b) (*bedeutend*) *Ereignis* significant; (*lobenswert*) *Leistung* considerable, excellent; (*zu berücksichtigend*) relevant ◆ **~!** (*dated*) well done; **er hat im Leben/Beruf B~es geleistet** he has achieved a considerable amount in life/ his job.
[2] *adv* (*sehr*) significantly, considerably.
Be|achtung *f siehe vt* **(a)** heeding; following; observance, compliance (*gen* with) ◆ **die ~ der Vorschriften** observance of *or* compliance with the regulations; **unter ~ der Vorschriften** in accordance with the regulations.
(b) consideration ◆ **unter ~ aller Umstände** considering *or* taking into consideration all the circumstances.
(c) notice, attention (*gen* to) ◆ **„zur ~"** please note; **~ finden** to receive attention; **jdm/einer Sache ~ schenken** to pay attention to *or* take notice of sb/sth; **jdm keine ~ schenken** to ignore sb, to take no notice of sb.
be|ackern* *vt* **(a)** *Feld* to till, to work. **(b)** (*inf*) *Thema, Wissensgebiet* to go into, to examine.
Beagle [biːgl] *m* **-s, -(s)** beagle.
Be|amte *m siehe* **Beamte(r).**
Be|amten-: ~anwärter *m* civil service trainee; **~apparat** *m* bureaucracy; **~beleidigung** *f* insulting an official; **~bestechung** *f* bribing an official; **~deutsch** *nt siehe* **Amtsdeutsch; ~herrschaft** *f* bureaucracy; **~laufbahn** *f* career in the civil service; **die ~laufbahn einschlagen** to enter *or* join the civil service; **~mentalität** *f* bureaucratic mentality; **~recht** *nt* civil service law; **~schaft** *f* civil servants *pl*, civil service; **~seele** *f* (*pej*) petty official; **~stand** *m* (*dated*) civil service; **~status** *m* civil servant status; **~tum** *nt, no pl* **(a)** civil service; (*~schaft auch*) civil servants *pl*; **(b)** (*Wesen*) **sein ~tum** the civil servant in him; **es ist Kennzeichen des ~tums, daß ...** it is the mark of civil servants that ...; **~verhältnis** *nt* **im ~verhältnis stehen/ins ~verhältnis übernommen werden** to be/become a civil servant; **~willkür** *f* arbitrariness of officials; **das war ~willkür** that was an arbitrary bureaucratic decision.
Be|amte(r) *m decl as adj* official; (*Staats~*) civil servant; (*Zoll~ auch, Polizei~*) officer; (*dated: Büro~, Schalter~*) clerk ◆ **politischer ~r** politically-appointed civil servant; **er ist ~r** (*bei Land, Bund*) he is a civil servant *or* in the civil service; **er ist ein typischer ~r** he is a typical petty official *or* bureaucrat; **ein kleiner ~r** a minor *or* (*esp pej*) petty official.
be|amtet *adj* (*form*) established, appointed on a permanent basis (*by the state*).
Be|amtin *f siehe* **Beamte(r).**
be|ängstigen* *vt* (*geh*) to alarm, to frighten, to scare.
be|ängstigend *adj* alarming, frightening ◆ **sein Zustand ist ~** his condition is giving cause for concern.
Be|ängstigung *f* alarm, fear ◆ **in großer ~** in (a state of) great alarm.
be|anspruchen* *vt* **(a)** (*fordern*) to claim; *Gebiet auch* to lay claim to ◆ **etw ~ können** to be entitled to sth.
(b) (*erfordern*) to take; *Zeit auch* to take up; *Platz auch* to take up, to occupy; *Kräfte auch, Aufmerksamkeit* to demand; (*benötigen*) to need.
(c) (*ausnützen*) to use; *jds Gastfreundschaft* to take advantage of; *jds Geduld* to demand; *jds Hilfe* to ask for ◆ **ich möchte Ihre Geduld nicht zu sehr ~** I don't want to try your patience.
(d) (*strapazieren*) *Maschine etc* to use; *jdn* to occupy, to keep busy ◆ **etw/jdn stark** *or* **sehr ~** to put sth under a lot of stress *etc*/keep sb very busy *or* occupied; **eine höchst beanspruchte Maschine** a heavily used machine; **ihr Beruf beansprucht sie ganz** her job is very demanding *or* takes up all her time and energy.
Be|anspruchung *f* **(a)** (*Forderung*) claim (*gen* to); (*Anforderung*) demand. **(b)** (*Ausnutzung: von jds Geduld, Hilfe etc*) demand (*von* on). **(c)** (*Belastung, Abnutzung*) use; (*von Beruf auch*) demands *pl*.
be|anstanden* *vt* to query, to complain about ◆ **das ist beanstandet worden** there has been a query *or* complaint about that; **er hat an allem etwas zu ~** he has complaints about everything; **die beanstandete Ware** the goods complained about *or* queried.
Be|anstandung *f* complaint (*gen* about) ◆ **zu ~en Anlaß geben** (*form*) to give cause for complaint; **er hat jahrelang ohne jede ~ seine Pflicht getan** for years he did his duty without giving any cause for complaint.
be|antragen* *vt* to apply for (*bei* to); (*Jur*) *Strafe* to demand, to ask for; (*vorschlagen: in Debatte etc*) to move, to propose ◆ **er beantragte, versetzt zu werden** he applied for a transfer *or* to be transferred; **etw bei der Behörde ~** to apply to the authorities for sth.
Be|antragung *f siehe vt* application (*gen* for); demand (*gen* for); proposal.
be|antworten* *vt* to answer; *Anfrage, Brief auch* to reply to; *Gruß, Beleidigung, Herausforderung auch* to respond to ◆ **jdm eine Frage ~** to answer sb's question; **eine Frage mit Nein ~** to answer a question in the negative; **leicht zu ~** easily answered.
Be|antwortung *f siehe vt* (*gen* to) answer; reply; response.
be|arbeiten* *vt* **(a)** (*behandeln*) to work on; *Stein, Holz* to work, to dress; (*inf: mit Chemikalien*) to treat ◆ **etw mit dem Hammer/Meißel ~** to hammer/chisel sth.
(b) (*sich befassen mit*) to deal with; *Fall auch* to handle; *Bestellungen etc* to process.
(c) (*redigieren*) to edit; (*neu ~*) to revise; (*umändern*) *Roman etc* to adapt; *Musik* to arrange ◆ **etw für die Drucklegung ~** to prepare sth for press.
(d) (*inf: einschlagen auf*); *Klavier, Trommel etc* to hammer *or* bash away at; *Geige* to saw away at ◆ **jdn mit Fußtritten/Fäusten ~** to kick sb about/thump sb.
(e) (*inf: einreden auf*) *jdn* to work on.
(f) *Land* to cultivate.
Be|arbeiter(in *f*) *m* **(a)** *siehe vt* (*b*) person dealing with *etc* sth ◆ **wer war der ~ der Akte?** who dealt with the file? **(b)** *siehe vt* (*c*) editor; reviser; adapter; arranger.
Be|arbeitung *f siehe vt* **(a)** working (on); dressing; treating ◆ **die ~ von Granit ist schwierig** it is difficult to work *or* dress granite.
(b) dealing with; handling; processing ◆ **die ~ meines Antrags hat lange gedauert** it took a long time to deal with my claim.
(c) editing; revising; adapting; arranging; (*bearbeitete Ausgabe etc*) edition; revision, revised edition; adaptation; arrangement ◆ **neue ~** (*von Film etc*) new version; **die deutsche ~** the German version.
Be|arbeitungs-: ~gebühr *f* handling charge; **~zeit** *f* (*Admin*) (time for) processing; **die ~zeit beträgt zwei Wochen** processing will take two weeks.
be|argwöhnen* *vt* to be suspicious of.
Beat [biːt] *m* **-(s),** *no pl* **(a)** (*Musik*) beat *or* pop music. **(b)** (*Rhythmus*) beat.
Beatband *f* beat *or* pop group.
Beatgeneration *f* beat generation.
Beatifikation *f* (*Eccl*) beatification.
beatifizieren* *vt* (*Eccl*) to beatify.
be|atmen* *vt* *Ertrunkenen* to give artificial respiration to ◆ **jdn künstlich ~** to keep sb breathing artificially.
Be|atmung *f* artificial respiration.
Beatmusik *f* beat *or* pop music.
Beatnik ['biːtnɪk] *m* **-s, -s** beatnik.
Beatschuppen *m* (*inf*) beat club.
Beau [boː] *m* **-, -s** good looker (*inf*).
be|aufsichtigen* *vt* *Arbeit, Bau* to supervise; *Klasse, Schüler, Häftlinge auch* to keep under supervision; *Kind* to mind; *Prüfung* to invigilate at ◆ **jdn bei einer Arbeit/beim Arbeiten ~** to supervise sb's work/sb working; **staatlich beaufsichtigt** state-controlled, under state control.
Be|aufsichtigung *f siehe vt* supervision, supervising; minding; invigilation.
be|auftragen* *vt* **(a)** (*heranziehen*) to engage; *Firma auch* to hire; *Architekten, Künstler etc, Forschungsinstitut* to commission; *Ausschuß etc* to appoint, to set up ◆ **jdn mit etw ~** to engage *etc* sb to do sth; **mit der Wahrnehmung beauftragt** temporarily in charge. **(b)** (*anweisen*) *Untergebenen etc* to instruct. **wir sind beauftragt, das zu tun** we have been instructed to do that.
Be|auftragte(r) *mf decl as adj* representative.
be|augapfeln* *vt* (*hum*) to eye.
be|äugeln* *vt* (*hum*) to make eyes at (*inf*), to ogle.
be|äugen* *vt* (*inf*) to gaze *or* look at.
Beauté [bo'teː] *f* **-, -s** (*geh*), **Beauty** ['bjuːti] *f* **-, -s** (*Press sl*) stunner (*inf*), beauty.
bebändern* *vt usu ptp* to decorate with ribbons, to beribbon (*liter*).
bebartet *adj* (*usu hum*) bearded.
bebaubar *adj* **(a)** *Boden* cultiv(at)able. **(b)** *Grundstück* suitable for building; (*zum Bau freigegeben*) available for building.
bebauen* *vt* **(a)** *Grundstück* to build on, to develop ◆ **das Grundstück ist jetzt mit einer Schule bebaut** the piece of land has had a school built on it; **das Viertel war dicht bebaut** the area was heavily built-up; **ein Gelände mit etw ~** to build sth on a piece of land.
(b) (*Agr*) to cultivate; *Land* to farm.
Bebauung *f, no pl* **(a)** (*Vorgang*) building (*gen* on); (*von Gelände*) development; (*Bauten*) buildings *pl* ◆ **Viertel mit dichter ~** densely built-up area. **(b)** (*Agr*) cultivation; (*von Land*) farming.
Bebauungs-: ~dichte *f* density of building *or* development; **für geringere ~dichte sorgen** to ensure development is less dense; **~plan** *m* development plan *or* scheme.
Bébé [be'beː] *nt* **-s, -s** (*Sw*) baby.
beben *vi* to shake, to tremble; (*Stimme auch*) to quiver (*vor +dat* with) ◆ **am ganzen Leib** *or* **an allen Gliedern ~** to tremble *or* shake all over; **vor jdm ~**

(*liter*) to be in fear and trembling of sb; **um jdn ~** (*liter*) to tremble for sb.

Beben *nt* **-s, -** (*Zittern*) shaking, trembling; (*von Stimme auch*) quivering; (*Erd~*) earthquake.

bebildern* *vt Buch, Vortrag* to illustrate.

Bebilderung *f* illustrations *pl* (*gen* in).

bebrillt *adj* (*hum inf*) bespectacled.

bebrüten* *vt Eier* to incubate ♦ **die Lage ~** (*fig inf*) to brood over the situation.

Becher *m* **-s, -** **(a)** cup; (*old: Kelch auch*) goblet; (*Glas~*) glass, tumbler; (*esp Porzellan~, Ton~ auch*) mug; (*Plastik~ auch*) beaker; (*Joghurt~ etc*) carton, tub; (*Eis~*) (*aus Pappe*) tub; (*aus Metall*) sundae dish ♦ **ein ~ Eis** a tub of icecream/an icecream sundae. **(b)** (*Bot: Eichel~*) cup, cupule (*spec*).

Becher-: b~förmig *adj* cup-shaped; **~glas** *nt* **(a)** (*Trinkglas*) glass, tumbler; **(b)** (*Chem*) glass, beaker.

bechern *vi* (*hum inf*) to have a few (*inf*).

becircen* [bəˈtsɪrtsn] *vt* (*inf*) to bewitch.

Becken *nt* **-s, -** **(a)** (*Brunnen~, Hafen~, Wasch~, Geol*) basin; (*Abwasch~*) sink; (*Toiletten~*) bowl, pan; (*Schwimm~*) pool; (*Stau~*) reservoir; (*Fisch~*) pond; (*Tauf~*) font. **(b)** (*Anat*) pelvis, pelvic girdle ♦ **ein breites ~** broad hips. **(c)** (*Mus*) cymbal.

Becken- (*Anat, Med*): **~bruch** *m* fractured pelvis, pelvic fracture; **~endlage** *f* breech position *or* presentation; **~knochen** *m* hip-bone.

Beckmesser *m* **-s, -** (*pej*) caviller, carper.

Beckmesserei *f* (*pej*) cavilling, carping.

beckmessern *vi* (*pej*) to cavil, to carp.

Becquerel [bɛkəˈrɛl] *nt* **-(s), -** becquerel.

bedachen* *vt* to roof.

bedacht[1] *ptp of* **bedenken, bedachen.**

bedacht[2] *adj* **(a)** (*überlegt*) prudent, careful, cautious. **(b) auf etw** (*acc*) **~ sein** to be concerned about sth; **er ist nur auf sich ~** he only thinks about himself; **darauf ~ sein, etw zu tun** to be concerned about doing sth *or* to do sth.

Bedacht *m* **-s,** *no pl* (*geh*) **mit ~** (*vorsichtig*) prudently, carefully, with care; (*absichtlich*) deliberately; **voll ~** very prudently *or* carefully, with great care; **ohne ~** without thinking, imprudently; **etw mit (gutem) ~ tun** to do sth (quite) deliberately.

Bedachte(r) *mf decl as adj* (*Jur*) beneficiary.

bedächtig *adj* (*gemessen*) *Schritt, Sprache* measured *no adv*, deliberate; *Wesen* deliberate, steady; (*besonnen*) thoughtful, reflective ♦ **~** *or* **mit ~en Schritten** *or* **~en Schrittes** (*liter*) **gehen** to walk with measured *or* deliberate steps; **langsam und ~ sprechen** to speak in slow, measured tones.

Bedächtigkeit *f, no pl siehe adj* measuredness, deliberateness; steadiness; thoughtfulness, reflectiveness ♦ **etw mit großer ~ tun** to do sth with great deliberation/very thoughtfully *or* reflectively.

bedachtsam *adj* (*geh*) careful, deliberate.

Bedachtsamkeit *f, no pl* (*geh*) care, deliberation.

Bedachung *f* roofing; (*Dach auch*) roof.

bedang *pret of* **bedingen 2.**

bedanken* [1] *vr* **(a)** to say thank-you, to express one's thanks (*form*) ♦ **sich bei jdm (für etw) ~** to thank sb (for sth), to say thank-you to sb (for sth); **ich bedanke mich herzlich** thank you very much, (very) many thanks; **dafür können Sie sich bei Herrn Weitz ~** (*iro inf*) you've got Mr Weitz to thank *or* you can thank Mr Weitz for that (*iro*).

(b) (*iro inf*) **ich bedanke mich, dafür bedanke ich mich (bestens)** no thank you (very much); **dafür/für dergleichen wird er sich ~** he refuses point-blank.

[2] *vt* (*form*) **seien Sie (herzlich) bedankt!** please accept my/our (grateful *or* deepest) thanks (*form*).

Bedarf *m* **-(e)s,** *no pl* **(a)** (*Bedürfnis*) need (*an +dat* for); (*~smenge*) requirements *pl*, requisites *pl* ♦ **bei ~** as *or* when required; **bei dringendem ~** in cases of urgent need; **der Bus hält hier nur bei ~** the bus stops here only on request; **Dinge des täglichen ~s** basic *or* everyday necessities; **alles für den häuslichen ~** all household requirements *or* requisites; **seinen ~ an Wein/Lebensmitteln** *etc* **einkaufen** to buy one's supply of wine/food *etc or* the wine/food *etc* one needs; **einem ~ abhelfen** to meet a need; **an etw** (*dat*) **~ haben** to need sth, to be in need of sth; **danke, kein ~** (*iro inf*) no thank you, not on your life (*inf*); *siehe* **decken.**

(b) (*Comm: Nachfrage*) demand (*an +dat* for) ♦ **(je) nach ~** according to demand; **den ~ übersteigen** to exceed demand; **über ~** in excess of demand.

Bedarfs-: ~artikel *m* requisite; **~befriedigung, ~deckung** *f* satisfaction of the/sb's needs; **~fall** *m* (*form*) need; **im ~fall** if necessary; (*wenn gebraucht*) as necessary *or* required; **für den ~fall vorsorgen** to provide for a time of need; **wir wissen nicht, wann der ~fall eintritt** we don't know when the need will arise; **b~gerecht** *adj* **b~gerecht produzieren** to match production and demand; **ein b~gerechtes Warenangebot** a range of goods which meets consumer demands; **~güter** *pl* consumer goods *pl*; **~haltestelle** *f* request (bus/tram) stop; **~träger** *m* (*Comm*) consumer; **~weckung** *f* stimulation of demand.

bedauerlich *adj* regrettable, unfortunate ♦ **~!** how unfortunate.

bedauerlicherweise *adv* regrettably, unfortunately.

bedauern* *vt* **(a)** *etw* to regret ♦ **einen Irrtum ~** to regret one's mistake *or* having made a mistake; **wir ~, Ihnen mitteilen zu müssen, ...** we regret to have to inform you ...; **er hat sehr bedauert, daß ...** he was very sorry that ...; **er schüttelte ~d den Kopf** he shook his head regretfully; **(ich) bedau(e)re!** I am sorry.

(b) (*bemitleiden*) *jdn* to feel *or* be sorry for ♦ **sich selbst ~** to feel sorry for oneself; **er ist zu ~** he is to be pitied, one *or* you should feel sorry for him; **er läßt sich gerne ~, er will immer bedauert sein** he always wants people to feel sorry for him.

Bedauern *nt* **-s,** *no pl* regret ♦ **(sehr) zu meinem ~** (much) to my regret; **zu meinem ~ kann ich nicht kommen** I regret that *or* to my regret I will not be able to come; **zu meinem größten ~ muß ich Ihnen mitteilen ...** it is with the deepest regret that I must inform you ...; **mit ~ habe ich ...** it is with regret that I ...

bedauerns-: ~wert, ~würdig (*geh*) *adj Mensch* pitiful; *Zustand* deplorable.

bedecken* [1] *vt* **(a)** to cover ♦ **von etw bedeckt sein** to be covered in sth; **mit einem Tuch/mit Papieren/Pickeln/Staub bedeckt sein** to be covered with a cloth/with *or* in papers/spots/dust; **sie hat ihre Familie mit Schande bedeckt** (*liter*) she brought shame upon her family; **sich bedeckt halten** (*fig*) to keep a low profile.

(b) (*Astron*) *Stern* to eclipse, to occult (*spec*).

[2] *vr* **(a)** (*sich zudecken*) to cover oneself.

(b) (*Himmel*) to become overcast, to cloud over ♦ **der Himmel bedeckte sich mit Wolken** it *or* the sky clouded over *or* became overcast.

bedeckt *adj* **(a)** covered ♦ **~en Hauptes** (*old*) with one's head covered. **(b)** (*bewölkt*) overcast, cloudy ♦ **bei ~em Himmel** when the sky *or* it is overcast *or* cloudy.

Bedecktsamer [-zaː-] *m*, **Bedecktsamige** [-zaː-] *pl* (*Bot*) angiospermae *pl*.

Bedeckung *f* **(a)** (*das Bedecken*) covering. **(b)** (*Deckendes*) cover, covering. **(c)** (*Mil*) (*Geleitschutz*) guard, escort; (*Leibwache*) guard ♦ **der Konvoi hatte drei Fregatten zur ~** the convoy was escorted by *or* had an escort of three frigates. **(d)** (*Astron: von Stern*) eclipse, occultation (*spec*).

bedenken* *irreg* [1] *vt* **(a)** (*überlegen*) *Sache, Lage, Maßnahme etc* to consider, to think about ♦ **das will wohl bedacht sein** (*geh*) that calls for careful consideration; **wenn man es recht bedenkt, ...** if you think about it properly ...

(b) (*in Betracht ziehen*) *Umstand, Folgen etc* to consider, to take into consideration ♦ **man muß ~, daß ...** one must take into consideration the fact that ...; **das hättest du früher** *or* **vorher ~ sollen** you should have thought about that sooner *or* before; **ich gebe (es) zu ~, daß ...** (*geh*) I would ask you to consider that ...; **bedenke, daß du sterben mußt** remember you are mortal.

(c) (*in Testament*) to remember ♦ **jdn mit einem Geschenk ~** (*geh*) to give sb a present; **jdn reich ~** (*geh*) to be generous to sb; **mit etw bedacht werden** to receive sth; **auch ich wurde bedacht** I was not forgotten (either), there was something for me too; **ich wurde auch diesmal reich bedacht** (*geh*) I did very well this time; *siehe* **Bedachte(r).**

[2] *vr* (*geh*) to think (about it), to reflect ♦ **bedenke dich gut, ehe du ...** think well before you ...; **ohne sich lange zu ~** without stopping to think *or* reflect; *siehe* **bedacht[2].**

Bedenken *nt* **-s, -** **(a)** *usu pl* (*Zweifel, Einwand*) doubt, reservation, misgiving ♦ **moralische ~** moral scruples; **~ haben** *or* **tragen** (*geh*) to have one's doubts (*bei* about); **ihm kommen ~** he is having second thoughts; **ohne ~ vorgehen** to act relentlessly *or* unrelentingly. **(b)** *no pl* (*das Überlegen*) consideration (*gen* of), reflection (*gen* (up)on) ♦ **nach langem ~** after much thought; **ohne ~** without thinking.

bedenkenlos *adj* **(a)** (*ohne Zögern*) *Zustimmung* unhesitating, prompt ♦ **ich würde ~ hingehen** I would not hesitate to go *or* would have no hesitation in going; **~ zustimmen** to agree without hesitation. **(b)** (*skrupellos*) heedless of others; (*unüberlegt*) thoughtless ♦ **etw ~ tun** to do sth without thinking.

Bedenkenlosigkeit *f, no pl* **(a)** (*Bereitwilligkeit*) readiness, promptness. **(b)** (*Skrupellosigkeit*) unscrupulousness, lack of scruples; (*Unüberlegtheit*) thoughtlessness, lack of thought.

bedenkenswert *adj* worth thinking about *or* considering.

Bedenkenträger *m* doubter ♦ **alle ~ gegen den Beschluß** all those with misgivings about the decision.

bedenklich *adj* **(a)** (*zweifelhaft*) *Geschäfte, Mittel etc* dubious, questionable.

(b) (*besorgniserregend*) *Lage, Verschlimmerung etc* serious, disturbing, alarming; *Gesundheitszustand* serious ♦ **der Zustand des Kranken ist ~** the patient's condition is giving cause for concern; **der Himmel sah ~ aus** the sky looked ominous.

(c) (*besorgt*) apprehensive, anxious ♦ **ein ~es Gesicht machen** to look apprehensive; **jdn ~ stimmen** to make sb (feel) apprehensive.

Bedenklichkeit *f siehe adj* **(a)** dubiousness, questionableness. **(b)** seriousness, disturbing *or* alarming nature. **(c)** apprehension, anxiety.

Bedenkzeit *f* **jdm zwei Tage/bis Freitag ~ geben** to give sb two days/until Friday to think about it; **sich** (*dat*) **(eine) ~ ausbitten** *or* **erbitten, um ~ bitten** to ask for time to think about it.

bedeppert *adj* (*inf*) **(a)** (*ratlos*) dazed, stunned. **(b)** (*trottelig*) dopey (*inf*), daft.

bedeuten* *vt* **(a)** (*gleichzusetzen sein mit, heißen, bezeichnen*) to mean; (*Math, Ling*) to stand for, to denote; (*versinnbildlichen*) to signify, to symbolize ♦ **was bedeutet dieses Wort?** what does this word mean?, what's the meaning of this word?; **was soll das ~?** what does that mean?; **was soll denn das ~!** what's the meaning of that?; **das hat nichts zu ~** it doesn't mean anything; (*macht nichts aus*) it doesn't matter.

(b) (*ankündigen, zur Folge haben*) to mean ♦ **diese Wolken ~ schlechtes Wetter** these clouds mean *or* spell bad weather; **das bedeutet nichts Gutes** that spells trouble, that bodes ill.

(c) (*gelten*) to mean (*dat, für* to); (*sein, gelten als auch*) to be ♦ **Geld bedeutet mir nichts** money doesn't mean anything *or* means nothing to me; **sein Name bedeutet etwas in der Medizin** his name means something *or* he is a

➤ SPRACHE AKTIV: **bedanken: 1a** → 47.5, 49, 52.1 **bedauern: a** → 39.2, 45.3 **Bedauern** → 45.3, 51.4, 52.1, 52.4 **bedeuten: a** → 53.3

name in the field of medicine.

(d) (*geh: einen Hinweis geben*) to indicate, to intimate; (*mit Geste*) to indicate, to gesture; *Abneigung, Zustimmung auch* to signify ◆ **ich bedeutete ihm, das zu tun** I indicated *or* intimated that he should do that; **man bedeutete mir, daß ...** I was given to understand that ...

bedeutend [1] *adj* (a) (*wichtig, bemerkenswert*) *Persönlichkeit* important, distinguished, eminent; *Leistung, Rolle* significant, important ◆ **etwas B~es leisten** to achieve something important *or* significant. (b) (*groß*) *Summe, Erfolg* considerable, significant.

[2] *adv* (*beträchtlich*) considerably.

bedeutsam *adj* (a) (*vielsagend*) meaningful, significant; *Rede, Blick auch* eloquent ◆ **jdm ~ zulächeln** to smile meaning(ful)ly at sb. (b) (*wichtig*) *Gespräch, Fortschritt etc* important; (*folgenschwer*) significant (*für* for).

Bedeutsamkeit *f siehe adj* (a) meaningfulness, significance; eloquence. (b) importance; significance.

Bedeutung *f* (a) (*Sinn, Wortsinn*) meaning ◆ **in wörtlicher/übertragener ~** in the literal/figurative sense.

(b) (*Wichtigkeit*) importance, significance; (*Tragweite*) significance ◆ **von ~ sein** to be important *or* significant *or* of significance; **von (großer *or* tiefer/geringer) ~ sein** to be of (great/little) importance *or* (very/not very) important; **ein Mann von ~** an important figure; **nichts von ~** nothing of any importance; **ohne ~** of no importance; **große ~ besitzen** to be of great importance.

Bedeutungs-: ~erweiterung *f* (*Ling*) extension of meaning; **~gehalt** *m* meaning; **~lehre** *f* (*Ling*) semantics *sing*, science of meaning (*old*); **b~los** *adj* (a) (*unwichtig*) insignificant, unimportant; (b) (*nichts besagend*) meaningless; **~losigkeit** *f* insignificance, unimportance; **zur ~losigkeit verurteilt sein** to be condemned to insignificance; **b~schwer** *adj* (*geh*) meaningful, laden *or* pregnant with meaning (*liter*); (*folgenschwer*) momentous; **~verengung** *f* (*Ling*) narrowing of meaning; **~verschiebung** *f* (*Ling*) shift of meaning, sense *or* semantic shift; **b~verwandt** *adj* (*Ling*) semantically related; **b~voll** *adj siehe* **bedeutsam**; **~wandel** *m* change in meaning, semantic change; **~wörterbuch** *nt* (defining) dictionary.

bedienbar *adj* **leicht/schwer ~** easy/hard to use.

Bedienbarkeit *f, no pl* usability ◆ **leichte ~** ease of use.

bedienen* [1] *vt* (a) (*Verkäufer*) to serve, to attend to; (*Kellner auch*) to wait on; (*Handlanger*) to assist; (*Diener etc*) to serve, to wait on ◆ **werden Sie schon bedient?** are you being attended to *or* served?; **hier wird man gut bedient** the service is good here; **er läßt sich gern ~** he likes to be waited on; **mit diesem Ratschlag war ich schlecht bedient** I was ill-served by that advice; **mit dieser Ware/damit sind Sie sehr gut bedient** these goods/that should serve you very well; **ich bin bedient!** (*inf*) I've had enough, I've had all I can take.

(b) (*Verkehrsmittel*) to serve ◆ **diese Flugroute wird von X bedient** X operate (on) this route; **Concorde soll demnächst New York ~** Concorde is due to operate to New York soon.

(c) (*handhaben*) *Maschine, Geschütz etc* to operate; *Telefon* to answer.

(d) (*Sport*) to pass *or* feed (the ball) to.

(e) (*Cards*) **eine Farbe/Karo ~** to follow suit/to follow suit in diamonds.

[2] *vi* (a) to serve; (*Kellner auch*) to wait (at table); (*als Beruf*) to wait, to be a waiter/waitress.

(b) (*Cards*) **du mußt ~** you must follow suit; **falsch ~** to revoke, to fail to follow suit.

[3] *vr* (a) (*bei Tisch*) to help *or* serve oneself (*mit* to) ◆ **bitte ~ Sie sich** please help *or* serve yourself.

(b) (*geh: gebrauchen*) **sich jds/einer Sache ~** to use sb/sth.

Bediener *m* **-s, -** (*Comput*) operator.

Bediener-: b~freundlich *adj* user-friendly; **~führung** *f, no pl* (*Comput*) context-sensitive help.

Bedienerin *f* (*Aus*) charwoman.

Bedieneroberfläche *f* (*Comput*) = **Benutzeroberfläche**.

bedienstet *adj*: **bei jdm ~ sein** to be in service with sb; **~ sein** (*Aus: im öffentlichen Dienst*) to be in the civil service.

Bedienstete(r) *mf decl as adj* (a) (*im öffentlichen Dienst*) public employee. (b) (*old: Diener*) servant.

Bedienung *f* (a) *no pl* (*in Restaurant etc*) service; (*von Maschinen*) operation ◆ **die ~ der Kunden** serving the customers; **eine Tankstelle/ein Restaurant mit ~** a petrol station with forecourt service/a restaurant with waiter service; **zur freien *or* gefälligen** (*old*) **~** please take one *or* help yourself; **die ~ des Geräts erlernen** to learn how to operate the machine.

(b) (*~sgeld*) service (charge).

(c) (*~spersonal*) staff; (*Kellner etc*) waiter/waitress ◆ **kommt denn hier keine ~?** isn't anyone serving here?; **hallo, ~!, ~ bitte!** waiter/waitress!

(d) (*Mil: ~smannschaft*) crew.

Bedienungs-: ~anleitung, ~anweisung *f* operating instructions *pl or* directions *pl*; **~aufschlag** *m*, **~geld** *nt* service charge; **~fehler** *m* mistake in operating a/the machine; **~hebel** *m* operating lever; **~komfort** *m* (*Comput, Tech*) ease of operation; **~mannschaft** *f* (*Mil*) crew; **~vorschrift** *f* operating instructions *pl*; **~zuschlag** *m* service charge.

bedingen *pret* **bedingte**, *ptp* **bedingt** *vt* (a) (*bewirken*) to cause; (*notwendig machen*) to necessitate; (*Psych, Physiol*) to condition; (*logisch voraussetzen*) to presuppose ◆ **sich gegenseitig ~** to be mutually dependent; **~de Konjunktion** conditional conjunction; *siehe* **bedingt**. (b) (*voraussetzen, verlangen*) to call for, to demand.

bedingt *adj* (a) (*eingeschränkt*) limited; *Lob auch* qualified ◆ **(nur) ~ richtig** (only) partly *or* partially right; **(nur) ~ gelten** to be (only) partly *or* partially valid; **~ tauglich** (*Mil*) fit for limited duties; **gefällt es Ihnen hier? — ~!** do you like it here? — with some reservations.

(b) (*an Bedingung geknüpft*) *Annahme, Straferlaß, Strafaussetzung* conditional.

(c) (*Physiol*) *Reflex* conditioned.

Bedingtheit *f* (a) (*von Lob, Anerkennung*) limitedness. (b) (*von Existenz etc*) determinedness.

Bedingung *f* (a) (*Voraussetzung*) condition; (*Erfordernis*) requirement ◆ **die erste ~ für etw** the basic requirement for sth; **mit *or* unter der ~, daß ...** on condition *or* with the proviso that ...; **unter keiner ~** in *or* under no circumstances, on no condition; **(nur) unter einer ~** (only) on one condition; **unter jeder anderen ~** in any other circumstances; **von einer ~ abhängen *or* abhängig sein** to be conditional on one thing; **~ (für meine Zustimmung) ist, daß ...** it is a condition (of my consent) that ...; **es zur ~ machen, daß ...** to stipulate that ...

(b) (*Forderung*) term, condition ◆ **zu günstigen ~en** (*Comm*) on favourable terms.

(c) **~en** *pl* (*Umstände*) conditions *pl* ◆ **unter guten/harten ~en arbeiten** to work in good/under *or* in difficult conditions.

Bedingungs-: ~form *f* (*Gram*) conditional (form); **b~los** *adj Kapitulation* unconditional; *Hingabe, Gehorsam, Gefolgschaft* unquestioning; **b~los für etw eintreten** to support sth without reservation; **~satz** *m* conditional clause.

bedrängen* *vt Feind* to attack; *gegnerische Mannschaft* to put pressure on, to pressurize; (*belästigen*) to plague, to badger; *Schuldner* to press (for payment); *Passanten, Mädchen* to pester; (*bedrücken: Sorgen*) to beset; (*heimsuchen*) to haunt ◆ **ein bedrängtes Herz** (*liter*) a troubled heart; **sich in einer bedrängten Lage/in bedrängten Verhältnissen finden** to be in dire *or* desperate straits; **die Bedrängten und Verzweifelten** people in distress and despair.

Bedrängnis *f* (*geh*) (*seelische ~*) distress, torment ◆ **in arger *or* großer/einer argen *or* großen ~** in dire *or* desperate straits; **jdn/etw in ~ bringen** to get sb/sth into trouble; **in ~ geraten** to get into difficulties.

Bedrängung *f* (a) *siehe vt* attacking; pressurizing; plaguing, badgering; pressing; pestering; besetting; haunting. (b) *siehe* **Bedrängnis**.

bedripst *adj* (*N Ger*) stunned, dazed.

bedrohen* *vt* to threaten; (*gefährden*) to endanger ◆ **den Frieden ~** to be a threat to peace; **vom Tode/von Überschwemmung bedroht** in mortal danger/in danger of being flooded; **vom Aussterben bedroht** threatened with extinction, in danger of becoming extinct.

bedrohlich *adj* (*gefährlich*) dangerous, alarming; (*unheilverkündend*) ominous, menacing, threatening ◆ **sich ~ verschlechtern** to deteriorate alarmingly; **in ~e Nähe rücken *or* kommen** to get dangerously *or* perilously close.

Bedrohung *f* threat (*gen* to); (*das Bedrohen auch*) threatening (*gen* of) ◆ **in ständiger ~ leben** to live under a constant threat.

bedrucken* *vt* to print on ◆ **ein bedrucktes Kleid** a print dress; **bedruckter Stoff** print, printed fabric; **etw mit einem Muster ~** to print a pattern on sth.

bedrücken* *vt* (a) to depress ◆ **jdn ~** to depress sb, to make sb feel depressed; **was bedrückt dich?** what is (weighing) on your mind?; **Sorgen bedrückten ihn** cares were weighing upon him. (b) (*old: unterdrücken*) to oppress.

bedrückend *adj Anblick, Nachrichten, Vorstellung* depressing; (*lastend*) oppressive; *Sorge, Not* pressing.

Bedrücker *m* **-s, -** (*old*) oppressor.

bedrückt *adj* (*niedergeschlagen*) depressed, dejected; *Schweigen* oppressive.

Bedrückung *f siehe adj* (a) depression, dejection; oppressiveness. (b) (*old*) oppression.

Beduine *m* **-n, -n, Beduinin** *f* Bedouin.

bedungen *ptp of* **bedingen 2**.

bedürfen* *vi irreg +gen* (*geh*) to need, to require ◆ **das bedarf keiner weiteren Erklärung** there's no need for any further explanation; **es hätte nur eines Wortes bedurft, um ...** it would only have taken a word to ...; **es bedarf nur eines Wortes von Ihnen** you only have to *or* need to say the word; **es bedarf einiger Mühe** some effort is called for *or* required; **ohne daß es eines Hinweises bedurft hätte, ...** without having to be asked ...

Bedürfnis *nt* (a) (*Notwendigkeit*) need; (*no pl: Bedarf auch*) necessity ◆ **die ~se des täglichen Lebens** everyday needs; **dafür liegt kein ~ vor *or* besteht kein ~** there is no need *or* necessity for that.

(b) *no pl* (*Verlangen*) need; (*form: Anliegen*) wish, desire ◆ **es war ihm ein ~, ...** it was his wish *or* desire to ..., he wished *or* desired to ...; **ich hatte das ~/das dringende ~, das zu tun** I felt the need/an urgent need to do that; **das ~ nach Schlaf haben *or* fühlen** to be *or* feel in need of sleep.

(c) (*old: Notdurft*) call of nature ◆ **(s)ein ~ verrichten** to relieve oneself.

Bedürfnis-: ~anstalt *f* (*dated form, hum*) **öffentliche ~anstalt** public convenience *or* restroom (*US*); **~befriedigung** *f* satisfaction of one's/sb's needs; **b~los** *adj Mensch etc* undemanding, modest in one's needs; *Leben* humble, simple.

bedurft *ptp of* **bedürfen**.

bedurfte *pret of* **bedürfen**.

bedürftig *adj* (a) (*hilfs~*) needy, in need ◆ **die B~en** the needy *pl*, those in need. (b) **einer Sache** (*gen*) **~ sein** (*geh*) to be *or* stand in need of sth, to have need of sth.

Bedürftigkeit *f, no pl* need ◆ **jds ~ (amtlich) feststellen** to give sb a means test.

beduseln* *vr* (*inf*) to get sozzled (*inf*) *or* tipsy (*inf*).

⚠: Informationen zur Rechtschreibreform im Anhang

beduselt *adj (inf) (angetrunken)* sozzled *(inf)*, tipsy *(inf)*; *(benommen)* bemused, befuddled.
Beefsteak ['bi:fste:k] *nt* steak ◆ **deutsches ~** hamburger, beefburger.
be|ehren* [1] *vt (geh)* to honour ◆ **wann ~ Sie uns (mit einem Besuch)?** when will you honour us with a visit?; **bitte ~ Sie uns bald wieder** *(Kellner etc)* I hope you'll do us the honour of coming again soon.
[2] *vr* **sich ~, etw zu tun** *(form)* to have the honour *or* privilege of doing sth *(form)*.
be|eiden* *vt (beschwören) Sache, Aussage* to swear to.
be|eidigen* *vt* **(a)** *siehe* **beeiden. (b)** *(old) siehe* **vereidigen.**
Be|eidigung *f siehe* **Vereidigung.**
be|eilen* *vr* to hurry (up), to get a move on *(inf)* ◆ **sich sehr** *or* **mächtig** *(inf)* **~** to get a real move on *(inf)*; **er beeilte sich hinzuzufügen ...** *(form)* he hastened to add ...
Be|eilung *interj (inf)* get a move on *(inf)*, step on it *(inf)*.
be|eindrucken* *vt* to impress; *(Eindruck hinterlassen auch)* to make an impression on ◆ **davon lasse ich mich nicht ~** I won't be impressed by that.
be|eindruckend *adj* impressive.
⚠**be|einflußbar** *adj Mensch* impressionable, suggestible ◆ **er ist nur schwer ~** he is hard to influence *or* sway; **diese Vorgänge sind nicht ~** these events cannot be influenced *or* changed.
be|einflussen* *vt jdn* to influence; *Urteil, Meinung, Aussage auch* to sway; *Ereignisse, Vorgänge auch* to affect ◆ **jdn günstig/nachhaltig ~** to have a favourable *or* good/lasting influence on sb; **er ist leicht/schwer zu ~** he is easily influenced/hard to influence; **kannst du deinen Freund nicht ~?** can't you persuade your friend?; **durch etw beeinflußt sein** to be *or* to have been influenced *or* affected by sth.
Be|einflussung *f (das Beeinflussen)* influencing; *(Einfluß)* influence *(durch* of) ◆ **~ der Rechtspflege** *(Jur)* prejudicing the outcome of a trial.
be|einträchtigen* *vt (stören)* to spoil; *Vergnügen, Genuß auch* to detract from; *Konzentration auch* to disturb; *Rundfunkempfang* to interfere with, to impair; *(schädigen) jds Ruf* to damage, to harm; *(vermindern) Qualität, Wert, Absatz, Energie, Appetit* to reduce; *Sehvermögen etc* to impair; *Reaktionen, Leistung* to reduce, to impair; *(hemmen) Entscheidung* to interfere with; *Freiheit, Entschlußkraft* to restrict, to interfere with, to curb ◆ **dadurch wird der Wert erheblich beeinträchtigt** that reduces the value considerably; **sich (gegenseitig) ~** to have an adverse effect on one another; *(Empfangsgeräte)* to interfere with one another; **jdn in seiner Freiheit** *or* **jds Freiheit ~** to restrict *or* interfere with *or* curb sb's freedom.
Be|einträchtigung *f siehe vt* spoiling; detracting *(gen* from); disturbance; interference *(gen* with), impairment; damage, harm *(gen* to); reduction *(gen* of, in); restriction, curbing ◆ **ohne ~ seiner Rechte** without restricting his rights.
be|elenden* *vt (Sw)* to upset, to distress.
Beelzebub [be'ɛltsəbu:p, 'be:l-] *m* **-s** *(Bibl)* Beelzebub; *siehe* **Teufel.**
be|enden* *vt* to end; *Arbeit, Aufgabe etc* to finish, to complete; *Vortrag, Brief, Schulstunde, Versammlung auch* to bring to an end, to conclude; *Streik, Streit, Krieg, Verhältnis auch* to bring to an end; *Studium* to complete ◆ **der Abend wurde mit einer Diskussion beendet** the evening ended with *or* finished with a discussion; **etw vorzeitig ~** to cut sth short; **sein Leben ~** *(geh)* to end one's days; *(durch Selbstmord)* to take one's life; **damit ist unser Konzert/ unser heutiges Programm beendet** that concludes *or* brings to an end our concert/our programmes for today.
Be|endigung, Be|endung *f, no pl* ending; *(Ende)* end; *(Fertigstellung)* completion; *(Schluß)* conclusion ◆ **zur ~ dieser Arbeit** to finish this piece of work; **zur ~ des heutigen Abends ...** to round off this evening ...; **nach ~ des Unterrichts** after school (ends).
be|engen* *vt (lit) Bewegung* to restrict, to cramp; *(Möbel etc) Zimmer* to make cramped; *(fig)* to stifle, to inhibit ◆ **das Zimmer/Kleid beengt mich** the room is too cramped/the dress is too tight for me; **~de Kleidung** tight *or* restricting clothing.
be|engt *adj* cramped, confined; *(fig auch)* stifled ◆ **~ wohnen** to live in cramped conditions; **sich ~ fühlen** to feel confined *etc*; **~e Verhältnisse** *(fig)* restricted circumstances.
Be|engtheit *f (Eingeschränktheit)* restriction, confinement; *(von Räumen)* cramped conditions *pl* ◆ **ein Gefühl der ~ haben** to feel restricted *or* confined *or (fig auch)* stifled.
be|erben* *vt* **jdn ~** to inherit sb's estate, to be heir to sb.
be|erdigen* *vt* to bury ◆ **jdn kirchlich ~** to give sb a Christian burial.
Be|erdigung *f* burial; *(~sfeier)* funeral ◆ **auf der falschen ~ sein** *(hum sl)* to have come to the wrong place.
Be|erdigungs- *in cpds siehe auch* **Bestattungs-** funeral; **~feier** *f* funeral service.
Beere *f* **-, -n** berry; *(Wein~)* grape ◆ **~n tragen** to bear fruit; **~n sammeln, in die ~n gehen** *(dial)* to go berry-picking; *(Brombeeren)* to go blackberrying.
Beeren-: ~auslese *f (Wein) wine made from specially selected grapes*; **~frucht** *f* berry; **~lese** *f* fruit picking; **~obst** *nt* soft fruit.
Beet *nt* **-(e)s, -e** *(Blumen~, Spargel~)* bed; *(Gemüse~)* patch; *(Rabatte)* border *(mit* of).
Beete *f* **-, -n** *siehe* **Bete.**
befähigen* *vt* to enable; *(Ausbildung)* to qualify, to equip ◆ **jdn zu etw ~** to enable sb to do sth; to qualify *or* equip sb to do sth.
befähigt *adj* capable, competent; *(durch Ausbildung)* qualified ◆ **sie ist zum Richteramt ~** she is qualified to be *or* become a judge; **zu etw ~ sein** to be capable of doing sth *or* competent to do sth.

Befähigung *f, no pl* **(a)** *(durch Ausbildung, Voraussetzung)* qualifications *pl* ◆ **die ~ zum Richteramt** the qualifications to be *or* become a judge.
(b) *(Können, Eignung)* capability, ability ◆ **er hat nicht die ~ dazu** he does not have the ability to do that; **~ zu etw zeigen** to show talent *or* a gift for sth.
Befähigungsnachweis *m* certificate of qualifications.
befahl *pret of* **befehlen.**
befahrbar *adj Straße, Weg* passable; *Seeweg, Fluß* navigable ◆ **~ sein** *(Straße)* to be open to traffic; **nicht ~ sein** *(Straße, Weg)* to be closed (to traffic); *(wegen Schnee etc auch)* to be impassable; *(Seeweg, Fluß)* to be unnavigable *or* not navigable; *siehe* **Bankette, Seitenstreifen.**
befahren[1]* *vt irreg* **(a)** *Straße, Weg* to use, to drive on *or* along; *Paßstraße* to drive over; *Gegend, Land* to drive *or* travel through; *Kreuzung, Seitenstreifen* to drive onto; *Eisenbahnstrecke* to travel on ◆ **der Paß kann nur im Sommer ~ werden** the pass is only open to traffic *or* passable in summer; **die Strecke darf nur in einer Richtung ~ werden** this stretch of road is only open in one direction; **dieser Weg kann nur mit dem Fahrrad ~ werden** you can only use a bicycle on this path; **die Straße darf nicht ~ werden/wird von Panzern ~** the road is closed/tanks use this road; **diese Straße wird stark/wenig ~** this road is used a lot/isn't used much, there is a lot of/not much traffic on this road.
(b) *(Schiff, Seemann)* to sail; *Fluß auch* to sail up/down; *Seeweg auch* to navigate; *Küste* to sail along ◆ **der See wird von vielen Booten ~** many boats sail on *or* use this lake; **diese Route wird nicht mehr von Schiffen ~** ships no longer sail this route.
(c) *(Min) Schacht* to go down ◆ **die Grube wird nicht mehr ~** the mine is not worked any more.
(d) *(abladen auf)* to spread ◆ **ein Feld mit Dung ~** to spread manure on a field.
befahren[2] *adj* **(a)** *Straße, Seeweg, Kanal* used ◆ **eine viel** *or* **stark/wenig ~e Straße** *etc* a much/little used road *etc.* **(b)** *(Naut: erprobt)* seasoned *attr*, experienced ◆ **(ein) ~es Volk** seasoned *or* experienced sailors *pl or* seamen *pl.*
(c) *(Hunt: bewohnt)* inhabited.
Befahren *nt* **-s,** *no pl* use *(gen* of); *(Vorgang)* using ◆ **beim ~ der Brücke** when using the bridge; **„~ verboten"** "road closed"; **„~ der Brücke verboten"** "bridge closed".
Befall *m* **-(e)s,** *no pl* attack; *(mit Schädlingen)* infestation ◆ **es kam zum ~ aller Organe** all organs were affected; **der ~ (des Kohls) mit Raupen** the blight of caterpillars (on the cabbage).
befallen[1]* *vt irreg* **(a)** *(geh: überkommen)* to overcome; *(Angst auch)* to grip, to seize; *(Durst, Hunger auch)* to assail; *(Fieber, Krankheit, Seuche)* to attack, to strike; *(Mißgeschick, Schicksal etc)* to befall, to affect ◆ **eine Schwäche/eine Ohnmacht befiel sie** she felt faint/she fainted. **(b)** *(angreifen, infizieren)* to affect; *(Schädlinge, Ungeziefer)* to infest.
befallen[2] *adj* affected *(von* by); *(von Schädlingen)* infested *(von* with).
befangen *adj* **(a)** *Mensch, Lächeln* bashful, diffident; *Schweigen, Stille* awkward.
(b) *(esp Jur: voreingenommen) Richter, Zeuge* prejudiced, bias(s)ed ◆ **als ~ gelten** to be considered (to be) prejudiced *etc or (Jur auch)* an interested party; **sich für ~ erklären** *(Jur)* to declare one's interest; **jdn als ~ ablehnen** *(Jur)* to object to sb on grounds of interest.
(c) *(geh: verstrickt)* **in der Vorstellung ~ sein, daß ...** *or* **... zu ...** to have the impression that ...; **er ist in seinen eigenen Anschauungen ~** he can only see his own point of view; **in einem Irrtum ~ sein** to labour under a misapprehension.
Befangenheit *f, no pl siehe adj* **(a)** bashfulness, diffidence; awkwardness.
(b) bias, prejudice; *(Jur)* interest ◆ **jdn wegen (Besorgnis der) ~ ablehnen** *(Jur)* to object to sb on grounds of interest.
befassen* [1] *vr* **(a)** *(sich beschäftigen)* **sich mit etw ~** to deal with sth; *mit Problem, Frage auch* to look into sth; *mit Fall, Angelegenheit auch* to attend to sth; *mit Arbeit auch, Forschungsbereich etc* to work on sth; **sich mit jds Vorleben ~** to look into sb's past; **damit haben wir uns jetzt lange genug befaßt** we have spent long enough on *or* over that; **er hat sich lange damit befaßt, alle Einzelheiten auszuarbeiten** he spent a long time working out all the details; **mit solchen Kleinigkeiten hat er sich nie befaßt** he has never bothered with *or* concerned himself with such trivialities.
(b) *(sich annehmen)* **sich mit jdm ~** to deal with sb, to attend to sb; *mit Kindern auch* to see to sb; **sich mit jdm sehr ~** to give sb a lot of attention.
[2] *vt* **(a)** *(dial: anfassen)* to touch.
(b) *(form)* **jdn mit etw ~** to get sb to deal with sth; **mit etw befaßt sein** to be dealing with sth; **die mit diesem Fall befaßten Richter** the judges engaged on this case.
befehden* [1] *vt (Hist)* to be feuding with; *(fig)* to attack.
[2] *vr* to be feuding ◆ **sich mit Worten ~** to attack each other verbally.
Befehl *m* **-(e)s, -e (a)** *(Anordnung)* order, command *(an +acc* to, *von* from); *(Physiol)* command; *(Comput)* command ◆ **einen ~ verweigern** to refuse to obey an order *etc*; **er gab (uns) den ~, ...** he ordered us to ...; **wir hatten den ~, ...** we had orders *or* were ordered to ...; **wir haben ~, Sie festzunehmen** we have orders *or* have been ordered to arrest you; **auf seinen ~ (hin)** on his orders, at his command; **auf ~** to order; *(sofort)* at the drop of a hat *(inf)*; **auf ~ handeln** to act under *or* according to orders; **auf höheren ~** on orders from above; **zu ~, Herr Hauptmann** *(Mil)* yes, sir; *(nach erhaltenem Befehl auch)* very good, sir; **zu ~, Herr Kapitän** aye-aye, sir; **~ ausgeführt!** mission accomplished; **~ ist ~** orders are orders; **~ vom Chef!** boss's orders; **dein Wunsch ist mir ~** *(hum)* your wish is my command.
(b) *(Befehlsgewalt)* command ◆ **den ~ haben** *or* **führen** to have command, to

⚠: for details of spelling reform, see supplement

be in command (*über +acc* of); **den ~ übernehmen** to take *or* assume command.

befehlen *pret* **befahl,** *ptp* **befohlen** *vti* **(a)** to order; (*vi: Befehle erteilen*) to give orders ◆ **er befahl Stillschweigen** *or* **zu schweigen** he ordered them/us *etc* to be silent; **sie befahl ihm Stillschweigen** *or* **zu schweigen** she ordered him to keep quiet; **schweigen Sie, befahl er** be quiet, he ordered; **er befahl, den Mann zu erschießen** *or* **die Erschießung des Mannes** he ordered the man to be shot; **sie befahl, daß ...** she ordered *or* gave orders that ...; **du hast mir gar nichts zu ~, von dir lasse ich mir nichts ~** I won't take orders from you; **gnädige Frau ~?, was ~ gnädige Frau?** (*old form*) yes, Madam?, what can I do for you, Madam?; **er befiehlt gern** he likes giving orders; **hier habe nur ich zu ~** I give the orders around here; **wie Sie ~** as you wish; **wer ~ will, muß erst gehorchen lernen** (*prov*) if you wish to command you must first learn to obey.
(b) (*beordern*) (*an die Front etc*) to order, to send; (*zu sich auch*) to summon.
(c) *vi only* (*Mil: den Befehl haben*) to be in command, to have command (*über +acc* of) ◆ **über Leben und Tod ~** to be in absolute command.
(d) (*liter: anvertrauen*) to entrust, to commend (*liter*) ◆ **seine Seele Gott/in die Hände Gottes ~** to commend *or* entrust one's soul to God/into God's hands.

befehlerisch *adj Ton, Wesen* imperious, dictatorial.

befehligen* *vt* (*Mil*) to command, to be in command of, to have command of *or* over.

Befehls-: ~ausgabe *f* (*Mil*) issuing of orders; **um 15 Uhr ist ~ausgabe** orders will be issued at 15^{00} hours; **~bereich** *m* (*Mil*) (area of) command; **~code** *m* (*Comput*) command code; **~empfänger** *m* recipient of an order; **~empfänger sein** to follow orders (*gen* from); **jdn zum ~empfänger degradieren** (*fig*) to lower sb to the level of just following orders; **~folge** *f* (*Comput*) command sequence; **~form** *f* (*Gram*) imperative; **b~gemäß** *adj* as ordered, in accordance with (sb's) orders; **~gewalt** *f* (*Mil*) command; **~gewalt haben** to be in *or* to have command (*über +acc* over); **jds ~gewalt** (*dat*) **unterstehen** to be under sb's command; **~haber** *m* **-s, -** commander; **b~haberisch** *adj* dictatorial; **~notstand** *m* (*Jur*) compulsion *or* necessity to obey orders; **unter ~notstand handeln** to be acting under orders; **~satz** *m* (*Gram*) imperative, command; **~sprache** *f* (*Comput*) command language; **~ton** *m* peremptory tone; **~verweigerung** *f* (*Mil*) refusal to obey orders; **b~widrig** *adj* contrary to orders, against orders; **~zeile** *f* (*Comput*) command line.

befeinden* [1] *vt* (*geh*) *Land* to be hostile towards; *Ideologie, Schriften, Schriftsteller* to attack.
[2] *vr* to be hostile (towards each other).

befestigen* *vt* **(a)** (*an +dat* to) (*anbringen*) to fasten; (*festmachen auch*) to secure; *Boot* to tie up ◆ **etw durch Nähen/Kleben** *etc* **~** to sew/glue *etc* sth; **etw an der Wand/Tür ~** to attach *or* fix sth to the wall/door; **die beiden Enden/Teile werden (aneinander) befestigt** the two ends/parts are fastened together; **die Wäsche mit Klammern an der Leine ~** to peg the washing on the line; **ein loses Brett ~** to fasten down *or* secure a loose board.
(b) (*fest, haltbar machen*) *Böschung, Deich* to reinforce; *Fahrbahn, Straße* to make up; (*fig: stärken*) *Herrschaft, Ruhm* to consolidate ◆ **eine Straße gut ~** to make up a road with good foundations.
(c) (*Mil: mit Festungsanlagen versehen*) to fortify.

Befestigung *f* **(a)** (*das Befestigen*) fastening; (*das Festmachen auch*) securing; (*von Boot*) tying up ◆ **zur ~ des Plakats ...** in order to attach the poster ...
(b) (*Vorrichtung zum Befestigen*) fastening, catch.
(c) (*das Haltbarmachen*) reinforcement; (*fig: Stärkung*) consolidation ◆ **zur ~ der Macht des ...** in order to consolidate the power of ...
(d) (*Mil*) fortification.

Befestigungs-: ~anlage *f*, **~bau** *m*, **~werk** *nt* fortification, defence.

befeuchten* *vt* to moisten; *Finger auch* to wet; *Wäsche* to damp(en) ◆ **das vom Tau befeuchtete Gras** the grass moistened by the dew.

befeuern* *vt* **(a)** (*beheizen*) to fuel. **(b)** (*Naut, Aviat*) *Wasserstraße, Untiefen* to light *or* mark with beacons; *Start- und Landebahn* to light, to mark with lights. **(c)** (*lit, fig: mit Geschossen*) to bombard. **(d)** (*geh: anspornen*) to fire with enthusiasm.

Befeuerung *f* (*Aviat, Naut*) lights *pl*, beacons *pl*.

Beffchen *nt* Geneva band.

befiedert *adj* feathered.

befiehl *imper sing of* **befehlen.**

befinden* *irreg* [1] *vr* **(a)** (*sein*) to be; (*liegen auch*) to be situated; (*esp in Maschine, Körper etc auch*) to be located ◆ **sich auf Reisen ~** to be away; **unter ihnen befanden sich einige, die ...** there were some amongst them who ...; **die Abbildung befindet sich im Katalog** the illustration can be found *or* is in the catalogue; **sich in Verwirrung/guter Laune/im Irrtum ~** to be confused/in a good mood/mistaken; **sich auf dem Weg der Besserung ~** to be on the road to recovery; **wenn man sich in schlechter Gesellschaft befindet ...** if you find yourself in bad company ...
(b) (*form: sich fühlen*) to feel ◆ **wie ~ Sie sich heute?** how are you (feeling) *or* how do you feel today?
[2] *vt* (*form: erachten*) to deem (*form*), to find ◆ **etw für nötig/angemessen/für** *or* **als gut ~** to deem *or* find sth (to be) necessary/appropriate/good; **Ihre Papiere wurden in Ordnung befunden** your papers were found to be in order; **jdn für schuldig ~** to find sb guilty; *siehe* **wiegen²**.
[3] *vi* (*geh: entscheiden*) to come to *or* make a decision, to decide (*über +acc* about, *in +dat* on) ◆ **darüber hat der Arzt zu ~/habe ich nicht zu ~** that is for the doctor/not for me to decide; **über jdn/etw ~** to pass judgement *or* reach a verdict on sb/sth.

Befinden *nt* **-s,** *no pl* **(a)** (*form: Gesundheitszustand*) (state of) health; (*eines Kranken*) condition ◆ **seelisches ~** mental state *or* condition; **wie ist Ihr ~?** (*form*) how are you (feeling)?
(b) (*geh: das Dafürhalten*) view, opinion ◆ **nach meinem ~** in my view *or* opinion; **nach eigenem ~ entscheiden** to decide according to one's own judgement.

befindlich *adj usu attr* (*form*) **(a)** (*an einem Ort*) *Gebäude, Park* situated, located; (*in Behälter*) contained ◆ **der hinter dem Hause ~e Garten** the garden (situated) behind the house; **alle in der Bibliothek ~en Bücher** all the books in the library.
(b) (*in einem Zustand*) **das im Umbau ~e Hotel** the hotel which is being renovated; **das im Umlauf ~e Geld** the money in circulation; **die in Kraft ~e Verordnung** the regulation which is in force.

Befindlichkeit *f* **-, -en** state of mind ◆ **nationale ~en** national mentalities.

befingern* *vt* (*inf*) (*betasten*) to finger ◆ **eine Sache ~** (*sl*) to deal with a matter.

beflaggen* *vt Häuser* to (be)deck *or* decorate with flags; *Schiff* to dress ◆ **die beflaggten Straßen** the flag-decked streets, the streets (be)decked *or* decorated with flags; **anläßlich seines Todes wurden alle öffentlichen Gebäude beflaggt** flags were flown on all public buildings to mark his death.

Beflaggung *f* **(a)** (*das Beflaggen*) (*von Gebäuden*) decoration with flags; (*von Schiffen*) dressing. **(b)** (*Fahnenschmuck*) flags *pl*.

beflecken* *vt* **(a)** (*lit*) to stain ◆ **er hat seinen Anzug mit Farbe befleckt** he got paint on his suit; **er hat sich** *or* **seine Hände mit Blut befleckt** (*fig*) he has blood on his hands.
(b) (*fig geh*) *Ruf, Ehre* to cast a slur on, to besmirch, to sully; *Heiligtum* to defile, to desecrate.

befleckt *adj* **(a)** stained ◆ **sein mit Blut ~er Anzug** his blood-stained suit. **(b)** *Ruf, Ehre* sullied, besmirched.

Befleckung *f siehe vt* **(a)** staining. **(b)** besmirching, sullying; defilement, desecration.

befleißen *pret* **befliß,** *ptp* **beflissen** *vr* (*old*) *siehe* **befleißigen.**

befleißigen* *vr* (*geh*) **sich einer Sache** (*gen*) **~** to cultivate sth; **sich ~, etw zu tun** to make a great effort to do sth; **sich größter** *or* **der größten Höflichkeit ~** to go out of one's way to be polite.

befliegen* *vt irreg* (*Aviat*) *Strecke* to fly, to operate (on); *Gegend* to fly over; *Raum* to fly through *or* in ◆ **eine viel beflogene Strecke** a heavily used route.

⚠ **befliß** *pret of* **befleißen.**

beflissen [1] *ptp of* **befleißen.**
[2] *adj* (*geh*) (*bemüht*) zealous, keen; (*pej: unterwürfig*) obsequious ◆ **um etw ~ sein** to be concerned for sth; **er war sehr um die Zufriedenheit seiner Gäste ~** he was very anxious *or* concerned to please his guests; **~ sein, etw zu tun** to be concerned to do sth; **ängstlich ~** anxious.

Beflissenheit *f siehe adj* zeal, keenness; obsequiousness.

beflissentlich *adv siehe* **geflissentlich.**

beflügeln* *vt* (*geh*) to inspire, to fire ◆ **die Angst beflügelte seine Schritte** (*liter*) fear winged his steps (*liter*); **der Gedanke an Erfolg beflügelte ihn** the thought of success spurred him on.

befohlen *ptp of* **befehlen.**

befolgen* *vt Vorschrift, Befehl etc* to obey, to comply with; *grammatische Regel* to follow, to obey; *Rat(schlag)* to follow, to take.

Befolgung *f siehe vt* obeying, compliance (*gen* with); following, obeying; following, taking ◆ **~ der Vorschriften** obeying the rules, compliance with the rules.

Beförderer *m* (*form*) carrier.

befördern* *vt* **(a)** *Waren, Gepäck* to transport, to carry; *Personen* to carry; *Post* to handle ◆ **etw mit der Post/per Luftpost/Bahn/Schiff ~** to send sth by post/airmail/rail/ship; to ship sth; **jdn/etw von A nach B ~** to transport *or* convey sb/sth from A to B; **jdn an die (frische) Luft** *or* **zur Tür hinaus** *or* **ins Freie ~** (*fig*) to fling *or* chuck sb out (*inf*); **jdn ins Jenseits ~** (*inf*) to bump sb off (*inf*), to do sb in (*inf*).
(b) (*dienstlich aufrücken lassen*) to promote ◆ **er wurde zum Major befördert** he was promoted to (the rank of) major.

Beförderung *f siehe vt* **(a)** transportation, carriage; carriage; handling ◆ **die ~ der Post/eines Briefes dauert drei Tage** the post/a letter takes three days (to arrive); **für die ~ von 35 Personen zugelassen** permitted to carry 35 persons; **für die ~ der Kursteilnehmer wird gesorgt** transport will be arranged for course participants; **~ zu Lande/zur Luft/per Bahn** land/air/rail transportation. **(b)** promotion.

Beförderungs-: ~bedingungen *pl* terms *pl or* conditions *pl* of carriage; **~dauer** *f* delivery time; **~kosten** *pl* transport costs *pl*; **~liste** *f* promotion list; **~mittel** *nt* means of transport; **~pflicht** *f obligation of taxis, buses etc to accept passengers*; **~steuer** *f* transport tax; **~tarif** *m* transportation *or* (*Post~*) postage charge.

befrachten* *vt Fahrzeug, Schiff* to load; (*fig geh auch*) to burden ◆ **ein schwer befrachtetes Schiff** a heavily laden ship; **seine übermäßig mit Emotionen befrachtete Rede** his speech, overladen with emotion.

Befrachter *m* **-s, -** shipper, freighter.

Befrachtung *f* loading.

befrackt *adj* in tails, tail-coated.

befragen* [1] *vt* **(a)** (*über +acc, zu, nach* about) to question; *Zeugen auch* to examine ◆ **jdn im Kreuzverhör ~** to cross-question *or* (*esp Jur*) to cross-examine sb; **auf B~** when questioned.

⚠: Informationen zur Rechtschreibreform im Anhang

(b) *(um Stellungnahme bitten)* to consult *(über +acc, nach* about*)* ◆ **jdn um Rat/nach seiner Meinung ~** to ask sb for advice/his opinion, to ask sb's advice/opinion; **jdn in einer Angelegenheit ~** to consult sb about *or* on a matter.
[2] *vr (dated)* to consult; *(sich erkundigen)* to make enquiries ◆ **sich bei jdm/etw ~** to consult sb/sth.

Befragte(r) *mf decl as adj* person asked; *(in Umfrage auch)* interviewee ◆ **alle ~n** all those asked.

Befragung *f siehe vt* **(a)** questioning; examining, examination. **(b)** consultation *(gen* with *or* of*)*. **(c)** *(Umfrage)* survey.

befranst *adj* fringed, with a fringe.

befreien* [1] *vt* **(a)** *(frei machen)* to free, to release; *Volk, Land* to liberate, to free; *(freilassen) Gefangenen, Tier, Vogel* to set free, to free ◆ **jdn aus einer schwierigen Lage ~** to rescue sb from *or* get sb out of a tricky situation.
(b) *(freistellen) (von* from*)* to excuse; *(von Militärdienst, Steuern)* to exempt; *(von Eid etc)* to absolve; *(von Pflicht auch)* to release ◆ **sich vom Religionsunterricht ~ lassen** to be excused religious instruction.
(c) *(erlösen: von Schmerz etc)* to release, to free ◆ **jdn von einer Last ~** to take a weight off sb's mind.
(d) *(reinigen) (von* of*) (von Ungeziefer etc)* to rid; *(von Schnee, Eis)* to free ◆ **seine Schuhe von Schmutz ~** to remove the dirt from one's shoes; **ein ~des Lachen** a healthy *or* an unrepressed laugh.
[2] *vr* **(a)** *(Volk, Land)* to free oneself; *(entkommen)* to escape *(von, aus* from*)* ◆ **sich aus einer schwierigen Lage ~** to get oneself out of a difficult situation.
(b) *(erleichtern)* to rid oneself *(von* of*)*, to free oneself *(von* from*)*.

Befreier(in *f***)** *m* **-s, -** liberator.

befreit *adj (erleichtert)* relieved ◆ **~ aufatmen** to heave *or* breathe a sigh of relief.

Befreiung *f siehe vt* **(a)** freeing, releasing; liberation, freeing; setting free, freeing. **(b)** excusing; exemption; absolving; releasing ◆ **um ~ von etw bitten** to ask to be excused/exempted from sth. **(c)** releasing; *(Erleichterung)* relief. **(d)** ridding; freeing.

Befreiungs-: ~bewegung *f* liberation movement; **~front** *f* liberation front; **~kampf** *m* struggle for liberation; **~krieg** *m* war of liberation; **~organisation** *f* liberation organization; **~schlag** *m (Eishockey, Ftbl)* clearance; *(fig)* coup; **~versuch** *m* escape attempt.

befremden* [1] *vt* to disconcert ◆ **es befremdet mich, daß ...** I'm rather taken aback that ...; **das befremdet mich an ihr** that (side of her) disconcerts me.
[2] *vi* to cause disconcertment.

Befremden *nt* **-s,** *no pl* disconcertment ◆ **nicht ohne ~ ...** it is with some disconcertment that ...

befremdend *adj* disconcerting.

befremdet *adj* disconcerted, taken aback.

befremdlich *adj (geh) siehe* **befremdend.**

Befremdung *f siehe* **Befremden.**

befreunden* *vr* **(a)** *(sich anfreunden)* to make *or* become friends ◆ **ich habe mich schnell mit ihm befreundet** I quickly made friends with him, he and I quickly became friends; **die beiden haben sich (miteinander) befreundet** the pair made *or* became friends.
(b) *(fig: mit einem Gedanken etc)* to get used to, to get *or* grow accustomed to.

befreundet *adj* **wir/sie sind schon lange (miteinander) ~** we/they have been friends *or* friendly for a long time; **gut** *or* **eng ~ sein** to be good *or* close friends; **alle ~en Familien** all the families we etc are friendly with; **ein uns ~er Staat** a friendly nation; **das ~e Ausland** friendly (foreign) countries; **ein uns ~er Arzt** a doctor (who is a) friend of ours; **~e Zahlen** *(Math)* amicable numbers.

befrieden* *vt (geh)* to pacify.

befriedigen* [1] *vt* to satisfy; *Gläubiger auch* to pay; *Hunger, Durst, Appetit auch* to assuage *(form)*; *Gelüste auch* to gratify; *Ansprüche, Forderungen, Verlangen auch* to meet ◆ **jdn (sexuell) ~** to satisfy sb (sexually); **er ist leicht/schwer zu ~** he's easily/not easily satisfied, he's easy/hard to satisfy.
[2] *vi* to be satisfactory ◆ **Ihre Leistung hat nicht befriedigt** your performance was unsatisfactory.
[3] *vr* **sich (selbst) ~** to masturbate.

befriedigend *adj* satisfactory; *Verhältnisse, Leistung, Arbeit, Antwort auch* adequate; *Gefühl* satisfying; *Lösung auch* acceptable; *(Schulnote)* fair ◆ **nicht ~ sein** to be unsatisfactory/inadequate/unacceptable.

befriedigt *adj* satisfied, contented ◆ **bist du nun endlich ~?** are you satisfied at last?; **er lächelte ~** he smiled with satisfaction.

Befriedigung *f* **(a)** *siehe vt* satisfaction, satisfying; payment; assuagement *(form)*; gratification; meeting ◆ **sexuelle ~** sexual satisfaction; **zur ~ deiner Neugier ...** to satisfy your curiosity ... **(b)** *(Genugtuung)* satisfaction ◆ **seine ~ in etw** *(dat)* **suchen** to look for *or* seek satisfaction in sth.

Befriedung *f (geh)* pacification.

befristen* *vt* to limit, to restrict *(auf +acc* to*)*; *Aufgabe, Projekt* to put a time limit on.

befristet *adj Genehmigung, Visum* restricted, limited *(auf +acc* to*)*; *Arbeitsverhältnis, Anstellung* temporary ◆ **mein Arbeitsverhältnis ist auf zwei Jahre ~** my appointment is limited *or* restricted to two years; **~ sein/auf zwei Jahre ~ sein** *(Paß etc)* to be valid for a limited time/for two years.

Befristung *f* limitation, restriction *(auf +acc* to*)*.

befruchten* *vt* **(a)** *(lit) Eizelle* to fertilize; *(schwängern auch)* to impregnate *(form)*; *Blüte* to pollinate ◆ **künstlich ~** to inseminate artificially. **(b)** *(fig: fruchtbar machen)* to make fertile. **(c)** *(fig: geistig anregen)* to stimulate, to have a stimulating effect on.

Befruchtung *f siehe vt (a)* fertilization; impregnation; pollination ◆ **künstliche ~** artificial insemination.

befugen* *vt (form)* to authorize ◆ **wer hat Sie dazu befugt?** who authorized you to do that?

Befugnis *f (form)* authority *no pl*; *(Erlaubnis)* authorization *no pl* ◆ **eine ~ erhalten/erteilen** to receive/give authorization *or* authority; **besondere ~se erhalten** to receive *or* be given special authority; **Zutritt ohne ~ nicht gestattet** no entry to unauthorized persons.

befugt *adj (form)* **~ sein(, etw zu tun)** to have the authority *or (ermächtigt worden sein)* be authorized (to do sth).

befühlen* *vt* to feel; *(hinstreichen über auch)* to run one's hands over.

befummeln* *vt (inf) (betasten)* to paw *(inf)*.

Befund *m* **-(e)s, -e** results *pl*, findings *pl* ◆ **der ~ war positiv/negativ** *(Med)* the results were positive/negative; **ohne ~** *(Med)* (results) negative.

befürchten* *vt* to fear, to be afraid of ◆ **ich befürchte das Schlimmste** I fear the worst; **es ist zu ~, daß ...** it is (to be) feared that ...; **dabei sind Komplikationen/ist gar nichts zu ~** it is feared there may be complications/there's nothing to fear with that.

Befürchtung *f* fear *usu pl* ◆ **~en** *or* **die ~ haben, daß ...** to fear *or* be afraid that ...; **die schlimmsten ~en haben** *or* **hegen** *(geh)* to fear the worst.

▼ **befürworten*** *vt* to approve.

Befürworter(in *f***)** *m* **-s, -** supporter; *(von Idee auch)* advocate.

Befürwortung *f* approval, support.

begab *pret of* **begeben.**

begaben* *vt usu pass (liter)* to endow ◆ **mit etw begabt sein** to be endowed with sth.

begabt *adj* talented; *(esp geistig, musisch auch)* gifted ◆ **für etw ~ sein** to be talented at sth; *für Musik, Kunst etc auch* to have a gift for sth.

Begabten-: ~auslese *f* selection of the most gifted *or* talented people; **~förderung** *f* (educational) grant.

Begabte(r) *mf decl as adj* talented *or* gifted person/man/woman *etc.*

Begabung *f* **(a)** *(Anlage)* talent; *(geistig, musisch auch)* gift ◆ **er hat eine ~ dafür, immer das Falsche zu sagen** he has a gift for *or* a knack of always saying the wrong thing; **er hat ~ zum Lehrer** he has a gift for teaching; **mangelnde ~** a lack of talent, insufficient talent.
(b) *(begabter Mensch)* talented person ◆ **sie ist eine musikalische ~** she has a talent for music.

begaffen* *vt (pej inf)* to gape *or* goggle at *(inf)*.

begangen *ptp of* **begehen.**

begann *pret of* **beginnen.**

begasen* *vt (Agr)* to gas.

begatten* *(esp Zool)* [1] *vt* to mate *or* copulate with; *(geh, hum)* to copulate with.
[2] *vr* to mate, to copulate; *(geh, hum)* to copulate.

Begattung *f (esp Zool)* mating, copulation; *(geh, hum)* copulation.

Begattungs- *in cpds* mating; **~organe** *pl* reproductive organs *pl.*

begaunern* *vt* to swindle, to cheat.

begeben* *irreg* [1] *vr* **(a)** *(geh: gehen)* to betake oneself *(liter)*, to go ◆ **sich nach Hause** *or* **auf den Heimweg ~** to wend *(liter) or* make one's way home; **sich auf eine Reise ~** to undertake a journey; **sich zu Bett/zur Ruhe ~** to repair to one's bed *(liter)*/to retire; **sich an seinen Platz ~** to take one's place; **sich in ärztliche Behandlung ~** to undergo medical treatment; **sich an die Arbeit ~** to commence work.
(b) *(sich einer Sache aussetzen)* **sich in Gefahr ~** to expose oneself to *or* put oneself in danger; **sich in jds Schutz** *(acc)* **~** to place oneself under sb's protection; *siehe* **Gefahr.**
(c) *(old liter: geschehen)* to come to pass *(old liter)* ◆ **es begab sich aber zu der Zeit, daß ...** *(Bibl)* and it came to pass at that time that ...; **es hatte sich vieles ~** many things had happened.
(d) *(geh: aufgeben) +gen* to relinquish, to renounce.
[2] *vt (Fin)* to issue.

Begebenheit *f (geh)*, **Begebnis** *nt (old)* occurrence, event.

begegnen* *vi aux sein +dat* **(a)** *(treffen)* to meet ◆ **sich** *or* **einander** *(geh)* **~** to meet; **ihre Augen** *or* **Blicke begegneten sich** their eyes met; **unsere Wünsche ~ sich** *(liter)* our wishes coincide *(form)*; **sie ~ sich in dem Wunsch/in der Ansicht, ...** they are united in the wish/opinion ... *(form)*.
(b) *(stoßen auf)* to encounter; *Schwierigkeiten auch* to run into ◆ **dieses Wort wird uns später noch einmal ~** we will encounter this word again later.
(c) *(widerfahren)* **jdm ist etw begegnet** sth has happened to sb; **es war mir schon einmal begegnet, daß ...** it had happened to me once already that ...
(d) *(geh: behandeln)* to treat ◆ **man begegnete mir nur mit Spott** I only met with derision.
(e) *(geh) (entgegentreten) einer Krankheit, Seuche, der Not* to combat; *einem Übel, Angriff, Unrecht auch* to oppose, to resist; *(überwinden) einer Gefahr, Schwierigkeiten, dem Schicksal* to confront, to meet, to face; *(reagieren auf) einem Wunsch, Vorschlag, einer Ansicht* to meet, to respond to ◆ **man begegnete seinen Vorschlägen mit Zurückhaltung** his suggestions met with reserve.
(f) *(geh: einwenden gegen) Behauptungen etc* to counter.

Begegnung *f* **(a)** *(Treffen)* meeting, encounter; *(fig: mit Idee etc)* encounter ◆ **bei der ersten/letzten ~ der beiden** at the first/last meeting between the two; **ein Ort internationaler ~** an international meeting place.
(b) *(Sport)* encounter, match ◆ **die ~ Spanien-Italien findet nächsten Monat statt** Spain and Italy meet next month.

Begegnungsstätte *f* meeting place.

➤ SPRACHE AKTIV: **befürworten** → 40.1, 40.2

begehen* *vt irreg* (a) (*verüben*) *Selbstmord, Ehebruch, Sünde* to commit; *Verbrechen auch* to perpetrate (*form*); *Fehler* to make ◆ **eine Indiskretion (gegenüber jdm) ~** to be indiscreet (about sb); **einen Mord an jdm ~** to murder sb; **eine Dummheit/Taktlosigkeit/Unvorsichtigkeit ~** to do something stupid/tactless/careless; **die Dummheit/Taktlosigkeit/Unvorsichtigkeit ~, ...** to be so stupid/tactless/careless as to ...; **an jdm ein Unrecht ~** to wrong sb, to be unjust to sb; **Verrat an jdm/etw ~** to betray sb/sth; **ein oft begangener Fehler** a frequent mistake.
(b) (*entlanggehen*) *Weg* to use ◆ **der Weg wird viel begangen** the path is used a lot, it is a much-used path; **„B~ der Brücke auf eigene Gefahr"** "persons using this bridge do so at their own risk".
(c) (*abschreiten*) *Bahnstrecke, Felder* to inspect (on foot).
(d) (*geh: feiern*) to celebrate; (*Eccl*) *Fest auch* to observe.

Begehr *m or nt* **-s,** *no pl* (*old*) wish, desire ◆ **er fragte nach meinem ~** he inquired after my wishes.

begehren* *vt* (a) (*liter: Verlangen haben nach*) to desire, to crave; *Frau* to desire; *Gegenstände, Besitz eines andern* to covet ◆ **ein Mädchen zur Frau ~** to desire a girl's hand in marriage; **sie bekam die von ihr so begehrte Rolle** she was given the role she desired so much; **du sollst nicht ~ ...** (*Bibl*) thou shalt not covet ...; *siehe* **begehrt.**
(b) (*old: wollen*) to desire.

Begehren *nt* **-s,** (*rare*) **-** (a) (*geh: Verlangen*) desire (*nach* for) ◆ **das ~ fühlen** *or* **haben, etw zu tun** to feel the *or* a desire to do sth; **heißes ~** burning desire.
(b) (*old: Wunsch, Forderung*) wish ◆ **nach jds ~ fragen** to inquire after sb's wishes, to ask what sb wants; **auf mein ~ (hin)** at my request.

begehrenswert *adj* desirable, attractive; *Frau* desirable.

begehrlich *adj* (*geh*) covetous.

Begehrlichkeit *f* (*geh*) covetousness.

begehrt *adj* much *or* very sought-after; *Partner etc auch, Ferienziel* popular; *Junggeselle* eligible; *Posten auch* desirable.

Begehung *f* (a) (*form*) (*einer Sünde*) committing; (*eines Verbrechens auch*) perpetrating (*form*) ◆ **nach ~ des Verbrechens** after committing *etc* the crime. (b) (*das Abschreiten*) inspection (on foot).

begeifern* *vt* (*fig pej*) to run down, to slam (*inf*); (*lit*) to dribble on.

begeistern* [1] *vt jdn* to fill with enthusiasm; (*inspirieren*) to inspire ◆ **er begeistert alle durch sein** *or* **mit seinem Talent** everybody is enthusiastic about his talent; **er ist für nichts zu ~** he's never enthusiastic about anything.
[2] *vr* to be *or* feel enthusiastic (*an +dat, für* about).

begeisternd *adj* inspiring; *Rede auch* stirring.

▼ **begeistert** *adj* enthusiastic (*von* about).

Begeisterung *f, no pl* enthusiasm (*über +acc* about, *für* for) ◆ **etw mit ~ tun** to do sth enthusiastically *or* with enthusiasm; **in ~ geraten** to become enthusiastic *or* be filled with enthusiasm; **sich in ~ reden** to get carried away with what one is saying.

Begeisterungs-: b~fähig *adj* able to get enthusiastic; *Publikum etc* quick to show one's enthusiasm; **sie ist zwar b~fähig, aber ...** her enthusiasm is easily aroused but ...; **~fähigkeit** *f* capacity for enthusiasm; **ein Pessimist, dem jegliche ~fähigkeit abgeht** a pessimist who never shows enthusiasm for anything; **~sturm** *m* storm of enthusiasm; **~taumel** *m* frenzy of enthusiasm.

Begier *f* **-,** *no pl* (*liter*), **Begierde** *f* **-, -n** (*geh*) desire (*nach* for); (*Sehnsucht*) longing, yearning ◆ **vor ~ brennen, etw zu tun** to be longing *or* burning to do sth.

begierig *adj* (*voll Verlangen*) hungry, greedy; (*gespannt*) eager, keen; *Leser* avid ◆ **auf etw** (*acc*) **~ sein** to be eager for sth; **~ (darauf) sein, etw zu tun** to be eager *or* keen to do sth.

begießen* *vt irreg* (a) (*mit Wasser*) to pour water on; *Blumen, Beet* to water; (*mit Fett*) *Braten etc* to baste; *siehe* **begossen.** (b) (*fig inf*) *freudiges Ereignis, Vereinbarung* to celebrate ◆ **das muß begossen werden!** that calls for a drink!

beging *pret of* **begehen.**

Beginn *m* **-(e)s,** *no pl* beginning, start ◆ **am** *or* **bei** *or* **zu ~** at the beginning; **mit ~ der Ferien** at the beginning *or* start of the holidays, when the holidays begin *or* start; **gleich zu ~** right at the beginning *or* start, at the very beginning *or* start.

▼ **beginnen** *pret* **begann,** *ptp* **begonnen** [1] *vi* to start, to begin, to commence (*form*); (*in Beruf etc auch*) to start off ◆ **mit einer Arbeit ~** to start *or* begin (to do) a job; **mit der Arbeit ~** to start *or* begin work; **es beginnt zu regnen** it's starting *or* beginning to rain; **er hat als Lehrling/mit nichts begonnen** he started (off) *or* began as an apprentice/with nothing.
[2] *vt* (a) (*anfangen*) to start, to begin; *Gespräch, Verhandlungen, Rede auch* to open ◆ **~, etw zu tun** to start *or* begin to do sth, to start doing sth.
(b) (*anpacken*) *Aufgabe etc* to tackle, to go *or* set about.
(c) (*geh: unternehmen*) to do ◆ **ich wußte nicht, was ich ~ sollte** I didn't know what to do.

Beginnen *nt* **-s,** *no pl* (*geh: Vorhaben*) enterprise, plan, scheme.

beginnend *adj attr* incipient (*form*) ◆ **eine ~e Erkältung** the beginnings of a cold; **bei ~er Dämmerung/Nacht** at dusk/nightfall; **im ~en 19. Jahrhundert** in the early 19th century.

beglänzen* *vt* (*poet*) to light up, to illumine (*poet*).

beglaubigen* *vt* (a) *Testament, Unterschrift* to witness; *Zeugnisabschrift* to authenticate; *Echtheit* to attest (to) ◆ **etw behördlich/notariell ~ lassen** to have sth witnessed *etc* officially/by a notary. (b) *Gesandten, Botschafter* to accredit (*bei* to).

Beglaubigung *f siehe vt* (a) witnessing; authentication; attestation. (b) accrediting, accreditation (*form*).

Beglaubigungsschreiben *nt* credentials *pl*.

▼ **begleichen*** *vt irreg* (*lit: bezahlen*) *Rechnung, Zeche* to settle, to pay; *Schulden auch* to discharge (*form*); (*fig*) *Schuld* to pay (off), to discharge ◆ **mit Ihnen habe ich noch eine Rechnung zu ~** (*fig*) I've a score to settle with you.

▼ **Begleichung** *f siehe vt* settlement, payment; discharging ◆ **vollständige/teilweise ~** payment in full/part payment.

Begleit-: ~adresse *f siehe* **~schein; ~brief** *m* covering letter.

begleiten* *vt* (a) to accompany; (*zu Veranstaltung auch*) to go/come with; (*zum Schutz auch*) to escort; *esp Schiff auch* to escort, to convoy ◆ **er wurde stets von seinem Hund begleitet** his dog always went everywhere with him.
(b) (*fig*) to accompany; (*Glück, Erfolg auch*) to attend ◆ **ein paar ~de Worte** a few accompanying words; **meine Wünsche ~ Sie** my best wishes go with you; **~de Umstände** attendant *or* accompanying circumstances (*form*).
(c) (*Mus*) to accompany (*an or auf +dat* on).

Begleiter(in *f*) *m* **-s, -** (a) companion; (*zum Schutz*) escort; (*von Reisenden*) courier ◆ **ständiger ~** constant companion. (b) (*Mus*) accompanist.

Begleit-: ~erscheinung *f* concomitant (*form*); (*Med*) side effect; **ist Jugendkriminalität eine ~erscheinung der Wohlstandsgesellschaft?** does juvenile delinquency go hand-in-hand with an affluent society?; **~flugzeug** *nt* escort plane; **~instrument** *nt* accompanying instrument; **~musik** *f* accompaniment; (*in Film etc*) incidental music; **~papiere** *pl* (*Comm*) accompanying documents *pl*; **~person** *f* escort; **die ~person eines Jugendlichen** the person accompanying a minor; **~personal** *nt* escort; **~schein** *m* dispatch note; **~schiff** *nt* (*Mil*) escort (ship); **~schreiben** *nt* covering letter; (*für Waren auch*) advice note; **~text** *m* (accompanying) text; **~umstände** *pl* attendant circumstances *pl*.

Begleitung *f* (a) *no pl* company ◆ **er bot ihr seine ~ an** he offered to accompany *or* (*zum Schutz auch*) escort her; **in ~ seines Vaters/in Peters ~** accompanied by his father/Peter; **ich bin in ~ hier** I'm with someone.
(b) (*Begleiter*) companion; (*zum Schutz*) escort; (*Gefolge*) entourage, retinue ◆ **ohne ~** unaccompanied.
(c) (*Mus*) (*Begleitmusik*) accompaniment; (*das Begleiten auch*) accompanying; (*Begleitstimme*) harmony ◆ **ohne ~ spielen** to play unaccompanied.

beglotzen* *vt* (*inf*) to goggle *or* gawp *or* gape at (*all inf*).

beglücken* *vt* **jdn ~** to make sb happy; **er hat uns gestern mit seinem Besuch beglückt** (*iro*) he honoured us with a visit yesterday; **Casanova hat Tausende von Frauen beglückt** (*hum*) Casanova bestowed his favours upon thousands of women; **ein ~des Gefühl/Erlebnis** a cheering feeling/experience; **er ist sehr beglückt darüber** he's very happy *or* pleased about it; **beglückt lächeln** to smile happily.

Beglücker *m* **-s, -** (*liter, iro*) benefactor ◆ **er fühlt sich als ~ aller Frauen** (*hum*) he thinks he's God's gift to women.

beglückwünschen* *vt* to congratulate, to offer one's congratulations (*form*) (*zu* on) ◆ **laß dich ~!** congratulations!

begnaden* *vt* (*liter*) to bless (*liter*), to endow ◆ **ein begnadeter Künstler/Musiker** a gifted artist/musician.

begnadigen* *vt* to reprieve; (*Strafe erlassen*) to pardon.

Begnadigung *f siehe vt* reprieve; pardon ◆ **um (jds) ~ ersuchen** to seek a reprieve (for sb).

Begnadigungs-: ~gesuch *nt* plea for (a) reprieve; **~recht** *nt* right of reprieve.

begnügen* *vr* **sich mit etw ~** to be content *or* satisfied with sth, to content oneself with sth; **sich damit ~, etw zu tun** to be content *or* satisfied with doing sth *or* to do sth, to content oneself with doing sth; **damit begnüge ich mich nicht** that doesn't satisfy me, I'm not satisfied with that.

Begonie [-niə] *f* begonia.

begonnen *ptp of* **beginnen.**

begossen [1] *ptp of* **begießen.**
[2] *adj* **er stand da wie ein ~er Pudel** (*inf*) he looked that small, he looked so sheepish.

begraben* *vt irreg* (a) (*beerdigen*) to bury ◆ **dort möchte ich nicht ~ sein** (*inf*) I wouldn't like to be stuck in that hole (*inf*); **der kann sich ~ lassen** (*inf*) he is worse than useless; **damit kannst du dich ~ lassen** (*inf*) you can stuff that (*sl*); *siehe* **Hund.**
(b) (*verschütten*) to bury ◆ **beim Einsturz begrub das Gebäude alle Bewohner unter sich** when the building collapsed all the residents were buried.
(c) (*aufgeben*) *Hoffnung, Wunsch* to abandon, to relinquish; (*beenden*) *Streit, Angelegenheit, Feindschaft* to end ◆ **ein längst ~er Wunsch** a long-abandoned wish; **diese Angelegenheit ist längst ~** this matter was over (and done with) long ago.

Begräbnis *nt* burial; (*~feier*) funeral.

Begräbnis-: ~kosten *pl* funeral costs *pl*; **~stätte** *f* (*geh*) burial place.

begradigen* *vt* to straighten.

Begradigung *f* straightening.

begrast *adj* grassy, grass-covered.

begreifbar *adj* conceivable.

begreifen* *irreg* [1] *vt* (a) (*verstehen*) to understand; *Aufgabe, Problem(stellung), Zusammenhang auch* to grasp, to comprehend; *jdn, jds Handlung or Haltung auch* to comprehend; *Sinn, Notwendigkeit,* (*Schwierigkeit einer*) *Lage auch* to see, to appreciate ◆ **~, daß ...** (*einsehen*) to realize that ...; **er begriff nicht, worum es ging** he didn't understand *or* comprehend what it was about; **hast du mich begriffen?** did you understand what I said?; **es ist kaum zu ~** it's almost incomprehensible; **es läßt sich leicht ~, daß ...** it's easy to understand that ...; **wie kann man Gott/die Unendlichkeit ~?** how can one

comprehend God/infinity?; **ich begreife mich selbst nicht** I don't understand myself.
(b) (*auffassen, interpretieren*) to view, to see.
(c) (*geh: einschließen*) **etw in sich** (*dat*) ~ to encompass *or* include sth; *siehe auch* **begriffen.**
(d) (*dial: anfassen*) to touch.
2 *vi* to understand, to comprehend ◆ **leicht/schnell** ~ to be quick on the uptake; **schwer/langsam** ~ to be slow on the uptake.
3 *vr* to be understandable ◆ **eine solche Tat läßt sich nicht leicht** ~ such an action cannot be easily understood.
begreiflich *adj* understandable ◆ **es wird mir allmählich ~, warum** ... I'm beginning to understand why ...; **ich kann mich ihm nicht ~ machen** I can't make myself clear to him; **ich habe ihm das ~ gemacht** I've made it clear to him.
begreiflicherweise *adv* understandably.
begrenzen* *vt* **(a)** (*Grenze sein von*) to mark *or* form the boundary of *no pass*; *Horizont* to mark; *Straße etc* to line ◆ **das Gebiet wird durch** *or* **von einem Wald begrenzt** a forest marks *or* forms the boundary of the area. **(b)** (*beschränken*) to restrict, to limit (*auf +acc* to).
begrenzt *adj* (*beschränkt*) restricted, limited; (*geistig beschränkt*) limited ◆ **meine Aufenthaltsdauer ist nicht zeitlich ~** there's no time limit on (the length of) my stay; **eine genau ~e Aufgabe** a clearly defined task.
Begrenztheit *f, no pl* (*von Möglichkeiten, Talent etc*) limitedness; (*von Menschen*) limitations *pl.*
Begrenzung *f* **(a)** (*das Begrenzen*) (*von Gebiet, Straße etc*) demarcation; (*von Horizont*) marking; (*von Geschwindigkeit, Redezeit*) restriction. **(b)** (*Grenze*) boundary.
begriff *pret of* **begreifen.**
Begriff *m* **-(e)s, -e (a)** (*objektiv: Bedeutungsgehalt*) concept; (*Terminus*) term ◆ **etw in ~en ausdrücken** *or* **in ~e fassen** to put sth into words; **in neuen ~en denken** to think in new terms; **sein Name ist mir ein/kein ~** his name means something/doesn't mean anything to me; **sein Name ist in aller Welt ein ~** his name is known all over the world; **ein ~ für Qualität!** a byword for quality.
(b) (*subjektiv: Vorstellung, Eindruck*) idea ◆ **sein ~ von** *or* **der Freiheit** his idea *or* conception of freedom; **falsche ~e von etw haben** to have the wrong ideas about sth; **sich** (*dat*) **einen ~ von etw machen** to imagine sth; **du machst dir keinen ~ (davon)** (*inf*) you've no idea (about it) (*inf*); **das geht über meine ~e** that's beyond me; **es war über alle ~e schön** it was incredibly beautiful; **einen hohen ~ von jdm/etw haben** to have a high opinion of sb/sth; **nach unseren heutigen ~en** by today's standards; **nach menschlichen ~en** in human terms; **für meine ~e** in my opinion.
(c) im ~ sein *or* **stehen** (*form*), **etw zu tun** to be on the point of doing sth, to be about to do sth.
(d) schwer *or* **langsam/schnell von ~ sein** (*inf*) to be slow/quick on the uptake; **sei doch nicht so schwer von ~!** (*inf*) don't be so dense (*inf*).
begriffen 1 *ptp of* **begreifen.**
2 *adj* : **in etw** (*dat*) **~ sein** (*form*) to be in the process of doing sth; **ein noch in der Entwicklung ~er Plan** a plan still in the process of being developed.
begrifflich *adj* **(a)** *attr* (*bedeutungsmäßig*) conceptual ◆ **~e Klärung** clarification of one's terms; **~ bestimmen** to define (in clear terms); **~ ordnen** to arrange according to conceptual groups. **(b)** (*gedanklich, abstrakt*) abstract. **etw ~ erfassen** to understand sth in the abstract.
Begriffs-: ~bestimmung *f* definition; **~bildung** *f* formation of a concept/concepts; **~inhalt** *m* meaning; (*in der Logik*) connotation; **b~mäßig** *adj* conceptual; **b~stutzig, b~stützig** (*Aus*) *adj* (*inf*) dense (*inf*); **~stutzigkeit** *f* (*inf*) denseness; **~vermögen** *nt* understanding; **das ging über ihr ~vermögen** that was beyond her grasp *or* understanding; **~verwirrung** *f* confusion of concepts/terms; **~welt** *f* (*einer Person*) conceptual range.
begründen* *vt* **(a)** (*Gründe anführen für*) to give reasons for; (*rechtfertigend*) *Forderung, Meinung, Ansicht* to justify; *Verhalten* to account for; *Verdacht, Behauptung* to substantiate ◆ **wie** *or* **womit begründete er seine Ablehnung?** how did he account for *or* justify his refusal?, what reason(s) did he give for his refusal?; **etw eingehend/näher ~** to give detailed/specific reasons for sth; **ein ~der Satz** (*Gram*) a causal clause; *siehe* **begründet.**
(b) (*beginnen, gründen*) to establish; *Schule, Verein, Geschäft auch* to found; *Hausstand* to set up.
Begründer *m* founder.
begründet *adj* well-founded; (*berechtigt*) justified; (*bewiesen*) *Tatsache etc* proven ◆ **es besteht ~e/keine ~e Hoffnung, daß** ... there is reason/no reason to hope that ...; **das halte ich für nicht ~** I think that's unfounded/unjustified; **sachlich ~** founded on fact; **etw liegt** *or* **ist in etw** (*dat*) **~** sth has its roots in sth.
▼ **Begründung** *f* **(a)** reason (*für, gen* for), grounds *pl* (*für, gen* for); (*von Anklage, Behauptung etc*) grounds *pl* (*gen* for) ◆ **etwas zur** *or* **als ~ sagen** to say something in explanation. **(b)** (*Gründung*) establishment; (*von Schule, Verein, Geschäft auch*) foundation; (*von Hausstand*) setting up.
Begründungssatz *m* (*Gram*) causal clause.
begrünen* *vt Hinterhöfe, Plätze* to cover with greenery, to landscape.
Begrünung *f* planting with trees and grass, landscaping.
▼ **begrüßen*** *vt* **(a)** to greet; (*als Gastgeber auch*) to welcome ◆ **jdn herzlich ~** to greet sb heartily, to give sb a hearty welcome; **es ist mir eine große Ehre, Sie bei mir ~ zu dürfen** (*form*) it's a great honour to (be able to) welcome you here; **wir würden uns freuen, Sie bei uns ~ zu dürfen** (*form*) we would be delighted to have the pleasure of your company (*form*).
▼ **(b)** (*gut finden*) *Kritik, Entschluß etc* to welcome; (*esp iro, form*) to appreciate ◆ **es ist zu ~, daß** ... it's a good thing that ...
(c) (*Sw: um Erlaubnis fragen*) to ask (*um* for, *wegen* about).
begrüßenswert *adj* welcome ◆ **es wäre ~, wenn** ... it would be desirable if ...
Begrüßung *f* greeting; (*der Gäste*) (*das Begrüßen*) welcoming; (*Zeremonie*) welcome ◆ **er nickte zur ~ mit dem Kopf** he nodded his head in greeting; **jdm einen Blumenstrauß zur ~ überreichen** to welcome sb with a bouquet of flowers; **jdm die Hand zur ~ reichen** to hold out one's hand to sb in welcome.
Begrüßungs-: ~ansprache *f* welcoming speech; **⚠~kuß** *m* welcoming kiss; **~trank** *m* welcoming drink.
begucken* *vt* (*inf*) to look at ◆ **laß dich mal ~** let's (have *or* take a) look at you!
begünstigen* *vt* **(a)** (*förderlich sein für*) to favour; *Wachstum, Handel* to encourage; *Pläne, Beziehungen* to further; (*Jur*) to aid and abet ◆ **vom Schicksal begünstigt** smiled upon by fate; **durch die Dunkelheit begünstigt** assisted by the darkness. **(b)** (*bevorzugen*) **jdn ~** to favour sb; **von jdm begünstigt werden** to be favoured *or* shown favour by sb.
Begünstigung *f* **(a)** (*Jur*) aiding and abetting ◆ **persönliche ~** aiding and abetting; **sachliche ~** (acting as an) accessory; **~ im Amt** connivance.
(b) (*Bevorzugung*) preferential treatment; (*Vorteil*) advantage.
(c) (*Förderung*) favouring; (*von Wachstum, Handel*) encouragement; (*von Plänen, Beziehungen*) furthering.
begut|achten* *vt* (*beurteilen, Gutachten abgeben*) to give expert advice about; *Kunstwerk, Stipendiaten* to examine; *Projekte, Leistung* to judge; *Gelände, Haus* to survey; (*inf: ansehen*) to have *or* take a look at ◆ **etw ~ lassen** to get *or* obtain expert advice about sth.
Begut|achter *m* **-s, -** expert; (*von Haus, Gelände*) surveyor.
Begut|achtung *f* (expert) assessment; (*von Haus, Gelände*) survey; (*das Begutachten*) surveying ◆ **psychologische/graphologische** *etc* **~** (expert) psychological/graphological *etc* assessment.
begütert *adj* **(a)** (*dated: Landgüter besitzend*) landed *attr*, propertied. **(b)** (*reich*) wealthy, affluent ◆ **die ~e Klasse/Schicht** the rich *pl.*
begütigen* *vt* to pacify, to placate, to appease.
begütigend *adj Worte etc* soothing ◆ **~ auf jdn einreden** to calm sb down.
behaart *adj* hairy, hirsute ◆ **stark/dicht/schwarz ~** very hairy/(thickly) covered with hair/covered with black hair.
Behaarung *f* covering of hair, hairs *pl* (*+gen, an +dat* on).
behäbig *adj* **(a)** *Mensch* portly; (*phlegmatisch, geruhsam*) stolid; (*fig*) *Leben, Möbel, Auto* comfortable; *Architektur* solid; *Sprache, Ton* complacent ◆ **(breit und) ~ in der Ecke sitzen** to sit on one's fat backside (*inf*). **(b)** (*old liter, Sw: wohlhabend*) well-to-do, affluent.
Behäbigkeit *f, no pl siehe adj (a)* portliness; stolidity; comfortableness; solidness; complacency.
behacken* *vt* **(a)** (*mit der Hacke*) to hoe. **(b)** (*Vogel*) to peck at. **(c)** (*inf: betrügen*) to do (*um* out of) (*inf*).
behaftet *adj*: **mit etw ~ sein** (*mit Krankheit etc*) to be afflicted with sth; (*mit Fehlern/Vorurteilen etc*) to be full of sth; (*mit einer schweren Last/Sorgen/Schulden etc*) to be encumbered with sth; (*mit Makel*) to be tainted with sth.
Behagen *nt* **-s,** *no pl* contentment ◆ **mit sichtlichem ~** with visible *or* obvious pleasure; **mit ~ essen** to eat with relish; **er findet sein ~ daran** *or* **darin** it gives him pleasure.
behagen* *vi* **etw behagt jdm** sth pleases sb, sb likes sth; **etw behagt jdm nicht** (*nicht gefallen*) sth doesn't please sb, sb doesn't like sth; (*beunruhigen*) sb feels uneasy about sth; **er behagt ihr nicht** she doesn't like him.
behaglich *adj* cosy; (*heimelig auch*) snug, homely; (*bequem*) comfortable; (*zufrieden*) contented ◆ **~ warm** comfortably warm; **es sich** (*dat*) **~ machen** to make oneself comfortable; **~ in der Sonne sitzen** to sit comfortably in the sun.
Behaglichkeit *f, no pl siehe adj* cosiness; snugness, homeliness; comfortableness; contentment ◆ **es stört meine ~** it disturbs my sense of comfort.
behalten* *vt irreg* **(a)** (*nicht weggeben, nicht zurückgeben*) to keep.
(b) (*lassen, wo es ist*) to keep ◆ **~ Sie (doch) Platz!** please don't get up!; **den Hut auf dem Kopf ~** to keep one's hat on; **jdn an der Hand ~** to keep hold of sb's hand; **der Kranke kann nichts bei sich ~** the patient can't keep anything down; *siehe* **Auge.**
(c) (*nicht verlieren*) to keep; *Wert auch* to retain ◆ **die Ruhe/Nerven ~** to keep one's cool/nerve; **wenn wir solches Wetter ~** if this weather lasts; *siehe* **Fassung, Kopf, Zügel** *etc.*
(d) (*nicht vergessen*) to remember ◆ **im Gedächtnis/im Kopf ~** to remember, to keep in one's head; **er behielt die Melodie im Ohr** he kept the tune in his head; **ich habe die Zahl/seine Adresse nicht ~** I've forgotten the number/his address.
(e) (*nicht weitersagen*) **etw für sich ~** to keep sth to oneself.
(f) (*nicht weggehen lassen*) to keep; *Mitarbeiter auch* to keep on ◆ **jdn bei sich ~** to keep sb with one; **einen Gast zum Abendbrot bei sich ~** to invite a guest to stay on to supper.
(g) (*nicht aufgeben*) *Stellung, Namen, Staatsangehörigkeit* to keep ◆ **sie muß immer ihren Willen ~** she always has to have her own way; *siehe* **lieb.**
(h) (*aufbewahren, versorgen*) *Kinder, Katze, Gegenstand* to look after; (*nicht wegwerfen*) *Briefe etc* to keep ◆ **jdn/etw in guter/schlechter Erinnerung ~** to have happy/unhappy memories of sb/sth; *siehe* **Andenken.**
(i) (*zurückbehalten, nicht loswerden*) to be left with; *Schock, Schaden* to suffer

◆ **vom Unfall hat er ein steifes Knie ~** after the accident he was left with a stiff knee.

Behälter *m* **-s, -** **(a)** container, receptacle (*form*). **(b)** (*Container*) container.

Behälterschiff *nt* container ship.

behämmern* *vt* (*lit, fig*) to hammer.

behämmert *adj* (*sl*) screwy (*sl*).

behandeln* *vt* **(a)** *Material, Stoff, Materie* to treat.
(b) *Thema, Frage, Problem, Antrag* to deal with.
(c) (*in bestimmter Weise umgehen mit*) to treat; (*verfahren mit*) to handle ◆ **jdn/etw gut/schlecht ~** to treat sb/sth well/badly; **er weiß, wie man Kinder/die Maschine ~ muß** he knows how to handle children/the machine; **eine Angelegenheit diskret ~** to treat *or* handle a matter with discretion; **jdn/etw ungeschickt ~** to handle sb/sth clumsily.
(d) (*ärztlich*) *Patienten, Krankheit* to treat; *Zähne* to attend to ◆ **jdn/etw operativ ~** to operate on sb/sth; **der ~de Arzt** the doctor in attendance.

Behandlung *f siehe vt* **(a)** treatment.
(b) treatment ◆ **wir sind jetzt bei der ~ dieses Themas** we are now dealing with this theme; **um schnelle ~ des Antrags wird gebeten** please deal with the application as quickly as possible.
(c) treatment; handling ◆ **die schlechte ~ seiner Frau und Kinder** the ill-treatment *or* maltreatment of his wife and children.
(d) treatment; attention (*gen* to) ◆ **waren Sie deswegen schon früher in ~?** have you had treatment *or* been treated for this before?; **bei wem sind Sie in ~?** who's treating you?

Behandlungs-: **~art** *f* type of treatment; **b~bedürftig** *adj* in need of treatment; **~form** *f* form of treatment; **~kosten** *pl* cost *sing* of treatment; **~methode** *f* (method of) treatment; **~raum** *m* treatment room; **~stuhl** *m* doctor's/dentist's chair; **~verfahren** *nt* therapy; **~weise** *f* treatment.

behandschuht *adj* gloved.

Behang *m* **-(e)s, ¨-e** **(a)** curtain; (*Wand~*) hanging; (*Schmuck*) decorations *pl* ◆ **der Birnbaum hat einen guten ~** the pear tree promises a good crop. **(b)** (*Hunt: von Hund*) lop-ears *pl*.

behangen *adj* laden.

behängen* [1] *vt* to decorate; *Wände auch* to hang.
[2] *vr* (*pej*) to deck oneself out (*mit* in *or* with).

beharren* *vi* **(a)** (*hartnäckig sein*) to insist (*auf +dat* on); (*nicht aufgeben*) to persist, to persevere (*bei* in). **(b)** (*bleiben*) **in etw** (*dat*) **~** (*in Zustand*) to persist in sth; (*an Ort*) to remain in sth.

Beharren *nt* **-s,** *no pl siehe vi* **(a)** insistence (*auf* on); persistence, perseverance (*bei* in). **(b)** (*in +dat* in) persistence, perseverance; remaining.

beharrlich *adj* (*hartnäckig*) insistent; (*ausdauernd*) persistent; *Glaube, Liebe* steadfast, unwavering ◆ **~er Fleiß** perseverance; **~ fortfahren, etw zu tun** to persist in doing sth.

Beharrlichkeit *f siehe adj* insistence; persistence; steadfastness.

Beharrung *f* (*Phys*) inertia.

Beharrungsvermögen *nt* (*Phys*) inertia.

behauchen* *vt* to breathe on; (*Ling*) to aspirate ◆ **behauchte Laute** (*Ling*) aspirates.

behauen* *vt irreg Holz* to hew; *Stein* to cut; (*mit dem Meißel*) to carve.

▼ **behaupten*** [1] *vt* **(a)** (*sagen*) to claim; (*bestimmte Aussage aufstellen auch*) to maintain; (*Unerwiesenes ~ auch*) to assert ◆ **steif und fest ~** to insist; **von jdm ~, daß ...** to say (of sb) that ...; **es wird behauptet, daß ...** it is said *or* claimed that ...
(b) (*erfolgreich verteidigen*) *Stellung, Recht* to maintain; *Meinung* to assert; *Markt* to keep one's share of; *siehe* **Feld**.
[2] *vr* to assert oneself; (*bei Diskussion*) to hold one's own *or* one's ground (*gegenüber, gegen* against) ◆ **sich auf dem Markt ~** to maintain one's hold on the market.

▼ **Behauptung** *f* **(a)** claim; (*esp unerwiesene ~*) assertion. **(b)** (*Aufrechterhaltung*) assertion; (*von Stellung*) successful defence. **(c)** (*das Sich-Behaupten*) assertion ◆ **die ~ der Firma auf dem Markt** the firm's ability to maintain its hold on the market.

Behausung *f* **(a)** *no pl* (*liter: das Behausen*) accommodation, housing. **(b)** (*geh, hum: Wohnung*) dwelling.

Behaviorismus [biheviə'rɪsmʊs] *m, no pl* behaviourism.

Behaviorist [biheviə'rɪst] *m* behaviourist.

behavioristisch [biheviə'rɪstɪʃ] *adj* behaviouristic.

beheben* *vt irreg* **(a)** (*beseitigen*) to remove; *Mängel, Mißstände* to rectify, to remedy; *Schaden* to repair, to put right; *Störung* to clear. **(b)** (*Aus: abheben*) *Geld* to withdraw.

Behebung *f, no pl siehe vt* **(a)** removal; rectification, remedying; repairing, putting right; clearing. **(b)** (*Aus*) withdrawal.

beheimaten* *vt* to find a home for.

beheimatet *adj* (*ansässig*) resident (*in +dat* in); (*heimisch*) indigenous, native (*in +dat* to) ◆ **wo sind Sie ~?** where is your home?

beheizbar *adj* heatable; *Heckscheibe* heated.

beheizen* *vt* to heat.

Behelf *m* **-(e)s, -e** **(a)** (*Ersatz*) substitute; (*Notlösung*) makeshift ◆ **als ~ dienen** to serve *or* act as a substitute/makeshift. **(b)** (*Jur: Rechtsbehelf*) (legal) remedy.

behelfen* *vr irreg* **(a)** (*Ersatz verwenden*) to manage, to make do ◆ **sich mit Ausreden/Ausflüchten ~** to resort to excuses/to be evasive. **(b)** (*auskommen*) to manage, to get by. **er weiß sich allein nicht zu ~** he can't manage *or* get by alone.

Behelfs- *in cpds* temporary; **~ausfahrt** *f* (*auf Autobahn*) temporary exit; **~heim** *nt* temporary accommodation; **b~mäßig** *adj* makeshift; (*zeitlich begrenzt*) *Straßenbelag, Ausweis* temporary; **b~weise** *adv* temporarily; **er hat sich b~weise eingerichtet** his furnishings are only makeshift.

behelligen* *vt* to bother.

Behelligung *f* bother *no pl* ◆ **jds ~ mit Fragen** (*das Behelligen*) bothering sb with questions; (*das Behelligtwerden*) sb being bothered with questions.

behelmt *adj* helmeted.

behend(e) *adj* (*geh*) (*flink*) swift, quick; (*gewandt*) nimble, agile.

Behendigkeit *f, no pl siehe adj* swiftness, quickness; nimbleness, agility.

beherbergen* *vt* (*lit, fig*) to house; *Gäste* to accommodate; *Flüchtlinge auch* to give shelter to.

Beherbergung *f* housing; (*Unterkunft*) accommodation.

beherrschen* [1] *vt* **(a)** (*herrschen über*) to rule, to govern; (*fig: Gefühle, Vorstellungen*) to dominate.
(b) (*fig: das Übergewicht haben*) *Stadtbild, Landschaft, Ebene, Markt* to dominate; *siehe* **Feld, Szene**.
(c) (*zügeln*) to control; *Zunge* to curb.
(d) (*gut können*) *Handwerk, Sprache, Instrument, Tricks, Spielregeln* to master; (*bewältigen*) *Fahrzeug, Situation* to have control of.
[2] *vr* to control oneself ◆ **ich kann mich ~!** (*iro inf*) not likely! (*inf*).

Beherrscher *m* (*liter*) ruler.

beherrscht *adj* (*fig*) self-controlled.

Beherrschtheit *f, no pl* (*fig*) self-control.

Beherrschung *f, no pl* control; (*Selbst~*) self-control; (*des Markts*) domination; (*eines Fachs*) mastery ◆ **die ~ verlieren** to lose one's temper.

beherzigen* *vt* to take to heart, to heed.

Beherzigung *f* heeding ◆ **dies zur ~!** (*old*) heed this!, take heed!

beherzt *adj* (*geh*) courageous, brave.

Beherztheit *f, no pl* (*geh*) courage, bravery.

behexen* *vt* to bewitch.

behielt *pret of* **behalten**.

behilflich *adj* helpful ◆ **jdm (bei etw) ~ sein** to help sb (with sth).

behindern* *vt* to hinder; *Sicht* to impede; (*bei Sport, im Verkehr*) to obstruct ◆ **jdn bei etw ~** to hinder sb in sth; **eine behinderte Person** a handicapped person.

Behinderte(r) *mf decl as adj* disabled *or* handicapped person ◆ **die ~n** the handicapped *pl or* disabled *pl*.

behindertengerecht *adj* adapted to the needs of the handicapped ◆ **etw ~ umbauen/gestalten** to alter/design sth to fit the needs of the handicapped.

Behindertenwerkstatt *f* sheltered workshop.

Behinderung *f* hindrance; (*im Sport, Verkehr*) obstruction; (*körperlich, Nachteil*) handicap ◆ **mit ~en muß gerechnet werden** delays *or* hold-ups are likely to occur.

behorchen* *vt* **(a)** to listen in on. **(b)** (*Med inf*) to listen to.

Behörde *f* **-, -n** authority *usu pl*; (*Amtsgebäude*) office *usu pl* ◆ **die ~n** the authorities; **die zuständige ~** the appropriate *or* proper authorities.

Behörden- *in cpds* official; **~unwesen** *nt* sprawling bureaucracy; **~wesen** *nt* bureaucracy.

behördlich *adj* official.

behördlicherseits *adv* (*form*) by the authorities; (*auf behördlicher Seite*) on the part of the authorities.

Behuf *m* **-(e)s, -e** (*old form*) **zu diesem ~** to this end, for this purpose.

behuft *adj* hoofed.

behüten* *vt* (*beschützen, bewachen*) to look after; (*esp Engel etc*) to watch over; *Geheimnis* to keep ◆ **jdn vor etw** (*dat*) **~** to save *or* protect sb from sth; **(Gott) behüte!** (*inf*) God *or* Heaven forbid!; **behüt' dich Gott!** (*old, S Ger*) (may) God be with you!

Behüter *m* **-s, -** (*geh*) protector.

behütet *adj* *Mädchen* carefully brought up; *Jugend* sheltered ◆ **~ aufwachsen** to have a sheltered upbringing.

behutsam *adj* cautious, careful; (*zart auch*) gentle ◆ **man muß es ihr ~ beibringen** it will have to be broken to her gently.

Behutsamkeit *f, no pl* care(fulness), cautiousness; (*Zartheit auch*) gentleness; (*Feingefühl*) delicacy.

bei *prep +dat* **(a)** (*räumlich*) (*in der Nähe von*) near; (*zum Aufenthalt*) at, with; (*Tätigkeitsbereich angebend, in Institutionen*) at; (*in Werken*) in; (*jdn betreffend*) with; (*Teilnahme bezeichnend*) at; (*unter, zwischen Menge*) among; (*Ort der Berührung bezeichnend*) by ◆ **die Schlacht ~ Leipzig** the Battle of Leipzig; **dicht ~ dem Ort, wo ...** very near the place where ...; **ich stand/saß ~ ihm** I stood/sat beside him *or* next to him; **der Wert liegt ~ tausend Mark** the value is around a thousand marks; **~ seinen Eltern wohnen** to live with one's parents; **ich war ~ meiner Tante** I was at my aunt's; **~ Müller** (*auf Briefen*) care of *or* c/o Müller; **~ uns** at our place; **~ uns in Deutschland** in Germany; **~ uns zu Hause** (*im Haus*) at our house; (*im Land, in Familie*) back *or* at home; **~ Tisch** at table; **sie sind ~ uns eingeladen** they're invited to our house; **er ist** *or* **arbeitet ~ der Post** he works for the post office; **~ jdm Unterricht haben/Vorlesungen hören** to have lessons with *or* from sb/lectures from sb; **~m Militär** in the army; **~m Fleischer** at the butcher's; **ein Konto ~ der Bank** an account at the bank; **~ Shakespeare liest man ...** in Shakespeare it says ...; **~ Collins erschienen** published by Collins; **~ Kühen findet man das nicht** one doesn't find *or* get that with cows; **~ den Franzosen ißt man ...** in France one eats ...; **~ mir hast du damit kein Glück** you're wasting your time with me; **~ ihm ist es 8 Uhr** he makes it *or* he has (*esp US*) 8 o'clock; **~ mir ist Schluß für heute** I've had enough for today; **das war ~ ihm der Fall** that was

the case with him; **man weiß nicht, woran man ~ ihm ist** (*inf*) one never knows where one is with him; **~ einer Hochzeit sein** to be at a wedding; **er hat ~ der Aufführung der Elektra mitgewirkt** he took part in the performance of Elektra; **er nahm mich ~ der Hand** he took me by the hand; **jdn ~ sich haben** to have sb with one; **ich habe kein Geld ~ mir** I have no money on me; *siehe* **weit, Wort, Name.**
(b) (*zeitlich*) (*Zeitspanne: während*) during; (*Zeitpunkt*) (up)on; (*bestimmten Zeitpunkt betreffend*) at ◆ **~m letzten Gewitter** during the last storm; **~ meiner Ankunft** on my arrival; **~m Erwachen** (up)on waking; **~m Erscheinen der Königin ...** when the queen appeared ...; **~ Beginn und Ende der Vorstellung** at the beginning and end of the performance; **~ Tag/Nacht** by day/at night; **~ Tag und Nacht** day and night.
(c) (*Tätigkeit, Geschehen ausdrückend*) in, during ◆ **~ reiflicher Überlegung** upon mature reflection; **ich habe ihm ~m Arbeiten/~ der Arbeit geholfen** I helped him with the work; **~m Arbeiten/~ der Arbeit** when I'm *etc* working; **~m Lesen (dieses Artikels) ...** when reading (this article) ...; **~ dem Zugunglück starben viele Menschen** a lot of people died in the train crash; **~ dieser Schlacht** in *or* during this battle; **er verliert ~m Kartenspiel immer** he always loses at cards; **er ist gerade ~m Anziehen seiner Schuhe** he's just putting his shoes on.
(d) (*Zustand, Umstand bezeichnend*) in ◆ **~ Kerzenlicht essen** to eat by candlelight; **etw ~ einer Flasche Wein bereden** to discuss sth over a bottle of wine; **~ guter Gesundheit sein** to be in good health; **~ zehn Grad unter Null** when it's ten degrees below zero; **~ Regen** in the rain; **das Schönste ~ der Sache** the best thing about it; **nicht ~ sich sein** (*inf*) to be out of one's mind (*inf*); **~ offenem Fenster schlafen** to sleep with the window open; **~ alledem ...** in spite of everything, for all that; *siehe* **Bewußtsein, Kraft, Verstand** *etc.*
(e) (*konditionaler Nebensinn*) in case of ◆ **~ Feuer Scheibe einschlagen** in case of fire break glass; **~ Nebel und Glatteis muß man vorsichtig fahren** when there is fog and ice one must drive carefully; **~ einer Erkältung sollte man sich warm halten** when one has a cold one should keep warm.
(f) (*kausaler Nebensinn*) with ◆ **~ dieser Sturheit/so vielen Schwierigkeiten** with this stubbornness/so many difficulties; **~ solcher Hitze/solchem Wind** in such heat/such a wind; **~ seinem Talent** with his talent.
(g) (*konzessiver Nebensinn*) in spite of, despite ◆ **~ aller Vorsicht** in spite of *or* despite all one's caution; **es geht ~m besten Willen nicht** with the best will in the world it's not possible; **~ all seinen Bemühungen hat er es trotzdem nicht geschafft** in spite of *or* despite *or* for all his efforts he still didn't manage it.
(h) (*in Schwurformeln*) by ◆ **~ Gott** by God; **~ meiner Ehre** upon my honour.

beibehalten* *vt sep irreg* to keep; *Bräuche, Regelung auch* to retain; *Leitsatz, Richtung* to keep to; *Gewohnheit* to keep up.

Beibehaltung *f, no pl siehe vt* keeping; retention; keeping to; keeping up.

beibiegen *vt sep irreg* **jdm etw ~** (*inf*) to get sth through to sb (*inf*).

Beibl. *abbr of* **Beiblatt.**

Beiblatt *nt* (*Press*) insert, supplement.

Beiboot *nt* (*Naut*) dinghy.

beibringen *vt sep irreg* **(a) jdm etw ~** (*mitteilen*) to break sth to sb; (*zu verstehen geben*) to get sth across to sb, to get sb to understand sth.
(b) (*unterweisen in*) to teach (*jdm etw* sb sth).
(c) (*zufügen*) *Verluste, Wunde, Niederlage, Schläge* to inflict (*jdm etw* sth on sb).
(d) (*herbeischaffen*) to produce; *Dokumente, Beweis, Geld etc* to furnish, to supply.

Beibringung *f, no pl siehe vt (c, d)* infliction; production; furnishing, supplying.

Beichte *f -, -n* confession ◆ **zur ~ gehen** to go to confession; **(bei jdm) die ~ ablegen** to make one's confession (to sb); **eine ~ ablegen** (*fig*) to make a confession; **jdm die ~ abnehmen** to hear sb's confession; **~ hören** *or* **sitzen** (*inf*) to hear *or* take confession.

beichten *vti* (*lit, fig*) to confess (*jdm etw* sth to sb) ◆ **~ gehen** to go to confession.

Beicht-: **~formel** *f form of words used at confession;* **~geheimnis** *nt* seal of confession *or* of the confessional; **b~hören** *vi sep* (*inf, Aus*) to hear confession; **~stuhl** *m* confessional; **~vater** *m* father confessor; **~zettel** *m* (*Aufstellung*) list of sins; (*Bescheinigung*) absolution.

beid-: **~armig** *adj* with both arms; *Lähmung* of *or* in both arms; **~beinig** *adj* with both legs; *Lähmung* of *or* in both legs; *Absprung* double-footed; **~beinig abspringen** to take off with both feet.

beide *pron* **(a)** (*adjektivisch*) (*ohne Artikel*) both; (*mit Artikel*) two ◆ **alle ~n Teller** both plates; **seine ~n Brüder** both his brothers, his two brothers.
(b) (*als Apposition*) both ◆ **ihr ~(n)/euch ~** you two; **euch ~n herzlichen Dank** many thanks to both of you.
(c) (*substantivisch*) (*ohne Artikel*) both (of them); (*mit Artikel*) two (of them) ◆ **alle ~** both (of them); **alle ~ wollten gleichzeitig Urlaub haben** both of them *or* they both wanted holidays at the same time; **keiner/keines** *etc* **von ~n** neither of them; **ich habe ~ nicht gesehen** I haven't seen either of them.
(d) ~s (*substantivisch: zwei verschiedene Dinge*) both; **(alles) ~s ist erlaubt** both are permitted.

beidemal *adv* both times.

beider-: **~lei** *adj attr inv* both; **das Abendmahl in** *or* **unter ~lei Gestalt** Communion of bread and wine; **~seitig** *adj* (*auf beiden Seiten*) on both sides; (*gegenseitig*) *Abkommen, Vertrag etc* bilateral; *Versicherungen, Einverständnis etc* mutual; **~seits** [1] *adv* on both sides; **sie haben ~seits versichert ...** they have given mutual assurances *or* assurances on both sides ...; [2] *prep +gen* on both sides of.

Beiderwand *f or nt* **-(e)s,** *no pl* (*Tex*) linsey-woolsey.

Beid-: **b~füßig** *adj* two-footed; *Absprung* double-footed; **b~füßig abspringen** to take off with both feet; **~händer** *m* **-s, -** (*Mensch*) ambidextrous person; (*Schwert*) two-handed sword; **b~händig** *adj* (*mit beiden Händen gleich geschickt*) ambidextrous; (*mit beiden Händen zugleich*) two-handed; **b~händig schießen/schreiben können** to be able to shoot/write with either hand *or* both hands.

beidrehen *vi sep* (*Naut*) to heave to.

beid-: **~seitig** [1] *adj* (*auf beiden Seiten*) on both sides; (*gegenseitig*) mutual; **~seitige Zufriedenheit** satisfaction on both sides/mutual satisfaction; [2] *adv* on both sides; **~seits** *prep +gen* (*Sw, S Ger*) on both sides of.

bei|einander *adv* together.

bei|einander- *pref* together; ⚠**~haben** *vt sep irreg* (*inf*) to have together; **du hast sie nicht richtig** *or* **alle ~** you can't be all there (*inf*); ⚠**~halten** *vt sep irreg* to keep together; ⚠**~sein** *vi sep irreg aux sein* (*inf*) (*gesundheitlich*) to be in good shape (*inf*); (*geistig*) to be all there (*inf*); **gut ~sein** to be in good shape/to be all there; (*S Ger: dick*) to be a bit chubby (*inf*); **B~sein** *nt siehe* **Zusammensein.**

Beifahrer *m* (*Aut*) (front-seat) passenger; (*bei einem Motorrad*) (*im Beiwagen*) sidecar passenger; (*auf dem Soziussitz*) pillion rider *or* passenger; (*berufsmäßiger Mitfahrer, Sport*) co-driver; (*bei einem LKW*) co-driver, driver's mate.

Beifahrer-: **~airbag** *m* (*Aut*) passenger airbag; **~platz** *m* passenger seat; **~sitz** *m* passenger seat; (*auf Motorrad*) pillion.

Beifall *m* **-(e)s,** *no pl* (*Zustimmung*) approval; (*Händeklatschen*) applause; (*Zuruf*) cheering, cheers *pl* ◆ **~ finden** to meet with approval; **~ spenden/klatschen/klopfen** *etc* to applaud.

⚠**beifallheischend** *adj* looking for approval/applause.

beifällig *adj* approving ◆ **~e Worte/Laute** words/noises of approval; **er nickte ~ mit dem Kopf** he nodded his head approvingly *or* in approval; **dieser Vorschlag wurde ~ aufgenommen** this suggestion was favourably received *or* met with approval.

Beifalls-: **~äußerung** *f* expression of (one's) approval; **~bekundung** *f* show *or* demonstration of (one's) approval; **~bezeigung, ~kundgebung** *f* applause *no pl.*

⚠**beifallspendend** *adj* applauding.

Beifalls-: **~ruf** *m* cheer; **~sturm** *m* storm of applause.

Beifang *m no pl* unwanted catch.

Beifangquote *f* quota of unwanted catch.

Beifilm *m* supporting film.

beifügen *vt sep* (*mitschicken*) to enclose (*dat* with); (*beiläufig sagen*) to add.

Beifügung *f* **(a)** *no pl* (*form*) enclosure ◆ **unter ~ eines Schecks** enclosing a cheque. **(b)** (*Gram*) attribute.

Beifügungssatz *m* (*Gram*) attributive clause.

Beifuß *m* **-es,** *no pl* (*Bot*) mugwort.

Beifutter *nt* supplementary fodder.

Beigabe *f* **(a)** (*das Beigeben*) addition ◆ **eine ~ von etw empfehlen** to recommend adding sth *or* the addition of sth; **unter ~ eines Löffels Senf** adding a spoonful of mustard.
(b) (*Beigefügtes, Begleiterscheinung*) addition; (*Beilage: Gemüse, Salat etc*) side-dish; (*Comm: Zugabe*) free gift; (*Grab~*) burial gift.

beige [beːʃ, 'bɛːʒə] *adj* (*geh: inv*) beige.

Beige[1] [beːʃ, 'bɛːʒə] *nt* **-, -** *or* (*inf*) **-s** beige.

Beige[2] *f* **-, -n** (*S Ger, Aus, Sw*) pile.

beigeben *sep irreg* [1] *vt* (*zufügen*) to add (*dat* to); (*mitgeben*) *jdn* to assign (*jdm* to sb).
[2] *vi*: **klein ~** (*inf*) to give in.

beigebunden *adj* (*Typ*) bound in.

beigefarben ['beːʃ-, 'bɛːʒə-] *adj* beige(-coloured).

beigehen *vi sep irreg aux sein* (*dial*) to start.

beige|ordnet *adj* (*Gram*) *Nebensatz* co-ordinate.

Beige|ordnete(r) *mf decl as adj* (town) councillor.

Beigeschmack *m* aftertaste; (*fig: von Worten*) flavour ◆ **es hat einen unangenehmen ~** (*lit, fig*) it has a nasty *or* an unpleasant taste (to it).

beigesellen* *sep* (*geh*) [1] *vt* **ihr wurde ein Beschützer beigesellt** she was provided with an escort.
[2] *vr* **sich jdm ~** to join sb.

Beignet [bɛn'jeː] *m* **-s, -s** (*Cook*) fritter.

Beiheft *nt* supplement; (*Lösungsheft*) answer book.

beiheften *vt sep* to append, to attach.

Beihilfe *f* **(a)** (*finanzielle Unterstützung*) financial assistance *no indef art;* (*Zuschuß, Kleidungs ~*) allowance; (*für Arztkosten*) contribution; (*Studien~*) grant; (*Subvention*) subsidy. **(b)** (*Jur*) abetment ◆ **wegen ~ zum Mord** because of being an *or* acting as an accessory to the murder.

beihilfefähig *adj* (*form*) eligible for financial assistance/a contribution/contributions *etc.*

Beiklang *m* (*lit*) (accompanying) sound; (*fig*) overtone *usu pl.*

beikommen *vi sep irreg aux sein* **(a) jdm ~** (*zu fassen bekommen*) to get hold of sb; (*fertig werden mit*) to get the better of sb; **einer Sache** (*dat*) **~** (*bewältigen*) to deal with sth.
(b) (*old inf: einfallen*) **jdm ~** to occur to sb; **laß dir das ja nicht ~!** don't even think of it!
(c) (*dial: herkommen*) to come.
(d) (*dial*) **ich komme da nicht bei** I can't reach it.

Beikost *f* supplementary diet.

⚠: for details of spelling reform, see supplement

Beil *nt* **-(e)s, -e** axe; (*kleiner*) hatchet; (*Fleischer~*) cleaver; (*zum Hinrichten*) axe; (*Fall~*) blade (of a/the guillotine).

beil. *abbr of* **beiliegend.**

beiladen *vt sep irreg* **(a)** to add (*dat* to). **(b)** (*Jur*) to call in.

Beiladung *f* **(a)** (*das Beiladen*) additional loading; (*zusätzliche Ladung*) extra *or* additional load. **(b)** (*Jur*) calling in ◆ **notwendige ~** subpoena.

Beilage *f* **-, -n (a)** (*Gedrucktes*) insert; (*Beiheft*) supplement.
(b) (*das Beilegen*) enclosure; (*in Buch*) insertion; (*Aus: Anlage zu Brief*) enclosure.
(c) (*Cook*) side-dish; (*Gemüse~*) vegetables *pl*; (*Salat~*) side-salad ◆ **Erbsen und Pommes frites als ~ zum Hähnchen** chicken with peas and chips.

Beilager *nt* (*Hist*) consummation; (*obs: Beischlaf*) sexual relations *pl*.

beiläufig *adj* **(a)** casual; *Bemerkung, Erwähnung auch* passing *attr* ◆ **etw ~ erwähnen** to mention sth in passing *or* casually. **(b)** (*Aus: ungefähr*) approximate.

Beiläufigkeit *f* (*von Bemerkung, in Benehmen etc*) casualness; (*Nebensächlichkeit*) triviality ◆ **~en** trivia *pl*.

beilegen *vt sep* **(a)** (*hinzulegen*) to insert (*dat* in); (*einem Brief, Paket*) to enclose (*dat* with, in).
(b) (*beimessen*) to attribute, to ascribe (*dat* to) ◆ **einer Sache** (*dat*) **Bedeutung** *or* **Gewicht/Wert ~** to attach importance/value to sth.
(c) (*schlichten*) to settle.
(d) (*Naut: anlegen*) to moor.

Beilegung *f siehe vt* **(a)** insertion; enclosure. **(b)** attribution, ascription; (*von Bedeutung, Wert*) attaching. **(c)** settlement. **(d)** mooring.

beileibe *adv*: **~ nicht!** certainly not; **das darf ~ nicht passieren** that mustn't happen under any circumstances; **~ kein ...** by no means a ..., certainly no ...

▼ **Beileid** *nt* **-(e)s,** *no pl* condolence(s), sympathy ◆ **jdm sein ~ aussprechen** *or* **ausdrücken** *or* **bezeigen** to offer sb one's condolences, to express one's sympathy with sb; **mein ~!** (*iro*) you have my sympathy!

Beileids- *in cpds* of condolence *or* sympathy; **~bekundung** *f siehe* **~bezeigung**; **~besuch** *m* visit of condolence; **~bezeigung, ~bezeugung** *f* expression of sympathy; (*Brief, Telegramm etc*) condolence; **~karte** *f* sympathy *or* condolence card.

Beilhieb *m* blow with *or* from an axe.

beiliegen *vi sep irreg* **(a)** (*beigefügt sein*) to be enclosed (*dat* with, in); (*einer Zeitschrift etc*) to be inserted (*dat* in). **(b)** (*Naut*) to lie to. **(c)** (*obs*) **jdm ~** to lie with sb (*obs*).

beiliegend *adj* enclosed ◆ **~ senden wir Ihnen ...** please find enclosed ...

beim *contr of* **bei dem.**

beimachen *vr sep* (*dial*) to get down to it.

beimengen *vt sep* to add (*dat* to).

beimessen *vt sep irreg* **jdm/einer Sache Bedeutung** *or* **Gewicht/Wert ~** to attach importance/value to sb/sth.

beimischen *vt sep* to add (*dat* to) ◆ **unserer Freude war eine leichte Traurigkeit beigemischt** our joy was tinged with sadness.

Beimischung *f* addition ◆ **eine leichte ~ von ...** (*fig*) a touch of ...

Bein *nt* **-(e)s, -e (a)** leg ◆ **mit übereinandergeschlagenen ~en** cross-legged; **von einem ~ aufs andere treten** to shift from one leg *or* foot to the other; **sich kaum auf den ~en halten können** to be hardly able to stay on one's feet; **er ist noch gut auf den ~en** he's still sprightly; **jdm ein ~ stellen** (*lit, fig*) to trip sb up; **jdm wieder auf die ~e helfen** (*lit, fig*) to help sb back on his feet; **auf den ~en sein** (*nicht krank, in Bewegung*) to be on one's feet; (*unterwegs sein*) to be out and about; **sich auf die ~e machen** (*inf*) to make tracks (*inf*); **jdm ~e machen** (*inf*) (*antreiben*) to make sb get a move on (*inf*); (*wegjagen*) to make sb clear off (*inf*); **die ~e unter den Arm** *or* **in die Hand nehmen** (*inf*) to take to one's heels; **mein Geldbeutel hat ~e bekommen** (*fig*) my purse has vanished into thin air *or* seems to have grown legs and walked; **sich** (*dat*) **die ~e in den Bauch** *or* **Leib stehen** (*inf*) to stand about until one is fit to drop (*inf*); **mit beiden ~en im Leben** *or* **auf der Erde stehen** (*fig*) to have both feet (firmly) on the ground; **mit einem ~ im Grab/im Gefängnis stehen** (*fig*) to have one foot in the grave/to be likely to end up in jail; **das steht auf schwachen ~en** (*fig*) that isn't very sound; **auf eigenen ~en stehen** (*fig*) to be able to stand on one's own two feet; **auf einem ~ kann man nicht stehen!** (*fig inf*) you can't stop at one!; **er fällt immer wieder auf die ~e** (*fig*) he always falls on his feet; **wieder auf die ~e kommen** (*fig*) to get back on one's feet again; **jdn/etw wieder auf die ~e bringen** *or* **stellen** (*fig*) to get sb/sth back on his/its feet again; **etw auf die ~e stellen** (*fig*) to get sth off the ground; *Geld etc* to raise sth; **sich** (*dat*) **etw ans ~ binden** (*fig*) to saddle oneself with sth; **jdn/etw am ~ haben** (*fig inf*) to have sb/sth round one's neck (*inf*); *siehe* **ausreißen, Knüppel, Lüge, Klotz** *etc*.
(b) (*Knochen*) bone ◆ **der Schreck ist ihm in die ~e gefahren** the shock went right through him; **Fleisch am ~** (*old*) meat on the bone; *siehe* **Stein, Mark[1]**.
(c) (*Elfenbein*) ivory.
(d) (*dial: Fuß*) foot.

beinah(e) *adv* almost, nearly ◆ **~ in allen Fällen, in ~ allen Fällen** in almost *or* nearly every case; **das kommt ~ auf dasselbe heraus** that comes to almost *or* nearly the same thing.

Beiname *m* epithet; (*Spitzname*) nickname.

Bein-: ~amputation *f* leg amputation; **b~amputiert** *adj* with an amputated leg/amputated legs; **b~amputiert sein** to have had a leg/both legs amputated; **~arbeit** *f* (*Sport*) footwork; (*beim Schwimmen*) legwork; **~bruch** *m* fracture of the leg; **das ist kein ~bruch** (*fig inf*) it could be worse (*inf*); *siehe* **Hals- und Beinbruch.**

beinern *adj* (*aus Knochen*) made of bone; (*aus Elfenbein*) ivory.

Beinfreiheit *f no pl* legroom.

be|inhalten* *vt insep* (*form*) to comprise.

Bein-: b~hart *adj Mensch* hard as nails; *Erde, Piste, Kuchen* rock-hard; *Wettstreit, Kampf* fierce; *Druck, Streß* intense; *Argument, Bemerkung* scathing; **die Gewerkschaft ging den Minister b~hart an** the union gave the minister a rough ride; **~haus** *nt* charnel-house.

-beinig *adj suf* -legged.

Bein-: ~kleid *nt usu pl* (*old, hum*) breeches *pl* (*old*); **~ling** *m* leg; **~prothese** *f* artificial leg; **~raum** *m* leg room; **~schiene** *f* (*Hist*) greave; (*Sport*) shin pad; (*bei Cricket*) (leg)pad; (*Med*) splint; **~stumpf** *m* stump.

bei|ordnen *vt sep* **(a)** (*Gram*) *siehe* **nebenordnen. (b)** (*beigeben*) **jdm/einer Sache beigeordnet sein** to be assigned to sb/appointed to sth; **bei einer Prüfung beigeordnet sein** to sit in on an examination.

Beipack *m* additional consignment *or* order; (*Frachtgut*) part load (*zu* with).

beipacken *vt sep* to enclose; *Frachtgut* to add (*dat* to).

Beipackzettel *m* instruction leaflet; (*Inhaltsverzeichnis*) list of contents.

beipflichten *vi sep* **jdm/einer Sache in etw** (*dat*) **~** to agree with sb/sth on sth.

Beiprogramm *nt* supporting programme.

Beirat *m* (*Person*) adviser; (*Körperschaft*) advisory council *or* committee *or* body.

Beiratschaft *f* (*Sw Jur*) (legal) care and protection.

be|irren* *vt* (*verwirren*) to disconcert ◆ **sich nicht in etw** (*dat*) **~ lassen** not to let oneself be shaken *or* swayed in sth; **sich (durch etw) ~/nicht ~ lassen** to let/not to let oneself be put off (by sth); **er läßt sich nicht ~** he won't be put off; **nichts konnte ihn (in seinem Vorhaben) ~** nothing could shake him (in his intentions).

beisammen *adv* together.

beisammen- *pref* together; **~haben** *vt sep irreg* (*inf*) *Geld, Leute* to have got together; **seine Gedanken ~haben** to have one's wits about one; **seinen Verstand** *or* **seine fünf Sinne ~haben** to have all one's wits about one; **(sie) nicht alle ~haben** not to be all there; ⚠**~sein** *vi sep irreg aux sein* (*Zusammenschreibung nur bei infin und ptp*) (*fig*) (*körperlich*) to be in good shape; (*geistig*) to be all there; **gut ~sein** to be in good shape; (*kräftig gebaut sein*) to be well built; **B~sein** *nt* get-together.

Beisasse *m* **-n, -n** (*Hist*) *citizen without full civic rights.*

Beisatz *m* (*Gram*) appositive.

beischaffen *vt sep* (*dial*) to bring.

beischießen *vt sep irreg* (*inf*) to chip in with (*inf*).

Beischlaf *m* (*Jur*) sexual intercourse *or* relations *pl*.

beischlafen *vi sep irreg* (*form*) to have sexual intercourse *or* relations *pl* (*dat* with).

beischließen *vt sep irreg* (*Aus*) to enclose (*dat* with).

⚠ **Beischluß** *m* (*Aus*) enclosure ◆ **unter ~ von ...** enclosing ...

Beisegel *nt* studdingsail.

Beisein *nt* presence ◆ **in/ohne jds ~** in sb's presence/without sb being present.

beiseite *adv* aside (*auch Theat*); *treten, gehen, stehen auch* to one side; *legen,* (*fig*) *lassen auch* on one side; *setzen,* (*fig*) *schieben auch* to *or* on one side ◆ **Spaß** *or* **Scherz ~!** joking aside *or* apart!; **jdn/etw ~ schaffen** *or* **bringen** to get rid of sb/sth.

Beiseiteschaffung *f* removal.

Beis(e)l *nt* **-s, -n** (*Aus inf*) pub (*Brit*).

beisetzen *vt sep* **(a)** (*beerdigen*) to inter (*form*), to bury; *Urne* to install (in its resting place). **(b)** (*Naut*) *Segel* to set, to spread. **(c)** (*old*) *siehe* **zusetzen.**

Beisetzung *f* funeral; (*von Urne*) installing in its resting place.

beisitzen *vi sep irreg* (*in Versammlung*) to attend; (*einem Ausschuß*) to have a seat (*dat* on), to sit (*dat* on); (*bei Prüfung*) to sit in (*bei* on).

Beisitzer(in *f*) *m* **-s, - (a)** (*Jur*) assessor. **(b)** (*Ausschußmitglied*) committee member; (*bei Prüfung*) observer.

▼ **Beispiel** *nt* **-(e)s, -e** example ◆ **zum ~** for example *or* instance; **wie zum ~** such as; **jdm als ~ dienen** to be an example to sb; **jdm ein ~ geben** to set sb an example; **sich** (*dat*) **ein ~ an jdm/etw nehmen** to take a leaf out of sb's book/to take sth as an example; **mit gutem ~ vorangehen** to set a good example; **schlechte ~e verderben gute Sitten** (*Prov*) you shouldn't set a bad example.

Beispiel-: b~gebend *adj* exemplary; **b~gebend für etw sein** to serve as an example for sth; **b~haft** *adj* exemplary; **b~halber** *adv* by way of example; **b~los** *adj* unprecedented; (*unerhört*) outrageous; **~satz** *m* example.

beispielsweise *adv* for example *or* instance.

beispringen *vi sep irreg aux sein* **jdm ~** to rush to sb's aid; (*mit Geldbeträgen*) to help sb out.

beißen *pret* **biß,** *ptp* **gebissen** [1] *vti* to bite; (*brennen: Geschmack, Geruch, Schmerzen*) to sting; (*kauen*) to chew ◆ **in den Apfel ~** to bite into *or* take a bite out of the apple; **der Hund hat mich** *or* **mir ins Bein gebissen** the dog has bitten my leg *or* me in the leg; **der Rauch/Wind beißt in den Augen/mich in die Augen** (*inf*) the smoke/wind makes one's/my eyes sting; **er wird dich schon nicht ~** (*fig*) he won't eat *or* bite you; **etwas/nichts zu ~** (*inf: essen*) something/nothing to eat; **an etw** (*dat*) **zu ~ haben** (*fig*) to have sth to chew over; *siehe* **Gras, sauer, letzte(r, s).**
[2] *vr* (*Farben*) to clash ◆ **sich** (*acc or dat*) **auf die Zunge/Lippen ~** to bite one's tongue/lips; **sich in den Arsch** (*vulg*) *or* **Hintern** (*sl*) **~** to kick oneself (*inf*).

beißend *adj* (*lit, fig*) biting; *Wind auch, Bemerkung* cutting; *Geschmack, Geruch* pungent, sharp; *Schmerz* gnawing; *Ironie, Hohn, Spott* bitter.

➤ SPRACHE AKTIV: **Beileid** → 51.4 **Beispiel** → 53.1, 53.5

Beißerchen *pl (baby-talk)* toothy-pegs *pl (baby-talk)*.
Beiß-: **~ring** *m* teething ring; **~zange** *f* (pair of) pincers *or* pliers; *(pej inf)* shrew; **das würde ich nicht mit der ~zange anfassen** *or* **anpacken** *(inf)* I wouldn't touch that with a barge pole *(inf)*.
Beistand *m* **-(e)s, ¨-e (a)** *no pl (Hilfe)* help, assistance; *(Unterstützung)* support; *(von Priester)* attendance, presence ◆ **jdm ~ leisten** to give sb help *or* assistance/give *or* lend sb one's support/attend sb.
(b) *(Jur)* legal adviser *or* representative; *(in Duell)* aid, representative, second ◆ **einen ~ stellen** *(Jur)* to appoint a legal adviser *or* representative.
Beistands-: **~abkommen** *nt*, **~pakt** *m* mutual assistance pact; **~vertrag** *m* treaty of mutual assistance.
beistehen *vi sep irreg* **jdm ~** to stand by sb.
beistellen *vt sep* **(a)** to put *or* place beside. **(b)** *(Aus: zur Verfügung stellen) (dat* for) to make available, to provide. **(c)** *(Rail: bereitstellen)* to put on.
Beistell- *in cpds* side; **~herd** *m* auxiliary cooker; **~möbel** *pl* occasional furniture *sing*; **~tisch** *m* occasional table.
beisteuern *vt sep* to contribute.
beistimmen *vi sep siehe* **zustimmen**.
Beistrich *m (esp Aus)* comma.
Beitel *m* **-s, -** chisel.
Beitrag *m* **-(e)s, ¨-e (a)** *(Anteil)* contribution; *(Aufsatz auch)* article ◆ **einen ~ zu etw leisten** to make a contribution to sth, to contribute to sth. **(b)** *(Betrag)* contribution; *(Versicherungs~)* premium; *(Mitglieds~)* fee.
beitragen *vti sep irreg* to contribute *(zu* to); *(mithelfen auch)* to help *(zu* to) ◆ **das trägt nur dazu bei, die Lage zu verschlimmern** that only helps to make the position worse.
Beitrags-: **~bemessungsgrenze** *f (Insur)* income threshold *(for insurance contributions)*; **b~frei** *adj* non-contributory; **~gruppe, ~klasse** *f* insurance group; *(bei Verein etc)* class of membership; **~marke** *f* stamp; **b~pflichtig** *adj Arbeitsentgelt* contributory; **b~pflichtig sein** *(Mensch)* to have to pay contributions; **~rückstand** *m* arrears *pl*; **~satz** *m* membership rate; **~schlüssel** *m*, **~system** *nt* contributory system; **~zahlende(r)** *mf decl as adj* fee-paying member.
beitreiben *vt sep irreg Steuern* to collect; *Schulden auch* to recover; *(esp Jur)* to enforce (the) payment of.
Beitreibung *f (Jur)* collection.
beitreten *vi sep irreg aux sein +dat* to join; *einem Pakt, Abkommen* to enter into; *einem Vertrag* to accede to.
Beitritt *m* joining *(zu etw* sth); *(zu einem Pakt, Abkommen)* agreement *(zu* to); *(zu einem Vertrag)* accession *(zu* to) ◆ **seinen ~ erklären** to become a member.
Beitritts-: **~erklärung** *f* confirmation of membership; **~gesuch** *nt* application for membership.
Beiwagen *m* **(a)** *(beim Motorrad)* sidecar. **(b)** *(dated: Anhänger)* carriage.
Beiwerk *nt* additions *pl*; *(bei Aufsatz etc)* details *pl*; *(modisch)* accessories *pl*.
beiwilligen *vi sep (Sw) siehe* **zustimmen**.
beiwohnen *vi sep +dat (geh)* **(a)** *(dabeisein)* to be present at. **(b)** *(dated euph)* to have sexual relations with.
Beiwohnung *f* **(a)** *(form: Anwesenheit)* presence. **(b)** *(Jur)* intimacy *no art*.
Beiwort *nt* **-(e)s,** *(rare)* **¨-er (a)** *(Adjektiv)* adjective. **(b)** *(beschreibendes Wort)* epithet.
Beiz *f* **-, -en** *(Sw, S Ger inf)* pub *(Brit)*.
Beize[1] *f* **-, -n (a)** *(Beizmittel)* corrosive fluid; *(Metall~)* pickling solution, pickle; *(Holz~)* stain; *(zum Gerben)* lye; *(Tabak~)* sauce; *(Agr)* disinfectant; *(Färbemittel, Typ)* mordant; *(Cook)* marinade. **(b)** *(das Beizen)* steeping in a/the corrosive fluid *etc*. **(c)** *(Hunt)* hawking.
Beize[2] *f* **-, -n** *(dial)* pub *(Brit)*.
beizeiten *adv* in good time.
beizen *vt* **(a)** to steep in corrosive fluid; *(Metal)* to pickle; *Holz* to stain; *Häute* to bate, to master; *Tabak* to steep in sauce; *Saatgut* to disinfect, to treat; *Kupfer* to etch; *(Cook)* to marinate. **(b)** *(Hunt)* to hawk.
Beiz-: **~mittel** *nt siehe* **Beize**[1] **(a)**; **~vogel** *m* falcon, hawk.
bejahen* *vti* to answer in the affirmative; *(gutheißen)* to approve of ◆ **das Leben ~** to have a positive attitude towards life.
bejahend *adj* positive, affirmative; *Einstellung* positive ◆ **etw ~ beantworten** *(form)* to answer sth in the affirmative.
bejahrt *adj* elderly, advanced in years.
Bejahung *f* affirmative answer *(gen* to); *(Gutheißung)* approval.
Bejahungsfall *m (form)* **im ~e** in the event of an affirmative answer.
bejammern* *vt* to lament; *Schicksal, Los auch* to bewail *(liter)*; *jdn* to lament for.
bejammerns-: **~wert, ~würdig** *(rare) adj* deplorable, lamentable; *Mensch* pitiable; *Schicksal* pitiable, dreadful.
bejubeln* *vt* to cheer; *Ereignis* to rejoice at ◆ **sie wurden als Befreier bejubelt** they were acclaimed as liberators.
bekacken* *(vulg)* [1] *vt* to shit on *(sl)*.
[2] *vr* to shit oneself *(sl)*.
bekakeln* *vt (N Ger inf)* to talk over, to discuss.
bekalmen* *vt (Naut)* to becalm.
bekam *pret of* **bekommen**.
bekämpfen* *vt* to fight; *(fig auch)* to combat; *Ungeziefer* to control ◆ **sich gegenseitig ~** to fight one another.
Bekämpfung *f* fight, battle *(von, gen* against); *(von Ungeziefer)* controlling ◆ **zur/bei ~ der Terroristen** to fight *or* combat/in fighting *or* combatting the terrorists.
Bekämpfungsmittel *nt (Insekten~)* pesticide, insecticide; *(Unkraut~)* weed-killer.
bekannt [1] *ptp of* **bekennen**.
[2] *adj* **(a)** *(allgemein gekannt, gewußt)* well-known *(wegen* for); *Mensch auch* famous ◆ **die ~eren/~esten Spieler** the better-/best-known *or* more/most famous players; **wie ist er ~ geworden?** how did he become famous?; **sie ist in Wien ~** she is (well-)known in Vienna; **er ist ~ dafür, daß er seine Schulden nicht bezahlt** he is well-known for not paying his debts; **das/sie ist mir ~** I know about that/I know her, she is known to me; **es ist allgemein/durchaus ~, daß ...** it is common knowledge/a known fact that ...; **ich darf diese Tatsachen als ~ voraussetzen** I assume that these facts are known.
(b) *(nicht fremd)* familiar ◆ **jdn mit etw ~ machen** *mit Aufgabe etc* to show sb how to do sth; *mit Gebiet, Fach etc* to introduce sb to sth; *mit Problem* to familiarize sb with sth; **sich mit etw ~ machen** to familiarize *or* acquaint oneself with sth; **jdn/sich (mit jdm) ~ machen** to introduce sb/oneself (to sb); **wir sind miteinander ~** we already know each other, we have already met.
bekannte *pret of* **bekennen**.
Bekanntenkreis *m* circle of acquaintances.
Bekannte(r) *mf decl as adj* friend; *(entfernter ~r)* acquaintance.
bekanntermaßen *adv (form)* as is known.
Bekanntgabe *f* announcement; *(in Zeitung etc)* publication.
⚠ **bekanntgeben** *vt sep irreg* to announce; *(in Zeitung etc)* to publish ◆ **ihre Verlobung geben bekannt ...** the engagement is announced between ... ▼
Bekanntheit *f* fame; *(von Fakten)* knowledge ◆ **aufgrund der ~ dieser Tatsachen** because these facts are known.
Bekanntheitsgrad *m* **einen hohen/niedrigen ~ haben** to be well-/little-known.
bekanntlich *adv* **~ gibt es ...** it is known that there are ...; **er hat ~ eine Schwäche für Frauen** he is known to have a weakness for women; **London ist ~ die Hauptstadt Englands** London is known to be the capital of England.
⚠ **bekanntmachen** *vt sep* to announce; *(der Allgemeinheit mitteilen)* to publicize; *(in Zeitung auch)* to publish; *(durch Rundfunk, Fernsehen auch)* to broadcast; *siehe auch* **bekannt (b)**.
Bekanntmachung *f* **(a)** *(das Bekanntmachen) siehe vt* announcement; publicizing; publication; broadcasting. **(b)** *(Anschlag etc)* announcement, notice.
Bekanntschaft *f* **(a)** *(das Bekanntwerden)* acquaintance; *(mit Materie, Gebiet)* knowledge *(mit* of) ◆ **jds ~ machen** to make sb's acquaintance; **mit etw ~ machen** to come into contact with sth; **bei näherer ~** on closer acquaintance.
(b) *(inf: Bekannte)* acquaintance ◆ **meine ganze ~** all my acquaintances; **ich habe gestern eine nette ~ gemacht** I met a nice person yesterday.
⚠ **bekanntwerden** *vi sep irreg aux sein* to become known; *(Geheimnis)* to leak out.
bekehren* [1] *vt* to convert *(zu* to).
[2] *vr* to be(come) converted *(zu* to) ◆ **er hat sich endlich bekehrt** *(fig)* he has finally turned over a new leaf *or* mended his ways.
Bekehrer(in *f*) *m* **-s, -** apostle *(gen* to); *(Missionar)* missionary *(gen* to); *(fig)* proselytizer.
Bekehrte(r) *mf decl as adj* convert, proselyte.
Bekehrung *f* conversion.
bekennen* *irreg* [1] *vt* to confess, to admit; *Sünde* to confess; *Wahrheit* to admit; *(Rel) Glauben* to bear witness to ◆ **Farbe ~** *(fig)* to put one's cards on the table.
[2] *vr* **sich (als** *or* **für) schuldig ~** to admit *or* confess one's guilt; **sich zum Christentum/zu einem Glauben/zu Jesus ~** to profess Christianity/a faith/one's faith in Jesus; **sich zu jdm/etw ~** to declare oneself *or* one's support for sb/sth; **sich nicht zu jdm ~** to deny sb; **die B~de Kirche** the (German) Confessional Church.
bekennend *adj Katholik, Homosexueller* professed.
Bekenner(in *f*) *m* **-s, -** confessor.
Bekenner-: **~anruf** *m* call claiming responsibility; **~brief** *m* letter claiming responsibility; **~geist, ~mut** *m* courage of one's convictions.
Bekenntnis *nt* **(a)** *(Geständnis)* confession *(zu* of); *(zum religiösen Glauben auch)* profession *(zu* of) ◆ **ein ~ zu den Menschenrechten** a declaration of belief in human rights; **sein ~ zum Sozialismus** his declared belief in socialism; **ein ~ zur Demokratie/zum Christentum ablegen** to declare one's belief in democracy/profess one's Christianity.
(b) *(Rel: Konfession)* denomination.
Bekenntnis-: **~christ** *m* member of the Confessional Church; **~freiheit** *f* freedom of religious belief; **b~freudig** *adj* eager to make confessions; **~kirche** *f* (German) Confessional Church; **b~los** *adj* uncommitted to any religious denomination; **~schule** *f* denominational school.
bekieken* *(N Ger inf)* [1] *vt* to look at.
[2] *vr* to (have a) look at oneself; *(gegenseitig)* to look at each other.
bekiest *adj* gravelled, gravel *attr*.
bekiffen* *vr (sl)* to get stoned *(sl)* ◆ **bekifft sein** to be stoned *(sl)*.
bekindert *adj (form)* with children.
beklagen* [1] *vt* to lament; *Los* to bewail; *Tod, Verlust* to mourn ◆ **Menschenleben sind nicht zu ~** there are no casualties.
[2] *vr* to complain *(über +acc, wegen* about) ◆ **sich bei jdm über etw** *(acc)* **~** to complain *or* make a complaint to sb about sth; **ich kann mich nicht ~** I can't complain, I've nothing to complain about.
beklagenswert, beklagenswürdig *(geh) adj Mensch* pitiful; *Zustand*

lamentable, deplorable; *Mißerfolg, Vorfall, Scheitern* regrettable, unfortunate; *Unfall* terrible.

beklagt *adj (Jur)* **die ~e Partei** the defendant; (*bei Scheidung*) the respondent; **der ~e Ehegatte** the respondent.

Beklagte(r) *mf decl as adj (Jur)* defendant; (*bei Scheidung*) respondent.

beklatschen* *vt* **(a)** (*applaudieren*) to clap, to applaud. **(b)** (*inf: Klatsch verbreiten über*) to gossip about.

beklauen* *vt (inf) jdn* to rob.

bekleben* *vt* **etw (mit Papier/Plakaten** *etc*) ~ to stick paper/posters *etc* on(to) sth; **etw mit Etiketten ~** to stick labels on(to) *or* to label sth.

bekleckern* *(inf)* [1] *vt* to stain ◆ **ich habe mir das Kleid bekleckert** I've made a mess on my dress; **einen Bekleckerten machen** (*sl*) to give oneself airs and graces.
[2] *vr* **sich (mit Saft** *etc*) ~ to spill juice *etc* all down *or* over oneself; **er hat sich nicht gerade mit Ruhm bekleckert** he didn't exactly cover himself with glory.

beklecksen* [1] *vt (inf)* to splatter (*mit* with) ◆ **etw (mit Tinte/Farbe) ~** to splatter ink/paint on sth; **ein bekleckstes Heft** an ink-/paint- *etc* besplattered exercise book; **du bist ja von oben bis unten bekleckst!** (*inf*) you're covered in ink/paint *etc*!
[2] *vr* to splatter oneself with ink/paint *etc*.

bekleiden* *(geh)* [1] *vt* **(a)** (*anziehen*) to dress (*mit* in); (*Kleidung geben*) to clothe ◆ **er war nur mit einer Hose bekleidet** he was only wearing a pair of trousers; **etw mit etw ~** (*geh*) to cover sth in sth.
(b) (*innehaben*) *Amt etc* to occupy, to hold ◆ **jdn mit einem Amt/einer Würde ~** to bestow an office/a title on sb.
[2] *vr* to get dressed.

bekleidet *adj* dressed, clad (*mit* in) ◆ **sie war nur leicht ~** she was only lightly *or* (*spärlich*) scantily dressed *or* clad; **nur mit einer Hose ~ sein** to be clad in *or* wearing only a pair of trousers.

Bekleidung *f* **(a)** (*Kleider*) clothes *pl*, clothing; (*Aufmachung*) dress, attire ◆ **ohne ~** without any clothes on. **(b)** (*form: eines Amtes*) tenure; (*rare: mit einem Amt*) honouring.

Bekleidungs-: ~amt *nt (Mil)* quartermaster's store; **~gegenstand** *m* garment, article of clothing; **~gewerbe** *nt* clothing *or* garment (*esp US*) trade; **~industrie** *f* clothing *or* garment (*esp US*) industry, rag trade (*inf*); **~stück** *nt* garment, article of clothing; **~vorschriften** *pl* clothing/uniform regulations.

bekleistern* *vt* **(a)** *Tapete etc* to paste. **(b)** (*bekleben*) **eine Wand (mit Plakaten) ~** to stick posters all over a wall.

beklemmen* *vt (fig)* to oppress; (*Schuld auch*) to weigh upon.

beklemmend *adj* (*beengend*) oppressive, constricting; (*beängstigend*) tormenting, oppressive.

Beklemmnis *f* feeling of oppressiveness; (*Gefühl der Angst*) feeling of apprehension *or* trepidation.

Beklemmung *f usu pl* feeling of oppressiveness; (*Gefühl der Angst*) feeling of apprehension *or* trepidation ◆ **~en bekommen/haben** to start to feel/to feel oppressed/full of apprehension *or* trepidation; (*bei enger Kleidung*) to start to feel/to feel restricted.

beklommen *adj* apprehensive, anxious; *Mensch auch* full of trepidation.

Beklommenheit *f* trepidation, apprehensiveness.

beklönen* *vt (N Ger inf)* to talk over.

beklopfen* *vt* to tap; *Brust auch* to sound.

bekloppt *adj (sl) Mensch* loony, crazy, mad (*all inf*); *Sache* lousy (*inf*), stupid (*inf*), crappy (*sl*).

beknackt *adj (sl) siehe* **bekloppt**.

beknien* *vt (inf) jdn* to beg.

bekochen* *vt (inf)* to cook for.

beködern* *vt* to bait.

bekommen* *irreg* [1] *vt* **(a)** to get; *Genehmigung, Stimmen, Nachricht auch* to obtain; *Geschenk, Brief, Lob, Belohnung auch* to receive; *Zug, Bus, Krankheit auch* to catch; *gutes Essen, Verpflegung auch, Schlaganfall, Junges, ein Kind, Besuch* to have; *Spritze, Tadel* to be given ◆ **ein Jahr Gefängnis ~** to be given one year in prison; **wir ~ Kälte/anderes Wetter** the weather is turning cold/is changing; **wir ~ Regen/Schnee** we're going to have rain/snow; **einen Stein/Ball** *etc* **an den Kopf ~** to be hit on the head by a stone/ball *etc*; **kann ich das schriftlich ~?** can I have that in writing?; **wir haben das große Bett nicht nach oben ~** we couldn't get the big bed upstairs; **jdn ins/aus dem Bett ~** to get sb into/out of bed; **was bekommt der Herr?** what will you have, sir?; **ich bekomme bitte ein Glas Wein** I'll have a glass of wine, please; **was ~ Sie dafür/von mir?** how much is that/how much do I owe you for that?; **jdn dazu ~, etw zu tun** to get sb to do sth; **er bekam es einfach nicht über sich, ...** he just could not bring himself to ...; **ich bekomme den Deckel nicht abgeschraubt** (*inf*) I can't unscrew the lid.
(b) (*entwickeln*) *Fieber, Schmerzen, Vorliebe, Komplexe* to get, to develop; *Zähne* to get, to cut; *Übung, neue Hoffnung* to gain ◆ **Rost/Flecken/Risse ~** to get *or* become rusty/spotty/cracked, to develop rust/spots/cracks; **Heimweh ~** to get *or* become homesick; **Sehnsucht ~** to develop a longing (*nach* for); **graue Haare/eine Glatze ~** to go grey/bald; **Hunger/Durst ~** to get *or* become hungry/thirsty; **Angst ~** to get *or* become afraid; **einen roten Kopf ~** to go red.
(c) *mit Infinitivkonstruktion* to get ◆ **etw zu essen ~** to get sth to eat; **etw zu sehen/hören ~** to get to see/hear sth; **was muß ich denn da zu hören ~?** what's all this I've been hearing?; **es mit jdm zu tun ~** to get into trouble with sb; **etw zu fassen ~** to catch hold of sth; **wenn ich ihn zu fassen bekomme ...** if I get my hands on him ...
(d) *mit ptp oder adj siehe auch dort* **etw gemacht ~** to get *or* have sth done; **seine Arbeit fertig** *or* **gemacht** (*inf*) **~** to get one's work finished *or* done; **etw geschenkt ~** to be given sth (as a present); **ich habe das Buch geliehen ~** I have been lent the book; **etw bezahlt ~** to get paid for sth; **einen Wunsch erfüllt ~** to have a wish fulfilled; **das Haus sauber ~** to get the house clean; **etw satt** *or* **über** (*inf*) **~** to have enough of sth.
(e) *in Verbindung mit n siehe auch dort* **Lust ~, etw zu tun** to feel like doing sth; **es mit der Angst/Wut ~** to become afraid/angry; **Ärger ~** to get into trouble; **eine Ohrfeige** *or* **eine** (*inf*) **~** to catch it (*inf*); **Prügel** *or* **sie** (*inf*) *or* **es** (*inf*) **~** to be given *or* to get a hiding.
[2] *vi* **(a)** *aux sein +dat* (*zuträglich sein*) **jdm (gut) ~** to do sb good; (*Essen*) to agree with sb; **jdm nicht** *or* **schlecht ~** not to do sb any good; (*Essen*) to disagree *or* not to agree with sb; **wie ist Ihnen das Bad ~?** how was your bath?; **wie bekommt ihm die Ehe?** how is he enjoying married life?; **es ist ihm schlecht ~, daß er nicht gearbeitet hat** not working did him no good; **wohl bekomm's!** your health!
(b) (*bedient werden*) **~ Sie schon?** are you being attended to *or* served?

bekömmlich *adj Mahlzeit, Speisen* (easily) digestible; *Luft, Klima* beneficial ◆ **leicht/schwer/besser ~ sein** to be easily digestible/difficult/easier to digest.

Bekömmlichkeit *f siehe adj* digestibility; beneficial quality.

beköstigen* *vt* to cater for.

Beköstigung *f* (*das Beköstigen*) catering (*gen* for); (*Kost*) food.

bekotzen* (*vulg*) *vt* to spew *or* puke over (*sl*).

bekräftigen* *vt* to confirm; *Vorschlag* to support, to back up ◆ **etw nochmals ~** to reaffirm sth; **seine Aussage mit einem Eid ~** to reinforce one's evidence by swearing an oath; **eine Vereinbarung mit einem Handschlag ~** to seal an agreement by shaking hands; **er nickte ~d** he nodded in support.

Bekräftigung *f* confirmation; (*Versicherung*) assurance ◆ **zur ~ seiner Worte** to reinforce his words.

bekränzen* *vt* to crown with a wreath; (*mit Blumen*) to garland.

bekreuzen* [1] *vt (Eccl)* to bless (with the sign of the cross).
[2] *vr siehe* **bekreuzigen**.

bekreuzigen* *vr* to cross oneself.

bekriegen* *vt* to wage war on; (*fig*) to fight ◆ **sie ~ sich (gegenseitig) schon seit Jahren** they have been at war with one another for years; **bekriegt werden** to be attacked.

bekritteln* *vt* to criticize; *Arbeit auch* to find fault with.

bekritzeln* *vt* to scribble over ◆ **das Buch mit Bemerkungen ~** to scribble comments over the book.

bekrönen* *vt* to crown (*auch fig*); (*Archit*) to surmount.

bekucken* *vt (N Ger) siehe* **begucken**.

bekümmern* [1] *vt* to worry ◆ **das braucht dich nicht zu ~** there is no need for you to worry about that.
[2] *vr* **sich über etw** (*acc*) **~** to worry about sth; **sich um etw ~** to concern oneself with sth.

Bekümmernis *f (geh)* distress.

bekümmert *adj* worried (*über +acc* about).

bekunden* [1] *vt* to show, to express; (*in Worten auch*) to state; (*Jur: bezeugen*) to testify to ◆ **~, daß ...** (*Jur*) to testify that ...
[2] *vr (geh)* to manifest itself.

Bekundung *f* expression, manifestation; (*in Worten auch*) statement; (*Jur*) testimony.

belabern* *vt (inf)* **jdn ~** to keep on at sb; (*überreden*) **er hat mich belabert** he talked me into it.

belächeln* *vt* to smile at.

belachen* *vt* to laugh at.

beladen* *irreg* [1] *vt Schiff, Zug* to load (up); (*fig: mit Sorgen etc*) *jdn* to burden ◆ **etw mit Holz** *etc* **~** to load sth with wood *etc*, to load wood *etc* onto sth; **ein Tier mit einer schweren Last ~** to put a heavy load on an animal.
[2] *vr* (*mit Gepäck etc*) to load oneself up ◆ **sich mit Verantwortung/Sorgen ~** to take on responsibilities/worries; **sich mit Schuld ~** to incur guilt.
[3] *adj* loaded; *Mensch* laden; (*mit Schuld*) laden, burdened ◆ **mit etw ~ sein** to be loaded with sth; (*Mensch*) to be loaded down *or* laden with sth; (*mit Schuld etc*) to be weighed down *or* laden *or* burdened with sth.

Belag *m* **-(e)s, ¨e** coating; (*Schicht*) layer; (*Ölfilm etc*) film; (*auf Pizza, Brot*) topping; (*auf Tortenboden, zwischen zwei Brotscheiben*) filling; (*auf Zahn*) film; (*Zungen~*) fur; (*Brems~*) lining; (*Fußboden~*) covering; (*Straßen~*) surface.

Belagerer *m* **-s, -** besieger.

belagern* *vt (Mil)* to besiege (*auch fig*), to lay siege to.

Belagerung *f* siege.

Belagerungs-: ~krieg *m* siege warfare; **~maschine** *f* siege machine; **~zustand** *m* state of siege; **den ~zustand ausrufen** to declare a state of siege.

Belami *m* **-(s), -s** (*dated*) ladykiller (*inf*).

belämmern* *vt*, **belämmert** *adj siehe* **belemmert**.

Belang *m* **-(e)s, -e** **(a)** (*no pl: Wichtigkeit*) importance, significance ◆ **von/ohne ~ (für jdn/etw) sein** to be of importance/of no importance (to sb/for *or* to sth). **(b)** **~e** *pl* interests. **(c)** (*form: Sache*) matter. **in diesem ~** as regards this matter.

belangen* *vt* **(a)** (*Jur*) to prosecute (*wegen* for); (*wegen Beleidigung, Verleumdung*) to sue ◆ **dafür kann man belangt werden** you could be prosecuted for that. **(b)** (*dated: betreffen*) **was mich belangt** as far as I am concerned.

belanglos *adj* inconsequential, trivial ◆ **das ist für das Ergebnis ~** that is irrelevant to the result.
Belanglosigkeit *f* **(a)** *no pl* inconsequentiality, triviality. **(b)** (*Bemerkung*) triviality.
Belangung *f* prosecution; (*wegen Beleidigung, Verleumdung*) suing.
belangvoll *adj* relevant (*für* to).
belassen* *vt irreg* to leave ◆ **wir wollen es dabei ~** let's leave it at that; **jdn in dem Glauben ~, daß ...** to allow sb to go on believing that ...; **jdn in seinem Amt ~** to allow sb to remain in office; **etw an seinem Ort ~** to leave sth in its place; **das muß ihm ~ bleiben** that must be left up to him.
belastbar *adj* **(a)** (*mit Last, Gewicht*) **bis zu 500 Kilogramm ~ sein** to have a maximum load of *or* load-bearing capacity of 500 kilogrammes; **wie hoch ist diese Brücke ~?** what is the maximum load of this bridge?
(b) (*fig*) **daran habe ich bemerkt, wie ~ ein Mensch ist** that made me see how much a person can take; **das Gedächtnis ist nur bis zu einem gewissen Grad ~** the memory can only absorb a certain amount; **weiter waren seine Nerven nicht ~** his nerves could take no more *or* were at breaking point.
(c) (*beanspruchbar*) (*Med*) *Mensch, Körper, Organe, Kreislauf* resilient ◆ **der Steuerzahler ist nicht weiter ~** the tax payer cannot be burdened any more; **die Atmosphäre ist nicht unbegrenzt (durch Schadstoffe) ~** the atmosphere cannot stand an unlimited degree of contamination; **da wird sich zeigen, wie ~ das Stromnetz/unser Wasserhaushalt ist** that will show how much pressure our electricity/water supply will take.
(d) wie hoch ist mein Konto ~? what is the limit on my account?; **der Etat ist nicht unbegrenzt ~** the budget is not unlimited.
Belastbarkeit *f* **(a)** (*von Brücke, Aufzug*) load-bearing capacity.
(b) (*von Menschen, Nerven*) ability to take stress; (*von Gedächtnis*) capacity.
(c) (*von Stromnetz etc*) maximum capacity; (*von Menschen, Organ*) maximum resilience ◆ **die höhere physische ~ eines Sportlers** an athlete's higher degree of physical resilience.
(d) (*von Haushalt*) (maximum) limit (*gen* of, on).
belasten* [1] *vt* **(a)** (*lit*) (*mit Gewicht*) *Brücke, Balken, Träger, Ski* to put weight on; (*mit Last*) *Fahrzeug, Fahrstuhl* to load ◆ **etw mit 50 Tonnen ~** to put a 50 ton load on sth, to put a weight of 50 tons on sth; **den Träger gleichmäßig ~** to distribute weight evenly over the girder; **das darf nur mit maximal 5 Personen/Tonnen belastet werden** its maximum load is 5 people/tons; **die Brücke/das Fahrzeug** *etc* **zu sehr ~** to put too much weight on the bridge/to overload the vehicle.
(b) (*fig*) **jdn mit etw ~** *mit Arbeit* to load sb with sth; *mit Verantwortung, Sorgen, Wissen* to burden sb with sth; **das Gedächtnis mit unnützem Wissen ~** to burden one's memory with useless knowledge; **jdn ~** (*mit Arbeit, Verantwortung, Sorgen*) to burden sb; (*nervlich, körperlich anstrengen*) to put a strain on sb; **jdn mit zu viel Arbeit/Verantwortung** *etc* **~** to overload/overburden sb with work/responsibility; *siehe* **erblich**.
(c) (*fig: bedrücken*) **jdn/jds Gewissen/Seele mit etw ~** (*Mensch*) to burden sb/sb's conscience/soul with sth; **jdn/jds Gewissen** *etc* **~** (*Schuld etc*) to weigh upon sb *or* sb's mind/conscience *etc*; **das belastet ihn sehr** that is weighing heavily on his mind; **mit einer Schuld belastet sein** to be burdened (down) by guilt; **von Sorgen belastet** weighed down with cares.
(d) (*beanspruchen*) *Wasserhaushalt, Stromnetz, Leitung* to put pressure on, to stretch; *Atmosphäre* to pollute; (*Med*) *Kreislauf, Magen, Organe, Körper, Menschen* to put a strain on, to strain; *Nerven* to strain, to tax; *Steuerzahler* to burden ◆ **jdn/etw zu sehr** *or* **stark ~** to overstrain sb/sth; *Wasserhaushalt etc* to put too much pressure on *or* to overstretch sth.
(e) (*Jur*) *Angeklagten* to incriminate ◆ **~des Material** incriminating evidence.
(f) (*Fin*) *Konto* to charge; *Etat* to be a burden on; (*steuerlich*) *jdn* to burden ◆ **etw (mit einer Hypothek) ~** to mortgage sth; **das Konto mit einem Betrag ~** to debit a sum from the account; **jdn mit den Kosten ~** to charge the costs to sb; **dafür werden wir Sie mit DM 50 ~** we will charge you 50 marks for that.
[2] *vr* **(a) sich mit etw ~** *mit Arbeit* to take sth on; *mit Verantwortung* to take sth upon oneself; *mit Sorgen* to burden oneself with sth; **sich mit Schuld ~** to incur guilt; **damit belaste ich mich nicht** (*mit Arbeit, Verantwortung*) I don't want to take that on; **ich will mich nicht ~** (*mit Wissen*) I don't want to know (about it).
(b) (*Jur*) to incriminate oneself.
belästigen* *vt* (*zur Last fallen*) to bother; (*zudringlich werden*) to pester; (*körperlich*) to molest; (*Licht, Geräusch, Geruch*) to irritate.
belästigend *adj* annoying, aggravating; *Licht etc* irritating.
Belästigung *f* annoyance; (*durch Lärm etc*) irritation; (*Zudringlichkeit auch*) pestering; (*körperlich*) molesting ◆ **etw als eine ~ empfinden** to find sth an annoyance *or* a nuisance; **sie beklagte sich über die ~en durch ihren Chef** she complained about being pestered by her boss.
Belastung *f siehe vt* **(a)** (*das Belasten*) putting weight on; loading; (*Last, Gewicht*) weight; (*in Fahrzeug, Fahrstuhl etc*) load ◆ **die erhöhte ~ der Brücke** the increased weight put on the bridge; **maximale ~ der Brücke/des Fahrstuhls** weight limit of the bridge/maximum load of the lift.
(b) (*fig*) (*das Belasten*) (*mit Arbeit*) loading; (*mit Verantwortung etc*) burdening; (*Anstrengung*) strain; (*Last, Bürde*) burden.
(c) burden (*gen* on).
(d) pressure (*gen* on); pollution (*gen* of); strain (*gen* on).
(e) incrimination.
(f) (*Fin*) charge (*gen* on); (*von Etat, steuerlich*) burden (*gen* on); (*mit Hypothek*) mortgage (*gen* on).
Belastungs-: b~fähig *adj siehe* **belastbar**; **~grenze** *f* (*von Brücke, Fahrzeug, Balken etc*) weight limit; (*von Atmosphäre, Wasserhaushalt*) maximum capacity; (*seelisch, physisch*) limit; (*Elec*) level of peak load; **ich habe meine ~grenze erreicht/überschritten** I've reached my limit *or* had enough/I've overdone it; **~material** *nt* (*Jur*) incriminating evidence; **~probe** *f* endurance test; **~spitze** *f* (*Elec*) peak load; **~zeuge** *m* (*Jur*) witness for the prosecution.
belatschern* *vt* (*dial inf*) to talk round, to persuade.
belauben* *vr* to come into leaf ◆ **spärlich/dicht belaubt sein** to have sparse/thick foliage.
Belaubung *f, no pl* (*Laub*) leaves *pl*, foliage; (*das Sichbelauben*) coming into leaf.
belauern* *vt* to eye; *Wild* to observe secretly; (*fig: Gefahr etc*) to menace.
belaufen* *irreg* [1] *vr* **sich auf etw** (*acc*) **~** to come *or* amount to sth.
[2] *vt* (*rare: begehen*) to walk ◆ **ein viel ~er Weg** a well-trodden path.
[3] *vi aux sein* (*dial: anlaufen*) to become covered in condensation; (*Fenster auch*) to steam up, to become steamed up.
belauschen* *vt* to eavesdrop on; (*genau beobachten*) to observe.
beleben* [1] *vt* **(a)** (*anregen*) to liven up; (*neu ~*) *Natur* to revive; (*aufmuntern auch*) to brighten up; *Absatz, Konjunktur, jds Hoffnungen* to stimulate ◆ **eine kalte Dusche wird dich neu ~** a cold shower will refresh you.
(b) (*lebendiger gestalten*) to brighten up; *Unterhaltung auch* to animate.
(c) (*zum Leben erwecken*) to bring to life.
[2] *vr* (*Konjunktur*) to be stimulated; (*Augen, Gesicht*) to light up; (*Natur, Stadt*) to come to life; (*geschäftiger werden*) to liven up.
[3] *vi* **das belebt** that livens you up.
belebend *adj* invigorating.
belebt *adj* **(a)** *Straße, Stadt etc* busy. **(b)** (*lebendig*) living ◆ **die ~e Natur** the living world; **~er Schlamm** activated sludge.
Belebtheit *f siehe adj* **(a)** bustle. **(b)** life.
Belebung *f* revival; (*der Wirtschaft, Konjunktur*) stimulation ◆ **zur ~ trank er einen starken Kaffee** to revive himself he drank a cup of strong coffee.
Belebungsversuch *m* (*Med*) resuscitation attempt.
belecken* *vt* to lick.
Beleg *m* **-(e)s, -e (a)** (*Beweis*) instance, piece of evidence; (*Quellennachweis*) reference ◆ **~e für den Gebrauch eines Wortes** instances of the use of a word. **(b)** (*Quittung*) receipt.
Beleg|arzt *m general practitioner, who also looks after a certain number of patients in a hospital.*
belegbar *adj* verifiable.
Belegbett *nt hospital bed at the disposal of a general practitioner, GP bed.*
belegen* *vt* **(a)** (*bedecken*) to cover; *Brote, Tortenboden* to fill ◆ **etw mit Fliesen/Teppich ~** to tile/carpet sth; **mit Beschuß/Bomben ~** to bombard/bomb *or* bombard; *siehe* **belegt**.
(b) (*besetzen*) *Wohnung, Hotelbett* to occupy; (*reservieren*) to reserve, to book; (*Univ*) *Fach* to take; *Seminar, Vorlesung* to enrol for ◆ **den fünften Platz ~** to take fifth place, to come fifth.
(c) (*beweisen*) to verify.
(d) (*auferlegen*) **jdn mit etw ~** to impose sth on sb; **jdn mit dem Bann ~** to proscribe sb; (*Eccl*) to excommunicate sb; **etw mit einem Namen ~** to give sth a name.
Beleg-: ~exemplar *nt* specimen copy; **~frist** *f* (*Univ*) enrolment period; **~leser** *m* OCR reader; **~material** *nt* documentation.
Belegschaft *f* **(a)** (*Beschäftigte*) staff; (*esp in Fabriken etc*) workforce. **(b)** (*inf: die Anwesenden*) **die ganze ~** the whole mob (*inf*) *or* gang (*inf*).
Belegschafts-: ~aktien *pl* employees' shares; **~mitglied** *nt* employee; **~versammlung** *f* meeting of employees.
Beleg-: ~stelle *f* reference; **~stück** *nt* piece of evidence.
belegt *adj Zunge* furred; *Stimme* hoarse; *Zimmer, Bett, Wohnung* occupied ◆ **~e Brote** open sandwiches.
belehnen* *vt* **(a)** (*Hist*) to enfeoff. **(b)** (*Sw*) *Haus* to mortgage.
belehrbar *adj* teachable.
belehren* *vt* (*unterweisen*) to teach, to instruct; (*aufklären*) to inform, to advise (*form*) (*über +acc* of) ◆ **jdn eines anderen ~** to teach sb otherwise; **sich eines anderen ~ lassen** to learn *or* be taught otherwise; **da mußte ich mich ~ lassen** I realized I was wrong; **er ist nicht zu** *or* **läßt sich nicht ~** he won't be told; **ich bin belehrt!** I've learned my lesson; *siehe* **besser**.
belehrend *adj* didactic.
Belehrung *f* explanation, lecture (*inf*); (*Anweisung*) instruction (*über +acc* about); (*von Zeugen, Angeklagten*) caution ◆ **deine ~en kannst du dir sparen** there's no need to lecture me.
beleibt *adj* stout, corpulent, portly.
Beleibtheit *f* corpulence, stoutness.
beleidigen* *vt jdn* to insult; (*Verhalten, Anblick, Geruch etc*) to offend; (*Jur*) (*mündlich*) to slander; (*schriftlich*) to libel.
beleidigt *adj* insulted; (*gekränkt*) offended; *Gesicht, Miene auch* hurt ◆ **~ weggehen** to go off in a huff (*inf*); **er fühlt sich in seiner Ehre ~** he feels his honour has been insulted; **die ~e Leberwurst spielen** (*inf*) to be in a huff (*inf*); **bist du jetzt ~?** have I offended you?; **jetzt ist er ~** now he's in a huff (*inf*).
Beleidigung *f* insult; (*Jur*) (*mündliche*) slander; (*schriftliche*) libel ◆ **eine ~ für den Geschmack/das Auge** an insult to one's taste/an eyesore; **etw als ~ auffassen** to take sth as an insult, to take offence at sth.
Beleidigungs-: ~klage *f* (*Jur*) slander/libel action, action for slander/libel; ⚠**~prozeß** *m* (*Jur*) slander/libel trial.
beleihen* *vt irreg* **(a)** (*Comm*) to lend money on; *Haus, Grundstück auch* to

mortgage, to give a mortgage on. **(b)** (*Hist*) *siehe* **belehnen.**

⚠**belemmert** *adj* (*inf*) (*betreten*) sheepish; (*niedergeschlagen*) miserable; (*scheußlich*) *Wetter, Angelegenheit* lousy (*inf*).

belesen *adj* well-read.

Belesenheit *f* wide reading ◆ **eine gewisse ~** a certain degree of erudition.

Beletage [bɛle'ta:ʒə] *f* (*old*) first floor (*Brit*), second floor (*US*).

beleuchten* *vt* (*Licht werfen auf*) to light up, to illuminate; (*mit Licht versehen*) *Straße, Bühne etc* to light; (*fig: betrachten*) to examine.

Beleuchter(in *f*) *m* **-s, -** lighting technician.

Beleuchterbrücke *f* lighting bridge.

Beleuchtung *f* **(a)** (*das Beleuchten*) lighting; (*das Bestrahlen*) illumination; (*fig*) examination, investigation. **(b)** (*Licht*) light; (*das Beleuchtetsein*) lighting; (*Lichter*) lights *pl* ◆ **die ~ der Straßen/Fahrzeuge** street lighting/lights *pl* on vehicles.

Beleuchtungs-: ~anlage *f* lighting (installation); **~körper** *m* lighting appliance; **~stärke** *f* intensity of light; **~technik** *f* lighting engineering.

beleumdet, beleumundet *adj* **gut/schlecht ~ sein** to have a good/bad reputation; **ein schlecht ~es Etablissement** an establishment with a bad reputation.

belfern *vti* to bark; (*Kanone*) to boom.

Belgien [-iən] *nt* **-s** Belgium.

Belgier(in *f*) [-iɐ, -iərɪn] *m* **-s, -** Belgian.

belgisch *adj* Belgian.

Belgrad *nt* **-s** Belgrade.

Belgrader *adj attr* Belgrade.

Belgrader(in *f*) *m* native of Belgrade; (*Einwohner*) inhabitant of Belgrade.

belichten* *vt* (*Phot*) to expose ◆ **wie lange muß ich das Bild ~?** what exposure should I give the shot?

Belichtung *f* (*Phot*) exposure.

Belichtungs-: ~automatik *f* automatic exposure; **~dauer** *f siehe* **~zeit**; **~messer** *m* light meter; **~tabelle** *f* exposure chart *or* table; **~zeit** *f* exposure (time).

Belieben *nt* **-s,** *no pl* **nach ~** just as you/they *etc* like, any way you *etc* want (to); **das steht** *or* **liegt in Ihrem ~** that is up to you *or* left to your discretion.

belieben* [1] *vi impers* (*geh*) **wie es Ihnen beliebt** as you like *or* wish; **was beliebt?** (*old: wird gewünscht*) what can I do for you?

[2] *vt* (*old, iro*) **es beliebt jdm, etw zu tun** (*hat Lust*) sb feels like doing sth; (*iro*) sb deigns *or* condescends to do sth; **jd beliebt, etw zu tun** (*neigt dazu*) sb likes doing sth; **er beliebt zu scherzen** (*iro*) he must be joking.

beliebig [1] *adj* any ◆ **(irgend)eine/jede ~e Farbe** any colour at all *or* whatever *or* you like; **nicht jede ~e Farbe** not every colour; **jeder B~e** anyone at all; **eine ganz ~e Reihe von Beispielen** a quite arbitrary series of examples; **in ~er Reihenfolge** in any order whatever; **alles B~e** anything whatever; **die Auswahl ist ~** the choice is open *or* free.

[2] *adv* as you *etc* like ◆ **Sie können ~ lange bleiben** you can stay as long as you like; **die Farben können ~ ausgewählt werden** you can choose any colour you like.

beliebt *adj* popular (*bei* with) ◆ **sich bei jdm ~ machen** to make oneself popular with sb.

Beliebtheit *f* popularity.

beliefern* *vt* to supply ◆ **jdn (mit etw) ~** to supply sb with sth.

Belieferung *f* supplying ◆ **die ~ einer Firma einstellen** to stop supplying a firm.

Belladonna *f* **-, Belladonnen** deadly nightshade, belladonna; (*Extrakt*) belladonna.

bellen [1] *vi* to bark; (*Kanonen*) to boom; (*Maschinengewehr*) to crack; (*Donner*) to crash.

[2] *vt* to bark; *Befehle* to bark out.

bellend *adj Husten* hacking; *Stimme* gruff; *Maschinengewehre* cracking; *Kanonen* booming.

Belletristik *f* fiction and poetry, belles lettres *pl*.

belletristisch *adj Zeitschrift, Neigung* literary ◆ **~e Literatur/Bücher** fiction and poetry/books of fiction and poetry; **~e Abteilung** department for fiction and poetry.

belobigen* *vt* to commend, to praise.

Belobigung *f* (*form*) commendation.

Belobigungsschreiben *nt* commendation.

belohnen*, belöhnen* (*Sw*) *vt* to reward; *jds Treue, gute Tat auch* to repay ◆ **starker Beifall belohnte den Schauspieler** the actor received hearty applause.

Belohnung, Belöhnung (*Sw*) *f* reward; (*das Belohnen*) rewarding ◆ **zur** *or* **als ~ (für)** as a reward (for); **eine ~ aussetzen** to offer a reward; **zur ~ der Kinder für ihr gutes Benehmen** in order to reward the children for their good behaviour.

Belt *m* **-s, -e der Große/Kleine ~** the Great/Little Belt.

belüften* *vt* to ventilate; *Kleider* to air.

Belüftung *f* **(a)** (*das Belüften*) ventilating; airing. **(b)** (*inf: die Anlage*) ventilation.

belügen* *vt irreg* to lie *or* tell lies/a lie to ◆ **sich selbst ~** to deceive oneself.

belustigen* [1] *vt* to amuse.

[2] *vr* (*geh*) **sich über jdn/etw ~** to make fun of sb/sth; **sich an etw** (*dat*) **~** to laugh at sth; **sich mit etw ~** to amuse oneself by (doing) sth.

belustigt [1] *adj Gesichtsausdruck, Ton, Stimme* amused.

[2] *adv* in amusement.

Belustigung *f* (*geh: Veranstaltung*) entertainment; (*das Belustigtsein*) amusement.

Belzebub *m siehe* **Beelzebub.**

bemachen* *vr* (*inf*) **(a)** (*sich beschmutzen*) to make oneself dirty *or* filthy. **(b)** (*sich aufregen*) to get het-up (*inf*).

bemächtigen* *vr* (*geh*) **(a)** (*in seine Gewalt bringen*) **sich eines Menschen/einer Sache ~** to take *or* seize hold of sb/sth; **sich des Thrones ~** to seize *or* take the throne; (*durch Intrige*) to usurp the throne. **(b)** (*Gefühl, Gedanke*) **sich jds ~** to come over sb.

bemähnt *adj Tier* maned; (*hum*) *Jugendliche* shaggy-haired.

bemäkeln* *vt* to find fault with, to pick holes in.

bemalen* [1] *vt* to paint; (*verzieren auch*) to decorate ◆ **etw mit Blumen ~** to paint flowers on sth; **bemalt sein** (*pej*) to be heavily made up.

[2] *vr* to paint oneself; (*pej: schminken*) to put on one's war paint (*inf*).

Bemalung *f siehe vt* painting; decoration.

bemängeln* *vt* to find fault with, to fault ◆ **was die Kritiker an dem Buch ~ ist ...** the fault the critics find with the book is ...

Bemängelung *f* finding fault (*gen* with), faulting (*gen* of).

bemannen* *vt U-Boot, Raumschiff* to man ◆ **sie ist seit neuestem wieder bemannt** (*inf*) she has just recently got herself a man again *or* a new boyfriend.

Bemannung *f* manning; (*rare: Mannschaft*) crew.

bemänteln* *vt* to cover up.

Bemäntelung *f* covering-up.

Bembel *m* **-s, -** (*dial*) pitcher.

bemeistern* (*geh*) [1] *vt* to master; *Wut, Erregung auch* to control

[2] *vr* **(a)** to control oneself. **(b) sich einer Sache** (*gen*) **~** to take *or* seize hold of sth.

bemerkbar *adj* noticeable, perceptible ◆ **sich ~ machen** (*sich zeigen*) to make itself felt, to become noticeable; (*auf sich aufmerksam machen*) to draw attention to oneself, to attract attention; **mach dich ~, wenn du etwas brauchst** let me know if you need anything.

Bemerken *nt* (*form*): **mit dem ~** with the observation.

➤ **bemerken*** *vt* **(a)** (*wahrnehmen*) to notice; *Schmerzen auch* to feel ◆ **er bemerkte rechtzeitig/zu spät, daß ...** he realized in time/too late that ...

➤ **(b)** (*äußern*) to remark, to comment (*zu* on) ◆ **hör auf, bemerkte sie** stop that, she said; **nebenbei bemerkt** by the way; **ich möchte dazu ~, daß ...** I would like to say *or* add, that ...; **er hatte einiges zu ~** he had a few comments *or* remarks to make.

bemerkenswert *adj* remarkable.

Bemerkung *f* **(a)** remark, comment (*zu* on). **(b)** (*old: Wahrnehmung*) observation.

bemessen* *irreg* [1] *vt* (*zuteilen*) to allocate; (*einteilen*) to calculate ◆ **der Raum ist für eine kleine Gruppe ~** the room is designed for a small group of people; **reichlich/knapp ~** generous/not very generous; **meine Zeit ist kurz** *or* **knapp ~** my time is limited *or* restricted.

[2] *vr* (*form*) to be proportionate (*nach* to).

Bemessung *f* **(a)** *siehe vt* allocation; calculation. **(b)** (*Build*) building specification.

Bemessungsgrundlage *f* (*Fin*) basis of assessment.

bemitleiden* *vt* to pity, to feel pity *or* feel sorry for ◆ **er ist zu ~** he is to be pitied; **sich selbst ~** to feel sorry for oneself.

bemitleidenswert *adj* pitiable, pitiful.

bemittelt *adj* well-to-do, well-off.

Bemme *f* **-, -n** (*dial*) slice of buttered bread; (*zusammengeklappt*) sandwich.

bemogeln* *vt* (*inf*) to cheat.

bemoosen* *vr* to become overgrown with moss.

bemoost *adj* mossy ◆ **~es Haupt** (*inf*) old fogey; (*Student*) perpetual student.

Bemühen *nt* **-s,** *no pl* (*geh*) efforts *pl*, endeavours *pl* (*um* for).

bemühen* [1] *vt* to trouble, to bother; *Rechtsanwalt etc* to engage ◆ **jdn zu sich ~** to call in sb, to call upon the services of sb; **die Bibel** *or* **Bibelstellen ~** to quote from the Bible.

[2] *vr* **(a)** (*sich Mühe geben*) to try hard, to endeavour ◆ **sich um gute Beziehungen/eine Stelle ~** to try to get good relations/a job; **sich um jds Wohl/jds Vertrauen/jds Gunst ~** to take trouble over sb's well-being/try to win sb's trust/court sb's favour; **sich um eine Verbesserung der Lage ~** to try to improve the situation; **sich um jdn ~** (*für eine Stelle*) to try to get sb; (*um Kranken etc*) to look after sb; (*um jds Gunst*) to court sb; **bitte ~ Sie sich nicht** please don't trouble yourself *or* put yourself out; **sich redlich ~** to make a genuine effort.

(b) (*geh: gehen*) to go, to proceed (*form*) ◆ **sich ins Nebenzimmer ~** to proceed to the next room (*form*); **sich zu jdm ~** to go to sb; **sich auf die Polizei ~** to go to the police.

bemüht *adj* **~ sein, etw zu tun** to try hard *or* endeavour to do sth; **um etw ~ sein, darum ~ sein, etw zu tun** to endeavour *or* be at pains to do sth.

Bemühung *f* effort, endeavour ◆ **vielen Dank für Ihre (freundlichen) ~en** (*form*) thank you for your efforts *or* trouble.

bemüßigen* *vr* (*geh*) **sich einer Sache** (*gen*) **~** to avail oneself of sth.

bemüßigt *adj* **sich ~ fühlen/sehen/finden** (*geh, usu iro*) to feel called upon *or* obliged.

bemuttern* *vt* to mother.

bemützt *adj* wearing a cap/hat ◆ **weiß ~e Bergkuppen** snow-capped mountains.

benachbart *adj* neighbouring *attr*; *Haus, Familie auch* next door; *Staat auch* adjoining ◆ **die Häuser sind ~** the houses adjoin one another *or* are next (door) to one another.

benachrichtigen* *vt* to inform (*von* of); (*amtlich auch*) to notify (*von* of).

Benachrichtigung *f* (*Nachricht*) notification; (*Comm*) advice note ◆ **die ~ der Eltern ist in solchen Fällen vorgeschrieben** the parents must be notified in such cases.

Benachrichtigungsschreiben *nt* letter of notification.

benachteiligen* *vt* to put at a disadvantage; (*wegen Geschlecht, Klasse, Rasse, Glauben etc auch*) to discriminate against; (*körperliches Leiden auch*) to handicap ◆ **benachteiligt sein** to be at a disadvantage/discriminated against/handicapped.

Benachteiligte(r) *mf decl as adj* victim ◆ **der/die ~ sein** to be at a disadvantage.

Benachteiligung *f siehe vt* (*das Benachteiligen*) disadvantaging; discrimination (*gen* against); (*Zustand*) disadvantage; discrimination *no pl*.

benageln* *vt* **eine Wand/das Dach** *etc* **mit etw ~** to nail sth onto a wall/the roof *etc*.

benagen* *vt* to gnaw at.

benähen* *vt* **das Kleid** *etc* **mit etw ~** to sew sth onto the dress.

benässen* *vt* (*geh*) to moisten.

⚠ **Bendel** *m or nt* **-s, -** *siehe* **Bändel**.

benebeln* *vt* (*inf*) **jdn/jds Sinne/jds Kopf ~** to make sb's head swim *or* reel; (*Narkose, Sturz*) to daze sb, to make sb feel dazed; **benebelt sein** to be feeling dazed *or* (*von Alkohol auch*) muzzy (*inf*).

benedeien *vt* (*Eccl*) to bless; *Gott* to glorify.

Benediktiner *m* **-s, -** **(a)** (*Eccl auch* **~in** *f*) Benedictine (friar/nun). **(b)** (*Likör*) Benedictine.

Benediktiner- *in cpds* Benedictine.

Benediktus *nt* **-, -** (*Eccl*) Benedictus.

Benefiz *nt* **-es, -e** benefit.

Benefizium *nt* **(a)** benefice. **(b)** (*Hist*) fee, feoff.

Benefiz-: ~spiel *nt* benefit match; **~vorstellung** *f* charity performance.

Benehmen *nt* **-s,** *no pl* **(a)** behaviour ◆ **kein ~ haben** to have no manners, to be bad-mannered. **(b) sich mit jdm ins ~ setzen** (*form*) to get in touch with sb.

benehmen* *irreg* [1] *vt* (*geh*) **(a)** (*rauben*) to take away ◆ **jdm den Atem ~** to take sb's breath away.
(b) (*rare: die Sinne trüben*) **jdn/jdm die Sinne** *or* **den Kopf ~** to make sb feel dazed; *siehe* **benommen**.
[2] *vr* to behave; (*in bezug auf Umgangsformen auch*) to behave oneself ◆ **benimm dich!** behave yourself!; **sich gut ~** to behave oneself, to behave well; **sich schlecht ~** to behave (oneself) badly, to misbehave.

beneiden* *vt* to envy ◆ **jdn um etw ~** to envy sb sth; **er ist nicht zu ~** I don't envy him.

beneidenswert *adj* enviable ◆ **~ naiv** (*iro*) amazingly naïve.

BENELUX *abbr of* **Belgien, Niederlande, Luxemburg.**

Benelux- [*auch* - -'-]: **~länder, ~staaten** *pl* Benelux countries *pl*.

benennen* *vt irreg* to name; *jdn auch* to call ◆ **jdn/etw nach jdm ~** to name *or* call sb/sth after *or* for (*US*) sb.

Benennung *f* (*das Benennen*) naming; (*von Mensch auch*) calling; (*Bezeichnung*) name, designation (*form*).

benetzen* *vt* (*geh*) to moisten; (*Tau, Tränen auch*) to cover.

Bengale *m* **-n, -n, Bengalin** *f* Bengalese, Bengali.

Bengalen *nt* **-s** Bengal.

Bengalin *f siehe* **Bengale**.

bengalisch *adj* **(a)** Bengalese; *Mensch, Sprache auch* Bengali. **(b) ~es Feuer** *brightly coloured flames from burning certain substances*, Bengal light; **~es Hölzchen** Bengal match; **~e Beleuchtung** subdued multicoloured lighting.

Bengel *m* **-s, -(s)** **(a)** boy, lad; (*frecher Junge*) rascal ◆ **ein süßer ~** (*inf*) a dear little boy. **(b)** (*dial: Knüppel*) stick ◆ **den ~ wegwerfen** (*dial*) to lose courage.

Benimm *m* **-s,** *no pl* (*inf*) manners *pl*.

Benimmregel *f, usu pl* etiquette *sing* ◆ **eine ~** a rule of etiquette.

Benin *m* **-s** Benin.

Benjamin [-miːn] *m* **-s, -e** Benjamin ◆ **er ist der ~** he is the baby of the family.

benommen [1] *ptp of* **benehmen**.
[2] *adj* dazed; (*von Ereignissen auch*) bemused.

Benommenheit *f* daze, dazed state.

benoten* *vt* to mark ◆ **etw mit „gut" ~** to mark sth "good".

➤ **benötigen*** *vt* to need, to require ◆ **das benötigte Geld** *etc* the necessary money *etc*, the money *etc* needed.

Benotung *f* mark; (*das Benoten*) marking.

benutzbar *adj* usable; *Weg* passable.

benutzen*, benützen* (*dial*) *vt* (*verwenden*) to use; *Literatur* to consult; *Gelegenheit auch* to make use of, to take advantage of ◆ **etw als Schlafzimmer/Vorwand ~** to use sth as a bedroom/an excuse; **das benutzte Geschirr** the dirty dishes.

Benutzer(in *f***), Benützer(in** *f***)** (*dial*) *m* **-s, -** user; (*von Leihbücherei*) borrower.

Benutzer-: b~freundlich *adj Computer, Telefonsystem* user-friendly; **etw b~freundlich gestalten** to make sth user-friendly; **~freundlichkeit** *f* user-friendliness; **~handbuch** *nt* user's guide, user handbook; **~oberfläche** *f* (*Comput*) user *or* system interface; **~sprache** *f* (*Comput*) user language.

Benutzung, Benützung (*dial*) *f* use ◆ **etw in ~ haben/nehmen** to be/start using sth; **jdm etw zur ~ überlassen** to put sth at sb's disposal; **etw zur ~ freigeben** *or* **bereitstellen** to open sth.

Benutzungsgebühr *f* charge; (*Leihgebühr*) hire charge.

benzen *vi* (*Aus inf*) **(a)** (*betteln*) to beg. **(b)** (*klagen*) to complain.

Benzin *nt* **-s, -e** (*für Auto*) petrol (*Brit*), gasoline (*US*), gas (*US*); (*Reinigungs~*) benzine; (*Feuerzeug~*) lighter fuel.

Benzin-: ~abscheider *m* **-s, -** petrol separator; **~einspritzung** *f* fuel injection.

Benziner *m* **-s, -** (*inf*) car which runs on petrol (*Brit*) *or* gasoline (*US*).

Benzin-: ~feuerzeug *nt* petrol/gasoline lighter; **~gutschein** *m* petrol/gasoline coupon; **~hahn** *m* fuel cock; **den ~hahn zudrehen** (*fig*) to stop the supply of petrol; **~kanister** *m* petrol/gasoline can; **~leitung** *f* fuel *or* petrol/gasoline pipe; **~motor** *m* petrol/gasoline engine; **~pumpe** *f* (*Aut*) fuel pump; (*an Tankstellen*) petrol/gasoline pump; **~uhr** *f* fuel gauge; **~verbrauch** *m* fuel *or* petrol/gasoline consumption.

Benzoe [-tsoe] *f* **-,** *no pl* benzoin.

Benzoesäure *f* benzoic acid.

Benzol *nt* **-s, -e** benzol(e).

be|obachtbar *adj* observable.

be|obachten* *vt* to observe; (*bemerken auch*) to notice, to see; (*genau verfolgen, betrachten auch*) to watch ◆ **etw an jdm ~** to notice sth in sb; **jdn ~ lassen** (*Polizei etc*) to put sb under surveillance; **er wird von der Polizei beobachtet** he's under police surveillance.

Be|obachter(in *f***)** *m* **-s, -** observer.

Be|obachtung *f* observation; (*polizeilich*) surveillance ◆ **die ~ habe ich oft gemacht** I've often noticed that; **bei der ~ der Vorgänge ...** as I *etc* observed *or* watched these developments ...

Be|obachtungs-: ~ballon *m* observation balloon; **~gabe** *f* talent for observation; **er hat eine gute ~gabe** he has a very observant eye; **~posten** *m* (*Mil*) observation post; (*Mensch*) lookout; **auf ~posten sein** to be on lookout duty; **~satellit** *m* (*Mil*) observation satellite; **~station** *f* **(a)** (*Med*) observation ward; (*nach Operation*) post-operative ward; **(b)** (*Met*) weather station.

be|ölen* *vr* (*sl*) to piss (*sl*) *or* wet (*inf*) oneself (laughing).

be|ordern* *vt* to order; (*kommen lassen*) to summon, to send for; (*an andern Ort*) to instruct *or* order to go ◆ **jdn zu sich ~** to send for sb.

bepacken* [1] *vt* to load (up) ◆ **jdn/etw mit etw ~** to load sb/sth up with sth.
[2] *vr* to load oneself up.

bepflanzen* *vt* to plant ◆ **das Blumenbeet mit etw ~** to plant sth in the flower bed.

Bepflanzung *f* **(a)** (*das Bepflanzen*) planting. **(b)** (*Gesamtheit der Pflanzen*) plants *pl* (*gen* in).

bepflastern* *vt* **(a)** *Straße* to pave; (*fig: behängen*) to plaster. **(b)** (*inf*) *Wunde etc* to put a plaster on. **(c)** (*Mil sl: bombardieren*) to plaster (*inf*); (*fig: bewerfen*) to bombard.

bepinkeln* (*inf*) [1] *vt* to pee on (*inf*).
[2] *vr* to wet oneself (*inf*).

bepinseln* *vt* to paint (*auch fig*); (*Cook, Med*) to brush; *Zahnfleisch* to paint; *Wand* to brush down; (*vollschreiben*) to scribble on.

bepissen* (*vulg*) [1] *vt* to piss on (*sl*).
[2] *vr* to piss oneself (*sl*).

Beplankung *f* (*Tech*) planking.

bepudern* *vt* to powder (*auch fig*).

bequasseln* *vt* (*inf*) to talk over.

bequatschen* *vt* (*sl*) **(a)** *etw* to talk over. **(b)** (*überreden*) *jdn* to persuade ◆ **wir haben sie bequatscht, daß sie kommt** we talked her into coming.

bequem *adj* (*angenehm*) comfortable; *Gast, Schüler etc* (*leicht, mühelos*) *Weg, Methode* easy; *Ausrede* convenient; (*träge*) *Mensch* idle ◆ **es ~ haben** to have an easy time of it; **es sich** (*dat*) **~ machen** to make oneself comfortable; **machen Sie es sich ~** make yourself at home.

bequemen* *vr* **sich zu etw ~, sich (dazu) ~, etw zu tun** to bring oneself to do sth; **endlich bequemten sie sich nach Hause** they finally forced themselves to go home.

bequemlich *adj* (*dated*) *siehe* **bequem**.

Bequemlichkeit *f* **(a)** *no pl* (*Behaglichkeit*) comfort; (*Trägheit*) idleness. **(b)** (*Einrichtung*) convenience.

berappen* *vti* (*inf*) to fork *or* shell out (*inf*) ◆ **er mußte schwer ~** he had to fork out a lot.

➤ **beraten*** *irreg* [1] *vt* **(a) jdn ~** to advise sb, to give sb advice; **gut/schlecht ~ sein** to be well-/ill-advised; **jdn gut/schlecht ~** to give sb good/bad advice; **sich von jdm ~ lassen(, wie ...)** to ask sb's advice (on how ...), to consult sb (about how ...).
(b) (*besprechen*) to discuss.
[2] *vi* to discuss ◆ **mit jdm über etw** (*acc*) **~** to discuss sth with sb; **sie ~ noch** they are still in discussion, they are still discussing it.
[3] *vr* (*gegenseitig Rat spenden*) to give each other advice; (*sich besprechen*) to discuss ◆ **sich mit jdm ~** to consult (with) sb (*über +acc* about); **das Kabinett tritt heute zusammen, um sich zu ~** the cabinet meets today for talks.

beratend *adj* advisory, consultative; *Ingenieur* consultant ◆ **jdm ~ zur Seite stehen** to act in an advisory capacity to sb; **er hat nur eine ~e Stimme** he is only in an advisory capacity; **~ an einer Konferenz teilnehmen** to attend a conference in a consultative *or* an advisory capacity.

Berater(in *f***)** *m* **-s, -** adviser.

Beratervertrag *m* consultative contract.

beratschlagen* *vti insep* to discuss.

Beratschlagung *f* discussion.

Beratung *f* **(a)** (*das Beraten*) advice; (*bei Rechtsanwalt, Arzt etc*) consultation.

⚠: for details of spelling reform, see supplement

➤ SPRACHE AKTIV: **benötigen** → 37.1 **beraten: 1a** → 29.2

(b) (*Besprechung*) discussion ◆ **eine ~ haben/abhalten** to have *or* hold talks *or* discussions.
Beratungs-: ~dienst *m* advice *or* advisory service; (*esp Comm, Fin auch*) consultancy; **~gebühr** *f* consultancy fee; **~stelle** *f* advice centre; **~zimmer** *nt* consultation room.
berauben* *vt* to rob ◆ **jdn einer Sache** (*gen*) **~** to rob sb of sth; *seiner Freiheit, seines Rechtes* to deprive sb of sth; **aller Hoffnung beraubt** having lost all hope.
berauschen* [1] *vt* (*trunken machen*) to intoxicate; (*Alkohol etc auch*) to inebriate; (*Droge auch*) to make euphoric; (*in Verzückung versetzen*) to intoxicate, to enrapture (*liter*); (*Geschwindigkeit*) to exhilarate; (*Blut, Greueltat etc*) to put in a frenzy ◆ **der Erfolg hat ihn völlig berauscht** he was drunk *or* carried away with success; **von Glück/Leidenschaft berauscht ...** in transports of happiness/passion ...; **berauscht von dem Wein/der Poesie/den Klängen** intoxicated by the wine/intoxicated *or* enraptured by the poetry/the sounds.
[2] *vr* **sich an etw** (*dat*) **~** *an Wein, Drogen* to become intoxicated with sth; (*in Ekstase geraten*) to be intoxicated *or* enraptured (*liter*) *or an Geschwindigkeit* exhilarated by sth; *an Blut, Greueltat etc* to be in a frenzy over sth.
berauschend *adj Getränke, Drogen* intoxicating ◆ **das war nicht sehr ~** (*iro*) that wasn't very enthralling *or* exciting.
Berber *m* **-s, -** **(a)** Berber. **(b)** (*auch* **~teppich)** Berber carpet.
Berberitze *f* **-, -n** (*Bot*) berberis.
berechenbar *adj Kosten* calculable; *Verhalten etc* predictable.
Berechenbarkeit *f siehe adj* calculability; predictability.
berechnen* *vt* **(a)** (*ausrechnen*) to calculate; *Umfang auch* to estimate; *Worte, Gesten* to calculate the effect of ◆ **alles, was sie tut, ist berechnet** everything she does is calculated.
(b) (*in Rechnung stellen*) to charge ◆ **das ~ wir Ihnen nicht** we will not charge you for it; **das hat er mir mit DM 75 berechnet** he charged me 75 marks for it.
(c) (*vorsehen*) to intend, to mean ◆ **alle Rezepte sind für 4 Personen berechnet** all the recipes are (calculated) for 4 persons; **auf eine bestimmte Wirkung berechnet sein** to be intended *or* calculated to have a particular effect.
berechnend *adj* (*pej*) *Mensch* calculating.
Berechnung *f siehe vt* **(a)** calculation; estimation ◆ **meiner ~ nach, nach meiner ~** according to my calculations, by my reckoning; **aus ~ handeln** to act calculatingly *or* in a calculating manner; **mit kühler ~ vorgehen** to act in a cool and calculating manner; **es war alles genaue ~** it was all calculated exactly.
(b) charge ◆ **ohne ~** without any charge.
berechtigen* *vti* to entitle ◆ **(jdn) zu etw ~** to entitle sb to sth; **diese Karte berechtigt nicht zum Eintritt** this ticket does not entitle the bearer to admittance; **er/seine Begabung berechtigt zu den größten Hoffnungen** he/his talent gives grounds for the greatest hopes; **das berechtigt zu der Annahme, daß ...** this justifies the assumption that ...
berechtigt *adj* justifiable; *Frage, Hoffnung* legitimate; *Anspruch* legitimate, rightful; *Vorwurf auch* just; *Forderung, Einwand auch* justified ◆ **~ sein, etw zu tun** to be entitled to do sth; **einen ~en Anspruch auf etw** (*acc*) **haben** to have a legitimate *or* rightful claim to sth, to be fully entitled to sth.
berechtigterweise *adv* legitimately; (*verständlicherweise*) justifiably.
Berechtigung *f* **(a)** (*Befugnis*) entitlement; (*Recht*) right ◆ **die ~/keine ~ haben, etw zu tun** to be entitled/not to be entitled to do sth. **(b)** (*Rechtmäßigkeit*) legitimacy; (*Verständlichkeit*) justifiability.
Berechtigungsschein *m* authorization.
bereden* [1] *vt* **(a)** (*besprechen*) to discuss, to talk over.
(b) (*überreden*) **jdn zu etw ~** to talk sb into sth; **jdn dazu ~, etw zu tun** to talk sb into doing sth; **bleib bei deiner Entscheidung, laß dich nicht ~** stick to your decision, don't let anybody talk you out of it.
(c) (*inf: beklatschen*) to gossip about.
[2] *vr* **sich mit jdm über etw** (*acc*) **~** to talk sth over with sb, to discuss sth with sb; **die beiden haben sich miteinander beredet** the two of them talked it over.
beredsam *adj* (*liter*) eloquent; (*iro: redefreudig*) talkative.
Beredsamkeit *f siehe adj* eloquence; talkativeness.
beredt *adj* (*geh*) eloquent ◆ **mit ~en Worten** eloquently.
Beredtheit *f* eloquence.
beregnen* *vt* to water, to sprinkle; (*vom Flugzeug aus*) to spray (with water) ◆ **beregnet werden** to be watered *etc*; (*natürlich*) to get rain.
Beregnung *f siehe vt* watering, sprinkling; spraying (with water); (*natürliche*) rain(fall).
Beregnungs|anlage *f* sprinkler.
Bereich *m* **-(e)s, -e** **(a)** area ◆ **in nördlicheren ~en** in more northerly regions; **im ~ der Kaserne** inside the barracks; **im ~ des Domes** in the precincts of the cathedral; **im ~ der Innenstadt** in the town centre (area).
(b) (*Einfluß~, Aufgaben~*) sphere; (*Sach~*) area, sphere, field; (*Sektor*) sector ◆ **im ~ des Möglichen liegen** to be within the realms *or* bounds of possibility; **Musik aus dem ~ der Oper** music from the realm of opera; **in jds ~** (*acc*) **fallen** to be within sb's province.
bereichern* [1] *vt* (*lit, fig*) to enrich; *Sammlung etc auch* to enlarge ◆ **das Gespräch hat mich sehr bereichert** I gained a great deal from the conversation.
[2] *vr* to make a lot of money (*an +dat* out of) ◆ **sich auf Kosten anderer ~** to feather one's nest at the expense of other people.
Bereicherung *f* **(a)** (*das Bereichern*) enrichment; (*von Sammlung auch*) enlargement.
(b) (*das Reichwerden*) moneymaking ◆ **seine eigene ~** making money for oneself.
(c) (*Gewinn*) boon ◆ **das Gespräch mit Ihnen war mir eine ~** I gained a lot from my conversation with you; **das ist eine wertvolle ~** that is a valuable addition.
bereifen* *vt* (*Aut*) *Wagen* to put tyres on; *Rad* to put a tyre on; *Faß* to hoop ◆ **gut/richtig bereift sein** (*Auto*) to have good/the right tyres.
Bereifung *f* (*Aut*) set of tyres ◆ **eine neue ~** new tyres, a new set of tyres; **die ~ bei diesem Auto** the tyres on this car.
bereinigen* *vt* to clear up, to resolve; *Meinungsverschiedenheiten auch* to settle ◆ **ich habe mit ihr noch etwas zu ~** I have something to clear up with her; **die Sache hat sich von selbst bereinigt** the matter resolved itself *or* cleared itself up.
Bereinigung *f siehe vt* clearing up, resolving; settlement.
bereisen* *vt ein Land* to travel around; (*Comm*) *Gebiet* to travel, to cover ◆ **die Welt/fremde Länder ~** to travel the world/in foreign countries.
bereit *adj usu pred* **(a)** (*fertig*) ready; (*vorbereitet auch*) prepared ◆ **es ist alles zum Essen/Aufbruch ~** the meal is all ready *or* prepared/we're all ready to go; **zum Einsatz ~e Truppen** troops ready *or* prepared to go into action; **sich ~ halten** to be ready *or* prepared; **eine Antwort/Ausrede ~ haben** to have an answer/excuse ready *or* a ready answer/excuse.
(b) (*willens*) willing, prepared ◆ **zu Zugeständnissen/Verhandlungen ~ sein** to be prepared to make concessions/to negotiate; **~ sein, etw zu tun** to be willing *or* prepared to do sth; **sich ~ zeigen, etw zu tun** to show oneself willing *or* prepared *or* ready to do sth; **sich ~ erklären, etw zu tun** to agree to do sth; **sich zu etw ~ finden** to be willing *or* prepared to do sth; **sich zur Ausführung einer Arbeit ~ finden, sich ~ finden, eine Arbeit auszuführen** to be willing *or* prepared to carry out a piece of work.
bereiten¹* [1] *vt* **(a)** (*zu~*) (*dat* for) to prepare; *Arznei* to make up; *Bett* to make (up).
(b) (*verursachen*) to cause; *Überraschung, Empfang, Freude, Kopfschmerzen* to give ◆ **jdm Kummer/Ärger ~** to cause sb grief/trouble; **er hat mir Schwierigkeiten bereitet** he made difficulties for me; **das bereitet mir Schwierigkeiten** it causes me difficulties; **einer Sache** (*dat*) **ein Ende ~** to put an end to sth; **es bereitet mir (viel *or* ein großes) Vergnügen** (*form*) it gives me (the greatest) pleasure.
[2] *vr* **sich zu etw ~** (*geh*) to prepare oneself for sth.
bereiten²* *vt irreg* **(a)** (*rare: einreiten*) to break in. **(b)** *Gebiet* to ride over.
bereit-: ~halten *vt sep irreg Fahrkarten etc* to have ready; (*für den Notfall*) to keep ready; *Überraschung* to have in store; **wer weiß, was das Schicksal für uns ~hält?** who knows what fate has in store for us?; **~legen** *vt sep* to lay out ready; **~liegen** *vi sep irreg* to be ready; **~machen** *vt sep* to get ready.
bereits *adv* already ◆ **~ vor drei Wochen/vor 100 Jahren/damals/damals, als ...** even three weeks/100 years ago/then/when ...; **das haben wir ~ gestern** *or* **gestern ~ gemacht** we did that yesterday; **er ist ~ vor zwei Stunden angekommen** he arrived two hours ago; **ich warte ~ seit einer Stunde** I've (already) been waiting for an hour; **der Bus ist ~ abgefahren** the bus has already left; **das hat man mir ~ gesagt** I've been told that already; **~ am nächsten Tage** on the very next day.
Bereitschaft *f* **(a)** *no pl* readiness; (*Bereitwilligkeit auch*) willingness, preparedness ◆ **in ~ sein** to be ready; (*Polizei, Feuerwehr, Soldaten etc*) to be on stand-by; (*Arzt*) to be on call *or* (*im Krankenhaus*) on duty; **etw in ~ haben** to have sth ready *or* in readiness.
(b) *no pl* (*~sdienst*) **~ haben** (*Arzt etc*) to be on call *or* (*im Krankenhaus*) on duty; (*Apotheke*) to provide emergency *or* after-hours service; (*Polizei etc*) to be on stand-by.
(c) (*Mannschaft*) squad.
Bereitschafts-: ~arzt *m* doctor on call; (*im Krankenhaus*) duty doctor; **~dienst** *m* emergency service; **~dienst haben** *siehe* **Bereitschaft (b)**; **~polizei** *f* riot police.
Bereit-: b~stehen *vi sep irreg* to be ready; (*Flugzeug auch, Truppen*) to stand by; **die Truppen stehen b~** the troops are standing by; **etw b~stehen haben** to have sth ready; **Ihr Wagen steht b~** your car is waiting; **zur Abfahrt b~stehen** to be ready to depart; **b~stellen** *vt sep* to get ready; *Material, Fahrzeug, Mittel* to provide, to supply; (*Rail*) to make available; *Truppen* to put on stand-by; **~stellung** *f* preparation; (*von Auto, Material, Mitteln*) provision, supply; (*von Truppen*) putting on stand-by.
Bereitung *f* preparation.
Bereit-: b~willig *adj* (*entgegenkommend*) willing; (*eifrig*) eager; **b~willig** *or* **b~willige Auskunft erteilen** to give information willingly; **~willigkeit** *f siehe adj* willingness; eagerness.
berennen* *vt irreg* (*Mil*) to charge, to assault; (*Sport*) to rush, to storm.
berenten* *vt* (*Admin sl*) **berentet werden** to retire and receive a pension; **sich ~ lassen** to retire with a pension.
bereuen* [1] *vt* to regret; *Schuld, Sünden* to repent of ◆ **~, etw getan zu haben** to regret having done sth; **das wirst du noch ~!** you will be sorry (for that)!
[2] *vi* to repent.
Berg *m* **-(e)s, -e** **(a)** hill; (*größer*) mountain ◆ **wenn der ~ nicht zum Propheten kommt, muß der Prophet zum ~ kommen** (*Prov*) if the mountain won't come to Mahomet, then Mahomet must go to the mountain (*Prov*); **~e versetzen (können)** to (be able to) move mountains; **mit etw hinterm ~ halten** (*fig*) to keep sth to oneself, to keep quiet about sth; *mit seinem Alter* to be cagey about sth; **in die ~e fahren** to go to the hills *etc*; **über ~ und Tal** up hill and down dale; **über den ~ sein** (*inf*) to be out of the woods; **über alle ~e sein** (*inf*) to be long gone *or* miles away (*inf*); **die Haare standen ihm zu ~e**

his hair stood on end; **da stehen einem ja die Haare zu ~e** it's enough to make your hair stand on end; *siehe* **kreißen, Ochse.**
(b) *(große Menge)* heap, pile; *(von Sorgen)* mass; *(von Papieren auch)* mountain.
(c) *(inf: ~werk)* pit ◆ **im ~ arbeiten** to work down the pit.

Berg- *in cpds* mountain; *(Bergbau-)* mining; **b~ab(wärts)** *adv* downhill; **es geht mit ihm b~ab(wärts)** *(fig)* he is going downhill; **~abhang** *m* side of a mountain, mountainside; **~absatz** *m* ledge; **~absturz** *m* drop; **~ahorn** *m* sycamore (tree); **~akademie** *f* mining college.

Bergamotte *f* -, -n bergamot.

Berg-: ~amt *nt* mining authority; **b~an** *adv siehe* **b~auf**; **~arbeiter** *m* miner; **b~auf(wärts)** *adv* uphill; **es geht wieder b~auf** *(fig)* things are getting better *or* looking up; **es geht mit seinem Geschäft/seiner Gesundheit wieder b~auf** his business/health is looking up; **~bahn** *f* mountain railway; *(Seilbahn auch)* cable railway; **~bau** *m* mining; **~bewohner** *m* mountain dweller.

Berge-: b~hoch *adj siehe* **berghoch**; **~lohn** *m (Naut)* salvage (money).

bergen *pret* **barg,** *ptp* **geborgen** *vt* **(a)** *(retten) Menschen* to save, to rescue; *Leichen* to recover; *Ladung, Schiff, Fahrzeug* to salvage; *Ernte* to get *or* gather (in); *(Naut) Segel* to furl ◆ **aus dem Wasser/brennenden Haus tot/lebend geborgen werden** to be brought out of the water/burning house dead/alive.
(b) *(geh: enthalten)* to hold; *Schätze auch* to hide ◆ **das birgt viele Gefahren in sich** that holds many dangers; **diese Möglichkeit birgt die Gefahr/das Risiko in sich, daß** ... this possibility involves the danger/risk that ...
(c) *(liter: verbergen) Gesicht* to hide; *Verfolgten etc* to shelter ◆ **sie barg ihren Kopf an seiner Schulter** she buried her face on his shoulder; *siehe* **geborgen.**

berge-: ⚠~versetzend *adj Glaube* colossal; **~weise** *adv* by the ton.

Berg-: ~fach *nt* mining; **~fahrt** *f* **(a)** mountaineering *or* climbing expedition; **auf ~fahrt gehen** to go mountaineering *etc or* on a mountaineering *etc* expedition; **(b)** *(auf Fluß)* upstream passage; *(von Seilbahn)* uphill *or* upward journey; **~fex** *m (inf)* mountaineering enthusiast *or* freak *(sl)*; **~fried** *m* keep; **~führer** *m* mountain guide; **~geist** *m* mountain troll; **~gipfel** *m* mountain top/peak; **~grat** *m* mountain ridge; **~hang** *m* mountain slope; **b~hoch** *adj Wellen, Haufen* mountainous; **b~hoher Müll** mountains of rubbish; **die Wellen stiegen b~hoch** the waves reached mountainous heights; **~hütte** *f* mountain hut *or* refuge, bothy *(Scot)*.

bergig *adj* hilly; *(hoch~)* mountainous.

Berg-: ~ingenieur *m* mining engineer; **~kamm** *m* mountain crest; **~kessel** *m* cirque, corrie; **~kette** *f* mountain range *or* chain, range *or* chain of mountains; **b~krank** *adj* affected by mountain sickness; **~krankheit** *f* mountain sickness; **~kraxler** *m* **-s, -** *(esp Aus, inf)* mountaineer; **~kristall** *m* rock crystal; **~kuppe** *f* (round) mountain top; **~land** *nt* hilly *or (Gebirgsland)* mountainous country/region; *(Landschaft)* hilly *etc* scenery.

Bergmann *m, pl* **Bergleute** miner.

bergmännisch *adj* miner's *attr.*

Bergmanns-: ~gruß *m* miner's greeting; **~sprache** *f* mining terminology.

Berg-: ~not *f* **in ~not sein/geraten** to be in/get into difficulties while climbing; **jdn aus ~not retten** to rescue sb who was in difficulties while climbing; **~plateau** *nt* mountain plateau; **~predigt** *f (Bibl)* Sermon on the Mount; **b~reich** *adj* mountainous; **~rennen** *nt (Sport)* hill climbing; **ein ~rennen** a hill climb; **~rettungsdienst** *m* mountain rescue service; **~riese** *m* gigantic mountain; **~rücken** *m* mountain ridge *or* crest; **~rutsch** *m* landslide *(auch fig)*, landslip; **~sattel** *m* (mountain) saddle, col; **~schrund** *m* bergschrund *(spec)*; **~schuh** *m* climbing boot; **b~seits** *adv* on the mountain side; **~spitze** *f* mountain peak; **~sport** *m* mountaineering, mountain climbing; **~station** *f* top station, summit station; **b~steigen** *vi sep irreg aux sein or haben, infin and ptp only* to go mountain climbing *or* mountaineering, to mountaineer; **b~steigen gehen** to go mountain climbing *or* mountaineering; **(das) ~steigen** mountaineering, mountain climbing; **~steiger(in** *f***)** *m* mountaineer, mountain climber; **~steigerei** *f (inf)* mountaineering, mountain climbing; **b~steigerisch** [1] *adj* mountaineering, mountain-climbing; [2] *adv* from a mountaineering point of view; **~stock** *m* **(a)** alpenstock; **(b)** *(Geol)* massif; **~straße** *f* mountain road; **die ~straße** *(Geog) wine-producing area north of Heidelberg*; **~sturz** *m siehe* **~rutsch**; **~tour** *f* trip round the mountains; *(~besteigung)* (mountain) climb; **~-und-Tal-Bahn** *f* big dipper, roller-coaster *(esp US)*, switchback; **~-und-Tal-Fahrt** *f* ride on the big dipper *etc*; **das war die reinste ~-und-Tal-Fahrt** *(fig)* it was like being on a switchback *or* big dipper.

Bergung *f, no pl* **(a)** *siehe* **bergen (a)** saving, rescue; recovery; salvage, salvaging; gathering (in). **(b)** *(liter: von Verfolgten)* sheltering.

Bergungs-: ~arbeit *f* rescue work; *(bei Schiffen etc)* salvage work; **~dampfer** *m* salvage vessel; **~kommando** *nt (esp Mil)*, **~mannschaft** *f*, **~trupp** *m* rescue team.

Berg-: ~volk *nt* **(a)** mountain race; **(b)** *(rare: ~leute)* miners *pl*; **~vorsprung** *m* (mountain) ledge; **~wacht** *f* mountain rescue service; **~wand** *f* mountain face; **~wanderung** *f* walk *or* hike in the mountains; **b~wärts** *adv* uphill; **~welt** *f* mountains *pl*; **~werk** *nt* mine; **im ~werk arbeiten** to work down the mine; **~wiese** *f* mountain pasture; **~zinne** *f (geh)* mountain pinnacle.

Beriberi *f* -, *no pl (Med)* beriberi.

Bericht *m* **-(e)s, -e** report *(über +acc* about, on, *von* on); *(Erzählung auch)* account; *(Zeitungs~ auch)* story; *(Sch: Aufsatzform)* commentary ◆ **der ~ eines Augenzeugen** an eyewitness account; **~e zum Tagesgeschehen** news reports; **eigener ~** from our correspondent; **(über etw** *acc***) ~ erstatten** to report *or* give a report (on sth); **jdm über etw** *(acc)* **~ erstatten** to give sb a report (on sth).

berichten* *vti* to report; *(erzählen)* to tell ◆ **jdm über etw** *(acc)* **~** to report to sb about sth; to tell sb about sth; **mir ist (darüber) berichtet worden, daß** ... I have received reports *or* been told that ...; **uns wird soeben berichtet, daß** ... *(Rad, TV)* news is just coming in that ...; **wie unser Korrespondent berichtet** according to our correspondent; **wie soeben berichtet wird, sind die Verhandlungen abgebrochen worden** we are just receiving reports that negotiations have been broken off; **gibt es Neues zu ~?** has anything new happened?; **sie berichtete, daß** ... she said *or* reported that ...; **sie hat bestimmt vieles zu ~** she is sure to have a lot to tell us.

Bericht-: ~erstatter(in *f***)** *m* reporter; *(Korrespondent)* correspondent; **~erstatter ist** ... *(bei Jahresversammlung etc)* the report will be given by ...; **~erstattung** *f* reporting; **eine objektive ~erstattung** objective reporting; **~erstattung durch Presse/Rundfunk** press/radio reporting; **die ~erstattung über diese Vorgänge in der Presse** press coverage of these events; **zur ~erstattung zurückgerufen werden** to be called back to report *or* make a report.

▼ **berichtigen*** *vt* to correct; *Fehler auch, (Jur)* to rectify; *Text, Aussage auch* to amend.

Berichtigung *f siehe vt* correction; rectification; amendment.

Berichts-: ~heft *nt* apprentice's record book; **~jahr** *nt (Comm)* year under review *or* report.

beriechen* *vt irreg* to sniff at, to smell ◆ **sich (gegenseitig) ~** *(fig inf)* to size each other up.

berieseln* *vt* **(a)** to spray with water *etc*; *(durch Sprinkleranlage)* to sprinkle. **(b)** *(fig inf)* **von etw berieselt werden** *(fig)* to be exposed to a constant stream of sth; **sich von Musik ~ lassen** to have (a constant stream of) music going on in the background.

Berieselung *f* watering ◆ **die ständige ~ der Kunden mit Musik/Werbung** exposing the customers to a constant stream of music/advertisements; **die ~ mit** *or* **durch etw** *(fig)* the constant stream of sth.

Berieselungs|anlage *f* sprinkler (system).

beringen* *vt* to put a ring on; *Vogel auch* to ring ◆ **mit Diamanten beringte Finger** fingers ringed with diamonds.

Beringmeer *nt* Bering Sea.

Beringung *f siehe vt* putting a ring on; ringing; *(Ring)* ring.

beritten *adj* mounted, on horseback ◆ **~e Polizei** mounted police.

Berkelium *nt, no pl (abbr* **Bk***)* berkelium.

Berlin *nt* **-s** Berlin.

Berliner[1] *m* **-s, -** *(auch* **~ Pfannkuchen***)* doughnut.

Berliner[2] *adj attr* Berlin ◆ **~ Weiße (mit Schuß)** *light, fizzy beer (with fruit juice added)*.

Berliner(in *f***)** *m* **-s, -** Berliner.

berlinerisch *adj (inf) Dialekt* Berlin *attr* ◆ **er spricht B~** he speaks the Berlin dialect.

berlinern* *vi (inf)* to speak in the Berlin dialect.

berlinisch *adj* Berlin *attr.*

Bermuda-Dreieck *nt* Bermuda triangle.

Bermuda|inseln, Bermudas *pl* Bermuda *sing, no def art* ◆ **auf den ~** in Bermuda *or* the Bermudas.

Bermudas, Bermudashorts *pl* Bermuda shorts *pl*, Bermudas *pl.*

Bern *nt* **-s** Bern(e).

Berner *adj attr* Berne(se).

Berner(in *f***)** *m* **-s, -** Bernese.

Bernhardiner *m* **-s, -** Saint Bernard (dog).

Bernstein *m, no pl* amber.

bernstein-: ~farben, ~gelb *adj* amber(-coloured).

berockt *adj (hum)* (dressed) in a skirt.

Berserker *m* **-s, -** *(Hist)* berserker ◆ **wie ein ~ arbeiten/kämpfen** to work/fight like mad *or* fury; **wie ein ~ toben** to go berserk; **auf jdn einschlagen wie ein ~** to go berserk and attack sb.

bersten *pret* **barst,** *ptp* **geborsten** *vi aux sein (geh)* to crack; *(auf~, zerbrechen)* to break; *(zerplatzen)* to burst; *(fig: vor Wut etc)* to burst *(vor* with) ◆ **als wollte ihm das Herz in der Seele ~** as if his heart would burst; **die Erde barst** the earth broke asunder *(liter)*; **vor Ungeduld/Neugier/Zorn** *etc* **~** to be bursting with impatience/curiosity/anger *etc*; **sie barst vor Lachen** she was helpless with laughter; **zum B~ voll** *(auch inf)* full to bursting.

Berstschutz *m (im Kernreaktor)* safety containment.

berüchtigt *adj* notorious, infamous.

berücken* *vt (geh)* to charm, to enchant.

berückend *adj* charming, enchanting ◆ **das ist nicht gerade ~** *(iro inf)* it's not exactly stunning.

berücksichtigen* *vt (beachten, bedenken)* to take into account *or* consideration; *Mangel, Alter, geringe Erfahrung, körperliches Leiden* to make allowances for; *(in Betracht ziehen) Antrag, Bewerbung, Bewerber* to consider ◆ **das ist zu ~** that must be taken into account *or* consideration; **meine Vorschläge wurden nicht berücksichtigt** my suggestions were disregarded.

Berücksichtigung *f* consideration ◆ **in** *or* **unter ~ der Umstände/der Tatsache, daß** ... in view of the circumstances/the fact that ...; **eine ~ Ihres Antrags ist zur Zeit nicht möglich** it is impossible for us to consider your application at present.

Beruf *m* **-(e)s, -e** *(Tätigkeit)* occupation; *(akademischer auch)* profession; *(handwerklicher)* trade; *(Stellung)* job ◆ **was sind Sie von ~?** what is your occupation *etc*?, what do you do for a living?; **von ~ Arzt/Bäcker/Hausfrau sein** to be a doctor by profession/baker by trade/housewife by occupation; **ihr stehen viele ~e offen** many careers are open to her; **seinen ~ verfehlt haben** to have missed one's vocation; **im ~ stehen** to be working; **von ~s wegen** on account of one's job.

berufen* *irreg* [1] *vt* **(a)** (*ernennen, einsetzen*) to appoint ◆ **jdn auf einen Lehrstuhl/zu einem Amt ~** to appoint sb to a chair/an office.
(b) (*old: kommen lassen*) **jdn zu sich/an einen Ort ~** to call *or* summon sb to one/a place; **Gott hat ihn zu sich ~** he has been called to his Maker.
(c) (*inf: beschwören*) **ich will/wir wollen** *etc* **es nicht ~** touch wood (*inf*); **ich will es nicht ~, aber ...** I don't want to tempt fate, but ...
(d) (*dial: ermahnen*) to tell off, to reproach.
[2] *vr* **sich auf jdn/etw ~** to refer to sb/sth.
[3] *vi* (*Aus Jur: Berufung einlegen*) to appeal.
[4] *adj* **(a)** (*befähigt*) *Kritiker* competent, capable ◆ **von ~er Seite, aus ~em Mund** from an authoritative source; **zu etw ~ sein, ~ sein, etw zu tun** to be competent to do sth.
(b) (*ausersehen*) **zu etw ~ sein** to have a vocation for sth; (*esp Rel*) to be called to sth; **viele sind ~** (*Bibl*) many are called; **sich zu etw ~ fühlen** to feel one has a mission to be/do sth.

beruflich *adj* (*esp auf akademische Berufe bezüglich*) professional; *Weiterbildung auch* job *or* career orientated ◆ **sein ~er Werdegang** his career; **im ~en Leben** in my *etc* working life, in my *etc* career; **meine ~en Probleme** my problems at work *or* in my job; **was das B~e betrifft, bin ich zufrieden** as far as my job is concerned I am satisfied; **~ ist sie sehr erfolgreich** she is very successful in her career; **sich ~ weiterbilden** to undertake further job *or* career orientated *or* professional training; **er ist ~ viel unterwegs** he is away a lot on business.

Berufs- *in cpds* professional; **~ausbildung** *f* training (*for an occupation*); (*für Handwerk*) vocational training; **~aussichten** *pl* job prospects *pl*; **~beamtentum** *nt* civil service with tenure; **~beamte(r)** *m* civil servant with tenure; **b~bedingt** *adj* occupational, caused by one's occupation; **~berater** *m* careers adviser; **~beratung** *f* careers guidance; **~bezeichnung** *f* job title; **b~bezogen** *adj* relevant to one's job; *Unterricht* vocationally orientated; **~bild** *nt* job outline; **~boxen** *nt* professional boxing; **b~erfahren** *adj* (professionally) experienced; **~erfahrung** *f* (professional) experience; **~ethos** *nt* professional ethics *pl*; **~fachschule** *f* training college (*attended full-time*); **~feuerwehr** *f* fire service; **~freiheit** *f* freedom to choose and carry out one's career; **b~fremd** *adj* unconnected with one's occupation; *Mensch* without relevant experience; **eine b~fremde Tätigkeit** a job outside one's profession/trade; **~fremde(r)** *mf decl as adj* person without relevant experience. **~fußball** *m* professional football; **~geheimnis** *nt* professional secret; (*Schweigepflicht*) professional secrecy, confidentiality; **das ~geheimnis wahren** to observe professional secrecy *or* confidentiality; **~genossenschaft** *f* professional/trade association; **~gruppe** *f* occupational group; **~heer** *nt* professional *or* regular army; **~kleidung** *f* working clothes *pl*; **~krankheit** *f* occupational disease; **~kriminalität** *f* professional crime; **~leben** *nt* working *or* professional life; **im ~leben stehen** to be working *or* in employment; **b~los** *adj* without a profession/trade; **b~mäßig** *adj* professional; **etw b~mäßig betreiben** to do sth professionally *or* on a professional basis; **~offizier** *m* regular officer; **~pflicht** *f* professional duty; **~revolutionär** *m* (*esp pej*) professional revolutionary; **~risiko** *nt* occupational hazard *or* risk; **~schule** *f* vocational school, ≃ technical college (*Brit*); **~schüler** *m* student at vocational school *etc*; **~soldat** *m* regular *or* professional soldier; **~spieler** *m* professional player; **~sport** *m* professional sport; **~sportler** *m* professional sportsman; **~stand** *m* profession, professional group; (*Gewerbe*) trade; **b~tätig** *adj* working; **b~tätig sein** to be working, to work; **halbtags b~tätig sein** to work part-time; **ich bin auch b~tätig** I go out to work too; **nicht mehr b~tätig sein** to have left work; **~tätige(r)** *mf decl as adj* working person; **b~unfähig** *adj* unable to work; **~unfähigkeit** *f* inability to work; **~unfall** *m* occupational accident; **~verband** *m* professional/trade organization *or* association; **~verbot** *nt exclusion from a civil service profession by government ruling*; **jdm ~verbot erteilen** to ban sb from a profession; **unter das ~verbot fallen** to be banned from a profession; **~verbrecher** *m* professional criminal; **~verkehr** *m* commuter traffic; **~wahl** *f* choice of occupation/profession/trade; **~wechsel** *m* change of occupation; **~ziel** *nt* profession one is aiming for; **~zweig** *m siehe* **Beruf** branch of an occupation *etc*; (*~gruppe*) occupation/profession/trade.

Berufung *f* **(a)** (*Jur*) appeal ◆ **in die ~ gehen/~ einlegen** to appeal (*bei* to).
(b) (*in ein Amt etc*) appointment (*auf or an +acc* to).
(c) (*innerer Auftrag*) vocation; (*Rel auch*) mission, calling ◆ **die ~ zu etw in sich** (*dat*) **fühlen** to feel one has a vocation *etc* to be sth.
(d) (*form*) **die ~ auf jdn/etw** reference to sb/sth; **unter ~ auf etw** (*acc*) with reference to sth.

Berufungs-: ⚠**~ausschuß** *m* appeal tribunal; **~frist** *f* period in which an appeal must be submitted; **~gericht** *nt* appeal court, court of appeal; **~instanz** *f* court of appeal; **~klage** *f* appeal; **~kläger** *m* appellant.

beruhen* *vi* to be based *or* founded (*auf +dat* on) ◆ **das beruht auf Gegenseitigkeit** (*inf*) the feeling is mutual; **etw auf sich ~ lassen** to let sth rest.

beruhigen* [1] *vt* to calm (down); *Baby* to quieten; (*trösten*) to soothe, to comfort; (*versichern*) to reassure; *Magen* to settle; *Nerven auch* to soothe; *Gewissen* to soothe, to salve; *Schmerzen* to ease, to relieve ◆ **na, dann bin ich ja beruhigt** well I must say I'm quite relieved; **dann kann ich ja beruhigt schlafen/nach Hause gehen** then I can go to sleep/go home with my mind at rest; **~d** (*körperlich, beschwichtigend*) soothing; (*tröstlich*) reassuring; **es ist ~d zu wissen, daß ...** it is reassuring to know that ...
[2] *vr* to calm down; (*Krise auch*) to ease off, to lessen; (*Gewissen*) to be eased; (*Andrang, Verkehr, Kämpfe*) to subside, to lessen; (*Börse, Preise, Magen*) to settle down; (*Krämpfe, Schmerzen*) to lessen, to ease; (*Meer*) to become calm; (*Sturm*) to die down, to abate ◆ **sie konnte sich gar nicht darüber ~, daß ...** she could not get over the fact that ...; **beruhige dich doch!** calm down!

Beruhigung *f, no pl* **(a)** *siehe vt* calming (down); quietening; soothing, comforting; reassuring; settling; placating, appeasing; soothing; soothing, salving; easing, relieving ◆ **zu Ihrer ~ kann ich sagen ...** you'll be reassured to know that ...
(b) *siehe vr* calming down; easing off, lessening; easing; subsiding, lessening; settling down; settling; lessening, easing; calming; abatement ◆ **ein Gefühl der ~** a reassuring feeling.

Beruhigungs-: **~mittel** *nt* sedative, tranquillizer; **~pille, ~tablette** *f* sedative (pill), tranquillizer, downer (*sl*); **~spritze** *f* sedative (injection).

berühmt *adj* famous ◆ **wegen** *or* **für etw ~ sein** to be famous *or* renowned for sth; **das war nicht ~** (*inf*) it was nothing to write home about (*inf*).

berühmt-berüchtigt *adj* infamous, notorious.

Berühmtheit *f* **(a)** fame ◆ **~ erlangen** to become famous; **zu trauriger ~ gelangen** to become notorious *or* infamous. **(b)** (*Mensch*) celebrity.

berühren* [1] *vt* **(a)** (*anfassen, streifen, Math*) to touch; (*grenzen an*) to border on; (*auf Reise streifen*) *Länder* to touch; *Hafen* to stop at, to put in *or* call at; (*erwähnen*) *Thema, Punkt* to touch on ◆ **B~ verboten** do not touch.
(b) (*seelisch bewegen*) to move; (*auf jdn wirken*) to affect; (*betreffen*) to affect, to concern ◆ **das berührt mich gar nicht!** that's nothing to do with me; **von etw peinlich/schmerzlich berührt sein** to be embarrassed/pained by sth; **es berührt mich angenehm/seltsam, daß ...** I am pleased/surprised that ...
[2] *vr* to touch; (*Menschen auch*) to touch each other; (*Drähte etc auch*) to be in/come into contact; (*Ideen, Vorstellungen, Interessen*) to coincide.

Berührung *f* touch; (*zwischen Drähten etc, menschlicher Kontakt*) contact; (*Erwähnung*) mention ◆ **mit jdm/etw in ~ kommen** to come into contact with sb/sth; **jdn mit jdm/etw in ~ bringen** to bring sb into contact with sb/sth; **körperliche ~** physical *or* bodily contact; **die ~ der Instrumente ist zu vermeiden** avoid touching the instruments; **bei ~ Lebensgefahr!** danger! do not touch!; **Ansteckung durch ~** contagion, infection by contact.

Berührungs-: **~angst** *f usu pl* reservation (*mit* about); **die ~ängste vor diesem Thema sind noch groß** there is still great reluctance to deal with this subject; **~bildschirm** *m* touch screen; **~gift** *nt* contact poison; **~punkt** *m* point of contact; (*Math auch*) tangential point; **unsere Interessen haben keinerlei ~punkte** there are no points of contact between our interests.

Beryllium *nt, no pl* (*abbr* **Be**) beryllium.

bes. *abbr of* **besonders.**

besabbern* (*inf*) [1] *vt* to slobber on *or* all over.
[2] *vr* to slobber all over oneself.

besäen* *vt* (*lit*) to sow; *siehe* **besät.**

besagen* *vt* to say; (*bedeuten*) to mean, to imply ◆ **das besagt nichts/viel** that does not mean anything/that means a lot; **das besagt nicht, daß ...** that does not mean (to say) that ...

besagt *adj attr* (*form*) said (*form*), aforementioned (*form*).

besaiten* *vt* to string ◆ **etw neu ~** to restring sth; *siehe* **zart.**

besamen* *vt* to fertilize; (*künstlich*) to inseminate; (*Bot*) to pollinate.

besammeln* *vr* (*esp Sw*) to assemble, to gather.

Besammlung *f* (*esp Sw*) assembly.

Besamung *f siehe vt* fertilization; insemination; pollination.

Besan *m* **-s, -e** (*Naut*) mizzen (sail/mast).

besänftigen* [1] *vt* to calm down, to soothe; *Menge auch* to pacify; *jds Zorn, Erregung, Gemüt* to soothe ◆ **er war nicht zu ~** it was impossible to calm him down.
[2] *vr* (*Mensch*) to calm down; (*Meer, Elemente*) to become calm.

Besänftigung *f siehe vt* calming (down), soothing; pacifying; soothing.

Besanmast *m* (*Naut*) mizzen mast.

besaß *pret of* **besitzen.**

besät [1] *ptp of* **besäen.**
[2] *adj* covered; (*mit Blättern etc*) strewn; (*iro: mit Orden*) studded ◆ **der mit Sternen ~e Himmel** the star-spangled sky.

Besatz *m* **-es, ¨-e** **(a)** edging, trimming; (*an Tischtuch auch*) border ◆ **einen ~ aus etw haben** to be trimmed with sth. **(b)** (*Bestand*) stock.

Besatzer *m* **-s, -** (*pej inf*) occupying forces *pl*.

Besatzung *f* **(a)** (*Mannschaft*) crew; (*Verteidigungstruppe*) garrison. **(b)** (*~sarmee*) occupying army *or* forces *pl*.

Besatzungs-: **~armee** *f* occupying army, army of occupation; **~kind** *nt illegitimate child of member of the occupying forces*; **~macht** *f* occupying power; **~statut** *nt* statute of occupation; **~streitkräfte, ~truppen** *pl* occupying forces *pl*; **~zone** *f* occupation zone; **die amerikanische ~zone** the American (-occupied) zone.

besaufen* *vr irreg* (*sl*) to get plastered (*sl*) *or* pissed (*Brit sl*).

Besäufnis *nt* (*inf*) booze-up (*inf*).

besäuseln* *vr* (*inf*) to get tipsy *or* merry ◆ **besäuselt** tipsy, merry.

beschädigen* *vt* to damage ◆ **beschädigt** damaged; *Schiff auch* disabled.

Beschädigte(r) *mf decl as adj* disabled person.

Beschädigung *f* damage (*von* to) ◆ **das Auto hat mehrere ~en** the car is damaged in several places.

beschaffen* [1] *vt* to procure (*form*), to get (hold of), to obtain ◆ **jdm etw ~** to get (hold of) *or* obtain sth for sb; **jdm/sich eine Stelle ~** to get sb/oneself a job; **das ist schwer zu ~** that is difficult to get (hold of).

[2] *adj* (*form*) **wie ist es mit seiner Gesundheit ~?** what about his health?; **mit jdm/damit ist es gut/schlecht ~** sb/it is in a good/bad way; **so ~ sein wie ...** to be the same as ...; **das ist so ~, daß ...** that is such that ...

Beschaffenheit *f, no pl* composition; (*von Mensch*) (*körperlich*) constitution; (*seelisch*) nature, qualities *pl* ♦ **die glatte ~ des Steins** the smoothness of the stone; **von sensibler seelischer ~ sein** to be of a very sensitive nature *or* disposition; **er hat für diesen Beruf nicht die seelische/körperliche ~** he doesn't have the right sort of psychological make-up/physique for this job; **je nach ~ der Lage** according to the situation.

Beschaffung *f, no pl* procuring, obtaining.

Beschaffungskriminalität *f* drug-related crime.

beschäftigen* [1] *vr* **sich mit etw ~** to occupy oneself with sth; (*sich befassen, abhandeln*) to deal with sth; **sich mit dem Tod ~** to think about death; **sich mit Literatur ~** to study literature; **sich mit der Frage ~, ob ...** to consider the question of whether ...; **sich mit jdm ~** to devote one's attention to sb; **sie beschäftigt sich viel mit den Kindern** she devotes a lot of her time to the children; **sie beschäftigt sich gerade mit den Kindern** she is busy with the children just now.

[2] *vt* **(a)** (*innerlich ~*) **jdn ~** to be on sb's mind; **die Frage beschäftigt sie sehr** she is very preoccupied with that question, that question has been on her mind a lot.

(b) (*anstellen*) to employ.

(c) (*eine Tätigkeit geben*) to occupy, to keep occupied ♦ **jdn mit etw ~** to give sb sth to do.

beschäftigt *adj* **(a)** busy ♦ **mit dem Nähen/jdm ~ sein** to be busy sewing/with sb; **mit sich selbst/seinen Problemen ~ sein** to be preoccupied with oneself/one's problems. **(b)** (*angestellt*) employed (*bei* by).

Beschäftigte(r) *mf decl as adj* employee.

Beschäftigung *f* **(a)** (*berufliche Arbeit*) work *no indef art*, job; (*Anstellung, Angestelltsein*) employment ♦ **eine ~ suchen** to be looking for work *or* a job, to seek employment (*form*); **einer ~ nachgehen** (*form*) to be employed; **ohne ~ sein** to be unemployed *or* out of work.

(b) (*Tätigkeit*) activity, occupation ♦ **jdm eine ~ geben** to give sb something to do; **~ haben** to have something to do.

(c) (*geistige ~*) preoccupation; (*mit Frage*) consideration; (*mit Thema*) treatment; (*mit Literatur*) study (*mit* of); (*mit sich, seinen Problemen*) preoccupation.

(d) (*von Kindern, Patienten etc*) occupying, keeping occupied ♦ **die ~ der Patienten** keeping the patients occupied.

Beschäftigungs-: b~los *adj* unoccupied; (*arbeitslos*) unemployed, out-of-work; **~offensive** *f* job creation campaign; **~programm** *nt* job creation scheme; **~therapeut** *m* occupational therapist; **~therapie** *f* occupational therapy.

beschälen* *vt* (*form*) to cover, to serve.

Beschäler *m* **-s, -** (*form*) stallion, stud.

Beschälung *f* (*form*) covering, service.

beschämen* *vt* to shame; (*jds Großzügigkeit*) to embarrass ♦ **es beschämt mich, zu sagen ...** I feel ashamed to have to say ...

beschämend *adj* **(a)** (*schändlich*) shameful ♦ **es war ~ für seine ganze Familie** it brought shame on *or* to his whole family. **(b)** (*vorbildlich*) shaming; *Großzügigkeit auch* embarrassing. **(c)** (*demütigend*) humiliating, shaming.

beschämt *adj* ashamed, abashed ♦ **ich fühle mich durch deine Großzügigkeit ~** I am embarrassed by your generosity.

Beschämung *f* shame; (*Verlegenheit*) embarrassment ♦ **zu meiner ~** to my shame; **in tiefer ~ ging er nach Hause** he went home feeling very ashamed; **seine Güte war eine ~ für uns alle** his kindness put us all to shame.

beschatten* *vt* **(a)** (*geh: Schatten geben*) to shade; (*fig: trüben*) to overshadow. **(b)** (*überwachen*) to shadow, to tail ♦ **jdn ~ lassen** to have sb shadowed *or* tailed. **(c)** (*Sport*) to mark closely.

Beschatter *m* **-s, - (a)** (*Polizist etc*) tail. **(b)** (*Sport*) marker.

Beschattung *f siehe vt* **(a)** shading; overshadowing. **(b)** shadowing, tailing. **(c)** marking.

Beschau *f* **-**, *no pl* inspection.

beschauen* *vt* **(a)** *Fleisch etc* to inspect. **(b)** (*dial: betrachten*) to look at ♦ **sich** (*dat*) **etw ~** to look at sth.

Beschauer *m* **-s, - (a)** inspector. **(b)** (*Betrachter*) spectator; (*von Bild*) viewer.

beschaulich *adj* **(a)** (*geruhsam*) *Leben, Abend* quiet, tranquil; *Charakter, Mensch* pensive, contemplative ♦ **~ dasitzen** to sit contemplating. **(b)** (*Rel*) contemplative.

Beschaulichkeit *f siehe adj* **(a)** quietness, tranquillity; pensiveness, contemplation. **(b)** (*Rel*) contemplativeness.

Beschauung *f* inspection.

Bescheid *m* **-(e)s, -e (a)** (*Auskunft*) information; (*Nachricht*) notification; (*Entscheidung auf Antrag etc*) decision ♦ **wir erwarten Ihren ~** we look forward to hearing from you; **ich warte noch auf ~** I am still waiting to hear, I still have not heard anything; **jdm (über etw** *acc or* **von etw) ~ sagen/geben** to let sb know (about sth), to tell sb (about sth); **jdm ordentlich ~ sagen** *or* **gründlich ~ stoßen** (*inf*) to tell sb where to get off (*inf*); **~ hinterlassen** to leave word.

(b) (**über etw** *acc or* **in etw** *dat*) **~ wissen** to know (about sth); **weißt du ~ wegen Samstagabend?** do you know about Saturday evening?; **weißt du ~ mit den Maschinen?** do you know how to deal with these machines?, do you know about these machines?; **ich weiß hier nicht ~** I don't know about things around here; **er weiß gut ~** he is well informed; **auf dem Gebiet weiß ich nicht ~** I don't know much about that sort of thing; **weißt du schon ~?** do you know?, have you heard?; **sag ihr, Egon habe angerufen, dann weiß sie schon ~** if you tell her Egon phoned she'll understand.

bescheiden[1] *pret* **beschied**, *ptp* **beschieden** [1] *vt* **(a)** (*form: bestellen*) to summon (*form*) (*zu jdm* to sb).

(b) (*form: entscheiden*) *Gesuch, Antrag* to decide upon ♦ **etw abschlägig ~** to turn sth down.

(c) (*form: informieren*) **jdn dahin gehend ~, daß ...** to inform *or* notify sb that ...

(d) (*geh: zuteil werden lassen*) **jdm etw ~** to grant sb sth; **es war ihr nicht beschieden, den Erfolg zu genießen** she was not granted the opportunity to *or* it was not given to her to (*liter*) enjoy the success.

[2] *vr* (*geh*) to be content ♦ **sich mit wenigem ~** to be content *or* to content oneself with little.

bescheiden[2] *adj* **(a)** modest; *Mensch, Verhalten auch* unassuming ♦ **~** *or* **in ~en Verhältnissen leben** to live modestly; **darf ich mal ~ fragen, ob ...** may I venture to ask whether ...; **eine ~e Frage** one small question; **aus ~en Anfängen** from humble beginnings.

(b) (*euph: beschissen*) awful, terrible; (*inf: mäßig*) mediocre.

Bescheidenheit *f siehe adj (a)* modesty; unassumingness ♦ **nur keine falsche ~** no false modesty now; **~ ist eine Zier, doch weiter kommt man ohne ihr** (*hum inf*) modesty is fine but it doesn't get you very far.

bescheinen* *vt irreg* to shine on; (*Feuer*) to light up ♦ **vom Mond/von der Sonne beschienen** moonlit/sunlit.

bescheinigen* *vt* to certify; *Gesundheit, Tauglichkeit* to confirm in writing; *Empfang* to confirm, to acknowledge; (*durch Quittung*) to sign *or* give a receipt for; (*inf: mündlich bestätigen*) to confirm ♦ **sich** (*dat*) **die Arbeit/Überstunden ~ lassen** to get written confirmation of having done the work/overtime; **können Sie mir ~, daß ...** can you confirm in writing that ... *or* give me written confirmation that ...; **hiermit wird bescheinigt, daß ...** this is to certify that ...; **jdm äußerste Kompetenz ~** to confirm sb's extreme competence.

Bescheinigung *f siehe vt* (*das Bescheinigen*) certification; confirmation; (*Schriftstück*) certificate; written confirmation; (*Quittung*) receipt.

bescheißen* *irreg* [1] *vt* (*sl*) *jdn* to swindle, to cheat, to do (*um* out of).

[2] *vi* (*sl*) to cheat.

beschenken* *vt jdn* to give presents/a present to ♦ **jdn mit etw ~** to give sb sth (as a present); **sich (gegenseitig) ~** to give each other presents; **jdn reich ~** to shower sb with presents; **damit bin ich reich beschenkt** that's very generous.

bescheren* *vti* **(a) jdn ~** to give sb a Christmas present/presents; **jdn mit etw ~** to give sb sth for Christmas; **um 5 Uhr wird beschert** the Christmas presents will be given out at 5 o'clock; **jdm eine Überraschung ~** to give sb a nice surprise.

(b) (*zuteil werden lassen*) **jdm etw ~** to grant sb sth, to bestow sth upon sb; (*Gott*) to bless sb with sth.

Bescherung *f* **(a)** (*Feier*) giving out of Christmas presents. **(b)** (*iro inf*) **das ist ja eine schöne ~!** this is a nice mess; **die (ganze) ~** the (whole) mess; **da haben wir die ~!** I told you so, what did I tell you!

bescheuert *adj* (*inf*) stupid; *Mensch auch* dumb (*inf*).

beschichten* *vt* (*Tech*) to coat, to cover ♦ **mit Kunststoff beschichtet** laminated; **PVC-beschichtet** PVC coated.

beschicken* *vt* **(a)** (*Vertreter schicken auf*) to send representatives to; (*Exemplare schicken auf*) to send exhibits to ♦ **eine Ausstellung mit jdm/etw ~** to send sb/sth to an exhibition; **die Firma hat die Messe beschickt** the firm exhibited at the fair; **der Kongreß wurde von den meisten Ländern beschickt** most countries sent representatives to the congress.

(b) (*Tech*) *Hochofen* to charge; *Kessel* to fire.

beschickert *adj* (*inf*) tipsy.

Beschickung *f* (*Tech*) (*von Hochofen*) charging; (*von Kessel*) firing; (*Ladung*) load.

beschied *pret of* **bescheiden**[1].

beschieden *ptp of* **bescheiden**[1].

beschießen* *vt irreg* **(a)** to shoot at, to fire on *or* at; (*mit Geschützen*) to bombard; (*aus Flugzeug auch*) to strafe; (*fig: mit Fragen, Vorwürfen, Argumenten*) to bombard. **(b)** (*Phys*) *Atomkern* to bombard.

Beschießung *f siehe vt* **(a)** shooting (*gen* at), firing (*gen* on, at); bombardment (*gen* of); strafing (*gen* of). **(b)** bombarding.

beschildern* *vt* to put a sign *or* notice/signs *or* notices on; (*mit Schildchen*) *Ausstellungsgegenstand, Käfig etc* to label; (*mit Verkehrsschildern*) to signpost.

Beschilderung *f siehe vt* putting a sign *etc* (*von* on); labelling; signposting; (*Schilder*) signs *pl*; labels *pl*; signposts *pl*.

beschimpfen* *vt jdn* to swear at, to abuse; *Ruf, guten Namen* to slander.

Beschimpfung *f* **(a)** (*das Beschimpfen*) abusing, swearing (*gen* at); (*Jur*) slander (*gen* on). **(b)** (*Schimpfwort*) insult.

beschirmen* *vt* **(a)** (*geh: beschützen*) to shield, to protect. **(b)** (*geh: sich breiten über*) to shade. **(c)** (*mit Schirm versehen*) *Lampe* to put a shade on ♦ **ich werde dich ~** (*hum inf*) I'll let you share my umbrella.

⚠ **Beschiß** *m* **-sses, -sse** (*sl*) swindle, rip off (*sl*) ♦ **das ist ~** it's a swindle *or* swizz (*inf*).

beschissen *adj* (*sl*) bloody awful (*Brit inf*), lousy (*inf*), shit-awful (*sl*).

beschlafen* *vt irreg* (*inf*) **(a)** *Sache* to sleep on. **(b)** *Mädchen* to sleep with.

Beschlag *m* **-(e)s, ¨e (a)** (*an Koffer, Truhe, Buch*) (ornamental) fitting; (*an Tür, Fenster, Möbelstück, Sattel*) (ornamental) mounting; (*Scharnier/Schließe*) ornamental hinge/clasp; (*von Pferd*) shoes *pl*.

(b) (*das Beschlagen: von Pferd*) shoeing.

(c) (*auf Metall*) tarnish; (*auf Speisen*) layer of mould; (*auf Glas, Spiegel etc*)

➤ SPRACHE AKTIV: beschäftigen: 1 → 33.3

condensation ◆ **der Löffel hat einen ~** the spoon is tarnished.
(d) jdn/etw mit ~ belegen, jdn/etw in ~ nehmen to monopolize sb/sth; **mit ~ belegt sein** to be being used; (*Mensch*) to be occupied.

beschlagen* *irreg* [1] *vt* **(a)** (*mit Beschlägen versehen*) *Truhen, Möbel, Türen* to put (metal) fittings on; *Huftiere* to shoe; *Schuhe* to put metal tips on; (*mit Ziernägeln*) to stud ◆ **ein Faß mit Reifen ~** to put hoops on a barrel, to hoop a barrel; **ist das Pferd ~?** is the horse shod?
(b) (*Hunt*) *Wild* to cover, to serve.
(c) (*anlaufen lassen*) (*Dampf*) to steam up; (*Rost*) to cover; (*Patina*) to tarnish; (*Pilz*) to cover, to grow over *or* on.
(d) (*Sw: betreffen*) to concern.
[2] *vir* (*vi: aux sein*) (*Brille, Glas, Fenster*) to steam up, to get steamed up, to mist up *or* over; (*Wand*) to get covered in condensation, to get steamed up; (*Silber etc*) to tarnish; (*einen Pilzbelag bekommen*) to go mouldy ◆ **würden Sie bitte die ~en Scheiben abwischen?** the windows are getting steamed up *etc*, could you give them a wipe?
[3] *adj* (*erfahren*) well-versed ◆ **in etw** (*dat*) **(gut) ~ sein** to be (well-)versed in sth; **auf einem Gebiet ~ sein** to be well-versed in a subject.

Beschlagenheit *f, no pl* sound knowledge *or* grasp (*in +dat* of).

Beschlagnahme *f -, -n* confiscation, seizure, impounding.

beschlagnahmen* *vt insep* **(a)** to confiscate, to seize, to impound. **(b)** (*inf: in Anspruch nehmen*) (*Mensch*) to monopolize, to hog (*inf*); (*Arbeit*) *Zeit* to take up.

Beschlagnahmung *f siehe* **Beschlagnahme.**

beschleichen* *vt irreg* to creep *or* steal up to *or* up on; *Wild* to stalk; (*fig*) to creep over.

beschleunigen* [1] *vt* to accelerate, to speed up; *Arbeit, Lieferung etc auch* to expedite; *Tempo auch* to increase; *Atem, Puls auch* to quicken; *Verfall, wirtschaftlichen Zusammenbruch etc* to precipitate, to hasten, to accelerate ◆ **die Angst beschleunigte ihre Schritte** fear quickened *or* hastened her steps.
[2] *vr siehe vt* to accelerate, to speed up; to increase; to quicken; to be precipitated *or* hastened.
[3] *vi* (*Fahrzeug, Fahrer*) to accelerate.

Beschleuniger *m -s, -* (*Phys, Chem*) accelerator.

beschleunigt *adj* faster ◆ **~es Verfahren** (*Jur*) summary proceedings *pl*.

Beschleunigung *f* **(a)** acceleration (*auch Aut, Phys*), speeding up; (*von Tempo auch*) increase; (*von Atem, Puls auch*) quickening; (*von Verfall etc*) precipitation, hastening ◆ **wir tun alles, was zur ~ der Arbeit führen könnte** we are doing everything we can towards speeding up *or* in order to speed up the work. **(b)** (*Eile*) speed.

Beschleunigungs-: ~anlage, ~maschine *f* accelerator; **~vermögen** *nt* accelerating power, acceleration; **~wert** *m* (*Aut*) acceleration ratio.

➤ **beschließen*** *irreg* [1] *vt* **(a)** (*Entschluß fassen*) to decide on; *Gesetz* to pass; *Statuten* to establish ◆ **~, etw zu tun** to decide *or* resolve to do sth. **(b)** (*beenden*) to end; *Brief, Abend, Programm auch* to conclude, to wind up.
[2] *vi* **über etw** (*acc*) **~** to decide on sth.

beschlossen [1] *ptp of* **beschließen.**
[2] *adj* (*entschieden*) decided, agreed ◆ **das ist ~e Sache** that's settled.

⚠ **Beschluß** *m -sses, -̈sse* **(a)** (*Entschluß*) decision, resolution ◆ **einen ~ fassen** to pass a resolution; **auf ~ des Gerichts** by order of the court; **wie lautete der ~ des Gerichts?** what was the court's decision? **(b)** (*obs: Schluß*) conclusion, end.

⚠ **Beschluß-: b~fähig** *adj* **b~fähig sein** to have a quorum; **b~fähige Anzahl** quorum; **~fähigkeit** *f, no pl* quorum; **~fassung** *f* (passing of a) resolution; **~recht** *nt* competence (to pass *or* make a resolution); **b~reif** *adj Gesetz* ready to be voted on, ready for the vote; **b~unfähig** *adj* **b~unfähig sein** not to have a quorum.

beschmeißen* *vt irreg* (*inf*) to pelt, to bombard; (*mit Vorwürfen etc*) to bombard.

beschmieren* [1] *vt* **(a)** (*bestreichen*) *Brot* to spread; *Körperteil, Maschinenteil* to smear, to cover ◆ **Brot mit Butter/Käse ~** to butter bread/to spread cheese on the bread.
(b) *Kleidung* to (be)smear; *Wand auch* to bedaub; *Tafel* to scribble *or* scrawl all over ◆ **ein Buch mit Bemerkungen ~** to scrawl comments all over a book.
[2] *vr* to get (all) dirty, to get oneself in a mess ◆ **sich von oben bis unten mit etw ~** to get sth all over oneself, to cover oneself with sth.

beschmunzeln* *vt* to smile (quietly) at ◆ **der alte Scherz wird immer noch beschmunzelt** the old joke still raises a smile.

beschmutzen* [1] *vt* to (make *or* get) dirty, to soil; (*fig*) *Ruf, Namen* to besmirch, to sully; *Ehre* to stain; *siehe* **Nest.**
[2] *vr* to make *or* get oneself dirty.

Beschmutzung *f siehe vt* dirtying, soiling; besmirching, sullying; staining.

beschneiden* *vt irreg* **(a)** (*zurechtschneiden, stutzen*) to trim; *Sträucher, Reben* to prune; *Bäume auch* to lop; *Flügel* to clip; *Fingernägel auch* to cut, to pare. **(b)** (*Med, Rel*) to circumcise. **(c)** (*fig: beschränken*) to cut back, to curtail.

Beschneidung *f, no pl siehe vt* **(a)** trimming; pruning; lopping; clipping; cutting, paring. **(b)** circumcision. **(c)** (*von Unterstützung etc*) cut-back; (*von Rechten*) curtailing, curtailment.

beschneien* *vt* to cover with artificial snow.

beschneit *adj* snow-covered; *Berge auch* snow-capped.

Beschneiungsanlage *f* artificial snow spreader.

beschnüffeln* [1] *vt* to sniff at; (*fig*) (*vorsichtig untersuchen*) to sniff out, to suss out (*sl*); *jdn* to size up; (*bespitzeln*) to spy out.
[2] *vr* (*Hunde*) to have a sniff at each other, to sniff each other; (*fig*) to size each other up.

beschnuppern* *vtr siehe* **beschnüffeln.**

beschönigen* *vt* to gloss over ◆ **~der Ausdruck** euphemism; **... sagte er ~d** ... he said, trying to make things seem better.

Beschönigung *f* glossing over ◆ **was er zur ~ angeführt hat,** ... what he said to make things seem better ...

beschottern* *vt Straße* to macadamize, to metal; (*Rail*) to ballast.

beschranken* *vt Bahnübergang* to provide with gates, to put gates on.

➤ **beschränken*** [1] *vt* (*auf +acc* to) to limit, to restrict; *Anzahl, Ausgaben, Bedeutung eines Wortes etc auch* to confine.
➤ [2] *vr* (*auf +acc* to) to limit *or* restrict; (*esp Jur, Rede, Aufsatz etc auch*) to confine oneself; (*sich einschränken*) to restrict oneself ◆ **das Wort beschränkt sich auf regionalen Gebrauch** the word is limited *or* restricted *or* confined to regional usage.

beschrankt *adj siehe* **Bahnübergang.**

beschränkt *adj* **(a)** (*eingeschränkt, knapp*) limited; *Gebrauch auch* restricted ◆ **wir sind räumlich/zeitlich/finanziell ~** we have only a limited amount of space/time/money; **~e Haftung** limited liability; **Gesellschaft mit ~er Haftung** limited company (*Brit*), corporation (*US*).
(b) (*pej*) (*geistig*) *Mensch, Intelligenz* limited; (*engstirnig auch*) narrow ◆ **wie kann man nur so ~ sein?** how can anyone be so dim *or* stupid?

Beschränktheit *f siehe adj* **(a)** limitedness; restriction. **(b)** limitedness, limited intelligence; (*Engstirnigkeit*) narrowness ◆ **er konnte in seiner ~ nicht begreifen** ... his simple mind could not grasp ...

Beschränkung *f* **(a)** *siehe vt* limitation, restriction; confinement ◆ **eine ~ der Teilnehmerzahl scheint unvermeidbar zu sein** it seems unavoidable that the number of participants will have to be limited *or* restricted. **(b)** *siehe vr* (*auf +acc* to) limitation, restriction; confinement. **(c)** (*Maßnahme*) restriction, limitation ◆ **jdm ~en auferlegen** to impose restrictions on sb.

beschreiben* *vt irreg* **(a)** (*darstellen*) to describe, to give a description of ◆ **sein Glück/Schmerz war nicht zu ~** his happiness/pain was indescribable *or* beyond (all) description; **ich kann dir nicht ~, wie erleichtert ich war** I can't tell you how relieved I was; **~de Psychologie/Pädagogik** descriptive psychology/theory of education; **~de Grammatik** descriptive grammar.
(b) (*vollschreiben*) to write on.
(c) *Kreis, Bahn* to describe.

Beschreibung *f* **(a)** description. **(b)** (*Gebrauchsanweisung*) instructions *pl*.

beschreien* *vt irreg* (*inf*) *siehe* **berufen 1 (c).**

beschreiten* *vt irreg* (*lit geh*) *Pfad* to walk *or* step along; *Brücke* to walk *or* step across; (*fig*) *neue Wege* to follow, to pursue, to take; *neue Methode* to follow, to pursue.

beschriften* *vt* to write on; *Grabstein, Sockel etc* to inscribe; (*mit Aufschrift*) to label; *Umschlag* to address; *Karikatur* to give a caption (to) ◆ **etw mit seinem Namen ~** to write one's name on sth; **die Funde waren mit Tusche beschriftet** the finds were marked with ink.

Beschriftung *f siehe vt* **(a)** (*das Beschriften*) inscribing; labelling; addressing; giving a caption to; marking ◆ **bei der ~ der Etiketten** while filling in the labels. **(b)** (*Aufschrift*) writing; inscription; label; caption.

beschuhen* *vt* to shoe; (*Tech*) *Pfahl, Spitze etc* to tip with metal.

beschuht *adj* wearing shoes, shod.

beschuldigen* *vt* to accuse; (*esp Jur auch, liter*) to charge ◆ **jdn einer Sache** (*gen*) **~** to accuse sb of sth, to charge sb with sth.

Beschuldigte(r) *mf decl as adj* accused.

Beschuldigung *f* accusation; (*esp Jur auch, liter*) charge.

Beschulung *f, no pl* provision of school(ing) facilities (*gen* for).

beschummeln*, beschuppen* *vti* (*inf*) to cheat ◆ **jdn um etw ~** to cheat *or* diddle (*inf*) sb out of sth.

beschuppt *adj* scaly ◆ **dick ~** thick-scaled, with thick scales.

beschupsen* *vti* (*inf*) *siehe* **beschummeln.**

⚠ **Beschuß** *m -sses, no pl* (*Mil*) fire; (*mit Granaten auch*) shelling, bombardment; (*Phys*) bombardment, bombarding ◆ **jdn/etw unter ~ nehmen** (*Mil*) to (start to) bombard *or* shell sb/sth; *Stellung auch* to fire on sth; (*fig*) to attack sb/sth, to launch an attack on sb/sth; **unter ~ hängen** *or* **stehen** (*Mil*) to be under fire; **unter ~ geraten** (*Mil, fig*) to come under fire.

beschütten* *vt* (*mit Sand etc*) to cover ◆ **jdn/etw (mit Wasser** *etc*) **~** to pour water *etc* on *or* over sb/sth; **die Straße mit Sand ~** to throw *or* put sand on the road; **eine Feld mit Jauche ~** to put liquid manure on a field.

beschützen* *vt* to protect, to shield, to shelter (*vor +dat* from) ◆ **~d** protective; **~de Werkstätte** sheltered workshop.

Beschützer(in *f*) *m -s, -* protector/protectress.

beschwatzen*, beschwätzen* (*dial*) *vt* (*inf*) **(a)** (*überreden*) to talk over ◆ **jdn zu etw ~** to talk sb into sth; **sich zu etw ~ lassen** to get talked into sth. **(b)** (*bereden*) to chat about, to have a chat about.

Beschwer *f - or nt -s, no pl* (*obs*) hardship.

Beschwerde *f -, -n* **(a)** (*Mühe*) hardship.
(b) ~n *pl* (*Leiden*) trouble ◆ **das macht mir immer noch ~n** it's still causing *or* giving me trouble; **mit etw ~n haben** to have trouble with sth; **wenn Sie wieder ganz ohne ~n sind** when the trouble's cleared up completely.
(c) (*Klage*) complaint; (*Jur*) appeal ◆ **eine ~ gegen jdn** a complaint about sb; **wenn Sie eine ~ haben** if you have a complaint *or* grievance; **~ führen** *or* **einlegen** *or* **erheben** (*form*) to lodge a complaint; **jdm Grund zur ~ geben** to give sb grounds *or* cause for complaint.

Beschwerde-: ~buch *nt* complaints book; **b~frei** *adj* (*Med*) fit and healthy; **er war nie wieder ganz b~frei** the symptoms never completely disappeared; **~frist** *f* (*Jur*) *period of time during which an appeal may be lodged or filed*; **~führende(r)** *mf decl as adj*, **~führer** *m* (*form*) person who lodges a complaint, complainant; (*Jur*) appellant; **~schrift** *f* written (*or* formal) complaint, petition; **~weg** *m* (*form*) *possibility of lodging a complaint with sb (in authority)*; **auf dem ~weg** by (means of) lodging *or* making a complaint; **den ~weg beschreiten** to lodge a complaint.

beschweren* [1] *vt* (*mit Gewicht*) to weigh(t) down; (*fig: belasten*) (*Problem, Kummer*) to weigh on; (*Mensch*) to burden ♦ **von Kummer beschwert** weighed down with sorrow.
[2] *vr* **(a)** (*sich belasten*) (*lit*) to weigh oneself down; (*fig*) to encumber oneself. **(b)** (*sich beklagen*) to complain.

beschwerlich *adj* laborious, arduous; *Reise* arduous ♦ **jdm ~ fallen** (*old*)/**werden** to be/become a burden to sb; **das Gehen/Atmen ist für ihn ~** he finds walking/breathing hard work.

Beschwerlichkeit *f* difficulty; (*von Reise, Aufgabe auch*) laboriousness *no pl*, arduousness *no pl*.

Beschwernis *f or nt* (*geh*) (*Mühsal*) hardship.

Beschwerung *f* **(a)** (*das Beschweren*) weigh(t)ing down. **(b)** (*Gegenstand*) weight.

beschwichtigen* *vt jdn* to appease, to pacify; *Kinder* to calm down, to soothe; *jds Zorn, Gewissen* to soothe, to appease, to calm.

Beschwichtigung *f siehe vt* appeasement, pacification; calming down, soothing; soothing, appeasement, calming; (*beschwichtigende Worte*) calming *or* soothing words *pl*.

Beschwichtigungspolitik *f* policy of appeasement.

beschwindeln* *vt* (*inf*) **(a)** (*belügen*) **jdn ~** to tell sb a lie or a fib (*inf*). **(b)** (*betrügen*) to cheat, to swindle, to do (*inf*).

beschwingen* *vt* to exhilarate, to elate.

beschwingt *adj* elated, exhilarated; *Musik, Mensch* vibrant ♦ **sich ~ fühlen** to walk on air; **ein ~es Gefühl** a feeling of elation *or* exhilaration; **~en Schrittes** (*geh*) *or* **Fußes** (*liter*) with a spring *or* bounce in one's step, lightly tripping (*liter*).

Beschwingtheit *f siehe adj* elation, exhilaration; vibrancy.

beschwipsen* (*inf*) [1] *vt* to make tipsy, to go to sb's head.
[2] *vr* to get tipsy.

beschwipst *adj* (*inf*) tipsy.

beschwören* *vt irreg* **(a)** (*beeiden*) to swear to; (*Jur auch*) to swear on oath.
(b) (*anflehen*) to implore, to beseech ♦ **sie hob ~d die Hände** she raised her hands imploringly *or* beseechingly.
(c) (*erscheinen lassen*) to conjure up; *Verstorbene auch* to raise, to call up; (*bannen*) *böse Geister* to exorcise, to lay; *Schlangen* to charm.
(d) (*geh: hervorrufen*) *Erinnerung etc* to conjure up ♦ **das beschwor Erinnerungen in mir** that conjured up memories.

Beschwörung *f* **(a)** (*das Flehen*) entreaty. **(b)** *siehe vt (c)* conjuring up, conjuration; raising, calling up; exorcising, exorcism, laying; charming. **(c)** (*auch* **~sformel**) incantation.

beseelen* *vt* **(a)** (*lit: mit Seele versehen*) to give a soul to; *Natur, Kunstwerk* to breathe life into ♦ **das beseelte Spiel des Pianisten** (*geh*) the pianist's inspired playing.
(b) (*erfüllen*) to fill ♦ **neuer Mut beseelte ihn** he was filled *or* imbued with fresh courage; **ein neuer Geist beseelt unser Jahrhundert** a new spirit pervades *or* informs (*liter*) our century.

besehen* *irreg* [1] *vt* (*auch:* **sich dat ~**) to take a look at, to look at.
[2] *vr* to (take a) look at oneself.

beseibeln*, beseibern* *vt* (*dial*) to dribble all over, to slobber all over.

beseitigen* *vt* **(a)** (*entfernen*) to remove, to get rid of; *Abfall, Schnee auch* to clear (away); *Atommüll* to dispose of; *Schwierigkeiten auch* to sort *or* smooth out; *Fehler auch* to eliminate; *Mißstände* to get rid of, to do away with. **(b)** (*euph: umbringen*) to get rid of, to eliminate.

Beseitigung *f, no pl siehe vt* **(a)** removal, getting rid of; clearing (away); disposal; sorting *or* smoothing out; elimination; doing away with. **(b)** getting rid of, elimination.

beseligen* *vt* to make blissfully happy ♦ **~d/beseligt** blissful.

Besen *m* **-s, - (a)** (*Kehr~*) broom; (*Reisig~*) besom; (*zum Rühren*) whisk; (*von Hexe*) broomstick ♦ **jdn auf den ~ laden** (*inf*) to pull sb's leg (*inf*), to have sb on (*inf*); **ich fresse einen ~, wenn das stimmt** (*inf*) if that's right, I'll eat my hat (*inf*); **neue ~ kehren gut** (*Prov*) a new broom sweeps clean (*Prov*).
(b) (*pej inf: Frau*) old bag (*inf*), old boot (*inf*), besom (*dial inf*).

Besen-: ~binder *m* broom-maker; **~kammer** *f* broom cupboard; **~macher** *m siehe* **~binder**; **b~rein** *adj* well-swept; **eine Wohnung b~rein verlassen** to leave a flat in a clean and tidy condition (for the next tenant); **~schrank** *m* broom cupboard; **~stiel** *m* broom-stick, broom-handle; **steif wie ein ~stiel** as stiff as a poker; **er sitzt da/tanzt als hätte er einen ~stiel verschluckt** (*inf*) he's sitting there as stiff as a poker/he dances so stiffly.

besessen [1] *ptp of* **besitzen**.
[2] *adj* (*von bösen Geistern*) possessed (*von* by); (*von einer Idee, Leidenschaft etc*) obsessed (*von* with) ♦ **wie ~** like a thing *or* like one possessed.

Besessene(r) *mf decl as adj* one possessed *no art* ♦ **die ~n** the possessed; **wie ein ~r** like one possessed.

Besessenheit *f, no pl siehe adj* possession; obsession.

besetzen* *vt* **(a)** (*dekorieren*) to trim; (*mit Edelsteinen*) to stud.
(b) (*belegen*) to occupy; (*reservieren*) to reserve; (*füllen*) *Plätze, Stühle* to fill ♦ **ist hier** *or* **dieser Platz besetzt?** is this place taken?; **irgend jemand hat die (Telefon)leitung stundenlang besetzt** somebody was on the line for hours, somebody was keeping the line busy for hours; **viele Autos besetzten den Parkplatz** there were a lot of cars in the car-park; *siehe auch* **besetzt**.
(c) (*esp Mil: eingenommen haben*) to occupy; (*Hausbesetzer*) to squat in.
(d) (*mit Person*) *Stelle, Amt, Posten* to fill; (*Theat*) *Rolle* to cast; (*mit Tieren*) to stock ♦ **eine Stelle** *etc* **neu ~** to find a new person to fill a job.

Besetzer(in *f*) *m* (*Haus~*) squatter.

➤ **besetzt** *adj* (*belegt*) *Telefon, Nummer, Leitung* engaged (*Brit*), busy (*esp US*); (*in Gebrauch*) *Spielautomat, Waschmaschinen etc* being used, taken, busy; *WC* occupied, engaged; *Abteil, Tisch* taken; *Hörsaal* being used; (*vorgebucht*) booked; (*voll*) *Bus, Wagen, Abteil etc* full (up); (*anderweitig beschäftigt, verplant*) *Mensch* busy ♦ **Freitag ist schon ~** Friday I'm/he's *etc* busy, Friday's out.

Besetztton *m*, **Besetztzeichen** *nt* (*Telec*) engaged (*Brit*) *or* busy (*esp US*) tone.

Besetzung *f* **(a)** (*das Besetzen*) (*von Stelle*) filling; (*von Rolle*) casting; (*mit Tieren*) stocking; (*Theat: Schauspieler*) cast; (*Sport: Mannschaft*) team, side ♦ **die Nationalelf in der neuen ~** the new line-up for the international side; **das Stück in der neuen ~** the play with the new cast; **zweite ~** (*Theat*) understudy. **(b)** (*esp Mil*) occupation.

Besetzungsliste *f* (*Theat, Film*) cast list.

besichtigen* *vt* (*ansehen*) *Stadt, Kirche* to have a look at, to visit; *Betrieb* to tour, to have a look over *or* round; (*zur Prüfung*) *Haus* to view, to have a look at, to look over; *Ware* to have a look at, to inspect; *Schule auch* to inspect; (*inspizieren*) *Truppen* to inspect, to review; (*hum*) *Baby, zukünftigen Schwiegersohn etc* to inspect.

Besichtigung *f* (*von Sehenswürdigkeiten*) sight-seeing tour; (*von Museum, Kirche, Betrieb*) tour; (*zur Prüfung*) (*von Haus*) viewing; (*von Waren, Schule, Baby*) inspection; (*von Truppen*) inspection, review ♦ **nach einer kurzen ~ der Kirche/des Museums/Betriebs** *etc* after a short look round the church/museum/factory *etc*; **die Waren liegen zur ~ aus** the goods are on display.

Besichtigungs-: ~reise *f* (*zum Vergnügen*) sight-seeing tour *or* trip; (*zur Überprüfung*) tour of inspection; **~zeiten** *pl* hours *pl* of opening.

besiedeln* *vt* (*ansiedeln*) to populate, to settle (*mit* with); (*sich niederlassen in*) to settle; (*kolonisieren*) to colonize; (*Tiere*) to populate, to inhabit; (*Pflanzen*) to be found in, to inhabit ♦ **dicht/dünn/schwach besiedelt** densely/thinly/sparsely populated.

Besied(e)lung *f, no pl siehe vt* settlement; colonization ♦ **dichte/dünne/schwache ~** dense/thin/sparse population.

Besiedlungsdichte *f* population density.

besiegeln* *vt* to seal.

Besiegelung *f* sealing.

besiegen* *vt* (*schlagen*) to defeat, to beat; *Feind auch* to conquer, to vanquish (*liter*); (*überwinden*) to overcome, to conquer ♦ **sich selbst ~** to overcome one's fears/doubts *etc*; (*seine Triebe* **~**) to repress the urge.

Besiegte(r) *mf decl as adj* defeated *or* vanquished person, loser.

Besiegung *f, no pl siehe vt* defeat; conquest, vanquishing; overcoming.

besingen* *vt irreg* **(a)** (*rühmen*) to sing of, to sing (*poet*) ♦ **jdn/etw ~** to sing the praises of sb/sth. **(b)** *Schallplatte, Tonband* to record.

besinnen* *irreg* [1] *vr* (*überlegen*) to reflect, to think; (*erinnern*) to remember (*auf jdn/etw* sb/sth); (*es sich anders überlegen*) to have second thoughts ♦ **besinne dich, mein Kind!** take thought, my child; **sich anders** *or* **eines anderen/eines Besseren ~** to change one's mind/to think better of sth; **er hat sich besonnen** he has seen the light; **ohne sich (viel) zu ~, ohne langes B~** without a moment's thought *or* hesitation; **wenn ich mich recht besinne** if I remember correctly.
[2] *vt* (*geh: bedenken*) to reflect on, to ponder, to consider.

besinnlich *adj* contemplative ♦ **eine ~e Zeit** a time of contemplation; **~ werden** to become thoughtful *or* pensive.

Besinnlichkeit *f, no pl* contemplativeness, thoughtfulness.

Besinnung *f, no pl* **(a)** (*Bewußtsein*) consciousness ♦ **bei/ohne ~ sein** to be conscious/unconscious; **die ~ verlieren** to lose consciousness; (*fig*) to lose one's head; **wieder zur ~ kommen** to regain consciousness, to come to; (*fig*) to come to one's senses; **jdn zur ~ bringen** to bring sb round; (*fig*) to bring sb to his senses.
(b) (*das Sich-Besinnen*) contemplation (*auf +acc* of), reflection (*auf +acc* upon).
(c) (*das Nachdenken*) reflection ♦ **ich brauche Zeit, zur ~ zu kommen** I need time to reflect *or* for reflection.

Besinnungs-: ~aufsatz *m* discursive essay; **b~los** *adj* unconscious, insensible; (*fig*) blind; *Wut* blind, insensate; **b~los werden** to lose consciousness; **~losigkeit** *f, no pl* (*lit*) unconsciousness.

Besitz *m* **-es,** *no pl* **(a)** (*das Besitzen*) possession ♦ **im ~ von etw sein** to be in possession of sth; **ich bin im ~ Ihres Schreibens** I am in receipt of your letter; **etw in ~ nehmen** to take possession of sth; **von etw ~ ergreifen** to seize possession of sth; **von jdm ~ ergreifen** to take *or* seize hold of sb; (*Zweifel, Wahnsinn etc*) to take possession of sb's mind; **in privatem ~** in private ownership.
(b) (*Eigentum*) property; (*Landgut*) estate.

Besitz-: ~anspruch *m* claim of ownership; (*Jur*) title; **einen ~anspruch auf etw** (*acc*) **haben** to have a claim to sth; **seine ~ansprüche (auf etw** *acc*) **anmelden** to make one's claims (to sth), to lay claim to sth; **b~anzeigend** *adj* (*Gram*) possessive; **~bürgertum** *nt* middle-class property owners *pl*, property-owning bourgeoisie.

besitzen* *vt irreg* to have, to possess; *käufliche Güter auch* to own; *Vermögen* to possess, to own; *Wertpapiere auch* to hold; *Narbe, grüne Augen* to have; *Rechte, jds Zuneigung etc auch* to enjoy ♦ **große Schönheit/Fähigkeiten** *etc* **~** to be possessed of great beauty/abilities *etc*; **die ~den Klassen** the propertied classes.

Besitzer(in *f*) *m* **-s, -** owner; (*von Wertpapieren auch, von Führerschein etc*)

holder; (*Inhaber auch*) proprietor ◆ **den ~ wechseln** to change hands.
Besitz|ergreifung *f* seizure.
Besitzer-: ~stolz *m* pride of possession; **voller ~stolz** proudly; **~wechsel** *m* change of ownership.
Besitz-: ~gier *f* acquisitive greed, acquisitiveness; **b~los** *adj* having no possessions; **sie ist nicht völlig b~los** she is not completely without possessions; **~nahme** *f* -, *no pl* seizure; **~stand** *m* (*form*) assets *pl*; (*fig*) vested rights *pl*; **~standswahrung** *f* (*fig*) protection of vested rights; **~tum** *nt* (*Eigentum*) possession, property *no pl*; (*Grundbesitz*) estate(s *pl*), property.
Besitzung *f* possession; (*privater Land- und Grundbesitz*) estate(s *pl*).
Besitz-: ~verhältnisse *pl* property situation *or* conditions *pl*; **~verteilung** *f* distribution of property.
besoffen *adj* (*sl*) (*betrunken*) pissed (*Brit*), stoned, smashed (*all sl*).
Besoffene(r) *mf decl as adj* (*inf*) drunk.
besohlen* *vt* to sole; (*neu ~*) to resole.
Besohlung *f siehe vt* soling *no pl*; resoling.
besolden* *vt* to pay.
Besoldung *f* pay.
Besoldungs-: ~gruppe *f* pay *or* salary group; **~ordnung** *f* pay *or* salary regulations *pl*.
besondere(r, s) *adj* **(a)** (*ungewöhnlich, eine Ausnahme bildend*) special; (*hervorragend*) *Qualität, Schönheit etc* exceptional ◆ **er ist ein ganz ~r Freund** he is a very special friend; **es ist eine ~ Freude** it is a special *or* particular pleasure; **das sind ~ Umstände** those are special circumstances; **das ist eine ganz ~ Augenfarbe** that is a very unusual eye colour.
(b) (*speziell*) special, particular; (*bestimmt*) particular ◆ **unser ~s Interesse gilt ...** we are particularly *or* (e)specially interested in ...; **wir legen ~n Wert auf ...** we place particular *or* special emphasis on ...; **ohne ~ Begeisterung** without any particular enthusiasm; **er hat sich mit ~m Eifer darangemacht** he set about it with particular enthusiasm; **es ist mein ganz ~r Wunsch, daß ...** it is my very special wish that ..., I particularly wish that ...; **in diesem ~n Fall** in this particular case; **keine ~n Vorlieben** no special *or* particular preferences; **das ist von ~r Bedeutung** it is of (e)special *or* particular importance.
(c) (*zusätzlich, separat, gesondert*) special, separate.
Besondere(s) *nt decl as adj* **(a) das ~ und das Allgemeine** the particular and the general; **im b~n** (*im einzelnen*) in particular cases; (*vor allem*) in particular.
(b) etwas/nichts ~s something/nothing special; **er möchte etwas ~s sein** he thinks he's something special; **das ist doch nichts ~s** that's nothing special *or* out of the ordinary, what's special about that?; **das ~ daran** the special thing about it.
Besonderheit *f* exceptional *or* unusual quality *or* feature; (*besondere Eigenschaft*) peculiarity.
besonders *adv gut, hübsch, teuer etc* particularly, (e)specially; (*ausdrücklich, vor allem*) particularly, in particular, (e)specially; (*gesondert*) separately, individually; (*speziell*) *anfertigen etc* specially ◆ **~ du müßtest das wissen** you particularly *or* in particular *or* especially should know that; **nicht ~ (lustig/kalt)** not particularly *or* not (e)specially (funny/cold); **nicht ~ viel Geld** not a particularly *or* not a(n) (e)specially large amount of money; **ich habe nicht ~ wenig Geld** I'm not particularly badly off; **das Essen/der Film war nicht ~** (*inf*) the food/film was nothing special *or* nothing to write home about (*inf*); **wie geht's dir? — nicht ~** (*inf*) how are you? — not too hot (*inf*); **~ wenig Fehler** an exceptionally *or* a particularly low number of mistakes; **er hat ~ viel/wenig gearbeitet/gegessen** he did a particularly large/small amount of work/he ate a particularly large amount of food/he ate particularly little.
besonnen [1] *ptp of* **besinnen**.
[2] *adj* considered, level-headed ◆ **ihre ruhige, ~e Art** her calm and collected way; **die Polizei ist ~ vorgegangen** the police proceeded in a careful and thoughtful way.
Besonnenheit *f, no pl* level-headedness, calm ◆ **durch seine ~ hat er eine Katastrophe verhindert** by staying calm and collected he avoided a disaster.
besonnt *adj* sunny.
besorgen* *vt* **(a)** (*kaufen, beschaffen etc*) to get; (*euph inf: stehlen*) to acquire (*euph inf*) ◆ **jdm/sich etw ~** to get sth for sb/oneself, to get sb/oneself sth; **jdm eine Stelle/einen neuen Anzug ~** to get *or* find a job for sb *or* to fix sb up with a job/new suit.
(b) (*erledigen*) to attend *or* see to ◆ **was du heute kannst ~, das verschiebe nicht auf morgen** (*Prov*) never put off until tomorrow what you can do today.
(c) (*versorgen*) to take care of, to look after.
(d) (*inf*) **es jdm ~** to sort sb out (*inf*), to fix sb (*inf*).
(e) (*sl: sexuell*) **es jdm ~** to have it off with sb (*sl*), to give sb one (*inf*).
Besorgnis *f* anxiety, worry, apprehension.
besorgnis|erregend *adj* alarming, disquieting, worrying.
besorgt *adj* **(a)** (*voller Sorge*) anxious, worried (*wegen* about). **(b) um jdn/etw ~ sein** to be concerned about sb/sth.
Besorgtheit *f, no pl* concern, solicitude.
Besorgung *f* **(a)** (*das Kaufen*) purchase ◆ **er wurde mit der ~ von ... beauftragt** he was asked to get ... **(b)** (*Erledigung*) **jdn mit der ~ seiner Geschäfte betrauen** to entrust sb with looking after one's affairs. **(c)** (*Einkauf*) errand (*dial*). **~en** shopping; **~en machen** to do some shopping.
bespannen* *vt* **(a)** (*überziehen*) (*mit Material*) to cover; (*mit Saiten, Fäden etc*) to string. **(b)** (*mit Zugtieren*) *Wagen* to harness up ◆ **den Wagen mit zwei Pferden ~** to harness two horses to the cart.
Bespannung *f* **(a)** *no pl* (*das Bespannen*) covering; (*mit Saiten etc*) stringing; (*mit Pferden*) harnessing. **(b)** (*Material*) covering; (*Saiten, Fäden etc*) strings *pl*.
bespeien* *vt irreg* (*geh*) to spit at *or* (up)on.
bespicken* *vt* (*mit Fett*) to lard; (*mit Nägeln*) to stud, to spike; (*fig: dicht bestecken*) to cover ◆ **seine mit Orden bespickte Brust** his chest bristling with medals.
bespiegeln* [1] *vr* (*lit: im Spiegel*) to look at oneself in a/the mirror; (*fig: Selbstbetrachtung machen*) to contemplate oneself *or* one's own navel (*hum*).
[2] *vt* (*geh*) *das eigene Ich* to contemplate; (*darstellen, verarbeiten*) *Vergangenheit, Gefühle, Nöte* to portray, to give a picture of.
bespielbar *adj Rasen etc* playable; *Kassette* capable of being recorded on.
bespielen* *vt* **(a)** *Schallplatte, Tonband* to record on, to make a recording on ◆ **das Band ist mit klassischer Musik bespielt** the tape has a recording of classical music on it. **(b)** (*Theat*) *Ort* to play. **(c)** (*Sport*) to play on.
bespitzeln* *vt* to spy on.
Bespitz(e)lung *f* spying.
bespötteln* *vt* to mock (at), to scoff at, to ridicule.
besprechen* *irreg* [1] *vt* **(a)** (*über etw sprechen*) to discuss, to talk about ◆ **wie besprochen** as arranged.
(b) (*rezensieren*) to review.
(c) *Schallplatte, Tonband* to make a recording on ◆ **ein besprochenes Band** a tape of sb's voice *or* of sb talking.
(d) (*beschwören*) to (attempt a) cure by magic *or* incantation.
[2] *vr* **sich mit jdm ~** to confer with sb, to consult (with) sb (*über +acc* about); **sich über etw** (*acc*) **~** to discuss sth.
Besprechung *f* **(a)** (*Unterredung*) discussion, talk; (*Konferenz*) meeting ◆ **nach ~ mit ...** after discussion with ..., after talking with ...; **er ist bei einer ~, er hat eine ~** he's in a meeting. **(b)** (*Rezension*) review, notice. **(c)** (*von Tonbändern, Schallplatten*) recording. **(d)** (*Beschwörung*) conjuring away.
Besprechungs-: ~exemplar *nt* review copy; **~zimmer** *nt* boardroom.
besprengen* *vt* to sprinkle.
besprenkeln* *vt* (*mit Farbe, Schmutz*) to speckle; (*fig: übersäen*) to stud.
bespringen* *vt irreg* (*Tier*) to mount, to cover.
bespritzen* [1] *vt* to spray; (*beschmutzen*) to (be)spatter, to splash.
[2] *vr* to spray oneself; (*sich beschmutzen*) to (be)spatter oneself, to splash oneself.
besprühen* [1] *vt* to spray.
[2] *vr* to spray oneself.
bespucken* *vt* to spit at *or* (up)on.
bespülen* *vt* (*Wellen*) to wash against.
▼ **besser** *adj, adv, comp of* **gut, wohl (a)** better ◆ **~e Kreise/Gegend** better circles/neighbourhood; **~e Leute** better class of people; **er hat ~e Tage** *or* **Zeiten gesehen** (*iro*) he has seen better days; **du willst wohl etwas B~es sein!** (*inf*) I suppose you think you're better than other people *or* think yourself superior; **soll es etwas B~es sein?** did you have something of rather better quality in mind?; **~ ist ~** (it is) better to be on the safe side; **um so ~!** (*inf*) so much the better!; **~ (gesagt)** or rather, or better; **~ werden** to improve, to get better; **sie will immer alles ~ wissen** she always thinks she knows better; **das ist auch ~ so** it's better that way; **das macht nichts ~** that doesn't improve matters, that doesn't make things any (the) better; **es kommt noch ~** there's worse *or* more to come *or* follow; **das wäre noch ~** (*iro*) no way; **es ~ haben** to have a better life; **B~es zu tun haben** (*inf*) to have better things to do; **eine Wendung zum B~en nehmen** to take a turn for the better; **jdn eines B~en belehren** to teach sb otherwise *or* better; *siehe* **besinnen**.
▼ **(b) laß das ~ bleiben** you had better leave well alone; **das solltest du ~ nicht tun** you had better not do that; **du tätest ~ daran ...** you would do better to ..., you had better ...; **dann geh ich ~** then I'd better go.
(c) das Essen war nur ein ~er Imbiß the meal was just a glorified snack.
Besser-: b~gehen *vi impers sep irreg aux sein* **es geht jdm b~** sb is feeling better; **jetzt geht's der Firma wieder b~** the firm is doing better again now, things are going better again for the firm now; **b~gestellt** *adj* better-off.
bessern [1] *vt* **(a)** to improve, to (make) better; *Verbrecher etc* to reform. **(b)** (*old*) (*ausbessern*) to mend; (*verbessern*) to improve.
[2] *vr* (*moralisch, im Benehmen*) to mend one's ways ◆ **bessere dich** (*hum inf*) mend your ways!
besser-: ~stehen *vr sep irreg* (*inf*) to be better off; **~stellen** *sep* [1] *vt* **jdn ~stellen** to improve sb's financial position; [2] *vr* to be better off.
▼ **Besserung** *f, no pl* improvement; (*von Verbrecher etc*) reformation; (*Genesung*) recovery ◆ **(ich wünsche dir) gute ~!** I wish you a speedy recovery, I hope you get better soon; **auf dem Wege der ~ sein** to be getting better, to be improving; (*Patient auch*) to be on the road to recovery.
Besserungs-: ~anstalt *f* (*dated*) reformatory, approved school; **b~fähig** *adj* improvable; *Verbrecher* capable of being reformed, reformable; **~maßnahme** *f* (*Jur*) corrective measure; **b~willig** *adj* willing to reform (oneself).
Besser-: ~wisser *m* -s, - (*inf*) know-all, know-it-all (*US*), smart-aleck (*inf*), smart-ass (*esp US inf*); **~wisserei** *f* (*inf*) know-all *etc* manner; **b~wisserisch** *adj* (*inf*) *Einstellung, Art* know-all *etc attr*.
best- *in cpds mit adj* best.
bestach *pret of* **bestechen**.
bestallen* *vt* (*form*) to install, to appoint (*zu* as).
Bestallung *f* (*form*) installation, appointment.
Bestallungs|urkunde *f* certificate of appointment.
bestand *pret of* **bestehen**.
Bestand *m* -(e)s, ¨e **(a)** (*Fortdauer*) continued existence, continuance ◆ **von**

~ sein/~ haben to be permanent, to endure; **das Gesetz hat noch immer ~** the law still continues to exist; **zum 100-jährigen ~ des Vereins** (*Aus*) on the (occasion of the) 100th anniversary of the society.
(b) (*vorhandene Menge, Tiere*) stock (*an +dat* of); (*Forst~ auch*) forest *or* timber stand (*US*) ◆ **~ aufnehmen** to take stock.
(c) (*Aus: Pacht*) lease, tenure ◆ **in ~ geben** to let (out) *or* put out on lease.

bestanden [1] *ptp of* **bestehen.**
[2] *adj* **(a)** (*bewachsen*) covered with trees; *Allee* lined with trees ◆ **die mit Bäumen ~en Alleen/Abhänge** the tree-lined avenues/tree-covered slopes; **der Wald ist gut ~** the forest is well stocked.
(b) nach ~er/mit „sehr gut" ~er Prüfung after passing the/an exam/after getting a "very good" in the exam; **bei nicht ~er Prüfung** if you *etc* don't pass the exam; **sie feiert die ~e Prüfung** she's celebrating passing her exam.
(c) (*Sw: alt*) advanced (in years).

beständig *adj* **(a)** *no pred* (*dauernd*) constant, continual ◆ **ich mache mir ~ Sorgen** I am constantly *or* continually worried. **(b)** (*gleichbleibend*) constant; *Mitarbeiter* steady; *Wetter* settled. **(c)** *no adv* (*widerstandsfähig*) resistant (*gegen* to); *Farbe* fast; (*dauerhaft*) *Freundschaft, Beziehung* lasting, durable.

-beständig *adj suf* -resistant.

Beständigkeit *f, no pl siehe adj* **(a)** continualness ◆ **er fragt mit einer ~ ...** he asks so constantly ... **(b)** constancy; steadiness; settledness. **(c)** resistance; fastness; lastingness, durability.

Bestands|aufnahme *f* stock-taking.

Bestandteil *m* component, part, element; (*fig*) essential *or* integral part ◆ **sich in seine ~e auflösen** to fall to pieces, to come apart; **etw in seine ~e zerlegen** to take sth apart *or* to pieces.

Best|arbeiter *m* (*DDR*) worker with the highest output.

bestärken* *vt* to confirm; *Verdacht auch* to reinforce ◆ **jdn in seinem Vorsatz/Wunsch ~** to confirm sb in his intention/desire, to make sb's intention/desire firmer *or* stronger; **das hat mich nur darin bestärkt, es zu tun** that merely made me all the more determined to do it.

Bestärkung *f* confirmation; (*von Verdacht auch*) reinforcement.

bestätigen* [1] *vt* **(a)** to confirm; *Theorie, Beweise, Alibi etc* to bear out, to corroborate; (*Jur*) *Urteil* to uphold ◆ **sich in etw (*dat*) bestätigt finden** to be confirmed in sth; **ich hatte angenommen, daß ... und fand mich darin bestätigt** I had assumed that ... and my assumption was confirmed *or* borne out; **~d** confirmative, confirmatory; **ein ~des Kopfnicken** a nod of confirmation; **... sagte er ~d** ... he said in confirmation.
(b) (*Comm*) *Empfang, Brief* to acknowledge (receipt of).
(c) (*beurkunden*) to confirm, to certify, to attest ◆ **hiermit wird bestätigt, daß ...** this is to confirm *or* certify that ...
(d) (*anerkennen*) to acknowledge, to recognize ◆ **jdn (im Amt) ~** to confirm sb's appointment.
[2] *vr* to be confirmed, to prove true, to be proved true ◆ **das tut er nur, um sich selbst zu ~** he only does it to boost his ego.

Bestätigung *f siehe vt* **(a)** confirmation (*auch Dokument*); bearing out, corroboration; upholding. **(b)** (*auch Dokument*) acknowledgement (of receipt). **(c)** (*auch Dokument*) confirmation, certification, attestation. **(d)** recognition; confirmation of appointment.

Bestätigungsschreiben *nt* letter of confirmation.

bestatten* *vt* to bury ◆ **bestattet liegen** to be *or* lie buried (*in +dat* in); **wann wird er bestattet?** when is the funeral (service)?

Bestatter *m* **-s, -** undertaker, mortician (*US*).

Bestattung *f* burial; (*Feuer~*) cremation; (*Feier auch*) funeral ◆ **kirchliche/weltliche ~** Christian/secular burial.

Bestattungs-: ~institut, ~unternehmen *nt* undertaker's, mortician's (*US*); **~unternehmer** *m* undertaker, funeral director, mortician (*US*).

bestäuben* *vt* to dust (*auch Cook*), to sprinkle; (*Bot*) to pollinate; (*Agr*) to dust, to spray.

Bestäubung *f* dusting, sprinkling; (*Bot*) pollination; (*Agr*) dusting, spraying.

bestaunen* *vt* to marvel at, to gaze at in wonder *or* admiration; (*verblüfft*) to gape at, to stare at in astonishment ◆ **laß dich ~** let's have a good look at you; **sie wurde von allen bestaunt** they all gazed at her in admiration/gaped at her.

best-: ~bemittelt *adj* (*Aus*) extremely well-off; **~bewährt** *adj attr* well-proven; **~bezahlt** *adj attr* best-paid.

beste *siehe* **beste(r, s).**

bestechen* *irreg* [1] *vt* **(a)** (*mit Geld, Geschenken etc*) to bribe; *Beamte auch* to corrupt ◆ **ich lasse mich nicht ~** I'm not open to bribery; (*mit Geld etc auch*) I don't take bribes.
(b) (*beeindrucken*) to captivate.
[2] *vi* (*Eindruck machen*) to be impressive (*durch* because of) ◆ **ein Mädchen, das durch Schönheit besticht** a girl of captivating beauty.

bestechend *adj Schönheit, Eindruck* captivating; *Angebot* tempting, enticing; *Klarheit* irresistible; *Geist, Kondition* winning.

bestechlich *adj* bribable, corruptible, venal.

Bestechlichkeit *f, no pl* corruptibility, venality.

Bestechung *f* bribery; (*von Beamten etc auch*) corruption ◆ **aktive ~** (*Jur*) offering of bribes/a bribe (to an official); **passive ~** (*Jur*) taking of bribes/a bribe (by an official).

Bestechungs-: ~geld *nt usu pl* bribe; **~skandal** *m* bribery scandal; **~summe** *f* bribe; **~versuch** *m* attempted bribery.

Besteck *nt* **-(e)s, -e (a)** (*Eß~*) knives and forks *pl*, cutlery *sing* (*esp Brit*), flatware *sing* (*US*); (*Set, für ein Gedeck*) set of cutlery/flatware ◆ **ein silbernes ~** a set of silver cutlery/flatware; **Herr Ober, ich habe kein ~** waiter, I haven't any cutlery/flatware.
(b) (*Instrumentensatz*) set of instruments; (*Raucher~*) pipe-cleaning implements *pl*, smoker's set ◆ **chirurgisches ~** (set of) surgical instruments.
(c) (*Naut*) reckoning, ship's position.

bestecken* *vt* to decorate.

Besteck-: ~kasten *m* cutlery tray; (*mit Deckel*) cutlery canteen, flatware chest (*US*); **~(schub)fach** *nt* cutlery drawer.

bestehen* *irreg* [1] *vt* **(a)** *Examen, Probe* to pass ◆ **eine Prüfung mit Auszeichnung/„sehr gut" ~** to get a distinction/"very good" (in an exam), to pass an exam with distinction/"very good"; *siehe auch* **bestanden.**
(b) (*durchstehen*) *Schicksalsschläge* to withstand; *schwere Zeit* to come through, to pull through; *Gefahr* to overcome; *Kampf* to win.
[2] *vi* **(a)** (*existieren*) to exist, to be in existence; (*Zweifel, Hoffnung, Aussicht, Gefahr, Probleme etc*) to exist; (*Brauch auch*) to be extant ◆ **~ bleiben** (*Frage, Hoffnung etc*) to remain; **die Universität/Firma besteht seit hundert Jahren** the university/firm has been in existence *or* has existed for a hundred years; **es besteht die Hoffnung/die Aussicht/der Verdacht, daß ...** there is (a) hope/a prospect/a suspicion that ...
(b) (*Bestand haben*) to continue to exist; (*Zweifel, Problem etc auch*) to persist.
(c) (*sich zusammensetzen*) to consist (*aus* of) ◆ **in etw (*dat*) ~** to consist in sth; (*Aufgabe*) to involve sth; **seine einzige Chance besteht darin, ...** his only chance is to ...; **die Schwierigkeit/das Problem besteht darin, daß ...** the difficulty/problem consists *or* lies in the fact that ..., the difficulty/problem is that ...; **das Problem besteht darin, zu zeigen ...** the problem consists in showing ...
(d) (*standhalten, sich bewähren*) to hold one's own (*in +dat* in) ◆ **vor etw (*dat*) ~** to stand up to *or* against sth.
(e) (*durchkommen*) to pass ◆ **(in einer Prüfung) mit „sehr gut" ~** to get a "very good" (in an exam).
(f) auf etw (*dat*) ~ to insist on sth; **ich bestehe darauf** I insist.

Bestehen *nt* **-s,** *no pl* **(a)** (*Vorhandensein, Dauer*) existence ◆ **seit ~ der Firma/des Staates** ever since the firm/state came into existence *or* has existed; **das 100-jährige ~ von etw feiern** to celebrate the hundredth anniversary *or* first hundred years of (the existence of) sth.
(b) (*Beharren*) insistence (*auf +dat* on).
(c) *siehe vt (a, b)* passing; withstanding; coming *or* pulling through; overcoming ◆ **bei ~ der Prüfung** on passing the exam.

bestehenbleiben *vi sep irreg aux sein* to last, to endure; (*Hoffnung*) to remain; (*Versprechen, Vereinbarungen*) to hold good.

bestehend *adj* existing; *Gesetze auch* present, current; *Preise* current; *Umstände, Verhältnisse auch* prevailing ◆ **die seit 1887 ~en Gesetze** the laws which have existed since 1887.

bestehenlassen *vt sep irreg* to keep, to retain.

bestehlen* *vt irreg* to rob ◆ **jdn (um etw) ~** (*lit, fig*) to rob sb of sth.

besteigen* *vt irreg* **(a)** *Berg, Turm, Leiter* to climb (up), to ascend (*liter*); *Fahrrad, Pferd* to mount, to get *or* climb on(to); *Bus, Flugzeug* to get on, to enter; *Auto, Segelflugzeug, Hubschrauber* to get into; *Schiff* to go on *or* aboard; *Thron* to ascend. **(b)** *siehe* **bespringen.**

Besteigung *f* (*von Berg*) climbing, ascent; (*von Thron*) accession (*gen* to).

Bestell-: ~block *m* order pad, pad of order forms; **~buch** *nt* order book.

bestellen* [1] *vt* **(a)** (*anfordern, in Restaurant*) to order; (*abonnieren auch*) to subscribe to ◆ **sich (*dat*) etw ~** to order sth; **das Material ist bestellt** the material has been ordered *or* is on order; **wie bestellt und nicht abgeholt** (*hum inf*) like orphan Annie (*inf*).
(b) (*reservieren*) to book, to reserve.
(c) (*ausrichten*) **bestell ihm (von mir), daß ...** tell him (from me) that ...; **soll ich irgend etwas ~?** can I take a message?, can I give him/her a message?; **~ Sie ihm schöne Grüße von mir** give him my regards; **er hat nicht viel/nichts zu ~** he doesn't have much/any say here.
(d) (*kommen lassen*) *jdn* to send for, to summon ◆ **jdn zu jdm/an einen Ort ~** to summon sb to sb/a place, to ask sb to go/come to sb/a place; **ich bin um** *or* **für 10 Uhr bestellt** I have an appointment for *or* at 10 o'clock.
(e) (*einsetzen, ernennen*) to nominate, to appoint.
(f) (*bearbeiten*) *Land* to till; (*old*) *Haus* to set in order.
(g) (*fig*) **es ist schlecht um ihn/mit seinen Finanzen bestellt** he is/his finances are in a bad way; **damit ist es schlecht bestellt** that's rather difficult.
[2] *vi* (*in Restaurant*) to order.

Besteller *m* **-s, -** customer; (*Abonnent*) subscriber ◆ **Hinweise für den ~** ordering instructions, instructions on how to order.

Bestellgeld *nt* price including postage and packing; (*für Zeitungen etc*) subscription rate *or* charge.

Bestelliste *f getrennt:* **Bestell-liste** order list.

Bestell-: ~karte *f* order form; **~liste** *f siehe* **Bestelliste**; **~menge** *f* order quantity; **~nummer** *f* order number *or* code; **~schein** *m* order form *or* slip.

Bestellung *f siehe vt (a-c, e, f)* **(a)** (*Anforderung, das Angeforderte*) order; (*das Bestellen*) ordering; subscription. **(b)** booking, reservation. **(c)** message. **(d)** nomination, appointment. **(e)** tilling.

Bestellzettel *m siehe* **Bestellschein.**

besten *adv:* **am ~** *siehe* **beste(r, s) 2.**

bestenfalls *adv* at best.

bestens *adv* (*sehr gut*) very well; (*herzlich*) *danken* very warmly ◆ **sie läßt ~ grüßen** she sends her best regards.

beste(r, s) [1] *adj, superl of* **gut, wohl (a)** *attr* best ◆ **im ~n Fall** at (the) best; **im**

~n Alter, in den ~n Jahren in the prime of (one's) life; **mit (den) ~n Grüßen/Wünschen** with best wishes; **in ~n Händen** in the best of hands; **aus ~m Hause sein** to come from the very best of homes; **das kommt in den ~n Familien vor** (*hum*) that can happen in the best of families.
(b) der/die/das erste *or* **nächste ~** the first (person/job *etc*) that comes along; the first (hotel/cinema *etc*) one comes to; **ich hielte es für das ~, wenn ...** I thought it (would be) best if ...; **das ~ wäre, wir ...** the best thing would be for us to ..., it would be best for us to ...; **aufs** *or* **auf das ~** very well; **zum ~n** for the best; **es steht nicht zum ~n** it does not look too promising *or* good *or* hopeful; **jdn zum ~n haben** *or* **halten** to pull sb's leg, to have sb on (*inf*); **etw zum ~n geben** (*erzählen*) to tell sth; **jdm eine Geschichte/ein Liedchen zum ~n geben** to entertain sb with a story/song.
(c) der/die/das B~ the best; **der/die B~ sein** to be the best; (*in der Klasse auch*) to be top (of the class); **meine B~/mein B~r!** (*dated inf*) (my) dear lady/my dear fellow; **zu deinem B~n** for your good; **ich will nur dein B~s** I've your best interests at heart; **sein B~s tun** to do one's best; **sein B~s geben** to give of one's best; **wir wollen das B~ hoffen** let's hope for the best.
▼[2] *adv* **am ~n** best; **ich hielt es für am ~n, wenn ...** I thought it (would be) best if ...; **am ~n würden wir gleich gehen** we'd be best to go immediately; **am ~n gehe ich jetzt** I'd *or* I had best go *or* be going now.

besternt *adj* (*geh*) star-studded, starry.
Beste(s) *nt siehe* **beste(r, s) 1 (c).**
besteuern* *vt* to tax ◆ **Luxusartikel sind sehr hoch besteuert** there is a high tax on luxury goods, luxury goods are heavily taxed.
Besteuerung *f* taxation; (*Steuersatz*) tax.
Best-: ~form *f* (*esp Sport*) top *or* best form; **in ~form sein** to be in top form *or* on one's best form; ⚠**b~gehaßt** *adj attr* (*iro*) most hated.
bestialisch *adj* bestial; (*inf*) awful, beastly (*inf*) ◆ **~ kalt** beastly cold; **~ stinken** to stink to high heaven (*inf*).
Bestialität *f* bestiality.
besticken* *vt* to embroider.
Bestie [-tiə] *f* beast; (*fig*) animal.
bestimmbar *adj* determinable.
bestimmen* [1] *vt* **(a)** (*festsetzen*) to determine; *Grenze, Ort, Zeit etc auch* to fix, to set; (*entscheiden auch*) to decide ◆ **sie will immer alles ~** she always wants to decide the way things are to be done.
(b) (*prägen*) *Stadtbild, Landschaft* to characterize; (*beeinflussen*) *Preis, Anzahl* to determine; *Entwicklung, Werk, Stil etc* to have a determining influence on; (*Gram*) *Kasus, Tempus* to determine ◆ **näher ~** (*Gram: Adverb*) to qualify.
(c) (*wissenschaftlich feststellen*) *Alter, Standort* to determine, to ascertain; *Pflanze, Funde* to classify; (*definieren*) *Wort, Bedeutung* to define.
(d) (*vorsehen*) to intend, to mean (*für* for) ◆ **jdn zu etw ~** to choose *or* designate sb as sth; **er ist zu Höherem bestimmt** he is destined for higher things; **wir waren füreinander bestimmt** we were meant for each other.
[2] *vi* **(a)** to decide (*über +acc* on) ◆ **du hast hier nicht zu ~** you don't make the decisions here.
(b) (*verfügen*) **er kann über sein Geld allein ~** it is up to him what he does with his money; **du kannst nicht über ihn/seine Zeit ~** it's not up to you to decide what he's going to do/how his time is to be spent.
[3] *vr* **sich nach etw ~** to be determined by sth.
bestimmend *adj* (*entscheidend*) *Faktor, Einfluß* determining, decisive, determinant ◆ **an etw** (*dat*) **~ mitwirken** to play a determining *or* decisive part in sth; **für etw ~ sein** to be characteristic of sth; (*entscheidend*) to have a determining influence on sth.
bestimmt [1] *adj* **(a)** (*gewiß, nicht genau genannt*) *Leute, Dinge, Vorstellungen, Aussagen etc* certain; (*speziell, genau genannt*) particular, definite; (*festgesetzt*) *Preis, Tag* set, fixed; (*klar, deutlich*) *Angaben, Ausdruck* definite, precise; (*Gram*) *Artikel, Zahlwort* definite ◆ **suchen Sie etwas B~es?** are you looking for anything in particular?; **den ganz ~en Eindruck gewinnen, daß ...** to get *or* have a definite *or* the distinct impression that ...
(b) (*entschieden*) *Auftreten, Ton, Mensch* firm, resolute, decisive ◆ **höflich, aber ~** polite but firm.
[2] *adv* **(a)** (*sicher*) definitely, certainly ◆ **ich weiß ganz ~, daß ...** I know for sure *or* for certain that ...; **kommst du? — ja — ~?** are you coming? — yes — definitely?; **ich schaffe es ~** I'll manage it all right; **er schafft es ~ nicht** he definitely won't manage it.
(b) (*wahrscheinlich*) no doubt ◆ **das hat er ~ verloren** he's bound to have lost it; **er kommt ~ wieder zu spät** he's bound to be late again.
Bestimmtheit *f* **(a)** (*Sicherheit*) certainty ◆ **ich kann mit ~ sagen, daß ...** I can say with certainty *or* definitely that ...; **ich weiß aber mit ~, daß ...** but I know for sure *or* for certain that ... **(b)** (*Entschiedenheit*) firmness ◆ **in** *or* **mit aller ~** quite categorically.
Bestimmung *f* **(a)** (*Vorschrift*) regulation ◆ **gesetzliche ~en** legal requirements.
(b) *no pl* (*Zweck*) purpose ◆ **eine Brücke/Straße/Anlage ihrer ~ übergeben** to open a new bridge/road/plant officially.
(c) (*Schicksal*) destiny.
(d) (*old: Ort*) destination.
(e) (*Gram*) modifier.
(f) (*das Bestimmen*) determination, determining; (*von Grenze, Zeit etc*) fixing, setting; (*Gram, von Preis, Anzahl*) determining, determination; (*von Alter, Standort*) determining, determination, ascertaining, ascertainment; (*von Pflanze, Funden*) classification; (*Definition*) definition ◆ **seine ~ zu dieser Aufgabe** choosing him for this task; **nähere ~** (*durch Adverb*) qualifying, qualification.

Bestimmungs-: ~bahnhof *m* (station of) destination; **b~gemäß** *adj* as agreed; **~gleichung** *f* (*Math*) conditional equation; **~hafen** *m* (port of) destination; **~land** *nt* (country of) destination; **~ort** *m* (place of) destination; **~wort** *nt* (*Gram*) modifier.
Best-: ~leistung *f* (*esp Sport*) best performance; **seine persönliche ~leistung** his personal best; **~marke** *f* record; **b~möglich** *adj no pred* best possible; **wir haben unser ~mögliches getan** we did our (level) best.
Best. Nr. *abbr of* **Bestellnummer.**
bestochen *ptp of* **bestechen.**
bestocken* *vt* to stock ◆ **der Wald ist gut bestockt** the forest is well timbered.
Bestockung *f* (*das Bestocken*) stocking; (*Bestand*) stock.
bestrafen* *vt* to punish; (*Jur*) *jdn* to sentence (*mit* to); (*Sport*) *Spieler, Foul* to penalize ◆ **der Schiedsrichter bestrafte das Foul mit einem Elfmeter** the referee awarded *or* gave a penalty for the foul.
Bestrafung *f siehe vt* punishment; sentencing; penalization ◆ **wir fordern eine strengere ~ von ...** we demand more severe punishments *or* (*Jur auch*) sentences for ...
bestrahlen* *vt* to shine on; (*beleuchten*) *Gebäude, Bühne* to light up, to illuminate; (*Med*) to give ray *or* radiation treatment *or* radiotherapy to ◆ **er ließ sich von der Sonne ~** he was soaking up the sun.
Bestrahlung *f* illumination; (*Med*) ray *or* radiation treatment, radiotherapy ◆ **Pflanzen der direkten ~ der Sonne aussetzen** to expose plants to direct sunlight *or* directly to the sun's rays; **15 ~en verordnen** to prescribe (a course of) 15 doses of ray treatment *etc.*
Bestrahlungslampe *f* radiation *or* ray lamp.
bestreben* *vr* (*geh*) *siehe* **bestrebt.**
Bestreben *nt* **-s,** *no pl* endeavour ◆ **im** *or* **in seinem ~, dem Fußgänger auszuweichen** in his efforts *or* attempts *or* endeavours to avoid the pedestrian.
bestrebt *adj* **~ sein, etw zu tun** to endeavour to do sth; **wir waren immer ~, ...** we have always endeavoured ..., it has always been our endeavour ...
Bestrebung *f usu pl* endeavour, attempt, effort.
bestreichen* *vt irreg* **(a)** to spread; (*Cook*) (*mit Milch etc*) to coat; (*mit Butter auch*) to butter; (*mit Farbe*) to paint ◆ **etw mit Butter/Fett/Öl ~** to butter/grease/oil sth; **etw mit Butter/Salbe/Klebstoff ~** to spread butter/ointment/glue on sth; **etw mit Farbe ~** to put a coat of paint on sth.
(b) (*Mil*) to rake, to sweep.
(c) (*Scheinwerfer, Strahl*) to sweep (over); (*in der Elektronik: abtasten*) to scan.
bestreiken* *vt* to black ◆ **bestreikt** strikebound; **die Fabrik wird zur Zeit bestreikt** there's a strike on in the factory at the moment; **„dieser Betrieb wird bestreikt"** "please do not cross the picket line".
Bestreikung *f* blacking ◆ **die ~ einer Fabrik beschließen** to decide to take strike action against *or* to black a factory.
bestreitbar *adj* disputable, contestable.
bestreiten* *vt irreg* **(a)** (*abstreiten*) to dispute, to contest, to challenge; (*leugnen*) to deny ◆ **jdm das Recht auf ... ~** to dispute *etc* sb's right to ...; **das möchte ich nicht ~** I'm not disputing *or* denying it.
(b) (*finanzieren*) to pay for, to finance; *Kosten* to carry, to defray (*form*).
(c) (*tragen, gestalten*) to provide for, to carry ◆ **er hat das ganze Gespräch allein bestritten** he did all the talking.
Bestreitung *f siehe vt* **(a)** contestation, challenge; denial. **(b)** financing; carrying, defrayal (*form*).
bestrenommiert ['bɛst-] *adj attr* most renowned.
bestreuen* *vt* to cover (*mit* with); (*Cook*) to sprinkle.
bestricken* *vt* **(a)** (*fig*) to charm, to captivate ◆ **~der Charme** alluring charms. **(b)** (*hum inf*) to knit things for.
bestrumpft *adj* in stockings; *Beine* stockinged.
Bestseller ['bɛst-] *m* **-s, -** best-seller.
Bestseller-: ~autor *m* best-selling author, best-seller; **~liste** *f* best-seller list; (*von Schallplatten*) charts *pl.*
bestsituiert ['bɛst-] *adj attr* (*esp Aus*) well-to-do, well-off.
bestücken* *vt* to fit, to equip; (*Mil*) to arm; *Lager* to stock ◆ **sie ist gut bestückt** (*hum inf*) she's pretty well stacked (*inf*).
Bestückung *f* **(a)** *siehe vt* fitting, equipping; arming; stocking. **(b)** (*Ausstattung*) equipment; (*Geschütze*) guns *pl*, armaments *pl.*
Bestuhlung *f* seating *no indef art.*
bestürmen* *vt* to storm; (*mit Fragen, Bitten*) to bombard; (*mit Anfragen, Briefen, Anrufen*) to inundate.
Bestürmung *f siehe vt* storming; bombardment; inundation.
bestürzen* *vt* to shake, to fill with consternation.
bestürzend *adj* alarming ◆ **ich finde es ~, wie wenig die Schüler wissen** it fills me with consternation *or* it dismays me to see how little the children know.
bestürzt *adj* filled with consternation ◆ **sie machte ein ~es Gesicht** a look of consternation came over her face; **er sah mich ~ an** he looked at me in consternation.
Bestürzung *f* consternation.
⚠**bestußt** *adj* (*inf*) *Kerl, Ausrede, Behauptung* crazy.
Best-: ~wert *m* (*Fin*) top value; (*Tech, Sport*) best performance; **~zeit** *f* (*esp Sport*) best time; **~zustand** *m* perfect condition.
Besuch *m* **-(e)s, -e (a)** (*das Besuchen*) visit (*des Museums etc* to the museum *etc*); (*von Schule, Veranstaltung*) attendance (*gen* at) ◆ **ein ~ (von) meiner Tante** a visit from my aunt; **zu seinen Aufgaben gehört auch der ~ der Klienten** his jobs include visiting clients; **bei jdm auf** *or* **zu ~ sein** to be visiting sb; **(von jdm) ~ erhalten** to have *or* get a visit (from sb); **jdm einen ~ abstatten** to pay

➤ SPRACHE AKTIV: **beste(r, s) : 2 → 29.2**

sb a visit.
(b) *(Besucher)* visitor; visitors *pl* ♦ **ist dein ~ wieder abgefahren?** have your visitors/has your visitor gone?; **er hat ~** he has company *or* visitors/a visitor; **er bekommt viel ~** he has a lot of visitors, he often has visitors.

besuchen* *vt jdn* to visit, to pay a visit to; *(Arzt) Patienten* to visit; *Vortrag, Schule, Seminar, Gottesdienst* to attend, to go to; *Kino, Theater, Lokal* to go to; *Bordell, Museum* to go to, to visit ♦ **du kannst mich mal am Abend/im Mondschein ~** *(euph inf)* you know what you can do *(inf)*.

Besucher(in *f*) *m* **-s, -** visitor; *(von Kino, Theater)* patron *(form)* ♦ **etwa 1.000 ~ waren zu der Veranstaltung/dem Vortrag/der Ausstellung gekommen** about 1,000 people attended *or* went to the function/lecture/visited the exhibition; **ein regelmäßiger ~ der Oper** a regular opera-goer, an habitué of the opera.

Besucher-: ~ritze *f (hum inf) crack between the two mattresses of twin beds;* **~zahl** *f* attendance figures *pl*; *(bei Schloß, Museum, Ausstellung etc)* number of visitors.

Besuchs-: ~erlaubnis *f* visitor's card; *(für Land)* visitor's visa; **~erlaubnis haben/bekommen** to be allowed to receive visitors/to obtain permission to visit sb; **~recht** *nt (Jur: nach Scheidung)* (right of) access ♦ **das ~recht bei ihrem Sohn** the right to visit her son; **~tag** *m* visiting day; **b~weise** *adv* on a visit; **~zeit** *f* visiting time; **jetzt ist keine ~zeit** it's not visiting time; **~zimmer** *nt* visitor's room.

besucht *adj* **gut/schlecht/schwach ~ sein** to be well/badly/poorly attended; *(Schloß etc)* to get a lot of/not many/only a handful of visitors.

besudeln* *(geh)* [1] *vt Wände* to besmear; *Kleidung, Hände* to soil; *(fig) Andenken, Namen, Ehre* to besmirch, to sully.
[2] *vr* **sich mit Blut ~** to get blood on one's hands.

Beta *nt* **-(s), -s** beta.

Betablocker *m* **-s, -** *(Med)* beta-blocker.

betagt *adj (geh)* aged, well advanced in years.

Betagtheit *f, no pl (geh)* old age, advancing years *pl*.

betakeln* *vt (Aus: betrügen)* to swindle.

betanken* *vt Fahrzeug* to fill up; *Flugzeug* to refuel.

betasten* *vt* to feel; *(Med auch)* to palpate *(form)*.

Beta-: ~strahlen *pl* beta rays *pl*; **~strahlung** *f* beta radiation; **~teilchen** *nt* beta particle.

betätigen* [1] *vt* **(a)** to operate, to work; *Muskeln, Gehirn, Darm* to activate; *Bremse auch* to apply, to put on; *Mechanismus auch* to activate, to actuate *(form)*; *Knopf auch* to press; *(drehen)* to turn; *Schalter auch* to turn on; *Hebel* to move, to operate; *Sirene* to operate, to sound.
(b) *(liter: bewirken)* to bring about, to effect.
(c) *(liter: einsetzen)* to put into effect.
[2] *vr* to busy oneself; *(körperlich)* to get some exercise ♦ **sich politisch ~** to be active in politics; **sich wissenschaftlich/literarisch/künstlerisch ~** to do (some) scientific work/some writing/painting; **sich geistig und körperlich ~** to stay active in body and mind; **wenn man sich längere Zeit nicht geistig betätigt hat** if you haven't used your mind for months.

Betätigung *f* **(a)** *(Tätigkeit)* activity ♦ **an ~ fehlt es mir nicht** I've no lack of things to do.
(b) *siehe vt (a)* operation; activation; applying, application; actuation; pressing; turning; turning on; moving; sounding ♦ **etw zur ~ der Muskeln tun** to do sth to exercise one's muscles; **die ~ des Mechanismus erfolgt durch Knopfdruck** pressing the button activates the mechanism *or* sets the mechanism in motion.

Betätigungs-: ~drang *m* need for activity; **~feld** *nt* sphere *or* field of activity.

Betatron *nt* **-s, -e** betatron.

betatschen* *vt (inf)* to paw *(inf)*.

betäuben* *vt (unempfindlich machen) Körperteil* to (be)numb, to deaden; *Nerv, Schmerzen* to deaden; *Schmerzen* to kill; *(durch Narkose)* to anaesthetize; *(mit einem Schlag)* to stun, to daze; *(fig) Kummer, Gewissen* to ease; *(fig: benommen machen)* to stun ♦ **er versuchte, seinen Kummer mit Alkohol zu ~** he tried to drown his sorrows with alcohol; **~der Lärm** deafening noise; **ein ~der Duft** an overpowering smell; **der Duft betäubte mich fast** I was almost overcome by the smell.

Betäubung *f* **(a)** *siehe vt* (be)numbing, deadening; killing; anaesthetization; stunning, dazing; easing. **(b)** *(Narkose)* anaesthetic. **örtliche** *or* **lokale ~** local anaesthetic.

Betäubungsmittel *nt* anaesthetic.

betaut *adj* dewy, bedewed.

Bet-: ~bank *f* kneeler; **~bruder** *m (pej inf)* churchy type, holy Joe *(pej inf)*.

Bete *f* **-,** *(rare)* **-n** beet ♦ **rote ~** beetroot.

beteilen* *vt (Aus)* to give presents to; *Flüchtlinge etc* to give gifts to ♦ **jdn mit etw ~** to give sb sth.

beteiligen* [1] *vt* **jdn an etw** *(dat)* **~** to let sb take part in sth, to involve sb in sth; *(finanziell)* to give sb a share in sth.
[2] *vr* to take part, to participate *(an +dat* in); *(finanziell)* to have a share *(an +dat* in) ♦ **sich an den Unkosten ~** to contribute to the expenses; **ich möchte mich bei** *or* **an dem Geschenk ~** I would like to put something towards the present.

beteiligt *adj* **an etw** *(dat)* **~ sein/werden** to be involved in sth, to have a part in sth; *(finanziell)* to have a share in sth; *am Gewinn auch* to have a slice of sth; **an einem Unfall/einer Schlägerei ~ sein** to be involved in an accident/a fight; **an einer Tat/Sache ~ sein** to be party to a deed/cause; **er war an dem Gelingen der Aktion maßgeblich ~** he made a major contribution to the success of the campaign; **er ist an dem Geschäft (mit 500.000 Mark) ~** he has a (500,000-mark) share in the business.

Beteiligte(r) *mf decl as adj* person involved; *(Teilhaber)* partner; *(Jur)* party ♦ **die an der Diskussion ~n** those taking part in *or* involved in the discussion; **die am Unfall ~n** those involved in the accident; **an alle ~n** to all concerned.

Beteiligung *f, no pl* **(a)** *(Teilnahme) (an +dat* in) participation; *(finanziell)* share; *(an Unfall)* involvement. **(b)** *(das Beteiligen)* involvement *(an +dat* in) ♦ **die ~ der Arbeiter am Gewinn** giving the workers a share in the profits.

Beteilung *f (Aus)* giving ♦ **die ~ der Armen mit ...** the giving of ... to the poor.

Betel *m* **-s,** *no pl* betel.

⚠ **Betelnuß** *f* betel nut.

beten [1] *vi* to pray *(um, für* for, *zu* to), to say one's prayers; *(bei Tisch)* to say grace.
[2] *vt* to say.

beteuern* *vt* to declare, to aver, to asseverate *(liter)*; *Unschuld auch* to protest, to affirm ♦ **er beteuerte mir seine Liebe** he declared his love to me, he professed his love for me.

Beteuerung *f siehe vt* declaration, averment, asseveration *(liter)*; protestation.

betexten* *vt Bild* to write a caption for; *Lied* to write the words *or* lyric(s) for.

Bet-: ~glocke *f* church bell; **~haus** *nt* temple.

betiteln* *vt* to entitle; *(anreden) jdn* to address as, to call; *(beschimpfen)* to call ♦ **die Sendung ist betitelt ...** the broadcast is entitled ...; **wie ist das Buch betitelt?** what is the book called?, what's the book's title?; **er betitelte seinen Beitrag ...** he called his article *or* gave his article the title ... *or* entitled his article ...

Betitelung *f* **(a)** *no pl (das Betiteln)* **eine andere ~ des Films wäre besser** it would be better to call the film something else *or* to find a different title for the film.
(b) *(Titel)* title; *(Anrede)* form of address; *(Benennung)* name ♦ **ich verbitte mir eine solche ~** I refuse to be called names like that.

Beton [be'tɔŋ, be'tõ:, *(esp Aus)* be'to:n] *m* **-s,** *(rare)* **-s** concrete.

Beton- *in cpds* concrete; **~bau** *m* **(a)** concrete building *or* structure; **(b)** *no pl (Bauweise)* concrete construction; **~bauer** *m* builder; **~burg** *f (pej)* pile of concrete, concrete blockhouse; **~decke** *f* concrete ceiling; *(von Straße)* concrete surface.

▼ **betonen*** *vt* **(a)** *(hervorheben)* to emphasize; *Hüften, Augen auch* to accentuate; *(Gewicht legen auf auch)* to stress ♦ **ich möchte noch einmal ~, daß ...** I want to stress *or* emphasize once again that ...; *siehe auch* **betont**.
(b) *(Ling, Mus: einen Akzent legen auf)* to stress; *(Tonfall gebrauchen)* to intonate *(form)* ♦ **ein Wort falsch ~** to give a word the wrong stress, to stress a word wrongly; **du mußt den Satz anders ~** you must stress the sentence differently; *(mit Tonfall)* you must say the sentence with a different intonation.

betonieren* [1] *vt* **(a)** to concrete ♦ **betoniert** concrete. **(b)** *(fig: festlegen)* to firm up.
[2] *vi* **(a)** to concrete. **(b)** *(Sport sl)* to block the goal (area).

Betonierung *f (das Betonieren)* concreting; *(Betondecke auch)* concrete surface.

Beton-: ~klotz *m (lit)* block of concrete, concrete block; *(fig pej)* concrete block; **~kopf** *m (pej inf)* reactionary die-hard; **~mischmaschine** *f* concrete-mixer; **~silo** *m (pej inf)* high-rise block, concrete block *(pej)*.

betont [1] *ptp of* **betonen.**
[2] *adj Höflichkeit* emphatic, deliberate; *Kühle, Sachlichkeit* pointed; *Eleganz* pronounced ♦ **sich ~ einfach kleiden** to dress with marked *or* pronounced simplicity.

Betonung *f* **(a)** *no pl siehe vt* emphasis; accentuation; stressing; intonation.
(b) *(Akzent)* stress; *(fig: Gewicht)* emphasis, stress, accent ♦ **die ~ liegt auf der ersten Silbe** the stress is on the first syllable.

Betonungszeichen *nt* stress mark.

Betonwüste *f (pej)* concrete jungle.

Betophalt *m* concrete and asphalt road surface.

betören* *vt* to bewitch, to beguile.

Betörer(in *f*) *m* **-s, -** *(geh)* bewitcher, beguiler.

Betörung *f* bewitchment.

Betpult *nt* prie-dieu, kneeler.

Betr. *abbr of* **Betreff, betrifft.**

betr. *abbr of* **betreffend, betrifft, betreffs.**

Betracht *m* **-(e)s,** *no pl* **(a) außer ~ bleiben** to be left out of consideration, to be disregarded; **etw außer ~ lassen** to leave sth out of consideration, to disregard sth; **in ~ kommen** to be considered; **nicht in ~ kommen** to be out of the question; **jdn in ~ ziehen** to take sb into consideration, to consider sb; **etw in ~ ziehen** to take sth into account *or* consideration.
(b) *(dated: Hinsicht)* **in diesem ~** in this respect; **in gewissem ~** in certain respects.

▼ **betrachten*** *vt* **(a)** *(sehen, beurteilen)* to look at; *Verhältnisse, Situation etc auch* to view ♦ **sich** *(dat)* **etw ~** to have a look at sth; **bei näherem B~** on closer examination.
▼ **(b)** *(halten für)* **als jd** *or* **jdn/etw ~** to regard *or* look upon *or* consider as sb/sth; **ich betrachte ihn als Freund** I regard *etc* him as a friend.

Betrachter(in *f*) *m* **-s, -** *(von Anblick)* observer, beholder *(liter)*; *(von Situation)* observer ♦ **der aufmerksame ~ wird bei diesem Bild festgestellt haben ...** to

the alert eye it will have become apparent that in this picture ...
beträchtlich *adj* considerable ◆ **um ein ~es** considerably.
Betrachtung *f* (a) (*das Betrachten*) contemplation ◆ **bei näherer ~** on closer examination, when you look more closely; **eine neuartige ~ des Problems** a new way of looking at the problem.
(b) (*Überlegung, Untersuchung*) reflection ◆ **über etw** (*acc*) **~en anstellen** to reflect on *or* contemplate sth; **in ~en versunken** lost in thought *or* meditation.
Betrachtungsweise *f* **verschiedene ~n der Lage** different ways of looking at the situation; **er hat eine völlig andere ~** he has a completely different way of looking at things.
Betrag *m* -(e)s, ¨e amount, sum ◆ **der gesamte ~** the total (amount); **~ dankend erhalten** (payment) received with thanks.
betragen* *irreg* [1] *vi* to be; (*Kosten, Rechnung auch*) to come to, to amount to ◆ **die Entfernung betrug 25 km** the distance was 25 km; **der Unterschied beträgt 100 DM** the difference is *or* amounts to 100 DM.
[2] *vr* to behave ◆ **sich gut/schlecht/unhöflich ~** to behave (oneself) well/badly/to behave impolitely.
Betragen *nt* -s, *no pl* behaviour; (*esp im Zeugnis*) conduct.
betrauen* *vt* **jdn mit etw ~** to entrust sb with sth; **jdn damit ~, etw zu tun** to give sb the task of doing sth; **jdn mit einem öffentlichen Amt ~** to appoint sb to public office.
betrauern* *vt* to mourn; *jdn auch* to mourn for.
beträufeln* *vt* **den Fisch mit Zitrone ~** to sprinkle lemon juice over the fish; **die Wunde mit der Lösung ~** to put drops of the solution on the wound.
Betrauung *f* entrustment, entrusting.
Betreff *m* -(e)s, -e (*form*) **~: Ihr Schreiben vom ...** re your letter of ...; **den ~ angeben** to state the reference *or* subject matter; **in ~ dieser Frage** with respect *or* regard to this question; **in diesem ~** (*old*) in this regard (*old*) *or* respect.
betreffen* *vt irreg* (a) (*angehen*) to concern ◆ **das betrifft dich** it concerns you; **von dieser Regelung werde ich nicht betroffen** this rule does not concern *or* affect me; **was mich betrifft** ... as far as I'm concerned ...; **was das betrifft** ... as far as that goes *or* is concerned ...; **betrifft** re; *siehe auch* **betreffend, betroffen.**
(b) (*geh: widerfahren*) to befall.
(c) (*geh: seelisch treffen*) to affect, to touch ◆ **jdn schwer ~** to affect sb deeply; *siehe auch* **betroffen.**
betreffend *adj attr* (*erwähnt*) in question; (*zuständig, für etw relevant*) relevant ◆ **das ~e Wort richtig einsetzen** to insert the appropriate word in the right place; **alle (mein Fach) ~en Artikel** all the articles relevant to my subject, all the relevant articles.
Betreffende(r) *mf decl as adj* person concerned ◆ **die ~n** those concerned.
betreffs *prep +gen* (*form*) concerning, re (*esp Comm*).
betreiben* *vt irreg* (a) (*vorantreiben*) to push ahead *or* forward; *Geschäft, Untersuchung, Angelegenheit auch* to prosecute ◆ **auf jds B~** (*acc*) **hin** at sb's instigation.
(b) (*ausüben*) *Gewerbe, Handwerk* to carry on; *Geschäft auch* to conduct; *Handel auch, Sport* to do; *Studium, Politik* to pursue.
(c) (*Tech*) to operate.
(d) (*Sw*) to obtain a writ of account against.
Betreiber(in *f*) *m* -s, - operating authority.
Betreibung *f siehe vt (b)* carrying on; conduct; pursuit ◆ **bei der ~ einer Klage** in the pursuit of a legal action.
⚠ **betreßt** *adj* braided.
betreten[1]* *vt irreg* (*hineingehen in*) to enter, to go/come into; (*auf etw treten*) *Rasen, Spielfeld etc* to walk on; *feuchten Zementboden* to step *or* walk on; *Bühne, Brücke* to walk *or* step onto; *Podium* to step (up) onto; (*fig*) *Zeitalter etc* to enter ◆ **wir ~ damit ein noch unerforschtes Gebiet** we are here entering unknown *or* unexplored territory; **„B~ (des Rasens) verboten!"** "keep off (the grass)"; **„B~ für Unbefugte verboten"** "no entry to unauthorized persons".
betreten[2] *adj* embarrassed.
Betretenheit *f* embarrassment.
betreuen* *vt* to look after; *Reisegruppe, Abteilung auch* to be in charge of.
Betreuer(in *f*) *m* -s, - person who is in charge of *or* looking after sb; (*Kinder~*) child-minder; (*von alten Leuten, Kranken*) nurse ◆ **wir suchen noch ~ für** ... we are still looking for people to look after *or* take charge of ...; **der medizinische ~ der Nationalelf** the doctor who looks after the international team.
Betreuung *f* looking after; (*von Patienten, Tieren etc*) care ◆ **er wurde mit der ~ der Gruppe beauftragt** he was put in charge of the group, the group was put in his care.
Betrieb *m* -(e)s, -e (a) (*Firma*) business, concern; (*DDR auch*) enterprise; (*Fabrik*) factory, works *sing or pl*; (*Arbeitsstelle*) place of work ◆ **wir kommen um 5 Uhr aus dem ~** we leave work at 5 o'clock; **der Direktor ist heute nicht im ~** the director isn't at work *or* in (the office) today.
(b) (*Tätigkeit*) work; (*von Maschine, Fabrik*) working, operation; (*von Eisenbahn*) running; (*von Bergwerk*) working ◆ **den ~ stören** to be disruptive, to cause disruption; **er hält den ganzen ~ auf** he's holding everything up; **der ganze ~ stand still** everything stopped *or* came to a stop; **außer ~** out of order; **die Maschinen sind in ~** the machines are running; **eine Maschine in/außer ~ setzen** to start a machine up/to stop a machine; **eine Fabrik außer ~ setzen** to put a factory out of operation; **eine Maschine/Fabrik in ~ nehmen** to put a machine/factory into operation, to start operating a machine/in a factory; **einen Bus in ~ nehmen** to put a bus into service; **etw dem ~ übergeben** to open sth.
(c) (*Betriebsamkeit*) bustle ◆ **in den Geschäften herrscht großer ~** the shops are very busy; **auf den Straßen ist noch kein ~** there is nobody about in the streets yet; **bei dem ~ soll sich ein Mensch konzentrieren können!** how can anybody concentrate with all that (bustle) going on?
(d) (*inf*) **ich habe den ganzen ~ satt!** I'm fed up with the whole business! (*inf*); **ich schmeiß den ganzen ~ hin!** I'm going to chuck it all up! (*inf*), I'm going to chuck the whole business in (*inf*).
betrieblich *adj attr* internal company *attr* ; *Nutzungsdauer etc* operational ◆ **eine Sache ~ regeln** to settle a matter within the company.
Betriebs- *in cpds* (*Fabrik-*) factory, works; (*Firmen-*) company.
betriebsam *adj* busy, bustling *no adv* ◆ **seine Assistenten huschten ~ herum** his assistants bustled around.
Betriebsamkeit *f* bustle; (*von Mensch*) active nature ◆ **wegen der ständigen ~ meiner Mutter** ... because my mother is a very busy *or* active person ...
Betriebs-: ~angehörige(r) *mf* employee; **~anleitung** *f* operating instructions *pl*; **~art** *f* operating mode; **~begehung** *f* (*DDR*) round of inspection; **b~bereit** *adj* operational; **b~blind** *adj* blind to the shortcomings of one's company; **~blindheit** *f* organizational blindness *or* myopia; **~daten** *pl* operational data *sing*; operating *or* trading results *pl*; **b~eigen** *adj* company *attr*; **b~fähig** *adj* in working condition, operational; **~ferien** *pl* (annual) holiday, vacation close-down (*US*); **wegen ~ferien geschlossen** closed for holidays; **b~fremd** *adj* outside; **b~fremde Personen** non-company employees; **~frieden** *m* industrial peace; **~führung** *f* management; **~geheimnis** *nt* trade secret; **~gemeinschaft** *f* staff and management *pl*; **~gewerkschaftsleitung** *f* (*DDR*) company trade union committee; (*in Industrie*) works trade union committee; **~ingenieur** *m* production engineer; **b~intern** *adj* internal company *attr*; **etw b~intern regeln** to settle sth within the company; **~kampfgruppe** *f* (*DDR*) workers' militia branch; **~kapital** *nt* (*laufendes Kapital*) working capital; (*Anfangskapital*) initial capital; **~kindergarten** *m* company kindergarten; **~klima** *nt* atmosphere at work, working atmosphere; **~kollektivvertrag** *m* (*DDR*) union agreement; **~kosten** *pl* (*von Firma etc*) overheads *pl*, overhead expenses *pl*; (*von Maschine*) running costs *pl*; **~krankenkasse** *f* company health insurance scheme; **~leiter** *m* (works *or* factory) manager; **~leitung** *f* management; **~mittel** *nt siehe* **Produktionsmittel; ~nudel** *f* (*inf*) live wire (*inf*); (*Frau auch*) busy Lizzie (*inf*); (*Witzbold*) office/club *etc* clown; **~prüfung** *f* (government) audit; **~psychologie** *f* industrial psychology; **~rat** *m* (a) (*Gremium*) works *or* factory committee; (b) (*Person*) works *or* factory committee member; **~ratsvorsitzende(r)** *mf decl as adj* chair of works *or* factory committee; **~ruhe** *f* shutdown; ⚠**~schluß** *m* (*von Firma*) end of business hours; (*von Fabrik*) end of factory hours; **nach ~schluß** after business/factory hours; **was macht der Durchschnittsbürger nach ~schluß?** what does the average citizen do after work?; **~schutz** *m* (*von Anlagen*) factory *or* works security; (*Arbeitsschutz*) industrial safety; **b~sicher** *adj* safe (to operate); **~sicherheit** *f* (a) (operational) safety; (b) (*von Betrieb*) factory *or* works security; **~soziologie** *f* industrial sociology; **~stockung** *f* hold-up (in production); **~stoff** *m* (a) (*Treibstoff etc*) fuel; (b) (*Rohstoff*) raw *or* working materials *pl*; **~störung** *f* breakdown; **~system** *nt* (*Comput*) operating system; **~treue** *f* faithful service to the company; **~unfall** *m* industrial accident; (*hum sl*) accident; **~vereinbarung** *f* internal agreement; **~verfassung** *f regulations governing industrial relations*; **~verfassungsgesetz** *nt* Industrial Constitution Law; **~versammlung** *f* company meeting; **~wirt** *m* management expert; **~wirtschaft** *f* business management; **b~wirtschaftlich** *adj* business management *attr*; **~wirtschaftslehre** *f* business management.
betrinken* *vr irreg* to get drunk; *siehe* **betrunken.**
betroffen [1] *ptp of* **betreffen.**
[2] *adj* (a) affected (*von* by). (b) (*bestürzt*) full of consternation; *Schweigen* embarrassed, awkward ◆ **jdn ~ ansehen** to look at sb in consternation.
Betroffene(r) *mf decl as adj* person affected ◆ **schließlich sind wir die ~n** after all we are the ones who are affected *or* on the receiving end (*inf*).
Betroffenheit *f* consternation ◆ **stumme ~** embarrassed *or* awkward silence.
betrog *pret of* **betrügen.**
betrogen *ptp of* **betrügen.**
betrüben* [1] *vt* to sadden, to distress ◆ **es betrübt mich sehr** ... it grieves *or* saddens me greatly ...
[2] *vr* (*dated, hum*) to grieve (*über +acc* over); *siehe* **betrübt.**
betrüblich *adj* sad, distressing; *Zustände, Unwissenheit, Unfähigkeit* deplorable ◆ **die Lage sieht ~ aus** things look bad.
betrüblicherweise *adv* lamentably.
Betrübnis *f* (*geh*) grief, sadness *no pl*, distress *no pl* ◆ **~se** sorrows.
betrübt [1] *ptp of* **betrüben.**
[2] *adj* saddened, distressed.
Betrübtheit *f* sadness, distress, grief.
betrug *pret of* **betragen.**
Betrug *m* -(e)s, *no pl* deceit, deception; (*Jur*) fraud ◆ **das ist ja (alles) ~** it's (all) a cheat *or* fraud; **das ist ja ~, du hast geguckt!** that's cheating, you looked!; *siehe* **fromm.**
betrügen *pret* **betrog**, *ptp* **betrogen** [1] *vt* to deceive; (*geschäftlich auch*) to cheat; *Freund(in), Ehepartner auch* to be unfaithful to, to cheat (on); (*Jur*) to defraud ◆ **jdn um etw ~** to cheat *or* swindle sb out of sth; (*Jur*) to defraud sb of sth; **sie betrügt mich mit meinem besten Freund** she is having an affair with my best friend; **ich fühle mich betrogen** I feel betrayed; **sich um etw be-**

➤ SPRACHE AKTIV: **Betrachtung: a** → 53.2 **Betrag** → 47.5 **betreffen: a** → 33.2, 38.1, 53.2

trogen sehen to feel deprived of *or* done out of sth; **ich sah mich in ihm betrogen** he disappointed me, he let me down, I was deceived in him; **sich in seinen Hoffnungen/seinem Vertrauen betrogen sehen** to be disappointed in one's hopes/to be proved wrong in trusting sb.

[2] *vr* to deceive oneself.

Betrüger(in *f***)** *m* **-s, -** (*beim Spiel*) cheat; (*geschäftlich*) swindler; (*Jur*) defrauder; (*Hochstapler*) confidence trickster, con-man.

Betrügerei *f* deceit; (*geschäftlich*) cheating *no pl*, swindling *no pl*; (*von Ehepartner*) deceiving *no pl*; (*Jur*) fraud ◆ **seine Frau ist nie hinter seine ~en gekommen** (*inf*) his wife never found out that he was deceiving her *or* being unfaithful to her.

betrügerisch *adj* deceitful; (*Jur*) fraudulent ◆ **in ~er Absicht** with intent to defraud.

betrunken [1] *ptp of* **betrinken.**

[2] *adj* drunk *no adv*, drunken *attr* ◆ **er torkelte ~ nach Hause** he staggered home drunk; he staggered drunkenly home; **Fahren in ~em Zustand** driving while under the influence of drink *or* alcohol (*form*), drunk driving.

Betrunkene(r) *mf decl as adj* drunk.

Betrunkenheit *f* drunkenness.

Bet-: ~schemel *m siehe* **~bank**; **~schwester** *f* (*pej*) churchy type; **~stuhl** *m siehe* **~pult**; **~stunde** *f* prayer meeting.

Bett *nt* **-(e)s, -en** (*alle Bedeutungen*) bed; (*Feder~*) (continental) quilt, duvet ◆ **Frühstück ans ~** breakfast in bed; **an jds ~** (*dat*) **sitzen** to sit at sb's bedside *or* by sb's bed; **im ~** in bed; **jdn ins** *or* **zu ~ bringen** to put sb to bed; **mit jdm ins ~ gehen/steigen** (*euph*) to go to/jump into bed with sb; **mit jdm das ~ teilen** to share sb's bed; **er hat sich ins gemachte ~ gelegt** (*fig*) he had everything handed to him on a plate; *siehe* **französisch.**

Bettag ['be:tta:k] *m siehe* **Buß- und Bettag.**

Bett-: ~anzug *m* (*Sw*) *siehe* **~bezug**; **~bank** *f* (*Aus*) *siehe* **~couch**; **~bezug** *m* duvet *or* (continental) quilt cover; **~couch** *f* bed settee; **~decke** *f* blanket; (*gesteppt*) (continental) quilt, duvet; **sich unter der ~decke verstecken** to hide under the bedclothes.

Bettel *m* **-s,** *no pl* **(a)** (*obs: das Betteln*) begging. **(b)** (*dial*) (*Gerümpel*) rubbish, lumber, junk.

Bettel-: b~arm *adj* destitute; **~brief** *m* begging letter; **~bruder** *m* **(a)** (*~mönch*) mendicant *or* begging friar; **(b)** (*pej*) beggar, panhandler (*US inf*).

Bettelei *f* begging.

Bettel-: ~geld *nt* (*pej*) pittance; **~kram** *m siehe* **Bettel (b)**; **~lohn** *m* (*pej*) pittance; **~mönch** *m* mendicant *or* begging monk; **~musikant** *m* (*dated*) street musician.

betteln *vi* to beg ◆ **um ein Almosen ~** to beg (for) alms; **„B~ verboten"** "no begging"; **(bei jdm) um etw ~** to beg (sb) for sth.

Bettel-: ~orden *m* mendicant order; **~sack** *m* beggar's sack; **~stab** *m*: **an den ~stab kommen** to be reduced to beggary; **jdn an den ~stab bringen** to reduce sb to beggary; **~weib** *nt* (*old*) beggarwoman (*dated*).

betten [1] *vt* **(a)** (*legen*) to make a bed for, to bed down; *Unfallopfer* to lay *or* bed down; *Kopf* to lay ◆ **jdn weich/flach ~** to put sb on a soft bed/to lay sb down flat; **die Patienten werden zweimal am Tag gebettet** the patients have their beds made up twice a day; **das Dorf liegt ins** *or* **im Tal gebettet** (*liter*) the village nestles *or* lies nestling in the valley; *siehe* **Rose.**

(b) (*rare*) (*einlassen*) *Steine* to bed; (*einpflanzen*) to bed.

[2] *vr* to make a bed for oneself, to bed oneself down ◆ **wie man sich bettet, so liegt man** (*Prov*) as you make your bed so you must lie on it (*Prov*); **sich weich ~** to sleep on a soft mattress; **er hat sich schön weich gebettet** (*mit Heirat*) he's feathered his nest very nicely; (*in Stellung*) he's got a nice cushy little number for himself (*inf*).

Bett-: ~feder *f* bedspring; **~federn** *pl* (*Daunen*) bed feathers *pl*; **~flasche** *f* hot-water bottle; **~geflüster** *nt* pillow talk; **~genosse** *m* (*dated, iro*) bedfellow; **~geschichte** *f* (love) affair; **~geschichten** bedroom antics; **~gestell** *nt* bedstead; **~häschen** *nt*, **~hase** *m* (*inf*) sexy piece (*inf*); **~himmel** *m* canopy; **~hupferl** *nt* **-s, -** (*S Ger*) bed-time sweets; **~jacke** *f* bed jacket; **~kante** *f* edge of the bed; **~kasten** *m* linen drawer; **~lade** *f* (*S Ger, Aus*) bedstead; **b~lägerig** *adj* bedridden, confined to bed; **~lägerigkeit** *f*, *no pl* confinement to bed; **~laken** *nt* sheet; **~lektüre** *f* bedtime reading.

Bettler(in *f***)** *m* **-s, -** beggar, mendicant (*form*).

Bett-: ~nachbar *m* neighbour, person in the next bed; **~nässen** *nt* **-s,** *no pl* bed-wetting; **~nässer** *m* **-s, -** bed-wetter; **~pfanne** *f* bedpan; **~pfosten** *m* bedpost; **~platz** *m* (*Rail*) sleeping berth; **~rand** *m* edge of the bed; **b~reif** *adj* ready for bed; **~rost** *m* (bed) base; **~ruhe** *f* confinement to bed, bed rest; **der Arzt hat eine Woche ~ruhe verordnet** the doctor ordered him *etc* to stay in bed for one week; **~schüssel** *f* bedpan; **~schwere** *f* (*inf*) **die nötige ~schwere haben/bekommen** to be/get tired enough to sleep; **~statt, ~stelle** *f* bed; **~szene** *f* bedroom scene; **~tuch** *nt siehe* **Bettuch**; **~überwurf** *m* bedspread, counterpane; **~überzug** *m siehe* **~bezug.**

⚠ **Bettuch** *nt getrennt:* **Bett-tuch** sheet.

Bettumrandung *f* bed surround.

Bettung *f* (*Tech*) bed(ding); (*Rail*) ballast; (*Mil: Geschütze~*) platform.

Bett-: ~vorlage *f* (*dial*), **~vorleger** *m* bedside rug; **~wanze** *f* bedbug; **~wärme** *f* warmth of one's bed; **~wäsche** *f* bed linen; **~zeug** *nt* bedding; **~zipfel** *m* corner of the bed cover; **nach dem ~zipfel schielen** (*hum*) to be longing for one's bed.

betucht *adj* (*inf*) well-to-do.

betulich *adj* **(a)** (*übertrieben besorgt*) fussing *attr; Redeweise* twee ◆ **sei doch nicht so ~** don't be such an old mother hen (*inf*). **(b)** (*beschaulich*) leisurely *no adv*.

Betulichkeit *f siehe adj* **(a)** fussing nature; tweeness. **(b)** leisureliness.

betun* *vr irreg* (*inf*) **(a)** (*sich zieren*) to make a song and dance (*inf*). **(b)** (*übertrieben besorgt sein*) to make a fuss, to fuss about.

betupfen* *vt* to dab; (*Med*) to swab.

betuppen* *vt* (*dial inf*) to cheat, to trick.

betütern* (*N Ger inf*) [1] *vt* to mollycoddle.

[2] *vr* to get tipsy.

betütert *adj* (*N Ger inf*) (*betrunken*) tipsy; (*verwirrt*) dazed.

beugbar *adj* (*Gram*) *Substantiv, Adjektiv etc* declinable; *Verb* conjugable.

Beuge *f* **-, -n** bend; (*von Arm auch*) crook; (*Rumpf~*) forward bend; (*seitlich*) sideways bend; (*Knie~*) knee-bend ◆ **in die ~ gehen** to bend.

Beugehaft *f* (*Jur*) coercive detention.

Beugel *m* **-s, -** (*Aus*) croissant.

Beuge-: ~mann *m* (*hum*) bow; **~muskel** *m* flexor.

beugen [1] *vt* **(a)** (*krümmen*) to bend; (*Phys*) *Wellen* to diffract; *Strahlen, Licht* to deflect; (*fig*) *Stolz, Starrsinn* to break ◆ **das Recht ~** to pervert the course of justice; **vom Alter gebeugt** bent *or* bowed by age; **von der Last gebeugt** bowed down with the weight; **von Kummer/Gram gebeugt** bowed down with grief/sorrow; *siehe auch* **gebeugt.**

(b) (*Gram*) *Substantiv, Adjektiv etc* to decline; *Verb* to conjugate.

[2] *vr* to bend; (*fig*) to submit, to bow (*dat* to) ◆ **sich nach vorn ~** to bend *or* lean forward; **sich aus dem Fenster ~** to lean out of the window; **er beugte sich zu mir herüber** he leant across to me; **über seine Bücher/seinen Teller gebeugt** hunched over his books/his plate; **sich der Mehrheit ~** to bow *or* submit to the will of the majority.

Beuger *m* **-s, -** (*Anat*) flexor.

Beugestellung *f* bent position.

Beugung *f siehe vt* **(a)** (*Krümmung*) bending; diffraction; deflection; breaking ◆ **eine ~ des Rechts** a perversion of (the course of) justice. **(b)** (*Gram*) declension; conjugation.

Beule *f* **-, -n** (*von Stoß etc*) bump; (*eiternd*) boil; (*Delle*) dent.

beulen *vi* to bag.

Beulenpest *f* bubonic plague.

be|unruhigen* [1] *vt* to worry; (*Nachricht etc auch*) to disquiet, to disturb; (*Mil*) to harass ◆ **über etw** (*acc*) **beunruhigt sein** to be worried *or* disturbed about sth; **es ist ~d** it's worrying *or* disturbing, it gives cause for concern.

[2] *vr* to worry (oneself) (*über +acc, um, wegen* about).

Be|unruhigung *f* concern, disquiet; (*Mil*) harassment.

be|urkunden* *vt* **(a)** to certify; *Vertrag* to record; *Geschäft* to document. **(b)** (*old: bezeugen*) *Gefühle, Gesinnung, Haltung* to give evidence of.

Be|urkundung *f* **(a)** *siehe vt (a)* certification; recording; documentation. **(b)** (*Dokument*) documentary proof *or* evidence *no indef art no pl*.

be|urlauben* [1] *vt* to give *or* grant leave (of absence); (*Univ*) *Studenten* to give time off; *Lehrpersonal auch* to give *or* grant sabbatical leave; (*von Pflichten befreien*) to excuse (*von* from) ◆ **beurlaubt sein** to be on leave, to have leave of absence; to have time off; to be on sabbatical leave; (*suspendiert sein*) to have been relieved of one's duties; **sich ~ lassen** to take leave (of absence)/time off/sabbatical leave.

[2] *vr* (*dated: sich zurückziehen*) to excuse oneself.

Be|urlaubung *f siehe vt* (*gen* to) granting of leave (of absence); giving time off; granting of sabbatical leave; (*Beurlaubtsein*) leave (of absence); time off; sabbatical leave ◆ **seine ~ vom Dienst** (*Befreiung*) his being excused (from) his duties; (*Suspendierung*) his being relieved of his duties.

be|urteilen* *vt* to judge (*nach* by, from); *Leistung, Wert* to assess; *Buch, Bild etc auch* to give an opinion of ◆ **etw richtig/falsch ~** to judge sth correctly/to misjudge sth; **du kannst das doch gar nicht ~** you are not in a position to judge.

Be|urteiler(in *f***)** *m* **-s, -** judge.

Be|urteilung *f siehe vt* judging, judgement; assessing, assessment; (*Urteil*) assessment; (*Kritik: von Stück etc*) review.

Be|urteilungs-: ~gespräch *nt* appraisal interview; **~maßstab** *m* criterion.

Beuschel *nt* **-s, -** (*Aus*) **(a)** *dish made of offal.* **(b)** (*sl*) lungs *pl*; (*Eingeweide*) entrails *pl*.

Beute[1] *f* **-,** *no pl* **(a)** (*Kriegs~, fig hum*) spoils *pl*, booty, loot *no indef art*; (*Diebes~*) haul, loot (*inf*); (*von Raubtieren etc*) prey; (*getötete*) kill; (*Jagd~*) bag; (*beim Fischen*) catch ◆ **~ machen** to capture booty/make a haul/kill/get a bag/catch; **ohne ~/mit reicher ~** (*Hunt*) empty-handed/with a good bag.

(b) (*liter: Opfer*) prey ◆ **eine leichte ~** easy prey; **jdm/einer Sache zur ~ fallen** (*liter*) to fall (a) prey to sb/sth.

Beute[2] *f* **-, -n** (*Bienenkasten*) (bee)hive.

beutegierig *adj Tier* eager for the kill, ravening *attr*; (*fig*) eager for booty *or* a haul.

Beutel *m* **-s, - (a)** (*Behälter*) bag; (*Tasche*) (draw-string) bag *or* purse; (*Tragetasche*) carrier bag; (*Tabaks~, Zool*) pouch; (*dial*) (*Tüte*) paper bag; (*Päckchen*) packet.

(b) (*inf: Geld~*) (*von Frau*) purse; (*von Mann*) wallet ◆ **tief in den ~ greifen** to put one's hand in one's pocket, to dig deep into one's pocket(s); **jds ~ ist leer** sb has no money *or* is broke (*inf*); (*von Staat etc*) sb's coffers are empty; **das geht an den ~** that costs money!; **die Hand auf dem ~ haben, den ~ zuhalten** (*dated*) to be tight-fisted; *siehe* **Loch.**

beuteln [1] *vt* **(a)** (*old*) *Mehl* to sieve. **(b)** (*dial*) to shake; (*fig*) to shake about ◆ **mich hat's gebeutelt!** (*inf*) (*bin gefallen*) I fell, I came a cropper (*inf*); (*bin krank geworden*) I've come down with it/with flu *etc.*

⚠: for details of spelling reform, see supplement

2 *vi* (*sich bauschen*) to bag.
Beutel-: ~ratte *f* opossum; **~schneider** *m* (*obs: Gauner*) cutpurse (*obs*), pickpocket; (*dated geh: Wucherer*) swindler; **~schneiderei** *f* (*obs*) theft, thievery (*old*); (*geh: Nepp*) swindling; **~tier** *nt* marsupial.
Beute-: ~recht *nt* right of plunder; **~stück** *nt* booty; **~zug** *m* raid (*auch fig*); **auf ~zug durch die Geschäfte gehen** (*fig*) to go on a foray of the shops.
Beutler *m* **-s, -** (*Zool*) marsupial.
bevölkern* 1 *vt* **(a)** (*bewohnen*) to inhabit; (*beleben*) to crowd, to fill ◆ **schwach/stark** *or* **dicht bevölkert** thinly *or* sparsely/densely *or* thickly populated; **Tausende bevölkerten den Marktplatz** the marketplace was crowded with thousands of people. **(b)** (*besiedeln*) to populate.
2 *vr* to become inhabited; (*fig*) to fill up.
Bevölkerung *f* **(a)** (*die Bewohner*) population. **(b)** *no pl* (*das Bevölkern*) peopling, populating.
Bevölkerungs-: ~abnahme *f* fall *or* decrease in population; **~dichte** *f* density of population, population density; **~explosion** *f* population explosion; **~gruppe** *f* section of the population; **~politik** *f* population policy; **~schicht** *f* class of society, social stratum *or* class; **~statistik** *f* population statistics *pl*; **~zahl** *f* (total) population; **~zunahme** *f* rise *or* increase in population.
➤ **bevollmächtigen*** *vt* to authorize (*zu etw* to do sth).
Bevollmächtigte(r) *mf decl as adj* authorized representative; (*Pol*) plenipotentiary.
Bevollmächtigung *f* authorization (*durch* from).
bevor *conj* before ◆ **~ Sie (nicht) die Rechnung bezahlt haben** until you pay *or* you have paid the bill.
bevormunden* *vt* to treat like a child ◆ **jdn ~** to make sb's decisions (for him/her), to make up sb's mind for him/her; **ich lasse mich von niemandem ~** I shan't let anyone make my decisions (for me) *or* make up my mind for me.
Bevormundung *f* **seine Schüler/Untergebenen** *etc* **wehren sich gegen die ständige ~** his pupils/subordinates *etc* object to his constantly making up their minds for them; **unsere ~ durch den Staat** the State's making up our minds for us.
bevorraten* *vt insep* (*form*) to stock up.
bevorrechtigt *adj* (*privilegiert*) privileged; (*wichtig*) high-priority.
Bevorrechtigung *f* preferential treatment *no pl*.
bevorschussen* *vt insep* (*rare*) to make an advance to.
bevorstehen *vi sep irreg* to be imminent; (*Winter etc*) to be near, to approach ◆ **jdm ~** to be in store for sb; **ihm steht eine Überraschung bevor** there's a surprise in store for him; **das Schlimmste steht uns noch bevor** the worst is yet *or* still to come; **die Prüfung stand ihm noch bevor** the exam was yet *or* still to come, the exam still lay ahead.
bevorstehend *adj* forthcoming; *Gefahr, Krise* imminent; *Winter* approaching.
bevorzugen* *vt* to prefer; (*begünstigen*) to favour, to give preference *or* preferential treatment to ◆ **keines unserer Kinder wird bevorzugt** we don't give preference to any of our children; **hier wird niemand bevorzugt** there's no favouritism here.
bevorzugt 1 *adj* preferred; *Behandlung* preferential; (*privilegiert*) privileged ◆ **die von mir ~en Bücher** the books I prefer.
2 *adv* **jdn ~ abfertigen/bedienen** *etc* to give sb preferential treatment; **etw ~ abfertigen/bedienen** *etc* to give sth priority.
Bevorzugung *f* preference (*gen* for); (*vorrangige Behandlung*) preferential treatment (*bei* in).
bewachen* *vt* to guard; (*Sport*) *Tor* to guard; *Spieler* to mark.
Bewacher(in *f***)** *m* **-s, -** guard; (*Sport: von Spieler*) marker.
bewachsen* 1 *vt irreg* to grow over, to cover.
2 *adj* overgrown, covered (*mit* in, with).
Bewachung *f* guarding; (*Wachmannschaft*) guard; (*Sport*) marking ◆ **jdn unter ~ halten/stellen** to keep/put sb under guard.
bewaffnen* 1 *vt* to arm.
2 *vr* (*lit, fig*) to arm oneself.
bewaffnet *adj* armed ◆ **bis an die Zähne ~** armed to the teeth; **~e Organe** (*DDR*) armed forces.
Bewaffnete(r) *mf decl as adj* armed man/woman/person *etc*.
Bewaffnung *f* **(a)** *no pl* (*das Bewaffnen*) arming ◆ **man hat die ~ der Polizei beschlossen** it was decided to arm the police. **(b)** (*Waffen*) weapons *pl*.
bewahren* *vt* **(a)** (*beschützen*) to protect (*vor +dat* from) ◆ **jdn vor etw ~** to protect *or* save *or* preserve sb from sth; **(i** *or* **Gott) bewahre!** (*inf*) heaven *or* God forbid!, heaven *or* saints preserve us!
(b) (*geh: auf~*) to keep ◆ **sich für jdn ~** (*liter*) to keep oneself for sb; **jdn/etw in guter Erinnerung ~** to have happy memories of sb/sth.
(c) (*beibehalten*) to keep, to retain, to preserve; *Denkmal* to conserve ◆ **sich** (*dat*) **etw ~** to keep *or* retain *or* preserve sth.
bewähren* *vr* to prove oneself/itself, to prove one's/its worth; (*Methode, Plan, Investition, Sparsamkeit, Fleiß*) to pay off, to prove (to be) worthwhile; (*Auto, Gerät etc*) to prove (to be) a good investment ◆ **sich im Leben ~** to make something of one's life; **wenn sich der Straftäter bewährt** if the offender proves he has reformed; **die Methode/das Gerät hat sich gut/schlecht bewährt** the method proved/didn't prove (to be) very worthwhile/the appliance proved/didn't prove (to be) a very good investment; **es bewährt sich immer, das zu tun** it's always worthwhile doing that; **ihre Freundschaft hat sich bewährt** their friendship stood the test of time; *siehe* **bewährt**.

Bewahrer *m* **-s, -** (*rare*) guardian, custodian, keeper.
bewahrheiten* *vr* (*Befürchtung, Hoffnung, Gerücht*) to prove (to be) well-founded; (*Prophezeiung*) to come true.
bewährt 1 *ptp of* **bewähren.**
2 *adj* proven, tried and tested, reliable; *Geldanlage* worthwhile; *Rezept* tried and tested ◆ **vielfach/seit langem ~** tried and tested/well-established.
Bewährtheit *f, no pl* reliability.
Bewahrung *f siehe vt* **(a)** protection. **(b)** keeping. **(c)** keeping, retaining, preservation; conservation.
Bewährung *f* **(a)** *siehe vr* proving oneself/itself, proving one's/its worth; proving oneself/itself worthwhile ◆ **bei ~ der Methode ...** if the method proves (to be) worthwhile ...
(b) (*Jur*) probation ◆ **eine Strafe zur ~ aussetzen** to impose a suspended sentence; **ein Jahr Gefängnis mit ~** a suspended sentence of one year with probation; *siehe* **Bewährungsfrist.**
Bewährungs-: ~auflage *f* (*Jur*) probation order; **~frist** *f* (*Jur*) probation(ary) period, (period of) probation; **~heim** *nt* home for young offenders; **~helfer** *m* probation officer; **~hilfe** *f* probation service; **~probe** *f* test; **etw einer ~probe** (*dat*) **unterziehen** to put sth to the test; **~zeit** *f* time spent on probation.
bewalden* 1 *vt* to plant with trees, to afforest (*form*).
2 *vr* **allmählich bewaldet sich das Gebiet** trees are gradually beginning to grow in the area.
bewaldet *adj* wooded.
Bewaldung *f* (*das Bewalden*) planting with trees, afforestation (*form*); (*Baumbestand*) trees *pl*, woodlands *pl* ◆ **spärliche/dichte ~** few trees/dense woodlands.
bewältigen* *vt* (*meistern*) *Schwierigkeiten, Problem* to cope with; *Arbeit, Aufgabe auch, Strecke* to manage; (*überwinden*) *Vergangenheit, Erlebnis etc* to get over; *Schüchternheit auch* to overcome; (*erledigen, beenden*) to deal with; (*aufessen*) to manage.
Bewältigung *f siehe vt* **die ~ der Schwierigkeiten/der Arbeit/eines Erlebnisses** *etc* coping with the difficulties/managing the work/getting over an experience *etc*.
bewandert *adj* experienced ◆ **in etw** (*dat*)**/auf einem Gebiet ~ sein** to be familiar with *or* well-versed in sth/to be experienced *or* well-versed in a field.
bewandt *adj* (*old*) **es ist so ~, daß ...** the situation *or* position is such that ...; **wie ist es damit ~?** how does the matter lie?
Bewandtnis *f* reason, explanation ◆ **das hat** *or* **damit hat es eine andere ~** there's another reason *or* explanation for that; **das hat** *or* **damit hat es seine eigene ~** that's a long story; **das hat** *or* **damit hat es folgende ~** the fact/facts of the matter is/are this/these.
bewässern* *vt* to irrigate; (*mit Sprühanlage*) to water.
Bewässerung *f siehe vt* irrigation; watering.
Bewässerungs-: ~anlage *f* irrigation plant; **~graben** *m* irrigation channel, feeder; **~kanal** *m* irrigation canal; **~system** *nt* irrigation system.
bewegbar *adj siehe* **beweglich (a).**
bewegen[1]* 1 *vt* **(a)** (*Lage verändern, regen*) to move; *Erdmassen, Möbelstück auch* to shift; *Hund, Pferd* to exercise.
(b) (*innerlich ~*) to move; (*beschäftigen, angehen*) to concern ◆ **dieser Gedanke bewegt mich seit langem** this has been on my mind a long time; **~d** moving; *siehe auch* **bewegt.**
(c) (*bewirken, ändern*) to change.
2 *vr* **(a)** to move ◆ **beide Reden bewegten sich in der gleichen Richtung** both speeches were along the same lines.
(b) (*Bewegung haben: Mensch*) to get some exercise; (*inf: spazierengehen*) to stretch one's legs, to take some exercise.
(c) (*fig*) (*variieren, schwanken*) to vary, to range (*zwischen* between) ◆ **der Preis bewegt sich um die 50 Mark** the price is about 50 marks; **die Verluste ~ sich in den Tausenden** losses are in the thousands.
(d) (*sich ändern, Fortschritte machen*) to change ◆ **es bewegt sich etwas** things are beginning to happen.
(e) (*auftreten, sich benehmen*) to behave, to act.
bewegen[2] *pret* **bewog,** *ptp* **bewogen** *vt* **jdn zu etw ~** to induce *or* persuade sb to do sth; **was hat dich dazu bewogen?** what induced you to do that?; **sich dazu ~ lassen, etw zu tun** to allow oneself to be persuaded to do sth.
Beweggrund *m* motive.
beweglich *adj* **(a)** (*bewegbar*) movable; *Hebel, Griff auch* mobile; *Truppe* mobile. **(b)** (*wendig*) agile; *Fahrzeug* manoeuvrable; (*geistig ~*) agile-minded, nimble-minded; (*fig*) *Geist auch* nimble ◆ **mit einem Kleinwagen ist man in der Stadt ~er** you're more mobile in town with a small car.
Beweglichkeit *f, no pl siehe adj* **(a)** movability; mobility. **(b)** agility; manoeuvrability; agility *or* nimbleness of mind; nimbleness.
bewegt 1 *ptp of* **bewegen**[1].
2 *adj* **(a)** (*unruhig*) *Wasser, See* choppy; *Zeiten, Vergangenheit, Leben* eventful; *Jugend* eventful, turbulent ◆ **die See war stark ~/kaum ~** the sea was rough/fairly calm. **(b)** (*gerührt*) *Stimme, Worte, Stille* emotional ◆ **~ sein** to be moved.
Bewegung *f* **(a)** movement; (*Hand~ auch*) gesture; (*Sci, Tech auch*) motion ◆ **eine falsche ~!** one false move!; **keine ~!** freeze! (*inf*), don't move!; **in ~ sein** (*Fahrzeug*) to be moving, to be in motion; (*Menge*) to mill around; **sich in ~ setzen** to start moving, to begin to move; **etw in ~ setzen/bringen** to set sth in motion, to start sth moving; **jdn in ~ bringen** to get sb moving;

alle Hebel *or* **Himmel und Hölle in ~ setzen** to move heaven and earth; **jdn in ~ halten** to keep sb moving, to keep sb on the go (*inf*).
(b) (*körperliche ~*) exercise ◆ **sich** (*dat*) **~ verschaffen** *or* **machen** to get (some) exercise.
(c) (*Unruhe*) agitation ◆ **in ~ geraten** to get into a state of agitation; **diese Nachricht ließ die ganze Stadt in ~ geraten** this news caused a commotion throughout the whole town *or* threw the whole town into a state of agitation.
(d) (*Entwicklung*) progress ◆ **etw kommt in ~** sth gets moving; **endlich kam ~ in die Verhandlungen** at last there was some progress in the negotiations.
(e) (*Ergriffenheit*) emotion.
(f) (*Pol, Art etc*) movement.

Bewegungs-: ~bild *nt* (*Admin*) record of (sb's) movements; **~drang** *m* urge *or* impulse to be active; **~energie** *f* kinetic energy; **b~fähig** *adj* mobile; **~freiheit** *f* freedom of movement; (*fig*) freedom of action; **~krieg** *m* mobile warfare; **b~los** *adj* motionless, immobile; **~losigkeit** *f* motionlessness, immobility; **~mangel** *m* lack of exercise; **~nerv** *m* motor nerve; **~spiel** *nt* (*Sport*) active game; **~studie** *f* (a) (*Ind*) time and motion study; (b) (*Art*) study in movement; **~therapie** *f* (*aktiv*) therapeutic exercise; (*passiv*) manipulation; **~trieb** *m* urge *or* impulse to be active; **b~unfähig** *adj* unable to move; (*gehunfähig*) unable to move *or* get about; **~unfähigkeit** *f siehe adj* inability to move; inability to move *or* get about; **~unschärfe** *f* (*Phot*) camera-shake; **~zustand** *m* state of motion.

bewehren* (*old*) [1] *vt* to fortify; (*bewaffnen*) to arm.
[2] *vr* (*auch iro*) to arm oneself.

Bewehrung *f* (a) *siehe vt* fortifying; arming. (b) (*Wehranlagen*) fortifications *pl*; (*Waffen*) arms *pl*.

beweiben* *vr* (*dated*) to take a wife (*dated*), to wed (*dated*).

beweiden* *vt* (*Agr*) *Land* to pasture; (*Kühe*) to graze on.

beweihräuchern* *vt* to (in)cense; (*fig*) to praise to the skies ◆ **sich (selbst) ~** to indulge in self-adulation.

beweinen* *vt* to mourn (for), to weep for.

beweinenswert *adj* (*geh*) lamentable.

Beweinung *f* mourning ◆ **die ~ Christi** (*Art*) the Mourning of Christ.

Beweis *m* **-es, -e** proof (*für* of); (*Zeugnis*) evidence *no pl* ◆ **als** *or* **zum ~** as proof *or* evidence; **das ist kein ~ für das, was du behauptest** that doesn't prove *or* that's no proof of what you have been claiming; **ein eindeutiger ~** clear evidence; **sein Schweigen ist ein ~ seines Schuldgefühls** his silence is proof *or* evidence of his feeling of guilt; **den ~ antreten** to offer evidence *or* proof; **einen/den ~ führen** to offer evidence *or* proof; **den ~ für etw/seiner Unschuld erbringen** to produce *or* supply evidence *or* proof of sth/one's innocence; **~ erheben** (*Jur*) to hear *or* take evidence; **jdm einen ~ seiner Hochachtung geben** to give sb a token of one's respect.

Beweis-: ~antrag *m* (*Jur*) motion to take *or* hear evidence; **~aufnahme** *f* (*Jur*) taking *or* hearing of evidence; **b~bar** *adj* provable, demonstrable, capable of being proved.

▼ **beweisen*** *irreg* [1] *vt* (a) (*nachweisen*) to prove ◆ **was zu ~ war** QED, quod
▼ erat demonstrandum; **was noch zu ~ wäre** that remains to be seen. (b) (*erkennen lassen, dated: erweisen*) to show.
[2] *vr* to prove oneself/itself.

Beweis-: b~erheblich *adj* (*Jur*) evidentiary (*spec*); **~führung** *f* (*Jur*) presentation of one's case; (*Math*) proof; (*Argumentation*) (line of) argumentation *or* reasoning; **~gang** *m* argumentation (*in proving sth*); **~gegenstand** *m* (*esp Jur*) point at issue; **~grund** *m* argument; **~kette** *f* chain of proof; (*Jur auch*) chain of evidence; **~kraft** *f* evidential value, value as evidence; **b~kräftig** *adj* evidential, probative (*form*); **~lage** *f* (*Jur*) body of evidence; **~last** *f* (*Jur*) onus, burden of proof; **~material** *nt* (body of) evidence; **~mittel** *nt* evidence *no pl*; **~not** *f* (*Jur*) lack of evidence; **in ~not sein** to be lacking evidence; **~pflicht** *f* (*Jur*) onus, burden of proof; **~stück** *nt* exhibit; **~würdigung** *f* (*Jur*) assessment of the evidence.

bewenden *vt impers*: **es bei** *or* **mit etw ~ lassen** to be content with sth; **wir wollen es dabei ~ lassen** let's leave it at that.

Bewenden *nt*: **damit hatte es sein/die Angelegenheit ihr ~** the matter rested there, that was the end of the matter.

Bewerb *m* **-(e)s, -e** (*Aus Sport*) *siehe* **Wettbewerb**.

▼ **bewerben*** *irreg* [1] *vr* to apply (*um* for, *als* for the post/job of) ◆ **sich bei einer Firma ~** to apply to a firm (for a job); **sich um jdn ~** (*dated*) to ask for sb's hand in marriage.
[2] *vt Produkte, Firmen* to promote.

Bewerber(in *f*) *m* **-s, -** applicant; (*dated: Freier*) suitor (*dated*).

Bewerbung *f* application; (*dated: um Mädchen*) wooing (*dated*), courting (*dated*).

Bewerbungs-: ~bogen *m*, **~formular** *nt* application form; **~gespräch** *nt* (job) interview; **~schreiben** *nt* (letter of) application; **~unterlagen** *pl* application documents *pl*; **~verfahren** *nt* application procedure.

bewerfen* *vt irreg* (a) **jdn/etw mit etw ~** to throw sth at sb/sth; *mit Steinen, Pfeilen etc auch* to pelt sb with sth; (*fig*) to hurl sth at sb/sth; **jdn/jds guten Namen mit Schmutz** *or* **Dreck ~** to throw *or* sling mud at sb/sb's good name.
(b) (*Build*) to face, to cover; (*mit Rauhputz auch*) to roughcast; (*mit Gips auch*) to plaster; (*mit Zement auch*) to cement ◆ **mit Kies beworfen** pebble-dashed.

bewerkstelligen* *vt* to manage; *Geschäft* to effect, to bring off ◆ **es ~, daß jd etw tut** to manage *or* contrive to get sb to do sth.

Bewerkstelligung *f, no pl* managing.

bewerten* *vt jdn* to judge; *Gegenstand* to value, to put a value on; *Leistung auch, Schularbeit* to assess ◆ **etw zu hoch/niedrig ~** to overvalue/undervalue sth; **jdn/etw nach einem Maßstab ~** to judge sb/measure sth against a yardstick; **etw mit der Note 5 ~** to give sth a mark of 5; **eine Arbeit mit (der Note) „gut" ~** to mark a piece of work "good", to give a "good" for a piece of work.

Bewertung *f siehe vt* judgement; valuation; assessment.

Bewertungs-: ~kriterium *nt* criterion; **~maßstab** *m* set of criteria.

bewies *pret of* **beweisen**.

bewiesen *ptp of* **beweisen**.

bewiesenermaßen *adv* **was er sagt, ist ~ unwahr** it has been proved that *or* there is evidence to show that what he is saying is untrue; **er ist ~ ein Betrüger** he has been proved to be a fraud.

bewilligen* *vt* to allow; *Planstelle auch, Etat, Steuererhöhung etc* to approve; *Mittel, Geld, Darlehen etc auch* to grant; *Stipendium* to award ◆ **jdm etw ~** to allow/grant/award sb sth.

Bewilligung *f siehe vt* allowing; approving, approval; granting; awarding; (*Genehmigung*) approval ◆ **dafür brauchen Sie eine ~** you need approval for that; **die ~ für einen Kredit bekommen** to be allowed *or* granted credit.

Bewilligungs-: ~bescheid *m* approval; **b~pflichtig** *adj* subject to approval.

bewillkommnen* *vt insep* (*geh*) to welcome.

Bewillkommnung *f* (*rare*) welcoming *no pl*, reception.

bewimpert *adj Auge* lashed; (*Zool*) ciliate(d) (*spec*).

bewirken* *vt* (a) (*verursachen*) to cause, to bring about, to produce ◆ **~, daß etw passiert** to cause sth to happen.
(b) (*erreichen*) to achieve ◆ **mit so einem Auftreten kannst du bei ihm nichts ~** you won't get anywhere *or* achieve anything with him if you behave like that; **damit bewirkst du bei ihm nur das Gegenteil** that way you'll only achieve the opposite effect.

bewirten* *vt jdn* **~** to feed sb; (*bei offiziellem Besuch etc*) to entertain sb to a meal; **wir wurden während der ganzen Zeit köstlich bewirtet** we were very well fed all the time, we were given excellent food all the time; **jdn mit Kaffee und Kuchen ~** to entertain sb to coffee and cakes; **wenn man so viele Leute zu ~ hat** if you have so many people to cater for *or* feed.

bewirtschaften* *vt* (a) *Betrieb etc* to manage, to run ◆ **die Berghütte wird im Winter nicht/wird von Herrn und Frau X bewirtschaftet** the mountain hut is not serviced in the winter/is managed *or* run by Mr and Mrs X.
(b) *Land* to farm, to cultivate, to work.
(c) (*staatlich kontrollieren*) *Waren* to ration; *Devisen, Wohnraum* to control.

Bewirtschaftung *f siehe vt* (a) management, running; servicing. (b) farming, cultivation, working. (c) rationing; control.

Bewirtung *f* (*das Bewirten*) hospitality; (*im Hotel*) (food and) service; (*rare: Essen und Getränke*) food (and drink) ◆ **die ~ so vieler Gäste** catering for *or* feeding so many guests.

bewitzeln* *vt* to make fun of.

bewog *pret of* **bewegen[2]**.

bewogen *ptp of* **bewegen[2]**.

bewohnbar *adj* (a) *Gegend, Land etc* habitable. (b) *Haus, Wohnung etc* habitable, fit to live in; (*beziehbar*) habitable, ready to live in.

Bewohnbarkeit *f* habitability.

bewohnen* *vt* to live in; *Haus, Zimmer, Bau, Nest auch* to occupy; (*Volk*) to inhabit; (*Krankheit*) to be carried by ◆ **das Zimmer/das Haus war jahrelang nicht bewohnt** the room was unoccupied/the house was uninhabited *or* unoccupied for years; *siehe auch* **bewohnt**.

Bewohner(in *f*) *m* **-s, -** (*von Land, Gebiet*) inhabitant; (*von Haus etc*) occupier ◆ **dieser Vogel ist ein ~ der Wälder** this bird is a forest-dweller *or* a denizen of the forest (*liter*).

Bewohnerschaft *f* occupants *pl*.

bewohnt *adj Land, Gebiet* inhabited; *Haus etc auch* occupied.

bewölken* *vr* (*lit, fig*) to cloud over, to darken.

bewölkt *adj* cloudy ◆ **~ bis bedeckt** (*Met*) cloudy, perhaps overcast.

Bewölkung *f* (*das Sich-Bewölken*) clouding over, darkening; (*das Bewölktsein*) cloud ◆ **wechselnde bis zunehmende ~** (*Met*) variable amounts of cloud, becoming cloudier.

Bewölkungs-: ~auflockerung *f* break-up of the cloud; **~zunahme** *f* increase in cloud.

bewuchern* *vt* to grow over, to cover.

Bewuchs *m, no pl* vegetation.

Bewund(e)rer(in *f*) *m* **-s, -** admirer.

bewundern* *vt* to admire (*wegen* for) ◆ **~d** admiring; **ein überall bewunderter Künstler** a universally admired artist.

bewundernswert, bewundernswürdig *adj* admirable.

▼ **Bewunderung** *f* admiration.

bewunderungswert, bewunderungswürdig *adj* admirable.

Bewundrer(in *f*) *m siehe* **Bewund(e)rer(in)**.

Bewurf *m* (a) (*das Bewerfen*) **der ~ der Feinde/Mauern mit Steinen** throwing stones at the enemy/walls, pelting the enemy/walls with stones. (b) (*Build*) facing, covering; (*Rauhputz*) roughcast; (*Kies~*) pebble dash.

bewurzeln* *vr* to root, to grow roots.

⚠ **bewußt** [1] *adj* (a) *usu attr* (*Philos, Psych*) conscious.
(b) *attr* (*überlegt*) conscious; *Mensch* self-aware ◆ **er führte ein sehr ~es Leben** he lived a life of total awareness.
(c) *pred* **sich** (*dat*) **einer Sache** (*gen*) **~ sein/werden** to be/become aware *or* conscious of sth, to realize sth; **etw ist jdm ~** sb is aware *or* conscious of sth; **es wurde ihm allmählich ~, daß** ... he gradually realized (that) ..., it gradually dawned on him (that) ...

(d) *attr* (*willentlich*) deliberate, intentional; *Lüge* deliberate.
(e) *attr* (*überzeugt*) convinced ◆ **er ist ein ~er Kommunist** he is a convinced communist.
(f) *attr* (*bekannt, besagt*) in question; *Zeit* agreed ◆ **die ~e Kreuzung** the crossroads in question.
[2] *adv* **(a)** consciously; *leben* in total awareness.
(b) (*willentlich*) deliberately, intentionally.

⚠**Bewußtheit** *f, no pl siehe adj* (*a, b, d, e*) **(a)** consciousness. **(b)** consciousness; self-awareness. **(c)** deliberate *or* intentional nature. **(d)** conviction.

⚠**Bewußt-: b~los** *adj* unconscious, senseless; **b~los werden** to lose consciousness, to become unconscious; **b~los zusammenbrechen** to fall senseless; **~lose(r)** *mf decl as adj* unconscious man/woman/person *etc*; **die ~losen** the unconscious; **~losigkeit** *f* unconsciousness; **bis zur ~losigkeit** (*inf*) ad nauseam; **b~machen** *vt sep* **jdm etw b~machen** to make sb aware *or* conscious of sth, to make sb realize sth; **sich** (*dat*) **etw b~machen** to realize sth.

⚠**Bewußtsein** *nt* **-s,** *no pl* **(a)** (*Wissen*) awareness, consciousness ◆ **etw kommt jdm zu(m) ~** sb becomes aware *or* conscious of sth *or* realizes sth; **jdm etw zu ~ bringen/ins ~ rufen** to make sb (fully) conscious *or* aware of sth; **etw tritt in jds ~** (*acc*) sth occurs to sb; **das allgemeine ~** general awareness; **im ~** *+gen*/**daß** ... in the knowledge of/that ...
(b) (*Philos, Psych, Med*) consciousness ◆ **das ~ verlieren/wiedererlangen** to lose/regain consciousness; **bei ~ sein** to be conscious; **zu(m) ~ kommen** to regain consciousness; **bei vollem ~** fully conscious; **jdm schwindet das ~** (*geh*) sb faints *or* swoons (*liter*).
(c) er tat es mit (vollem)/ohne ~ he was (fully) aware/he was not aware of what he was doing.
(d) (*Anschauungen*) convictions *pl*.

⚠**Bewußtseins-: ~bildung** *f* (*Pol*) shaping of political ideas; **b~erweiternd** *adj* **b~erweiternde Drogen** mind-expanding drugs, drugs that heighten (one's) awareness; **~erweiterung** *f* heightening of (one's) awareness; **~inhalt** *m usu pl* (*Philos*) content of consciousness; **~kunst** *f* (*Liter*) stream-of-consciousness technique; **~lage** *f* (*Pol*) state of political awareness; **~lenkung** *f* (*Sociol*) manipulation of consciousness; **~schwelle** *f* (*Psych*) threshold of consciousness; **~spaltung** *f* (*Med, Psych*) splitting of the consciousness; **~störung** *f* (*Psych*) disturbance of consciousness; **~strom** *m* (*Liter*) stream of consciousness; **~trübung** *f* (*Psych*) dimming of consciousness; **b~verändernd** *adj* (*Psych*) **b~verändernde Drogen** drugs which alter one's (state of) awareness; **b~verändernde Erfahrungen** experiences which alter one's outlook; **~veränderung** *f siehe adj* change in the state of mind; change in outlook; **(politische) ~veränderung** change in political outlook.

⚠**Bewußtwerdung** *f* dawning of consciousness.

bez. *abbr of* **(a) bezahlt** paid. **(b) bezüglich** with reference to, re.

Bez. *abbr of* **Bezirk**.

bezahlbar *adj* payable ◆ **das ist zwar recht teuer, aber für die meisten doch durchaus ~** although it's quite expensive most people can certainly afford it.

bezahlen* [1] *vt* **(a)** to pay; *Rechnung, Schuld auch* to pay off, to settle ◆ **jdm 10 Mark ~** to pay sb 10 marks;**etw an jdn ~** to pay sb sth.
(b) *Sache, Leistung, Schaden* to pay for; *Zeche* to pay, to foot (*inf*) ◆ **etw bezahlt bekommen** *or* **kriegen** (*inf*)/**für etw nichts bezahlt bekommen** *or* **kriegen** (*inf*) to get/not to get paid for sth; **jdm etw ~** (*für jdn kaufen*) to pay for sth for sb; (*Geld geben für*) to pay sb for sth; **laß mal, ich bezahl' das** it's OK, I'll pay for that *or* I'll get that; **er hat seinen Fehler mit seinem Leben bezahlt** he paid for his mistake with his life; **... als ob er es bezahlt bekäme** (*inf*) like mad *or* crazy (*inf*), like hell (*sl*); **Liebe ist nicht mit Geld zu ~** money can't buy love, love cannot be bought.
[2] *vi* to pay ◆ **Herr Ober, ~ bitte!** waiter, the bill *or* check (*esp US*) please!

bezahlt *adj* paid ◆ **sich ~ machen** to be worth it, to pay off.

Bezahlung *f* **(a)** *siehe vt* payment; paying off, settlement; paying for (*einer Sache* (*gen*) sth). **(b)** (*Lohn, Gehalt*) pay; (*für Dienste*) payment ◆ **ohne/gegen/für ~** without/for/for payment.

bezähmen* [1] *vt* **(a)** (*fig geh*) *Begierden, Leidenschaften* to master, to control, to curb. **(b)** (*lit obs*) *siehe* **zähmen**.
[2] *vr* to control *or* restrain oneself.

bezaubern* [1] *vt* (*fig*) to charm, to captivate.
[2] *vi* to be bewitching *or* captivating.

bezaubernd *adj* enchanting, charming.

Bezauberung *f* bewitchment, captivation; (*Entzücken*) enchantment, delight.

bezechen* *vr* (*inf*) to get drunk.

bezecht (*inf*) *adj* drunk ◆ **völlig ~** dead drunk (*inf*).

bezeichnen* *vt* **(a)** (*kennzeichnen*) (*durch, mit* by) to mark; *Takt, Tonart* to indicate.
(b) (*genau beschreiben*) to describe ◆ **er bezeichnete uns den Weg** he described the way to us.
(c) (*benennen*) to call, to describe ◆ **ich weiß nicht, wie man das bezeichnet** I don't know what that's called; **das würde ich schlicht als eine Unverschämtheit ~** I would describe that as *or* call that sheer effrontery; **so kann man es natürlich auch ~** of course, you can call it that *or* describe it that way too; **jd/etw wird mit dem Wort ... bezeichnet** sb/sth is described by the word ..., the word ... describes sb/sth; **er bezeichnet sich gern als Künstler** he likes to call himself an artist.
(d) (*bedeuten*) to mean, to denote.
(e) (*geh: typisch sein für*) to epitomize.

bezeichnend *adj* (*für* of) characteristic, typical ◆ **es ist ~ für ihre Unfähigkeit, daß ...** (*ist ein Beweis für*) it's indicative of her incompetence that ...

bezeichnenderweise *adv* typically (enough) ◆ **die Regierung hat ~ die Wahlversprechen wieder nicht eingehalten** typically (enough), the government hasn't kept its election promises again.

Bezeichnung *f* **(a)** *siehe vt* (*a, b*) marking, indication; description. **(b)** (*Ausdruck*) expression, term.

Bezeichnungslehre *f* (*Ling*) *siehe* **Onomasiologie**.

bezeugen* *vt* **(a)** (*Sache*) to attest; (*Person auch*) to testify to ◆ **~, daß** ... to attest the fact that ...; to testify that ... **(b)** (*geh*) **jdm etw ~** to show sb sth.

Bezeugung *f* attestation ◆ **urkundliche ~** documentary proof *or* evidence.

bezichtigen* *vt* to accuse ◆ **jdn einer Sache** (*gen*) **~** to accuse sb of sth, to charge sb with sth; **jdn ~, etw getan zu haben** to accuse sb of having done sth.

Bezichtigung *f* accusation, charge.

beziehbar *adj* **(a)** (*bezugsfertig*) *Wohnung etc* ready to move into. **(b)** (*erhältlich*) *Waren etc* obtainable. **(c)** relatable, referable ◆ **das ist auf einen Vorfall in seiner Jugend ~** that can be related to an incident in his youth.

beziehen* *irreg* [1] *vt* **(a)** (*überziehen*) *Polster, Regenschirm* to (re)cover; *Bettdecke, Kissen* to put a cover on; (*mit Saiten*) *Geige etc* to string ◆ **die Betten frisch ~** to put clean sheets on *or* to change the beds.
(b) (*einziehen in*) *Wohnung* to move into.
(c) (*esp Mil: einnehmen*) *Posten, Position, Stellung* to take up; (*old*) *Universität* to enter, to go up to; (*fig*) *Standpunkt* to take up, to adopt ◆ **ein Lager ~** to encamp; **Wache ~** to mount guard, to go on guard.
(d) (*sich beschaffen*) to get, to obtain; *Zeitungen etc* to take, to get.
(e) (*erhalten*) to get, to receive; *Einkommen, Rente auch* to draw; *Prügel etc* to get.
(f) (*in Beziehung setzen*) **etw auf jdn/etw ~** to apply sth to sb/sth; **warum bezieht er (bloß) immer alles auf sich?** why does he always take everything personally?; *siehe* **bezogen**.
(g) (*Sw: einfordern*) *Steuern* to collect.
[2] *vr* **(a)** (*sich bedecken*) (*Himmel*) to cloud over, to darken.
(b) (*betreffen*) **sich auf jdn/etw ~** to refer to sb/sth; **diese Bemerkung bezog sich nicht auf dich/auf den gestrigen Vorfall** this remark wasn't meant to refer to you *or* wasn't intended for you/wasn't meant to refer to what happened yesterday.
(c) (*sich berufen*) **sich ~ auf** (*+acc*) to refer to.

Bezieher(in *f*) *m* **-s, -** (*von Zeitung*) regular reader; (*Abonnent, von Aktien*) subscriber; (*von Waren*) purchaser; (*von Einkommen, Rente*) drawer.

Beziehung *f* **(a)** (*Verhältnis*) relationship; (*Philos, Math*) relation.
(b) *usu pl* (*Kontakt*) relations *pl* ◆ **diplomatische ~en aufnehmen/abbrechen** to establish/break off diplomatic relations; **intime ~en zu jdm haben** to have intimate relations with sb; **menschliche ~en** human relations *or* intercourse.
(c) (*Zusammenhang*) connection (*zu* with), relation ◆ **etw zu etw in ~ setzen** to relate sth to sth; **zwischen den beiden Dingen besteht keinerlei ~** there is absolutely no connection between the two (things), the two (things) are totally unconnected *or* unrelated; **etw hat keine ~ zu etw** sth has no bearing on sth *or* no relationship to sth; **jd verliert die ~ zur Wirklichkeit** sb feels cut off from reality.
(d) *usu pl* (*Verbindung*) connections *pl* (*zu* with) ◆ **er hat die Stelle durch ~en bekommen** he got the post through his connections *or* through knowing the right people; **seine ~en spielen lassen** to pull strings; **~en muß/müßte man haben** you need to know the right people, you need to be able to pull strings.
(e) (*Sympathie*) (*zu etw*) feeling (*zu* for); (*zu jdm*) affinity (*zu* for), rapport (*zu* with) ◆ **ich habe keine ~ zu abstrakter Malerei** I have no feeling for abstract art, abstract painting doesn't do anything for me; **er hat überhaupt keine ~ zu seinen Kindern** he just doesn't relate to his children, he has no affinity for his children.
(f) (*Bezug*) *siehe* **Bezug (g)**.
(g) (*Hinsicht*) **in einer/keiner ~** in one/no respect *or* way; **in jeder ~** in every respect, in all respects; **in mancher ~** in some *or* certain respects; **in dieser ~** in this respect.

Beziehungs-: ~kiste *f* (*inf*) relationship; **b~los** *adj* unrelated, unconnected; **~losigkeit** *f* unrelatedness, unconnectedness; **b~reich** *adj* having many associations; **b~voll** *adj* suggestive; **~wahn** *m* (*Psych*) paranoia.

beziehungsweise *conj* **(a)** (*oder aber*) or.
(b) (*im anderen Fall*) and ... respectively ◆ **zwei Briefmarken, die 50 ~ 70 Pfennig kosten** two stamps costing 50 and 70 Pfennig respectively; **geben Sie in Ihrer Bestellung rot ~ blau als gewünschte Farbe an** state your choice of colour in your order: red or blue.
(c) (*genauer gesagt*) or rather, or that is to say.

Beziehungswort *nt* (*Gram*) antecedent.

beziffern* [1] *vt* **(a)** (*mit Ziffern versehen*) to number; *Baß* to figure.
(b) (*angeben*) to estimate (*auf +acc, mit* at) ◆ **man bezifferte den Schaden auf 750.000 Mark** the damage was estimated at *or* was put at 750,000 marks.
[2] *vr* **sich ~ auf** (*+acc*) (*Verluste, Schaden, Gewinn*) to amount to, to come to; (*Teilnehmer, Besucher*) to number.

beziffert *adj* (*Mus*) *Baß* figured.

Bezifferung *f* **(a)** (*das Beziffern*) numbering; (*Mus*) figuring. **(b)** (*Zahlen*) numbers *pl*, figures *pl*.

Bezirk *m* **-(e)s, -e (a)** (*Gebiet*) district; (*fig: Bereich*) sphere, realm. **(b)** (*Verwaltungseinheit*) (*Stadt*) ≃ district; (*von Land*) ≃ region; (*DDR*) state. **(c)** (*DDR inf: Bezirksdienststelle*) local government office.

Bezirks-: ~arzt *m* district medical officer; **~beamte(r)** *m* local government officer; **~gericht** *nt* **(a)** (*DDR*) state court; **(b)** (*Aus, Sw*) district court; **~hauptmann** *m* (*Aus*) *chief officer of local government;* **~kabinett** *nt* (*DDR*) cabinet of a/the *Bezirkstag;* **~klasse** *f* (*Sport*) regional division; **~leiter** *m* (*DDR*) chief administration officer, chief officer of the state administration; **~liga** *f* (*Sport*) regional league; **~regierung** *f* regional administration; **~richter** *m* judge at a/the *Bezirksgericht;* **~spital** *nt* (*esp Sw*) district hospital; **~stadt** *f* ≃ county town; (*DDR*) state *or* regional capital; **~tag** *m* (*DDR*) state parliament (*operating at regional level*).

bezirzen* *vt siehe* **becircen.**

bezog *pret of* **beziehen.**

bezogen [1] *ptp of* **beziehen.**
[2] *adj* **auf jdn/etw ~** referring to sb/sth.

Bezogene(r) *mf decl as adj* (*Fin*) (*von Scheck*) drawee; (*von Wechsel*) acceptor.

⚠ **bezug** *siehe* **Bezug (h).**

Bezug *m* **-(e)s, ⸚e (a)** (*Überzug*) (*für Kissen, Polster etc*) cover; (*für Kopfkissen*) pillow-case, pillow-slip.
(b) (*Bespannung*) strings *pl.*
(c) (*Erwerb*) (*von Waren etc*) buying, purchase; (*von Zeitung*) taking ◆ **der ~ der diversen Magazine kostet uns ...** the various magazines we take cost (us) ...
(d) (*Erhalt*) (*von Einkommen, Rente etc*) drawing.
(e) **⸚e** *pl* (*Einkünfte*) income, earnings *pl* ◆ **⸚e aus Nebenerwerb** income *or* earnings from secondary sources.
(f) (*Zusammenhang*) *siehe* **Beziehung (c).**
(g) (*form: Berufung*) reference ◆ **~ nehmen auf** (+*acc*) to refer to, to make reference to; **~ nehmend auf** (+*acc*) referring to, with reference to; **mit** *or* **unter ~ auf** (+*acc*) with reference to.
(h) (*Hinsicht*): **in b~ auf** (+*acc*) regarding, with regard to, concerning; **in b~ darauf** regarding that.

Bezüger(in *f*) *m* **-s, -** (*Sw*) **(a)** *siehe* **Bezieher(in). (b)** (*von Steuern*) collector.

bezüglich [1] *prep +gen* (*form*) regarding, with regard to, concerning, re (*Comm*).
[2] *adj* (*sich beziehend*) **das ~e Fürwort** (*Gram*) the relative pronoun; **auf etw** (*acc*) **~** relating to sth; **alle darauf ~en Fragen** all questions relating to that.

Bezugnahme *f* **-, -n** (*form*) reference ◆ **unter ~ auf** (+*acc*) with reference to.

Bezugs-: ~bedingungen *pl* (*von Zeitschriften*) terms of delivery *or* subscription; (*bei Katalogbestellungen etc*) conditions of purchase; **b~berechtigt** *adj* entitled to draw; **~berechtigte(r)** *mf* (*von Rente etc*) authorized drawer; (*von Versicherung*) beneficiary; **b~bereit, b~fertig** *adj Haus etc* ready to move into, ready for occupation.

Bezugschein *m siehe* **Bezugsschein.**

Bezugs-: ~person *f* **die wichtigste ~person des Kleinkindes** the person to whom the small child relates most closely; **~preis** *m* (*von Zeitungsabonnement etc*) subscription charge; **~punkt** *m* (*lit, fig*) point of reference; **~quelle** *f* source of supply; **~rahmen** *m* terms *pl* of reference; **~recht** *nt* (*Fin*) option (on a new share issue), subscription right; **~satz** *m* (*Gram*) *siehe* **Relativsatz; ~schein** *m* (ration) coupon; **etw auf** *or* **durch ~schein bekommen** to get sth on coupons; **b~scheinpflichtig** *adj* rationed, available only on coupons; **~system** *nt* frame of reference; (*Statistics*) reference system; **~(wort)satz** *m siehe* **Relativsatz.**

bezuschussen* *vt* to subsidize.

Bezuschussung *f* subsidizing; (*Betrag*) subsidy.

bezwecken* *vt* to aim at; (*Regelung, Maßnahme auch*) to have as its object ◆ **etw mit etw ~** (*Mensch*) to intend sth by sth; **das bezweckt doch gar nichts** that doesn't get one/you anywhere (at all); **was soll das ~?** what's the point of that?

➤ **bezweifeln*** *vt* to doubt, to question, to have one's doubts about ◆ **das ist nicht zu ~** that's unquestionable *or* beyond question; **~, daß ...** to doubt that ..., to question whether ...

bezwingbar *adj siehe vt* conquerable; defeatable; beatable; that can be conquered/defeated/overcome/beaten *etc.*

bezwingen* *irreg* [1] *vt* to conquer; *Feind auch* to defeat, to overcome, to vanquish (*liter*); (*Sport*) to beat, to defeat; *Festung* to capture; *Zorn, Gefühle* to master, to overcome; *Berg* to conquer, to vanquish (*liter*); *Strecke* to do.
[2] *vr* to overcome *or* master one's emotions/desires *etc.*

bezwingend *adj* compelling.

Bezwinger(in *f*) *m* **-s, -** (*von Berg, Feind*) conqueror, vanquisher (*liter*); (*Sport*) winner (*gen* over); (*von Festung, Burg*) captor.

Bezwingung *f siehe vt* conquering, conquest; defeat(ing), overcoming; vanquishing (*liter*); beating, defeat(ing); capture, capturing; mastering, overcoming; conquering, vanquishing (*liter*).

Bf. *abbr of* **Bahnhof; Brief.**

BfA [be:|ɛf'|a:] *f* - *abbr of* **Bundesversicherungsanstalt für Angestellte** *federal pensions office for salaried employees.*

BGB ['be:ge:'be:] *nt* **-,** *no pl abbr of* **Bürgerliches Gesetzbuch.**

BGBl ['be:ge:be:'ɛl] *nt* **-,** *no pl abbr of* **Bundesgesetzblatt.**

BGH [be:ge:'ha:] *m* **-s** *abbr of* **Bundesgerichtshof.**

BGS [be:ge:'|ɛs] *m* - *abbr of* **Bundesgrenzschutz.**

BH [be:'ha:] *m* **-(s), -(s)** *abbr of* **Büstenhalter** bra.

Bhagwan *m* **-s,** *no pl* Bhagwan.

Bhf. *abbr of* **Bahnhof.**

bi [bi:] *adj pred* (*sl*) ac/dc (*sl*), bi (*sl*).

bi- *pref* bi-.

Bias *nt* **-, -** (*form*) bias.

Biathlon *nt* **-s, -s** (*Sport*) biathlon.

bibbern *vi* (*inf*) (*vor Angst*) to tremble, to shake; (*vor Kälte*) to shiver ◆ **um jdn/etw ~** to fear for sb/sth.

Bibel *f* **-, -n** (*lit*) Bible; (*fig*) bible.

Bibel|auslegung *f* interpretation of the Bible.

Bibeleskäs(e) *m* (*dial*) *siehe* **Quark.**

Bibel-: b~fest *adj* well versed in the Bible; **~forscher** *m* (*dated*) Jehovah's witness; **~sprache** *f* biblical language; **~spruch** *m* biblical saying, quotation from the Bible; **~stelle** *f* passage *or* text from the Bible; **~stunde** *f* Bible study *no pl;* **~text** *m* text of the Bible; (*Auszug*) text *or* passage from the Bible; **~vers** *m* verse from/of the Bible; **~wort** *nt, pl* **~worte** biblical saying.

Biber *m* **-s, - (a)** (*Tier, Pelz, Tuch*) beaver. **(b)** *auch nt* (*Tuch*) flannelette. **(c)** (*inf*) (*Vollbart*) full beard; (*Mensch*) man with a beard, bearded man.

Biber-: ~bau *m, pl* **~baue** beaver's lodge; **~bettuch** *nt* flannelette; **~burg** *f* beaver's lodge; **~geil** *nt* **-(e)s,** *no pl* castor(eum); **~pelz** *m* beaver (fur); **~schwanz** *m* **(a)** beaver's tail; **(b)** (*Build: Dachziegel*) flat tile, plain tile; **~tuch** *nt* flannelette.

Biblio-: ⚠**~graph(in** *f*) *m* bibliographer; ⚠**~graphie** *f* bibliography; ⚠**b~graphieren*** *insep* [1] *vt* **(a)** (*verzeichnen*) to record in a/the bibliography; **(b)** (*einordnen*) to take (the) bibliographical details of; [2] *vi* to take bibliographical details; ⚠**b~graphisch** *adj* bibliographic(al); **~mane** *m* **-n, -n** bibliomaniac; **~manie** *f* bibliomania; **b~manisch** *adj* bibliomaniac(al) (*form*); **b~phil** *adj Mensch* bibliophilic (*form*), bibliophil(e) (*form*), book-loving *attr; Ausgabe* for bibliophil(e)s *or* book-lovers; **~phile(r)** *mf decl as adj* book-lover, lover of books, bibliophil(e); **~philie** *f* love of books, bibliophily (*form*).

Bibliothek *f* **-, -en** library.

Bibliothekar(in *f*) *m* librarian.

bibliothekarisch *adj* library *attr* ◆ **~e Ausbildung** training in librarianship *or* as a librarian; **sich ~ betätigen** to work as a librarian.

Bibliotheks-: ~katalog *m* library catalogue; **~kunde** *f* librarianship; **b~kundlich** *adj* library *attr;* **~lehre** *f* (practical aspects of) librarianship; **~wesen** *nt, no pl* libraries *pl;* (*als Fach*) librarianship; **~wissenschaft** *f* librarianship.

biblisch *adj* biblical ◆ **ein ~es Alter** a great age, a ripe old age.

Bickbeere *f* (*N Ger*) *siehe* **Heidelbeere.**

Bidet [bi'de:] *nt* **-s, -s** bidet.

bieder *adj* **(a)** (*rechtschaffen*) honest; *Mensch, Leben auch* upright. **(b)** (*pej*) conventional, conservative; *Miene* worthy (*iro*).

Biederkeit *f siehe adj* **(a)** honesty; uprightness. **(b)** conventionality, conservatism, conservativeness; worthiness.

Bieder-: ~mann *m, pl* **~männer (a)** (*dated, iro*) honest man; **(b)** (*pej geh*) petty bourgeois; **b~männisch** *adj* **(a)** (*dated*) honest; **(b)** (*pej geh*) petty bourgeois; *Geschmack, Gesinnung auch* philistine.

Biedermeier *nt* **-s,** *no pl* Biedermeier period.

Biedermeier- *in cpds* Biedermeier; **~sträußchen** *nt* posy (with paper frill).

Bieder-: ~miene *f* (*geh*) worthy air; **~sinn** *m* (*geh*) **(a)** (*dated*) honest mentality; **(b)** (*pej*) middle-class *or* petty-bourgeois mentality.

biegbar *adj Lampenarm, Metall etc* flexible; *Material auch* pliable.

Biege *f* **-, -n** (*dial*) bend, curve ◆ **eine ~ drehen/fahren/fliegen** (*inf*) to go for a walk/a short ride *or* a spin (*inf*)/a short flight *or* a spin (*inf*); **die ~ machen** (*inf*) to disappear.

Biegefestigkeit *f* (*Tech*) bending strength.

biegen *pret* **bog,** *ptp* **gebogen** [1] *vt* **(a)** to bend; *Glieder auch* to flex; (*fig: manipulieren*) to wangle (*inf*) ◆ **das Recht ~** (*fig dated*) to bend the law; **auf B~ oder Brechen** (*inf*) by hook or by crook (*inf*), come hell or high water (*inf*); **es geht auf B~ oder Brechen** (*inf*) it's do or die; *siehe* **gebogen.**
(b) (*Aus Gram: flektieren*) to inflect.
[2] *vi aux sein* (*Mensch, Wagen*) to turn; (*Weg, Straße auch*) to curve ◆ **der Fahrer bog zur Seite** the driver turned; (*als Ausweichmanöver*) the driver pulled over to one side.
[3] *vr* to bend; (*sich verziehen*) (*Schallplatte, Holz*) to warp; (*Metall*) to buckle ◆ **seine Nase biegt sich leicht nach oben** his nose turns up slightly *or* is slightly turned-up; **sich vor Lachen ~** (*fig*) to double up *or* crease up (*inf*) with laughter.

biegsam *adj* flexible; *Holz auch* pliable; *Stock, Gerte auch* pliant; *Metall auch* malleable, ductile; *Glieder, Körper* supple, lithe; *Einband* limp; (*fig*) pliable, pliant.

Biegsamkeit *f siehe adj* flexibility; pliability; pliancy; malleability, ductility; suppleness, litheness.

Biegung *f* **(a)** bend; (*von Weg, Fluß auch, Wirbelsäule*) curve (*gen* in) ◆ **die ~en der Straße** the (twists and) turns *or* the curves in the road; **der Fluß/die Straße macht eine ~** the river/road curves *or* bends. **(b)** (*Aus Gram*) inflection.

Biene *f* **-, -n (a)** bee. **(b)** (*dated sl: Mädchen*) bird (*Brit sl*), chick (*esp US sl*).

Bienen-: b~artig *adj Insekt* bee-like; (*fig*) bustling *attr;* **~fleiß** *m* bustling industriousness; **b~fleißig** *adj* industrious; **~gift** *nt* bee poison; **~haltung** *f* beekeeping; **~haube** *f* bee veil(s); **~haus** *nt* apiary; **~honig** *m* real *or* natural honey; **~kasten** *m* (bee)hive; **~königin** *f* queen bee; **~korb** *m* (bee)hive; **~schwarm** *m* swarm (of bees); **~sprache** *f* language of bees; **~staat** *m* bee colony; **~stich** *m* **(a)** bee sting; **(b)** (*Cook*) *cake coated with* *sugar and almonds filled with custard or cream;* **~stock** *m* (bee)hive; **~volk** *nt* bee colony, colony of bees; **~wachs** *nt* beeswax; **~zucht** *f* beekeeping, apiculture; **~züchter** *m* beekeeper, apiarist.

Biennale [biɛ'na:lə] *f* **-, -n** biennial film/art festival.

Bier *nt* **-(e)s, -e** beer ♦ **zwei ~, bitte!** two beers, please; **zwanzig verschiedene ~e** twenty different kinds of beer, twenty different beers; **das ist mein** *etc* **~** *(fig inf)* that's my *etc* business.

Bier- *in cpds* beer; **~arsch** *m (sl)* fat arse *(sl)*; ⚠**~baß** *m (inf)* deep bass voice; **~bauch** *m (inf)* beer gut *(inf)*, beer belly *(inf)*, pot-belly; **~brauerei** *f (das Brauen)* (beer-)brewing; *(Betrieb)* brewery.

Bierchen *nt* (glass of) beer.

Bier-: ~deckel *m* beer mat; **~dose** *f* beer can; **~durst** *m (inf)* **~durst haben** to feel like a beer; **~eifer, ~ernst** *m (inf)* deadly seriousness; ⚠**~faß** *nt* keg; **~filz** *m* beer mat; **~flasche** *f* beer bottle; **~garten** *m* beer garden; **~kasten** *m* beer crate; **~keller** *m (Lager)* beer cellar; *(Gaststätte auch)* bierkeller; **~krug** *m* tankard, beer mug; *(aus Steingut)* (beer) stein; **~kutscher** *m* **(a)** brewer's drayman; **(b)** *(inf)* beer-lorry *(Brit) or* -truck *(US)* driver; **~laune** *f (inf)* **in einer ~laune, aus einer ~laune heraus** after a few beers; **~leiche** *f (inf)* drunk; **es lagen noch einige ~leichen herum** there were still a few drunks lying around dead to the world; **~reise** *f (hum)* pub-crawl; **~ruhe** *f (inf)* cool *(inf)*; **~schinken** *m* ham sausage; **~seidel** *nt* tankard; **b~selig** *adj Mensch* boozed up *(inf)*; **er kam in einer b~seligen Stimmung nach Hause** he came home pretty merry; **~ulk** *m (inf)* drunken prank; **~verlag, ~vertrieb** *m* beer wholesaler's; **~wärmer** *m* beer-warmer; **~wurst** *f* ham sausage; **~zeitung** *f (inf)* comic newspaper; **~zelt** *nt* beer tent.

Biese *f* **-, -n (a)** *(an Hose)* braid. **(b)** *(Sew)* tuck; *(an Schuh)* decorative seam.

Biest *nt* **-(e)s, -er** *(pej inf)* **(a)** *(Tier)* creature; *(Insekt auch)* bug. **(b)** *(Mensch)* (little) wretch; *(Frau)* bitch *(sl)*, cow *(sl)* ♦ **sie ist ein süßes ~** she looks a sweet little thing but she can be a bitch at times *(sl)*. **(c)** *(Sache)* beast (of a thing) *(inf)*.

Biesterei *f (inf)* **(a)** *(Gemeinheit)* horrible thing. **(b)** *(Anstoßendes)* obscenity. **(c)** *(Schinderei)* beast of a job *(inf)*.

biestig *adj (inf)* beastly *(inf)*, horrible; *(schlechter Laune)* ratty *(inf)*.

Biet *nt* **-(e)s, -e** *(Sw)* area.

▼ **bieten** *pret* **bot,** *ptp* **geboten** [1] *vt* **(a)** *(anbieten)* to offer *(jdm etw* sb sth, sth to sb); *(bei Auktion)* to bid *(auf +acc* for); *Möglichkeit, Gelegenheit auch* to give *(jdm etw* sb sth, sth to sb) ♦ **jdm die Hand ~** to hold out one's hand to sb, to offer sb one's hand; *(fig auch)* to make a conciliatory gesture to sb; **jdm die Hand zur Versöhnung ~** *(fig)* to hold out the olive branch to sb; **jdm den Arm ~** to offer sb one's arm; **wer bietet mehr?** will anyone offer me *etc* more?; *(bei Auktion)* any more bids?; **mehr bietet dir niemand** no-one will give *or* offer you more *or* make you a higher offer; **diese Stadt/dieser Mann hat nichts zu ~** this town/man has nothing to offer.

(b) *(geben)* to give *(jdm etw* sb sth); *Gewähr, Sicherheit, Anlaß etc auch* to provide *(etw* sth, *jdm etw* sb with sth); *Asyl* to grant *(jdm etw* sb sth).

▼ **(c)** *(haben, aufweisen)* to have; *Problem, Schwierigkeit* to present ♦ **das Hochhaus bietet fünfzig Familien Wohnung/Wohnungen für fünfzig Familien** the tower block provides accommodation/flats for fifty families.

(d) *(zeigen, darbieten) Anblick, Bild* to present; *Film* to show; *Leistung* to give ♦ **die Mannschaft bot den Zuschauern ein hervorragendes Spiel** the team put on an excellent game for the spectators; *siehe* **Blöße, Stirn, Trotz.**

(e) *(zumuten)* **sich** *(dat)* **etw ~ lassen** to stand for sth; **so etwas könnte man mir nicht ~** I wouldn't stand for that sort of thing; **ist dir so etwas schon einmal geboten worden?** have you ever known the like *(inf) or* anything like it?

(f) *(geh: sagen)* **jdm einen Gruß ~** to greet sb; **jdm einen guten Morgen ~** to bid sb good morning *(old, liter)*; *siehe* **Paroli, geboten.**

[2] *vi (Cards)* to bid; *(bei Auktion auch)* to make a bid *(auf +acc* for).

[3] *vr (Gelegenheit, Lösung, Anblick etc)* to present itself *(jdm* to sb) ♦ **ein grauenhaftes Schauspiel bot sich unseren Augen** a terrible scene met our eyes.

Bieter(in *f***)** *m* **-s, -** bidder.

Bigamie *f* bigamy.

Bigamist(in *f***)** *m* bigamist.

bigamistisch *adj* bigamous.

bigott *adj* overly pious.

Bigotterie *f (pej)* **(a)** *no pl* excessive piousness. **(b)** *(Handlung)* overly pious behaviour *no pl*; *(Bemerkung)* overly pious remark.

Bijouterie [biʒutə'ri:] *f* **(a)** *(Schmuck)* jewellery. **(b)** *(Sw, obs: Geschäft)* jeweller's shop.

Bikarbonat *nt* bicarbonate.

Bikini *m* **-s, -s** bikini.

bikonkav *adj* biconcave.

bikonvex *adj* biconvex.

Bilanz *f* **(a)** *(Econ, Comm: Lage)* balance; *(Abrechnung)* balance sheet ♦ **eine ~ aufstellen** to draw up a balance sheet; **~ machen** *(fig inf)* to check one's finances. **(b)** *(fig: Ergebnis)* end result ♦ **(die) ~ ziehen** to take stock *(aus* of).

Bilanzbuchhalter *m* accountant.

bilanzieren* *vti* to balance; *(fig)* to assess.

Bilanz-: ~prüfer *m* auditor; **~summe** *f* balance.

bilateral *adj* bilateral.

Bild *nt* **-(e)s, -er (a)** *(lit, fig)* picture; *(Fotografie auch)* photo; *(Film)* frame; *(Art: Zeichnung)* drawing; *(Gemälde)* painting; *(Cards)* court *or* face *(US)* card, picture card *(inf)* ♦ **~ oder Wappen** heads or tails; **ein ~ machen** to take a photo *or* picture; **etw im ~ festhalten** to photograph/paint/draw sth as a permanent record; **sie ist ein ~ von einer Frau** she's a fine specimen of a woman; **ein ~ des Elends** a picture of misery; **~: Hans Schwarz** *(TV, Film)* camera: Hans Schwarz; *siehe* **schwach.**

(b) *(Abbild)* image; *(Spiegel~ auch)* reflection ♦ **sie ist ganz das ~ ihrer Mutter** she is the image of her mother; **Gott schuf den Menschen ihm zum ~e** *(Bibl)* God created man in His own image.

(c) *(Anblick, Ansicht)* sight ♦ **das äußere ~ der Stadt** the appearance of the town.

(d) *(Opt)* image.

(e) *(Theat: Szene)* scene; *siehe* **lebend.**

(f) *(Metapher)* metaphor, image ♦ **um mit einem** *or* **im ~ zu sprechen ...** to use a metaphor ...; **etw mit einem ~ sagen** to say *or* express sth metaphorically; **im ~ bleiben** to use the same metaphor.

(g) *(Erscheinungs~)* character ♦ **sie gehören zum ~ dieser Stadt** they are part of the scene in this town.

(h) *(fig: Vorstellung)* image, picture ♦ **im ~e sein** to be in the picture *(über +acc* about); **jdn ins ~ setzen** to put sb in the picture *(über +acc* about); **sich** *(dat)* **von jdm/etw ein ~ machen** to get an idea of sb/sth; **du machst dir kein ~ davon, wie schwer das war** you've no idea *or* conception how hard it was; **das ~ des Deutschen/Juden** the image of the German/Jew.

Bild-: ~archiv *nt* picture library; **~atlas** *m* pictorial atlas; **~auflösung** *f (TV, Comput)* resolution; **~ausfall** *m (TV)* loss of vision; **~autor** *m* photographer; **~band** *m* illustrated book, coffee-table book.

bildbar *adj (lit, fig)* malleable ♦ **der Charakter des Kindes ist noch ~** the child's character can still be shaped.

Bild-: ~beilage *f* colour supplement; **~bericht** *m* photographic report; **~beschreibung** *f (Sch)* description of a picture; **~betrachtung** *f* art appreciation.

Bildchen *nt, pl auch* **Bilderchen** *dim of* **Bild.**

Bild-: ~dokument *nt* photograph/painting/drawing of documentary value; **~ebene** *f (Phot)* focal plane; **~empfänger** *m (Tech)* picture receiver.

bilden [1] *vt* **(a)** *(formen)* to form; *Figuren etc auch* to fashion; *(fig) Charakter auch* to shape, to mould; *Körper, Figur* to shape ♦ **sich** *(dat)* **ein Urteil/eine Meinung ~** to form a judgement/an opinion.

(b) *(hervorbringen, Gram)* to form ♦ **der Magen hat ein Geschwür gebildet** an ulcer formed in the stomach, the stomach developed an ulcer.

(c) *(einrichten) Fond, Institution etc* to set up.

(d) *(zusammenstellen) Kabinett, Regierung* to form; *Ausschuß, Gruppe auch* to set up; *Vermögen* to acquire.

(e) *(ausmachen) Höhepunkt, Regel, Ausnahme, Problem, Gefahr etc* to constitute; *Dreieck, Kreis etc* to form ♦ **die Teile ~ ein Ganzes** the parts make up *or* form a whole; **die drei ~ ein hervorragendes Team** the three of them make (up) an excellent team.

(f) *(erziehen)* to educate.

[2] *vr* **(a)** *(entstehen)* to form, to develop ♦ **damit sich keine Vorurteile ~ ...** so that no prejudices are allowed to form ...

(b) *(lernen)* to educate oneself; *(durch Lesen etc)* to improve one's mind; *(durch Reisen etc)* to broaden one's mind.

[3] *vi siehe vr (b)* to be educational; to improve the *or* one's mind; to broaden the *or* one's mind.

bildend *adj*: **die ~e Kunst** art; **die ~en Künste** the fine arts; **~er Künstler** artist.

Bilderbogen *m* illustrated broadsheet.

Bilderbuch *nt* **(a)** picture book ♦ **eine Landschaft wie im ~** a picturesque landscape. **(b)** *(rare) siehe* **Bildband.**

Bilderbuch- *in cpds (lit)* picture-book; *(fig)* perfect; **~autor/-verlag** author/publisher of picture-books; **~landung** *f* **eine ~landung** a textbook landing.

Bilder-: ~geschichte *f* **(a)** picture story; **(b)** *(in Comic, Zeitung)* strip cartoon; *(lustig auch)* comic strip; **~kult** *m (Rel)* image-worship, iconolatry *(form)*; **~rahmen** *m* picture-frame; **~rätsel** *nt* picture-puzzle; **b~reich** *adj Buch etc* full of pictures; *(fig) Sprache* rich in imagery; **b~reich sprechen** to use a lot of images; **~schrift** *f* pictographic writing system; **~sprache** *f* metaphorical language; **~streit** *m (Eccl Hist)* controversy over image-worship, iconographic controversy; **~sturm** *m (Eccl Hist)* iconoclasm; **~stürmer** *m (lit, fig)* iconoclast; **b~stürmerisch** *adj (lit, fig)* iconoclastic; **~verehrung** *f siehe* **~kult.**

Bild-: ~fernsprecher *m* video-phone; **~fläche** *f* **(a)** *(Leinwand)* projection surface; *(von Fotoapparat)* film plane; **(b)** *(fig inf)* **auf der ~fläche erscheinen** to appear on the scene; **von der ~fläche verschwinden** to disappear (from the scene); **~folge** *f* sequence of pictures; *(Film)* sequence of shots; **~frequenz** *f* filming speed; **~funk** *m* radio photography; **~geschichte** *f* strip cartoon; **b~haft** *adj* pictorial; *Beschreibung, Vorstellung, Sprache* vivid; **~haftigkeit** *f siehe adj* pictorial nature; vividness; **~hauer** *m* sculptor; **~hauerei** *f* sculpture; **~hauerin** *f* sculptress; **b~hauerisch** *adj* sculptural; **~hauerkunst** *f* sculpture; **b~hauern** *vti insep (inf)* to sculpt; **b~hübsch** *adj Mädchen* (as) pretty as a picture; *Kleid, Garten etc* really lovely; **~journalist** *m* photojournalist; **~karte** *f* court *or* face *(US)* card, picture card *(inf)*; **~konserve** *f* film recording.

bildlich *adj* pictorial; *Ausdruck etc* metaphorical, figurative ♦ **sich** *(dat)* **etw ~ vorstellen** to picture sth in one's mind's eye; **stell dir das mal ~ vor!** just picture it.

Bildlichkeit *f (von Sprache)* figurativeness; *(von Beschreibung)* graphicness.

➤ SPRACHE AKTIV: **bieten: 1c** → 40.2, 53.1

Bild-: ~material *nt* pictures *pl;* (*für Vortrag*) visual material, photographic and film material; (*für Buch*) pictorial material; (*Sch*) visual aids *pl;* **~mischer** *m* **-s, -** (*TV*) vision mixer.

Bildner(in *f*) *m* **-s, -** (*geh: Schöpfer*) creator.

bildnerisch *adj Begabung, Fähigkeit, Wille* artistic; *Element, Mittel, Gestaltung* visual.

Bildnis *nt* (*liter*) portrait.

Bild-: ~platte *f* video disc; **~plattenspieler** *m* video disc player; **~punkt** *m* pixel; **~qualität** *f* (*TV, Film*) picture quality; (*Phot*) print quality; **~redakteur** *m* picture editor; **~röhre** *f* (*TV*) picture tube; **~schärfe** *f* definition *no indef art.*

Bildschirm *m* (*TV, Comput*) screen.

Bildschirm-: ~abstrahlung *f, no pl* screen radiation; **~arbeiter(in** *f*) *m* VDU operator; **~arbeitsplatz** *m* work station; **~gerät** *nt* visual display unit, VDU; **~schoner** *m* (*Comput*) screen saver; **~text** *m* viewdata *sing,* Prestel ®.

Bild-: ~schnitzer *m* wood-carver; **~schnitzerei** *f* (wood) carving; **b~schön** *adj* beautiful; **~seite** *f* **(a)** face, obverse (*form*); **(b)** (*von Buch*) picture page; **~stelle** *f* educational film hire service; **~stock** *m* **(a)** wayside shrine; **(b)** (*Typ*) block; **~störung** *f* (*TV*) interference (on vision *or* the picture); **~suchlauf** *m* picture search; **b~synchron** *adj* (*Film, TV*) synchronized (with the picture); **~tafel** *f* plate; **~telefon** *nt siehe* **~fernsprecher; ~telegramm** *nt* phototelegram; **~text** *m* caption.

Bildung *f* **(a)** (*Erziehung*) education; (*Kultur*) culture ◆ **zu seiner ~ macht er Abendkurse/liest er viel/reist er** he does evening classes to try and educate himself/reads to improve his mind/travels to broaden his mind; **die allgemeine ~** general education; (*eines Menschen*) one's general education; **~ haben** to be educated.
(b) *no pl* (*das Formen*) formation, forming; (*von Figuren etc auch*) fashioning; (*fig: von Charakter etc auch*) shaping ◆ **zur ~ des Passivs** to form the passive.
(c) (*Form: von Baum, Hand etc, Ling: Wort etc*) form.
(d) *no pl* (*Entstehung: von Rost etc*) formation.
(e) *no pl* (*Einrichtung*) setting-up.
(f) *no pl* (*Zusammenstellung*) (*von Kabinett, Regierung*) formation, forming; (*von Ausschuß, Gruppe auch*) setting-up; (*von Vermögen*) acquisition.

Bildungs-: ~anstalt *f* (*form*) educational establishment; **~arbeit** *f* work in the field of education; **b~beflissen** *adj* eager to improve one's mind; **~bürger** *m* member of the educated classes; **~bürgertum** *nt* educated classes *pl;* **~chancen** *pl* educational opportunities *pl;* **~drang** *m* desire for education; **~dünkel** *m* intellectual snobbery; **~eifer** *m* desire to be educated; **b~eifrig** *adj* keen to be educated; **~einrichtung** *f* educational institution; (*Kulturstätte*) cultural institution; **b~fähig** *adj* educable; **b~feindlich** *adj* anti-education; **~gang** *m* school (and university/college) career; **~grad** *m* level of education; **~gut** *nt* established part of one's general education; **das gehört zum deutschen ~gut** that is part of the German cultural heritage; **~hunger** *m* thirst for education; **b~hungrig** *adj* thirsting for education; **der b~hungrige Student** the eager student; **~ideal** *nt* educational ideal; **~institut** *nt siehe* **~einrichtung; ~lücke** *f* gap in one's education; **~monopol** *nt* monopoly on education; **~niveau** *nt* standard *or* level of education; **~notstand** *m* chronic shortage of educational facilities; **~planung** *f* education(al) planning *no indef art;* **~politik** *f* education policy; **~politiker** *m politician with a special interest in or responsibility for education;* **b~politisch** *adj* politico-educational; **~reform** *f* educational reform; **~reise** *f* educational trip *or* journey; **~roman** *m* (*Liter*) Bildungsroman (*form*), *novel concerned with the intellectual or spiritual development of the main character;* **~stand** *m* level of education, educational level; **~stätte** *f* (*geh*) place *or* seat of learning; **~streben** *nt* striving after education; **~stufe** *f* level of education; **eine hohe/niedrige ~stufe haben** to be highly/not very educated; **~urlaub** *m* educational holiday; (*in Firma*) study leave; **~weg** *m* **jds ~weg** the course of sb's education; **auf dem zweiten ~weg** through night school; **einen anderen ~weg einschlagen** to opt for a different type of education; **~wesen** *nt* education system.

Bild-: ~unterschrift *f* caption; **~wand** *f* projection wall; **~werfer** *m* projector; **~winkel** *m* (*Opt, Phot*) angle of view; **~wörterbuch** *nt* pictorial *or* picture dictionary; **~zuschrift** *f* reply enclosing photograph.

Bilge *f* **-, -n** (*Naut*) bilge.

bilingual [bilɪŋ'guaːl], **bilinguisch** [bi'lɪŋguɪʃ] *adj* (*form*) bilingual.

Bilirubin *nt* **-s,** *no pl* bilirubin.

Billard ['bɪljart] *nt* **-s, -e** *or* (*Aus*) **-s (a)** (*Spiel*) billiards *sing.* **(b)** (*inf: Spieltisch*) billiard table.

Billard- *in cpds* billiard; **~ball** *m,* **~kugel** *f* billiard ball; **~queue** *nt or* (*Aus inf*) *m,* **~stock** *m* billiard cue; **~tisch** *m* billiard table.

Billet(t) [bɪl'jɛt] *nt* **-(e)s, -e** *or* **-s (a)** (*Sw, dated: Fahr~, Eintrittskarte*) ticket. **(b)** (*Aus, obs: Schreiben*) note; (*Briefkarte*) letter-card.

Billet(t)eur [bɪljɛ'tøːɐ] *m* **(a)** (*Aus: Platzanweiser*) usher. **(b)** (*Sw: Schaffner*) conductor.

Billet(t)eurin [bɪljɛ'tøːrɪn] *f* (*Aus*) usherette.

Billet(t)euse [bɪljɛ'tøːzə] *f* (*Sw*) conductress.

Billettsteuer *f* (*Sw*) *siehe* **Vergnügungssteuer.**

Billiarde *f* **-, -n** thousand billion (*Brit*), thousand trillion (*US*).

billig *adj* **(a)** (*preisgünstig*) cheap; *Preis* low; (*minderwertig auch*) cheapjack *attr* ◆ **~ abzugeben** going cheap; **~es Geld** (*inf: leicht verdient*) easy money; **etw für ~es Geld kaufen** to buy sth cheap; **~ davonkommen** (*inf*) to get off lightly.
(b) (*pej: primitiv*) cheap; *Trick, Masche auch* shabby; *Ausrede* feeble ◆ **ein ~er Trost** cold comfort.
(c) (*old*) (*angemessen*) proper, meet (*old*); (*gerecht, berechtigt*) just, fair; *siehe* **recht.**

Billig- *in cpds* cheap; **~anbieter** *m* supplier of cheap goods.

billigen *vt* to approve ◆ **etw stillschweigend ~** to condone sth; **~, daß jd etw tut** to approve of sb's doing sth.

billigermaßen, billigerweise *adv* (*old*) (*mit Recht*) rightly; (*gerechterweise*) by rights.

Billigflagge *f* (*Naut, Comm*) flag of convenience.

Billigkeit *f siehe adj* **(a)** cheapness; lowness. **(b)** cheapness; shabbiness; feebleness; cheapjack nature. **(c)** (*old*) properness, meetness (*old*); justness, fairness.

Billig-: ~land *nt* country with low production costs; **~lohnland** *nt* low-wage country; **~preis** *m* low price.

Billigung *f* approval ◆ **jds ~ finden** to meet with sb's approval.

Billion *f* billion (*Brit*), trillion (*US*).

bim *interj* ding.

bimbam *interj* ding-dong.

Bimbam *m*: **ach, du heiliger ~!** (*inf*) hell's bells! (*inf*).

Bimbim *f* **-, -s** (*baby-talk*) tram.

Bimetall *nt* (*Material*) bimetal; (*~streifen*) bimetal strip.

Bimmel *f* **-, -n** (*inf*) bell.

Bimmelbahn *f* (*inf*) *small train with a warning bell.*

Bimmelei *f* (*pej*) ringing.

bimmeln *vi* (*inf*) to ring.

Bims *m* **-es, -e** *siehe* **Bimsstein.**

Bimse *f* **-,** *no pl* (*inf*) **~ kriegen** to get a walloping (*inf*).

bimsen *vt* (*inf*) **(a)** (*drillen*) to drill. **(b)** (*einüben*) *Vokabeln etc* to swot (*inf*), to cram (*inf*); *Griffe etc* to practise.

Bimsstein *m* **(a)** pumice stone. **(b)** (*Build*) breezeblock.

bin *1. pers sing present of* **sein.**

binar, binär, binarisch *adj* binary.

Binärcode [-koːd] *m* binary code.

Binde *f* **-, -n (a)** (*Med*) bandage; (*Schlinge*) sling. **(b)** (*Band*) strip of material; (*Schnur*) cord; (*Arm~*) armband; (*Augen~*) blindfold. **(c)** (*Monats~*) (sanitary) towel *or* napkin (*US*). **(d)** (*dated: Krawatte*) tie ◆ **sich** (*dat*) **einen hinter die ~ gießen** *or* **kippen** (*inf*) to put a few drinks away.

Binde-: ~gewebe *nt* (*Anat*) connective tissue; **~glied** *nt* connecting link; **~haut** *f* (*Anat*) conjunctiva; **~hautentzündung** *f* conjunctivitis; **~mittel** *nt* binder.

binden *pret* **band,** *ptp* **gebunden** [1] *vt* **(a)** (*zusammen~*) to tie; (*fest~*) to bind; (*fig geh*) to bind, to unite ◆ **etw zu etw** *or* **in etw** (*acc*) **~** to tie *or* bind sth into sth.
(b) (*durch Binden herstellen*) to bind; *Strauß, Kranz* to make up; *Knoten etc* to tie; *Faß* to hoop.
(c) (*zu~*) *Schal* to tie; *Krawatte* to knot ◆ **sich** (*dat*) **die Schuhe ~** to tie (up) one's shoelaces.
(d) (*fesseln, befestigen*) (*an +acc* to) to tie (up); *Menschen auch* to bind; *Ziege, Pferd auch* to tether; *Boot auch* to moor; (*fig*) *Menschen* to bind, to tie; (*an einen Ort*) to tie; (*Versprechen, Vertrag, Eid etc*) to bind ◆ **jdn an Händen und Füßen ~** to tie *or* bind sb hand and foot; **jdm die Hände auf den Rücken ~** to tie sb's hands behind his back; **mir sind die Hände gebunden** (*fig*) my hands are tied; **nichts bindet mich an Glasgow** I have no special ties to keep me in Glasgow; **sie versuchte, ihn an sich zu ~** she tried to tie him to her; *siehe* **gebunden, Nase.**
(e) (*festhalten*) *Staub, Erdreich* to bind; (*Chem*) (*aufnehmen*) to absorb; (*sich verbinden mit*) to combine with.
(f) (*zusammenhalten, Cook*) *Farbe, Soße* to bind.
(g) (*verbinden*) (*Poet*) to bind; (*fig geh auch*) to unite; (*Mus*) *Töne* to slur; *gleiche Note* to tie ◆ **was Gott gebunden hat, soll der Mensch nicht trennen** what God has joined together let no man put asunder.
[2] *vi* (*Mehl, Zement, Soße etc*) to bind; (*Klebstoff*) to bond; (*fig*) to be tying, to tie one down; (*Erlebnisse*) to create a bond.
[3] *vr* (*sich verpflichten*) to commit oneself (*an +acc* to) ◆ **ich will mich nicht ~** I don't want to get involved.

bindend *adj* binding (*für* on); *Zusage* definite.

Binder *m* **-s, - (a)** (*Krawatte*) tie. **(b)** (*Agr*) (*Bindemaschine*) binder; (*Mähbinder*) reaper-binder. **(c)** (*Build*) (*Stein*) header; (*Balken*) truss beam. **(d)** (*Bindemittel*) binder. **(e)** (*S Ger, Aus*) *siehe* **Böttcher.**

Binderei *f* (*Buch~*) bindery; (*Blumen~*) wreath and bouquet department.

Binde-: ~strich *m* hyphen; **~vokal** *m* thematic vowel; **~wort** *nt* (*Gram*) conjunction.

Bindfaden *m* string ◆ **ein (Stück) ~** a piece of string; **es regnet ~** (*inf*) it's sheeting down (*inf*).

-bindig *adj suf* **dieses Element ist vier~** this element has a valency of four.

Bindigkeit *f* valency.

Bindung *f* **(a)** (*Beziehung zu einem Partner*) relationship (*an +acc* with); (*Verbundenheit mit einem Menschen, Ort*) tie, bond (*an +acc* with); (*Verpflichtung: an Beruf etc, durch Vertrag*) commitment (*an +acc* to) ◆ **seine enge ~ an die Heimat** his close ties with his home country.
(b) (*Ski~*) binding.
(c) (*Chem*) bond.
(d) (*Tex*) weave.

Binkel *m* **-s, -(n)** (*Aus inf*) **(a)** *siehe* **Bündel. (b)** (*Dummkopf*) twit (*inf*). **(c)** *siehe* **Beule.**

binnen *prep +dat or (geh) gen (form)* within ◆ **~ kurzem** shortly.
Binnen-: b~bords *adv (Naut)* inboard; **~deich** *m* inner dyke; **b~deutsch** *adj Ausdruck, Wort* used in Germany; *Sprache, Dialekt* spoken in Germany; **~fischerei** *f* freshwater fishing; **~gewässer** *nt* inland water; **~hafen** *m* river port; **~handel** *m* domestic trade; **~land** *nt* **(a)** *(Landesinneres)* interior; **(b)** *(N Ger: eingedeichtes Gebiet)* dyked land; **~länder** *m* **-s, -** inlander; **b~ländisch** *adj* inland; **~markt** *m* home market; **~meer** *nt* **(a)** inland sea; **(b)** *siehe* **~see**; **~reim** *m (Poet)* internal rhyme; **~schiffahrt** *f* inland navigation; **~schiffer** *m* sailor on inland waterways; *(auf Schleppkahn)* bargeman; **~see** *m* lake, continental lake *(form)*; **~staat** *m* landlocked country *or* state; **~verkehr** *m* inland traffic; **~währung** *f* internal currency; **~wasserstraße** *f* inland waterway; **~wirtschaft** *f* domestic economy; **~zoll** *m* internal duty.
Binom *nt* **-s, -e** binomial.
binomisch *adj* binomial.
Binse *f* **-, -n** *usu pl* rush ◆ **in die ~n gehen** *(fig inf) (mißlingen)* to be a wash-out *(inf)*; *(verlorengehen)* to go west *(inf)*, to go for a burton *(inf)*; *(kaputtgehen)* to give out *(inf)*.
Binsenwahrheit, Binsenweisheit *f* truism.
Bio *f* **-,** *no pl (Sch sl)* biol *(sl)*, bio *(esp US sl)*, bilge *(hum sl)*.
Bio- *in cpds* bio-; **b~aktiv** *adj Waschmittel* biological; **~chemie** *f* biochemistry; **b~dynamisch** *adj* biodynamic; **~gas** *nt* methane gas; **~genese** *f* biogenesis; **b~genetisch** *adj* biogenetic.
⚠ **Biograph(in** *f)* *m* biographer.
⚠ **Biographie** *f* biography.
⚠ **biographisch** *adj* biographical.
Bioladen *m* whole-food shop.
Biologe *m*, **Biologin** *f* biologist.
Biologie *f* biology.
biologisch *adj* biological ◆ **~-technische Assistentin, ~-technischer Assistent** laboratory technician.
Bio-: ~masse *f, no pl (Chem)* organic substances *pl*; **~müll** *m* organic waste; **~physik** *f* biophysics *sing*; **b~physikalisch** *adj* biophysical.
Biopsie *f (Med)* biopsy.
Bio-: ~rhythmus *m* biorhythm; **das verlangt mein ~rhythmus** my internal clock tells me it's necessary; **~technik** *f* biotechnology; **b~technisch** *adj* biotechnological; **~top** *nt* **-s, -e** biotope; **~-Waschmittel** *nt* biological detergent; **~wissenschaft** *f* biological science.
BIP [be:|i'pe:] *nt - abbr of* **Bruttoinlandsprodukt** GDP.
biquadratisch *adj* biquadratic.
Bircher-: ~müesli *(Sw)*, **~müsli** *nt* muesli *(with fresh fruit)*.
birg *imper sing of* **bergen.**
Birke *f* **-, -n** birch; *(Baum auch)* birch tree.
Birken-: ~pilz *m* boletus (scaber); **~wald** *m* birch wood *or* forest; **~wasser** *nt* hair lotion *(made from birch sap)*.
Birk-: ~hahn *m* black cock; **~huhn** *nt* black grouse.
Birma *nt* **-s** Burma.
Birmane *m* **-n, -n, Birmanin** *f* Burmese.
birmanisch *adj* Burmese.
Birnbaum *m (Baum)* pear tree; *(Holz)* pear-wood.
Birne *f* **-, -n (a)** pear. **(b)** *(Glühlampe)* (light) bulb. **(c)** *(inf: Kopf)* nut *(inf)* ◆ **eine weiche ~ haben** *(sl)* to be soft in the head *(inf)*.
birnenförmig *adj* pear-shaped.
bis[1] *adv (Mus)* bis, twice.
bis[2] [1] *prep +acc* **(a)** *(zeitlich)* until, till; *(die ganze Zeit über bis zu einem bestimmtem Zeitpunkt auch)* up to, up until, up till; *(bis spätestens, nicht später als)* by ◆ **das muß ~ Ende Mai warten** that will have to wait until *or* till the end of May; **~ Ende Mai bin ich wieder in Berlin/damit fertig** I'll be in Berlin again/I'll have finished it by the end of May; **~ 5 Uhr mache ich Hausaufgaben, und dann ...** I do my homework until 5 o'clock, and then ...; **~ 5 Uhr kann ich das unmöglich machen/gemacht haben, das ist viel zu früh** I can't possibly do it/get it done by 5 o'clock, that's much too early; **~ jetzt hat er nichts gesagt** up to now *or* so far he has said nothing; **das hätte eigentlich ~ jetzt fertig sein müssen** that should really have been finished by now; **~ dato** *(form)* to date; **~ anhin** *(Sw)* hitherto; **~ dahin** *or* **dann** until *etc*/up to *etc*/by then; **~ dahin bin ich alt und grau/ist er längst weg** I'll be old and grey by then/he will have gone long before then; **~ wann gilt der Fahrplan/ist das fertig/können Sie das machen?** when is the timetable valid till/will that be finished by/can you do that for me by?; **~ wann?** when till/by?, till/by when?; **~ wann bleibt ihr hier?** how long are you staying here?, when are you staying here till?; **~ dann!** see you then!; **~ bald/später/morgen** *etc*! see you soon/later/tomorrow *etc*!; **von ... ~ (einschließlich)** ... from ... to *or* till *or* through *(US) or* thru *(US)* ...; **von ... ~ ...** *(mit Uhrzeiten)* from ... till *or* to ...; **Montag ~ Freitag** Monday to *or* thru *(US)* Friday; **~ einschließlich** *or (dial)* **mit/ausschließlich 5. Mai** up to and including/but not including 5th May; **~ spätestens Montag brauche ich das Geld** I need the money by Monday at the latest; **~ spätestens Montag darfst du es behalten** you can keep it until Monday at the latest; **die Wäsche ist frühestens ~ nächsten Montag fertig** the laundry won't be ready until *or* before next Monday at the earliest *or* will be ready by next Monday at the earliest; **es dauert mindestens/höchstens ~ nächste Woche** it will take until *etc* next week at the very least/most; **ich kann nur (noch) ~ nächste Woche warten** I can only wait until *etc* next week, no longer.
(b) *(räumlich)* to; *(in Buch, Film etc auch)* up to ◆ **ich fahre nur ~ München** I'm only going to *or* as far as Munich; **ich habe das Buch nur ~ Seite 35 gelesen** I've only read up to *or* as far as page 35; **~ wo/wohin ...?** where ... to?; **~ dort/dorthin/dahin** (to) there; **~ dorthin sind es nur 5 km** it's only 5 km there; **höchstens ~ dahin stimme ich mit dir überein** I would only agree with you up to that point; **~ hierher** *(lit)* (to) here; *(fig)* this *or* so *or* thus far; **~ hierher und nicht weiter** *(lit, fig)* this far and no further; **~ höchstens Carlisle** to Carlisle at the furthest; **~ mindestens Carlisle** at least to *or* as far as Carlisle; **~ einschließlich/ausschließlich** up to and including/but not including.
(c) *(bei Alters-, Maß-, Mengen-, Temperaturangaben) (bis zu einer oberen Grenze von)* up to; *(bis zu einer unteren Grenze von)* to ◆ **Kinder ~ sechs Jahre, ~ sechs Jahre alte Kinder** children up to the age of six.
[2] *adv* **(a)** *(zeitlich)* until, till; *(bis spätestens)* by ◆ **~ zu diesem Zeitpunkt war alles ...** up to this time everything was ...; **das sollte ~ zum nächsten Sommer fertig sein** that should be finished by next summer; **dieser Brauch hat sich ~ ins 19. Jh. gehalten** this custom continued until *or* till into the 19th century; **~ in den Sommer/die Nacht hinein** (until *or* till) into the summer/night; **er ist ~ gegen 5 Uhr noch da** he'll be there (up) until *or* till about 5 o'clock; **~ gegen 5 Uhr ist das bestimmt fertig** it'll certainly be ready by about 5 o'clock; **~ auf weiteres** until further notice.
(b) *(räumlich)* to; *durch, über, unter* right ◆ **~ an unser Grundstück** (right *or* up) to our plot; **~ vor den Baum** (up) to the tree; **~ hinter den Baum** (to) beyond the tree; **es sind noch 10 km ~ nach Schlüchtern** it's another 10 km to Schlüchtern; **~ ins letzte/kleinste** (right) down to the last/smallest detail.
(c) *(bei Alters-, Maß-, Mengen-, Temperaturangaben)* **~ zu** *(bis zu einer oberen Grenze von)* up to; *(bis zu einer unteren Grenze von)* (down) to; **er ist genau ~ zur Haarspalterei** he is exact to the point of hair-splitting; **Gefängnis ~ zu 8 Jahren** a maximum of 8 years' imprisonment.
(d) ~ auf *(+acc) (außer)* except (for); *(einschließlich)* (right) down to.
[3] *conj* **(a)** *(beiordnend)* to ◆ **zehn ~ zwanzig Stück** ten to twenty; **bewölkt ~ bedeckt** cloudy or overcast.
(b) *(unterordnend: zeitlich)* until, till; *(nicht später als)* by the time ◆ **ich warte noch, ~ es dunkel wird,** I'll wait until *or* till it gets dark; **~ es dunkel wird, möchte ich zu Hause sein** I want to get home by the time it's dark; **~ daß der Tod euch scheide(t)** *(form)* until *or* till death you do part *(form)*; **~ das einer merkt!** it'll be ages before anyone realizes *(inf)*; **du gehst hier nicht weg, ~ das (nicht) gemacht ist** you're not leaving until *or* before that's done.
(c) *(Aus inf: sobald)* when ◆ **gleich ~ er kommt** the moment *(inf) or* as soon as he comes.
Bisam *m* **-s, -e** *or* **-s (a)** *(Pelz)* musquash. **(b)** *no pl siehe* **Moschus.**
Bisamratte *f* muskrat (beaver).
Bischof *m* **-s, ⸚e** bishop.
bischöflich *adj* episcopal.
Bischofs- *in cpds* episcopal; **~amt** *nt* episcopate; **~mütze** *f* **(a)** (bishop's) mitre; **(b)** *(Kaktus)* bishop's mitre; **~sitz** *m* diocesan town; **~stab** *m* crosier, (bishop's) crook.
Bisexualität *f* bisexuality, bisexualism.
bisexuell *adj* bisexual.
bisher *adv* until *or* till now, hitherto; *(und immer noch)* up to now ◆ **~ nicht** not until *or* till now, not before; *(und immer noch nicht)* not as yet; **das wußte ich ~ nicht** I didn't know that before; **~ habe ich es ihm nicht gesagt** I haven't told him as yet; **ein ~ unbekannter Stern** a hitherto *or* previously unknown star, a star unknown until *or* till now; **alle ~ bekannten Sterne** all the known stars.
bisherig *adj attr (vorherig)* previous; *(momentan)* present, up to now ◆ **der ~e Außenminister ist jetzt Kanzler** the previous minister for foreign affairs is now chancellor; **der ~e Außenminister wird jetzt Kanzler** the present minister for foreign affairs *or* the person who was minister for foreign affairs up to now will become chancellor; **wegen unserer ~en Arbeitsweise war das unmöglich** because of our previous way of working *or* the way we worked before that wasn't possible; **wegen unserer ~en Arbeitsweise ist das unmöglich** because of our present way of working *or* the way we have worked up to now that isn't possible; **wir müssen unsere ~en Anschauungen revidieren** we will have to revise our present views; **das ist mir in meiner ~en Karriere noch nicht vorgekommen** I've never known that in my career up to now; **die ~en Bestimmungen gelten seit letzter Woche/ab nächster Woche nicht mehr** the regulations previously/presently in force ceased to be valid last week/cease to be valid next week.
Biskaya [bɪs'ka:ja] *f* **die ~** (the) Biscay; **Golf von ~** Bay of Biscay.
Biskuit [bɪs'kvi:t, bɪs'kui:t] *nt or m* **-(e)s, -s** *or* **-e** (fatless) sponge.
Biskuit-: ~gebäck *nt* sponge cake/cakes; **~rolle** *f* Swiss roll; **~teig** *m* sponge mixture.
bislang *adv siehe* **bisher.**
Bismarckhering *m* Bismarck herring *(filleted pickled herring)*.
Bison *m* **-s, -s** bison.
⚠ **biß** *pret of* **beißen.**
⚠ **Biß** *m* **-sses, -sse** bite; *(Zahnmedizin auch)* occlusion; *(fig)* vigour, spirit ◆ **mit einem ~ war das Törtchen verschwunden** the tart disappeared in one mouthful; **Spaghetti/Bohnen mit ~** spaghetti/beans al dente; **~ haben** *(fig sl)* to have punch; **einer Sache den ~ nehmen** to take the sting out of sth.
⚠ **Bißchen** *nt dim of* **Biß, Bissen.**
⚠ **bißchen** [1] *adj inv* **ein ~ Geld/Liebe/Wärme** a bit of *or* a little money/love/warmth; **ein ~ Milch/Wasser** a drop *or* bit of milk/water, a little milk/water; **ein klein ~ ...** a little bit/drop of ...; **kein ~ ...** not one (little) bit/not a drop of ...; **das ~ Geld/Whisky** that little bit of money/drop of whisky; **ich habe kein ~ Hunger** I'm not a bit hungry.

⚠: Informationen zur Rechtschreibreform im Anhang

[2] *adv* **ein ~** a bit, a little; **ein klein ~** a little bit; **ein ~ wenig** not very much; **ein ~ mehr/viel/teuer** *etc* a bit more/much/expensive *etc*; **ein ~ zu wenig** not quite enough; **ein ~ sehr** (*inf*) a little bit too much; **ein ~ sehr teuer** *etc* (*inf*) a (little) bit too expensive *etc*.
[3] *nt inv*: **ein ~** a bit, a little; (*Flüssigkeit*) a drop, a little; **ein ganz ~** (*inf*) just a tiny bit/drop; *siehe* **lieb**.

bissel (*dial inf*) *siehe* **bißchen**.

Bissen *m* **-s, -** mouthful; (*Imbiß*) bite (to eat) ◆ **er will keinen ~ anrühren** he won't eat a thing; **einen ~ zu sich nehmen** to have a bite to eat; **sich** (*dat*) **den letzten/jeden ~ vom** *or* **am Munde absparen** to go short onself/to watch every penny one spends.

bissenweise *adv* mouthful by mouthful; (*fig*) bit by bit.

bisserl (*dial*) *siehe* **bißchen**.

bissig *adj* **(a)** (*lit, fig*) vicious ◆ **~ sein** to bite; **„Vorsicht, ~er Hund"** "beware of the dog". **(b)** (*übellaunig*) waspish. **du brauchst nicht gleich ~ zu werden** there's no need to bite my *etc* head off.

Bissigkeit *f siehe adj* **(a)** viciousness; (*Bemerkung*) vicious remark. **(b)** waspishness; (*Bemerkung*) waspish remark.

bissl *adj, adv, nt inv* (*dial*) *siehe* **bißchen**.

⚠ **Bißwunde** *f* bite.

bist *2. pers sing present of* **sein**.

biste (*dial inf*) *contr of* **bist du**.

Bistro *nt* **-s, -s** bistro.

Bistum ['bɪstuːm] *nt* diocese, bishopric.

bisweilen *adv* (*geh*) from time to time, now and then.

Bit *nt* **-(s), -(s)** (*Comput*) bit.

Bittbrief *m* petition.

Bitte *f* **-, -n** request; (*inständig*) plea ◆ **auf seine ~ hin** at his request; **ich habe eine große ~ an dich** I have a (great) favour to ask you; **sich mit einer ~ an jdn wenden** to make a request to sb; **er kann ihr keine ~ ausschlagen** he can't refuse her anything; **er gab den ~n der Kinder nach** he gave in to the children's pleas.

bitte *interj* **(a)** (*bittend, auffordernd*) please ◆ **~ schön** please; **nun hör mir doch mal ~ zu** listen to me please; **~ sei so gut und ruf mich an** would you phone me, please *or* please phone me; **wo ist ~ das nächste Telefon?** could you please tell me where the nearest telephone is?; **~ nicht!** no, please!, please don't!; **ja ~!, ~ ja!** yes please; **~ ~ machen** (*inf*) (*Kind*) ≃ to say pretty please (*inf*); (*Hund*) to (sit up and) beg; **~ zahlen, zahlen ~!** (could I/we have) the bill, please; **~ nach Ihnen!** after you.
(b) (*bei höflicher Frage, Aufforderung*) *meist nicht übersetzt* **~ schön?, ~(, was darf es sein)?** (*in Geschäft*) can I help you?; (*in Gaststätte*) what would you like?; **~(, Sie wünschen)?** what can I do for you?; **~ (schön** *or* **sehr)(, Ihr Bier/Kaffee)!** *meist nicht übersetzt* your beer/coffee, here you are (*inf*); **ja ~?** yes?; **~(, treten Sie ein)!** come in!, come!; **~(, nehmen Sie doch Platz)!** (*form*) please *or* do sit down; **~ hier, hier ~!** (over) here, please; **Entschuldigung! — ~!** I'm sorry! — that's all right; **~, mit (dem größten) Vergnügen!** (*form*) with pleasure; **aber ~!** sure (*inf*), go (right) ahead (*inf*), please do; **~, nur zu!** help yourself; **na ~!** there you are!
(c) (*sarkastisch: nun gut*) all right ◆ **~, wie du willst** (all right,) just as you like; **~, soll er doch kommen, mir ist das egal** (all right,) let him come, it's all the same to me.
(d) (*Dank erwidernd*) you're welcome, not at all (*Brit*), sure (*US inf*) ◆ **~ sehr** *or* **schön** you're welcome, not at all (*Brit*); **~(, gern geschehen)** (not at all,) my pleasure; **~, keine Ursache** it was nothing; **~, nichts zu danken** don't mention it; **aber ~!** there's no need to thank me.
(e) (*nachfragend*) **(wie) ~?** (I beg your) pardon? (*auch iro*), sorry(, what did you say)?

➤ **bitten** *pret* **bat**, *ptp* **gebeten** [1] *vt* **(a)** to ask; (*inständig*) to beg; (*Eccl*) to beseech ◆ **jdn um etw ~** to ask/beg/beseech sb for sth; **jdn (darum) ~, etw zu tun** *or* **daß er etw tut** to ask *etc* sb to do sth; **jdn etw** (*acc*) **~** (*dated*) to ask sth of sb; **darf ich Sie um Ihren Namen ~?** might I ask your name?; **um Ruhe wird gebeten** silence is requested; (*auf Schild*) silence please; **darf ich Sie um den nächsten Tanz ~?** may I have the pleasure of the next dance?; **wir ~ dich, erhöre uns!** (*Eccl*) we beseech Thee to hear us; (*katholisch*) Lord hear us; **ich bitte dich um alles in der Welt** I beg *or* implore you; **er läßt sich gerne ~** he likes people to keep asking him; **er läßt sich nicht (lange) ~** you don't have to ask him twice; **aber ich bitte dich!** not at all; **ich bitte dich, wie kann man nur so dumm sein?** I ask you, how can anyone be so stupid?; **wenn ich ~ darf** (*form*) if you please, if you wouldn't mind; **ich bitte darum** (*form*) I'd be glad if you would, if you wouldn't mind; **(keineswegs,) ich bitte sogar darum** (*form*) (not at all,) I should be glad; **darum möchte ich doch sehr gebeten haben!** (*form*) I should hope so indeed; **ich muß doch (sehr) ~!** well I must say!
(b) (*einladen*) to ask, to invite ◆ **jdn auf ein Glas Wein ~** to invite sb to have a glass of wine; **jdn zum Abendessen (zu sich) ~** to ask *or* invite sb to dinner; **jdn zu Tisch ~** to ask sb to come to table; **jdn ins Zimmer ~** to ask *or* invite sb to come in.
(c) (*bestellen*) **jdn an einen Ort ~** to ask sb (to come) somewhere; **jdn zu sich ~** to ask sb to come and see one.
[2] *vi* **(a)** to ask; (*inständig*) to plead, to beg ◆ **um etw ~** to ask (for) *or* request sth; to plead *or* beg for sth; **bei jdm um etw ~** to ask sb for sth; **~ und betteln** to beg and plead.
(b) (*einladen*) **der Herr Professor läßt ~** the Professor will see you now; **ich lasse ~** he/she can come in now, would you ask him/her to come in now?; **darf ich zu Tisch ~?** lunch/dinner is served; **darf ich (um den nächsten Tanz) ~?** may I have the pleasure (of the next dance)?

Bitten *nt* **-s,** *no pl* pleading ◆ **sich aufs ~ verlegen** to resort to pleas *or* pleading; **auf ~ von** at the request of.

bittend *adj* pleading ◆ **mit ~en Augen** with a look of pleading.

bitter *adj* **(a)** bitter; *Schokolade* plain; (*fig*) *Geschmack* nasty; *siehe* **Pille.**
(b) (*fig*) *Enttäuschung, Erfahrung, Ironie* bitter; *Wahrheit, Lehre, Verlust* hard, painful; *Zeit, Schicksal* hard; *Ernst, Feind* deadly; *Hohn, Spott* cruel ◆ **ein ~es Gefühl** a feeling of bitterness; **bis zum ~en Ende** to the bitter end.
(c) (*fig: verbittert*) bitter ◆ **jdn ~ machen** to embitter sb, to make sb bitter; **~e Klagen führen** to complain bitterly.
(d) (*stark*) *Kälte, Frost, Reue, Tränen* bitter; *Not, Notwendigkeit* dire; *Leid, Unrecht* grievous ◆ **jdn/etw ~ entbehren/vermissen** to miss sb/sth sadly; **etw ~ nötig haben** to be in dire need of sth; **~ wenig Geld haben** to be desperately short of money; **solche Fehler rächen sich ~** one pays dearly for mistakes like that.

Bitter *m* **-s, -** bitters *pl*.

bitterböse *adj* furious.

Bittere(r) *m decl as adj siehe* **Bitter.**

Bitter-: b~ernst *adj Situation etc* extremely serious; *Mensch* deadly serious; **damit ist es mir b~ernst** I am deadly serious *or* in deadly earnest; **b~kalt** *adj attr* bitterly cold, bitter; **~keit** *f* (*lit, fig*) bitterness; **b~lich** [1] *adj* bitter; [2] *adv* bitterly; **~mandel** *f* bitter almond.

Bitternis *f* (*geh*) bitterness *no pl*; (*fig: von Mensch auch*) embitterment *no pl*; (*Leiden*) adversity, hardship.

Bitter-: ~salz *nt* Epsom salts *pl*; **b~süß** *adj* (*lit, fig*) bitter-sweet.

Bitteschön *nt* **-s, -s** (*bittend, auffordernd*) please; (*Dank erwidernd*) not at all; (*anbietend*) (*von Verkäufer*) can I help you?; (*von Kellner*) what would you like?

Bitt-: ~gang *m* **(a)** (*geh*) **einen ~gang zu jdm machen** to go to sb with a request; **das war ein schwerer ~gang** it was hard (for him *etc*) to ask that; **(b)** (*Eccl*) pilgrimage; (*~ prozession*) rogation procession; **~gebet** *nt* (prayer of) supplication; **~gesuch** *nt* petition; **~gottesdienst** *m* rogation service.

bittschön *interj* = **bitte schön.**

Bitt-: ~schrift *f* (*dated*) *siehe* **~gesuch; ~steller(in** *f*) *m* **-s, -** petitioner, supplicant.

Bitumen *nt* **-s, -** *or* **Bitumina** bitumen.

bivalent [-va-] *adj* bivalent.

Biwak *nt* **-s, -s** *or* **-e** bivouac.

biwakieren* *vi* to bivouac.

bizarr *adj* bizarre; *Form, Gestalt etc auch* fantastic.

Bizarrerie *f* (*geh*) **(a)** *no pl* bizarreness. **(b)** (*Gedanke, Verhalten*) bizarre idea/behaviour *no pl*/comment *etc*.

Bizeps *m* **-(es), -e** biceps.

Bj. *abbr of* **Baujahr.**

BKA [beːkaˈ|aː] *nt* - *abbr of* **Bundeskriminalamt.**

blabla *interj* (*inf*) blah blah blah (*inf*).

Blabla *nt* **-s,** *no pl* (*inf*) waffle (*inf*).

Blackout [ˈblɛkaut] *nt or m* **-(s), -s** blackout.

blaffen, bläffen *vi* to yelp; (*schimpfen*) to snap.

Blag *nt* **-s, -en, Blage** *f* **-, -n** (*pej inf*) brat.

blähen [1] *vt* to swell; *Segel auch* to belly (out), to fill; *Anorak, Gardine, Windsack* to fill; *Nüstern* to dilate; *Bauch* to swell, to distend (*form*) ◆ **voller Stolz blähte er seine Brust** his chest swelled with pride.
[2] *vr* to swell; (*Segel auch*) to belly out, to billow; (*Anorak, Gardine*) to billow; (*Nüstern*) to dilate; (*fig: Mensch*) to puff oneself up (*inf*).
[3] *vi* to cause flatulence *or* wind.

blähend *adj* (*Med*) flatulent (*form*).

Blähung *f usu pl* (*Med*) wind *no pl*, flatulence *no pl* ◆ **eine ~ abgehen lassen** to break wind.

blakig *adj* (*verrußt*) sooty; (*rußend*) smoky.

blamabel *adj* shameful.

Blamage [blaˈmaːʒə] *f* **-, -n** disgrace.

blamieren* [1] *vt* to disgrace; *siehe* **Innung.**
[2] *vr* to make a fool of oneself; (*durch Benehmen*) to disgrace oneself.

⚠ **blanchieren*** [blãˈʃiːrən] *vt* (*Cook*) to blanch.

blank *adj* **(a)** (*glänzend, sauber*) shiny, shining; (*abgescheuert*) *Hosenboden etc* shiny ◆ **etw ~ scheuern/polieren, etw scheuern/polieren, bis es ~ wird** to clean/polish sth till it shines; **der ~e Hans** (*poet*) the wild North Sea.
(b) (*poet: strahlend*) *Licht* bright; *Augen auch* shining ◆ **der ~e Tag** broad daylight.
(c) (*nackt*) bare; *Schwert etc auch* naked; (*Aus: ohne Mantel*) coatless; (*inf: ohne Geld*) broke; (*Cards: einzeln*) single ◆ **eine Karte ~ haben** to have only one card of a suit; **die Herzzehn habe ich ~** the ten of hearts is the only heart I have; *siehe* **blankziehen.**
(d) (*rein*) pure, sheer; *Hohn* utter.

Blankett *nt* **-s, -e** (*Fin*) blank form.

⚠ **blankgewetzt** *adj attr* shiny, worn shiny.

blanko *adj pred* **(a)** *Papier* plain. **(b)** *Scheck etc* blank.

Blanko- *in cpds* blank; **~akzept** *nt* (*Fin*) blank acceptance; **~kredit** *m* open *or* blank credit; **~scheck** *m* blank cheque; **jdm einen ~scheck ausstellen** (*fig*) to give sb carte blanche; **~vollmacht** *f* carte blanche.

⚠ **blankpoliert** *adj attr* brightly polished.

Blankvers *m* blank verse.

blankziehen *sep irreg* [1] *vt* to draw.
[2] *vi* (*sl*) to draw (one's gun).

Bläschen *nt* **(a)** *dim of* **Blase. (b)** (*Med*) vesicle (*form*), small blister.

Bläschen|ausschlag *m* herpes *sing*, blistery rash (*inf*).
Blase *f* **-, -n (a)** (*Seifen~, Luft~*) bubble; (*Sprech~*) balloon ◆ **~n werfen** *or* **ziehen** (*Farbe*) to blister; (*Teig*) to become light and frothy.
(b) (*Med*) blister; (*Fieber~ auch*) vesicle (*form*) ◆ **sich** (*dat*) **~n laufen** *etc* to get blisters from walking *etc*.
(c) (*Anat*) bladder ◆ **sich** (*dat*) **die ~ erkälten** to get a chill on the bladder.
(d) (*pej inf: Clique*) gang (*inf*), mob (*inf*).
Blasebalg *m* (pair of) bellows.
blasen *pret* **blies**, *ptp* **geblasen** [1] *vi* to blow; (*Posaunenbläser etc*) to play; (*auf Essen*) to blow on it; (*auf Wunde etc*) ≃ to kiss it better ◆ **zum Rückzug ~** (*lit, fig*) to sound the retreat; **zum Aufbruch ~** (*lit*) to sound the departure; (*fig*) to say it's time to go; **es bläst** (*inf*) it's blowy (*inf*) *or* windy, there's a wind blowing; *siehe* **tuten, Horn.**
[2] *vt* **(a)** to blow; *Essen* to blow on; *Wunde etc* ≃ to kiss better.
(b) *Melodie, Posaune etc* to play.
(c) (*inf*) **dir/ihm werd ich was ~!** I'll give you/him a piece of my mind; *siehe* **Marsch¹, Trübsal.**
(d) (*inf: mitteilen*) to tell ◆ **jdm etw ins Ohr ~** to whisper sth in sb's ear.
(e) (*sl: fellieren*) **jdm einen ~** to give sb a blow-job (*sl*).
Blasen-: ~bildung *f* formation of bubbles; (*bei Anstrich, an Fuß etc*) blistering; **~entzündung** *f*, ⚠**~katarrh** *m* cystitis; **~leiden** *nt* bladder trouble *no art*; **~stein** *m* bladder stone; **~tee** *m herb tea beneficial in cases of bladder trouble*.
Bläser(in *f*) *m* **-s, -** (*Mus*) wind player ◆ **die ~** the wind (section).
Bläserquartett *nt* wind quartet.
blasiert *adj* (*pej geh*) blasé.
Blasiertheit *f* (*pej geh*) blasé character; (*von Mensch*) blasé attitude.
blasig *adj* full of bubbles; *Flüssigkeit etc* aerated; *Teig* light and frothy; (*Med*) blistered.
Blas-: ~instrument *nt* wind instrument; **~kapelle** *f* brass band; **~musik** *f* brass band music.
Blasphemie *f* blasphemy.
blasphemisch *adj* blasphemous.
Blasrohr *nt* **(a)** (*Waffe*) blow-pipe. **(b)** (*Tech*) blast pipe.
⚠ **blaß** *adj* **(a)** *Gesicht, Haut etc* pale ◆ **~ werden** to go *or* grow pale, to pale; (*vor Schreck auch*) to blanch; **~ wie der Tod** (*geh*) deathly pale; **~ wie Kreide** white as chalk; **~ vor Neid werden** to go green with envy; **etw macht jdn ~** sth makes sb look pale.
(b) *Farbe, Schrift etc* pale.
(c) (*geh*) *Licht, Mond* pale, wan.
(d) (*fig*) faint; *Ahnung, Vorstellung auch* vague; *Erinnerung auch* dim, vague; *Ausdruck, Sprache, Schilderung* colourless ◆ **ich habe keinen blassen Schimmer** *or* **Dunst (davon)** (*inf*) I haven't a clue *or* the faintest (idea) (about it) (*inf*).
(e) (*rare: pur*) sheer, pure.
⚠ **blaß-** *in cpds* pale.
Blässe *f* **-, -n (a)** paleness; (*von Haut, Gesicht etc auch*) pallor; (*von Licht auch*) wanness; (*fig: von Ausdruck, Schilderung etc*) colourlessness. **(b)** *siehe* **Blesse.**
⚠ **Bläßhuhn** *nt* coot.
⚠ **bläßlich** *adj* palish, rather pale.
Blatt *nt* **-(e)s, ¨er (a)** (*Bot*) leaf ◆ **kein ~ vor den Mund nehmen** not to mince one's words.
(b) (*Papier etc*) sheet ◆ **ein ~ Papier** a sheet of paper; **(noch) ein unbeschriebenes ~ sein** (*unerfahren*) to be inexperienced; (*ohne Image*) to be an unknown quantity; **er ist kein unbeschriebenes ~** he's been around (*inf*); (*Krimineller*) he's got a record; *siehe* **fliegend.**
(c) (*Seite*) page ◆ **das steht auf einem anderen ~** (*fig*) that's another story; **ein neues ~ in der Geschichte** *or* **im Buch der Geschichte** a new chapter of history.
(d) (*Noten~*) sheet ◆ **vom ~ singen/spielen** to sight-read.
(e) (*Kunst~*) print; (*Reproduktion*) reproduction.
(f) (*bei Landkartenserien*) sheet.
(g) (*Zeitung*) paper.
(h) (*von Messer, Ruder, Propeller*) blade.
(i) (*Cards*) hand; (*Einzelkarte*) card ◆ **das ~ hat sich gewendet** (*fig*) the tables have been turned.
(j) (*Hunt, Cook*) shoulder.
Blatt|ader *f* (*Bot*) leaf vein.
Blättchen *nt dim of* **Blatt** (*pej: Zeitung*) rag (*inf*).
Blatter *f* **-, -n** (*dated Med*) (*Pocke*) pock, pustule. **~n** *pl* (*Krankheit*) smallpox.
blatt(e)rig *adj siehe* **blatternarbig.**
blätt(e)rig *adj Teig* flaky; *Farbe etc* flaking ◆ **~ werden** (*Farbe etc*) to start flaking.
-blätt(e)rig *adj suf* -leaved.
Blättermagen *m* (*Zool*) omasum (*spec*).
blättern [1] *vi* **(a)** (*in Buch*) to leaf *or* (*schnell*) flick through it/them; (*Comput*) to scroll ◆ **in etw** (*dat*) **~** to leaf *or* flick through sth.
(b) *aux sein* (*rare*) (*in Schichten zerfallen*) to flake; (*abblättern*) to flake off.
[2] *vt Geldscheine, Spielkarten* to put down one by one ◆ **er blätterte mir die 100 Mark auf den Tisch** he put the 100 marks down note by note on the table for me.
Blatter-: ~narbe *f* (*dated*) pockmark; **b~narbig** *adj* (*dated*) pockmarked.
Blätter-: ~pilz *m* agaric; **~schmuck** *m* (*poet*) beautiful foliage; **~teig** *m* puff pastry *or* paste (*US*); **~teiggebäck** *nt* puff pastry; (*Backwaren*) puff pastries *pl*; **~wald** *m* (*Press hum*) press; **es rauscht im deutschen ~wald** there are murmurings in the German press; **~werk** *nt, no pl siehe* **Blattwerk.**
Blatt-: ~feder *f* (*Tech*) leaf spring; **~form** *f* (*Bot*) leafshape; **b~förmig** *adj* leaf-shaped, foliar (*form*); **~gemüse** *nt* greens *pl*, green *or* leaf (*form*) vegetables *pl*; **ein ~gemüse** a leaf vegetable; **~gewächs** *nt siehe* **~pflanze;** **~gold** *nt* gold leaf; **~grün** *nt* chlorophyll; **~knospe** *f* leafbud; **~laus** *f* greenfly, aphid; **b~los** *adj* leafless; **~pflanze** *f* foliate plant; **~rippe** *f* (*Bot*) (leaf) rib *or* vein; **~salat** *m* green salad; ⚠**~schuß** *m* (*Hunt*) shot through the shoulder to the heart; **~silber** *nt* silver leaf; **~stellung** *f* leaf arrangement; ⚠**~stengel, ~stiel** *m* petiole, leafstalk; **~trieb** *m* leaf shoot; **~vergoldung** *f* gilding; **b~weise** *adv* leaf by leaf; (*bei Papier*) sheet by sheet; **~werk** *nt, no pl* foliage.
Blätz *m* **-, -** (*Sw*) cloth.
Blätzli *nt* **-(s), -(s)** (*Sw*) cutlet.
blau *adj* **(a)** blue ◆ **Forelle** *etc* **~** (*Cook*) trout *etc* au bleu; **~er Anton** (*inf*) boilersuit; **ein ~es Auge** (*inf*) a black eye; **ich tu das nicht wegen deiner schönen ~en Augen** (*fig*) I'm not doing it for the sake of your bonny blue eyes; **mit einem ~en Auge davonkommen** (*fig*) to get off lightly; **die ~e Blume** (*Liter*) the Blue Flower; **~es Blut in den Adern haben** to have blue blood in one's veins; **ein ~er Brief** (*Sch*) *letter informing parents that their child must repeat a year*; (*von Hauswirt*) notice to quit; (*von der Firma*) one's cards; **ein ~er Fleck** a bruise; **~e Flecken haben** to be bruised; **die ~en Jungs** (*inf*) the boys in blue (*inf*), the navy; **~er Lappen** (*sl*) hundred mark note *or* bill (*US*), blue one (*inf*); **der B~e Nil** the Blue Nile; **der ~e Planet** the blue planet; **der B~e Reiter** (*Art*) the Blaue Reiter; **die ~e Stunde** (*poet*) the twilight hour; **er wird sein ~es Wunder erleben** (*inf*) he won't know what's hit him (*inf*); *siehe* **Dunst.**
(b) *usu pred* (*inf: betrunken*) drunk, tight (*inf*), canned (*inf*); *siehe* **Veilchen.**
(c) (*inf: geschwänzt*) **einen ~en Montag machen** to skip work on Monday (*inf*); **der letzte Freitag war für mich ~** I skipped work last Friday (*inf*).
Blau *nt* **-s, -** *or* (*inf*) **-s** blue; *siehe auch* **Blaue².**
Blau-: ~algen *pl* blue-green algae *pl*; **b~äugig** *adj* blue-eyed; (*fig*) naïve; **~äugigkeit** *f* (*lit*) blue eyes *pl*; (*fig*) naïvety; **~bart** *m* (*geh*) Bluebeard; **~beere** *f siehe* **Heidelbeere;** **b~blütig** *adj* blue-blooded; **~blütigkeit** *f* blue blood.
Blaue¹ *m*: **der ~** *siehe* **Blaue(r).**
Blaue² *nt* **-n,** *no pl* **(a) das ~** (*Farbe*) the blue; **es spielt ins ~** it has a touch of blue in it; **das ~ vom Himmel (herunter) lügen** (*inf*) to tell a pack of lies; **das ~ vom Himmel (herunter) reden** (*inf*) to talk one's head off (*inf*), to prattle away nineteen to the dozen (*inf*); **jdm das ~ vom Himmel (herunter) versprechen** (*inf*) to promise sb the moon.
(b) (*ohne Ziel*) **ins ~ hinein** (*inf*) at random; *arbeiten* with no particular goal; **wir wollen ins ~ fahren** we'll just set off and see where we end up; **eine Fahrt ins ~** a trip to nowhere in particular; (*Veranstaltung*) a mystery tour.
Bläue *f* **-,** *no pl* blueness; (*des Himmels auch*) blue.
blauen *vi* (*liter*) (*Himmel*) to turn blue.
bläuen [1] *vt* **(a)** to dye blue; *Lackmuspapier etc* to turn blue. **(b)** *Wäsche* to blue.
[2] *vr* to turn *or* go blue.
Blaue(r) *m decl as adj* **(a)** (*inf: Polizist*) cop (*inf*), copper (*inf*). **(b)** (*sl: Geldschein*) blue one (*inf*) ◆ **ein kleiner/großer ~r** a ten/hundred mark note.
Blau-: ~felchen *m* whitefish, powan (*spec*); **~filter** *m or nt* (*Phot*) blue filter; **~fuchs** *m* arctic fox; **b~grau** *adj* blue-grey, bluish *or* bluey grey; **b~grün** *adj* blue-green, bluish *or* bluey green; **~helm** *m* (*Press sl*) UN soldier; **~hemd** *nt* (*DDR*) **(a)** blue shirt (*worn by members of the Free German Youth*); **(b)** (*inf: Mensch*) member of the Free German Youth; **~jacke** *f* (*inf*) bluejacket (*inf*), sailor; **~kabis** *m* (*Sw*), **~kohl** *m* (*dial*), **~kraut** *nt* (*S Ger, Aus*) *siehe* **Rotkohl;** **~kreuz(l)er(in** *f*) *m* **-s, -** member of the Blue Cross Temperance League.
bläulich *adj* bluish, bluey.
Blau-: ~licht *nt* (*von Polizei etc*) flashing blue light; (*Lampe*) blue light; **mit ~licht** with its blue light flashing; **b~machen** *sep* (*inf*) [1] *vi* to skip work; [2] *vt* **den Freitag/zwei Tage b~machen** to skip work on Friday/for two days; **~mann** *m, pl* **~männer** (*inf*) boilersuit; **~meise** *f* bluetit; **~papier** *nt* carbon paper; **~pause** *f* blueprint; **b~rot** *adj* purple; **~säure** *f* prussic *or* hydrocyanic acid; **~schimmelkäse** *m* blue cheese; **b~schwarz** *adj* blue-black, bluey black; **~stich** *m* (*Phot*) blue cast; **b~stichig** *adj* (*Phot*) with a blue cast; **~stift** *m* blue pencil; (*zum Malen*) blue crayon; **~strumpf** *m* bluestocking; **b~strümpfig** *adj* bluestocking *attr*; **~tanne** *f* blue *or* colorado spruce; **b~violett** *adj* (dark) bluish *or* bluey purple; **~wal** *m* blue whale.
Blazer ['ble:zɐ] *m* **-s, -, Blazerjacke** *f* blazer.
Blech *nt* **-(e)s, -e (a)** *no pl* (sheet) metal; (*von Auto*) body ◆ **eine Dose aus ~** a tin (*Brit*), a metal container; **das ist doch nur ~** it's just ordinary metal.
(b) (*Blechstück*) metal plate.
(c) (*Backblech*) (baking) tray.
(d) *no pl* (*inf: Blechinstrumente*) brass.
(e) *no pl* (*pej inf: Orden etc*) gongs *pl* (*inf*), fruit salad (*US inf*).
(f) *no pl* (*inf: Unsinn*) rubbish *no art* (*inf*), trash *no art* (*inf*) ◆ **red' kein ~** don't talk crap (*sl*).
Blech-: ~bläser *m* brass player; **die ~bläser** the brass (section); **~blasinstrument** *nt* brass instrument; **~büchse** *f* tin (*Brit*), can; **~dose** *f* tin container; (*esp für Konserven*) tin (*Brit*), can.
blechen *vti* (*inf*) to cough *or* pay up (*inf*), to fork out (*inf*).
blechern *adj* **(a)** *attr* metal. **(b)** *Geräusch, Stimme etc* tinny; (*fig: hohl*) hollow, empty.
Blech-: ~geschirr *nt* metal pots and pans *pl or* utensils *pl* (*form*); **~instrument** *nt* brass instrument; **~kanister** *m* metal can; **~kiste** *f* (*pej inf*) (old)

crate (*inf*); **~lawine** *f* (*pej inf*) vast column of cars; **~lehre** *f* metal gauge; **~musik** *f* (*usu pej*) brass (band) music; **~napf** *m* metal bowl; **~schaden** *m* damage to the bodywork; **~schere** *f* (pair of) metal shears; (*Maschine*) metal shearer; **~trommel** *f* tin drum; **~walzwerk** *nt* sheet (rolling) mill.

blecken [1] *vt* **die Zähne ~** to bare *or* show one's teeth.
[2] *vi* (*rare*) to flash; (*Flammen*) to dart, to leap.

Blei *nt* **-(e)s, -e (a)** *no pl* (*abbr* **Pb**) lead ♦ **jdm wie ~ in den Gliedern** *or* **Knochen liegen** (*Schreck*) to paralyse sb; (*Depression*) to weigh sb down; **die Müdigkeit/Anstrengung lag ihm wie ~ in den Gliedern** *or* **Knochen** his whole body ached with tiredness/the exertion; *siehe* **Magen**.
(b) (*Lot*) plumb, (plumb-)bob.
(c) (*Munition*) lead; (*Typ*) hot metal.

Blei- *in cpds* lead; **~ader** *f* lead vein.

Bleibe *f* **-, -n (a)** (*Unterkunft*) place to stay ♦ **eine/keine ~ haben** to have somewhere/nowhere to stay. **(b)** (*Institution*) remand home.

bleiben *pret* **blieb**, *ptp* **geblieben** *vi aux sein* **(a)** (*sich nicht verändern*) to stay, to remain ♦ **unbelohnt/unbestraft ~** to go unrewarded/unpunished; **unbeachtet ~** to go unnoticed, to escape notice; **unbeantwortet ~** to be left *or* to remain unanswered; **unvergessen ~** to continue to be remembered; **an Samstagen bleibt unser Geschäft geschlossen** this shop is closed on Saturdays; **in Verbindung ~** to keep *or* stay *or* remain in touch; **in Übung/Form ~** to keep in practice/form; **jdm in** *or* **in jds Erinnerung ~** to stay *or* remain in sb's mind; **ruhig/still ~** to keep calm/quiet; **wach ~** to stay *or* keep awake; **Freunde ~** to stay *or* remain friends, to go on being friends.
(b) (*sich nicht bewegen, zu Besuch ~*) to stay; (*nicht weggehen, nicht zurückkommen auch*) to remain ♦ **sitzen/stehen ~** to stay sitting down/ standing up, to remain seated/standing; **bitte, ~ Sie doch sitzen** please don't get up; **jdn zum B~ einladen** *or* **auffordern** to invite sb to stay; **von etw ~** to stay *or* keep away from sth; **wo bleibst du so lange?** (*inf*) what's keeping you (all this time)?; **wo bleibt er so lange?** (*inf*) where has he got to?; **wo sind denn all die alten Häuser geblieben?** what (has) happened to all the old houses?, where have all the old houses gone (to)?; **bleibe im Lande und nähre dich redlich** (*Prov*) east, west, home's best (*prov*); **hier ist meines B~s nicht (mehr** *or* **länger)** (*geh*) I cannot remain here (any longer); *siehe* **Ball[1]**, **Apparat**.
(c) (*fig*) **bei etw ~** to keep *or* stick (*inf*) to sth; **das bleibt unter uns** that's (just) between ourselves; **wir möchten für** *or* **unter uns ~** we want to keep ourselves to ourselves; *siehe* **dabei, Sache**.
(d) (*übrigbleiben*) to be left, to remain ♦ **es blieb mir/es blieb keine andere Wahl/Möglichkeit** I had/there was no other choice/possibility; **es blieb mir keine Hoffnung** I lost all hope.
(e) (*sein*) **es bleibt abzuwarten** it remains to be seen; **es bleibt zu hoffen/ wünschen, daß ...** I/we can only hope that ...
(f) (*inf: versorgt werden*) **sie können (selber) sehen, wo sie ~** they'll just have to look out for themselves (*inf*); **und wo bleibe ich?** and what about me?; **sieh zu, wo du bleibst!** you're on your own! (*inf*), you'd better look out for yourself! (*inf*).
(g) (*euph: umkommen*) **er ist auf See/im Krieg geblieben** he died at sea/didn't come back from the war.

bleibend *adj Wert, Erinnerung etc* lasting; *Schaden, Zähne* permanent.

⚠ **bleibenlassen** *vt sep irreg* (*inf*) **(a)** (*unterlassen*) **etw ~** to give sth a miss (*inf*); **das werde ich/wirst du ganz schön ~** I'll/you'll do nothing of the sort! **(b)** (*aufgeben*) to give up ♦ **das Rauchen/Nägelkauen ~** to give up *or* stop smoking/chewing one's nails.

bleich *adj* pale; (*fig*) *Grauen, Entsetzen* sheer ♦ **~ wie der Tod** deathly pale, pale as death.

Bleiche *f* **-, -n (a)** *no pl* paleness; (*von Mensch auch*) pallor. **(b)** (*Bleichplatz*) bleachery (*obs*), *green where sheets etc were laid out to be bleached by the sun.*

bleichen [1] *vt* to bleach.
[2] *vi pret* **bleichte** *or* (*old*) **blich**, *ptp* **gebleicht** *or* (*old*) **geblicht** to be *or* become bleached ♦ **in der Sonne ~** to be bleached by the sun.

Bleich-: **~gesicht** *nt* **(a)** (*inf: blasser Mensch*) pasty-face (*inf*), pale-faced person; **(b)** (*Weißer*) paleface; **b~gesichtig** *adj* (*inf*) pale-faced, pasty-faced (*inf*); **~mittel** *nt* bleach, bleaching agent; **~sucht** *f* (*old Med*) anaemia; **b~süchtig** *adj* (*old Med*) anaemic.

bleiern *adj* **(a)** *attr* (*aus Blei*) lead; (*fig*) *Farbe, Himmel* leaden ♦ **wie eine ~e Ente schwimmen** (*hum*) to swim like a brick.
(b) (*fig*) leaden; *Verantwortung* onerous ♦ **die Verantwortung lastete ~ auf ihm/seiner Seele** the responsibility weighed heavily upon him/his mind; **es lag ihr ~ in den Gliedern** her limbs were like lead; *siehe* **Magen**.

Blei-: **~erz** *nt* lead ore; **~farbe** *f* lead paint; **b~farbig, b~farben** *adj* lead-coloured, lead-grey; *Himmel* leaden; **b~frei** *adj Benzin etc* lead-free, unleaded; **b~frei fahren** to drive on lead-free petrol; **~fuß** *m*: **mit ~fuß fahren** (*inf*) to keep one's foot down; **~gehalt** *m* lead content; **~gewicht** *nt* lead weight; (*Angeln*) sinker; **~gießen** *nt New Year's Eve custom of telling fortunes by the shapes made by molten lead dropped into cold water;* **~glanz** *m* galena, galenite; **b~grau** *adj* lead-grey; **b~haltig** *adj* containing lead; *Erz, Gestein* plumbiferous (*spec*); *Benzin etc* leaded; **b~haltig/zu b~haltig sein** to contain lead/too much lead; **~hütte** *f* lead works *pl*; **~kristall** *nt* lead crystal; **~kugel** *f* lead bullet; lead ball; **~lot** *nt* plumbline; **~menninge** *f siehe* **Menninge**; **~oxid, ~oxyd** *nt* lead oxide; **gelbes ~oxid** lead monoxide; **rotes ~oxid** red lead; **~satz** *m* (*Typ*) hot-metal setting; **~schürze** *f* lead apron; **b~schwer** *adj siehe* **bleiern (b)**; **~soldat** *m* ≃ tin soldier.

Bleistift *m* pencil; (*zum Malen*) crayon ♦ **mit/in ~** with a/in pencil.

Bleistift- *in cpds* pencil; **~absatz** *m* stiletto heel; **~spitzer** *m* pencil sharpener.

Blei-: **~vergiftung** *f* lead poisoning; **b~verglast** *adj* leaded; **~verglasung** *f* lead glazing; **Fenster mit ~verglasung** leaded windows; **b~verseucht** *adj* lead-polluted; **~weiß** *nt* white lead.

Blende *f* **-, -n (a)** (*Lichtschutz*) shade, screen; (*Aut*) (sun) visor; (*an Fenster*) blind.
(b) (*Opt*) filter.
(c) (*Phot*) (*Öffnung*) aperture; (*Einstellungsposition*) f-stop; (*Vorrichtung*) diaphragm ♦ **die ~ schließen** to stop down; **bei** *or* **mit ~ 2.8** at (an aperture setting of) f/2.8.
(d) (*Film, TV, Tontechnik: Aufblende, Abblende*) fade.
(e) (*Naut*) deadlight.
(f) (*Archit*) blind window/arch *etc.*
(g) (*Sew*) trim.
(h) (*Verkleidung*) cover.
(i) (*Geol*) blende.

blenden [1] *vt* **(a)** (*lit, fig: bezaubern*) to dazzle; (*fig geh: täuschen auch*) to blind, to hoodwink. **(b)** (*blind machen*) to blind.
[2] *vi* **(a)** to be dazzling ♦ **~d weiß sein** to be shining *or* dazzling white. **(b)** (*fig: täuschen*) to dazzle.

Blenden|automatik *f* (*Phot*) automatic diaphragm.

blendend [1] *prp of* **blenden**.
[2] *adj* splendid; *Pianist, Schüler etc* brilliant; *Laune, Stimmung* sparkling ♦ **es geht mir ~** I feel wonderful; **sich ~ amüsieren** to have a splendid *or* wonderful time.

⚠ **blendendweiß** *adj attr* shining *or* dazzling white.

Blenden- (*Phot*): **~einstellung** *f* aperture (setting); (*Vorrichtung*) aperture control; **~öffnung** *f* aperture.

Blender(in *f***)** *m* **-s, -** phoney (*inf*).

Blend-: **b~frei** *adj* dazzle-free; *Glas, Fernsehschirm* non-reflective; **~laterne** *f* signalling lantern; **~rahmen** *m* **(a)** (*Art*) canvas-stretcher; **(b)** (*Build*) frame; **~schutz** *m* **(a)** protection against dazzle; **(b)** (*Vorrichtung*) anti-dazzle device; **~schutzgitter** *nt*, **~schutzzaun** *m* anti-dazzle barrier.

Blendung *f siehe vt* **(a)** dazzling; blinding. **(b)** blinding.

Blend-: **~werk** *nt* (*liter*) illusion; (*Vortäuschung*) deception; **hinter einem ~werk schöner Worte** *or* **aus schönen Worten** behind a screen of pretty words; **ein ~werk des Teufels** *or* **der Hölle** a trap set by the devil; **~zaun** *m* anti-dazzle barrier.

Blesse *f* **-, -n (a)** (*Fleck*) blaze. **(b)** (*Tier*) *horse with a blaze.*

blessieren* *vt* (*old: verwunden*) to wound.

Blessur *f* (*old*) wound.

bleu [blø:] *adj inv* (*Fashion*) light blue.

⚠ **bleuen** *vti siehe* **prügeln**.

blich (*old*) *pret of* **bleichen 2**.

▼ **Blick** *m* **-(e)s, -e (a)** (*das Blicken*) look; (*flüchtiger ~*) glance ♦ **auf den ersten ~** at first glance; **Liebe auf den ersten ~** love at first sight; **auf den zweiten ~** when one looks (at it) again, the second time one looks (at it); **mit einem ~** at a glance; **jds ~ (*dat*) ausweichen** to avoid sb's eye; **jds ~ erwidern** to return sb's gaze; **~e miteinander wechseln** to exchange glances; **jdn mit seinen ~en verschlingen** to devour sb with one's eyes; **er folgte ihr mit ~en** *or* **dem ~** his eyes followed her; **sie zog alle ~e auf sich** everybody's eyes were drawn to her; **einen ~ auf etw** (*acc*) **tun** *or* **werfen** to throw a glance at sth; **einen ~ hinter die Kulissen tun** *or* **werfen** (*fig*) to take a look behind the scenes; **sie würdigte ihn keines ~es** she did not deign to look at him; **jdm einen/keinen ~ schenken** to look at sb/not to spare sb a glance; **wenn ~e töten könnten!** if looks could kill!; *siehe* **durchbohren**.
(b) (*~richtung*) eyes *pl* ♦ **mein ~ fiel auf sein leeres Glas** my eye fell on his empty glass; **von hier aus fällt der ~ auf den Dom** from here one can see the cathedral; **den ~ heben** to raise one's eyes, to look up; **den ~ senken** to look down.
(c) (*Augenausdruck*) expression *or* look in one's eyes ♦ **den bösen ~ haben** to have the evil eye; **in ihrem ~ lag Verzweiflung** there was a look of despair in her eyes; **er musterte sie mit durchdringendem/finsterem ~** he looked at her penetratingly/darkly.
(d) (*Ausblick*) view ♦ **ein Zimmer mit ~ auf den Park** a room with a view of the park, a room overlooking the park; **dem ~ entschwinden** to disappear from view *or* sight, to go out of sight.
▼ **(e)** (*Verständnis*) **seinen ~ für etw schärfen** to increase one's awareness of sth; **einen klaren ~ haben** to see things clearly; **einen (guten) ~ für etw haben** to have an eye *or* a good eye for sth; **er hat keinen ~ dafür** he doesn't see *or* notice that sort of thing.

blickdicht *adj Strümpfe* opaque.

blicken *vi* (*auf + acc* at) to look; (*flüchtig ~*) to glance; (*fig: hervorsehen*) to peep ♦ **sich ~ lassen** to put in an appearance; **laß dich hier ja nicht mehr ~!** don't let me see you here again!, don't show your face here again!; **laß dich doch mal wieder ~!** why don't you drop in some time?; **danach hat er sich nie wieder ~ lassen** after that he was never seen again; **das läßt tief ~** that's very revealing.

Blick-: **~fang** *m* eye-catcher; **als ~fang** to catch the eye; **~feld** *nt* field of vision; **ein enges ~feld haben** (*fig*) to have narrow horizons; **ins ~feld (der Öffentlichkeit) rücken** to become the focus of (public) attention; **~kontakt** *m* visual contact; **~punkt** *m* **(a)** (*Zentrum der Aufmerksamkeit*) centre of one's field of vision; (*fig*) limelight; **im ~punkt der Öffentlichkeit stehen** to be in the public eye; **(b)** (*fig: Standpunkt*) viewpoint, point of view; **~richtung** *f* line of vision *or* sight; (*fig*) outlook; **in ~richtung (nach) links** looking to the left; **~wechsel** *m* exchange of glances; (*fig*) change in one's viewpoint; **~winkel** *m* angle of vision; (*fig*) viewpoint.

blind *adj* **(a)** (*lit, fig*) blind (*für* to); *Zufall* pure, sheer; *Alarm* false ◆ **~ für etw** *or* **in bezug auf etw** (*acc*) **sein** (*fig*) to be blind to sth; **ich bin doch nicht ~!** (*fig*) I'm not blind; **jdn ~ machen** (*lit, fig*) to blind sb, to make sb blind; **ein ~es Huhn findet auch mal ein Korn** (*Prov*) anyone can be lucky now and again; **jdm ~ gehorchen** to obey sb blindly; **~ landen** (*Aviat*) to make a blind landing, to land blind; **~ (Schach) spielen** to play (chess) blind; **~er Fleck** (*Anat*) blind spot; **in ~er Liebe** blinded with love; **ihr Blick war von** *or* **vor Tränen ~** she was blinded with tears; **~e Gewalt** brute force; **~er Eifer** blind enthusiasm; **~er Eifer schadet nur** (*Prov*) it's not a good thing to be overenthusiastic; **ein ~er Schuß** (*nicht scharf*) a shot with a blank cartridge; (*nicht gezielt*) a blind shot; **etw ~ herausgreifen** to take *or* pick sth at random; **~ in etw** (*acc*) **hineingreifen** to put one's hand in sth without looking.
(b) (*getrübt*) dull; *Spiegel, Glasscheibe* clouded; *Metall auch* tarnished; *Fleck* blind.
(c) (*verdeckt*) *Naht etc* invisible; (*vorgetäuscht*) (*Archit*) false; *Fenster* blind, false ◆ **ein ~er Passagier** a stowaway.

Blind-: ~band *m* (*Typ*) dummy; **~boden** *m* (*Archit*) subfloor.

Blinddarm *m* (*Anat*) caecum; (*inf: Wurmfortsatz*) appendix.

Blinddarm-: ~entzündung *f* appendicitis; **~operation** *f* append(ic)ectomy; **~reizung** *f* grumbling appendix.

Blindekuh(spiel *nt*) *f no art* blind man's buff.

Blinden-: ~anstalt *f* home for the blind; **~führer** *m* blind person's guide; **~hund** *m* guide-dog; **~schrift** *f* braille.

Blinde(r) *mf decl as adj* blind person/man/woman *etc* ◆ **die ~n** the blind; **die ~n und die Lahmen** (*Bibl*) the lame and the blind; **das sieht doch ein ~r (mit dem Krückstock)** (*hum inf*) any fool can see that; **unter den ~n ist der Einäugige König** (*Prov*) in the country of the blind the one-eyed man is king; **der ~ verlacht den Lahmen** (*Prov*) the pot calling the kettle black; **von etw reden, wie der ~ von der Farbe** (*prov*) to talk about sth when one knows nothing about it.

Blind-: ⚠**b~fliegen** *vi sep irreg aux sein* to fly blind; **~flug** *m* blind flight; (*das ~fliegen*) blind flying; **~gänger** *m* (*Mil*) dud (shot); (*inf: Versager*) dud (*inf*), dead loss (*inf*); **b~geboren** *adj attr* blind from birth; **~geborene(r)** *mf decl as adj* person blind from birth; **b~gläubig** *adj* credulous; **~heit** *f* (*lit, fig*) blindness; **jdn mit ~heit schlagen** (*Bibl, liter*) to strike sb blind; **wie mit ~heit geschlagen** (*fig*) as though blind; **mit ~heit geschlagen sein** (*fig*) to be blind; **~landung** *f* blind landing; **b~lings** *adv* blindly; **~material** *nt* (*Typ*) leads *pl*; **~schleiche** *f* slow-worm; ⚠**b~schreiben** *vti sep irreg* to touch-type; **~schreibverfahren** *nt* touch-typing; **~spiel** *nt* (*Chess*) blind game; ⚠**b~spielen** *vi sep* to play blind; **~start** *m* (*Aviat*) blind take-off; **b~wütend, b~wütig** *adj* in a blind rage.

blinken [1] *vi* **(a)** (*funkeln*) to gleam.
(b) (*Blinkzeichen geben*) (*Boje, Leuchtturm*) to flash; (*Aut*) to indicate.
[2] *vt Signal* to flash ◆ **SOS ~** to flash an SOS (signal); **rechts/links ~** to indicate right/left; **er hat mir geblinkt, daß ich überholen kann** he signalled for me to overtake.

Blinker *m* **-s, - (a)** (*Aut*) indicator, winker (*inf*). **(b)** (*Angeln*) spinner.

blinkern *vi* **(a)** (*inf: blinken*) to flash ◆ **er blinkerte mit den Augen** he blinked. **(b)** (*Angeln*) to use a spinner.

Blink-: ~feuer *nt* flashing light; **~leuchte** *f* indicator; **~licht** *nt* flashing light; (*inf: ~leuchte*) indicator, winker (*inf*); **~lichtanlage** *f* warning light system; **~zeichen** *nt* signal.

blinzeln, blinzen (*dated*) *vi* to blink; (*zwinkern*) to wink; (*geblendet*) to squint.

Blitz *m* **-es, -e (a)** (*das Blitzen*) lightning *no pl, no indef art*; (*~strahl*) flash of lightning; (*Lichtstrahl*) flash (of light) ◆ **vom ~ getroffen/erschlagen werden** to be struck by lightning; **wie vom ~ getroffen** (*fig*) thunderstruck; **aus ihren Augen schossen** *or* **sprühten ~e** her eyes flashed; **einschlagen wie ein ~** (*fig*) to be a bombshell; **die Nachricht schlug überall wie ein ~ ein** the news came as a bombshell to everyone; **wie ein ~ aus heiterem Himmel** (*fig*) like a bolt from the blue; **wie der ~** (*inf*) like lightning; **laufen wie ein geölter ~** (*inf*) to run like greased lightning; **die Antwort kam wie ein geölter ~** (*inf*) the answer came in a flash.
(b) (*Phot inf*) flash; (*Blitzlichtgerät auch*) flashgun.

Blitz- *in cpds* (*esp Mil: schnell*) lightning; **~ableiter** *m* lightning conductor; **jdn als ~ableiter benutzen** *or* **mißbrauchen** to vent one's anger on sb; **~aktion** *f* lightning operation; **~angriff** *m* (*Mil*) lightning attack; **der ~angriff auf London** the London Blitz; **b~artig** [1] *adj* lightning *attr*; [2] *adv* (*schnell*) *reagieren* like lightning; (*plötzlich*) *verschwinden* in a flash; **b~(e)blank** *adj* (*inf*) spick and span.

blitzen [1] *vi impers* **es blitzt** there is lightning; (*mehrmals auch*) there are flashes of lightning; **es blitzt und donnert** there is thunder and lightning; **hat es eben geblitzt?** was that (a flash of) lightning?; **es fing an zu ~** lightning began; **bei dir blitzt es** (*hum inf*) your slip is showing, Charlie's dead (*Brit inf*); **gleich blitzt es!** (*dial*) there'll be trouble.
[2] *vi* **(a)** (*strahlen*) to flash; (*Gold, Zähne*) to sparkle ◆ **vor Sauberkeit ~** to be sparkling clean; **Zorn blitzte aus seinen Augen** his eyes flashed with anger.
(b) (*inf: unbekleidet flitzen*) to streak.
(c) (*Phot inf*) to use (a) flash.
[3] *vt* (*Phot inf*) to take a flash photograph of.

Blitzer(in *f*) *m* **-s, -** (*inf*) streaker.

Blitzesschnelle *f* lightning speed ◆ **mit ~** at lightning speed; **in ~** in a flash.

Blitz-: ~gerät *nt* (*Phot*) flash(gun); **b~gescheit** *adj* (*inf*) brilliant; **~gespräch** *nt* special priority telephone call; **~kaffee** *m* (*Sw*) instant coffee; **~karriere** *f* rapid rise; **eine ~karriere machen** to rise rapidly; **~krieg** *m* blitzkrieg.

Blitzlicht *nt* (*Phot*) flash(light).

Blitzlicht-: ~birne *f* flashbulb; **~gewitter** *nt* popping of flashbulbs; **~würfel** *m* flash cube.

Blitz-: ~merker(in *f*) *m* **-s, -** (*inf: usu iro*) bright spark (*inf*); **~reise** *f* flying visit; **b~sauber** *adj* spick and span; **~schaden** *m* damage caused by lightning; **~schlag** *m* flash of lightning; **vom ~schlag getroffen** struck by lightning; **b~schnell** [1] *adj* lightning *attr*; [2] *adv* like lightning; (*plötzlich*) *verschwinden* in a flash; **~schutzanlage** *f* lightning protection equipment; **~sieg** *m* lightning victory; **~strahl** *m* flash of lightning; **~umfrage** *f* quick poll; **~würfel** *m* (*Phot*) flashcube.

Blizzard ['blɪzət] *m* **-s, -s** blizzard.

Bloch *m or nt* **-(e)s, -e** *or* **¨-er** (*S Ger, Aus*) log.

Block *m* **-(e)s, ¨-e (a)** block (*von, aus* of); (*von Seife, Schokolade*) bar.
(b) *pl auch* **-s** (*Häuser~, Haus*) block.
(c) *pl auch* **-s** (*Papier~*) pad; (*Briefmarken~*) block; (*von Fahrkarten*) book.
(d) *pl* **-s** (*Rail*) block.
(e) (*Zusammengefaßtes*) block ◆ **etw im ~ kaufen** to buy sth in bulk.
(f) *pl auch* **-s** (*Pol*) (*Staaten~*) bloc; (*Fraktion*) faction.
(g) (*NS*) *smallest organizational unit of Nazi party based on a block of houses.*
(h) (*Sport*) wall.
(i) *pl auch* **-s** (*inf: Blockierung*) (mental) block.
(j) (*Folter~*) stocks *pl*.
(k) (*Comput*) block.

Blockade *f* (*Absperrung*) blockade ◆ **eine ~ brechen** to run *or* break a blockade.

Blockadebrecher *m* blockade runner.

Block-: ~bau *m* **(a)** (*Gebäude*) log cabin; **(b)** (*auch* **~bauweise**) method of building houses from logs; **~bildung** *f* (*Pol*) formation of blocs/factions; **~buchstabe** *m* block letter *or* capital.

blocken *vti* **(a)** (*Rail*) to block. **(b)** (*Hunt*) to perch. **(c)** (*abfangen*) to block, to stop. **(d)** (*Sport: sperren*) to block. **(e)** (*dial: bohnern*) to polish. **(f)** (*Comput*) to block.

Blocker *m* **-s, -** (*S Ger*) *siehe* **Blocher.**

Block-: ~flöte *f* recorder; **b~frei** *adj* non-aligned; **~freiheit** *f* non-alignment; **~haus** *nt* log cabin; **~heizkraftwerk** *nt* block heating and generating plant; **~hütte** *f* log cabin.

blockieren* [1] *vt* **(a)** (*sperren, hemmen*) to block; *Verkehr, Verhandlung* to obstruct; *Flugverkehr* to halt; *Gesetz* to block the passage of; *Rad, Lenkung* to lock. **(b)** (*mit Blockade belegen*) to blockade.
[2] *vi* to jam; (*Bremsen, Rad etc*) to lock.

Blockierung *f siehe vt* blocking; obstruction; locking; blockade.

Block-: ~leiter *m* (*NS*) block leader; **~malz** *nt type of cough sweet*; **~partei** *f* (*esp DDR*) party in a faction; **~politik** *f* joint policy; **~satz** *m* (*Typ*) justification; **~schokolade** *f, no pl* cooking chocolate; **~schrift** *f* block capitals *pl or* letters *pl*; **~staat** *m* aligned state; **~station, ~stelle** *f* (*Rail*) block signal; **~stunde** *f* (*Sch*) double period; **~system** *nt* **(a)** (*Rail*) block system; **(b)** (*Pol*) system of factions; **~unterricht** *m* (*Sch*) teaching by topics; **~wart** *m* (*NS*) block leader; **~werk** *nt* (*Rail*) block signal.

blöd(e) *adj* (*inf*) **(a)** (*dumm*) silly, stupid, idiotic; *Wetter* terrible; *Gefühl* funny ◆ **das B~e daran ist, daß ...** the silly *etc* thing about it is that ... **(b)** (*Med: schwachsinnig*) imbecilic. **(c)** (*Sw: schüchtern*) shy. **(d)** (*S Ger: abgescheuert*) worn.

Blödel *m* **-s, -** (*inf*) stupid fool (*inf*) *or* idiot (*inf*); (*ungeschickter Mensch*) clumsy fool (*inf*) *or* idiot (*inf*).

Blödelei *f* (*inf*) (*Albernheit*) messing (*inf*) *or* fooling about *or* around; (*Witz*) joke; (*dumme Streiche*) pranks *pl* ◆ **laß die ~** stop messing (*inf*) *or* fooling about.

blödeln *vi* (*inf*) to mess (*inf*) *or* fool about *or* around; (*Witze machen*) to make jokes ◆ **mit jdm ~** to have fun with sb.

blöderweise *adv* (*inf*) stupidly.

Blödhammel *m* (*sl*) bloody fool (*Brit sl*), mother (*US sl*).

Blödheit *f* **(a)** (*Dummheit*) stupidity. **(b)** (*blödes Verhalten*) stupid thing; (*alberne Bemerkung*) silly *or* stupid remark ◆ **es ist eine ~, das zu machen** it's stupid to do that. **(c)** (*Med: Schwachsinnigkeit*) imbecility. **(d)** (*Sw: Schüchternheit*) shyness.

Blödian *m* **-(e)s, -e** (*inf*) idiot.

Blödmann *m, pl* **-männer** (*inf*) stupid fool (*inf*).

Blödsinn *m, no pl* **(a)** (*Unsinn*) nonsense, rubbish; (*Unfug*) stupid tricks *pl* ◆ **so ein ~** what nonsense *or* rubbish/how stupid; **das ist doch ~** that's nonsense *or* rubbish/stupid; **~ machen** to fool *or* mess about; **wer hat diesen ~ hier gemacht?** what fool did this?; **mach keinen ~** don't fool *or* mess about.
(b) (*Schwachsinn*) imbecility.

blödsinnig *adj* **(a)** stupid, idiotic. **(b)** (*Med*) imbecilic.

Blödsinnigkeit *f* (*inf*) **(a)** (*Eigenschaft*) stupidity, idiocy. **(b)** (*Verhalten*) stupid thing ◆ **laß diese ~en** stop being stupid.

blöken *vi* (*Schaf*) to bleat; (*geh: Rinder*) to low.

blond *adj* **(a)** (*blondhaarig*) fair(-haired); (*bei Frauen auch*) blonde; (*bei Männern, Menschenrasse auch*) blond ◆ **~es Gift** (*hum inf*) blonde bombshell (*inf*). **(b)** (*hum inf: hellfarbig*) light-coloured; *Bier* light, pale.

Blond *nt* **-s,** *no pl* blonde; blond.

Blonde(s) *nt decl as adj* (*inf: Bier*) lager.

Blond-: ⚠**b~gefärbt** *adj attr* dyed blonde/blond; ⚠**b~gelockt** *adj* with fair curly hair; *Haar* fair curly *attr*; **b~gelockt sein** to have fair curly hair; **b~haarig** *adj* fair-haired, blonde/blond.

blondieren* *vt* to bleach ◆ **blondiert** *Haare* bleached.

Blondierung *f* **(a)** (*Vorgang*) bleaching. **(b)** (*Zustand*) bleachedness.

Blondine *f* blonde.

Blond-: **~kopf** *m* **(a)** (*Haare*) fair *or* blonde/blond hair *or* head; **(b)** (*Mensch*) fair-haired *or* blonde/blond person/girl/boy *etc*; **b~lockig** *adj* with fair *or* blonde/blond curly hair; **~schopf** *m siehe* **~kopf.**

bloß [1] *adj* **(a)** (*unbedeckt*) bare ◆ **etw auf der ~en Haut tragen** to wear sth without anything on underneath; **mit ~en Füßen** bare-footed, barefoot; **mit der ~en Hand** with one's bare hand; *siehe* **Oberkörper**.
(b) *attr* (*alleinig*) mere; *Neid, Dummheit* sheer; (*allein schon auch*) *Gedanke, Anblick* very ◆ **im ~en Hemd dastehen** to stand there with nothing on over one's shirt/vest; **er kam mit dem ~en Schrecken davon** he got off with no more than a fright.
[2] *adv* only ◆ **ich möchte es schon machen, ~ weiß ich nicht wie** I'd like to but *or* only I don't know how; **wie kann so etwas ~ geschehen?** how on earth can something like that happen?; **was er ~ hat?** what on earth *or* whatever is wrong with him?; **tu das ~ nicht wieder!** don't you dare do that again; **geh mir ~ aus dem Weg** just get out of my way; **nicht ~ ..., sondern auch ...** not only ... but also ...

Blöße *f* **-, -n** **(a)** (*geh*) (*Unbedecktheit*) bareness; (*Nacktheit*) nakedness. **(b)** (*im Wald*) clearing. **(c)** (*Sport*) opening ◆ **jdm eine ~ bieten** (*lit*) to drop one's guard; (*fig*) to show sb one's ignorance; **sich** (*dat*) **eine ~ geben** (*fig*) to reveal *or* show one's ignorance.

Bloß-: **b~legen** *vt sep* to uncover; (*ausgraben auch, Med*) to expose; (*fig*) *Geheimnis* to reveal; *Hintergründe* to bring to light; **b~liegen** *vi sep irreg aux sein* to be *or* lie uncovered; (*Ausgegrabenes auch, Med*) to be exposed; (*fig geh: Geheimnis*) to be revealed; **b~stellen** *sep* [1] *vt jdn* to show up; *Lügner, Betrüger* to unmask, to expose; [2] *vr* to show oneself up; to expose oneself; **~stellung** *f siehe vt* showing up; unmasking, exposing; **b~strampeln** *vr sep* to kick one's covers off.

Blouson [blu'zõ:] *m or nt* **-(s), -s** blouson, bomber jacket.

Blowout ['blouaut] *m* **-s, -s** (*von Bohrinsel etc*) blowout.

blubbern *vi* (*inf*) to bubble; (*dial: undeutlich sprechen*) to gabble; (*inf: Blödsinn reden*) to waffle (*inf*).

Blücher *m*: **er geht ran wie ~** (*inf*) he doesn't hang about (*inf*).

Blue jeans ['blu:dʒi:ns] *pl* (pair of) (blue) jeans *or* denims.

Blues [blu:s] *m* **-, -** blues *sing or pl* ◆ **(einen) ~ tanzen** to smooch (*inf*).

Bluff [blʊf, (*dated*) blœf] *m* **-(e)s, -s** bluff.

bluffen ['blʊfn, (*dated*) 'blœfn] *vti* to bluff.

blühen [1] *vi* **(a)** (*Blume*) to be in flower *or* bloom, to bloom, to flower; (*Bäume*) to be in blossom, to blossom; (*Garten, Wiese*) to be full of flowers; (*fig: gedeihen*) to flourish, to thrive ◆ **weiß ~** to have *or* bear white flowers.
(b) (*inf: bevorstehen*) to be in store (*jdm* for sb) ◆ **... dann blüht dir aber was ...** then you'll be in for it (*inf*); **das kann mir auch noch ~** that may happen to me too.
[2] *vi impers* **es blüht** there are flowers.

blühend *adj Baum* blossoming; *Pflanze* blooming; *Frau, Aussehen* radiant; *Gesichtsfarbe, Gesundheit* glowing; *Garten, Wiese* full of flowers; (*fig*) *Geschäft, Stadt etc* flourishing, thriving; *Unsinn* absolute; *Phantasie* vivid, lively ◆ **im ~en Alter von 18 Jahren** at the early age of 18; **wie das ~e Leben** *or* **~ aussehen** to look the very picture of health.

Blümchen *nt dim of* **Blume.**

Blümchenkaffee *m* (*hum*) weak coffee.

Blume *f* **-, -n** **(a)** (*Blüte, Pflanze*) flower; (*Topfblume*) (flowering) pot plant; (*poet: Frau*) pearl ◆ **vielen Dank für die ~n** (*iro*) thanks for nothing, thank you very much (*iro*); **jdm etw durch die ~ sagen/zu verstehen geben** to say/put sth in a roundabout way to sb.
(b) (*von Wein, Weinbrand*) bouquet; (*von Bier*) head.
(c) (*Hunt*) (*von Kaninchen, Hasen*) scut; (*von Fuchs*) tag.

Blumen- *in cpds* flower; **~bank** *f* (*am Fenster*) windowsill; (*~ständer*) flower stand; **~beet** *nt* flowerbed; **~binder(in *f*)** *m* florist; **~blatt** *nt* petal; **~bukett** *nt* (*old*) bouquet (of flowers); **~draht** *m* florist's wire; **~erde** *f* potting compost; **~fenster** *nt* window full of flowers; (*Archit*) *window for keeping and displaying flowers and pot plants*; **~flor** *m* (*liter*) abundance of flowers; **~frau** *f* flower woman; **~geschäft** *nt* florist's, flower shop; **b~geschmückt** *adj* adorned with flowers; **~gruß** *m* **jdm einen ~gruß übermitteln** to send sb flowers; **~händler** *m* florist; **~igel** *m* pinholder; **~kasten** *m* window box; **~kind** *nt* (*inf*) flower child, hippie; **~kinder** flower children *or* people, hippies; **~kohl** *m* **-s,** *no pl* cauliflower; **~kohlohr** *nt* (*inf*) cauliflower ear; **~korso** *m* flower carnival; **~kranz** *m* floral wreath; **~kübel** *m* flower tub; **~mädchen** *nt* flower girl; **~meer** *nt* sea of flowers; **~muster** *nt* floral pattern; **~pracht** *f* brilliant display of flowers; **~rabatte** *f* herbaceous border; **b~reich** *adj* full of flowers, flowery; (*fig*) *Stil, Sprache etc* flowery, ornate; **~sprache** *f* language of flowers; **~ständer** *m* flower stand; **~stock** *m* flowering plant; **~strauß** *m* bouquet *or* bunch of flowers; **~stück** *nt* (*Art*) flower painting; **~teppich** *m* carpet of flowers; **~topf** *m* flowerpot; (*Pflanze*) flowering plant; **damit ist kein ~topf zu gewinnen** (*inf*) that's nothing to write home about (*inf*); **~vase** *f* (flower) vase; **~zucht** *f* growing of flowers, floriculture (*form*); **~züchter** *m* flower-grower, floriculturist (*form*); **~zwiebel** *f* bulb.

blümerant *adj Gefühl* queer ◆ **jdm wird es ~** sb feels queer.

blumig *adj Parfüm* flowery; *Wein* with a flowery bouquet; (*fig*) *Stil, Sprache auch* ornate.

Blüschen ['bly:sçən] *nt dim of* **Bluse.**

Bluse *f* **-, -n** blouse ◆ **ganz schön was in** *or* **unter der ~ haben** (*sl*) to have a nice pair (*sl*); **jdm an die ~ gehen** (*sl*) to touch sb up (*sl*).

Blüse *f* **-, -n** (*Naut*) flare.

blusig *adj* bloused, blouse *attr.*

Blut *nt* **-(e)s,** *no pl* (*lit, fig*) blood ◆ **er lag in seinem ~** he lay in a pool of blood; **es ist viel ~ vergossen worden** *or* **geflossen** there was a lot of bloodshed; **nach ~ lechzen** *or* **dürsten** to thirst for blood; **er kann kein ~ sehen** he can't stand the sight of blood; **~ lecken** (*lit: Hund*) to taste blood; (*fig*) to develop a taste *or* liking for it; **etw mit seinem ~ besiegeln** to lay down one's life for sth; **böses ~ machen** *or* **schaffen** *or* **geben** to cause bad blood *or* ill feeling; **jdm steigt das ~ in den Kopf** the blood rushes to sb's head; **ihnen gefror** *or* **stockte** *or* **gerann das ~ in den Adern** their blood froze; **vor Scham/Zorn schoß ihr das ~ ins Gesicht** she blushed with shame/went red with anger; **alles ~ wich aus ihrem Gesicht** she went deathly pale; **heißes** *or* **feuriges ~ haben** to be hot-blooded; **kaltes ~ bewahren** to remain unmoved; **kalten ~es** cold-bloodedly; **(nur) ruhig ~** keep your shirt on (*inf*); **jdn bis aufs ~ hassen** to loathe (and detest) sb; **jdn/sich bis aufs ~ bekämpfen** to fight sb/fight bitterly; **ein junges ~** (*liter*) a young blood (*dated*) *or* (*Mädchen*) thing; **frisches ~** (*fig*) new blood; **~ und Eisen** blood and iron; **~ und Boden** (*NS*) blood and soil, *idea that political stability and power depend on unification of race and territory*; **~ und Wasser schwitzen** (*inf*) to sweat blood; **die Stimme des ~es** the call of the blood; **das liegt mir/ihm** *etc* **im ~** that's in my/his *etc* blood; **es geht (einem) ins ~** it gets into your blood.

Blut-: **~acker** *m* (*Bibl*) field of blood; **~ader** *f* vein; **~algen** *pl* red algae *pl*; **~alkohol(gehalt)** *m* blood alcohol level *or* content; **~andrang** *m* congestion; **~apfelsine** *f* blood orange; **b~arm** *adj* **(a)** ['blu:t-] (*Med*) anaemic; (*fig auch*) colourless; **(b)** [-'arm] (*liter*) very poor, penniless; **~armut** *f* (*Med*) anaemia; **~auffrischung** *f* blood replacement; **~austausch** *m* (*Med*) exchange transfusion; **~bad** *nt* bloodbath; **~bahn** *f* bloodstream; **~bank** *f* blood bank; **~bann** *m* power over life and death; **b~befleckt** *adj* bloodstained; **b~beschmiert** *adj* smeared with blood; **~bild** *nt* blood count; ⚠**b~bildend** *adj* haematinic (*spec*); *Nahrung* full of iron; **~bildung** *f* formation of blood, blood formation; **~blase** *f* blood blister; **~buche** *f* copper beech; **~druck** *m* blood pressure; **b~drucksenkend** *adj* hypotensive; *Mittel* anti-hypertensive; **~durst** *m* (*geh*) blood lust; **b~dürstig** *adj* (*geh*) bloodthirsty.

Blüte *f* **-, -n** **(a)** (*Bot: Pflanzenteil*) (*von Blume*) flower, bloom; (*von Baum*) blossom ◆ **~n treiben** to be in flower *or* bloom, to be flowering *or* blooming; (*Baum*) to be blossoming *or* in blossom; **merkwürdige ~n treiben** to produce strange effects; (*Phantasie, Angst*) to produce strange fancies; **eine ~ seiner Phantasie** a figment of his imagination.
(b) (*das Blühen, Blütezeit*) **zur ~ des Klees/der Kirschbäume** when the clover is in flower *or* bloom/cherry trees are blossoming *or* in blossom; **die ~ beginnt** the flowers/trees are coming into bloom/blossom; **die ~ der Apfelbäume ist vorüber** the apple trees are no longer blossoming *or* in blossom; **in (voller) ~ stehen** to be in (full) flower/blossom; (*Kultur, Geschäft*) to be flourishing; **sich zur vollen ~ entfalten** to come into full flower; (*Mädchen, Kultur*) to blossom; **seine ~ erreichen** *or* **erleben** (*Kultur etc*) to reach its peak; **ein Zeitalter kultureller ~** an age of cultural ascendency; **in der ~ seiner Jahre** in his prime, in the prime of his life; **eine neue ~ erleben** to undergo a revival.
(c) (*Med: Ausschlag*) rash, efflorescence (*spec*).
(d) (*inf: gefälschte Note*) dud (*inf*).

Blut|egel *m* leech.

bluten *vi* to bleed (*an +dat, aus* from) ◆ **mir blutet das Herz** my heart bleeds; **~den Herzens** with heavy heart; **für etw (schwer) ~** (*inf*) to cough up a lot of money for sth (*inf*).

Blüten-: **~blatt** *nt* petal; **~honig** *m* honey (*made from flowers*); **~kelch** *m* calyx; **~knospe** *f* flower bud; **b~los** *adj* non-flowering; **~stand** *m* inflorescence; **~staub** *m* pollen.

Blut|entnahme *f* taking of a blood sample.

Blütenzweig *m* flowering twig.

Bluter *m* **-s, -** (*Med*) haemophiliac.

⚠**Blut|erguß** *m* haematoma (*spec*); (*blauer Fleck*) bruise.

Bluterkrankheit *f* haemophilia.

Blütezeit *f* **(a)** **während der ~ der Kirschbäume** while the cherries were in blossom; **die ~ der Obstbäume ist vorbei** the fruit trees are no longer in blossom. **(b)** (*fig*) heyday; (*von Mensch*) prime.

Blut-: **~farbstoff** *m* haemoglobin; **~faserstoff** *m* fibrin; **~fehde** *f* blood feud; **~fleck** *m* bloodstain; **~flüssigkeit** *f siehe* **~plasma**; **~gefäß** *nt* blood vessel; **~geld** *nt* blood money; **~gerinnsel** *nt* blood clot; **~gerinnung** *f* clotting of the blood; **~gerüst** *nt* (*liter*) scaffold; **b~getränkt** *adj* blood-soaked, soaked in blood; **~gier** *f* blood lust; **b~gierig** *adj* bloodthirsty.

Blutgruppe *f* blood group ◆ **die ~ O haben** to be blood group O; **jds ~ bestimmen** to type *or* group sb's blood.

Blutgruppen-: **~bestimmung** *f* blood-typing; **~untersuchung** *f* (*Jur*) blood test (*to determine paternity*).

Blut-: **~hochdruck** *m* high blood pressure; **~hochzeit** *f siehe* **Bartholomäusnacht**; **~hund** *m* (*lit, fig*) bloodhound; **~husten** *m* haemoptysis (*spec*); **er hat ~husten** he is coughing (up) blood.

blutig *adj* **(a)** (*lit, fig*) bloody ◆ **jdn ~ schlagen** to beat sb to a pulp; **sich ~ machen** to get blood on oneself; **~e Tränen weinen** (*liter*) to shed bitter tears. **(b)** (*inf*) *Anfänger* absolute; *Ernst* deadly.

⚠: for details of spelling reform, see supplement

-blütig *adj suf* (a) (*Tier*) -blooded. (b) (*Pflanze*) -blossomed.

Blut-: b~jung *adj* very young; **~konserve** *f* unit *or* pint of stored blood; **~kontakt** *m* contact through blood; **~körperchen** *nt* blood corpuscle; **~krankheit** *f* blood disease; **~krebs** *m* leukaemia; **~kreislauf** *m* blood circulation; **~lache** *f* pool of blood; **b~leer** *adj* bloodless; **~leere** *f, no pl* lack of blood; **b~los** *adj* bloodless; (*fig*) *Stil* colourless, anaemic; **~opfer** *nt* (a) (*Opferung*) blood sacrifice; (b) (*Geopferter*) victim; (*fig*) casualty; **~-orange** *f* blood orange; ⚠**~paß** *m card giving blood group etc*; **~pfropf** *m* clot of blood; **~plasma** *nt* blood plasma; **~plättchen** *nt* platelet; **~probe** *f* blood test; **~rache** *f* blood feud; **~rausch** *m* frenzy; **b~reinigend** *adj* blood-cleansing, depurative (*spec*); **~reinigung** *f* cleansing of the blood; **b~rot** *adj* (*liter*) blood-red; **b~rünstig** *adj* bloodthirsty; **~sauger** *m* (*lit, fig*) bloodsucker; (*Vampir*) vampire.

Bluts-: ~bande *pl* (*geh*) bonds *or* ties of blood *pl*; **~bruder** *m* blood brother; **~brüderschaft** *f* blood brotherhood.

Blut-: ~schande *f* incest; **~schuld** *f* (*liter*) blood guilt; **eine ~schuld auf sich** (*acc*) **laden** to sully one's hands with blood (*liter*); **~schwamm** *m* (*Med*) strawberry mark; **~senkung** *f* (*Med*) sedimentation of the blood; **eine ~senkung machen** to test the sedimentation rate of the blood; **~serum** *nt* blood serum; **~spende** *f* unit *or* pint of blood (*given by a donor*); **~spenden** *nt* giving blood *no art*; **zum ~spenden aufrufen** to appeal for blood donors; **~spender** *m* blood donor; **~spur** *f* trail of blood; **~spuren** traces of blood; **~stauung** *f* congestion; **~stein** *m* haematite; **b~stillend** *adj* styptic; **~strahl** *m* stream of blood; **~strom** *m* bloodstream; (*aus Wunde*) stream of blood.

Blutstropfen ['blu:ts-] *m* drop of blood.

Blut-: ~stuhl *m* (*Med*) blood in the faeces; **~sturz** *m* haemorrhage.

Bluts-: b~verwandt *adj* related by blood; **~verwandte(r)** *mf* blood relation *or* relative; **~verwandtschaft** *f* blood relationship.

blutt *adj* (*Sw: nackt*) bare.

Blut-: ~tat *f* bloody deed; **~transfusion** *f* blood transfusion; **b~triefend** *adj attr* bloody, dripping with blood; **b~überströmt** *adj* streaming with blood; **~übertragung** *f* blood transfusion.

Blutung *f* bleeding *no pl*; (*starke*) haemorrhage; (*monatliche*) period ◆ **eine/die ~ stillen** to stop the bleeding.

Blut-: b~unterlaufen *adj* suffused with blood; *Augen* bloodshot; **~untersuchung** *f* blood test; **~vergießen** *nt* **-s,** *no pl* bloodshed *no indef art*; **~vergiftung** *f* blood-poisoning *no indef art*; **~verlust** *m* loss of blood; **b~verschmiert** *adj* bloody, smeared with blood; **b~voll** *adj* vivid, lively; **~wallung** *f* congestion; (*bei Frau*) hot flush; **~wäsche** *f* (*Med*) detoxification of the blood; **~wasser** *nt siehe* **~serum; ~wurst** *f* blutwurst (*US*), blood sausage; (*zum Warmmachen*) black pudding (*Brit*); **~zelle** *f* blood corpuscle *or* cell; **~zeuge** *m* (*old*) martyr; **~zirkulation** *f* blood circulation; **~zoll** *m* (*geh*) toll (of lives); **~zucker** *m* blood sugar; **~zuckerspiegel** *m* blood sugar level; **~zufuhr** *f* blood supply.

BLZ [be:|ɛl'tsɛt] *f* **-, -s** *abbr of* **Bankleitzahl.**

BMX-Rad *nt* BMX bike.

BND [be:|ɛn'de:] *m* **-s** *or* **-** *abbr of* **Bundesnachrichtendienst.**

Bö *f* **-, -en** gust (of wind); (*stärker, mit Regen*) squall.

Boa *f* **-, -s** (*Schlange, Schal*) boa.

Bob *m* **-s, -s** bob(sleigh).

Bob-: ~bahn *f* bob(sleigh) run; **~fahrer** *m* bobber.

Boccia ['bɔtʃa] *nt* **-(s)** *or f* **-,** *no pl* bowls *sing*.

Bock¹ *m* **-(e)s, ¨-e** (a) (*Reh~, Kaninchen~*) buck; (*Schafs~*) ram; (*Ziegen~*) he-goat, billy-goat ◆ **alter ~** (*inf*) old goat (*inf*); **sturer/geiler ~** (*inf*) stubborn old devil (*inf*)/randy (*Brit*) *or* horny old goat (*inf*); **wie ein ~ stinken** to smell like a pig (*inf*), to stink to high heaven (*inf*); **die ¨~e von den Schafen scheiden** *or* **trennen** (*fig*) to separate the sheep from the goats; **den ~ zum Gärtner machen** (*fig*) to be asking for trouble; **ihn stößt der ~** (*inf*) he's (just) being awkward *or* difficult; **einen ~ schießen** (*fig inf*) to (make a) boob (*inf*); (*Fauxpas auch*) to drop a clanger (*inf*).

(b) (*inf: Trotz*) stubbornness ◆ **(s)einen ~ haben** to be awkward *or* difficult, to play up (*inf*).

(c) (*Gestell*) stand; (*Stützgerät*) support; (*für Auto*) ramp; (*aus Holzbalken, mit Beinen*) trestle; (*Säge~*) sawhorse.

(d) (*Sport*) vaulting horse ◆ **den** *or* **einen ~ machen** to bend over (*for someone to vault over*).

(e) (*Schemel*) (high) stool.

(f) (*Kutsch~*) box (seat).

(g) (*Ramme*) (battering) ram.

(h) (*sl: Lust, Spaß*) **null ~!** couldn't be buggered! (*sl*); **¨~e** *or* **(einen) ~ auf etw** (*acc*) **haben** to fancy sth (*inf*); **¨~e** *or* **(einen) ~ haben, etw zu tun** to fancy doing sth; **ich hab' keinen** *or* **null ~, das zu tun** I couldn't be buggered doing that (*sl*); **null ~ auf nichts** pissed off with everything (*sl*).

Bock² *nt* **-s, -** *siehe* **Bockbier.**

Bock-: b~beinig *adj* (*inf*) contrary, awkward; **~bier** *nt* bock (beer) (*type of strong beer*).

bocken *vi* (a) (*Zugtier etc*) to refuse to move; (*nicht springen wollen: Pferd*) to refuse; (*fig inf: Auto, Motor etc*) to refuse to start/go properly ◆ **vor einer Hürde ~** to refuse a jump. (b) (*inf: trotzen*) to play *or* act up (*inf*).

bockig *adj* (*inf*) stubborn, awkward.

Bock-: ~leiter *f* stepladder; **~mist** *m* (*inf*) (*dummes Gerede*) bullshit (*sl*); **~mist machen** to make a balls-up (*sl*).

Bocks-: ~beutel *m wide, rounded bottle containing Franconian wine*; **~horn** *nt*: **jdn ins ~horn jagen** to put the wind up sb (*inf*); **sich von jdm ins ~horn jagen lassen** to let sb upset one; **sie ließ sich nicht ins ~horn jagen** she didn't let herself get into a state.

Bock-: ~springen *nt* **-s** leapfrog; (*Sport*) vaulting; **~springen machen** to play leapfrog; **~sprung** *m* (a) (*Sprung über Menschen*) leapfrog; (*Sport*) vault; (b) (*ungeschickter Sprung*) leap, bound; **~wurst** *f* bockwurst (*type of sausage*).

Boden *m* **-s, ¨** (a) (*Erde, Grundfläche*) ground; (*Erdreich auch*) soil; (*Fuß~*) floor; (*Grundbesitz*) land; (*no pl: Terrain*) soil ◆ **auf spanischem ~** on Spanish soil; **zu ~ fallen** to fall to the ground; **jdn zu ~ schlagen** *or* **strecken** to knock sb down, to floor sb; **festen ~ unter den Füßen haben, auf festem ~ sein** to be *or* stand on firm ground, to be on terra firma; (*fig*) (*finanziell abgesichert*) to be secure; (*fundierte Argumente haben*) to be on firm ground; **den ~ unter den Füßen verlieren** (*lit*) to lose one's footing; (*fig: in Diskussion*) to get out of one's depth; **der ~ brannte ihm unter den Füßen, ihm wurde der ~ (unter den Füßen) zu heiß** (*fig*) things were getting too hot for him; **jdm den ~ unter den Füßen wegziehen** (*fig*) to cut the ground from under sb's feet; **ich hätte (vor Scham) im ~ versinken können** (*fig*) I was so ashamed that I wished the ground would (open and) swallow me up; **am ~ zerstört sein** (*inf*) to be shattered (*fig inf*); **(an) ~ gewinnen/verlieren** (*fig*) to gain/lose ground; **~ gutmachen** *or* **wettmachen** (*fig*) to make up ground, to catch up; **etw aus dem ~ stampfen** (*fig*) to conjure sth up out of nothing; *Häuser auch* to build overnight; **er stand wie aus dem ~ gewachsen vor mir** he appeared in front of me as if by magic; **auf fruchtbaren ~ fallen** (*fig*) to fall on fertile ground; **jdm/einer Sache den ~ bereiten** (*fig*) to prepare the ground for sb/sth; *siehe* **Faß, Grund, schießen.**

(b) (*unterste Fläche*) (*von Behälter*) bottom; (*von Meer auch*) seabed; (*von Hose*) seat; (*Torten~*) base; *siehe* **doppelt.**

(c) (*Raum*) (*Dach~, Heu~*) loft; (*Trocken~*) (*für Getreide*) drying floor/room; (*für Wäsche*) drying room.

(d) (*fig: Grundlage*) **auf dem ~ der Wissenschaft/Tatsachen/Wirklichkeit stehen** to base oneself on scientific fact/on fact/on reality; (*Behauptung*) to be based *or* founded on scientific fact/on fact/on reality; **sie wurde hart auf den ~ der Wirklichkeit zurückgeholt** she was brought down to earth with a bump; **auf dem ~ der Tatsachen bleiben** to stick to the facts; **den ~ der Tatsachen verlassen** to go into the realm of fantasy; **sich auf unsicherem ~ bewegen** to be on shaky ground; **er steht auf dem ~ des Gesetzes** (*nicht ungesetzlich*) he is within the law; (*hat Gesetz hinter sich*) he has the backing of the law; **einem Gerücht den ~ entziehen** to knock the bottom out of a rumour, to show a rumour to be unfounded.

Boden-: ~abwehr *f* ground defence; **~belag** *m* floor covering; **~beschaffenheit** *f* condition of the ground; (*von Acker etc*) condition of the soil; **~erhebung** *f* elevation; **~ertrag** *m* (*Agr*) crop yield; **~feuchtigkeit** *f* (*Hort, Agr*) soil *or* ground humidity; (*im Haus*) rising damp; **~fläche** *f* (*Agr*) area of land; (*von Zimmer*) floor space *or* area; **~frost** *m* ground frost; **b~gestützt** *adj Flugkörper* ground-launched; **~gruppe** *f* (*Aut*) substructure, floorpan; **~haftung** *f* (*Aut*) road holding *no indef art*; **~haltung** *f* (*Agr: von Hühnern etc*) *keeping (of hens etc) in free-range conditions* ◆ **„aus ~haltung"** "free-range"; **~heizung** *f* underfloor (central) heating; **~kammer** *f* attic; **~kontrolle** *f* (*Space*) ground control; **~leger** *m* **-s, -** floor layer; **b~los** *adj* bottomless; (*inf: unerhört*) indescribable, incredible; **ins ~lose fallen** to fall into an abyss; **~nebel** *m* ground mist; **~nutzung** *f* land utilization; **~organisation** *f* (*Aviat*) ground organization; **~personal** *nt* (*Aviat*) ground personnel *pl or* staff *pl*; **~reform** *f* land *or* agrarian reform; **~satz** *m* sediment; (*von Kaffee*) grounds *pl*, dregs *pl*; **~schätze** *pl* mineral resources *pl*; **~schicht** *f* layer of soil; (*Geol*) stratum; **~see** *m*: **der ~see** Lake Constance; **~senke** *f* depression, hollow; **~sicht** *f* (*Aviat*) ground visibility; **~spekulation** *f* land speculation; **b~ständig** *adj* (*einheimisch*) native (*in +dat* to); (*lang ansässig*) long-established; (*fig: mit dem Boden verwurzelt*) rooted in the soil; **~station** *f* (*Space*) ground station; **~streitkräfte** *pl* ground forces *pl*; **~turnen** *nt* floor exercises *pl*; **~übung** *f* (*Sport*) floor exercise; **~vase** *f* floor vase; **~welle** *f* (a) bump; (b) (*Rad*) ground wave.

Bodmerei *f* (*Naut*) bottomry.

Body ['bɔdɪ] *m* **-, Bodies** body stocking *or* suit.

Bodybuilder(in *f*) *m* ['bɔdibɪldɐ, -ərɪn] bodybuilder.

Bodybuilding ['bɔdibɪldɪŋ] *nt* **-s,** *no pl* bodybuilding ◆ **~ machen** to do bodybuilding exercises.

Bodycheck ['bɔditʃɛk] *m* **-s, -s** (*Sport*) bodycheck.

Bodysuit ['bɔdɪsu:t] *m* **-, -s** *siehe* **Body.**

Böe *f* **-, -n** *siehe* **Bö.**

bog *pret of* **biegen.**

Bogen *m* **-s, -** *or* **¨** (a) (*gekrümmte Linie*) curve; (*Kurve*) bend; (*Umweg*) detour; (*Math*) arc; (*Mus*) (*zwischen zwei Noten gleicher Höhe*) tie; (*zur Bindung von verschiedenen Noten*) slur (mark); (*Ski*) turn ◆ **einen ~ fahren** (*Ski*) to do *or* execute a turn; **den ~ heraushaben** (*inf*) to have got the hang of it (*inf*); **den ~ heraushaben, wie ...** (*inf*) to have got the hang of how ... (*inf*); **einen ~ machen** (*Fluß etc*) to curve, to describe a curve (*form*); (*einen Umweg machen*) to make a detour; **einen großen ~ um jdn/etw machen** (*meiden*) to keep well clear of sb/sth, to give sb/sth a wide berth; **jdn in hohem ~ hinauswerfen** (*inf*) to send sb flying out.

(b) (*Archit*) arch.

(c) (*Waffe, Mus: Geigen~ etc*) bow ◆ **den ~ überspannen** (*fig*) to overstep the mark, to go too far.

(d) (*Papier~*) sheet (of paper).

Bogen-: ~fenster *nt* bow window; **b~förmig** *adj* arched; **~führung** *f* (*Mus*) bowing; **~gang** *m* (a) (*Archit*) arcade; (b) (*Anat: von Ohr*) semicircular canal; **~lampe** *f* arc lamp *or* light; **~pfeiler** *m* pillar, column (*supporting an arch*); **~schießen** *nt* archery; **~schütze** *m* archer, bowman; **~sehne** *f* bowstring; **~strich** *m* (*Mus*) bowing.

Boheme [bo'eːm, bo'ɛːm] *f* **-,** *no pl* bohemian world.

Bohemien [boe'miɛ̃ː, bohe'miɛ̃ː] *m* **-s, -s** bohemian.

Bohle *f* **-, -n** (thick) board; (*Rail*) sleeper.

böhmakeln* *vi* (*Aus inf*) to speak with a dreadful accent.

Böhme *m* **-n, -n,** Bohemian (*inhabitant of Bohemia*).

Böhmen *nt* **-s** Bohemia.

Böhmerwald *m* Bohemian Forest.

Böhmin *f siehe* **Böhme**.

böhmisch *adj* Bohemian ◆ **das sind für mich ~e Dörfer** (*inf*) that's all Greek to me (*inf*); **das kommt mir ~ vor** (*inf*) that sounds a bit Irish to me (*inf*); **~ einkaufen** (*Aus inf*) to shoplift.

Böhnchen *nt dim of* **Bohne**.

Bohne *f* **-, -n** bean; (*inf: Kot des Kaninchens, Rehs*) droppings *pl* ◆ **dicke/grüne/weiße ~n** broad/green *or* French *or* runner/haricot beans; **blaue ~** (*dated Mil sl*) bullet; **nicht die ~** (*inf*) not a scrap (*inf*), not one little bit; **das kümmert mich nicht die ~** I don't care a fig about that (*inf*); **du hast wohl ~n in den Ohren** (*inf*) are you deaf?; *siehe* **scheren[2]**.

Bohnen-: ~eintopf *m* bean stew; **~kaffee** *m* real coffee; **gemahlener ~kaffee** ground coffee; **~kraut** *nt* savo(u)ry; **~ranke** *f* tendril; **~stange** *f* bean support; (*fig inf*) beanpole (*inf*); **~stroh** *nt*: **dumm wie ~stroh** (*inf*) (as) thick as two (short) planks (*inf*); **~suppe** *f* bean soup.

Bohner *m* **-s, -, Bohnerbesen** *m*, **Bohnerbürste** *f* floor-polishing brush.

bohnern *vti* to polish.

Bohnerwachs *nt* floor polish *or* wax.

Bohr|arbeiten *pl* drillings *pl*.

bohren [1] *vt* to bore; (*mit Bohrer, Bohrmaschine auch*) to drill; *Brunnen* to sink; (*hineindrücken*) *Stange, Pfahl, Schwert etc* to sink (*in +acc* into) ◆ **ein Schiff in den Grund ~** to send a ship to the bottom (of the sea).

[2] *vi* **(a)** to bore (*in +dat* into); to drill (*nach* for) ◆ **in einem Zahn ~** to drill a tooth; **in der Nase ~** to pick one's nose.

(b) (*fig*) (*drängen*) to keep on; (*peinigen: Schmerz, Zweifel etc*) to gnaw ◆ **er bohrte und bohrte, bekam aber keine Antwort** he kept on and on but got no reply; **der Schmerz bohrte ihm im Magen** he had a gnawing pain in his stomach.

[3] *vr* **sich in/durch etw** (*acc*) **~** to bore its way into/through sth; **ein grelles Licht bohrte sich durchs Dunkel** a glaring light pierced the darkness.

bohrend *adj* (*fig*) *Blick* piercing; *Schmerz, Zweifel, Hunger, Reue* gnawing; *Frage* probing.

Bohrer *m* **-s, - (a)** (*elektrisch, Drill~*) drill; (*Hand~*) gimlet, auger. **(b)** (*Arbeiter*) driller.

Bohr-: ~futterschlüssel *m* chuck key; **~insel** *f* drilling rig; (*für Öl auch*) oilrig; **~loch** *nt* borehole; (*in Holz, Metall etc*) drill-hole; **~maschine** *f* drill; **~probe** *f* drilling; **~turm** *m* derrick.

Bohrung *f* **(a)** *siehe vt* boring; drilling; sinking. **(b)** (*Loch*) bore(-hole); (*in Holz, Metall etc*) drill-hole.

böig *adj siehe* **Bö** gusty; squally.

Boiler ['bɔylɐ] *m* **-s, -** (hot-water) tank ◆ **den ~ anstellen** to put the water heater on.

Boje *f* **-, -n** buoy.

Bolero *m* **-s, -s** (*Tanz, Jäckchen*) bolero.

Bolivianer(in *f*) [bolivi'aːnɐ, -ərın] *m* Bolivian.

Bolivien [bo'liːviən] *nt* **-s** Bolivia.

Böller *m* **-s, -** (small) cannon (*for ceremonial use*).

bollern *vi* **(a)** *aux sein* (*dial: poltern*) to thud. **(b)** (*Ftbl sl*) to slam the ball blindly towards the goal.

böllern *vi* to fire ◆ **es böllert** there is firing.

⚠**Böllerschuß** *m* gun salute ◆ **5 Böllerschüsse** 5 shots from the cannon.

Bollwerk *nt* (*lit, fig*) bulwark (*usu fig*), bastion, stronghold; (*Kai*) bulwark.

Bolschewik *m* **-en, -en** *or* **-i** Bolshevik.

Bolschewismus *m* Bolshevism.

Bolschewist *m* Bolshevist.

bolschewistisch *adj* Bolshevist, Bolshevik *attr*.

Bolzen *m* **-s, - (a)** (*Tech*) pin; (*esp mit Gewinde*) bolt. **(b)** (*Geschoß*) bolt.

bolzen (*inf*) [1] *vi* to kick about ◆ **es wurde mehr gebolzt als gespielt** they just kicked (the ball) about instead of playing football.

[2] *vt Ball* to slam.

Bolzenschneider *m* bolt croppers *pl*.

Bombardement [bɔmbardə'mãː, (*Aus*) bɔmbard'mãː] *nt* **-s, -s** bombardment; (*mit Bomben*) bombing ◆ **ein ~ von** (*fig*) a deluge *or* shower of.

bombardieren* *vt* (*mit Bomben belegen*) to bomb; (*mit Granaten beschießen, fig*) to bombard.

Bombardierung *f* (*mit Bomben*) bombing; (*mit Granaten, fig*) bombardment.

Bombast *m* **-(e)s,** *no pl* bombast.

bombastisch *adj Sprache* bombastic; *Kleidung, Architektur, Hauseinrichtung* overdone *pred*.

Bombay ['bɔmbeı] *nt* **-s** Bombay.

Bombe *f* **-, -n** bomb; (*dated: Könner*) ace (*in +dat* at); (*Sport inf: Schuß*) cracker (*inf*) ◆ **mit ~n belegen** to bomb; **wie eine ~ einschlagen** to come as a (real) bombshell; **eine/die ~ platzen lassen** (*fig*) to drop a/the bombshell.

bomben *vt* (*Sport inf*) *Ball* to smash (*inf*), to slam (*inf*).

Bomben- *in cpds* (*Mil*) bomb; (*inf: hervorragend*) fantastic (*inf*), great (*inf*); **~alarm** *m* bomb scare; **~angriff** *m* bomb attack *or* raid; **~anschlag** *m* bomb attack; **~besetzung** *f* (*inf*) fantastic *or* great cast (*inf*); **~erfolg** *m* (*inf*) smash hit (*inf*); **b~fest** *adj* **(a)** (*Mil*) bombproof; **(b)** (*inf*) *Klebestelle, Naht* absolutely secure; *Entschluß* unshakeable; **~flugzeug** *nt* bomber; **~geschädigte(r)** *mf decl as adj* person who has been bombed out; **~geschäft** *nt* (*inf*) **ein ~geschäft sein** to be a gold mine (*fig inf*); **ein ~geschäft machen** to do a roaring trade (*inf*) (*mit* in); **~geschwader** *nt* bomber squadron; **~hitze** *f* (*inf*) sweltering heat *no indef art*; **~krater** *m* bomb crater; **~leger(in** *f*) *m* bomber; **~nacht** *f* night of bombing; **~schaden** *m* bomb damage; ⚠**~schuß** *m* (*inf*) unstoppable shot; **b~sicher** *adj* **(a)** (*Mil*) bombproof; **(b)** (*inf*) dead certain (*inf*); **~splitter** *m* bomb fragment; **~stellung** *f* (*inf*) job in a million (*inf*), fantastic job (*inf*); **~teppich** *m* **einen ~teppich legen** to blanket-bomb an/the area; **~terror** *m* terror bombing; **~trichter** *m* bomb crater.

Bomber *m* **-s, -** bomber.

Bomberjacke *f* bomber jacket.

Bommel *f* **-, -n** bobble.

Bon [bɔŋ] *m* **-s, -s** voucher, coupon; (*Kassenzettel*) receipt, (sales) slip.

Bonbon [bɔŋ'bɔŋ] *nt or m* **-s, -s** sweet (*Brit*), candy (*US*); (*fig*) treat.

bonbonfarben, bonbonfarbig *adj* candy-coloured.

⚠**Bonbonniere** [bɔŋbɔ'nieːrə] *f* **-, -n** box of chocolates.

Bonbonpapier *nt* sweet *or* candy (*US*) wrapper.

bongen *vt* (*inf*) *Betrag etc* to ring up ◆ **das ist gebongt** (*inf*) okey-doke, righto (*inf*).

Bongo ['bɔŋgo] *nt* **-(s), -s,** *f* **-, -s, Bongotrommel** *f* bongo (drum).

Bonität *f* **-,** *no pl* (*Fin*) financial standing, creditworthiness.

Bonitätsprüfung *f* (*Fin*) credit investigation.

Bonmot [bõ'moː] *nt* **-s, -s** bon mot.

Bonn *nt* **-s** Bonn.

Bonner *adj attr* Bonn.

Bonner(in *f*) *m* **-s, -** native of Bonn; (*Einwohner*) inhabitant of Bonn.

Bonsai *nt* **-s, -s** bonsai.

Bonus *m* **-** *or* **-ses, -** *or* **-se** (*Comm, bei Versicherung*) bonus; (*Univ, Sport: Punktvorteil*) bonus points *pl*.

Bonze *m* **-n, -n (a)** (*Rel*) bonze. **(b)** (*pej*) bigwig (*inf*), big shot (*inf*).

Boogie(-Woogie) ['bʊgi('vʊgi)] *m* **-(s), -s** boogie-woogie.

Boom [buːm] *m* **-s, -s** boom.

boomen ['buːmən] *vi* to boom.

Boot *nt* **-(e)s, -e** boat ◆ **~ fahren** to go out in a boat; (*zum Vergnügen*) to go boating; **wir sitzen alle in einem** *or* **im selben ~** (*fig*) we're all in the same boat.

Boots-: ~bauer *m* boatbuilder; **~deck** *nt* boat-deck; **~fahrt** *f* boat trip; **~flüchtlinge** *pl* boat people; **~haus** *nt* boathouse; **~länge** *f* (*Sport*) (boat's) length; **~mann** *m, pl* **~leute** (*Naut*) bo'sun, boatswain; (*Dienstgrad*) petty officer; **~steg** *m* landing-stage; **~verleih** *m* boat hire business; **~verleiher** *m* boat hirer.

Bor *nt* **-s,** *no pl* (*abbr* **B**) boron.

Borax *m* **-(es),** *no pl* borax.

Bord[1] *m* **-(e)s,** *no pl* **an ~ (eines Schiffes/der „Bremen")** aboard *or* on board (a ship/the "Bremen"); **alle Mann an ~!** all aboard!; **frei an ~** (*Comm*) free on board, f.o.b.; **an ~ gehen** to board *or* go aboard (the ship/plane), to go on board; **über ~** overboard; **Mann über ~!** man overboard!; **über ~ gehen** to go overboard; (*fig*) to go by the board; **über ~ werfen** (*lit, fig*) to throw overboard, to jettison; **die Vorsicht über ~ werfen** to throw caution to the winds; **von ~ gehen** to leave (the) ship/the plane; (*esp Passagiere am Ziel*) to disembark.

Bord[2] *nt* **-(e)s, -e** (*Wandbrett*) shelf.

Bord[3] *nt* **-(e)s, -e** (*Sw*) (*Rand*) ledge, raised edge; (*Böschung*) embankment, bank.

Bord-: ~buch *nt* log(book); **~computer** *m* on-board computer; **b~eigen** *adj* ship's/plane's *etc*.

Bordell *nt* **-s, -e** brothel.

Bordellier [-'lieː] *m* **-s, -s** brothel-keeper.

Bordellwirtin *f* brothel-keeper, madam.

Bord-: ~funk *m* (*Naut*) (ship's) radio; (*Aviat*) (aircraft) radio equipment; **~funker** *m* (*Naut, Aviat*) radio operator.

bordieren* *vt* (*Sew*) to edge, to border.

Bord-: ~kante *f* kerb; **~karte** *f* boarding pass *or* card; **~mechaniker** *m* ship's/aircraft mechanic; **~stein** *m* kerb; **den ~stein mitnehmen** (*inf*) to hit the kerb; **~steinkante** *f*, **~steinrand** *m* kerb.

Bordüre *f* **-, -n** edging, border.

Bord-: ~waffen *pl* (*Mil*) aircraft/tank/ship armaments *pl*; **~wand** *f* (*Naut*) ship's side; (*Aviat*) side of the aircraft.

Boretsch *m* **-(e)s,** *no pl siehe* **Bor(r)etsch**.

borgen *vti* **(a)** (*erhalten*) to borrow (*von* from). **(b)** (*geben*) to lend, to loan (*jdm etw* sb sth, sth to sb).

Borke *f* **-, -n** bark.

Borken-: ~flechte *f* (*Med*) ringworm; **~käfer** *m* bark beetle; **~krepp** *m* (*Tex*) crepe.

Born *m* **-(e)s, -e** (*old, liter*) (*Brunnen*) well; (*Quelle*) spring; (*fig*) fountain, fount (*liter*).

borniert *adj* bigoted, narrow-minded.

Bor(r)etsch *m* **-(e)s,** *no pl* borage.

Borsalbe *f* boric acid ointment.

Börse *f* **-, -n (a)** (*Geld~*) (*für Frauen*) purse; (*für Männer*) wallet. **(b)** (*Wertpapierhandel*) stock market; (*Ort*) stock exchange.

⚠: for details of spelling reform, see supplement

Börsen-: **~beginn** *m* opening of the stock market; **bei ~beginn** when the stock market opens/opened; **~bericht** *m* stock market report; **~einführung** *f* flotation on the stock exchange; **b~fähig** *adj* negotiable on the stock exchange; **~geschäft** *nt* (*Wertpapierhandel*) stockbroking; (*Transaktion*) stock market transaction; **~krach** *m* stock market crash; **~krise** *f* crisis on the stock market; **~kurs** *m* stock market price; **~makler** *m* stockbroker; **b~notiert** *adj Firma* listed; **~notierung** *f* quotation (on the stock exchange); **~platz** *m* stock exchange; ⚠**~schluß** *m, no pl* close of the stock market; **~schwankungen** *pl* fluctuations on the stock market; **~schwindel** *m* stock market swindle *or* fiddle (*inf*); **~spekulant** *m* speculator on the stock market; **~spekulation** *f* speculation on the stock market; **~sturz** *m* collapse of the market; **~tendenz** *f* stock market trend; ⚠**~tip** *m* market tip; **~verkehr** *m* stock market dealings *pl or* transactions *pl*; **~wesen** *nt* stock market.

Börsianer(in *f*) *m* **-s, -** (*inf*) (*Makler*) broker; (*Spekulant*) speculator.

Borste *f* **-, -n** bristle.

Borsten-: **~tier** *nt* pig, swine; **~vieh** *nt* pigs *pl*, swine *pl*.

borstig *adj* bristly; (*fig*) snappish.

Borte *f* **-, -n** braid trimming.

Borwasser *nt* boric acid lotion.

bös *adj siehe* **böse**.

bös|artig *adj* malicious, nasty; *Tier, (stärker) Mensch, Wesen* vicious; (*Med*) *Geschwür* malignant.

Bös|artigkeit *f siehe adj* maliciousness, nastiness; viciousness; malignancy.

Böschung *f* (*von Straße*) bank, embankment; (*von Bahndamm*) embankment; (*von Fluß*) bank.

Böschungswinkel *m* gradient.

böse *adj* **(a)** (*sittlich schlecht*) bad; (*stärker*) evil, wicked; (*inf: unartig auch*) naughty ◆ **die ~ Fee/Stiefmutter** the Wicked Fairy/Stepmother; **ein ~r Geist** an evil spirit; **das war keine ~ Absicht** there was no harm intended; **das war nicht ~ gemeint** I/he *etc* didn't mean it nastily; **eine ~ Zunge** *or* **ein ~s Mundwerk haben** to have a malicious *or* wicked tongue; *siehe* **Blick**.

(b) *no pred* (*unangenehm, übel*) *Traum, Angelegenheit, Krankheit* bad; *Überraschung, Streich, Geschichte* nasty ◆ **ein ~s Erwachen** a rude awakening; **~ Folgen** dire consequences; **~ Zeiten** bad times; **er ist ~ dran** life's not easy for him; (*gesundheitlich*) he's in a bad way; **das/es sieht ~ aus** things look/it looks bad; *siehe* **Blut, Ende, Wetter²**.

(c) (*verärgert*) angry, cross (*+dat, auf +acc, mit* with) ◆ **ein ~s Gesicht machen** to scowl; **im ~n auseinandergehen** to part on bad terms.

(d) (*inf*) (*schmerzend, entzündet*) bad *attr*, sore; (*krank, schlimm*) bad; *Wunde, Husten* nasty, bad.

(e) (*inf: verstärkend*) real (*inf*); *Enttäuschung, Gewitter, Sturz* bad, terrible ◆ **er hat ~ geschimpft** he didn't half curse (*Brit inf*), he cursed like hell (*inf*).

Böse(r) *mf decl as adj* wicked *or* evil person; (*Film, Theat*) villain, baddy (*inf*) ◆ **die ~n** the wicked; **der ~** (*Teufel*) the Evil One.

Böse(s) *nt decl as adj* evil; (*Schaden, Leid*) harm ◆ **jdm ~s antun** to do sb harm; **ich will dir doch nichts ~s** I don't mean you any harm; **mir schwant ~s** it sounds/looks ominous (to me); **ich dachte an gar nichts ~s, als ...** I was quite unsuspecting when ...; **ich habe mir gar nichts ~s dabei gedacht, als ich das sagte** I didn't mean any harm when I said that; *siehe* **ahnen**.

Bösewicht *m* **-(e)s, -e** *or* **-er** (*old, hum*) villain.

Bos-: **b~haft** *adj* malicious, spiteful, nasty; **~haftigkeit** *f* maliciousness, spitefulness, nastiness; **~heit** *f* malice, nastiness; (*Bemerkung, Handlung*) malicious *or* nasty remark/thing to do; **er hat es mit konstanter ~heit getan** maliciously he kept on doing it.

Boskop *m* **-s, -** ≃ russet.

Bosnien *nt* **-s** Bosnia.

Bosnien-Herzegowina *n* **-s** Bosnia-Herzegovina.

Bosnier(in) *m(f)* **-s, -** Bosnian.

bosnisch *adj* Bosnian.

⚠**Boß** *m* **Bosses, Bosse** (*inf*) boss (*inf*).

Bossa Nova *m* **- -, - -s** bossanova.

bosseln (*inf*) 1 *vi* to tinker *or* fiddle about (*inf*) (*an +dat* with).
2 *vt* (*zusammenbasteln*) to rig up (*inf*) (*jdm* for sb).

böswillig *adj* malicious; (*Jur auch*) wilful ◆ **in ~er Absicht** with malicious intent.

Böswilligkeit *f* malice, maliciousness.

bot *pret of* **bieten**.

Botanik *f* botany.

Botaniker(in *f*) *m* **-s, -** botanist.

botanisch *adj* botanic.

botanisieren* *vi* to collect and study plants, to botanize (*rare*).

Botanisiertrommel *f* (botanist's) specimen container.

Bötchen *nt dim of* **Boot** little boat.

Bote *m* **-n, -n (a)** (*usu mit Nachricht*) messenger; (*Kurier*) courier; (*Post~*) postman; (*Zeitungs~*) paperboy; (*Laufbursche*) errand boy; (*Gerichts~*) messenger-at-arms. **(b)** (*fig: Anzeichen*) herald, harbinger (*liter*).

Boten-: **~bericht** *m* (*Liter*) report by messenger; **~dienst** *m* errand; (*Einrichtung*) messenger service; **~gang** *m* errand; **einen ~gang machen** to run an errand; **~lohn** *m* delivery fee; (*Bezahlung des Boten*) messenger's/errand boy's fee; **~stoff** *m* (*Med*) neurotransmitter.

Botin *f siehe* **Bote (a)** messenger; courier; postwoman; papergirl; errand girl.

botmäßig *adj* (*old, geh*) (*untertänig*) compliant, submissive; (*gehorsam*) obedient ◆ **jdm ~ sein** to be at sb's command.

Botmäßigkeit *f, no pl* (*old, geh*) **(a)** (*Herrschaft*) dominion, rule. **(b)** *siehe adj* compliance, submissiveness; obedience.

Botschaft *f* **(a)** (*Mitteilung*) message; (*esp amtlich*) communication; (*Neuigkeit*) piece of news, news *no indef art or pl* ◆ **ein freudige ~** good news, glad tidings *pl* (*liter, hum*); **die ~ in ihren Protestliedern** the message in her protest songs; **die Frohe ~** the Gospel. **(b)** (*Pol: Vertretung*) embassy.

Botschafter *m* **-s, -** ambassador.

Botschafter|ebene *f*: **auf ~** at ambassadorial level.

Botschafterin *f* ambassador; (*Ehefrau*) ambassadress.

Botschaftssekretär *m* secretary (*in the diplomatic service*).

Böttcher *m* **-s, -** cooper.

Böttcherei *f* (*no pl: Gewerbe*) cooper's trade, cooperage; (*Werkstatt*) cooper's (work)shop, cooperage.

Bottich *m* **-(e)s, -e** tub.

Bottle-Party ['bɔtl-] *f* bottle party.

⚠**Bouclé** [bu'kle:] *nt* **-s, -s** bouclé (yarn).

Boudoir [bu'doa:ɐ] *nt* **-s, -s** (*dated geh*) boudoir.

Bouillon [bʊl'jɔn, bʊl'jõ:, (*Aus*) bu'jõ:] *f* **-, -s** stock, bouillon; (*auf Speisekarte*) bouillon, consommé.

Bouillonwürfel *m* stock *or* bouillon cube.

Boulevard [bulə'va:ɐ, (*Aus*) bul'va:ɐ] *m* **-s, -s** boulevard.

Boulevard-: **~blatt** *nt* (*inf*) popular daily, tabloid; **~presse** *f* (*inf*) popular press; **~stück** *nt* light play/comedy; **~theater** *nt* light theatre; **~zeitung** *f siehe* **~blatt**.

Bouquet [bu'ke:] *nt* **-s, -s** *siehe* **Bukett**.

Bourgeois [bʊr'ʒoa] *m* **-, -** (*geh*) bourgeois.

bourgeois [bʊr'ʒoa] *adj* (*geh*) bourgeois, middle-class.

Bourgeoisie [bʊrʒoa'zi:] *f* (*geh*) bourgeoisie.

Boutique [bu'ti:k] *f* **-, -n** boutique.

Bovist [*auch* 'bo:vɪst] *m* **-s, -e** (*Bot*) puffball, bovista (*spec*).

Bowle ['bo:lə] *f* **-, -n (a)** (*Getränk*) punch ◆ **eine ~ ansetzen** to prepare (some) punch. **(b)** (*Gefäß, Schüssel*) punchbowl; (*Garnitur*) punch set (*punchbowl and cups*).

Bowlen-: **~schüssel** *f* punchbowl; **~service** *nt* punch set (*punchbowl and cups*).

Bowling ['bo:lɪŋ] *nt* **-s, -s** (*Spiel*) (tenpin) bowling; (*Ort*) bowling alley ◆ **~ spielen gehen** to go bowling.

Bowlingkugel *f* bowl.

Box *f* **-, -en (a)** (*abgeteilter Raum*) compartment; (*für Pferde*) box; (*in Großgarage*) (partitioned-off) parking place; (*für Rennwagen*) pit; (*bei Ausstellungen*) stand. **(b)** (*Kamera*) box camera. **(c)** (*Behälter*) box. **(d)** (*Lautsprecher~*) speaker (unit).

Boxen *nt* **-s,** *no pl* (*Sport*) boxing.

boxen 1 *vi* (*Sport*) to box; (*zur Übung*) to spar; (*mit Fäusten zuschlagen*) to hit out, to punch ◆ **um einen Titel ~** to fight for a title; **gegen jdn ~** to fight sb.
2 *vt* **(a)** (*schlagen*) *jdn* to punch, to hit ◆ **ich box dir gleich eine** (*inf*) I'll hit you one (*inf*).
(b) (*Sport sl: antreten gegen*) to fight.
(c) (*mit der Faust*) *Ball* to punch, to thump.
(d) (*fig: durchsetzen*) to push, to force ◆ **ein Produkt auf den Markt ~** to push a product.
3 *vr* **(a)** (*inf: sich schlagen*) to have a punch-up (*inf*) *or* a fight.
(b) (*sich einen Weg bahnen*) to fight one's way ◆ **sich durchs Leben/nach oben ~** (*fig inf*) to fight one's way through life/up.

Boxer *m* **-s, -** (*Sportler, Hund*) boxer.

Boxer-: **~aufstand** *m* (*Hist*) Boxer Rebellion; **~motor** *m* (*Tech*) opposed cylinder engine; **~nase** *f* boxer's nose, broken nose; **~-Shorts** [-ʃo:ɐts, -ʃɔrts] *pl* boxer shorts; **~stellung** *f* boxer's stance.

Box-: **~handschuh** *m* boxing glove; **~kalf** *nt* **-s,** *no pl* box calf; **~kamera** *f* box camera; **~kampf** *m* (*Disziplin*) boxing *no art*; (*Einzelkampf*) fight, bout, (boxing) match; **~ring** *m* boxing ring; **~sport** *m* (sport of) boxing.

Boy [bɔy] *m* **-s, -s** pageboy (*Brit*), bellhop (*esp US*).

Boykott [bɔy'kɔt] *m* **-(e)s, -e** *or* **-s** boycott.

boykottieren* [bɔykɔ'ti:rən] *vt* to boycott.

BP *abbr of* **Bundespost**.

brabbeln *vi* (*inf*) to mumble, to mutter; (*Baby*) to babble.

brach¹ *pret of* **brechen**.

brach² *adj attr* (*old*) fallow.

Brache *f* **-, -n** (*old*) (*Land*) fallow (land); (*Zeit*) fallow period.

Brachfeld *nt* fallow field.

brachial *adj* **mit ~er Gewalt** by brute force.

Brachialgewalt *f* brute force.

Brach-: **~land** *nt* fallow (land); **b~legen** *vt sep* to leave fallow; **b~liegen** *vi sep irreg* to lie fallow; (*fig*) to be left unexploited; **b~liegende Kenntnisse/Kräfte** unexploited knowledge/powers; **~monat, ~mond** (*obs*) *m* June.

brachte *pret of* **bringen**.

Brachvogel *m* curlew.

Brack *nt* **-s, -s** *siehe* **Brackwasser**.

brackig *adj* brackish.

Brackwasser *nt* brackish water.

Brahman *nt* **-s,** *no pl* Brahma.

Brahmane *m* **-n, -n** Brahman, Brahmin.

brahmanisch *adj* Brahminical, Brahman *attr*.

Brahmanismus *m* Brahmanism.

Brainstorming ['breɪnstɔ:mɪŋ] *n* **-s, -s** brainstorming session.

bramarbasieren* *vi* (*geh*) to brag (*von* about), to boast (*von* about), to swagger.

Bram-: ~segel *nt* topgallant sail; **~stenge** *f* topgallant stay.

Branche ['brã:ʃə] *f* **-, -n** (*Fach*) field, department; (*Gewerbe*) trade; (*Geschäftszweig*) area of business, trade; (*Wirtschaftszweig*) (branch of) industry ◆ **das gehört in seine ~** that's in his line *or* department *or* field.

Branchen-: ⚠**~adreßbuch** *nt* classified directory; **b~fremd** *adj Waren* foreign to the trade/industry; *Kollege* not familiar with the trade; **~führer** *m* market leader; **~kenner** *m* **er ist ~kenner** he knows the trade/industry, he has a good knowledge of the trade/industry; **~kenntnis** *f* knowledge of the trade/industry; **b~kundig** *adj* experienced *or* well-versed in the trade/industry; **b~üblich** *adj* usual in the trade/industry; **b~unüblich** *adj* not usual in the trade/industry; **~verzeichnis** *nt* yellow pages.

Brand *m* **-(e)s, ¨e** **(a)** (*Feuer*) fire; (*lodernd auch*) blaze, conflagration (*liter*) ◆ **in ~ geraten** to catch fire; (*in Flammen aufgehen*) to burst into flames; **in ~ stehen** to be on fire, to be ablaze; **etw in ~ setzen** *or* **stecken** to set fire to sth, to set sth alight *or* on fire.
(b) *usu pl* (*brennendes Holz etc*) firebrand.
(c) (*fig geh: der Liebe, des Hasses*) burning passion.
(d) (*das Brennen, von Porzellan etc*) firing.
(e) (*fig inf: großer Durst*) raging thirst.
(f) (*dial inf*) (*Brennstoff*) fuel; (*Holz auch*) firewood.
(g) (*Med*) gangrene *no art*.
(h) (*Pflanzenkrankheit*) blight.

Brand-: b~aktuell *adj* (*inf*) *Thema, Frage* red-hot (*inf*); *Buch* hot from the presses; *Platte etc* the latest thing (*inf*); **~anschlag** *m* arson attack; **~bekämpfung** *f* firefighting; **~binde** *f* bandage for burns; **~blase** *f* (burn) blister; **~bombe** *f* firebomb, incendiary bomb *or* device; **~brief** *m* (*inf*) (*Bettelbrief*) begging letter; (*Mahnbrief*) urgent reminder; **~direktor** *m* ≃ fire chief; **b~eilig** *adj* (*inf*) extremely urgent.

branden *vi* to surge (*auch fig*) ◆ **an** *or* **gegen etw** (*acc*) **~** to break against sth; **~der Beifall** thunderous applause.

Brandenburg *nt* **-s** Brandenburg.

Brand-: ~fackel *f* firebrand; **~fleck** *m* burn; **~gans** *f* shelduck; **~gefahr** *f* danger of fire; **bei ~gefahr** when there is danger of fire; **~geruch** *m* smell of burning; **~herd** *m* source of the fire *or* blaze; (*fig*) source.

brandig *adj* **(a)** (*Bot*) suffering from blight; (*Med*) gangrenous. **(b) ~ riechen** to smell of burning; (*bei ausgegangenem Brand*) to have a burnt smell.

Brand-: ~inspektor *m* fire inspector; **~kasse** *f* fire insurance company; **~katastrophe** *f* fire disaster; **~leger** *m* **-s, -** (*esp Aus*) *siehe* **~stifter**; **~loch** *nt* burn hole; **~mal** *nt* **-s, -e** brand; (*fig auch*) stigma; **b~marken** *vt insep* to brand; (*fig*) to denounce; **jdn als etw b~marken** (*fig*) to brand sb (as) sth; **~mauer** *f* fire(proof) wall; **~meister** *m* fire chief; **b~neu** *adj* (*inf*) brand-new, spanking new (*inf*); **~opfer** *nt* **(a)** (*Rel*) burnt offering; **(b)** (*Mensch*) fire victim; **~rede** *f* harangue; **~rodung** *f* slash-and-burn; **~salbe** *f* ointment for burns; **~satz** *m* incendiary compound; **~schaden** *m* fire damage; **b~schatzen** *vt insep* to sack, to lay waste to; **die b~schatzenden Horden** the pillaging mob; **~schatzung** *f* (*Hist*) sack, pillage; **~schutz** *m* protection against fire; **~sohle** *f* insole; **~stelle** *f* (*Ort des Brandes*) fire, blaze; (*verbrannte Stelle*) burnt patch; **~stifter** *m* fire-raiser, arsonist (*esp Jur*), incendiary (*Jur*); **~stiftung** *f* arson (*auch Jur*), fire-raising; **~teig** *m* choux pastry.

Brandung *f* surf, breakers *pl*; (*fig geh*) surge.

Brandungswelle *f* breaker.

Brand-: ~ursache *f* cause of a/the fire *or* blaze; **~wache** *f* **(a)** (*Überwachung der ~stelle*) firewatch; **(b)** (*Personen*) firewatch team; **~wunde** *f* burn; (*durch Flüssigkeit*) scald; **~zeichen** *nt* brand.

brannte *pret of* **brennen.**

Branntwein *m* spirits *pl* ◆ **jede Art von ~** all types *or* every type of spirit(s); **Whisky ist ein ~** whisky is a (type of) spirit.

Branntwein-: ~brenner *m* distiller; **~brennerei** *f* distillery; (*~brennen*) distilling *or* distillation of spirits; **~schank** *f* **-, -en** (*Aus*) ≃ public house (*Brit*), bar; **~steuer** *f* tax on spirits.

Brasil[1] *f* **-, -(s)** Brazil cigar.

Brasil[2] *m* **-s, -e** *or* **-s** (*Tabak*) Brazil(ian) tobacco.

Brasilholz *nt* brazilwood.

Brasilianer(in *f***)** *m* **-s, -** Brazilian.

brasilianisch *adj* Brazilian.

Brasilien [-iən] *nt* **-s** Brazil.

Brasse *f* **-, -n (a)** (*Naut*) brace. **(b)** (*Fisch*) bream.

brassen *vt* (*Naut*) to brace.

Brät *nt* **-s,** *no pl* sausage meat.

Brat|apfel *m* baked apple.

braten *pret* **briet,** *ptp* **gebraten** [1] *vti* (*am Spieß, im Ofen: mit Fett*) to roast; (*im Ofen: ohne Fett*) to bake; (*in der Pfanne*) to fry ◆ **etw braun/knusprig ~** to roast/fry sth until it is brown/crispy.
[2] *vi* (*inf: in der Sonne*) to roast (*inf*) ◆ **sich ~ lassen** to roast oneself (*inf*).

Braten *m* **-s, -** ≃ pot-roast meat *no indef art, no pl*; (*im Ofen gebraten*) joint, roast, roast meat *no indef art, no pl* ◆ **kalter ~** cold meat; **ein fetter ~** (*fig*) a prize catch; **den ~ riechen** *or* **schmecken** (*inf*) to smell a rat (*inf*), to get wind of it/something.

Braten-: ~fett *nt* meat fat and juices *pl*; **~fleisch** *nt* meat for roasting/frying, roasting/frying meat; **~rock** *m* frock coat, Prince Albert (coat) (*US*); **~soße** *f* gravy; **~wender** *m* **-s, -** fishslice.

Brat-: b~fertig *adj* oven-ready; **~fett** *nt* fat for frying/roasting; **~fisch** *m* fried fish; **~hähnchen** *nt,* **~hendl** *nt* **-s, -(n)** (*Aus, S Ger*) roast chicken; **~hering** *m* fried herring (*sold cold*); **~huhn, ~hühnchen** *nt* roast chicken; (*Huhn zum Braten*) roasting chicken; **~kartoffeln** *pl* fried *or* sauté potatoes; **~kartoffelverhältnis** *nt* (*hum*) **er hat ein ~kartoffelverhältnis mit ihr** he only sees her because she feeds and waters him (*hum*); **er sucht ein ~kartoffelverhältnis** he's looking for a meal ticket; **~ofen** *m* oven; **~pfanne** *f* frying pan; **~röhre** *f* oven; **~rost** *m* grill; (*über offenem Feuer auch*) gridiron.

Bratsche *f* **-, -n** viola.

Bratscher *m* **-s, -, Bratschist(in** *f***)** *m* violist, viola player.

Brat-: ~spieß *m* skewer; (*Teil des Grills*) spit; (*Gericht*) kebab; **~wurst** *f* (*zum Braten*) (frying) sausage; (*gebraten*) (fried) sausage.

Bräu *nt* **-(e)s, -e** (*esp SGer*) (*Biersorte*) brew, beer; (*Brauerei*) brewery; (*rare: Schenke*) inn (*old*), pub (*Brit*).

Brauch *m* **-(e)s, Bräuche** custom, tradition ◆ **nach altem ~** according to (established) custom *or* tradition; **etw ist ~** sth is traditional, sth is the custom; **so ist es ~, so will es der ~** that's the tradition *or* custom; **das ist bei uns so ~** (*inf*) that's traditional with us.

brauchbar *adj* **(a)** (*benutzbar*) useable; *Plan* workable; (*nützlich*) useful. **(b)** (*ordentlich*) *Schüler, Idee* decent, reasonable; *Arbeit, Arbeiter etc auch* useful *attr* (*inf*).

Brauchbarkeit *f* usefulness; (*von Plan*) workableness, workability.

brauchen [1] *vt* **(a)** (*nötig haben*) to need, to require (*form*) (*für, zu* for).
(b) (*bei Zeitangaben*) **Zeit/zwei Minuten** *etc* **~** to need time/two minutes *etc*; **normalerweise brauche ich zwei Stunden dafür** I normally take two hours to do it; **wenn 5 Männer 3 Stunden ~, ...** if 5 men take 3 hours ...; **es braucht alles seine Zeit** everything takes time; **wie lange braucht man, um ...?** how long does it take to ...?; **er hat zwei Tage dafür gebraucht** he took two days over it, he needed two days to do it.
(c) (*dated, geh: bedürfen*) **es braucht einer Sache** (*gen*) sth is necessary.
(d) (*inf: nützlich finden*) **das könnte ich ~** I could do with *or* use that; **wir können das/ihn nicht ~** we could *or* can do without that/him, we don't need that/him; **das kann ich gerade ~!** (*iro*) that's all I need!; **kannst du die Sachen ~?** have you any use for the things?, are the things of any use to you?; **er ist zu allem zu ~** (*inf*) he's a really useful type (to have around) (*inf*); **heute bin ich zu nichts zu ~** (*inf*) I'm useless today (*inf*).
(e) (*benutzen*) *Waffe, Verstand, Gerät* to use.
(f) (*inf: verbrauchen*) to use (up); *Strom etc* to use.
[2] *v aux* to need ◆ **du brauchst das nicht tun** you needn't do that, you've no need to do that, you don't have *or* need to do that; **du brauchst es ihm nicht (zu) sagen** you needn't tell *or* don't need to tell him that; (*er weiß das schon*) you don't need to tell him that; **du hättest das nicht (zu) tun ~** you needn't have done that, you didn't need to *or* had no need to do that; **du brauchst nur an(zu)rufen** you only have *or* need to call, you need only call; **es braucht nicht besonders betont zu werden, daß ...** there's no need to stress the fact that ...; **es hätte nicht sein ~** there was no need for that; (*das hätte nicht geschehen müssen*) that needn't have happened.

Brauchtum *nt* customs *pl*, traditions *pl* ◆ **zum ~ in diesem Land gehört ...** one of the customs in this country is ...

Braue *f* **-, -n** (eye)brow.

brauen [1] *vti Bier* to brew; (*inf: zubereiten*) *Tee* to brew up; *Kaffee* to make; *Zaubertrank, Punsch etc* to concoct.
[2] *vi* (*old liter*) (*Nebel*) to build up.

Brauer *m* **-s, -** brewer.

Brauerei *f* **(a)** brewery. **(b)** *no pl* (*das Brauen*) brewing.

Brauereiwesen *nt* brewing trade *or* industry.

Brau-: ~haus *nt* brewery; **~meister** *m* master brewer.

braun *adj* brown; (*von Sonne auch*) *Mensch, Haut* (sun-)tanned; (*inf: ~haarig*) brown-haired; (*pej: Nazi~*) Nazi ◆ **~ werden** (*Mensch*) to get a (sun-)tan, to go *or* get brown, to tan; **von der Sonne ~ gebrannt sein** to be tanned (by the sun); **die B~en** (*old: Pferde*) the brown *or* bay horses; (*Nazis*) the Brownshirts.

Braun *nt* **-s, -** brown.

Braun-: b~äugig *adj* brown-eyed; **~bär** *m* brown bear.

Bräune *f* **-,** *no pl* (*braune Färbung*) brown(ness); (*von Sonne*) (sun-)tan.

bräunen [1] *vt* (*Cook*) to brown; (*Sonne etc*) to tan.
[2] *vi* (*Cook*) to go *or* turn brown; (*Mensch*) to tan, to go brown; (*Sonne*) to tan ◆ **sich in der Sonne ~ lassen** to get a (sun-)tan.
[3] *vr* (*Haut*) to go brown; (*Mensch auch*) to tan.

Braun-: ⚠**b~gebrannt** *adj attr* (sun-)tanned, bronzed, brown; **b~haarig** *adj* brown-haired; *Frau auch* brunette; **~kohl** *m* (*dial*) *siehe* **Grünkohl**; **~kohle** *f* brown coal.

bräunlich *adj* brownish, browny.

braunrot *adj* reddish brown.

Braunschweig *nt* **-s** Brunswick.

Bräunung *f* browning; (*von Haut*) bronzing ◆ **eine tiefe ~ der Haut** a deep (sun-)tan.

Bräunungsstudio *nt* tanning studio.

Braus *m siehe* **Saus.**

Brause *f* **-, -n (a)** (*Dusche, Duschvorrichtung*) shower ◆ **sich unter die ~ stellen** to have a shower. **(b)** (*~aufsatz*) shower attachment; (*an Schlauch, Gießkanne*) rose, spray (attachment). **(c)** (*Getränk*) pop; (*Limonade*) (fizzy) lemonade; (*~pulver*) lemonade powder.

Brause-: ~bad *nt* shower(bath); **~kopf** *m* (*dated*) hothead.

brausen [1] *vi* **(a)** (*tosen*) to roar; (*Orgel, Beifall*) to thunder; (*Jubel*) to ring out; (*Ohren*) to ring, to buzz; (*sprudeln*) (*Wasser, Brandung*) to foam; (*geh: Blut*) to pound ◆ **es brauste mir in den Ohren** *or* **in meinen Ohren** my ears were ring-

ing *or* buzzing; **~der Beifall** thunderous applause.
(b) *aux sein (rasen, rennen, schnell fahren)* to race; *(Mensch auch)* to storm.
(c) *auch vr (duschen)* to (have a) shower.
[2] *vt (abspülen) Gegenstände* to rinse (off); *(abduschen) Körperteil, Kinder* to put under the shower.

Brause-: ~pulver *nt* sherbet; **~tablette** *f* lemonade tablet; **~würfel** *m* tablet of lemonade powder.

Braut *f* **-, Bräute** bride; *(dated) (Verlobte)* fiancée, betrothed *(old)*, bride-to-be; *(Freundin)* girl(-friend) ◆ **~ Christi** bride of Christ.

-braut *f in cpds (inf)* **Rocker~/Motorrad~** rocker/motor-cycle queen *(sl)*; **Fußball~/Tennis~** footballer's/tennis player's girl *or* moll *(hum sl)*.

Braut-: ~bett *nt* nuptial *or* marital bed; **~führer** *m* person who gives away the bride; **~gemach** *nt (Hist)* nuptial chamber.

Bräutigam *m* **-s, -e** (bride)groom; *(dated: Verlobter)* fiancé, betrothed *(old)*, husband-to-be.

Braut-: ~jungfer *f* bridesmaid; **~kleid** *nt* wedding dress; **~kranz** *m headdress of myrtle leaves traditionally worn by a bride;* **~leute** *pl siehe* **~paar**; **~mutter** *f* bride's mother; **~paar** *nt* bride and (bride)groom, bridal pair *or* couple; *(dated: Verlobte)* engaged couple; **~schau** *f*: **auf (die) ~schau gehen/auf ~schau sein** to go looking/be looking for a bride *or* wife; *(hum sl)* to be out to make a kill *(inf)*; **~schleier** *m* wedding *or* bridal veil; **~staat** *m* wedding finery; **~stand** *m, no pl (dated)* engagement; **~unterricht** *m in RC church, religious instruction of engaged couple prior to marriage;* **~vater** *m* bride's father; **~werbung** *f* courtship, wooing; **~zeit** *f* last few weeks before the wedding.

brav *adj* **(a)** *(gehorsam) Kind* good, well-behaved ◆ **sei schön ~!** be a good boy/girl; **~ (gemacht)!** *(zu Tier)* good boy!, well done; **iß das ~ leer** be a good boy/girl and eat it up, eat it up like a good boy/girl.
(b) *(rechtschaffen)* upright, worthy, (good) honest; *(bieder) Frisur, Kleid* plain ◆ **~ seine Pflicht tun** to do one's duty worthily; **etw ~ spielen** to give an uninspired rendition of sth.
(c) *(dated: tapfer)* brave.

Bravheit *f siehe adj* **(a)** good behaviour. **(b)** uprightness, worthiness, honesty; plainness. **(c)** bravery.

bravo ['bra:vo] *interj* well done; *(für Künstler)* bravo.

Bravoruf *m* cheer.

⚠**Bravour** [bra'vu:ɐ] *f* **-,** *no pl (geh)* bravura; *(old: Kühnheit)* bravery, daring ◆ **mit ~** with style.

⚠**Bravourleistung** *f (geh)* brilliant performance.

⚠**bravourös** [bravu'rø:s] *adj* **(a)** *(meisterhaft)* brilliant. **(b)** *(forsch)* **mit ~em Tempo** with verve; **etw ~ in Angriff nehmen** to attack *or* tackle sth with verve *or* gusto.

⚠**Bravourstück** *nt (geh)* brilliant coup; *(Mus)* bravura.

BRD [be:|ɛr'de:] *f* **-** *abbr of* **Bundesrepublik Deutschland** FRG.

Break-even-point [breɪk'i:vnpɔynt] *m* **-s, -s** *(Econ)* break-even point.

Brech-: b~bar *adj* breakable; **~bohnen** *pl* French beans *pl*; **~durchfall** *m* diarrhoea and sickness; **~eisen** *nt* crowbar; *(von Dieb)* jemmy, jimmy *(US)*.

brechen *pret* **brach,** *ptp* **gebrochen** [1] *vt* **(a)** to break; *Schiefer, Stein, Marmor* to cut; *Widerstand, Trotz auch* to overcome; *Licht* to refract; *(geh: pflücken) Blumen* to pluck, to pick ◆ **sich/jdm den Arm ~** to break one's/sb's arm; **einer Flasche den Hals ~** to crack (open) a bottle; **das wird ihm das Genick** *or* **den Hals ~** *(fig)* that will bring about his downfall; **jdm die Treue ~** to break trust with sb; *(Liebhaber etc)* to be unfaithful to sb; *siehe* **Bahn, Eis, Ehe.**
(b) *(erbrechen)* to vomit up, to bring up.
[2] *vi* **(a)** *aux sein* to break ◆ **seine Augen brachen** *(old, liter)* he passed away; **mir bricht das Herz** it breaks my heart; **zum B~** *or* **~d voll sein** to be full to bursting.
(b) mit jdm/etw ~ to break with sb/sth.
(c) *(sich erbrechen)* to be sick, to throw up.
[3] *vr (Wellen)* to break; *(Lichtstrahl)* to be refracted; *(Schall)* to rebound *(an +dat* off).

Brecher *m* **-s, - (a)** *(Welle)* breaker. **(b)** *(Tech)* crusher.

Brech-: ~mittel *nt* emetic; **er/das ist das reinste ~mittel (für mich)** he/it makes me feel ill; **~reiz** *m* nausea; **ein leichter ~reiz** a slight touch of nausea; **~stange** *f* crowbar.

Brechung *f* **(a)** *(der Wellen)* breaking; *(des Lichts)* refraction; *(des Schalls)* rebounding. **(b)** *(Ling)* mutation.

Brechungswinkel *m* angle of refraction.

Bredouille [bre'dʊljə] *f* **in der ~ sein** *or* **sitzen/in die ~ geraten** *or* **kommen** to be in/get into a scrape *(inf)*.

Brei *m* **-(e)s, -e** mush, paste, goo *(inf)*; *(für Kinder, Kranke)* mash, semi-solid food; *(Hafer~)* porridge; *(Grieß~)* semolina; *(Reis~)* rice pudding; *(Papier~)* pulp ◆ **verrühren Sie die Zutaten zu einem dünnen ~** mix the ingredients to a thin paste; **die Lava fließt wie ein zäher ~** the lava flows like a sluggish pulp; **jdn zu ~ schlagen** *(inf)* to beat sb to a pulp *(inf)*; **um den heißen ~ herumreden** *(inf)* to beat about the bush *(inf)*; **jdm ~ um den Mund** *or* **ums Maul schmieren** *(inf)* to soft-soap sb *(inf)*; *siehe* **Katze, Koch.**

breiig *adj* mushy ◆ **eine ~e Masse** a paste, a paste-like substance.

breit [1] *adj* broad; *(esp bei Maßangabe)* wide; *Bekanntenkreis, Publikum, Interessen auch* wide; *Schrift* broadly spaced, sprawling ◆ **etw ~er machen** to broaden *or* widen sth; **den Stoff ~ nehmen** to take the material widthways; **~es Lachen** guffaw; **er hat ein ~es Lachen** he guffaws; **die ~e Masse** the masses *pl*, the broad mass of the population; **ein ~es Angebot** a broad *or* wide selection; **~e Streuung des Eigentums** widespread distribution of property, distribution of property on a broad basis; **er hat einen ~en Rücken** *or* **Buckel** *(fig inf)* he has a broad back, his shoulders are broad.
[2] *adv* **~ lachen** to guffaw; **~ sprechen** to speak with a broad accent; **~ gebaut** sturdily built; **die Schuhe ~ treten** to wear one's shoes out of shape; **der Stoff liegt doppelt ~** the material is double width; **sich ~ hinsetzen** to sit down squarely; **setz dich doch nicht so ~ hin** don't take up so much room.

Breitband-: ~kabel *nt* broadband cable; **~verteiler** *m* broadband distributor.

breit-: ~beinig [1] *adj* **in ~beiniger Stellung** with one's legs apart; **~beiniger Gang** rolling gait; [2] *adv* with one's legs apart; **~drücken** *vt sep* to press flat.

Breite *f* **-, -n (a)** breadth; *(von Dialekt, Aussprache)* broadness; *(esp bei Maßangaben)* width; *(von Angebot)* breadth; *(von Interessen)* breadth, wide range ◆ **der ~ nach** widthways; **etw in aller ~ erklären** to explain sth in great detail; **in voller ~ vor jdm** smack in front of sb; **in die ~ gehen** to go into detail; *(inf: dick werden)* to put on weight, to put it on a bit *(inf)*.
(b) *(Geog)* latitude; *(Gebiet)* part of the world ◆ **in südlichere ~n fahren** *(inf)* to travel to more southerly climes *or* parts; **es liegt (auf) 20° nördlicher ~** it lies 20° north.

breiten *vtr* to spread ◆ **jdm etw über die Beine** *etc* **~** to spread sth across sb's legs *etc*; **sich über das Tal/jds Gesicht ~** to spread across the valley/across *or* over sb's face.

Breiten-: ~arbeit *f* broader *or* more general work; **~grad** *m* (degree of) latitude; **~kreis** *m* parallel; **~sport** *m* popular sport; **~wirkung** *f (von Roman etc)* large *or* widespread impact.

Breit-: b~flächig *adj Gesicht* wide; **b~flächig malen** to paint with broad strokes; ⚠**b~gefächert** *adj* **ein b~gefächertes Angebot** a wide range; **b~krempig** *adj* broad-brimmed; ⚠**b~machen** *vr sep (inf)* **wenn er sich auf dem Sofa b~macht...** when he plants himself on the sofa ...; **mach dich doch nicht so b~!** don't take up so much room; **die Touristen haben sich im Hotel b~gemacht** the tourists in the hotel behaved as if they owned the place; **b~randig** *adj Hut* broad-brimmed; *Schwimmbecken, Gefäß, Brille* broad-rimmed; **b~schlagen** *vt sep irreg (inf)* **jdn (zu etw) b~schlagen** to talk sb round (to sth); **sich b~schlagen lassen** to let oneself be talked round; **b~schult(e)rig** *adj* broad-shouldered; **~schwanz** *m, no pl* caracul; **~seite** *f (Naut)* broadside; *(von Tisch)* short end; **eine ~seite abgeben** to fire a broadside; **~spurbahn** *f* broad-gauge railway; **b~spurig** *adj* broad-gauge *attr*; **b~treten** *vt sep irreg (inf)* to go on about *(inf)*; *Thema, Witz* to flog to death *(inf)*; **~wand** *f* wide screen; **etw in ~wand drehen** to film sth for the wide screen; **~wandfilm** *m* film for the wide screen.

Bremen *nt* **-s** Bremen.

Bremer *adj attr* Bremen.

Bremer(in *f*) *m* **-s, -** native of Bremen; *(Einwohner)* inhabitant of Bremen.

bremisch *adj* Bremen *attr.*

Brems-: ~backe *f* brake block; **~belag** *m* brake lining.

Bremse[1] *f* **-, -n** *(bei Fahrzeugen)* brake ◆ **auf die ~(n) treten/steigen** *(inf) or* **latschen** *(sl)* to put on *or* apply/slam on *(inf)* the brake(s).

Bremse[2] *f* **-, -n** *(Insekt)* horsefly.

bremsen [1] *vi* **(a)** to brake; *(Vorrichtung)* to function as a brake ◆ **der Dynamo/Wind bremst** the dynamo acts as a brake/the wind slows you *etc* down.
(b) *(inf: zurückstecken)* to ease off, to put on the brakes *(inf)* ◆ **mit etw ~** to cut down (on) sth; **jetzt sollten wir mit den Ausgaben ~** it's time to apply the (financial) brakes.
[2] *vt* **(a)** *Fahrzeug* to brake.
(b) *(fig)* to restrict, to limit; *Entwicklung* to slow down; *Begeisterung* to dampen; *(inf) jdn* to check ◆ **er ist nicht zu ~** *(inf)* there's no stopping him.
[3] *vr (inf)* **sich in seiner Ausdrucksweise ~** to moderate one's language; **ich kann** *or* **werd' mich ~** not likely!, no fear!

Bremser *m* **-s, -** *(Rail, Sport)* brakeman.

Brems-: ~fallschirm *m* brake parachute; **~flüssigkeit** *f* brake fluid; **~hebel** *m* brake lever; **~klappe** *f (Aviat)* brake flap; **~klotz** *m (Aut)* brake pad; **~kraft** *f* braking power; **~kraftverstärker** *m* servo brake; **~leistung** *f* braking efficiency; **~leuchte** *f*, **~licht** *nt* brake light; **~pedal** *nt* brake pedal; **~probe** *f* brake test; **eine ~probe machen** to test one's brakes; **~rakete** *f* retro-rocket; **~schlauch** *m* brake hose; **~schuh** *m* brake shoe; **~spur** *f* skid mark *usu pl.*

Bremsung *f* braking.

Brems-: ~vorrichtung *f* brake mechanism; **~weg** *m* braking distance.

Brenn-: b~bar *adj* combustible, inflammable, flammable; **leicht b~bar** highly combustible *or* inflammable; **~dauer** *f (von Glühbirnen)* life; **~element** *nt* fuel element.

brennen *pret* **brannte,** *ptp* **gebrannt** [1] *vi* to burn; *(Haus, Wald auch)* to be on fire; *(elektrisches Gerät, Glühbirne etc)* to be on; *(Zigarette, Sparflamme)* to be alight; *(Stich)* to sting; *(Füße)* to hurt, to be sore ◆ **das Streichholz/Feuerzeug brennt nicht** the match/lighter won't light; **auf der Haut/in den Augen ~** to burn *or* sting the skin/eyes; **das Licht ~ lassen** to leave the light on; **im Zimmer brennt noch Licht** the light is still on in the room; **es brennt!** fire, fire!; *(fig)* it's urgent; **wo brennt's denn?** *(inf)* what's the panic?; **darauf ~, etw zu tun** to be dying to do sth; **das brennt mir auf der Seele** that is preying on my mind; **es brennt mir unter den Nägeln ...** *(fig)* I am itching *or* dying ...; *siehe* **Boden.**
[2] *vt* to burn; *Branntwein* to distil; *Mandeln, Kaffee* to roast; *Porzellan, Ton, Ziegel* to fire, to bake; *Tier* to brand ◆ **sich** *(dat)* **Locken ins Haar ~** to curl one's hair with curling tongs; **ein gebranntes Kind scheut das Feuer** *(Prov)*

once bitten, twice shy (*Prov*).
3 *vr* (*lit*) to burn oneself (*an +dat* on); (*inf: sich täuschen*) to be very much mistaken.
brennend *adj* (*lit, fig*) burning; *Zigarette* lighted; *Durst* raging; *Haß* consuming ◆ **das interessiert mich ~** (*inf*) I would be incredibly interested; **ich wüßte ja ~ gern ...** (*inf*) I'm dying *or* itching to know ... (*inf*).
Brenner *m* **-s, -** (**a**) (*Tech*) burner. (**b**) (*Beruf*) (*Branntwein~*) distiller; (*Kaffee~*) coffee-roaster; (*Ziegel~*) brick-firer.
Brennerei *f* distillery; (*Kaffee~*) coffee-roasting plant; (*Ziegel~*) brickworks *sing or pl*.
⚠ **Brennessel** *f getrennt*: **Brenn-nessel** stinging nettle.
Brenn-: **~glas** *nt* burning glass; **~holz** *nt* firewood; **~kammer** *f* combustion chamber; **~material** *nt* fuel (for heating); **~nessel** *f siehe* **Brennessel**; **~ofen** *m* kiln; **~punkt** *m* (*Math, Opt*) focus; **im ~punkt des Interesses stehen** to be the focus *or* focal point of attention; **etw in den ~punkt rücken** (*fig*) to focus attention on sth; **~schere** *f* curling tongs *pl*; **~spiegel** *m* burning glass; **~spiritus** *m* methylated spirits *sing or pl*; **~stab** *m* fuel rod; **~stoff** *m* fuel; **~weite** *f* (*Opt*) focal length.
brenzlig *adj* (**a**) **ein ~er Geruch** a smell of burning. (**b**) (*inf*) *Situation, Angelegenheit* precarious, dicey (*Brit inf*) ◆ **die Sache/die Lage wurde ihm zu ~** things got too hot for him.
Bresche *f* **-, -n** breach, gap ◆ **in etw** (*acc*) **eine ~ schießen** to breach sth; **in die ~ springen** (*fig*) to step into *or* fill the breach; **für jdn/etw eine ~ schlagen** (*fig*) to stand up for sb/sth.
Bretagne [bre'tanjə] *f* **- die ~** Brittany.
Bretone *m* **-n, -n**, **Bretonin** *f* Breton.
bretonisch *adj* Breton.
Brett *nt* **-(e)s, -er** (**a**) (*Holzplatte*) board; (*länger und dicker*) plank; (*Spiel~, Sprung~*) board; (*Bücher~, Gewürz~*) shelf; (*inf: Tablett*) tray; (*Frühstücks~*) platter, wooden plate ◆ **Schwarzes ~** noticeboard (*Brit*), bulletin board (*US*); **etw mit ~ern vernageln** to board sth up; **hier ist die Welt mit ~ern vernagelt** this is a parochial little place; **ich habe heute ein ~ vor dem Kopf** (*inf*) I can't think straight today; *siehe* **Stein**.
(**b**) **~er** *pl* (*fig*) (*Bühne*) stage, boards *pl*, planks *pl* (*inf*); (*Boden des Boxrings*) floor, canvas; (*Skier*) planks *pl* (*sl*) ◆ **über die ~er gehen** (*Theat*) to be put on; **die ~er, die die Welt bedeuten** the stage; **auf den ~ern (stehen)** (to be) on the stage; (*auf Skiern*) to ski; **jdn auf die ~er schicken** (*Sport*) to send sb to the canvas, to floor sb.
Brettchen *nt* (*inf*) platter, wooden plate; (*zum Schneiden*) board.
Bretter-: **~boden** *m* wooden floor (*made from floorboards*); **~bude** *f* booth; (*pej*) shack.
brettern *vi* (*inf: Fahrzeug, Fahrer*) to race (along); **über die Autobahn ~** to tear along the motorway.
Bretter-: **~wand** *f* wooden wall; (*Trennwand*) wooden partition; (*Zaun, für Reklame*) hoarding; **~zaun** *m* wooden fence; (*an Baustellen auch*) hoarding.
Brettspiel *nt* board game.
Brevier [bre'viːɐ] *nt* **-s, -e** (**a**) (*Eccl*) breviary. (**b**) (*Auswahl von Texten*) extracts *pl*; (*Leitfaden*) guide (*gen* to).
Brezel *f* **-, -n** pretzel ◆ **das geht wie's ~ backen** it's no trouble at all.
brich *imper sing of* **brechen**.
Bridge [brɪtʃ] *nt* **-**, *no pl* (*Cards*) bridge.
Brief *m* **-(e)s, -e** (**a**) letter; (*Bibl*) epistle ◆ **aus seinen ~en** from his letters *or* correspondence; **etw als ~ schicken** to send sth (by) letter post; **jdm ~ und Siegel auf etw** (*acc*) **geben** to give sb one's word. (**b**) (*St Ex*) *siehe* **Briefkurs**.
Brief- *in cpds* letter; **~adel** *m* title conferred by letters patent; (*Leute*) non-hereditary nobility; **~beschwerer** *m* **-s, -** paperweight; **~block** *m* writing *or* letter pad; **~bogen** *m* (sheet of) writing *or* letter *or* note paper; **~bombe** *f* letter bomb.
Briefchen *nt* (**a**) note. (**b**) (*für Shampoo, Creme, Pulver*) sachet ◆ **ein ~ Streichhölzer** a book of matches; **ein ~ Nadeln** a packet *or* paper of needles/pins.
Brief-: **~drucksache** *f* circular; **~einwurf** *m* (*in Tür*) letter-box; (*in Postamt etc*) post-box; **~fach** *nt* pigeon-hole; **~freund** *m* penfriend, pen-pal (*inf*); **~freundschaft** *f* correspondence with a penfriend; **eine ~freundschaft mit jdm haben** to be penfriends with sb; **~geheimnis** *nt* privacy of the post; **~karte** *f* correspondence card.
Briefkasten *m* (*am Haus*) letter box, mail box (*US*); (*der Post*) post- *or* pillar-box, mail box (*US*); (*in Zeitungen*) problem column, agony column ◆ **elektronischer ~** (*Comput*) electronic mailbox; *siehe* **tot**.
Briefkasten-: **~firma** *f* **das ist nur eine ~firma** that firm is just an accommodation address; **~onkel** *m* (*inf*) agony columnist; **~tante** *f* (*inf*) agony columnist *or* aunt (*inf*).
Brief-: **~kopf** *m* letterhead; (*handgeschrieben*) heading; **~kurs** *m* (*St Ex*) selling rate, offer price.
brieflich **1** *adj* by letter ◆ **wir bitten um ~e Mitteilung** please inform us by letter; **~er Verkehr** correspondence.
2 *adv* by letter ◆ **mit jdm ~ verkehren** to correspond with sb.
Briefmarke *f* stamp.
Briefmarken- *in cpds* stamp; **~automat** *m* stamp machine; **~bogen** *m* sheet of stamps; **~kunde** *f* philately; **~sammler** *m* stamp collector, philatelist; **~sammlung** *f* stamp collection.
Brief-: **~öffner** *m* letter opener, paper knife; **~papier** *nt* letter *or* writing *or* note paper; **~porto** *nt* postage; (*Gebühr*) postage rate for letters, letter rate; **~post** *f* letter post; **~qualität** *f* (*Comput*) letter quality; **~roman** *m* epistolary novel, novel in letter form; **~sendung** *f* letter, item sent by letter post; **~tasche** *f* wallet, billfold (*US*); **~taube** *f* carrier pigeon; **~träger(in** *f*) *m* postman/-woman, mailman/-woman (*US*); **~umschlag** *m* envelope; **~verkehr** *m* correspondence; **~waage** *f* letter scales *pl*; **~wahl** *f* postal vote; **seine Stimme durch ~wahl abgeben** to use the postal vote, to vote by post; **~wähler** *m* postal voter; **~wechsel** *m* correspondence; **im ~wechsel mit jdm stehen, einen ~wechsel mit jdm führen** to be in correspondence *or* corresponding with sb; **~zusteller** *m* (*form*) postman, mailman (*US*).
Briekäse *m* brie.
Bries *nt* **-es, -e** (*Physiol*) thymus; (*Cook*) sweetbread.
briet *pret of* **braten**.
Brigade *f* (**a**) (*Mil*) brigade. (**b**) (*DDR*) (work) team *or* group.
Brigadegeneral *m* brigadier (*Brit*), brigadier general (*US*); (*in Luftwaffe*) air commodore (*Brit*).
Brigadier [-'dieː] *m* **-s, -e** (*DDR*) (work) team leader.
Brigg *f* **-, -s** (*Naut: Schiff*) brig.
Brikett *nt* **-s, -s** *or* (*rare*) **-e** briquette.
Brikettzange *f* fire tongs *pl*.
brillant [brɪl'jant] *adj* brilliant ◆ **~ aussehen** to look beautiful.
Brillant [brɪl'jant] *m* brilliant, diamond.
Brillant- *in cpds* diamond; **~feuerwerk** *nt* cascade; **~kollier** *nt* diamond necklace; **~schmuck** *m* diamonds *pl*.
Brillanz [brɪl'jants] *f* brilliance.
Brille *f* **-, -n** (**a**) (*Opt*) glasses *pl*, spectacles *pl*, specs (*inf*) *pl*; (*Schutz~*) goggles *pl*; (*Sonnen~*) glasses *pl* ◆ **eine ~** a pair of glasses *or* spectacles; **eine ~ tragen** to wear glasses; *siehe* **rosa**. (**b**) (*Klosett~*) (toilet) seat.
Brillen-: **~etui, ~futteral** *nt* glasses *or* spectacle case; **~glas** *nt* lens; **~schlange** *f* (*pej*) four-eyes (*pej inf*), woman who wears glasses; **~träger(in** *f*) *m* person who wears glasses; **er ist ~träger** he wears glasses.
Brilli *m* **-s, -s** (*inf*) diamond, rock (*inf*).
brillieren* [brɪl'jiːrən] *vi* (*geh*) to be brilliant ◆ **sie brillierte mit ihrem Gesang** her singing was brilliant.
Brimborium *nt* (*inf*) fuss.
bringen *pret* **brachte**, *ptp* **gebracht** *vt* (**a**) (*her~*) to bring; (*holen auch*) to get (*jdm* for sb); (*mitnehmen*) to take ◆ **der Besuch hat mir Blumen gebracht** my visitors brought me flowers; **wir haben der Gastgeberin Blumen gebracht** we took our hostess flowers; **alle Gäste hatten Blumen gebracht** all the guests had taken *or* brought flowers; **sich** (*dat*) **etw ~ lassen** to have sth brought to one; **das Essen auf den Tisch ~** to serve the food; **jdm eine Nachricht ~** to give sb some news; **was für Nachricht ~ Sie?** what news have you got?; **der letzte Sommer brachte uns viel Regen** last summer brought us a lot of rain; **jdn/etw unter** *or* **in seine Gewalt ~** to gain control over *or* of sb/sth; **er bringt es nicht übers Herz** *or* **über sich** he can't bring himself to do it; **etw an sich** (*acc*) **~** to acquire sth; **etw mit sich ~** to involve *or* imply *or* mean sth; **die Liebe bringt es mit sich, daß man leiden muß** love brings *or* involves suffering; **etw hinter sich** (*acc*) **~** to get sth over and done with, to get sth behind one; **diese Wolken ~ schönes Wetter** these clouds mean fine weather; **Unglück über jdn ~** to bring unhappiness upon sb; **(jdm) Glück/Unglück ~** to bring sb good/bad luck.
(**b**) (*weg~, begleiten*) to take; (*im Auto mitnehmen auch*) to give a lift ◆ **bring das Auto in die Garage** put the car in the garage; **jdn ins Krankenhaus/zum Bahnhof/nach Hause ~** to take sb to hospital/to the station/home; **die Kinder zu** *or* **ins Bett ~** to put the children to bed.
(**c**) (*inf: entfernen*) to get ◆ **ich bringe den Ring nicht vom Finger** I can't get the ring off my finger.
(**d**) (*ein~*) *Geld, Gewinn* to bring in, to make, to earn; (*Boden, Mine etc*) to produce; *Ärger* to cause; *Freude* to give, to bring; *Vorteile* to bring ◆ **das Bild brachte DM 100** the picture went for *or* fetched 100 marks; **das bringt nichts** (*fig inf*) it's pointless.
(**e**) (*lenken, bewirken*) to bring ◆ **etw in die richtige Form ~** to get *or* put sth in the right form; **etw zum Stehen ~** to bring sth to a stop; **das bringt dich vors Gericht/ins Gefängnis** you'll end up in court/prison if you do that; **das Gespräch/die Rede auf etw** (*acc*) **~** to bring the conversation/talk round to sth; **jdn auf die schiefe Bahn/auf den rechten Weg ~** (*fig*) to lead sb astray/to bring *or* get sb back on the straight and narrow; **jdn in Gefahr ~** to put sb in danger; **jdn zum Lachen/Weinen ~** to make sb laugh/cry; **jdn zur Verzweiflung ~** to drive sb to despair; **jdn außer sich** (*acc*) **~** to upset sb; **jdn dazu ~, etw zu tun** to get sb to do sth; **jdn so weit** *or* **dahin ~, daß ...** to force sb to ...; **du wirst es noch so weit** *or* **dahin ~, daß man dich hinauswirft** you will make them throw you out.
(**f**) (*leisten, erreichen*) **es auf 80 Jahre ~** to reach the age of 80; **der Motor hat es auf 180.000 km gebracht** the engine has kept going for 180,000 km; **das Auto bringt 180 km/h** (*inf*) the car can do 180 km/h; **er hat es auf 25 Punkte gebracht** he got *or* received 25 points; **es zu etwas/nichts ~** to get somewhere/nowhere *or* achieve something/nothing; **es weit (im Leben) ~** to do very well (for oneself), to get far; **es zu Ehren** *etc* **~** to achieve honours *etc*; **er hat es bis zum Hauptmann/Direktor gebracht** he became a captain/director, he made it to captain/director.
(**g**) (*darbieten*) *Opfer* to offer ◆ **welche Sprünge bringst du in deiner Übung?** what leaps are you doing in your exercise?
(**h**) (*senden*) *Bericht etc* to broadcast; *Sonderbericht* to present; (*im Fernsehen auch*) to show ◆ **das Fernsehen brachte nichts darüber** there was nothing on television about it; **wir ~ Nachrichten!** here is the news; **um zehn Uhr ~ wir Nachrichten** at ten o'clock we have the news; **die nächsten Nachrichten ~ wir um ...** the next news will be at ...; **was bringt das Radio/Fernsehen heute**

abend? what's on television/the radio tonight?
(i) (*veröffentlichen*) (*Verlag*) to publish; (*Zeitung*) to print, to publish ◆ **etw in die Zeitung ~** to publish *or* put sth in the paper; *Verlobung, Angebot* to announce *or* put in the paper; **die Zeitung brachte nichts/einen Artikel darüber** there was nothing/an article in the paper about it, the paper had an article about it; **alle Zeitungen brachten es auf der ersten Seite** all the papers had it on the front page.
(j) (*aufführen*) *Stück* to do.
(k) **jdn um etw ~** to make sb lose sth, to do sb out of sth; **das bringt mich noch um den Verstand** it's driving me mad; **der Lärm hat mich um den Schlaf gebracht** the noise stopped me getting any sleep; **jdn ums Leben ~** to kill sb.
(l) (*sl: schaffen, können*) **ich bringe diese Übung nicht** I can't do *or* manage this exercise; **das bringt er nicht** he's not up to it; **er bringt's** he's got what it takes; **der Motor bringt's nicht mehr** the engine has had it (*inf*); **ihr Typ bringt's nicht mehr** her boyfriend can't make it *or* can't stand the pace any more (*inf*); **das bringt's doch nicht!** that's no damn use (*inf*)!; **das kannst du doch nicht ~** that's not on (*inf*); **hat er das tatsächlich gebracht?** did he really do it?

Bringschuld *f* (*Jur*) *obligation to be performed at creditor's habitual residence.*

brisant *adj* (*lit, fig*) explosive.

Brisanz *f* explosive force; (*fig*) explosive nature ◆ **ein Thema von äußerster ~** an extremely explosive subject.

Brise *f* **-, -n** breeze.

Britannien [-iən] *nt* **-s** (*Hist*) Britain, Britannia (*Hist*).

britannisch *adj* (*Hist*) Britannic.

Brite *m* **-n, -n, Britin** *f* Briton, Britisher (*US*), Brit (*inf*) ◆ **er ist ~** he is British; **die ~n** the British.

britisch *adj* British ◆ **die B~en Inseln** the British Isles.

Bröckchen *nt dim of* **Brocken.**

bröckelig *adj* crumbly; *Mauer* crumbling ◆ **~ werden** to (start to) crumble.

bröckeln *vti* to crumble; (*Gestein auch*) to crumble away.

Brocken *m* **-s, -** lump, chunk; (*fig: Bruchstück*) scrap; (*Hunt*) bait; (*inf: Person*) lump (*inf*) ◆ **das Baby ist ein richtiger ~** the baby's a regular little dumpling (*inf*); **ein paar ~ Spanisch/Psychologie** a smattering of Spanish/psychology; **er schnappte den anderen die besten ~ weg** he snapped up all the best titbits; **das ist ein harter ~** that's a tough nut to crack.

brocken *vt Brot* to break.

brockenweise *adv* bit by bit.

brodeln *vi* (*Wasser, Suppe*) to bubble; (*in Krater auch*) to seethe; (*Dämpfe, liter: Nebel*) to swirl, to seethe ◆ **es brodelt** (*fig*) there is seething unrest.

Brodem *m* **-s, -** (*liter*) foul-smelling vapour.

Broiler ['brɔylɐ] *m* **-s, -** (*dial*) roast chicken.

Brokat *m* **-(e)s, -e** brocade.

Brokkoli *pl* broccoli *sing.*

Brom *nt* **-s,** *no pl* (*abbr* **Br**) bromine.

Brombeere *f* blackberry, bramble.

Brombeerstrauch *m* bramble *or* blackberry bush.

Bromsilber *nt* silver bromide.

bronchial *adj* bronchial.

Bronchial-: ~asthma *nt* bronchial asthma; ⚠**~katarrh** *m* bronchial catarrh.

Bronchie [-iə] *f usu pl* bronchial tube, bronchus (*form*).

Bronchitis *f* **-, Bronchitiden** bronchitis.

Bronn *m* **-s, -en, Bronnen** *m* **-s, -** (*obs, liter*) fount (*liter*).

Brontosaurus *m* **-, -se, Brontosaurier** *m* brontosaurus.

Bronze ['brõːsə] *f* **-, -n** bronze.

Bronzemedaille ['brõːsə-] *f* bronze medal.

bronzen ['brõːsn] *adj* bronze ◆ **~ schimmern** to glint like bronze.

Bronzezeit ['brõːsə-] *f, no pl* Bronze Age.

Brosame *f* **-, -n** (*liter*) crumb.

Brosche *f* **-, -n** brooch.

broschiert *adj Ausgabe* paperback; (*geheftet*) sewn; (*geklammert*) wire-stitched ◆ **jetzt auch ~ erhältlich** now also available in paperback; **~es Heftchen** booklet.

Broschur *f* **-, -en** (*Typ*) cut flush binding.

Broschurarbeit *f* (*Typ*) cut flush work.

Broschüre *f* **-, -n** brochure.

Broschureinband *m* (*Typ*) cut flush binding.

Brösel *m* **-s, -** crumb.

brös(e)lig *adj* crumbly ◆ **~ werden** to (start to) crumble.

bröseln *vi* (*Kuchen, Stein*) to crumble; (*Mensch*) to make crumbs.

Brot *nt* **-(e)s, -e** bread; (*Laib*) loaf (of bread); (*Scheibe*) slice (of bread); (*Stulle*) sandwich; (*fig: Unterhalt*) daily bread (*hum*), living ◆ **ein ~ mit Käse** a slice of bread and cheese; **das ist ein hartes** *or* **schweres ~** (*fig*) that's a hard way to earn one's living; **wes ~ ich ess', des Lied ich sing'** (*Prov*) he who pays the piper calls the tune (*Prov*); **der Mensch lebt nicht vom ~ allein** (*Prov*) man does not live by bread alone; *siehe* **Butterbrot, täglich.**

Brot-: ~aufstrich *m* spread (*for bread*); **~belag** *m* topping (*for bread*); **~beutel** *m* haversack.

Brötchen *nt* roll ◆ **(sich** *dat*) **seine ~ verdienen** (*inf*) to earn one's living *or* one's daily bread (*hum*); **kleine ~ backen** (*inf*) to set one's sights lower.

Brötchengeber *m* (*inf*) employer, provider (*hum*).

Brot-: ~einheit *f* carbohydrate exchange (*Brit*), bread unit (*US*); **~erwerb** *m* (way of earning one's) living; **etw zum ~erwerb betreiben** to do sth for a living; **~geber** (*hum*), **~herr** (*obs*) *m* employer, provider (*hum*); **~kasten** *m* bread bin; **~korb** *m* bread basket; **jdm den ~korb höher hängen** (*fig*) to keep sb short; **~krume** *f* breadcrumb; **~kruste** *f* crust; **b~los** *adj* unemployed, out of work; **jdn b~los machen** to put sb out of work; *siehe* **Kunst**; **~maschine** *f* bread slicer; **~messer** *nt* bread knife; **~neid** *m* envy of other people's incomes/jobs; **das ist der reine ~neid** he *etc* is just jealous of your salary/job; **~rinde** *f* crust; **~schneidemaschine** *f* bread slicer; **~schnitte** *f* slice of bread; **~suppe** *f soup made from bread, stock etc*; **~teig** *m* bread dough; **~zeit** *f* **(a)** (*SGer: Pause*) tea break; **(b)** (*Essen*) sandwiches *pl.*

brr *interj* (*Befehl an Zugtiere*) whoa; (*Zeichen des Ekels*) ugh, yuck; (*bei Kälte*) brr.

Bruch[1] *m* **-(e)s, ¨-e (a)** (*~stelle*) break; (*in Porzellan etc auch*) crack; (*im Damm*) breach; (*das Brechen*) breaking; (*von Fels*) breaking-off; (*von Damm*) breaching ◆ **das führte zu einem ~ an der Achse** it caused the axle to break; **zu ~ gehen** to get broken; **zu ~ fahren** to smash; **~ machen** (*inf*) (*mit Flugzeug, Auto*) to crash (*mit etw* sth); (*beim Abwaschen*) to break something.
(b) (*fig*) (*von Vertrag, Eid etc*) breaking; (*von Gesetz, Abkommen auch*) violation, infringement; (*mit Vergangenheit, Partei, in einer Entwicklung*) break; (*des Vertrauens*) breach; (*von Freundschaft*) break-up; (*im Stil*) discontinuity, break; (*von Verlöbnis*) breaking-off ◆ **in die ¨-e gehen** (*Ehe, Freundschaft*) to break up; **es kam zum ~ zwischen ihnen** they broke up.
(c) (*zerbrochene Ware*) broken biscuits/chocolate *etc*; (*Porzellan*) breakage.
(d) (*Med*) (*Knochen~*) fracture, break; (*Eingeweide~*) hernia, rupture ◆ **sich** (*dat*) **einen ~ heben** to rupture oneself (by lifting something), to give oneself a hernia.
(e) (*Stein~*) quarry.
(f) (*Geol*) fault.
(g) (*Knick*) fold.
(h) (*Math*) fraction.
(i) (*sl: Einbruch*) break-in ◆ **(einen) ~ in einem Geschäft machen** to break into a shop; **einen ~ machen** to do a break-in.

Bruch[2] *m or nt* **-(e)s, ¨-e** marsh(land), bog.

Bruch-: ~band *nt* truss; **~bude** *f* (*pej*) hovel; **b~fest** *adj* unbreakable; **~fläche** *f* surface of the break; **die ~flächen zusammendrücken** press the two broken edges together.

brüchig *adj* brittle, fragile; *Gestein, Mauerwerk* crumbling; *Leder* cracked, split; (*fig*) *Stimme* cracked, rough; *Verhältnisse, Ehe, Moral* crumbling ◆ **~ werden** (*Gestein, Macht etc*) to (begin to) crumble; (*Ehe, Verhältnisse auch*) to (begin to) break up; (*Leder*) to crack *or* split.

Brüchigkeit *f* brittleness, fragility; (*von Gestein etc*) crumbliness.

Bruch-: ~kante *f* edge (of break/split *etc*); **~landung** *f* crash-landing; **eine ~landung machen** to crash-land; **b~rechnen** *vi infin only* to do fractions; **~rechnen** *nt* fractions *sing or pl*; **~rechnung** *f* fractions *sing or pl*; (*Aufgabe*) sum with fractions; **~schrift** *f* gothic script; **~stein** *m* rough, undressed stone; **~stelle** *f* break; (*von Knochen auch*) fracture; **~strich** *m* (*Math*) line (of a fraction); **~stück** *nt* fragment; (*von Lied, Rede etc auch*) snatch; **b~stückhaft** *adj* fragmentary; **ich kenne die Geschichte nur b~stückhaft** I only know parts *or* fragments of the story; **~teil** *m* fraction; **im ~teil einer Sekunde** in a split second; **~zahl** *f* (*Math*) fraction.

Brücke *f* **-, -n (a)** (*lit, fig*) bridge ◆ **alle ~n hinter sich** (*dat*) **abbrechen** (*fig*) to burn one's bridges *or* boats behind one; **jdm eine ~ bauen** (*fig*) to give sb a helping hand; **jdm goldene ~n bauen** to make things easy for sb; **eine ~ schlagen** (*liter*) to build *or* throw (*liter*) a bridge (*über +acc* across); **~n schlagen** (*fig*) to forge links.
(b) (*Turnen*) crab; (*Ringen*) bridge.
(c) (*Anat*) pons Varolii.
(d) (*Naut*) bridge; (*Landungs~*) gangway, gangplank.
(e) (*Zahn~*) bridge.
(f) (*Elec*) bridge.
(g) (*Teppich*) rug.

Brücken-: ~bau *m* **(a)** *no pl* bridge-building; **(b)** (*Brücke*) bridge; **~bogen** *m* arch (of a/the bridge); **~gebühr** *f* toll; **~geländer** *nt* parapet; **~kopf** *m* (*Mil, fig*) bridgehead; **~pfeiler** *m* pier (*of a/the bridge*); **~schlag** *m* (*fig*) **das war der erste ~schlag** that forged the first link; **~waage** *f* scale platform; **~zoll** *m* bridge toll.

Bruder *m* **-s, ¨ (a)** brother ◆ **der große ~** (*fig*) Big Brother; **die ¨ Müller/Grimm** the Müller brothers/the Brothers Grimm; **¨** (*Rel*) brothers *pl*, brethren *pl*; **unter ¨n** (*inf*) between friends; **¨ im Geiste** (*geh*) spiritual brothers; **und willst du nicht mein ~ sein, so schlag' ich dir den Schädel ein** (*prov*) if you're not prepared to agree with me, then you'd better watch out!
(b) (*Mönch*) friar, brother ◆ **~ Franziskus** (*als Anrede*) Brother Francis; **die ¨** the brothers *pl*, the brethren *pl.*
(c) (*inf: Mann*) guy (*inf*), bloke (*Brit inf*) ◆ **ein warmer ~** (*dated*) a poof (*sl*), a pansy (*sl*); **ein zwielichtiger ~** a shady character *or* customer (*inf*); **das sind alles ganz windige ¨** (*pej*) they're a shady lot *or* crew (*inf*) *or* bunch (*inf*); **euch ¨ kenn' ich** (*pej*) I know *you* lot.

Bruderbund *m* (*geh, esp DDR*) (link of) comradeship, fraternal *or* brotherly link.

Brüderchen *nt* little brother, baby brother.

Bruder-: ~hand *f* (*liter*) hand of brotherhood; ⚠**~haß** *m* fraternal hatred, hatred between brothers; **~herz** *nt* (*hum*) dear brother; **na ~herz, wie geht's?** well, brother dear *or* dear brother, how are you?; **~krieg** *m* war between brothers, fratricidal war; ⚠**~kuß** *m* (*fig*) fraternal *or* brotherly kiss; **~land** *nt* (*DDR*) brother nation.

Brüderlein *nt siehe* **Brüderchen.**

brüderlich *adj* fraternal, brotherly *no adv* ♦ **~ teilen** to share and share alike; **mit jdm ~ teilen** to share generously with sb.

Bruder-: ~liebe *f* brotherly love; **~mord** *m* fratricide; **~mörder** *m* fratricide; **~partei** *f* (*DDR*) brother party.

Brüderschaft, Bruderschaft (*esp Eccl*) *f* **(a)** (*Eccl*) brotherhood. **(b)** (*Freundschaft*) close *or* intimate friendship (*in which the familiar 'du' is used*) ♦ **mit jdm ~ trinken** to agree to use the familiar 'du' (*over a drink*).

Bruder-: ~volk *nt* (*geh*) sister people; **unser ~volk in Kuba** our Cuban brothers; **~zwist** *m* (*liter*) fraternal feud.

Brügge *nt* **-s** Bruges.

Brühe *f* **-, -n** (*Suppe*) (clear) soup; (*als Suppengrundlage*) stock; (*dial: von Gemüse*) vegetable water; (*pej*) (*schmutzige Flüssigkeit*) sludge; (*Getränk*) dish-water (*inf*), muck (*inf*).

brühen *vt* **(a)** to blanch, to pour boiling water over. **(b)** *Tee* to brew; *Kaffee* to make in the jug *or* pot.

Brüh-: b~heiß *adj* scalding (hot), boiling hot; **~kartoffeln** *pl* potatoes boiled in meat stock; **b~warm** *adj* (*inf*) hot from the press (*inf*); **er hat das sofort b~warm weitererzählt** he promptly went straight off and spread it around; **~würfel** *m* stock cube; **~wurst** *f* sausage (*to be heated in water*).

Brüll|affe *m* howling monkey, howler; (*inf: Mensch*) loudmouth (*inf*).

brüllen *vti* to shout, to roar; (*pej: laut weinen*) to yell, to bawl; (*Stier*) to bellow; (*Elefant*) to trumpet ♦ **brüll doch nicht so!** don't shout; **er brüllte vor Schmerzen** he screamed with pain; **vor Lachen ~** to roar *or* howl *or* scream with laughter; **~des Gelächter** roars *or* howls *or* screams of laughter (*all pl*); **~ wie am Spieß** to cry *or* scream blue murder (*inf*); **das ist zum B~** (*inf*) it's a scream (*inf*).

Brumm-: ~bär *m* (*inf*) **(a)** (*baby-talk*) teddy bear (*baby-talk*); **(b)** (*brummiger Mann*) crosspatch (*inf*), grouch (*inf*); **~bart** *m* (*inf*) *siehe* **~bär (b)**; ⚠**~baß** *m* (*inf*) (*Baßgeige*) (double) bass; (*Baßstimme*) deep bass (voice).

brummeln *vti* (*inf*) to mumble, to mutter.

brummen *vti* **(a)** (*Insekt*) to buzz; (*Bär*) to growl; (*Motor, Baß*) to drone; (*Kreisel etc*) to hum ♦ **mir brummt der Kopf** *or* **Schädel** my head is throbbing.
(b) (*beim Singen*) to drone.
(c) (*murren*) to grumble, to grouch (*inf*), to grouse (*inf*).
(d) (*brummeln*) to mumble, to mutter.
(e) (*inf*) (*in Haft sein*) to be locked up (*inf*); (*Sch: nachsitzen*) to be kept in ♦ **vier Monate ~** to do four months (*inf*).

Brummer *m* **-s, - (a)** (*Schmeißfliege*) bluebottle; (*hum inf: Sänger*) droner. **(b)** (*inf*) (*etwas Großes*) whopper (*inf*); (*Lastwagen*) juggernaut.

Brummi *m* **-s, -s** (*inf: Lastwagen*) lorry (*Brit*), truck.

brummig *adj* grumpy, grouchy (*inf*), sour-tempered.

Brumm-: ~kreisel *m* (*inf*) humming-top; **~schädel** *m* (*inf*) thick head (*inf*).

brünett *adj* dark(-haired) ♦ **~es Mädchen** dark-haired girl, brunette; **sie ist ~** she is (a) brunette.

Brünette *f* brunette.

Brunft *f* **-, ¨e** (*Hunt*) rut; (*~zeit auch*) rutting season ♦ **in der ~ sein** to be rutting.

brunften *vi* (*Hunt*) to rut.

brunftig *adj* (*Hunt*) rutting.

Brunft-: ~platz *m* rutting ground; **~schrei** *m* bell, mating *or* rutting call (*auch fig*); **~zeit** *f* rutting season, rut.

Brunnen *m* **-s, - (a)** well; (*fig liter*) fountain, fount (*liter*) ♦ **den ~ erst zudecken, wenn das Kind hineingefallen ist** (*fig*) to lock the stable door after the horse has bolted (*prov*); **erst, wenn das Kind in den ~ gefallen ist** (*fig*) but not until things had gone wrong.
(b) (*Spring~*) fountain.
(c) (*Heilquelle*) spring ♦ **~ trinken** to take the waters.

Brunnen-: ~bauer(in *f*) *m* **-s, -** well-digger *or* -borer; **~becken** *nt* basin (of a well/fountain); **~figur** *f* (decorative) sculpture on a fountain; **~haus** *nt* pump room; **~kresse** *f* watercress; **~kur** *f* (course of) spa treatment, cure; **~schacht** *m* well shaft; **~vergifter(in *f*)** *m* **-s, - (a)** well-poisoner; **(b)** (*fig pej*) (political) trouble-maker; **~vergiftung** *f* well-poisoning; **politische ~vergiftung** political calumny; **~wasser** *nt* well water.

Brünnlein *nt dim of* **Brunnen**.

Brunst *f* **-, ¨e** (*von männlichen Tieren*) rut; (*von weiblichen Tieren*) heat; (*~zeit*) rutting season/heat; (*hum: von Mensch*) lust, sexual appetite ♦ **in der ~** rutting/on *or* in heat.

brünstig *adj* **(a)** *siehe* **Brunst** rutting/on *or* in heat; (*hum: von Mensch*) (feeling) sexy (*hum*). **(b)** (*liter: inbrünstig*) ardent, fervent.

Brunst-: ~schrei *m* mating call; **~zeit** *f siehe* **Brunst**.

brunzen *vi* (*S Ger sl*) to (have a) piss (*sl*) *or* slash (*Brit sl*).

brüsk *adj* brusque, abrupt, curt ♦ **sich ~ abwenden** to turn away abruptly *or* brusquely.

brüskieren* *vt* to snub.

Brüskierung *f* snub.

Brüssel *nt* **-s** Brussels.

Brüsseler, ⚠**Brüßler** *adj attr* Brussels ♦ **~ Spitzen** Brussels lace; **~ Salat** (*Sw: Chicorée*) chicory.

Brüsseler(in *f*), ⚠**Brüßler(in *f*)** *m* **-s, -** inhabitant *or* (*gebürtiger*) native of Brussels ♦ **er ist ~** he lives in/comes from Brussels.

Brust *f* **-, ¨e (a)** (*Körperteil*) chest; (*fig: Inneres*) breast, heart ♦ **einen zur ~ nehmen** (*inf*) to have a quick drink *or* quick one *or* quickie (*inf*); **~ (he)raus!** chest out!; **~ an ~** face to face; **sich an jds ~** (*dat*) **ausweinen** to weep on sb's shoulder; **sich** (*dat*) **an die ~ schlagen** (*fig*) to beat one's breast; **sich in die ~ werfen** (*fig*) to puff oneself up; **mit geschwellter ~** (*fig*) as proud as Punch *or* a peacock; **schwach auf der ~ sein** (*inf*) to have a weak chest; (*hum: an Geldmangel leiden*) to be a bit short (*inf*).
(b) (*weibliche ~*) breast ♦ **einem Kind die ~ geben, ein Kind an die ~ legen** to feed a baby (*at the breast*), to nurse a baby.
(c) (*Cook*) breast.
(d) (*~schwimmen*) breast-stroke.

Brust-: ~bein *nt* (*Anat*) breastbone, sternum; **~beutel** *m* money bag (*worn around the neck*); **~bild** *nt* half-length portrait; **~breite** *f* **um ~breite** by a whisker.

Brüstchen *nt dim of* **Brust**.

Brustdrüse *f* mammary gland.

brüsten *vr* to boast, to brag (*mit* about).

Brust-: ~fell *nt* (*Anat*) pleura; **~fellentzündung** *f* pleurisy; **~flosse** *f* pectoral fin; **~gegend** *f* thoracic region; **~haar** *nt* hair on the chest, chest hair; **~harnisch** *m* breastplate; **b~hoch** *adj* chest-high; **~höhe** *f*: **in ~höhe** chest high; **~höhle** *f* thoracic cavity; **~kasten** (*inf*), **~korb** *m* (*Anat*) thorax; **~krebs** *m* breast cancer, cancer of the breast; **~kreuz** *nt* (*Eccl*) pectoral cross; **~lage** *f* prone position; **in ~lage schwimmen** to swim in the prone position; **~muskel** *m* pectoral muscle; **~panzer** *m* breastplate; **~plastik** *f* cosmetic breast surgery; **~schutz** *m* (*esp Fechten*) breast *or* chest protector, plastron; **~schwimmen** *nt* breast-stroke; **b~schwimmen** *vi infin only* to swim *or* do the breast-stroke; **~schwimmer** *m* breast-stroke swimmer; **~stimme** *f* chest-voice; **~stück** *nt* (*Cook*) breast; **~tasche** *f* breast pocket; (*Innentasche*) inside (breast) pocket; **~tee** *m* herbal tea (*for infections of the respiratory tract*); **b~tief** *adj* chest-deep, up to one's chest; **~ton** *m* (*Mus*) chest note; **im ~ton der Überzeugung, (daß ...)** in a tone of utter conviction (that ...); **~umfang** *m* chest measurement; (*von Frau*) bust measurement.

Brüstung *f* parapet; (*Balkon~ etc auch*) balustrade; (*Fenster~*) breast.

Brust-: ~wand *f* (*Anat*) thoracic *or* chest wall; **~warze** *f* nipple; **~wehr** *f* (*Mil*) breastwork; (*Hist*) parapet; **~weite** *f siehe* **~umfang**; **~wickel** *m* chest compress; **~wirbel** *m* thoracic *or* dorsal vertebra.

Brut *f* **-, -en (a)** *no pl* (*das Brüten*) brooding, sitting, incubating. **(b)** (*die Jungen*) brood; (*pej*) lot, mob (*inf*). **(c)** (*bei Pflanzen*) offset, offshoot.

brutal *adj* brutal; (*gewalttätig auch*) violent ♦ **jdm etw ganz ~ sagen** to be brutally *or* cruelly frank to sb about sth, to tell sb sth (quite) brutally; **das tut ~ weh** (*inf*) that hurts like hell (*inf*).

brutalisieren* *vt* to brutalize.

Brutalisierung *f* brutalization.

Brutalität *f* **(a)** *no pl siehe adj* brutality; violence. **(b)** (*Gewalttat*) act of violence *or* brutality ♦ **~en** brutalities, acts of violence *or* brutality.

Brutalo *m* **-s, -s** (*sl*) bruiser (*inf*), thug.

Brut|apparat *m* incubator.

brüten [1] *vi* to brood, to sit, to incubate; (*fig*) to ponder (*über +dat* over) ♦ **~de Hitze** oppressive *or* stifling heat.
[2] *vt* **(a)** (*künstlich*) to incubate; (*Tech*) to breed. **(b)** (*geh*) *Rache, Verrat* to plot.

brütendheiß *adj attr* sweltering, boiling (hot) (*inf*).

Brüter *m* **-s, -** (*Tech*) breeder (reactor) ♦ **schneller ~** fast-breeder (reactor).

Brut-: ~henne *f* sitting hen; **~hitze** *f* (*inf*) stifling *or* sweltering heat; **~kasten** *m* (*Med*) incubator; **hier ist eine Hitze wie in einem ~kasten** (*inf*) it's like an oven *or* a furnace in here (*inf*); **~ofen** *m* (*fig*) furnace; **~pflege** *f* care of the brood; **~platz** *m* breeding ground; **~reaktor** *m* breeder (reactor); **~stätte** *f* breeding ground (*gen* for); (*fig auch*) hotbed (*gen* of); **~teich** *m* spawning pond.

brutto *adv* gross ♦ **~ 1000 DM, 1000 DM ~** DM 1000 gross.

Brutto-: ~einkommen *nt* gross *or* before-tax income; **~ertrag** *m* gross *or* before-tax profit; **~gehalt** *nt* gross salary; **~gewinn** *m* gross *or* before-tax profit; **~inlandsprodukt** *nt* gross domestic product; **~lohn** *m* gross *or* before-tax wage(s); **~registertonne** *f* register ton; **~sozialprodukt** *nt* gross national product, GNP; **~verdienst** *m* gross *or* before-tax earnings *pl*.

Brutzeit *f* incubation (period).

brutzeln (*inf*) [1] *vi* to sizzle (away).
[2] *vt* to fry (up).

Bruyère [bry'jɛ:r] *nt* **-s,** *no pl*, **Bruyèreholz** *nt* briar *or* brier (wood).

Bruyère(pfeife) *f* **-, -s** briar *or* brier (pipe).

BSE [be:|ɛs'|e:] *abbr of* **Bovine Spongiforme Enzephalopathie** BSE.

BSE- *in cpds* BSE.

BSE-Erreger *m* BSE virus.

BSE-frei *adj Betrieb, Fleisch, Tiere* free from BSE.

B-Seite ['be:-] *f* (*von Schallplatte*) B-side.

BTA [be:te:'|a:] *mf abbr of* **biologisch-technische Assistentin, biologisch-technischer Assistent**.

Btx [be:te:'|iks] *m* **-,** *no pl abbr of* **Bildschirmtext**.

Bub *m* **-en, -en** (*S Ger, Aus, Sw*) boy, lad.

Bübchen *nt dim of* **Bub**.

Bube *m* **-n, -n (a)** (*old*) rogue, knave (*old*). **(b)** (*Cards*) jack, knave.

Bubenstreich *m*, **Bubenstück** *nt*, **Büberei** *f* **(a)** (*old*) piece of knavery (*old*) *or* villainy, knavish trick (*old*). **(b)** *siehe* **Dummejungenstreich**.

Bubi *m* **-s, -s** (*inf*) little boy *or* lad, laddie (*inf*); (*pej inf*) (school)boy; (*als Anrede*) laddie (*inf*).

Bubi-: ~kopf *m* bobbed hair *no pl*, bob; **sich** (*dat*) **einen ~kopf machen lassen** to have one's hair bobbed *or* cut in a bob; **~kragen** *m* Peter Pan collar.

bübisch *adj* **(a)** (*old: schurkenhaft*) villainous, knavish (*old*). **(b)** (*verschmitzt*) roguish, mischievous.

Buch *nt* **-(e)s, ¨er (a)** book; (*Band*) volume; (*Dreh~*) script ◆ **über den ¨ern sitzen** to pore over one's books; **er redet wie ein ~** (*inf*) he never stops talking; **ein Gentleman, wie er im ~e steht** a perfect example of a gentleman; **ein Tor, wie es im ~e steht** a textbook *or* copybook goal; **das ~ der ¨er** the Book of Books; **die ¨er Mose** the Pentateuch; **das erste/zweite/dritte/vierte/fünfte ~ Mose** Genesis/Exodus/Leviticus/Numbers/Deuteronomy; **ein ~ mit sieben Siegeln** (*fig*) a closed book; **er ist für mich ein offenes** *or* **aufgeschlagenes ~** I can read him like a book; **sich ins ~ der Geschichte eintragen** (*geh*) to enter one's name in the annals *or* book of history; **~ machen** (*Pferderennen*) to make a book.

(b) *usu pl* (*Comm: Geschäfts~*) books *pl*, accounts *pl* ◆ **über etw** (*acc*) **~ führen** to keep a record of sth; **jdm die ¨er führen** to keep sb's accounts *or* books; **zu ~(e) schlagen** to make a (significant) difference; **das schlägt mit 1000 DM zu ~(e)** that gives you DM 1000; **zu ~ stehen mit** to be valued at.

Buch-: ~besprechung *f* book review; **~binder(in** *f*) *m* bookbinder; **~binderei** *f* (*Betrieb*) bookbindery; (*Handwerk*) bookbinding; **~block** *m* **-s, -s** book block; **~deckel** *m* book cover; **~druck** *m, no pl* letterpress (printing); **~drucker** *m* printer; **~druckerei** *f* (*Betrieb*) printing works *sing or pl*; (*Handwerk*) printing; **~druckerkunst** *f* art of printing.

Buche *f* **-, -n** beech (tree).

Buch|ecker *f* **-, -n** beechnut.

Buch|einband *m* binding, (book) cover.

buchen¹ *vt* **(a)** (*Comm*) to enter, to post (*spec*); (*Kasse*) to register; (*fig: registrieren*) to register, to record ◆ **einen Erfolg für sich ~** to chalk (*inf*) *or* mark up a success (for oneself); **etw als Erfolg ~** to put sth down as a success. **(b)** (*vorbestellen*) to book, to reserve.

buchen² *adj* (*rare*) (made) of beech(wood), beech.

Buchen-: ~holz *nt* beech wood; **~wald** *m* beech wood.

Bücher-: ~bord, ~brett *nt* bookshelf; **~bus** *m* mobile library.

Bücherei *f* (lending) library.

Bücher-: ~freund *m* book-lover, bibliophile; **~gestell** *nt* bookcase; **~gutschein** *m* book token; **~narr** *m* book-fan, book-freak (*inf*); **er ist ein richtiger ~narr** he's book mad *or* crazy about books, he's a real book-freak (*inf*); **~reff** *nt* case for transporting books; **~regal** *nt* bookshelf; **~revision** *f* audit; **~schrank** *m* bookcase; **~sendung** *f* consignment of books; (*im Postwesen*) books (sent) at printed paper rate; **~stube** *f* bookshop; **~stütze** *f* book-end; **~verbot** *nt* ban on books; **~verbrennung** *f* burning of books; **~verzeichnis** *nt* bibliography; **~wand** *f* wall of book shelves; (*als Möbelstück*) (large) set of book shelves; **~weisheit** *f* book learning; **~wurm** *m* (*lit, fig hum*) bookworm.

Buchfink *m* chaffinch.

Buch-: ~form *f*: **in ~form** in book form; **~format** *nt* format for a book; **~führung** *f* book-keeping, accounting; **einfache/doppelte ~führung** single/double entry book-keeping; **~geld** *nt* (*Fin*) bank deposit money; **~gelehrsamkeit** *f* book-learning; **~gemeinschaft** *f* book club; **~halter(in** *f*) *m* book-keeper; **b~halterisch** *adj* book-keeping; **sich b~halterisch ausbilden lassen** to be trained in book-keeping *or* as a book-keeper; **ein Problem b~halterisch sehen** to see something as a book-keeping problem, to view a problem in terms of book-keeping; **~haltung** *f* **(a)** *siehe* **~führung**; **(b)** (*Abteilung einer Firma*) accounts department; **~handel** *m* book trade; **im ~handel erhältlich** available *or* on sale in bookshops; **~händler** *m* bookseller; **b~händlerisch** *adj* of *or* connected with the book trade; **eine b~händlerische Ausbildung haben** to be a trained bookseller; **~handlung** *f* bookshop, bookstore (*US*); **~hülle** *f* dust jacket *or* cover; **~kritik** *f* **(a)** (*das Rezensieren*) book reviewing; (*Rezension*) book review; **(b)** *no pl* (*die Rezensenten*) book reviewers *pl or* critics *pl*.

Buch-: ~laden *m* bookshop, bookstore (*US*); **~macher** *m* bookmaker, bookie (*inf*); **~malerei** *f* illumination; **~messe** *f* book fair; **~prüfer** *m* auditor; **~prüfung** *f* audit; **~rücken** *m* spine.

Buchs ['bʊks] *m* **-es, -e, Buchsbaum** *m* box(tree).

Büchschen ['byksçən] *nt dim of* **Büchse**.

Buchse ['bʊksə] *f* **-, -n** (*Elec*) socket; (*Tech*) (*von Zylinder*) liner; (*von Lager*) bush.

Büchse ['byksə] *f* **-, -n (a)** tin; (*Konserven~*) can, tin (*Brit*); (*Sammel~*) collecting box ◆ **die ~ der Pandora** (*Myth, liter*) Pandora's box. **(b)** (*Gewehr*) rifle, (shot)gun.

Büchsen-: ~fleisch *nt* canned *or* tinned (*Brit*) meat; **~macher** *m* gunsmith; **~milch** *f* tinned (*Brit*) *or* evaporated milk; **~öffner** *m* can *or* tin (*Brit*) opener.

Buchstabe *m* **-n(s), -n** letter; (*esp Druck~*) character ◆ **kleiner ~** small letter; **großer ~** capital (letter); **ein fetter ~** a bold character, a character in bold (face); **in fetten ~n** in bold (face); **Betrag in ~n** amount in words; **dem ~n nach** (*fig*) literally; **auf den ~n genau** (*fig*), **bis auf den letzten ~n** (*fig*) to the letter; **nach dem ~n des Gesetzes ist das verboten, aber ...** according to the letter of the law that's illegal but ...; *siehe* **vier**.

Buchstaben-: b~getreu *adj* literal; **etw b~getreu befolgen** to follow sth to the letter; **~glaube** *m* literalism; **b~gläubig** *adj* literalist(ic); **~kombination** *f* combination (of letters); **~rätsel** *nt* word-puzzle, anagram; **~schrift** *f* alphabetic script; **~treue** *f* adherence to the letter.

buchstabieren* *vt* **(a)** to spell. **(b)** (*mühsam lesen*) to spell out.

Buchstabier-: ~methode *f* alphabetical method; **~tafel** *f* word spelling alphabet.

buchstäblich *adj* literal.

Buchstütze *f siehe* **Bücherstütze**.

Bucht *f* **-, -en (a)** (*im Meer*) bay; (*kleiner*) cove. **(b)** (*für Schweine etc*) stall.

Buchteln *pl* (*Aus Cook*) jam-filled yeast dumplings.

buchtenreich, buchtig *adj* indented.

Buch-: ~titel *m* (book) title; **~umschlag** *m* dust jacket *or* cover.

Buchung *f* (*Comm*) entry; (*Reservierung*) booking, reservation.

Buchungs-: ~karte *f* charge card; **~maschine** *f* accounting machine; **~system** *nt* booking system.

Buchweizen *m* buckwheat.

Buch-: ~wert *m* (*Comm*) book value; **~wissen** *nt* (*pej*) book learning.

Buckel *m* **-s, - (a)** hump(back), hunchback; (*inf: Rücken*) back ◆ **einen ~ machen** (*Katze*) to arch its back; **steh gerade, mach nicht so einen ~!** stand up (straight), don't hunch your back *or* shoulders like that!; **einen krummen ~ machen** (*fig inf*) to bow and scrape, to kowtow; **den ~ voll kriegen** (*inf*) to get a good hiding, to get a belting (*inf*); **er kann mir den ~ (he)runterrutschen** (*inf*) he can (go and) take a running jump, he can get lost *or* knotted (*all inf*); **viel/genug auf dem ~ haben** (*inf*) to have a lot/enough on one's plate (*inf*); **den ~ voll Schulden haben** (*inf*) to be up to one's neck *or* eyes in debt (*inf*); **den ~ hinhalten** (*fig inf*) to carry the can (*inf*); **seine 80 Jahre auf dem ~ haben** (*inf*) to be 80 (years old), to have seen 80 summers; *siehe* **jucken, breit**.

(b) (*inf: Hügel*) hummock, hillock.

(c) (*inf: Auswölbung*) bulge, hump.

(d) (*von Schild*) boss.

buck(e)lig *adj* hunchbacked, humpbacked; (*inf*) *Straße* bumpy; *Landschaft* undulating, hilly.

Buck(e)lige(r) *mf decl as adj* hunchback, humpback.

buckeln *vi* (*pej*) to bow and scrape, to kowtow ◆ **nach oben ~ und nach unten treten** to bow to superiors and tread inferiors underfoot.

Buckelpiste *f* (*Ski*) mogul piste.

Buckelrind *nt* zebu.

bücken *vr* to bend (down), to stoop ◆ **sich nach etw ~** to bend down *or* to stoop to pick sth up; *siehe* **gebückt**.

Buckerl *nt* **-s, -(n)** (*Aus inf*) *siehe* **Bückling (b)**.

bucklig *adj etc siehe* **buck(e)lig**.

Bückling *m* **(a)** (*Cook*) smoked herring. **(b)** (*hum inf: Verbeugung*) bow.

Budapest *nt* **-s** Budapest.

Büdchen *nt dim of* **Bude (a)**.

Buddel *f* **-, -n** (*N Ger inf*) bottle.

Buddelei *f* (*im Sand*) digging; (*inf: Tiefbauarbeiten*) constant digging (up) (*of road etc*).

Buddelkasten *m* (*dial*) sand-box.

buddeln [1] *vi* (*inf*) to dig ◆ **in der Straße wird dauernd gebuddelt** they're always digging up the road.

[2] *vt* (*dial*) (*ausgraben*) *Kartoffeln* to dig up; *Loch* to dig.

Buddha ['bʊda] *m* **-s, -s** Buddha.

Buddhismus *m* Buddhism.

Buddhist(in *f*) *m* Buddhist.

buddhistisch *adj* Buddhist(ic).

Bude *f* **-, -n (a)** (*Bretterbau*) hut; (*Bau~*) (workmen's) hut; (*Markt~, Verkaufs~*) stall, stand, booth; (*Zeitungs~*) kiosk.

(b) (*pej inf: Laden, Lokal etc*) dump (*inf*).

(c) (*inf*) (*Zimmer*) room; (*von Untermieter auch*) digs *pl* (*inf*); (*Wohnung*) pad (*inf*) ◆ **Leben in die ~ bringen** to liven *or* brighten up the place; **jdm die ~ einrennen** *or* **einlaufen** to pester *or* badger sb; **jdm auf die ~ rücken** (*als Besucher*) to drop in on sb, to land on sb (*inf*); (*aus einem bestimmten Grund*) to pay sb a visit, to go/come round to sb's place; **jdm die ~ auf den Kopf stellen** to turn sb's place upside down.

Budel *f* **-, -n** (*Aus inf*) (shop) counter.

Buden-: ~besitzer *m* (market) stall-holder; **~zauber** *m* (*dated inf*) knees-up (*dated sl*), jamboree (*dated inf*).

Budget [by'dʒeː] *nt* **-s, -s** budget.

budgetär [bydʒe'tɛːɐ] *adj* budgetary.

Budget- (*Pol*): **~beratung** *f* budget debate; **~entwurf** *m* draft budget; **~vorlage** *f* presentation of the budget.

Budike *f* **-, -n** (*dial*) bar, pub (*Brit*), saloon (*US*).

Budiker(in *f*) *m* **-s, -** (*dial*) bar keeper, landlord (*Brit*).

Buenos Aires *nt* Buenos Aires.

Büfett *nt* **-(e)s, -e** *or* **-s (a)** (*Geschirrschrank*) sideboard. **(b)** (*Schanktisch*) bar; (*Verkaufstisch*) counter. **(c) kaltes ~** cold buffet. **(d)** (*Sw: Bahnhofsgaststätte*) (station) buffet.

Büfett-: ~dame *f*, **~fräulein** *nt*, **~mamsell** *f* (*dated*) (*in Gastwirtschaft*) barmaid; (*in Konditorei*) (counter) assistant.

Büfettier [byfɛ'tieː] *m* **-s, -s** barman.

Büffel *m* **-s, -** buffalo.

Büffel-: ~herde *f* herd of buffalo; **~leder** *nt* buff (leather), buffalo skin.

Büffelei *f* (*inf*) swotting (*inf*), cramming (*inf*).

büffeln (*inf*) [1] *vi* to swot (*inf*), to cram (*inf*).

[2] *vt* *Lernstoff* to swot up (*inf*).

Buffet, Büffet [by'feː] (*esp Aus*) *nt* **-s, -s** *siehe* **Büfett**.

Buffo *m* **-s, -s** *or* **Buffi** buffo.

Bug *m* **-(e)s, ¨e** *or* **-e (a)** (*Schiffs~*) bow *usu pl*; (*Flugzeug~*) nose ◆ **jdm eins vor den ~ knallen** (*sl*) to sock sb one (*sl*). **(b)** (*Cook: Schultergegend*) shoulder. **(c)** (*Tech*) brace, strut.

Bügel *m* **-s, - (a)** (*Kleider~*) (coat-)hanger. **(b)** (*Steig~*) stirrup. **(c)** (*Stromabnehmer*) bow (collector). **(d)** (*von Säge*) frame; (*von Handtasche*) frame;

➤ SPRACHE AKTIV: buchen: b → 48.3

(*Brillen~*) side *or* ear-piece, bow; (*von Gewehr*) trigger-guard; (*für Einweckgläser*) clip, clamp; (*am Lift*) T-bar.

Bügel-: ~automat *m* rotary iron; **~brett** *nt* ironing board; **b~echt** *adj* ironable; **~eisen** *nt* iron; **~falte** *f* crease in one's trousers; **b~fertig** *adj* ready for ironing; **b~frei** *adj* non-iron; **~maschine** *f* rotary iron.

bügeln [1] *vt Wäsche* to iron; *Hose* to press; (*Sport sl*) to lick, to hammer, to thrash (*all inf*); *siehe* **gebügelt.**
[2] *vi* to iron.

Buggy ['bagi] *m* **-s, -s** buggy.

Bügler(in *f*) *m* **-s, -** ironer.

Bug-: ~mann *m* (*Sport*) bow(man); **~rad** *nt* (*Aviat*) nose wheel; **~see** *f* (*Naut*) *siehe* **~welle.**

Bugsier- (*Naut*): **~dampfer, ~schlepper** *m* tug(boat).

bugsieren* [1] *vt* **(a)** (*Naut*) to tow. **(b)** (*inf*) *Möbelstück etc* to manoeuvre, to edge ◆ **jdn aus dem Zimmer ~** to steer *or* hustle sb out of the room. **(c)** (*inf: lancieren*) **jdn in einen Posten ~** to wangle *or* fiddle a job for sb (*inf*).
[2] *vi* (*Naut*) to tow ◆ **Schlepper, die im Hafen ~** tugs that do the towing in the port.

Bugsierer *m* **-s, -** (*Naut*) *siehe* **Bugsierdampfer.**

Bugsier- (*Naut*): **~tau** *nt*, **~trosse** *f* towline, towrope.

Bug- (*Naut*): **~ spriet** *nt* bowsprit; **~welle** *f* bow wave.

buh *interj* boo.

Buh *nt* **-s, -s** (*inf*) boo.

Bühel, Bühl *m* **-s, -** (*S Ger, Aus, Sw*) hill.

buhen *vi* (*inf*) to boo.

Buhle[1] *m* **-n, -n** (*old liter*) paramour (*obs, liter*), lover.

Buhle[2] *f* **-, -n** (*old liter*) paramour (*obs, liter*), mistress.

buhlen *vi* **(a)** (*pej: werben*) **um jdn/Anerkennung ~** to woo sb/recognition; **um jds Gunst ~** to woo *or* court sb's favour. **(b)** (*obs*) **mit jdm ~** to have a love affair with sb.

Buhler(in *f*) *m* **-s, - (a)** (*old liter*) *siehe* **Buhle. (b)** (*pej: Werbender*) wooer.

Buhlerei *f* (*pej*) wooing (*um jdn/etw* of sb/sth).

Buhmann *m*, *pl* **-männer** (*inf*) bogeyman (*inf*).

Buhne *f* **-, -n** groyne, breakwater.

Bühne *f* **-, -n (a)** (*lit, fig*) stage; (*von Konzertsaal, Aula etc auch*) platform ◆ **über die ~ gehen** (*inf*) to go *or* pass off; **etw über die ~ bringen** (*inf*) to stage sth; **wie haben Sie Ihren ersten Elternabend/Ihre Antrittsvorlesung über die ~ gebracht?** how did you manage your first parents' evening/your inaugural lecture?; **hinter der ~** (*lit, fig*) behind the scenes; **von der ~ abtreten** *or* **verschwinden** (*inf*), **die ~ verlassen** to make one's exit, to leave the scene.
(b) (*Theater*) theatre; (*als Beruf*) stage ◆ **Städtische ~n** Municipal Theatres; **zur ~ gehen** to go on the stage, to go into the theatre; **an** *or* **bei der ~ sein** to be on the stage, to be in the theatre; **sie steht seit zwanzig Jahren auf der ~** she has been on the stage *or* in the theatre for twenty years; **das Stück ging über alle ~n** the play was put on *or* staged everywhere *or* in all the theatres.
(c) (*dial: Dachboden*) loft.
(d) (*Tech: Hebe~*) ramp.

Bühnen-: ~anweisung *f* stage direction; **~arbeiter** *m* stagehand; **~ausbildung** *f* dramatic training; **~(aus)sprache** *f* standard *or* received pronunciation; **~ausstattung** *f* stage property *or* props *pl*; **~autor** *m* playwright, dramatist; **~bearbeitung** *f* stage adaptation; **~beleuchter** *m* lighting man; **~beleuchtung** *f* stage lighting; **~bild** *nt* (stage) set; **~bildner** *m* set-designer; **~dichter** *m siehe* **~autor; ~dichtung** *f* dramatic verse; **~effekt** *m* stage effect; **~erfahrung** *f* stage experience; **~erfolg** *m* success; (*Stück auch*) (stage) hit; **~fassung** *f* stage adaptation; **b~gerecht** *adj* suitable for the stage; **etw b~gerecht bearbeiten** to adapt sth for the stage; **~gestalt** *f* (dramatic) character; **~haus** *nt* fly tower; **~himmel** *m* cyclorama; **~maler** *m* scene painter; **~malerei** *f* scene painting; **~manuskript** *nt* script; **~meister** *m* stage manager; **~musik** *f* incidental music; **~personal** *nt* theatre staff; **~raum** *m* stage and backstage area; **b~reif** *adj* ready for the stage; **~schaffende(r)** *mf decl as adj* (*geh*) dramatic artist; **~sprache** *f siehe* **~(aus)sprache; ~stück** *nt* (stage) play; **~technik** *f* stage technique; **~techniker** *m* stage-technician; **~werk** *nt* stage entertainment, dramatic work; **b~wirksam** *adj* effective on the stage; **läßt sich dieser Stoff b~wirksam gestalten?** would this material be effective on the stage?; **~wirkung** *f* dramatic effect.

Buh-: ~ruf *m* boo, catcall; **~rufer** *m* **der Redner wurde von ~rufern empfangen** the speaker was booed *or* greeted by boos *or* booing; **die ~rufer wurden aus dem Saal entfernt** those who had booed were removed from the auditorium.

buk (*old*) *pret of* **backen.**

Bukarest *nt* **-s** Bucharest.

Bukett *nt* **-s, -s** *or* **-e** (*geh*) **(a)** (*Blumen~*) bouquet. **(b)** (*von Wein*) bouquet, nose.

Bukolik *f* (*Liter*) bucolic *or* pastoral poetry.

bukolisch *adj* (*Liter*) bucolic, pastoral.

Bulette *f* (*dial*) meat ball ◆ **ran an die ~n** (*inf*) go right ahead!

Bulgare *m* **-n, -n, Bulgarin** *f* Bulgarian.

Bulgarien [-iən] *nt* **-s** Bulgaria.

bulgarisch *adj* Bulgarian.

Bulgarisch(e) *nt decl as adj* Bulgarian; *siehe* **Deutsch(e).**

Bulimie *f* **-,** *no pl* (*Med*) bulimia (*spec*).

Bulkladung *f* (*Naut*) bulk cargo.

Bull|auge *nt* (*Naut*) porthole.

Bulldogge *f* bulldog.

Bulldozer ['bʊldo:zɐ] *m* **-s, -** bulldozer.

Bulle[1] *m* **-n, -n (a)** bull. **(b)** (*inf: starker Mann*) great ox of a man. **(c)** (*pej sl: Polizist*) cop (*inf*) ◆ **die ~n** the fuzz (*pej sl*), the cops (*inf*).

Bulle[2] *f* **-, -n** (*Hist, Eccl*) bull.

Bullen-: ~beißer *m* **-s, - (a)** (*fig pej*) cantankerous *or* sour-tempered character; **(b)** (*lit: Bulldogge*) bulldog; **~hitze** *f* (*inf*) sweltering *or* boiling (*inf*) heat; **b~stark** *adj* (*inf*) beefy (*inf*), brawny, strong as an ox.

bull(e)rig *adj* (*dial*) sour-tempered, cantankerous.

bullern *vi* (*inf*) **(a)** (*poltern*) to thud, to rumble; (*Wasser, Flüssigkeit*) to bubble; (*Ofen*) to roar. **(b)** (*dial: schimpfen*) to bellyache (*inf*), to moan and groan (*inf*).

Bulletin [byl'tɛ̃:] *nt* **-s, -s** bulletin.

bullig *adj* (*inf*) **(a)** brawny, beefy (*inf*). **(b)** *Hitze* sweltering, boiling (*inf*).

Bullterrier *m* bull-terrier.

bum *interj* bang; (*tiefer*) boom.

Bumerang *m* **-s, -s** *or* **-e** (*lit, fig*) boomerang.

Bumerang|effekt *m* boomerang effect.

Bummel *m* **-s, -** stroll; (*durch Lokale*) wander (*durch* around), tour (*durch* of) ◆ **einen ~ machen, auf einen ~ gehen** to go for *or* take a stroll; **einen ~ durch die Stadt/Nachtlokale machen** to go for *or* take a stroll round (the) town, to (go for a) wander round (the) town/to take in a few nightclubs.

Bummelant(in *f*) *m* (*inf*) **(a)** (*Trödler*) slowcoach (*Brit inf*), slowpoke (*US inf*), dawdler. **(b)** (*Faulenzer*) loafer (*inf*), idler.

Bummelantentum *nt* (*pej*) absenteeism.

Bummelei *f* (*inf*) (*Trödelei*) dawdling; (*Faulenzerei*) loafing about (*inf*), idling.

Bummelfritze *m* (*inf*) loafer (*inf*), idler.

bumm(e)lig *adj* (*trödelnd*) slow; (*faul*) idle.

Bummelleben *nt* (*inf*) life of idleness.

bummeln *vi* **(a)** *aux sein* (*spazierengehen*) to stroll; (*Lokale besuchen*) to go round the pubs/bars *etc*; (*ausgehen*) to go out on the town ◆ **im Park ~ gehen** to go for *or* take a stroll in the park. **(b)** (*trödeln*) to dawdle, to hang about (*inf*). **(c)** (*faulenzen*) to idle *or* fritter one's time away, to take it easy.

Bummel-: ~streik *m* go-slow; **~zug** *m* (*inf*) slow *or* stopping train.

Bummerl *nt* **-s, -(n)** (*Aus inf*) point against.

bummern *vi* (*dial*) to hammer, to bang.

Bummler(in *f*) *m* **-s, - (a)** (*Spaziergänger*) stroller. **(b)** *siehe* **Bummelant.**

bummlig *adj* (*inf*) *siehe* **bumm(e)lig.**

bums *interj* thump, thud ◆ **~, da fiel der Kleine hin** bang! down went the little one.

Bums *m* **-es, -e** (*inf*) **(a)** (*Schlag*) bang, thump; (*Ftbl sl*) kick. **(b)** (*sl*) (*Tanzvergnügen*) hop (*inf*); (*Tanzlokal*) dance hall.

Bumsbomber *m* (*sl*) plane carrying sex tourists.

bumsen [1] *vi impers* (*inf: dröhnen*) **..., daß es bumste ...** with a bang; **er schlug gegen die Tür, daß es bumste** he hammered *or* thumped on the door; **es bumste, als ...** there was a thump *or* thud when ...; **es hat gebumst** (*von Fahrzeugen*) there's been a smash-up (*inf*) *or* crash.
[2] *vi* **(a)** (*schlagen*) to thump, to hammer; (*Ftbl sl*) to kick.
(b) *aux sein* (*prallen, stoßen*) to bump, to bang, to clout (*inf*); (*fallen*) to fall with a bang *or* bump ◆ **mit dem Kopf gegen etw ~** to bump *or* bang *or* clout (*inf*) one's head on sth.
(c) (*inf: koitieren*) to have it off (*Brit sl*), to have sex *or* nookie (*hum inf*).
[3] *vt* **(a)** (*Ftbl sl*) *Ball* to thump, to bang, to hammer.
(b) (*inf*) **jdn ~** to lay sb, to have it off with sb (*Brit sl*), to have sex *or* a bit of nookie (*hum inf*) with sb; **gebumst werden** to get laid (*sl*).

Bums-: ~kneipe *f* (*pej inf*), **~lokal** *nt* (*pej inf*) (low) dive; **~musik** *f* (*inf*) loud (vulgar) music; **b~voll** *adj* (*inf*) full to bursting.

Bund[1] *m* **-(e)s, ¨-e (a)** (*Vereinigung, Gemeinschaft*) bond; (*Bündnis*) alliance ◆ **der Alte/Neue ~** (*Bibl*) the Old/New Testament *or* Covenant; **mit jdm im ~e stehen** *or* **sein** to be in league with sb; **sich** (*dat*) **die Hand zum ~e reichen** (*geh*) to enter into a bond of friendship; **den ~ der Ehe eingehen** to enter (into) the bond of marriage; **ein ~ der Freundschaft** a bond of friendship; **den ~ fürs Leben schließen** to take the marriage vows; *siehe* **australisch.**
(b) (*Organisation*) association, (con)federation; (*Staaten~*) league, alliance.
(c) (*Pol: Bundesstaat*) Federal Government ◆ **~ und Länder** the Federal Government and the/its Länder.
(d) (*inf: Bundeswehr*) **der ~** the army, the services *pl*.
(e) (*an Kleidern*) waist-band.
(f) (*Mus: bei Saiteninstrumenten*) fret.

Bund[2] *nt* **-(e)s, -e** (*von Stroh, Flachs, Reisig etc*) bundle; (*von Radieschen, Spargel etc*) bunch.

Bündchen *nt* neck- *or* sleeve-band.

Bündel *nt* **-s, -** bundle, sheaf; (*Stroh~*) sheaf; (*von Banknoten auch*) wad; (*von Karotten, Radieschen etc*) bunch; (*Opt: Strahlen~*) pencil; (*Math*) sheaf; (*fig*) (*von Fragen, Problemen etc*) cluster; (*von Vorschlägen etc*) set ◆ **ein hilfloses/schreiendes ~** a helpless/howling (little) bundle; **sein ~ schnüren** *or* **packen** (*dated*) to pack one's bags; **jeder hat sein ~ zu tragen** everybody has his cross to bear.

bündeln *vt Zeitungen etc* to bundle up, to tie into bundles/a bundle; *Garben, Stroh* to sheave; *Karotten etc* to tie into bunches/a bunch; (*Opt*) *Strahlen* to focus, to concentrate.

bündelweise *adv* by the bundle, in bundles ◆ **er holte ~ Banknoten aus der Tasche** he pulled wads of banknotes out of his pocket.

Bünden *nt* **-s** *siehe* **Graubünden.**

Bundes- *in cpds* federal; **~amt** *nt* Federal Office; **~angestelltentarif** *m* (*BRD*) statutory salary scale; **~anleihe** *f* government bond; **~anstalt** *f*

Federal Institute; **~anwalt** *m* **(a)** *(BRD)* attorney of the Federal Supreme Court; **(b)** *(Sw)* ≃ Public Prosecutor; **~anwaltschaft** *f (BRD)* Federal German Prosecutor's Office; *(Gesamtheit der Anwälte)* Federal German bar; **~anzeiger** *m (BRD)* Federal legal gazette; **~ärztekammer** *f* professional organization of German doctors; **~aufsicht** *f (BRD)* Government supervision; **~ausbildungsförderungsgesetz** *nt law regarding grants for higher education*; **~autobahn** *f (BRD, Aus)* Federal autobahn *(maintained by the Federal Government)*; **~bahn** *f (BRD, Aus, Sw)* Federal Railway(s *pl*); **~bank** *f* Federal bank; **Deutsche ~bank** Federal Bank of Germany; **~behörde** *f* Federal authority; **~blatt** *nt (Sw)* Federal Law gazette; **~bruder** *m (Univ)* fellow member (of a/the student fraternity); **~bürger** *m* (West) German, citizen of (West) Germany; **b~deutsch** *adj* (West) German; **~deutsche(r)** *mf* (West) German; **~ebene** *f*: **auf ~ebene** at a national level; **b~eigen** *adj* Federal(-owned), national; **b~einheitlich** *adj* Federal, national; **~fernstraße** *f* trunk road *(maintained by the Federal Government)*; **~gebiet** *nt (BRD)* Federal territory; **~genosse** *m* ally, confederate; **~gericht** *nt* **(a)** Federal Court; **(b)** *(Sw)* Federal Appeal Court; **~gerichtshof** *m (BRD)* Federal Supreme Court; **~gesetzblatt** *nt (BRD, Aus)* Federal Law Gazette; **~grenzschutz** *m (BRD)* Federal Border Guard; **~hauptstadt** *f* Federal capital; **~haus** *nt (BRD, Sw)* Federal Houses of Parliament; **~haushalt** *m* Federal budget; **~heer** *nt (Aus)* services *pl*, army, (federal) armed forces; **~kabinett** *nt* Federal cabinet; **~kanzlei** *f* **(a)** *(BRD)* Federal Chancellery; **(b)** *(Sw)* Federal Chancellery; **~kanzler** *m* **(a)** *(BRD, Aus)* Federal *or* (West) German Chancellor; **(b)** *(Sw)* Head of the Federal Chancellery; **~kanzleramt** *nt (BRD, Aus)* Federal Chancellery; **~kriminalamt** *nt (BRD)* Federal Criminal Police Office; **~lade** *f (Bibl)* Ark of the Covenant; **~land** *nt* **(a)** state; **(b)** Land of the Federal Republic of Germany; **~liga** *f (BRD Sport)* national league; **~ligist** *m (BRD Sport)* national league team; **~minister** *m (BRD, Aus)* Federal Minister; **~ministerium** *nt (BRD, Aus)* Federal Ministry; **~mittel** *pl* Federal funds *pl*; **~nachrichtendienst** *m (BRD)* Federal Intelligence Service; **~post** *f*: **die (Deutsche) ~post** the (German) Federal Post (Office); **~präsident** *m (BRD, Aus)* (Federal) President; *(Sw)* President of the Federal Council; **~presseamt** *nt (BRD)* Federal Government's Press and Information Office; **~rat** *m* Bundesrat *(upper house of the (West) German Parliament)*; *(Sw)* Council of Ministers; *(Sw Beamter)* Minister of State; **~rechnungshof** *m* Federal Audit Office, Federal Accounting Office; **~recht** *nt* Federal law; **~regierung** *f (BRD, Aus)* Federal Government; **~republik** *f* Federal Republic; **~republik Deutschland** Federal Republic of Germany; **~republikaner** *m* citizen of the Federal Republic of Germany; **b~republikanisch** *adj* (West) German; **~schatzbrief** *m (Fin)* Federal treasury bill; **~staat** *m (Staatenbund, Gliedstaat)* Federal state; **~straße** *f* Federal road *(maintained by the Federal Government)*.

Bundestag *m* Bundestag, *(lower house of the (West) German Parliament)*; *(Hist)* Diet of the German Confederation.

Bundestags- *(BRD)*: **~abgeordnete(r)** *m* German member of Parliament, member of the *Bundestag*; **~fraktion** *f* group *or* faction in the *Bundestag*; **~präsident** *m* President of the *Bundestag or* (West) German Parliament; **~wahl** *f* (federal) parliamentary elections *pl*.

Bundes-: **~trainer** *m (BRD Sport)* national coach; **~verdienstkreuz** *nt (BRD)* order of the Federal Republic of Germany, ≃ OBE *(Brit)*; **~verfassung** *f* Federal constitution; **~verfassungsgericht** *nt (BRD)* Federal Constitutional Court; **~versammlung** *f* **(a)** *(BRD)* Federal Convention; **(b)** *(Sw)* Federal Assembly; **~verwaltungsgericht** *nt (BRD)* Supreme Administrative Court; **~wehr** *f (BRD)* services *pl*, army, ((West) German) Federal Armed Forces *pl*; **b~weit** *adj* nationwide.

Bund-: **~faltenhose** *f* pleated trousers *pl*; **~hose** *f* knee breeches *pl*.

bündig *adj* **(a)** *(schlüssig)* conclusive; *(kurz, bestimmt)* concise, succinct, terse; *siehe* **kurz**. **(b)** *(in gleicher Ebene)* flush *pred*, level.

Bündigkeit *f (Schlüssigkeit)* conclusiveness; *(Kürze, Bestimmtheit)* conciseness, succinctness, terseness.

bündisch *adj*: **die ~e Jugend** *(Hist)* members of the "free youth movement".

Bündnis *nt* alliance.

Bündnis-: **~block** *m* allied bloc; **~politik** *f* policy vis-à-vis one's allies; **~system** *nt* system of alliances; **~treue** *f* loyalty to the alliance; **die ~treue der Ruritanier** the loyalty of the Ruritanians to the *or* their alliance; **~verpflichtung** *f* commitment to one's allies; **~vertrag** *m* pact of alliance.

Bund-: **~weite** *f* waist measurement; **~zeichen** *nt* jointing mark.

Bungalow ['bʊŋgalo] *m* **-s, -s** bungalow.

Bungee-Springen ['bʌndʒi-] *nt* bungee-jumping.

Bunker *m* **-s, -** **(a)** *(Mil)* bunker; *(Luftschutz~)* air-raid shelter. **(b)** *(Sammelbehälter)* bin; *(Kohlen~)* bunker; *(Getreide~)* silo. **(c)** *(Golf)* bunker. **(d)** *(Mil sl: Gefängnis)* clink *(sl)*, jankers *(Brit Mil sl)*.

bunkern *vti* **(a)** *Kohle* to bunker; *Öl* to refuel. **(b)** *(sl: verstecken)* to stash (away) *(sl)*.

Bunker|öl *nt* bunker oil *or* fuel.

Bunsenbrenner *m* Bunsen burner.

bunt *adj* **(a)** *(farbig)* coloured; *(mehrfarbig)* colourful; *(vielfarbig)* multicoloured, many-coloured; *(gefleckt)* mottled, spotted ◆ **~ gestreift** *pred* colourfully striped; **zu ~e Kleidung** loud *or* gaudy clothing; **~e Farben** bright *or* gay colours; **~es Glas** stained glass; **etw ~ anstreichen** to paint sth colourfully; **etw ~ bekleben** to stick coloured paper on sth; **~ gekleidet sein** to be colourfully *or* brightly dressed, to have colourful clothes on; **Abzüge in B~, ~e Abzüge** *(Phot)* colour prints; **ich sehe lieber Filme in B~** I prefer seeing films in colour; **~ fotografieren** *(inf)* to photograph in colour; *siehe* **Hund**.

(b) *(fig: abwechslungsreich)* varied ◆ **eine ~e Menge** an assorted *or* a motley crowd; **ein ~es Bild** a colourful picture; **in ~er Reihenfolge** in a varied sequence; **ein ~er Teller** a plate of cakes and sweets *(Brit) or* candy *(US)*; **ein ~er Abend** a social; *(Rad, TV)* a variety programme.

(c) *(fig: wirr)* confused, higgledy-piggledy ◆ **es geht hier ~ zu** *(inf)* it's lively here, this is some sort of mad-house *(pej inf)*; **jetzt wird's mir aber zu ~!** *(inf)* that's going too far!, that's too much; **es zu ~ treiben** *(inf)* to carry things *or* go too far, to overstep the mark.

Bunt-: ⚠**b~bemalt** *adj attr* colourfully *or* brightly *or* gaily painted, painted in bright colours; **~druck** *m* colour print; **b~farbig** *adj* colourful, brightly coloured; **~film** *m (inf) siehe* **Farbfilm**; **b~geblümt** *adj attr Stoff* with a colourful flower design or pattern; ⚠**b~gefärbt** *adj attr* multicoloured, many-coloured; **b~gefiedert** *adj attr* with multicoloured *or* bright feathers *or* plumage; **b~gefleckt** *adj attr Tier* spotted, mottled; ⚠**b~gemischt** *adj attr Programm* varied; ⚠**b~gestreift** *adj attr* with coloured stripes; **~heit** *f* colourfulness, gay *or* bright colours *pl*; **b~kariert** *adj attr* with a coloured check (pattern); **~metall** *nt* non-ferrous metal; **~papier** *nt* coloured paper; **~sandstein** *m* new red sandstone; **b~scheckig** *adj* spotted; *Pferd* dappled; ⚠**b~schillernd** *adj attr* **(a)** iridescent; **(b)** *(fig)* colourful; *Vergangenheit auch* chequered *(Brit) or* checkered *(US)*; **~specht** *m* spotted woodpecker; **~stift** *m* coloured pencil; **~wäsche** *f* coloureds *pl*.

Bürde *f* **-, -n** *(geh)* load, weight; *(fig)* burden ◆ **jdm eine ~ aufladen** *(fig)* to impose a burden on sb.

bürden *vt (dated geh)* **etw auf jdn ~** *(lit, fig)* to load sth upon sb.

Bure *m* **-n, -n, Burin** *f* Boer.

Burenkrieg *m* Boer War.

Burg *f* **-, -en** **(a)** castle; *(Strand~)* wall of sand *(built on beach by holiday-maker to demarcate his chosen spot)*. **(b)** *(Biberbau)* (beaver's) lodge.

Burg-: **~anlage** *f* castle buildings *pl or* complex; **~berg** *m* castle hill *or* mound.

Bürge *m* **-n, -n** guarantor; *(fig)* guarantee *(für* of) ◆ **für jdn ~ sein** to be sb's guarantor, to stand surety for sb; **einen ~n stellen** *(Fin)* to offer surety.

bürgen *vi* **für etw ~** to guarantee sth, to vouch for sth; *(fig)* to guarantee sth, to be a guarantee of sth; **für jdn ~** *(Fin)* to stand surety for sb; *(fig)* to vouch for sb; **Sie ~ mir persönlich dafür, daß** ... you are personally responsible *or* answerable to me that ...

Bürger *m* **-s, -** *(von Staat, Gemeinde)* citizen, burgher *(Hist)*; *(Sociol, pej)* bourgeois; *(im Gegensatz zu Landbewohner)* town/city-dweller ◆ **die ~ von Ulm** the townsfolk of Ulm.

Bürger-: **~aktion** *f siehe* **~initiative**; **~beauftragte(r)** *mf* ombudsman; **~begehren** *nt (BRD)* public petition; **~block** *m* conservative alliance; **~brief** *m* patent of citizenship; **~eid** *m* civic oath; **~entscheid** *m (BRD)* citizens' *or* public decision; **~familie** *f* merchant family; **b~fern** *adj* non-populist; **~forum** *nt* open *or* public debate; **~haus** *nt* **(a)** town house *or* residence; **(b)** *(dated: ~familie)* merchant family; **~initiative** *f* citizens' initiative *or* action group; **~komitee** *nt* citizens' committee; **~krieg** *m* civil war.

bürgerlich *adj* **(a)** *attr Ehe, Recht etc* civil; *Pflicht* civic ◆ **B~es Gesetzbuch** Civil Code.

(b) *(dem Bürgerstand angehörend)* middle-class *(auch pej)*, bourgeois *(esp pej)*; *(Hist)* bourgeois ◆ **aus guter ~er Familie** from a good respectable *or* middle-class family; **~es Essen/Küche** good plain food/cooking; **~ essen** to eat good plain food; **~es Trauerspiel** *(Liter)* domestic tragedy.

Bürgerliche(r) *mf decl as adj* commoner.

Bürgerlichkeit *f (von Lebensstil)* middle-class way of life; *(von Denkweise)* middle-class mentality.

Bürger-: **~meister** *m* mayor; **~meisteramt** *nt* **(a)** *(Aufgabe)* office of mayor; **(b)** *(Behörde, Gebäude)* town hall; **~meisterei** *f (old)* **(a)** district council; *(Gebäude)* district council offices *pl*; **(b)** *(dial) siehe* **~meisteramt (b)**; **~meisterin** *f* mayor(ess); *(Frau eines ~meisters)* mayoress; **b~nah** *adj* populist; **~nähe** *f* populism; **~pflicht** *f* civic duty; **Ruhe ist die erste ~pflicht** law and order is the citizen's first duty, the first duty of the citizen is law and order; **~recht** *nt usu pl* civil rights *pl*; **jdm die ~rechte aberkennen** *or* **entziehen** to strip sb of his civil rights; **~rechtler** *m* **-s, -** civil rights campaigner.

Bürgerrechts-: **~bewegung** *f* civil rights movement; **~kämpfer** *m siehe* **Bürgerrechtler**.

Bürger-: **~schaft** *f* citizens *pl*; *(Vertretung)* City Parliament; **~schaftswahl** *f* metropolitan council election *(in Hamburg and Bremen)*; **~schreck** *m* bog(e)y of the middle classes.

Bürgersfrau *f (old)* middle-class woman, bourgeoise *(Hist)*.

Bürgersmann *m, pl* **-leute** *(old)* citizen, bourgeois *(Hist)*.

Bürger(s)sohn *m (usu iro)* son of the middle classes.

Bürgerstand *m (old)* middle class(es), bourgeoisie *(Hist)*.

Bürgersteig *m* pavement *(Brit)*, sidewalk *(US)*.

Bürgerstochter *f (usu iro)* daughter of the middle classes.

Bürger-: **~tum** *nt, no pl (Hist)* bourgeoisie *(Hist)*; **~wehr** *f (Hist)* militia.

Burg-: **~fräulein** *nt* damsel of the/a castle *(old)*; **~fried** *m* **-(e)s, -e** keep; **~friede(n)** *m* **(a)** *(fig)* truce; **(b)** *(Hist)* castle precincts *pl*, castellany; **~herr** *m* lord of the/a castle.

Bürgin *f siehe* **Bürge**.

Bürgschaft *f (Jur) (gegenüber Gläubigern)* security, surety; *(Haftungssumme)* penalty; (*old liter*) pledge (*old liter*) ♦ **~ für jdn leisten** to stand surety for sb, to act as guarantor for sb; (*fig*) to vouch for sb; **er verlangte eine ~** he demanded (a) security *or* surety; he demanded that someone (should) vouch for him/her.

Bürgschafts-: ~erklärung *f* declaration of suretyship; **~nehmer** *m siehe* **Gläubiger.**

Burgund *nt* **-(s)** Burgundy.

Burgunder *m* **-s, -** **(a)** (*Einwohner*) Burgundian. **(b)** (*auch:* **~wein**) burgundy.

burgundisch *adj* Burgundian ♦ **die B~e Pforte** the Belfort Gap.

Burgverlies *nt* (castle) dungeon.

burlesk *adj* burlesque *no adv.*

Burleske *f* **-, -n** burlesque.

Burma *nt* **-** *siehe* **Birma.**

Burmese *m* **-n, -n, Burmesin** *f siehe* **Birmane.**

burmesisch *adj siehe* **birmanisch.**

Burnout, Burn-out ['bøːɐnaut] *m* **-s** *no pl* (*Med*) burnout.

Burnout-Syndrom *nt* (*Med*) burnout syndrome.

Burnus *m* **-** *or* **-ses, -se** burnous(e).

Büro *nt* **-s, -s** office.

Büro- *in cpds* office; **~angestellte(r)** *mf* office worker; **~arbeit** *f* office work; **~artikel** *m* item of office equipment; *pl* office supplies *pl or* equipment; **~automation** *f* office automation; **~bedarf** *m* office supplies *pl or* equipment; **~gebäude** *nt* office building; **~gehilfe** *m* (office) junior, office boy; **~haus** *nt* office block; **~hengst** *m* (*pej inf*) office worker; **all die ~hengste** all the office mob (*inf*); **~kauffrau** *f*, **~kaufmann** *m* office administrator; **~klammer** *f* paper clip; **~kraft** *f* (office) clerk.

Bürokrat *m* **-en, -en** bureaucrat.

Bürokratie *f* bureaucracy.

bürokratisieren* *vt* to bureaucratize.

Bürokratismus *m, no pl* bureaucracy.

Büro-: ~maschine *f* office machine; **~mensch** *m* (*inf*) office worker, pen pusher (*pej inf*); ⚠**~schluß** *m* office closing time; **nach ~schluß** after office hours; **~stunden** *pl* office hours *pl*; **~tätigkeit** *f* office work; **~technik** *f* office technology; **~turm** *m* office block; **~vorsteher** *m* (*dated*) senior *or* chief clerk; **~zeit** *f siehe* **~stunden.**

Bürschchen *nt dim of* **Bursche** little lad *or* fellow ♦ **freches ~** cheeky little devil; **mein ~!** laddie!

Bursche *m* **-n, -n** **(a)** (*old, dial*) boy, lad ♦ **ein toller ~** quite a lad.
(b) (*inf: Kerl*) fellow, guy (*inf*), so-and-so (*pej inf*) ♦ **ein übler ~** a bad lot.
(c) (*Univ: Verbindungsmitglied*) member of a student fraternity.
(d) (*Lauf~*) boy.
(e) (*old Mil*) batman (*Brit*), orderly.
(f) (*inf: großes Exemplar*) **das ist vielleicht ein ~** what a whopper! (*inf*); **da haben wir den ~n** that's got it *or* him! (*inf*).

Burschen-: ~herrlichkeit *f* good old student days; **~schaft** *f* student fraternity; **~schaft(l)er** *m* **-s, -** member of a student fraternity; **b~schaftlich** *adj attr* of a/the (student) fraternity.

burschikos *adj* **(a)** (*jungenhaft*) (tom)boyish ♦ **benimm dich doch nicht so ~** stop behaving like a tomboy. **(b)** (*unbekümmert*) casual.

Burschikosität *f siehe adj* **(a)** (tom)boyishness. **(b)** casualness.

Burse *f* **-, -n** hostel.

Bürste *f* **-, -n** brush; (*inf: Bürstenfrisur*) crew cut.

bürsten *vt* to brush; (*vulg: koitieren*) to screw (*sl.*).

Bürsten-: ~binder *m* (*old*) brushmaker; **wie ein ~binder** (*inf*) like mad (*inf*); *siehe* **saufen; ~frisur** *f*, **~(haar)schnitt** *m* crew cut; **~macher** *m siehe* **~binder; ~massage** *f* brush massage.

Burundi *nt* **-s** Burundi.

Burundier(in *f*) [-iɐ, -iərɪn] *m* **-s, -** Burundian.

burundisch *adj* Burundian.

Bürzel *m* **-s -** **(a)** (*Orn*) rump. **(b)** (*Hunt*) tail. **(c)** (*Cook*) parson's nose.

Bus[1] *m* **-ses, -se** bus; (*Privat- und Überland~ auch*) coach (*Brit*).

Bus[2] *m* **-, -se** (*Elec*) bus.

Busbahnhof *m* bus/coach (*Brit*) station.

Busch *m* **-(e)s, ¨-e** **(a)** (*Strauch*) bush, shrub ♦ **etwas ist im ~** (*inf*) there's something up; **mit etw hinter dem ~ halten** (*inf*) to keep sth quiet *or* to oneself; **auf den ~ klopfen** (*inf*) to fish (about) for information (*inf*); **bei jdm auf den ~ klopfen** (*inf*) to sound sb out; **sich (seitwärts) in die ¨~e schlagen** (*inf*) to slip away; (*euph hum*) to go behind a tree (*euph hum*).
(b) (*Geog: in den Tropen*) bush; (*inf: Wildnis*) jungle.
(c) (*Strauß*) bunch; (*rare: Büschel*) tuft.

Buschbohne *f* dwarf bean.

Büschel *nt* **-s, -** (*von Gras, Haaren*) tuft; (*von Heu, Stroh*) bundle; (*von Blumen, Rettichen*) bunch ♦ **in ~n wachsen** to grow in tufts; (*Blumen*) to grow in clumps.

büsch(e)lig *adj* in tufts; (*Blüten*) in clusters.

büscheln *vt* (*S Ger, Sw*) to tie into bunches.

büschelweise *adv siehe n* in tufts/bundles/bunches/clumps.

Buschen *m* **-s, -** (*dial*) bunch of leaves *etc.*

⚠ **Buschenschenke** *f* (*Aus*) inn.

Buschi *nt* **-s, -s** (*Sw*) baby.

buschig *adj* bushy.

büschlig *adj siehe* **büsch(e)lig.**

Busch-: ~mann *m, pl* **-männer** bushman; **~messer** *nt* machete; **~neger** *m* maroon; **~werk** *nt* bushes *pl*; **~windröschen** *nt* (wood) anemone.

Busen *m* **-s, -** (*von Frau*) bust, bosom; (*old: Oberteil des Kleides*) bodice; (*liter*) (*von Mann*) breast (*liter*); (*fig geh: Innerstes, von Natur*) bosom (*liter*) ♦ **ein Geheimnis in seinem ~ wahren** to keep a secret deep in one's heart (*liter*).

Busen-: b~frei *adj* topless; **~freund** *m* (*iro*) bosom friend; **~star** *m* (*inf*) busty filmstar (*inf*).

Bus-: ~fahrer *m* bus/coach (*Brit*) driver; **~fahrt** *f* bus/coach (*Brit*) ride; **~haltestelle** *f* bus stop; **~linie** *f* bus route; **welche ~linie fährt zum Bahnhof?** which bus goes to the station?

Bussard *m* **-s, -e** buzzard.

Buße *f* **-, -n** **(a)** (*Rel*) (*Reue*) repentance, penitence; (*Bußauflage*) penance; (*tätige ~*) atonement ♦ **~ tun** to do penance; **zur ~** as a penance; **zur ~ bereit sein** to be ready to do penance *or* to atone; **das Sakrament der ~** the sacrament of penance.
(b) (*Jur*) (*Schadenersatz*) damages *pl*; (*Geldstrafe*) fine ♦ **eine ~ von DM 100** a 100 mark fine; **jdn zu einer ~ verurteilen** to make sb pay (the) damages; to fine sb, to impose a fine on sb.

Bussel *nt* **-s, -(n)** (*Aus*) *siehe* **Busse(r)l.**

busseln, bussen *vti* (*S Ger, Aus*) *siehe* **busse(r)ln.**

büßen [1] *vt* to pay for; *Sünden* to atone for, to expiate ♦ **das wirst** *or* **sollst du mir ~** I'll make you *or* you'll pay for that.
[2] *vi* **für etw ~** (*auch Rel*) to atone for sth; (*wiedergutmachen*) to make amends for sth; *für Leichtsinn etc* to pay for sth; **schwer (für etw) ~ müssen** to have to pay dearly (for sth).

Büßer(in *f*) *m* **-s, -** penitent.

Büßer-: ~gewand, ~hemd, ~kleid *nt* penitential robe, hairshirt.

Busse(r)l *nt* **-s, -(n)** (*S Ger, Aus*) kiss.

busse(r)ln *vti* (*S Ger, Aus*) to kiss.

Büßerschnee *m* (*spec*) penitent snow (*spec*).

Buß-: b~fertig *adj* repentant, contrite; (*Rel auch*) penitent; **~fertigkeit** *f* repentance, contrition; **~gang** *m* penitential pilgrimage; **einen ~gang antreten** (*fig*) to don sackcloth and ashes; **~gebet** *nt* prayer of repentance.

Bußgeld *nt* fine.

Bußgeld-: ~bescheid *m* notice of payment due (*for traffic offence etc*); **~katalog** *m* list of offences punishable by fines; **~verfahren** *nt* fining system.

Bußgesang *m*, **Bußlied** *nt* penitential hymn.

Bussole *f* **-, -n** compass; (*Elec*) galvanometer.

Buß-: ~prediger *m* preacher of repentance; **~predigt** *f* sermon calling to repentance; **~sakrament** *nt* sacrament of penance; **~tag** *m* **(a)** day of repentance; **(b)** *siehe* **~- und Bettag; ~übung** *f* act of penance; **~- und Bettag** *m* day of prayer and repentance.

Büste *f* **-, -n** bust; (*Schneider~*) tailor's dummy; (*weibliche*) dressmaker's dummy.

Büstenhalter *m* bra, brassière (*dated*).

Busuki *f* **-, -s** bouzouki.

Busverbindung *f* bus connection.

Butan *nt* **-s, -e, Butangas** *nt* butane (gas).

Butt *m* **-(e)s, -e** flounder, butt ♦ **die ~e** the bothidae (*form*), flounders.

Bütt *f* **-, -en** (*dial*) speaker's platform ♦ **in die ~ steigen** to mount the platform.

Butte *f* **-, -n** **(a)** *siehe* **Bütte. (b)** grape container.

Bütte *f* **-, -n** vat; (*dial: Wanne*) tub.

Buttel *f* **-, -n** *siehe* **Buddel.**

Büttel *m* **-s, -** (*old*) bailiff; (*pej*) henchman (*pej*); (*Polizist*) cop(per) (*inf*) ♦ **die ~** the law (*inf*), the cops (*inf*); **ich bin doch nicht dein ~** (*inf*) I'm not going to do your dirty work (*pej inf*), I'm not your henchman.

Bütteldienst *m* dirty work (*pej inf*).

Bütten(papier) *nt* **-s,** *no pl* handmade paper (*with deckle edge*).

Bütten-: ~rand *m* deckle edge; **~rede** *f* carnival speech.

Butter *f* **-,** *no pl* butter ♦ **braune ~** browned (melted) butter; **gute ~** real butter; **es schmolz wie ~ in der Sonne** it vanished into thin air; **alles (ist) in ~** (*inf*) everything is fine *or* OK *or* hunky-dory (*inf*); **sein Herz ist weich wie ~** his heart is as soft as butter; **jdm die ~ auf dem Brot nicht gönnen** (*fig inf*) to begrudge sb the very air he breathes; **wir lassen uns** (*dat*) **nicht die ~ vom Brot nehmen** (*inf*) we're not going to let somebody put one over on us (*inf*), we're going to stick up for our rights.

Butter- *in cpds* butter; **~bemme** *f* (*dial*) *siehe* **~brot; ~berg** *m* (*inf*) butter mountain; **~blume** *f* buttercup; **~brot** *nt* bread and butter *no art, no pl*, slice *or* piece of bread and butter; (*inf: Sandwich*) sandwich; **für ein ~brot** (*inf*) for next to nothing; *kaufen, verkaufen auch* for a song; **das mußt du mir nicht ständig aufs ~brot streichen** *or* **schmieren** there's no need to keep rubbing it in; **~brotpapier** *nt* greaseproof paper; **~creme** *f* butter cream; **~cremetorte** *f* cream cake; **~dose** *f* butterdish; ⚠**~faß** *nt* butter churn; **~fett** *nt* butterfat; **~flöckchen** *nt* (*Cook*) (small knob of) butter.

Butterfly(stil) ['bʌtəflaɪ-] *m* **-s,** *no pl* butterfly (stroke).

Butter-: ~gelb *nt* **(a)** (*Farbe*) butter yellow; **(b)** (*Farbstoff*) butter colour; **b~gelb** *adj* butter yellow.

butterig *adj* buttery.

Butter-: ~käse *m* (full fat) soft cheese; **~keks** *m* ≃ Rich Tea ® biscuit; **~krem** *f siehe* **~creme; ~milch** *f* buttermilk.

buttern [1] *vt* **(a)** *Brot* to butter. **(b)** *Milch* to make into butter. **(c)** (*inf: investieren*) to put (*in +acc* into). **(d)** (*Sport sl*) to slam (*inf*).
[2] *vi* to make butter.

Butter-: ~pilz *m* boletus luteus (*form*); **~säure** *f* butyric acid; **~schmalz** *nt* clarified butter; **~seite** *f* (*lit*) buttered side; **auf die ~seite fallen** (*fig inf*) to fall on one's feet (*inf*); **b~weich** *adj Frucht, Landung* beautifully soft; (*Sport*

⚠: for details of spelling reform, see supplement

sl) Abgabe, Paß, Aufschlag gentle.
Buttje(r) *m* **-s, -s** (*N Ger*) kid (*inf*), child.
Büttner *m* **-s, -** (*dial*) *siehe* **Böttcher.**
Button ['batn] *m* **-s, -s** badge.
buttrig *adj siehe* **butterig.**
Butz[1] *m* **-en, -en** (*dial*) (*Zwerg*) hobgoblin; (*Schreckgestalt*) bog(e)y(man).
Butz[2] *m* **-en, -en** (*dial*) (apple) core.
Butzemann *m siehe* **Butz**[1].
Butzen *m* **-s, -** (*dial*) **(a)** *siehe* **Butz**[2]. **(b)** (*in ~scheibe*) bulge (*in a bull's-eye pane*).
bützen *vti* (*dial*) to kiss.
Butzenscheibe *f* bulls'-eye (window) pane.
Büx *f* **-, -en, Buxe** *f* **-, -n** (*N Ger*) trousers *pl* (*Brit*), pants *pl* ◆ **fünf ~en** five pairs of trousers *or* pants.
Buxtehude *nt* **(a)** Buxtehude (*town near Hamburg*). **(b)** (*inf*): **aus/nach ~** from/to the back of beyond (*inf*); **in ~ leben** to live in the back of beyond (*inf*); **das macht man vielleicht noch in ~** perhaps they still do that in the provincial backwaters.
BVG [be:fau'ge:] *nt* **-** *abbr of* **Bundesverfassungsgericht.**
Bw *abbr of* **Bundeswehr.**
b.w. *abbr of* **bitte wenden** pto.
BWL [be:ve:'|ɛl] *f* **-** *abbr of* **Betriebswirtschaftslehre.**
Bypass-Operation ['baɪpa:s-] *f* bypass operation.
Byte ['baɪt] *nt* **-s, -s** byte.
Byzantiner(in *f*) *m* **-s, -** Byzantine.
byzantinisch *adj* **(a)** Byzantine. **(b)** (*üppig*) extravagant.
Byzantinist(in *f*) *m* Byzantine scholar.
Byzantinistik *f* Byzantine studies *pl.*
Byzanz *nt* **-'** Byzantium.
bzgl. *abbr of* **bezüglich.**
bzw. *abbr of* **beziehungsweise.**

(*siehe auch* **K, Z;** *für* **CH** *siehe auch* **SCH**)

C, c [tseː] *nt* -, - C, c ◆ **C-Schlüssel** *m* alto *or* C clef.
C *abbr of* **Celsius.**
ca. *abbr of* **circa** approx.
Cabrio *nt* **-s, -s** *siehe* **Kabrio.**
Cabriolet [-'leː] *nt* **-s, -s** *siehe* **Kabriolett.**
Cachou [ka'ʃuː] *nt* **-s, -s, Cachoubonbon** *nt* cachou.
CAD [kat] *nt* **-s,** *no pl abbr of* **computer aided design** CAD.
Cadmium *nt, no pl* (*abbr* **Cd**) cadmium.
Caesar ['tseːzar] *m* **-s** *siehe* **Cäsar**[1].
Café [ka'feː] *nt* **-s, -s** café.
Cafeteria *f* **-, -s** cafeteria.
Cafetier [kafe'tieː] *m* **-s, -s** (*old, Aus*) coffee-house proprietor.
cal *abbr of* **(Gramm)kalorie** (gramme-)calorie.
Calais [ka'leː] *nt* **-'** Calais ◆ **die Straße von ~** the Straits of Dover.
Calcium ['kaltsiʊm] *nt, no pl siehe* **Kalzium.**
Californium *nt, no pl* (*abbr* **Cf**) californium.
Callboy ['kɔːlbɔy] *m* **-s, -s** male prostitute.
Callgirl ['kɔːlgøːɐl] *nt* **-s, -s** callgirl.
Calvados [kalva'doːs] *m* **-, -** calvados.
calvinisch *adj etc siehe* **kalvinisch.**
Calypso *m* **-(s), -s** calypso.
CAM [kam] *nt* **-s,** *no pl abbr of* **computer-aided manufacture** CAM.
Camcorder *m* **-s, -** camcorder.
Camembert ['kamɑmbeːɐ] *m* **-s, -s** Camembert.
Camion [ka'miõː] *m* **-s, -s** (*Sw*) *siehe* **Lastwagen.**
Camouflage [kamu'flaːʒə] *f* **-, -n** (*dated, geh*) camouflage.
Camp [kɛmp] *nt* **-s, -s** camp; (*Gefangenenlager auch*) compound.
campen ['kɛmpn] *vi* to camp.
Camper(in *f***)** ['kɛmpɐ, -ərɪn] *m* **-s, -** camper.
campieren* [kam'piːrən] *vi* **(a)** *siehe* **kampieren. (b)** (*Aus, Sw*) *siehe* **campen.**
Camping ['kɛmpɪŋ] *nt* **-s,** *no pl* camping *no art* ◆ **zum ~ fahren** to go camping.
Camping- *in cpds* camping; **~artikel** *m* piece *or* item of camping equipment; *pl* camping equipment *sing*; **~bus** *m* dormobile ® (*Brit*), camper (*esp US*); **~führer** *m* camping *or* camper's guide(book); **~platz** *m* camp site; **~zubehör** *nt* camping equipment.
Campus *m* **-,** *no pl* (*Univ*) campus ◆ **auf dem ~** on (the) campus.
Canasta *nt* **-s,** *no pl* canasta.
Cancan [kā'kāː] *m* **-s, -s** cancan.
cand. *abbr of* **candidatus** *siehe* **Kandidat** ◆ **~ phil./med.** *etc* final year arts/medical *etc* student.
Cannabis *m* **-,** *no pl* cannabis.
Cannelloni *pl* cannelloni *sing or pl.*
Cañon ['kanjɔn] *m* **-s, -s** canyon.
Canossa *nt* **-(s)** *siehe* **Kanossa.**
Canto *m* **-s, -s** (*Liter*) canto.
Cape [keːp] *nt* **-s, -s** cape.
Capriccio [ka'prɪtʃo] *nt* **-s, -s** (*Mus*) caprice, capriccio.
Capuccino [kapu'tʃiːno] *m* **-s, -s** cappuccino.
Car *m* **-s, -s** (*Sw*) *abbr of* **Autocar.**
Caravan ['ka(ː)ravan] *m* **-s, -s (a)** (*Kombiwagen*) estate car (*Brit*), station wagon. **(b)** (*Wohnwagen*) caravan (*Brit*), trailer (*US*).
CARE-Paket ['kɛə-] *nt* CARE packet *or* parcel.
carrarisch *adj Marmor* Carrara.
Car-sharing ['kaːʃɛːərɪŋ] *nt* **-s** *no pl* car-sharing.
cartesianisch *adj etc siehe* **kartesianisch.**
Cartoon [kar'tuːn] *m or nt* cartoon; (*Bildergeschichte auch*) strip cartoon.
Casanova [kaza'noːva] *m* **-(s), -s** (*fig*) Casanova.
Cäsar[1] ['tsɛːzar] *m* **-s** Caesar.
Cäsar[2] ['tsɛːzar] *m* **-en, -en** [tsɛ'zaːrən] (*Titel*) Caesar.
Cäsaren-: ~herrschaft *f* autocratic rule, dictatorship; **~wahn(sinn)** *m* megalomania.
Cäsarismus [tsɛza'rɪsmʊs] *m* Caesarism, autocracy.
⚠ **Cashewnuß** ['kɛʃu-] *f* cashew (nut).

⚠: for details of spelling reform, see supplement

Cash-flow ['kɛʃfloː] *m* **-s,** *no pl* cash flow.
Casino *nt* **-s, -s** *siehe* **Kasino.**
Cäsium ['tsɛːziʊm] *nt, no pl* (*abbr* **Cs**) caesium (*Brit*), cesium (*US*).
Casting ['kaːstɪŋ] *nt* **-s, -s** (*für Filmrolle etc*) casting session.
Castor ® *m* **-s, -, Castor-Behälter** *m* spent fuel rod container.
Casus belli *m* **- -, - -** (*geh*) casus belli (*form*).
Catch-as-catch-can ['kætʃ əz 'kætʃ'kæn] *nt* **-,** *no pl* (*lit*) catch-as-catch-can, all-in wrestling; (*fig*) free-for-all.
catchen ['kɛtʃn] *vi* to do catch(-as-catch-can)-wrestling, to do all-in wrestling ◆ **er catcht gegen X** he has an all-in *or* catch bout against X; **er catcht gut** he's a good all-in *or* catch wrestler.
Catcher(in *f***)** ['kɛtʃɐ, -ərɪn] *m* **-s, -** all-in wrestler, catch(-as-catch-can) wrestler.
Catull *m* **-s** Catullus.
Cause célèbre [kozse'lɛbr] *f* **- -, -s -s** (*geh*) cause célèbre.
Cayennepfeffer [ka'jɛn-] *m* cayenne (pepper).
CB-Funk [tseː'beː-] *m* **-s,** *no pl* citizens' band, CB.
cbm *abbr of* **Kubikmeter** cubic metre.
ccm *abbr of* **Kubikzentimeter** cc, cubic centimetre.
CD [tseː'deː] *f* **-, -s** *abbr of* **Compact Disc** CD.
CD- *in cpds* CD; **~-Gerät** *nt* CD player; **~-I** *f abbr of* **Compact Disc-Interactive** (*Comput*) CD-I; **~-ROM** [-rɔm] *f* **-, -s** CD ROM; **~-ROM-Laufwerk** *nt* CD ROM drive; **~-Spieler** *m* CD player.
CDU ['tseːdeː'|uː] *f* **-** *abbr of* **Christlich-Demokratische Union** Christian Democratic Union.
CD-: ~-Video *f* video disc; **~-Videogerät** *nt* video disc player, CD-video; **~-Wechsler** *m* CD changer.
Cedille [se'diːj(ə)] *f* **-, -n** cedilla.
Celesta [tʃe'lɛsta] *f* **-, -s** *or* **Celesten** celeste, celesta.
Cellist(in *f***)** [tʃɛ'lɪst(ɪn)] *m* cellist.
Cello ['tʃɛlo] *nt* **-s, -s** *or* **Celli** cello.
Cellophan ® [tselo'faːn] *nt* **-s,** *no pl,* **Cellophanpapier** *nt* (*inf*) cellophane (paper).
Celsius ['tsɛlziʊs] *no art, inv* centigrade.
Celsiusskala *f* centigrade scale.
Cembalo ['tʃɛmbalo] *nt* **-s, -s** cembalo, harpsichord.
Cent [tsɛnt] *m* **-(s), -(s)** cent.
cerise [sə'riːz] *adj* (*Fashion*) cerise, cherry.
Cervelat [tsɛrvə'laːt] *m* **-s, -s** (*Sw*) *siehe* **Zervelatwurst.**
ces, Ces [tsɛs] *nt* **-, -** (*Mus*) C flat.
Ceylon ['tsailɔn] *nt* **-s** Ceylon.
Ceylonese [tsai-] *m* **-n, -n, Ceylonesin** *f* Ceylonese, Sin(g)halese.
ceylonesisch [tsai-] *adj* Ceylonese, Sin(g)halese.
Cha-Cha-Cha ['tʃa'tʃa'tʃa] *m* **-(s), -s** cha-cha(-cha).
Chagrinleder [ʃa'grɛː-] *nt* shagreen.
Chaise ['ʃɛːzə] *f* **-, -n (a)** (*old*) (*Kutsche*) (post)chaise (*old*); (*Stuhl*) chair. **(b)** (*inf*) jaloppy (*inf*), banger (*Brit inf*).
Chaiselongue [ʃɛzə'lɔŋ] *f* **-, -s** chaise longue.
Chalet [ʃa'leː] *nt* **-s, -s** chalet.
Chamäleon [ka'mɛːleɔn] *nt* **-s, -s** (*lit, fig*) chameleon.
chamäleon|artig [1] *adj* (*lit, fig*) chameleon-like.
[2] *adv* like a chameleon.
Chambre séparée [ʃābrəsepa're] *nt* **- -, -s -s** (*dated*) private room.
Chamois [ʃa'moa] *nt* **-,** *no pl* **(a)** (*Farbe*) buff (colour), (light) tan (colour). **(b)** (*auch* **~leder**) chamois (leather).
Champagner [ʃam'panjɐ] *m* **-s, -** champagne.
Champignon ['ʃampɪnjɔŋ] *m* **-s, -s** mushroom.
Champignon- ['ʃampɪnjɔŋ-]: **~kultur** *f* mushroom culture; **~zucht** *f* mushroom cultivation *or* growing.
Champion ['tʃɛmpiən] *m* **-s, -s** champion; (*Mannschaft*) champions *pl.*
Chance ['ʃāːsə, (*Aus*) 'ʃāːs] *f* **-, -n (a)** chance; (*bei Wetten*) odds *pl* ◆ **keine ~ haben** not to have *or* stand a chance; **nicht die geringste ~ haben** not to have an earthly (chance) (*inf*); **ich sehe keine ~, das noch rechtzeitig zu schaffen** I don't see any chance of being able to do it in time; **die ~n, von**

einem Auto überfahren zu werden the chances of being run over by a car; **jdm eine (letzte) ~ geben** to give sb one (last) chance; **die ~n stehen 100:1** the odds are a hundred to one; **die ~n steigen/verringern sich** the odds are shortening/lengthening; (*fig auch*) the chances are improving/getting worse.

(b) **~n** *pl (Aussichten)* prospects *pl* ♦ **im Beruf ~n haben** to have good career prospects; **(bei jdm) ~n haben** (*inf*) to stand a chance (with sb) (*inf*).

Chancen-: ~gleichheit *f* equal opportunities *pl*; **c~los** *adj Spieler, Partei* bound to lose; *Plan, Produkt* bound to fail.

changieren* [ʃã'ʒi:rən] *vi* (a) (*schillern*) to be iridescent ♦ **changierende Seide** shot silk. (b) (*Pferd*) to change step.

Chanson [ʃã'sõ:] *nt* **-s, -s** (political *or* satirical) song.

Chanson(n)ette [ʃãso'nɛtə] *f*, ⚠**Chansonnier** [ʃãsɔ'nie:] *m* **-s, -s** political/satirical song-writer; singer of political/satirical songs.

Chaos ['ka:ɔs] *nt* **-,** *no pl* chaos ♦ **einem ~ gleichen/ein einziges ~ sein** to be in utter chaos.

Chaot(in *f*) [ka'o:t(ɪn)] *m* **-en, -en** (*Pol pej*) anarchist (*pej*); (*unordentlicher Mensch*) scatterbrain (*pej*) ♦ **er ist ein richtiger ~** he's completely chaotic.

chaotisch [ka'o:tɪʃ] *adj* chaotic ♦ **~e Zustände** a state of (utter) chaos; **es geht ~ zu** there is utter chaos.

Chapeau claque [ʃapo'klak] *m* **- -, -x -s** opera hat.

Charakter [ka'raktɐ] *m* **-s, -e** [-'te:rə] (a) (*Wesen, Eigenart*) character ♦ **er ist ein Mann von ~** he is a man of character; **etw prägt den ~** sth is character-forming; **keinen ~ haben** (*ohne Prägung*) to have no *or* to lack character; (*nicht ehrenhaft auch*) to have no principles; **die Party bekam immer mehr den ~ einer Orgie** the party became more and more like an orgy; **seine Warnung hatte mehr den ~ einer Drohung** his warning was more like a threat; **der vertrauliche ~ dieses Gespräches** the confidential nature of this conversation.

(b) (*Person*) character, personality; (*Liter, Theat*) character ♦ **sie sind ganz gegensätzliche ~e** their characters are entirely different, they have entirely different personalities.

(c) *siehe* **Charakterkopf**.

(d) (*dated Typ*) *siehe* **Schriftzeichen**.

Charakter-: ~anlage *f* characteristic, trait; **angeborene ~anlagen** innate characteristics; **jds gute ~anlagen fördern** to encourage sb's good (character) traits *or* qualities; **~bild** *nt* character (image); (*~schilderung*) character study; ⚠**c~bildend** *adj* character-forming; **~bildung** *f* character formation; **~darsteller** *m* character actor; **~eigenschaft** *f* character trait; **~fehler** *m* character defect; **c~fest** *adj* strong-minded, of firm *or* strong character; **ein c~fester Mann** a man of firm *or* strong character; **~festigkeit** *f* strength of character, strong-mindedness.

charakterisieren* [ka-] *vt* to characterize ♦ **jdn als etw ~** to portray *or* characterize sb as sth.

Charakterisierung *f* characterization.

Charakteristik [ka-] *f* (a) description; (*typische Eigenschaften*) characteristics *pl*. (b) (*Tech*) characteristic curve.

Charakteristikum [ka-] *nt* **-s, Charakteristika** (*geh*) characteristic (feature).

charakteristisch [ka-] *adj* characteristic (*für* of).

charakteristischerweise *adv* characteristically.

Charakter-: ~kopf *m* (*Kopf*) distinctive *or* striking features *pl*; **c~lich** [1] *adj* (of) character, personal; **c~liche Stärke/Mängel/Qualitäten** strength of character/character defects/personal qualities; [2] *adv* in character; **sie hat sich c~lich sehr verändert** her character has changed a lot; **jdn c~lich stark prägen** to have a strong influence on sb's character; **c~los** *adj* (a) (*niederträchtig*) *Mensch, Verhalten etc* unprincipled; **c~los handeln** to act in an unprincipled way; (b) (*ohne Prägung*) characterless; *Spiel, Vortrag* colourless, insipid; **~losigkeit** *f* (a) (*Niederträchtigkeit*) lack of principle; (*Handlung*) unprincipled behaviour *no pl*; (b) (*Prägungslosigkeit*) characterlessness; colourlessness; insipidity; **~merkmal** *nt* characteristic.

Charakterologe [ka-] *m*, **Charakterologin** *f* characterologist.

Charakterologie [karakterolo'gi:] *f* characterology.

charakterologisch [ka-] *adj* characterological.

Charakter-: ~rolle *f* character part *or* role; **~sache** *f* (*inf*) **das ist ~sache** it's a matter of character; **~schauspieler** *m siehe* **~darsteller**; **c~schwach** *adj* weak, of weak character; **~schwäche** *f* weakness of character; **~schwein** *nt* (*inf*) unprincipled character; **c~stark** *adj* strong, of strong character; **~stärke** *f* strength of character; **~stück** *nt* (*Mus*) mood piece; **~studie** *f* character study; **c~voll** *adj* (a) (*anständig*) *Verhalten* which shows character; **dazu ist er zu c~voll** he has too much character for that; (b) (*ausgeprägt*) full of character; **eine c~volle Stadt** a town (full) of character; **~zug** *m* characteristic; (*von Menschen auch*) (character) trait; **es ist kein sehr schöner ~zug von ihm, ...** it is not very nice of him ...

Charge ['ʃarʒə] *f* **-, -n** (a) (*Mil, fig: Dienstgrad, Person*) rank. (b) (*Theat*) minor character part.

chargieren* [ʃar'ʒi:rən] *vi* (*Theat*) (*übertreiben*) to overact, to ham (*inf*); (*eine Charge spielen*) to play a minor character part.

Charisma ['ça:rɪsma] *nt* **-s, Charismen** *or* **Charismata** (*Rel, fig*) charisma.

charismatisch [ça-] *adj* charismatic.

Charleston ['tʃarlstn] *m* **-, -s** charleston.

Charlottenburger [ʃa-] *m*: **einen ~ machen** (*dial sl*) to snot oneself with one's fingers (*sl*).

charmant [ʃar'mant] *adj* charming.

Charme [ʃarm] *m* **-s,** *no pl* charm.

Charmeur [ʃar'mø:ɐ] *m* charmer; (*Schmeichler*) flatterer ♦ **du alter ~!** you old smoothy! (*inf*).

Charmeuse [ʃar'mø:z] *f, no pl* (*Tex*) charmeuse.

Chart [tʃart] *m or nt* **-, -s** (a) (*Comput*) chart. (b) **die ~s** (*Hitparade*) the charts.

Charta ['karta] *f* **-, -s** charter ♦ **Magna ~** Magna Carta.

Charter ['tʃartɐ] *m* **-s, -s** charter.

Charter-: ~flug *m* charter flight; **~(flug)gesellschaft** *f* charter(flight) company; **~maschine** *f* charter plane.

chartern ['tʃartɐn] *vt Schiff, Flugzeug* to charter; (*fig inf*) *Taxi, Arbeitskräfte etc* to hire.

Chassis [ʃa'si:] *nt* **-, -** [-i:(s), -i:s] (*Aut, Rad, TV*) chassis.

Chauffeur [ʃɔ'fø:ɐ] *m* chauffeur.

chauffieren* [ʃɔ-] *vti* (*dated*) to chauffeur, to drive.

Chaussee [ʃo'se:] *f* **-, -n** [-e:ən] (*dated*) high road; (*in Straßennamen*) Avenue.

Chaussee-: ~baum *m* (*dated*) roadside tree; **~graben** *m* (*dated*) *siehe* **Straßengraben**.

Chauvi(e) ['ʃo:vi] *m* **-s, -s** (*inf*) male chauvinist pig, MCP.

Chauvinismus [ʃovi-] *m* chauvinism; (*männlicher ~*) male chauvinism; (*Benehmen, Äußerung*) chauvinist(ic) action/remark.

Chauvinist(in *f*) *m* (*Pol*) chauvinist; (*männlicher ~*) male chauvinist (pig).

chauvinistisch [ʃovi-] *adj* (*Pol*) chauvinist(ic) ♦ **er ist sehr ~** he is a real chauvinist.

checken ['tʃɛkn] [1] *vt* (a) (*überprüfen*) to check.

(b) (*sl: verstehen*) to get (*inf*).

(c) (*sl: merken*) to cotton on to (*inf*), to wise up to (*sl*) ♦ **er hat das nicht gecheckt** he didn't cotton on (*inf*), he didn't wise up to it (*sl*).

(d) (*sl: schaffen*) to make (*inf*), to get.

[2] *vti* (*Eishockey*) to block; (*anrempeln*) to barge.

Check- ['tʃɛk-]: **~liste** *f* check list; **~point** [-pɔynt] *m* **-s, -s** checkpoint.

Chef [ʃɛf, (*Aus*) ʃe:f] *m* **-s, -s** boss; (*von Bande, Delegation etc*) leader; (*von Organisation, inf: Schuldirektor*) head; (*der Polizei*) chief; (*Mil: von Kompanie*) commander ♦ **~ des Stabes** Chief of Staff; **er ist der ~ vom ganzen** he's in charge *or* the boss here; **hallo ~!** (*inf*) hey, gov(ernor) *or* chief *or* squire (*all Brit inf*) *or* mac (*US inf*).

Chef-: ~arzt *m* senior consultant; **~etage** *f* management *or* executive floor.

Chef|ideologe *m* (*inf*) chief ideologist.

Chefin ['ʃɛfɪn, (*Aus*) 'ʃe:fɪn] *f* (a) boss; (*Sch*) head; (*von Delegation etc*) head. (b) (*inf: Frau des Chefs*) boss's wife ♦ **Frau ~!** ma'am (*US*), ≃ excuse me.

Chef-: ~koch *m* chef, head cook; **~redakteur** *m* editor-in-chief; (*einer Zeitung*) editor; **~redaktion** *f* (a) (*Aufgabe*) (chief) editorship; (b) (*Büro*) main editorial office; *siehe* **Redaktion**; **~sache** *f* **etw zur ~sache erklären** to make sth a matter for decision at the top level; **das ist ~sache** it's a matter for the boss; **~sekretärin** *f* personal assistant/secretary; **~visite** *f* (*Med*) consultant's round.

chem. *abbr of* **chemisch**.

Chemie [çe'mi:, (*esp S Ger*) ke'mi:] *f* **-,** *no pl* (*lit, fig*) chemistry; (*inf: Chemikalien*) chemicals *pl* ♦ **was die so essen, ist alles ~** they just eat synthetic food.

Chemie-: ~arbeiter *m* chemical worker; **~beruf** *m* job in industrial chemistry; **~faser** *f* synthetic *or* man-made fibre; **~unfall** *m* chemical accident; **~unterricht** *m* chemistry; **c~waffenfrei** *adj* free of chemical weapons; **c~waffenfreie Zone** chemical-weapon free zone.

Chemikal [çe-] *nt* **-s, -ien** [-iən], **Chemikalie** [çemi'ka:liə] *f* **-, -n** *usu pl* chemical.

Chemiker(in *f*) ['çe:-, (*esp S Ger*) 'ke:-] *m* **-s, -** chemist.

Cheminée ['ʃmɪne] *nt* **-s, -s** (*Sw*) fireplace.

chemisch ['çe:-, (*esp S Ger*) 'ke:-] *adj* chemical; *siehe* **Reinigung**.

chemisieren* [çe-] *vti* (*DDR*) to make increasing use of chemistry (in).

Chemo- [çemo-]: **~technik** *f* chemical engineering, technochemistry; **~techniker** *m* chemical engineer; **~therapie** *f* chemotherapy.

-chen *nt suf dim* little.

Cherub ['çe:rʊp] *m* **-s, -im** ['-bi:m] *or* **-inen** [-'bi:nən] cherub.

chevaleresk [ʃəvalə'rɛsk] *adj* (*geh*) chivalrous.

Chiasmus ['çiasmʊs] *m* (*Ling*) chiasmus.

chic [ʃɪk] *adj siehe* **schick**.

⚠**Chicorée** [ʃiko're:] *f* **-** *or m* **-s,** *no pl* chicory.

Chiffon ['ʃɪfõ(:)] *m* **-s, -s** chiffon.

Chiffre ['ʃɪfɐ, 'ʃɪfrə] *f* **-, -n** (a) cipher. (b) (*in Zeitung*) box number.

Chiffreschrift *f* cipher, code.

chiffrieren* [ʃɪf-] *vti* to encipher, to code ♦ **chiffriert** coded.

Chile ['tʃi:le] *nt* **-s** Chile.

Chilene [tʃi'le:nə] *m* **-n, -n, Chilenin** *f* Chilean.

chilenisch [tʃi-] *adj* Chilean.

Chilesalpeter *m* chile saltpetre, sodium nitrate.

Chili ['tʃi:li] *m* **-s,** *no pl* chil(l)i (pepper).

China ['çi:na, (*esp S Ger*) 'ki:na] *nt* **-s** China.

China-: ~cracker *m siehe* **~kracher**; **~kohl** *m* Chinese cabbage; **~kracher** *m* banger (*Brit*), firecracker (*US*); **~krepp** *m* crêpe de Chine; **~restaurant** *nt* Chinese restaurant.

Chinchilla¹ [tʃɪn'tʃɪla] *f* **-, -s** (*Tier*) chinchilla.

Chinchilla² [tʃɪn'tʃɪla] *nt* **-s, -s** (a) (*Pelz*) chinchilla. (b) (*auch* **~kaninchen**) chinchilla rabbit.

Chinese [çi-, (*esp S Ger*) ki-] *m* **-n, -n** Chinaman; (*heutig auch*) Chinese.

Chinesin [çi-, (*esp S Ger*) ki-] *f* Chinese woman; (*heutig auch*) Chinese.

chinesisch [çi-, (*esp S Ger*) ki-] *adj* Chinese ◆ **die C~e Mauer** the Great Wall of China; **das ist ~ für mich** (*inf*) that's all Greek *or* Chinese to me (*inf*).

Chinesisch(e) [çi-, (*esp S Ger*) ki-] *nt decl as adj* Chinese; *siehe auch* **Deutsch(e)**.

Chinin [çi'ni:n] *nt* **-s,** *no pl* quinine.

Chinoiserie [ʃinoazə'ri:] *f* chinoiserie.

Chip [tʃɪp] *m* **-s, -s** **(a)** (*Spiel~*) chip. **(b)** *usu pl* (*Kartoffel~*) (potato) crisp (*Brit*), potato chip (*US*). **(c)** (*Comput*) chip.

Chipkarte *f* smart card.

Chiromant(in *f***)** [çi-] *m* chiromancer.

Chiromantie [çiroman'ti:] *f* chiromancy.

Chiro- [çiro-]: **~praktik** *f* chiropractic; **~praktiker** *m* chiropractor.

Chirurg(in *f***)** [çi'rʊrg(ɪn)] *m* **-en, -en** surgeon.

Chirurgie [çirʊr'gi:] *f* surgery ◆ **er liegt in der ~** he's in surgery.

chirurgisch [çi-] *adj* surgical ◆ **ein ~er Eingriff** surgery.

Chitin [çi'ti:n] *nt* **-s,** *no pl* chitin.

Chlor [klo:ɐ] *nt* **-s,** *no pl* (*abbr* **Cl**) chlorine.

Chlorakne ['klo:ɐ|aknə] *f* chloracne.

chloren, chlorieren* [klo-] *vt* to chlorinate.

chlorig ['klo:-] *adj* (*Chem*) chlorous.

Chloro- [kloro-]: **~form** *nt* **-s,** *no pl* chloroform; **c~formieren*** *vt insep* to chloroform; **~phyll** *nt* **-s,** *no pl* chlorophyll.

Chlorwasser *nt* **(a)** (*Chem*) chlorine water. **(b)** (*im Hallenbad*) chlorinated water.

Choke [tʃo:k] *m* **-s, -s, Choker** ['tʃo:kɐ] *m* **-s, -** choke.

Cholera ['ko:lera] *f* **-,** *no pl* cholera.

Choleriker(in *f***)** [ko-] *m* **-s, -** choleric person; (*fig*) irascible *or* hot-tempered person.

cholerisch [ko-] *adj* choleric.

Cholesterin [ko-] *nt* **-s,** *no pl* cholesterol.

Cholesterinspiegel *m* cholesterol level.

Chor[1] [ko:ɐ] *m* **-(e)s, ¨-e** **(a)** (*Sänger~*) choir; (*Bläser~ etc*) section ◆ **im ~ singen** to sing in the choir; (*zusammen singen*) to sing in chorus, to chorus; **im ~ sprechen/rufen** to speak/shout in chorus; **ja, riefen sie im ~** yes, they chorused.
(b) (*Theat*) chorus.
(c) (*Komposition*) choral work *or* composition.
(d) (*bei Orgel*) rank.
(e) (*bei Klavier, Laute etc*) group of strings tuned in unison *or* to the same pitch.

Chor[2] [ko:ɐ] *m or* (*rare*) *nt* **-(e)s, -e** *or* **¨-e** (*Archit*) **(a)** (*Altarraum*) chancel, choir. **(b)** (*Chorempore*) loft, gallery.

Choral [ko'ra:l] *m* **-s, Choräle** (*Mus*) **(a)** (*Gregorianischer*) chant, plainsong. **(b)** (*Kirchenlied*) hymn.

Choreo- [koreo-]: ⚠**~graph(in** *f***)** *m* choreographer; ⚠**~graphie** *f* choreography; ⚠**c~graphieren*** [1] *vt* to choreograph, to write *or* do the choreography for; [2] *vi* to write *or* do (the) choreography; ⚠**c~graphisch** *adj* choreographic(al).

Chor- ['ko:ɐ]: **~frau** *f* (*Eccl*) canoness; **~gebet** *nt* Divine office; **~gesang** *m* (*Lied*) choral music; (*das Singen*) choral singing; **~gestühl** *nt* choir stalls *pl*; **~herr** *m* (*Eccl*) *siehe* **Kanoniker**.

chorisch ['ko:-] *adj* choral.

Chorist(in *f***)** [ko-] *m siehe* **Chorsänger(in)**.

Chor- ['ko:ɐ]: **~knabe** *m* choirboy; **~leiter** *m* choirmaster; **~sänger(in** *f***)** *m* member of a choir; (*im Kirchenchor*) chorister; (*im Opernchor etc*) member of the chorus; **~schranke** *f* choir *or* rood screen; **~stuhl** *m* choirstall.

Chorus ['ko:rʊs] *m* **-, -se** (*Mus*) **(a)** (*obs*) *siehe* **Chor**[1] **(a)**. **(b)** (*Jazz: Variationsthema*) theme.

Chose ['ʃo:zə] *f* **-, -n** (*inf*) **(a)** (*Angelegenheit*) business, thing. **(b)** (*Zeug*) stuff ◆ **die ganze ~** the whole lot.

Chow-Chow [tʃau'tʃau] *m* **-s, -s** chow.

Chr. *abbr of* **Christus**.

Christ[1] [krɪst] *m* **-s** (*old, geh*) *siehe* **Christus**.

Christ[2] [krɪst] *m* **-en, -en** Christian.

Christbaum *m* Christmas tree; (*Mil inf*) flares *pl*.

Christbaum- *in cpds siehe auch* **Weihnachtsbaum-**; **~kugel** *f* Christmas tree ball; **~schmuck** *m* **(a)** Christmas tree decorations *pl*; **(b)** (*iro: Orden*) gongs *pl* (*Brit inf*), fruit salad (*US inf*).

Christ- ['krɪst-]: **~demokrat** *m* Christian Democrat; **c~demokratisch** *adj* Christian Democratic.

Christen- ['krɪstn-]: **~gemeinde** *f* Christian community; **~glaube(n)** *m* Christian faith; **~heit** *f* Christendom; **~pflicht** *f* (one's) duty as a Christian, (one's) Christian duty; **~tum** *nt, no pl* Christianity; **~verfolgung** *f* persecution of the Christians.

Christfest *nt* (*dated, dial*) *siehe* **Weihnachtsfest**.

Christi *gen of* **Christus**.

christianisieren* [krɪ-] [1] *vt* to convert to Christianity, to christianize. [2] *vi* to convert people to Christianity.

Christianisierung *f* conversion to Christianity, Christianization.

Christin ['krɪstɪn] *f* Christian.

Christ- ['krɪst-]: **~kind(chen)** *nt, no pl* baby *or* infant Jesus, Christ Child; (*Sinnbild für Weihnachten*) Christmas; (*das Geschenke bringt*) Father Christmas; (*fig inf: Dummerchen*) little innocent; **~kindl(e)** *nt* (*dial*) **(a)** *siehe* **~kind(chen)**; **(b)** (*dial: Geschenk*) Christmas present; **zum ~kindl(e)** as a Christmas present, for Christmas.

christlich ['krɪ-] [1] *adj* Christian ◆ **er ist bei der ~en Seefahrt** (*hum*) he is a seafaring man; **C~er Verein Junger Männer** Young Men's Christian Association.
[2] *adv* like *or* as a Christian ◆ **~ leben** to live a Christian life; **~ handeln** to act like a Christian; **~ aufwachsen/jdn ~ erziehen** to grow up/bring sb up as a Christian; **eine ~ orientierte Moral** a Christian(-orientated) morality; **etw ~ teilen** to let the other person have the larger share.

Christlichkeit *f* Christianity.

Christ- ['krɪst-]: **~messe** *f* Midnight Mass; **~mette** *f* (*katholisch*) Midnight Mass; (*evangelisch*) Midnight Service.

Christoph ['krɪ-] *m* **-s** Christopher.

Christophorus [krɪ-] *m* **-** Saint Christopher.

Christrose ['krɪst-] *f* Christmas rose.

Christus ['krɪstʊs] *m* **Christi,** *dat* **-** *or* (*form*) **Christo,** *acc* **-** *or* (*form*) **Christum** Christ; (*~figur auch*) figure of Christ ◆ **vor Christi Geburt, vor Christo** (*form*) *or* **~** before Christ, BC; **nach Christi Geburt, nach Christo** (*form*) AD, Anno Domini, in the year of our Lord (*liter*); **Christi Himmelfahrt** the Ascension of Christ; (*Himmelfahrtstag*) Ascension Day.

Chrom [kro:m] *nt* **-s,** *no pl* chrome; (*Chem: abbr* **Cr**) chromium.

Chromatik [kro-] *f* **(a)** (*Mus*) chromaticism. **(b)** (*Opt*) chromatics *sing*.

chromatisch [kro-] *adj* (*Mus, Opt*) chromatic.

chromblitzend *adj* gleaming with chrome.

Chromosom [kro-] *nt* **-s, -en** chromosome.

Chromosomen-: **~paar** *nt* pair of chromosomes; **~satz** *m* set of chromosomes.

Chronik ['kro:-] *f* chronicle ◆ **etw in einer ~ aufzeichnen** to chronicle sth, to record sth in a chronicle.

chronisch ['kro:-] *adj* (*Med, fig*) chronic.

Chronist(in *f***)** [kro-] *m* chronicler.

Chronologie [kronolo'gi:] *f* chronology.

chronologisch [kro-] *adj* chronological.

Chronometer [kro-] *nt* **-s, -** chronometer.

Chrysantheme [kryzan'te:mə] *f* **-, -n** chrysanthemum.

chthonisch ['çto:nɪʃ] *adj* (*liter*) chthonian (*liter*), chthonic (*liter*).

Chuzpe ['xʊtspə] *f* **-,** *no pl* (*sl*) chutzpa(h) (*sl*), audacity.

CIA ['si:ai'ei] *f or m* **-s** CIA.

Cicero[1] ['tsi:tsero] *m* **-s** Cicero.

Cicero[2] ['tsi:tsero] *f or m* **-,** *no pl* (*Typ*) twelve-point type, pica.

Cicerone [tʃitʃe'ro:nə] *m* **-(s), -s** *or* (*geh*) **Ciceroni** **(a)** (*Mensch*) cicerone (*form*), guide. **(b)** (*Buch*) (travel) guide(book).

Cie. *abbr of* **Kompanie**.

Cineast(in *f***)** [sine'ast(ɪn)] *m* **-en, -en** cineast(e).

Cinemathek [sinema'te:k] *f siehe* **Kinemathek**.

circa ['tsɪrka] *adv siehe* **zirka**.

Circe ['tsɪrtsə] *f* **-, -n** (*Myth*) Circe; (*fig geh*) femme fatale.

circensisch [tsɪr'tsɛnzɪʃ] *adj siehe* **zirzensisch**.

Circulus vitiosus ['tsɪrkulʊs vi'tsio:zʊs] *m* **- -, Circuli vitiosi** (*geh*) (*Teufelskreis*) vicious circle; (*Zirkelschluß auch*) circular argument, petitio principii (*form*).

cis, Cis [tsɪs] *nt* **-, -** (*Mus*) C sharp.

City ['sɪti] *f* **-, -s** city centre.

City-Bahn ['sɪti-] *f* express commuter train.

Clair-obscur [klɛrɔps'ky:ɐ] *nt* **-s,** *no pl* (*Art*) chiaroscuro.

Clan [kla:n] *m* **-s, -s** *or* (*rare*) **-e** (*lit, fig*) clan.

Claqueur [kla'kø:ɐ] *m* hired applauder, claqueur.

Clavicembalo [klavi'tʃembalo] *nt* **-s, -s** *or* **Clavicembali** clavicembalo, harpsichord.

clean [kli:n] *adj pred* (*sl*) off drugs ◆ **~ werden** to kick (the habit) (*sl*).

Clearing ['kli:rɪŋ] *nt* **-s, -s** (*Econ*) clearing.

Clematis *f* **-, -** (*Bot*) clematis.

Clementine *f siehe* **Klementine**.

clever ['klevɐ] *adj* (*intelligent*) clever, bright; (*raffiniert*) sharp, shrewd; (*gerissen*) crafty, cunning; (*geschickt*) clever.

Cleverness, ⚠**Cleverneß** ['klevɐnɛs] *f* **-,** *no pl siehe adj* cleverness, brightness; sharpness, shrewdness; craftiness, cunning; cleverness.

Clinch [klɪntʃ] *m* **-(e)s,** *no pl* (*Boxen, fig*) clinch ◆ **in den ~ gehen** (*lit, fig*) to go into a clinch; (*fig: Verhandlungspartner*) to get stuck into each other (*inf*); **jdn in den ~ nehmen** (*lit*) to go into a clinch with sb; (*fig*) to get stuck into sb (*inf*); **sich aus dem ~ lösen, den ~ lösen** to break the clinch.

clinchen ['klɪntʃn] *vi* to clinch.

Clip *m* **-s, -s** (*Haar~, am Füller etc*) clip; (*Brosche*) clip-on brooch; (*Ohr~*) (clip-on) earring.

Clips *m* **-, -e** *siehe* **Clip**.

Clique ['klɪkə] *f* **-, -n** **(a)** (*Freundeskreis*) group, set ◆ **wir fahren mit der ganzen ~ in Urlaub** the whole gang *or* crowd of us are going on holiday together; **Thomas und seine ~** Thomas and his set. **(b)** (*pej*) clique.

Cliquen-: **~bildung** *f* forming of cliques; **da kam es natürlich zur ~bildung** then of course it started getting cliquey (*inf*) *or* people started forming cliques; **~(un)wesen** *nt* (*pej*) cliquishness; **~wirtschaft** *f* (*pej inf*) cliquey set-up (*inf*).

Clochard [klɔ'ʃa:r] *m* **-s, -s** tramp.

Clou [klu:] *m* **-s, -s** (*von Geschichte*) (whole) point; (*von Show*) highlight, high spot; (*von Begebenheit*) show-stopper; (*Witz*) real laugh (*inf*) ◆ **und jetzt kommt der ~ der Geschichte** and now, wait for it, ...; **das ist doch gerade der ~** but that's just it, but that's the whole point; **das wäre der ~** that'd be a

⚠: for details of spelling reform, see supplement

real laugh (*inf*).

Clown [klaun] *m* **-s, -s** (*lit, fig*) clown ◆ **den ~ spielen** to clown around, to play the fool; **sich/jdn zum ~ machen** to make a clown of oneself/sb.

Clownerie [klaunəˈriː] *f* clowning (around) *no pl.*

Club *m* **-s, -s** *siehe* **Klub.**

cm *abbr of* **Zentimeter** cm.

Co. *abbr of* **Kompagnon; Kompanie** Co.

Co-, co- *in cpds* co-.

Coach [koːtʃ] *m* **-(s), -s** (*Sport*) coach.

coachen [ˈkoːtʃn] *vti* (*Sport*) to coach.

Coca *f* **-, -s** (*inf*) Coke ® (*inf*).

Cockerspaniel *m* cocker spaniel.

Cockpit *nt* **-s, -s** cockpit.

Cocktail [ˈkɔkteːl] *m* **-s, -s** **(a)** (*Getränk*) cocktail. **(b)** (*DDR: Empfang*) reception. **(c)** (*~party*) cocktail party ◆ **jdn zum ~ einladen** to invite sb for cocktails, to invite sb to a cocktail party.

Cocktail-: ~kleid *nt* cocktail dress; **~party** *f* cocktail party; **~tomate** *f* cherry tomato.

Cocom *nt* - Cocom.

Code [koːt] *m* **-s, -s** *siehe* **Kode.**

Codex *m* **-es** *or* **-, -e** *or* **Codizes** [ˈkoːditseːs] *siehe* **Kodex.**

Cognac ® [ˈkɔnjak] *m* **-s, -s** cognac.

Coiffeur [koaˈføːɐ] *m,* **Coiffeuse** [koaˈføːzə] *f* (*Sw*) hairdresser; (*geh*) hair stylist.

Coiffure [koaˈfyːɐ] *f* **-, -n** **(a)** (*geh*) hairstyling. **(b)** (*Sw*) hairdressing salon.

Cola *f* **-, -s** (*inf*) Coke ® (*inf*).

⚠ **Colanuß** *f* cola nut.

Collage [kɔˈlaːʒə] *f* **-, -n** (*Art, fig*) collage; (*Musik*) medley.

Collie *m* **-s, -s** collie.

Collier [kɔˈlieː] *nt* **-s, -s** *siehe* **Kollier.**

Colloquium *nt siehe* **Kolloquium.**

Colonia-: ~kübel *m* (*Aus*) *siehe* **Koloniakübel; ~wagen** *m* (*Aus*) *siehe* **Koloniawagen.**

color *adv* (*inf*) in colour.

Color *nt:* **in ~** in colour.

Color- *in cpds* colour.

Colt ® *m* **-s, -s** Colt ®.

Combo *f* **-, -s** combo.

Comeback [kamˈbɛk] *nt* **-(s), -s** comeback.

Comecon, COMECON [ˈkɔmekɔn] *m or nt* - Comecon.

Comic [ˈkɔmɪk] *m* **-s, -s** comic strip.

Coming-out [ˈkʌmɪŋˈ|aut] *nt* **-s** *no pl* (*inf: als Homosexueller, Aids-Kranker etc*) coming out ◆ **er erlebte sein ~ als Schlagersänger** he emerged as a pop singer.

⚠ **Communiqué** [kɔmyniˈkeː] *nt* **-s, -s** *siehe* **Kommuniqué.**

Compact Disc *f* **-, -s, Compact Platte** *f* compact disc.

Compiler [kɔmˈpaile] *m* **-s, -** (*Comput*) compiler.

Computer [kɔmˈpjuːtɐ] *m* **-s, -** computer ◆ **auf ~** on computer; **per ~** by computer.

Computer- *in cpds* computer-; **~arbeitsplatz** *m* computer work station; **~blitz** *m* (*Phot*) *siehe* **Elektronenblitz; ~diagnostik** *f* (*Med*) computer diagnosis; **~freak** *m* **-s, -s** computer freak; **~generation** *f* computer generation; **c~gerecht** *adj* (ready) for the computer; **c~gesteuert** *adj* controlled by computer, computer-controlled; **~grafik** *f* computer graphics *pl.*

computerisieren* [kɔmpjutəriˈziːrən] *vti* to computerize.

Computer-: ~kriminalität *f* computer crime; **c~lesbar** *adj* machine-readable; **~linguistik** *f* computational linguistics *sing*; **~satz** *m* computer typesetting; **~simulation** *f* computer simulation; **~spiel** *nt* computer game; **~sprache** *f* computer language; **~tomogramm** *nt* (*Med*) computer tomogram; ⚠**~tomograph** *m* (*Med*) computer tomograph; ⚠**~tomographie** *f* **-, -n** computer tomography; **~-Virus** *nt or m* computer virus.

Comtesse *f* countess.

Conditio sine qua non [kɔnˈdiːtsio] *f* **- - - -,** *no pl* (*geh*) sine qua non.

Conférencier [kõferãˈsieː] *m* **-s, -s** compère, MC.

Confiserie [kɔnfizəˈriː] *f siehe* **Konditorei.**

Connaisseur [kɔnɛˈsøːɐ] *m* (*geh*) connoisseur.

Consensus *m* **-, -** (*geh*) *siehe* **Konsens.**

Container [kɔnˈteːnɐ] *m* **-s, -** container; (*Blumentrog*) plant box; (*Bauschutt~*) skip; (*Müll~*) waste container; (*Transport~*) container; (*Wohn~*) prefabricated hut, Portakabin ®.

Container- *in cpds* container; **~bahnhof** *m* container depot; **~dorf** *nt* village of prefabricated huts; **~hafen** *m* container port; **~schiff** *nt* container ship; **~terminal** *m or nt* **-s, -s** container terminal; **~verkehr** *m* container traffic; **auf ~verkehr umstellen** to containerize.

Containment [kɔnˈteːnmənt] *nt* **-s, -s** containment.

Contenance [kõtəˈnãːs(ə)] *f* **-,** *no pl* (*geh*) composure.

Contergan ® *nt* **-s** thalidomide.

Contergankind *nt* (*inf*) thalidomide child/baby.

Contra *m* **-s, -s** (*Pol*) Contra.

Controller *m* **-s, -** **(a)** (*Fin: Finanzbuchhalter*) cost controller. **(b)** (*Computer*) controller.

Controlling *nt* **-s** *no pl* (*Fin*) cost control.

cool [ˈkuːl] *adj* (*sl*) **(a)** (*gefaßt*) cool, laid-back (*sl*) ◆ **du mußt ~ bleiben** you must keep your cool (*inf*) *or* stay cool (*inf*). **(b)** (*angenehm*) cool (*sl*) ◆ **die Party war ~** the party was (real) cool (*sl*). **(c)** (*ungefährlich*) safe. **(d)** (*fair*) on the level (*inf*), fair ◆ **er ist ein ~er Dealer** he is a fair dealer, as a dealer he is on the level.

Copilot, Co-Pilot *m siehe* **Kopilot.**

Copyright [ˈkɔpirait] *nt* **-s, -s** copyright.

coram publico *adv* (*geh*) publicly.

Cord *m* **-s, -e** *or* **-s** (*Tex*) cord, corduroy.

Cord- *in cpds* cord, corduroy; **~jeans** *pl* cords *pl.*

Cordon bleu [kɔrdõˈblø] *nt* **- -, -s -s** (*Cook*) veal cordon bleu.

Corner [ˈkoːɐnɐ] *m* **-s, -** (*Aus Sport*) corner.

Corn-flakes, Corn Flakes ® [ˈkoːɐnfleːks] *pl* cornflakes *pl.*

Cornichon [kɔrniˈʃõː] *nt* **-s, -s** gherkin.

Corpora delicti *pl of* **Corpus delicti.**

Corps [koːɐ] *nt* **-, -** *siehe* **Korps.**

Corpus *nt* **-, Corpora** (*Ling*) *siehe* **Korpus.**

Corpus delicti *nt* **- -, Corpora -** corpus delicti; (*hum*) culprit (*inf*).

cos. *abbr of* **Kosinus** cos.

Costa Rica *nt* **-s** Costa Rica.

Costaricaner(in *f***)** *m* **-s, -** Costa Rican.

costaricanisch *adj* Costa Rican.

Couch [kautʃ] *f or* (*Sw*) *m* **-, -es** *or* **-en** couch.

Couch-: ~garnitur *f* three-piece suite; **~tisch** *m* coffee table.

Couleur [kuˈløːɐ] *f* **-, -s** **(a)** (*geh*) kind, sort ◆ **Faschisten/Sozialisten jeder ~** Fascists/Socialists of every shade. **(b)** (*Univ*) colours *pl* ◆ **~ tragen** to wear the colours of one's student society (*Brit*) *or* fraternity (*US*).

Countdown [ˈkauntˈdaun] *m or nt* **-s, -s** (*Space, fig*) countdown.

Coup [kuː] *m* **-s, -s** coup ◆ **einen ~ (gegen jdn/etw) landen** to bring *or* pull (*inf*) off a coup (against sb/sth).

⚠ **Coupé** [kuˈpeː] *nt* **-s, -s** coupé.

Couplet [kuˈpleː] *nt* **-s, -s** political/cabaret/ music-hall song.

Coupon [kuˈpõː] *m* **-s, -s** **(a)** (*Zettel*) coupon. **(b)** (*Fin*) (interest) coupon. **(c)** (*Stoff~*) length (of material).

Cour [kuːɐ] *f* (*dated*): **einem Mädchen die ~ machen** *or* **schneiden** to court a young lady (*dated*).

Courage [kuˈraːʒə] *f* **-,** *no pl* (*geh*) courage, pluck.

couragiert [kuraˈʒiːɐt] *adj* (*geh*) courageous, plucky.

Courtage [kʊrˈtaːʒə] *f* **-, -n** (*Fin*) commission.

Cousin [kuˈzɛ̃ː] *m* **-s, -s, Cousine** [kuˈziːnə] *f* cousin.

Couvert [kuˈveːɐ] *nt* **-s, -s** *siehe* **Kuvert.**

Cover [ˈkavɐ] *nt* **-s, -s** cover.

Crack[1] [kræk] *m* **-s, -s** (*Sportler*) ace.

Crack[2] [kræk] *nt* **-,** *no pl* (*Droge*) crack.

Cracker [ˈkrɛkɐ] *m* **-s, -(s)** **(a)** (*Keks*) cracker. **(b)** (*Feuerwerkskörper*) banger (*Brit*), fire-cracker (*US*).

Craquelé [krakəˈleː] *nt* **-s, -s** crackle.

Crash-Kurs [ˈkræʃ-] *m* crash course.

Crash-Test *m* (*Aut*) crash test.

Credo *nt* **-s, -s** *siehe* **Kredo.**

Creme [kreːm] *f* **-, -s** (*Haut~, Cook, fig*) cream ◆ **die ~ der Gesellschaft** the cream of society, the crème de la crème (*liter*).

creme [kreːm] *adj pred* (*Fashion*) cream.

creme-: ~artig *adj* cream-like; **~farben** *adj* cream-coloured.

Crème fraîche [krɛmˈfrɛʃ] *f* **-,** *no pl* (*Cook*) crème fraîche.

Cremetorte *f* cream gateau.

cremig *adj* creamy.

Crêpe de Chine [krɛpdəˈʃin] *m* **- - -, -s - -** crêpe de Chine.

Crescendo [krɛˈʃɛndo] *nt* **-s, -s** *or* **Crescendi** **(a)** (*Mus*) crescendo. **(b)** (*Sport*) final spurt.

Creutzfeldt-Jakob-: ~-Krankheit *f* Creutzfeldt-Jakob disease; **~-Syndrom** *nt* Creutzfeldt-Jakob syndrome.

Crew [kruː] *f* **-, -s** crew; (*Kadettenjahrgang*) cadets of the same year/age.

Croissant [kroaˈsãː] *nt* **-s, -s** croissant.

Cromargan ® [kro-] *nt* **-s,** *no pl* stainless steel.

Croupier [kruˈpieː] *m* **-s, -s** croupier.

Croutonwecken [kruˈtõː-] *m* (*Aus*) *siehe* **Stangenbrot.**

Crux *f* **-,** *no pl* **(a)** (*Last*) nuisance. **(b)** (*Schwierigkeit*) trouble, problem ◆ **die ~ bei der Sache ist, ...** the trouble *or* problem (with that) is ...

CS-Gas [tseːˈ|ɛs-] *nt* CS gas.

CSSR [tʃeː|ɛs|ɛsˈ|ɛr] *f* **-** = **Tschechoslowakei.**

CSU [tseː|ɛsˈ|uː] *f* **-** *abbr of* **Christlich-Soziale Union** Christian Social Union.

c.t. [ˈtseːˈteː] *abbr of* **cum tempore** *adv* within fifteen minutes of the time stated ◆ **18.30 ~** 6.30 for 6.45.

cum grano salis *adv* (*geh*) with a pinch of salt.

cum laude *adv* (*Univ*) cum laude (*form*), with distinction.

Cunnilingus [-ˈlɪŋgʊs] *m* **-, Cunnilingi** [-ˈlɪŋgi] cunnilingus, cunnilinctus.

Cup [kap] *m* **-s, -s** (*Sport*) cup.

Cupido *m* **-s** Cupid.

Curie [kyˈriː] *nt* **-, -** (*abbr* **Ci**) Curie.

Curium *nt, no pl* (*abbr* **Cu**) curium.

Curling [ˈkøːɐlɪŋ] *nt* **-s,** *no pl* curling.

Curricula (*geh*) *pl of* **Curriculum.**

curricular *adj attr* (*geh*) curricular.

Curriculum *nt* **-s, Curricula** (*geh*) curriculum.

Curriculumforschung *f* curriculum development.
Curry ['kari] *m or nt* **-s,** *no pl* curry.
Currywurst *f* curried sausage.
Cursor ['kø:rsɐ] *m* **-s, -s** (*Comput*) cursor.
Cut [kœt], **Cutaway** ['kœtəve] *m* **-s, -s** (*dated*) cutaway.
cutten ['katn] *vti* (*Film, Rad, TV*) to cut, to edit.
Cutter(in *f*) ['katɐ, -ərın] *m* **-s, -** (*Film, Rad, TV*) editor.
C.V.J.F. [tse:faujɔt'|ɛf] *m* **-s** *abbr of* **Christlicher Verein Junger Frauen** YWCA.
C.V.J.M. [tse:faujɔt'|ɛm] *m* **-s** *abbr of* **Christlicher Verein Junger Männer** YMCA.
C-Waffe ['tse:-] *f abbr of* **chemische Waffe.**
Cyberspace ['saıbɐspeıs] *m* **-** *no pl* (*Comput*) cyberspace.
Cypern ['tsy:pɐn] *nt* **-s** *siehe* **Zypern.**
cystisch *adj siehe* **zystisch.**

D, d [de:] *nt* -, - D, d.

d.Ä. *abbr of* **der Ältere** sen.

▼ **da** 1 *adv* **(a)** (*örtlich*) (*dort*) there; (*hier*) here ◆ **es liegt ~ draußen/drinnen/drüben/vorn** it's out there/in there/over there/there in front; **das liegt etwa ~ herum** it's somewhere round about there *or* thereabouts; **geh ~ herum** go round there; **~ und ~** what's-its-name (*inf*); **hier und ~, ~ und dort** here and there; **wer ~?** who goes there?; **he, Sie ~!** hey, you there!; **die Frau ~** that woman (over) there; **~ bin ich/sind wir** here I am/we are; **~ bist du ja!** there you are!; **~ kommt er ja** here he comes; **wir sind gleich ~** we'll soon be there, we're almost there; **~, wo ...** where ...; **wo die Straße über den Fluß geht, ~ fängt Schottland an** Scotland begins where the road crosses the river, where the road crosses the river, that's where Scotland begins; **ach, ~ war der Brief!** so that's where the letter was; **~ möchte ich auch einmal hinfahren** (*inf*) I'd like to go there one day; **geben Sie mir ein halbes Pfund von dem ~** give me half a pound of that one (there); **~ haben wir's** *or* **den Salat** (*inf*) that had to happen; **~ hast du deinen Kram/dein Geld!** (there you are,) there's your stuff/money; **~**, nimm schon! here, take it!; *siehe* **als**.
(b) (*zeitlich: dann, damals*) then ◆ **ich ging gerade aus dem Haus, ~ schlug es zwei** I was just going out of the house when the clock struck two; **vor vielen, vielen Jahren, ~ lebte ein König** (*liter*) long, long ago there lived a king *or* there once was a king; **~ werden wir uns den Schaden mal ansehen** (*inf*) let's have a look at the damage; **~ kommen Sie mal gleich mit** (*inf*) you just come along with me; **~ siehst du, was du angerichtet hast** now see what you've done.
(c) (*daraufhin*) *sagen* to that; *lachen* at that ◆ **sie weinte, ~ ließ er sich erweichen** when she started to cry he softened, she started to cry, whereupon he softened (*liter*); **als er das Elend der Leute sah, ~ nahm er sich vor ...** when he saw the people's suffering he decided ...
(d) (*folglich*) so; (*dann*) then ◆ **es war niemand im Zimmer, ~ habe ich ...** there was nobody in the room, so I ...; **wenn ich schon gehen muß, ~ gehe ich lieber gleich** if I have to go, (then) I'd rather go straight away.
(e) (*inf: in diesem Fall*) there ◆ **~ haben wir aber Glück gehabt!** we were lucky there!; **~ muß man vorsichtig sein** you've got to be careful there; **was gibt's denn ~ zu lachen/fragen?** what's funny about that?/what is there to ask?; **~ kann man nichts mehr machen** there's nothing more to be done (there *or* about it); **~ kann man** *or* **läßt sich nichts machen** nothing can be done about it; **~ könnte man aus der Haut fahren** it would drive you mad *or* crazy; **~ kann man nur lachen/sich nur fragen, warum/sich nur wundern** you can't help laughing/asking yourself why/being amazed; **~ kann man nur noch still sein/nur den Kopf schütteln** you can't say anything/you can only shake your head in despair/bewilderment *etc*; **und ~ fragst du noch?** and you still have to ask?; **und ~ soll einer** *or* **ein Mensch wissen, warum!** and you're meant to know why!; **~ fragt man sich (doch), ob der Mann noch normal ist** it makes you wonder if the man's normal; **~ hat doch jemand gelacht/alle Kekse gegessen** somebody laughed/has eaten all the biscuits.
(f) (*zur Hervorhebung*) **wir haben ~ eine neue Mitschülerin/Ausführung des Artikels** *etc* we've got this new girl in our school/this new model *etc*; **~ fällt mir gerade ein** ... it's just occurred to me ...
(g) (*N Ger*) *siehe* **dabei, dafür** *etc*.
▼ 2 *conj* **(a)** (*weil*) as, since, seeing that.
(b) (*liter: als*) when ◆ **die Stunde, ~ du ...** the hour when you ...; **nun** *or* **jetzt, ~** now that.

DAAD [de:|a:|a:'de:] *m* - *abbr of* **Deutscher Akademischer Austauschdienst** German Academic Exchange Service.

dabehalten* *vt sep irreg* to keep (here/there); (*in Haft auch*) to detain (there); *Schüler* to keep behind.

dabei *adv* **(a)** (*örtlich*) with it; (*bei Gruppe von Menschen, Dingen*) there ◆ **ein Häuschen mit einem Garten ~** a little house with a garden (attached to it *or* attached); **ist die Lösung ~?** is the solution given (there)?; **nahe ~** nearby.
(b) (*zeitlich*) (*gleichzeitig*) at the same time; (*währenddessen, wodurch*) in the course of this ◆ **er aß weiter und blätterte ~ in dem Buch** he went on eating, leafing through the book as he did so *or* at the same time; **warum arbeiten Sie im Stehen? Sie können doch auch ~ sitzen** why are you working standing up? you can sit down while you're doing it; **nach der Explosion entstand eine Panik; ~ wurden drei Kinder verletzt** there was a general panic after the explosion, in the course of which *or* during which three children were injured; ... **orkanartige Winde; ~ kam es zu schweren Schäden** ... gale-force winds, which have resulted in serious damage.
(c) (*außerdem*) as well, into the bargain (*inf*), with it (*inf*) ◆ **sie ist schön und ~ auch noch klug** she's pretty, and clever as well *etc*.
(d) (*wenn, während man etw tut*) in the process; *ertappen, erwischen* at it ◆ **er wollte helfen und wurde ~ selbst verletzt** he wanted to help and got injured in the process *or* (in) doing so *or* while he was about it (*inf*); **du warst bei einem Jugendtreffen? hast du denn ~ etwas gelernt?** you were at a youth meeting? did you learn anything there *or* from it?; **~ darf man nicht vergessen, daß** ... it shouldn't be forgotten that ...; (*Einschränkung eines Arguments*) it should not be forgotten here that ...; **die ~ entstehenden Kosten** the expenses arising from this/that; **als er das tat, hat er ~** ... when he did that he ...; **wenn man das tut, muß man ~** ... when you do that you have to ...; **wir haben ihn ~ ertappt, wie er über den Zaun stieg** we caught him in the act of climbing over the fence.
(e) (*in dieser Angelegenheit*) **das Schwierigste ~** the most difficult part of it; **wichtig ~ ist** ... the important thing here *or* about it is ...; **mir ist nicht ganz wohl ~** I don't really feel happy about it; **~ kann man viel Geld verdienen, da kann man viel Geld bei verdienen** (*N Ger*) there's a lot of money in that; **er hat ~ einen Fehler gemacht** he's made a mistake; **sie hat sich ~ sehr dumm benommen** she behaved very stupidly; **es kommt doch nichts ~ heraus** nothing will come of it.
(f) (*einräumend: doch*) (and) yet ◆ **er hat mich geschlagen, ~ hatte ich gar nichts gemacht** he hit me and I hadn't even done anything *or* and yet I hadn't done anything; **ich habe fünf Stück gegessen, ~ hatte ich gar keinen Hunger** I've eaten five pieces, and I wasn't even hungry.
(g) du gehst sofort nach Hause, und ~ bleibt es! you're going straight home and that's that *or* that's the end of it!; **es bleibt ~, daß ihr morgen alle mitkommt** we'll stick to that *or* keep it like that, you're all coming tomorrow; **ich bleibe ~** I'm not changing my mind; **er bleibt ~, daß er es nicht gewesen ist** he still insists *or* he's still sticking to his guns that he didn't do it; **aber ~ sollte es nicht bleiben** but it shouldn't stop there *or* at that; **lassen wir es ~** let's leave it at that!; **was ist schon ~?** so what? (*inf*), what of it? (*inf*); **was ist schon ~, wenn man das tut?** what harm is there in doing that?; **ich finde gar nichts ~** I don't see any harm in it; **es ist nichts ~** *or* (*N Ger*) **da ist nichts bei, wenn man das tut** (*schadet nichts*) there's no harm in doing that; (*will nichts bedeuten*) doing that doesn't mean anything; **nimm meine Bemerkung nicht so ernst, ich habe mir nichts ~ gedacht** don't take my remark so seriously, I didn't mean anything by it; **ich habe mir nichts ~ gedacht, als ich den Mann aus der Bank kommen sah** I didn't think anything of it when I saw the man coming out of the bank; **was hast du dir denn ~ gedacht?** what were you thinking of?; **~ kann er sich nicht viel gedacht haben, da kann er sich nicht viel bei gedacht haben** (*N Ger*) he can't have thought about it much.

dabeibleiben *vi sep irreg aux sein* to stay *or* stick (*inf*) with it; (*bei Firma, Stelle, Armee etc*) to stay on; *siehe auch* **dabei (g)**.

dabeihaben *vt sep irreg* (*Zusammenschreibung nur bei infin und ptp*) (*inf*) to have with one; *Geld, Paß, Schirm etc auch* to have on one.

⚠ **dabeisein** *vi sep irreg aux sein* (*Zusammenschreibung nur bei infin und ptp*) **(a)** to be there (*bei* at); (*mitmachen*) to be involved (*bei* in) ◆ **ich bin dabei!** count me in!; **er war bei der Flugzeugentführung dabei** he was there when the plane was hijacked, he was there at the hijacking; **ein wenig Furcht ist immer dabei** I'm/you're *etc* always a bit scared; **er will überall ~** he wants to be in on everything.
(b) (*im Begriff sein*) **~, etw zu tun** to be just doing sth; **ich bin (gerade) dabei** I'm just doing it.

dabeisitzen *vi sep irreg aux haben or* (*S Ger, Aus, Sw*) *sein* to sit there ◆ **bei einer Besprechung ~** to sit in on a discussion.

dabeistehen *vi sep irreg aux haben or* (*S Ger, Aus, Sw*) *sein* to stand there.

dableiben *vi sep irreg aux sein* to stay (on); (*nachsitzen*) to stay behind ◆ **(jetzt wird) dageblieben!** (you just) stay right there!

da capo *adv* da capo ◆ **~ ~ rufen** to call for an encore.

Dach *nt* **-(e)s, ¨er (a)** roof; (*Aut auch*) top ◆ **das ~ der Welt** the roof of the world; **ein/kein ~ über dem Kopf haben** (*inf*) to have a/no roof over one's head; **mit jdm unter einem ~ wohnen** to live under the same roof as sb; **jdm das ~ überm Kopf anzünden** to burn down sb's house; **unterm ~ juchhe** (*inf*) right under the eaves; **unterm ~ wohnen** (*inf*) to live in an attic room/flat

➤ SPRACHE AKTIV: **da: 2a** → 44.1

(*Brit*) *or* apartment; (*im obersten Stock*) to live right on the top floor; **unter ~ und Fach sein** (*abgeschlossen*) to be all wrapped up *or* in the bag (*inf*); (*Vertrag, Geschäft auch*) to be signed and sealed; (*in Sicherheit*) to be safely under cover; (*Ernte*) to be safely in; **etw unter ~ und Fach bringen** to get sth all wrapped up/signed and sealed/safely under cover/to bring sth in.
(b) (*fig inf*) **jdm eins aufs ~ geben** (*schlagen*) to smash sb on the head (*inf*); (*ausschimpfen*) to give sb a (good) talking-to; **eins aufs ~ bekommen** *or* **kriegen** (*geschlagen werden*) to get hit on the head; (*ausgeschimpft werden*) to be given a (good) talking-to; **jdm aufs ~ steigen** (*inf*) to get onto sb (*inf*).

Dach- *in cpds* roof; **~balken** *m* roof joist *or* beam; **~bedeckung** *f*, **~belag** *m* roofing; **~boden** *m* attic, loft; (*von Scheune*) loft; **auf dem ~boden** in the attic; **~decker** *m* **-s, -** roofer; (*mit Ziegeln*) tiler; (*mit Schiefer*) slater; (*mit Stroh*) thatcher; **das kannst du halten wie ein ~decker** (*fig inf*) it doesn't matter two ha'pence (*Brit inf*) *or* one jot (*inf*); **~deckerarbeiten** *pl* roofing; tiling; slating; thatching.

dachen *vt* (*obs*) to roof.

Dach-: ~erker *m* dormer window; **~fenster** *nt* skylight; (*ausgestellt*) dormer window; **~first** *m* ridge of the roof; **d~förmig** *adj* rooflike; **~garten** *m* roof garden; **~gebälk** *nt* roof timbers *pl*; **~gepäckträger** *m* (*Aut*) roof rack; ⚠**~geschoß** *nt* attic storey; (*oberster Stock*) top floor *or* storey; **~gesellschaft** *f* parent company; **~gesims** *nt* (roof) cornice; **~gestühl** *nt* roof truss; **~giebel** *m* gable; **~gleiche(nfeier)** *f* **-, -n** (*Aus*) topping-out ceremony; **~hase** *m* (*hum*) cat; **~kammer** *f* attic room, garret (*dated*); **~latte** *f* tile *or* roof batten; **~luke** *f* skylight; **~neigung** *f* slope of the roof; **~organisation** *f* umbrella *or* (*Comm*) parent organization; **~pappe** *f* roofing felt; **~pfanne** *f* (roof) tile; **~reiter** *m* (*Archit*) roof *or* ridge turret; **~rinne** *f* gutter.

Dachs *m* **-es, -e (a)** (*Zool*) badger ◆ **schlafen wie ein ~** (*inf*) to sleep like a log (*inf*). **(b)** (*inf: Mensch*) **ein frecher ~!** a cheeky devil!; **ein junger ~** a young whippersnapper.

Dachsbau *m* badger's sett.

Dach-: ~schaden *m* **(a)** (*lit*) damage to the roof; **(b)** (*inf*) **einen (kleinen) ~schaden haben** to have a slate loose (*inf*); **~schiefer** *m* roofing slate; **~schindel** *f* (roof) shingle.

Dachshund *m* dachshund.

Dachsilhouette *f* outline of the roof.

Dächsin *f* female badger.

Dach-: ~sparren *m* rafter; **~stein** *m* (cement) roofing slab; **~stroh** *nt* thatch; **~stube** *f*, **~stübchen** *nt* attic room, garret (*dated*); **~stuhl** *m siehe* **~gestühl**; **~stuhlbrand** *m* roof fire.

dachte *pret of* **denken**.

Dach-: ~terrasse *f* roof terrace; **~träger** *m* (*Aut*) roof rack; **~traufe** *f* rain spout; (*dial:* **~rinne**) gutter; **~verband** *m* umbrella organization; **~wohnung** *f* attic flat (*Brit*) *or* apartment; **~ziegel** *m* roofing tile; **~zimmer** *nt* attic room, garret.

Dackel *m* **-s, -** dachshund, sausage dog (*inf*); (*inf: Person*) silly clot (*inf*).

Dackelbeine *pl* (*inf*) short stumpy legs *pl*.

Dadaismus *m* Dadaism, Dada.

Dadaist(in *f***)** *m* Dadaist ◆ **die ~en** the Dada group, the Dadaists.

dadaistisch *adj* dadaist.

Daddelhalle *f* (*inf*) amusement arcade.

daddeln *vi* (*inf*) to play the fruit machines.

dadurch *adv* (*emph* **dadurch**) **(a)** (*örtlich*) through there; (*wenn Bezugsobjekt vorher erwähnt*) through it; (*geh: in Relativsatz*) through which.
(b) (*kausal*) thereby (*form*); (*mit Hilfe von, aus diesem Grund auch*) because of this/that, through this/that; (*durch diesen Umstand, diese Tat etc auch*) by *or* with that; (*auf diese Weise*) in this/that way ◆ **was willst du ~ gewinnen?** what do you hope to gain by *or* from that?; **meinst du, ~ wird alles wieder gut?** do you think that will make everything all right again?; **~ kam es, daß er nicht dabeisein konnte** that was why he couldn't be there.
(c) ~, daß er das tat, hat er ... (*durch diesen Umstand, diese Tat*) by doing that he ...; (*deswegen, weil*) because he did that he ...; **~, daß ich das tat, hat er ...** by my doing that he ..., because I did that he ...; **~, daß er den zweiten Satz gewonnen hat, sind seine Chancen wieder gestiegen** his chances improved again with him *or* his winning the second set; **~, daß das Haus isoliert ist, ist es viel wärmer** the house is much warmer because it's insulated *or* for being insulated.

dafür *adv* (*emph* **dafür**) **(a)** (*für das, diese Tat etc*) for that/it ◆ **wir haben kein Geld ~** we've no money for that; **~ haben wir kein Geld, da haben wir kein Geld für** (*N Ger inf*) we've no money for that sort of thing; **der Grund ~ ist, daß ...** the reason for that is (that) ...; **warum ist er so böse? er hat doch keinen Grund ~** why is he so angry? there's no reason for it *or* he has no reason to be; **~ war er nicht zu haben** it wasn't his scene (*inf*); (*erlaubte es nicht*) he wouldn't have it; **~ ist er immer zu haben** he never says no to that; **ich bin nicht ~ verantwortlich, was mein Bruder macht** I'm not responsible for what my brother does; **~ bin ich ja hier** that's what I'm here for, that's why I'm here; **er ist ~ bestraft worden, daß er frech zum Lehrer war** he was punished for being cheeky to the teacher.
(b) (*Zustimmung*) for that/it, in favour (of that/it) ◆ **ich bin ganz ~** I'm all for it (*inf*), I'm all in favour; **ich bin (ganz) ~, daß wir/sie das machen** I'm (all) for *or* in favour of doing that/them doing that; **~ stimmen** to vote for it; **ich bin nicht ~, daß das so gemacht wird** I don't think it should be done like that, I'm not in favour of it being done that way.
(c) (*als Ersatz*) instead, in its place; (*als Bezahlung*) for that/it; (*bei Tausch*) in exchange; (*als Gegenleistung*) in return ◆ **... ich mache dir ~ deine Hausaufgaben** ... and I'll do your homework in return.
(d) (*zum Ausgleich*) but ... to make up ◆ **in Mathematik ist er schlecht, ~ kann er gut Fußball spielen** he's very bad at maths but he makes up for it at football *or* but he's good at football to make up; **ich hatte diesmal immer nur Kurzferien, ~ habe ich um so mehr gesehen** I've only had short holidays this time but I've seen a lot more for all that.
(e) (*im Hinblick darauf*) **der Junge ist erst drei Jahre, ~ ist er sehr klug** the boy is only three, (so) considering that he's very clever; **~, daß er erst drei Jahre ist, ist er sehr klug** seeing *or* considering that he's only three he's very clever.
(f) *in Verbindung mit n, vb etc siehe auch dort* **er interessiert sich nicht ~** he's not interested in that/it; **~ interessiert er sich nicht** he's not interested in that sort of thing; **er gibt sein ganzes Geld ~ aus** he spends all his money on that/it; **ein Beispiel ~ wäre ...** an example of that would be ...; **ich kann mich nicht ~ begeistern** I can't get enthusiastic about it, I can't rouse any enthusiasm for it; **sie ist dreißig/sehr intelligent — ~ hätte ich sie nicht gehalten** she's thirty/very intelligent — I would never have thought it *or* thought she was; **~ werde ich schon sorgen** I'll see to *or* take care of that; **ich werde ~ sorgen, daß ...** I'll see to it that ...

dafür-: ~halten *vi sep irreg* (*geh*) to be of the opinion; **ich halte ~, daß wir zu Hause bleiben** I am of the opinion that we should stay at home; **nach meinem D~halten** in my opinion; ⚠**~können** *vt sep irreg* **er kann nichts ~** he can't help it, it's not his fault; **er kann nichts ~, daß er dumm ist** he can't help being stupid, it's not his fault that he's stupid; **er kann nichts/etwas ~, daß es kaputtgegangen ist** it's not/it was his fault that it broke, he couldn't help it breaking; **was kann ich ~, daß es heute regnet?** it's not my fault (that) *or* I can't help that it's raining today; **als ob ich da was für könnte!** (*N Ger inf*) as if I could help it!, as if it were my fault!; **~stehen** *vir sep irreg* (*Aus*) to be worth it *or* worthwhile.

DAG [deːǀaːˈgeː] *f* - *abbr of* **Deutsche Angestellten-Gewerkschaft** Trade Union of German Employees.

▼ **dagegen** [1] *adv* (*emph* **dagegen**) **(a)** (*örtlich*) against it ◆ **es stand ein Baum im Weg und der Vogel/Wagen prallte ~** there was a tree in the way and the bird/car crashed into it; **die Tür war verschlossen, also pochte er ~** the door was locked, so he hammered on it; **mache das Licht an und halte das Dia ~** put the light on and hold the slide up to it *or* against it.
▼ **(b)** (*als Einwand, Ablehnung*) against that/it ◆ **~ sein** to be against it *or* opposed (to it); **etwas/nichts ~ haben** to object/not to object; **ich habe etwas ~, da habe ich was gegen** (*N Ger inf*) I object to that; **was hat er ~, daß wir früher anfangen?** what has he got against us starting earlier?, why does he object to us *or* our starting earlier?; **haben Sie was ~, wenn ich rauche?** do you mind if I smoke?, would you mind *or* object if I smoked?; **sollen wir ins Kino gehen? — ich hätte nichts ~ (einzuwenden)** shall we go to the cinema? — that's okay by me (*inf*); **ich hätte nichts ~, wenn er nicht kommen würde** I wouldn't mind at all if he didn't come; **ich werde ~ protestieren** I will protest against that/it; **ich werde ~ protestieren, daß das gemacht wird** I will protest against that being done.
(c) (*als Gegenmaßnahme*) *tun, unternehmen* about it; (*Medikamente einnehmen etc*) for it ◆ **~ läßt sich nichts machen** nothing can be done about it; **bei mir regnet es herein, aber ich kann nichts ~ machen** the rain comes in, but I can't do anything to stop it *or* about it.
(d) (*verglichen damit*) compared with that/it/them, in comparison ◆ **die Stürme letztes Jahr waren furchtbar, ~ sind die jetzigen nicht so schlimm** the gales last year were terrible, compared with them *or* those, these aren't so bad *or* these aren't so bad in comparison.
(e) (*als Ersatz, Gegenwert*) for that/it/them.
[2] *conj* (*im Gegensatz dazu*) on the other hand, however ◆ **er sprach fließend Französisch, ~ konnte er kein Deutsch** he spoke French fluently, but (on the other hand) he could not speak any German.

dagegen-: ~halten *vt sep irreg* **(a)** (*vergleichen*) to compare it/them with; **wenn wir das Original ~halten ...** if we compare the original with it ...; **(b)** (*einwenden*) *siehe* **~setzen**; **~setzen** *vt sep* (*fig*) **seine eigene Meinung ~setzen** to put forward one's own opinion in opposition; **das einzige, was Sie ~setzen könnten, wäre ...** the only objection you could put forward would be ...; **er setzte ~, daß ...** he put forward the objection that ...; **~sprechen** *vi sep irreg* to be against it; **was spricht ~?** what is there against it?; **was spricht ~, daß wir es so machen?** what is there against us doing it that way?, why shouldn't we do it that way?; **es spricht nichts ~, es so zu machen** there's no reason not to do it that way; **~stellen** *vr sep* to oppose it; **warum mußt du dich immer ~stellen?** why must you always oppose everything?; **~stemmen** *vr sep* to fight it, to oppose it bitterly; **~wirken** *vi sep* to act against it.

dahaben *vt sep irreg* (*Zusammenschreibung nur bei infin und ptp*) **(a)** (*vorrätig haben*) to have here/there; (*in Geschäft etc*) to have in stock. **(b)** (*zu Besuch haben*) to have here/there; (*zum Essen etc*) to have in.

daheim *adv* at home; (*nach prep*) home ◆ **bei uns ~** back home (where I/we come from); **das Buch liegt bei mir ~** *or* **~ bei mir** I've got the book at home; **wir haben bei mir ~** *or* **~ bei mir gefeiert** we had a celebration at my place; **~ sein** (*lit, fig*) to be at home; (*nach Reise*) to be home; **wo bist du ~?** where's your home?; **ich bin für niemanden ~** I'm not at home to anybody; **~ ist ~** (*Prov*) east, west, home's best (*prov*), there's no place like home (*prov*).

Daheim *nt* **-s**, *no pl* home.

Daheim-: ~gebliebene(r) *mf decl as adj* person/friend/son *etc* (left) at home; **die/alle ~gebliebenen** those/all those at home; **~sein** *nt* **das ~sein ist auch schön** being (at) home is nice too, it's nice being (at) home.

➤ SPRACHE AKTIV: **dagegen: 1b** → 36.1, 36.2, 39.2

▼ **daher** [1] *adv* (*auch* **daher**) **(a)** (*von dort*) from there ♦ **von ~** from there; **~ habe ich das** that's where I got it from.
(b) (*dial: hierher*) here.
(c) (*durch diesen Umstand*) that is why ♦ **~ weiß ich das** that's how *or* why I know that; **~ die große Eile/all der Lärm** that's why there's *or* that's the reason for all this hurry/noise; **~ der Name X** that's why it's called X; **~ kommt es, daß ...** that is (the reason) why ...; **ich bin überzeugt, daß seine Krankheit ~ kommt** I'm sure that's why he's ill; **das kommt** *or* **rührt ~, daß ...** that is because ...
▼[2] *conj* (*deshalb*) that is why ♦ **~ die Verspätung** that's what is causing the delay, hence the delay.
daher-: ~bringen *vt sep irreg* (*Aus*) to produce, to bring along; **~fliegen** *vi sep irreg aux sein* to fly along; **~gelaufen** *adj* **jeder D~gelaufene, jeder ~gelaufene Kerl** any Tom, Dick or Harry, any guy who comes/came along; **diese ~gelaufenen Kerle in der Politik** these jumped-up nobodies in politics; **sie hat so einen ~gelaufenen Kerl geheiratet** she married some fellow who just happened along (*inf*); **~kommen** *vi sep irreg aux sein* to come along; **da kommt so einer ~ ...** this guy comes along (*inf*); **wie kann man nur so geschminkt/schlampig ~kommen?** (*inf*) how can anybody go around with make-up like that/looking so scruffy?; **~laufen** *vi sep irreg aux sein* (*gehen*) to walk up; (*laufen*) to run up; **~gelaufen kommen** to come running up; **~reden** *sep* [1] *vi* to talk away; **red doch nicht so (dumm) ~!** don't talk such rubbish!; [2] *vt* to say without thinking; **was er alles/für ein blödes Zeug ~redet** the things/the rubbish he comes out with! (*inf*); **das war nur so ~geredet** I/he *etc* just said that; **~sagen** *vt sep* to say without thinking.
daherum *adv* round there.
dahin [1] *adv* (*emph* **dahin**) **(a)** (*räumlich*) there; (*hierhin*) here ♦ **kommst du auch~?** are you coming too?; **~ und dorthin blicken** to look here and there; **~ gehe ich nie wieder, da gehe ich nie wieder hin** (*inf*) I'm never going there again; **bis ~** as far as there, up to that point; **ist es noch weit bis ~?** is it still a long way?; **bis ~ dauert es noch zwei Stunden** it'll take us another two hours to get there; **es steht mir bis ~** I've had it up to here (*inf*).
(b) (*fig: so weit*) **~ kommen** to come to that, to reach such a pass; **es ist ~ gekommen, daß ...** things have got to the stage where *or* have reached such a pass that ...; **du wirst es ~ bringen, daß ...** you'll bring things to such a pass that ...
(c) (*in dem Sinne, in die Richtung*) **er äußerte sich ~ gehend, daß ...** he said something to the effect that ...; **eine ~ gehende Aussage/Änderung** *etc* a statement/change to that effect; **ein ~ gehender Befehl, daß ...** an order to the effect that ...; **wir sind ~ gehend verblieben, daß ...** we agreed that ...; **er hat den Bericht ~ (gehend) interpretiert, daß ...** he interpreted the report as saying ...; **wir haben uns ~ geeinigt/abgesprochen, daß ...** we have agreed that ...; **alle meine Hoffnungen/Bemühungen gehen ~, daß ich dieses Ziel bald erreiche** all my hopes/efforts are directed towards (my) reaching this goal soon; **seine Meinung geht ~, daß ...** he tends to feel that *or* to the opinion that ...
(d) (*zeitlich*) then; *siehe* **bis**[2].
[2] *adj pred* **~ sein** to have gone; **sein Leben** *or* **er ist ~** (*geh*) his life is over; **das Auto ist ~** (*hum inf*) the car has had it (*inf*).
da-: ~hinab *adv siehe* **dorthinab**; **~hinauf** *adv siehe* **dorthinauf**; **~hinaus** *adv* there; *transportieren, bringen* out that way; **~hinaus muß der Dieb entkommen sein** that must be where the thief escaped; **~hinaus will er also!** (*fig*) so that's what he's getting at!
dahin-: ~bewegen* *vr sep* to move on one's way; (*Fluß*) to flow on its way; **~dämmern** *vi sep aux sein* to lie/sit there in a stupor; **~eilen** *vi sep aux sein* (*liter*) to hurry along; (*Zeit*) to pass swiftly.
dahinein *adv siehe* **dorthinein**.
dahin-: ~fahren *vi sep irreg aux sein* (*liter: sterben*) to pass away *or* over; **~fliegen** *vi sep irreg aux sein* (*liter*) (*wegfliegen*) to fly off; (*fig*) (*schnell fahren, vergehen*) to fly along *or* past; **~geben** *vt sep irreg* (*liter*) *Leben, Gut, Besitz* to give up; **D~gegangene(r)** *mf decl as adj* (*liter*) departed.
dahingegen *adv* on the other hand.
dahingehen *vi sep irreg aux sein* (*geh*) **(a)** (*vergehen*) (*Zeit, Jahre*) to pass (*jdm* for sb). **(b)** (*vorbeigehen, entlanggehen*) to pass. **(c)** (*sterben*) to pass away *or* on.
dahingehend *adv siehe* **dahin 1 (c)**.
dahin-: ~gestellt *adj* **~gestellt sein lassen, ob ...** to leave it open whether ...; **es bleibt** *or* **sei ~gestellt, ob ...** it is an open question whether ...; **~leben** *vi sep* to exist, to vegetate (*pej*); **~raffen** *vt sep* (*liter*) to carry off; **~reden** *vi sep* to say the first thing that comes into one's head; **~sagen** *vt sep* to say without (really) thinking; **das war nur so ~gesagt** I/he *etc* just said that (without thinking); **~scheiden** *vi sep irreg aux sein* (*geh*) to pass away; **~schleppen** *vr sep* (*lit: sich fortbewegen*) to drag oneself along; (*fig: Verhandlungen, Zeit*) to drag on; **~schwinden** *vi sep irreg aux sein* (*geh*) (*Vorräte, Geld, Kraft*) to dwindle (away); (*Interesse, Gefühle etc*) to dwindle; (*vergehen: Zeit*) to go past; **~siechen** *vi sep aux sein* (*geh*) to waste away; **vor Kummer ~siechen** to pine away; **jahrelang siechte er in einem dunklen Keller ~** for years he languished in a dark cellar; **~stehen** *vi sep irreg* to be debatable.
dahinten *adv* (*emph* **dahinten**) over there; (*hinter Sprecher*) back there ♦ **ganz weit ~** right *or* way (*inf*) over there.
dahinter *adv* (*emph* **dahinter**) **(a)** (*räumlich*) behind (it/that/him *etc*) ♦ **was sich wohl ~ verbirgt?** (*lit, fig*) I wonder what's behind that?; **da ist schon etwas ~** (*fig*) there's something in that; **(da ist) nichts ~** (*fig*) there's nothing behind it. **(b)** (*danach*) beyond.
dahinterher *adj*: **~ sein** (*inf*) to push (*daß* to see that); **die Polizei ist ~, die Jugendkriminalität einzudämmen** the police are pretty hot on trying to keep juvenile delinquency under control (*inf*).
⚠**dahinter-: ~klemmen, ~knien** *vr sep* (*inf*) to put one's back into it, to get *or* pull one's finger out (*sl*); **klemm'** *or* **knie dich mal ein bißchen ~** make a bit of an effort; **~kommen** *vi sep irreg aux sein* (*inf*) to find out; (*langsam verstehen*) to get it (*inf*); **~setzen** *vr sep siehe* **~klemmen**; **~stecken** *vi sep* (*inf*) to be behind it/that; **da steckt doch etwas ~** there's something behind it; **da steckt doch etwas ~, daß er jetzt gehen will** there's something behind his *or* him wanting to go now; **da werden die Eltern ~stecken, daß er nicht mehr kommen will** his parents must be behind his *or* him not wanting to come any more; **er redet viel, es steckt aber nichts ~** he talks a lot but there's nothing behind it; **~stehen** *vi sep irreg* **(a)** (*unterstützen*) to back it/that, to be behind it/that; **(b)** (*zugrunde liegen*) to underlie it/that.
dahinunter *adv siehe* **dorthinunter**.
dahinvegetieren* *vi sep* to vegetate.
Dahlie [-iə] *f* dahlia.
DAK [deːǀaˈkaː] *f* - *abbr of* **Deutsche Angestellten-Krankenkasse** Employees' Health Insurance.
Dakapo *nt* **-s, -s** encore.
Dakaporuf *m* call for an encore.
daktylisch *adj* (*Poet*) dactylic.
Daktylo-: ~gramm *nt* (*von einem Finger*) fingerprint; (*von ganzer Hand*) fingerprints *pl*; ⚠**~graphie** *f* (*Sw*) typing; **~skopie** *f* fingerprinting.
Daktylus *m* **-, Daktylen** (*Poet*) dactyl.
da-: ~lassen *vt sep irreg* to leave (here/there); **~liegen** *vi sep irreg* to lie there; **... sonst liegst du nachher ~ mit einer schweren Grippe** (*inf*) otherwise you'll be in bed with a bad dose of flu.
Dalk *m* **-(e)s, -e** (*Aus inf*) (*Dummkopf*) fathead (*inf*); (*ungeschickter Mensch*) clumsy oaf (*inf*).
dalke(r)t *adj* (*Aus inf*) daft (*inf*).
dalli *adv* (*inf*) **~, ~!** on the double! (*inf*), look smart! (*inf*); **mach ein bißchen ~!** get a move on! (*inf*); **verzieh dich, aber ~!** beat it, go on, quick!
Dalmatiner *m* **-s, -** (*Hund*) dalmatian.
damalig *adj attr* at that *or* the time; *Inhaber eines Amtes auch* then *attr*; *Sitten auch* in those days.
damals *adv* at that time, then ♦ **seit ~** since then, since that time; **von ~** of that time; **~, als ...** at the time when ...; **wenn ich daran denke, was ~ war** when I think of that time *or* of what things were like then.
Damast *m* **-(e)s, -e** damask.
Damast- *in cpds* damask.
damasten *adj attr* (*liter*) damask.
Damaszenerklinge *f* damascene sword.
Dambock *m siehe* **Damhirsch**.
Dämchen *nt* (*pej*) precocious young madam; (*Dirne*) tart (*inf*).
Dame *f* **-, -n** **(a)** lady ♦ **sehr verehrte** (*form*) *or* **meine ~n und Herren!** ladies and gentlemen!; **guten Abend, die ~n** (*old, hum*) good evening, ladies; „**~n**" (*Toilette*) "Ladies"; **die ~ wünscht?** (*old*) can I be of assistance, madam? (*form*); **ganz ~ sein** to be the perfect lady *or* every inch a lady.
(b) (*allgemein gesehen: Tanzpartnerin, Begleiterin*) lady; (*auf einen bestimmten Herrn bezogen*) partner; (*bei Cocktailparty, Theaterbesuch etc*) (lady) companion ♦ **seine ~ ist eben mit einem anderen weggegangen** the lady he came with has just left with someone else; **bringen Sie ruhig Ihre ~n mit** do by all means bring your wives and girlfriends.
(c) (*Sport*) woman, lady ♦ **Hundert-Meter-Staffel der ~n** women's *or* ladies' hundred metre relay.
(d) (*Spiel*) draughts *sing*, checkers *sing* (*US*); (*Doppelstein*) king.
Damebrett *nt* draught(s)board, checkerboard (*US*).
Dämel *m* **-s, -** (*inf*) *siehe* **Dämlack**.
Damen- *in cpds* ladies'; **~bart** *m* facial hair; **~begleitung** *f* **~begleitung erwünscht** please bring a lady *or* (*bei Ball*) partner; **in ~begleitung** in the company of a lady; **~bekanntschaft** *f* female acquaintance (*inf*); **eine ~bekanntschaft machen** to make the acquaintance of a lady/young lady; **~besuch** *m* lady visitor/visitors; **~binde** *f* sanitary towel *or* napkin (*US*); **~doppel** *nt* (*Tennis etc*) ladies' doubles *sing*; **~einzel** *nt* (*Tennis etc*) ladies' singles *sing*; **~(fahr)rad** *nt* ladies' bicycle or bike (*inf*); **~gesellschaft** *f* **(a)** *no pl* (*Begleitung von Dame*) company of ladies/a lady; **(b)** (*gesellige Runde*) ladies' gathering; **d~haft** *adj* ladylike *no adv*; **sich d~haft benehmen/kleiden** to behave/dress in a ladylike way; **~konfektion** *f* ladies' wear (department); **~mangel** *m* shortage of ladies; **~oberbekleidung** *f* ladies' wear; **~sattel** *m* side-saddle; **im ~sattel reiten** to ride side-saddle; **~schneider** *m* dressmaker; **~schneiderei** *f* **(a)** dressmaking; **(b)** (*Werkstatt*) dressmaker's; **~sitz** *m* side-saddle style of riding; **im ~sitz** side-saddle; **~toilette** *f* **(a)** (*WC*) ladies, ladies' toilet *or* restroom (*US*); **(b)** (*Kleidung*) ladies' toilette; **~unterwäsche** *f* ladies' underwear, lingerie; **~wahl** *f* ladies' choice; **~welt** *f* (*dated hum*) ladies *pl*; **in** *or* **bei der ~welt beliebt** popular with the ladies.
Dame-: ~spiel *nt* draughts *sing*, checkers *sing* (*US*); **~stein** *m* draughtsman, checker (*US*).
Damhirsch *m* fallow deer.
damisch (*S Ger, Aus*) [1] *adj* **(a)** (*dämlich*) daft (*inf*). **(b)** (*pred: schwindelig*) dizzy, giddy.
[2] *adv* (*sehr*) terribly (*inf*).
damit [1] *adv* (*emph auch* **damit**) *siehe auch* **mit**, *vbs +mit* **(a)** (*mit diesem Gegenstand, dieser Tätigkeit, mit Hilfe davon*) with it/that ♦ **sie hatte zwei Koffer und stand ~ am Bahnhof** she had two cases and was standing there with them

in the station; **sie hat Ärger mit der Waschmaschine — ~ habe ich auch Probleme** she's got trouble with the washing machine — I've got problems with mine too; **was will er ~?** what does he want that for?, what does he want with that?; **was soll ich ~?** what am I meant to do with that?; **ist Ihre Frage ~ beantwortet?** does that answer your question?; **~ kann er mich ärgern, da kann er mich mit ärgern** (*N Ger inf*) I get really annoyed when he does that.
(b) (*mit, in dieser Angelegenheit*) **meint er mich ~?** does he mean me?; **weißt du, was er ~ meint?** do you know what he means by that?; **was ist ~?** what about it?; **wie wäre es ~?** how about it?; **er konnte mir nicht sagen, was es ~ auf sich hat** he couldn't tell me what it was all about; **wie sieht es ~ aus?** what's happening about it?; **muß er denn immer wieder ~ ankommen?** (*davon reden*) must he keep on about it?; (*mit Bitten, Forderungen etc*) must he keep coming back about it?; **das/er hat gar nichts ~ zu tun** that/he has nothing to do with it; **~ ist nichts** (*inf*) it's no go (*inf*); **hör auf ~!** (*inf*) lay off! (*inf*); **~ hat es noch Zeit** there's no hurry for that.
(c) (*bei Verben*) *siehe vb +mit* **was willst du ~ sagen?** what's that supposed *or* meant to mean?; **~ will ich nicht sagen, daß ...** I don't mean to say that ...; **sind Sie ~ einverstanden?** do you agree to that?; **er hatte nicht ~ gerechnet** he hadn't reckoned on *or* with that; **~, daß du dich jetzt aufregst, machst du den Schaden auch nicht wieder gut** you're not making anything better by getting excited; **sie fangen schon ~ an** they're already starting on it; **sie fangen schon ~ an, das Haus abzureißen** they're already starting to pull down the house; **~ fing der Streit an** the argument started with that; **der Streit fing ~ an, daß er behauptete ...** the argument started when he said ...; **er fing ~ an, daß er ... sagte** he began by saying that ...
(d) (*bei Befehlen*) with it ◆ **weg/heraus ~!** away/out with it; **her ~!** give it here! (*inf*); **Schluß/genug ~!** that's enough (of that)!
(e) (*begründend*) because of that ◆ **er verlor den zweiten Satz und ~ das Spiel** he lost the second set and because of that the match; **~ ist es klar, daß er es war** from that it's clear that it was he (*form*) *or* him.
(f) (*daraufhin, dann, jetzt*) with that ◆ **~ schließe ich für heute** I'll close with that for today; **~ kommen wir zum Ende des Programms** that brings us to the end of our programmes.
[2] *conj* so that ◆ **~ er nicht fällt** so that he does not fall, lest he (should) fall (*old*).

Dämlack *m* **-s, -e** *or* **-s** (*inf*) sap (*sl*), jerk (*sl*).

dämlich *adj* (*inf*) stupid, dumb (*inf*) ◆ **komm mir nicht so ~!** don't give me that! (*inf*), don't come that with me! (*inf*); **er ist mir vielleicht ~ gekommen** he acted really dumb (*inf*) *or* stupid; **~ fragen** to ask stupid *or* dumb (*inf*) questions/a stupid *or* dumb (*inf*) question.

Dämlichkeit *f* **(a)** stupidity, dumbness (*inf*). **(b)** (*dumme Handlung*) stupid *or* dumb (*inf*) thing.

Damm *m* **-(e)s, ¨-e (a)** (*Deich*) dyke; (*Stau~*) dam; (*Hafen~*) wall; (*Ufer~*) embankment, levee (*esp US*); (*Verkehrsverbindung zu Insel*) causeway; (*fig*) barrier ◆ **einen ~ gegen etw aufbauen, einer Sache** (*dat*) **einen ~ (entgegen) setzen** (*fig*) to check sth; **wenn wir das kleinste bißchen nachgeben, werden alle ¨~e brechen** if we give way at all, the floodgates will open wide.
(b) (*Bahn~, Straßen~*) embankment.
(c) (*dial: Fahr~*) road.
(d) (*Anat*) perineum.
(e) (*fig inf*) **wieder auf dem ~ sein** to be back to normal; **geistig auf dem ~ sein** to be with it (*inf*); **nicht recht auf dem ~ sein** not to be up to the mark (*inf*).

Dammbruch *m* breach in a/the dyke *etc*.

dämmen *vt* **(a)** (*geh*) (*lit*) to dam; (*fig*) to check; *Tränen, Gefühle* to (hold in) check; *Umtriebe, Gefühle, Seuche* to curb, to check. **(b)** (*Tech*) *Wärme* to keep in; *Schall* to absorb.

Dämmer *m* **-s,** *no pl* **(a)** (*poet*) *siehe* **Dämmerung. (b)** (*fig geh*) nebulousness.

dämmerhaft *adj* (*liter*) hazy, nebulous.

dämm(e)rig *adj Licht* dim, faint; *Stunden* twilight *attr* ◆ **es wird ~** (*abends*) dusk is falling; (*morgens*) dawn is breaking.

Dämmerlicht *nt* twilight; (*abends auch*) dusk; (*Halbdunkel*) half-light, gloom.

dämmern [1] *vi* **(a)** (*Tag, Morgen*) to dawn; (*Abend*) to fall ◆ **als der Tag** *or* **Morgen/Abend dämmerte ...** as dawn was breaking/dusk was falling; **die Erkenntnis/es dämmerte ihm, daß ...** (*inf*) he began to realize that ...
(b) (*im Halbschlaf sein*) to doze; (*Kranker*) to be dopey ◆ **vor sich hin ~** (*im Halbschlaf sein*) to doze; (*nicht bei klarem Verstand sein*) to be dopey.
[2] *vi impers* **es dämmert** (*morgens*) dawn is breaking; (*abends*) dusk is falling; **jetzt dämmert's (bei) mir!** (*inf*) now it's dawning (on me)!

Dämmer-: ~schein *m* (*liter*) glow; **~schlaf** *m* doze; **ich war nur im ~schlaf** I was only dozing; **~schoppen** *m* early evening drink; **~stunde** *f* twilight, dusk.

Dämmerung *f* twilight; (*Abend~ auch*) dusk; (*Morgen~ auch*) dawn; (*Halbdunkel*) half-light ◆ **in der ~ des Morgens** at dawn, when dawn came/comes; **bei** *or* **mit Anbruch der ~** when dusk began/begins to fall/dawn began/begins to break; **in der ~** at dusk/dawn.

Dämmerzustand *m* (*Halbschlaf*) dozy state; (*Bewußtseinstrübung*) dopey state.

dämmrig *adj siehe* **dämm(e)rig.**

⚠**Damm-: ~riß** *m* (*Med*) tear of the perineum; **~rutsch** *m landslide which destroys a dyke etc*; **~schnitt** *m* (*Med*) episiotomy.

Dämmstoffe *pl* insulating materials *pl*.

Dämmung *f* insulation.

⚠: for details of spelling reform, see supplement

Dammweg *m* causeway.

Damnum *nt* **-s, Damna** (*Fin*) debt discount.

Damoklesschwert *nt* (*lit, fig*) sword of Damocles.

Dämon *m* **-s, Dämonen** demon ◆ **ein böser ~** an evil spirit, a demon.

Dämonie *f* demonic nature.

dämonisch *adj* demonic.

dämonisieren* *vt* to demonize.

Dämonismus *m* (*Rel*) demonism.

Dampf *m* **-(e)s, ¨-e (a)** vapour; (*Wasser~*) steam ◆ **~ ablassen** *or* **abblasen** (*lit, fig*) to let off steam; **unter ~ sein** *or* **stehen** to have (its) steam up; **aus dem Schornstein quoll der ~ in weißen Wolken** clouds of white smoke poured from the chimney.
(b) (*inf: Wucht, Schwung*)) force ◆ **jdm ~ machen** (*inf*) to make sb get a move on (*inf*); **~ dahinter machen** *or* **setzen** to get a move on (*inf*); **mit ~** (*inf*) at full tilt; **vorm Chef hat sie unheimlich ~** the boss really puts the wind up her (*inf*); **~ drauf haben** (*dated inf*) to be going at full steam.

Dampf- *in cpds* steam; **~antrieb** *m* steam drive; **Maschine mit ~antrieb** steam-driven engine; **~bad** *nt* steam bath; **~boot** *nt* steamboat; **~bügeleisen** *nt* steam iron; **~druck** *m* steam pressure.

dampfen *vi* **(a)** (*Dampf abgeben*) to steam; (*Badezimmer etc*) to be full of steam; (*Pferd*) to be in a lather ◆ **ein ~des Bad/Essen** a steaming hot bath/meal.
(b) *aux sein* (*Zug, Schiff*) to steam.
(c) *aux sein* (*inf*) (*mit Dampfer fahren*) to sail, to steam; (*mit Zug fahren*) to go by (steam) train.

dämpfen *vt* **(a)** (*abschwächen*) to muffle; *Geräusch, Lärm, Schall auch* to deaden, to dampen; *Geige, Trompete, Farbe* to mute; *Licht, Stimme* to lower; *Wut* to calm; *Freude, Begeisterung, Stimmung* to dampen; *Aufprall* to deaden; (*fig*) *jdn* to subdue; *Konjunktur* to depress; *siehe auch* **gedämpft.**
(b) (*Cook*) to steam.
(c) (*bügeln*) to press with a damp cloth/steam iron.

Dampfer *m* **-s, -** steamer, steamship ◆ **auf dem falschen ~ sein** *or* **sitzen** (*fig inf*) to have got the wrong idea.

Dämpfer *m* **-s, - (a)** (*Mus: bei Klavier*) damper; (*bei Geige, Trompete*) mute ◆ **dadurch hat er/sein Optimismus einen ~ bekommen** that dampened his spirits/optimism; **jdm einen ~ aufsetzen** to dampen sb's spirits; **einer Sache** (*dat*) **einen ~ aufsetzen** (*inf*) to put a damper on sth (*inf*).
(b) (*Cook: Dampfkochtopf*) steamer.

Dampfer-: ~anlegestelle *f* steamer jetty; **~fahrt** *f* boat trip; **~linie** *f* steamship line.

Dampf-: d~förmig *adj* vaporous; **~hammer** *m* steam hammer; **~heizung** *f* steam heating.

dampfig *adj* steamy.

dämpfig *adj* **(a)** (*Vet*) broken-winded. **(b)** (*dial: schwül*) muggy.

Dampf-: ~kessel *m* (*Tech*) steam-boiler; (*Cook*) steamer; **~kocher, ~(koch)topf** *m* pressure cooker; **~kraft** *f* steam power; **~kraftwerk** *nt* steam power station; **~lokomotive, ~lok** (*inf*) *f* steam engine *or* locomotive; **~maschine** *f* steam(-driven) engine; **~nudel** *f* (*Cook*) *sweet yeast dumpling cooked in milk and sugar*; **aufgehen wie eine ~nudel** (*fig inf*) to blow up like a balloon (*inf*); **~pfeife** *f* steam whistle; (*von Schiff*) siren; **~schiff** *nt* steamship, steamer; **~schiffahrt** *f* steam navigation; **~schiffahrtgesellschaft** *f* steamship company; **~turbine** *f* steam turbine.

Dämpfung *f* (*Mus*) damping; (*Phys, Rad, TV*) attenuation.

Dampfwalze *f* steamroller.

Damwild *nt* fallow deer.

danach *adv* (*emph auch* **danach**) **(a)** (*zeitlich*) after that/it; (*nachher auch*) afterwards, after (*inf*) ◆ **ich habe einen Whisky getrunken, ~ fühlte ich mich schon besser** I had a whisky and after that *or* afterwards felt better, I had a whisky and felt better after that *or* afterwards *or* after (*inf*); **ich las das Buch zu Ende, erst ~ konnte ich einschlafen** only when I had finished reading the book could I get to sleep; **zehn Minuten ~ war sie schon wieder da** ten minutes later she was back; **um die Zwanziger und ~** around the twenties and after.
(b) (*in der Reihenfolge*) (*örtlich*) behind (that/it/him/them *etc*); (*zeitlich*) after that/it/him/them *etc* ◆ **als erster ging der Engländer durchs Ziel und gleich ~ der Russe** the Englishman finished first, immediately followed by the Russian *or* and the Russian immediately after him; **bei ihm kommt als erstes die Arbeit, ~ lange nichts und dann das Privatleben** work comes first with him, and then, a long long way behind, his private life.
(c) (*dementsprechend*) accordingly; (*laut diesem*) according to that; (*im Einklang damit*) in accordance with that/it ◆ **wir haben hier einen Bericht; ~ war die Stimmung damals ganz anders** we have a report here, according to which the atmosphere at the time was quite different; **~ sein** (*Wetter, Bedingungen, Stimmung* etc) to be right; **er hat den Aufsatz in zehn Minuten geschrieben — ~ ist er auch** (*inf*) he wrote the essay in ten minutes — it looks like it too; **sie sieht auch/nicht ~ aus** she looks/doesn't look (like) it; (*als ob sie so was getan hätte*) she looks/doesn't look the type; **~ siehst du gerade aus** (*iro*) I can just see that (*iro*); **lesen Sie Paragraph 218; ~ ist es verboten** read paragraph 218, under that it is illegal; **~ zu urteilen** judging by *or* from that; **mir war nicht ~** (*inf*) *or* **~ zumute** I didn't feel like it; **mir steht der Sinn nicht ~** (*geh*) I don't feel inclined to.
(d) (*in bestimmte Richtung*) towards it ◆ **er griff schnell ~** he grabbed at it, he made a grab for it; **hinter ihm war etwas, aber er hat sich nicht ~ umgesehen** there was something behind him, but he didn't look round to see what it was.
(e) *in Verbindung mit n, vb etc siehe auch dort* **sie sehnte sich ~** she longed for

that/it; **sie sehnte sich ~, ihren Sohn wiederzusehen** she longed to see her son again; **er hatte großes Verlangen ~** he felt a great desire for it; **er hatte großes Verlangen ~, wieder einmal die Heimat zu sehen** he felt a great desire to see his home again; **~ kann man nicht gehen** you can't go by that; **wenn es ~ ginge, was ich sage/was mir Spaß macht, dann ...** if it were a matter of what I say/enjoy then ...; **sich ~ erkundigen, ob ...** to enquire whether ...

Danaergeschenk ['da:naɐ-] *nt (fig)* two-edged gift.

Dandy ['dɛndi] *m* **-s, -s** dandy.

Däne *m* **-n, -n** Dane, Danish man/boy.

daneben *adv (emph auch* **daneben***)* **(a)** *(räumlich) (in unmittelbarer Nähe von jdm/etw)* next to him/her/that/it *etc*; *(seitlich von jdm/etw auch, zum Vergleich)* beside him/her/that/it *etc* ♦ **links/rechts ~** *(neben Sache)* to the left/right of it; *(neben Mensch)* to his/her *etc* left/right; **ich stand direkt ~, als die Bombe losging** the bomb went off right next to me; **wir wohnen im Haus ~** we live in the house next door.
(b) *(verglichen damit)* compared with that/it/him/them *etc*, in comparison.
(c) *(außerdem)* besides that, as well as that, in addition (to that); *(gleichzeitig)* at the same time.

daneben-: ~benehmen* *vr sep irreg (inf)* to make an exhibition of oneself; **~fallen** *vi sep irreg aux sein* to miss (it *or* one's mark); **~gehen** *vi sep irreg aux sein* **(a)** *(verfehlen: Schuß etc)* to miss; **(b)** *(inf: scheitern)* to go wrong; *(Witz)* to fall flat; **~geraten*** *vi sep irreg aux sein* to go wrong; *(Übersetzung)* not to hit the mark; **~greifen** *vi sep irreg* **(a)** *(verfehlen) (auf dem Klavier etc)* to play a wrong note/some wrong notes; *(beim Fangen)* to miss (the mark), to be wide of the mark; **(b)** *(fig inf) (mit Schätzung, Prognose etc)* to be wide of the mark *or* way out *(inf)*; **im Ton ~greifen** to strike the wrong note; **im Ausdruck ~greifen** to put things the wrong way; **mit seiner Bemerkung hat er aber ganz schön ~gegriffen** he really put his foot in it with that remark *(inf)*; **~halten** *sep irreg* [1] *vt* **jdn/etw ~halten** to compare him/her/it *etc* with sb/sth; [2] *vi siehe* **~zielen**; **~hauen** *vi sep irreg* **(a)** *(beim Schlagen)* to miss; *(beim Klavierspielen)* to play a wrong note/some wrong notes; **(b)** *(inf: sich irren)* to miss the mark, to be wide of the mark; *(beim Berechnen, Raten, Schätzen auch)* to be way out *(inf)*; **~liegen** *vi sep irreg (inf: sich irren)* to be quite wrong *or* way out *(inf)*; **~raten** *vi sep irreg (inf)* to guess wrong; **~schießen** *vi sep irreg* **(a)** *(verfehlen)* to miss; **(b)** *(absichtlich vorbeischießen)* to shoot to miss; ⚠**~sein** *vi sep irreg aux sein (Zusammenschreibung nur bei infin und ptp) (inf) (verwirrt sein)* to be completely confused; *(sich nicht wohl fühlen)* not to feel up to it *(inf)*; **~tippen** *vi sep (inf)* to guess wrong; **~treffen** *vi sep irreg siehe* **~schießen (a)**; **~zielen** *vi sep* to aim to miss.

Dänemark *nt* **-s** Denmark.

danieden *adv (obs)* down below ♦ **~ auf Erden** on earth below.

daniederliegen *vi sep irreg* **(a)** *(old liter: krank sein)* to be laid low, to be ill. **(b)** *(fig geh: schwach sein)* to be depressed.

Dänin *f* Dane, Danish woman/girl.

dänisch *adj* Danish.

Dänisch(e) *nt decl as adj* Danish; *siehe auch* **Deutsch(e)**.

▼ **Dank** *m* **-(e)s,** *no pl (ausgedrückt)* thanks *pl*; *(Gefühl der Dankbarkeit)* gratitude ♦ **besten** *or* **herzlichen** *or* **schönen** *or* **vielen ~** many thanks, thank you very much, thanks a lot *(inf)*; **vielen herzlichen/tausend ~!** many/very many thanks!, thanks a million! *(inf)*; **~ sei dem Herrn** *(Eccl)* thanks be to God; **haben Sie/hab ~!** *(geh)* thank you!; *(für Hilfe auch)* I'm much obliged to you; **jdm für etw ~ sagen** *(liter)* to express one's *or* give *(esp Eccl)* thanks to sb for sth; **~ sagen** *(Aus)* to express one's thanks; *(Eccl)* to give thanks; **jdm ~ schulden** *(form)*, **jdm zu ~ verpflichtet sein** *(form)* to owe sb a debt of gratitude; **jdm für etw ~ wissen** *(form)* to be indebted to sb for sth; **etw mit ~ annehmen** to accept sth with thanks; **mit bestem ~ zurück!** many thanks for lending it/them to me; *(iro: Retourkutsche)* thank you — the same to you!; **das war ein schlechter ~** that was poor thanks; **das ist der (ganze) ~ dafür** that's all the thanks one gets; **als ~ für seine Dienste** in grateful recognition of his service; **zum ~ (dafür)** as a way of saying thank you; **das ist der ~ des Vaterlandes!** *(iro)* that's all the thanks one gets!; **der ~ des Vaterlandes ist dir gewiß** *(iro)* you'll get a medal for that.

dank *prep +gen or dat* thanks to.

Dank|adresse *f* official letter of thanks.

▼ **dankbar** *adj* **(a)** *(dankerfüllt)* grateful; *(erleichtert, froh)* thankful; *Publikum, Zuhörer* appreciative ♦ **jdm ~ sein** to be grateful to sb *(für* for); *(für Rat, Hilfe etc auch)* to be indebted to sb *(für* for); **sich ~ erweisen** *or* **zeigen** to show one's gratitude *(gegenüber* to); **ich wäre dir ~, wenn du ...** I would be grateful *or* I would appreciate it if you ...
(b) *(lohnend) Arbeit, Aufgabe, Rolle* rewarding; *Stoff* easy-care *attr*; *Opfer* worthwhile; *(haltbar)* hard-wearing ♦ **eine ~e Pflanze** a plant which doesn't need much attention.

▼ **Dankbarkeit** *f* gratitude *(gegen, gegenüber* to); *(Gefühl der Erleichterung)* thankfulness.

Dankbrief *m* thank-you letter.

danke *interj* **(a)** thank you, thanks *(inf)*, ta *(Brit inf)*; *(ablehnend)* no thank you ♦ **~ ja, ja, ~** yes please, yes, thank you; **~ nein, nein, ~** no thank you; **~ schön** *or* **sehr** thank you *or* thanks *(inf)* very much; **(zu jdm) ~ (schön) sagen** to say thank you (to sb); **ich soll dir von meiner Schwester ~ schön sagen** my sister sends (you) her thanks; **~ vielmals** many thanks; *(iro)* thanks a million *(inf)*; **~ der Nachfrage** *(form)* thank you for your concern; **wie geht's? — ~, ich kann nicht klagen** how's it going? — (I) can't complain; **soll ich helfen? — ~, ich glaube, ich komme allein zurecht** can I help? — thanks (all the same), but I think I can manage; *siehe auch* **danken**.
(b) *(inf)* **mir geht's ~** I'm OK *(inf)*; **sonst geht's dir (wohl) ~!** *(iro)* are you feeling all right?

▼ **danken** [1] *vi* **(a)** *(Dankbarkeit zeigen)* to express one's thanks ♦ **jdm ~** to thank sb *(für* for); **mit überschwenglichen Worten/einem Strauß Blumen ~** to be effusive in one's thanks/to express one's thanks with a bunch of flowers; **ich danke dir für das Geschenk/die Gastfreundschaft** *etc* thank you for your *or* the present/your hospitality; **wir ~ für die Einladung** thank you for your *or* the invitation; **(ich) danke!** yes please; *(ablehnend)* no thank you, no thanks *(inf)*; **(ich) danke bestens** *(iro)* thanks a million *(inf)*, thanks for nothing *(inf)*; **man dankt** *(inf)* thanks *(inf)*, ta *(Brit inf)*; **ich danke Ihnen (dafür), daß Sie mir den Betrag überwiesen haben** thank you for transferring the money (to me); **jdm ~ lassen** to send sb one's thanks; **bestellen Sie bitte Ihrem Vater, ich lasse herzlich ~** please give your father my thanks; **nichts zu ~** don't mention it, not at all, you're welcome; **dafür** *or* **für so was danke ich** *(iro)* not on your life!, not a chance! *(inf)*; **na, ich danke** *(iro)* no thank you; **ich danke für Obst und Südfrüchte** *(sl)* no thank you very much *(iro)*; **~d erhalten/annehmen/ablehnen** to receive/accept/decline with thanks.
(b) *(ablehnen)* to decline.
(c) *(Gruß erwidern)* to return a/the greeting.
[2] *vt* **(a)** *(geh: verdanken)* **jdm/einer Sache etw ~** to owe sth to sb/sth; **ihm danke ich es, daß ...** I owe it to him that ...; **nur dem rechtzeitigen Erscheinen der Feuerwehr ist es zu ~, daß ...** it was only thanks to the prompt turn-out of the fire brigade that ...
(b) jdm etw ~ *(jdm dankbar sein für)* to thank sb for sth; *(jdm etw lohnen)* to repay sb for sth; **man wird es dir nicht ~/nicht zu ~ wissen** you won't be thanked for it/it won't be appreciated; **sie werden es mir später einmal ~, daß ich das getan habe** they'll thank me for doing that one day; **all meine Hilfe wurde mir mit keinem Wort/mit Beschimpfungen gedankt** I didn't get a single word of thanks for all my help/all my help was just repaid with insults; **man hat es mir schlecht gedankt, daß ich das getan habe** I got small thanks *or* I didn't get a lot of thanks for doing it; **wie kann ich Ihnen das jemals ~?** how can I ever thank you?

dankenswert *adj Bemühung, Hingabe* commendable; *Hilfe* kind; *(lohnenswert) Aufgabe, Arbeit* rewarding ♦ **in ~er Weise** *(löblich)* (most) commendably; *(freundlicherweise)* very kindly.

dankenswerterweise *adv* generously.

dank|erfüllt *adj (liter)* grateful.

Dankesbezeigung *f* demonstration of one's gratitude *or* thanks.

▼ **Dankeschön** *nt* **-s,** *no pl* thank-you.

Dankesworte *pl* words *pl* of thanks; *(von Redner)* vote *sing* of thanks.

Dank-: ~gebet *nt* prayer of thanksgiving; **~gottesdienst** *m* service of thanksgiving; **~opfer** *nt* thanks-offering; **d~sagen** *pret* **d~sagte**, *ptp* **d~gesagt**, *infin auch* **d~zusagen** *vi (geh)* to express one's thanks *(jdm* to sb); *(Eccl)* to give thanks *(jdm* to sb); **~sagung** *f* **(a)** *(Eccl)* thanksgiving; **(b)** *(Brief)* note of thanks; **~schreiben** *nt* letter of thanks.

dann *adv* **(a)** *(Reihenfolge ausdrückend, später)* then ♦ **~ und ~** round about then; **von ~ bis ~** for some time around then; **~ und wann** now and then; **gerade ~, wenn ...** just when ...; **wenn das gemacht ist, ~ kannst du gehen** when that's done you can go; **noch eine Woche, ~ ist Weihnachten** another week till Christmas, another week and (then) it's Christmas; *siehe* **bis²**.
(b) *(unter diesen Umständen)* then ♦ **wenn ..., ~ if ...**, (then); **wenn du was brauchst, ~ sagst du's mir, nicht?** just tell me if you need anything, if you need anything (then) just tell me; **ja, selbst ~** yes, even then; **nein, selbst ~ nicht** no, not even then; **selbst ~/selbst ~ nicht, wenn ...** even/not even if ...; **erst ~, wenn ...** only when ...; **ja, ~!** (oh) well then!; **ich habe keine Lust mehr — ~ hör doch auf!** I'm not in the mood any more — well stop then!; **und wie es ~ so geht** *or* **ist, kommt natürlich Besuch** and as was bound to happen, I got visitors, but you know how it is, I got visitors; **wenn er seine Gedichte selbst nicht versteht, wer ~?** if he can't understand his own poems, who else could (understand them)?; **wenn man nicht einmal in Schottland echten Whisky bekommt, wo ~?** if you can't get real whisky in Scotland, where *can* you expect to find it?; **wenn ich nicht einmal das Einmaleins bei euch voraussetzen kann, was ~?** if I can't even assume you know your tables, what can I assume you know?; **~ eben nicht** well, in that case (there's no more to be said); **~ erst recht nicht!** in that case no way *(sl) or* not a chance *(inf)*!; **~ ist ja alles in Ordnung** (oh well,) everything's all right then, in that case everything 's all right; **~ will ich lieber gehen** well, I'd better be getting along (then); **ja ~, auf Wiedersehen** well then, good-bye; **also ~ bis morgen** right then, see you tomorrow, see you tomorrow then.
(c) *(außerdem)* **~ ... noch** on top of that; **strohdumm und ~ auch noch frech** as thick as they come and cheeky into the bargain; **kommandiert mich herum und meint ~ auch noch ...** orders me around and then on top of that thinks ...

dannen *adv:* **von ~** *(obs: von woher)* thence *(old)*, from thence *(Eccl)*; *(liter: weg)* away.

dantesk *adj* Dantesque.

dantisch *adj* Dantean.

daran *adv (auch* **daran***)* **(a)** *(räumlich: an dieser Stelle, diesem Ort, Gegenstand)* on it/that; *schieben, lehnen, stellen* against it/that; *legen* next to it/that; *kleben, befestigen, machen, gehen* to it/that; *sich setzen* at it/that ♦ **nahe** *or* **dicht ~** right up against *or* up close against it; **nahe ~ sein** *(fig)* to be on the point of it, to be just about to; **nahe ~ sein, etw zu tun** to be on the point of doing sth *or* just about to do sth; **zu nahe ~** too close (to it); **~ vorbei** past it; **er hat dicht ~ vorbeigeschossen** his shot just missed it; **~ kommen** *or* **fassen/riechen/schlagen** to touch/smell/hit it/that; **er hielt seine Hand ~** he touched it with his hand; **das Telefon klingelte, er ging aber nicht ~** the

➤ SPRACHE AKTIV: **Dank** → 48.1, 49, 52.3 **dankbar: a** → 29.1, 31, 46.5, 47.1, 47.5, 49 **Dankbarkeit** → 49 **danken: 1a** → 47.1, 47.2, 49

phone rang but he didn't answer it; **die Kinder sind wieder ~ gewesen** (*inf*) the children have been at it again.
(b) (*zeitlich: danach anschließend*) **im Anschluß ~, ~ anschließend** following that/this; **im Anschluß ~ findet eine Diskussion statt** it/this/that will be followed by a discussion; **erst fand ein Vortrag statt, ~ schloß sich eine Diskussion** first there was a lecture which was followed by a discussion *or* and after that a discussion.
(c) (*inf*) **er ist schlecht/gut ~** (*gesundheitlich, finanziell*) he's in a bad way (*inf*)/ he's OK (*inf*); **ich weiß nie, wie ich (bei ihm) ~ bin** I never know where I am with him; **sie sind sehr arm ~** (*haben wenig Geld*) they're not at all well-off; (*sind bedauernswert*) they are poor creatures.
(d) *in Verbindung mit n, adj, vb siehe auch dort; arbeiten* on it/that; *sterben, erinnern, Bedarf, Mangel* of it/that; *interessieren, sich beteiligen, arm, reich* in it/ that; *sich klammern* to it/that ◆ **~ sticken/bauen** to embroider/build it/that; **was macht der Aufsatz? — ich bin zur Zeit ~** how's the essay doing? — I'm (working) on it now; **er war ~ interessiert** he was interested in it; **er war ~ interessiert, es zu tun** he was interested in doing it; **ich zweifle nicht ~** I don't doubt it; **ich zweifle nicht ~, daß ...** I don't doubt that ...; **erinnere mich ~** remind me about *or* of that; **erinnere mich ~, daß ich das machen soll** remind me to do that *or* that I must do that; **~ wird er zugrunde gehen** that will be the ruin of him; **wir haben großen Anteil ~ genommen** we sympathized deeply; **wird sich etwas ~ ändern?** will that change at all?; **wir können nichts ~ machen** we can't do anything about it; **~ sieht man, wie ...** there you (can) see how ...; **Sie würden gut ~ tun, dieses Angebot anzunehmen** you would do well *or* would be well-advised to accept this offer; **das Beste/Schönste/Schlimmste** *etc* **~** the best/nicest/worst *etc* thing about it; **es ist kein wahres Wort ~** there isn't a word of truth in it, not a word of it is true; **an den Gerüchten ist nichts ~** there's nothing in those rumours; **es ist nichts ~** (*ist nicht fundiert*) there's nothing in it; (*ist nichts Besonderes*) it's nothing special; *siehe auch* **dran**.

daran-: ~geben *vt sep irreg* (*geh*) to sacrifice; **~gehen** *vi sep irreg aux sein* to set about it; **~gehen, etw zu tun** to set about doing sth; **~machen** *vr sep* (*inf*) to set about it; (*endlich in Angriff nehmen*) to get down to it; **sich ~machen, etw zu tun** to set about doing sth/to get down to doing sth; **~setzen** *sep* [1] *vt* (*einsetzen*) to exert; (*aufs Spiel setzen*) to stake, to risk; **seine ganzen Kräfte ~setzen, etw zu tun** to spare no effort to do sth; [2] *vr* to sit down to it; **~wenden** *vt sep irreg* (*geh*) to exert; **seine ganzen Kräfte ~wenden, etw zu tun** to spare no effort to do sth.

darauf *adv* (*emph* **darauf**) (a) (*räumlich*) on it/that/them *etc*; (*in Richtung*) towards it/that/them *etc*; *schießen, zielen, losfahren* at it/that/them *etc*; (*fig*) *fußen, basieren, aufbauen* on it/that; *zurückführen, beziehen* to it/that ◆ **da er es nicht wagte herunterzuklettern, mußte er ~ sitzen bleiben** since he didn't dare climb down he just had to sit (up) there; **er hielt den Nagel fest und schlug mit dem Hammer ~** he held the nail in place and hit it with the hammer; **seine Behauptungen stützen sich ~, daß der Mensch von Natur aus gut ist** his claims are based on the supposition that man is naturally good.
(b) (*Reihenfolge: zeitlich, örtlich*) after that ◆ **die Tage, die ~ folgten** the days which followed; **~ folgte ...** that was followed by ..., after that came ...; **zuerst kam der Wagen des Premiers, ~ folgten Polizisten** the prime minister's car came first, followed by policemen; **am Tag/Abend/Jahr ~** the next day/evening/year, the day/evening/year after (that).
(c) (*infolgedessen*) because of that ◆ **er hat gestohlen und wurde ~ von der Schule verwiesen** he was caught stealing and because of that was expelled.
(d) (*als Reaktion*) *sagen, reagieren* to that ◆ **~ antworten** to answer that; **eine Antwort ~** an answer to that; **er hat ein Gedicht ~ geschrieben** that prompted him to write a poem; **~ wurde er ganz beschämt** that made him feel quite ashamed; **~ haben sich viele Interessenten gemeldet** a lot of people have shown an interest in it/that; **nimm die Marke, ~ bekommst du ein Essen in der Kantine** take this token, you'll get a meal in the canteen for *or* with it; **~ steht die Todesstrafe/stehen mindestens fünf Jahre Gefängnis** that carries the death penalty/a minimum sentence of five years' imprisonment.
(e) *in Verbindung mit n, adj, vb siehe auch dort; bestehen, verlassen, wetten, Zeit/ Mühe verschwenden, Einfluß* on that/it; *hoffen, warten, sich vorbereiten, gefaßt sein, reinfallen* for that/it; *trinken* to that/it; *stolz sein* of that/it ◆ **ich bin stolz ~, daß sie gewonnen hat** I'm proud that she won *or* of her winning; **ich bestehe ~, daß du kommst** I insist that you come *or* on your coming; **wir müssen ~ Rücksicht nehmen/Rücksicht ~ nehmen, daß ...** we must take that into consideration/take into consideration that ...; **ich möchte ~ hinweisen, daß ...** I would like to point out that ...; **gib mir die Hand ~** shake on it; **~ freuen wir uns schon** we're looking forward to it already; **~ kommen** (*auffinden*) to come (up)on that/it; (*sich erinnern*) to think of that/it; **wir kamen auch ~ zu sprechen** we talked about that too; **wie kommst du ~?** what makes you think that?, how do you work that out? (*inf*); **~ willst du hinaus!** that's what you're getting at!; **er war nur ~ aus** he was only after that *or* interested in that; **er war nur ~ aus, möglichst viel Geld zu verdienen** he was only interested in earning as much money as possible.

⚠**darauffolgend** *adj attr* after him/it/that *etc*; *Tag etc* following; *Wagen etc* behind *pred*.

daraufhin *adv* (*emph* **daraufhin**) (a) (*aus diesem Anlaß, deshalb*) as a result (of that/this); (*danach*) after that, thereupon. (b) (*im Hinblick darauf*) with regard to that/this ◆ **wir müssen es ~ prüfen, ob es für unsere Zwecke geeignet ist** we must test it with a view to whether it is suitable for our purposes.

daraus *adv* (*emph auch* **daraus**) (a) (*räumlich*) out of that/it/them ◆ **~ kann man nicht trinken!** you can't drink out of that/it!
(b) (*aus diesem Material etc*) from *or* out of that/it/them ◆ **~ kann man Wein herstellen** you can make wine from that.
(c) (*aus dieser Sache, Angelegenheit*) from that/it/them; *in Verbindung mit n, vb siehe auch dort* ◆ **~ ergibt sich/folgt, daß ...** it follows from that that ...; **~ sieht man ...** from this it can be seen ...

darben *vi* (*geh*) (*entbehren*)) to live in want; (*hungern*) to starve.

darbieten *sep irreg* [1] *vt* (*geh*) (a) (*vorführen*) *Tänze, Schauspiel* to perform; (*vortragen*) *Lehrstoff* to present. (b) (*anbieten*) to offer; *Speisen* to serve; (*reichen*) *Hand, Geschenk etc auch* to proffer.
[2] *vr* to present itself; (*Gelegenheit, Möglichkeit auch*) to offer itself ◆ **dort bot sich (ihnen) ein schauerlicher Anblick dar** a horrible sight met their eyes, they were faced with a horrible sight.

Darbietung *f* (*das Darbieten*) performance; (*das Dargebotene*) act.

darbringen *vt sep irreg* (*geh*) *Opfer* to offer.

Dardanellen *pl* **die ~** the Dardanelles *pl*.

darein *adv* (*emph auch* **darein**) (a) (*räumlich: hinein*) in there; (*wenn Bezugsobjekt vorher erwähnt*) in it/them ◆ **hierein? — nein, ~!** in here? — no, in there.
(b) (*old: in diese Lage*) *einwilligen, sich ergeben* to that ◆ **wir müssen uns ~ fügen** we must accept that *or* bow to that.

darein- *pref siehe auch* **drein-**; **~finden** *vr sep irreg* (*geh*) to come to terms with it, to learn to accept it; **sich ~finden, etw zu tun** to come to terms with *or* learn to accept doing sth; **~legen** *vt sep* (*fig geh*) *siehe* **~setzen**; **~reden** *vi sep* (*in Angelegenheiten*) to interfere (*jdm* in sb's affairs); **~setzen** *vt sep* (*fig geh*) *Energie* to put into it, to devote to it; **seine ganze Energie ~setzen, etw zu tun** to put all one's energy into *or* devote all one's energy to doing sth; **er setzte seinen ganzen Stolz ~** it was a matter of pride with him.

darin *adv* (*emph auch* **darin**) (a) (*räumlich*) in there; (*wenn Bezugsobjekt vorher erwähnt*) in it/them; (*fig*) in that/it ◆ **~ liegt ein Widerspruch** there is a contradiction in that.
(b) (*in dieser Beziehung*) in that respect ◆ **~ ist er ganz groß** (*inf*) he's very good at that; **~ unterscheiden sich die beiden** the two of them differ in that (respect); **die beiden unterscheiden sich ~, daß ...** the two of them differ in that ...; **~ liegt der Unterschied** that is the difference, that is where the difference is; **der Unterschied liegt ~, daß ...** the difference is that ...; **wir stimmen ~ überein, daß ...** we agree that ...; *in Verbindung mit vb siehe auch dort.*
(c) (*old: worin*) in which.

darinnen *adv* (*old*) therein (*old*).

darlegen *vt sep* to explain (*jdm* to sb); *Theorie, Plan, Ansichten auch* to expound (*jdm* to sb).

Darlegung *f* explanation.

Darleh(e)n *nt* **-s, -** loan ◆ **als ~** as a loan.

Darleh(e)ns-: ~bank *f* lending *or* credit bank; **~geber** *m* lender; **~kasse** *f* credit bank; **~konto** *nt* loan account; **~nehmer** *m* borrower; **~schuld** *f* loan; **~summe** *f* **die ~summe** the amount of the/a loan; **eine ~summe** a loan.

Darm *m* **-(e)s, ⸚e** intestine(s *pl*), bowel(s *pl*), gut(s *pl*); (*für Wurst*) (sausage) skin or case; (*Material: für Saiten, Schläger etc*) gut ◆ **Wurst in echtem/ künstlichem ~** sausage in real/synthetic skin.

Darm- *in cpds* intestinal; **~ausgang** *m* anus; **~bewegung** *f* peristalsis *no art, no pl*, peristaltic movement; **~entleerung** *f* evacuation of the bowels; **~grippe** *f* gastric influenza *or* 'flu; ⚠**~katarrh** *m* enteritis; **~krebs** *m* cancer of the intestine; **~leiden** *nt* intestinal trouble *no art*; **~saite** *f* gut string; **~spülung** *f* enema; **~tätigkeit** *f* peristalsis *no art*; **die ~tätigkeit fördern/regulieren** to stimulate/regulate the movement of the bowels; **~trägheit** *f* under-activity of the intestines; **~verschlingung** *f* volvulus (*form*), twisting of the intestine; ⚠**~verschluß** *m* obstruction of the bowels *or* intestines.

darnach *adv* (*old*) *siehe* **danach**.

darneben *adv* (*old*) *siehe* **daneben**.

darob *adv* (*old*) (a) *siehe* **darüber**. (b) (*deswegen*) **er war ~ sehr erstaunt** he was very surprised by that; **er wurde ~ sehr bewundert** he was much admired for that *or* on that account.

Darre *f* **-, -n** drying kiln *or* oven; (*Hopfen~, Malz~*) oast.

darreichen *vt sep* (*liter*) (*anbieten*) to offer (*jdm etw* sb sth, sth to sb); (*reichen auch*) to proffer (*jdm etw* sth to sb).

darren *vt* to (kiln-)dry; *Malz, Hopfen* to (oast-)dry.

Darr|ofen *m siehe* **Darre**.

darstellbar *adj* (*in Literaturwerk etc*) portrayable; (*in Bild etc auch*) depictable; (*durch Diagramm etc*) representable; (*beschreibbar*) describable ◆ **schwer/leicht ~** hard/easy to portray/depict/show/describe; **dieses Phänomen ist graphisch ~** this phenomenon can be shown on a graph.

darstellen *sep* [1] *vt* (a) to show; (*ein Bild entwerfen von*) to portray, to depict; (*Theat*) to portray; *Rolle* to play; (*beschreiben*) to describe ◆ **etw in einem möglichst günstigen Licht ~** to show sth in the best possible light; **etw kurz** *or* **knapp ~** to give a short description of sth; **was sollen diese verworrenen Striche ~?** what are these confused lines supposed to show *or* (*in Zeichnung*) be?; **die ~den Künste** (*Theater*) the dramatic *or* performing arts; (*Malerei, Plastik*) the visual arts; **er stellt etwas/nichts dar** (*fig*) he has a certain air/ doesn't have much of an air about him.
(b) (*Math*) *Funktion* to plot; (*Chem*) to produce ◆ **~de Geometrie** projective geometry.
(c) (*bedeuten*) to constitute, to represent.
[2] *vr* (*Eindruck vermitteln*) to appear (*jdm* to sb); (*sich erweisen*) to show oneself ◆ **die Sache stellte sich (als) sehr fragwürdig dar** the matter appeared (to be)

very dubious; bei dem Talentwettbewerb stellte er sich als begabter Sänger dar at the talent competition he showed himself to be a gifted singer.

Darsteller *m* -s, - (*Theat*) actor ◆ der ~ des Hamlet the actor playing Hamlet; ein hervorragender ~ tragischer Rollen an excellent actor in tragic roles.

Darstellerin *f* (*Theat*) actress; *siehe auch* Darsteller.

darstellerisch *adj* dramatic ◆ ~ war die Weber der Klein weit überlegen as an actress Weber was much superior to Klein; eine ~e Höchstleistung a magnificent piece of acting.

Darstellung *f* (a) portrayal; (*in Buch, Bild auch*) depiction; (*durch Diagramm etc*) representation; (*Beschreibung*) description; (*Bericht*) account ◆ an den Wänden fand man ~en der Heldentaten des Königs on the walls one could see the King's heroic deeds depicted; eine falsche ~ der Fakten a misrepresentation of the facts; er gab eine großartige ~ des Hamlet his performance as Hamlet was superb; der Stoff war in *or* durch ~en von Wanderbühnen bekannt geworden the material became known through being performed by travelling theatre groups.
(b) (*Math*) graphische ~ graph.
(c) (*Chem*) preparation.

Darstellungs-: **~form** *f* form of expression; (*Theat*) dramatic art form; **~kunst** *f* skills *pl* of portrayal; (*von Schauspieler*) acting technique; **~mittel** *nt* technique (of representation).

dartun *vt sep irreg* (*geh*) to set forth; *Überlegenheit* to demonstrate.

▼ **darüber** *adv* (*emph* darüber) (a) (*räumlich*) over that/it/them; (*quer* ~) across *or* over there; (*wenn Bezugsobjekt vorher erwähnt*) across *or* over it/them; (*höher als etw*) above (there/it/them); (*direkt auf etw*) on top (of it/them) ◆ geh ~, nicht hierüber! go across *or* over there, not here!; die Aufgabe war sehr schwer, ich habe lange ~ gesessen the exercise was very difficult, I sat over it for a long time; ~ hinweg sein (*fig*) to have got over it; ~ hinaus apart from this/that, in addition; ~ hinaus kann ich nichts sagen over and above that I can't say anything; ~ hinaus log sie mich auch noch an on top of that she also lied to me; jetzt ist er ~ hinaus (*fig*) he is past that now.
(b) (*deswegen, in dieser Beziehung*) about that/it ◆ sich ~ beschweren/beklagen *etc* to complain/moan *etc* about it; sich ~ beschweren/beklagen *etc*, daß ... to complain/moan *etc* that ...; wir wollen nicht ~ streiten, ob ... we don't want to argue *or* disagree about whether ...
(c) (*davon*) about that/it ◆ Rechenschaft ~ ablegen to account for it; sie führt eine Liste ~ she keeps a list of it; *in Verbindung mit n, vb siehe auch dort.*
(d) (*währenddessen*) in the meantime ◆ Wochen gingen ~ hin meanwhile *or* in the meantime weeks went past.
(e) (*mehr, höher*) above *or* over that ◆ 21 Jahre/4 DM und ~ 21 years/4 DM and above *or* over; kein Pfennig ~ not a penny over (that) *or* more; ~ hinaus over and above that; es geht nichts ~ there is nothing to beat it.

⚠ **darüber-:** **~fahren** *vi sep irreg aux sein* (*fig*) to run over it; wenn du mit der Hand ~fährst, ... if you run your hand over it ...; **~liegen** *vi sep irreg* (*fig*) to be higher; **~machen** *vr sep* (*inf*) to get to work on it (*inf*), to set about it (*inf*); **~schreiben** *vt sep irreg* to write above it; **~stehen** *vi sep irreg* (*fig*) to be above such things.

darum *adv* (*emph* darum) (a) (*räumlich*) round that/it/him/her/them ◆ ~ herum round about (it/him/her/them); ~, wo ... round where ...
(b) (*um diese Angelegenheit*) *in Verbindung mit n, vb siehe auch dort* ◆ es geht ~, daß ... the thing is that ...; ~ geht es gar nicht that isn't the point; ~ geht es that is what it is about, that's it; ~ geht es mir/geht es mir nicht that's my point/that's not the point for me; es geht mir ~, Ihnen das klarzumachen I'm trying to make it clear to you; wir kommen leider nicht ~ herum, die Preise heraufzusetzen unfortunately we cannot avoid raising prices; wir wollen nicht lange ~ herumreden we don't want to spend a long time talking around the subject; ich gäbe viel ~, die Wahrheit zu erfahren I would give a lot to learn the truth; ich habe ihn schon ein paarmal ~ gebeten, aber ... I've asked him a few times (for it/to do it), but ...; könntest du ihn ~ bitten, zu mir zu kommen? could you ask him to come to me?; sie haben sich ~ gestritten they argued over it; sie haben sich ~ gestritten, wer ... they argued over who ...
(c) (*liter: darüber, davon*) about that/it ◆ nur wenige wissen ~, wie ... (*geh*) few people know how ...
(d) (*deshalb*) that's why, because of that ◆ ~, daß *or* weil ... because of that; eben ~ that is exactly why; ach ~! so that's why!; ~? because of that?; warum willst du nicht mitkommen? — ~! (*inf*) why don't you want to come? — (just) 'cos! (*inf*); er ist faul, aber ~ nicht dumm he's lazy but that doesn't mean he's stupid; *siehe auch* drum.

darum-: **~kommen** *vi sep irreg aux sein* to lose it/them; ~kommen, etw zu tun to lose the opportunity of doing sth; **~legen** *vt sep* to put around it/them; **~stehen** *vi sep irreg aux haben or sein* to stand around; **~wickeln** *vt sep* to wrap round it/them.

darunter *adv* (*emph auch* darunter) (a) (*räumlich*) under that/it/them, underneath *or* beneath (that/it/them); (*niedriger als etw auch*) below (that/it/them) ◆ ~ hervorkommen to appear from underneath; als weitere Belastung kam der Tod seiner Mutter, ~ ist er dann zusammengebrochen his mother's death was an added burden and he broke down under this strain.
(b) (*weniger*) under that ◆ Leute im Alter von 35 Jahren und ~ people aged 35 and under; der Preis beträgt 50 DM, ~ kann ich die Ware nicht abgeben the price is 50 marks, I can't sell for less; kein Pfennig ~ not a penny under that *or* less; ~ macht sie's nicht (*inf*) she won't do it for less.
(c) (*dabei*) among them ◆ ~ waren viele Ausländer there were a lot of foreigners among them.
(d) (*unter dieser Angelegenheit*) *in Verbindung mit n, vb siehe auch dort* ◆ was verstehen Sie ~? what do you understand by that/it?; ~ kann ich mir nichts vorstellen that doesn't mean anything to me; *siehe auch* drunter.

⚠ **darunter-:** **~bleiben** *vi sep irreg aux sein* (*fig*) to be lower; Sie kennen die Anforderungen, wenn Sie mit *or* in Ihrer Leistung ~bleiben, werden Sie entlassen you are aware of the requirements, if you fail to meet them you will be dismissed; **~fallen** *vi sep irreg aux sein* (*fig*) (*dazugerechnet werden*) to be included; (*davon betroffen werden*) to come *or* fall under it/them; **~gehen** *vi sep irreg aux sein* (*~passen*) to fit underneath; **~liegen** *vi sep irreg* (a) *aux haben or sein* (*lit*) to lie underneath; (b) (*fig*) *siehe* ~bleiben; **~mischen** *sep* [1] *vt Mehl etc* to mix in; [2] *vr* (*Mensch*) to mingle with them; **~schreiben** *vt sep irreg* to write underneath; *Namen auch* to sign at the bottom; **~setzen** *vt sep Unterschrift* to put to it.

das *art etc siehe* der[2].

Dasein *nt* -s, *no pl* (*Leben, Existenz, Philos*) existence; (*Anwesendsein*) presence ◆ der Kampf ums ~ the struggle for existence; etw ins ~ rufen (*liter*) to bring sth into existence, to call sth into being.

⚠ **dasein** *vi sep irreg aux sein* (*Zusammenschreibung nur bei infin und ptp*) (*lit, fig inf*) to be there ◆ noch ~ to be still there; (*übrig sein auch*) to be left; wieder ~ to be back; ich bin gleich wieder da I'll be right *or* straight back; sind Sie schon lange da? have you been here/there long?; ist Post/sind Besucher für mich da? is there any mail/are there visitors for me?; war der Briefträger schon da? has the postman been yet?; für jdn ~ to be there *or* available for sb; ein Arzt, der immer für seine Patienten da ist a doctor who always has time for his patients; voll ~ (*inf*) to be all there (*inf*); so etwas ist noch nie dagewesen it's quite unprecedented; es ist alles schon mal dagewesen it's all been done before; das übertrifft alles bisher Dagewesene that beats everything; ein nie dagewesener Erfolg an unprecedented success.

Daseins-: **~angst** *f* (*Philos*) existential fear, angst; **~bedingungen** *pl* living conditions *pl*; **~berechtigung** *f siehe* Existenzberechtigung; **~form** *f* form of life *or* existence; **~freude** *f* zest for life, joie de vivre; **~kampf** *m* struggle for survival; **~weise** *f* mode of being.

daselbst *adv* (*old*) in said place; (*bei Quellenangaben*) ibidem, ibid *abbr* ◆ geboren 1714 zu Florenz, gestorben 1768 ~ born in Florence 1714, died there 1768.

dasitzen *vi sep irreg aux haben or sein* to sit there ◆ wie die Kinder heutzutage ~! the way children sit nowadays!; ohne Hilfe/einen Pfennig ~ (*inf*) to be left without any help/without a penny.

dasjenige *dem pron siehe* derjenige.

⚠ **daß** *conj* (a) (*mit Subjektsatz*) that ◆ ~ wir alle sterben müssen, ist sicher that we all must die is certain (*liter*), it is certain (that) we all must die.
(b) (*mit Objektsatz*) (that) ◆ ich bin überzeugt, ~ du das Richtige getan hast I'm sure (that) you have done the right thing; ich verstehe nicht, ~ man ihn als Bewerber abgelehnt hat I don't understand why he was turned down; ich sehe nicht ein, ~ wir hungern sollen I don't see why we should starve.
(c) (*mit Attributivsatz*) that ◆ angenommen/vorausgesetzt, ~ ... given/provided that ...; ich bin mir dessen bewußt, ~ ... I am aware (that) *or* of the fact that ...; unter der Bedingung, ~ ... on (the) condition that ...
(d) (*mit Kausalsatz*) that ◆ ich war böse, ~ ... I was annoyed that ...; ich freue mich darüber, ~ ... I'm glad (that) ...; das kommt daher, ~ ... that comes because ...; das liegt daran, ~ ... that is because ...; das kommt davon, ~ er niemals aufpaßt that comes from him *or* his never paying attention.
(e) (*mit Konsekutivsatz*) that ◆ er fuhr so schnell, ~ er sich überschlug he drove so fast that he overturned.
(f) (*geh: mit Finalsatz*) so that ◆ ich gab ihm den Brief, ~ er ihn selbst lesen konnte I gave him the letter so that he could read it himself.
(g) (*als Einleitung eines Instrumentalsatzes*) er verbringt seine Freizeit damit, ~ er Rosen züchtet he spends his free time breeding roses.
(h) (*geh*) (*mit Wunschsatz*) if only, would that (*liter*); (*in Befehl*) see that ◆ ~ er immer da wäre! would that he were always there (*liter*), if only he were always there; ~ du es mir nicht verlierst! see that you don't lose it!
(i) *siehe* als, auf, außer, ohne, so *etc.*

dasselbe, dasselbige *dem pron siehe* derselbe.

dastehen *vi sep irreg aux haben or sein* (a) to stand there ◆ wie stehst denn du wieder da! what sort of a way do you call that to stand!; steh nicht so dumm da! don't just stand there looking stupid.
(b) (*fig*) anders/glänzend/gut/schlecht ~ to be in a different/splendid/good/bad position; die Firma/Regierung steht wieder gut da the company/government is doing all right again (*inf*) *or* is in a good position again; allein ~ to be on one's own; einzig ~ to be unique *or* unparalleled; jetzt stehe ich ohne Mittel/als Lügner da now I'm left with no money/looking like a liar; wenn die Sache schiefgeht, stehst du dumm da if things go wrong you'll be left looking stupid; wie stehe ich jetzt da! (*Selbstlob*) just look at me now!; (*Vorwurf*) what kind of fool do I look now!

DAT [de:|a:'te:] *nt* -, -s DAT.

Datei *f* (*Comput*) file.

Datei- *in cpds* file; **~name** *m* file name; **~verwaltung** *f* file management; **~verwaltungsprogramm** *nt* file manager; **~verzeichnis** *nt* directory.

Daten (a) *pl of* Datum. (b) (*Comput*) data *sing*.

Daten- *in cpds* data; **~abruf** *m* data retrieval; **~aufbereitung** *f* data preparation; **~austausch** *m* data exchange *or* interchange; **~autobahn** *f* information highway; **~band** *nt* data tape; **~bank** *f* database; (*Zentralstelle*) data bank; **~bankverwaltung** *f* database management; **~bestand** *m* database; **~eingabe** *f* data input; **~erfassung** *f* data capture; **~fernübertragung** *f* data transmission; **~fernverarbeitung** *f* teleprocessing; **~handschuh** *m* data glove; **~kompression** *f* data compres-

➤ SPRACHE AKTIV: darüber → 53.5

sion; **~kompressionsprogramm** *nt* data compression program; **⚠~mißbrauch** *m* misuse of data, data abuse; **~netz** *nt* data network; **~satz** *m* record; **~schrott** *m* (*inf*) rubbish data; **~schutz** *m* data protection; **~schutzbeauftragte(r)** *mf* data protection official; **~schützer** *m* data protectionist; **~schutzgesetz** *nt* data protection act; **~sicherung** *f* data storage *or* saving; **~sichtgerät** *nt* visual display unit; **~träger** *m* data carrier; **~transfer** *m* data transfer; **~typist(in** *f*) *m* keyboarder; **~übertragung** *f* data transmission; **~verarbeitung** *f* data processing; **~verarbeitungsanlage** *f* data processing equipment; **~verbund** *m* data network; **~zentrale** *f*, **~zentrum** *nt* data centre.

datieren* [1] *vt Brief, Fund* to date ◆ **der Brief ist vom 20. April datiert** the letter is dated 20th April.

[2] *vi* (*stammen*) to date (*aus* from) ◆ **dieser Brief datiert vom 1. Januar** this letter is dated January 1st; **unsere Freundschaft datiert seit einem Urlaub vor zehn Jahren** our friendship dates from *or* dates back to a holiday ten years ago.

Dativ *m* (*Gram*) dative (case).

Dativ|objekt *nt* (*Gram*) indirect object.

DAT-Kassette *f* DAT *or* digital audio tape cassette.

dato *adv*: **bis ~** (*Comm, inf*) to date.

Datowechsel *m* (*Comm*) time bill.

DAT-Recorder *m* DAT *or* digital audio tape recorder.

Datscha *f* **-, Datschen, Datsche** *f* **-, -n** (*esp DDR*) country cottage ◆ **auf seiner ~** in his country cottage.

DAT-Streamer [deː|aˈteːstriːmɐ] *m* (*Comput*) DAT streamer.

Dattel *f* **-, -n** date.

Dattel- *in cpds* date; **~palme** *f* date palm.

Datterich *m siehe* **Tatterich.**

Datum *nt* **-s, Daten (a)** date ◆ **was für ein ~ haben wir heute?** what is the date today?; **das heutige/gestrige/morgige ~** today's/yesterday's/tomorrow's date; **sich im ~ irren** to get the date wrong; **ein Brief gleichen ~s** a letter of the same date; **gleichen ~s übersandten wir Ihnen ...** (*form*) on the same date we sent you ...; **etw mit dem ~ versehen** to date sth; **der Brief trägt das ~ vom 1. April** the letter is dated 1st April; **ein Brief ohne ~** an undated letter; **~ des Poststempels** date as postmark; **ein Nachschlagewerk neueren ~s** a recent reference work.

(b) *usu pl* (*Faktum*) fact; (*statistische Zahlenangabe etc*) datum (*form*), piece of data ◆ **technische Daten** technical data *pl*.

Datums-: ~grenze *f* (*Geog*) (international) date line; **~stempel** *m* date stamp.

Daube *f* **-, -n** stave; (*beim Eisschießen*) tee.

Dauer *f* **-,** *no pl* (*das Andauern*) duration; (*Zeitspanne*) period, term; (*Länge: einer Sendung etc*) length ◆ **während der ~ des Vertrages/Krieges** for the duration of the contract/war; **für die ~ eines Monats** *or* **von einem Monat** for a period of one month; **ein Gefängnisaufenthalt von zehnjähriger ~** a ten-year term of imprisonment; **von ~ sein** to be long-lasting; **seine Begeisterung war nicht von ~** his enthusiasm was short-lived *or* wasn't long-lasting; **keine ~ haben** to be short-lived; **von langer/kurzer ~ sein** to last a long time/not to last long; **auf die ~** in the long term; **auf die ~ wird das langweilig** it gets boring in the long run; **das kann man auf die ~ nicht ertragen** you can't stand it for any length of time; **das kann auf die ~ nicht so weitergehen** it can't go on like that indefinitely; **auf ~** permanently; **auf ~ gearbeitet** made to last; **für die ~ Ihres Aufenthaltes in unserem Hause** as long as you stay with us, for the period *or* duration of your stay with us (*form*); **man konnte sich nicht über die ~ der Regelung einigen** they could not decide on the duration of the agreement.

Dauer- *in cpds* permanent; **~arbeitslose(r)** *mf* long-term unemployed person; **die ~arbeitslosen** the long-term unemployed; **~auftrag** *m* (*Fin*) standing order; **~ausweis** *m* (permanent) identity card; (*Fahrkarte etc*) season ticket; **~belastung** *f* continual pressure *no indef art*; (*von Maschine*) constant load; **unter ~belastung** under continual pressure/a constant load; **~beschäftigung** *f* (*Stellung*) permanent position; **~betrieb** *m* continuous operation; **~beziehung** *f* permanent relationship; **~brandofen** *m* slow-burning stove; **~brenner** *m* **(a)** *siehe* **~brandofen; (b)** (*inf: Dauererfolg*) long runner; (*hum: Kuß*) long passionate kiss; **~bügelfalte** *f* permanent crease; **~einrichtung** *f* permanent institution; **~emittent** *m* **-en, -en** (*Fin*) constant issuer; **~erfolg** *m* long-running success; **~festigkeit** *f siehe* **~(schwing)festigkeit; ~feuer** *nt* (*Mil*) sustained fire; **~flug** *m* (*Aviat*) long haul flight; **~frostboden** *m* permafrost; **~funktion** *f* (*bei Schreibmaschine etc*) locking function; **~gast** *m* permanent guest; (*häufiger Gast*) regular visitor, permanent fixture (*hum*); **er scheint sich hier als ~gast einrichten zu wollen** (*iro inf*) he seems to be settling down for a long stay; **~geschwindigkeit** *f* cruising speed.

dauerhaft *adj Zustand, Einrichtung, Farbe* permanent; *Bündnis, Frieden, Beziehung* lasting *attr*, long-lasting, durable ◆ **durch eine Impfung sind Sie gegen diese Krankheit ~ geschützt** one vaccination gives you lasting immunity to this disease.

Dauerhaftigkeit *f* permanence; (*von Material*) durability.

Dauer-: ~karte *f* season ticket; **~lauf** *m* (*Sport*) jog; (*das Laufen*) jogging; **im ~lauf** at a jog *or* trot; **einen ~lauf machen** to jog, to go jogging *or* for a jog; **~laut** *m* (*Phon*) continuant; **~lutscher** *m* lollipop; **~marsch** *m* (*Mil*) forced march; **~miete** *f* long lease *or* tenancy; **er hat das Haus in ~miete** he has the house on a long lease; **~mieter** *m* long-term tenant; **~milch** *f* long-life milk.

dauern[1] *vi* **(a)** (*an~*) to last, to go on ◆ **das Gewitter dauerte zwei Stunden** the thunderstorm lasted (for) *or* went on for two hours; **die Verhandlungen ~ schon drei Wochen** the negotiations have already been going on for three weeks; **wie lange soll dieser Zustand noch ~?** how long will this situation last *or* go on (for) *or* continue?

(b) (*Zeit benötigen*) to take a while *or* some time; (*lange*) to take a long time ◆ **das dauert noch** (*inf*) it'll be a while *or* some time yet; **warum dauert das Anziehen bei dir immer so lange?** why do you always take so long to get dressed?; **es dauerte lange, bis er sich befreit hatte** it took him a long time to get free; **das dauert mir zu lange** it takes too long for me; **muß das so lange ~?** does it have to take so long?; **das dauert immer, bis er fertig ist** (*inf*) it always takes ages for him to get ready; **das dauert und dauert** (*inf*) it takes forever (*inf*); **es dauert jetzt nicht mehr lange** it won't take much longer; **das dauert heute vielleicht wieder einmal** (*inf*) it's taking ages again today.

(c) (*geh: dauerhaft sein*) to last.

dauern[2] *vt* (*old, liter*) **etw dauert jdn** sb regrets sth; **er/sie dauert mich** I feel sorry for him/her; **es dauert mich, daß ...** I regret *or* I'm sorry that ...; **es dauerte ihn im Alter, seine Jugend so vergeudet zu haben** in his old age he regretted having squandered his youth like that; **das arme Tier kann einen ~** you can't help feeling sorry for the poor animal.

dauernd [1] *adj* (*anhaltend*) *Frieden, Regelung* lasting; (*ständig*) *Wohnsitz, Ausstellung* permanent; (*fortwährend*) *Unterbrechung, Nörgelei, Sorge* constant, perpetual.

[2] *adv* **etw ~ tun** to keep doing sth; (*stärker*) to be always *or* forever (*inf*) doing sth, to do sth the whole time (*inf*); **sie mußte ~ auf die Toilette** she had to keep going to the toilet; **er beschwert sich ~ darüber** he's always *or* forever (*inf*) complaining about it, he complains about it the whole time (*inf*); **frag nicht ~ so dumm!** don't keep asking stupid questions.

Dauer-: ~obst *nt* fruit suitable for storing; **~parker** *m* **-s, -** long-stay parker; **Parkplatz für ~parker** long-stay car park; **~redner** *m* (*pej*) interminable speaker; **~regen** *m* continuous rain; **ein mehrtägiger ~regen** several days of continuous rain; **~schlaf** *m* prolonged sleep; **ich fiel in einen 24-stündigen ~schlaf** I fell asleep for 24 hours solid; **~(schwing)festigkeit** *f* (*Tech*) fatigue strength; **~schwingung** *f* continuous oscillation; **~sitzung** *f* prolonged *or* lengthy session; **~spannung** *f* (*Elec*) continuous voltage; **~speicher** *m* (*Comput*) permanent memory; **~stellung** *f* permanent position; **in ~stellung beschäftigt** employed in a permanent capacity; **~streit** *m* permanent conflict; **⚠~streß** *m* **im ~streß sein** to be in a state of permanent stress; **~strom** *m* (*Elec*) constant current; **~test** *m* long-term test; **~ton** *m* continuous tone; **~wald** *m* permanent forest; **~welle** *f* perm, permanent wave; **~wirkung** *f* (long-)lasting effect; **~wohnrecht** *nt* permanent right of tenure; **~wurst** *f* German salami; **~zustand** *m* permanent state of affairs; **ich möchte das nicht zum ~zustand werden lassen** I don't want that to become permanent.

Däumchen *nt* **(a)** *dim of* **Daumen. (b)** (*inf*) **~ drehen** to twiddle one's thumbs; **und da mußten wir ~ drehen** and we were left twiddling our thumbs.

Daumen *m* **-s, -** thumb ◆ **am ~ lutschen** to suck one's thumb; **jdm** *or* **für jdn die ~ drücken** *or* **halten** to keep one's fingers crossed for sb; **den ~ auf etw** (*acc*) **halten** (*inf*) to hold on to sth; *siehe* **peilen.**

Daumen-: ~abdruck *m* thumbprint; **~ballen** *m* ball of the/one's thumb; **d~breit** *adj* as broad as your thumb; **~breite** *f* thumb's width; **~index** *m siehe* **~register; ~lutscher** *m* thumb-sucker; **~nagel** *m* thumbnail; **~register** *nt* thumb index; **~schraube** *f* (*Hist*) thumbscrew; **jdm die ~schrauben anlegen** (*lit, fig inf*) to put the (thumb)screws on sb; **die ~schrauben ansetzen** (*fig*) to put the screws on.

Däumling *m* **(a)** (*im Märchen*) **der ~** Tom Thumb. **(b)** (*von Handschuh*) thumb; (*Med*) thumbstall.

Daune *f* **-, -n** down feather ◆ **~n** down *sing*; **ich schlief dort wie auf ~n** it was like sleeping on air; **weich wie ~n** as soft as thistledown.

Daunen-: ~bett *nt*, **~decke** *f* (down-filled) duvet; **~feder** *f* down feather; **~jacke** *f* quilted jacket; **~kissen** *nt* down-filled cushion; (*Kopfkissen*) down pillow; **d~weich** *adj* soft as down.

Dauphin [doˈfɛ̃ː] *m* **-s, -s** (*Hist*) dauphin.

Daus[1] *m*: **(ei) der ~!** (*old*), **was der ~!** (*old*) what the devil *or* deuce! (*dated*).

Daus[2] *nt* **-es, Däuse(r) (a)** (*beim Würfel*) deuce. **(b)** (*Cards*) ace (*in German pack*).

David(s)stern *m* star of David.

Davis- [ˈdeɪvɪs]: **~cup** [-kap], **~pokal** *m* Davis cup.

davon *adv* (*emph* **davon**) **(a)** (*räumlich*) from there; (*wenn Bezugsobjekt vorher erwähnt*) from it/them; (*mit Entfernungsangabe*) away (from there/it/them) ◆ **weg ~!** (*inf*) get away from there/it/them; **~ zweigt ein Weg ab** a path branches off it; *siehe* **auf.**

(b) (*fig*) *in Verbindung mit n, vb siehe auch dort* **es unterscheidet sich ~ nur in der Farbe** it only differs from it in the colour; **nein, weit ~ entfernt!** no, far from it!; **ich bin weit ~ entfernt, Ihnen Vorwürfe machen zu wollen** the last thing I want to do is reproach you; **wenn wir einmal ~ absehen, daß ...** if for once we overlook the fact that ...; **wir möchten in diesem Fall ~ absehen, Ihnen den Betrag zu berechnen** in this case we shall not invoice you; **in ihren Berechnungen sind sie ~ ausgegangen, daß ...** they made their calculations on the basis that ...

(c) (*fig: dadurch*) *leben, abhängen* on that/it/them; *sterben* of that/it; *krank/braun werden* from that/it/them ◆ **... und ~ kommt die rote Farbe ...** and that's where the red colour comes from, ... and the red colour comes from that; **die rote Farbe kommt ~, daß das Holz im Wasser gelegen hat** the red colour comes from the wood lying in the water; **das kommt ~!** that's what

you get; ... **und ~ hängt es ab** and it depends on that; **das hängt ~ ab, ob ...** that depends on whether ...; **~ hat man nur Ärger** you get nothing but trouble with it; **~ wird man müde** that makes you tired; **gib ihr ein bißchen mehr, ~ kann sie doch nicht satt werden** give her a bit more, that won't fill her up; **~ stirbst du nicht** it won't kill you; **was habe *ich* denn ~?** what do I get out of it?; **was *habe* ich denn ~?** why should I?; **was hast du denn ~, daß du so schuftest?** what do you get out of slaving away like that?
(d) (*mit Passiv*) by that/it/them ◆ **~ betroffen werden** *or* **sein** to be affected by it/them.
(e) (*Anteil, Ausgangsstoff*) of that/it/them ◆ **~ essen/trinken/nehmen** to eat/drink/take some of that/it/them; **nehmen Sie doch noch etwas ~!** do have some more!; **die Hälfte ~** half of that/it/them; **das Doppelte ~** twice *or* double that; **zwei/ein Viertelpfund ~, bitte!** would you give me two of those/a quarter of a pound of that/those, please; **er hat drei Schwestern, ~ sind zwei älter als er** he has three sisters, two of whom are older than he is; **früher war er sehr reich, aber nach dem Krieg ist ihm nichts ~ geblieben** he used to be very rich but after the war nothing was left of his earlier wealth.
(f) (*darüber*) *hören, wissen, sprechen* about that/it/them; *verstehen, halten* of that/it/them ◆ **genug ~!** enough of this!; **ich habe keine Ahnung ~** I've no idea about that/it; **nichts mehr ~!** no more of that!; **nichts ~ halten** not to think much of it; **ich halte viel ~** I think it is quite good; **was wissen Sie ~!** what do you know about it anyway?; *in Verbindung mit n, vb siehe auch dort.*

davon-: ~bleiben *vi sep irreg aux sein* (*inf*) to keep away; (*nicht anfassen*) to keep one's hands off; **~eilen** *vi sep aux sein* (*geh*) to hurry *or* hasten away; **~fahren** *vi sep irreg aux sein* **(a)** to drive away; (*auf Fahrrad etc*) to ride away; (*Zug*) to pull away; **(b) jdm ~fahren** to pull away from sb; **~fliegen** *vi sep irreg aux sein* to fly away; **~gehen** *vi sep irreg aux sein* (*geh*) to walk away; **~jagen** *vt sep* to chase off *or* away; **~kommen** *vi sep irreg aux sein* (*entkommen*) to get away, to escape; (*nicht bestraft werden*) to get away with it; (*freigesprochen werden*) to get off; **mit dem Schrecken/dem Leben/einer Geldstrafe ~kommen** to escape with no more than a shock/with one's life/to get off with a fine; **~lassen** *vt sep irreg* **die Hände** *or* **Finger ~lassen** (*inf*) to leave it/them well alone; **du sollst die Hände** *or* **Finger ~lassen** keep your hands *or* fingers off (it/them); **~laufen** *vi sep irreg aux sein* **(a)** to run away (*jdm/vor jdm* from sb); (*verlassen*) to walk out (*jdm* on sb); **den Eltern** *or* **von zu Hause ~laufen** to run away from home; **das Hausmädchen/ihr Mann ist ihr ~gelaufen** (*inf*) the maid/her husband walked out on her; **es ist zum D~laufen!** (*inf*) it's all too much!; **(b)** (*außer Kontrolle geraten*) to get out of hand; **die Preise sind ~gelaufen** prices have run away with themselves *or* have got out of hand; **die Preise sind uns/den Löhnen ~gelaufen** prices are beyond our control/have outstripped wages; **~machen** *vr sep* to make off; **~rennen** *vi sep irreg aux sein* (*inf*) *siehe* **~laufen**; **~schleichen** *vir sep irreg* (*vi: aux sein*) to creep *or* slink away *or* off; **~schwimmen** *vi sep irreg aux sein* **jdm ~schwimmen** to outswim *or* outstrip sb; **~stehlen** *vr sep irreg* (*geh*) to steal away; **~tragen** *vt sep irreg* **(a)** (*wegtragen*) *Gegenstände, Verletzte* to carry away; *Preis* to carry off; *Sieg, Ruhm* to win; **(b)** (*erleiden*) *Schaden, Verletzung* to suffer; **~ziehen** *vi sep irreg aux sein* (*liter*) to leave; (*Prozession etc*) to move off; (*Sport inf*) to pull away (*jdm* from sb).

davor *adv* (*emph* **davor**) **(a)** (*räumlich*) in front (of that/it/them); (*wenn Bezugsobjekt vorher erwähnt*) in front of it/them ◆ **ein Haus mit einem großen Rasen ~** a house with a big front lawn *or* with a big lawn in front.
(b) (*zeitlich*) (*vor einem bestimmten Datum*) before that; (*bevor man etw tut*) beforehand ◆ **ist er 1950 ausgewandert? — nein, schon ~** did he emigrate in 1950? — no, before that.
(c) *in Verbindung mit n, vb siehe auch dort; bewahren, schützen* from that/it; *warnen* of *or* about that/it; *Angst haben* of that/it; *sich ekeln* by that/it ◆ **ich habe Angst ~, das zu tun** I'm afraid of doing that; **ich habe Angst ~, daß der Hund beißen könnte** I'm afraid that the dog might bite; **sein Ekel ~** his disgust of it; **ich warne Sie ~!** I warn you!; **ich habe ihn ~ gewarnt, sich in Gefahr zu begeben** I warned him not to get into danger.

⚠ **davor-: ~hängen** *vt sep* to hang in front of it/them; **sie hängte das Schloß ~** she put the lock on it; **~legen** *sep* [1] *vt* to put in front of it/them; **leg doch eine Kette ~** put a chain on it/them; [2] *vr* to lie down in front of it/them; **~liegen** *vi sep irreg aux haben or sein* to lie in front of it/them; **~stehen** *vi sep irreg aux haben or sein* to stand in front of it/them; **~stellen** *sep* [1] *vt* to put in front of it/them; [2] *vr* to stand in front of it/them.

dawider *adv* (*old*) against it ◆ **dafür und ~** for and against.

dazu *adv* (*emph* **dazu**) **(a)** (*räumlich*) there ◆ **wozu gehört das? — ~!** where does that belong? — there!
(b) (*dabei, damit*) with it; (*außerdem, obendrein auch*) into the bargain (*inf*), at the same time ◆ **er ist dumm und ~ auch noch faul** he's stupid and lazy with it *or* into the bargain (*inf*) *or* as well; **sie ist hübsch und ~ nicht unintelligent** she's pretty and not unintelligent either; **noch ~** as well, too; **noch ~, wo ...** when ... too; **~ reicht** *or* **serviert man am besten Reis** it's best to serve rice with it; **er singt und spielt Gitarre ~** he sings and accompanies himself on the guitar.
(c) (*dahin*) to that/it ◆ **auf dem besten Wege ~ sein, etw zu tun** to be well on the way to doing sth; **er ist auf dem besten Wege ~** he's well on the way to it; **das führt ~, daß weitere Forderungen gestellt werden** that will lead to further demands being made; **~ führt das dann** that's what it leads to; **wie konnte es nur ~ kommen?** how could that happen?; **wer weiß, wie sie ~ gekommen ist** (*zu diesem Auto etc*) who knows how she came by it; **wie komme ich ~?** (*empört*) why on earth should I?; **... aber ich bin nicht ~ gekommen** ... but I didn't get round to it; *in Verbindung mit n, vb siehe auch dort.*
(d) (*dafür, zu diesem Zweck*) for that/it ◆ **~ bin ich zu alt** I'm too old for that; **ich bin zu alt ~, noch tanzen zu gehen** I'm too old to go dancing; **~ habe ich dich nicht studieren lassen, daß du ...** I didn't send you to university so that you could *or* for you to ...; **ich habe ihm ~ geraten** I advised him to (do that); **Sie sind/die Maschine ist ~ wie geschaffen** it's as if you were/the machine was made for it; **~ fähig/bereit sein, etw zu tun** to be capable of doing sth/prepared to do sth; **er war nicht ~ fähig/bereit** he wasn't capable of it/prepared to; **~ gehört viel Geld** that takes a lot of money; **~ ist er da** that's what he's there for, that's why he's there; **die Erlaubnis/die Mittel/das Recht ~** permission/the means/the right to do it; **ich habe keine Lust ~** I don't feel like it; **ich habe keine Lust ~, mitzugehen** I don't feel like going along; **~ habe ich keine Zeit, da habe ich keine Zeit zu** (*N Ger inf*) I haven't the time (for that); **ich habe keine Zeit ~, die Fenster zu putzen** I haven't (the) time to clean the windows; **ich bin nicht ~ in der Lage** I'm not in a position to; *in Verbindung mit n, vb siehe auch dort.*
(e) (*darüber, zum Thema*) about that/it ◆ **was sagst/meinst du ~?** what do you say to/think about that?; **meine Gedanken/Meinung ~** my thoughts about/opinion of that; **..., ~ hören Sie jetzt einen Kommentar ...** we now bring you a commentary; **das Hauptthema war die Inflation; ~ schreibt die Zeitung: ...** the main subject was inflation — the paper has this to say about it ...; **er hat sich nur kurz ~ geäußert** he only commented briefly on that/it.
(f) (*in Wendungen*) **im Gegensatz/Vergleich ~** in contrast to/comparison with that; **früher war sie nicht so hysterisch, er hat sie ~ gemacht** she never used to be so hysterical, he made her like that; **er war nicht immer Lord, er wurde erst ~ gemacht** he wasn't born a Lord, he was made *or* created one; **~ wird man nicht gewählt, sondern ernannt** one is appointed rather than elected to that; *in Verbindung mit n, vb siehe auch dort.*

dazu-: ~geben *vt sep irreg* to add; *siehe* **Senf**; **~gehören*** *vi sep* to belong (to it/us *etc*); (*als Ergänzung*) to go with it/them; (*eingeschlossen sein*) to be included (in it/them); **bei einer Familienfeier gehört Onkel Otto auch ~** Uncle Otto should be part of any family gathering too; **das gehört mit ~** that belongs to/goes with/is included in it; (*versteht sich von selbst*) it's all part of it; **es gehört schon einiges ~** that takes a lot; **es gehört schon einiges ~, das zu tun** it takes a lot to do that; **~gehörig** *adj attr* which goes/go with it/them; *Schlüssel etc* belonging to it/them; (*zu dieser Arbeit gehörend*) *Werkzeuge, Material* necessary; (*gebührlich*) obligatory; **~kommen** *vi sep irreg aux sein* **(a)** (*ankommen*) to arrive (on the scene); **er kam zufällig ~** he happened to arrive on the scene; **(b)** (*hinzugefügt werden*) to be added; **es kommen laufend neue Bücher ~** new books are always being added; **es kamen noch mehrere Straftaten ~** there were several other offences; **kommt noch etwas ~?** is there *or* will there be anything else?; **es kommt noch ~, daß er faul ist** on top of that *or* in addition to that he's lazy; **(c)** (*Aus, Sw: Zeit dafür finden*) to get round to it; **~legen** *sep* [1] *vt* to add to it; **jdm/sich noch ein Stückchen Fleisch ~legen** to give sb/oneself another piece of meat; **leg die Sachen ruhig ~** just put the things with it/them; [2] *vr* to lie down with him/them *etc*; **~lernen** *vt sep* **viel/nichts ~lernen** to learn a lot more/nothing new; **man kann immer was ~lernen** there's always something to learn; **schon wieder was ~gelernt!** you learn something (new) every day!

dazumal *adv* (*old*) in those days; *siehe* **Anno.**

dazu-: ~rechnen *vt sep* **(a)** *Kosten, Betrag, Zahl* to add on; **(b)** (*mit berücksichtigen*) to consider also; **~schauen** *vi sep* (*Aus*) *siehe* **zusehen**; **~schreiben** *vt sep irreg* to add; **~setzen** *sep* [1] *vt* **(a) können wir den Jungen hier noch ~setzen?** could the boy sit here too?; **(b)** (*~schreiben*) to add; [2] *vr* to join him/us *etc*; **komm, setz dich doch ~** come and sit with *or* join us; **~tun** *vt sep irreg* (*inf*) to add.

Dazutun *nt* **er hat es ohne dein ~ geschafft** he managed it without your doing/saying anything; **ohne dein ~ hätte er es nicht geschafft** he wouldn't have managed it if you hadn't done/said something *or* without your doing/saying anything.

dazwischen *adv* (*räumlich, zeitlich*) in between; (*in der betreffenden Menge, Gruppe*) amongst them, in with them ◆ **die Betten standen dicht nebeneinander, es hing nur ein Vorhang ~** the beds were very close together, there was only a curtain between them.

dazwischen-: ~fahren *vi sep irreg aux sein* **(a)** (*eingreifen*) to step in and put a stop to things, to intervene; **(b)** (*unterbrechen*) to break in, to interrupt; **jdm ~fahren** to interrupt sb; **~funken** *vi sep* (*Rad*) to jam the signal; (*inf: eingreifen*) to put one's oar in (*inf*); (*etw vereiteln*) to put a spoke in it (*inf*); **~kommen** *vi sep irreg aux sein* **(a) mit der Hand/der Hose** *etc* **~kommen** to get one's hand/trousers *etc* caught in it/them; **(b)** (*störend erscheinen*) to get in the way; **... wenn nichts ~kommt!** ... if all goes well; **leider ist** *or* **mir ist leider etwas ~gekommen, ich kann nicht dabeisein** something has come *or* cropped up, I'm afraid I can't be there; **~legen** *vt sep* to put in between; **~liegend** *adj attr* **die ~liegenden Seiten/Monate/Bahnhöfe** *etc* the pages/months/stations in between; **~reden** *vi sep* **(a)** (*unterbrechen*) to interrupt (*jdm* sb); **(b)** *siehe* **dreinreden**; **~rufen** *vti sep irreg* to yell out; **~schlagen** *vi sep irreg* to wade in, to lam in (*esp US inf*); **~stehen** *vi sep irreg aux haben or sein* **(a)** (*lit*) to be amongst *or* (*zwischen zweien*) between them; **(b)** (*zwischen den Parteien*) to be neutral; **(c)** (*geh: hindernd*) to be in the way; **~treten** *vi sep irreg aux sein* **(a)** (*schlichtend*) to intervene; **sein D~treten** his intervention; **(b)** (*geh: störend*) to come between them.

DB [deː'beː] *f* - *abbr of* **Deutsche Bundesbahn.**

DD-Diskette [deː'deː-] *f* (*Comput*) DD diskette.

DDR [deːdeː'|ɛr] *f* - *abbr of* **Deutsche Demokratische Republik** GDR, German Democratic Republic, East Germany.

DDR-Bürger *m* East German, citizen of the German Democratic Republic.
DDT ® [de:de:'te:] *nt* - *abbr of* **Dichlordiphenyltrichloräthan** DDT.
Deal [di:l] *m* **-s, -s** (*Geschäft etc, inf: Drogen*) deal.
dealen ['di:lən] (*inf*) [1] *vt Drogen* to push ◆ **er kann alles für dich ~** he can fix you up with anything.
[2] *vi* **er dealt** he is a dealer; **mit Kokain ~** to deal in *or* to push cocaine.
Dealer(in *f*) ['di:lɐ, -ərın] *m* **-s, -** (*inf*) (drug) dealer, pusher; (*international auch*) trafficker.
Debakel *nt* **-s, -** debacle ◆ **ein ~ erleiden** (*Stück etc*) to be a debacle; **damit hat die Regierung ein ~ erlitten** that turned into something of a debacle for the government.
Debatte *f* **-, -n** debate ◆ **etw in die ~ werfen** to throw sth into the discussion; **etw zur ~ stellen** to put sth up for discussion *or* (*Parl*) debate; **was steht zur ~?** what is being discussed *or* is under discussion?; (*Parl*) what is being debated?; **das steht hier nicht zur ~** that's not the issue; **sich in eine ~ (über etw** *acc*) **einlassen** to enter into a discussion (about sth).
debattelos *adj* (*Parl*) without debate.
debattieren* *vti* to debate ◆ **über etw** (*acc*) **(mit jdm) ~** to discuss sth (with sb); **mit ihm kann man schlecht ~** you can't have a good discussion with him.
Debattierklub *m* debating society.
Debet *nt* **-s, -s** (*Fin*) debits *pl*.
Debetseite *f* (*Fin*) debit side.
debil *adj* (*Med*) feeble-minded.
Debilität *f* (*Med*) feeble-mindedness.
debitieren* *vt* (*Fin*) to debit ◆ **jdn mit einem Betrag ~** to debit an amount to sb, to debit sb with an amount.
Debitor *m* (*Fin*) debtor.
Debüt [de'by:] *nt* **-s, -s** debut ◆ **sein ~ als etw geben** to make one's debut as sth.
Debütant *m person making his debut*; (*fig: Anfänger, Neuling*) novice.
Debütantin *f* **(a)** *siehe* **Debütant. (b)** (*in der Gesellschaft*) debutante, deb.
Debütantinnenball *m* debutantes' ball.
debütieren* *vi* (*Theat, fig*) to make one's debut.
Dechanat *nt* (*Eccl*) deanery.
Dechanei *f* (*Eccl*) deanery, dean's residence.
Dechant *m* (*Eccl*) dean.
dechiffrieren* [deʃı'fri:rən] *vt* to decode; *Text, Geheimschrift auch* to decipher.
Dechiffrierung *f siehe vt* decoding; deciphering.
Deck *nt* **-(e)s, -s** deck; (*in Parkhaus*) level ◆ **auf ~** on deck; **an ~ gehen** to go on deck; **alle Mann an ~!** all hands on deck!; **unter** *or* **von ~ gehen** to go below deck; **nicht ganz auf ~ sein** (*inf*) to feel under the weather (*inf*).
Deck-: ~adresse, ~anschrift *f* accommodation *or* cover (*US*) address; **~anstrich** *m* top *or* final coat; **~aufbauten** *pl* (*Naut*) superstructure *sing*; **~bett** *nt* feather quilt; **~blatt** *nt* (*Bot*) bract; (*von Zigarre*) wrapper; (*Schutzblatt*) cover; (*Einlageblatt*) overlay.
Deckchen *nt* mat; (*auf Tablett*) traycloth; (*Torten~*) doily; (*auf Sessel etc*) antimacassar; (*für Lehne*) arm-cover.
Deckdienst *m* (*Naut*) deck duty.
Decke *f* **-, -n (a)** cloth; (*Woll~*) blanket; (*kleiner*) rug; (*Stepp~*) quilt; (*Bett~*) cover; (*fig: Schnee~, Staub~ etc*) blanket ◆ **unter die ~ kriechen** to pull the bedclothes up over one's head; **sich nach der ~ strecken** (*fig*) to cut one's coat according to one's cloth; **mit jdm unter einer ~ stecken** (*fig*) to be in league *or* in cahoots (*inf*) *or* hand in glove with sb.
(b) (*Zimmer~*) ceiling; (*Min*) roof ◆ **es tropft von der ~** there's water coming through the ceiling; **an die ~ gehen** (*inf*) to hit the roof (*inf*); **vor Freude an die ~ springen** (*inf*) to jump for joy; **mir fällt die ~ auf den Kopf** (*fig inf*) I feel really claustrophobic *or* shut in.
(c) (*Schicht*) layer; (*Straßen~*) surface; (*Reifen~*) outer tyre *or* cover *or* casing.
(d) (*Hunt*) skin.
Deckel *m* **-s, -** lid; (*von Schachtel, Glas auch, von Flasche*) top; (*Buch~, Uhr~*) cover; (*inf: Hut, Mütze*) titfer (*Brit inf*), hat ◆ **eins auf den ~ kriegen** (*inf*) (*geschlagen werden*) to get hit on the head; (*ausgeschimpft werden*) to be given a (good) talking-to (*inf*); **jdm eins auf den ~ geben** (*inf*) (*schlagen*) to smash sb on the head; (*ausschimpfen*) to give sb a (good) talking-to (*inf*); *siehe* **Topf.**
Deckel- *in cpds* with a lid.
decken [1] *vt* **(a)** (*zu~*) to cover ◆ **ein Dach mit Schiefer/Ziegeln ~** to roof a building with slate/tiles; **ein Dach mit Stroh/Reet ~** to thatch a roof (with straw/reeds); **gedeckter Gang/Wagen** covered walk/hard-topped car; *siehe auch* **gedeckt.**
(b) (*zurechtmachen*) *Tisch, Tafel* to set, to lay ◆ **es ist für vier Personen gedeckt** the table is laid *or* set for four (people); **sich an einen gedeckten Tisch setzen** (*lit*) to find one's meal ready and waiting; (*fig*) to be handed everything on a plate.
(c) (*breiten*) **die Hand/ein Tuch über etw** (*acc*) **~** to cover sth with one's hand/a cloth, to put one's hand/a cloth over sth.
(d) (*schützen*) to cover; (*Ftbl*) *Spieler auch* to mark; *Komplizen* to cover up for.
(e) *Kosten, Schulden, Bedarf* to cover, to meet ◆ **mein Bedarf ist gedeckt** I have all I need; (*fig inf*) I've had enough (to last me some time); **damit ist unser Bedarf gedeckt** that will meet *or* cover our needs; **wir haben sofort unseren Bedarf gedeckt** we immediately obtained enough to meet *or* cover our needs.
(f) (*Comm, Fin: absichern*) *Scheck, Darlehen* to cover; *Defizit* to offset ◆ **der Schaden wird voll durch die Versicherung gedeckt** the cost of the damage will be fully met by the insurance.
(g) (*begatten*) *Stute, Ziege* to cover.
[2] *vi* to cover; (*Boxen*) to guard; (*Ftbl: Spieler ~ auch*) to mark; (*Tisch~*) to lay a/the table ◆ **du mußt besser ~** (*Ftbl*) you must mark your opponent better; (*Boxen*) you must improve your guard; **es ist gedeckt** luncheon/dinner is served.
[3] *vr* **(a)** (*Standpunkte, Interessen, Begriffe*) to coincide; (*Aussagen*) to correspond, to agree; (*Math: Dreiecke, Figur*) to be congruent ◆ **sich ~de Dreiecke** congruent triangles; **sich ~de Begriffe/Interessen** concepts/interests which coincide.
(b) (*sich schützen*) to defend oneself; (*mit Schild etc*) to protect oneself; (*Boxer etc*) to cover oneself; (*sich absichern*) to cover oneself.
Decken-: ~balken *m* ceiling beam; **~beleuchtung** *f* ceiling lighting; **~gemälde** *nt* ceiling fresco; **~gewölbe** *nt* (*Archit*) vaulting; **~heizung** *f* overhead heating; **~konstruktion** *f* roof construction; **~lampe** *f* ceiling light; **~malerei** *f* ceiling fresco; **~träger** *m* ceiling girder.
Deck-: ~farbe *f* opaque water colour; **~flügel** *m* (*Zool*) wing case; **~fracht** *f* (*Naut*) deck cargo; **~geld** *nt* (*Agr*) stud fee; **~glas** *nt* (*Opt*) cover glass; **~haar** *nt* top hair; **~haus** *nt* (*Naut*) deckhouse; **~hengst** *m* stud(horse), stallion; **~mantel** *m* (*fig*) mask, blind; **unter dem ~mantel von ...** under the guise of ...; **~name** *m* assumed name; (*Mil*) code name; **~offizier** *m* (*Naut*) ≃ warrant officer; **~passagier** *m* (*Naut*) first-class passenger; **~plane** *f* (*Aut*) tarpaulin; **~platte** *f* (*Build*) slab; (*von Mauer*) coping stone; (*von Grab*) covering stone *or* slab; **~salon** *m* (*Naut*) first-class lounge; **~schicht** *f* surface layer; (*von Straße*) surface; (*Geol*) top layer *or* stratum; **~station** *f* stud (farm); **~stein** *m* (*Build*) coping stone; (*von Grab*) covering stone.
Deckung *f* **(a)** (*Schutz*) cover; (*Ftbl, Chess*) defence; (*Boxen, Fechten*) guard ◆ **in ~ gehen** to take cover; **~ suchen** to seek cover; **volle ~!** (*Mil*) take cover!; **jdm ~ geben** to cover sb; (*Feuerschutz auch*) to give sb cover.
(b) (*Verheimlichung*) **die ~ von etw** covering up for sth; **er kann mit ~ durch den Minister rechnen** he can count on the minister covering up for him.
(c) (*Comm, Fin*) (*von Scheck, Wechsel*) cover; (*das Decken*) covering; (*von Darlehen*) security; (*das Begleichen*) meeting ◆ **der Scheck ist ohne ~** the cheque is not covered; **ein Darlehen ohne ~** an unsecured loan; **zur ~ seiner Schulden** to meet his debts; **als ~ für seine Schulden** as security *or* surety for his debts; **dafür ist auf meinem Konto keine ~** there are no funds to cover that in my account; **die Versicherung übernahm die ~ des Schadens** the insurance company agreed to meet the cost of the damage.
(d) (*Befriedigung*) meeting ◆ **eine ~ der Nachfrage ist unmöglich** demand cannot possibly be met.
(e) (*Übereinstimmung*) (*Math*) congruence ◆ **zur ~ bringen** (*Math*) to make congruent; **lassen sich diese Standpunkte/Interessen zur ~ bringen?** can these points of view/interests be made to coincide?; **diese beiden Zeugenaussagen lassen sich schwer zur ~ bringen** these two statements can't be made to agree.
Deckungs-: ~auflage *f* (*Typ*) break-even quantity; **~fehler** *m* (*Ftbl*) error by the defence; **~feuer** *nt* (*Mil*) covering fire; **im ~feuer der Kameraden** under covering fire from their *etc* comrades; **d~gleich** *adj* (*Math*) congruent; **d~gleich sein** (*fig*) to coincide; (*Aussagen*) to agree; **~gleichheit** *f* (*Math*) congruence; **wegen der ~gleichheit der Ansichten/Aussagen** because of the degree to which these views coincide/these statements agree; **~graben** *m* (*Mil*) shelter trench; **~kapital** *nt* (*Insur*) covering funds *pl*; **~loch** *nt* (*Mil*) foxhole; **~zusage** *f* (*von Versicherung*) cover note.
Deck-: ~weiß *nt* opaque white; **~wort** *nt* code word.
Decoder [de'ko:dɐ, dı'koudə] *m* **-s, -** decoder.
decodieren* *vt* to decode.
⚠ **Décolleté** [dekɔl'te:] *nt* **-s, -s** *siehe* ⚠**Dekolleté.**
decouragiert [dekura'ʒi:ɐt] *adj* (*dated geh*) disheartened, dispirited.
Decrescendo [dekre'ʃɛndo] *nt* **-s, -s** *or* **Decrescendi** (*Mus*) diminuendo.
Dedikation *f* (*geh*) **(a)** (*Widmung*) dedication. **(b)** (*Schenkung*) gift.
Dedikations|exemplar *nt* presentation copy.
dedizieren* *vt* (*geh*) **(a)** (*widmen*) to dedicate. **(b)** (*schenken*) **jdm etw ~** to present sth to sb.
Deduktion *f* deduction.
deduktiv *adj* deductive.
deduzieren* *vt* to deduce (*aus* from).
Deern [de:ɐn] *f* **-, -s** (*N Ger inf*) lass(ie).
De|eskalation *f* (*Mil*) de-escalation.
Deez *m* **-es, -e** (*hum inf*) *siehe* **Dez.**
de facto *adv* de facto.
De-facto-Anerkennung *f* (*Pol*) de facto recognition.
defäkieren* *vi* (*form*) to defecate.
Defätismus *m, no pl* defeatism.
Defätist *m* defeatist.
defätistisch *adj* defeatist *no adv*.
defäzieren* *vi* (*form*) *siehe* **defäkieren.**
defekt *adj Gerät etc* faulty, defective ◆ **geistig/moralisch ~ sein** to be mentally/morally deficient.
Defekt *m* **-(e)s, -e** fault, defect; (*Med*) deficiency ◆ **körperlicher/geistiger ~** physical defect/mental deficiency; **einen ~ haben** to be faulty *or* defective; (*inf: von Mensch*) to be a bit lacking (*inf*).
defektiv *adj* (*Gram*) defective.
Defektivum *nt* **-s, Defektiva** (*Gram*) defective.
defensiv *adj Maßnahmen, Taktik* defensive; *Fahrweise auch* (*US*), non-aggressive ◆ **sich ~ verhalten** to be on the defensive.

Defensivbündnis *nt* defence alliance.
Defensive [-'ziːvə] *f, no pl* defensive ♦ **in der ~ bleiben** to remain on the defensive; **jdn in die ~ drängen** to force sb onto the defensive.
Defensivität [-vi'teːt] *f* defensiveness; (*von Fahrweise*) defensiveness (*US*) (*gen* of), lack of aggression (*gen* in).
Defensiv- *in cpds* defensive; **~krieg** *m* defensive warfare; **~spiel** *nt* defensive game; **~stellung** *f* defensive position, position of defence.
Defilee [defi'leː] *nt* **-s, -s** *or* **-n** [-eːən] (*Mil*) march-past; (*fig*) parade.
defilieren* *vi aux haben or sein* (*Mil*) to march past; (*fig*) to parade past.
definierbar *adj* definable ♦ **schwer/leicht ~** hard/easy to define.
definieren* *vt* to define ♦ **etw neu ~** to redefine sth.
Definition *f* definition.
definitiv *adj* definite.
definitorisch *adj* (*geh*) *Frage, Problem* of definition ♦ **ein ~ schwieriges Problem** a problem which is hard to define.
defizient *adj* deficient.
Defizit *nt* **-s, -e** (*Fehlbetrag*) deficit; (*Mangel*) deficiency (*an +dat* of).
defizitär *adj* in deficit ♦ **das Bahnwesen entwickelt sich immer ~er** the railways have a larger deficit every year; **die ~e Entwicklung der Organisation** the trend in the organization to run to a deficit; **eine ~e Haushaltspolitik führen** to follow an economic policy which can only lead to deficit.
Deflation *f* (*Econ*) deflation.
deflationär, deflationistisch *adj* deflationary *no adv*.
Deflationspolitik *f* deflationary policy.
deflatorisch *adj* (*Econ*) *siehe* **deflationär**.
Defloration *f* defloration.
deflorieren* *vt* to deflower.
Deformation *f* deformation, distortion; (*Mißbildung*) deformity; (*Entstellung*) disfigurement.
deformieren* *vt* (*Tech*) to deform, to contort; (*lit, fig: mißbilden*) to deform; (*entstellen*) to disfigure ♦ **in einer Schlägerei haben sie ihm die Nase deformiert** they flattened his nose (for him) in a fight; **eine deformierte Nase** a misshapen nose.
Deformierung *f* **(a)** (*das Deformieren*) deformation; (*Entstellung*) disfigurement. **(b)** *siehe* **Deformation.**
Deformität *f* (*Med*) deformity.
Defroster *m* **-s, -** (*Aut*) heated windscreen; (*Sprühmittel*) de-icer; (*im Kühlschrank*) defroster.
deftig *adj* **(a)** (*derb, urwüchsig*) *Witz, Humor* ribald.
(b) (*kräftig*) *Lüge* whopping (*inf*), huge; *Mahlzeit* solid; *Wurst etc* substantial, good solid *attr; Ohrfeige* cracking (*inf*) ♦ **er hat sich ganz ~ ins Zeug gelegt** he really got going (*inf*); **dann langten die Kinder ~ zu** then the kids really got stuck in (*inf*).
Deftigkeit *f, no pl siehe adj* **(a)** ribaldry. **(b)** hugeness; solidness; substantialness; soundness.
degagieren* [dega'ʒiːrən] *vt* (*Fechten*) to disengage.
Degen *m* **-s, -** rapier; (*Sportfechten*) épée ♦ **mit bloßem** *or* **nacktem ~** with one's rapier drawn; *siehe* **kreuzen.**
Degeneration *f* degeneration.
Degenerationserscheinung *f* sign of degeneration.
degenerativ *adj Schäden* degenerative.
degenerieren* *vi aux sein* to degenerate (*zu* into).
degeneriert *adj* degenerate.
Degen-: **~fechten** *nt* épée fencing; **~klinge** *f* rapier blade; **~knauf** *m* pommel; **~korb** *m* guard; **~stoß** *m* thrust from one's/a rapier.
degoutant [degu'tant] *adj* (*geh*) distasteful, disgusting.
degoutieren* [degu'tiːrən] *vt* (*geh*) to disgust.
Degradation *f* (*Phys*) **~ der Energie** degradation of energy.
degradieren* *vt* (*Mil*) to demote (*zu* to); (*fig: herabwürdigen*) to degrade ♦ **jdn/etw zu etw ~** (*fig*) to lower sb/sth to the level of sth.
Degradierung *f* (*Mil*) demotion (*zu* to); (*fig*) degradation ♦ **diese Behandlung empfand er als (eine) ~** he felt such treatment to be degrading.
Degression *f* (*Fin*) degression.
degressiv *adj* (*Fin*) degressive.
Degustation *f* (*esp Sw*) tasting.
degustieren* *vti* (*esp Sw*) *Wein* to taste.
dehnbar *adj* (*lit*) elastic; (*fig auch*) flexible; *Stoff* stretch *attr*, stretchy (*inf*), elastic; *Metall* ductile ♦ **ein ~er Vokal** a vowel which can be lengthened.
Dehnbarkeit *f, no pl siehe adj* elasticity; flexibility; stretchiness (*inf*), elasticity; ductility ♦ **Eisen hat eine geringere ~ als Blei** iron is less ductile than lead; **die ~ der Vokale** the degree *or* extent to which the vowels can be lengthened.
dehnen [1] *vt* to stretch; (*Med auch*) to dilate; *Laut, Silbe* to lengthen ♦ **seine gedehnte Sprechweise** his drawling way of speaking; **Vokale gedehnt aussprechen** to pronounce one's vowels long.
[2] *vr* to stretch ♦ **er dehnte und streckte sich** he had a good stretch; **die Minuten dehnten sich zu Stunden** (*geh*) the minutes seemed like hours; **vor ihnen dehnte sich der Ozean** (*geh*) the ocean stretched out before them; **der Weg dehnte sich endlos** the road seemed to go on for ever.
Dehn- (*Ling*): **~strich** *m* length mark; **~stufe** *f* lengthened grade, dehnstufe (*form*).
Dehnung *f siehe vt* stretching; dilation; lengthening.
Dehnungs- (*Ling*): **~-h** *nt* h with a lengthening effect on the preceding vowel; **~strich** *m siehe* **Dehnstrich.**
dehydrieren* *vt* (*Chem*) to dehydrate.
Dehydrierung *f* (*Chem*) dehydration.
Deibel *m* **-s, -** (*N Ger inf*) *siehe* **Teufel, pfui.**
Deich *m* **-(e)s, -e** dyke, dike (*esp US*).
Deich-: **~bau** *m* dyke; (*das Bauen*) dyke building; **~bruch** *m* breach in the dyke; **~genossenschaft** *f siehe* **~verband**; **~graf, ~hauptmann** *m* dyke reeve (*old*) *or* warden; **~krone** *f* dyke top.
Deichsel [-ks-] *f* **-, -n** shaft, whiffletree (*US*); (*Doppel~*) shafts *pl* ♦ **ein Pferd in der ~** a horse in *or* between the shafts; **Ochsen an die ~ spannen** to yoke oxen into *or* between the shafts.
Deichsel-: **~bruch** *m* broken shaft/shafts; **~kreuz** *nt* **(a)** handle; **(b)** (*Rel*) Y-shaped cross.
deichseln [-ks-] *vt* (*inf*) to wangle (*inf*) ♦ **das werden wir schon ~** we'll wangle it somehow.
Deich-: **~verband** *m association of owners of dyked land*; **~vogt** *m* (*old*) *siehe* **~graf**; **~vorland** *nt land to the seaward side of a dyke.*
Deifikation [deifika'tsioːn] *f* (*Philos*) deification.
deifizieren* [dei-] *vt* (*Philos*) to deify.
dein [1] *poss pron* **(a)** (*adjektivisch*) (*in Briefen:* **D~**) your, thy (*obs, dial*) ♦ **~ doofes/schönes Gesicht** that stupid/beautiful face of yours, your stupid/beautiful face; **rauchst du immer noch ~e 20 Zigaretten pro Tag?** are you still smoking your 20 cigarettes a day?; **herzliche Grüße, D~e Elke** with best wishes, yours *or* (*herzlicher*) love Elke; **stets** *or* **immer D~ Otto** yours ever, Otto; **D~ Wille geschehe** (*Bibl*) Thy will be done. **(b)** (*old: substantivisch*) yours ♦ **behalte, was ~ ist** keep what is yours.
[2] *pers pron gen of* **du** (*old, poet*) **ich werde ewig ~ gedenken** I shall remember you forever.
deiner *pers pron gen of* **du** (*geh*) of you ♦ **wir werden ~ gedenken** we will remember you.
deine(r, s) *poss pron* (*substantivisch*) yours ♦ **der/die/das ~** (*geh*) yours; **tu du das D~** (*geh*) you do your bit; **stets** *or* **immer der D~** (*form*) yours ever; **die D~n** (*geh*) your family, your people; **du und die D~n** (*geh: Familie*) you and yours; **das D~** (*geh: Besitz*) what is yours.
deinerseits *adv* (*auf deiner Seite*) for your part; (*von deiner Seite*) on your part ♦ **den Vorschlag hast du ~ gemacht** you made the suggestion yourself.
deinesgleichen *pron inv* people like you *or* yourself; (*pej auch*) your sort, the likes of you ♦ **an Schönheit ist keine ~** (*liter*) in beauty there is none to equal you (*liter*).
deinet-: **~halben** (*dated*), **~wegen** *adv* (*wegen dir*) because of you, on account of you, on your account; (*dir zuliebe*) for your sake; (*um dich*) about you; (*für dich*) on your behalf; **~willen** *adv* **um ~willen** for your sake.
deinige *poss pron* (*old, geh*) **der/die/das ~** yours; **die D~n** your family *or* people; **das D~** (*Besitz*) what is yours; **tu du das D~** you do your bit.
deins *poss pron* yours.
Deismus *m, no pl* (*Philos*) deism.
Deist *m* (*Philos*) deist.
deistisch *adj* (*Philos*) deistic.
Deiwel (*N Ger*), **Deixel** (*S Ger*) *m* **-s, -** *siehe* **Teufel.**
Déjà-vu-Erlebnis [deʒa'vyː-] *nt* (*Psych*) sense *or* feeling of déjà vu.
de jure *adv* de jure.
De-jure-Anerkennung *f* de jure recognition.
Deka *nt* **-(s), -** (*Aus*) *siehe* **Dekagramm.**
Dekade *f* (*10 Tage*) ten days, ten-day period; (*10 Jahre*) decade.
dekadent *adj* decadent.
Dekadenz *f, no pl* decadence.
dekadisch *adj Zahlensystem* decimal ♦ **~er Logarithmus** common logarithm.
Deka-: **~eder** *m* **-s, -** decahedron; **~gon** *nt* **-s, -e** decagon; **~gramm** [(aus) 'dɛka-] *nt* decagram(me); **10 ~gramm Schinken** (*Aus*) 100 grams of ham; **~liter** *m* decalitre.
Dekalog *m* **-(e)s** (*Bibl*) decalogue.
Dekameron [de'kaːmerɔn] *nt* **-s** Decameron.
Dekameter *m* decametre.
Dekan *m* **-s, -e** (*Univ, Eccl*) dean.
Dekanat *nt* **(a)** (*Univ, Eccl: Amt, Amtszeit*) deanship. **(b)** (*Amtssitz*) (*Univ*) office of the dean; (*Eccl*) deanery.
Dekanei *f* (*Eccl*) deanery.
dekarbonisieren* *vt* to decarbonize; (*Aut*) to decoke.
dekartellieren*, dekartellisieren* *vt* to decartelize.
Deklamation *f* declamation ♦ **~en** (*pej*) (empty) rhetoric *sing*.
deklamatorisch *adj* declamatory, rhetorical.
deklamieren* *vti* to declaim.
Deklaration *f* (*alle Bedeutungen*) declaration.
deklarieren* *vt* (*alle Bedeutungen*) to declare.
Deklarierung *f* declaration.
deklassieren* *vt* **(a)** (*Sociol, herabsetzen*) to downgrade. **(b)** (*Sport: weit übertreffen*) to outclass.
Deklassierung *f siehe vt* downgrading; outclassing.
deklinabel *adj* (*Gram*) declinable.
Deklination *f* **(a)** (*Gram*) declension. **(b)** (*Astron, Phys*) declination.
deklinierbar *adj* (*Gram*) declinable.
deklinieren* *vt* (*Gram*) to decline.
dekodieren* *vt siehe* **decodieren.**
⚠ **Dekolleté** [dekɔl'teː] *nt* **-s, -s** low-cut *or* décolleté neckline, décolletage ♦ **ein Kleid mit einem tiefen/gewagten ~** a very/daringly low-cut *or* décolleté dress; **ihr ~ war so tief, ...** she was wearing such a low-cut *or* plunging neckline ...

dekolletieren* [dekɔl'ti:rən] *vt* to give a *or* cut with a low neckline.
dekolletiert [dekɔl'ti:ɐt] *adj Kleid* low-cut, décolleté ◆ **eine ~e Dame** a woman in a low-cut dress.
Dekolonisation *f* decolonization.
dekolonisieren* *vt* to decolonize.
Dekomposition *f* decomposition.
Dekompositum *nt* **-s, Dekomposita** (*Ling*) (*zusammengesetztes Wort*) multiple compound, decomposite (*form*), decompound (*form*); (*Ableitung*) compound derivative.
Dekompression *f* decompression.
Dekompressionskammer *f* decompression chamber.
Dekontamination *f* decontamination.
dekontaminieren* *vt* to decontaminate.
Dekonzentration *f* deconcentration, decentralization.
Dekor *m or nt* **-s, -s** *or* **-e (a)** decoration; (*von Raum auch*) décor; (*Muster*) pattern. **(b)** (*Theat, Film etc*) décor.
Dekorateur(in *f*) [dekora'tø:ɐ, -ø:rɪn] *m* (*Schaufenster~*) window-dresser; (*von Innenräumen*) interior designer.
Dekoration *f* **(a)** *no pl* (*das Ausschmücken*) decorating, decoration.
(b) (*Einrichtung*) décor *no pl*; (*Fenster~*) window dressing *or* decoration; (*Theat: Bühnenbild*) set ◆ **zur ~ dienen** to be decorative; **zu Weihnachten haben viele Kaufhäuser schöne ~en** many department stores have beautifully decorated windows for Christmas.
(c) (*Orden, Ordensverleihung*) decoration.
Dekorations-: ~arbeiten *pl* decorating *no pl*; **~maler** *m* (interior) decorator; (*Theat*) scene-painter; **~stoff** *m* (*Tex*) furnishing fabric; **~stück** *nt* piece of the décor; **das ist nur ein ~stück** that's just for decoration.
dekorativ *adj* decorative.
dekorieren* *vt* to decorate; *Schaufenster* to dress.
Dekorierung *f siehe vt* decoration; dressing.
Dekorum *nt* **-s,** *no pl* (*liter*) propriety, decorum ◆ **das ~ wahren** to maintain *or* observe the proprieties; **das ~ verletzen** to go against *or* infringe the proprieties.
Dekostoff *m siehe* **Dekorationsstoff.**
Dekret *nt* **-(e)s, -e** decree.
dekretieren* *vt* to decree.
dekuvrieren* [deku'vri:rən] (*geh*) [1] *vt Skandal, Machenschaften* to expose, to uncover; *Person, Betrüger etc* to expose.
[2] *vr* to reveal oneself.
Deleatur(zeichen) *nt* **-s, -** (*Typ*) deletion mark.
Delegat *m* **-en, -en** delegate.
Delegation *f* (*alle Bedeutungen*) delegation.
Delegationschef *m* head of a delegation ◆ **der koreanische ~** the head of the Korean delegation.
delegieren* *vt* (*alle Bedeutungen*) to delegate (*an +acc* to).
Delegierten-: ~konferenz, ~versammlung *f* delegates' conference.
Delegierte(r) *mf decl as adj* delegate.
delektieren* (*geh*) [1] *vr* **sich an etw** (*dat*) **~** to delight in sth.
[2] *vt* **jdn mit etw ~** to delight sb with sth; **sie delektierten den Sultan mit Tänzen** they danced for the sultan's delectation (*liter*).
Delfter *adj attr Porzellan etc* Delft.
delikat *adj* **(a)** (*wohlschmeckend*) exquisite, delicious. **(b)** (*behutsam*) delicate; *Andeutung auch* gentle. **(c)** (*heikel*) *Problem, Frage* delicate, sensitive; (*gewagt*) risqué. **(d)** (*geh: empfindlich*) delicate.
⚠ **Delikateß-** *in cpds* top-quality.
Delikatesse *f* **(a)** (*Leckerbissen, fig*) delicacy ◆ **ein Geschäft für Obst und ~n** a fruit shop and delicatessen *sing*. **(b)** *no pl* (*geh: Feinfühligkeit*) delicacy, sensitivity.
Delikatessen-: ~geschäft *nt*, **~handlung** *f* delicatessen, deli (*inf*).
Delikt *nt* **-(e)s, -e** (*Jur*) offence; (*schwerer*) crime.
Delinquent [delɪŋ'kvɛnt] *m* (*geh*) offender.
delinquent [delɪŋ'kvɛnt] *adj* (*Sociol, Psych*) delinquent.
Delinquenz [delɪŋ'kvɛnts] *f* (*Sociol, Psych*) delinquency.
delirieren* *vi* (*geh, Med*) to be delirious ◆ **er delirierte im Fieber** he was delirious with fever.
Delirium *nt* delirium ◆ **im ~ sein** to be delirious *or* in a state of delirium; (*inf: betrunken*) to be paralytic (*inf*); **im ~ redete der Kranke wirr und konfus** the sick man raved deliriously; **in seinen Delirien** whenever he was delirious *or* (*betrunken*) paralytic (*inf*); **~ tremens** delirium tremens, the DT's.
deliziös *adj* (*liter*) most delectable.
Delle *f* **-, -n (a)** (*inf*) dent ◆ **eine ~ bekommen** to get a dent, to get *or* be dented. **(b)** (*Boden~*) hollow, dip.
delogieren* [delo'ʒi:rən] *vt* (*Aus*) *Mieter* to evict.
Delogierung *f* (*Aus*) eviction.
Delphi *nt* **-s** Delphi ◆ **das Orakel von ~** the Delphic oracle, the oracle of Delphi.
⚠ **Delphin**[1] *m* **-s, -e** (*Zool*) dolphin.
⚠ **Delphin**[2] *nt* **-s,** *no pl siehe* **Delphinschwimmen.**
⚠ **Delphinarium** *nt* dolphinarium.
⚠ **Delphinschwimmen** *nt* butterfly.
delphisch *adj* Delphic ◆ **das D~e Orakel** the Delphic oracle.
Delta[1] *nt* **-s, -s** *or* **Delten** (*Geog*) delta.
Delta[2] *nt* **-(s), -s** (*Buchstabe*) delta.
Delta-: d~förmig *adj* delta-shaped, deltaic (*rare*); *Muskel* deltoid; **~mündung** *f* delta estuary; **~muskel** *m* deltoid; **~strahlen** *pl* (*Phys*) delta rays *pl*.
de Luxe [də'lyks] *adj* (*Comm*) de luxe.
De-Luxe-Ausführung *f* (*Comm*) de-luxe version.
dem [1] *dat of def art* **der, das (a)** to the; (*mit Präposition*) the.
(b) es ist nicht an ~ that is not the case *or* how it is; **wenn ~ so ist** if that is the way it is; **wie ~ auch sei** be that as it may.
[2] *dat of dem pron* **der, das (a)** *attr* to that; (*mit Präposition*) that.
(b) (*substantivisch*) to that one; that one; (*Menschen*) to him; him; (*von mehreren*) to that one; that one.
[3] *dat of rel pron* **der, das** to whom, that *or* who(m) ... to; (*mit Präposition*) who(m); (*von Sachen*) to which, which *or* that ... to; which ◆ **~ der Fehler unterlaufen ist,** ... whoever made that mistake ...
Demagoge *m* demagogue.
Demagogentum *nt*, **Demagogie** *f* demagogy, demagoguery.
demagogisch *adj Rede etc* demagogic ◆ **er hat in seiner Rede die Tatsachen ~ verzerrt** in his speech he twisted the facts to demagogic ends; **leider lassen sich die Wähler immer noch ~ beeinflussen** sadly voters can still be swayed by demagogues *or* by demagogic ploys.
demanten *adj* (*poet*) *siehe* **diamanten.**
Demarche [de'marʃə] *f* **-, -n** (*Pol*) (diplomatic) representation, démarche ◆ **eine ~ unternehmen** to lodge a diplomatic protest.
Demarkation *f* demarcation.
Demarkationslinie *f* (*Pol, Mil*) demarcation line ◆ **die ~ des Waffenstillstands** the cease-fire line.
demarkieren* *vt Grenze, Bereiche* to demarcate.
demaskieren* [1] *vt* to unmask, to expose ◆ **jdn als etw ~** to expose sb as sth.
[2] *vr* to unmask oneself, to take off one's mask ◆ **sich als etw ~** to show oneself to be sth.
Dementi *nt* **-s, -s** denial.
dementieren* [1] *vt* to deny.
[2] *vi* to deny it.
Dementierung *f* denial, denying.
dem|entsprechend [1] *adv* correspondingly; (*demnach*) accordingly; *bezahlt* commensurately.
[2] *adj* appropriate; *Bemerkung auch* apposite; *Gehalt* commensurate ◆ **er nennt sich Christ, aber sein Verhalten ist nicht ~** he says he is a Christian but he does not behave accordingly *or* correspondingly.
Demenz *f* (*Med*) dementia.
dem-: ~gegenüber *adv* (*wohingegen*) on the other hand; (*im Vergleich dazu*) in contrast; **~gemäß** *adv, adj siehe* **~entsprechend.**
demilitarisieren* *vt* to demilitarize.
Demilitarisierung *f* demilitarization.
Demimonde [dəmi'mõ:d] *f* **-,** *no pl* (*pej geh*) demimonde.
Demission *f* (*Pol*) (*Rücktritt*) resignation; (*Entlassung*) dismissal ◆ **um seine ~ bitten** to ask to be relieved of one's duties; **er wurde zur ~ gezwungen** he was forced to resign.
demissionieren* *vi* (*Pol, Sw: kündigen*) to resign.
Demissions|angebot *nt* offer of resignation *or* to resign.
Demiurg *m* **-en** *or* **-s,** *no pl* (*Myth, liter*) demiurge.
dem-: ~nach *adv* therefore; (*~entsprechend*) accordingly; **~nächst** *adv* soon; **~nächst (in diesem Kino)** coming soon.
Demo *f* **-, -s** (*inf*) demo (*inf*).
Demobilisation *f* (*Mil*) demobilization.
demobilisieren* [1] *vt* to demobilize; *Soldaten auch* to demob (*Brit inf*).
[2] *vi* to demobilize; (*Soldat auch*) to get *or* be demobbed (*Brit inf*).
Demobilisierung *f* demobilization; (*von Soldaten auch*) demob (*Brit inf*).
démodé [de:mo'de:] *adj attr* (*geh*) outmoded.
Demodiskette *f* (*Comput*) demo disk.
⚠ **Demograph(in** *f*) *m* demographer.
⚠ **Demographie** *f* demography.
⚠ **demographisch** *adj* demographic.
Demokrat(in *f*) *m* **-en, -en** democrat.
Demokratie *f* democracy.
Demokratieverständnis *nt* understanding of (the meaning of) democracy.
demokratisch *adj* democratic.
demokratisieren* *vt* to democratize, to make democratic.
Demokratisierung *f* democratization.
demolieren* *vt* to wreck, to smash up; (*Rowdy auch*) to vandalize ◆ **nach dem Unfall war das Auto total demoliert** after the accident the car was a complete wreck; **er sah ganz schön demoliert aus** (*inf*) he was a real mess, he looked pretty badly bashed about.
Demolierung *f siehe vt* wrecking, smashing-up; vandalizing.
Demonstrant(in *f*) *m* demonstrator.
Demonstration *f* (*alle Bedeutungen*) demonstration ◆ **zur ~ seiner Friedfertigkeit** ... as a demonstration of *or* to demonstrate his peaceful intentions ...; **eine ~ für/gegen etw** a demonstration in support of/against sth.
Demonstrations-: ~marsch *m* march; **~material** *nt* teaching material *or* aids *pl*; **~objekt** *nt* teaching aid; **~recht** *nt* right to demonstrate *or* hold demonstrations; **~strafrecht** *nt* criminal law as it relates to demonstrations; **~zug** *m* demonstration, (protest) march.
demonstrativ *adj* demonstrative (*auch Gram*); *Beifall* acclamatory; *Protest, Fehlen* pointed; *Beispiel* clear ◆ **war seine Abwesenheit ~ oder reiner Zufall?**

was his absence a deliberate *or* pointed gesture or pure chance?; **der Botschafter verließ während der Rede ~ den Saal** during the speech the ambassador pointedly left the room.

Demonstrativ- *in cpds (Gram)* demonstrative.

demonstrieren* *vti (alle Bedeutungen)* to demonstrate ◆ **für/gegen etw ~** to demonstrate in support of/against sth; **die Regierung hat ihre Entschlossenheit demonstriert** the government gave a demonstration of *or* demonstrated its determination.

Demontage [-'ta:ʒə] *f* -, **-n** *(lit, fig)* dismantling.

demontieren* *vt (lit, fig)* to dismantle; *Räder* to take off.

Demoralisation *f (Entmutigung)* demoralization; *(Sittenverfall)* moral decline.

demoralisieren* *vt (entmutigen)* to demoralize; *(korrumpieren)* to corrupt ◆ **die römische Gesellschaft war am Ende so demoralisiert, daß ...** ultimately Roman society had suffered such a moral decline that ...

Demoralisierung *f siehe* **Demoralisation.**

Demoskop(in *f***)** *m* **-en -en** (opinion) pollster.

Demoskopie *f, no pl* (public) opinion research.

demoskopisch *adj* **~es Institut** (public) opinion research institute; **alle ~en Voraussagen waren falsch** all the predictions in the opinion polls were wrong; **eine ~e Untersuchung** a (public) opinion poll.

dem-: ~selben *dat of* **derselbe, dasselbe; ≈unerachtet, ≈ungeachtet** *adv (old) siehe* **des(sen)ungeachtet.**

Demut *f* -, *no pl* humility ◆ **in ~** with humility.

demütig *adj Bitte, Blick* humble.

demütigen [1] *vt Gefangenen, Besiegten, Volk* to humiliate; *(eine Lektion erteilen) stolzen Menschen etc* to humble.
[2] *vr* to humble oneself (*vor +dat* before).

Demütigung *f* humiliation ◆ **jdm ~en/eine ~ zufügen** to humiliate sb.

Demuts-: ~gebärde, ~haltung *f (esp Zool)* submissive posture; **d~voll** *adj* humble.

demzufolge *adv* therefore.

den [1] (a) *acc of def art* **der** the. **(b)** *dat pl of def art* **der, die, das** the; to the.
[2] *acc of dem pron* **der (a)** *attr* that. **(b)** *(substantivisch)* that one; *(Menschen)* him; *(von mehreren)* that one.
[3] *acc of rel pron* **der** who(m), that; *(von Sachen)* which, that.

denaturalisieren* *vt* to denaturalize.

denaturieren* [1] *vt* to denature.
[2] *vi* **zu etw ~** *(fig geh)* to degenerate into sth.

Dendrit *m* **-en, -en** *(Geol, Med)* dendrite.

denen [1] *dat pl of dem pron* **der, die, das** to them; *(mit Präposition)* them.
[2] *dat pl of rel pron* **der, die, das** to whom, that *or* who(m) ... to; *(mit Präposition)* whom; *(von Sachen)* to which, that *or* which ... to; which.

dengeln *vt Sense* to sharpen, to hone.

Denk-: ~ansatz *m* starting point; **~anstoß** *m* something to start one thinking; **jdm ~anstöße geben** to give sb something to think about, to give sb food for thought; **~art** *f* way of thinking; **eine edle/niedrige ~art** high-mindedness/low-mindedness; **~aufgabe** *f* brain-teaser; **d~bar** [1] *adj* conceivable; **es ist durchaus d~bar, daß er kommt** it's very possible *or* likely that he'll come; [2] *adv* extremely; *(ziemlich)* rather; **den d~bar schlechtesten/besten Eindruck machen** to make the worst/best possible impression.

Denken *nt* **-s,** *no pl* **(a)** *(Gedankenwelt)* thought; *(Denkweise)* thinking ◆ **ich kann seinem ~ nicht folgen** I can't follow his thinking *or* train of thought; **im ~ Goethes/der Aufklärung** in Goethe's thought/in the thinking of the Enlightenment; **abstraktes ~** abstract thought *or* thinking; **klares ~** clear thinking, clarity of thought.
(b) *(Gedanken)* thoughts *pl*, thinking.
(c) *(Denkvermögen)* mind.

▼ **denken** *pret* **dachte,** *ptp* **gedacht** [1] *vi* **(a)** *(überlegen)* to think ◆ **bei sich ~** to think to oneself; **hin und her ~** to rack one's brains (*über +acc* over); **wo ~ Sie hin!** what an idea!; **ich denke, also bin ich** I think, therefore I am; **der Mensch denkt, (und) Gott lenkt** *(Prov)* man proposes, God disposes *(Prov)*; **das gibt mir/einem zu ~** it starts you thinking, it makes you think; **langsam/schnell ~** to be a slow/quick thinker; **so darf man eben nicht ~** you shouldn't think like that.
▼ **(b)** *(urteilen)* to think (*über +acc* about, of) ◆ **wie ~ Sie darüber?** what do you think about it?; **schlecht von jdm** *or* **über jdn ~** to think badly of sb; **ich denke genauso** I think the same (way); **wieviel soll ich spenden? — wie Sie ~** how much should I donate? — it's up to you *or* as much as you think fit.
(c) *(gesinnt sein)* to think ◆ **edel ~** to be of a noble frame of mind, to be noble-minded; **kleinlich ~** to be petty-minded; **alle, die damals liberal gedacht haben, ...** all those who were thinking along liberal lines ...; **da muß man etwas großzügiger ~** one must be more liberally minded *or* liberal.
(d) *(im Sinn haben)* **an jdn/etw ~** to think of sb/sth, to have sb/sth in mind; **daran ist gar nicht zu ~** that's (quite) out of the question; **ich denke nicht daran!** no way! *(inf)*, not on your life!; **ich denke nicht daran, das zu tun** there's no way I'm going to do that *(inf)*, I wouldn't dream of doing that.
(e) *(besorgt sein)* **an jdn/etw ~** to think of *or* about sb/sth; **an die bevorstehende Prüfung denke ich mit gemischten Gefühlen** I'm looking ahead to the coming exam with mixed feelings.
(f) *(sich erinnern)* **an jdn/etw ~** to think of sb/sth; **solange ich ~ kann** (for) as long as I can remember *or* recall; **denk daran!** don't forget!; **an das Geld habe ich gar nicht mehr gedacht** I had forgotten about the money; **~ Sie zum Beispiel an England im 19. Jahrhundert** look at *or* think of England in the 19th century, for example; **wenn ich so an früher denke** when I cast my mind back, when I think back; **~ Sie mal an die Kriegsjahre** think of the war; **die viele Arbeit, ich darf gar nicht daran ~** all that work, it doesn't bear thinking about.
▼ **(g)** *(Einfall haben)* **an etw** *(acc)* **~** to think of sth; **das erste, woran ich dachte** the first thing I thought of, the first thing that came *or* sprang to (my) mind.
[2] *vt* **(a)** *Gedanken* to think; *(sich vorstellen)* to conceive of ◆ **er war der erste, der diesen Gedanken gedacht hat** he was the first to conceive of this idea; **was denkst du jetzt?** what are you thinking (about)?; **ich denke gar nichts** I'm not thinking about anything; **... das wage ich kaum zu ~** ... I hardly dare think; **wieviel Trinkgeld gibt man? — soviel, wie Sie ~** how big a tip does one give? — it's up to you *or* as much as you think fit; **sagen, was man denkt** to say what one thinks, to speak one's mind.
▼ **(b)** *(annehmen, glauben)* to think ◆ **(nur) Schlechtes/Gutes von jdm ~** to think ill/well of sb; **wer hätte das (von ihr) gedacht!** who'd have thought *or* believed it (of her)!; **was sollen bloß die Leute ~!** what will people think!; **ich dächte, ...** I would have thought ...; **ich denke schon** I think so; **ich denke nicht** I don't think so, I think not; **denkste!** *(inf)* that's what you think!
(c) *(vorsehen)* **für jdn/etw gedacht sein** to be intended *or* meant for sb/sth; **so war das nicht gedacht** that wasn't what I/he *etc* had in mind.
[3] *vr* **(a)** *(vorstellen)* **sich** *(dat)* **etw ~** to imagine; **das kann ich mir ~** I can imagine; **wieviel soll ich Ihnen zahlen? — was Sie sich** *(dat)* **so gedacht haben** what shall I pay you? — whatever you had in mind; **ich könnte ihn mir gut als Direktor ~** I could just imagine him *or* see him as director; **wie denkst du dir das eigentlich?** *(inf)* what's the big idea? *(inf)*; **ich habe mir das so gedacht: ...** this is what I had in mind: ..., this is what I'd thought: ...; **das habe ich mir** *gleich* **gedacht** I thought that from the first; **das habe ich mir** *gedacht* I thought so; **das habe ich mir beinahe** *gedacht* I thought as much; *dachte* **ich mir's doch!** I knew it!; **ich denke mir mein Teil** I have my own thoughts on the matter; **das läßt sich ~!** that's very likely; *siehe* **gedacht.**
(b) *(beabsichtigen)* **sich** *(dat)* **etw bei etw ~** to mean sth by sth; **ich habe mir nichts Böses dabei gedacht** I meant no harm (in it); **was hast du dir bei dieser Bemerkung bloß gedacht?** what were you thinking of when you made that remark?; **sie läuft zu Hause immer nackt herum und denkt sich nichts dabei** she runs around the house with nothing on and doesn't think anything of it.

Denker(in *f***)** *m* **-s, -** thinker ◆ **das Volk der Dichter und ~** the nation of poets and philosophers.

Denkerfalte *f usu pl (hum)* furrow on one's brow ◆ **er zog seine Stirn in ~n** *(acc)* he furrowed his brow.

denkerisch *adj* intellectual.

Denkerstirn *f (hum)* lofty brow.

Denk-: ~fabrik *f* think tank; **d~fähig** *adj* capable of thinking; **nicht mehr d~fähig** incapable of thinking (straight) (any more); **als d~fähiger Mensch** as an intelligent person; **~fähigkeit** *f* ability to think, intelligence; **d~faul** *adj* (mentally) lazy; **sei nicht so d~faul!** get your brain working!; **~fehler** *m* mistake in the/one's logic, flaw in the/one's reasoning; **ein ~fehler in der Beurteilung der Lage** an error in the assessment of the situation; **~gewohnheit** *f usu pl* thought habit, habitual way of thinking; **~hemmung** *f* mental block; **~hilfe** *f* clue, hint; *(Merkhilfe)* reminder; **~horizont** *m* mental horizon; **~inhalt** *m* idea; **~kategorie** *f usu pl* thought category; **in veralteten ~kategorien erzogen** brought up to think in outmoded categories; **~kraft** *f* mental capacity.

Denkmal [-ma:l] *nt* **-s, ¨er** *or (liter)* **-e (a)** *(Gedenkstätte)* monument, memorial (*für* to); *(Standbild)* statue ◆ **die Stadt hat ihm ein ~ gesetzt** the town put up *or* erected a memorial/statue to him; **er hat sich** *(dat)* **ein ~ gesetzt** he has left a memorial (to himself). **(b)** *(Zeugnis: literarisch etc)* monument (*gen* to).

Denkmal(s)-: ~kunde *f* study of historical monuments; **~pflege** *f* preservation of historical monuments; **~pfleger** *m* curator of monuments; **~schändung** *f* defacing a monument *no art*; **~schändungen** defacing monuments; **~schutz** *m* protection of historical monuments; **etw unter ~schutz stellen** to classify sth as a historical monument; **unter ~schutz stehen** to be listed *or* under a preservation order *or* classified as a historical monument.

Denk-: ~modell *nt (Entwurf)* plan for further discussion; *(wissenschaftlich)* working hypothesis; *(~muster)* thought pattern; **~muster** *nt* pattern of thought; **~pause** *f* break, adjournment; **eine ~pause einlegen** to have a break *or* to adjourn to think things over; ⚠**~prozeß** *m* thought-process; **~psychologie** *f* psychology of thought; **~schablone** *f (pej)* (set *or* hackneyed) thought pattern; **~schema** *nt* thought pattern; **~schrift** *f* memorandum; **~schritt** *m* step (in one's/sb's/the thinking); **~spiel** *nt* mental *or* mind game; **~sport** *m* mental exercise; **„~sport"** "puzzle corner"; **er ist ein Liebhaber des ~sports** he loves doing puzzles and brain-teasers; **~sportaufgabe** *f* brain-teaser; **~spruch** *m* motto.

denkste *interj siehe* **denken 2 (b).**

Denk-: ~system *nt* system of thought; **~übung** *f* mental exercise.

Denkungs-: ~art, ~weise *f siehe* **Denkart.**

Denk-: ~vermögen *nt* capacity for thought, intellectual capacity; **~vers** *m* mnemonic (verse); **~vorgang** *m siehe* **~prozeß; ~weise** *f siehe* **~art; d~würdig** *adj* memorable, notable; **~würdigkeit** *f* **(a)** *(von Ereignis)* memorability, notability; **(b)** *(liter: Ereignis)* memorable *or* notable event; **~zentrum** *nt* thought centre; **~zettel** *m (inf)* warning; **jdm einen ~zettel**

verpassen to give sb a warning.

denn [1] *conj* (a) (*kausal*) because, for (*esp liter*).
(b) (*geh: vergleichend*) than ◆ **schöner ~ je** more beautiful than ever.
(c) (*konzessiv*) **es sei ~, (daß)** unless; **..., du segnest mich ~** (*Bibl*) ... except thou blessest me (*obs, Bibl*); *siehe* **geschweige**.
[2] *adv* (a) (*verstärkend*) **wann/woran/wer/wie/wo ~?** when/why/who/how/where?; **ich habe ihn gestern gesehen — wo ~?** I saw him yesterday — oh, where?; **wieso ~?** why?, how come?; **warum ~ nicht?** why not?; **wie geht's ~?** how are you or things then?, how's it going then?; **wo bleibt er ~?** where has he got to?; **was soll das ~?** what's all this then?; **das ist ~ doch die Höhe!** (well,) that really is the limit!
(b) (*N Ger inf: dann*) then ◆ **na, ~ man los!** right then, let's go!; **na, ~ prost!** well, cheers (then).

dennoch *adv* nevertheless, nonetheless, still ◆ **~ liebte er sie** yet he still loved her *or* he loved her nevertheless; **er hat es ~ getan** (but *or* yet) he still did it, he did it nonetheless *or* nevertheless; **und ~, ...** and yet ...; **schön und ~ häßlich** beautiful and yet ugly.

Denominativ *nt* (*Ling*) denominative.

Denotat *nt* (*Ling*) denotation.

Denotation *f* (*Ling*) denotation.

denselben [1] *acc of* **derselbe**.
[2] *dat of* **dieselben**.

dental *adj* (*Med, Ling*) dental.

Dental(laut) *m* **-s, -e** (*Ling*) dental.

Dentist(in *f*) *m* (*dated*) dentist.

Denunziant(in *f*) *m* (*pej*) informer.

Denunziantentum *nt* (*pej*) informing.

Denunziation *f* (*pej*) informing *no pl* (*von* on, against); (*Anzeige*) denunciation (*von* of).

denunzieren* *vt* (*pej*) (a) (*verraten*) to inform on *or* against, to denounce (*bei* to). (b) (*geh: verunglimpfen*) to denounce, to condemn.

Deo *nt* **-(s), -s** *abbr of* **Deodorant**.

Deodorant *nt* **-s, -s** *or* **-e** deodorant.

Deodorantspray *nt or m* deodorant spray.

deodorierend *adj* deodorant.

Deo-: ~roller *m* roll-on (deodorant); **~spray** *nt or m siehe* **Deodorantspray**; **~stift** *m* stick deodorant.

Departement [departə'mã:] *nt* **-s, -s** (*esp Sw*) department.

Dependance [depã'dã:s] *f* **-, -n** (a) (*geh*) branch. (b) (*Hotel~*) annexe.

Dependenz *f* (*Philos*) dependence.

Dependenzgrammatik *f* dependence grammar.

Depersonalisation *f* (*Psych*) depersonalization.

Depesche *f* **-, -n** (*dated*) dispatch.

⚠**deplaciert** [depla'si:ɐt], ⚠**deplaziert** *adj* out of place.

Deponie *f* dump, disposal site.

deponieren* *vt* (*geh*) to deposit.

Deponierung *f* (*geh*) depository.

Deportation *f* deportation.

deportieren* *vt* to deport.

Deportierte(r) *mf decl as adj* deportee.

Depositar, Depositär *m* (*Fin*) depositary.

Depositen *pl* (*Fin*) deposits *pl*.

Depositen- (*Fin*): **~bank** *f* deposit bank; **~gelder** *pl* deposits *pl*, deposit(ed) money; **~geschäft** *nt* deposit banking; **~konto** *nt* deposit account.

Depot [de'po:] *nt* **-s, -s** depot; (*Aufbewahrungsort auch*) depository; (*in Bank*) strong room; (*aufbewahrte Gegenstände*) deposits *pl*; (*Schließfach*) safety deposit box; (*Med*) deposit.

Depot-: ~behandlung *f* (*Med*) depot treatment; **~fett** *nt* (*Med*) adipose fat; **~geschäft** *nt* (*Fin*) security deposit business.

Depp *m* **-en** *or* **-s, -e(n)** (*S Ger, Aus, Sw pej*) twit (*inf*).

deppert *adj* (*S Ger, Aus inf*) dopey (*inf*).

depraviert [depra'vi:ɐt] *adj* (*geh*) depraved.

Depression *f* (*alle Bedeutungen*) depression ◆ **~en haben** to suffer from depression.

depressiv *adj* depressive; (*Econ*) depressed.

Depressivität *f* depressiveness.

deprimieren* *vt* to depress.

deprimierend *adj* depressing.

deprimiert *adj* depressed.

Deprivation [depriva'tsio:n] *f* (*Psych*) deprivation.

deprivieren* [-'vi:rən] *vt* (*Psych*) to deprive.

Deputat *nt* (a) (*esp Agr*) payment in kind. (b) (*Sch*) teaching load.

Deputation *f* deputation.

deputieren* *vt* to deputize.

Deputierte(r) *mf decl as adj* deputy.

Deputiertenkammer *f* (*Pol*) Chamber of Deputies.

der[1] [1] (a) *gen of def art* **die** *sing, pl* of the ◆ **das Miauen ~ Katze** the miaowing of the cat, the cat's miaowing.
(b) *dat of def art* **die** *sing* to the; (*mit Präposition*) the.
[2] *dat of dem pron* **die** *sing* (a) (*adjektivisch*) to that; (*mit Präpositionen*) that.
(b) (*substantivisch*) to her; her.
[3] *dat of rel pron* **die** *sing* to whom, that *or* who(m) ... to; (*mit Präposition*) who(m); (*von Sachen*) to which, which ... to; which.

der[2], **die, das**, *pl* **die** [1] *def art gen* **des, der, des,** *pl* **der**; *dat* **dem, der, dem,** *pl* **den**; *acc* **den, die, das,** *pl* **die** the ◆ **der/die Arme!** the poor man/woman *or* girl!; **die Toten** the dead *pl*; **die Engländer** the English *pl*; **der Engländer** (*dated inf: die Engländer*) the Englishman; **der Hans** (*inf*)/**der Faust** Hans/Faust; **der kleine Hans** little Hans; **der Rhein** the Rhine; **der Michigansee** Lake Michigan; **die Domstraße** Cathedral Street; **die „Bismarck"** the "Bismarck"; **der Lehrer/die Frau** (*im allgemeinen*) teachers *pl*/women *pl*; **der Tod/die Liebe/das Leben** death/love/life; **der Tod des Sokrates** the death of Socrates; **das Viktorianische England** Victorian England; **in dem England, das ich kannte** in the England (that *or* which) I knew; **er liebt den Jazz/die Oper/das Kino** he likes jazz/(the) opera/the cinema; **das Singen macht ihm Freude** singing gives him pleasure; **das Singen meines Opas** my grandpa's singing; **mir fiel das Atmen schwer** I found breathing difficult; **das Herstellen von Waffen ist ...** manufacturing weapons is ..., the manufacturing of weapons is ...; **die Callas** Callas; **der spätere Wittgenstein** the later Wittgenstein; **er war nicht mehr der Hans, den ...** he was no longer the Hans who ...; **er hat sich den Fuß verletzt** he has hurt his foot; **wascht euch** (*dat*) **mal das Gesicht!** wash your face; **er nimmt den Hut ab** he takes his hat off; **eine Mark das Stück** one mark apiece *or* each; **10 Mark die Stunde** 10 marks an *or* per hour; **der und der Wissenschaftler** such and such a scientist.
[2] *dem pron gen* **dessen** *or* (*old*) **des, deren, dessen,** *pl* **deren**; *dat* **dem, der, dem,** *pl* **denen**; *acc* **den, die, das,** *pl* **die** (a) (*attr*) (*jener, dieser*) that; *pl* those, them (*inf*) ◆ **zu der und der Zeit** at such and such a time; **an dem und dem Ort** at such and such a place.
(b) (*substantivisch*) he/she/it; *pl* those, them (*inf*) ◆ **der/die war es** it was him/her; **der/die mit der großen Nase** the one *or* him/her (*inf*) with the big nose; **die** (*pl*) **mit den roten Haaren** those *or* them (*inf*) with red hair; **deine Schwester, die war nicht da** (*inf*) your sister, she wasn't there; **der und schwimmen?** him, swimming?, swimming?, (what) him?; **der/die hier/da** (*von Menschen*) he/she, this/that man/woman *etc*; (*von Gegenständen*) this/that (one); (*von mehreren*) this one/that one; **die hier/da** *pl* they, these/those men/women *etc*; these/those, them (*inf*); **der, den ich meine** the one I mean; **der und der/die und die** so-and-so; **das und das** such and such.
[3] *rel pron* (*decl as* [2]) (*Mensch*) who, that; (*Gegenstand, Tier*) which, that.
[4] *rel +dem pron* (*decl as* [2]) **der/die dafür verantwortlich war, ...** the man/woman who was responsible for it; **die so etwas tun, ...** those *or* people who do that sort of thing ...

der|art *adv* (a) (*Art und Weise*) in such a way ◆ **er hat sich ~ benommen, daß ...** he behaved so badly that ...; **sein Benehmen war ~, daß ...** his behaviour was so bad that ...; **~ vorbereitet, ...** thus prepared ...
(b) (*Ausmaß*) (*vor adj*) so; (*vor vb*) so much, to such an extent ◆ **ein ~ unzuverlässiger Mensch** such an unreliable person, so unreliable a person; **er hat mich ~ geärgert, daß ...** he annoyed me so much that ...; **es hat ~ geregnet, daß ...** it rained so much that ...

der|artig [1] *adj* such, of that kind ◆ **bei ~en Versuchen** in such experiments, in experiments of that kind; **(etwas) D~es** something like that *or* of the kind.
[2] *adv siehe* **derart**.

derb *adj* (a) (*kräftig*) strong; *Stoff, Leder auch* tough; *Schuhe auch* stout; *Kost* coarse ◆ **jdn ~ anfassen** to manhandle sb; (*fig*) to be rough with sb.
(b) (*grob*) coarse; *Manieren, Kerl auch* uncouth; *Witz, Sprache, Ausdrucksweise auch* earthy, crude (*pej*) ◆ **um mich einmal ~ auszudrücken ...** to put it crudely ...
(c) (*unfreundlich*) gruff.

Derbheit *f siehe adj* (a) strength; toughness; stoutness; coarseness. (b) coarseness; uncouthness; earthiness, crudeness ◆ **~en** crudities. (c) gruffness.

Derby ['dɛrbi] *nt* **-s, -s** horse-race for three-year-olds, derby (*US*); (*fig: sportliche Begegnung*) derby ◆ **das (englische) ~** the Derby.

Derbyrennen *nt siehe* **Derby**.

Deregulierung *f* deregulation.

der|einst *adv* (*liter*) (a) (*in der Zukunft*) one day. (b) (*rare: früher*) at one time, once.

der|einstig *adj* (*liter*) (a) (*künftig*) future, tomorrow's ◆ **im ~en vereinten Europa** in tomorrow's united Europe, in the united Europe of tomorrow.
(b) (*damalig*) of former times.

deren [1] *gen pl of dem pron* **der, die, das** their.
[2] (a) *gen sing of rel pron* **die** whose. (b) *gen pl of rel pron* **der, die, das** whose, of whom; (*von Sachen*) of which.

derent-: ~halben (*dated*), **~wegen** *adv* (*weswegen*) because of whom, on whose account; (*von Sachen*) because of which, on account of which; (*welcher zuliebe auch*) for whose sake; for the sake of which; (*um welche*) about whom; (*von Sachen*) about which; (*für welche*) on whose behalf; **~willen** *adv* **um ~willen** (a) (*rel*) for whose sake; (*von Sachen*) for the sake of which; (b) (*dem*) *sing* for her/its sake; *pl* for their sake.

derer *gen pl of dem pron* **der, die, das** of those ◆ **das Geschlecht ~ von Hohenstein** (*geh*) the von Hohenstein family.

deret- *in cpds siehe* **derent-**.

dergestalt *adv* (*geh*) in such a way; (*Ausmaß*) so much; to such an extent ◆ **~ ausgerüstet, ...** thus equipped ...; **dann gab er dem Pferde die Sporen ~, daß ...** then he spurred his horse on so forcefully that ...

dergleichen *inv* [1] *dem pron* (a) (*adjektivisch*) of that kind, such, like that ◆ **~ Dinge** things of that kind *or* like that, such things.
(b) (*substantivisch*) that sort of thing ◆ **nichts ~** nothing of that kind *or* like it; **er tat nichts ~** he did nothing of the kind; **und ~ (mehr)** and suchlike.
[2] *rel pron* (*old*) of the kind that ◆ **Juwelen, ~ man selten sieht** jewels whose

like *or* the like of which one rarely sees.

Derivat [-'vaːt] *nt* (*Chem, Ling*) derivative.

Derivation [-va'tsioːn] *f* (*Ling*) derivation.

Derivativ *nt* (*Ling*) derivative.

derjenige, diejenige, dasjenige, *pl* **diejenigen** *dem pron* **(a)** (*substantivisch*) the one; *pl* those ◆ **sie ist immer diejenige, welche** (*inf*) it's always her; **du warst also derjenige, welcher!** (*inf*) so it was you!, so you're the one! **(b)** (*adjektivisch*) the; *pl* those.

derlei *dem pron inv* **(a)** (*adjektivisch*) such, like that, that kind of ◆ **~ Probleme** problems like that, that kind of *or* such problems. **(b)** (*substantivisch*) that sort *or* kind of thing ◆ **und ~ (mehr)** and suchlike.

dermalen *adv* (*old, Aus form*) presently, at present, now.

dermalig *adj* (*old, Aus form*) present, actual.

dermaßen *adv* (*mit adj*) so; (*mit vb*) so much ◆ **~ dumm** so stupid; **ein ~ dummer Kerl** such a stupid fellow; **sie hatte ~ Angst, daß** ... she was so afraid that ...; **er hat sich geärgert, und zwar ~, daß** ... he was angry, so much so that ...

Dermato-: ~loge *m*, **~login** *f* dermatologist; **~logie** *f* dermatology; **~plastik** *f* plastic surgery, dermatoplasty (*spec*).

Dernier cri [dɛrnje'kri] *m* - -, **-s -s** dernier cri.

dero *poss pron* (*obs*) her; *pl* their ◆ **D~ Gnaden** Your Grace.

derselbe, dieselbe, dasselbe, *pl* **dieselben** *dem pron.* **(a)** (*substantivisch*) the same; (*old: er, sie, es*) he/she/it; (*inf: der, die, das gleiche*) the same ◆ **er sagt in jeder Vorlesung dasselbe** he says the same (thing) in every lecture; **jedes Jahr kriegen dieselben mehr Geld** every year the same people get more money; **sie/er ist immer noch ganz dieselbe/derselbe** she/he is still exactly the same; **es sind immer dieselben** it's always the same ones *or* people; **noch mal dasselbe, bitte!** (*inf*) same again, please. **(b)** (*adjektivisch*) the same ◆ **ein und derselbe Mensch** one and the same person.

derselbige *etc dem pron* (*old*) *siehe* **derselbe** *etc.*

derweil(en) **1** *adv* in the meantime, meanwhile. **2** *conj* (*old*) whilst, while.

Derwisch *m* **-es, -e** dervish.

derzeit *adv* **(a)** (*jetzt*) at present, at the moment. **(b)** (*dated: damals*) at that *or* the time, then.

derzeitig *adj attr* **(a)** (*jetzig*) present, current. **(b)** (*dated: damalig*) of that *or* the time.

des¹ (a) *gen of def art* **der, das** of the ◆ **das Bellen ~ Hundes** the barking of the dog, the dog's barking. **(b)** (*old*) *siehe* **dessen.**

des², Des *nt* **-,** *no pl* (*Mus*) D flat.

Desaster [de'zastɐ] *nt* **-s,** - disaster.

desavouieren* [dɛs|avu'iːrən] *vt* (*geh*) to disavow; *Bemühungen, Pläne* to compromise.

Desensibilisator *m* (*Phot*) desensitizer.

desensibilisieren* *vt* (*Phot, Med*) to desensitize.

Deserteur(in *f*) [-'tøːɐ, -'tøːrɪn] *m* (*Mil, fig*) deserter.

desertieren* *vi aux sein or* (*rare*) *haben* (*Mil, fig*) to desert.

Desertion *f* (*Mil, fig*) desertion.

desgleichen **1** *adv* (*ebenso*) likewise, also ◆ **er ist Vegetarier, ~ seine Frau** he is a vegetarian, as is his wife. **2** *dem pron inv* (*old: dasselbe*) the same ◆ **~ habe ich noch nie gehört** I have never heard the like. **3** *rel pron inv* (*old*) the like of which.

deshalb *adv, conj* therefore; (*aus diesem Grunde, darüber*) because of that; (*dafür*) for that ◆ **es ist schon spät, ~ wollen wir anfangen** it is late, so let us start; **~ bin ich hergekommen** that is what I came here for, that is why I came here; **ich bin ~ hergekommen, weil ich dich sprechen wollte** what I came here for was to speak to you, the reason I came here was that I wanted to speak to you; **~ also!** so that's why *or* the reason!; **~ muß er nicht dumm sein** that does not (necessarily) mean (to say) he is stupid; **~ frage ich ja** that's exactly why I'm asking.

desiderabel *adj* (*geh*) desirable.

Desiderat *nt*, **Desideratum** *nt* **-s, Desiderata** desideratum; (*Anschaffungsvorschlag*) suggestion.

Design [di'zaɪn] *nt* **-s, -s** design.

Designat [dezɪ'gnaːt] *nt* (*Philos, Ling*) referendum.

Designation [dezɪgna'tsioːn] *f* designation.

Designator [dezi'gnaːtɔr] *m* (*Philos, Ling*) referens.

designen* [di'zaɪnən] to design.

Designer(in *f*) [di'zaɪnɐ, -ərɪn] *m* **-s,** - designer.

Designer-: ~droge *f* designer drug; **~-Jeans** *pl* designer jeans *pl*; **~-Mode** *f* designer fashion.

designieren* [dezɪ'gniːrən] *vt* to designate (*jdn zu etw* sb as sth).

designiert [dezɪ'gniːɐt] *adj attr* **der ~e Vorsitzende** the chairman elect *or* designate.

des|illusionieren* *vt* to disillusion.

Des|illusionierung *f* disillusionment.

Des|infektion *f* disinfection.

Des|infektions-: ~lösung *f* antiseptic solution; **~mittel** *nt* disinfectant.

des|infizieren* *vt Zimmer, Bett etc* to disinfect; *Spritze, Gefäß etc* to sterilize.

Des|infizierung *f siehe vt* disinfection; sterilization.

Des|information *f* (*Pol*) disinformation *no pl.*

Des|informationskampagne *f* campaign of disinformation.

Des|integration *f* (*Sociol, Psych*) disintegration.

Des|interesse *nt* lack of interest (*an +dat* in).

des|interessiert *adj* uninterested; *Gesicht* bored.

Deskription *f* (*geh*) description.

deskriptiv *adj* descriptive.

Desktop Publishing ['dɛsktɔp 'pablɪʃɪŋ] *nt* **-,** *no pl* desktop publishing, DTP.

Desodorant *nt* **-s, -s** *or* **-e** *siehe* **Deodorant.**

desolat *adj* (*geh*) desolate; *Zustand, wirtschaftliche Lage* desperate.

Des|organisation *f* disorganization; (*Auflösung auch*) disruption ◆ **auf der Tagung herrschte eine völlige ~** there was complete chaos at the conference.

des|organisieren* *vt* to disorganize.

des|orientieren* *vt* to disorient(ate).

Des|orientiertheit, Des|orientierung *f* disorientation.

Desoxyribonukleinsäure *f* (*abbr* **DNS**) deoxyribonucleic acid, DNA.

despektierlich [despɛk'tiːɐlɪç] *adj* (*old, hum*) disrespectful.

Desperado [dɛspe'raːdo] *m* **-s, -s** desperado.

desperat [dɛspe'raːt] *adj* (*geh*) desperate.

Despot [dɛs'poːt] *m* **-en, -en** despot.

Despotie [dɛspo'tiː] *f* despotism.

despotisch [dɛs'poːtɪʃ] *adj* despotic.

Despotismus [dɛspo-] *m, no pl* despotism.

desselben *gen of* **derselbe, dasselbe.**

dessen **1** *gen of dem pron* **der², das** his; (*von Sachen, Tieren*) its. **2** *gen of rel pron* **der², das** whose; (*von Sachen*) of which, which ... of.

dessent-: ~halben (*dated*), **~wegen** *siehe* **derenthalben** *etc*; **~willen** *adv*: **um ~willen (a)** (*rel*) for whose sake; **(b)** (*dem*) for his/its sake.

⚠ **des(sen)|unge|achtet** *adv* (*geh*) nevertheless, notwithstanding (this).

Dessert [de'seːɐ] *nt* **-s, -s** dessert.

Dessert-: *in cpds* dessert.

Dessin [dɛ'sɛ̃ː] *nt* **-s, -s** (*Tex*) pattern, design.

Dessous [dɛ'suː] *nt* **-, -** [dɛ'suːs] *usu pl* (*dated*) undergarment, underwear *no pl.*

destabilisieren* *vt* to destabilize.

Destabilisierung *f* destabilization.

Destillat [dɛstɪ'laːt] *nt* (*Chem*) distillation, distillate; (*fig*) distillation.

Destillateur [dɛstɪla'tøːɐ] *m* distiller.

Destillation [dɛstɪla'tsioːn] *f* **(a)** (*Chem*) distillation. **(b)** (*Branntweinbrennerei*) distillery. **(c)** (*dated dial: Großgaststätte*) drinking establishment, ≃ gin palace (*old*), brandy shop (*old*).

Destillations-: ~anlage *f* distilling *or* distillation plant; **~produkt** *nt* distillate.

Destille [dɛs'tɪlə] *f* **-, -n (a)** (*dial inf: Gaststätte*) (big) pub (*Brit*), bar. **(b)** (*Brennerei*) distillery.

destillieren* [dɛstɪ'liːrən] *vt* to distil; (*fig*) to condense.

Destillierkolben [dɛstɪ'liːɐ-] *m* (*Chem*) retort.

desto *conj* **~ mehr/besser** all the more/better; **~ grausamer/schneller** all the more cruel/all the faster; **~ wahrscheinlicher ist es, daß wir** ... that makes it all the more probable that we ...; *siehe* **je.**

Destruktion [dɛstrʊk'tsioːn] *f* destruction.

Destruktionstrieb *m* (*Psych*) destructive instinct.

destruktiv [dɛstrʊk'tiːf] *adj* destructive.

Destruktivität *f* destructiveness.

⚠ **des|unge|achtet** *adv* (*old*) *siehe* **des(sen)ungeachtet.**

deswegen *adv siehe* **deshalb.**

deszendent *adj* (*Astron*) descendent (*spec*), setting.

Deszendent *m* **im ~en sein** (*Astrol*) to be in the descendent.

Deszendenz *f* **(a)** (*Abstammung*) descent; (*Nachkommenschaft*) descendants *pl.* **(b)** (*Astron*) descendence (*spec*), setting.

Deszendenztheorie *f* (*Biol*) theory of evolution.

deszendieren* *vi aux sein* (*Astron, liter*) to descend.

Detail [de'tai, de'taj] *nt* **-s, -s** detail; (*Filmeinstellung*) big close-up ◆ **ins ~ gehen** to go into detail(s); **im ~** in detail; **bis ins kleinste ~** (right) down to the smallest *or* last detail; **in allen ~s** in the greatest detail; **etw mit allen ~s berichten** to report sth in full detail, to give a fully detailed account of sth; **die Schwierigkeiten liegen im ~** it is the details that are most difficult.

Detail-: ~bericht *m* detailed report; **~frage** *f* question of detail; **~handel** *m* (*dated*) *siehe* **Einzelhandel**; **~händler** *m* (*dated*) *siehe* **Einzelhändler**; **~kenntnisse** *pl* detailed knowledge *no pl.*

detaillieren* [deta'jiːrən] *vt* (*genau beschreiben*) to specify, to give full particulars of ◆ **etw genauer ~** to specify sth more precisely.

detailliert [deta'jiːɐt] *adj* detailed.

Detailliertheit *f* detail.

Detail-: d~reich *adj* fully detailed; **etw d~reich schildern** to describe sth in great detail; **~schilderung** *f* detailed account; **die beiden Versionen unterscheiden sich in der ~schilderung** the two versions differ in their account of the details; **~verkauf** *m* (*dated Comm*) *siehe* **Einzelverkauf**; **~zeichnung** *f* detail drawing.

Detektei *f* (private) detective agency, firm of (private) investigators ◆ **„~ R.B. von Halske"** "R.B. von Halske, private investigator".

Detektiv(in *f*) *m* private investigator *or* detective *or* eye (*inf*).

Detektivbüro *nt siehe* **Detektei.**

detektivisch *adj* **in ~er Kleinarbeit** with detailed detection work; **bei etw ~ vorgehen** to go about sth like a detective.

Detektivroman *m* detective novel.

⚠: Informationen zur Rechtschreibreform im Anhang

Detektor *m (Tech)* detector.

Detektor|empfänger *m (Rad)* crystal set.

Détente [de'tã:t] *f -, no pl (rare) (Pol)* détente.

Determinante *f -, -n (Math, Biol)* determinant.

determinieren* *vt* to (pre)determine; *(Gram)* to govern.

Determinismus *m, no pl (Philos)* determinism.

Determinist(in *f***)** *m (Philos)* determinist.

deterministisch *adj (Philos)* deterministic.

Detonation *f* explosion, blast ◆ **etw** *(acc)* **zur ~ bringen** to detonate sth.

detonieren* *vi aux sein* to explode, to go off.

Deubel *m* **-s, -** *(dial) siehe* **Teufel.**

deucht *3rd pers sing of* **dünken.**

Deus ex machina ['de:ʊs ɛks 'maxina] *m* **- - -, Dei - -** *(rare)* deus ex machina.

Deut *m* **um keinen ~** not one iota *or* jot; **seine Ratschläge sind keinen ~ wert** his advice is not worth tuppence; **er versteht nicht einen ~ davon** he does not know the first thing about it; **daran ist kein ~ wahr** there is not a grain of truth in it; **du bist keinen ~ besser** you're not one jot *or* iota *or* whit better.

deutbar *adj* interpretable ◆ **..., ob Nietzsche theologisch ~ ist ...** whether Nietzsche can be interpreted *or* understood theologically; **nicht/schwer ~** impossible/difficult to interpret; **es ist nicht anders ~** it cannot be explained in any other way.

Deutelei *f (pej geh)* quibbling, quibbles *pl*, cavilling.

deuteln *vi (geh)* to quibble, to cavil ◆ **an jedem Wort ~** to quibble over every word; **daran gibt es nichts zu ~!** there are no ifs and buts about it!

deuten [1] *vt (auslegen)* to interpret; *Zukunft auch* to read ◆ **sich** *(dat)* **etw ~** *(geh)* to understand sth; **etw falsch ~** to misinterpret sth.
[2] *vi* **(a)** *(zeigen)* **(mit dem Finger) auf etw** *(acc)* **~** to point (one's finger) at sth.
(b) *(fig: hinweisen)* to indicate ◆ **alles deutet auf Regen/Schnee** all the signs are that it is going to rain/snow, everything points to rain/snow; **alles deutet darauf, daß ...** all the indications are that ..., everything indicates that ...

Deuter *m* **-s, - (a)** interpreter. **(b)** *(Aus: Wink)* sign.

deutlich *adj* **(a)** *(klar)* clear ◆ **~ erkennbar/sichtbar/hörbar/wahrnehmbar** clearly *or* plainly recognizable/visible/audible/perceptible; **~ sehen** to see clearly; **~ fühlen** to feel distinctly; **ich fühle ~, daß ...** I have the distinct feeling ...; **~ unterscheiden** to distinguish clearly; **~ sprechen** to speak clearly.
(b) *(unmißverständlich)* clear, plain ◆ **jdm etw ~ vor Augen führen** to make sth perfectly clear *or* plain to sb; **eine ~e Sprache mit jdm reden** to speak plainly *or* bluntly with sb; **sich ~ ausdrücken, ~ werden** to make oneself clear *or* plain; **das war ~!** *(taktlos)* that was clear *or* plain enough; **muß ich ~er werden?** have I not made myself clear *or* plain enough?; **ich muß es einmal ~ sagen** let me make myself clear *or* plain; **jdm ~ zu verstehen geben, daß** to make it clear *or* plain to sb that.

Deutlichkeit *f* clarity ◆ **etw mit aller ~ sagen** to make sth perfectly clear *or* plain; **seine Antwort ließ an ~ nichts zu wünschen übrig** his answer was perfectly clear *or* plain and left no possible doubt.

deutlichkeitshalber *adv* for the sake of clarity.

deutsch *adj* **(a)** German ◆ **~e Schrift** Gothic script; **~er Schäferhund** Alsatian *(Brit)*, German shepherd; **~e Gründlichkeit** *etc* German *or* Teutonic efficiency *etc*; **die D~e Bucht** the German Bight; **D~e Mark** deutschmark, German mark; **der D~e Orden** *(Hist)* the Teutonic Order (of Knights).
(b) *(in bezug auf Sprache)* German ◆ **er hat ~, nicht englisch gesprochen** he spoke German not English; **sich (auf) ~ unterhalten** to speak (in) German; **auf** *or* **zu ~ heißt das ...** in German it means ...; **der Text ist (in) ~ geschrieben** the text is written in German; **der Vortrag wird in** *or* **auf ~ gehalten** the lecture will be given in German; **etw ~ aussprechen** to pronounce sth in a German(ic) way, to give sth a German pronunciation; **~ denken** to think in German; **mit jdm ~ reden** *(fig inf: deutlich)* to speak bluntly with sb; **auf gut ~ (gesagt)** *(fig inf)* in plain English.

Deutsch *nt* **-(s),** *dat* **-,** *no pl* German ◆ **das ~ Thomas Manns** Thomas Mann's German; **gut(es) ~ sprechen** to speak good German; *(Ausländer auch)* to speak German well; **~ lernen/verstehen** to learn/understand German; **der Unterricht/die Schulnote in ~** German lessons *pl*/school mark in *or* for German; *siehe auch* **deutsch (b).**

Deutsch-: ~amerikaner *m* German American; **d~amerikanisch** *adj* German-American; **d~-d~** *adj* intra-German.

Deutsch(e) *nt* **-n,** *dat* **-n,** *no pl* **(a)** *(Sprache)* German ◆ **aus dem ~en/ins ~e übersetzt** translated from the/into (the) German; **das ~ des Mittelalters** medieval German, the German of the Middle Ages; **die Aussprache des ~en** the pronunciation of German, German pronunciation.
(b) *(Charakteristik)* Germanness ◆ **manchmal kommt noch das ~e in ihm durch** sometimes the German in him *or* his Germanness shows through.

Deutsche Demokratische Republik *f (abbr* **DDR***)* German Democratic Republic, East Germany *no art*, GDR.

Deutschen-: ~feind, ~fresser *(inf) m* anti-German, Germanophobe; **~freund** *m* Germanophile.

deutsch-|englisch *adj* **(a)** *(Pol)* Anglo-German. **(b)** *(Ling)* German-English.

Deutschen-: ⚠~haß *m* Germanophobia; **~hasser** *m* **-s, -** Germanophobe, German-hater.

Deutsche(r) *mf decl as adj* **er ist ~r** he is (a) German; **die ~n** the Germans.

Deutsch-: d~feindlich *adj* anti-German, Germanophobic; **~feindlichkeit** *f* Germanophobia; **d~-französisch** *adj* **(a)** *(Pol)* Franco-German; **der D~-Französische Krieg** the Franco-Prussian war; **(b)** *(Ling)* German-French; **d~freundlich** *adj* pro-German, Germanophile; **~freundlichkeit** *f* Germanophilia; **d~gesinnt** *adj* **d~gesinnt sein** to feel oneself to be German, to think of oneself as being German; **~herren** *pl (Hist)* Teutonic Knights *pl*; **~herrenorden** *m (Hist)* Teutonic Order of Knights.

Deutschland *nt* **-s** Germany ◆ **die beiden ~(s)** the two Germanys.

Deutschland-: ~frage *f (Pol)* German question; **~lied** *nt* (West) German national anthem; **~politik** *f* home *or* domestic policy; *(von fremdem Staat)* policy on *or* towards Germany; **~tournee** *f* tour of Germany.

Deutsch-: ~lehrer *m* German teacher; **d~national** *adj (Hist)* German National; **~ordensritter** *m (Hist)* Teutonic Knight; **~ritterorden** *m (Hist) siehe* **~herrenorden**; **~schweiz** *f* **die ~schweiz** German-speaking Switzerland; **~schweizer** *m* German Swiss; **d~schweizerisch** *adj* German-Swiss; **d~sprachig** *adj Bevölkerung, Gebiete* German-speaking; *Zeitung, Ausgabe* German language; *Literatur* German; **d~sprachlich** *adj* German(-language); **~sprechen** *nt* speaking German; **⚠d~sprechend** *adj* German-speaking; **d~stämmig** *adj* of German origin *or* stock; **~stämmige(r)** *mf decl as adj* ethnic German; **~stunde** *f* German lesson; **~tum** *nt, no pl* Germanness; *(die ~en)* Germans *pl*; **~tümelei** *f (pej)* hyper-Germanness.

Deutung *f* interpretation ◆ **eine falsche ~** a misinterpretation.

Deutungsversuch *m* attempt at an interpretation ◆ **er unternimmt einen neuen ~ des ...** he attempts a new interpretation of ...

Devise [de'vi:zə] *f* **-, -n (a)** *(Wahlspruch)* maxim, motto; *(Her auch)* device. **(b)** *(Fin)* **~n** *pl* foreign exchange *or* currency.

Devisen-: ~abkommen *nt* foreign exchange agreement; **~ausgleich** *m* foreign exchange offset; **~beschränkungen** *pl* foreign exchange restrictions *pl*; **~bestimmungen** *pl* foreign exchange control regulations *pl*; **~bewirtschaftung** *f* foreign exchange control; **~bilanz** *f* foreign exchange balance; **~börse** *f* foreign exchange market; **~bringer** *m* **-s, -** bringer *or (Geschäft etc)* earner of foreign exchange *or* currency; **~geschäft** *nt* foreign exchange dealing; **~handel** *m* foreign currency *or* exchange dealings *pl*, sale and purchase of currencies; **~knappheit** *f* shortage of foreign exchange; **~kurs** *m* exchange rate, rate of exchange; **~markt** *m* foreign exchange market; **~politik** *f* foreign exchange policy; **~schmuggel** *m* currency smuggling; **d~schwach** *adj* **d~schwache Länder** countries with limited foreign currency reserves; **~termingeschäft** *nt* forward exchange; **~vergehen** *nt* breach of exchange control regulations; **~vorschriften** *pl siehe* **~bestimmungen.**

devot [de'vo:t] *adj (geh)* **(a)** *(pej: unterwürfig)* obsequious. **(b)** *(old: demütig)* humble.

Devotion [devo'tsio:n] *f siehe adj (geh)* **(a)** obsequiousness. **(b)** humility.

Devotionalien [devotsio'na:liən] *pl* devotional objects *pl*.

Dextrose *f* **-,** *no pl (Chem)* dextrose.

Dez *m* **-es, -e** *(dial inf)* bonce *(inf)*.

Dezember *m* **-s, -** December; *siehe auch* **März.**

Dezennium *nt (geh)* decade, decennium *(form)*.

dezent *adj* discreet.

dezentral *adj* decentralized.

Dezentralisation *f* decentralization.

dezentralisieren* *vt* to decentralize.

Dezentralisierung *f siehe* **Dezentralisation.**

Dezenz *f, no pl (geh)* **(a)** *(old: Anstand)* sense of decency. **(b)** *(von Geschmack, Kleidung etc)* discreetness; *(von Benehmen auch)* discretion.

Dezernat *nt (Admin)* department.

Dezernent(in *f***)** *m (Admin)* head of department.

Dezibel ['de:tsibɛl, -'bɛl] *nt* **-s, -** *(Phys)* decibel.

dezidiert *adj (geh)* firm, determined.

Dezi- [*(esp Aus)* 'de:tsi-]: **~gramm** *nt* decigram(me); **~liter** *m or nt* decilitre.

dezimal *adj* decimal.

Dezimalbruch *m* decimal fraction.

Dezimale *f* decimal.

dezimalisieren* *vt* to decimalize ◆ **als in Großbritannien dezimalisiert wurde** when Great Britain went decimal.

Dezimalisierung *f* decimalization.

Dezimal-: ~klassifikation *f* decimal classification; **~maß** *nt* decimal measure; **~rechnung** *f* decimals *pl*; **~stelle** *f* decimal place; **auf zwei ~stellen genau** correct to two decimal places; **~system** *nt* decimal system; **~waage** *f* decimal balance; **~zahl** *f* decimal number.

Dezime *f* **-, -n** *(Mus)* tenth.

Dezimeter *m or nt* decimetre.

dezimieren* *(fig)* [1] *vt* to decimate.
[2] *vr* to be decimated.

Dezimierung *f (fig)* decimation.

DFB [de:|ɛf'be:] *m* **-s** *abbr of* **Deutscher Fußball-Bund** German Football Association.

DFÜ [de:|ɛf'|y:] **-** *abbr of* **Datenfernübertragung.**

DGB [de:ge:'be:] *m* **-s** *abbr of* **Deutscher Gewerkschaftsbund** Federation of German Trade Unions.

dgl. *abbr of* **dergleichen, desgleichen** the like.

d. Gr. *abbr of* **der Große.**

d.h. *abbr of* **das heißt** i.e.

d.i. *abbr of* **das ist** i.e.

Dia *nt* **-s, -s** (*Phot*) slide, transparency.
Diabetes [dia'beːtɛs] *m* **-,** *no pl* diabetes.
Diabetiker- *in cpds* diabetic.
Diabetiker(in *f*) *m* **-s, -** diabetic.
diabetisch *adj* diabetic.
Diabetrachter *m* slide viewer.
Diabolik *f* (*geh*) diabolicalness, fiendishness.
diabolisch *adj* (*geh*) diabolical, fiendish.
Diachronie [diakro'niː] *f* (*Ling*) diachrony.
diachron(isch) [-kr-] *adj* (*Ling*) diachronic.
Diadem *nt* **-s, -e** diadem.
Diadochen *pl* (*Hist*) diadochi *pl*; (*fig*) rivals *pl* in a power struggle.
Diadochenkämpfe *pl* (*fig*) power struggle.
Diagnose *f* **-, -n** diagnosis ◆ **eine ~ stellen** to make a diagnosis.
Diagnose-: ~stand *m* diagnostic test bay; **~verfahren** *nt* diagnostic method, method of diagnosis; **~zentrum** *nt* diagnostic centre.
Diagnostik *f* diagnosis.
Diagnostiker(in *f*) *m* **-s, -** diagnostician.
diagnostisch *adj* diagnostic.
diagnostizieren* *vti* (*Med, fig*) to diagnose ◆ **(auf) etw** (*acc*) **~** to diagnose sth.
diagonal *adj* diagonal ◆ **ein Buch ~ lesen** (*inf*) to skim *or* flick through a book.
Diagonale *f* **-, -n** diagonal.
Diagonalreifen *m* (*Aut*) cross-ply (tyre).
Diagramm *nt* **-s, -e** diagram.
Diagramm-: ~form *f* **in ~form** diagrammatically; **~papier** *nt* graph paper.
Diakon [dia'koːn, (*Aus*) 'diːakoːn] *m* **-s** *or* **-en, -e(n)** (*Eccl*) deacon.
Diakonat *nt* (*Eccl*) **(a)** (*Amt*) deaconry, deaconship, diaconate. **(b)** (*Wohnung*) deacon's house.
Diakonie *f* (*Eccl*) social welfare work.
Diakonisse *f* **-, -n, Diakonissin** *f* (*Eccl*) deaconess.
diakritisch *adj* diacritic ◆ **~e Zeichen** diacritics, diacritic(al) marks *or* signs.
Dialekt *m* **-(e)s, -e** dialect.
dialektal *adj* dialectal.
Dialekt- *in cpds* dialect; **~färbung** *f* accent, dialect features *pl*; **~forscher** *m* dialectologist, dialectician; **~forschung** *f* dialect research, dialectology; **d~frei** *adj* accent-free, without an accent, without a trace of dialect.
Dialektik *f* (*Philos*) dialectics *sing or pl*.
Dialektiker(in *f*) *m* **-s, -** (*Philos*) dialectician.
dialektisch *adj* **(a)** (*Philos*) dialectic(al) ◆ **~er Materialismus** dialectical materialism. **(b)** (*Ling*) *siehe* **dialektal**.
Dialektismus *m* (*Ling*) dialecticism.
Dialog *m* **-(e)s, -e** dialogue, dialog (*US also*).
Dialog-: ~autor *m* (*Film*) script-writer; **~betrieb** *m* (*Comput*) conversation mode; **~fähig** *adj* (*Comput*) **~fähig sein** to be capable of two-way communication; **~form** *f* dialogue form.
dialogisch *adj* dialogue *attr*.
Dialog-: ~regie *f* (*Film*) script supervision; **~stück** *nt* (*Theat*) dialogue play.
Dialyse *f* **-, -n** (*Med*) dialysis.
Diamant[1] *m* **-en, -en** diamond.
Diamant[2] *f* **-,** *no pl* (*Typ*) four-point, diamond (4½ *point*).
diamantbesetzt *adj attr* diamond-studded.
diamanten *adj attr* diamond ◆ **von ~er Härte** as hard as diamond; **~er Glanz** adamantine lustre (*liter*).
Diamant-: ~nadel *f* **(a)** diamond brooch; **(b)** (*an Tonarm*) diamond (stylus); **~schleifer** *m* diamond polisher; **~schliff** *m* diamond polishing; **~schmuck** *m* diamonds *pl*, diamond jewellery; **~stahl** *m* diamond plate; **~staub** *m* diamond dust.
Diameter *m* **-s, -** (*Geom*) diameter.
diametral *adj* diametral; (*fig*) *Ansichten* diametrically opposed ◆ **~ entgegengesetzt sein, sich ~ gegenüberliegen** to be diametrically opposite; **~ entgegengesetzt** (*fig*) diametrically opposed.
Diana *f* **-s** (*Myth*) Diana.
Diaphragma [dia'fragma] *nt* **-s, Diaphragmen** (*Tech, Med*) diaphragm.
Dia- (*Phot*): **~positiv** *nt* slide, transparency; **~projektor** *m* slide projector; **~rahmen** *m* slide frame.
⚠ **Diarrhö(e)** [dia'røː] *f* **-, -en** (*Med*) diarrhoea.
Diaspora *f* **-,** *no pl* (*Eccl*) diaspora.
Diastole [di'astole, dia'stoːlə] *f* **-, -n** (*Med*) diastole.
diastolisch *adj* diastolic.
⚠ **diät** *adv kochen, essen* according to a diet; *leben* on a special diet.
Diät *f* **-, -en** (*Med*) diet ◆ **~ halten** to keep to *or* observe a strict diet; **nach einer ~ leben** to be on a diet *or* (*wegen Krankheit*) special diet; **jdn auf ~ setzen** (*inf*) to put sb on a diet.
Diät-: ~assistent *m* dietician; **~bier** *nt* diabetic beer.
Diäten *pl* (*Parl*) parliamentary allowance.
Diätetik *f* dietetics *sing*.
diätetisch *adj* dietetic.
Diätfahrplan *m* (*hum*) dieting course *or* schedule.
Diathek *f* slide collection *or* library.
Diätist(in *f*) *m* dietician.
Diät-: ~kost *f* dietary foods *pl*; **~kost bekommen** to be on a special diet; **~kur** *f* dietary *or* dietetic treatment.

Diatonik *f* (*Mus*) diatonicism.
diatonisch *adj* (*Mus*) diatonic.
Diavortrag *m* slide presentation.
dich [1] *pers pron acc of* **du** you; (*obs, dial*) thee.
[2] *refl pron* yourself ◆ **wie fühlst du ~?** how do you feel?
Dichotomie *f* dichotomy.
dicht [1] *adj* **(a)** *Gefieder, Haar, Hecke* thick; *Laub, Nebel auch, Wald, (Menschen)menge, Gewühl* dense; *Verkehr auch* heavy, dense; *Gewebe* close; *Stoff* closely-woven; (*fig: konzentriert*) *Stil* dense; *Szene* full, compact ◆ **in ~er Folge** in rapid *or* quick succession; **sie standen in ~en Reihen** they were standing row upon row close together.
(b) (*undurchlässig*) watertight; airtight; *Vorhänge* thick, heavy; *Rolladen* heavy ◆ **~ machen** to seal, to make watertight/airtight; *Fenster* to seal; **~ halten** to be watertight; **~ schließen** to shut tightly; **~ verhängen** to curtain heavily; **er ist nicht ganz ~** (*inf*) he's crackers (*inf*).
(c) (*inf: zu*) shut, closed.
[2] *adv* **(a)** (*nahe*) closely ◆ **(~ an) ~ stehen** to stand close together; **~ gefolgt von** closely followed by.
(b) (*sehr stark*) *bevölkert* densely; *bewaldet auch* thickly ◆ **~ mit Efeu bewachsen** with ivy growing thickly over it; **~/~er behaart sein** to be very hairy/have more hair.
(c) (*mit Präpositionen*) **~ an/bei** close to; **~ dahinter/darüber/davor** right behind/above/in front; **~ daneben** right *or* close beside it; **~ bevor** right before; **~ daran** hard by it; **~ hintereinander** close(ly) *or* right behind one another; **~ beieinander** *or* **beisammen** close together; **~ am Winde halten** (*Naut*) to sail close to *or* to hug the wind; **~ hinter jdm her sein** to be right *or* hard *or* close behind sb.
dicht-: ~auf *adv* closely; **~auf folgen** to follow close behind *or* closely; ⚠**~behaart** *adj attr* (very) hairy; ⚠**~belaubt** *adj attr* thick with leaves, densely foliated; ⚠**~bevölkert** *adj attr* densely populated; **~bewachsen** *adj attr Baumstämme* grown over with moss and lichen; *Ufer* thickly covered with vegetation; *Landstriche* rich in vegetation; ⚠**~bewölkt** *adj attr* heavily overcast.
Dichte *f* **-, -n (a)** *no pl siehe adj (a)* thickness; denseness; heaviness, denseness; closeness; close weave; denseness; fullness, compactness. **(b)** (*Phys*) density. **(c)** (*Comput*) **Diskette mit einfacher/doppelter ~** single-density/double-density diskette.
Dichtemesser *m* **-s, -** (*Phys*) densimeter.
dichten[1] [1] *vt* to write, to compose ◆ **sein Glückwunsch war gedichtet** his congratulations were (written) in verse.
[2] *vi* to write poems/a poem.
dichten[2] *vt* (*undurchlässig machen*) to seal, to make watertight/airtight; (*Naut auch*) to caulk.
Dichter *m* **-s, -** poet; (*Schriftsteller*) writer, author.
Dichterfürst *m* prince among poets.
Dichterin *f siehe* **Dichter** poet(ess); writer, author(ess).
dichterisch *adj* poetic; (*schriftstellerisch*) literary ◆ **~e Freiheit** poetic licence.
Dichter-: ~kreis *m* circle of poets; **~lesung** *f* reading (*by a poet/writer from his own works*); **~ling** *m* (*pej*) rhymester (*pej*), poetaster (*pej*); **~schule** *f* school of poets/writers; **~sprache** *f* poetic language; **~wort** *nt, pl* **~worte** (literary) quotation.
Dicht-: ⚠**d~gedrängt** *adj attr* closely packed; **d~halten** *vi sep irreg* (*inf*) to hold one's tongue (*inf*), to keep one's mouth shut (*inf*); **~heit** *f siehe* **Dichte (a)**.
Dichtkunst *f* art of poetry; (*Schriftstellerei*) creative writing.
dichtmachen *vti sep* (*inf*) *Laden etc* to shut up, to close; *Fabrik, Betrieb etc* to close *or* shut down ◆ **(den Laden) ~** to shut up shop (and go home) (*inf*); **er hat (sich) völlig dichtgemacht** (*fig inf*) he's pulled down the shutters (*inf*).
Dichtung[1] *f* **(a)** *no pl* (*Dichtkunst, Gesamtwerk*) literature; (*in Versform*) poetry ◆ **~ und Wahrheit** (*Liter*) poetry and truth; (*fig*) fact and fantasy *or* fiction. **(b)** (*Dichtwerk*) poem, poetic work; literary work ◆ **dramatische ~** dramatic poem.
Dichtung[2] *f* (*Tech*) seal; (*in Wasserhahn etc*) washer; (*Aut: von Zylinder, Vergaser*) gasket; (*das Abdichten*) sealing.
Dichtungs-: ~art, ~gattung *f* literary genre; **~manschette** *f* seal; **~masse** *f* sealant; **~material, ~mittel** *nt* sealing compound; **~ring** *m*, **~scheibe** *f* seal, sealing ring; (*in Wasserhahn*) washer.
dick *adj* **(a)** thick; *Mensch, Körperteil, Band, Buch, Brieftasche* fat; *Baum, Stamm* big, large, thick; (*inf*) *Gehalt, Belohnung, Rechnung, Gewinn* fat, hefty; (*inf*) *Tränen, Geschäft* big ◆ **einen ~en Mercedes fahren** (*inf*) to drive a big Mercedes; **eine ~e Zigarre** a big fat cigar; **die ~e Berta** Big Bertha; **ein ~er Brocken** (*inf*) a hard *or* tough nut (to crack); **~ machen** (*Speisen*) to be fattening; **~ werden** (*Mensch: zunehmen*) to get fat; **sich/jdn ~ anziehen** to wrap up/sb up warmly; **~(e) kommen** (*inf*) to come thick and fast; **etw ~ unterstreichen** to underline sth heavily; **~e** (*inf: ausreichend*) easily; **er hat es ~(e)** (*inf*) (*satt*) he's had enough of it; (*viel*) he's got enough and to spare.
(b) (*nach Maßangaben*) thick; *Erdschicht* deep ◆ **3 m ~e Wände** walls 3 metres thick, 3 metre thick walls.
(c) (*inf: schwerwiegend*) *Fehler, Verweis* big ◆ **das ist ein ~er Tadel/ein ~es Lob** that's heavy criticism/high praise; **ach, du ~es Ei!** (*sl*) bloody hell! (*Brit sl*); **das ist ein ~er Hund** (*sl*) that's a bit much (*inf*); **das ~e Ende kommt noch** (*prov*) the worst is yet to come.
(d) (*geschwollen*) *Backe, Beine, Finger, Mandeln* swollen; *Beule* big ◆ **ein ~er Kopf** (*inf*) a thick head (*inf*); *siehe* **Bauch**.
(e) (*zähflüssig, dicht*) thick ◆ **eine ~e Suppe** (*inf: Nebel*) a real pea-souper (*inf*);

⚠: Informationen zur Rechtschreibreform im Anhang

~e Milch sour milk; **durch ~ und dünn** through thick and thin; *siehe* **Luft.**
(f) (*inf: herzlich*) *Freundschaft, Freund* close ◆ **mit jdm ~ befreundet** *or* **~e sein** to be thick with sb (*inf*).

Dick-: d~bauchig *adj Vase, Krug* bulbous; *Mann* potbellied; **d~bäuchig** *adj Mensch* potbellied; (*krankhaft auch*) swollen-bellied; **~darm** *m* (*Anat*) colon.

Dicke *f* **-, -n (a)** (*Stärke, Durchmesser*) thickness; (*bei Maßangaben auch*) depth. **(b)** (*von Menschen, Körperteilen*) fatness.

dicke *adv* (*inf*) *siehe* **dick (a, f).**

Dicken-: ~messer *m* **-s, -** thickness gauge; **~wachstum** *nt* lateral growth.

Dicke(r) *mf decl as adj* (*inf*) fatty (*inf*), fatso (*inf*).

Dickerchen *nt* (*inf*) chubby chops (*inf*).

dicketun *vr sep irreg siehe* **dicktun.**

Dick-: d~fellig *adj* (*inf*) thick-skinned; **~felligkeit** *f* (*inf*) insensitivity, rhinoceros hide (*inf*); **d~flüssig** *adj* thick, viscous; **~flüssigkeit** *f* thickness, viscosity; **~häuter** *m* **-s, -** pachyderm; (*fig*) thick-skinned person; **d~häutig** *adj* (*fig*) thick-skinned.

Dickicht *nt* **-(e)s, -e** (*Gebüsch*) thicket; (*fig*) jungle, maze.

Dick-: ~kopf *m* **(a)** (*Starrsinn*) obstinacy, stubbornness, mulishness; **einen ~kopf haben** to be obstinate *or* stubborn *or* mulish; **sie setzt ihren ~kopf immer durch** she always gets what she wants; **(b)** (*Mensch*) mule (*inf*); **d~köpfig** *adj* (*fig*) stubborn; **d~leibig** *adj Buch* massive; *Mensch* corpulent; **~leibigkeit** *f siehe adj* massiveness; corpulence; **d~lich** *adj* plump; *Mensch auch* plumpish, tubby (*inf*); **~milch** *f* (*Cook*) sour milk; **~schädel** *m* (*inf*) *siehe* **~kopf**; **d~schalig** *adj* thick-skinned, with a thick skin *or* peel; **~sein** *nt* fatness.

Dick-: ~tuer(in *f*) *m* **-s, -** (*inf*) swank; **~tuerei** *f* (*inf*) swanking *no pl*; **d~tun** *vir sep irreg* (*inf*) to swank; **(sich) mit etw d~tun** to go swanking around (the place) with sth (*inf*); **d~wandig** *adj Gebäude, Bunker, etc* with thick walls, thick-walled; *Gefäß, Schale* with thick sides, thick; **~wanst** *m* (*pej inf*) fatso (*inf*).

Didaktik *f* didactics (*form*), teaching methods *pl*.

Didaktiker(in *f*) *m* **-s, -** (*Univ*) lecturer in teaching methods ◆ **er ist ein miserabler ~** his teaching methods are terrible.

didaktisch *adj* didactic.

dideldum, dideldumdei *interj* tum-ti-tum.

die *art etc siehe* **der²**.

Dieb *m* **-(e)s, -e** thief ◆ **haltet den ~!** stop thief!; **sich wie ein ~ davonschleichen** to steal *or* slink away like a thief in the night.

Dieberei *f* thievery *no pl*, thieving *no pl*.

Diebes-: ~bande *f* gang of thieves; **~gesindel** *nt siehe* **~pack**; **~gut** *nt* stolen property *or* goods *pl*; **~höhle** *f* thieves' den; **~nest** *nt* den of thieves; **~pack** *nt* (*pej*) thieving riff-raff (*pej*) *or* trash (*pej*); **d~sicher** *adj* thief-proof.

Diebin *f* thief.

diebisch *adj* **(a)** (*Gesindel*) thieving *attr*. **(b)** (*inf*) *Freude, Vergnügen* impish, mischievous.

Diebstahl ['di:p-ʃta:l] *m* **-(e)s, ¨e** theft; (*Jur auch*) larceny ◆ **einfacher/schwerer ~** petty/grand larceny; **bewaffneter ~** armed robbery; **geistiger ~** plagiarism.

Diebstahl-: d~sicher *adj* theft-proof; **~sicherung** *f* (*Aut*) anti-theft device; **~versicherung** *f* insurance against theft.

diejenige *dem pron siehe* **derjenige.**

Diele *f* **-, -n (a)** (*Fußbodenbrett*) floorboard. **(b)** (*Vorraum*) hall, hallway; *siehe* **Eis~, Tanz~**. **(c)** (*N Ger*) *siehe* **Tenne.**

dielen *vt Zimmer* to lay floorboards in.

Dielenbrett *nt* floorboard.

dienen *vi* **(a)** (*Dienste tun, sich einsetzen*) to serve (*jdm* sb); (*old: angestellt sein*) to be in service (*bei* with) ◆ **bei Hof ~** to serve *or* wait at court; **bei der Messe** *or* **am Altar ~** to serve at mass.
(b) (*Mil*) (*beim Militär sein*) to serve; (*Militärdienst leisten*) to do (one's) military service ◆ **bei der Kavallerie/unter jdm ~** to serve in the cavalry/under sb; **ein gedienter Soldat** an ex-soldier; *siehe* **Pike.**
(c) (*fördern*) (*einer Sache (dat)* sth) to serve; *dem Fortschritt, der Erforschung* to aid; *dem Verständnis* to promote; (*nützlich sein*) to be of use *or* service (*jdm* to sb) ◆ **es dient einem guten Zweck/einer guten Sache** it serves a useful purpose/it is in a good cause; **der Verbesserung der Arbeitsbedingungen ~** to serve to improve working conditions; **das wird dir später ~** that will be *or* come in useful to you later.
(d) (*behilflich sein*) to help (*jdm* sb), to be of help *or* service (*jdm* to sb) ◆ **womit kann ich Ihnen ~?** what can I do for you?; (*im Geschäft auch*) can I help you?; **damit kann ich leider nicht ~** I'm afraid I can't help you there; **damit ist mir wenig gedient** that's no use *or* good to me.
(e) (*verwendet werden*) **als/zu etw ~** to serve *or* be used as/for sth; **laß dir das als Warnung ~!** let that serve as *or* be a warning to you!

Diener *m* **-s, - (a)** (*Mensch*) (*lit, fig*) servant; (*Lakai auch*) valet ◆ **~ Gottes** servant of God; **Ihr ergebenster ~** (*old*) (*in Briefen*) your (most) obedient servant; *siehe* **stumm. (b)** (*inf: Verbeugung*) bow.

Dienerin *f* maid(-servant *old*).

dienern *vi* (*vor +dat* to) (*lit*) to bow; (*fig pej*) to bow and scrape.

Dienerschaft *f* servants *pl*, domestic staff.

dienlich *adj* useful, helpful; (*ratsam*) expedient, advisable ◆ **jdm/einer Sache ~ sein** to help sb/sth, to be of use *or* help to sb/sth.

Dienst *m* **-(e)s, -e (a)** (*Arbeitsverhältnis, Tätigkeitsbereich*) service; (*Arbeitsstelle*) position ◆ **diplomatischer/öffentlicher ~** diplomatic /civil service; **bei jdm in ~(en)** *or* **in jds ~(en)** (*dat*) **sein** *or* **stehen** to be in sb's service; **jdn in (seinen) ~ nehmen** to engage sb; **in jds ~(e)** (*acc*) **treten** to enter sb's service; **Oberst** *etc* **außer ~** (*abbr* **a.D.**) retired colonel *etc*; **den ~ quittieren, aus dem ~ (aus)scheiden** to resign one's post; (*Mil*) to leave the service; **~ mit der Waffe** (*Mil*) armed service; **nicht mehr im ~ sein** to have left the service; **im ~ ergraut sein** to have many years of faithful service behind one.
(b) (*Berufsausübung, Amtspflicht*) duty; (*Arbeit, Arbeitszeit*) work ◆ **im ~ sein, ~ haben** (*Arzt, Feuerwehrmann etc*) to be on duty; (*Apotheke*) to be open; **im ~ sein** (*Angestellter etc*) to be working; **außer ~ sein** to be off duty; **nach ~** after work; **zum ~ gehen** to go to work; **~ tun** to serve (*bei* in, *als* as); **jdn vom ~ beurlauben** to grant sb leave of absence; **jdn vom ~ befreien** to exempt sb from his duties; **~ nach Vorschrift** work to rule; **~ ist ~ und Schnaps ist Schnaps** (*Prov inf*) you can't mix business with pleasure, there's a time for everything.
(c) (*Tätigkeit, Leistung, Hilfe*) service ◆ **im ~(e) einer Sache/der Menschheit** in the service of sth/humanity; **sich in den ~ der Sache stellen** to embrace the cause; **jdm einen ~/einen schlechten ~ erweisen** to do sb a good/bad turn *or* a service/disservice; **jdm gute ~e leisten** *or* **tun** to serve sb well; **jdm den ~ verweigern** to refuse to work for sb; **die Stimme** *etc* **versagte ihr den ~** her voice *etc* failed (her) *or* gave way; **~ am Vaterland** service to one's country; **~ am Kunden** customer service; **etw in ~ stellen** to put sth into commission *or* service; **jdm zu ~en** *or* **zu jds ~en stehen** to be at sb's disposal; (*Mensch auch*) to be at sb's service; **(ich stehe) zu ~en!** (*old*) at your service!; **was steht zu ~en?** (*old*) you wish, sir/madam?
(d) (*Einrichtung: oft in cpds*) service.
(e) (*Archit*) engaged column *or* shaft.

-dienst *m in cpds* service.

Dienst-: ~abteil *nt* (*Rail*) ≈ guard's compartment, conductor's car (*US*); **~adel** *m* (*Hist*) *nobility whose titles derive from being in the king's service.*

Dienstag *m* Tuesday ◆ **~ abend/morgen/nachmittag** (on) Tuesday evening/morning/afternoon; **~ abends/nachts/vormittags** on Tuesday evenings/nights/mornings; **am ~** on Tuesday; **hast du ~ Zeit?** have you time on Tuesday?; **heute ist ~, der 10. Juni** today is Tuesday the tenth of June *or* Tuesday June the tenth; **alle ~e** every Tuesday; **eines ~s** one Tuesday; **des ~s** (*geh*) on Tuesdays; **die Nacht von ~ auf** *or* **zum Mittwoch** the night of Tuesday to Wednesday; **den (ganzen) ~ über** all (day) Tuesday, the whole of Tuesday; **ab nächsten** *or* **nächstem ~** from next Tuesday; **~ in 8 Tagen** *or* **in einer Woche** a week on Tuesday, Tuesday week; **seit letzten** *or* **letztem ~** since last Tuesday; **~ vor einer Woche** *or* **acht Tagen** a week (ago) last Tuesday.

Dienstag-: ~abend *m* Tuesday evening; **~nachmittag** *m* Tuesday afternoon.

dienstags *adv* on Tuesdays, on a Tuesday ◆ **~ abends** on Tuesday evenings, on a Tuesday evening.

dienstagsnachmittags *adv* on Tuesday afternoons.

Dienst-: ~alter *nt* length of service; **~älteste(r)** *mf* (most) senior member of staff; **d~älteste(r, s)** *adj* longest-serving, most senior; **~antritt** *m* assumption of one's duties; (*jeden Tag*) commencement of work; **bei ~antritt** on taking up one's duties/on commencing work; **~anweisung** *f* instructions *pl*, regulations *pl*; **~anzug** *m* (*Mil*) service uniform *or* dress; **~auffassung** *f* conception of one's duties; **was ist denn das für eine ~auffassung?** have you no sense of duty!; **~aufsicht** *f* supervision; **die ~aufsicht über etw** (*acc*) **haben** to be in charge of sth; **~aufsichtsbeschwerde** *f* complaint about a ruling; **d~bar** *adj* **(a)** (*Hist*) subject; **(b)** (*fig: helfend*) **d~barer Geist** helpful soul; **d~bare Geister** willing hands; **sich** (*dat*) **etw d~bar machen** to utilize sth; **~barkeit** *f* **(a)** (*Jur*) servitude; **(b)** (*Hist: Leibeigenschaft*) servitude; **etw in seine ~barkeit bringen** (*fig geh*) to utilize sth; **(c)** (*Gefälligkeit*) service; **(d)** (*rare: Tätigsein als Diener*) service; **d~beflissen** *adj* zealous, assiduous; **~beflissenheit** *f* zealousness, assiduousness, assiduity; **~befreiung** *f* (*Mil*) leave, furlough (*US*); **d~bereit** *adj* **(a)** (*geöffnet*) *Apotheke* open *pred*; *Arzt* on duty; **(b)** (*hilfsbereit*) willing to be of service, obliging; **~bereitschaft** *f* **(a) in ~bereitschaft sein** to be on stand-by duty; **welche Apotheke hat dieses Wochenende ~bereitschaft?** which chemist is open this weekend?; **(b)** willingness to be of service; **~bezüge** *pl* salary *sing*; **~bote** *m* servant; **~boteneingang** *m* tradesmen's *or* service entrance; **~eid** *m* oath of service; **~eifer** *m* zeal; **d~eifrig** *adj* zealous, assiduous; **d~fähig** *adj* (*Mil*) fit for duty; **d~fertig** *adj siehe* **d~beflissen**; **d~frei** *adj* free; **d~freier Tag** day off, free day; **d~frei haben/bekommen** to have/be given a day off; **~gebrauch** *m* (*Mil, Admin*) **nur für den ~gebrauch** for official use only; **~geheimnis** *nt* official secret; **~gespräch** *nt* business call; (*von Beamten*) official call; **~grad** *m* (*Mil*) **(a)** (*Rangstufe*) rank; **(b)** (*Mensch*) **ein höherer ~grad** a person of higher rank, a higher ranking person; **~gradabzeichen** *nt* (*Mil*) insignia; ⚠**d~habend** *adj attr Arzt, Offizier* duty *attr*, on duty; **der ~habende** (*Mil*) the duty officer; **~herr** *m* employer; **~jahr** *nt usu pl* (*Mil, Admin*) year of service; **~kleidung** *f* working dress; uniform; (*Mil*) service dress; **~leistung** *f* service; **~leistungsabend** *m* late-closing night; **~leistungsberuf** *m* job in the services sector; **~leistungsbetrieb** *m* service industry; **~leistungsgewerbe** *nt* services trade; **d~lich** **1** *adj Angelegenheiten* business *attr*; *Schreiben, Befehl* official; **d~lich werden** (*inf*) to become businesslike; **2** *adv* on business; **wir haben hier d~lich zu tun** we have business here; **~mädchen** *nt* maid; **~mann** *m* **(a)** *pl* **-männer** *or* **-leute** (*Gepäckträger*) porter; **(b)** *pl* **-mannen** *or* **-leute** (*Hist: Vasall*) liegeman, vassal; **~mütze** *f* uniform cap; **~ordnung** *f* (*Admin*) official regulations *pl*; (*Mil*) service regulations *pl*; **~personal** *nt* staff, personnel; **~pflicht** *f* compulsory service; **d~pflichtig** *adj* liable for compulsory service;

⚠: for details of spelling reform, see supplement

~pistole *f* service revolver *or* pistol; **~plan** *m* duty rota; **~rang** *m* grade; (*Mil*) rank; **~reise** *f* business trip; **auf ~reise** on a business trip; **~sache** *f* (*Post*) **gebührenfreie ~sache** official matter sent postage paid; ⚠**~schluß** *m* end of work; **nach ~schluß** (*von Arbeiter etc*) after work; (*von Büro, Firma etc auch*) after working hours; **wir haben jetzt ~schluß** we finish work now; **~siegel** *nt*, **~stempel** *m* official stamp; **~stelle** *f* (*Admin*) department; (*Mil*) section; **~stunden** *pl* working hours *pl*; **d~tauglich** *adj* (*Mil*) fit for service; ⚠**d~tuend** *adj Arzt* duty *attr*, on duty; **d~unfähig** *adj* unfit for work; (*Mil*) unfit for duty; **d~untauglich** *adj* (*Mil*) unfit for service; **~vergehen** *nt* breach of duty; **~verhältnis** *nt* **im ~verhältnis stehen** to be a public employee; **ein ~verhältnis eingehen/ins ~verhältnis übernommen werden** to become a public employee; **d~verpflichten*** *vt insep* to call up *or* draft (*US*) for essential service; **~vertrag** *m* contract of employment; **~vorschrift** *f* official regulations *pl*; (*Mil*) service regulations *pl*; **~wagen** *m* company car; (*von Beamten*) official car; (*Mil*) staff car; (*Rail*) ≃ guard's carriage, conductor's car (*US*); **~weg** *m* **den ~weg einhalten** to go through the proper *or* official channels *pl*; **auf dem ~weg** through the proper *or* official channels *pl*; **d~willig** *adj* willing to be of service; (*Mil*) willing to do one's duty; **~wohnung** *f* police/army *etc* house, house provided by the police/army *etc*; **~zeit** *f* **(a)** period of service; **(b)** (*Arbeitszeit*) working hours *pl*; (*Mil*) hours *pl* of duty; **~zeugnis** *nt* testimonial.

dies *dem pron inv* this; *pl* these ◆ **~ sind** these are; *siehe auch* **dieser**.

diesbezüglich *adj* (*form*) relating to *or* regarding this ◆ **sich ~ äußern** to give one's views regarding this *or* on this matter.

diese *dem pron siehe* **dieser**.

Diesel *m* **-s, -** (*inf*) diesel.

dieselbe, dieselbige *dem pron siehe* **derselbe**.

Diesel-: d~elektrisch *adj* diesel-electric; **~lok(omotive)** *f* diesel locomotive; **~motor** *m* diesel engine; **~öl** *nt* diesel oil.

dieser, diese, dies(es), *pl* **diese** *dem pron* **(a)** (*substantivisch*) this; (*~ dort, da*) that; *pl* these; (*~ dort, da*) those ◆ **diese(r, s) hier** this (one); **diese(r, s) da** that (one); **wer hat es getan? — dieser!** which one did it? — this/that one!; **dieser ist es!** this/that is the one!; **dieser ..., jener ...** the latter ..., the former ...; **schließlich fragte ich einen Polizisten; dieser sagte mir ...** in the end I asked a policeman, he told me ...; **dies und das, dieses und jenes** this and that; **dieser und jener** this person and that; **dieser oder jener** someone or other; **... oder dem Überbringer dieses** (*form*) ... or to the bearer of this.
(b) *attr* this; (*~ dort, da*) that; *pl* these; (*~ dort, da*) those ◆ **gib mir dieses Buch** give me that book; **dies(es) Jahr/dieser Monat** this year/month; **Anfang dieses Jahres/Monats** at the beginning of the *or* this *or* the current (*form*) year/month; **in diesen Wochen/Jahren habe ich viel erlebt** I experienced a lot in those weeks/years; **ich fahre diese Woche/dieses Jahr noch weg** I'm going away this week/year; **am 5. dieses Monats** on the 5th of this month; (*in Briefen auch*) on the 5th inst. (*form*); **dieser Tage** (*vergangen*) the other day; (*zukünftig*) one of these days; **(nur) dieses eine Mal** just this/that once; **dies alles, alles dies** all this/that; **dieser Maier** (*inf*) that *or* this Maier; *siehe* **Nacht**.

dieserart *adv* (*Aus, old*) thus, in this way.

dieses *dem pron siehe* **dieser**.

diesig *adj Wetter, Luft* hazy, misty.

Diesigkeit *f* haziness, mistiness.

dies-: ~jährig *adj attr* this year's; **die ~jährige Ernte** this year's harvest; **~mal** *adv* this time; **~malig** *adj attr* **der ~malige Preis** the price this time; **~seitig** *adj* **(a)** *Ufer* near(side) *attr*, (on) this side; **(b)** (*irdisch*) of this world; *Leben* in this world; **~seits** *prep +gen* on this side of; **D~seits** *nt* **-**, *no pl* **das D~seits** this life; **im D~seits** in this life, on earth.

Dietrich *m* **-s, -e** picklock, skeleton key.

dieweil (*obs*) [1] *adv* meanwhile, in the meantime, the while (*dial*).
[2] *conj* whilst, while.

Diffamation *f siehe* **Diffamierung**.

diffamieren* *vt* to defame.

diffamierend *adj* defamatory.

Diffamierung *f* (*das Diffamieren*) defamation (of character); (*Bemerkung etc*) defamatory statement.

Diffamierungskampagne *f* smear campaign.

⚠**Differential** [-'tsia:l] *nt* **-s, -e (a)** (*Math*) differential. **(b)** (*Aut: auch* **~getriebe** *nt*) differential (gear).

⚠**Differential-** *in cpds* (*Tech, Math*) differential; ⚠**~rechnung** *f* (*Math*) differential calculus.

Differenz *f* **(a)** (*Unterschied, fehlender Betrag, Math*) difference; (*Abweichung*) discrepancy. **(b)** (*usu pl: Meinungsverschiedenheit*) difference (of opinion), disagreement.

Differenzbetrag *m* difference, balance.

differenzieren* [1] *vt* **(a)** to make distinctions/a distinction in; *Behauptung, Urteil* to be discriminating in; (*abändern*) to make changes/a change in, to modify ◆ **zwischen zwei Dingen ~** to differentiate between two things; **die Gesetze wurden immer stärker differenziert** the laws became more and more sophisticated.
(b) (*Math*) to differentiate.
[2] *vi* to make distinctions/a distinction (*zwischen +dat* between, *bei* in); (*den Unterschied verstehen*) to differentiate (*zwischen +dat* between, *bei* in); (*bei Behauptung, Urteil*) to be discriminating, to discriminate (*bei* in) ◆ **~de Methoden** discriminative methods; **genau ~** to make a precise distinction.
[3] *vr* to become sophisticated; (*sich auseinanderentwickeln*) to become differentiated.

differenziert *adj* (*fein unterscheidend*) subtly differentiated; (*verfeinert*) sophisticated; *Charakter, Mensch, Gefühlsleben* complex; (*verschiedenartig*) *Farbgebung, Anschauungen* subtly diversified; *Warenangebot* diverse.

Differenzierung *f* **(a)** *siehe vt (a)* distinction; modification; differentiation. **(b)** (*Math*) differentiation. **(c)** *siehe vr* sophistication; differentiation.

differieren* *vi* to differ.

diffizil *adj* (*geh*) difficult, awkward; *Mensch* complicated.

diffus *adj Licht* diffuse; *Gedanken, Ausdrucksweise* confused.

Diffusion *f* diffusion.

digital *adj* digital.

Digital- *in cpds* digital; **~band** *nt* digital tape; **~baustein** *m* integrated circuit element.

digitalisieren* *vt* to digitalize.

Digitalisierung *f* **-**, *no pl* digitalization.

Digital-: ~rechner *m* (*Comput*) digital calculator; **~technik** *f* (*Comput*) digital technology; **~tonband** *nt* (*abbr* **DAT**) digital audio tape; **~uhr** *f* digital clock/watch.

Dikta (*geh*) *pl of* **Diktum**.

⚠**Diktaphon** *nt* **-s, -e** dictaphone ®.

Diktat *nt* **(a)** dictation ◆ **etw nach ~ schreiben** to write sth from dictation; **Fräulein, bitte zum ~!** take a letter, please; **nach ~ verreist** dictated by X and signed in his absence. **(b)** (*fig: Gebot*) dictate; (*Pol auch*) diktat.

Diktator *m* dictator.

diktatorisch *adj* dictatorial.

Diktatur *f* dictatorship.

diktieren* *vt Brief*, (*fig*) *Bedingungen* to dictate.

Diktiergerät *nt*, **Diktiermaschine** *f* dictating machine.

Diktion *f* style.

Diktionär [dɪktsio'nɛ:ɐ] *nt or m* **-s, -e** (*old*) dictionary.

Diktum *nt* **-s, Dikta** (*geh*) dictum, adage.

Dilemma *nt* **-s, -s** *or* (*geh*) **-ta** dilemma.

Dilettant(in *f*) *m* amateur; (*pej auch*) dilettante.

dilettantisch *adj* amateurish.

Dilettantismus *m* amateurism.

dilettieren* *vi* (*geh*) to dabble (*in +dat* in).

Dill *m* **-(e)s, -e** (*Bot, Cook*) dill.

diluvial [dilu'via:l] *adj* (*Geol*) diluvial.

Diluvium *nt* (*Geol*) glacial epoch, ice age.

Dimension *f* (*Phys, Math, fig*) dimension.

-dimensional *adj suf* -dimensional.

Diminuendo *nt* **-s, -s** (*Mus*) diminuendo.

diminutiv *adj Form, Endung* diminutive (*zu, von* of).

Diminutivform *f* diminutive form.

Diminutiv(um) *nt* diminutive (*zu, von* of).

Dimmer *m* **-s, -** dimmer (switch).

DIN[1] ® [dɪn, di:n] *f* **-**, *no pl abbr of* **Deutsche Industrie-Norm** German Industrial Standard ◆ **~ A4** A4; **~-Format** German standard paper size.

DIN[2] [di:n] *nt* **-(s)**, *no pl* (*Phot*) DIN ◆ **~-Grad** DIN-speed.

dinarisch *adj Rasse* Dinaric ◆ **D~es Gebirge** Dinaric Alps.

Diner [di'ne:] *nt* **-s, -s** (*form*) (*Mittagessen*) luncheon; (*Abendessen*) dinner.

Ding[1] *nt* **-(e)s, -e** *or* (*inf*) **-er (a)** (*Sache, Gegenstand*) thing ◆ **Gläser, Flaschen und ähnliche ~e** glasses, bottles and that sort of thing *or* and things of that kind; **die Welt der ~e** (*Philos*) the world of material objects; **das ~ an sich** (*Philos*) the thing-in-itself; **das ist ein ~ der Unmöglichkeit** that is quite impossible; **guter ~e sein** (*geh*) to be in good spirits *or* of good cheer (*old*); **die ~e beim (rechten) Namen nennen** to call a spade a spade (*prov*); **jedes ~ hat zwei Seiten** (*Prov*) there are two sides to everything; **gut ~ will Weile haben** (*Prov*) it takes time to do a thing well; *siehe* **drei**.
(b) (*Gegebenheit*) thing; (*Angelegenheit, Thema auch*) matter; (*Ereignis auch*) event ◆ **in diesen ~en** about these things *or* matters; **vergangene/berufliche ~e** past events/professional matters; **reden wir von andern ~en** let's talk about something else; **wir harrten der ~e, die da kommen sollten** we waited to see what would happen; **die ~e sind nun mal nicht so** things aren't like that; **so wie die ~e liegen** as things are, as matters lie; **wie ich die ~e sehe** as I see things *or* matters; **über den ~en stehen** to be above things; **die ~e stehen schlecht** things are bad; **nach Lage der ~e** the way things are; **vor allen ~en** above all (things), first and foremost; **es müßte nicht mit rechten ~en zugehen, wenn ...** it would be more than a little strange if ...; *siehe* **Lauf, Natur, unverrichtet** *etc*.
(c) (*inf*) *auch* **~s** (*unbestimmtes Etwas*) thing; (*Vorrichtung auch*) gadget; **was ist das für ein ~?** what's that thing?; **das ~(s) da** (*inf*) that thing (over) there; **das ist ein ~!** now there's a thing! (*inf*); **ein tolles ~!** great! (*inf*); **das ~ ist gut!** that's a good one! (*inf*).
(d) *pl* **-er** (*sl: Verbrechen*) job; **sich** (*dat*) **ein ~ leisten** to get up to something; **da hast du dir aber ein ~ geleistet** that was quite something you got up to (*inf*); **~er machen** to get up to all sorts of tricks (*inf*); **was macht ihr bloß für ~er?** the things you do! (*inf*); **das war vielleicht ein ~** (*inf*) that was quite something (*inf*); **jdm ein ~ verpassen** to get one's own back on sb; *siehe* **drehen**.
(e) (*inf: Mädchen*) thing, creature.
(f) (*sl: Penis*) tool (*sl*), dong (*US sl*).

Ding[2] *nt* **-(e)s, -e** (*Hist*) thing.

dingen *pret* **dingte**, *ptp* **gedungen** *vt* (*old*) *Diener* to hire, to engage ◆ **gedungener Mörder** hired assassin.

Dingens *nt* **-, -** (*dial inf*) *siehe* **Ding**[1].

dingfest *adj* **jdn ~ machen** to take sb into custody, to arrest sb.
Dingi ['dɪŋgi] *nt* **-s, -s** dinghy.
dinglich [1] *adj* material ◆ **~er Anspruch/Klage** (*Jur*) claim/action in rem.
[2] *adv* (*Fin*) **~ gesicherte Forderungen** claims covered by assets.
Dinglichkeit *f* materiality.
Dings, Dingsbums, Dingsda *nt* **-**, *no pl* (*inf*) (*Sache*) what'sit, doo-dah, thingummy(-bob *or* -jig) (*all inf*); (*Person: auch* **der/die ~**) what's-his-/-her-name (*inf*).
Dingwort *nt* **-(e)s, ¨er** (*Gram*) noun.
dinieren* *vi* (*geh*) to dine (*form*).
Dinkel *m* **-s, -** (*Bot*) spelt.
Dinner *nt* **-s, -** (*geh*) dinner.
Dinosaurier *m* dinosaur.
Diode *f* **-, -n** diode.
dionysisch *adj* Dionysian.
Diopter *nt* **-s, -** (*old*) (*Phot*) viewfinder; (*am Gewehr*) (peep) sight.
Dioptrie *f* **-, -n** (*Opt: abbr* **dpt**) diopter.
Dioskuren *pl* (*Myth*) heavenly twins (*auch fig*), Dioscuri (*form*).
Dioxin *nt* **-s, -e** dioxin.
dioxinhaltig *adj* dioxinated.
Dioxyd *nt* **-s, -e** dioxide.
Diözesan *m* **-en, -en** diocesan.
Diözese *f* **-, -n** diocese ◆ **die ~ Münster** the diocese of Münster.
Diphtherie [dɪfte'ri:] *f* diphtheria.
Diphtherie(schutz)impfung *f* diphtheria immunization; (*eine Impfung*) diphtheria injection.
Diphthong [dɪf'tɔŋ] *m* **-s, -e** diphthong.
diphthongieren* [dɪftɔŋ'gi:rən] *vt* to diphthongize.
Diphthongierung *f* diphthongization.
diphthongisch [dɪf'tɔŋɪʃ] *adj* diphthongized ◆ **~ aussprechen** to pronounce as a diphthong.
Dipl. *abbr of* **Diplom.**
Dipl.-Ing. *abbr of* **Diplomingenieur** academically trained engineer.
Dipl.-Kfm. *abbr of* **Diplomkaufmann.**
Diplom *nt* **-s, -e** diploma; (*Zeugnis auch*) certificate ◆ **ein ~ machen** to take *or* do one's diploma.
Diplom- *in cpds* (*vor Berufsbezeichnung*) qualified.
Diplomand *m* **-en, -en** *student about to take his diploma.*
Diplom|arbeit *f* dissertation (*submitted for a diploma*).
Diplomat *m* **-en, -en** diplomat.
Diplomatenkoffer *m* executive case.
Diplomatie *f* (*lit, fig*) diplomacy.
diplomatisch *adj* (*Pol, fig*) diplomatic.
diplomiert *adj* qualified.
Diplom-: ~kauffrau *f*, **~kaufmann** *m* business school graduate.
Dipol ['di:po:l] *m* **-s, -e (a)** (*Phys*) dipole. **(b)** (*auch* **~antenne**) dipole (aerial *or* antenna).
dippen *vt* (*Naut*) *Flagge* to dip.
DIP-Schalter *n* (*Comput*) dip-switch.
Dir. *abbr of* **Direktion; Direktor; Dirigent.**
dir *pers pron dat of* **du** to you; (*obs, dial*) to thee; (*nach Präpositionen*) you; (*obs, dial*) thou; *siehe* **ihm.**
direkt [1] *adj* **(a)** (*unmittelbar, gerade*) direct; *Erledigung* immediate ◆ **eine ~e Verbindung** a through train/direct flight; **~e Rede** direct speech.
(b) (*unverblümt*) *Mensch, Frage, Ausdrucksweise* direct, blunt; (*genau*) *Hinweis* plain; *Vorstellungen, Antwort, Auskunft* clear.
(c) (*inf: ausgesprochen*) perfect, sheer ◆ **es war keine ~e Katastrophe** it wasn't exactly a catastrophe.
[2] *adv* **(a)** (*unmittelbar*) directly; (*geradewegs auch*) straight ◆ **~ aus** *or* **von/zu** *or* **nach** straight *or* direct from/to; **~ an/neben/unter/über** directly *or* right by/next to/under/over; **~ gegenüber** right *or* directly *or* straight opposite; **jdm ~ ins Gesicht/in die Augen sehen** to look sb straight in the face/the eyes; **~ übertragen** *or* **senden** to transmit live; **ich kann von hier nicht ~ telefonieren** I can't dial direct from here.
(b) (*unverblümt*) bluntly ◆ **jdm etw ~ ins Gesicht sagen** to tell sb sth (straight) to his face; **~ fragen** to ask outright *or* straight out.
(c) (*inf: geradezu*) really ◆ **nicht ~** not exactly *or* really.
Direkt- *in cpds* direct; (*Rad, TV*) live.
Direktion *f* **(a)** (*Leitung*) management, administration; (*von Schule*) headship (*Brit*), principalship (*US*). **(b)** (*Direktoren, Vorstand*) management. **(c)** (*Direktionsbüro*) manager's office.
Direktionsrecht *nt* right to give directives.
Direktive *f* (*geh*) directive.
Direktmandat *nt* (*Pol*) direct mandate.
Direktor *m* director; (*von Gefängnis*) governor, warden (*US*); (*von Krankenhaus*) ≃ senior consultant; (*von Hochschule*) principal; (*von Schule*) head (teacher), headmaster/mistress, principal (*esp US*) ◆ **geschäftsführender ~** (*Univ*) head of department; **~ der Bank von England** governor of the Bank of England.
Direktorat *nt* **(a)** (*Amt*) directorship; (*von Schule*) headship, principalship (*esp US*); (*von Gefängnis*) governorship, wardenship (*US*).
(b) (*Diensträume*) (*von Firma, Museum*) director's office; (*von Hochschule etc*) principal's office; (*von Schule*) head(master/mistress)'s *or* principal's (*esp US*) study *or* room; (*von Gefängnis*) governor's *or* warden's (*US*) office.
Direktorin *f siehe* **Direktor.**

Direktorium *nt* **(a)** board of directors, directorate. **(b)** (*Hist*) Directory, Directoire.
Direktrice [dirɛk'tri:sə] *f* **-, -n** manageress.
Direkt-: ~strahlung *f* direct radiation; **~übertragung** *f* (*Rad, TV*) live transmission; **~verbindung** *f* (*Rail*) through train; (*Aviat*) direct flight; **~vertrieb** *m* direct marketing; **~zugriff** *m* direct access; **~zugriffsspeicher** *m* random access memory, RAM.
Direx *m* **-, -e** (*Sch sl*) head, principal (*esp US*).
Dirigent(in *f*) *m* (*Mus*) conductor; (*fig*) leader.
Dirigenten-: ~stab, ~stock (*inf*) *m* (conductor's) bâton.
dirigieren* *vt* **(a)** (*auch vi*) (*Mus*) to conduct; (*fig*) to lead. **(b)** (*leiten, einweisen*) *Verkehr etc* to direct.
Dirigismus *m* (*Pol*) dirigism.
dirigistisch *adj Maßnahmen* dirigiste.
Dirn *f* **-, -en (a)** (*S Ger, Aus: Magd*) maid. **(b)** (*N Ger: Mädchen*) girl, lass (*dial inf*).
Dirndl *nt* **-s, - (a)** (*auch* **~kleid**) dirndl. **(b)** (*S Ger, Aus: Mädchen*) girl, lass (*dial inf*).
Dirne *f* **-, -n (a)** (*Prostituierte*) prostitute, hooker (*US inf*). **(b)** (*obs: Mädchen*) lass (*old, dial*).
Dirnenviertel *nt* red light district.
dis, Dis *nt* **-, -** (*Mus*) D sharp.
Disagio [dɪs'|a:dʒo] *nt* **-s, -s** *or* **Disagien** (*Fin*) discount.
Disc-Kamera *f* disc camera.
Discman ® *m* **-s, -** Discman ®.
Disco *f* **-, -s** disco.
Discount- [dɪs'kaunt] *in cpds* discount.
Discounter *m* **-s, -** (*inf*) **(a)** *siehe* **Discounthändler. (b)** *siehe* **Discountladen.**
Discount-: ~händler *m* discount dealer; **~laden** *m* discount shop.
Disharmonie *f* (*Mus*) discord, dissonance, disharmony; (*fig: Unstimmigkeit*) discord *no pl*, friction *no pl*, disagreement; (*von Farben*) clash.
disharmonieren* *vi* (*geh*) (*Mus*) to be discordant *or* dissonant; (*Farben*) to clash; (*Menschen*) to be at variance, to disaccord (*form*) ◆ **die beiden ~ so offensichtlich** the two of them are so obviously out of tune with one another.
disharmonisch *adj Akkord* discordant, dissonant, disharmonious; *Farbzusammenstellung* clashing; *Ehe, Verbindung, Atmosphäre* discordant.
Diskant *m* **-s, -e** (*Stimmlage*) treble; (*Gegenstimme*) descant.
Diskantschlüssel *m* soprano clef.
Diskette *f* disk, diskette.
Diskettenlaufwerk *nt* disk drive.
Diskjockey ['dɪskdʒɔke] *m* **-s, -s** disc jockey, deejay (*inf*), DJ (*inf*).
Disko *f* **-, -s** *siehe* **Disco.**
Diskont *m* **-s, -e** (*Fin*) discount.
Diskonten *pl* (*Fin*) discounted bills *pl.*
diskontieren* *vt* (*Fin*) to discount.
diskontinuierlich *adj* (*geh*) discontinuous.
Diskontinuität *f* (*geh*) discontinuity.
Diskontsatz *m* (*Fin*) minimum lending rate.
Diskothek *f* **-, -en (a)** (*Tanzbar*) discotheque. **(b)** (*Plattensammlung*) record collection.
diskreditieren* *vt* (*geh*) to discredit.
Diskrepanz *f* discrepancy.
diskret *adj* **(a)** (*taktvoll, unaufdringlich*) discreet; (*vertraulich*) *Angelegenheit, Gespräch* confidential ◆ **er ist sehr ~** (*verschwiegen*) he's not one to betray a confidence; **du mußt lernen, etwas ~er zu sein** you must learn to be more discreet about confidential matters.
(b) (*Math*) discrete.
Diskretion *f* discretion; (*vertrauliche Behandlung*) confidentiality ◆ **~ üben** to be discreet; **strengste ~ wahren** to preserve the strictest confidence; **jdn um ~ in einer Angelegenheit bitten** to ask sb to treat an affair as a matter of confidence; **~ ist Ehrensache!** you can count on my discretion.
Diskriminante *f* **-, -n** (*Math*) discriminant.
diskriminieren* *vt* to discriminate against.
diskriminierend *adj* discriminatory.
Diskriminierung *f* discrimination.
Diskurs *m* **-es, -e** (*geh*) discourse.
diskursiv *adj* (*Philos*) discursive.
Diskus *m* **-, -se** *or* **Disken** discus.
Diskussion *f* discussion ◆ **zur ~ stehen** to be under discussion; **etw zur ~ stellen** to put *or* bring sth up for discussion; **sich mit jdm auf eine ~ einlassen** to be drawn *or* to get into discussion with sb; **da gibt's gar keine ~, du ...** I'm not having any discussion about it, you ...
Diskussions-: ~beitrag *m* contribution to the discussion; **~redner** *m* speaker (in a discussion); **~teilnehmer** *m* participant (in a discussion).
Diskus-: ~werfen *nt* **-s**, *no pl* throwing the discus; **~werfer(in** *f*) *m* discus-thrower.
diskutabel, diskutierbar *adj* worth discussing ◆ **das ist überhaupt nicht ~** that's not even worth talking about.
diskutieren* *vti* to discuss ◆ **über etw** (*acc*) **~** to discuss sth; **darüber läßt sich ~** that's debatable; **er diskutiert gern** he's a great one for discussing (everything); **wir haben stundenlang diskutiert** we've spent hours in discussion; **was gibt's denn da zu ~?** what is there to talk about *or* to discuss?
Dispens [dɪs'pɛns] *f* **-, -en** *or m* **-es, -e** (*Eccl*) dispensation.
dispensieren* [dɪspɛn'zi:rən] *vt* **(a)** *jdn* to excuse (*von* from); (*Eccl*) to dis-

pense. **(b)** *(zubereiten) Arznei* to dispense.
Dispersion [dɪspɛr'zio:n] *f (Chem, Opt)* dispersion.
Dispersionsfarbe *f* emulsion paint.
Display [dɪs'pleɪ] *nt* **-s, -s** *(Comput, Waren)* display.
Dispo-Kredit *m (Fin inf) siehe* **Dispositionskredit.**
disponibel *adj* available.
disponieren* [dɪspo'ni:rən] *vi (geh)* **(a)** *(verfügen)* **über jdn ~** to command sb's services *(form)*; **willkürlich über jdn ~** to deal with sb high-handedly; **ich kann nicht über sie ~** I can't tell her what to do; **über etw** *(acc)* **(frei) ~** to do as one wishes *or* likes with sth; **über etw** *(acc)* **~ können** *(zur Verfügung haben)* to have sth at one's disposal; **ich kann über meine Zeit frei ~** my time is my own (to do with as I wish).
(b) *(planen)* to make arrangements *or* plans.
disponiert [dɪspo'ni:ɐt] *adj (geh)* **gut/schlecht ~ sein** to be on/off form *or* in good/bad form; **zu** *or* **für etw ~ sein** *(Med)* to be prone to sth; **so ~e Leute** people with this kind of disposition.
Disposition [dɪspozi'tsio:n] *f (geh)* **(a)** *(Verfügung)* **jdm zur** *or* **zu jds ~ stehen** to be at sb's disposal; **jdm etw zur ~ stellen** to place sth at sb's disposal.
(b) *(Anordnung)* arrangement, provision ♦ **seine ~en treffen** to make (one's) arrangements *or* plans.
(c) *(Gliederung)* layout, plan.
(d) *(Med: Anlage)* susceptibility, proneness *(zu* to).
Dispositionskredit *m (Fin)* drawing credit.
disproportioniert [dɪsproportsio'ni:ɐt] *adj* ill-proportioned.
Disput [dɪs'pu:t] *m* **-(e)s, -e** *(geh)* dispute.
disputabel [dɪspu'ta:bl] *adj (dated)* disputable.
Disputant [dɪspu'tant] *m* disputant.
Disputation [dɪsputa'tsio:n] *f (old)* disputation.
disputieren* [dɪspu'ti:rən] *vi (geh)* to dispute *(über etw (acc)* sth).
Disqualifikation *f* disqualification.
disqualifizieren* *vt* to disqualify.
Disqualifizierung *f* disqualification.
Dissens *m* **-es, -e** *(Jur)* dissent, disagreement *no indef art.*
Dissertation *f* dissertation; *(Doktorarbeit)* thesis.
dissertieren* *vi* to write a dissertation/thesis *(über +acc* on).
Dissident(in *f)* *m* dissident.
Dissimilation *f (Ling)* dissimilation; *(Biol auch)* catabolism.
dissimilieren* *vt (Ling) Laut* to dissimilate; *(Biol) Stoffe* to break down.
dissonant *adj* dissonant.
Dissonanz *f (Mus)* dissonance; *(fig)* (note of) discord.
Distanz *f* **(a)** *(lit)* distance; *(fig) (Abstand, Entfernung)* detachment; *(Zurückhaltung)* reserve ♦ **~ halten** *or* **wahren** *(lit, fig)* to keep one's distance; **auf ~ gehen** *(fig)* to become distant; **die nötige ~ zu etw finden/haben** to become/be sufficiently detached from sth. **(b)** *(Sport)* distance.
distanzieren* [1] *vr* **sich von jdm/etw ~** to distance oneself from sb/sth; *(jdn/etw zurückweisen)* to dissociate oneself from sb/sth.
[2] *vt (Sport)* to outdistance.
distanziert *adj Verhalten* distant.
Distanzwaffe *f (Mil)* long-range weapon.
Distel *f* **-, -n** thistle.
Distelfink *m* goldfinch.
Distichon ['dɪstɪçɔn] *nt* **-s, Distichen** *(Poet)* distich.
distinguiert [dɪstɪŋ'gi:ɐt] *adj (geh)* distinguished.
distinkt *adj (old)* distinct, clear.
Distinktion *f (geh)* **(a)** *(Auszeichnung)* distinction. **(b)** *(Rang)* distinction; *(Aus: Rangabzeichen)* insignia *pl.*
Distribution *f* distribution.
distributiv *adj (Gram, Math)* distributive.
Distrikt *m* **-(e)s, -e** district.
Disziplin *f* **-, -en (a)** *no pl (Zucht, Ordnung)* discipline ♦ **~ halten** *(Lehrer)* to keep *or* maintain discipline; *(Klasse)* to behave in a disciplined manner. **(b)** *(Fachrichtung, Sportart)* discipline.
Disziplinar- *in cpds* disciplinary; **~gesetz** *nt* disciplinary code; **~gewalt** *f* disciplinary powers *pl.*
disziplinarisch *adj* disciplinary ♦ **jdn ~ bestrafen** to take disciplinary action against sb; **jdm ~ unterstellt sein** to be answerable to sb.
Disziplinar-: ~strafe *f* punishment; **mit einer ~strafe rechnen** to expect disciplinary action; **eine ~strafe bekommen** to be disciplined; **~verfahren** *nt* disciplinary proceedings *pl.*
disziplinieren* [1] *vt* to discipline.
[2] *vr* to discipline oneself.
diszipliniert [1] *adj* disciplined.
[2] *adv* in a disciplined manner.
Disziplin-: d~los [1] *adj* undisciplined; [2] *adv* in an undisciplined manner; **~losigkeit** *f* lack *no pl* of discipline.
dito *adv (Comm, hum)* ditto.
Diva ['di:va] *f* **-, -s** *or* **Diven** star; *(Film)* screen goddess.
divergent [divɛr'gɛnt] *adj* divergent.
Divergenz [divɛr'gɛnts] *f* **(a)** *no pl* divergence. **(b)** *usu pl (Meinungsverschiedenheit)* difference (of opinion).
divergieren* [divɛr'gi:rən] *vi* to diverge.
divers [di'vɛrs] *adj attr* various ♦ **die ~esten ...** the most diverse ...; **~es Angebot von ...** an assortment of ...; **~e** *(mehrere der gleichen Art)* several; **„D~es"** "miscellaneous"; **wir haben noch D~es zu erledigen** we still have various *or* several things to see to.
Diversant [divɛr'zant] *m (DDR)* subversive.
Diversifikation *f* diversification.
diversifizieren* *vti* to diversify.
Divertimento [divɛrti'mento] *nt* **-s, -s** *or* **Divertimenti, Divertissement** [divɛrtɪsə'mã:] *nt* **-s, -s** *(Mus)* divertimento, divertissement.
Dividend [divi'dɛnt] *m* **-en, -en** *(Math)* dividend.
Dividende [divi'dɛndə] *f* **-, -n** *(Fin)* dividend.
Dividenden|ausschüttung *f (Fin)* distribution of dividends.
dividieren* [divi'di:rən] *vti* to divide *(durch* by).
divinatorisch [divina'to:rɪʃ] *adj (geh)* divinatory.
Divis [di'vi:s] *nt* **-es, -e** *(Typ)* hyphen.
Division [divi'zio:n] *f (Math, Mil)* division.
Divisionär [divizio'nɛ:ɐ] *m (Sw)* divisional commander.
Divisions- *in cpds (Math)* division; *(Mil)* divisional; **~stab** *m* divisional headquarters *pl.*
Divisor [di'vi:zɔr] *m (Math)* divisor.
Diwan *m* **-s, -e** divan.
d. J. *abbr of* **(a) dieses Jahres** of this year. **(b) der Jüngere** jun.
DJH [de:jɔt'ha:] *nt* **-(s)** *abbr of* **Deutsches Jugendherbergswerk** German Youth Hostel Association.
DKP [de:ka:'pe:] *f* **-** *abbr of* **Deutsche Kommunistische Partei.**
DM ['de:'|ɛm] *no art* **-, -** *abbr of* **Deutsche Mark.**
d. M. *abbr of* **dieses Monats** inst.
D-Mark ['de:mark] *f* **-, -** deutschmark, (West) German mark.
DNA [de:|ɛn'|a:] *abbr of* **Deutscher Normenausschuß** German Committee of Standards.
DNS [de:|ɛn'|ɛs] *f abbr of* **Desoxyribonukleinsäure** DNA.
DNS-: ~-Code *m* DNA-code; **~-Strickleiter** *f* DNA-ladder; **~-Zeile** *f* line of DNA.
Dobermann *m* **-(s), -männer** Doberman (Pinscher).
doch [1] *conj (aber, allein)* but; *(jedoch, trotzdem)* but still, yet ♦ **und ~ hat er es getan** but he still *or* but still he did it.
[2] *adv* **(a)** *(betont: dennoch)* after all; *(trotzdem)* anyway, all the same; *(sowieso)* anyway ♦ **jetzt ist er ~ nicht gekommen** now he hasn't come after all; **..., aber ich bin ~ hingegangen** ... but I went anyway *or* all the same *or* after all; **du weißt es ja ~ besser** you always know better than I do anyway; **das geht denn ~ zu weit!** that really is going too far; **und ~, ...** and yet ...
(b) *(betont: tatsächlich)* really ♦ **ja ~!** of course!, sure! *(esp US)*; **nein ~!** of course *or* certainly not!; **also ~!** so it *is*/so he *did*! *etc*; **er hat es gestohlen — also ~!** he stole it — so it *was* him!; **er hat es also ~ gesagt** so he *did* say it; **es ist ~ so, wie ich vermutet hatte** so it (really) *is* as I thought; **das ist er ~!** (why,) that *is* him!; **das ist ~ interessant, was er da sagt** what he's saying is really interesting; **was es ~ alles für Leute gibt!** the people you get!
(c) *(als bejahende Antwort)* yes I do/it does *etc* ♦ **hat es dir nicht gefallen? — (~,) ~!** didn't you like it? — (oh) yes I did! *or* oh I did, I did!; **will er nicht mitkommen? — ~!** doesn't he want to come? — (oh) yes, he does; **~, schon, aber ...** yes it does/I do *etc* but ...
(d) *(auffordernd) nicht übersetzt, aber emphatisches „to do" wird oft gebraucht* ♦ **komm ~** do come; **kommen Sie ~ bitte morgen wieder** won't you come back tomorrow?; **gib ~ mal her** (come on,) give it to me; **seid ~ endlich still!** do keep quiet!, keep quiet, can't you?; **sei ~ nicht so frech!** don't you be so cheeky!; **laß ihn ~!** just leave him!; **soll er ~!** well let him!, let him then!; **nicht ~!** don't (do that)!
(e) *(verstärkend)* but; *(Bestätigung erwartend)* isn't it/haven't you *etc?* ♦ **sie ist ~ noch so jung** but she's still so young; **es wäre ~ schön, wenn ...** (but) it *would* be nice if ...; **daß sie ~ immer widersprechen muß!** why must she always contradict everything?; **das ist ~ die Höhe** *or* **das Letzte!** well, that's the limit!, that really is the limit!; **das ist ~ gar nicht wahr!** (but) that's just not true!; **das ist ~ wohl nicht wahr?** that's not true, is it? **du hast ~ nicht etwa ...?** you haven't ..., have you?, surely you haven't *or* you haven't by any chance ...(, have you)?; **ich habe ~ (aber) gefragt** (but) I did ask.
(f) *(eigentlich)* really, actually ♦ **es war ~ ganz interessant** it was really *or* actually quite interesting; **hier ist es ~ ganz nett** it's actually quite nice here.
(g) *(als bekannt Angenommenes wiederholend) nicht übersetzt* ♦ **Sie wissen ~, wie das so ist** (well,) you know how it is, don't you?; **du kennst dich ~ hier aus, wo ist denn ...?** you know your way around here, where is ...?; **wie war ~ Ihr Name?** (I'm sorry,) *what* was your name?; **hier darf man ~ nicht rauchen** you can't smoke here(, you know).
(h) *(in Wunschsätzen)* **wenn ~** if only; **o wäre es ~ schon Frühling!** oh if only it were spring!; **daß dich ~ der Teufel holte!** (oh) go to blazes!, the devil take you *(old)*.
(i) *(geh: begründet)* but then ♦ **er sprach etwas verwirrt, war er ~ eben erst aus dem Bett aufgestanden** he spoke in a somewhat confused manner, but then he had only just got out of bed.
Docht *m* **-(e)s, -e** wick.
Docht-: ~halter *m* wick-holder; **~schere** *f* wick trimmer.
Dock *nt* **-s, -s** *or* **-e** dock.
Docke *f* **-, -n (a)** *(Korn)* stook; *(Wolle, Garn)* hank, skein; *(Tabak)* bundle. **(b)** *(dial: Puppe)* doll.
docken[1] *vti* to dock.
docken[2] *vt Korn etc* to stook; *Wolle etc* to wind into a hank *or* skein; *Tabak* to bundle.
Docker *m* **-s, -** docker.
Docking *nt* **-s, -s** *(Space)* docking.

Doge ['do:ʒə] *m* **-n, -n** (*Hist*) doge.
Dogenpalast *m* Doge's Palace.
Dogge *f* **-, -n** mastiff ◆ **englische ~** (English) mastiff; **deutsche ~** great Dane.
Dogger[1] *m* **-s, -** (*Naut*) dogger.
Dogger[2] *m* **-s** (*Geol*) Middle Jurassic, Dogger; (*Gestein*) dogger.
Doggerbank *f* (*Geog*) **die ~** the Dogger Bank.
Dogma *nt* **-s, Dogmen** dogma ◆ **etw zum ~ erheben** to make sth into dogma.
Dogmatik *f* dogmatics *sing*; (*fig: usu pej*) dogmatism.
Dogmatiker(in *f*) *m* **-s, -** dogmatist.
dogmatisch *adj* (*Rel, fig*) dogmatic.
dogmatisieren* [1] *vt* to make into a dogma, to dogmatize.
[2] *vi* (*fig pej*) to be dogmatic.
Dogmatismus *m* (*pej*) dogmatism.
Dohle[1] *f* **-, -n** (*Orn*) jackdaw.
Dohle[2] *f* **-, -n** *siehe* **Dole.**
Döhnkes *pl* (*N Ger*) *siehe* **Döntjes.**
Doktor *m* (*auch inf: Arzt*) doctor ◆ **ja, Herr/Frau ~** yes, Doctor; **er ist ~ der Philosophie/Theologie** he is a doctor of philosophy/theology; **sie hat den ~, sie ist ~** she has a doctorate *or* PhD, she has *or* is a PhD; **den** *or* **seinen ~ machen** *or* **bauen** (*inf*) to do a doctorate *or* PhD; **zum ~ promoviert werden** to receive one's doctorate *or* PhD; **~ spielen** (*inf*) to play doctors and nurses.
Doktorand(in *f*) *m* **-en, -en** graduate student studying for a doctorate.
Doktor|arbeit *f* doctoral *or* PhD thesis.
Doktorat *nt* (**a**) (*dated*) doctorate. (**b**) (*Aus*) *siehe* **Doktorprüfung.**
Doktor-: ~diplom *nt* doctor's diploma; **~examen** *nt siehe* **~prüfung; ~grad** *m* doctorate, doctor's degree, PhD; **den ~grad erwerben** to obtain one's doctorate; **~hut** *m* doctor's cap; (*fig*) doctorate.
Doktorin *f* doctor.
Doktor-: ~prüfung *f* examination for a/one's doctorate; **~schrift** *f* (*inf: Handschrift*) doctor's *or* illegible handwriting; **~spiele** *pl* doctors and nurses *sing*; **~titel** *m* doctorate; **den ~titel führen** to have the title of doctor; **jdm den ~titel verleihen** to confer a doctorate *or* the degree of doctor (up)on sb; **~vater** *m* supervisor; **~würde** *f siehe* **~titel.**
Doktrin *f* **-, -en** doctrine.
doktrinär *adj* doctrinal; (*pej: stur*) doctrinaire.
Dokument *nt* document; (*fig: Zeugnis*) record.
Dokumentar(in *f*) *m* documentalist.
Dokumentar- *in cpds* documentary; **~film** *m* documentary (film).
dokumentarisch [1] *adj* documentary.
[2] *adv* (*mit Dokumenten*) with documents ◆ **etw ~ belegen/festhalten** to provide documentary evidence for *or* of sth/to document sth.
Dokumentar-: ~literatur *f* documentary literature; **~sendung** *f* documentary; **~spiel** *nt* docudrama.
Dokumentation *f* documentation; (*Sammlung auch*) records *pl*.
Dokumenten-: d~echt, d~fest *adj Tinte* waterproof; **d~echtes Papier** *siehe* **~papier; ~papier** *nt good quality paper used for documents, certificates etc.*
dokumentieren* [1] *vt* to document; (*fig: zu erkennen geben*) to reveal, to show.
[2] *vr* (*fig*) to become evident.
Dolce vita ['dɔltʃə 'vi:ta] *nt or f* **- -,** *no pl* life of ease, dolce vita ◆ **~ ~ machen** (*inf*) to live a life of ease.
Dolch *m* **-(e)s, -e** dagger; (*inf: Messer*) knife.
Dolchstich, Dolchstoß (*esp fig*) *m* stab (*auch fig*), dagger thrust ◆ **ein ~ (von hinten)** (*fig*) a stab in the back.
Dolchstoßlegende *f* (*Hist*) myth of the stab in the back (*betrayal of Germany in the First World War by its own politicians*).
Dolde *f* **-, -n** umbel.
Dolden-: ~blütler *m* **-s, -** umbellifer, umbelliferous plant; **d~förmig** *adj* umbellate; **~gewächs** *nt* umbellifer; **die ~gewächse** the umbelliferae.
Dole *f* **-, -n** drain.
doll *adj* (*dial, sl*) (**a**) *siehe* **toll.** (**b**) (*unerhört*) incredible ◆ **das hat ~ weh getan** that hurt like hell (*inf*).
Dollar *m* **-(s), -s** dollar ◆ **hundert ~** a hundred dollars.
Dollar-: ~kurs *m* dollar rate; **~note** *f* dollar bill; **~zeichen** *nt* dollar sign.
Dollbord *nt* (*Naut*) gunwale.
Dolle *f* **-, -n** (*Naut*) rowlock, oarlock (*US*).
Dolly ['dɔli] *m* **-(s), -s** (*Film*) dolly.
Dolm *m* **-s, -** (*Aus*) idiot, clot (*inf*).
Dolmen *m* **-s, -** (*Archeol*) dolmen.
Dolmetsch *m* **-(e)s, -e** (**a**) (*Aus, old*) interpreter. (**b**) (*geh: Fürsprecher*) spokesman (*gen, von* for).
dolmetschen *vti* to interpret.
Dolmetscher(in *f*) *m* **-s, -** interpreter.
Dolmetscher-: ~institut *nt*, **~schule** *f* school *or* institute of interpreting.
Dolomit *m* **-s, -e** (*Geol, Chem*) dolomite.
Dolomiten *pl* (*Geog*) **die ~** the Dolomites *pl*.
Dom *m* **-(e)s, -e** (**a**) cathedral. (**b**) (*fig poet*) vault (*poet*), dome (*poet*).
Domäne *f* **-, -n** (*Hist, Jur*) demesne; (*fig*) domain, province.
Domestikation *f* domestication.
Domestik(e) *m* **-en, -en** (*pej old*) (domestic) servant, domestic; (*Sport*) pace-maker.
domestizieren* *vt* to domesticate; (*fig auch*) to tame.
Dom-: ~freiheit *f* (*Hist*) cathedral close *or* precincts *pl*; **~herr** *m* (*Eccl*) canon.

dominant *adj* dominant (*auch Biol*), dominating.
Dominant- *in cpds* (*Mus*) dominant.
Dominante *f* **-, -n** (**a**) (*Mus*) dominant. (**b**) (*wichtigster Faktor*) dominant *or* dominating feature.
Dominanz *f* (*Biol, Psych*) dominance.
dominieren* [1] *vi* (*vorherrschen*) to be (pre)dominant, to predominate; (*Mensch*) to dominate.
[2] *vt* to dominate.
dominierend *adj* dominating, dominant.
Dominikaner(in *f*) *m* **-s, -** (**a**) (*Eccl*) Dominican. (**b**) (*Geog*) Dominican.
Dominikaner-: ~kloster *nt* Dominican monastery; **~orden** *m* Order of St Dominic, Dominicans *pl*.
dominikanisch *adj* (**a**) (*Eccl*) Dominican. (**b**) (*Geog*) **die D~e Republik** the Dominican Republic.
Domino[1] *m* **-s, -s** domino.
Domino[2] *nt* **-s, -s** (*Spiel*) dominoes *sing*.
Domino: ~effekt *m* domino effect; **dann tritt ein ~effekt ein** then the domino theory comes into play; **einen ~effekt auslösen** to have a knock-on effect; **~spiel** *nt* dominoes *sing*; (*Spielmaterial*) set of dominoes; (*Partie*) game of dominoes; **~stein** *m* (**a**) domino; (**b**) (*Cook*) *small chocolate biscuit with layers of marzipan and gingerbread.*
Domizil *nt* **-s, -e** domicile (*form*).
Dom-: ~kapitel *nt* cathedral chapter; **~kapitular** *m* canon; **~pfaff** *m* (*Orn*) bullfinch; **~propst** *m* dean of a/the cathedral.
Dompteur [dɔmp'tø:ɐ] *m*, **Dompteuse** [-'tø:zə] *f* trainer; (*von Raubtieren*) tamer.
Don *m* **-(s)** (*Geog*) Don.
Donar *m* **-s** Thor.
Donau *f* **- die ~** the (river) Danube.
Donau- *in cpds* Danube *attr*, Danubian; **~monarchie** *f* (*Hist*) Austria-Hungary, Austro-Hungarian Empire; **~schwaben** *pl Swabian settlers on the Danube in Hungary.*
Döner (Kebab) *m* **-(s), -, Dönerkebab** *m* doner kebab.
Don Juan [dɔn'xuan, dɔn'ju:an] *m* **- -s, - -s** Don Juan.
Dönkes *pl* (*N Ger*) *siehe* **Döntjes.**
Donkosaken ['dɔn-] *pl* Don Cossacks *pl*.
Donner *m* **-s,** (*rare*) **-** (*lit, fig*) thunder *no indef art, no pl*; (*~schlag*) peal *or* clap of thunder ◆ **wie vom ~ gerührt** (*fig inf*) thunderstruck; **~ und Doria** *or* **Blitz!** (*dated inf*) by thunder! (*dated inf*), by Jove! (*dated inf*).
Donner-: ~balken *m* (*Mil sl*) thunderbox (*old sl*); **~blech** *nt* (*Theat*) thunder sheet; **~büchse** *f* (*hum dated*) shotgun; **~gepolter, ~getöse** *nt* thunderous *or* deafening crash; **mit ~getöse** with a thunderous *or* deafening crash; **~gott** *m* god of thunder; **~grollen** *nt* **-s,** *no pl* rolling thunder; **~keil** *m* (*Geol*) thunderstone; (*Archeol*) flintstone; (*Myth, poet*) thunderbolt; **~keil!** (*dated*), **~kiel!** (*dated*) my word!, heavens!, **~maschine** *f* (*Theat*) thunder machine.
donnern [1] *vi impers* to thunder ◆ **es donnerte in der Ferne** there was (the sound of) thunder in the distance.
[2] *vi aux haben or* (*bei Bewegung*) *sein* to thunder ◆ **gegen etw ~** (*prallen*) to crash into sth; (*schlagen*) to hammer on sth; (*schimpfen*) to thunder against sth; **er hat furchtbar gedonnert** he really thundered on.
[3] *vt* (*inf*) (*brüllen*) to thunder out; (*schleudern, schlagen*) to slam, to crash ◆ **jdm eine ~** to thump sb (*inf*).
donnernd *adj* (*fig*) *Beifall* thunderous.
Donner-: ~rollen *nt* **-s,** *no pl* rolling of thunder; **~schlag** *m* clap *or* peal of thunder, thunderclap; **die Nachricht traf mich wie ein ~schlag** the news left me thunderstruck, the news came like a thunderclap to me.
Donnerstag *m* Thursday; *siehe* **Dienstag.**
donnerstags *adv* on Thursdays.
Donner-: ~stimme *f* thunderous voice; **~wetter** *nt* (*lit old*) thunderstorm; (*fig inf: Schelte*) row; **das wird ein schönes ~wetter geben** *or* **setzen** (*inf*) all hell will be let loose (*inf*); **~wetter!** (*inf: anerkennend*) my word!; **(zum) ~wetter!** (*inf: zornig*) damn *or* blast (it)! (*inf*).
Don Quichotte [dɔnki'ʃɔt] *m* **- -s, - -s** *siehe* **Don Quixote.**
Donquichot(t)erie [dɔnkiʃɔtə'ri:] *f* (*geh*) quixotism; (*Handlung*) quixotic gesture *or* act.
Don Quijote, Don Quixote [dɔnki'xo:tə] *m* **- -s, - -s** (*Liter, fig*) Don Quixote.
Döntjes *pl* (*N Ger*) story, anecdote.
doof *adj* (*inf*) stupid, daft (*inf*), dumb (*esp US inf*).
Doofheit *f* (*inf*) stupidity, daftness (*inf*), dumbness (*esp US inf*).
Doofi *m* **-(s), -s** (*inf*) thicky, dummy, dumb-dumb (*all inf*) ◆ **wie klein ~ mit Plüschohren aussehen** to look a proper charlie (*inf*).
Doofkopp (*sl*), **Doofmann** (*inf*) *m* thickhead (*inf*), blockhead (*inf*).
Dope [do:p] *nt* **-s, -s** (*sl*) dope (*sl*).
dopen ['dɔpn, 'do:pn] (*Sport*) [1] *vt* to dope ◆ **er war gedopt** he had taken drugs.
[2] *vir* to take drugs.
Doping ['dɔpɪŋ, 'do:pɪŋ] *nt* **-s, -s** (*Sport*) drug-taking; (*bei Pferden*) doping.
Doping-: ~kontrolle *f* (*Sport*) drug(s) test; **~sünder(in)** *m(f)* (*Sport*) drug-taker; **~test** *m* (*Sport*) drug(s) test; **~verdacht** *m* (*Sport*) **bei ihm besteht ~verdacht** he is suspected of having taken drugs.
Doppel *nt* **-s, -** (**a**) (*Duplikat*) duplicate (copy) (*gen, zu* of). (**b**) (*Tennis etc*) doubles *sing*; (*Mannschaft*) doubles pair.
Doppel- *in cpds* double; **~adler** *m* double eagle; **~agent** *m* double agent;

~-b *nt (Mus)* double flat; **~band** *m (von doppeltem Umfang)* double-sized volume; *(zwei Bände)* two volumes *pl*; **~bauer** *m (Chess)* doubled pawn; **~belastung** *f* double *or* dual load *or* burden *(gen* on); **steuerliche ~belastung** double taxation; ⚠**~beschluß** *m (Pol)* two-track *or* twin-track decision; **~besteuerung** *f* double taxation; **~bett** *nt* double bed; *(zwei Betten)* twin beds *pl*; **~bilder** *pl (Med)* **~bilder wahrnehmen** *or* **sehen** to have double vision; **~blindversuch** *m (Psych)* experiment using a double blind; **~bock** *nt or m* double(-strength) bock beer; **d~bödig** *adj Koffer etc* false-bottomed; *(d~deutig)* ambiguous; **~bödigkeit** *f (fig)* ambiguity; **~bogen** *m* double sheet (of paper); **~brief** *m letter weighing over 20 g*; **~bruch** *m (Math)* compound fraction; **~büchse** *f* double-barrelled gun *or (Schrotbüchse)* shotgun; **~buchstabe** *m* double letter; **~decker** *m* **-s, - (a)** *(Aviat)* biplane; **(b)** *(auch* **~deckerbus**) double-decker (bus); **d~deutig** *adj* ambiguous; **~deutigkeit** *f* ambiguity; **~ehe** *f* bigamous marriage; *(Tatbestand)* bigamy *no pl*; **eine ~ehe führen** to live bigamously; **~fehler** *m (Tennis)* double fault; *(Sch)* double mistake; **einen ~fehler machen** *(Tennis)* to (serve a) double-fault; **~fenster** *nt* double window; **~fenster haben** to have double-glazing; **~flinte** *f siehe* **~büchse**; **~funktion** *f* dual *or* twin function; **~gänger(in** *f)* *m* **-s, -** double, doppelgänger *(esp Liter)*; **ein ~gänger von Boris Becker** a Boris Becker lookalike, a double of Boris Becker; **d~geschlechtig** *adj (Bot)* hermaphrodite; **~gesicht** *nt* two faces *pl*; *(fig)* two sides *pl*; **d~gesichtig** *adj* two-faced, having two faces; *(fig)* two-sided; **~gestirn** *nt siehe* **~stern**; **d~gleisig** *adj (Rail)* double-track, twin-track; *(fig)* double; **d~gleisig sein** *(lit)* to have two tracks; **d~gleisig fahren** *(fig)* to play a double game; **~griff** *m (Mus)* double-stop; **~haus** *nt* semi-detached house, semi *(Brit inf)*, duplex (house) *(US)*; **er bewohnt eine Hälfte eines ~hauses** he lives in a semi(-detached house); **~haushälfte** *f* semi-detached house; **~heft** *nt (von Zeitschrift)* double number *or* edition; *(Sch)* exercise book of double thickness; **~kabine** *f* double *or* twin cabin *or (von LKW)* cab; **~kinn** *nt* double chin; **~klebeband** *nt* double-sided adhesive tape; **~klick** *m (Comput)* double click *(auf* on); **~kolbenmotor** *m* two cylinder engine; **~konsonant** *m* double *or* geminate *(spec)* consonant; **~kopf** *m German card game*; **~korn** *m type of schnapps*; **~kreuz** *nt (Mus)* double sharp; *(Typ)* double dagger; **~lauf** *m* double barrel; **d~läufig** *adj* double-barrelled; **~laut** *m (Ling) (Konsonant)* double *or* geminate *(spec)* consonant; *(Vokal)* double vowel; *(Diphthong)* diphthong; **~leben** *nt* double life; **~moral** *f* double (moral) standard(s *pl)*; **~mord** *m* double murder.

doppeln *vt* **(a)** *siehe* **verdoppeln. (b)** *(Aus: besohlen)* to resole.

Doppel-: ~naht *f* double-stitched seam; **~name** *m (Nachname)* double-barrelled name; *(Vorname)* double name; **~natur** *f* dual nature; **~nelson** *m (Ringen)* full nelson; **~-Null-Lösung** *f (Pol)* double zero option; **~nummer** *f (von Zeitschrift)* double issue; **~partner** *m (Sport)* doubles partner; ⚠**~paß** *m (Ftbl)* one-two; **~punkt** *m* colon; **d~reihig** *adj* in two rows; *Jacke* double-breasted; **d~reihige Perlenkette** double string of pearls; **d~reihige Nietung** two rows of rivets; **~rolle** *f (Theat)* double role; *(fig)* dual capacity; **d~schläfrig** *adj Bett* double; **~schlag** *m (Mus)* turn; **d~seitig** *adj* two-sided, double-sided; *Diskette* double-sided; *Lungenentzündung* double; **d~seitige Anzeige** double page spread; **d~seitige Lähmung** diplegia; **~sinn** *m* double meaning, ambiguity; **d~sinnig** *adj* ambiguous; **~spiel** *nt* **(a)** *(Tennis)* (game of) doubles *sing*; **(b)** *(fig)* double game; **~spielfeld** *nt (Tennis)* doubles court; **d~spurig** *adj siehe* **zweispurig**; **~steckdose** *f* double socket; **~stecker** *m* two-way adaptor; **~stern** *m* double star; **~steuerabkommen** *nt* reciprocal taxation agreement; **d~stöckig** *adj Haus* two-storey, twin-storey; *Bus* double-decker *attr*; *(hum inf) Schnaps* double; **ein d~stöckiges Bett** bunk beds *pl*; **~strategie** *f* dual strategy. **~strich** *m (Mus)* double bar; **~studium** *nt* joint course (of study); **~stunde** *f (esp Sch)* double period.

doppelt [1] *adj* double; *(verstärkt) Enthusiasmus* redoubled; *(mit zwei identischen Teilen)* twin *attr*; *(zweimal soviel)* twice; *(Comm) Buchführung* double-entry; *Staatsbürgerschaft* dual ◆ **die ~e Freude/Länge/Menge** double or twice the pleasure/length/amount; **~e Negation** *or* **Verneinung** double negative; **~er Boden** *(von Koffer)* false bottom; *(von Boot)* double bottom; **~e Moral, eine Moral mit ~em Boden** double standards *pl*, a double standard; **in ~er Hinsicht** in two respects; **ein ~es Spiel spielen** *or* **treiben** to play a double game; *siehe* **Ausfertigung**.

[2] *adv sehen, zählen* double; *(zweimal)* twice; *(direkt vor Adjektiv)* doubly ◆ **~ so schön/soviel** *etc* twice as nice/much *etc*; **sie ist ~ so alt wie ich** she is twice as old as I am *or* twice my age; **das/die Karte habe ich ~** I have two of them/these cards; **das freut mich ~** that gives me double *or* twice the pleasure; **~ gemoppelt** *(inf)* saying the same thing twice over; **sich ~ in acht nehmen** to be doubly careful; **~ und dreifach** *bereuen, leid tun* deeply; *sich entschuldigen* profusely; *prüfen* thoroughly; *versichern* absolutely; **seine Schuld ~ und dreifach bezahlen** to pay back one's debt with interest; **der Stoff liegt ~** the material is double width; **~ genäht hält besser** *(prov)* ≃ better safe than sorry *(prov)*.

Doppelte(r) *m decl as adj (inf)* double.

Doppelte(s) *nt decl as adj* double ◆ **um das ~ größer** twice as large; *(Gegenstand auch)* double the size; **das ~ bezahlen** to pay twice as much *or* double the amount; **etw um das ~ erhöhen** to double sth.

Doppelt-: d~kohlensauer *adj* **d~kohlensaures Natron** sodium bicarbonate, bicarbonate of soda; **~sehen** *nt* double vision.

Doppelung *f* doubling.

Doppel-: ~verdiener *m* person with two incomes; *(pl: Paar)* couple with two incomes, two-income *or* double-income family; **~vergaser** *m* twin carburettors *pl or* carbs *pl (inf)*; **~versicherung** *f* double insurance; *(Police)* double insurance policy; **~vierer** *m (Sport)* quadruple skulls *pl*; **~vokal** *m* double vowel; **~währung** *f* bimetallism; **~zentner** *m* 100 kilos, (metric) quintal; **~zimmer** *nt* double room; **d~züngig** *adj (fig)* devious; *(stärker)* deceitful; *Mensch auch* two-faced; **d~züngig reden** to say one thing and mean another; **~züngigkeit** *f* **(a)** *no pl siehe adj* deviousness; deceitfulness; two-facedness; **(b)** *(Äußerung)* devious remark; **~zweier** *m (Sport)* double skulls *pl*.

Doppler|effekt *m (Phys)* Doppler effect.

Dorado *nt* **-s, -s** *siehe* **Eldorado.**

Dorf *nt* **-(e)s, ⸗er** village; *(fig)* backwater ◆ **auf dem ~(e)** *(in einem bestimmten Dorf)* in the village; *(auf dem Land)* in the country; **das Leben auf dem ~e** village life; **er ist vom ~(e)** he's from the/our village; *(vom Lande)* he's from the country; **nie aus seinem ~ herausgekommen sein** *(fig)* to be parochial *or* insular; *siehe* **böhmisch, Kirche.**

Dorf- *in cpds* village; **~akademie** *f (DDR) village college for adult further education through evening classes*; **~älteste(r)** *mf* village elder; **~anger** *m (dated)* village green; **~bewohner** *m* villager.

Dörfchen *nt dim of* **Dorf** small village, hamlet.

Dorf-: ~gasthaus *nt*, **~gasthof** *m* village inn; **~gemeinde** *f* village community; *(Admin)* rural district; *(Eccl)* village parish; **~geschichte** *f* **(a)** *(Liter: Erzählung)* story of village life; **(b)** *no pl* village history; **~jugend** *f* young people *pl* of the village, village youth *pl*; **~krug** *m* village inn *or* pub *(Brit)*.

Dörflein *nt dim of* **Dorf.**

Dörfler(in *f)* *m* **-s, -** *(dated)* villager.

Dorfleute *pl* villagers *pl*.

dörflich *adj* village *attr*; *(ländlich)* rustic, rural.

Dorf-: ~platz *m* village square; **~schaft** *f (Sw)* hamlet; **~schöne, ~schönheit** *f (iro)* village beauty; **~schulze** *m (Hist)* village mayor; **~trottel** *m (inf)* village idiot.

Doria *interj siehe* **Donner.**

dorisch *adj (Archit)* Doric; *(Hist auch, Mus)* Dorian.

Dorisch(e) *nt* **-en,** *no pl* Doric.

Dormitorium *nt (Eccl)* dormitory.

Dorn *m* **-(e)s, -en** *or (inf)* **⸗er (a)** *(Bot, fig)* thorn ◆ **das ist mir ein ~ im Auge** *(fig)* that is a thorn in my flesh; *(Anblick)* I find that an eyesore. **(b)** *pl* **-e** *(poet: ~busch)* briar, thornbush. **(c)** *pl* **-e** *(Sporn)* spike; *(von Schnalle)* tongue; *(von Scharnier)* pin; *(Tech; Werkzeug)* awl.

Dornbusch *m* briar, thornbush ◆ **der brennende ~** *(Bibl)* the burning bush.

Dornen-: d~gekrönt *adj (Bibl)* wearing a crown of thorns, crowned with thorns; **~gestrüpp** *nt* thorny bushes *pl or* undergrowth; **~hecke** *f* thorn(y) hedge; **~krone** *f (Bibl)* crown of thorns; **~pfad** *m* thorny path; *(fig)* path fraught with difficulties, path of tribulation; **d~reich** *adj* thorny; *(fig)* fraught with difficulty; **d~voll** *adj (fig)* fraught with difficulty.

Dornfortsatz *m (Anat)* spiny *or* spinous *(spec)* process.

dornig *adj* thorny; *(fig auch)* fraught with difficulty.

Dorn-: ~röschen *nt* the Sleeping Beauty; **~röschenschlaf** *f (fig)* torpor, slumber; **~strauch** *m siehe* **~busch.**

Dörre *f* **-, -n** *(dial) siehe* **Darre.**

dorren *vi aux sein (geh) siehe* **dörren 2.**

dörren [1] *vt* to dry.

[2] *vi aux sein* to dry; *(austrocknen)* to dry up.

Dörr- *in cpds* dried; **~fisch** *m* dried fish; **~fleisch** *nt* dried meat; **~obst** *nt* dried fruit; **~pflaume** *f* prune.

dorsal *adj (Zool, Ling)* dorsal; *Verkrümmung, Schwäche* spinal.

Dorsal *m* **-s, -e, Dorsallaut** *m (Ling)* dorsal (consonant).

Dorsch *m* **-(e)s, -e** fish of the cod group; *(Kabeljau)* cod(fish).

Dorschleber *f* cod liver.

dort *adv* there; *siehe* **da 1 (a).**

⚠**dort-: ~behalten*** *vt sep irreg* to keep there; **~bleiben** *vi sep irreg aux sein* to stay *or* remain there.

dorten *adv (old, Aus)* there.

dort-: ~her *adv* **von ~her** from there, thence *(old, liter)*; **~herum** *adv* around (there), thereabouts; **~hin** *adv* there, thither *(old, liter)*; **bis ~hin** as far as there, up to that place; **wie komme ich ~hin?** how do I get there?; **~hinab** *adv* down there; **~hinauf** *adv* up there; **~hinaus** *adv* out there; **frech bis ~hinaus** *(inf)* really cheeky; **das ärgert mich bis ~hinaus** *(inf)* that really gets me *(inf)*, that doesn't half annoy me *(Brit inf)*; **~hinein** *adv* in there; **~hinunter** *adv* down there.

dortig *adj* there *(nachgestellt)* ◆ **die ~en Behörden** the authorities there.

⚠**dortzuland(e)** *adv* in that country, (over) there.

DOS *nt abbr of* **Disk Operating System** *(Comput)* DOS.

Döschen ['dø:sçən] *nt dim of* **Dose.**

Dose *f* **-, -n (a)** *(Blech~)* tin; *(Konserven~)* can, tin *(Brit)*; *(Bier~)* can; *(esp aus Holz)* box; *(mit Deckel)* jar; *(Pillen~, für Schmuck)* box; *(Butter~)* dish; *(Zucker~)* bowl; *(für Gesichtspuder)* compact; *(Plastik~, Streu~)* pack *(inf)* ◆ **in ~n** *(Konserven)* canned, tinned *(Brit)*.

(b) *(Elec)* socket.

(c) *(Pharm) siehe* **Dosis.**

(d) *(sl: Vagina)* hole *(sl)*.

dösen *vi (inf)* to doze.

Dosen- *in cpds* canned, tinned *(Brit)*; **~bier** *nt* canned beer; **~blech** *nt* tin for making cans *or* tins; **~öffner** *m* can-opener, tin-opener *(Brit)*.

dosierbar *adj* **leichter ~ sein** to be more easily measured into exact doses; **etw in ~en Mengen verabreichen** to administer sth in exact doses.

dosieren* *vt Arznei* to measure into doses; *Menge* to measure out; *(fig) Rat, Liebe, Geschenke, Lob* to dispense, to measure *or* hand out; *Stoff, Hinweise* to dispense ♦ **ein Medikament genau ~** to measure out an exact dose of a medicine; **etw dosiert verteilen** *(fig)* to dispense *etc* sth in small amounts *or* doses.
Dosierung *f* **(a)** *(Dosis)* dosage, dose. **(b)** *siehe vt* measuring into doses; measuring out; dispensing, handing out; dispensing.
dösig *adj (inf)* dozy *(inf)*, drowsy.
Dosimeter *nt* **-s, -** dosage meter, dosimeter.
Dosis *f* **-, Dosen** dose ♦ **in kleinen Dosen** *(lit, fig)* in small doses.
Döskopp *m (N Ger inf)* dozy idiot *(inf)*.
Dossier [dɔ'sie:] *nt or (dated) m* **-s, -s** dossier.
Dotation *f* endowment.
dotieren* *vt Posten* to remunerate *(mit* with); *Preis* to endow *(mit* with) ♦ **eine gut dotierte Stellung** a remunerative position.
Dotierung *f* endowment; *(von Posten)* remuneration.
Dotter *m or nt* **-s, -** yolk.
Dotter-: ~blume *f* globe flower; *(Sumpf~)* marsh marigold; **d~gelb** *adj* golden yellow; **~sack** *m (Zool)* yolk sac.
doubeln ['du:bln] **1** *vt jdn* to stand in for; *Szene* to shoot with a stand-in ♦ **er läßt sich nie ~** he never has a stand-in; **ein Stuntman hat die Szene für ihn gedoubelt** a stuntman doubled for him in the scene.
2 *vi* to stand in; *(als Double arbeiten)* to work as a stand-in.
Double ['du:bl] *nt* **-s, -s** *(Film etc)* stand-in; *(für Gesang)* dubber.
⚠**Doublé,** ⚠**Doublee** [du'ble:] *nt* **-s, -s** *siehe* **Dublee.**
doublieren* [du'bli:rən] *vt siehe* **dublieren.**
Douglasie [du'gla:ziə], **Douglasfichte, Douglastanne** ['du:glas-] *f* Douglas fir *or* pine.
Dow-Jones-Index ['daʊ'dʒoʊnz-] *m, no pl (Econ)* Dow-Jones Index.
down [daʊn] *adj pred (sl)* **~ sein** to be (feeling) down *or* blue *(inf)*.
Down-Syndrom ['daʊn-] *nt, no pl (Med)* Down's syndrome ♦ **ein Kind mit ~** a Down's syndrome child.
Doyen [doa'jɛ̃:] *m* **-s, -s** *(lit, fig)* doyen.
Doyenne [doa'jɛn] *f* **-, -n** doyenne.
Doz. *abbr of* **Dozent.**
Dozent(in *f)* *m* lecturer *(für* in), (assistant) professor *(US)* *(für* of).
Dozentur *f* lectureship *(für* in), (assistant) professorship *(US)* *(für* of).
dozieren* *(Univ)* **1** *vi* to lecture *(über +acc* on, *an +dat* at); *(pej auch)* to hold forth *(über +acc* on), to pontificate *(über +acc* about).
2 *vt* to lecture in.
dozierend *adj (pej)* pontificating, lecturing.
Dozierton *m (pej)* pontificating tone.
dpa ['de:pe:'|a:] *f* - *abbr of* **Deutsche Presse-Agentur.**
dpt *abbr of* **Dioptrie.**
Dr. ['dɔktɔr] *abbr of* **Doktor. Dr. rer. nat./rer. pol./phil.** PhD; **Dr. theol./jur.** DD/LLD; **Dr. med.** M.D.
Drache *m* **-n, -n** *siehe auch* **Drachen (a)** *(Myth)* dragon. **(b)** *(Astron)* Draco.
Drachen *m* **-s, - (a)** *(Papier~)* kite; *(Sport: Fluggerät)* hang-glider ♦ **einen ~ steigen lassen** to fly a kite. **(b)** *(pej inf: zänkisches Weib)* dragon *(inf)*, battleaxe *(inf)*. **(c)** *(Wikingerschiff)* longship; *(Segelschiff)* dragon class yacht.
Drachen-: ~blut *nt (Myth)* dragon's blood; **~fliegen** *nt (Sport)* hang-gliding; **~flieger** *m (Sport)* hang-glider; **~saat** *f (pej geh)* seeds of discord *pl*; **~töter** *m* dragon-killer.
Drachme *f* **-, -n** drachma; *(Pharm old)* drachm.
Dragée, Dragee [dra'ʒe:] *nt* **-s, -s (a)** *(Bonbon)* sugar-coated chocolate sweet; *(Nuß~, Mandel~)* dragee. **(b)** *(Pharm)* dragee, sugar-coated pill *or* tablet.
Drageeform *f* **in ~** coated with sugar, in sugar-coated form.
dragieren* [dra'ʒi:rən] *vt (Pharm)* to sugar-coat, to coat with sugar.
Dragoman *m* **-s, -e** dragoman.
Dragoner *m* **-s, -** *(Hist)* dragoon; *(pej: Frau)* battleaxe, dragon ♦ **fluchen wie ein ~** *(inf)* to swear like a trooper *(inf)*.
Draht *m* **-(e)s, ⸚e** wire ♦ **per** *or* **über ~** by wire *or (ins Ausland)* cable; **auf ~ sein** *(inf)* to be on the ball *(inf)*; *(wissensmäßig auch)* to know one's stuff; **du bist wohl heute nicht ganz auf ~** *(inf)* you're not quite with it today *(inf)*; **jdn auf ~ bringen** *(inf)* to bring sb up to scratch; *siehe* **heiß.**
Draht- *in cpds* wire; **~auslöser** *m (Phot)* cable release; **~bürste** *f* wire brush.
drahten *vt (dated)* to wire, to cable.
Draht-: ~esel *m (dated hum)* trusty bicycle; *(alt auch)* boneshaker *(inf)*; **~fernsehen** *nt* cable television; **~funk** *m* wire *or* line broadcasting; **~geflecht** *nt* wire mesh; **~gewebe** *nt* wire gauze; **~gitter** *nt* wire netting; **~haar(dackel)** *m* wire-haired dachshund; **d~haarig** *adj* wire-haired; **~haarterrier** *m* wire-haired terrier.
drahtig *adj Haar, Mensch* wiry.
Draht-: d~los *adj Telegrafie* wireless; *Telefon, Nachrichtenübermittlung* cordless; **~saite** *f (Mus)* steel string; **~schere** *f* wire cutters *pl*; **~schneider** *m* **-s, -** wire cutters *pl*.
Drahtseil *nt* wire cable ♦ **Nerven wie ~e** *(inf)* nerves of steel.
Drahtseil-: ~akt *m (lit, fig)* balancing act; **~bahn** *f* cable railway; **~künstler** *m (Seiltänzer)* tightrope artist *or* walker.
Draht-: ~sieb *nt* wire sieve; **~stift** *m* panel pin; **~verhau** *m* wire entanglement; *(Käfig)* wire enclosure; **~zaun** *m* wire fence; **~ziehen** *nt* **-s,** *no pl* wire-drawing; **~zieher(in** *f)* *m* **-s, -** wire-drawer; *(fig)* wire-puller.
Drainage [drɛ'na:ʒə, *(Aus)* drɛ'na:ʒ] *f* **-, -n** drainage *(auch Med etc)*.
drainieren* [drɛ'ni:rən] *vti* to drain *(auch Med)*.
Draisine [drai'zi:nə, drɛ'zi:nə] *f (Rail)* trolley; *(Fahrrad)* dandy horse.
drakonisch *adj* draconian.
drall *adj Mädchen, Arme* strapping, sturdy; *Busen, Hintern* ample; *Backen* rounded.
Drall *m* **-(e)s, -e (a)** *(von Kugel, Ball)* spin; *(um Längsachse auch)* twist; *(Abweichung von Bahn)* swerve; *(inf: von Auto)* pull ♦ **einem Ball einen ~ geben** to give a ball (some) spin, to spin a ball; **einen ~ nach links haben** *(Auto)* to pull to the left.
(b) *(fig: Hang)* tendency, inclination ♦ **sie hat einen ~ nach links/zum Moralisieren** she inclines *or* leans to the left/tends to moralize.
Dralon ® *nt* **-(s),** *no pl* dralon.
Drama *nt* **-s, Dramen** *(lit: Stück, Gattung, fig: dramatisches Geschehen)* drama; *(fig) (Katastrophe)* disaster; *(Aufheben)* to-do *(inf)*.
Dramatik *f (lit, fig)* drama.
Dramatiker(in *f)* *m* **-s, -** dramatist.
dramatisch *adj (lit, fig)* dramatic.
dramatisieren* *vt (lit, fig)* to dramatize.
Dramatisierung *f* dramatization.
Dramaturg(in *f)* *m* **-en, -en** dramaturge *(form)*, literary manager.
Dramaturgie *f* dramaturgy; *(Abteilung)* drama department.
dramaturgisch *adj* dramatic, dramaturgical *(rare)*; *Abteilung* drama *attr.*
dran *adv (inf) siehe auch* **daran (a)** *(an der Reihe)* **jetzt bist du ~** it's your turn now; *(beim Spielen auch)* it's your go now; **(wenn er erwischt wird,) dann ist er ~** *or (hum)* **am ~sten** (if he gets caught) he'll be for it *or* for the high jump *(inf)*; **er war ~** *(mußte sterben)* his time had come; **morgen ist Mathematik ~** we've got maths tomorrow; *siehe* **drauf, drum, glauben.**
(b) schlecht ~ sein to be in a bad way; *(unglücklich auch)* to be unfortunate; **gut ~ sein** to be well-off; *(glücklich)* to be fortunate; *(gesundheitlich)* to be well; **früh/spät ~ sein** to be early/late.
(c) an ihm ist nichts ~ *(sehr dünn)* he's nothing but skin and bone; *(nicht attraktiv, nicht interessant)* there is nothing to him; **an dem Hühnchen ist nichts ~** there is no meat on that chicken; **was ist an ihm ~, daß ...?** what is there about him that ...?; **da ist alles ~!** that's got everything; **da wird schon etwas (Wahres) ~ sein** there must be something *or* some truth in that; **an dem Auto ist irgendetwas ~** there is something wrong *or* the matter with the car; **ich weiß nicht, wie ich (bei ihm) ~ bin** I don't know where I stand (with him).
Dränage [drɛ'na:ʒə] *f* **-, -n** *(esp Aus, Sw) siehe* **Drainage.**
dranbleiben *vi sep irreg aux sein (inf)* **(a)** *(sich nicht entfernen)* to stay close; *(am Apparat)* to hang on; *(an der Arbeit)* to stick at it ♦ **am Gegner/an der Arbeit ~** to stick to one's opponent/at one's work.
(b) *(sterben)* to kick the bucket *(inf)* ♦ **er ist bei der Operation drangeblieben** the operation did for him *(inf)*.
Drang *m* **-(e)s, ⸚e (a)** *(Antrieb)* urge *(auch Physiol)*, impulse; *(Sehnsucht)* yearning *(nach* for); *(nach Wissen)* thirst *(nach* for) ♦ **~ nach Bewegung** urge *or* impulse to move; **ich habe einen ~** *(inf: zur Toilette)* I'm dying to go *(inf)*; *siehe* **Sturm.**
(b) der ~ zum Tor *(Sport)* the surge towards the goal; **der ~ nach Osten** the drive towards the East.
(c) *(geh: Druck)* pressure; *(des Augenblicks auch)* stress ♦ **im ~ der Ereignisse** under the pressure of events.
drang *pret of* **dringen.**
drangeben *vt sep irreg (inf)* **(a)** *(zufügen)* to add *(an +acc* to) ♦ **ich geb' noch 10 Minuten dran** I'll wait another ten minutes, I'll give you/him *etc* another ten minutes. **(b)** *(opfern)* to give up; *Leben auch* to sacrifice; *Geld* to fork out *(inf)* ♦ **sein Leben für etw ~** to give one's life for sth.
drangehen *vi sep irreg aux sein (inf)* **(a)** *(berühren, sich zu schaffen machen an)* to touch *(an etw (acc)* sth) ♦ **an etw (acc) (zu nahe) ~** *(sich nähern)* to go too close to sth.
(b) *(in Angriff nehmen)* **~, etw zu tun** to get down to doing sth; **es wird Zeit, daß ich drangehe** it's time I got down to it.
Drängelei *f (inf)* pushing, jostling; *(Bettelei)* pestering.
drängeln *(inf)* **1** *vi* to push, to jostle.
2 *vti (betteln)* to pester.
3 *vr* **sich nach vorne** *etc* **~** to push one's way to the front *etc*; **sich ~, etw zu tun** *(fig)* to fall over oneself to do sth *(inf)*.
drängen **1** *vi* **(a)** *(in Menge)* to push, to press ♦ **die Menge drängte zum Ausgang** the crowd pressed towards the exit.
(b) *(Sport: offensiv spielen)* to press *or* push forward.
(c) *(fordern)* to press *(auf +acc* for) ♦ **darauf ~, eine Antwort zu erhalten, auf Antwort ~** to press for an answer; **darauf ~, daß jd etw tut/etw getan wird** to press for sb to do sth/for sth to be done; **zum Aufbruch/zur Eile ~** to be insistent that one should leave/hurry.
(d) *(zeitlich)* to be pressing, to press ♦ **die Zeit drängt** time is pressing *or* presses; **es drängt/drängt nicht** it's/it's not pressing *or* urgent.
2 *vt* **(a)** *(mit Ortsangabe)* to push.
(b) *(auffordern)* to press, to urge ♦ **es drängt mich, das zu tun** I feel moved *or* the urge to do that.
3 *vr (Menge)* to throng *or* crowd; *(fig: Termine etc)* to mount up ♦ **sich nach vorn/durch die Menge ~** to push *or* force one's way to the front/through the crowd; *siehe* **gedrängt.**
Drängen *nt* **-s,** *no pl* urging; *(Bitten)* requests *pl*; *(Bestehen)* insistence.
drängend *adj* pressing, urgent.
Drangsal ['draŋza:l] *f* **-, -e** *(old, liter) (Not)* hardship; *(Leiden)* suffering, dis-

tress.

drangsalieren* vt (plagen) to pester, to plague; (unterdrücken) to oppress.

dranhalten sep irreg (inf) [1] vt to hold up (dat, an +acc to) ◆ etw näher an etw (acc) ~ to hold sth closer to sth.
[2] vr (sich beeilen) to hurry up, to get a move on (inf); (sich anstrengen) to make an effort, to get one's finger out (sl); (nahe dranbleiben) to keep close to it.

dranhängen sep (inf) [1] vt etw an etw (acc) ~ to hang sth onto sth; viel Zeit etc ~, etw zu tun to put a lot of time etc into doing sth.
[2] vi irreg an etw (dat) ~ to hang from sth; es hing ein Zettel dran a tag was attached (an +dat to).
[3] vr to hang on; (verfolgen) to stay close behind, to stick to sb's tail (inf); (ständig begleiten) to latch on (bei to); (jds Beispiel folgen) to follow suit.

dränieren* vt siehe drainieren.

drankommen vi sep irreg aux sein (inf) (a) (berühren) to touch.
(b) (erreichen können) to be able to reach (an etw (acc) sth).
(c) (an die Reihe kommen) to have one's turn or (bei Spielen auch) go; (Sch: beim Melden) to be called; (Frage, Aufgabe etc) to come up ◆ jetzt kommst du dran now it's your turn/go; du kommst als erster/nächster dran it's your turn/go first/next; nun kommt das Schlafzimmer dran it's the bedroom next.

drankriegen vt sep (inf) jdn ~ to get sb (inf); (zu einer Arbeit) to get sb to do it/sth; (mit Witz, Streich) to catch sb out.

Dranktonne f (N Ger) swill bucket; (fig inf) walking dustbin (hum).

dranlassen vt sep irreg (inf) etw (an etw dat) ~ to leave sth on (sth).

dranmachen sep (inf) [1] vr siehe daranmachen.
[2] vt etw (an etw acc) ~ to put sth on (sth).

drannehmen vt sep irreg (inf) Schüler to ask, to question; Patienten to take, to see.

dransetzen sep (inf) [1] vt (a) (anfügen) ein Stück/ein Teil etc (an etw acc) ~ to add a piece/part (to sth).
(b) (einsetzen) seine Kraft/sein Vermögen etc ~ to put one's effort/money into it; alles ~ to make every effort; jdn ~ to put sb onto the job or it.
[2] vr (a) (nahe an etw) sich (an etw acc) ~ to sit (down) next to sth.
(b) (Arbeit anfangen) to get down to work or it.

dransten adv (hum) superl of dran.

dranwollen vi sep (inf) (drankommen wollen) to want to have one's turn; (probieren wollen) to want to have a go.

Draperie [drapə'ri:] f (old) drapery; (Faltenwurf) drapes pl.

drapieren* vt to drape; (fig) to cloak.

Drapierung f (a) (das Drapieren) siehe vt draping; cloaking. (b) (Schmuck, kunstvolle Falten) drape ◆ ~en (fig: beschönigende Worte) fine phrases.

Drastik f, no pl (Derbheit) drasticness; (Deutlichkeit) graphicness ◆ etw mit besonderer ~ beschreiben to describe sth particularly graphically or in very extreme tones.

drastisch adj (derb) drastic; (deutlich) graphic.

dräuen vi (poet) siehe drohen.

drauf adv (inf) siehe auch darauf ◆ immer feste ~! get stuck in there! (inf), let him have it! (inf); ~ und dran sein, etw zu tun to be on the point or verge of doing sth; etw ~ haben (sl) (können) to be able to do sth no bother (inf); Kenntnisse to be well up on sth (inf); Witze, Sprüche to have sth off pat (inf); schwer was ~ haben (sl) to know one's stuff or onions (inf); 160 Sachen ~ haben (inf) to be doing 160.

Drauf-: d~bekommen* vt sep irreg (inf) eins d~bekommen to be given a smack; **~gabe** f (a) (Comm) deposit; (b) (Aus) siehe Zugabe; **~gänger** m -s, - daredevil, adventurous type; (bei Frauen) wolf; **d~gängerisch** adj daring, adventurous; (negativ) reckless; (bei Frauen) wolfish; **d~geben** vt irreg sep (a) jdm eins d~geben (inf) to give sb a smack; (b) (dazugeben) noch etwas d~geben to add some extra (inf); (c) (Aus: als Zugabe anfügen) to sing/play etc as an encore; **d~gehen** vi sep irreg aux sein (inf) (entzweigehen) to fall to bits or apart; (sterben) to bite the dust (inf); (Geld) to disappear; **~geld** nt extra payment; **d~haben** vt sep irreg (inf) Sprüche, Antwort to come out with ◆ er hat es d~ he's got what it takes; jetzt hat sie es endlich d~ she's finally got it; zeigen, was man d~ hat to show what one is made of; den Chauvi d~haben to be a real chauvinist; **d~halten** sep irreg (inf) [1] vt etw (auf etw acc) d~halten to hold sth on (sth); [2] vi (als Ziel angehen) to aim for it; **d~hauen** sep irreg [1] vi (inf: schlagen) to hit hard; [2] vt (sl) einen d~hauen to have a booze-up (inf); **d~kommen** vi sep irreg aux sein (inf) (sich erinnern) to remember; (begreifen) to catch on, to get it (inf); jdm d~kommen to get on to sb (inf); **d~kriegen** vt sep (inf) etw (auf etw acc) d~kriegen to get or fit sth on(to sth); eins d~kriegen to be given what-for (inf); (geschlagen werden) to be given a smack; (Schicksalsschlag erhalten) to receive a blow; (besiegt werden) to be given a thrashing; **d~lassen** vt sep irreg (inf) etw (auf etw dat) d~lassen to leave sth on (sth); **d~legen** vt sep (inf) (a) auch vi to lay out; 20 Mark d~legen to lay out an extra 20 marks; (b) etw (auf etw acc) d~legen to put or lay sth on(to sth).

drauflos adv (nur) immer feste or munter ~! (just) keep at it!, keep it up!

drauflos-: ~arbeiten vi sep (inf) to work away, to beaver away (inf); (anfangen) to start working; **~gehen** vi sep irreg aux sein (inf) (auf ein Ziel) to make straight for it; (ohne Ziel) to set off; (nicht zögern) to set to work; **~malen** vi sep (inf) to paint away; (anfangen) to start painting; **~reden** vi sep (inf) to talk away; (anfangen) to start talking; **~schießen** vi sep irreg (inf) to fire away; **~schlagen** vi sep irreg (inf) to hit out, to let fly (inf).

drauf-: ~machen vt sep (inf) etw (auf etw acc) ~machen to put sth on(to sth); einen ~machen to make a night of it (inf); **~satteln** vt sep (inf) to slap on (top); ⚠**~sein** vi sep irreg aux sein (inf) schlecht/gut ~sein to be in a bad/good mood; wie ist der denn ~? what kind of trip is he on? (inf); **~setzen** vt sep (inf) eins or einen ~setzen to go one step further; **D~sicht** f top view; **~stehen** vi sep irreg (inf) aux haben or (dial) sein etw steht ~ sth is on it; auf etw (dat) ~stehen (Mensch, Sache) to stand on sth; (Aufschrift) to be on sth; (da) stehe ich nicht ~ (fig sl) it doesn't turn me on (sl); **~stoßen** sep irreg (inf) [1] vi aux sein to come or hit upon it; (gegen etw stoßen) to bump or run into it; (finden) to come across it; [2] vt jdn ~stoßen to point it out to sb; **~stürzen** vr sep (inf) to swoop or pounce on it/them, to rush to get one's hands on it/them; **~zahlen** vi sep (inf) (a) auch vt siehe ~legen (a); (b) (fig: Einbußen erleiden) to pay the price.

draus adv siehe daraus.

draus-: ~bringen vt sep irreg (dial) jdn ~bringen (Konzentration stören) to make sb lose track, to distract sb; (irremachen) to put sb off; **~kommen** vi sep irreg aux sein (a) (dial, Aus: aus dem Konzept kommen) to lose track; (b) (Sw: verstehen) to see, to get it (inf).

draußen adv outside; (im Freien auch) out of doors, outdoors; (da ~, weit weg von hier) out there; (im Ausland) abroad ◆ ~ (an der Front) out there (on the front); ~ auf dem Lande/dem Balkon/im Garten out in the country/on the balcony/in the garden; ~ (auf dem Meer) out at sea; da/hier ~ out there/here; ganz da ~ way out there; ~ (vor der Tür) at the door; nach ~ outside; (ferner weg) out there; weit/weiter ~ far/further out; ~ bleiben/lassen to stay/leave out (auch fig inf) or outside; „Hunde müssen ~ bleiben" "no dogs (please)", "please leave your dog outside"; etw ~ tragen to wear sth outside.

Drechselbank f wood(-turning) lathe.

drechseln [1] vt to turn (on a wood lathe); (fig pej) to over-elaborate; Vers to turn; siehe auch gedrechselt.
[2] vi to work the (wood) lathe.

Drechsler(in f) m -s, - (wood) turner.

Drechsler|arbeit f (wood) turning; (Gegenstand) piece turned on the lathe.

Drechslerei f (Werkstatt) (wood-)turner's workshop; (Handwerk) (wood) turning.

Dreck m -(e)s, no pl (a) dirt; (esp ekelhaft) filth; (Schlamm) mud; (Kot) muck; (fig) (Schund) rubbish; (Schmutz, Obszönes) dirt, muck; (stärker) filth; (inf: schlimme Lage) mess, jam (inf) ◆ ~ machen to make a mess; in/mit ~ und Speck (ungewaschen) unwashed; im ~ sitzen or stecken (inf) to be in a mess or jam (inf); aus dem größten or gröbsten ~ heraus sein (inf) to be through or past the worst; jdn wie den letzten ~ behandeln (inf) to treat sb like dirt; der letzte ~ sein (inf: Mensch) to be the lowest of the low; ~ am Stecken haben (fig) to have a skeleton in the cupboard; etw in den ~ ziehen or treten (fig) to drag sth through the mud; siehe Karren, bewerfen.
(b) (inf) (Angelegenheit, Kram) business, stuff (inf); (Kleinigkeit) little thing ◆ sich einen ~ um jdn/etw kümmern or scheren not to care or give a damn about sb/sth (inf); mach deinen ~ alleine! do it yourself; die Nase in jeden ~ stecken (inf) to poke one's nose into everyone's business or into everything; das geht ihn einen ~ an that's none of his business, that's got damn all to do with him (sl); einen ~ ist er/hast du like hell he is/you have (sl).

Dreck-: ~arbeit f (inf) (a) (lit, fig: schmutzige Arbeit) dirty work; (b) (pej: niedere Arbeit) drudgery no pl; **~eimer** m (inf) (im Haus) rubbish bin; (im Freien) dustbin, trash can (US); **~finger** pl (inf) (lit, fig) dirty fingers pl; **~fink** m (inf) siehe ~spatz.

dreckig adj (lit, fig) dirty; (stärker) filthy ◆ ~ lachen to give or laugh a dirty laugh; es geht mir ~ (inf) I'm in a bad way; (finanziell) I'm badly off; wenn man ihn erwischt, geht es ihm ~ (inf) if they catch him, he'll be sorry or in for it (inf).

Dreck-: ~loch nt (pej) hole (inf), hovel; **~nest** nt (pej) dump (inf), hole (inf); **~pfoten** pl (inf) (lit, fig) dirty or filthy paws pl; **~sack** m (pej inf) dirty bastard (sl); **~sau** f (vulg) filthy swine (inf); **~schleuder** f (pej) (Mundwerk) foul mouth; (Mensch) foul-mouthed person; (Kraftwerk, Auto) environmental hazard; **~schwein** nt (vulg) dirty pig (inf).

Dreckskerl m (inf) dirty swine (inf), louse (inf).

Dreckspatz m (inf) (Kind) mucky pup (inf); (Schimpfwort) filthy beggar (inf).

Dreck(s)zeug nt (inf) damn or blasted stuff (inf) ◆ das ist doch ein ~ damn this stuff (inf).

Dreckwetter nt (inf) filthy weather (inf).

Dreh m -s, -s or -e (a) (List) dodge; (Kunstgriff) trick ◆ den ~ heraushaben, etw zu tun to have got the knack of doing sth; den (richtigen) ~ heraushaben or weghaben (inf) to have got the hang of it. (b) siehe Drehe.

Dreh-: ~achse f axis of rotation; **~arbeit** f (a) (von Dreher) lathe work; (Gegenstand) piece turned on the lathe; (b) **~arbeiten** pl (Film) shooting sing; **~bank** f lathe; **d~bar** adj (rundum) rotating, revolving attr; (um einen Festpunkt) swivelling attr; (~gelagert) pivoted; d~bar sein to rotate or revolve/swivel; **~beginn** m (Film) start of shooting; **~bewegung** f turn(ing motion); (esp Tech) rotation, rotary motion; eine ~bewegung machen to turn/rotate/revolve once; **~bleistift** m propelling (Brit) or mechanical (US) pencil; **~brücke** f swing bridge; **~buch** nt (Film) screenplay, (film) script; **~buchautor** m scriptwriter, screenplay writer; **~bühne** f revolving stage.

Drehe f -, no pl (inf) (so) um die ~ (zeitlich) or thereabouts, round about then; (so) in der ~ (örtlich) (there) or thereabouts, round about there.

drehen [1] vt to turn (auch Tech: auf Drehbank); (um eine Achse auch) to rotate; (um Mittelpunkt auch) to revolve, to rotate; Stuhl to swivel; Kreisel to spin; Kopf auch to twist; Zwirne to twist; Zigaretten, Pillen to roll; Film to shoot; (fig: verdrehen) to twist; (inf: schaffen) to fix (inf), to work (inf) ◆ jdm den Rücken ~

to turn one's back on sb; **das Gas hoch/auf klein ~** to turn the gas up high/down low; **Fleisch durch den Wolf ~** to put meat through the mincer; **ein Ding ~** (*sl*) to play a *or* to pull off a prank; (*Verbrecher*) to pull a job (*inf*) *or* caper (*sl*); **wie man es auch dreht und wendet** no matter how you look at it; *siehe* **Däumchen, Runde, Strick[1].**

[2] *vi* to turn; (*Wind*) to shift, to change; (*Film*) to shoot, to film; (*Zigaretten* ~) to roll one's own ◆ **an etw** (*dat*) **~** to turn sth; **am Radio ~** to turn a knob on the radio; **daran ist nichts zu ~ und deuteln** (*fig*) there are no two ways about it.

[3] *vr* **(a)** to turn (*um* about); (*um Mittelpunkt auch*) to revolve, to rotate; (*um Achse auch*) to rotate; (*sehr schnell: Kreisel*) to spin; (*Wind*) to shift, to change ◆ **sich auf den Rücken ~** to turn on(to) one's back; **sich um etw ~** to revolve *or* rotate around sth; **sich um sich (selbst) ~** to rotate, to revolve on its own axis; (*Mensch*) to turn round; (*Auto*) to spin; **sich im Kreise ~** to turn round and round; **mir drehte sich alles** everything's spinning about me; **mir dreht sich alles im Kopf** my head is spinning *or* swimming; **sich ~ und winden** (*fig*) to twist and turn.

(b) sich um etw ~ (*betreffen*) to concern sth, to be about sth; (*um zentrale Frage*) to centre on sth; **alles dreht sich um sie** everything revolves around her; (*steht im Mittelpunkt*) she's the centre of attention *or* interest; **es dreht sich darum, daß ...** the point is that ...; **in meiner Frage dreht es sich darum, ob ...** my question is whether ...; **in dieser Sendung drehte es sich um ..., die Sendung drehte sich um ...** the broadcast was about ... *or* concerned ...

Dreher *m* **-s, -** **(a)** lathe operator; (*Drechsler auch*) (wood) turner. **(b)** (*Tanz*) country waltz.

Dreherin *f siehe* **Dreher (a).**

Dreh-: ~geschwindigkeit *f* rotary *or* rotating speed; **~gestell** *nt* (*Rail*) bogie; **~impuls** *m* angular momentum; **~knopf** *m* knob; **~kran** *m* slewing *or* rotary crane; **~kreuz** *nt* turnstile; **~leier** *f* barrel-organ, hurdy-gurdy; **~maschine** *f* motorized (metal-turning) lathe; **~moment** *nt* torque; **~orgel** *f* barrel-organ, hurdy-gurdy; **~orgelspieler** *m* organ-grinder, hurdy-gurdy man; **~ort** *m* (*Film*) location; **~pause** *f* (*Film*) break in shooting; **~punkt** *m* pivot; **~restaurant** *nt* revolving restaurant; **~schalter** *m* rotary switch; **~scheibe** *f* **(a)** (*Rail*) turntable; **(b)** *siehe* **Töpferscheibe; ~strom** *m* three-phase current; **~stuhl** *m* swivel-chair; **~tag** *m* (*Film*) day of shooting; **~tür** *f* revolving door.

Drehung *f* **(a)** turn; (*ganze ~ um eigene Achse auch*) rotation; (*um einen Punkt auch*) revolution ◆ **eine halbe/ganze ~** a half/complete turn; **eine ~ um 180°** a 180° turn, a turn through 180°.

(b) (*das Drehen*) turning; (*um eigene Achse auch*) rotation; (*um einen Punkt auch*) revolving.

Drehwurm *m* (*inf*): **einen** *or* **den ~ kriegen/haben** to get giddy.

Drehzahl *f* number of revolutions *or* revs; (*pro Minute*) revolutions *or* revs *pl* per minute, rpm.

Drehzahl-: ~bereich *m* (*Aut*) engine speed range; **im niederen/hohen ~bereich** at low/high revs; **~messer** *m* rev counter.

drei *num* three ◆ **von uns ~en** from the three of us; **die (Heiligen) D~ Könige, die ~ Weisen aus dem Morgenland** the Three Kings *or* Wise Men (from the East), the Magi; **die ~ tollen Tage** *the last three days of Fasching in Germany*; **aller guten Dinge sind ~!** (*prov*) all good things/disasters come in threes!; (*nach zwei mißglückten Versuchen*) third time lucky!; **er arbeitet/ißt für ~** (*inf*) he does the work of/eats enough for three; **etw in ~ Worten erklären** (*inf*) to explain sth briefly *or* in a few words; **ehe man bis ~ zählen konnte** (*inf*) in a trice, before you could say Jack Robinson (*inf*); **sie sieht aus, als ob sie nicht bis ~ zählen könnte** (*inf*) she looks pretty vacuous *or* empty-headed; (*unschuldig*) she looks as if butter wouldn't melt in her mouth; *siehe* **vier.**

Drei *f* **-, -en** three; *siehe auch* **Vier.**

Drei- *in cpds* three-, tri-; **~achteltakt** *m* three-eight time; **d~ad(e)rig** *adj* (*Elec*) three-core; **d~beinig** *adj* three-legged; **~bund** *m* (*Hist*) Triple Alliance (*between Germany, Austria-Hungary and Italy in 1882*).

Drei-D- [drai'de:] *in cpds* 3-D.

Drei-: ~decker *m* **-s, -** (*Aviat*) triplane; (*Naut*) three-decker; **d~dimensional** *adj* three-dimensional; **~dimensionalität** *f* three-dimensionality.

Drei|eck *nt* **-(e)s, -e** triangle; (*Zeichen~*) set-square; (*Sport: Winkel*) top left/right hand corner of the goal.

drei|eckig *adj* triangular, three-sided.

Drei|ecks-: ~tuch *nt* triangular scarf; (*um die Schultern getragen*) triangular shawl; (*Med*) triangular bandage; **~verhältnis** *nt* (eternal) triangle; **ein ~verhältnis haben** to be involved in an eternal triangle.

drei|einig *adj* triune, three in one *pred* ◆ **der ~e Gott** the Holy Trinity, the Triune God.

Drei|einigkeit *f* Trinity ◆ **die ~ Gottes** the Holy Trinity.

Dreier *m* **-s, -** **(a)** (*Münze*) three pfennig piece, ≃ thruppence (*Brit*). **(b)** (*Aus, S Ger: Ziffer, Note*) three. **(c)** (*Sport*) (*Eislauf etc*) three; (*Golf*) threesome.

Dreier- *in cpds siehe* **Vierer-, vierer-.**

dreifach [1] *adj* triple, threefold (*liter*) ◆ **die ~e Menge** triple *or* treble *or* three times the amount; **ein ~es Hoch!** three cheers!; *siehe* **Ausfertigung.**

[2] *adv* three times ◆ **~ abgesichert/verstärkt** trebly secure/reinforced; *siehe* **vierfach.**

Dreifache(s) *nt decl as adj* **das ~** triple *or* treble *or* three times the amount, three times as much; **9 ist das ~ von 3** 9 is *or* equals three times 3; **ein ~s kosten** to cost three times as much; **er verdient das ~ von dem, was ich bekomme** he earns three times as much as *or* treble the amount that I do; **etw um das ~ vermehren** to multiply sth three times *or Zahl auch* by three.

Dreifach- *in cpds* triple; **~stecker** *m* three-way adapter.

Drei-: d~faltig *adj siehe* **d~einig; d~fältig** *adj siehe* **d~fach; ~faltigkeit** *f* Trinity; **~faltigkeitsfest** *nt*, **~faltigkeitssonntag** *m* Trinity Sunday; **~farbendruck** *m* **(a)** (*Verfahren*) three-colour printing; **(b)** (*Gedrucktes*) three-colour print; **d~farbig, d~färbig** (*Aus*) *adj* three-colour *attr*, three-coloured, trichromatic (*form*); **~felderwirtschaft** *f* three-field system; **~fuß** *m* tripod; (*Gestell für Kessel*) trivet; (*Schemel*) three-legged stool; **d~füßig** *adj Vers* three-foot *attr.*

Dreigang *m* (*inf*) *siehe* **Dreigangschaltung.**

Dreigang-: ~getriebe *nt* three-speed gear; **~rad** *nt* three-speed bike; **~schaltung** *f* three-speed gear; **ein Fahrrad mit ~schaltung** a three-speed bicycle.

Drei-: ~gespann *nt* troika; (*fig*) threesome; (*an leitender Stelle*) triumvirate; **~gestirn** *nt* (*lit*) triple star; (*fig geh*) big three; **d~gestrichen** *adj* (*Mus*) **das d~gestrichene C/F** the C/F two octaves above middle C; **d~geteilt** *adj* divided into three (parts); **d~glied(e)rig** *adj* (*Math*) trinomial; **~gliederung** *f* (*Gegliedertsein*) three-part *or* tripartite structure; (*das Gliedern*) division into three (parts); **~groschenheft(chen)** *nt* (*pej*) penny-dreadful (*dated inf*).

Dreiheit *f* trinity.

Drei-: d~hundert *num* three hundred; *siehe* **vierhundert; ~kampf** *m* three-part competition (*100m sprint, long jump and shot-put*); **~kant** *nt or m* **-(e)s, -e** trihedron; **~käsehoch** *m* **-s, -s** (*inf*) tiny tot (*inf*); **~klang** *m* triad; **~klassenwahlsystem** *nt* (*Hist*) three-class electoral system (*in Prussia 1850-1918*); **~könige** *pl* Epiphany *sing*; **~königsfest** *nt* (feast of) Epiphany; **~königstag** *m* feast of Epiphany; **~ländereck** *nt* place where three countries meet; **~mächtepakt** *m* (*Hist*) three-power *or* tripartite pact (*between Germany, Italy and Japan*), Axis pact.

dreimal *adv* three times, thrice (*old*); *siehe auch* **viermal.**

Drei-: ~master *m* **-s, -** three-master; **~meilengrenze** *f* three-mile limit; **~meilenzone** *f* three-mile zone; **~meterbrett** *nt* three-metre board.

drein *adv* (*inf*) *siehe* **darein.**

drein- *in cpds siehe auch* **darein-; ~blicken** *vi sep* **traurig** *etc* **~blicken** to look sad *etc*; **~fahren** *vi sep irreg aux sein* (*dial*) to intervene; **~fügen** *vr sep* to resign oneself (to it), to come to terms with it; **~reden** *vi sep* (*dazwischenreden*) to interrupt; (*sich einmischen*) to interfere (*bei* in, with); **ich lasse mir in dieser Angelegenheit von niemandem ~reden** I won't have anyone interfering (with this); **er ließ sich nirgends ~reden** he would never be told; **~schauen** *vi sep siehe* **~blicken; ~schlagen** *vi sep irreg* (*dial*) to weigh in (*inf*).

Drei-: ~phasenstrom *m* three-phase current; **d~polig** *adj* three-pole *attr*, with three poles; *Kabel* three-core; *Steckdose, Stecker* three-pin; **~punkt(sicherheits)gurt** *m* lap and diagonal seatbelt; **~rad** *nt* tricycle; (*inf: Auto*) three-wheeler; **d~räd(e)rig** *adj* three-wheeled; **~radwagen** *m* three-wheeled vehicle, three-wheeler.

Dreisatz *m* (*Math*) rule of three.

Dreisatz-: ~aufgabe *f* problem using the rule of three; **~rechnung** *f* calculation using the rule of three; **~tisch** *m* nest of tables.

Drei-: d~schiffig *adj Kirche* with three naves; **~spitz** *m* three-cornered hat, tricorn; **~springer** *m* triple-jumper; **~sprung** *m* triple jump, hop, step and jump.

dreißig *num* thirty; *siehe auch* **vierzig.**

dreißig- *in cpds siehe auch* **vierzig-; ~jährig** *adj* (*dreißig Jahre dauernd*) thirty years' *attr*, lasting thirty years; (*dreißig Jahre alt*) thirty years old, thirty-year-old *attr*; **der D~jährige Krieg** the Thirty Years' War.

Dreißigstel[1] *nt* **-s, -** thirtieth; *siehe* **Viertel[1].**

Dreißigstel[2] *f* **-,** *no pl* (*Phot inf*) thirtieth (of a second).

dreißigste(r, s) *adj* thirtieth.

dreist *adj* bold; *Handlung auch* audacious.

Dreistigkeit *f* **(a)** *no pl siehe adj* boldness; audacity. **(b)** (*Bemerkung*) bold remark; (*Handlung*) bold *or* audacious act.

Drei-: ~stufenrakete *f* three-stage rocket; **d~stufig** *adj Rakete* three-stage *attr*, with three stages; *Plan auch* three-phase *attr*; **eine d~stufige Treppe** three steps; **d~teilig** *adj* (*aus 3 Teilen*) *Kostüm etc* three-piece *attr*; (*in 3 Teile geteilt*) three-part *attr*, tripartite (*form*); **~teilung** *f* division into three; **die ~teilung der Streitkräfte** dividing the armed forces into three.

⚠ **dreiviertel** ['drai'fɪrtl] *siehe auch* **viertel** [1] *adj inv* threequarter ◆ **eine ~ Stunde** threequarters of an hour; **~ zwei** (*dial*) a quarter to two.

[2] *adv* threequarters.

Dreiviertel ['drai'fɪrtl] *nt* threequarters ◆ **in einem ~ der Zeit** in threequarters of the time; **das Saal war zu einem ~ leer** the room was threequarters empty.

Dreiviertel-: ~arm (*inf*), **~ärmel** *m* threequarter(-length) sleeve; **~jacke** *f* threequarter-length coat; **d~lang** *adj* threequarter-length; **~mehrheit** *f* threequarters majority; **~spieler** *m* (*Rugby*) three-quarter; **~stunde** *f* threequarters of an hour *no indef art*; **~takt** *m* three-four time; **im ~takt** in three-four time.

Dreiweg- *in cpds* (*Elec*) three-way; **~(lautsprecher)-box** *f* three-way loudspeaker system; **~schalter** *m* three-way switch; **~stecker** *m* three-way adapter.

Drei-: d~wertig *adj* (*Chem*) trivalent; (*Ling*) three-place; **d~wöchentlich** [1] *adj attr* three-weekly; [2] *adv* every three weeks, at three-weekly intervals; **d~wöchig** *adj attr* three-week; **~zack** *m* **-s, -e** trident; **d~zackig** *adj* three-pointed.

dreizehn *adj num* thirteen ◆ **jetzt schlägt's aber ~** (*inf*) that's a bit much *or*

thick (*inf*); *siehe auch* **vierzehn.**
Dresch-: ~boden *m*, **~diele** *f* threshing floor.
Dresche *f* **-**, *no pl* (*inf*) thrashing ♦ **~ kriegen** to get a thrashing.
dreschen *pret* **drosch**, *ptp* **gedroschen** [1] *vt* **(a)** *Korn* to thresh; (*inf*) *Phrasen* to bandy ♦ **leeres Stroh ~** (*fig*) to talk a lot of hot air (*inf*), to talk/write a lot of claptrap (*inf*); **Skat ~** (*inf*) to play skat.
(b) (*inf: prügeln*) to thrash.
(c) (*Sport inf: treten, schlagen*) to slam (*inf*), to wallop (*inf*).
[2] *vi* **(a)** to thresh.
(b) (*inf: schlagen, treten*) to hit violently ♦ **auf die Tasten ~** to thump *or* pound the keys.
[3] *vr* (*inf: sich prügeln*) to have a fight.
Drescher *m* **-s, -** thresher.
Dresch-: ~flegel *m* flail; **~maschine** *f* threshing machine; **~tenne** *f* threshing floor.
⚠ **Dreß** *m* **-sses, -sse,** (*Aus*) *f* **-, -ssen** (*Sport*) (sports) kit; (*für Fußball auch*) strip.
Dresseur [-'søːɐ] *m* trainer.
dressierbar *adj Tier* trainable; (*pej*) *Mensch auch* susceptible to conditioning ♦ **leicht/schwer ~** easy/difficult to train/condition.
dressieren* *vt* **(a)** *Tier* to train; (*pej*) *Mensch auch* to condition, to discipline ♦ **auf jdn/etw dressiert sein** to be trained to respond to sb/sth; **auf den Mann dressiert sein** to be trained to attack people; **auf das Zusammentreiben von Tieren dressiert** trained to round up animals; **zu etw dressiert sein** to be trained *etc* to do sth.
(b) (*Cook*) *Geflügel* to dress; *Braten* to prepare; (*esp Aus*) *Torte etc* to decorate; *Teig, Creme* to pipe.
Dressman ['drɛsmən] *m* **-s, Dressmen** male model.
Dressur *f* training; (*für ~reiten*) dressage; (*fig*) conditioning.
Dressur-: ~prüfung *f* dressage test; **~reiten** *nt* dressage; **~reiter** *m* dressage rider.
dribbeln *vi* to dribble ♦ **mit dem Ball ~** to dribble the ball.
Dribbling *nt* **-s, -s** dribbling ♦ **ein ~** a piece of dribbling.
Drift *f* **-, -en** (*Naut*) drift.
driften *vi aux sein* (*Naut, fig*) to drift.
Drill *m* **-(e)s,** *no pl* (*Mil, fig*) drill; (*Sch auch*) drills *pl*.
Drillbohrer *m* drill.
drillen *vti* **(a)** (*Mil, fig*) to drill ♦ **jdn auf etw** (*acc*) **~** to drill sb in sth; **auf etw** (*acc*) **gedrillt sein** (*fig inf*) to be practised at doing sth. **(b)** *Loch* to drill. **(c)** (*Agr*) to drill, to sow *or* plant in drills. **(d)** (*beim Angeln*) to play.
Drillich *m* **-s, -e** drill; (*für Matratzen etc*) ticking; (*für Markisen*) canvas.
Drillich-: ~anzug *m* overalls *pl*, dungarees *pl*; **~zeug** *nt* overalls *pl*.
Drilling *m* **(a)** triplet. **(b)** (*Angelhaken*) three-pronged hook. **(c)** (*Jagdgewehr*) triple-barrelled shotgun.
Drillingsgeburt *f* triple birth.
Drill-: ~maschine *f* (*Agr*) seed drill; **~übung** *f* drill.
drin *adv* **(a)** (*inf*) *siehe* **darin (a), drinnen.**
(b) (*inf*) **da ~** *siehe* **darin (b).**
(c) in it ♦ **er/es ist da ~** he/it is in there; **in der Flasche ist noch etwas ~** there's still something in the bottle; **hallo, ist da jemand ~?** hello, is (there) anyone in there?; *siehe* **~sitzen** *etc.*
(d) (*inf: in Redewendungen*) **das ist** *or* **liegt bei dem alles ~** anything's possible with him; **bis jetzt ist** *or* **liegt noch alles ~** everything is still quite open; **~ sein** (*in der Arbeit*) to be into it; **für sie ist doch (gegen ihn) nichts ~** she hasn't a hope (against him); **das ist doch nicht ~** (*geht nicht*) that's not on (*inf*).
dringen *pret* **drang,** *ptp* **gedrungen** *vi* **(a)** *aux sein* to penetrate, to come through; (*fig: Nachricht, Geheimnis*) to penetrate, to get through (*an or in +acc* to) ♦ **(durch etw) ~** to come through (sth), to penetrate (sth); **jdm ans Herz ~** to go to *or* touch sb's heart; **an** *or* **in die Öffentlichkeit ~** to leak *or* get out, to become public knowledge; **der Pfeil drang ihm in die Brust** the arrow penetrated (into) his chest; **durch eine Menschenmenge ~** to push (one's way) through a crowd of people; **hinter die Ursache/ein Rätsel ~** to get to the bottom of this/a puzzle.
(b) *aux sein* (*geh*) **in jdn ~** to press *or* urge sb; **mit Bitten/Fragen in jdn ~** to ply *or* press sb with requests/questions.
(c) auf etw (*acc*) **~** to insist on sth; **er drang darauf, einen Arzt zu holen** *or* **daß man einen Arzt holte** he insisted on fetching a doctor.
dringend *adj* (*eilig, wichtig*) urgent, pressing; (*nachdrücklich, zwingend*) strong; *Abraten, Anraten* strong, strenuous; *Gründe* compelling ♦ **etw ~ machen** (*inf*) to treat sth as urgent; **ein ~er Fall** (*Med*) an emergency; **jdn ~ bitten, etw zu unterlassen** to ask sb in the strongest terms *or* to urge sb to stop doing sth; **~ notwendig/erforderlich** urgently needed, essential; **~ verdächtig** strongly suspected.
dringlich *adj* urgent, pressing.
Dringlichkeit *f* urgency.
Dringlichkeits-: ~anfrage *f* (*Parl*) emergency question; **~antrag** *m* (*Parl*) emergency motion; **~stufe** *f* priority; **~stufe 1** top priority.
drinhängen *vi sep irreg* (*inf*) *siehe* **drinstecken (b, c).**
Drink *m* **-s, -s** drink.
drinnen *adv* (*in geschlossenem Raum*) inside; (*im Haus auch*) indoors; (*fig: im Inland*) internally, at home ♦ **~ und draußen** inside and outside; (*im Inland etc*) at home and abroad; **hier/dort ~** in here/there; **ich gehe nach ~** (*inf*) I'm going in(side).
drinsitzen *vi sep irreg* (*inf*) to be in trouble.
drinstecken *vi sep* (*inf*) **(a)** (*verborgen sein*) to be (contained) ♦ **auch bei ihm muß ein guter Kern ~** there must be some good even in him.
(b) (*investiert sein*) **da steckt eine Menge Geld/Arbeit** *etc* **drin** a lot of money/work *etc* has gone into it.
(c) (*verwickelt sein*) to be involved in it ♦ **er steckt bis über die Ohren drin** he's up to his ears in it.
(d) (*voraussehen können*) **da steckt man nicht drin** one never knows *or* can never tell (what will happen).
drinstehen *vi sep irreg aux haben or* (*dial*) *sein* (*inf*) to be in it.
drisch *imper sing of* **dreschen.**
dritt *adv* **wir kommen zu ~** three of us are coming together; *siehe* **viert.**
dritt- *in cpds* third; **~älteste(r, s)** *adj* third oldest.
Drittel *nt* **-s, -** third; *siehe* **Viertel**[1].
dritteln *vt* to divide into three (parts); *Zahl* to divide by three.
Drittelparität *f* equal say in decision-making for students/workers ♦ **die ~ verlangen** to demand an equal say in decision-making.
Dritten|abschlagen *nt children's game,* ≃ tag.
drittens *adv* thirdly; *siehe* **viertens.**
Dritte(r) *mf decl as adj* third person, third man/woman *etc*; (*Unbeteiligter*) third party ♦ **der lachende ~** *the third party who benefits from a division between two others*; **in dieser Angelegenheit ist er der lachende ~** he comes off best from this matter; **wenn zwei sich streiten, freut sich der ~** (*prov*) when two people quarrel a third one rejoices; **der ~ im Bunde** the third in *or* of the trio; *siehe* **Vierte(r).**
dritte(r, s) *adj* third ♦ **der ~ Fall** the dative case; **an einem ~n Ort** on neutral territory; **von ~r Seite (eine Neuigkeit erfahren)** (to learn a piece of news) from a third party; **Menschen ~r Klasse** third-class citizens; **ein D~s** a third thing; *siehe* **vierte(r, s).**
Dritte-Welt- *in cpds* Third World; **~-Bewegung** *f* Third World movement; **~-Laden** *m* ≃ OXFAM shop (*Brit*), thrift store (*US*), charity shop for the Third World.
Dritt-: d~größte(r, s) *adj* third-biggest *or* -largest; **d~höchste(r, s)** *adj* third highest; **~interesse** *nt* interest of a third party; **d~klassig** *adj* third-rate (*pej*), third-class; ⚠**~kläßler(in** *f*) *m* **-s, -** (*Sch*) third-former; **d~letzte(r, s)** *adj* third from last, last but two; **an d~letzter Stelle** third from last, last but two; **~person** *f* third person *or* party; **d~rangig** *adj* third-rate; **~schaden** *m* damage suffered by a third party.
Drive [draif] *m* **-s, -s** drive.
DRK ['deː|ɛr'kaː] *nt* **-** *abbr of* **Deutsches Rotes Kreuz.**
drob *adv* (*obs*) *siehe* **darob.**
droben *adv* (*old, dial*) up there ♦ **dort ~** up there.
Droge *f* **-, -n** drug.
dröge *adj* (*N Ger*) *siehe* **trocken.**
Drogen-: d~abhängig *adj* addicted to drugs; **er ist d~abhängig** he's a drug addict; **~abhängige(r)** *mf decl as adj* drug addict; **~abhängigkeit** *f* drug addiction *no art*; **~baron** *m* (*inf*) drug baron (*inf*); **~benutzer(in** *f*) *m* drug user; **~fahnder** *m* **-s, -** drug squad officer, narcotics officer; **~fahndungsbehörde** *f* drug squad; **~geschäft** *nt* drug trade; **~handel** *m* drug traffic *or* trade; **~konsum** *m* drug consumption; ⚠**~mißbrauch** *m* drug abuse *no art*; **~sucht** *f* drug addiction; **d~süchtig** *adj* addicted to drugs; **~süchtige(r)** *mf* drug addict; **~szene** *f* drug scene; **~tote(r)** *mf* drug death.
Drogerie *f* chemist's (shop), drugstore (*US*).
Drogist(in *f*) *m* chemist, druggist (*US*).
Drohbrief *m* threatening letter.
drohen [1] *vi* **(a)** to threaten (*jdm* sb) ♦ **er drohte dem Kind mit erhobenem Zeigefinger** he raised a warning finger to the child.
(b) (jdm) mit etw ~ to threaten (sb with) sth; **er droht mit Selbstmord** he threatens to commit suicide; **(jdm) ~, etw zu tun** to threaten to do sth.
(c) (*bevorstehen*) (*Gefahr*) to threaten; (*Gewitter*) to be imminent *or* in the offing; (*Streik, Krieg*) to be imminent *or* looming ♦ **jdm droht etw** sb is being threatened by sth; **jdm droht Gefahr/der Tod** sb is in danger/in danger of dying; **es droht Gefahr/ein Streik** there is the threat of danger/a strike.
[2] *v aux* to threaten ♦ **das Schiff drohte zu sinken** the ship threatened to sink, the ship was in danger of sinking.
drohend *adj* **(a)** *Handbewegung, Haltung, Blick, Wolken* threatening, menacing. **(b)** (*bevorstehend*) *Unheil, Gefahr, Krieg* imminent, impending.
Drohgebärde *f* threatening gesture.
Drohn *m* **-en, -en** (*form*), **Drohne** *f* **-, -n** drone; (*fig pej auch*) idler, parasite.
dröhnen [1] *vi* **(a)** to roar; (*Donner*) to rumble; (*Lautsprecher, Musik, Stimme*) to boom ♦ **etw dröhnt jdm in den Ohren/im Kopf** sth roars *etc* in sb's ears/head.
(b) (*Raum etc*) to resound, to echo ♦ **mir ~ die Ohren/dröhnt der Kopf** my ears are/head is ringing.
[2] *vt* **jdm eine ~** (*sl*) to sock sb (*inf*).
dröhnend *adj Lärm, Applaus* resounding, echoing; *Stimme* booming; *Gelächter* roaring.
Drohnen-: ~dasein *nt* (*fig pej*) idle *or* parasitic life; **d~haft** *adj* drone-like; (*fig auch*) idle, parasitic; **~schlacht** *f* (*Zool*) slaughter of the drones.
Dröhnung *f* (*sl*) beating.
Drohung *f* threat.
Droh-: ~verhalten *nt* threatening *or* aggressive behaviour; **~wort** *nt* threat.
drollig *adj* **(a)** funny, comical, droll. **(b)** (*seltsam*) odd, strange ♦ **werd' nicht ~!** don't be funny!; **ein ~er Kauz** an odd bod (*inf*), an oddball (*esp US inf*).
Dromedar [*auch:* 'droː-] *nt* **-s, -e** dromedary.
Dropout ['drɔp|aʊt] *m* **-s, -s (a)** (*Mensch*) dropout. **(b)** (*in Bandaufzeichnung*) fade.

Drops *m or nt* **-, -** *or* **-e** fruit drop.
drosch *pret of* **dreschen.**
Droschke *f* **-, -n (a)** *(Pferde~)* (hackney) cab, hackney-carriage. **(b)** *(dated: Taxi)* (taxi-)cab.
Droschken-: ~(halte)platz *m (dated)* cab rank; **~kutscher** *m* cab driver.
Drossel[1] *f* **-, -n** *(Orn)* thrush.
Drossel[2] *f* **-, -n** *siehe* **Drosselspule, Drosselventil.**
Drosselklappe *f (Tech)* throttle valve.
drosseln *vt* **(a)** *Motor, Dampf etc* to throttle, to choke; *Heizung, Wärme* to turn down; *Strom* to reduce; *Tempo, Produktion etc* to cut down. **(b)** *(dated: würgen)* to throttle, to strangle.
Drosselspule *f (Elec)* choking coil.
Drosselung, ⚠Droßlung *f siehe vt (a)* throttling, choking; turning down; reducing; cutting down.
Drosselventil *nt* throttle valve.
drüben *adv* over there; *(auf der anderen Seite, inf: auf die DDR bezogen)* on the other side; *(inf: auf Amerika bezogen)* over the water ♦ **hier/dort** *or* **da ~** over here/there; **nach ~** over there; **bei der Nachbarin ~** over at my neighbour's; **~ über dem Rhein** on the other side of the Rhine; **nach/von ~** over/from over there; *siehe* **hüben.**
Drüben *nt* **-s,** *no pl siehe* **Jenseits.**
drüber *adv (inf)* **(a)** *siehe* **darüber, hinüber. (b) da ~** *siehe* **darüber.**
Druck[1] *m* **-(e)s, ¨e (a)** *(Phys, fig)* pressure ♦ **unter ~ stehen** *(lit, fig)* to be under pressure; **jdn unter ~ setzen** *(fig)* to put pressure on sb, to pressurize sb; **(fürchterlich) in ~ sein** *(fig)* to be under (terrible) pressure; **~ auf jdn/etw ausüben** *(lit, fig)* to exert *or* put pressure on sb/sth; **~ hinter etw** *(acc)* **machen** *(inf)* to put some pressure on sth; **~ und Gegendruck** pressure and resistance; **ein ~ im Kopf/Magen** a feeling of pressure in one's head/stomach.
(b) *(das Drücken)* pressure *(gen* from) *no indef art* ♦ **durch einen ~ auf den Knopf** by pressing the button.
(c) *(Drogen sl)* fix ♦ **sich** *(dat)* **einen ~ machen** to have a fix.
Druck[2] *m* **-(e)s, -e (a)** *(das Drucken)* printing; *(Art des Drucks, Schriftart)* print; *(Druckwerk)* copy ♦ **~ und Satz** setting and printing; **das Buch ist im ~** the book is in the press *or* is being printed; **im ~ erscheinen** to appear in print; **in ~ gehen** to go into print; **etw in ~ geben** to send sth to press *or* to be printed; **~ und Verlag von ...** printed and published by ...
(b) *(Kunst~)* print.
(c) *pl* **-s** *(Tex)* print.
Druck-: ~abfall *m* drop *or* fall in pressure; **~anstieg** *m* rise in pressure; **~anzug** *m* pressure suit; **~ausgleich** *m* pressure balance; **~behälter** *m* pressure vessel; **~belastung** *f* pressure load; **~bleistift** *m* retractable pencil; **~bogen** *m (Typ)* printed sheet; **~buchstabe** *m* printed character *or* letter; **den Bogen bitte in ~buchstaben ausfüllen** please fill out the form in block capitals *or* block letters; **in ~buchstaben schreiben** to print.
Drückeberger *m* **-s, -** *(pej inf)* *(fauler Mensch)* shirker, idle so-and-so *(inf)*; *(in der Schule auch)* skiver *(Brit inf)*; *(Feigling)* coward.
Drückebergerei *f, no pl (pej inf)* shirking; *(in der Schule auch)* skiving *(Brit inf)*.
drückebergerisch *adj (pej inf) Mensch* idle ♦ **sein ~es Verhalten** his idling *or* shirking.
druck|empfindlich *adj* sensitive (to pressure).
drucken *vti (Typ, Tex)* to print ♦ **ein Buch ~ lassen** to have a book printed; **ein Buch in 1000 Exemplaren/einer hohen Auflage ~** to print 1000 copies/a large edition of a book; *siehe* **gedruckt.**
drücken, *(dial)* **drucken** **1** *vt* **(a)** *Hand, Klinke, Hebel* to press; *Knopf auch* to push; *Obst, Saft, Eiter* to squeeze ♦ **jdm etw in die Hand ~** to press *or* slip sth into sb's hand; **jdn ~** to squeeze sb; *(umarmen)* to hug sb; **jdn/etw an sich/ans Herz ~** to press *or* clasp sb/sth to one/one's breast; **jdn zur Seite/nach hinten/in einen Stuhl ~** to push sb aside/back/into a chair; **den Hut in die Stirn ~** to pull one's hat down over one's brow *or* forehead.
(b) *(geh: bedrücken)* to weigh heavily upon ♦ **was drückt dich denn?** what's on your mind?
(c) *(Druckgefühl erzeugen: Schuhe, Korsett etc)* to pinch, to nip ♦ **jdn im Magen ~** *(Essen)* to lie *or* weigh heavily on sb's stomach; **mich drückt der Magen** my stomach feels heavy.
(d) *(verringern, herabsetzen)* to force down; *Rekord* to beat; *Leistung, Niveau* to lower; *Steuern* to bring down.
(e) *(inf: unterdrücken) jdn* to keep down; *Stimmung* to dampen.
(f) *(Sport) Gewicht* to press; *Handstand* to press into.
(g) *(Aviat)* to point down.
(h) *(Cards)* to discard.
(i) *(Econ)* **etw in** *or* **auf den Markt ~** to push sth.
(j) *(inf) Heroin* to shoot.
2 *vi* **(a)** to press; *(Wetter, Hitze)* to be oppressive; *(Brille, Schuhe, Korsett etc)* to pinch; *(Essen)* to weigh (on one's stomach) ♦ **„bitte ~"** "push"; **auf etw** *(acc)***/an etw** *(acc)* **~** to press sth; **aufs Gemüt ~** to dampen *or* depress one's spirits, to get one down; **auf die Stimmung ~** to dampen one's mood.
(b) *(drängeln, stoßen)* to push.
(c) *(bei Stuhlentleerung)* to strain, to push.
(d) *(inf: Heroin injizieren)* to shoot up.
(e) *(sl: Abonnements etc verkaufen)* to hawk (subscriptions *etc*) *(inf)*, to go on the knocker *(sl)*.
3 *vr* **(a)** *(mit Ortsangabe)* *(in +acc* into, *an +acc* against) *(sich quetschen)* to squeeze; *(schutzsuchend)* to huddle ♦ **sich aus dem Zimmer ~** to slip out of the room.
(b) *(inf)* to shirk, to dodge; *(vor Militärdienst)* to dodge ♦ **sich vor etw** *(dat)* **~** to shirk *or* dodge sth; **sich (um etw) ~** to get out of (doing) sth; *(esp in Schule auch)* to skive off *or* out of (doing) sth *(Brit inf)*.
drückend *adj Last, Steuern* heavy; *Sorgen* serious; *Armut* grinding; *Wetter, Hitze* oppressive, close ♦ **es ist ~ heiß** it's oppressively hot.
⚠**drückendheiß** *adj attr* oppressively hot.
Drucker *m* **-s, - (a)** *(Beruf)* printer. **(b)** *(Comput)* printer.
Drücker *m* **-s, - (a)** *(Knopf)* (push) button; *(inf: von Pistole etc)* trigger; *(von Klingel)* push ♦ **die Hand am ~ haben** *(fig inf)* to be ready to act; **am ~ sein** *or* **sitzen** *(fig inf)* *(in Machtposition)* to be in a key position; *(an der Quelle)* to be ideally placed *or* in an ideal position; **auf den letzten ~** *(fig inf)* at the last minute.
(b) *(Türklinke)* handle; *(von Schnappschloß)* latch.
(c) *(sl: Abonnementverkäufer)* hawker *(inf)*.
Druckerei *f* **(a)** printing works *pl*, printery; *(Firma auch)* printer's. **(b)** *(Druckwesen)* printing *no art.*
Druckerin *f siehe* **Drucker (a).**
Drückerin *f siehe* **Drücker (c).**
Drückerkolonne *f (sl)* door-to-door sales team.
Druck|erlaubnis *f* imprimatur.
Drucker-: ~presse *f* printing press; **~schwärze** *f* printer's ink; **~sprache** *f* printer's language; **~treiber** *m (Comput)* printer driver; **~zeichen** *nt* printer's mark.
Druck-: ~erzeugnis *nt* printed material; **~fahne** *f* galley(-proof), proof; **~farbe** *f* coloured printing ink; **~fehler** *m* misprint, typographical *or* printer's error; **~fehlerteufel** *m (hum)* gremlin *(which causes misprints)*; **d~fertig** *adj* ready to print *or* for the press; **d~fest** *adj Werkstoff* resistant to pressure; **~form** *f (Typ)* printing forme, quoin; **d~frisch** *adj* hot from the press; **~gefälle** *nt (Phys)* difference in pressure; **~gefühl** *nt* feeling of pressure; **~geschwindigkeit** *f (Comput)* print speed; **~kabine** *f* pressurized cabin; **~knopf** *m* **(a)** *(Sew)* press-stud, snap fastener; **(b)** *(Tech)* push-button; **~kopf** *m (Comput)* print head; **~kosten** *pl* printing costs *pl*; **~legung** *f* printing; **mit der ~legung beginnen** to begin printing, to go to press.
Druckluft *f* compressed air.
Druckluft-: ~bohrer *m* pneumatic drill; **~bremse** *f* air-brake.
Druck-: ~maschine *f (Typ)* printing press; **~menü** *nt (Comput)* print menu; **~messer** *m* **-s, -** pressure gauge; **~mittel** *nt (fig)* form of pressure, means of exerting pressure; **als politisches ~mittel** as a form of political pressure, as a means of exerting political pressure; **~muster** *nt* print(ed pattern *or* design); **Stoffe mit ~muster** prints, printed materials; **~ort** *m* place of printing; **~papier** *nt* printing paper; **~platte** *f* printing plate; **~posten** *m (inf)* cushy job *or* number *(inf)*; **~presse** *f* printing press; **~pumpe** *f* pressure pump; **d~reif** *adj* ready for printing, passed for press; *(fig)* polished; **d~reif sprechen** to speak in a polished style; **~sache** *f* **(a)** *(Post)* business letter; *(Werbematerial)* circular; *(als Portoklasse)* printed matter; **„~sache"** "printed matter"; **etw als ~sache schicken** ≃ to send sth at printed-paper rate; **(b)** *(Typ)* *(Auftrag)* stationery printing job; **~sachen** *pl (Akzidenz)* stationery printing *sing*; **~schalter** *m* push-button switch; **~schott** *nt (Aviat)* bulkhead; **~schrift** *f* **(a)** *(Schriftart)* printing; **in ~schrift schreiben** to print; **bitte das Formular in** *or* **mit ~schrift ausfüllen** please fill out the form in block capitals *or* block letters; **die ~schrift lernen** to learn printing, to learn to print; **(b)** *(gedrucktes Werk)* pamphlet; **~seite** *f* printed page.
drucksen *vi (inf)* to hum and haw *(inf)*.
Druck-: ~sorten *pl (Aus)* printed forms *pl*; **~stelle** *f* place *or* *(Mal)* mark *(where pressure has been applied)*; *(Fleck auf Pfirsich, Haut)* bruise; **~stock** *m (Typ)* relief plate; **~taste** *f* push-button; **~technik** *f* printing technology *or* *(Verfahren)* technique; **d~technisch** *adj* typographical; *(in bezug auf mechanischen Vorgang)* printing *attr*; **d~technisch verfeinert** improved from the printing point of view; **~trommel** *f (Comput)* print drum; **~type** *f* type; **d~unempfindlich** *adj* insensitive to pressure; **~unterschied** *m* difference in pressure; **~verband** *m (Med)* pressure bandage; **~verbot** *nt* printing ban; **~verfahren** *nt* printing process; **~verlust** *m (Tech)* loss of pressure, reduction in pressure; **~vorlage** *f (Typ)* setting copy; **~wasserreaktor** *m* pressurized water reactor; **~welle** *f* shock wave; **~werk** *nt* printed work, publication; **~wesen** *nt* printing *no art*; **~zeile** *f* line of print.
Drude *f* **-, -n** *(Myth)* witch.
Drudenfuß *m (Myth)* pentagram.
druff *adv (dial inf) siehe* **drauf.**
Druide *m* **-n, -n** Druid.
druidisch *adj* druidic(al), druid *attr.*
drum *adv (inf)* around, round *(Brit)* ♦ **~ rum** all around *or* round *(Brit)*; **~ rumreden** to beat about the bush; **da wirst du nicht ~ rumkommen** there's no getting out of it; **sei's ~!** *(geh)* never mind; **das D~ und Dran** the paraphernalia; *(Begleiterscheinungen)* the fuss and bother; **mit allem D~ und Dran** with all the bits and pieces *(inf)* *or* *(Mahlzeit)* trimmings *pl*; *siehe* **darum.**
Drumherum *nt* **-s** *no pl* trappings *pl.*
drunten *adv (old, dial)* down there.
drunter *adv* under(neath) ♦ **da kann ich mir nichts ~ vorstellen** that means nothing to me; **~ und drüber** upside down, topsy-turvy; **alles ging** *or* **es ging alles ~ und drüber** everything was upside down *or* topsy-turvy; **das D~ und Drüber** the confusion, the muddle; *siehe* **darunter.**
Drusch *m* **-(e)s, -e** *(Agr)* threshing; *(Produkt)* threshed corn.
Druse[1] *f* **-, -n** *(Min, Geol)* druse.
Druse[2] *m* **-n, -n** *(Rel)* Druse.

Drüse *f* **-, -n** gland.
Drüsen-: d~artig *adj* glandular; **~fieber** *nt* glandular fever, mono(nucleosis) (*US*); **~funktion** *f* glandular function; **~krankheit** *f*, **~leiden** *nt* glandular disorder; **~schwellung** *f* glandular swelling, swollen glands *pl*; **~überfunktion** *f* hyperactivity *or* overactivity of the glands; **~unterfunktion** *f* underactivity of the glands.
DSB [de:|ɛs'be:] *m* **-s** *abbr of* **Deutscher Sportbund** German Sports Association.
Dschungel *m* **-s, -** (*lit, fig*) jungle ◆ **sich im ~ der Paragraphen zurechtfinden** to wade one's way through the verbiage.
Dschungel-: d~artig *adj Wald* jungle-like; **~fieber** *nt* yellow fever; **~gesetz** *nt* law of the jungle; **~krieg** *m* jungle war/warfare.
Dschunke *f* **-, -n** (*Naut*) junk.
DSG [de:|ɛs'ge:] *f* - *abbr of* **Deutsche Schlafwagen- und Speisewagen-Gesellschaft.**
dt(sch). *abbr of* **deutsch.**
DTP [de:te:'pe:] *abbr of* **Desktop Publishing** DTP.
DTP- *in cpds* DTP; **~-Anwender** *m* DTP user; **~-Fachmann** *m* DTP specialist; **~-Software** *f* DTP software.
Dtzd. *abbr of* **Dutzend.**
du *pers pron gen* **deiner**, *dat* **dir**, *acc* **dich** you (*familiar form of address*), thou (*obs, dial*); (*man*) you ◆ **D~** (*in Briefen*) you; **ich gehe heute ins Kino und ~?** I'm going to the cinema today, how about you? **~ (zu jdm) sagen, jdn mit ~ anreden** to use the familiar form of address (with sb), to say "du" (to sb); **~**, der **~ es erlebt hast** you who have experienced it; **mit jdm auf ~ und ~ stehen** to be pals with sb; **mit jdm per ~ sein** to be on familiar *or* friendly terms with sb; **~ bist es** it's you; **bist ~ es** *or* **das?** is it *or* that you?; **Vater unser, der ~ bist im Himmel** our Father, who *or* which art in heaven; **mach ~ das doch!** *you* do it!, do it yourself!; **~**, meine Heimat! (*poet*) thou, my homeland!; **~ Glücklicher!/Idiot!** lucky you *or* you lucky thing/you idiot; **~ Schlingel/Schuft(, ~)!** you rascal/scoundrel *etc*, (you)! **ach ~ lieber Gott** *or* **liebe Güte** good Lord!, good heavens!; **~ (Mutti), kannst ~ mir mal helfen?** hey (mummy), can you help me?; **~**, ich muß jetzt aber gehen listen, I have to go now; **~, ~!** (*hum: drohend*) naughty, naughty; *siehe* **mir.**
Du *nt* **-(s), -(s)** "du", familiar form of address ◆ **jdm das ~ anbieten** to suggest that sb uses "du" *or* the familiar form of address.
dual *adj* dual.
Dual *m* **-s, -e, Dualis** *m* **-, Duale** dual.
Dualismus *m* (*Philos, Pol, geh*) dualism.
Dualist(in *f*) *m* (*Philos*) dualist.
dualistisch *adj* (*Philos, Pol, geh*) dualistic.
Dualität *f* (*geh*) duality.
Dualsystem *nt* (*Math*) binary system.
Dübel *m* **-s, -** rawlplug ®; (*Holz~*) dowel.
Dübelmasse *f* plugging compound, filler.
dübeln *vti* to plug.
dubios, dubiös *adj* (*geh*) dubious.
Dublee *nt* **-s, -s** rolled gold *no pl*; (*Gegenstand*) article made of rolled gold.
Dubleegold *nt* rolled gold.
Dublette *f* **(a)** (*doppelt vorhandenes Stück*) duplicate. **(b)** (*Hunt*) right and left. **(c)** (*Edelstein*) doublet. **(d)** (*Boxen*) one-two.
dublieren* *vt Metall* to coat with gold; *Garn* to twist.
Dublin ['dablɪn] *nt* **-s** Dublin.
Dubliner ['dablɪnɐ] *adj attr* Dublin.
Dubliner(in *f*) ['dablinɐ, -ərɪn] *m* Dubliner.
ducken [1] *vr* to duck; (*fig pej*) to cringe, to cower; (*fig: Bäume, Häuser*) to nestle ◆ **ich duckte mich vor dem Hieb** I ducked the blow; **sich in eine Ecke/hinter eine Deckung ~** to duck *or* dodge into a corner/behind cover; *siehe* **geduckt.**
[2] *vt Kopf, Menschen* to duck; (*fig*) to humiliate.
[3] *vi* (*fig pej*) to cower.
Duckmäuser *m* **-s, -** (*pej*) moral coward.
Duckmäuserei *f* (*pej*) moral cowardice ◆ **Erziehung zur ~** bringing up to be moral cowards.
duckmäuserisch *adj* (*pej*) showing moral cowardice.
duckmäusern *vi insep* (*pej*) to be moral cowards/a moral coward.
Duckmäusertum *nt* (*pej*) chicken-heartedness ◆ **jdn zum ~ erziehen** to bring sb up to be chicken-hearted.
Dudelei *f* (*pej*) humming; (*auf Flöte*) tootling.
Dudelkasten *m* (*pej inf*) noise-box.
dudeln (*pej inf*) [1] *vi* to hum; (*auf Flöte*) to tootle (*auf +dat* on).
[2] *vt* **(a)** *Lied* to hum; (*auf Flöte*) to toot. **(b)** (*dial*) **einen ~** to have a wee dram (*dial*).
Dudelsack *m* bagpipes *pl*.
Dudelsack-: ~pfeifer, ~spieler *m* (bag)piper.
Duell *nt* **-s, -e** (*lit, fig*) duel (*um* over) ◆ **ein ~ auf Degen** a duel with swords; **ein ~ (mit jdm) austragen** to fight *or* have a duel (with sb); **jdn zum ~ (heraus)fordern/ins ~ fordern** to challenge sb to a duel.
Duellant [due'lant] *m* dueller, duellist.
duellieren* [due'li:rən] *vr* to (fight a) duel.
Duellpistole *f* duelling pistol.
Duett *nt* **-(e)s, -e (a)** (*Mus, fig*) duet ◆ **im ~ singen** to sing a duet; **etw im ~ singen** to sing sth as a duet. **(b)** (*fig inf: Paar*) duo (*inf*).
duff *adj* (*N Ger*) matt; *Glas, Fenster* dull.
Dufflecoat ['daflko:t] *m* **-s, -s** dufflecoat.
Duft *m* **-(e)s, ¨e (a)** (pleasant) smell, scent; (*von Blumen, Parfüm auch*) fragrance, perfume; (*von Essen, Kaffee etc*) smell, aroma; (*Absonderung von Tieren*) scent; (*fig*) allure ◆ **den ~ der großen weiten Welt verspüren** (*usu iro*) to get a taste of the big, wide world. **(b)** (*liter: Dunst*) haze.
Duftdrüse *f* scent gland.
dufte *adj, adv* (*sl*) smashing (*inf*), great (*inf*).
duften [1] *vi* to smell ◆ **nach etw ~** to smell *or* have a smell of sth.
[2] *vi impers* **hier duftet es nach Kaffee** there is a smell *or* it smells of coffee here.
duftend *adj attr* nice-smelling; *Parfüm, Blumen etc* fragrant.
duftig *adj* **(a)** *Kleid, Stoff* gossamery; *Spitzen* frothy; *Wolken* fluffy. **(b)** (*poet: zart dunstig*) hazy.
Duftigkeit *f siehe adj (a)* gossamer lightness; frothiness; fluffiness; lightness.
Duft-: d~los *adj* odourless, unscented; **~marke** *f* scent mark; **~note** *f* (*von Parfüm*) scent; (*von Mensch*) smell; **~organ** *nt* scent gland; **~probe** *f* **(a)** (*Vorgang*) perfume test; **(b)** (*Probeflasche*) free sample of perfume; **~stoff** *m* scent; (*für Parfüm, Waschmittel etc*) fragrance; **~wasser** *nt, pl* **~wässer** toilet water; (*hum: Parfüm*) perfume, scent; **~wolke** *f* (*iro*) fragrance (*iro*); (*von Parfüm*) cloud of perfume.
duhn *adj* (*N Ger inf*) sloshed (*inf*).
Dukaten *m* **-s, -** ducat.
Dukaten-: ~esel *m* (*hum*) *siehe* **~scheißer**; **~gold** *nt* fine gold; **~scheißer** *m* (*inf*) **einen ~scheißer haben, ein ~scheißer sein** to be a goldmine, to be made of money.
Duktus *m* **-**, *no pl* (*geh*) characteristic style; (*von Handschrift*) characteristics *pl*, flow.
dulden [1] *vi* (*geh: leiden*) to suffer.
[2] *vt* **(a)** (*zulassen*) to tolerate; *Widerspruch auch* to countenance ◆ **ich dulde das nicht** I won't tolerate that; **die Sache duldet keinen Aufschub** the matter cannot be delayed *or* postponed; **etw stillschweigend ~/stillschweigend ~, daß ...** to connive at sth.
(b) (*nicht vertreiben*) to tolerate ◆ **er ist hier nur geduldet** he's only tolerated here, he's only here on sufferance.
(c) (*geh: erdulden*) *Not, Schmerz* to suffer.
Dulder(in *f*) *m* **-s, -** silent sufferer.
Duldermiene *f* (*iro*) air of patient suffering ◆ **mit ~** with an air of patient suffering.
duldsam *adj* tolerant (*gegenüber* of, *jdm gegenüber* towards sb).
Duldsamkeit *f* tolerance.
Duldung *f* toleration ◆ **solche Zustände erlauben keine weitere ~** such conditions can be tolerated no longer; **unter** *or* **bei** *or* **mit stillschweigender ~ der Behörden** *etc* with the (tacit) connivance of the authorities *etc*.
Dulliäh *m* **-**, *no pl* (*Aus inf*) tipsiness (*inf*) ◆ **im ~** (when one is/was) tipsy.
Dulzinea *f* **-, Dulzineen** (*hum*) ladylove.
Dumdum *nt* **-(s), -(s)**, ⚠**Dumdumgeschoß** *nt* dumdum (bullet).
dumm *adj comp* **¨er**, *superl* **¨ste(r, s)**, *adv* **am ¨sten (a)** stupid, dumb (*esp US*); *Mensch auch* thick (*inf*); (*unklug, unvernünftig auch*) silly, foolish ◆ **der ~e August** (*inf*) the clown; **~e Gans** silly goose; **~es Zeug (reden)** (to talk) nonsense *or* rubbish; **ein ~es Gesicht machen, ~ gucken** to look stupid; **jdn wie einen ~en Jungen behandeln** (*inf*) to treat sb like a child; **jdn für ~ verkaufen** (*inf*) to think sb is stupid; **du willst mich wohl für ~ verkaufen** you must think I'm stupid; **ich lasse mich nicht für ~ verkaufen** I'm not so stupid (*inf*); **das ist gar nicht (so) ~** that's not a bad idea; **sich ~ anstellen** to behave stupidly; **sich ~ stellen** to act stupid *or* dumb (*esp US*); **~ fragen** to ask a silly question/silly questions; **~ dastehen** to look stupid *or* foolish; **sich ~ und dämlich reden** (*inf*) to talk till one is blue in the face (*inf*); **sich ~ und dämlich suchen** to search high and low; **sich ~ und dämlich verdienen** to earn the earth (*inf*); **~ geboren, nichts dazugelernt** (*prov*) he/she *etc* hasn't got the sense he/she *etc* was born with (*prov*); **jetzt wird's mir zu ~** I've had enough; **der Krach macht mich ganz ~ (im Kopf)** the noise is making my head spin.
(b) (*ärgerlich, unangenehm*) annoying; *Gefühl auch* nagging; *Sache, Geschichte, Angelegenheit auch* silly ◆ **es ist zu ~, daß er nicht kommen kann** it's too bad that he can't come; **jdm ~ kommen** to get funny with sb (*inf*); **etw D~es** a silly *or* stupid thing; **so etwas D~es** how silly *or* stupid; (*wie ärgerlich*) what a nuisance.
Dumm-: ~bach *nt* (*inf*) **ich bin doch nicht aus ~bach** you can't fool me that easily, I'm not stupid; **~bart, ~beutel** *m* (*inf*) fool (*inf*), dumbbell (*US inf*).
Dummchen *nt* (*inf*) silly-billy (*inf*).
dummdreist *adj* insolent.
Dummdreistigkeit *f* insolence.
Dummejungenstreich *m* silly *or* foolish *or* childish prank.
Dummenfang *m* **das ist der reinste ~** that's just a con (*inf*); **auf ~ ausgehen** to try to catch fools.
Dumme(r) *mf decl as adj* (*inf*) mug (*inf*), fool, sucker (*inf*) ◆ **der ~ sein** to be left to carry the can (*inf*), to be left holding the baby (*inf*); **einen ~n finden** to find a mug (*inf*) *or* a sucker (*inf*).
Dummerchen *nt* (*inf*) silly-billy (*inf*) ◆ **mein ~** you silly-billy.
Dummerjan *m* **-s, -e** (*inf*) silly dope (*inf*).
dummerweise *adv* unfortunately; (*aus Dummheit*) stupidly, foolishly.
Dummheit *f* **(a)** *no pl* stupidity; (*von Menschen auch*) foolishness. **(b)** (*dumme Handlung*) stupid *or* foolish thing ◆ **mach bloß keine ~en!** just don't do anything stupid *or* foolish.
Dummkopf *m* (*inf*) idiot, fool.
dümmlich *adj* silly, stupid; *Mensch auch* foolish, dumb (*esp US*) ◆ **eine ~e Blondine** a dumb blonde.

Dümmling *m* fool.
dümpeln *vi* **(a)** (*Naut*) to bob up and down. **(b)** (*fig*) to hover ◆ **die Partei dümpelt bei 40%** the party is hovering around the 40% mark.
dumpf *adj* **(a)** *Geräusch, Ton* muffled ◆ **~ aufprallen** to land with a thud. **(b)** *Luft, Geruch, Keller, Geschmack etc* musty; (*fig*) *Atmosphäre* stifling. **(c)** *Gefühl, Ahnung, Erinnerung* vague; *Schmerz* dull; (*bedrückend*) gloomy; (*stumpfsinnig*) dull; *Mensch, Geist, Sinn* dulled.
Dumpfbacke *f* (*sl*) dimwit (*inf*), bonehead (*inf*).
Dumpfheit *f, no pl siehe adj* **(a)** muffledness. **(b)** mustiness; stiflingness. **(c)** vagueness; dullness; gloominess; dulledness.
dumpfig *adj* (*feucht*) dank, damp; (*muffig*) musty; (*moderig*) mouldy.
Dumpfigkeit *f, no pl siehe adj* dankness, dampness; mustiness; mouldiness.
Dumping ['dampɪŋ] *nt* **-s,** *no pl* (*Econ*) dumping.
Dumpingpreis *m* give-away price.
dun *adj* (*N Ger inf*) sloshed (*inf*).
Düne *f* **-, -n** (sand-)dune.
Dünen-: ~bildung *f* formation of dunes; **~gras** *nt* marram (grass); **~sand** *m* dune-sand.
Dung *m* **-(e)s,** *no pl* dung, manure.
Düngemittel *nt* fertilizer.
düngen [1] *vt* to fertilize.
[2] *vi* (*Stoff*) to act as a fertilizer; (*Mensch*) to apply fertilizer ◆ **im Garten ~** to put fertilizer on the garden.
Dünger *m* **-s, -** fertilizer.
Dung-: ~fliege *f* dung fly; **~grube** *f* manure pit; **~haufen** *m* dung *or* manure heap.
Düngung *f* **(a)** (*das Düngen*) fertilizing. **(b)** *siehe* **Dünger**.
dunkel *adj* **(a)** (*finster*) dark; (*fig auch*) black ◆ **im D~n** in the dark; **in dunkler Nacht** at dead of night; **im Zimmer ~ machen** (*inf*) to make the room dark, to darken the room.
(b) (*farblich*) dark ◆ **~ gefärbt sein** to be a dark colour; **sich ~ kleiden** to dress in dark colours; **etw ~ anmalen** to paint sth a dark colour; **ein Dunkles, bitte!** ≃ a brown ale (*Brit*) *or* dark beer, please.
(c) (*tief*) *Stimme, Ton* deep.
(d) (*unbestimmt, unklar*) vague; *Erinnerung auch* dim; *Textstelle* unclear ◆ **in dunkler Vergangenheit/Vorzeit** in the dim and distant past; **im ~n tappen** (*fig*) to grope (about) in the dark; **jdn im ~n lassen** to leave sb in the dark; **das liegt noch im ~n** that remains to be seen.
(e) (*pej: zweifelhaft, zwielichtig*) shady (*inf*), dubious.
Dunkel *nt* **-s,** *no pl* (*lit, fig*) darkness ◆ **im ~ der Vergangenheit** in the dim and distant past; **das verliert sich im ~ der Geschichte** it is lost in the mists of history; **in ~ gehüllt sein** (*fig*) to be shrouded in mystery; **im ~ der Nacht** at dead of night.
Dünkel *m* **-s,** *no pl* (*pej geh*) conceit, arrogance.
dunkel- *in cpds* dark; **~blau** *adj* dark blue; **~blond** *adj* light brown; **~gekleidet** *adj attr* dressed in dark(-coloured) clothes; **~haarig** *adj* dark-haired.
dünkelhaft *adj* (*pej geh*) arrogant, conceited.
Dunkel-: d~häutig *adj* dark-skinned; **~heit** *f* (*lit, fig*) darkness; **bei Einbruch** *or* **Eintritt der ~heit** at nightfall; **~kammer** *f* (*Phot*) darkroom; **~kammerleuchte, ~kammerlampe** *f* safelight; **~mann** *m, pl* **-männer** (*pej*) **(a)** shady character; **(b)** (*liter*) obscurant(ist).
dunkeln [1] *vi impers* **es dunkelt** (*geh*) darkness is falling, it is growing dark.
[2] *vi* **(a)** (*poet: Nacht, Abend*) to grow dark. **(b)** *aux sein* (*dunkel werden*) to become darker, to darken.
[3] *vt Holz, Leder, Haar* to darken.
Dunkel-: d~rot *adj* dark red, maroon; **d~weiß** *adj* (*hum*) off-white; **~werden** *nt* nightfall; **~ziffer** *f estimated number of unreported/undetected cases*; **~zone** *f* twilight zone.
dünken (*geh*) *pret* **dünkte** *or* (*obs*) **deuchte**, *ptp* **gedünkt** *or* (*obs*) **gedeucht** [1] *vti impers* **das dünkt mich gut, das dünkt mich** *or* **mir gut zu sein, mich dünkt, daß das gut ist** it seems good to me; **mich dünkt, er kommt nicht mehr** I think *or* methinks (*obs*) he will not come.
[2] *vi* to seem, to appear.
[3] *vr* to think *or* imagine (oneself) ◆ **sie dünkt sich sehr klug** she thinks herself very clever.
dünn *adj* thin; *Suppe, Bier auch* watery; *Kaffee, Tee* watery, weak; (*fein*) *Schleier, Regen, Strümpfe* fine; *Haarwuchs, Besiedlung auch* sparse ◆ **~ gesät** (*fig*) thin on the ground, few and far between; **sich ~ machen** (*hum*) to breathe in; *siehe* **dick, dünnmachen.**
Dünn-: ⚠d~behaart *adj attr Mensch* with thin hair; *Haupt* thinly covered in hair; **⚠d~besiedelt, ⚠d~bevölkert** *adj attr* sparsely populated; **~bier** *nt* weak beer; **~brettbohrer** *m* (*pej inf*) slacker, skiver (*inf*); **geistiger ~brettbohrer** dimwit (*inf*); **~darm** *m* small intestine; **~druckausgabe** *f* India paper edition; **~druckpapier** *nt* India paper.
dünne *adj pred* (*dial*) *siehe* **dünn.**
Dünne *f* **-,** *no pl siehe* **Dünnheit.**
dünnemachen *vr sep* (*dial, inf*) *siehe* **dünnmachen.**
dunnemals *adv* (*dated, hum*) *siehe* **damals.**
Dünn-: d~flüssig *adj Farbe, Öl* thin; *Teig, Honig* runny; *Stuhlgang* loose; **~flüssigkeit** *f siehe adj* thinness; runniness; looseness; **⚠d~gesät** *adj attr* sparse; **d~häutig** *adj* thin-skinned; (*fig auch*) sensitive; **~heit** *f siehe adj* thinness; wateriness; weakness; fineness; sparseness; **d~lippig** *adj* thin-lipped; **d~machen** *vr sep* (*inf*) to make oneself scarce; **~pfiff** *m* (*inf*) the runs (*inf*); **~säure** *f* dilute acid; **~säureverklappung** *f* dumping of dilute acids; **d~schalig** *adj Obst* thin-skinned; *Nüsse, Ei etc* thin-shelled; **⚠~schiß** *m* (*sl*) *siehe* **~pfiff; d~wandig** *adj Haus* thin-walled, with thin walls; *Behälter* thin.
Dunst *m* **-(e)s, ¨-e** (*leichter Nebel*) mist, haze; (*Dampf*) steam; (*Smog*) smog; (*dumpfe Luft*) fug; (*Geruch*) smell ◆ **blauer ~** (*fig inf*) sheer invention; **jdm blauen ~ vormachen** (*inf*) to throw dust in sb's eyes; **sich in ~ auflösen** to go up in smoke; *siehe* **blaß.**
Dunst-: ~abzugshaube *f* extractor hood (*over a cooker*); **d~artig** *adj Rauch, Nebel* vapoury, vaporous.
dunsten *vi* **(a)** (*dampfen*) to steam. **(b)** (*Dunst ausströmen*) to give off a smell, to smell.
dünsten *vt* (*Cook*) *Gemüse, Fisch, Fleisch* to steam; *Obst* to stew.
Dunst-: ~glocke, ~haube *f* haze; pall of smog.
dunstig *adj* **(a)** hazy, misty. **(b)** (*schlecht belüftet*) stuffy; (*verräuchert*) smoky.
Dunstkreis *m* atmosphere; (*von Mensch*) society.
Dünst|obst *nt* (*Cook*) stewed fruit.
Dunst-: ~schicht *f* layer of haze *or* mist; **~schleier** *m* veil of haze *or* mist; **~schwaden** *pl* clouds *pl* of haze/steam; (*Nebel*) haze *sing*; (*Dampf*) clouds *pl* of steam; (*Rauch*) clouds *pl* of smoke; **~wolke** *f* cloud of smog.
Dünung *f* (*Naut*) swell.
Duo *nt* **-s, -s** **(a)** (*Mus*) (*Musikstück*) duet, duo; (*Ausführende*) duo. **(b)** (*Paar*) duo.
Duodez-: ~ausgabe *f* duodecimo edition; **~band** *m* duodecimo volume; **~fürst** *m* (*pej geh*) princeling, minor *or* petty prince; **~fürstentum** *nt* (*pej geh*) minor *or* petty princedom.
Duodezimalsystem *nt* duodecimal system.
Duodezstaat *m* (*pej geh*) miniature state.
düpieren* *vt* (*geh*) to dupe.
düpiert *adj* duped.
Duplikat *nt* duplicate (copy).
Duplikation *f* (*geh*) duplication.
duplizieren* *vt* (*geh*) to duplicate.
Duplizität *f* (*geh*) duplication.
Dur *nt* **-,** *no pl* (*Mus*) major ◆ **ein Stück in ~/in G-~** a piece in a major key/in G major.
durabel *adj* (*geh*) durable.
Dur|akkord *m* major chord.
durch [1] *prep +acc* **(a)** (*räumlich: hindurch*) through ◆ **quer ~** right across; **mitten ~ die Stadt** through the middle of the town; **~ den Fluß waten** to wade across the river; **~ die ganze Welt reisen** to travel all over the world *or* throughout the world.
(b) (*mittels, von*) through, by (means of); (*in Passivkonstruktion: von*) by; (*über jdn/etw, mit jds Hilfe*) through, via; (*den Grund, die Ursache nennend*) through, because of ◆ **Tod ~ Ertrinken/den Strang** death by drowning/hanging; **Tod ~ Erfrieren/Herzschlag** *etc* death from exposure/a heart attack *etc*; **neun (geteilt) ~ drei** nine divided by three, three into nine; **~ Zufall/das Los** by chance/lot; **~ die Post** by post; **etw ~ die Zeitung bekanntgeben** to announce sth in the press; **~ den Lautsprecher** through the loudspeaker.
(c) (*aufgrund, infolge von*) due *or* owing to.
(d) (*Aus: zeitlich*) for.
[2] *adv* **(a)** (*hin~*) through ◆ **die ganze Nacht ~** all through the night, throughout the night; **es ist 4 Uhr ~** it's past *or* gone 4 o'clock; **~ und ~** *kennen* through and through; *verlogen, überzeugt* completely, utterly; **~ und ~ ehrlich** honest through and through; **~ und ~ naß** wet through; **das geht mir ~ und ~** that goes right through me.
(b) (*Cook inf*) *Steak* well-done ◆ **das Fleisch ist noch nicht ~** the meat isn't done yet.
durch- *in Verbindung mit Verben* through.
durch|ackern *sep* (*inf*) [1] *vt* to plough through.
[2] *vr* to plough one's way through (*durch etw* sth).
durch|arbeiten *sep* [1] *vt* **(a)** *Buch, Stoff etc* to work *or* go through. **(b)** (*ausarbeiten*) to work out (in detail). **(c)** (*durchkneten*) *Teig, Knetmasse* to work *or* knead thoroughly; *Muskeln* to massage *or* knead thoroughly.
[2] *vi* to work through.
[3] *vr* **sich durch etw ~** to work one's way through sth.
durch|arbeitet *adj* **nach fünf ~en Nächten** after being up working five whole nights.
durch|atmen[1] *vi sep* to breathe deeply, to take deep breaths.
durch|atmen[2]* *vt insep* (*poet*) to pervade, to inform (*liter*).
durch|aus *adv* (*emph auch* **durch|aus**) **(a)** (*in bejahten Sätzen: unbedingt*) **das muß ~ sein** that definitely has to be; **sie wollte ~ mitgehen/ein neues Auto haben** she insisted on going too/having a new car; **wenn du das ~ willst** if you insist, if you absolutely must; **das ist ~ nötig** that is absolutely necessary; **du mußt ~ mitkommen** you really must come; **muß das sein? — ja ~** is that necessary? — yes, definitely *or* absolutely; **hat er sich anständig benommen? — ja ~** did he behave himself properly? — yes, perfectly *or* absolutely; **es mußte ~ dieses Kleid sein** it absolutely had to be this dress; **er will ~ recht haben** he (absolutely) insists that he is right.
(b) (*bekräftigend in bejahten Sätzen*) quite; *verständlich, richtig, korrekt, möglich auch* perfectly; *passen, annehmen* perfectly well; *sich freuen, gefallen* really ◆ **das könnte man ~ machen, das läßt sich ~ machen** that sounds feasible, I/we *etc* could do that; **ich bin ~ Ihrer Meinung** I quite *or* absolutely agree with you; **ich hätte ~ Lust/Zeit ...** I *would* like to/I would have time; **es ist mir ~ ernst damit** I am quite *or* perfectly *or* absolutely serious about it; **es ist ~ anzunehmen, daß sie kommt** it's highly likely that she'll be coming; **das ist**

zwar ~ möglich, aber ... that is quite *or* perfectly possible, but ...
(c) (*in bejahten Sätzen: ganz und gar*) *ehrlich, zufrieden, unerfreulich* thoroughly, completely ♦ **ein ~ gelungener Abend** a thoroughly successful evening; **ein ~ beneidenswerter Mensch** a thoroughly enviable person.
(d) (*in verneinten Sätzen*) **~ nicht** (*als Verstärkung*) by no means; (*als Antwort*) not at all; (*stärker*) absolutely not; **~ nicht reich/so klug** by no means rich/as clever; **etw ~ nicht tun wollen** to refuse absolutely to do sth; **das braucht ~ nicht schlecht zu sein** that does not *have* to be bad; **das ist ~ kein Witz** that's no joke at all; **er ist ~ kein schlechter Mensch** he is by no means a bad person; **es ist ~ nicht so einfach wie ...** it is by no means as easy as ...

dụrchbacken *sep* [1] *vt Kuchen* to bake through.
[2] *vi* (*Kuchen*) to bake thoroughly.

durchbeben* *vt insep* (*geh*) to run through.

dụrchbeißen¹ *sep irreg* [1] *vt* (*in zwei Teile*) to bite through.
[2] *vr* (*inf*) (*durch etw* sth) to struggle through; (*mit Erfolg*) to win through.

durchbeißen²* *vt insep irreg* **jdm die Kehle ~** to tear sb's throat open.

dụrchbekommen* *vt sep irreg* (*inf*) to get through.

dụrchbetteln *vr sep* to beg one's way.

dụrchbeuteln *vt sep* (*S Ger inf*) to shake thoroughly (*auch fig*), to give a good shaking.

dụrchbiegen *sep irreg* [1] *vt Knie* to bend.
[2] *vr* to sag.

dụrchblasen¹ *sep irreg* [1] *vt* **(a)** to blow through (*durch etw* sth); *Eileiter, Rohr, Ohren etc* to clear (by blowing). **(b)** (*Wind*) to blow.
[2] *vi* to blow through (*durch etw* sth).

durchblasen²* *vt insep irreg* to blow (through).

dụrchblättern *vt sep or* **durchblạttern*** *insep Buch etc* to leaf *or* flick through.

⚠ **dụrchbleuen** *vt sep* (*inf*) to beat black and blue.

Dụrchblick *m* vista (*auf +acc* of); (*Ausblick*) view (*auf +acc* of); (*fig inf: Verständnis, Überblick*) knowledge ♦ **den ~ haben** (*inf*) to know what's what (*inf*); **den ~ verlieren** to lose track (*bei* of).

dụrchblicken *vi sep* **(a)** (*lit*) to look through (*durch etw* sth); (*zum Vorschein kommen*) to shine through. **(b)** (*fig*) **etw ~ lassen** to hint at sth, to intimate sth. **(c)** (*fig inf: verstehen*) to understand ♦ **blickst du da durch?** do you get it? (*inf*).

durchblịtzen* *vt insep* to flash through ♦ **jdn ~** to flash through sb's mind.

durchbluten¹* *vt insep* to supply with blood.

dụrchbluten² *vti sep* **die Wunde hat durchgeblutet** the wound has bled through (the bandage), blood from the wound has soaked through (the bandage); **es blutet durch** the blood is soaking through; **der Verband ist durchgeblutet** the bandage is soaked through with blood.

durchblutet *adj* supplied with blood.

Durchblutung *f* circulation (of the blood) (*gen* to).

Durchblutungsstörung *f* circulatory disturbance, disturbance of the circulation.

durchbohren¹* *vt insep Wand, Brett* to drill through; (*mit Schwert etc*) to run through; (*Kugel*) to go through ♦ **jdn mit Blicken ~** (*fig*) to look piercingly at sb; (*haßerfüllt*) to look daggers at sb.

dụrchbohren² *sep* [1] *vt* **etw durch etw ~** *Loch, Tunnel* to drill sth through sth; *Schwert etc* to run sth through sth; *Nagel* to pierce sth through sth.
[2] *vi* to drill through (*durch etw* sth).
[3] *vr* (*durch etw* sth) to bore one's way through; (*Speer*) to go through.

durchbohrend *adj* piercing; *Blicke auch* penetrating.

dụrchboxen *sep* (*fig inf*) (*durch etw* sth) [1] *vt* to push *or* force through.
[2] *vr* to fight one's way through.

dụrchbraten *vti sep irreg* to cook through ♦ **durchgebraten** well done.

dụrchbrausen *vi sep aux sein* to tear *or* roar through (*durch etw* sth).

dụrchbrechen¹ *sep irreg* [1] *vt* (*in zwei Teile*) to break (in two).
[2] *vi aux sein* **(a)** (*in zwei Teile*) to break (in two).
(b) (*einbrechen: Mensch*) to fall through (*durch etw* sth).
(c) (*hervorbrechen*) (*Knospen*) to appear; (*Zahn*) to come through; (*Sonne auch*) to break through (*durch etw* sth); (*Charakter*) to reveal itself.
(d) (*Med: Blinddarm etc*) to burst, to perforate.

durchbrẹchen²* *vt insep irreg Schallmauer* to break; *Mauer, Blockade etc* to break through; (*fig*) to break.

Durchbrẹchung *f siehe vt insep* breaking; breaking through; breaking.

dụrchbrennen *vi sep irreg* **(a)** (*nicht ausgehen: Ofen, Feuer, Licht etc*) to stay alight. **(b)** *aux sein* (*Sicherung, Glühbirne*) to blow, to burn out; (*inf: davonlaufen*) to run off *or* away, to abscond ♦ **jdm ~** (*inf*) to run away from sb. **(c)** *aux sein* (*vollständig brennen: Kohlen, Holz, Feuer*) to burn through.

Dụrchbrenner(in *f*) *m* (*inf*) *siehe* **Ausreißer(in)**.

dụrchbringen *sep irreg* [1] *vt* **(a)** (*durch etw* sth) (*durchsetzen, durch Prüfung, Kontrolle*) to get through; (*durch Krankheit*) to pull through; (*für Unterhalt sorgen*) to provide for, to support. **(b)** *Geld* to get through, to blow (*inf*). **(c)** (*dial*) *siehe* **durchbekommen**.
[2] *vr* to get by ♦ **sich kümmerlich ~** to scrape by.

durchbrọchen [1] *ptp of* **durchbrechen²**.
[2] *adj* open; *Stickerei etc* openwork *attr*.

Dụrchbruch *m* **(a)** (*durch etw* sth) (*durch Eis*) falling through *no art*; (*von Knospen*) appearance; (*von Zahn*) coming through; (*von Sonne*) breaking through; (*von Charakter*) revelation; (*von Blinddarm*) perforation ♦ **zum ~ kommen** (*fig*) (*Gewohnheit etc*) to assert *or* show itself; (*Natur*) to reveal itself; **der Patient wurde mit einem ~ (des Blinddarms) eingeliefert** the patient was admitted with a perforated appendix.
(b) (*Mil*) breakthrough; (*Sport auch*) break; (*fig: Erfolg*) breakthrough ♦ **eine Idee kommt zum ~** an idea comes to the fore *or* emerges; **jdm/etw zum ~ verhelfen** to help sb/sth on the road to success.
(c) (*durchbrochene Stelle*) breach; (*Öffnung*) opening; (*Geog: von Fluß*) rise, resurgence.

dụrchbuchstabieren* *vt sep* to spell out.

dụrchbummeln¹ *vi sep aux sein* (*inf*) (*durchschlendern*) to stroll through (*durch etw* sth) ♦ **die Nacht ~** to spend the night on the tiles (*inf*).

durchbụmmeln²* *vt insep Nacht* to spend on the tiles (*inf*).

dụrchbürsten *vt sep* to brush thoroughly.

dụrchchecken [-tʃɛkn] *vt sep* **(a)** *Gepäck* to check through. **(b)** (*inf: überprüfen*) to check through.

durchdạcht *adj* thought-out ♦ **gut/schlecht ~** well/badly thought-out.

durchdẹnken* *insep*, **dụrchdenken** *sep vt irreg* to think out *or* through.

dụrchdiskutieren* *vt sep* to discuss thoroughly, to talk through.

dụrchdrängeln (*inf*), **dụrchdrängen** *vr sep* to push *or* force one's way through (*durch etw* sth).

dụrchdrehen *sep* [1] *vt Fleisch etc* to mince.
[2] *vi* **(a)** (*Rad*) to spin. **(b)** (*inf*) to do one's nut (*sl*), to flip (*inf*); (*nervlich*) to crack up (*inf*) ♦ **ganz durchgedreht sein** (*inf*) to be really uptight (*inf*) *or* (*aus dem Gleichgewicht*) confused.

dụrchdringen¹ *vi sep irreg aux sein* **(a)** to penetrate (*durch etw* sth); (*Flüssigkeit, Kälte auch, Sonne*) to come through (*durch etw* sth); (*Stimme, Geräusch auch*) to be heard (*durch etw* through sth) ♦ **bis zu jdm ~** (*fig*) to go *or* get as far as sb.
(b) (*sich durchsetzen, sich verständlich machen*) to get through ♦ **zu jdm ~** to get through to sb; **mit einem Vorschlag ~** to get a suggestion accepted (*bei, in +dat* by).

durchdrịngen²* *vt insep irreg Materie, Dunkelheit etc* to penetrate; (*Gefühl, Idee, Gedanke*) to pervade; *siehe* **durchdrungen**.

dụrchdringend *adj* piercing; *Kälte, Wind auch* biting; *Stimme, Geräusch, Blick auch* penetrating; *Geruch* pungent, sharp.

Durchdrịngung *f* **(a)** penetration; (*Sättigung*) saturation; (*Verschmelzung*) fusion. **(b)** (*fig: Erfassen*) investigation, exploration.

dụrchdrücken *sep* [1] *vt* **(a)** (*durch Sieb*) to rub through; (*durch Presse*) to press through; *Creme, Teig* to pipe.
(b) (*fig*) *Gesetz, Reformen, Neuerungen etc* to push *or* force through; *seinen Willen* to get ♦ **es ~, daß ...** to get the decision that ... through.
(c) *Knie, Ellbogen etc* to straighten.
(d) *Wäsche* to wash through.
[2] *vr* to squeeze *or* push (one's way) through (*durch etw* sth) ♦ **sich in der Menge ~** to squeeze *or* push (one's way) through the crowd.

durchdrụngen [1] *ptp of* **durchdringen²**.
[2] *adj pred* imbued (*von* with) ♦ **ganz von einer Idee ~ sein** to be taken with an idea; **von einem Gefühl der Freude ~ sein** to be full of *or* imbued with a feeling of joy.

dụrchdürfen *vi sep irreg* (*inf*) to be allowed through ♦ **darf ich mal ~?** can I get through?; **Sie dürfen hier nicht durch** you can't come through here.

durch|einạnder [1] *adv* mixed *or* muddled up, in a muddle *or* mess ♦ **Gemüse ~** vegetable stew; **alles ~ essen/trinken** to eat/drink indiscriminately.
[2] *adj pred* **~ sein** (*inf*) (*Mensch*) to be confused *or* (*aufgeregt*) in a state (*inf*); (*Zimmer, Papier*) to be in a mess *or* muddle.

Durch|einạnder *nt* **-s,** *no pl* (*Unordnung*) mess, muddle; (*Wirrwarr*) confusion ♦ **in dem Zimmer herrscht ein wüstes ~** the room is in a terrible mess *or* muddle.

durch|einạnder-: ⚠**~bringen** *vt sep irreg* to muddle *or* mix up; (*in Unordnung bringen auch*) to get into a mess *or* muddle; (*verwirren*) *jdn* to confuse; ⚠**~gehen** *vi sep irreg aux sein* to get confused *or* into a muddle; ⚠**~geraten*** *vi sep irreg aux sein* to get mixed *or* muddled up; **jetzt bin ich mit dem Datum völlig ~geraten** now I've got completely mixed *or* muddled up about the date; ⚠**~kommen** *vi sep irreg aux sein* **(a)** (*vermischt werden*) to get mixed *or* muddled up; **(b)** (*inf*) *siehe* **~geraten**; ⚠**~laufen** *vi sep irreg aux sein* to run about *or* around all over the place; ⚠**~liegen** *vi sep irreg aux haben or sein* to be in a muddle, to be all over the place; ⚠**~mengen**, ⚠**~mischen** *vt sep* to mix (up); ⚠**~reden** *vi sep* to all speak *or* talk at once *or* at the same time; ⚠**~rennen** *vi sep irreg aux sein siehe* **~laufen**; ⚠**~rufen**, ⚠**~schreien** *vi sep irreg* to all shout out at once *or* at the same time; ⚠**~werfen** *vt sep irreg* to muddle up; (*fig inf: verwechseln*) to mix up, to confuse; ⚠**~wirbeln** *vt sep Blätter* to whirl around; (*fig*) to shake up.

dụrch|essen *vr sep irreg* **(a) sich bei jdm ~** to eat at sb's expense. **(b) sich durch etw ~** to eat one's way through sth.

dụrch|exerzieren* *vt sep* to rehearse, to run *or* go through.

dụrchfahren¹ *vi sep irreg aux sein* **(a)** to go through (*durch etw* sth). **(b)** (*nicht anhalten/umsteigen*) to go straight through (without stopping/changing) ♦ **er ist bei Rot durchgefahren** he jumped the lights; **die Nacht ~** to travel through the night.

durchfạhren²* *vt insep irreg* to travel through; (*fig: Schreck, Zittern etc*) to shoot through ♦ **ein Gedanke durchfuhr ihn blitzartig** a (sudden) thought flashed through his mind.

Dụrchfahrt *f* **(a)** (*Durchreise*) way through ♦ **auf der ~ sein** to be passing through; **auf** *or* **bei der ~ sieht man ja nicht viel** one doesn't see much when one is just passing through.
(b) (*Passage*) thoroughfare; (*Naut*) thoroughfare, channel ♦ **~ bitte freihalten!** please keep access free.

(c) (*das Durchfahren*) thoroughfare ◆ **~ verboten!** no through road, no thoroughfare; **der Polizist gab endlich die ~ frei/gab das Zeichen zur ~** the policeman finally allowed/signalled the traffic through.

Durchfahrts-: ~höhe *f* headroom, clearance; **~recht** *nt* right of way; **~straße** *f* through road; **~verbot** *nt* **seit wann besteht hier ~verbot?** since when has this been a no through road?; **die Anwohner haben das ~verbot durchgesetzt** the residents managed to get through traffic banned.

Durchfall *m* **(a)** (*Med*) diarrhoea, diarrhea (*US*) *no art.* **(b)** (*Mißerfolg*) failure; (*von Theaterstück auch*) flop.

durchfallen *vi sep irreg aux sein* **(a)** to fall through (*durch etw* sth). **(b)** (*inf: nicht bestehen*) to fail; (*Theaterstück etc auch*) to (be a) flop; (*Wahlkandidat*) to lose, to be defeated ◆ **in** *or* **bei der Prüfung ~** to fail the exam; **jdn ~ lassen** to fail sb; **beim Publikum/bei der Kritik ~** to be a failure *or* flop with the public/critics; **bei der Wahl ~** to lose the election, to be defeated in the election.

durchfärben *sep* [1] *vt* to dye *or* colour (evenly).
[2] *vi* to come *or* seep through (*durch etw* sth).

durchfaulen *vi sep aux sein* to rot through.

durchfechten *sep irreg* [1] *vt* **etw ~** to fight to get sth through.
[2] *vr* **sich (im Leben) ~** to struggle through (in life).

durchfedern *vi sep* to bend one's knees.

durchfegen[1] *sep* [1] *vt* to sweep out.
[2] *vi* to sweep up.

durchfegen[2]* *vt insep* to sweep through.

durchfeiern[1] *vi sep* to stay up all night celebrating.

durchfeiern[2]* *vt insep* **die Nacht ~** to stay up all night celebrating; **nach durchfeierter Nacht** after celebrating all night.

durchfeilen *sep or* **durchfeilen*** *insep vt* to file through; (*fig*) *Aufsatz* to polish up.

durchfeuchten* *vt insep* to soak ◆ **von etw durchfeuchtet sein** to be soaked (through) with sth.

durchfinden *vir sep irreg* (*lit, fig*) to find one's way through (*durch etw* sth) ◆ **ich finde (mich) hier nicht mehr durch** (*fig*) I am simply lost; **ich kann mich bei diesem Kram nicht ~** (*fig*) I can't make head nor tail of this mess.

durchflechten* *vt insep irreg* **etw mit etw ~** (*lit*) to thread *or* weave sth through sth, to intertwine sth with sth; (*fig*) to interweave sth with sth.

durchfliegen[1] *vi sep irreg aux sein* **(a)** to fly through (*durch etw* sth); (*ohne Landung*) to fly non-stop *or* direct. **(b)** (*inf*) (*durch Prüfung*) to fail, to flunk (*inf*) (*durch etw, in etw (dat)* (in) sth).

durchfliegen[2]* *vt insep irreg Luft, Wolken* to fly through; *Land* to fly over; *Luftkorridor* to fly along; *Strecke* to cover; (*flüchtig lesen*) to skim through.

durchfließen[1] *vi sep irreg aux sein* to flow *or* run through (*durch etw* sth).

durchfließen[2]* *vt insep irreg* (*lit, fig*) to flow *or* run through.

Durchflug *m* flight through; (*das Durchfliegen*) flying through (*durch etw* sth).

⚠**Durchfluß** *m* (*das Fließen, ~menge*) flow; (*Öffnung*) opening.

durchfluten[1] *vi sep aux sein* (*geh*) to flow through (*durch etw* sth).

durchfluten[2]* *vt insep* (*geh*) (*Fluß*) to flow through; (*fig*) (*Licht, Sonne*) to flood; (*Wärme, Gefühl*) to flow *or* flood through ◆ **Licht durchflutete das Zimmer** the room was flooded with *or* bathed in light, light flooded the room.

durchformen *vt sep* to work out (down) to the last detail.

durchforschen* *vt insep Gegend* to search; *Land, Wissensgebiet* to explore; *Akten, Bücher* to search through.

durchforsten* *vt insep*, **durchforsten** *vt sep Wald* to thin out; (*fig*) *Bücher, Akten etc* to go through.

durchfragen *vr sep* to ask one's way.

durchfressen[1] *sep irreg* [1] *vr* (*durch etw* sth) (*Säure, Rost, Tier*) to eat (its way) through ◆ **sich (bei jdm) ~** (*pej inf*) to live on sb's hospitality; **sich durch ein Buch ~** (*inf*) to plough *or* wade through a book.
[2] *vt* (*Rost, Maus*) to eat (its way) through; (*Motten*) to eat holes in ◆ **ein Loch durch etw ~** to eat a hole in sth.

durchfressen[2]* *vt insep irreg* to eat through; (*Motten*) to eat holes in ◆ **ein von Motten ~er Pullover** a moth-eaten pullover.

durchfretten *vr sep* (*Aus, S Ger*) to eke out an existence.

durchfrieren *vi sep irreg aux sein* (*See, Fluß*) to freeze through, to freeze solid; (*Mensch*) to get frozen stiff, to get chilled to the bone.

durchfroren *adj siehe* **durchgefroren**.

Durchfuhr *f* transit, passage.

durchführbar *adj* practicable, feasible, workable.

Durchführbarkeit *f* feasibility, practicability, workability.

durchführen *sep* [1] *vt* **(a)** (*durchleiten*) (*durch etw* sth) *jdn* to lead through, to take through; *Fluß* to lead through; *Leitung, Rohr* to run through; *Straße* to build through, to lay through; *Kanal, Tunnel* to dig through ◆ **etw durch etw ~** to lead *etc* sth through sth; **jdn durch eine Stadt/eine Wohnung ~** to show sb around a town/a flat.
(b) (*verwirklichen*) *Vorhaben, Beschluß, Plan* to carry out; *Gesetz* to implement, to enforce; (*unternehmen, veranstalten*) *Experiment, Haussuchung, Sammlung, Untersuchung, Reform* to carry out; *Test auch* to run; *Expedition, Reise* to undertake; *Messung* to take; *Kursus* to run; *Wahl, Prüfung* to hold; *Unterrichtsstunde* to take, to give.
(c) (*konsequent zu Ende bringen*) to carry through; *Gedankengang* to carry through (to its conclusion).
[2] *vi* (*durch etw* sth) to lead through; (*Straße*) to go through ◆ **zwischen/unter etw** (*dat*) **~** to lead/go between/under sth.

Durchfuhr-: ~erlaubnis *f* transit permit; **~handel** *m* transit trade; **~land** *nt* country of transit.

Durchführung *f siehe vt* **(a)** leading (through); running (through); building (through); digging (through).
(b) (*fig*) carrying out; implementation, enforcement; undertaking; taking; running; holding; giving ◆ **zur ~ kommen** (*form*) (*Reform, Gesetz, Maßnahme*) to come into force; **zur ~ bringen** (*form*) *Reform, Gesetz, Maßnahme* to bring into force.
(c) carrying through.
(d) (*Mus*) (*von Sonate*) development; (*von Fuge*) exposition.

Durchfuhr-: ~verbot *nt* transit embargo; **~zoll** *m* transit duty.

durchfurchen* *vt insep* (*geh*) *Land* to plough; *Wogen* to plough through.

durchfüttern *vt sep* (*inf*) to feed ◆ **sich von jdm ~ lassen** to live off sb.

Durchgabe *f* **(a)** (*von Nachricht, Lottozahlen etc*) announcement; (*von Hinweis, Bericht*) giving ◆ **bei der ~ der Zahlen übers Telefon kommen oft Fehler vor** when numbers are given over the telephone mistakes are often made.
(b) (*Nachricht, Ankündigung*) announcement; (*telefonisch*) message (over the telephone).

Durchgang *m* **(a)** (*Weg, Passage*) way; (*schmaler auch*) passage(way); (*Torweg*) gateway.
(b) (*das Durchgehen*) **kein ~!, ~ verboten!** no right of way; **beim ~ durch das Tal** going through the valley; **der ~ zur Höhle/zum anderen Tal ist beschwerlich** it's difficult to get through to the cave/other valley; **er hat mir den ~ versperrt** he blocked my passage.
(c) (*von Experiment, bei Arbeit, Parl*) stage.
(d) (*bei Wettbewerb, von Wahl, Sport*) round; (*beim Rennen*) heat.
(e) (*Astron*) transit.

Durchgänger *m* **-s, -** (*Pferd*) bolter.

durchgängig *adj* universal, general ◆ **eine ~e Eigenschaft in seinen Romanen** a constant feature in *or* of his novels.

Durchgangs-: ~bahnhof *m* through station; **~handel** *m* transit trade; **~lager** *nt* transit camp; **~stadium** *nt* transition stage; **~station** *f* (*fig*) stopping-off place; **~straße** *f* through road, thoroughfare; **~verkehr** *m* (*Mot*) through traffic; (*Transitverkehr*) transit traffic.

durchgaren *sep* [1] *vt* to cook thoroughly.
[2] *vi aux sein* to cook through.

durchgeben *vt sep irreg* **(a)** to pass through (*durch etw* sth).
(b) (*Rad, TV*) *Hinweis, Meldung, Wetter, Straßenzustandsbericht* to give; *Nachricht, Lottozahlen* to announce ◆ **jdm etw telefonisch ~** to let sb know sth by telephone, to telephone sth to sb; **ein Telegramm telefonisch ~** to telephone a telegram; **jdm ~, daß ...** to let sb know that ..., to tell sb that ...; **es wurde im Radio durchgegeben** it was announced on the radio; **wir geben (Ihnen) nun den Wetterbericht durch** and now we bring you the weather forecast.

durchgefroren *adj Mensch* frozen stiff, perishing (cold) (*inf*) *pred.*

durchgehen *sep irreg aux sein* [1] *vi* **(a)** (*lit*) (*durch etw* sth) to go through, to walk through; (*durch Kontrolle, Zoll*) to pass through; (*weitergehen, inf: sich durchstecken lassen*) to go through ◆ **bitte ~!** (*im Bus*) pass right down (the bus) please!
(b) (*Fluß, Weg, Linie etc*) (*durch etw* sth) to run through, to go through; (*fig: Thema*) to run through.
(c) (*durchdringen*) to come through (*durch etw* sth).
(d) (*nicht zurückgewiesen werden*) (*Gesetz*) to be passed, to go through; (*Antrag auch*) to be carried; (*Postsendung*) to get through.
(e) (*toleriert werden*) to be allowed (to pass), to be tolerated ◆ **jdm etw ~ lassen** to let sb get away with sth, to overlook sth; **das lasse ich nochmal ~** I'll let it pass.
(f) (*gehalten werden für*) **für etw ~** to pass for sth, to be taken for sth.
(g) (*durchpassen*) to go through (*durch etw* sth) ◆ **zwischen/unter etw** (*dat*) **~** to go (through) between/under sth.
(h) (*ohne Unterbrechung*) to go straight through; (*Fußgänger auch*) to walk straight through; (*Flug*) to be non-stop *or* direct; (*zeitlich: Party, Unterricht; örtlich: Straße, Linie auch*) to run (right) through ◆ **die ganze Nacht ~** (*Mensch*) to walk all night long, to walk through(out) the night.
(i) (*Pferd etc*) to bolt; (*inf: sich davonmachen*) to run off *or* away ◆ **mit jdm ~** to run *or* go off with sb, to elope with sb; **jdm ~** to run away from sb; **seine Frau ist ihm durchgegangen** his wife has run off and left him; **mit etw ~** to run *or* make off with sth.
(j) (*außer Kontrolle geraten*) **mit jdm ~** (*Temperament, Nerven*) to get the better of sb; (*Gefühle auch*) to run away with sb.
[2] *vt auch aux haben* (*durchsehen, -sprechen etc*) to go *or* run through, to go *or* run over.
[3] *vi impers* **es geht durch/nicht durch** there's a/no way through; **wo geht es durch?** where's the way through?

durchgehend [1] *adj Öffnungszeiten* round-the-clock *attr*, continuous; *Straße* straight; *Verkehrsverbindung* direct; *Zug* non-stop, through *attr*, direct; *Fahrkarte* through *attr*; *Muster* continuous; *Eigenschaft* constant ◆ **~e Güter** goods in transit.
[2] *adv* throughout, right through ◆ **~ geöffnet** open right through; open 24 hours; **~ gefüttert** fully lined, lined throughout.

durchgeistigt *adj* cerebral.

durchgeknallt *adj* (*inf: verrückt*) cuckoo (*inf*), loopy (*inf*).

durchgeregnet *adj* soaked ◆ **ich war völlig ~** I was soaked to the skin *or* soaked through.

durchgeschwitzt *adj Mensch* bathed in sweat; *Kleidung* soaked in sweat, sweat-soaked *attr.*

durchgestalten* *vt sep* to work out (down) to the last detail.
durchgießen *vt sep irreg* to pour through (*durch etw* sth) ◆ **etw durch ein Sieb ~** to strain sth, to pour sth through a sieve.
durchgliedern *vt sep* to subdivide.
durchglühen[1] *sep* [1] *vi aux sein* to glow red-hot; (*Lampe, Draht, Sicherung*) to burn out.
[2] *vt Eisen* to heat until red-hot *or* to red heat.
durchglühen[2]* *vt insep* (*liter: Gefühl*) to glow through ◆ **von Begeisterung durchglüht** aglow with enthusiasm.
durchgraben *sep irreg* [1] *vt* to dig through (*durch etw* sth).
[2] *vr* to dig one's way through (*durch etw* sth).
durchgreifen *vi sep irreg* to reach through (*durch etw* sth); (*fig*) to take vigorous action, to resort to drastic measures ◆ **hier muß viel strenger durchgegriffen werden** much more vigorous action is needed here.
durchgreifend *adj Änderung, Maßnahme* drastic; (*weitreichend*) *Änderung* far-reaching, radical, sweeping *attr.*
durchgucken *vi sep* **(a)** (*durch etw* sth) (*Mensch*) to look through, to peep through; (*durchscheinen*) to show through. **(b)** (*fig inf*) *siehe* **durchblicken (c).**
durchhaben *vt sep irreg* (*inf*) **etw ~** (*hindurchbekommen haben*) to have got sth through (*durch etw* sth); (*durchgelesen etc haben*) to have got through sth, to have finished sth; (*zerteilt haben*) to have got through sth, to be through sth.
durchhacken *vt sep* to chop *or* hack through.
Durchhalte|appell *m* appeal to hold out, rallying call.
durchhalten *sep irreg* [1] *vt* (*durchstehen*) *Zeit, Ehe, Kampf etc* to survive; *Streik* to hold out till the end of, to see through; *Belastung* to (with)stand; (*Sport*) *Strecke* to stay; *Tempo* (*beibehalten*) to keep up; (*aushalten*) to stand ◆ **das Rennen ~** to stay the course.
[2] *vi* to hold out, to stick it out (*inf*); (*beharren*) to persevere, to stick it out (*inf*); (*bei Rennen auch*) to stay the course ◆ **bis zum Äußersten ~** to hold out *or* stick it out (*inf*) to the last; **eisern ~** to hold out grimly.
Durchhalte-: ~parole *f* appeal to hold out, rallying call; **~vermögen** *nt* staying power, (powers *pl* of) endurance *no indef art.*
Durchhang *m* sag, slack.
durchhängen *vi sep irreg aux haben or sein* to sag.
Durchhänger *m* **-s, -** (*inf: schlechte Phase*) bad patch; (*an bestimmtem Tag*) off-day; **sich** (*dat*) **einen ~ leisten** to have a bad patch/an off-day.
durchhauen[1] *sep irreg or* (*inf*) *reg* [1] *vt* **(a)** to chop *or* hack in two; (*spalten*) to split, to cleave.
(b) (*inf: verprügeln*) **jdn ~** to give sb a thrashing *or* walloping (*inf*), to thrash *or* wallop (*inf*) sb.
(c) (*inf*) *Sicherung* to blow.
[2] *vr* (*lit*) to hack one's way through (*durch etw* sth); (*fig: sich durchschlagen*) to get by.
durchhauen[2]* *vt insep irreg* to chop *or* hack in two.
durchhecheln *vt sep* **(a)** *Flachs etc* to hackle. **(b)** (*fig inf*) to gossip about, to pull to pieces (*inf*) ◆ **in allen Zeitungen durchgehechelt** dragged through all the papers.
durchheizen *sep* [1] *vt* (*gründlich heizen*) to heat right through; (*ohne Unterbrechung heizen*) to heat continuously, to heat day and night.
[2] *vi* (*ohne Unterbrechung*) to keep the heating on.
durchhelfen *sep irreg* [1] *vi* **jdm (durch etw) ~** to help sb through (sth).
[2] *vr* to get by, to get along, to manage.
durchhören *vt sep* **(a) etw (durch etw) ~** (*lit*) *Lärm* to hear sth (through sth); (*fig*) *Gefühl, Enttäuschung auch* to discern sth (through sth); **ich konnte ~, daß** ... I could hear *or* tell that ... **(b)** *Schallplatte, Konzert etc* to hear (all the way) through, to hear all of.
durchhungern *vr sep* to struggle along on the breadline, to scrape by.
durch|irren* *vt insep* to wander *or* rove *or* roam through.
durch|ixen *vt sep* (*inf*) to ex out.
durchjagen[1] *sep* [1] *vt* **(a)** to chase through (*durch etw* sth). **(b)** (*fig*) *Gesetz, Prozeß etc* to rush *or* push through.
[2] *vi aux sein* to race *or* tear through ◆ **zwischen/unter etw** (*dat*) **~** to race *or* tear between/under sth.
durchjagen[2]* *vt insep Land etc* to race *or* tear through.
durchkämmen *vt sep* **(a)** *Haare* to comb out. **(b)** *auch* **durchkämmen*** *insep* (*absuchen*) to comb (through).
durchkämpfen *sep* [1] *vt* (*durchsetzen*) to push *or* force through.
[2] *vr* **(a)** (*durch etw* sth) to fight *or* battle one's way through; (*fig*) to struggle through.
(b) *siehe* **durchringen.**
[3] *vi* (*Kampf nicht aufgeben*) (*Soldaten*) to carry on fighting; (*Sportler, Bergsteiger*) to battle on, to carry on the battle *or* struggle ◆ **es wurde selbst über die Weihnachtszeit durchgekämpft** the fighting continued even over Christmas.
durchkauen *vt sep Essen* to chew (thoroughly); (*inf: besprechen*) to go over *or* through.
durchklettern *vi sep aux sein* to climb through (*durch etw* sth).
durchklingen[1] *vi sep irreg aux haben or sein* (*durch etw* sth) to sound through; (*fig*) to come through (*durch etw* sth), to come across (*durch etw* through sth) ◆ **die Musik klang durch den Lärm durch** the music could be heard above the noise.
durchklingen[2]* *vt insep irreg* to ring through.
durchkneifen *vt sep irreg Draht* to snip through.
durchkneten *vt sep Teig etc* to knead thoroughly; (*bei Massage*) to massage thoroughly ◆ **sich ~ lassen** to have a thorough massage.
durchknöpfen *vt sep* to button all the way up ◆ **ein durchgeknöpftes Kleid** a button-through dress.
durchkochen *vti sep* to boil thoroughly.
durchkommen *vi sep irreg aux sein* **(a)** (*durch etw* sth) (*durchfahren*) to come through; (*vorbeikommen, passieren auch*) to come past ◆ **er ist durch diese Straße/Stadt/unter dieser Brücke durchgekommen** he came through this street/town/under *or* through this bridge.
(b) (*durch etw* sth) to get through; (*Sonne, Wasser etc*) to come through; (*Sender, Farbe*) to come through; (*Charakterzug*) to show through, to come out *or* through; (*sichtbar werden*) (*Sonne*) to come out; (*Blumen*) to come through ◆ **kommst du durch?** can you get through?; **es kommt immer wieder durch, daß sie Ausländerin ist** the fact that she is a foreigner keeps showing *or* coming through.
(c) (*lit, fig: mit Erfolg ~*) to succeed (*durch etw* in sth), to get through (*durch etw* sth); (*sich durchsetzen*) (*telefonisch*) to get through; (*finanziell*) to get by ◆ **ich komme mit meiner Hand nicht (durch das Loch) durch** I can't get my hand through (the hole); **mit etw ~** (*mit Forderungen etc*) to succeed with sth; (*mit Betrug, Schmeichelei etc*) to get away with sth; **er kam (bei dem Lärm) mit seiner Stimme nicht durch** he couldn't make his voice heard (above the noise); **damit kommt er bei mir nicht durch** he won't get away with that with me.
(d) (*Prüfung bestehen*) to get through, to pass.
(e) (*überleben*) to come through; (*Patient auch*) to pull through.
(f) (*im Radio*) to be announced.
durchkomponieren* *vt sep* **(a)** (*Mus*) *Libretto* to set to music; *Gedicht* to set to music (with a different setting for each stanza). **(b)** (*fig*) *Bild, Text* to work out in detail. **(c)** (*ohne Unterbrechung*) to compose right through.
durchkönnen *vi sep irreg* (*inf*) to be able to get through (*durch etw* sth).
durchkonstruieren* *vt sep* **ein Auto ~** to construct a car well throughout; **gut durchkonstruiert** well constructed throughout.
durchkosten *vt sep* (*geh*) to taste (one after the other); (*fig*) *Freuden* to taste; *Leiden* to endure, to experience.
durchkreuzen[1]* *vt insep* **(a)** *Land, Wüste, Ozean* to cross, to travel across. **(b)** (*fig*) *Pläne etc* to thwart, to foil, to frustrate.
durchkreuzen[2] *vt sep* to cross out, to cross through.
Durchkreuzung *f* **(a)** (*von Land etc*) crossing. **(b)** (*von Plänen etc*) thwarting, foiling, frustrating.
durchkriechen *vi sep irreg aux sein* to crawl through, to creep through (*durch etw* sth).
durchkriegen *vt sep* (*inf*) *siehe* **durchbekommen.**
durchladen *vti sep irreg Gewehr* to reload.
durchlangen *sep* (*inf*) [1] *vi* (*durch etw* sth) to reach through, to put one's hand through.
[2] *vt* (*durchreichen*) to pass through.
⚠ **Durchlaß** *m* **-sses, Durchlässe (a)** (*Durchgang*) passage, way through; (*für Wasser*) duct. **(b)** *no pl* (*geh*) permission to pass ◆ **jdm/sich ~ verschaffen** to obtain permission for sb/to obtain permission to pass; (*mit Gewalt*) to force a way through for sb/to force one's way through.
durchlassen *vt sep irreg* (*durch etw* sth) (*passieren lassen*) to allow *or* let through; *Licht, Wasser etc* (*durchdringen lassen*) to let through; (*eindringen lassen*) to let in; (*inf: durch Prüfung*) to let through, to pass; (*inf: durchgehen lassen*) *Fehler etc* to let pass, to overlook.
durchlässig *adj Material* permeable; (*porös*) porous; *Zelt, Regenmantel, Schuh* that lets water in; *Zelt, Schuh* leaky; *Krug, Vase* that lets water out *or* through; *Grenze* open ◆ **eine ~e Stelle** (*fig*) a leak; **die Bildungswege ~ machen** to make the elements of the education programme interchangeable.
Durchlässigkeit *f* permeability; (*Porosität*) porosity ◆ **die ~ des Zelts/Krugs** the fact that the tent/jug leaks *or* lets water in/out *or* through; **die ~ der Bildungswege** the interchangeability of the elements of the education programme.
Durchlaucht *f* **-, -en** serenity ◆ **Seine ~** His (Serene) Highness; **(Euer) ~** Your Highness.
durchlauchtig *adj attr* (*old*) serene.
Durchlauf *m* **(a)** (*das Durchlaufen*) flow. **(b)** (*Comput*) run. **(c)** (*TV, Rad, Comput*) run, run-through. **(d)** (*Sport*) heat.
durchlaufen[1] *sep irreg* [1] *vt Schuhe, Sohlen* to go *or* wear through.
[2] *vi aux sein* **(a)** (*durch etw* sth) (*durch Straße/Öffnung etc gehen*) to go through; (*passieren auch*) to pass through; (*Straße, Rohr etc auch*) to run through; (*Flüssigkeit*) to run through.
(b) (*ohne Unterbrechung: Mensch*) to run without stopping ◆ **8 Stunden lang ohne Pause ~** to run for 8 hours without stopping; **der Fries/das Geländer läuft von der einen Seite des Gebäudes zur anderen durch** the frieze/railing runs uninterrupted *or* without a break from one end of the building to the other.
durchlaufen[2]* *vt insep irreg* **(a)** *Gebiet* to run through; *Strecke* to cover, to run; (*Astron*) *Bahn* to describe; *Lehrzeit, Schule, Phase* to pass *or* go through. **(b)** (*erfassen, erfüllen*) (*Gerücht*) to spread through; (*Gefühl*) to run through ◆ **es durchlief mich heiß** I felt hot all over.
durchlaufend *adj* continuous.
Durchlauf-: ~erhitzer *m* **-s, -** continuous-flow water heater; **~zeit** *f* (*Datenverarbeitung*) length of a/the run.
durchlavieren* [-laviːrən] *vr sep* to steer *or* manoeuvre one's way through (*durch etw* sth).
durchleben* *vt insep Jugend, Gefühl* to go through, to experience; *Zeit* to go

or live through.
durchleiden* *vt insep irreg* to suffer, to endure.
durchleiten *vt sep* to lead through (*durch etw* sth).
durchlesen *vt sep irreg* to read through ◆ **etw ganz ~** to read sth all the way through; **etw flüchtig ~** to skim *or* glance through sth; **etw auf Fehler (hin) ~** to read sth through (looking) for mistakes; **sich** (*dat*) **etw ~** to read sth through.
durchleuchten[1]* *vt insep* **(a)** (*untersuchen*) *Patienten* to X-ray; *Eier* to candle; (*fig*) *Angelegenheit etc* to investigate, to probe ◆ **jdm die Lunge ~** to X-ray sb's lungs; **sich ~ lassen** to have an X-ray.
(b) (*geh: Schein, Sonne etc*) to light up, to flood with light.
durchleuchten[2] *vi sep* to shine through (*durch etw* sth).
Durchleuchtung *f* (*Med: mit Röntgenstrahlen*) X-ray examination; (*fig: von Angelegenheit etc*) investigation.
durchliegen *sep irreg* [1] *vt Matratze, Bett* to wear down (in the middle).
[2] *vr* to get *or* develop bedsores.
durchlöchern* *vt insep* to make holes in; (*Motten auch, Rost*) to eat holes in; *Socken etc* to wear holes in; (*fig*) to undermine completely; *Argumente auch* to shoot down ◆ **(mit Schüssen) ~** to riddle with bullets; **eine völlig durchlöcherte Leiche** a corpse riddled with bullet holes; **er hatte völlig durchlöcherte Socken/Kleidung an** his socks/clothes were full of holes; **von Würmern durchlöchert** worm-eaten; **von Rost durchlöchert** eaten away with rust.
durchlotsen *vt sep* (*durch etw* sth) *Schiff* to pilot through; *Autofahrer* to guide through; (*fig*) to steer through ◆ **jdn durch etw ~** to pilot *etc* sb through sth.
durchlüften[1] *vti sep* to air thoroughly; *Wäsche auch* to air through ◆ **ich muß mich mal wieder ~ lassen** I must (go and) get some fresh air (in my lungs).
durchlüften[2]* *vt insep* to air thoroughly.
durchlügen *vr sep irreg* (*inf*) to lie one's way through (*durch etw* sth).
durchmachen *sep* [1] *vt* **(a)** (*erdulden*) to go through; *Krankheit* to have; *Operation* to undergo, to have ◆ **er hat viel durchgemacht** he has been *or* gone through a lot.
(b) (*durchlaufen*) to go through; *Lehre* to serve; (*fig*) *Entwicklung* to undergo; *Wandlung* to undergo, to experience.
(c) (*inf: durchbewegen, durchstecken etc*) *Faden, Nadel, Stange etc* to put through (*durch etw* sth).
(d) (*inf: durchtrennen*) **(in der Mitte) ~** to cut in half.
(e) (*inf*) (*durcharbeiten*) to work through ◆ **eine ganze Nacht/Woche ~** (*durchfeiern*) to have an all-night/week-long party, to make a night/week of it (*inf*).
[2] *vi* (*inf*) (*durcharbeiten*) to work right through; (*durchfeiern*) to keep going all night/day *etc.*
durchmanövrieren* *vt sep* to manoeuvre through (*durch etw* sth).
Durchmarsch *m* **(a)** march(ing) through; (*fig: problemloser Durchbruch*) (*Sport, von Politiker*) walkover; (*von Partei*) landslide; **der ~ durch die Stadt** the march through the town; **auf dem ~** when marching through; **sich zum ~ entschließen** (*fig*) to resolve to push (on) through. **(b)** (*inf: Durchfall*) runs *pl* (*inf*) ◆ **den ~ haben** to have the runs (*inf*). **(c)** (*Cards*) grand slam.
durchmarschieren* *vi sep aux sein* to march through (*durch etw* sth).
durchmengen *vt sep siehe* **durchmischen**[1].
durchmessen* *vt insep irreg* (*geh*) *Raum* to stride across; *Strecke* to cover.
Durchmesser *m* **-s, -** diameter ◆ **120 cm im ~** 120 cm in diameter.
durchmischen[1] *vt sep* to mix thoroughly.
durchmischen[2]* *vt insep* to (inter)mix ◆ **etw mit etw ~** to mix sth with sth.
durchmogeln *sep* (*inf*) [1] *vr* to wangle (*inf*) *or* fiddle (*inf*) one's way through.
[2] *vt* to fiddle through (*inf*) (*durch etw* sth).
durchmüssen *vi sep irreg* (*inf*) (*durch etw* sth) to have to go *or* get through; (*fig*) (*durch schwere Zeit*) to have to go through; (*durch Unangenehmes*) to have to go through with (*inf*); **da mußt du eben durch** (*fig*) you'll just have to see it through.
durchnagen *sep* [1] *vt* to gnaw through.
[2] *vr* to gnaw one's way through (*durch etw* sth).
durchnässen[1]* *vt insep* to soak, to drench, to make wet through ◆ **völlig durchnäßt** wet through, soaking wet, drenched.
durchnässen[2] *vi sep* (*Flüssigkeit*) to come *or* seep through (*durch etw* sth) ◆ **die Zeltplane/Wunde näßt durch** wet is coming *or* seeping through the canvas/moisture from the wound is coming *or* seeping through.
durchnehmen *vt sep irreg* **(a)** (*Sch*) to go through, to do (*inf*). **(b)** (*pej inf*) to gossip about.
⚠ **durchnumerieren*** *vt sep* to number consecutively (all the way through).
durch|organisieren* *vt sep* to organize down to the last detail.
durchpassieren* *vt sep* to (rub through a) sieve.
durchpauken *vt sep* (*inf*) **(a)** (*Schüler*) to cram (*inf*), to swot up (*inf*) ◆ **etw mit jdm ~** to drum sth into sb (*inf*).
(b) (*durchsetzen*) *Gesetz, Änderungen* to force *or* push through.
(c) (*durch Schwierigkeiten bringen*) *Schüler* to push through ◆ **dein Anwalt wird dich schon irgendwie ~** your lawyer will get you off somehow.
durchpausen *vt sep* to trace.
durchpeitschen *vt sep* to flog; (*fig*) to rush through, to railroad through (*inf*).
durchpflügen[1] *sep* [1] *vt* to plough thoroughly.
[2] *vr* to plough (one's/its way) through (*durch etw* sth).
durchpflügen[2]* *vt insep* to plough through.
durchplanen *vt sep* to plan (down) to the last detail.

⚠: for details of spelling reform, see supplement

durchplumpsen *vi sep aux sein* (*inf*) (*lit*) to fall through (*durch etw* sth); (*bei Prüfung*) to fail, to flunk (*inf*) (*durch etw, in etw* (*dat*) (in) sth).
durchpressen *vt sep* to press through, to squeeze through; *Knoblauch* to crush; *Kartoffeln* to mash (*by pushing through a press*); *Teig* to pipe.
durchproben *vt sep* to rehearse right through.
durchprobieren* *vt sep* to try one after the other.
durchprügeln *vt sep* to thrash, to beat.
durchpulsen* *vt insep* (*geh*) to pulsate through ◆ **von etw durchpulst sein** to be pulsating *or* vibrating with sth; **von Leben durchpulst** pulsating *or* throbbing with life.
durchpusten *vt sep* (*inf*) *Rohr, Düse* to blow through ◆ **etw (durch etw) ~** to blow sth through (sth); **der Wind hat uns kräftig durchgepustet** the wind blew right through us.
durchqueren* *vt insep* to cross; *Land, Gebiet auch* to pass through, to traverse (*form*).
durchquetschen *sep* (*inf*) [1] *vt siehe* **durchpressen.**
[2] *vr* (*inf*) to squeeze (one's way) through.
durchrasen[1] *vi sep aux sein* (*durch etw* sth) to race *or* tear through; (*inf: durchrennen auch*) to dash through.
durchrasen[2]* *vt insep* to race through, to tear through; (*liter: Schmerz*) to shoot through.
durchrasseln *vi sep aux sein* (*inf*) to fail, to flunk (*inf*) (*durch etw, in etw* (*dat*) (in) sth).
durchrauschen *vi sep aux sein* (*inf*) (*durch etw* sth) **(a)** to sweep through. **(b)** (*bei Prüfung*) *siehe* **durchrasseln.**
durchrechnen *vt sep* to calculate ◆ **eine Rechnung noch einmal ~** to go over *or* through a calculation (again).
durchregnen *vi impers sep* **(a)** (*durchkommen*) **hier regnet es durch** the rain is coming through here; **es regnet durchs Dach durch** the rain is coming through the roof.
(b) (*ununterbrochen regnen*) to rain continuously ◆ **während des ganzen Urlaubs hat es durchgeregnet** it rained throughout the whole holiday; **es hat die Nacht durchgeregnet** it rained all night long, it rained all through the night; *siehe* **durchgeregnet.**
durchreiben *sep irreg* [1] *vt* to rub through; *Material* to wear through.
[2] *vr* (*Material*) to wear through.
Durchreiche *f* **-, -n** (serving) hatch, pass-through (*US*).
durchreichen *vt sep* to pass *or* hand through (*durch etw* sth).
Durchreise *f* journey through ◆ **auf der ~ sein** to be on the way through, to be passing through.
Durchreise|erlaubnis *f* permission to travel through.
durchreisen[1] *vi sep aux sein* (*durch etw* sth) to travel through, to pass through ◆ **wir reisen nur durch** we are just passing through, we are just on the way through.
durchreisen[2]* *vt insep* to travel through, to traverse (*form*).
Durchreisende(r) *mf decl as adj* traveller (passing through), transient (*US*) ◆ **~ nach München** through passengers to Munich.
Durchreisevisum *nt* transit visa.
durchreißen *sep irreg* [1] *vt* to tear in two *or* in half ◆ **etw (in der Mitte) ~** to tear sth in two *or* in half *or* down the middle.
[2] *vi aux sein* to tear in two *or* in half; (*Seil*) to snap (in two *or* in half).
durchreiten[1] *sep irreg* [1] *vi aux sein* to ride through (*durch etw* sth) ◆ **die Nacht ~** to ride through(out) the night, to ride all night long.
[2] *vt Hose* to wear out (through riding).
durchreiten[2]* *vt insep irreg* to ride through; *Land auch* to ride across.
durchrennen[1] *vi sep irreg aux sein* to run *or* race through (*durch etw* sth).
durchrennen[2]* *vt insep irreg* to run *or* race through.
durchrieseln[1] *vi sep aux sein* to trickle through (*durch etw* sth) ◆ **jdm zwischen den Fingern ~** to trickle between *or* through sb's fingers.
durchrieseln[2]* *vt insep* (*fig: Gefühl, Schauer*) to run through.
durchringen *vr sep irreg* to make up one's mind finally ◆ **er hat sich endlich durchgerungen** after much hesitation, he has finally made up his mind *or* come to a decision; **sich zu einem Entschluß ~** to force oneself to take a decision; **sich dazu ~, etw zu tun** to bring *or* force oneself to do sth.
durchrinnen *vi sep irreg aux sein* to run through (*durch etw* sth); (*durchsickern*) to trickle through ◆ **zwischen etw** (*dat*) **~** to run between sth; **das Geld rinnt mir nur so zwischen den Fingern durch** (*fig inf*) money just runs through my fingers *or* burns a hole in my pockets (*inf*).
Durchritt *m* ride through ◆ **beim ~, auf dem ~** on the ride through.
durchrosten *vi sep aux sein* to rust through.
durchrufen *vi sep irreg* (*inf*) to ring.
durchrühren *vt sep* to mix thoroughly.
durchrutschen *vi sep aux sein* (*lit*) to slip through (*durch etw* sth); (*fig*) (*Fehler etc*) to slip through; (*bei Prüfung*) to scrape through ◆ **ein Brei, der einfach (durch die Speiseröhre) durchrutscht** a purée that simply slides *or* slips down the throat; **zwischen etw** (*dat*) **~** to slip between sth; **einige Fehler sind ihm durchgerutscht** a few mistakes slipped past him, he let a few mistakes slip through.
durchrütteln *vt sep* to shake about.
durchs = durch das.
durchsäbeln *vt sep* (*inf*) to hack through.
durchsacken *vi sep aux sein* **(a)** (*durchhängen*) (*Bett etc*) to sag; (*durchbrechen*) (*Dach, Sitz*) to give way; (*nach unten sinken*) to sink ◆ **durch etw ~** (*Mensch*) to fall (down) through sth. **(b)** (*Aviat: Flugzeug*) to pancake.
Durchsage *f* message; (*im Radio*) announcement ◆ **eine ~ der Polizei** a police

announcement.
durchsagen *vt sep* **(a)** *siehe* **durchgeben (b)**. **(b)** *Parole, Losung* to pass on.
durchsägen *vt sep* to saw through.
Durchsatz *m (Ind, Comput)* throughput.
durchsaufen[1] *sep irreg (sl)* [1] *vi* to booze the whole night/day long *(inf)* ◆ **die Nacht** *etc* ~ to booze all the night *etc* long *(inf)*.
[2] *vr* to booze at somebody else's expense *(inf)* ◆ **sich durch etw ~** to booze one's way through sth *(inf)*.
durchsaufen[2]* *vt insep irreg (sl) siehe* **durchsoffen**.
durchsausen *vi sep aux sein (inf)* **(a)** to rush *or* whizz *(inf)* through. **(b)** *(inf: nicht bestehen)* to fail, to flunk *(inf) (durch etw, in etw (dat))* (in) sth).
durchschalten *sep* [1] *vt (Elec)* to connect through.
[2] *vi* **(a)** *(Elec)* to connect through. **(b)** *(Aut)* to change through the gears.
durchschaubar *adj (fig) Hintergründe, Plan, Ereignisse* clear; *Lüge* transparent ◆ **gut/leicht ~** *(verständlich)* easily comprehensible *or* understood; *(erkennbar, offensichtlich)* perfectly clear ◆ **eine leicht ~e Lüge** a lie that is easy to see through; **schwer ~er Charakter/Mensch** inscrutable *or* enigmatic character/person.
durchschauen[1]* *vt insep (erkennen) Absichten, Lüge, jdn, Spiel* to see through; *Sachlage* to see clearly; *(begreifen)* to understand, to comprehend ◆ **du bist durchschaut!** I've/we've seen through you, I/we know what you're up to *(inf) or* what your little game is *(inf)*.
durchschauen[2] *vti sep siehe* **durchsehen 1 (a), 2 (a, b)**.
durchschauern* *vt insep* to run through ◆ **es durchschauert mich** a shiver *or* shudder runs through me.
durchscheinen[1] *vi sep irreg (durch etw* sth) *(Licht, Sonne)* to shine through; *(Farbe, Muster)* to show through; *(fig)* to shine through.
durchscheinen[2]* *vt insep irreg (Sonne)* to flood with light.
durchscheinend *adj* transparent; *Bluse etc* see-through; *Porzellan, Papier auch* translucent; *Stoff auch* diaphanous.
durchscheuern *sep* [1] *vt* to wear through ◆ **sich** *(dat)* **die Haut ~** to graze one's skin; **durchgescheuert sein** to be *or* have worn through.
[2] *vr* to wear through.
durchschieben *sep irreg* [1] *vt* to push *or* shove *(inf)* through *(durch etw* sth).
[2] *vr* to push *or* shove *(inf)* (one's way) through *(durch etw* sth).
durchschießen[1] *vi sep irreg* **(a) durch etw ~** to shoot through sth; **zwischen etw** *(dat)* ~ to shoot between sth. **(b)** *aux sein (schnell fahren, rennen)* to shoot *or* flash through ◆ **zwischen etw** *(dat)* ~ to shoot between sth.
durchschießen[2]* *vt insep irreg* **(a)** *(mit Kugeln)* to shoot through; *(fig)* to shoot *or* flash through ◆ **die Lunge ~** to shoot through the lung; **ein Gedanke durchschoß mich/mein Gehirn** a thought flashed through my mind.
(b) *(Typ: leere Seiten einfügen)* to interleave.
(c) *auch vi (Typ: Zeilenabstand vergrößern)* to set *or* space out; *siehe* **durchschossen**.
(d) *(Tex) Stoff* to interweave.
durchschiffen* *vt insep* to sail across, to cross.
durchschimmern *vi sep (durch etw* sth) to shimmer through; *(Farbe, fig)* to show through.
durchschlafen *vi sep irreg* to sleep through.
Durchschlag *m* **(a)** *(Kopie)* carbon (copy), copy. **(b)** *(Küchengerät)* sieve, strainer. **(c)** *(Lochgerät)* punch. **(d)** *(Loch)* hole; *(in Reifen auch)* puncture. **(e)** *(Elec)* disruptive discharge.
durchschlagen[1] *sep irreg* [1] *vt* **(a) etw ~** *(entzweischlagen)* to chop through sth; *(durchtreiben)* to knock sth through *(durch etw* sth); *(Cook)* to rub sth through a sieve, to sieve sth.
(b) *(Elec) Sicherung* to blow.
[2] *vi* **(a)** *aux sein (durchkommen) (durch etw* sth) to come through; *(fig: Charakter, Eigenschaft, Untugend)* to show through ◆ **bei ihm schlägt der Vater durch** you can see his father in him.
(b) *aux sein (Loch verursachen)* to come/go through *(durch etw* sth).
(c) *aux haben (abführen)* to have a laxative effect ◆ **grüne Äpfel schlagen (bei mir/ihm) durch** *(inf)* green apples run *or* go straight through me/him.
(d) *aux sein (Wirkung haben)* to catch on ◆ **auf etw** *(acc)* ~ to make one's/its mark on sth; **auf jdn ~** to rub off on sb; **alte Werte schlagen wieder voll durch** old values are reasserting themselves in a big way; **Investitionen schlagen auf die Nachfrage durch** investments have a marked effect on demand.
(e) *aux sein (Sicherung)* to blow, to go.
(f) *aux sein (Tech) (Federung, Stoßdämpfer)* to seize up ◆ **das Auto schlug durch** the suspension went.
[3] *vr* **(a)** *(sich durchbringen)* to fight one's way through; *(im Leben)* to struggle through *or* along.
(b) *(ein Ziel erreichen)* to fight one's way through.
[4] *vt impers (Elec)* **es hat die Sicherung durchgeschlagen** the fuse has blown *or* gone.
durchschlagen[2]* *vt insep irreg* to blast a hole in.
durchschlagend *adj Sieg, Erfolg* sweeping; *Maßnahmen* effective, decisive; *Argument, Beweis* decisive, conclusive; *Grund* compelling, cogent ◆ **eine ~e Wirkung haben** to be totally effective.
Durchschlagpapier *nt* copy paper; *(Kohlepapier)* carbon paper.
Durchschlags-: ~kraft *f (von Geschoß)* penetration; *(fig) (von Argument)* decisiveness, conclusiveness; *(von Maßnahmen)* effectiveness; *(von Grund)* cogency; **d~kräftig** *adj (fig) Argument, Beweis* decisive, conclusive; *Grund* compelling, cogent; *Maßnahme* effective, decisive.
durchschlängeln *vr sep (durch etw* sth) *(Fluß)* to wind (its way) through, to meander through; *(Mensch)* to thread one's way through; *(fig)* to manoeuvre one's way through.
durchschleichen *vir sep irreg (vi: aux sein)* to slip through *(durch etw* sth).
durchschleppen *sep* [1] *vt* to drag *or* haul through *(durch etw* sth); *(fig) jdn* to drag along; *Kollegen, Mitglied etc* to carry (along) (with one).
[2] *vr (lit: mühsam gehen)* to drag oneself along; *(fig)* to struggle through *(durch etw* sth).
durchschleusen *vt sep* **(a) ein Schiff ~** to pass a ship through a lock. **(b)** *(fig) (durch etw* sth) *(durch schmale Stelle)* to guide *or* lead through; *(durchschmuggeln) Menschen, Gegenstand* to smuggle *or* get through.
Durchschlupf *m* **-(e)s, Durchschlüpfe** way through.
durchschlüpfen *vi sep aux sein* to slip through, to creep through *(durch etw* sth) ◆ **er ist der Polizei durchgeschlüpft** he slipped through the fingers of the police; **durch Lücken im Gesetz ~** to slip through loopholes in the law.
durchschmecken *sep* [1] *vt* to taste ◆ **man kann den Essig ~** one can taste the vinegar through the other flavours.
[2] *vi* to come through ◆ **der Knoblauch schmeckt deutlich durch** the taste of the garlic comes through strongly.
durchschmuggeln *vt sep* to smuggle through *(durch etw* sth).
durchschneiden[1] *vt sep irreg* to cut through, to cut in two ◆ **etw in der Mitte ~** to cut sth (down) through the middle; **etw mitten ~** to cut sth in two *or* in half.
durchschneiden[2]* *vt insep irreg* to cut through, to cut in two; *(Schiff) Wellen* to plough through; *(Straße, Weg)* to cut through; *(fig: Schrei)* to pierce ◆ **Wasserwege ~ das Land** the country is criss-crossed by waterways.
Durchschnitt *m* **(a)** *(Mittelwert, Mittelmaß)* average; *(in Statistik)* mean; *(Math)* average, (arithmetic) mean ◆ **der ~** *(normale Menschen)* the average person; *(die Mehrheit)* the majority; **im ~** on average; **im ~ 100 km/h fahren/im ~ 8 Stunden täglich arbeiten** to average 100 kmph/8 hours a day, to work on average 8 hours a day; **über/unter dem ~** above/below average; **~ sein** to be average; **guter ~ sein, zum guten ~ gehören** to be a good average.
(b) *(form: Querschnitt)* (cross-)section.
durchschnittlich [1] *adj* average; *Wert auch* mean *attr*; *(mittelmäßig auch)* ordinary.
[2] *adv (im Durchschnitt) verdienen, schlafen, essen etc* on (an) average ◆ **~ begabt/groß** *etc* of average ability/height *etc*; **~ gut** good on average; **die Mannschaft hat sehr ~ gespielt** the team played a very average game.
Durchschnitts- *in cpds* average; **~alter** *nt* average age; **~bildung** *f* average education; **~bürger** *m* average citizen; **~ehe** *f* average *or* normal marriage; **~einkommen** *nt* average income; **~geschwindigkeit** *f* average speed; **~gesicht** *nt* ordinary *or* nondescript *(pej)* face; **~leser** *m* average reader; **~mensch** *m* average person; **~schüler** *m* average pupil; **~temperatur** *f* average *or* mean *(spec)* temperature; **~wert** *m* average *or* mean *(Math)* value; **~zeichnung** *f* sectional drawing; **~zeit** *f* average time.
durchschnüffeln *sep or* **durchschnüffeln*** *insep vt (pej inf) Post, Tasche* to nose through *(inf)*; *Wohnung* to sniff *or* nose around in *(inf)* ◆ **alle Winkel ~** to poke one's nose into every corner *(inf)*.
durchschossen [1] *ptp of* **durchschießen**[2].
[2] *adj (Typ) Buch* interleaved; *Satz* spaced.
Durchschreibeblock *m* duplicating pad.
durchschreiben *sep irreg* [1] *vt* to make a (carbon) copy of ◆ **alles wird durchgeschrieben** copies are *or* a copy is made of everything.
[2] *vi* **(a)** *(Kopie anfertigen)* to make a (carbon) copy. **(b)** *(Kopie liefern)* to print through, to produce a copy.
Durchschreibe-: ~papier *nt* carbon paper; **~satz** *m* carbon pad.
durchschreiten[1] *vi sep irreg aux sein (geh)* to stride through.
durchschreiten[2]* *vt insep irreg (geh)* to stride through.
Durchschrift *f* (carbon) copy.
⚠ **Durchschuß** *m* **(a)** *(durchgehender Schuß)* shot passing right through ◆ **bei einem ~** ... when a shot passes right through ...
(b) *(Loch)* bullet hole; *(Wunde)* gunshot wound *where the bullet has passed right through* ◆ **ein ~ durch den Darm** a gunshot wound right through the intestine.
(c) *(Tex: Schußfaden)* weft.
(d) *(Typ: Zwischenraum)* leading ◆ **ohne ~** unspaced, unleaded; **mit viel/wenig ~** widely/lightly leaded *or* spaced.
durchschütteln *vt sep Mischung* to shake thoroughly; *jdn (zur Strafe)* to give a good shaking; *(in Auto, Bus etc)* to shake about.
durchschwärmen* *vt insep (geh) Gebäude, Gelände* to swarm through ◆ **die Nacht ~** to make a merry night of it.
durchschweben[1] *vi sep aux sein (Vogel)* to glide through; *(Wolken auch, Ballon)* to float through.
durchschweben[2]* *vt insep (poet) (Vogel)* to glide through; *(Wolken auch)* to float through.
durchschweifen* *vt insep (liter)* to roam *or* wander through.
durchschweißen *vt sep* to through-weld.
durchschwimmen[1] *vi sep irreg aux sein* **(a)** *(durch etw* sth) to swim through; *(Dinge)* to float through ◆ **unter/zwischen etw** *(dat)* ~ to swim/float under/between sth. **(b)** *(ohne Pause schwimmen)* to swim without stopping.
durchschwimmen[2]* *vt insep irreg* to swim through; *Strecke* to swim.
durchschwindeln *vr sep* to trick *or* cheat one's way through.
durchschwitzen *sep or* **durchschwitzen*** *insep vt* to soak with *or* in sweat; *siehe* **durchgeschwitzt**.

⚠: Informationen zur Rechtschreibreform im Anhang

durchsegeln[1] *vi sep aux sein* **(a)** (*Schiff*) to sail through (*durch etw* sth) ◆ **unter/zwischen etw** (*dat*) ~ to sail under/between sth. **(b)** (*inf: nicht bestehen*) to fail, to flunk (*inf*) (*durch etw, bei etw* sth). **(c)** (*inf: durchlaufen*) to sail *or* sweep through (*durch etw* sth).

durchsegeln[2]* *vt insep Meer, See* to sail across ◆ **die Meere** ~ to sail (across) the seas.

durchsehen *sep irreg* [1] *vi* (*hindurchschauen*) to look through (*durch etw* sth) ◆ **ein Stoff, durch den man ~ kann** material one can see through.
[2] *vt* **(a)** (*nachsehen, überprüfen*) **etw** ~ to look *or* check sth through *or* over, to have a look through sth, to go *or* look *or* check through *or* over sth (*auf +acc* for); **etw flüchtig** ~ to glance *or* skim through sth.
(b) (*durch etw hindurch*) to see through (*durch etw* sth).

durchseihen *vt sep* (*Cook*) to strain.

⚠**durchsein** *vi sep irreg aux sein* (*Zusammenschreibung nur bei infin und ptp*) (*inf*) **(a)** (*hindurchgekommen sein*) to be through (*durch etw* sth); (*vorbeigekommen sein*) to have gone.
(b) (*fertig sein*) to have finished, to be through (*esp US*) ◆ **durch etw** ~ to have got through sth, to have finished sth.
(c) (*durchgetrennt sein*) to be through, to be in half; (*durchgescheuert sein*) to have worn *or* gone through.
(d) (*Gesetz, Antrag*) to have gone *or* got through.
(e) (*eine Krankheit überstanden haben*) to have pulled through; (*eine Prüfung bestanden haben*) to be through, to have got through ◆ **durch die Krise** ~ to be over the crisis.
(f) (*Cook*) (*Steak, Gemüse, Kuchen*) to be done.

durchsetzen[1] *sep* [1] *vt Maßnahmen, Reformen* to put *or* carry through; *Anspruch, Forderung* to push through; *Vorschlag, Plan, Vorhaben* to carry through; *Ziel* to achieve, to accomplish ◆ **etw bei jdm** ~ to get sb to agree to sth; **etw bei dem Aufsichtsrat** ~ to get sth through the board; **seinen Willen (bei jdm)** ~ to impose one's will (on sb), to get one's (own) way (with sb); *siehe* **Dickkopf, Kopf.**
[2] *vr* **(a)** (*Mensch*) to assert oneself (*bei jdm* with sb); (*Partei etc*) to be successful, to win through ◆ **sich gegen etw** ~ to win through against sth; **sich gegen jdn** ~ to assert oneself against sb, to have one's way despite sb; **sich mit etw** ~ to be successful with sth; **sich im Leben** ~ to make one's way in life, to be a success in life.
(b) (*Idee, Meinung, Neuheit*) to be (generally) accepted, to gain acceptance, to catch on.

durchsetzen[2]* *vt insep* **etw mit etw** ~ to intersperse sth with sth; **ein Land mit Spionen** ~ to infiltrate spies into a country; **die Armee war von subversiven Elementen durchsetzt** the army was infiltrated by subversive elements.

Durchsetzung[1] *f siehe* **durchsetzen**[1] **1** putting *or* carrying through; pushing through; carrying through; achievement, accomplishment.

Durchsetzung[2] *f* **die ~ des Laubwaldes mit Nadelbäumen** the fact that the deciduous forest is interspersed with conifers.

Durchsetzungsvermögen *nt* ability to assert oneself, drive.

durchseuchen* *vt insep* (*verseuchen*) to infect.

Durchseuchung *f -, no pl* spread of infection ◆ **die ~ der Bevölkerung** the spread of the infection throughout the population.

Durchseuchungs-: ~grad *m* degree of infection; **~rate** *f* rate of infection.

Durchsicht *f* examination, inspection, check; (*von Examensarbeiten*) checking through ◆ **jdm etw zur ~ geben/vorlegen** to give sb sth to look through *or* over, to give sb sth to check (through) *or* to examine; **bei ~ der Bücher** on checking the books.

durchsichtig *adj Material* transparent; *Bluse etc auch* see-through; *Wasser, Luft* clear; (*fig*) transparent, obvious; *Stil* clear, lucid, transparent.

Durchsichtigkeit *f, no pl siehe adj* transparency; clarity; transparency, obviousness; clarity, lucidity, transparency.

durchsickern *vi sep aux sein* (*lit, fig*) to trickle through, to seep through; (*fig: trotz Geheimhaltung*) to leak out *or* through ◆ **Informationen ~ lassen** to leak information.

durchsieben[1] *vt sep* to sieve, to sift; (*fig*) *Bewerber, Prüflinge* to sift through.

durchsieben[2]* *vt insep* (*inf*) **etw (mit etw)** ~ to riddle sth with sth.

durchsitzen *sep irreg* [1] *vt Sessel* to wear out (the seat of) ◆ **ich habe mir die Hose durchgesessen** I've worn out *or* through the seat of my trousers.
[2] *vr* (*Sessel, Polster*) to wear out ◆ **der neue Sessel hat sich schon durchgesessen** the seat of the new armchair is *or* has already worn out.

durchsoffen *adj attr* (*sl*) drunken ◆ **eine ~e Nacht** a night of drinking, a drunken night.

durchsonnt *adj* (*poet*) sunny, sun-drenched, sun-soaked.

durchspielen *sep* [1] *vt Szene, Spiel, Stück* to play through; *Rolle* to act through; (*fig*) to go through.
[2] *vi* (*zu Ende spielen*) to play through.
[3] *vr* (*Sport*) to get through.

durchsprechen *sep irreg* [1] *vi* **(a)** to speak *or* talk through (*durch* sth). **(b)** (*durchgehend sprechen*) to speak without a break, to speak solidly.
[2] *vt* **(a)** *Problem, Möglichkeiten, Taktik* to talk over *or* through, to go over *or* through. **(b)** (*Theat*) *Rolle* to read through.

durchsprengen *sep* [1] *vt Mauer etc* to blast through; *Tunnel, Schneise* to blast.
[2] *vi aux sein* (*liter*) to gallop through.

durchspringen[1] *vi sep irreg aux sein* to jump *or* leap *or* spring through (*durch etw* sth).

durchspringen[2]* *vt insep irreg* to jump *or* leap *or* spring through.

durchspülen *vt sep* to rinse *or* flush *or* wash (out) thoroughly; *Mund, Wäsche* to rinse (out) thoroughly.

durchstarten *sep* [1] *vi* (*Aviat*) to overshoot; (*Aut*) to accelerate off again; (*beim, vorm Anfahren*) to rev up.
[2] *vt Flugzeug* to pull up; *Motor, Auto* to rev (up).

durchstechen[1] *sep irreg* [1] *vt Nadel, Spieß* to stick through (*durch etw* sth); *Ohren* to pierce; *Deich, Damm, Grassode* to cut through; *Kanal, Tunnel* to build *or* put through (*durch etw* sth).
[2] *vi* to pierce; (*mit einer dünnen Nadel*) to prick ◆ **die Nadel sticht durch** the needle is sticking through.

durchstechen[2]* *vt insep irreg* to pierce; (*mit Degen, Spieß etc*) to run through; (*mit Nadel*) to prick.

durchstecken *vt sep* (*durch etw* sth) to put *or* stick (*inf*) through; *Nadel etc* to stick through.

durchstehen *sep or* **durchstehen*** *insep vt irreg Zeit, Prüfung* to get through; *Krankheit* to pull *or* come through, to get over; *Tempo, Test, Qualen* to (with)stand; *Abenteuer* to have; *Schwierigkeiten, Situation* to get through.

Durchstehvermögen *nt* endurance, staying power.

durchsteigen *vi sep irreg aux sein* to climb through (*durch etw* sth); (*fig sl*) to get (*inf*), to see ◆ **da steigt doch kein Mensch durch** (*fig sl*) you couldn't expect anyone to get that (*inf*).

➤ **durchstellen** *vt sep* to put through; (*durchreichen auch*) to pass through ◆ **einen Moment, ich stelle durch** one moment, I'll put you through.

Durchstich *m* (*Vorgang*) cut(ting); (*Öffnung*) cut.

Durchstieg *m* passage.

durchstöbern* *insep or* **durchstöbern** *sep vt* to hunt through (*nach* for), to rummage through (*nach* for); *Stadt, Gegend* to scour (*nach* for); (*durchwühlen*) to ransack (*nach* looking for, in search of).

Durchstoß *m* breakthrough.

durchstoßen[1]* *vt insep irreg* to break through; (*Mil auch*) to penetrate.

durchstoßen[2] *sep irreg* [1] *vi aux sein* (*zu einem Ziel gelangen*) to break through (*esp Mil*).
[2] *vt* (*durchbrechen*) to break through; (*abnutzen*) *Schuhe, Ärmel* to wear through ◆ **etw (durch etw)** ~ to push sth through (sth); *Tunnel* to drive sth through sth.
[3] *vr* (*Kragen, Manschetten, Schuhe*) to wear through.

durchstreichen[1] *vt sep irreg* to cross out *or* through, to strike out, to delete.

durchstreichen[2]* *vt insep irreg* (*liter*) to roam *or* wander *or* rove through.

durchstreifen* *vt insep* (*geh*) to roam *or* wander *or* rove through.

durchströmen[1] *vi sep aux sein* to flow *or* run through; (*fig: Menschenmenge*) to stream *or* pour through.

durchströmen[2]* *vt insep* (*lit, fig*) to flow *or* run through.

durchstrukturieren* *vt sep Aufsatz* to give a polished structure to; *Gesetzesvorlage* to work out in detail ◆ **ein gut durchstrukturierter Aufsatz** a well-structured essay.

durchstylen [-stailan] *vt sep* to give style to ◆ **durchgestylt** fully styled.

durchsuchen[1]* *vt insep* (*nach* for) to search (through); *jdn* to search, to frisk; *Stadt, Gegend auch* to scour.

durchsuchen[2] *vt sep* to search (through).

Durchsuchung *f* search (*auf +dat* for).

Durchsuchungsbefehl *m* search warrant ◆ **richterlicher ~** official search warrant.

durchtanzen[1] *sep* [1] *vi* to dance through ◆ **die Nacht ~** to dance through the night, to dance all night, to dance the night away.
[2] *vt Schuhe* to wear out (by *or* with) dancing.

durchtanzen[2]* *vt insep* to dance through ◆ **eine durchtanzte Nacht** a night of dancing.

durchtasten *vr sep* to feel *or* grope one's way through (*durch etw* sth).

durchtesten *vt sep* to test out.

durchtragen *vt sep irreg* to carry *or* take through (*durch etw* sth).

durchtrainieren* *sep* [1] *vt Sportler, Mannschaft, Körper, Muskeln* to get fit ◆ **(gut) durchtrainiert** *Sportler* completely *or* thoroughly fit; *Muskeln, Körper* in superb condition.
[2] *vi* (*ohne Pause trainieren*) to train without a break, to train non-stop.

durchtränken* *vt insep* to soak *or* saturate (completely) ◆ **mit/von etw durchtränkt sein** (*fig geh*) to be imbued with sth.

durchtreiben *vt sep irreg* **etw (durch etw)** ~ to drive sth through (sth).

durchtrennen *sep or* **durchtrennen*** *insep vt Stoff, Papier* to tear (through), to tear in two; (*schneiden*) to cut (through), to cut in two; *Nerv, Sehne* to sever; *Nabelschnur* to cut (through).

durchtreten *sep irreg* [1] *vt* **(a)** *Pedal* to step on; (*am Fahrrad*) to press down; *Starter* to kick.
(b) (*abnutzen*) *Teppich, Schuh, Sohle* to go *or* wear through.
(c) (*durchkicken*) to kick through (*durch etw* sth).
[2] *vi* **(a)** (*Aut: Pedal ~*) to step on the accelerator/brake/clutch; (*Radfahrer*) to pedal (hard).
(b) (*Ftbl*) to kick out.
(c) *aux sein* (*durchsickern, durchdringen*) to come through (*durch etw* sth).
(d) *aux sein* (*form: weitergehen*) to go *or* walk through.
[3] *vr* to wear through.

durchtrieben *adj* cunning, crafty, sly.

Durchtriebenheit *f, no pl* cunning, craftiness, slyness.

Durchtritt *m* (*das Durchtreten*) passage; (*~sstelle*) place where the gas/water *etc* comes through.

➤ SPRACHE AKTIV: **durchstellen** → 27.4

durchtropfen *vi sep aux sein* to drip through (*durch etw* sth).
durchwachen* *vt insep* **die Nacht ~** to stay awake all through the night.
durchwachsen[1] *vi sep irreg aux sein* to grow through (*durch etw* sth).
durchwachsen[2] *adj* (a) (*lit*) *Speck* streaky; *Fleisch, Schinken* with fat running through (it). (b) *pred* (*hum inf: mittelmäßig*) so-so (*inf*), like the curate's egg (*hum*), fair to middling ◆ **ihm geht es ~** he's having his ups and downs.
durchwagen *vr sep* to venture through (*durch etw* sth).
Durchwahl *f* (*Telec*) direct dialling.
▼ **durchwählen** *vi sep* to dial direct ◆ **nach London ~** to dial London direct, to dial through to London (direct).
Durchwahlnummer *f* dialling code (*Brit*), dial code (*US*); (*in Firma*) extension.
durchwalken *vt sep* (*inf*) (a) (*verprügeln*) **jdn ~** to give sb a belting (*inf*) or hammering (*inf*), to belt sb (*inf*). (b) (*dated: durchkneten*) to knead thoroughly.
durchwandern[1] *vi sep aux sein* (*durch Gegend*) to hike through (*durch etw* sth); (*ohne Unterbrechung wandern*) to carry on *or* continue hiking.
durchwandern[2]* *vt insep Gegend* to walk through; (*hum*) *Zimmer, Straßen etc* to wander through ◆ **die halbe Welt ~** to wander half way round the world.
durchwaschen *vt sep irreg* to wash through.
durchwaten[1] *vi sep aux sein* to wade through (*durch etw* sth).
durchwaten[2]* *vt insep* to wade through.
durchweben* *vt insep irreg* (*mit, von* with) to interweave; (*fig liter auch*) to intersperse.
durchweg, (*esp Aus*) **durchwegs** *adv* (*bei adj*) (*ausnahmslos*) without exception; (*in jeder Hinsicht*) in every way *or* respect; (*bei n*) without exception; (*bei vb*) (*völlig*) totally; (*ausnahmslos*) without exception ◆ **~ gut** good without exception/in every way *or* respect.
durchwehen[1]* *vt insep* (*geh*) to waft through.
durchwehen[2] *vti sep* to blow through ◆ **(etw) durch etw ~** to blow (sth) through sth.
durchweichen[1] *sep* [1] *vi aux sein* (*sehr naß werden*) to get wet through, to get soaked *or* drenched; (*weich werden: Karton, Boden*) to go soggy.
[2] *vt Kleidung, jdn* to soak, to drench; *Boden, Karton* to make soggy.
durchweichen[2]* *vt insep* (*geh*) *Boden, Karton* to soften.
durchwerfen *sep irreg* (*durch etw* sth) [1] *vt* to throw through.
[2] *vr* to throw oneself through.
durchwetzen *vtr sep* to wear through.
durchwinden *vr sep irreg* (*Fluß*) to wind its way, to meander (*durch etw* through sth); (*Mensch*) to thread *or* worm one's way through (*durch etw* sth); (*fig*) to worm one's way through (*durch etw* sth) ◆ **sich zwischen etw** (*dat*) **~** to wind its way/to thread *or* worm one's way between sth.
durchwirken* *vt insep* (*geh*) *Gewebe* to interweave.
durchwitschen *vi sep aux sein* (*inf*) to slip through (*durch etw* sth).
durchwogen* *vt insep* (*fig geh*) to surge through.
durchwollen *vi sep* (*inf*) to want to go/come through (*durch etw* sth) ◆ **zwischen/unter etw** (*dat*) **~** to want to pass between/under sth; **der Bohrer/Faden will nicht (durch den Beton/das Öhr) durch** the drill/thread doesn't want to go through (the concrete/eye).
durchwühlen[1] *sep* [1] *vt* to rummage through, to rummage about in (*nach* for); *Zimmer, Haus auch* to ransack (*nach* looking for, in search of).
[2] *vr* (*durch etw* sth) to burrow through; (*fig*) to work one's way through, to plough through.
durchwühlen[2]* *vt insep* to rummage through, to rummage about in (*nach* for); *Zimmer auch* to ransack (*nach* looking for, in search of); *Boden* to dig up.
durchwurschteln, durchwursteln *vr sep* (*inf*) to muddle through.
durchzählen *sep* [1] *vt* to count through *or* up.
[2] *vi* to count *or* number off.
durchzechen[1] *vi sep* to carry on drinking.
durchzechen[2]* *vt insep* **die Nacht ~** to drink through the night, to carry on drinking all night; **eine durchzechte Nacht** a night of drinking.
durchzeichnen *vt sep siehe* **durchpausen.**
durchziehen[1] *sep irreg* [1] *vt* (a) (*durch etw hindurchziehen*) to pull *or* draw through (*durch etw* sth).
(b) (*inf: erledigen, vollenden*) to get through.
(c) (*sl: rauchen*) *Joint* to smoke ◆ **einen ~** to have *or* smoke a joint (*sl*).
(d) (*durchbauen*) (*durch etw* sth) *Graben* to dig through; *Mauer* to build through.
[2] *vi aux sein* (a) (*durchkommen*) (*durch etw* sth) to pass *or* go/come through; (*Truppe auch*) to march through; (*Schmerz*) to go through; (*Kälte*) to come through.
(b) to soak ◆ **etw in etw** (*dat*) **~ lassen** to steep *or* soak sth in sth; (*in Marinade*) to marinate sth in sth.
[3] *vr* to run through (*durch etw* sth).
durchziehen[2]* *vt insep irreg* (*durchwandern*) to pass through, to go/come through; (*Straße, Fluß, fig: Thema*) to run through; (*Geruch*) to fill, to pervade; (*Graben*) to cut through ◆ **sein Haar ist von grauen Fäden durchzogen** his hair is streaked with grey; **die Welt ~** to travel (round) the world; **ein Feld mit Gräben ~** to crisscross a field with ditches; **ein mit Goldfäden durchzogener Stoff** material with a gold thread running through it.
durchzucken* *vt insep* (*Blitz*) to flash across; (*fig: Gedanke*) to flash through.
Durchzug *m* (a) *no pl* (*Luftzug*) draught ◆ **~ machen** to create a draught; (*zur Lüftung*) to get the air moving. (b) (*durch ein Gebiet*) passage; (*von Truppen*) march through ◆ **auf dem/beim ~ durch ein Land** while passing through a country.
Durchzugsrecht *nt* right of passage.
durchzwängen *sep* (*durch etw* sth) [1] *vt* to force *or* squeeze through.
[2] *vr* to force one's way through, to squeeze (one's way) through.
▼ **dürfen** *pret* **durfte,** *ptp* **gedurft** *or* (*modal aux vb*) **dürfen** *vi* (a) (*Erlaubnis haben*) **etw tun ~** to be allowed to do sth, to be permitted to do sth; **darf ich/man das tun?** may I/one do it?, am I/is one allowed to do it?; **darf ich? — ja, Sie ~** may I? — yes, you may; **darf ich ins Kino?** may I go to the cinema?; **er hat nicht gedurft** he wasn't allowed to.
▼ (b) (*verneint*) **man darf etw nicht (tun)** (*sollte, muß nicht*) one must not *or* mustn't do sth; (*hat keine Erlaubnis*) one isn't allowed to do sth, one may not do sth; (*kann nicht*) one may not do sth; **hier darf man nicht rauchen/durchfahren** (*ist verboten*) smoking is prohibited here/driving through here is prohibited, it is prohibited to smoke/drive through here; **diesen Zug darf ich nicht verpassen** I must not miss this train; **du darfst ihm das nicht übelnehmen** you must not take offence at him; **die Kinder ~ hier nicht spielen** the children aren't allowed to *or* may not play here; **der Patient darf noch nicht transportiert werden** the patient may not be moved yet; **das darf doch nicht wahr sein!** that can't be true!; **da darf er sich nicht wundern** that shouldn't surprise him.
▼ (c) (*in Höflichkeitsformeln*) **darf ich das tun?** may I do that?; **Ruhe, wenn ich bitten darf!** quiet, (if you) please!, will you please be quiet!; **darf ich um den nächsten Tanz bitten?** may I have (the pleasure of) the next dance?; **darf ich Sie bitten, das zu tun?** may *or* could I ask you to do that?; **was darf es sein?** can I help you, what can I do for you?; (*vom Gastgeber gesagt*) what can I get you?, what'll you have?; **dürfte ich bitte Ihren Ausweis sehen** (*als Aufforderung*) may *or* might I see your identity card, please.
(d) (*Veranlassung haben, können*) **wir freuen uns, Ihnen mitteilen zu ~** we are pleased to be able to tell you; **ich darf wohl sagen, daß ...** I think I can say that ...; **man darf doch wohl fragen** one can *or* may ask, surely?; **Sie ~ mir das ruhig glauben** you can *or* may take my word for it.
(e) (*im Konjunktiv*) **das dürfte ...** (*als Annahme*) that must ...; (*sollte*) that should *or* ought to ...; (*könnte*) that could ...; **das dürfte Emil sein** that must be Emil; **das dürfte wohl das Beste sein** that is probably the best thing; **das dürfte reichen** that should be enough, that ought to be enough; **das Essen dürfte stärker gewürzt sein** the food could have been more highly spiced.
dürftig *adj* (a) (*ärmlich*) wretched, miserable; *Essen auch* meagre.
(b) (*pej: unzureichend*) miserable, pathetic (*inf*); *Kenntnisse auch* sketchy, scanty; *Ausrede auch* feeble, lame; *Einkommen auch* paltry; *Ersatz* poor *attr*; (*spärlich*) *Haarwuchs, Pflanzenwuchs* sparse; *Bekleidung* scanty, skimpy ◆ **ein paar ~e Tannen** a few scrawny fir trees.
Dürftigkeit *f -, no pl siehe adj* (a) wretchedness, miserableness; meagreness. (b) (*pej*) miserableness, patheticness; sketchiness, scantiness; feebleness, lameness; paltriness; poorness; sparseness; skimpiness.
dürr *adj* (a) (*trocken*) dry; (*ausgetrocknet*) *Boden* arid, barren; *Ast, Strauch* dried up, withered. (b) (*pej: mager*) skinny, scrawny, scraggy. (c) (*fig*) **mit ~en Worten** in plain terms, plainly, bluntly; **die ~en Jahre** (*Bibl, fig*) the lean years.
Dürre *f -, -n* (a) (*Zeit der ~*) drought. (b) *siehe* **Dürrheit.**
Dürre-: ~jahr *nt* year of drought; **~katastrophe** *f* catastrophic *or* disastrous drought; **~periode** *f* (period of) drought; (*fig*) barren period.
Dürrheit *f, no pl* (*Trockenheit*) dryness; (*von Boden auch*) aridity, barrenness; (*pej: Magerkeit*) skinniness, scrawniness, scragginess.
Durst *m -(e)s, no pl* (*lit, fig*) thirst (*nach* for) ◆ **~ haben** to be thirsty; **~ bekommen** to get *or* become thirsty; **den ~ löschen** *or* **stillen** to quench one's thirst; **das macht ~** that makes you thirsty, that gives you a thirst; **einen** *or* **ein Glas über den ~ getrunken haben** (*inf*) to have had one too many *or* one over the eight (*inf*).
dursten [1] *vi* (a) (*geh*) to be thirsty, to thirst (*liter*) ◆ **er mußte ~** he had to go thirsty. (b) (*fig*) *siehe* **dürsten 2.**
[2] *vt impers siehe* **dürsten 1.**
dürsten [1] *vt impers* (*liter*) **es dürstet mich, mich dürstet** I thirst (*liter*); **es dürstet ihn nach Rache/Wissen/Wahrheit** he thirsts for revenge/knowledge/(the) truth; *siehe* **Blut.**
[2] *vi* (*fig*) **er dürstet nach Rache/Wahrheit** he is thirsty for revenge/truth.
Durstgefühl *nt* feeling of thirst.
durstig *adj* thirsty ◆ **jdn ~ machen** to make sb thirsty, to give sb a thirst; **diese Arbeit macht ~** this is thirsty work (*inf*), this work makes you thirsty; **nach etw ~ sein** (*fig geh*) to be thirsty for sth, to thirst for sth (*liter*); **sie ist eine ~e Seele** (*hum inf*) she likes the bottle (*hum*).
Durst-: d~löschend, d~stillend *adj* thirst-quenching; **~strecke** *f* hard times *pl*; (*Mangel an Inspiration*) barren period; **~streik** *m* thirst strike.
Dur-: ~tonart *f* major key; **~tonleiter** *f* major scale.
Duschbad *nt* (a) shower(-bath) ◆ **ein ~ nehmen** to have *or* take a shower(-bath). (b) (*Gel*) shower gel.
Dusche *f -, -n* shower ◆ **unter der ~ sein** *or* **stehen** to be in the shower, to be taking a shower; **eine ~ nehmen** to have *or* take a shower; **das war eine kalte ~** (*fig*) that really brought him/her *etc* down with a bump; **bei ihrem Enthusiasmus wirkten seine Worte wie eine kalte ~** (*fig*) his words poured cold water on her enthusiasm.
Dusch|ecke *f* shower (cubicle).
duschen [1] *vir* to have *or* take a shower, to shower ◆ **(sich) kalt ~** to have *or* take a cold shower.
[2] *vt* **jdn ~** to give sb a shower; **jdm/sich den Kopf/Rücken ~** to spray sb's/one's head/back.

➤ SPRACHE AKTIV: **durchwählen** → 27.1, 27.3 **dürfen: a** → 36.1, 46.5 **b** → 36.3, 37.4, 45.2 **c** → 27.5, 28.1, 29.2, 30, 52.2

Dusch-: ~gel *nt* shower gel; **~gelegenheit** *f* shower facilities *pl*; **~haube** *f* shower cap; **~kabine** *f* shower (cubicle); **~raum** *m* shower room, showers *pl*; **~vorhang** *m* shower curtain; **~wanne** *f* shower tray.

Düse *f* **-, -n** nozzle; (*Mech auch*) jet; (*von Flugzeug*) jet.

Dusel *m* **-s,** *no pl* (*inf*) **(a)** (*Glück*) luck ◆ **~ haben** to be lucky; **da hat er (einen) ~ gehabt** his luck was in (*inf*), he was lucky; **so ein ~!** that was lucky!, that was a fluke! (*inf*). **(b)** (*Trancezustand*) daze, dream; (*durch Alkohol*) fuddle ◆ **im ~** in a daze *or* dream/in a fuddle.

duselig *adj* (*schlaftrunken*) drowsy; (*benommen*) dizzy, giddy; (*esp durch Alkohol*) (be)fuddled ◆ **mir ist ganz ~ (im Kopfe), ich habe ein ~es Gefühl** my head is swimming, I feel quite dizzy *or* giddy.

duseln *vi* (*inf*) to doze.

düsen *vi aux sein* (*inf*) to dash; (*mit Flugzeug*) to jet ◆ **nach Hause ~** to dash *or* whizz off home; **durch die Welt ~** to jet around the world.

Düsen-: ~antrieb *m* jet propulsion; **mit ~antrieb** jet-propelled, with jet propulsion; **~bomber** *m* jet bomber; **~flugzeug** *nt* jet aircraft *or* plane, jet; **d~getrieben** *adj* jet-propelled, jet-powered; **~jäger** *m* **(a)** (*Mil*) jet fighter; **(b)** (*inf*) *siehe* **~flugzeug**; **~klipper** *m* jet airliner; **~maschine** *f* jet (aircraft *or* plane); **~motor** *m* jet engine; **~treibstoff** *m* jet fuel; **~triebwerk** *nt* jet power-unit.

duslig *adj* (*inf*) *siehe* **duselig.**

Dussel *m* **-s, -** (*inf*) twit (*Brit inf*), twerp (*inf*), dope (*inf*).

Dusselei *f* (*inf*) stupidity.

dusselig, ⚠dußlig *adj* (*inf*) stupid.

Dusseligkeit, ⚠Dußligkeit *f* (*inf*) stupidity.

duster *adj siehe* **dunkel.**

düster *adj* gloomy; *Nacht auch* murky; *Tag, Wetter auch* dismal, murky; *Musik auch* funereal, lugubrious; *Farbe, Gesicht auch* sombre, dismal; *Bild, Gedanken, Zukunftsvisionen* sombre, dismal, dark; *Miene, Stimmung auch* dark, black; (*unheimlich*) *Gestalten, Stadtteil* sinister, (dark and) forbidding.

Düstere(s) *nt decl as adj* gloom, dark(ness); (*fig: von Gedanken, Stimmung*) gloominess.

Düsterkeit *f* gloominess; (*Dunkelheit*) gloom, darkness.

Dutt *m* **-(e)s, -s** *or* **-e** (*dial*) bun.

Dutte *f* **-, -n** (*Aus*) teat, nipple.

Duty-free-Shop ['dju:tɪ'fri:ʃɔp] *m* **-s, -s** duty-free shop.

Dutzend *nt* **-s, -e** dozen ◆ **ein halbes ~** half-a-dozen, a half-dozen; **zwei/drei ~** two/three dozen; **ein ~ frische** *or* **frischer** (*geh*) **Eier kostet** *or* **kosten ...** a dozen fresh eggs cost(s) ...; **das ~ kostet 4 Mark** they cost 4 marks a dozen; **~e** *pl* (*inf*) dozens *pl*; **sie kamen in** *or* **zu ~en** they came in (their) dozens; **im ~ billiger** (*inf*) (*bei größerer Menge*) the more you buy, the more you save; (*bei mehr Leuten*) the more you are, the more you save (*inf*); *siehe* **zwölf.**

dutzend(e)mal *adv* (*inf*) dozens of times.

Dutzend-: d~fach [1] *adj* dozens of; **in d~fachen Variationen** in dozens of variations; [2] *adv* in dozens of ways; **~mensch** *m* (*pej*) ordinary *or* run-of-the-mill sort of person; **~preis** *m* price per dozen; **~ware** *f* (*pej*) (cheap) mass-produced item; **~waren** (cheap) mass-produced goods; **d~weise** *adv* in dozens, by the dozen.

Duzbruder *m* good friend *or* pal (*inf*) ◆ **alte Duzbrüder** old friends *or* pals (*inf*) *or* mates (*inf*).

duzen *vt* to address with the familiar "du"-form ◆ **wir ~ uns** we use "du" *or* the "du"-form (to each other).

Duz-: ~freund *m* good friend; **alte ~freunde** old friends; **~fuß** *m*: **mit jdm auf dem ~fuß stehen** (*inf*) to be on familiar terms with sb.

DV [de:'fau] *f* - *abbr of* **Datenverarbeitung** DP.

d. Verf. *abbr of* **der Verfasser.**

dwars *adv* (*N Ger Naut*) abeam.

Dynamik *f, no pl* **(a)** (*Phys*) dynamics *sing.* **(b)** (*fig*) dynamism ◆ **Menschen mit einer solchen ~** people with such dynamism.

Dynamiker *m* **-s, -** go-getter.

dynamisch *adj* **(a)** dynamic ◆ **~e Gesetze** laws of dynamics. **(b)** (*fig*) dynamic; *Renten* ≃ index-linked.

dynamisieren* *vt* (*geh*) *Politik* to make dynamic; (*vorantreiben*) *Prozeß, Reform* to speed up; *Renten* ≃ to index-link.

Dynamisierung *f* (*geh*) (*von Reform etc*) speeding up; (*von Renten*) ≃ index-linking ◆ **sie streben eine ~ ihrer Politik an** they are seeking to make their policy more dynamic.

Dynamit *nt* **-s,** *no pl* (*lit, fig*) dynamite.

Dynamo(maschine *f*) *m* **-s, -s** dynamo; (*fig*) powerhouse.

Dynast *m* **-en, -en** dynast.

Dynastie *f* dynasty.

dynastisch *adj* dynastic.

Dysprosium *nt, no pl* (*abbr* **Dy**) dysprosium.

D-Zug ['de:tsu:k] *m* fast train; (*hält nur in großen Städten*) non-stop *or* through train ◆ **ein alter Mann/eine alte Frau ist doch kein ~** (*inf*) I am going as fast as I can, I can't go any faster.

D-Zug-: ~-Tempo *nt* (*inf*) fantastic speed (*inf*); **im ~-Tempo** like greased lightning (*inf*), in double-quick time (*inf*); **~-Zuschlag** *m* express travel supplement, supplement payable on fast trains; (*inf: Karte*) supplementary ticket.

E, e [eː] *nt* -, - E, e.

Eau de Cologne ['oː də ko'lɔnjə] *nt* - - -, *no pl* eau de Cologne.

Ebbe *f* -, **-n** **(a)** (*ablaufendes Wasser*) ebb tide; (*Niedrigwasser*) low tide ◆ **~ und Flut** the tides, ebb and flow; **bei ~ baden/auslaufen** to swim when the tide is going out/to go out on the (ebb) tide; (*bei Niedrigwasser*) to swim/go out at low tide; **mit der ~** on *or* with the ebb tide; **die ~ tritt um 15³⁰ ein** the tide starts to go out *or* turns at 3.30 p.m.; **es ist ~** the tide is going out; (*es ist Niedrigwasser*) it's low tide, the tide is out.
(b) (*fig*) **bei mir** *or* **in meinem Geldbeutel ist** *or* **herrscht ~** I'm a bit hard up (*inf*) *or* my finances are at a pretty low ebb at the moment; **in den Beziehungen der beiden Staaten herrscht zur Zeit ~** *or* **ist eine ~ eingetreten** relations between the two countries are at a low ebb at the moment *or* have fallen off recently.

ebd. *abbr of* **ebenda**.

eben [1] *adj* (*glatt*) smooth; (*gleichmäßig*) even; (*gleich hoch*) level; (*flach*) flat; (*Math*) plane ◆ **zu ~er Erde** at ground level; **auf ~er Strecke** on the flat.
[2] *adv* **(a)** (*zeitlich: so~*) just; (*schnell, kurz*) for a minute *or* second ◆ **das wollte ich ~ sagen** I was just about to say that; **mein Bleistift war doch ~ noch da** my pencil was there (just) a minute ago; **kommst du ~ mal mit?** will you come with me for a minute *or* second?; **ich gehe ~ zur Bank** I'll just pop to the bank (*inf*).
(b) (*gerade or genau das*) exactly, precisely ◆ **(na) ~!** exactly!, quite!, precisely!; **das ist es ja ~!** that's just *or* precisely it!; **das ~ nicht!** no, not that!; **das ist es ~ nicht!** that's just *or* exactly what it isn't!; **~ das wollte ich sagen** that's just *or* exactly what I wanted to say; **nicht ~ billig/viel/angenehm** *etc* not exactly cheap/a lot/pleasant *etc.*
(c) (*gerade noch*) just ◆ **das reicht so** *or* **nur ~ aus** it's only just enough; **wir haben den Zug ~ noch erreicht** we just caught the train.
(d) (*nun einmal, einfach*) just, simply ◆ **das ist ~ so** that's just the way it is *or* things are; **dann bleibst du ~ zu Hause** then you'll just have to stay at home; *siehe* **dann**.

Ebenbild *nt* image ◆ **dein ~** the image of you; **das genaue ~ seines Vaters** the spitting image of his father.

ebenbürtig *adj* **(a)** (*Hist: gleichrangig*) of equal birth.
(b) (*gleichwertig*) equal; *Gegner* evenly matched ◆ **jdm an Kraft/Ausdauer ~ sein** to be sb's equal in strength/endurance; **sie war ihm an Kenntnissen ~** her knowledge equalled his *or* was equal to his; **wir sind einander ~** we are equal(s).

Ebenbürtigkeit *f* **(a)** (*Hist*) equality of birth. **(b)** (*Gleichwertigkeit*) equality ◆ **die ~ dieser beiden Gegner wurde deutlich** it became clear that the two opponents were evenly matched.

eben-: ~da *adv* **(a)** (*gerade dort*) **~da will auch ich hin** that is exactly where I am bound too; **(b)** (*bei Zitat*) ibid, ibidem; **~dahin** *adv* **~dahin zieht es auch mich** that is exactly where *or* whither (*old*) I am bound too; **~dann** *adv* **~dann soll ich zum Arzt** that is exactly when I have to go to the doctor; **~darum** *adv* that is why, for that reason; **~darum!** (*zu Kind*) because I say so!; **~der, ~die, ~das** *pron* he; she; it; **~der hat auch gesagt, daß ...** he was also the one who said that ..., it was he who also said that ...; **~deshalb, ~deswegen** *adv* that is exactly why; **~die** *pron siehe* **~der**; **~diese(r, s)** [1] *pron* (*liter*) he; she; it; **und ~dieser wurde später ermordet** and this same man was later murdered; [2] *adj* this very *or* same; **und ~diesen Mann hat sie geheiratet** and this was the very man she married; **~dort** *adv* (*old*) at that very *or* same place.

Ebene *f* -, **-n** (*Tief~*) plain; (*Hoch~*) plateau; (*Math, Phys*) plane; (*fig*) level ◆ **auf höchster/der gleichen ~** (*fig*) at the highest/the same level; **seine Beleidigungen liegen auf der gleichen ~ wie ...** his insults are on a par with ...; *siehe* **schief**.

eben-: ~erdig *adj* at ground level; **~falls** *adv* as well, likewise; (*bei Verneinungen*) either; **er hat ~falls nichts davon gewußt** he knew nothing about it either; **danke, ~falls!** thank you, the same to you!

Ebenheit *f siehe* **eben 1** smoothness; evenness; levelness; flatness; planeness.

Ebenholz *nt* ebony.

Eben-: e~jene(r, s) (*liter*) [1] *pron* he; she; it; **e~jener wurde später Präsident** this same man later became president; [2] *adj* that very *or* same; **~maß** *nt* (*von Gestalt, Gesichtszügen*) elegant proportions *pl*; (*von Zähnen*) evenness; (*von Versen*) even flow; **e~mäßig** *adj siehe* **~maß** elegantly proportioned; even; evenly flowing; **e~mäßig geformt** elegantly proportioned; **~mäßigkeit** *f siehe* **~maß**.

ebenso *adv* (*genauso*) just as; (*auch, ebenfalls*) as well ◆ **das kann doch ~ eine Frau machen** a woman can do that just as well; **die Geschäfte sind geschlossen, ~ alle Kinos** the shops are closed, as are all the cinemas; **viele Leute haben sich ~ wie wir beschwert** a lot of people complained just like *or* just as we did *or* just like us; **er freute sich ~ wie ich** he was just as pleased as I was; **er hat ein ~ großes Zimmer wie wir** he has just as big a room as we have.

⚠**ebenso-: ~gern** *adv* **ich mag sie ~gern** I like her just as much *or* equally well; **ich esse ~gern Reis** I like rice just as much, I'd just as soon eat rice; **ich komme ~gern morgen** I'd just as soon come tomorrow; **~gut** *adv* (just) as well; **ich kann ~gut Französisch wie Italienisch** I can speak French (just) as well as I can speak Italian, my French is (just) as good as my Italian; **~häufig** *adv siehe* ⚠**~oft**; **~lang(e)** *adv* just as long.

ebensolche(r, s) *adj* (exactly) the same.

⚠**ebenso-: ~oft** *adv* just as often *or* frequently; **~sehr** *adv* just as much; **~viel** *adv* just as much; **~wenig** *adv* just as little; **~wenig, wie man dies sagen kann, kann man behaupten, ...** there is just as little ground for saying this as for claiming ...

Eber *m* **-s, -** boar.

Eber|esche *f* rowan, mountain ash.

ebnen *vt* to level (off), to make level ◆ **jdm/einer Sache den Weg ~** (*fig*) to smooth the way for sb/sth.

EC [eː'tseː] *m* **-, -s** (*Rail*) *abbr of* **Euro-City-Zug**.

echauffieren* [eʃɔ'fiːrən] *vr* (*dated*) to get into a taking (*dated*), to get het-up.

Echo *nt* **-s, -s** echo; (*fig*) response (*auf +acc* to) ◆ **er war nur das ~ seines Chefs** (*fig*) he was only an echo of his boss; **ein starkes** *or* **lebhaftes ~ finden** (*fig*) to meet with *or* attract a lively *or* positive response (*bei* from).

echoen ['ɛçoən] *vi* (*rare*) to echo ◆ **hallooo ...!, echote es** hallooo ...!, came the echo.

Echolot *nt* (*Naut*) echo-sounder, sonar; (*Aviat*) sonic altimeter.

Echse ['ɛksə] *f* **-, -n** (*Zool*) lizard.

echt [1] *adj, adv* **(a)** real, genuine; *Gefühle auch* sincere; *Haar, Perlen, Gold* real; *Unterschrift, Geldschein, Gemälde* genuine; *Haarfarbe* natural ◆ **der Geldschein war nicht ~** the note was a forgery *or* was forged; **der Ring ist ~ golden** the ring is real gold.
(b) (*typisch*) typical ◆ **ein ~er Bayer** a real *or* typical Bavarian; **~ englisch** typically English; **~ Shakespeare** typical of Shakespeare, typically Shakespearean; **~ Franz/Frau** typical of *or* just like Franz/a woman, Franz/a woman all over (*inf*).
(c) *Farbe* fast.
(d) (*Math*) **~er Bruch** proper fraction.
[2] *adv* (*inf*) really ◆ **meinst du das ~?** do you really *or* honestly mean that?; **der spinnt doch ~** he must be cracked (*inf*) *or* round the bend (*inf*); **ich hab's ~ eilig** I'm really in a hurry.

Echt-: e~golden *adj attr* real gold; **~haarperücke** *f* real hair wig.

Echtheit *f* genuineness; (*von Unterschrift, Dokument auch*) authenticity; (*von Gefühlen, Glauben auch*) sincerity; (*von Haarfarbe*) naturalness; (*von Farbe*) fastness.

Echt-: e~silbern *adj attr* real silver; **~zeit** *f* (*Comput*) real time.

Eck *nt* **-(e)s, -e** **(a)** (*esp Aus, S Ger*) *siehe* **Ecke**.
(b) (*Sport*) **das kurze/lange ~** the near/far corner of the goal.
(c) **über ~** diagonally across *or* opposite; **die Schrauben über ~ anziehen** to tighten the nuts working diagonally across; **im ~ sein** (*Aus*) to be out of form; **da hat's ein ~** (*Aus inf*) you've/she's *etc* got problems there.

Eckart *m* **-s der getreue ~** (*liter*) the faithful Eckart *mythical figure in medieval German literature*; (*fig*) the old faithful.

Eck- *in cpds* corner; **~ball** *m* (*Sport*) corner; **einen ~ball schießen** *or* **treten/geben** to take/give a corner; **~bank** *f* corner seat.

Ecke *f* **-, -n** **(a)** corner; (*Kante*) edge; (*von Kragen*) point; (*Sport: Eckball*) corner ◆ **Kantstraße ~ Goethestraße** at the corner of Kantstraße and Goethestraße; **er wohnt gleich um die ~** he lives just round the corner; **ein Kind in die ~ stellen** to make a child stand in the corner; **etw in allen ~n und Winkeln su-**

chen to search *or* look high and low for sth; **jdn in die ~ drängen** (*fig*) to push sb into the background; **an allen ~n und Enden sparen** to pinch and scrape (*inf*); **jdn um die ~ bringen** (*inf*) to bump sb off (*inf*), to do away with sb (*inf*); **mit jdm um ein paar** *or* **sieben ~n herum verwandt sein** (*inf*) to be distantly related to sb, to be sb's second cousin twice removed (*hum inf*); **die neutrale ~** (*Boxen*) the neutral corner; **~n und Kanten** (*fig*) rough edges; *siehe* **fehlen.**
(b) (*Käse~, Kuchen~*) wedge.
(c) (*inf*) (*Gegend*) corner, area; (*von Stadt auch*) quarter; (*Strecke*) way ◆ **eine ~** (*fig: viel*) quite a bit; **eine ganze ~ entfernt** quite a (long) way away, a fair way away; **eine (ganze) ~ älter/billiger/größer** (quite) a bit older/cheaper/bigger; **ich komme noch eine ~ mit** I'll come with you for a (little) way; **aus welcher ~ kommst du?** what part of the world are you from?

Ecken-: ~steher *m* (*inf*) loafer (*inf*); **~verhältnis** *nt* (*Ftbl*) number of corners per team; **sie liegen nach dem ~verhältnis vorn** they're ahead on corners.

Ecker *f* -, -n (*Bot*) beechnut.

Eck-: ~fahne *f* (*Sport*) corner flag; **~fenster** *nt* corner window; **~haus** *nt* house at *or* on the corner; (*Reihen~*) end house.

eckig *adj* angular; *Tisch, Brot, Klammer* square; (*spitz*) sharp; (*fig*) *Bewegung, Gang* jerky.

-eckig *adj suf* -cornered.

Eck-: ~kneipe *f* (*inf*) pub on the corner (*Brit*); **~laden** *m* shop on a corner, corner shop; **~lohn** *m* basic rate of pay; **~pfeiler** *m* corner pillar; (*fig*) cornerstone; **~pfosten** *m* corner post; **~platz** *m* (*in Zug etc*) corner seat; (*in Theater etc*) end seat, seat at the end of a row; **~schrank** *m* corner cupboard; **~stein** *m* **(a)** (*lit, fig*) cornerstone; **(b)** (*Cards*) diamonds *pl*; **~stoß** *m* *siehe* **~ball**; **~turm** *m* corner tower; **~wert** *m* (*Econ*) benchmark figure; (*fig*) basis; **~wurf** *m* (*beim Handball*) corner (throw); **~zahn** *m* canine tooth; **~zins** *m* (*Fin*) minimum lending rate.

Eclair [e'klɛːɐ] *nt* -s, -s (*Cook*) eclair.

Economyklasse [i'kɔnəmɪ-] *f* economy class.

Ecstasy ['ɛkstəsi] *nt* -, *no pl* (Droge) ecstasy.

Ecstasy - Tablette *f* ecstasy tablet.

Ecu [e:'ku:] *m* -(s), -(s) ecu.

Ecuador [ekua'do:ɐ] *nt* -s Ecuador.

ecuadorianisch *adj* Ecuadorian.

Ed. *abbr of* **Edition.**

ed. *abbr of* **edidit = herausgegeben.**

Edamer (Käse) *m* -s, - Edam (cheese).

Edda *f* -, **Edden** (*Liter*) Edda.

edel *adj* **(a)** (*attr: vornehm, adlig*) noble. **(b)** (*hochwertig*) precious; *Hölzer auch, Rosen* fine; *Wein* noble, fine; *Pferd* thoroughbred. **(c)** (*~ geformt, harmonisch*) noble; *Nase* regal, aristocratic. **(d)** (*fig*) *Gesinnung, Mensch, Tat* noble; (*großherzig auch*) generous ◆ **er denkt ~** he has noble thoughts; *siehe* **Spender(in).**

Edel-: ~fäule *f* (*bei Weintrauben*) noble rot; (*bei Käse*) (veins *pl* of) mould; **~frau** *f* (*Hist*) noblewoman; **~fräulein** *nt* (*Hist*) unmarried noblewoman; **~gas** *nt* rare gas; **~holz** *nt* precious wood.

Edeling *m* (*Hist*) (Germanic) nobleman.

Edel-: ~kastanie *f* sweet *or* Spanish chestnut; **~kitsch** *m* (*iro*) pretentious rubbish *or* kitsch; **~knappe** *m* (*Hist*) squire; **~mann** *m, pl* **-leute** (*Hist*) noble(man); **~metall** *nt* precious metal; **~mut** *m* (*liter*) magnanimity; **e~mütig** *adj* (*liter*) magnanimous; **~nutte** *f* (*iro*) high-class tart; **~pilzkäse** *m* blue (vein) cheese, mould-ripened cheese (*spec*); **~reis** *nt* scion; **~rost** *m* patina; **~schnulze** *f* (*iro*) sentimental ballad; **~stahl** *m* high-grade steel; **~stein** *m* precious stone; (*geschliffener auch*) jewel, gem; **~tanne** *f* noble fir; **~weiß** *nt* -(es), -e edelweiss.

Eden *nt* -s, *no pl* Eden ◆ **der Garten ~** (*Bibl*) the Garden of Eden.

edieren* *vt* to edit.

Edikt *nt* -(e)s, -e (*Hist*) edict.

editierbar *adj* editable.

editieren* *vt* to edit.

Edition *f* (*das Herausgeben*) editing; (*die Ausgabe*) edition.

Editor(in *f*) [-'to:rɪn] *m* editor.

Editorial *nt* -s, -s editorial.

editorisch *adj* editorial.

Edle(r) *mf decl as adj* **(a)** *siehe* **Edelfrau, Edelmann. (b)** (*in Namen*) **Ulf ~r von Trautenau** Lord Ulf von Trautenau; **Johanna ~ von Fürstenberg** Lady Johanna von Fürstenberg.

Eduard *m* -s Edward.

EDV [e:de:'fau] *f* - *abbr of* **elektronische Datenverarbeitung** EDP; **~-Anlage** *f* EDP *or* computer system; **~-Branche** *f* data-processing business; **~-Fachmann** *m* computer specialist.

EEG [e:|e:'ge:] *nt abbr of* **Elektroenzephalogramm** EEG.

Efeu *m* -s, *no pl* ivy ◆ **mit ~ bewachsen** covered in ivy, ivy-clad (*liter*), ivy-covered.

Eff|eff *nt* -, *no pl* (*inf*) **etw aus dem ~ können** to be able to do sth standing on one's head (*inf*), *or* just like that (*inf*); **etw aus dem ~ beherrschen/kennen** to know sth inside out.

Effekt *m* -(e)s, -e effect ◆ **der ~ war gleich Null** it had absolutely nil effect *or* no effect whatsoever.

Effektbeleuchtung *f* special lighting; (*Theat*) special effect lighting.

Effekten *pl* (*Fin*) stocks and bonds *pl*.

Effekten-: ~börse *f* stock exchange; **~handel** *m* stock dealing; **im ~handel läßt sich viel Geld verdienen** there's a lot of money to be made in dealing on the stock exchange; **~makler** *m* stockbroker; **~markt** *m* stock market.

Effekthascherei *f* (*inf*) cheap showmanship.

effektiv [1] *adj* **(a)** effective ◆ **~e Verzinsung** *or* **Rendite** net yield. **(b)** (*tatsächlich*) actual.
[2] *adv* (*bestimmt*) actually ◆ **ich weiß ~, daß ...** I know for a fact that ...; **~nicht/kein** absolutely not/no.

Effektivgeschäft *nt* (*Comm*) spot transaction.

Effektivität *f* effectiveness.

Effektiv-: ~lohn *m* actual wage; **~verzinsung** *f* redemption yield.

effektvoll *adj* effective.

effeminiert *adj* (*geh*) effeminate.

Effet [ɛ'fe:] *m or nt* -s, -s (*Billard*) side ◆ **den Ball mit ~ schießen** to put side on a ball.

effizient *adj* efficient.

Effizienz *f* efficiency.

EG [e:'ge:] *f abbr of* **Europäische Gemeinschaft** EC.

➤ **egal** [1] *adj, adv* **(a)** *pred* (*gleichgültig*) **das ist ~** that doesn't matter, that doesn't make any difference; **das ist mir ganz ~** it's all the same to me; (*beides ist mir gleich*) I don't mind (either way), it doesn't make any difference to me; (*es kümmert mich nicht*) I don't care, I couldn't care less; **ob du willst oder nicht, das ist mir ganz ~** I don't care whether you want to or not; **~ ob/wo/wie** it doesn't matter whether/where/how, no matter whether/where/how; **ihm ist alles ~** he doesn't care about anything.
(b) (*inf*) (*gleichartig*) the same, identical; (*gleich groß*) the same size; (*gleichmäßig*) *Rocksaum* even ◆ **~ gearbeitet sein** to be the same, to match; **die Bretter ~ schneiden** to cut the planks (to) the same size.
(c) (*inf: glatt*) *Holzfläche* smooth.
[2] *adv* (*dial inf: ständig*) non-stop.

egalisieren* *vt* (*Sport*) *Rekord* to equal ◆ **er egalisierte den Vorsprung des Gegners** he levelled with his opponent, he closed his opponent's lead.

egalitär *adj* (*geh*) egalitarian.

Egalität *f* (*liter*) equality.

egalweg *adv* (*dial inf*) *siehe* **egal 2.**

EG-: ~-Beamte(r) *m* EC official; **~-Behörde** *f* EC institution; **~-einheitlich** *adj* harmonized within the EC.

Egel *m* -s, - (*Zool*) leech.

Egge *f* -, -n **(a)** (*Agr*) harrow. **(b)** (*Tex*) selvedge.

eggen *vt* (*Agr*) to harrow.

EG-: ~-Kommission *f* EC Commission; **~-Ministerrat** *m* Council of Ministers; **~-Mitgliedsland** *nt* EC member state; **~-Norm** *f* EC standard.

Ego *nt* -s, -s (*Psych*) ego.

Egoismus *m* ego(t)ism.

Egoist(in *f*) *m* ego(t)ist.

egoistisch *adj* ego(t)istical.

Ego-: ~mane *m* -n, -n egomaniac; **~manie** *f* egomania; **~manin** *f* *siehe* **~mane**; **~trip** *m* (*inf*) ego-trip (*inf*); **~zentrik** *f, no pl* egocentricity; **~zentriker(in** *f*) *m* -s, - egocentric; **e~zentrisch** *adj* egocentric.

EG-Staat *m* EC country.

e.h. *abbr of* **ehrenhalber.**

eh [1] *interj* hey.
[2] *conj siehe* **ehe.**
[3] *adv* **(a)** (*früher, damals*) **seit ~ und je** for ages, since the year dot (*inf*); **wie ~ und je** just as *or* like before; **es war alles wie ~ und je** everything was just as it always had been.
(b) (*esp S Ger, Aus: sowieso*) anyway ◆ **ich komme ~ nicht dazu** I won't get round to it anyway.

ehe *conj* (*bevor*) before, ere (*old, liter*) ◆ **~ ich es vergesse ...** before I forget ...; **wir können nichts tun, ~ wir (nicht) Nachricht haben** we can't do anything until *or* before we get some news; **~ (daß) ich mich auf andere verlasse, mache ich lieber alles selbst** rather than rely on others, I would prefer to do everything myself.

Ehe *f* -, -n marriage ◆ **er versprach ihr die ~** he promised to marry her; **in den Stand der ~ treten** (*form*), **die ~ eingehen** (*form*) to enter into matrimony (*form*) *or* the estate of matrimony (*form*); **mit jdm die ~ eingehen** *or* **schließen** (*form*) to marry sb, to enter into marriage with sb (*form*); **die ~ vollziehen** to consummate a/their/the marriage; **eine glückliche/unglückliche ~ führen** to have a happy/an unhappy marriage; **die ~ brechen** (*form*) to commit adultery; **~ zur linken Hand, morganatische ~** (*Hist*) morganatic *or* left-handed marriage; **sie hat drei Kinder aus erster ~** she has three children from her first marriage; **Kinder in die ~ mitbringen** to bring children into the marriage; **ein außerhalb der ~ geborenes Kind** a child born out of wedlock; **er ist in zweiter ~ mit einer Adligen verheiratet** his second wife is an aristocrat; **ihre ~ ist 1975 geschieden worden** they were divorced in 1975; **sie leben in wilder ~** (*dated, hum*) they are living in sin; *siehe* **Hafen[1], Bund[1].**

Ehe-: e~ähnlich *adj* (*form*) similar to marriage; **in einer e~ähnlichen Gemeinschaft leben** to cohabit (*form*), to live together as man and wife; **~anbahnung** *f* marriage-broking; (*Institut*) marriage bureau; **~anbahnungsinstitut** *nt* marriage bureau; **~berater(in** *f*) *m* marriage guidance counsellor; **~beratung** *f* (*das Beraten*) marriage guidance (counselling); (*Stelle*) marriage guidance council; **~bett** *nt* double bed; (*fig*) marital bed; **e~brechen** *vi* (*infin only*) to commit adultery; **~brecher** *m* -s, - adulterer; **~brecherin** *f* adulteress; **e~brecherisch** *adj* adulterous; **~bruch** *m* adultery; **~bund** *m*, **~bündnis** *nt* (*form*) bond of matrimony.

ehedem *adv* (*old*) formerly ◆ **seit ~** since time immemorial.

Ehe-: ~fähigkeit *f* (*Jur*) marriageability; **~frau** *f* wife; **~frauen haben es**

nicht leicht married women have a hard time; **~gatte** *m (form)* husband, spouse *(form)*; **~gattin** *f (form)* wife, spouse *(form)*; **~gemeinschaft** *f (form)* wedlock *(form)*, matrimony; **~gespons** *m or nt (hum)* spouse *(hum)*; **~glück** *nt* married bliss *or* happiness; **~hafen** *m (hum)*: **in den ~hafen einlaufen** to plight one's troth *(old, hum)*; **~hälfte** *f (hum inf)* **meine bessere ~hälfte** my better half *(inf)*; **~hindernis** *nt (Jur)* impediment to marriage; **~komödie** *f* marital comedy; **~krach** *m* marital row; **~krise** *f* marital crisis; **~krüppel** *m (hum inf)* henpecked husband *(inf)*; **~leben** *nt* married life; **~leute** *pl (form)* married couple; **ich vermiete diese Wohnung an die ~leute A. und P. Meier** I hereby let this flat to Mr and Mrs Meier; **die jungen ~leute** the young couple.

ehelich *adj* marital; *Pflichten, Rechte auch* conjugal; *Kind* legitimate ◆ **für ~ erklären** to (declare *or* make) legitimate; **das ~e Leben** married life; **die ~en Freuden** the joys of marriage.

ehelichen *vt (old, hum)* to wed *(old)*, to espouse *(old, form)*.

Ehelichkeit *f, no pl (von Kind)* legitimacy.

Ehelichkeits|erklärung *f (Jur)* declaration of legitimacy.

ehelos *adj* unmarried, single.

Ehelosigkeit *f, no pl* unmarried state; *(Rel)* celibacy ◆ **~ hat auch ihre Vorteile** being single *or* unmarried also has its advantages.

ehem., ehm. *abbr of* **ehemals**.

ehemalig *adj attr* former ◆ **die E~en seiner/einer Schulklasse** his former classmates/the ex-pupils *or* former pupils of a class; **ein ~er Häftling** an ex-convict; **ein E~r** *(inf)* an old lag *(Brit sl)*, an ex-con *(inf)*; **mein E~er/meine E~e** *(hum inf)* my ex *(inf)*.

ehemals *adv (form)* formerly, previously ◆ **die ~ deutschen Ostgebiete** the eastern territories which were formerly German.

Ehe-: ~mann *m, pl* **-männer** married man; *(Partner)* husband; **seitdem er ~mann ist** since he has been married; **e~mündig** *adj (Jur)* of marriageable age; **~mündigkeit** *f, no pl (Jur)* marriageable age; **die ~mündigkeit tritt im Alter von 18 Jahren ein** a person becomes legally marriageable at the age of 18; **~paar** *nt* (married) couple; **~partner** *m* husband; wife; **beide ~partner** both partners (in the marriage).

eher *adv* **(a)** *(früher)* earlier, sooner ◆ **je ~, je** *or* **desto lieber** the sooner the better; **nicht ~ als bis/als** not until/before.

(b) *(lieber)* rather, sooner; *(wahrscheinlicher)* more likely; *(leichter)* more easily ◆ **alles ~ als das!** anything but that!; **~ verzichte ich** *or* **will ich verzichten, als daß** ... I would rather *or* sooner do without than ...; **um so ~, als** the more so *or* all the more because *or* as; **das läßt sich schon ~ hören** that sounds more like it *(inf) or* better; **das könnte man schon ~ sagen, das ist ~ möglich** that is more likely *or* probable; **diese Prüfung kannst du ~ bestehen** this exam will be easier for you to pass.

(c) *(vielmehr)* more ◆ **er ist ~ faul als dumm** he's more lazy than stupid, he's lazy rather than stupid; **er ist alles ~ als das/ein Engel/dumm** he's anything but that/an angel/stupid.

Ehe-: ~recht *nt* marriage law; **~ring** *m* wedding ring.

ehern *adj (liter) (lit)* made of ore; *(fig)* iron ◆ **mit ~er Stirn** boldly; *(tollkühn auch)* brazenly.

Ehe-: ~roman *m novel about marriage*; **~sache** *f (Jur)* matrimonial matter; **~sakrament** *nt* marriage sacrament, sacrament of marriage; **~scheidung** *f* divorce; **~scheidungsklage** *f (Prozeß)* divorce case; **die ~scheidungsklage einreichen** to file a divorce petition *or* a petition for divorce; **~schließung** *f* marriage ceremony, wedding.

ehest *adv (Aus)* as soon as possible.

Ehe-: ~stand *m, no pl* matrimony, marriage; **~standsdarlehen** *nt low interest bank loan given to newly married couples.*

ehestens *adv* **(a)** *(frühestens)* **~ morgen** tomorrow at the earliest; **ich kann ~ heute abend kommen** the earliest I can come is this evening.

(b) *(Aus: baldigst)* as soon as possible, at the earliest opportunity.

eheste(r, s) [1] *adj* **bei ~r Gelegenheit** at the earliest opportunity.

[2] *adv* **am ~n** *(am liebsten)* best of all; *(am wahrscheinlichsten)* most likely; *(am leichtesten)* the easiest; *(zuerst)* first; **am ~n würde ich mir ein Auto kaufen** what I'd like best (of all) would be to buy myself a car; **keins der Kleider gefällt mir so richtig, am ~n würde ich noch das rote nehmen** I don't really like any of the dresses, but if I had to choose I'd take the red one; **das geht wohl am ~n** that's probably the best way; **er ist am ~n gekommen** he was the first (person) to come.

Ehe-: ~stifter *m* matchmaker; **~streit** *m* marital row *or* argument; **~tragödie** *f* marital tragedy; **~vermittlung** *f* marriage-broking; *(Büro)* marriage bureau; **~versprechen** *nt (Jur)* promise to marry; **Bruch des ~versprechens** breach of promise; **~vertrag** *m* marriage contract; **~weib** *nt (old: ~frau)* wife; *(hum inf)* old woman *(inf)*; **e~widrig** *adj (form) Beziehungen* extramarital, adulterous; *Verhalten* constituting a matrimonial offence.

Ehr|abschneider(in *f***)** *m* **-s, -** calumniator *(form)*.

ehrbar *adj (achtenswert)* respectable; *(ehrenhaft)* honourable; *Beruf auch* reputable.

Ehrbarkeit *f, no pl siehe adj* respectability; honourableness; reputability.

Ehrbegriff *m* sense of honour.

Ehre *f* **-, -n** honour; *(Ruhm)* glory ◆ **etw in ~n halten** to treasure *or* cherish sth; **damit/mit ihm können Sie ~ einlegen** that/he does you credit *or* is a credit to you; **er wollte mit dieser Rede ~ einlegen** he was wanting to gain kudos with this speech; **für jdn/etw ~ einlegen** to bring honour on sb/sth; **bei jdm mit etw ~ einlegen** to make a good impression on sb with sth; **jdm ~/wenig ~ machen** to do sb credit/not do sb any credit; **auf ~!, bei meiner ~!** *(obs)* by my troth! *(obs)*, 'pon my oath! *(obs)*; **auf ~ und Gewissen** on my/his *etc* honour; **auf ~ und Gewissen?** cross your heart? *(inf)*, on your honour?; **auf ~ und Gewissen: ich bin es nicht gewesen!** cross my heart *(inf) or* I promise you, it wasn't me; **zu seiner ~ muß ich sagen, daß** ... in his favour I must say (that) ...; **etw um der ~ willen tun** to do sth for the honour of it; **das mußt du schon um deiner ~ willen machen** you should do that as a matter of honour; **ein Mann von ~** a man of honour; **keine ~ im Leib haben** *(dated)* to have not a shred of self-respect; **er ist in ~n ergraut** *(geh) or* **in ~n alt geworden** he has had a long and honourable life; **sein Wort/seine Kenntnisse in allen ~n, aber** ... I don't doubt his word/his knowledge, but ...; **sich** *(dat)* **etw zur ~ anrechnen** to count sth an honour; **sich** *(dat)* **es zur ~ anrechnen, daß** ... to feel honoured that ..., to count it an honour that ...; **das rechne ich ihm zur ~ an** I consider that a point in his honour *or* favour; **mit wem habe ich die ~?** *(iro, form)* with whom do I have the pleasure of speaking? *(form)*; **was verschafft mir die ~?** *(iro, form)* to what do I owe the honour (of your visit)?; **es ist mir eine besondere ~,** ... *(form)* it is a great honour for me ...; **um der Wahrheit die ~ zu geben** ... *(geh)* to be perfectly honest ..., to tell you the truth ...; **wir geben uns die ~, Sie zu ... einzuladen** *(form)* we request the honour of your company at ... *(form)*; **zu ~n** *(+gen)* in honour of; **darf ich um die ~ bitten, Sie zu begleiten?** *(form)* may I have the honour of accompanying you? *(form)*, would you do me the honour of allowing me to accompany you? *(form)*; **habe die ~!** *(Aus, S Ger)* hullo; goodbye; **~, wem ~ gebührt** *(prov)* honour where honour is due *(prov)*; *siehe* **Feld, letzte(r, s)**.

ehren *vt (Achtung erweisen, würdigen)* to honour ◆ **etw ehrt jdn** sth does sb credit *or* honour; **dein Besuch/Ihr Vertrauen ehrt mich** I am honoured by your visit/trust; **der Präsident ehrte den Preisträger in einer Rede** the president made a speech in honour of the prizewinner; **der Preisträger wurde in einer Rede geehrt** a speech was made *or* there was a speech in honour of the prizewinner; **jdm ein ~des Andenken bewahren** to treasure sb's memory; **du sollst Vater und Mutter ~** *(Bibl)* honour thy father and thy mother; *siehe* **geehrt**.

Ehren-: ~amt *nt* honorary office *or* post; **e~amtlich** [1] *adj* honorary; **e~amtlicher Richter** ≃ member of the jury; [2] *adv* in an honorary capacity; **~bezeigung** *f (Mil)* salute; **jdm die ~bezeigung erweisen/verweigern** to salute/refuse to salute sb, to give/refuse to give sb a salute.

Ehrenbürger *m* freeman ◆ **er wurde zum ~ der Stadt ernannt** he was given the freedom of the city/town.

Ehrenbürgerrecht *nt* freedom ◆ **die Stadt verlieh ihm das ~** he was given the freedom of the city/town.

Ehren-: ~doktor *m* honorary doctor; **~doktorwürde** *f* honorary doctorate; **ihm wurde die ~doktorwürde der Universität Wien verliehen** he was made an honorary doctor of *or* given an honorary doctorate by the University of Vienna; **~erklärung** *f (von Beleidiger)* (formal) apology; *(von dritter Seite) statement in defence* (*of sb's honour*); **ich werde eine ~erklärung für Sie abgeben** I will make a statement in your defence; *(nach erfolgter Beleidigung)* I will make (you) a formal apology; **~garde** *f* guard of honour; **~gast** *m* guest of honour; **~geleit** *nt* guard of honour; **~gericht** *nt* tribunal; **e~haft** *adj* honourable; **~haftigkeit** *f* honourableness; **e~halber** *adv* **er wurde e~halber zum Vorsitzenden auf Lebenszeit ernannt** he was made honorary president for life; **Doktor e~halber** *(abbr* **e.h.**) Doctor honoris causa *(form)*, honorary doctor; **~handel** *m, pl* **-händel** *(old)* **eine Form des ~handels war das Duell** the duel was one way of settling an affair of honour; **~karte** *f* complimentary ticket; **~kodex** *m* code of honour; **~kompanie** *f (Mil)* guard of honour; **~kränkung** *f* insult, affront; **~legion** *f* legion of honour; **~loge** *f* royal/VIP box; *(in Stadion)* directors' box; **~mal** *nt* memorial; **~mann** *m, pl* **-männer** man of honour; **ein sauberer ~mann** *(pej)* a blackguard *(pej)*; **~mitglied** *nt* honorary member; **~mitgliedschaft** *f* honorary membership; **~nadel** *f* badge of honour; **~pflicht** *f* bounden duty; **~platz** *m (lit)* place *or* seat of honour; *(fig)* special place; **~preis** *m* **(a)** *(Auszeichnung)* prize; *(Anerkennung)* consolation prize; **(b)** *(Bot)* speedwell, veronica; **~rechte** *pl (Jur)* civil rights *pl*; **Verlust/Aberkennung der bürgerlichen ~rechte** loss/forfeiture of one's civil rights; **~rettung** *f* retrieval of one's honour; **eine ~rettung versuchen** to attempt to retrieve one's honour; **zu seiner ~rettung sei gesagt, daß** ... in his favour it must be said that ...; **e~rührig** *adj* defamatory; **etw als e~rührig empfinden** to regard sth as an insult to one's honour; **~runde** *f (Sport)* lap of honour; **~sache** *f* matter of honour; **~sache!** *(inf)* you can count on me; **das ist für mich ~sache!** that's a matter of honour for me; **~salut** *m*, **~salve** *f* salute; **~schuld** *f* debt of honour; **~sold** *m* honorarium; **~tafel** *f* **(a)** *(Tisch)* top table; **(b)** *(Gedenktafel)* roll of honour; **~tag** *m (Geburtstag)* birthday; *(großer Tag)* big *or* great day; **zum heutigen ~tag** on this special day; **~titel** *m* honorary title; **~tor** *nt*, **~treffer** *m (Sport)* consolation goal; **~tribüne** *f* VIP rostrum; **~urkunde** *f* certificate *(for outstanding performance in sport)*; **e~voll** *adj Friede* honourable; *Aufgabe auch* noble; **~vorsitzende(r)** *mf* honorary chairman/chairwoman; **~wache** *f* guard of honour; **e~wert** *adj Mensch* honourable, worthy; **die E~werte Gesellschaft** *(hum)* the Mafia; **~wort** *nt* word of honour; **~wort!** *(inf)* cross my heart! *(inf)*; **~wort?** *(inf)* cross your heart? *(inf)*; **mein ~wort!** you have my word; **sein ~wort geben/halten/brechen** to give/keep/break one's word; **Urlaub auf ~wort** parole; **e~wörtlich** [1] *adj Versprechen* solemn, faithful; [2] *adv* on one's honour; **~zeichen** *nt* decoration.

Ehr-: e~erbietig *adj* respectful, deferential; **~erbietung** *f* respect, deference.

Ehrfurcht *f, no pl* great *or* deep respect *(vor +dat* for); *(fromme Scheu)* reverence *(vor +dat* for) ◆ **vor jdm/etw ~ haben** to respect/revere sb/sth, to have

➤ SPRACHE AKTIV: **Ehre** → 52.1

(great) respect for sb/sth; **von ~ ergriffen** overawed.
ehrfurchtgebietend *adj Stimme, Geste* authoritative ◆ **er ist eine ~e Persönlichkeit** he's the kind of person who commands (one's) respect.
ehrfürchtig, ehrfurchtsvoll *adj* reverent.
ehrfurchtslos *adj* irreverent.
Ehrgefühl *nt* sense of honour; (*Selbstachtung*) self-respect ◆ **etw aus falschem ~ heraus tun** to do sth out of a misplaced sense of honour.
Ehrgeiz *m, no pl* ambition.
ehrgeizig *adj* ambitious.
Ehrgeizling *m* (*pej inf*) pusher (*inf*).
ehrlich [1] *adj, adv* honest; *Name* good; *Absicht, Zuneigung* sincere ◆ **der ~e Finder bekommt 100 Mark** a reward of 100 marks will be given to anyone finding and returning this; **eine ~e Haut** (*inf*) an honest soul; **ich hatte die ~e Absicht zu kommen** I honestly did intend to come; **er hat ~e Absichten** (*inf*) his intentions are honourable; **~ verdientes Geld** hard-earned money; **~ gesagt** ... quite frankly *or* honestly ..., to be quite frank ...; **er meint es ~ mit uns** he is being honest with us; **~ spielen** (*Cards*) to play straight; **~ währt am längsten** (*Prov*) honesty is the best policy (*Prov*).
[2] *adv* (*wirklich*) honestly, really (and truly), truly ◆ **ich bin ~ begeistert** I'm really thrilled; **~, ich habe nichts damit zu tun** honestly, I've got nothing to do with it; **~!** honestly!, really!
ehrlicherweise *adv* honestly, truly, in all honesty.
Ehrlichkeit *f, no pl* honesty; (*von Absicht, Zuneigung*) sincerity ◆ **sie zweifelte an der ~ seiner Absichten** she doubted the sincerity of his intentions; (*in bezug auf Heirat*) she doubted that his intentions were honourable.
Ehr-: e~los *adj* dishonourable; **~losigkeit** *f* dishonourableness; (*Schlechtigkeit*) infamy; **die ~losigkeit seines Verhaltens** his dishonourable conduct; **e~pusselig, ⚠e~pußlig** *adj* (*inf*) sensitive about one's reputation; **e~sam** *adj* (*old*) *siehe* **e~bar**; **~sucht** *f* (*old*) inordinate ambitiousness *or* ambition; **e~süchtig** *adj* (*old*) inordinately ambitious.
Ehrung *f* honour.
Ehr-: e~verletzend *adj* (*geh*) insulting; **~verletzung** *f* (*geh*) insult (to one's honour); **~verlust** *m* loss of honour; (*Jur*) loss of one's civil rights.
Ehrwürden *m* **-s,** *no pl* Reverend ◆ **Euer ~** Reverend Father/Mother.
ehrwürdig *adj* venerable ◆ **~e Mutter/~er Vater** (*Eccl*) Reverend Mother/Father.
Ehrwürdigkeit *f* venerability, venerableness.
ei *interj* (*zärtlich*) there (there); (*old*) (*spöttisch*) well; (*bekräftigend*) oh ◆ **(bei einem Kind/Tier) ~ ~ machen** to pet a child/an animal; **~ freilich** *or* **gewiß!** (*old*) but of course!
Ei *nt* **-(e)s, -er** (a) (*Vogel~, Schlangen~*) egg; (*Physiol auch*) ovum ◆ **das ~ des Kolumbus finden** to come up with just the thing; **das ist das ~ des Kolumbus** that's just the thing *or* just what we want; **das ~ will klüger sein als die Henne** you're trying to teach your grandmother to suck eggs (*prov*); **jdn wie ein rohes ~ behandeln** (*fig*) to handle sb with kid gloves; **wie auf ~ern gehen** (*inf*) to step gingerly; **wie aus dem ~ gepellt aussehen** (*inf*) to look spruce; **sie gleichen sich** *or* **einander wie ein ~ dem anderen** they are as alike as two peas (in a pod); **kümmere dich nicht um ungelegte ~er!** (*inf*) don't cross your bridges before you come to them! (*prov*); **das sind ungelegte ~er!** (*inf*) we'll cross that bridge when we come to it; **~er** *pl* (*sl: Hoden*) balls *pl* (*sl*); **jdm die ~er polieren** (*sl*) to kick sb in the balls (*sl*); *siehe* **dick**.
(b) ~er *pl* (*sl: Geld*) marks; (*in GB*) quid (*inf*); (*in US*) bucks (*inf*) ◆ **das kostet seine 50 ~er** that'll cost a good 50 marks.
(c) (*Rugby sl*) ball, pill (*sl*).
eiapopeia *interj* lullaby baby.
Eibe *f* **-, -n** (*Bot*) yew.
Eibisch *m* **-(e)s, -e** (*Bot*) marshmallow.
Eich|amt *nt* ≃ Weights and Measures Office (*Brit*).
Eichbaum *m siehe* **Eich(en)baum**.
Eiche *f* **-, -n** oak; (*Baum auch*) oak tree.
Eichel *f* **-, -n (a)** (*Bot*) acorn. **(b)** (*Anat*) glans. **(c)** (*Cards*) *suit in German playing cards equivalent to clubs.*
Eichelhäher *m* jay.
eichen[1] *adj* oak, oaken (*old*).
eichen[2] *vt* to calibrate; (*prüfen auch*) to check against official specifications ◆ **darauf bin ich geeicht!** (*inf*) that's right up my street (*inf*).
Eich(en)baum *m* oak tree.
Eichen-: ~holz *nt* oak; **ein Tisch aus ~holz** an oak table; **~laub** *nt* oak leaves *pl*; *siehe* **Ritterkreuz**; **~sarg** *m* oak(en) coffin; **~wald** *m* oakwood.
Eichhörnchen, Eichkätzchen *nt* squirrel ◆ **mühsam nährt sich das Eichhörnchen** (*inf*) one struggles on and little by little.
Eich-: ~maß *nt* standard measure; (*Gewicht*) standard weight; **~pfahl** *m calibrated pole marking the maximum safe water level of a reservoir etc*; **~strich** *m* official calibration; (*an Gläsern*) line measure; **ein Glas mit ~strich** a lined glass.
Eichung *f* calibration; (*Prüfung auch*) official verification.
Eid *m* **-(e)s, -e** oath ◆ **einen ~ ablegen** *or* **leisten** *or* **schwören** to take *or* swear an oath; **einen ~ auf die Bibel/Verfassung leisten** to swear an oath on the Bible/the constitution; **darauf kann ich einen ~ schwören** I can swear to that *or* take my oath on that; **ich nehme es auf meinen ~, daß** ... I would be prepared to swear that ...; **jdm den ~ abnehmen** to administer the oath to sb, to take the oath from sb; **unter ~** under *or* on oath; **eine Erklärung an ~es Statt abgeben** (*Jur*) to make a declaration in lieu of oath; **ich erkläre an ~es Statt, daß** ... I do solemnly declare that ...
Eidam *m* **-(e)s, -e** (*obs*) son-in-law.

Eid-: ~bruch *m* breach of one's oath; **einen ~bruch begehen** to break one's oath; **e~brüchig** *adj* **e~brüchig werden** to break one's oath.
Eidechse ['aidɛksə] *f* **-, -n** (*Zool*) lizard; (*Astron auch*) Lacerta; (*inf: Hubwagen*) fork-lift truck.
Eider-: ~d(a)unen *pl* eiderdown *no pl*; **~ente** *f* eider (duck).
Eides-: ~belehrung *f* (*Jur*) *caution as to the consequences of committing perjury*; **~formel** *f* wording of the oath; **die ~formel nachsprechen** to repeat the oath; **~leistung** *f* swearing of the oath; **niemand kann zur ~leistung gezwungen werden** no-one can be forced to swear *or* take the oath; **e~stattlich** *adj* solemn; **etw e~stattlich erklären** to affirm sth; **eine e~stattliche Erklärung abgeben** to make a solemn declaration, to swear an affidavit.
Eidetik *f* (*Psych*) eidetic ability.
Eidetiker(in *f*) *m* **-s, -** eidetic, eidetiker.
eidetisch *adj* eidetic.
Eidgenosse *m* confederate; (*Schweizer ~*) Swiss citizen.
Eidgenossenschaft *f* confederation ◆ **Schweizerische ~** Swiss Confederation.
Eidgenossin *f siehe* **Eidgenosse**.
eidgenössisch *adj* confederate; (*schweizerisch*) Swiss.
eidlich [1] *adj* sworn *attr*, given on *or* under oath ◆ **er gab eine ~e Erklärung ab** he made a declaration on *or* under oath; (*schriftlich*) he swore an affidavit.
[2] *adv* on *or* under oath ◆ **~ gebunden** bound by (one's) oath.
Eidotter *m or nt* egg yolk.
Eier-: ~becher *m* eggcup; **~brikett** *nt* ovoid (*of coal*); **~farbe** *f paint used to decorate Easter eggs*; **~handgranate** *f* (*Mil*) (pineapple) hand grenade, pineapple (*sl*); **~kognak** *m siehe* **~likör**; **~kopf** *m* (*inf*) egghead (*inf*); (*sl: Idiot*) blockhead (*inf*), numbskull (*inf*); **~kuchen** *m* pancake; (*Omelette*) *omelette made with a mixture containing flour*; **~laufen** *nt* egg and spoon race; **~laufen machen** to have an egg and spoon race; **~likör** *m* advocaat; **~löffel** *m* eggspoon.
eiern *vi* (*inf*) to wobble.
Eier-: ~pflaume *f* (large oval) plum; **~schale** *f* eggshell; **er hat noch die ~schalen hinter den Ohren** (*inf*) he's still wet behind the ears (*inf*); **e~schalenfarben** *adj* cream, off-white; **~schaum, ~schnee** *m* (*Cook*) beaten egg white; **~schwamm** *m* (*Bot: esp Aus*) chanterelle; **~speise** *f* **(a)** egg dish; **(b)** (*Aus: Rührei*) scrambled egg; **~stock** *m* (*Anat*) ovary; **~tanz** *m* **einen regelrechten ~tanz aufführen** (*fig inf*) to go through all kinds of contortions; **~uhr** *f* egg timer.
Eifer *m* **-s,** *no pl* (*Begeisterung*) enthusiasm; (*Eifrigkeit*) eagerness, keenness ◆ **mit ~** enthusiastically; eagerly, keenly; **mit ~ arbeiten** to work with a will *or* with great zeal; **in ~ geraten** to get agitated, to get into a state; **mit großem ~ bei der Sache sein** to put one's heart into it; **im ~ des Gefechts** (*fig inf*) in the heat of the moment.
Eiferer *m* **-s, -** (*liter*) fanatic; (*Rel auch*) zealot.
eifern *vi* (*liter*) **(a) gegen jdn/etw ~** to rail *or* inveigh against sb/sth; **für etw ~** to crusade *or* campaign for sth. **(b)** (*streben*) **nach etw ~** to strive for sth. **(c)** (*wett~*) **um etw ~** to compete *or* vie for sth.
Eifersucht *f* jealousy (*auf +acc* of) ◆ **aus/vor (lauter) ~** out of/for (pure) jealousy.
Eifersüchtelei *f* petty jealousy.
eifersüchtig *adj* jealous (*auf +acc* of).
Eifersuchts-: ~szene *f* **ihr Mann hat ihr wieder eine ~szene gemacht** her husband's jealousy caused another scene; **~tragödie** *f* **„~tragödie in München"** "jealousy causes tragedy in Munich".
eiförmig *adj* egg-shaped, oval.
eifrig *adj* eager; *Befürworter auch* keen; *Leser, Sammler* keen, avid; (*begeistert*) enthusiastic; (*emsig*) assiduous, industrious, zealous; (*heftig*) vehement ◆ **er putzte gerade ~ sein Auto, als ich ankam** he was busy *or* busily cleaning his car when I arrived; **sie diskutierten ~** they were involved in an animated discussion; **die E~en** the eager beavers (*inf*).
Eifrigkeit *f siehe adj* eagerness; keenness, avidity; enthusiasm; assiduity, industriousness, zeal; vehemence.
Eigelb *nt* **-s, -e** *or* (*bei Zahlenangabe*) **-** egg yolk ◆ **vier ~** the yolks of four eggs, four egg yolks.
eigen *adj* **(a)** own; (*selbständig*) separate ◆ **seine ~e Wohnung/Meinung haben** to have a flat/an opinion of one's own, to have one's own flat/opinion; **etw sein ~ nennen** (*geh*) to have sth to one's name, to have sth to call one's own; **er ist stolz, zwölf Kinder sein ~ nennen zu können** he is proud of being blessed with twelve children; **jdm etw zu ~ geben** (*liter*) to give sb sth; **meiner Mutter zu ~** (*liter*) for *or* (dedicated) to my mother; **~er Bericht** (*Press*) from *or* by our (own) correspondent; **Zimmer mit ~em Eingang** room with its own *or* a separate entrance; **San Marino ist ein ~er Staat** San Marino is an independent *or* a separate state; **sein ~ Fleisch und Blut** (*liter*) his own flesh and blood; **sich** (*dat*) **etw zu ~ machen** to adopt sth; (*zur Gewohnheit machen*) to make sth a habit, to make a habit of sth; **übergeben Sie diesen Brief dem Anwalt zu ~en Händen** (*form*) give this letter to the lawyer in person; **ich habe das Papier auf ~e Rechnung gekauft** I paid for the paper myself; **ich möchte kurz in ~er Sache sprechen** I would like to say something on my own account; *siehe* **Fuß, Nest, Tasche** *etc.*
(b) (*typisch, kennzeichnend*) typical ◆ **das ist ihm ~** that is typical of him; **er antwortete mit dem ihm ~en Zynismus** he answered with (his) characteristic cynicism; **ein Menschenschlag von ganz ~er Prägung** a race apart.
(c) (*seltsam*) strange, peculiar ◆ **es ist eine Landschaft von ganz ~em Reiz** the

➤ SPRACHE AKTIV: **Ehrgeiz** → 35.2, 35.4

country is strangely attractive in its own way *or* has its own strange attractions; *siehe* **Ding[1] (b).**

(d) (*ordentlich*) particular; (*übergenau*) fussy ◆ **in Gelddingen** *or* **was Geld anbetrifft ist er sehr ~** he is very particular about money matters.

-eigen *adj suf* -owned.

Eigen|antrieb *m* **Fahrzeuge mit ~** self-propelled vehicles; **~ haben** to be self-propelled.

Eigen|art *f* (*Besonderheit*) peculiarity; (*Eigenschaft*) characteristic; (*Individualität*) individuality; (*Eigentümlichkeit von Personen*) idiosyncrasy ◆ **das gehört zur ~ der Bayern** that's a typically Bavarian characteristic.

eigen|artig *adj* peculiar; (*sonderbar auch*) strange; (*persönlich kennzeichnend*) idiosyncratic.

Eigen-: ~bau *m, no pl* **Tabak/Gemüse im ~bau züchten** to grow one's own tobacco/vegetables; **er fährt ein Fahrrad/raucht Zigaretten Marke ~bau** (*hum inf*) he rides a home-made bike/smokes home-grown cigarettes (*hum*); **~bedarf** *m* (*von Mensch*) personal use; (*von Staat*) domestic requirements *pl*; **zum ~bedarf** for (one's own) personal use/domestic requirements; **der Hausbesitzer machte ~bedarf geltend** the landlord showed that he needed the house/flat for himself; **~bericht** *m* (*Press*) **diese Zeitung bringt kaum ~berichte** this paper rarely carries articles by its own journalists; **~bewegung** *f* (*Astron*) proper motion; **~blut** *nt* (*Med*) own blood; **dem Patienten wird vorher ~ blut abgenommen** some of the patient's own blood is taken beforehand; **~blutbehandlung** *f* (*Med*) autohaemotherapy; **~brötelei** [aignbrø:tə'lai] *f* (*inf*) eccentricity; (*Einzelgängertum*) solitary ways *pl*; **~brötler(in** *f*) *m* **-s, -** (*inf*) loner, lone wolf; (*komischer Kauz*) queer fish (*inf*), oddball (*esp US inf*); **e~brötlerisch** *adj* (*inf*) solitary; (*komisch*) eccentric; **~dünkel** *m* sense of superiority; **~dynamik** *f* momentum; **eine ~dynamik entwickeln** to gather momentum; **~finanzierung** *f* self-financing; **wir bauen die neue Fabrik in ~finanzierung** we are financing the building of the new factory ourselves; **e~gesetzlich** *adj* autonomous; **jede Revolution entwickelt sich e~gesetzlich** every revolution develops according to laws of its own; **~gesetzlichkeit** *f* autonomous laws *pl*; **sein Handeln folgte einer geheimnisvollen ~gesetzlichkeit** his behaviour followed its own mysterious laws; **~gewicht** *nt* (*von LKW etc*) unladen weight; (*Comm*) net weight; (*Sci*) dead weight; **~goal** *nt* (*Aus Sport*) own goal; **~gruppe** *f* (*Sociol*) in-group; **e~händig** *adj Brief, Unterschrift etc* in one's own hand, handwritten; *Übergabe* personal; **eine Arbeit e~händig machen** to do a job oneself *or* personally *or* with one's own hands; **~heim** *nt* one's own home; **sparen Sie für ein ~heim!** save for a home of your own!; **~heit** *f siehe* **~art**; **~initiative** *f* initiative of one's own; **auf ~initiative** on one's own initiative; **~kapital** *nt* (*von Person*) personal capital; (*von Firma*) company capital; **10.000 DM ~kapital** 10,000 DM of one's own capital; **~leben** *nt, no pl* one's own life; (*selbständige Existenz*) independent existence; (*Privatleben*) private life; **~leistung** *f* (*bei Hausbau*) borrower's own funding, personal contribution; **~liebe** *f* amour-propre; (*Selbstverliebtheit*) self-love, love of self; **~lob** *nt* self-importance, vaingloriousness; **~lob stinkt!** (*inf*) don't blow your own trumpet! (*prov*); **e~mächtig** [1] *adj* (*selbstherrlich*) high-handed; (*e~verantwortlich*) taken/done *etc* on one's own authority; (*unbefugt*) unauthorized; **e~mächtige Abwesenheit** (*Mil*) absence without leave; [2] *adv* high-handedly; (entirely) on one's own authority; without any authorization; **e~mächtigerweise** *adv* (*selbstherrlich*) high-handedly; (*unbefugt*) without any authorization; **~mächtigkeit** *f* (*Selbstherrlichkeit*) high-handedness *no pl*; (*unbefugtes Handeln*) unauthorized behaviour *no pl*; **die ~mächtigkeit seines Vorgehens wurde von allen kritisiert** everyone criticized him for having acted high-handedly/without authorization; **~mittel** *pl* (*form*) one's own resources; **die ~mittel der Körperschaft** the corporation's (own) resources; **man braucht nur 20% ~mittel** you only need to find 20% yourself *or* from your own resources; **~name** *m* proper name; **~nutz** *m, no pl* self-interest; **das habe ich ohne jeden ~nutz getan** I did that with no thought of myself *or* of furthering my own interests; **e~nützig** *adj* selfish; **~nützigkeit** *f siehe* **~nutz**; **~produktion** *f* **das ist eine ~produktion** we/they *etc* made it ourselves/themselves *etc*; **etw in ~produktion herstellen** to make sth oneself, to make one's own sth; **aus ~produktion** (*hausgemacht*) home-made; *Tabak etc* home-grown; **das war eine ~produktion des Irischen Fernsehens** that was one of Irish Television's own productions.

eigens *adv* (e)specially; (*ausdrücklich auch*) specifically.

Eigenschaft *f* (*Attribut*) quality; (*Chem, Phys etc*) property; (*Merkmal*) characteristic, feature; (*Funktion*) capacity.

Eigenschaftswort *nt* adjective.

Eigen-: ~schwingung *f* (*Sci*) free vibration; **~sinn** *m, no pl* stubbornness, obstinacy; (*inf: Trotzkopf*) stubborn child; **e~sinnig** *adj* stubborn, obstinate; **~sinnigkeit** *f* stubbornness, obstinacy; **~sinnigkeiten** *pl* stubborn *or* obstinate behaviour; **e~staatlich** *adj* sovereign; **~staatlichkeit** *f* sovereignty; **e~ständig** *adj* original; (*unabhängig*) independent; (*e~gesetzlich*) autonomous; **~ständigkeit** *f siehe adj* originality; independence; autonomy; **~sucht** *f, no pl* selfishness; (*Egotismus auch*) self-centredness; **e~süchtig** *adj siehe n* selfish; self-centred.

eigentlich [1] *adj* (*wirklich, tatsächlich*) real, actual; *Wert* true, real; (*ursprünglich*) original ◆ **im ~en Sinne bedeutet das ...** that really means ...; **im ~en Sinne des Wortes ...** in the original meaning of the word ...

[2] *adv* actually; (*tatsächlich, wirklich auch*) really; (*überhaupt*) anyway ◆ **~ wollte ich nur fünf Minuten bleiben** actually I was only *or* I was really only going to stay five minutes; **was willst du ~ hier?** what do you want here anyway?; **wissen Sie ~, wer ich bin?** do you know who I am?; **was ist ~ mit dir los?** what's the matter with you (anyway)?; **ich bin ~ froh, daß ...** really *or* actually I'm happy that ...; **~ müßtest du das wissen** you should really know that; **~ dürftest du das nicht tun** you shouldn't really do that.

Eigentlichkeit *f* (*Philos*) essentiality.

Eigentor *nt* (*Sport, fig*) own goal ◆ **ein ~ schießen** to score an own goal.

Eigentum *nt, no pl* property ◆ **bewegliches ~** movables *pl*, movable property; **unbewegliches ~** immovables *pl*, real property; **~ an etw** (*dat*) **erwerben** to acquire possession of sth; **~ an den Produktionsmitteln** private ownership of the means of production.

Eigentümer(in *f*) *m* **-s, -** owner.

eigentümlich *adj* **(a)** (*sonderbar, seltsam*) strange, curious, odd. **(b)** (*geh: typisch*) **jdm/einer Sache ~ sein** to be characteristic *or* typical of sb/sth.

eigentümlicherweise *adv* strangely *or* curiously *or* oddly enough.

Eigentümlichkeit *f* **(a)** (*Kennzeichen, Besonderheit*) characteristic. **(b)** (*Eigenheit*) peculiarity.

Eigentums-: ~anspruch *m* claim of ownership; **einen ~anspruch auf etw** (*acc*) **geltend machen** to claim ownership of sth; **~begriff** *m* concept of property; **~bildung** *f* private acquisition of property; **~delikt** *nt* (*Jur*) *offence against property*; **~denken** *nt* (*Theorie*) property ethic; (*Gesinnung*) property-mindedness; **~recht** *nt* right of ownership; (*Urheberrecht*) copyright; **~streuung** *f* dispersal of property; **~vergehen** *nt siehe* **~delikt**; **~verhältnisse** *pl* distribution *sing* of property; **~vorbehalt** *m* (*Jur*) reservation of proprietary rights; **~wohnung** *f* owner-occupied flat (*Brit*) *or* apartment; **er kaufte sich** (*dat*) **eine ~wohnung** he bought a flat (of his own); **~wohnungen bauen** to build flats for owner-occupation.

Eigen-: e~verantwortlich [1] *adj* autonomous; [2] *adv* on one's own authority; **e~verantwortlich für etw sorgen müssen** to be personally responsible for sth; **er hat e~verantwortlich dafür gesorgt** he saw to it personally *or* himself; **~verantwortlichkeit** *f* autonomy; **jds ~verantwortlichkeit für etw** sb's personal responsibility for sth; **~wärme** *f* body heat; **~wert** *m* intrinsic value; **e~willig** *adj* with a mind of one's own; (*e~sinnig*) self-willed; (*unkonventionell*) unconventional, original; **sie ist in allem recht e~willig** she has a mind of her own in everything; **~willigkeit** *f siehe adj* independence of mind; self-will; unconventionality, originality; **~zeit** *f* (*Phys*) proper time.

eignen [1] *vr* to be suitable (*für, zu* for, *als* as) ◆ **er eignet sich nicht zum Lehrer** he's not suited to teaching, he doesn't/wouldn't make a good teacher; *siehe* **geeignet.**

[2] *vi* (*geh*) **ihm eignet der Charme des Österreichers** he has *or* possesses all the charm of an Austrian; **seinen Büchern eignet ein präziser Prosastil** his books are characterized by a precise narrative style.

Eigner(in *f*) *m* **-s, -** (*form*) owner.

Eignung *f* suitability; (*Befähigung*) aptitude.

Eignungs-: ~prüfung *f*, **~test** *m* aptitude test.

eigtl. *abbr of* **eigentlich.**

Eiklar *nt* **-s, -** (*Aus, S Ger*) egg white.

Eiland *nt* **-(e)s, -e** (*liter*) isle (*liter*).

Eil-: ~angebot *nt* (*Comm*) express offer; **~bote** *m* messenger; **per** *or* **durch ~boten** express; **~brief** *m* express letter; **ich schicke diesen Brief als ~brief** I am sending this letter express.

Eile *f* **-,** *no pl* hurry ◆ **in ~ sein** to be in a hurry; **~ haben** (*Mensch*) to be in a hurry *or* rush; (*Sache*) to be urgent; **damit hat es keine ~, das hat keine ~** there is no hurry *or* rush about it, it's not urgent; **er trieb uns zur ~ an** he hurried us up; **in aller ~** hurriedly, hastily; **in höchster ~ laufen/fahren** to rush/drive in a tremendous hurry; **mit ~/mit fieberhafter ~ arbeiten** to work very quickly/feverishly; **in der/meiner ~** in the hurry/my haste; **nur keine ~!** don't rush!

Eileiter *m* (*Anat*) Fallopian tube.

Eileiterschwangerschaft *f* ectopic pregnancy.

eilen [1] *vi* **(a)** *aux sein* to rush, to hasten (*liter*), to hurry ◆ **er eilte dem Ertrinkenden zu Hilfe** he rushed *or* hastened to help the drowning man; **eile mit Weile** (*Prov*) more haste less speed (*Prov*).

(b) (*dringlich sein*) to be urgent *or* pressing ◆ **eilt!** (*auf Briefen etc*) urgent; **die Sache eilt** it's urgent, it's an urgent matter.

[2] *vr* (*inf*) to rush.

[3] *vi impers* **es eilt** it's urgent *or* pressing; **damit eilt es nicht** there's no great hurry *or* rush about it; **mit dieser Arbeit eilt es sehr/nicht** this work is very/is not urgent.

eilends *adv* hurriedly, hastily.

Eil-: e~fertig *adj* (*geh*) zealous; **~fertigkeit** *f* (*geh*) zeal, zealousness; **~fracht** *f*, **~gut** *nt* express freight; **etw als ~gut senden** to send sth express freight.

eilig *adj* **(a)** (*schnell, rasch*) quick, hurried, hasty ◆ **es ~ haben** to be in a hurry *or* rush; **er bat den Arzt, ~st zu kommen** he asked the doctor to come as quickly as possible; **nur nicht so ~!** don't be in such a hurry *or* rush!

(b) (*dringend*) urgent ◆ **er hatte nichts E~eres zu tun, als ...** (*iro*) he had nothing better to do than ... (*iro*).

Eil-: ~marsch *m* (*Mil*) fast march; **~meldung** *f* (*Press*) flash; **~paket** *nt* express parcel; **~sendung** *f* express delivery *or* letter/parcel; **~sendungen** *pl* express mail *or* post; **~tempo** *nt*: **etw im ~tempo machen** to do sth in a real rush; **er kam im ~tempo auf mich zugerannt** he came rushing *or* tearing up to me; **~zug** *m* fast stopping train; **~zustellung** *f* special delivery; **mit ~zustellung** (by) special delivery.

Eimer *m* **-s, - (a)** bucket, pail; (*Milch~*) pail; (*Müll~*) (rubbish) bin ◆ **ein ~ (voll) Wasser** a bucket(ful) of water; **es gießt wie mit** *or* **aus ~n** (*inf*) it's

bucketing down (*inf*), it's raining cats and dogs (*inf*). **(b) im ~ sein** (*inf*) to be up the spout (*sl*); (*kaputt auch*) to be bust (*inf*).
eimerweise *adv* in bucketfuls, by the bucket(ful).
ein¹ *adv* (*an Geräten*) **E~/Aus** on/off; **~ und aus gehen** to come and go; **er geht bei uns ~ und aus** he is always round at our place; **ich weiß (mit ihm) nicht mehr ~ noch aus** I'm at my wits' end (with him).
ein², eine, ein [1] *num* one ◆ **das kostet nur ~e Mark** it only costs one mark; **~ Uhr** one (o'clock); **~ Uhr zwanzig** twenty past one; **~ für allemal** once and for all; **~ und derselbe/dieselbe/dasselbe** one and the same; **er ist ihr ~ und alles** he means everything to her; *siehe* **eins.**
[2] *indef art* a; (*vor Vokalen*) an ◆ **~ Mann/~e Frau/~ Kind** a man/woman/child; **~ Europäer** a European; **~ Hotel** a *or* an hotel; **der Sohn ~es Lehrers** the son of a teacher, a teacher's son; **nur ~ Hegel konnte das schreiben** only a Hegel could have written that; **~e Hitze ist das hier!** the *or* some heat here!; **was für ~ Wetter/Lärm!** some weather/noise, what a noise; **wir hatten ~en Durst!** (*inf*) we were parched!, were we thirsty!; *siehe auch* **eine(r, s).**
ein|achsig *adj* two-wheeled, single-axle *attr.*
Ein|akter *m* **-s, -** (*Theat*) one-act play.
einander *pron* one another, each other ◆ **zwei ~ widersprechende Zeugenberichte** two (mutually) contradictory eye-witness reports.
ein|arbeiten *sep* [1] *vr* to get used to the work ◆ **sie muß sich in ihr neues Gebiet ~** she has to get used to her new area of work.
[2] *vt* **(a)** *jdn* to train. **(b)** (*einfügen*) to incorporate, to include. **(c)** (*einnähen*) to sew in; *Futter, Polster auch* to attach.
Ein|arbeitung *f siehe vt* **(a)** training. **(b)** incorporation, inclusion. **(c)** sewing in; attachment.
Ein|arbeitungszeit *f* training period.
ein|armig *adj* one-armed; *Turnübungen* single-arm ◆ **~er Bandit** one-armed bandit.
ein|äschern *vt sep Leichnam* to cremate; *Stadt etc* to burn to the ground *or* down, to reduce to ashes.
Ein|äscherung *f siehe vt* cremation; burning down.
ein|atmen *vti sep* to breathe in.
ein|ätzen *vt sep* to etch (in).
ein|äugig *adj* one-eyed; *Spiegelreflexkamera* single-lens.
Einbahnstraße *f* one-way street.
einbalsamieren* *vt sep* to embalm.
Einbalsamierung *f* embalming, embalmment.
Einband *m* book cover, case (*spec*).
einbändig *adj* one-volume *attr*, in one volume.
einbasisch *adj* (*Chem*) monobasic.
Einbau *m* **-(e)s, -ten (a)** *no pl siehe vt* installation; fitting; working-in. **(b)** (*usu pl: Schrank etc*) fixture.
einbauen *vt sep* to install, to put in; *Motor auch* to fit; (*inf: einfügen*) *Zitat etc* to work in, to incorporate ◆ **eingebaute Möbel/eingebauter Belichtungsmesser** built-in furniture/exposure meter.
Einbauküche *f* (fully-)fitted kitchen.
Einbaum *m* dug-out (canoe).
Einbau-: ~möbel *pl* built-in *or* fitted furniture; (*Schränke*) fitted cupboards *pl*; **~schrank** *m* built-in *or* fitted cupboard.
einbegriffen *adj* included.
einbehalten* *vt sep irreg* to keep back.
einbeinig *adj* one-legged.
einbekennen* *vt sep* (*geh*) *Schuld* to admit.
Einbekenntnis *nt* (*geh*) admission.
einberechnen* *vt sep* to allow for (in one's calculations) ◆ **~, daß** ... to allow for the fact that ...
einberufen* *vt sep irreg Parlament* to summon; *Versammlung* to convene, to call; (*Mil*) to call up, to conscript, to draft (*US*) ◆ **Leute zu einer Versammlung ~** to summon *or* call people to a meeting.
Einberufene(r) *mf decl as adj* (*Mil*) conscript, draftee (*US*).
Einberufung *f* **(a)** (*einer Versammlung*) convention, calling; (*des Parlaments*) summoning. **(b)** (*Mil*) conscription; (*~sbescheid*) call-up.
Einberufungs-: ~bescheid, ~befehl *m* (*Mil*) call-up *or* draft (*US*) papers *pl*.
einbeschrieben *adj* (*Math*) *Kreis* inscribed.
einbetonieren* *vt sep* to cement in (*in +acc* -to).
einbetten *vt sep* to embed (*in +acc* in); *Rohr, Kabel* to lay (*in +acc* in); *siehe* **eingebettet.**
Einbettzimmer *nt* single room.
einbeulen *vt sep* to dent (in).
einbeziehen* *vt sep irreg* to include (*in +acc* in).
Einbeziehung *f* inclusion ◆ **unter ~ von etw** including sth; **unter ~ sämtlicher Gesichtspunkte** having regard to all points.
einbiegen *sep irreg* [1] *vi aux sein* to turn (off) (*in +acc* into) ◆ **du mußt hier links ~** you have to turn (off to the) left here; **diese Straße biegt in die Hauptstraße ein** this road joins the main road.
[2] *vt* to bend in.
einbilden *vr sep* **(a) sich** (*dat*) **etw ~** to imagine sth; **er bildet sich** (*dat*) **ein, daß** ... he's got hold of the idea that ...; **sich** (*dat*) **steif und fest ~, daß** ... (*inf*) to get it fixed in one's head that ... (*inf*); **das bildest du dir nur ein** that's just your imagination; **ich bilde mir nicht ein, ich sei** ... I don't have any illusions about being ..., I'm not pretending to be ...; **er bildet sich** (*dat*) **viel ein!** he imagines a lot of things!; **bilde dir (doch) nichts ein!** don't kid (*inf*) *or* delude yourself!; **was bildest du dir eigentlich ein?** what's got into you?; **bilde dir bloß nicht ein, daß ich das glaube!** don't kid yourself (*inf*) *or* don't go thinking that I believe that!
(b) (*stolz sein*) **sich** (*dat*) **viel auf etw** (*acc*) **~** to be conceited about *or* vain about sth; **darauf kann ich mir etwas ~** (*iro*) praise indeed!; **darauf können Sie sich etwas ~!** that's something to be proud of!, that's a feather in your cap!; **darauf brauchst du dir nichts einzubilden!** that's nothing to crow about (*inf*) *or* be proud of; **auf diesen bescheidenen Erfolg brauchst du dir nichts einzubilden** don't go getting any big ideas just because of this little success; *siehe* **eingebildet.**
Einbildung *f* **(a)** (*Vorstellung*) imagination; (*irrige Vorstellung*) illusion ◆ **das sind ~en** that's pure imagination; **das ist alles nur ~** it's all in the mind, it's just (your/his) imagination; **krank ist er bloß in seiner ~** he just imagines *or* thinks he's ill.
(b) (*Dünkel*) conceit ◆ **an ~en leiden** (*hum inf*) to be (pretty) stuck on oneself (*inf*), to really fancy oneself (*inf*).
Einbildungs-: ~kraft *f*, **~vermögen** *nt* (powers *pl* of) imagination.
einbimsen *vt sep* (*inf*) **jdm etw ~** to drum *or* din sth into sb (*inf*).
einbinden *vt sep irreg Buch* to bind; (*in Schutzhülle*) to cover; (*fig: einbeziehen*) to integrate ◆ **neu ~** to rebind.
Einbindung *f* (*fig*) integration.
einblasen *vt sep irreg* to blow in (*in +acc* -to); *Kaltluft auch* to blast in (*in +acc* -to); (*Mus*) *Blasinstrument* to play *or* blow (*inf*) in ◆ **Gott blies Adam den Lebenshauch ein** God breathed the breath of life into Adam; **jdm etw ~** (*fig inf*) to whisper sth to sb.
einblenden *sep* (*Film, TV, Rad*) [1] *vt* to insert, to slot in; (*allmählich*) to fade in; (*nachträglich*) *Musik etc* to dub on.
[2] *vr* **sich in etw** (*acc*) **~** to link up with sth; **sich bei jdm/etw ~** to go over to sb/sth.
Einblendung *f siehe vt* insert; (*das Einblenden*) insertion; dubbing on.
⚠**einbleuen** *vt sep* (*inf*) **jdm etw ~** (*durch Schläge*) to beat sth into sb; (*einschärfen*) to drum sth into sb, to ram sth into sb's head (*inf*); **ich habe ihm eingebleut, das ja nicht zu vergessen** I told him time and again not to forget it.
Einblick *m* **(a)** (*rare: Blick in etw hinein*) view (*in +acc* of).
(b) (*fig: Kenntnis*) insight ◆ **~ in etw** (*acc*) **gewinnen** to gain an insight into sth; **~ in die Akten nehmen** to look at *or* examine the files; **jdm ~ in etw** (*acc*) **gewähren** to allow sb to look at sth; **er hat ~ in diese Vorgänge** he has some knowledge of these events.
einbrechen *sep irreg* [1] *vt Tür, Wand etc* to break down; *Eis* to break through.
[2] *vi* **(a)** *aux sein* (*einstürzen*) to fall *or* cave in ◆ **er ist (auf dem Eis) eingebrochen** he went *or* fell through the ice.
(b) *aux sein or haben* (*Einbruch verüben*) to break in ◆ **in unser** *or* **unserem Haus sind Diebe eingebrochen** thieves broke into our house; **bei mir ist eingebrochen worden, man hat bei mir eingebrochen** I've had a break-in, I've been burgled *or* burglarized (*US*); **in neue Absatzmärkte** *etc* **~** to make inroads into new markets *etc.*
(c) *aux sein* (*Nacht, Dämmerung, Dunkelheit*) to fall; *Winter* to set in ◆ **bei ~der Nacht** at nightfall.
Einbrecher(in f) *m* **-s, -** burglar.
einbrennen *sep irreg* [1] *vt Mal* to brand ◆ **Buchstaben/Muster in Holz ~** to burn letters/patterns into wood.
[2] *vr* (*liter*) to engrave *or* etch itself.
einbringen *vt sep irreg* **(a)** (*Parl*) to introduce.
(b) (*Ertrag bringen*) *Geld, Nutzen* to bring in; *Ruhm* to bring; *Zinsen* to earn ◆ **jdm etw ~** to bring/earn sb sth; **das bringt nichts ein** (*fig*) it's not worth it.
(c) etw in die Ehe ~ to bring sth into the marriage; **etw in die Firma ~** to put sth into the firm.
(d) (*hineinbringen, -schaffen*) to put in (*in +acc* -to); *Schiff* to bring in (*in +acc* -to); *Ernte* to bring *or* gather in; *Geflohene* to bring back.
(e) (*wettmachen*) *Zeit, Verlust* to make up.
(f) (*Typ*) *Zeilen* to take in.
(g) sich in etw (*acc*) **~** to play a part in sth; **jdn in etw** (*acc*) **~** to get sb involved in sth; **sie brachte ihre Kenntnis in die Diskussion ein** she brought her knowledge to bear in the discussion.
einbrocken *vt sep* to crumble (*in +acc* into) ◆ **jdm/sich etwas ~** (*inf*) to land sb/oneself in it (*inf*) *or* in the soup (*inf*); **da hast du dir etwas Schönes eingebrockt!** (*inf*) you've really let yourself in for it there; **was man sich eingebrockt hat, das muß man auch auslöffeln** (*prov*) you've made your bed, now you must lie on it (*prov*); *siehe* **Suppe.**
Einbruch *m* **(a)** (*~diebstahl*) burglary (*in +acc* in), breaking and entering (*form*) ◆ **ein ~** a break-in *or* burglary; **der ~ in die Bank** the bank break-in.
(b) (*von Wasser*) penetration ◆ **~ kühler Meeresluft** (*Met*) a stream of cold air moving inland.
(c) (*Einsturz: einer Mauer etc*) collapse; (*Geol*) rift valley; (*Verlust*) setback ◆ **~ der Kurse/der Konjunktur** (*Fin*) stock exchange/economic crash.
(d) (*fig*) (*der Nacht*) fall; (*des Winters*) onset ◆ **bei/vor ~ der Nacht/Dämmerung** at/before nightfall/dusk.
Einbruch(s)-: ~diebstahl *m* (*Jur*) burglary, breaking and entering (*form*); **e~sicher** *adj* burglar-proof; **~stelle** *f* (*im Damm*) breach; (*im Eis*) hole; **~tal** *nt* (*Geol*) rift valley; **~versicherung** *f* burglary insurance; **~werkzeug** *nt* housebreaking tool.
einbuchten *vt sep* (*lit*) to indent; (*inf*) to put away (*inf*), to lock up.
Einbuchtung *f* indentation; (*Bucht*) inlet, bay.
einbuddeln *sep* (*inf*) [1] *vt* to bury (*in +acc* in).
[2] *vr* **sich (in den Sand) ~** to dig oneself in(to the sand).

➤ SPRACHE AKTIV: **Einband** → 28.1, 36.1, 36.2, 38.1

einbürgern *sep* [1] *vt Person* to naturalize; *Fremdwort, Gewohnheit, Pflanze* to introduce ◆ **er ist in die** *or* **der Türkei eingebürgert worden** he has become a naturalized Turk.
[2] *vr (Person)* to become *or* be naturalized; *(Brauch, Tier, Pflanze)* to become established; *(Fremdwort)* to gain currency, to become established ◆ **das hat sich so eingebürgert** *(Brauch)* it's just the way we/they *etc* have come to do things; *(Wort)* it's been adopted into the language; **es hat sich bei uns so eingebürgert, daß wir uns abwechseln** we've got into the habit of taking turns.
Einbürgerung *f siehe vt* naturalization; introduction.
Einbuße *f* loss *(an +dat* to) ◆ **der Skandal hat seinem Ansehen schwere ~ getan** he lost a considerable amount of respect because of the scandal.
einbüßen *sep* [1] *vt* to lose; *(durch eigene Schuld)* to forfeit.
[2] *vi* to lose something ◆ **an Klarheit** *(dat)* ~ to lose some of its clarity.
einchecken ['-tʃɛkn] *vti sep (am Flughafen)* to check in *(an +dat* at); *(im Hotel auch)* to register.
eincremen *vt sep* to put cream on; *Gesicht etc auch* to cream.
eindämmen *vt sep Fluß* to dam; *(fig: halten, vermindern)* to check, to stem; *(im Zaum halten)* to contain.
Eindämmung *f* **(a)** *(Damm)* dam. **(b)** *siehe vt* damming; checking, stemming; containing.
eindampfen *vt sep* to evaporate.
eindecken *sep* [1] *vr* **sich (mit etw)** ~ to stock up (with sth); *(für den Haushalt)* to get in supplies (of sth); **wir haben uns ausreichend mit Geld eingedeckt** we've got enough money; **ich bin gut eingedeckt, ich habe mich eingedeckt** I am well supplied.
[2] *vt* **(a)** *(Build, Mil, fig)* to cover ◆ **ein Dach mit Ziegeln/Stroh ~** to tile/thatch a roof.
(b) *(inf: überhäufen)* to inundate ◆ **mit Arbeit eingedeckt sein** to be snowed under *or* inundated with work.
Eindecker *m* **-s, -** *(Aviat)* monoplane; *(Autobus)* single decker.
eindeichen *vt sep* to dyke; *Fluß auch* to embank.
eindellen *vt sep (inf)* to dent (in).
eindeutig *adj* clear; *Beweis auch* definite; *(nicht zweideutig)* unambiguous; *Witz* explicit ◆ **jdm etw ~ sagen** to tell sb sth quite plainly *or* straight *(inf)*; **das ist ~ der Fall** it's clearly *or* obviously the case.
Eindeutigkeit *f siehe adj* clearness; definiteness; unambiguity; explicitness.
eindeutschen *vt sep Fremdwort* to Germanize ◆ **Clips, ~d auch Klips** Clips, sometimes Germanized as Klips.
Eindeutschung *f* Germanization.
eindicken *vti sep (vi: aux sein)* to thicken.
eindimensional *adj* one-dimensional, unidimensional.
eindosen *vt sep* to can, to tin *(Brit)*.
eindösen *vi sep aux sein (inf)* to doze off, to drop off *(inf)*.
eindrängen *sep* [1] *vr* to crowd in *(in +acc* -to); *(fig)* to intrude *(in +acc* upon); *(sich einmischen) (in +acc* in) to interfere, to meddle *(inf)*.
[2] *vi aux sein (lit, fig)* to crowd in *(auf +acc* on).
eindrecken *vt sep (inf)* to get dirty *or* muddy.
eindrehen *vt sep* **(a)** *(einschrauben)* to screw in *(in +acc* -to). **(b)** *Haar* to put in rollers.
eindreschen *vi sep irreg (inf)* **auf jdn ~** to lay into *(inf) or* lambaste sb.
eindrillen *vt sep (inf)* **jdm etw ~** to drill sb in sth; *Verhalten, Manieren etc* to din *or* drum sth into sb *(inf)*.
eindringen *vi sep irreg aux sein* **(a)** *(einbrechen)* **in etw** *(acc)* **~** to force one's way into sth; *(Dieb etc auch)* to force an entry into sth; **in unsere Linien/das Land ~** *(Mil)* to penetrate our lines/into the country.
(b) in etw *(acc)* **~** *(Messer, Schwert)* to go into *or* penetrate (into) sth; *(Wasser, Gas auch)* to get into *or* find its way into sth; *(Fremdwörter, Amerikanismen)* to find its way into sth; **der Nagel drang tief ins Holz ein** the nail went deep into the wood; **eine Stimmung in sich ~ lassen** to let oneself be carried away by a mood.
(c) *(bestürmen)* **auf jdn ~** to go for *or* attack sb *(mit* with); *(mit Fragen, Bitten etc)* to besiege sb.
eindringlich *adj (nachdrücklich)* insistent; *(dringend auch)* urgent; *Schilderung* vivid ◆ **mit ~en Worten** insistently, with insistence; vividly, in vivid words; **ich habe ihn ~ gebeten, zu Hause zu bleiben** I urged him to stay at home; **jdm ~ nahelegen, etw zu tun** to urge sb *or* advise sb most strongly to do sth.
Eindringlichkeit *f siehe adj* insistence; urgency; vividness.
Eindringling *m* intruder; *(in Gesellschaft etc)* interloper.
▼ **Eindruck** *m* **-(e)s, ¨e** **(a)** impression ◆ **den ~ erwecken, als ob** *or* **daß ...** to give the impression that ...; **die ¨e, die wir gewonnen hatten** our impressions; **ich habe den ~, daß ..., ich kann mich des ~s nicht erwehren, daß ...** *(geh)* I have the impression that ..., I can't help thinking that ... *(inf)*; **großen ~ auf jdn machen** to make a great *or* big impression on sb; **er macht einen heiteren ~/den ~ eines heiteren Menschen** he gives the impression of being cheerful/a cheerful person; **die Rede hat ihren ~ auf ihn nicht verfehlt** the speech made a strong impression on him; **er will ~ (bei ihr) machen** *or* **schinden** *(inf)* he's out to impress (her); **ich stehe noch ganz unter dem ~ der Ereignisse** I'm still too close to it all; **viele (neue) ¨e sammeln** to gain a whole host of new impressions; **du solltest einmal neue ¨e sammeln** you should broaden your horizons.
(b) *(rare: Spur)* impression, imprint.
eindrücken *sep* [1] *vt* **(a)** to push in; *Fenster* to break; *Tür, Mauer* to push down; *(Sturm, Explosion)* to blow in/down; *(einbeulen)* to dent, to bash in *(inf)*; *Brustkorb* to crush; *Nase* to flatten. **(b)** *Fußspuren etc* to impress.
[2] *vr* to make *or* leave an impression.

Eindrucks-: **e~fähig** *adj* receptive; **~fähigkeit** *f, no pl* receptiveness; **e~los** *adj* unimpressive; **e~voll** *adj* impressive.
eind(r)useln *vi sep aux sein (inf)* to doze off, to drop off *(inf)*.
eindübeln *vt sep Haken* to plug *(in +acc* into).
einduseln *vi sep aux sein siehe* **eind(r)useln.**
eine *siehe* **ein, eine(r, s).**
ein|ebnen *vt sep (lit)* to level (off); *(fig)* to level (out).
Ein|ebnung *f, no pl* levelling.
Ein|ehe *f* monogamy.
ein|eiig *adj Zwillinge* identical.
ein|einhalb *num* one and a half; *siehe* **anderthalb.**
ein|einhalbmal *adv* one and a half times.
Ein|eltern(teil)familie *f* single-parent family.
einen *vtr (geh)* to unite.
ein|engen *vt sep (lit)* to constrict; *(fig) Begriff* to restrict, to narrow down; *Freiheit* to curb, to restrict ◆ **sich (in seiner Freiheit) eingeengt fühlen** to feel cramped *or* restricted; **jdn in seiner Freiheit ~** to curb sb's freedom; **eingeengt sitzen/stehen/liegen** to sit/stand/lie (all) squashed up.
ein|engend *adj (lit)* constricting; *(fig)* restricting ◆ **einen Begriff ~ interpretieren** to interpret a concept narrowly.
Ein|engung *f (lit)* constriction; *(fig)* restriction.
einer *adv (Aus) siehe* **herein.**
eine(r, s) *indef pron adj* **(a)** one; *(jemand)* somebody, someone ◆ **der/die/das ~** the one; **das ~ Buch habe ich schon gelesen** I've already read one of the books *or* the one book; **das ~ Gute war** ... the one good thing was ...; **sein ~r Sohn** *(inf)* one of his sons; **weder der ~ noch der andere** neither (one) of them; **die ~n sagen so, die anderen gerade das Gegenteil** some (people) say one thing and others *or* some say just the opposite; **~r für alle, alle für ~n** *(Prov)* all for one and one for all *(Prov)*; **dumm/geschickt** *etc* **wie nur ~r** *(dated)* thick/skilful *etc* as they come *(inf)*; **das ist ~r!** *(inf)* he's a (right) one! *(inf)*; **du bist mir vielleicht ~!** *(inf)* you're a fine *or* right one *(inf)*; **sieh mal ~r an!** *(iro)* well what do you know! *(inf)*, surprise, surprise! *(inf)*; **alles in ~m abmachen** to do everything in one go; **in ~m fort, in ~r Tour** *(inf)* non-stop; *siehe* **andere(r, s).**
(b) *(man)* one *(form)*, you ◆ **und das soll ~r glauben!** *(inf)* and we're/you're meant to believe that!; **wie kann ~r nur so unklug sein!** how could anybody be so stupid!; **wenn ~m so etwas gegeben wird** if such a thing is given (to) one *(form) or* (to) you.
(c) ~s *(auch* **eins)** one thing; **~s gefällt mir nicht an ihm** (there's) one thing I don't like about him; **~s sag' ich dir** I'll tell you one thing; **noch ~s!** another one!; *(Lied etc)* more!; **noch ~s, bevor ich's vergesse:** (there's) something else *or* one other thing before I forget; **es kam ~s nach dem** *or* **zum anderen** it was (just) one thing after another; **es läuft alles auf ~s hinaus, es kommt alles auf ~s heraus** it all comes to the same (thing) in the end.
(d) *(inf)* **sich** *(dat)* **~n genehmigen** to have a quick one *(inf) or* drink; **jdm ~ kleben** to thump sb one *(inf)*; *siehe* **abbrechen.**
Einer *m* **-s, -** **(a)** *(Math)* unit. **(b)** *(Ruderboot)* single scull ◆ **Weltmeister im ~** world champion in the single sculls.
Einerkajak *m* single seater *or* one-man canoe *or* kayak; *(Disziplin)* single kayak *or* canoe.
einerlei *adj inv* **(a)** *pred (gleichgültig)* all the same ◆ **das ist mir ganz ~** it's all the same *or* all one to me; **was du machst ist mir ~** it's all the same to me what you do; **~, ob er kommt** no matter whether he comes or not; **~, was/wer** ... it doesn't matter what/who ...
(b) Stoff von ~ Farbe self-coloured material; **sie kocht immer nur ~ Essen** she always cooks the same kind *or* sort of food; **es gab für alle nur ~ zu essen** everyone had to eat the same thing.
Einerlei *nt* **-s,** *no pl* monotony.
▼ **einerseits** *adv* **~ ... andererseits** ... on the one hand ... on the other hand ...
Einerstelle *f (Math)* unit (place).
einesteils *adv* **~ ... ander(e)nteils** on the one hand ... on the other hand.
einfach [1] *adj* **(a)** simple; *Mensch* ordinary; *Essen* plain.
(b) *(nicht doppelt) Knoten, Schleife* simple; *Fahrkarte, Fahrt* one-way, single *(Brit)*; *Rockfalten* knife; *Buchführung* single-entry ◆ **einmal ~!** *(in Bus etc)* one (ordinary) single; **das ist nicht so ~ zu verstehen** that is not so easy to understand *or* so easily understood.
[2] *adv* **(a)** simply ◆ **~ gefaltet** folded once.
(b) *(verstärkend: geradezu)* simply, just ◆ **~ gemein** downright mean; **das ist doch ~ dumm** that's (just) plain stupid.
Einfachheit *f siehe adj* simplicity; ordinariness; plainness ◆ **der ~ halber** for the sake of simplicity.
einfädeln *sep* [1] *vt* **(a)** *Nadel, Faden* to thread *(in +acc* through); *Nähmaschine* to thread up. **(b)** *(inf) Intrige, Plan etc* to set up *(inf)*.
[2] *vr* **sich in eine Verkehrskolonne ~** to filter into a stream of traffic.
einfahren *sep irreg* [1] *vi* **(a)** *aux sein (Zug, Schiff)* to come in *(in +acc* -to); *(Hunt: Fuchs, Dachs etc)* to go to earth ◆ **in die Grube/den Schacht ~** *(Min)* to go down (to the face); **auf Bahnsteig 2 fährt der Zug aus München ein** the train from Munich is arriving at *or* coming in at platform 2.
(b) *(inf: essen)* to tuck in.
[2] *vt* **(a)** *(kaputtfahren) Mauer, Zaun* to knock down.
(b) *Ernte* to bring in.
(c) *Fahrgestell, Periskop* to retract.
(d) *(ans Fahren etc gewöhnen)* to break in; *Wagen* to run in *(Brit)*, to break in *(US)* ◆ **„wird eingefahren"** "running in" *(Brit)*, "being broken in" *(US)*.
(e) *Verluste* to make; *Gewinne auch* to bring in.

➤ SPRACHE AKTIV: **Eindruck: a** → 33.2, 45.4, 53.4 **einerseits** → 53.5

[3] *vr* to get used to driving ◆ **ich muß mich erst mit dem neuen Auto ~** I have to get used to (driving) the new car; **das hat sich so eingefahren** (*fig*) it has just become a habit; *siehe* **eingefahren**.

Einfahrsignal *nt* (*Rail*) home signal.

Einfahrt *f* **(a)** *no pl* (*das Einfahren*) entry (*in +acc* to); (*Min*) descent ◆ **Vorsicht bei (der) ~ des Zuges!** stand well back, the train is arriving; **der Schnellzug hat ~ auf Gleis 3** the express is arriving at platform 3; **der Zug hat noch keine ~** the train can't enter the station.
(b) (*Eingang*) entrance; (*Tor~*) entry; (*Hunt*) tunnel.

Einfall *m* **(a)** (*fig*) (*plötzlicher Gedanke*) idea; (*Grille, Laune*) notion ◆ **jdn auf den ~ bringen, etw zu tun** to give sb the idea of doing sth; **auf den ~ kommen, etw zu tun** to get the idea of doing sth; **es war ein bloßer** *or* **nur so ein ~** it was just an idea; **er hat ¨~e wie ein altes Haus** (*hum inf*) he has some weird ideas.
(b) (*Mil*) invasion (*in +acc* of).
(c) (*des Lichts*) incidence (*spec*) ◆ **je nach (dem) ~ des Lichts** according to how the light falls.
(d) (*liter*) (*der Nacht*) fall; (*des Winters*) onset ◆ **vor ~ der Nacht** before nightfall.

einfallen *vi sep irreg aux sein* **(a)** to collapse, to cave in; (*Gesicht, Wangen*) to become sunken *or* haggard; *siehe* **eingefallen**.
(b) (*eindringen*) **in ein Land ~** to invade a country; **in die feindlichen Reihen ~** to penetrate the enemy lines; **Wölfe sind in die Schafherde eingefallen** (*liter*) wolves fell upon the flock of sheep (*liter*).
(c) (*liter*) (*Nacht*) to fall; (*Winter*) to set in.
(d) (*Lichtstrahlen*) to fall, to be incident (*spec*); (*in ein Zimmer etc*) to come in (*in +acc* -to).
(e) (*Hunt: Federwild*) to come in, to settle.
(f) (*mitsingen, mitreden*) to join in; (*einsetzen: Chor, Stimmen*) to come in; (*dazwischenreden*) to break in (*in +acc* on).
(g) (*Gedanke*) **jdm ~** to occur to sb; **das ist mir nicht eingefallen** I didn't think of that, that didn't occur to me; **mir fällt nichts ein, was ich schreiben kann** I can't think of anything to write; **jetzt fällt mir ein, wie/warum ...** I've just thought of how/why ..., it's just occurred to me how/why ...; **ihm fällt immer eine Ausrede ein** he can always think of an excuse; **das fällt mir nicht im Traum ein!** I wouldn't dream of it!; **hast du dir etwas ~ lassen?** have you had any ideas?, have you thought of anything?; **da mußt du dir schon etwas anderes/Besseres ~ lassen!** you'll really have to think of something else/better; **was fällt Ihnen ein!** what are you thinking of!
(h) (*in Erinnerung kommen*) **jdm ~** to come to sb; **dabei fällt mir mein Onkel ein, der ...** that reminds me of my uncle, who ...; **es fällt mir jetzt nicht ein** I can't think of it *or* it won't come to me at the moment; **es wird Ihnen schon wieder ~** it will come back to you.

Einfalls-: **e~los** *adj* unimaginative; **~losigkeit** *f* unimaginativeness; **e~reich** *adj* imaginative; **~reichtum** *m* imaginativeness; **~tor** *nt* gateway; **~winkel** *m* (*Phys*) angle of incidence.

Einfalt *f* -, *no pl* (*Arglosigkeit*) simplicity, naivety; (*Dummheit*) simple-mindedness, simpleness.

einfältig *adj siehe* **Einfalt** simple, naive; simple(-minded).

Einfältigkeit *f* simple-mindedness, simpleness.

Einfaltspinsel *m* (*inf*) simpleton.

Einfamilienhaus *nt* detached family house.

einfangen *vt sep irreg* (*lit, fig*) to catch, to capture.

einfärben *vt sep* **(a)** *Stoff, Haar* to dye. **(b)** (*Typ*) *Druckwalze* to ink.

einfarbig, einfärbig (*Aus*) *adj* all one colour; (*Tex*) self-coloured.

einfassen *vt sep* **(a)** (*umsäumen*) *Beet, Grab* to border, to edge; *Kleid, Naht, Knopfloch* to trim.
(b) ein Grundstück (mit einem Zaun/einer Mauer/Hecke) ~ to put a fence/wall/hedge *etc* round a plot of land, to fence/wall/hedge a plot of land round.
(c) *Edelstein* to set (*mit* in); *Bild* to mount; *Quelle* to put a wall round.

Einfassung *f siehe vt* **(a)** border, edging; trimming. **(b)** fence; wall; hedge. **(c)** setting; mount; wall.

einfetten *vt sep* to grease; *Leder, Schuhe* to dubbin; *Haut, Gesicht* to cream, to rub cream into.

einfinden *vr sep irreg* to come; (*eintreffen*) to arrive; (*zu Prüfung etc*) to present oneself ◆ **ich bitte alle, sich pünktlich in meinem Büro einzufinden** I would ask you all to be in my office punctually; **ich werde mich also um 10 Uhr bei euch ~** I'll be *or* arrive at your place at 10 o'clock.

einflechten *vt sep irreg Band, Blumen* to twine; (*fig: ins Gespräch etc*) to work in (*in +acc* -to), to introduce (*in +acc* in, into) ◆ **darf ich an dieser Stelle kurz ~, daß ...** I would just like to say at this point that ...; **in das Buch sind viele witzige Anekdoten eingeflochten** many amusing anecdotes have been woven into the book.

einfliegen *sep irreg* [1] *vt* **(a)** *Flugzeug* to test-fly. **(b)** *Proviant, Truppen* to fly in (*in +acc* -to). **(c)** *Verluste* to make; *Gewinne auch* to bring in.
[2] *vi aux sein* to fly in (*in +acc* -to).

einfließen *vi sep irreg aux sein* to flow in; (*Gelder auch*) to pour in; (*Wasser auch*) to run in; (*fig*) to have some influence (*in +acc* on), to leave its mark (*in +acc* on) ◆ **er ließ nebenbei ~, daß er Professor sei** he let it drop that he was a professor.

einflößen *vt sep* **jdm etw ~** to pour sth down sb's throat; *Medizin auch* to give sb sth; *Ehrfurcht, Mut etc* to instil sth into sb, to instil sb with a sense of sth.

Einflug *m* **er beobachtete das Flugzeug beim ~** he watched the plane coming in; **er wurde beim ~ in Feindgebiet abgeschossen** he was shot down when flying into enemy territory.

Einflugschneise *f* (*Aviat*) approach path.

⚠ **Einfluß** *m* **(a)** influence ◆ **unter dem ~ von jdm/etw** under the influence of sb/sth; **~ auf jdn haben/ausüben** to have/exert an influence on sb; **~ nehmen** to bring an influence to bear; **das Wetter steht unter dem ~ eines atlantischen Tiefs** the weather is being affected *or* influenced by an Atlantic depression; **auf die Entscheidung hat es keinen ~** it has no influence *or* bearing on the decision, it won't influence the decision; **darauf habe ich keinen ~** I can't influence that, I've no influence over that.
(b) (*lit: das Einfließen*) (*von Luft, fig*) influx; (*von Gas, Abwässern*) inflow.

⚠ **Einfluß-**: **~bereich** *m*, **~gebiet** *nt* sphere of influence; **England liegt im ~bereich eines atlantischen Tiefs** England is being affected by an Atlantic depression; **e~los** *adj* uninfluential; **~losigkeit** *f* lack of influence; **~möglichkeit** *f* influence; **unsere ~möglichkeiten sind begrenzt** we don't have much scope for influence; **~nahme** *f* -, (*rare*) **-n** exertion of influence (*gen* by); **e~reich** *adj* influential; **~sphäre** *f siehe* ⚠**~bereich**.

einflüstern *vt sep* **jdm etw ~** to whisper sth to sb; (*fig*) to insinuate sth to sb.

Einflüsterung *f* (*fig*) insinuation.

einfordern *vt sep Schulden* to demand payment of, to call (in).

einförmig *adj* uniform; (*eintönig*) monotonous.

Einförmigkeit *f siehe adj* uniformity; monotony.

einfressen *vr sep irreg* to eat in (*in +acc* -to) ◆ **der Haß hatte sich tief in ihn eingefressen** hate had eaten deep into his heart.

einfrieden *vt sep* (*geh*) to enclose.

Einfriedung *f* (*geh*) fence; wall; hedge.

einfrieren *sep irreg* [1] *vi aux sein* to freeze; (*Wasserleitung, Schiff*) to freeze up ◆ **im Eis eingefroren** frozen into the ice; **die Beziehungen ~ lassen** to suspend relations.
[2] *vt* (*lit, fig*) *Nahrungsmittel, Löhne etc* to freeze; (*Pol*) *Beziehungen* to suspend ◆ **sich ~ lassen** to allow oneself to be put into deep-freeze.

Einfrierung *f* (*fig*) (*von Löhnen etc*) freezing; (*von Beziehungen*) suspension.

einfrosten *vt sep Gemüse, Fleisch* to freeze.

Einfügemodus *m* (*Comput*) insert mode.

einfügen *sep* [1] *vt Steine, Maschinenteile* to fit (*in +acc* into); (*Comput*) to insert (*in +acc* in); (*nachtragen*) to add (*in +acc* to) ◆ **darf ich an dieser Stelle ~, daß ...** may I add at this point that ...
[2] *vr* to fit in (*in +acc* -to); (*sich anpassen*) to adapt (*in +acc* to); (*Haus in Umgebung etc*) to fit in (*in +acc* with).

Einfügetaste *f* (*Comput*) insert key.

Einfügung *f* insertion, addition.

einfühlen *vr sep* **sich in jdn ~** to empathize with sb; (*Theat*) to feel oneself into (the role of) sb; **er kann sich gut in andere Leute ~** he's good at putting himself in other people's shoes (*inf*) *or* places *or* at empathizing with other people; **sich in etw** (*acc*) **~** to understand sth; **sich in die Atmosphäre des 17. Jahrhunderts ~** to get into *or* project oneself into the atmosphere of the 17th century; **sich in ein Gedicht ~** to experience a poem.

einfühlsam *adj Interpretation* sensitive; *Mensch auch* understanding, empath(et)ic (*form*).

Einfühlung *f* understanding (*in +acc* of); (*in einen Menschen auch*) empathy (*in +acc* with); (*einer Interpretation*) sensitivity.

Einfühlungsvermögen *nt* capacity for understanding, empathy ◆ **ein Buch mit großem ~ interpretieren** to interpret a book with a great deal of sensitivity.

Einfuhr *f* **-, -en** import; (*das Einführen auch*) importing.

Einfuhr- *in cpds* import; **~artikel** *m* import; **ein ~artikel sein** to be imported.

einführen *sep* [1] *vt* **(a)** (*hineinstecken*) to insert, to introduce (*in +acc* into).
(b) (*bekannt machen*) to introduce (*in +acc* into); (*Comm*) *Firma, Artikel* to establish ◆ **jdn in sein Amt/seine Arbeit ~** to install sb (in office)/introduce sb to his work; **jdn bei Hofe ~** to present sb at court; **~de Worte** introductory words, words of introduction.
(c) (*als Neuerung*) to introduce, to bring in; *neue Mode* to set, to start; *Sitte* to start.
(d) (*Comm*) *Waren, Devisen* to import.
[2] *vr* to introduce oneself ◆ **sich gut/nicht gut ~** to make a good/bad (initial) impression, to get off to a good/bad start (*inf*).

Einfuhr-: **~genehmigung** *f* import permit; **~hafen** *m* port of entry; **~kontingent** *nt* import quota; **~land** *nt* importing country; **~sperre** *f*, **~stopp** *m* ban on imports; **eine ~sperre für etw** a ban on the import of sth.

Einführung *f* introduction (*in +acc* to); (*Amts~*) installation; (*das Hineinstecken*) insertion (*in +acc* into); (*bei Hof*) presentation.

Einführungs- *in cpds* introductory.

Einfuhr-: **~verbot** *nt siehe* **~sperre**; **~zoll** *m* import duty.

einfüllen *vt sep* to pour in ◆ **etw in Flaschen/Säcke/Fässer ~** to put sth into bottles/sacks/barrels, to bottle/sack/barrel sth.

Einfüll-: **~öffnung** *f* opening; **~stutzen** *m* (*Aut*) filler pipe.

einfurchen *sep* [1] *vt* to furrow.
[2] *vr* **sich in etw** (*acc*) **~** to carve itself deep into sth.

Eingabe *f* **(a)** (*form: Gesuch*) petition (*an +acc* to). **(b)** (*von Medizin*) administration. **(c)** (*Comput*) input.

Eingabe-: **~daten** *pl* input data *sing.* **~frist** *f* time limit for the filing of petitions; **~gerät** *nt* input device; **~taste** *f* (*Comput*) enter key.

Eingang *m* **(a)** entrance (*in +acc* to); (*Zutritt, Aufnahme*) entry ◆ **„kein ~!"** "no entrance"; **jdm/sich ~ in etw** (*acc*)/**zu etw verschaffen** to gain entry into/to

⚠: for details of spelling reform, see supplement

➤ SPRACHE AKTIV: **einfallen: g** → 39.3, 41 **Einführung** → 53.1

sth; **in etw** (*acc*) **~ finden** to find one's way into sth.
(b) (*Comm: Waren~, Post~*) delivery; (*Erhalt*) receipt ◆ **wir bestätigen den ~ Ihres Schreibens vom ...** we acknowledge receipt of your communication of the ...; **die Waren werden beim ~ gezählt** the goods are counted on delivery; **den ~** *or* **die ~e bearbeiten** to deal with the in-coming post *or* mail.
(c) (*Beginn*) start, beginning ◆ **zum ~ möchte ich bemerken ...** I would like to start by saying ...

eingängig *adj Melodie, Spruch* catchy; *Theorie* neat.

eingangs [1] *adv* at the start *or* beginning.
[2] *prep +gen* (*form*) at the start *or* beginning of.

Eingangs-: ~bestätigung *f* (*Comm*) acknowledgement of receipt; **~buch** *nt* (*Comm*) receipt book, book of receipts; **~datum** *nt* date of receipt; **~formel** *f* (*Jur*) preamble; (*in Brief*) opening phrase; **~halle** *f* entrance hall; **~pforte** *f* (*lit, fig*) gateway; **~stempel** *m* (*Comm*) receipt stamp; **mit einem ~stempel versehen** stamped with the date of receipt; **~tor** *nt* entrance, main gate; **~tür** *f* entrance, door; **~vermerk** *m* (*Comm*) notice of receipt.

eingeben *vt sep irreg* **(a)** (*verabreichen*) to give ◆ **jdm das Essen ~** to feed sb.
(b) (*Comput*) *Text, Befehl* to enter; (*eintippen auch*) to key in ◆ **dem Computer Daten ~** to feed *or* enter data into the computer.
(c) (*dated: einreichen*) *Gesuch etc* to submit (*an +acc* to).
(d) (*liter*) *Gedanken etc* **jdm etw ~** to inspire sb with sth; **das hat uns Gott eingegeben** it comes from God.

eingebettet *adj* **in** *or* **zwischen Wäldern/Hügeln ~** nestling among the woods/hills.

eingebildet [1] *ptp of* **einbilden**.
[2] *adj* **(a)** (*hochmütig*) conceited. **(b)** (*imaginär*) imaginary; *Schwangerschaft* false ◆ **ein ~er Kranker** a hypochondriac.

Eingebildetheit *f* conceit.

eingeboren *adj* (*einheimisch*) native; (*angeboren*) innate, inborn (*dat* in) ◆ **Gottes ~er Sohn** the only begotten Son of God.

Eingeborenensprache *f* native language.

Eingeborene(r) *mf decl as adj* native (*auch hum*).

Eingebung *f* inspiration.

eingedenk (*old, liter*) [1] *prep +gen* bearing in mind, remembering ◆ **~ dessen, daß ...** bearing in mind *or* remembering that ...
[2] *adj pred* **einer Sache** (*gen*) **~ sein** to bear sth in mind, to be mindful of sth (*old, liter*).

eingefahren *adj Verhaltensweise* well-worn ◆ **die Diskussion bewegte sich in ~en Gleisen** the discussion stayed in the same old groove *or* covered the same old well-worn topics.

eingefallen *adj Wangen* hollow, sunken; *Augen* sunken, deep-set; *Gesicht* haggard, gaunt.

eingefleischt *adj* **(a)** *attr* (*überzeugt*) confirmed; (*unverbesserlich*) dyed-in-the-wool ◆ **~er Junggeselle** (*hum*) confirmed bachelor. **(b)** (*zur zweiten Natur geworden*) ingrained, deep-rooted.

eingefuchst *adj* (*inf*) **~ sein** to have it all at one's fingertips.

▼ **eingehen** *sep irreg aux sein* [1] *vi* **(a)** (*old: eintreten*) to enter (*in +acc* into); (*Aufnahme finden: Wort, Sitte*) to be adopted (*in +acc* in) ◆ **in die Geschichte ~** to go down in (the annals of) history; **in die Unsterblichkeit ~** to attain immortality; **zur ewigen Ruhe** *or* **in den ewigen Frieden ~** to go to (one's) rest.
(b) etw geht jdm ein (*wird verstanden*) sb grasps *or* understands sth; **wann wird es dir endlich ~, daß ...?** when will it finally sink in *or* when will you finally understand that ...?; **es will mir einfach nicht ~, wie ...** it's beyond me how ..., I just cannot understand how ...
(c) (*wirken*) **diese Musik geht einem leicht ein** this music is very catchy; **diese Worte gingen ihm glatt ein** these words were music to his ears.
(d) (*fig: einfließen*) to leave its mark, to have some influence (*in +acc* on) ◆ **die verschiedensten Einflüsse sind in das Werk eingegangen** there have been the most diverse influences on his work.
(e) (*ankommen*) (*Briefe, Waren etc*) to arrive, to be received; (*Meldung, Spenden, Bewerbungen auch*) to come in ◆ **~de Post/Waren** incoming mail/goods; **eingegangene Post/Spenden** mail/donations received.
(f) (*einlaufen: Stoff*) to shrink.
(g) (*sterben: Tiere, Pflanze*) to die (*an +dat* of); (*inf: Firma etc*) to fold ◆ **bei dieser Hitze/Kälte geht man ja ein!** (*inf*) this heat/cold is just too much (*inf*) *or* is killing (*inf*); **da/bei diesem Geschäft bist du ja schön eingegangen!** (*sl*) you really came unstuck there/with that deal, didn't you? (*inf*); **bei dem Boxkampf ist er mächtig eingegangen** (*sl*) he got a clobbering in the fight (*inf*).
▼ **(h) auf etw** (*acc*) **~** (*behandeln*) *Frage, Punkt etc* to go into sth; **darauf gehe ich noch näher ein** I will go into that in more detail; **niemand ging auf meine Frage/mich ein** nobody took any notice of my question/me.
(i) (*sich widmen, einfühlen*) **auf jdn/etw ~** to give (one's) time and attention to sb/sth.
(j) (*zustimmen*) **auf einen Vorschlag/Plan ~** to agree to *or* fall in with a suggestion/plan.
[2] *vt* (*abmachen, abschließen*) to enter into; *Risiko* to take; *Wette* to make ◆ **er gewinnt, darauf gehe ich jede Wette ein** I bet you anything he wins; **einen Vergleich ~** (*Jur*) to reach a settlement.

eingehend *adj* (*ausführlich*) detailed; (*gründlich*) thorough; *Bericht, Studien, Untersuchungen auch* in-depth *attr*.

eingekeilt *adj* hemmed in; *Auto auch* boxed in; (*fig*) trapped.

Eingemachte(s) *nt decl as adj* bottled fruit/vegetables; (*Marmelade*) preserves *pl*; (*inf: Erspartes*) one's own resources *pl* ◆ **ans ~ gehen** (*fig inf*) to get down to the nitty-gritty (*inf*).

eingemeinden* *vt sep* to incorporate (*in +acc, nach* into).

Eingemeindung *f* incorporation.

eingenommen *adj* **für jdn/etw ~ sein** to be taken with sb/sth, to be enamoured of sb/sth; **gegen jdn/etw ~ sein** to be prejudiced *or* biased against sb/sth; **er ist sehr von sich** (*dat*) **selbst ~** he thinks a lot of himself, he really fancies himself.

Eingenommenheit *f* partiality (*für, von* to).

eingeschlechtig *adj* (*Bot*) unisexual, diclinous (*form*).

eingeschlechtlich *adj Gruppe* single-sex.

eingeschnappt *adj* (*inf*) cross ◆ **~ sein** to be in a huff; **sie ist immer gleich ~** she always gets into a huff.

eingeschossig ['aɪngəʃɔsɪç] *adj Haus* single-storey.

eingeschränkt *adj* (*eingeengt*) restricted, limited; (*sparsam*) careful ◆ **in ~en Verhältnissen leben** to live in straitened circumstances.

Eingeschränktheit *f* restriction; (*finanziell*) straitened circumstances *pl*.

eingeschrieben *adj Mitglied, Brief* registered.

eingeschworen *adj* confirmed; *Gemeinschaft* close ◆ **auf etw** (*acc*) **~ sein** to swear by sth; **auf eine Politik ~ sein** to be committed to a policy; **er ist auf diese Art von Malerei ~** he is a great fan of this type of painting; **die beiden sind aufeinander ~** the two of them are very close (to one another).

eingesessen *adj Einwohner, Familie* old-established; *Firma auch* long-established ◆ **die Firma/Familie ist dort seit Generationen ~** the firm/family has been (established) there for generations; **die E~en** the old established inhabitants/families/firms.

Eingesottene(s) *nt decl as adj* (*Aus*) bottled fruit.

eingespannt *adj* busy.

eingespielt *adj Mannschaft, Team* (well-)adjusted to playing/working together ◆ **aufeinander ~ sein** to be used to one another.

eingestand(e)nermaßen *adv* admittedly.

Eingeständnis *nt* admission, confession.

eingestehen* *vt sep irreg* to admit, to confess ◆ **sie hat den Diebstahl eingestanden** she admitted (to) *or* confessed to the theft; **sich** (*dat*) **~, daß ...** to admit to oneself that ...

eingestellt *adj* **materialistisch/fortschrittlich ~ sein** to be materialistically/progressively minded *or* materialistic/progressive; **links/rechts ~ sein** to have leanings to the left/right; **die links/rechts E~en** leftists, left-/right-wingers; **wer so ~ ist wie er** anyone who thinks as he does, anyone like him; **gegen jdn ~ sein** to be set against sb; **ich bin im Moment nicht auf Besuch ~** I'm not prepared for visitors; **wir sind nur auf kleinere Reisegesellschaften ~** we can only cater for small parties; **auf Export ~ sein** to be geared to exports *or* tailored to the export market.

eingestrichen *adj* (*Mus*): **das ~e C/A** middle C/the A above middle C.

eingetragen *adj Mitglied, Warenzeichen, Verein* registered.

Eingeweide *nt* **-s, -** *usu pl* entrails *pl*, innards *pl* ◆ **der Schreck fuhr mir bis in die ~** (*liter*) my blood froze.

Eingeweidebruch *m* (*Med*) hernia.

Eingeweihte(r) *mf decl as adj* initiate ◆ **seine Lyrik ist nur ~n verständlich** his poetry can only be understood by the initiated; **ein paar ~** a chosen few.

eingewöhnen* *vr sep* to settle down *or* in (*in +dat* in).

Eingewöhnung *f* settling down *or* in.

eingewurzelt *adj* deep-rooted, deep-seated ◆ **tief bei jdm ~ sein** to be deeply ingrained in sb.

Eingezogene(r) *mf decl as adj* (*Mil*) conscript, draftee (*US*).

eingießen *vt sep irreg* (*hineinschütten*) to pour in (*in +acc* -to); (*einschenken*) to pour (out) ◆ **darf ich Ihnen noch Kaffee ~?** can I give you *or* pour you some more coffee?

eingipsen *vt sep Arm, Bein* to put in plaster; *Dübel etc* to plaster in (*in +acc* -to).

Einglas *nt* (*dated*) monocle.

eingleisig *adj* single-track ◆ **der Zug/die Straßenbahn fährt hier nur ~** the railway/tram-line is only single-track here; **er denkt sehr ~** (*fig*) he's completely single-minded.

Eingleisigkeit *f* (*fig*) single-mindedness.

eingliedern *sep* [1] *vt Firma, Gebiet* to incorporate (*dat* into, with); *jdn* to integrate (*in +acc* into); (*einordnen*) to include (*unter +acc* under, in).
[2] *vr* to fit in (*dat, in +acc* -to, in), to integrate oneself (*dat, in +acc* into) (*form*).

Eingliederung *f* (*von Firma, Gebiet*) incorporation; (*von Behinderten, von Straffälligen*) integration.

eingraben *sep irreg* [1] *vt Pfahl, Pflanze, Krallen* to dig in (*in +acc* -to); (*vergraben*) *Schatz, Leiche* to bury (*in +acc* in) ◆ **eine Inschrift in Granit ~** (*geh*) to carve an inscription into granite.
[2] *vr* to dig oneself in (*auch Mil*) ◆ **der Fluß hat sich ins Gestein eingegraben** the river carved itself a channel in the rock; **dieses Erlebnis hat sich seinem Gedächtnis eingegraben** this experience has carved itself on his memory.

eingravieren* *vt sep* to engrave (*in +acc* in).

eingreifen *vi sep irreg* **(a)** (*Tech*) to mesh (*in +acc* with). **(b)** (*einschreiten, Mil*) to intervene ◆ **in jds Rechte** (*acc*) **~** to intrude (up)on sb's rights; **wenn nicht sofort ein Arzt eingreift, ...** without immediate medical intervention ...; **E~** intervention.

eingrenzen *vt sep* (*lit*) to enclose; (*fig*) *Problem, Thema* to delimit, to circumscribe; (*verringern*) to narrow *or* cut down.

Eingrenzung *f siehe vt* enclosure; delimitation, circumscription; narrowing down.

Eingriff *m* **(a)** *(Med)* operation ◆ **ein verbotener ~** an illegal abortion. **(b)** *(Übergriff)* intervention ◆ **ein ~ in jds Rechte/Privatsphäre** an intrusion (up)on sb's rights/privacy.

Eingriffsmöglichkeit *f* possibility of intervention.

eingruppieren* *vt sep* to group *(in +acc* in).

Eingruppierung *f* grouping.

einhacken *vi sep* to peck *(auf +acc* at) ◆ **auf jdn ~** *(fig)* to pick on sb.

einhaken *sep* [1] *vt* to hook in *(in +acc* -to).
[2] *vi (inf: Punkt aufgreifen)* to intervene; *(in Unterhaltung auch)* to break in ◆ **wenn ich an diesem Punkt vielleicht ~ darf** if I might just take up that point.
[3] *vr* **sie hakte sich bei ihm ein** she put *or* slipped her arm through his; **eingehakt gehen** to walk arm in arm.

Einhalt *m* **-(e)s,** *no pl* **jdm/einer Sache ~ gebieten** to stop *or* halt sb/sth; *einem Mißbrauch auch* to put an end *or* a stop to sth.

einhalten *sep irreg* [1] *vt* **(a)** *(beachten)* to keep; *Spielregeln* to follow; *Diät, Vertrag* to keep to; *Verpflichtungen* to carry out ◆ **die Zeit ~** to keep to time *or* schedule; **den Kurs ~** *(Aviat)* to maintain (its) course, to stay on course; **er hält seine Zahlungsverpflichtungen immer pünktlich ein** he's always prompt about payments.
(b) *(old: aufhalten) Schwungrad* to stop.
(c) *(Sew)* to gather.
[2] *vi* **(a)** *(geh: aufhören)* to stop *or* halt; *(innehalten)* to pause ◆ **halt ein!** stop!
(b) *(dial: Harn, Stuhlgang zurückhalten)* to wait.

Einhaltung *f siehe vt (a)* keeping *(gen* of); following *(gen* of); keeping *(gen* to); carrying out *(gen* of) ◆ **ich werde ihn zur ~ des Vertrages zwingen** I will force him to keep (to) the contract.

einhämmern *sep* [1] *vt Nagel etc* to hammer in *(in +acc* -to); *Inschrift etc* to chisel in *(in +acc* -to), to engrave *(in +acc* into) ◆ **jdm etw ~** *(fig)* to hammer *or* drum sth into sb.
[2] *vi* **auf etw** *(acc)* **~** to hammer on sth; **auf jdn ~** *(lit, fig)* to pound sb; **die laute Musik hämmerte auf uns ein** the loud music pounded in our ears.

einhamstern *vt sep (inf)* to collect.

einhandeln *vt sep* **(a)** *(gegen, für* for) to trade, to swop, to exchange. **(b)** *(bekommen)* **sich** *(dat)* **etw ~** *(inf)* to get sth.

einhändig *adj* one-handed.

einhändigen *vt sep (form)* to hand in, to submit *(form)*.

Einhändigung *f (form)* handing in, submission *(form)*.

Einhandsegler *m* **(a)** single-handed yachtsman ◆ **als ~ um die Welt fahren** to sail single-handed round the world. **(b)** *(Boot)* single-handed yacht, single-hander.

einhängen *sep* [1] *vt Tür* to hang; *Fenster* to put in; *(Telec) Hörer* to put down; *Lampe, Girlande* to hang up ◆ **er hat eingehängt** he's hung up.
[2] *vr* **sich bei jdm ~** to slip *or* put one's arm through sb's; **sie gingen eingehängt** they walked arm in arm.

einhauchen *vt sep (liter)* **jdm/einer Sache etw ~** to breathe sth into sb/sth; **einer Sache** *(dat)* **neues Leben ~** to breathe new life into sth, to bring new life to sth.

einhauen *sep irreg* [1] *vt* **(a)** *Nagel etc* to knock *or* drive *or* bash *(inf)* in *(in +acc* -to).
(b) *(zertrümmern)* to smash *or* bash *(inf)* in.
(c) *(einmeißeln) Kerbe* to cut in *(in +acc* -to); *Inschrift etc auch* to carve in *(in +acc* -to).
[2] *vi* **(a) auf jdn ~** to lay into sb, to go for sb; **auf etw** *(acc)* **~** to go at sth.
(b) *(inf: beim Essen)* to tuck *or* pitch in *(inf)*.

einheben *vt sep irreg* **(a)** *(einhängen) Tür* to hang. **(b)** *(esp Aus) Steuern* to levy; *Geld* to collect.

Einhebung *f (esp Aus) (von Steuern)* levying; *(von Geldern)* collection.

einheften *vt sep* **(a)** *Buchseiten* to stitch in; *(mit Heftmaschine)* to staple in; *(Sew) Futter* to tack in. **(b)** *(einordnen) Akten etc* to file.

einhegen *vt sep* to enclose.

einheimisch *adj Mensch, Tier, Pflanze* native, indigenous; *Produkt, Industrie, Mannschaft* local.

Einheimische(r) *mf decl as adj* local.

einheimsen *vt sep (inf)* to collect; *Erfolg, Ruhm auch* to walk off with; *Geld auch* to rake in *(inf)* ◆ **er hat den Ruhm für sich allein eingeheimst** he took the credit himself.

Einheirat *f* marriage *(in +acc* into).

einheiraten *vi sep* **in einen Betrieb ~** to marry into a business.

Einheit *f* **(a)** *(von Land etc, Einheitlichkeit)* unity; *(das Ganze)* whole ◆ **die drei ~en** *(Liter)* the three unities; **eine geschlossene ~ bilden** to form an integrated whole; **~ von Forschung und Lehre** indivisibility of teaching and research. **(b)** *(Mil, Sci)* unit.

einheitlich *adj (gleich)* the same, uniform; *(genormt)* standard(ized); *(in sich geschlossen)* unified ◆ **~ gekleidet** dressed alike *or* the same; **wir müssen ~ vorgehen** we must act consistently with one another; **alle Spielplätze sind ~ gestaltet** all the playgrounds are built on the same lines; **die Pausenzeiten sind in allen Werken ~ geregelt** the times of breaks are laid down to be the same in all the works.

Einheitlichkeit *f siehe adj* uniformity; standardization; unity.

Einheits-: ~essen *nt* institution food; **~format** *nt* standard format; **~front** *f (Pol)* united front; *(Volksfront)* popular front; **~gewerkschaft** *f* unified trade *or* labor *(US)* union; **~kleidung** *f* uniform; **~kurzschrift** *f* standard shorthand; **~liste** *f (Pol)* single *or* unified list of candidates; **~partei** *f* united party; **in einigen Staaten gibt es nur eine ~partei** in some countries there is only a single *or* only one political party; **~preis** *m* standard *or* flat price; **~schule** *f* comprehensive (school); **~sozialist** *m (DDR)* SED member; **~staat** *m (Pol)* united state; **~tarif** *m* flat rate.

einheizen *sep* [1] *vi* to put the heating on ◆ **bei dieser Kälte muß man tüchtig ~** you have to have the heating going full blast in this cold weather; **jdm (tüchtig) ~** *(inf) (die Meinung sagen)* to haul sb over the coals; *(zu schaffen machen)* to make things hot for sb; **er hat ganz schön eingeheizt** *(fig inf)* he's knocked back a few *(inf)*.
[2] *vt Ofen* to put on; *Zimmer* to heat (up).

einhelfen *vi sep irreg (dial)* to help out.

einhellig *adj* unanimous.

Einhelligkeit *f* unanimity.

ein(h)er *adv (Aus) siehe* **herein.**

einher- *pref (entlang)* along; *(hin und her)* up and down ◆ **~reden** *siehe* **daherreden.**

einhin *adv (Aus) siehe* **hinein.**

einhöck(e)rig *adj Kamel* one-humped.

einholen *vt sep* **(a)** *(einziehen) Boot, Netz, Tau* to pull *or* haul in; *Fahne, Segel* to lower, to take down.
(b) *Rat, Gutachten, Erlaubnis* to obtain ◆ **bei jdm Rat ~** to obtain sb's advice *or* advice from sb.
(c) *(erreichen, nachholen) Laufenden* to catch up; *Vorsprung, Versäumtes, Zeit* to make up; *Verlust* to make good ◆ **der Alltag/die Vergangenheit hat mich eingeholt** the daily routine/the past has caught up with me.
(d) *auch vi (dial) siehe* **einkaufen.**

Einhol- *(dial)*: **~netz** *nt* string bag; **~tasche** *f* shopping bag.

Einholung *f* **(a)** *(von Fahne)* lowering. **(b)** *(von Rat, Gutachten etc)* obtaining.

Einhorn *nt (Myth, Astron)* unicorn.

Einhufer *m* **-s, -** *(Zool)* solidungulate *(spec)*.

einhufig *adj* solidungulate *(spec)*.

einhüllen *sep* [1] *vt Kind, Leichnam* to wrap (up), to swathe *(liter) (in +acc* in) ◆ **in Nebel/Wolken eingehüllt** shrouded *or* enveloped in mist/clouds.
[2] *vr (geh)* to wrap oneself up.

einhundert *num (form) siehe* **hundert.**

einhüten *vi sep (N Ger)* to keep house *(bei* for); *(Kinder hüten)* to babysit *(bei* for).

eini *adv (Aus) siehe* **hinein.**

einig *adj* **(a)** *(geeint)* united.
(b) *(einer Meinung)* agreed, in agreement *(über +acc* on, about, *in +dat* on) ◆ **ich weiß mich in dieser Sache mit ihm ~** *(geh)* I know I am in agreement with him on this; **sich** *(dat)* **über etw** *(acc)* **~ werden** to agree on sth; **darüber** *or* **darin sind wir uns ~, daß ...** we are agreed that ...; **wir werden schon miteinander ~ werden** we will manage to come to an agreement; **ich bin mir selbst noch nicht ganz ~, was ...** I am still somewhat undecided as to what ...

einige *indef pron siehe* **einige(r, s).**

ein|igeln *vr sep (Mil)* to take up a position of all-round defence; *(fig)* to hide (oneself) away.

einigemal *adv* a few times.

einigen [1] *vt Volk etc* to unite; *Streitende* to reconcile.
[2] *vr* to reach (an) agreement *(über +acc* about) ◆ **sich über den Preis/eine gemeinsame Politik ~** to reach agreement *or* to agree on the price/a common policy; **sich auf einen Kompromiß/Vergleich ~** to agree to a compromise/settlement; **sich dahin (gehend) ~, daß ...** to agree that ...

Einiger *m* **-s, -** unifier.

einige(r, s) *indef pron* **(a)** *sing (etwas)* some; *(ziemlich viel)* (quite) some ◆ **in ~r Entfernung** some distance away; **nach ~r Zeit** after a while *or* some time; **ich könnte dir ~s über ihn erzählen, was ...** I could tell you a thing or two about him that ...; **das wird ~s kosten** that will cost something; **dazu ist noch ~s zu sagen** there are still one or two things to say about that; **dazu gehört schon ~s/~ Frechheit/~r Mut** that really takes something/that takes some cheek/some courage; **mit ~m guten Willen** *(mit Anstrengung)* with a bit of effort; **mit ~m guten Willen hätte der Richter ihn freisprechen können** the judge could have given him the benefit of the doubt and acquitted him.
(b) *pl* some; *(mehrere)* several; *(ein paar auch)* a few ◆ **mit ~n anderen** with several/a few others; **mit Ausnahme ~r weniger** with a few exceptions; **~ Male** several times; **~ hundert Menschen** a few hundred people; **~ Hunderte von Flaschen** hundreds of bottles, several hundred bottles; **an ~n Stellen** in some places; **in ~n Tagen** in a few days; **vor ~n Tagen** the other day, a few days ago.

einigermaßen [1] *adv (ziemlich)* rather, somewhat; *(vor adj)* fairly; *(ungefähr)* to some extent *or* degree ◆ **ein ~ gutes Angebot** a fairly good offer, not a bad offer; **~ Bescheid wissen** to have a fair idea; **er hat die Prüfung so ~ geschafft** he did so-so in the exam; **wie geht's dir? — ~** how are you? — all right *or* so-so *or* not too bad.
[2] *adj pred (inf: leidlich)* all right, fair, reasonable ◆ **wie ist denn das Hotel? — na ja, ~** what's the hotel like? — oh, fair *or* all right.

einiges *indef pron siehe* **einige(r, s).**

einiggehen *vi sep irreg aux sein* to agree, to be agreed *(in +dat* on) ◆ **ich gehe mit ihm darin einig, daß ...** I am agreed with him that ...; **wir gehen einig in der Überzeugung, daß ...** we are one in our conviction that ...

Einigkeit *f, no pl (Eintracht)* unity; *(Übereinstimmung)* agreement ◆ **in diesem** *or* **über diesen Punkt herrschte** *or* **bestand ~** there was agreement on this point; **~ macht stark** *(Prov)* unity gives strength, strength through unity (*prov*).

Einigung *f* **(a)** (*Pol*) unification. **(b)** (*Übereinstimmung*) agreement; (*Jur: Vergleich*) settlement ◆ **über etw** (*acc*) **~ erzielen** to come to *or* reach agreement on sth.

ein|impfen *vt sep* **jdm etw ~** (*lit*) to inject *or* inoculate sb with sth; **er hat seinen Kindern diese Ansichten eingeimpft** he dinned these ideas into his children.

einjagen *vt sep* **jdm Furcht/einen Schrecken ~** to frighten sb/to give sb a fright *or* a shock.

einjährig *adj Kind, Tier* one-year-old; *Pflanze* annual. **E~e** *pl* one-year-olds ◆ **nach ~er Pause** after a break of one *or* a year; **~e Frist/Dauer** a period of one *or* a year.

Einjährige(r), Einjährig-Freiwillige(r) *m decl as adj* (*Mil Hist*) one-year army volunteer.

Einjährige(s) *nt decl as adj* (*old Sch*) ≃ lower school certificate (*old*).

einkalkulieren* *vt sep* to reckon with *or* on; *Kosten* to include, to take into account.

Einkammersystem *nt* (*Pol*) single-chamber *or* unicameral (*form*) system.

einkapseln *sep* [1] *vt Tabletten* to encapsulate.
[2] *vr* (*Med*) to encapsulate (*form*); (*fig*) to withdraw *or* go into one's shell.

einkassieren* *vt sep* **(a)** *Geld, Schulden* to collect. **(b)** (*inf: wegnehmen*) to take ◆ **die Polizei hat den Dieb einkassiert** the police nabbed the criminal (*inf*); **er hat eine Ohrfeige einkassiert** he earned himself a clip on the ear.

einkasteln *vt sep* (*Aus, S Ger*) *Straftäter* to put away (*inf*), to lock up.

Einkauf *m* **(a)** (*das Einkaufen*) buying (*auch Comm*), purchase ◆ **der Sommer ist die beste Zeit für den ~ von Kohlen** summer is the best time to buy *or* for buying (in) coal; **Einkäufe machen** to go shopping; **ich muß noch ein paar Einkäufe machen** I still have a few things to buy *or* a few purchases to make.
(b) (*usu pl: Gekauftes*) purchase ◆ **ein guter** *or* **vorteilhafter/schlechter ~** a good/bad buy.
(c) *no pl* (*Comm: Abteilung*) buying (department).
(d) (*in Altersheim, Firma etc*) **durch den ~ in ein Seniorenheim** by buying oneself into an old people's home; **er versucht durch Einkäufe in diese Firma in Europa Fuß zu fassen** he is trying to get a foothold in Europe by buying up shares in this firm.
(e) (*Ftbl*) transfer.

einkaufen *sep* [1] *vt* to buy; *Vorräte* to buy (in).
[2] *vi* to shop; (*Comm*) to buy, to do the buying ◆ **~ gehen** to go shopping; **ich kaufe nur bei Müller ein** I only shop at Müllers.
[3] *vr* to buy one's way (*in +acc* into).

Einkäufer *m* (*Comm*) buyer.

Einkaufs- *in cpds* shopping; **~bummel** *m* shopping spree; **einen ~bummel machen** to go on a shopping spree; **~genossenschaft** *f* consumers' co-operative society; **~leiter** *m* (*Comm*) chief buyer; **~netz** *nt* string bag, shopping net; **~passage** *f* shopping arcade; **~preis** *m* wholesale price; (*Kaufpreis*) purchase price; **~quelle** *f* **eine gute ~quelle für etw** a good place to buy sth; **~straße** *f* shopping street; **~tasche** *f* shopping bag; **~viertel** *nt* shopping area; **~wagen** *m* shopping trolley (*Brit*) *or* cart (*US*); **~zentrum** *nt* shopping centre; **~zettel** *m* shopping list.

Einkehr *f* **-**, *no pl* **(a)** (*in Gasthaus*) stop ◆ **in einem Gasthaus ~ halten** to (make a) stop at an inn. **(b)** (*geh: Besinnung*) self-examination, reflection ◆ **bei sich ~ halten** to look into *or* search one's heart.

einkehren *vi sep aux sein* **(a)** (*in Gasthof*) to (make a) stop, to stop off (*in +dat* at); (*bei Freunden*) to call in (*bei* on). **(b)** (*Ruhe, Friede*) to come (*bei* to); (*Not, Sorge*) to come (*bei* upon, to) ◆ **wieder ~** to return (*bei* to).

einkeilen *vt sep siehe* **eingekeilt**.

einkellern *vt sep* to store in a cellar.

einkerben *vt sep* to cut a notch/notches in, to notch; (*schnitzen*) to cut, to chip.

Einkerbung *f* notch.

einkerkern *vt sep* to incarcerate.

Einkerkerung *f* incarceration.

einkesseln *vt sep* to encircle, to surround.

Einkesselung *f* encirclement, surrounding.

einkitten *vt sep* to fix with putty (*in +acc* in).

einklagbar *adj Schulden* (legally) recoverable.

einklagen *vt sep Schulden* to sue for (the recovery of).

einklammern *vt sep* to put in brackets, to put brackets around; (*fig*) *Thema, Frage* to leave aside.

Einklang *m* **(a)** (*Mus*) unison.
(b) (*geh: Übereinstimmung*) harmony ◆ **in ~ bringen** to bring into line; **in** *or* **im ~ mit etw stehen** to be in accord with sth; **seine Worte und Taten stehen nicht miteinander im** *or* **in ~** his words and deeds were at variance *or* not in accord with one another.

Einklassenschule *f* one-class school.

einklassig *adj Schule* one-class *attr*.

einkleben *vt sep* to stick in (*in +acc* -to).

einkleiden *vt sep Soldaten* to fit *or* kit out (with a uniform); *Novizen* to accept (as a novice); (*fig*) *Gedanken* to couch ◆ **jdn/sich völlig neu ~** to buy sb/oneself a completely new wardrobe.

Einkleidung *f* **(a)** (*das Einkleiden*) fitting out; acceptance as a novice; (*von Gedanken*) couching. **(b)** (*Verhüllung*) veil ◆ **in mystischer ~** veiled in mysticism.

einklemmen *vt sep* **(a)** (*quetschen*) to jam; *Finger etc* to catch, to get caught ◆ **er hat sich/mir die Hand in der Tür eingeklemmt** he caught his/my hand in the door; **der Fahrer war hinter dem Steuer eingeklemmt** the driver was pinned behind the wheel.
(b) (*festdrücken*) to clamp ◆ **der Hund klemmte den Schwanz ein** the dog put his tail between his legs; **eingeklemmter Bruch** (*Med*) strangulated hernia.

einklinken *sep* [1] *vt Tür etc* to latch; *Segelflugzeug, Leine* to hitch up ◆ **die Tür ist eingeklinkt** the door is on the latch.
[2] *vi* (*Verschluß, Sicherheitsgurt*) to click shut; (*Tech: einrasten*) to engage.

einklopfen *vt sep Nagel etc* to knock in (*in +acc* -to); *Hautcreme etc* to pat in (*in +acc* -to).

einkneifen *vt sep irreg Lippen* to press together; *Schwanz* (*lit*) to put between its legs ◆ **mit eingekniffenem Schwanz** (*lit, fig inf*) with his *etc* tail between his *etc* legs.

einknicken *sep* [1] *vt Papier* to crease (over); *Streichholz, Äste* to snap.
[2] *vi aux sein* (*Strohhalm*) to get bent; (*Äste*) to snap; (*Knie*) to give way, to buckle ◆ **er knickt immer mit den Knien ein** his knees are always giving way; **mein Knöchel** *or* **Fuß knickt dauernd ein** I'm always going over on my ankle.

einknöpfbar *adj Futter* attachable.

einknöpfen *vt sep Futter* to button in.

einknüppeln *vi sep* **auf jdn ~** to beat sb (up) with cudgels; (*Polizei*) to beat sb (up) with batons *or* truncheons; (*fig*) to lash sb.

einkochen *sep* [1] *vt Gemüse* to preserve; *Obst auch, Marmelade* to bottle.
[2] *vi aux sein* (*Marmelade etc*) to boil down; (*Wasser*) to boil away; (*Soße*) to thicken.

Einkochtopf *m* preserving pan.

einkommen *vi sep irreg aux sein* (*form*) **(a)** (*eingenommen werden: Geld*) to come in. **(b)** **(bei jdm) um etw ~** to apply (to sb) for sth. **(c)** (*Sport, Naut*) to come in.

Einkommen *nt* **-s, -** income.

Einkommens-: ~ausfall *m* loss of income; **~gefälle** *nt* income differential; **~grenze** *f* income limit; **~klasse** *f* income bracket; **e~los** *adj* (*form*) **e~los sein** to have no income, to be without an income; **e~schwach** *adj* low-income *attr*; **e~stark** *adj* high-income *attr*; **die ~starken** people in a high-income bracket.

Einkommen(s)steuer *f* income tax.

Einkommen(s)steuer-: ~erklärung *f* income tax return; **e~pflichtig** *adj* liable to income tax; **~veranlagung** *f* income tax coding.

Einkommens-: ~verhältnisse *pl* (level of) income; **~verteilung** *f* distribution of income; **~zuwachs** *m* increase in income.

einköpfen *vti sep* (*Ftbl*) to head in (*in +acc* -to) ◆ **Müller köpfte zum 1:0 ein** Müller's header made the score 1-0.

einkrachen *vi sep aux sein* (*inf*) to crash down.

einkreisen *vt sep Feind, Wild* to surround; (*fig*) *Frage, Problem* to consider from all sides; (*Pol*) to isolate.

Einkreisung *f* surrounding; (*von Frage, Problem*) systematic consideration; (*Pol*) isolation.

Einkreisungspolitik *f* policy of isolation.

einkremen *vt sep siehe* **eincremen**.

einkriegen *sep* (*inf*) [1] *vt* to catch up.
[2] *vr* **sie konnte sich gar nicht mehr darüber ~, wie/daß** ... she couldn't get over how/the fact that ...; **krieg dich mal wieder ein!** control yourself!

Einkünfte *pl* income *sing*; (*einer Firma auch*) receipts.

einkuppeln *sep* [1] *vi* (*Aut*) to let the clutch in, to engage the clutch.
[2] *vt Eisenbahnwaggon* to couple (up).

➤ **einladen** *vt sep irreg* **(a)** *Waren* to load (*in +acc* into).
➤ **(b)** to invite ◆ **jdn zu einer Party/ins Kino ~** to invite *or* ask sb to a party/to ask sb to the cinema; **jdn auf ein Bier ~** to invite sb for a beer; **laß mal, ich lade dich ein** come on, this one's on me; **wir sind heute abend eingeladen** we've been invited out this evening; **er traut sich nicht, das Mädchen einzuladen** he doesn't dare ask the girl out; **dieses hübsche Plätzchen lädt zum Bleiben ein** it's very tempting to linger in this pretty spot; **das lädt ja geradezu zum Stehlen/Einbrechen ein** that's inviting theft/a break-in, that's asking to be stolen/broken into.
(c) (*Sw*) *siehe* **auffordern**.

einladend *adj* inviting; *Speisen* appetizing.

➤ **Einladung** *f* **(a)** invitation ◆ **einer ~ Folge leisten** (*form*) to accept an invitation. **(b)** (*Sw*) *siehe* **Aufforderung**.

Einladungs-: ~karte *f* invitation (card); **~schreiben** *nt* (official) invitation.

Einlage *f* **-, -n (a)** (*Zahn~*) temporary filling.
(b) (*Schuh~*) insole; (*zum Stützen*) (arch) support.
(c) (*Sew*) padding; (*Versteifung*) interfacing.
(d) (*in Brief, Paket*) enclosure ◆ **einen Prospekt als ~ beilegen** to enclose a pamphlet.
(e) (*Cook*) *noodles, vegetables, egg etc added to a clear soup*.
(f) (*Zwischenspiel*) interlude.
(g) (*Fin: Kapital~*) investment; (*Spar~ auch*) deposit; (*Spiel~*) stake.

einlagern *sep* [1] *vt* to store.
[2] *vr* to become deposited (*in +acc or dat* in); (*Met*) to settle.

Einlagerung *f* **(a)** storage. **(b)** (*Geol*) deposit.

einlangen *vi sep aux sein* (*Aus*) to arrive.

⚠ **Einlaß** *m* **-sses, ¨-sse (a)** *no pl* (*Zutritt*) admission ◆ **jdm ~ gewähren** to admit sb; **sich** (*dat*) **~ in etw** (*acc*) **verschaffen** to gain entry *or* admission to sth. **(b)** (*Tech: Öffnung*) inlet, opening.

einlassen *sep irreg* [1] *vt* **(a)** (*eintreten lassen*) to let in, to admit.
(b) (*einlaufen lassen*) *Wasser* to run (*in +acc* into) ◆ **er ließ sich** (*dat*) **ein Bad ein**

he ran himself a bath.
(c) (*einpassen, einfügen*) to let in (*in +acc* -to); (*in Holz, Metall auch*) to set in (*in +acc* -to) ◆ **ein eingelassener Schrank** a built-in cupboard, a cupboard let into the wall; **eingelassene Schraube** countersunk screw.
(d) (*Aus*) *Boden, Möbel* to varnish.
2 *vr* **(a) sich auf etw** (*acc*) ~ (*auf Angelegenheit, Abenteuer, Diskussion, Liebschaft*) to get involved in sth; (*auf Streit, zwielichtiges Unternehmen auch*) to get mixed up in sth, to get into sth; (*sich zu etw verpflichten*) to let oneself in for sth; **sich auf einen Kompromiß** ~ to agree to a compromise; **sich in ein Gespräch** ~ to get into (a) *or* get involved in a conversation; **ich lasse mich auf keine Diskussion ein** I'm not having any discussion about it; **darauf lasse ich mich nicht ein!** (*bei Geschäft, Angelegenheit*) I don't want anything to do with it; (*bei Kompromiß, Handel etc*) I'm not agreeing to that; **lasse dich in keine Schlägerei ein!** don't you go getting mixed up in any rough stuff; **da habe ich mich aber auf etwas eingelassen!** I've let myself in for something there!
(b) sich mit jdm ~ (*pej: Umgang pflegen mit*) to get mixed up *or* involved with sb; **er ließ sich mit diesem Flittchen ein** he was carrying on with this tarty little bit (*pej inf*); **sie läßt sich mit jedem ein!** she'll go with anyone.
(c) (*Jur: sich äußern*) to testify (*zu* on).

Einlassung *f* (*Jur*) testimony.

Einlauf *m* **(a)** *no pl* (*Sport*) (*am Ziel*) finish; (*ins Stadion etc*) entry ◆ **beim** ~ **in die Zielgerade ...** coming into the final straight ...
(b) (*Med*) enema ◆ **jdm einen** ~ **machen** to give sb an enema.
(c) (*Cook*) (~*suppe*) *soup with egg and/or beurre manié added.*
(d) (*Comm: Post*) *siehe* **Eingang (b).**
(e) (*rare:* ~*öffnung*) opening.

einlaufen *sep irreg* **1** *vi aux sein* **(a)** to come in (*in +acc* -to); (*ankommen auch*) to arrive (*in +acc* in); (*Sport*) (*ins Stadion*) to come *or* run in (*in +acc* -to), to enter (*in etw* (*acc*) sth); (*durchs Ziel*) to finish ◆ **das Schiff läuft in den Hafen ein** the ship is coming into *or* entering the harbour; *siehe* **Zielgerade.**
(b) (*hineinlaufen: Wasser*) to run in (*in +acc* -to).
(c) (*eintreffen*) *Post* to arrive; *Bewerbungen, Spenden* to be received, to come in.
(d) (*eingehen: Stoff*) to shrink ◆ **garantiert kein E~** guaranteed non-shrink.
2 *vt Schuhe* to wear in.
3 *vr* (*Motor, Maschine*) to run in, to be broken in (*US*); (*Sport*) to warm *or* limber up; (*fig: Geschäfte*) to settle down.

Einlaufwette *f* (*Pferderennen*) three-way bet.

einläuten *vt sep Sonntag etc* to ring in; (*Sport*) *Runde* to sound the bell for.

einleben *vr sep* to settle down (*in or an +dat* in); (*fig: sich hineinversetzen*) to immerse oneself (*in +acc* in).

Einlege|arbeit *f* inlay work *no pl.*

einlegen *vt sep* **(a)** (*in Holz etc*) to inlay ◆ **eingelegte Arbeit** inlay work.
(b) (*hineintun*) to insert (*in +acc* in), to put in (*in +acc* -to); *Film auch* to load (*in +acc* into); (*in Brief*) to enclose (*in +acc* in) ◆ **einen Pfeil (in den Bogen)** ~ to fit an arrow (into the bow).
(c) (*einfügen*) *Sonderschicht, Spurt, Sonderzug* to put on; *Lied, Kunststück, Pause* to have; (*Aut*) *Gang* to engage; (*Hist*) *Lanze* to couch.
(d) (*Fin: einzahlen*) to pay in, to deposit.
(e) (*fig: geltend machen*) *Protest* to register ◆ **ein gutes Wort für jdn** ~ to put in a good word for sb (*bei* with); **sein Veto** ~ to exercise *or* use one's veto; *siehe* **Ehre, Berufung.**
(f) (*Cook*) *Heringe, Gurken etc* to pickle.
(g) *Haare* to set, to put in rollers.

Einleger(in *f***)** *m* **-s, -** investor.

Einlege-: ~sohle *f* insole; **~tisch** *m* inlaid table.

einleiten *sep* **1** *vt* **(a)** (*in Gang setzen*) to initiate; *Maßnahmen auch, Schritte* to introduce, to take; *neues Zeitalter* to mark the start of, to inaugurate; (*Jur*) *Verfahren* to institute; (*Med*) *Geburt* to induce.
(b) (*beginnen*) to start; (*eröffnen*) to open.
(c) *Buch* (*durch Vorwort*) to write an introduction to, to introduce; (*Mus*) to prelude.
(d) *Abwässer etc* to discharge (*in +acc* into).
2 *vi* to give an introduction (*in +acc* to).

einleitend *adj* introductory; *Worte auch* of introduction ◆ **er sagte ~, daß ...** he said by way of introduction that ...

Einleitung *f* **(a)** *siehe vt* (*a*) initiation; introduction; inauguration; institution; induction. **(b)** (*Vorwort*) introduction; (*Mus*) prelude. **(c)** (*von Abwässern*) discharge (*in +acc* into).

einlenken *sep* **1** *vi* **(a)** (*fig*) to yield, to give way. **(b)** (*einbiegen*) to turn in (*in +acc* -to).
2 *vt Rakete* to steer (*in +acc* onto).

einlesen *sep irreg* **1** *vr* **sich in ein Buch/Gebiet** *etc* ~ to get into a book/ subject *etc.*
2 *vt Daten* to read in (*in +acc* -to).

einleuchten *vi sep* to be clear (*jdm* to sb) ◆ **der Grund seiner Abneigung leuchtet mir nicht ein** I don't see *or* understand *or* it's not clear to me why he doesn't like me; **ja, das leuchtet mir ein!** yes, I see that, yes, that's clear (to me); **das will mir nicht** ~ I just don't understand *or* see that.

einleuchtend *adj* reasonable, plausible.

einliefern *vt sep Waren* to deliver ◆ **jdn ins Krankenhaus** ~ to admit sb to hospital; **jdn ins Gefängnis** ~ to put sb in *or* commit sb to prison; **ein Paket bei der Post** ~ to take a parcel to the post.

Einlieferung *f* (*von Waren*) delivery; (*ins Krankenhaus*) admission (*in +acc* to); (*ins Gefängnis*) committal (*in +acc* to); (*von Briefen etc*) sending ◆ **die** ~ **von Paketen ist nur bis 17⁰⁰ möglich** parcels are not accepted after 5 pm.

Einlieferungsschein *m* certificate of posting.

einliegend *adj pred* (*form*) enclosed ◆ ~ **erhalten Sie ...** please find enclosed ...

einlochen *vt sep* **(a)** (*inf: einsperren*) to lock up, to put behind bars. **(b)** (*Golf*) to hole out.

einloggen *vr* (*Comput*) to log in *or* on ◆ **sich in das System** ~ to log into the system.

einlogieren* [-loʒiːrən] *sep* **1** *vt* to put up, to lodge.
2 *vr* **sich (bei jdm)** ~ to lodge (with sb); (*Mil*) to be billeted (with *or* on sb).

einlösbar *adj* redeemable.

einlösen *vt sep Pfand* to redeem; *Scheck, Wechsel* to cash (in); (*fig*) *Wort, Versprechen* to keep ◆ **in der Praxis läßt sich das nicht problemlos** ~ in practice that cannot easily be realized.

Einlösung *f siehe vt* redemption; cashing (in); keeping.

einlöten *vt sep* to solder in (*in +acc* -to).

einlullen *vt sep* (*inf*) *Kind* to lull to sleep; (*fig*) *Mißtrauen, Wachsamkeit* to allay, to quiet ◆ **jdn mit Versprechungen/schönen Worten** ~ to lull sb with (soothing) promises/soft words.

Einmach(e) [-max(ə)] *f* **-**, *no pl* (*Aus Cook*) roux.

einmachen *vt sep Obst, Gemüse* to preserve; (*in Gläser auch*) to bottle; (*in Dosen*) to can, to tin (*Brit*).

Einmach-: ~glas *nt* bottling jar; **~topf** *m* preserving pan; **~zucker** *m* preserving sugar.

einmahnen *vt sep* (*form*) to demand payment of.

einmal *adv* **(a)** (*ein einziges Mal*) once; (*erstens*) first of all, firstly, for a start ◆ ~ **eins ist eins** once one *or* one times one is one; ~ **sagt er dies,** ~ **das** sometimes he says one thing, sometimes another; ~ **sagte sie, wir sollten bleiben,** ~ **wir sollten gehen** first of all she says that we should stay, then that we should go; **auf** ~ (*plötzlich*) suddenly, all of a sudden, all at once; (*zugleich*) at once; ~ **mehr** once again; ~ **und nicht** *or* **nie wieder** once and never again; **noch** ~ again; **versuch's noch** ~ (*wieder*) try once more *or* again; **versuch's noch** ***einmal*** (*ein letztes Mal*) try one last time *or* just once again; **noch** ~ **so groß wie** as big again as; **wenn sie da ist, ist es noch** ~ **so schön** it's twice as nice when she's there; ~ **ist keinmal** (*Prov*) (*schadet nicht*) once won't hurt *or* do any harm; (*zählt nicht*) once doesn't count.
(b) (*früher, vorher*) once; (*später, in Zukunft*) one *or* some day ◆ **waren Sie schon** ~ **in Rom?** have you ever been to Rome?; **er hat schon** ~ **bessere Zeiten gesehen** he has seen better days; **sie waren** ~ **glücklich, aber jetzt ...** they were happy once *or* at one time, but now ...; **es war** ~ **...** once upon a time there was ...; **das war** ~**!** that was then; **besuchen Sie mich doch** ~**!** come and visit me some time!; **das wird** ~ **anders werden** things will be different some *or* one day.
(c) (*verstärkend, eingrenzend*) *meist nicht übersetzt* ◆ **nicht** ~ not even; **auch** ~ also, too; **wieder** ~ again; **ich bin/die Frauen sind nun** ~ **so** that's the way I am/women are, I'm just/women are like that; **wie die Lage nun** ~ **ist** with things as *or* the way they are; **wenn er nun** ~ **hier ist ...** seeing he's here ...; **alle** ~ **herhören!** listen everyone!; **sag** ~**, ist das wahr?** tell me, is it true?; *siehe* **erst (a).**

Einmal|eins *nt* **-**, *no pl* (multiplication) tables *pl*; (*fig*) ABC, basics *pl* ◆ **das** ~ **lernen/aufsagen** to learn/say one's tables; **das kleine/große** ~ (multiplication) tables up to/over ten.

Einmalhandtuch *nt* disposable towel.

einmalig *adj* **(a)** *Gelegenheit, Angebot, Fall* unique.
(b) (*nur einmal erforderlich*) single; *Anschaffung, Zahlung* one-off *attr* ◆ **beim ~en Durchlesen des Textes** on a single reading of the text, on reading the text through once.
(c) (*inf: hervorragend*) fantastic, amazing ◆ **dieser Film ist etwas E~es** this film is really something (*inf*); **der Bursche ist wirklich** ~ that guy is really something (*inf*).

Einmaligkeit *f* uniqueness ◆ **alle lobten die** ~ **dieses Films** everyone said how fantastic the film was.

Einmann-: ~betrieb *m* **(a)** one-man business *or* band (*inf*); **(b) die Busse auf ~betrieb umstellen** to convert the buses for one-man operation; **~bus** *m* one-man bus, driver-operated bus; **~kapelle** *f* one-man band; **~wagen** *m* one-man tram.

Einmarkstück *nt* one-mark piece.

Einmarsch *m* entry (*in +acc* into); (*in ein Land*) invasion (*in +acc* of).

einmarschieren* *vi sep aux sein* to march in (*in +acc* -to).

einmassieren* *vt sep* to massage *or* rub in (*in +acc* -to).

Einmaster *m* **-s, -** (*Naut*) single-masted ship, single-master.

einmastig *adj* single-masted.

einmauern *vt sep* **(a)** (*ummauern*) to wall in, to immure (*liter*) (*in +acc* in). **(b)** (*einfügen*) to fix into the wall.

einmeißeln *vt sep* to chisel in (*in +acc* -to).

Einmeterbrett *nt* one-metre (diving) board.

einmieten *sep* **1** *vt* (*Agr*) to clamp.
2 *vr* **sich bei jdm** ~ to take lodgings with sb; **er hat sich in der Wohnung unter uns eingemietet** he has taken the flat below us.

einmischen *sep vr* to interfere (*in +acc* in), to stick one's oar in (*inf*) ◆ **sie muß sich bei allem** ~ she has to interfere *or* meddle in everything; **wenn ich mich kurz** ~ **darf ...** if I can butt in a moment ...

Einmischung *f* interference, meddling (*in +acc* in).

einmonatig *adj attr* one-month.

einmonatlich *adj* monthly.

einmontieren* *vt sep* to slot in (*in +acc* -to); (*Tech*) to fit in (*in +acc* -to).
einmotorig *adj Flugzeug* single-engine(d).
einmotten *vt sep Kleider etc* to put in mothballs; (*fig auch*) to mothball; *Schiff, Flugzeug* to mothball.
einmumme(l)n *vt sep* (*inf*) to muffle up.
einmünden *vi sep aux sein* (*Fluß*) to flow in (*in +acc* -to); (*Straße*) to run *or* lead in (*in +acc* -to) ◆ **in etw** (*acc*) ~ *auch* to join sth; (*fig*) to end up in sth; (*Elemente, Einflüsse*) to go into sth.
Einmündung *f* (*von Fluß*) confluence; (*von Straße*) junction ◆ **die ~ der Isar in die Donau** the confluence of the Isar and the Danube.
einmütig *adj* unanimous ◆ **~ zusammenstehen** to stand together solidly *or* as a man.
Einmütigkeit *f* unanimity ◆ **darüber besteht ~** there is complete agreement on that.
einnachten *vi impers sep* (*Sw*) **es nachtet ein** it's getting dark.
einnageln *vt sep* to nail in (*in +acc* -to); (*einhämmern*) to hammer in (*in +acc* -to).
einnähen *vt sep* to sew in (*in +acc* -to); (*enger machen*) to take in.
Einnahme *f* **-, -n (a)** (*Mil*) seizure; (*einer Stellung, Stadt auch*) capture.
(b) (*Ertrag*) receipt. **~n** *pl* income *sing*; (*Geschäfts~*) takings *pl*; (*aus Einzelverkauf*) proceeds *pl*; (*Gewinn*) earnings *pl*; (*eines Staates*) revenue *sing* ◆ **~n und Ausgaben** income and expenditure.
(c) (*das Einnehmen*) taking ◆ **durch ~ von etw** by taking sth.
Einnahme-: **~ausfall** *m* loss of income; (*von Geschäften*) loss of takings; **~buch** *nt* (*Comm*) book of receipts, receipt book; **~posten** *m* item of receipt; **~quelle** *f* source of income; (*eines Staates*) source of revenue.
einnässen *sep* (*form*) [1] *vt* to wet.
[2] *vr* to wet oneself; (*nachtsüber*) to wet the bed.
einnebeln *sep* [1] *vt* (*Mil*) to put up a smokescreen round; (*fig*) to befog, to obfuscate (*liter*).
[2] *vr* (*Mil*) to put up a smokescreen (around oneself) ◆ **es nebelt sich ein** (*Met*) it's getting misty, there's a mist coming down.
einnehmen *vt sep irreg* **(a)** *Geld* (*Geschäft etc*) to take; (*Freiberufler*) to earn; *Steuern* to collect ◆ **die eingenommenen Gelder** the takings.
(b) (*Mil: erobern*) to take; *Stadt, Festung auch* to capture.
(c) (*lit, fig*) *Platz etc* to take (up), to occupy; *Stelle* (*innehaben*) to have, to occupy (*form*); *Haltung, Standpunkt etc* to take up ◆ **er nimmt vorübergehend die Stelle des Chefs ein** he is acting for the boss; **bitte, nehmen Sie Ihre Plätze ein!** (*form*) please take your seats!; **die Plätze ~** (*Sport*) to take one's marks.
(d) (*zu sich nehmen*) *Mahlzeit, Arznei* to take.
(e) er nahm uns alle für sich ein he won us all over; **er hat alle für seine Pläne eingenommen** he won everyone over to his plans; **jdn gegen sich/jdn/etw ~** to set *or* put sb against oneself/sb/sth; **das nimmt mich sehr für sie ein** that makes me think highly of her; *siehe* **eingenommen.**
einnehmend *adj* likeable ◆ **er hat etwas E~es** there is something likeable about him; **er hat ein ~es Wesen** (*gewinnend*) he's a likeable character; (*hum inf: habgierig*) he has taking ways (*hum inf*).
Einnehmer *m* (*old*) collector.
einnicken *vi sep aux sein* (*inf*) to doze *or* nod off.
einnisten *vr sep* (*lit*) to nest; (*Parasiten, Ei*) to lodge; (*fig*) to park oneself (*bei* on) ◆ **in unserem Land haben sich so viele Kriminelle eingenistet** we have so many criminals settled in this country.
Ein|öd *f* **-, -en** (*Aus*) *siehe* **Einöde.**
Ein|ödbauer *m* farmer of an isolated farm.
Ein|öde *f* **Moore/Wüsten und ~** moors and wasteland/deserts and barren wastes *pl*; **die weiße ~ der Antarktis** the white wastes of the Antarctic; **er lebt in der ~ des schottischen Hochlands** he lives in the wilds of the Scottish Highlands; **er verließ die ~ seines Schwarzwaldhofes** he left the isolation of his Black Forest farm.
Ein|ödhof *m* ≃ croft.
ein|ölen *sep* [1] *vt* to oil.
[2] *vr* to rub oneself with oil, to oil oneself.
ein|ordnen *sep* [1] *vt* **(a)** (*der Reihe nach*) *Bücher etc* to (put in) order; *Akten, Karteikarten* to file.
(b) (*klassifizieren*) to classify; *Begriff, Theorie, Denker auch* to categorize.
[2] *vr* **(a)** (*in Gemeinschaft etc*) to fit in (*in +acc* -to).
(b) (*Aut*) to get in(to) lane ◆ **sich links/rechts ~** to get into the left/right lane; **„E~"** "get in lane".
einpacken *sep* [1] *vt* **(a)** (*einwickeln*) to wrap (up) (*in +acc* in) ◆ **jdn warm ~** (*fig*) to wrap sb up warmly.
(b) (*hineintun*) to pack (*in +acc* in) ◆ **laß dich damit ~** (*inf*) forget it!; (*mit altem Witz etc*) cut it out! (*inf*); **mit deinen Witzen kannst du dich ~ lassen!** (*inf*) stuff you and your jokes! (*sl*).
(c) (*packen*) *Paket* to pack up.
[2] *vi* to pack, to do one's packing ◆ **dann können wir ~** (*inf*) in that case we may as well pack it all in (*inf*) *or* give up.
einparken *vti sep* to park ◆ **(in eine Parklücke) ~** to get into a parking space.
Einparteien- *in cpds* one-party.
einpassen *sep* [1] *vt* to fit in (*in +acc* -to).
[2] *vr* to adjust, to adapt oneself (*in +acc* to).
einpauken *vt sep* (*inf*) to mug up (on) (*Brit inf*), to cram ◆ **jdm etw ~** to drum sth into sb.
Einpauker *m* (*inf*) crammer (*pej*).
Einpeitscher *m* **-s, -** (*Pol*) whip (*Brit*), floor leader (*US*); (*inf: Antreiber*) slave-driver (*inf*).
einpendeln *sep* [1] *vi* to commute in (*in +acc* -to).
[2] *vr* (*fig*) to settle down; (*Währung, Preise etc*) to find its level, to level off.
Einpendler(in *f*) *m* commuter.
einpennen *vi sep aux sein* (*sl*) to doze off, to drop off (*inf*).
Einpersonen-: **~haushalt** *m* single-person household; **~stück** *nt* (*Theat*) one-man play.
Einpfennigstück *nt* one-pfennig piece.
einpferchen *vt sep Vieh* to pen in (*in +acc* -to); (*fig*) to coop up (*in +acc* in) ◆ **eingepfercht stehen** to be hemmed in.
einpflanzen *vt sep* to plant (*in +dat* in); (*Med*) to implant (*jdm* in(to) sb) ◆ **einem Patienten eine fremde Niere ~** to give sb a kidney transplant; **jdm etw ~** (*fig*) to imbue sb with a sense of sth, to instil (a sense of) sth into sb.
einpfropfen *vt sep* **(a)** *Korken* to put *or* bung in (*in +acc* -to). **(b)** (*fig inf*) **jdm Wissen ~** to cram knowledge into sb.
Einphasenstrom, Einphasenwechselstrom *m* single-phase current.
einphasig *adj* single-phase.
einpinseln *vt sep Wunde, Mandeln* to paint; (*Cook*) to brush.
einplanen *vt sep* to plan (on), to include in one's plans; *Verzögerungen, Verluste* to allow for; *Baby* to plan.
einpökeln *vt sep Fisch, Fleisch* to salt ◆ **eingepökeltes Rindfleisch** salt beef.
einpolig *adj* single-pole.
einprägen *sep* [1] *vt Muster, Spuren* to imprint, to impress; *Inschrift* to stamp ◆ **ein Muster in Papier ~** to emboss paper with a pattern; **sich** (*dat*) **etw ~** to remember sth; (*auswendig lernen*) to memorize sth, to commit sth to memory.
[2] *vr* **sich jdm ins Gedächtnis/sich jdm ~** to make an impression on sb's mind/sb; **die Worte haben sich mir unauslöschlich eingeprägt** the words made an indelible impression on me.
einprägsam *adj* easily remembered; *Slogan, Melodie auch* catchy ◆ **er kann sehr ~ formulieren** he can put things in a way that is easy to remember.
einprasseln *vi sep aux sein* **auf jdn ~** to rain down on sb, to come pouring down on sb; (*Fragen*) to be showered upon sb; **von allen Seiten prasselten Geschosse auf uns ein** we were caught in a hail of shots from all sides.
einpressen *vt sep* to press in (*in +acc* -to).
einproben *vt sep* to rehearse.
einprogrammieren* *vt sep Daten* to feed in; (*fig*) to take into account ◆ **jdm etw ~** (*fig*) to inculcate sth in sb.
einprügeln *sep* (*inf*) [1] *vt* **jdm etw ~** to din (*inf*) *or* drum sth into sb.
[2] *vi* **auf jdn ~** to lay into sb.
einpudern *sep* [1] *vr* to powder oneself.
[2] *vt* to powder.
einpuppen *vr sep* (*Zool*) to pupate.
einquartieren* *sep* [1] *vt* to quarter; (*Mil auch*) to billet ◆ **Gäste bei Freunden ~** to put visitors up with friends.
[2] *vr* to be quartered (*bei* with); (*Mil auch*) to be billeted (*bei* on); (*Gäste*) to stop (*bei* with) (*inf*) ◆ **er hat sich bei uns anscheinend für ewig einquartiert** he seems to have dumped himself on us for good (*inf*).
Einquartierung *f* **(a)** (*das Einquartieren*) quartering; (*Mil auch*) billeting. **(b) wir haben ~** (*inf*) (*Soldaten*) we have soldiers billeted on us; (*Besuch*) we've got people staying *or* stopping (*inf*) (with us).
einquetschen *vt sep siehe* **einklemmen (a).**
Einrad *nt* unicycle.
einräd(e)rig *adj* (*Schub*)*karren* one-wheeled.
einrahmen *vt sep* (*lit, fig*) to frame ◆ **von zwei Schönen eingerahmt** with a beauty on either side; **das kannst du dir ~ lassen!** (*inf*) you ought to get that framed!
einrammen *vt sep Stadttor* to batter down *or* in; *Pfähle* to ram in (*in +acc* -to).
einrasten *vti sep* (*vi: aux sein*) to engage.
einräuchern *vt sep* **(a)** to envelop in smoke ◆ **die Polizei räucherte die Demonstranten mit Tränengas ein** the police used tear gas against the demonstrators. **(b)** (*inf*) *Zimmer* to fill with smoke, to smoke up; *Gardinen* to make reek of smoke.
einräumen *vt sep* **(a)** *Wäsche, Bücher etc* to put away; *Schrank, Regal etc* to fill; *Wohnung, Zimmer* to arrange; *Möbel* to move in (*in +acc* -to) ◆ **Bücher ins Regal/in einen Schrank ~** to put books on the shelf/in the cupboard; **er war mir beim E~ behilflich** he helped me sort things out; (*der Wohnung*) he helped me move in.
(b) (*zugestehen*) to concede, to admit; *Freiheiten etc* to allow; *Frist, Kredit* to give, to grant, to allow ◆ **jdm das Recht ~, etw zu tun** to give *or* grant sb the right to do sth, to allow sb to do sth; **~de Konjunktion** concessive conjunction.
Einräumungssatz *m* (*Gram*) concessive clause.
einrechnen *vt sep* to include ◆ **ihn (mit) eingerechnet** including him; **Mehrwertsteuer eingerechnet** including VAT, inclusive of VAT.
Einrede *f* (*form*) *siehe* **Einspruch.**
einreden *sep* [1] *vt* **jdm etw ~** to talk sb into believing sth, to persuade sb of sth; **sie hat ihm eingeredet, er sei dumm** she persuaded him that *or* talked him into believing that he was stupid; **das lasse ich mir nicht ~** you're not going to make me believe that; **wer hat dir denn diesen Unsinn eingeredet?** who put that rubbish into your head?; **er will mir ~, daß ...** he'd have me believe *or* he wants me to believe that ...; **sich** (*dat*) **etw ~** to talk oneself into believing sth, to make oneself believe sth; **das redest du dir nur ein!** you're only imagining it.
[2] *vi* **auf jdn ~** to keep on and on at sb.
einregnen *sep* [1] *vi aux sein* **(a)** to get soaked (through).

(b) (*fig*) (*Vorwürfe*) to rain down (*auf +acc* onto, on) ◆ **wilde Drohungen regneten auf uns ein** wild threats were hurled at us.
[2] *vr* **es hat sich eingeregnet** the rain has set in.
einreiben *vt sep irreg* **er rieb sich** (*dat*) **das Gesicht mit Schnee/Creme ein** he rubbed snow over/cream into his face.
Einreibung *f* **~en verordnen** to prescribe embrocation.
einreichen *vt sep* (a) *Antrag, Unterlagen* to submit (*bei* to); (*Jur*) *Klage* to file; *siehe* **Abschied (b).**
(b) (*bitten um*) *Versetzung, Pensionierung* to apply for, to request.
(c) (*inf*) **jdn für/zu etw ~** to recommend sb for sth, to put sb up for sth (*inf*).
Einreichung *f, no pl siehe vt* (*a, b*) submission; filing; application, request.
einreihen *sep* [1] *vt* (*einordnen, einfügen*) to put in (*in +acc* -to); (*klassifizieren*) to class, to classify ◆ **dieses Buch verdient, in die bedeutendste medizinische Fachliteratur eingereiht zu werden** this book deserves to be awarded a place amongst the most important works of medical literature; **er wurde in den Arbeitsprozeß eingereiht** he was fitted into *or* given a place in the work process.
[2] *vr* **sich in etw** (*acc*) **~** to join sth.
Einreiher *m* **-s, -** single-breasted suit/jacket/coat.
einreihig *adj Anzug, Jackett, Mantel* single-breasted.
Einreise *f* entry (*in +acc* into, to) ◆ **bei der ~ in die DDR** when entering the GDR, on entry to the GDR.
Einreise-: ~erlaubnis, ~genehmigung *f* entry permit.
einreisen *vi sep aux sein* to enter the country ◆ **er reiste in die Schweiz ein** he entered Switzerland; **ein- und ausreisen** to enter and leave the country.
Einreise-: ~verbot *nt* refusal of entry; **~verbot haben** to have been refused entry; **~visum** *nt* entry visa.
einreißen *sep irreg* [1] *vt* (a) *Papier, Stoff, Nagel* to tear ◆ **ich habe mir einen Splitter in den Zeh eingerissen** I've got a splinter in my toe. (b) *Zaun, Barrikaden* to tear *or* pull down.
[2] *vi aux sein* (*Papier*) to tear; (*fig inf: Unsitte etc*) to catch on (*inf*), to get to be a habit (*inf*).
einreiten *sep irreg* [1] *vt Pferd* to break in.
[2] *vi aux sein* (*in die Manege etc*) to ride in (*in +acc* -to).
[3] *vr* to warm up ◆ **sich mit einem Pferd ~** to get used to riding a particular horse.
einrenken *sep* [1] *vt Gelenk, Knie* to put back in place, to reduce (*spec*); (*fig inf*) to sort out.
[2] *vr* (*fig inf*) to sort itself out.
einrennen *vt sep irreg* (*inf*) *Mauer, Tür etc* to batter *or* break down ◆ **sich** (*dat*) **den Kopf an der Wand ~** to bang *or* bash (*inf*) one's head against the wall; *siehe* **offen.**
einrichten *sep* [1] *vt* (a) (*möblieren*) *Wohnung, Zimmer* to furnish; (*ausstatten*) *Hobbyraum, Spielzimmer* to fit out; *Praxis, Labor* to equip, to fit out ◆ **eine Wohnung antik/modern ~** to furnish a flat in an old/a modern style; **seine Wohnung neu ~** to refurnish one's flat; **Wohnungen im Dachgeschoß ~** to convert the attic into flats.
(b) (*gründen, eröffnen*) to set up; *Lehrstuhl* to establish; *Konto* to open; *Katalog, Buslinie etc* to start.
(c) (*einstellen*) *Maschine* to set up; *Motor* to set (*auf +acc* for); (*Mil*) *Geschütz* to aim (*auf +acc* at).
(d) (*bearbeiten*) *Musikstück* to arrange; *Theaterstück* to adapt.
(e) (*fig: arrangieren*) to arrange, to fix (*inf*) ◆ **ich werde es ~, daß wir um zwei Uhr da sind** I'll see to it that we're there at two; **das läßt sich ~** that can be arranged; **das Leben/die Welt ist nun einmal nicht so eingerichtet** life/the world isn't like that.
(f) (*Med*) *Arm, Knochen* to set.
[2] *vr* (a) (*sich möblieren*) **sich ~/neu ~** to furnish/refurnish one's flat/house; *siehe* **häuslich.**
(b) (*sich der Lage anpassen*) to get along *or* by, to manage; (*sparsam sein*) to cut down ◆ **er hat sich im bürgerlichen Leben eingerichtet** he has settled down into middle-class life.
(c) **sich auf etw** (*acc*) **~** to prepare oneself for sth; **sich auf eine lange Wartezeit ~** to be prepared for a long wait; **auf Tourismus/warme Speisen eingerichtet sein** to be geared to tourism/equipped for hot meals.
Einrichtung *f* (a) (*das Einrichten*) (*von Wohnung, Zimmer*) furnishing; (*von Hobbyraum, Spielzimmer*) fitting-out; (*von Labor, Praxis*) equipping; (*von Maschine*) setting-up; (*von Geschütz*) aiming; (*Med*) setting.
(b) (*Bearbeitung*) (*Mus*) arrangement; (*Theat*) adaptation.
(c) (*Wohnungs~*) furnishings *pl*; (*Geschäfts~ etc*) fittings *pl*; (*Labor~ etc*) equipment *no pl*.
(d) (*Gründung, Eröffnung*) setting-up; (*von Lehrstuhl*) establishment; (*von Konto*) opening; (*von Katalog, Busverkehr*) starting.
(e) (*behördlich, wohltätig*) institution; (*Schwimmbäder, Transportmittel etc*) facility.
(f) (*Gewohnheit*) **zur ständigen ~ werden** to become an institution.
Einrichtungs-: ~gegenstand *m* item of furniture; (*Geschäftseinrichtung*) fitment; **~haus** *nt* furnishing house.
einriegeln *vtr sep* **jdn/sich ~** to lock sb/oneself in (*in +dat* -to).
Einritt *m* entry (*in +acc* into).
einritzen *vt sep* to carve in (*in +acc* -to).
einrollen *sep* [1] *vt* (*einwickeln*) to roll up (*in +acc* in); (*Hockey*) to roll on (*in +acc* -to) ◆ **sich** (*dat*) **das Haar ~** to put one's hair in rollers.
[2] *vi aux sein* to roll in (*in +acc* -to).
[3] *vr* to roll up; (*Tier etc auch*) to roll oneself up.

einrosten *vi sep aux sein* to rust up; (*fig: Glieder*) to stiffen up ◆ **mein Latein ist ziemlich eingerostet** my Latin has got pretty rusty.
einrücken *sep* [1] *vt Zeile* to indent; *Anzeige* (*in Zeitung*) to insert.
[2] *vi aux sein* (*Mil*) (a) (*in ein Land*) to move in (*in +acc* -to); (*wieder ~*) to return (*in +acc* to). (b) (*eingezogen werden*) to report for duty; (*nach Urlaub etc*) to report back.
einrühren *vt sep* to stir *or* mix in (*in +acc* -to); (*Cook*) *Ei* to beat in (*in +acc* -to).
einrüsten *vt sep Haus* to put scaffolding around.
eins *num* one ◆ **es ist/schlägt ~** it's one/just striking one (o'clock); **~, zwei, drei** (*lit*) one, two, three; (*fig*) in a trice, in no time; **das ist ~, zwei, drei geschehen** (*fig*) it doesn't/won't take a second; **~ zu ~** (*Sport*) one all; **~ mit jdm sein** to be one with sb; (*übereinstimmen*) to be in agreement with sb; **sich mit jdm ~ wissen** to know one is in agreement with sb; **das ist doch alles ~** (*inf*) it's all one *or* all the same; **es ist mir alles ~** (*inf*) it's all one *or* all the same to me; **sehen und handeln waren ~** to see was to act; **~ a** (*inf*) A 1 (*inf*), first-rate (*inf*); *siehe auch* **ein[2], eine(r, s), vier.**
Eins *f* **-, -en** one; (*Sch auch*) A, alpha ◆ **er würfelte zwei ~en** he threw two ones; **eine ~ schreiben/bekommen** to get an A *or* alpha *or* a one; *siehe* **Vier.**
einsacken[1] *vt sep* (a) (*in Säcke füllen*) to put in sacks, to sack. (b) (*inf*) (*erbeuten*) to grab (*inf*); *Geld, Gewinne* to rake in (*inf*).
einsacken[2] *vi sep aux sein* (*einsinken*) to sink; (*Bürgersteig, Boden etc auch*) to subside.
einsagen *sep* (*dial*) [1] *vi* **jdm ~** to prompt sb.
[2] *vt* **jdm etw ~** to whisper sth to sb.
einsalben *vt sep* to rub with ointment; *Wunde, Hände auch* to rub ointment into.
einsalzen *vt sep irreg Fisch, Fleisch* to salt ◆ **laß dich ~!** (*inf*) get stuffed (*sl*) *or* knotted! (*inf*).
einsam *adj* (a) *Mensch, Leben, Gefühl* (*allein, verlassen*) lonely; (*einzeln*) solitary ◆ **~ leben** to live a lonely/solitary life; **sich ~ fühlen** to feel lonely *or* lonesome (*esp US*); **ein ~es Boot/ein ~er Schwimmer** a lone *or* solitary boat/swimmer; **~ überragt dieser Gipfel die anderen** this peak towers over the others in solitary splendour.
(b) (*abgelegen*) *Haus, Insel* secluded; *Dorf* isolated; (*menschenleer*) empty; *Strände* lonely, empty ◆ **~ liegen** to be secluded/isolated.
(c) (*inf: hervorragend*) **~e Klasse/Spitze** absolutely fantastic (*inf*), really great (*inf*).
Einsamkeit *f siehe adj* (a) loneliness; solitariness ◆ **er liebt die ~** he likes solitude; **die ~ vieler alter Leute** the loneliness of many old people. (b) seclusion; isolation; emptiness; loneliness ◆ **die ~ der Bergwelt** the solitude of the mountains.
Einsamkeitsgefühl *nt* feeling of loneliness.
einsammeln *vt sep* to collect (in); *Obst* to gather (in).
einsargen *vt sep* to put in a coffin ◆ **laß dich (doch) ~!** (*inf*) (go and) take a running jump! (*inf*), get stuffed! (*sl*).
Einsatz *m* (a) (*~teil*) inset; (*Schubladen~, Koffer~*) tray; (*Topf~*) compartment; (*Blusen~*) *false blouse etc collar and neck to wear under pullover*; (*Hemd~*) dicky (*dated*).
(b) (*Spiel~*) stake; (*Kapital~*) investment ◆ **den ~ erhöhen** to raise the stakes; **mit dem ~ herauskommen, den ~ heraushaben** (*inf*) to recover one's stake.
(c) (*Mus*) entry; (*Theat*) entrance ◆ **der Dirigent gab den ~** the conductor raised his bâton and brought in the orchestra; **der Dirigent gab den Geigern den ~** the conductor brought in the violins; **der ~ der Streicher war verfrüht** the strings came in too early.
(d) (*Verwendung*) use; (*esp Mil*) deployment; (*von Arbeitskräften*) employment ◆ **im ~** in use; **die Ersatzspieler kamen nicht zum ~** the reserves weren't put in *or* used; **unter ~ von Schlagstöcken** using truncheons; **unter ~ aller Kräfte** by making a supreme effort.
(e) (*Aktion*) (*Mil*) action, operation; (*von Polizei*) operation ◆ **im ~** in action; **wo war er im ~?** where did he see action?; **zum ~ kommen** to go into action; **bei seinem ersten ~** the first time he went into action; **sich zum ~ melden** to report for duty; **die Pfadfinder halfen in freiwilligen ~en** the scouts helped on a voluntary basis.
(f) (*Hingabe*) commitment ◆ **in selbstlosem ~ ihres Lebens** with a complete disregard for her own life; **etw unter ~ seines Lebens tun** to risk one's life to do sth, to do sth at the risk of one's life; **den ~ des eigenen Lebens nicht scheuen** (*geh*) not to hesitate to sacrifice one's own life.
Einsatz-: ~befehl *m* order to go into action; **e~bereit** *adj* ready for use; (*Mil*) ready for action; *Rakete etc* operational; **~bereitschaft** *f* readiness for use; (*Mil*) readiness for action; (*Bereitschaftsdienst*) stand-by (duty); **e~fähig** *adj* fit for use; (*Mil*) fit for action; *Sportler* fit; **~freude** *f* willing application; **e~freudig** *adj* eager (for action), enthusiastic; **~gruppe** *f*, **~kommando** (*Mil*) *nt* task force; **~leiter** *m* head of operations; **~plan** *m* plan of action; **~stück** *nt* (*Tech*) insert; (*Zubehörteil*) attachment; **~wagen** *m* police car; fire engine; ambulance; (*bei Straßenbahn, Bus*) extra tram/bus.
einsaugen *vt sep* (*lit, fig*) to soak up, to absorb; (*durch Strohhalm etc*) to suck; (*einatmen*) to breathe in; *frische Luft* to draw *or* suck in; *siehe* **Muttermilch.**
einsäumen *vt sep* (*Sew*) to hem; (*fig*) to edge, to line.
einschalten *sep* [1] *vt* (a) (*in Betrieb setzen*) to switch *or* turn *or* put on; *Sender* to tune in to.
(b) (*einfügen*) to interpolate; *Zitat, Erklärung etc auch* to include (*in +acc* in).
(c) **jdn ~** to call sb in; **jdn in etw** (*acc*) **~** to bring sb into sth *or* in on sth.
[2] *vr* to intervene; (*teilnehmen*) to join in ◆ **wir schalten uns jetzt in die Sendungen von Radio Bremen ein** we now go over to *or* join Radio Bremen.

Einschalt-: ~hebel *m* starting lever *or* handle; **~quote** *f* (*Rad, TV*) viewing figures *pl*.
Einschaltung *f* (**a**) (*von Licht, Motor etc*) switching *or* turning on. (**b**) (*von Nebensatz etc*) interpolation; (*von Zitat*) inclusion. (**c**) (*von Person, Organisation*) calling *or* bringing in.
Einschalung(sarbeit) *f* (*Build*) formwork.
einschärfen *vt sep* **jdm etw ~** to impress sth (up)on sb; *Höflichkeit, Rücksichtnahme etc* to inculcate sth in sb; **er hat uns Vorsicht eingeschärft** he impressed on us the need for caution; **ich habe den Kindern eingeschärft, Fremden gegenüber vorsichtig zu sein** I have impressed upon the children to be careful of strangers; **schärf dir das ein!** get that firmly fixed in your mind.
einscharren *vt sep* to cover with earth.
➤ **einschätzen** *vt sep* to assess (*auch Fin*), to evaluate; (*schätzen auch*) to estimate ◆ **falsch ~** to misjudge; (*falsch schätzen*) to miscalculate; **wie ich die Lage einschätze** as I see the situation; **jdn sehr hoch/niedrig ~** to have a very high/low opinion of sb; **etw zu hoch/niedrig ~** to overestimate/underestimate sth; **jdn/sich zu hoch/niedrig ~** to overrate/underrate sb/oneself, to have too high/low an opinion of sb/oneself.
Einschätzung *f siehe vt* assessment, evaluation; estimation ◆ **falsche ~** misjudgement; miscalculation; **nach meiner ~** in my estimation.
einschäumen *sep* [1] *vt* (**a**) to lather. (**b**) (*Tech*) to pack in plastic foam.
[2] *vr* to lather oneself.
einschenken *vt sep* to pour (out) ◆ **darf ich Ihnen noch Wein ~?** can I give *or* pour you some more wine?
einscheren *sep* [1] *vi aux sein* to get back.
[2] *vt Tau* to reeve.
einschichtig *adj* (**a**) single-layered. (**b**) *Arbeitstag* single-shift ◆ **unsere Fabrik arbeitet ~** our factory works a single shift.
einschicken *vt sep* to send in (*an +acc* to).
einschieben *vt sep irreg* (**a**) (*hineinschieben*) to put in (*in +acc* -to) ◆ **lässig schob er zum 2:0 ein** (*Ftbl sl*) he casually put it away to make it 2-0 (*inf*).
(**b**) (*einfügen*) to put in; *Sonderzüge* to put on; (*dazwischenschieben*) *Diskussion, Schüler, Patienten* to fit *or* squeeze (*inf*) in (*in +acc* -to) ◆ **eine Pause ~** to have a break.
Einschiebsel *nt* insertion.
Einschienenbahn *f* monorail.
einschießen *sep irreg* [1] *vt* (**a**) (*zertrümmern*) *Fenster* to shoot in; (*mit Ball etc*) to smash (in).
(**b**) *Gewehr* to try out and adjust.
(**c**) (*Tech*) *Dübel etc* to insert.
(**d**) *Fäden* to weave in ◆ **ein Gewebe mit eingeschossenen Goldfäden** a cloth shot with gold (thread).
(**e**) (*Typ*) *Seiten, Blätter* to interleave.
(**f**) *Fußball* to kick in ◆ **Müller schoß den Ball zum 2:0 ein** Müller scored to make it 2-0.
(**g**) (*Comm*) *Geld* to inject (*in +acc* into).
[2] *vr* to find one's range, to get one's eye in ◆ **sich auf ein Ziel ~** to get the range of a target; **sich auf jdn ~** (*fig*) to line sb up for the kill.
[3] *vi* (**a**) (*Sport*) to score ◆ **er schoß zum 1:0 ein** he scored to make it 1-0.
(**b**) *aux sein* (*Med*) **die Milch schießt in die Brust ein** the milk comes in.
(**c**) **auf jdn ~** to shoot at sb.
einschiffen *sep* [1] *vt* to ship.
[2] *vr* to embark ◆ **er schiffte sich in London nach Amerika ein** he boarded a ship in London for America.
Einschiffung *f* (*von Personen*) boarding, embarkation; (*von Gütern*) loading.
einschirren *vt sep Pferd* to harness.
einschl. *abbr of* **einschließlich** incl.
einschlafen *vi sep irreg aux sein* to fall asleep, to go to sleep, to drop off (*inf*); (*Bein, Arm*) to go to sleep; (*euph: sterben*) to pass away; (*fig: Gewohnheit, Freundschaft*) to peter out, to tail off ◆ **ich kann nicht ~** I can't get to sleep; **bei** *or* **über seiner Arbeit ~** to fall asleep over one's work; **vor dem E~ zu nehmen** (*Medizin*) to be taken before retiring.
einschläferig *adj Bett* single.
einschläfern *vt sep* (**a**) (*zum Schlafen bringen*) to send to sleep; (*schläfrig machen*) to make sleepy *or* drowsy; (*fig*) *Gewissen* to soothe, to quiet ◆ **das kann unsere Wachsamkeit nicht ~** that won't lull us into a false sense of security.
(**b**) (*narkotisieren*) to give a soporific.
(**c**) (*töten*) *Tier* to put to sleep, to put down, to destroy.
einschläfernd *adj* soporific; (*langweilig*) monotonous ◆ **ein ~es Mittel** a soporific (drug).
einschläf(r)ig *adj Bett* single.
Einschlafstörung *f* problem in getting to sleep.
Einschlag *m* (**a**) (*von Geschoß*) impact; (*von Blitz*) striking ◆ **dieses Loch ist der ~ eines Geschosses** this hole was made by a bullet; **der ~ der Granate war deutlich zu sehen** the place where the grenade had landed was clearly visible.
(**b**) (*Sew*) hem.
(**c**) (*Tex*) weft, woof.
(**d**) (*von Bäumen*) felling; (*gefällte Bäume*) timber.
(**e**) (*Aut: des Lenkrads*) lock ◆ **das Lenkrad bis zum (vollen) ~ drehen** to put the wheel on full lock.
(**f**) (*Zusatz, Beimischung*) element ◆ **einen stark(en) autoritären/südländischen ~ haben** to have more than a hint of authoritarianism/the Mediterranean about it/one *etc*.
einschlagen *sep irreg* [1] *vt* (**a**) *Nagel* to hammer *or* knock in; *Pfahl* to drive in; *Krallen* to sink in (*in +acc* -to).
(**b**) (*zertrümmern*) to smash (in); *Tür auch* to smash down; *Schädel auch* to bash in (*inf*); *Zähne* to knock out ◆ **mit eingeschlagenem Schädel** with one's head bashed in.
(**c**) *Bäume* to fell.
(**d**) (*einwickeln*) *Ware* to wrap up; *Buch* to cover.
(**e**) (*umlegen*) *Stoff, Decke* to turn up.
(**f**) (*Aut*) *Räder* to turn.
(**g**) (*wählen*) *Weg* to take; *Kurs* (*lit*) to follow; (*fig*) to pursue, to adopt; *Laufbahn etc* to enter on ◆ **das Schiff änderte den eingeschlagenen Kurs** the ship changed from its previous course; **Peking schlägt einen weicheren/härteren Kurs ein** Peking is taking a softer/harder line.
[2] *vi* (**a**) (**in etw** *acc*) **~** (*Blitz*) to strike (sth); (*Geschoß etc auch*) to hit (sth); **es muß irgendwo eingeschlagen haben** something must have been struck by lightning; **gut ~** (*inf*) to go down well, to be a big hit (*inf*); (*Schüler, Arbeiter*) to get on all right.
(**b**) **auf jdn/etw ~** to hit out at sb/sth.
(**c**) (*zur Bekräftigung*) to shake on it.
einschlägig (**a**) *adj* appropriate; *Literatur, Paragraph auch* relevant ◆ **er ist ~ vorbestraft** (*Jur*) he has a previous conviction for a similar offence. (**b**) (*zwielichtig*) *Lokal* dubious.
einschleichen *vr sep irreg* (*in +acc* -to) to creep in; (*lit auch*) to steal *or* sneak (*inf*) in; (*fig: Fehler auch*) to slip in ◆ **sich in jds Vertrauen ~** (*fig*) to worm one's way into sb's confidence.
einschleifen *vt sep irreg* to grind; (*eingravieren*) to cut in (*in +acc* -to) ◆ **eingeschliffene Reaktionen/Verhaltensweisen** (*Psych, geh*) established reactions/patterns of behaviour.
einschleppen *vt sep* (*Naut*) *Schiff* to tow in (*in +acc* -to); (*fig*) *Krankheit, Ungeziefer* to bring in.
Einschleppung *f* (*fig*) introduction, bringing-in.
einschleusen *vt sep* to smuggle in (*in +acc, nach* -to).
einschließen *vt sep irreg* (**a**) to lock up (*in +acc* in); (*Mil*) to confine to quarters ◆ **er schloß sich/mich in dem** *or* **das Zimmer ein** he locked himself/me in the room.
(**b**) (*umgeben*) to surround; (*Mil*) *Stadt, Feind auch* to encircle ◆ **einen Satz in Klammern ~** to put a sentence in brackets.
(**c**) (*fig: einbegreifen, beinhalten*) to include.
einschließlich [1] *prep +gen* including, inclusive of ◆ **~ Porto** postage included; **Preis ~ Porto** price including postage *or* inclusive of postage.
[2] *adv* **er hat das Buch bis S. 205 ~ gelesen** he has read up to and including p.205; **vom 1. bis ~ 31. Oktober** *or* **bis 31. Oktober ~ geschlossen** closed from 1st to 31st October inclusive.
Einschließung *f* (*esp Mil*) confinement.
einschlummern *vi sep aux sein* (*geh*) to fall asleep; (*euph: sterben*) to pass away.
⚠ **Einschluß** *m* (**a**) (*von Gefangenen*) locking of the cells. (**b**) **mit** *or* **unter ~ von** (*form*) with the inclusion of, including. (**c**) (*Geol*) inclusion.
einschmeicheln *vr sep* **sich bei jdm ~** to ingratiate oneself with sb, to insinuate oneself into sb's good graces; **~de Musik** enticing music; **~de Stimme** silky voice.
Einschmeich(e)lung *f* attempt to ingratiate oneself.
einschmeißen *vt sep irreg* (*inf*) *Fenster* to smash (in).
einschmelzen *sep irreg* [1] *vt* to melt down; (*fig: integrieren*) to put in the melting pot ◆ **diese Unterschiede sind weitgehend eingeschmolzen** these differences have for the most part fused and coalesced.
[2] *vi aux sein* to melt.
Einschmelzung *f* melting (down); (*fig*) coalescence.
einschmieren *vt sep* (**a**) (*mit Fett*) to grease; (*mit Öl*) to oil; *Gesicht* (*mit Creme*) to cream, to put cream on ◆ **er schmierte mir den Rücken mit Heilsalbe/Sonnenöl ein** he rubbed my back with ointment/sun-tan lotion. (**b**) (*inf: beschmutzen*) to get dirty ◆ **er hat sich ganz mit Dreck/Marmelade eingeschmiert** he has covered himself in dirt/jam.
einschmuggeln *vt sep* to smuggle in (*in +acc* -to) ◆ **er hat sich in den Saal eingeschmuggelt** he sneaked into the hall.
einschnappen *vi sep aux sein* (**a**) (*Schloß, Tür*) to click shut. (**b**) (*inf: beleidigt sein*) to take offence, to get into a huff (*inf*) ◆ **er schnappt wegen jeder Kleinigkeit ein** he takes offence at every little thing; *siehe* **eingeschnappt**.
einschneiden *sep irreg* [1] *vt* (**a**) *Stoff, Papier* to cut ◆ **er schnitt das Papier an den Ecken einige Zentimeter ein** he cut a few centimetres into the corners of the paper; **die Fesseln schneiden mir die Handgelenke ein** the bonds are cutting into my wrists.
(**b**) (*einkerben*) *Namen, Zeichen* to carve (*in +acc* in, into) ◆ **der Fluß hat ein Tal in das Gestein eingeschnitten** the river has carved out *or* cut a valley in the rock; **tief eingeschnittene Felsen** steep cliffs; **eine tief eingeschnittene Schlucht** a deep ravine.
(**c**) (*Cook*) **Zwiebeln in die Suppe ~** to cut up some onions and put them in the soup.
(**d**) (*Film*) to cut in (*in +acc* -to).
[2] *vi* to cut in (*in +acc* -to).
einschneidend *adj* (*fig*) drastic, radical; *Maßnahmen auch* trenchant; *Bedeutung, Wirkung* far-reaching.
einschneien *vi sep aux sein* to get snowed up; (*Auto, Mensch auch*) to get snowed in ◆ **eingeschneit sein** to be snowed up/in.

➤ SPRACHE AKTIV: **einschätzen** → 33.1

⚠: Informationen zur Rechtschreibreform im Anhang

Einschnitt *m* cut; (*Med*) incision; (*im Tal, Gebirge*) cleft; (*Zäsur*) break; (*im Leben*) decisive point.

einschnitzen *vt sep* to carve (*in +acc* into).

einschnüren *sep* [1] *vt* (a) (*einengen*) to cut into; *Taille* (*mit Mieder*) to lace in ◆ **dieser Kragen schnürt mir den Hals ein** this collar is nearly choking *or* strangling me.
(b) (*zusammenbinden*) *Paket* to tie up.
[2] *vr* to lace oneself up *or* in.

einschränken *sep* [1] *vt* to reduce, to cut back *or* down; *Bewegungsfreiheit, Recht* to limit, to restrict; *Wünsche* to moderate; *Behauptung* to qualify ◆ **jdn in seinen Rechten ~** to limit *or* restrict sb's rights; **~d möchte ich sagen, daß** ... I'd like to qualify that by saying ...; **das Rauchen/Trinken/Essen ~** to cut down on smoking/on drinking/on what one eats.
[2] *vr* (*sparen*) to economize ◆ **sich im Essen/Trinken ~** to cut down on what one eats/on one's drinking; *siehe* **eingeschränkt.**

Einschränkung *f* (a) *siehe vt* reduction; limitation, restriction; moderation; qualification; (*Vorbehalt*) reservation ◆ **ohne ~** without reservations, unreservedly. (b) (*Sparmaßnahme*) economy; (*das Einsparen*) economizing.

einschrauben *vt sep* to screw in (*in +acc* -to).

Einschreib(e)-: ~brief *m* recorded delivery (*Brit*) *or* certified (*US*) letter; **~gebühr** *f* (a) (*Post*) charge for recorded delivery (*Brit*) *or* certified mail (*US*); (b) (*Univ*) registration fee; (c) (*für Verein*) membership fee.

einschreiben *sep irreg* [1] *vt* (*eintragen*) to enter; *Post* to send recorded delivery (*Brit*) *or* certified mail (*US*); *siehe* **eingeschrieben.**
[2] *vr* (*in Verein, für Abendkurse etc*) to enrol; (*Univ*) to register ◆ **er schrieb sich in die Liste ein** he put his name on the list.

Einschreiben *nt* recorded delivery (*Brit*) *or* certified (*US*) letter/parcel. ~ *pl* recorded delivery (*Brit*) *or* certified (*US*) mail *sing* ◆ **einen Brief als** *or* **per ~ schicken** to send a letter recorded delivery (*Brit*) *or* certified mail (*US*).

Einschreib(e)sendung *f* letter/parcel sent recorded delivery (*Brit*) *or* certified mail (*US*).

Einschreibung *f* enrolment; (*Univ*) registration.

einschreien *vi sep irreg* **auf jdn ~** to yell *or* bawl at sb.

einschreiten *vi sep irreg aux sein* to take action (*gegen* against); (*dazwischentreten*) to intervene, to step in.

Einschreiten *nt* **-s,** *no pl* intervention.

einschrumpeln (*inf*), **einschrumpfen** *vi sep aux sein* to shrivel (up).

Einschub *m* insertion.

einschüchtern *vt sep* to intimidate.

Einschüchterung *f* intimidation.

Einschüchterungsversuch *m* attempt at intimidation.

einschulen *vti sep* **eingeschult werden** (*Kind*) to start school; **wir müssen unseren Sohn dieses Jahr ~** our son has to start school this year; **wir schulen dieses Jahr weniger Kinder ein** we have fewer children starting school this year.

Einschulung *f* first day at school ◆ **die ~ findet im Alter von 6 Jahren statt** children start school at the age of 6.

⚠ **Einschuß** *m* (a) (*~stelle*) bullet hole; (*Med*) point of entry ◆ **Tod durch ~ in die Schläfe** death caused by a shot *or* a bullet through the side of the head.
(b) (*Space*) **nach ~ der Rakete in die Erdumlaufbahn** after the rocket had been shot into orbit round the earth.
(c) (*Ftbl*) shot into goal.
(d) (*Tex*) weft, woof.

⚠ **Einschuß-: ~loch** *nt* bullet hole; **~stelle** *f* bullet hole; (*Med*) point of entry.

einschütten *vt sep* to tip in (*in +acc* -to); *Flüssigkeiten* to pour in (*in +acc* -to) ◆ **dem Pferd Futter ~** to give the horse some fodder; **er hat sich** (*dat*) **noch etwas Kaffee eingeschüttet** (*inf*) he poured himself (out) *or* gave himself some more coffee.

einschwärzen *vt sep* to blacken, to make black.

einschweben *vi sep aux sein* to glide in (*in +acc* -to).

einschweißen *vt sep* (*Tech*) (*hineinschweißen*) to weld in (*in +acc* -to); (*zuschweißen*) *Buch, Schallplatte* to shrink-wrap, to heat-seal (*spec*).

Einschweißfolie *f* shrink-wrapping.

einschwenken *vi sep aux sein* to turn *or* swing in (*in +acc* -to) ◆ **links/rechts ~** (*Mil*) to wheel left/right; **auf etw** (*acc*) **~** (*fig*) to fall in with *or* go along with sth.

einschwören *vt sep irreg* **jdn auf etw** (*acc*) **~** to swear sb to sth; *siehe* **eingeschworen.**

einsegnen *vt sep* (a) (*konfirmieren*) to confirm. (b) *Altar, Kirche* to consecrate; *Feld, Haus, Gläubige* to bless.

Einsegnung *f siehe vt* confirmation; consecration; blessing.

einsehen *sep irreg* [1] *vt* (a) *Gelände* to see; (*Mil*) to observe.
(b) (*prüfen*) *Akte* to see, to look at.
(c) (*verstehen, begreifen*) to see; *Fehler, Schuld auch* to recognize ◆ **das sehe ich nicht ein** I don't see why; (*verstehe ich nicht*) I don't see that.
[2] *vi* (a) **in etw** (*acc*) **~** to see sth; (*Mil*) to observe sth.
(b) (*prüfen*) to look (*in +acc* at).

Einsehen *nt*: **ein ~ haben** to have some understanding (*mit, für* for); (*Vernunft, Einsicht*) to see reason *or* sense; **hab doch ein ~!** have a heart!; be reasonable!; **hast du kein ~?** have you no understanding?; can't you see sense?

einseifen *vt sep* to soap; (*inf: betrügen*) to con (*inf*), to take for a ride (*inf*); (*inf: mit Schnee*) to rub with snow.

einseitig *adj* (a) on one side; (*Jur, Pol*) *Erklärung, Kündigung* unilateral; *Diskette* single-sided ◆ **~e Lungenentzündung** single pneumonia; **~e Lähmung** hemiplegia (*form*), paralysis of one side of the body.
(b) *Freundschaft, Zuneigung* one-sided.
(c) (*beschränkt*) *Ausbildung* one-sided; (*parteiisch*) *Bericht, Standpunkt, Zeitung auch* biased; *Ernährung* unbalanced ◆ **etw ~ schildern** to give a one-sided portrayal of sth, to portray sth one-sidedly.

Einseitigkeit *f* (*fig*) one-sidedness; (*von Bericht, Zeitung etc auch*) biasedness; (*von Ernährung*) imbalance.

einsenden *vt sep irreg* to send in, to submit (*an +acc* to).

Einsender(in *f*) *m* sender; (*bei Preisausschreiben*) competitor ◆ **wir bitten die ~ von Artikeln** ... we would ask those (people) who send in *or* submit articles ...

⚠ **Einsendeschluß** *m* last date for entries, closing date.

Einsendung *f* (a) *no pl* (*das Einsenden*) sending in, submission. (b) (*das Eingesandte*) letter/article/manuscript *etc*; (*bei Preisausschreiben*) entry.

einsenken *sep* [1] *vt sep* to sink in (*in +acc* -to).
[2] *vr* (*liter*) **dieses Bild senkte sich tief in seine Seele ein** this image made a deep impression on him *or* his mind.

Einser *m* **-s, -** (*esp S Ger*) (*Sch*) A (grade), alpha, one; (*Autobus*) (number) one ◆ **er hat einen ~ geschrieben** he got an A.

einsetzen *sep* [1] *vt* (a) (*einfügen*) to put in (*in +acc* -to); *Maschinenteil auch* to insert (*in +acc* into), to fit in (*in +acc* -to); *Ärmel auch* to set in (*in +acc* -to); *Stück Stoff* to let in (*in +acc* -to); (*einschreiben auch*) to enter (*in +acc* in); *Stiftzahn* to put on (*in +acc* -to); *Gebiß* to fit ◆ **Fische in einen Teich ~** to stock a pond with fish; **jdm einen Goldzahn ~** to give sb a gold tooth; **eingesetzte Taschen** pockets let *or* set into the seams.
(b) (*ernennen, bestimmen*) to appoint; *Ausschuß auch* to set up; *Erben, Nachfolger* to name ◆ **jdn in ein Amt ~** to appoint sb to an office; **jdn als** *or* **zum Richter ~** to appoint sb judge.
(c) (*verwenden*) to use (*auch Sport*), to employ; *Truppen, Polizei, Feuerwehr* to deploy, to bring into action; *Schlagstöcke* to use; *Busse, Sonderzüge* to put on; (*Chess*) *König etc* to bring into play ◆ **etw als** *or* **zum Pfand ~** to give sth as a deposit.
(d) (*beim Glücksspiel*) to stake; (*geh*) *Leben* to risk ◆ **seine ganze Energie** *or* **Kraft für etw ~** to devote all one's energies to sth.
[2] *vi* (*beginnen*) to start, to begin; (*Mus*) to come in; (*am Anfang*) to start to play/sing ◆ **die Ebbe/Flut setzt um 3 Uhr ein** the tide turns at 3 o'clock, the tide starts to go out/come in at 3 o'clock; **gegen Abend setzte stärkeres Fieber ein** the fever increased towards evening.
[3] *vr* (a) **sich (voll) ~** to show (complete) commitment (*in +dat* to); **die Mannschaft setzte sich bis an den Rand ihrer Kraft ein** the team did their absolute utmost.
(b) **sich für jdn ~** to fight for sb, to support sb's cause; (*sich verwenden für*) to give *or* lend sb one's support; **sie hat sich so sehr für ihn eingesetzt** she did so much for him; **sie hat sich voll für die Armen/Verwundeten eingesetzt** she lent her aid unreservedly to the poor/wounded; **sich für etw ~** to support sth; **ich werde mich dafür ~, daß** ... I will do what I can to see that ...; **er setzte sich für die Freilassung seines Bruders ein** he did what he could to secure the release of his brother.

Einsetzung *f* appointment (*in +acc* to) ◆ **die ~ des Bischofs in sein Amt** the Bishop's investiture; *siehe auch* **Einsatz.**

Einsicht *f* (a) (*in Akten, Bücher*) **~ in etw** (*acc*) **haben/nehmen/verlangen** to look/take a look/ask to look at sth; **jdm ~ in etw** (*acc*) **gewähren** to allow sb to look at *or* to see sth; **sie legte ihm die Akte zur ~ vor** she gave him the file to look at.
(b) (*Vernunft*) sense, reason; (*Erkenntnis*) insight; (*Kenntnis*) knowledge; (*Verständnis*) understanding; (*euph: Reue*) remorse ◆ **zur ~ kommen** to come to one's senses; **ich bin zu der ~ gekommen, daß** ... I have come to the conclusion that ...; **~ ist der erste Schritt zur Besserung** a fault confessed is half redressed (*Prov*); **haben Sie doch ~!** have a heart!; (*seien Sie vernünftig*) be reasonable!; **jdn zur ~ bringen** to bring sb to his/her senses; **er hat ~ in die internen Vorgänge der Firma** he has some knowledge of the internal affairs of the firm.

einsichtig *adj* (a) (*vernünftig*) reasonable; (*verständnisvoll*) understanding ◆ **er war so ~, seinen Fehler zuzugeben** he was reasonable enough to admit his mistake.
(b) (*verständlich, begreiflich*) understandable, comprehensible ◆ **etw ~ erklären** to explain sth clearly; **jdm etw ~ machen** to make sb understand *or* see sth.

Einsichtnahme *f* **-, -n** (*form*) inspection ◆ **er bat um ~ in die Akten** he asked to see the files; **nach ~ in die Akten** after seeing *or* inspecting the files; **„zur ~"** "for attention".

einsichts-: ~los *adj* (*unvernünftig*) unreasonable; **~voll** *adj siehe* **einsichtig** (a).

einsickern *vi sep aux sein* to seep in (*in +acc* -to); (*fig*) to filter in (*in +acc* -to) ◆ **Spione sickerten in unser Land ein** spies infiltrated (into) our country.

Einsiedelei *f* hermitage; (*fig hum: einsames Haus*) country retreat *or* hideaway.

einsieden *vt sep irreg* (*S Ger, Aus*) *Obst* to bottle; *Marmelade* to make.

Einsiedler(in *f*) *m* hermit; (*fig auch*) recluse.

einsiedlerisch *adj* hermit-like *no adv.*

Einsiedlerkrebs *m* hermit crab.

Einsilber *m* **-s, -** *siehe* **Einsilb(l)er.**

einsilbig *adj Wort* monosyllabic; *Reim* masculine, single; (*fig*) *Mensch* uncommunicative; *Antwort* monosyllabic.

Einsilbigkeit *f* (*lit*) monosyllabism; (*von Reim*) masculinity; (*fig: von Mensch*) uncommunicativeness.

Einsilb(l)er *m* **-s, -** monosyllable.

einsingen *vr sep irreg* to get oneself into voice.

einsinken *vi sep irreg aux sein* (*im Morast, Schnee*) to sink in (*in +acc or dat* -to); (*Boden etc*) to subside, to cave in; (*Knie*) to give way ◆ **er sank bis zu den Knien im Schlamm ein** he sank up to his knees in the mud; **ein Stück eingesunkenen Bodens** an area where the ground has subsided *or* caved in; **eingesunkene Schläfen/Wangen** sunken *or* hollow temples/cheeks.

einsitzen *vi sep irreg* (*form*) to serve a prison sentence ◆ **drei Jahre ~** to serve three years *or* a three-year sentence.

Einsitzer *m* **-s, -** single-seater.

einsitzig *adj Fahrzeug* single-seater.

einsortieren* *vt sep* to sort and put away; (*Dokumente*) to file away ◆ **in Schachteln/Körbe ~** to sort into boxes/baskets.

einspaltig *adj* (*Typ*) single-column ◆ **etw ~ setzen** to set sth in a single column/in single columns.

einspannen *vt sep* **(a)** (*in Rahmen*) *Leinwand* to fit *or* put in (*in +acc* -to) ◆ **Saiten in einen Schläger ~** to string a racket.
(b) (*in Schraubstock*) to clamp in (*in +acc* -to).
(c) (*in Kamera*) to put in (*in +acc* -to); (*in Schreibmaschine auch*) to insert (*in +acc* in, into).
(d) *Pferde* to harness.
(e) (*fig: arbeiten lassen*) to rope in (*für etw* to do sth) ◆ **jdn für seine Zwecke ~** to use sb for one's own ends; *siehe* **eingespannt.**

Einspänner *m* **-s, -** one-horse carriage; (*hum: Junggeselle*) bachelor; (*Aus*) *black coffee in a glass served with whipped cream.*

einspännig *adj Wagen* one-horse ◆ **der Wagen ist/fährt ~** the carriage is pulled by one horse.

einsparen *vt sep* to save; *Energie, Strom auch* to save *or* economize on; *Kosten, Ausgaben* to cut down on, to reduce; *Posten* to dispense with, to eliminate.

Einsparung *f* economy; *siehe vt* (*von* of) saving; reduction; elimination.

einspeicheln *vt sep* to insalivate.

einspeichern *vt sep Daten* to feed in (*in +acc* -to), to enter (*in +acc* into).

einspeisen *vt sep* to feed in (*in +acc* -to); *Daten auch* to enter (*in +acc* into).

einsperren *vt sep* to lock up (*in +acc or dat* in), to lock in (*in +acc or dat* -to); (*versehentlich*) to lock in (*in +acc or dat* in); (*inf: ins Gefängnis*) to put away (*inf*), to lock up.

einspielen *sep* [1] *vr* (*Mus, Sport*) to warm up; (*nach Sommerpause etc*) to get into practice; (*Regelung, Arbeit*) to work out ◆ **... aber das spielt sich alles noch ein** ... but things should sort themselves out all right; **ich fahre jetzt mit dem Bus, das hat sich gut eingespielt** I come by bus now, it's working out well; **sich aufeinander ~** to become attuned to *or* to get used to one another; *siehe* **eingespielt.**
[2] *vt* **(a)** (*Mus, Sport*) *Instrument, Schläger* to play in.
(b) (*Film, Theat*) to bring in, to gross; *Kosten* to recover.
(c) (*aufnehmen*) *Lied* to record; *Schallplatte auch* to cut.

Einspiel|ergebnis *nt* (*von Film*) box-office takings *pl or* receipts *pl.*

einspinnen *sep irreg* [1] *vr* (*Spinne*) to spin a web around itself; (*Larve*) to spin a cocoon around itself ◆ **sich in seine Gedanken ~** to wrap oneself up in one's thoughts.
[2] *vt* (*Spinne*) to spin a web around.

Einsprache *f* (*Aus, Sw*) *siehe* **Einspruch.**

einsprachig *adj* monolingual.

einsprechen *sep irreg* [1] *vi* **auf jdn ~** to harangue sb.
[2] *vt Text* to speak.

einsprengen *vt sep* (*mit Wasser*) to sprinkle with water, to dampen; *siehe* **eingesprengt.**

Einsprengsel *nt* (*Geol*) xenocryst (*spec*), embedded crystal ◆ **ein Buch mit einigen lyrischen ~n** a book with the odd moment of lyricism.

einspringen *sep irreg* [1] *vi aux sein* **(a)** (*Tech*) to lock shut *or* into place; (*Maschinenteile*) to engage. **(b)** (*inf: aushelfen*) to stand in; (*mit Geld etc*) to help out.
[2] *vr* (*Sport*) to do some practice jumps.

Einspritz- *in cpds* (*Aut, Med*) injection.

Einspritzdüse *f* (*Aut*) injector.

einspritzen *vt sep* **(a)** (*Aut, Med*) to inject ◆ **er spritzte ihr/sich Insulin ein** he gave her/himself an insulin injection, he injected her/himself with insulin. **(b)** (*einsprengen*) *Wäsche* to dampen, to sprinkle with water. **(c)** (*inf: mit Schmutz*) to splash, to spray.

Einspritzer *m* (*Aut*) fuel injection engine.

Einspritz-: ~motor *m* (*Aut*) fuel injection engine; **~pumpe** *f* (*Aut*) fuel injector, fuel injection pump.

Einspritzung *f* injection.

Einspruch *m* objection (*auch Jur*) ◆ **~ einlegen** (*Admin*) to file an objection, to register a protest; **gegen etw ~ erheben** to object to sth, to raise an objection to sth; **ich erhebe ~!** (*Jur*) objection!; **~ abgelehnt!** (*Jur*) objection overruled!; **dem ~ wird stattgegeben!** (*Jur*) objection sustained!

Einspruchs-: ~frist *f* (*Jur*) period for filing an objection; **~recht** *nt* right to object *or* protest.

einspurig *adj* (*Rail*) single-track; (*Aut*) single-lane ◆ **die Straße ist nur ~ befahrbar** only one lane of the road is open, it's single-lane traffic only; **er denkt sehr ~** his mind runs in well-worn grooves.

Einssein *nt* (*liter*) oneness.

einst *adv* **(a)** (*früher, damals*) once ◆ **Preußen ~ und heute** Prussia past and present *or* yesterday and today *or* then and now; **das E~ und das Heute** *or* **Jetzt** the past and the present. **(b)** (*geh: in ferner Zukunft*) one *or* some day.

einstampfen *vt sep Papier* to pulp (down); *Trauben, Kohl* to tread.

Einstand *m* **(a) ein guter ~** a good start to a new job; **er hat gestern seinen ~ gegeben** *or* **gefeiert** yesterday he celebrated starting his new job. **(b)** (*Tennis*) deuce.

Einstandspreis *m* (*Comm*) introductory price.

einstanzen *vt sep* to stamp in (*in +acc* -to).

einstauben *sep* [1] *vi aux sein* to get covered in dust ◆ **eingestaubt sein** to be covered in dust.
[2] *vt* (*Aus*) **sich** (*dat*) **das Gesicht (mit Puder) ~** to powder one's face, to dust one's face with powder.

einstäuben *vt sep* (*mit Puder*) to dust with powder, to powder; (*mit Parfüm etc*) to spray.

einstechen *sep irreg* [1] *vt* to pierce; *Gummi, Haut, Membran auch* to puncture; *Nadel* to put *or* stick (*inf*) in (*in +acc* -to), to insert (*in +acc* in, into); (*Cook*) to prick; (*eingravieren*) to engrave.
[2] *vi* **auf jdn/etw ~** to stab at sb/sth.

Einsteck|album *nt* (stamp) stock book (*spec*), stamp album.

einstecken *vt sep* **(a)** (*in etw stecken*) to put in (*in +acc* -to); *Stecker auch, Gerät* to plug in; *Schwert* to sheathe.
(b) (*in die Tasche etc*) **(sich** *dat*) **etw ~** to take sth; **hast du deinen Paß/ein Taschentuch/deine Brieftasche eingesteckt?** have you got your passport/a handkerchief/your briefcase with you?; **er steckte (sich) die Zeitung ein und ging los** he put the paper in his briefcase/pocket *etc or* he took the paper and left; **warte mal, ich habe mir meine Zigaretten noch nicht eingesteckt** hang on, I haven't got my cigarettes yet; **ich habe kein Geld eingesteckt** *or* (*incorrect*) **~** I haven't any money on me; **kannst du meinen Geldbeutel für mich ~?** can you take my purse for me?; **steck deine Pistole wieder ein** put away your pistol.
(c) (*in den Briefkasten*) to post, to mail (*esp US*).
(d) (*inf*) *Kritik etc* to take; *Beleidigung auch* to swallow; (*verdienen*) *Geld, Profit* to pocket (*inf*) ◆ **der Boxer mußte viel ~** the boxer had to take a lot of punishment; **er steckt sie alle ein** he beats the lot of them (*inf*).

Einsteck-: ~kamm *m* (decorative) comb; **~tuch** *nt* breast pocket handkerchief.

einstehen *vi sep irreg aux sein* **(a)** (*sich verbürgen*) **für jdn/etw ~** to vouch for sb/sth; **ich stehe dafür ein, daß ...** I will vouch that ...; **er stand mit seinem Wort dafür ein** he vouched for it personally.
(b) für etw ~ (*Ersatz leisten*) to make good sth; (*sich bekennen*) to answer for sth, to take responsibility for sth; **für jdn ~** to assume liability *or* responsibility for sb; **ich habe das immer behauptet, und dafür stehe ich auch ein** I've always said that, and I'll stand by it.

einsteigen *vi sep irreg aux sein* **(a)** (*in ein Fahrzeug etc*) to get in (*in +acc* -to); (*umständlich, mit viel Gepäck etc auch*) to climb *or* clamber in (*in +acc* -to); (*in Zug auch, in Bus*) to get on (*in +acc* -to) ◆ **~!** (*Rail etc*) all aboard!; **in eine Felswand ~** to attack a rockface; **er ist in die Problematik dieses Buchs noch nicht so richtig eingestiegen** he hasn't really got to grips with the problems in this book.
(b) (*in ein Haus etc*) to climb *or* get in (*in +acc* -to).
(c) (*Sport sl*) **hart ~** to go in hard.
(d) (*inf*) **in die Politik/ins Verlagsgeschäft ~** to go into politics/publishing; **er ist mit einer Million in diese Firma/ins Börsengeschäft eingestiegen** he put a million into this firm/invested a million on the stock exchange; **er ist ganz groß in dieses Geschäft eingestiegen** he's (gone) into that business in a big way (*inf*); **der Verlag ist jetzt in Lexika eingestiegen** the publishing company has branched out into dictionaries *or* into the dictionary market.

Einsteiger(in *f*) *m* (*inf*) beginner ◆ **ein Modell für PC-~** an entry-level PC.

Einsteigekarte *f* (*Aviat*) boarding pass *or* card.

Einsteinium *nt* **-s,** *no pl* (*abbr* **Es**) einsteinium.

einstellbar *adj* adjustable.

Einstellbereich *m* (*Aut*) adjustment range.

einstellen *sep* [1] *vt* **(a)** (*hineinstellen*) to put in ◆ **das Auto in die** *or* **der Garage ~** to put the car in(to) the garage; **das Buch ist falsch eingestellt** the book has been put in the wrong place.
(b) (*anstellen*) *Arbeitskräfte* to take on ◆ **„wir stellen ein: Sekretärinnen"** "we have vacancies for *or* are looking for secretaries".
(c) (*beenden*) to stop; (*endgültig auch*) to discontinue; *Expedition, Suche* to call off; (*Mil*) *Feindseligkeiten, Feuer* to cease; (*Jur*) *Prozeß, Verfahren* to abandon ◆ **die Arbeit ist eingestellt worden** work has stopped; (*vorübergehend auch*) work has been halted; **die Zeitung hat ihr Erscheinen eingestellt** the paper has ceased publication; **die Arbeit ~** (*in den Ausstand treten*) to withdraw one's labour.
(d) (*regulieren*) to adjust (*auf +acc* to); *Kanone* to aim (*auf +acc* at); *Fernglas, Fotoapparat* (*auf Entfernung*) to focus (*auf +acc* on); *Wecker, Zünder* to set (*auf +acc* for); *Radio* to tune (in) (*auf +acc* to); *Sender* to tune in to ◆ **die Steuerung auf Automatik ~** to switch over to *or* put the plane on the automatic pilot; **den Hebel auf Start ~** to set the lever to start.
(e) (*fig: abstimmen*) to tailor (*auf +acc* to).
(f) (*Sport*) *Rekord* to equal.
[2] *vr* **(a)** (*Besucher etc*) to appear, to present oneself; (*Fieber, Regen*) to set in; (*Symptome*) to appear; (*Folgen*) to become apparent, to appear; (*Wort, Gedanke*) to come to mind; (*Jahreszeiten*) to come, to arrive ◆ **wenn es kalt ist, stellen sich bei mir regelmäßig heftige Kopfschmerzen ein** I always suffer from bad headaches when it's cold.

(b) sich auf jdn/etw ~ (*sich richten nach*) to adapt oneself to sb/sth; (*sich vorbereiten auf*) to prepare oneself for sb/sth; *siehe* **eingestellt**.
[3] *vi* to take on staff/workers.

einstellig *adj Zahl* single-digit.

Einstell-: ~knopf *m* (*an Radio etc*) tuning knob; **~platz** *m* (*auf Hof*) carport; (*in großer Garage*) (covered) parking accommodation *no indef art*; **~schraube** *f* adjustment screw.

Einstellung *f* **(a)** (*Anstellung*) employment.
(b) (*Beendigung*) *siehe vt* (*c*) stopping; discontinuation; calling-off; cessation; abandonment ◆ **der Sturm zwang uns zur ~ der Suche/Bauarbeiten** the storm forced us to call off *or* abandon the search/to stop work on the building; **die Lackierer beschlossen die ~ der Arbeit** the paint-sprayers decided to withdraw their labour *or* to down tools.
(c) (*Regulierung*) *siehe vt* (*d*) adjustment; aiming; focusing; setting; tuning (in); (*Film: Szene*) take.
(d) (*Gesinnung, Haltung*) attitude; (*politisch, religiös etc*) views *pl* ◆ **er hat eine falsche ~ zum Leben** he doesn't have the right attitude to *or* outlook on life; **das ist doch keine ~!** what kind of attitude is that!, that's not the right attitude!

Einstellungs-: ~gespräch *nt* interview; **~stopp** *m* halt in recruitment; **~termin** *m* starting date; **~untersuchung** *f medical examination when starting a new job.*

einstens *adv* (*obs*) *siehe* **einst**.

Einstich *m* (*~stelle*) puncture, prick; (*Vorgang*) insertion.

Einstichstelle *f* puncture (mark).

Einstieg *m* **-(e)s, -e (a)** *no pl* (*das Einsteigen*) getting in; (*in Bus*) getting on; (*von Dieb: in Haus etc*) entry; (*fig: zu einem Thema etc*) lead-in (*zu* to) ◆ **~ nur vorn!** enter only at the front; **kein ~** exit only; **er stürzte beim ~ in die Eigernordwand ab** he fell during the assault on the north face of the Eiger.
(b) (*von Bahn*) door; (*von Bus auch*) entrance.

Einstiegsdroge *f* starter drug, drug leading to further addiction.

einstig *adj attr* former.

einstimmen *sep* [1] *vi* (*in ein Lied*) to join in; (*fig*) (*beistimmen*) to agree (*in +acc* with); (*zustimmen*) to agree (*in +acc* to) ◆ **in den Gesang/die Buhrufe (mit) ~** to join in the singing/booing.
[2] *vt* (*Mus*) *Instrument* to tune ◆ **jdn/sich auf etw** (*acc*) **~** (*fig*) to get *or* put sb/oneself in the (right) mood for sth; *auf eine Atmosphäre etc* to attune sb/oneself to sth.

einstimmig *adj* **(a)** *Lied* for one voice ◆ **~ singen** to sing in unison; **riefen sie ~** they called in unison. **(b)** (*einmütig*) unanimous.

Einstimmigkeit *f* unanimity.

Einstimmung *f* (*Mus: von Instrumenten*) tuning ◆ **für die richtige ~ der Zuhörer sorgen** (*fig*) to get the audience in the right mood.

einstippen *vt sep* (*dial*) to dunk.

einstmals *adv siehe* **einst**.

einstöckig *adj Haus* two-storey (*Brit*), two-story (*US*) ◆ **~ (gebaut) sein** to have two storeys *or* stories.

einstöpseln *vt sep* (*Elec*) to plug in (*in +acc* -to).

einstoßen *vt sep irreg Tür, Mauer* to knock *or* break down; *Scheibe* to push in, to break.

einstrahlen *vi sep* to irradiate (*spec*), to shine.

Einstrahlung *f* (*Sonnen~*) irradiation (*spec*), shining.

einstreichen *vt sep irreg* **(a) eine Wunde (mit Salbe) ~** to put ointment on a wound; **eine Kuchenform (mit Fett) ~** to grease a baking tin. **(b)** (*inf*) *Geld, Gewinn* to pocket (*inf*).

einstreuen *vt sep* to sprinkle in (*in +acc* -to); (*fig*) *Bemerkung etc* to slip in (*in +acc* -to).

einströmen *vi sep aux sein* to pour *or* flood in (*in +acc* -to); (*Licht, fig auch*) to stream in (*in +acc* -to) ◆ **kältere Luftschichten strömen nach Bayern ein** a stream of cooler air is moving in towards Bavaria; **~de Kaltluft** a stream of cold air.

einstrophig *adj* one-verse *attr*.

einstudieren* *vt sep Lied, Theaterstück* to rehearse ◆ **einstudierte Antworten** (*fig*) well-rehearsed answers.

Einstudierung *f* (*Theat*) production.

einstufen *vt sep* to classify ◆ **in eine Klasse/Kategorie** *etc* **~** to put into a class/category *etc*.

einstufig *adj Rakete* single-stage.

Einstufung *f* classification ◆ **nach seiner ~ in eine höhere Gehaltsklasse** after he was put on a higher salary grade.

einstündig *adj attr* one-hour ◆ **mehr als ~e Verspätungen** delays of more than an hour; **nach ~er Pause** after an hour's *or* a one-hour break, after a break of an hour.

einstürmen *vi sep aux sein* **auf jdn ~** (*Mil*) to storm sb; (*fig*) to assail sb; **mit Fragen auf jdn ~** to bombard *or* besiege sb with questions.

Einsturz *m* collapse; (*von Mauer, Boden, Decke auch*) caving-in.

einstürzen *vi sep aux sein* to collapse; (*Mauer, Boden, Decke auch*) to cave in; (*Theorie, Gedankengebäude auch*) to crumble ◆ **auf jdn ~** (*fig*) to overwhelm sb; **es stürzte viel auf ihn ein** he was overwhelmed by events.

Einsturzgefahr *f* danger of collapse.

einstweilen *adv* in the meantime; (*vorläufig*) temporarily.

einstweilig *adj attr* temporary ◆ **~e Verfügung/Anordnung** (*Jur*) temporary *or* interim injunction/order; **~ verfügen** (*Jur*) to issue a temporary *or* an interim injunction.

einsuggerieren* *vt sep* **jdm etw ~** to suggest sth to sb; (*inf*) to brainwash sb into believing sth.

Einswerden *nt* (*geh*) becoming one *no art*.

eintägig *adj attr* one-day; *siehe* **viertägig**.

Eintagsfliege *f* (*Zool*) mayfly; (*fig*) nine-day wonder; (*Mode, Idee*) passing craze.

eintanzen *vr sep* to get used to dancing with sb; (*vor Turnier etc*) to dance a few practice steps.

Eintänzer *m* gigolo.

eintätowieren* *vt sep* to tattoo (*in/auf +acc* on).

eintauchen *sep* [1] *vt* to dip (*in +acc* in, into); (*völlig*) to immerse (*in +acc* in); *Brot* (*in Kaffee etc*) to dunk (*in +acc* in).
[2] *vi aux sein* (*Schwimmer*) to dive in; (*Springer*) to enter the water; (*U-Boot*) to dive ◆ **das U-Boot ist jetzt ganz eingetaucht** the submarine is now completely submerged.

Eintausch *m* exchange, swap (*inf*) ◆ **„~ von Gutscheinen"** "coupons exchanged here".

eintauschen *vt sep* to exchange, to swap (*inf*) (*gegen, für* for); (*umtauschen*) *Devisen* to change.

eintausend *num* (*form*) *siehe* **tausend**.

einteilen *sep* [1] *vt* **(a)** to divide (up) (*in +acc* into); (*aufgliedern auch*) to split (up) (*in +acc* into); (*in Grade*) *Thermometer* to graduate, to calibrate.
(b) (*sinnvoll aufteilen*) *Zeit, Arbeit* to plan (out), to organize; *Geld auch* to budget ◆ **wenn ich mir eine Flasche gut einteile, reicht sie eine Woche** if I plan it well a bottle lasts me a week.
(c) (*dienstlich verpflichten*) to detail (*zu* for) ◆ **er ist heute als Aufseher/zur Aufsicht eingeteilt** he has been allocated the job of supervisor/detailed for *or* assigned supervisory duties today.
[2] *vi* (*inf: haushalten*) to budget.

Einteiler *m* **-s, -** (*Fashion*) one-piece (swimsuit).

einteilig *adj Badeanzug* one-piece *attr*.

Einteilung *f siehe vt* **(a)** division; splitting up; gradation, calibration. **(b)** planning, organization; budgeting. **(c)** detailment (*esp Mil*), assignment.

Eintel *nt* (*Sw auch m*) **-s, -** (*Math*) whole.

eintippen *vt sep* to type in (*in +acc* -to).

eintönig *adj* monotonous ◆ **~ reden** to talk in a monotone.

Eintönigkeit *f* monotony; (*von Stimme*) monotonousness.

Eintopf *m*, **Eintopfgericht** *or* **-essen** *nt* stew.

Eintracht *f, no pl* harmony, concord ◆ **er hat zwischen den beiden wieder ~ gestiftet** he restored peaceful relations between the two of them; **~ X** (*Sport*) ≃ X United.

einträchtig *adj* peaceable.

Eintrag *m* **-(e)s, ¨e (a)** (*schriftlich*) entry (*in +acc* in). **(b)** (*geh*) **das tut der Sache keinen ~** that does/will do no harm. **(c)** (*Tex*) weft, woof.

eintragen *sep irreg* [1] *vt* **(a)** (*in Liste, auf Konto etc*) to enter; (*amtlich registrieren*) to register ◆ **sich ~ lassen** to have one's name put down; *siehe* **eingetragen**.
(b) jdm Haß/Undank/Gewinn ~ to bring sb hatred/ingratitude/profit; **das trägt nur Schaden ein** that will only do harm.
[2] *vr* to sign; (*sich vormerken lassen*) to put one's name down ◆ **er trug sich ins Gästebuch/in die Warteliste ein** he signed the guest book/put his name (down) on the waiting list.

einträglich *adj* profitable; *Geschäft, Arbeit auch* lucrative, remunerative.

Einträglichkeit *f* profitability, profitableness.

Eintragung *f siehe* **Eintrag (a)**.

eintrainieren* *vt sep* to practise.

einträufeln *vt sep* **jdm Medizin in die Nase/ins Ohr ~** to put drops up sb's nose/in sb's ear; **jdm Haß ~** (*geh*) to infuse sb with hatred.

eintreffen *vi sep irreg aux sein* **(a)** (*ankommen*) to arrive ◆ **„Bananen frisch eingetroffen"** "bananas — just in". **(b)** (*fig: Wirklichkeit werden*) to come true; (*Prophezeiung auch*) to be fulfilled.

eintreibbar *adj Schulden* recoverable; *Steuern, Zinsen* exactable.

eintreiben *vt sep irreg* **(a)** *Vieh, Nagel, Pfahl* to drive in (*in +acc* -to). **(b)** (*einziehen*) *Geldbeträge* to collect; *Schulden auch* to recover.

Eintreibung *f* (*von Geldbeträgen*) collection; (*von Schulden auch*) recovery.

eintreten *sep irreg* [1] *vi* **(a)** *aux sein* (*hineingehen*) (*ins Zimmer etc*) to go/come in (*in +acc* -to); (*in Verein, Partei etc*) to join (*in etw* (*acc*) sth) ◆ **ins Haus ~** to go into *or* enter the house; **in eine Firma ~** to go into *or* join a firm; **in die Politik/den diplomatischen Dienst ~** to go into *or* enter politics/the diplomatic service; **ins Heer ~** to join the army, to join up; **in den Krieg ~** to enter the war; **in Verhandlungen ~** (*form*) to enter into negotiations; **ins 30. Lebensjahr ~** (*form*) to enter upon (*form*) *or* go into one's 30th year; **die Verhandlungen sind in eine kritische Phase eingetreten** the negotiations have entered a critical phase; **die Rakete trat in ihre Umlaufbahn ein** the rocket went into its orbit; **bitte treten Sie ein!** (*form*) (please) do come in.
(b) auf jdn ~ to boot *or* kick sb, to put the boot in on sb (*sl*).
(c) *aux sein* (*sich ereignen*) (*Tod*) to occur; (*Zeitpunkt*) to come; (*beginnen*) (*Dunkelheit, Nacht*) to fall; (*Besserung, Tauwetter*) to set in ◆ **bei E~ der Dunkelheit** at nightfall; **gegen Abend trat starkes Fieber ein** towards evening the patient started to run a high temperature; **es ist eine Besserung eingetreten** there has been an improvement; **wenn der Fall eintritt, daß ...** if it happens that ...; **es ist der Fall eingetreten, den wir befürchtet hatten** what we had feared has in fact happened.
(d) *aux sein* **für jdn/etw ~** to stand *or* speak up for sb/sth; **sein mutiges E~ für seine Überzeugung** his courageous defence of his conviction *or* belief.
(e) (*Sw*) **auf etw** (*acc*) **~** to follow sth up.

[2] *vt* (a) (*zertrümmern*) to kick in; *Tür auch* to kick down.
(b) (*hineintreten*) *Stein etc* to tread in (*in +acc* -to).
(c) *Schuhe* to wear *or* break in.
(d) **sich** (*dat*) **etw (in den Fuß) ~** to run sth into one's foot.

eintrichtern, eintrimmen *vt sep* (*inf*) **jdm etw ~** to drum sth into sb; **jdm ~, daß ...** to drum it into sb that ...

Eintritt *m* (a) (*das Eintreten*) entry (*in +acc* (in)to); (*ins Zimmer etc auch*) entrance; (*in Verein, Partei etc*) joining (*in +acc* of) ◆ **beim ~ ins Zimmer** when *or* on entering the room; **„~ im Sekretariat"** "entrance through the office"; **seine Beziehungen erleichterten ihm den ~ ins Geschäftsleben** his connections made it easier for him to get into the business world; **der ~ in den Staatsdienst** entry (in)to the civil service; **die Schule soll auf den ~ ins Leben vorbereiten** school should prepare you for going out into life; **der ~ in die EG** entry to the EC; **der ~ ins Gymnasium** starting at grammar school; **seit seinem ~ in die Armee** since joining the army *or* joining up.
(b) (*~sgeld*) admission (*in +acc* to); (*Einlaß auch*) admittance (*in +acc* to) ◆ **was kostet der ~?** how much *or* what is the admission?; **~ frei!** admission free; **~ DM 4,50** admission DM 4.50; **„~ verboten"** "no admittance"; **jdm ~ in etw** (*acc*) **gewähren** (*form*) to allow *or* permit sb to enter sth, to grant sb admission to sth (*form*).
(c) (*von Winter, Dunkelheit*) onset ◆ **bei ~ eines solchen Falles** in such an event; **der ~ des Todes** the moment when death occurs; **bei ~ der Dunkelheit** at nightfall, as darkness fell/falls.

Eintritts-: ~geld *nt* entrance money, admission charge; **die Zuschauer verlangten ihr ~geld zurück** the audience asked for their money back; **~karte** *f* ticket (of admission), entrance ticket; **~preis** *m* admission charge.

eintrocknen *vi sep aux sein* (*Fluß, Farbe*) to dry up; (*Wasser, Blut*) to dry.

eintrommeln *sep* (*inf*) [1] *vt siehe* **eintrichtern**.
[2] *vi* **auf jdn ~** (*lit, fig*) to pound sb.

eintrüben *vr sep* (*Met*) to cloud over, to become overcast.

Eintrübung *f* (*Met*) cloudiness *no pl*.

eintrudeln *vi sep aux sein* (*inf*) to drift in (*inf*) ◆ **... bis alle eingetrudelt sind ...** until everyone has turned up.

eintunken *vt sep Brot* to dunk (*in +acc* in).

eintüten *vt sep* (*form*) to put into (paper) bags.

ein|üben *vt sep* to practise; *Theaterstück, Rolle etc* to rehearse; *Rücksichtnahme, Solidarität* to learn *or* acquire (through practice) ◆ **sich** (*dat*) **etw ~** to practise sth.

Ein|übung *f* practice; (*Theat etc*) rehearsal.

Einung *f* (*geh*) *siehe* **Einigung**.

einverleiben* *vt sep and insep* (a) *Gebiet, Land* to annex (*dat* to); *Firma, Ministerium* to incorporate (*dat* into). (b) (*hum inf*) **sich** (*dat*) **etw ~** (*essen, trinken*) to put sth away (*inf*), to polish sth off (*inf*); (*sich aneignen, begreifen*) to assimilate sth, to take sth in.

Einverleibung *f, no pl siehe vt* (*a*) annexation; incorporation.

Einvernahme *f* **-, -n** (*Jur: esp Aus, Sw*) *siehe* **Vernehmung**.

einvernehmen* *vt insep irreg* (*Jur: esp Aus, Sw*) *siehe* **vernehmen**.

Einvernehmen *nt* **-s,** *no pl* (*Eintracht*) amity, harmony; (*Übereinstimmung*) agreement ◆ **in gutem** *or* **bestem ~ leben** to live in perfect amity *or* harmony; **wir arbeiten in gutem ~ (miteinander)** we work in perfect harmony (together); **im ~ mit jdm** in agreement with sb; **in gegenseitigem** *or* **beiderseitigem ~** by mutual agreement; **sich mit jdm ins ~ setzen** (*form*) to come to *or* reach an agreement *or* understanding with sb.

einvernehmlich (*esp Aus form*) [1] *adj Regelung* joint.
[2] *adv* in conjunction, jointly.

Einvernehmung *f* (*Jur: esp Aus, Sw*) *siehe* **Vernehmung**.

▼ **einverstanden** *adj* **~!** okay! (*inf*), agreed!; **~ sein** to agree, to consent, to be agreed; **ich bin ~** that's okay *or* all right by me (*inf*), I'm agreed; **mit jdm/etw ~ sein** to agree to sb/sth; (*übereinstimmen*) to agree *or* be in agreement with sb/sth; **sie ist damit ~, daß sie nur 10% bekommt** she has agreed *or* consented to take only 10%; **ich bin mit deinem Verhalten/mit dir gar nicht ~** I don't approve of your behaviour; **sich mit etw ~ erklären** to give one's agreement to sth.

einverständlich *adj* mutually agreed; *Ehescheidung* by mutual consent ◆ **diese Frage wurde ~ geklärt** this question was settled to the satisfaction of both parties.

Einverständnis *nt* agreement; (*Zustimmung*) consent ◆ **wir haben uns in gegenseitigem ~ scheiden lassen** we were divorced by mutual consent; **er erklärte sein ~ mit dem Plan** he gave his agreement to the plan; **das geschieht mit meinem ~** that has my consent *or* agreement; **im ~ mit jdm handeln** to act with sb's consent.

Einverständnis|erklärung *f* declaration of consent ◆ **die schriftliche ~ der Eltern** the parents' written consent.

Einw. *abbr of* **Einwohner**.

Einwaage *f, no pl* (*Comm*) (a) (*Reingewicht*) *weight of contents of can or jar excluding juice etc* ◆ **Frucht-~/Fleisch-~ 200 g** fruit/meat content 200g. (b) (*Comm: Gewichtsverlust*) weight loss.

einwachsen[1] *vt sep Boden, Skier* to wax.

einwachsen[2] *vi sep irreg aux sein* (*Baum, Staude*) to establish itself; (*Finger-, Zehennagel*) to become ingrown ◆ **der Zehennagel ist mir eingewachsen** I have an ingrowing toenail.

▼ **Einwand** *m* **-(e)s, ¨e** objection ◆ **einen ~ erheben** *or* **vorbringen** *or* **geltend machen** (*form*) to put forward *or* raise an objection.

Einwanderer *m* immigrant.

einwandern *vi sep aux sein* (*nach, in +acc* to) to immigrate; (*Volk*) to migrate.

Einwanderung *f* immigration (*nach, in +acc* to) ◆ **vor seiner ~ in die USA** before he came *or* immigrated to the USA.

Einwanderungs- *in cpds* immigration.

Einwanderungsland *nt* immigration country.

einwandfrei *adj* (a) (*ohne Fehler*) perfect; *Sprache, Arbeit auch* faultless; *Benehmen, Leumund* irreproachable, impeccable; *Lebensmittel* perfectly fresh ◆ **er arbeitet sehr genau und ~** his work is very precise and absolutely faultless; **er spricht ~** *or* **ein ~es Spanisch** he speaks perfect Spanish, he speaks Spanish perfectly.
(b) (*unzweifelhaft*) indisputable; *Beweis auch* definite ◆ **etw ~ beweisen** to prove sth beyond doubt, to give definite proof of sth; **es steht ~ fest, daß ...** it is beyond question *or* quite indisputable that ...; **das ist ~ Betrug/Unterschlagung** that is a clear case of fraud/embezzlement.

einwärts *adv* inwards.

⚠ **einwärtsgebogen** *adj attr* bent inwards.

einwässern *vt sep* (*Cook*) to steep.

einweben *vt sep irreg* to weave in (*in +acc* -to); (*fig auch*) to work in (*in +acc* -to).

einwechseln *vt sep Geld* to change (*in +acc, gegen* into) ◆ **jdm Geld ~** to change money for sb.

einwecken *vt sep* to preserve; *Obst etc auch* to bottle; (*rare: in Büchsen*) to can, to tin (*Brit*).

Einweck-: ~glas *nt* preserving jar; **~gummi, ~ring** *m* rubber seal (*for preserving jar*).

Einweg- ['ainve:k]: **~flasche** *f* non-returnable bottle; **~scheibe** *f* one-way glass; **~spiegel** *m* one-way mirror; **~spritze** *f* disposable syringe; **~verpackung** *f* disposable wrapping.

einweichen *vt sep* to soak.

einweihen *vt sep* (a) (*feierlich eröffnen*) to open (officially); (*fig*) to christen, to baptize. (b) **jdn in etw** (*acc*) **~** to initiate sb into sth; **er ist eingeweiht** he knows all about it; *siehe* **Eingeweihte(r)**.

Einweihung(sfeier) *f* (official) opening.

einweisen *vt sep irreg* (a) (*in Wohnung, Haus*) to send, to assign (*in +acc* to).
(b) (*in Krankenhaus, Heilanstalt*) to admit (*in +acc* to).
(c) (*in Arbeit unterweisen*) **jdn ~** to introduce sb to his job *or* work; **er wurde von seinem Vorgänger (in die Arbeit) eingewiesen** his predecessor showed him what the job involved.
(d) (*in ein Amt*) to install (*in +acc* in).
(e) (*Aut*) to guide in (*in +acc* -to).

Einweisung *f siehe vt* (a) accommodation (*in +acc* in). (b) admission (*in +acc* to). (c) **die ~ der neuen Mitarbeiter übernehmen** to assume responsibility for introducing new employees to their jobs *or* work. (d) installation (*in +acc* in). (e) guiding in.

einwenden *vt sep irreg* **etwas/nichts gegen etw einzuwenden haben** to have an objection/no objection to sth, to object/not to object to sth; **dagegen läßt sich ~, daß ...** one objection to this is that ...; **dagegen läßt sich nichts ~** there can be no objection to that; **er wandte ein, daß ...** he objected *or* raised the objection that ...; **er hat immer etwas einzuwenden** he always finds something to object to, he always has some objection to make.

Einwendung *f* objection (*auch Jur*) ◆ **gegen etw ~en erheben** *or* **haben** *or* **vorbringen** to raise objections to sth.

einwerfen *sep irreg* [1] *vt* (a) *Fensterscheibe etc* to break, to smash.
(b) (*Sport*) *Ball* to throw in.
(c) *Brief* to post, to mail (*esp US*); *Münze* to insert.
(d) (*fig*) *Bemerkung* to make, to throw in ◆ **er warf ein, daß ...** he made the point that ...; **ja, warf er ein** yes, he interjected.
[2] *vi* (*Sport*) to throw in, to take the throw-in ◆ **er hat falsch eingeworfen** he fouled when he was throwing in.

einwertig *adj* (*Chem*) monovalent; (*Ling*) one place.

einwickeln *vt sep* (a) to wrap (up) ◆ **er wickelte sich fest in seinen Mantel ein** he wrapped himself up well in his coat.
(b) (*inf: übervorteilen, überlisten*) to fool (*inf*), to take in; (*durch Schmeicheleien*) to butter up (*inf*).

Einwickelpapier *nt* wrapping paper.

einwiegen *vt sep irreg* (*Comm*) *Mehl etc* to weigh out.

einwilligen *vi sep* (*in +acc* to) to consent, to agree.

Einwilligung *f* (*in +acc* to) consent, agreement.

einwinken *vt sep* to guide *or* direct in.

einwintern *vt sep* to winter.

einwirken *sep* [1] *vi* **auf jdn/etw ~** to have an effect on sb/sth; (*beeinflussen*) to influence sb/sth; **diese Maßnahmen wirken günstig auf die Marktsituation ein** these measures are having a favourable effect on the market situation; **etw ~ lassen** (*Med*) to let sth work in; (*Chem*) to let sth react; *Beize* to let sth soak *or* work in.
[2] *vt* to work in (*in +acc* -to).

Einwirkung *f* influence; (*einer Sache auch*) effect; (*eines Katalysators*) effect ◆ **Bayern steht unter ~ eines atlantischen Hochs** Bavaria is being affected by an anticyclone over the Atlantic; **unter (der) ~ von Drogen** *etc* under the influence of drugs *etc*; **unter (der) ~ eines Schocks stehen** to be suffering (from) the effects of shock; **nach ~ der Salbe ...** when the ointment has worked in ...

Einwirkungsmöglichkeit *f* influence ◆ **dadurch haben wir eine gute ~** this has made it possible for us to have some influence *or* to bring some influence to bear.

einwöchig *adj* one-week *attr*.

➤ SPRACHE AKTIV: **einverstanden** → 41 **Einwand** → 28.1, 36.1, 36.2, 38.1

Einwohner(in *f*) *m* **-s,** - inhabitant.

Einwohner-: ~meldeamt *nt residents' registration office;* **sich beim ~meldeamt (an)melden** ≃ to register with the police; **~schaft** *f, no pl* population, inhabitants *pl;* **~verzeichnis** *nt list of inhabitants' names and addresses;* **~zahl** *f* population, number of inhabitants.

Einwurf *m* **(a)** (*das Hineinwerfen*) (*von Münze*) insertion; (*von Brief*) posting, mailing (*esp US*) ◆ **~ 2 Mark** insert 2 marks. **(b)** (*Sport*) throw-in ◆ **falscher ~** foul throw. **(c)** (*Schlitz*) slot; (*von Briefkasten*) slit. **(d)** (*fig*) interjection; (*Einwand*) objection.

einwurzeln *vir sep* (*vi: aux sein*) (*Pflanzen*) to take root; (*fig auch*) to become rooted (*bei* in); *siehe* **eingewurzelt.**

Einzahl *f* singular.

einzahlen *vt sep* to pay in ◆ **Geld auf ein Konto ~** to pay money into an account.

Einzahlung *f* payment; (*auf Bankkonto auch*) deposit (*auf +acc* into).

Einzahlungs-: ~schalter *m* (*Post*) paying-in counter; **~schein** *m* paying-in slip, deposit slip (*US*).

einzäunen *vt sep* to fence in.

Einzäunung *f* (*Zaun*) fence, fencing; (*das Umzäunen*) fencing-in.

einzeichnen *vt sep* to draw *or* mark in ◆ **ist der Ort eingezeichnet?** is the place marked?

Einzeichnung *f* **(a)** *no pl* (*das Einzeichnen*) drawing *or* marking in. **(b)** (*Markierung*) marking.

Einzeiler *m* **-s,** - (*Liter*) one-line poem, one-liner (*inf*), monostich (*form*).

einzeilig *adj* one-line *attr.*

Einzel *nt* **-s,** - (*Tennis*) singles *sing.*

Einzel-: ~aktion *f* independent action; (*Sport*) solo performance *or* effort; **~antrieb** *m* (*Tech*) independent drive; **~aufhängung** *f* (*Aut*) independent suspension; **~aufstellung** *f* (*Comm*) itemized list; **~ausgabe** *f* separate edition; **~behandlung** *f* individual treatment; **~blatteinzug** *m* cut-sheet feed; **~darstellung** *f* individual treatment; **eine Geschichte unseres Jahrhunderts in ~darstellungen** a history of our century in individual portraits; **~erscheinung** *f* isolated occurrence; **~fahrer** *m* (*Motorradrennen*) solo rider; **~fahrschein** *m* single (*Brit*) *or* one-way ticket.

Einzelfall *m* individual case; (*Sonderfall*) isolated case, exception.

Einzelfallstudie *f* (*Sociol, Psych*) (individual) case study.

Einzel-: ~fertigung *f* special order; **in ~ fertigung hergestellt** made to order, custom-made (*esp US*); **~gänger(in** *f*) *m* **-s,** - loner, lone wolf; (*Elefant*) rogue; **~haft** *f* solitary confinement.

Einzelhandel *m* retail trade ◆ **das ist im ~ teurer als im Großhandel** that is dearer (to buy) retail than wholesale; **im ~ erhältlich** available retail; **im ~ kostet das ...** it retails at ...

Einzelhandels-: ~geschäft *nt* retail shop; **~kauffrau** *f,* **~kaufmann** *m* trained retail saleswoman/salesman; **~preis** *m* retail price; **~spanne** *f* retail profit margin.

▼ **Einzel-: ~händler** *m* retailer, retail trader; **~haus** *nt* detached house; **~heit** *f* detail, particular; **auf ~heiten eingehen** to go into detail(s); **etw in allen/bis in die kleinsten ~heiten schildern** to describe sth in great detail/ right down to the last detail; **sich in ~heiten verlieren** to get bogged down in details; **~hof** *m* isolated farm; **~kabine** *f* (individual) cubicle; **~kampf** *m* **(a)** (*Mil*) single combat; **(b)** (*Sport*) individual competition; **~kauffrau** *f,* **~kaufmann** *m* small businesswoman/businessman; **~kind** *nt* only child.

Einzeller *m* **-s,** - (*Biol*) single-celled *or* unicellular organism.

einzellig *adj* single-cell(ed) *attr,* unicellular.

einzeln [1] *adj* **(a)** individual; (*getrennt*) separate; (*von Paar*) odd ◆ **~e Teile des Bestecks kann man nicht kaufen** you cannot buy individual *or* separate *or* single pieces of this cutlery; **wir kamen ~** we came separately; **die Gäste kamen ~ herein** the guests came in separately *or* singly *or* one by one; **bitte ~ eintreten** please come in one (person) at a time; **die ~en Städte, die wir besucht haben** the individual cities which we visited; **~ aufführen** to list separately *or* individually *or* singly; **im ~en Fall** in the particular case.

(b) *Mensch* individual.

(c) (*alleinstehend*) *Baum, Haus* single, solitary.

(d) (*mit pl n: einige, vereinzelte*) some; (*Met*) *Schauer* scattered ◆ **~e Firmen haben ...** some firms have ..., the odd firm has ..., a few odd firms have ...; **~e Besucher kamen schon früher** a few *or* one or two visitors came earlier.

[2] *adj* (*substantivisch*) **(a)** (*Mensch*) **der/die ~e** the individual; **ein ~er** an individual, a single person; (*ein einziger Mensch*) one single person; **~e** some (people), a few (people), one or two (people); **jeder ~e/jede ~e** each individual; **jeder ~e muß dabei helfen** (each and) every one of you/them *etc* must help; **als ~er kann man nichts machen** as an individual one can do nothing.

(b) ~es some; **~es hat mir gefallen** I liked parts *or* some of it; **~e haben mir gefallen** I liked some of them.

(c) das ~e the particular; **er kam vom E~en zum Allgemeinen** he went from the particular to the general; **jedes ~e** each one; **im ~en auf etw** (*acc*) **eingehen** to go into detail(s) *or* particulars about sth; **etw im ~en besprechen** to discuss sth in detail; **bis ins ~e** right down to the last detail.

⚠ **einzelnstehend** *adj attr* solitary ◆ **ein paar ~e Bäume** a few scattered trees, a few trees here and there; **ein ~er Baum** a tree (standing) all by itself, a solitary tree.

Einzel-: ~nummer *f* (*von Zeitung*) single issue; **~person** *f* single person; **für eine ~person kochen** to cook for one (person) *or* a single person; **~personen haben es auf Reisen meist schwer, ein Hotelzimmer zu bekommen** people travelling alone usually find it hard to get a hotel room; **~preis** *m* price, unit price (*Comm*); (*von Zeitung*) price per copy; **~radaufhängung** *f* (*Aut*) independent suspension; **~reisende(r)** *mf* single traveller; **~richter** *m* judge sitting singly; **~sieger** *m* individual winner; **~spiel** *nt* (*Tennis*) singles *sing;* **~staat** *m* individual state; **~stehende(r)** *mf decl as adj siehe* **Alleinstehende(r); ~stück** *nt* **ein schönes ~stück** a beautiful piece; **~stücke verkaufen wir nicht** we don't sell them singly; **~stunde** *f* private *or* individual lesson; **~teil** *nt* individual *or* separate part; (*Ersatzteil*) spare *or* replacement part; **etw in seine ~teile zerlegen** to take sth to pieces; **~unterricht** *m* private lessons *pl or* tuition; **~verkauf** *m* (*Comm*) retail sale; (*das Verkaufen*) retailing, retail selling; **~verpackung** *f* individual packing; **~wertung** *f* (*Sport*) individual placings *pl;* (*bei Kür*) individual marks *pl;* **~wesen** *nt* individual; **~wettbewerb** *m* (*Sport*) individual competition; **~zelle** *f* single cell (*auch Biol*); **~zimmer** *nt* single room.

einzementieren* *vt sep Stein* to cement; *Safe* to build *or* set into (the) concrete; *Kachel* to cement on.

Einzieh-: e~bar *adj* retractable; *Schulden* recoverable; **~decke** *f* duvet, continental quilt.

einziehen *sep irreg* [1] *vt* **(a)** (*hineinziehen, einfügen*) *Gummiband, Faden* to thread; (*in einen Bezug etc*) to put in; (*Build: einbauen*) *Wand, Balken* to put in; (*Kopiergerät*) *Papier* to take in.

(b) (*einsaugen*) *Flüssigkeit* to soak up; (*durch Strohhalm*) to draw up; *Duft* to breathe in; *Luft, Rauch* to draw in.

(c) (*zurückziehen*) *Fühler, Krallen, Fahrgestell* to retract, to draw in; *Bauch, Netz* to pull *or* draw in; *Antenne* to retract; *Schultern* to hunch; *Periskop, Flagge, Segel* to lower, to take down; *Ruder* to ship, to take in ◆ **den Kopf ~** to duck (one's head); **zieh den Bauch ein!** keep *or* tuck (*inf*) your tummy in; **der Hund zog den Schwanz ein** the dog put his tail between his legs; **mit eingezogenem Schwanz** (*lit, fig*) with its/his/her tail between its/his/her legs.

(d) (*Mil*) (*zu* into) *Personen* to conscript, to call up, to draft (*esp US*); *Fahrzeuge etc* to requisition.

(e) (*kassieren*) *Steuern, Gelder* to collect; (*fig*) *Erkundigungen* to make (*über +acc* about).

(f) (*aus dem Verkehr ziehen*) *Banknoten, Münzen* to withdraw (from circulation), to call in; (*beschlagnahmen*) *Führerschein* to take away, to withdraw; *Vermögen* to confiscate.

(g) (*Typ*) *Wörter, Zeilen* to indent.

[2] *vi aux sein* **(a)** (*in Wohnung, Haus*) to move in ◆ **wer ist im dritten Stock eingezogen?** who has moved into the third floor?; **er zog bei Bekannten ein** he moved in with friends; **ins Parlament ~** to take office; (*Abgeordneter*) to take up one's seat (in parliament).

(b) (*auch Mil: einmarschieren*) to march in (*in +acc* -to).

(c) (*einkehren*) to come (*in +dat* to) ◆ **mit ihm zog eine fröhliche Stimmung bei uns ein** he brought a happy atmosphere with him; **wenn der Friede im Lande einzieht** when peace comes to our country, when we have peace; **Ruhe und Ordnung zogen wieder ein** law and order returned.

(d) (*eindringen*) to soak in (*in +acc* -to).

Einziehung *f* **(a)** (*Mil*) (*von Personen*) conscription, call-up, drafting (*esp US*); (*von Fahrzeugen*) requisitioning. **(b)** (*Beschlagnahme*) (*von Vermögen, Publikationen*) confiscation; (*Rücknahme: von Banknoten, Führerschein etc*) withdrawal. **(c)** (*Eintreiben: von Steuern etc*) collection.

einzig [1] *adj* **(a)** *attr* only, sole ◆ **ich sehe nur eine ~e Möglichkeit** I can see only one (single) possibility; **ich habe nicht einen ~en Brief bekommen** I haven't had a single *or* solitary letter; **kein** *or* **nicht ein ~es Mal** not once, not one single time.

(b) (*emphatisch*) absolute, complete ◆ **dieses Fußballspiel war eine ~e Schlammschlacht** this football match was just one big mudbath.

(c) *pred* (*~artig*) unique ◆ **es ist ~ in seiner Art** it is quite unique; **sein Können steht ~ da** his skill is unmatched, his skill is second to none.

[2] *adj* (*substantivisch*) **der/die ~e** the only one; **das ~e** the only thing; **das ist das ~e, was wir tun können** that's the only thing we can do; **ein ~er hat geantwortet** only one (person) answered; **kein ~er wußte es** nobody *or* not a single *or* solitary person knew; **die ~en, die es wußten ...** the only ones who knew ...; **er hat als ~er das Ziel erreicht** he was the only one *or* the sole person to reach the finish; **Hans ist unser E~er** Hans is our only child *or* our one and only.

[3] *adv* **(a)** (*allein*) only, solely ◆ **seine Beförderung hat er ~ dir zu verdanken** he owes his promotion entirely to you; **die ~ mögliche Lösung** the only possible solution, the only solution possible; **~ und allein** solely; **~ und allein deshalb hat er gewonnen** he owes his victory solely *or* entirely to that, that's the only *or* sole reason he won; **das ~ Wahre** *or* **Senkrechte** (*inf*) the only thing; (*das beste*) the real McCoy; **jetzt Ferien machen/ein Bier trinken, das wäre das ~ Wahre** *etc* to take a holiday/have a beer, that's just what the doctor ordered (*inf*) *or* that would be just the job.

(b) (*inf: außerordentlich*) fantastically.

einzig|artig *adj* unique ◆ **der Film war ~ schön** the film was astoundingly beautiful.

Einzig|artigkeit *f* uniqueness.

Einzigkeit *f* uniqueness.

Einzimmer- *in cpds* one-room.

Einzug *m* **(a)** (*in Haus etc*) move (*in +acc* into) ◆ **vor dem ~** before moving in *or* the move; **der ~ in das neue Haus** moving *or* the move into the new house; **der ~ ins Parlament** taking office; (*Abgeordneter*) taking up one's seat.

(b) (*Einmarsch*) entry (*in +acc* into).

(c) (*fig: von Stimmung, Winter etc*) advent ◆ **der Winter hielt seinen ~ mit Schnee und Frost** winter arrived amid snow and frost; **der Frühling** *etc* **hält**

⚠: for details of spelling reform, see supplement

➤ SPRACHE AKTIV: **Einzelheit** → 47.1

seinen ~ spring *etc* is coming.
(d) (*von Feuchtigkeit*) penetration ♦ **der ~ kühlerer Meeresluft ...** a low trough moving in from the sea ...
(e) (*von Steuern, Geldern*) collection; (*von Banknoten*) withdrawal, calling-in.
(f) (*Typ*) indentation.

Einzugs-: ~auftrag *m* (*Fin*) direct debit; **~bereich** *m* catchment area; **~feier** *f* house-warming (party); **~gebiet** *nt* (*lit, fig*) catchment area; **~verfahren** *nt* (*Fin*) direct debit.

einzwängen *vt sep* (*lit*) to squeeze *or* jam *or* wedge in; (*fig*) *jdn* to constrain, to constrict; *Idee* to force ♦ **ich fühle mich eingezwängt** (*in Kleidung, Ehe etc*) I feel constricted.

Einzylindermotor *m* one- *or* single-cylinder engine.

Eipulver *nt* dried *or* powdered egg.

Eis *nt* **-es, -** (a) *no pl* (*gefrorenes Wasser*) ice ♦ **zu ~ gefrieren** to freeze, to turn to ice; **vom ~ eingeschlossen sein** to be iced in *or* icebound; **das ~ brechen** (*fig*) to break the ice; **jdn aufs ~ führen** (*fig*) to take sb for a ride (*inf*), to lead sb up the garden path; **etw auf ~ legen** (*lit*) to chill sth, to put sth on ice; (*fig inf*) to put sth on ice *or* into cold storage.
(b) (*Speise~*) ice(-cream) ♦ **er kaufte 3 ~** he bought 3 icecreams *or* ices; **~ am Stiel** ice(d)-lolly (*Brit*), Popsicle ® (*US*).

Eis-: ~bahn *f* ice-rink; **~bär** *m* polar bear; **~becher** *m* (*aus Pappe*) ice-cream tub; (*aus Metall*) sundae dish; (*Eis*) sundae; **e~bedeckt** *adj attr* ice-covered, covered in ice; **~bein** *nt* (a) (*Cook*) knuckle of pork (*boiled and served with sauerkraut*); (b) (*hum inf*) **wenn ich noch länger hier in dieser Kälte stehe, bekomme ich ~beine** if I stand around here in this cold any longer my feet will turn to ice; **~berg** *m* iceberg; **die Spitze des ~bergs** (*fig*) the tip of the iceberg; **~beutel** *m* ice pack; **~bildung** *f* **es kam zur ~bildung auf den Flüssen** ice formed on the rivers; **zur Verhinderung der ~bildung auf Fahrbahndecken** to prevent icing on *or* ice forming on road surfaces; **e~blau** *adj*, **~blau** *nt* ice-blue; **~block** *m* block of ice; **~blume** *f usu pl* frost pattern; **~bombe** *f* (*Cook*) bombe glacée; **~brecher** *m* icebreaker; **~bude** *f* ice-cream stall.

Eischnee *m* (*Cook*) beaten white of egg.

Eis-: ~creme *f* ice(-cream); **~decke** *f* ice sheet, sheet of ice; **~diele** *f* ice-cream parlour.

eisen *vt Tee, Wodka* to ice, to chill; *siehe* **geeist**.

Eisen *nt* **-s, -** (a) *no pl* (*Chem: abbr* **Fe**) iron ♦ **ein Mann aus ~** a man of iron; **mehrere/noch ein ~ im Feuer haben** (*fig*) to have more than one/another iron in the fire; **Muskeln von ~ haben** to have muscles of steel; **bei jdm auf ~ beißen** (*fig*) to get nowhere with sb; **zum alten ~ gehören** *or* **zählen** (*fig*) to be on the scrap heap; **jdn/etw zum alten ~ werfen** (*fig*) to throw sb/sth on the scrap heap; **man muß das ~ schmieden, solange es heiß** *or* **warm ist** (*Prov*) one must strike while the iron is hot (*prov*); *siehe* **Blut, heiß**.
(b) (*Bügel~, Golf*) iron; (*~beschlag*) iron fitting; (*~band*) iron band *or* hoop; (*Huf~*) shoe; (*Fang~*) trap; (*obs: Fesseln*) fetters *pl* (*obs*), irons *pl*; (*obs: Schwert*) iron (*obs*) ♦ **jdn in ~ legen** (*obs*) to put *or* clap sb in irons.
(c) (*no pl: Med*) iron.

Eisen-: ~ader *f* vein of iron ore; **e~artig** *adj* ironlike.

Eisenbahn *f* railway (*Brit*), railroad (*US*); (*~wesen*) railways *pl*, railroad (*US*); (*inf: Zug*) train; (*Spielzeug~*) train set ♦ **ich fahre lieber (mit der) ~ als (mit dem) Bus** I prefer to travel by train *or* rail than by bus; **Onkel Alfred arbeitet bei der ~** uncle Alfred works for the railways/railroad; **es ist (aller)höchste ~** (*inf*) it's getting late.

Eisenbahn-: ~abteil *nt* (railway/railroad) compartment; **~anlagen** *pl* railway/railroad installations *pl*; **~brücke** *f* railway/railroad bridge.

Eisenbahner(in *f*) *m* **-s, -** railwayman (*Brit*), railway employee (*Brit*), railroader (*US*).

Eisenbahn-: ~fähre *f* train ferry; **~fahrkarte** *f* rail ticket; **~fahrt** *f* train *or* rail journey *or* ride; **~gesellschaft** *f* railway/railroad company; **~gleis** *nt* railway/railroad track; **~knotenpunkt** *m* railway/railroad junction; **~netz** *nt* rail(way)/railroad network; **~schaffner** *m* (railway) guard, (railroad) conductor (*US*); **~schiene** *f* railway/railroad track; **~schwelle** *f* (railway/railroad) sleeper; **~signal** *nt* railway/railroad signal; **~station** *f* railway/railroad station; **~strecke** *f* railway line, railroad (*US*); **~überführung** *f* (railway/railroad) footbridge; **~unglück** *nt* railway/railroad accident, train crash; **~unterführung** *f* railway/railroad underpass; **~verbindung** *f* rail link; (*Anschluß*) connection; **~verkehr** *m* rail(way)/railroad traffic; **~wagen** *m* (*Personen~*) railway/railroad carriage; (*Güter~*) goods wagon *or* truck; **~wesen** *nt* railway/railroad system; **~zug** *m* railway/railroad train.

Eisenbart(h) *m*: **Doktor ~** (*fig*) quack, horse-doctor (*inf*).

Eisen-: ~bereifung *f* iron hooping; (*Reif*) iron hoop; **~bergwerk** *nt* iron mine; **~beschlag** *m* ironwork *no pl*; (*zum Verstärken*) iron band; **e~beschlagen** *adj* with iron fittings; *Stiefel* steel-tipped; **~beton** *m* (*dated*) ferroconcrete, reinforced concrete; **~blech** *nt* sheet iron; **~block** *m* iron block, block of iron; **~bohrer** *m* (*Tech*) iron *or* steel drill; **~chlorid** *nt* ($FeCl_2$) ferrous chloride; ($FeCl_3$) ferric chloride; **~draht** *m* steel wire; **~erz** *nt* iron ore; **~feile** *f* iron file; **~feilspäne** *pl* iron filings *pl*; **~flecken** *pl* (*in Kartoffeln*) discoloured patches *pl*; **~fresser** *m* (*pej*) tough guy; **~garn** *nt* steel thread; **~gehalt** *m* iron content; **~gießerei** *f* (*Vorgang*) iron smelting; (*Werkstatt*) iron foundry; **~glanz, ~glimmer** *m* ferric oxide, iron glance; ⚠**~guß** *m* iron casting; **e~haltig** *adj Gestein* iron-bearing, ferruginous (*form*); **das Wasser ist e~haltig** the water contains iron; **~hammer** *m* steam hammer; (*Werkstatt*) forge; **e~hart** *adj* (*lit*) as hard as iron; **ein e~harter Mann/Wille** a man/will of iron; **~hut** *m* (a) (*Bot*) monk's hood, aconite; (b) (*Hist*) iron helmet; **~hütte** *f* ironworks *pl or sing*, iron foundry; **~hüttenkombinat** *nt* (*DDR*) iron processing combine; **~industrie** *f* iron industry; **~karbid** *nt* cementite; **~kern** *m* iron core; **~kies** *m* iron pyrites *sing*; **~kitt** *m* iron-cement; **~kur** *f* course of iron treatment; **~legierung** *f* iron alloy; **~mangel** *m* iron deficiency; **~oxyd** *nt* ferric oxide; **~präparat** *nt* (*Med*) iron tonic/tablets *pl*; **e~schüssig** *adj Boden* iron-bearing, ferruginous (*form*); **~späne** *pl* iron filings *pl*; **~stange** *f* iron bar; ⚠**~sulphat** *nt* ferric sulphate; **~träger** *m* iron girder; ⚠**e~verarbeitend** *adj attr* iron processing; **~verbindung** *f* (*Chem*) iron compound; **~vitriol** *nt* iron *or* ferrous sulphate, green vitriol; **~waren** *pl* ironmongery *sing* (*Brit*), hardware *sing*; **~warenhändler** *m* ironmonger; **~warenhandlung** *f* ironmonger's (shop) (*Brit*), hardware store; **~werk** *nt* (a) (*Art*) ironwork; (b) *siehe* **~hütte**; **~zeit** *f* (*Hist*) Iron Age.

eisern *adj* (a) *attr* (*aus Eisen*) iron ♦ **das E~e Kreuz** (*Mil*) the Iron Cross; **der E~e Kanzler** the Iron Chancellor; **der ~e Vorhang** (*Theat*) the safety curtain; **der E~e Vorhang** (*Pol*) the Iron Curtain; **~e Lunge** (*Med*) iron lung; **die E~e Jungfrau** (*Hist*) the Iron Maiden; **~e Hochzeit** 65th wedding anniversary.
(b) (*fest, unnachgiebig*) *Disziplin* iron *attr*, strict; *Wille* iron *attr*, of iron; *Energie* unflagging, indefatigable; *Ruhe* unshakeable ♦ **~e Gesundheit** iron constitution; **sein Griff war ~** his grip was like iron; **er schwieg ~** he remained resolutely silent; **mit ~er Stirn** (*unverschämt*) brazenly; (*unerschütterlich*) resolutely; **er ist ~ bei seinem Entschluß geblieben** he stuck steadfastly *or* firmly to his decision; **mit ~er Faust** with an iron hand; **es ist ein ~es Gesetz, daß ...** it's a hard and fast rule that ...; **ein ~es Regiment führen** to rule with a rod of iron; **in etw** (*dat*) **~ sein/bleiben** to be/remain resolute about sth; **da bin** *or* **bleibe ich ~!** (*inf*) that's definite; **(aber) ~!** (*inf*) (but) of course!, absolutely!; **mit ~em Besen auskehren** to make a clean sweep, to be ruthless in creating order; **~ trainieren/sparen** to train/save resolutely *or* with iron determination.
(c) *attr* (*unantastbar*) *Reserve* emergency; *Ration auch* iron.

Eiseskälte *f* icy cold.

Eis-: ~fach *nt* freezer compartment, ice-box; **~fischerei** *f* fishing through ice; **~fläche** *f* (surface of the) ice; **die ~fläche des Sees** the (sheet of) ice covering the lake; **e~frei** *adj* ice-free *attr*, free of ice *pred*; **~gang** *m* ice drift; **e~gekühlt** *adj* chilled; **~getränk** *nt* iced drink; **~glätte** *f* black ice; **e~grau** *adj* (*liter*) steel(y) grey; **~heiligen** *pl*: **die drei ~heiligen** *three Saints' Days, 12th-14th May, which are usually particularly cold and after which further frost is rare*; **~hockey** *nt* ice hockey, hockey (*US*).

eisig *adj* (a) (*kalt*) *Wasser, Wind* icy (cold); *Kälte* icy. (b) (*jäh*) *Schreck, Grauen* chilling ♦ **es durchzuckte mich ~** a cold shiver ran through me. (c) (*fig: abweisend*) icy, glacial; *Schweigen auch* frosty, chilly; *Ablehnung* cold; *Blick* icy, cold; *Lächeln* frosty.

Eis-: ~jacht *f* ice-yacht; **~kaffee** *m* iced coffee; **e~kalt** *adj* (a) icy-cold; (b) *siehe* **eisig (b)**; (c) (*fig*) (*abweisend*) icy, cold, frosty; (*kalt und berechnend*) cold-blooded, cold and calculating; (*dreist*) cool; **davor habe ich keine Angst, das mache ich e~kalt** I'm not afraid of that, I can do it without turning a hair; **machst du das? — ja! e~kalt** will you do it? — no problem; **~kappe** *f* icecap; **~kasten** *m* (*S Ger, Aus*) refrigerator, fridge (*Brit*), icebox (*US*); **~keller** *m* cold store, cold room; **unser Schlafzimmer ist ein ~keller** our bedroom is like an icebox; **~kristall** *nt* ice crystal; **~kunstlauf** *m* figure skating; **~kunstläufer** *m* figure skater; **~lauf** *m* ice-skating; ⚠**e~laufen** *vi sep irreg aux sein* to ice-skate; **sie läuft e~** she ice-skates; **~läufer** *m* ice-skater; **~männer** *pl* (*S Ger, Aus*) *siehe* **~heiligen**; **~maschine** *f* ice-cream machine; **~meer** *nt* polar sea; **Nördliches/Südliches ~meer** Arctic/Antarctic Ocean; **~monat, ~mond** *m* (*obs*) January; **~nadeln** *pl* ice needles *pl*; **~nebel** *m* freezing fog; **~palast** *m* ice rink; (*hum inf*) icebox; **~pickel** *m* ice axe, ice pick.

Eisprung *m* (*Physiol*) ovulation *no art*.

Eis-: ~pulver *nt* (*Cook*) ice-cream mix; **~punkt** *m* (*Phys*) freezing point; **~regen** *m* sleet; **~revue** *f* ice revue, ice show; **~schießen** *nt* curling; **~schmelze** *f* thaw; **~schnellauf** *m* speed skating; **~schnelläufer** *m* speed skater; **~scholle** *f* ice floe; **~schrank** *m* refrigerator, fridge (*Brit*), icebox (*US*); **~segeln** *nt* ice-sailing; **~sport** *m* ice sports *pl*; **~(sport)stadion** *nt* ice rink; **~stock** *m* (*Sport*) curling stone; **~(stock)schießen** *nt* curling; **~tanz** *m* ice-dancing; **~torte** *f* ice-cream cake; **~verkäufer** *m* ice-cream seller *or* man (*inf*); **~vogel** *m* (a) kingfisher; (b) (*Schmetterling*) white admiral; **~wasser** *nt* icy water; (*Getränk*) iced water; **~wein** *m sweet wine made from grapes which have been exposed to frost*; **~würfel** *m* ice cube; **~zapfen** *m* icicle; **~zeit** *f* Ice Age, glacial epoch (*form*); (*fig*) cold war; **e~zeitlich** *adj* ice-age, of the Ice Age.

eitel *adj* (a) *Mensch* vain; (*eingebildet auch*) conceited ♦ **~ wie ein Pfau** vain as a peacock.
(b) (*liter*) *Hoffnung, Wahn, Versuch, Gerede* vain ♦ **seine Hoffnungen erwiesen sich als ~** his hopes proved to be all in vain; **alles ist ~** all is vanity.
(c) *inv* (*obs: rein*) *Gold* pure ♦ **es herrschte ~ Freude** (*obs, hum*) there was absolute joy; **er denkt, das ganze Leben sei ~ Freude und Sonnenschein** he thinks the whole of life is nothing but sweetness and light.

Eitelkeit *f siehe adj* (*a, b*) vanity; vainness.

Eiter *m* **-s,** *no pl* pus.

Eiter-: ~beule *f* boil; (*fig*) canker; **~bläschen** *nt*, **~blase** *f* pustule; **~erreger** *m* pyogenic organism (*spec*); **~herd** *m* suppurative focus (*spec*).

eit(e)rig *adj Ausfluß* purulent; *Wunde* festering, suppurating; *Binde* pus-covered.

eitern *vi* to fester, to discharge pus, to suppurate.

Eiter-: ~pfropf *m* core (*of a boil*); (*von Pickel*) head; **~pickel** *m* pimple (con-

taining pus).
Eiterung *f* discharge of pus, suppuration.
eitrig *adj siehe* **eit(e)rig.**
Eiweiß *nt* (egg-)white, white of egg, albumen (*spec*); (*Chem*) protein.
Eiweiß-: e~arm *adj* low in protein; **e~arme Kost** a low-protein diet; **~bedarf** *m* protein requirement; **~gehalt** *m* protein content; **e~haltig** *adj* protein-containing *attr*; **Fleisch ist sehr e~haltig** meat is high in protein *or* contains a lot of protein; **~haushalt** *m* (*Physiol*) protein metabolism; **~mangel** *m* protein deficiency; **~präparat** *nt* protein preparation; **~stoffwechsel** *m* protein metabolism.
Eizelle *f* (*Biol*) egg cell.
Ejakulat *nt* (*Med*) ejaculated semen, ejaculate (*spec*).
Ejakulation *f* ejaculation.
ejakulieren* *vi* to ejaculate.
EK [e:'ka:] *nt* **-s, -s** *abbr of* **Eisernes Kreuz ◆ EK I/II** Iron Cross First/Second Class.
EKD [e:ka:'de:] *f* - *abbr of* **Evangelische Kirche in Deutschland.**
Ekel¹ *m* **-s,** *no pl* disgust, revulsion, loathing; (*Übelkeit*) nausea ◆ **vor jdm/etw einen ~ haben** *or* **empfinden** to have a loathing of sb/sth, to loathe sb/sth; **dabei empfinde ich ~** it gives me a feeling of disgust *etc*; **~ überkommt mich** a feeling of disgust *etc* overcomes me; **diese Heuchelei ist mir ein ~** this hypocrisy is just nauseating *or* disgusting, I find this hypocrisy nauseating *or* disgusting; **er hat das Essen vor ~ ausgespuckt** he spat out the food in disgust *or* revulsion; **er mußte sich vor ~ übergeben** he was so nauseated that he vomited.
Ekel² *nt* **-s,** - (*inf*) obnoxious person, horror (*inf*).
⚠ **ekel|erregend** *adj* nauseating, revolting, disgusting.
ekelhaft, ek(e)lig *adj* disgusting, revolting; (*inf*) *Schmerzen, Problem, Chef* nasty (*inf*), horrible, vile ◆ **sei nicht so ~ zu ihr!** don't be so nasty to her.
ekeln [1] *vt* to disgust, to revolt, to nauseate.
[2] *vt impers* **es ekelt mich vor diesem Geruch/Anblick, mich** *or* **mir ekelt vor diesem Geruch/Anblick** the smell/sight of it fills me with disgust *or* revulsion, this smell/sight is disgusting *or* revolting *or* nauseating.
[3] *vr* to be *or* feel disgusted *or* revolted *or* nauseated ◆ **sich vor etw** (*dat*) **~** to find sth disgusting *or* revolting *or* nauseating.
EKG, Ekg [e:ka:'ge:] *nt* **-s, -s** *abbr of* **Elektrokardiogramm** ECG ◆ **ein ~ machen lassen** to have an ECG.
Eklat [e'kla(:)] *m* **-s, -s** (*geh*) (*Aufsehen*) sensation, stir; (*Zusammenstoß*) row, (major) altercation (*form*) ◆ **mit großem ~** causing a great stir *or* sensation, spectacularly; **mit (großem) ~ durchfallen** to be a resounding flop *or* a spectacular failure.
eklatant *adj* (*aufsehenerregend*) *Fall* sensational, spectacular; (*offenkundig*) *Beispiel* striking; *Verletzung* flagrant.
Eklektiker(in *f***)** *m* **-s,** - eclectic.
eklektisch *adj* eclectic.
Eklektizismus *m* eclecticism.
eklig *adj siehe* **ek(e)lig.**
Eklipse *f* **-, -n** eclipse.
Ekliptik *f* ecliptic.
ekliptisch *adj* ecliptical.
Ekstase *f* **-, -n** ecstasy ◆ **in ~ geraten** to go into ecstasies; **jdn in ~ versetzen** to send sb into ecstasies.
ekstatisch *adj* ecstatic, full of ecstasy.
Ekzem *nt* **-s, -e** (*Med*) eczema.
Elaborat *nt* (*pej*) concoction (*pej*).
Elan [*auch* e'lã:] *m* **-s,** *no pl* élan, zest, vigour.
Elast *m* **-(e)s, -e** (*esp DDR*) rubber, elastomer (*spec*).
Elastikbinde *f* elasticated bandage.
elastisch *adj* elastic; *Gang auch* springy; *Metall, Holz* springy, flexible; *Stoff auch* stretchy; (*fig*) (*spannkräftig*) *Muskel, Mensch* strong and supple; (*flexibel*) flexible, elastic ◆ **der Baum bog sich ~ im Wind** the tree bent supply in the wind; **er federte ~** he bent supply at the knees; **der Bügel schnellte ~ zurück** the bow sprang back.
Elastizität *f siehe* **elastisch** elasticity; springiness; flexibility; stretchiness; flexibility, elasticity ◆ **die ~ seines Körpers** the supple strength of his body.
Elativ *m* (*Gram*) absolute superlative.
Elbkähne *pl* (*N Ger hum*) beetle-crushers *pl* (*inf*), clodhoppers *pl* (*inf*).
Elch *m* **-(e)s, -e** elk.
Eldorado *nt* **-s, -s** (*lit, fig*) eldorado.
Elefant *m* elephant ◆ **wie ein ~ im Porzellanladen** (*inf*) like a bull in a china shop (*prov*); *siehe* **Mücke.**
Elefanten-: ~baby *nt* (*inf*) baby elephant (*auch fig hum*); **~bulle** *m* bull elephant; **~hochzeit** *f* (*Comm inf*) mega-merger (*inf*); **~kuh** *f* cow elephant; **~rennen** *nt* (*hum inf*) duel between two lorries (*Brit*) *or* trucks; **~robbe** *f* elephant seal; **~rüssel** *m* elephant's trunk; **~schlacht** *f* (*fig*) battle of the giants.
Elefantiasis *f* **-,** *no pl* (*Med*) elephantiasis.
elegant *adj* elegant ◆ **die ~e Welt** (*dated*) high society.
Eleganz *f* elegance.
Elegie *f* elegy.
Elegiendichter [-'gi:ən-], **Elegiker(in** *f***)** *m* **-s,** - elegist.
elegisch *adj* elegiac; (*melancholisch auch*) melancholy ◆ **~ gestimmt** in a melancholy mood.
Eleison *nt* **-s, -s** (*Eccl*) Kyrie eleison.
Elektrifikation *f* (*Sw*) *siehe* **Elektrifizierung.**

elektrifizieren* *vt* to electrify.
Elektrifizierung *f* electrification.
Elektrik *f* **(a)** (*elektrische Anlagen*) electrical equipment. **(b)** (*inf: Elektrizitätslehre*) electricity.
Elektriker(in *f***)** *m* **-s,** - electrician.
elektrisch *adj* electric; *Entladung, Feld, Widerstand* electrical ◆ **~e Geräte** electrical appliances; **~er Schlag/Strom** electric shock/current; **der ~e Stuhl** the electric chair; **~ betrieben** electrically driven, driven *or* run by electricity, electric; **wir kochen/heizen ~** we cook/heat by *or* with electricity; **bei uns ist alles ~** we're all electric; **das geht alles ~** (*inf*) it's all automatic.
Elektrische *f* **-n, -n** (*dated*) tram, streetcar (*US*).
elektrisieren* [1] *vt* (*lit, fig*) to electrify; (*aufladen*) to charge with electricity; (*Med*) to treat with electricity ◆ **der Plattenspieler hat mich elektrisiert** the record-player gave me a shock *or* an electric shock; **ich habe mich elektrisiert** I gave myself *or* got an electric shock; **die elektrisierte Atmosphäre** the electrically-charged atmosphere; **wie elektrisiert** (as if) electrified.
[2] *vi* to give an electric shock.
Elektrisiermaschine *f* electrostatic generator.
Elektrizität *f* electricity.
Elektrizitäts-: ~gesellschaft *f* electric power company; **~lehre** *f* (science of) electricity; **~versorgung** *f* (electric) power supply; **~werk** *nt* (electric) power station; (*Gesellschaft*) electric power company; **~zähler** *m* (*form*) electricity meter.
Elektro- [e'lɛktro] *in cpds* electro- (*auch Sci*), electric; **~analyse** *f* electroanalysis; **~antrieb** *m* electric drive; **~artikel** *m* electrical appliance; **~auto** *nt* electric car; **~chemie** *f* electrochemistry; **e~chemisch** *adj* electrochemical.
Elektrode *f* **-, -n** electrode.
Elektrodenspannung *f* electrode potential.
Elektro-: ~diagnostik *f* (*Med*) electrodiagnosis; **~dynamik** *f* electrodynamics *sing*; **e~dynamisch** *adj* electrodynamic; **~enzephalogramm** *nt* (*Med*) electroencephalogram, EEG; **~fahrzeug** *nt* electric vehicle; **~gerät** *nt* electrical appliance; **~geschäft** *nt* electrical shop; **~herd** *m* electric cooker; **~industrie** *f* electrical industry; **~ingenieur** *m* electrical engineer; **~installateur** *m* electrician; **~kardiogramm** *nt* (*Med*) electrocardiogram, ECG; **~karren** *m* small electric truck; (*des Milchmannes etc*) electric float; **~lok** *f* electric locomotive; **~lyse** *f* **-, -n** electrolysis; **~lyt** *m* **-en, -en** electrolyte; **e~lytisch** *adj* electrolytic; **~magnet** *m* electromagnet; **e~magnetisch** *adj* electromagnetic; **~mechaniker** *m* electrician; **e~mechanisch** *adj* electromechanical; **~meister** *m* master electrician; **~messer** *nt* electric carving knife; **~meter** *nt* electrometer; **~motor** *m* electric motor.
Elektron [elɛk'tro:n] *nt* **-s, -en** [elɛk'tro:nən] electron.
Elektronen-: ~blitz(gerät *nt***)** *m* (*Phot*) electronic flash; **~(ge)hirn** *nt* electronic brain; **~hülle** *f* (*Phys*) electron shell *or* cloud; **~laser** *m* electron laser; **~mikroskop** *nt* electron microscope; **~orgel** *f* (*Mus*) electronic organ; **~rechner** *m* (electronic) computer; **~röhre** *f* valve, electron tube (*US*); **~schale** *f* electron shell; **~schleuder** *f* (*Phys*) electron accelerator, betatron (*spec*); **~strahlen** *pl* electron *or* cathode rays *pl*; **~theorie** *f* electron theory.
Electronic Banking ['elɛktrɔnɪk'bɛŋkɪŋ] *nt* - *no pl* electronic *or* home banking.
Elektronik *f* electronics *sing*; (*elektronische Teile*) electronics *pl*.
Elektronik- *in cpds* electronics.
elektronisch *adj* electronic ◆ **~e Post** electronic mail, E-mail; **~er Briefkasten** electronic mailbox.
Elektro-: ~ofen *m* (*Metal*) electric furnace; (*Heizofen*) electric heater; **~rasenmäher** *m* electric lawn mower; **~rasierer** *m* electric shaver *or* razor; **~schock** *m* (*Med*) electric shock, electroshock; **~schockbehandlung** *f* electric shock treatment; **~schweißung** *f* electric welding; **~smog** *m* electromagnetic radiation; **~stahl** *m* (*Metal*) electrosteel, electric steel; **~statik** *f* (*Phys*) electrostatics *sing*; **e~statisch** *adj* electrostatic; **~technik** *f* electrical engineering; **~techniker** *m* electrician; (*Ingenieur*) electrical engineer; **e~technisch** *adj* electrical, electrotechnical (*rare*); **~therapie** *f* (*Med*) electrotherapy.
Element *nt* element; (*Elec*) cell, battery ◆ **~e** *pl* (*fig: Anfangsgründe*) elements *pl*, rudiments *pl* ◆ **das Toben der ~e** (*liter*) the raging of the elements; **kriminelle ~e** (*pej*) criminal elements; **in seinem ~ sein** to be in one's element.
elementar *adj* (*grundlegend, wesentlich*) elementary; (*naturhaft, urwüchsig*) *Gewalt, Trieb* elemental; *Haß* strong, violent ◆ **~ hervorbrechen** to erupt with elemental force.
Elementar- *in cpds* (*grundlegend*) elementary; (*naturhaft*) elemental; **~begriff** *m* elementary *or* basic concept; **~gewalt** *f* (*liter*) elemental force; **~kenntnisse** *pl* elementary knowledge *sing*; **~ladung** *f* (*Phys*) elementary charge; **~schule** *f* (*rare*) primary *or* elementary school; **~teilchen** *nt* (*Phys*) elementary particle.
Elen *m or nt* (*rare*) **-s,** - *siehe* **Elch.**
elend *adj* **(a)** (*unglücklich, jämmerlich, pej: gemein*) wretched, miserable; (*krank*) wretched, awful (*inf*), ill *pred* ◆ **~ aussehen/sich ~ fühlen** to look/feel awful (*inf*) *or* wretched; **mir ist ganz ~** I feel really awful (*inf*) *or* wretched; **mir wird ganz ~, wenn ich daran denke** I feel quite ill when I think about it, thinking about it makes me feel quite ill.
(b) (*inf*) (*sehr groß*) *Hunger, Hitze* awful, dreadful; (*sehr schlecht*) *Wetter, Kälte, Leistung* wretched, dreadful, miserable ◆ **ich habe ~ gefroren** I was miserably cold; **da bin ich ~ betrogen worden** I was cheated wretchedly; **es war ~**

heiß/kalt it was awfully *or* dreadfully hot/miserably *or* dreadfully cold.
Elend *nt* **-(e)s,** *no pl* (*Unglück, Not*) misery, distress; (*Verwahrlosung*) squalor; (*Armut*) poverty, penury ◆ **ein Bild des ~s** a picture of misery/squalor; **ins ~ geraten** to fall into poverty, to be reduced to penury, to become destitute; **im (tiefsten) ~ leben** to live in (abject) misery/squalor/poverty; **jdn/sich (selbst) ins ~ stürzen** to plunge sb/oneself into misery/poverty; **wie das leibhaftige ~ aussehen** (*inf*) to look really awful (*inf*) *or* terrible (*inf*); **(wie) ein Häufchen ~** (*inf*) (looking) a picture of misery; **das heulende ~** (*inf*) the blues *pl* (*inf*); **da kann man das heulende ~ kriegen** (*inf*) it's enough to make you scream (*inf*); **es ist ein ~ mit ihm** (*inf*) he makes you want to weep (*inf*), he's hopeless; **es ist ein ~, ...** (*inf*) it's heart-breaking ...; *siehe* **lang.**
elendig(lich) *adv* (*geh*) miserably, wretchedly ◆ **~ zugrunde gehen** *or* **verrecken** (*sl*) to come to a wretched *or* miserable *or* dismal end.
Elends-: ~gestalt *f* (poor) wretch, wretched figure; **~quartier** *nt* slum (dwelling), squalid dwelling; **~viertel** *nt* slums *pl*, slum area.
Elephantiasis *f* (*Med*) *siehe* **Elefantiasis.**
Eleve [e'le:və] *m* **-n, -n, Elevin** [e'le:vɪn] *f* (*Theat*) student; (*old: Schüler*) pupil.
elf *num* eleven; *siehe auch* **vier.**
Elf[1] *f* **-, -en** (*Sport*) team, eleven.
Elf[2] *m* **-en, -en, Elfe** *f* **-, -n** elf.
Elf-: ~eck *nt* undecagon, eleven-sided figure; **e~eckig** *adj* eleven-sided.
Elfenbein *nt* ivory.
Elfenbein|arbeit *f* ivory (carving).
elfenbeine(r)n [1] *adj* ivory, made of ivory ◆ **~er Turm** (*Rel*) Tower of Ivory.
[2] *adv* ivory-like.
Elfenbein-: e~farben, e~farbig *adj* ivory-coloured; **~küste** *f* Ivory Coast; **~turm** *m* (*fig*) ivory tower.
Elfen-: e~haft *adj* (*liter*) elfish, elfin; **~reich** *nt* fairyland.
Elfer *m* **-s, -** (*Ftbl inf*) *siehe* **Elfmeter.**
Elfer-: ~probe *f* (*Math*) casting out of elevens; **~rat** *m* committee of eleven.
elf-: ~fach *adj* elevenfold; *siehe* **vierfach**; **~mal** *adv* eleven times; *siehe* **viermal.**
Elfmeter *m* (*Ftbl*) penalty (kick) (*für* to, for) ◆ **einen ~ schießen** to take a penalty.
Elfmeter-: ~marke *f*, **~punkt** *m* (*Ftbl*) penalty spot; **~schießen** *nt* (*Ftbl*) sudden-death play-off; **durch ~schießen entschieden** decided on penalties; ⚠**~schuß** *m* (*Ftbl*) penalty (kick); **~schütze** *m* (*Ftbl*) penalty-taker.
Elftel *nt* **-s, -** eleventh; *siehe* **Viertel**[1].
elftens *adv* eleventh, in the eleventh place.
elfte(r, s) *adj* eleventh; *siehe* **vierte(r, s).**
Elimination *f* elimination (*auch Math*).
eliminieren* *vt* to eliminate (*auch Math*).
Eliminierung *f* elimination.
elisabethanisch *adj* Elizabethan.
Elision *f* (*Gram*) elision.
elitär [1] *adj* elitist.
[2] *adv* in an elitist fashion.
Elite *f* **-, -n** elite.
Elite-: ~denken *nt* elitism; **~truppe** *f* (*Mil*) crack *or* elite troops *pl.*
Elixier *nt* **-s, -e** elixir (*liter*), tonic.
Ellbogen *m siehe* **Ell(en)bogen.**
Elle *f* **-, -n** (**a**) (*Anat*) ulna (*spec*). (**b**) (*Hist*) (*Measure*) cubit; (*Maßstock*) ≃ yardstick ◆ **alles mit der gleichen** *or* **mit gleicher ~ messen** (*fig*) to measure everything by the same yardstick *or* standards.
Ell(en)bogen *m* **-s, -** elbow; (*fig*) push ◆ **er bahnte sich seinen Weg mit den ~ durch die Menge** he elbowed his way through the crowd; **die ~ gebrauchen** (*fig*) to use one's elbows, to be ruthless; **er hat keine ~** (*fig*) he's not ruthless enough, he has no push (*inf*).
Ell(en)bogen-: ~freiheit *f* (*fig*) elbow room; **~gesellschaft** *f* dog-eat-dog society; **~mensch** *m* ruthless *or* pushy (*inf*) person, pusher (*inf*); **~taktik** *f* pushiness (*inf*); **~taktik anwenden** to be pushy (*inf*).
ellen-: ~lang *adj* (*fig inf*) incredibly long (*inf*); *Liste, Weg auch* mile-long *attr* (*inf*), a mile long *pred* (*inf*); *Geschichte etc auch* lengthy, interminable; *Kerl* incredibly tall (*inf*); **~weise** *adv* ≃ by the yard.
Ellipse *f* **-, -n** (*Math*) ellipse; (*Gram*) ellipsis.
elliptisch *adj* (*Math, Gram*) elliptic(al).
Elmsfeuer *nt* (*Met*) St Elmo's fire, corposant.
Eloge [e'lo:ʒə] *f* **-, -n** eulogy.
E-Lok ['e:lɔk] *f* **-, -s** *abbr of* **elektrische Lokomotive** electric locomotive *or* engine.
eloquent *adj* (*geh*) eloquent.
Eloquenz *f* (*geh*) eloquence.
⚠ **Elsaß** *nt* **-** *or* **-sses das ~** Alsace.
Elsässer(in *f*) *m* **-s, -** Alsatian, inhabitant of Alsace.
Elsässer, elsässisch *adj* Alsatian.
⚠ **Elsaß-Lothringen** *nt* Alsace-Lorraine.
⚠ **elsaß-lothringisch** *adj* Alsace-Lorraine *attr*, of Alsace-Lorraine.
Elster *f* **-, -n** magpie ◆ **wie eine ~ stehlen** to be always stealing things, to have sticky fingers (*inf*); **eine diebische ~ sein** (*fig*) to be a thief *or* pilferer; **geschwätzig wie eine ~ sein** to chatter like a magpie.
Elter *m or nt* **-s, -n** (*Sci, Statistics*) parent.
elterlich *adj* parental.
Eltern *pl* parents *pl* ◆ **nicht von schlechten ~ sein** (*inf*) to be quite something (*inf*), to be a good one (*inf*).
Eltern-: ~abend *m* (*Sch*) parents' evening; **~beirat** *m* parents' council; **~haus** *nt* (*lit, fig*) (parental) home; **aus gutem ~haus stammen** to come from a good home; **~liebe** *f* parental love; **e~los** *adj* orphaned, parentless; **~schaft** *f* parents *pl*; **~sprechstunde** *f* (*Sch*) consultation hour (for parents); **~sprechtag** *m* open *or* visiting day (for parents); **~teil** *m* parent; **~urlaub** *m unpaid leave given to new mother or father.*
Elysium *nt* **-s,** *no pl* (*Myth, fig*) **das ~** Elysium.
Email [e'mai, e'ma:j] *nt* **-s, -s** enamel.
E-Mail *f* **-** *no pl* (*Comput*) E-mail, e-mail.
Emaillack [e'mailak] *m* enamel paint.
Emaille [e'maljə, e'mai, e'ma:j] *f* **-, -n** *siehe* **Email.**
emaillieren* [ema'ji:rən, emal'ji:rən] *vt* to enamel.
Email-: ~malerei *f* enamel painting, enamelling; **~schmuck** *m* enamel jewellery.
Emanation *f* (*Philos, Chem*) emanation.
Emanze *f* **-, -n** (*usu pej*) women's libber (*inf*).
Emanzipation *f* emancipation.
Emanzipationsbewegung *f* emancipation movement.
emanzipatorisch *adj* emancipatory.
emanzipieren* [1] *vt* to emancipate.
[2] *vr* to emancipate oneself.
Emanzipierung *f siehe* **Emanzipation.**
Embargo *nt* **-s, -s** embargo ◆ **etw mit einem ~ belegen, ein ~ über etw** (*acc*) **verhängen** to put *or* place an embargo on sth.
Emblem *nt* **-(e)s, -e** emblem; (*Firmen~*) logo.
emblematisch *adj* emblematic.
Embolie *f* (*Med*) embolism.
Embryo *m* (*Aus auch nt*) **-s, -s** *or* **-nen** [-y'o:nən] embryo.
Embryologe *m*, **Embryologin** *f* embryologist.
Embryologie *f* embryology.
embryonal *adj attr* (*Biol, fig*) embryonic.
Emendation *f* (*Liter*) emendation.
emeritieren* *vt* (*Univ*) to give emeritus status (to) ◆ **emeritierter Professor** emeritus professor.
Emeritus *m* **-, Emeriti** (*Univ*) emeritus.
Emigrant(in *f*) *m* emigrant; (*politischer Flüchtling*) émigré.
Emigration *f* emigration; (*die Emigranten*) emigrant/émigré community ◆ **in der ~ leben** to live in (self-imposed) exile; **in die ~ gehen** to emigrate; *siehe* **innere(r, s).**
emigrieren* *vi aux sein* to emigrate.
eminent *adj* (*geh*) *Person* eminent ◆ **~ wichtig** of the utmost importance; **von ~er Bedeutung** of the utmost significance; **er hat E~es geleistet** he is a man of eminent achievements.
Eminenz *f* (*Eccl*) **(Seine/Eure) ~** (His/Your) Eminence; *siehe* **grau.**
Emir *m* **-s, -e** emir.
Emirat *nt* emirate.
Emissär *m* (*old*) emissary.
Emission *f* (**a**) (*Fin*) issue. (**b**) (*Phys*) emission. (**c**) (*Sw: Radiosendung*) (radio) broadcast.
Emissions-: ~bank *f* issuing bank; **~kurs** *m* rate of issue, issuing price.
emittieren* *vt* (**a**) (*Fin*) to issue. (**b**) (*Phys*) to emit.
Emmchen *nt* (*hum inf*) mark, ≃ quid (*Brit inf*), buck (*US inf*).
Emmentaler *m* **-s, -** Emment(h)aler.
Emotion *f* emotion.
emotional *adj* emotional; *Ausdrucksweise* emotive.
emotionalisieren* *vt* to emotionalize.
emotionell *adj siehe* **emotional.**
emotions-: ~arm *adj* lacking in emotion, unfeeling; **~geladen** *adj* emotionally charged; **~los** *adj* free of emotion, unemotional.
Empf. *abbr of* **Empfänger; Empfohlen(er Preis).**
empfahl *pret of* **empfehlen.**
empfand *pret of* **empfinden.**
Empfang *m* **-(e)s, ⸚e** reception; (*von Brief, Ware etc*) receipt; (*von Sakramenten*) receiving ◆ **jdm einen guten ~ bereiten** to give sb a good reception; **zu jds ~ kommen** (*jdn begrüßen*) to (come to) receive sb; **einen ~ geben** *or* **veranstalten** to give *or* hold a reception; **jdn/etw in ~ nehmen** to receive sb/sth; (*Comm*) to take delivery of sth; **(zahlbar) nach/bei ~** (*+gen*) (payable) on receipt (of); **auf ~ bleiben** (*Rad*) to stand by; **auf ~ schalten** (*Rad*) to switch over to "receive".
empfangen *pret* **empfing,** *ptp* **empfangen** [1] *vt* to receive; (*begrüßen*) to greet, to receive (*form*); (*herzlich*) to welcome; (*abholen*) *Besuch* to meet ◆ **die Weihen ~** (*Eccl*) to take Holy Orders; **die Polizisten wurden mit einem Steinhagel ~** the police were greeted by a shower of stones.
[2] *vti* (*schwanger werden*) to conceive.
Empfänger(in *f*) *m* **-s, -** recipient, receiver (*auch Rad*); (*Adressat*) addressee; (*Waren~*) consignee ◆ **~ unbekannt** (*auf Briefen*) not known at this address; **~ verzogen** gone away.
Empfänger|abschnitt *m* receipt slip.
empfänglich *adj* (*aufnahmebereit*) receptive (*für* to); (*beeinflußbar, anfällig*) susceptible (*für* to).
Empfänglichkeit *f siehe adj* receptivity; susceptibility.
Empfängnis *f* conception; *siehe* **unbefleckt.**
Empfängnis-: e~verhütend *adj* contraceptive; **e~verhütende Mittel** *pl*

⚠: Informationen zur Rechtschreibreform im Anhang

contraceptives *pl*; **~verhütung** *f* contraception.

Empfangs-: ~antenne *f* receiving aerial; **e~berechtigt** *adj* authorized to receive payment/goods *etc*; **~berechtigte(r)** *mf* authorized recipient; **~bereich** *m* (*Rad, TV*) reception area; **~bescheinigung, ~bestätigung** *f* (acknowledgment of) receipt; **~chef** *m* (*von Hotel*) head porter; **~dame** *f* receptionist; **~gerät** *nt* (*Rad, TV*) (radio/TV) set, receiver; **~kopie** *f* incoming document; **~station** *f* (*Rad*) receiving station; (*Space*) tracking station; (*Comm*) destination; **~störung** *f* (*Rad, TV*) interference *no pl*; **~zimmer** *nt* reception room.

empfehlen *pret* **empfahl,** *ptp* **empfohlen** [1] *vt* to recommend; (*liter: anvertrauen*) to commend (*form*), to entrust ◆ **(jdm) etw/jdn ~** to recommend sth/sb (to sb); **~, etw zu tun** to recommend *or* advise doing sth; **jdm ~, etw zu tun** to recommend *or* advise sb to do sth; **diese Methode/dieses Restaurant ist sehr zu ~** I would recommend this method/restaurant, this method/restaurant is to be recommended; **ich würde dir Vorsicht/Geduld ~** I would recommend caution/patience, I would advise *or* recommend you to be cautious/patient; **seinen Geist (dem Herrn) ~** (*liter*) to commend one's soul to the Lord; **bitte, ~ Sie mich Ihrer Frau Gemahlin** (*form*) please convey my respects to your wife (*form*); *siehe* **empfohlen.**
[2] *vr* **(a)** to recommend itself/oneself ◆ **sich für Reparaturen/als Experte** *etc* **~** to offer one's services for repairs/as an expert *etc*; **diese Ware empfiehlt sich von selbst** this product is its own recommendation; **es empfiehlt sich, das zu tun** it is advisable to do that.
(b) (*dated, hum: sich verabschieden*) to take one's leave ◆ **ich empfehle mich!** I'll take my leave; **ich empfehle mich Ihnen** (*am Briefende*) please be sure of my best wishes (*dated form*); *siehe* **französisch.**

empfehlenswert *adj* to be recommended, recommendable.

Empfehlung *f* recommendation; (*Referenz*) testimonial, reference; (*form: Gruß*) regards *pl*, respects *pl* ◆ **auf ~ von** on the recommendation of; **mit freundlichen** *or* **den besten ~en** (*am Briefende*) with best regards; **meine ~ an Ihre Frau Gemahlin!** (*form*) my regards *or* respects to your wife (*form*).

Empfehlungsschreiben *nt* letter of recommendation, testimonial.

empfiehl *imper sing of* **empfehlen.**

empfinden *pret* **empfand,** *ptp* **empfunden** *vt* to feel ◆ **etw als kränkend/Beleidigung ~** to feel sth as an insult, to find sth insulting; **er hat noch nie Hunger empfunden** he has never experienced *or* known hunger; **er empfand einen solch starken Hunger, daß ...** his hunger was so great that ...; **bei Musik Freude ~** to experience pleasure from music; **ich habe dabei viel Freude empfunden** it gave me great pleasure; **viel/nichts für jdn ~** to feel a lot/nothing for sb; **jdn als (einen) Störenfried ~** to think of sb as *or* feel sb to be a troublemaker.

Empfinden *nt* **-s,** *no pl* feeling ◆ **meinem ~ nach** to my mind, the way I feel about it.

empfindlich *adj* **(a)** sensitive (*auch Phot, Tech*); *Gesundheit, Stoff, Glas, Keramik etc* delicate; (*leicht reizbar*) touchy (*inf*), (over)sensitive ◆ **~ reagieren** to be sensitive (*auf +acc* to); **wenn man ihren geschiedenen Mann erwähnt, reagiert sie sehr ~** she is very sensitive to references to her ex-husband; **~e Stelle** (*lit*) sensitive spot; (*fig auch*) sore point; **gegen etw ~ sein** to be sensitive to sth; **Kupfer ist sehr ~** copper discolours/dents *etc* easily.
(b) (*spürbar, schmerzlich*) *Verlust, Kälte, Strafe* severe; *Mangel* appreciable ◆ **deine Kritik hat ihn ~ getroffen** your criticism cut him to the quick; **es ist ~ kalt** it is bitterly cold.

Empfindlichkeit *f siehe adj* (*a*) sensitivity (*auch Phot, Tech*), sensitiveness; delicateness, delicate nature; touchiness (*inf*), (over)sensitivity.

empfindsam *adj Mensch* sensitive; (*gefühlvoll, Liter*) sentimental.

Empfindsamkeit *f siehe adj* sensitivity; sentimentality ◆ **das Zeitalter der ~** (*Liter*) the age of sentimentalism.

Empfindung *f* feeling; (*Sinnes~ auch*) sensation; (*Eindruck, Ahnung auch*) impression.

Empfindungs-: e~los *adj* (*lit, fig*) insensitive (*für, gegen* to); *Glieder* numb, without sensation; **~losigkeit** *f* (*lit, fig*) insensitivity; (*der Glieder*) numbness, loss of sensation; **~nerven** *pl* (*Physiol*) sensory nerves *pl*; **~vermögen** *nt* faculty of sensation; (*in Gliedern*) sensation; (*fig*) sensitivity, ability to feel; **~vermögen für etw** ability to feel *or* sense sth; (*fig*) sensitivity to sth; **~wort** *nt* (*Gram*) interjection.

empfing *pret of* **empfangen.**

empfohlen [1] *ptp of* **empfehlen.**
[2] *adj* **(sehr** *or* **gut) ~** (highly) recommended.

empfunden *ptp of* **empfinden.**

Emphase *f* **-, -n** emphasis.

emphatisch *adj* emphatic.

Empire[1] [ã'piːɐ] *nt* **-(s),** *no pl* (*Hist*) Empire; (*~stil*) Empire style.

Empire[2] ['ɛmpaɪə] *nt* **-(s),** *no pl* (British) Empire.

Empirestil *m* Empire style.

Empirik *f* **-,** *no pl* empirical experience.

Empiriker(in *f*) *m* **-s, -** empiricist.

empirisch *adj* empirical.

Empirismus *m* (*Philos, Sci*) empiricism.

empor *adv* (*liter*) upwards, up ◆ **zum Licht ~** up(wards) towards the light; **~ die Herzen/Blicke!** lift up your hearts/eyes! (*liter*); *siehe auch* **hinauf.**

empor-: ~arbeiten *vr sep* (*geh*) to work one's way up; **~blicken** *vi sep* (*liter*) to raise one's eyes; (*fig*) to look up (*zu* to).

Empore *f* **-, -n** (*Archit*) gallery.

empören* [1] *vt* to fill with indignation, to outrage; (*stärker*) to incense; *siehe* **empört.**
[2] *vr* **(a)** (*über +acc* at) to be indignant *or* outraged; (*stärker*) to be incensed ◆ **das ist unerhört! empörte sich der Schulmeister** that's scandalous!, said the schoolmaster indignantly.
(b) (*liter: sich auflehnen*) to rise (up) *or* rebel (*gegen* against).

empörend *adj* outrageous, scandalous.

Empörer(in *f*) *m* **-s, -** (*liter*) rebel, insurrectionist.

empörerisch *adj* (*liter*) rebellious, insurrectionary.

empor-: ~heben *vt sep irreg* (*geh*) to raise, to lift up; **jdn über andere ~heben** (*fig*) to raise *or* elevate sb above others; **~kommen** *vi sep irreg aux sein* (*geh*) to rise (up); (*fig*) (*aufkommen*) to come to the fore; (*vorankommen*) to rise *or* go up in the world, to get on; **nur an sein E~kommen denken** (*fig*) to think only of one's advancement; **E~kömmling** *m* (*pej*) upstart, parvenu; **~lodern** *vi sep aux sein or haben* (*liter*) to blaze *or* flare upwards; **~ragen** *vi sep aux haben or sein* (*geh: lit, fig*) to tower (*über +acc* above); **~recken** *sep* [1] *vt* (*liter*) *Faust* to raise aloft; [2] *vr* to stretch upwards; **~schauen** *vi sep* (*geh*) *siehe* **~blicken**; **~schweben** *vi sep aux sein* (*geh*) to float upwards *or* aloft (*liter*); **~schwingen** *vr sep irreg* (*geh*) to soar upwards *or* aloft (*liter*); (*Turnern*) to swing upwards; **sich zu etw ~schwingen** (*fig*) to (come to) achieve sth; *zu einer Stellung* to reach sth; **~steigen** *sep irreg aux sein* (*geh*) [1] *vt* to climb (up); [2] *vi* to climb (up); (*Mond, Angst etc*) to rise (up); (*fig: Karriere machen*) to climb, to rise; **~streben** *vi sep aux sein* to soar upwards; (*fig*) *aux haben* to be ambitious.

empört *adj* **(a)** (highly) indignant, outraged (*über +acc* at); (*schockiert*) outraged, scandalized. **(b)** (*liter: in Auflehnung*) rebellious.

emportreiben *vt sep irreg* (*geh*) to drive up.

Empörung *f* **(a)** *no pl* (*Entrüstung*) indignation (*über +acc* at) ◆ **über etw in ~ geraten** to become *or* get indignant about sth. **(b)** (*liter: Aufstand*) rebellion, uprising.

empor-: ~ziehen *sep irreg* (*geh*) [1] *vt* to draw *or* pull up; [2] *vi aux sein* to drift upwards; **~züngeln** *vi sep aux sein* (*liter: Flammen*) to leap up(wards) *or* aloft (*liter*).

emsig *adj* busy, industrious; (*eifrig*) eager, keen; (*geschäftig*) bustling *attr*, busy.

Emsigkeit *f siehe adj* industry, industriousness; eagerness, zeal; bustle.

Emu *m* **-s, -s** emu.

Emulation *f* (*esp Comput*) emulation.

emulieren* *vt* (*esp Comput*) to emulate.

emulgieren* *vti* to emulsify.

Emulsion *f* emulsion.

Emulsions-: ~farbe *f* emulsion (paint); **~mittel** *nt* emulsifier.

E-Musik *f* serious music.

en bloc [ã'blɔk] *adv* en bloc.

End- *in cpds* final; **~abnehmer** *m* end buyer; **~abrechnung** *f* final account; **~bahnhof** *m* terminus; **~benutzer** *m* end-user; **e~betont** *adj Wort* with final stress; **~betrag** *m* final amount.

Endchen *nt* (*inf*) (small) piece, bit; (*eines Weges*) short distance, little way.

Ende *nt* **-s, -n** end; (*eines Jahrhunderts etc auch*) close; (*Ausgang, Ergebnis*) outcome, result; (*Ausgang eines Films, Romans etc*) ending; (*Hunt: Geweih~*) point; (*inf: Stückchen*) (small) piece; (*Strecke*) way, stretch; (*Naut: Tau*) (rope's) end ◆ **~ Mai/der Woche** at the end of May/the week; **~ der zwanziger Jahre** in the late twenties; **er ist ~ vierzig** he is in his late forties; **das ~ der Welt** the end of the world; **er wohnt am ~ der Welt** (*inf*) he lives at the back of beyond *or* in the middle of nowhere; **bis ans ~ der Welt** to the ends of the earth; **ein ~ mit Schrecken** a terrible *or* dreadful end; **lieber ein ~ mit Schrecken als ein Schrecken ohne ~** (*Prov*) it's best to get unpleasant things over and done with; **letzten ~es** when all is said and done, after all; (*am ~*) in the end, at the end of the day; **einer Sache** (*dat*) **ein ~ machen** to put an end to sth; **(bei** *or* **mit etw) kein ~ finden** (*inf*) to be unable (to bring oneself) to stop (sth *or* telling/doing *etc* sth); **damit muß es jetzt ein ~ haben** there has to be an end to this now, this must stop now; **ein ~ nehmen** to come to an end; **das nimmt** *or* **findet gar kein ~** (*inf*) there's no sign of it stopping, there's no end to it; **ein böses ~ nehmen** to come to a bad end; **kein ~ ist abzusehen** there's no end in sight; **da ist das ~ von weg!** (*N Ger inf*) it's incredible! (*inf*); **... und kein ~** ... with no end in sight, ... without end; **es war des Staunens/Jubels** *etc* **kein ~** (*old, liter*) there was no end to the surprise/celebrations *etc*; **es ist noch ein gutes** *or* **ganzes ~** (*inf*) there's still quite a way to go (yet); **am ~** at the end; (*schließlich*) in the end; (*inf: möglicherweise*) perhaps; **(am) ~ des Monats** at the end of the month; **am ~ sein** (*fig*) to be at the end of one's tether; **mit etw am ~ sein** to be at *or* have reached the end of sth; (*Vorrat*) to have run out of sth; **ich bin mit meiner Weisheit am ~** I'm at my wits' end; **meine Geduld ist am ~** my patience is at an end; **ein Problem am richtigen/falschen** *or* **verkehrten ~ anfassen** to tackle a problem from the right/wrong end; **Leiden ohne ~** endless suffering, suffering without end; **das ist eine Kette** *or* **Schraube ohne ~** (*fig*) it's an endless spiral; **zu ~** finished, over, at an end; **etw zu ~ bringen** *or* **führen** to finish (off) sth; **ein Buch/einen Brief zu ~ lesen/schreiben** to finish (reading/writing) a book/letter; **etw zu einem guten ~ bringen** *or* **führen** to bring sth to a satisfactory conclusion; **zu ~ gehen** to come to an end; (*Vorräte*) to run out; **zu dem ~, daß ...** (*obs*) to the end that ... (*form*); **zu diesem ~** (*obs*) to this end (*form*); **~ gut, alles gut** (*Prov*) all's well that ends well (*Prov*); **es hat alles einmal** *or* **alles hat einmal ein ~** (*Prov*) everything must come to an end sometime; (*angenehme Dinge*) all good things must come to an end (*Prov*); *siehe* **dick.**

End|effekt *m*: **im ~** (*inf*) in the end, in the final analysis.

endeln *vt* (*Aus*) *Saum* to whip, to oversew.

Endemie *f* (*Med*) endemic disease.

➤ SPRACHE AKTIV: **empfehlen: 1** → 29.1, 40.4, 46.5 **Ende** → 53.4

endemisch *adj* (*Med*) endemic.
enden *vi* to end, to finish; (*Frist auch*) to run out, to expire; (*Zug*) to terminate; (*sterben*) to meet one's end ♦ **auf** (+*acc*) *or* **mit etw ~** (*Wort*) to end with sth; **mit den Worten ... ~** (*bei Rede*) to close with the words ...; **es endete damit, daß** ... the outcome was that ...; **der Streit endete vor Gericht** the quarrel ended up in court; **er endete im Gefängnis** he ended up in prison; **wie wird das noch mit ihm ~?** what will become of him?; **das wird böse ~!** no good will come of it!; **er wird schlimm ~** he will come to a bad end; **nicht ~ wollend** unending.
-ender *m suf* **-s, -** (*Hunt*) -pointer.
End-: ~ergebnis *nt* final result; **~gehalt** *nt* final salary; **~gerät** *nt* (*Telec etc*) terminal; **~geschwindigkeit** *f* terminal velocity.
endgültig *adj* final; *Beweis auch* conclusive; *Antwort* definite; (*geh: vorbildlich*) definitive ♦ **damit ist die Sache ~ entschieden** that settles the matter once and for all; **das ist ~ aus** *or* **vorbei** that's (all) over and done with; **sie haben sich jetzt ~ getrennt** they've separated for good; **jetzt ist ~ Schluß!** that's the end!, that's it!; **etwas E~es läßt sich noch nicht sagen** I/we *etc* cannot say anything definite at this stage.
Endgültigkeit *f siehe adj* finality; conclusiveness; definitiveness.
Endivie [-viə] *f* endive.
End-: ~kampf *m* (*Mil*) final battle; (*Sport*) final; (*~phase: Mil, Sport*) final stages *pl* (of a battle/contest); **~lager** *nt* (*für Atommüll etc*) permanent (waste) disposal site; **~lagerung** *f* (*von Atommüll etc*) permanent (waste) disposal; **~lauf** *m* final; **~laufteilnehmer** *m* finalist.
endlich [1] *adj* **(a)** (*Math, Philos*) finite.
(b) (*rare: langerwartet, schließlich*) eventual.
[2] *adv* finally, at last; (*am Ende*) eventually, in the end, finally ♦ **na ~!** at (long) last!; **hör ~ damit auf!** will you stop that!; **komm doch ~!** come on, get a move on!; **~ kam er doch** he eventually came after all, in the end he came (after all).
Endlichkeit *f* (*Math, Philos*) finiteness, finite nature.
endlos *adj* endless; (*langwierig auch*) interminable ♦ **ich mußte ~ lange warten** I had to wait for an interminably long time, I had to wait for ages (*inf*); **(sich) bis ins E~e (erstrecken)** (to stretch) to infinity.
Endlosigkeit *f* endlessness, infinite nature; (*Langwierigkeit*) interminableness, interminable nature.
End-: ~lospapier *nt, no pl* continuous paper; **~lösung** *f*: **die ~lösung** the Final Solution (*extermination of the Jews by the Nazis*); **~montage** *f* final assembly; **~moräne** *f* terminal moraine.
Endo- *in cpds* endo-; **e~gen** *adj* (*Biol, Psych*) endogenous; **e~krin** *adj* (*Med*) endocrine; **~krinologie** *f* (*Med*) endocrinology.
Endorphin *nt* **-s, -e** endorphin.
Endoskop *nt* **-s, -e** (*Med*) endoscope.
End-: ~phase *f* final stage(s *pl*); **~preis** *m* final price; **~produkt** *nt* end *or* final product; **~punkt** *m* (*lit, fig*) end; (*von Buslinie etc auch*) terminus; **~reim** *m* (*Liter*) end rhyme; **~resultat** *nt* final result.
Endrunde *f* (*Sport*) finals *pl*; (*Leichtathletik, Autorennen*) final lap; (*Boxen, fig*) final round.
Endrunden-: ~spiel *nt* final (match); **~teilnehmer** *m* finalist.
End-: ~see *m* (*Geog*) lake without an outlet; **~sieg** *m* final *or* ultimate victory; **~silbe** *f* final syllable; **~spiel** *nt* (*Sport*) final; (*Chess*) end game; **~spurt** *m* (*Sport, fig*) final spurt; **~stadium** *nt* final *or* (*Med*) terminal stage; **~station** *f* (*Rail etc*) terminus; (*fig*) end of the line; **~stelle** *f* (*Tech*) terminal apparatus; **~stufe** *f* final stage; **~summe** *f* (sum) total.
Endung *f* (*Gram*) ending.
endungslos *adj* (*Gram*) without an ending.
End-: ~ursache *f* ultimate cause; (*Philos*) final cause; **~urteil** *nt* final verdict or judgement; **~verbraucher** *m* consumer, end-user; **~vierziger** *m* (*inf*) man in his late forties; **~zeit** *f* last days *pl*; **e~zeitlich** *adj attr Phase* final; *Stimmung, Prophezeiung* apocalyptic; **~zeitstimmung** *f* apocalyptic mood; **~ziel** *nt* ultimate goal *or* aim; **~ziffer** *f* final number; **~zustand** *m* final state; **~zweck** *m* ultimate aim *or* purpose.
Energetik *f* (*Phys*) energetics *sing*.
energetisch *adj* (*Phys*) energetic.
Energie *f* (*Sci, fig*) energy; (*Schwung auch*) vigour, vitality ♦ **seine ganze ~ für etw einsetzen** *or* **aufbieten** to devote all one's energies to sth; **mit aller** *or* **ganzer ~** with all one's energy *or* energies.
Energie-: ~bedarf *m* energy requirement; ⚠**e~bewußt** *adj* energy-conscious; **~farm** *f* (*Tech*) energy farm; **~gewinnung** *f* generation of energy; **~haushalt** *m* (*Physiol*) energy balance; **~knappheit** *f* energy shortage; **~krise** *f* energy crisis; **e~los** *adj* lacking in energy, weak; **~losigkeit** *f* lack of energy; **~politik** *f* energy policy/politics *sing or pl*; **~prinzip** *nt siehe* **~satz**; **~quelle** *f* energy source; **~satz** *m* (*Phys*) principle of the conservation of energy; ⚠**e~sparend** *adj* energy-saving; **~sparlampe** *f* energy-saving bulb; **~sparmaßnahmen** *pl* energy-saving measures *pl*; **~träger** *m* energy source; **~verbrauch** *m* energy consumption; **~versorgung** *f* supply of energy; **~versorgungsunternehmen** *nt* energy supply company; **~wirtschaft** *f* energy economy; (*Wirtschaftszweige*) energy industry; **~zufuhr** *f* energy supply.
energisch *adj* (*voller Energie*) energetic; (*entschlossen, streng*) forceful, firm; *Griff, Maßnahmen* vigorous, firm; *Worte* forceful, strong; *Protest* energetic, strong ♦ **~ durchgreifen** to take vigorous *or* firm action, to act vigorously *or* firmly; **~ werden** to assert oneself *or* one's authority; **wenn das nicht aufhört, werde ich ~!** if this doesn't stop I'll have to put my foot down!; **etw ~ sagen** to say sth forcefully; **etw ~ betonen** to stress *or* emphasize sth strongly; **etw ~ verteidigen** to defend sth vigorously; **etw ~ dementieren** to deny sth strongly *or* strenuously *or* emphatically.
enervieren* [enɛr'vi:rən] *vt* (*old*) to enervate (*form*).
en famille [ãfa'mij] *adv* (*geh*) en famille.
Enfant terrible [ãfãtɛ'ribl] *nt* **- -, -s -s** (*geh*) enfant terrible.
eng *adj* **(a)** (*schmal*) *Straße etc* narrow; (*beengt*) *Raum* cramped, confined; (*~ anliegend*) *Kleidung* tight, close-fitting; (*ärmlich*) *Verhältnisse* straitened, reduced; (*beschränkt*) *Horizont, Moralbegriff* narrow, limited, restricted ♦ **ein Kleid ~er machen** to take a dress in; **im ~eren Sinne** in the narrow sense; **in dem Zimmer standen wir sehr ~** we were very crowded in the room; **~ zusammengedrängt sein** to be crowded together; **in die ~ere Wahl kommen** to be put on the short list, to be short-listed; **ein ~erer Ausschuß** a select committee; **das darfst du nicht so ~ sehen** (*fig inf*) don't take it so seriously.
(b) (*nah, dicht, vertraut*) close ♦ **~ nebeneinander** *or* **zusammen** close together; **aufs ~ste befreundet sein** to be on the closest possible terms; **eine Feier im ~sten Kreise** a small party for close friends; **die Hochzeit fand im ~sten Kreise der Familie statt** the wedding was celebrated with just the immediate family present; **~ befreundet sein** to be close friends; **mit jdm ~ befreundet sein** to be a close friend of sb; **die ~ere Heimat** one's home area, the area (where) one comes from.
Engadin ['ɛŋgadi:n] *nt* **-s das ~** the Engadine.
Engagement [ãgaʒə'mã:] *nt* **-s, -s (a)** (*Theat*) engagement. **(b)** (*geh: Aktivität*) involvement, engagement; (*politisches ~*) commitment (*für* to).
engagieren* [ãga'ʒi:rən] [1] *vt* to engage.
[2] *vr* to be/become committed (*für* to); (*in einer Bekanntschaft*) to become involved ♦ **er hat sich sehr dafür engagiert, daß** ... he completely committed himself to ...; **engagierte Literatur** (politically/socially) committed literature.
engagiert [ãga'ʒi:ɐt] *adj* committed.
Engagiertheit [ãga'ʒi:ɐthait] *f siehe vr* commitment; involvement.
eng-: ⚠**~anliegend** *adj attr* tight(-fitting), close-fitting; ⚠**~bedruckt** *adj attr* close-printed; ⚠**~befreundet** *adj attr* close; **die ~befreundeten Mädchen/Männer** *etc* the close friends; ⚠**~begrenzt** *adj attr* restricted, narrow; ⚠**~beschrieben** *adj attr* closely written; **~brüstig** *adj* narrow-chested.
Enge *f* **-, -n (a)** *no pl* (*von Straße etc*) narrowness; (*von Wohnung*) confinement, crampedness; (*Gedrängtheit*) crush; (*von Kleid etc*) tightness; (*fig*) (*Ärmlichkeit*) straitened circumstances *pl*, poverty; (*Beschränktheit*) narrowness, limited *or* restricted nature. **(b)** (*Meeres~*) strait; (*Engpaß*) pass, defile ♦ **jdn in die ~ treiben** (*fig*) to drive sb into a corner.
Engel *m* **-s, -** (*lit, fig*) angel ♦ **ein rettender/guter ~** (*fig*) a saviour/a guardian angel; **ich hörte die ~ im Himmel singen** (*inf*) it hurt like anything (*inf*), it was agony; **er ist auch nicht gerade ein ~** (*inf*) he's no angel (*inf*); **wir sind alle keine ~** (*prov*) none of us is perfect.
Engelchen, Eng(e)lein *nt* little angel.
Engel-: e~gleich *adj siehe* **engel(s)gleich**; **~macher(in** *f*) *m* (*euph inf*) back-street abortionist; **~schar** *f* host of angels, angelic host.
Engel(s)-: ~geduld *f* saintly patience; **sie hat eine ~geduld** she has the patience of a saint; **e~gleich** *adj* angelic; **~haar** *nt* angel's hair; **e~rein** *adj* pure as the driven snow; **~zungen** *pl*: **(wie) mit ~zungen reden** to use all one's powers of persuasion.
Engelwurz *f* **-, -en** (*Bot*) angelica.
Engerling *m* (*Zool*) grub *or* larva of the May bug *or* cockchafer.
Eng-: e~herzig *adj* petty, hidebound; **~herzigkeit** *f* pettiness.
engl. *abbr of* **englisch**.
England *nt* **-s** England.
Engländer *m* **-s, - (a)** Englishman; English boy ♦ **die ~** *pl* the English, the Britishers (*US*); **er ist ~** he's English. **(b)** (*Tech*) adjustable spanner, monkey wrench.
Engländerin *f* Englishwoman; English girl.
englisch[1] *adj* English; *Steak* rare ♦ **die ~e Krankheit** (*dated Med*) rickets *sing*; (*fig*) the English disease *or* sickness; **die E~e Kirche** the Anglican Church, the Church of England; **die E~en Fräulein** (*Eccl*) *institute of Catholic nuns for the education of girls*; **~e Broschur** case binding; *siehe auch* **deutsch**.
englisch[2] *adj* (*Bibl*) angelic ♦ **der E~e Gruß** the Angelic Salutation, the Ave Maria *or* Hail Mary.
Englisch(e) *nt* English; *siehe auch* **Deutsch(e)**.
englisch-deutsch/-französisch *etc adj* Anglo-German/-French *etc*; *Wörterbuch* English-German/-French *etc*.
Englisch-: ~horn *nt* (*Mus*) cor anglais; **~leder** *nt* (*Tex*) moleskin; **e~sprachig** *adj Gebiet* English-speaking; **~traben** *nt* rising trot.
Eng-: e~maschig *adj* close-meshed; (*fig, Sport*) close; **e~maschig stricken** to knit to a fine tension; ⚠**~paß** *m* (narrow) pass, defile; (*Fahrbahnverengung, fig*) bottleneck.
Engramm [ɛn'gram] *nt* (*Physiol*) engram.
en gros [ã'gro] *adv* wholesale.
Engros- *siehe* **Großhandels-**.
Engrossist [ãgrɔ'sɪst] *m* (*Aus*) wholesale dealer, wholesaler.
engstirnig *adj* narrow-minded, insular, parochial.
enigmatisch *adj* (*liter*) *siehe* **änigmatisch**.
Enjambement [ãʒãbə'mã:] *nt* **-s, -s** (*Poet*) enjambement.
Enkel[1] *m* **-s, -** (*~kind*) grandchild; (*~sohn*) grandson; (*Nachfahr*) descendant; (*fig*) heir ♦ **er ist ~ eines berühmten Geschlechts** (*geh*) he comes from a famous family *or* line.
Enkel[2] *m* **-s, -** (*dial*) ankle.

⚠: Informationen zur Rechtschreibreform im Anhang

Enkelin *f* granddaughter.
Enkel-: ~kind *nt* grandchild; **~sohn** *m* grandson; **~tochter** *f* granddaughter.
Enklave [ɛn'klaːvə] *f* **-, -n** enclave.
en masse [ã'mas] *adv* en masse.
en miniature [ãminja'tyːr] *adv* (*geh*) in miniature.
enorm *adj* (*riesig*) enormous; (*inf: herrlich, kolossal*) tremendous (*inf*) ◆ **er verdient ~** *or* **~ viel (Geld)** (*inf*) he earns an enormous amount (of money); **~e Hitze/Kälte** tremendous heat/cold.
en passant [ãpa'sã] *adv* en passant, in passing.
Enquete [ã'keːt(ə), ã'kɛːt(ə)] *f* **-, -n** (*form*) survey; (*Aus auch: Arbeitstagung*) symposium.
Enquetekommission [ã'keːt-] *f* (*BRD*) commission of enquiry, select committee.
Ensemble [ã'sãbl] *nt* **-s, -s** ensemble; (*Besetzung*) cast.
Ensemblespiel *nt* (*Theat*) ensemble.
ent|arten* *vi aux sein* to degenerate (*zu* into).
ent|artet *adj* degenerate.
Ent|artung *f* degeneration.
Ent|artungs|erscheinung *f* symptom *or* sign of degeneration.
ent|äußern* *vr* **sich einer Sache** (*gen*) **~** (*geh*) to relinquish sth, to divest oneself of sth (*form*); **sich ~** (*Philos*) to be realized.
entbehren* 1 *vt* (*vermissen*) to miss; (*auch vi: verzichten*) to do *or* manage without; (*zur Verfügung stellen*) to spare ◆ **wir haben jahrelang ~ müssen** for years we had/we have had to do *or* go without; **wir können ihn heute nicht ~** we cannot spare him/it today.
2 *vi* (*fehlen*) **einer Sache** (*gen*) **~** (*geh*) to lack sth, to be devoid of sth.
entbehrlich *adj* dispensable, unnecessary.
Entbehrung *f* privation, deprivation, want *no pl* ◆ **~en auf sich** (*acc*) **nehmen** to make sacrifices.
entbehrungs-: ~reich, ~voll *adj* full of privation; **die ~reichen Kriegsjahre** the deprivation of the war years.
entbieten* *vt irreg* (*form*) **(jdm) seinen Gruß ~** (*old*) to present one's compliments (to sb) (*form*); **der Vorsitzende entbot der Delegation herzliche Willkommensgrüße** the Chairman welcomed the delegation cordially.
entbinden* *irreg* 1 *vt* **(a)** *Frau* to deliver ◆ **sie ist von einem Sohn entbunden worden** she has given birth to a son, she has been delivered of a son (*liter, old*). **(b)** (*befreien: von Versprechen, Amt etc*) to release (*von* from).
2 *vi* (*Frau*) to give birth.
Entbindung *f* delivery, birth; (*von Amt etc*) release.
Entbindungs-: ~heim *nt* maternity home *or* hospital; **~klinik** *f* maternity clinic; **~pfleger** *m* obstetric nurse; **~station** *f* maternity ward.
entblättern* 1 *vt* to strip (of leaves).
2 *vr* to shed its/their leaves; (*hum inf*) to strip, to shed one's clothes.
entblöden* *vr* **sich nicht ~, etw zu tun** to have the effrontery *or* audacity to do sth, to do sth unashamedly.
entblößen* *vt* (*form*) **(a)** to bare, to expose (*auch Mil*); *Kopf* to bare, to uncover; *Schwert* to draw, to unsheathe; (*fig*) *sein Innenleben* to lay bare, to reveal ◆ **er hat sich entblößt** (*Exhibitionist*) he exposed himself; (*seinen wahren Charakter*) he showed his true colours.
(b) (*liter: des Schutzes berauben*) to divest, to denude (*form*).
entblößt *adj* bare.
Entblößung *f siehe vt* **(a)** baring, exposing; (*Mil*) exposure; drawing; laying bare, revelation. **(b)** divesting, stripping.
entbrennen* *vi irreg aux sein* (*liter*) (*Kampf, Streit, Zorn*) to flare up, to erupt; (*Leidenschaft, Liebe*) to be (a)roused; (*Begeisterung*) to be fired ◆ **in heißer Liebe zu jdm** *or* **für jdn ~** to fall passionately in love with sb; **in** *or* **von Leidenschaft/Wut ~** to become inflamed with passion/anger.
entbürokratisieren* *vt* to free of *or* from bureaucracy, to debureaucratize.
Entbürokratisierung *f* freeing from bureaucracy, debureaucratization.
Entchen *nt dim of* **Ente** duckling.
entdecken* 1 *vt* **(a)** to discover; *Fehler, Anzeichen, Lücke auch* to detect, to spot; (*in der Ferne*) to discern, to spot; (*in einer Menge*) to spot. **(b)** (*old: offenbaren*) **jdm etw ~** to reveal *or* discover (*obs*) sth to sb.
2 *vr* **sich jdm ~** (*old*) to reveal *or* discover (*obs*) oneself to sb (*form*).
Entdecker(in *f***)** *m* **-s, -** discoverer.
Entdeckung *f* discovery; (*von Fehler, Anzeichen auch*) detection, spotting; (*etw Entdecktes auch*) find.
Entdeckungs-: ~fahrt, ~reise *f* voyage of discovery; (*zu Lande*) expedition of discovery; **auf ~reise gehen** (*hum inf*) to go exploring.
Ente *f* **-, -n** duck; (*Press inf*) canard, hoax, false report; (*Med sl: Harngefäß*) (bed) urinal; (*Aut inf*) Citroën 2CV, deux-chevaux ◆ **die ~ ist geplatzt** (*Press inf*) the story has turned out to be a hoax *or* canard *or* false report.
ent|ehren* *vt* to dishonour; (*entwürdigen*) to degrade; (*verleumden*) to defame; (*entjungfern*) to deflower ◆ **~d** degrading; **sich ~** to degrade *or* disgrace oneself.
Ent|ehrung *f siehe vt* dishonouring; degradation; defamation; defloration.
ent|eignen* *vt* to expropriate; *Besitzer* to dispossess.
Ent|eignung *f siehe vt* expropriation; dispossession.
ent|eilen* *vi aux sein* (*old*) to hasten away (*liter*); (*liter: Zeit*) to fly by.
ent|eisen* *vt* to de-ice; *Kühlschrank* to defrost.
Ent|eisung *f siehe vt* de-icing; defrosting.
Ent|eisungs|anlage *f* de-icing unit.
Entelechie *f* (*Philos*) entelechy.
ent|emotionalisieren* *vt* to de-emotionalize.

Enten-: ~braten *m* roast duck; **~brust** *f* breast of duck; **~ei** *nt* duck's egg; **~flott** *nt*, **~grieß** *m*, **~grün** *nt*, **~grütze** *f* duckweed; **~küken** *nt* duckling.
Entente [ã'tãːt(ə)] *f* **-, -n** (*Pol*) entente.
Enterbeil *nt* boarding axe.
ent|erben* *vt* to disinherit.
Enterbrücke *f* boarding plank.
Ent|erbung *f* disinheriting.
Enterhaken *m* grappling iron *or* hook.
Enterich *m* drake.
entern (*Naut*) 1 *vti Schiff* to board.
2 *vi aux sein* to climb.
Entertainer(in *f***)** [entə'teinɐ, -ərin] *m* **-s, -** entertainer.
ENTER-Taste *f* (*Comput*) enter key.
entf. *abbr of* **entfällt** n/a.
entfachen* *vt* (*geh*) *Feuer* to kindle; *Leidenschaft, Begierde* to arouse, to kindle (the flames of); *Krieg, Streit* to provoke.
entfahren* *vi irreg aux sein* **jdm ~** to slip out, to escape sb's lips; **Blödsinn! entfuhr es ihm** nonsense, he cried inadvertently; **ihr ist ein kleiner Furz entfahren** (*inf*) she accidentally broke wind *or* let off a little fart (*vulg*).
entfallen* *vi irreg aux sein +dat* **(a)** (*form: herunterfallen*) **jds Händen ~** to slip *or* fall *or* drop from sb's hands; **das Glas entfiel ihm** he dropped the glass.
(b) (*fig: aus dem Gedächtnis*) **jdm ~** to slip sb's mind, to escape sb; **der Name ist mir ~** the name has slipped my mind *or* escapes me.
(c) (*nicht in Betracht kommen*) not to apply, to be inapplicable; (*wegfallen*) to be dropped; (*erlöschen*) to lapse ◆ **dieser Punkt der Tagesordnung entfällt** this point on the agenda has been dropped.
(d) auf jdn/etw ~ (*Geld, Kosten*) to be allotted *or* apportioned to sb/sth; **auf jeden ~ 100 Mark** each person will receive/pay 100 marks.
entfalten* 1 *vt* **(a)** (*auseinanderlegen*) to unfold, to open *or* spread out.
(b) (*fig*) (*entwickeln*) *Kräfte, Begabung, Theorie* to develop; (*beginnen*) *Tätigkeit* to launch into; (*darlegen*) *Plan, Gedankengänge* to set forth *or* out, to unfold, to expound ◆ **seine Fähigkeiten voll ~** to develop one's abilities to the full.
(c) (*fig: zeigen*) *Pracht, Prunk* to display, to exhibit.
2 *vr* (*Knospe, Blüte*) to open, to unfold; (*fig*) to develop, to unfold, to blossom (out) ◆ **der Garten hat sich zu voller Pracht entfaltet** the garden blossomed (out) into its full magnificence; **hier kann ich mich nicht ~** I can't make full use of my abilities here, I'm held back here.
Entfaltung *f* unfolding; (*von Blüte auch*) opening; (*fig*) (*Entwicklung*) development; (*einer Tätigkeit*) launching into; (*Darstellung*) (*eines Planes, Gedankens*) exposition, setting out, unfolding; (*von Prunk, Tatkraft*) display ◆ **zur ~ kommen** to develop, to blossom.
entfärben* 1 *vt* to take the colour out of, to decolour (*Tech*), to decolorize (*Tech*); (*bleichen*) to bleach ◆ **das E~** the removal of colour, decolorization (*Tech*).
2 *vr* (*Stoff, Blätter*) to lose (its/their) colour; (*Mensch*) to turn *or* go pale.
Entfärber *m*, **Entfärbungsmittel** *nt* colour *or* dye remover, decolorant (*Tech*).
entfernen* 1 *vt* to remove (*von, aus* from) ◆ **jdn aus der Schule ~** to expel sb from school; **das entfernt uns (weit) vom Thema** that takes us a long way from our subject.
2 *vr* **(a) sich (von** *or* **aus etw) ~** (*weggehen*) to go away (from sth), to leave (sth); (*abfahren, abziehen*) to move off (from sth), to depart (from sth); **sich von seinem Posten/Arbeitsplatz ~** to leave one's post/position; **sich unerlaubt von der Truppe ~** (*Mil*) to go absent without leave; **sich zu weit ~** to go too far away.
(b) (*fig*) (*von* from) (*von jdm*) to become estranged; (*von Thema*) to depart, to digress; (*von Wahrheit*) to depart, to deviate ◆ **er hat sich sehr weit von seinen früheren Ansichten entfernt** he has come a long way from his earlier views.
entfernt 1 *adj Ort, Verwandter* distant; (*abgelegen*) remote; (*gering*) *Ähnlichkeit* distant, remote, vague ◆ **10 km ~ von** 10km (away) from; **das Haus liegt 2 km ~** the house is 2km away; **aus den ~esten Ländern** from the furthest corners of the globe; **ich hatte nicht den ~esten Verdacht** I didn't have the slightest *or* remotest suspicion; *siehe* **weit.**
2 *adv* remotely, slightly ◆ **nicht einmal ~ (so gut/hübsch** *etc***)** not even remotely (as good/pretty *etc*); **~ verwandt** distantly related; **er erinnert mich ~ an meinen Onkel** he reminds me slightly *or* vaguely of my uncle; **das hat nur ~ mit dieser Angelegenheit zu tun** that has only a distant bearing on this matter *or* is only vaguely related *or* has only a remote connection with this matter; **nicht im ~esten!** not in the slightest *or* least!;
Entfernung *f* **(a)** distance; (*Mil: bei Waffen*) range ◆ **man hört das Echo auf große ~ (hin)** you can hear the echo from a great distance *or* a long way away; **aus** *or* **in der ~ (hörte er ...)** in the distance (he heard ...); **aus kurzer/großer ~ (schießen)** (to fire) at *or* from close/long range; **aus einiger ~** from a distance; **in einiger ~** at a distance; **etw auf eine ~ von 50 Meter treffen** to hit sth at a distance of 50 metres.
(b) (*das Entfernen*) removal; (*aus der Schule*) expulsion ◆ **unerlaubte ~ (von der Truppe)** absence without leave; **unerlaubte ~ von der Schule/vom Posten** *etc* absence from school/one's post *etc* without permission.
Entfernungsmesser *m* **-s, -** (*Mil, Phot*) rangefinder.
Entfernungstaste *f* (*Comput*) delete key.
entfesseln* *vt* (*fig*) to unleash.
entfesselt *adj* unleashed; *Leidenschaft, Trieb* unbridled, uncontrolled; *Mensch* wild; *Naturgewalten* raging ◆ **vor Zorn/Begeisterung ~** wild with rage/enthusiasm; **der ~e Prometheus** Prometheus Unbound.

entfetten* *vt* to remove the grease from, to degrease (*Tech*); *Wolle* to scour.
Entfettung *f* **(a)** *siehe vt* removal of grease (from), degreasing; scouring. **(b)** (*Gewichtsabnahme*) losing fat.
Entfettungskur *f* weight-reducing course.
entflammbar *adj* inflammable.
entflammen* [1] *vt* (*fig*) to (a)rouse; *Leidenschaft, Haß auch* to inflame; *Begeisterung* to fire.
[2] *vr* (*fig*) to be (a)roused *or* fired *or* inflamed.
[3] *vi aux sein* to burst into flames, to catch fire, to ignite (*Chem etc*); (*fig*) (*Zorn, Streit*) to flare up; (*Leidenschaft, Liebe*) to be (a)roused *or* inflamed ◆ **für etw entflammt sein** to be fired with enthusiasm for sth; **in Liebe ~/entflammt sein** to fall/be passionately in love.
entflechten* *vt irreg Konzern, Kartell etc* to break up.
Entflechtung *f* (*von Konzern, Kartell*) breaking up.
entflecken* *vt* to remove the stain(s) from.
entfleuchen* *vi aux sein* (*obs: wegfliegen*) to fly away; (*hum: weggehen*) to be off (*inf*).
entfliegen* *vi irreg aux sein* to fly away, to escape (*dat or aus* from).
entfliehen* *vi irreg aux sein* (*geh*) **(a)** to escape, to flee (*dat or aus* from) ◆ **dem Lärm/der Unrast** *etc* **~** to escape *or* flee (from) the noise/unrest *etc*. **(b)** (*vergehen: Zeit, Jugend etc*) to fly past.
entfremden* [1] *vt* to alienate (*auch Sociol, Philos*), to estrange ◆ **jdn einer Person/Sache** (*dat*) **~, jdm eine Person/Sache ~** to alienate *or* estrange sb from sb/sth; **die lange Trennung hat die Freunde (einander) entfremdet** the long separation estranged the friends from each other *or* made the two friends strangers to each other; **entfremdete Arbeit** (*Sociol*) alienated work; **etw seinem Zweck ~** to use sth for the wrong purpose, not to use sth for its intended purpose.
[2] *vr* to become alienated *or* estranged (*dat* from) ◆ **er hat sich seiner Frau ganz entfremdet** he has become completely alienated from his wife, he has become a complete stranger to his wife; **durch die lange Abwesenheit habe ich mich** *or* **bin ich der Stadt ganz entfremdet** my long absence has made me a stranger to the city.
Entfremdung *f* estrangement; (*Sociol, Philos*) alienation.
entfrosten* *vt* to defrost.
Entfroster *m* **-s, -** defroster.
entführen* *vt jdn* to abduct, to kidnap; *Beute etc* to carry off, to make off with; *LKW, Flugzeug* to hijack; *Mädchen* (*mit Zustimmung zur Heirat*) to elope with, to run off with; (*hum inf: wegnehmen*) to borrow (*often hum*) ◆ **sie ließ sich von ihrem Liebhaber ~** she eloped with her lover; **wer hat mir denn meinen Bleistift entführt?** (*inf*) who's made off with my pencil? (*inf*).
Entführer(in *f*) *m* **(a)** abductor, kidnapper. **(b)** (*Flugzeug~ etc*) hijacker; (*Flugzeug~ auch*) skyjacker (*inf*).
Entführung *f siehe vt* abduction, kidnapping; hijacking; elopement ◆ **„Die ~ aus dem Serail"** "The Abduction from the Seraglio".
entgasen* *vt* (*Chem*) to degas.
entgegen [1] *adv* (*liter*) **dem Licht/der Zukunft** *etc* **~!** on towards the light/future *etc*!; **neuen Ufern/Abenteuern ~!** on to new shores/adventures!; **dem Wind ~!** into the (teeth of the) wind!
[2] *prep +dat* contrary to, against ◆ **~ meiner Bitte** contrary to my request; **~ allen Erwartungen, allen Erwartungen ~** contrary to all *or* against all expectation(s).
entgegen|arbeiten *vi sep +dat* to oppose, to work against.
entgegenblicken *vi sep siehe* **entgegensehen.**
entgegenbringen *vt sep irreg* **jdm etw ~** to bring sth to sb; (*fig*) *Achtung, Freundschaft etc* to show *or* evince sth for sb.
entgegen|eilen *vi sep aux sein +dat* to rush towards; (*um jdn zu treffen*) to rush to meet.
entgegenfahren *vi sep irreg aux sein +dat* to travel towards, to approach; (*um jdn zu treffen*) to travel to meet; (*mit dem Auto*) to drive towards/to meet.
entgegengehen *vi sep irreg aux sein +dat* to go towards, to approach; (*um jdn zu treffen*) to go to meet; (*fig*) *einer Gefahr, dem Tode, der Zukunft* to face ◆ **dem Ende ~** (*Leben, Krieg*) to draw to a close, to approach its end; **seinem Untergang/Schwierigkeiten ~** to be heading for disaster/difficulties; **seiner Vollendung ~** to near *or* approach completion.
entgegengesetzt *adj Richtung, Meinung* opposite; *Charakter auch* contrasting; (*fig: einander widersprechend*) *Interessen, Meinungen* opposing *attr*, opposed, conflicting *attr* ◆ **einander ~e Interessen/Meinungen** *etc* opposing *or* conflicting interests/views *etc*; **genau ~ denken/handeln** *etc* to think/do *etc* exactly the opposite.
entgegenhalten *vt sep irreg +dat* **(a) jdm etw ~** to hold sth out towards sb. **(b)** (*fig*) **einer Sache ~, daß ...** to object to sth that ...; **dieser Ansicht muß man ~, daß ...** against this view it must be objected that ...
entgegenhandeln *vi sep siehe* **zuwiderhandeln.**
entgegenkommen *vi sep irreg aux sein +dat* to come towards, to approach; (*um jdn zu treffen*) to (come to) meet; (*fig*) to accommodate; *Wünschen, Bitten auch* to meet, to comply with ◆ **jdm auf halbem Wege ~** (*lit, fig*) to meet sb halfway; **das kommt unseren Plänen/Vorstellungen** *etc* **sehr entgegen** that fits in very well with our plans/ideas *etc*; **Ihr Vorschlag kommt mir sehr entgegen** I find your suggestion very congenial; **können Sie uns preislich etwas ~?** can you adjust your price a little?
Entgegenkommen *nt* (*Gefälligkeit*) kindness, obligingness; (*Zugeständnis*) concession, accommodation.
entgegenkommend *adj* (*fig*) obliging, accommodating.
entgegenkommenderweise *adv* obligingly, accommodatingly; (*als Zugeständnis*) as a concession.
entgegenlaufen *vi sep irreg aux sein +dat* to run towards; (*um jdn zu treffen*) to run to meet; (*fig*) to run contrary *or* counter to.
Entgegennahme *f* **-,** *no pl* (*form*) (*Empfang*) receipt; (*Annahme*) acceptance ◆ **bei ~** on receipt/acceptance.
entgegennehmen *vt sep irreg* (*empfangen*) to receive; (*annehmen*) to accept ◆ **nehmen Sie meinen Dank entgegen** (*form*) please accept my thanks.
entgegenschauen *vi sep siehe* **entgegensehen.**
entgegenschlagen *vi sep irreg aux sein +dat* (*Geruch, Haß*) to confront, to meet; (*Flammen auch*) to leap towards; (*Jubel, Begeisterung*) to meet, to greet ◆ **ihm schlug Jubel/ein widerlicher Geruch entgegen** he was greeted with jubilation/confronted by a nauseating smell.
entgegensehen *vi sep irreg* **(a) jdm ~** to see sb coming. **(b)** (*fig*) **einer Sache** (*dat*) **~** to await sth; (*freudig*) to look forward to sth; **einer Sache ~ müssen** to have to expect *or* face sth; **Ihrer baldigen Antwort ~d** (*form*) in anticipation of *or* looking forward to your early reply.
entgegensetzen *vt sep +dat* **etw einer Sache ~** to set sth against sth; **wir können diesen Forderungen nichts ~** we have nothing to counter these claims with; **einer Sache Alternativen ~** to put *or* pose alternatives to sth; **dem habe ich entgegenzusetzen, daß ...** against that I'd like to say that ...; **die Gewerkschaften hatten den Regierungsvorschlägen nichts entgegenzusetzen** the unions had nothing to offer in reply to the government's suggestions; **jdm/einer Sache Widerstand ~** to put up *or* offer resistance to sb/sth; **ihren Anklagen konnte er nichts ~** he could find no reply to her accusations; *siehe* **entgegengesetzt.**
entgegenstehen *vi sep irreg +dat* (*fig*) to stand in the way of, to be an obstacle to ◆ **dem steht entgegen, daß ...** what stands in the way of that is that ...; **dem steht nichts entgegen** there's no obstacle to that, there's nothing against that; **was steht dem entgegen?** what obstacle is there to that?
entgegenstellen *sep +dat* [1] *vt siehe* **entgegensetzen.**
[2] *vr* **sich jdm/einer Sache ~** to resist sb/sth, to oppose sb/sth.
entgegenstemmen *vr sep* **sich jdm/einer Sache ~** to pit oneself against sb/sth, to oppose sb/sth.
entgegenstrecken *vt sep* **jdm etw ~** to hold out sth to sb.
entgegenstürzen *vi sep aux sein +dat* to fall upon; (*zueilen auf*) to rush towards.
entgegentreten *vi sep irreg aux sein +dat* to step *or* walk up to; *dem Feind* to go into action against; *einer Politik, Forderungen* to oppose; *Behauptungen, Vorurteilen* to counter; *einer Gefahr, Unsitten* to take steps against, to act against.
entgegenwirken *vi sep +dat* to counteract.
entgegnen* *vti* to reply; (*kurz, barsch*) to retort (*auf +acc* to) ◆ **er entgegnete nichts** he made no reply; **darauf wußte er nichts zu ~** he didn't know what to reply to that.
Entgegnung *f* reply; (*kurz, barsch*) retort.
entgehen* *vi irreg aux sein +dat* **(a)** (*entkommen*) *Verfolgern, dem Feind* to elude, to escape (from); *dem Schicksal, der Gefahr, Strafe* to escape, to avoid.
(b) (*fig: nicht bemerkt werden*) **dieser Fehler ist mir entgangen** I failed to notice *or* I missed this mistake, this mistake escaped my notice; **mir ist kein Wort entgangen** I didn't miss a word (of it); **es ist meiner Aufmerksamkeit nicht entgangen, daß ...** it has not escaped my attention that ...; **ihr entgeht nichts** she doesn't miss anything *or* a thing; **es ist ihm nicht entgangen, daß ...** he didn't fail to notice that ..., it didn't escape him that ...; **sich** (*dat*) **etw ~ lassen** to miss sth.
entgeistert *adj* dumbfounded, thunderstruck, flabbergasted (*inf*) ◆ **er starrte mich ganz ~ an** he stared at me quite dumbfounded *or* thunderstruck *or* flabbergasted (*inf*); **er reagierte ~** he reacted with complete astonishment.
Entgelt *nt* **-(e)s,** *no pl* (*form*) **(a)** (*Bezahlung*) remuneration (*form*); (*Entschädigung*) recompense (*form*), compensation; (*Anerkennung*) reward. **(b)** (*Gebühr*) fee, consideration ◆ **gegen ~** for a fee *or* consideration; **etw gegen ~ abgeben** to give sb sth for a consideration.
entgelten* *vt irreg* (*geh*) **(a)** (*büßen*) to pay for ◆ **jdn etw ~ lassen** to make sb pay *or* suffer for sth. **(b)** (*vergüten*) **jdm etw ~** to repay sb for sth.
entgiften* *vt* to decontaminate; (*Med*) to detoxicate, to detoxify.
Entgiftung *f* decontamination; (*Med*) detoxication.
entgleisen* *vi aux sein* **(a)** (*Rail*) to be derailed; to leave *or* run off *or* jump the rails ◆ **einen Zug zum E~ bringen** *or* **~ lassen** to derail a train. **(b)** (*fig: Mensch*) to misbehave; (*einen Fauxpas begehen*) to commit a faux pas, to drop a clanger (*inf*).
Entgleisung *f* derailment; (*fig*) faux pas, gaffe, clanger (*inf*).
entgleiten* *vi irreg aux sein +dat* to slip ◆ **jdm** *or* **jds Hand ~** to slip from *or* out of sb's grasp; **jdm/einer Sache ~** (*fig*) to slip away from sb/sth.
entgotten*, entgöttern* *vt* (*liter*) to remove god(s) from ◆ **die entgötterte Welt** the godless world, the world without god(s).
Entgötterung, Entgottung *f* (*liter*) removal of god(s) (*gen* from) ◆ **die ~ des Olymp** the banishing of the gods from Olympus.
entgräten* *vt Fisch* to fillet, to bone.
enthaaren* *vt* to remove unwanted hair from, to depilate (*form*).
Enthaarungs-: ~creme *f* depilatory cream; **~mittel** *nt* depilatory.
enthalten* *irreg* [1] *vt* to contain ◆ **(mit) ~ sein in** (*+dat*) to be included in.
[2] *vr* **(a)** (*geh*) **sich einer Sache** (*gen*) **~** to abstain from sth; **sich nicht ~ können, etw zu tun** to be unable to refrain from doing sth; **sich einer Bemerkung nicht ~ können** to be unable to refrain from making a remark.
(b) sich (der Stimme) ~ to abstain.
enthaltsam *adj* abstemious; (*geschlechtlich*) chaste, continent; (*mäßig*)

moderate.
Enthaltsamkeit *f siehe adj* abstinence; chastity, continence; moderation.
Enthaltung *f* abstinence; (*Stimm~*) abstention.
enthärten* *vt Wasser* to soften; *Metall* to anneal.
Enthärter *m*, **Enthärtungsmittel** *nt* (water) softener.
Enthärtung *f siehe vt* softening; annealing.
enthaupten* *vt* to decapitate; (*als Hinrichtung auch*) to behead.
Enthauptung *f siehe vt* decapitation; beheading.
enthäuten* *vt* to skin; (*als Folter etc*) to flay.
entheben* *vt irreg* **jdn einer Sache** (*gen*) **~** to relieve sb of sth.
entheiligen* *vt* to desecrate, to profane.
Entheiligung *f* desecration, profanation.
enthemmen* *vti* **jdn ~** to make sb lose his inhibitions, to free sb from his inhibitions; **Alkohol wirkt ~d** alcohol has a disinhibiting effect; **(moralisch** *etc*) **völlig enthemmt sein** to have no (moral *etc*) inhibitions whatsoever; to have lost one's (moral) inhibitions.
Enthemmtheit, Enthemmung *f* loss of inhibitions.
enthüllen* [1] *vt* to uncover, to reveal; *Skandal, Lüge auch* to expose; *Denkmal, Gesicht* to unveil; *Geheimnis, Plan, Hintergründe* to reveal.
[2] *vr* (*lit, hum*) to reveal oneself ◆ **er hat sich in seiner ganzen Gemeinheit enthüllt** he revealed himself for the villain he was.
Enthüllung *f siehe vt* uncovering, revealing; exposure; unveiling ◆ **noch eine sensationelle ~** another sensational revelation *or* disclosure.
Enthüllungs-: ~autor *m* investigative author; **~journalismus** *m* investigative journalism.
enthülsen* *vt* to shell; *Getreide* to husk.
Enthusiasmus *m* enthusiasm.
Enthusiast(in *f*) *m* enthusiast.
enthusiastisch *adj* enthusiastic.
ent|ideologisieren* [1] *vt* to free from ideology.
[2] *vr* (*Partei*) to dispense with one's ideology.
Ent|ideologisierung *f* freeing from ideology; (*das Entideologisiertwerden*) decreasing ideological commitment.
Entität *f* (*Philos*) entity.
entjungfern* *vt* to deflower.
Entjungferung *f* defloration.
entkalken* *vt* to decalcify.
entkeimen* [1] *vt* **(a)** *Kartoffeln* to remove the buds from. **(b)** (*keimfrei machen*) to sterilize.
[2] *vi aux sein +dat* (*liter*) to burgeon forth from (*liter*).
entkernen* *vt* **(a)** *Orangen etc* to remove the pips from; *Kernobst* to core; *Steinobst* to stone; (*Biol*) *Zellen* to denucleate. **(b)** *Wohngebiet* (*Dichte reduzieren*) to reduce the density of; (*dezentralisieren*) to decentralize, to disperse.
Entkerner *m* **-s, -** *siehe vt* corer; stoner.
entkleiden* (*geh*) [1] *vt* to undress ◆ **jdn einer Sache** (*gen*) **~** (*fig*) to strip *or* divest sb of sth.
[2] *vr* to undress, to take one's clothes off.
entknoten* *vt* to untie, to undo; (*fig: entwirren*) to unravel.
entkoffe|iniert *adj* decaffeinated.
entkolonialisieren* *vt* to decolonialize.
Entkolonialisierung *f* decolonialization.
entkommen* *vi irreg aux sein* to escape, to get away (*+dat, aus* from).
Entkommen *nt* escape.
Entkonservierung *f* (*von Auto*) de-waxing.
entkorken* *vt Flasche* to uncork.
entkörperlicht *adj* (*liter*) incorporeal.
entkräften* *vt* (*schwächen*) to weaken, to debilitate, to enfeeble; (*erschöpfen*) to exhaust, to wear out; (*fig: widerlegen*) *Behauptung etc* to refute, to invalidate.
Entkräftung *f siehe vt* weakening, debilitation, enfeeblement; exhaustion; refutation, invalidation.
entkrampfen* *vt* (*fig*) to relax, to ease; *Lage* to ease ◆ **eine entkrampfte Atmosphäre** a relaxed atmosphere.
Entkrampfung *f* (*fig*) relaxation, easing.
entkriminalisieren *vt* to decriminalize.
entladen* *irreg* [1] *vt* to unload; *Batterie etc* to discharge.
[2] *vr* (*Gewitter*) to break; (*Schußwaffe*) to go off, to discharge (*form*); (*elektrische Spannung, Batterie etc*) to discharge; (*langsam*) to run down; (*Sprengladung*) to explode, to go off; (*fig: Emotion*) to vent itself/themselves ◆ **sein Zorn entlud sich über mir** he vented his anger on me.
Entladung *f* **(a)** (*das Entladen*) unloading. **(b)** *siehe vr* breaking; discharge; running down; explosion; venting ◆ **etw zur ~ bringen** (*Mil, fig*) to detonate sth.
entlang [1] *prep nach n +acc or* (*rare*) *+dat, vor n +dat or* (*rare*) *+gen* along ◆ **den** *or* (*rare*) **dem Fluß ~** along the river.
[2] *adv* along ◆ **am Bach ~** along (by the side of) the stream; **am Haus ~** along (by) the side of the house; **hier ~** this way.
entlang- *pref* along; **~gehen** *vti sep irreg aux sein* to walk along, to go along (*auch fig*); **am Haus ~gehen** to walk along by the side of the house; **~schrammen** *vi* (*fig*) to scrape by; **haarscharf an etw** (*dat*) **~schrammen** to escape sth by the skin of one's teeth.
entlarven* *vt* (*fig*) *Spion, Dieb etc* to unmask, to expose; *Pläne, Betrug etc* to uncover, to expose ◆ **sich ~** to reveal one's true colours *or* character; **sich als Schuft** *etc* **~** to reveal *or* show oneself to be a scoundrel *etc*.
Entlarvung *f siehe vt* unmasking, exposure; uncovering, exposure.

entlassen* *vt irreg* (*aus* from) (*gehen lassen, kündigen*) to dismiss; (*nach Streichungen*) to make redundant; (*aus dem Krankenhaus*) to discharge; *Soldaten* to discharge; (*in den Ruhestand versetzen*) to retire, to pension off; (*aus dem Gefängnis, aus Verpflichtungen*) to release, to discharge, to free; (*aus der Schule: als Strafe*) to expel ◆ **aus der Schule ~ werden** to leave school; to be expelled from school; **jdn mit ein paar freundlichen Worten ~** to dismiss sb *or* send sb away with a few kind words; **jdn in den Ruhestand ~** to retire sb, to pension sb off; **Soldaten ins Zivilleben ~** to demobilize soldiers; **jdn aus der Verantwortung ~** to free sb from responsibility.
Entlassung *f siehe vt* dismissal; making redundant; discharge; discharge; retirement, pensioning off; release, discharge; expulsion ◆ **um seine ~ einreichen** to tender one's resignation; **es gab 20 ~en** there were 20 redundancies.
Entlassungs-: ~gesuch *nt* (letter of) resignation; (*Jur*) petition for release; **ein ~gesuch stellen** *or* **einreichen** to tender one's resignation; (*Jur*) to petition for one's/sb's release; **~schein** *m* certificate of discharge; (*Mil auch*) discharge papers *pl*; **~zeugnis** *nt* (*Sch*) school leaving certificate.
entlasten* *vt Achse, Telefonleitungen etc* to relieve the strain *or* load on; *Herz* to relieve the strain on; (*Mil, Rail*), *Gewissen* to relieve; *Verkehr* to ease; *Stadtzentrum* to relieve congestion in; (*Arbeit abnehmen*) *Chef, Hausfrau* to take some of the load off, to relieve; (*Jur*) *Angeklagten* (*völlig*) to exonerate; (*teilweise*) to support the case of; (*Comm: gutheißen*) *Vorstand* to approve the activities of; (*von Verpflichtungen, Schulden*) *jdn* to discharge, to release ◆ **jdn finanziell ~** to ease sb's financial burden; **jdn** *or* **jds Konto um** *or* **für einen Betrag ~** to credit sb *or* sb's account with a sum, to credit a sum to sb's account.
Entlastung *f* relief (*auch Mil, Rail etc*); (*von Achse etc, Herz*) relief of the strain (*+gen* on); (*Jur*) exoneration; (*Comm: des Vorstands*) approval; (*Fin*) credit; (*von Verpflichtungen etc*) release, discharge ◆ **zu jds ~** (in order) to take some of the load off sb; (*Mil*) (in order) to relieve sb ...; **eine Aussage zur ~ des Angeklagten** a statement supporting the case of the defendant; **zu seiner ~ führte der Angeklagte an, daß** ... in his defence the defendant stated that ...
Entlastungs-: ~material *nt* (*Jur*) evidence for the defence; **~zeuge** *m* (*Jur*) witness for the defence, defence witness; **~zug** *m* relief train.
entlauben* *vt* to strip of leaves; (*Sci*) to defoliate.
Entlaubung *f* defoliation.
Entlaubungsmittel *nt* defoliant.
entlaufen* *vi irreg aux sein* to run away (*dat, von* from) ◆ **ein ~er Sklave/~es Kind** *etc* a runaway slave/child *etc*; **ein ~er Sträfling** an escaped convict; **ein ~er Hund** a lost *or* missing dog; „**Hund ~**" "dog missing".
entlausen* *vt* to delouse.
Entlausung *f* delousing.
entledigen* (*form*) [1] *vr* **sich einer Person/Sache** (*gen*) **~** to rid oneself of sb/sth; **sich einer Pflicht ~** to discharge a duty; **sich eines Komplizen ~** (*euph*) to eliminate *or* dispose of an accomplice (*euph*); **sich seiner Schulden ~** to discharge (*form*) *or* pay off one's debts; **sich seiner Kleidung ~** to remove one's clothes.
[2] *vt* **jdn einer Pflicht** (*gen*) **~** to release sb from a duty.
entleeren* *vt* to empty; *Darm*, (*Sci*) *Glasglocke* to evacuate.
Entleerung *f siehe vt* emptying; evacuation.
entlegen *adj Ort, Haus* (*abgelegen*) remote, out-of-the-way; (*weit weg*) far away *or* off, remote; (*fig*) *Gedanke etc* odd, out-of-the-way.
Entlegenheit *f* remoteness; (*fig*) oddness.
entlehnen* *vt* (*fig*) to borrow (*dat, von* from).
Entlehnung *f* (*fig*) borrowing.
entleiben* *vr* (*obs*) to take one's own life.
entleihen* *vt irreg* to borrow (*von, aus* from).
Entleiher *m* **-s, -** borrower.
Entleihung *f* borrowing.
Entlein *nt* duckling ◆ **das häßliche ~** the Ugly Duckling.
entloben* *vr* to break off one's engagement.
Entlobung *f* breaking off of one's engagement; broken engagement.
entlocken* *vt* **jdm/einer Sache etw ~** to elicit sth from sb/sth; (*durch Überredung auch*) to coax sth out of sb; (*durch ständige Befragung auch*) to worm sth out of sb.
entlohnen*, entlöhnen* (*Sw*) *vt* to pay; (*fig*) to reward.
Entlohnung, Entlöhnung (*Sw*) *f* pay(ment); (*fig*) reward ◆ **etw gegen ~ tun** to do sth for payment.
entlüften* *vt* to ventilate, to air; *Bremsen* to bleed.
Entlüfter *m* **-s, -** ventilator.
Entlüftung *f siehe vt* ventilation, airing; bleeding.
Entlüftungs|anlage *f* ventilation system.
entmachten* *vt* to deprive of power.
Entmachtung *f* deprivation of power.
entmagnetisieren* *vt* to demagnetize.
entmannen* *vt* to castrate; (*fig*) to emasculate, to unman.
Entmannung *f* castration; (*fig*) emasculation.
entmaterialisieren* *vt* to dematerialize.
entmenschlichen* *vt* to dehumanize.
entmenscht *adj* bestial, inhuman.
entmieten* *vt* (*form*) to clear *or* evict tenants from.
Entmietung *f* (*form*) clearance.
entmilitarisieren* *vt* to demilitarize.
Entmilitarisierung *f* demilitarization.
entminen* *vt* (*Mil*) to clear of mines.

entmotten* *vt* (*fig*) to take out of mothballs.

entmündigen* *vt* (*Jur*) to (legally) incapacitate, to declare incapable of managing one's own affairs; (*wegen Geisteskrankheit auch*) to certify ♦ **das Fernsehen entmündigt die Zuschauer, wenn ...** television takes away the viewer's right to form an independent opinion when ...

Entmündigung *f siehe vt* (*Jur*) (legal) incapacitation; certification.

entmutigen* *vt* to discourage, to dishearten ♦ **sich nicht ~ lassen** not to be discouraged *or* disheartened.

Entmutigung *f* discouragement.

entmythologisieren* *vt* to demythologize.

Entnahme *f* **-, -n** (*form*) removal, taking out; (*von Blut*) extraction; (*von Geld*) withdrawal ♦ **vor** *etc* **~ einer Sache** (*gen*) before *etc* removing *or* extracting/withdrawing sth.

entnazifizieren* *vt* to denazify.

Entnazifizierung *f* denazification.

entnehmen* *vt irreg* (*aus, dat*) to take out (of), to take (from); (*aus Kasse*) *Geld* to withdraw (from); (*einem Buch etc*) *Zitat* to take (from); (*fig: erkennen, folgern*) to infer (from), to gather (from) ♦ **wie ich Ihren Worten entnehme, ...** I gather from what you say that ...

entnerven* *vt* to unnerve ♦ **~d** unnerving; (*nervtötend*) nerve-racking; **entnervt** unnerved, nervous.

Entoderm *nt* **-s, -e** (*Biol*) entoderm, endoderm.

ent|ölen* *vt Kakao* to extract the oil from.

Entomologie *f* entomology.

entomologisch *adj* entomological.

Entourage [ãtu:ra:ʒ(ə)] *f* **-** (*geh*) entourage.

entpersönlichen* *vt* to depersonalize.

entpflichten* *vt* (*form*) *Pfarrer, Professor* to retire.

entpolitisieren* *vt* to depoliticize.

Entpolitisierung *f* depoliticizing, depoliticization.

entpuppen* *vr* (*Schmetterling*) to emerge from its cocoon *or* chrysalis ♦ **sich als Betrüger** *etc* **~** to turn out to be a cheat *etc*; **mal sehen, wie er sich entpuppt** we'll see how he turns out.

entrahmen* *vt Milch* to remove the cream from, to skim; (*mit Zentrifuge*) to separate.

Entrahmung *f* skimming; (*mit Zentrifuge*) separation.

entraten* *vi irreg* (*geh, old*) **einer Sache** (*gen*) **~** to be devoid of sth; **einer Person/Sache** (*gen*) **~/nicht ~ können** to be able/unable to dispense with sb/sth.

enträtseln* *vt* to solve; *Sinn* to work out; *Schrift* to decipher.

entrechten* *vt* **jdn ~** to deprive sb of his rights; **die Entrechteten** those who have lost *or* been deprived of their rights.

Entrechtung *f* deprivation of rights ♦ **die ~ des Parlaments** depriving parliament of its rights.

Entree [ã'tre:] *nt* **-s, -s** (*dated*) (*Eingang*) entrance; (*obs: Vorraum*) (entrance) hall; (*Eintrittsgeld*) entrance *or* admission fee; (*Mus: Vorspiel*) introduction; (*Cook: Vorspeise*) entrée; (*Theat: Auftritt*) solo entrance.

entreißen* *vt irreg* **jdm etw ~** (*lit, fig liter*) to snatch sth (away) from sb; **jdn dem Tode ~** (*liter*) to snatch sb from the jaws of death.

entrichten* *vt* (*form*) to pay.

Entrichtung *f* (*form*) payment.

entrinden* *vt* to remove the bark from, to decorticate (*form*).

entringen* *irreg* [1] *vt* (*geh*) **jdm etw ~** to wrench *or* wrest sth from sb; **jdm ein Geheimnis** *etc* **~** to wring a secret *etc* out of sb, to wrest a secret *etc* from sb.
[2] *vr* (*liter*) **sich jds Lippen** (*dat*) **~** to escape from sb's lips; **ein Seufzer entrang sich seiner Brust** he heaved a sigh.

entrinnen* *vi irreg aux sein* (*geh*) **(a)** +*dat* to escape from; *dem Tod* to escape ♦ **es gibt kein E~** there is no escape. **(b)** (*entfliehen: Zeit*) to fly by.

entrollen* [1] *vt Landkarte etc* to unroll; *Fahne, Segel* to unfurl ♦ **ein Bild des Schreckens ~** (*fig*) to reveal a picture of horror.
[2] *vr* to unroll/unfurl ♦ **ein Bild des Schreckens entrollte sich** (*fig*) a picture of horror unfolded.
[3] *vi aux sein* +*dat* (*rare*) to roll out of.

Entropie *f* (*Phys*) entropy.

entrosten* *vt* to derust.

Entroster *m* **-s, -, Entrostungsmittel** *nt* deruster.

entrücken* *vt* (*geh*) **jdn jdm/einer Sache ~** (*lit, fig*) to carry *or* bear (*liter*) sb away from sb/sth, to transport sb (away) from sb/sth; **jdn (in den Himmel) ~** (*Rel*) to translate sb (into heaven); **der Tod hat sie allen Sorgen entrückt** death has put her beyond all tribulation; **einer Sache weit entrückt sein** (*fig*) to be far removed from sth; **jdn jds Blicken ~** to remove sb from sb's sight; **jds Blicken entrückt (sein)** (to be) out of (sb's) sight.

entrückt *adj* (*geh*) (*verzückt*) enraptured, transported; (*versunken*) lost in reverie, rapt.

Entrückung *f* (*geh, Rel*) rapture, ecstasy; (*Versunkenheit*) rapt absorption; (*Rel: Versetzung*) translation.

entrümpeln* *vt* to clear out; (*fig*) to tidy up.

Entrümp(e)lung *f* clear-out; (*das Entrümpeln*) clearing out; (*fig*) tidying up.

entrüsten* [1] *vt* (*empören*) to fill with indignation, to outrage; (*zornig machen*) to incense, to anger; (*schockieren*) to outrage, to scandalize.
[2] *vr* **sich ~ über** (+*acc*) (*sich empören*) to be filled with indignation at, to be outraged at; (*zornig werden*) to be incensed at; (*schockiert sein*) to be outraged *or* scandalized at; **das ist unerhört!, entrüstete sich die alte Dame** that is scandalous!, said the old lady incensed.

entrüstet *adj siehe vt* (highly) indignant, outraged; incensed; outraged, scandalized.

Entrüstung *f* (*über* +*acc* at) indignation; (*Zorn*) anger ♦ **ein Sturm der ~ brach los** a storm of indignation broke out.

entsaften* *vt* to extract the juice from.

Entsafter *m* **-s, -** juice extractor.

entsagen* *vi* +*dat* (*geh*) to renounce ♦ **der Welt ~** to renounce the world; **sie hat vielen Freuden ~ müssen** she had to forgo many pleasures; **dem muß ich ~** I shall have to forgo that.

Entsagung *f* (*geh*) (*von der Welt etc*) renunciation (of worldly things) ♦ **Armut und ~ sind die Grundprinzipien des Klosterlebens** poverty and the renunciation of worldly things are the basic principles of monastic life.

entsagungsvoll *adj* (*geh*) *Leben* (full) of privation; *Blick, Geste* resigned.

entsalzen* *vt irreg* to desalinate.

Entsalzung *f* desalination.

Entsatz *m* **-es,** *no pl* (*Mil*) relief.

entschädigen* [1] *vt* (*für* for) (*lit, fig*) to compensate, to recompense, to indemnify (*form*); (*für Dienste etc*) to reward; (*mit Geld auch*) to remunerate; (*Kosten erstatten*) to reimburse, to indemnify (*form*) ♦ **das Theaterstück entschädigte uns für das lange Warten** the play made up for the long wait.
[2] *vr* **sich (für etw) ~** to compensate oneself for sth; **ihr Mann ist fremdgegangen, aber sie hat sich reichlich dafür entschädigt** her husband was unfaithful to her but she got her own back with a vengeance.

Entschädigung *f siehe vt* compensation, recompense, indemnification (*form*); reward; remuneration; reimbursement ♦ **jdm eine ~ zahlen** to pay sb compensation.

Entschädigungs-: ~klage *f* claim for compensation; **~summe** *f* amount of compensation.

entschärfen* *vt* **(a)** *Bombe etc* to defuse, to de-activate. **(b)** (*fig*) *Kurve* to straighten out; *Krise, Lage* to defuse; *Argument* to neutralize; *Buch, Film* to tone down.

Entscheid *m* **-(e)s, -e** (*Sw, form*) *siehe* **Entscheidung.**

▼ **entscheiden*** *pret* **entschied,** *ptp* **entschieden** [1] *vt* to decide ♦ **das Gericht entschied, daß ...** the court decided *or* ruled that ...; **~ Sie, wie es gemacht werden soll!** you decide how it is to be done; **das Spiel/die Wahl ist entschieden/schon entschieden** the game/election has been decided/is already decided; **den Kampf/Krieg (um etw) für sich ~** to secure victory in the struggle/battle (for sth); **das hat das Spiel zu unseren Gunsten entschieden** that decided the game in our favour; **es ist noch nichts entschieden** nothing has been decided (as) yet.
[2] *vi* (*über* +*acc*) to decide (on); (*Jur auch*) to rule (on) ♦ **darüber habe ich nicht zu ~** that is not for me to decide; **der Richter hat für/gegen den Kläger entschieden** the judge decided *or* ruled for/against the plaintiff.
▼ [3] *vr* (*Mensch*) to decide, to make up one's mind, to come to a decision; (*Angelegenheit*) to be decided ♦ **sich für etw ~** to decide in favour of sth, to decide on sth; **sich für jdn ~** to decide in favour of sb; **sich gegen jdn/etw ~** to decide against sb/sth; **jetzt wird es sich ~, wer der Schnellere ist** now we'll see *or* settle who is the quicker.

entscheidend *adj* decisive; *Faktor auch* deciding *attr*; *Argument, Aussage auch* conclusive; *Augenblick auch* crucial, critical; *Fehler, Irrtum auch* crucial ♦ **die ~e Stimme** (*bei Wahlen etc*) the deciding *or* casting vote; **für jdn/etw ~ sein** to be decisive *or* crucial for sb/sth; **der alles ~e Augenblick** the all-decisive moment; **das E~e** the decisive *or* deciding factor.

Entscheidung *f* decision; (*Jur auch*) ruling; (*der Geschworenen auch*) verdict ♦ **um die ~ spielen** (*Sport*) to play the deciding match *or* the decider; (*bei gleichem Tor-, Punktverhältnis auch*) to play off; **Spiel um die ~** (*Sport*) deciding match, decider; play-off; **mit den finanziellen ~en habe ich nichts zu tun** I have nothing to do with the financial decision-making *or* decisions; **wie ist die ~ ausgefallen?** which way did the decision go?; **es geht um die ~** it's going to be decisive, it's going to decide things; **die Lage drängt zur ~** the situation is coming to a head; **die Frage kommt heute zur ~** the question will be decided today.

Entscheidungs-: ~bedarf *m* need for a decision; **~befugnis** *f* decision-making powers *pl*; **~findung** *f* decision-making; **~frage** *f* (*Gram*) yes-no question; **~freiheit** *f* freedom of decision-making; **e~freudig** *adj* able to make decisions, decisive; **~gremium** *nt* decision-making body; **~hilfe** *f* aid to decision-making; **~kampf** *m* decisive encounter, show-down (*inf, auch fig*); (*Sport*) decider; **~kriterium** *nt* deciding factor; **~schlacht** *f* decisive battle; (*fig*) show-down (*inf*); **e~schwach** *adj* indecisive; **~schwäche** *f* indecision; **~spiel** *nt* decider, deciding match; (*bei gleichem Punkt-, Torverhältnis auch*) play-off; **~spielraum** *m* room for manoeuvre in making a decision; **wir haben hierbei keinen ~spielraum** we don't have much choice in this; **~träger** *m* decision-maker; **~unfähigkeit** *f* inability to make decisions, indecision.

entschieden *adj* **(a)** (*entschlossen*) determined, resolute; *Befürworter* staunch; *Ablehnung* firm, uncompromising ♦ **etw ~ ablehnen** to reject sth firmly.
(b) *no pred* (*eindeutig*) decided, distinct ♦ **er ist ein ~er Könner in seinem Fach** he is unquestionably *or* decidedly an expert in his subject; **das geht ~ zu weit** that's definitely going too far.

Entschiedenheit *f siehe adj* (*a*) determination, resolution; staunchness; firmness, uncompromising nature ♦ **etw mit aller ~ dementieren/ablehnen** to deny sth categorically/reject sth flatly.

entschlacken* *vt* (*Metal*) to remove the slag from; (*Med*) *Körper* to purify.

Entschlackung *f* (*Metal*) removal of slag (*gen* from); (*Med*) purification.

entschlafen* *vi irreg aux sein* (*geh*) to fall asleep; (*euph auch: sterben*) to pass away ◆ **der/die E~e/die E~en** the deceased, the departed.

entschleiern* [1] *vt* to unveil; (*fig auch*) to uncover, to reveal.
[2] *vr* to unveil (oneself); (*hum*) to strip, to disrobe (*hum, form*); (*fig: Geheimnis etc*) to be unveiled *or* revealed.

entschließen* *pret* **entschlọß,** *ptp* **entschlọssen** *vr* to decide (*für, zu* on) ◆ **sich ~, etw zu tun** to decide *or* determine *or* resolve to do sth; **ich entschloß mich zum Kauf dieses Hauses** I decided to buy this house; **ich weiß nicht, wozu ich mich ~ soll** I don't know what to decide; **sich anders ~** to change one's mind; **sich zu nichts ~ können** to be unable to make up one's mind; **ich bin fest entschlossen** I am absolutely determined; **zu allem entschlossen sein** to be ready for anything; **er ist zum Schlimmsten entschlossen** he will stop at nothing, he's prepared to do anything; **kurz entschlossen** straight away, without further ado.

Entschließung *f* resolution.

Entschließungsantrag *m* (*Pol*) resolution proposal.

⚠ **entschlọß** *pret of* **entschließen.**

▼ **entschlọssen** *adj* determined, resolute ◆ **~ handeln** to act resolutely *or* with determination.

Entschlọssenheit *f* determination, resolution ◆ **in wilder ~** with fierce determination.

entschlụmmern* *vi aux sein* (*liter, auch euph: sterben*) to fall asleep.

entschlüpfen* *vi aux sein* to escape (*dat* from), to slip away (*dat* from); (*Küken*) to be hatched; (*fig: Wort etc*) to slip out (*dat* from) ◆ **mir ist eine unüberlegte Bemerkung entschlüpft** I let slip an ill-considered remark.

⚠ **Entschlụß** *m* (*Entscheidung*) decision; (*Vorsatz*) resolution, resolve ◆ **zu keinem ~ kommen können** to be unable to make up one's mind *or* come to a decision; **mein ~ ist gefaßt** my decision is made, my mind is made up; **aus eigenem ~ handeln** to act on one's own initiative; **seinen ~ ändern** to change one's mind; **es ist mein fester ~** ... it is my firm intention ..., I firmly intend ...; **ein Mann von schnellen ~̈ssen sein** to be good at decision-making, to be able to decide quickly.

entschlüsseln* *vt* to decipher; *Funkspruch auch* to decode.

Entschlüsselung *f siehe vt* deciphering; decoding.

⚠ **Entschlụß-: e~freudig** *adj* decisive; **~kraft** *f* decisiveness, determination; **e~los** *adj* indecisive, irresolute.

entschụldbar *adj* excusable, pardonable.

▼ **entschụldigen*** [1] *vt* to excuse ◆ **etw mit etw ~** to excuse sth as due to sth; **das ist durch nichts zu ~!, das läßt sich nicht ~!** that is inexcusable!; **der Lehrer entschuldigte das Kind** the teacher excused the child (from attendance); **das entschuldigt nicht, daß er sich so benimmt** that is no excuse for *or* doesn't excuse his behaving like that; **jdn bei jdm/einem Treffen ~** to make *or* present sb's excuses *or* apologies to sb/a meeting; **einen Schüler ~ lassen** *or* **~** to ask for a pupil to be excused; **ich möchte meine Tochter für morgen ~** I would like to have my daughter excused for tomorrow; **ich bitte mich zu ~** I beg to be excused; **bitte entschuldigt die Störung, aber** ... please excuse *or* forgive the interruption, but ...
[2] *vi* **entschuldige/~ Sie (bitte)!** (do *or* please) excuse me!, sorry!; (*bei Bitte, Frage etc*) excuse me (please), pardon me (*US*); **(na) ~ Sie/entschuldige mal!** excuse me!
[3] *vr* **sich (bei jdm) ~** (*sich abmelden, sich rechtfertigen*) to excuse oneself, to make one's excuses (to sb); (*sich bei Lehrer, Chef abmelden*) to ask (sb) to be excused; **sich (bei jdm) (wegen etw) ~** (*um Verzeihung bitten*) to apologize (to sb) (for sth); **sich (von jdm) ~ lassen** to send *or* convey (*form*) one's excuses *or* apologies (via sb); **sich mit Krankheit ~** to excuse oneself on account of illness.

entschụldigend *adj* apologetic.

▼ **Entschụldigung** *f* (*Grund*) excuse; (*Bitte um ~*) apology; (*Sch: Brief*) letter of excuse, note ◆ **~!** excuse me!; (*Verzeihung auch*) sorry!; **als** *or* **zur ~ für** ... as an excuse/apology for ..., in excuse of ... (*form*); **zu seiner ~ sagte er** ... he said in his defence that ...; **ohne ~ fehlen** to be absent without an excuse; **(jdn) (wegen einer Sache) um ~ bitten** to apologize (to sb) (for sth); **ich bitte vielmals um ~(, daß ich mich verspätet habe)!** I do apologize *or* beg your pardon (for being late)!

Entschụldigungs-: ~brief *m* letter of apology; (*Sch*) excuse note; **~grund** *m* excuse.

entschweben* *vi aux sein* (*geh, hum: weggehen*) to float *or* waft away (*dat* from).

entschwefeln* *vt* to desulphurize.

Entschwefelung *f* desulphurization.

Entschwefelungsanlage *f* desulphurization plant.

entschwịnden* *vi irreg aux sein* (*geh: lit, fig*) to vanish, to disappear (*dat* from, *in +acc* into) ◆ **dem Gedächtnis ~** to fade from one's memory; **die Tage entschwanden wie im Flug** the days flew *or* raced by.

entseelt *adj* (*liter*) lifeless, dead.

entsẹnden* *vt irreg or reg Abgeordnete etc* to send; *Boten auch* to dispatch.

Entsẹndung *f siehe vt* sending; dispatch.

entsẹtzen* [1] *vt* **(a)** (*Mil*) *Festung, Truppen* to relieve. **(b)** (*in Grauen versetzen*) to horrify, to appal.
[2] *vr* **sich über jdn/etw ~** to be horrified *or* appalled at *or* by sb/sth; **sich vor etw** (*dat*) **~** to be horrified *or* appalled at sth; *siehe* **entsetzt.**

Entsẹtzen *nt* **-s,** *no pl* horror; (*Bestürzung auch*) dismay; (*Erschrecken*) terror ◆ **von ~ erfaßt** *or* **ergriffen** *or* **gepackt werden** to be seized with horror/terror/dismay, to be horror-stricken; **zu meinem größten ~ bemerkte ich, daß** ... to my horror *or* great dismay I noticed that ...; **mit ~ sehen/hören, daß** ... to be horrified/terrified/dismayed to see/hear that ...

Entsẹtzensschrei *m* cry of horror.

entsẹtzlich *adj* dreadful, appalling, hideous; (*inf: sehr unangenehm auch*) terrible, awful ◆ **~ viel (Geld)** an awful lot (of money) (*inf*).

Entsẹtzlichkeit *f* dreadfulness, appallingness, hideousness.

entsẹtzt *adj* horrified, appalled (*über +acc* at, by) ◆ **ein ~er Schrei** a horrified scream, a cry *or* scream of horror.

Entsẹtzung *f* (*Mil*) relief.

entseuchen* *vt* (*desinfizieren*) to disinfect; (*dekontaminieren*) to decontaminate.

Entseuchung *f* decontamination.

entsịchern* *vt* **eine Pistole ~** to release the safety catch of a pistol; **eine entsicherte Pistole** a pistol with the safety catch off.

entsịnnen* *vr irreg* (*einer Sache (gen), an etw (acc)* sth) to remember, to recall, to recollect ◆ **wenn ich mich recht entsinne** if my memory serves me correctly *or* right.

entsọrgen* [1] *vt Atomkraftwerk* to remove the waste from ◆ **eine Stadt ~** to dispose of a town's refuse and sewage.
[2] *vi* to dispose of refuse and sewage.

Entsọrgung *f* waste disposal ◆ **die ~ von Chemikalien** the disposal of chemicals.

Entsọrgungspark *m* (nuclear) waste dump.

entspạnnen* [1] *vt Muskeln, Nerven etc* to relax; *Bogen* to unbend; *Seil, Saite* to slacken, to untighten; *Wasser* to reduce the surface tension of; (*Tech*) *Feder* to relax the tension of; (*fig*) *Lage, Beziehungen* to ease (up).
[2] *vr* to relax (*auch fig*); (*ausruhen*) to rest; (*nach der Arbeit etc*) to unwind, to unbend; (*Lage etc*) to ease; (*Feder etc*) to lose tension; (*Bogen*) to unbend.

entspạnnt *adj* relaxed ◆ **die Lage hier ist wieder etwas ~er** the situation here is now less tense again.

Entspạnnung *f* relaxation (*auch fig*); (*von Lage, Fin: an der Börse*) easing(-up); (*Pol*) easing *or* reduction of tension (*+gen* in), détente; (*Tech: von Feder etc*) reduction of tension (*+gen* on); (*des Wassers*) reduction of surface tension; (*von Bogen*) unbending; (*von Seil etc*) slackening, untightening ◆ **nach der Arbeit sehe ich zur ~ etwas fern** after work I watch television for a bit to help me unwind.

Entspạnnungs-: ~bemühungen *pl* efforts aimed at easing (political) tension; **~politik** *f* policy of détente; **~übungen** *pl* (*Med etc*) relaxation exercises.

entspịnnen* *vr irreg* to develop, to arise.

entspr. *abbr of* **entsprechend.**

▼ **entsprẹchen*** *vi irreg +dat* to correspond to; *der Wahrheit, den Tatsachen auch* to be in accordance with; *den Tatsachen auch* to fit; (*genügen*) *Anforderungen, Kriterien* to fulfil, to meet; *einem Anlaß* to be in keeping with; *Erwartungen* to come *or* live up to; *einer Beschreibung* to answer, to fit; *einer Bitte, einem Wunsch etc* to meet, to comply with ◆ **sich** *or* **einander ~** to correspond (with each other), to tally; **ihre Ausrüstung entsprach nicht den alpinen Bedingungen** her outfit wasn't suitable for the alpine conditions; **seinem Zweck ~** to fulfil its purpose.

entsprẹchend [1] *adj* corresponding; (*zuständig*) relevant; (*angemessen*) appropriate ◆ **der Film war besonders geschmacklos, und die Kritiken waren dann auch ~** the film was particularly tasteless and the reviews of it were correspondingly harsh; **ein der Leistung ~es Gehalt** a salary commensurate with one's performance.
[2] *adv* accordingly; (*ähnlich, gleich*) correspondingly ◆ **er wurde ~ bestraft** he was suitably *or* appropriately punished; **etw ~ würdigen** to show suitable appreciation for sth.
[3] *prep +dat* in accordance with, according to; (*ähnlich, gleich*) corresponding to ◆ **er wird seiner Leistung ~ bezahlt** he is paid according to output; **er hat sich den Erwartungen ~ entwickelt** he has progressed as we had hoped; *siehe* **Umstand.**

Entsprẹchung *f* (*Äquivalent*) equivalent; (*Gegenstück*) counterpart; (*Analogie*) parallel; (*Übereinstimmung*) correspondence.

entsprießen* *vi irreg aux sein* (*liter: lit, fig*) **einer Sache** (*dat*) *or* **aus etw ~** to spring forth from sth (*liter*); (*old, hum*) *aus Ehe, Familie etc* to issue from sth (*old, form*).

entsprịngen* *vi irreg aux sein* **(a)** (*Fluß*) to rise. **(b)** (*entfliehen*) to escape (*dat, aus* from). **(c)** (*sich herleiten von*) *+dat* to spring from, to arise from.

entstaatlichen* *vt* to denationalize.

Entstalinisierung *f* destalinization.

entstạmmen* *vi aux sein +dat* to stem *or* come from; *einer Familie auch* to be descended from; (*fig auch*) to originate in *or* from.

entstauben* *vt* to remove the dust from, to free from dust.

entstehen* *vi irreg aux sein* (*ins Dasein treten*) to come into being; (*seinen Ursprung haben*) to originate; (*sich entwickeln*) to arise, to develop (*aus, durch* from); (*hervorkommen*) to emerge (*aus, durch* from); (*verursacht werden*) to result (*aus, durch* from); (*Chem: Verbindungen*) to be produced (*aus* from, *durch* through, via); (*Kunstwerk: geschrieben/gebaut etc werden*) to be written/built *etc* ◆ **das Feuer war durch Nachlässigkeit entstanden** the fire was caused by negligence; **bei E~ eines Feuers** in the event of (a) fire; **wir wollen nicht den Eindruck ~ lassen, ...** we don't want to give (rise to) the impression that ..., we don't want to let the impression emerge that ...; **im E~ begriffen sein** to be in the process of formation *or* development, to be emerging; **für ~den** *or* **entstandenen Schaden** for damages incurred.

Entstehung *f* (*das Werden*) genesis, coming into being; (*das Hervorkommen*) emergence; (*Ursprung*) origin; (*Bildung*) formation.

Entstehungs-: ~geschichte *f* genesis; (*Bibl*) Genesis; **~ort** *m* place of ori-

➤ SPRACHE AKTIV: **entschlossen** → 35.2 **entschuldigen** → 45.1 **Entschuldigung** → 45.1, 45.2 **entsprechen** → 32.4, 38.1, 53.6

gin; ~**ursache** *f* original cause; ~**zeit** *f* time of origin.

entsteigen* *vi irreg aux sein +dat (geh) einem Wagen* to alight from *(form)*; *dem Wasser, dem Bad* to emerge from; *(fig: Dampf etc)* to rise from.

entsteinen* *vt* to stone.

entstellen* *vt (verunstalten) Gesicht* to disfigure; *(verzerren) Gesicht(szüge)* to distort, to contort; *(fig) Bericht, Wahrheit etc* to distort ♦ **etw entstellt wiedergeben** to distort *or* misrepresent sth; **sein von Haß/Schmerz entstelltes Gesicht** his face distorted *or* contorted with hate/pain.

Entstellung *f* disfigurement; *(fig)* distortion; *(der Wahrheit)* perversion, distortion.

entstempeln* *vt (Aut)* to cancel the registration of.

Entstickung *f* denitrification.

Entstickungsanlage *f* denitrification plant.

entstielen* *vt Obst* to remove the stalk(s) from.

entstofflichen* *vt* to dematerialize.

entstören* *vt Radio, Telefon* to free from interference; *Auto, Staubsauger* to fit a suppressor to, to suppress.

Entstörer *m*, **Entstörgerät** *nt (für Auto etc)* suppressor; *(für Radio, Telefon)* anti-interference device.

Entstörung *f siehe vt* freeing from interference, suppression of interference; fitting of a suppressor *(gen* to), suppressing.

Entstörungs-: ~**dienst** *m*, ~**stelle** *f* telephone maintenance service.

entströmen* *vi aux sein* to pour *or* gush out *(+dat, aus* of); *(Gas, Geruch etc)* to issue *or* escape *(+dat, aus* from).

Entsublimierung *f (Psych, Sociol)* **repressive ~** repressive desublimation.

entsumpfen* *vt Gebiet* to drain.

enttabuisieren* [ɛnttabuiˈziːrən] *vt* to free from taboos, to remove the taboos from.

Enttabuisierung *f* removal of taboos *(+gen* from).

enttarnen* *vt Spion* to blow the cover of *(inf)*; *(fig: entlarven)* to expose ♦ **er wurde enttarnt** *(Spion)* his cover was blown, he was exposed.

Enttarnung *f* exposure.

enttäuschen* [1] *vt* to disappoint; *Vertrauen* to betray ♦ **enttäuscht sein über** *(+acc)***/von** to be disappointed at/by *or* in; **er ging enttäuscht nach Hause** he went home disappointed; **sie ist im Leben oft enttäuscht worden** she has had many disappointments in life; **du hast uns sehr enttäuscht** you have really let us down *or* disappointed us; **angenehm enttäuscht sein** to be pleasantly surprised.

[2] *vi* **unsere Mannschaft hat sehr enttäuscht** our team were very disappointing *or* played very disappointingly; **der neue Wagen hat enttäuscht** the new car is a disappointment *or* let-down *(inf)*.

Enttäuschung *f* disappointment ♦ **das Theaterstück war eine große ~** the play was a big disappointment *or* let-down *(inf)*; **jdm eine ~ bereiten** to disappoint sb.

entthronen* *vt (lit, fig)* to dethrone.

Entthronung *f (lit, fig)* dethronement, dethroning.

enttrümmern* [1] *vt* to clear of rubble.

[2] *vi* to clear the rubble (away).

entvölkern* *vt* to depopulate.

Entvölkerung *f* depopulation.

entw. *abbr of* **entweder**.

entwachsen* *vi irreg aux sein +dat* **(a)** *(geh: herauswachsen aus)* to spring from. **(b)** *(zu groß werden für)* to outgrow, to grow out of.

entwaffnen* *vt (lit, fig)* to disarm.

entwaffnend *adj (fig)* disarming.

Entwaffnung *f* disarming; *(eines Landes)* disarmament.

entwalden* *vt* to deforest.

entwanzen *vt (Comput)* to debug.

entwarnen* *vi* to sound *or* give the all-clear.

Entwarnung *f* sounding of the all-clear; *(Signal)* all-clear.

entwässern* *vt Grundstück, Moor* to drain; *Gewebe, Ödem* to dehydrate.

Entwässerung *f* drainage; *(Chem)* dehydration.

Entwässerungs-: ~**anlage** *f* drainage system; ~**graben** *m* drainage ditch.

entweder [*auch* ˈɛntweːdɐ] *conj* **~ ... oder ...** either ... or ...; **~ oder!** make up your mind (one way or the other)!, yes or no; **~ gleich oder gar nicht, ~ jetzt oder nie** it's now or never.

Entweder-Oder *nt* -, - **hier gibt es kein ~** there is no alternative; **hier gibt es nur ein ~** there has to be a definite decision one way or the other.

entweichen* *vi irreg aux sein (geh: fliehen)* to escape *or* run away *(+dat, aus* from); *(sich verflüchtigen: Gas, Flüssigkeit)* to leak *or* escape *(+dat, aus* from, out of).

entweihen* *vt* to violate *(auch fig)*; *(entheiligen)* to profane, to desecrate.

Entweihung *f siehe vt* violation; profanation, desecration.

entwenden* *vt (form)* **jdm etw/etw aus etw ~** to steal *or* purloin *(hum, form)* sth from sb/sth.

Entwendung *f (form)* theft, stealing, purloining *(hum, form)*.

entwerfen* *vt irreg* **(a)** *(zeichnen, gestalten) Zeichnung etc* to sketch; *Muster, Modell etc* to design. **(b)** *(ausarbeiten) Gesetz, Vortrag, Schreiben etc* to draft, to draw up; *Plan* to devise, to draw up. **(c)** *(fig) (darstellen, darlegen) Bild* to depict, to draw; *(in Umrissen darstellen)* to outline.

entwerten* *vt* **(a)** *(im Wert mindern)* to devalue, to depreciate; *Zeugenaussage, Argument etc auch* to undermine. **(b)** *(ungültig machen)* to make *or* render invalid; *Münzen* to demonetize; *Briefmarke, Fahrschein* to cancel.

Entwerter *m* -s, - (ticket-)cancelling machine.

Entwertung *f siehe vt* devaluation, depreciation; undermining; invalidation; demonetization; cancellation.

entwickeln* [1] *vt* to develop *(auch Phot)*; *(Phot) esp Diapositive* to process; *Methode, Verfahren auch* to evolve; *(Math auch) Formel* to expand; *(Chem) Gas etc* to produce, to generate; *Mut, Energie* to show, to display ♦ **jdm etw ~** to set out *or* expound sth to sb; **etw zu etw ~** to develop sth into sth.

[2] *vr* to develop *(zu* into); *(Chem: Gase etc)* to be produced *or* generated ♦ **das Projekt/der neue Angestellte entwickelt sich gut** the project/the new employee is coming along *or* shaping up nicely; **das Kind entwickelt sich gut** the baby is coming along nicely; **er hat sich ganz schön entwickelt** *(inf)* he's turned out really nicely.

Entwickler *m* -s, - *(Phot)* developer.

Entwicklerbad *nt (Phot)* developing bath.

Entwicklung *f* development; *(von Methoden, Verfahren, Gattung auch)* evolution; *(Math: von Formel auch)* expansion; *(Erzeugung, Chem: von Gasen etc)* production, generation; *(von Mut, Energie)* show, display; *(Phot)* developing; *(esp von Diapositiven)* processing ♦ **das Flugzeug ist noch in der ~** the plane is still being developed *or* is still in the development stage; **Jugendliche, die noch in der ~ sind** young people who are still in their adolescence *or* still developing; **das Flugzeug ist zur ~ höchster Geschwindigkeiten fähig** this plane is capable of reaching extremely high speeds.

Entwicklungs-: ~**alter** *nt* adolescence; ~**arbeit** *f* development (work); ~**beschleunigung** *f (Physiol)* acceleration (in development); ~**dienst** *m* voluntary service overseas *(Brit)*, VSO *(Brit)*, Peace Corps *(US)*; **e~fähig** *adj* capable of development; **der Plan/die Idee ist durchaus e~fähig** this plan/idea is definitely worth following up *or* expanding; **diese Stelle ist e~fähig** this position has prospects; ~**fähigkeit** *f* capability of development, capacity for development; *(einer Stelle)* prospects *pl*; ~**gang** *m* development; ~**gebiet** *nt* development area; ~**geschichte** *f* developmental history, evolution; **e~geschichtlich** *adj* evolutionary *attr*, with respect to evolution *or* developmental history; ~**helfer** *m* person doing Voluntary Service Overseas *(Brit)*, VSO worker *(Brit)*, Peace Corps worker *(US)*; **e~hemmend** *adj* restricting *or* impeding development; ~**hilfe** *f* foreign aid; ~**jahre** *pl* adolescent *or* formative *(auch fig)* years, adolescence; ~**land** *nt* developing *or* third-world country; ~**möglichkeit** *f* possibility for development; ~**phase** *f (Psych)* developmental stage; ~**psychologie** *f* developmental psychology; ~**roman** *m (Liter)* novel showing the development of a character; ~**stadium** *nt* stage of development; *(der Menschheit etc)* evolutionary stage; ~**störung** *f* developmental disturbance, disturbance in development; ~**stufe** *f* stage of development; *(der Menschheit etc)* evolutionary stage; ~**zeit** *f* period of development; *(Biol, Psych)* developmental period; *(Phot)* developing time.

entwinden* *vt irreg (geh)* **jdm etw ~** to wrest sth from sb.

entwirrbar *adj (fig)* extricable, soluble.

entwirren* *vt (lit, fig)* to disentangle, to unravel.

entwischen* *vi aux sein (inf)* to escape, to get away *(dat, aus* from).

entwöhnen* *vt* **jdn ~** *(einer Gewohnheit, Sucht)* to break sb of the habit *(+dat, von* of), to cure sb *(+dat, von* of), to wean sb *(+dat, von* from); *Säugling, Jungtier* to wean; **sich einer Sache** *(gen)* **~** *(geh)* to lose the habit of doing sth, to disaccustom oneself from sth *(form)*.

Entwöhnung *f siehe vt* cure, curing; weaning.

entwölken* *vr (lit, fig liter)* to clear.

entwürdigen* [1] *vt* to degrade; *(Schande bringen über)* to disgrace.

[2] *vr* to degrade *or* abase oneself.

entwürdigend *adj* degrading.

Entwürdigung *f* degradation, abasement; *(Entehrung)* disgrace *(gen* to).

Entwurf *m* -s, ⸚e **(a)** *(Skizze, Abriß)* outline, sketch; *(Design)* design; *(Archit, fig)* blueprint.

(b) *(Vertrags~, von Plan, Gesetz etc, Konzept)* draft (version), framework; *(einer Theorie auch)* outline; *(Parl: Gesetz~)* bill ♦ **das Bild/die Doktorarbeit ist im ~ fertig** the sketch/the framework for the picture/PhD is finished.

Entwurfsstadium *nt* **sich im ~ befinden** to be in the planning stage, to be on the drawing board.

entwurmen* *vt Katze etc* to worm.

entwurzeln* *vt (lit, fig)* to uproot.

Entwurzelung *f (lit, fig: das Entwurzeln)* uprooting; *(fig: das Entwurzeltsein)* rootlessness.

entzaubern* *vt* **jdn/etw ~** to break the spell on sb/sth; *(fig auch)* to deprive sb/sth of his/its mystique; **ihre romantischen Vorstellungen wurden entzaubert** her romantic illusions were shattered.

Entzauberung *f* breaking of the/a spell *(gen* on); *(fig auch)* deprivation of mystique; *(von Vorstellungen)* shattering, destruction.

entzerren* *vt* to correct, to rectify.

Entzerrung *f* correction, rectification ♦ **zeitliche ~** staggering.

entziehen* *irreg* [1] *vt (+dat* from) to withdraw, to take away; *Gunst etc* to withdraw; *Flüssigkeit* to draw, to extract; *(Chem)* to extract ♦ **jdm Alkohol/Nikotin ~** to deprive sb of alcohol/nicotine; **die Ärzte versuchten ihn zu ~** *(inf)* the doctors tried to cure him of his addiction; **jdm die Erlaubnis** *etc* **~** to withdraw *or* revoke sb's permit *etc*, to take sb's permit *etc* away; **jdm die Rente** *etc* **~** to cut off *or* stop sb's pension *etc*; **jdm sein Vertrauen ~** to withdraw one's confidence *or* trust in sb; **dem Redner das Wort ~** to ask the speaker to stop.

[2] *vr* **sich jdm/einer Sache ~** to evade *or* elude sb/sth; *(entkommen auch)* to escape (from) sb/sth; **sich seiner Verantwortung ~** to shirk one's re-

sponsibilities; **sich jds Verständnis/Kontrolle ~** to be beyond sb's understanding/control; **das entzieht sich meiner Kenntnis/Zuständigkeit** that is beyond my knowledge/authority; **das hat sich meiner Aufmerksamkeit entzogen** that escaped my attention; **sich jds Blicken ~** to be hidden from sight.
[3] *vi* (*inf*) to undergo treatment for (drug) addiction; (*Alkoholiker*) to dry out (*inf*).

Entziehung *f* **(a)** (*von Lizenz etc*) withdrawal, revocation (*form*). **(b)** (*von Rauschgift etc*) (*Wegnahme*) withdrawal, deprivation; (*Behandlung*) treatment for drug addiction/alcoholism.

Entziehungs-: ~anstalt *f* treatment centre for drug addicts/alcoholics; **~kur** *f* cure for drug addiction/alcoholism cure.

entzifferbar *adj siehe vt* decipherable; decodable.

entziffern* *vt* to decipher; *Funkspruch etc* to decode.

Entzifferung *f siehe vt* deciphering; decoding.

entzücken* *vt* to delight ◆ **von jdm/über etw** (*acc*) **entzückt sein** to be delighted by sb/at sth.

Entzücken *nt* **-s**, *no pl* delight, joy ◆ **zu meinem (größten) ~** to my (great) delight *or* joy; **in ~ geraten** to go into raptures; **jdn in (helles) ~ versetzen** to send sb into raptures.

entzückend *adj* delightful, charming ◆ **das ist ja ~!** how delightful *or* charming!

Entzückung *f siehe* **Entzücken.**

Entzug *m* **-(e)s**, *no pl* **(a)** (*einer Lizenz etc*) withdrawal, revocation (*form*). **(b)** (*Med: von Rauschgift etc*) withdrawal; (*Behandlung*) cure for drug addiction/alcoholism ◆ **er ist auf ~** (*Med sl*) he is being treated for drug addiction; (*Alkoholiker*) he is being dried out (*inf*).

Entzugs-: ~erscheinung *f*, **~symptom** *nt* withdrawal symptom.

entzündbar *adj* (*lit, fig*) inflammable ◆ **leicht ~** highly inflammable; (*fig*) easily roused *or* excited.

Entzündbarkeit *f* inflammability.

entzünden* [1] *vt* **(a)** *Feuer* to light; *Holz etc auch* to set light to, to ignite (*esp Sci, Tech*); *Streichholz auch* to strike; (*fig*) *Streit etc* to start, to spark off; *Haß* to inflame; *Phantasie* to fire; *Begeisterung* to fire, to kindle.
(b) (*Med*) to inflame.
[2] *vr* **(a)** to catch fire, to ignite (*esp Sci, Tech*); (*fig*) (*Streit*) to be sparked off; (*Haß*) to be inflamed; (*Phantasie*) to be fired; (*Begeisterung*) to be kindled.
(b) (*Med*) to become inflamed ◆ **entzündet** inflamed.

entzündlich *adj Gase, Brennstoff* inflammable; (*Med*) inflammatory ◆ **~e Haut** skin which easily becomes inflamed.

Entzündung *f* **(a)** (*Med*) inflammation. **(b)** ignition (*esp Sci, Tech*). **Funken führten zur ~ des Heus** sparks led to the hay catching fire.

Entzündungs- (*Med*): **e~hemmend** *adj* anti-inflammatory, antiphlogistic (*form*); **~herd** *m* focus of inflammation.

entzwei *adj pred* in two (pieces), in half, asunder (*old, poet*); (*kaputt*) broken; (*zerrissen*) torn.

entzweibrechen *vti sep irreg* (*vi: aux sein*) to break in two; (*zerbrechen*) to break.

entzweien* [1] *vt* to turn against each other, to divide, to set at variance.
[2] *vr* **sich (mit jdm) ~** to fall out (with sb); (*sich streiten auch*) to quarrel (with sb).

entzwei-: ~gehen *vi sep irreg aux sein* to break (in two *or* half), to break asunder (*poet*); **~reißen** *vt sep irreg* to tear *or* rend in two *or* in half *or* asunder (*poet*); (*zerreißen*) to tear to pieces; **~schlagen** *vt sep irreg* to strike in half *or* in two *or* asunder (*poet*); (*zerschlagen*) to smash (to pieces); **~schneiden** *vt sep irreg* to cut in two *or* half; (*zerschneiden*) to cut to pieces.

Entzweiung *f* (*fig*) (*Bruch*) split, rupture, break; (*Streit*) quarrel.

en vogue [ã'vo:k] *adj pred* (*geh*) in vogue *or* fashion.

Enzephalogramm *nt* **-s, -e** (*Med*) encephalogram.

Enzian ['ɛntsia:n] *m* **-s, -e** gentian; (*Branntwein*) *spirit distilled from the roots of gentian*.

Enzyklika *f* **-, Enzykliken** (*Eccl*) encyclical.

Enzyklopädie *f* encyclop(a)edia.

enzyklopädisch *adj* encyclop(a)edic.

Enzym *nt* **-s, -e** enzyme.

eo ipso *adv* (*geh*) ipso facto.

Epaulette [epo'lɛtə] *f* epaulette.

Epen *pl of* **Epos.**

Ephebe *m* **-n, -n** (*Hist*) ephebe, ephebus.

ephemer(isch) *adj* (*geh*) ephemeral.

Epheser *m* **-s, -** Ephesian.

Epheserbrief *m* Epistle to the Ephesians, Ephesians *sing*.

Epidemie *f* (*Med, fig*) epidemic.

Epidemio-: ~loge *m*, **~login** *f* epidemiologist; **~logie** *f* epidemiology; **e~logisch** *adj* epidemiological.

epidemisch *adj* (*Med, fig*) epidemic.

Epidermis *f* **-, Epidermen** epidermis.

Epidiaskop *nt* **-s, -e** epidiascope.

Epigone *m* **-n, -n** epigone (*liter*); (*Nachahmer*) imitator.

epigonenhaft *adj* epigonic (*liter, rare*); (*nachahmend*) imitative.

Epigramm *nt* **-s, -e** epigram.

epigrammatisch *adj* epigrammatic.

⚠ **Epigraph** *nt* **-s, -e** epigraph.

Epik *f* epic poetry.

Epiker(in *f*) *m* **-s, -** epic poet.

Epikur *m* **-s** Epicurus.

Epikureer [epiku're:ɐ] *m* **-s, -** (*Philos*) Epicurean; (*fig*) epicure(an).

epikureisch [epiku're:ɪʃ] *adj* (*Philos*) Epicurean; (*fig*) epicurean.

Epilepsie *f* epilepsy.

Epileptiker(in *f*) *m* **-s, -** epileptic.

epileptisch *adj* epileptic.

Epilog *m* **-s, -e** epilogue.

episch *adj* (*lit, fig*) epic.

Episkop *nt* **-s, -e** episcope.

Episkopat *m or nt* episcopacy, episcopate.

Episode *f* **-, -n** episode.

episodenhaft, episodisch *adj* episodic.

Epistel *f* **-, -n** epistle (*auch inf*); (*old: Lesung*) lesson ◆ **jdm die ~ lesen** (*old inf*) to read sb the riot act (*inf*).

Epistemologie *f* epistemology.

Epitaph *nt* **-s, -e** (*liter*) epitaph.

Epitheton [e'pi:tetɔn] *nt* **-s, Epitheta** (*Poet*) epithet.

Epizentrum *nt* epicentre.

epochal *adj* **(a)** epochal. **(b)** *siehe* **epochemachend.**

Epoche *f* **-, -n** epoch ◆ **~ machen** to be epoch-making, to mark a new epoch.

⚠ **epochemachend** *adj* epoch-making.

Epos *nt* **-, Epen** epic (poem), epos.

Epoxydharz [epɔ'ksy:t-] *nt* epoxy resin.

Eprouvette [epru'vɛt] *f* (*Aus Chem*) test tube.

Equipage [ek(v)i'pa:ʒə] *f* **-, -n** (*old*) equipage.

Equipe [e'kɪp] *f* **-, -n** team.

er *pers pron gen* **seiner**, *dat* **ihm**, *acc* **ihn** he; (*von Dingen*) it; (*von Hund etc*) it, he; (*vom Mond*) it, she (*poet*) ◆ **wenn ich ~ wäre** if I were him *or* he (*form*); **~ ist es** it's him, it is he (*form*); **wer hat das gemacht/ist der Täter? — ~/~ (ist es)!** who did that/is the person responsible? — he did/is!, him (*inf*)!; **~ war es nicht, ich war's** it wasn't him, it was me; **sie ist größer als ~** she is taller than he is *or* him; **E~** (*obs*) you; (*Bibl*) He; **ein E~ und eine Sie** (*hum inf*) a he and a she.

er|achten* *vt* (*geh*) **jdn/etw für** *or* **als etw ~** to consider *or* deem (*form*) sb/sth (to be) sth.

Er|achten *nt* **-s**, *no pl*: **meines ~s, nach meinem ~** in my opinion.

er|ahnen* *vt siehe* **ahnen 1.**

er|arbeiten* *vt* **(a)** (*erwerben*) *Vermögen etc* to work for; *Wissen etc* to acquire.
(b) (*erstellen*) *Entwurf etc* to work out, to elaborate.

Erb-: ~adel *m* hereditary nobility; **~anlage** *f usu pl* hereditary factor(s *pl*); **~anspruch** *m* claim to an/the inheritance; **~anteil** *m* share *or* portion of an/the inheritance.

erbarmen* [1] *vt* **jdn ~** to arouse sb's pity, to move sb to pity; **es kann einen ~** it's pitiable; **er sieht zum E~ aus** he's a pitiful sight; **das ist zum E~** it's pitiful; **sie singt zum E~** she sings appallingly, she's an appalling singer; **es möchte einen Hund ~** (*inf*) it would melt a heart of stone.
[2] *vr* (*+gen*) to have *or* take pity (on) (*auch hum inf*); (*verzeihen, verschonen*) to have mercy (on) ◆ **Herr, erbarme dich (unser)!** Lord, have mercy (upon us)!

Erbarmen *nt* **-s**, *no pl* (*Mitleid*) pity, compassion (*mit* on); (*Gnade*) mercy (*mit* on) ◆ **aus ~** out of pity; **ohne ~** pitiless(ly), merciless(ly); **er kennt kein ~** he knows no mercy; **kein ~ mit jdm kennen** to be merciless with sb, to show sb no mercy.

erbarmenswert *adj* pitiable, wretched, pitiful.

erbärmlich *adj* (*erbarmenswert, pej: dürftig*) pitiful, wretched; (*gemein, schlecht*) wretched, miserable; (*inf: furchtbar*) *Kälte* terrible, hideous ◆ **~ aussehen** to look wretched *or* terrible; **sich ~ verhalten** to behave abominably *or* wretchedly; **sie hat ~ gesungen** she sang wretchedly *or* appallingly.

Erbärmlichkeit *f* (*Elend*) wretchedness, misery; (*fig: Dürftigkeit, Gemeinheit etc*) wretchedness, miserableness.

Erbarmungs-: e~los *adj* (*lit, fig*) pitiless, merciless; **~losigkeit** *f* (*lit, fig*) pitilessness, mercilessness; **e~voll** *adj* compassionate, full of pity; **e~würdig** *adj siehe* **erbarmenswert.**

erbauen* [1] *vt* **(a)** (*lit, fig: errichten*) to build.
(b) (*fig: seelisch bereichern*) to edify, to uplift ◆ **wir waren von der Nachricht nicht gerade erbaut** (*inf*) we weren't exactly delighted by the news; **der Chef ist von meinem Plan nicht besonders erbaut** (*inf*) the boss isn't particularly enthusiastic about my plan.
[2] *vr* **sich ~ an** (*+dat*) to be uplifted *or* edified by; **abends erbaut er sich an Bachschen Kantaten** in the evenings he finds uplift *or* spiritual edification in Bach's cantatas.

Erbauer(in *f*) *m* **-s, -** builder; (*fig auch*) architect.

erbaulich *adj* edifying (*auch iro*), uplifting; (*Rel*) *Buch, Schriften* devotional.

Erbauung *f siehe vt* building; edification ◆ **zur ~** for one's edification.

Erb-: ~bauer *m farmer with a hereditary right to his property*; **~begräbnis** *nt* family grave *or* (*Gruft*) vault; **e~berechtigt** *adj* entitled to inherit; **die ~berechtigten** the legal heirs; **e~biologisch** *adj* (*Jur*) **e~biologisches Gutachten** blood test (*to establish paternity*).

Erbe[1] *m* **-n, -n** (*lit, fig*) heir (*einer Person* (*gen*) of *or* to sb, *einer Sache* (*gen*) to sth) ◆ **gesetzlicher ~** legal heir, heir at law (*Jur*), heir apparent (*Jur*); **leiblicher ~** blood-related heir, heir according to bloodright; **direkter ~** direct *or* lineal heir, heir of the body (*Jur*); **mutmaßlicher ~** presumptive heir, heir presumptive (*Jur*); **jdn zum** *or* **als ~n einsetzen** to appoint sb as *or* make sb one's/sb's heir.

Erbe[2] *nt* **-s**, *no pl* inheritance; (*fig*) heritage; (*esp Unerwünschtes*) legacy ◆ **das**

~ **des Faschismus** the legacy of fascism.

erbeben* *vi aux sein* (*geh: Erde, Mensch etc*) to tremble, to shake, to shudder.

erbeigen *adj* (*geerbt, vererbt*) inherited; (*erblich*) hereditary.

erben [1] *vt* (*lit, fig*) to inherit (*von* from); *Vermögen auch* to come into; (*inf: geschenkt bekommen*) to get, to be given ◆ **bei ihm ist nichts zu** *or* **kann man nichts ~** (*inf*) you won't get anything *or* a sausage (*inf*) out of him.
[2] *vi* to inherit.

Erbengemeinschaft *f* community of heirs.

erbetteln* *vt* to get by begging ◆ **die Kinder müssen alles auf der Straße ~** the children have to go begging on the streets for everything; **seine Möbel hat er (sich** *dat***) alle bei seinen Bekannten erbettelt** he cadged all his furniture off his friends; **die Kinder erbettelten sich die Erlaubnis, ...** the children managed to wheedle permission ...

erbeuten* *vt* (*Tier*) *Opfer* to carry off; (*Dieb*) to get away with; (*im Krieg*) to capture, to take.

Erb-: e~fähig *adj* entitled to inherit, heritable (*spec*); **~faktor** *m* (*Biol*) (hereditary) factor, gene; **~fall** *m* (*Jur*) **im ~fall** in the case of inheritance; **~fehler** *m* (*lit, fig*) hereditary defect; **~feind** *m* traditional *or* arch enemy; **der ~feind** (*Teufel*) the Arch-Fiend; **~folge** *f* (line of) succession; **~folgekrieg** *m* war of succession.

Erbgut *nt* **(a)** (*Hof*) ancestral estate. **(b)** (*Nachlaß*) estate, inheritance; (*fig*) heritage. **(c)** (*Biol*) genotype, genetic make-up.

⚠**erbgut-: ~schädigend** *adj* genetically harmful; **~verändernd** *adj Wirkung* hereditary; **das hat eine ~verändernde Wirkung** it causes genetic changes.

erbieten* *vr irreg* (*geh*) **sich ~, etw zu tun** to offer *or* volunteer to do sth; **sich zu etw ~** to offer one's services for sth.

Erbin *f* heiress.

Erbinformation *f* genetic information.

erbitten* *vt irreg* to ask for, to request ◆ **sich (nicht) ~ lassen** (not) to be prevailed upon.

erbittern* *vt* to enrage, to incense.

erbittert *adj Widerstand, Gegner etc* bitter.

Erbitterung *f* rage; (*rare: Heftigkeit*) fierceness, bitterness.

Erbium *nt, no pl* (*abbr* **Er**) erbium.

Erbkrankheit *f* hereditary disease.

erblassen* *vi aux sein* to (go *or* turn) pale, to blanch ◆ **vor Neid ~** to turn *or* go green with envy.

Erblasser(in *f***)** *m* **-s, -** **(a)** person who leaves an inheritance. **(b)** (*Testator*) testator; testatrix.

erbleichen* *vi aux sein* **(a)** (*geh*) to (go *or* turn) pale, to blanch. **(b)** *pret* **erblich,** *ptp* **erblichen** (*obs, liter: sterben*) to expire.

erblich *adj* hereditary ◆ **er ist ~ belastet, auch sein Vater** ... it's inherited, his father too ...; **er ist ~ schwer (vor)belastet** it runs in the family.

Erblichkeit *f* heritability, hereditability.

erblicken* *vt* (*geh*) to see, to perceive; (*erspähen*) to spot, to catch sight of ◆ **in jdm/etw eine Gefahr** *etc* **~** to see sb/sth as a danger *etc*, to see a danger *etc* in sb/sth; *siehe* **Licht.**

erblinden* *vi aux sein* to go blind, to lose one's sight.

Erblindung *f* loss of sight.

erblonden* *vi aux sein* (*hum*) to go blond(e).

erblühen* *vi aux sein* (*geh*) to bloom, to blossom ◆ **zu voller Schönheit ~** (*fig*) to blossom out.

Erb-: ~masse *f* estate, inheritance; (*Biol*) genotype, genetic make-up; **~onkel** *m* (*inf*) rich uncle.

erbosen* (*geh*) [1] *vt* to infuriate, to anger ◆ **erbost sein über** (*+acc*) to be furious *or* infuriated at.
[2] *vr* **sich ~ über** (*+acc*) to get *or* become furious *or* infuriated at.

erbötig *adj* **~ sein, etw zu tun** (*obs*) to be willing *or* prepared to do sth.

Erb-: ~pacht *f* hereditary lease(hold); **~pächter** *m* hereditary leaseholder; **~pflege** *f siehe* **Eugenik; ~prinz** *m* hereditary prince; (*Thronfolger*) heir to the throne.

erbrechen* *irreg* [1] *vt* (*liter*) *Schloß, Siegel* to break open; *Tür auch* to force (open).
[2] *vtir* **(sich) ~** (*Med*) to vomit, to be sick (*not vt*) ◆ **etw bis zum E~ tun** (*fig*) to do sth ad nauseam; **etw zum E~ satt haben** (*fig*) to be absolutely sick of sth.

Erbrecht *nt* law of inheritance; (*Erbanspruch*) right of inheritance (*auf +acc* to).

erbringen* *vt irreg* to produce, to furnish, to adduce.

Erbrochene(s) *nt* **-n,** *no pl* vomit.

Erbschaden *m* hereditary defect.

Erbschaft *f* inheritance ◆ **eine ~ machen** *or* **antreten** to come into an inheritance; **die ~ des Faschismus** the legacy of fascism.

Erbschafts-: ~auseinandersetzung *f* dispute over an inheritance; **~klage** *f* (*Jur*) action for recovery of an/the inheritance; **~steuer** *f* estate *or* death duty *or* duties *pl.*

Erb-: ~schein *m* certificate of inheritance; **~schleicher(in** *f***)** *m* legacy-hunter; **~schleicherei** *f* legacy-hunting; **~schuld** *f* inherited debt.

Erbse *f* **-, -n** pea ◆ **gelbe** *or* **getrocknete ~n** dried peas.

Erbsen-: e~groß *adj* pea-size, the size of a pea; **~püree** *nt* ≃ pease pudding; **~suppe** *f* pea soup.

Erb-: ~stück *nt* heirloom; **~sünde** *f* (*Rel*) original sin.

Erbswurst *f pea meal compressed into the form of a sausage.*

Erb-: ~tante *f* (*inf*) rich aunt; **~teil** *nt* **(a)** (*Jur: auch m*) (portion of an/the) inheritance; **(b)** (*Veranlagung*) inherited trait; **~vertrag** *m* testamentary contract; **~verzicht** *m* renunciation of one's claim to an inheritance; **~walter** *m* (*geh*) trustee.

Erdachse *f* earth's axis.

erdacht *adj Geschichte* made-up.

Erd-: ~altertum *nt* (*Geol*) Palaeozoic; **~anziehung** *f* gravitational pull of the earth; **~apfel** *m* (*Aus, S Ger*) potato; **~arbeiten** *pl* excavation(s *pl*), earthwork *sing*; **~atmosphäre** *f* earth's atmosphere; **~bahn** *f* orbit of the earth, earth's orbit; **~ball** *m* (*liter*) globe, world.

Erdbeben *nt* earthquake.

Erdbeben-: ~gebiet *nt* earthquake area; **e~gefährdet** *adj* at risk from earthquakes; **~gürtel** *m* earthquake belt *or* zone; **~herd** *m* seismic focus *or* centre; **~messer** *m,* ⚠**~meßgerät** *nt* seismograph; **e~sicher** *adj* earthquake-proof; **~warte** *f* seismological station.

Erd-: ~beere *f* strawberry; **e~beerfarben** *adj* strawberry-colour(ed); **~bestattung** *f* burial, interment; **~bevölkerung** *f* population of the earth, earth's population; **~bewohner** *m* inhabitant of the earth; (*gegenüber Marsbewohnern etc*) terrestrial, earthling (*pej*); **~birne** *f* (*dial*) potato.

Erdboden *m* ground, earth ◆ **etw dem ~ gleichmachen** to level sth, to raze sth to the ground; **vom ~ verschwinden** to disappear from *or* off the face of the earth; **als hätte ihn der ~ verschluckt** as if the earth had swallowed him up.

Erde *f* **-, -n** **(a)** (*Welt*) earth, world ◆ **unsere Mutter ~** (*liter*) Mother Earth; **auf ~n** (*old, liter*) on earth; **auf der ganzen ~** all over the world; **niemand auf der ganzen ~** nobody in the whole world.
(b) (*Boden*) ground ◆ **in fremder ~ ruhen** (*liter*) to lie *or* rest in foreign soil (*liter*); **unter der ~** underground, below ground; (*fig*) beneath the soil; **du wirst mich noch unter die ~ bringen** (*inf*) you'll be the death of me yet (*inf*); **über der ~** above ground; **auf die ~ fallen** to fall to the ground; **auf nackter** *or* **bloßer ~** on the bare ground; **mit beiden Beinen** *or* **Füßen (fest) auf der ~ stehen** (*fig*) to have both feet firmly on the ground; *siehe* **eben.**
(c) (*Erdreich, Bodenart*) soil, earth (*auch Chem*) ◆ **fette/trockene ~** rich/dry soil; **zu ~ werden** to turn to dust; **~ zu ~** (*Eccl*) dust to dust; **seltene ~n** (*Chem*) rare earths.
(d) (*Elec: Erdung*) earth, ground (*US*).

erden *vt* (*Elec*) to earth, to ground (*US*).

Erden-: ~bürger *m* (*geh*) mortal; **ein neuer ~bürger** a new addition to the human race; **e~fern** *adj* (*liter*) far from the earth; **~glück** *nt* (*liter*) earthly happiness.

erdenken* *vt irreg* to devise, to think up.

Erdenkind *nt* (*geh*) child of the earth (*liter*).

erdenklich *adj attr* conceivable, imaginable ◆ **alles ~(e) Gute** all the very best; **sich** (*dat*) **alle ~e Mühe geben** to take the greatest (possible) pains; **alles E~e tun** to do everything conceivable *or* imaginable.

Erden- (*liter*): **~leben** *nt* earthly life, life on earth; **~rund** *nt* **-s,** *no pl* world.

Erd-: e~farben, e~farbig *adj* earth-coloured; **e~fern** *adj* (*Astron*) far from the earth; **~ferne** *f* (*Astron*) apogee; **~gas** *nt* natural gas; **~geborene(r)** *mf* (*liter*) mortal; **e~gebunden** *adj* (*liter*) earthbound; **~geist** *m* earth-spirit; **~geruch** *m* earthy smell; **~geschichte** *f* geological history, history of the earth; **e~geschichtlich** *adj no pred* geological; ⚠**~geschoß** *nt* ground floor, first floor (*US*); **im ~geschoß** on the ground/first floor; **e~haltig** *adj* containing earth; **~harz** *nt* bitumen; **~haufen** *m* mound of earth; **~hörnchen** *nt* ground squirrel.

erdichten* *vt* to invent, to fabricate, to make up ◆ **das ist alles erdichtet und erlogen** it's all pure fabrication.

erdig *adj* earthy.

Erd-: ~innere(s) *nt* interior *or* bowels *pl* of the earth; **~kabel** *nt* underground cable; **~karte** *f* map of the earth; **~kern** *m* earth's core; **~klumpen** *m* clod of earth; **~kreis** *m* globe, world; **auf dem ganzen ~kreis** all over the world; **~kruste** *f* earth's crust; **~kugel** *f* world, earth, globe; **~kunde** *f* geography; **e~kundlich** *adj* geographical; **~leitung** *f* (*Elec*) earth *or* ground (*US*) (connection); (*Kabel*) underground wire; **~loch** *nt* (*Mil*) foxhole; **e~magnetisch** *adj* geomagnetic; **~magnetismus** *m* geomagnetism; **~mantel** *m* mantle; **~metalle** *pl* earth metals *pl*; **~mittelalter** *nt* (*Geol*) Mesozoic; **e~nah** *adj* (*Astron*) near to the earth; **~nähe** *f* (*Astron*) perigee; ⚠**~nuß** *f* peanut, groundnut; **~oberfläche** *f* surface of the earth, earth's surface; **~öl** *nt* (mineral) oil, petroleum.

erdolchen* *vt* to stab (to death) ◆ **jdn mit Blicken ~** to look daggers at sb.

Erdöl-: ⚠**e~exportierend** *adj attr* oil-exporting, petroleum-exporting; **~leitung** *f* oil pipeline; **~preise** *pl* oil prices *pl*; **~raffination** *f* petroleum refining; **~verarbeitung** *f* processing of crude oil.

Erd-: ~pech *nt* bitumen, asphalt, mineral pitch; **~pol** *m* (*Geog*) (terrestrial) pole; **~reich** *nt* soil, earth.

erdreisten* *vr* **sich ~, etw zu tun** to have the audacity to do sth; **wie können Sie sich ~!** how dare you!; **er hat sich zu dieser Eigenmächtigkeit erdreistet** he had the audacity to act in this high-handed way.

Erdrinde *f siehe* **Erdkruste.**

erdröhnen* *vi aux sein* to boom out, to thunder out; (*Kanonen auch*) to roar; (*Luft, Raum*) to resound (*von* with).

erdrosseln* *vt* to strangle, to throttle.

Erdrosselung *f* strangulation, throttling.

erdrücken* *vt* to crush (to death); (*fig: überwältigen*) to overwhelm ◆ **ein ~des Gefühl** a stifling feeling; **~de Übermacht/~des Beweismaterial** overwhelming superiority/evidence; **die Schuld erdrückte ihn beinahe** the sense of guilt oppressed him *or* weighed down on him.

Erd-: ~rutsch *m* landslide, landslip; **politischer ~rutsch** political upheaval; (*überwältigender Wahlsieg*) (political) landslide; **~rutschsieg** *m* landslide (victory); **~satellit** *m* earth satellite; **~schatten** *m* shadow of the earth; **~schicht** *f* layer (of the earth), stratum; ⚠**~schluß** *m* (*Elec*) accidental earth *or* ground (*US*); **~scholle** *f* clod of earth; **~sicht** *f* (*Aviat*) ground visibility; **~spalte** *f* crevice; **~stoß** *m* (seismic) shock; **~strahlen** *pl* field lines *pl*; **~strich** *m* region, area; **~teil** *m* continent; **~trabant** *m* moon.

erdulden* *vt* to endure, to suffer.

Erd-: ~umdrehung *f* rotation *or* revolution of the earth; **~umfang** *m* circumference of the earth; **~umkreisung** *siehe* **~umrundung**; **~umlaufbahn** *f* earth orbit; **~umrundung** *f* (*durch Satelliten*) orbit(ing) of the earth; **~umsegelung** *f* voyage around the world, circumnavigation of the globe; **~umsegler** *m* round-the-world sailor, circumnavigator of the globe.

Erdung *f* (*Elec*) earth(ing), ground(ing) (*US*).

Erd-: e~verbunden, e~verwachsen *adj* earthy; **~wall** *m* earthwork, earth bank *or* wall; **~wärme** *f* natural heat of the earth; **e~wärts** *adv* earthward(s); **~zeitalter** *nt* geological era.

er|eifern* *vr* to get excited *or* worked up (*über +acc* over).

er|eignen* *vr* to occur, to happen.

Er|eignis *nt* event, occurrence; (*Vorfall*) incident, event; (*besonderes*) occasion, event; *siehe* **freudig**.

er|eignis-: ~los *adj* uneventful; **~reich** *adj* eventful.

er|eilen* *vt* (*geh*) to overtake.

erektil *adj* (*Physiol*) erectile.

Erektion *f* (*Physiol*) erection.

Eremit *m* **-en, -en** hermit.

Eremitage [eremi'taːʒə] *f* **-, -n** hermitage.

er|erben* *vt* to inherit.

erfahren[1] *irreg* [1] *vt* **(a)** *Nachricht etc* to learn, to find out; (*hören*) to hear (*von* about, of) ◆ **wenn der Chef das erfährt, wird er wütend** if the boss gets to hear about it *or* finds that out he'll be furious; **etw zu ~ suchen** to try to find out sth; **darf man Ihre Absichten ~?** might one inquire as to your intentions?
(b) (*erleben*) to experience; (*erleiden auch*) *Rückschlag* to suffer; (*empfangen*) *Liebe, Verständnis* to receive; *Veränderungen etc* to undergo.
[2] *vi* to hear (*von* about, of).

erfahren[2] *adj* experienced.

Erfahrenheit *f* experience.

Erfahrung *f* experience; (*Übung auch*) practical knowledge; (*Philos auch*) empirical knowledge ◆ **aus (eigener) ~** from (one's own) experience; **nach meiner ~** in my experience; **~en sammeln** to gain experience; **die ~ hat gezeigt, daß ...** experience has shown that ...; **etw in ~ bringen** to learn *or* to find out sth; **eine ~ machen** to have an experience; **seine ~en machen** to learn (things) the hard way; **jeder muß seine ~en selber machen** everyone has to learn by experience; **ich habe die ~ gemacht, daß ...** I have found that ...; **mit dieser neuen Maschine/Mitarbeiterin haben wir nur gute/schlechte ~en gemacht** we have found this new machine/employee (to be) completely satisfactory/unsatisfactory; **was für ~en haben Sie mit ihm/damit gemacht?** how did you find him/it?; **ich habe mit der Ehe nur schlechte ~en gemacht** I've had a very bad experience of marriage; **durch ~ wird man klug** (*Prov*) one learns by experience.

Erfahrungs-: ~austausch *m* (*Pol*) exchange of experiences; **e~gemäß** *adv* **e~gemäß ist es ...** experience shows ...; **~medizin** *f* alternative medicine; **~tatsache** *f* empirical fact; **~wert** *m* figure based on experience, empirically established figure; **~wissenschaft** *f* empirical science.

⚠**erfaßbar** *adj* ascertainable.

erfassen* *vt* **(a)** (*rare: ergreifen*) to seize, to catch (hold of).
(b) (*mitreißen: Auto, Strömung*) to catch.
(c) (*Furcht, Verlangen etc*) to seize ◆ **Angst erfaßte sie** she was seized by fear; **Mitleid erfaßte sie** she was filled with compassion.
(d) (*begreifen*) to grasp, to comprehend, to understand ◆ **er hat's endlich erfaßt** he's caught on at last.
(e) (*einbeziehen*) to include; (*registrieren*) to record, to register; *Daten* to capture ◆ **alle Fälle werden statistisch erfaßt** statistics of all cases are being recorded; **das ist noch nicht statistisch erfaßt worden** there are no statistics on it yet.

Erfassung *f* registration, recording; (*von Daten*) capture; (*Miteinbeziehung*) inclusion.

erfechten* *vt irreg Sieg* to gain; *Rechte* to fight for and win.

erfinden* *vt irreg* to invent; (*erdichten auch*) to make up, to fabricate ◆ **das hat sie glatt erfunden** she made it all up; **frei erfunden** completely fictitious; **er hat die Arbeit auch nicht erfunden** (*inf*) he's not exactly crazy about work (*inf*); *siehe* **Pulver**.

Erfinder(in *f*) *m* **-s, -** inventor.

Erfindergeist *m* inventive genius.

erfinderisch *adj* inventive; (*phantasievoll auch*) imaginative; (*findig auch*) ingenious; *siehe* **Not**.

Erfinderschutz *m* (*Jur*) protection of inventors.

Erfindung *f* invention; (*Erdichtung, Lüge auch*) fiction, fabrication ◆ **eine ~ machen** to invent something.

Erfindungs-: ~gabe *f* inventiveness, invention; **e~reich** *adj siehe* **erfinderisch**; **~reichtum** *m* inventiveness, ingenuity.

erflehen* *vt* (*geh*) to beg for ◆ **etw von jdm ~** to beg *or* beseech (*liter*) sb for sth, to beg sth of sb.

Erfolg *m* **-(e)s, -e** success; (*Ergebnis, Folge*) result, outcome ◆ **mit/ohne ~** successfully/without success *or* unsuccessfully; **~/keinen ~ haben** to be successful/have no success *or* be unsuccessful; **ohne ~ bleiben** *or* **sein** to be unsuccessful; **ein voller ~** a great success; (*Stück, Roman, Vorschlag etc auch*) a hit; **ein kläglicher ~** not much of a success, a bit of a failure; **~(e) bei Frauen haben** to be successful with women; **sie warnte mich mit dem ~, daß ...** the effect *or* result of her warning me was that ...

erfolgen* *vi aux sein* (*form*) (*folgen*) to follow, to ensue; (*sich ergeben*) to result; (*vollzogen werden*) to be effected (*form*) *or* carried out; (*stattfinden*) to take place, to occur; (*Zahlung*) to be effected (*form*) *or* made ◆ **nach erfolgter Zahlung** after payment has been effected (*form*) *or* made; **es erfolgte keine Antwort** no answer was forthcoming.

Erfolg-: ~hascherei *f* (*pej*) striving *or* angling for success; **e~los** *adj* unsuccessful, without success; **~losigkeit** *f* lack of success, unsuccessfulness; **e~reich** *adj* successful.

Erfolgs-: e~abhängig *adj* success-related; (*Econ*) profit-related; **e~arm** *adj* short on success; **~aussicht** *f* prospect of success; **~autor** *m* successful author; **~bilanz** *f* record of success; **~buch** *nt* bestseller, successful book; **~denken** *nt* positive way of thinking; **~druck** *m* pressure to succeed; **~erlebnis** *nt* feeling of success, sense of achievement; **~film** *m* successful *or* hit film; **e~gewohnt** *adj* used to success *pred*; **~honorar** *nt* performance-related *or* success-related fee; **~kurve** *f* success curve; **~leiter** *f* (*fig*) ladder to success; **~marke** *f* successful brand; **~meldung** *f* news *sing* of success; **endlich eine ~meldung!** good news at last!; **~mensch** *m* success, successful person; **als einem ~menschen widerstrebt ihm so etwas** being used to success *or* succeeding, he reacts against that sort of thing; **e~orientiert** *adj* achievement-oriented; **~rezept** *nt* recipe for success; **~roman** *m* successful novel; **~serie** *f* string of successes; **~strategie** *f* strategy for success.

⚠**erfolgversprechend** *adj* promising.

erforderlich *adj* necessary, required, requisite ◆ **es ist dringend ~, daß ...** it is a matter of urgent necessity that ...; **etw ~ machen** to make sth necessary, to necessitate sth; **unbedingt ~** (absolutely) essential *or* imperative.

erforderlichenfalls *adv* (*form*) if required, if necessary, if need be.

erfordern* *vt* to require, to demand, to call for.

Erfordernis *nt* requirement; (*Voraussetzung auch*) prerequisite.

erforschen* *vt* **(a)** *Land, Weltraum etc* to explore.
(b) *Probleme etc* to explore, to investigate, to inquire into; (*in der Wissenschaft auch*) to research into; *Thema etc* to research; *Lage, Meinung, Wahrheit* to ascertain, to find out ◆ **sein Gewissen ~** to search *or* examine one's conscience.

Erforscher *m* (*eines Landes*) explorer; (*in Wissenschaft*) investigator, researcher.

Erforschung *f siehe vt* **(a)** exploration. **(b)** investigation, inquiry (*+gen* into); research (*+gen* into); researching; ascertaining.

erfragen* *vt Weg* to ask, to inquire; *Einzelheiten etc* to obtain, to ascertain ◆ **Einzelheiten zu ~ bei ...** for details apply to ..., details can be obtained from ...

erfrechen* *vr* **sich ~, etw zu tun** to have the audacity to do sth; **wie können Sie sich zu so einer Behauptung ~?** how dare you (have the audacity to) claim such a thing!

erfreuen* [1] *vt* to please, to delight; *Herz* to gladden ◆ **sehr erfreut!** (*dated: bei Vorstellung*) pleased to meet you!, delighted! (*dated*); **er wollte damit die Menschen ~** he wanted to give people pleasure; **ja, sagte er erfreut** yes, he said delighted(ly); **über jdn/etw erfreut sein** to be pleased *or* delighted about *or* at sb/sth.
[2] *vr* **sich einer Sache** (*gen*) **~** (*geh*) to enjoy sth; **sich an etw** (*dat*) **~** to enjoy sth, to take pleasure in sth.

erfreulich *adj* pleasant; *Neuerung, Besserung etc* welcome; (*befriedigend*) gratifying ◆ **es ist wenig ~, daß wir ...** it's not very satisfactory that we ...; **es wäre ~, wenn die Regierung ...** it would be good *or* nice if the government ...; **ich habe diesmal keine Sechs in Latein — das ist ja sehr ~** I didn't get the lowest grade in Latin this time — that's good to hear *or* I'm so glad; **sehr ~!** very nice!; **er hat sich ~ wenig beklagt** it was pleasant *or* nice how little he complained.

erfreulicherweise *adv* happily ◆ **wir haben ~ einmal ein Spiel gewonnen** I'm pleased *or* glad to say that we've won a game at last.

erfrieren* [1] *vi irreg aux sein* to freeze to death, to die of exposure; (*Pflanzen*) to be killed by frost ◆ **erfrorene Glieder** frostbitten limbs.
[2] *vt* **sich** (*dat*) **die Füße/Finger ~** to suffer frostbite in one's feet/fingers.

Erfrierung *f usu pl* frostbite *no pl* ◆ **Tod durch ~** death from exposure.

erfrischen* [1] *vti* to refresh.
[2] *vr* to refresh oneself; (*sich waschen*) to freshen up.

erfrischend *adj* (*lit, fig*) refreshing.

Erfrischung *f* refreshment ◆ **es ist eine ~, das zu sehen** it is refreshing to see it.

Erfrischungs-: ~getränk *nt* refreshment; **~raum** *m* refreshment room, cafeteria, snack bar; **~tuch** *nt* towelette, tissue wipe.

erfüllen* [1] *vt* **(a)** *Raum etc* to fill ◆ **Haß/Liebe/Ekel** *etc* **erfüllte ihn** he was full of hate/love/disgust *etc*, he was filled with hate/love/disgust *etc*; **Schmerz erfüllte ihn** he was grief-stricken; **Freude erfüllte ihn** his heart was full of *or* filled with joy; **er/sein Leben war von einem starken Pflichtgefühl erfüllt** he/his life was impregnated with a strong sense of duty; **es erfüllt mich mit Genugtuung, daß ...** it gives me great satisfaction to see that ...; **ein erfülltes Leben** a full life.
(b) (*ausführen, einhalten*) to fulfil; *Bedingungen auch* to meet, to comply with;

⚠: for details of spelling reform, see supplement

➤ SPRACHE AKTIV: **Erfahrung** → 38.1, 46.2

Wunsch, Bitte auch to carry out; *Pflicht, Aufgabe auch* to carry out, to perform; *Erwartungen auch* to come up to; *(Jur) Soll* to achieve; *Plan* to carry through; *Formalitäten* to comply with; *Zweck, Funktion* to serve ◆ **die Fee erfüllte ihm seinen Wunsch** the fairy granted him his wish; **ihr Wunsch nach einem Kind wurde erfüllt** their wish for a child came true *or* was granted; **erfüllst du mir einen Wunsch?** will you do something for me?; *siehe* **Tatbestand.**
[2] *vr (Wunsch, Voraussagung)* to be fulfilled, to come true ◆ **als er diesen Titel bekam, hatte sich sein Leben erfüllt** when he received this title his life had reached fulfilment.
[3] *vi (Jur)* to discharge one's debts.

Erfüllung *f* fulfilment; *(einer Bitte, eines Wunsches auch)* carrying out; *(einer Pflicht, Aufgabe, eines Vertrags auch)* performance; *(von Erwartungen)* realization; *(eines Solls)* achievement; *(eines Plans)* execution; *(Jur: Tilgung)* discharge ◆ **in ~ gehen** to be fulfilled; **in etw** *(dat)* **~ finden** to find fulfilment in sth.

Erfüllungs-: ~gehilfe *m* accomplice, henchman *(pej)*; **~ort** *m (Jur) (von Vertrag) place where a contract is to be fulfilled*; *(von Scheck)* place of payment; **~politik** *f (Hist)* policy of fulfilment; *(pej)* (policy of) appeasement; **~politiker** *m (Hist)* politician supporting the policy of fulfilment; *(pej)* appeaser.

erg. *abbr of* **ergänze** supply, add.

Erg *nt* **-s, -** *(Sci)* erg.

ergänzen* *vt* to supplement; *(vervollständigen)* to complete; *Fehlendes* to supply; *Lager, Vorräte* to replenish; *Bericht auch* to add (sth) to; *Ausführungen* to amplify; *Worte, Summe* to add; *Gesetz, Gesetzentwurf* to amend ◆ **seine Sammlung ~** to add to *or* build up one's collection; **einander** *or* **sich ~** to complement one another; **um das Team zu ~** to make up the numbers of the team; **~d hinzufügen** *or* **bemerken** to make an additional remark *(zu* to).

ergänzt *adj Ausgabe* expanded.

Ergänzung *f* **(a)** *(das Ergänzen)* supplementing; *(Vervollständigung)* completion; *(von Fehlendem)* supply(ing); *(eines Berichts)* addition (+*gen* to); *(von Summe)* addition; *(von Gesetz)* amendment; *(von Lager, Vorräten)* replenishment ◆ **zur ~ meiner Sammlung** to add to *or* build up my collection; **zur ~ des vorher Gesagten möchte ich hinzufügen, daß ...** let me amplify the previous remarks by adding that ...; **zur ~ des Teams** to make up the numbers of the team.
(b) *(Zusatz, zu Buch etc)* supplement; *(Hinzugefügtes, Person)* addition; *(zu einem Gesetz)* amendment; *(Gram)* complement.

Ergänzungs-: ~abgabe *f* supplementary tax; **~antrag** *m (Parl)* amendment; **~band** *m* supplement(ary volume); **~bindestrich** *m* hyphen; **~menge** *f (Math)* complementary set; **~satz** *m (Gram)* complementary clause.

ergattern* *vt (inf)* to get hold of.

ergaunern* *vt (inf)* **(sich** *dat***) etw ~** to get by dishonest means.

ergeben* *irreg* [1] *vt* to yield, to produce; *(zum Ergebnis haben)* to result in; *(zeigen)* to reveal; *Betrag, Summe* to amount to, to come to.
[2] *vr* **(a)** *(kapitulieren) (dat* to) to surrender, to yield, to capitulate ◆ **sich auf Gnade oder Ungnade ~** to surrender unconditionally; **sich in etw** *(acc)* **~** to submit to sth.
(b) sich einer Sache *(dat)* **~** *(sich hingeben)* to take to sth, to give oneself up to sth; *der Schwermut* to sink into sth; *dem Dienst etc auch* to devote oneself to sth; **sich dem Trunk** *or* **Suff** *(sl)* **~** to take to drink *or* the bottle *(inf)*.
(c) *(folgen)* to result, to arise, to ensue *(aus* from) ◆ **daraus können sich Nachteile ~** this could turn out to be disadvantageous; **das eine ergibt sich aus dem anderen** the one (thing) follows from the other.
(d) *(sich herausstellen)* to come to light ◆ **es ergab sich, daß unsere Befürchtungen ...** it turned out that our fears ...
[3] *adj (hingegeben, treu)* devoted; *(demütig)* humble; *(unterwürfig)* submissive ◆ **jdm treu ~ sein** to be loyally devoted to sb; **einem Laster ~ sein** to be addicted to a vice; **Ihr (sehr) ~er ..., Ihr ~ster ...** *(old form)* respectfully yours ... *(form)*, your (most) obedient *or* humble servant ... *(old form)*.

Ergebenheit *f (Hingabe, Treue)* devotion; *(Demut)* humility; *(Unterwürfigkeit)* submissiveness.

Ergebnis *nt* result; *(Auswirkung auch)* consequence, outcome ◆ **die Verhandlungen führten zu keinem ~** the negotiations led nowhere *or* were inconclusive; **die Verhandlungen führten zu dem ~, daß ...** the negotiations led to the conclusion that ...; **zu einem ~ kommen** to come to *or* reach a conclusion; **unsere Anstrengungen blieben ohne ~** our efforts produced no results.

ergebnislos *adj* unsuccessful, without result, fruitless; *Verhandlungen auch* inconclusive ◆ **~ bleiben/verlaufen** to come to nothing; **Verhandlungen ~ abbrechen** to break off negotiations without having reached any conclusions.

Ergebung *f (Mil, fig)* surrender, capitulation; *(fig: Demut)* humility.

ergehen* *irreg* [1] *vi aux sein* **(a)** *(form) (an +acc* to) *(erteilt, erlassen werden)* to go out, to be issued; *(Einladung)* to go out, to be sent; *(Gesetz)* to be enacted ◆ **~ lassen** to issue; to send; to enact.
(b) sie ließ seine Vorwürfe/alles über sich *(acc)* **~** she let his reproaches/everything simply wash over her; **sie ließ seine Zärtlichkeiten über sich** *(acc)* **~** she submitted to his intimacies.
[2] *vi impers aux sein* **es ist ihm schlecht/gut ergangen** he fared badly/well; **es wird ihm schlecht ~** he will suffer; **wie ist es ihm in der Prüfung ergangen?** how did he fare in the exam?
[3] *vr* **(a)** *(geh)* to go for a walk *or* stroll, to take the air.
(b) *(fig)* **sich in etw** *(dat)* **~** to indulge in sth; **er erging sich in Lobreden** he indulged in lavish *or* profuse praise; **er erging sich in Schmähungen** he poured forth abuse; **sich (in langen Reden) über ein Thema ~** to hold forth at length on sth, to expatiate on sth.

Ergehen *nt* **-s,** *no pl (geh)* (state of) health.

ergiebig *adj (lit, fig)* productive; *Geschäft* profitable, lucrative; *(fruchtbar)* fertile; *(sparsam im Verbrauch)* economical.

Ergiebigkeit *f siehe adj* productiveness, productivity; profitability; fertility; economicalness.

ergießen* *irreg* [1] *vt (liter)* to pour (out *or* forth *liter*).
[2] *vr (geh)* to pour forth *(liter) or* out *(auch fig)*.

erglänzen* *vi aux sein* to shine, to gleam; *(Licht auch)* to shine out.

erglühen* *vi aux sein (liter)* to glow; *(fig) (vor Scham, Zorn)* to burn; *(vor Freude)* to glow ◆ **in Liebe für jdn ~** *(liter)* to fall passionately in love with sb.

ergo *conj* therefore, ergo *(liter, hum)*.

Ergo-: ~meter *nt* **-s, -** ergometer; **~nomie** *f* ergonomics *sing*; **e~nomisch** *adj* ergonomic; **~therapie** *f* ergotherapy.

ergötzen* [1] *vt* to delight ◆ **zum E~ aller** to everyone's delight.
[2] *vr* **sich an etw** *(dat)* **~** to be amused by sth, to take delight in sth; *(schadenfroh auch, böswillig)* to gloat over sth.

ergötzlich *adj* delightful.

ergrauen* *vi aux sein* to turn *or* go grey; *siehe* **Dienst, Ehre.**

ergreifen* *vt irreg* **(a)** to seize; *(fassen auch)* to grasp, to grip; *(Krankheit)* to overcome; *Feder, Schwert auch* to take up; *Verbrecher* to seize, to apprehend ◆ **das Feuer ergriff den ganzen Wald** the fire engulfed the whole forest; *siehe* **Besitz.**
(b) *(fig) Gelegenheit, Macht* to seize; *Beruf* to take up; *Maßnahmen* to take, to resort to ◆ **er ergriff das Wort** he began to speak; *(Parl, bei Versammlung etc)* he took the floor; *siehe* **Flucht, Partei.**
(c) *(fig) jdn (packen)* to seize, to grip; *(bewegen)* to move ◆ **von Furcht/Sehnsucht** *etc* **ergriffen werden** to be seized with fear/longing *etc*.

ergreifend *adj (fig)* moving, stirring, touching *(auch iro)*.

ergriffen *adj (fig)* moved, deeply stirred.

Ergriffenheit *f* emotion.

ergrimmen* *(old, liter)* [1] *vi aux sein* to become angry *or* furious.
[2] *vt* to incense, to anger.

ergründen* *vt Sinn etc* to fathom; *Geheimnis auch* to penetrate; *Ursache, Motiv* to discover ◆ **ich muß ~, ob ...** I have to discover whether ...

⚠ **Erguß** *m* **-sses, ⸚sse** effusion; *(Blut~)* bruise, contusion *(form)*; *(Samen~)* ejaculation, emission; *(fig)* outpouring, effusion.

erhaben *adj* **(a)** *Druck, Muster* raised, embossed.
(b) *(fig) Gedanken, Stil* lofty, elevated, exalted; *Schönheit, Anblick* sublime; *Augenblick* solemn; *Herrscher* illustrious, eminent ◆ **vom E~en zum Lächerlichen ist nur ein Schritt** it is but a step from the sublime to the ridiculous.
(c) *(überlegen)* superior ◆ **~ lächeln** to smile in a superior way; **er dünkt sich über alles/alle ~** he thinks himself to be above it all/superior to everybody; **über etw** *(acc)* **~ (sein)** (to be) above sth; **über jeden Tadel/Verdacht ~ sein** to be above *or* beyond reproach/suspicion; **~ tun** to act superior.

Erhabenheit *f siehe adj* **(a)** *(rare)* elevation, relief. **(b)** *(fig)* loftiness, elevation, sublimity; solemnity; illustriousness, eminence. **(c)** superiority.

Erhalt *m* **-(e)s,** *no pl* receipt; *(das Erhalten)* preservation ◆ **der ~ der Macht** the preservation of power.

erhalten* *irreg* [1] *vt* **(a)** to get, to receive; *Preis, Orden auch* to be awarded; *Strafe, neuen Namen, fünf Jahre Gefängnis auch* to be given; *Resultat, Produkt, Genehmigung* to obtain, to get ◆ **das Wort ~** to receive permission to speak; **(Betrag) dankend ~** *(form)* received with thanks (the sum of...); *siehe* **Besuch, Kenntnis.**
(b) *(bewahren)* to preserve; *Gesundheit etc auch* to maintain ◆ **jdn am Leben/bei guter Laune ~** to keep sb alive/in a good mood; **ich hoffe, daß du uns noch lange ~ bleibst** I hope you'll be with us for a long time yet; *(nicht sterben)* I hope you'll have many more happy days; **erhalte dir deinen Frohsinn/Optimismus** stay cheerful/optimistic; **er hat sich** *(dat)* **seinen Frohsinn/Optimismus ~** he kept up *or* retained his cheerfulness/optimism; **unser Kind ist uns ~ geblieben** our child was spared; **gut ~** well preserved *(auch hum inf)*, in good condition; **von der Altstadt sind nur noch ein paar Kirchen ~** of the old town only a few churches remain *or* still stand.
(c) *(unterhalten) Familie* to support, to keep, to maintain.
[2] *vr (Brauch etc)* to be preserved, to remain ◆ **sich frisch und gesund ~** to keep *or* stay bright and healthy.

Erhalter(in *f***)** *m* **-s, -** preserver, maintainer; *(der Familie)* breadwinner, supporter.

erhältlich *adj* obtainable, available ◆ **schwer ~** difficult to obtain, hard to come by.

Erhaltung *f (Bewahrung)* preservation; *(Unterhaltung)* support ◆ **die ~ der Energie** *(Phys)* the conservation of energy.

erhandeln* *vt* to get by bargaining, to bargain for.

erhängen* *vt* to hang ◆ **Tod durch E~** death by hanging; **sich ~** to hang oneself.

erhärten* [1] *vt* to harden; *(fig) Behauptung etc* to substantiate, to corroborate; *(Verdacht)* to harden ◆ **etw durch Eid ~** to affirm sth on oath.
[2] *vr (fig: Verdacht)* to harden.

Erhärtung *f (fig) siehe vt* substantiation, corroboration; hardening.

erhaschen* *vt* to catch *(auch fig)*, to seize, to grab.

▼ **erheben*** *irreg* [1] *vt* **(a)** to raise *(auch Math)*, to lift (up); *Glas, Stimme* to raise ◆ **die Hand zum Gruß ~** to raise one's hand in greeting; **seinen** *or* **den Blick ~**

➤ SPRACHE AKTIV: **erheben: 1 → 36.2**

to look up; **jdn in den Adelsstand ~** to raise *or* elevate sb to the peerage; **etw zu einem Prinzip/einer Regel** *etc* **~** to make sth into a principle/a rule *etc*, to raise *or* elevate sth to (the level of) a principle/a rule *etc*; **jdn zum Herrscher ~** to install sb as a/the ruler; *siehe* **Anklage, Anspruch, Einspruch, Geschrei, Potenz.**
(b) *Gebühren* to charge, to levy; *Steuern* (*einziehen*) to raise, to levy; (*auferlegen*) to impose.
(c) *Fakten, Daten* to ascertain.
(d) (*liter: loben*) to laud (*liter*), to extol (*liter*).
[2] *vr* **(a)** (*aufstehen*) to get up, to rise; (*Flugzeug, Vogel*) to rise.
(b) (*sich auflehnen*) to rise (up) (in revolt), to revolt.
(c) (*aufragen*) to rise (*über +dat* above).
(d) **sich über eine Schwierigkeit ~** to overcome *or* rise above a difficulty; **sich über andere ~** to elevate *or* place oneself above others.
(e) (*aufkommen*) (*Wind etc, form: Frage etc*) to arise.

erhebend *adj* elevating, uplifting; (*beeindruckend*) impressive; (*erbaulich*) edifying.

erheblich *adj* (*beträchtlich*) considerable; (*wichtig*) important; (*relevant*) relevant, pertinent; *Verletzung* serious, severe.

Erhebung *f* **(a)** (*Boden~*) elevation.
(b) (*Aufstand*) uprising, revolt; (*Meuterei*) mutiny.
(c) (*von Gebühren*) levying, imposition.
(d) (*amtliche Ermittlung*) investigation, inquiry; (*Umfrage*) survey ♦ **~en machen** *or* **anstellen über** (*+acc*) to make inquiries about *or* into.
(e) (*das Erheben*) raising; (*in den Adelsstand*) elevation; (*zum Herrscher*) installation (*zu* as) ♦ **~ ins Quadrat/in die dritte Potenz** squaring/cubing, raising to the power of three.
(f) (*fig: Erbauung*) uplift, elevation.

erheischen* *vt* (*old, liter*) to require, to demand; *Achtung* to command.

erheitern* [1] *vt* to cheer (up); (*belustigen*) to entertain, to amuse.
[2] *vr* to be amused (*über +acc* by); (*Gesicht*) to brighten, to cheer up.

Erheiterung *f* amusement ♦ **zur allgemeinen ~** to the general amusement.

erhellen* [1] *vt* to light up (*auch fig*), to illuminate; (*fig: klären*) to elucidate, to illuminate; *Geheimnis* to shed light on.
[2] *vr* (*lit, fig*) to brighten; (*plötzlich*) to light up.
[3] *vi* (*geh: hervorgehen*) to be evident *or* manifest ♦ **daraus erhellt, daß ...** from that it is evident *or* manifest that ...

Erhellung *f* (*fig*) elucidation, illumination.

erhitzen* [1] *vt* to heat (up) (*auf +acc* to) ♦ **die Gemüter ~** to inflame passions, to whip up feeling.
[2] *vr* to get hot, to heat up; (*fig: sich erregen*) to become heated (*an +dat* over); (*Phantasie etc*) to be inflamed *or* aroused (*an +dat* at) ♦ **die Gemüter erhitzten sich** feelings were running high; **erhitzt aussehen** to look hot; (*fig*) to look hot and bothered; **vom Tanzen erhitzt** hot from the dancing.

Erhitzung *f* heating up; (*fig*) (*Erregung*) excitement; (*der Gemüter, Phantasie*) inflammation.

erhoffen* *vt* to hope for ♦ **sich** (*dat*) **etw ~** to hope for sth (*von* from); **was erhoffst du dir davon?** what do you hope to gain from it?

erhöhen* [1] *vt* to raise; *Preise etc auch* to increase, to put up; *Zahl auch, Produktion, Kraft* to increase; *Wirkung, Schönheit* to increase, to heighten, to enhance; *Spannung* to increase, to heighten; (*Mus*) *Note* to sharpen ♦ **die Mauern wurden um zwei Meter erhöht** the walls were made two metres higher *or* were raised (by) two metres; **etw um 10% ~** to raise *or* put up *or* increase sth by 10%; **um das Doppelte ~** increase sth by twice as much again; **erhöhte Temperatur haben** to have a temperature; **erhöhte Wachsamkeit/Anstrengungen** *etc* increased vigilance/efforts *etc.*
[2] *vr* to rise, to increase; (*Spannung etc auch*) to heighten, to intensify ♦ **wer sich selbst erhöht, der wird erniedrigt (werden)** (*Bibl*) whosoever shall exalt himself shall be abased.

Erhöhung *f* **(a)** (*das Erhöhen*) *siehe vt* raising; increase, heightening, enhancement; (*von Spannung*) heightening, intensification. **(b)** (*Lohn~*) rise (*Brit*), raise (*US*); (*Preis~*) increase. **(c)** (*Hügel*) hill, elevation.

Erhöhungszeichen *nt* (*Mus*) sharp (sign).

erholen* *vr* (*von* from) to recover; (*von Krankheit auch*) to recuperate; (*sich entspannen auch*) to relax, to have a rest; (*fig: Preise, Aktien*) to recover, to rally, to pick up ♦ **er hat sich von dem Schreck(en) noch nicht erholt** he hasn't got over the shock yet; **du siehst sehr erholt aus** you look very rested.

erholsam *adj* restful, refreshing.

Erholung *f siehe vr* recovery; recuperation; relaxation, rest; (*der Wirtschaft*) recovery, rallying ♦ **der Direktor ist zur ~ in der Schweiz** the director has gone to Switzerland for a holiday (*esp Brit*) *or* a vacation (*US*) and a rest; (*zur Genesung*) the director is convalescing in Switzerland; **zur ~ an die See fahren** to go to the seaside in order to recover *or* recuperate *or* convalesce; **er braucht dringend ~** he badly needs a holiday (*esp Brit*) *or* a vacation (*US*) *or* a break; **Urlaub ist zur ~ da** holidays are for relaxation; **gute ~!** have a good rest.

Erholungs-: ~aufenthalt *m* holiday (*esp Brit*), vacation (*US*); **e~bedürftig** *adj* in need of a rest, run-down; **~gebiet** *nt* recreation area; **~heim** *nt* rest home; (*Ferienheim*) holiday home; (*Sanatorium*) convalescent home; **~kur** *f* rest cure; **~ort** *m* spa, health resort; **~pause** *f* break; **~reise** *f* holiday/vacation trip; **~urlaub** *m* holiday/vacation; (*nach Krankheit*) convalescent leave *or* holiday; **~wert** *m* recreational value.

erhören* *vt Gebet etc* to hear; *Bitte, Liebhaber* to yield to.

Eriesee *m* Lake Erie *no art.*

erigibel *adj* (*Physiol*) erectile.

erigieren* *vi* to become erect ♦ **erigiert** erect.

Erika *f* -, **Eriken** (*Bot*) heather.

er|innerlich *adj pred* **soviel mir ~ ist** as far as I (can) remember *or* recall.

er|innern* [1] *vt* **jdn an etw** (*acc*) **~** to remind sb of sth; **jdn daran ~, etw zu tun/daß ...** to remind sb to do sth/that ...; **etw ~** (*dial, sl*) to remember *or* recall sth.
[2] *vr* **sich an jdn/etw ~, sich einer Sache** (*gen*) **~** (*old*) to remember *or* recall *or* recollect sb/sth; **sich nur noch dunkel ~ an** (*+acc*) to have only a faint *or* dim recollection *or* memory of; **soweit** *or* **soviel ich mich ~ kann** as far as I remember *etc*, to the best of my recollection; **wenn ich mich recht erinnere, ...** if my memory serves me right *or* correctly ..., if I remember rightly ...
[3] *vi* **(a) ~ an** (*+acc*) to be reminiscent of, to call to mind, to recall; **sie erinnert sehr an ihre Mutter** she reminds one very much of her mother.
(b) (*erwähnen*) **daran ~, daß ...** to point out that ...

Er|innerung *f* (*an +acc* of) memory, recollection; (*euph: Mahnung*) reminder; (*Andenken*) memento, remembrance, keepsake. **~en** *pl* (*Lebens~*) reminiscences *pl*; (*Liter*) memoirs *pl* ♦ **~en austauschen** to reminisce; **zur ~ an** (*+acc*) in memory of; (*an Ereignis*) in commemoration of; (*als Andenken*) as a memento of; **jdn/etw in guter/schlechter ~ haben** *or* **behalten** to have pleasant/unpleasant memories of sb/sth; **sich** (*dat*) **etw in die ~ zurückrufen** to call sth to mind; **wenn mich meine ~ nicht täuscht** if my memory doesn't deceive me.

Er|innerungs-: ~bild *nt* visual memento (*an +acc* of); **~feier** *f* commemoration; **~lücke** *f* gap in one's memory; **~schreiben** *nt* (*Comm*) reminder; **~stück** *nt* keepsake (*an +acc* from); **~tafel** *f* commemorative plaque; **~vermögen** *nt* memory, powers *pl* of recollection; **~wert** *m* sentimental value.

Erinnyen *pl* (*Myth*) Furies *pl*, Erin(n)yes *pl.*

Eritrea *nt* **-s** Eritrea.

Eritreer(in *f*) *m* **-s, -** Eritrean.

erjagen* *vt* to bag, to catch; (*fig: ergattern*) to get hold of, to hunt down ♦ **um sich dort Reichtum zu ~** to make his fortune.

erkalten* *vi aux sein* (*lit, fig*) to cool (down *or* off), to go cold.

erkälten* *vr* to catch (a) cold; (*esp sich verkühlen*) to catch a chill ♦ **sich stark** *or* **sehr/leicht erkältet haben** to have (caught) a heavy/slight cold/chill; **sich** (*dat*) **die Blase ~** to catch a chill in one's bladder.

erkältet *adj* with a cold ♦ **(stark) ~ sein** to have a (bad *or* heavy) cold; **wir sind alle ~** we all have colds.

Erkältung *f* cold; (*leicht*) chill ♦ **sich** (*dat*) **eine ~ zuziehen** to catch a cold/chill.

Erkältungskrankheiten *pl* coughs and sneezes *pl.*

erkämpfen* *vt* to win, to secure ♦ **sich** (*dat*) **etw ~** to win sth; **hart erkämpft** hard-won; **er hat sich** (*dat*) **seine Position hart erkämpft** he fought hard for his *or* to secure his position.

erkaufen* *vt* to buy ♦ **etw teuer ~** to pay dearly for sth; **den Erfolg mit seiner Gesundheit ~** to pay for one's success with one's health, to buy success at the price of one's health.

erkennbar *adj* (*wieder~*) recognizable; (*sichtbar*) visible; (*wahrnehmbar, ersichtlich*) discernible.

Erkennbarkeit *f siehe adj* recognizability; visibility; discernibility.

erkennen* *irreg* [1] *vt* **(a)** (*wieder~, an~, einsehen*) to recognize (*an +dat* by); (*wahrnehmen*) to see, to make out, to discern; *Unterschied* to see; *Situation* to see, to understand ♦ **ich erkannte die Lage sofort** I immediately realized what the situation was; **er hat erkannt, daß das nicht stimmte** he realized that it wasn't right; **kannst du ~, ob das da drüben X ist?** can you see *or* tell if that's X over there?; **jdn für schuldig ~** (*Jur*) to find sb guilty; **(jdm) etw zu ~ geben** to indicate sth (to sb); **jdm zu ~ geben, daß ...** to give sb to understand that ...; **sich zu ~ geben** to reveal oneself (*als* to be), to disclose one's identity; **~ lassen** to show, to reveal; **erkenne dich selbst!** know thyself!; **du bist erkannt!** I see what you're after, I know your game.
(b) (*Bibl, obs*) to know (*Bibl*).
[2] *vi* **~ auf** (*+acc*) (*Jur*) *Freispruch* to grant; *Strafe* to impose, to inflict; (*Sport*) *Freistoß etc* to give, to award; **auf drei Jahre Haft ~** to impose a sentence of three years' imprisonment.

erkenntlich *adj* **(a) sich (für etw) ~ zeigen** to show one's gratitude *or* appreciation (for sth). **(b)** (*rare*) *siehe* **erkennbar.**

Erkenntlichkeit *f* (*Dankbarkeit*) gratitude; (*Gegenleistung*) token of one's gratitude *or* appreciation.

Erkenntnis[1] *f* (*Wissen*) knowledge *no pl*; (*das Erkennen*) recognition, realization; (*Philos, Psych*) cognition *no pl*; (*Einsicht*) insight, realization; (*Entdekkung*) finding, discovery ♦ **zur ~ kommen** to see the light; **zu der ~ kommen** *or* **gelangen, daß ...** to come to the realization that ..., to realize that ...

Erkenntnis[2] *nt* (*Jur*) decision, finding; (*der Geschworenen*) verdict.

Erkenntnis-: ~drang *m* thirst for knowledge; **~fähigkeit** *f* cognitive faculty; **~lage** *f siehe* **~stand**; **~lehre** *f siehe* **~theorie**; **~schub** *m* wealth of new knowledge; **~stand** *m* level of knowledge; **e~theoretisch** *adj* epistemological; **~theorie** *f* epistemology, theory of knowledge; **~vermögen** *nt* cognitive capacity.

Erkennung *f* recognition, identification.

Erkennungs-: ~dienst *m* police records department; **e~dienstlich** *adv* **jdn e~dienstlich behandeln** to fingerprint and photograph sb; **~marke** *f* identity disc *or* tag; **~melodie** *f* signature tune; **~wort** *nt* password; **~zeichen** *nt* identification; (*Mil: Abzeichen*) badge; (*Aviat*) markings *pl*; (*Med*) sign (*für* of) ♦ **das ist mein ~zeichen** that's what you'll recognize me by.

Erker *m* **-s, -** bay; (*kleiner Vorbau*) oriel.

Erker-: ~fenster *nt* bay window; oriel window; **~zimmer** *nt* room with a bay *or* oriel window (recess).

erkiesen *pret* **erkor**, *ptp* **erkoren** *vt* (*obs, liter*) to choose, to elect (*zu* as, to be).

erklärbar *adj* explicable, explainable ♦ **leicht ~** easily explained; **schwer ~** hard to explain; **nicht ~** inexplicable.

erklären* 1 *vt* **(a)** (*erläutern*) to explain (*jdm etw* sth to sb); (*begründen auch*) to account for ♦ **ich kann mir nicht ~, warum** ... I can't understand why ...; **wie erklärt ihr euch das?** how can *or* do you explain that?, what do you make of that?; **ich erkläre mir die Sache so:** ... the way I see it, ...
(b) (*äußern, bekanntgeben*) to declare (*als* to be); *Rücktritt* to announce; (*Politiker, Pressesprecher etc*) to say ♦ **einem Staat den Krieg ~** to declare war on a country; **er erklärte ihr seine Liebe** he declared his love for her; **eine Ausstellung** *etc* **für** *or* **als eröffnet ~** to declare an exhibition *etc* open; **jdn für schuldig/tot/gesund** *etc* **~** to pronounce sb guilty/dead/healthy *etc*.
2 *vr* **(a)** (*Sache*) to be explained ♦ **das erklärt sich daraus, daß** ... it can be explained by the fact that ...; **damit hat sich die Sache von selbst erklärt** the affair thereby explained itself; **das erklärt sich (von) selbst** that's self-explanatory.
(b) (*Mensch*) to declare oneself; (*Liebe gestehen auch*) to declare one's love ♦ **sich für bankrott** *etc* **~** to declare oneself bankrupt *etc*; **sich für gesund/diensttauglich ~** to pronounce *or* declare oneself healthy/fit for service; **sich für/gegen jdn/etw ~** to declare oneself *or* come out for/against sb/sth.
3 *vi* to explain ♦ **er kann sehr gut ~** he's very good at explaining things.

erklärend *adj* explanatory ♦ **einige ~e Worte** a few words of explanation; **er fügte ~ hinzu** ... he added in explanation ...

erklärlich *adj* **(a)** *siehe* **erklärbar. (b)** (*verständlich*) understandable. **ist Ihnen das ~?** can you find an explanation for that?; **mir ist einfach nicht ~, wie** ... I simply cannot understand how ...

erklärlicherweise *adv* understandably.

erklärt *adj attr Ziel* professed; *Gegner auch* avowed; *Favorit, Liebling* acknowledged.

erklärtermaßen *adv* avowedly.

Erklärung *f* **(a)** explanation. **(b)** (*Mitteilung, Bekanntgabe*) declaration; (*eines Politikers, Pressesprechers etc*) statement ♦ **eine ~ (zu etw) abgeben** to make a statement (about *or* concerning sth).

Erklärungs-: ~frist *f period of time granted to sb to explain sth to a commission etc*; **~notstand** *m* **im ~notstand sein** to have a lot of explaining to do.

erklecklich *adj* considerable.

erklettern* *vt* to climb (up); *Berg auch* to scale; *Alpengebiet* to climb.

erklimmen* *vt irreg* (*geh*) to scale; (*fig*) *Spitze, höchste Stufe* to climb to; (*fig*) *Leiter* to climb *or* ascend to the top of.

erklingen* *vi irreg* (*geh*) *aux sein* to ring out, to resound ♦ **eine Harfe/ein Glöckchen/Stimmchen erklang** (the sound of) a harp/bell/voice was heard, I *etc* heard (the sound of) a harp/bell/voice; **ein Lied ~ lassen** to burst (forth) into song; **die Gläser ~ lassen** to clink glasses.

erkor *pret of* **erkiesen, erküren.**

erkoren *ptp of* **erkiesen, erküren.**

erkranken* *vi aux sein* (*krank werden*) to be taken ill, to fall ill (*an +dat* with); (*Organ, Pflanze, Tier*) to become diseased (*an +dat* with) ♦ **erkrankt sein** (*krank sein*) to be ill/diseased; **die an Krebs erkrankten Menschen** people with *or* suffering from cancer; **die erkrankten Stellen** the diseased *or* affected areas.

Erkrankung *f* illness; (*von Organ, Pflanze, Tier*) disease ♦ **wegen einer plötzlichen ~ des Viehbestandes** because the livestock suddenly became diseased.

Erkrankungsfall *m* case of illness ♦ **im ~** in case of illness.

erkühnen* *vr* (*old, liter*) **sich ~, etw zu tun** to dare to do sth, to make so bold as to do sth.

erkunden* *vt* (*esp Mil*) *Gelände, Stellungen* to reconnoitre, to scout; (*feststellen*) to find out, to establish, to ascertain.

▼ **erkundigen*** *vr* **sich (nach etw/über jdn) ~** to ask *or* inquire (about sth/sb); **sich nach jdm ~** to ask after sb; **sich bei jdm (nach etw) ~** to ask sb (about sth); **ich werde mich ~** I'll find out.

Erkundigung *f* inquiry; (*Nachforschung auch*) investigation ♦ **~en einholen** *or* **einziehen** to make inquiries.

Erkundung *f* (*Mil*) reconnaissance.

Erkundungsgang *m* (*Mil, fig*) reconnaissance expedition.

erküren* *pret* **erkor**, *ptp* **erkoren** *vt* (*obs, liter*) *siehe* **erkiesen.**

Erlagschein *m* (*Aus*) *siehe* **Zahlkarte.**

erlahmen* *vi aux sein* to tire, to grow weary; (*Kräfte, fig: Interesse, Eifer*) to flag, to wane.

erlangen* *vt* to attain, to achieve; *Alter, Ziel auch* to reach; *Bedeutung auch, Eintritt* to gain.

Erlangung *f* attainment.

⚠ **Erlaß** *m* **-sses, -sse** *or* (*Aus*) **¨sse (a)** (*Verfügung*) decree, edict; (*der Regierung*) enactment, edict. **(b)** (*Straf~, Schulden~, Sünden~ etc*) remission.

erlassen* *vt irreg* **(a)** *Verfügung* to pass; *Gesetz* to enact; *Embargo etc* to impose; *Dekret* to issue.
(b) (*von etw entbinden*) *Strafe, Schulden etc* to remit; *Gebühren* to waive ♦ **jdm etw ~** *Schulden etc* to release sb from sth; *Gebühren* to waive sth for sb; **bitte ~ Sie es mir, darüber zu sprechen** please don't ask me to talk about that; **jdm die Strafarbeit/eine Pflicht ~** to let sb off a punishment/to release sb from a duty; **ich erlasse ihm den Rest (des Geldes)** I'll waive the rest *or* let him off paying the rest (of the money).

▼ **erlauben*** 1 *vt* (*gestatten*) to allow, to permit ♦ **jdm etw ~** to allow *or* permit sb (to do) sth; **mein Vater erlaubt mir nicht, daß ich mit Mädchen ausgehe** my father doesn't *or* won't allow me to go out with girls; **es ist mir nicht erlaubt, das zu tun** I am not allowed *or* permitted to do that; **du erlaubst deinem Kind zuviel** you allow your child too much freedom; **~ Sie?, Sie ~?** (*form*) may I?; **~ Sie, daß ich das Fenster öffne?** do you mind if I open the window?; **~ Sie, daß ich mich vorstelle** allow *or* permit me to introduce myself; **~ Sie mal!** do you mind!; **soweit es meine Zeit/das Wetter erlaubt** (*form*) time/weather permitting; **erlaubt ist, was gefällt** (*prov*) a little of what you fancy does you good (*prov*); **erlaubt ist, was sich ziemt** (*prov*) you must only do what is proper.
2 *vr* **sich (dat) etw ~** (*gestatten, sich gönnen*) to allow *or* permit oneself sth; (*wagen*) *Bemerkung, Vorschlag* to venture sth; (*sich leisten*) to afford sth; **sich (dat) ~, etw zu tun** (*so frei sein*) to take the liberty of doing sth; (*sich leisten*) to afford to do sth; **darf ich mir ~ ...?** might I possibly ...?; **wenn ich mir die folgende Bemerkung ~ darf** ... if I might venture *or* be allowed the following remark ...; **sich (dat) Frechheiten ~** to take liberties, to be cheeky; **sich (dat) einen Scherz ~** to have a joke; **was die Jugend sich heutzutage alles erlaubt!** the things young people get up to nowadays!; **was ~ Sie sich (eigentlich)!** how dare you!

▼ **Erlaubnis** *f* permission; (*Schriftstück*) permit ♦ **mit Ihrer (freundlichen) ~** (*form*) with your (kind) permission, by your leave (*form*); **du brauchst eine elterliche ~** you need your parents' (written) permission; **(jdn) um ~ bitten** to ask (sb) (for) permission, to ask *or* beg leave (of sb) (*form*); **jdm zu etw die ~ geben** *or* **erteilen** (*form*) to give sb permission *or* leave (*form*) for sth/to do sth.

Erlaubnisschein *m* permit.

erlaucht *adj* (*obs, iro*) illustrious ♦ **ein ~er Kreis** a select circle.

Erlaucht *f* **-, -en** (*Hist*) Lordship.

erläutern* *vt* to explain, to elucidate; (*klarstellen auch*) to clarify; *Text* to comment on ♦ **~d** explanatory; **~d fügte er hinzu** he added in explanation *or* clarification; **etw anhand von Beispielen ~** to illustrate sth with examples.

Erläuterung *f siehe vt* explanation, elucidation; clarification; comment, commentary ♦ **zur ~** in explanation.

Erle *f* **-, -n** alder.

erleben* *vt* to experience; (*noch lebend erreichen*) to live to see; (*durchmachen*) *schwere Zeiten, Sturm* to go through; *Aufstieg, Abenteuer, Enttäuschung* to have; *Erfolg* to have, to enjoy; *Mißerfolg, Niederlage* to have, to suffer; *Aufführung* to have, to receive; *Jahrhundertwende, erste Mondlandung* to see; *Schauspieler* to see (perform); *Musik, Gedicht, Fußballspiel, Landschaft* to experience ♦ **im Urlaub habe ich viel erlebt** I had an eventful time on holiday; **was haben Sie im Ausland erlebt?** what sort of experiences did you have abroad?; **Deutschland, wie ich es erlebt habe, war** ... I remember Germany as being ...; **wir haben wunderschöne Tage in Spanien erlebt** we had a lovely time in Spain; **etwas Angenehmes** *etc* **~** to have a pleasant *etc* experience; **er hat schon viel Schlimmes erlebt** he's had a lot of bad times *or* experiences; **wir haben mit unseren Kindern viel Freude erlebt** our children have given us much pleasure; **ich habe es oft erlebt** ... I've often known *or* seen it happen ...; **so wütend habe ich ihn noch nie erlebt** I've never seen *or* known him so furious; **unser Land hat schon bessere Zeiten erlebt** our country has seen *or* known better times; **ich möchte mal ~, daß du rechtzeitig kommst** I'd like to see you come on time; **er hat gesagt, er würde helfen — das möchte ich ~!** he said he'd like to help — that I'd like to see!; **das werde ich nicht mehr ~** I shan't live to see that; **er möchte mal etwas ~** he wants to have a good time; **er hat viel erlebt** he has been around (*inf*), he has experienced a lot; **das muß man erlebt haben** you've got to have experienced it (for) yourself; **erlebte Rede** (*Liter*) interior monologue; **na, der kann was ~!** (*inf*) he's going to be (in) for it! (*inf*); **hat man so (et)was schon (mal) erlebt!** (*inf*) I've never heard anything like it!; **daß ich das ~ muß!** I never thought I'd see the day!; **so was Dummes habe ich noch nie erlebt!** I've never seen/heard anything so stupid in all my life!

Erlebensfall *m* **im ~** in case of survival; **Versicherung auf den ~** pure endowment insurance.

Erlebnis *nt* experience; (*Abenteuer*) adventure; (*Liebschaft*) affair ♦ **(jdm) zu einem ~ werden** to be (quite) an experience (for sb).

Erlebnis-: ~aufsatz *m* (*Sch*) essay based on personal experience; **~fähigkeit** *f* receptivity to experiences, ability to experience things (deeply); **~lyrik** *f* poetry based on personal experience; **e~reich** *adj* eventful.

erledigen* 1 *vt* **(a)** to deal with, to take care of; *Akte etc* to process; (*ausführen*) *Auftrag* to carry out; (*beenden*) *Arbeit* to finish off, to deal with; *Sache* to settle ♦ **Einkäufe ~** to do the shopping; **ich habe noch einiges in der Stadt zu ~** I've still got a few things to do in town; **ich muß noch schnell was ~** I've just got something to do; **die Sache/er ist für mich erledigt** as far as I'm concerned the matter's closed/I'm finished with him; **erledigt!** (*Stempel*) dealt with, processed; **erledigt, reden wir nicht mehr darüber!** OK, let's say no more about it!; **das ist (damit) erledigt** that's settled *or* taken care of; **wird erledigt!** shall *or* will do! (*inf*), right-ho! (*Brit inf*), sure thing! (*US inf*); **zu ~** (*Vermerk auf Akten*) for attention; **schon erledigt!** I've already done it; (*mache ich sofort*) consider it done.
(b) (*inf: ermüden*) to wear *or* knock (*inf*) out; (*inf: ruinieren*) to finish, to ruin; (*sl: töten*) to do in (*sl*); (*sl: k.o. schlagen*) to finish off, to knock out.
2 *vr* **damit erledigt sich das Problem** that disposes of *or* settles the problem;

➤ SPRACHE AKTIV: **erkundigen** → 46.1, 48.1 **erlauben: 1** → 36.3 **Erlaubnis** → 36.1, 36.2

das hat sich erledigt that's all settled; **sich von selbst ~** to take care of itself.

erledigt *adj* **(a)** (*obs*) *Stelle* vacant. **(b)** (*inf*) (*erschöpft*) shattered (*inf*), done in *pred* (*inf*); (*ruiniert*) finished, ruined ◆ **wenn jetzt die Bullen kommen, sind wir ~** if the cops come now, we've had it (*inf*); *siehe auch vt* **(a).**

Erledigung *f* (*Ausführung*) execution, carrying out; (*Durchführung, Beendung*) completion; (*einer Sache, eines Geschäfts*) settlement ◆ **die ~ von Einkäufen** (*form*) shopping; **die ~ meiner Korrespondenz** dealing with my correspondence; **sie betraute ihn mit der ~ ihrer Geschäfte** she entrusted him with the execution of *or* with dealing with her business affairs; **einige ~en in der Stadt** a few things to do in town; **um rasche ~ wird gebeten** please give this your immediate attention; **in ~ Ihres Auftrages/Ihrer Anfrage** (*form*) in execution of your order/further to your inquiry (*form*).

Erledigungsvermerk *m* actioned stamp.

erlegen* *vt* **(a)** *Wild* to shoot, to bag (*Hunt*). **(b)** (*Aus, Sw: bezahlen*) to pay.

erleichtern* [1] *vt* (*einfacher machen*) to make easier; (*fig*) *Last, Los* to lighten; (*beruhigen*) to relieve; (*lindern*) *Not, Schmerz etc* to relieve, to alleviate ◆ **sein Herz/Gewissen** *or* **sich** (*dat*) **das Gewissen ~** to unburden one's heart/conscience; **es würde mein Gewissen ~, wenn ...** it would ease my mind *or* conscience if ...; **jdm etw ~** to make sth easier for sb; **jdn um etw ~** (*hum*) to relieve sb of sth; **erleichtert aufatmen** to breathe a sigh of relief.
[2] *vr* (*old*) to relieve oneself.

Erleichterung *f* (*von Last etc*) lightening; (*Linderung*) relief, alleviation; (*Beruhigung*) relief; (*Zahlungs~*) facility ◆ **das trägt zur ~ meiner Aufgabe bei** it makes my work easier; **einem Kranken ~ verschaffen** to give relief to a sick person.

erleiden* *vt irreg* to suffer; *Verluste, Schaden auch* to sustain, to incur ◆ **den Tod ~** (*old*) to suffer death (*old*); *siehe* **Schiffbruch.**

Erlenmeierkolben *m* (*Phys*) Erlenmeyer flask.

erlernbar *adj* learnable.

erlernen* *vt* to learn.

erlesen *adj* exquisite ◆ **ein ~er Kreis** a select circle.

Erlesenheit *f* exquisiteness; (*von Kreis*) selectness.

erleuchten* *vt* to light (up), to illuminate; (*fig*) to enlighten, to inspire ◆ **Herr, erleuchte uns!** Lord, let thy light shine upon us; **hell erleuchtet** brightly lit; *Stadt* brightly illuminated.

Erleuchtung *f* (*Eingebung*) inspiration; (*religiöse auch*) enlightenment *no pl.*

erliegen* *vi irreg aux sein +dat* (*lit, fig*) to succumb to; *einem Irrtum* to be the victim of ◆ **zum E~ kommen/bringen** to come/bring to a standstill.

erlisch *imper sing of* **erlöschen.**

Erlös *m* **-es, -e** proceeds *pl.*

erlöschen *pret* **erlosch,** *ptp* **erloschen** *vi aux sein* (*Feuer*) to go out; (*Gefühle, Interesse*) to die; (*Vulkan*) to become extinct; (*Leben*) to come to an end; (*Vertrag, Anspruch etc*) to expire, to lapse; (*Firma*) to be dissolved; (*Geschlecht, Name*) to die out ◆ **ein erloschener Vulkan** an extinct volcano; **mit ~der Stimme** (*liter*) in a dying voice; **seine Augen waren erloschen** (*liter*) his eyes were lifeless.

erlösen* *vt* **(a)** (*retten*) to save, to rescue (*aus, von* from); (*Rel*) to redeem, to save; (*von Sünden, Qualen*) to deliver (*esp Bibl*), to release ◆ **erlöse uns von dem Bösen** (*Rel*) deliver us from evil. **(b)** (*Comm: aus Verkauf*) *Geld* to realize.

erlösend *adj* relieving, liberating ◆ **sie sprach das ~e Wort** she spoke the word he/she/everybody *etc* was waiting for; **~ wirken** to come as a relief; **er empfand es beinahe ~, als ...** it was almost a relief for him when ...

Erlöser(in *f***)** *m* **-s, -** (*Rel*) Redeemer; (*Befreier*) saviour.

Erlösung *f* release, deliverance; (*Erleichterung*) relief; (*Rel*) redemption ◆ **der Tod war für sie eine ~** death was a release for her.

erlügen* *vt irreg* to fabricate, to make up, to invent ◆ **eine erlogene Geschichte** a fabrication, a fiction.

ermächtigen* *vt* to authorize, to empower (*zu etw* to do sth).

ermächtigt *adj* authorized, empowered ◆ **zur Unterschrift ~** authorized to sign.

Ermächtigung *f* authorization.

Ermächtigungsgesetz *nt* (*Pol*) Enabling Act (*esp that of Nazis in 1933*).

ermahnen* *vt* to exhort (*form*), to admonish, to urge; (*warnend*) to warn; (*Jur*) to caution ◆ **jdn zum Fleiß/zur Aufmerksamkeit** *etc* **~** to exhort (*form*) *or* urge sb to work hard/to be attentive *etc*; **muß ich dich immer erst ~?** do I always have to remind *or* tell you first?; **jdn im Guten ~** to give sb a friendly warning.

Ermahnung *f* exhortation, admonition, urging; (*warnend*) warning; (*Jur*) caution.

ermangeln* *vi* **einer Sache** (*gen*) **~** (*geh*) to lack sth.

Ermang(e)lung *f*: **in ~** *+gen* because of the lack of; **in ~ eines Besseren** for lack of something better.

ermannen* *vr* to pluck up courage.

ermäßigen* [1] *vt* to reduce.
[2] *vr* to be reduced.

Ermäßigung *f* reduction; (*Steuer~*) relief.

Ermäßigungsfahrschein *m* concessionary ticket.

ermatten* (*geh*) [1] *vt* to tire, to exhaust.
[2] *vi aux sein* to tire, to become exhausted.

ermattet *adj* (*geh*) exhausted, weary.

Ermattung *f* (*geh*) exhaustion, weariness, fatigue.

ermessen* *vt irreg* (*einschätzen*) *Größe, Weite, Wert* to gauge, to estimate; (*erfassen, begreifen können*) to appreciate, to realize.

Ermessen *nt* **-s,** *no pl* (*Urteil*) judgement, estimation; (*Gutdünken*) discretion ◆ **nach meinem ~** in my estimation; **nach menschlichem ~** as far as anyone can judge; **nach bestem ~ handeln** to act according to one's best judgement; **nach freiem ~** at one's discretion; **nach eigenem ~ handeln** to act on one's own discretion; **etw in jds ~** (*acc*) **stellen, etw jds ~** (*dat*) **anheimstellen** to leave sth to sb's discretion; **in jds ~** (*dat*) **liegen** *or* **stehen** to be within sb's discretion.

Ermessens-: ~entscheidung *f* (*Jur*) discretionary decision; **~frage** *f* matter of discretion; ⚠**~mißbrauch** *m* abuse of (one's powers of) discretion; **~spielraum** *m* discretionary powers *pl.*

ermitteln* [1] *vt* to determine (*auch Chem, Math*), to ascertain; *Person* to trace; *Tatsache, Identität* to establish.
[2] *vi* to investigate ◆ **gegen jdn ~** to investigate sb; **in einem Fall ~** to investigate a case.

Ermittlung *f* **(a)** *no pl siehe vt* determination, ascertaining; tracing; establishing, establishment. **(b)** (*esp Jur: Erkundigung*) investigation, inquiry ◆ **~en anstellen** to make inquiries (*über +acc* about).

Ermittlungs-: ⚠**~ausschuß** *m* committee of inquiry; **~richter** *m* (*Jur*) examining magistrate; **~stand** *m* stage of the investigation; **~verfahren** *nt* (*Jur*) preliminary proceedings *pl.*

ermöglichen* *vt* to facilitate, to make possible ◆ **es jdm ~, etw zu tun** to make it possible for sb *or* to enable sb to do sth; **um uns den freien Austausch von Informationen zu ~** to facilitate the free exchange of information, to make it possible for us *or* to enable us to exchange information freely; **jdm das Studium/eine Reise ~** to make it possible for sb to study/to go on a journey; **(nur,) wenn Sie es ~ können** (*form*) (only) if you are able (to); **können Sie es ~, morgen zu kommen?** (*form*) would it be possible for you to *or* are you able to come tomorrow?

ermorden* *vt* to murder; (*esp aus politischen Gründen*) to assassinate.

Ermordung *f* murder; (*esp politisch*) assassination.

ermüden* [1] *vt* to tire.
[2] *vi aux sein* to tire, to become tired; (*Tech*) to fatigue.

ermüdend *adj* tiring.

Ermüdung *f* fatigue (*auch Tech*), tiredness, weariness.

Ermüdungs-: ~erscheinung *f* sign *or* symptom of fatigue; **~zustand** *m* feeling of tiredness.

ermuntern* [1] *vt* (*ermutigen*) to encourage (*jdn zu etw* sb to do sth); (*beleben, erfrischen*) to liven up, to stimulate, to invigorate; (*aufmuntern*) to cheer up ◆ **seine Gegenwart wirkt ~d auf mich** his presence has an enlivening effect on me *or* stimulates me.
[2] *vr* (*rare*) to wake up, to rouse oneself.

Ermunterung *f siehe vt* encouragement; enlivening, stimulation; cheering-up.

ermutigen* *vt* (*ermuntern*) to encourage; (*Mut geben*) to give courage, to embolden (*form*) ◆ **jdn zu etw ~** to encourage sb to do sth/give sb the courage *or* embolden (*form*) sb to do sth.

Ermutigung *f* encouragement.

Ern *m* **-(e)s, -e** (*dial*) *siehe* **Hausflur.**

ernähren* [1] *vt* to feed; (*unterhalten*) to support, to keep, to maintain ◆ **schlecht/gut ernährt** undernourished/well-nourished *or* -fed; **dieser Beruf ernährt seinen Mann** you can make a good living in this profession.
[2] *vr* to eat ◆ **sich von etw ~** to live *or* subsist on sth; **sich von Übersetzungen ~** to earn one's living by doing translations; **sich selbst ~ müssen** to have to earn one's own living; **der Arzt klärte ihn auf, wie er sich ~ sollte** the doctor advised him on his diet.

Ernährer(in *f***)** *m* **-s, -** breadwinner, provider.

Ernährung *f* (*das Ernähren*) feeding; (*Nahrung*) food, nourishment, nutrition (*esp Med*); (*Unterhalt*) maintenance ◆ **auf vernünftige ~ achten** to eat sensibly; **die ~ einer großen Familie** feeding a big family; **falsche/richtige/pflanzliche ~** the wrong/a proper/a vegetarian diet.

Ernährungs- *in cpds* nutritional; **~forschung** *f* nutritional research; **~gewohnheiten** *pl* eating habits *pl*; **~krankheit** *f* nutritional disease; **~weise** *f* diet, form of nutrition; **~wissenschaft** *f* dietetics *sing*; **~wissenschaftler** *m* dietician, nutritionist.

ernennen* *vt irreg* to appoint ◆ **jdn zu etw ~** to make *or* appoint sb sth.

Ernennung *f* appointment (*zum* as).

Ernennungs-: ~schreiben *nt* letter of appointment; **~urkunde** *f* certificate of appointment.

erneuerbar *adj* renewable.

Erneuerer *m* **-s, -, Erneuerin** *f* innovator.

erneuern* *vt* to renew; (*renovieren*) to renovate; (*restaurieren*) to restore; (*auswechseln*) *Öl* to change; *Maschinenteile* to replace; (*wiederbeleben*) to revive ◆ **Reifen/Bettwäsche/Schnürsenkel** *etc* **~** to buy *or* get new tyres/sheets/shoelaces *etc.*

Erneuerung *f siehe vt* renewal; renovation; restoration; changing; replacement; revival.

erneut [1] *adj attr* renewed.
[2] *adv* (once) again, once more.

erniedrigen* [1] *vt* (*demütigen*) to humiliate; (*herabsetzen*) to degrade; (*Mus*) to flatten, to flat (*US*).
[2] *vr* to humble oneself; (*pej*) to demean *or* lower oneself.

Erniedrigung *f siehe vt* humiliation; degradation, abasement; flattening, flatting (*US*).

Erniedrigungszeichen *nt* (*Mus*) flat (sign).

Ernst[1] *m* **-s** Ernest.

Ernst[2] *m* **-(e)s,** *no pl* seriousness; (*Bedenklichkeit auch*) gravity; (*Dringlichkeit, Ernsthaftigkeit von Gesinnung*) earnestness ◆ **feierlicher ~** solemnity; **im ~** seriously; **allen ~es** in all seriousness, quite seriously; **meinen Sie das allen ~es?, ist das Ihr ~?** are you (really) serious?, you're not serious, are you?; **das kann doch nicht dein ~ sein!** you can't mean that seriously!, you can't be serious!; **das ist mein (völliger** *or* **voller) ~** I'm quite serious; **dieses Angebot ist im ~ gemeint** this offer is meant seriously; **es ist mir ~ damit** I'm serious about it, I'm in earnest; **mit etw ~ machen** to be serious about sth; **mit einer Drohung ~ machen** to carry out a threat; **der ~ des Lebens** the serious side of life, the real world; **damit wird es jetzt ~** now it's serious, now it's for real (*inf*); **mit ~ bei der Sache sein** to do sth seriously.

ernst *adj* serious; (*bedenklich, bedrohlich, würdevoll auch*) grave; (*eifrig, ~haft*) *Mensch, Gesinnung* earnest; (*feierlich, elegisch*) solemn ◆ **~e Absichten haben** (*inf*) to have honourable intentions; **es (mit jdm/etw) ~ meinen** to be serious (about sb/sth); **jdn/etw ~ nehmen** to take sb/sth seriously; **es steht ~ um ihn/die Sache** things look bad for him/it; (*wegen Krankheit*) he's in a bad way; **es ist nichts E~es** it's nothing serious; **~ bleiben** to remain *or* be serious; (*sich das Lachen verbeißen*) to keep a straight face.

Ernst-: ~fall *m* emergency; **im ~fall** in case of emergency; ⚠**e~gemeint** *adj attr* serious; **e~haft** *adj* serious; (*bedenklich, gewichtig auch*) grave; (*eindringlich, eifrig*) earnest; **etw e~haft tun** to do sth seriously *or* in earnest; **~haftigkeit** *f siehe adj* seriousness; gravity; earnestness; **e~lich** *adj* serious; (*bedrohlich auch*) grave; (*attr: eindringlich*) earnest; **e~lich besorgt um** seriously *or* gravely concerned about; **e~lich böse werden** to get really angry.

Ernte *f* **-, -n (a)** (*das Ernten*) (*von Getreide*) harvest(ing); (*von Kartoffeln*) digging; (*von Äpfeln etc*) picking.
(b) (*Ertrag*) harvest (*an +dat* of); (*von Kartoffeln etc auch, von Äpfeln, fig*) crop ◆ **die ~ bergen** (*form*) *or* **einbringen** to bring in the harvest, to harvest the crop(s); **die ~ seines Fleißes** the fruits of his industry; **der Tod hielt grausige ~** (*liter*) death took a heavy toll; **du siehst aus, als sei dir die ganze ~ verhagelt** (*fig inf*) you look as though you've lost a shilling and found sixpence.

Ernte-: ~arbeiter *m* (*von Getreide*) reaper, harvester; (*von Kartoffeln, Obst, Hopfen*) picker; **~ausfall** *m* crop shortfall (*spec*) *or* failure; **~(dank)fest** *nt* harvest festival; **~maschine** *f* reaper, harvester.

ernten *vt* **(a)** *Getreide* to harvest, to reap; *Kartoffeln* to dig, to get in; *Äpfel, Erbsen* to pick ◆ **ich muß jetzt meinen Apfelbaum ~** it's time I picked my apples. **(b)** (*fig*) *Früchte, Lohn, Unfrieden* to reap; *(Un)dank, Applaus, Spott* to get.

ernüchtern* *vt* to sober up; (*fig*) to bring down to earth, to sober ◆ **~d** sobering.

Ernüchterung *f* sobering-up; (*fig*) disillusionment.

Er|oberer *m* **-s, -** conqueror.

er|obern* *vt* to conquer; *Festung, Stadt* to take, to capture; (*fig*) *Sympathie etc* to win, to capture; *neue Märkte* to win, to move into; *Herz, Mädchen* to conquer; (*inf: ergattern*) to get hold of ◆ **im Sturm ~** (*Mil, fig*) to take by storm.

Er|oberung *f* (*lit, fig*) conquest; (*einer Festung, Stadt*) capture, taking ◆ **eine ~ machen** (*fig inf*) to make a conquest; **auf ~en ausgehen** (*fig inf*) to be out to make conquests.

Er|oberungs-: ~krieg *m* war of conquest; **~zug** *m* campaign of conquest.

er|öffnen* [1] *vt* **(a)** to open (*auch Fin, Mil etc*); *Ausstellung auch* to inaugurate (*form*); *Konkursverfahren* to institute, to initiate; *Testament* to open ◆ **etw für eröffnet erklären** to declare sth open.
(b) (*Med*) *Geschwür* to lance; (*rare*) *Geburt* to induce.
(c) (*hum, geh*) **jdm etw ~** to disclose *or* reveal sth to sb; **ich habe dir etwas zu ~** I have something to tell you.
[2] *vr* **(a)** (*Aussichten etc*) to open up, to present itself/themselves.
(b) (*geh*) **sich jdm ~** to open one's heart to sb.
[3] *vi* (*Währungskurs*) to open (*mit* at).

Er|öffnung *f siehe vt* **(a)** opening; inauguration; institution, initiation. **(b)** lancing; induction. **(c)** (*hum, geh*) disclosure, revelation ◆ **jdm eine ~ machen** to disclose *or* reveal sth to sb; **ich habe dir eine ~ zu machen** I have something to tell you.

Er|öffnungs-: ~ansprache *f* inaugural *or* opening address; **~kurs** *m* opening price; **~wehen** *pl* (*Med*) labour pains *pl*.

erogen *adj* erogenous.

➤ **er|örtern*** *vt* to discuss (in detail).

Er|örterung *f* discussion ◆ **zur ~ stehen** (*form*) to be under discussion.

Eros *m* **-,** *no pl* (*esp Philos*) Eros.

Eros-Center ['eːrɔssɛntɐ] *nt* **-s, -** eros centre.

Erosion *f* (*Geol, Med*) erosion.

Eroten *pl* (*Art*) Cupids *pl*.

Erotik *f* eroticism.

Erotika *pl* (*Liter*) erotica *sing*.

Erotiker(in *f*) *m* **-s, -** eroticist.

erotisch *adj* erotic.

Erotomane *m* **-n, -n** sex maniac.

Erotomanie *f* (*Psych*) erotomania (*spec*).

Erotomanin *f* nymphomaniac.

Erpel *m* **-s, -** drake.

erpicht *adj* **auf etw** (*acc*) **~ sein** to be keen on sth; **er ist nur auf Geld ~** he's only after money.

erpressen* *vt Geld etc* to extort (*von* from); *jdn* to blackmail ◆ **die Kidnapper haben den Vater erpreßt** the kidnappers tried to extort money from the father.

Erpresser(in *f*) *m* **-s, -** blackmailer; (*bei Entführung*) kidnapper.

Erpresserbrief *m* blackmail letter.

erpresserisch *adj* blackmailing *attr*.

Erpressermethoden *pl* blackmail *sing*.

Erpressung *f* (*von Geld, Zugeständnissen*) extortion; (*eines Menschen*) blackmail ◆ **die Kidnapper hatten keinen Erfolg mit ihrer ~** the kidnappers failed to get their ransom money *or* failed in their ransom attempt.

Erpressungsversuch *m* blackmail attempt; (*durch Gewaltandrohung*) attempt at obtaining money by menaces; (*bei Entführung*) attempt at getting a ransom.

erproben* *vt* to test; (*fig*) to (put to the) test ◆ **erprobt** tried and tested, proven; (*zuverlässig*) reliable; (*erfahren*) experienced.

erquicken* *vt* (*old, liter*) to refresh.

erquicklich *adj* (*angenehm*) pleasant; (*anregend*) stimulating.

Erquickung *f* (*old*) refreshment.

Errata *pl* (*Typ*) errata *pl*.

erraten* *vt irreg* to guess; *Rätsel* to guess (the answer to) ◆ **du hast es ~!** how did you guess?, you guessed!

erratisch *adj* (*Geol*) erratic ◆ **ein ~er Block** an erratic.

errechnen* *vt* to calculate, to work out.

erregbar *adj* excitable; (*sexuell*) easily aroused; (*empfindlich*) sensitive ◆ **schwer ~** not easily aroused.

Erregbarkeit *f siehe adj* excitability; ability to be aroused; sensitivity.

erregen* [1] *vt* **(a)** (*aufregen*) *jdn, Nerven etc* to excite; (*sexuell auch*) to arouse; (*fig*) *Wellen, Meer* to agitate; (*erzürnen*) to infuriate, to annoy ◆ **er war vor Wut ganz erregt** he was in a rage *or* fury; **in der Debatte ging es erregt zu** feelings ran high in the debate, the debate was quite heated; **erregte Diskussionen** heated discussions; **erregt lief er hin und her** he paced to and fro in a state of agitation; **freudig erregt** excited; *siehe* **Gemüt**.
(b) (*hervorrufen, erzeugen*) to arouse; *Zorn auch* to provoke; *Leidenschaften auch* to excite; *Aufsehen, öffentliches Ärgernis, Heiterkeit* to cause, to create; *Aufmerksamkeit* to attract; *Zweifel* to raise; (*Elec*) *Strom* to produce, to generate.
[2] *vr* to get worked up *or* excited (*über +acc* about, over); (*sich ärgern*) to get annoyed (*über +acc* at).

Erreger *m* **-s, -** (*Med*) cause, causative agent (*spec*); (*Bazillus etc*) pathogene (*spec*).

Erregtheit *f siehe* **Erregung (c)**.

Erregung *f* **(a)** *no pl siehe vt* (*a*) excitation; arousal, arousing; agitation; infuriation, infuriating.
(b) *no pl siehe vt* (*b*) arousal, arousing; excitation; causing, creating; attracting; raising; generation; *siehe* **Ärgernis**.
(c) (*Zustand*) (*esp angenehm*) excitement; (*sexuell auch*) arousal; (*Beunruhigung*) agitation; (*Wut*) rage; (*liter: des Meeres, der Wellen*) turbulence ◆ **in ~ geraten** to get excited/aroused/agitated/into a rage; **jdn in ~ versetzen** to get sb excited/aroused/agitated/put sb into a rage; **das Meer in ~ versetzen** to make the sea churn.

erreichbar *adj* reachable, able to be reached; (*nicht weit*) within reach; (*Telec*) obtainable; *Glück, Ziel* attainable ◆ **leicht ~** easily reached/within easy reach/easily attainable; **schwer ~ sein** (*Ort*) not to be very accessible; (*Mensch*) to be difficult to get hold of; (*Gegenstand*) to be difficult to reach; **zu Fuß ~** able to be reached on foot; (*nicht weit*) within walking distance; **in ~er Nähe** near at hand (*+gen* to); **der Direktor ist nie ~** the director is never available; (*telefonisch*) the director can never be reached; **sind Sie morgen zu Hause ~?** can I get in touch with you at home tomorrow?, are you contactable at home tomorrow?; *siehe* **telefonisch**.

erreichen* *vt* to reach; *Ort auch* to get to, to arrive at; *Festland, Hafen auch* to make; *Zug* to catch; *Alter, Geschwindigkeit auch* to attain; *Absicht, Zweck* to achieve, to attain; (*einholen*) to catch up with; (*sich in Verbindung setzen mit*) *jdn, Büro etc* to contact, to get, to reach ◆ **ein hohes Alter ~** to live to a great age; **vom Bahnhof leicht zu ~** within easy reach of the station; **zu Fuß zu ~** able to be reached on foot; (*nicht weit*) within walking distance; **wann kann ich Sie morgen ~?** when can I get in touch with you tomorrow?; **du erreichst damit nur, daß ...** all you'll achieve that way is that ...; **wir haben nichts erreicht** we achieved nothing; **bei ihm war nichts zu ~** you couldn't get anywhere with him *or* anything out of him.

Erreichung *f* (*form*) attainment; (*eines Ziels auch*) achievement ◆ **bei ~ des 60. Lebensjahres** on reaching the age of 60.

erretten* *vt* (*liter, esp Rel*) to save, to deliver (*liter*).

Erretter *m* (*liter, esp Rel*) saviour (*esp Rel*), deliverer (*liter*).

Errettung *f, no pl* (*liter*) rescue, deliverance (*liter*); (*Rel*) salvation.

errichten* *vt* to erect (*auch Math*), to put up; (*fig: gründen*) to establish, to set up.

Errichtung *f, no pl* erection, construction; (*fig: Gründung*) establishment, setting-up.

erringen* *vt irreg* to gain, to win; *den 3. Platz, Erfolg* to gain, to achieve; *Rekord* to set ◆ **ein hart errungener Sieg** a hard-won victory.

Er-Roman *m* (*Liter*) third-person novel.

erröten* *vi aux sein* (*über +acc* at) to flush; (*esp aus Verlegenheit, Scham*) to blush; (*Gesicht*) to go *or* turn red, to redden ◆ **jdn zum E~ bringen** to make sb flush/blush.

Errungenschaft *f* achievement; (*inf: Anschaffung*) acquisition.

Ersatz *m* **-es,** *no pl* substitute (*auch Sport*); (*für Altes, Zerbrochenes, Mitarbeiter*) replacement; (*inf: die ~spieler*) substitutes *pl*; (*Mil: ~truppen*) replacements *pl*; (*Reserveheer*) reserves *pl*; (*das Ersetzen*) replacement, substitution; (*durch Geld*) compensation; (*von Kosten*) reimbursement ◆ **als** *or* **zum ~** as a substitute/replacement; **zum ~ der beschädigten Ware verpflichtet** obliged to replace the damaged item; **als ~ für jdn einspringen** to stand in for sb; **für etw ~ leisten** (*Jur*) to pay *or* provide compensation *or* restitution for sth; **~ schaffen**

➤ SPRACHE AKTIV: **erörtern** → 53.1

für to find replacements/a replacement for, to replace.

Ersatz-: ~anspruch *m (Jur)* entitlement to compensation; **~anspruch haben** to be entitled to compensation; **~befriedigung** *f (Psych)* vicarious satisfaction; **das Rauchen ist eine ~befriedigung** smoking is a substitute; **~dienst** *m (Mil)* alternative service; **~handlung** *f (Psych)* substitute (act); **~kaffee** *m siehe* **Kaffee-Ersatz**; **~kasse** *f* private health insurance; **~mann** *m, pl* **-männer** *or* **-leute** replacement; *(Sport)* substitute; **~mine** *f* refill; **~objekt** *nt (Psych)* substitute, surrogate; **~pflicht** *f* obligation to pay compensation; **e~pflichtig** *adj* liable to pay compensation; **~rad** *nt (Aut)* spare wheel; **~reifen** *m (Aut)* spare tyre; **~spieler** *m (Sport)* substitute; **~teil** *nt* spare (part); **~truppen** *pl* replacements *pl*; *(Reserveheer)* reserve troops *pl*; **e~weise** *adv* as an alternative.

ersaufen* *vi irreg aux sein (sl)* **(a)** *(ertrinken)* to drown, to be drowned. **(b)** *(überschwemmt werden, Aut)* to be flooded, to flood.

ersäufen* *vt* to drown ◆ **seinen Kummer im Alkohol ~** *(inf)* to drown one's sorrows (in drink) *(inf)*.

erschaffen *pret* **erschuf**, *ptp* **erschaffen** *vt* to create.

Erschaffer *m* **-s, -** creator.

Erschaffung *f* creation.

erschallen *pret* **erscholl** *or* **erschallte**, *ptp* **erschollen** *or* **erschallt** *vi aux sein (geh) (Stimme, Lachen)* to ring out; *(Trompete)* to sound.

erschaudern* *vi aux sein (geh)* to shudder *(bei* at).

erschauen* *vt (liter)* to see, to espy *(liter)*.

erschauern* *vi aux sein (geh) (vor Kälte)* to shiver; *(vor Erregung, Ehrfurcht)* to tremble, to shudder.

➤ **erscheinen*** *vi irreg aux sein* to appear; *(vorkommen, wirken wie auch)* to seem *(dat* to); *(sich sehen lassen: auf Party etc auch)* to put in an appearance *(auf +dat* at); *(zur Arbeit auch)* to turn up *(zu* for); *(Buch auch)* to come out ◆ **in einem anderen Licht ~** to appear in a different light; **es erscheint (mir) wünschenswert** it seems *or* appears desirable (to me); **das Buch ist in** *or* **bei einem anderen Verlag erschienen** the book was published by *or* brought out by another publisher; **das Buch erscheint nicht mehr** the book is no longer published.

Erscheinen *nt* **-s,** *no pl* appearance; *(von Geist auch)* apparition; *(von Buch auch)* publication ◆ **um rechtzeitiges ~ wird gebeten** you are kindly requested to attend punctually; **er dankte den Besuchern für ihr (zahlreiches) ~** he thanked his (many) guests for coming; **mit seinem ~ hatte ich nicht mehr gerechnet** I no longer reckoned on his turning up *or* appearing.

Erscheinung *f* **(a)** *no pl (das Erscheinen)* appearance ◆ **das Fest der ~** *(Eccl)* (the Feast of) the Epiphany; **in ~ treten** *(Merkmale)* to appear, to manifest themselves *(form)*; *(Gefühle)* to show themselves, to become visible *or* obvious; **sie tritt (persönlich) fast nie in ~** she hardly ever appears (in person).

(b) *(äußere ~)* appearance; *(Philos auch, Natur~, Vorkommnis)* phenomenon; *(Krankheits~, Alters~)* symptom; *(Zeichen)* sign, manifestation ◆ **es ist eine bekannte ~, daß** ... it is (a) well-known (phenomenon) that ...

(c) *(Gestalt)* figure ◆ **seiner äußeren ~ nach** judging by his appearance; **er ist eine stattliche ~** he is a fine figure of a man; **eine elegante ~ sein** to cut an elegant figure.

(d) *(Geister~)* apparition; *(Traumbild)* vision.

Erscheinungs-: ~bild *nt (Biol)* phenotype; **~form** *f* manifestation; **~jahr** *nt (von Buch)* year of publication; **~ort** *m (von Buch)* place of publication; **~weise** *f (von Zeitschrift)* publication dates *pl*; **~weise: monatlich** appearing monthly.

erschießen* *irreg* [1] *vt* to shoot (dead).

[2] *vr* to shoot oneself ◆ **dann kannst du dich ~** you might as well stick your head in a gas oven; *siehe* **erschossen**.

Erschießung *f* shooting; *(Jur: als Todesstrafe)* execution ◆ **die Verurteilten wurden zur ~ abgeführt** the condemned were led off to be shot; **er drohte mit ~ der Geiseln** he threatened to shoot the hostages; **Tod durch ~** *(Jur)* death by firing squad.

erschlaffen* [1] *vi aux sein (ermüden)* to tire, to grow weary; *(schlaff werden)* to go limp; *(Seil)* to slacken, to go slack; *(Interesse, Eifer)* to wane, to flag.

[2] *vt* to tire; *(Medikament)* to relax.

Erschlaffung *f siehe vi* tiredness, weariness; limpness; slackness; waning, flagging.

erschlagen* [1] *vt irreg* to kill, to strike dead *(liter)* ◆ **vom Blitz ~ werden** to be struck (dead) by lightning.

[2] *adj* **~ sein** *(inf) (todmüde)* to be worn out *or* dead beat *(inf)*; *(erstaunt)* to be thunderstruck *or* flabbergasted *(inf)*.

erschleichen* *vt irreg* **(sich** *dat***) etw ~** to obtain sth by devious means *or* in an underhand way; **sich** *(dat)* **jds Gunst/Vertrauen ~** to worm oneself into sb's favour *or* good graces/confidence.

erschließen* *irreg* [1] *vt* **(a)** *Gebiet, Absatzmarkt, Baugelände* to develop, to open up; *Einnahmequelle* to find, to acquire; *Rohstoffquellen, Bodenschätze* to tap.

(b) *(folgern)* to deduce, to infer *(aus* from); *Gedicht* to decipher, to work out the meaning of ◆ **daraus ist zu ~, daß** ... it can be deduced *or* inferred from this, that ...

(c) *(Ling, Liter)* to reconstruct.

[2] *vr (liter) (Blüte)* to open (out) ◆ **sich jdm ~** *(verständlich werden)* to disclose itself to sb *(liter)*; **sich** *(dat)* **etw ~** to master sth.

Erschließungskosten *pl* development costs *pl*.

erschlossen *adj Gebiet* developed; *(Ling, Liter)* reconstructed.

erscholl *pret of* **erschallen**.

erschollen *ptp of* **erschallen**.

erschöpfbar *adj* exhaustible.

erschöpfen* [1] *vt Mittel, Thema, Geduld* to exhaust; *(ermüden auch)* to tire out ◆ **in erschöpftem Zustand** in a state of exhaustion.

[2] *vr* **(a)** *(körperlich)* to exhaust oneself.

(b) *(fig) (in etw (dat)* ~ to amount to nothing more than sth; **darin erschöpft sich seine Bildung** that's the sum total of his education; **ein Schriftsteller, der sich erschöpft hat** an author who has run out of ideas *or* expended his talent.

erschöpfend *adj* **(a)** *(ermüdend)* exhausting. **(b)** *(ausführlich)* exhaustive.

Erschöpfung *f* **(a)** *(völlige Ermüdung)* exhaustion, fatigue ◆ **bis zur ~ arbeiten** to work to the point of exhaustion. **(b)** *(der Mittel, Vorräte etc)* exhaustion.

Erschöpfungszustand *m* state of exhaustion *no pl*.

erschossen [1] *ptp of* **erschießen**.

[2] *adj (inf)* **(völlig) ~ sein** to be whacked *(inf)*, to be dead (beat) *(inf)*.

erschrak *pret of* **erschrecken 2**.

erschrecken [1] *pret* **erschreckte**, *ptp* **erschreckt** *vt* to frighten, to scare; *(bestürzen)* to startle, to give a shock *or* a start; *(zusammenzucken lassen)* to make jump, to give a start, to startle ◆ **es hat mich erschreckt, wie schlecht er aussah** it gave me a shock *or* a start *or* it startled me to see how bad he looked.

[2] *pret* **erschreckte** *or* **erschrak**, *ptp* **erschreckt** *or* **erschrocken** *vir (vi: aux sein)* to be frightened *(vor +dat* by); *(bestürzt sein)* to be startled; *(zusammenzucken)* to jump, to start ◆ **ich bin erschrocken, wie schlecht er aussah** it gave me a shock *or* a start *or* I was shocked *or* startled to see how bad he looked; **sie erschrak beim Gedanken, daß** ... the thought that ... gave her a start *or* a scare; **sie erschrak bei dem Knall** the bang made her jump; **~ Sie nicht, ich bin's nur** don't be frightened *or* afraid, it's only me; **~ Sie nicht, wenn Sie ihn sehen, er ist sehr alt geworden** don't be alarmed when you see him, he's grown very old; *siehe* **erschrocken**.

Erschrecken *nt* **-s,** *no pl* fright, shock.

erschreckend *adj* alarming, frightening ◆ **~ aussehen** to look dreadful *or* terrible; **~ wenig Leute** alarmingly few people; **~ viele** an alarmingly large number.

erschrick *imper sing of* **erschrecken**.

erschrocken *adj* frightened, scared; *(bestürzt)* startled ◆ **~ hochspringen/zusammenzucken** to jump, to (give a) start.

erschuf *pret of* **erschaffen**.

erschüttern* *vt Boden, Gebäude, (fig) Vertrauen, Glauben etc* to shake; *(fig) Glaubwürdigkeit* to cast doubt upon; *(fig) Gesundheit* to unsettle, to upset; *(fig: bewegen, Schock versetzen)* to shake severely ◆ **jdn in seinem Glauben ~** to shake *or* shatter sb's faith; **sie war von seinem Tod tief erschüttert** she was severely shaken by his death; **seine Geschichte hat mich erschüttert** I was shattered *(inf)* by his story; **über etw** *(acc)* **erschüttert sein** to be shaken *or* shattered *(inf)* by sth; **mich kann nichts mehr ~** nothing surprises me any more; **er läßt sich durch nichts ~, ihn kann nichts ~** he always keeps his cool *(inf)*.

erschütternd *adj* shattering *(inf)*; *Nachricht auch* distressing; *Verhältnisse auch* shocking.

Erschütterung *f (des Bodens etc)* tremor, vibration; *(fig) (der Ruhe, Wirtschaftslage)* disruption; *(des Selbstvertrauens)* blow *(gen* to); *(seelische Ergriffenheit)* emotion, shock ◆ **bei der ~ des Gebäudes** when the building shook; **die Krise kann zu einer ~ des Staates führen** the crisis could rock the state; **ihr Tod löste allgemeine ~ aus** her death shocked everyone.

erschweren* *vt* to make more difficult; *Sachlage auch* to aggravate; *Fortschritt etc auch* to impede, to hinder ◆ **jdm etw ~** to make sth more difficult for sb; **~de Umstände** *(Jur)* aggravating circumstances; **es kommt noch ~d hinzu, daß** ... to compound matters, ...

Erschwernis *f* difficulty.

Erschwerung *f* impediment *(gen* to), obstruction *(gen* to) ◆ **das bedeutet eine ~ meiner Arbeit** that will make my job more difficult.

erschwindeln* *vt* to obtain by fraud ◆ **sich** *(dat)* **(von jdm) etw ~** to swindle *or* do *(inf)* sb out of sth.

erschwingen* *vt irreg* to afford.

erschwinglich *adj Preise* within one's means, reasonable ◆ **das Haus ist für uns nicht ~** the house is not within our means.

ersehen* *vt irreg (form)* **etw aus etw ~** to see *or* gather sth from sth.

ersehnen* *vt (geh)* to long for.

ersehnt *adj* longed-for ◆ **heiß** *or* **lang ~** much-longed-for.

ersetzbar *adj* replaceable; *Schaden* reparable.

ersetzen* *vt* to replace *(auch Comput)*; *(als Ersatz dienen für, an die Stelle treten von auch)* to take the place of ◆ **niemand kann Kindern die Mutter ~** no-one can take the place of *or* replace a child's mother; **diese Vase kannst du mir nie ~** you'll never be able to replace that vase.

Ersetzung *f, no pl* replacing; *(von Schaden, Verlust)* compensation, reparation *(gen* for); *(von Unkosten)* reimbursement, repayment.

ersichtlich *adj* obvious, clear, apparent ◆ **hieraus ist klar ~, daß** ... it is obvious *etc* from this that ..., this shows clearly that ...

ersinnen* *vt irreg* to devise, to think up; *(erfinden)* to invent.

ersitzen* *vt irreg (Jur) Anspruch* to acquire by prescription.

erspähen* *vt* to catch sight of, to spot, to espy *(liter)*.

ersparen* [1] *vt Vermögen, Zeit, Kummer etc* to save ◆ **jdm/sich etw ~** to spare *or* save sb/oneself sth; **ich kann mir jeglichen Kommentar ~** I don't think I need to comment; **jdm eine Demütigung ~** to spare sb a humiliation; **~ Sie sich die Mühe!** save *or* spare yourself the trouble; **Sie können sich alles**

Weitere ~ you don't need to say any more; **ihr blieb auch nichts erspart** she was spared nothing; **das Ersparte** the savings *pl*.
[2] *vr* to be superfluous *or* unnecessary.

Ersparnis *f or (Aus) nt* **(a)** *no pl (an Zeit etc)* saving *(an +dat* of). **(b)** *usu pl* savings *pl*.

erspielen* *vt (Sport) Punkte, Sieg* to win, to gain.

ersprießlich *adj (förderlich)* beneficial, advantageous; *(nützlich)* fruitful, profitable; *(angenehm)* pleasant.

erst *adv* **(a)** first; *(anfänglich)* at first ◆ **mach ~ (ein)mal die Arbeit fertig** finish your work first; **~ mal ist das gar nicht wahr ...** first *or* for one thing it's just not true...; **~ einmal mußt du an deine Pflicht denken** you should consider your duty first; **wenn du das ~ einmal hinter dir hast** once you've got that behind you; **~ wollte er, dann wieder nicht** first he wanted to, then he didn't; *siehe* **Arbeit**.
(b) *(nicht früher als, nicht mehr als, bloß)* only; *(nicht früher als auch)* not until ◆ **eben** *or* **gerade ~** just; **~ gestern** only yesterday; **~ jetzt** *(gerade eben)* only just; **~ jetzt verstehe ich ...** I have only just understood ...; **~ jetzt wissen wir ...** it is only now that we know ...; **~ morgen** not until *or* before tomorrow; **~ vor kurzem** only a short time ago; **es ist ~ 6 Uhr** it is only 6 o'clock; **wir fahren ~ übermorgen/~ später** we're not going until the day after tomorrow/until later; **sie war ~ 6 Jahre** she was only 6; **~ als** only when, not until; **~ wenn** only if *or* when, not until.
(c) *(emph: gar, nun gar)* **da ging's ~ richtig los** then it really got going; **was wird Mutter ~ sagen!** whatever will mother say!; **was wird dann ~ passieren?** whatever will happen then?; **sie ist schon ziemlich blöd, aber ~ ihre Schwester!** she is fairly stupid, but you should see her sister!; **da fange ich ~ gar nicht an** I simply won't (bother to) begin; **wie wird er sich ~ ärgern, wenn er das noch erfährt** he really will be annoyed when he finds out about that; **jetzt ~ recht/recht nicht!** that just makes me all the more determined; **da tat er es ~ recht!** so he did it deliberately; **das macht es ~ recht schlimm** that makes it even worse *or* all the worse; **da habe ich mich ~ recht geärgert** then I really did get annoyed.
(d) wäre er doch ~ zurück! if only he were back!; **diese Gerüchte darf man gar nicht ~ aufkommen lassen** these rumours mustn't even be allowed to start.

erstarken* *vi aux sein (geh)* to gain strength, to become stronger.

erstarren* *vi aux sein (Finger)* to grow stiff *or* numb; *(Flüssigkeit)* to solidify; *(Gips, Zement etc)* to set, to solidify; *(Blut, Fett etc)* to congeal; *(fig: Blut)* to freeze, to run cold; *(Lächeln)* to freeze; *(vor Schrecken, Entsetzen etc)* to be paralyzed *or* petrified *(vor +dat* with); *(Haltung, Meinung)* to become rigid *or* fixed; *(Ideen, Kunstform etc)* to ossify, to become rigid ◆ **erstarrte Formen** fossilized forms.

Erstarrung *f, no pl siehe vi* stiffness, numbness; solidification; congelation, congealment; freezing; paralysis, petrification; ossification; fossilization.

erstatten* *vt* **(a)** *Unkosten* to refund, to reimburse. **(b)** *(form)* **(Straf)anzeige gegen jdn ~** to report sb; **Meldung ~** to report; **Bericht ~** to (give a) report *(über +acc* on).

Erstattung *f, no pl (von Unkosten)* refund, reimbursement.

Erst-: e~aufführen *ptp* **e~aufgeführt** *vt infin, ptp only (Theat)* to give the first public performance of; **~aufführung** *f (Theat)* first performance *or* night, première; **~auflage** *f* first printing.

erstaunen* [1] *vt* to astonish, to amaze; *siehe* **erstaunt**.
[2] *vi* **(a)** *aux sein (old: überrascht sein)* to be astonished *or* amazed. **(b)** *(Erstaunen erregen)* to cause astonishment *or* amazement, to astonish *or* amaze (people) ◆ **seine Körperbeherrschung erstaunt immer wieder** his physical control never fails to amaze.

Erstaunen *nt* **-s,** *no pl* astonishment, amazement ◆ **jdn in ~ (ver)setzen** to astonish *or* amaze sb.

erstaunlich *adj* astonishing, amazing.

erstaunt *adj* astonished, amazed *(über +acc* about) ◆ **er sah mich ~ an** he looked at me in astonishment *or* amazement.

Erst-: ~ausgabe *f* first edition; **~besteigung** *f* first ascent; **e~beste(r, s)** *adj attr siehe* **erste(r, s) (b)**; **~druck** *m* first edition.

erstechen* *vt irreg* to stab to death.

erstehen* *irreg* [1] *vt (inf)* to buy, to get.
[2] *vi aux sein (form)* to arise; *(Städte)* to rise up; *(Bibl: auf~)* to rise.

Erste-Hilfe-Leistung *f* administering first aid.

ersteigen* *vt irreg* to climb; *Felswand auch, Stadtmauer* to scale.

ersteigern* *vt* to buy at an auction.

Ersteigung *f siehe vt* ascent; scaling.

Erst|einsatz *m* **~ (von Atomwaffen)** first strike.

erstellen* *vt* **(a)** *(bauen)* to construct, to erect. **(b)** *(anfertigen) Liste etc* to draw up, to make out.

Erstellung *f siehe vt* construction, erection; drawing up, making out.

⚠**erstemal** *adv* **das ~** the first time; **das tue ich das ~** I'm doing this for the first time, it's the first time I've done this.

⚠**erstenmal** *adv* **zum ~** for the first time.

erstens *adv* first(ly), in the first place.

erste(r, s) *adj* **(a)** first; *(fig: führend auch)* best, foremost; *Seite der Zeitung* front ◆ **~r Stock, ~ Etage** first floor, second floor *(US)*; **die ~ Klasse** *(Rail)* the first class (compartment); **~r Klasse fahren** to travel first class; **der ~ Rang** *(Theat)* the dress-circle, the (first) balcony *(US)*; **~ Güte** *or* **Qualität** top quality; **E~ Hilfe** first aid; **die drei ~n/die ~n drei** the first three/the first three (from each group); **der E~ in der Klasse** the top of *or* best in the class; **die E~n werden die Letzten sein** *(Bibl)* the first shall be last; **E~r unter Gleichen** first among equals; **der E~ des Monats** the first (day) of the month; **vom nächsten E~n an** as of the first of next month; **~ Kontakte anknüpfen** to establish preliminary contacts; **das ist das ~, was ich höre** that's the first I've heard of it; **er kam als ~r** he was the first to come; **als ~s** first of all; **am ~n** first; **an ~r Stelle** in the first place; **dieses Thema steht an ~r Stelle unserer Tagesordnung** this subject comes first on our agenda; **fürs ~** for the time being, for the present; **in ~r Linie** first and foremost; **zum ~n, zum zweiten, zum dritten** *(bei Auktionen)* going, going, gone!; *siehe* **Blick, Hand, Mal** *etc, siehe auch* **vierte(r, s)**.
(b) nimm das ~ beste! take anything!; **er hat den ~n besten Kühlschrank gekauft** he bought the first fridge he saw, he bought any old fridge *(inf)*; *siehe* **beste(r, s)**.

ersterben* *vi irreg aux sein (liter)* to die; *(Lärm, Wort)* to die away.

erstere(r, s) *adj* the former ◆ **der/die/das ~** the former.

Erste(r)-Klasse- *(Rail)*: **~-Abteil** *nt* first class compartment; **~-Wagen** *m* first class carriage *(Brit) or* car *(US)*.

Erst-: ~gebärende *f* primigravida *(spec)*; **e~geboren** *adj attr* first-born; **~geburt** *f (Kind)* first-born (child); *(Tier)* first young; *(Hist: auch* **~geburtsrecht)** birthright, right of primogeniture *(Jur)*; **e~genannt** *adj attr* first-mentioned; *(wichtigster)* first to be mentioned.

ersticken* [1] *vt jdn* to suffocate, to smother; *Feuer* to smother; *Geräusche* to stifle, to smother; *(fig: unterdrücken) Aufruhr etc* to suppress ◆ **mit erstickter Stimme** in a choked voice.
[2] *vi aux sein* to suffocate; *(Feuer)* to die, to go out; *(Stimme)* to become choked ◆ **an etw** *(dat)* **~** to be suffocated by sth; **an einer Gräte ~** to choke (to death) on a bone; **vor Lachen ~** to choke with laughter; **das Kind erstickt förmlich unter der Liebe der Mutter** the child is smothered by mother-love; **unsere Städte ~ im Verkehr** our cities are being choked by traffic; **in der Arbeit ~** *(inf)* to be snowed under with work, to be up to one's neck in work *(inf)*; **er erstickt im Geld** *(inf)* he's rolling in money *(inf)*; **die Luft im Zimmer war zum E~** the air in the room was suffocating *or* stifling.

Erstickung *f* suffocation, asphyxiation.

Erstickungs-: ~gefahr *f* danger of suffocation; **~tod** *m* death from *or* by suffocation, asphyxia.

erst|instanzlich *adj (Jur)* first-instance.

erstkl. *abbr of* **erstklassig**.

Erst-: e~klassig *adj* first-class, first-rate; ⚠**~kläßler(in** *f) m (esp S Ger, Sw)* pupil in the first class of primary school, first-grader *(US)*; **~kommunion** *f* first communion; **~lagerung** *f (von Atommüll)* initial storage.

Erstling *m (Kind)* first (child); *(Tier)* first young; *(Werk)* first work *or* baby *(inf)*.

Erstlingswerk *nt* first work.

erst-: ~malig [1] *adj* first; [2] *adv* for the first time; **~mals** *adv* for the first time.

erstrahlen* *vi aux sein (liter)* to shine ◆ **im Lichterglanz ~** to be aglitter (with lights).

erstrangig ['eːɐstraŋıç] *adj* first-rate.

erstreben* *vt* to strive for *or* after, to aspire to.

erstrebenswert *adj* worthwhile, desirable; *Beruf* desirable.

erstrecken* *vr* to extend *(auf, über +acc* over); *(räumlich auch)* to reach, to stretch *(auf, über +acc* over); *(zeitlich auch)* to carry on, to last *(auf, über +acc* for) ◆ **sich auf jdn/etw ~** *(betreffen)* to apply to sb/sth.

Erst-: ~schlag *m (mit Atomwaffen)* first strike; **~schlagwaffe** *f* first-strike weapon; **~semester(in** *f) m* first-year student, fresher *(inf)*; *(männlich auch)* freshman; **~sendung** *f (Rad, TV)* first broadcast; **~stimme** *f* first vote; **~tagsbrief** *m* first-day cover; **~tagsstempel** *m* date stamp *or* postmark from a first-day cover; **~täter** *m* first offender.

erstunken *adj:* **das ist ~ und erlogen** *(inf)* that's a pack of lies.

erstürmen* *vt (Mil)* to (take by) storm; *(liter) Gipfel* to conquer.

Erstürmung *f (Mil)* storming.

Erst-: ~veröffentlichung *f* first publication; **~wähler** *m* first-time voter.

ersuchen* *vt (form)* to request *(jdn um etw* sth of sb).

Ersuchen *nt* **-s, -** *(form)* request ◆ **auf ~ von** at the request of; **ein ~ an jdn richten** *or* **stellen** to make a request of sb.

ertappen* *vt* to catch ◆ **jdn/sich bei etw ~** to catch sb/oneself at *or* doing sth; **ich habe ihn dabei ertappt** I caught him at it *or* doing it.

ertasten* *vt* to feel, to make out by touch(ing); *(um zu finden)* to feel for.

erteilen* *vt* to give; *Genehmigung auch* to grant; *Lizenz* to issue; *Auftrag auch* to place *(jdm* with sb) ◆ **jdm einen Verweis ~** to reproach sb; **Unterricht ~** to teach, to give lessons; *siehe* **Wort**.

Erteilung *f siehe vt* giving; granting; issue; placing ◆ **für die ~ von Auskünften zuständig** responsible for giving information.

ertönen* *vi aux sein (geh)* to sound, to ring out ◆ **von etw ~** to resound with sth; **~ lassen** to sound; **er ließ seine tiefe Baßstimme ~** his deep bass voice rang out.

Ertrag *m* **-(e)s, ¨-e** *(von Acker)* yield; *(Ergebnis einer Arbeit)* return; *(Einnahmen)* proceeds *pl*, return ◆ **~ abwerfen** *or* **bringen** to bring in a return; **vom ~ seiner Bücher/seines Kapitals leben** to live on the proceeds from one's books/the return on one's capital.

▼ **ertragen*** *vt irreg* to bear; *Schmerzen, Leiden, Schicksal auch* to endure; *Ungewißheit, Zweifel auch* to tolerate; *(esp in Frage, Verneinung auch)* to stand ◆ **das ist nicht mehr zu ~** it's unbearable *or* intolerable; **wie erträgst du nur seine Launen?** how do you put up with *or* stand his moods?

erträglich *adj* bearable, endurable; *(leidlich)* tolerable.

Erträglichkeit *f* bearableness, endurableness.

ertrag-: ~los *adj Acker* unproductive, infertile; *Geschäft* unprofitable;

➤ SPRACHE AKTIV: **ertragen** → 34.3

~reich *adj Acker* productive, fertile; *Geschäft* profitable, lucrative.

Ertrags-: e~arm *adj Boden* poor, infertile; **~ausschüttung** *f* dividend distribution; **~lage** *f* returns *pl*, profits *pl*, profit situation; **~minderung** *f* decrease in profit(s) *or* return(s); **~schein** *m* dividend coupon; **~steigerung** *f* increase in profit(s) *or* return(s); **~steuer** *f* profit(s) tax, tax on profit(s); **~wert** *m* capitalized value of potential yield/return(s).

ertränken* [1] *vt* to drown ♦ **seinen Kummer** *or* **seine Sorgen im Alkohol ~** to drown one's sorrows.
[2] *vr* to drown oneself.

erträumen* *vt* to dream of, to imagine ♦ **eine erträumte Welt** an imaginary world; **das war alles nur erträumt** it was all in the mind; **sich** (*dat*) **etw ~** to dream of sth, to imagine sth.

ertrinken* *vi irreg aux sein* to drown, to be drowned.

Ertrinken *nt* **-s**, *no pl* drowning.

ertrotzen* *vt* (*geh*) **(sich** *dat***) etw ~** to obtain sth by sheer obstinacy *or* defiance.

ertüchtigen* (*geh*) [1] *vt* to get in (good) trim, to toughen up.
[2] *vr* to keep fit, to train.

Ertüchtigung *f* (*geh*) getting in (good) trim, toughening up ♦ **körperliche ~** physical training.

er|übrigen* [1] *vt Zeit, Geld* to spare.
[2] *vr* to be unnecessary *or* superfluous ♦ **jedes weitere Wort erübrigt sich** there's nothing more to be said.

eruieren* *vt* (*form*) *Sachverhalt* to investigate, to find out; (*esp Aus*) *Person* to trace.

Eruption *f* (*Geol, Med, fig*) eruption.

Eruptivgestein *nt* volcanic rock.

erw. *abbr of* **erweitert** extended.

erwachen* *vi aux sein* to awake, to wake (up); (*aus Ohnmacht etc*) to come to *or* round (*aus* from); (*fig: Gefühle, Verdacht*) to be aroused; (*liter: Tag*) to dawn ♦ **von etw ~** to be awoken *or* woken up by sth; **ein böses E~** (*fig*) a rude awakening.

erwachsen* [1] *vi irreg aux sein* (*geh*) to arise, to develop; (*Vorteil, Kosten etc*) to result, to accrue; (*Stadt auch*) to grow ♦ **daraus erwuchsen ihm Unannehmlichkeiten** that caused him some trouble; **daraus wird ihm kein Nutzen ~** no advantage will accrue to him (from this); **mir sind Zweifel ~** I have come to have doubts.
[2] *adj* grown-up, adult ♦ **~ sein** (*Mensch*) to be grown-up *or* an adult.

Erwachsenen-: ~bildung *f* adult education; **~taufe** *f* adult baptism.

Erwachsene(r) *mf decl as adj* adult, grown-up.

erwägen* *vt irreg* (*überlegen*) to consider, to deliberate; (*prüfen*) to consider, to examine; (*in Betracht ziehen*) to consider, to take into consideration.

erwägenswert *adj* worthy of consideration, worth considering.

Erwägung *f* consideration ♦ **aus folgenden ~en (heraus)** for the following reasons *or* considerations; **etw in ~ ziehen** to consider sth, to take sth into consideration.

erwählen* *vt* to choose.

erwähnen* *vt* to mention, to refer to, to make mention of *or* reference to ♦ **ich möchte nur kurz erwähnt haben, daß ...** I would just briefly like to mention that ...; **davon hat er nichts erwähnt, das hat er mit keinem Wort erwähnt** he did not mention *or* refer to it at all, he made no mention of *or* reference to it; **beiläufig** *or* **nebenbei ~** to mention in passing, to make a passing reference to.

erwähnenswert *adj* worth mentioning.

Erwähnung *f* mention (*gen* of), reference (*gen* to) ♦ **~ finden** (*form*) to be mentioned, to be referred to.

erwandern* *vt* **er hat sich** (*dat*) **die ganze Insel erwandert** he's walked all over the island and knows it inside out.

erwärmen* [1] *vt* to warm, to heat; (*fig*) to warm.
[2] *vr* to warm up ♦ **sich für jdn/etw ~** (*fig*) to take to sb/sth; **ich kann mich für Goethe/Geometrie nicht ~** Goethe/geometry leaves me cold.

erwarten* *vt Gäste, Ereignis* to expect ♦ **etw von jdm/etw ~** to expect sth from *or* of sb/sth; **ein Kind** *or* **Baby ~** to be expecting a child *or* baby; **das war zu ~** that was to be expected; **etw sehnsüchtig ~** to long for sth; **sie kann den Sommer kaum noch ~** she can hardly wait for the summer, she's really looking forward to the summer; **sie kann es kaum ~, daß Vater heimkommt** she can hardly wait for father to come home, she's really looking forward to father coming home; **was mich da wohl erwartet?** I wonder what awaits me there; **von ihr ist nicht viel Gutes zu ~** no good can come of her; **da hast du (et)was zu ~!** (*iro*) then you'll have something to think about!; **es steht zu ~, daß ...** (*form*) it is to be expected that ...; **über E~** beyond expectation; *siehe* **wider**.

Erwartung *f* expectation; (*Spannung, Ungeduld*) anticipation ♦ **in ~ Ihrer baldigen Antwort** (*form*) in anticipation of *or* looking forward to *or* awaiting your early reply; **zu großen ~en berechtigen** to show great promise; **den ~en entsprechen** to come up to expectations; (*Voraussetzung erfüllen*) to meet the requirements.

Erwartungs-: ~druck *m* **unter ~druck sein** *or* **stehen** to be under pressure as a result of people's expectations; **e~gemäß** *adv* as expected; **~haltung** *f* expectations *pl*; **~horizont** *m* level of expectations; **e~voll** *adj* expectant.

erwecken* *vt* **(a)** (*liter: aus Schlaf, Lethargie*) to wake, to rouse; (*Bibl: vom Tode*) to raise (from the dead) ♦ **etw zu neuem Leben ~** to resurrect *or* revive sth.
(b) (*fig*) *Freude, Begeisterung etc* to arouse; *Hoffnungen, Zweifel* to raise; *Erinnerungen* to bring back ♦ **(bei jdm) den Eindruck ~, als ob ...** to give (sb) the impression that ...

Erweckung *f, no pl* (*Bibl: vom Tode*) resurrection, raising (from the dead); (*Rel*) revival; (*fig*) arousal, awakening.

Erweckungsbewegung *f* (*Rel*) revivalist movement, revivalism.

erwehren* *vr* (*+gen*) (*geh*) to ward *or* fend off ♦ **er konnte sich kaum der Tränen ~** he could hardly keep *or* hold back his tears; *siehe* **Eindruck**.

erweichen* *vt* to soften; (*fig: überreden auch*) to move ♦ **jds Herz ~** to touch sb's heart; **sich (durch Bitten) nicht ~ lassen** to be unmoved (by entreaties), not to give in *or* yield (to entreaties).

Erweis *m* **-es, -e** (*form*) proof.

erweisen* *irreg* [1] *vt* **(a)** (*nachweisen*) to prove ♦ **eine erwiesene Tatsache** a proven fact; **es ist noch nicht erwiesen** it has not been proved yet.
(b) (*zuteil werden lassen*) to show ♦ **jdm einen Gefallen/Dienst ~** to do sb a favour/service; **jdm Achtung ~** to pay respect to sb; **jdm Gutes ~** to be good to sb; **wir danken für die erwiesene Anteilnahme** we thank you for the sympathy you have shown.
[2] *vr* **sich als etw ~** to prove to be sth, to turn out to be sth; **sich als zuverlässig ~** to prove to be reliable, to prove oneself reliable; **sich jdm gegenüber dankbar ~** to show *or* prove one's gratitude to sb, to show *or* prove oneself grateful to sb; **es hat sich erwiesen, daß ...** it turned out that ...

erweislich *adj* (*geh*) provable, demonstrable ♦ **das ist ~ falsch** that is demonstrably false.

erweiterbar *adj* (*auch Comput*) expandable.

erweitern* *vtr* to widen, to enlarge; *Absatzgebiet auch, Geschäft, Abteilung* to expand; *Kleid* to let out; (*Med*) to dilate; (*Math*) *Bruch* to reduce to the lowest common denominator; (*fig*) *Interessen, Kenntnisse, Horizont* to broaden; *Macht* to extend ♦ **im erweiterten Sinn** in an extended sense.

Erweiterung *f siehe vtr* widening, enlargement; expansion; letting out; dilation; reduction to the lowest common denominator; broadening; extension.

Erweiterungsbau *m* extension.

Erwerb *m* **-(e)s, -e** **(a)** *no pl* acquisition; (*Kauf*) purchase ♦ **beim ~ eines Autos** when buying a car. **(b)** (*Brot~, Beruf*) living; (*Verdienst, Lohn*) earnings *pl*, income ♦ **einem ~ nachgehen** to follow a profession.

erwerben* *vt irreg* to acquire; *Achtung, Ehre, Vertrauen* to earn, to gain, to win; *Pokal* to win; (*Sport*) *Titel* to win, to gain; (*käuflich*) to purchase ♦ **sich** (*dat*) **etw ~** to acquire *etc* sth; **er hat sich** (*dat*) **große Verdienste um die Firma erworben** he has done great service for the firm.

Erwerbermodell *nt scheme by which tax relief is obtained on investment in property.*

Erwerbs-: ~arbeit *f* gainful employment; **e~fähig** *adj* (*form*) capable of gainful employment; **~fähige(r)** *mf* (*form*) person capable of gainful employment; **~fähigkeit** *f* (*form*) fitness for work; **e~gemindert** *adj* suffering a reduction in (one's) earning capacity; **~kampf** *m* rat-race; **~leben** *nt* working life; **e~los** *adj siehe* **arbeitslos**; **~minderung** *f* reduction in (one's) earning capacity; **~quelle** *f* source of income; **e~tätig** *adj* (gainfully) employed; **~tätigkeit** *f* gainful employment; **e~unfähig** *adj* unable to work, incapacitated; **~unfähigkeit** *f* inability to work, incapacitation; **~zweig** *m* line of business.

Erwerbung *f* acquisition.

erwidern* *vt* **(a)** (*antworten*) to reply (*auf +acc* to); (*schroff*) to retort ♦ **darauf konnte er nichts ~** he couldn't answer that, he had no answer to that; **auf meine Frage erwiderte sie, daß ...** in reply *or* answer to my question, she said that ...
(b) (*entgegnen, entgelten*) *Besuch, Grüße, Komplimente, Gefühle* to return, to reciprocate; *Blick*, (*Mil*) *Feuer* to return.

Erwiderung *f* **(a)** (*Antwort*) reply, answer; (*schroff*) retort, rejoinder ♦ **in ~ Ihres Schreibens vom ...** (*form*) in reply *or* answer to your letter of the ... **(b)** return, reciprocation; (*von Gefühlen*) reciprocation; (*Mil: des Feuers*) return ♦ **ihre Liebe fand bei ihm keine ~** he did not return her love.

erwiesen *ptp of* **erweisen**.

erwiesenermaßen *adv* as has been proved *or* shown ♦ **er hat dich ~ betrogen** it has been proved *or* shown that he has deceived you; **der Angeklagte ist ~ schuldig** the accused has been proved guilty.

erwirken* *vt* (*form*) to obtain.

erwirtschaften* *vt* to make *or* obtain through good *or* careful management ♦ **Gewinne ~** to make profits; **seine Frau hat ein kleines Auto erwirtschaftet** his wife has bought a little car with her savings.

erwischen* *vt* (*inf*) (*erreichen, ertappen*) to catch; (*ergattern*) to get (hold of) ♦ **jdn beim Stehlen ~** to catch sb stealing; **du darfst dich nicht ~ lassen** you mustn't get caught; **ihn hat's erwischt!** (*verliebt*) he's got it bad (*inf*); (*krank*) he's got it, he's caught it; (*gestorben*) he's had it (*inf*); **die Kugel/der Hund hat ihn am Bein erwischt** the bullet got *or* caught/the dog got him in the leg.

erworben *adj* acquired (*auch Med, Jur*).

erwünscht *adj Wirkung etc* desired; *Eigenschaft, Kenntnisse* desirable; (*willkommen*) *Gelegenheit, Anwesenheit* welcome ♦ **persönliche Vorstellung ~** applications should be made in person; **du bist hier nicht ~!** you're not welcome *or* wanted here!

erwürgen* *vt* to strangle, to throttle.

Erz *nt* **-es, -e** ore; (*Bronze*) bronze.

Erz- *in cpds* (*Geol*) mineral, ore; (*Rang bezeichnend*) arch-; **~ader** *f* mineral vein, vein of ore.

Erzähl- (*Liter*): **~absicht** *f* narrative intent; **~ebene** *f* narrative level.

erzählen* [1] *vt* (a) *Geschichte, Witz etc* to tell; (*berichten*) *Traum, Vorfall, Erlebnis etc auch* to relate, to recount, to give an account of ♦ **er hat seinen Traum/den Vorfall erzählt** he told (*us etc*) about his dream/the incident; **jdm etw ~** to tell sth to sb; **man erzählt sich, daß ...** people say *or* it is said that ...; **erzähl mal, was/wie ...** tell me/us what/how ...; **Mutti, erzähl mir was** tell me a story, mummy; **erzähl mal was** (*inf*) say something; **wem ~ Sie das!** (*inf*) you're telling me!; **das kannst du einem anderen ~** (*inf*) pull the other one (*inf*), tell that to the marines (*inf*); **mir kannst du viel** *or* **nichts ~** (*inf*) don't give *or* tell me that! (*inf*); **davon kann ich etwas ~!** (*inf*) I can tell you a thing or two about it; **dem werd' ich was ~!** (*inf*) I'll have something to say to him, I'll give him a piece of my mind (*inf*); *siehe* **Großmutter**.
(b) (*Liter*) to narrate ♦ **~de Dichtung** narrative fiction; **Grundformen des E~s** basic forms of narrative; **erzählte Zeit** narrated time.
[2] *vi* (a) to tell (*von* about, of *liter*) ♦ **er kann gut ~** he tells good stories, he's a good story-teller; **er hat die ganze Nacht erzählt** he told stories all night.
(b) (*Liter*) to narrate.

erzählenswert *adj* worth telling.

Erzähler(in *f*) *m* **-s, -** narrator (*auch Liter*); (*Geschichten~*) story-teller; (*Schriftsteller*) narrative writer.

erzählerisch *adj* narrative.

Erzählerstandpunkt *m* (*Liter*) point of view of the narrator.

Erzählformen *pl* (*Liter*) narrative forms *pl*.

Erzählung *f* (*Liter*) story, tale; (*das Erzählen*) narration, relation; (*Bericht, Schilderung*) account ♦ **in Form einer ~** in narrative form; **Dialog und ~ wechseln sich ab** dialogue alternates with narrative.

Erzählzeit *f* (*Liter*) narrative time.

Erz-: **~bergbau** *m* ore mining; **~bischof** *m* archbishop; **e~bischöflich** *adj attr* archiepiscopal; **~bistum** *nt* archbishopric; **~bösewicht** *m* arrant rogue (*old*), arch-villain; **~diözese** *f* archbishopric; **e~dumm** *adj* (*inf*) extremely stupid.

erzeigen* (*geh*) *vr* **sich dankbar ~** to show *or* prove oneself grateful.

erzen *adj* (*liter*) bronze.

Erz|engel *m* archangel.

erzeugen* *vt* (*Chem, Elec, Phys*) to generate, to produce; (*Comm*) *Produkt* to produce, to manufacture; *Wein, Butter etc* to produce; (*rare*) *Kinder* to beget (*old*); (*fig: bewirken*) to cause, to engender, to give rise to ♦ **Mißtrauen/Angst** *etc* **in** *or* **bei jdm ~** to give rise to *or* produce *or* engender a sense of mistrust/fear *etc* in sb; **der Autor versteht es, Spannung zu ~** the author knows how to create *or* generate tension.

Erzeuger *m* **-s, -** (*form: Vater*) begetter (*old*), progenitor (*form*); (*Comm*) producer, manufacturer; (*von Naturprodukten*) producer.

Erzeuger-: **~land** *nt* country of origin; **~preis** *m* manufacturer's price.

Erzeugnis *nt* product; (*Industrieprodukt auch*) manufacture (*esp Comm*); (*Agr*) produce *no indef art, no pl*; (*fig: geistiges, künstlerisches auch*) creation ♦ **deutsches ~** made in Germany; **~ seiner Phantasie** figment of his imagination.

Erzeugung *f, no pl* (*Chem, Elec, Phys*) generation, production; (*von Waren*) manufacture, production; (*eines Kindes*) procreation (*form*); (*geistige, künstlerische*) creation.

Erzeugungsgrammatik *f* (*Ling*) generative grammar.

Erz-: **e~faul** *adj* bone-idle; **~feind** *m* arch-enemy; (*Theologie auch*) arch-fiend; **~gauner** *m* (*inf*) cunning *or* sly rascal (*inf*); **~gießer** *m* brass-founder; **~gießerei** *f* brass-foundry; **~grube** *f* ore mine; **e~haltig** *adj* ore-bearing, metalliferous (*spec*); **~herzog** *m* archduke; **~herzogin** *f* archduchess; **e~herzoglich** *adj attr* archducal; **~herzogtum** *nt* archduchy; **~hütte** *f* smelting works *sing or pl*.

erziehbar *adj Kind* educable; *Tier* trainable ♦ **schwer ~** *Kind* difficult; *Hund* difficult to train; **das Kind ist schwer ~** he/she is a problem *or* a difficult child; **ein Heim für schwer ~e Kinder** a home for problem *or* difficult children.

erziehen* *vt irreg Kind* to bring up; *Tier, Körper, Gehör* to train; (*ausbilden*) to educate ♦ **ein Tier/ein Kind zur Sauberkeit** *etc* **~** to train an animal/to teach *or* bring up a child to be clean *etc*; **jdn zu einem tüchtigen Menschen ~** to bring sb up to be a fine, upstanding person; **ein gut/schlecht erzogenes Kind** a well-/badly-brought-up child, a well-/ill-bred child.

Erzieher *m* **-s, -** educator, teacher; (*in Kindergarten*) nursery school teacher (*Privatlehrer*) tutor ♦ **der Vater war ein strenger ~** the father brought his children up strictly.

Erzieherin *f* educator, teacher; (*in Kindergarten*) nursery school teacher (*Gouvernante*) governess.

erzieherisch *adj* educational ♦ **ein Vater mit wenig ~em Können** a father with little skill in bringing up children; **verschiedene ~e Methoden** different ways of bringing up children; **das ist ~ falsch** that is no way to bring up children.

Erziehung *f, no pl* upbringing; (*Ausbildung*) education; (*das Erziehen*) bringing up; (*von Tieren, Körper, Gehör*) training; (*Manieren*) upbringing, (good) breeding ♦ **die ~ zu(r) Höflichkeit** teaching (sb) good manners *or* politeness; (*durch Eltern auch*) bringing (sb) up to be polite *or* well-mannered.

Erziehungs-: **~anstalt** *f* approved school, borstal (*Brit*), reformatory (*US*); **~beihilfe** *f* (*dated*) *siehe* **Ausbildungsbeihilfe**; **~beratung** *f* educational guidance *or* counselling; **e~berechtigt** *adj* having parental authority; **~berechtigte(r)** *mf* parent or (legal) guardian; **~geld** *nt* ≃ child benefit; **~gewalt** *f* parental authority; **~heim** *nt siehe* **~anstalt**; **~methode** *f* educational method; **~mittel** *nt* aid to education; **~urlaub** *m* paid leave for new parent; **~wesen** *nt* educational system; **~wissenschaft** *f* educational science; **~wissenschaftler** *m* educationalist.

erzielen* *vt Erfolg, Ergebnis* to achieve, to attain, to obtain; *Kompromiß, Einigung* to reach, to arrive at; *Geschwindigkeit* to reach; *Gewinn* to make, to realize; *Preis* (*Mensch*) to secure; (*Gegenstand*) to fetch; (*Sport*) *Tor, Punkte* to score; *Rekord* to set ♦ **was willst du damit ~?** what do you hope to achieve by that?

erzittern* *vi aux sein* (*liter*) to tremble, to shake, to quake.

Erz-: **e~konservativ** *adj* ultraconservative; (*Pol auch*) dyed-in-the-wool conservative; **~lager** *nt* ore deposit; **~lügner** *m* (*inf*) inveterate *or* unmitigated liar; **~reaktionär** *m* ultrareactionary.

erzürnen* (*geh*) [1] *vt* to anger, to incense.
[2] *vr* to become *or* grow angry (*über +acc* about).

Erzvater *m* (*Bibl*) patriarch; (*fig*) forefather.

erzwingen* *vt irreg* to force; (*gerichtlich*) to enforce ♦ **etw von jdm ~** to force sth from *or* out of sb; **sie erzwangen den Zutritt zur Wohnung mit Gewalt** they forced entry into the flat.

es[1] *pers pron gen* **seiner**, *dat* **ihm**, *acc* **es** (a) (*auf Dinge bezogen*) it; (*auf männliches Wesen bezogen*) (*nom*) he; (*acc*) him; (*auf weibliches Wesen bezogen*) (*nom*) she; (*acc*) her.
(b) (*auf vorangehende Substantive, Adjektive bezüglich*) **wer ist da? — ich bin ~** who's there? — it's me *or* I (*form*); **sie ist klug, er ist ~ auch** she is clever, so is he; **ich höre jemanden klopfen, ~ sind die Kinder** I can hear somebody knocking, it's the children; **wer ist die Dame? — ~ ist meine Frau** who's the lady? — it's *or* she's my wife.
(c) (*auf vorangehenden Satzinhalt bezüglich*) **das Glas wurde zerbrochen, keiner will ~ getan haben** the glass had been broken, but nobody will admit to doing it; **alle dachten, daß das ungerecht war, aber niemand sagte ~** everyone thought it was unjust, but nobody said so.
(d) (*rein formales Subjekt*) **~ ist kalt/8 Uhr/Sonntag** it's cold/8 o'clock/Sunday; **~ friert mich** I am cold; **~ freut mich, daß ...** I am pleased *or* glad that ...; **~ sei denn, daß ...** unless ...
(e) (*rein formales Objekt*) **ich halte ~ für richtig, daß ...** I think it (is) right that ...; **ich hoffe ~** I hope so; **ich habe ~ satt, zu** (*+infin*), **ich bin ~ müde, zu** (*+infin*) I've had enough of (*+prp*), I'm tired of (*+prp*).
(f) (*bei unpersönlichem Gebrauch des Verbs*) **~ gefällt mir** I like it; **~ klopft** there's a knock (at the door); **~ regnet** it's raining; **~ sich** (*dat*) **schön machen** to have a good time; **bei dem Licht liest ~ sich gut** this light is good for reading; **~ sitzt sich bequem hier** it's comfortable sitting here; **~ darf geraucht werden** smoking is permitted; **~ wurde gesagt, daß ...** it was said that ...; **~ wurde getanzt** there was dancing; **er läßt ~ nicht zu, daß ich länger bleibe** he won't allow me to stay any longer.
(g) (*Einleitewort mit folgendem Subjekt*) **~ geschah ein Unglück** there was an accident; **~ gibt viel Arbeit** there's a lot of work; **~ gibt viele Leute, die ...** there are a lot of people who ...; **~ kamen viele Leute** a lot of people came; **~ lebe der König!** long live the king!; **~ meldete sich niemand** nobody replied; **~ war einmal eine Königin** once upon a time there was a queen.

es[2] *nt* **-, -** (*Mus*) E flat minor.

Es *nt* **-, -** (a) (*Mus: Dur*) E flat. (b) (*Psych*) id, Id.

Escape-Taste [ɛsˈkeːp-] *f* (*Comput*) escape key.

Eschatologie *f* **-** (*Rel*) eschatology.

Esche *f* **-, -n** ash-tree.

Eschenholz *nt* ash.

Esel *m* **-s, -** donkey, ass (*old, esp Bibl*); (*inf: Dummkopf*) (silly) ass ♦ **du alter ~!** you are an ass (*inf*) *or* a fool; **ich ~!** I am an ass *or* a fool!, silly (old) me!; **störrisch wie ein ~** as stubborn as a mule; **der ~ nennt sich selbst zuerst** it's rude to put yourself first; **ein ~ schimpft den andern Langohr** (*prov*) (it's a case of) the pot calling the kettle black (*prov*); **wenn es dem ~ zu wohl wird, geht er aufs Eis (tanzen)** (*Prov*) complacency makes one *or* you reckless.

Eselei *f* (*inf*) stupidity; (*Streich*) silly prank.

Eselin *f* she-ass.

Esels-: **~brücke** *f* (*Gedächtnishilfe*) mnemonic, aide-mémoire; (*gereimt*) jingle; (*Sch sl: Klatsche*) crib (*inf*), pony (*US*); **~ohr** *nt* (*fig*) dog-ear, turned-down corner; **ein Buch mit ~ohren** a dog-eared book.

Eskalation *f* escalation.

eskalieren* *vti* (*vi: aux sein*) to escalate.

Eskalierung *f* escalation.

Eskamotage [ɛskamoˈtaːʒə] *f* **-, -n** sleight of hand.

eskamotieren* *vt* to spirit *or* conjure away.

Eskapade *f* (*von Pferd*) caper; (*fig*) escapade.

Eskapismus *m* (*Psych, Sociol*) escapism.

Eskimo *m* **-s, -s** Eskimo.

eskimotieren* *vi* (*Sport*) to roll.

eskomptieren* *vt* (*Fin*) (*diskontieren*) to discount; (*St Ex*) to preempt.

Eskorte *f* **-, -n** (*Mil*) escort.

eskortieren* *vt* to escort.

Esoterik *f* esotericism.

Esoteriker(in *f*) *m* **-s, -** esoteric.

esoterisch *adj* esoteric.

Espe *f* **-, -n** aspen.

Espenlaub *nt* aspen leaves *pl* ♦ **zittern wie ~** to shake like a leaf.

Esperanto *nt* **-s,** *no pl* Esperanto.

Espresso[1] *m* **-(s), -s** *or* **Espressi** espresso.

Espresso[2] *nt* **-(s), -(s), Espressobar** *f* (*Café*) coffee *or* espresso bar.

Espressomaschine *f* espresso machine.

Esprit [ɛsˈpriː] *m* **-s,** *no pl* wit ♦ **ein Mann von ~** a wit, a witty man.

⚠ **Eß|apfel** *m* eating apple, eater.

Essay [ˈɛse, ɛˈseː] *m or nt* **-s, -s** (*Liter*) essay.

⚠: Informationen zur Rechtschreibreform im Anhang

Essayist(in *f*) [ɛse'ɪst] *m* (*Liter*) essayist.
essayistisch [ɛse'ɪstɪʃ] *adj* (*Liter*) *Roman* essayistic ◆ **das ~e Werk Thomas Manns** the essays of Thomas Mann.
⚠ **Eß-: e~bar** *adj* edible, eatable; *Pilz* edible; **habt ihr irgend etwas ~bares im Haus?** have you got anything to eat in the house?; **nicht e~bar** inedible, uneatable; **~besteck** *nt* knife, fork and spoon, eating irons *pl* (*hum*).
Esse *f* -, -**n** (*dial: Schornstein*) chimney; (*Schmiede~*) hearth.
essen *pret* **aß**, *ptp* **gegessen** *vti* to eat ◆ **gut/schlecht ~** (*Appetit haben*) to have a good/poor appetite; **in dem Restaurant kann man gut ~** that's a good restaurant; **die Franzosen ~ gut** the French eat well, French food is good; **da ißt es sich gut** the food is good there, you can eat well there, they do good food there; **warm/kalt ~** to have a hot/cold meal; **tüchtig** *or* **ordentlich ~** to eat well *or* properly; **iß mal tüchtig!** tuck in!, eat up!; **sich satt ~** to eat one's fill; **sich krank ~** to overeat, to overindulge (in food); **jdn arm ~** to eat sb out of house and home; **den Teller leer ~** to eat everything up, to empty one's plate; **~ Sie gern Äpfel?** do you like apples?; **wer hat davon/von meinem Teller gegessen?** who has been eating that/who's been eating off my plate?; **gerade ~, beim E~ sein** to be in the middle of eating *or* a meal; **~ gehen** (*auswärts*) to eat out, to go out to eat; **wann gehst du ~?** when are you going to eat?; (*normalerweise*) when do you eat?; **ich bin ~** (*inf*) I've gone to eat; **nach dem Kino gingen wir noch ~** after the cinema we went for a meal; **das Thema ist schon lange/noch nicht gegessen** (*fig inf*) the subject is dead and buried/still alive; **selber ~ macht fett** (*prov*) I'm all right, Jack (*prov*); **E~ und Trinken hält Leib und Seele zusammen** (*prov*) food and drink keep body and soul together; *siehe* **heiß, Tisch.**
Essen *nt* -**s**, - (*Mahlzeit*) meal; (*Nahrung*) food; (*Küche*) cooking; (*Fest~*) luncheon; dinner ◆ **bleib doch zum ~** stay for lunch/supper, stay for a meal; **das ~ kochen** *or* **machen** (*inf*) to cook *or* get the meal; **jdn zum ~ einladen** to invite sb for a meal; **(bitte) zum ~** lunch/dinner is ready; *siehe* **ruhen.**
Essen(s)-: ~ausgabe *f* serving of meals; (*Stelle*) serving counter; **ab 12[30] ist in der Kantine ~ausgabe** meals are served in the canteen from 12.30; **~marke** *f* meal voucher; **~zeit** *f* mealtime; **bei uns ist um 12[00] ~zeit** we have lunch at 12; **die Kinder müssen abends zur ~zeit zu Hause sein** the children have to be at home in time for their evening meal; ⚠**~zuschuß** *m* meal subsidy.
⚠ **essentiell** [ɛsɛn'tsiɛl] *adj* (*Philos*) essential.
Essenz *f* **(a)** *no pl* (*Philos*) essence. **(b)** (*Cook etc*) essence.
Esser *m* -**s**, - diner; *pl auch* people eating ◆ **ein guter** *or* **starker/schlechter ~ sein** to be a good *or* great/poor eater; **auf einen ~ mehr kommt es nicht an** one more person won't make any difference.
Esserei *f* (*inf*) guzzling (*inf*); (*Mahl*) blow-out (*inf*), nosh-up (*Brit sl*) ◆ **die ~ im Stehen ist nicht gut** it's not good to eat standing up.
⚠ **Eß-: ~geschirr** *nt* dinner service; (*Mil*) mess tin; **~gewohnheiten** *pl* eating habits *pl.*
Essig *m* -**s**, -**e** vinegar ◆ **damit ist es ~** (*inf*) it's all off, it's up the spout (*Brit sl*).
Essig-: ~äther *m siehe* **~ester**; **~essenz** *f* vinegar concentrate; **~ester** *m* ethyl acetate; **~gurke** *f* (pickled) gherkin; **e~sauer** *adj* (*Chem*) acetic; **e~saure Tonerde** aluminium acetate; **~säure** *f* acetic acid.
⚠ **Eß-: ~kastanie** *f* sweet chestnut; **~kultur** *f* gastronomic culture; **~löffel** *m* soup/dessert spoon; (*in Rezept*) tablespoon; **e~löffelweise** *adv* in tablespoonfuls; (*inf*) by the spoonful; **~lust** *f* appetite; **~stäbchen** *pl* chopsticks *pl.*
⚠ **eßt** *imper pl of* **essen.**
⚠ **Eß-: ~tisch** *m* dining table; **~unlust** *f* loss of appetite; **~waren** *pl* food, provisions *pl*; **~zimmer** *nt* dining room; **~zwang** *m* (*Psych*) compulsive eating; **an ~zwang leiden** to be a compulsive eater.
Establishment [ɪs'tæblɪʃmənt] *nt* -**s**, -**s** (*Sociol, Press*) establishment.
Este *m* -**n**, -**n**, **Estin** *f* Est(h)onian.
Ester *m* -**s**, - (*Chem*) ester.
Estland *nt* Est(h)onia.
estländisch *adj* Est(h)onian.
Estnisch(e) *nt decl as adj* Est(h)onian; *siehe auch* **Deutsch(e).**
Estrade *f* (*esp DDR*) **(a)** podium. **(b)** (*auch* **~nkonzert**) *concert of light music etc, especially performed out of doors.*
Estragon *m* -**s**, *no pl* tarragon.
Estrich *m* -**s**, -**e** **(a)** stone/clay *etc* floor. **(b)** (*Sw: Dachboden*) attic.
Eszett *nt* -, - eszett, ß.
etablieren* [1] *vt* (*dated*) to establish.
[2] *vr* to establish oneself; (*als Geschäftsmann auch*) to set up.
etabliert *adj* established ◆ **er gehört jetzt zu den E~en** he is now part of the establishment; **die ~e Oberschicht** the upper echelons of the establishment.
Etablissement [etablɪsə'mã:] *nt* -**s**, -**s** establishment.
Etage [e'ta:ʒə] *f* -, -**n** floor ◆ **in** *or* **auf der 2. ~** on the 2nd *or* 3rd (*US*) floor; **er bewohnt im 5. Stock die ganze ~** he lives in *or* occupies the whole of the 5th *or* 6th (*US*) floor.
Etagen-: ~bad *nt* (*im Hotel*) shared bath; **~bett** *nt* bunk bed; **~dusche** *f* (*im Hotel*) shared shower; **~heizung** *f heating system which covers one floor of a building*; **~kellner** *m* waiter on room-service; **~wohnung** *f flat occupying the whole of one floor of a building.*
Etagere [eta'ʒɛ:rə] *f* -, -**n** (*dated*) étagère.
Etappe *f* -, -**n** **(a)** (*Abschnitt, Stufe, beim Radrennen*) stage; (*einer Strecke auch*) leg. **(b)** (*Mil*) communications zone ◆ **in der ~ liegen/sein** to be behind the lines.
Etappen-: ~hengst *m*, **~schwein** *nt* (*Mil sl*) base wallah (*Mil sl*); **~sieg** *m* (*Sport*) stage-win; (*fig*) partial victory; **~sieger** *m* (*Sport*) stage-winner; **e~weise** [1] *adj* step-by-step, stage-by-stage; [2] *adv* step by step, stage by stage.
Etat [e'ta:] *m* -**s**, -**s** budget.
Etat-: ~jahr *nt* financial year; **e~mäßig** *adj* (*Admin*) budgetary; **das Geld wurde e~mäßig ausgegeben** the money was spent as budgeted; **nicht e~mäßig erfaßt** not in the budget, not budgeted for; **~posten** *m* item in the budget, budgetary item.
etc *abbr of* **et cetera** [ɛt'tse:tera] etc, et cetera.
etc pp [ɛt'tse:tera'pe:'pe :] *adv* (*hum*) and so on and so forth.
etepetete [e:təpe'te:tə] *adj pred* (*inf*) fussy, finicky (*inf*), pernickety (*inf*).
Eternit ® *m or nt* -**s**, *no pl* fibre cement.
Ethan *nt* -**s** (*Chem*) ethane.
Ethik *f* ethics *pl* (*als Fach sing*) ◆ **die ~ Kants** Kantian ethics; **die christliche ~** the Christian ethic, Christian ethics.
Ethiker *m* -**s**, - moral philosopher.
Ethikunterricht *m* (*Sch*) (teaching of) ethics.
ethisch *adj* ethical.
ethnisch *adj* ethnic.
⚠ **Ethnograph(in** *f*) *m* ethnographer.
⚠ **Ethnographie** *f* ethnography.
Ethnologe *m*, **Ethnologin** *f* ethnologist.
Ethnologie *f* ethnology.
Ethologe *m*, **Ethologin** *f* ethologist.
Ethologie *f* ethology.
Ethos ['e:tɔs] *nt* -, *no pl* ethos; (*Berufs~*) professional ethics *pl.*
Etikett *nt* -**(e)s**, -**e** (*lit, fig*) label.
Etikette *f* **(a)** etiquette ◆ **gegen die ~ (bei Hofe) verstoßen** to offend against (court) etiquette, to commit a breach of (court) etiquette. **(b)** (*Aus: Etikett*) label.
Etikettenschwindel *m* (*Pol*) juggling with names ◆ **es ist reinster ~, wenn** ... it is just playing *or* juggling with names if ...
etikettieren* *vt* (*lit, fig*) to label.
etlichemal *adv* quite a few times.
etliche(r, s) *indef pron* **(a)** *sing attr* quite a lot of ◆ **nachdem ~ Zeit verstrichen war** after quite some time.
(b) **etliche** *pl* (*substantivisch*) quite a few, several people/things; (*attr*) several, quite a few.
(c) **~s** *sing* (*substantivisch*) quite a lot; **ich habe ~s daran auszusetzen, aber im großen und ganzen** ... I have one or two objections to make but by and large ...; **um ~s älter als ich** quite a lot *or* considerably older than me.
Etrurien [-iən] *nt* -**s** (*Hist*) Etruria.
Etrusker(in *f*) *m* -**s**, - Etruscan.
etruskisch *adj* Etruscan.
Etsch *f* - Adige.
Etüde *f* -, -**n** (*Mus*) étude.
Etui [ɛt'vi:, e'tyi:] *nt* -**s**, -**s** case.
Etuikleid *nt* box dress.
etwa *adv* **(a)** (*ungefähr, annähernd*) about, approximately ◆ **so ~, ~ so** roughly *or* more or less like this; **wann ~ ...?** about *or* approximately *or* roughly when ...?
(b) (*zum Beispiel*) for instance ◆ **wenn man ~ behauptet, daß** ... for instance if one maintains that ...
(c) (*entrüstet, erstaunt*) **hast du ~ schon wieder kein Geld dabei?** don't tell me *or* you don't mean to say you haven't got any money again!; **soll das ~ heißen, daß** ... is that supposed to mean ...?; **willst du ~ schon gehen?** (surely) you don't want to go already!
(d) (*zur Bestätigung*) **Sie kommen doch, oder ~ nicht?** you are coming, aren't you?; **das haben Sie wohl nicht mit Absicht gesagt, oder ~ doch?** surely you didn't say that on purpose, you didn't say that on purpose — or did you?; **sind Sie ~ nicht einverstanden?** do you mean to say that you don't agree?; **ist das ~ wahr?** (surely) it's not true!, (surely) it can't be true!; **ist das ~ nicht wahr?** do you mean to say it's not true?
(e) (*in Gegenüberstellung, einschränkend*) **nicht ~, daß** ... (it's) not that ...; **er ist nicht ~ dumm, sondern nur faul** it's not that he's stupid, he's simply lazy; **das hat Fritz getan und nicht ~ sein Bruder** Fritz did it and not his brother; **ich wollte dich nicht ~ beleidigen** I didn't intend to insult you.
etwaig ['ɛtvaɪç, ɛt'va:ɪç] *adj attr* possible ◆ **~e Einwände/Unkosten** any objections/costs arising *or* which might arise; **bei ~en Beschwerden/Schäden** *etc* in the event of (any) complaints/damage *etc*; **eine Liege für ~e Besucher** a campbed for possible visitors *or* in case there should be visitors.
etwas *indef pron* **(a)** (*substantivisch*) something; (*fragend, bedingend auch, verneinend*) anything; (*unbestimmter Teil einer Menge*) some; any ◆ **kannst du mir ~ (davon) leihen?** can you lend me some (of it)?; **ohne ~ zu erwähnen** without saying anything; **~ habe ich doch vergessen** there is something I've forgotten; **~ anderes** something else; **das ist ~ (ganz) anderes** that's something (quite) different; **~ sein** (*inf*) to be somebody (*inf*); **~ werden** (*inf*), **es zu ~ bringen** (*inf*) to make something of oneself, to get somewhere (*inf*); **aus ihm wird nie ~** (*inf*) he'll never become anything; **er kann ~** he's good; **das ist immerhin ~** at least that's something; **sein Wort gilt ~ beim Chef** what he says counts for something with the boss; **hast du ~?** is (there) something wrong *or* the matter (with you)?; **sie hat ~ mit ihm** (*inf*) she's got something going on with him; **das ist sicher, wie nur ~** (*inf*) that's as sure as (sure) can be (*inf*); **er hat ~ vom Schulmeister an sich** he has *or* there is some-

thing of the schoolmaster about him; **da ist ~ (Richtiges) dran** there's something in that; **da ist ~ Wahres dran** there is some truth in that.
(b) (*adjektivisch*) some; (*fragend, bedingend auch*) any ◆ **~ Salz?** some salt?; **kannst du mir vielleicht ~ Geld leihen?** could you possibly lend me some money?; **~ Nettes** something nice; **~ Schöneres habe ich noch nie gesehen** I have never seen anything more beautiful.
(c) (*adverbial*) somewhat, a little.

Etwas *nt -, no pl* something ◆ **das gewisse ~** that certain something; **ein winziges ~** a tiny little thing.

Etymologe *m*, **Etymologin** *f* etymologist.

Etymologie *f* etymology.

etymologisch *adj* etymological.

Et-Zeichen *nt* ampersand.

Etzel *m -s* Attila the Hun.

EU [eːˈ|uː] *f - abbr of* **Europäische Union** EU.

euch *pers pron dat, acc of* **ihr** (*in Briefen:* **E~**) you; (*obs, dial*) thee; (*dat auch*) to/ for you; to/for thee; (*refl*) yourselves ◆ **wie ist das bei ~ (in Frankreich) mit den Ferien?** what are your holidays like in France?; **ein Freund von ~** a friend of yours; **wascht ~!** wash yourselves; **setzt ~!** sit (yourselves *inf*) down!; **vertragt ~!** stop quarrelling!

Eucharistie *f* (*Eccl*) Eucharist.

eucharistisch *adj Kongreß* Eucharistic.

euer [1] *poss pron* **(a)** (*adjektivisch*) (*in Briefen:* **E~**) your ◆ **E~** (*Briefschluß*) yours; (*obs, dial*) thy; **viele Grüße, E~ Hans** best wishes, yours, Hans; **das sind ~e** *or* **eure Bücher** those are your books; **ist das ~ Haus?** is that your house?; **E~** *or* **Eure Gnaden/Exzellenz/Majestät** your Grace/Excellency/Majesty.
(b) (*old: substantivisch*) yours ◆ **behaltet, was ~ ist** keep what is yours.
[2] *pers pron gen of* **ihr** ◆ **wir werden ~ gedenken** we will think of you; **~ beider gemeinsame Zukunft** your common future; **~ aller heimlicher Wunsch** the secret wish of all of you.

euere(r, s) *poss pron siehe* **eure(r, s)**.

euersgleichen *in cpds siehe* **euresgleichen**.

euert- *in cpds siehe* **euret-**.

Eugenik *f* (*Biol*) eugenics *sing*.

eugenisch *adj* (*Biol*) eugenic.

Eukalyptus *m -*, **Eukalypten** (*Baum*) eucalyptus (tree); (*Öl*) eucalyptus oil.

Eukalyptusbonbon *m or nt* eucalyptus sweet (*Brit*) *or* candy (*US*).

Euklid *m -s* Euclid.

euklidisch *adj* Euclidean.

Eule *f -, -n* owl; (*pej: häßliche Frau*) crow ◆ **~n nach Athen tragen** (*prov*) to carry coals to Newcastle (*prov*).

Eulen-: **≈spiegel** *m* **Till ~spiegel** (*lit*) Till Eulenspiegel; **unser Sohn ist ein richtiger ~spiegel** (*fig*) our son is a real scamp (*inf*) *or* rascal (*inf*); **~spiegelei** *f*, **≈spiegelstreich** *m* trick, caper.

Eunuch *m -en, -en* eunuch.

Euphemismus *m* euphemism.

euphemistisch *adj* euphemistic.

Euphorie *f* euphoria.

euphorisch *adj* euphoric.

Euphrat [ˈɔyfrat] *m -(s)* Euphrates.

Eurasien [-iən] *nt -s* Eurasia.

Eurasier(in *f*) [-iɐ, -iərɪn] *m -s, -* Eurasian.

eurasisch *adj* Eurasian.

Euratom *abbr of* **Europäische Atomgemeinschaft** European Atomic Community, Euratom.

eure(r, s) *poss pron* **(a)** (*substantivisch*) yours ◆ **der/die/das ~** (*geh*) yours; **tut ihr das E~** (*geh*) you do your bit; **stets** *or* **immer der E~** (*form*) yours ever; **die E~n** (*geh*) your family, your people; **ihr und die E~n** (*geh: Familie*) you and yours; **der/die E~** (*old: Ehepartner*) your spouse (*old*); **das E~** (*geh: Besitz*) what is yours. **(b)** (*adjektivisch*) *siehe* **euer 1 (a)**.

eurerseits *adv* (*auf eurer Seite*) for your part; (*von eurer Seite*) from *or* on your part ◆ **den Vorschlag habt ihr ~ gemacht** you made the suggestion yourselves.

euresgleichen *pron inv* people like you *or* yourselves; (*pej auch*) the likes of you, your sort.

euret-: **~halben** (*dated*), **~wegen** *adv* (*wegen euch*) because of you, on account of you, on your account; (*euch zuliebe auch*) for your sake; (*um euch*) about you; (*für euch*) on your behalf *or* behalves.

Eur(h)ythmie *f* eurhythmics.

eurige *poss pron* (*old, geh*) **der/die/das ~** yours; **die E~n** your families; **das E~** (*Besitz*) what is yours; **tut ihr das E~** you do your bit.

Euro *m -, -* (*Währung*) euro.

Euro- *in cpds* Euro-; **≈cheque** *m siehe* **~scheck**; **~-City-Zug** [-ˈsɪtɪ-] *m* European Inter-City train; **≈dollar** *m* eurodollar; **~krat** *m -en, -en* (*Press sl*) Eurocrat.

Europa *nt -s* Europe.

Europacup [-kap] *m siehe* **Europapokal**.

Europäer(in *f*) *m -s, -* European.

europäisch *adj* European ◆ **das E~e Parlament** the European Parliament; **E~er Gerichtshof** European Court of Justice; **E~es Währungssystem** European Monetary System; **E~e Wirtschaftsgemeinschaft** European Economic Community, Common Market; **die E~en Gemeinschaften** the European Community.

europäisieren* *vt* to Europeanize.

Europa-: **~meister** *m* (*Sport*) European champion; (*Team, Land*) European champions *pl*; **~meisterschaft** *f* European championship; **~parlament** *nt* European Parliament; ⚠**~paß** *m* European passport; **~pokal** *m* (*Sport*) European cup; **~pokal der Landesmeister** European Champions cup; **~rat** *m* Council of Europe; **~straße** *f* through-route in Europe; **~wahlen** *pl* European elections *pl*; **e~weit** *adj* Europe-wide.

europid *adj Rasse* Caucasian.

Europide *mf -n, -n* Caucasian.

Europium *nt, no pl* (*abbr* **Eu**) europium.

Euro-: **≈scheck** *m* Eurocheque; **≈scheckkarte** *f* Eurocheque card; **~tunnel** *m* (*Kanaltunnel*) Channel Tunnel; **~vision** *f* Eurovision; **~visionssendung** *f* Eurovision broadcast *or* programme.

Eurythmie *f siehe* **Eur(h)ythmie**.

⚠**Eustachische Röhre** *f* (*Anat*) Eustachian tube.

Euter *nt -s, -* udder.

Euthanasie *f* euthanasia.

ev. *abbr of* **evangelisch**.

e.V., E.V. *abbr of* **eingetragener Verein**.

Eva [ˈeːfa, ˈeːva] *f -s* Eve ◆ **sie ist eine echte ~** (*hum*) she is the archetypal woman.

evakuieren* [evakuˈiːrən] *vt* to evacuate.

Evakuierte(r) [evakuˈiːɐtə] *mf decl as adj* evacuee.

Evakuierung [evakuˈiːrʊŋ] *f* evacuation.

Evangeliar [evaŋgeliˈaːr], **Evangelienbuch** [evaŋˈgeːliən-] *nt* book of the Gospels, Gospel.

Evangelikale(r) [evaŋgeliˈkaːlə] *mf decl as adj* evangelical.

evangelisch [evaŋˈgeːlɪʃ] *adj* Protestant.

Evangelist [evaŋgeˈlɪst] *m* evangelist.

Evangelium [evaŋˈgeːliʊm] *nt* Gospel; (*fig*) gospel ◆ **alles, was er sagt, ist für sie (ein) ~** (*fig*) everything he says is gospel to her.

evaporieren* [evapoˈriːrən] *vi aux sein* to evaporate.

Eva(s)kostüm *nt* (*dated hum*) **im ~** in the altogether (*hum*), in her birthday suit (*hum*).

Evastochter [ˈeːfas-, ˈeːvas-] *f* (*dated hum*) coquette.

Eventual- [evɛntuˈaːl]: **~fall** *m* eventuality; **~haushalt** *m* (*Parl*) emergency *or* contingency budget.

Eventualität [evɛntualiˈtɛːt] *f* eventuality, contingency.

eventuell [evɛntuˈɛl] [1] *adj attr* possible.
[2] *adv* possibly, perhaps ◆ **~ rufe ich Sie später an** I may possibly call you later; **ich komme ~ ein bißchen später** I might (possibly) come a little later.

Evergreen [ˈɛvɐgriːn] *m -s, -s* evergreen.

evident [eviˈdɛnt] *adj* (*geh: offenbar*) obvious, clear.

Evidenz [eviˈdɛnts] *f* **(a)** (*Philos*) evidence. **(b)** (*Aus*) **etw in ~ halten** to keep a current record of sth, to keep sth up-to-date.

Evidenzbüro *nt* (*Aus*) registry.

ev.-luth. *abbr of* **evangelisch-lutherisch** Lutheran Protestant.

Evolution [evoluˈtsioːn] *f* evolution.

evolutionär, evolutionistisch [evolutsio-] *adj* evolutionary.

Evolutionstheorie *f* theory of evolution.

evtl. *abbr of* **eventuell**.

E-Werk [ˈeːvɛrk] *nt abbr of* **Elektrizitätswerk** generating *or* power station.

EWG [eːveːˈgeː] *f - abbr of* **Europäische Wirtschaftsgemeinschaft** EEC, Common Market.

ewig [1] *adj* eternal; *Leben auch* everlasting; *Eis, Schnee* perpetual; (*inf*) *Nörgelei etc auch* never-ending ◆ **der E~e Jude** the Wandering Jew; **das E~e Licht, die E~e Lampe** (*Eccl*) the sanctuary lamp; **in den ~en Frieden** *or* **die ~e Ruhe eingehen** to find eternal peace; **die E~e Stadt** the Eternal City; **(Gott,) der E~e** God, the Eternal; *siehe* **Jagdgründe**.
[2] *adv* for ever, eternally ◆ **auf ~** for ever; **das dauert ja ~ (und drei Tage** *hum*) it goes on for ever (and a day); **das dauert ja ~, bis ...** it'll take ages until ...; **er muß sich ~ beklagen** he's eternally *or* for ever complaining; **es ist ~ schade, daß ...** (*inf*) it's an enormous pity *or* shame that ...; **~ dankbar** eternally grateful; **ich habe Sie ~ lange nicht gesehen** (*inf*) I haven't seen you for absolutely ages *or* for an eternity; *siehe* **immer**.

Ewiggestrige(r) *mf decl as adj* person living in the past; (*gegen alles Neue*) stick in the mud (*inf*).

Ewigkeit *f* eternity; (*der Naturgesetze*) immutability; (*inf*) ages ◆ **in die ~ eingehen** to go to eternal rest; **bis in alle ~** *or* **von ~ zu ~ amen** for ever and ever, amen; **bis in alle ~** for ever, for all eternity (*liter*); **eine ~** *or* **eine halbe ~** (*hum*) **dauern** (*inf*) to last an age *or* an eternity; **es dauert eine ~** *or* **eine halbe ~** (*hum*), **bis ...** it'll take absolutely ages until ...; **ich habe sie seit ~en** *or* **einer ~ nicht gesehen** (*inf*) I've not seen her for ages.

ewiglich (*liter*) [1] *adj attr* eternal, everlasting.
[2] *adv* eternally, for ever, to the end of time (*liter*).

EWR [eːveːˈɛr] *m - abbr of* **Europäischer Wirtschaftsraum** EEA.

EWS [eːveːˈ|ɛs] *nt abbr of* **Europäisches Währungssystem** EMS.

EWU [eːveːˈ|uː] *f abbr of* **Europäische Währungsunion** EMU.

e.Wz. *abbr of* **eingetragenes Warenzeichen**.

ex *adv* (*inf*) **(a)** (*leer*) **(trink) ~!** down the hatch! (*inf*); **etw ~ trinken** to drink sth down in one. **(b)** (*Schluß, vorbei*) (all) over, finished ◆ **~ und hopp** here today, gone tomorrow.

Ex- *in cpds* ex-.

exakt *adj* exact ◆ **eine ~e Wissenschaft** an exact science; **~ arbeiten** to work accurately.

Exaktheit *f* exactness, precision.

exaltiert *adj* exaggerated, effusive.

⚠: Informationen zur Rechtschreibreform im Anhang

Exaltiertheit *f* exaggeratedness, effusiveness.
Examen *nt* **-s, -** *or* **Examina** exam, examination; (*Univ*) final examinations, finals *pl* ◆ **~ machen** to do *or* take one's exams *or* finals; **das ~ mit Eins machen** to get top marks in an exam; (*Univ*) ≃ to get a First; **das mündliche ~** oral examination; (*Univ*) viva (voce).
Examens-: ~angst *f* exam nerves *pl*; **~arbeit** *f* dissertation; **~kandidat** *m* candidate (for an examination), examinee.
examinieren* *vt* (*geh*) to examine ◆ **jdn über etw** (*acc*) **~** (*lit, fig*) to question sb about sth.
Exegese *f* **-, -n** exegesis.
Exeget *m* **-en, -en** exegete.
exegetisch *adj* exegetic(al).
exekutieren* *vt* (*form*) to execute ◆ **jdn ~** (*Aus: pfänden*) to seize *or* impound sb's possessions.
Exekution *f* execution; (*Aus: Pfändung*) seizing, impounding.
Exekutionskommando *nt* firing squad.
exekutiv *adj* executive.
⚠ **Exekutiv|ausschuß** *m* executive committee.
Exekutive [-'ti:və], **Exekutivgewalt** *f* executive; (*Aus*) forces *pl* of law and order.
Exekutor *m* (*Aus*) bailiff.
Exempel *nt* **-s, -** (*geh*) example; (*dated Math: Rechen~*) example (*dated*) ◆ **die Probe aufs ~ machen** to put it to the test; *siehe* **statuieren.**
Exemplar *nt* **-s, -e** specimen; (*Buch~, Zeitschriften~*) copy.
exemplarisch *adj* exemplary ◆ **~es Lehren/Lernen** teaching/learning by example; **etw ~ durcharbeiten** to work through sth as an example; **jdn ~ bestrafen** to punish sb as an example (to others); **das Urteil wurde ~ für alle folgenden Fälle** the verdict set a precedent for all subsequent cases.
Exemplifikation *f* (*geh*) exemplification.
exemplifizieren* *vt* (*geh*) to exemplify.
exerzieren* *vti* to drill; (*fig*) to practise.
Exerzierplatz *m* (*Mil*) parade ground.
Exerzitien [ɛksɛr'tsi:tsiən] *pl* (*Eccl*) spiritual exercises *pl.*
Exhibitionismus [ɛkshibitsio'nɪsmʊs] *m* exhibitionism.
Exhibitionist(in *f*) [ɛkshibitsio'nɪst(ɪn)] *m* exhibitionist.
exhibitionistisch [ɛkshibitsio'nɪstɪʃ] *adj* exhibitionist.
exhumieren* *vt* to exhume.
Exhumierung *f* exhumation.
Exil *nt* **-s, -e** exile ◆ **im (amerikanischen) ~ leben** to live in exile (in America); **ins ~ gehen** to go into exile.
Exil-: ~literatur *f* literature written in exile (*esp by Germans exiled during the 3rd Reich*); **~regierung** *f* government in exile.
existent *adj* (*geh*) existing, existent.
⚠ **Existentialismus** [ɛksɪstɛntsia'lɪsmʊs] *m* existentialism.
⚠ **Existentialist(in** *f*) [ɛksɪstɛntsia'lɪst(ɪn)] *m* existentialist.
⚠ **existentialistisch** [-tsia'lɪstɪʃ] *adj* existential(ist).
⚠ **Existentialphilosophie** [ɛksɪstɛn'tsia:l-] *f* existential(ist) philosophy.
⚠ **existentiell** [ɛksɪstɛn'tsiɛl] *adj* (*geh*) existential ◆ **das Problem der Umweltverschmutzung ist ~** the problem of environmental pollution is of vital significance; **von ~er Bedeutung** of vital significance.
Existenz *f* existence; (*Lebensgrundlage, Auskommen*) livelihood; (*pej inf: Person*) character, customer (*inf*) ◆ **eine gescheiterte** *or* **verkrachte ~** (*inf*) a failure; **sich eine (neue) ~ aufbauen** to make a (new) life for oneself; **keine sichere ~ haben** to have no secure livelihood.
Existenz-: ~angst *f* (*Philos*) existential fear, angst; (*wirtschaftlich*) fear for one's livelihood *or* existence; **~berechtigung** *f* right to exist; **hat die UNO noch eine ~berechtigung?** can the UN still justify its existence?; **e~fähig** *adj* able to exist; *Firma* viable; **~fähigkeit** *f* ability to exist; (*von Firma*) viability; **~gründer** *m* (*Econ*) founder of a new business; **~grundlage** *f* basis of one's livelihood; **~gründung** *f* establishing one's livelihood; **~gründungskredit** *m* small business loan; **~kampf** *m* struggle for survival; **~minimum** *nt* subsistence level; (*Lohn*) minimal living wage *or* income; **das Gehalt liegt noch unter dem ~minimum** that salary is not enough to live on, that is not even a living wage; **er verdient nicht einmal das ~minimum** he does not even earn enough to live on *or* a living wage; **das gibt uns gerade das ~minimum** we just have enough to get by on; **~philosophie** *f* existentialism.
existieren* [ɛksɪs'ti:rən] *vi* to exist; (*Gesetz, Schule etc auch*) to be in existence.
Exitus *m* **-**, *no pl* (*Med*) death.
exkl. *abbr of* **exklusive.**
Exklave [ɛks'kla:və] *f* **-, -n** (*Pol*) exclave.
exklusiv *adj* exclusive.
Exklusivbericht *m* (*Press*) exclusive (report).
exklusive [-'zi:və] [1] *prep* +*gen* exclusive of, excluding.
[2] *adv* **Getränke ~** excluding drinks ◆ **bis zum 20. ~** to the 20th exclusively.
Exklusiv|interview *nt* (*Press*) exclusive interview.
Exklusivität [-zivi'tɛ:t] *f* exclusiveness.
Exklusivrecht *nt* exclusive rights *pl.*
Exkommunikation *f* (*Eccl*) excommunication.
exkommunizieren* *vt* to excommunicate.
Exkrement *usu pl nt* (*geh*) excrement *no pl*, excreta *pl.*
Exkretion *f* (*Med*) excretion.
Exkurs *m* **-es, -e** digression.
Exkursion *f* (study) trip.

⚠: for details of spelling reform, see supplement

Exlibris *nt* **-, -** ex libris, bookplate.
Exmatrikulation *f* (*Univ*) being taken off the university register.
exmatrikulieren* *vt* (*Univ*) to take off the university register ◆ **sich ~ lassen** to withdraw from the university register.
exmittieren* *vt* (*Admin*) *Mieter* to evict.
Exmittierung *f* (*Admin*) eviction.
Exodus *m* **-** (*Bibl, fig*) exodus.
exogen *adj* (*Biol, Geol*) exogenous.
exorbitant *adj* (*geh*) *Preise* exorbitant.
exorz(is)ieren* *vt* to exorcize.
Exorzismus *m* exorcism.
Exorzist *m* exorcist.
Exot(e) *m* **-en, -en, Exotin** *f* exotic *or* tropical animal/plant *etc*; (*Mensch*) exotic foreigner.
exotisch *adj* exotic.
Expander *m* **-s, -** (*Sport*) chest-expander.
expandieren* *vi* to expand.
Expansion *f* (*Phys, Pol*) expansion.
Expansionspolitik *f* expansionism, expansionist policies *pl.*
expansiv *adj* *Politik* expansionist; *Wirtschaftszweige* expanding; *Gase* expansile, expansive.
expatriieren* *vt* to expatriate.
Expedient *m* (*Comm*) dispatch clerk.
expedieren* *vt* to dispatch, to send (off).
Expedition *f* **(a)** (*Forschungs~, Mil*) expedition. **(b)** (*Versendung*) dispatch; (*Versandabteilung*) dispatch office.
Experiment *nt* experiment ◆ **~e machen** *or* **anstellen** to carry out *or* do experiments.
Experimental- *in cpds* experimental.
experimentell *adj* experimental ◆ **etw ~ nachweisen** to prove sth by experiment.
experimentieren* *vi* to experiment (*mit* with).
Experte *m* **-n, -n, Expertin** *f* expert (*für* in).
Experten-: ~anhörung *f* specialist evidence; **~kommission** *f* think tank; **~system** *nt* (*Comput*) expert system.
Expertise *f* **-, -n** (expert's) report.
Expl. *abbr of* **Exemplar.**
Explikation *f* (*geh*) explication (*form*).
explizieren* *vt* (*geh*) to explicate (*form*).
explizit *adj* explicit.
explizite *adv* explicitly.
explodieren* *vi aux sein* (*lit, fig*) to explode.
Exploration *f* (*eines Landes*) exploration; (*Psych*) examination.
Explorationsfond *m* exploratory investment.
explorieren* *vt* *Gelände* to explore; *Person* to examine.
Explosion *f* explosion ◆ **etw zur ~ bringen** to detonate *or* explode sth.
Explosions-: e~artig *adj* *Geräusch* like an explosion; *Wirkung* explosive; **das Gerücht verbreitete sich e~artig** the rumour spread like wildfire; **~gefahr** *f* danger of explosion; **~motor** *m* internal combustion engine.
explosiv *adj* (*lit, fig*) explosive.
Explosiv(laut) *m* **-s, -e** (*Ling*) plosive.
Explosivstoff *m* explosive.
Exponat *nt* exhibit.
Exponent *m* (*Math*) exponent; (*fig auch*) spokesman.
⚠ **Exponential-** [ɛksponɛn'tsia:l-]: **~funktion** *f* (*Math*) exponential function; **~gleichung** *f* (*Math*) exponential equation.
exponieren* [1] *vt* (*herausheben, dated Phot*) to expose ◆ **jdn zu sehr ~** to overexpose sb; **an exponierter Stelle stehen** to be in an exposed position.
[2] *vr* (*sich auffällig benehmen*) to behave boisterously; (*in der Politik*) to take a prominent stance; (*in Diskussion*) to make one's presence felt, to come on strong (*inf*) ◆ **die Studenten wollen sich nicht mehr ~** the students are keeping a low profile.
Export *m* **-(e)s, -e** export (*an* +*dat* of); (*~waren*) exports *pl.*
Export- *in cpds* export; **~abteilung** *f* export department; **~anreiz** *m* export incentive; **~artikel** *m* export; **~ausführung** *f* export model.
Exporteur [ɛkspɔr'tø:ɐ] *m* exporter.
Export-: ~geschäft *nt* **(a)** (*Firma*) export business; **(b)** (*Handel*) export business *or* trade; **~handel** *m* export business *or* trade.
exportieren* *vti* (*auch Comput*) to export.
Export-: ~kaufmann *m* exporter; **~quote** *f* export ratio; **~ware** *f* export.
⚠ **Exposé** [ɛkspo'ze:] *nt* **-s, -s** (*für Film, Buch etc*) outline, plan; (*Denkschrift*) memo(randum).
Exposition *f* (*Liter, Mus*) exposition; (*Gliederung eines Aufsatzes*) outline, plan.
Expositur *f* (*Aus*) (*Zweigstelle*) branch; (*Sch*) annexe.
⚠ **expreß** *adv* (*dated*) quickly, expeditiously (*form*); (*Post*) express.
⚠ **Expreß** *m* **-sses,** *pl* **Expreßzüge** (*old Rail, Aus*) express (train).
⚠ **Expreß-: ~brief** *m* express letter; **~gut** *nt* express goods *pl.*
Expressionismus *m* expressionism.
Expressionist(in *f*) *m* expressionist.
expressionistisch *adj* expressionist *no adv*, expressionistic.
expressis verbis *adv* explicitly, expressly.
expressiv *adj* expressive.
⚠ **Expreß-: ~reinigung** *f* express dry-cleaning service; **~zug** *m* *siehe* **Expreß.**
Expropriation *f* expropriation.
exquisit *adj* exquisite.

extemporieren* *vti (geh)* to improvise, to extemporize.
extensiv *adj (auch Agr)* extensive.
extern *adj (Sch, Comput)* external ◆ **ein ~er Schüler** a day boy
Externe(r) *mf decl as adj (Sch)* day boy/girl.
Externist *m (Aus)* **(a)** *(Schüler)* day boy. **(b)** *pupil educated by private tuition, not at school.*
exterritorial *adj* extraterritorial.
Exterritorialität *f* extraterritoriality.
extra [1] *adj inv (inf)* extra ◆ **etwas E~es** *(inf)* something special.
[2] *adv (besonders, außerordentlich)* extra, (e)specially; *(eigens, ausschließlich)* (e)specially, just; *(gesondert)* separately; *(zusätzlich)* extra, in addition; *(inf: absichtlich)* on purpose, deliberately ◆ **etw ~ legen** to put sth in a separate place; **ich gebe Ihnen noch ein Exemplar ~** I'll give you an extra copy; **jetzt tu ich's ~!** *(inf)* just for that I will do it!
Extra *nt* **-s, -s** extra.
Extra-: ~ausgabe *f* special edition; **~ausstattung** *f* extras *pl*; **~blatt** *nt* special edition; *(zusätzlich zur Zeitung)* special supplement; **e~fein** *adj* superfine; **e~fein gemahlener Kaffee** extra finely ground coffee.
extrahieren* [ɛkstra'hi:rən] *vt* to extract.
Extrakt *m* **-(e)s, -e** *(Med, Pharm auch nt)* extract; *(von Buch etc)* synopsis ◆ **etw im ~ wiedergeben** to summarize sth, to give a summary of sth.
Extra-: ~ordinarius *m (Univ)* ≃ reader *(Brit)*, associate professor *(US)*; **~polation** *f (Math, fig)* extrapolation; **e~polieren*** *vti (Math, fig)* to extrapolate; **~tour** *f (fig inf) siehe* **~wurst**; **e~uterin** *adj* extra-uterine.
extravagant [-va'gant] *adj* extravagant; *Kleidung auch* flamboyant.
Extravaganz [-va'gants] *f siehe adj* extravagance; flamboyance.
extravertiert [-vɛrti:ɐt] *adj (Psych)* extrovert.
Extrawurst *f* **(a)** *(inf: Sonderwunsch)* special favour ◆ **jdm eine ~ braten** to make an exception of *or* for sb; **er will immer eine ~ (gebraten haben)** he always wants something different *or* special. **(b)** *(Aus) siehe* **Lyoner**.
extrem *adj* extreme; *Belastung* excessive; *(sl)* way-out *(sl)* ◆ **~ schlecht/gut** *etc* extremely badly/well *etc*; **die Lage hat sich ~ verschlechtert** the situation has deteriorated enormously; **ich habe mich ~ beeilt** I hurried as much as I could; **du bist immer so ~** you always go to extremes; **~e Zeit!** *(sl)* have a great time.
Extrem *nt* **-s, -e** extreme ◆ **von einem ~ ins andere fallen** to go from one extreme to the other.
Extremfall *m* extreme (case).
Extremist(in *f*) *m* extremist.
extremistisch *adj* extremist.
Extremität *f usu pl* extremity *usu pl.*
Extremsport *m* extreme sport.
Extremwert *m* extreme (value).
extrovertiert [-vɛr'ti:ɐt] *adj siehe* **extravertiert**.
exzellent *adj (geh)* excellent.
Exzellenz *f* Excellency.
exzentrisch *adj (Math, fig)* eccentric.
Exzentrizität *f (Math, Tech, fig)* eccentricity.
exzerpieren* *vt* to select *or* extract *(aus* from).
Exzerpt *nt* **-(e)s, -e** excerpt.
⚠**Exzeß** *m* **-sses, -sse** **(a)** excess ◆ **bis zum ~** excessively, to excess; **etw bis zum ~ treiben** to take sth to excess *or* extremes; **bis zum ~ gesteigerter Haß** excessive hate. **(b)** *usu pl (Ausschreitung)* excess.
exzessiv *adj* excessive.
Eyeliner ['aɪlaɪnə] *m* **-s, -** eyeliner.
E-Zug ['e:tsu:k] *m abbr of* **Eilzug**.

F

F, f [ɛf] *nt* **-, -** F, f ◆ **nach Schema F** (*inf*) in the usual way.
F *abbr of* **Fahrenheit; Farad; Fernschnellzug.**
f. *abbr of* **und folgende(r, s).**
Fa. *abbr of* **Firma.**
fa *interj* (*Mus*) fa(h).
Fabel *f* **-, -n (a)** fable. **(b)** (*inf*) fantastic story. **(c)** (*Liter: Handlung*) plot.
Fabel-: ~buch *nt* book of fables; **~dichter** *m* writer of fables, fabulist (*form*).
Fabelei *f* **(a)** (*das Fabeln*) romancing. **(b)** (*Geschichte*) fantastic story.
Fabel-: ~geschöpf *nt*, **~gestalt** *f siehe* **~wesen; f~haft** *adj* splendid, magnificent; **ein f~haft niedriger Preis** a fabulously *or* fantastically low price.
fabeln [1] *vi* to romance.
[2] *vt Unsinn* to concoct, to fabricate.
Fabel-: ~tier *nt* mythical creature; **der Fuchs als ~tier** the fox (as he appears) in fables; **~welt** *f* world *or* realm of fantasy; **~wesen** *nt* mythical creature.
Fabrik *f* **-, -en** factory; (*Papier~*) mill ◆ **in die ~ gehen** (*inf*) to work in a factory.
Fabrik|anlage *f* (manufacturing) plant; (*Fabrikgelände*) factory premises *pl*.
Fabrikant(in *f*) *m* **(a)** (*Fabrikbesitzer*) industrialist. **(b)** (*Hersteller*) manufacturer.
Fabrik-: ~arbeit *f, no pl* factory work; **das ist ~arbeit** that is factory-made; **~arbeiter** *m* factory worker.
Fabrikat *nt* **(a)** (*Marke*) make; (*von Nahrungs- und Genußmitteln*) brand. **(b)** (*Produkt*) product; (*Ausführung*) model.
Fabrikation *f* manufacture, production.
Fabrikations-: ~fehler *m* manufacturing fault; **~stätte** *f* manufacturing *or* production plant.
Fabrik- *in cpds* factory; **~bau** *m, pl* **-ten** factory (building); **~direktor** *m* managing director (of a factory); **f~frisch** *adj* straight from the factory; **~gelände** *nt* factory site; **~halle** *f* factory building.
Fabrikler(in *f*) *m* **-s, -** (*Sw*) factory worker.
fabrik-: ~mäßig *adj* **~mäßige Herstellung** mass production; **~mäßig hergestellt** mass-produced; **~neu** *adj* straight from the factory; (*nagelneu*) brand-new; **~neu aussehen** to be in mint condition.
Fabriks- *in cpds* (*Aus*) *siehe* **Fabrik-.**
Fabrikschiff *nt* factory ship.
fabrizieren* *vt* **(a)** (*dated*) (*industriell produzieren*) to manufacture, to produce, to fabricate (*dated*). **(b)** (*inf*) *Möbelstück etc* to make; *geistiges Produkt* to produce; *Alibi, Lügengeschichte* to concoct, to fabricate. **(c)** (*inf: anstellen*) to get up to (*inf*).
Fabulant(in *f*) *m* (*geh*) **(a)** (*pej*) fabulist. **(b)** *siehe* **Fabulierer(in).**
fabulieren* *vi* (*geh*) **(a)** (*pej: schwätzen*) to romance. **(b)** (*phantasievoll erzählen*) to spin a yarn ◆ **er fabulierte, wie ...** he spun some yarns about how ...
Fabulierer(in *f*) *m* **-s, -** (*geh*) romancer, storyteller.
fabulös *adj* (*geh*) fabulous (*liter*); (*unglaubwürdig, hum: großartig*) fantastic.
Facelifting [ˈfeːsliftiŋ] *nt* **-s, -s** (*lit, fig*) facelift.
⚠**Facette** [faˈsɛtə] *f* facet.
⚠**Facetten-: f~artig** [1] *adj* facet(t)ed; [2] *adv schleifen* in facets; **~auge** *nt* compound eye; **~schliff** *m* facet(t)ing; **ein Amethyst mit ~schliff** a facet(t)ed amethyst.
⚠**facettieren*** [faseˈtiːrən] *vt* to facet ◆ **facettiert** (*lit, fig*) facet(t)ed.
Fach *nt* **-(e)s, ⸚er (a)** compartment; (*in Tasche, Brieftasche, Portemonnaie etc auch*) pocket; (*in Schrank, Regal etc*) shelf; (*für Briefe etc*) pigeonhole.
(b) (*Wissens-, Sachgebiet*) subject; (*Gebiet*) field; (*Handwerk*) trade ◆ **ein Mann vom ~** an expert; **sein ~ verstehen** to know one's stuff (*inf*) *or* one's subject/trade; **das ~ Medizin** *etc* medicine *etc*.
(c) (*Theat*) mode.
-fach *adj suf* -fold; (*-mal*) times; *siehe* **vier~** *etc*.
Fach-: ~arbeiter *m* skilled worker; **Bau-/Brauerei-** *etc* **~arbeiter** construction/brewery *etc* workers; **~arbeiterbrief** *m* certificate of proficiency; **~arzt** *m* specialist (*für* in); **f~ärztlich** *adj Behandlung* specialist *attr; Untersuchung* by a specialist; **ein f~ärztliches Attest/Gutachten** a certificate from *or* signed by a specialist/a specialist's opinion; **~ausbildung** *f* specialist training; **~ausdruck** *m* technical *or* specialist term; ⚠**~ausschuß** *m* committee of experts; **~berater** *m* technical consultant; **~bereich** *m* **(a)** *siehe* **~gebiet; (b)** (*Univ*) school, faculty; **f~bezogen** *adj* specifically related to one's/the subject; (*fachlich beschränkt*) specialized; **~bibliothek** *f* specialist library; **~blatt** *nt* (specialist) journal; **ein medizinisches ~blatt** a medical journal; **~buch** *nt* reference book; **wasserbautechnische ~bücher** specialist books on hydraulic engineering; **~buchhandlung** *f* specialist bookshop; **~buchhandlung für Medizin/Mathematik** *etc* bookshop specializing in medical/mathematical *etc* books; **~buchverlag** *m* specialist publishing company; **~buchverlag für Geographie/Fremdsprachen** *etc* publisher of geography/modern language *etc* books; **~chinesisch** *nt* (*inf*) technical jargon *or* mumbo-jumbo (*inf*).
fächeln (*geh*) [1] *vt* to fan; *Blätter etc* to stir.
[2] *vi* to stir.
Fächer *m* **-s, -** fan; (*fig*) range, array.
Fächer-: f~artig [1] *adj* fanlike; [2] *adv* like a fan; **~besen** *m* (*Hort*) wire rake; **f~förmig** [1] *adj* fan-shaped; [2] *adv* like a fan; **~gewölbe** *nt* fan vaulting; **ein ~gewölbe** a fan vault.
fächern [1] *vt* to fan (out); (*fig*) to diversify ◆ **gefächert** diverse; *Auswahl auch* varied; *Unterricht* diversified.
[2] *vr* to fan out.
[3] *vti* (*rare*) *siehe* **fächeln.**
Fächerpalme *f* fan palm.
Fächerung *f, no pl* variety, range, diversity.
Fach-: ~frau *f* expert; **f~fremd** *adj Lektüre, Aufgaben etc* unconnected with the/one's subject; *Mitarbeiter* with no background in the subject; *Methode* foreign to the subject; **~gebiet** *nt* (special) field; **f~gebunden** *adj* related (to the field/subject); **~gelehrte(r)** *mf* specialist; **f~gemäß, f~gerecht** *adj* expert; *Ausbildung* specialist *attr*; **~geschäft** *nt* specialist shop *or* store (*esp US*); **~geschäft für Lederwaren** leather shop, shop *or* store specializing in leather goods; **~gespräch** *nt* professional *or* technical discussion; **~größe** *f* authority; **~gruppe** *f* professional group; (*Univ*) study group; (*Gruppe von Experten*) team of specialists; **~handel** *m* specialist shops *pl or* stores *pl* (*esp US*); **~händler** *m* specialist supplier; ⚠**~hochschulabschluß** *m* diploma from university for applied science; **~hochschule** *f* university for applied science; **~idiot** *m* (*sl*) person who can think of nothing but his/her subject, philosophy/chemistry *etc* freak (*sl*); **~jargon** *m* technical jargon; **~kenntnisse** *pl* specialized knowledge; **~kollege** *m* professional colleague; **~kraft** *f* qualified employee; **~kreise** *pl*: **in ~kreisen** among experts; **f~kundig** *adj* informed *no adv*; (*erfahren*) with a knowledge of the subject; (*fachmännisch*) proficient; **jdn f~kundig beraten** to give sb informed advice; **f~kundlich** *adj* **f~kundlicher Unterricht** teaching of technical subjects; **~lehrer** *m* specialist subject teacher; **~leiter** *m* head of department.
fachlich *adj* technical; *Ausbildung* specialist *attr*; *Spezialisierung* in one aspect of a/the subject; (*beruflich*) professional ◆ **ein ~ ausgezeichneter Lehrer** a teacher who is academically excellent; **~ hochqualifizierte Mitarbeiter** staff members who are highly qualified in their field; **sich ~ qualifizieren** to gain qualifications in one's field; **~ auf dem laufenden bleiben** to keep up to date in one's subject.
Fach-: ~literatur *f* specialist literature; **~mann** *m, pl* **-leute** *or* (*rare*) **-männer** expert; **f~männisch** *adj* expert; **~männisch ausgeführt** expertly done; **~oberschule** *f* College of Further Education; **~personal** *nt* specialist staff; **~presse** *f* specialist publications *pl*; **die medizinische/philologische** *etc* **~presse** the medical/philological *etc* publications *pl*; **~prüfung** *f* professional examination; **~redakteur** *m* (special) editor; **~redakteur für Sport/Naturwissenschaft** *etc* sports/science *etc* editor; **~richtung** *f* subject area; **die ~richtung Mathematik** mathematics; **~schaft** *f* (*Univ*) students *pl* of the/a department; **~schule** *f* technical college; **~schulreife** *f* entrance qualification for a technical college; **~simpelei** *f* (*inf*) shop-talk; **f~simpeln** *vi insep* (*inf*) to talk shop; **f~spezifisch** *adj* technical, subject-specific; **~sprache** *f* technical terminology; **f~sprachlich** [1] *adj* technical; [2] *adv* in technical terminology; **~studium** *nt course of study at a polytechnic or technical college*; **~terminus** *m* technical term; **~text** *m* specialist text; **f~übergreifend** [1] *adj Problematik, Lernziel etc* inter-disciplinary, which extends across the disciplines; [2] *adv* across the disci-

⚠: for details of spelling reform, see supplement

plines; ~**verband** *m* (*im Handel*) trade association; (*von Ärzten etc*) association; ~**vokabular** *nt* technical vocabulary; ~**welt** *f* experts *pl*; ~**werk** *nt, no pl* half-timbering; ~**werkbauweise** *f* half-timbering; ~**werkhaus** *nt* half-timbered house; ~**wissen** *nt* (specialized) knowledge of the/one's subject; ~**wissenschaft** *f* specialists *pl or* experts *pl* (in a particular/the subject); ~**wissenschaftler** *m* specialist *or* expert (in a particular/the subject); **f~wissenschaftlich** *adj* technical; *Publikation auch* specialist; ~**wort** *nt* specialist term; ~**wörterbuch** *nt* specialist dictionary; (*wissenschaftliches auch*) technical dictionary; ~**zeitschrift** *f* specialist journal; (*technisch*) technical journal; (*naturwissenschaftlich*) scientific journal; (*für Berufe*) trade journal.

Fackel *f* **-, -n** (*lit, fig*) torch; (*der Revolution auch, des Glaubens*) flame.

Fackellauf *m* torch race.

fackeln *vi* (*inf*) to shilly-shally (*inf*) ♦ **nicht lange gefackelt!** no shilly-shallying!; **da wird nicht lange gefackelt** there won't be any shilly-shallying.

Fackel-: ~**schein** *m* torchlight; **im ~schein** by torchlight; **im ~schein sah man ...** you could see by the light of the torches ...; ~**zug** *m* torchlight procession.

Factoring ['fɛktərɪŋ] *nt* **-s** *no pl* (*Fin*) factoring.

fad *adj pred* **(a)** *siehe* **fad(e) (a, b)**. **(b)** (*Aus, S Ger*) (*zimperlich*) soft (*inf*), wet (*inf*), soppy (*inf*).

Fädchen *nt dim of* **Faden[1]**.

fad(e) *adj* **(a)** *Geschmack* insipid; *Essen auch* tasteless. **(b)** (*fig: langweilig*) dull. **(c)** (*Aus, S Ger*) *siehe* **fad (b)**.

fädeln *vt* **(a)** to thread. **(b)** (*fig*) *siehe* **einfädeln 1(b)**.

Faden[1] *m* **-s, ¨** **(a)** (*lit, fig*) thread; (*an Marionetten*) string; (*Med*) stitch ♦ **der rote ~** (*fig*) the leitmotif, the central theme; **den ~ verlieren** (*fig*) to lose the thread; **alle ¨ laufen in seiner Hand/hier zusammen** he is at the hub of the whole business/this is the hub *or* the nerve centre of the whole business; **er hält alle ¨ (fest) in der Hand** he holds the reins; **sein Leben hing an einem (dünnen *or* seidenen) ~** his life was hanging by a thread; **keinen guten ~ an jdm/etw lassen** (*inf*) to tear sb/sth to shreds (*inf*) *or* pieces (*inf*).
(b) (*Spinnen~ etc*) thread; (*Bohnen~*) string ♦ **der Klebstoff/Käse zieht ¨** the glue is tacky/the cheese has gone stringy; **die Bohnen haben ¨** the beans are stringy.

Faden[2] *m* **-s, -** (*Naut*) fathom.

Faden-: **f~förmig** *adj* thread-like; ~**kreuz** *nt* crosshair; **jdn/etw im ~kreuz haben** to have sb/sth in one's sights; ~**nudeln** *pl* vermicelli *pl*; **f~scheinig** *adj* **(a)** threadbare; **(b)** (*fig*) flimsy; *Argument auch, Moral* threadbare *no adv*; *Ausrede auch* transparent; *Trost* poor; ~**schlag** *m* (*Sw Sew*) basted *or* tacked seam; ~**wurm** *m* threadworm.

Fadheit *f siehe* **fad(e) (a)** insipidness, insipidity; tastelessness. **(b)** (*fig*) dullness.

Fading ['fe:dɪŋ] *nt* **-(s),** *no pl* (*Rad*) fading.

fadisieren* *vr* (*Aus*) *siehe* **langweilen 3**.

Fagott *nt* **-(e)s, -e** bassoon.

Fagottbläser(in *f*), Fagottist(in *f*) *m* bassoonist.

Fähe *f* **-, -n** (*Hunt*) (*Füchsin*) vixen; (*Dächsin*) sow.

fähig *adj* **(a)** (*tüchtig*) *Mensch, Mitarbeiter etc* capable, competent, able ♦ **sie ist ein ~er Kopf** she has an able mind. **(b)** (*sl: gut*) great (*inf*). **(c)** *pred* (*befähigt, bereit*) capable (*zu, gen* of) ♦ **(dazu) ~ sein, etw zu tun** to be capable of doing sth; **bei dem Lärm bin ich keines klaren Gedankens ~** I can't think straight *or* hear myself think with all this noise; **zu allem ~ sein** to be capable of anything.

Fähigkeit *f* (*Begabung*) ability; (*Tüchtigkeit auch*) capability; (*Geschicklichkeit auch*) aptitude; (*praktisches Können*) skill ♦ **die ~ haben, etw zu tun** to be capable of doing sth; **eine Frau von großen ~en** a women of great ability; **bei deinen ~en ...** with your talents ...

fahl *adj* pale; *Mondlicht auch* wan (*liter*).

Fahlheit *f siehe adj* paleness; wanness (*liter*).

Fähnchen *nt* **(a)** *dim of* **Fahne**; *siehe* **Wind**. **(b)** (*Wimpel*) pennant. **(c)** (*usu pej, inf*) flimsy dress.

fahnden *vi* to search (*nach* for).

Fahndung *f* search.

Fahndungs-: ~**aktion** *f* search; ~**buch** *nt siehe* ~**liste**; ~**dienst** *m* CID (*Brit*), detective branch; ~**liste** *f* wanted (persons) list.

Fahne *f* **-, -n** **(a)** flag; (*von Verein etc auch*) banner; (*Mil, von Pfadfinder etc auch*) colours *pl* ♦ **die ~ hochhalten** (*fig*) to keep the flag flying; **die ~ des Glaubens** *etc* **hochhalten** (*fig geh*) to hold aloft the flag *or* banner of faith *etc*; **etw auf seine ~ schreiben** (*fig*) to take up the cause of sth; **mit fliegenden *or* wehenden ~n** with beat of drum and flourish of trumpets (*liter*); **mit fliegenden *or* wehenden ~n untergehen** to go down with all flags flying; **zu den ~n eilen** (*old, geh*) to join the colours (*old*); **jdn zu den ~n rufen** (*old, geh*) to call sb up (for military service); **unter der ~ stehen** (*old, geh*), **der ~ folgen** (*old, geh*) to follow the flag (*old*), to serve with the colours (*old*); **unter jds ~n fechten *or* kämpfen** (*old, geh*) to fight under sb's flag; *siehe* **Wind**.
(b) (*inf*) **eine ~ haben** to reek of alcohol; **man konnte seine ~ schon aus drei Meter Entfernung riechen** you could smell the alcohol on his breath ten feet away.
(c) (*Typ*) galley (proof).

Fahnen-: ~**abzug** *m* (*Typ*) galley (proof); ~**eid** *m* oath of allegiance; ~**flucht** *f* (*Mil, fig*) desertion; **f~flüchtig** *adj* **f~flüchtig sein/werden** (*Mil, fig*) to be a deserter, to have deserted/to desert; **ein f~flüchtiger Soldat** a deserter; ~**flüchtige(r)** *mf* (*Mil, fig*) deserter; **f~geschmückt** *adj* beflagged, decorated with flags; ~**junker** *m* (*Mil, Hist*) officer cadet; ~**mast** *m* flagpole; ~**schmuck** *m* drapery of flags and bunting; **im ~schmuck** decked out with flags and bunting; ~**stange** *f* flagpole; ~**träger** *m* standard-bearer, colour-bearer; ~**tuch** *nt* **(a)** (*Tex*) bunting; **(b)** (*Fahne*) flag; ~**weihe** *f* consecration of the flag.

Fähnlein *nt* **(a)** *dim of* **Fahne**. **(b)** (*kleine Gruppe*) troop.

Fähnrich *m* (*Hist*) standard-bearer; (*Mil*) sergeant ♦ **~ zur See** petty officer.

Fahrausweis *m* **(a)** (*Sw, form*) ticket. **(b)** (*Sw*) *siehe* **Führerschein**.

Fahrbahn *f* carriageway (*Brit*), highway (*US*), roadway; (*Fahrspur*) lane ♦ **„Betreten der ~ verboten"** "pedestrians keep off the road".

Fahrbahn-: ~**markierung** *f* road marking; ~**verengung** *f* lane closures *pl*; (*auf Schildern*) "road narrows"; ~**verschmutzung** *f* dirt on the road.

Fahr-: **f~bar** *adj* **(a)** on castors; *Kran* mobile; **f~barer Untersatz** (*hum*) wheels *pl* (*hum*); **(b)** (*dated*) *siehe* **befahrbar**; **f~bereit** *adj* in running order; **etw f~bereit machen** to get sth in(to) running order; ~**bereitschaft** *f* **~bereitschaft haben** to be the driver on duty.

Fähr-: ~**betrieb** *m* ferry service; **es herrschte reger ~betrieb** there were a lot of ferries running; ~**boot** *nt* ferry (boat).

Fahrbücherei *f* mobile *or* travelling library.

Fahrdamm *m* (*dial*) *siehe* **Fahrbahn**.

Fahrdienst *m* **(a) ~ haben** to have crew duty. **(b)** (*Rail*) rail service.

Fährdienst *m* ferry service.

Fahrdienstleiter *m* area manager.

Fahrdraht *m* (*Rail etc*) overhead contact wire *or* line.

Fähre *f* **-, -n** ferry.

Fahr|eigenschaft *f usu pl* handling characteristic ♦ **die ~en eines Wagens** the handling of a car; **der Wagen hat hervorragende ~en** the car handles excellently.

fahren *pret* **fuhr**, *ptp* **gefahren** [1] *vi* **(a)** *aux sein* (*sich fortbewegen*) (*Fahrzeug, Fahrgast*) to go; (*Fahrer*) to drive; (*Schiff*) to sail; (*Kran, Kamera, Rolltreppe etc*) to move ♦ **mit dem Auto/Rad ~** to drive/cycle, to go by car/bike; **mit dem Zug/Motorrad/Bus/Taxi ~** to go by train *or* rail/motorbike/bus/taxi; **mit dem Aufzug ~** to take the lift, to ride the elevator (*US*); **wollen wir ~ oder zu Fuß gehen?** shall we go by car/bus *etc* or walk?; **links/rechts ~** to drive on the left/right; **wie lange fährt man von hier nach Basel?** how long does it take to get to Basle from here?; **wie fährt man von hier/am schnellsten zum Bahnhof?** how does one get to the station from here/what is the quickest way to the station (by car/bus *etc*)?; **ich fahre lieber auf der Autobahn** I'd rather go on *or* take the motorway; **zweiter Klasse ~** to travel *or* go *or* ride (*US*) second class; **per Anhalter *or* Autostop ~** to hitch(hike); **gegen einen Baum ~** to drive *or* go into a tree; **über den See ~** to cross the lake; **die Lok fährt elektrisch/mit Dampf** the engine is electric *or* powered by electricity/is steam-driven; **der Wagen fährt sehr ruhig** the car is very quiet *or* is a very quiet runner; **gen Himmel/zur Hölle ~** (*liter*) to ascend into heaven/descend into hell; **fahr zur Hölle *or* zum Teufel!** (*old*) the devil take you! (*old*); *siehe* **fahrend, Grube** *etc*.
(b) *aux sein or haben* (*ein Fahrzeug lenken, Fahrer sein*) to drive.
(c) *aux sein* (*los~*) (*Verkehrsmittel, Fahrer, Mitfahrer*) to go, to leave ♦ **einen ~ lassen** (*inf*) to let off (*inf*), to fart (*vulg*).
(d) *aux sein* (*verkehren*) to run ♦ **es ~ täglich zwei Fähren** there are two ferries a day; **~ da keine Züge?** don't any trains go there?; **~ Sie bis Walterplatz?** do you go as far as *or* all the way to Walterplatz?; **die U-Bahn fährt alle fünf Minuten** the underground goes *or* runs every five minutes.
(e) *aux sein* (*reisen*) to go ♦ **ich fahre mit dem Auto nach Schweden** I'm taking the car to Sweden, I'm going to Sweden by car.
(f) *aux sein* (*sich rasch bewegen*) **blitzartig fuhr es ihm durch den Kopf, daß ...** the thought suddenly flashed through his mind that ...; **was ist (denn) in dich gefahren?** what's got into you?; **in den Mantel ~** to fling on one's coat; **in seine Kleider ~** to fling on *or* leap into one's clothes; **der Blitz fuhr in die Eiche** the lightning struck the oak; **die Katze fuhr ihm ins Gesicht** the cat leapt *or* sprang at his face; **der Hexenschuß fuhr ihm durch den Rücken** a twinge of lumbago shot down his back; *siehe* **Glied** *etc*.
(g) *aux sein or haben* (*streichen*) **er fuhr mit der Hand/einem Tuch/einer raschen Handbewegung über den Tisch** he ran his hand/a cloth over the table/he swept his hand over the table; **ihre Hand fuhr sanft über ...** she gently ran her hand over ...; **jdm/sich durchs Haar ~** to run one's fingers through sb's/one's hair; **sich (*dat*) mit der Hand über die Stirn ~** to pass one's hand over one's brow.
(h) *aux sein* (*zurechtkommen*) **(mit jdm/etw) gut/schlecht ~** to get on all right/not very well (with sb/sth), not to fare very well (with sb/sth); **(bei etw) gut/schlecht ~** to do well/badly (with sth); **du fährst besser, wenn ...** you would do *or* fare better if ...
(i) (*Film: eine Kamerafahrt machen*) to track.
[2] *vt* **(a)** (*lenken*) *Auto, Bus, Zug etc* to drive; *Fahrrad, Motorrad* to ride.
(b) *aux sein* (*zum F~ benutzen*) *Straße, Strecke, Buslinie etc* to take ♦ **welche Strecke fährt der 59er?** which way does the 59 go?, which route does the 59 take?; **einen Umweg ~** to go a long way round; **wir sind die Umleitung gefahren** we took *or* followed the diversion; **ich fahre lieber Autobahn als Landstraße** I prefer (driving on) motorways to ordinary roads; *siehe* **Eisenbahn, Karussell, Schlitten** *etc*.
(c) (*benutzen*) *Kraftstoff etc* to use; *Reifen* to drive on.
(d) (*befördern*) to take; (*hierher~*) to bring; (*Lastwagen, Taxi: gewerbsmäßig*) to carry; *Personen auch* to drive ♦ **ich fahre dich nach Hause** I'll take *or* drive you *or* give you a lift home; **jdn in den Tod ~** (*geh*) to kill sb.
(e) **schrottreif *or* zu Schrott ~** *Fahrzeug* (*durch Unfall*) to write off; (*durch*

Verschleiß) to drive into the ground.
(f) *aux sein Straße, Strecke* to drive; *Kurve, Gefälle etc* to take.
(g) *aux sein Geschwindigkeit* to do.
(h) *aux haben or sein* (*Sport*) *Rennen* to take part in; *Runde etc* to do; *Zeit, Rekord etc* to clock up.
(i) (*Tech*) (*steuern, betreiben*) to run; (*abspielen*) *Platten, Tonbandspulen etc* to play; (*senden*) to broadcast; (*durchführen*) *Sonderschicht* to put on; *Überstunden* to do, to work; *Angriff* to launch ◆ **einen harten Kurs ~** to follow a hard line; **die Produktion nach oben/unten ~** to step up/cut down production.
(j) (*Film*) *Aufnahme* to track.
3 *vr* (a) *impers* **mit diesem Wagen/bei solchem Wetter/auf dieser Straße fährt es sich gut** it's good driving this car/in that kind of weather/on this road.
(b) (*Fahrzeug, Straße etc*) **der neue Wagen fährt sich gut** the new car is nice to drive.

fahrend *adj* itinerant; *Musikant auch* travelling; *Zug, Auto* in motion ◆ **~es Volk** travelling people; **ein ~er Sänger** a wandering minstrel.

Fahrenheit *no art* Fahrenheit.

fahrenlassen* *vt sep irreg* (*lit*) to let go of, to relinquish one's hold on; (*fig*) to abandon; *siehe* **fahren 1 (c)**.

Fahrer *m* **-s, -** (a) driver; (*Chauffeur auch*) chauffeur/chauffeuse. (b) (*Sport inf*) (*Rad~*) cyclist; (*Motorrad~*) motorcyclist.

Fahrerei *f* driving.

Fahrer-: ~flucht *f* hit-and-run driving; **~flucht begehen** to fail to stop after being involved in an accident, to be involved in a hit-and-run; *siehe* **Unfallflucht**; **f~flüchtig** *adj* (*form*) hit-and-run *attr*; **f~flüchtig sein** to have failed to stop after being involved in an accident, to have committed a hit-and-run offence; **~haus** *nt* (driver's) cab.

Fahrerin *f siehe* **Fahrer**.

fahrerisch *adj* driving *attr* ◆ **er ist mir ~ weit überlegen** he is a far better driver than I am.

Fahrerlaubnis *f* (*form*) driving licence (*Brit*), driver's license (*US*).

Fahrersitz *m* driver's seat.

Fahrgast *m* passenger.

Fahrgast-: ~raum *m* (*von Auto*) interior; (*Rail etc*) compartment; **~schiff** *nt* passenger boat.

Fahr-: ~gefühl *nt* **unser neues Modell vermittelt Ihnen ein völlig neues ~gefühl** our new model offers you a completely new driving experience; **~geld** *nt* fares *pl*; (*für einzelne Fahrt*) fare; **„das ~geld bitte passend** *or* **abgezählt bereithalten"** "please tender exact fare" (*form*), "please have the exact fare ready"; **~gelegenheit** *f* transport *no indef art*, means of transport; **~gemeinschaft** *f* carpool; **~geschwindigkeit** *f* (*form*) speed; **~gestell** *nt* (a) (*Aut*) chassis; (b) *siehe* **~werk (a)**; (c) (*hum inf*) legs *pl*; **ein hohes ~gestell** long legs.

Fähr-: ~hafen *m* ferry terminal; **~haus** *nt* ferry house.

fahrig *adj* nervous; (*unkonzentriert*) distracted.

Fahrigkeit *f siehe adj* nervousness; distractedness, distraction.

Fahrkarte *f* (a) ticket; (*Zeit~, Streckenkarte*) season ticket; (*fig*) passport (*nach* to) ◆ **mit diesem Sieg hatten sie die ~ zum Endspiel in der Tasche** this victory was their passport to the final. (b) (*Schießsport*) miss.

Fahrkarten-: ~ausgabe *f* ticket office; **~automat** *m* ticket machine; **~kontrolle** *f* ticket inspection; **~schalter** *m* ticket office.

Fahr-: ~komfort *m* (motoring) comfort; **~kosten** *pl siehe* **Fahrtkosten**; **~künste** *pl* driving skills *pl*; **f~lässig** *adj* negligent (*auch Jur*); **f~lässig handeln** to be guilty of negligence, to be negligent; *siehe* **Körperverletzung, Tötung**; **~lässigkeit** *f* negligence (*auch Jur*); **~lehrer** *m* driving instructor; **~leistung** *f* road performance.

Fährmann *m, pl* **-männer** *or* **-leute** ferryman.

Fahrnis *f* (*Jur*) chattels *pl*, moveables *pl*.

Fährnis *f* (*obs*) peril.

Fahr-: ~personal *nt* drivers and conductors *pl*; (*Rail*) footplatemen *pl* (*Brit*), railroad crews *pl* (*US*); (*von Einzelfahrzeug*) bus/tram/train crew; **~plan** *m* timetable, schedule (*US*); (*fig*) schedule; **~planauszug** *m* (*Rail*) timetable (*for a particular service*); **f~planmäßig** *adj* scheduled *attr, pred*; **f~planmäßig verkehren/ankommen** to run/arrive on schedule; **es verlief alles f~planmäßig** everything went according to schedule; **~praxis** *f, no pl* driving experience *no indef art*.

Fahrpreis *m* fare.

Fahrpreis-: ~anzeiger *m* taxi meter; **~ermäßigung** *f* fare reduction.

Fahrprüfung *f* driving test.

Fahrrad *nt* bicycle, cycle, bike (*inf*).

Fahrrad-: ~fahrer *m* cyclist, bicyclist (*form*); **~händler** *m* bicycle dealer; (*Geschäft*) cycle shop; **~helm** *m* cycle helmet; **~kurier** *m* cycle courier; **~ständer** *m* (bi)cycle stand; **~weg** *m* cycle path, cycleway.

Fahrrinne *f* (*Naut*) shipping channel, fairway.

Fahrschein *m* ticket.

Fahrschein-: ~automat *m* ticket machine; **~block** *m siehe* **~heft**; **~entwerter** *m* automatic ticket stamping machine (*in bus/trams etc*); **~heft** *nt* book of tickets.

Fährschiff *nt* ferry(boat).

Fahr-: ~schule *f* driving school; **~schüler** *m* (a) (*bei Fahrschule*) learner driver, student driver (*US*); (b) *pupil who has to travel some distance to and from school*; **~schullehrer** *m* driving instructor; **~sicherheit** *f* safe driving *or* motoring *no art*; **erhöhte ~sicherheit** safer driving *or* motoring; **~spur** *f* lane; **~stil** *m* style of driving/riding/skiing *etc*; **~streifen** *m siehe* **~spur**; **~stuhl** *m* lift (*Brit*), elevator (*US*); **~stuhlschacht** *m* lift (*Brit*) *or* elevator (*US*) shaft; **~stunde** *f* driving lesson.

Fahrt *f* **-, -en** (a) (*das Fahren*) journey ◆ **„während der ~ nicht hinauslehnen"** "do not lean out of the window while the train/bus *etc* is in motion"; **nach zwei Stunden ~** after travelling for two hours; (*mit dem Auto auch*) after two hours' drive; *siehe* **frei**.
(b) (*Fahrgeschwindigkeit*) speed ◆ **volle/halbe ~ voraus!** (*Naut*) full/half speed ahead!; **30 Knoten ~ machen** to do 30 knots; **~ aufnehmen** to pick up speed; **jdn in ~ bringen** to get sb going; **in ~ kommen** *or* **geraten/sein** to get/have got going.
(c) (*Reise*) journey ◆ **was kostet eine ~/eine einfache ~ nach London?** how much is it to London/how much is a single to London?, what is the fare/the single fare to London?; **gute ~!** bon voyage!, safe journey!; **auf ~ gehen** (*dated*) to take to the road.
(d) (*Ausflug, Wanderung*) trip ◆ **eine ~ machen** to go on a trip.
(e) (*Naut*) voyage; (*Über~*) crossing ◆ **für große/kleine ~ zugelassen sein** to be licensed for long/short voyages.
(f) (*Film*) tracking shot.

Fahrtantritt *m* start of the journey.

Fahr-: f~tauglich *adj* fit to drive; **~tauglichkeit** *f* fitness to drive; **jdm die ~tauglichkeit bescheinigen** to certify sb fit to drive.

Fahrtdauer *f* time for the journey ◆ **bei einer ~** von fünf Stunden on a five-hour journey; **man muß für diese Strecke mit einer ~ von drei Stunden rechnen** you have to allow three hours for this stretch.

Fährte *f* **-, -n** tracks *pl*; (*Hunt auch*) spoor; (*Witterung*) scent; (*Spuren*) trail ◆ **auf der richtigen/falschen ~ sein** (*fig*) to be on the right/wrong track; **jdn auf die richtige ~ bringen** (*fig*) to put sb on the right track; **jdn auf eine falsche ~ locken** (*fig*) to put sb off the scent; **eine ~ verfolgen** (*fig*) to follow up a lead; **eine falsche ~ verfolgen** (*fig*) to be on the wrong track.

Fahr-: ~technik *f* driving technique; **f~technisch** *adj* as regards the technicalities of driving; **eine gute f~technische Ausbildung bekommen** to learn to drive well; **eine f~technisch schwierige Strecke** a difficult stretch of road (to drive).

Fahrten-: ~buch *nt* (a) (*Kontrollbuch*) driver's log; (b) (*Wandertagebuch*) diary of a trip; **~messer** *nt* sheath knife; **~schreiber** *m siehe* **Fahrtschreiber**; **~schwimmer** *m person who has passed an advanced swimming test*; **seinen ~schwimmer machen** (*inf*) to do one's advanced swimming test.

Fahrtest *m* road test.

Fahrtkosten *pl* travelling expenses *pl*.

Fahrtreppe *f* escalator.

Fahrt-: ~richtung *f* direction of travel; (*im Verkehr*) direction of the traffic; **entgegen der/in ~richtung** (*im Zug*) with one's back to the engine/facing the engine; (*im Bus etc*) facing backwards/the front; **die Züge in ~richtung Norden/Süden** *etc* the northbound/southbound *etc* trains; **in ~richtung Norden sind Stauungen zu erwarten** long delays are affecting northbound traffic; **die Autobahn ist in ~richtung Norden gesperrt** the northbound carriageway of the motorway is closed; **~richtungsanzeiger** *m* (*Aut*) indicator; **~route** *f* route; **~schreiber** *m* tachograph.

Fahr-: f~tüchtig *adj* fit to drive; *Wagen etc* roadworthy; **~tüchtigkeit** *f* driving ability; roadworthiness.

Fahrt-: ~unterbrechung *f* break in the journey, stop; **~wind** *m* airstream.

Fahr-: f~untauglich *adj* unfit to drive; *Wagen etc* unroadworthy; **~untauglichkeit** *f* unfitness to drive; unroadworthiness; **~verbot** *nt* loss of one's licence, driving ban; **jdn mit ~verbot belegen** to ban sb from driving, to take sb's licence away; **~verbot für Privatwagen** ban on private vehicles; **~verhalten** *nt* (*von Fahrer*) behaviour behind the wheel; (*von Wagen*) road performance.

Fährverkehr *m* ferry traffic.

Fahr-: ~wasser *nt* (a) (*Naut*) *siehe* **~rinne**; (b) (*fig*) **in jds ~wasser geraten** to get in with sb; **in ein gefährliches ~wasser geraten** to get onto dangerous ground; **in ein politisches/kommunistisches ~wasser geraten** to get tied up with politics/communism; **in jds ~wasser segeln** *or* **schwimmen** to follow in sb's wake; **in seinem** *or* **im richtigen ~wasser sein** to be in one's element; **~weise** *f* **seine ~weise** his driving, the way he drives; **~werk** *nt* (a) (*Aviat*) undercarriage, landing gear; (b) *siehe* **~gestell (a)**; **~wind** *m* (a) (*Naut*) wind; (b) *siehe* **Fahrtwind**; **~zeit** *f siehe* **Fahrtdauer**.

Fahrzeug *nt* vehicle; (*Luft~*) aircraft; (*Wasser~*) vessel.

Fahrzeug-: ~ausfall *m* vehicle breakdown; **~ausstattung** *f* vehicle accessories *pl*; **~brief** *m* registration document, log book (*Brit inf*); **~führer** *m* (*form*) driver of a vehicle; **~halter** *m* vehicle owner; **~kolonne** *f* (a) (*Schlange*) queue (*Brit*) *or* line of vehicles *etc*; (b) (*auch* **~konvoi**) convoy; (*bei Staatsbesuchen etc*) motorcade; **~lenker** *m* (*form*) *siehe* **~führer**; **~papiere** *pl* vehicle documents *pl*; **~park** *m* (*form*) fleet.

Faible ['fɛːbl] *nt* **-s, -s** (*geh*) liking; (*Schwäche auch*) weakness; (*Vorliebe auch*) penchant.

fair [fɛːɐ] 1 *adj* fair (*gegen* to).
2 *adv* fairly ◆ **~ spielen** (*Sport*) to play fairly; (*fig*) to play fair.

⚠ **Fairneß, Fairness** ['fɛːɐnɛs] *f* **-**, *no pl* fairness.

Fair play ['fɛːɐ 'pleː] *nt* **- -**, *no pl* fair play.

fäkal *adj* (*geh*) faecal.

Fäkaldünger *m* natural manure, dung.

Fäkalien [-iən] *pl* faeces *pl*.

Fäkalsprache *f* scatological language, scatology.

Fakir *m* **-s, -e** fakir.

Faksimile [fak'ziːmile] *nt* **-s, -s** facsimile.

Faksimile-: ~ausgabe *f* facsimile edition; **~druck** *m* **(a)** printed facsimile; **(b)** *(Verfahren)* autotype; **~stempel** *m* signature stamp; **~unterschrift** *f* facsimile signature.

faksimilieren* *vt* to make a facsimile of, to reproduce in facsimile, to facsimile.

Fakt *nt or m* **-(e)s, -en** *siehe* **Faktum.**

Fakten *pl of* **Fakt, Faktum.**

Fakten-: ~material *nt, no pl* facts *pl*; **~sammlung** *f* collection of facts; **~wissen** *nt* factual knowledge.

Faktion *f (old, Sw) siehe* **Fraktion.**

faktisch [1] *adj attr* actual, real.
[2] *adv* **(a)** in reality *or* actuality *(form)*. **(b)** *(esp Aus inf: praktisch)* more or less.

faktitiv *adj (Gram)* factitive.

Faktitiv(um) *nt (Gram)* factitive verb.

Faktizität *f (geh)* factuality.

Faktor *m* **(a)** factor *(auch Math)*. **(b)** *(Typ)* case-room/bookbindery *etc* supervisor.

Faktorei *f (Comm)* trading post.

Faktoren|analyse *f* factor analysis.

Faktotum *nt* **-s, -s** *or* **Faktoten** factotum.

Faktum *nt* **-s, Fakten** fact.

Faktur *f* **(a)** *(dated)* invoice. **(b)** *(Mus)* structure.

Faktura *f* **-, Fakturen** *(Aus, dated) siehe* **Faktur (a).**

fakturieren* *vt (Comm)* to invoice.

Fakturist(in *f***)** *m (Comm)* **(a)** bookkeeper. **(b)** *(Aus: Rechnungsprüfer)* invoice clerk.

Fakultas *f* **-, Fakultäten: die ~ für ein Fach haben** to be qualified to teach a subject.

Fakultät *f* **(a)** *(Univ: Fachbereich)* faculty ◆ **(ein Kollege) von der anderen ~ sein** *(hum inf) (homosexuell sein)* to be one of them *(inf)*, to be the other way round *(inf)*; *(rare: eine andere Weltanschauung haben)* to be of another school of thought. **(b)** *(obs: Begabung)* faculty. **(c)** *(Math)* factorial.

fakultativ *adj (geh)* optional.

Falange [fa'laŋge] *f* **-,** *no pl (Pol)* Falange.

Falangist(in *f***)** [falaŋ'gɪst(ɪn)] *m (Pol)* Falangist.

falb *adj (geh)* dun.

Falbe *m* **-n, -n** dun.

Falke *m* **-n, -n** falcon; *(fig)* hawk.

Falken-: ~auge *nt (Miner)* hawk's-eye; **~beize, ~jagd** *f* falconry.

Falkland-: ~-Inseln *pl* Falkland Islands *pl*; **~-Krieg** *m* Falklands War.

Falkner(in *f***)** *m* **-s, -** falconer.

Falknerei *f* **(a)** falconry. **(b)** *(Anlage)* falcon house.

Fall[1] *m* **-(e)s, ⸚e (a)** *(das Hinunterfallen)* fall ◆ **im/beim ~ hat er ...** when/as he fell he ...; *siehe* **frei.**
(b) *(das Zufallkommen)* fall; *(fig) (von Menschen, Regierung)* downfall; *(von Plänen, Gesetz etc)* failure ◆ **zu ~ kommen** *(lit geh)* to fall; **über die Affäre ist er zu ~ gekommen** *(fig)* the affair was *or* caused his downfall; **zu ~ bringen** *(lit geh)* to make fall, to trip up; *(fig) Menschen* to cause the downfall of; *Regierung* to bring down; *Gesetz, Plan etc* to thwart; *Tabu* to break down.
(c) *(fig: Untergang, Sturz)* fall.
(d) *(von Kurs, Temperatur etc)* drop, fall *(gen* in).
(e) *(von Gardine etc)* hang, drape.

▼ **Fall**[2] *m* **-(e)s, ⸚e (a)** *(Umstand)* **gesetzt den ~** assuming *or* supposing (that); **für den ~, daß ich ...** in case I ...; **für den ~ meines Todes, im ~e meines Todes** in case I die; **für alle ⸚e** just in case; **in jedem/keinem ~(e)** always/never; **auf jeden/keinen ~** at any rate, at all events/on no account; **auf alle ⸚e** in any case, anyway; **für solche ⸚e** for such occasions; **im äußersten ~(e)** if the worst comes to the worst; **im anderen ~(e)** if not, if that is not the case; **im günstigsten/schlimmsten ~(e)** at best/worst; **im ~e eines ~es** if it comes to it; **wenn dieser ~ eintritt** if this should be the case, if this should arise.
▼ **(b)** *(gegebener Sachverhalt)* case ◆ **in diesem ~** in this case *or* instance; **ein ~ von ...** a case *or* an instance of ...; **von ~ zu ~** from case to case, from one case to the next; *(hin und wieder)* periodically; **in diesem ~(e) will ich noch einmal von einer Bestrafung absehen, aber ...** I won't punish you on this occasion either, but ...; **jds ~ sein** *(inf)* to be sb's cup of tea *(inf)*; **klarer ~!** *(inf)* sure thing! *(esp US inf)*, you bet! *(inf)*.
(c) *(Jur, Med: Beispiel, Person)* case.
(d) *(Gram: Kasus)* case ◆ **der erste/zweite/dritte/vierte/fünfte/sechste ~** the nominative/genitive/dative/accusative/ablative/vocative case.

Fall[3] *nt* **-(e)s, -en** *(Naut)* halyard.

fällbar *adj (Chem)* precipitable.

Fall-: ~beil *nt* guillotine; **~bericht** *m* case report; **~beschleunigung** *f* gravitational acceleration, acceleration due to gravity; **~bö** *f* down gust; **~brücke** *f* drawbridge; *(Enterbrücke)* gangplank.

Falle *f* **-, -n (a)** *(lit, fig)* trap ◆ **in eine ~ geraten** *or* **gehen** *(lit)* to get caught in a trap; *(fig)* to fall into a trap; **jdm in die ~ gehen, in jds ~ geraten** to walk *or* fall into sb's trap; **in der ~ sitzen** to be trapped; **jdn in eine ~ locken** *(fig)* to trick sb; **jdm eine ~ stellen** *(fig)* to set a trap for sb.
(b) *(Tech)* catch, latch.
(c) *(inf: Bett)* bed ◆ **in der ~ sein/liegen** to be in bed; **sich in die ~ hauen, in die ~ gehen** to hit the hay *(inf)*, to turn in; **ab (mit euch) in die ~!** off to beddy-byes *(baby-talk)* *or* bed!

fallen *pret* **fiel,** *ptp* **gefallen** *vi aux sein* **(a)** *(hinabfallen, umfallen)* to fall; *(Gegenstand, Wassermassen auch)* to drop; *(Theat, Vorhang auch)* to come down; *(Klappe auch)* to come down, to drop ◆ **etw ~ lassen** to drop sth; **über etw** *(acc)* **~** to trip over sth; **sich ~ lassen** to drop; *(fig)* to give up; **durch eine Prüfung** *etc* **~** to fail an exam *etc*; **ein gefallenes Mädchen** *(dated)* a fallen woman *(dated)*; *siehe auch* **fallenlassen, Nase, Groschen** *etc.*
(b) *(hängen: Vorhang, Kleid etc)* to hang; *(reichen)* to come down *(bis auf +acc* to) ◆ **die Haare ~ ihr bis auf die Schultern/über die Augen/ins Gesicht/in die Stirn** her hair comes down to *or* reaches her shoulders/falls into her eyes/face/onto her forehead.
(c) *(abfallen, sinken)* to drop; *(Wasserstand, Preise, Fieber auch, Thermometer)* to go down; *(Fluß, Kurse, Wert, Aktien auch, Barometer)* to fall; *(Nachfrage, Ansehen)* to fall off, to decrease ◆ **im Preis/Wert ~** to go down *or* drop *or* fall in price/value; **im Kurs ~** to go down, to drop.
(d) *(im Krieg ums Leben kommen)* to fall, to be killed ◆ **mein Mann ist gefallen** my husband was killed in the war.
(e) *(erobert werden: Festung, Stadt etc)* to fall.
(f) *(fig) (Regierung)* to fall; *(Gesetz etc)* to be dropped; *(Tabu, Brauch etc)* to disappear.
(g) *(mit schneller Bewegung)* **jdm ins Lenkrad ~** to grab the steering wheel from sb; **einem Pferd in die Zügel ~** to grab a horse's reins; **die Tür fällt ins Schloß** the door clicks shut; **die Tür ins Schloß ~ lassen** to let the door shut; **der Tiger fiel dem Elefanten in die Flanke** the tiger pounced on the elephant's flank; *siehe* **Hals**[1]**, Wort.**
(h) *(treffen)* to fall; *(Wahl, Verdacht auch)* to light *(form)* ◆ **das Licht fällt durch die Luke** the light comes in through the skylight; **das Los, das zu tun, fiel auf ihn** it fell to his lot to do that.
(i) *(stattfinden, sich ereignen: Weihnachten, Datum etc)* to fall *(auf +acc* on); *(gehören)* to come *(unter +acc* under, *in +acc* within, under) ◆ **in eine Zeit ~** to belong to an era; **unter einen Begriff ~** to be part of a concept; **aus einer Gruppe/Kategorie** *etc* **~** to come outside *or* be excluded from a group/category *etc.*
(j) *(zufallen: Erbschaft etc)* to go *(an +acc* to) ◆ **das Elsaß fiel an Frankreich** Alsace fell to France; *(nach Verhandlungen)* Alsace went to France.
(k) *(gemacht, erzielt werden) (Entscheidung)* to be made; *(Urteil)* to be passed *or* pronounced; *(Schuß)* to be fired; *(Sport: Tor)* to be scored.
(l) *(Wort)* to be uttered *or* spoken; *(Name)* to be mentioned; *(Bemerkung)* to be made.
(m) *(geraten)* **in Schlaf ~** to fall asleep; **in eine andere Tonart ~** to speak in *or* *(absichtlich)* adopt a different tone (of voice); **in eine andere Sprache ~** to lapse *or* drop into another language; **in eine andere Gangart ~** to change one's pace; *siehe* **Opfer, Rahmen, Rolle** *etc.*
(n) *(sein)* **das fällt ihm leicht/schwer** he finds that easy/difficult; *siehe* **Last, lästig** *etc.*

fällen *vt* **(a)** *(umschlagen)* to fell.
(b) *(fig) Entscheidung* to make, to come to; *Urteil* to pass, to pronounce.
(c) *(zum Angriff senken) Lanze* to lower, to level ◆ **mit gefälltem Bajonett** with bayonet(s) at the ready.
(d) *(Chem)* to precipitate.
(e) *(Math) siehe* **Lot**[1] **(d).**

⚠ **fallenlassen*** *vt sep irreg* **(a)** *(aufgeben) Plan, Mitarbeiter* to drop. **(b)** *(äußern) Bemerkung* to let drop ◆ **hat er irgend etwas darüber ~?** *(inf)* has he let anything drop about it?

Fallensteller *m* **-s, -** *(Hunt)* trapper.

Fall-: ~gatter *nt siehe* **~gitter**; **~geschwindigkeit** *f (Phys)* speed of fall; **~gesetz** *nt (Phys)* law of falling bodies; **~gitter** *nt* portcullis; **~grube** *f (Hunt)* pit; *(fig rare)* pitfall; **~hammer** *m* pile-driver; **~höhe** *f (Phys)* (height *or* depth of) drop; *(beim Wasserkraftwerk)* head.

fallieren* *vi (Fin)* to fail, to go bankrupt.

fällig *adj* due *pred*; *(Fin) Rechnung, Betrag etc auch* payable; *Wechsel* mature(d) ◆ **längst ~** long overdue; **die ~en Zinsen** the interest due; **~ werden** to become *or* fall due; *(Wechsel)* to mature; **am Wochenende ist endlich Rasenmähen/eine Party ~** the lawn is about due for a cut/a party is about due at the weekend; **der Kerl ist ~** *(inf)* he's for it *(inf)*.

Fälligkeit *f (Fin)* settlement date; *(von Wechseln)* maturity ◆ **zahlbar bei ~** payable by settlement date; payable at *or* on maturity.

Fälligkeits-: ~tag, ~termin *m* settlement date; *(von Wechsel)* date of maturity.

Fall|obst *nt* windfalls *pl*; *(sl: Hängebrüste)* floppy boobs *(sl)* ◆ **ein Stück ~** a windfall.

Fallout, Fall-out [fɔ'laut] *m* **-s, -s** fall-out.

Fall-: ~reep *nt (Naut)* rope ladder; *(Treppe)* gangway; **~rohr** *nt* drainpipe, downpipe *(form)*; **~rückzieher** *m (Ftbl)* overhead kick, bicycle kick.

falls *conj (wenn)* if; *(für den Fall, daß)* in case ◆ **~ möglich** if possible; **~ du Lust hast** if you (happen to) want to, if you should (happen to) want to; **gib mir deine Telefonnummer, ~ ich mich verspäten sollte** give me your phone number in case I'm late; **~ ich mich verspäten sollte, rufe ich vorher an** if I'm late *or* in the event of my being late *(form)* I'll phone you first.

Fallschirm *m* parachute ◆ **mit dem ~ abspringen** to parachute, to make a parachute jump; **mit dem ~ über Frankreich abspringen** to parachute out over France; *(in Kriegszeit)* to parachute into France; **etw mit dem ~ abwerfen** to drop sth by parachute.

Fallschirm-: ~absprung *m* parachute jump; **~jäger** *m (Mil)* paratrooper; **die ~jäger** *(Einheit)* the paratroop(er)s; **~springen** *nt* parachuting; **~springer** *m* parachutist; **~truppe** *f (Mil)* paratroops *pl.*

Fall-: ~strick *m (fig)* trap, snare; **jdm ~stricke** *or* **einen ~strick legen** to set a trap *or* snare for sb (to walk into); **~studie** *f* case study; **~sucht** *f (old)* falling sickness *(old)*; **f~süchtig** *adj (old)* epileptic; **~tür** *f* trapdoor.

Fällung *f, no pl* (a) (*von Bäumen etc*) felling. (b) (*Jur: eines Urteils*) pronouncement; (*einer Entscheidung*) reaching. (c) (*Chem*) precipitation.

Fällungsmittel *nt* (*Chem*) precipitant.

Fall-: f~weise *adv* (a) from case to case; (b) (*esp Aus: gelegentlich*) now and again, occasionally; **~wind** *m* katabatic (*form*) *or* fall wind; **~wurf** *m* (*Sport*) diving throw.

falsch *adj* (a) (*verkehrt, fehlerhaft*) wrong; (*in der Logik etc*) false ♦ **richtig/wahr oder ~** right or wrong/true or false; **alles ~ machen** to do everything wrong; **wie man's macht, ist es ~** (*inf*) whatever I/you *etc* do it's bound to be wrong; **mach dir keine ~en Vorstellungen darüber/davon** don't get the wrong idea (*inf*) *or* any misconceptions about it; **du machst dir völlig ~e Vorstellungen** you have *or* you've got quite the wrong idea *or* some misconceptions; **~es Bewußtsein** (*Philos, Sociol*) false consciousness; **~er Alarm** (*lit, fig*) false alarm; **etw ~ verstehen** to misunderstand sth, to get sth wrong (*inf*); **etw ~ schreiben/aussprechen** to spell/pronounce sth wrongly, to misspell/mispronounce sth; **die Uhr geht ~** the clock is wrong; **Kinder ~ erziehen** to bring children up badly; **~ spielen** (*Mus*) to play the wrong note/notes; (*unrein*) to play off key *or* out of tune; (*Cards*) to cheat; **~ singen** to sing out of tune *or* off key; **Sie sind hier ~** you're in the wrong place; **bei jdm an den F~en geraten** *or* **kommen** to pick the wrong person in sb; **~ liegen** (*inf*) to be wrong (*bei, in +dat* about, *mit* in); **am ~en Ort** *or* **Platz sein** to have come to the wrong place; **~ verbunden sein** to have the wrong number; **~ verstandene Freundschaft** misinterpreted friendship; *siehe* **Licht, Pferd** *etc*.
(b) (*unecht, nachgemacht*) *Zähne etc* false; *Perlen auch* fake; *Würfel* loaded; (*gefälscht*) *Paß etc* forged, fake; *Geld* counterfeit; (*betrügerisch*) bogus, fake ♦ **~er Zopf** hairpiece, switch.
(c) (*unaufrichtig, unangebracht*) *Gefühl, Freund, Scham, Pathos etc* false ♦ **ein ~er Hund, eine ~e Schlange** (*inf*) a snake-in-the-grass; **ein ~es Spiel (mit jdm) treiben** to play (sb) false; **~ lachen** to give a false laugh; **unter ~er Flagge segeln** (*lit, fig*) to sail under false colours; *siehe* **Bescheidenheit**.
(d) (*dial: tückisch*) nasty.

Falsch *m* (*old*): **ohne ~ sein** to be without guile *or* artifice.

Falsch|aussage *f* (*Jur*) (**uneidliche**) **~** false statement, false evidence.

Falsch|eid *m* (*Jur*) (unintentional) false statement *or* oath.

fälschen *vt* to forge, to fake; *Geld, Briefmarken auch* to counterfeit; (*Comm*) *Bücher* to falsify; *Geschichte, Tatsachen* to falsify; *siehe* **gefälscht**.

Fälscher(in *f*) *m* **-s, -** forger; (*von Geld, Briefmarken auch*) counterfeiter.

Falsch-: ~fahrer *m* ghost-driver (*esp US inf*), *person driving in the wrong direction*; **~geld** *nt* counterfeit *or* forged money; **f~gläubig** *adj* (*old Rel*) heterodox; **~heit** *f, no pl* falsity, falseness; (*dial: von Menschen*) nastiness.

fälschlich [1] *adj* false; *Behauptung auch* erroneous; *Annahme, Glaube auch* mistaken, erroneous.
[2] *adv* wrongly, falsely; *behaupten, annehmen, glauben auch* mistakenly, erroneously; (*versehentlich*) by mistake.

fälschlicherweise *adv* wrongly, falsely; *behaupten, annehmen, glauben auch* mistakenly, erroneously.

Falsch-: ~meldung *f* (*Press*) false report; **~münzer(in *f*)** *m* **-s, -** forger, counterfeiter; **~münzerei** *f* forgery, counterfeiting; **~parker(in *f*)** *m* **-s, -** parking offender; **f~spielen** *vi sep* (*Cards*) to cheat; **~spieler** *m* (*Cards*) cheat; (*professionell*) cardsharp(er).

Fälschung *f* (a) *no pl* (*das Fälschen*) forgery, forging, faking; (*von Geld, Briefmarken auch*) counterfeiting. (b) (*gefälschter Gegenstand*) forgery, fake.

fälschungssicher *adj* forgery-proof.

Falsett *nt* **-(e)s, -e** falsetto ♦ **~ singen, mit ~stimme singen** to sing falsetto.

Falsifikat *nt* forgery, fake.

Falsifikation *f* falsification.

falsifizieren* *vt* to falsify.

Falt-: f~bar *adj* foldable; (*zusammenklappbar*) collapsible; *Stuhl, Tisch, Fahrrad* folding *attr*, collapsible; **~blatt** *nt* leaflet; (*in Zeitschrift etc auch*) insert; **~boot** *nt* collapsible boat.

Fältchen *nt dim of* **Falte**.

Falte *f* **-, -n** (a) (*in Stoff, Papier*) fold; (*Knitter~, Bügel~*) crease ♦ **in ~n legen** to fold; **~n schlagen** to get creased, to crease; **~n werfen** to fall in folds, to drape.
(b) (*in Haut*) wrinkle ♦ **strenge ~n** harsh lines; **die Stirn in ~n ziehen** *or* **legen** to knit *or* furrow one's brow.
(c) (*Geol*) fold.

fälteln *vt* to pleat.

falten [1] *vt* to fold ♦ **die Stirn ~** to knit one's brow.
[2] *vr* to fold.

Falten-: ~gebirge *nt* fold mountains *pl*; **f~los** *adj Gesicht* unlined; *Haut auch* smooth; **f~reich** *adj Haut* wrinkled; *Gesicht auch* lined; **~rock** *m* pleated skirt; **~wurf** *m* fall of the folds.

Falter *m* **-s, -** (*Tag~*) butterfly; (*Nacht~*) moth.

faltig *adj* (*zerknittert*) creased; (*in Falten gelegt*) hanging in folds; *Gesicht, Haut* wrinkled ♦ **~ fallen** to hang in folds; **~ gerafft sein** to be gathered into folds.

-fältig *adj suf* -fold.

Falt-: ~kalender *m siehe* **~planer**; **~karte** *f* folding *or* fold-up map; **~karton** *m siehe* **~schachtel**; **~kinderwagen** *m* collapsible pram (*Brit*) *or* baby carriage (*US*); (*Sportwagen*) baby buggy (*Brit*), babywalker (*US*); **~planer** *m* fold-out planner; **~schachtel** *f* collapsible box; **~tür** *f* folding door.

Falz *m* **-es, -e** (*Kniff, Faltlinie*) fold; (*zwischen Buchrücken und -deckel*) joint; (*Tech*) rabbet; (*zwischen Blechrändern*) join, lock seam (*spec*); (*Briefmarken~*) hinge.

falzen *vt Papierbogen* to fold; *Holz* to rabbet; *Blechränder* to join with a lock seam.

Fam. *abbr of* **Familie**.

familiär *adj* (a) family *attr*. (b) (*zwanglos*) informal; (*freundschaftlich*) close; (*pej: plump-vertraulich*) familiar ♦ **ein ~er Ausdruck** a colloquialism; **mit jdm ~ verkehren** to be on close terms with sb.

Familiarität *f siehe adj (b)* informality; closeness; familiarity.

Familie [fa'mi:liə] *f* family ♦ **~ Müller** the Müller family; **~ Otto Francke** (*als Anschrift*) Mr. & Mrs. Otto Francke and family; **eine ~ gründen** to start a family; **~ haben** (*inf*) to have a family; **aus guter ~ sein** to come from a good family; **es liegt in der ~** it runs in the family; **zur ~ gehören** to be one of the family; **es bleibt in der ~** it'll stay in the family; *siehe* **beste(r, s)**.

Familien- [-iən-] *in cpds* family; **~ähnlichkeit** *f* family resemblance; **~angehörige(r)** *mf* dependant; ⚠**~anschluß** *m* **Unterkunft/Stellung mit ~anschluß** *accommodation/job where one is treated as one of the family*; **~anschluß suchen** to wish to be treated as one of the family; **~anzeigen** *pl* personal announcements *pl*; **~ausweis** *m* family pass; **~beratungsstelle** *f* family planning office; **~besitz** *m* family property; **in ~besitz sein** to be owned by the family; **~betrieb** *m* family concern *or* business; **~buch** *nt book of family events with some legal documents*; **~feier** *f*, **~fest** *nt* family party; **~forschung** *f* genealogy; **~glück** *nt* happy family life; **~grab** *nt* family grave; **~gruft** *f* family vault; **~klüngel** *m* (*inf*) **der ganze ~klüngel** the whole tribe (*inf*); **~kreis** *m* family circle; **die Trauung fand im engsten ~kreis statt** only the immediate family were present at the wedding; **~leben** *nt* family life; **~mitglied** *nt* member of the family; **~nachrichten** *pl* births, marriages and deaths, personal announcements; **~name** *m* surname, family name (*US*); **~oberhaupt** *nt* head of the family; **~packung** *f* family(-size) pack; ⚠**~paß** *m* family passport; **~planung** *f* family planning; **~rat** *m* family council; **~recht** *nt* family law; **~roman** *m* (family) saga; **~schmuck** *m* family jewels *pl*; **~serie** *f* (*TV*) family series; **~sinn** *m* sense of family; **~stand** *m* marital status; **~unterhalt** *m* family upkeep *or* maintenance; **den ~unterhalt verdienen** to support the family; **~vater** *m* father (of a family); **~verhältnisse** *pl* family circumstances *pl or* background *sing*; **aus was für ~verhältnissen kommt sie?** what is her family background?, what kind of family does she come from?; **~vorstand** *m* (*form*) head of the family; **~wappen** *nt* family arms *pl*; **~zulage** *f* dependants' allowance (*in unemployment benefit*); **~zusammenführung** *f* (*Pol*) *principle of allowing families to be united*; **~zuwachs** *m* addition to the family.

famos *adj* (*dated inf*) capital (*dated inf*), splendid.

Famulatur *f period when a medical student does practical work in a hospital*, clinical practice.

famulieren* *vi* (*Med*) to do some practical work.

Famulus *m* **-, Famuli** (a) (*Med*) *student doing practical work*. (b) (*old*) professor's assistant, student.

Fan [fɛn] *m* **-s, -s** fan; (*Ftbl auch*) supporter.

Fanal *nt* **-s, -e** (*liter*) signal (*gen* for).

Fanatiker(in *f*) *m* **-s, -** fanatic.

-fanatiker(in *f*) *m in cpds* -fiend (*inf*), -fanatic, -maniac.

fanatisch *adj* fanatical.

fanatisiert *adj* (*geh*) rabid.

Fanatismus *m* fanaticism.

Fanclub ['fɛn-] *m* fan club.

fand *pret of* **finden**.

Fanfare *f* **-, -n** (a) (*Mus*) fanfare. (b) (*Aut*) horn.

Fanfaren-: ~stoß *m* flourish (of trumpets), fanfare; **~zug** *m* trumpeters *pl*.

Fang *m* **-(e)s, ¨e** (a) *no pl* (*das Fangen*) hunting; (*mit Fallen*) trapping; (*Fischen*) fishing ♦ **auf ~ gehen** to go hunting/trapping/fishing; **zum ~ auslaufen** to go fishing.
(b) *no pl* (*Beute*) (*lit, fig*) catch; (*von Wild auch*) bag; (*fig: von Gegenständen*) haul ♦ **einen guten ~ machen** to make a good catch/get a good bag/haul.
(c) *no pl* (*Hunt: Todesstoß*) coup de grâce.
(d) *usu pl* (*Hunt*) (*Kralle*) talon; (*Reißzahn*) fang ♦ **in den ¨~en** *+gen* (*fig*) in the clutches of.

Fang-: ~arm *m* (*Zool*) tentacle; **~ball** *m* catch; **~eisen** *nt* (*Hunt*) gin trap.

fangen *pret* **fing**, *ptp* **gefangen** [1] *vt Tier, Fisch, Verbrecher* to catch; *Wild auch* to bag; (*mit Fallen*) to trap; (*fig: überlisten*) (*durch geschickte Fragen*) to trap; (*durch Versprechungen etc*) to trick ♦ **(sich** *dat*) **eine (Ohrfeige** *etc*) **~** (*inf*) to catch it (*inf*); *siehe* **gefangen**.
[2] *vi* to catch ♦ **F~ spielen** to play tag *or* it.
[3] *vr* (a) (*in einer Falle*) to get caught ♦ **er hat sich in der eigenen Schlinge** *or* **Falle gefangen** (*fig*) he was hoist with his own petard.
(b) (*das Gleichgewicht wiederfinden*) to steady oneself; (*beim Reden etc*) to recover oneself; (*Flugzeug*) to straighten out; (*seelisch*) to get on an even keel again.
(c) (*sich verfangen*) to get caught (up); (*Wind*) to get trapped ♦ **ich fing mich mit dem Hosenbein in der Fahrradkette** I got my trouser leg caught (up) in the bicycle chain.

Fänger *m* **-s, -** (a) (*Tier~*) hunter; (*mit Fallen*) trapper; (*Wal~*) whaler; (*Robben~*) sealer. (b) (*Sport*) catcher.

Fang-: ~flotte *f* fishing fleet; **~frage** *f* catch *or* trick question; **~gründe** *pl* fishing grounds *pl*; **~korb** *m* lifeguard, cowcatcher (*inf*); **~leine** *f* (a) (*Naut*) hawser; (b) (*Aviat*) arresting gear cable; (c) (*von Fallschirm*) rigging line;

⚠: for details of spelling reform, see supplement

~**messer** *nt* hunting knife; ~**netz** *nt* **(a)** (*Hunt, Fishing*) net; **(b)** (*Aviat*) arresting gear; ~**quote** *f* (fishing) quota; ~**schaltung** *f* (*Telec*) interception circuit; ~**schiff** *nt* fishing boat; (*mit Netzen*) trawler; (*Walfangschiff*) whaler; ~**schnur** *f* (*Mil*) aiguillette; ⚠~**schuß** *m* (*Hunt, fig*) coup de grâce (*with a gun*); **f~sicher** *adj* safe; **f~sicher sein** to be a good catch; ~**stoß** *m* coup de grâce (*with a knife*); ~**tuch** *nt* life-net (*US*), jumping-sheet, blanket (*inf*); **f~unsicher** *adj* butter-fingered; ~**vorrichtung** *f* arresting device; ~**zahn** *m* canine (tooth), fang; (*von Eber*) tusk.

Fant *m* **-(e)s, -e** (*old pej*) jackanapes (*old*).

Fantasie *f* **(a)** (*Mus*) fantasia. **(b)** *siehe* **Phantasie.**

fantastisch *adj* fantastic.

Farad *nt* **-(s), -** farad.

Faradaysch *adj* ~**er Käfig** Faraday cage.

Farb- *in cpds* colour; ~**abstimmung** *f* colour scheme; (*TV*) colour adjustment; ~**aufnahme** *f* colour photo(graph); ~**bad** *nt* dye-bath; ~**band**[1] *nt* (*von Schreibmaschine*) (typewriter) ribbon; ~**band**[2] *m* (*Buch*) book with colour illustrations; ~**bandkassette** *f* typewriter ribbon cassette.

färbbar *adj* colourable.

Farb-: ~**bericht** *m* (*Press, TV*) report in colour; (*in Zeitschriften auch*) colour feature; ~**beutel** *m* paint bomb; ~**bild** *nt* (*Phot*) colour photo(graph); ~**druck** *m* colour print; ~**drucker** *m* colour printer.

Farbe *f* **-, -n (a)** (*Farbton, Tönung*) colour, color (*US*); (*Tönung auch*) shade ◆ **~ bekommen** to get a bit of colour, to catch the sun (*inf*); **~ verlieren** to go pale; **in ~** in colour; **einer Sache** (*dat*) **mehr ~ geben** (*fig*) to give sth more colour; **etw in den dunkelsten** *or* **schwärzesten/glänzendsten ~n schildern** *or* **ausmalen** to paint a black/rosy picture of sth, to paint sth in glowing colours.

(b) (*Maler~, Anstrich~*) paint; (*für Farbbad*) dye; (*Druck~*) ink.

(c) (*Fahne, Univ*) **~n** *pl* colours *pl*.

(d) (*Cards*) suit ◆ **~ bedienen** to follow suit; **~ bekennen** (*fig*) (*alles zugeben*) to make a clean breast of it, to come clean; (*sich entscheiden*) to nail one's colours to the mast.

farb|echt *adj* colourfast.

Färbemittel *nt* dye.

farb|empfindlich *adj* (*Phot*) colour-sensitive.

färben [1] *vt* to colour; *Stoff, Haar* to dye; *siehe* **gefärbt.**

[2] *vi* (*ab~*) to run (*inf*).

[3] *vr* to change colour ◆ **ihre Wangen färbten sich leicht** she coloured slightly; **sich grün/blau** *etc* **~** to turn green/blue *etc.*

Farben- *in cpds* colour; **f~blind** *adj* colour-blind; ~**druck** *m* (*Typ*) colour printing; **f~freudig** *adj* colourful; *Mensch* keen on bright colours; **f~froh** *adj* colourful; ~**lehre** *f* theory of colour; (*Fach auch*) chromatics *sing*; ~**pracht** *f* blaze of colour; **in seiner ganzen ~pracht** in all its glory; **f~prächtig** *adj* gloriously colourful; **f~reich** *adj* colourful; ~**reichtum** *m* wealth of colours; ~**sinn** *m* sense of colour (*auch Biol*), colour sense; ~**spiel** *nt* play *or* kaleidoscope of colours; ⚠**f~tragend** *adj* (*Univ*) **f~tragende Verbindung** *society with traditional heraldic colours*; ~**zusammenstellung** *f* colour combination.

Färber *m* **-s, -** dyer.

Färberei *f* **(a)** (*Betrieb*) dyeing works *sing or pl*. **(b)** *no pl* (*Verfahren*) dyeing.

Farb-: ~**fernsehen** *nt* colour television *or* TV; ~**fernseher** *m*, ~**fernsehgerät** *nt* colour television (set); ~**film** *m* colour film; ~**filter** *m* (*Phot*) colour filter; ~**foto** *nt* colour photo(graph); ~**fotografie** *f* (*Verfahren*) colour photography; (*Bild*) colour photo(graph); ~**gebung** *f* colouring, coloration.

farbig *adj* **(a)** coloured; (*fig*) *Schilderung* vivid, colourful ◆ **ein ~er Druck/eine ~e Postkarte** a colour print/postcard; **~ fotografieren** to take colour photographs. **(b)** *attr* (*Hautfarbe*) coloured.

färbig *adj* (*Aus*) *siehe* **farbig (a).**

Farbige(r) *mf decl as adj* coloured man/woman/person *etc* ◆ **die ~n** the coloureds *pl*, coloured people *pl*.

Farb-: ~**kasten** *m* paintbox; ~**kissen** *nt* inkpad; ~**klecks** *m* blob of paint, paint spot; ~**kopierer** *m* colour copier; **f~lich** *adj* colour; **f~lich einwandfrei** with perfect colour; **zwei Sachen f~lich aufeinander abstimmen** to match two things up for colour; **f~los** *adj* (*lit, fig*) colourless; ~**losigkeit** *f* (*lit, fig*) colourlessness; ~**mine** *f* coloured-ink cartridge; ~**mischung** *f* (*gemischte Farbe*) mixture of colours; ~**roller** *m* paint roller; ~**sinn** *m siehe* **Farbensinn**; ~**stich** *m* (*Phot, TV*) colour fault; ~**stift** *m* coloured pen; (*Buntstift*) crayon, coloured pencil; ~**stoff** *m* (*Lebensmittel~*) (artificial) colouring; (*Haut~*) pigment; (*für Textilien etc*) dye; ~**tafel** *f* colour plate; (*Tabelle*) colour chart; ~**ton** *m* shade, hue; (*Tönung*) tint; ~**tupfer** *m* spot of colour.

Färbung *f* (*das Färben, Farbgebung*) colouring; (*Tönung*) tinge, hue; (*fig*) slant, bias.

Farce ['farsə] *f* **-, -n (a)** (*Theat, fig*) farce. **(b)** (*Cook*) stuffing; (*Fleisch auch*) forcemeat.

farcieren* [far'si:rən] *vt* (*Cook*) to stuff.

Farm *f* **-, -en** farm.

Farmer *m* **-s, -** farmer.

Farmhaus *nt* farmhouse.

Farn *m* **-(e)s, -e, Farnkraut** *nt* fern; (*Adler~*) bracken.

Färöer *pl* Faeroes *pl*, Faeroe Islands *pl*.

Färse *f* **-, -n** heifer.

Fasan *m* **-s, -e** *or* **-en** pheasant.

Fasanerie *f* pheasant-house; (*im Freien*) pheasant-run.

Fasche *f* **-, -n** (*Aus*) bandage.

faschen *vt* (*Aus*) to bandage.

faschieren* *vt* (*Aus Cook*) to mince ◆ **Faschiertes** mince, minced meat.

Faschine *f* fascine.

Fasching *m* **-s, -e** *or* **-s** *Shrovetide carnival*, Fasching.

Faschings- *in cpds* carnival; ~**dienstag** *m* Shrove Tuesday, Pancake Day; ~**zeit** *f* carnival period.

Faschismus *m* fascism.

Faschist(in *f*) *m* fascist.

faschistisch *adj* fascist.

faschistoid *adj* fascistic.

Fase *f* **-, -n** bevel, chamfer.

Faselei *f* (*pej*) *siehe* **Gefasel.**

Fas(e)ler *m* **-s, -** (*pej*) drivelling idiot (*pej*).

faseln (*pej*) [1] *vi* to drivel (*inf*).

[2] *vt* **Blödsinn** *etc* **~** to talk drivel; **das ist alles gefaselt** that's drivel (*inf*), that's just (so much) twaddle (*inf*); **was hat er gefaselt?** what was he drivelling about?

Faser *f* **-, -n** fibre ◆ **ein Pullover aus synthetischen ~n** a pullover made of synthetic fibre; **er hat keine trockene ~ am Leib** he's soaked through *or* drenched; **mit allen ~n des Herzens** (*liter*) with every fibre of one's being (*liter*).

Faser-: **f~artig** *adj* fibrous; ~**gewebe** *nt* (*Biol*) fibrous tissue.

fas(e)rig *adj* fibrous; *Fleisch, Spargel auch* stringy (*pej*); (*zerfasert*) frayed.

fasern *vi* to fray.

Faser-: **f~nackt** *adj siehe* **splitter(faser)nackt**; ~**optik** *f* fibre optics *sing*; ~**pflanze** *f* fibre plant; ~**platte** *f* fibre-board; **f~schonend** *adj* gentle (*to fabrics*); ~**stoff** *m* fibrous material.

Fasnacht *f siehe* **Fastnacht.**

⚠**Faß** *nt* **Fasses, Fässer** barrel; (*kleines Bier~*) keg; (*zum Gären, Einlegen*) vat; (*zum Buttern*) (barrel) churn; (*für Öl, Benzin, Chemikalien*) drum ◆ **etw in Fässer füllen** to put sth into barrels/drums, to barrel sth; **drei Fässer/~ Bier** three barrels of beer; **vom ~** on tap; *Bier auch* on draught (*esp Brit*); *Sherry, Wein auch* from the wood (*esp Brit*); **er trinkt nur Bier vom ~** he only drinks draught beer; **ein ~ ohne Boden** (*fig*) a bottomless pit; **ein ~ aufmachen** (*fig inf*) to kick up a shindy (*inf*) *or* a dust (*inf*); **das schlägt dem ~ den Boden aus** (*inf*) that beats everything!, that takes the biscuit! (*inf*); **das brachte das ~ zum Überlaufen** (*fig*) that put the tin lid on it (*inf*).

Fassade *f* (*lit, fig*) façade; (*inf: Gesicht*) face ◆ **das ist doch nur ~** (*fig*) that's just a façade.

Fassaden-: ~**kletterer** *m* cat burglar; ~**reinigung** *f* exterior cleaning.

⚠**Faß-:** ~**band** *nt* hoop (of a barrel); **f~bar** *adj* comprehensible, understandable; **das ist doch nicht f~bar!** that's incomprehensible!; ~**bier** *nt* draught beer; ~**binder** *m* (*old, Aus*) cooper.

⚠**Fäßchen** *nt dim of* **Faß** cask.

⚠**Faßdaube** *f* stave.

fassen [1] *vt* **(a)** (*ergreifen*) to take hold of; (*hastig, kräftig*) to grab, to seize; (*festnehmen*) *Einbrecher etc* to apprehend (*form*), to seize; (*Mil*) *Munition* to draw ◆ **jdn beim** *or* **am Arm ~** to take/grab sb by the arm; **er faßte ihre Hand** he took her hand; **Schauder/Grauen/Entsetzen faßte ihn** he was seized with horror; **faß!** seize!

(b) (*fig*) *Beschluß, Entschluß* to make, to take; *Mut* to take ◆ **Vertrauen zu jdm ~** to come to trust sb; **den Gedanken ~, etw zu tun** to form *or* have the idea of doing sth; **den Vorsatz ~, etw zu tun** to make a resolution to do sth; *siehe* **Auge, Fuß, Herz** *etc.*

(c) (*begreifen*) to grasp, to understand ◆ **es ist nicht zu ~** it's unbelievable *or* incredible.

(d) (*enthalten*) to hold.

(e) (*aufnehmen*) *Essen* to get; (*Rail, Naut*) *Wasser, Kohlen* to take on ◆ **Essen ~!** come and get it!

(f) (*ein~*) *Edelsteine* to set; *Bild* to frame; *Quelle* to surround; (*fig: ausdrücken*) to express ◆ **in Verse/Worte ~** to put into verse/words; **neu ~** *Manuskript, Rede, Erzählung* to revise; **etw weit/eng ~** to interpret sth broadly/narrowly.

[2] *vi* **(a)** (*nicht abrutschen*) to grip; (*Zahnrad*) to bite.

(b) (*greifen*) **an/in etw** (*acc*) **~** to feel sth; (*berühren*) to touch sth; **faß mal unter den Tisch** feel under the table; **da faßt man sich** (*dat*) **an den Kopf** (*inf*) you wouldn't believe it, would you?

[3] *vr* (*sich beherrschen*) to compose oneself ◆ **faß dich!** pull yourself together!; **sich vor Freude kaum ~ können** to be beside oneself with joy; **sich** (*dat*) **an den Kopf ~** (*fig*) to shake one's head in disbelief; **sich in Geduld ~** to be patient, to possess one's soul in patience; **sich kurz ~** to be brief; *siehe* **gefaßt.**

fässerweise *adv* (*in großen Mengen*) by the gallon; (*in Fässern*) by the barrel.

⚠**faßlich** *adj* comprehensible, understandable.

⚠**Faßlichkeit** *f, no pl* comprehensibility.

Fasson [fa'sõ:] *f* **-, -s** (*von Kleidung*) style; (*von Frisur*) shape ◆ **aus der ~ geraten** (*lit*) to go out of shape, to lose its shape; (*dated: dick werden*) to get a spare tyre (*inf*), to get (a bit) broad in the beam (*inf*); **jeder soll nach seiner ~ selig werden** (*prov*) everyone has to find his own salvation.

fassonieren* *vt* (*Aus*) *Haare* to (cut and) shape.

Fassonschnitt [fa'sõ:-] *m style in which the hair is shaped into the neck*; (*für Herren*) short back and sides.

⚠**Faßreif(en)** *m* hoop.

Fassung *f* **(a)** (*von Juwelen*) setting; (*von Bild*) frame; (*Elec*) holder.

(b) (*Bearbeitung, Wortlaut*) version ◆ **ein Film/Buch in ungekürzter ~** the uncut/unabridged version of a film/book; **ein Film in deutscher ~** a film

with German dubbing.
(c) *no pl (Ruhe, Besonnenheit)* composure ◆ **die ~ bewahren** *or* **behalten** to maintain one's composure; **etw mit ~ tragen** to take sth calmly *or* with equanimity; **die ~ verlieren** to lose one's composure; **völlig außer ~ geraten** to lose all self-control; **jdn aus der ~ bringen** to disconcert *or* throw *(inf)* sb; *Redner auch* to put sb off.

Fassungs-: ~kraft *f (liter)* (powers of) comprehension *or* understanding; **die menschliche ~kraft übersteigen** to be beyond human understanding; **f~los** *adj* aghast, stunned; **~losigkeit** *f* complete bewilderment; **~vermögen** *nt (lit, fig)* capacity; **das übersteigt mein ~vermögen** that is beyond me *or* beyond the limits of my comprehension.

⚠**Faß-: ~wein** *m* wine from the wood; **f~weise** *adv* by the barrel; *(in Fässern)* in barrels.

fast *adv* almost, nearly ◆ **~ nie** hardly ever, almost never; **~ nichts** hardly anything, almost nothing; **ich wäre ~ überfahren worden** I was almost *or* nearly run over.

fasten *vi* to fast.

Fasten-: ~kur *f* diet; **eine ~kur machen/anfangen** to be/go on a diet; **~zeit** *f* period of fasting; *(Eccl)* Lent.

Fast-Food [fa:st'fu:d] *nt -, no pl* fast food.

Fastnacht *f, no pl* **(a)** *siehe* **Faschingsdienstag. (b)** *siehe* **Fasching.**

Fastnachts-: ~narr *m disguised figure in Shrove Tuesday celebrations;* **~spiel** *nt (Liter)* Shrovetide play; **~umzug** *m* Shrove Tuesday procession.

Fasttag *m* day of fasting.

Faszikel *m -s, - (old, form)* section of manuscript, fascicle *(spec)*.

Faszination *f* fascination ◆ **~ ausstrahlen** to radiate charm; **jds ~** *(dat)* **erlegen sein** to succumb to sb's fascinating power.

faszinieren* *vti* to fascinate *(an +dat* about) ◆ **~d** fascinating; **mich fasziniert der Gedanke, das zu tun** I'm very attracted by *or* to the idea of doing that.

fatal *adj (geh) (verhängnisvoll)* fatal, fateful, dire; *(peinlich)* embarrassing, awkward.

Fatalismus *m* fatalism.

Fatalist(in *f)* *m* fatalist.

fatalistisch *adj* fatalistic.

Fatalität *f* great misfortune.

Fata Morgana *f - -, - Morganen or -s (lit, fig)* Fata Morgana *(liter)*, mirage.

Fatsche *f -, -n (Aus) siehe* **Fasche.**

fatschen *vt (Aus) siehe* **faschen.**

Fatzke *m -n or -s, -n or -s (inf)* stuck-up twit *(inf)*.

fauchen *vti* to hiss.

faul *adj* **(a)** *(verfault)* bad; *Lebensmittel auch* off *pred; Eier, Obst auch, Holz, Gesellschaftsordnung* rotten; *Geschmack, Geruch auch* foul, putrid; *Zahn auch* decayed; *Laub* rotting; *Wasser* foul.
(b) *(verdächtig)* fishy *(inf)*, suspicious, dubious; *(Comm) Wechsel, Scheck* dud *(inf)*; *Kredit* bad; *(fadenscheinig) Ausreden* flimsy, feeble; *Kompromiß* uneasy; *Friede* empty; *(dumm) Witz* bad ◆ **hier ist etwas ~** *(inf)* there's something fishy here *(inf)*; **etwas ist ~ daran, an der Sache ist etwas ~** *(inf)* there's something fishy about the whole business *(inf)*; **etwas ist ~ im Staate Dänemark** *(prov)* there's something rotten in the State of Denmark *(prov)*.
(c) *(träge)* lazy, idle ◆ **~ wie die Sünde** bone-idle; **nicht ~** *(reaktionsschnell)* quick as you please; **er hat seinen ~en Tag** *(müßiger Tag)* he's having a lazy day; *(~e Stimmung)* he's in a lazy mood; *siehe* **Haut, Strick[1].**

Fäule *f -, no pl* **(a)** *(Vet)* (liver) rot. **(b)** *siehe* **Fäulnis.**

faulen *vi aux sein or haben* to rot; *(Aas auch)* to putrefy; *(Zahn)* to decay; *(Lebensmittel)* to go bad.

faulenzen *vi* to laze *or* loaf *(esp pej inf)* about.

Faulenzer *m -s, -* **(a)** layabout. **(b)** *(Aus: Linienblatt)* sheet of ruled paper.

Faulenzerei *f* lazing *or* loafing *(esp pej inf)* about.

Faulheit *f* laziness, idleness ◆ **er stinkt vor ~** *(inf)* he's bone-idle.

faulig *adj* going bad; *Lebensmittel auch* going off; *Eier, Obst auch* going rotten; *Wasser* stale; *(in Teich, See etc)* stagnating; *Geruch, Geschmack* foul, putrid ◆ **~ riechen/schmecken** to taste/smell bad; *(Wasser)* to taste/smell foul.

Fäulnis *f, no pl* rot; *(von Fleisch auch)* putrefaction; *(von Zahn)* decay; *(fig)* decadence, degeneracy ◆ **von ~ befallen** rotting, decaying.

Fäulnis-: ⚠**f~erregend** *adj* putrefactive; **~erreger** *m* putrefier.

Faul-: ~pelz *m (inf)* lazybones *sing (inf)*; **~schlamm** *m* sapropel *(spec)*, sludge; **~tier** *nt* sloth; *(inf: Mensch)* lazybones *sing (inf)*.

Faun *m -(e)s, -e (Myth)* faun.

Fauna *f -, Faunen* fauna.

Faust *f -, Fäuste* fist ◆ **die (Hand zur) ~ ballen** to clench one's fist; **jdm eine ~ machen** *(inf)* to shake one's fist at sb; **jdm mit der ~ ins Gesicht schlagen** to punch sb in the face; **jdm die ~ unter die Nase halten** to shake one's fist in sb's face *or* under sb's nose; **mit der ~ auf den Tisch schlagen** *(lit)* to thump on the table (with one's fist); *(fig)* to take a hard line, to put one's foot down; **etw aus der ~ essen** to eat sth with one's hands; **ein Butterbrot auf die ~** a sandwich in one's hand; **die ~/Fäuste in der Tasche ballen** *(fig)* to bottle up *or* choke back one's anger; **mit geballten Fäusten zusehen müssen** *(fig)* to watch in helpless anger; **das paßt wie die ~ aufs Auge** *(paßt nicht)* it's all wrong; *(Farbe)* it clashes horribly; *(ist fehl am Platz)* it's completely out of place; *(paßt gut)* it's just the thing *(inf) or* job *(inf)*; **jds ~ im Nacken spüren** *(fig)* to have sb breathing down one's neck; **auf eigene ~** *(fig)* off one's own bat *(inf)*; *reisen, fahren* under one's own steam; *siehe* **eisern.**

Faust-: ~abwehr *f (Sport)* save using the fists; **herrlich, diese ~abwehr des Torwarts!** the goalkeeper punches the ball clear beautifully!; **~ball** *m form of volleyball.*

Fäustchen *nt dim of* **Faust; sich** *(dat)* **ins ~ lachen** to laugh up one's sleeve; *(bei finanziellem Vorteil)* to laugh all the way to the bank *(inf)*.

faustdick *adj (inf)* **eine ~e Lüge** a whopper *(inf)*, a whopping (great) lie *(inf)*; **das ist ~ gelogen** that's a whopping lie *(inf) or* a whopper *(inf)*; **er hat es ~ hinter den Ohren** he's a fly *or* crafty one *(inf)*; **~ auftragen** to lay it on thick.

Fäustel *m or nt -s, -* sledgehammer.

fausten *vt Ball* to punch; *(Ftbl auch)* to fist.

Faust-: ~feuerwaffe *f* handgun; **f~groß** *adj* as big as a fist, the size of a fist; **~handschuh** *m* mitt(en).

faustisch *adj* Faustian.

Faust-: ~kampf *m* fist-fight; **~kämpfer** *m (old)* pugilist *(old)*; **~keil** *m* hand-axe.

Fäustling *m* mitt(en).

Faust-: ~pfand *nt* security; **~recht** *nt, no pl* law of the jungle; **~regel** *f* rule of thumb; **~schlag** *m* punch.

Fauteuil [fo'tø:j] *m -s, -s (old, Aus)* leather armchair.

Fauxpas [fo'pa] *m -, -* gaffe, faux pas.

favorisieren* [favori'zi:rən] *vt* to favour ◆ **die Wettbüros ~ X als Sieger** the betting shops show X as favourite *or* have X to win; **favorisiert werden** to be favourite.

Favorit(in *f)* [favo'ri:t(ɪn)] *m -en, -en* favourite.

Fax *nt -, -e (Telec) siehe* **Telefax.**

faxen *vt* to fax, to send by fax.

Faxen *pl* **(a)** *(Alberei)* fooling about *or* around ◆ **~ machen** to fool about *or* around. **(b)** *(Grimassen)* **~ schneiden** to pull faces.

Faxgerät *nt* fax machine.

Faxnummer *f* fax number.

Fayence [fa'jã:s] *f -, -n* faïence.

FAZ [ɛf|a:'tset, fats] *f abbr of* **Frankfurter Allgemeine Zeitung.**

Fazit *nt -s, -s or -e* **das ~ der Untersuchungen war ...** on balance the result of the investigations was ...; **wenn wir aus diesen vier Jahren das ~ ziehen** if we take stock of these four years; **wenn ich das ~ ziehen müßte, würde ich sagen ...** on balance I would say ...

FCKW [ɛftse:ka:'ve:] *m -s, -s abbr of* **Fluorchlorkohlenwasserstoff** CFC.

FDGB [ɛfde:ge:'be:] *m -(s) (DDR) abbr of* **Freier Deutscher Gewerkschaftsbund** Free German Trades Union Congress.

FDJ [ɛfde:'jɔt] *f - (DDR) abbr of* **Freie Deutsche Jugend** Free German Youth.

FDJler(in *f)* *m -s, - (DDR)* member of the Free German Youth.

FDP [ɛfde:'pe:] *f - abbr of* **Freie Demokratische Partei.**

Feature ['fi:tʃɐ] *nt -s, -s (Rad, TV)* feature programme.

Feber *m -s, - (Aus)* February.

Februar *m -(s), -e* February; *siehe auch* **März.**

Fechtbahn *f (Sport)* piste.

fechten *pret* **focht,** *ptp* **gefochten** [1] *vi (Sport)* to fence; *(geh: kämpfen)* to fight ◆ **das F~** fencing.
[2] *vt* **Degen/Säbel/Florett ~** to fence with épées/sabres/foils; **einen Gang ~** to fence a bout.

Fechter(in *f)* *m -s, -* fencer.

Fechterstellung *f* fencing stance.

Fecht-: ~handschuh *m* fencing glove; **~hieb** *m* (fencing) cut; **~kunst** *f* art of fencing; *(Geschick)* skill in fencing; **~meister** *m* fencing master; **~sport** *m* fencing.

Feder *f -, -n* **(a)** *(Vogel~)* feather; *(Gänse~ etc)* quill; *(lange Hut~)* plume ◆ **leicht wie eine ~** as light as a feather; **~n lassen müssen** *(inf)* not to escape unscathed; **in den ~n stecken** *or* **liegen** *(inf)* to be/stay in one's bed *or* pit *(inf)*; **jdn aus den ~n holen** *(inf)* to drag *or* turf sb out of bed *(inf)*; **raus aus den ~n!** *(inf)* rise and shine! *(inf)*, show a leg! *(inf)*; *siehe* **fremd.**
(b) *(Schreib~)* quill; *(an ~halter)* nib ◆ **ich greife zur ~ ...** I take up my pen ...; **aus jds ~ fließen** to flow from sb's pen; **eine scharfe** *or* **spitze ~ führen** to wield a wicked *or* deadly pen; **mit spitzer ~** with a deadly pen, with a pen dipped in vitriol *(liter)*; **ein Mann der ~** *(dated geh)* a man of letters.
(c) *(Tech)* spring.
(d) *(in Holz)* tongue.

Feder-: ~antrieb *m* clockwork; **mit ~antrieb** clockwork-driven, driven by clockwork; **~ball** *m (Ball)* shuttlecock; *(Spiel)* badminton; **~bein** *nt (Tech)* suspension strut; **~besen** *m* feather duster; **~bett** *nt* quilt; *(in heutigen Zusammenhängen)* continental quilt, duvet; **~blatt** *nt* leaf of a spring; **~busch** *m (von Vögeln)* crest; *(von Hut, Helm)* plume; **~decke** *f siehe* **~bett; ~fuchser** *m -s, - (pej)* petty-minded pedant *(pej)*; *(Schreiberling)* pettifogging penpusher *(pej)*; **f~führend** *adj Behörde* in overall charge *(für* of); **~führung** *f* **unter der ~führung** *+gen* under the overall control of; **die ~führung haben** to be in *or* have overall charge; **~gewicht** *nt (Sport)* featherweight (class); **~gewichtler** *m -s, - (Sport)* featherweight; **~halter** *m* (dip) pen; *(Füll~)* (fountain) pen; *(ohne Feder)* pen(holder); **~hut** *m* plumed hat; **~kasten** *m (Sch)* pencil box; **~kernmatratze** *f* interior sprung mattress, innerspring mattress *(US)*; **~kiel** *m* quill; **~kissen** *nt* feather cushion; *(in Bett)* feather pillow; **~kleid** *nt (liter)* plumage; **~krieg** *m (fig)* war of words; **f~leicht** *adj* light as a feather; **~lesen** *nt*: **nicht viel ~lesens mit jdm/etw machen** to waste no time on sb/sth, to make short work of sb/sth; **ohne langes ~lesen, ohne viel ~lesens** without ceremony *or* any (further) ado; **~mäppchen** *nt,* **~mappe** *f* pencil case; **~messer** *nt* penknife.

federn [1] *vi* **(a)** *(Eigenschaft)* to be springy.
(b) *(hoch~, zurück~)* to spring back; *(Fahrzeug)* to bounce (up and down); *(Knie)* to give; *(Springer, Turner: hochgeschleudert werden)* to bounce ◆ **(in den**

⚠: for details of spelling reform, see supplement

Knien) ~ (*Sport*) to bend *or* give at the knees.
(c) (*Kissen etc*) to shed (feathers); (*Vogel*) to moult, to shed its feathers.
[2] *vr* to moult, to shed its feathers.
[3] *vt* to spring; *Auto, Räder auch* to fit with suspension ◆ **ein Auto hydraulisch ~** to fit a car with hydraulic suspension; *siehe* **gefedert.**

federnd *adj* (*Tech*) sprung ◆ **~e Radaufhängung** spring suspension; **einen ~en Gang haben** to have a jaunty *or* springy step *or* gait; **mit ~en Schritten** with a spring in one's step.

Feder-: ~pennal *nt* (*Aus*) pencil case; **~ring** *m* spring washer; **~schmuck** *m* feather trimming; (*von Indianern etc*) headdress; (*~busch*) plume; (*von Vogel*) plumage; **~skizze** *f* pen-and-ink sketch; **~spiel** *nt* (*Hist*) lure; **~strich** *m* pen-stroke, stroke of the pen; **mit einem** *or* **durch einen ~strich** with a single stroke of the pen.

Federung *f* springs *pl*, springing; (*Aut auch*) suspension.

Feder-: ~vieh *nt* poultry; **~waage** *f* spring balance; **~weiße(r)** *m decl as adj* (*dial*) new wine; **~wild** *nt* (*Hunt*) game birds *pl*; **~wisch** *m* (*old*) feather duster; **~wölkchen** *nt*, **~wolke** *f* fleecy cloud; **~zeichnung** *f* pen-and-ink drawing.

Fee *f* -, -n ['fe:ən] fairy.

Feedback ['fi:dbæk] *nt* -s, -s feedback.

feenhaft ['fe:ən-] *adj* (*liter*) fairylike.

Fegefeuer *nt* **das ~** purgatory.

fegen [1] *vt* (a) to sweep; (*auf~*) to sweep up ◆ **den Schmutz von etw ~** to sweep sth (clean). (b) (*Hunt*) *Geweih* to fray.
[2] *vi* (a) (*ausfegen*) to sweep (up). (b) *aux sein* (*inf: jagen*) to sweep; (*Wind auch*) to race.

Feger *m* -s, - (a) (*inf*) brush. (b) (*sl: Mädchen*) little tigress.

Fehde *f* -, -n (*Hist*) feud ◆ **mit jdm eine ~ ausfechten** to feud *or* carry on a feud with sb; **mit jdm in ~ liegen** (*lit, fig*) to be feuding *or* in a state of feud with sb.

Fehdehandschuh *m*: **jdm den ~ hinwerfen** (*lit, fig*) to throw down the gauntlet (to sb); **den ~ aufheben** (*lit, fig*) to take up the gauntlet.

fehl *adj*: **~ am Platz(e)** out of place.

Fehl *m* (*old, liter*): **ohne ~** without (a) blemish.

Fehl-: ~anflug *m* (*Aviat*) failed approach (to landing); **~anpassung** *f* (a) (*Psych*) maladjustment; (b) (*Elec*) mismatch; **~anzeige** *f* (*inf*) dead loss (*inf*); **~anzeige!** wrong!; **~aufschlag** *m* (*Sport*) fault; **einen ~aufschlag machen** to serve a fault; **f~bar** *adj* fallible; (*Sw*) guilty; **~bedarf** *m* uncovered demand; **f~besetzen*** *vt sep* to miscast; **~besetzung** *f* miscasting; **eine ~besetzung** a piece *or* bit of miscasting; **~bestand** *m* deficiency; **~betrag** *m* (*form*) deficit, shortfall; **~bitte** *f* (*form*) vain request; **~deutung** *f* misinterpretation; **~diagnose** *f* wrong *or* false diagnosis; **~disposition** *f* miscalculation; **~druck** *m* (*Typ*) misprint; **~einschätzung** *f* false estimation; (*der Lage auch*) misjudgement.

fehlen [1] *vi* (a) (*mangeln*) to be lacking; (*nicht vorhanden sein*) to be missing; (*in der Schule etc*) to be away *or* absent (*in +dat* from); (*schmerzlich vermißt werden*) to be missed ◆ **das Geld fehlt** (*ist nicht vorhanden*) there is no money; (*ist zuwenig vorhanden*) there isn't enough money; **etwas fehlt** there's something missing; **jdm fehlt etw** sb lacks *or* doesn't have sth; (*wird schmerzlich vermißt*) sb misses sth; **mir fehlt Geld** I'm missing some money; **mir ~ 20 Pfennig am Fahrgeld** I'm 20 pfennigs short *or* I'm short of 20 pfennigs for my fare; **mir ~ die Worte** words fail me; **meine Bibliothek fehlt/du fehlst mir sehr** I miss my library/you a lot; **der/das hat mir gerade noch gefehlt!** (*inf*) he/that was all I needed (*iro*); **das durfte nicht ~** that had to happen.
(b) (*los sein*) **was fehlt dir?** what's the matter *or* what's up (with you)?; **fehlt dir (et)was?** is something the matter (with you)?; **mir fehlt nichts** there's nothing the matter (with me); **dem Hund scheint etwas zu ~** the dog seems to have something the matter with it, there seems to be something wrong *or* the matter with the dog.
(c) (*old: etwas falsch machen*) to err.
[2] *vi impers* **es fehlt etw** *or* **an etw** (*dat*) there is a lack of sth; (*völlig*) there is no sth, sth is missing; **es ~ drei Messer** there are three knives missing; **es fehlt jdm an etw** (*dat*) sb lacks sth; **es an etw** (*dat*) **~ lassen** to be lacking in sth, to lack sth; **er ließ es uns an nichts ~** (*geh*) he let us want for nothing; **es fehlt hinten und vorn(e)** *or* **an allen Ecken und Enden** *or* **Kanten** we/they *etc* are short of everything; (*bei Kenntnissen*) he/she *etc* has a lot to learn *or* a long way to go; (*bei Klassenarbeit etc*) it's a long way from perfect; **wo fehlt es?** what's the trouble?, what's up? (*inf*); **es fehlte nicht viel, und ich hätte ihn verprügelt** I almost hit him; **es fehlt(e) nur noch, daß wir sonntags arbeiten sollen** working Sundays is all we need (*iro*).
[3] *vt* (*old Hunt*) to miss ◆ **weit gefehlt!** (*fig*) you're way out! (*inf*); (*ganz im Gegenteil*) far from it!

Fehl-: ~entscheidung *f* wrong decision; **~entwicklung** *f* mistake; **um ~entwicklungen zu vermeiden** to stop things going off course *or* taking a wrong turn.

➤ **Fehler** *m* -s, - (a) (*Irrtum, Unrichtigkeit*) mistake, error; (*Sport*) fault ◆ **einen ~ machen** *or* **begehen** to make a mistake *or* error; **ihr ist ein ~ unterlaufen** she's made a mistake; **~!** (*Sport*) fault!
➤ (b) (*Mangel*) fault, defect; (*Charakter~ auch*) failing ◆ **einen ~ aufweisen** to prove faulty; **jeder hat seine ~** we all have our faults, nobody's perfect; **das ist nicht mein ~** that's not my fault; **einen ~ an sich** (*dat*) **haben** to have a fault; **er hat den ~ an sich, immer dazwischenzureden** *or* **daß er immer dazwischenredet** the trouble with him is that he's always interrupting; **in den ~ verfallen, etw zu tun** to make the mistake of doing sth.

Fehler-: ~analyse *f* error analysis; **f~anfällig** *adj* error-prone; **~anzeige** *f* (*Comput*) error message; **~code** *m* error code; **f~frei** *adj* perfect; *Arbeit, Übersetzung, Aussprache etc auch* faultless, flawless; *Messung, Rechnung* correct; **f~freier Lauf/Sprung** (*Sport*) clear round/jump; **~grenze** *f* margin of error; **f~haft** *adj* (*Mech, Tech*) faulty, defective; *Ware* substandard, imperfect; *Messung, Rechnung* incorrect; *Arbeit, Übersetzung, Aussprache* poor; **~korrekturprogramm** *nt* (*Comput*) debugging program; **f~los** *adj siehe* **f~frei**; **~meldung** *f* (*Comput*) error message.

Fehlernährung *f* malnutrition.

Fehler-: ~quelle *f* cause of the fault; (*in Statistik*) source of error; **~quote** *f* error rate; **~verzeichnis** *nt* errata *pl*.

Fehl-: ~farbe *f* (*Cards*) missing suit; (*Nicht-Trumpf*) plain *or* side suit; (*Zigarre*) cigar with a discoloured wrapper; **~geburt** *f* miscarriage.

fehlgehen *vi sep irreg aux sein* (a) (*geh: sich verirren*) to go wrong, to miss the way; (*Schuß*) to go wide. (b) (*sich irren*) to be wrong *or* mistaken, to err (*form*) ◆ **ich hoffe, ich gehe nicht fehl in der Annahme, daß ...** I trust I am not mistaken in assuming that ...

Fehl-: f~gesteuert *adj* misdirected; **~griff** *m* mistake; **einen ~griff tun** to make a mistake; **~information** *f* incorrect information *no pl*; **~interpretation** *f* misinterpretation; **~investition** *f* bad investment; **~kalkulation** *f* miscalculation; **~konstruktion** *f* bad design; **der Stuhl ist eine ~konstruktion** this chair is badly designed; **~landung** *f* bad landing; **~leistung** *f* slip, mistake; **Freudsche ~leistung** Freudian slip; **f~leiten** *vt sep* to misdirect; **die Akte wurde f~geleitet** the file was sent to the wrong place; **~leitung** *f* misdirection; ⚠**~paß** *m* (*Ftbl*) bad pass; **~planung** *f* misplanning, bad planning; **eine ~planung** a piece of bad planning *or* misplanning; ⚠**f~plaziert** *adj Empörung etc* misplaced; **~prägung** *f* (*einer Münze*) mis-strike; **~prognose** *f* incorrect prognosis; **~reaktion** *f* incorrect response; **~schaltung** *f* faulty circuit; **f~schießen** *vi sep irreg* to shoot wide; **~schlag** *m* (*fig*) failure; **f~schlagen** *vi sep irreg aux sein* to go wrong; (*Hoffnung*) to be misplaced, to come to nothing; ⚠**~schluß** *m* false conclusion; ⚠**~schuß** *m* miss; **f~sichtig** *adj* (*form*) with defective vision; **~sichtigkeit** *f* (*form*) defective vision; **~spekulation** *f* bad speculation; **~start** *m* false start; (*Space*) faulty launch; **~stoß** *m* (*Ftbl*) miskick; (*Billard*) miscue; **f~stoßen** *vi sep irreg* (*Ftbl, Billard*) to miskick/miscue; **f~treten** *vi sep irreg aux sein* (*geh*) to miss one's footing; (*fig*) to err, to lapse; **~tritt** *m* (*geh*) false step; (*fig*) (*Vergehen*) slip, lapse; (*Affäre*) indiscretion; **~urteil** *nt* miscarriage of justice; **~verhalten** *nt* inappropriate behaviour; (*Psych*) abnormal behaviour; **~versuch** *m* unsuccessful *or* abortive attempt; **f~verwenden** *vt sep* to misappropriate; **~wurf** *m* (*Sport*) misthrow, bad throw; (*ungültig*) no-throw; **~zeiten** *pl* working hours *pl* lost through absenteeism; **~zug** *m* (*Chess*) bad move; **~zündung** *f* misfiring *no pl*; **eine ~zündung** a backfire; **das war bei mir eine ~zündung** (*fig inf*) I got hold of the wrong end of the stick (*inf*).

feien *vt* (*old*) to protect (*gegen* from), to make proof (*gegen* against); *siehe* **gefeit.**

Feier *f* -, -n celebration; (*Party*) party; (*Zeremonie*) ceremony; (*Hochzeits~*) reception ◆ **zur ~ von etw** to celebrate sth; **zur ~ des Tages** in honour of the occasion.

Feierabend *m* (a) (*Arbeitsschluß*) end of work; (*Geschäftsschluß*) closing time ◆ **~ machen** to finish work, to knock off (work) (*inf*); (*Geschäfte*) to close; **ich mache jetzt ~** I think I'll call it a day (*inf*) *or* I'll knock off now (*inf*); **~!** (*in Gaststätte*) time, please!; **nach ~** after work; **jetzt ist aber ~!** (*fig inf*) enough is enough; **damit ist jetzt ~** (*fig inf*) that's all over now; **dann ist ~** (*fig inf*) then it's all over, then it's the end of the road; **für mich ist ~** (*fig inf*) I've had enough.
(b) (*Zeit nach Arbeitsschluß*) evening ◆ **schönen ~!** have a nice evening!

Feierabendheim *nt* (*DDR*) old people's home.

feierlich *adj* (*ernsthaft, würdig*) solemn; (*festlich*) festive; (*förmlich*) ceremonial ◆ **einen Tag ~ begehen** to celebrate a day; **das ist ja nicht mehr ~** (*inf*) that's beyond a joke (*inf*).

Feierlichkeit *f* (a) *siehe adj* solemnity; festiveness; ceremony. (b) *usu pl* (*Veranstaltungen*) celebrations *pl*, festivities *pl*.

feiern [1] *vt* (a) to celebrate; *Party, Fest, Orgie* to hold ◆ **das muß gefeiert werden!** that calls for a celebration; **Triumphe ~** to achieve a great triumph, to make one's mark.
(b) (*umjubeln*) to fête.
[2] *vi* (a) to celebrate ◆ **die ganze Nacht ~** to make a night of it.
(b) (*nicht arbeiten*) to stay off work.

Feier-: ~schicht *f* cancelled shift; **eine ~schicht fahren/einlegen** to miss/cancel a shift; **~stunde** *f* ceremony; **~tag** *m* holiday; **f~täglich** *adj* holiday *attr*; **f~tägliche Stimmung** holiday mood; **f~täglich angezogen** in one's Sunday best.

feig(e) [1] *adj* cowardly ◆ **~ wie er war** like the coward he was.
[2] *adv* in a cowardly way ◆ **er zog sich ~ zurück** he retreated like a coward.

Feige *f* -, -n fig.

Feigen-: ~baum *m* fig tree; **~blatt** *nt* fig leaf; **ein ~blatt für etw** (*fig*) a front to hide sth; **als demokratisches ~blatt** (*fig*) to give a veneer of democracy.

Feigheit *f* cowardice, cowardliness.

Feigling *m* coward.

feil *adj* (*old, geh*) (up) for sale ◆ **der Schmuck war ihr um** *or* **für nichts auf der Welt ~** not for all the world would she have sold the jewellery.

feilbieten *vt sep irreg* (*old*) to offer for sale.

Feile *f* -, -n file.

feilen [1] *vt* to file.
[2] *vi* to file; (*fig*) to make some improvements ◆ **an etw** (*dat*) **~** (*lit*) to file

(away at) sth; (*fig*) to hone sth, to polish sth up.
feilhalten *vt sep irreg* (*old*) to offer for sale; *siehe* **Maulaffen.**
feilschen *vi* (*pej*) to haggle (*um* over).
Feil-: ~span *m* filing; **~staub** *m* (fine) filings *pl.*
fein 1 *adj* **(a)** (*nicht grob*) fine; *Humor, Ironie* delicate; (*fig: listig*) cunning.
(b) (*erlesen*) excellent, choice *attr*; *Geruch, Geschmack* delicate; *Gold, Silber* refined; *Mensch, Charakter* thoroughly nice; (*prima*) great (*inf*), splendid, swell (*esp US inf*); (*iro*) fine ◆ **~ säuberlich** (nice and) neat; **etw ~ machen** to do sth beautifully; **ein ~er Kerl** a great guy (*inf*), a splendid person; **das war von dir aber wieder ~ bemerkt** you have such a nice way of putting things; **~!** great! (*inf*), marvellous!; (*in Ordnung*) fine!; **~, daß ...** great that ... (*inf*), (I'm) so glad that ...; **das ist etwas F~es** that's really something (*inf or* nice; **~ (he)raussein** to be sitting pretty.
(c) (*scharf*) sensitive, keen; *Gehör, Gefühl auch* acute ◆ **etw ~ einstellen** to adjust sth accurately.
(d) (*vornehm*) refined, fine (*esp iro*), posh (*inf*) ◆ **nicht ~ genug sein** not to be good enough; **er/sie hat sich ~ gemacht** he's dressed to kill/she's all dolled up; **dazu ist sie sich** (*dat*) **zu ~** that's beneath her.
2 *adv* (*baby-talk*) just; (*vor adj, adv*) nice and ... **du gehst jetzt ~ nach Hause** now just you go straight home; **sei jetzt mal ~ still** now keep nice and quiet.
Fein- *in cpds* fine; **~abstimmung** *f* (*Rad, TV*) fine tuning; **~arbeit** *f* precision work; **~ausgleich** *m* (*Comput*) microspacing; **~bäckerei** *f* cake shop, patisserie; **~blech** *nt* thin sheet metal.
⚠**feind** *adj pred* (*old*) **jdm/einer Sache ~ sein** to be hostile to sb/sth.
Feind *m* **-(e)s, -e** enemy, foe (*liter*) ◆ **jdn zum ~ haben** to have sb as an enemy; **sich** (*dat*) **jdn zum ~ machen** to make an enemy of sb; **sich** (*dat*) **~e schaffen** to make enemies; **er war ein ~ jeden Fortschritts** he was opposed to progress in any shape or form; **ran an den ~** (*inf*) let's get stuck in (*inf*); **der böse ~** (*Bibl*) the Evil One, the Enemy; **liebet eure ~e** (*Bibl*) love thine enemy (*Bibl*).
-feind *m in cpds* -hater.
Feind- *in cpds* enemy; **~berührung** *f* contact with the enemy; **~bild** *nt* concept of an/the enemy.
Feindes-: ~hand *f* (*old, liter*) the hands of the foe (*liter*); **~land** *nt* (*old, liter*) enemy territory.
Feindin *f siehe* **Feind.**
feindlich *adj* **(a)** (*Mil: gegnerisch*) enemy ◆ **im ~en Lager** (*lit, fig*) in the enemy camp. **(b)** (*feindselig*) hostile. **jdm/einer Sache ~ gegenüberstehen** to be hostile to sb/sth.
-feindlich *adj suf* anti- ◆ **deutsch~** anti-German.
Feindmacht *f* enemy power ◆ **eine ~ unseres Landes** an enemy of our country.
Feindschaft *f* hostility, enmity ◆ **sich** (*dat*) **jds ~ zuziehen** to make an enemy of sb; **mit jdm in ~ leben** *or* **liegen** to be at daggers drawn *or* to live in enmity with sb; **eine ~ auf Leben und Tod** mortal enmity.
feindselig *adj* hostile.
Feindseligkeit *f* hostility.
Fein-: f~fühlend, f~fühlig *adj* sensitive; (*taktvoll*) tactful; **~gebäck** *nt* cakes and pastries *pl*; **~gefühl** *nt, no pl* sensitivity; (*Takt*) delicacy, tact(fulness); **jds ~gefühl verletzen** to hurt sb's feelings; ⚠**f~gemahlen** *adj attr* finely ground; **f~glied(e)rig** *adj* delicate, slender; **~gold** *nt* refined gold.
Feinheit *f siehe adj* **(a)** fineness; delicacy. **(b)** excellence; delicateness; refinement; niceness. **(c)** keenness; acuteness. **(d)** refinement, fineness, poshness (*inf*). **(e) ~en** *pl* niceties *pl*, finer points *pl*; (*Nuancen*) subtleties *pl* ◆ **das sind eben die ~en** it's the little things that make the difference.
Fein-: ~kohle *f* slack; **f~körnig** *adj Film* fine-grain; *Sand, Salz auch* fine; **~kost** *f* delicacies *pl*; **„~kost"** "Delicatessen"; **~kostgeschäft** *nt* delicatessen; **f~maschig** *adj* with a fine mesh; *Strickwaren* finely knitted; **~mechanik** *f* precision engineering; **~mechaniker** *m* precision engineer; ⚠**~meßgerät** *nt* precision instrument; **f~nervig** *adj* sensitive; **~positionierung** *f* microjustification. **~schliff** *m* fine finish(ing); **~schmecker** *m* **-s, -** gourmet, epicure; (*fig*) connoisseur; **~schnitt** *m* (*Tabak*) fine cut; (*Film*) final editing; **~silber** *nt* refined silver; **f~sinnig** *adj* sensitive; **~sinnigkeit** *f* sensitivity.
Feinsliebchen *nt* (*poet*) lady-love (*poet*), sweetheart.
Fein-: ~struktur *f* fine structure; **~unze** *f* troy ounce; **~wäsche** *f* delicates *pl*; **~waschmittel** *nt* mild(-action) detergent.
feist *adj* fat; *Mensch auch* gross, obese ◆ **ein ~es Lachen** an obscene chuckle.
Feistheit, Feistigkeit *f siehe adj* fatness; grossness, obesity.
Feitel *m* **-s, -** (*Aus*) penknife.
feixen *vi* (*inf*) to smirk.
Felchen *m* **-s, -** whitefish.
Feld *nt* **-(e)s, -er (a)** (*offenes Gelände*) open country ◆ **auf freiem ~** in the open country; *siehe* **Wald.**
(b) (*Acker*) field.
(c) (*Flächenstück: auf Spielbrett*) square; (*an Zielscheibe*) ring; (*Her*) field.
(d) (*Sport: Spiel~*) field, pitch ◆ **das ~ beherrschen** to be on top.
(e) (*Kriegsschauplatz*) (battle)field ◆ **ins ~ ziehen** *or* **rücken** (*old*) to take the field, to march into battle; **auf dem ~e der Ehre fallen** (*euph old*) to fall on the field of honour; **gegen jdn/etw zu ~e ziehen** (*fig*) to crusade against sb/sth; **Argumente ins ~ führen** to bring arguments to bear; **das ~ behaupten** (*fig*) to stand *or* stay one's ground; **das ~ räumen** (*fig*) to quit the field, to bow out; **jdm/einer Sache das ~ überlassen** *or* **räumen** to give way *or* yield to sb/sth; (*freiwillig*) to hand over to sb/sth.
(f) (*fig: Bereich*) field, area.
(g) (*Ling, Min, Phys, Comput*) field.
(h) (*Sport: Gruppe*) field ◆ **er ließ das ~ hinter sich** (*dat*) he left the rest of the field behind (him); **das ~ ist geschlossen** the field is bunched (up).
Feld- *in cpds* field; **~arbeit** *f* (*Agr*) work in the fields; (*Sci, Sociol*) fieldwork; **~arbeiter** *m* fieldworker; **~arzt** *m* (*old Mil*) army doctor; **~besteck** *nt* eating irons *pl*; **~bett** *nt* campbed; **~binde** *f* **(a)** (*old: Schärpe*) sash; **(b)** (*Med Mil*) Red Cross armband; **~blume** *f* wild flower; **~dienst** *m* (*old Mil*) active service; **~elektronen** *pl* (*Elec*) field electrons *pl*; **~energie** *f* (*Phys*) field energy.
Felderwirtschaft *f* (*Agr*) crop rotation.
Feld-: ~flasche *f* canteen (*Mil*), water bottle; **~flugplatz** *m* (military) airstrip (*near the front*); **~frucht** *f* (*Agr*) agricultural crop; **~geistliche(r)** *m* (*old Mil*) army chaplain, padre; **~gendarmerie** *f* (*old Mil*) military police; **~gleichung** *f* (*Math*) field equation; **~gottesdienst** *m* (*Mil*) camp service; **~handball** *m* European (outdoor) handball; **~hase** *m* European hare; **~haubitze** *f* (*Mil*) (field) howitzer; **~heer** *nt* (*Mil*) army in the field; **~herr** *m* (*old*) commander; **~herrnkunst** *f* (*old*) strategy; **~herrnstab** *m* (*old*) (general's) baton *or* swagger stick; **~heuschrecke** *f* grasshopper; (*schädlich*) locust; **~huhn** *nt* partridge; **~hüter** *m* watchman (*in charge of fields*); **~jäger** *m* **(a)** (*old Mil*) (*Kurier*) courier; (*Infanterist*) infantryman; **(b)** (*Mil*) military police; (*bei der Marine*) shore patrol; **~konstante** *f* (*Phys*) space constant; **~kraft** *f* (*Phys*) field intensity *or* strength; **~krähe** *f* rook; **~küche** *f* (*Mil*) field kitchen; **~lager** *nt* (*old Mil*) camp, encampment; **~lazarett** *nt* (*Mil*) field hospital; **~lerche** *f* skylark; **~linie** *f* (*Phys*) line of force; **~mark** *f* (*von Gemeinde*) parish land; (*von Gut*) estate; **~marschall** *m* (*old*) field marshal; **~maus** *f* field mouse (*loosely*), common vole (*spec*); **~messer** *m* **-s, -** (land) surveyor; **~pflanze** *f* agricultural crop; **~post** *f* (*Mil*) forces' postal service; **~postbrief** *m* (*Mil*) forces' letter; **~rain** *m* edge of the field; **~salat** *m* lamb's lettuce; **~schlacht** *f* (*old*) battle; **~schütz** *m* **-es, -e** *siehe* **~hüter**; **~spat** *m* (*Geol*) fel(d)spar; **~spieler** *m* (*Sport*) player (on the field); **~stärke** *f* (*Phys*) field strength *or* intensity; (*Rad, TV*) strength of the signal; **~stecher** *m* **-s, -** (pair of) binoculars *or* field glasses; **~stuhl** *m* folding stool; **~telefon** *nt* (*Mil*) field telephone; ⚠**~telegraph** *m* (*Mil*) field telegraph; **~theorie** *f* (*Ling, Phys, Psych*) field theory; **~versuch** *m* field test; **~verweis** *m siehe* **Platzverweis**; **~wache** *f* (*old Mil*) outpost.
Feld-, Wald- und Wiesen- *in cpds* (*inf*) common-or-garden, run-of-the-mill.
Feld-: ~webel *m* sergeant; (*fig inf*) sergeant-major (type); **~weg** *m* track across the fields; **~weibel** *m* (*Sw*) sergeant; **~zeichen** *nt* (*old Mil*) standard, ensign; **~zug** *m* (*old, fig*) campaign.
Felg|aufschwung *m* (*Sport*) upward circle forwards.
Felge *f* **-, -n (a)** (*Tech*) (wheel) rim. **(b)** (*Sport*) circle.
Felgenbremse *f* calliper brake.
Felg|umschwung *m* (*Sport*) circle.
Fell *nt* **-(e)s, -e (a)** fur; (*von Schaf, Lamm*) fleece; (*von toten Tieren*) skin, fell ◆ **ein gesundes ~** a healthy coat; **einem Tier das ~ abziehen** to skin an animal; **ihm sind alle** *or* **die ~e weggeschwommen** (*fig*) all his hopes were dashed.
(b) (*fig inf: Menschenhaut*) skin, hide (*inf*) ◆ **ein dickes ~ haben** to be thickskinned *or* have a thick skin; **jdm das ~ gerben** to tan sb's hide; **jdm das ~ über die Ohren ziehen** to dupe sb, to pull the wool over sb's eyes; **ihn** *or* **ihm juckt das ~** he's asking for a good hiding; **das ~ versaufen** to hold the wake.
(c) (*von Trommel*) skin.
Fell- *in cpds* fur; (*Ziegen~/Schaf~ etc*) goatskin/sheepskin *etc.*
Fellache *m* **-n, -n** fellah.
Fellatio [fe'la:tsio] *f* **-,** *no pl* fellatio.
Fell-: ~eisen *nt* (*obs*) knapsack; **~handel** *m* trade in skins.
Fels *m* **-en, -en, Felsen** *m* **-s, -** rock; (*Klippe*) cliff.
Fels-: ~block *m* boulder; **~brocken** *m* (lump of) rock.
Fels(en)-: ~bild *nt* rock-scape; **~burg** *f* mountain fortress.
Felsen-: f~fest *adj* firm; **f~fest überzeugt sein** to be absolutely *or* firmly convinced; **sich f~fest auf jdn verlassen** to put one's complete trust in sb; **~gebirge** *nt* **(a)** rocky mountain range; **(b)** (*Geog*) Rocky Mountains *pl*, Rockies *pl*; **~grab** *nt* rock tomb.
Fels(en)-: ~grund *m* rockbed; (*poet: Tal*) rocky vale (*poet*) *or* glen; **~höhle** *f* rock cave; **~klippe** *f* rocky cliff; (*im Meer*) stack; **~nest** *nt* mountain lair *or* hideout; **~riff** *nt* (rocky) reef; **~schlucht** *f* rocky valley *or* glen.
Felsentor *nt* **-(e)s, -e** arch in the rock.
Fels-: ~gestein *nt* (*Geol*) (solid) rock; **~glimmer** *m* (*Geol*) mica; **~grat** *m* (rocky) ridge.
felsig *adj* rocky; (*steil abfallend*) *Küste* cliff-lined, cliffy.
Fels-: ~kessel *m* corrie; **~malerei** *f* rock painting; **~massiv** *nt* rock massif; **~nase** *f* rock overhang *or* shelf; **~spalte** *f* crevice; **~vorsprung** *m* ledge; **~wand** *f* rock face; **~wüste** *f* rock desert; **~zacke** *f* crag.
Feluke *f* **-, -n** felucca.
Feme *f* **-, -n, Fem(e)gericht** *nt* (*Hist*) Vehmgericht; (*Bandengericht*) kangaroo court.
Fememord *m* (*Hist*) *killing ordered by a Vehmgericht*; (*fig*) lynch-law killing; (*bei Gangstern*) underworld killing.
Feminat *nt* female power base.
feminin *adj* **(a)** (*Gram*) feminine. **(b)** (*fraulich*) feminine; (*pej*) effeminate.
Femininum *nt* **-s, Feminina** (*Gram*) feminine noun.

⚠: for details of spelling reform, see supplement

Feminịsmus *m* feminism.
Feminịst(in *f*) *m* feminist.
feminịstisch *adj* feminist.
Femme fatale [famfa'tal] *f* - -, **-s -s** femme fatale.
Fẹnchel *m* **-s,** *no pl* fennel.
Fẹnchel- *in cpds* fennel; **~holz** *nt* sassafras wood.
Fẹnder *m* **-s,** - fender.
Fẹnn *nt* **-(e)s, -e** *siehe* **Fehn.**
Fẹnster *nt* **-s,** - window (*auch Comput*) ◆ **weg vom ~** (*inf*) out of the game (*inf*), finished; **~ der Gelegenheit** window of opportunity; *siehe* **Geld.**
Fẹnster- *in cpds* window; **~bank** *f*, **~brett** *nt* window-sill, window ledge; **~briefumschlag** *m* window envelope; **~flügel** *m* side of a window; **~front** *f* glass façade; **~glas** *nt* window glass; (*in Brille*) plain glass; **~griff** *m* window catch; **~heber** *m* (*Aut*) window winder; (*elektronisch*) window control; **~kitt** *m* (window) putty; **~klappe** *f* fanlight; **~kreuz** *nt* mullion and transom (*of a cross window*); **~kurbel** *f* window handle (*for winding car windows*); **~laden** *m* shutter; **~leder** *nt* chamois, shammy (leather).
fẹnsterln *vi* (*S Ger, Aus*) to climb through one's sweetheart's bedroom window.
Fẹnster-: f~los *adj* windowless; **~pfosten** *m* mullion; **~platz** *m* seat by the window, window seat; **~putzer** *m* window cleaner; **~rahmen** *m* window frame; **~rede** *f* soapbox speech; **~rose** *f* rose window; **~scheibe** *f* window pane; **~sims** *m* window ledge, windowsill; **~stock** *m* window frame; **~sturz** *m* **(a)** (*Build*) window lintel; **(b)** (*Hist*) **der Prager ~sturz** the Prague defenestration; **~technik** *f* (*Comput*) windowing technique; **~umschlag** *m* window envelope.
-fenstrig *adj suf* -windowed.
Fẹrge *m* **-n, -n** (*poet*) ferryman.
Ferial- *in cpds* (*Aus*) *siehe* **Ferien-.**
Ferien ['fe:riən] *pl* holidays *pl* (*Brit*), vacation *sing* (*US, Univ*); (*~reise*) holiday *sing* (*Brit*), vacation *sing* (*US*); (*Parlaments~, Jur*) recess *sing* ◆ **die großen ~** the summer holidays (*Brit*) *or* long vacation (*US, Univ*); **~ haben** to be on holiday *or* vacation; **~ machen** to have *or* take a holiday *or* vacation; **~ vom Ich machen** to get away from it all; **in die ~ gehen** *or* **fahren** to go on holiday *or* vacation.
Ferien- *in cpds* holiday (*Brit*), vacation (*US*); **~gast** *m* holiday-maker; (*Besuch*) person staying on holiday; **~haus** *nt* holiday home; **~kind** *nt child from a town on a state-subsidized holiday*; **~kolonie** *f* children's holiday camp; **~ordnung** *f* holiday dates *pl*; **~ort** *m* holiday resort; **~reise** *f* holiday (*Brit*), vacation (*US*); **~tag** *m* day of one's holidays (*Brit*) *or* vacation (*US*); **~wohnung** *f* holiday flat (*Brit*), vacation apartment (*US*); **~zeit** *f* holiday period.
Fẹrkel *nt* **-s,** - piglet; (*fig*) (*unsauber*) pig, mucky pup (*inf*); (*unanständig*) dirty pig (*inf*).
Ferkelei *f* (*inf*) (*Schmutz*) mess; (*Witz*) dirty joke; (*Handlung*) dirty *or* filthy *or* disgusting thing to do.
fẹrkeln *vi* **(a)** (*Zool*) to litter. **(b)** (*inf*) *siehe* **Ferkelei** to make a mess; to tell dirty jokes; to be dirty *or* filthy *or* disgusting.
Fermate *f* **-, -n** (*Mus*) pause.
Fermẹnt *nt* **-s, -e** enzyme.
Fermentation *f* fermentation.
fermentieren* *vt* to ferment.
Fermẹntmangel *m* enzyme deficiency.
Fẹrmium *nt, no pl* (*abbr* **Fm**) fermium.
fẹrn [1] *adj* **(a)** (*räumlich*) distant, far-off, faraway ◆ **~ von hier** a long way (away) from *or* far away from here; **von ~(e) betrachtet** seen from a distance; **sich ~ sein** (*fig*) to be not at all close (to one another); **der F~e Osten** the Far East; **von ~(e) kennen** (*fig*) to know (only) slightly; **das sei ~ von mir** (*fig*) nothing is further from my thoughts, heaven forbid.
(b) (*zeitlich entfernt*) far-off ◆ **~e Vergangenheit** (dim and) distant past; **in nicht zu ~er Zeit** in the not-too-distant future; **der Tag ist nicht mehr ~, wo** ... the day is not far off when ...
[2] *prep +gen* far (away) from ◆ **~ der Heimat** (*liter*) far from home; **unrasiert und ~ der Heimat** (*hum inf*) down on one's luck and a long way from home.
Fern-: f~ạb *adv* far away; **f~ab gelegen** far away; **~abfrage** *f* (*Telec*) remote control facility; **~amt** *nt* (telephone) exchange; **das Gespräch wurde vom ~amt vermittelt** the call was connected by the operator; **~aufnahme** *f* (*Phot*) long shot; **~auslöser** *m* (*Phot*) cable release; **~bahn** *f* (*Rail*) main-line service; **~beben** *nt* distant earthquake; **~bedienung** *f* remote control; **f~bleiben** *vi sep irreg aux sein* to stay away (*dat, von* from); **~bleiben** *nt* **-s,** *no pl* absence (*von* from); (*Nichtteilnahme*) non-attendance; **~blick** *m* good view; **ein herrlicher ~blick** a splendid view for miles around.
fẹrne *adv* (*poet, geh*) *siehe* **fern 1.**
Fẹrne *f* **-, -n (a)** (*räumlich*) distance; (*old: ferne Länder*) distant lands *pl or* shores *pl* (*liter*) ◆ **in der ~** in the distance; **aus der ~** from a distance; **in die ~ ziehen** (*old*) to seek out far-off shores *or* distant climes (*liter*). **(b)** (*zeitlich*) (*Zukunft*) future; (*Vergangenheit*) (distant) past ◆ **in weiter ~ liegen** to be a long time off *or* in the distant future.
Fern|empfang *m* (*Rad, TV*) long-distance reception.
fẹrner [1] *adj comp of* **fern** further ◆ **Ihre ~en Aufträge** (*Comm*) your future *or* further orders; **für die ~e Zukunft** for the long term.
[2] *adv* **(a)** further ◆ **~ liefen ...** (*Sport*) also-rans ...; **unter ~ liefen rangieren** *or* **kommen** (*inf*) to be among the also-rans.
(b) (*künftig*) in future ◆ **(auch) ~ etw machen** to continue to do sth; **auch ~ im Amt bleiben** to continue in office.
fẹrnerhin *adv siehe* **ferner 2 (b).**
fẹrnerliegen *vi sep irreg* (*fig*) **nichts läge mir ferner, als ...** nothing could be further from my thoughts *or* mind than ...; **kein Gedanke könnte ~ als ...** nothing could be further from my thoughts than ...
Fẹrn-: ⚠**~expreß** *m* (*Rail*) long-distance express train; **~fahrer** *m* long-distance lorry (*Brit*) *or* truck driver, trucker (*US*); **~fahrerlokal** *nt* transport café (*Brit*), truckstop (*US*); **~flug** *m* long-distance *or* long-haul flight; **~gas** *nt gas piped over a long distance*; **f~gelenkt** *adj* remote-controlled; (*fig*) manipulated (*von* by); **~geschütz** *nt* (*Mil*) long-range weapon; **~gespräch** *nt* trunk (*Brit*) *or* long-distance call; **f~gesteuert** *adj* remote-controlled; (*durch Funk auch*) radio-controlled; **~glas** *nt* (pair of) binoculars *or* field glasses.
⚠**fẹrnhalten** *sep irreg* [1] *vt* to keep away.
[2] *vr* to keep *or* stay away.
Fẹrn-: ~heizung *f* district heating (*spec*); **f~her** *adv* (*old*) **(von) f~her** from afar (*old, liter*); **~kopie** *f* (*Telec*) *siehe* **Telefax (a)**; **~kopieren** *vti siehe* **faxen**; **~kopierer** *m siehe* **Telefax (b)**; **~kurs(us)** *m* correspondence course.
Fẹrnlaster *m* long-distance lorry (*Brit*) *or* truck, juggernaut.
Fẹrnlast-: ~fahrer *m* (*inf*) long-distance lorry (*Brit*) *or* truck driver, trucker (*US*); **~verkehr** *m* long-distance goods traffic; **~zug** *m* long-distance truck-trailer.
Fẹrn-: ~lehrgang *m* correspondence course; **~leitung** *f* **(a)** (*Telec*) trunk (*Brit*) *or* long-distance line(s); **(b)** (*Röhren*) pipeline; **f~lenken** *vt sep* to operate by remote control; **~lenkung** *f* remote control; **~lenkwaffen** *pl* (*Mil*) guided missiles; **~licht** *nt* (*Aut*) full *or* main *or* high (*esp US*) beam; **mit ~licht fahren, (das) ~licht anhaben** to be *or* drive on full beam; ⚠**f~liegen** *vi sep irreg* (*fig*) **(jdm) f~liegen** to be far from sb's thoughts *or* mind; **es liegt mir f~, das zu tun** far be it from me to do that; **nichts liegt mir f~er** nothing could be further from my mind.
Fẹrnmelde- *in cpds* telecommunications; telephone; (*Mil*) signals; **~amt** *nt* telephone exchange; **~dienst** *m* telecommunications/telephone service; **~geheimnis** *nt* (*Jur*) secrecy of telecommunications.
Fẹrnmelder *m* **-s,** - **(a)** (*Apparat*) telephone. **(b)** (*Mil inf*) signaller.
Fẹrnmelde-: ~satellit *m* communication satellite; **~technik** *f* telecommunications/telephone engineering; **~truppe** *f* (*Mil*) signals corps *sing*; **~wesen** *nt* telecommunications *sing.*
Fẹrn-: ~messung *f* telemetering; **f~mündlich** [1] *adj* telephone *attr*; [2] *adv* by telephone.
Fern|ọst *no art* **aus/in/nach ~** from/in/to the Far East.
Fern|ọst- *in cpds* Far East; **~exporte** *pl* exports *pl* to the Far East; **~handel** *m* trade with the Far East.
fẹrn|östlich *adj* Far Eastern *attr.*
Fern|ọstreise *f* journey to the Far East.
Fẹrn-: ~rakete *f* long-range missile; **~reise** *f* long-haul journey; **~rohr** *nt* telescope; (*Doppel~*) (pair of) binoculars *or* field glasses; **~ruf** *m* (*form*) telephone number; **~ruf 68190** Tel. 68190; **~schalter** *m* (*Elec*) remote-control switch; **~schnellzug** *m* long-distance express (train); **~schreiben** *nt* telex; **~schreiber** *m* **(a)** teleprinter; (*Comm*) telex(-machine); **(b)** (*Mensch*) teleprinter/telex operator; **~schreibnetz** *nt* telex network; **f~schriftlich** *adj* by telex.
Fẹrnseh- *in cpds* television, TV; **~ansager** *m* television announcer; **~ansprache** *f* television speech; **~anstalt** *f* television company; **~apparat** *m* television *or* TV (set); **~debatte** *f* televised debate; **~empfänger** *m* (*form*) television receiver.
fẹrnsehen *vi sep irreg* to watch television *or* TV *or* telly (*Brit inf*).
Fẹrnsehen *nt* **-s,** *no pl* television, TV, telly (*Brit inf*) ◆ **~ haben** (*Familie etc*) to have a television; (*Staat etc*) to have television *or* TV; **beim ~ arbeiten** to work *or* be in television; **vom ~ übertragen werden** to be televised; **im ~** on television *or* TV *or* (the) telly (*Brit inf*); **das ~ bringt etw** sth is on television, they're showing sth on television.
Fẹrnseher *m* **-s,** - (*inf*) **(a)** (*Gerät*) television, TV, telly (*Brit inf*). **(b)** (*Zuschauer*) (television) viewer.
Fẹrnseh-: ~gebühr *f* television licence fee; **~genehmigung** *f* television licence; **~gerät** *nt* television *or* TV set; **f~gerecht** *adj* suitable for television; **etw f~gerecht aufbereiten** to adapt sth for television; **~journalist** *m* television *or* TV reporter; **~kamera** *f* television *or* TV camera; **wir haben Herrn Schmidt vor die ~kamera gebeten** we've asked Herr Schmidt to speak to us; **~kanal** *m* (television) channel; **~konserve** *f* (tele)recording; **~norm** *f* television standard; **~programm** *nt* **(a)** (*Kanal*) channel, station (*US*); **(b)** (*Sendung*) programme; (*Sendefolge*) programmes *pl*; **(c)** (*~zeitschrift*) (television) programme guide; **~publikum** *nt* viewers *pl*, viewing public; **~rechte** *pl* television rights *pl*; **~satellit** *m* TV satellite; **~schirm** *m* television *or* TV screen; **~sender** *m* television transmitter; **~sendung** *f* television programme; **~spiel** *nt* television play; **~sprecher** *m* television announcer; **~spot** *m* **(a)** (*Werbespot*) TV ad(vertisement); **(b)** (*Kurzfilm*) TV short; **~teilnehmer** *m* (*form*) television viewer; **~truhe** *f* cabinet TV; **~turm** *m* television tower; **~übertragung** *f* television broadcast; (*von außerhalb des Studios*) outside broadcast; **~übertragungswagen** *m* outside broadcast vehicle *or* van; **~zeitschrift** *f* TV guide; **~zuschauer** *m* (television) viewer.
Fẹrnsicht *f* clear view ◆ **(eine) gute ~ haben** to be able to see a long way.
Fẹrnsprech- *in cpds* (*form*) telephone; ⚠**~anschluß** *m* telephone; **15 ~anschlüsse haben** to have 15 lines; **~apparat** *m* telephone; **~auftragsdienst** *m* telephone services *pl*; **~buch** *nt* telephone directory.
Fẹrnsprecher *m* **-s,** - (*form*) (public) telephone.

⚠: Informationen zur Rechtschreibreform im Anhang

Fẹrnsprech- *in cpds siehe auch* **Telefon-**; **~gebühr** *f* telephone charges *pl*; **~geheimnis** *nt siehe* **Fernmeldegeheimnis**; **~leitung** *f* (*per Draht*) (telephone) line; (*per Radio, Satellit*) telephone link; **~netz** *nt* telephone system; **~teilnehmer** *m* (*form*) telephone subscriber; **~verkehr** *m* telephone traffic; **~wesen** *nt* telephone system; **~zelle** *f* (tele)phone box *or* booth (*US*), callbox; **~zentrale** *f* telephone exchange.

Fẹrn-: ⚠**f~stehen** *vi sep irreg* **jdm/einer Sache f~stehen** to have no connection with sb/sth; **ich stehe ihm ziemlich f~** I'm not on very close terms with him; **f~steuern** *vt sep* to operate by remote control; (*per Funk auch*) to control by radio; **~steuerung** *f* remote/radio control; **~steuerung haben** to be remote-/radio-controlled; **~straße** *f* trunk *or* major road, highway (*US*); **~studium** *nt* correspondence degree course (*also with radio, TV etc*), ≃ Open University course (*Brit*); **~tourismus** *m* long-haul tourism; **~trauung** *f* marriage by proxy; **~überwachung** *f* remote monitoring; **~universität** *f* ≃ Open University (*Brit*); **~unterricht** *m correspondence course also using radio, TV etc*, multi-media course; **~verkehr** *m* **(a)** (*Transport*) long-distance traffic; **(b)** (*Telec*) trunk (*Brit*) *or* long-distance traffic; **~verkehrsstraße** *f siehe* **~straße**; **~vermittlung(sstelle)** *f* telephone exchange; **~versorgung** *f* long-distance supply; **~wärme** *f* district heating (*spec*); **~weh** *nt* wanderlust; **~wirkung** *f* (*Phys*) long-distance effect; **~ziel** *nt* long-term goal; **~zug** *m* long-distance train; **~zündung** *f* long-range *or* remote ignition.

Ferrat *nt* (*Chem*) ferrate.

Ferrit *m* **-s, -e** (*Chem*) ferrite.

Fẹrro- *in cpds* ferro-.

Fẹrse *f* **-, -n** heel ◆ **jdm (dicht) auf den ~n sein** *or* **folgen/bleiben** to be/stay hard *or* close on sb's heels; *siehe* **heften.**

Fẹrsen-: **~automatik** *f* (*Ski*) automatic heel release; **~bein** *nt* (*Anat*) heel bone, calcaneus (*spec*); **~geld** *nt*: **~geld geben** to take to one's heels.

fẹrtig *adj* **(a)** (*abgeschlossen, vollendet*) finished; (*ausgebildet*) qualified; (*reif*) *Mensch, Charakter* mature ◆ **etw ~ kaufen** to buy sth ready-made; *Essen* to buy sth ready-prepared *or* ready to eat; **~ ausgebildet** fully qualified; **mit der Ausbildung ~ sein** to have completed one's training; **~ ist die Laube** (*inf*) *or* **der Lack** (*inf*) (and) there we are!, (and) Bob's your uncle! (*inf*).
(b) (*zu Ende*) finished ◆ **wird das/werden wir rechtzeitig ~ werden?** will it/we be finished in time?; **mit etw ~ sein, etw ~ haben** to have finished sth; **~ essen/lesen** to finish eating/reading; **mit jdm ~ sein** (*fig*) to be finished *or* through with sb; **mit jdm/etw ~ werden** to cope with sb/sth; **ich werde damit nicht ~** I can't cope with it; **du darfst nicht gehen, ~!** you're not going and that's that *or* and that's the end of it!
(c) (*bereit*) ready ◆ **~ zur Abfahrt** ready to go *or* leave; **bist du/ist das Essen ~?** are you/is the meal ready?; *siehe* **Achtung, Platz.**
(d) (*inf*) shattered (*inf*), all in (*inf*); (*ruiniert*) finished; (*erstaunt*) knocked for six (*inf*) ◆ **mit den Nerven ~ sein** to be at the end of one's tether; **da bin ich ~!** (*erstaunt*) my God!, well I never!; *siehe* **fix.**

Fẹrtig- *in cpds* finished; (*Build*) prefabricated; **~bau** *m* (*Build*) (*no pl: Bauweise*) prefabricated building; (*Gebäude auch*) *pl* **-bauten** prefab; ⚠**f~bekommen*** *vt sep irreg* to finish, to get finished; ⚠**f~bringen** *vt sep irreg* **(a)** (*vollenden*) to get done; **(b)** (*imstande sein*) to manage; (*iro*) to be capable of; **ich habe es nicht f~gebracht, ihr die Wahrheit zu sagen** I couldn't bring myself to tell her the truth; **er bringt das f~** (*iro*) I wouldn't put it past him; **er bringt es f~, und sagt ihr das** he's quite capable of saying that to her.

fẹrtigen *vt* (*form*) to manufacture.

Fẹrtig-: **~erzeugnis** *nt* finished product; **~fabrikat** *nt* finished product; **~gericht** *nt* ready-to-serve meal; **~haus** *nt* prefabricated house.

Fẹrtigkeit *f* skill ◆ **wenig/eine große ~ in etw** (*dat*) **haben** to be not very/to be very skilled at *or* in sth.

Fẹrtig-: ⚠**f~kriegen** *vt sep* (*inf*) *siehe* **f~bringen**; ⚠**f~machen** *vt sep* **(a)** (*vollenden*) to finish; **(b)** (*bereit machen*) to get ready; **sich f~machen** to get ready; **f~machen!** get ready!; (*Sport*) get set!, steady!; **(c)** (*inf*) **jdn f~machen** (*erledigen*) to do for sb; (*ermüden*) to take it out of sb; (*deprimieren*) to get sb down; (*abkanzeln*) to tear sb off a strip, to lay into sb (*inf*); **sich f~machen** to do oneself in; **~produkt** *nt* finished product; ⚠**f~stellen** *vt sep* to complete; **~stellung** *f* completion; **~teil** *nt* finished part.

Fẹrtigung *f* production ◆ **in der ~ arbeiten** to work in production *or* in the production department.

Fẹrtigungs- *in cpds* production; **~straße** *f* production line; **~technik** *f* production engineering.

Fẹrtigware *f* finished product.

Fẹs¹, fẹs *nt* **-,** *no pl* (*Mus*) F flat.

Fẹs² [feːs] *m* **-(es), -(e)** fez.

fẹsch *adj* (*S Ger, Aus: inf*) (*modisch*) smart; (*hübsch*) attractive ◆ **das ist ~** that's great (*inf*); **sei ~!** (*Aus*) (*sei brav*) be good; (*sei kein Frosch*) be a sport (*inf*).

Fẹssel *f* **-, -n (a)** (*Bande*) (*lit, fig*) bond, fetter, shackle; (*Kette*) chain ◆ **sich von den ~n befreien** to free oneself, to loose one's bonds (*liter*); **jdm ~n anlegen, jdn in ~n legen** to fetter *or* shackle sb/put sb in chains; **jdn in ~n schlagen** (*liter, fig*) to put sb in fetters, to enchain sb (*liter*); **die ~n der Ehe/Liebe** the shackles of marriage/love.
(b) (*Anat*) (*von Huftieren*) pastern; (*von Menschen*) ankle.

Fẹssel-: **~ballon** *m* captive balloon; **~gelenk** *nt* pastern; (*von Menschen*) ankle joint; **~griff** *m* lock.

fẹsseln *vt* **(a)** (*mit Tau etc*) to tie (up), to bind; (*Hist: mit Hand~, Fußschellen*) to fetter, to shackle; (*mit Handschellen*) to handcuff; (*mit Ketten*) to chain (up) ◆ **jdn (an Händen und Füßen) ~** to tie/fetter/chain sb (hand and foot); **jdm die Hände auf dem Rücken ~** to tie sb's hands behind his back; **der Gefangene wurde gefesselt vorgeführt** the prisoner was brought in handcuffed/in chains; **jdn ans Bett ~** (*fig*) to confine sb to (his) bed, to keep sb in bed; **jdn ans Haus ~** (*fig*) to tie sb to the house; **jdn an jdn/sich ~** (*fig*) to bind sb to sb/oneself.
(b) (*faszinieren*) to grip; *Aufmerksamkeit* to hold.

fẹsselnd *adj* gripping.

fẹst [1] *adj* **(a)** (*hart*) solid ◆ **~e Nahrung** solid food, solids *pl*; **~e Form** *or* **Gestalt annehmen** (*fig*) to take shape.
(b) (*stabil*) solid; *Gewebe, Schuhe* tough, sturdy; (*Comm, Fin*) stable; *Zuneigung* strong; *siehe* **Boden.**
(c) (*sicher, entschlossen*) firm; *Plan auch* definite; *Stimme* steady ◆ **~ versprechen** to promise faithfully; **~ verankert** (*lit*) firmly *or* securely anchored; (*fig*) firmly rooted; **eine ~e Meinung von etw haben** to have definite views on sth; **etw ist ~** sth is definite; **~ entschlossen sein** to be absolutely determined.
(d) (*kräftig*) firm; *Schlag* hard, heavy ◆ **~ zuschlagen** to hit hard.
(e) (*nicht locker*) tight; *Griff* firm; (*fig*) *Schlaf* sound ◆ **~ packen** to grip tightly *or* firmly; **etw ~ anziehen/zudrehen** to pull/screw sth tight; **die Handbremse ~ anziehen** to put the handbrake on firmly; **die Tür ~ schließen** to shut the door tight; **~ schlafen** to sleep soundly; **er hat schon ~ geschlafen** he was sound asleep; **jdn/etw ~ in der Hand haben** to have sb under one's thumb/have sth firmly under control.
(f) (*ständig*) regular; *Freund(in)* steady; *Bindung, Stellung, Mitarbeiter* permanent; *Kosten, Tarif, Einkommen* fixed; *Redewendung* set ◆ **~ befreundet sein** to be good friends; (*Freund und Freundin*) to be going steady; **jdn ~ anstellen** to employ sb as a regular member of staff; **Geld ~ anlegen** to tie up money; **in ~en Händen sein** *or* **sich befinden** (*Besitz*) to be in private hands; (*inf: Mädchen*) to be spoken for; **seinen ~en Platz gewinnen** to establish oneself; **sie hat keinen ~en Platz im Büro** she doesn't have her own desk in the office; **er hat einen ~en Platz in ihrem Herzen** he has a special place in her affections; *siehe auch* **Platz.**
[2] *adv* (*inf: tüchtig, kräftig*) *helfen, arbeiten* with a will.

Fẹst *nt* **-(e)s, -e (a)** (*Feier*) celebration; (*historische Begebenheit*) celebrations *pl*; (*Party*) party; (*Hochzeits~*) reception; (*Bankett*) banquet, feast (*old*); (*Ball~*) ball; (*Kinder~, Schützen~*) carnival ◆ **ein ~ zum hundertjährigen Bestehen des Vereins** the club's centenary celebrations, celebrations to mark the club's centenary; **das war ein ~!** (*inf*) it was great fun; **man soll die ~e feiern, wie sie fallen** (*prov*) make hay while the sun shines (*Prov*).
(b) (*kirchlicher Feiertag*) feast, festival; (*Weihnachts~*) Christmas ◆ **bewegliches/unbewegliches ~** movable/immovable feast; **frohes ~!** Merry *or* Happy Christmas!

Fẹst-: **~akt** *m* ceremony; ⚠**f~angestellt** *adj* employed on a regular basis; **~angestellte(r)** *mf* regular member of staff; **~ansprache** *f* speech; **~aufführung** *f* festival production; **f~backen** *vi sep irreg aux sein* (*dial*) *siehe* **f~kleben**; **~bankett** *nt* ceremonial banquet; **f~beißen** *vr sep irreg* (*Hund etc*) to get a firm hold with its teeth (*an +dat* on); (*Zecke etc*) to attach itself firmly (*an +dat* to); (*fig: nicht weiterkommen*) to get bogged down (*inf*) (*an +dat* in); **der Hund biß sich an ihrem Bein f~** the dog sank its teeth firmly into her leg; **~beleuchtung** *f* festive lighting *or* lights *pl*; (*inf: im Haus*) blazing lights *pl*; **was soll denn diese ~beleuchtung?** (*inf*) why is the place lit up like a Christmas tree? (*inf*); ⚠**f~besoldet** *adj* on a regular salary; **f~binden** *vt sep irreg* to tie up; **jdn/etw an etw** (*dat*) **f~binden** to tie sb/sth to sth; **f~bleiben** *vi sep irreg aux sein* to stand firm, to remain resolute; **f~drehen** *vt sep* to screw up tightly; **f~drücken** *vt sep* to press in/down/together firmly.

fẹste *adv* (*inf*) *siehe* **fest 2**; **immer ~ druff!** let him/her *etc* have it! (*inf*), give it to him/her *etc*! (*inf*).

Fẹste *f* **-, -n** (*old*) **(a)** *siehe* **Festung. (b)** (*Erde*) dry land, terra firma ◆ **die ~ des Himmels** (*Bibl*) the firmament.

Fẹst-: **~essen** *nt* banquet; Christmas dinner; **f~fahren** *vr sep irreg* (*fig*) to get bogged down; (*lit auch*) to get stuck, to stick fast; **f~fressen** *vr sep irreg* to seize up; **f~frieren** *vi sep irreg aux sein* to freeze solid; **~gabe** *f* **(a)** (*Geschenk*) presentation gift; **(b)** (*~schrift*) commemorative paper, festschrift; **~gedicht** *nt* celebratory *or* occasional poem; **~gelage** *nt* banquet; **~geläute** *nt* festive peal of bells; **~geld** *nt* (*Fin*) time deposit; **~gewand** *nt* (*liter*) festive garb (*liter*); **f~gewurzelt** *adj*: **wie f~gewurzelt** rooted to the spot; **~gottesdienst** *m* festival service; **f~gurten** *sep* [1] *vr* to strap oneself in; [2] *vt* to strap in; **f~haken** *sep* [1] *vt* to hook up (*an +dat* on); [2] *vr* to get caught (up) (*an +dat* on); **~halle** *f* festival hall.

fẹsthalten *sep irreg* [1] *vt* **(a)** to keep a firm hold on, to keep hold of, to hold on to ◆ **jdn am Arm/Rockzipfel ~** to hold on to sb's arm/the hem of sb's coat.
(b) (*bemerken*) to stress, to emphasize.
(c) (*inhaftieren*) to hold, to detain.
(d) (*speichern*) to record; *Atmosphäre etc* to capture ◆ **etw schriftlich/im Gedächtnis ~** to record sth/bear sth firmly in mind; **etw in Wort und Bild ~** to record sth in words and pictures.
[2] *vi* **an etw** (*dat*) **~** to hold *or* stick (*inf*) to sth; **am Glauben ~** to hold to the faith.
[3] *vr* to hold on (*an +dat* to) ◆ **sich irgendwo ~** to hold on to something; **halt dich fest!** (*lit*) hold tight!; **halt dich fest, und hör dir das an!** (*inf*) brace yourself and listen to this!

fẹstheften *vt sep* (*mit Nadel*) to pin (*an +dat* (on)to); (*mit Faden*) to tack (*an +dat* (on)to).

⚠: for details of spelling reform, see supplement

festigen [1] *vt* to strengthen; *Freundschaft, Macht, Ruf auch* to consolidate ◆ **ein gefestigter Charakter** a firm *or* resolute character; **sittlich gefestigt sein** to have a sense of moral responsibility.
[2] *vr* to become stronger; (*Freundschaft, Macht, Ruf auch*) to consolidate.

Festiger *m* **-s, -** setting lotion.

Festigkeit *f, no pl* strength; (*fig*) steadfastness; (*von Meinung*) firmness ◆ **die ~ seines Charakters** his moral strength, his strength of character.

Festigung *f siehe vb* strengthening; consolidation.

Festival ['fɛstivəl, 'fɛstival] *nt* **-s, -s** festival.

Festivität [fɛstivi'tɛːt] *f* (*old, hum inf*) celebration, festivity.

Fest-: f~keilen *vt sep* to wedge; **f~klammern** *sep* [1] *vt* to clip on (*an +dat* to); **Wäsche an** *or* **auf der Leine f~klammern** to peg washing on the line; [2] *vr* to cling (*an +dat* to); **f~kleben** *vti sep* (*vi: aux sein*) to stick (firmly) (*an +dat* (on)to); **~kleid** *nt* formal dress; **die Stadt legte ihr ~kleid an** (*liter*) the town decked itself out in all its finery; **f~klemmen** *sep* [1] *vt* to wedge fast; (*mit Klammer, Klemme*) to clip; **f~geklemmt werden** (*aus Versehen*) to get stuck *or* jammed; [2] *vir* (*vi: aux sein*) to jam, to stick (fast); **f~klopfen** *vt sep* to pack down; **f~knoten** *vt sep siehe* **f~binden**; **~komma** *nt* (*auch Comput*) fixed point; **~körper** *m* (*Phys*) solid; **~körperphysik** *f* solid-state physics *sing*; **f~krallen** *vr sep* (*Tier*) to dig one's claws in (*an +dat* -to); (*Mensch*) to dig one's nails in (*an +dat* -to); (*fig*) to cling (*an +dat* to).

Festland *nt* (*nicht Insel*) mainland; (*nicht Meer*) dry land; (*europäisches ~*) Continent, Europe.

festländisch *adj* mainland *attr*; Continental, European.

Festlands-: ~masse *f* continent; **~sockel** *m* continental shelf.

festlaufen *sep irreg* [1] *vr* (*Schiff*) to run aground; (*fig*) (*Verhandlungen*) to founder ◆ **die Stürmer liefen sich (an der Verteidigung) immer wieder fest** the forwards kept coming up against a solid line of defence.
[2] *vi aux sein* (*Schiff*) to run aground.

festlegen *sep* [1] *vt* **(a)** (*festsetzen*) *Reihenfolge, Termin, Kurs etc* to fix (*auf +acc, bei* for); *Grenze auch* to establish; *Sprachgebrauch* to establish, to lay down; (*bestimmen*) *Regelung, Arbeitszeiten* to lay down; (*feststellen*) *Geburtsdatum* to determine ◆ **etw schriftlich/testamentarisch ~** to stipulate *or* specify sth in writing/in one's will.
(b) jdn auf etw (*acc*) **~/darauf ~, etw zu tun** (*festnageln*) to tie sb (down) to sth/to doing sth; (*einschränken auch*) to restrict *or* limit sb to sth/to doing sth; (*verpflichten*) to commit sb to sth/to doing sth.
(c) *Geld* to put on time deposit, to tie up.
[2] *vr* **(a)** to tie oneself down (*auf +acc* to); (*sich verpflichten*) to commit oneself (*auf +acc* to) ◆ **ich kann mich darauf nicht ~, ich kann mich auch irren** I can't swear to it, I might be wrong; **sich darauf ~, etw zu tun** to tie oneself down/commit oneself to doing sth.
(b) (*einen Entschluß fassen*) to decide (*auf +acc* on) ◆ **sich darauf ~, etw zu tun** to decide on doing sth *or* to do sth.

Festlegung *f siehe vt (a, b)* **(a)** fixing; establishing; laying-down; determining. **(b)** tying-down; restriction, limiting; commitment.

festlich *adj* festive; (*feierlich*) solemn; (*prächtig*) splendid, magnificent ◆ **ein ~er Tag** a special *or* red-letter day; **etw ~ begehen** to celebrate sth.

Festlichkeit *f* celebration; (*Stimmung*) festiveness.

Fest-: f~liegen *vi sep irreg* **(a)** (*f~gesetzt sein*) to have been fixed *or* definitely decided; (*Sprachgebrauch, Grenze*) to have been established; (*Arbeitszeiten, Regelung*) to have been laid down; **(b)** (*Fin: Geld*) to be on time deposit *or* tied up; **(c)** (*nicht weiterkönnen*) to be stuck; (*Naut*) to be aground; **f~machen** *sep* [1] *vt* **(a)** (*befestigen*) to fix on (*an +dat* -to); (*f~binden*) to fasten (*an +dat* (on)to); (*Naut*) to moor; **(b)** (*vereinbaren*) to arrange; **ein Geschäft f~machen** to clinch a deal; **(c)** (*Hunt: aufspüren*) to bring to bay; **(d)** (*beweisen, zeigen*) to demonstrate, to exemplify; **etw an etw/jdm f~machen** (*fig*) to link sth to sth/sb; [2] *vi* (*Naut*) to moor; **~mahl** *nt* (*geh*) banquet, feast; **~meter** *m or nt* cubic metre of solid timber; **f~nageln** *vt sep* **(a)** to nail (down/up/on); **etw an/auf etw** (*dat*) **f~nageln** to nail sth to sth; **(b)** (*fig inf*) *jdn* to tie down (*auf +acc* to); **f~nähen** *vt sep* to sew up/on; **~nahme** *f* **-, -n** arrest, apprehension; **vorläufige ~nahme** temporary detention; **f~nehmen** *vt sep irreg* to apprehend, to arrest; **vorläufig f~nehmen** to take into custody; **Sie sind f~genommen** you are under arrest; **~offerte** *f* (*Comm*) firm offer; **~ordner** *m* steward; **~platte** *f* (*Comput*) hard disk; **~plattenlaufwerk** *nt* hard disk drive; **~platz** *m* festival ground; (*für Volksfest*) fairground; **~predigt** *f* feast-day sermon; **~preis** *m* (*Comm*) fixed price; **~programm** *nt* festival programme; **~punkt** *m* (*auch Comput*) fixed point; **~rede** *f* speech; **eine ~rede halten** to make a speech on a special occasion; **f~reden** *vr sep* to get involved in a conversation; **~redner** *m* (main) speaker; **f~rennen** *vr sep irreg* (*inf*) to get bogged down (*inf*); **unsere Spieler rannten sich (an der gegnerischen Abwehr) f~** our players came up against the solid line of the opponents' defence; **~saal** *m* hall; (*Speisesaal*) banqueting hall; (*Tanzsaal*) ballroom; **f~saufen** *vr sep irreg* (*inf*) to get stuck in (*inf*), to make a night of it (*inf*); **f~saugen** *vr sep* to attach itself firmly (*an +dat* to); **~schmaus** *m* (*old*) *siehe* **~mahl**; **~schmuck** *m* festive decorations *pl*; **im ~schmuck** festively decorated; **f~schnallen** *vtr sep siehe* **anschnallen**; **f~schnüren** *vt sep siehe* **f~binden**; **f~schrauben** *vt sep* to screw (in/on/down/up) tight; **f~schreiben** *vt sep irreg* (*fig*) to establish; (*Jur*) to enact; **~schreibung** *f* establishment; (*Jur*) enactment; **~schrift** *f* commemorative publication; (*für Gelehrten*) festschrift.

festsetzen *sep* [1] *vt* **(a)** (*bestimmen*) *Preis, Rente, Grenze* to fix (*bei, auf +acc* at); *Ort, Termin auch* to arrange (*auf +acc, bei* for); *Frist auch* to set; *Arbeitszeiten* to lay down ◆ **der Beginn der Veranstaltung wurde auf zwei Uhr festgesetzt** the event was scheduled to begin at 2 o'clock.
(b) (*inhaftieren*) to detain.
[2] *vr* (*Staub, Schmutz*) to collect; (*Rost, Ungeziefer, unerwünschte Personen*) to get a foothold; (*Mil*) to take up one's position; (*fig: Gedanke*) to take root, to implant itself.

Festsetzung *f* **(a)** *siehe vt (a)* fixing; arrangement; setting; laying-down. **(b)** (*Inhaftierung*) detention.

festsitzen *vi sep irreg* **(a)** (*klemmen, haften*) to be stuck; (*Schmutz*) to cling; (*in Zwischenräumen*) to be trapped. **(b)** (*steckengeblieben sein*) to be stuck (*bei* on); (*Naut*) to be aground.

Festspiel *nt* (*einzelnes Stück*) festival production ◆ **~e** *pl* (*Veranstaltung*) festival *sing*.

Festspiel-: ~haus *nt* festival theatre; **~stadt** *f* festival city/town.

fest-: ~stampfen *vt sep* to pound down; (*mit den Füßen auch*) to stamp *or* tread down; **~stecken** *sep* [1] *vt* to pin (*an +dat* (on)to, *in +dat* in); *Haare, Rocksaum* to pin up; [2] *vi* (*steckengeblieben sein*) to be stuck; **~stehen** *vi sep irreg* (*sicher sein*) to be certain; (*beschlossen sein*) to have been settled *or* fixed; (*unveränderlich sein*) to be definite; **~ steht** *or* **eines steht ~, daß** ... one thing's (for) certain *or* sure and that is that ...; **soviel steht ~** this *or* so much is certain; **~stehend** *adj* **(a)** (*Mech*) fixed; **(b)** *attr* (*bestimmt, verbindlich*) definite; *Redewendung, Reihenfolge* set; *Brauch* (well-)established; **~stellbar** *adj* **(a)** (*Mech: arretierbar*) **der Wagen der Schreibmaschine ist ~stellbar** the typewriter carriage can be locked in position; **(b)** (*herauszufinden*) ascertainable.

➤ **feststellen** *vt sep* **(a)** (*Mech*) to lock (fast).
(b) (*ermitteln*) to ascertain, to find out; *Personalien, Sachverhalt, Datum etc auch* to establish; *Ursache, Grund auch* to establish, to determine; *Schaden* to assess; *Krankheit* to diagnose ◆ **einen Totalschaden an einem Wagen ~** to assess a car as a total write-off; **der Arzt konnte nur noch den Tod ~** the doctor found him to be dead.
➤ **(c)** (*erkennen*) to tell (*an +dat* from); *Fehler, Unterschied* to find, to detect; (*bemerken*) to discover; (*einsehen*) to realize ◆ **wir mußten ~, daß wir uns geirrt hatten** we were forced to realize that we had made a mistake; **ich mußte entsetzt/überrascht** *etc* **~, daß** ... I was horrified/surprised *etc* to find that ...
(d) (*aussprechen*) to stress, to emphasize.

Feststelltaste *f* shift lock.

Feststellung *f* **(a)** *siehe vt (b)* ascertainment; establishment; assessment; diagnosis.
(b) (*Erkenntnis*) conclusion ◆ **zu der ~ kommen** *or* **gelangen, daß** ... to come to the conclusion that ...
(c) (*Wahrnehmung*) observation ◆ **die ~ machen** *or* **treffen daß** ... to realize that ...; **wir mußten leider die ~ machen, daß** ... (*form*) it has come to our notice that ...; **ist das eine Frage oder eine ~?** is that a question or a statement (of fact)?
(d) (*Bemerkung*) remark, comment, observation ◆ **die abschließende ~** one's closing remarks; **die ~ machen, daß** ... to remark *or* observe that ...

Feststellungsklage *f* action for a declaratory judgement.

Fest-: ~stimmung *f* festive atmosphere; (*~laune*) festive mood; **~stoffrakete** *f* solid-fuel rocket; **~tafel** *f* banquet table; (*bei Familienanlässen*) (dinner) table.

Festtag *m* **(a)** (*Ehrentag*) special *or* red-letter day. **(b)** (*Feiertag*) holiday, feast (day) (*Eccl*) ◆ **angenehme ~e!** happy Christmas/Easter *etc*!

festtäglich *adj* holiday *attr* ◆ **~ gestimmt sein** to be in a holiday mood; **~ gekleidet** festively dressed.

Festtags-: ~kleidung *f* **~kleidung tragen** to be festively dressed; **~laune** *f* festive mood; **~stimmung** *f* festive atmosphere; **in ~stimmung** in a festive mood.

Fest-: ~treibstoffrakete *f* solid fuel rocket; **f~treten** *sep irreg* [1] *vt* to tread down; (*in Teppich etc*) to tread in (*in +acc* -to); [2] *vr* to get trodden down/in; **das tritt sich f~!** (*hum inf*) don't worry, it's good for the carpet (*hum*); **f~trocknen** *vi sep aux sein* to dry (on); **f~umrissen** *adj attr* clear-cut; **~umzug** *m* procession.

Festung *f* (*Befestigung*) fortress; (*Burgfeste*) castle.

Festungs-: ~graben *m* moat; **~haft** *f* imprisonment in a fortress; **~wall** *m* rampart.

Fest-: ~veranstaltung *f* function ; **~versammlung** *f* assembled company; ⚠**f~verwurzelt** *adj attr* deep-rooted, deep-seated; **f~verzinslich** *adj* fixed-interest *attr*; **~vorstellung** *f* gala performance; **~vortrag** *m* lecture, talk; **f~wachsen** *vi sep irreg aux sein siehe* **anwachsen** (*lit*); **~wertspeicher** *m* (*Comput*) read-only memory; **~wiese** *f* festival ground; (*für Volksfest*) fairground; **~woche** *f* festival week; **die ~wochen** the festival *sing*; **f~wurzeln** *vi sep aux sein* to take root; *siehe* **f~gewurzelt**; **~zeit** *f* holiday period; (*~spielzeit*) festival (period); **~zelt** *nt* carnival marquee; **f~ziehen** *vt sep irreg* to pull tight; *Schraube* to tighten (up); **~zins** *m* fixed interest; **~zinssatz** *m* fixed rate of interest; **~zug** *m* carnival procession; **f~zurren** *vt sep* (*Naut*) to lash up.

fetal *adj attr siehe* **fötal**.

Fete, Fête ['feːtə, 'fɛːtə] *f* **-, -n** party ◆ **eine ~ feiern** (*als Gastgeber*) to have *or* give *or* throw a party; (*als Gast*) to go to a party.

Feten *pl of* **Fetus**.

Fetisch *m* **-(e)s, -e** fetish.

fetischisieren* *vt* (*geh*) to make a fetish of.

Fetischismus *m* fetishism.

Fetischist *m* fetishist.

fett *adj* **(a)** (*~haltig*) *Speisen, Kost* fatty; (*fig inf: ölig*) *Stimme* fat ◆ **~ essen** to eat fatty food; **~ kochen** to cook fatty food; (*viel Fett gebrauchen*) to use a lot of fat; **ein ~er Bissen** *or* **Brocken** *or* **Happen** (*lit*) a juicy morsel; (*fig*) a lucrative deal.

(b) (*dick*) fat; (*Typ*) *Überschrift, Schlagzeilen* bold ◆ **~ gedruckt** (*Typ*) (in) bold, printed in bold; **sich dick und ~ fressen** (*sl*) to stuff oneself (*inf*) *or* one's face (*sl*); **~ dasitzen** (*inf*)/**sich ~ hinsetzen** (*inf*) to sit there/plump oneself down like a sack of potatoes (*inf*).

(c) (*üppig*) *Boden, Weide, Klee* rich, luxuriant; (*fig inf*) rich; *Beute, Gewinn* fat; *Geschäft* lucrative ◆ **~e Jahre** fat years; **ein ~er Posten** (*inf*) a cushy job *or* number (*inf*); *siehe* **sieben²**.

(d) (*Aut*) *Gemisch etc* rich.

Fett *nt* **-(e)s, -e** fat; (*zum Schmieren*) grease ◆ **~ ansetzen** to put on weight, to get fat; (*Tiere*) to fatten up; **mit heißem ~ übergießen** to baste (with hot fat); **in schwimmendem ~ backen** to deep-fry; **sein ~ bekommen** (*inf*) *or* **kriegen** (*inf*)/**weghaben** (*inf*) to get/have got what was coming to one (*inf*) *or* one's come-uppance (*inf*); **~ schwimmt oben** (*prov*) (*hum: Dicke im Wasser*) fat floats; *siehe* **abschöpfen, schmoren.**

Fett-: ~ablagerung *f, no pl* deposition of fat; **~ablagerungen** fatty deposits; **~ansatz** *m* layer of fat; **zu ~ansatz neigen** to tend to corpulence; **f~arm** *adj* low-fat, with a low fat content; **f~arm essen** to eat foods with a low fat content; **~auge** *nt* globule of fat; **~bauch** *m* paunch; (*inf: fetter Mann*) fatso (*inf*); **f~bäuchig** *adj* (*inf*) paunchy, fat-bellied (*inf*); **~bedarf** *m* fat requirements *pl*; **~creme** *f* skin cream with oil; **~druck** *m* (*Typ*) bold type.

Fette Henne *f* (*Bot*) stonecrop.

Fett|embolie *f* (*Med*) fat-embolism.

fetten [1] *vt* to grease.

[2] *vi* to be greasy; (*Fett absondern*) to get greasy.

Fett-: ~film *m* greasy film; **~fleck(en)** *m* grease spot, greasy mark; **f~frei** *adj* fat-free; *Milch* non-fat; *Kost* non-fatty; *Creme* non-greasy; **f~füttern** *vt sep* to fatten up; **f~gedruckt** *adj attr* (*Typ*) bold, in bold face; **~gehalt** *m* fat content; **~geschwulst** *f* (*Med*) fatty tumour; **~gewebe** *nt* (*Anat*) fat(ty) tissue; **f~glänzend** *adj* **die f~glänzenden Ringer** the wrestlers with their oiled bodies glistening; **f~haltig, f~hältig** (*Aus*) *adj* fatty; **~haushalt** *m* fat balance; **ein gestörter ~haushalt** a fat imbalance.

Fettheit *f, no pl* (*inf: Dickheit*) fatness; (*Fetthaltigkeit*) fattiness.

fettig *adj* greasy; *Haut auch* oily.

Fettigkeit *f siehe adj* greasiness; oiliness.

Fett-: ~kloß *m* (*pej*) fatty (*inf*), dumpling (*inf*); **~klumpen** *m* globule of fat; **~leber** *f* fatty liver; **f~leibig** *adj* (*geh*) obese, corpulent; **~leibigkeit** *f* (*geh*) obesity, corpulence; **f~los** *adj* fat-free; **völlig f~los essen** to eat no fats at all; **f~löslich** *adj* fat-soluble; **~massen** *pl* (*inf*) mass *sing* of fat; **~mops** *m* (*inf*) roly-poly (*inf*), dumpling (*inf*); **~näpfchen** *nt* (*inf*): **ins ~näpfchen treten** to put one's foot in it (*bei jdm* with sb), to drop a clanger (*inf*); **~polster** *nt* (*Anat*) (layer of) subcutaneous fat; (*hum inf*) flab *no pl*, padding *no pl*; **~polster haben** to be well-padded; **~pölsterchen** *nt* padding *no pl*; **~presse** *f* grease gun; **f~reich** *adj* high-fat, with a high fat content; **f~reich essen** to eat foods with a high fat content; **~sack** *m* (*sl*) fatso (*inf*); **~salbe** *f* fat-based ointment; **~sau** *f* (*vulg*) fat slob (*sl*); **~säure** *f* (*Chem*) fatty acid; **~schicht** *f* layer of fat; **~schrift** *f* bold (type *or* face); **~steiß** *m* (*Anat*) steatopygia (*spec*); **~stift** *m* grease pencil, lithographic crayon; (*für Lippen*) lip salve; **~sucht** *f, no pl* (*Med*) obesity; **f~süchtig** *adj* (*Med*) obese; **f~triefend** *adj* greasy, dripping with fat; **~wanst** *m* (*pej*) potbelly; (*Mensch*) paunchy man, fatso (*inf*).

Fetus *m* - *or* **-sses, -sse** *or* **Feten** *siehe* **Fötus.**

Fetzen *m* **-s, - (a)** (*abgerissen*) shred; (*zerrissen auch*) tatter; (*Stoff~, Papier~, Gesprächs~*) scrap; (*Kleidung*) rag; (*Nebel~*) wisp ◆ **in ~ sein, nur noch ~ sein** to be in tatters *or* shreds; **in ~ gekleidet** dressed in rags; **das Kleid ist in ~ gegangen** the dress has fallen to pieces; **etw in ~/in tausend ~ (zer)reißen** to tear sth to shreds/into a thousand pieces; **..., daß die ~ fliegen** (*inf*) ... like mad (*inf*) *or* crazy (*inf*).

(b) (*Aus*) (*Scheuertuch*) rag.

fetzen [1] *vi* (*sl*) **(a)** (*mitreißen*) to be mind-blowing (*sl*); (*Musik*) to have a driving beat. **(b)** *aux sein* (*rasen*) to hare (*inf*), to tear (*inf*) ◆ **gegen jdn/etw ~** to tear into sb/sth.

[2] *vt* to rip ◆ **der Sturm fetzte das Dach vom Haus** the storm tore the roof off the house; **Klamotten durchs Zimmer ~** to fling clothes about the room; **die beiden ~ sich den ganzen Tag** they are tearing into each other all day long.

Fetzenball *m* (*Aus*) *siehe* **Maskenball.**

Fetzer *m* **-s, -** (*sl*) wow (*sl*).

fetzig *adj* (*sl*) wild, crazy; *Musik auch* hot.

feucht *adj* damp; (*schlüpfrig*) moist; (*feuchtheiß*) *Klima* humid; *Hände* sweaty; *Tinte, Farbe* not quite dry ◆ **sich ins ~e Element stürzen** (*hum*) to plunge into the water; **sie kriegte/hatte ~e Augen** her eyes moistened/were moist; **ein ~er Abend** (*hum*) a boozy night; **eine ~e Aussprache haben** (*hum inf*) to splutter when one speaks; **das geht dich einen ~en Kehricht** (*inf*) *or* **Dreck** (*sl*) *or* **Schmutz** (*sl*) **an** that's none of your goddamn (*sl*) *or* bloody (*Brit sl*) business; *siehe* **Ohr.**

Feucht-: ~biotop *nt* damp biotope; **f~fröhlich** *adj* (*hum*) merry, convivial; **ein f~fröhlicher Abend** an evening of convivial drinking; **~gebiet** *nt* marshland; **f~heiß** *adj* hot and damp, muggy.

Feuchtigkeit *f, no pl* **(a)** *siehe adj* dampness; moistness; humidity; sweatiness; wetness. **(b)** (*Flüssigkeit*) moisture; (*Luft~*) humidity.

Feuchtigkeits-: ~creme *f* moisturizer, moisturizing cream; **~gehalt, ~grad** *m* moisture level *or* content; **~messer** *m* hygrometer.

feucht-: ~kalt *adj* cold and damp; *Höhle, Keller etc auch* dank; **~warm** *adj* muggy, humid.

feudal *adj* **(a)** (*Pol, Hist*) feudal. **(b)** (*inf: prächtig*) plush (*inf*).

Feudal- *in cpds* feudal; **~herrschaft** *f* feudalism.

Feudalismus *m* feudalism.

feudalistisch *adj* feudalistic.

Feudalität *f* **(a)** (*Hist*) feudality. **(b)** (*inf*) plushness (*inf*).

Feudal-: ~system, ~wesen *nt* feudalism, feudal system.

Feudel *m* **-s, -** (*N Ger*) (floor)cloth.

feudeln *vt* (*N Ger*) to wash, to wipe.

Feuer *nt* **-s, - (a)** (*Flamme, Kamin~*) fire; (*olympisches ~*) flame ◆ **am ~** by the fire; **~ machen** to light a/the fire; **~ schlagen** to make fire, to strike a spark; **~ speien** to spew flames *or* fire; **das brennt wie ~** (*fig*) that burns; **~ hinter etw** (*acc*) **machen** (*fig*) to chase sth up; **jdm ~ unter den Hintern** (*inf*) *or* **Arsch** (*sl*) **machen** to put a bomb under sb; **mit dem ~ spielen** (*fig*) to play with fire; **sie sind wie ~ und Wasser** they're as different as chalk and cheese.

(b) (*Funk~*) beacon; (*von Leuchtturm*) light.

(c) (*Herd*) fire ◆ **auf offenem ~ kochen** to cook on an open fire.

(d) (*für Zigarette etc*) light ◆ **haben Sie ~?** have you got a light?; **jdm ~ geben** to give sb a light.

(e) (*Brand*) fire ◆ **~!** fire!; **~ legen** to start a fire; **an etw** (*acc*)/**in etw** (*dat*) **~ legen** to set fire to sth; **~ fangen** to catch fire; **für jdn durchs ~ gehen** to go through fire and water for sb.

(f) (*Schwung*) (*von Frau*) passion; (*von Liebhaber auch*) ardour; (*von Pferd*) mettle; (*von Wein*) vigour ◆ **~ haben** to be passionate/ardent/mettlesome/ full of vigour; **~ fangen** to be really taken (*bei* with); **bei jdm ~ fangen** to fall for sb; **~ und Flamme sein** (*inf*) to be dead keen (*inf*) (*für* on).

(g) (*liter: Glanz*) sparkle, glitter ◆ **das ~ ihrer Augen** her flashing *or* fiery eyes.

(h) (*Schießen*) fire ◆ **~!** fire!; **~ frei!** open fire!; **~ geben/das ~ eröffnen** to open fire; **das ~ einstellen** to cease fire *or* firing; **etw unter ~** (*acc*) **nehmen** to open fire on sth; **unter ~** (*dat*) **liegen** to be under fire; **zwischen zwei ~** (*acc*) **geraten** (*fig*) to be caught between the Devil and the deep blue sea (*prov*).

Feuer- *in cpds* fire; **~alarm** *m* fire alarm; **~anzünder** *m* firelighter; **~bake** *f* (*Naut*) light beacon; **~ball** *m* fireball; **~befehl** *m* (*Mil*) order to fire; **~bekämpfung** *f* fire-fighting; **~bereich** *m* (*Mil*) firing range; **f~bereit** *adj* (*Mil*) ready to fire; **f~beständig** *adj* fire-resistant; **~bestattung** *f* cremation; **~eifer** *m* zeal; **mit ~eifer spielen/diskutieren** to play/discuss with zest; **~eimer** *m* fire-bucket; **~einstellung** *f* cessation of fire; (*Waffenstillstand*) ceasefire; **f~fest** *adj* fireproof; *Geschirr* heat-resistant; **f~fester Ton/Ziegel** fireclay/firebrick; **~fresser** *m* fire-eater; **~garbe** *f siehe* **~stoß;** **~gasse** *f* fire lane; **~gefahr** *f* fire hazard *or* risk; **bei ~gefahr** in the event of fire; **f~gefährlich** *adj* (highly) (in)flammable *or* combustible; **~gefährlichkeit** *f* (in)flammability, combustibility; **~gefecht** *nt* gun fight, shoot-out (*inf*); **~geist** *m* (*liter*) volatile young genius, fireball; **~glocke** *f* fire bell; **~gott** *m* god of fire; **~haken** *m* poker; **~holz** *nt, no pl* firewood; **~käfer** *m* cardinal beetle; **~kopf** *m* (*geh*) fireball; **~kult** *m* (*Rel*) fire cult; **~land** *nt* Tierra del Fuego; **~länder(in** *f*) *m* **-s, -** Fuegian; **~leiter** *f* (*am Haus*) fire escape; (*bei ~wehrauto*) (fireman's) ladder; (*fahrbar*) turntable ladder; **~linie** *f* (*Mil*) firing line.

Feuerlösch-: ~apparat *m siehe* **~gerät; ~boot** *nt* fireboat.

Feuerlöscher *m* fire extinguisher.

Feuerlösch-: ~gerät *nt* fire-fighting appliance; **~teich** *m* emergency water reserve; **~zug** *m* convoy of fire engines, set of appliances (*form*).

Feuer-: ~meer *nt* sea of flames, blazing inferno; **~melder** *m* **-s, -** fire alarm; **er hat ein Gesicht wie ein ~melder(, so schön zum Reinschlagen)** (*sl*) he's got the kind of face that just makes you want to hit it.

feuern [1] *vi* **(a)** (*heizen*) **mit Öl/Holz ~** to have oil heating/use wood for one's heating.

(b) (*Mil*) to fire.

[2] *vt* **(a)** *Zimmer* to heat; *Ofen* to light ◆ **Öl/Briketts ~** to have oil heating/use briquettes for one's heating.

(b) (*inf*) (*werfen*) to fling (*inf*), to sling (*inf*); (*Ftbl*) *Ball* to slam (*inf*); (*ins Tor*) to slam home (*inf*) *or* in (*inf*) ◆ **du kriegst gleich eine gefeuert!** (*sl*) I'll thump you one in a minute (*inf*).

(c) (*inf: entlassen*) to fire (*inf*), to sack (*inf*) ◆ **gefeuert werden** to get the sack, to be fired *or* sacked.

Feuer-: ~ofen *m* (*Bibl*) fiery furnace; **~patsche** *f* fire-beater; **~pause** *f* break in the firing; (*vereinbarf*) ceasefire; **f~polizeilich** *adj Bestimmungen* laid down by the fire authorities; **f~polizeilich verboten** prohibited by order of the fire authorities; **~probe** *f* (*Hist: Gottesurteil*) ordeal by fire; **die ~probe bestehen** (*fig*) to pass the (acid) test; **das war seine ~probe** (*fig*) that was the acid test for him; **~qualle** *f* stinging jellyfish; **~rad** *nt* fire-wheel; (*~werkskörper*) catherine wheel; **f~rot** *adj* fiery red; *Haar auch* flaming; *Kleidung, Auto* scarlet; **f~rot werden** (*vor Verlegenheit etc*) to turn crimson *or* scarlet; **~salamander** *m* fire *or* European salamander; **~säule** *f* (*Bibl*) pillar of fire.

Feuersbrunst *f* (*geh*) conflagration.

Feuer-: ~schaden *m* fire damage *no pl*; **~schein** *m* glow of the fire; **~schiff** *nt* lightship; **~schlucker** *m* **-s, -** *siehe* **~fresser;** ⚠**f~schnaubend** *adj attr* (*poet*) fire-breathing; **~schneise** *f* fire break; **~schutz** *m* **(a)** (*Vorbeugung*) fire prevention; **(b)** (*Mil: Deckung*) covering fire; **~schutztür** *f* fire door; **~schweif** *m* fiery tail; **f~sicher** *adj siehe* **f~fest; ~sirene** *f* fire siren.

Feuersnot *f* (*liter*) fiery peril (*poet*).

Feuer-: ⚠**f~speiend** *adj attr Drache* fire-breathing; *Berg* spewing (forth) fire; **~spritze** *f* fire hose; ⚠**f~sprühend** *adj* (*liter*) *siehe* **funkensprühend;** **~stätte** *f* (*form*) **(a)** (*Koch-, Heizstelle*) fireplace, hearth; **(b)** (*Brandstelle*) scene

⚠: for details of spelling reform, see supplement

of the fire; **~stein** *m* flint; **~stelle** *f* campfire site; (*Spuren eines Feuers*) burnt spot, remains *pl* of a fire; (*Herd*) fireplace; **~stellung** *f* (*Mil*) firing position; **~stoß** *m* burst of fire; **~strahl** *m* (*geh*) jet of flame *or* fire; (*poet: Blitz*) thunderbolt; **~stuhl** *m* (*sl*) (motor)bike; **~sturm** *m* fire storm; **~taufe** *f* baptism of fire; **die ~taufe bestehen/erhalten** to go through/have one's baptism of fire; **~tod** *m* (*Hist*) (death at) the stake; **den ~tod erleiden** to be burnt *or* to die at the stake; **~treppe** *f* fire escape; **~tür** *f* fire door; **~überfall** *m* armed attack.

Feuerung *f* **(a)** (*das Beheizen*) heating. **(b)** (*Brennstoff*) fuel. **(c)** (*Heizanlage*) heating system.

Feuer-: ~verhütung *f* fire prevention; **~versicherung** *f* fire insurance; **f~verzinkt** *adj* galvanized; **~wache** *f* fire station; **~waffe** *f* firearm; **~wasser** *nt* (*inf*) firewater (*inf*); **~wechsel** *m* exchange of fire.

Feuerwehr *f* fire brigade ◆ **fahren wie die ~** (*inf*) to drive like the clappers (*Brit inf*).

Feuerwehr-: ~auto *nt* fire engine; **~ball** *m* firemen's ball; **~frau** *f* firewoman; **~mann** *m* fireman; **~schlauch** *m* fire hose; **~übung** *f* fire-fighting exercise; **~wagen** *m* fire engine.

Feuer-: ~werk *nt* fireworks *pl*; (*Schauspiel auch*) firework display; (*fig*) cavalcade; **~werker** *m* **-s, -** firework-maker; **~werkskörper** *m* firework; **~zange** *f* fire tongs *pl*; **~zangenbowle** *f red wine punch containing rum which has been flamed off*; **~zeichen** *nt* **(a)** (*Signal*) beacon; **(b)** (*Astrol*) fire sign; **~zeug** *nt* (cigarette) lighter; **~zeugbenzin** *nt* lighter fuel; **~zeuggas** *nt* lighter gas; **~zone** *f* (*Mil*) firing zone; **~zunge** *f* (*Bibl*) tongue of flame.

Feuilleton [fœjəˈtõ, ˈfœjətõ] *nt* **-s, -s** (*Press*) **(a)** (*Zeitungsteil*) feature pages *pl or* section. **(b)** (*Artikel*) feature (article).

Feuilletonismus [fœjətoˈnɪsmʊs] *m style of writing used in feature articles, often regarded as facile.*

Feuilletonist(in *f*) [fœjətoˈnɪst(ɪn)] *m* feature writer.

feuilletonistisch [fœjətoˈnɪstɪʃ] *adj* **dieser Journalist ist ein ~es Talent** this journalist has a natural flair for writing feature articles; **dieser Aufsatz ist zu ~** (*pej*) this essay is too glib *or* facile.

Feuilleton-: ~schreiber *m siehe* **Feuilletonist(in)**; **~stil** *m* style used in feature articles; (*pej*) facile *or* glib style.

feurig *adj* fiery; (*old: glühend*) glowing.

feurio *interj* (*old*) (fire,) fire.

Fex *m* **-es** *or* **-en, -e** *or* **-en** (*S Ger, Aus*) enthusiast.

Fez[1] [fɛːs] *m* **-(es), -(e)** fez.

Fez[2] *m* **-(e)s,** *no pl* (*dated inf*) larking about (*inf*) ◆ **~ machen** to lark about (*inf*).

ff [ɛfˈ|ɛf] *adj inv* first-class, top-grade; *siehe* **Effeff.**

ff. *abbr of* **folgende Seiten.**

Ffm. *abbr of* **Frankfurt am Main.**

Fiaker *m* **-s, -** (*Aus*) **(a)** (*Kutsche*) (hackney) cab. **(b)** (*Kutscher*) cab driver, cabby (*inf*).

Fiale *f* **-, -n** (*Archit*) pinnacle.

Fiasko *nt* **-s, -s** (*inf*) fiasco ◆ **mit seinem Buch erlebte er ein ~** his book was a complete failure *or* flop *or* fiasco; **dann gibt es ein ~** it'll be disastrous *or* a fiasco.

Fibel[1] *f* **-, -n** (*Sch*) primer.

Fibel[2] *f* **-, -n** (*Archeol*) fibula (*spec*), clasp.

Fiber *f* **-, -n** fibre.

Fibrin *nt* **-s,** *no pl* (*Physiol*) fibrin.

Fibrom *nt* **-s, -e** (*Med*) fibroma (*spec*).

fibrös *adj* (*Med*) fibrous.

Fiche [fiːʃ] *m or nt* **-(s), -s** (micro)fiche.

Fichte *f* **-, -n** (*Bot*) spruce.

fichten *adj* spruce(wood).

Fichten- *in cpds* spruce; **~nadelextrakt** *m* pine essence; **~zapfen** *m* spruce cone.

Fick *m* **-s, -s** (*vulg*) fuck (*vulg*).

ficken *vti* (*vulg*) to fuck (*vulg*) ◆ **mit jdm ~** to fuck sb (*vulg*).

fick(e)rig *adj* (*dial*) fidgety.

Ficus *m* **-, Fici** (*Zierpflanze*) weeping fig.

⚠**Fideikommiß** [fideikɔˈmɪs, ˈfiːdeɪkɔmɪs] *nt* **-sses, -sse** (*old Jur*) entail (*form*), entailed estate.

fidel *adj* jolly, merry.

Fidel *f* **-, -n** *siehe* **Fiedel.**

Fidibus *m* **-** *or* **-ses, -** *or* **-se** spill.

Fidschi [ˈfɪdʒi] *nt* **-s** Fiji.

Fidschianer(in *f*) *m* **-s, -** Fijian.

Fidschi|inseln *pl* Fiji Islands.

Fieber *nt* **-s, - (a)** temperature; (*sehr hoch, mit Phantasieren*) fever ◆ **~ haben** to have *or* be running a temperature; to be feverish *or* running a fever; **40° ~ haben** to have a temperature of 40; **(jdm) das ~ messen** to take sb's temperature; **im ~ seiner Leidenschaft** in a fever of passion.
(b) (*Krankheit*) fever.

Fieber- *in cpds* feverish, febrile (*form*); **~anfall** *m* attack *or* bout of fever; **~flecken** *pl* fever spots *pl*; **f~frei** *adj* free of fever; **~frost** *m* feverish shivering; **f~haft** *adj* **(a)** (*fiebrig*) feverish, febrile (*form*); **(b)** (*hektisch*) feverish.

fieb(e)rig *adj* feverish, febrile (*form*).

Fieber-: ~kurve *f* temperature curve; **~messer** *m* **-s, -** (*dated, Sw*) thermometer; **~mittel** *nt* anti-fever drug, antipyretic (*spec*); **~mücke** *f* malarial mosquito.

fiebern *vi* **(a)** to have a fever *or* temperature; (*schwer*) to be feverish *or* febrile (*form*). **(b)** (*fig*) **nach etw ~** to long feverishly for sth; **vor Ungeduld/Erregung** (*dat*) **~** to be in a fever of impatience/excitement.

Fieber-: ⚠~phantasien *pl* feverish *or* febrile (*form*) wanderings *pl or* ravings *pl*; **⚠f~senkend** *adj* fever-reducing; **~senkung** *f* reduction of fever; **ein Mittel zur ~senkung** a medicine for reducing fever; **~tabelle** *f* temperature chart; **~thermometer** *nt* (clinical) thermometer; **~wahn** *m* (feverish *or* febrile) delirium.

fiebrig *adj siehe* **fieb(e)rig.**

Fiedel *f* **-, -n** fiddle.

Fiedelbogen *m* fiddle bow.

fiedeln (*hum, pej*) *vti* to fiddle ◆ **ein Liedchen ~** to play a song on the fiddle.

fiedern *vr* (*Orn*) to acquire its plumage; *siehe* **gefiedert.**

Fiederung *f* **(a)** (*Orn*) plumage. **(b)** (*Bot*) pinnation (*spec*).

Fiedler *m* **-s, -** (*hum, pej: Geiger*) fiddler.

fiel *pret of* **fallen.**

fiepen *vi* (*Reh*) to call; (*Hund, Mensch*) to whimper; (*Vogel*) to cheep.

fieren *vt* (*Naut*) *Segel, Last* to lower; *Tau* to pay out.

fies *adj* (*inf*) (*abstoßend, unangenehm*) *Mensch, Gesicht, Geruch, Arbeit* nasty, horrid, horrible; (*gemein*) *Charakter, Methoden auch* mean ◆ **benimm dich nicht so ~!** don't be so horrid!; (*ordinär*) don't behave so horribly!; *siehe* **Möp.**

Fiesling *m* (*inf*) (*abstoßender Mensch*) slob (*sl*); (*gemeiner Mensch*) sod (*sl*), bastard (*sl*).

Fifa, FIFA *f* **-** FIFA.

fifty-fifty [ˈfɪftɪˈfɪftɪ] *adv* (*inf*) fifty-fifty (*inf*) ◆ **~ machen** to go fifty-fifty; **die Sache steht ~** there's a fifty-fifty chance.

Figaro *m* **-s, -s** (*hum*) hairdresser.

Fight [fait] *m* **-s, -s** fight.

fighten [ˈfaitn] *vi* to fight.

Fighter [ˈfaitɐ] *m* **-s, -** fighter.

Figur *f* **(a)** (*Bildwerk, Abbildung, Math*) figure; (*gedankenlos hingezeichnet*) doodle.
(b) (*Gestalt, Persönlichkeit*) figure; (*Körperform*) (*von Frauen*) figure; (*von Männern*) physique; (*inf: Mensch*) character ◆ **in ganzer ~** (*Phot, Art*) full-figure; **auf seine ~ achten** to watch one's figure; **eine gute/schlechte/traurige ~ machen** *or* **abgeben** to cut a good/poor/sorry figure.
(c) (*Roman~, Film~ etc*) character.
(d) (*Sport, Mus*) figure; (*rhetorische ~*) figure of speech.

figural *adj* (*Art*) figured.

Figuralmusik *f* figural *or* florid music.

Figuration *f* figuration.

figurativ *adj* figurative.

figurbetont *adj* figure-hugging.

Figürchen *nt dim of* **Figur.**

Figurenlaufen *nt* figure skating.

figurieren* [1] *vi* (*geh*) to figure.
[2] *vt* (*Mus*) to figure.

Figurine *f* (*Art*) figure; (*kleine Statue*) figurine; (*Theat*) costume design *or* sketch.

figürlich *adj* **(a)** (*übertragen*) figurative. **(b)** (*figurmäßig*) as regards the/her figure; (*von Männern*) as regards physique.

Fiktion *f* fiction.

fiktiv *adj* fictitious.

Filet [fiˈleː] *nt* **-s, -s (a)** (*Cook*) (*Schweine~, Geflügel~, Fisch~*) fillet; (*Rinder~*) fillet steak; (*zum Braten*) piece of sirloin *or* tenderloin (*US*). **(b)** (*Tex*) *siehe* **Filetarbeit.**

Filet|arbeit [fiˈleː-] *f* (*Tex*) netting.

filetieren* *vt* to fillet.

Filet- [fiˈleː-]: **~steak** *nt* fillet steak; **~stück** *nt* piece of sirloin *or* tenderloin (*US*).

Filialbetrieb *m* branch.

Filiale *f* **-, -n** branch.

Filial-: ~generation *f* (*Biol*) (first) filial generation; **~geschäft** *nt* branch; **~kirche** *f* daughter church; **~leiter** *m* branch manager; **~netz** *nt* network of branches.

Filibuster[1] *m* **-s, -** *siehe* **Flibustier.**

Filibuster[2] [filiˈbastɐ] *nt* **-(s), -** (*Pol*) filibuster.

filigran *adj* filigree.

Filigran *nt* **-s, -e** filigree.

Filigran|arbeit *f* filigree work; (*Schmuckstück*) piece of filigree work.

Filipino *m* **-s, -s** Filipino.

Filius *m* **-, -se** (*hum*) son, offspring (*hum*).

Film *m* **-(e)s, -e (a)** (*alle Bedeutungen*) film; (*Spiel~ auch*) movie (*esp US*), motion picture (*US*); (*Dokumentar~ auch*) documentary (film) ◆ **ein ~ nach dem Roman von E. Marlitt** a film of *or* based on the novel by E. Marlitt; **in einen ~ gehen** to go and see a film, to go to a film; **da ist bei mir der ~ gerissen** (*fig sl*) I had a mental blackout (*inf*).
(b) (*~branche*) films *pl*, movie (*esp US*) *or* motion-picture (*esp US*) business ◆ **zum ~ gehen/kommen** to go/get *or* break into films *or* movies (*esp US*); **beim ~ arbeiten** *or* **sein** (*inf*) to work in films *or* the movie business (*esp US*).

Film- *in cpds* film, movie (*esp US*); **~amateur** *m* home-movie enthusiast *or* buff (*inf*); **~archiv** *nt* film archives *pl*; **~atelier** *nt* film studio; **~autor** *m* scriptwriter, screen-writer; **~ball** *m* film festival ball; **~bauten** *pl* film sets *pl*; **~bearbeitung** *f* (screen) adaptation; **~bericht** *m* film report; **~bewertungsstelle** *f* ≃ board of film classification; **~bühne** *f* (*dated*) picture house (*dated*), movie house (*US*); **~diva** *f* (*dated*) screen goddess; **~drama** *nt* film drama.

Filmemacher(in *f*) *m* film-maker.

Film|empfindlichkeit *f* film speed.

filmen *vti* to film.

Film-: ~entwickler *m* developer; **~epos** *nt* epic film.

Filmer *m* **-s, -** (*inf*) film *or* movie (*esp US*) director.

Filmerei *f* filming.

Film-: ~festival *nt*, **~festspiele** *pl* film festival; **~förderungsgesetz** *nt* *law on film subsidies*; **~format** *nt* (*für Fotoapparat*) film size; (*für ~kamera*) film gauge; **~fritze** *m* **-n, -n** (*inf*) film *or* movie (*esp US*) guy (*inf*); **f~gerecht** *adj* filmable; **der Roman muß f~gerecht bearbeitet werden** the novel will have to be adapted for the cinema *or* for film; **~geschäft** *nt* film *or* movie (*esp US*) *or* motion-picture (*esp US*) industry; **~geschichte** *f* history of the cinema; **~geschichte machen** to make film history; **~größe** *f* great star of the screen; **~held** *m* screen *or* movie (*esp US*) hero.

filmisch *adj* cinematic.

Film-: ~kamera *f* film *or* movie (*esp US*) camera; (*Schmalfilmkamera*) cine-camera (*Brit*); **~kassette** *f* film cassette; **~komponist** *m* composer of film music; **~kritik** *f* film criticism *or* reviewing; (*Artikel*) film review; (*Kritiker*) film critics *pl*; **~kulisse** *f* setting for a film; **~kunst** *f* cinematic art; **~material** *nt* film; **~musik** *f* film music; **die originale ~musik** the original soundtrack.

Filmo-: ⚠~graphie *f* biopic; **~thek** *f* **-, -en** *siehe* **Kinemathek.**

Film-: ~palast *m* picture *or* movie (*esp US*) palace; **~preis** *m* film *or* movie (*esp US*) award; **~produzent** *m* film *or* movie (*esp US*) producer; **~projektor** *m* film projector; **~prüfstelle** *f* film censorship office; **~publikum** *nt* filmgoing public; **~rechte** *pl* film rights *pl*; **~regie** *f* direction of a/the film; **~regisseur** *m* film *or* movie (*esp US*) director; **~reportage** *f* film report; **⚠~riß** *m* (*lit*) tear in a film; (*fig sl*) mental blackout (*inf*); **~rolle** *f* (*Spule*) spool of film; (*für Fotoapparat*) roll of film; (*Part*) film part *or* role; **~satz** *m* (*Typ*) *siehe* **Lichtsatz**; **~schaffende(r)** *mf decl as adj* film-maker; **~schauplatz** *m* setting of a film; **~schauspieler** *m* film *or* movie (*esp US*) actor; **~schauspielerin** *f* film *or* movie (*esp US*) actress; **~schönheit** *f* screen beauty; **~serie** *f* (*esp TV*) film series *sing*; **~spule** *f* film spool; **~star** *m* filmstar; **~sternchen** *nt* starlet; **~studio** *nt* film *or* movie (*esp US*) studio; **~szene** *f* scene of a film; **~theater** *nt* (*form*) cinema, movie theater (*US*); **~- und Fernsehakademie, ~- und Fernsehhochschule** *f* college of film and television technology; **~verleih** *m* film distributors *pl*; **~vorführer** *m* projectionist; **~vorstellung** *f* film show; **~welt** *f* film *or* movie (*esp US*) world; **~zensur** *f* film censorship; (*Zensoren*) film censors *pl*.

Filou [fi'lu:] *m* **-s, -s** (*dated inf*) devil (*inf*).

Filter *nt or m* **-s, -** filter ◆ **eine Zigarette mit/ohne ~** a (filter-) tipped/plain cigarette.

Filter-: ~einsatz *m* filter pad; **f~fein** *adj* finely ground; **f~fein mahlen** to grind finely; **~glas** *nt* tinted glass; **~kaffee** *m* filter *or* drip (*US*) coffee; **~mundstück** *nt* filter-tip.

filtern *vti* to filter.

Filter-: ~papier *nt* filter paper; **~rückstand** *m* residue (*after filtering*); **~tuch** *nt* filter cloth; **~tüte** *f* filter bag.

Filterung *f* filtering.

Filterzigarette *f* tipped *or* filter(-tipped) cigarette.

Filtrat *nt* filtrate.

Filtration *f* filtration.

filtrierbar *adj* filterable.

filtrieren* *vt* to filter.

Filtrierung *f siehe* **Filterung.**

Filz *m* **-es, -e (a)** (*Tex*) felt; (*inf: ~hut*) felt hat ◆ **grüner ~** green baize. **(b)** (*inf: Bierdeckel*) beermat. **(c)** (*Pol pej*) *siehe* **Filzokratie.**

filzen 1 *vi* (*Tex*) to felt, to go felty.
2 *vt* (*inf*) (*durchsuchen*) *jdn* to frisk, to search; *Gepäck etc* to search, to go through; (*berauben*) to do over (*inf*).

Filzhut *m* felt hat.

filzig *adj* (*wie Filz*) felty, feltlike.

Filz-: ~latschen *m* (*inf*) carpet slipper; **~laus** *f* crab louse.

Filzokrat *m* **-en, -en** (*Pol pej*) corrupt nepotist.

Filzokratie *f* (*Pol pej*) web of patronage and nepotism, spoils system (*US*).

filzokratisch *adj* (*Pol pej*) nepotically corrupt.

Filz-: ~pantoffel *m* (carpet) slipper; **~schreiber** *m* felt(-tip) pen, felt-tip; **~sohle** *f* felt insole; **~stiefel** *m* felt boot; **~stift** *m siehe* **~schreiber.**

Fimmel *m* **-s, -** (*inf*) **(a)** (*Tick*) mania ◆ **er hat diesen ~ mit dem Unkrautjäten** he's got this thing about weeding (*inf*). **(b)** (*Spleen*) obsession (*mit* about). **du hast wohl einen ~!** you're crazy (*inf*) *or* mad (*inf*).

final *adj* final.

Finale *nt* **-s, -s** *or* **-** (*Mus*) finale; (*Sport*) final, finals *pl*.

Finalist *m* finalist.

Finalität *f* (*Philos*) finality.

Finalsatz *m* final clause.

Financier [finã'sie:] *m* **-s, -s** financier.

Finanz *f, no pl* financial world ◆ **die hohe ~** the world of high finance; **Kreise der ~** financial circles.

Finanz- *in cpds* financial; **~adel** *m* plutocrats *pl*, plutocracy; **~amt** *nt* tax office; **~aristokratie** *f* plutocrats *pl*, plutocracy; **~ausgleich** *m redistribution of income between 'Bund', 'Länder' and 'Gemeinden'*; **⚠~ausschuß** *m* finance committee; **~autonomie** *f siehe* **~hoheit**; **~beamte(r)** *m* tax official; **~behörde** *f* tax authority; **~dinge** *pl* financial matters *pl*.

Finanzen *pl* finances *pl* ◆ **das übersteigt meine ~** that's beyond my means.

Finanzer *m* **-s, -** (*Aus*) *siehe* **Zollbeamte(r).**

Finanz-: ~frage *f* question of finance; **~gebaren** *nt* management of public finances; **~genie** *nt* financial genius *or* wizard (*inf*); **~gericht** *nt tribunal dealing with tax and other financial matters*; **~hai** *m* (*pej*) (financial) shark; **~hoheit** *f* financial autonomy.

finanziell *adj* financial ◆ **sich ~ an etw** (*dat*) **beteiligen** to take a (financial) stake in sth.

Finanzier [finan'tsie:] *m* **-s, -s** financier.

finanzieren* *vt* to finance, to fund ◆ **frei ~** to finance privately; **ich kann meinen Urlaub nicht ~** I can't afford a holiday.

Finanzierung *f* financing ◆ **zur ~ von etw** to finance sth; **die ~ meines Urlaubs ist noch nicht gesichert** it isn't certain whether I will have the money for my holiday.

Finanzierungs-: ~defizit *nt* budget deficit; **~gesellschaft** *f* finance company; **~lücke** *f* financing gap; **~plan** *m* finance plan *or* scheme; **~platz** *m* financial centre.

Finanz-: ~jahr *nt* financial year; **f~kräftig** *adj* financially strong; **~minister** *m* minister of finance; **~plan** *m* financial plan; **~planung** *f* financial planning; **~politik** *f* financial policy; (*Wissenschaft, Disziplin*) politics of finance; **f~politisch** *adj Fragen, Probleme* relating to financial policy; **f~politisch unklug** unwise as regards financial policy; **~recht** *nt* financial law; **f~schwach** *adj* financially weak; **~spritze** *f* capital injection/injection of capital; **ich brauche eine kleine ~spritze** I need something to boost my cashflow, I could do with a little cash; **f~stark** *adj* financially strong; **~welt** *f* financial world; **~wesen** *nt* financial system; **ein Ausdruck aus dem ~wesen** a financial term.

finassieren* *vi* (*pej*) to machinate, to do some finagling (*inf*).

Findelkind *nt* (*old*) foundling (*old*).

▼ **finden** *pret* **fand**, *ptp* **gefunden** 1 *vt* **(a)** (*entdecken*) to find ◆ **ich finde es nicht** I can't find it; **es war nicht/nirgends zu ~** it was not/nowhere to be found; **das muß zu ~ sein** it must be somewhere (to be found); **es ließ sich niemand ~** we/they *etc* couldn't find anybody, there was nobody to be found; **der Grund/die Ursache läßt sich nicht ~** we/they *etc* couldn't find the reason/cause; **etwas an jdm ~** to see something in sb; **nichts dabei ~** to think nothing of it.
(b) (*vor~*) to find ◆ **jdn schlafend/bei der Arbeit ~** to find sb asleep/working.
▼ **(c)** *in Verbindung mit n siehe auch dort. Trost, Hilfe, Ruhe, Schlaf etc* to find; *Anklang, Zustimmung auch* to meet with; *Beifall* to meet *or* be met with; *Berücksichtigung, Beachtung* to receive ◆ **(den) Mut/(die) Kraft ~, etw zu tun** to find the courage/strength to do sth; **(bei jdm) Anerkennung ~** to find recognition (with sb); **Bestätigung ~** to be confirmed.
▼ **(d)** (*ansehen, betrachten*) to think ◆ **es kalt/warm/ganz erträglich** *etc* **~** to find it cold/warm/quite tolerable *etc*; **etw gut/zu teuer/eine Frechheit** *etc* **~** to think (that) sth is good/too expensive/a cheek *etc*; **jdn blöd/nett** *etc* **~** to think (that) sb is stupid/nice *etc*; **wie findest du das?** what do you think?; **wie finde ich denn das?** what do I think (of that)?
2 *vi* (*lit, fig: den Weg ~*) to find one's way ◆ **er findet nicht nach Hause** (*lit*) he can't find his *or* the way home; (*fig*) he can't tear *or* drag himself away (*inf*); **zu sich selbst ~** to sort oneself out.
3 *vti* (*meinen*) to think ◆ **~ Sie (das)?** do you think so?; **ich finde (das) nicht** I don't think so; **~ Sie (das) nicht auch?** don't you agree?, don't you think so too?; **ich finde, wir sollten/daß wir ...** I think we should/that we ...; **ich kann das** *or* **das kann ich nicht ~** I don't think so; **ich fände es besser, wenn ...** I think it would be better if ...
4 *vr* **(a)** (*zum Vorschein kommen*) to be found; (*wiederauftauchen auch*) to turn up; (*sich befinden auch*) to be ◆ **das wird sich (alles) ~** it will (all) turn up; (*sich herausstellen*) it'll all come out (*inf*); **es fand sich niemand, der sich freiwillig gemeldet hätte** there was nobody who volunteered.
(b) (*in Ordnung kommen: Angelegenheit etc*) to sort itself out; (*Mensch: zu sich ~*) to sort oneself out ◆ **das wird sich alles ~** it'll all sort itself out.
(c) (*sich fügen*) **sich in etw** (*acc*) **~** to reconcile oneself *or* become reconciled to sth.
(d) (*sich treffen*) (*lit*) to find each other; (*fig*) to meet ◆ **da haben sich aber zwei gefunden!** (*iro*) they'll make a fine pair.

Finder(in *f*) *m* **-s, -** finder.

Finderlohn *m* reward for the finder.

Fin de siècle [fɛ̃d'sjɛkl] *nt* **- - -**, *no pl* fin de siècle ◆ **die Kunst des ~ ~ ~** fin de siècle art.

findig *adj* resourceful.

Findigkeit *f* resourcefulness.

Findling *m* **(a)** (*Geol*) erratic (boulder). **(b)** (*Findelkind*) foundling (*old*).

Finesse *f* **(a)** (*Feinheit*) refinement; (*no pl: Kunstfertigkeit*) finesse ◆ **mit allen ~n** with every refinement. **(b)** (*Trick*) trick.

finessenreich *adj* artful.

fing *pret of* **fangen.**

Finger *m* **-s, -** finger ◆ **der kleine ~** one's little finger, one's pinkie (*US, Scot inf*); **der elfte ~** (*hum*) one's third leg (*inf*); **mit dem ~ auf jdn/etw zeigen** *or* **weisen** (*geh*) to point to sb/sth; **mit ~n auf jdn zeigen** (*fig*) to look askance at

➤ SPRACHE AKTIV: **finden: 1a** → 27.1 **1c** → 40.2 **1d** → 34.3, 40.3

sb; **jdm mit dem ~ drohen** to wag one's finger at sb; **jdm eins/was auf die ~ geben** to give sb a rap/to rap sb across the knuckles; **jdm auf die ~ schlagen** *or* **hauen** (*lit*)/**klopfen** (*fig*) to rap sb's knuckles, to give sb a rap on the knuckles; **zwei ~ breit** the width of two fingers, two fingers wide; **(nimm/laß die) ~ weg!** (get/keep your) hands off!; **sich** (*dat*) **nicht die ~ schmutzig machen** (*lit, fig*) not to get one's hands dirty, not to dirty one's hands; **das kann sich jeder an den (fünf** *or* **zehn) ~n abzählen** (*inf*) it sticks out a mile (to anybody) (*inf*); **das läßt er nicht mehr aus den ~n** he won't let it out of his hands; **jdn/etw in die ~ bekommen** *or* **kriegen** (*inf*) to get one's hands on sb/sth, to get hold of sb/sth; **bei etw die ~ drin haben** (*sl*) to have a hand in sth; **er hat überall seine ~ drin** (*sl*) he has a finger in every pie (*inf*); **sich** (*dat*) **die ~ abschreiben** *or* **wund schreiben/arbeiten** *etc* to write/work *etc* one's fingers to the bone; **wenn man ihm/dem Teufel den kleinen ~ gibt, (dann) nimmt er (gleich) die ganze Hand** (*prov*) give him an inch and he'll take a mile (*inf*); **lange ~ machen** (*hum inf*) to be light-fingered; **jdm in** *or* **zwischen die ~ geraten** *or* **fallen** to fall into sb's hands *or* clutches; **die ~ von jdm/etw lassen** (*inf*) to keep away from sb/sth; **sich** (*dat*) **bei** *or* **an etw** (*dat*) **die ~ verbrennen** to burn one's fingers *or* get one's fingers burnt over sth; **jdm (scharf) auf die ~ sehen** to keep an eye *or* a close eye on sb; **sich** (*dat*) **etw aus den ~n saugen** to conjure sth up (*inf*), to dream sth up; **sich** (*dat*) **die** *or* **alle ~ nach etw lecken** (*inf*) to be panting *or* dying for sth (*inf*); **für jdn keinen ~ rühren** not to lift a finger to help sb; **keinen ~ krumm machen** (*inf*) not to lift a finger (*inf*); **den ~ auf eine/die Wunde legen** to touch on a sore point; **mich** *or* **mir juckt es in den ~n(, etw zu tun)** (*inf*) I'm itching *or* dying to (do sth); **da hast du dich in den ~ geschnitten** (*inf*) you've made a big mistake; **er hat eine** *or* **zehn an jedem ~** he's got a woman for every day of the week; **jdn um den kleinen ~ wickeln** to twist sb round one's little finger; **etw im kleinen ~ haben** (*perfekt beherrschen*) to have sth at one's fingertips; (*sicher im Gefühl haben*) to have a feel for sth; **man zeigt nicht mit nacktem ~ auf angezogene Leute** (*inf*) it's rude to point.

Finger-: ~abdruck *m* fingerprint; **jds ~abdrücke nehmen** to take sb's fingerprints, to fingerprint sb; **~alphabet** *nt* manual alphabet; **f~breit** *adj* the width of a finger; **~breit** *m* -, - finger's breadth, fingerbreadth; (*fig*) inch; **keinen ~breit nachgeben** *or* **weichen** not to give an inch; **f~dick** *adj* as thick as a finger; **~druck** *m* touch of the finger; **~farbe** *f* finger paint; **f~fertig** *adj* nimble-fingered, dexterous; **~fertigkeit** *f* dexterity; **~gelenk** *nt* finger joint; **~glied** *nt* phalanx (of the finger) (*form*); **~hakeln** *nt* finger-wrestling; **~handschuh** *m* glove; **~hut** *m* (a) (*Sew*) thimble; **ein ~hut (voll)** (*fig*) a thimbleful; (b) (*Bot*) foxglove; **~knochen, ~knöchel** *m* knucklebone; **~kuppe** *f* fingertip; **f~lang** *adj Narbe etc* the length of a finger; **~ling** *m* fingerstall.

fingern [1] *vi* **an** *or* **mit etw** (*dat*) **~** to fiddle with sth; **nach etw ~** to fumble (around) for sth; **... als eine Hand über die Decke fingerte** ... as a hand moved over the bedclothes.
[2] *vt* (*hervorholen*) to fumble around and produce; (*sl: manipulieren*) to fiddle (*inf*); (*bewerkstelligen*) *Projekt* to wangle (*inf*).

Finger-: ~nagel *m* fingernail; **~nägel kauen** to bite one's (finger)nails; **~ring** *m* ring (for one's finger); **~schale** *f* fingerbowl; **~spitze** *f* fingertip, tip of one's finger; **er ist musikalisch bis in die ~spitzen** he's musical right down to his fingertips *or* the tips of his fingers; **das muß man in den ~spitzen haben** you have to have a feel for it; **mir juckt** *or* **kribbelt es in den ~spitzen, das zu tun** I'm itching to do that; **~spitzengefühl** *nt, no pl* (*Einfühlungsgabe*) instinctive feel *or* feeling; (*im Umgang mit Menschen*) tact and sensitivity, fine feeling; **~sprache** *f* manual alphabet, sign language; **~übung** *f* (*Mus*) finger exercise; (*Übungsstück*) étude; (*fig*) (*erste Arbeit*) first stage of one's apprenticeship; (*Anfangswerk*) apprentice piece; **~zeig** *m* **-s, -e** hint; **etw als ~zeig Gottes/des Schicksals empfinden** to regard sth as a sign from God/as meant.

fingieren* [fɪŋ'giːrən] *vt* (*vortäuschen*) to fake; (*erdichten*) to fabricate.

fingiert [fɪŋ'giːɐt] *adj* (*vorgetäuscht*) bogus; (*erfunden*) fictitious.

fini ['fiːni] *adj pred* (*inf*): **jetzt/dann ist ~** that's it, finito (*inf*).

Finish ['fɪnɪʃ] *nt* **-s, -s** (a) (*Endverarbeitung*) finish; (*Vorgang*) finishing. (b) (*Sport: Endspurt*) final spurt.

finit *adj* (*Gram*) finite.

Fink *m* **-en, -en** finch.

Finkenschlag *m, no pl* finch's song.

Finne[1] *f* **-, -n** (a) (*Zool: Stadium des Bandwurms*) bladder worm, cysticercus (*form*). (b) (*Med: Mitesser*) pimple. (c) (*Rückenflosse*) fin. (d) (*von Hammer*) peen.

Finne[2] *m* **-n, -n, Finnin** *f* Finn, Finnish man/woman/boy/girl.

finnisch *adj* Finnish ♦ **der F~e Meerbusen** the Gulf of Finland; *siehe auch* **deutsch.**

Finnisch(e) *nt* **-n** Finnish; *siehe auch* **Deutsch(e).**

finnisch-ugrisch *adj siehe* **finnougrisch.**

Finnland *nt* Finland.

Finnländer(in *f*) *m* **-s, -** Finn.

finnländisch *adj* Finnish.

finnlandisieren* *vt* (*Pol sl*) to Finlandize.

Finnlandisierung *f* (*Pol sl*) Finlandization.

Finnmark *f* (*Währung*) Finnish mark, markka (*form*).

finnougrisch, finno-ugrisch *adj* Finno-Ugric, Finno-Ugrian.

Finno-Ugristik *f* Finno-Ugric studies *pl.*

Finnwal *m* finback, finwhale.

finster *adj* (a) (*ohne Licht*) dark; *Zimmer, Wald, Nacht* dark (and gloomy) ♦ **im F~n** in the dark; **im F~n liegen** to be in darkness; (*zumachen*) to put up the shutters; **es sieht ~ aus** (*fig*) things look bleak.
(b) (*dubios*) shady.
(c) (*mürrisch, verdrossen, düster*) grim; *Wolken* dark, black ♦ **~ entschlossen sein** to be grimly determined; **jdn ~ ansehen** to give sb a black look.
(d) (*fig: unaufgeklärt*) dark ♦ **das ~(st)e Mittelalter** the Dark Ages *pl.*
(e) (*unheimlich*) *Gestalt, Blick, Gedanken* sinister.

Finsterling *m* sinister character; (*Dunkelmann*) obscurantist.

Finsternis *f* (a) (*Dunkelheit, Bibl: Hölle*) darkness. (b) (*Astron*) eclipse.

Finte *f* **-, -n** (a) (*Sport*) feint; (*im Rugby*) dummy. (b) (*List*) ruse, subterfuge.

fintenreich *adj* artful, crafty.

finz(e)lig *adj* (*N Ger inf*) (a) (*winzig*) *Schrift* tiny, weeny (*inf*). (b) (*knifflig*) fiddly.

Fips *m* **-es, -e** (*dial*) little chap (*Brit inf*) *or* fellow (*inf*).

fipsig *adj* (*dial*) titchy (*inf*).

Firlefanz *m* **-es,** *no pl* (*inf*) (a) (*Kram*) frippery, trumpery. (b) (*Albernheit*) clowning *or* fooling around ♦ **~ machen** to play the fool, to clown *or* fool around.

firm *adj pred* **ich bin noch nicht ~** I don't really know it yet; **in einem Fachgebiet ~ sein** to have a sound knowledge of an area.

Firma *f* **-, Firmen** (a) company, firm; (*Kleinbetrieb*) business ♦ **die ~ Wahlster/Lexomat** Wahlster(s)/Lexomat; **die ~ dankt** (*hum*) much obliged (to you).
(b) (*Geschäfts- or Handelsname*) **eine ~ löschen** to strike a company's name/the name of a business from the register; **eine ~ eintragen** to register a company name/the name of a business; **unter der ~ Smith** under the name of Smith; **unter eigener ~** under one's own name.

Firmament *nt* **-s,** *no pl* (*liter*) heavens *pl* (*liter*), firmament (*Bibl*).

firmen *vt* (*Rel*) to confirm.

Firmen *pl of* **Firma.**

Firmen-: ~aufdruck *m* company stamp; **~bücher** *pl siehe* **Geschäftsbücher**; **~chef** *m* head of the company *or* firm/business; **f~eigen** *adj* company *attr*; **f~eigen sein** to belong to the company; **~gründung** *f* formation of a company; **~inhaber** *m* owner of the company/business; **f~intern** *adj* internal company *attr*; **f~intern geregelt** decided internally by the company; **f~intern sein** to be an internal company matter; **~kopf** *m* company/business letterhead; **~logo** *nt* company logo; **~name** *m* company name/name of a business; **~register** *nt* register of companies/businesses; **~schild** *nt* company/business plaque; **~schließung** *f* closing down (of a firm); **~stempel** *m* company/business stamp; **~verzeichnis** *nt* trade directory; **~wagen** *m* company car; **~wert** *m* (*Comm*) goodwill; **~zeichen** *nt* trademark.

firmieren* *vi*: **als** *or* **mit ... ~** (*Comm, fig*) to trade under the name of ...

Firmling *m* (*Rel*) candidate for confirmation.

Firm-: ~pate *m*, **~patin** *f* sponsor.

Firmung *f* (*Rel*) confirmation ♦ **jdm die ~ erteilen** to confirm sb.

Firmware ['fɜːmwɛə] *f* (*Comput*) firmware.

firn *adj Wein* old.

Firn *m* **-(e)s, -e** névé, firn.

Firne *f* **-,** *no pl* well-seasoned taste.

firnig *adj Schnee* névé *attr.*

Firnis *m* **-ses, -se** (*Öl~*) oil; (*Lack~*) varnish.

firnissen *vt* to oil; to varnish.

Firnschnee *m* névé, firn.

First *m* **-(e)s, -e** (a) (*Dach~*) (roof) ridge. (b) (*geh: Gebirgskamm*) crest, ridge.

First-: ~feier *f* (*Aus*) topping-out ceremony; **~ziegel** *m* ridge tile.

Fis *nt* **-, -** (*Mus*) F sharp ♦ **in ~/f ~** in F sharp major/minor.

Fisch *m* **-(e)s, -e** (a) (*Zool, Cook*) fish ♦ **~e/drei ~e fangen** to catch fish/three fish(es); **das sind kleine ~e** (*fig inf*) that's child's play (*inf*) (*für* to, for); **ein großer** *or* **dicker ~** (*fig inf*) a big fish; **ein paar kleine ~e/ein kleiner ~** some of/one of the small fry; **ein (kalter) ~ sein** (*fig*) to be a cold fish; **munter** *or* **gesund sein wie ein ~ im Wasser** to be in fine fettle; **sich wohl fühlen wie ein ~ im Wasser** to be in one's element; **stumm wie ein ~ sein** to be as silent as a post; **weder ~ noch Fleisch** neither fish nor fowl; **die ~e füttern** (*hum*) to be sick; **~ will schwimmen** (*prov*) fish gives you a thirst; **der ~ stinkt vom Kopf her** the problems are at the top.
(b) (*Astrol*) Pisces ♦ **die ~e** (*Astron*) Pisces *sing*, the Fish *sing*; **ein ~ sein** to be Pisces *or* a Piscean.
(c) (*Typ*) character from the wrong fount.

Fisch- *in cpds* fish; **~adler** *m* osprey; **f~ähnlich** *adj* fish-like; **f~arm** *adj* low in fish; **~armut** *f* scarcity of fish; **f~artig** *adj* (*Zool*) fish-like; *Geschmack, Geruch* fishy; **~auge** *nt* (*Phot*) fish-eye lens; **f~äugig** *adj* fish-eyed; **~becken** *nt* fishpond; **~bein** *nt, no pl* whalebone; **~bestand** *m* fish population; **~blase** *f* (a) (*Zool*) air-bladder, swim bladder; (b) (*Archit*) foil; **~blut** *nt* (*fig*): **~blut in den Adern haben** to be a cold fish; **~boulette** *f* fishcake; **~braterei, ~bratküche** *f* fish and chip shop; **~brut** *f* fry *pl*, young fish *pl*; **~bude** *f* fish and chip stand; **~dampfer** *m* trawler.

fischen *vti* (*lit, fig*) to fish ♦ **mit (dem) Netz ~** to trawl; **(auf) Heringe ~** to fish for herring; *siehe* **trüb(e).**

Fischer *m* **-s, -** fisherman.

Fischer-: ~boot *nt* fishing boat; **~dorf** *nt* fishing village.

Fischerei *f* (a) (*das Fangen*) fishing. (b) (*~gewerbe*) fishing industry, fisheries *pl.*

Fischerei- *in cpds* fishing; **~frevel** *m* (*Jur*) poaching; **~gerät** *nt* fishing tackle; (*einzelnes Stück*) piece of fishing tackle; **~grenze** *f* fishing limit; **~hafen** *m* fishing port; **~recht** *nt, no pl* (a) fishing rights *pl*; (b) (*Jur*) law on fishing; **~schutzboot** *nt* fishery protection vessel; **~wesen** *nt* fishing *no art*; **Ministerium für ~wesen** ministry of fisheries.

Fischer-: ~netz *nt* fishing net; **~ring** *m (Rel)* Ring of the Fisherman.

Fischfang *m, no pl* **vom ~ leben** to live by fishing; **zum ~ auslaufen** to set off for the fishing grounds.

Fischfang-: ~flotte *f* fishing fleet; **~gebiet** *nt* fishing grounds *pl.*

Fisch-: ~filet *nt* fish fillet; **~frikadelle** *f* fishcake; **~futter** *nt* fish food; **~geruch** *m* smell of fish, fishy smell; **~geschäft** *nt* fishmonger's (shop) *(Brit)*, fish shop *(Brit) or* dealer *(US)*; **~gräte** *f* fish bone; **~grätenmuster** *nt* herringbone (pattern); **~gründe** *pl* fishing grounds *pl*, fisheries *pl*; **~halle** *f* fish market hall; **~händler** *m* fishmonger *(Brit)*, fish dealer *(US)*; *(Großhändler)* fish merchant; **~köder** *m* bait; **~konserve** *f* canned *or* tinned *(Brit)* fish; **~kutter** *m* fishing cutter; **~laden** *m* fish shop *(Brit) or* dealer *(US)*; **~leder** *nt* shagreen; **~leim** *m* isinglass; **~markt** *m* fish market; **~mehl** *nt* fish meal; **~milch** *f* milt, soft roe; **~otter** *m* otter; **f~reich** *adj* rich in fish; **~reichtum** *m* richness in fish; **~reiher** *m* grey heron; **~reuse** *f* fish trap, weir basket; **~rogen** *m* (hard) roe; **~schuppe** *f* (fish) scale; **~schuppenkrankheit** *f* ichthyosis *(spec)*; **~schwarm** *m* shoal of fish; **~stäbchen** *nt* fish finger *(Brit)*, fish stick *(US)*; **~sterben** *nt* death of fish; **~tran** *m* train oil; **~trawler** *m* trawler; ⚠**f~verarbeitend** *adj attr* fish-processing; **~verarbeitung** *f* fish processing; **~waren** *pl* fish products *pl*; **~wasser** *nt (Cook)* fish stock; **~wehr** *nt* fish weir; **~weib** *nt (dated)* fish seller, fishwoman; *(pej)* fishwife; **~wilderei** *f* poaching; **~wirtschaft** *f* fishing industry; **~zaun** *m* fish weir; **~zucht** *f* fish-farming; *(inf: auch* **~zuchtanstalt)** fish farm; **~zug** *m* **(a)** *(Bibl)* **der ~zug des Petrus, Petri ~zug** the miraculous draught of fishes; **(b)** *(fig: Beutezug)* raid, foray.

Fisimatenten *pl (inf) (Ausflüchte)* excuses *pl*; *(Umstände)* fuss; *(Albernheiten)* nonsense ◆ **~ machen** to make excuses/a fuss/to get up to a lot of nonsense; **mit jdm/etw ~ machen** to mess about with sb/sth *(inf)*.

fiskalisch *adj* fiscal.

Fiskal-: ~politik *f, no pl* fiscal politics *sing*/policy; **f~politisch** *adj* politico-economic.

Fiskus *m* **-, -se** *or* **Fisken** *(Staatsvermögen)* treasury, exchequer *(Brit)*; *(fig: Staat)* Treasury.

Fisolen *pl (Aus)* green beans *pl.*

fisselig *adj (dial)* fine; *(empfindlich zu handhaben)* fiddly.

Fisselregen *m (dial) siehe* **Nieselregen.**

Fission *f* fission.

Fissur *f (Anat)* fissure; *(Med)* crack.

Fistel *f* **-, -n** *(Med)* fistula *(spec)*.

fisteln *vi* to speak in a falsetto (voice) *or* piping voice.

Fistelstimme *f* **(a)** *(Mus)* falsetto. **(b)** *(hohes Sprechstimmchen)* falsetto (voice), piping voice.

fit *adj pred, no comp* fit ◆ **sich ~ halten/machen** to keep/get fit.

Fitness, ⚠**Fitneß** *f* **-,** *no pl* physical fitness.

Fitness-: ~-Center *nt* health *or* fitness centre; **~training** *nt* fitness training.

fitten *vt (Tech)* to fit.

Fittich *m* **-(e)s, -e** *(liter)* wing, pinion *(liter)* ◆ **jdn unter seine ~e nehmen** *(hum)* to take sb under one's wing *(fig)*.

Fitting *nt* **-s, -s** *(Tech)* fitting.

Fitzchen *nt (dial)*, **Fitzel** *m or nt* **-s, -, Fitzelchen** *nt* little bit.

fix *adj* **(a)** *(inf) (flink)* quick; *(intelligent auch)* bright, smart ◆ **in etw** *(dat)* **~ sein** to be quick at sth; **mach ~!** be quick!, look lively! *(inf)*; **das geht ganz ~** that doesn't/won't take long at all; **geht das nicht ~er?** does it have to take so long?

(b) *(inf)* **~ und fertig** *or* **alle** *or* **foxi sein** *(nervös)* to be at the end of one's tether; *(erschöpft)* to be worn out *or* done in *(inf) or* all in *(inf)*; *(emotional, seelisch)* to be shattered; *(ruiniert)* to be done for *(inf)*; **jdn ~ und fertig** *or* **alle** *or* **foxi machen** *(nervös machen)* to drive sb mad; *(erschöpfen)* to wear sb out, to do sb in *(inf)*; *(emotional, seelisch)* to shatter sb; *(in Prüfung, Wettbewerb, Kampf etc)* to give sb a thrashing *(inf)*; *(ruinieren)* to do for sb *(inf)*.

(c) *(feststehend)* fixed ◆ **~e Idee** obsession, idée fixe.

Fix *m* **-(es), -e** *(sl)* fix *(sl)*.

Fixa *pl of* **Fixum.**

fixen *vi* **(a)** *(sl: Drogen spritzen)* to fix *(sl)*, to shoot *(sl)*. **(b)** *(St Ex)* to bear.

Fixer(in *f***)** *m* **-s, - (a)** *(sl)* fixer *(sl)*. **(b)** *(St Ex)* bear.

Fixerstube *f (inf)* junkies' centre *(inf)*.

Fixgeschäft *nt (Comm)* transaction for delivery by a fixed date; *(St Ex)* time bargain.

Fixierbad *nt* fixer.

fixierbar *adj* specifiable, definable.

fixieren* *vt* **(a)** *(anstarren)* **jdn/etw (mit seinem Blick/seinen Augen) ~** to fix one's gaze/eyes on sb/sth.

(b) *(festlegen)* to specify, to define; *Gehälter, Termin etc* to set *(auf +acc* for); *(schriftlich niederlegen)* to record ◆ **er ist zu stark auf seine Mutter fixiert** *(Psych)* he has a mother fixation; **seine Interessen sind auf Fußball fixiert** he has a fixation about football.

(c) *(haltbar machen)* to fix.

(d) *(Gewichtheben)* to lock; *(Ringen)* to get in a lock ◆ **er fixierte seinen Gegner auf den Schultern** he pinned his opponent/his opponent's shoulders to the canvas.

Fixier-: ~mittel *nt* fixer, fixative; **~natron, ~salz** *nt* hypo.

Fixierung *f* **(a)** *(Festlegung) siehe vt (b)* specification, definition; setting; recording; *(Psych)* fixation. **(b)** *(Anstarren)* fixing of one's gaze *(gen* on).

Fixigkeit *f (inf)* speed.

Fixing *nt* **-s,** *no pl (Fin)* fixing.

Fix-: ~kosten *pl* fixed costs *pl*; **~punkt** *m siehe* **Festpunkt**; **~stern** *m* fixed star.

Fixum *nt* **-s, Fixa** basic salary, basic.

Fixzeit *f siehe* **Kernzeit.**

Fjord *m* **-(e)s, -e** fiord.

FKK [ɛfka:'ka:] *no art abbr of* **Freikörperkultur** ◆ **~-Anhänger sein** to be a nudist *or* naturist.

FKK-Strand [ɛfka:'ka:-] *m* nudist beach.

Fla *f* **-,** *no pl (Mil) abbr of* **Flugabwehr.**

Flab *f* **-,** *no pl (Sw) siehe* **Flak.**

flach *adj* **(a)** *(eben, platt, niedrig)* flat; *Gebäude* low; *Abhang* gentle; *Boot* flat-bottomed ◆ **sich ~ hinlegen/~ liegen** to lie down/lie flat; **~ schlafen** to sleep without a pillow; **die ~e Klinge/Hand** the flat of the blade/one's hand; **eine ~e Brust** a hollow chest; *(Busen)* a flat chest; **auf dem ~en Land** in the middle of the country.

(b) *(untief)* shallow.

(c) *(fig)* flat; *Geschmack* insipid; *(oberflächlich)* shallow ◆ **~ atmen** to take shallow breaths.

Flach *nt* **-(e)s, -e** *(Naut)* shallows *pl.*

Flach-: ~bau *m* low building; **~bauweise** *f* low style of building; **~bildschirm** *m (TV)* flat screen; **f~brüstig** *adj* flat-chested; **~dach** *nt* flat roof; **~druck** *m* **(a)** *(Verfahren)* planography; **(b)** *(Produkt)* planograph; **~drucker** *m* planographic printer.

Fläche *f* **-, -n** *(Ausdehnung, Flächeninhalt, Math)* area; *(Ober~)* surface; *(von Würfel)* face; *(Gelände, Land~, Wasser~)* expanse (of ground/water).

Flach|eisen *nt* flat bar; *(Werkzeug)* flat-bladed chisel.

Flächen-: ~ausdehnung *f* surface area; **~brand** *m* extensive fire; **sich zu einem ~brand ausweiten** *(fig)* to spread to epidemic proportions; **f~deckend** *adj* **wir müssen f~deckend arbeiten** we need blanket coverage; **~ertrag** *m* yield per acre/hectare *etc*; **f~gleich** *adj (Math)* equal in area; **f~haft** *adj* two-dimensional; *(ausgedehnt)* extensive; **~inhalt** *m* area; **~land** *nt siehe* **~staat**; **~maß** *nt* unit of square measure; **~nutzung** *f* land utilization; **~staat** *m* state *(as opposed to city state)*; **f~treu** *adj Projektion* equal-area.

Flach-: f~fallen *vi sep irreg aux sein (inf)* not to come off; *(Regelung)* to end; **~feile** *f* flat file; **~glas** *nt* sheet-glass; **~hang** *m* gentle slope.

Flachheit *f siehe adj* **(a)** flatness; lowness; gentleness. **(b)** shallowness. **(c)** flatness; insipidity, insipidness; shallowness.

flächig *adj Gesicht* flat; *Aufforstungen* extensive.

Flach-: ~kopf *m (inf)* dunderhead *(inf)*, numskull *(inf)*; **~kopfschraube** *f* countersunk screw; **~küste** *f* flat coast; **~land** *nt* lowland; *(Tiefland)* plains *pl*; **~länder(in** *f***)** *m* **-s, -** lowlander; plainsman; **~landtiroler** *m (inf)* pseudo-Tyrolean type; **f~legen** *sep (inf)* **1** *vt* to lay out; **2** *vr* to lie down; **f~liegen** *vi sep irreg (inf)* to be laid up *(inf)*; **~mann** *m, pl* **-männer** *(inf)* hipflask; **~meißel** *m* flat chisel; **~moor** *nt* fen; ⚠**~paß** *m (Ftbl)* low pass; **~relief** *nt* bas-relief; **~rennen** *nt* flat (race).

Flachs [flaks] *m* **-es,** *no pl* **(a)** *(Bot, Tex)* flax. **(b)** *(inf: Neckerei, Witzelei)* kidding *(inf)*; *(Bemerkung)* joke ◆ **~ machen** to kid around *(inf)*; **das war nur ~** I/he *etc* was only kidding *(inf)*; **jetzt mal ganz ohne ~** joking *or* kidding *(inf)* apart.

flachsblond *adj* flaxen.

⚠ **Flachschuß** *m (Ftbl)* low shot.

Flachse ['flaksə] *f* **-, -n** *(Aus) siehe* **Flechse.**

flachsen ['flaksn] *vi (inf)* to kid around *(inf)* ◆ **mit jdm ~** to kid sb (on) *(inf)*.

Flachserei [flaksə'rai] *f (inf) siehe* **Flachs (b).**

Flachs-: f~farben *adj* flaxen; **~haar** *nt* flaxen hair.

Flachsinn *m, no pl* shallowness.

Flachskopf *m* flaxen-haired child/youth.

Flachzange *f* flat-nosed pliers *pl.*

flackern *vi (lit, fig)* to flicker.

Flackerschein *m* flicker, flickering light.

Fladen *m* **-s, - (a)** *(Cook)* round flat dough-cake. **(b)** *(inf: Kuh~)* cowpat.

Fladenbrot *nt* round flat loaf.

Flader *f* **-, -n** grain *no pl*; *(Jahresring)* ring.

fladern *vti (Aus inf)* to steal, to nick *(Brit inf)*.

Flagellant *m* flagellant.

Flagellantentum *nt (Rel)* self-flagellation, flagellantism.

Flagellantismus *m (Psych)* flagellantism.

Flagellat *m* **-en, -en** *(Biol)* flagellate.

Flagellation *f (Psych)* flagellation.

Flagge *f* **-, -n** flag ◆ **die belgische ~ führen** to fly the Belgian flag *or* colours; **die ~ streichen** *(lit)* to strike the flag; *(fig)* to capitulate, to show the white flag; **~ zeigen** to nail one's colours to the mast.

flaggen *vi* to fly flags/a flag ◆ **geflaggt haben** to fly flags/a flag; *siehe* **halbmast, Topp.**

Flaggen-: ~alphabet *nt* semaphore *no art*; **~gruß** *m* dipping of the flag; **~leine** *f siehe* **Flaggleine**; **~mast** *m* flagpole, flagstaff; **~parade** *f* morning/evening colours *sing*; **~signal** *nt* flag signal; **~tuch** *nt, no pl* bunting.

Flagg-: ~leine *f* (flag) halyard; **~offizier** *m* flag officer; **~schiff** *nt (lit, fig)* flagship.

flagrant *adj* flagrant; *siehe* **in flagranti.**

Flair [flɛ:ɐ] *nt or (rare) m* **-s,** *no pl (geh)* atmosphere; *(Nimbus)* aura; *(esp Sw: Gespür)* flair.

Flak *f* -, - *or* **-s** *abbr of* **Flug(zeug)abwehrkanone (a)** anti-aircraft *or* ack-ack gun. **(b)** (*Einheit*) anti-aircraft *or* ack-ack unit.
Flak-: ~batterie *f* anti-aircraft *or* ack-ack battery; **~helfer(in** *f*) *m* (*Hist*) anti-aircraft auxiliary.
Flakon [fla'kõ:] *nt or m* **-s, -s** bottle, flacon.
Flakstellung *f* anti-aircraft *or* ack-ack (*inf*) artillery position.
Flambeau [flã'bo:] *m* **-s, -s** (*geh*) chandelier.
flambieren* *vt* (*Cook*) to flambé.
flamboyant [flãboa'jã:] *adj* (*geh, Archit*) flamboyant.
Flamboyantstil [flãboa'jã:-] *m* flamboyant style.
Flame *m* **-n, -n** Fleming, Flemish man/boy.
Flamenco *m* **-(s), -s** flamenco.
Flamin, Flämin *f* Fleming, Flemish woman/girl.
Flamingo [fla'mɪŋgo] *m* **-s, -s** flamingo.
flämisch *adj* Flemish.
Flämisch(e) *nt* **-en** Flemish; *siehe auch* **Deutsch(e)**.
Flämmchen *nt dim of* **Flamme**.
Flamme *f* **-, -n (a)** (*lit, fig*) flame ◆ **mit ruhiger/flackernder ~ brennen** to burn with a steady/flickering flame; **in ~n aufgehen** to go up in flames; **in (hellen) ~n stehen** to be ablaze *or* in flames; **etw den ~n übergeben** (*liter*) to consign sth to the flames; **etw auf kleiner ~ kochen** (*lit*) to cook sth on a low flame; (*fig*) to let sth just tick over; **etw auf großer ~ kochen** to cook sth fast.
(b) (*Brennstelle*) flame, burner.
(c) (*dated inf: Geliebte*) flame (*inf*).
flammen *vi* (*old, fig*) to blaze; *siehe* **flammend**.
flammend *adj* fiery ◆ **mit ~em Gesicht** blazing.
flammendrot *adj* (*geh*) flame red, blazing red.
Flammen-: ~meer *nt* sea of flames; **~tod** *m* death by burning; **den ~tod erleiden** to be burnt to death; **jdn zum ~tod verurteilen** to sentence sb to be burnt to death; **~werfer** *m* flame-thrower; **~zeichen** *nt* (*geh*) *siehe* **Feuerzeichen**.
Flandern *nt* **-s** Flanders *sing*.
flandrisch *adj* Flemish.
Flanell *m* **-s, -e** flannel.
flanellen *adj attr* flannel.
Flaneur [fla'nø:ɐ] *m* **-s, -e** (*geh*) stroller.
flanieren* *vi* to stroll, to saunter.
Flanke *f* **-, -n (a)** (*Anat, Mil, Chess*) flank; (*von Bus, Lastzug etc*) side ◆ **dem Feind in die ~n fallen** to attack the enemy on the flank. **(b)** (*Sport*) (*Turnen*) flank-vault; (*Ftbl*) cross; (*Spielfeldseite*) wing.
flanken *vi* (*Turnen*) to flank-vault; (*Ftbl*) to centre.
Flanken-: ~angriff *m* (*Mil, Chess*) flank attack; **~ball** *m* (*Ftbl*) cross, centre; **~deckung** *f* (*Mil*) flank defence; **~schutz** *m* (*Mil*) protection on the flank; **jdm ~schutz geben** (*fig*) to give sb added support; **~sicherung** *f* (*Mil*) *siehe* **~deckung**.
flankieren* *vt* (*Mil, Chess, fig*) to flank; (*fig: ergänzen*) to accompany ◆ **~de Maßnahmen** supporting measures.
Flansch *m* **-(e)s, -e** flange.
Flappe *f* **-, -n** (*dial*) pout ◆ **eine ~ ziehen** to look petulant, to pout.
flappen *vi* (*N Ger*) to flap.
Flaps *m* **-es, -e** (*dial inf*) *siehe* **Flegel**.
flapsig *adj* (*dial inf*) *Benehmen* cheeky; *Bemerkung* offhand.
Fläschchen *nt* bottle.
Flasche *f* **-, -n (a)** bottle ◆ **einem Baby die ~ geben** to give a baby its bottle; **mit der ~ aufziehen** to bottle-feed; **das Kind bekommt die ~** (*momentan*) the child is having its bottle; (*generell*) the child is bottle-fed; **eine ~ Wein/Bier** *etc* a bottle of wine/beer *etc*; **aus der ~ trinken** to drink (straight) from *or* out of the bottle; **zur ~ greifen** (*fig*) to take to the bottle.
(b) (*inf: Versager*) dead loss (*inf*) ◆ **du ~!** you're a dead loss! (*inf*).
Flaschen-: ~batterie *f* array of bottles; **~bier** *nt* bottled beer; **~bürste** *f* bottle-brush; **~etikett** *nt* label on a/the bottle; **~fach** *nt* bottle compartment; **~gärung** *f* fermentation in the bottle; **~gestell** *nt* bottle rack; **f~grün** *adj* bottle-green; **~hals** *m* neck of a bottle; (*fig*) bottleneck; **~kind** *nt* bottle-fed baby; **er ist ein ~kind** (*hum*) he's a straight-from-the-bottle man (*inf*), he always drinks straight from the bottle; **~kürbis** *m* calabash, bottle gourd; **~milch** *f* bottled milk; **~nahrung** *f* baby milk; **~öffner** *m* bottle-opener; **~pfand** *nt* deposit on a/the bottle; **~post** *f* message in a/ the bottle; **mit der ~post** in a bottle; **~regal** *nt* wine rack; **f~reif** *adj Wein* ready for bottling; ⚠**~verschluß** *m* bottle top; **~wein** *m* bottled wine; **f~weise** *adv* by the bottle; **~zug** *m* block and tackle.
Flaschner *m* **-s, -** (*S Ger*) plumber.
Flash [flɛʃ] *m* **-s, -s** (*Film*) flash, intercut scene (*form*); (*Rückblende*) flashback; (*sl*) flash (*sl*).
Flatter *f*: **die ~ machen** (*sl*) to beat it (*inf*).
Flatter-: ~geist *m* butterfly; **f~haft** *adj* butterfly *attr*, fickle; **sie ist ziemlich f~haft** she's a bit of a butterfly; **~haftigkeit** *f* fickleness.
flatterig *adj* fluttery; *Puls* fluttering.
Flattermann *m, pl* **-männer** (*inf*) **(a) einen ~ haben** (*Zittern der Hände*) to have the shakes; (*Lampenfieber*) to have stage-fright. **(b)** (*hum: Hähnchen*) chicken.
flattern *vi bei Richtungsangabe aux sein* (*lit, fig*) to flutter; (*mit den Flügeln schlagen*) to flap its wings; (*Fahne, Segel beim Sturm, Hose*) to flap; (*Haar*) to stream, to fly; (*Blick*) to flicker; (*inf: Mensch*) to be in a flap (*inf*); (*Lenkung, Autorad*) to wobble ◆ **ein Brief flatterte mir auf den Schreibtisch** a letter turned up *or* arrived on my desk.
Flattersatz *m* (*Typ*) unjustified print, ragged right.
Flatulenz *f* (*Med*) flatulence.
flau *adj* **(a)** *Brise, Wind* slack. **(b)** *Farbe* weak; *Geschmack* insipid; *Stimmung*, (*Phot inf*) *Negativ* flat. **(c)** (*übel*) queasy; (*vor Hunger*) faint ◆ **mir ist ~ (im Magen)** I feel queasy. **(d)** (*Comm*) *Markt, Börse* slack ◆ **in meiner Kasse sieht es ~ aus** (*inf*) my finances aren't too healthy (*inf*).
Flauheit *f siehe adj (b-d)* weakness; insipidity, insipidness; flatness; queasiness; faintness; slackness.
Flaum *m* **-(e)s,** *no pl* **(a)** (*~federn, Härchen, auf Obst*) down. **(b)** (*dial: Schweinebauchfett*) lard.
Flaum-: ~bart *m* downy beard, bum-fluff (*sl*) *no indef art*; **~feder** *f* down feather, plumule (*spec*).
flaumig *adj* downy; (*Aus: flockig*) light and creamy.
flaumweich *adj* (*fig inf*) *Mensch* soft; *Haltung* milk-and-water *attr*, lukewarm.
Flausch *m* **-(e)s, -e** fleece.
flauschig *adj* fleecy; (*weich*) soft.
Flausen *pl* (*inf*) (*Unsinn*) nonsense; (*Illusionen*) fancy ideas *pl* (*inf*) ◆ **macht keine ~!** don't try anything! (*inf*).
Flaute *f* **-, -n (a)** (*Met*) calm ◆ **das Schiff geriet in eine ~** the ship was becalmed. **(b)** (*fig*) (*Comm*) lull, slack period; (*der Stimmung*) fit of the doldrums (*inf*); (*der Leistung*) period of slackness.
Flaxe *f* **-, -n** (*Aus*) *siehe* **Flechse**.
Fläz *m* **-es, -e** (*dial inf*) lout, roughneck.
fläzen *vr* (*inf*) to sprawl (*in +acc* in).
Flechse ['flɛksə] *f* **-, -n** tendon.
flechsig ['flɛksɪç] *adj Fleisch* stringy (*inf*), sinewy.
Flecht|arbeit *f* wickerwork, basketwork; (*aus Rohr*) canework.
Flechte *f* **-, -n (a)** (*Bot, Med*) lichen. **(b)** (*geh: Zopf*) plait, braid (*dated*).
flechten *pret* **flocht,** *ptp* **geflochten** *vt Haar* to plait, to braid (*dated*); *Kranz, Korb, Matte* to weave, to make; *Seil* to make; *Stuhl* to cane ◆ **sich/jdm das Haar zu Zöpfen** *or* **in Zöpfe ~** to plait *or* braid (*dated*) one's/sb's hair; **Zitate in eine Rede ~** to punctuate a speech with quotations; *siehe* **Rad**.
Flechtwerk *nt* **(a)** (*Art*) interlace. **(b)** *siehe* **Geflecht**.
Fleck *m* **-(e)s, -e** *or* **-en (a)** (*Schmutz~*) stain ◆ **dieses Zeug macht ~en** this stuff stains (*in/auf etw (acc)* sth); **einen ~ auf der (weißen) Weste haben** (*fig*) to have blotted one's copybook; **einen ~ auf der Ehre haben** to have a stain on one's honour *or* a blot on one's escutcheon.
(b) (*Farb~*) splodge (*Brit*), splotch, blob; (*auf Arm etc*) blotch; (*auf Obst*) blemish ◆ **ein grüner/gelber** *etc* **~** a patch of green/yellow *etc*, a green/ yellow *etc* patch; **weißer ~** white patch; (*auf Stirn von Pferd*) star, blaze; (*auf Landkarte*) blank area; *siehe* **blau**.
(c) (*Stelle*) spot, place ◆ **auf demselben ~** in the same place; **sich nicht vom ~ rühren** not to move *or* budge (*inf*); **nicht vom ~ kommen** not to get any further; **er hat das Herz auf dem rechten ~** (*fig*) his heart is in the right place; **am falschen ~** (*fig*) in the wrong way; *sparen* in the wrong places; **vom ~ weg** on the spot.
(d) (*dial: Flicken*) patch.
(e) *no pl* (*Cook dial*) *siehe* **Kaldaune**.
Fleckchen *nt* **(a)** *dim of* **Fleck**. **(b) ein schönes ~ (Erde)** a lovely little spot.
flecken *vi* (*dial*) to stain.
Flecken *m* **-s, - (a)** (*old: Markt~*) small town. **(b)** *siehe* **Fleck (a, b, d)**.
fleckenlos *adj* (*lit, fig*) spotless.
Fleck-: ~entferner *m*, **~entfernungsmittel** *nt* stain-remover.
Fleckenwasser *nt* stain-remover.
Fleckerlteppich *m* (*S Ger, Aus*) rag rug.
Fleckfieber *nt* typhus fever.
fleckig *adj* marked; (*mit Flüssigkeit auch*) stained; *Obst* blemished; *Tierfell* speckled; *Gesichtshaut* blotchy.
Flecktyphus *m siehe* **Fleckfieber (a)**.
Fledderer *m* **-s, -** *siehe* **Leichenfledderer**.
fleddern *vt Leichen* to rob; (*inf: durchwühlen*) to rummage *or* ferret (*inf*) through.
Fleder-: ~maus *f* bat; **~mausärmel** *m* (*Fashion*) **Mantel mit ~mausärmel** batwing coat; **~wisch** *m* feather duster.
Fleet [fle:t] *nt* **-(e)s, -e** (*N Ger*) canal.
Flegel *m* **-s, - (a)** (*Lümmel*) lout, yob (*inf*); (*Kind*) brat (*inf*). **(b)** (*Dresch~, old: Kriegs~*) flail.
Flegel|alter *nt* awkward adolescent phase.
Flegelei *f* uncouthness; (*Benehmen, Bemerkung*) uncouth behaviour *no pl*/ remark ◆ **so eine ~!** how rude *or* uncouth!
Flegel-: f~haft *adj* uncouth; **~haftigkeit** *f* uncouthness; **~jahre** *pl siehe* **~alter**.
flegeln *vr* to loll, to sprawl ◆ **sich in die Bank/den Sessel ~** to loll *or* sprawl all over the bench/in the armchair.
flehen *vi* (*geh*) to plead (*um +acc* for, *zu* with) ◆ **..., flehte er zu Gott** ..., he beseeched *or* besought God (*liter, old*).
flehentlich *adj* imploring, pleading, beseeching (*liter, old*) ◆ **eine ~e Bitte** an earnest entreaty *or* plea; **jdn ~ bitten** to plead with sb; **jdn ~ bitten, etw zu tun** to entreat *or* implore sb to do sth.
Fleisch *nt* **-(e)s,** *no pl* **(a)** (*Gewebe, Muskel~*) flesh ◆ **nacktes ~** (*lit, fig hum*) bare flesh; **vom ~ fallen** to lose (a lot of) weight; **sich** (*dat or acc*) **ins eigene ~ schneiden** to cut off one's nose to spite one's face; **den Weg allen ~es gehen** (*liter*) to go the way of all flesh; **Menschen von ~ und Blut** flesh and blood; **sein eigen ~ und Blut** (*liter*) his own flesh and blood; **jdm in ~ und Blut über-**

gehen to become second nature to sb; **und das Wort ward ~** (*Bibl*) and the Word was made flesh.

(b) (*Nahrungsmittel*) meat; (*Frucht~*) flesh.

Fleisch- *in cpds* (*Cook*) meat; (*Anat*) flesh; **~abfälle** *pl* (meat) scraps *pl*; **f~arm** *adj* containing little meat; **f~arm sein** to contain little meat; **~berg** *m* (*pej inf*) mountain of flesh; **~beschau** *f* (a) meat inspection; (b) (*hum inf*) cattle market (*inf*); **~beschauer(in** *f*) *m* meat inspector; **~brocken** *m* lump of meat; **~brühe** *f* (*Gericht*) bouillon; (*Fond*) meat stock; **~brühwürfel** *m* (meat) stock cube; **~einlage** *f* meat; **~einwaage** *f* meat content, weight of meat.

Fleischer *m* **-s, -** butcher; (*pej inf: Chirurg*) sawbones *sing* (*inf*).

Fleischerbeil *nt* meat cleaver.

Fleischerei *f* butcher's (shop).

Fleischer-: ~haken *m* meat hook; **~handwerk** *nt* butcher's trade, butchery; **~hund** *m* (*lit*) butcher's dog; (*fig*) brute of a dog; **ein Gemüt wie ein ~hund haben** (*inf*) to be a callous brute; **~innung** *f* butchers' guild; **~laden** *m siehe* **Fleischerei**; **~messer** *nt* butcher's knife.

Fleischerne(s) *nt decl as adj* (*S Ger*) meat.

Fleischeslust *f* (*old liter*) carnal lust, lusts *pl* of the flesh.

Fleisch-: ≈esser *m* meat-eater; **≈extrakt** *m* beef extract; **≈farbe** *f* flesh colour; **f≈farben, f≈farbig** *adj* flesh-coloured; **≈fliege** *f* flesh-fly; ⚠**f≈fressend** *adj* (*Biol*) **f~fressende Pflanzen** carnivorous plants, carnivores; **f~fressende Tiere** carnivores, carnivorous animals; **≈fresser** *m* (*Zool*) carnivore; ⚠**≈genuß** *m* consumption of meat; ⚠**f≈geworden** *adj attr* (*liter*) incarnate; **der f~gewordene Sohn Gottes** the Son of God incarnate; **≈hauer** *m* (*Aus*) butcher; **≈hauerei** *f* (*Aus*) butcher's (shop).

fleischig *adj* fleshy.

Fleisch-: ~käse *m* meat loaf; **~klopfer** *m* steak hammer; **~kloß** *m*, **~klößchen** *nt* (a) meatball; (b) (*pej inf*) mountain of flesh; **~konserve** *f* can *or* tin (*Brit*) of meat; (*in Glas*) pot *or* jar of meat; **~konserven** *pl* (*als Gattung*) canned *or* tinned (*Brit*) meat; (*in Glas*) potted meat.

fleischlich *adj attr Speisen, Kost* meat; (*old liter: Lüste, Genüsse, Begierden*) carnal, of the flesh.

Fleisch-: f~los *adj* (a) (*ohne Fleisch*) meatless; *Kost, Ernährung* vegetarian; **f~los essen/kochen** to eat no meat/to cook without meat; (b) (*mager*) thin, lean; **~maschine** *f* (*Aus, S Ger*) *siehe* **~wolf**; **~pastete** *f* meat vol-au-vent; **~reste** *pl* left-over meat *sing*; **~saft** *m* meat juices *pl*; **~salat** *m* diced meat salad with mayonnaise; **~spieß** *m* (*Cook*) meat skewer; **~stück(chen)** *nt* piece of meat; **~suppe** *f* meat soup; **~tomate** *f* beef tomato; **~ton** *m* (*Art*) flesh-colour; **~topf** *m* (a) (*Cook*) meat pan; (b) **~töpfe** (*Bibl*) fleshpots *pl*; (*fig*) good life; ⚠**f~verarbeitend** *adj attr* meat-processing; **~vergiftung** *f* food poisoning (*from meat*); **~waren** *pl* meat products *pl*; **~werdung** *f* (*Rel, liter*) incarnation; **~wolf** *m* mincer, meat grinder (*esp US*); **Rekruten/Prüflinge durch den ~wolf drehen** (*inf*) to put new recruits/exam candidates through the mill; **~wunde** *f* flesh wound; **~wurst** *f* pork sausage.

Fleiß *m* **-(e)s,** *no pl* diligence; (*eifriges Tätigsein*) industry; (*Beharrlichkeit*) application; (*als Charaktereigenschaft*) industriousness ◆ **~ aufwenden** to apply oneself; **ihm fehlt der ~** he lacks application; **mit ~ kann es jeder zu etwas bringen** anybody can succeed if he works hard; **er hat die Prüfung ausschließlich durch ~ geschafft** he passed the exam by sheer hard work *or* simply by working hard; **mit ~ bei der Sache sein** to work hard; **mit** (*S Ger*) *or* **zu** (*N Ger*) **~** (*absichtlich*) deliberately, on purpose; **ohne ~ kein Preis** (*Prov*) success never comes easily.

Fleiß|arbeit *f* industrious piece of work; (*nichts als Fleiß erfordernd*) laborious task ◆ **eine (reine) ~** (*pej*) an industrious but uninspired piece of work.

fleißig *adj* (a) (*arbeitsam*) hard-working *no adv*, industrious, diligent ◆ **~ studieren/arbeiten** to study/work hard; **~ wie die Bienen sein** to work like beavers; **~e Hände** busy hands; **~es Lieschen** (*Bot*) busy Lizzie.

(b) (*Fleiß zeigend*) diligent, painstaking.

(c) (*inf: unverdrossen*) assiduous, diligent; *Theaterbesucher, Sammler etc* keen ◆ **wir haben immer ~ getrunken bis 12 Uhr** we were drinking away till 12 o'clock.

flektierbar *adj* (in)flectional (*form*); *Verbum* conjugable; *Substantiv, Adjektiv* declinable.

flektieren* [1] *vt* to inflect (*form*); *Substantiv, Adjektiv* to decline; *Verbum* to conjugate.

[2] *vi* to inflect; to be declined; to be conjugated ◆ **„schwimmen" flektiert stark** "schwimmen" is (conjugated as) a strong verb; **~d** *siehe* **flektierbar**.

flennen *vi* (*pej inf*) to blubb(er) (*inf*).

Flennerei *f* (*pej inf*) blubb(er)ing (*inf*).

fletschen *vti* **die Zähne** *or* **mit den Zähnen ~** to bare *or* show one's teeth.

fleucht (*obs, poet*) *3. pers sing of* **fliegen**; *siehe* **kreucht**.

Fleurist(in *f*) [flø'rɪst(ɪn)] *m* **-en, -en** florist.

Fleurop ® ['flɔyrɔp, 'flø:rɔp, flɔy'ro:p, flø'ro:p] *f* - Interflora ®.

flexibel *adj* (*lit, fig*) flexible; *Holz, Kunststoff auch* pliable.

Flexibilisierung *f, no pl* **~ der Arbeitszeit** transition to flexible working hours.

Flexibilität *f siehe adj* flexibility; pliability.

Flexion *f* (*Gram*) inflection.

Flexions-: ~endung *f* inflectional ending *or* suffix; **f~fähig** *adj siehe* **flektierbar**; **f~los** *adj* uninflected.

Flibustier [fli'bʊstiɐ] *m* **-s, -** (*old, fig*) buccaneer.

flicht *imper sing and 3. pers sing present of* **flechten**.

Flick|arbeit *f* (*Sew*) mending.

flicken *vt* to mend; *Wäsche* (*stopfen auch*) to darn; (*mit Flicken*) to patch; *siehe* **Zeug**.

Flicken *m* **-s, -** patch ◆ **eine Jacke mit ~** a patched jacket; (*als Schmuck*) a patchwork jacket.

Flickenteppich *m* rag rug.

Flick-: ~flack *m* (*Sport*) backflip; **~schneider** *m* (*dated*) mender; (*pej*) bungler (*inf*), bungling tailor; **~schuster** *m* (*old*) cobbler; (*fig pej*) bungler (*inf*), botcher (*inf*); **~schusterei** *f* cobbler's (shop); **das ist ~schusterei** (*fig pej*) that's a patch-up job; **~wäsche** *f* mending; **~werk** *nt* **die Reform war reinstes ~werk** the reform had been carried out piecemeal; **~wort** *nt* filler; **~zeug** *nt* (*Nähzeug*) sewing kit; (*Reifen~*) (puncture) repair outfit.

Flieder *m* **-s, -** (a) lilac; (*dial: Holunder*) elder. (b) (*Aus inf: Geld*) money.

Flieder-: ~beere *f* (*dial*) elderberry; **~busch** *m* lilac; **f~farben, f~farbig** *adj* lilac; **~tee** *m* elderflower tea.

Fliege *f* **-, -n** (a) fly ◆ **sie fielen um wie die ~n** they went down like ninepins; **sie starben wie die ~n** they fell like flies; **er tut keiner ~ etwas zuleide, er würde keiner ~ ein Bein ausreißen** (*fig*) he wouldn't hurt a fly; **zwei ~n mit einer Klappe schlagen** to kill two birds with one stone; **ihn stört die ~ an der Wand, er ärgert sich über die ~ an der Wand** every little thing irritates him; **die** *or* **~ machen** (*sl*) to beat it (*inf*).

(b) (*Bärtchen*) imperial.

(c) (*Schlips*) bow tie.

fliegen *pret* **flog**, *ptp* **geflogen** [1] *vi aux sein* (a) to fly; (*Raumschiff, Raumfahrer*) to go, to travel (*form*) ◆ **mit General Air ~** to fly (with *or* by) General Air; **in den Urlaub ~** to fly on holiday; **nach Köln fliegt man zwei Stunden** it takes two hours to fly to Cologne, it's a two-hour flight to Cologne; **ich kann doch nicht ~!** I haven't got wings (*inf*).

(b) (*eilen*) to fly ◆ **jdm/einander in die Arme ~** to fly into sb's/each other's arms; **jdm an den Hals ~** to hurl oneself at sb; **ein Lächeln flog über sein Gesicht** a brief smile lit up his face; **die Zeit fliegt** time flies; **auf jdn/etw ~** (*inf*) to be mad *or* wild about sb/sth (*inf*).

(c) (*inf: fallen*) to fall ◆ **von der Leiter ~** to fall off the ladder; **ich bin von der Treppe geflogen** I went flying down the stairs; **durchs Examen ~** to fail *or* flunk (*inf*) one's exam.

(d) (*sl: hinausgeworfen werden*) to be chucked *or* slung *or* kicked out (*inf*) (*aus, von* of) ◆ **aus der Firma ~** to get the sack *or* the boot (*inf*).

(e) (*bewegt werden*) (*Fahne, Haare*) to fly; (*Puls*) to race ◆ **das Tier flog am ganzen Körper** the animal was quivering *or* trembling all over.

(f) (*geworfen werden*) to be thrown *or* flung (*inf*) *or* chucked (*inf*) ◆ **geflogen kommen** to come flying; **in den Papierkorb ~** to go into the wastepaper basket, to be immediately consigned to the wastepaper basket; **die Tür flog ins Schloß** the door flew shut; **ein Schuh flog ihm an den Kopf** he had a shoe flung at him; **der Hut flog ihm vom Kopf** his hat flew off his head; **aus der Kurve ~** to skid off the bend; *siehe* **Luft**.

[2] *vt Flugzeug, Güter, Personen, Route, Einsatz etc* to fly.

[3] *vr* **in dieser Maschine/nachts fliegt es sich angenehm** flying in this plane/at night is pleasant; **das Flugzeug fliegt sich leicht/schwer** this plane is easy/difficult to fly, flying this plane is easy/difficult; *siehe auch* **fliegend**.

fliegend *adj attr Fische, Untertasse, Start* flying; *Personal* flight; *Würstchenbuden* mobile ◆ **~er Hund** flying fox; **in ~er Eile** *or* **Hast** in a tremendous hurry; **~er Händler** travelling hawker; (*mit Lieferwagen*) mobile trader; **~e Brigade** (*DDR*) mobile work brigade; **Der F~e Holländer** The Flying Dutchman; **~e Hitze** hot flushes *pl*; **~e Blätter** loose leaves *or* sheets; (*Hist*) broadsheets.

Fliegen-: ~draht *m* wire mesh; **~dreck** *m* fly droppings *pl*; **~fänger** *m* (*Klebestreifen*) fly-paper; **~fenster** *nt* wire-mesh window; **~gewicht** *nt* (*Sport, fig*) flyweight; **~gewichtler** *m* **-s, -** (*Sport*) flyweight; **~gitter** *nt* fly screen; **~klatsche** *f* fly-swat; **~kopf** *m* (*Typ*) turn; **~netz** *nt* fly-net; **~pilz** *m* fly agaric; **~rute** *f* fly rod; ⚠**~schiß** *m* (*inf*) **sich wegen jedem ~schiß an der Wand aufregen** to get one's knickers in a twist about nothing.

Flieger *m* **-s, -** (a) (*Pilot*) airman, aviator (*dated*), flier (*dated*); (*Mil: Rang*) aircraftman (*Brit*), airman basic (*US*) ◆ **er ist bei den ~n** (*dated*) he's in the air force. (b) (*inf: Flugzeug*) plane. (c) (*Vogel*) flier. (d) (*Sport*) (*Radrennen*) sprinter; (*Pferderennen*) flier.

Flieger- (*Mil*): **~abwehr** *f siehe* **Flugabwehr**; **~abzeichen** *nt* wings *pl*; **~alarm** *m* air-raid warning; **~angriff** *m* air-raid; **~bombe** *f* aerial bomb.

Fliegerei *f, no pl* flying.

Fliegerhorst *m* (*Mil*) military airfield *or* aerodrome (*Brit*).

Fliegerin *f siehe* **Flieger (a)**.

fliegerisch *adj attr* aeronautical.

Flieger-: ~jacke *f* bomber jacket; **~karte** *f* aviation chart; **~offizier** *m* (*Mil, Aviat*) air force officer; **~schule** *f* flying school; **~sprache** *f* pilots' jargon; **~staffel** *f* (*Mil*) (air force) squadron; **~truppe** *f* (*Mil*) air corps *sing*.

Fliehburg *f* refuge.

fliehen *pret* **floh**, *ptp* **geflohen** [1] *vi aux sein* to flee; (*entkommen*) to escape (*aus* from) ◆ **vor jdm/der Polizei/einem Gewitter ~** to flee from sb/the police/before a storm; **aus dem Lande ~** to flee the country; *siehe* **geflohen, fliehend**.

[2] *vt* (*liter*) (*meiden*) to shun; (*entkommen*) to flee from ◆ **jds Gegenwart ~** to shun/flee sb's presence.

fliehend *adj Kinn* receding; *Stirn* sloping.

Fliehende(r) *mf decl as adj* fugitive.

Flieh-: ~kraft *f* centrifugal force; **~kraftkupplung** *f* centrifugal clutch.

Fliese *f* **-, -n** tile ◆ **~n legen** to lay tiles; **etw mit ~n auslegen** to tile sth.

fliesen *vt* to tile.

Fliesen-: ~(fuß)boden *m* tiled floor; **~leger** *m* tiler.

Fließ-: ~band *nt* conveyor-belt; (*als Einrichtung*) assembly *or* production

⚠: for details of spelling reform, see supplement

line; **am ~band arbeiten** *or* **stehen** *(inf)* to work on the assembly *or* production line; **~bandfertigung** *f* belt production.

fließen *pret* **floß**, *ptp* **geflossen** *vi aux sein* to flow; *(Verkehr, Luftmassen auch)* to move; *(Fluß auch, Tränen)* to run ◆ **es ist genug Blut geflossen** enough blood has been shed *or* spilled; **der Schweiß floß ihm von der Stirn** sweat was pouring off his forehead; **die Steuergelder flossen in finstere Kanäle** the taxes were diverted along rather dubious channels; **die Mittel für Jugendarbeit ~ immer spärlicher** less and less money is being made available for youth work; **aus der Feder ~** *(geh)* to flow from the pen; **Nachrichten ~ spärlich** the flow of news is minimal; **alles fließt** *(Philos)* all is in a state of flux; *siehe* **Strom**.

fließend *adj* flowing; *Leitungswasser, Gewässer* running; *Verkehr* moving; *Rede, Vortrag, Sprache* fluent; *Grenze, Übergang* fluid ◆ **sie spricht ~ Französisch** *or* **ein ~es Französisch** she speaks fluent French, she speaks French fluently.

Fließ-: **~heck** *nt* fastback; **~komma** *nt (auch Comput)* floating point; **~laut** *m* liquid; **~punkt** *m (auch Comput)* floating point; **~satz** *m (Typ)* word-wrap; **~straße** *f (Tech)* assembly *or* production line; **~wasser** *nt (esp Aus)* running water.

Flimmer *m* **-s, -** **(a)** *(Anat)* cilium. **(b)** *no pl (liter: zitternder Glanz)* shimmer.

Flimmer-: **f~frei** *adj (Opt, Phot)* flicker-free; **~härchen** *nt* cilium; **~kasten** *m*, **~kiste** *f (inf)* TV *(inf)*, (goggle)box *(Brit inf)*, telly *(Brit inf)*.

flimmern [1] *vi* to shimmer; *(Film, TV)* to flicker ◆ **es flimmert mir vor den Augen** everything is swimming *or* dancing in front of my eyes; **über den Bildschirm ~** *(inf)* to be on the box *(Brit inf) or* on TV.
[2] *vt (dial: blank putzen)* to polish, to shine *(inf)*.

flink *adj (geschickt)* nimble; *Bewegung, Finger auch* deft; *(schnell, dated: aufgeweckt)* quick; *Mundwerk, Zunge* quick, ready; *Augen* sharp, bright ◆ **ein bißchen ~!** *(inf)* get a move on!, make it snappy! *(inf)*; **mit etw ~ bei der Hand sein** to be quick (off the mark) with sth.

Flinkheit *f siehe adj* nimbleness; deftness; quickness; readiness; sharpness, brightness.

Flint *m* **-(e)s, -e** *(old)* flint.

Flinte *f* **-, -n** *(Schrot~)* shotgun ◆ **jdn/etw vor die ~ bekommen** *(fig)* to get hold of sb/sth; **wenn der mir vor die ~ kommt ...** *(fig)* just wait till I get hold of him ...; **die ~ ins Korn werfen** *(fig)* to throw in the sponge *or* towel.

Flinten-: **~lauf** *m* (shot)gun barrel; **~weib** *nt (pej)* gunwoman.

Flintglas *nt* flint glass.

Flip *m* **-s, -s** *(Eiskunstlauf)* flip.

Flip-Chart ['-tʃɑːt] *f* **-, -s** flipchart.

Flipflopschaltung ['flɪpflɔp-] *f* flip-flop circuit.

Flipper *m* **-s, -**, **Flipperautomat** *m* pinball machine.

flippern [1] *vt* to flip ◆ **eine heiße Kugel ~** *(sl)* to be a pinball wizard *(inf)*.
[2] *vi* to play pinball.

flippig *adj (sl) Typ, Klamotten* hip *(sl)*.

flirren *vi* to whirr; *(Luft, Hitze)* to shimmer.

Flirt [flɪrt, *auch* flœːɐt, flœrt] *m* **-s, -s** **(a)** *(Flirten)* flirtation. **(b)** *(dated) (Schwarm)* flame *(dated)*; *(Mann auch)* beau *(dated)*.

flirten ['flɪrtn, *auch* 'flœːɐtn, 'flœrtn] *vi* to flirt ◆ **mit einem Gedanken ~** *(inf)* to toy with an idea.

Flitscherl *nt* **-s, -(n)** *(Aus)*, **Flittchen** *nt (pej inf)* slut.

Flitter *m* **-s, -** **(a)** *(~schmuck)* sequins *pl*, spangles *pl*. **(b)** *no pl (pej: Tand)* trumpery.

Flittergold *nt* gold foil.

flittern *vi* **(a)** to glitter, to sparkle. **(b)** *(hum)* to honeymoon.

Flitter-: **~werk** *nt siehe* **Flitter (b)**; **~wochen** *pl* honeymoon *sing*; **in die ~wochen fahren/in den ~wochen sein** to go/be on one's honeymoon; **~wöchner** *m* **-s, -** *(hum)* honeymooner.

Flitz(e)bogen *m* bow and arrow ◆ **ich bin gespannt wie ein ~** *(inf)* the suspense is killing me *(inf)*; **gespannt wie ein ~ sein, ob ...** *(inf)* to be on tenterhooks waiting to see whether ...

flitzen *vi aux sein (inf)* **(a)** to whizz *(inf)*, to dash. **(b)** *(nackt rennen)* to streak ◆ **(das) F~** streaking.

Flitzer *m* **-s, -** *(inf)* **(a)** *(Fahrzeug)* sporty little job *(inf)*; *(Schnelläufer)* streak of lightning *(inf)*. **(b)** *(nackter Läufer)* streaker.

floaten ['floːtn] *vti (Fin)* to float ◆ **~ (lassen)** to float.

Floating ['floːtɪŋ] *nt (Fin)* floating.

F-Loch ['ɛflɔx] *nt (Mus)* f-hole.

flocht *pret of* **flechten**.

Flöckchen *nt dim of* **Flocke**.

Flocke *f* **-, -n** **(a)** flake; *(Woll~)* piece of wool; *(Schaum~)* blob (of foam); *(Staub~)* ball (of fluff). **(b)** **~n** *pl (inf: Geld)* dough *(inf)*.

flockig *adj* fluffy.

flog *pret of* **fliegen**.

floh *pret of* **fliehen**.

Floh *m* **-(e)s, ¨-e** **(a)** *(Zool)* flea ◆ **von ¨-en zerbissen** *or* **zerstochen** flea-bitten *attr*, bitten by fleas; **es ist leichter, einen Sack ¨-e zu hüten, als ...** I'd as soon jump in the lake as ...; **jdm einen ~ ins Ohr setzen** *(inf)* to put an idea into sb's head; **die ¨-e husten hören** *(inf)* to imagine things.
(b) *(sl: Geld)* **¨-e** *pl* dough *(sl)*, bread *(sl)*.

⚠ **Flohbiß** *m* fleabite.

flöhe *pres subjunc of* **fliehen**.

flöhen *vt* **jdn/sich ~** to get rid of sb's/one's fleas, to debug sb/oneself *(inf)*.

Floh-: **~halsband** *nt* flea collar; **~hüpfen** *nt* tiddl(e)ywinks *sing, no art*; **~kino** *nt (inf)* local fleapit *(inf)*; **~kiste** *f (inf)* pit *(sl)*, bed; **~markt** *m* flea market; **~spiel** *nt siehe* **~hüpfen**; **~zirkus** *m* flea circus.

Flokati *m* **-s, -s** flokati.

Flom(en) *m* **-s,** *no pl (Cook) siehe* **Flaum**.

Flop *m* **-s, -s** flop *(inf)*.

Floppy Disk ['flɒpɪ-] *f* floppy disk.

Flor[1] *m* **-s, -e** *(liter)* array of flowers ◆ **in ~ stehen** to be in full bloom.

Flor[2] *m* **-s, -e** *or (rare)* **¨-e** **(a)** *(dünnes Gewebe)* gauze; *(Trauer~)* crêpe; *(liter: Schleier)* veil. **(b)** *(Teppich~, Samt~)* pile.

Flora *f* **-, Floren** flora.

Florentiner [1] *m* **-s, -** **(a)** *(Geog, Cook)* Florentine. **(b)** *(auch* **~hut***)* picture hat.
[2] *adj* Florentine.

florentinisch *adj* Florentine.

Florenz *nt* **-'** *or* **-ens** Florence.

Florett *nt* **-(e)s, -e** **(a)** *(Waffe)* foil ◆ **~ fechten** to fence with a foil. **(b)** *(auch* **~fechten***)* foil-fencing.

Florfliege *f* lacewing.

florieren* *vi* to flourish, to bloom.

Florist(in *f***)** *m* **-en, -en** florist.

Florpost *f*, **Florpostpapier** *nt* bank paper.

Floskel *f* **-, -n** set phrase ◆ **eine höfliche/abgedroschene ~** a polite but meaningless/a hackneyed phrase.

floskelhaft *adj Stil* cliché-ridden; *Rede, Brief auch* full of set phrases; *Phrasen, Ausdrucksweise* stereotyped.

⚠ **floß** *pret of* **fließen**.

Floß *nt* **-es, ¨-e** raft; *(Fishing)* float.

flößbar *adj* navigable by raft.

Floßbrücke *f* floating bridge.

Flosse *f* **-, -n** **(a)** *(Zool) (Fisch~)* fin; *(Wal~, Robben~)* flipper. **(b)** *(Aviat, Naut: Leitwerk)* fin. **(c)** *(Taucher~)* flipper. **(d)** *(sl: Hand)* paw *(inf)*, mauler *(inf)* ◆ **reich mir die ~, Genosse!** *(hum)* shake, pal! *(inf)*.

flößen *vti* to raft.

Flößer(in *f***)** *m* **-s, -** raftsman.

Flößerei *f, no pl* rafting.

Flöte *f* **-, -n** **(a)** pipe; *(Quer~, in Zusammensetzungen)* flute; *(Block~)* recorder; *(Pikkolo~)* piccolo; *(des Pan)* pipes *pl*; *(Orgel~)* flute; *(dial: Pfeife, Kessel~)* whistle ◆ **die ~** *or* **auf der ~ spielen** *or* **blasen** to play the pipe *etc*. **(b)** *(Kelchglas)* flute glass. **(c)** *(Cards)* flush. **(d)** *(sl: Penis)* cock *(sl)*.

flöten [1] *vt (Mus)* to play on the flute.
[2] *vi* **(a)** *(Mus)* to play the flute. **(b)** *(sl: fellieren)* to do a blow-job *(sl)*.
[3] *vti* **(a)** *(Vogel)* to warble; *(dial: pfeifen)* to whistle. **(b)** *(hum inf: süß sprechen)* to flute, to warble.

Flöten-: **~bläser** *m siehe* **~spieler**; ⚠**f~gehen** *vi sep aux sein (sl)* to go west *(inf)*, to go for a burton *(inf)*; **~kessel** *m* whistling kettle; **~register** *nt* flue-stop; **~spiel** *nt* pipe-/flute- *etc* playing; *(~musik)* pipe-/flute- *etc* music; **~spieler** *m* piper; flautist; recorder/piccolo player; **~ton** *m* **(a)** *(lit)* sound of flutes/a flute; **(b)** *(inf)* **jdm die ~töne beibringen** to teach sb what's what *(inf)*; **~werk** *nt* flue-work.

Flötist(in *f***)** *m* **-en, -en** flautist; piccolo player.

flott *adj* **(a)** *(zügig) Fahrt* quick; *Tempo, Geschäft* brisk; *Arbeiter, Bedienung* speedy *(inf)*, quick and efficient; *Tänzer* good; *(flüssig) Stil, Artikel* racy *(inf)*; *(schwungvoll) Musik* lively ◆ **aber ein bißchen ~!** and look lively!, and make it snappy!; **den ~en Otto** *or* **Heinrich haben** *(hum inf)* to have the runs *(inf)*; **~ auftreten** to cut a dash.
(b) *(schick)* smart.
(c) *(lebenslustig)* fun-loving, fast-living ◆ **~ leben, ein ~es Leben führen** to be a fast liver.
(d) *pred* **~/wieder ~ werden** *(Schiff)* to be floated off/refloated; *(fig inf) (Auto etc)* to be/get back on the road; *(Flugzeug)* to be working/working again; *(Mensch)* to be out of the woods/back on top; *(Unternehmen)* to be/get back on its feet; **wieder ~ sein** *(Schiff)* to be afloat again; *(fig inf) (Auto etc)* to be back on the road; *(Flugzeug)* to be working again; *(Mensch) (gesundheitlich)* to be in the pink again *(inf)*; *(finanziell)* to be in funds again; *(Unternehmen)* to be back on its feet.

Flott *nt* **-(e)s,** *no pl* **(a)** *(N Ger)* skin of the milk. **(b)** *(Enten~)* duckweed.

flottbekommen* *vt sep irreg Schiff* to float off; *(fig inf) Auto etc* to get on the road; *Flugzeug* to get working; *Unternehmen* to get on its feet.

Flotte *f* **-, -n** **(a)** *(Naut, Aviat)* fleet. **(b)** *(Tex) (Färbebad)* dye (solution); *(Bleichlösung)* bleach (solution); *(Einweichlösung)* soaking solution.

Flotten-: **~abkommen** *nt* naval treaty; **~basis** *f* naval base; **~chef** *m* commander-in-chief of the fleet; **~kommando** *nt* fleet command; **~parade** *f* naval review; **die ~parade abnehmen** to review the fleet; **~stützpunkt** *m* naval base; **~verband** *m* naval unit.

Flottille [flɔtɪl(j)ə] *f* **-, -n** *(Mil)* flotilla; *(Fischfang~)* fleet.

Flottillen|admiral *m (Mil)* commodore.

flott-: **~kriegen, ~machen** *vt sep siehe* **~bekommen**; **~weg** [-vɛk] *adv (inf)* non-stop; **das geht immer ~weg** there's no hanging about *(inf)*.

Flöz *nt* **-es, -e** *(Min)* seam.

Fluch *m* **-(e)s, ¨-e** curse; *(Schimpfwort auch)* oath ◆ **ein ~ liegt über** *or* **lastet auf diesem Haus** there is a curse on this house, this house lies under a curse; **~ dem Alkohol!** a curse on alcohol!; **das (eben) ist der ~ der bösen Tat** *(prov)* evil begets evil *(Prov)*.

fluchbeladen *adj (liter)* accursed, cursed.

fluchen [1] *vi (Flüche ausstoßen, schimpfen)* to curse (and swear) ◆ **auf** *or* **über jdn/etw ~** to curse sb/sth.
[2] *vt (old)* **jdm/etw ~** to curse sb/sth.

⚠: Informationen zur Rechtschreibreform im Anhang

Flucht *f* **-, -en (a)** (*Fliehen*) flight; (*geglückt auch*) escape ◆ **die ~ ergreifen** to take flight, to flee; (*erfolgreich auch*) to (make one's) escape; **ihm glückte die ~** he escaped, he succeeded in escaping; **auf der ~ sein** to be fleeing; (*Gesetzesbrecher*) to be on the run; **jdn/etw in die ~ treiben** *or* **jagen** *or* **schlagen** to put sb/sth to flight; **in wilder** *or* **heilloser ~ davonjagen** to stampede; **jdm zur ~ verhelfen** to help sb to escape; **auf der ~ erschossen werden** to be shot while attempting to escape; **sein Heil in der ~ suchen** (*geh*) to take refuge in flight; **die ~ nach vorn antreten** to take the bull by the horns; **die ~ in die Anonymität/die Krankheit/den Trotz/die Öffentlichkeit antreten** to take refuge in anonymity/illness/to resort to defiance/publicity; **die ~ nach Ägypten** (*Bibl*) the flight into Egypt.
(b) (*Hunt*) leap, bound ◆ **eine ~ machen** to make a leap *or* bound.
(c) (*Häuser~*) row; (*~linie*) alignment.
(d) (*Zimmer~*) suite.

Flucht-: f~artig *adj* hasty, hurried, precipitate (*form*); **in f~artiger Eile** in great haste; **~auto** *nt* escape car; (*von Gesetzesbrecher*) getaway car; **~burg** *f* refuge.

fluchten (*Archit*) **1** *vt* to align.
2 *vi* to be aligned.

flüchten *vi* **(a)** *aux sein* (*davonlaufen*) to flee; (*erfolgreich auch*) to escape ◆ **aus dem Land/Südafrika ~** to flee the country/from South Africa; **vor der Wirklichkeit ~** to escape reality; **sich in Alkohol ~** to take refuge in alcohol; **sich in Ausreden ~** to resort to excuses.
(b) *auch vr* (*vi: aux sein*) (*Schutz suchen*) to take refuge.

Flucht-: ~fahrzeug *nt* escape vehicle; (*von Gesetzesbrecher*) getaway vehicle; **~gefahr** *f* risk of escape *or* an escape attempt; **~geschwindigkeit** *f* (*Phys*) escape velocity; **~helfer** *m* escape helper; **~hilfe** *f* escape aid; **~hilfe leisten** to aid an escape; **~hilfeorganisation** *f* escape organization.

flüchtig *adj* **(a)** (*geflüchtet*) fugitive ◆ **~ sein** to be still at large; **ein ~er Verbrecher** a criminal who hasn't been caught.
(b) (*kurz, schnell vorübergehend*) fleeting, brief; *Gruß* brief ◆ **~ erwähnen** to mention in passing.
(c) (*oberflächlich*) cursory, sketchy ◆ **etw ~ lesen** to glance *or* skim through sth; **~ arbeiten** to work hurriedly *or* hastily; **jdn ~ kennen** to have met sb briefly.
(d) (*Chem*) volatile.
(e) (*Comput*) **~er Speicher** volatile memory.

Flüchtige(r) *mf decl as adj* fugitive; (*Ausbrecher*) escaper.

Flüchtigkeit *f* **(a)** (*Kürze*) briefness, brevity. **(b)** (*Oberflächlichkeit*) cursoriness, sketchiness; (*von Arbeit*) hastiness; (*~sfehler*) careless mistake. **(c)** (*Vergänglichkeit*) fleetingness, briefness. **(d)** (*Chem*) volatility.

Flüchtigkeitsfehler *m* careless mistake; (*beim Schreiben auch*) slip of the pen.

Flüchtling *m* refugee.

Flüchtlings- *in cpds* refugee; *siehe auch* **Vertriebenen-**; **~ausweis** *m* refugee's identity card; **~hilfe** *f* aid to refugees; (*inf: ~organisation*) (refugee) relief agency; **~lager** *nt* refugee camp.

Flucht-: ~linie *f* alignment; (*einer Straße*) building line; **~punkt** *m* vanishing point; **~tunnel** *m* escape tunnel; **~verdacht** *m* **bei ~verdacht** if an attempt to abscond is thought likely; **es besteht ~verdacht** there are grounds for suspecting that he/she *etc* will try to abscond; **f~verdächtig** *adj* suspected of planning to abscond; **~versuch** *m* escape attempt *or* bid; **~weg** *m* escape route.

fluchwürdig *adj* (*liter*) dastardly (*old*) *no adv*, execrable (*liter*).

Flug *m* **-(e)s, ¨-e** (*alle Bedeutungen*) flight; (*Ski~*) jump ◆ **im ~(e)** in the air; (*bei Vögeln auch*) in flight, on the wing; **einen ~ antreten** to take off (*nach* for); **einen ~ stornieren** to cancel a booking; **der ~ zum Mond** (*Fliegen*) travel to the moon; (*spezifische Fahrt*) the moon flight *or* trip; **wie im ~(e)** (*fig*) in a twinkling *or* flash.

Flugabwehr *f* air defence.

Flugabwehr-: ~kanone *f* anti-aircraft gun; **~körper** *m* air defence missile; **~rakete** *f* anti-aircraft missile.

Flug-: ~angel *f* fly rod; **~angst** *f* fear of flying; **~asche** *f* flying ashes *pl*; **~aufkommen** *nt* air traffic; **~bahn** *f* (*von Vogel, Flugzeug*) flight path; (*von Rakete, Satelliten auch, von Kugel*) trajectory; (*Kreisbahn*) orbit; **~ball** *m* (*Sport*) high ball; (*Tennis etc*) volley; **~basis** *f* (*Mil*) air base; **~begleiter(in *f*)** *m* steward/stewardess *or* air hostess; **~begleitpersonal** *nt* cabin crew; **~benzin** *nt* aviation fuel; **~bereich** *m* operational range *no pl*; **f~bereit** *adj* ready for take-off; **~betrieb** *m* air traffic; **den ~betrieb auf einem Flughafen einstellen** to close an airport; **~bewegungen** *pl* aircraft movements *pl*; **~bild** *nt* (*Zool*) flight silhouette.

Flugblatt *nt* leaflet; (*als Werbung auch*) handbill.

Flugblatt-: ~aktion *f* leafletting campaign; **~verteiler** *m* distributor of leaflets/handbills.

Flug-: ~boot *nt* flying boat; **~buch** *nt* logbook; **~(daten)schreiber** *m* flight recorder; **~dauer** *f* flying time; **~deck** *nt* flight deck; **~dichte** *f* density of air traffic; **~dienst** *m* air traffic services *pl*; (*~verkehr*) air service; **~drachen** *m* hang-glider; **~echse** *f siehe* **~saurier**; **~eigenschaft** *f usu pl* handling characteristic.

Flügel *m* **-s, - (a)** (*Anat, Aviat*) wing ◆ **mit den ~n schlagen** to beat *or* flap its wings; **einem Vogel/jdm die ~ stutzen** *or* **beschneiden** to clip a bird's/sb's wings; **die Hoffnung/der Gedanke verlieh ihm ~** (*liter*) hope/the thought lent him wings (*liter*).
(b) (*von Hubschrauber, Ventilator*) blade; (*Propeller~ auch*) vane; (*Windmühlen~*) sail, vane.
(c) (*Altar~*) sidepiece, wing; (*Fenster~*) casement (*form*), side; (*Tür~*) door (*of double doors*), leaf (*form*); (*Lungen~*) lung; (*Nasen~*) nostril.
(d) (*Mil, Sport: Teil einer Truppe*) wing ◆ **über den/auf dem linken ~ angreifen** to attack up/on the left wing.
(e) (*Gebäude~*) wing.
(f) (*Konzert~*) grand piano, grand (*inf*) ◆ **auf dem ~ spielen** to play the piano; **am ~:** ... at *or* on the piano: ...

Flügel-: ~adjutant *m* (*Mil, Hist*) aide-de-camp (*often of the rank of general*); **~altar** *m* winged altar; **~ärmel** *m* hanging sleeve; **~fenster** *nt* casement window; (*Verandafenster*) French window; **f~förmig** *adj* wing-shaped; **~haube** *f* pinner, cap with upturned lappets; **~horn** *nt* (*Mus*) flugelhorn; **~kampf** *m* (*Pol*) factional dispute, party in-fighting; **~klappe** *f* (*Aviat*) wing flap, aileron (*spec*); **f~lahm** *adj* with injured wings/an injured wing; (*fig*) *Industrie etc* ailing; *Mensch* feeble; **f~lahm sein** (*lit*) to have an injured wing/its wings injured; **einen Vogel f~lahm schießen** to wing a bird; **f~los** *adj* wingless; **~mann** *m* (*Ftbl*) wing forward, winger; (*Mil*) flank man; (*Pol*) person on the wing of a party; **~mutter** *f* wing *or* butterfly nut; **~rad** *nt* (*Rail fig*) winged wheel (*symbol of the West German railways*); ⚠**~roß** *nt* (*Myth*) winged horse; **~schlag** *m* (*liter*) beat of its wings; **den ~schlag der Zeit spüren** (*liter*) to feel the life-pulse of history; **f~schlagend** *adj* beating its wings; **~schraube** *f* **(a)** wing bolt; **(b)** *siehe* **~mutter**; **~spanne, ~spannweite** *f* wing span; **~stürmer** *m* (*Sport*) wing forward; **~tür** *f* leaved door (*form*); (*mit zwei Flügeln*) double door; (*Verandatür*) French door.

Flug-: ~entfernung *f* air *or* flying distance; **~erfahrung** *f* flying experience; **f~erprobt** *adj* flight-tested; **f~fähig** *adj* able to fly; *Flugzeug* (*in Ordnung*) airworthy; **~fähigkeit** *f* ability to fly; airworthiness; **~feld** *nt* airfield; **~frequenz** *f* frequency of flights; **~fuchs** *m* (Indian) flying fox; **~funk** *m* air radio.

Fluggast *m* (airline) passenger.

Fluggast-: ~kontrolle *f* airport security check; **~raum** *m* passenger cabin.

flügge *adj* fully-fledged; (*fig*) *Jugendlicher* independent ◆ **~ werden** (*lit*) to be able to fly; (*fig*) to leave the nest.

Flug-: ~gelände *nt* airfield; **~gepäck** *nt* baggage; **erlaubtes ~gepäck 15 Kilo** baggage allowance 15 kilos; **~gerät** *nt, no pl* aircraft; **~geschwindigkeit** *f* (*von Vögeln, Insekten*) speed of flight; (*von Flugzeug*) flying speed; (*von Rakete, Geschoß, Ball*) velocity; **~gesellschaft** *f* airline (company); **~gewicht** *nt* all-up weight.

Flughafen *m* airport; (*Mil*) aerodrome (*Brit*), airdrome (*US*) ◆ **der ~ Hamburg** Hamburg airport; **auf dem ~** at the airport.

Flughafen-: ~bus *m* airport bus; **~feuerwehr** *f* airport fire fighting service; **~gebühr** *f* airport charges *pl*; **~gelände** *nt* airport grounds *pl*; **~steuer** *f* airport tax.

Flug-: ~höhe *f* flying height (*auch Orn*); altitude; **unsere** *or* **die ~höhe beträgt 10.000 Meter** we are flying at an altitude of 10,000 metres; **die ~höhe erreichen** to reach one's cruising altitude *or* flying height; **~hörnchen** *nt* flying squirrel; **~hund** *m* flying fox; **~ingenieur** *m* flight engineer; **~kanzel** *f* cockpit; **~kapitän** *m* captain (of an/the aircraft); **~karte** *f* **(a)** (*Luftfahrtkarte*) flight *or* aviation chart; **(b)** (*rare: ~schein*) plane ticket; **~kilometer** *m* (air) kilometre; **~körper** *m* flying object; **~korridor** *m siehe* **Luftkorridor**; **~kunst** *f* airmanship, flying skill; **~künste** *pl* flying skills *pl*; (*Kunststücke*) aerobatic feats *pl*; **~lärm** *m* aircraft noise; **~lage** *f* flying position *or* attitude (*spec*); **~lehrer** *m* flying instructor; **~leitsystem** *nt* flight control system; **~leitung** *f* air-traffic *or* flight control; **~linie** *f* **(a)** (*Strecke*) airway, air route; **(b)** *siehe* **~gesellschaft**; **~loch** *nt* entrance hole; (*bei Bienenstock*) (hive) entrance; **~lotse** *m* air-traffic *or* flight controller; **~manöver** *nt* aerial manoeuvre; **~meldedienst** *m* (*Mil*) enemy aircraft warning service; **~meteorologie** *f* aeronautical meteorology; **~minute** *f* **nach fünf ~minuten** after flying for five minutes; **dreißig ~minuten von hier** thirty minutes by air from here; **~mission** *f* space mission; **~motor** *m* aircraft engine; **~netz** *nt* network of air routes; **~nummer** *f* flight number; **~objekt** *nt*: **ein unbekanntes ~objekt** an unidentified flying object, a UFO; **~ordnung** *f* flight formation; **~passagier** *m siehe* **~gast**; **~personal** *nt* flight personnel *pl*; **~plan** *m* flight schedule; **~platz** *m* airfield; (*größer*) airport; **~preis** *m* air fare; **~prüfung** *f* examination for one's pilot's licence; **~reise** *f* flight; **eine ~reise machen** to travel by air; **~reisende(r)** *mf* (airline) passenger; **~richtung** *f* direction of flight; **die ~richtung ändern** to change one's flight course; **~route** *f* air-route.

flugs [flʊks] *adv* (*dated*) without delay, speedily.

Flug-: ~sand *m* drifting sand; **~saurier** *m* pterodactyl; **die ~saurier** the pterosauria; **~schanze** *f* (*Sport*) ski-jump; **~schein** *m* **(a)** pilot's licence; **(b)** (*~karte*) plane *or* air ticket; **~schneise** *f* flight path; **~schreiber** *m siehe* **~(daten)schreiber**; **~schrift** *f* pamphlet; **~schüler** *m* trainee pilot; **~sicherheit** *f* air safety; **~sicherung** *f* air traffic control; **~simulator** *m* flight simulator; **~sport** *m* flying, aviation; **~staub** *m* flue dust; **~steig** *m* gate; **~strecke** *f* **(a)** flying distance; **eine große ~strecke zurücklegen** to fly a long distance; **(b)** (*Route*) route; **~stunde** *f* **(a)** flying hour; **zehn ~stunden entfernt** ten hours away by air; **(b)** (*Unterricht*) flying lesson; **f~tauglich** *adj Pilot* fit to fly; **~technik** *f* **(a)** aircraft engineering; **(b)** (*~fertigkeit*) flying technique; **f~technisch** *adj* aeronautical; *Bedeutung, Entwicklung, Prinzipien auch* aerotechnical; *Erfahrung, Fehler* flying *attr*; **eine f~technische Ausbildung haben** to have been trained in flying; **f~technisch ist er perfekt** his flying is perfect; **~ticket** *nt* plane ticket; **~touristik** *f* holiday air travel; **f~tüchtig** *adj* airworthy; **~tüchtigkeit** *f* airworthiness; **f~unfähig** *adj* unable to fly; *Flugzeug* (*nicht in Ordnung*) unairworthy; **f~untauglich** *adj* unfit to fly; **~unterbrechung** *f* stop; (*mit Übernachtung* *auch*) stopover; **f~untüchtig** *adj* unairworthy; **~veranstaltung** *f* air display *or* show; **~verbindung** *f* air connection; **es gibt auch eine ~verbindung** there are flights there too; **~verbot** *nt* flying ban; **nachts besteht ~verbot auf dem Flughafen** the airport is closed to air traffic at night; **ein ~verbot erlassen** to ground; (*über bestimmten Gebieten*) to ban from flying; **~verkehr** *m* air traffic; **~versuch** *m* attempt to fly *or* at flight; **~warndienst** *m siehe* **~meldedienst; ~wesen** *nt, no pl* aviation *no art*; (*mit Ballons etc*) aeronautics *sing no art*; **~wetter** *nt* flying weather; **~zeit** *f* flying time; **~zettel** *m* (*Aus*) *siehe* **~blatt.**

Flugzeug *nt* **-(e)s, -e** plane, aircraft, aeroplane (*Brit*), airplane (*US*); (*Düsen~ auch*) jet; (*Segel~*) glider ◆ **im** *or* **mit dem** *or* **per ~** by air *or* plane; **ein ~ der Lufthansa** a Lufthansa plane/jet.

Flugzeug- *in cpds* aircraft; **~absturz** *m* plane *or* air crash; **~abwehr** *f* (*Mil*) *siehe* **Flugabwehr; ~bau** *m* aircraft construction *no art*; **~besatzung** *f* air *or* plane crew; **~entführer** *m* (aircraft) hijacker, skyjacker; **~entführung** *f* (aircraft) hijacking, skyjacking; **~führer** *m* (aircraft) pilot; **~halle** *f* (aircraft) hangar; **~katastrophe** *f* air disaster; **~modell** *nt* model plane; **~park** *m* fleet of aircraft; **~rumpf** *m* fuselage; **~schleuder** *f* catapult; **~start** *m* aeroplane *or* airplane (*US*) take-off; **~träger** *m* aircraft carrier; **~typ** *m* model of aircraft; **~unglück** *nt* plane *or* air crash; **~verband** *m* (*Mil*) aircraft formation; **~wrack** *nt* **ein ~wrack/zwei ~wracks** the wreckage of a plane/two planes.

Flugziel *nt* destination.

Fluidum *nt* **-s, Fluida (a)** (*fig*) aura; (*von Städten, Orten*) atmosphere ◆ **von ihr ging ein geheimnisvolles ~ aus** she was surrounded by an aura of mystery.
(b) (*Chem*) fluid.

Fluktuation *f* fluctuation (*gen* in).

fluktuieren* *vi* to fluctuate.

Flunder *f* **-, -n** flounder ◆ **da war ich platt wie eine ~** (*inf*) you could have knocked me down with a feather (*inf*).

Flunkerei *f* (*inf*) **(a)** (*no pl: Flunkern*) story-telling. **(b)** (*kleine Lüge*) story.

Flunkerer *m* **-s, -** (*inf*) story-teller.

flunkern (*inf*) [1] *vi* to tell stories.
[2] *vt* to make up.

Flunsch *m or f* **-(e)s, -e** (*inf*) pout ◆ **eine(n) ~ ziehen** *or* **machen** to pout.

Fluor[1] *nt* **-s,** *no pl* (*abbr* **F**) fluorine; (*~verbindung*) fluoride.

Fluor[2] *m* **-s,** *no pl* (*Med*) (vaginal) discharge.

Fluorchlorkohlenwasserstoff *m* chlorofluorocarbon.

Fluoreszenz *f* fluorescence.

Fluoreszenzfarbe *f* luminous paint.

fluoreszieren* *vi* to be luminous, to fluoresce (*form*).

Fluorid *nt* **-(e)s, -e** (*Chem*) fluoride.

Fluorit *m* **-s, -e** *siehe* **Flußspat.**

Fluorkohlenwasserstoff *m* fluorocarbon.

Flur[1] *m* **-(e)s, -e** corridor; (*Haus ~*) hall.

Flur[2] *f* **-, -en** (*liter*) (*unbewaldetes Land*) open fields *pl*; (*Wiese*) meadow, mead (*poet*); (*Agr*) *agricultural land of a community* ◆ **durch Wald/Feld und ~** through woods/fields and meadows; **allein auf weiter ~ stehen** (*fig*) to be out on a limb.

Flurbeleuchtung *f* corridor/hall light/lights *pl*.

Flurbereinigung *f reparcelling of the agricultural land of a community.*

Flurfenster *nt* corridor/hall window.

Flur-: ~form *f layout of the agricultural land of a community*; **~gang** *m siehe* **~umgang.**

Flurgarderobe *f* hall-stand.

Flurlicht *nt* corridor/hall light.

Flur-: ~name *m* field-name; **~schaden** *m damage to an agricultural area*; (*fig*) damage; **~toilette** *f* toilet on the landing; **~tür** *f* door to the corridor, hall door.

Fluse *f* **-, -n** (*N Ger*) bit of fluff; (*Woll~*) bobble ◆ **~n** fluff/bobbles.

⚠ **Fluß** *m* **-sses, ¨sse (a)** (*Gewässer*) river ◆ **am ~** by the river; *Stadt* on the river; **unten am ~** down by the river(side); **den ~ aufwärts/abwärts fahren** to go upstream *or* upriver/downstream *or* downriver.
(b) *no pl* (*Tech: Schmelz~*) molten mass ◆ **im ~ sein** to be molten.
(c) (*kontinuierlicher Verlauf: von Verkehr, Rede, Strom, Elektronen*) flow; (*von Verhandlungen auch*) continuity ◆ **etw in ~** (*acc*) **bringen** to get sth moving *or* going; **etw kommt** *or* **gerät in ~** sth gets underway *or* going; (*sich verändern*) sth moves into a state of flux; **im ~ sein** (*sich verändern*) to be in a state of flux; (*im Gange sein*) to be in progress *or* going on.

⚠ **Fluß-** *in cpds* river; **~aal** *m* common eel; **f~ab(wärts)** *adv* downstream, downriver; **~arm** *m* arm of a/the river; **f~aufwärts** *adv* upstream, upriver; **~bau** *m siehe* **~regelung; ~bett** *nt* riverbed.

⚠ **Flüßchen** *nt dim of* **Fluß (a).**

⚠ **Fluß-: ~diagramm** *nt* flow chart *or* diagram; **~ebene** *f* fluvial plain; **~gebiet** *nt* river basin; **~gefälle** *nt* gradient of a/the river; **~geschiebe** *nt, no pl* silt; **~hafen** *m* river port.

flüssig *adj* **(a)** (*nicht fest*) liquid; *Honig, Lack* runny; (*geschmolzen*) *Glas, Metall auch* molten; *Butter* melted ◆ **~e Nahrung** liquids *pl*, liquid food; **~ ernährt werden** to be fed on liquids; **~ machen** to liquefy; *Glas, Metall, Wachs, Fett* to melt; **~ werden** to turn *or* become liquid, to liquefy; (*Lack*) to become runny; (*Glas, Metall*) to become molten; (*Wachs, Fett*) to melt.
(b) (*fließend*) *Stil, Spiel* flowing, fluid ◆ **~ lesen/schreiben/sprechen** to read/write/talk fluently; **die Polizei meldete ~en Verkehr** the police reported that the traffic was flowing smoothly; **den Verkehr ~ halten** to keep the traffic flowing.
(c) (*verfügbar*) *Geld* available ◆ **~es Vermögen** liquid assets *pl*; **Wertpapiere ~ machen** to convert *or* realize securities; **ich bin im Moment nicht ~** (*inf*) I haven't much money *or* I'm out of funds at the moment; **wenn ich wieder ~ bin** when I'm in funds again.

Flüssiggas *nt* liquid gas.

Flüssigkeit *f* **(a)** (*flüssiger Stoff*) liquid. **(b)** *no pl* (*von Metall*) liquidity; (*von Geldern*) availability; (*von Stil*) fluidity.

Flüssigkeits-: ~aufnahme *f* fluid *or* liquid intake; **~maß** *nt* liquid measure; **~menge** *f* quantity *or* amount of liquid.

Flüssig-: ~kristall *m* liquid crystal; **~kristallanzeige** *f* liquid-crystal display, LCD; ⚠**f~machen** *vt sep* to realize; (*in Geld umwandeln auch*) to convert (into cash).

⚠ **Fluß-: ~krebs** *m* crayfish (*Brit*), crawfish (*US*); **~landschaft** *f* countryside by a/the river; (*Art*) riverscape; **~lauf** *m* course of a/the river; **~mündung** *f* river mouth; (*Gezeiten~*) estuary; **~niederung** *f* fluvial plain; **~nixe** *f* river sprite; **~pferd** *nt* hippopotamus; **~regelung, ~regulierung** *f* river control *no art, no pl*; **~sand** *m* river *or* fluvial sand; **~schiff** *nt* river boat; **~schiffahrt** *f, no pl* river navigation; (*Verkehr*) river traffic; **~spat** *m* fluorspar, fluorite (*US*); **~stahl** *m* ingot steel; **~ufer** *nt* river bank.

Flüster-: ~galerie *f*, **~gewölbe** *nt* whispering gallery; **~laut** *m* whisper.

flüstern *vti* to whisper; (*etwas lauter tuscheln*) to mutter ◆ **jdm etw ins Ohr ~** to whisper sth in sb's ear; **sich ~d unterhalten** to talk in whispers; **miteinander ~** to whisper together; **wer hat da geflüstert?** who was that whispering?; **das kann ich dir ~** (*inf*) take it from me (*inf*); (*Zustimmung heischend auch*) I can tell you (*inf*); **dem werde ich was ~** (*inf*) I'll tell him a thing or two (*inf*).

Flüster-: ~parole *f* rumour, whisper (*inf*); **~propaganda** *f* underground rumours *pl*; **~stimme** *f* whisper; **mit ~stimme sprechen** to talk in a whisper *or* in whispers; **~ton** *m* whisper; **sich im ~ton unterhalten** to talk in whispers; **~tüte** *f* (*hum inf*) megaphone.

Flut *f* **-, -en (a)** (*ansteigender Wasserstand*) incoming *or* flood tide; (*angestiegener Wasserstand*) high tide ◆ **es ist ~** the tide is coming in; it's high tide, the tide's in; **die ~ kommt** *or* **steigt** (*form*) the tide's coming in *or* rising; **bei ~ baden/einlaufen** to swim when the tide is coming in/to come in on the tide; to swim/come in at high tide; **mit der ~** with the tide *or* flood tide (*spec*); **die ~ tritt um 16[30] ein** the tide starts to come in *or* turns at 4.30 p.m.; **die ~ geht zurück** the tide has started to go out *or* has turned; *siehe* **Ebbe.**
(b) *usu pl* (*Wassermasse*) waters *pl* ◆ **sich in die kühlen ~en stürzen** (*hum*) to plunge into the water.
(c) (*fig: Menge*) flood ◆ **eine ~ von Tränen** floods of tears.

fluten [1] *vi aux sein* (*geh*) (*Wasser, Licht*) to flood, to stream, to pour; (*Verkehr*) to stream, to pour; (*Musik*) to flood, to pour ◆ **~des Licht** streaming light.
[2] *vt* (*Naut*) to flood.

Flut-: ~hafen *m* tidal harbour; **~katastrophe** *f* flood disaster; **~kraftwerk** *nt siehe* **Gezeitenkraftwerk; ~licht** *nt* floodlight; **~lichtspiel** *nt* match played by floodlight, floodlit match.

flutschen *vi* (*N Ger*) **(a)** *aux sein* (*rutschen*) to slide. **(b)** (*funktionieren*) to go smoothly *or* well *or* swimmingly (*dated inf*).

Flut-: ~tor *nt* floodgate; **~ventil** *nt* antiflood valve; **~welle** *f* tidal wave.

fl.W. *abbr of* **fließendes Wasser.**

focht *pret of* **fechten.**

Fock *f* **-, -en** (*Naut*) foresail.

Fock-: ~mast *m* foremast; **~rah(e)** *f* foreyard; **~segel** *nt siehe* **Fock.**

föderal *adj siehe* **föderativ.**

Föderalismus *m* federalism.

Föderalist(in *f*) *m* **-en, -en** federalist.

föderalistisch *adj* federalist.

Föderation *f* federation.

föderativ *adj* federal.

föderieren* *vr* to federate ◆ **föderierte Staaten** federated states.

fohlen *vi* to foal.

Fohlen *nt* **-s, -** foal; (*männliches Pferd auch*) colt; (*weibliches Pferd auch*) filly.

Föhn *m* **-(e)s, -e** foehn, föhn ◆ **wir haben ~** the foehn is blowing.

föhnig *adj* foehn *attr* ◆ **es ist ~** there's a foehn (wind).

Föhre *f* **-, -n** Scots pine (tree).

fokal *adj* focal.

Fokus *m* **-, -se** focus.

fokussieren* *vti* to focus.

Folge *f* **-, -n (a)** (*Reihen~*) order; (*Aufeinander~*) succession; (*zusammengehörige Reihe, Math*) sequence; (*Cards*) run, sequence; (*Lieferung einer Zeitschrift*) issue; (*Fortsetzung*) instalment; (*TV, Rad*) episode; (*Serie*) series ◆ **in chronologischer/zwangloser ~** in chronological/no particular order; **in rascher/dichter ~** in rapid *or* quick/close succession; **Musik in bunter ~** a musical potpourri; **in der** *or* **für die ~** (*form*) in future.
(b) (*Ergebnis*) consequence; (*unmittelbare ~*) result; (*Auswirkung*) effect ◆ **als ~ davon** in consequence, as a result (of that); **dies hatte zur ~, daß ...** the consequence *or* result of this was that ...; **dies hatte seine Entlassung zur ~** this resulted in his dismissal *or* in his being dismissed; **bedenke die ~n!** think of the consequences!; **die ~n werden nicht ausbleiben** there will be repercussions; **die ~n für den Tourismus** the effect on *or* the consequences for tourism; **für die ~n aufkommen** to take the consequences; **an den ~n eines Unfalls/einer Krankheit sterben** to die as a result of an accident/illness; **das wird ~n haben** that will have serious consequences; **ohne ~n bleiben** to have no consequences; **ihr Verhältnis blieb nicht ohne ~n** (*euph*) their relationship was not exactly unfruitful.
(c) (*form*) **einem Befehl/einer Einladung ~ leisten** to comply with *or* obey an

order/to accept an invitation.

Folge-: ~einrichtung *f* facility *or* utility (*US*) for the community; **~erscheinung** *f* result, consequence; **~kosten** *pl* subsequent costs *pl*; **~lasten** *pl* resultant costs *pl*.

folgen *vi aux sein* **(a)** to follow (*jdm/einer Sache* sb/sth) ◆ **auf etw** (*acc*) **~** to follow sth, to come after sth; **auf jdn (im Rang) ~** to come *or* rank after sb; **~ Sie mir (bitte/unauffällig)!** come with me please; **es folgt nun** *or* **nun folgt ein Konzert** we now have a concert, a concert now follows; **... dann ~ die Meldungen im einzelnen** ... followed by the news in detail; **dem** (*liter*) *or* **auf den Sommer folgt der Herbst** summer is followed by autumn, autumn follows summer; **Fortsetzung folgt** (to be) continued; **wie folgt** as follows; *siehe* **Tod**.
(b) (*verstehen*) to follow (*jdm/einer Sache* sb/sth) ◆ **können Sie mir ~?** are you with me? (*inf*), do you follow (me)?
(c) (*gehorchen*) to do as *or* what one is told ◆ **einem Befehl/einer Anordnung~** to follow an order/instruction; **jdm ~** (*inf*) to do what sb tells one.
(d) *+dat* (*sich richten nach*) *einer Mode, einem Vorschlag* to follow; *jdm* to agree with, to go along with (*inf*).
(e) (*hervorgehen*) to follow (*aus* from) ◆ **was folgt daraus für die Zukunft?** what are the consequences of this for the future?

folgend *adj* following ◆ **~es** the following; **er schreibt ~es** *or* **das F~e** he writes (as follows *or* the following); **im ~en** in the following; (*schriftlich auch*) below; **es handelt sich um ~es** it's like this; (*schriftlich*) it concerns the following.

folgendermaßen, folgenderweise (*rare*) *adv* like this, as follows ◆ **wir werden das ~ machen** we'll do it like this *or* in the following way.

Folgen-: f~los *adj* without consequences; (*wirkungslos*) ineffective; **f~los bleiben** not to have any consequences; to be ineffective; **das konnte nicht f~los bleiben** that was bound to have serious consequences/could not fail to be effective; **f~reich** *adj* (*bedeutsam*) momentous; (*f~schwer*) serious; (*wirkungsvoll*) effective; **f~schwer** *adj* serious; **die Maßnahme erwies sich als f~schwer** the measure had serious consequences; **~schwere** *f* seriousness.

Folge-: ~problem *nt* resultant problem; **die ~probleme einer Sache** (*gen*) the problems arising from *or* out of sth; **f~recht** (*rare*), **f~richtig** *adj* (logically) consistent; **das einzig ~richtige in dieser Situation** the only logical *or* consistent thing to do in this situation; **~richtigkeit** *f* logical consistency.

folgern [1] *vti* to conclude ◆ **aus diesem Brief läßt sich ~, daß** ... it can be concluded *or* we can conclude from this letter that ...
[2] *vi* to draw a/the conclusion ◆ **logisch ~ lernen** to learn to think logically.

Folgerung *f* conclusion ◆ **daraus ergibt sich die ~, daß** ... from this it can be concluded that ...

Folge-: ~satz *m* (*Gram*) consecutive clause; **~tonhorn** *nt* (*Aus*) *siehe* **Martinshorn**; **f~widrig** *adj* (*geh*) logically inconsistent; **~widrigkeit** *f* (*geh*) logical inconsistency; **~zeit** *f* following period, period following.

folglich *adv, conj* consequently, therefore.

folgsam *adj* obedient.

Folgsamkeit *f* obedience.

Foliant *m* folio (volume); (*dicker Band*) tome.

Folie ['fo:liə] *f* **(a)** (*Plastik~*) film; (*für Projektor*) transparency; (*Metall~, Typ, Cook*) foil; (*Schicht*) layer of film/foil ◆ **eine ~ aus Kupfer** a thin layer of copper. **(b)** (*fig: Hintergrund*) background ◆ **etw als ~ benutzen** to use sth as a model.

Folien ['fo:liən] *pl of* **Folie, Folio**.

Folio *nt* **-s, -s** *or* **Folien** folio.

Folklore *f* **-,** *no pl* folklore; (*Volksmusik*) folk music.

Folklorist(in *f*) *m* folklorist.

folkloristisch *adj* folkloric; *Kleidung* ethnic.

Folksänger *m* folk singer.

Follikel *m* **-s, -** follicle.

Follikelsprung *m* ovulation.

Folter *f* **-, -n** **(a)** (*lit, fig*) torture; (*fig auch*) torment ◆ **die ~ anwenden** to use torture. **(b)** (*old: ~bank*) rack ◆ **jdn auf die ~ spannen** (*fig*) to keep sb on tenterhooks, to keep sb in an agony of suspense.

Folterbank *f* rack.

Folterer *m* **-s, -** torturer.

Folter-: ~gerät, ~instrument *nt* instrument of torture; **~kammer** *f*, **~keller** *m* torture chamber; **~knecht** *m* torturer; **~methode** *f* method of torture.

foltern [1] *vt* to torture; (*quälen auch*) to torment ◆ **jdn ~ lassen** to have sb tortured.
[2] *vi* to use torture.

Folterqual *f* (*lit*) agony of torture; (*fig*) agony of torment.

Folterung *f* torture.

Folterwerkzeug *nt* instrument of torture.

⚠ **Fön** ® *m* **-(e)s, -e** hair-dryer.

Fond [fõ:] *m* **-s, -s** **(a)** (*geh: Wagen~*) back, rear. **(b)** (*Hintergrund*) (*Art*) background; (*Tex*) (back)ground ◆ **im ~ der Bühne** (*Theat*) at the back of the stage. **(c)** (*geh: Basis*) foundation (*zu* for). **(d)** (*Cook: Fleischsaft*) meat juices *pl*.

Fondant [fõ'dã:] *m or* (*Aus*) *nt* **-s, -s** (*Cook*) fondant.

Fonds [fõ:] *m* **-, -** **(a)** (*Geldreserve, fig geh*) fund ◆ **keinen ~ für etw haben** to have no funds for sth. **(b)** (*Fin: Schuldverschreibung*) government bond.

Fonds- [fõ:]: (*Fin*) **~börse** *f*, **~geschäft** *nt* market of government bonds.

Fondue [fõ'dy:] *nt* **-s, -s** *or f* **-, -s** fondue.

⚠ **fönen** *vt* to dry.

Fono- *siehe* **Phono-**.

Fontäne *f* **-, -n** jet, fount (*poet*); (*geh: Springbrunnen*) fountain, fount (*poet*).

Fontanelle *f* **-, -n** (*Anat*) fontanelle.

foppen *vt* (*inf*) **jdn ~** to make a fool of sb; (*necken*) to pull sb's leg (*inf*); **er fühlte sich gefoppt** he felt he'd been made a fool of.

Fopperei *f* (*inf*) leg-pulling *no pl* (*inf*).

Fora (*Hist*) *pl of* **Forum**.

forcieren* [fɔr'si:rən] *vt* to push; *Entwicklung auch, Tempo* to force; *Konsum, Produktion* to push *or* force up ◆ **seine Anstrengungen ~** to increase one's efforts.

forciert [fɔr'si:ɐt] *adj* forced.

Förde *f* **-, -n** firth (*esp Scot*) *narrow coastal inlet.*

Förder-: ~anlage *f* conveyor; **~band** *nt* conveyor belt.

Förderbetrag *m* (*Univ*) grant.

Förderbetrieb *m* (*Min*) production ◆ **den ~ aufnehmen** to start production.

Förderer *m* **-s, -, Förderin** *f* sponsor; (*Gönner*) patron.

Förder-: ~klasse *f* (*Sch*) special class; **~kohle** *f* run of mine (coal), through-and-through coal (*Brit*); **~korb** *m* mine cage; **~kurs(us)** *m* (*Sch*) special classes *pl*; **~land** *nt* producing country; **~leistung** *f* output.

förderlich *adj* beneficial (*dat* to) ◆ **guten Beziehungen/jds Gesundung/der Krebsbekämpfung ~ sein** to be conducive to *or* to promote good relations/to aid sb's recovery/to contribute to *or* to help in the fight against cancer; **ein der Weiterbildung ~er Kursus** a course which contributes to one's further education.

Fördermaschine *f* winding engine.

fordern [1] *vt* **(a)** (*verlangen*) to demand; *Preis* to ask; (*in Appell, Aufrufen etc, erfordern*) to call for; (*Anspruch erheben auf*) *Entschädigung, Lohnerhöhung* to claim ◆ **viel/zuviel von jdm ~** to ask *or* demand a lot/too much of sb, to make too many demands on sb; *siehe* **Rechenschaft**.
(b) (*fig: kosten*) *Menschenleben, Opfer* to claim.
(c) (*lit, fig: herausfordern*) to challenge ◆ **er ist noch nie im Leben richtig gefordert worden** he has never been faced with a real challenge.
(d) (*Sport*) to make demands on; (*das Äußerste abverlangen*) to stretch.
[2] *vi* to make demands ◆ **er fordert nur, ohne selbst zu geben** he demands everything as a right, without giving anything himself.

fördern *vt* **(a)** (*unterstützen*) *Handel, Projekt, Entwicklung, Arbeit, Kunst, Wissenschaft* to support; (*propagieren*) to promote; (*finanziell*) *bestimmtes Projekt* to sponsor; *Nachwuchs, Künstler* to support, to help; *jds Talent, Kunstverständnis, Neigung* to encourage, to foster; (*voranbringen*) *Freundschaft, Frieden* to foster, to promote; *Verdauung* to aid; *Appetit* to stimulate; *Untersuchung, Wahrheitsfindung* to further ◆ **jdn beruflich ~** to help sb in his career.
(b) (*steigern*) *Wachstum* to promote; *Umsatz, Absatz, Produktion, Verbrauch auch* to boost, to increase.
(c) *Bodenschätze* to extract; *Kohle, Erz auch* to mine.

fordernd *adj* imperious.

Förder- (*Min*): **~plattform** *f* production platform; **~quote** *f* production level; **~schacht** *m* winding shaft; **~seil** *nt* winding rope; **~sohle** *f* haulage level; **~staaten** *pl* producing countries *pl*.

Förderstufe *f* (*Sch*) *mixed ability class(es) intended to foster the particular talents of each pupil.*

Förderturm *m* (*Min*) winding tower; (*auf Bohrstelle*) derrick.

Forderung *f* **(a)** (*Verlangen*) demand (*nach* for); (*Lohn~, Entschädigungs~ etc*) claim (*nach* for); (*in Appell, Aufrufen etc*) call (*nach* for) ◆ **~en/hohe ~en an jdn stellen** to make demands on sb/to demand a lot of sb; **eine ~ nach etw erheben** to call for sth; **jds ~** *or* **jdm eine ~ erfüllen** to meet sb's demands/claim.
(b) (*geh: Erfordernis*) requirement ◆ **die ~ des Tages sein** to be the/our *etc* number one priority.
(c) (*Comm: Anspruch*) claim (*an +acc, gegen* on, against) ◆ **eine ~ einklagen/eintreiben** *or* **einziehen** to sue for payment of a debt/to collect a debt.
(d) (*Herausforderung*) challenge.

Förderung *f* **(a)** *siehe* **fördern (a)** support; promotion; sponsorship; support, help; encouragement, fostering; fostering, promotion; aid; stimulation; furtherance ◆ **Maßnahmen zur ~ des Fremdenverkehrs** measures to promote tourism *or* for the promotion of tourism.
(b) (*inf: Förderungsbetrag*) grant.
(c) (*Gewinnung*) extraction; (*von Kohle, Erz auch*) mining.

Forderungsabtretung *f* (*Jur*) assignment of a claim.

Förderungs-: ~maßnahme *f* supportive measure; **~maßnahmen** *pl* assistance *sing*; **~mittel** *pl* aid *sing*; **~programm** *nt* aid programme; **f~würdig** *adj* (*unterstützungswürdig*) deserving aid; (*f~berechtigt*) entitled to aid; (*Univ*) eligible for a grant.

Förder|unterricht *m* special instruction.

Förderwagen *m* (*Min*) tram, mine car.

Forelle *f* trout; *siehe* **blau**.

Forellen-: ~teich *m* trout hatchery; **~zucht** *f* trout farming; (*Anlage*) trout farm.

Foren *pl of* **Forum**.

forensisch *adj Medizin* forensic; (*old: rhetorisch*) oratorical.

Forke *f* **-, -n** (*N Ger*) pitch fork.

Form *f* **-, -en** **(a)** form; (*Gestalt, Umriß*) shape ◆ **in ~ von Regen/Steuerermäßigungen** in the form of rain/tax reductions; **in ~ von Dragees/Salbe** in pill/cream form, in the form of pills/cream; **in ~ eines Dreiecks** shaped like *or* in the shape of a triangle; **eine bestimmte ~ haben** to be in a

certain form; to be a certain shape; **seine ~ verlieren/aus der ~ geraten** to lose its shape; (*Kleidung auch*) to go out of shape; **einer Sache** (*dat*) **~ (und Gestalt) geben** (*lit*) to shape sth; (*fig*) to give sth a coherent shape; **Sie müssen Ihr Gesuch in die geeignete ~ kleiden** your application must be in the proper form; **feste ~ annehmen** (*fig*) to take shape; **häßliche/gewalttätige ~en annehmen** (*fig*) to become ugly/violent; **(weibliche) ~en** feminine figure; *siehe* **bringen.**
(b) (*Gestaltung*) form ◆ **~ und Inhalt** form and content.
(c) (*Umgangs~en*) **~en** *pl* manners *pl* ◆ **die ~ wahren** to observe the proprieties; **der ~ wegen** *or* **halber, um der ~ zu genügen** for form's sake, as a matter of form; **in aller ~** formally; **ein Mann mit/ohne ~en** a well-/ill-mannered gentleman.
(d) (*Kondition*) form ◆ **in bester ~ sein** to be in great form *or* shape; **in ~ bleiben/kommen** to keep/get (oneself) fit *or* in condition; (*Sportler*) to keep/get in form; **hoch in ~** in great form *or* shape; **außer ~** out of condition.
(e) (*Gieß~*) mould; (*Kuchen~, Back~*) baking tin (*Brit*) *or* pan (*US*); (*Hut~, Schuh~*) block.

formal *adj* **(a)** formal ◆ **~-ästhetisch** formal aesthetic. **(b)** (*äußerlich*) *Besitzer, Fehler, Grund* technical.

Formal|ausbildung *f* drill.

Form|aldehyd *m* **-s,** *no pl* formaldehyde.

Formalie [-liə] *f usu pl* formality; (*Äußerlichkeit*) technicality.

Formalin ® *nt* **-s** formalin.

formalisieren* *vt* to formalize.

Formalismus *m* formalism *no pl.*

Formalist(in *f*) *m* formalist.

formalistisch *adj* formalistic.

Formalität *f* formality; (*Äußerlichkeit*) technicality ◆ **alle ~en erledigen** to go through all the formalities.

formaliter *adv* (*geh*) in form; (*äußerlich*) technically.

formal-: ~juristisch, ~rechtlich *adj* technical.

Formans *nt* **-, -manzien** [-tsiən] *or* **-zie** [-tsiə] (*Ling*) formative (element).

Format *nt* **-(e)s, -e (a)** (*Größenverhältnis*) size; (*von Zeitung, Papierbogen, Photographie, Buch, Film*) format ◆ **im ~ DIN A4** in A4 (format). **(b)** (*Rang, Persönlichkeit*) stature. **(c)** (*fig: Niveau*) class (*inf*), quality ◆ **internationales ~ haben** to be of international quality.

formatieren* *vti* (*Comput*) to format.

Formatierung *f* (*Comput*) formatting.

Formation *f* formation; (*Gruppe*) group.

Formationsflug *m* (*Mil*) formation flying.

formativ *adj* formative.

Formativ *nt* **-s, -e** (*Ling*) syntactic morpheme; (*Formans*) formative (element).

Form-: f~bar *adj* (*lit, fig*) malleable; **~barkeit** *f* (*lit, fig*) malleability; **f~beständig** *adj* **(a) f~beständig sein** to hold *or* retain its shape; **(b)** (*Sport*) consistent in form; **~blatt** *nt* form; **~brief** *m* form letter; **~eisen** *nt* structural steel.

Formel *f* **-, -n** formula; (*von Eid etc*) wording; (*Floskel*) set phrase ◆ **etw auf eine ~ bringen** to reduce sth to a formula.

Formel-1-Rennen ['fɔrml'|ains-] *nt* formula-one race/racing.

Form|element *nt* (*esp Art*) formal element, element of form.

Formel-: f~haft *adj* **(a)** (*floskelhaft*) *Sprache, Stil* stereotyped; **f~hafte Wendung** set phrase; **f~haft reden** to talk in set phrases; **(b)** (*als ~*) formulistic; **etw f~haft zusammenfassen** to summarize sth in a formula; **~haftigkeit** *f* **(a)** stereotyped nature; (*einer Wendung*) setness; **(b)** formulism.

formell *adj* formal ◆ **als Bürgermeister mußte er den Vorfall ~ verurteilen** as mayor he had to deplore the incident as a matter of form.

Formel-: ~sammlung *f* (*Math*) formulary; **~sprache** *f* system of notation.

formen [1] *vt* to form, to shape; *Charakter auch, Eisen* to mould; *Wörter* to articulate ◆ **schön geformte Glieder** beautifully shaped limbs; **der Krieg hat ihn geformt** the war shaped his character; **~de Kraft** formative power.
[2] *vr* (*lit*) to form *or* shape itself; (*fig*) to mature.

Formen-: ~fülle *f* wealth of forms; **~lehre** *f* morphology; (*Mus*) theory of musical form; **f~reich** *adj* with a great variety *or* wealth of forms; **f~reich sein** to have a great variety *or* wealth of forms; **~reichtum** *m* wealth of forms; **~sinn** *m* sense of *or* feeling for form; **~sprache** *f* (*geh*) use of forms.

Former(in *f*) *m* **-s, -** moulder.

Formerei *f* moulding shop.

Form-: ~fehler *m* irregularity; (*gesellschaftlich*) breach of etiquette; **~fleisch** *nt* pressed meat; **~gebung** *f* (*geh*) design; **~gefühl** *nt* sense of form; **f~gerecht** *adj* (*lit, fig*) correct, proper; **~gestalter** *m* (*geh*) designer; **~gestaltung** *f* design; **f~gewandt** *adj* urbane, suave.

formidabel *adj* (*dated*) formidable.

formieren* [1] *vt Truppen* to draw up; *Kolonne, Zug* to form (into), to fall into; (*bilden*) to form.
[2] *vr* to form up.

Formierung *f* formation; (*Mil: von Truppen*) drawing-up.

-förmig *adj suf* -shaped.

Formkrise *f* (*esp Sport*) loss of form.

förmlich *adj* **(a)** (*formell*) formal. **(b)** (*regelrecht*) positive ◆ **ich hätte ~ weinen können** I really could have cried.

Förmlichkeit *f* **(a)** *no pl* (*Benehmen*) formality. **(b)** *usu pl* (*Äußerlichkeit*) social convention ◆ **bitte keine ~en!** please don't stand on ceremony.

formlos *adj* **(a)** (*ohne Form*) shapeless; *Vortrag, Aufsatz auch* unstructured. **(b)** (*zwanglos*) informal, casual. **(c)** (*Admin*) *Antrag* unaccompanied by a form/any forms.

Formlosigkeit *f* **(a)** (*Gestaltlosigkeit*) shapelessness, lack of shape; (*von Vortrag, Aufsatz auch*) lack of structure. **(b)** (*Zwanglosigkeit*) informality, casualness.

Form-: ~sache *f* matter of form, formality; **f~schön** *adj* elegant, elegantly proportioned; **~schönheit** *f* elegant proportions *pl*, elegance; **~schwäche** *f* poor form; **~schwächen zeigen** to be in *or* on poor form; **~strenge** *f* strict observance of form; **~tief** *nt* loss of form; **sich in einem ~tief befinden** to be badly off form; **f~treu** *adj siehe* **f~beständig.**

Formular *nt* **-s, -e** form.

Formularvorschub *m* (*Comput*) form feed.

formulieren* [1] *vt* to word, to phrase, to formulate ◆ **... wenn ich es mal so ~ darf** ... if I might put it like that.
[2] *vi* to use words skilfully ◆ **..., wie der Kanzler formulierte ...** as the chancellor put it; **wenn ich mal so ~ darf** if I might put it like that.

Formulierung *f* **(a)** *no pl* wording, phrasing, formulation. **(b)** phraseology *no pl* ◆ **eine bestimmte ~** a particular phrase.

Formung *f* **(a)** *no pl* (*Formen*) forming, shaping; (*von Eisen*) moulding; (*von Charakter auch*) moulding, formation; (*von Wörtern*) articulation ◆ **zur ~ muß das Eisen erhitzt werden** the iron has to be heated before it can be moulded. **(b)** (*Form*) shape; (*von Felsen, Dünen etc auch*) formation.

Form-: ~veränderung *f* change in the form; (*einer Sprache*) change in the forms; (*Gestaltveränderung*) change in the shape; **eine kleine ~veränderung vornehmen** to make a small modification; **~verstoß** *m* breach of form; **f~vollendet** *adj* perfect; *Vase etc* perfectly shaped; *Gedicht, Musikstück* perfectly structured; **er verabschiedete/verneigte sich f~vollendet** he took his leave/bowed with perfect elegance; **~vorschrift** *f* formal requirement; **f~widrig** *adj* incorrect; (*Admin, Jur*) irregular; *Urkunde* incorrectly drawn up; **~wille** *m* (*geh*) striving for form.

forsch *adj* dynamic; (*dated: schneidig*) dashing ◆ **eine Sache ~ anpacken** to attack sth energetically *or* with vigour.

forschen [1] *vi* **(a)** (*suchen*) to search (*nach* for), to seek (*liter*) (*nach jdm/etw* sb/sth) ◆ **in alten Papieren ~** to search in old papers; **nach der Wahrheit ~** to seek *or* search after truth. **(b)** (*Forschung betreiben*) to research ◆ **über etw** (*acc*) **~** to research on *or* into sth.
[2] *vt* (*Sw*) *siehe* **erforschen (b).**

forschend *adj* inquiring; (*musternd*) searching.

Forscher *m* **-s, - (a)** (*Wissenschaftler*) researcher; (*in Medizin, Naturwissenschaften*) research scientist. **(b)** (*Forschungsreisender*) explorer.

Forscher-: ~arbeit *f siehe* **Forschungsarbeit; ~blick** *m, no pl* (*geh*) scientific eye; **~geist** *m* (*geh*) inquiring mind; (*Entdekkungsreisender*) explorer; (*Entdeckergeist*) exploratory spirit; **der Mensch in seinem angeborenen ~geist ist bestrebt, ...** man, with his inquiring mind, strives ...

Forscherin *f siehe* **Forscher.**

forscherisch *adj* (*als Wissenschaftler*) research *attr*; (*als Forschungsreisender*) explorative, exploratory ◆ **eine ~e Höchstleistung** a triumph for research/exploration.

forscherlich *adj attr* scholarly.

Forschheit *f siehe* **forsch** brashness; dash.

Forschung *f* **(a)** research *no pl* ◆ **eingehende ~en** intensive research; **ältere/verschiedene ~en** older/various studies; **~en betreiben** to research, to be engaged in research. **(b)** *no pl* (*Wissenschaft*) research *no art* ◆ **~ und Lehre** research and teaching; **~ und Entwicklung** research and development, R&D.

Forschungs- *in cpds* research; **~arbeit** *f, no pl* research; **~aufgabe** *f* research assignment; (*~auftrag eines Wissenschaftlers*) research duty; **~auftrag** *m* research assignment *or* contract; **~ballon** *m* observation balloon; **~bereich** *m siehe* **~gebiet; ~bericht** *m* research report; **~drang** *m* exploratory urge; **~ergebnis** *nt* result of the research; **neueste ~ergebnisse** results of the latest research; **~gebiet** *nt* field of research; **ein/das ~gebiet der Medizin** a/the field of medical research; **~gegenstand** *m* object of research; **~gemeinschaft** *f* research council; **~methode** *f* method of research; **~minister** *m* minister of science; **~ministerium** *nt* ministry of research and development; **~objekt** *nt siehe* **~gegenstand; ~reise** *f* expedition; **~reisende(r)** *mf decl as adj* explorer; **~satellit** *m* research satellite; **~schiff** *nt* research vessel; **~semester** *nt* sabbatical term; **~station** *f* research station; **~stipendium** *nt* research fellowship; **~tätigkeit** *f* research *no indef art*; **~vorhaben** *nt* research project; **~zentrum** *nt* research centre; **~zweig** *m* branch of research.

Forst *m* **-(e)s, -e(n)** forest.

Forst-: ~akademie *f* school of forestry; **~amt** *nt* forestry office; **~assessor** *m graduate forestry official who has completed the probationary period*; **~beamte(r)** *m* forestry official.

forsten *vt* (*form*) to forest.

Förster(in *f*) *m* **-s, -** forest warden *or* ranger (*US*).

Försterei *f* forest warden's *or* ranger's (*US*) lodge.

Forst-: ~frevel *m* (*Jur*) offence against the forest laws; **~haus** *nt* forester's lodge; **~meister** *m* forestry commissioner, chief (forest) ranger (*US*); **~recht** *nt* forest law; **~revier** *nt* forestry district; **~schaden** *m* forest damage *no pl*; **~schädling** *m* forest pest; **~schule** *f* school of forestry; **~verwaltung** *f* forestry commission; **~wesen** *nt* forestry *no art*; **~wirt** *m* graduate in forestry; **~wirtschaft** *f* forestry; **~wissenschaft** *f* forestry.

Forsythie [fɔr'zy:tsiə, *Aus* fɔr'zy:tiə] *f* **-, -n** forsythia.

Fort [foːɐ] *nt* **-s, -s** fort.

fort *adv* **(a)** (*weg*) away; (*verschwunden*) gone ◆ **~ mit ihm/damit!** away with

him/it!, take him/it away!; ... und dann ~! ... and then away with you/we'll get away; etw ist ~ sth has gone *or* disappeared; es war plötzlich ~ it suddenly disappeared; die Katze ist schon seit gestern ~ the cat has been missing since yesterday; er ist ~ he has left *or* gone; (*dial: ist nicht zu Hause*) he isn't here; weit ~ far away, a long way away; von zu Hause ~ away from home; wann sind Sie von zu Hause ~? (*dial*) when did you leave home?; nur ~ von hier! (*geh*) let us begone (*old*); ~ von hier! (*geh*) begone! (*old*), hence! (*old*).
(b) (*weiter*) on ◆ und so ~ and so on, and so forth; das ging immer so weiter und so ~ und so ~ (*inf*) that went on and on and on; in einem ~, ~ und ~ (*old*) incessantly, continually.

fort- *pref in cpd vbs* (*weg*) away; *siehe auch* weg-.

Fort-: **f~ab** (*rare*), **f~an** (*geh*) *adv* from this time on, henceforth (*old, liter*), henceforward (*old*); **f~begeben*** *vr sep irreg* (*geh*) to depart, to leave; sich aus dem Schloß *etc* f~begeben to depart from (*form*) *or* to leave the castle *etc*; **~bestand** *m, no pl* continuance; (*von Staat, Institution*) continued existence; (*von Gattung etc*) survival; **f~bestehen*** *vi sep irreg* to continue; (*Staat, Institution*) to continue in existence; (*Zustand*) to continue (to exist); **f~bewegen*** *sep* [1] *vt* to move away; [2] *vr* to move; **~bewegung** *f, no pl* locomotion; **~bewegungsmittel** *nt* means of locomotion; **f~bilden** *vt sep* jdn/sich f~bilden to continue sb's/one's education; **~bildung** *f, no pl* further education; berufliche ~bildung further vocational training; **~bildungskurs(us)** *m* in-service training course; **f~bleiben** *vi sep irreg aux sein* to stay away; **~bleiben** *nt* **-s,** *no pl* absence; **f~bringen** *vt sep irreg* to take away; (*zur Reparatur, Reinigung etc*) to take in; *Brief, Paket etc* to post; (*zurückbringen*) to take back; (*bewegen*) to move; **~dauer** *f* continuance, continuation; **f~dauern** *vi sep* to continue; **f~dauernd** [1] *adj* continuing; (*in der Vergangenheit*) continued; [2] *adv* constantly, continuously.

forte *adv* (*Mus, Pharm*) forte.

Forte *nt* **-s, -s** *or* **Forti** forte.

Fort-: **f~eilen** *vi sep* (*geh*) to hurry *or* hasten away; **f~entwickeln*** *sep* [1] *vt* to develop; [2] *vr* to develop; **~entwicklung** *f, no pl* development; **f~existieren*** *vi sep siehe* f~bestehen; **f~fahren** *sep* [1] *vi* (a) *aux sein* (*wegfahren*) to go away; (*abfahren*) to leave, to go; (*einen Ausflug machen*) to go out; (b) *aux haben or sein* (*weitermachen*) to continue; f~fahren, etw zu tun to continue doing sth *or* to do sth; in einer Tätigkeit f~fahren to continue with an activity; ich fahre f~ ... as I was about to say ...; [2] *vt* (*wegbringen*) to take away; *Wagen* to drive away; **~fall** *m* discontinuance; **f~fallen** *vi sep irreg aux sein* to cease to exist; (*nicht mehr zutreffend sein*) to cease to apply; (*Zuschuß etc*) to be discontinued *or* stopped; (*abgeschafft werden*) to be abolished; **f~fliegen** *vi sep aux sein* to fly away *or* off; **f~führen** *sep* [1] *vt* (a) (*fortsetzen*) to continue, to carry on; (b) (*wegführen*) to take away; (*zu Fuß, fig*) to lead away; [2] *vi* (*fig*) to lead away; **~führung** *f* continuation; **~gang** *m, no pl* (a) (*Weggang*) departure (*aus* from); bei/nach seinem ~gang when he left/after he had left, on/after his departure; (b) (*Verlauf*) progress; seinen ~gang nehmen to progress; **f~gehen** *vi sep aux sein* (a) to leave; von zu Hause f~gehen to leave home; geh ~/nicht ~! go away/don't go (away)!; (b) *siehe* weitergehen; **f~geschritten** *adj* advanced; zu f~geschrittener Stunde wurden sie fröhlich as the night wore on they got quite merry; er kam zu f~geschrittener Stunde he came at a late hour; **~geschrittenenkurs(us)** *m* advanced course; **~geschrittene(r)** *mf decl as adj* advanced student; **f~gesetzt** *adj* continual, constant, incessant; *Betrug, Steuerhinterziehung* repeated; **f~hin** *adv* (*dated*) from this time on, henceforth (*old, liter*), henceforward (*old*).

Forti *pl of* Forte.

Fortifikation *f* (*old Mil*) fortification.

Fortissimo *nt* **-s, -s** *or* **-tissimi** fortissimo ◆ im ~ spielen to play fortissimo.

Fort-: **f~jagen** *sep* [1] *vt Menschen* to throw out (*aus, von* of); *Tier, Kinder* to chase out (*aus, von* of); [2] *vi aux sein* to race *or* career off; **f~kommen** *vi aux sein* (a) (*wegkommen*) to get away; (*weggebracht werden*) to be taken away; mach, daß du f~kommst! begone! (*old*), be off!; (b) (*abhanden kommen*) to disappear, to vanish; (c) (*vorankommen*) to get on well; im Leben f~kommen to get on in life *or* the world; **~kommen** *nt* (a) (*lit, fig: Weiterkommen*) progress; jdn am ~kommen hindern to hold sb back, to hinder sb's progress; (b) (*Auskommen*) sein ~kommen finden to find a means of earning one's living; **f~können** *vi sep irreg* to be able to get away; **f~lassen** *vt sep irreg* (a) (*weggehen lassen*) jdn f~lassen to let sb go, to allow sb to go; (b) (*auslassen*) to leave out, to omit; **f~laufen** *vi sep irreg aux sein* to run away; der Hund/meine Freundin ist mir f~gelaufen the dog has run away from me/my girlfriend has (gone off and) left me; **f~laufend** *adj Handlung* ongoing *no adv*; *Erscheinen* serial *attr*; *Zahlungen* regular; (*andauernd*) continual; die Handlung geht f~laufend weiter the storyline unfolds steadily; f~laufend numeriert *Geldscheine, Motoren* serially numbered; *Bücher, Zeitschriften* consecutively paginated; **f~leben** *vi sep* (*liter*) to live on; **f~loben** *vt* jdn auf einen Posten f~loben to kick sb upstairs; **f~locken** *vt sep* to lure away; **f~machen** *vr sep* (*inf*) to clear out *or* off (*inf*); **f~müssen** *vi sep irreg* to have to go *or* leave; (*ausgehen müssen*) to have to go out; (*Brief*) to have to go (off); **f~nehmen** *vt sep irreg* to take away (*jdm* from sb); **f~pflanzen** *vr sep* (*Mensch*) to reproduce; (*Pflanzen auch*) to propagate (itself); (*Schall, Wellen, Licht*) to travel, to be transmitted; (*Gerücht*) to spread.

Fortpflanzung *f* **-,** *no pl* reproduction; (*von Pflanzen*) propagation.

Fortpflanzungs-: **f~fähig** *adj* capable of reproduction; *Pflanze* capable of propagation; **~geschwindigkeit** *f* (*Phys*) speed of propagation; **~organ** *nt* reproductive organ; **~trieb** *m* reproductive instinct; **f~unfähig** *adj* incapable of reproduction; *Pflanze* incapable of propagation.

⚠: for details of spelling reform, see supplement

Fort-: **f~räumen** *vt sep* (*lit, fig*) to clear away; **f~reisen** *vi sep aux sein* to go away; **f~reißen** *vt sep irreg* to snatch *or* tear away; (*Menge, Flut, Strom*) to sweep *or* carry away; (*fig*) to carry away; jdn/etw mit sich f~reißen (*lit*) to carry *or* sweep sb/sth along; **f~rennen** *vi sep irreg aux sein* to race *or* tear (*inf*) off *or* away; **f~rücken** *sep* [1] *vt* to move away; [2] *vi aux sein* to move away; **~satz** *m* (*Anat*) process; **f~schaffen** *vt sep* to remove; **f~scheren** *vr sep* (*inf*) to clear off (*aus* out of) *or* out (*aus* of) (*inf*); **f~schicken** *vt sep* to send away; *Brief etc* to send off; **f~schleppen** *sep* [1] *vt* to drag away; (*fig*) *Fehler, Traditionen* to perpetuate; [2] *vr* to drag oneself along; (*fig*) (*Fehler, Traditionen*) to be perpetuated; (*Beziehung, Unterhaltung*) to limp along; **f~schreiben** *vt sep irreg* (a) *Statistik etc* to extrapolate; (b) (*weiterführend aktualisieren*) *Programm etc* to continue; **~schreibung** *f siehe vt* extrapolation; continuation; **f~schreiten** *vi sep irreg aux sein* (*vorwärtsschreiten*) to progress; (*weitergehen*) to continue; (*Entwicklung, Sprache*) to develop; (*Wissenschaft*) to advance; (*Zeit*) to go *or* march (*liter*) on; die Ausbreitung der Epidemie schreitet weiter f~ the epidemic is continuing to spread; *siehe auch* f~geschritten; **f~schreitend** *adj* progressive; *Alter, Wissenschaft* advancing.

Fortschritt *m* advance; (*esp Pol*) progress *no pl* ◆ gute ~e machen to make good progress, to get on (*inf*) *or* progress well; ~e erzielen to make progress; ~e in der Medizin advances in medicine; das ist ein wesentlicher ~ that's a considerable step forward *or* improvement; dem ~ dienen to further progress.

fortschrittlich *adj* progressive (*auch Pol*); *Mensch, Ideen auch* forward-looking.

Fortschrittlichkeit *f* progressiveness.

Fortschritts-: **~fanatiker** *m* fanatical progressive; **f~feindlich** *adj* anti-progressive; **~feindlichkeit** *f* anti-progressiveness; **~glaube** *m* belief in progress; **f~gläubig** *adj* f~gläubig sein to believe in progress; das f~gläubige 19. Jh. the 19th century with its belief in progress; **~gläubigkeit** *f* naïve belief in progress; **~optimismus** *m* belief in progress.

fort-: **~sehnen** *vr sep* to long *or* yearn to be away (*aus* from); **~setzen** *sep* [1] *vt* to continue; (*nach Unterbrechung auch*) to resume; den Weg zu Fuß ~setzen to continue on foot; „wird ~gesetzt" "to be continued"; [2] *vr* (*zeitlich*) to continue; (*räumlich*) to extend.

Fortsetzung *f* (a) *no pl* (*das Fortsetzen*) continuation; (*nach Unterbrechung auch*) resumption. (b) (*folgender Teil*) (*Rad, TV*) episode; (*eines Romans*) instalment ◆ ein Film in drei ~en a film in three parts; „~ folgt" "to be continued". (c) (*Anschlußstück*) continuation.

Fortsetzungs-: **~geschichte** *f* serial; **~roman** *m* serialized novel; **~serie** *f* series.

fort-: **~stehlen** *vr sep irreg* (*geh*) to steal *or* slip away; sich aus etw ~stehlen to steal *or* slip out of sth; **~streben** *vi sep* (*geh*) to attempt *or* try to get away (*aus* from); **~stürzen** *vi sep aux sein* (*geh*) to rush off *or* away; (*Pferd*) to bolt; **~treiben** *sep irreg* [1] *vt* (a) (*verjagen*) to drive away; (b) (*weitertragen*) to carry away; (c) (*fig: weitermachen*) to go *or* keep *or* carry on with; wenn er es weiter so ~treibt wie bisher ... if he goes *or* keeps *or* carries on as he has been (doing) ...; [2] *vi aux sein* to be carried away.

Fortuna *f* - (*Myth*) Fortuna; (*fig*) Fortune.

Fortune [fɔr'ty:n(ə)] (*geh*), **Fortüne** *f* **-,** *no pl* good fortune ◆ politische ~ haben to have good fortune in politics; keine ~ haben to have no luck.

fort-: **~währen** *vi sep* (*geh*) to continue, to persist; **~während** *adj no pred* constant, continual, incessant; **~wälzen** *sep* [1] *vt* to roll away; mit sich ~wälzen to carry away (with it); [2] *vr* to roll on; **~weg** [-vɛk] *adv* (*rare*) the whole time, all the time; er hat ~weg geschwatzt he was chattering the whole time *or* all the time; **~wirken** *vi sep* to continue to have an effect; das wirkt noch bis heute ~ that still has an effect today; das Gesehene wirkte noch lange in ihm ~ what he had seen affected him *or* went on having an effect on him for a long time; das F~wirken klassischer Ideale the continued effect of classical ideals; **~wollen** *vi sep* to want to get away (*aus* from); **~zeugen** *vi sep* (*liter*) to continue to have an effect; **~ziehen** *sep irreg* [1] *vt* to pull away; (*mit großer Anstrengung*) to drag away; (*Strom, Strudel*) to carry away; er zog den widerstrebenden Hund mit sich ~ he dragged *or* pulled the unwilling dog along *or* off *or* away; [2] *vi aux sein* (a) (*weiterziehen*) to move on; (*Vögel*) to migrate; (b) (*von einem Ort*) to move away (*aus* from); (*aus einer Wohnung*) to move out (*aus* of).

Forum *nt* **-s, Foren** *or* (*Hist*) **Fora** forum ◆ etw vor das ~ der Öffentlichkeit bringen to bring sth before the forum of public opinion.

Forums-: **~diskussion** *f*, **~gespräch** *nt* forum (discussion).

Forward ['fɔ:wəd] *m* **-(s), -s** (*esp Aus Ftbl*) forward.

Forz *m* **-es, -e** (*dial inf*) *siehe* Furz.

Fosbury-Flop ['fɔsbərɪflɔp] *m* **-s, -s** Fosbury flop.

fossil *adj attr* fossil *attr*, fossilized.

Fossil *nt* **-s, -ien** [iən] fossil.

fötal *adj* foetal.

Föten *pl of* Fötus.

Foto[1] *nt* **-s, -s** photo(graph), snap(shot) (*inf*) ◆ ein ~ machen to take a photo(graph); *siehe auch* Photo[1].

Foto[2] *m* **-s, -s** (*dial inf*) camera.

Foto- *in cpds* (*Sci*) photo; *siehe auch* Photo-; **~album** *nt* photograph album; **~amateur** *m* amateur photographer; **~apparat** *m* camera; **~arbeiten** *pl* photographic work *sing*; **~archiv** *nt* photo archives *pl*; **~artikel** *pl* photographic equipment *sing*; **~atelier** *nt* (photographic) studio; **~ecke** *f* corner; **~finish** *nt* (*Sport*) photo finish.

fotogen *adj* photogenic.

Fotogeschäft *nt* photographic shop.
Fotograf *m* **-en, -en** photographer.
Fotografie *f* (a) photography. (b) (*Bild*) photo(graph).
fotografieren* [1] *vt* to photograph, to take a photo(graph) of ◆ **sich ~ lassen** to have one's photo(graph) *or* picture taken; **sie läßt sich gut ~** she photographs well, she comes out well in photos.
[2] *vi* to take photos *or* photographs.
Fotografin *f* photographer.
fotografisch [1] *adj* photographic.
[2] *adv* photographically.
Foto-: **~industrie** *f* photographic industry; **~journalist(in *f*)** *m* photo journalist; **~kopie** *f* photocopy; **~kopierautomat, ~kopierer** (*inf*) *m* photocopying machine, photocopier; **f~kopieren*** *vt insep* to photocopy, to make a photocopy of; **~labor** *nt* darkroom; **~laborant** *m* photographic lab(oratory) assistant; **~material** *nt* photographic materials *pl*; **f~mechanisch** *adj* photomechanical; **~modell** *nt* photographic model; **~montage** *f* photomontage; **~papier** *nt* photographic paper; **~reporter** *m* press photographer; **~satz** *m* (*Typ*) *siehe* **Lichtsatz**.
Fotothek *f* **-, -en** photographic collection.
Fotozeitschrift *f* photographic magazine.
Fötus *m* **-, Föten** *or* **-ses, -se** foetus.
Fotze *f* **-, -n** (*vulg*) cunt (*vulg*).
Fotzel *m* **-s, -** (*Sw*) scoundrel, rogue.
foul [faul] *adj* (*Sport*): **~ spielen** to foul; **das war aber ~** (*inf*) that was a foul.
Foul [faul] *nt* **-s, -s** (*Sport*) foul.
Foul|elfmeter ['faul-] *m* (*Ftbl*) penalty (kick).
foulen ['faulən] *vti* (*Sport*) to foul ◆ **es wurde viel gefoult** there was a lot of fouling.
Foulspiel ['faul-] *nt* (*Sport*) foul play.
Fourage [fu'ra:ʒə] *f* **-**, *no pl siehe* **Furage**.
Fox *m* **-(es), -e, Foxterrier** *m* fox-terrier.
Foxtrott *m* **-s, -e** *or* **-s** foxtrot.
Foyer [foa'je:] *nt* **-s, -s** foyer; (*in Hotel auch*) lobby, entrance hall.
Fr. *abbr of* **Frau**.
Fracht *f* **-, -en** (a) (*Ladung*) freight *no pl*; (*von Flugzeug, Schiff auch*) cargo; (*Güter auch*) payload ◆ **etw per ~ schicken** to send sth freight, to freight sth. (b) (*~preis*) freight *no pl*, freightage *no pl*; (*bei Lastwagen*) carriage *no pl*; (*~tarif*) freight/carriage rate.
Fracht-: **~brief** *m* consignment note, waybill; **~dampfer** *m* (*dated*) cargo *or* freight steamer.
Frachtenbahnhof *m* (*Aus*) *siehe* **Güterbahnhof**.
Frachter *m* **-s, -** freighter.
Fracht-: **~flugzeug** *nt* cargo *or* freight plane, (air) freighter; **f~frei** *adj* carriage paid *or* free; **~führer** *m* (*form*) carrier; **~geld** *nt* freight, freightage; (*bei Lastwagen*) carriage; **~gut** *nt* (ordinary) freight *no pl*; **etw als ~gut schicken** to send sth freight *or* as ordinary freight; **~kosten** *pl* freight charges *pl*; **~raum** *m* hold; (*Ladefähigkeit*) cargo space; **~schiff** *nt* cargo ship, freighter; **~schiffahrt** *f* cargo shipping; **~sendung** *f* freight load; (*Aviat, Naut*) cargo of freight; **als ~sendung** (as) freight; **~tarif** *m* freight rate *or* charge; **~verkehr** *m* goods traffic; **~zettel** *m siehe* **Frachtbrief**.
Frack *m* **-(e)s, -s** (*inf*) *or* **¨-e** tails *pl*, tail coat ◆ **im ~** in tails.
Frack-: **~hemd** *nt* dress shirt; **~hose** *f* dress trousers *pl*; **~jacke** *f* tails *pl*, tail coat; **~sausen** *nt*: **~sausen haben** (*inf*) to be in a funk (*inf*); **~schoß** *m* coat-tail; **~verleih** *m* dress hire (service); **~weste** *f* waistcoat *or* vest (*US*) *worn with tails*; **~zwang** *m* requirement to wear tails; **(es herrscht) ~zwang** tails are obligatory, you have to wear tails; „**~zwang**" "tails".
▼ **Frage** *f* **-, -n** question; (*Rück~, Zwischen~ auch*) query; (*Problem auch*) problem; (*Angelegenheit auch*) matter, issue (*esp Pol*) ◆ **eine ~ zu etw** a question on sth; **jdm eine ~ stellen, an jdn eine ~ stellen** *or* **richten** to ask sb a question; **an jdn eine ~ haben** to have a question for sb; **gestatten Sie mir eine ~?** (*form*) might I ask a question?; (*in Diskussionen auch*) permit me to ask you a question (*form*); **auf eine ~ mit Ja oder Nein antworten** to answer a question with a straight yes or no; **sind noch ~n?, hat jemand noch eine ~?** does anyone have *or* are there any more *or* any further questions?; **auf eine dumme ~ (bekommt man) eine dumme Antwort** (*prov*) ask a silly question (get a silly answer) (*prov*); **die deutsche ~** the German question *or* issue; **das ist (doch sehr) die ~** that's (just *or* precisely) the question/problem, that's the whole question/problem; **das ist die große ~** that's the big *or* sixty-four thousand dollar (*inf*) question; **das ist gar keine ~, das steht** *or* **ist außer ~** there's no question *or* doubt about it; **daß ..., steht** *or* **ist außer ~** that ... is beyond question, ..., there's no question *or* doubt about it; **ohne ~** without question *or* doubt; **in ~ kommen** to be possible; **sollte er für diese Stelle in ~ kommen, ...** if he should be considered for this post ...; **für jdn/etw nicht in ~ kommen** to be out of the question for sb/sth; **das kommt (überhaupt) nicht in ~!** that's (quite) out of the question!; **in ~ kommend** possible; *Bewerber* worth considering; **etw in ~ stellen** to question sth, to query sth, to call sth into question; **eine ~ der Zeit/des Geldes** a question *or* matter of time/money.
-frage *f in cpds* question of; (*Problem auch*) problem of ◆ **die ...~** the ... question/problem, the question/problem of ...; (*Angelegenheit auch*) the ... issue.
Frage-: **~bogen** *m* questionnaire; (*Formular*) form; **~fürwort** *nt* interrogative pronoun.
▼ **fragen** [1] *vti* to ask ◆ **nach** *or* **wegen** (*inf*) **jdm ~** to ask after sb; (*in Hotel etc*) to ask for sb; **ich fragte sie nach den Kindern** I asked her how the children were doing; **nach jds Namen/Alter/dem Weg ~** to ask sb's name/age/the way; **nach Arbeit/Post ~** to ask whether there is/was any work/mail; **nach den Ursachen ~** to inquire as to the causes; **ich fragte sie nach ihren Wünschen** I asked her what she wanted; **ich habe nicht nach Einzelheiten gefragt** I didn't ask any details; **nach den Folgen ~** to bother *or* care about the consequences; **er fragte nicht danach, ob ...** he didn't bother *or* care whether ...; **wegen etw ~** to ask about sth; **frag (mich/ihn) lieber nicht** I'd rather you didn't ask (that), you'd better not ask (him) that; **das frage ich dich!** I could ask you the same; **da fragst du noch?** you still have to ask?, you still don't know?; **frag nicht so dumm!** don't ask silly questions; **du fragst zuviel** you ask too many questions; **da fragst du mich zuviel** (*inf*) I really couldn't say; **man wird ja wohl noch ~ dürfen** (*inf*) I was only asking (*inf*), there's no law against asking, is there? (*inf*); **wenn ich (mal) ~ darf?** if I may *or* might ask?; **ohne lange zu ~** without asking a lot of questions.
[2] *vr* to wonder ◆ **das/da frage ich mich** I wonder; **das frage ich mich auch** that's just what I was wondering; **ja, das fragt man sich** yes, that's the question; **es/man fragt sich, ob ...** it's debatable *or* questionable/one wonders whether ...; **da muß man sich ~, ob ...** you can't help wondering if ...; **ich frage mich, wie/wo ...** I'd like to know how/where ..., I really wonder how/where ...
fragend *adj* questioning, inquiring; (*Gram*) interrogative.
Fragen-: **~komplex, ~kreis** *m* complex of questions.
Frager(in *f*) *m* **-s, -** questioner ◆ **wer ist denn der lästige ~?** who is this wretched person who keeps asking questions?
Fragerei *f* questions *pl*.
Frage-: **~satz** *m* (*Gram*) interrogative sentence/clause; **~steller(in *f*)** *m* **-s, -** questioner; (*Interviewer*) interviewer; **~stellung** *f* (a) formulation of a question; **das ist eine falsche ~stellung** the question is wrongly put *or* stated *or* formulated; (b) (*Frage*) question; **~stunde** *f* (*Parl*) question time; **~-und-Antwort-Spiel** *nt* question and answer game; **~wort** *nt* interrogative (particle); **~zeichen** *nt* question mark (*auch fig*), interrogation mark *or* point (*form*); **hinter diese Behauptung muß man ein dickes** *or* **großes ~zeichen setzen** (*fig*) this statement should be taken with a large pinch of salt; **dastehen/dasitzen wie ein ~zeichen** to slouch.
fragil *adj* (*geh*) fragile.
Fragilität *f, no pl* (*geh*) fragility.
▼ **fraglich** *adj* (a) (*zweifelhaft*) uncertain; (*fragwürdig*) doubtful, questionable ◆ **eine ~e Sache** a moot point. (b) *attr* (*betreffend*) in question; *Angelegenheit* under discussion ◆ **zu der ~en Zeit** at the time in question.
Fraglichkeit *f, no pl siehe adj (a)* uncertainty; doubtfulness.
fraglos *adv* undoubtedly, unquestionably.
Fragment *nt* fragment ◆ **~ bleiben** to remain a fragment.
fragmentarisch *adj* fragmentary ◆ **die Manuskripte sind nur ~ erhalten** only fragments of the manuscript have been preserved.
fragwürdig *adj* (a) doubtful, dubious. (b) (*pej*) *Lokal, Mensch, Kreise* dubious.
Fragwürdigkeit *f siehe adj* doubtful *or* dubious nature, doubtfulness; dubiousness, dubious nature.
fraise ['frɛ:zə] *adj inv* (*Aus Fashion*) strawberry(-coloured).
Fraisen ['frɛ:zən] *pl* (*Aus Med*) **die ~** (infant) spasms *pl*.
Fraktion *f* (a) (*Pol*) ≃ parliamentary *or* congressional (*US*) party; (*von mehreren Parteien*) ≃ coalition party; (*Sondergruppe*) group, faction. (b) (*Aus: Ortsteil*) area. (c) (*Chem*) fraction.
fraktionell [fraktsio'nɛl] *adj* (*Pol*) **~ entschieden** decided by the parliamentary *etc* party; **~e Gruppen** factions within the parliamentary *etc* party.
fraktionieren* [fraktsio'ni:rən] *vt* (*Chem*) to fractionate.
Fraktions- *in cpds* (*Pol*) party; **~bildung** *f* formation of factions/a faction; **~führer** *m* party whip, floor leader (*US*); **f~los** *adj* independent; **~mitglied** *nt* member of a parliamentary *etc* party; **~sitzung** *f* party meeting; **~spaltung** *f* party split; (*auf Dauer*) split into two parties; **~sprecher(in *f*)** *m* party spokesperson; **~stärke** *f* (a) numerical strength of a/the parliamentary *etc* party; (b) (*erforderliche Mitgliederzahl*) *numerical strength required for recognition of a parliamentary party*; **~status** *m* party status; **~vorsitzende(r)** *mf* party whip; **~vorstand** *m* party executive; **~zwang** *m* requirement to vote in accordance with party policy; **unter ~zwang stehen** to be under the whip.
Fraktur *f* (a) (*Typ*) Gothic print, Fraktur ◆ **(mit jdm) ~ reden** (*inf*) to be blunt (with sb). (b) (*Med*) fracture.
Frakturschrift *f* Gothic script.
Franc [frɑ̃:] *m* **-, -s** franc.
Franchise ['frɛntʃaiz] *m* **-**, *no pl* franchise.
Franchise-: **~-Geber** *m* franchisor; **~-Nehmer** *m* franchisee.
Franchising ['frɛntʃaiziŋ] *nt* **-s**, *no pl* franchising.
Francium ['frantsiʊm] *nt, no pl* (*abbr* **Fr**) francium.
frank *adv*: **~ und frei** frankly, openly.
Franke *m* **-n, -n** (*Geog*) Franconian; (*Hist*) Frank.
Franken[1] *nt* **-s** Franconia.
Franken[2] *m* **-s, -** **(Schweizer) ~** (Swiss) franc.
Frankenwein *m* Franken wine.
Frankfurt *nt* **-s** **~ (am Main)** Frankfurt (on the Main); **~ (Oder)** Frankfurt on the Oder.
Frankfurter *m* **-s, -** (a) (*Einwohner Frankfurts*) Frankfurter. (b) (*inf: Würstchen*) frankfurter.
frankfurterisch (*inf*), **frankfurtisch** *adj* Frankfurt *attr* ◆ **er spricht F~** he speaks the Frankfurt dialect.

➤ SPRACHE AKTIV: **Frage** → 39.3, 42.1, 43.3, 53.1, 53.2, 53.5, 53.6, 3 **fragen: 1** → 28.1, 29.1, 29.2, 33.2 **fraglich: a** → 53.6

frankieren* *vt* to stamp; (*mit Maschine*) to frank.
Frankiermaschine *f* franking machine.
Frankierung *f* franking; (*Porto auch*) postage.
Fränkin *f* Franconian (woman).
fränkisch *adj* Franconian.
Fränkler *m* **-s, -, Fränkli** *nt* **-s, -** (*inf*) (*Sw*) franc (piece).
franko *adj inv* (*Comm*) carriage paid; (*von Postsendungen*) post-free, postpaid.
Franko-: ~kanadier *m* French-Canadian; **f~kanadisch** *adj* French-Canadian; **~manie** *f* (*geh*) Francomania; **f~phil** *adj* (*geh*) Francophile; **f~phob** *adj* (*geh*) Francophobe; **f~phon** *adj* francophone.
Frankreich *nt* France.
Fränschen ['frɛnsçən] *nt dim of* **Franse**.
Franse *f* **-, -n** (*lose*) (loose) thread; (*von Haar*) strand of hair ◆ **~n** (*als Besatz, Pony*) fringe; **ein mit ~n besetzter Schal** a shawl with a fringe, a fringed shawl; **sich in ~n auflösen** to fray (out).
fransen *vi* to fray (out).
fransig *adj* (*Sew*) fringed *no adv; Haar* straggly *no adv;* (*ausgefasert*) frayed *no adv*.
Franz *m* **-' or -ens** Francis; (*bei Deutschen*) Franz.
Franz-: ~band *m* leather binding; **ein ~band-Buchrücken** a leather spine; **~branntwein** *m* alcoholic liniment.
Franziskaner *m* **-s, -** (*Eccl*) Franciscan (friar).
Franziskanerin *f* (*Eccl*) Franciscan (nun).
Franziskaner|orden *m* (*Eccl*) Franciscan Order, Order of St. Francis.
Franzmann *m, pl* **Franzmänner** (*dated sl*) Frenchie (*inf*), frog (*pej inf*).
Franzose *m* **-n, -n (a)** Frenchman/French boy ◆ **er ist ~** he's French; **die ~n** the French. **(b)** (*Werkzeug*) adjustable spanner, monkey wrench.
Franzosen-: f~feindlich *adj* anti-French; **~krankheit** *f* (*old*) French disease (*old*), syphilis.
Französin *f* Frenchwoman/French girl ◆ **sie ist ~** she's French.
französisch *adj* French ◆ **die ~e Schweiz** French-speaking Switzerland; **die F~e Revolution** the French Revolution; **die ~e Krankheit** (*old*) the French disease (*old*), syphilis; **~es Bett** double bed; **~e Spielkarten** ordinary playing cards; **~ kochen** to do French cooking; **(auf) ~ Abschied nehmen** to leave without saying goodbye; **sich (auf) ~ empfehlen** to leave without saying good-bye/paying; (*sich unerlaubt entfernen*) to take French leave; *siehe auch* **deutsch**.
Französisch(e) *nt* French; *siehe auch* **Deutsch(e)**.
frappant *adj* (*geh*) *Schnelligkeit, Entdeckung* remarkable, astounding; *Verbesserung, Wirkung, Ähnlichkeit auch* striking ◆ **auf jdn ~ wirken** to astound sb.
frappieren* **1** *vt* (*verblüffen*) to astound, to astonish, to amaze.
2 *vi* (*Sache*) to be astounding *or* astonishing.
frappierend *adj siehe* **frappant**.
Fräse *f* **-, -n (a)** (*Werkzeug*) milling cutter; (*für Holz*) moulding cutter; (*Boden~*) rotary hoe. **(b)** (*Bart*) chinstrap (beard).
fräsen *vt* to mill, to mill-cut; *Holz* to mould.
Fräser *m* **-s, - (a)** (*Beruf*) milling cutter. **(b)** (*Maschinenteil*) milling cutter; (*für Holz*) moulding cutter.
Fräsmaschine *f* milling machine.
fraß *pret of* **fressen**.
Fraß *m* **-es, -e (a)** food; (*pej inf*) muck (*inf*) *no indef art* ◆ **etw einem Tier zum ~ vorwerfen** to feed sth to an animal; **jdn den Kritikern zum ~ vorwerfen** to throw sb to the critics. **(b)** (*Abfressen*) **vom ~ befallen** eaten away.
Frater *m* **-s, Fratres** (*Eccl*) Brother.
fraternisieren* *vi* to fraternize.
Fraternisierung *f* fraternization.
Fratz *m* **-es, -e** *or* (*Aus*) **-en, -en (a)** (*pej*) brat. **(b)** (*schelmisches Mädchen*) rascal, scallywag (*inf*).
Frätzchen *nt dim of* **Fratz, Fratze**.
Fratze *f* **-, -n (a)** grotesque face. **(b)** (*Grimasse*) grimace; (*inf: Gesicht*) face, phiz (*dated inf*); (*fig: Zerrbild*) caricature ◆ **jdm eine ~ schneiden** to pull *or* make a face at sb; **eine ~ ziehen, das Gesicht zu einer ~ verziehen** to pull *or* make a face, to grimace.
fratzenhaft *adj* grotesque.
frau *indef pron proposed feminist alternative to 'man'; siehe* **man**[1].
Frau *f* **-, -en (a)** (*weiblicher Mensch*) woman ◆ **zur ~ werden** to become a woman; **von ~ zu ~** woman to woman; **Unsere Liebe ~** (*Eccl*) our blessed Lady, the blessed Virgin.
(b) (*Ehe~*) wife ◆ **sich** (*dat*) **eine ~ nehmen** (*dated*) to marry, to take a wife (*old*); **willst du meine ~ werden?** will you marry me?, will you be my wife?; **jdn zur ~ haben** to be married to sb; **seine zukünftige/geschiedene ~** his bride-to-be/his ex-wife; **die junge ~** (*dated*) the son's wife/the daughter-in-law.
(c) (*Anrede*) madam; (*mit Namen*) Mrs; (*für eine unverheiratete ~*) Miss, Ms (*feministisch*) ◆ **liebe ~!** (*dated*) my dear lady!; **~ Doktor/Direktor** doctor/headmistress; **Ihre (liebe) ~ Mutter/Schwester** your good mother/sister; **~ Nachbarin** (*old*) neighbour (*old*).
Frauchen *nt dim of* **Frau** (*inf*) (*Herrin von Hund*) mistress ◆ **geh zum ~** go to your mistress.
Frauen- *in cpds* women's; (*einer bestimmten Frau*) woman's; (*Sport auch*) ladies'; **~arbeit** *f* **(a)** (*Arbeit für Frauen, von Frauen*) female *or* women's labour; **das ist keine ~arbeit** that's no job for a woman; **niedrig bezahlte ~arbeit** badly paid jobs for women; **(b)** (*Arbeit zugunsten der Frau*) work among women; **in der ~arbeit tätig sein** to be involved in work among women; **~art** *f*: **nach ~art** (*dated*) as women do; **~arzt** *m* gynaecologist; **~beauftragte** *f* (*in Gewerkschaft etc*) women's representative; (*Beamtin*) commissioner for women's issues; **~beruf** *m* career for women; **f~bewegt** *adj* feminist; **~bewegte(r)** *mf decl as adj* feminist; **~bewegung** *f* women's (*auch Hist*) *or* feminist movement; **~blatt** *nt* women's magazine; **~buch** *nt* women's book; **~chor** *m* ladies' *or* female choir; **~emanzipation** *f* female emancipation *no art*, emancipation of women; (*in der heutigen Zeit auch*) women's lib(eration); **~fachschule** *f* domestic science college; **~feind** *m* misogynist; **f~feindlich** *adj* anti-women *pred; Mensch, Verhalten auch* misogynous; **~frage** *f* question of women's rights; **f~freundlich** *adj* pro-women *pred*; **~front** *f* women's front; **~funk** *m* woman's radio, ≃ Woman's Hour (*Brit*); **~gefängnis** *nt* women's prison; **~geschichte** *f* affair with a woman; **~geschichten** (*Affären*) womanizing; (*Erlebnisse*) sexploits *pl* (*hum inf*), experiences with women *pl*; **~gestalt** *f* female figure; (*Liter, Art*) female character; **~gruppe** *f* women's group; **~haar** *nt* **(a)** woman's hair; **(b)** (*Bot*) maidenhair (fern); **f~haft** *adj* womanly *no adv*; **~hand** *f*: **von (zarter) ~hand** by a woman's fair hand; **~hasser** *m* **-s, -** misogynist, woman-hater; **~haus** *nt* **(a)** women's refuge; **(b)** (*Ethnologie*) women's house; **~heilkunde** *f* gynaecology; **~held** *m* lady-killer; **~kenner** *m* connoisseur of women; **~kleider** *pl* women's clothes *pl or* clothing *sing*; **~klinik** *f* gynaecological hospital *or* clinic; **~kloster** *nt* convent, nunnery (*old*); **~krankheit** *f*, **~leiden** *nt* gynaecological disorder; **Facharzt für ~krankheiten und Geburtshilfe** gynaecologist and obstetrician; **~mantel** *m* (*Bot*) lady's mantle; **~mörder** *m* murderer *of women/a woman*; **~orden** *m* (*Eccl*) women's order; **~politik** *f* feminist politics; **~rechtlerin** *f* feminist; (*in der heutigen Zeit auch*) Women's Libber (*inf*); **f~rechtlerisch** *adj* feminist; **sich f~rechtlerisch betätigen** to be involved in women's rights *or* (*in der heutigen Zeit auch*) Women's Lib; **~referat** *nt* women's department; **~referentin** *f* consultant on women's issues; **~schänder** *m* **-s, -** rapist; **~schuh** *m no pl* (*Bot*) lady's slipper *no pl*.
Frauens-: ~leute *pl* (*hum inf*) womenfolk *pl*; **~person** *f* female person; (*hum inf*) female (*inf*), broad (*US inf*).
Frauen-: ~sport *m* women's sport; **~station** *f* women's ward; **~stimme** *f* woman's voice; (*Parl*) woman's vote; **~stimmen** women's voices/votes; **~stimmrecht** *nt siehe* **~wahlrecht**; **~tausch** *m* wife-swapping; (*Anthropologie*) exchange of partners; **~typ** *m* **(a)** feminine type (of woman); **mütterlicher ~typ** motherly type of woman; **(b)** (*inf*) ladies' man; ⚠**~überschuß** *m* surplus of women; **~verband, ~verein** *m* women's association *or* society; **~wahlrecht** *nt* vote for women, female suffrage *no art*; **~zeitschrift** *f* women's magazine; **~zentrum** *nt* women's advice centre; **~zimmer** *nt* (*old, dated*) woman; (*hum*) woman, female (*inf*), broad (*US inf*).
Fräulein *nt* **-s, - or -s (a)** (*unverheiratete weibliche Person*) young lady ◆ **ein altes** *or* **älteres ~** an elderly spinster.
(b) (*Anrede*) Miss ◆ **Ihr ~ Tochter/Braut** your daughter/bride.
(c) (*weibliche Angestellte*) young lady; (*Verkäuferin auch*) assistant; (*Kellnerin*) waitress; (*dated: Lehrerin*) teacher, mistress ◆ **~!** Miss!; (*Kellnerin auch*) waitress!; **das ~ vom Amt** (*dated*) the operator, the switchboard girl.
fraulich *adj* feminine; (*reif*) womanly *no adv*.
Fraulichkeit *f, no pl siehe adj* femininity; womanliness.
Freak ['fri:k] *m* **-s, -s** (*sl*) freak (*sl*).
freakig ['fri:kɪç] *adj* (*sl*) freaky (*sl*).
frech *adj* **(a)** (*unverschämt*) cheeky (*esp Brit*), fresh *pred* (*esp US*), impudent; *Lüge* brazen, bare-faced *no adv* ◆ **~ werden** to get cheeky *etc*; **jdm ~ kommen** to get cheeky *etc* with sb; **sich ~ benehmen** to be cheeky *etc*; **halt deinen ~en Mund!** (you) shut up and stop being cheeky *etc*; **~ wie Oskar** (*inf*) *or* **wie ein Spatz sein** (*inf*) to be a cheeky little devil (*Brit inf*), to be a little monkey.
(b) (*herausfordernd*) *Kleidung etc* saucy (*inf*), cheeky (*Brit inf*).
Frechdachs *m* (*inf*) cheeky monkey (*Brit inf*) *or* devil (*Brit inf*), monkey.
Frechheit *f* **(a)** *no pl* (*Verhalten*) impudence; (*esp von Kindern auch*) cheekiness (*esp Brit*) ◆ **das ist der Gipfel der ~** that's the height of impudence; **die ~ haben** *or* **besitzen, ... zu ...** to have the cheek (*esp Brit*) *or* nerve (*inf*) *or* impudence to ...
(b) (*Äußerung, Handlung*) piece *or* bit of cheek (*esp Brit*) *or* impudence ◆ **sich** (*dat*) **einige ~en erlauben** to be a bit cheeky (*esp Brit*) *or* fresh (*esp US*); **solche ~en** what cheek (*esp Brit*) *or* impudence.
Freesie ['fre:ziə] *f* freesia.
Fregatte *f* frigate.
Fregattenkapitän *m* commander.
Fregattvogel *m* frigate-bird.
frei *adj* **(a)** (*uneingeschränkt, unbehindert*) free; *Blick* clear ◆ **~e Rhythmen** free verse; **~e Hand haben** to have a free hand; **jdm ~e Hand lassen** to give sb free rein *or* a free hand; **aus ~er Hand** *or* **aus der ~en Hand** *or* **~ Hand zeichnen** to draw freehand; **jdm zur ~en Verfügung stehen** to be completely at sb's disposal; **aus ~en Stücken** *or* **~em Willen** of one's own free will; **das Recht der ~en Rede** the right of free speech *or* to freedom of speech; **~ schalten und walten** to do what one wants *or* pleases; **das ist ~ wählbar** you can choose as you please, it's completely optional; **~ definierbare Zeichen** (*Comput*) user-definable characters; **~ nach ...** based on ...; **~ nach Goethe** (*Zitat*) as Goethe didn't say; **ich bin so ~** (*form*) may I?; **von Kiel nach Hamburg hatten wir ~e Fahrt** we had a clear run from Kiel to Hamburg; **einem Zug ~e Fahrt geben** to give a train the "go" signal; **der Polizist gab uns ~e Fahrt** the policeman signalled us on; **für etw ~e Fahrt geben** (*fig*) to give sth the go-ahead *or* green light; **die Straße ~ machen** to clear the road; **der ~e Fall** (*Phys*) free fall; **~er Durchgang** thoroughfare; **~er Zutritt** entry; **~er**

⚠: for details of spelling reform, see supplement

Zugang unlimited *or* unrestricted access; **der Film ist ~ (für Jugendliche) ab 16 (Jahren)** the film may be seen by people over (the age of) 16; **~es Geleit** safe conduct; **auf ~er Wildbahn** in its natural surroundings *or* habitat; **auf ~em Fuß sein, ~ herumlaufen** (*inf*) to be free, to be running around free (*inf*); **jdn auf ~en Fuß setzen** to set sb free; **sich von etw ~ machen** to rid oneself of *or* free oneself from sth; **~ von etw** free of sth; *siehe* **frank, Lauf.**

(b) (*unabhängig*) free; *Schriftsteller etc* freelance; (*nicht staatlich*) private ◆ **~er Beruf** independent profession; **~er Mitarbeiter sein** to be freelance; **als ~er Mitarbeiter arbeiten** to work freelance; **~er Mitarbeiter** freelance collaborator; **~er Markt** open market; **~e Marktwirtschaft** free-market *or* open market economy; **die ~e Wirtschaft** private enterprise; **in die ~e Wirtschaft gehen** to go into industry; **~e Tankstelle** independent petrol station; **~ machen** to have a liberating effect; **~e Reichsstadt** (*Hist*) free city of the Empire; **F~e und Hansestadt Hamburg/F~e Hansestadt Bremen** Free Hansa Town of Hamburg/Bremen; **F~er Deutscher Gewerkschaftsbund** (*DDR*) Free German Trades Union Congress; **F~e Deutsche Jugend** (*DDR*) Free German Youth; **F~e Demokratische Partei** (*BRD*) Free Democratic Party.

(c) (*ohne Hilfsmittel*) *Rede* extemporary ◆ **das Kind kann ~ stehen** the child can stand on its own *or* without any help; **~ schwimmen** to swim unaided *or* on one's own; **~ in der Luft schweben** to hang in mid-air; **ein Vortrag in ~er Rede** a talk given without notes, an extemporary talk; **~ sprechen** to speak extempore *or* without notes, to extemporize.

(d) (*verfügbar*) *Mittel, Geld* available; *Zeit, Mensch* free ◆ **morgen/Mittwoch ist ~** tomorrow/Wednesday is a holiday; **einen Tag ~ nehmen/haben** to take/have a day off; **Herr Mayer ist jetzt ~** Mr Mayer is free now; **ich bin jetzt ~ für ihn** I can see him now; **fünf Minuten ~ haben** to have five minutes (free).

(e) (*unbesetzt*) *Zimmer, Toilette* vacant, empty; *Platz* free; *Stelle* vacant, free; *Taxi* for hire, free ◆ **ist hier** *or* **ist dieser Platz noch ~?** is anyone sitting here?, is this anyone's seat?, is this seat taken *or* free?; **„~"** (*an Taxi*) "for hire"; (*an Toilettentür*) "vacant"; **„Zimmer ~"** "vacancies"; **haben Sie noch etwas ~?** do you have anything?; (*in Hotel*) have you got any vacancies *or* any rooms left *or* free?; (*in Restaurant*) do you have a table (free)?; **einen Platz ~ machen** (*aufstehen*) to vacate a seat; (*leer räumen*) to clear a seat; **für etw Platz ~ lassen/machen** to leave/make room *or* space for sth; **eine Wohnung ~ machen** to vacate a flat; **einen Platz für jdn ~ lassen** to leave a seat for sb; *siehe* **Bahn, Ring.**

(f) (*offen*) open ◆ **unter ~em Himmel** in the open (air), out of doors, outdoors; **im ~en Raum** (*Astron*) in (outer) space; **eine Frage/Aussage im ~en Raum stehenlassen** to leave a question/statement hanging (in mid-air *or* in the air); **auf ~er Strecke** (*Rail*) between stations; (*Aut*) on the road; **~ stehen** (*Haus*) to stand by itself; **~ stehen** *or* **sein** (*Sport*) to be free *or* not marked; *siehe* **Freie.**

(g) (*kostenlos*) free ◆ **Eintritt ~** admission free; **~ Grenze** free frontier; *siehe* **Haus.**

(h) (*unkonventionell*) free, liberal ◆ **sie benimmt sich etwas zu ~** she's rather free in her behaviour.

(i) (*unbekleidet*) bare ◆ **sich ~ machen** to take one's clothes off, to strip; **~ lassen** to leave bare.

(j) (*ungeschützt*) *Autor* out of copyright ◆ **seit die Rechte an Karl May ~ geworden sind** since Karl May's books have been out of copyright.

Frei-: ≈anlage *f* (*im Zoo*) outdoor *or* open-air enclosure; (*Sport*) sports ground *pl*, playing fields *pl*; (*Park*) park grounds *pl*; **≈bad** *nt* open-air (swimming) pool, lido; **≈ballon** *m* free balloon; **≈bank** *f stall or shop selling substandard meat*; **f≈bekommen*** *vt sep irreg* **(a)** (*befreien*) **jdn f~bekommen** to get sb freed *or* released; **etw f~bekommen** to get sth free, to free sth; **(b) einen Tag/eine Woche f~bekommen** to get a day/a week off; **~berufler(in** *f*) *m* **-s, -** self-employed person; **f≈beruflich** *adj* self-employed; **f~beruflich arbeiten** to be self-employed; **f~beruflich für eine Firma arbeiten** to work freelance *or* do freelance work for a company; **≈betrag** *m* tax allowance; **≈beuter** *m* **-s, -** pirate, buccaneer, freebooter (*old*); (*fig*) exploiter; **~beuterei** *f* piracy, buccaneering, freebooting (*old*); (*fig*) exploitation; **f≈beweglich** *adj* free-moving; **≈bier** *nt* free beer; **f≈bleibend** *adj* subject to alteration; **≈bord** *m* (*Naut*) freeboard; **≈brief** *m* **(a)** (*Hist*) (*Privileg*) royal charter; (*~lassung*) letter of manumission; **(b)** (*fig*) licence.

Freiburg *nt* **(a)** (*Deutschland*) Freiburg. **(b)** (*Schweiz, Kanton, Stadt*) Fribourg.

Frei-: ≈deck *nt* uncovered level (*of multistorey car park*); **≈denker** *m* freethinker; **f≈denkerisch** *adj* freethinking.

freien (*old*) **1** *vt* to wed (*old, liter*).
2 *vi* **um ein Mädchen ~** to woo (*old*) *or* court (*dated*) a girl; **jung gefreit hat nie gereut** (*Prov*) marry young and you'll never regret it.

Freie(r) *mf decl as adj* (*Hist*) freeman.

Freie(s) *nt decl as adj* **das ~** the open (air); **im ~n** in the open (air); **ins ~ gehen** to go outside *or* into the open (air); **ins ~ gelangen** to get out; **im ~n übernachten** to sleep out in the open.

Freier *m* **-s, - (a)** (*dated, hum*) suitor. **(b)** (*inf: von Dirne*) (prostitute's) client, john (*US inf*).

Freiersfüße *pl*: **auf ~n gehen** (*hum*) to be courting (*dated*).

Frei-: ~exemplar *nt* free copy; **~fahrschein** *m* free ticket; **~fahrt** *f* free journey; **~fahrt haben** to travel free; **f~finanziert** *adj Wohnungsbau* privately financed; **~fläche** *f* open space; **~flug** *m* free flight; **~frau** *f* baroness (*by marriage*); **~fräulein** *nt* baroness (*in her own right*); **~gabe** *f siehe vt* release; decontrol, lifting of controls (*gen* on); opening; passing; putting back into play; **~gang** *m* (*von Strafgefangenen*) day release, day parole ◆ **~gang bekommen** to be let out on parole; **während des ~gangs** while on parole; **~gänger** *m* **-s, -** day release prisoner; **f~geben** *sep irreg* **1** *vt* to release (*an +acc* to); *Gefangene, Ehepartner auch* to set free; *Preise, Wechselkurse* to decontrol, to lift controls on; *Straße, Strecke, Flugbahn* to open; *Film* to pass; (*Ftbl*) *Ball* to put back into play; *Spieler* to release; **etw zum Verkauf f~geben** to allow sth to be sold on the open market; **jdm den Weg f~geben** to let sb past *or* by; **2** *vi* **jdm f~geben** to give sb a holiday; **jdm zwei Tage f~geben** to give sb two days off; **f~gebig** *adj* generous; (*iro auch*) free, liberal; **~gebigkeit** *f* generosity; (*iro*) liberalness; **~gehege** *nt* open-air *or* outdoor enclosure; **~geist** *m* freethinker; **f~geistig** *adj* freethinking; **~gelände** *nt* open-air exhibition ground; **~gelassene(r)** *mf decl as adj* (*Hist*) freedman; freedwoman; **~gepäck** *nt* baggage allowance; **~gericht** *nt* (*Hist*) Vehmgericht; **~graf** *m* (*Hist*) Vehmic judge; **~grenze** *f* (*bei Steuer*) tax exemption limit; **f~haben** *vi sep irreg* to have a holiday; **ich habe heute/zwei Tage f~** I have today/two days off; **eine Stunde/die sechste Stunde f~haben** (*Sch*) to have a free period/have the sixth period free; **er hat mittags eine Stunde f~** he has an hour free at midday; **~hafen** *m* free port; **f~halten** *sep irreg* **1** *vt* **(a)** (*nicht besetzen*) to keep free *or* clear; **(b)** (*reservieren*) to keep, to save; **(c)** (*jds Zeche begleichen*) to pay for; **sich von jdm f~halten lassen** to let sb pay for one; **2** *vr* **sich von etw f~halten** to avoid sth; *von Vorurteilen etc* to be free of sth; *von Verpflich- tungen* to keep oneself free of sth; **~handbücherei** *f* open-shelf library; **~handel** *m* free trade; **~handelszone** *f* free trade area; **die kleine ~handelszone** EFTA, the European Free Trade Area; **f~händig** *adj Zeichnung* freehand; *Radfahren* without hands, (with) no hands; *Schießen* offhand (*spec*), without support; **~handzeichnung** *f* freehand drawing; **f~hängend** *adj attr* suspended.

Freiheit *f* **(a)** *no pl* freedom ◆ **die ~** freedom; (*persönliche ~ als politisches Ideal*) liberty; **~, Gleichheit, Brüderlichkeit** liberty, equality, fraternity; **persönliche ~** personal freedom; **in ~ (*dat*) sein** to be free; (*Tier*) to be in the wild; **in ~ leben** (*Tier*) to live in the wild; **in ~ geboren** born free; **jdn in ~ (*acc*) setzen** to set sb free; **jdm die ~ schenken** to give sb his/her *etc* freedom, to free sb; **der Weg in die ~** the path to freedom.

(b) (*Vorrecht*) freedom *no pl* ◆ **dichterische ~** poetic licence; **alle ~en haben** to have all the freedom possible; **die ~ haben** *or* **genießen** (*geh*), **etw zu tun** to be free *or* at liberty to do sth, to have *or* enjoy the freedom to do sth; **sich (*dat*) die ~ nehmen, etw zu tun** to take the liberty of doing sth; **sich (*dat*) zu viele ~en erlauben** to take too many liberties.

freiheitlich *adj* liberal; *Verfassung* based on the principle of liberty; *Demokratie* free ◆ **die ~-demokratische Grundordnung** (*BRD*) the free democratic constitutional structure; **~ gesinnt** liberal.

Freiheits-: ~begriff *m* concept of freedom; **~beraubung** *f* (*Jur*) wrongful deprivation of personal liberty; **~bewegung** *f* liberation movement; **~delikt** *nt* (*Jur*) offence against personal liberty; **~drang** *m, no pl* urge *or* desire for freedom; **~entzug** *m* imprisonment; **f~feindlich** *adj* operating against freedom; *Kräfte auch* anti-freedom *attr*; **~kampf** *m* fight for freedom; **~kämpfer** *m* freedom-fighter; **~krieg** *m* war of liberation; **f~liebend** *adj* freedom-loving; **~rechte** *pl* civil rights and liberties *pl*; **~statue** *f* Statue of Liberty; **~strafe** *f* prison sentence; **er erhielt eine ~strafe von zwei Jahren** he was sentenced to two years' imprisonment *or* given a two-year prison sentence.

Frei-: f~heraus *adv* candidly, frankly; **≈herr** *m* baron; **f≈herrlich** *adj attr* baronial.

Freiin *f siehe* **Freifräulein.**

Frei-: f~kämpfen *sep* **1** *vt* to get free; (*durch Gewaltanwendung*) to free by force; **2** *vr* to get free; to free oneself by force; **~karte** *f* free *or* complimentary ticket; **f~kaufen** *vt sep* **jdn/sich f~kaufen** to buy sb's/one's freedom; **~kirche** *f* Free Church; **~klettern** *nt* free climbing; **f~kommen** *vi sep irreg aux sein* **(a)** (*entkommen*) to get out (*aus* of); (*befreit werden*) to be released *or* freed (*aus, von* from); **(b)** (*sich bewegen lassen: Boot*) to come free; **~konzert** *nt* (*Sw*) *siehe* **Platzkonzert**; **~körperkultur** *f, no pl* nudism, naturism; **~korps** *nt* (*Mil*) volunteer corps *sing*.

Freiland *nt* (*Hort*) open beds *pl* ◆ **auf/im ~** outdoors.

Freiland-: ~gemüse *nt* outdoor vegetables *pl*; **~kultur** *f* outdoor cultivation.

Frei-: f~lassen *vt sep irreg* to set free, to free; (*aus Haft, Gefangenschaft auch*) to release; *Hund* to let off the lead *or* leash; **~lassung** *f* release; (*von Sklaven*) setting free; **~lauf** *m* (*Aut*) neutral; (*bei Fahrrad*) freewheel; **im ~lauf fahren** to coast (in neutral); to freewheel; **f~laufen** *vr sep irreg* (*Sport*) to get free; **~laufend** *adj Huhn* free-range; **Eier von ~laufenden Hühnern** free-range eggs; **f~lebend** *adj* living free; **f~legen** *vt sep* to expose; *Ruinen, Trümmer* to uncover; (*fig auch*) to lay bare; **~legung** *f siehe vt* exposure; uncovering; laying bare; **~leitung** *f* overhead cable.

freilich *adv* **(a)** (*allerdings*) admittedly ◆ **es scheint ~ nicht leicht zu sein** admittedly *or* certainly it doesn't seem easy. **(b)** (*esp S Ger: natürlich*) of course, certainly, sure (*esp US*) ◆ **aber ~!** of course!; **ja ~** yes of course.

Freilicht- *in cpds* open-air; **~bühne** *f* open-air theatre; **~kino** *nt* open-air cinema; (*Autokino*) drive-in cinema.

Frei-: ≈los *nt* free lottery ticket; (*Sport*) bye; **f≈machen** *sep* **1** *vt* to stamp; (*mit Frankiermaschine*) to frank; **einen Brief mit 1 Mark f~machen** to put stamps to the value of 1 mark on a letter; *siehe auch* **frei (a, d)**; **2** *vi* to take time/a day/a week *etc* off; **ich habe eine Woche/gestern f~gemacht** I took a week off/the day off yesterday; **3** *vr* to arrange to be free; *siehe* **frei (h)**; **≈machung** *f, no pl siehe vt* stamping; franking; **≈marke** *f* (postage) stamp; **≈maurer** *m* Mason, Freemason; **≈maurerei** *f* Freemasonry; **f≈maurerisch** *adj* Masonic; **≈maurerloge** *f* Masonic Lodge.

⚠: Informationen zur Rechtschreibreform im Anhang

Freimut *m, no pl* frankness, honesty, openness ◆ **mit allem ~** perfectly frankly *or* honestly *or* openly.

freimütig *adj* frank, honest, open.

Freimütigkeit *f* frankness, honesty, openness.

Frei-: ~platz *m* **(a)** free *or* complimentary seat; **(b)** (*Univ*) scholarship; (*Sch auch*) free place; **f~pressen** *vt sep* **jdn f~pressen** to obtain sb's release, to get sb set free; **versuchen, jdn f~zupressen** to demand sb's release; **~raum** *m* (*fig*) freedom *no art, no pl* (*zu* for); **~raum brauchen, in dem man sich entwickeln kann** to need freedom to develop *or* in which to develop; **die Universität ist kein gesellschaftlicher ~raum** university isn't a social vacuum; **f~religiös** *adj* non-denominational; ⚠**~saß** [-zas], **~sasse** *m*, **-sassen, -sassen** (*Hist*) yeoman; **f~schaffend** *adj attr* freelance; **~schaffende(r)** *mf decl as adj* freelance; **~schar** *f* (*Hist*) (irregular) volunteer corps *sing*; **~schärler** *m* **-s, -** guerrilla; (*Hist*) irregular (volunteer); **f~schaufeln** *vt sep* to clear, to dig clear; **f~schießen** *vt sep irreg* **sich** (*dat*) **den Weg f~schießen** to shoot one's way out; **jdn f~schießen** to shoot sb free; ⚠**~schuß** *m* free shot; **f~schwimmen** *vr sep irreg* (*Sport*) *to pass a test by swimming for 15 minutes*; (*fig*) to learn to stand on one's own two feet; **~schwimmen** *nt 15 minute swimming test*; **f~setzen** *vt sep* to release; (*euph*) *Arbeitskräfte* to make redundant; (*vorübergehend*) to lay off; **~setzung** *f* release; (*euph*) dismissal; (*vorübergehend*) laying off; **~sinn** *m, no pl* (*dated*) liberalism; **f~sinnig** *adj* (*dated*) liberal; **~spiel** *nt* free game; **f~sprechen** *vt sep irreg* **(a)** to acquit; **jdn von einer Schuld/von einem Verdacht f~sprechen** to acquit sb of guilt/clear sb of suspicion; **jdn wegen erwiesener Unschuld f~sprechen** to prove sb not guilty; **(b)** (*Handwerk*) *Auszubildende* to qualify; **~spruch** *m* acquittal; **es ergeht ~spruch** the verdict is "not guilty"; **auf ~spruch plädieren** to plead not guilty; **~staat** *m* free state; **der ~staat Bayern** the Free State of Bavaria; **~statt, ~stätte** *f* (*liter*) sanctuary; **f~stehen** *vi sep irreg* **(a)** (*überlassen sein*) **es steht jdm f~, etw zu tun** sb is free *or* at liberty to do sth; **das steht Ihnen völlig f~** that is completely up to you; **es steht Ihnen f~, ob ...** it is up to you whether ...; **(b)** (*leerstehen*) to stand empty; **f~stellen** *vt sep* **(a)** (*anheimstellen*) **jdm etw f~stellen** to leave sth (up) to sb; **(b)** (*zur Verfügung stellen*) *Mittel* to make available; *Personal* to release; **(c)** (*befreien*) to exempt; **einen Schüler vom Unterricht f~stellen** to excuse a pupil from a lesson/his lessons; **~stempel** *m* frank.

Freistil- *in cpds* freestyle; **~ringen** *nt* all-in *or* freestyle wrestling.

Frei-: ~stoß *m* (*Ftbl*) free kick (*für* to, for); **~stück** *nt* free copy; **~stunde** *f* free hour; (*Sch*) free period.

Freitag *m* Friday ◆ **der Schwarze ~** *the day of the Wall Street crash*; **ein schwarzer ~** a black day; *siehe auch* **Dienstag**.

freitäglich *adj attr* Friday.

freitags *adv* on Fridays, on a Friday.

Frei-: ~tisch *m* free meals *pl*; **~tod** *m* suicide; **den ~tod wählen** *or* **suchen** to decide to put an end to one's life; **f~tragend** *adj* self-supporting; *Konstruktion, Flügel* cantilever *attr*; *Treppe* hanging, cantilever *attr*; **~treppe** *f* (flight of) steps (*gen* leading up to); **~übung** *f* exercise; **~übungen machen** to do one's exercises; **~umschlag** *m* stamped addressed envelope, s.a.e.

freiweg ['frai'vɛk] *adv* openly; (*freiheraus*) straight out, frankly ◆ **er fing an, ~ zu erzählen** he started talking away.

Frei-: ~wild *nt* (*fig*) fair game; **f~willig** *adj* voluntary; (*Jur*) *Gerichtsbarkeit auch* non-contentious; (*freigestellt*) *Versicherung, Unterricht* optional; **f~willige Feuerwehr** voluntary fire brigade; **sich f~willig melden** to volunteer (*zu, für* for); **etw f~willig machen** to do sth voluntarily *or* of one's own free will; **f~willig in den Tod gehen** to take one's own life; **~willige(r)** *mf decl as adj* volunteer; **~willige vor!** volunteers, one pace forwards!; **~willigkeit** *f* voluntary nature, voluntariness; **~wurf** *m* free throw; **~zeichen** *nt* ringing tone; **~zeichnungsklausel** *f* (*Jur, Comm*) exemption from liability clause.

Freizeit *f* **(a)** (*arbeitsfreie Zeit*) free *or* spare *or* leisure time. **(b)** (*Zusammenkunft*) weekend/holiday course; (*Eccl*) retreat.

Freizeit-: ~anzug *m* jogging suit; **~ausgleich** *m* time off in lieu; **~bekleidung** *f siehe* **~kleidung**; **~gestaltung** *f* organization of one's leisure time; **das Problem der ~gestaltung** the leisure problem; **~hemd** *nt* sports shirt; **~industrie** *f* leisure industry; **~kleidung** *f* casual clothes *pl*; (*Warengattung*) leisurewear *no pl*; **~park** *m* amusement park; **~problem** *nt* problem of leisure, leisure problem; **~wert** *m* **München hat einen hohen ~wert** Munich has a lot to offer in the way of recreational and leisure-time facilities.

Frei-: f~zügig *adj* **(a)** (*reichlich*) *Gebrauch, Anwendung* liberal; **f~zügig Geld ausgeben** to spend money freely *or* liberally; **(b)** (*in moralischer Hinsicht*) permissive; **(c)** (*den Wohnort frei wählen könnend*) free to move; **~zügigkeit** *f siehe adj* **(a)** liberalness; **(b)** permissiveness; **(c)** freedom of movement.

fremd *adj* **(a)** (*andern gehörig*) someone else's; *Bank, Bibliothek, Firma* different; (*Comm, Fin, Pol*) outside *attr* ◆ **ohne ~e Hilfe** without anyone else's/outside help, without help from anyone else/outside; **ich schlafe nicht gern in ~en Betten** I don't like sleeping in strange beds; **~es Eigentum** someone else's property, property not one's own (*form*); **das ist nicht für ~e Ohren** that is not for other people to hear; **etw geht in ~e Hände über** sth passes into the hands of strangers *or* into strange hands; **sich mit ~en Federn schmücken** to claim all the glory for oneself.
(b) (*~ländisch*) foreign, alien (*esp Admin, Pol*).
(c) (*andersartig*) strange; *Planeten* other; *Welt* different.
(d) (*unvertraut*) strange ◆ **jdm ~ sein** (*unbekannt*) to be unknown to sb; (*unverständlich*) to be foreign *or* alien to sb; (*nicht in jds Art*) to be foreign *or* alien to sb *or* to sb's nature; **es ist mir ~, wie ...** I don't understand how ...; **das ist eine ~e/mir ~e Seite seines Wesens** that is a side of his character which nobody has/I haven't seen before; **ich bin hier/in London ~** I'm a stranger here/to London; **meine Heimat ist mir ~ geworden** I've become a stranger in my own country, my own country has become quite foreign *or* alien to me; **sich** *or* **einander** (*dat*) **~ werden** to grow apart, to become strangers (to one another); **sich ~ fühlen** to feel alien, to feel like a stranger; **~ tun** to be reserved.

Fremd-: ~arbeiter *m* foreign worker; **f~artig** *adj* strange; (*exotisch*) exotic; **~artigkeit** *f siehe adj* strangeness; exoticism; **~bestäubung** *f* cross-fertilization; **f~bestimmt** *adj* heteronomous; **f~bestimmt handeln** to act under orders; **~bestimmung** *f* heteronomy.

Fremde *f* -, *no pl* (*liter*) **die ~** foreign parts *pl*; **in die ~ gehen/in der ~ sein** to go to/be in foreign parts, to go/be abroad.

fremde(l)n *vi* (*S Ger, Sw*) to be scared of strangers.

Fremden-: ~bett *nt* spare *or* guest bed; (*in Hotel*) hotel bed; **f~feindlich** *adj* hostile to strangers; (*ausländerfeindlich*) hostile to foreigners, xenophobic (*form*); **~führer** *m* **(a)** (*Mensch*) (tourist) guide; **(b)** (*Buch*) guide(book); ⚠**~haß** *m* xenophobia; **~legion** *f* Foreign Legion; **~legionär** *m* Foreign Legionnaire; ⚠**~paß** *m* alien's passport; **~polizei** *f* aliens branch (of the police); (*Aviat*) aliens office.

Fremdenverkehr *m* tourism *no def art*.

Fremdenverkehrs-: ~ort *m* tourist resort *or* centre; **~verein** *m* tourist association.

Fremdenzimmer *nt* guest room.

Fremde(r) *mf decl as adj* (*Unbekannter, Orts~*) stranger; (*Ausländer*) foreigner; (*Admin, Pol*) alien; (*Tourist*) visitor.

Fremd-: ~finanzierung *f* outside financing; **f~gehen** *vi sep irreg aux sein* (*inf*) to be unfaithful; **~heit** *f, no pl* (*ausländische Natur*) foreignness; (*Unvertrautheit*) strangeness; (*Entfremdung*) alienation; (*zwischen Menschen*) reserve; **~herrschaft** *f, no pl* foreign rule; **~kapital** *nt* outside capital; **~körper** *m* foreign body; (*fig*) alien element; **sich als ~körper fühlen** to feel out of place; **f~ländisch** *adj* foreign *no adv*; (*exotisch*) exotic; **~ling** *m* (*liter*) stranger.

Fremdsprache *f* foreign language ◆ **eine Begabung für ~n** a gift for languages.

Fremdsprachen-: ~korrespondent(in *f*) *m* bilingual secretary; **~sekretärin** *f* bilingual secretary; **~unterricht** *m* language teaching; **~unterricht haben/erteilen** to have/give language classes.

Fremd-: f~sprachig *adj* in a foreign language; *Fähigkeiten* (foreign) language; **die f~sprachige Bevölkerung** non-English/non-German *etc* speakers; **f~sprachlich** *adj* foreign; **f~sprachlicher Unterricht** language teaching; **~stoff** *m* foreign matter *no pl or* substance; **~verschulden** *nt* third-party responsibility; **~währung** *f* foreign currency; **~wort** *nt* borrowed *or* foreign word, borrowing; **Rücksichtnahme ist für ihn ein ~wort** (*fig*) he's never heard of the word consideration; **~wörterbuch** *nt* dictionary of borrowed *or* foreign words.

frenetisch *adj* frenetic, frenzied; *Beifall auch* wild.

frequentieren* *vt* (*geh*) to frequent.

Frequenz *f* **(a)** (*Häufigkeit*) frequency (*auch Phys*); (*Med*) (pulse) rate. **(b)** (*Stärke*) numbers *pl*; (*Verkehrsdichte*) volume of traffic.

Frequenz- *in cpds* frequency.

Freske *f* -, **-n** (*rare*), **Fresko** *nt* **-s, Fresken** fresco.

Fressalien [-iən] *pl* (*inf*) grub *sing* (*inf*), eats *pl* (*inf*).

⚠**Freßbeutel** *m* (*für Pferd*) nosebag.

Fresse *f* -, **-n** (*sl*) (*Mund*) trap (*sl*), gob (*sl*), cakehole (*Brit sl*); (*Gesicht*) mug (*inf*) ◆ **die ~ halten** to shut one's trap *or* gob *or* face (*all sl*); **eine große ~ haben** to be a loud-mouth (*inf*); **jdn** *or* **jdm in die ~ hauen, jdm die ~ polieren** to smash sb's face in (*inf*); **ach du meine ~!** bloody hell! (*Brit sl*), Jesus Christ! (*sl*).

fressen *pret* **fraß**, *ptp* **gefressen** [1] *vi* **(a)** to feed, to eat; (*sl: Menschen*) to eat; (*gierig*) to guzzle ◆ **jdm aus der Hand ~** (*lit, fig inf*) to eat out of sb's hand; **für drei ~** to eat enough for a whole army (*inf*); **er ißt nicht, er frißt (wie ein Schwein)** he eats like a pig; *siehe* **Vogel, Scheunendrescher**.
(b) (*zerstören*) to eat away (*an etw* (*dat*) sth).
[2] *vt* **(a)** (*verzehren: Tier, sl: Mensch*) to eat; (*sich ernähren von*) to feed *or* live on; (*sl: gierig essen*) to guzzle, to scoff ◆ **etwas zu ~** something to eat; **den Napf leer ~** (*Tiere*) to lick the bowl clean; (*Menschen*) to polish everything off (*inf*); **jdn arm ~, jdm die Haare vom Kopf ~** to eat sb out of house and home; *siehe* **Bauer**[1], **Not**.
(b) (*in Wendungen*) **Kilometer ~** to burn up the kilometres; **Löcher in etw** (*acc*) **~** (*lit*) to eat holes in sth; **ein Loch in den Geldbeutel ~** to make a big hole in one's pocket; **ich habe dich zum F~ gern** (*inf*) you're good enough to eat (*inf*); **ich könnte dich ~** (*inf*) I could eat you (*inf*); **ich will dich doch nicht ~** (*inf*) I'm not going to eat you (*inf*); **ich fresse einen Besen** *or* **meinen Hut, wenn ...** (*inf*) I'll eat my hat if ...; **jdn/etw gefressen haben** (*inf*) to have had one's fill *or* as much as one can take of sb/sth; **jetzt hat er es endlich gefressen** (*inf*) he's got it *or* got there at last (*inf*), at last the penny's dropped; **einen Narren** *or* **Affen an jdm/etw gefressen haben** to dote on sb/sth; *siehe* **Weisheit**.
(c) (*verbrauchen*) *Benzin, Ersparnisse* to eat *or* gobble up; *Zeit* to take up.
(d) (*geh: Neid, Haß*) to eat up.
[3] *vr* **(a)** (*sich bohren*) to eat one's way (*in +acc* into, *durch* through).
(b) **sich voll/satt ~** to gorge oneself/eat one's fill; (*Mensch auch*) to stuff oneself (*inf*); **sich krank ~** to eat oneself sick.

Fressen *nt* **-s**, *no pl* food; (*sl*) grub (*sl*); (*sl: Schmaus*) blow-out (*inf*); *siehe* **gefunden**.

Fresser *m* **-s, -** (*Tier*) eater; (*sl: gieriger Mensch*) glutton, greedyguts (*inf*)

⚠: for details of spelling reform, see supplement

♦ **wenn man fünf ~ im Haus hat** (*inf*) when you have five hungry mouths to feed.

Fresserei *f* (*inf*) **(a)** *no pl* (*übermäßiges Essen*) guzzling; (*Gefräßigkeit*) piggishness (*inf*), gluttony. **(b)** (*Schmaus*) blow-out (*inf*), nosh-up (*Brit sl*).

⚠ **Freß-: ~gier** *f* voraciousness; (*pej: von Menschen*) gluttony, piggishness (*inf*); **~korb** *m* (*inf*) (*für Picknick*) picnic hamper; (*Geschenkkorb*) food hamper; **~napf** *m* feeding bowl; **~paket** *nt* (*inf*) food parcel; **~sack** *m* (*sl*) greedyguts (*inf*), glutton; **~sucht** *f* (*inf*) gluttony; (*krankhaft*) craving for food.

⚠ **freßt** *imper pl of* **fressen.**

⚠ **Freß-: ~welle** *f* (*hum inf*) wave of gluttony; **~werkzeuge** *pl* feeding equipment *no pl or* organs *pl*; (*von Insekten*) mouthpart.

Frettchen *nt* ferret.

Freude *f* -, -n **(a)** *no pl* pleasure; (*innig*) joy (*über +acc* at); (*Erfreutheit*) delight (*über +acc* at) ♦ **~ an etw** (*dat*) **haben** to get *or* derive pleasure from sth; **er hat ~ an seinen Kindern** his children give him pleasure; **~ am Leben haben** to enjoy life; **wenn man an der Arbeit keine ~ hat** if you don't get any pleasure out of *or* if you don't enjoy your work; **die ~ an der Natur** the joy one gets from nature; **daran hat er seine ~** that gives him pleasure; (*iro*) he thinks that's fun; **es ist eine (wahre** *or* **reine) ~, zu ...** it's a (real) joy *or* pleasure to ...; **es war eine reine ~, das mit anzusehen** it was a joy to see; **es ist keine (reine) ~, das zu tun** (*iro*) it's not exactly fun doing that; **es ist mir eine ~, zu ...** it's a real pleasure for me to ...; **das Kind macht seinen Eltern viel/nur ~** the child gives his parents a lot of/nothing but joy; **er macht ihnen keine/wenig ~** he's no joy/not much of a joy to them; **es macht ihnen keine/wenig ~** they don't enjoy it (at all)/much; **jdm eine ~ machen** *or* **bereiten** to make sb happy; **jdm eine ~ machen wollen** to want to do something to please sb; **zu meiner großen ~** to my great delight; **zu unserer größten ~ können wir Ihnen mitteilen ...** we are pleased to be able to inform you ...; **Sie hätten seine ~ sehen sollen** you should have seen how happy he was; **aus ~ an der Sache** for the love of it *or* the thing; **aus Spaß an der ~** (*inf*) for the fun *or* hell (*inf*) of it *or* the thing; **in Freud und Leid zu jdm halten** (*dated*) to stand by sb come rain, come shine.

(b) (*Vergnügung*) joy ♦ **die kleinen ~n des Lebens** the pleasures of life; **herrlich und in ~n leben** to live a life of ease; **mit ~n** with pleasure; **da kommt ~ auf** this is where the fun starts.

Freuden-: ~botschaft *f* good news *sing*, glad tidings *pl* (*old, Bibl*); **~fest** *nt* celebration; **~feuer** *nt* bonfire; **~geheul, ~geschrei** *nt* howls *pl or* shrieks *pl* of joy; **~haus** *nt* (*dated, hum*) house of pleasure *or* ill-repute; **~junge** *m* (*hum*) male prostitute; **~mädchen** *nt* (*dated, hum*) lady of easy virtue (*euph*), prostitute; **~mahl** *nt* celebration meal, banquet (*old*), feast; **f~reich** *adj* (*geh*) joyful, joyous; **~ruf, ~schrei** *m* joyful cry, cry of joy; **~sprung** *m* joyful leap; **einen ~sprung machen** to jump for joy; **~tag** *m* happy *or* joyful (*esp liter*) day; **~tanz** *m* dance of joy; **einen ~tanz auf-** *or* **vollführen** to dance with joy; **~taumel** *m* ecstasy (of joy); **~tränen** *pl* tears *pl* of joy; **f~voll** *adj siehe* **freudvoll.**

freude-: ~strahlend *adj no pred* beaming with delight; *Gesicht auch* beaming; **~trunken** *adj* (*liter*) delirious with joy.

Freudianer *m* -s, - Freudian.

freudig *adj* **(a)** (*frohgestimmt*) joyful; (*gern bereit*) willing; (*begeistert*) enthusiastic ♦ **einen Vorschlag ~ begrüßen** to greet a suggestion with delight; **jdn ~ stimmen** to raise sb's spirits; **etw ~ erwarten** to look forward to sth with great pleasure; **~ überrascht sein** to have a delightful surprise.

(b) (*beglückend*) happy, joyful (*liter*) ♦ **eine ~e Nachricht** some good *or* joyful (*liter*) news, some glad tidings *pl* (*old, Bibl*); **ein ~es Ereignis** (*euph*) a happy *or* blessed event (*euph*).

Freud-: f~los *adj* joyless, cheerless; **f~los dahinleben** to lead a joyless *or* cheerless existence; **~losigkeit** *f, no pl* joylessness, cheerlessness.

Freudsch *adj attr* Freudian.

freudvoll *adj* (*geh*) joyful, joyous (*liter*); *Tage, Leben* filled with joy.

▼ **freuen** 1 *vr* **(a)** to be glad *or* pleased (*über +acc,* (*geh*) *+gen* about) ♦ **sich über ein Geschenk ~** to be pleased with a present; **sich sehr** *or* **riesig** (*inf*) **~** to be delighted *or* ever so pleased (*inf*) (*über +acc* about); **ich habe es bekommen, freute sie sich** I've got it, she said happily *or* (*stärker*) joyfully; **sich an etw** (*dat*) **~** to get *or* derive a lot of pleasure from sth; **er freut sich sehr an seinen Kindern** his children give him a lot of pleasure; **sich für jdn ~** to be glad *or* pleased for sb *or* for sb's sake; **sich mit jdm ~** to share sb's happiness; **sich seines Lebens ~** to enjoy life; **ich freue mich, Ihnen mitteilen zu können, ...** I'm pleased to be able to tell you ...; *siehe* **Kind.**

▼ **(b) sich auf jdn/etw ~** to look forward to seeing sb/to sth; **sich auf das Kind ~** to look forward to the child being born *or* to the child's birth; **sich zu früh ~** to get one's hopes up too soon.

2 *vt impers* to please ♦ **es freut mich/ihn, daß ...** I'm/he's pleased *or* glad that ...; **es freut mich/ihn sehr, daß ...** I'm/he's delighted *or* very pleased *or* glad that ...; **das freut mich** I'm really pleased; **es freut mich sehr/es hat mich sehr gefreut, Ihre Bekanntschaft zu machen** (*form*) (I'm) pleased to meet/have met you.

freund *adj pred* (*old*) **jdm ~ sein/bleiben/werden** to be/remain/become sb's friend.

Freund *m* -(e)s, -e **(a)** (*Kamerad*) friend ♦ **wir sind schon seit 1954 ~e** we've been friends since 1954; **mit jdm gut ~ sein** to be good friends with sb; **das habe ich ihm unter ~en gesagt** that was just between ourselves; **10 Mark unter ~en** 10 marks to a friend; **~ und Feind** friend and foe; **ein schöner ~** (*iro inf*) a fine friend; **jdn zum ~ haben** to have sb for *or* as a friend; **guter ~!** (*liter*) my dear man; *siehe* **alt.**

(b) (*Liebhaber*) boyfriend; (*älter auch*) gentleman-friend.

(c) (*fig*) (*Anhänger*) lover; (*Förderer*) friend ♦ **ein ~ der Kunst** an art-lover, a lover/friend of art; **ich bin kein ~ von Hunden** I'm no lover of dogs; **er ist kein ~ von vielen Worten** he's not one for talking much, he's a man of few words; **ich bin kein ~ von so etwas** I'm not one for that sort of thing; **ein ~ des Alkohols sein** to like one's drink.

-freund *m in cpds* **(a)** (*Kamerad*) friend. **(b)** (*fig: Liebhaber*) lover of.

Freundchen *nt* (*inf*) my friend (*iro*) ♦ **~! ~!** watch it, mate (*Brit inf*) *or* my friend!

Freundes-: ~hand *f* (*geh*) **jdm die ~hand reichen** to extend the hand *or* arm of friendship to sb; **von ~hand** by the hand of a friend; **~kreis** *m* circle of friends; **etw im engsten ~kreis feiern** to celebrate sth with one's closest friends.

Freund-Feind-Denken *nt* attitude that if you're not for us you're against us.

Freundin *f* **(a)** friend; (*Liebhaberin*) girlfriend; (*älter auch*) lady-friend. **(b)** (*fig: Anhänger, Förderer*) *siehe* **Freund (c).**

freundlich *adj* **(a)** (*wohlgesinnt*) friendly *no adv* ♦ **jdn ~ behandeln** to treat sb in a friendly way, to be friendly towards sb; **bitte recht ~!** say cheese! (*inf*), smile please!; **mit ~en Grüßen** *or* **~em Gruß** (with) best wishes; **einem Vorschlag ~ gegenüberstehen** to be in favour of *or* be well-disposed to a suggestion.

(b) (*liebenswürdig*) kind (*zu* to) ♦ **würden Sie bitte so ~ sein und das tun?** would you be so kind *or* good as to do that?, would you be kind *or* good enough to do that?; **das ist sehr ~ von Ihnen** that's very kind *or* good of you.

(c) (*ansprechend*) *Aussehen, Landschaft, Wetter etc* pleasant; *Zimmer, Einrichtung, Farben* cheerful; *Atmosphäre* friendly, congenial; (*Fin, Comm: günstig*) favourable.

-freundlich *adj suf* (*wohlgesinnt*) pro-; (*liebend*) fond of; (*schonend*) kind to.

freundlicherweise *adv* kindly ♦ **er trug uns ~ die Koffer** he was kind enough to carry our cases for us, he kindly carried our cases (for us).

Freundlichkeit *f* **(a)** *no pl siehe adj (a-c)* friendliness; kindness; kindliness; pleasantness; cheerfulness; friendliness, congeniality; favourableness ♦ **würden Sie (wohl) die ~ haben, das zu tun?** would you be so kind *or* good as to *or* be kind *or* good enough to do that? **(b)** (*freundliche Handlung, Gefälligkeit*) kindness, favour; (*freundliche Bemerkung*) kind remark ♦ **jdm ~en erweisen** to be kind to sb; **jdm ein paar ~en sagen** to say a few kind words *or* make a few kind remarks to sb.

Freundschaft *f* **(a)** (*freundschaftliches Verhältnis*) friendship ♦ **mit jdm ~ schließen** to make *or* become friends with sb, to form a friendship with sb; **jdm die ~ anbieten** to offer sb one's friendship; **in aller ~** in all friendliness; **da hört die ~ auf** (*inf*) friendship doesn't go that far; **in Geldsachen hört die ~ auf** friendship doesn't extend to money matters; **~!** (*DDR*) *greeting used by the Free German Youth; siehe* **kündigen, Geschenk.**

(b) *no pl* (*dial: Verwandtschaft*) relatives *pl*, relations *pl*.

(c) (*DDR*) *the Pioneer groups in one school.*

freundschaftlich *adj* friendly *no adv* ♦ **jdm ~ gesinnt sein** to feel friendly towards sb; **jdm ~ auf die Schulter klopfen** to give sb a friendly slap on the back; **~e Gefühle** feelings of friendship.

Freundschafts-: ~bande *pl* (*liter*) ties *pl* of friendship; **~besuch** *m* (*Pol*) goodwill visit; **~bund** *m* friendly alliance; **~dienst** *m* favour to a friend; **jdm einen ~dienst erweisen** to do sb a favour; **~preis** *m* (special) price for a friend; **er überließ mir sein Auto zu einem ~preis/einem ~preis von 100 DM** he let me have his car cheaply/for 100 DM because we're friends; **ich mache dir einen ~preis** (*inf*) seeing we're friends I'll let you have it for a special price; **~spiel** *nt* (*Sport*) friendly game *or* match, friendly (*inf*); **~vertrag** *m* (*Pol*) treaty of friendship.

Frevel *m* -s, - (*geh*) sin (*gegen* against); (*Tat auch*) heinous deed (*liter*); (*fig*) crime (*an +dat* against).

Frevel-: f~haft *adj* (*geh*) (*verwerflich*) sinful; *Leichtsinn, Verschwendung* wanton; **~haftigkeit** *f* (*geh*) *siehe adj* sinfulness; wantonness.

freveln *vi* (*liter*) to sin (*gegen, an +dat* against).

Freveltat *f* (*liter*) heinous deed (*liter*).

Frevler(in *f*) *m* -s, - (*liter*) sinner ♦ **die Strafe für den ~ an der Natur/gegen Gott** the punishment for someone who sins against nature/God.

frevlerisch *adj* (*liter*) *siehe* **frevelhaft.**

friderizianisch *adj* of Frederick the Great.

Friede *m* -ns, -n (*old*) peace ♦ **der ~ der Natur** the tranquillity of nature; **~ auf Erden** peace on earth; **~ sei mit euch** peace be with you; **~ seiner Asche** God rest his soul; **~, Freude, Eierkuchen** (*inf*) everything is rosy.

Frieden *m* -s, - **(a)** peace ♦ **ein langer, ungestörter ~** a long period of uninterrupted peace; **im ~** in peacetime, in time of peace; **in ~ und Freiheit leben** to live at peace and in freedom; **im tiefsten ~** (living) in perfect tranquillity; **seit letztem Jahr herrscht in dieser Gegend ~** this region has been at peace since last year; **~ schließen** to make one's peace; (*Pol*) to conclude (*form*) *or* make peace; **~ stiften** to make peace (*zwischen +dat* between).

(b) (*Friedensschluß*) peace; (*Vertrag*) peace treaty ♦ **der Westfälische ~** (*Hist*) the Peace of Westphalia; **den ~ diktieren** to dictate the peace terms; **über den ~ verhandeln** to hold peace negotiations; **den ~ einhalten** to keep the peace, to keep to the peace agreement.

(c) (*Harmonie*) peace, tranquillity ♦ **sozialer ~** social harmony; **der häusliche ~** domestic harmony; **in ~ und Freundschaft** *or* **Eintracht leben** to live in peace and harmony *or* tranquillity.

(d) (*Ruhe*) peace ♦ **jdn in ~ lassen** to leave sb in peace; **um des lieben ~s**

willen (*inf*) for the sake of peace and quiet; **sein schlechtes Gewissen ließ ihn keinen ~ mehr finden** his guilty conscience gave him no peace; **ich traue dem ~ nicht** (*inf*) something (fishy) is going on (*inf*); **(er) ruhe in ~** rest in peace.

Friedens- *in cpds* peace; **~bedingungen** *pl* peace terms *pl*; **~bemühung** *f usu pl* effort to achieve peace; (*~angebot*) peace move; **f~bewegt** *adj Kreise, Gruppen* pacifist; **ein f~bewegtes Thema** a peace issue; **~bewegte(r)** *mf decl as adj* peace activist; **~bewegung** *f* peace movement; **~bruch** *m* violation of the peace; **~engel** *m* (*lit, fig*) angel of peace; **~fahrt** *f* (*DDR*) peace race, *international cycling race through East Germany, Czechoslovakia and Poland*; **~forscher** *m* peace researcher; **~forschung** *f* peace studies *sing*; **~fühler** *pl*: **die ~fühler ausstrecken** (*inf*) to make a tentative move towards peace (*in Richtung* with); **~initiative** *f* peace initiative; **~kämpfer** *m* pacifist; **~konferenz** *f* peace conference; ⚠**~kuß** *m* (*Eccl*) pax, kiss of peace; **~lager** *nt* (*DDR*) *nations of the Socialist bloc*; **~liebe** *f* love of peace; **~nobelpreis** *m* Nobel peace prize; **~pfeife** *f* peace-pipe; **mit jdm/miteinander die ~pfeife rauchen** (*lit*) to smoke a peace-pipe with sb/together; (*fig*) to make (one's) peace with sb/to bury the hatchet; **~pflicht** *f* (*Ind*) *obligation binding on employers and unions to avoid industrial action during wages negotiations*; **~politik** *f* policy of peace; **~produktion** *f* peacetime production; ⚠**~prozeß** *m* peace process; **~richter** *m* justice of the peace, JP; ⚠**~schluß** *m* peace agreement; **f~sichernd** *adj* **f~sichernde Maßnahmen** measures to ensure peace; **~sicherung** *f* maintenance of peace; **Maßnahmen zur ~sicherung** measures to ensure peace; **~stärke** *f* (*Mil*) peacetime strength; **f~stiftend** *adj* peacemaking; **~stifter** *m* peacemaker; **~taube** *f* dove of peace; **~truppen** *pl* peacekeeping forces *pl*; **~verhandlungen** *pl* peace negotiations *pl*; **~vertrag** *m* peace treaty; **~vorschlag** *m* peace proposal; **~wille** *m* desire *or* wish for peace; **~wirtschaft** *f* peacetime economy; **~zeit** *f* period of peace; **in ~zeiten** in peacetime, in times of peace; **~zustand** *m* state of peace; **im ~zustand** at peace.

friedfertig *adj* peaceable; *Hund* placid ◆ **selig sind die F~en** (*Bibl*) blessed are the peacemakers.

Friedfertigkeit *f* peaceableness; (*von Hund*) placidness ◆ **in seiner ~/aus reiner ~ hat er ...** peaceable as he is/because of his peaceable nature, he ...

Friedhof *m* (*Kirchhof*) graveyard; (*Stadt~ etc*) cemetery ◆ **auf dem ~** in the graveyard/cemetery.

Friedhofs-: ~atmosphäre *f* gloomy atmosphere; **es herrscht im Haus eine ~atmosphäre** the house is like a graveyard; **~gärtnerei** *f* cemetery flower shop; **~kapelle** *f* cemetery chapel; **~ruhe** *f* (*lit*) peace of the graveyard/cemetery; (*fig*) deathly quiet.

friedlich *adj* **(a)** (*nicht kriegerisch, ohne Gewalt*) *Lösung, Demonstration, Volk, Zeiten* peaceful; (*friedfertig, ohne Streit*) *Mensch, Abschied* peaceable; *Hund* placid ◆ **etw auf ~em Wege lösen** to find a peaceful solution to sth, to solve sth peacefully *or* by peaceful means; **damit er endlich ~ ist** (*inf*) to keep him happy; **nun sei doch endlich ~!** (*fig inf*) give it a rest! (*inf*); **sei ~, ich will keinen Streit** take it easy *or* calm down, I don't want any trouble.
(b) (*friedvoll*) peaceful ◆ **~ sterben** *or* **einschlafen** (*euph*) to die peacefully.

Friedlichkeit *f, no pl siehe adj* **(a)** peacefulness; peaceableness; placidness, placidity. **(b)** peacefulness.

fried-: ~liebend *adj* peace-loving; **~los** *adj* **(a)** (*Hist*) *Person* outlawed; **(b)** (*liter: ruhelos*) *Leben* without peace; *Mensch* unable to find peace; **~sam** *adj* (*old*) *siehe* **friedlich**.

Friedrich *m* **-s** Frederick ◆ **~ der Große** Frederick the Great; **seinen ~ Wilhelm unter etw** (*acc*) **setzen** (*inf*) to put one's signature *or* monicker (*inf*) to sth.

frieren *pret* **fror**, *ptp* **gefroren** [1] *vi* **(a)** *auch vt impers* (*sich kalt fühlen*) to be/get cold ◆ **ich friere, mich friert, es friert mich** (*geh*) I'm cold; **wie ein Schneider ~** (*inf*) to be/get frozen to the marrow (*inf*); **mir** *or* **mich ~ die Zehen, mich friert es** *or* **ich friere an den Zehen** my toes are/get cold.
(b) *aux sein* (*gefrieren*) to freeze; (*Fluß auch*) to freeze over.
[2] *vi impers* to freeze ◆ **heute nacht hat es gefroren** it was below freezing last night.

Fries *m* **-es, -e** (*Archit, Tex*) frieze.

Friese *m* **-n, -n**, **Friesin** *f* Fri(e)sian.

friesisch *adj* Fri(e)sian.

Friesland *nt* Friesland.

frigid(e) *adj* frigid.

Frigidität *f* frigidity.

Frika(n)delle *f* (*Cook*) rissole.

Frikassee *nt* **-s, -s** (*Cook*) fricassee.

frikassieren* *vt* (*Cook*) to fricassee.

Frikativ(laut) *m* (*Ling*) fricative.

Friktion *f* (*Tech, fig geh*) friction *no pl*.

Frisbee ['frɪzbi] *nt* **-, -s** (*Scheibe*) frisbee; **Frisbee spielen** to play with a frisbee.

Frisbeescheibe *f* frisbee disk.

frisch *adj* **(a)** fresh; (*feucht*) *Farbe, Fleck* wet ◆ **~es Obst** fresh-picked fruit; **~e Eier** new-laid eggs; **Bier ~ vom Faß** beer (straight) from the barrel; **~ gestrichen** newly painted; (*auf Schild*) wet paint; **~ geschlachtet** fresh(ly) slaughtered; *Geflügel* fresh(ly) killed; **~ gefallener Schnee** freshly *or* newly fallen snow; **~ gewaschen** *Kind* clean; *Hemd etc auch* freshly washed *or* laundered; **das Bett ~ beziehen** to change the bed, to make the bed up with fresh sheets; **sich ~ machen** to freshen up; **mit ~en Kräften** with renewed vigour *or* strength; **~en Mut fassen** to gain new courage; **~e Luft schöpfen** to get some fresh air; **jdn an die ~e Luft setzen** (*inf*) to show sb the door; **das ist mir noch ~ in Erinnerung** that is still fresh in my mind *or* memory; **jdn auf ~er Tat ertappen** to catch sb in the act *or* red-handed.
(b) (*munter*) *Wesen, Art* bright, cheery; *Erzählung* bright; (*gesund*) *Aussehen, Gesichtsfarbe* fresh; *Mädchen* fresh-looking ◆ **~ und munter sein** (*inf*) to be bright and lively; **~, fromm, fröhlich, frei** (*prov*) *motto of a 19th century gymnastic movement*; (*iro*) cheerfully, gaily; **immer ~ drauflos!** don't hold back!; **er geht immer ~ drauflos** he doesn't hang about; **er redet/schreibt immer ~ drauflos** he just talks/writes away; **~ begonnen, halb gewonnen** (*Prov*), **~ gewagt ist halb gewonnen** (*Prov*) a good start is half the battle.
(c) (*kühl*) cool, chilly; *Luft, Wind auch* fresh ◆ **es weht ein ~er Wind** (*lit*) there's a fresh wind; (*fig*) the wind of change is blowing.

frisch|auf *interj* (*old*) let us away (*old*).

Frische *f* **-**, *no pl* **(a)** freshness; (*Feuchtigkeit: von Farbe, Fleck*) wetness.
(b) (*Munterkeit: von Wesen, Erzählung*) brightness; (*gesundes Aussehen*) freshness ◆ **in voller körperlicher und geistiger ~** in perfect health both physically and mentally; **in alter ~** (*inf*) as always.
(c) (*Kühle*) coolness, chilliness; (*von Luft, Wind auch*) freshness.

Frische-Datum *nt* sell-by date.

Frisch|ei *nt* new-laid egg.

frischen [1] *vt Metall* to refine.
[2] *vi* (*Wildschwein*) to farrow.

Frisch-: ~fisch *m* fresh fish; **~fleisch** *nt* fresh meat; **f~fröhlich** *adj* bright and cheerful; ⚠**f~gebacken** *adj* (*inf*) *Ehepaar* newly wed; **~gemüse** *nt* fresh vegetables *pl*.

Frischhalte-: ~beutel *m* airtight bag; **~datum** *nt* sell-by date; **~folie** *f* cling film; **~packung** *f* airtight pack.

Frisch-: ~käse *m* cream cheese; **~ling** *m* **(a)** (*Hunt*) *young wild boar*; **(b)** (*hum: Neuling*) raw beginner; **~luft** *f* fresh air; **~milch** *f* fresh milk; **~wasser** *nt* fresh water; **f~weg** *adv* (*ohne Hemmungen*) straight out (*inf*); **die Kinder fingen f~weg an zu singen** the children started to sing right off (*inf*); **~wurst** *f* sausage (*unsmoked, undried etc*); **~zelle** *f* (*Med*) live cell; **~zellentherapie** *f* (*Med*) cellular *or* live-cell therapy.

Friseur [fri'zøːɐ] *m* hairdresser; (*Herren~ auch*) barber; (*Geschäft*) hairdresser's; barber's.

Friseurin [fri'zøːrɪn] *f* (female) hairdresser.

Friseursalon *m* hairdresser's, hairdressing salon.

Friseuse [fri'zøːzə] *f* (female) hairdresser.

Frisiercreme *f* haircream.

frisieren* [1] *vt* **(a)** (*kämmen*) **jdn ~, jdm das Haar ~** to do sb's hair; (*nach dem Legen*) to comb sb's hair *or* sb (*inf*) out; **ihr elegant frisierter Kopf** her elegant hairdo; **sie ist stets gut frisiert** her hair is always beautifully done; **eine modisch frisierte Dame** a lady with a fashionable hairstyle *or* hairdo.
(b) (*inf: abändern*) *Abrechnung* to fiddle; *Bericht, Meldung* to doctor (*inf*) ◆ **die Bilanzen ~** to cook the books (*inf*).
(c) *Auto* to hot *or* soup up (*inf*); *Motor auch* to tweak (*sl*).
[2] *vr* to do one's hair.

Frisier-: ~haube *f* (*Trockner*) hairdryer hood; (*beim Friseur*) hairdryer; **~kommode** *f* dressing table; **~salon** *m* hairdressing salon; (*für Herren*) barber's shop; **~spiegel** *m* dressing (table) mirror; **~stab** *m* styling brush; **~tisch** *m* dressing table; **~umhang** *m* hairdressing cape.

Frisör *m* **-s, -e**, **Frisöse** *f* **-, -n** *siehe* **Friseur, Friseuse**.

⚠**friß** *imper sing of* **fressen**.

Frist *f* **-, -en** **(a)** (*Zeitraum*) period; (*Kündigungs~*) period of notice ◆ **eine ~ von vier Tagen/Wochen** *etc* four days/weeks *etc*; **eine ~ einhalten** to meet a deadline; (*bei Rechnung*) to pay within the period stipulated; **jds ~ verlängern/um zwei Tage verlängern** to give sb more time/two more days; **die Bibliothek hat mir die ~ für die Rückgabe der Bücher verlängert** the library extended the loan-period on my books; **eine ~ verstreichen lassen** to let a deadline pass; (*bei Rechnung*) not to pay within the period stipulated; **innerhalb kürzester ~** without delay.
(b) (*Zeitpunkt*) deadline (*zu* for); (*bei Rechnung*) last date for payment ◆ **eine ~ versäumen** *or* **verpassen** to miss a deadline/the last date for payment.
(c) (*Aufschub*) extension, period of grace ◆ **jdm eine ~ von vier Tagen/Wochen geben** to give sb four days/weeks grace.

Frist|ablauf *m* **nach ~** after the deadline has/had expired; (*bei Rechnung*) after expiry of the stipulated period.

fristen *vt* **sein Leben** *or* **Dasein ~/mit etw ~** to eke out an existence/one's existence with sth; **ein kümmerliches Dasein ~** to eke out a miserable existence; (*Partei, Institution*) to exist on the fringes; **die Bauern mußten in Armut ihr Leben ~** the peasants barely managed to scrape a living.

Fristenlösung, Fristenregelung *f law allowing the termination of a pregnancy within the first three months*.

Frist-: f~gerecht *adj* within the period stipulated; **f~los** *adj* instant, without notice; **Sie sind f~los entlassen** you are dismissed without notice; **~verlängerung** *f* extension.

Frisur *f* hairstyle.

⚠**Friteuse** [fri'tøːzə] *f* chip pan, deep-fat fryer.

⚠**fritieren*** *vt* to (deep-)fry.

Fritten *pl* (*inf*) chips *pl* (*Brit*), fries *pl* (*esp US inf*).

Frittenbude *f* (*inf*) chip shop (*Brit*), chippie (*Brit inf*), ≃ hotdog stand.

⚠**Fritüre** *f* **-, -n** **(a)** *siehe* **Friteuse**. **(b)** (*Fett*) fat. **(c)** (*Speise*) fried food.

-fritze *m in cpds* **-n, -n** (*inf*) chap (*Brit inf*), guy (*inf*).

frivol [fri'voːl] *adj* (*leichtfertig*) frivolous; (*anzüglich*) *Witz, Bemerkung* risqué, suggestive; (*verantwortungslos*) irresponsible.

Frivolität [frivoli'tɛːt] *f* **(a)** *no pl siehe adj* frivolity; suggestiveness; irrespon-

⚠: for details of spelling reform, see supplement

sibility. **(b)** (*Bemerkung*) risqué remark.
Frivolitäten|arbeit *f* (*Sew*) tatting.
Frl. *abbr of* **Fräulein.**
froh *adj* **(a)** (*heiter*) happy; (*dankbar auch*) glad; (*erfreut auch*) glad, pleased ♦ **über etw** (*acc*) **~ sein** to be pleased with sth; **(darüber) ~ sein, daß ...** to be glad *or* pleased that ...; **um etw ~ sein** to be grateful for sth; **~en Mutes** *or* **Sinnes sein** (*old, geh*) to be cheerful, to be of good cheer (*old*); **~en Mutes machte sie sich an die Arbeit** (*old, geh*) cheerfully *or* with a light heart she set herself to work; **seines Lebens nicht (mehr) ~ werden** not to enjoy life any more; **da wird man seines Lebens nicht mehr ~!** it makes your life a misery.
(b) (*erfreulich*) happy, joyful; *Nachricht auch* good ♦ **~e Ostern!** Happy Easter!; **~e Weihnachten!** Happy *or* Merry Christmas!; *siehe* **Botschaft.**
froh-: ~gelaunt *adj* joyful (*liter*), cheerful, happy; **~gemut** *adj* (*old*) with a cheerful heart; **~gestimmt** *adj* (*geh*) happy, joyful (*liter*).
fröhlich [1] *adj* happy, cheerful, merry; *Lieder, Lachen, Stimme auch* gay ♦ **~e Weihnachten!** Happy *or* Merry Christmas!; **~es Treiben** gaiety.
[2] *adv* (*unbekümmert*) merrily, blithely, gaily ♦ **er kam einfach so ~ ins Zimmer marschiert** he came waltzing into the room (*inf*).
Fröhlichkeit *f, no pl* happiness; (*fröhliches Wesen*) happy *or* cheerful nature; (*gesellige Stimmung*) merriment, gaiety.
frohlocken* *vi* (*geh*) to rejoice (*über +acc* over, at); (*vor Schadenfreude auch*) to gloat (*über +acc* over, *bei* at).
Froh-: ~natur *f* (*geh*) **(a)** (*Mensch*) happy *or* cheerful soul *or* person; **(b)** (*Wesensart*) happy *or* cheerful nature; **~sinn** *m, no pl* cheerfulness; (*fröhliches Wesen*) cheerful nature; **f~sinnig** *adj* cheerful.
fromm *adj, comp* **¨er** *or* **-er,** *superl* **¨ste(r, s)** *or* **-ste(r, s)** *or* **am ¨sten (a)** (*gläubig*) religious; *Christ* devout; *Werke* good; *Leben, Tun, Versenkung etc* godly, pious; (*scheinheilig*) sanctimonious ♦ **~ werden** to become religious, to turn to *or* get (*inf*) religion; **mit ~em Augenaufschlag/Blick** looking as if butter wouldn't melt in his/her mouth; **~e Sprüche** pious words.
(b) (*old: rechtschaffen*) *Bürger, Leute, Denkungsart* god-fearing, upright ♦ **es kann der F¨ste nicht in Frieden leben, wenn es dem bösen Nachbarn nicht gefällt** (*Prov*) you can't be on good terms with a bad neighbour however hard you try.
(c) (*old: gehorsam*) meek, docile; *Tier* quiet, docile ♦ **~ wie ein Lamm sein** to be as meek *or* (*Tier*) gentle as a lamb.
(d) (*fig*) **eine ~e Lüge, ein ~er Betrug** self-deception; **das ist ja wohl nur ein ~er Wunsch** that's just a pipe-dream.
Frömmelei *f* (*pej*) false piety.
frömmeln *vi* (*pej*) to act piously, to affect piety.
frommen *vi* (*old*) **jdm/nichts ~** to avail sb (*form*)/avail sb naught (*old*); **was frommt ihm das Geld?** of what avail is the money to him? (*form*).
Frömmigkeit *f siehe* **fromm (a, b)** religiousness; devoutness; goodness; godliness, piousness; piousness, sanctimony; uprightness.
Frömmler(in *f***)** *m* **-s, -** (*pej*) sanctimonious hypocrite.
frömmlerisch *adj* (*pej*) pious, sanctimonious.
Fron *f* **-, -en, Fron|arbeit** *f* (*Hist*) socage *no pl*; (*fig*) drudgery *no pl*; (*Sklavenarbeit*) slavery.
Fronde ['frõ:də] *f* **-, -n** (*Pol*) faction.
Frondeur [frõdø:ʁ] *m* factionist.
Frondienst *m* (*Hist*) socage *no pl* ♦ **jdm ~e leisten** to do socage (work) for sb.
fronen *vi* (*Hist*) to labour for one's feudal lord; (*fig geh*) to labour.
frönen *vi +dat* (*geh*) to indulge in; *seiner Eitelkeit* to indulge.
Fronleichnam *no art* **-(e)s,** *no pl* (the Feast of) Corpus Christi ♦ **zu** *or* **an ~** at the Feast of Corpus Christi, on Corpus Christi.
Fronleichnams-: ~fest *nt* Feast of Corpus Christi; **~prozession** *f*, **~zug** *m* Corpus Christi procession.
Front *f* **-, -en (a)** (*Vorderseite*) front; (*Vorderansicht*) frontage ♦ **die hintere/rückwärtige ~** the back/the rear; **der General schritt die ~ der wartenden Truppen ab** the general inspected the waiting troops.
(b) (*Kampflinie, -gebiet*) front ♦ **in vorderster ~ stehen** to be in the front line; **auf breiter ~** along a wide front; **an der ~** at the front; **klare ~en schaffen** (*fig*) to clarify the/one's position.
(c) (*Met*) front.
(d) (*Einheit*) ranks *pl*; (*in Namen*) front ♦ **sich einer geschlossenen ~ gegenübersehen** to be faced with a united front; **~ gegen jdn/etw machen** to make a stand against sb/sth.
(e) (*Sport: Führung*) **in ~ liegen/gehen** to be in/go into *or* take the lead.
Front|abschnitt *m* section of the front.
frontal [1] *adj no pred* frontal; *Zusammenstoß* head-on.
[2] *adv* frontally; *zusammenstoßen* head-on.
Frontal-: ~angriff *m* frontal attack; **~unterricht** *m* (*Sch*) didactic teaching, chalk and talk (*inf*); **~zusammenstoß** *m* head-on collision.
Front-: ~antrieb *m* (*Aut*) front-wheel drive; **~begradigung** *f* straightening of the front; (*fig*) streamlining operation; **~bericht** *m* report from the front; **~dienst, ~einsatz** *m* service at the front; **er wurde zum ~dienst nach Rumänien abkommandiert** he was posted to serve on the Rumanian front.
Frontispiz *nt* **-es, -e** (*Archit, Typ*) frontispiece.
Front-: ~kämpfer *m siehe* **~soldat; ~lader** *m* **-s, -** front loader; **~motor** *m* front-mounted engine; **~schwein** *nt* (*sl*), **~soldat** *m* front-line soldier; **~spoiler** *m* (*Aut*) front spoiler; **~stadt** *f* frontier town/city; **~urlaub** *m* leave from the front; **~wand** *f* frontage; **~wechsel** *m* (*fig*) about-turn; **~zulage** *f* supplement for service at the front.
Fronvogt *m* (*Hist*) (socage) overseer.
fror *pret of* **frieren.**
Frosch *m* **-(e)s, ¨e** frog; (*Feuerwerkskörper*) (fire)cracker, jumping jack (*Brit*) ♦ **einen ~ in der Kehle** *or* **im Hals haben** (*inf*) to have a frog in one's throat; **sei kein ~!** (*inf*) be a sport!
Frosch-: ~auge *nt* (*fig inf*) pop eye; **er hat ~augen** he has pop eyes *or* is pop-eyed; ⚠**~biß** *m* (*Bot*) frogbit; **~hüpfen** *nt* leapfrog; **~könig** *m* Frog Prince; **~konzert** *nt* (*hum*) frog chorus; **~laich** *m* frogspawn; **~lurch** *m* salientian (*form*), member of the frog family; **~mann** *m* frogman; **~maul** *nt* (*fig inf*) pout; **~perspektive** *f* worm's-eye view; (*fig*) blinkered view; **etw aus der ~perspektive fotografieren/sehen** to take/get a worm's-eye view of sth; **etw aus der ~perspektive betrachten** (*fig*) to have a blinkered view of sth; **~schenkel** *m* frog's leg; **~test** *m* (*Med*) Bickenbach (pregnancy) test.
Frost *m* **-(e)s, ¨e (a)** frost ♦ **es herrscht strenger/klirrender ~** there's a hard *or* heavy/crisp frost; **bei eisigem ~** in heavy frost; **~ (ab)bekommen** (*Hände, Ohren*) to get frostbitten; **~ vertragen (können)** to be able to stand (the) frost.
(b) (*Med: Schüttel~*) fit of shivering *or* the shivers (*inf*) ♦ **er wurde von einem heftigen ~ geschüttelt** he shivered violently.
Frost-: ~aufbruch *m* frost damage; **f~beständig** *adj* frost-resistant; **~beule** *f* chilblain; **~boden** *m* frozen ground; (*ständig gefroren*) permafrost.
fröst(e)lig *adj* (*inf*) chilly ♦ **er ist ein ~er Mensch** he's a chilly mortal (*inf*), he feels the cold.
frösteln [1] *vi* to shiver; (*vor Angst auch*) to tremble; (*vor Entsetzen auch*) to shudder ♦ **im Fieber ~** to shiver feverishly.
[2] *vt impers* **es fröstelte mich** I shivered/trembled/shuddered.
frosten *vt* to freeze.
Froster *m* **-s, -** (*im Kühlschrank*) icebox (*Brit*), freezer compartment; (*Gefriertruhe*) freezer, deep-freeze.
Frost-: f~frei *adj* frost-free, free from *or* of frost; **die Nacht war f~frei** there was no frost overnight; **~gefahr** *f* danger of frost.
frostig *adj* (*lit, fig*) frosty ♦ **ein ~er Hauch** an icy draught.
Frostigkeit *f* (*fig*) frostiness.
Frost-: f~klar *adj* clear and frosty; **f~klirrend** *adj attr* (*liter*) crisp and frosty; **~schaden** *m* frost damage; **~schutz** *m* protection against frost; **~schutzmittel** *nt* (*Aut*) antifreeze; **~warnung** *f* frost warning; **~wetter** *nt* frosty weather.
Frottee [frɔ'te:] *nt or m* **-s, -s** terry towelling ♦ **ein Kleid aus ~** a towelling dress.
Frottee-: ~(hand)tuch *nt* (terry) towel; **~kleid** *nt* towelling dress.
frottieren* *vt Haut* to rub; *jdn, sich* to rub down.
Frottier(hand)tuch *nt siehe* **Frottee(hand)tuch.**
Frotzelei *f* (*inf*) teasing; (*Bemerkung*) teasing remark.
frotzeln *vti* (*inf*) to tease ♦ **über jdn/etw ~** to make fun of sb/sth.
Frucht *f* **-, ¨e** (*Bot, fig*) fruit; (*Embryo*) foetus; (*no pl: Getreide*) crops *pl* ♦ **¨e** (*Obst*) fruit *sing*; **¨e tragen** (*lit, fig*) to bear fruit; **die ¨e des Feldes** (*liter*) the fruits of the earth (*liter*); **verbotene ¨e** forbidden fruits; **eine ~ der Liebe** (*old euph*) a love child; **an ihren ¨en sollt ihr sie erkennen** (*Bibl*) by their fruits ye shall know them (*Bibl*).
Frucht|ansatz *m* (*Bot*) fruit buds *pl*.
fruchtbar *adj* **(a)** (*lit, fig: zeugungsfähig, reiche Frucht bringend*) fertile; *siehe* **Boden. (b)** (*lit, fig: viele Nachkommen zeugend, viel schaffend*) prolific; (*Bibl*) fruitful. **(c)** (*fig: nutzbringend*) fruitful, productive ♦ **etw für jdn/etw ~ machen** to use sth for the good of sb/sth, to use sth to benefit sb/sth.
Fruchtbarkeit *f siehe adj* fertility; prolificness; fruitfulness, productiveness.
Fruchtbarkeits-: ~kult *m* fertility cult; **~symbol** *nt* fertility symbol; **~zauber** *m* fertility rite.
Fruchtbarmachung *f* (*von Wüste*) reclamation.
Frucht-: ~becher *m* fruit sundae; (*Bot*) cupule (*spec*), cup; **~blase** *f* amniotic sac; **~bonbon** *m or nt* fruit drop; **f~bringend** *adj* (*geh*) fruitful, productive.
Früchtchen *nt dim of* **Frucht** (*inf*) (*Tunichtgut*) good-for-nothing; (*Kind*) rascal (*inf*) ♦ **du bist mir ein sauberes** *or* **nettes ~** (*iro*) you're a right one (*inf*).
Früchtebrot *nt* fruit loaf.
fruchten *vi* to bear fruit ♦ **nichts ~** to be fruitless.
Früchtetee *m* fruit tea *or* infusion.
Frucht-: ~fleisch *nt* flesh (*of a fruit*); **~fliege** *f* fruit-fly; **~folge** *f* (*Agr*) rotation of crops.
fruchtig *adj* fruity.
Frucht-: ~kapsel *f* (*Bot*) capsule; **~knoten** *m* (*Bot*) ovary; **f~los** *adj* (*fig*) fruitless; **~mark** *nt* (*Cook*) fruit pulp; **~presse** *f* fruit press *or* squeezer; **~saft** *m* fruit juice; **~säure** *f* fruit acid; **~stand** *m* (*Bot*) multiple fruit; **f~tragend** *adj attr* fruit-bearing; **~wasser** *nt* (*Physiol*) amniotic fluid; **das ~wasser ist vorzeitig abgegangen** the waters broke early; **~wasseruntersuchung** *f* (*Med*) amniocentesis; **~wechsel** *m* crop rotation; **~zucker** *m* fructose.
frugal *adj* (*geh*) frugal.
früh [1] *adj* early ♦ **am ~en Morgen** early in the morning, in the early morning; **in ~er Jugend** in one's early youth; **in ~er/~ester Kindheit** in one's early childhood/very early in one's childhood; **der ~e Goethe** the young Goethe; **ein Werk des ~en Picasso** an early work by Picasso; **ein ~er Picasso** an early Picasso.
[2] *adv* **(a)** early; (*in jungen Jahren*) young, at an early age; (*in Entwicklung*) early on ♦ **es ist noch ~ am Tag/im Jahr** it is still early in the day/year; **von ~ bis spät** from morning till night, from dawn to dusk; **er hat schon ~ erkannt,**

daß ... he recognized early on that ...; **du hast dich nicht ~ genug angemeldet** you didn't apply early *or* soon enough; **zu ~ starten** to start too soon; **~ übt sich, was ein Meister werden will** (*Prov*) there's nothing like starting young.
(b) Freitag/morgen ~ Friday/tomorrow morning; **heute ~** this morning.

Früh- *in cpds* early; **~antike** *f* early classical period; ⚠**f~auf** *adv* **von f~auf** from an early age; **~aufsteher** *m* **-s, -** early riser, early bird (*inf*); **~beet** *nt* cold frame; **~behandlung** *f* early *or* prompt treatment *no indef art*; **f~christlich** *adj* early Christian; **~diagnose** *f* early diagnosis; **~dienst** *m* early duty; **~dienst haben** to be on early duty.

Frühe *f* **-,** *no pl* **(a)** (*liter: Frühzeit*) dawn ◆ **in der ~ des Tages** in the early morning. **(b)** (*Morgen*) **in der ~** early in the morning; **in aller** *or* **gleich in der ~** at break *or* (the) crack of dawn.

Früh-: ~ehe *f* young marriage; **~entwickler(in** *f*) *m* early developer.

früher *comp of* **früh** [1] *adj* **(a)** earlier ◆ **in ~en Jahren/Zeiten** in the past; **in ~em Alter** when he/she *etc* was younger; **in ~en Zeitaltern** in past ages.
(b) (*ehemalig*) former; (*vorherig*) *Besitzer, Wohnsitz* previous ◆ **der Kontakt zu seinen ~en Freunden ist abgebrochen** he lost contact with his old friends.
[2] *adv* **(a)** earlier ◆ **~ als 6 Uhr/Freitag kann ich nicht kommen** I can't come earlier than 6 o'clock/earlier *or* sooner than Friday; **~ geht's nicht** it can't be done any/I *etc* can't make it earlier *or* sooner; **~ am Abend hat er gesagt** ... earlier (on) in the evening he said ...; **alle, die sich ~ angemeldet haben, werden zuerst berücksichtigt** the first to apply will be the first to be considered; **das hättest du ~ sagen müssen/wissen sollen** you should have said that before *or* sooner/known that before; **~ oder später** sooner or later.
(b) (*in jüngeren Jahren, in vergangenen Zeiten*) **Herr X, ~ Direktor eines Industriebetriebs** Herr X, formerly director of an industrial concern; **ich habe ihn ~ mal gekannt** I used to know him; **~ habe ich so etwas nie gemacht** I never used to do that kind of thing; **~ stand hier eine Kirche** there used to be a church here; **~ war alles besser/war das alles anders** things were better/different in the old days, things used to be better/different; **genau wie ~** just as it/he *etc* used to be; **Erzählungen von/Erinnerungen an ~** stories/memories of times gone by *or* of bygone days (*liter*); **das habe ich noch von ~** I had it before; **ich kannte/kenne ihn von ~** I knew him before/I've known him some time; **wir kennen uns noch von ~** we got to know each other some time ago; **meine Freunde von ~** my old friends.

Früh|erkennung *f* (*Med*) early diagnosis.

frühestens *adv* at the earliest ◆ **~ am Sonntag** on Sunday at the earliest; **wann kann das ~ fertig sein?** what is the earliest that can be ready?

früheste(r, s) *adj superl of* **früh**.

frühestmöglich *adj attr* earliest possible.

Früh-: ~geburt *f* premature birth; (*Kind*) premature baby; **sie hatte/meine Tochter war eine ~geburt** her baby/my daughter was premature *or* born prematurely; **~gemüse** *nt* early vegetables *pl*; **~geschichte** *f* early history; **~gottesdienst** *m* early service; **~herbst** *m* early autumn *or* fall (*US*); **f~herbstlich** *adj* early autumn/fall *attr*; **~invalidität** *f* early retirement due to ill health.

Frühjahr *nt* spring.

Frühjahrs-: ~bote *m* (*liter*) harbinger of spring (*liter*); **~müdigkeit** *f* springtime lethargy; **~putz** *m* spring-cleaning.

Früh-: ~kapitalismus *m* early capitalism; **~kartoffeln** *pl* early potatoes *pl*; **f~kindlich** *adj* (*Psych*) of early childhood; *Sexualität, Entwicklung* in early childhood; *Trauma, Erlebnisse* from early childhood; **~konzert** *nt* early morning concert; (*von Vögeln*) dawn chorus; **~kultur** *f* **(a)** early culture; **(b)** (*Hort*) propagated seedlings *pl*.

Frühling *m* spring ◆ **es wird ~, der ~ kommt** spring is coming; **im ~** in spring; **die Stadt des ewigen ~s** (*poet*) the springtime city (*liter*); **im ~ des Lebens stehen** (*poet*) to be in the springtime of one's life (*liter*); **einem neuen ~ entgegengehen** (*fig*) to start to flourish again; **seinen zweiten ~ erleben** to go through one's second adolescence.

Frühlings- *in cpds* spring; **~anfang** *m* first day of spring; **~fest** *nt* spring festival; **~gefühle** *pl* (*hum inf*) **~gefühle haben/bekommen** to be/get frisky (*hum inf*); **wenn sich ~gefühle (bei ihm) regen** when he starts to feel frisky (*hum inf*), when the sap starts to rise (*hum*); **f~haft** *adj* springlike; **sich f~haft kleiden** to dress in spring clothes; **~rolle** *f* (*Cook*) spring roll; **~suppe** *f* spring vegetable soup; **~zeit** *f* springtime, springtide (*liter*).

Früh-: ≈messe *f* early mass; **f~morgens** *adv* early in the morning; **≈nebel** *m* early morning mist; **≈neuhochdeutsch** *nt* Early New High German; ⚠**f≈pensionieren*** *vt insep* **jdn f~pensionieren** to give sb early retirement; **≈pensionierung** *f* early retirement; **f≈reif** *adj* precocious; (*körperlich*) mature at an early age; **≈reife** *f siehe adj* precociousness; early maturity; **≈rentner** *m* person who has retired early; **≈schicht** *f* early shift; **ich gehöre zur ~schicht** (*inf*) I'm on the early shift; **≈schoppen** *m* morning/lunchtime drinking; **zum ~schoppen gehen** to go for a morning/lunchtime drink; **≈sommer** *m* early summer; **f≈sommerlich** *adj* early summer *attr*; **das Wetter ist schon f~sommerlich** the weather is already quite summery; **≈sport** *m* early morning exercise; **~sport treiben** to get some early morning exercise; **≈stadium** *nt* early stage; **im ~stadium** in the early stages; **≈start** *m* false start.

Frühstück *nt* **-s, -e** breakfast; (*~spause*) morning *or* coffee break ◆ **zweites ~** ≃ elevenses (*Brit inf*), midmorning snack; **um 9 Uhr ist ~** breakfast is at 9 o'clock; **was ißt du zum ~?** what do you have for breakfast?; **die ganze Familie saß beim ~** the whole family were having breakfast.

frühstücken *insep* [1] *vi* to have breakfast, to breakfast.
[2] *vt* to breakfast on.

⚠: for details of spelling reform, see supplement

Frühstücks-: ~brett *nt* wooden platter; **~brot** *nt* sandwich (*for one's morning snack*); **~buffet** *nt* breakfast buffet; **~fernsehen** *nt* breakfast television; **~fleisch** *nt* luncheon meat; **~pause** *f* morning *or* coffee break; **~pause machen** to have one's morning *or* coffee break; **~teller** *m* dessert plate.

Früh-: ⚠**f~verrenten*** *vt insep* **jdn f~verrenten** to give sb early retirement; **~verrentung** *f* early retirement; ⚠**f~vollendet** *adj attr* (*liter*) **ein f~vollendeter Maler/Dichter, ein ~vollendeter** a young artist/poet of genius whose life was soon over; **~warnsystem** *nt* early warning system; **~werk** *nt* early work; **~zeit** *f* early days *pl*; **die ~zeit des Christentums/der Menschheit** early Christian times/the early days of mankind; ⚠**f~zeitig** [1] *adj* early; (*vorzeitig auch*) premature; *Tod auch* premature, untimely; [2] *adv* early; (*vorzeitig*) prematurely; (*früh genug auch*) in good time; (*ziemlich am Anfang*) early on; **~zug** *m* early train; **~zündung** *f* (*Aut*) pre-ignition.

Frust *m* **-(e)s,** *no pl* (*sl*) frustration *no art* ◆ **das ist der totale ~, wenn** ... it's totally frustrating when ...

frusten *vti* (*inf*) **von etw gefrustet sein** to be frustrated by sth; **das frustet** it's frustrating.

Frustration *f* frustration.

frustrieren* *vt* to frustrate; (*inf: enttäuschen*) to upset.

frz. *abbr of* **französisch**.

F-Schlüssel ['ɛfʃlʏsl] *m* (*Mus*) F *or* bass clef.

FU [ɛf'|uː] *f* - *abbr of* **Freie Universität (Berlin)**.

Fuchs [fʊks] *m* **-es, ¨-e (a)** (*Tier*) fox; (*fig auch*) cunning devil (*inf*) ◆ **er ist ein alter** *or* **schlauer ~** (*inf*) he's a cunning old devil (*inf*) *or* fox (*inf*); **schlau wie ein ~** as cunning as a fox; **wo sich die ¨-e** *or* **wo sich Hase und ~ gute Nacht sagen** (*hum*) in the back of beyond *or* the middle of nowhere.
(b) (*~pelz*) fox (fur).
(c) (*Pferd*) chestnut; (*mit hellerem Schwanz und Mähne*) sorrel; (*inf: Mensch*) redhead.
(d) (*Univ*) *siehe* **Fux**.

Fuchs-: ~bau *m* fox's den; **~eisen** *nt* (*Hunt*) fox trap.

fuchsen ['fʊksn] (*inf*) [1] *vt* to vex, to annoy.
[2] *vr* to be annoyed *or* cross.

Fuchsie ['fʊksiə] *f* (*Bot*) fuchsia.

fuchsig ['fʊksɪç] *adj* (*inf*) **(a)** (*rotblond*) *Haar* ginger, carroty (*inf*). **(b)** (*wütend*) mad (*inf*).

Füchsin ['fʏksɪn] *f* vixen.

Fuchs-: ~jagd *f* fox-hunt/-hunting; **~loch** *nt* foxhole; **~pelz** *m* fox fur; **f~rot** *adj Fell* red; *Pferd* chestnut; *Haar* ginger, carroty (*inf*); **~schwanz** *m* **(a)** fox's tail; (*Hunt*) (fox's) brush; **(b)** (*Bot*) love-lies-bleeding, amaranth; **(c)** (*Tech: Säge*) handsaw; **f~teufelswild** *adj* (*inf*) hopping mad (*inf*).

Fuchtel *f* **-, -n (a)** (*Hist: Degen*) broadsword; (*fig inf: Knute*) control ◆ **unter jds ~** under sb's thumb; **er ist unter ihre ~ gekommen** *or* **geraten** she's got *or* gotten (*US*) him under her thumb; **er steht unter der ~** he's not his own master. **(b)** (*Aus, S Ger inf: zänkische Frau*) shrew, vixen.

fuchteln *vi* (*inf*) **(mit den Händen) ~** to wave one's hands about (*inf*); **mit etw ~** to wave sth about *or* around; (*drohend*) to brandish sth.

fuchtig *adj* (*inf*) (hopping) mad (*inf*).

Fuder *nt* **-s, - (a)** (*Wagenladung*) cartload. **(b)** (*Hohlmaß für Wein*) tun.

fuderweise *adv* by the cartload ◆ **~ Salat essen** (*hum*) to eat tons of salad (*inf*).

Fudschijama *m* **-s** Fujiyama.

fuffzehn *num* (*dial*) fifteen.

Fuffziger *m* **-s, -** (*dial*) fifty-pfennig piece ◆ **er ist ein falscher ~** (*sl*) he's a real crook (*inf*).

Fug *m*: **mit ~ und Recht** (*geh*) with complete justification; **etw mit ~ und Recht tun** to be completely justified in doing sth.

Fuge *f* **-, -n (a)** joint; (*Ritze*) gap, crack ◆ **in allen ~n krachen** to creak at the joints; **aus den ~n gehen** *or* **geraten** (*Auto etc*) to come apart at the seams; **die Menschheit/Welt ist/die Zeiten sind aus den ~n geraten** (*geh*) mankind has gone awry (*liter*)/the world is/the times are out of joint (*liter*).
(b) (*Mus*) fugue.

fugen *vt* to joint.

fügen [1] *vt* **(a)** (*setzen*) to put, to place; (*ein~ auch*) to fix; (*geh*) *Worte, Satz* to formulate ◆ **Wort an Wort ~** to string words together.
(b) (*geh: bewirken*) to ordain; (*Schicksal auch*) to decree ◆ **der Zufall fügte es, daß** ... fate decreed that ...
[2] *vr* **(a)** (*sich unterordnen*) to be obedient, to obey ◆ **sich jdm/einer Sache** *or* **in etw** (*acc*) (*geh*) **~** to bow to sb/sth; *Anordnungen etc* to obey sth; **sich dem** *or* **in das Schicksal ~** to accept one's fate, to bow to one's fate.
(b) *impers* (*geh: geschehen*) **es hat sich so gefügt** it was decreed by fate; **es fügte sich, daß** ... it so happened that ...

Fugen-: f~los *adj* smooth; **~-s** *nt* (*Ling*) linking 's'; **~zeichen** *nt* (*Ling*) linking letter.

füglich *adv* (*geh*) justifiably, reasonably.

fügsam *adj Mensch* obedient; *Haar* manageable.

Fügsamkeit *f siehe adj* obedience; manageability.

Fügung *f* **(a)** (*Bestimmung*) chance, stroke of fate ◆ **eine glückliche ~** a stroke of good fortune, a happy chance; **göttliche ~** divine providence; **eine ~ Gottes/des Schicksals** an act of divine providence/of fate; **eine seltsame ~ wollte es, daß er** ... by some *or* a strange chance he ...
(b) (*Ling: Wortgruppe*) construction.

fühlbar *adj* (*spürbar*) perceptible; (*beträchtlich auch*) marked ◆ **bald wird die Krise auch bei uns ~** the crisis will soon be felt here too.

fühlen [1] *vt* **(a)** *(spüren, empfinden)* to feel ◆ **Mitleid mit jdm ~** to feel sympathy for sb.
(b) *(ertasten) Beule, Erhebung* to feel; *Puls* to take.
[2] *vi* **(a)** *(geh: empfinden)* to feel.
(b) nach etw ~ to feel for sth.
[3] *vr* **(a)** *(empfinden, sich halten für)* to feel ◆ **sich krank/beleidigt/verantwortlich ~** to feel ill/insulted/responsible; **wie ~ Sie sich?** how are you feeling *or* do you feel?; **er fühlte sich als Held** he felt (like) a hero.
(b) *(inf: stolz sein)* to think one is so great *(inf)*.

Fühler *m* **-s, -** *(Zool)* feeler, antenna; *(von Schnecke)* horn ◆ **seine ~ ausstrecken** *(fig inf)* to put out feelers *(nach* towards).

Fühlerlehre *f* callipers *pl*.

fühllos *adj (geh) siehe* **gefühllos.**

Fühlung *f* contact ◆ **mit jdm in ~ bleiben/stehen** to remain *or* stay/be in contact *or* touch with sb.

Fühlungnahme *f* **-, -n die erste ~ der beiden Parteien** the initial contact between the two parties.

fuhr *pret of* **fahren.**

Fuhr-: ~amt *nt (form)* cleansing department; **~betrieb** *m* haulage business.

Fuhre *f* **-, -n** *(Ladung)* load; *(Taxieinsatz)* fare ◆ **eine ~ Stroh** a (cart- *or* waggon-)load of straw; **wir müssen die Leute in zwei ~n zum Bahnhof bringen** we'll have to take the people to the station in two batches.

führen [1] *vt* **(a)** *(geleiten)* to take; *(vorangehen, -fahren)* to lead ◆ **eine alte Dame über die Straße ~** to help an old lady over the road; **sie hat uns den richtigen Weg geführt** she showed us the right way; **er führte uns durch das Schloß/durch Italien** he showed us round the castle/he was our guide in Italy; **~ Sie mich zum Geschäftsführer!** take me to the manager!; **eine Klasse zum Abitur ~** to see a class through to A-levels; **jdn zum (Trau)altar ~** to lead sb to the altar.
(b) *(leiten) Geschäft, Betrieb etc* to run; *Gruppe, Expedition etc* to lead, to head; *Schiff* to captain; *Armee etc* to command.
(c) *(in eine Situation bringen)* to get *(inf)*, to lead; *(veranlassen zu kommen/gehen)* to bring/take ◆ **der Hinweis führte die Polizei auf die Spur des Diebes** that tip put the police on the trail of the thief; **das führt uns auf das Thema** ... that brings *or* leads us (on)to the subject ...; **was führt Sie zu mir?** *(form)* what brings you to me?; **ein Land ins Chaos ~** to reduce a country to chaos.
(d) *(registriert haben)* to have a record of ◆ **wir ~ keinen Meier in unserer Kartei** we have no (record of a) Meier on our files.
(e) *(handhaben) Pinsel, Bogen, Kamera etc* to wield ◆ **den Löffel zum Mund/das Glas an die Lippen ~** to raise one's spoon to one's mouth/one's glass to one's lips; **die Hand an die Mütze ~** to touch one's cap.
(f) *(entlangführen) Leitung, Draht* to carry.
(g) *(form: steuern) Kraftfahrzeug* to drive; *Flugzeug* to fly, to pilot; *Kran, Fahrstuhl* to operate; *Schiff* to sail.
(h) *(transportieren)* to carry; *(haben) Autokennzeichen, Wappen, Namen* to have, to bear; *Titel* to have; *(selbst gebrauchen)* to use ◆ **Geld/seine Papiere bei sich ~** *(form)* to carry money/one's papers on one's person; **der Fluß führt Hochwasser** the river is running high.
(i) *(im Angebot haben)* to stock, to carry *(spec)*, to keep ◆ **etw ständig im Munde ~** to be always talking about sth; **er führt diesen Spruch ständig im Munde** he is always using that phrase.
[2] *vi* **(a)** *(in Führung liegen)* to lead; *(bei Wettkämpfen auch)* to be in the lead ◆ **die Mannschaft führt mit 10 Punkten Vorsprung** the team has a lead of 10 points *or* is in the lead by 10 points; **die Firma XY führt in Tonbandgeräten** XY is the leading firm for tape recorders.
(b) *(verlaufen) (Straße)* to go; *(Kabel, Pipeline etc)* to run; *(Spur)* to lead ◆ **das Rennen führt über 10 Runden/durch ganz Frankreich** the race takes place over 10 laps/covers France; **die Autobahn führt nach Kiel/am Rhein entlang** the motorway goes to Kiel/runs *or* goes along the Rhine; **die Brücke führt über die Elbe** the bridge crosses *or* spans the Elbe; **der Waldweg führt zu einem Gasthof** the forest path leads *or* goes to an inn; **wohin soll das alles nur ~?** where is it all leading (us)?
(c) *(als Ergebnis haben)* **zu etw ~** to lead to sth, to result in sth; **das führt zu nichts** that will come to nothing; **es führte zu dem Ergebnis, daß er entlassen wurde** it resulted in *or* led to his being dismissed.
[3] *vr (form: sich benehmen)* to conduct oneself.

führend *adj* leading *attr; Rolle, Persönlichkeit auch* prominent ◆ **diese Firma ist im Stahlbau ~** that is one of the leading firms in steel construction; **die Sowjets sind im Schach ~** the Soviets lead the world in chess.

Führer *m* **-s, - (a)** *(Leiter)* leader; *(Oberhaupt)* head ◆ **der ~** *(Hist)* the Führer *or* Fuehrer. **(b)** *(Fremden~, Berg~)* guide. **(c)** *(Buch)* guide ◆ **~ durch England** guide to England. **(d)** *(form: Lenker)* driver; *(von Flugzeug)* pilot; *(von Kran, Fahrstuhl)* operator; *(von Schiff)* person in charge.

Führerhaus *nt* cab; *(von Kran auch)* cabin.

Führerin *f siehe* **Führer (a, b, d).**

Führer-: f~los *adj Gruppe, Partei* leaderless *no adv*, without a leader; *Wagen* driverless *no adv*, without a driver; *Flugzeug* pilotless *no adv*, without a pilot; *Schiff* with no-one at the helm; **~schein** *m (für Auto)* driving licence, driver's license *(US)*; *(für Flugzeug)* pilot's licence; *(für Motorboot)* motorboat licence; **den ~schein machen** *(Aut)* to learn to drive; *(die Prüfung ablegen)* to take one's (driving) test; **jdm den ~schein entziehen** to take away sb's driving licence, to disqualify sb from driving; **ihm ist der ~schein abgenommen worden** he's lost his licence; **~scheinentzug** *m* disqualification from driving; **~stand** *m (von Zug)* cab; *(von Kran auch)* cabin.

Fuhr-: ~geld *nt siehe* **~lohn; ~geschäft** *nt siehe* **~unternehmen.**

führig *adj Schnee* good for skiing.

Fuhr-: ~knecht *m (old) siehe* **~mann; ~leute** *pl of* **~mann; ~lohn** *m* delivery charge; **~mann** *m, pl* **-leute** carter; *(Kutscher)* coachman; **der ~mann** *(Astron)* Auriga, the Charioteer; **~park** *m* fleet (of vehicles).

Führung *f* **(a)** *no pl* guidance, direction; *(von Partei, Expedition etc)* leadership; *(Mil)* command; *(eines Unternehmens etc)* management ◆ **unter der ~** *+gen* under the direction/leadership/command/management of, directed/led *or* headed/commanded/managed by; **wer hat hier die ~?** *(Mil)* who is in command here?
(b) *no pl (die Führer)* leaders *pl*, leadership *sing*; *(Mil)* commanders *pl*; *(eines Unternehmens etc)* directors *pl*.
(c) *(Besichtigung)* guided tour *(durch* of).
(d) *no pl (Vorsprung)* lead ◆ **die klare ~ haben** *(bei Wettkämpfen)* to have a clear lead; **die Firma hat eine klare ~ auf diesem Gebiet** the firm clearly leads the field in this area; **in ~ gehen/liegen** to go into/be in the lead.
(e) *no pl (Betragen)* conduct.
(f) *no pl (Handhabung)* touch.
(g) *(Mech)* guide, guideway.
(h) *(form: Lenken)* **zur ~ eines Kraft-/Wasserfahrzeugs/Flugzeugs berechtigt sein** to be licensed to drive a motor vehicle/be in charge of a vessel/fly *or* pilot an aeroplane.
(i) *no pl (Betreuung)* running ◆ **die ~ der Akten/Bücher** keeping the files/books.

Führungs-: ~anspruch *m* claims *pl* to leadership; **seinen ~anspruch anmelden** to make a bid for the leadership; **~aufgabe** *f* executive duty; **~kraft** *f* executive; **~qualität** *f usu pl* leadership qualities *pl*; **~riege** *f* leadership; **~rolle** *f* role of leader; **~schicht** *f* ruling classes *pl*; **~schiene** *f* guide rail; **f~schwach** *adj* weak; **~schwäche** *f* weak leadership; **~spitze** *f* highest echelon of the leadership; *(eines Unternehmens etc)* top management; **~stab** *m (Mil)* command *no pl*; *(Comm)* top management; **~stärke** *f* strong leadership; **~stil** *m* style of leadership; *(Comm auch)* management style; **~tor** *nt (Ftbl)* goal which gives/gave a/the team the lead; **~wechsel** *m* change of leadership; **~zeugnis** *nt siehe* **polizeilich.**

Fuhr-: ~unternehmen *nt* haulage business; **~unternehmer** *m* haulier, haulage contractor, carrier; **~werk** *nt* wag(g)on; *(Pferde~)* horse and cart; *(Ochsen~)* oxcart; **f~werken** *vi insep* **(a)** *(inf)* **in der Küche f~werken** to bustle around in the kitchen; **mit den Armen f~werken** to wave one's arms about; **(b)** *(S Ger, Aus)* to drive a cart; **~wesen** *nt* cartage business.

Fülle *f* **-,** *no pl* **(a)** *(Körpermasse)* corpulence, portliness.
(b) *(Stärke)* fullness; *(von Stimme, Klang auch)* richness; *(von Wein auch)* full-bodiedness; *(von Haar)* body.
(c) *(Menge)* wealth ◆ **eine ~ von Fragen/Eindrücken** *etc* a whole host of questions/impressions *etc*; **in ~** in abundance; *siehe* **Hülle.**

füllen [1] *vt* **(a)** to fill; *(Cook)* to stuff ◆ **etw in Flaschen ~** to bottle sth; **etw in Säcke ~** to put sth into sacks; *siehe* **gefüllt. (b)** *(in Anspruch nehmen)* to fill, to occupy; *Regal auch* to take up.
[2] *vr (Theater, Badewanne)* to fill up ◆ **ihre Augen füllten sich mit Tränen** her eyes filled with tears.

Füllen *nt* **-s, -** *siehe* **Fohlen.**

Füller *m* **-s, - (a)** *(Füllfederhalter)* fountain pen. **(b)** *(Press)* filler.

Füll-: ~federhalter *m* fountain pen; **~gewicht** *nt* **(a)** *(Comm)* weight at time of packing; *(auf Dosen)* net weight; **(b)** *(von Waschmaschine)* maximum load, capacity; **~horn** *nt (liter)* cornucopia; *(fig auch)* horn of plenty.

füllig *adj Mensch* corpulent, portly; *Figur, Busen* generous, ample; *Frisur* bouffant *attr.*

Füllmasse *f* filler, filling material; *(Zahn~)* filling compound.

Füllsel *nt (in Paket etc)* packing; *(in Geschriebenem) (Wort)* filler; *(Floskel)* padding.

Füllung *f* filling; *(Geflügel~, Fleisch~, Stofftier~, Polster~)* stuffing; *(Tür~)* panel; *(von Pralinen)* centre.

Füllwort *nt* filler (word).

fulminant *adj (geh)* sparkling, brilliant.

Fummel *m* **-s, -** *(sl)* rag.

Fummelei *f (inf)* fidgeting, fiddling; *(sl: Petting)* petting, groping *(inf)*.

Fummelkram *m (inf)* fiddle *(inf)*, fiddly job *(inf)*.

fummeln *vi (inf)* to fiddle; *(hantieren)* to fumble; *(erotisch)* to pet, to grope *(inf)* ◆ **an etw** *(dat) or* **mit etw ~** to fiddle (about)/fumble around with sth.

Fund *m* **-(e)s, -e** find; *(das Entdecken)* discovery, finding ◆ **einen ~ machen** to make a find.

Fundament *nt (lit, fig)* foundation *(usu pl)* ◆ **das ~ zu etw legen** *or* **für etw schaffen** *(fig)* to lay the foundations for sth.

fundamental *adj* fundamental.

Fundamentalismus *m* fundamentalism.

Fundamentalist(in *f) m* fundamentalist.

fundamentalistisch *adj* fundamentalist.

fundamentieren* *vi* to lay the foundations.

Fund-: ~amt, ~büro *nt* lost property office *(Brit)*, lost and found *(US)*; **~grube** *f (fig)* treasure trove; **eine ~grube des Wissens** a treasury of knowledge.

Fundi *m* **-s, -s** *or f* **-, -s** *(Pol inf)* fundamentalist *(of the Green party)*.

fundieren* *vt (fig)* to back up.

fundiert *adj* sound ◆ **schlecht ~** unsound.

fündig *adj (Min) Sohle* rich ◆ **~ werden** to make a strike; *(fig)* to strike it lucky.

Fund-: ~ort *m* **der ~ort von etw** (the place) where sth is/was found;

~sachen *pl* lost property *sing*; **~stätte, ~stelle** *f* **die ~stätte von etw** (the place) where sth is/was found.

Fundus *m* -, - (*lit, fig*) fund; (*Theat*) basic equipment ◆ **der ~ seines reichen Wissens** his rich fund of knowledge.

fünf *num* five ◆ **es ist ~ Minuten vor zwölf** (*lit*) it's five to twelve; (*fig*) it's almost too late; **sie warteten bis ~ Minuten vor zwölf** (*fig*) they waited till the eleventh hour; **seine ~ Sinne beieinander-** *or* **beisammenhaben** to have all one's wits about one; **seine ~ Sinne zusammennehmen** to gather one's wits together; **man mußte seine ~ Sinne zusammennehmen** you had to have your wits about you; **~(e) gerade sein lassen** (*inf*) to turn a blind eye, to look the other way; *siehe auch* **Finger, vier.**

Fünf *f* -, **-en** five; *siehe auch* **Vier.**

Fünf- *in cpds* five; *siehe auch* **Vier-**; **~eck** *nt* pentagon; **f~eckig** *adj* pentagonal, five-cornered.

Fünfer *m* **-s,** - (*inf*) five-pfennig piece; five-marks; *siehe auch* **Vierer.**

Fünf-: f~fach *adj* fivefold; *siehe auch* **vierfach**; **f~füßig** *adj* (*Poet*) pentametrical; **f~füßiger Jambus** iambic pentameter; **~ganggetriebe** *nt* five-speed gearbox; **~gangschaltung** *f* five-speed gears *pl*; **f~hundert** *num* five hundred; *siehe auch* **vierhundert**; **~jahr(es)plan** *m* five-year plan; **f~jährig** *adj Frist, Plan etc* five-year, quinquennial (*form*); *Kind* five-year-old; **eine f~jährige Zeitspanne** a period of five years, a quinquennium (*form*); *siehe auch* **vierjährig**; **~kampf** *m* (*Sport*) pentathlon; **~ling** *m* quintuplet; **f~mal** *adv* five times; *siehe auch* **viermal**; **~markschein** *m* five-mark note; **~markstück** *nt* five-mark piece; **~pfennigstück** *nt* five-pfennig piece.

Fünfprozent-: ~grenze *f* (*Parl*) five-percent barrier; **~hürde** *f* (*Parl*) five-percent hurdle; **~klausel** *f* five-percent rule.

Fünf-: f~seitig *adj* (*Geom*) five-sided; (*Brief*) five-page *attr*; *siehe auch* **vierseitig**; **~stromland** *nt* (*Geog*) Punjab; **f~tägig** *adj* five-day *attr*; **f~tausend** *num* five thousand; *siehe auch* **viertausend.**

Fünftel *nt* **-s,** - fifth; *siehe auch* **Viertel**[1].

fünftens *adv* fifth(ly), in the fifth place.

fünfte(r, s) *adj* fifth ◆ **die ~ Kolonne** the fifth column; *siehe auch* **vierte(r, s), Rad.**

Fünf-: ~uhrtee *m* afternoon tea; **~unddreißig-Stunden-Woche** *f* thirty-five-hour week; **f~undzwanzig** *num* twenty-five; **f~zehn** *num* fifteen.

fünfzig *num* fifty; *siehe auch* **vierzig.**

Fünfzig *f* -, **-en** fifties; *siehe auch* **Vierzig.**

Fünfziger *m* **-s,** - (*inf*) (*Fünfzigjähriger*) fifty-year-old; (*Geld*) fifty-pfennig piece; fifty-mark note; *siehe auch* **Fuffziger, Vierziger(in).**

Fünfzig-: f~jährig *adj Person* fifty-year-old *attr*; *Zeitspanne* fifty-year; **er ist f~jährig verstorben** he died at (the age of) fifty; **~markschein** *m* fifty-mark note; **~pfennigstück** *nt* fifty-pfennig piece.

fungieren* [fʊŋ'giːrən] *vi* to function (*als* as a).

Fungizid *nt* **-(e)s, -e** fungicide.

Funk *m* **-s,** *no pl* radio, wireless (*dated*) ◆ **über** *or* **per ~** by radio; **er arbeitet beim ~** he works in radio *or* broadcasting.

-funk *in cpds* broadcasts *pl*.

Funk-: ~amateur *m* radio ham, amateur radio enthusiast; **~anlage** *f* radio set *or* transceiver; **~aufklärung** *f* (*Mil*) radio intelligence; **~ausstellung** *f* radio and television exhibition; **~bake** *f siehe* **~feuer**; **~bild** *nt* telephotograph (*spec*), radio picture.

Fünkchen *nt dim of* **Funke** ◆ **ein/kein ~ Wahrheit** a grain/not a particle *or* shred of truth.

Funkdienst *m* radio communication service.

Funke *m* **-ns, -n, Funken** *m* **-s,** - **(a)** (*lit, fig*) spark ◆ **~n sprühen** to spark, to send out *or* emit sparks; **ihre Augen sprühten ~n** her eyes flashed; **der zündende ~** (*fig*) the vital spark; **der ~ der Begeisterung sprang auf die Zuschauer über** the audience was infected by his/her *etc* enthusiasm; **arbeiten, daß die ~n fliegen** *or* **sprühen** (*inf*) to work like mad (*inf*) *or* crazy (*inf*); **zwischen den beiden sprang der ~ über** (*inf*) something clicked between them (*inf*).
(b) (*ein bißchen*) scrap; (*von Hoffnung auch*) gleam, ray, glimmer; (*von Anstand auch*) spark.

Funk|einrichtung *f* radio (equipment) ◆ **mit ~ versehen** radio-equipped, equipped with radio.

funkeln *vi* to sparkle; (*Sterne auch*) to twinkle; (*Augen*) (*vor Freude*) to gleam, to twinkle; (*vor Zorn auch*) to glitter, to flash; (*Edelsteine auch*) to glitter; (*Edelmetall*) to gleam.

funkelnagelneu *adj* (*inf*) brand-new.

Funken *m* **-s,** - *siehe* **Funke.**

funken [1] *vt Signal* to radio ◆ **SOS ~** to send out *or* radio an SOS.
[2] *vi* **(a)** (*senden*) to radio. **(b)** (*Funken sprühen*) to give off *or* emit sparks, to spark; (*fig inf: funktionieren*) to work.
[3] *vi impers* **endlich hat es bei ihm gefunkt** (*inf*) it finally clicked (with him) (*inf*), the light finally dawned (on him).

Funken-: ~entladung *f* spark discharge; **~flug** *m* **der Brand wurde durch ~flug von einer Lokomotive verursacht** the fire was caused by sparks from a locomotive; **~gitter** *nt* fireguard; ⚠**f~sprühend** *adj* giving off *or* emitting sparks; (*fig*) *Diskussion* lively; *Augen* flashing *attr*, fiery.

Funk|entstörung *f* suppression of interference.

Funker *m* **-s,** - radio *or* wireless operator.

Funk-: ~fernsteuerung *f* radio control; (*Anlage*) radio-control equipment *no pl*; **~feuer** *nt* radio beacon; **~gerät** *nt* **(a)** *no pl* radio equipment; **(b)** (*Sprechfunkgerät*) radio set, walkie-talkie; **~haus** *nt* broadcasting centre, studios *pl*; **~kolleg** *nt* educational radio broadcasts *pl*; **~kontakt** *m* radio contact; ⚠**~meßgerät** *nt* radar (equipment) *no pl*; **~navigation** *f* radio navigation; **~ortung** *f* radiolocation; **~peilung** *f* radio direction finding; **~sprechgerät** *nt* radio telephone; (*tragbar*) walkie-talkie; **~sprechverkehr** *m* radiotelephony; **~spruch** *m* radio signal; (*Mitteilung*) radio message; **~station** *f* radio station; **f~still** *adj* non-transmitting; **~stille** *f* radio silence; (*fig*) silence; **~streife** *f* police radio patrol; **~streifenwagen** *m* police radio patrol *or* squad car; **~taxi** *nt* radio taxi *or* cab; **~technik** *f* radio technology; **~telefon** *nt* cordless telephone.

Funktion *f* (*no pl: Tätigkeit*) functioning; (*Zweck, Aufgabe, Math*) function; (*Amt*) office; (*Stellung*) position ◆ **in ~ treten/sein** to come into/be in operation; (*Organ, Maschine etc*) to start to function/be functioning; **etw außer ~ setzen** to stop sth functioning; **dieser Bolzen hat die ~, den Apparat senkrecht zu halten** the function of this bolt is to hold the machine upright.

funktional [fʊŋktsio'naːl] *adj siehe* **funktionell.**

Funktionalismus [fʊŋktsiona'lɪsmʊs] *m* functionalism.

Funktionär(in *f*) [fʊŋktsio'nɛːɐ, -'nɛːərɪn] *m* functionary, official.

funktionell [fʊŋktsio'nɛl] *adj* functional (*auch Med*), practical.

funktionieren* [fʊŋktsio'niːrən] *vi* to work; (*Maschine etc auch*) to function, to operate; (*inf: gehorchen*) to obey.

Funktions-: ~bild *nt, no pl* job profile; **f~fähig** *adj* able to work/function *or* operate; **~störung** *f* (*Med*) malfunction, functional disorder; **~taste** *f* function key; **f~tüchtig** *adj* in working order; *Organ* sound; **~verb** *nt* (*Ling*) empty verb.

Funk-: ~turm *m* radio tower; **~uhr** *f* radio-controlled clock; **~universität** *f* university of the air; **~verbindung** *f* radio contact; **~verkehr** *m* radio communication *or* traffic; **~wagen** *m* radio car; **~weg** *m* **auf dem ~weg** by radio; **~werbung** *f* radio advertizing; **~wesen** *nt* radio; (*Sendesystem*) broadcasting system.

Funsel, Funzel *f* -, **-n** (*inf*) dim light, gloom.

Für *nt*: **das ~ und Wider** the pros and cons (*pl*).

für [1] *prep +acc* **(a)** for ◆ **~ was ist denn dieses Werkzeug?** (*inf*) what is this tool (used) for?; **kann ich sonst noch etwas ~ Sie tun?** will there be anything else?; **~ mich** for me; (*meiner Ansicht nach*) in my opinion *or* view; **diese Frage muß jeder ~ sich (alleine) entscheiden** everyone has to decide this question for *or* by themselves; **das ist gut ~ Migräne** that's good for migraine; **~ zwei arbeiten** (*fig*) to do the work of two people; **~ einen Deutschen ...** for a German ...; **~s erste** for the moment; **~s nächstemal** next time.
(b) (*Zustimmung*) for, in favour of ◆ **sich ~ etw entscheiden** to decide in favour of sth; **was Sie da sagen, hat etwas ~ sich** there's something in what you're saying; **er/das hat was ~ sich** he's not a bad person/it's not a bad thing.
(c) (*Gegenleistung*) (in exchange) for ◆ **das hat er ~ zehn Pfund gekauft** he bought it for ten pounds.
(d) (*Ersatz*) for, instead of, in place of ◆ **~ jdn einspringen** to stand in for sb.
(e) (*Aufeinanderfolge*) **Tag ~ Tag** day after day; **Schritt ~ Schritt** step by step.
(f) *in Verbindung mit vb, adj siehe auch dort* **etw ~ sich behalten** to keep sth to oneself; **~ etw bekannt sein** to be famous *or* known for sth; **ich halte sie ~ intelligent** I think she is intelligent.
(g) was ~ *siehe* **was.**
[2] *adv* (*old poet*): **~ und ~** for ever and ever.

Furage [fu'raːʒə] *f* -, *no pl* (*Mil old*) forage.

⚠**fürbaß** *adv* (*obs*) onwards ◆ **~ gehen/schreiten** to continue on one's way.

Fürbitte *f* (*Eccl, fig*) intercession ◆ **er legte beim Kaiser ~ für die Gefangenen ein** he interceded with the Emperor on behalf of the prisoners.

Fürbitten *nt* (*Eccl*) prayers *pl*; (*fig*) pleading.

Furche *f* -, **-n** (*Acker~, Gesichtsfalte*) furrow; (*Wagenspur*) rut ◆ **ein von ~n durchzogenes Gesicht** a deeply furrowed *or* lined face.

furchen *vt* to furrow; (*Gesicht etc auch*) to line ◆ **die Spuren des Traktors furchten den Weg** the tractor made ruts *or* furrows in the road; **eine gefurchte Stirn** a furrowed brow.

furchig *adj* furrowed; (*durch Wagenspuren etc auch*) rutted.

Furcht *f* -, *no pl* fear ◆ **aus ~ vor jdm/etw** for fear of sb/sth; **ohne ~ sein** to be fearless *or* without fear; **~ vor jdm/etw haben** *or* **empfinden** to be afraid of sb/sth, to fear sb/sth; **~ ergriff** *or* **packte ihn** fear seized him, he was seized with fear; **jdn in ~ versetzen, jdm ~ einflößen** to frighten *or* scare sb.

furchtbar *adj* terrible, awful, dreadful ◆ **ich habe einen ~en Hunger** I'm ever so *or* terribly hungry (*inf*).

⚠**furcht|einflößend** *adj* terrifying, fearful.

fürchten [1] *vt* **jdn/etw ~** to be afraid of sb/sth, to fear sb/sth; **das Schlimmste ~** to fear the worst; **~, daß ...** to be afraid *or* fear that ...; **es war schlimmer, als ich gefürchtet hatte** it was worse than I had feared; **Gott ~** to fear God; *siehe* **gefürchtet.**
[2] *vr* to be afraid (*vor +dat* of) ◆ **sich im Dunkeln ~** to be afraid *or* scared of the dark.
[3] *vi* **für** *or* **um jdn/jds Leben/etw ~** to fear for sb/sb's life/sth; **zum F~ aussehen** to look frightening *or* terrifying; **da kannst du das F~ lernen** that will scare you stiff; **jdn das F~ lehren** to put the fear of God into sb.

fürchterlich *adj siehe* **furchtbar.**

Furcht-: ⚠**f~erregend** *adj siehe* **f~einflößend**; **f~los** *adj* fearless, intrepid, dauntless; **~losigkeit** *f* fearlessness, intrepidity, dauntlessness; **f~sam** *adj* timorous; **~samkeit** *f* timorousness.

Furchung *f* (*Biol*) cleavage.

fürder(hin) *adv* (*obs*) hereafter (*old*), in future.

⚠: for details of spelling reform, see supplement

für|einander *adv* for each other, for one another.
Furie ['fu:riə] *f (Myth)* fury; *(fig)* hellcat, termagant ◆ **wie von ~n gejagt** *or* **gehetzt** *(liter)* as though the devil himself were after him/them *etc*; **sie gingen wie ~n aufeinander los** they went for each other like cats *or* wild things.
Furnier *nt* **-s, -e** veneer.
furnieren* *vt* to veneer ◆ **mit Mahagoni furniert** with a mahogany veneer.
Furore *f* **-** *or nt* **-s,** *no pl* sensation ◆ **~ machen** *(inf)* to cause a sensation.
Fürsorge *f, no pl* **(a)** *(Betreuung)* care; *(Sozial~)* welfare.
(b) *(inf: Sozialamt)* welfare *(inf)*, welfare services ◆ **der ~ zur Last fallen** to be a burden on the state.
(c) *(inf: Sozialunterstützung)* social security *(Brit)*, welfare *(US)* ◆ **von der ~ leben** to live on social security.
Fürsorge-: ~amt *nt* (church) welfare office; **~beruf** *m* job in one of the welfare services; **~erziehung** *f* education in a special school; **~pflicht** *f (Jur)* employer's obligation to provide for the welfare of his employees.
Fürsorger(in *f***)** *m* **-s, -** (church) welfare worker.
fürsorgerisch *adj* welfare *attr* ◆ **alte Menschen ~ betreuen** to look after the welfare of old people.
Fürsorge-: ~satz *m* rate of social security (benefit); **~unterstützung** *f* social security benefit.
fürsorglich *adj* careful; *Mensch auch* solicitous ◆ **jdn sehr ~ behandeln** to lavish care on sb.
Fürsorglichkeit *f siehe adj* care; solicitousness.
Fürsprache *f* recommendation ◆ **für jdn ~ einlegen** to recommend sb *(bei* to), to put in a word for sb *(inf) (bei* with); **auf ~ von jdm** on sb's recommendation.
Fürsprech *m* **-s, -e** **(a)** *(old: Rechtsbeistand)* counsel. **(b)** *(Sw: Rechtsanwalt)* barrister.
Fürsprecher(in *f***)** *m* **(a)** advocate. **(b)** *siehe* **Fürsprech.**
Fürst *m* **-en, -en** prince; *(Herrscher)* ruler ◆ **geistlicher ~** prince-bishop; **wie ein ~ leben** to live like a lord *or* king; **der ~ der Finsternis** *or* **dieser Welt** *(liter)* the Prince of Darkness *or* of this world *(Bibl)*.
Fürsten-: ~geschlecht, ~haus *nt* royal house; **~stand** *m* royal rank; **jdn in den ~stand erheben** to create sb prince; **~tum** *nt* principality, princedom *(old)*; **das ~tum Monaco/Liechtenstein** the principality of Monaco/ Liechtenstein.
Fürstin *f* princess; *(Herrscherin)* ruler.
fürstlich *adj (lit)* princely *no adv*; *(fig auch)* handsome, lavish ◆ **jdn ~ bewirten** to entertain sb right royally; **~ leben** to live like a lord.
Fürstlichkeit *f* **(a)** *no pl* princeliness, handsomeness, lavishness. **(b)** *(form: fürstl. Herrschaften)* royal personage *(form)*.
Furt *f* **-, -en** ford.
Furunkel *nt or m* **-s, -** boil.
fürwahr *adv (old)* forsooth *(old)*, in truth *(old)*.
Fürwort *nt* **-(e)s, ¨-er** *(Gram) siehe* **Pronomen.**
Furz *m* **-(e)s, ¨-e** *(inf)* fart *(inf)* ◆ **einen ~ (fahren) lassen** to let off a fart *(inf)*.
furzen *vi (inf)* to fart *(inf)*.
Fusel *m* **-s, -** *(pej)* rotgut *(inf)*, hooch *(esp US inf)*.
Fusel|öl *nt* fusel oil.
Füsilier *m* **-s, -e** *(old Mil, Sw)* fusilier.
füsilieren* *vt (old Mil)* to execute by firing squad.
Fusion *f* amalgamation; *(von Unternehmen auch)* merger; *(von Atomkernen, Zellen)* fusion.
fusionieren* *vti* to amalgamate; *(Unternehmen auch)* to merge.
Fusionsreaktor *m* fusion reactor.
Fuß *m* **-es, ¨-e** **(a)** *(Körperteil)* foot; *(S Ger, Aus: Bein)* leg ◆ **zu ~** on foot; **zu ~ gehen/kommen** to walk, to go/come on foot; **er ist gut/schlecht zu ~** he is steady/not so steady on his feet; **sich jdm zu ¨-en werfen** to prostrate oneself before sb; **jdm zu ¨-en fallen/liegen/sitzen/sinken** to fall/lie/sit at sb's feet/to sink to the ground at sb's feet; **jdm zu ¨-en fallen** *or* **sinken** *(fig: Bittsteller)* to go down on one's knees to *or* before sb; **das Publikum lag/sank ihm zu ¨-en** he had the audience at his feet; **den ~ in** *or* **zwischen die Tür stellen** to get *or* put one's foot in the door; **den ~ auf die Erde/den Mond setzen** to set foot on the earth/the moon; **über seine eigenen ¨-e stolpern** to trip over one's own feet; *(fig)* to get tied up in knots; **kalte ¨-e bekommen, sich** *(dat)* **kalte ¨-e holen** *(lit, fig)* to get cold feet; **so schnell/weit ihn seine ¨-e trugen** as fast/far as his legs would carry him; **bei ~!** heel!; **jdm zwischen die ¨-e geraten** *or* **kommen** to get under sb's feet; **jdm etw vor die ¨-e werfen** *or* **schmeißen** *(inf) (lit)* to throw sth at sb; *(fig)* to tell sb to keep *or* stuff *(sl)* sth; **jdn/etw mit ¨-en treten** *(fig)* to walk all over sb, to treat sb/sth with contempt; **(festen) ~ fassen** *(lit, fig)* to gain a foothold; *(sich niederlassen)* to settle down; **auf eigenen ¨-en stehen** *(lit)* to stand by oneself; *(fig)* to stand on one's own two feet; **jdn auf freien ~ setzen** to release sb, to set sb free; **auf großem ~ leben** to live the high life; **mit jdm auf gutem ~ stehen** to be on good terms with sb; **jdm/einer Sache auf dem ~e folgen** *(lit)* to be hot on the heels of sb/sth; *(fig)* to follow hard on sb/sth; **mit einem ~ im Grab stehen** to have one foot in the grave; *siehe* **Boden, Hand, Gewehr, frei.**
(b) *(von Gegenstand)* base; *(Tisch-, Stuhlbein)* leg; *(von Schrank, Gebirge)* foot ◆ **auf schwachen/tönernen ¨-en stehen** to be built on sand.
(c) *(Poet)* foot.
(d) *(von Strumpf)* foot.
(e) *pl* **-** *(Längenmaß)* foot ◆ **12 ~ lang** 12 foot *or* feet long.
Fuß-: ~abdruck *m* footprint; **~abstreifer** *m* **-s, -** footscraper; *(aus Gummi etc)* doormat; **~abtreter** *m* **-s, -** doormat; **~angel** *f (lit)* mantrap; *(fig)* catch, trap; **~arbeit** *f (Sport)* footwork; **~bad** *nt* foot bath.
Fußball *m* **(a)** *(no pl: ~spiel)* football; *(als Kampfsport auch)* soccer. **(b)** *(Ball)* football.
Fußballer(in *f***)** *m* **-s, -** *(inf)* footballer.
Fußball-: ~mannschaft *f* football team; **~match** *nt (Aus)* football *or* soccer match; **~meisterschaft** *f* football league championship; **~platz** *m* football *or* soccer pitch; **~rowdy** *m* football hooligan; **~schuh** *m* football boot; **~spiel** *nt* football *or* soccer match; *(Sportart)* football; **~spieler** *m* football *or* soccer player; **~toto** *m or nt* football pools *pl*; **~verein** *m* football club.
Fußbank *f* footstool.
Fußboden *m* floor.
Fußboden-: ~belag *m* floor covering; **~heizung** *f* (under)floor heating.
Fuß-: ~breit *m* **-,** *no pl* foot; **keinen ~breit weichen** *(lit, fig)* not to budge an inch *(inf)*; **f~breit** *adj* a foot wide; **~bremse** *f* footbrake; **~eisen** *nt* mantrap.
Fussel *f* **-, -n** *or m* **-s, -** fluff *no pl* ◆ **ein(e) ~** some fluff, a bit of fluff.
fusselig *adj* fluffy ◆ **sich** *(dat)* **den Mund ~ reden** *(inf)* to talk till one is blue in the face.
fusseln *vi (von Stoff, Kleid etc)* to go bobbly *(inf)*, to pill *(spec)*.
füßeln *vi* to play footsie *(inf) (mit* with).
fußen *vi* to rest, to be based *(auf +dat* on).
Fuß-: ~ende *nt (von Bett)* foot; **~fall** *m siehe* **Kniefall; f~fällig** *adj siehe* **kniefällig; ~fesseln** *pl* shackles *pl*.
Fußgänger(in *f***)** *m* **-s, -** pedestrian.
Fußgänger-: ~brücke *f* footbridge; **~insel** *f* traffic island; **~überweg** *m* pedestrian crossing *(Brit)*, crosswalk *(US)*; *(auch* **~überführung***)* pedestrian bridge; **~unterführung** *f* underpass, pedestrian subway *(Brit)*; **~zone** *f* pedestrian precinct.
Fuß-: ~gelenk *nt* ankle; **f~hoch** *adj* ankle-deep.
-füßig *adj suf Mensch* -footed; *Tisch, Insekt* -legged; *(Poet)* -foot.
Fuß-: f~kalt *adj* **die Wohnung ist immer f~kalt** there's always a draught around your feet in that flat; **f~krank** *adj* **f~krank sein** to have trouble with one's feet; **~lappen** *m* footcloth; **~leiden** *nt* foot complaint; **~leiste** *f* skirting (board) *(Brit)*, baseboard *(US)*.
fußlig *adj* fluffy.
Füßling *m (von Strumpf)* foot; *(Socke)* footlet.
Fuß-: ~marsch *m* walk; *(Mil)* march; **~matte** *f* doormat; **~note** *f* footnote; **~pflege** *f* chiropody; **zur ~pflege gehen** to go to the chiropodist; **~pfleger** *m* chiropodist; **~pilz** *m (Med)* athlete's foot; **~puder** *m* foot powder; **~punkt** *m* **(a)** *(Astron)* nadir; **(b)** *(Math)* foot *(of a perpendicular)*; **~schweiß** *m* foot perspiration; **~sohle** *f* sole of the foot; **~soldat** *m (Mil old)* foot soldier; **~spitze** *f* toes *pl*; **sich auf die ~spitzen stellen** to stand on tiptoe; **~sprung** *m* **einen ~sprung machen** to jump feet-first; **~spur** *f* footprint; **~stapfen** *m* footprint; **in jds ~ stapfen treten** *(fig)* to follow in sb's footsteps; **~steig** *m* **(a)** *(Weg)* footpath; **(b)** *(S Ger: Bürgersteig)* pavement *(Brit)*, sidewalk *(US)*; **~stütze** *f* footrest; **f~tief** *adj* ankle-deep; **~tritt** *m (Geräusch)* footstep; *(Spur auch)* footprint; *(Stoß)* kick; **jdm einen ~tritt geben** *or* **versetzen** to kick sb, to give sb a kick; **jdn mit einem ~tritt hinausbefördern** to kick sb out; **einen ~tritt bekommen** *(fig)* to be kicked out; **~truppe** *f* infantry *no pl*; **~volk** *nt* **(a)** *(Mil old)* footmen *pl*; **(b)** *(fig)* **das ~volk** the rank and file; **~wanderung** *f* walk; **~waschung** *f* foot-washing; **die ~waschung Christi** the washing of Christ's feet; **~weg** *m* **(a)** *(Pfad)* footpath; **(b)** *(Entfernung)* **es sind nur 15 Minuten ~weg** it's only 15 minutes walk; **~wurzel** *f (Anat)* tarsus; **~zeile** *f (Comput)* footer.
futsch *adj pred (inf) (weg)* gone, vanished; *(S Ger: kaputt)* bust *(inf)*, broken.
Futter *nt* **-s, -** **(a)** *no pl* (animal) food *or* feed; *(für Kühe, Pferde etc auch)* fodder ◆ **gut im ~ sein** to be well-fed. **(b)** *(Auskleidung) (Kleider~, Briefumschlag~)* lining; *(Tür~)* casing. **(c)** *(Spann~)* chuck.
Futteral *nt* **-s, -e** case.
Futter-: ~getreide *nt* forage cereal; **~häuschen** *nt* bird box; **~krippe** *f* manger; **an der ~krippe sitzen** *(inf)* to be well-placed.
futtern [1] *vi (hum inf)* to stuff oneself *(inf)*.
[2] *vt (hum inf)* to scoff.
füttern *vt* **(a)** *Tier, Kind, Kranke* to feed ◆ **„F~ verboten"** "do not feed the animals". **(b)** *Kleidungsstück* to line.
Futter-: ~napf *m* bowl; **~neid** *m (fig)* green-eyed monster *(hum)*, jealousy; **~pflanze** *f* forage plant; **~rübe** *f* root vegetable used for forage; **~sack** *m* nosebag; **~stoff** *m* lining (material); **~trog** *m* feeding trough.
Fütterung *f* feeding ◆ **die ~ der Nilpferde findet um 17⁰⁰ Uhr statt** feeding time for the hippos is 5 p.m.
Futterverwerter(in *f***)** *m* **-s, -** *(inf: Mensch)* **er ist ein guter ~** food goes straight to his figure.
Futur *nt* **-(e)s, -e** *(Gram)* future (tense).
Futura *pl of* **Futurum.**
futurisch *adj (Gram)* future.
Futurismus *m* futurism.
futuristisch *adj* futurist(ic).
Futurologe *m* futurologist.
Futurologie *f* futurology.
futurologisch *adj* futurological.
Futurum *nt* **-s, Futura** *(Gram) siehe* **Futur.**
Fux *m* **-es, ¨-e** *(Univ)* new member of a student fraternity.
Fuxmajor *m (Univ) student in charge of the new members of a fraternity.*
fuzeln *vi (Aus)* to write small.

G, g [geː] *nt* -, - G, g.
g *abbr of* **Gramm.**
gab *pret of* **geben.**
Gabardine ['gabardiːn, gabar'diːn(ə)] *m* **-s,** *no pl or f* -, *no pl* gaberdine, gabardine.
Gabe *f* -, **-n (a)** *(dated: Geschenk)* gift, present *(gen* of, from); *(Schenkung)* donation *(gen* from); *(Eccl: Opfer)* offering; *siehe* **mild(e). (b)** *(Begabung)* gift ◆ **die ~ haben, etw zu tun** to have a natural *or (auch iro)* (great) gift for doing sth. **(c)** *(Med) (das Verabreichen)* administering; *(Dosis)* dose.
Gabel *f* -, **-n** fork; *(Heu~, Mist~)* pitchfork; *(Deichsel)* shafts *pl*; *(Telec)* rest, cradle; *(Geweih mit zwei Enden)* two-pointed antler; *(zwei Enden des Geweihs)* branch, fork.
Gabel-: ~bissen *m* canapé; **~bock** *m (Hunt: Rehbock)* two-pointer; *(~antilope)* pronghorn (antelope); **~deichsel** *f* shafts *pl*; **g~förmig** *adj* forked *no adv*; **sich g~förmig teilen** to fork; **~frühstück** *nt* mid-morning snack; **~hirsch** *m (Hunt: Rothirsch)* two-pointer; *(Andenhirsch)* guemal.
gabelig *adj siehe* **gabelförmig.**
gabeln *vtr* to fork.
Gabelstapler *m* **-s,** - fork-lift truck.
Gabelung *f* fork.
Gabentisch *m table for Christmas or birthday presents.*
gackern *vi (lit, fig)* to cackle.
Gadolinium *nt, no pl (abbr* **Gd)** gadolinium.
Gaffel *f* -, **-n** *(Naut)* gaff.
Gaffel-: ~schoner *m (Naut)* fore-and-aft schooner; **~segel** *nt (Naut)* gaffsail.
gaffen *vi* to gape, to gawp *(inf)*, to stare *(nach* at), to rubberneck *(US sl)* ◆ **gaff nicht, sondern hilf mir lieber!** don't just stand there gaping *etc*, come and help!
Gaffer(in *f)* *m* **-s,** - gaper, gawper *(inf)*, starer, rubbernecker *(US sl)* ◆ **die neugierigen ~ bei einem Unfall** the nosy people standing gaping at an accident.
Gafferei *f* gaping, gawping *(inf)*, staring.
Gag [gɛ(ː)k] *m* **-s, -s** *(Film~)* gag; *(Werbe~)* gimmick; *(Witz)* joke; *(inf: Spaß)* laugh.
gaga *adj pred inv (sl)* gaga *(inf)*.
Gagat *m* **-(e)s, -e, Gagatkohle** *f* jet.
Gage ['gaːʒə] *f* -, **-n** *(esp Theat)* fee; *(regelmäßige ~)* salary.
gähnen *vi (lit, fig)* to yawn ◆ **~de Leere** total emptiness; **im Kino herrschte ~de Leere** the cinema was (totally) deserted; **ein ~der Abgrund/~des Loch** a yawning abyss/gaping hole; **ein G~** a yawn; **das G~ unterdrücken** to stop oneself (from) yawning; **das G~ der Schüler** the pupils' yawning; **das war zum G~ (langweilig)** it was one big yawn *(inf)*.
GAL [geː|aː'|ɛl] *f* - *abbr of* **Grün-Alternative Liste** *electoral pact of Greens and alternative parties.*
Gala *f* -, *no pl* formal *or* evening *or* gala dress; *(Mil)* full *or* ceremonial *or* gala dress ◆ **sich in ~ werfen** to get all dressed up (to the nines *inf*), to put on one's best bib and tucker *(inf)*.
Gala- *in cpds* formal, evening; *(Mil)* full ceremonial, gala; *(Theat)* gala; **~abend** *m* gala evening; **~anzug** *m* formal *or* evening dress; *(Mil)* full *or* ceremonial *or* gala dress; **~diner** *nt* formal dinner; **~empfang** *m* formal reception.
galaktisch *adj* galactic.
Galan *m* **-s, -e** *(old)* gallant; *(hum inf auch)* beau.
galant *adj (dated)* gallant ◆ **die ~e Dichtung** galant poetry; **~es Abenteuer** affair of the heart, amatory adventure.
Galanterie *f (dated)* gallantry.
Galanteriewaren *pl (old)* fashion accessories *pl*.
Gala-: ~uniform *f (Mil)* full dress *or* ceremonial *or* gala uniform; **~vorstellung** *f (Theat)* gala performance.
Gäle *m* **-n, -n** Gael.
Galeere *f* -, **-n** galley.
Galeerensklave, Galeerensträfling *m* galley slave.
Galeone *f* -, **-n** *(Hist)* galleon.
Galerie *f* **(a)** *(Empore, Gang, Kunst~, Mil, Naut)* gallery ◆ **auf der ~** in the gallery. **(b)** *(Geschäftspassage)* arcade.
Galerist(in *f)* *m* owner of a gallery.
Galgen *m* **-s,** - gallows *pl*, gibbet; *(Film)* boom; *(Tech)* crossbeam; *(Spiel)* hangman ◆ **jdn an den ~ bringen** to bring sb to the gallows; **an den ~ mit ihm!** let him swing!, to the gallows with him!; **jdn am ~ hinrichten** to hang sb (from the gallows).
Galgen-: ~frist *f (inf)* reprieve; **jdm eine ~frist geben** to give sb a reprieve, to reprieve sb; **~humor** *m* gallows humour; **sagte er mit ~humor** he said with a macabre sense of humour; **~strick, ~vogel** *m (inf)* gallows bird *(inf)*.
Galiläa *nt* **-s,** *no pl* Galilee.
Galiläer(in *f)* *m* **-s,** - Galilean.
galiläisch *adj* Galilean.
Galion *nt* **-s, -s** *(Hist)* cutwater.
Galionsfigur *f* figurehead.
gälisch *adj* Gaelic.
Gall|apfel *m* gallnut; *(an Eichen)* oak-apple, oak-gall.
Galle *f* -, **-n** *(Anat) (Organ)* gallbladder; *(Flüssigkeit)* bile, gall; *(Bot, Vet)* gall; *(fig: Bosheit)* gall, virulence ◆ **bitter wie ~** bitter as gall *or* wormwood; **seine ~ verspritzen** *(fig)* to pour out one's venom; **jdm kommt die ~ hoch** sb's blood begins to boil; **die ~ läuft ihm über** *(inf)* he's seething *or* livid; *siehe* **Gift.**
galle(n)bitter *adj* bitter as gall; *Wein, Geschmack auch* acid, acrid; *Arznei auch* bitter; *Bemerkung* caustic.
Gallen- *in cpds* gall; **~blase** *f* gall-bladder; **~gang** *m* bile duct; **~grieß** *m* small gall-stones *pl*; **~kolik** *f* gall-stone colic; **~leiden** *nt* trouble with one's gall-bladder; **~stein** *m* gall-stone.
Gallert *nt* **-(e)s, -e, Gallerte** *f* -, **-n** jelly.
gallert|artig *adj* jelly-like, gelatinous.
Gallien [-iən] *nt* **-s** Gaul.
Gallier(in *f)* [-iɐ, -iərɪn] *m* **-s,** - Gaul.
gallig *adj* gall-like *attr*; *(fig) Mensch, Bemerkung, Humor* caustic, acerbic.
gallisch *adj* Gallic.
Gallium *nt, no pl (abbr* **Ga)** gallium.
Gallizismus *m (Ling)* Gallicism.
Gallone *f* -, **-n** gallon.
Galopp *m* **-s, -s** *or* **-e** gallop; *(Tanz)* galop ◆ **im ~** *(lit)* at a gallop; *(fig)* at top *or* high speed; **langsamer ~** canter; **gestreckter/kurzer ~** full/checked gallop; **in den ~ verfallen** to break into a gallop; **das Pferd sprang in fliegendem ~ über die Mauer** the horse flew *or* soared over the wall in mid-gallop.
galoppieren* *vi aux haben or sein* to gallop ◆ **~de Inflation** galloping inflation.
Galopprennen *nt* horse race *(on the flat)* ◆ **zum ~ gehen** to go to the races.
Galosche *f* -, **-n** galosh *usu pl*, overshoe.
galt *pret of* **gelten.**
galvanisch [gal'vaːnɪʃ] *adj* galvanic.
Galvaniseur [galvani'zøːɐ] *m* electroplater.
Galvanisier|anstalt *f* electroplating works *sing or pl*.
galvanisieren* [galvani'ziːrən] *vt* to electroplate; *(mit Zink auch)* to galvanize.
Galvanisierung *f* electroplating; *(mit Zink auch)* galvanization, galvanizing.
Galvanismus [galva'nɪsmʊs] *m* galvanism.
Galvano [gal'vaːno] *nt* **-s, -s** *(Typ)* electrotype, electro *(inf)*.
Galvano-: ~meter *nt* galvanometer; **~plastik** *f (Tech)* electroforming, galvanoplasty *(form)*; *(Typ)* electrotype.
Gamasche *f* -, **-n** gaiter; *(kurze ~)* spat; *(Wickel~)* puttee ◆ **sie hat ~n vor ihm/davor** *(dated inf)* he/it makes her tremble in her boots *(inf)*.
Gamaschenhose *f* (pair *sing* of) leggings *pl*.
Gambe *f* -, **-n** viola da gamba.
Gambia *nt* **-s** (the) Gambia.
Gameboy ['geɪmbɔɪ] ® *m* -, **-s** *(Comput)* Gameboy ®.
Gameshow ['geɪmʃoʊ] *f* game show.
Gammastrahlen, Gamma-Strahlen *pl* gamma rays *pl*.
Gammastrahlung *f* gamma radiation.
Gammel *m* **-s,** *no pl (dial)* junk *(inf)*, rubbish.
Gammeldienst *m (Mil sl)* lazy spell of duty.
gammelig *adj (inf) Lebensmittel* old, ancient *(inf)*; *Kleidung* tatty *(inf)*; *Auto auch*

⚠: for details of spelling reform, see supplement

decrepit ◆ **das Fleisch ist ja schon ganz ~** the meat has already gone bad *or* off.

Gammelleben *nt (inf)* loafing *or* bumming around *(inf) no art.*

gammeln *vi (inf)* to laze *or* loaf *(inf)* about, to bum around *(inf).*

Gammler(in f) *m* **-s, -** long-haired layabout.

Gams *f* **-, -(en)** *(Aus, S Ger, Hunt) siehe* **Gemse.**

⚠**Gams-: ~bart** *m tuft of hair from a chamois worn as a hat decoration,* shaving-brush *(hum inf);* **~bock** *m* chamois buck; **~leder** *nt* chamois (leather).

gang *adj:* **~ und gäbe sein** to be the usual thing, to be quite usual.

Gang[1] *m* **-(e)s, ¨e** (a) *(no pl: ~art)* walk, way of walking, gait; *(eines Pferdes)* gait, pace ◆ **einen leichten/schnellen ~ haben** to be light on one's feet, to walk lightly/to be a fast walker; **jdn an seinem** *or* **am ~ erkennen/am aufrechten ~ erkennen** to recognize sb's walk *or* sb from the way he walks/ from his upright carriage; **seinen ~ verlangsamen/beschleunigen** to slow down/to speed up, to hasten one's step *(liter).*
(b) *(Besorgung)* errand; *(Spazier~)* walk ◆ **einen ~ machen** *or* **tun** to go on an errand/to go for a walk; **einen ~zum Anwalt/zur Bank machen** to go to *or* pay a visit to one's lawyer/the bank; **einen schweren ~ tun** to do something difficult; **das war für ihn immer ein schwerer ~** it was always hard for him; **ich muß einen schweren ~ tun** I have a difficult thing to do; **sein erster ~ war** ... the first thing he did was ...; **den ~ nach Canossa antreten** *(fig)* to eat humble pie; **der ~ nach Canossa** *(Hist)* the pilgrimage to Canossa.
(c) *(no pl: Bewegung eines Motors)* running; *(einer Maschine auch)* operation; *(Ablauf)* course; *(eines Dramas)* development ◆ **der Motor hat einen leisen ~** the engine runs quietly; **der ~ der Ereignisse/der Dinge** the course of events/things; **seinen gewohnten ~ gehen** *(fig)* to run its usual course; **etw in ~ bringen** *or* **setzen** to get *or* set sth going; *(fig auch)* to get sth off the ground *or* under way; **etw in ~ halten** *(lit, fig)* to keep sth going; *Maschine, Motor auch* to keep sth running; **in ~ kommen** to get going; *(fig auch)* to get off the ground *or* under way; **in ~ sein** to be going; *(eine Maschine auch)* to be in operation, to be running; *(Motor auch)* to be running; *(fig)* to be off the ground *or* under way; *(los sein)* to be going on *or* happening; **in vollem ~** in full swing; **es ist etwas im ~(e)** *(inf)* something's up *(inf); siehe* **tot.**
(d) *(Arbeits~)* operation; *(eines Essens)* course; *(Fechten, im Zweikampf)* bout; *(beim Rennen)* heat ◆ **ein Essen von** *or* **mit vier ¨en** a four-course meal.
(e) *(Verbindungs~)* passage(way); *(Rail, in Gebäuden)* corridor; *(Hausflur) (offen)* passage(way), close *(Scot); (hinter Eingangstür)* hallway; *(im oberen Stock)* landing; *(Theat, Aviat, in Kirche, in Geschäft, in Stadion)* aisle; *(Aviat, in Stadion)* gangway; *(Säulen~)* colonnade, passage; *(Bogen~)* arcade, passage; *(Wandel~)* walk; *(in einem Bergwerk)* tunnel, gallery; *(Durch~ zwischen Häusern)* passage(way); *(Anat)* duct; *(Gehör~)* meatus; *(Min: Erz~)* vein; *(Tech: eines Gewindes)* thread.
(f) *(Mech)* gear; *(bei Fahrrad auch)* speed ◆ **den ersten ~ einschalten** *or* **einlegen** to engage first (gear); **auf** *or* **in den dritten ~ schalten** to change *or* shift *(US)* into third (gear).

Gang[2] [gɛŋ] *f* **-, -s** gang.

Gang|art *f* (a) walk, way of walking, gait; *(von Pferd)* gait, pace; *(Haltung)* carriage, bearing; *(fig)* stance ◆ **Menschen haben eine aufrechte ~** humans walk upright; **eine leicht nach vorne gebeugte ~ haben** to walk with one's body bent slightly forward; **eine schnellere ~ vorlegen** to walk faster; **eine harte ~** *(fig)* a tough stance *or* line.
(b) *(Min)* gangue, matrix.

gangbar *adj (lit) Weg, Brücke etc* passable; *(fig) Lösung, Weg* practicable ◆ **nicht ~** impassable/impracticable.

Gängelband *nt:* **jdn am ~ führen** *(fig) (Lehrer etc)* to spoon-feed sb; *(Ehefrau, Mutter)* to keep sb tied to one's apron strings.

Gängelei *f* spoon-feeding ◆ **warum wehrt er sich nicht gegen die ~ seiner Mutter/Frau?** why doesn't he fight against being tied to his mother's/wife's apron strings?

gängeln *vt (fig)* **jdn ~** to spoon-feed sb, to treat sb like a child/children; *(Mutter, Ehefrau)* to keep sb tied to one's apron strings.

Ganghebel *m (Tech)* gear lever.

gängig *adj* (a) *(üblich)* common; *(aktuell)* current; *Münze* current; *(vertretbar)* possible.
(b) *(gut gehend) Waren* popular, in demand ◆ **die ~ste Ausführung** the best-selling model.
(c) *(rare: gut laufend)* **~ sein** *(Pferd)* to be a good goer; *(Hund)* to be well-trained; **ein ~es/schlecht ~es Gespann** a fast/slow team; **einen Hund ~ machen** *(Hunt)* to train a dog.

Ganglien [-iən] *pl (Anat)* ganglia *pl.*

Ganglien-: ~system *nt* gangliar *or* ganglionic system; **~zelle** *f* gangliocyte, ganglion cell.

Gangräne *f* **-, -n** *or* **Gangrän** *nt* **-s, -e** *(Med)* gangrene.

Gangschaltung *f* gears *pl.*

Gangster ['gɛŋstɐ, 'gaŋstɐ] *m* **-s, -** gangster.

Gangster-: ⚠**~boß** *m* gang boss; **~braut** *f* (gang) moll *(sl);* **~methoden** *pl* strong-arm tactics *pl.*

Gangway ['gæŋweɪ] *f* **-, -s** *(Naut)* gangway; *(Aviat)* steps *pl.*

Ganove [ga'no:və] *m* **-n, -n** *(inf)* crook; *(hum: listiger Kerl)* sly old fox.

Ganoven-: ~ehre *f* honour among(st) thieves; **das verbietet mir meine ~ehre** even crooks have some honour; **~sprache** *f* underworld slang.

Gans *f* **-, ¨e** goose ◆ **wie die ¨e schnattern** to cackle away, to cackle like a bunch of old hens *(inf).*

Gans- *in cpds (Aus) siehe* **Gänse-.**

Gänschen ['gɛnsçən] *nt* gosling; *(fig inf)* little goose *(inf).*

Gänse- *in cpds* goose; **~blümchen** *nt,* **~blume** *f* daisy; **~braten** *m* roast goose; **~brust** *f (Cook)* breast of goose; **~feder** *f* (goose-)quill; **~fett** *nt* goose-fat; **~füßchen** *pl (inf)* inverted commas *pl,* quotation marks *pl,* sixty-sixes and ninety-nines *pl (inf);* **~haut** *f (fig)* goose-pimples *pl,* goose-flesh; **eine ~haut bekommen** *or* **kriegen** *(inf)* to get goose-pimples *or* goose-flesh, to go all goose-pimply *(inf);* **~kiel** *m* (goose-)quill; **~klein** *nt* **-s,** *no pl* goose pieces *pl; (Innereien)* goose giblets *pl;* **~leberpastete** *f* pâté de foie gras; **~marsch** *m:* **im ~marsch** in single *or* Indian file.

Gänserich *m* **-s, -e, Ganser** *m* **-s, -** *(Aus)* gander.

Gänse-: ~schmalz *nt* goose-dripping; **~wein** *m (hum)* Adam's ale *(hum),* water.

Ganter *m* **-s, -** *(N Ger) siehe* **Gänserich.**

ganz [1] *adj* (a) whole, entire; *(vollständig)* complete; *Wahrheit* whole ◆ **eine ~e Zahl** a whole number, an integer; **eine ~e Note/Pause** *(Mus)* a semi-breve *(Brit),* a whole note *(US)*/a semi-breve *or* whole note rest; **die ~e Mannschaft war** ... the whole *or* entire team was ..., all the team were ...; **die ~en Tassen/Kinder** *(inf)* all the cups/children; **der ~e Vordergrund** the whole *or* entire foreground, the whole of the foreground, all the foreground; **~ England/London** the whole of England/London, all England/London; **wir fuhren durch ~ England** we travelled all over England; **in ~ England/London** in the whole of *or* in all England/London; **die ~e Zeit** all the time, the whole time; **der ~e Kram** the whole lot; **eine ~e Menge** quite a lot; **sein ~es Geld/Vermögen** all his money/fortune, his entire *or* whole fortune; **seine ~en Sachen** all his things; **seine ~e Kraft** all his strength; **sie ist seine ~e Freude** *(inf)* she's the apple of his eye *(inf);* **du bist ja mein ~es Leben** you're my whole life; **du hast mir den ~en Spaß verdorben** you've spoilt all my fun; **ein ~er Mann** a real *or* proper man.
(b) **Käse/eine Sammlung ~** *or* **im ~en kaufen** to buy a whole cheese/a collection as a whole; **im (großen und) ~en (genommen)** on the whole, by and large, (taken) all in all.
(c) *(inf: unbeschädigt)* intact ◆ **etw wieder ~ machen** to mend sth; **wieder ~ sein** to be mended.
(d) *(inf: nicht mehr als)* all of ◆ **ich verdiene im Monat ~e 200 DM** I earn all of 200 marks a month; **noch ~e zehn Minuten** all of ten minutes.
[2] *adv (völlig)* quite; *(vollständig, ausnahmslos)* completely; *(ziemlich, leidlich)* quite; *(sehr)* really; *(genau)* exactly, just ◆ **~ hinten/vorn** right at the back/ front; **nicht ~** not quite; **~ gewiß!** most certainly, absolutely; **ein ~ gutes Buch** *(ziemlich)* quite a good book; *(sehr gut)* a very *or* really good book; **ich habe mich ~ riesig gefreut** I was really enormously pleased; **du hast ihn ~ fürchterlich beleidigt** you've really insulted him very badly; **ein ~ billiger Trick/böser Kerl** a really cheap trick/evil character; **du bist ein ~ Schlauer** you're really a crafty one; **das war ~ lieb von dir** that was really nice of you; **das ist mir ~ gleich** it's all the same *or* all one to me; **er hat ~ recht** he's quite *or* absolutely right; **~ mit Ruß bedeckt** all *or* completely covered with soot; **~ allein** all alone; **du bist ja ~ naß** you're all wet; **so ~ vergnügt/traurig** *etc* so very happy/sad *etc;* **~ Aufmerksamkeit/Demut** *etc* **sein** to be all attention/ humility *etc;* **etwas ~ Intelligentes/Verrücktes** something really clever/ mad *etc;* **es ist ~ aus** it's all over; **~ wie Sie meinen** just as you think (best); **~ gleich wer** it doesn't matter who, no matter who; **eine Zeitschrift ~ lesen** to read a magazine right through *or* from cover to cover; **das habe ich nicht ~ gelesen** I haven't read it all yet, I haven't finished reading it yet; **ein ~ ~ hoher Berg** a very very *or* really really high mountain; **~ und gar** completely, utterly; **~ und gar nicht** not at all, not in the least; **noch nicht ~ zwei Uhr** not quite two o'clock yet; **ich habe ~ den Eindruck, daß ...** I've rather got the impression that ...; **ein ~ klein wenig** just a little *or* tiny bit; **das mag ich ~ besonders gerne** I'm particularly *or* especially fond of that; **sie ist ~ die Mutter** she's just *or* exactly like her mother; **etw ~ oder gar nicht machen** to do sth properly or not at all.

Ganz|aufnahme *f (Phot)* full-length photo(graph).

Gänze *f* **-,** *no pl (form, Aus)* entirety ◆ **zur ~** completely, fully, in its entirety.

Ganze(s) *nt decl as adj* whole; *(alle Sachen zusammen)* lot; *(ganzer Satz, ganze Ausrüstung)* complete set ◆ **etw als ~s sehen** to see sth as a whole; **das ~ kostet** ... altogether it costs ...; **das ~ alleine machen** to do the whole thing *or* it all on one's own; **das ~ halt!** *(Mil)* parade, halt!; **das ist nichts ~s und nichts Halbes** that's neither one thing nor the other; **das ~ gefällt mir gar nicht** I don't like it at all, I don't like anything about it; **aufs ~ gehen** *(inf)* to go all out; **es geht ums ~** everything's at stake.

Ganzheit *f (Einheit)* unity; *(Vollständigkeit)* entirety ◆ **als ~** as an integral whole; **in seiner ~** in its entirety.

ganzheitlich *adj (umfassend einheitlich)* integral ◆ **ein Problem ~ betrachten/ darstellen** to view/present a problem in its entirety.

Ganzheits-: ~medizin *f* holistic medicine; **~methode** *f* look-and-say method; **~psychologie** *f* holism.

Ganz-: g~jährig *adj* non-seasonal, all the year round; **~leder** *nt* **ein Buch in ~leder** a leather-bound book, a book with a leather binding; **~lederband** *m* leather-bound volume; **g~ledern** *adj* leather-bound, bound in leather; **~leinen** *nt* (a) *(Stoff)* pure linen; (b) *(~einband)* **ein Buch in ~leinen** a cloth-bound book, a book with a cloth binding; **~leinenband** *m* cloth-bound volume.

gänzlich [1] *adv* completely, totally.
[2] *adj (rare)* complete, total.

Ganz-: g~seiden *adj* pure silk; **g~seitig** *adj Anzeige etc* full-page; **g~tägig** *adj* all-day; *Arbeit, Stelle* full-time; **ein g~tägiger Ausflug** a day-trip; **g~tägig arbeiten** to work full-time; **sie ist jetzt g~tägig zu Hause** she's at home all day now; **das Schwimmbad ist g~tägig geöffnet** the swimming baths are open all day.

ganztags *adv arbeiten* full-time.

Ganztags-: ~beschäftigung *f* full-time occupation; **~schule** *f* all-day schooling *no pl or* schools *pl*; (*Gebäude*) all-day school; **~stelle** *f* full-time job.

Ganz-: ~ton *m* (*Mus*) (whole) tone; **g~wollen** *adj* all-wool.

gar [1] *adv* **(a)** (*überhaupt*) at all; (*ganz*) quite ♦ **~ keines** not a single one, none whatsoever *or* at all; **~ kein Grund** no reason whatsoever *or* at all, not the slightest reason; **~ niemand** not a soul, nobody at all *or* whatsoever; **~ nichts** nothing at all *or* whatsoever; **~ nicht schlecht** *or* **übel** not bad at all, not at all bad.
(b) (*old, S Ger, Aus: zur Verstärkung*) **es war ~ so kalt/warm** it was really *or* so cold/warm; **er wäre ~ zu gern noch länger geblieben** he would really *or* so have liked to stay longer; **es ist ~ zu dumm, daß er nicht gekommen ist** (*S Ger, Aus*) it's really *or* so *or* too stupid that he didn't come; *siehe* **ganz 2.**
(c) (*geh, S Ger, Aus: sogar*) even ♦ **er wird doch nicht ~ verunglückt sein?** he hasn't had an accident, has he?; **du hast das doch nicht ~ meinem Mann erzählt?** you haven't told my husband, have you?; **warum nicht ~!** (and) why not?, why not indeed?; **und nun will sie ~ ...** and now she even wants ...; **hast du eine Wohnung, oder ~ ein eigenes Haus?** do you have a flat, or perhaps even a house of your own?
(d) (*obs, Aus, S Ger: sehr*) really, indeed ♦ **ein ~ feiner Mensch** a really splendid person, a splendid person indeed; **~ schön** passing fair (*obs*); **er kommt ~ oft** he comes really frequently *or* very frequently indeed; **~ mancher** many a person; **~ manchmal** many a time, many a time and oft (*old*).
[2] *adj* **(a)** *Speise* done *pred*, cooked ♦ **das Steak ist ja nur halb ~** this steak is only half-cooked.
(b) (*form*) *Leder* tanned, dressed; (*Agr*) *Boden* well-prepared.
(c) (*S Ger, Aus*) (*verbraucht*) used up, finished; (*zu Ende*) at an end, over ♦ **das Öl wird ja nie ~** we'll never use all this oil.

Garage [ga'ra:ʒə] *f* **-, -n** garage; (*Hoch~, Tief~*) car-park ♦ **das Auto in einer ~ unterstellen** to garage one's car.

garagieren* [gara'ʒi:rən] *vt* (*Aus, Sw*) to park.

Garant *m* guarantor.

Garantie *f* (*lit, fig*) guarantee ♦ **die Uhr hat ein Jahr ~** the watch is guaranteed for a year *or* has a year's guarantee; **das fällt noch unter die ~** *or* **geht noch auf ~** that comes under *or* is covered by the guarantee; **ich gebe dir meine ~ darauf** (*fig inf*) I guarantee (you) that.

Garantie-: ~anspruch *m* right to claim under guarantee; **~frist** *f* guarantee period; **~lohn** *m* guaranteed minimum wage.

garantieren* [1] *vt* to guarantee (*jdm etw* sb sth) ♦ **der Name dieser Firma garantiert Qualität** the name of this firm is a guarantee of good quality *or* guarantees good quality; **er konnte mir nicht ~, daß ...** he couldn't give me any guarantee that ...
[2] *vi* to give a guarantee ♦ **für etw ~** to guarantee sth; **diese Marke garantiert für Qualität** this brand is a guarantee of quality; **er konnte für nichts ~** he couldn't guarantee anything.

garantiert *adv* guaranteed; (*inf*) I bet (*inf*) ♦ **er kommt garantiert nicht** I bet he won't come (*inf*), he's bound not to come.

Garantieschein *m* guarantee, certificate of guarantee (*form*).

Garaus *m*: (*inf*) **jdm den ~ machen** to do sb in (*inf*), to bump sb off (*inf*); **einer Sache den ~ machen** to put an end *or* a stop to a matter.

Garbe *f* **-, -n** (*Korn~*) sheaf; (*Licht~*) beam; (*Mil: Schuß~*) burst of fire; (*Metal*) faggot ♦ **das Getreide wurde in** *or* **zu ~n gebunden** the corn was bound into sheaves.

Garbenbindemaschine *f* (*Agr*) sheaf-binder, sheaf-binding machine.

Gärbottich *m* fermenting vat.

Garçonnière [garsɔ'nie:rə] *f* **-, -n** (*Aus*) one-room flat (*Brit*) *or* apartment.

Garde *f* **-, -n** guard ♦ **~ zu Fuß** (*Hist*) Foot Guards *pl*; **bei der ~** in the Guards; **die alte ~** (*fig*) the old guard.

Garde-: ~maß *nt height required for eligibility for the Guards*; **~maß haben** (*inf*) to be as tall as a tree; **~offizier** *m* Guards officer; **~regiment** *nt* Guards regiment.

Garderobe *f* **-, -n (a)** (*Kleiderbestand*) wardrobe ♦ **eine reiche ~ haben** to have a large wardrobe, to have a great many clothes.
(b) (*Kleiderablage*) hall-stand; (*im Theater, Kino etc*) cloakroom, checkroom (*US*) ♦ **seinen Mantel an der ~ abgeben** to leave one's coat in the cloakroom.
(c) (*Theat: Umkleideraum*) dressing-room.

Garderoben-: ~frau *f* cloakroom *or* checkroom (*US*) attendant; **~haken** *m* coat hook; **~marke** *f* cloakroom *or* checkroom (*US*) number; **~schein** *m* cloakroom *or* checkroom (*US*) ticket; **~schrank** *m* hall cupboard; **~ständer** *m* hat-stand, hat tree (*US*).

Garderobier [gardəro'bie:] *m* **-s, -s (a)** (*Theat: für Kostüme*) wardrobe master; (*im Umkleideraum*) dresser. **(b)** (*an der Abgabe*) cloakroom *or* checkroom (*US*) attendant.

Garderobiere [-'bie:rə] *f* **-, -n (a)** wardrobe mistress, dresser. **(b)** cloakroom *or* checkroom (*US*) attendant.

gardez [gar'de:] *interj* (*Chess*) gardez.

Gardine *f* curtain, drape (*US*); (*Scheiben~*) net curtain; *siehe* **schwedisch.**

Gardinen-: ~band *nt* curtain tape; **~blende** *f* pelmet; **~predigt** *f* (*inf*) dressing-down, talking-to; **jdm eine ~predigt halten** to give sb a dressing-down or a talking-to; **~rolle** *f*, **~röllchen** *nt* curtain runner; **~stange** *f* curtain rail; (*zum Ziehen*) curtain rod.

Gardist *m* (*Mil*) guardsman.

garen (*Cook*) *vti* to cook; (*auf kleiner Flamme*) to simmer.

gären [1] *vi aux haben or sein* to ferment; (*Hefe*) to work; (*fig: Gefühle etc*) to seethe ♦ **die Wut/das Unrecht gärte in ihm** he was seething with anger/a sense of injustice; **in ihm gärt es** he is in a state of inner turmoil.
[2] *vt* to ferment.

Gären *nt* **-s,** *no pl siehe* **Gärung.**

Garette *f* **-, -n** (*Sw: Schubkarren*) barrow.

Gärfutter *nt* (*Agr*) silage *no pl.*

Gar-: ⚠g~kochen *vt sep* to cook/boil *etc* sth (until done); *siehe* **kochen**; **~küche** *f* (*old*) hot food stall.

Gärmittel *nt* ferment.

Garn *nt* **-(e)s, -e (a)** thread; (*Baumwoll~ auch*) cotton; (*Häkel~, fig: Seemanns~*) yarn ♦ **ein ~ spinnen** (*fig*) to spin a yarn. **(b)** (*Netz*) net. **jdm ins ~ gehen** (*fig*) to fall into sb's snare, to fall *or* walk into sb's trap.

Garnele *f* **-, -n** (*Zool*) prawn; (*Granat*) shrimp.

garni *adj siehe* **Hotel ~.**

garnieren* *vt Kuchen, Kleid* to decorate; *Gericht*, (*fig*) *Reden etc* to garnish.

Garnierung *f siehe vt* **(a)** (*das Garnieren*) decoration; garnishing. **(b)** (*Material zur ~*) decoration; garnish ♦ **Zitate als ~ einer Rede** quotations to garnish a speech.

Garnison *f* (*Mil*) garrison ♦ **mit ~ belegen** to garrison; **in ~ liegen** to be garrisoned *or* in garrison.

Garnison(s)- *in cpds* garrison; **~kirche** *f* garrison church; **~stadt** *f* garrison town.

Garnitur *f* **(a)** (*Satz*) set; (*Unterwäsche*) set of (matching) underwear ♦ **die erste ~** (*fig*) the pick of the bunch, the top-notches *pl* (*inf*); **erste/zweite ~ sein, zur ersten/zweiten ~ gehören** to be first-rate *or* first-class/second-rate.
(b) (*Besatz*) trimming. **(c)** (*Mil: Uniform*) uniform. **erste ~** number one uniform *or* dress.

Garn-: ~knäuel *m or nt* ball of thread *or* yarn; **~rolle** *f* spool; (*von Baumwolle, Nähgarn*) cotton reel; **~spinnerei** *f* spinning mill.

Garotte *f* **-, -n** garrotte.

garottieren* *vt* to garrotte.

garstig *adj* (*dated*) nasty, horrible.

Gärstoff *m* ferment.

Garten *m* **-s, ¨** garden; (*Obst~*) orchard ♦ **öffentlicher/botanischer/zoologischer ~** public/botanic(al)/zoological gardens *pl*; **im ~ arbeiten** to work in the garden, to do some gardening; **das ist nicht in seinem ~ gewachsen** (*fig inf*) (*Ideen*) he didn't think of that himself, that's not his own idea; (*Leistungen*) he didn't do that by himself.

Garten- *in cpds* garden; **~arbeit** *f* gardening *no pl*; **~architekt** *m* landscape gardener; **~bau** *m* horticulture; **~bauausstellung** *f* horticultural exhibition; **~blume** *f* garden *or* cultivated flower; **~gerät** *nt* gardening tool *or* implement; **~haus** *nt* summer house; (*für Geräte*) garden shed; (*Hinterhaus*) back *or* rear building; **~kolonie** *f* allotments *pl*; **~laube** *f* (*~häuschen*) summer house; (*aus Blattwerk*) arbour, bower; (*für Geräte*) garden shed; **~lokal** *nt* beer garden; (*Restaurant*) garden café; **~möbel** *pl* garden furniture; **~schere** *f* secateurs *pl* (*Brit*), pruning-shears *pl*; (*Heckenschere*) shears *pl*; **~schlauch** *m* garden hose; **~tür** *f* garden gate; **~zwerg** *m* garden gnome; (*pej inf*) squirt (*inf*); **~zwiebel** *f* flower bulb.

Gärtner *m* **-s, -** gardener; *siehe* **Bock[1].**

Gärtnerei *f* **(a)** (*Baumschule, für Setzlinge*) nursery; (*für Obst, Gemüse, Schnittblumen*) market-garden (*Brit*), truck farm (*US*). **(b)** *no pl* (*Gartenarbeit*) gardening; (*Gartenbau*) horticulture.

Gärtnerin *f* gardener.

gärtnerisch [1] *adj attr* gardening; *Ausbildung* horticultural ♦ **~e Gestaltung** landscaping; **die ~en Kosten** the cost of the landscaping.
[2] *adv* **einen Park ~ gestalten** to landscape a park; **~ ausgebildet** trained in horticulture.

gärtnern *vi* to garden.

Gärung *f* fermentation; (*fig*) ferment, turmoil ♦ **in ~ kommen** to start fermenting; **in ~ sein** (*fig*) to be in ferment *or* in a turmoil.

Gärungs-: ~erreger *m* ferment; **⚠~prozeß** *m* process of fermentation.

Gas *nt* **-es, -e** gas; (*Aut: ~pedal*) accelerator, gas pedal (*esp US*) ♦ **~ geben** (*Aut*) to accelerate, to put one's foot down (*inf*), to step on the gas (*inf*); (*auf höhere Touren bringen*) to rev up; **~ wegnehmen** (*Aut*) to decelerate, to ease one's foot off the accelerator, to throttle back (*US*); **mit ~ vergiften** to gas.

Gas- *in cpds* gas; **~badeofen** *m* gas(-fired) water heater; **~behälter** *m* gasholder, gasometer; **g~beheizt** *adj* gas-heated; **~dichte** *f* (*Phys*) density of a/the gas; **~erzeugung** *f* generation of gas; (*Ind*) gas-production; **~fernversorgung** *f* (*System*) long-distance gas supply; **~feuerzeug** *nt* gas lighter; **~flasche** *f* bottle of gas, gas canister; **g~förmig** *adj* gaseous, gasiform; **~geruch** *m* smell of gas; **~hahn** *m* gas-tap; **den ~hahn aufdrehen** (*fig*) to put one's head in the gas oven; **~hebel** *m* (*Aut*) accelerator (pedal), gas pedal (*esp US*); (*Hand~*) (hand) throttle; **~heizung** *f* gas (central) heating; **~herd** *m* gas cooker; **~hülle** *f* atmosphere; **~installateur** *m* gas fitter; **~kammer** *f* gas chamber; **~kocher** *m* camping stove; **~kraftwerk** *nt* gas-fired power station; **~krieg** *m* chemical *or* gas war/warfare; **~laterne** *f* gas (street) lamp; **~leitung** *f* (*Rohr*) gas pipe; (*Hauptrohr*) gas main; **~licht** *nt* gaslight; (*Beleuchtung*) gaslighting; **~mann** *m* gasman; **~maske** *f* gasmask; **~ofen** *m* (*Heizofen*) gas fire *or* heater; (*Heizungsofen*) gas(-fired) boiler; (*Backofen*) gas oven; (*Herd*) gas cooker *or* stove.

Gasolin *nt* **-s,** *no pl* petroleum ether.

Gasometer *m* gasometer.
Gas-: ~pedal *nt (Aut)* accelerator (pedal), gas pedal *(esp US)*; **~pistole** *f* tear-gas gun; **~plasma** *nt* gas plasma; **~rohr** *nt siehe* **~leitung**.
⚠ **Gäßchen** *nt* alley(way).
Gasse *f* **-, -n** lane; *(Durchgang)* alley(way); *(S Ger, Aus: Stadtstraße)* street; *(Rugby)* line-out ◆ **die schmalen ~n der Altstadt** the narrow streets and alleys of the old town; **eine ~ bilden** to make a passage; *(Rugby)* to form a line-out; **eine ~ für jdn bilden** to make way or clear a path for sb; **sich** *(dat)* **eine ~ bahnen** to force one's way; **auf der ~** *(S Ger, Aus)* on the street; **etw über die ~ verkaufen** *(Aus)* to sell sth to take away.
Gassen-: ~hauer *m (old, inf)* popular melody; **~jargon** *m* gutter language; **~junge** *m (pej)* street urchin *or* arab; **~schänke** *f (S Ger)* off-sales *(Brit)*, package store *(US)*.
Gassi *adv (inf)* **~ gehen** to go walkies *(inf)*; **mit einem Hund ~ gehen** to take a dog (for) walkies *(inf)*.
Gast[1] *m* **-es, ¨-e** guest; *(Besucher auch, Tourist)* visitor; *(in einer ~stätte)* customer; *(Theat)* guest (star); *(Univ: ~hörer)* observer, auditor *(US)* ◆ **Vorstellung vor geladenen ¨-en** performance before an invited audience; **ungeladener ~** uninvited guest; *(bei einer Party auch)* gatecrasher; **jdn zu ~ bitten** *(form)* to request the pleasure of sb's company *(form)*; **wir haben heute abend ¨-e** we're having people round *or* company this evening; **bei jdm zu ~ sein** to be sb's guest(s); **in einem anderen Ort/bei einem anderen Sender zu ~ sein** *(Rad)* to visit another place/go over to another station.
Gast[2] *m* **-(e)s, -en** *(Naut) (Signal~)* signalman; *(Radio~)* operator.
Gastarbeiter *m* immigrant *or* foreign worker.
Gäste-: ~bett *nt* spare *or* guest bed; **~buch** *nt* visitors' book.
Gastechnik *f* gas-engineering.
Gäste-: ~handtuch *nt* guest towel; **~haus** *nt* guest house; **~heim** *nt (dated)* guest house, boarding house; **~zimmer** *nt* guest *or* spare room.
Gast-: g~frei, g~freundlich *adj* hospitable; **~freundlichkeit, ~freundschaft** *f* hospitality; **g~gebend** *adj attr Land* host; **~geber** *m* host; **~geberin** *f* hostess; **~geschenk** *nt* present *brought by a guest;* **~haus** *nt*, **~hof** *m* inn; **~hörer(in** *f***)** *m (Univ)* observer, auditor *(US)*.
gastieren* *vi* to guest, to make a guest appearance.
Gast-: ~land *nt* host country; **g~lich** *adj siehe* **g~freundlich; ~lichkeit** *f siehe* **~freundlichkeit; ~mahl** *nt (old)* banquet; **Platos „~mahl"** Plato's "Symposium".
Gastod *m* death by gassing ◆ **den ~ sterben** to be gassed.
Gast-: ~professor *m* visiting professor; **~recht** *nt* right to hospitality.
gastrisch *adj (Med)* gastric.
Gastritis *f* -, **Gastritiden** gastritis.
Gastrolle *f (Theat)* guest role ◆ **eine ~ geben** *or* **spielen** *(lit)* to make a guest appearance; *(fig)* to put in *or* make a fleeting appearance.
Gastronom(in *f***)** *m (Gastwirt)* restaurateur; *(Koch)* cuisinier, cordon-bleu cook.
Gastronomie *f (form: Gaststättengewerbe)* catering trade; *(geh: Kochkunst)* gastronomy.
gastronomisch *adj* gastronomic.
Gastroskopie *f (Med)* gastroscopy.
Gast-: ~spiel *nt (Theat)* guest performance; *(Sport)* away match; **ein ~spiel geben** *(lit)* to give a guest performance; *(fig inf)* to make *or* put in a fleeting *or* brief appearance; **~spielreise** *f (Theat)* tour; **auf ~spielreise** on tour; **~stätte** *f (Speise~)* restaurant; *(Trinklokal)* pub *(Brit)*, bar; **~stättengewerbe** *nt* catering trade; **~stube** *f* lounge.
Gasturbine *f* gas turbine.
Gast-: ~vorlesung *f (Univ)* guest lecture; **~vorstellung** *f (Theat) siehe* **~spiel; ~vortrag** *m* guest lecture; **~wirt(in** *f***)** *m (Besitzer)* restaurant owner *or* proprietor/proprietress; *(Pächter)* restaurant manager/manageress; *(von Trinklokal)* landlord/landlady; **~wirtschaft** *f siehe* **~stätte; ~zimmer** *nt* guest room.
Gas-: ~uhr *f siehe* **~zähler; ~verbrauch** *m* gas consumption; **~vergiftung** *f* gas poisoning; **~versorgung** *f (System)* gas supply *(gen* to); **~werk** *nt* gasworks *sing or pl*; *(~verwaltung)* gas board; **~wolke** *f* gas cloud; **~zähler** *m* gas meter; **~zentralheizung** *f* gas central heating.
Gatt *nt* **-(e)s, -en** *or* **-s** *(Naut) (Spei~)* scupper; *(Heckform)* stern; *(kleiner Raum)* locker; *(Loch)* clew; *(enge Durchfahrt)* strait.
GATT [gat] *nt* **-s** GATT.
Gatte *m* **-n, -n** *(form)* husband, spouse *(form)* ◆ **die (beiden) ~n** both partners, husband and wife.
Gatten-: ~liebe *f (form)* married *or* conjugal *(form)* love; **~mord** *m (form)* murder of one's husband/wife; **~wahl** *f (Biol)* choice of mate; **das Ritual der ~wahl** the complicated ritual of choosing a mate.
Gatter *nt* **-s, -** **(a)** *(Tür)* gate; *(Zaun)* fence; *(Rost)* grating, grid. **(b)** *(Tech: auch* **~säge***)* gangsaw, framesaw.
Gattin *f (form)* wife, spouse *(form)*.
Gattung *f (Biol)* genus; *(Liter, Mus, Art)* genre, form; *(fig: Sorte)* type, kind.
Gattungs-: ~begriff *m* generic concept; **~name** *m* generic term.
Gau *m or nt* **-(e)s, -e** **(a)** *(Hist)* gau, *a tribal district, later an administrative district under the Nazis.* **(b)** *(Bezirk)* district, region, area.
GAU [gau] *m* **-(s)** *abbr of* **größter anzunehmender Unfall** MCA, maximum credible accident.
Gaube *f* **-, -n** dormer window.
Gaudee *f* **-, -n** *(Aus)* fun *no pl* ◆ **auf der ~ sein** to be out gallivanting *(inf)*.
Gaudi *nt* **-s** *or (S Ger, Aus) f* **-,** *no pl (inf)* fun ◆ **das war eine ~** that was great fun; **das war eine ~ auf der Party** the party was great fun.
Gaudium *nt, no pl (old)* amusement, entertainment.
Gaukelei *f* trickery *no pl* ◆ **~en** tricks *pl*, trickery.
gaukeln [1] *vi (liter: Schmetterling)* to flutter; *(fig liter)* to flit.
[2] *vt siehe* **vor~**.
Gaukelspiel *nt (liter)* illusion ◆ **ein ~ mit jdm treiben** to play sb false *(liter)*, to deceive sb.
Gaukler *m* **-s, -** **(a)** *(liter)* travelling entertainer; *(fig)* story-teller. **(b)** *(Orn)* bateleur eagle.
Gaul *m* **-(e)s, Gäule** *(pej)* nag, hack; *(rare: Arbeitspferd)* work-horse; *siehe* **Schwanz, schenken, scheu.**
Gauleiter *m (Pol)* Gauleiter, *head of a Nazi administrative district.*
Gaullismus [go'lɪsmʊs] *m* Gaullism.
Gaullist [go'lɪst] *m* Gaullist.
gaullistisch [go'lɪstɪʃ] *adj* Gaullist *no adv.*
Gaumen *m* **-s, -** palate *(auch fig)*, roof of the/one's mouth ◆ **die Zunge klebte ihm vor Durst am ~** his tongue was hanging out (with thirst); **einen feinen ~ haben** *(fig)* to be (something of) a gourmet, to enjoy good food; **das kitzelt mir den ~** *(fig)* that tickles my taste-buds *or* my palate.
Gaumen-: ~kitzel *m (inf)* delight for the taste-buds; **~laut** *m* palatal (sound); **~platte** *f* (dental) plate; **~segel** *nt* soft palate, velum *(spec)*; **~zäpfchen** *nt* uvula.
Gauner *m* **-s, -** rogue, rascal, scoundrel; *(Betrüger)* crook; *(hum inf: Schelm auch)* scamp, scallywag *(inf)*; *(inf: gerissener Kerl)* cunning devil *(inf)*, sly customer *(inf)* ◆ **kleine ~** *(Kriminelle)* small-time crooks.
Gaunerbande *f* bunch of rogues *or* rascals *or* scoundrels/crooks; *(hum: Kinder auch)* bunch of scamps *or* scallywags *(inf)*.
Gaunerei *f* swindling *no pl*, cheating *no pl.*
gaunerhaft *adj* rascally *no adv.*
gaunern *(inf) vi (betrügen)* to swindle, to cheat; *(stehlen)* to thieve ◆ **er hat sich durchs Leben gegaunert** he cheated his way through life.
Gauner-: ~sprache *f* underworld jargon; **~zinken** *m tramp's or gypsy's sign written on wall etc.*
Gavotte [ga'vɔt(ə)] *f* **-, -n** *(Mus)* gavotte.
Gaza-Streifen ['ga:za:-] *m* Gaza Strip.
Gaze ['ga:zə] *f* **-, -n** gauze; *(Draht~ auch)* (wire) mesh.
Gazelle *f* gazelle.
Gazette *f (old, pej)* gazette *(old)*, (news)paper, rag *(pej inf)*.
g-Druck ['ge:-] *m (Aviat)* g-force.
Ge|ächtete(r) *mf decl as adj* outlaw; *(fig)* outcast.
Ge|ächze *nt* **-s,** *no pl* groaning *no pl*, groans *pl.*
ge|ädert *adj* veined.
ge|artet *adj* **gutmütig/freundlich ~ sein** to be good-natured/have a friendly nature; **er ist (eben) so ~(, daß ...)** it's (just) his nature (to ...); **sie ist ganz anders ~** she has a completely different nature, she's quite different; **so ~e Probleme** problems of this nature; **das Problem ist so ~, daß ...** the nature of the problem is such that ...
Ge|äst *nt* **-(e)s,** *no pl* branches *pl*, boughs *pl (liter)*; *(von Adern etc)* branches *pl.*
geb. *abbr of* **geboren.**
Gebabbel *nt* **-s,** *no pl (inf)* babbling.
Gebäck *nt* **-(e)s, -e** *(Kekse)* biscuits *pl (Brit)*, cookies *pl (US)*; *(süße Teilchen)* pastries *pl*; *(rundes Hefe~)* buns *pl*; *(Törtchen)* tarts *pl*, tartlets *pl* ◆ **allerlei (Kuchen und) ~** all kinds of cakes and pastries.
gebacken *ptp of* **backen**[1].
Gebälk *nt* **-(e)s, -e** timberwork *no pl*, timbers *pl*; *(Archit: Verbindung zu Säulen)* entablature ◆ **ein Partisan im ~** *(inf)* a nigger in the woodpile *(inf)*; *siehe* **knistern.**
geballt *adj (konzentriert) Energie, Kraft, Ladung*, *(fig)* concentrated; *Stil auch* concise; *Beschuß* massed.
gebannt *adj* spellbound ◆ **vor Schreck ~** rigid with fear; **wie ~** as if spellbound.
gebar *pret of* **gebären.**
Gebärde *f* **-, -n** gesture; *(lebhafte auch)* gesticulation.
gebärden* *vr* to behave, to conduct oneself *(form)*.
Gebärden-: ~spiel *nt, no pl* gestures *pl*, gesticulation(s); **das ~spiel der Sänger** the singers' use of gesture; **~sprache** *f* gestures *pl*; *(Zeichensprache)* sign language; *(in Stummfilmen etc)* gesturing; *(unbewußte ~sprache)* body language.
gebaren* *vr (rare) siehe* **gebärden.**
Gebaren *nt* **-s,** *no pl* **(a)** behaviour. **(b)** *(Comm: Geschäfts~)* conduct.
gebären *pret* **gebar**, *ptp* **geboren** [1] *vt* to give birth to; *Kind auch* to bear *(old, form)*, to be delivered of *(old)*; *(fig liter: erzeugen)* to breed ◆ **jdm ein Kind ~** to bear *or* give sb a child; **geboren werden** to be born; **wo sind Sie geboren?** where were you born?; **aus der Not geborene Ideen** ideas springing *or* stemming from necessity; *siehe* **geboren.**
[2] *vi* to give birth.
gebär-: ~fähig *adj* child-bearing; **~freudig** *adj*: **ein ~freudiges Becken haben** *(hum)* to have child-bearing hips.
Gebärmutter *f (Anat)* womb, uterus.
Gebärmutter-: ~hals *m* neck of the womb *or* uterus, cervix; **~krebs** *m* cancer of the uterus; **~mund** *m* mouth of the uterus.
Gebarung *f (Aus Comm) siehe* **Gebaren (b).**
Gebarungs- *(Aus Comm)*: **~bericht** *m* financial report; **~jahr** *nt* financial year; **~kontrolle** *f siehe* **Buchprüfung.**
Gebäu *nt* **-s, -e** *(obs) siehe* **Gebäude.**
gebauchpinselt *adj (hum inf)* **sich ~ fühlen** to be tickled pink *(inf)*, to feel

flattered.

Gebäude nt -s, - building; (Pracht~) edifice; (fig: Gefüge) structure; (von Ideen) edifice; construct; (von Lügen) web.

Gebäude-: **~komplex** m building complex; **~reiniger** m cleaner; (Fensterputzer) window cleaner; (Fassadenreiniger) building cleaner; **~reinigung** f (das Reinigen) commercial cleaning; (Firma) cleaning contractors pl; **~teil** m part of the building.

gebaut adj built ◆ **gut/stark ~ sein** to be well-built/to have a broad frame; **... so, wie du ~ bist** (inf) ... a big man/woman like you; **ein gut ~es Stück** a well-constructed play.

gebefreudig adj generous, open-handed.

Gebefreudigkeit f generosity, open-handedness.

Gebein nt -(e)s, -e (a) skeleton ◆ **der Schreck fuhr ihm ins ~** (old) his whole body trembled with fear. (b) **~e** pl (geh) bones pl, mortal remains pl (liter); (von Heiligen etc auch) relics pl.

Gebell(e) nt -s, no pl barking; (von Jagdhunden) baying; (fig inf: Geschimpfe) bawling (inf).

geben pret **gab**, ptp **gegeben** [1] vt (a) (auch vi) to give; (reichen auch) to pass, to hand; (her~) Leben to give up; (fig) Schatten, Kühle to provide; (machen, zusprechen) Mut, Hoffnung to give ◆ **wer hat dir das gegeben?** who gave you that?; **gib's mir!** give it to me!, give me it!; **jdm einen Tritt ~** to kick sb, to give sb a kick; (fig) to get rid of sb; **gib's ihm (tüchtig)!** (inf) let him have it! (inf); **sich (dat) (von jdm) etw ~ lassen** to ask sb for sth; **was darf ich Ihnen ~?** what can I get you?; **~ Sie mir bitte zwei Flaschen Bier** I'd like two bottles of beer, please; **ich gebe dir das Auto für 100 Mark/zwei Tage** I'll let you have or I'll give you the car for 100 marks/two days; **jdm etw zu verstehen ~** to let sb know sth; **ein gutes Beispiel ~** to set a good example; **jdn/etw verloren ~** to give sb/sth up for or as lost; **~ Sie mir bitte Herrn Braun** (Telec) can I speak to Mr Braun please?; **man kann nicht für alles ~** (spenden) you can't give to everything; **ich gäbe viel darum, zu ...** I'd give a lot to ...; **sie gaben ihr Leben fürs Vaterland** they gave or laid down their lives for their country; **~ or G~ ist seliger denn nehmen** or **Nehmen** (Bibl) it is more blessed to give than to receive.

(b) (stellen) to give; Thema, Aufgabe, Problem auch to set; (gewähren) Interview, Audienz auch to grant; Rabatt auch to allow; (vergönnen) to grant; (verleihen) Titel, Namen to give; Preis auch to award; (zusprechen) Verwarnung to give; Freistoß auch to award ◆ **Gott gebe, daß ...** God grant that ...; **Taktgefühl ist ihm nicht gegeben** he has not been endowed with tactfulness; **es war ihm nicht gegeben, seine Eltern lebend wiederzusehen** he was not to see his parents alive again.

(c) (schicken) to send; (dial: tun) to put ◆ **in die Post ~** to post; **ein Auto in Reparatur/ein Manuskript in Druck ~** to have a car repaired/to send a manuscript to be printed; **ein Kind in Pflege ~** to put or place a child in care; **Zucker über etw (acc) ~** (dial) to sprinkle sugar over sth; **Milch in den Teig ~** (dial) to add milk to the dough; siehe **Bescheid, Nachricht**.

(d) (ergeben, erzeugen) to produce ◆ **2 + 2 gibt 4** 2 + 2 makes 4; **fünf Manuskriptseiten ~ eine Druckseite** five pages of manuscript give or equal one page of print; **die Kuh gibt Milch** the cow produces or yields milk; **ein Pfund gibt fünf Klöße** you can get five dumplings from one pound; **ein Wort gab das andere** one word led to another; **das gibt keinen Sinn** that doesn't make sense; **Rotwein gibt Flecken** red wine leaves stains.

(e) (veranstalten) Konzert, Fest to give; Theaterstück etc to put on; (erteilen) Schulfach etc to teach ◆ **was wird heute im Theater gegeben?** what's on at the theatre today?; **Unterricht ~** to teach; **er gibt Nachhilfeunterricht/Tanzstunden** he gives private coaching/dancing lessons.

(f) **viel/nicht viel auf etw (acc) ~** to set great/not much store by sth; **auf die Meinung der Nachbarn brauchst du nichts zu ~** you shouldn't pay any attention to what the neighbours say; **ich gebe nicht viel auf seinen Rat** I don't think much of his advice; **das Buch hat mir viel gegeben** I got a lot out of the book.

(g) **etw von sich ~** Laut, Worte, Flüche to utter; Rede to deliver; Meinung to express; Lebenszeichen to show, to give; Essen to bring up; **was ich gestern von mir gegeben habe, war völlig unverständlich** what I said yesterday was completely incomprehensible.

[2] vi (rare vt) (Cards) to deal; (Sport: Aufschlag haben) to serve ◆ **wer gibt?** whose deal/serve is it?

[3] vt impers **es gibt** (+acc) there is/are; **was gibt's?** what's the matter?, what's up?, what is it?; **gibt es einen Gott?** is there a God?, does God exist?; **was gibt's zum Mittagessen?** what's (there) for lunch?; **wann gibt's was zu essen? — es gibt gleich was** when are we going to get something to eat? — in a minute; **freitags gibt es bei uns immer Fisch** we always have fish on Fridays; **heute gibt's noch Regen** it's going to rain today; **es wird noch Ärger ~** there'll be trouble (yet); **was wird das noch ~?** what will it come to?; **dafür gibt es 10% Rabatt** you get 10% discount for it; **ein Mensch mit zwei Köpfen? das gibt's nicht!** a two-headed person? there's no such thing!; **das gibt's nicht, daß ein Analphabet Lexikograph wird** it's impossible for an illiterate to become a lexicographer; **das gibt's doch nicht!, das darf es doch nicht ~!** I don't believe it!, that can't be true!; **das hat es ja noch nie gegeben/so was gibt's bei uns nicht!** that's just not on! (inf); **da gibt's nichts** (inf) there's no two ways about it (inf); **so was gibt's also!** (inf) who'd have thought it! (inf); **gleich gibt's was!** (inf) there'll be trouble in a minute!; **hat es sonst noch etwas gegeben?** was there anything else?; **was es nicht alles gibt!** it's a strange or funny world.

[4] vr (a) (nachlassen) to ease off, to let up; (Schmerz auch) to get less; (Leidenschaft auch) to cool.

(b) (sich erledigen) to sort itself out; (aufhören) to stop ◆ **er gab sich in sein Schicksal** he gave himself up to his fate; **sich gefangen/verloren ~** to give oneself up/to give oneself up for lost; **das wird sich schon ~** it'll all work out; **gibt sich das bald!** (inf) cut it out! (inf); siehe **schlagen, erkennen** etc.

(c) (sich benehmen, aufführen) to behave ◆ **sich als etw ~** to play sth; **sich von oben herab ~** to behave condescendingly; **sich von der besten Seite ~** to show one's best side; **nach außen gab er sich heiter** outwardly he seemed quite cheerful; **sie gibt sich, wie sie ist** she doesn't try to be anything she's not.

Gebenedeite f -n, no pl (Eccl) **die ~** the Blessed Virgin.

Geber m -s, - giver; (Cards) dealer; (Rad: Sender) transmitter.

Geberlaune f generous mood ◆ **in ~ sein** to be feeling generous, to be in a generous mood.

Gebet nt -(e)s, -e prayer ◆ **ein ~ sprechen** to say a prayer; **sein ~ sprechen** or **verrichten** to say one's prayers; **das ~ des Herrn** the Lord's Prayer; **die Hände zum ~ falten** to join one's hands in prayer; **jdn ins ~ nehmen** (fig) to take sb to task; (iro: bei Polizeiverhör etc) to put the pressure on sb.

Gebetbuch nt prayer-book, missal (US).

gebeten ptp of **bitten**.

Gebetläuten nt (Aus) angelus.

Gebets-: **~mantel** m prayer shawl, tallith; **~mühle** f prayer wheel; **g~mühlenhaft** adj constant, continual; **~riemen** m phylactery; **~stätte** f place of prayer; **~teppich** m prayer mat or rug.

Gebettel nt -s, no pl begging.

gebeugt adj (a) Haltung stooped; Kopf bowed; Schultern sloping ◆ **~ sitzen/stehen** to sit/stand hunched up. (b) (Gram) Verb, Substantiv inflected.

gebier (liter) imper sing of **gebären**.

Gebiet nt -(e)s, -e (a) area, region; (Fläche, Stadt~) area; (Staats~) territory. (b) (fig: Fach) field; (Teil~) branch ◆ **auf diesem ~** in this field.

gebieten pret **gebot**, ptp **geboten** (geh) [1] vt (verlangen) to demand; (befehlen) to command ◆ **jdm etw ~** to command sb to do sth; **der Ernst der Lage gebietet sofortiges Handeln** the seriousness of the situation demands immediate action; siehe **Einhalt, geboten, ehrfurchtgebietend**.

[2] vi (a) (liter: herrschen) to have command (über +acc over) ◆ **über ein Land/Volk ~** to have dominion over a country/nation.

(b) (geh: verfügen) **über etw** (acc) **~** Geld etc to have sth at one's disposal; Wissen etc to have sth at one's command.

Gebieter m -s, - (liter) master, lord; (über Heer) commander (über +acc of) ◆ **(mein) Herr und ~** (old) (my) lord and master.

Gebieterin f (liter, old) mistress, lady; (über Heer) commander.

gebieterisch [1] adj (geh) imperious; (herrisch) domineering; Ton peremptory.

[2] adv (unbedingt) absolutely.

Gebiets-: **~abtretung** f (form) cession of territory; **~anspruch** m territorial claim; **~erweiterung** f territorial expansion; **~hoheit** f territorial sovereignty; **~körperschaft** f regional administrative body; **~reform** f local government reform; **~teil** m area (of territory); **g~weise** adv locally.

Gebilde nt -s, - (Ding) thing; (Gegenstand) object; (Bauwerk) construction; (Schöpfung) creation; (Muster) pattern; (Form) shape; (Einrichtung) organization; (der Phantasie) figment.

gebildet adj educated; (gelehrt) learned, erudite; (wohlerzogen) well-bred; (kultiviert) cultured, cultivated; (belesen) well-read; Manieren refined ◆ **sich ~ unterhalten** to have a cultured conversation.

Gebildete(r) mf decl as adj educated person ◆ **die ~n** the intellectuals.

Gebimmel nt -s, no pl (inf) ting-a-ling (inf).

Gebinde nt -s, - (a) (Blumen~) arrangement; (Sträußchen) posy; (Blumenkranz) wreath; (Getreidegarbe) sheaf. (b) (von Garn) skein.

Gebirge nt -s, - (a) mountains pl, mountain range ◆ **im/ins ~** in/into the mountains. (b) (Min) rock.

gebirgig adj mountainous.

Gebirgler(in f) m -s, - mountain-dweller, highlander.

Gebirgs- in cpds mountain; **~bach** m mountain stream; **~bahn** f mountain railway crossing a mountain range; (in Alpen) transalpine railway; **~blume** f mountain flower, flower growing in the mountains; **~jäger** m (Mil) mountain soldier; pl auch mountain troops; **~landschaft** f (Gegend) mountainous region; (Gemälde) mountainscape; (Ausblick) mountain scenery; **~massiv** nt massif; **~rücken** m mountain ridge; **~stock** m massif; **~straße** f mountain road; **~truppen** pl mountain troops pl; **~wand** f mountain face; **~zug** m mountain range.

⚠ **Gebiß** nt -sses, -sse (a) (die Zähne) (set of) teeth; (künstliches ~) dentures pl ◆ **ich habe noch mein ganzes ~** I still have all my teeth. (b) (am Pferdezaum) bit.

⚠ **Gebiß-:** **~abdruck** m impression; **~anomalie** f deformity of the teeth.

gebissen ptp of **beißen**.

Gebläse nt -s, - fan, blower; (Motor~) supercharger; (Verdichter) compressor.

Gebläse-: **~luft** f air from a blower; **~motor** m supercharger (engine).

geblasen ptp of **blasen**.

geblichen ptp of **bleichen**.

geblieben ptp of **bleiben**.

Geblödel nt -s, no pl (inf) nonsense; (blödes Gerede auch) twaddle (inf), baloney (inf); (von Komiker) patter ◆ **die Unterhaltung artete in allgemeines ~ aus** the conversation degenerated into silliness.

Geblök(e) nt -(e)s, no pl (von Schaf, Kalb) bleating; (von Kuh) lowing; (inf: von Mensch) bawling (inf).

geblümt, geblumt (Aus) adj flowered; (Liter, fig) Stil flowery.

⚠: for details of spelling reform, see supplement

Geblüt *nt* **-(e)s,** *no pl (geh) (Abstammung)* descent, lineage; *(fig: Blut)* blood; *(liter: Geschlecht)* family ◆ **von edlem ~** of noble blood.

gebogen [1] *ptp of* **biegen.**
[2] *adj Nase* Roman.

geboren [1] *ptp of* **gebären.**
[2] *adj* born ◆ **blind ~ sein** to have been born blind; **er ist blind ~** he was born blind; **~er Engländer/Londoner sein** to be English/a Londoner by birth; **er ist der ~e Erfinder** he's a born inventor; **Hanna Schmidt ~e** *or* **geb. Müller** Hanna Schmidt, née Müller; **sie ist eine ~e Müller** she was born Müller, her maiden name was Müller.

Geborenzeichen *nt asterisk used to denote "date of birth".*

geborgen [1] *ptp of* **bergen.**
[2] *adj* **sich ~ fühlen/ ~ sein** to feel/be secure *or* safe.

Geborgenheit *f* security.

geborsten *ptp of* **bersten.**

gebot *pret of* **gebieten.**

Gebot *nt* **-(e)s, -e (a)** *(Gesetz)* law; *(Regel, Vorschrift)* rule; *(Bibl)* commandment; *(Grundsatz)* precept; *(old: Verordnung)* decree; *(old: Befehl)* command.
(b) *(geh: Erfordernis)* requirement ◆ **das ~ der Stunde** the needs of the moment; **Besonnenheit ist das ~ der Stunde** what is called for now is calm; **das ~ der Vernunft** the dictates of reason; **das ~ der Vernunft verlangt, daß** ... reason dictates that ...
(c) *(Verfügung)* command ◆ **jdm zu ~e stehen** to be at sb's command *or* *(Geld etc)* disposal.
(d) *(Comm: bei Auktionen)* bid.

geboten [1] *ptp of* **gebieten** *and* **bieten.**
[2] *adj (geh) (ratsam, angebracht)* advisable; *(notwendig)* necessary; *(dringend ~)* imperative ◆ **bei aller ~en Achtung** with all due respect.

Gebotsschild *nt* sign giving orders.

Gebr. *abbr of* **Gebrüder** Bros.

Gebrabbel *nt* **-s,** *no pl (inf)* jabbering *(inf)*, prattling *(inf)*.

gebracht *ptp of* **bringen.**

gebrannt [1] *ptp of* **brennen.**
[2] *adj* **~er Kalk** quicklime; **~e Mandeln** *pl* burnt almonds *pl*; **ein ~es Kind scheut das Feuer** *(Prov)* once bitten twice shy *(Prov)*.

gebraten *ptp of* **braten.**

Gebratene(s) *nt decl as adj* fried food.

Gebräu *nt* **-(e)s, -e** brew; *(pej)* strange concoction; *(fig)* concoction *(aus* of).

Gebrauch *m* **-(e)s, Gebräuche** *(Benutzung)* use; *(eines Wortes)* usage; *(Anwendung)* application; *(Brauch, Gepflogenheit)* custom ◆ **falscher ~** misuse; abuse; misapplication; **von etw ~ machen** to make use of sth; **in ~ sein** to be used *or* in use; *(Auto)* to be running; **etw in ~** *(dat)* **haben** to use sth; *Auto etc* to run sth; **allgemein in ~** *(dat)* in general use; **etw in ~ nehmen** *(form)* to put sth into use; **zum äußeren/inneren ~** to be taken externally/internally; **vor ~ (gut) schütteln** shake (well) before use.

gebrauchen* *vt (benutzen)* to use; *(anwenden)* to apply ◆ **sich zu etw ~ lassen** to be useful for sth; *(mißbrauchen)* to be used as sth; **nicht mehr zu ~ sein** to be no longer any use, to be useless; **er/das ist zu nichts zu ~** he's/that's (of) no use to anybody *or* absolutely useless; **das kann ich gut ~** I can make good use of that, I can really use that; **ich könnte ein neues Kleid/einen Whisky ~** I could use a new dress/a whisky; **Geld kann ich immer ~** money's always useful; *siehe* **gebraucht.**

gebräuchlich *adj (verbreitet)* common; *(gewöhnlich)* usual, customary; *(herkömmlich)* conventional ◆ **nicht mehr ~** *(Ausdruck etc)* no longer used.

Gebräuchlichkeit *f siehe adj* commonness; usualness, customariness; conventionality.

Gebrauchs-: ~anleitung *(form)*, **~anweisung** *f (für Arznei)* directions *pl*; *(für Geräte etc)* instructions *pl*; **~artikel** *m* article for everyday use; **~artikel** *pl (esp Comm)* basic consumer goods *pl*; **g~fähig** *adj* in working order, usable; **etw g~fähig machen** to put sth into working order; **g~fertig** *adj* ready for use; *Nahrungsmittel auch* instant; **~gegenstand** *m* commodity; *(Werkzeug, Küchengerät)* utensil; ⚠**~graphik** *f* commercial art; ⚠**~graphiker** *m* commercial artist; **~gut** *nt usu pl* consumer item; **Konsum- und ~güter** consumer and utility goods; **~lyrik** *f* everyday poetry; **~möbel** *pl* utility furniture *no pl*; **~muster** *nt* registered pattern *or* design; **~musterschutz** *m* protection of patterns and designs; **~wert** *m* utility value.

gebraucht *adj* second-hand, used ◆ **etw ~ kaufen** to buy sth second-hand.

Gebrauchtwagen *m* used *or* second-hand car.

Gebrauchtwaren *pl* second-hand goods *pl*.

Gebrauchtwaren-: ~händler *m* dealer in second-hand goods; **~handlung** *f* second-hand shop.

gebräunt *adj (braungebrannt)* (sun-)tanned.

Gebrechen *nt* **-s, -** *(geh)* affliction; *(fig)* weakness ◆ **die ~ des Alters** the afflictions *or* infirmities of old age.

gebrechen* *vi irreg (old liter)* **es gebricht an etw** *(dat)* sth is lacking; **es gebricht ihm an Mut** he lacks courage.

gebrechlich *adj* frail; *(altersschwach)* infirm; *(fig: unvollkommen)* weak.

Gebrechlichkeit *f siehe adj* frailty; infirmness; weakness.

gebrochen [1] *ptp of* **brechen.**
[2] *adj* broken; *Mensch auch* crushed ◆ **~e Zahl** *(Math)* fraction; **mit ~em Herzen, ~en Herzens** broken-hearted; **an ~em Herzen** of a broken heart; **~ Deutsch sprechen** to speak broken German.

Gebrüder *pl (Comm)* Brothers *pl* ◆ **~ Müller** Müller Brothers.

Gebrüll *nt* **-(e)s,** *no pl (von Rind)* bellowing; *(von Esel)* braying; *(von Löwe)* roar; *(in Todesangst)* screaming; *(von Mensch)* yelling ◆ **auf ihn mit ~!** *(inf)* go for him!, at him!

Gebrumm(e) *nt* **-es,** *no pl* buzzing; *(von Motor, von Baß, Singen)* droning; *(inf: Gebrummel)* grumping *(inf)*.

Gebrummel *nt* **-s,** *no pl* grumping.

gebückt *adj* **eine ~e Haltung** a stoop; **~ gehen** to stoop.

gebügelt *adj (inf: perplex)* knocked flat *(inf)*; *siehe* **geschniegelt.**

Gebühr *f* **-, -en (a)** charge; *(Post~)* postage *no pl*; *(Honorar, Beitrag)* fee; *(Schul~, Studien~)* fees *pl*; *(Vermittlungs~)* commission; *(Straßenbenutzungs~)* toll ◆ **~en erheben** to make *or* levy *(form)* a charge, to charge postage/a fee *etc*; **zu ermäßigter ~** at a reduced rate; **eine ~ von 50 DM** *or* **50 DM ~en bezahlen** to pay a fee/charge *etc* of DM 50; **~ (be)zahlt Empfänger** postage to be paid by addressee; **die ~en für Rundfunk/Fernsehen werden erhöht** radio/television licences are going up.
(b) *(Angemessenheit)* **nach ~** suitably, properly; **über ~** excessively.

gebühren* *(geh)* [1] *vi* to be due *(dat* to) ◆ **ihm gebührt Anerkennung/Achtung** he deserves *or* is due recognition/respect; **das gebührt ihm** *(steht ihm zu)* it is his (just) due; *(gehört sich für ihn)* it befits him.
[2] *vr* to be proper *or* seemly *or* fitting ◆ **wie es sich gebührt** as is proper.

Gebühren-: ~anhebung *f* augmentation in charges/fees *etc*; **~anzeiger** *m* call-fee indicator *(Brit)*, tollcharge meter *(US)*.

gebührend *adj (verdient)* due; *(angemessen)* suitable; *(geziemend)* proper ◆ **das ihm ~e Gehalt** the salary he deserves; **jdm die ~e Achtung erweisen/verweigern** to pay/deny sb the respect due to him.

Gebühren-: ~einheit *f (Telec)* (tariff) unit; **~erhöhung** *f* increase in charges/fees; ⚠**~erlaß** *m* remission of charges/fees; **g~frei** *adj* free of charge; *Brief, Paket* post-free; **~freiheit** *f* exemption from charges/fees/postage; **~marke** *f* revenue stamp; **~ordnung** *f* scale of charges, tariff; **g~pflichtig** *adj* subject *or* liable to a charge, chargeable; *Autobahnbenutzung* subject to a toll; **g~pflichtige Verwarnung** *(Jur)* fine; **jdn g~pflichtig verwarnen** to fine sb; **g~pflichtige Autobahn** toll road *(Brit)*, turnpike *(US)*; **~satz** *m* rate (of charge); **~zähler** *m* meter.

gebührlich *adj siehe* **gebührend.**

Gebums(e) *nt* **-es,** *no pl* **(a)** *(inf: Gepolter)* thumping, thudding. **(b)** *(sl: Koitieren)* screwing *(sl)*.

gebündelt *adj Strahlen* bundled; *(fig)* joint.

gebunden [1] *ptp of* **binden.**
[2] *adj* tied *(an +acc* to sth); *(durch Verpflichtungen etc)* tied down; *Kapital* tied up; *Preise* controlled; *(Ling, Phys)* bound; *Buch* cased, hardback; *Wärme* latent; *(Mus)* legato ◆ **in ~er Rede** in verse; **zeitlich/vertraglich ~ sein** to be restricted as regards time/to be bound by contract; **anderweitig ~ sein** to be otherwise engaged.

Gebundenheit *f* restriction; *(von Wärme)* latency ◆ **auf Grund der ~ unseres Kapitals** because our capital is tied up; **ein Gefühl der ~** a feeling of being tied.

➤ **Geburt** *f* **-, -en** *(lit, fig)* birth; *(fig: Produkt)* fruit, product ◆ **von ~** by birth; **von ~ an** from birth; **von hoher/adliger ~** of good/noble birth; **bei der ~ sterben** *(Mutter)* to die in childbirth; *(Kind)* to die at birth; **das war eine schwere ~!** *(fig inf)* that took some doing *(inf)*.

Geburten-: ~beschränkung *f* population control; **~buch** *nt* register of births; **~kontrolle, ~regelung** *f* birth control; **~rückgang** *m* drop in the birthrate; **g~schwach** *adj Jahrgang* with a low birthrate; **g~stark** *adj Jahrgang* with a high birthrate; **~statistik** *f* birth statistics *pl*; ⚠**~überschuß** *m* excess of births over deaths; **~zahlen** *pl*, **~ziffer** *f* number of births, birthrate; **~zuwachs** *m* increase in the birthrate.

gebürtig *adj* **~er Londoner** *or* **aus London ~ sein** to have been born in London, to be London-born, to be a native Londoner.

Geburts-: ~adel *m* hereditary nobility; **er stammt aus altem ~adel** he comes from a long line of nobility; **~anzeige** *f* birth announcement; **~datum** *nt* date of birth; **~fehler** *m* congenital defect; **~haus** *nt* **das ~haus Kleists** the house where Kleist was born; **~helfer(in** *f***)** *m (Arzt)* obstetrician; *(Laie)* assistant at a birth; **~hilfe** *f* **(a)** assistance at a birth; **~hilfe leisten** to assist at a birth; *(fig)* to help sth see the light of day; **(b)** *(als Fach)* obstetrics *sing*; *(von Hebamme auch)* midwifery; **~jahr** *nt* year of birth; **~lage** *f* presentation; **~land** *nt* native country; **~ort** *m* birthplace; **~stadt** *f* native town; **~stätte** *f (geh)* birthplace.

➤ **Geburtstag** *m* birthday; *(auf Formularen)* date of birth ◆ **herzlichen Glückwunsch zum ~!** happy birthday!, many happy returns (of the day)!; **jdm zum ~ gratulieren** to wish sb (a) happy birthday *or* many happy returns (of the day); **heute habe ich ~** it's my birthday today; **~ feiern** to celebrate one's/sb's birthday; **jdm etw zum ~ schenken** to give sb sth for his/her birthday.

Geburtstags- *in cpds* birthday; **~kind** *nt* birthday boy/girl.

Geburts-: ~urkunde *f* birth certificate; **~wehen** *pl* labour pains *pl*; *(fig auch)* birth pangs *pl*; **~zange** *f* (pair *sing* of) forceps *pl*.

Gebüsch *nt* **-(e)s, -e** bushes *pl*; *(Unterholz)* undergrowth, brush.

Geck *m* **-en, -en** *(pej)* fop, dandy.

geckenhaft *adj (pej)* foppish.

Gecko *m* **-s, -s** *(Zool)* gecko.

gedacht [1] *ptp of* **denken** *and* **gedenken.**
[2] *adj Linie, Größe, Fall* imaginary.

Gedächtnis *nt* memory; *(Andenken auch)* remembrance ◆ **etw aus dem ~ hersagen** to recite sth from memory; **das ist seinem ~ entfallen** it went out of his mind; **sich** *(dat)* **etw ins ~ zurückrufen** to recall sth, to call sth to mind; **wenn mich mein ~ nicht trügt** if my memory serves me right; **noch**

frisch in jds ~ (*dat*) **sein** to be still fresh in sb's mind; **zum ~ der** *or* **an die Toten** in memory *or* remembrance of the dead.

Gedächtnis-: ~fehler *m* lapse of memory; **~feier** *f* commemoration; (*kirchliche*) memorial *or* commemorative service; **~hilfe** *f* memory aid, mnemonic; **er machte sich ein paar Notizen als ~hilfe** he made a few notes to aid his memory; **~lücke** *f* gap in one's memory; (*Psych*) localized amnesia; **da habe ich eine ~lücke** I just don't remember anything about it; **~protokoll** *nt* record; **~rennen** *nt* memorial race; **~schulung** *f* memory training; **~schwund** *m* amnesia, loss of memory; **~störung** *f* partial *or* (*vorübergehend*) temporary amnesia; **~stütze** *f siehe* **~hilfe**; **~übung** *f* memory training exercise; **~verlust** *m* loss of memory.

gedämpft *adj Geräusch* muffled; *Farben, Musikinstrument, Stimmung* muted; *Optimismus* cautious; *Licht, Freude* subdued; *Wut* suppressed; (*Tech*) *Schwingung* damped ♦ **mit ~er Stimme** in a low voice.

▼ **Gedanke** *m* **-ns, -n** thought (*über +acc* on, about); (*Idee, Plan, Einfall*) idea; (*Konzept*) concept; (*Betrachtung*) reflection (*über +acc* on) ♦ **der bloße ~ an ...** the mere thought of ...; **da kam mir ein ~** then I had an idea, then something occurred to me; **einen ~n fassen** to formulate an idea; **bei diesem Lärm kann man ja keinen ~n fassen** you can't hear yourself think in this noise; **seine ~n beisammen haben** to have one's mind *or* thoughts concentrated; **in ~n vertieft** *or* **versunken/verloren sein** to be deep *or* sunk/lost in thought; **in ~n, Worten und Werken sündigen** to sin in thought, word and deed; **in ~n bin ich bei dir** in thought I am with you, my thoughts are with you; **jdn auf andere ~n bringen** to take sb's mind off things; **schwarzen ~n nachhängen** to think gloomy *or* dismal thoughts; **wo hat er nur seine ~n?** whatever is he thinking about?; **sich** (*dat*) **über etw** (*acc*) **~n machen** to think about sth; (*sich sorgen*) to worry *or* be worried about sth; **mach dir keine ~n (darüber)!** don't worry about it!; **man macht sich** (*dat*) **so seine ~n** (*inf*) I've got my ideas; **kein ~ (daran)!** (*stimmt nicht*) not a bit of it! (*inf*); (*kommt nicht in Frage*) (that's) out of the question; **etw ganz in ~n** (*dat*) **tun** to do sth (quite) without thinking; **jds ~n lesen** to read sb's mind *or* thoughts; **ich kann doch nicht ~n lesen!** I'm not a mind-reader!; **auf einen ~n kommen** to have *or* get an idea; **wie kommen Sie auf den ~n?** what gives you that idea?, what makes you think that?; **auf dumme ~n kommen** (*inf*) to get up to mischief; **jdn auf den ~n bringen, etw zu tun** to give sb the idea of doing sth; **sich mit dem ~n tragen, etw zu tun** (*geh*) to consider *or* entertain the idea of doing sth; **der Europa~** *or* **europäische/olympische ~** the European/Olympic Idea.

Gedanken-: ~armut *f* lack of thought; (*Ideenarmut*) lack of originality; **~austausch** *m* (*Pol*) exchange of ideas; **~flug** *m* (*geh*) flight(s) of thought; **~folge** *f* reasoning; **~freiheit** *f* freedom of thought; **~fülle** *f* wealth of ideas; **~gang** *m* train of thought; **~gebäude** *nt* edifice *or* construct of ideas; **~gut** *nt* body of thought; **~kette** *f* chain of thought; **~lesen** *nt* mind-reading; **g~los** *adj* (*unüberlegt*) unthinking; (*zerstreut*) absent-minded; (*rücksichtslos*) thoughtless; **etw g~los tun** to do sth without thinking; **~losigkeit** *f siehe adj* lack of thought; absent-mindedness; thoughtlessness; **~lyrik** *f* reflective poetry; **g~reich** *adj* full of ideas; **~reichtum** *m* wealth of ideas; **~reihe** *f siehe* **~kette**; **~splitter** *m* aphorism; **~sprung** *m* mental leap, jump from one idea to another; **~strich** *m* dash; **~tiefe** *f* depth of thought; **~übertragung** *f* telepathy (*auch fig*), thought transference; **~verbindung, ~verknüpfung** *f* association of ideas; **g~verloren** *adj* lost in thought; **g~voll** *adj* (*nachdenklich*) thoughtful, pensive; **~welt** *f* world of thought *or* (*Ideenwelt*) ideas; **die römische ~welt** (the world of) Roman thought; **er lebt in seiner eigenen ~welt** he lives in a world of his own.

gedanklich *adj* intellectual; (*vorgestellt*) imaginary ♦ **sich** (*dat*) **~** *or* **in ~er Hinsicht näherkommen** to find a common way of thinking; **in ~er Hinsicht übereinstimmen** to have an affinity of mind; **die große ~e Klarheit in seinem Werk** the great clarity of thought in his work.

Gedärm(e) *nt* **-(e)s, -e** (*old, liter*) bowels *pl*, entrails *pl*.

Gedärme *pl* intestines *pl* ♦ **da drehen sich einem ja die ~ um!** it's enough to make your insides *or* stomach turn over!

Gedeck *nt* **-(e)s, -e (a)** (*Tisch~*) cover ♦ **ein ~ auflegen** to lay *or* set a place; **ein ~ für drei Personen** places *or* covers for three people; **eine Tafel mit zehn ~en** a table laid for ten (people). **(b)** (*Menü*) set meal, table d'hôte. **(c)** (*im Nachtclub*) cover charge; drink with cover charge.

gedeckt *adj Farben* muted; *Basar, Gang* covered.

Gedeih *m*: **auf ~ und Verderb** for better or (for) worse; **jdm auf ~ und Verderb ausgeliefert sein** to be completely and utterly at sb's mercy.

gedeihen *pret* **gedieh**, *ptp* **gediehen** *vi aux sein* to thrive; (*wirtschaftlich auch*) to prosper, to flourish; (*geh: sich entwikkeln*) to develop; (*fig: vorankommen*) to make progress *or* headway, to progress ♦ **die Sache ist so weit gediehen, daß ...** the matter has reached the point *or* stage where ...

Gedeihen *nt* **-s**, *no pl siehe vi* thriving; prospering, flourishing; (*Gelingen*) success ♦ **zum ~ dieses Vorhabens braucht es Geduld und Glück** if this plan is to succeed patience and luck will be called for.

gedeihlich *adj* (*geh*) (*vorteilhaft*) beneficial, advantageous, salutary; (*erfolgreich*) successful.

Gedenk|ausstellung *f* commemorative exhibition.

Gedenken *nt* **-s**, *no pl* memory ♦ **zum** *or* **im ~ an jdn** in memory *or* remembrance of sb; **etw in gutem ~ behalten** to treasure the memory of sth; **jdm ein ehrendes ~ bewahren** to remember sb with honour.

▼ **gedenken*** *vi irreg +gen* **(a)** (*geh: denken an*) to remember, to think of; (*erwähnen*) to recall ♦ **in seiner Rede gedachte er ...** in his speech he recalled ▼ ... **(b)** (*feiern*) to commemorate, to remember. **(c) ~, etw zu tun** to propose to do sth.

Gedenk-: ~feier *f* commemoration; **~gottesdienst** *m* memorial *or* commemorative service; **~marke** *f* commemorative stamp; **~minute** *f* minute's silence; **~münze** *f* commemorative coin; **~rede** *f* commemorative speech; **~stätte** *f* memorial; **~stein** *m* commemorative *or* memorial stone; **~stunde** *f* hour of commemoration; **~tafel** *f* plaque; **~tag** *m* commemoration day.

Gedicht *nt* **-(e)s, -e** poem ♦ **die ~e Enzensbergers** Enzensberger's poetry *or* poems; **dieses Kleid/der Nachtisch ist ein ~** (*fig inf*) this dress/the dessert is sheer poetry.

Gedicht-: ~form *f* poetic form; **in ~form** in verse; **~sammlung** *f* collection of poems; (*von mehreren Dichtern auch*) anthology.

gediegen *adj* **(a)** *Metall* pure, native (*esp Min*). **(b)** (*von guter Qualität*) high-quality; (*geschmackvoll*) tasteful; (*rechtschaffen*) upright; *Verarbeitung* solid; *Kenntnisse* sound. **(c)** (*inf: wunderlich*) peculiar.

Gediegenheit *f siehe adj* **(a)** purity, nativeness. **(b)** high quality; tastefulness; uprightness; solidity; soundness.

gedieh *pret of* **gedeihen.**

gediehen *ptp of* **gedeihen.**

gedient *adj*: **ein ~er Soldat** *someone who has completed his military service.*

Gedinge *nt* **-s, -** (*Miner*): **im ~ arbeiten** to work on a piece-rate basis.

Gedöns *nt* **-es**, *no pl* (*dial inf*) fuss, hullabaloo (*inf*).

gedr. *abbr of* **gedruckt.**

Gedränge *nt* **-s**, *no pl* (*Menschenmenge*) crowd, crush; (*Drängeln*) jostling; (*Sport*) bunching; (*Rugby*) scrum(mage) ♦ **vor der Theaterkasse herrschte ~** there was a big crush at the ticket office; **ein offenes ~** (*Rugby*) a loose scrum; **ins ~ kommen** *or* **geraten** (*fig*) to get into a fix.

Gedrängel *nt* **-s**, *no pl* (*inf*) (*Menschenmenge*) crush; (*Drängeln*) shoving (*inf*).

gedrängt *adj* packed; (*fig*) *Stil* terse ♦ **~ voll** packed full, jam-packed (*inf*); **~e Übersicht** synopsis; **~ stehen** to be crowded together.

Gedrängtheit *f* (*von Stil*) terseness; (*von Übersicht*) conciseness.

gedrechselt *adj* (*pej*) *Rede, Sätze, Stil* stilted ♦ **wie ~ reden** to speak in a stilted fashion *or* stiltedly; **kunstvoll ~e Sätze** nicely turned phrases.

Gedröhn(e) *nt* **-es**, *no pl* (*von Motoren*) droning; (*von Kanonen, Lautsprecher, Hämmern etc*) booming.

gedroschen *ptp of* **dreschen.**

gedruckt *adj* printed ♦ **~e Schaltung** printed circuit board, PCB; **lügen wie ~** (*inf*) to lie right, left and centre (*inf*).

gedrückt *adj* depressed, dejected ♦ **~er Stimmung sein** to be in low spirits, to feel depressed.

Gedrücktheit *f* depression, dejection.

gedrungen 1 *ptp of* **dringen.**
2 *adj Gestalt* sturdy, stocky.

Gedrungenheit *f* sturdiness, stockiness.

geduckt *adj Haltung, Mensch* crouching; *Kopf* lowered ♦ **hinter einer Hecke ~** crouching down behind a hedge; **~ sitzen** to sit hunched up.

Gedudel *nt* **-s**, *no pl* (*inf*) (*von Klarinette etc*) tootling; (*von Dudelsack*) droning, whining; (*von Radio*) noise.

Geduld *f* **-**, *no pl* patience ♦ **mit jdm/etw ~ haben** to be patient *or* have patience with sb/sth; **sich mit ~ wappnen** to possess one's soul in patience; **mir geht die ~ aus, mir reißt die ~, ich verliere die ~** my patience is wearing thin, I'm losing my patience; **jds ~ auf eine harte Probe stellen** to try sb's patience.

gedulden* *vr* to be patient.

geduldig *adj* patient ♦ **~ wie ein Lamm** meek as a lamb.

Gedulds-: ~arbeit *f* job calling for patience; **~faden** *m* **jetzt reißt mir aber der ~faden!** (*inf*) I'm just about losing my patience; **einen langen ~faden haben** to have a lot of patience, to have the patience of Job; **~probe** *f* trial of (one's) patience; **das war eine harte ~probe** it was enough to try anyone's patience *or* to try the patience of a saint; **~spiel** *nt* puzzle.

gedungen *ptp of* **dingen.**

gedunsen *adj* bloated.

gedurft *ptp of* **dürfen.**

ge|ehrt *adj* honoured, esteemed ♦ **sehr ~e Damen und Herren!** Ladies and Gentlemen!; **sehr ~er Herr Kurz!** dear Mr Kurz; **Sehr ~e Damen und Herren** (*in Briefen*) Dear Sir or Madam.

ge|eicht *adj* (*inf*) **darauf ist er ~** that's right up his street (*inf*).

ge|eignet *adj* (*passend*) suitable; (*richtig*) right ♦ **sie ist für diesen Posten nicht ~** she's not the right person for this job; **er ist nicht der ~e Mann für meine Tochter** he's not the right *or* a suitable man for my daughter; **im ~en Augenblick** at the right moment; **er ist zu dieser Arbeit nicht ~** he's not suited to this work; **er wäre zum Lehrer gut/schlecht ~** he would/wouldn't make a good teacher.

ge|eigneten|orts *adv* (*form*) in an appropriate place.

ge|eist *adj Früchte, Getränke* iced.

Geest *f* **-, -en**, **Geestland** *nt coastal sandy moorlands of N.W. Germany.*

Gefahr *f* **-, -en (a)** danger (*für* to, for); (*Bedrohung*) threat (*für* to, for) ♦ **die ~en des Dschungels/Verkehrs/dieses Berufs** the dangers *or* perils *or* hazards of the jungle/traffic/this job; **in ~ sein/schweben** to be in danger *or* jeopardy; (*bedroht*) to feel threatened; **außer ~** (*nicht gefährdet*) not in danger; (*nicht mehr gefährdet*) out of danger; (*Patienten*) out of danger, off the danger list; **sich ~en** *or* **einer ~ aussetzen** to expose oneself to danger, to put oneself in danger; **es besteht die ~, daß ...** there's a risk *or* the danger that ...; **er liebt die ~** he likes living dangerously; **(nur) bei ~ (bedienen)!** (to be used only) in case of emergency!; **wer sich in ~ begibt, kommt darin um**

(*Prov*) if you play with fire, you must expect to get your fingers burned. **(b)** (*Wagnis, Risiko*) risk (*für* to, for) ◆ **auf eigene ~** at one's own risk *or* (*stärker*) peril; **auf die ~ hin, etw zu tun/daß jd etw tut** at the risk of doing sth/of sb doing sth; **~ laufen, etw zu tun** to run the risk of doing sth; **unter ~ seines eigenen Lebens** at the risk of one's own life; **auf eigene Rechnung und ~** (*Comm*) at one's own account and risk.

⚠**gefahrbringend** *adj* dangerous.

gefährden* *vt* to endanger; *Position, Wirtschaft, Chancen etc auch* to jeopardize; (*bedrohen*) to threaten; (*aufs Spiel setzen auch*) to put at risk ◆ **Versetzung** *or* **Vorrücken gefährdet** (*Sch*) *comment on a school report indicating that the pupil may have to repeat a year.*

gefährdet *adj Tierart* endangered; *Ehe, Jugend* at risk ◆ **G~e** people at risk.

Gefährdung *f no pl* **(a)** *siehe vt* endangering; jeopardizing; risking. **(b)** (*Gefahr*) danger (*gen* to).

Gefährdungshaftung *f* risk liability.

gefahren *ptp of* **fahren**.

Gefahren-: ~herd *m* danger area; **~moment**[1] *nt* potential danger; **~moment**[2] *m* (*Schrecksekunde*) moment of danger; **~quelle** *f* source of danger; **~stelle** *f* danger spot; **~zone** *f* danger zone *or* area; **~zulage** *f* danger money; **eine ~zulage von 200 Mark** 200 marks danger money.

Gefahr-: ~gut *nt* hazardous materials *pl*; **~guttransport** *m* transport of hazardous materials.

gefährlich *adj* dangerous; (*gewagt auch*) risky; (*lebens~ auch*) perilous ◆ **das ~e Alter** (*fig*) the dangerous age.

Gefährlichkeit *f siehe adj* dangerousness; riskiness; perilousness.

Gefahr-: g~los *adj* safe; (*harmlos*) harmless; **~losigkeit** *f* safety; harmlessness.

Gefahrstelle *f siehe* **Gefahrenstelle.**

Gefährt *nt* **-(e)s, -e** (*dated*) wagon, carriage; (*hum*) jalopy (*inf*).

Gefährte *m* **-n, -n, Gefährtin** *f* (*geh*) (*lit, fig*) companion; (*Lebens~ auch*) partner (through life).

Gefahr-: g~voll *adj* dangerous, full of danger; **~zeichen** *nt* danger sign.

Gefälle *nt* **-s, -** **(a)** (*Neigung*) (*von Fluß*) drop, fall; (*von Land, Straße*) slope; (*Neigungsgrad*) gradient ◆ **das Gelände/der Fluß hat ein starkes ~** the land slopes down steeply/the river drops sharply; **ein ~ von 10%** a gradient of 10%; **starkes ~!** steep hill. **(b)** (*fig: Unterschied*) difference.

➤ **gefallen**[1] *pret* **gefiel**, *ptp* **~** *vi* to please (*jdm* sb) ◆ **es gefällt mir (gut)** I like it (very much *or* a lot); **es gefällt ihm, wie sie spricht** he likes the way she talks; **das gefällt mir gar nicht, das will mir gar nicht ~** (*dated*) I don't like it at all *or* one little bit; **das könnte dir so ~!** (*inf*) no way! (*inf*); **das Stück hat ~** (*geh*) the play was well received; **das gefällt mir schon besser** (*inf*) that's more like it (*inf*); **er gefällt mir gar nicht** (*inf: gesundheitlich*) I don't like the look of him (*inf*); **sich** (*dat*) **in einer Rolle ~** to fancy oneself in a role; **er gefällt sich in der Rolle des Leidenden** he likes playing the martyr; **sich** (*dat*) **etw ~ lassen** (*dulden*) to put up with sth, to tolerate sth; **er läßt sich alles ~** he'll put up with anything; **das lasse ich mir (von Ihnen/denen) nicht ~!** I won't stand for *or* put up with that (from you/them)!; **das lasse ich mir ~!** that's just the job (*inf*) *or* thing (*inf*), there's nothing I'd like better.

gefallen[2] 1 *ptp of* **fallen** *and* **gefallen**[1].
2 *adj Engel, (dated) Mädchen* fallen; (*Mil*) killed in action ◆ **er ist ~** he was killed in action.

Gefallen[1] *nt* **-s,** *no pl* (*geh*) pleasure ◆ **an etw** (*dat*) **~ finden** to derive *or* get pleasure from sth, to delight in sth; **an jdm/aneinander (großes) ~ finden** to take a (great) fancy to sb/each other; **bei jdm ~ finden** to appeal to sb.

Gefallen[2] *m* **-s, -** favour ◆ **jdn um einen ~ bitten** to ask a favour of sb; **tun Sie mir den ~ und schreiben Sie** would you do me a favour and write, would you do me the favour of writing; **Sie würden mir einen ~ tun, wenn ...** you'd be doing me a favour if ...; **jdm etw zu ~ tun** (*geh*) to do sth to please sb; **ihm zu ~** to please him.

Gefallenendenkmal *nt* war memorial.

Gefallene(r) *mf decl as adj* soldier killed in action ◆ **die ~n und die Toten des Krieges** the soldiers and civilians who died in the war; **ein Denkmal für die ~n des Krieges** a memorial to those killed in the war.

Gefäll(e)strecke *f* incline.

gefällig *adj* **(a)** (*hilfsbereit*) helpful, obliging ◆ **sich ~ zeigen** to show oneself willing to oblige; **jdm ~ sein** to oblige *or* help sb. **(b)** (*ansprechend*) pleasing; (*freundlich*) pleasant. **(c) Zigarette ~?** (*form*) would you care for a cigarette?; *siehe* **gefälligst.**

Gefälligkeit *f* **(a)** (*Gefallen*) favour ◆ **jdm eine ~ erweisen** to do sb a favour. **(b)** *no pl* (*gefälliges Wesen*) pleasantness; (*Entgegenkommen*) helpfulness ◆ **etw aus ~ tun** to do sth out of the kindness of one's heart.

Gefälligkeits-: ~akzept *nt*, **~wechsel** *m* (*Fin*) accommodation bill *or* paper.

gefälligst *adv* (*inf*) kindly ◆ **sei ~ still!** kindly keep your mouth shut! (*inf*).

Gefällstrecke *f siehe* **Gefäll(e)strecke.**

Gefall-: ~sucht *f* craving for admiration; **g~süchtig** *adj* desperate to be liked.

gefälscht *adj* forged.

gefangen 1 *ptp of* **fangen.**
2 *adj* (*~genommen*) captured; (*fig*) captivated ◆ **sich ~ geben** to give oneself up, to surrender.

Gefangenen-: ~aufseher *m* guard; **~austausch** *m* exchange of prisoners; **~befreiung** *f* rescue of a prisoner/prisoners; (*als Delikt*) aiding and abetting the escape of a prisoner; **~fürsorge** *f* prison welfare; (*inf: Dienst*) prison welfare service; **~haus** *nt* (*Aus*) prison; **~hilfsorganisation** *f* prisoners' rights organization; **~lager** *nt* prison camp; **~wärter** *m* prison officer, (prison) warder, jailer (*old, inf*).

Gefangene(r) *mf decl as adj* captive; (*Sträfling, Kriegs~, fig*) prisoner ◆ **500 ~ machen** (*Mil*) to take 500 prisoners; **keine ~n machen** (*Mil*) to take no prisoners (alive).

Gefangen-: ⚠**g~halten** *vt sep irreg* to hold prisoner; *Tiere* to keep in captivity; (*fig*) to captivate; **~haus** *nt* (*form, Aus*) *siehe* **Gefangenenhaus**; **~nahme** *f* **-, -n** capture; (*Verhaftung*) arrest; **bei der ~nahme** on one's capture/arrest; ⚠**g~nehmen** *vt sep irreg Mensch* to take captive; *Geiseln auch* to capture; (*verhaften*) to arrest; (*Mil*) to take prisoner; (*fig*) to captivate; **~schaft** *f* captivity; **in ~schaft geraten** to be taken prisoner; ⚠**g~setzen** *vt sep* to take into captivity; (*verhaften*) to imprison.

Gefängnis *nt* prison, jail, gaol (*Brit*); (*~strafe*) imprisonment ◆ **im ~ sein** *or* **sitzen** (*inf*) to be in prison; **ins ~ kommen** to be sent to prison; **zwei Jahre ~ bekommen** to get two years' imprisonment *or* two years in prison; **auf Meineid steht ~** perjury is punishable by imprisonment *or* by a prison sentence.

Gefängnis- *in cpds* prison; **~aufseher** *m* warder, prison officer, jailer (*old, inf*); **~direktor** *m* prison governor, prison warden (*esp US*); **~gebäude** *nt* prison; **~geistlicher** *m* prison chaplain; **~haft** *f* imprisonment; **~hof** *m* prison yard; **~insasse** *m* inmate; **~strafe** *f* prison sentence; **eine ~strafe von zehn Jahren** ten years' imprisonment; **er wurde zu einer ~strafe verurteilt** he was sent to prison, he was given a prison sentence; **~tor** *nt* prison gate *usu pl*; **für ihn öffneten sich die ~tore** the prison gates were opened for him; **~wärter** *m siehe* **~aufseher**; **~zelle** *f* prison cell.

gefärbt *adj* dyed; *Lebensmittel* artificially coloured; (*fig*) *Aussprache* tinged; *Bericht* biased ◆ **ihre Sprache ist schottisch ~** her accent has a Scottish tinge *or* ring to it; **konservativ ~ sein** to have a conservative bias.

-gefärbt *adj suf* dyed; *Lebensmittel* coloured ◆ **rot~es Haar** dyed red hair, hair dyed red; **gelb~er Korn** spirit with yellow colouring.

Gefasel *nt* **-s,** *no pl* (*pej*) twaddle (*inf*), drivel (*inf*).

Gefäß *nt* **-es, -e** vessel (*auch Anat, Bot*); (*Behälter*) receptacle; (*Degenkorb*) coquille.

Gefäß- (*Med*): **g~erweiternd** *adj* vasodilatory; **~erweiterung** *f* vasodilatation, vascular dilatation; **~leiden** *nt* angiopathy, vascular disease.

⚠**gefaßt** *adj* (*ruhig*) composed, calm ◆ **einen sehr ~en Eindruck machen** to appear cool, calm and collected; **auf etw** (*acc*) **~ sein** to be prepared *or* ready for sth; **sich auf etw** (*acc*) **~ machen** to prepare oneself for sth; **er kann sich auf etwas ~ machen** (*inf*) I'll give him something to think about (*inf*).

⚠**Gefaßtheit** *f* composure, calmness.

Gefäß-: (*Med*) **g~verengend** *adj* vasoconstrictive; **~verengung** *f* vasoconstriction, vascular constriction; ⚠**~verschluß** *m*, **~verstopfung** *f* embolism; **~wand** *f* vascular wall.

Gefecht *nt* **-(e)s, -e** (*lit, fig*) battle; (*Mil*) encounter, engagement; (*Scharmützel*) skirmish ◆ **ein hartes ~** fierce fighting; **das ~ abbrechen/einleiten** to cease/open combat; **jdn/etw außer ~ setzen** (*lit, fig*) to put sb/sth out of action; **mit diesen Argumenten setzte er seinen Gegner außer ~** he spiked his opponent's guns with these arguments; **Argumente ins ~ führen** to advance arguments; **im Eifer** *or* **in der Hitze des ~s** (*fig*) in the heat of the moment; **klar zum ~!** (*Naut*) clear for action!; (*fig*) clear the decks!

Gefechts-: ~abschnitt *m* battle zone; **~aufklärung** *f* tactical reconnaissance; **~ausbildung** *f* combat training; **g~bereit** *adj* ready for action *or* battle; (*einsatzfähig*) (fully) operational; **~bereitschaft** *f* readiness for action *or* battle; **in ~bereitschaft** fully operational; **~feld** *nt* battleground; **~feldwaffe** *f* battleground weapon; **g~klar** *adj* (*Naut*) cleared for action; **ein Schiff g~klar machen** to clear a ship for action; **~kopf** *m* warhead; **~lärm** *m* noise of battle; **g~mäßig** *adj* combat *attr*, under combat conditions; **~pause** *f* break in the fighting; **~stand** *m* command post; **~stärke** *f* fighting strength; **~übung** *f* field exercise, manoeuvres *pl*.

gefedert *adj* (*Matratze*) sprung; (*Karosserie*) spring-suspended ◆ **ein gut ~es Auto/eine gut ~e Kutsche** a car with good suspension/a well-sprung carriage.

gefeiert *adj* celebrated.

Gefeilsche *nt* **-s,** *no pl* (*inf*) haggling.

gefeit *adj* **gegen etw ~ sein** to be immune to sth; **niemand ist gegen den Tod ~** nobody is immortal; **dagegen ist keiner ~** that could happen to anyone.

gefestigt *adj Tradition* established; *Charakter* steadfast.

Gefiedel *nt* **-s,** *no pl* (*inf*) fiddling (*inf*), scraping (*pej*).

Gefieder *nt* **-s, -** plumage, feathers *pl*; (*old: von Pfeil*) flight.

gefiedert *adj* feathered; *Blatt* pinnate ◆ **die ~en Sänger** (*poet*) the feathered songsters (*poet*); **unsere ~en Freunde** (*geh*) our feathered friends.

gefiel *pret of* **gefallen**[1].

Gefilde *nt* **-s, -** (*old, liter*) realm ◆ **die ~ der Seligen** the Elysian fields; **die heimatlichen ~** (*hum*) home pastures.

gefinkelt *adj* (*esp Aus*) cunning, crafty.

Geflacker *nt* **-s,** *no pl* flickering.

geflammt *adj Marmor* waved, rippled; *Holz* wavy-grained; *Stoff* watered.

Geflatter *nt* **-s,** *no pl* fluttering; (*von Fahne etc: bei starkem Wind*) flapping.

Geflecht *nt* **-(e)s, -e** (*lit, fig*) network; (*Gewebe*) weave; (*Rohr~*) wickerwork, basketwork; (*von Haaren*) plaiting.

gefleckt *adj* spotted; *Blume, Vogel* speckled; *Haut* blotchy.

Geflenn(e) *nt* **-s,** *no pl* (*pej inf*) blubbering (*inf*).

Geflimmer *nt* **-s,** *no pl* shimmering; (*Film, TV*) flicker(ing); (*heiße Luft*) heat-haze; (*von Stern*) twinkling.

Geflissenheit *f siehe* **Beflissenheit.**

➤ SPRACHE AKTIV: **gefallen**[1] → 34.3, 34.4, 40.2

geflissentlich *adj* (*geh*) deliberate, intentional ♦ **zur ~en Beachtung** (*form*) for your attention.
geflochten *ptp of* **flechten.**
geflogen *ptp of* **fliegen.**
geflohen *ptp of* **fliehen.**
geflossen *ptp of* **fließen.**
Geflügel *nt* **-s,** *no pl* (*Zool, Cook*) poultry *no pl*; (*Vögel auch*) fowl.
Geflügel- *in cpds* poultry; **~cremesuppe** *f* cream of chicken/turkey *etc* soup; **~fleisch** *nt* poultry; **~händler** *m* poulterer, poultry dealer; **~handlung** *f* poulterer's; **~klein** *nt* giblets *pl*; **~leber** *f* chicken/turkey *etc* liver; **~salat** *m* chicken/turkey *etc* salad; **~schere** *f* poultry shears *pl*.
geflügelt *adj* winged ♦ **~e Worte** familiar *or* standard quotations; **er spricht immer in ~en Worten** he always speaks in quotations.
Geflügelzucht *f* poultry farming.
Geflunker *nt* **-s,** *no pl* (*inf*) fibbing (*inf*) ♦ **das ist alles ~** it's all lies *or* fibs (*inf*).
Geflüster *nt* **-s,** *no pl* whispering; (*von Bäumen, Blättern auch*) rustling.
gefochten *ptp of* **fechten.**
Gefolge *nt* **-s, -** retinue, entourage; (*Trauer~*) cortege; (*fig*) wake ♦ **im ~** in the wake (*+gen* of); **etw im ~ haben** (*fig*) to result in sth, to bring sth in its wake.
Gefolgschaft *f* **(a)** (*die Anhänger*) following; (*NS: Betriebs~*) workforce; (*Hist: Gefolge*) retinue, entourage. **(b)** (*Treue*) fealty (*Hist*), allegiance (*auch Hist*), loyalty.
Gefolgschaftstreue *f siehe* **Gefolgschaft (b).**
Gefolgsmann *m, pl* **-leute** follower; (*Hist*) liegeman.
Gefrage *nt* **-s,** *no pl* (*inf*) questions *pl* ♦ **hör auf mit deinem ~!** stop pestering me with (your) questions!
gefragt *adj* in demand *pred*.
gefräßig *adj* gluttonous; (*fig geh*) voracious ♦ **~e Stille** (*hum*) the silence of people who enjoy their food.
Gefräßigkeit *f* gluttony; (*fig geh*) voracity.
Gefreite(r) *mf decl as adj* (*Mil*) lance corporal (*Brit*), private first class (*US*); (*Naut*) able seaman (*Brit*), seaman apprentice (*US*); (*Aviat*) leading aircraftman (*Brit*), airman first class (*US*).
gefressen *ptp of* **fressen** ♦ **jdn ~ haben** (*inf*) to be sick of sb (*inf*).
G(e)frett *nt* **-s,** *no pl* (*Aus*) worry.
Gefrier-: ~brand *m* (*Cook*) freezer burn; **~chirurgie** *f* cryosurgery.
gefrieren* *vi irreg aux sein* (*lit, fig*) to freeze; *siehe* **Blut.**
Gefrier-: ~fach *nt* freezer *or* ice compartment; **~fleisch** *nt* frozen meat; **~gemüse** *nt* frozen vegetables *pl*; **g~getrocknet** *adj* freeze-dried; **~kost** *f* frozen food; **~punkt** *m* freezing point; (*von Thermometer*) zero; **auf dem ~punkt stehen** to be at freezing point/zero; **Temperaturen unter dem ~punkt** temperatures below zero *or* freezing (point); **~raum** *m* deep-freeze room; **~schrank** *m* (upright) freezer; **~schutzmittel** *nt* (*Aut*) anti-freeze; **~temperatur** *f* freezing temperature; **~trocknung** *f* freeze-drying; **~truhe** *f* freezer, deep freeze; **~verfahren** *nt* freezing process.
gefroren *ptp of* **frieren, gefrieren.**
Gefuchtel *nt* **-s,** *no pl* gesticulating.
Gefüge *nt* **-s, -** (*lit, fig*) structure; (*Bau~ auch*) construction; (*Aufbau*) structure, make-up.
gefügig *adj* (*willfährig*) submissive; (*gehorsam*) obedient ♦ **jdn ~ machen** to make sb bend to one's will.
Gefügigkeit *f siehe adj* submissiveness; obedience.
Gefühl *nt* **-(e)s, -e (a)** (*Sinneswahrnehmung*) feeling ♦ **etw im ~ haben** to have a feel for sth; **sie hat mehr ~ in den Fingern als ich** she has a better sense of touch than I do; **er hat kein ~ für heiß und kalt/oben und unten** he can't feel the difference between hot and cold/tell the difference between above and below.
(b) (*seelische Empfindung, Ahnung*) feeling; (*Emotionalität*) sentiment ♦ **ich habe das ~, daß ...** I have the feeling that ...; **ich habe ein ~, als ob ...** I feel as though ...; **es geht gegen mein ~ ...** I don't like ...; **mein ~ täuscht mich nie** my instinct is never wrong; **jds ~e erwidern/verletzen** to return sb's affection/hurt sb's feelings; **ein Mensch ohne ~** (*hartherzig*) a person without any feelings; (*gefühlskalt*) a person without any emotions; **er ist zu keinem menschlichen ~ fähig** he is incapable of (feeling) any human emotion; **~ und Verstand** emotion and reason; **die Romantik war das Zeitalter des ~s** romanticism was the age of sensibility; **das höchste der ~e** (*inf*) the ultimate.
(c) (*Verständnis*) feeling; (*Sinn*) sense ♦ **ein ~ für Zahlen/Musik** a feeling for figures/music; **ein ~ für Gerechtigkeit/Anstand/Proportionen/Rhythmus** a sense of justice/decency/proportion/rhythm; **Tiere haben ein ~ dafür, wer sie mag** animals can sense who likes them; **einen Apparat mit ~ behandeln** to treat an appliance sensitively.
gefühlig *adj* (*pej geh*) mawkish.
gefühllos *adj* (*unempfindlich, hartherzig*) insensitive; (*mitleidlos*) callous, unfeeling; *Glieder* numb, dead *pred* ♦ **ich habe ganz ~e Finger** my fingers are quite numb *or* have gone dead.
Gefühllosigkeit *f siehe adj* insensitivity; callousness, unfeelingness; numbness, deadness.
Gefühls-: g~aktiv *adj* supersensitive; **~anwandlung** *f* (fit of) emotion; **g~arm** *adj* unemotional; **~armut** *f* lack of emotion *or* feeling; **~(auf)wallung** *f* emotional outburst; **~ausbruch** *m* emotional outburst; **~ausdruck** *m*, **~äußerung** *f* expression of one's emotions; **g~bedingt, g~bestimmt** *adj* emotional; **g~betont** *adj* emotional; *Rede, Äußerung auch* emotive; **~dinge** *pl* emotional matters *pl*; **~duselei** *f* (*pej*) mawkishness; **g~echt** *adj Kondom* ultrasensitive; **g~kalt** *adj* cold; **~kälte** *f* coldness; **~krüppel** *m* (*pej*) emotional cripple; **~lage** *f* emotional state; **~leben** *nt* emotional life; **g~mäßig** *adj* instinctive; **~mensch** *m* emotional person; **~nerv** *m* sensory nerve; **~regung** *f* stir of emotion; (*seelische Empfindung*) feeling; **g~roh** *adj* hard-hearted; **~sache** *f* (*Geschmacksache*) matter of feeling; **Kochen ist zum großen Teil ~sache** cooking is largely something you have a feel for; **~schwelgerei** *f* wallowing in one's emotions *no pl*; **g~selig** *adj* sentimental; **g~tief** *adj* intense; **~tiefe** *f* (emotional) intensity; **~überschwang** *m* flood of emotions; **~wallung** *f siehe* **~(auf)wallung**; **~welt** *f* emotions *pl*.
gefühlvoll *adj* **(a)** (*empfindsam*) sensitive; (*ausdrucksvoll*) expressive ♦ **sehr ~ singen** to sing with real feeling. **(b)** (*liebevoll*) loving.
gefüllt *adj Paprikaschoten etc* stuffed; *Brieftasche* full ♦ **~e Pralinen** chocolates *or* candies (*US*) with soft centres.
Gefummel *nt* **-s,** *no pl* (*inf*) fiddling (*inf*); (*Hantieren*) fumbling (*inf*); (*erotisch*) groping (*inf*) ♦ **diese Arbeit ist ein furchtbares ~** this work is a terrible fiddle.
gefunden [1] *ptp of* **finden.**
[2] *adj* **das war ein ~es Fressen für ihn** that was handing it to him on a plate.
Gefunkel *nt* **-s,** *no pl* (*von Sonne, Glas, Wein etc*) sparkling; (*von Sternen auch*) twinkling; (*von Augen*) (*vor Freude*) gleaming, twinkling; (*vor Zorn*) flashing; (*von Edelsteinen*) glittering; (*von Edelmetall*) gleaming.
gefurcht *adj* furrowed ♦ **eine von Sorgen ~e Stirn** a brow lined with cares.
gefürchtet *adj* dreaded *usu attr* ♦ **~ sein** to be feared.
gegabelt *adj* forked, bifurcate (*spec*).
Gegacker *nt* **-s,** *no pl* (*lit, fig*) cackle, cackling.
gegangen *ptp of* **gehen.**
gegeben [1] *ptp of* **geben.**
[2] *adj* **(a)** (*bekannt*) given. **(b)** (*vorhanden*) given *attr*; (*Philos: real*) factual; *Bedingung, Voraussetzung* fulfilled *pred* ♦ **im ~en Fall** ... should the situation arise ...; **bei den ~en Tatsachen/der ~en Situation** given these facts/this situation; **etw als ~ voraussetzen** to assume sth. **(c)** (*günstig*) **zu ~er Zeit** in due course.
gegebenenfalls *adv* should the situation arise; (*wenn nötig*) if need be, if necessary; (*eventuell*) possibly; (*Admin*) if applicable.
Gegebenheit *f usu pl* (actual) fact; (*Realität*) actuality; (*Zustand*) condition ♦ **sich mit den ~en abfinden** to come to terms with the facts as they are.
gegen *prep +acc* **(a)** (*wider*) against ♦ **X ~ Y** (*Sport, Jur*) X versus Y; **für oder ~** for or against; **~ seinen Befehl** contrary to *or* against his orders; **haben Sie ein Mittel ~ Schnupfen?** do you have anything for colds?; **etwas/nichts ~ jdn/etw haben** to have something/nothing against sb/sth; **~ etw sein** to be against sth *or* opposed to sth; **10 ~ 1 wetten** to bet 10 to 1.
(b) (*in Richtung auf*) towards, toward (*US*); (*nach*) to; (*an*) against ♦ **~ einen Baum rennen/prallen** to run/crash into a tree; **er pochte ~ das Tor** he hammered on the gate; **etw ~ das Licht halten** to hold sth to *or* against the light; **~ Osten** *etc* **fahren** to travel eastwards *etc*, to travel to(wards) the east *etc*; **es wird ~ abend kühler** it grows cooler towards evening.
(c) (*ungefähr*) round about, around; (*nicht mehr als*) getting on for; (*nicht später als*) towards.
(d) (*gegenüber*) towards, to ♦ **sie ist immer fair ~ mich gewesen** she's always been fair to me.
(e) (*im Austausch für*) for ♦ **~ bar** for cash; **~ Bezahlung/Quittung** against payment/a receipt.
(f) (*verglichen mit*) compared with, in comparison with.
Gegen-: ~aktion *f* counteraction; **~angebot** *nt* counteroffer; **~angriff** *m* (*Mil, fig*) counterattack; **~ansicht** *f* opposite opinion; **~antrag** *m* countermotion; (*Jur*) counterclaim; **~anzeige** *f* (*Med*) contraindication; **~argument** *nt* counterargument; **~aussage** *f* counterstatement; **~bedingung** *f* countercondition, counterstipulation; **~befehl** *m* (*Mil*) countermand, countercommand; **~behauptung** *f* counterclaim; **~beispiel** *nt* counterexample; **~besuch** *m* return visit; **jdm einen ~besuch machen** to return sb's visit; **~bewegung** *f* (*Tech, fig*) countermovement; (*Mus*) contramotion; **~beweis** *m* counterevidence *no indef art, no pl*; **den ~beweis zu etw erbringen** *or* **antreten** to produce evidence to counter sth; **bis zum ~beweis müssen wir** ... until we have evidence to the contrary we must ...; **~buchung** *f* cross entry.
Gegend *f* **-, -en** area; (*Wohn~ auch*) neighbourhood, district; (*geographisches Gebiet, Körper~*) region; (*Richtung*) direction; (*inf: Nähe*) area ♦ **die ~ von London, die Londoner ~** the London area; **er wohnt in der ~ des Bahnhofs** he lives in the area near the station; **Neuwied liegt in einer schönen ~** Neuwied is in a beautiful area; **eine schöne ~ Deutschlands** a beautiful part of Germany; **hier in der ~** (a)round here, in this area, hereabouts; **ungefähr in dieser ~** somewhere (a)round here *or* in this area/region; **die ganze ~ spricht davon** it's the talk of the neighbourhood; **ein bißchen durch die ~ laufen** (*inf*) to have a stroll around; **sie warfen die leeren Bierflaschen einfach in die ~** (*inf*) they just threw the empty beer bottles around anywhere; **brüll nicht so durch die ~** (*inf*) don't scream your head off (*inf*).
Gegen-: ~darstellung *f* reply; **~demonstration** *f* counterdemonstration; **~dienst** *m* favour in return; **jdm einen ~dienst leisten** *or* **erweisen** to return the favour, to do sb a favour in return; **~dreier** *m* (*Sport*) bracket; **~druck** *m* (*Tech*) counterpressure; (*fig*) resistance; *siehe* **Druck**[1].
gegen|einander *adv* against each other *or* one another; (*zueinander*) to(wards) each other *or* one another; (*im Austausch*) for each other *or* one another ♦ **sich ~ aufheben** to cancel each other *or* one another out; **sie haben etwas ~** they've got something against each other.

⚠: for details of spelling reform, see supplement

Gegen|einander *nt* **-s,** *no pl* conflict.

⚠ **gegen|einander-: ~halten** *vt sep irreg (lit)* to hold side by side *or* together; *(fig)* to compare; **~prallen** *vi sep aux sein* to collide; **~stehen** *vi sep irreg (fig)* to be on opposite sides; *(Aussagen)* to conflict; **~stellen** *vt sep (lit)* to put together; *(fig)* to compare; **~stoßen** *vi sep irreg aux sein* to bump into each other; *(kollidieren)* to collide.

Gegen-: ~entwurf *m* alternative plan; **~erklärung** *f* counterstatement; *(Dementi)* denial, disclaimer; **~fahrbahn** *f* oncoming carriageway *(Brit) or* highway *(US) or (Spur)* lane; **~feuer** *nt* backfire; **~forderung** *f* counterdemand; *(Comm)* counterclaim; **~frage** *f* counterquestion; **darf ich mit einer ~frage antworten?** may I answer your question with another (of my own)?; **jdm eine ~frage stellen** to ask sb a question in reply (to his); **~gabe** *f (geh) siehe* **~geschenk**; **~gerade** *f (Sport)* back straight, backstretch *(US)*; **~geschenk** *nt* present *or* gift in return; **jdm etw als ~geschenk überreichen** to give sb sth in return; **~gewalt** *f* counterviolence; **Gewalt mit ~gewalt beantworten** to counter violence with violence; **~gewicht** *nt* counterbalance *(auch fig)*, counterweight, counterpoise; **als (ausgleichendes) ~gewicht zu etw wirken** *(lit, fig)* to counterbalance sth; **~gift** *nt* antidote *(gegen* to); **~gleis** *nt* opposite track; **~grund** *m* reason against; **Gründe und ~gründe (für etw)** reasons for and against (sth); **g~halten** *vi sep (sich wehren)* to counter; *(standhalten)* to stand one's ground; **~kaiser** *m (Hist)* anti-emperor; **~kandidat** *m* rival candidate; **als ~kandidat zu jdm aufgestellt werden** to be put up as a candidate against sb; **~klage** *f (Jur)* countercharge; **~klage gegen jdn erheben** to put in a countercharge against sb, to countercharge sb; **~kläger** *m (Jur)* bringer of a countercharge; **~könig** *m (Hist)* anti-king; **~kraft** *f (lit, fig)* counterforce; **~kultur** *f* alternative culture; **~kurs** *m (lit, fig)* opposite course; **einen ~kurs steuern** to take an opposing course of action; **g~läufig** *adj (Tech) Bewegung* contrarotating; *(fig) Tendenz* contrary, opposite; **~leistung** *f* service in return; **als ~leistung für etw** in return for sth; **ich erwarte keine ~leistung** I don't expect anything in return; **g~lenken** *vi sep (Aut)* to steer in the opposite direction; **g~lesen** *vti sep irreg* countercheck.

Gegenlicht *nt* **bei ~ Auto fahren** to drive with the light in one's eyes; **etw bei** *or* **im ~ aufnehmen** *(Phot)* to take a backlit *or* contre-jour photo(graph) of sth.

Gegenlicht- *(Phot)*: **~aufnahme** *f* backlit *or* contre-jour photo(graph) *or* shot; **~blende** *f* lens hood.

Gegen-: ~liebe *f* requited love; *(fig: Zustimmung)* approval; **sie fand keine ~liebe** *(lit)* her love was not returned *or* reciprocated; *(fig)* she met with no approval; **auf ~liebe/wenig ~liebe stoßen** *(fig)* to be welcomed/hardly welcomed with open arms; **~macht** *f* hostile power; **~maßnahme** *f* countermeasure; **~maßnahmen zur Bekämpfung der Inflation** measures to counter inflation; **~meinung** *f* opposite view *or* opinion; **~mittel** *nt (Med)* antidote *(gegen* to); **~mutter** *f (Tech)* locknut; **~offensive** *f (lit, fig)* counteroffensive; **~papst** *m (Hist)* antipope; **~partei** *f* other side; *(Sport)* opposing side; *(Jur)* opposing party; **~pol** *m* counterpole; *(fig)* antithesis *(zu* of, to); **~position** *f* opposite standpoint; **~probe** *f* crosscheck; **die ~probe zu etw machen** to carry out a crosscheck on sth, to crosscheck sth; **~propaganda** *f* counterpropaganda; **~reaktion** *f* counter-reaction; **~rechnung** *f* **(a)** *(Math: ~probe)* crosscheck; **(b)** *(Comm)* set-off; *(~schuld)* offset; **die ~rechnung aufmachen** *(fig)* to present one's own reckoning; **~rede** *f (Antwort)* reply; *(Widerrede)* contradiction; **eine ~rede zu jds Rede halten** to reply to sb's speech; **keine ~rede!** no contradiction!; **Rede und ~rede** dialogue; **eine Diskussion, in der Rede und ~rede einander abwechseln** a discussion with a lively exchange between the speakers; **~reformation** *f (Hist)* Counter-Reformation; **~regierung** *f* rival government; **~revolution** *f siehe* **Konterrevolution**; **~richtung** *f* opposite direction; **~ruder** *nt* opposed control surfaces.

▼ **Gegensatz** *m* **-es, ¨-e** *(konträrer ~)* contrast; *(kontradiktorischer ~, Gegenteil)* opposite; *(Unvereinbarkeit)* conflict; *(Unterschied)* difference; *(Philos)* antithesis; *(Mus)* countersubject ◆ **¨-e** *(Meinungsverschiedenheiten)* differences *pl*; **im ~ zu** unlike, in contrast to; **Marx, im ~ zu ...** Marx, as against ...; **er, im ~ zu mir, ...** unlike me, he ...; **einen krassen ~ zu etw bilden** to contrast sharply with sth; **¨-e ziehen einander** *or* **sich an** *(prov)* opposites attract; **im ~ zu etw stehen** to conflict with sth; **¨-e ausgleichen** to even out differences; **unüberbrückbare ¨-e** irreconcilable differences.

gegensätzlich *adj (konträr)* contrasting; *(widersprüchlich)* opposing; *(unterschiedlich)* different; *(unvereinbar)* conflicting ◆ **Schwarz und Weiß sind ~e Begriffe** black and white are opposites; **eine ~e Meinung** a conflicting view; **sie verhalten sich völlig ~** they behave in totally different ways.

Gegensätzlichkeit *f (gen* between) *siehe adj* contrast; opposition; difference; conflict ◆ **die ~ dieser beiden Systeme** the contrast between *or* contrasting nature of these two systems; **bei aller ~ ...** in spite of all (the) differences ...

Gegensatzpaar *nt* pair of opposites.

Gegen-: ~schlag *m (Mil)* reprisal; *(fig)* retaliation *no pl*; **einen ~schlag (gegen jdn) führen** to strike back (at sb); **zum ~schlag ausholen** to prepare to retaliate; **~seite** *f (lit, fig)* other side; *(gegenüberliegende Seite auch)* opposite side; **g~seitig** *adj* mutual; *(wechselseitig auch)* reciprocal; **sie beschuldigten sich g~seitig** they (each) accused one another *or* each other; **sich g~seitig bedingen** to be contingent (up)on one another *or* each other; **sich g~seitig ausschließen** to be mutually exclusive, to exclude one another; **in g~seitigem Einverständnis** by mutual agreement; **~seitigkeit** *f siehe adj* mutuality; reciprocity; **ein Abkommen/Vertrag auf ~seitigkeit** a reciprocal agreement/treaty; **Versicherung auf ~seitigkeit** mutual insurance; **~sinn** *m* **im ~sinn** in the opposite direction; **g~sinnig** *adj (Tech)* in the opposite direction; **~spieler** *m* opponent; *(Liter)* antagonist; *(bei Mannschaftsspielen auch)* opposite number; **~spionage** *f* counterespionage; **~sprechanlage** *f* (two-way) intercom; *(Telec)* duplex (system); **~sprechverkehr** *m* two-way communication.

Gegenstand *m* **-(e)s, ¨-e** *(Ding)* object, thing; *(Econ: Artikel)* article; *(Thema, Angelegenheit, Stoff)* subject; *(von Gespräch, Diskussion)* subject, topic; *(der Neugier, des Hasses etc, Philos)* object; *(Aus: Schulfach)* subject ◆ **ein harter ~ fiel ihm auf den Kopf** something hard *or* a hard object fell on his head; **sie wurde mit einem stumpfen ~ erschlagen** she was killed by a blow from a blunt instrument; **~ des Gespötts** laughing-stock, object of ridicule; *(Mensch auch)* figure of fun.

gegenständlich *adj* concrete; *(Philos)* objective; *(Art)* representational; *(anschaulich)* graphical ◆ **die ~e Welt** the world of objects.

Gegenständlichkeit *f siehe adj* concreteness; objectivity; representationalism; graphicalness.

Gegenstandpunkt *m* opposite point of view.

Gegenstands-: g~los *adj (überflüssig)* redundant, unnecessary; *(grundlos)* unfounded, groundless; *(hinfällig)* irrelevant; *(Art)* non-representational, abstract; **bitte betrachten Sie dieses Schreiben als g~los, falls ...** please disregard this notice if ...; **~wort** *nt* concrete noun.

Gegen-: g~steuern *vi sep (Aut)* to steer in the opposite direction; *(fig)* to take countermeasures; **~stimme** *f (Parl)* vote against; **der Antrag wurde mit 250 Stimmen bei** *or* **und 30 ~stimmen/ohne ~stimmen angenommen** the motion was carried by 250 votes to 30/unanimously; **~stoß** *m (Mil, Sport)* counterattack; **~strömung** *f (lit, fig)* countercurrent; **~stück** *nt* opposite; *(passendes ~stück)* counterpart.

Gegenteil *nt* opposite *(von* of); *(Umkehrung)* reverse *(von* of) ◆ **im ~!** on the contrary!; **ganz im ~** quite the reverse; **das ~ bewirken** to have the opposite effect; *(Mensch)* to achieve the exact opposite; **ins ~ umschlagen** to swing to the other extreme; **eine Äußerung ins ~ um-** *or* **verkehren** to twist a statement to mean just the opposite.

gegenteilig *adj Ansicht, Wirkung* opposite, contrary ◆ **eine ~e Meinung** a different opinion; **sich ~ entscheiden** to come to a different decision; **~e Behauptungen** statements to the contrary; **ich habe nichts G~es gehört** I've heard nothing to the contrary.

Gegenteilsbeweis *m (Jur)* evidence to the contrary.

Gegentor *nt (esp Ftbl)*, **Gegentreffer** *m (Sport)* **sie konnten ein ~ verhindern** they managed to stop any goals being scored against them; **ein ~ hinnehmen müssen** to concede a goal; **ein ~ erzielen** to score.

gegen|über [1] *prep +dat* **(a)** *(örtlich)* opposite ◆ **er wohnt mir ~** he lives opposite me *or* across from me; **er saß mir genau/schräg ~** he sat directly opposite *or* facing me/diagonally across from me.

(b) *(zu)* to; *(in bezug auf)* with regard *or* respect to, as regards; *(angesichts, vor)* in the face of; *(im Vergleich zu)* in comparison with, compared with ◆ **mir ~ hat er das nicht geäußert** he didn't say that to me; **allem Politischen ~ ist er mißtrauisch** he's distrustful of anything political *or* as far as anything political is concerned; **er ist allem Neuen ~ wenig aufgeschlossen** he's not very open-minded about anything new *or* where anything new is concerned.

[2] *adv* opposite ◆ **der Park ~** the park opposite; **die Leute von ~** *(inf)* the people opposite *or* (from) across the way.

Gegen|über *nt* **-s, -** *(bei Kampf)* opponent; *(bei Diskussion)* opposite number ◆ **mein ~ im Zug/am Tisch** the person (sitting) opposite me in the train/at (the) table; **wir haben einen freien Ausblick und kein ~** we've an open view with no building opposite.

gegen|über-: ~gestellt *adj*: **sich einer Sache** *(dat)* **~gestellt sehen** to be faced *or* confronted with sth; **~liegen** *sep irreg* [1] *vi +dat* to be opposite, to face; [2] *vr* **sich** *(dat)* **~liegen** to face each other; **~liegend** *adj attr* opposite; **das ~liegende Grundstück** the plot of land opposite; **der der Hypotenuse ~liegende Winkel** the angle opposite *or* facing the hypotenuse; **~sehen** *vr sep irreg +dat* **sich einer Aufgabe ~sehen** to be faced *or* confronted with a task; **~sitzen** *vi sep irreg +dat* to sit opposite *or* facing; **~stehen** *vi sep irreg +dat* to be opposite, to face; *jdm* to stand opposite *or* facing; **jdm feindlich/freundlich/desinteressiert ~stehen** to have a hostile/friendly/disinterested attitude towards sb; **einem Plan freundlich ~stehen** to be favourably disposed to a plan; **einer Gefahr ~stehen** to be faced with a danger; **~stellen** *vt sep (konfrontieren mit)* to confront *(dat* with); *(fig: vergleichen)* to compare *(dat* with); **G~stellung** *f* confrontation; *(fig: Vergleich)* comparison; **~treten** *vi sep irreg aux sein* **jdm ~treten** to face sb.

Gegen-: ~verkehr *m* oncoming traffic; **~vorschlag** *m* counterproposal.

Gegenwart *f, - no pl* **(a)** *(jetziger Augenblick)* present; *(heutiges Zeitalter)* present (time *or* day); *(Gram)* present (tense) ◆ **in der ~ leben** to live in the present; *(den Augenblick genießen)* to live for the present *or* for today; **die Literatur/Musik der ~** contemporary literature/music; **die Probleme der ~** the problems of today, today's problems; **in der ~ stehen** *(Gram)* to be in the present (tense).

(b) *(Anwesenheit)* presence ◆ **in ~ des** in the presence of.

gegenwärtig [1] *adj* **(a)** *attr (jetzig)* present; *(heutig auch)* current, present-day ◆ **der ~e Minister/Preis** the present minister/current price. **(b)** *(geh: anwesend)* present *pred.* **es ist mir im Moment nicht ~** I can't recall it at the moment.

[2] *adv* **(a)** *(augenblicklich)* at present, at the moment; *(heutzutage auch)* currently. **(b)** **sich** *(dat)* **etw ~ halten** *(geh)* to bear sth in mind.

Gegenwarts-: g~bezogen *adj* relevant to present times; **ein sehr**

➤ SPRACHE AKTIV: **Gegensatz** → 32.1

g~bezogener Mensch a person whose life revolves very much around the present; ~bezug m relevance (to present times); ~deutsch nt modern German; ~form f (Gram) present (tense); g~fremd adj out-of-touch (with reality); g~nah(e) adj relevant (to the present); ~nähe f relevance (to the present); ~problem nt current or topical problem; ~roman m contemporary novel; ~schaffen nt contemporary scene; ~sprache f present-day language; die englische ~sprache modern English.

Gegen-: ~wehr f resistance; ~wert m equivalent; es wurden Waren im ~wert von 8.000 DM entwendet goods worth or to the value of 8,000 DM were taken; ~wind m headwind; wir hatten starken ~wind there was a strong headwind; ~winkel m (Geom) opposite angle; (korrespondierend) corresponding angle; ~wirkung f reaction, counteraction; diese Tabletten können eine ~wirkung haben these tablets can have the opposite effect; g~zeichnen vt sep to countersign; ~zeichnung f (Unterschrift) countersignature; (das Unterschreiben) countersigning; ~zeuge m witness for the other side; ~zug m (a) countermove; im ~zug zu etw as a countermove to sth; (b) (Luftzug) cross-draught; (c) (Rail) corresponding train in the other direction; (entgegenkommender Zug) oncoming train.

gegessen ptp of essen.

geglichen ptp of gleichen.

gegliedert adj jointed; (fig) structured; (organisiert) organized.

geglitten ptp of gleiten.

Geglitzer nt -s, no pl glitter(ing).

geglommen ptp of glimmen.

geglückt adj Feier successful; Wahl lucky; Überraschung real.

Gegner(in f) m -s, - opponent (auch Sport), adversary; (Rivale) rival; (Feind) enemy ♦ ein ~ der Todesstrafe sein to be against or opposed to capital punishment.

gegnerisch adj attr opposing; (Mil: feindlich) enemy attr, hostile; Übermacht of the enemy.

Gegnerschaft f opposition.

gegolten ptp of gelten.

gegoren ptp of gären.

gegossen ptp of gießen.

gegr. abbr of gegründet established, est.

gegraben ptp of graben.

gegriffen ptp of greifen.

Gegrinse nt -s, no pl (inf) grin(ning).

Gegröle nt -s, no pl (inf) raucous bawling.

Gegrübel nt -s, no pl (inf) worrying.

Gegrunze nt -s, no pl grunting.

Gehabe nt -s, no pl (inf) affected behaviour.

gehaben* vr (old, Aus) to behave, to deport oneself (old, form) ♦ gehab dich wohl! (old, dial) farewell! (old).

gehabt ptp of haben.

Gehackte(s) nt decl as adj mince (Brit), minced or ground (US) meat.

Gehalt[1] m -(e)s, -e (a) (Anteil) content ♦ der ~ an Eiweiß/Kohlenhydraten the protein/carbohydrate content; ein hoher ~ an Kohlenmonoxyd a high carbon monoxide content. (b) (fig: Inhalt) content; (Substanz) substance ♦ ~ und Gestalt (liter) form and content.

Gehalt[2] nt or (Aus) m -(e)s, ¨-er salary; (esp Eccl) stipend.

gehalten [1] ptp of halten.
[2] adj: ~ sein, etw zu tun (form) to be required to do sth.

Gehalt-: g~los adj Nahrung unnutritious; (fig) empty; (oberflächlich) shallow, empty; dieses Brot ist ziemlich g~los there's not much nourishment in this bread; ~losigkeit f siehe adj (fig) lack of content/substance; emptiness; shallowness; g~reich adj (a) Erz high-yield; (b) siehe g~voll.

Gehalts-: ~abrechnung f salary statement; die ~abrechnung ist abgeschlossen the salaries have been worked out; ~abzug m salary deduction; ~anspruch m salary claim; ~bescheinigung f salary declaration; ~empfänger m salary-earner; ~empfänger sein to receive a salary, to be salaried; die Firma hat 500 ~empfänger the firm has 500 salaried staff or employees; ~erhöhung f salary increase, rise in salary; (regelmäßig) increment; ~forderung f salary claim; ~gruppe, ~klasse f salary bracket; er ist in der ~gruppe 6 he's on grade 6 on the salary scale; ~konto nt current account (Brit), checking account (US); ~kürzung f cut in salary; ~nachzahlung f back-payment; ~pfändung f deduction of salary (at source); ~streifen m salary slip; ~stufe f siehe ~gruppe; ~verhandlung f salary negotiations pl; ~vorrückung f (Aus) siehe ~erhöhung; ~vorstellung f, ~wunsch m salary requirement; ~zahlung f salary payment; der Tag der ~zahlung ist der 28. salaries are paid on the 28th; ~zulage f (~erhöhung) salary increase, rise in salary; (regelmäßige) increment; (Extrazulage) salary bonus.

gehaltvoll adj Speise nutritious, nourishing; (fig) rich in content ♦ ein ~es Buch/eine ~e Rede a book/speech which says a great deal.

Gehämmer nt -s, no pl hammering.

gehandikapt [gə'hɛndikɛpt] adj handicapped (durch by).

Gehänge nt -s, - (a) garland; (Ohr~) drop, pendant. (b) (Wehr~) ammunition belt. (c) (Min: Abhang) declivity, incline. (d) (Build) system of fascines.

gehangen ptp of hängen.

Gehängte(r) mf decl as adj hanged man/woman ♦ die ~n the hanged.

Gehänsel nt -s, no pl (inf) mocking ♦ hört auf mit dem ~! stop making fun of me/him etc!

geharnischt adj (Hist: gepanzert) armour-clad; (fig) Brief, Abfuhr etc strong; Antwort sharp, sharply-worded ♦ ein ~er Ritter a knight in armour.

gehässig adj spiteful.

Gehässigkeit f spite, spitefulness ♦ ~en spiteful things; jdm ~en sagen to be spiteful to sb.

Gehaue nt -s, no pl (inf) fisticuffs (inf) ♦ Schluß mit dem ewigen ~! stop fighting all the time!

gehauen ptp of hauen.

gehäuft [1] adj Löffel heaped.
[2] adv in large numbers.

Gehäuse nt -s, - (a) case; (Radio~, Kamera~, Uhr~, Kompaß~ auch) casing; (Lautsprecher~) box; (großes Lautsprecher~, Radio~) cabinet. (b) (Schnecken~) shell. (c) (Obst~) core. (d) (Ftbl sl) goal.

gehbehindert adj disabled.

Gehege nt -s, - reserve; (im Zoo) enclosure, compound; (Wild~) preserve ♦ jdm ins ~ kommen (fig inf) to get under sb's feet (inf); (ein Recht streitig machen) to poach on sb's preserves.

geheiligt adj Brauch, Tradition, Recht sacred; Räume sacrosanct ♦ sein ~es Mittagsschläfchen (inf) his precious afternoon nap.

geheim adj secret ♦ seine ~sten Gefühle/Wünsche/Gedanken his innermost or most private feelings/wishes/thoughts; streng ~ top secret; „die ~en Verführer" "the hidden persuaders"; G~er Rat privy council; (Mitglied) privy councillor; ~ bleiben to remain (a) secret; ~ abstimmen to vote by secret ballot; im ~en in secret, secretly.

Geheim- in cpds secret; ≈bund m secret society; ~bündelei f organization/membership of illegal secret societies; ≈dienst m secret service; ≈dienstler m -s, - (inf) man from the secret service; ≈fach nt secret compartment; (Schublade) secret drawer; ≈favorit m personal favourite; ⚠g≈halten vt sep irreg etw (vor jdm) g~halten to keep sth a secret (from sb).

Geheimhaltung f secrecy ♦ zur ~ von etw verpflichtet sein to be sworn to secrecy about sth.

Geheimhaltungs-: ~pflicht f obligation to maintain secrecy; ~stufe f security classification.

Geheimkonto nt private or secret account.

Geheimlehre f esoteric doctrine.

Geheimnis nt secret; (rätselhaftes ~) mystery ♦ das ~ der Schönheit/des Erfolgs the secret of beauty/success; das ~ der Auferstehung/des Lebens the mystery of the Resurrection/of life; ein offenes or öffentliches (rare) ~ an open secret; das ist das ganze ~ (inf) that's all there is to it; aus etw ein/kein ~ machen to make a big secret about sth/no secret of sth; sie hat ein süßes ~ (inf) she's expecting a happy event.

Geheimnis-: ≈krämer m (inf) mystery-monger (inf); ~krämerei f (inf) secretiveness; ≈träger m bearer of secrets; ≈tuer(in f) m -s, - mystery-monger (inf); ~tuerei f secretiveness; g≈tuerisch adj secretive; g≈umwittert adj (geh) shrouded in mystery (liter); ≈verrat m offence under the Official Secrets Act; g≈voll adj mysterious; g~voll tun to be mysterious; mit etw g~voll tun to make a big mystery of sth.

Geheim-: ~nummer f (Telefon) secret number; (Konto) secret account; ~polizei f secret police; ~polizist m member of the secret police; ~rat m privy councillor; ~ratsecken pl (inf) receding hairline sing; er hat ~ratsecken he is going bald at the temples; ~rezept nt secret recipe; ⚠~schloß nt combination lock; ~schrift f code, secret writing; ~tinte f invisible ink; ⚠~tip m (personal) tip; ~treppe f secret staircase; ⚠g~tun vi sep irreg to be secretive; mit etw g~tun to be secretive about sth; ~tür f secret door; ~waffe f secret weapon; ~wissenschaft f secret or esoteric lore; ~zahl f (für Geldautomat) PIN number, personal identification number; ~zeichen nt secret sign; (Chiffre) cipher.

Geheiß nt -es, no pl (geh) behest (old, form) no pl ♦ auf jds ~ (acc) at sb's behest or bidding.

geheißen ptp of heißen.

gehemmt adj Mensch inhibited; Benehmen self-conscious ♦ ~ sprechen to have inhibitions in speaking.

▼ **gehen** pret ging, ptp gegangen aux sein [1] vi (a) to go; (zu Fuß) to walk; (Gerücht) to go around ♦ im Schritt/Trab ~ to walk/trot; über die Straße/Brücke ~ to cross the road/(over) the bridge; auf die andere Seite ~ to cross (over) to the other side; am Stock/auf Stelzen (dat) ~ to walk with a stick/on stilts; geh mal in die Küche go into the kitchen; zur Post/zum Fleischer ~ to go to the post office/the butcher; zur Schule ~ to go to school; zu jdm ~ to go to see sb; er ging im Zimmer auf und ab he walked or paced up and down the room; wie lange geht man bis zum Bus? how long a walk is it to the bus?; wie geht man dorthin? how do you get there?; das Kind lernt ~ the baby is learning to walk; wo er geht und steht wherever he goes or is; schwimmen/tanzen/spielen/schlafen ~ to go swimming/dancing/out to play/to bed; unter Menschen ~ to mix with people; bitte ~ Sie (höflich) please carry on; (bestimmt) please go; geh doch! go on (then)!; geh schon! go on!; ~ Sie (mir) nicht an meine Sachen! don't touch my things; ohne Hut/Schirm ~ not to wear a hat/take an umbrella; mit jdm ~ to go with sb; (befreundet sein) to go out with sb, to be with sb; mit der Zeit/Mode ~ to move with the times/follow the fashion; in sich (acc) ~ to think things over; (bereuen) to turn one's eyes inward; er geht ins siebzigste Jahr he's getting or going on for seventy; das Erbe ging an ihn the inheritance went to him; nach einer Regel ~ to follow a rule; das geht gegen meine Überzeugung that is contrary to or runs against my convictions; er ging so weit, zu behaupten ... (fig) he went so far as to claim ...; das geht zu weit (fig) that's going too far; wie geht das Lied/Gedicht? how does the song/poem go?; heute geht ein scharfer Wind there's a biting wind today; die See geht hoch there's a

⚠: for details of spelling reform, see supplement

high sea, the sea is running high; **der Schmerz ging sehr tief** the pain went very deep.
(b) (*führen*) (*Weg, Straße*) to go; (*Tür*) to lead (*auf +acc, nach* onto); (*blicken*) (*Fenster*) to look out (*auf +acc, nach* onto), to give (*auf +acc, nach* onto) ◆ **die Brücke geht dort über den Fluß** the bridge crosses the river there; **die Reise geht über Dresden** we/they *etc* are going via Dresden; **es ging schon auf den Winter** (*geh*) winter was drawing near.
(c) (*weg~*) to go; (*abfahren auch*) to leave; (*ausscheiden*) to leave, to go; (*aus einem Amt*) to go, to quit ◆ **ich muß ~** I must go *or* be going *or* be off; **~ wir!** let's go; **das Schiff geht nach Harwich** the boat is going to *or* is bound for Harwich; **jdm aus dem Licht/Weg ~** to get *or* move out of sb's light/way; **er ist gegangen worden** (*hum inf*) he was given a gentle push (*hum inf*); **er ist von uns gegangen** (*euph*) he has gone from us (*euph*).
(d) (*funktionieren*) to work; (*Auto, Uhr*) to go ◆ **die Uhr geht gut** the clock keeps good time; **die Uhr geht falsch/richtig** the clock is wrong/right.
(e) (*laufen*) (*Geschäft*) to go; (*verkauft werden auch*) to sell ◆ **wie ~ die Geschäfte?** how's business?
(f) (*hineinpassen*) to go ◆ **wieviele Leute ~ in deinen Wagen?** how many people can you get in your car?; **in diese Schachtel ~ 20 Zigaretten** this packet holds 20 cigarettes; **das Klavier geht nicht durch die Tür** the piano won't go through the door; **3 geht in 9 dreimal** 3 into 9 goes 3; **das geht mir nicht in den Kopf** I just can't understand it.
(g) (*dauern*) to go on ◆ **wie lange geht das denn noch?** how much longer is it going to go on?; **es geht schon eine halbe Stunde** it's been going (on) for half an hour; **mein Urlaub geht vom 2. bis 28. Juni** my holiday goes *or* runs from the 2nd to the 28th of June.
(h) (*reichen*) to go ◆ **das Wasser ging ihm bis zum Bauch** the water went up to his waist; **der Rock geht ihr bis zum Knie** her skirt goes *or* is down to her knee; **der Blick geht bis an den Horizont** the view extends right to the horizon; **in die Tausende ~** to run into (the) thousands.
(i) (*Teig*) to rise; (*vor dem Backen auch*) to prove.
(j) (*urteilen*) **nach etw ~** to go by sth.
(k) (*sich kleiden*) **in etw** (*dat*) **~** to wear sth; **als etw ~** (*sich verkleiden*) to go as sth.
(l) (*betreffen*) **der Artikel ging gegen ...** the article criticized ...; **das Buch ging um ...** the book was about ...; **die Wette geht um 100 Mark** the bet is for 100 marks; **das geht auf sein Konto** *or* **auf ihn** he's responsible for that; **das ging auf Sie!** that was aimed at you!; **mein Vorschlag geht dahin, daß ...** my suggestion is that ...
(m) (*sich bewegen*) **ich hörte, wie die Tür ging** I heard the door (go); **diese Tür/Schublade geht schwer** this door/drawer is very stiff; **mein Rasenmäher geht schwer** my lawnmower is very heavy to push.
(n) (*ertönen: Klingel, Glocke*) to ring.
▼**(o)** (*übertreffen*) **das geht über meine Kräfte** that's beyond my power; (*seelisch*) that's too much for me; **sein Garten geht ihm über alles** his garden means more to him than anything else; **nichts geht über** (*+acc*) **...** there's nothing to beat ..., there's nothing better than ...
(p) (*inf*) **(ach) geh (doch), das darf doch nicht wahr sein!** get along *or* on with you, that can't be true (*inf*); **geh, geh** *or* **(ach) geh, so schlimm ist das nicht!** (oh) come on, it's not as bad as all that; **~ Sie (mir) doch mit Ihren Ausreden!** none of your lame excuses!; **geh!** (*Aus: erstaunt*) get away! (*inf*).
(q) (*Beruf etc ergreifen*) **ins Kloster ~** to go into *or* join a monastery/convent; **zur See ~** to go to sea; **zum Militär ~** to join the army; **zum Theater/zur Universität ~** to go on the stage/become an academic; **in die Industrie/Politik ~** to go into industry/politics; **in die Gewerkschaft/Partei ~** to join the union/party; **unter die Lexikographen/Künstler/Säufer ~** (*usu hum*) to join the ranks of lexicographers/artists/alcoholics.
(r) (*sich betätigen, arbeiten*) **als etw ~** to work as sth.
(s) (*möglich, gut sein*) to be all right, to be OK (*inf*) ◆ **das geht doch nicht** that's not on; **Dienstag geht auch nicht** (*inf*) Tuesday's no good either.
(t) was geht hier vor sich? what's going on here?; **ich weiß nicht, wie das vor sich geht** I don't know the procedure.
[2] *vi impers* **(a)** (*gesundheitlich*) **wie geht es Ihnen?** how are you?; (*zu Patient*) how are you feeling?; **wie geht's denn (so)?** (*inf*) how are things (with you)? (*inf*); **(danke,) es geht** (*inf*) all right *or* not too bad(, thanks) (*inf*); **es geht ihm gut/schlecht** he's quite well/not at all well; **es geht mir (wieder) besser** I'm better (again) now; **nach einem Bad ging's mir gleich besser** I soon felt better after a bath; **sonst geht's dir gut?** (*iro*) are you sure you're feeling all right? (*iro*).
(b) (*ergehen*) **wie geht's?** how are things?; (*bei Arbeit etc*) how's it going?; **wie geht's sonst?** (*inf*) how are things otherwise?; **es geht** not too bad, so-so; **wie war denn die Prüfung? — ach, es ging ganz gut** how was the exam? — oh, it went quite well; **mir ist es genauso gegangen** (*ich habe dasselbe erlebt*) it was just the same *or* just like that with me; (*ich habe dasselbe empfunden*) I felt the same way; **laß es dir gut ~** look after yourself, take care of yourself.
(c) es geht (*läßt sich machen*) it's all right *or* OK (*inf*); (*funktioniert*) it works; **solange es geht** as long as possible; **geht es?** (*ohne Hilfe*) can you manage?; **es geht nicht** (*ist nicht möglich*) it can't be done, it's impossible; (*kommt nicht in Frage*) it's not on; (*funktioniert nicht*) it won't *or* doesn't work; **es wird schon ~** I'll/he'll *etc* manage; (*wird sich machen lassen*) it'll be all right; **wir müssen uns damit abfinden, es geht eben nicht anders** there's nothing else for it, we'll just have to put up with it; **so geht das, das geht so** that/this is how it's done; **so geht es** *or* **das, es** *or* **das geht so** that's all right *or* OK (*inf*); **so geht es** *or* **das (eben)** (*so ist das Leben*) that's how it goes, that's the way things go; **so geht es** *or* **das nicht** that's not how it's done; (*entrüstet*) it just won't do; **morgen geht es nicht** tomorrow's no good; **paßt dir Dienstag? — nein, Dienstag geht's nicht** is Tuesday all right for you? — no, I can't manage Tuesday.
▼**(d)** (*betreffen*) **worum geht's denn?** what's it about?; **ich weiß nicht, worum es geht** I don't know what this is about; **es geht um seinen Vertrag** it's about *or* it concerns his contract; **worum geht es in diesem Film/bei eurem Streit?** what is this film/your argument about?; **es geht um Leben und Tod** it's a matter of life and death; **das geht gegen meine Prinzipien** that goes against my principles; **es geht um meine Ehre** my honour is at stake; **es geht ihm nur um eins** he's only interested in one thing; **darum geht es mir nicht** that's not the point; (*spielt keine Rolle*) that's not important to me; **es geht um 5 Millionen bei diesem Geschäft** (*im Spiel sein*) the deal involves 5 million; (*auf dem Spiel stehen*) 5 million are at stake in the deal; **wenn es ums Lügen geht, ist er unübertrefflich** he is unbeatable when it comes to lying; **wenn es nach mir ginge ...** if it were *or* was up to me ..., if I had my way ...; **es kann nicht immer alles nach dir ~** you can't expect to have your own way all the time.
(e) (*führen*) **dann geht es immer geradeaus** (*Richtung, in der jd geht*) then you keep going straight on; (*Straßenrichtung*) then it just goes straight on; **dann ging es nach Süden/ins Gebirge** (*Richtung, in der jd geht*) then we/they *etc* were off to the south/the mountains; (*Straßenrichtung*) then it went south/into the mountains; **wohin geht es diesmal in Urlaub?** where are you off to on holiday this time?
(f) es geht ein starker Wind there's a strong wind (blowing); **es geht das Gerücht, daß ...** there's a rumour going around that ...; **es geht auf 9 Uhr** it is approaching 9 o'clock.
[3] *vt* **er ging eine Meile** he walked a mile; **ich gehe immer diesen Weg/diese Straße** I always walk *or* go this way/along this road.
[4] *vr* **es geht sich schlecht hier** it's hard to walk here, it's bad for walking here; **in diesen Schuhen geht es sich bequem** these shoes are comfortable to walk in *or* for walking in.

Gehen *nt* **-s,** *no pl* (*Zu-Fuß-~*) walking; (*Abschied*) leaving; (*Sport*) (*Disziplin*) walking; (*Wettbewerb*) walk.

Gehenk *nt* **-(e)s, -e** (*Hist*) (*für Schwert*) sword-belt; (*für Degen*) knife-belt; (*für Pistolen*) gun-belt.

Gehenkte(r) *mf decl as adj* hanged man/woman ◆ **die ~n** the hanged.

⚠ **gehenlassen*** *sep irreg* [1] *vt* (*inf: in Ruhe lassen*) to leave alone.
[2] *vr* **(a)** (*sich nicht beherrschen*) to lose one's self-control, to lose control of oneself. **(b)** (*nachlässig sein*) to let oneself go.

Geher(in *f***)** *m* **-s, -** (*Sport*) walker ◆ **er ist Weltmeister der ~** he's the world champion in walking.

Gehetze *nt* **-s,** *no pl* (*inf*) **(a)** (*Eile*) mad rush *or* dash. **(b)** (*pej: das Aufhetzen*) backbiting (*pej inf*).

gehetzt *adj* harassed.

geheuer *adj* **nicht ~** (*beängstigend*) scary (*inf*); (*spukhaft*) eerie, creepy (*inf*), spooky; (*verdächtig*) dubious, fishy; (*unwohl*) uneasy; **es ist mir nicht ganz ~** it is scary (*inf*); it is eerie etc *or* gives me the creeps (*inf*); it seems a bit dubious *or* fishy to me; I feel uneasy about it; **mir ist es hier nicht ~** (*mir ist unheimlich*) this place gives me the creeps (*inf*); (*mir ist unwohl*) I have got an uneasy feeling about this place.

Geheul(e) *nt* **-(e)s,** *no pl* howling.

Gehilfe *m* **-n, -n, Gehilfin** *f* **(a)** (*dated: Helfer*) assistant, helper. **(b)** (*kaufmännischer ~*) trainee. **(c)** (*Jur*) accomplice.

Gehilfenbrief *m* diploma.

Gehilfenschaft *f* (*Sw*) aiding and abetting.

Gehilfin *f siehe* **Gehilfe.**

Gehirn *nt* **-(e)s, -e** brain; (*Geist*) mind ◆ **das ist nicht seinem ~ entsprungen** (*inf*) he didn't think of that himself; **hast du denn kein ~ im Kopf?** (*inf*) haven't you got any brains? (*inf*).

Gehirn- *in cpds siehe auch* **Hirn-**; **~akrobatik** *f* (*inf*) mental acrobatics *pl*; **g~amputiert** *adj* (*pej sl*) dead from the neck up (*sl*); **~blutung** *f* brain *or* cerebral haemorrhage; **~chirurg** *m* brain surgeon; **~chirurgie** *f* brain surgery; **~erschütterung** *f* concussion; **~erweichung** *f* (*lit, fig inf*) softening of the brain; **~kasten** *m* (*inf*) thick skull; **~nerv** *m* cranial nerve; **~rinde** *f* cerebral cortex; **~schlag** *m* stroke; **~schwund** *m* atrophy of the brain; **~substanz** *f* brain matter; **graue ~substanz** grey matter; **~wäsche** *f* brainwashing *no pl*; **jdn einer ~wäsche unterziehen** to brainwash sb.

gehl *adj* (*dial*) yellow.

gehn *siehe* **gehen.**

gehoben [1] *ptp of* **heben.**
[2] *adj Sprache, Ausdrucksweise* elevated, lofty; (*anspruchsvoll*) sophisticated; *Stellung* senior, high; *Stimmung* elated ◆ **sich ~ ausdrücken** to use elevated language; **Güter des ~en Bedarfs** semi-luxuries; **~er Dienst** professional and executive levels of the civil service.

Gehöft *nt* **-(e)s, -e** farm(stead).

geholfen *ptp of* **helfen.**

Geholper(e) *nt* **-s,** *no pl* bumping.

Gehölz *nt* **-es, -e** (*geh*) copse, coppice, spinney; (*Dickicht*) undergrowth.

Geholze *nt* **-s,** *no pl* (*Sport inf*) bad play; (*unfair*) rough play.

Gehoppel(e) *nt* **-s,** *no pl* hopping.

Gehör *nt* **-(e)s,** (*rare*) **-e (a)** (*Hörvermögen*) hearing; (*Mus*) ear ◆ **kein musikalisches ~ haben** to have no ear for music; **ein schlechtes ~ haben** to be hard of hearing, to have bad hearing; (*Mus*) to have a bad ear (for music); **nach dem ~ singen/spielen** to sing/play by ear; **absolutes ~** perfect pitch; **das ~ verlieren** to go *or* become deaf.

➤ SPRACHE AKTIV: **gehen: 1o** → 43.4 **2d** → 53.1

(b) (*geh: Anhörung*) **ein Musikstück zu ~ bringen** to perform a piece of music; **~ finden** to gain a hearing; **jdm ~/kein ~ schenken** to listen/not to listen to sb; **schenkt mir ~!** (*old*) lend me your ears (*old*); **um ~ bitten** to request a hearing; **sich** (*dat*) **~ verschaffen** to obtain a hearing; (*Aufmerksamkeit*) to gain attention.

Gehörbildung *f* aural training.

gehorchen* *vi* to obey (*jdm* sb); (*Wagen, Maschine etc*) to respond (*jdm/einer Sache* to sb/sth) ◆ **seine Stimme gehorchte ihm nicht mehr** he lost control over his voice; **der Junge gehorcht überhaupt nicht** the boy is completely disobedient *or* is never obedient; *siehe* **Wort.**

gehören* [1] *vi* **(a) jdm ~** (*jds Eigentum sein*) to belong to sb, to be sb's; **das Haus gehört ihm** he owns the house, the house belongs to him; **ihm gehört meine ganze Liebe** he is the only one I love, he has all my love; **ihr Herz gehört einem anderen** her heart belongs to another.

(b) (*den richtigen Platz haben*) to go ; (*Mensch*) to belong; (*gebühren*) to deserve ◆ **das gehört nicht hierher** (*Gegenstand*) it doesn't go here; (*Vorschlag*) it is irrelevant here; **das Buch gehört ins Regal** the book belongs in *or* goes on the bookshelves; **das gehört nicht zur Sache/zum Thema** that is off the point *or* is irrelevant; **dieser Betrag gehört unter die Rubrik „Einnahmen"** this sum comes *or* belongs under the heading "credits"; **er gehört ins Bett** he should be in bed; **er gehört verprügelt** (*dial*) he needs a thrashing, he ought to be thrashed.

(c) ~ zu (*zählen zu*) to be amongst, to be one of; (*Bestandteil sein von*) to be part of; (*Mitglied sein von*) to belong to; **es gehört zu seiner Arbeit/zu seinen Pflichten** it's part of his work/one of his duties; **zur Familie ~** to be one of the family; **zu diesem Kleid gehört ein blauer Hut** (*ist Bestandteil von*) a blue hat goes with *or* belongs to this dress; (*würde dazu passen*) a blue hat would go with this dress; **zum Wild gehört einfach Rotwein** red wine is a must with venison.

(d) ~ zu (*Voraussetzung, nötig sein*) to be called for by; **zu dieser Arbeit gehört viel Konzentration** this work calls for *or* takes a lot of concentration; **dazu gehört Mut** that takes courage; **dazu gehört nicht viel** it doesn't take much; **dazu gehört (schon) einiges** *or* **etwas** that takes some doing (*inf*); **dazu gehört mehr** there's more to it than that.

[2] *vr* to be (right and) proper ◆ **das gehört sich einfach nicht** that's just not done; **wie es sich gehört** (*wie es sich schickt*) as is (right and) proper; (*wie es zünftig ist*) comme il faut; **benimm dich, wie es sich gehört!** behave yourself properly.

Gehör-: ~fehler *m* **ein ~fehler** a hearing defect, defective hearing; **~gang** *m* auditory canal.

gehörig *adj* **(a)** (*geh*) **jdm/zu etw ~** belonging to sb/sth; **zu etw ~ sein** to belong to sth; **nicht zur Sache ~** irrelevant; **alle nicht zum Thema ~en Vorschläge** all suggestions not pertaining to *or* relevant to the topic.

(b) *attr, adv* (*gebührend*) proper; (*notwendig auch*) necessary, requisite ◆ **er behandelt seinen Vater nicht mit dem ~en Respekt** he doesn't treat his father with proper respect *or* with the respect due to him.

(c) (*inf: beträchtlich, groß*) good *attr*, good and proper (*inf*) *adv*, well and truly *adv* ◆ **eine ~e Achtung vor jdm haben** to have a healthy respect for sb; **eine ~e Tracht Prügel** a good *or* proper thrashing; **ich hab's ihm ~ gegeben** (*inf*) I showed him what's what (*inf*), I gave him what for (*inf*); (*verbal*) I gave him a piece of my mind (*inf*).

gehörlos *adj* (*form*) deaf ◆ **~ sein** to have no hearing.

Gehörlosenschule *f* (*form*) school for the deaf.

Gehörlose(r) *mf decl as adj* (*form*) deaf person.

Gehörlosigkeit *f* (*form*) lack of hearing; (*Taubheit*) deafness.

Gehörn *nt* **-(e)s, -e** (*Hunt*) antlers *pl*, set of antlers.

Gehörnerv *m* auditory nerve.

gehörnt *adj* horned; (*mit Geweih*) antlered ◆ **ein ~er Ehemann** (*hum inf*) a cuckold; **der G~e** Satan.

gehorsam *adj* obedient ◆ **ich bitte ~st** (*old*) I respectfully beg; **Ihr ~ster Diener** (*old*) your most obedient servant (*old*), yours obediently (*old*); *siehe* **melden.**

Gehorsam *m* **-s,** *no pl* obedience ◆ **jdm den ~ verweigern** to refuse to obey sb.

Gehorsamkeit *f* obedience.

Gehorsams-: ~pflicht *f* duty to obey; **~verweigerung** *f* (*Mil*) insubordination, refusal to obey orders.

Gehör-: ~schutz *m* ear protectors *pl*, ear muffs *pl*; **~sinn** *m* sense of hearing.

gehren *vti* (*Tech*) to mitre.

Gehrock *m* frock coat.

Gehrung *f* (*Tech*) (*das Gehren*) mitring; (*Eckfuge*) mitre joint.

Gehsteig *m* pavement (*Brit*), sidewalk (*US*).

Gehtnichtmehr *nt* **trinken/tanzen bis zum ~** to drink/dance till one drops (*inf*); **sich bis zum ~ verschulden** to get up to one's ears in debt (*inf*).

Gehupe *nt* **-s,** *no pl* (*inf*) hooting, honking.

Gehuste *nt* **-s,** *no pl* (*inf*) coughing.

Geh-: ~verband *m* (*Med*) plaster cast *allowing the patient to walk*; **~weg** *m* footpath.

Gei *f* **-, -en** (*Naut*) *siehe* **Geitau.**

Geier *m* **-s, -** (*lit, fig*) vulture ◆ **weiß der ~!** (*inf*) God knows!

Geifer *m* **-s,** *no pl* slaver; (*Schaum vor dem Mund*) froth, foam; (*fig pej*) venom ◆ **seinen ~ (gegen etw) verspritzen** to pour out one's venom (on sth).

geifern *vi* to slaver; (*Schaum vor dem Mund haben*) to foam at the mouth; (*fig pej*) to be bursting with venom ◆ **vor Wut/Neid ~** to be bursting with rage/envy; **gegen jdn/etw ~** to revile sb/sth.

Geige *f* **-, -n** violin, fiddle (*inf*) ◆ **die erste/zweite ~ spielen** (*lit*) to play first/second violin; (*fig*) to call the tune/play second fiddle; **nach jds ~ tanzen** (*fig*) to dance to sb's tune.

geigen [1] *vi* to play the violin, to (play the) fiddle (*inf*).

[2] *vt Lied* to play on a/the violin *or* fiddle (*inf*) ◆ **jdm die Meinung ~** (*inf*) to give sb a piece of one's mind (*inf*).

Geigen-: ~bauer *m* violin-maker; **~bogen** *m* violin bow; **~harz** *nt* rosin; **~kasten** *m* violin-case; **~kästen** *pl* (*hum inf*) clodhoppers *pl* (*inf*); **~saite** *f* violin string; **~strich** *m* stroke of the violin bow.

Geiger(in *f*) *m* **-s, -** violinist, fiddler (*inf*) ◆ **erster ~** first violin.

Geigerzähler *m* Geiger counter.

geil *adj* **(a)** randy, horny; (*pej: lüstern*) lecherous ◆ **auf jdn ~ sein** to be lusting after sb. **(b)** (*Agr*) *Boden* rich, fertile; (*üppig*) luxuriant; *Vegetation* rank. **(c)** (*sl: prima*) brilliant (*inf*), wicked (*sl*) ◆ **der Typ ist ~** he's a cool guy (*inf*).

Geilheit *f siehe adj* **(a)** randiness (*Brit*), horniness; lecherousness. **(b)** richness, fertility; luxuriance; rankness.

Geisel *f* **-, -n** hostage ◆ **jdn als ~ nehmen** to take sb hostage; **~n stellen** to produce hostages.

Geisel-: ~drama *nt* hostage crisis; **~gangster** *m* (*Press sl*) gangster who takes/took *etc* hostages; **~haft** *f* captivity (as a hostage); **~nahme** *f* **-, -n** hostage-taking; **mit ~nahme der Besatzung** with the crew taken hostage; **~nehmer(in** *f*) *m* hostage-taker.

Geiser *m* **-s, -** *siehe* **Geysir.**

Geisha ['ge:ʃa] *f* **-, -s** geisha (girl).

Geiß *f* **-, -en (a)** (*S Ger, Aus, Sw: Ziege*) (nanny-)goat. **(b)** (*von Rehwild etc*) doe.

Geiß-: ~bart *m* (*Bot*) goatsbeard; (*esp S Ger inf: Spitzbart*) goatee (beard); **~blatt** *nt* honeysuckle, woodbine; **~bock** *m* billy-goat.

Geißel *f* **-, -n (a)** (*lit, fig*) scourge; (*dial: Peitsche*) whip. **(b)** (*Biol*) flagellum.

Geißelbruder *m* (*Eccl*) *siehe* **Geißler.**

geißeln *vt* **(a)** to whip, to flagellate (*esp Rel*). **(b)** (*fig*) (*kasteien*) to chastise; (*anprangern*) to castigate; (*heimsuchen*) to scourge.

Geißeltierchen *nt* flagellate.

Geiß(e)lung *f siehe vt* **(a)** whipping, flagellation. **(b)** chastisement; castigation; scourging.

Geiß-: ~fuß *m* (*Gehreisen*) parting tool; (*Brechstange*) crowbar; **~hirt** *m* goatherd; **~kitz** *nt* (female) kid; **~lein** *nt* kid.

Geißler *m* **-s, -** (*Rel*) flagellator.

Geist *m* **-(e)s, -er (a)** *no pl* (*Denken, Vernunft*) mind ◆ **der menschliche ~, der ~ des Menschen** the human mind; **~ und Materie** mind and matter; **mit ~ begabt** endowed with a mind; **„Phänomenologie des ~es"** "Phenomenology of the Spirit".

(b) (*Rel: Seele, außerirdisches Wesen*) spirit; (*Gespenst*) ghost ◆ **~ und Körper** mind and body; **seinen ~ aufgeben** *or* **aushauchen** (*liter, iro*) to give up the ghost; **der ~ ist willig, aber das Fleisch ist schwach** the spirit is willing, but the flesh is weak; **der Heilige ~** the Holy Ghost *or* Spirit; **der ~ Gottes** the Spirit of God; **der böse ~** the Evil One; **der ~ der Finsternis** the Prince of Darkness; **gute/böse ~er** good/evil spirits; **die Stunde der ~er** the witching hour; **der gute ~ des Hauses** (*geh*) the moving spirit in the household; **von allen guten ~ern verlassen sein** (*inf*) to have taken leave of one's senses (*inf*); **jdm auf den ~ gehen** (*inf*) to get on sb's nerves; **in dem Schloß gehen ~er um** the castle is haunted, the castle is walked by ghosts (*liter*); *siehe* **empfehlen.**

(c) (*no pl: Intellekt*) intellect, mind; (*fig: Denker, Genie*) mind ◆ **~ haben** to have a good mind *or* intellect; (*Witz*) to show wit; **einen regen/lebhaften ~ haben** to have an active/lively mind; **ein Mann von großem ~** a man of great intellect *or* with a great mind; **die Rede zeugte nicht von großem ~** the speech was not particularly brilliant; **das geht über meinen ~** (*inf*) that's way over my head (*inf*), that's beyond me (*inf*); **hier scheiden sich die ~er** this is the parting of the ways; **seinen ~ anstrengen** (*inf*) to use one's brains (*inf*); **sie sind verwandte ~er** they are kindred spirits; **kleine ~er** (*iro: ungebildet*) people of limited intellect; (*kleinmütig*) small- *or* petty-minded people; *siehe* **unruhig.**

(d) *no pl* (*Wesen, Sinn, Gesinnung*) spirit ◆ **in kameradschaftlichem ~** in a spirit of comradeship; **in diesem Büro herrscht ein kollegialer ~** this office has a friendly atmosphere; **in seinem/ihrem ~** in his/her spirit; **in jds ~ handeln** to act in the spirit of sb; **der ~ der Zeit/der russischen Sprache** the spirit *or* genius (*liter*) of the times/of the Russian language; **nach dem ~ des Gesetzes, nicht nach seinem Buchstaben gehen** to go by the spirit rather than the letter of the law; **daran zeigt sich, wes ~es Kind er ist** that (just) shows what kind of person he is.

(e) *no pl* (*Vorstellung*) mind ◆ **etw im ~(e) vor sich sehen** to see sth in one's mind's eye; **sich im ~(e) als etw/als jd/an einem Ort sehen** to see *or* picture oneself as sth/as sb/in a place; **im ~e bin ich bei Euch** I am with you in spirit, my thoughts are with you.

Geister-: ~bahn *f* ghost train; **~beschwörer(in** *f*) *m* **-s, - (a)** (*der Geister herbeiruft*) necromancer; **(b)** (*der Geister austreibt*) exorcist; **~beschwörung** *f* **(a)** (*Herbeirufung*) necromancy; **(b)** (*Austreibung*) exorcism; **~bild** *nt* (*TV*) ghost image; **~bilder** ghosting *no pl*; **~erscheinung** *f* (ghostly) apparition; (*im Traum etc*) vision; **eine ~erscheinung haben** to see a ghost *or* an apparition/to have a vision; **~fahrer** *m* (*inf*) ghost-driver (*US inf*), *person driving in the wrong direction*; **~geschichte** *f* ghost story; **~glaube** *m* belief in the supernatural; **g~haft** *adj* ghostly *no adv*, unearthly *no adv*; (*übernatürlich*) supernatural; **~hand** *f*: **wie von/durch ~hand** as if by magic.

geistern *vi aux sein* to wander like a ghost ◆ **der Gedanke geisterte in seinem Hirn/durch sein Hirn** the thought haunted him *or* his mind; **Lichter gei-**

sterten hinter den Fenstern ghostly lights shone through the windows; **Schatten geisterten an der Wand** ghostly *or* ghostlike shadows played on the wall.

Geister-: ~seher(in *f*) *m* visionary; **~stadt** *f* ghost town; **~stimme** *f* ghostly voice; **~stunde** *f* witching hour; **~welt** *f* spirit world.

Geistes-: g~abwesend *adj* absent-minded; **~abwesenheit** *f* absent-mindedness; **~arbeit** *f* brainwork (*inf*); **~arbeiter** *m* brain-worker (*inf*); **~armut** *f* dullness, intellectual poverty; (*von Mensch auch*) poverty of mind; **~art** *f* disposition; **~blitz** *m* brainwave (*Brit*), brainstorm (*US*), flash of inspiration; **~gabe** *f* intellectual gift; **~gegenwart** *f* presence of mind; **g~gegenwärtig** *adj* quick-witted; **g~gegenwärtig duckte er sich unter das Steuer** with great presence of mind he ducked below the steering wheel; **~geschichte** *f* history of ideas; **die ~geschichte der Goethezeit** the intellectual history of Goethe's time; **g~gestört** *adj* mentally disturbed *or* (*stärker*) deranged; **du bist wohl g~gestört!** (*inf*) are you out of your mind? (*inf*); **ein ~gestörter** a mentally disturbed/deranged person; **~gestörtheit** *f* mental instability *or* (*stärker*) derangement; **~größe** *f* **(a)** *no pl* (*Genialität*) greatness of mind; **(b)** (*genialer Mensch*) great mind, genius; **~haltung** *f* attitude of mind; **g~krank** *adj* mentally ill; **~kranke(r)** *mf* mentally ill person; **die ~kranken** the mentally ill; **~krankheit** *f* mental illness; (*Wahnsinn*) insanity; **~störung** *f* mental disturbance *or* (*stärker*) derangement; **~verfassung** *f* frame *or* state of mind; **g~verwandt** *adj* mentally akin (*mit* to); **die beiden sind g~verwandt** they are kindred spirits; **~verwandtschaft** *f* spiritual affinity (*mit* to); **~verwirrung** *f* mental confusion; **~welt** *f* (*liter*) world of thought; **~wissenschaft** *f* arts subject; **die ~wissenschaften** the arts; (*als Studium*) the humanities; **~wissenschaftler** *m* arts scholar; (*Student*) arts student; **g~wissenschaftlich** *adj Fach* arts *attr*; **g~wissenschaftliche Psychologie** humanistic psychology; **er ist mehr g~wissenschaftlich orientiert** he is more orientated towards the arts; **~zustand** *m* mental condition; **jdn auf seinen ~zustand untersuchen** to give sb a psychiatric examination; **du mußt dich mal auf deinen ~zustand untersuchen lassen** (*inf*) you need your head examined (*inf*).

Geist-: ~feindlichkeit *f* anti-intellectualism; **~heiler** *m* faith healer.

geistig *adj* **(a)** (*unkörperlich*) *Wesen, Liebe, Existenz* spiritual ♦ **ein ~es Band** a spiritual bond; **~-moralisch** spiritual and moral; **~-moralische Erneuerung** spiritual and moral renewal; **~-seelisch** mental and spiritual.

(b) (*intellektuell*) intellectual; (*Psych*) mental ♦ **~e Arbeit** intellectual work, brain-work (*inf*); **~e Nahrung** intellectual nourishment; **~ anspruchsvoll/anspruchslos** intellectually demanding/undemanding, highbrow/lowbrow (*inf*); **~ nicht mehr folgen können** to be unable to understand *or* follow any more; **~er Diebstahl** plagiarism *no pl*; **~es Eigentum** intellectual property; **der ~e Vater** the spiritual father; **~ behindert/zurückgeblieben** mentally handicapped *or* deficient/retarded.

(c) (*imaginär*) **sein ~es Auge** one's mind's eye; **etw vor seinem ~en Auge sehen** to see sth in one's mind's eye.

(d) *attr* (*alkoholisch*) spirituous.

Geistigkeit *f* intellectuality.

geistlich *adj Angelegenheit, Einstellung, Führer, Beistand* spiritual; (*religiös*) *Drama, Dichtung, Schrift* religious; *Musik* religious, sacred; (*kirchlich*) ecclesiastical; *Gewand* ecclesiastical, clerical ♦ **~es Amt/~er Orden** religious office/order; **~es Recht** canon law; **der ~e Stand** the clergy; **die ~en Weihen empfangen** to take holy orders.

Geistliche *f* **-n, -n** woman priest; (*von Freikirchen*) woman minister.

Geistliche(r) *m decl as adj* clergyman; (*Priester*) priest; (*Pastor, von Freikirchen*) minister; (*Gefängnis~, Militär~ etc*) chaplain.

Geistlichkeit *f siehe* **Geistliche(r)** clergy; priesthood; ministry.

Geist-: g~los *adj* (*dumm*) stupid; (*langweilig*) dull; (*einfallslos*) unimaginative; (*trivial*) inane; **~losigkeit** *f* **(a)** *no pl siehe adj* stupidity; dullness, unimaginativeness; inanity; **(b)** (*g~lose Äußerung*) dull/stupid *etc* remark; **g~reich** *adj* (*witzig*) witty; (*klug*) intelligent; (*einfallsreich*) ingenious; *Beschäftigung, Gespräch, Unterhaltung* intellectually stimulating; (*schlagfertig*) quick-witted; **das war sehr g~reich** (*iro*) that was bright (*iro*); **g~sprühend** *adj attr* (*geh*) scintillatingly *or* brilliantly witty; **g~tötend** *adj* soul-destroying; **g~voll** *adj Mensch, Äußerung* wise, sage; *Buch, Gespräch, Beschäftigung* intellectual.

Geitau *nt* (*Naut*) stay.

Geiz *m* **-es,** *no pl* meanness; (*Sparsamkeit, Knauserei auch*) miserliness.

geizen *vi* to be mean; (*sparsam, knausrig sein auch*) to be miserly; (*mit Worten, Zeit*) to be sparing ♦ **mit etw ~** to be mean *etc* with sth; **sie geizt nicht mit ihren Reizen** she doesn't mind showing what she's got; **nach etw ~** (*old*) to crave (for) sth.

Geizhals *m* miser.

geizig *adj* mean, stingy (*inf*); (*sparsam, knausrig auch*) miserly; (*mit Geld auch*) tight-fisted ♦ **„Der G~e"** "The Miser".

Geizkragen *m* (*inf*) skinflint.

Gejammer *nt* **-s,** *no pl* moaning (and groaning); (*inf: Klagen auch*) bellyaching (*inf*), griping (*inf*).

Gejauchze *nt* **-s,** *no pl* jubilation, exultation (*liter*), rejoicing.

Gejaule *nt* **-s,** *no pl* howling; (*von Tieren auch*) yowling.

Gejohle *nt* **-s,** *no pl* howling; (*von Betrunkenen etc*) caterwauling.

gek. *abbr of* **gekürzt** abbreviated.

gekannt *ptp of* **kennen.**

Gekeife *nt* **-s,** *no pl* carping, nagging.

Gekicher *nt* **-s,** *no pl* giggling, tittering; (*spöttisch*) sniggering, snickering.

Gekläff *nt* **-(e)s,** *no pl* yapping (*auch fig pej*), yelping.

Geklapper *nt* **-s,** *no pl* clatter(ing).

Geklatsche *nt* **-s,** *no pl* (*inf*) **(a)** (*von Händen*) clapping. **(b)** (*pej: Tratscherei*) gossiping, tittle-tattling.

gekleidet *adj* dressed ♦ **gut/schlecht ~ sein** to be well/badly dressed; **weiß/schwarz ~ sein** to be dressed in white/black.

Geklimper *nt* **-s,** *no pl* (*inf*) (*Klavier~*) tinkling; (*stümperhaft*) plonking (*inf*); (*Banjo~ etc*) twanging; (*von Geld*) jingling; (*von Wimpern*) fluttering.

Geklingel *nt* **-s,** *no pl* ringing; (*von Motor*) pinking, knocking.

Geklirr(e) *nt* **-(e)s,** *no pl* clinking; (*von Gläsern auch*) tinkling; (*von Fensterscheiben*) rattling; (*von Ketten etc*) clanging, clanking; (*von Waffen*) clashing; (*von Lautsprecher, Mikrophon*) crackling; (*von Eis*) crunching.

geklommen *ptp of* **klimmen.**

Geklön(e) *nt* **-(e)s,** *no pl* (*inf*) natter (*inf*).

Geklopfe *nt* **-s,** *no pl* knocking; (*von Fleisch, Teppich*) beating; (*des Spechts*) tapping, hammering; (*des Motors*) knocking, pinking.

geklungen *ptp of* **klingen.**

Geknall(e) *nt* **-(e)s,** *no pl* banging; (*von Tür auch*) slamming; (*von Schüssen*) cracking, ringing out; (*bei Feuerwerk*) banging; (*von Pfropfen*) popping; (*von Peitsche*) cracking.

Geknarr(e) *nt* **-(e)s,** *no pl* creaking; (*von Stimme*) rasping, grating.

Geknatter *nt* **-s,** *no pl* (*von Motorrad*) roaring; (*von Preßlufthammer*) hammering; (*von Maschinengewehr*) rattling, chattering; (*von Schüssen*) rattling (out).

geknickt *adj* (*inf*) glum, dejected.

gekniffen *ptp of* **kneifen.**

Geknipse *nt* **-(e)s,** *no pl* (*inf*) snap-taking (*inf*).

Geknister *nt* **-s,** *no pl* crackling, crackle; (*von Papier, Seide*) rustling.

geknüppelt *adj* **~ voll** (*inf*) packed (out), chock-a-block (*inf*).

gekommen *ptp of* **kommen.**

gekonnt [1] *ptp of* **können.**

[2] *adj* neat; (*meisterhaft*) masterly.

Gekrächz(e) *nt* **-es,** *no pl* croaking; (*von Mensch auch*) rasping.

Gekrakel *nt* **-s,** *no pl* (*inf*) scrawl, scribble; (*Krakeln*) scrawling, scribbling.

Gekratze *nt* **-s,** *no pl* scratching.

gekräuselt *adj* ruffled.

Gekreisch(e) *nt* **-s,** *no pl* screeching; (*von Vogel auch*) squawking; (*von Reifen, Bremsen auch*) squealing; (*von Mensch auch*) shrieking, squealing.

Gekreuzigte(r) *mf decl as adj* crucified (person) ♦ **Jesus der ~** Jesus the Crucified.

Gekrieche *nt* **-s,** *no pl* (*inf*) crawling, creeping.

gekrischen *ptp of* **kreischen.**

Gekritzel *nt* **-s,** *no pl* **(a)** scribbling, scrawling; (*Männchenmalen*) doodling. **(b)** (*Gekritzeltes*) scribble, scrawl, doodle.

gekrochen *ptp of* **kriechen.**

Gekröse *nt* **-s, -** (*Anat*) mesentery; (*Kutteln*) tripe; (*eßbare Eingeweide*) chitterlings *pl*; (*von Geflügel*) giblets *pl*.

gekühlt *adj* chilled.

gekünstelt *adj* artificial; *Sprache, Benehmen auch* affected ♦ **er spricht sehr ~** his speech is very affected.

Gekünsteltheit *f* artificiality; affectedness.

Gel *nt* **-s, -e** gel.

Gelaber(e) *nt* **-(s),** *no pl* (*inf*) jabbering (*inf*), prattling (*inf*).

Gelache *nt* **-s,** *no pl* (*inf*) silly laughter.

Gelächter *nt* **-s, -** laughter ♦ **in ~ ausbrechen** to burst into laughter, to burst out laughing; **sich dem ~ aussetzen** to make oneself a/the laughing-stock, to expose oneself to ridicule; **jdn dem ~ preisgeben** (*geh*) to make sb a/the laughing-stock.

gelackmeiert *adj* (*inf*) duped, conned (*inf*) ♦ **~** *or* **der G~e sein** (*hintergangen worden sein*) to have been duped *or* conned (*inf*); (*dumm dastehen*) to look a right fool (*inf*).

geladen [1] *ptp of* **laden[1], laden[2].**

[2] *adj* **(a)** loaded; (*Phys*) charged; (*inf: wütend*) (hopping *inf*) mad. **(b) ~ haben** (*inf*) to be tanked up (*inf*).

Gelage *nt* **-s, -** feast, banquet; (*Zech~*) carouse.

gelagert *adj* **in anders/ähnlich/besonders ~en Fällen** in different/similar/exceptional cases; **anders ~ sein** to be different.

gelähmt *adj* paralyzed ♦ **er ist seit seinem Unfall ~** his accident left him paralyzed, he's been paralyzed since his accident; **er hat ~e Beine** his legs are paralyzed, he's paralyzed in the legs.

Gelände *nt* **-s, - (a)** (*Land*) open country; (*Mil: Gebiet, Terrain*) ground ♦ **offenes ~** open country; **schwieriges ~** difficult terrain *or* country; **das ~ erkunden** (*Mil*) to reconnoitre. **(b)** (*Gebiet*) area. **(c)** (*Grundstück*) (*Fabrik~, Schul~ etc*) grounds *pl*; (*Bau~*) site; (*Ausstellungs~*) exhibition centre.

Gelände-: ~fahrt *f* cross-country drive; **für ~fahrten gut geeignet** well-suited to cross-country driving *or* to driving cross-country; **~fahrzeug** *nt* cross-country *or* all-terrain vehicle; **g~gängig** *adj Fahrzeug* suitable for cross-country work; **~lauf** *m* cross-country run; (*Wettbewerb*) cross-country race; **er macht gerne ~lauf** he enjoys cross-country running; **~marsch** *m* cross-country march; **einen ~marsch machen** to march cross-country.

Geländer *nt* **-s, -** railing(s *pl*); (*Treppen~*) banister(s *pl*).

Gelände-: ~rad *nt* all-terrain bike; **~rennen** *nt* cross-country race; **~ritt** *m* cross-country riding; **ein ~ritt** a cross-country ride; **für ~ritte ungeeignet** unsuitable for cross-country riding; **~spiel** *nt* scouting game; (*Mil*) field exercise; **~übung** *f* field exercise; **~wagen** *m* cross-country *or* general-purpose vehicle.

gelang *pret of* **gelingen.**

gelangen* *vi aux sein* **an/auf** *etc* **etw** *(acc)*/**zu etw ~** *(lit, fig)* to reach sth; *(fig: mit Mühe)* to attain sth; *(erwerben)* to acquire sth; **zum Ziel ~** to reach one's goal; *(fig auch)* to attain one's end *or* goal; **in jds Besitz ~** to come into sb's possession; **in die richtigen/falschen Hände ~** to fall into the right/wrong hands; **zu Reichtum ~** to come into a fortune; *(durch Arbeit)* to make a *or* one's fortune; **zu Ruhm ~** to achieve *or* acquire fame; **zur Reife ~** to reach *or* attain *(form)* maturity; **zu einer Überzeugung ~** to become convinced; **zum Abschluß/zur Abstimmung ~** *(form)* to reach a conclusion/be put to the vote; **zur Durchführung/Aufführung ~** *(form)* to be carried out/performed; **zur Auszahlung ~** *(form)* to be paid out; **an die Macht ~** to come to power.

gelangweilt *adj* bored *no adv* ◆ **die Zuschauer saßen ~ da** the audience sat there looking bored; **er hörte ihr ~ zu** he was bored listening to her.

gelappt *adj Blatt* lobate, lobed.

Gelärme *nt* **-s,** *no pl (inf) siehe* **Lärm.**

gelassen [1] *ptp of* **lassen.**

[2] *adj (ruhig)* calm; *(gefaßt auch)* cool, composed *no adv* ◆ **~ bleiben** to keep calm *or* cool; **etw ~ hinnehmen** to take sth calmly *or* with composure.

Gelassenheit *f siehe adj* calmness; coolness, composure.

Gelatine [ʒela'ti:nə] *f, no pl* gelatine.

gelatinieren* [ʒelati'ni:rən] *vti* to gelatinize.

Geläuf *nt* **-(e)s, -e (a)** *(Hunt)* tracks *pl (of game birds)*. **(b)** *(von Pferderennbahn)* turf.

Gelaufe *nt* **-s,** *no pl (inf)* running about ◆ **das war ein ~** that was a real run round *(inf)*.

gelaufen *ptp of* **laufen.**

geläufig *adj (üblich)* common; *(vertraut)* familiar; *(dated: fließend)* fluent ◆ **eine ~e Redensart** a common saying; **das ist mir nicht ~** I'm not familiar with that, that isn't familiar to me.

gelaunt *adj pred* **gut/schlecht ~** good-/bad-tempered, good-/ill-humoured; *(vorübergehend)* in a good/bad mood; **wie ist er ~?** what sort of mood is he in?

Geläut(e) *nt* **-(e)s,** *no pl* **(a)** *(Glockenläuten)* ringing; *(harmonisch auch)* chiming; *(Läutwerk)* chime. **(b)** *(Hunt)* baying.

gelb *adj* yellow; *(bei Verkehrsampel)* amber ◆ **die Blätter werden ~** the leaves are turning (yellow); **~er Fleck** *(Anat)* yellow spot; **~e Rübe** carrot; **die ~e Rasse** the yellow race, the Orientals *pl*; **die ~e Gefahr** *(Pol pej)* the yellow peril; **der G~e Fluß/das G~e Meer** the Yellow River/Sea; **~e Karte** *(Ftbl)* yellow card; **G~e Seiten** yellow pages; **die ~e Post** the postal service *(excluding telecommunications)*; **~ vor Neid** green with envy; **Löwenzahn blüht ~** the dandelion has a yellow flower.

Gelb *nt* **-s, -** *or (inf)* **-s** yellow; *(von Verkehrsampel)* amber ◆ **die Ampel stand auf ~** the lights were amber *or* had turned amber; **bei ~ stehenbleiben** to stop on amber.

Gelbe(r) *mf decl as adj* Oriental.

Gelbe(s) *nt decl as adj (vom Ei)* yolk ◆ **das ist nicht gerade das ~ vom Ei** *(inf)* it's not exactly brilliant.

Gelb-: ~fieber *nt* yellow fever; **~filter** *m (Phot)* yellow filter; **g~grün** *adj* yellowish-green; **~körperhormon** *nt* gestagen; **~kreuz** *nt (Chem)* mustard gas.

gelblich *adj* yellowish, yellowy; *Gesichtsfarbe* sallow.

Gelbling *m (Bot)* chanterelle.

Gelb-: ~sucht *f* jaundice; **g~süchtig** *adj* jaundiced; **er ist g~süchtig** he has jaundice; **~wurz** *f* turmeric.

Geld *nt* **-(e)s, -er (a)** *no pl (Zahlungsmittel)* money ◆ **bares/großes/kleines ~** cash/notes *pl*/change; **~ und Gut** wealth and possessions; **alles für unser ~!** and we're paying for it!; **~ aufnehmen** to raise money; **aus etw ~ machen** to make money out of sth; **zu ~ machen** to sell off; *Aktien* to cash in; **(mit etw) ~ machen** *(inf)* to make money (from sth); **um ~ spielen** to play for money; **ins ~ gehen** *(inf) or* **laufen** *(inf)* to cost a pretty penny *(inf)*; **das kostet ein (wahnsinniges) ~** *(inf)* that costs a fortune *or* a packet *(inf)*; **etw für teures ~ kaufen** to pay a lot for sth; **das habe ich für billiges ~ gekauft** I got it cheaply, I didn't pay much for it; **ich stand ohne ~ da** I was left penniless *or* without a penny; **in** *or* **im ~ schwimmen** *(inf)* to be rolling in it *(inf)*, to be loaded *(inf)*; **er hat ~ wie Heu** *(inf)* he's got stacks of money *(inf)*, he's filthy *or* stinking rich *(inf)*; **das ~ auf die Straße werfen** *(inf) or* **zum Fenster hinauswerfen** *(inf)* to spend money like water *or* like it was going out of fashion *(inf)*; **da hast du das Geld zum Fenster hinausgeworfen** *(inf)* that's money down the drain *(inf)*; **mit ~ um sich werfen** *or* **schmeißen** *(inf)* to chuck one's money around *(inf)*; **gutes ~ dem schlechten hinterher-** *or* **nachwerfen** *(inf)* to throw good money after bad; **jdm das ~ aus der Tasche ziehen** *or* **lotsen** *(inf)* to get *or* squeeze money out of sb; **am ~ hängen** *or* **kleben** to be tight with money; **hinterm ~ hersein** *(inf)* to be a money-grubber *(inf)*; **das ist nicht für ~ zu haben** *(inf)* that can't be bought; **sie/das ist nicht mit ~ zu bezahlen** *(inf)* she/that is priceless; **nicht für ~ und gute Worte** *(inf)* not for love nor money; **~ allein macht nicht glücklich(, aber es beruhigt)** *(Prov)* money isn't everything(, but it helps) *(prov)*; **~ oder Leben!** your money or your life!; **~ stinkt nicht** *(Prov)* there's nothing wrong with money; **~ regiert die Welt** *(Prov)* money makes the world go round *(prov)*.

(b) *(~summen)* **~er** *pl* money ◆ **tägliche ~er** day-to-day money *or* loans *pl*; **staatliche/öffentliche ~er** state/public funds *pl or* money.

(c) *(St Ex) siehe* **Geldkurs.**

Geld-: ~abwertung *f* currency devaluation; **~adel** *m* **der ~adel** the money aristocracy; *(hum: die Reichen)* the rich *pl*; **~angelegenheit** *f* financial matter; **jds ~angelegenheiten** sb's financial affairs; **~anlage** *f* (financial) investment; **~aristokratie** *f siehe* **~adel**; **~aufwertung** *f* currency revaluation; **~ausgabe** *f* (financial) expenditure; **~automat** *m (zum Geldabheben)* cash dispenser, automatic teller *(US)*; *(zum Geldwechseln)* change machine; **~beutel** *m* purse; **tief in den ~beutel greifen** *(inf)* to dig deep (into one's pocket) *(inf)*; **~bombe** *f* strongbox; **~börse** *f siehe* **~beutel**; **~bote** *m* security guard; **~brief** *m siehe* **Wertbrief**; **~briefträger** *m postman who delivers money orders*; **~buße** *f (Jur)* fine; **eine hohe ~buße** a heavy fine; **~dinge** *pl* financial matters; **~einlage** *f* capital invested *no pl*; **~einwurf** *m* slot; **beim ~einwurf müssen Sie ...** when inserting the money you should ...; **~entwertung** *f (Inflation)* currency depreciation; *(Abwertung)* currency devaluation; **~erwerb** *m* **zum ~erwerb arbeiten** to work to earn money; **etw zum ~erwerb machen** to make money out of sth; **~fälschung** *f* counterfeiting; **~geber(in** *f***)** *m* financial backer; *(esp Rad, TV)* sponsor; *(hum: Arbeitgeber)* employer; **~geschäft** *nt* financial transaction; **~geschenk** *nt* gift of money; **~gier** *f* avarice; **g~gierig** *adj* avaricious; **~heirat** *f* **das war eine reine ~heirat** she/he *etc* just got married for the money; **~herrschaft** *f* plutocracy.

geldig *adj (esp Aus)* moneyed.

Geld-: ~institut *nt* financial institution; **~kassette** *f* cash box; **~katze** *f (Hist)* money pouch; *(Gürtel)* money-belt; **~knappheit** *f* shortage of money; **~kurs** *m (St Ex)* buying rate, bid price.

geldlich *adj* financial.

Geld-: ~mangel *m* lack of money; **~markt** *m* money market; **~menge** *f* money supply; **~mittel** *pl* funds *pl*; **~not** *f (~mangel)* lack of money; *(~schwierigkeiten)* financial difficulties *pl*; **~politik** *f* financial policy; **etwas von ~politik verstehen** to know something about the politics of finance; **~prämie** *f* bonus; *(als Auszeichnung)* (financial) award; *(als Belohnung)* (financial) reward; **~preis** *m* cash prize; **~quelle** *f* source of income; **~rolle** *f* roll of money *or* coins; **~sache** *f* money *or* financial matter; **in ~sachen hört die Gemütlichkeit auf** *(prov)* business is business *(prov)*; **~sack** *m* money bag; *(pej inf: reicher Mann)* moneybags *sing*; **auf dem ~sack sitzen** *(inf)* to be sitting on a pile of money *(inf)*; **~säckel** *m (dial)* money bag; *(fig: von Kanton, Staat etc)* coffers *pl*; **~schein** *m* banknote, bill *(US)*; **~schöpfung** *f (Fin)* money creation; **~schrank** *m* safe; **~schrankknacker** *m (inf)* safeblower; **~schuld** *f* (financial) debt; **~schwierigkeiten** *pl* financial difficulties *pl*; **~sendung** *f* cash remittance; **~sorgen** *pl* financial worries *pl*, money troubles *pl*; **~sorgen haben, in ~sorgen sein** to have financial worries *or* money troubles; **~sorte** *f (Fin)* (type of) currency; **~spende** *f* donation, gift of money; **~spielautomat** *m* slot machine; **~spritze** *f (inf)* injection of money; **~strafe** *f* fine; **jdn zu einer ~strafe verurteilen** *or* **mit einer ~strafe belegen** to fine sb, to impose a fine on sb; **~stück** *nt* coin; **~summe** *f* sum of money; **~tasche** *f* purse, wallet *(US)*; *(Herren~)* wallet; *(sackartig)* money bag; **~umlauf** *m* circulation of money; **~umtausch** *m siehe* **~wechsel**; **~verdiener** *m (inf)* moneymaker *(inf)*; **~verkehr** *m* money transactions *pl*; **~verlegenheit** *f* financial embarrassment *no pl*; **in ~verlegenheit sein** to be short of money; **jdm aus einer ~verlegenheit helfen** to help sb out of his financial difficulties; **~verleiher** *m* moneylender; **~verschwendung** *f* waste of money; **~volumen** *nt (Fin) siehe* **~menge**; **~waschanlage** *f* money-laundering outfit; **~wäsche** *f* money laundering; **~wechsel** *m* exchange of money; **beim ~wechsel muß man eine Gebühr bezahlen** there is a charge for changing money; **„~wechsel"** "bureau de change"; **~wechselautomat** *m* change machine; **~wechsler** *m* moneychanger; *(Automat)* change machine; **g~wert** *adj* **g~werter Vorteil** perk, payment in kind; **~wert** *m* cash value; *(Fin: Kaufkraft)* (currency) value; **innerer/äußerer ~wert** an/the internal/external value of currency; **~wertstabilität** *f* stability of a/the currency; **~wesen** *nt* monetary system; **~wirtschaft** *f* money economy; **~zuwendungen** *pl* money *sing*; *(~geschenk)* gifts *pl* of money; *(regelmäßiges ~geschenk)* allowance *sing*; **private ~zuwendungen erhalten** to receive a private income.

geleckt *adj* **wie ~ aussehen** *Mann* to be spruced up; *Zimmer, Boden etc* to be spick and span.

Gelee [ʒe'le:] *m or nt* **-s, -s** jelly.

Gelege *nt* **-s, -** *(Vogel~)* clutch (of eggs); *(Frosch~)* spawn *no pl*; *(von Reptilien)* eggs *pl*.

gelegen [1] *ptp of* **liegen.**

[2] *adj* **(a)** *(befindlich, liegend) Haus* situated; *Grundstück auch* located ◆ **ein herrlich ~er Ort** a place in a magnificent area.

(b) *(passend)* opportune ◆ **zu ~er Zeit** at a convenient time; **wenn ich nicht ~ komme, gehe ich gleich wieder** if it's not convenient, I'll go immediately; **du kommst mir gerade ~** you've come at just the right time; *(iro)* you do pick your time well; **es kommt mir sehr/nicht sehr ~** it comes just at the right/wrong time.

(c) *pred (wichtig)* **mir ist viel/nichts daran ~** it matters a great deal/doesn't matter to me.

Gelegenheit *f* **(a)** *(günstiger Umstand)* opportunity ◆ **bei ~** some time (or other); **bei passender ~** when the opportunity arises; **bei passender/der ersten (besten) ~ werde ich ...** when I get the opportunity *or* chance/at the first opportunity I'll ...; **(die) ~ haben** to get an *or* the opportunity *or* a *or* the chance *(etw zu tun* to do sth); **jdm (die) ~ geben** *or* **bieten** to give sb an *or* the opportunity *or* a *or* the chance *(etw zu tun* to do sth); **~ macht Diebe** *(Prov)* opportunity makes a thief; *siehe* **wahrnehmen.**

(b) *(Anlaß)* occasion ◆ **bei dieser ~** on this occasion; **ein Kleid für alle ~en** a dress suitable for all occasions; *siehe* **Schopf.**

(c) *(Comm)* bargain.

Gelegenheits-: ~arbeit *f* **(a)** casual work *no pl*; **(b)** *(eines Autors)* minor work; **~arbeiter** *m* casual labourer; **~dichter** *m* occasional poet;

△: for details of spelling reform, see supplement

~**gedicht** *nt* occasional poem; ~**kauf** *m* bargain; ~**raucher** *m* occasional smoker; ~**trinker** *m* occasional drinker.

gelegentlich [1] *adj attr* occasional ◆ **von ~en Ausnahmen abgesehen** except for the odd occasion.
[2] *adv* (*manchmal*) occasionally, now and again; (*bei Gelegenheit*) some time (or other) ◆ **wenn Sie ~ dort sind** if you happen to be there; **lassen Sie ~ etwas von sich hören!** keep in touch.
[3] *prep +gen* (*geh*) ~ **seines 60. Geburtstags** on the occasion of his 60th birthday.

gelehrig *adj* quick to learn ◆ **sich bei etw ~ anstellen** to be quick to grasp sth.

Gelehrigkeit *f* quickness to learn.

gelehrsam *adj* **(a)** (*old*) *siehe* **gelehrt 2. (b)** (*rare*) *siehe* **gelehrig.**

Gelehrsamkeit *f* (*geh*) learning, erudition.

gelehrt [1] *ptp of* **lehren.**
[2] *adj* learned, erudite; (*wissenschaftlich*) scholarly ◆ **~e Gesellschaft** (*old*) learned society.

Gelehrte(r) *mf decl as adj* scholar ◆ **darüber sind sich die ~n noch nicht einig** that's a moot point.

Gelehrten-: ~**familie** *f* family of scholars; ~**kopf** *m* scholarly profile; ~**streit** *m* dispute amongst the scholars; ~**welt** *f* world of learning.

Gelehrtheit *f* learning, erudition.

Geleier *nt* **-s,** *no pl* droning.

Geleise *nt* **-s, -** (*geh, Aus*) *siehe* **Gleis.**

Geleit *nt* **-(e)s, -e** (*Hist: Gefolge*) retinue, entourage; (*Begleitung, Mil*) escort; (*Naut*) convoy, escort; (*Leichenzug*) cortege ◆ **freies** *or* **sicheres ~** safe-conduct; **jdm das ~ geben** to escort *or* accompany sb; **„zum ~"** "preface"; *siehe* **letzte(r, s).**

Geleit-: ~**boot** *nt* escort *or* convoy ship; ~**brief** *m* (*Hist*) letter of safe-conduct.

geleiten* *vt* (*geh*) to escort; (*begleiten auch*) to accompany; (*Naut*) to convoy, to escort.

Geleit-: ~**schiff** *nt siehe* ~**boot;** ~**schutz** *m* escort; (*Naut auch*) convoy; **jdm ~schutz gewähren** *or* **geben** to give sb an escort/a convoy; (*persönlich*) to escort/convoy sb; **im ~schutz (von Polizeifahrzeugen)** under (police) escort; ~**wort** *nt* (*geh*) preface; ~**zug** *m* (*Mil, Naut*) convoy; **im ~zug fahren** to drive in/sail under convoy.

Gelenk *nt* **-(e)s, -e** joint; (*Hand~*) wrist; (*Fuß~*) ankle; (*Ketten~*) link; (*Scharnier~*) hinge.

gelenk *adj* (*old*) *siehe* **gelenkig.**

Gelenk-, Gelenks- (*Aus*): ~**bus** *m* articulated bus; ~**entzündung** *f* arthritis; ~**fahrzeug** *nt* articulated vehicle.

gelenkig *adj* supple; *Mensch auch* agile ◆ ~ **verbunden sein** (*Tech*) to be jointed; (*zusammengefügt*) to be articulated; (*mit Kettengelenk*) to be linked; (*mit Scharniergelenk*) to be hinged.

Gelenkigkeit *f* suppleness; (*von Mensch auch*) agility.

Gelenk-, Gelenks- (*Aus*): ~**kopf** *m,* ~**kugel** *f* (*Anat*) head of a bone, condyle (*spec*); ~**leuchte** *f* Anglepoise ® (lamp); ~**omnibus** *m siehe* ~**bus;** ~**pfanne** *f* (*Anat*) glenoid cavity; ~**plastik** *f* (*Med*) anthroplasty; ~**puppe** *f siehe* **Gliederpuppe;** ~**rheumatismus** *m* rheumatic fever; ~**schmiere** *f* (*Anat*) synovial fluid; ~**welle** *f* (*Tech*) cardan shaft; ~**zug** *m* articulated train.

gelernt *adj* trained; *Arbeiter* skilled.

gelesen *ptp of* **lesen.**

geliebt *adj* dear, beloved (*liter, Eccl*).

Geliebte *f decl as adj* sweetheart; (*Mätresse*) mistress; (*liter: als Anrede*) beloved (*liter*).

Geliebte(r) *m decl as adj* sweetheart, lover (*old*); (*Liebhaber*) lover; (*liter: als Anrede*) beloved (*liter*).

geliefert *adj* ~ **sein** (*inf*) to have had it (*inf*); **jetzt sind wir ~** that's the end (*inf*).

geliehen *ptp of* **leihen.**

gelieren* [ʒe'liːrən] *vi* to gel.

Gelier- [ʒe'liːɐ]: ~**mittel** *nt* gelling agent; ~**zucker** *m* preserving sugar.

gelind(e) *adj* (*geh*) **(a)** (*mäßig, mild*) mild; (*schonend, vorsichtig*) gentle; *Wind, Frost, Regen* light; *Klima, Anhöhe* gentle ◆ **~e gesagt** putting it mildly, to put it mildly. **(b)** (*inf: heftig*) awful (*inf*) ◆ **da packte mich ~e Wut** I got pretty angry.

gelingen *pret* **gelang,** *ptp* **gelungen** *vi aux sein* (*glücken*) to succeed; (*erfolgreich sein*) to be successful ◆ **es gelang ihm, das zu tun** he succeeded in doing it; **es gelang ihm nicht, das zu tun** he failed to do it, he didn't succeed in doing it; **dem Häftling gelang die Flucht** the prisoner managed to escape *or* succeeded in escaping; **dein Plan wird dir nicht ~** you won't succeed with your plan; **es will mir nicht ~/~ ... zu ...** I can't seem to manage it/manage to ...; **das Bild ist ihr gut/schlecht gelungen** her picture turned out well/badly; *siehe* **gelungen.**

Gelingen *nt* **-s,** *no pl* (*geh*) (*Glück*) success; (*erfolgreiches Ergebnis*) successful outcome ◆ **gutes ~ für Ihren Plan!** good luck with your plan!; **auf gutes ~!** to success!

Gelispel *nt* **-s,** *no pl* (*das Lispeln*) lisping; (*Geflüster*) whispering.

gelitten *ptp of* **leiden.**

gell[1] *adj* shrill, piercing.

gell[2], **gelle** *interj* (*S Ger, Sw*) *siehe* **gelt.**

gellen *vi* to shrill; (*von lauten Tönen erfüllt sein*) to ring ◆ **der Lärm gellt mir in den Ohren** the noise makes my ears ring; **ein schriller Schrei gellte durch die Nacht** a shrill scream pierced the night.

gellend *adj* shrill, piercing ◆ ~ **um Hilfe schreien** to scream for help.

geloben* *vt* (*geh*) to vow, to swear ◆ **die Fürsten gelobten dem König Treue** the princes pledged their loyalty *or* vowed loyalty to the king; **ich habe mir gelobt, das Rauchen aufzugeben** I've vowed *or* sworn *or* made a pledge to give up smoking; **das Gelobte Land** (*Bibl*) the Promised Land; **ich schwöre und gelobe, ...** I (do) solemnly swear and promise ...

Gelöbnis *nt* (*geh*) vow ◆ **ein** *or* **das ~ ablegen** to take a vow.

Gelöbnisfeier *f* swearing-in ceremony.

gelockt *adj Haar* curly; *Mensch* curly-haired, curly-headed.

Geloder *nt* **-s,** *no pl* (*geh*) blaze.

gelogen *ptp of* **lügen.**

gelöst *adj* relaxed ◆ **danach war sie ~ und entspannt** afterwards she felt calm and relaxed.

Gelöstheit *f* feeling of relaxation; (*gelöste Stimmung*) relaxed mood.

Gelse *f* **-, -n** (*Aus*) gnat, mosquito.

gelt *interj* (*S Ger*) right ◆ **morgen kommst du wieder, ~?** you'll be back tomorrow, won't you *or* right?; **~, du leihst mir 5 Mark?** you'll lend me 5 marks, won't you *or* right?; **ich werde es mal versuchen, ~?** well, I'll give it a try; **es ist schön heute — ~?** it's nice today — isn't it just?

gelten *pret* **galt,** *ptp* **gegolten** [1] *vi* **(a)** (*gültig sein*) to be valid; (*Gesetz*) to be in force; (*Preise*) to be effective; (*Münze*) to be legal tender; (*erlaubt sein*) to be allowed *or* permitted; (*zählen*) to count ◆ **die Wette gilt!** the bet's on!, it's a bet!; **was ich sage, gilt!** what I say goes!; **das gilt nicht!** that doesn't count!; (*nicht erlaubt*) that's not allowed!; **das Gesetz gilt für alle** the law applies to everyone; **diese Karte gilt nur für eine Person** this ticket only admits one; *siehe* **geltend.**
(b) *+dat* (*bestimmt sein für*) to be meant for *or* aimed at.
(c) *+dat* (*geh: sich beziehen auf*) to be for ◆ **seine ganze Liebe galt der Musik** music was his only love; **sein letzter Gedanke galt seinem Volk** his last thought was for his people.
(d) (*zutreffen*) **für jdn/etw ~** to hold (good) for sb/sth, to go for sb/sth; **das gleiche gilt auch für ihn/von ihm** the same goes for him too/is true of him too.
(e) ~ **als** *or* **für** (*rare*) to be regarded as; **es gilt als sicher, daß ...** it seems certain that ...
(f) ~ **lassen** to accept; **das lasse ich ~!** I'll agree to that!, I accept that!; **für diesmal lasse ich es ~** I'll let it go this time; **etw als etw ~ lassen** to accept sth as sth; **er läßt nur seine eigene Meinung ~** he won't accept anybody's opinion but his own.
[2] *vti impers* (*geh*) **es gilt, ... zu ...** it is necessary to ...; **jetzt gilt es, Mut zu zeigen/zusammenzuhalten** it is now a question of courage/of sticking together; **jetzt gilt's!** this is it!; **was gilt's?** (*bei Wette*) what do you bet?; **es gilt!** done!, you're on!, it's a deal!
[3] *vt* (*wert sein*) to be worth; (*zählen*) to count for ◆ **was gilt die Wette?** what do you bet?

geltend *adj attr Preise, Tarife* current; *Gesetz, Regelung* in force; (*vorherrschend*) *Meinung etc* currently accepted, prevailing ◆ ~ **machen** (*form*) to assert; **einen Einwand ~ machen** to raise an objection; **~es Recht sein** to be the law of the land.

Geltendmachung *f* (*form*) enforcement.

Geltung *f* (*Gültigkeit*) validity; (*von Münzen*) currency; (*Wert*) value, worth; (*Einfluß*) influence; (*Ansehen*) prestige ◆ ~ **haben** to have validity; (*Münzen*) to be legal tender, to have currency; (*Gesetz*) to be in force; (*Preise*) to be effective; (*Auffassung etc*) to be prevalent; (*Einfluß haben*) to carry weight; (*angesehen sein*) to be recognized; **an ~ verlieren** to lose prestige; **einer Sache** (*dat*) **~ verschaffen** to enforce sth; **sich** (*dat*) **~ verschaffen** to establish one's position; **etw zur ~ bringen** to show sth (off) to advantage; (*durch Kontrast*) to set sth off; **zur ~ kommen** to show to advantage; (*durch Kontrast*) to be set off; **in diesem Konzertsaal kommt die Musik voll zur ~** the music can be heard to its best advantage in this concert hall.

Geltungs-: ~**bedürfnis** *nt, no pl* need for admiration; **g~bedürftig** *adj* desperate for admiration; ~**bereich** *m* **der ~bereich einer Fahrkarte/eines Gesetzes** the area within which a ticket is valid/a law is operative; ~**dauer** *f* (*einer Fahrkarte etc*) period of validity; **die ~dauer eines Vertrages/einer Genehmigung** the period during which a contract is in force/a licence is valid; ~**drang** *m,* ~**streben** *nt siehe* ~**bedürfnis;** ~**sucht** *f* craving for admiration; **g~süchtig** *adj* craving (for) admiration; ~**trieb** *m* (~*bedürfnis*) need for admiration; (~*sucht*) craving for admiration.

Gelübde *nt* **-s, -** (*Rel, geh*) vow ◆ **ein/das ~ ablegen** *or* **tun** to take a vow.

Gelump(e) *nt* **-s,** *no pl* (*inf: Plunder, Sachen*) junk, trash; (*pej: Gesindel*) trash.

gelungen [1] *ptp of* **gelingen.**
[2] *adj attr* **(a)** (*geglückt*) successful ◆ **ein gut ~er Abend/Braten** a very successful evening/a roast that turned out very well; **eine nicht so recht ~e Überraschung** a surprise that didn't quite come off. **(b)** (*inf: drollig*) priceless ◆ **du bist mir ein ~er Bursche** you're priceless, you *are* a funny chap.

Gelüst(e) *nt* **-(e)s, -e** (*geh*) desire; (*Sucht*) craving (*auf +acc, nach* for).

gelüsten* *vt impers* (*liter, iro*) **es gelüstet mich** *or* **mich gelüstet nach ...** I am overcome by desire for ...; (*süchtig nach*) I have a craving for ...; **es gelüstet mich, das zu tun** I'm more than tempted *or* I'm sorely tempted to do that.

Gelüsten *nt* **-s,** *no pl siehe* **Gelüst(e).**

GEMA ['geːma] *f* **-,** *no pl abbr of* **Gesellschaft für musikalische Aufführungs- und mechanische Vervielfältigungsrechte** *musical copyright watchdog body.*

gemach *adv* (*old*) slowly ◆ **~!** not so fast!; (*nichts übereilen*) one mustn't rush things!

Gemach *nt* -(e)s, ¨er (*geh*) chamber (*old, form*) ◆ **sich in seine ¨er zurückziehen** to repair to one's chamber (*old, hum*).
gemächlich *adj* leisurely *no adv*; *Mensch* unhurried ◆ **ein ~ fließender Strom** a gently flowing river; **er wanderte ~ durch die Wiesen** he strolled through the meadows, he took a leisurely stroll through the meadows; **ein ~es Leben führen** to lead a quiet life.
Gemächlichkeit *f* leisureliness; (*Ruhe*) peace.
gemacht *adj* (a) made ◆ **für etw ~ sein** to be made for sth; **ein ~er Mann sein** to be made *or* a made man; *siehe* **Bett**. (b) (*gewollt, gekünstelt*) false, contrived. (c) **(ist) ~!** (*inf*) done! (*inf*).
Gemahl[1] *m* -s, -e (*geh, form*) spouse (*old, form*), husband; (*Prinz~*) consort ◆ **bitte grüßen Sie Ihren Herrn ~** do give my regards to your husband.
Gemahl[2] *nt* - *or* -(e)s, -e (*obs*) spouse (*old, form*), wife.
Gemahlin *f* (*geh, form*) spouse (*old, form*), wife; (*von König auch*) consort ◆ **bitte empfehlen Sie mich Ihrer Frau ~** do give my regards to your lady wife (*form, hum*) *or* to your good lady.
gemahnen* *vt* (*geh*) **jdn an jdn/etw ~** to remind sb of sb/sth, to put sb in mind of sb/sth.
Gemälde *nt* -s, - painting; (*fig: Schilderung*) portrayal.
Gemälde-: **~ausstellung** *f* exhibition of paintings; **~galerie** *f* picture gallery; **~sammlung** *f* collection of paintings; (*~galerie*) art collection.
Gemansche *nt* -s, *no pl* (*dial*) mush ◆ **hör auf mit dem ~!** stop messing about with it!
Gemarkung *f* (*dated, form*) (*Feldmark*) bounds *pl*; (*Gemeindegebiet*) district.
gemasert [1] *ptp of* **masern**.
[2] *adj Holz* grained.
gemäß [1] *prep +dat* in accordance with ◆ **Ihren Anordnungen ~** as per your instructions, in accordance with your instructions; **~ den Bestimmungen** under the regulations; **~ § 209** under § 209.
[2] *adj* appropriate (*dat* to) ◆ **dieser Umgang ist seiner sozialen Stellung nicht ~** the company he is keeping ill befits *or* does not befit his social position; **eine ihren Fähigkeiten ~e Arbeit** a job suited to her abilities; **das einzig G~e** the only fitting thing.
gemäßigt *adj* moderate; *Klima, Zone* temperate; *Optimismus etc* qualified.
Gemäuer *nt* -s, - (*geh*) masonry, walls *pl*; (*Ruine*) ruins *pl*.
Gemauschel *nt* -s, *no pl* (*pej inf*) scheming.
Gemeck(e)re, Gemecker *nt* -s, *no pl* (*von Ziegen*) bleating; (*inf: Nörgelei*) moaning, belly-aching (*inf*); (*meckerndes Lachen*) cackling.
gemein *adj* (a) *pred, no comp* (*gemeinsam*) **etw ~ mit jdm/etw haben** to have sth in common with sb/sth; **Menschen/einer Sache** (*dat*) **~ sein** (*geh*) to be common to people/sth; **nichts mit jdm ~ haben wollen** to want nothing to do with sb; **das ist beiden ~** it is common to both of them.
(b) *attr, no comp* (*Biol, old: üblich, verbreitet, öffentlich*) common ◆ **~er Bruch** (*Math*) vulgar fraction; **~es Recht** common law; **ein ~er Soldat** a common soldier; **das ~e Volk/Wohl** the common people/good *or* weal (*old*); **der ~e Mann** the ordinary man.
(c) (*niederträchtig*) mean; (*roh, unverschämt auch*) nasty; *Verräter, Lüge* contemptible ◆ **das war ~ von dir!** that was mean *or* nasty of you; **ein ~er Streich** a dirty *or* rotten trick; **alles ins G~e ziehen** to cheapen *or* debase everything.
(d) (*ordinär*) vulgar; *Bemerkung, Witz auch* dirty, coarse.
(e) (*inf: unangenehm*) horrible, awful ◆ **die Prüfung war ~ schwer** the exam was horribly *or* awfully difficult.
Gemeinbesitz *m* common property.
Gemeinde *f* -, -n (a) (*Kommune*) municipality; (*~bewohner auch*) community; (*inf: ~amt*) local authority ◆ **die ~ Burg** the municipality of Burg. (b) (*Pfarr~*) parish; (*Gläubige auch*) parishioners *pl*; (*beim Gottesdienst*) congregation. (c) (*Anhängerschaft*) (*von Theater etc*) patrons *pl*; (*von Schriftsteller etc*) following.
Gemeinde-: **~abgaben** *pl* rates and local taxes *pl*; **~ammann** *m* (*Sw*) (a) *siehe* **~vorsteher**; (b) bailiff; **~amt** *nt* local authority; (*Gebäude*) local administrative office; **~bau** *m* (*Aus*) council house; **~beamte(r)** *m* local government officer; **~behörde** *f* local authority; ⚠**~beschluß** *m* local government decision; **~bezirk** *m* district; (*Aus*) ward; **im ~bezirk Dumfries** in the district of Dumfries; **~diener** *m* (*dated*) beadle; **g~eigen** *adj* local authority *attr*, (*esp städtisch*) municipal; **~eigentum** *nt* communal property; **~glied** *nt* (*Eccl*) parishioner; **~haus** *nt* (*Eccl*) parish rooms *pl*; (*von Freikirchen*) church rooms *pl*; (*katholisch*) parish house; **~helfer(in** *f*) *m* (*Eccl*) parish worker; **~mitglied** *nt* (*Eccl*) *siehe* **~glied**; **~ordnung** *f* bylaws *pl*, ordinances *pl* (*US*); **~präsident** *m* (*Sw*) mayor; **~rat** *m* district council; (*Mitglied*) district councillor (*Brit*), councilman (*US*); **~saal** *m* (*Eccl*) church hall; **~schwester** *f* district nurse; (*Eccl*) *nun working in a parish as a nurse or social worker*; **~spital** *nt* (*Aus*) local hospital; **~steuer** *f* local tax.
gemeindeutsch *adj* standard German.
Gemeinde-: **~väter** *pl* (*hum*) venerable councillors *pl* (*hum*); **~vertretung** *f siehe* **~rat**; **~vorstand** *m* ≃ aldermen *pl*; **~vorsteher** *m* head of the district council; (*Bürgermeister*) mayor; **~wahl** *f* local election; **~zentrum** *nt* community centre; (*Eccl*) parish rooms *pl*; (*von Freikirchen*) church rooms *pl*; (*katholisch*) parish house.
Gemein|eigentum *nt* common property.
Gemeine(r) *m decl as adj* (a) (*dated: Soldat*) common soldier ◆ **die ~n** the ranks. (b) (*Typ*) lower-case letter ◆ **in ~n** in lower case.
Gemein-: **g~gefährlich** *adj* constituting a public danger; **ein g~gefährlicher Verbrecher** a dangerous criminal; **g~gefährlich handeln** to endanger the public safety; **~gefährlichkeit** *f* danger to the public; **~geist** *m* public spirit; **g~gültig** *adj siehe* **allgemeingültig**; **~gut** *nt* (*lit, fig*) common property; **Schumanns Lieder gehören zum ~gut der Deutschen** Schumann's Lieder are part of the German heritage.
Gemeinheit *f* (a) *no pl* (*Niedertracht*) meanness; (*Roheit, Unverschämtheit auch*) nastiness. (b) *no pl* (*Vulgarität*) vulgarity; (*von Bemerkung, Witz auch*) coarseness. (c) (*Tat*) mean *or* dirty trick; (*Behandlung*) nasty treatment *no pl*; (*Worte*) mean thing ◆ **das war eine ~** that was a mean thing to do/say. (d) (*inf: ärgerlicher Umstand*) (blasted *inf*) nuisance.
Gemein-: **g~hin** *adv* generally; **~kosten** *pl* overheads *pl*, over head costs *pl*; **~nutz** *m* public *or* common good; **~nutz geht vor Eigennutz** (*dated prov*) service before self (*Prov*); **g~nützig** *adj* of benefit to the public *pred*; (*wohltätig*) charitable; **g~nütziger Verein** charitable *or* non-profit-making organization; **g~nützige Einrichtung** public utility; **Schulen und Parkanlagen sind g~nützige Einrichtungen** schools and parks are for the benefit of the public; **~nützigkeit** *f* benefit to the public; **die ~nützigkeit einer Organisation** the charitable status of an organization; **~platz** *m* commonplace.
gemeinsam [1] *adj* (*mehreren gehörend*) *Eigenschaft, Interesse, Zwecke, Politik* common; *Konto* joint; *Freund* mutual; (*von mehreren unternommen*) *Aktion, Ausflug* joint ◆ **sie haben vieles ~, ihnen ist vieles ~** they have a great deal in common; **die Firma ist ~es Eigentum** *or* **das ~e Eigentum der beiden Brüder** the firm belongs jointly to *or* is the joint property of the two brothers; **unser ~es Leben** our life together; **der G~e Markt** the Common Market; **mit jdm ~e Sache machen** to make common cause with sb; **er betonte das G~e** he stressed all that we/they had in common.
[2] *adv* together ◆ **etw ~ haben** to have sth in common; **es gehört den beiden ~** it belongs jointly to the two of them.
Gemeinsamkeit *f* (a) (*gemeinsame Interessen, Eigenschaft etc*) common ground *no pl* ◆ **die ~en zwischen ihnen sind sehr groß** they have a great deal in common.
(b) *no pl* (*gemeinsames Besitzen*) joint possession; (*von Freunden, Interessen*) mutuality ◆ **uns verbindet die ~ unserer Interessen** we are united by many common interests.
Gemeinschaft *f* community; (*Gruppe*) group; (*Zusammensein*) company; (*Zusammengehörigkeitsgefühl*) sense of community ◆ **die ~ der neun** (*Pol*) the nine; **in ~ mit** jointly with, together with; **in ~ mit jdm leben** to live in close companionship with sb; **die ~ der Heiligen/der Gläubigen** the communion of saints/of the faithful; **eheliche ~** (*Jur*) matrimony.
gemeinschaftlich *adj siehe* **gemeinsam**.
Gemeinschafts-: ⚠**~anschluß** *m* (*Telec*) party line; **~antenne** *f* block *or* party aerial *or* antenna (*esp US*); **~arbeit** *f* teamwork; **das Buch ist eine ~arbeit** the book is a team effort; (*von zwei Personen*) the book is a joint effort; **~aufgabe** *f* joint task; (*BRD: Aufgabe des Bundes*) federal project; **~beichte** *f* (*Eccl*) general confession; **g~bildend** *adj* community-building; (*einigend*) unifying; **~depot** *nt* (*Fin*) joint security deposit; **~ehe** *f* group *or* communal marriage; **~erziehung** *f* coeducation; (*soziale Erziehung*) social education; **~gefühl** *nt* sense of community; (*Uneigennützigkeit*) public-spiritedness; **~geist** *m* community spirit, esprit de corps; **~grab** *nt* communal grave; **~haft** *f* group confinement; **~küche** *f* (*Kantine*) canteen; (*gemeinsame Kochgelegenheit*) communal *or* (*kleiner*) shared kitchen; **~kunde** *f* social studies *pl*; **~leben** *nt* community life; **~leistung** *f* collective achievement; **~praxis** *f* joint practice; **~produktion** *f* (a) *siehe* **~arbeit**; (b) (*Rad, TV, Film*) co-production; **~raum** *m* common room; **g~schädigend** *adj Verhalten* antisocial; **~schule** *f* interdenominational school; **~sendung** *f* simultaneous broadcast; **~sinn** *m siehe* **~geist**; **~werbung** *f* joint advertising *no pl*; **~werbung machen** to advertise jointly, to run a joint advertisement; **~wohnung** *f* shared house/flat *etc*; **~zelle** *f* communal cell.
Gemein-: **~sinn** *m* public spirit; **~sprache** *f* standard language; **g~verständlich** *adj* generally comprehensible *no adv*; **sich g~verständlich ausdrücken** to make oneself generally understood; **wissenschaftliche Probleme g~verständlich darstellen** to present scientific problems in such a way that they are intelligible *or* comprehensible to the layman; **~werk** *nt* (*Sw*) voluntary work; **~wesen** *nt* community; (*Staat*) polity; **~wille** *m* collective will; **~wirtschaft** *f* co-operative economy; **g~wirtschaftlich** *adj* co-operative; **~wohl** *nt* public welfare; **das dient dem ~wohl** it is in the public interest.
Gemenge *nt* -s, - (a) (*Mischung*) mixture (*aus* of); (*Agr*) mixed crop; (*fig*) mixture; (*wirres Durcheinander*) jumble (*aus* of). (b) (*Gewühl*) bustle; (*Hand~*) scuffle ◆ **mit jdm ins ~ kommen** to come to blows with sb.
gemessen [1] *ptp of* **messen**.
[2] *adj* (a) (*würdevoll*) measured, studied ◆ **~en Schrittes** with measured tread. (b) (*dated: zurückhaltend*) reticent. (c) *attr* (*angemessen*) *Abstand, Entfernung* respectful.
Gemessenheit *f siehe adj* (a) measuredness, studiedness. (b) reticence. (c) respectfulness.
Gemetzel *nt* -s, - bloodbath; (*Massaker auch*) slaughter, massacre.
gemieden *ptp of* **meiden**.
Gemisch *nt* -(e)s, -e (a) (*lit, fig*) mixture (*aus* of). (b) *no pl* (*Durcheinander*) jumble (*aus* of).
gemischt *adj* mixed; (*inf: nicht sehr gut auch*) patchy ◆ **mit ~en Gefühlen** with mixed feelings.
Gemischt-: **g~rassig** *adj* of mixed race; (*mit mehreren Rassen*) multi-racial; **g~sprachig** *adj* multilingual; **~warenhandlung** *f* (*dated*) grocery and general store.

⚠: for details of spelling reform, see supplement

➤ SPRACHE AKTIV: **gemein: a → 32.5**

gemittelt *adj* standardized.
Gemme *f* -, -n (*erhaben*) cameo; (*vertieft*) intaglio.
gemocht *ptp of* **mögen.**
gemolken *ptp of* **melken.**
gemoppelt *adj siehe* **doppelt.**
Gemotze *nt* -s, *no pl* (*inf*) moaning, fault-finding.
Gems-: **~bart** *m siehe* **Gamsbart**; **~bock** *m* chamois buck.
⚠ **Gemse** *f* -, -n chamois.
Gemsleder *nt siehe* **Gamsleder.**
Gemunkel *nt* -s, *no pl* rumours; (*Klatsch*) gossip.
Gemurmel *nt* -s, *no pl* murmuring; (*unverständliches Reden auch*) mumbling ◆ **zustimmendes ~ ging durch den Saal** a murmur of approval ran through the hall.
Gemurre *nt* -s, *no pl* (*inf*) grumbling (*inf*).
Gemüse *nt* -s, (*rare*) - vegetables *pl* ◆ **frisches ~** fresh vegetables; **ein ~** a vegetable; **junges ~** (*hum inf*) whippersnappers *pl* (*inf*), green young things *pl* (*inf*).
Gemüse-: **~(an)bau** *m* vegetable-growing; (*für den Handel*) market gardening (*Brit*), truck farming (*US*); **~beet** *nt* vegetable bed *or* patch; **~beilage** *f* vegetables *pl*; **~beilage nach Wunsch** a choice of vegetables; **~eintopf** *m* vegetable stew; **~fach** *nt* vegetable compartment; **~frau** *f* (*inf*) vegetable woman (*inf*); **~fritze** *m* -n, -n (*inf*) vegetable seller; **~garten** *m* vegetable *or* kitchen garden; **quer durch den ~garten** (*hum inf*) a real assortment; **in dem Geschäft dort gibt es alles quer durch den ~garten** they have everything but the kitchen sink in that shop there (*inf*); **~händler** *m* greengrocer; (*Großhändler*) vegetable supplier; **~handlung** *f* greengrocer's (shop); **~konserve** *f* tinned (*Brit*) *or* canned vegetables *pl*; (*in Gläsern*) preserved vegetables *pl*; **~laden** *m* greengrocer's (shop); **~markt** *m* vegetable market; **~pflanze** *f* vegetable; **~platte** *f* (*Cook*) **eine ~platte** assorted vegetables *pl*; **~saft** *m* vegetable juice; **~sorte** *f* kind *or* type of vegetable; **~suppe** *f* vegetable soup.
gemüßigt *adv siehe* **bemüßigt.**
⚠ **gemußt** *ptp of* **müssen.**
gemustert *adj* patterned.
Gemüt *nt* -(e)s, -er (a) (*Geist*) mind; (*Charakter*) nature, disposition; (*Seele*) soul; (*Gefühl*) feeling; (*Gutmütigkeit*) warm-heartedness ◆ **viel ~ haben** to be very warm-hearted; **die Menschen hatten damals mehr ~** people had more soul in those days; **das denkst du (dir) so einfach in deinem kindlichen ~!** that's what you think in your innocence; **etwas fürs ~** (*hum*) something for the soul; (*Film, Buch etc*) something sentimental; **jds ~ bewegen** (*liter*) to stir sb's heart *or* emotions; **sich** (*dat*) **etw zu ~e führen** (*beherzigen*) to take sth to heart; (*hum inf*) *Glas Wein, Speise, Buch etc* to indulge in sth; **das ist ihr aufs ~ geschlagen** that made her worry her heart out.
(b) (*fig: Mensch*) person; (*pl*) people ◆ **sie ist ein ängstliches ~** she's a nervous soul, she has a nervous disposition; **die ~er erregen** to cause a stir; **wir müssen warten, bis sich die ~er beruhigt haben** we must wait until feelings have cooled down.
gemütlich *adj* (a) (*bequem, behaglich*) comfortable, comfy (*inf*); (*freundlich*) friendly *no adv*; (*zwanglos*) informal; (*klein und intim*) cosy, snug; *Schwatz, Beisammensein etc* cosy ◆ **wir verbrachten einen ~en Abend** we spent a very pleasant evening; **es sich/jdm ~ machen** to make oneself/sb comfortable.
(b) *Mensch* good-natured, pleasant; (*leutselig*) approachable, friendly; (*gelassen*) easy-going *no adv*, relaxed *no adv*.
(c) (*gemächlich*) unhurried, leisurely *no adv* ◆ **in ~em Tempo** at a comfortable *or* leisurely speed; **er arbeitete ~ vor sich hin** he worked away at a leisurely pace *or* unhurriedly.
Gemütlichkeit *f siehe adj* (a) comfortableness; friendliness; informality; cosiness, snugness.
(b) good-naturedness, pleasantness; approachability, friendliness; easy-going nature ◆ **da hört doch die ~ auf!** (*inf*) that's going too far; **da hört bei mir die ~ auf** I won't stand for that; **ein Prosit der ~!** happy days!
(c) unhurriedness, leisure ◆ **in aller ~** at one's leisure; **ihr sitzt da in aller ~, und ich arbeite wie ein Verrückter** you sit there as though there were all the time in the world and I'm working like mad.
Gemüts-: **g~arm** *adj* emotionally impoverished; **~armut** *f* emotional impoverishment; **~art** *f* disposition, nature; **ein Mensch von heiterer ~art** a person of cheerful disposition *or* nature; **~bewegung** *f* emotion; **bist du zu keiner ~bewegung fähig?** can't you show some emotion?; **g~kalt** *adj* cold; **g~krank** *adj* emotionally disturbed; **~kranke(r)** *mf* emotionally disturbed person; **~krankheit** *f* emotional disorder *or* disturbance; **~krüppel** *m* (*inf*) emotional cripple; **~lage** *f* mood; **je nach ~lage** as the mood takes me/him *etc*; **~leben** *nt* emotional life; **~leiden** *nt siehe* **~krankheit**; **~mensch** *m* good-natured, phlegmatic person; **du bist vielleicht ein ~mensch!** (*iro inf*) you're a fine one! (*inf*); (*das ist unmöglich*) you'll be lucky! (*inf*); **~regung** *f siehe* **~bewegung**; **~ruhe** *f* calmness; (*Kaltblütigkeit*) sang-froid, composure, coolness; (*Phlegma*) placidness; **in aller ~ruhe** (*inf*) (as) cool as a cucumber (*inf*) *or* as you please (*inf*); (*gemächlich*) at a leisurely pace; (*aufreizend langsam*) as if there were all the time in the world; **du hast eine ~ruhe!** you take everything so calmly; **deine ~ruhe möchte ich haben!** (*iro*) I like your cool! (*inf*); **~verfassung** *f*, **~zustand** *m* frame *or* state of mind.
gemütvoll *adj* sentimental; (*warmherzig*) warm-hearted.
gen *prep +acc* (*old, liter*) towards, toward ◆ **~ Norden/Osten** *etc* northwards/eastwards *etc*; **~ Himmel blicken** to look up to the sky, to look heavenwards; *siehe* **gegen.**

Gen *nt* -s, -e gene.
genannt *ptp of* **nennen.**
genant [ʒe'nant] *adj* (*dated*) (*schüchtern*) bashful, shy; (*peinlich*) embarrassing.
genarbt *adj Leder* grained.
genas *pret of* **genesen.**
Genäsel *nt* -s, *no pl* nasal voice.
▼ **genau** [1] *adj* exact; (*richtig auch*) accurate; (*präzis auch*) precise; (*sorgfältig auch*) meticulous; (*förmlich ~ auch*) punctilious ◆ **haben Sie die ~e Zeit?** have you got the right *or* exact time?; **G~eres** further details *pl or* particulars *pl*; **G~eres weiß ich nicht** I don't know any more than that; **man weiß nichts G~es über ihn** no-one knows anything definite about him.
▼ [2] *adv* **~!** (*inf*) exactly!, precisely!, quite!; **~ dasselbe** just *or* exactly the same; **~ das Gegenteil** just *or* exactly the opposite; **~ in der Mitte** right in the middle; **~ das wollte ich sagen** that's just *or* exactly what I wanted to say; **ich kenne ihn ~** I know just *or* exactly what he's like; **etw ~ wissen** to know sth for certain *or* for sure; **etw ~ nehmen** to take sth seriously; **er nimmt es sehr/nicht sehr ~** he's very/not very particular (*mit etw* about sth); **einen Entschluß ~ überlegen** to think a decision over very carefully; **meine Uhr geht ~** my watch keeps accurate time; **es stimmt auf den Millimeter ~** it's right to the millimetre; **die Schuhe paßten mir ~/nicht ganz ~** the shoes fitted me perfectly/didn't quite fit me; **das reicht ~** that's just enough; **~estens, aufs ~este** (right) down to the last (little) detail; **~ entgegengesetzt** diametrically opposed; **~ auf die Minute** dead (*inf*) *or* exactly on time; **so ~ wollte ich es (nun auch wieder) nicht wissen!** (*iro*) you can spare me the details; *siehe* **Wahrheit.**
⚠ **genaugenommen** *adv* strictly speaking.
Genauigkeit *f siehe adj* exactness, exactitude (*form*); accuracy; precision; meticulousness; punctiliousness.
genauso *adv* (*vor Adjektiv*) just as; (*alleinstehend*) just *or* exactly the same.
⚠ **genauso-** *siehe* **ebenso-.**
Gen-Bank *f* gene bank.
Gendarm [ʒan'darm, ʒã'd-] *m* -en, -en (*old, Aus*) gendarme.
Gendarmerie [ʒandarmə'ri:, ʒãd-] *f* (*old, Aus*) gendarmerie.
Genealoge *m*, **Genealogin** *f* genealogist.
Genealogie *f* genealogy.
genealogisch *adj* genealogical.
genehm *adj* (*geh*) suitable, acceptable ◆ **jdm ~ sein** to suit sb; **ist es so ~?** is that agreeable *or* acceptable to you?; **wenn es ~ ist** if you are agreeable.
genehmigen* *vt Baupläne, Antrag, Veränderungen* to approve; (*erlauben*) to sanction; (*Lizenz erteilen*) to license; *Durchreise, Aufenthalt* to authorize; (*zugestehen*) to grant; *Bitte auch* to agree to, to assent to ◆ **wer kann mir den Urlaub ~?** from whom do I get permission for my holiday?; **„genehmigt"** "approved"; (*inf*) permission granted (*hum*); **sich** (*dat*) **etw ~** to indulge in sth; (*kaufen*) to lash *or* splash out on sth; **sich** (*dat*) **einen ~** (*hum inf*) to have a little drink.
Genehmigung *f siehe vt* (a) (*das Genehmigen*) approval; sanctioning; licensing; authorization; granting. (b) (*Erlaubnis*) approval; sanction; licence; authorization; agreement (*gen* to), assent (*gen* to); (*Berechtigungsschein*) permit ◆ **mit freundlicher ~ von** by kind permission of.
Genehmigungs-: **~pflicht** *f* (*form*) licence requirement; **g~pflichtig** *adj* (*form*) requiring official approval; (*mit Visum, Stempel, Marke*) requiring official authorization; (*mit schriftlicher Genehmigung*) requiring a licence; **Radiosender sind g~pflichtig** a licence is required for radio transmitters.
geneigt *adj* (*geh*) *Zuhörer, Publikum* willing; *Aufmerksamkeit* kind; (*obs: huldvoll*) gracious ◆ **~er Leser!** gentle reader; **jdm/einer Sache ~ sein** to be well-disposed *or* favourably disposed to sb/sth; **zu etw ~ sein/~ sein, etw zu tun** to be inclined to do sth; **nicht ~ sein, etw zu tun** not to be inclined to do sth; *siehe* **Ohr.**
Geneigtheit *f* (*Bereitwilligkeit*) inclination; (*Wohlwollen*) goodwill (*gegenüber* towards); (*Huld*) favour (*gegenüber* to).
Genera *pl of* **Genus.**
General *m* -(e)s, -e *or* ¨-e (a) (*Mil, Eccl*) general ◆ **Herr ~** General. (b) (*inf: ~direktor*) head.
General-: **≈absolution** *f* general absolution; **≈agent** *m* general agent; **≈agentur** *f* general agency; **≈amnestie** *f* general amnesty; **≈angriff** *m* (*Mil, fig*) general attack; ⚠ **≈baß** *m* (basso) continuo; **≈beichte** *f* general confession; **≈bevollmächtigte(r)** *mf* plenipotentiary; (*Comm*) general representative; **~bundesanwalt** *m* (*BRD*) Chief Federal Prosecutor; **≈direktion** *f* head office; **≈direktor** *m* chairman, president (*US*); **~feldmarschall** *m* field marshal, general of the army (*US*); **≈gouverneur** *m* governor-general.
Generalin *f siehe* **General.**
General-: **~inspekteur** *m* (*BRD*) inspector general; **~intendant** *m* (*Theat, Mus*) director.
generalisieren* *vi* to generalize.
Generalisierung *f* generalization.
Generalissimus *m* -, **Generalissimi** *or* -se generalissimo.
Generalist *m* generalist.
Generalität *f* (*Mil*) generals *pl*.
General-: **≈klausel** *f* general *or* blanket clause; **≈konsul** *m* consul general; **≈konsulat** *nt* consulate general; **≈leutnant** *m* lieutenant general, major general (*US*); (*Brit Aviat*) air marshal; **≈major** *m* major general, brigadier-general (*US*); (*Brit Aviat*) air vice-marshal; **≈musikdirektor** *m* (chief) musical director; **≈nenner** *m siehe* **Hauptnenner**; **≈obere(r)** *m* (*Eccl*) gen-

eral (*of a religious order*); **≈oberst** *m* (*DDR*) senior general; **≈prävention** *f* (*Jur*) general deterrence; **≈probe** *f* (*Theat, fig*) dress rehearsal; (*Mus*) final rehearsal; **≈repräsentanz** *f* (*esp Aus*) sole *or* exclusive agency *or* distribution; **≈sekretär** *m* secretary-general; **~staatsanwalt** *m public prosecutor for a provincial court,* ≃ district attorney (*US*); **≈stab** *m* general staff; **≈stabskarte** *f* Ordnance Survey map (on the scale 1:100,000); **g~stabsmäßig** [1] *adj Aktion* planned with military precision; [2] *adv planen, organisieren* with military precision; **≈stabsoffizier** *m* general staff officer; **≈streik** *m* general strike; **≈synode** *f* general synod; **g≈überholen*** *vt infin and ptp only* **etw g~überholen** to give sth a general overhaul; **etw g~überholen lassen** to have sth generally overhauled; **≈überholung** *f* complete overhaul; **≈versammlung** *f* general meeting; **≈vertreter** *m* general representative; **≈vertretung** *f* sole agency; **≈vikar** *m* vicar-general; **≈vollmacht** *f* general *or* full power of attorney.

Generation *f* generation ◆ **ein technisches Gerät der ersten ~** a piece of first-generation technology.

Generationen-: ~konflikt *m* generation gap; **g~lang** [1] *adj* age-long; [2] *adv* for generations; **~vertrag** *m* (*Econ*) *system whereby old people receive a pension from their children.*

Generations-: ~konflikt *m siehe* **Generationenkonflikt**; **~problem** *nt* problem of one generation; **ein ~problem der Jugend** a problem of the younger generation; **~wechsel** *m* (*Biol*) alternation of generations; **wir brauchen einen ~wechsel in der Regierung** we need a new generation in government.

generativ *adj* generative ◆ **~e Zellen** reproductive cells; **~e (Transformations)grammatik** (transformational) generative grammar.

Generator *m* generator; (*Gas~ auch*) producer.

Generatorgas *nt* producer gas.

generell *adj* general ◆ **~ kann man sagen, daß** ... generally *or* in general one can say that ...

generieren* *vt* (*Ling, geh*) to generate.

Generikum *nt* **-s, Generika** generic drug.

generös *adj* (*geh*) generous; (*freigebig auch*) munificent (*liter*).

Generosität *f* (*geh*) *siehe adj* generosity; munificence (*liter*).

Genese *f* **-, -n** (*Biol, fig*) genesis.

genesen *pret* **genas,** *ptp* **~** *vi aux sein* (*geh*) to convalesce; (*fig*) to recuperate.

Genesende(r) *mf decl as adj* convalescent.

Genesis *f* **-,** *no pl* genesis ◆ **die ~** (*Bibl*) (the Book of) Genesis.

Genesung *f* convalescence, recovery (*auch fig*) ◆ **auf dem Wege der ~** on the road to recovery; **ich wünsche baldige ~** I wish you a speedy recovery; **er fuhr zur ~ ins Sanatorium** he went into a sanatorium to convalesce.

Genesungs-: ~heim *nt* (*dated*) convalescent home; ⚠**~prozeß** *m* convalescence; **der ~prozeß hat sich verzögert** his *etc* convalescence was protracted; **~urlaub** *m* convalescent leave.

Genetik *f* genetics *sing.*

Genetiker(in *f*) *m* **-s, -** geneticist.

genetisch *adj* genetic.

Genezareth: der See ~ the Sea of Galilee.

Genf *nt* **-s** Geneva.

Genfer(in *f*) *m* **-s, -** Genevan, native *or* (*Einwohner*) inhabitant of Geneva.

Genfer *adj attr* Genevan ◆ **der ~ See** Lake Geneva, Lake Leman; **~ Konvention** Geneva Convention.

Gen-: ~forscher *m* genetic researcher; **~forschung** *f* genetic research.

genial *adj Entdeckung, Einfall, Mensch* brilliant; *Künstler, Stil auch* inspired; (*erfinderisch*) ingenious ◆ **ein ~er Mensch, ein G~er** a genius; **ein ~es Werk** a work of genius; **das war eine ~e Idee** that idea was *or* showed a stroke of genius.

genialisch *adj* (*geh*) brilliant; (*unkonventionell*) eccentric.

Genialität *f* genius; (*Erfindungsreichtum*) ingenuity.

Genick *nt* **-(e)s, -e** neck ◆ **jdn am ~ packen** to grab sb by the scruff of the neck; **ein Schlag ins ~** a blow on the back of the neck; **seinen Hut ins ~ schieben** to push one's hat back (on one's head); **sich** (*dat*) **das ~ brechen** to break one's neck; (*fig*) to kill oneself; **jdm/einer Sache das ~ brechen** (*fig*) to finish sb/sth.

Genick-: ⚠**~schuß** *m* shot in the neck; **~starre** *f* stiffness of the neck; (*Med*) (cerebral) meningitis; **~starre haben** (*inf*) to have a stiff neck.

Genie[1] [ʒe'ni:] *nt* **-s, -s** genius ◆ **er ist ein ~** he's a (man of) genius; **er ist ein ~ im Taktieren** he's a genius when it comes to tactics, he has a genius for tactics.

Genie[2] *f* (*Sw Mil*) *siehe* **Genietruppe.**

Genien ['ge:niən] *pl of* **Genius.**

genieren* [ʒe'ni:rən] [1] *vr* to be embarrassed ◆ **sich vor Fremden ~** to be shy of *or* with strangers; **~ Sie sich nicht!** don't be shy!; **dabei geniere ich mich** I get embarrassed doing it; **ich geniere mich, das zu sagen** I don't like to say it; **er genierte sich (gar) nicht, das zu tun** it didn't bother him (at all) to do that.

[2] *vt* **jdn ~** (*peinlich berühren*) to embarrass sb; (*old, dial: stören*) to bother *or* disturb sb; **das geniert mich wenig!** that doesn't bother *or* worry me.

genierlich [ʒe'ni:ɐlɪç] *adj* (**a**) (*inf: lästig*) bothersome; (*genant*) embarrassing. (**b**) (*dated: schüchtern*) shy, bashful.

geniert [ʒe'ni:ɐt] [1] *ptp of* **genieren.**
[2] *adj* embarrassed.
[3] *adv* with embarrassment.

genießbar *adj* (*eßbar*) edible; (*trinkbar*) drinkable; (*fig: annehmbar*) acceptable ◆ **er ist heute nicht ~** (*fig inf*) he is unbearable today.

genießen *pret* **genoß,** *ptp* **genossen** *vt* (**a**) (*lit, fig: sich erfreuen an*) to enjoy ◆ **den Wein muß man ~** you must savour the wine; **er ist heute nicht zu ~** (*inf*) he is unbearable today.

(**b**) (*essen*) to eat; (*trinken*) to drink ◆ **das Essen/der Wein ist kaum zu ~** the meal/wine is scarcely edible/drinkable; *siehe* **Vorsicht, Kavalier.**

Genießer(in *f*) *m* **-s, -** connoisseur; (*des Lebens*) pleasure-lover; (*Feinschmecker*) gourmet, epicure ◆ **er ist ein richtiger/stiller ~** he really knows how to enjoy life/he really knows how to enjoy life in his quiet way.

genießerisch [1] *adj* appreciative ◆ **sein ~er Ausdruck** his expression of pleasure.
[2] *adv* appreciatively; (*mit Behagen*) pleasurably ◆ **~ schmatzte er mit den Lippen** he smacked his lips with relish; **~ zog er an seiner Zigarre** he puffed at his cigar with relish.

Genie- [ʒe'ni:]: **~streich** *m* stroke of genius; **~truppe** *f* (*Sw Mil*) engineer corps.

genital *adj* genital.

Genital- *in cpds* genital.

Genitale *nt* **-s, Genitalien** [-iən] genital ◆ **die Genitalien** the genitals *or* genitalia (*form*).

Genitiv *m* (*Fall*) genitive (case); (*Form*) genitive (form) ◆ **im ~** in the genitive.

Genitiv|objekt *nt* genitive object.

Genius *m* **-, Genien** ['ge:niən] (**a**) (*Myth*) genius, guardian spirit. (**b**) (*Genie*) genius ◆ **~ loci** (*geh*) genius loci. (**c**) (*Art*) genius.

Genmanipulation *f* genetic manipulation.

Genmutation *f* gene mutation.

Genom *nt* **-s, -e** genome.

Genomanalyse *f* genome analysis.

genommen *ptp of* **nehmen.**

genoppt *adj Teppich, Stoff, Wolle* nubbly; *Gummi* pimpled.

Genörgel *nt* **-s,** *no pl* (*inf*) moaning, grumbling, carping.

⚠**genoß** *pret of* **genießen.**

Genosse *m* **-n, -n** comrade; (*dated: Gefährte auch*) companion; (*Mitglied einer Genossenschaft*) member of a co-operative; (*pej: Kumpan*) mate (*Brit inf*), buddy (*US inf*), pal (*inf*) ◆ **X und ~n** (*Jur*) X and others; (*pej*) X and co (*inf*).

genossen *ptp of* **genießen.**

Genossen-: ~schaft *f* co-operative; **~schaft(l)er(in** *f*) *m* **-s, -** member of a co-operative; **g~schaftlich** *adj* co-operative; **g~schaftlich organisiert** organized as a co-operative.

Genossenschafts-: ~bank *f* co-operative bank; **~bauer** *m* co-operative farmer; **~betrieb** *m* co-operative; **~wesen** *nt* co-operative system.

Genossin *f siehe* **Genosse.**

genötigt *adj* **~ sein, etw zu tun** to be forced *or* obliged to do sth; **sich ~ sehen, etw zu tun** to feel (oneself) obliged to do sth.

Geno-: g~typisch *adj* genotypic; **~typ(us)** *m* genotype; **~zid** *m or nt* **-(e)s, -e** *or* **-ien** [-iən] (*geh*) genocide.

Genre [ʒã:ɐ, 'ʒã:rə] *nt* **-s, -s** genre.

Genre-: ~bild *nt* genre picture; **~malerei** *f* genre painting.

Gent *nt* **-s** Ghent.

Gen-: ~technik *f* genetic engineering; **~techniker** *m* genetic engineer; **g~technisch** *adj Fortschritte etc* in genetic engineering; **einen Stoff g~technisch produzieren** to produce a substance by means of genetic engineering; **~technologie** *f* genetic engineering; **g~technologisch** *adj Verfahren, Zeitalter* of genetic engineering; **~therapie** *f* gene therapy; **~transfer** *m* genetic transfer.

Genua *nt* **-s** Genoa.

Genuese [genu'e:zə] *m* **-n, -n, Genueser(in** *f*) *m* **-s, -** Genoese.

genuesisch [genu'e:zɪʃ] *adj* Genoese.

genug *adj inv* enough ◆ **~ Platz, Platz ~** enough *or* sufficient room; **groß/alt/reich ~** big/old/rich enough; **~ davon** enough of that; **~ der vielen Worte!** enough of words!; **danke, das ist ~** that's enough, thank you; **das ist wenig ~** that's precious little; **und damit noch nicht ~** and that's not/that wasn't all; **sie sind jetzt ~, um** ... there are enough of them now to ...; **sag, wenn's ~ ist!** (*beim Einschenken etc*) say when!; **jetzt ist('s) aber ~!** that's enough, that does it!; **(von etw) ~ haben** to have (got) enough (of sth); (*überdrüssig sein*) to have had enough (of sth); **er kann nicht ~ bekommen** *or* **kriegen** he can't get enough; **nicht ~, daß er sein ganzes Geld verspielt, außerdem ... er** ... not only does he gamble away all his money, he also ...; **er konnte sich nicht ~ darin tun, ihre Gastfreundschaft zu loben** (*geh*) he could not praise her hospitality enough *or* sufficiently; **sich** (*dat*) **selbst ~ sein** to be sufficient unto oneself; (*gern allein sein*) to be content with one's own company; **Manns ~ sein, um zu** ... to be man enough to ...

Genüge *f* **-,** *no pl* **zur ~** enough; **das habe ich zur ~ getan/gehört/gesehen** I have done/heard/seen it often enough *or* (*stärker, abwertend*) quite often enough; **etw zur ~ kennen** to know sth well enough; (*abwertender*) to know sth only too well, to be only too familiar with sth; **jdm ~ tun** (*geh*) to satisfy sb; **jds Forderungen** (*dat*) **~ tun** (*geh*) to satisfy *or* meet sb's demands; **jds Erwartungen** (*dat*) **~ tun** (*geh*) (*dat*) to fulfil sb's expectations.

genügen* *vi* (**a**) (*ausreichen*) to be enough *or* sufficient (*dat* for) ◆ **das genügt (mir)** that's enough *or* sufficient (for me), that will do (for me); **diese Wohnung genügt uns/für uns** we're happy with this flat/this flat is enough for us.

(**b**) +*dat* (*befriedigen, gerecht werden*) *den Anforderungen* to satisfy; *jds Wünschen, Erwartungen, den Anforderungen* to fulfil.

genügend [1] *adj* (**a**) *inv* (*ausreichend*) enough, sufficient. (**b**) (*befriedigend*)

➤ SPRACHE AKTIV: **Genesung** → 50.4

satisfactory.

2 *adv* (*reichlich*) enough, sufficiently ♦ **ich habe ~ oft versucht, zu ...** I have tried often enough *or* sufficiently often to ...

genugsam *adv* (*geh*) enough ♦ **es ist ~ bekannt** it is sufficiently well-known.

genügsam *adj* (*anspruchslos*) *Tier, Pflanze* undemanding; *Mensch auch* modest ♦ **~ leben, ein ~es Leben führen** to live modestly.

Genügsamkeit *f siehe adj* simple needs *pl*; undemandingness; modesty ♦ **die ~ einer Pflanze/eines Tieres** the modest requirements of a plant/an animal.

genugtun *vi sep irreg +dat* (*dated*) to satisfy ♦ **er konnte sich** (*dat*) **nicht ~, ihre Schönheit zu preisen** he couldn't praise her beauty enough, he never tired of praising her beauty.

Genugtuung *f* satisfaction (*über +acc* at) ♦ **für etw ~ leisten** to make amends for sth; **~ verlangen** *or* **fordern** to demand satisfaction; **ich hörte mit ~, daß ...** it gave me great satisfaction to hear that ...; **das hat mir ~ verschafft** that gave me a sense of satisfaction.

genuin *adj* (*geh*) genuine.

Genus *nt* **-, Genera** (a) (*Biol*) genus. (b) (*Gram*) gender ♦ **~ verbi** voice of the verb.

⚠**Genuß** *m* **-sses, ¨sse** (a) *no pl* (*das Zusichnehmen*) consumption; (*von Drogen*) taking, use; (*von Tabak*) smoking ♦ **der ~ von Alkohol ist Kindern verboten** children are forbidden to drink *or* consume (*form*) alcohol; **der übermäßige ~ von Tabak ist gesundheitsschädlich** excessive smoking is injurious to one's health; **nach dem ~ der Pilze** after eating the mushrooms.

(b) (*Vergnügen*) pleasure ♦ **die ¨sse des Lebens** the pleasures *or* joys of life; **etw mit ~ essen** to eat sth with relish; **den Wein hat er mit ~ getrunken** he really enjoyed the wine.

(c) *no pl* (*Nutznießung*) **in den ~ von etw kommen** (*von Vergünstigungen*) to enjoy sth; (*von Rente, Prämie etc*) to be in receipt of sth.

⚠**Genuß-: g~freudig** *adj* (*geh*) pleasure-loving *no adv*; **~gift** *nt* (*form*) social drug.

⚠**genüßlich** *adj* pleasurable ♦ **er grunzte ~** he grunted with obvious enjoyment; **er schmatzte ~** he smacked his lips with relish.

⚠**Genuß-: ~mensch** *m* hedonist; (*auf Essen und Trinken bezogen*) bon-vivant; **~mittel** *nt semi-luxury foods and tobacco*; **g~reich** *adj* enjoyable; **~schein** *m* (*Fin*) profit-participation certificate; **~sucht** *f* hedonism; **g~süchtig** *adj* hedonistic; **g~voll** *adj Aufenthalt, Urlaub, Erlebnis, Abend* delightful; *Schmatzen* appreciative; *Lächeln* gratified; **g~voll rekelte er sich vor dem warmen Feuer** he sprawled in front of the fire with obvious enjoyment.

Geodäsie *f* geodesy, geodetics *sing*.

Geodät(in *f*) *m* **-en, -en** geodesist.

Geo-Dreieck *nt* (*inf*) set square.

⚠**Geograph(in** *f*) *m* geographer.

⚠**Geographie** *f* geography.

⚠**geographisch** *adj no pred* geographic(al).

Geologe *m*, **Geologin** *f* geologist.

Geologie *f* geology.

geologisch *adj no pred* geological.

Geometer *m* **-s, -** (a) surveyor. (b) (*old*) geometrician.

Geometrie *f* geometry.

geometrisch *adj* geometric ♦ **~er Ort** locus.

Geomorphologie *f* geomorphology.

Geophysik *f* geophysics *sing*.

Geopolitik *f* geopolitics *pl or* (*Fach*) *sing*.

geopolitisch *adj no pred* geopolitical.

geordnet *adj Leben, Zustände* well-ordered ♦ **in ~en Verhältnissen leben** to live a well-ordered life; **Kinder aus ~en Verhältnissen** children from well-ordered backgrounds; **~e Verhältnisse schaffen** to put things on an orderly basis.

Georgette [ʒɔr'ʒɛt] *f* **-, -s**, *or nt* **-s, -s** georgette.

Georgien [ge'ɔrgiən] *nt* **-s** Georgia (*in Caucasia*).

Georgier(in *f*) [ge'ɔrgiɐ, -iərɪn] *m* **-s, -** Georgian.

georgisch *adj* Georgian.

Geo-: g~stationär *adj* geostationary; **g~strategisch** *adj* geostrategic; **~wissenschaft** *f* earth science; **g~zentrisch** *adj* geocentric.

Gepäck *nt* **-(e)s** *no pl* luggage *no pl* (*Brit*), baggage *no pl*; (*Mil: Marsch~*) baggage; (*von Soldat, Pfadfinder etc*) kit; (*von Bergsteiger*) pack ♦ **mit leichtem ~ reisen** to travel light.

Gepäck-, Gepäcks- (*Aus*): **~abfertigung** *f* (*Vorgang*) (*am Bahnhof*) luggage *or* baggage processing; (*am Flughafen*) checking-in of luggage *or* baggage; (*Stelle*) (*am Bahnhof*) luggage *or* baggage office; (*am Flughafen*) luggage *or* baggage check-in; **~ablage** *f* luggage *or* baggage rack; **~annahme** *f* (*Vorgang*) checking-in of luggage *or* baggage; (*auch* **~annahmestelle**) (*am Bahnhof*) (*zur Beförderung*) (in-counter of the) luggage *or* baggage office; (*zur Aufbewahrung*) (in-counter of the) left-luggage office (*Brit*) *or* baggage checkroom (*US*); (*am Flughafen*) luggage *or* baggage check-in; **~aufbewahrung** *f* (*das Aufbewahren*) looking after left luggage *no art*; (*auch* **~aufbewahrungsstelle**) left-luggage office (*Brit*), baggage checkroom (*US*); **~aufbewahrungsschein** *m* left-luggage ticket (*Brit*), check number (*US*); **~aufkleber** *m* luggage *or* baggage sticker; **~ausgabe** *f* (*auch* **~ausgabestelle**) (*am Bahnhof*) (*zur Beförderung*) (out-counter of the) luggage *or* baggage office; (*zur Aufbewahrung*) (out-counter of the) left-luggage office (*Brit*) *or* baggage checkroom (*US*); (*am Flughafen*) luggage *or* baggage reclaim; **wir müssen noch zur ~ausgabe** we still have to collect our luggage; **~band** *nt* luggage *or* baggage conveyor belt; **~karren** *m* luggage *or* baggage trolley; **~kontrolle** *f* luggage *or* baggage control *or* check; **~marsch** *m* (*Mil*) pack march; **~netz** *nt* luggage *or* baggage rack; **~raum** *m* luggage *or* baggage hold; **~schalter** *m siehe* **~annahme**; **~schein** *m* luggage *or* baggage ticket; **~schließfach** *nt* luggage *or* baggage locker; **~stück** *nt* piece *or* item of luggage *or* baggage; **~träger** *m* (a) (*Person*) porter (*Brit*), baggage handler; (b) (*am Fahrrad*) carrier; **~versicherung** *f* luggage *or* baggage insurance; **~wagen** *m* luggage van, baggage car (*US*).

Gepard *m* **-s, -e** cheetah.

gepfeffert *adj* (*inf*) (*hoch*) *Preise, Mieten* steep; *Preise auch* fancy (*inf*); (*schwierig*) *Fragen, Prüfung* tough; (*hart*) *Kritik* biting; *Strafpredigt* tough; (*anzüglich*) *Witz, Geschichte* spicy.

Gepfeife *nt* **-s,** *no pl* whistling.

gepfiffen *ptp of* **pfeifen.**

gepflegt 1 *adj* (a) (*nicht vernachlässigt*) well looked after; *Garten auch* well-tended; *Hände, Parkanlagen auch* well-kept; *Mensch, Äußeres, Hund* well-groomed; *Aussehen* well-groomed, soigné (*liter*).

(b) (*inf: kultiviert, niveauvoll*) civilized; *Atmosphäre, Restaurant* sophisticated; *Ausdrucksweise, Gespräche* cultured; *Sprache, Stil* cultured, refined; (*angenehm*) *Abend* pleasant ♦ **ein ganz ~es Bad nehmen** to have a nice long bath.

(c) (*erstklassig*) *Speisen, Weine* excellent; (*inf: von guter Qualität*) decent ♦ **„~e Küche"** "excellent cuisine".

2 *adv* (a) (*kultiviert*) **sich ~ unterhalten** to have a civilized conversation; **sich ~ ausdrücken** to have a cultured way of speaking; **drück dich gefälligst ein bißchen ~er aus** don't be so crude; **sehr ~ wohnen** to live in style; **so richtig ~ essen gehen** (*inf*) to go to a really nice restaurant.

(b) (*inf: gut, gründlich*) **ganz ~ ausschlafen/sich ganz ~ ausruhen** to have a good long sleep/rest.

Gepflegtheit *f* (a) well-looked-after state ♦ **die ~ seines Aussehens** his well-groomed appearance.

(b) **die ~ ihrer Aussprache/ihres Stils** her refined *or* cultured accent/style.

gepflogen (*old*) *ptp of* **pflegen.**

Gepflogenheit *f* (*geh*) (*Gewohnheit*) habit; (*Verfahrensweise*) practice; (*Brauch*) custom, tradition.

Geplänkel *nt* **-s, -** skirmish; (*fig*) squabble.

Geplapper *nt* **-s,** *no pl* babbling; (*fig: Geschwätz auch*) chatter(ing).

Geplärr(e) *nt* **-(e)s,** *no pl* bawling; (*von Radio*) blaring.

Geplätscher *nt* **-s,** *no pl* splashing; (*pej inf: Unterhaltung*) babbling.

geplättet *adj pred* (*sl*) floored (*inf*) ♦ **ich bin ganz ~** (*inf*) I'm flabbergasted (*inf*).

Geplauder *nt* **-s,** *no pl* (*geh*) chatting.

Gepolter *nt* **-s,** *no pl* (*Krach*) din; (*an Tür etc*) banging, thudding; (*von Kutsche etc*) clattering; (*inf: Geschimpfe*) ranting ♦ **die Fässer fielen mit ~ die Treppe hinunter** the barrels went thudding down the stairs.

gepr. *abbr of* **geprüft.**

Gepräge *nt* **-s,** *no pl* (*auf Münzen*) strike; (*fig: Eigentümlichkeit*) character; (*Aura*) aura ♦ **das hat den 60er Jahren ihr ~ gegeben** *or* **verliehen** it has left its mark *or* stamp on the sixties.

Geprahle *nt* **-s,** *no pl* (*inf*) boasting, bragging.

Gepränge *nt* **-s,** *no pl* (*geh*) splendour, magnificence.

Geprassel *nt* **-s,** *no pl* clatter(ing), rattle, rattling; (*von Regen, Hagel*) drumming; (*von Feuer*) crackle, crackling.

gepriesen *ptp of* **preisen.**

gepuffert *adj* (*Comput*) buffered.

gepunktet *adj Linie* dotted; *Stoff, Kleid* spotted; (*regelmäßig*) polka-dot.

Gequake *nt* **-s,** *no pl* croaking; (*pej inf: Geschwätz*) chatter.

Gequäke *nt* **-s,** *no pl* (*inf*) (*von Kind*) whining; (*von Radio*) blaring.

gequält *adj Lächeln* forced; *Miene, Ausdruck* pained; *Gesang, Stimme* strained.

Gequassel *nt* **-s,** *no pl* (*pej inf*) chattering.

Gequatsche *nt* **-s,** *no pl* (*pej sl*) gabbing (*inf*); (*Blödsinn*) twaddle (*inf*).

Gequengel(e), Gequengle *nt* **-s,** *no pl* whining.

Gequieke *nt* **-s,** *no pl* squealing.

Gequietsche *nt* **-s,** *no pl* squeaking; (*von Reifen, Mensch*) squealing.

gequollen *ptp of* **quellen.**

Ger *m* **-(e)s, -e** (*old*) javelin *used by the ancient Germanic peoples*.

gerade, grade (*inf*) 1 *adj* straight; *Zahl* even; (*aufrecht*) *Haltung* upright; (*fig: aufrichtig*) *Charakter* honest; *Mensch* upright, upstanding ♦ **~ gewachsen sein** (*Mensch*) to be clean-limbed; (*Baum*) to be straight; **eine ~ Körperhaltung haben** to hold oneself up straight; **in ~r Linie von jdm abstammen** to be directly descended from sb; **seinen ~n Weg gehen** (*fig*) to maintain one's integrity; **jdn mit ~m und offenem Blick ansehen** to look sb straight in the face; **das ~ Gegenteil** the exact *or* very opposite, exactly *or* just the opposite; **~ sitzen/stehen** to sit up/stand up straight; *siehe* **fünf.**

2 *adv* (a) (*im Augenblick, soeben*) just ♦ **wenn Sie ~ Zeit haben** if you have time just now; **wo Sie ~ da sind** just while you're here; **er wollte ~ aufstehen** he was just about to get up; **der Zug war ~ weg** the train had just gone; **~ erst** only just; **da wir ~ von Geld sprechen, ...** talking of money ...; **es macht uns ~ so viel Spaß** we're just enjoying it so much.

(b) (*knapp*) just ♦ **~ so viel, daß er davon leben kann** just enough for him to live on; **sie hat die Prüfung ~ so bestanden** she just about passed the exam; **~ noch** only just; **~ noch zur rechten Zeit** just in time; **das hat ~ noch gefehlt!** (*iro*) that's all we wanted!

(c) (*genau*) just; (*direkt*) right ♦ **es ist ~ 8 Uhr** it's just 8 o'clock; **~ zur rechten Zeit** at just *or* exactly the right time, just at the right time; **~ heute hab' ich an dich gedacht** I was thinking of you just *or* only today; **jdm ~ in die Augen sehen** to look sb straight *or* right in the eyes; **~ deshalb** that's just *or* exactly

why; **~ umgekehrt** *or* **das Gegenteil** exactly *or* just the opposite; **das ist es ja ~!** that's just *or* exactly it!; **so ist es ~ richtig** that's just *or* exactly right.
(d) (*speziell, besonders*) especially ♦ **~, weil** ... just because ...; **~ du solltest dafür Verständnis haben** you should be particularly understanding; **sie ist nicht ~ eine Schönheit** she's not exactly a beauty; **das war nicht ~ schön/interessant** that wasn't particularly *or* exactly nice/interesting; **du kannst dich ~ beklagen** (*iro*) what are you complaining about?, you've got a lot to complain about (*iro*).
(e) (*ausgerechnet*) **warum ~ das?** why that of all things?; **warum ~ heute/ich?** why today of all days/me of all people?; **warum ~ im Winter/in Venedig?** why in winter of all times/in Venice of all places?; **~ diesem Trottel mußte ich begegnen** of all people I would have to meet that idiot.
(f) (*inf: erst recht*) **nun ~!** you try and stop me now! (*inf*); **jetzt** *or* **nun ~ nicht!** I'll be damned if I will! (*inf*).

Gerade *f* **-n, -n (a)** (*Math*) straight line. **(b)** (*Sport*) (*von Renn-, Laufbahn*) straight; (*beim Boxen*) straight left/right ♦ **seine rechte ~ traf ihn genau am Kinn** he hit him with a straight right to the chin.

gerade-: ~aus *adv* straight ahead; *gehen, fahren auch* straight on; **≃biegen** *vt sep irreg* to straighten out; (*fig inf auch*) to put straight, to sort out; **⚠≃halten** *sep irreg* [1] *vt* to hold straight; [2] *vr* to hold oneself (up) straight; **~heraus** (*inf*) [1] *adj pred* forthright, frank, plain-spoken; [2] *adv* frankly; **~heraus gesagt** quite frankly; **⚠≃legen** *vt sep* to put straight; **⚠≃machen** *vt sep* to straighten (out); **≃nwegs** *adv siehe* **~(s)wegs**; **⚠≃richten** *vt sep* to straighten up; (*horizontal*) to straighten out.

gerädert *adj* (*inf*) **wie ~ sein, sich wie ~ fühlen** to be *or* feel (absolutely) whacked (*inf*).

gerade-: ⚠≃sitzen *vi sep irreg aux haben or sein* to sit up straight; **≃so** *adv siehe* **ebenso**; **⚠≃sogut** *adv siehe* **ebensogut**; **⚠≃soviel** *adv* just as much; **≃stehen** *vi sep irreg aux haben or sein* **(a)** (*aufrecht stehen*) to stand up straight; **(b) für jdn/etw ~stehen** (*fig*) to be answerable *or* to answer for sb/sth; **≃(s)wegs** *adv* straight; **~(s)wegs auf etw** (*acc*) **losgehen** (*fig*) to get straight down to sth; **er nahm ~(s)wegs dazu Stellung** he voiced his opinion about it straight away *or* immediately; **~zu** [1] *adv* **(a)** (*beinahe*) virtually, almost; (*wirklich, durchaus*) really; **das ist doch ~zu Selbstmord** that's nothing short of suicide, that's absolute suicide; **das ist ja ~zu verblüffend/lächerlich!** that is absolutely amazing/ridiculous!; **(b)** (*ohne Umschweife*) frankly; **er sagte mir ~zu, daß ...** he told me straight out *or* frankly that ...; **~zu aufs Ziel zusteuern** (*fig*) to go straight to the point; [2] *adj pred* (*inf: ehrlich*) frank, candid; (*unverblümt*) blunt.

Gerad-: ~führung *f* (*Tech*) guide; **~heit** *f* (*fig*) (*Aufrichtigkeit*) rectitude; (*Freimut*) frankness, candidness; **g~linig** *adj* straight; *Abkomme, Abstammung* direct; *Entwicklung etc* linear; (*fig: aufrichtig*) straight; **die Straße verläuft g~linig durch die Wiesen** the road runs in a straight line through the meadows; **g~linig denken/handeln** to be straight; **~linigkeit** *f* (*lit, fig*) straightness; **g~sinnig** *adj* (*geh*) upright.

G(e)raffel *nt* **-s,** *no pl* (*Aus, S Ger*) *siehe* **Gerümpel**.

gerammelt *adv*: **~ voll** (*inf*) (jam-)packed (*inf*), chock-a-block (*inf*).

Gerangel *nt* **-s,** *no pl* (*Balgerei*) scrapping; (*fig: zäher Kampf*) wrangling ♦ **ein kurzes ~ der beiden Spieler** a short scrap between the two players; **das ~ um die Sonderangebote** the tussle over the bargains.

Geranie [-iə] *f* geranium.

gerann *pret of* **gerinnen**.

gerannt *ptp of* **rennen**.

Geraschel *nt* **-s,** *no pl* rustle, rustling.

Gerassel *nt* **-s,** *no pl* rattle, rattling.

Gerät *nt* **-(e)s, -e (a)** piece of equipment; (*Vorrichtung*) device; (*Apparat*) gadget; (*landwirtschaftliches ~*) implement; (*elektrisches ~*) appliance; (*Radio~, Fernseh~, Telefon*) set; (*Meß~*) instrument; (*Küchen~*) utensil; (*Werkzeug, Garten~*) tool; (*Turn~*) piece of apparatus; (*sl: Penis*) tool (*sl*).
(b) *no pl* (*Ausrüstung*) equipment *no pl*; (*von Handwerker*) tools *pl*.

Geräte|anbieter *m* (*Leasinggeber*) lessor (of the equipment).

geraten[1] *pret* **geriet**, *ptp* **geraten** [1] *vi aux sein* **(a)** (*zufällig gelangen*) to get (*in +acc* into) ♦ **an jdn ~** (*jdn kennenlernen*) to come across sb; (*jdn bekommen*) to find sb, to dig sb up (*pej*); **an etw** (*acc*) **~** to get sth, to come by sth; **an einen Ort ~** to come to a place; **an den Richtigen/Falschen ~** to come to the right/wrong person; **unter ein Fahrzeug ~** to fall under a vehicle; **mit der Hand in eine Maschine ~** to get one's hand caught in a machine; **in Gefangenschaft ~** to be taken prisoner; **das Schiff ist in einen Sturm ~** the boat got caught in a storm; **in Bewegung ~** to begin to move; **ins Stocken/Schleudern ~** to come to a halt/get into a skid; **in Brand ~** to catch fire; **in Angst/Begeisterung/Schwierigkeiten ~** to get scared/enthusiastic/into difficulties; **in Vergessenheit ~** to fall into oblivion; **aus der Bahn ~** (*lit*) to come off *or* leave the track; (*fig*) to go off the rails; **auf krumme Wege** *or* **die schiefe Bahn ~** to stray from the straight and narrow; **aus der Fassung/der Form ~** to lose one's composure/one's shape; **außer sich** (*dat*) **~ (vor etw)** to be beside oneself (with sth); **unter schlechten Einfluß ~** to come under a bad influence; *siehe* **Abweg, Haar** *etc*.
(b) (*sich entwickeln, gelingen, ausfallen*) to turn out ♦ **ihm gerät einfach alles** everything he does turns out well *or* is a success, everything always goes right for him; **mein Aufsatz ist mir zu lang ~** my essay turned out too long; **der Junge/Kaktus ist gut ~** the boy/cactus turned out well; **nach jdm ~** to take after sb.
[2] *adj* (*geh: ratsam*) advisable.

geraten[2] *ptp of* **raten, geraten**[1].

Geräte-: ~raum *m* equipment room; **~schuppen** *m* toolshed; **~turnen** *nt* apparatus gymnastics *no pl*.

Geratewohl *nt*: **aufs ~** on the off-chance; (*aussuchen, auswählen etc*) at random; **er hat die Prüfung einfach aufs ~ versucht** he decided to have a go at the exam just on the off-chance of passing; **er ist aufs ~ nach Amerika ausgewandert** he emigrated to America just like that; **wir schlugen aufs ~ diesen Weg ein** we decided to trust to luck and come this way.

Gerätschaften *pl* (*Ausrüstung*) equipment *sing*; (*Werkzeug*) tools *pl*.

Geratter *nt* **-s,** *no pl* clatter(ing), rattle, rattling; (*von Maschinengewehr*) chatter(ing).

Geräucherte(s) *nt, no pl decl as adj* smoked meat *especially bacon and ham*.

geraum *adj attr* **vor ~er Zeit** some time ago; **seit ~er Zeit** for some time; **es dauerte eine ~e Weile** it took some time.

geräumig *adj Haus, Zimmer* spacious, roomy; *Koffer, Kofferraum auch* capacious.

Geräumigkeit *f, no pl siehe adj* spaciousness, roominess; capaciousness.

Geraune *nt* **-s,** *no pl* (*liter*) whispering.

Geraunze *nt* **-s,** *no pl* (*inf: S Ger, Aus*) grousing (*inf*), grouching (*inf*).

Geräusch *nt* **-(e)s, -e** sound; (*esp unangenehm*) noise ♦ **der Arzt horchte meine Brust auf ~e ab** the doctor listened to my chest for any unusual sounds; **die ~e des Verkehrs** the noise of the traffic; **aus dem Keller hörte man verdächtige ~e** suspicious noises came from the cellar; **mit einem dumpfen ~** with a dull thud.

Geräusch-: g~arm *adj* quiet; **~dämpfung** *f* sound damping; (*stärker*) deadening of sound; **g~empfindlich** *adj* sensitive to noise; (*Tech*) sound-sensitive; **~kulisse** *f* background noise; (*Film, Rad, TV*) sound effects *pl*; **g~los** *adj* silent; **g~los öffnete er die Tür** without a sound *or* noiselessly *or* silently he opened the door; **~losigkeit** *f, no pl* quietness, noiselessness, silence; **~messer** *m* **-s, -** sound level recorder; **~pegel** *m* sound level; **g~voll** *adj* (*laut*) loud; (*lärmend*) noisy.

Geräusper *nt* **-s,** *no pl* throat-clearing.

gerben *vt* to tan ♦ **vom Wetter gegerbte Haut** weather-beaten skin; *siehe* **Fell**.

Gerber(in *f*) *m* **-s, -** tanner.

Gerbera *f* **-, -(s)** (*Bot*) gerbera.

Gerberei *f* **(a)** *no pl* (*Gerben*) tanning. **(b)** (*Werkstatt*) tannery.

Gerberlohe *f* tanbark.

Gerbstoff *m* tannic acid.

Gerbung *f* tanning.

gerecht *adj* **(a)** (*rechtgemäß, verdient*) just; (*unparteiisch auch*) fair; (*rechtschaffen*) upright ♦ **~ gegen jdn sein** to be fair *or* just to sb; **~er Lohn für alle Arbeiter!** fair wages for all workers!; **seinen ~en Lohn bekommen** (*fig*) to get one's just deserts *or* reward; **das ist nur ~** that's only fair *or* right *or* just; **~er Gott** *or* **Himmel!** (*inf*) good heavens (above)!; **die G~en** the just; **Gott, der G~e** God the righteous; **der G~e muß viel leiden** (*prov*) no peace for the wicked (*iro prov*); **den Schlaf des G~en schlafen** (*usu hum*) to sleep the sleep of the just.
(b) (*berechtigt*) just, legitimate ♦ **~er Zorn** righteous anger; **sich für eine ~e Sache einsetzen** to fight for a just cause.
(c) jdm/einer Sache ~ werden to do justice to sb/sth; **den Bedingungen ~ werden** to fulfil the conditions; **jds Erwartungen** (*dat*) **~ werden** to come up to *or* fulfil sb's expectations; *siehe* **Sattel**.

-gerecht *adj suf* suitable for.

gerechterweise *adv* to be fair.

gerechtfertigt *adj* justified.

Gerechtigkeit *f* **(a)** justice; (*das Gerechtsein*) justness; (*Unparteilichkeit*) fairness; (*Rechtschaffenheit*) righteousness ♦ **die ~ nahm ihren Lauf** justice took its course; **jdm/einer Sache ~ widerfahren lassen** to be just to sb/sth; (*fig*) to do justice to sb/sth. **(b)** (*geh: Gerichtsbarkeit*) justice ♦ **jdn (den Händen) der ~ ausliefern** to bring sb to justice.

Gerechtigkeits-: ~fimmel *m* (*pej inf*) thing about justice (*inf*); **~gefühl** *nt* sense of justice; **~liebe** *f* love of justice; **g~liebend** *adj* **ein g~liebender Mensch** a lover of justice, a person with a love of justice; **g~liebend sein** to have a love of justice; **~sinn** *m* sense of justice.

Gerechtsame *f* **-, -n** (*Hist*) rights *pl*.

Gerede *nt* **-s,** *no pl* talk; (*Klatsch*) gossip(ing) ♦ **ins ~ kommen** *or* **geraten** to get oneself talked about; **jdn ins ~ bringen** to get sb talked about; **kümmere dich nicht um das ~ der Leute** don't worry about what people say.

geregelt *adj Arbeit(szeiten), Mahlzeiten* regular; *Leben* well-ordered.

gereichen* *vi* (*geh*) **jdm zur Ehre ~** to do sb honour, to redound to sb's honour (*form*); **jdm zum Schaden/Nutzen ~** to be damaging/beneficial to sb, to redound to sb's benefit (*form*); **jdm/einer Sache zum Vorteil ~** to be an advantage to sb/sth, to redound to sb's advantage (*form*); (*vorteilhaft erscheinen lassen*) to be advantageous for sb/sth.

gereift *adj* (*fig*) mature.

Gereiftheit *f* (*fig*) maturity.

gereizt *adj* (*verärgert*) irritated; (*reizbar*) irritable, touchy; (*nervös*) tetchy, edgy ♦ **im Zimmer herrschte ~e Stimmung** there was a strained atmosphere in the room.

Gereiztheit *f siehe adj* irritation; irritability, touchiness; tetchiness, edginess; strainedness.

Gerenne *nt* **-s,** *no pl* (*inf*) running, racing; (*das Umherlaufen*) running *or* racing about *or* around.

gereuen* (*old, geh*) [1] *vt impers* **es gereut mich, daß ...** I regret that ..., I am sorry that ...; **es wird Sie nicht ~** you will not regret it.
[2] *vt* **meine Tat gereut mich** I regret my action.

Gerfalke *m* gyrfalcon, gerfalcon.

⚠: for details of spelling reform, see supplement

Geriater *m* **-s, -** geriatrician.
Geriatrie *f* geriatrics *sing*.
geriatrisch *adj* geriatric.
Gericht[1] *nt* **-(e)s, -e** (*Speise*) dish ♦ **leckere ~e** delicious meals.
Gericht[2] *nt* **-(e)s, -e (a)** (*Behörde*) court (of justice); (*Gebäude*) court(house), law courts *pl*; (*die Richter*) court, bench ♦ **Hohes ~!** My Lord! (*Brit*), Your Honor! (*US*); **vor ~ erscheinen/aussagen** to appear/testify in court; **vor ~ kommen** (*Fall*) to come to court; (*Mensch*) to come *or* appear before a/the court; **vor ~ stehen** to stand trial; **jdn vor ~ laden** to summon *or* call sb to appear in court; **jdn/einen Fall vor ~ bringen** to take sb/sth to court; **mit etw vor ~ gehen** to go to court *or* take legal action about sth; **jdn bei ~ verklagen** to take sb to court; **jdn/einen Fall vor ~ vertreten** to represent sb/sth in court; **das ~ zieht sich zur Beratung zurück** the court will adjourn.
(b) das Jüngste *or* **Letzte ~** the Last Judgement; **über jdn/etw ~ halten** to pronounce judgement on sb/sth; **über jdn zu ~ sitzen** (*fig*) to sit in judgement on sb; **mit jdm (scharf) ins ~ gehen** (*fig*) to judge sb harshly.
gerichtlich *adj attr* judicial; *Bestimmung, Entscheidung etc* court; *Medizin, Psychologie* forensic; *Verhandlung* legal ♦ **laut ~em Beschluß** according to the decision of a/the court *or* a/the court decision; **ein ~es Nachspiel** a court sequel; **ein ~es Nachspiel haben** to finish up in court; **~ gegen jdn vorgehen** to take legal proceedings against sb, to litigate against sb; **eine Sache ~** *or* **auf ~em Weg klären** to settle a matter in court *or* by litigation; **Schulden ~ eintreiben** to recover debts through the courts; **jdn ~ für tot erklären lassen** to have sb legally declared dead; **~ vereidigt** sworn.
Gerichts-: ~akten *pl* court records *pl*; **~arzt** *m* court doctor; **~assessor** *m* ≃ junior barrister (*Brit*) *or* lawyer.
Gerichtsbarkeit *f* jurisdiction.
Gerichts-: ~berichterstatter *m* legal correspondent; ⚠**~beschluß** *m* decision of a/the court, court decision; **~bezirk** *m* juridical district; **~diener** *m* (*old*) court usher; **~entscheid** *m*, **~entscheidung** *f* court decision; **~ferien** *pl* court vacation, recess; **~gebühren** *pl siehe* **~kosten**; **~herr** *m* (*Hist*) lord of the manor; **~hof** *m* court (of justice), law court; **Oberster ~hof** Supreme Court (of Justice); **der Hohe ~hof** the high court; **~hoheit** *f* jurisdiction; **~kasse** *f* **den Betrag von DM 200 an die ~kasse zahlen** to pay the court DM 200; **~kosten** *pl* court costs *pl*; **jdn zum Tragen der ~kosten verurteilen, jdm die ~kosten auferlegen** (*form*) to order sb to pay costs; **g~kundig** *adj siehe* **g~notorisch**; **~medizin** *f* forensic medicine, medical jurisprudence; **~mediziner** *m* forensic doctor; **g~medizinisch** *adj* forensic medical *attr*; **die Leiche wurde g~medizinisch untersucht** the body was examined by an expert in forensic medicine; **g~notorisch** *adj* known to the court; **~ordnung** *f* rules *pl* of the court; **~ort** *m* town *etc* with a court; **~ort ist Stuttgart** (*Vertragsbedingung*) any legal case arising from this contract shall be heard in Stuttgart; **~präsident** *m* president of the court; **~referendar** *m law student who has passed the first State Examination*, ≃ articled barrister (*Brit*); **~reporter** *m* legal correspondent; **~saal** *m* courtroom; **~schreiber** *m* clerk of the court; **~sprache** *f* language of the courts; **~stand** *m* (*form*) court of jurisdiction; **~tafel** *f* court notice board; (*für öffentliche Bekanntmachungen*) ≃ public notice board; **~tag** *m* court day; **Montag ist ~tag** the court sits on Monday *or* is in session on Monday; **~termin** *m* date of a/the trial; (*für Zivilsachen*) date of a/the hearing; **einen ~termin ansetzen** to fix a date for a/the trial/hearing; **~verfahren** *nt* court *or* legal proceedings *pl*; **ein ~verfahren gegen jdn einleiten** to institute legal proceedings against sb; (*zivil auch*) to litigate against sb; **er wurde ohne ordentliches ~verfahren verurteilt** he was sentenced without a proper trial; **~verfassung** *f* legal constitution; **~verhandlung** *f* trial; (*zivil*) hearing; **~vollzieher** *m* bailiff; **~weg** *m* **auf dem ~weg** through the courts; **~wesen** *nt* judiciary, judicial system.
gerieben [1] *ptp of* **reiben**.
[2] *adj* (*fig inf*) smart, sharp; (*verschlagen auch*) tricky, sly, fly (*inf*) ♦ **der ist verdammt ~** (*inf*) there are no flies on him (*inf*).
gerieren* *vr* (*geh*) to project an image.
Geriesel *nt* **-s,** *no pl* (*von Sand*) trickling; (*von Schnee*) floating down.
geriet *pret of* **geraten**[1].
gering *adj* **(a)** (*nicht sehr groß, niedrig*) *Temperatur, Luftdruck, Leistung, Produktion* low; *Gehalt, Preis* low, modest; *Menge, Vorrat, Betrag, Entfernung*, small; *Wert* little *attr*; (*kurz*) *Zeit, Entfernung* short ♦ **mit ~en Ausnahmen** with few exceptions; **Berge von ~er Höhe** low hills; **etw in ~er Höhe anbringen** to fix sth fairly low down; **~ gerechnet** at a conservative estimate; **seine Leistung erhielt eine zu ~e Bewertung** his achievement wasn't rated highly enough.
(b) (*unbedeutend, unerheblich*) slight; *Chance auch* small, slim; *Bedeutung, Rolle* minor ♦ **die ~ste Kleinigkeit** the least *or* smallest *or* slightest little thing; **das ist meine ~ste Sorge** that's the least of my worries; **die Kosten sind nicht ~** the costs are not inconsiderable; **nicht das G~ste** nothing at all; **nicht im ~sten** not in the least *or* slightest; **das G~ste** the least thing; **nichts G~eres als** ... nothing less than ...
(c) (*unzulänglich*) *Qualität, Kenntnisse* poor; (*abschätzig*) *Meinung* low, poor ♦ **~ von jdm sprechen/denken** to speak badly/have a low opinion of sb.
(d) *attr* (*fig geh*) *Familie, Herkunft* humble ♦ **(auch) der G~ste** even the most humble person; **kein G~erer als Freud** ... no less a person than Freud.
⚠**gering|achten** *vt sep siehe* **geringschätzen**.
geringelt *adj* **(a)** *Muster* ringed; *Socken* hooped; *siehe* **ringeln. (b)** (*lockig*) *Haare* curly.
Gering-: g~fügig *adj* (*unwichtig*) insignificant; *Verbesserung, Unterschied* slight; *Vergehen, Verletzung* minor; *Einzelheiten* minor, trivial; *Betrag* small; **sein Zustand hat sich g~fügig gebessert** his condition is marginally *or* slightly improved; **~fügigkeit** *f* **(a)** insignificance; slightness; (*von Vergehen, Einzelheiten*) triviality; smallness; **ein Verfahren wegen ~fügigkeit einstellen** (*Jur*) to dismiss a case because of the trifling nature of the offence; **(b)** (*Kleinigkeit*) little *or* small thing, trifle; ⚠**g~schätzen** *vt sep* (*verachten*) *Menschen, Leistung* to think little of, to have a poor *or* low opinion of; *Erfolg, Reichtum* to set little store by, to place little value on; *menschliches Leben* to have scant regard for, to place little value on; (*mißachten*) *Gefahr, Folgen* to disregard; **eine Tugend, die man nicht g~schätzen sollte** a virtue not to be despised; **g~schätzig** *adj* contemptuous; *Bemerkung auch* disparaging; **~schätzigkeit** *f* contemptuousness; disparagement; **~schätzung** *f, no pl* (*Ablehnung*) disdain; (*von Bemerkung*) disparagement (*für, gen* of); (*schlechte Meinung*) poor *or* low opinion (*für, gen* of); (*für Erfolg, Reichtum, menschliches Leben*) low regard (*für, gen* for).
geringstenfalls *adj* (*geh*) at (the very) least.
geringwertig *adj* (*rare*) inferior; *Nahrung* low-value.
gerinnbar *adj siehe* **gerinnungsfähig**.
gerinnen *pret* **gerann**, *ptp* **geronnen** *vi aux sein* to coagulate; (*Blut auch*) to clot; (*Milch auch*) to curdle ♦ **mir gerann (vor Schreck) das Blut in den Adern** (*fig*) my blood ran cold; **zu etw ~** (*fig geh*) to develop into sth.
Gerinnsel *nt* **(a)** (*Blut~*) clot, coagulum (*spec*). **(b)** (*geh: Rinnsal*) rivulet, trickle.
Gerinnung *f siehe vi* coagulation; clotting; curdling.
Gerinnungs-: g~fähig *adj* coagulable; **~fähigkeit** *f* coagulability.
Gerippe *nt* **-s, -** skeleton; (*von Schiff, Flugzeug auch, von Schirm, Gebäude*) frame; (*von Blatt auch*) ribbing; (*fig: Grundplan*) framework ♦ **er ist nur noch ein ~** he's nothing but skin and bones.
gerippt *adj* ribbed *no adv*; *Säule* fluted *no adv*.
⚠**G(e)riß** *nt* **-sses,** *no pl* (*Aus inf*) crush.
gerissen [1] *ptp of* **reißen**.
[2] *adj* crafty, cunning.
Gerissenheit *f* cunning.
geritten *ptp of* **reiten**.
geritzt *adj pred* (*inf*) **die Sache ist ~** everything's fixed up *or* settled.
Germ *m or f* **-,** *no pl* (*Aus*) baker's yeast.
Germane *m* **-n, -n** Teuton ♦ **die alten ~n** the Teutons.
Germanentum *nt* Teutonicism; (*Kultur*) Teutonism; (*Gesamtheit der Germanen*) Teutonic world, Teutons *pl*.
Germanin *f* Teuton.
germanisch *adj* Germanic ♦ **G~es Seminar** Institute of Germanic Studies.
germanisieren* *vt* to Germanize.
Germanisierung *f* Germanization.
Germanismus *m* (*Ling*) Germanism.
Germanist(in *f*) *m* Gernmanist; (*Student auch*) German student; (*Wissenschaftler auch*) German specialist.
Germanistik *f* German (studies *pl*) ♦ **~ studieren** to do German studies, to study German; **Professor der ~** professor of German studies *or* German.
germanistisch *adj* German; *Zeitschrift* on Germanic/German studies.
Germanium *nt* **-s,** *no pl* (*abbr* **Ge**) germanium.
Germano- (*geh*): **g~phil** *adj* Germanophile; **~philie** *f* Germanophilia; **g~phob** *adj* Germanophobe; **~phobie** *f* Germanophobia.
gern(e) *adv, comp* **lieber**, *superl* **am liebsten (a)** (*freudig*) with pleasure; (*bereitwillig auch*) willingly, readily ♦ **(aber) ~!** of course!; **ja, ~!** (yes) please; **kommst du mit? — ja, ~** are you coming too? — oh yes, I'd like to; **darf ich das? — ja, ~** can I do that? — (yes,) of course; **~ geschehen!** you're welcome! (*esp US*), not at all!, my pleasure!; **„Witwer, 61, sucht Partnerin, ~ älter/mit Kindern"** "widower, aged 61, seeks partner, age not important/children not a problem"; **von mir aus kann er ja ~ älter sein** I don't mind if he's older; **etw ~ tun** to like doing sth *or* to do sth (*esp US*); **etw ~ essen/trinken** to like sth; **sie ißt am liebsten Spargel** asparagus is her favourite food; **~ ins Kino gehen** to like *or* enjoy going to the cinema; **das tue ich für mein Leben ~** I adore doing that; **etw ~ sehen** to like sth; **das sähe ich ~** I would welcome it; **das wird nicht ~ gesehen** that's frowned (up)on; **er sieht es nicht ~, wenn wir zu spät kommen** he doesn't like us coming too late; **ein ~ gesehener Gast** a welcome visitor; **das glaube ich ~** I can quite *or* well believe it, I'm quite willing to believe it; **das würde ich zu ~ tun** I'd really love to do that; **er macht seine Arbeit ~ und mit Freude** he does his work willingly and gets a lot of pleasure out of it; **ich stehe ~ zu Ihren Diensten** (*old form*) I am/would be happy *or* pleased to be of service to you; **ich bin ~ dazu bereit** I'm quite willing *or* happy to do it; **jdn/etw ~ haben** *or* **mögen** to like *or* be fond of sb/sth; **das kannst du ~ haben** you're welcome to it, you can have it with pleasure; **er hat es ~, wenn man ihm schmeichelt** he likes being flattered, he likes it when you flatter him; **ich hätte** *or* **möchte ~** ... I would like ...; **ich hätte ~ Herrn Kurtz gesprochen** could I speak to Mr Kurtz?, I would like to speak to Mr Kurtz, please; **wie hätten Sie's (denn) ~?** how would you like it?; **du kannst/er kann mich mal ~ haben!** (*inf*) (you can)/he can go to hell! (*inf*), stuff you/him! (*sl*); *siehe* **gut 2, lieber**.
(b) (*gewöhnlich, oft*) **etw ~ tun** to tend to do sth; **Weiden wachsen ~ an Flüssen** willows tend to grow by rivers; **morgens läßt er sich ~ viel Zeit** he likes to leave himself a lot of time in the mornings.
Gernegroß *m* **-, -e** (*hum*) **er war schon immer ein kleiner ~** he always did like to act big (*inf*).
Geröchel *nt* **-s,** *no pl* groans *pl*; (*von Sterbenden*) (death-)rattle.
gerochen *ptp of* **riechen**.
Geröll *nt* **-(e)s, -e, Gerölle** (*rare*) *nt* **-s, -** detritus *no pl*; (*im Gebirge auch*) scree *no pl*; (*größeres*) boulders *pl*.

Geröll-: ~halde *f* scree (slope); **~schutt** *m* rock debris.
geronnen *ptp of* **rinnen, gerinnen.**
Gerontokratie *f (Pol)* gerontocracy.
Gerontologe *m*, **Gerontologin** *f (Med)* gerontologist.
Gerontologie *f (Med)* gerontology.
gerontologisch *adj (Med)* gerontological.
Geröstete *pl decl as adj (S Ger, Aus: Cook)* sauté potatoes *pl.*
Gerste *f* **-, -n** barley.
Gersten- *in cpds* barley; **~graupen** *pl* pearl barley *sing*; **~grütze** *f* barley groats *pl*; *(Brei)* barley porridge; **~korn** *nt* **(a)** barleycorn; **(b)** *(Med)* stye; **~saft** *m (hum)* John Barleycorn *(hum)*, beer; **~zucker** *m* barley sugar.
Gerte *f* **-, -n** switch; *(Reit~ auch)* crop ◆ **sie ist schlank wie eine ~** she is slim and willowy, she is as slender as a reed.
gertenschlank *adj* slim and willowy.
Geruch *m* **-(e)s, ¨-e (a)** smell, odour *(nach* of); *(Duft auch)* fragrance, scent, perfume *(nach* of); *(von Kuchen etc auch)* aroma *(nach* of); *(unangenehm auch)* stench *(nach* of) ◆ **der starke ~ nach Alkohol/Knoblauch** the reek of alcohol/garlic.
(b) *no pl (~ssinn)* sense of smell.
(c) *no pl (fig: Ruf)* reputation ◆ **in den ~ von etw kommen** to get a reputation for sth.
Geruch-: g~los *adj* odourless; *(duftlos)* scentless; **g~los sein** not to have a smell, to be odourless; *(Blumen)* not to smell; **~losigkeit** *f* lack of smell.
Geruch(s)-: ~belästigung *f* **das ist eine ~belästigung** the smell is a real nuisance; **g~bindend** *adj* deodorizing *no adv*; **~empfindung** *f* **(a)** *(Riechempfindung)* smell; **(b)** *(~sinn)* sense of smell; **~nerv** *m* olfactory nerve; **g~neutral** *adj siehe* **geruchlos**; **~organ** *nt* organ of smell, olfactory organ; **~sinn** *m* sense of smell; ⚠**~verschluß** *m (Tech)* odour trap; **~werkzeuge** *pl* olfactory organs *pl.*
Gerücht *nt* **-(e)s, -e** rumour ◆ **es geht das ~, daß ...** there's a rumour (going round) that ..., it's rumoured that ...; **das halte ich für ein ~** *(inf)* I have my doubts about that.
Gerüchte-: ~küche *f (inf)* gossip factory *(inf)*; **die Pressestelle ist eine wahre ~küche** the press office is filled with rumour-mongers; **~macher** *m* rumour-monger.
geruchtilgend *adj* deodorizing *no adv*, deodorant *attr.*
gerüchtweise *adv* **etw ~ hören** to hear sth rumoured; **~ ist bekanntgeworden, daß ...** rumour has it that ...; **ich habe ~ erfahren, daß ...** I've heard a rumour *or* heard say that ...; **das ist mir ~ zu Ohren gekommen** I've heard it rumoured.
Geruckel *nt* **-s,** *no pl* jerking, jolting.
Gerufe *nt* **-s,** *no pl* calling.
gerufen *ptp of* **rufen.**
geruhen* *vt* **~, etw zu tun** *(dated form)* to deign *or* condescend to do sth *(auch iro)*, to be pleased to do sth.
geruhig *adj (old) siehe* **ruhig.**
geruhsam *adj* peaceful; *Spaziergang etc* leisurely *no adv* ◆ **~ essen** to eat in peace (and quiet).
Geruhsamkeit *f siehe adj* peacefulness; leisureliness.
Gerumpel *nt* **-s,** *no pl* rumbling, rumble.
Gerümpel *nt* **-s,** *no pl* junk.
Gerundium *nt* gerund.
gerundiv(isch) *adj* gerundival.
Gerundiv(um) *nt* **-s, -e** gerundive.
gerungen *ptp of* **ringen.**
Gerüst *nt* **-(e)s, -e** scaffolding *no pl*; *(Gestell)* trestle; *(Brücken~, Dach~)* truss; *(Hänge~)* cradle; *(fig: Gerippe)* framework *(zu* of) ◆ **ein ~ aufstellen** to put up *or* erect scaffolding.
Gerüst-: ~bau *m* erection of scaffolding; **„W. Friedrich GmbH, ~bau"** "W. Friedrich Ltd, Scaffolders"; **~bauer** *m* scaffolder; **~stange** *f* scaffolding pole.
Gerüttel *nt* **-s,** *no pl* shaking (about); *(im Zug, Wagen etc)* jolting (about).
gerüttelt *adj* **~ voll** chock-a-block *(inf)*, jam-packed *(inf)*, chock-full; **ein ~es Maß von** *or* **an etw** *(dat)* a fair amount of sth; **er besitzt ein ~es Maß Unverschämtheit** he has more than his fair share of cheek.
ges, Ges *nt* **-, -** *(Mus)* G flat.
Gesalbte(r) *m decl as adj (Rel)* **der ~** the Lord's Anointed.
gesalzen [1] *ptp of* **salzen.**
[2] *adj (fig inf) Witz* spicy; *Preis, Rechnung* steep, fancy *(inf)*, stiff.
Gesalzene(s) *nt decl as adj (Cook)* salted meat.
gesammelt *adj Aufmerksamkeit, Kraft* collective; *Werke* collected.
gesamt *adj attr* whole, entire ◆ **die ~e Familie** all the family, the whole *or* entire family; **die ~en Lehrkräfte** all the teachers; **im ~en** in all; **die ~en Kosten** the total costs.
Gesamt *nt* **-s,** *no pl (liter) siehe* **Gesamtheit.**
Gesamt-: ~ansicht *f* general *or* overall view; **~auflage** *f (von Zeitung etc)* total circulation; *(von Buch)* total edition; **bisherige ~auflage: 300.000 Stück** sales totalling 300,000; **~ausfuhr** *f* total exports *pl*; **~ausgabe** *f* complete edition; **~bedarf** *m* complete needs *pl*; **~betrag** *m* total (amount); **~bild** *nt* general *or* overall picture; **g~deutsch** *adj* all-German; **Ministerium für g~deutsche Fragen** *(Hist)* Ministry for all-German Affairs; **~deutschland** *nt* all Germany; **ein ~deutschland hat nur von 1871 bis 1945 bestanden** there was one Germany *or* a united Germany only from 1871 to 1945; **~eindruck** *m* general *or* overall impression; **~einfuhr** *f* total imports *pl*; **~einkommen** *nt* total income; **~ergebnis** *nt* overall result; **~erlös** *m* total proceeds *pl*; **~ertrag** *m* total yield; **~fläche** *f* total area; **~gesellschaft** *f (Sociol)* society as a whole; **g~gesellschaftlich** *adj (Sociol) Produktion* by society as a whole; **~gewicht** *nt* total weight; *(eines LKW etc auch)* laden weight; **~gläubiger** *pl (Jur)* joint creditors *pl*; **g~haft** *(esp Sw)* [1] *adj siehe* **gesamt**; [2] *adv siehe* **insgesamt**; **~haftung** *f (Jur)* joint liability.
Gesamtheit *f* totality ◆ **die ~ der ...** all the ...; *(die Summe)* the totality of ...; **die ~ (der Bevölkerung)** the population (as a whole); **die ~ der Studenten/Arbeiter** the entire student population/work-force, all the students/workers; **die ~ der Delegierten** all the delegates; **in seiner ~** in its entirety; **das Volk in seiner ~/die Steuerzahler in ihrer ~** the nation/taxpayers as a whole.
Gesamt-: ~hochschule *f* polytechnic; **~interesse** *nt* general interest; **~kapital** *nt* total capital; **~katalog** *m* union catalogue; **~klassement** *nt (Sport)* overall placings *pl*; **~kosten** *pl* total *or* overall costs *pl*; **~kunstwerk** *nt (bei Wagner)* synthesis of the arts; *(Show, Happening)* multi-media performance *or* show; **~lage** *f* general situation; **~masse** *f (Comm)* total assets *pl*; **~note** *f (Sch)* overall mark; **~nutzungsdauer** *f* useful life; **~planung** *f* overall planning; **~schaden** *m* total damage; **ein ~schaden von 5.000 Mark** damage totalling 5,000 marks; **~schau** *f* synopsis *(über +acc* of); **~schuldner** *pl (Jur)* (joint) debtors *pl*; **~schule** *f* comprehensive school; **~sieger** *m (Sport)* overall winner; **~stärke** *f* total strength; **~stimmenzahl** *f* total number of votes cast; **~strafe** *f (Jur)* overall sentence *(for a series of offences, longer than the maximum sentence for the most serious offence but less than the total sentences taken consecutively)*; **~summe** *f siehe* **~betrag**; **~übersicht** *f* general survey *(über +acc* of); **~umsatz** *m* total turnover; **~werk** *nt* complete works *pl*; **~wert** *m* total value; **im ~wert von ...** totalling ... in value; **~wertung** *f (Sport)* overall placings *pl*; **er liegt in der ~wertung vorn** he's leading overall, he has the overall lead; **~wirkung** *f* general *or* overall effect; **~wirtschaft** *f* national economy; **g~wirtschaftlich** *adj* national economic *attr*; **g~wirtschaftlich nicht vertretbar** not justifiable from the point of view of the national economy; **~zahl** *f* total number; **eine ~zahl von 8.000 Punkten** a total of 8,000 points; **~zusammenhang** *m* general view.
gesandt *ptp of* **senden**[1].
Gesandte(r) *mf decl as adj* envoy, legate; *(inf: Botschafter)* ambassador ◆ **päpstlicher ~** (papal) nuncio.
Gesandtschaft *f* legation; *(inf: Botschaft)* embassy; *(päpstliche ~)* nunciature.
Gesang *m* **-(e)s, ¨-e (a)** *(Lied, Vogel~)* song; *(Preislied)* hymn; *(gregorianischer ~ etc)* chant ◆ **erster ~ der Ilias/von Dantes Inferno** first book of the Iliad/first canto of Dante's Inferno; **geistliche ¨~e** religious hymns and chants. **(b)** *no pl (das Singen)* singing; *(von Mönchen etc)* chanting.
Gesang-, Gesangs- *(Aus)*: **~buch** *nt (Eccl)* hymnbook; **das richtige/falsche ~buch haben** *(inf)* to belong to the right/wrong denomination; **~lehrer** *m* singing teacher.
gesanglich *adj* vocal; *Begabung* for singing.
Gesangskunst *f* singing technique.
Gesang-, Gesangs- *(Aus)*: **~stunde** *f* singing lesson; **~unterricht** *m* singing lessons *pl*; **~verein** *m* choral society; **mein lieber Herr ~verein!** *(hum)* ye gods and little fishes! *(hum)*.
Gesäß *nt* **-es, -e** seat, bottom, posterior *(hum)*.
Gesäß-: ~backe *f* buttock, cheek; **~muskel** *m* gluteal muscle *(spec)*; **~spalte** *f (form)* cleft between the buttocks; **~tasche** *f* back pocket.
gesättigt *adj (Chem)* saturated.
Gesäusel *nt* **-s,** *no pl (von Blättern)* rustling, rustle, whisper; *(vom Wind)* murmur(ing), whisper(ing), sigh(ing); *(fig iro: von Menschen)* purring.
gesch. *abbr of* **geschieden** divorced.
Geschacher *nt* **-s,** *no pl (pej)* haggling *(um* about).
Geschädigte(r) *mf decl as adj* victim.
geschaffen *ptp of* **schaffen**[1].
Geschäft *nt* **-(e)s, -e (a)** *(Gewerbe, Handel)* business *no pl*; *(~sabschluß)* (business) deal *or* transaction ◆ **~ ist ~** business is business; **wie geht das ~?, wie gehen die ~e?** how's business?; **mit jdm ins ~ kommen** to do business with sb; **mit jdm ~e machen** to do business *or* have business dealings with sb; **im ~ sein** to be in business; **für jdn die ~e führen** to act for sb; *(im Gewerbe, Handel)* to run the business for sb; **ein ~ tätigen** to do a deal, to make *or* carry out a transaction; **dunkle ~e treiben** to be involved in some shady dealings *or* business; **ein gutes/schlechtes ~ machen** to make a good/bad deal; **dabei hat er ein ~ gemacht** he made a profit by it; **~e mit etw machen** to make money out of sth; **viel in ~en unterwegs sein** to travel a lot on business; **das ~ mit der Lust** the sex industry; **Boulevardzeitungen leben von dem ~ mit der Angst** the popular press make their living by trading on people's fears.
(b) *(Aufgabe)* duty ◆ **das gehört zu den ~en des Ministers** that is one of the minister's duties, that is part of the minister's work; **seinen ~en nachgehen** to go about one's business.
(c) *(Firma)* business (concern); *(Laden)* shop *(Brit)*, store; *(inf: Büro)* office ◆ **die ~e schließen um 17[30] Uhr** the shops *or* stores close at 5.30; **ich gehe um 8 Uhr ins ~** I go to work *or* to the office at 8.00; **im ~** at work, in the office; *(im Laden)* in the shop.
(d) *(baby-talk: Notdurft)* **kleines/großes ~** little/big job *(baby-talk)*, number one/two *(baby-talk)*; **ein ~ machen** to do a job *(baby-talk)*; **sein ~ verrichten** to do one's business *(euph)*.
Geschäfte-: g~halber *adv (in Geschäften)* on business; *(wegen Geschäften)* because of business; **~macher** *m (pej)* profiteer; **~macherei** *f (pej)* profiteering *no indef art.*

geschäftig *adj* (*betriebsam*) busy; (*emsig, eifrig auch*) industrious, assiduous, zealous (*esp pej*) ◆ **~ tun, sich ~ geben** to look busy; **~es Treiben** *or* **Hin und Her** hustle and bustle, bustling activity; **~ hin und her laufen** to bustle around (busily).

Geschäftigkeit *f* busyness; (*Emsigkeit, Eifer auch*) industriousness, assiduousness, zealousness (*esp pej*); (*geschäftiges Treiben auch*) (hustle and) bustle.

Geschaftlhuber *m* **-s, -** (*S Ger*) *siehe* **Gschaftlhuber**.

geschäftlich [1] *adj* (*das Geschäft betreffend*) business *attr*; (*sachlich*) *Ton* businesslike ◆ **ich habe mit ihm etwas G~es zu besprechen** I have some business *or* business matters to discuss with him.
[2] *adv* (*in Geschäften*) on business; (*wegen Geschäften*) because of business; (*~ gesehen*) from a business point of view ◆ **er hat morgen ~ in Berlin zu tun** he has business in Berlin tomorrow *or* has to be in Berlin on business tomorrow; **~ verhindert** prevented by business; **~ verreist** away on business; **~ mit jdm verkehren** to have business dealings with sb.

Geschäfts-: **~ablauf** *m* course of business; ⚠**~abschluß** *m* business deal *or* transaction; **~angelegenheit** *f siehe* **~sache**; **~anteil** *m* share of a/the business; **~aufgabe, ~auflösung** *f* closure of a/the business; **Räumungsverkauf wegen ~aufgabe** closing-down sale; **~auslage** *f* window display; **~auto** *nt* company car; **~bank** *f* commercial bank; **~bedingungen** *pl* terms of business *pl*; **~bereich** *m* (*Parl*) responsibilities *pl*; **Minister ohne ~bereich** minister without portfolio; **~bericht** *m* report; (*einer Gesellschaft*) company report; **~besitzer** *m siehe* **~inhaber**; **~beziehungen** *pl* business connections *pl* (*zu* with); **~brief** *m* business letter; **~bücher** *pl* books *pl*, accounts *pl*; **~eröffnung** *f* opening of a store *or* shop (*Brit*); **g~fähig** *adj* (*Jur*) capable of contracting (*form*), competent (*form*); **voll/beschränkt g~fähig sein** to have complete/limited competence; **~fähigkeit** *f* (*Jur*) (legal) competence; **~frau** *f* businesswoman; **~freund** *m* business associate; **g~führend** *adj attr* executive; (*stellvertretend*) acting; *Regierung* caretaker; **~führer** *m* (*von Laden*) manager; (*von GmbH*) managing director; (*von Verein*) secretary; (*von Partei*) whip; **~führung** *f* management; **mit der ~führung beauftragt** (*abbr* **m.d.G.b.**) in charge of administration; **~gang** *m* business *no art*; (*Besorgung*) errand; **~gebaren** *nt* business methods *pl or* practices *pl*; **~geheimnis** *nt* business secret; **~geist** *m siehe* **~sinn**; **~haus** *nt* **(a)** (*Gebäude*) business premises *pl*; (*von Büros*) office block; **(b)** (*Firma*) house, firm; **~herr** *m* (*Sw*) owner (of a business); **~inhaber** *m* owner (of a business); (*von Laden, Restaurant*) proprietor, owner; **~inhaberin** *f siehe* **~inhaber** owner; proprietress; **~interesse** *nt* business interest; **~jahr** *nt* financial year; **~kapital** *nt* working capital; **~kosten** *pl* business expenses *pl*; **das geht alles auf ~kosten** it's all on expenses; **~lage** *f* **(a)** (*Wirtschaftslage*) business situation; **(b) in erstklassiger ~lage** in a good business location; **~leben** *nt* business life; **er steht noch im ~leben** he's still active in the world of business; **~leitung** *f siehe* **~führung**; **~liste** *f* (*Sw*) *siehe* **Tagesordnung**; **~mann** *m, pl* **-leute** businessman; **g~mäßig** *adj* businesslike *no adv*; **~methoden** *pl* business methods *pl*; **~ordnung** *f* standing orders *pl*; **zur ~ordnung!** point of order!; **eine Frage zur ~ordnung** a question on a point of order; **~papiere** *pl* business papers *pl*; **~partner** *m* business partner; (*~freund*) business associate; **~räume** *pl* (business) premises *pl*; (*Büroräume*) offices *pl*; **in den ~räumen** on the premises/in the offices; **~reise** *f* business trip; **auf ~reise sein** to be on a business trip; **~rückgang** *m* decline in business; **~sache** *f* business matter *or* affair; **g~schädigend** *adj* bad for business; **g~schädigendes Verhalten** *siehe* **~schädigung**; **~schädigung** *f* conduct *no art* injurious to the interests of the company (*form*); ⚠**~schluß** *m* close of business; (*von Läden*) closing-time; **nach ~schluß** out of working hours/after closing-time; **~sinn** *m* business sense *or* acumen; **~sitz** *m* place of business; **~stelle** *f* offices *pl*; (*von Gericht*) administrative office; **~straße** *f* shopping street; **~stunden** *pl* office *or* working hours *pl*; (*von Läden*) (shop) opening hours; **„~stunden"** "hours of opening"; **~tätigkeit** *f* business activity; **~träger** *m* (*Pol*) chargé d'affaires; **g~tüchtig** *adj* business-minded; **~übernahme** *f* takeover of a/the business/store; **g~unfähig** *adj* (*Jur*) not capable of contracting (*form*), (legally) incompetent (*form*); **~unfähigkeit** *f* (*Jur*) (legal) incompetence; **~verbindung** *f* business connection; **in ~verbindung mit jdm stehen** to have business connections with sb; **~verkehr** *m* **(a)** business *no art*; **in regem ~verkehr mit einer Firma stehen** to do a considerable amount of business with a firm; **(b)** (*Straßenverkehr*) business traffic; **~viertel** *nt* (*Banken- und Versicherungsviertel*) business *or* commercial district; **~volumen** *nt* volume of trade; **~wagen** *m* company car; **~welt** *f* world of business, business world; **~wert** *m* value of a/the business; **~zimmer** *nt* office; **~zweig** *m* branch of a/the business.

geschah *pret of* **geschehen**.

Geschäker *nt* **-s,** *no pl* (*inf*) flirting.

geschamig *adj* (*esp Aus inf*) *siehe* **gschamig**.

Geschaukel *nt* **-s,** *no pl* (*im Schaukelstuhl*) swinging; (*in Bus, Wagen*) lurching; (*in Boot*) pitching, rolling.

gescheckt *adj* spotted; *Pferd* skewbald, pinto (*US*).

geschehen *pret* **geschah**, *ptp* **~** *vi aux sein* to happen (*jdm* to sb); (*vorkommen auch*) to occur; (*stattfinden auch*) to take place; (*ausgeführt werden*) to be done; (*Verbrechen*) to be committed ◆ **ihr Selbstmord geschah aus Verzweiflung** her despair led her to commit suicide; **es ist nun einmal ~** what's done is done; **Dein Wille geschehe** (*Bibl*) Thy *or* Your will be done; **es wird ihm nichts ~** nothing will happen to him; **das geschieht ihm (ganz) recht** it serves him (jolly well *inf*) right; **ihm ist ein Unrecht ~** he has been wronged; **ihm ist ein Mißgeschick ~** he had a mishap; **er wußte nicht, wie ihm geschah** he didn't know what was happening *or* going on; **was soll mit ihm/damit ~?** what is to be done with him/it?; **als er sie sah, war es um ihn ~** he was lost the moment he set eyes on her; **da war es um meine Seelenruhe ~** that was an end to my peace of mind; **es kann ~, daß ...** it could happen that ...; **und so geschah es, daß ...** and so it happened *or* came about that ...; **es muß etwas ~** something must be done; **so ~ am ...** such was the case on ...; **G~es ruhen lassen** (*geh*) to let bygones be bygones; *siehe* **gern**.

Geschehen *nt* **-s,** (*rare*) **-** events *pl*, happenings *pl*.

Geschehnis *nt* (*geh*) event; (*Vorfall auch*) incident.

gescheit *adj* **(a)** clever; *Mensch, Idee auch* bright; (*vernünftig*) sensible ◆ **du bist wohl nicht recht ~?** you must be out of your mind *or* off your head; **sei ~!** be sensible; **es wäre ~er ...** it would be wiser *or* more sensible ... ; **jetzt bin ich so ~ wie vorher** I'm none the wiser now.
(b) (*S Ger: tüchtig, ordentlich*) proper, good ◆ **ich habe ihm ~ die Meinung gesagt** (*S Ger*) I really gave him a piece of my mind; **wie ~** (*Aus inf*) like mad (*inf*).

Geschenk *nt* **-(e)s, -e** present, gift; (*Schenkung*) gift ◆ **jdm ein ~ machen** to give sb a present; **jdm etw zum ~ machen** to make sb a present of sth, to give sb sth (as a present); **ein ~ seiner Mutter** a present *or* gift from his mother; **ein ~ Gottes** a gift from *or* of God; **das war ein ~ des Himmels** it was a godsend; **kleine ~e erhalten die Freundschaft** (*prov*) little presents keep a friendship alive.

Geschenk-, Geschenks- (*Aus*) *in cpds* gift; **~artikel** *m* gift; **~idee** *f* idea for a present *or* gift; **~packung** *f* gift pack *or* box; (*von Pralinen*) gift box; **~papier** *nt* wrapping paper, giftwrap; **etw in ~papier einwickeln** to giftwrap sth; **~sendung** *f* gift parcel.

Gescherte(r) *mf decl as adj* (*Aus inf*) *siehe* **Gscherte(r)**.

Geschichtchen *nt* little story.

Geschichte *f* **-, -n** **(a)** *no pl* (*Historie*) history ◆ **~ des Altertums/der Neuzeit, Alte/Neuere ~** ancient/modern history; **die ~ Spaniens/der Menschheit** the history of Spain/mankind; **~ machen** to make history; **das ist längst ~** that's past history.
(b) (*Erzählung, Lügen~*) story; (*Märchen, Fabel etc auch*) tale; (*Kurz~*) short story ◆ **das sind alles bloß ~n** that's all just made up, that's just a story; **~n erzählen** to tell stories.
(c) (*inf: Angelegenheit, Sache*) affair, business *no pl* ◆ **das sind alte ~n** that's old hat (*inf*); **das ist (wieder) die alte ~** it's the same old *or* the old old story (all over again); **alte ~n wieder aufwärmen** to rake up the past; **die ganze ~** the whole business; **eine schöne ~!** (*iro*) a fine how-do-you-do! (*inf*); **das sind ja nette ~n!** (*iro*) this is a fine thing; **die ~ mit seinem Magen** the trouble *or* business with his stomach; **als er damals diese ~ mit der Tänzerin hatte** when he was having that affair with the dancer; **mach keine ~n!** don't be silly! (*inf*); (*Dummheiten*) don't get up to anything silly!

Geschichten-: **~buch** *nt* storybook; **~erzähler** *m* (*lit, fig*) storyteller.

geschichtlich *adj* (*historisch*) historical; (*bedeutungsvoll*) historic ◆ **~ bedeutsam** historic; **~ denken** to think in terms of history; **etw ~ betrachten** to consider sth from the historical point of view; **~ belegt** *or* **nachgewiesen sein** to be a historical fact.

Geschichts-: **~atlas** *m* historical atlas; **~auffassung, ~betrachtung** *f* conception of history; ⚠**~bewußtsein** *nt* awareness of history, historical awareness; **~buch** *nt* history book; **~deutung** *f* interpretation of history; **~drama** *nt* historical drama; **~epoche** *f* period of history; **~fälschung** *f* falsification of history; **~forscher** *m* historian; **~forschung** *f* historical research; **~kenntnis** *f* knowledge of history *no pl*, historical knowledge *no pl*; **~klitterung** *f* historical misrepresentation; **~lehrer** *m* history teacher; **g~los** *adj Land, Stadt* with no history; *Zeit* with no historical records; *Volk* with no sense of history, ahistorical; *Politik, Weltanschauung* ahistorical; **~losigkeit** *f siehe adj* lack of history; absence of historical records (*gen* for); historical unawareness; ahistoricity (*form*); **~philosoph** *m* philosopher of history; **~philosophie** *f* philosophy of history; **g~philosophisch** *adj Schrift etc* on the philosophy of history; *Interesse, Studien* in the philosophy of history; **~schreiber** *m* historian, historiographer; **~schreibung** *f* historiography; **~werk** *nt* historical work; **~wissenschaft** *f* (science of) history; **~wissenschaftler** *m* historian; **~zahl** *f* (historical) date.

Geschick[1] *nt* **-(e)s, -e** (*geh*) (*Schicksal*) fate; (*politische etc Entwicklung, Situation*) fortune ◆ **ein gütiges ~** good fortune, providence; **ein schlimmes/schweres/trauriges ~** a sad fate.

Geschick[2] *nt* **-s,** *no pl* skill.

Geschicklichkeit *f siehe* **geschickt** skill, skilfulness; cleverness, adroitness; dexterity; agility ◆ **für** *or* **zu etw ~ haben** *or* **zeigen** to be clever at sth.

Geschicklichkeits-: **~fahren** *nt* (*Sport*) skill tests *pl*; (*Aut*) manoeuvring tests *pl*; **~spiel** *nt* game of skill; **~übung** *f* exercise in skill/agility.

geschickt *adj* **(a)** skilful; (*taktisch auch*) clever, adroit; (*fingerfertig auch*) dexterous; (*beweglich*) agile. **(b)** (*S Ger*) *siehe* **praktisch** [1].

Geschicktheit *f siehe* **Geschicklichkeit**.

Geschiebe *nt* **-s,** *no pl* **(a)** (*Geol*) debris; (*in Flüssen*) deposit. **(b)** (*Gedränge*) pushing and shoving (*inf*).

geschieden *ptp of* **scheiden**.

Geschiedene *f decl as adj* divorcee ◆ **seine ~** (*inf*) his ex (*inf*).

Geschiedene(r) *m decl as adj* divorced man, divorcé ◆ **ihr ~r** (*inf*) her ex (*inf*).

geschienen *ptp of* **scheinen**.

Geschimpfe *nt* **-s,** *no pl* (*inf*) cursing; (*tadelnd*) scolding.

Geschirr *nt* **-(e)s, -e** **(a)** *no pl* (*Haushaltsgefäße*) crockery (*Brit*), tableware; (*Küchen~*) pots and pans *pl*, kitchenware; (*Teller etc*) china; (*zu einer Mahlzeit*

benutzt) dishes *pl* ◆ **(das) ~ (ab)spülen** to wash *or* do the dishes, to wash up; **feuerfestes ~** ovenware.
(b) (*Service*) (dinner/tea *etc*) service; (*Glas~*) set of glasses; (*feuerfestes ~*) set of ovenware ◆ **das gute ~** the best china.
(c) (*old*) (*Gefäß*) vessel, pot; (*Nacht~*) chamber-pot.
(d) (*von Zugtieren*) harness ◆ **einem Pferd das ~ anlegen** to harness (up) a horse; **sich ins ~ legen** *or* **werfen** (*Pferde, Ochsen*) to pull hard; (*fig*) to put one's shoulder to the wheel, to put one's back into it.

Geschirr-: ~aufzug *m* dumb waiter; **~handtuch** *nt* tea towel; **~macher** *m* harness-maker; **~schrank** *m* china cupboard; **~spülen** *nt* washing-up; **~spülmaschine** *f* dishwasher; **~spülmittel** *nt* washing-up liquid (*Brit*), dishwashing liquid (*US*); **~tuch** *nt* tea towel.

⚠ **Geschiß** *nt* **-sses,** *no pl* (*sl*) fuss and bother.

geschissen *ptp of* **scheißen.**

Geschlabber *nt* **-s,** *no pl* (*inf*) slurping.

geschlafen *ptp of* **schlafen.**

geschlagen *ptp of* **schlagen.**

Geschlecht *nt* **-(e)s, -er (a)** sex; (*Gram*) gender ◆ **Jugendliche beiderlei ~s** young people of both sexes; **das andere ~** the opposite sex; **das schwache/schöne/starke ~** the weaker/fair/stronger sex; **das dritte ~** transvestites *pl*; (*Homosexuelle*) homosexuals *pl*.
(b) (*geh: Geschlechtsteil*) sex (*liter*).
(c) (*liter*) (*Gattung*) race; (*Generation*) generation; (*Sippe*) house; (*Abstammung*) lineage ◆ **das menschliche ~, das ~ der Menschen** the human race; **das ~ der Götter** the gods; **er ist vornehmen ~s** he is of noble lineage.

Geschlechter-: ~folge *f* line; **~kampf** *m* battle of the sexes; **~kunde** *f* genealogy; **~trennung** *f* segregation of the sexes.

geschlechtlich *adj* sexual ◆ **~e Erziehung** sex education; **mit jdm ~ verkehren** to have sexual intercourse with sb.

Geschlechtlichkeit *f* sexuality.

Geschlechts-: g~abhängig *adj* sexually determined; **~akt** *m* sex(ual) act; **~bestimmung** *f* sex determination; **~chromosom** *nt* sex chromosome; **~drang** *m* sex(ual) urge; **~drüse** *f* sex gland; **~erziehung** *f* sex(ual) education; **g~gebunden** *adj siehe* **g~abhängig**; **~genosse** *m* person of the same sex; **jds ~genossen** those *or* people of the same sex as sb; **~hormon** *nt* sex hormone; **g~krank** *adj* suffering from VD *or* a venereal disease; **g~krank sein** to have VD; **ein ~kranker** a person with VD; **~krankheit** *f* venereal disease; **eine ~krankheit haben** to have VD *or* a venereal disease; **~leben** *nt* sex life; **~leiden** *nt* venereal disease; **g~los** *adj* asexual (*auch Biol*), sexless; **~losigkeit** *f* asexuality (*auch Biol*), sexlessness; **~lust** *f* (*geh*) lust; **~merkmal** *nt* sex(ual) characteristic; **~organ** *nt* sex(ual) organ; **g~reif** *adj* sexually mature; **~reife** *f* sexual maturity; **~rolle** *f* (*Sociol*) sex role; **g~spezifisch** *adj* (*Sociol*) sex-specific; **~teil** *nt* genitals *pl*; **~trieb** *m* sex(ual) urge; sex(ual) drive; **~umwandlung** *f* sex change; **~unterschied** *m* difference between the sexes; **~verirrung** *f* sexual perversion; **~verkehr** *m* sexual intercourse; **~wort** *nt* (*Gram*) article; **~zelle** *f* sexual cell.

geschlichen *ptp of* **schleichen.**

geschliffen [1] *ptp of* **schleifen²**.
[2] *adj Manieren, Ausdrucksweise* polished, refined; *Sätze* polished.

Geschliffenheit *f siehe adj* refinement; polish.

geschlossen [1] *ptp of* **schließen.**
[2] *adj* closed; (*vereint*) united, unified ◆ **in sich** (*dat*) **~** self-contained; *Mensch, Charakter* well-rounded; *Buch, Handlung* well-knit; *Systeme, Produktionskreisläufe* closed; **es war eine ~e Wolkendecke vorhanden** the sky was completely overcast; **ein ~es Ganzes** a unified whole; **~e Gesellschaft** closed society; (*Fest*) private party; **in ~er Sitzung** in closed session; (*Jur*) in camera; **ein ~er Wagen** a saloon car; **~e Ortschaft** built-up area; **in ~er Formation** (*Aviat*) in close formation.
[3] *adv* **~ für etw sein/stimmen** to be/vote unanimously in favour of sth; **wir protestierten ~ gegen das neue Gesetz** we were unanimous in our protest against the new law; **~ hinter jdm stehen** to stand solidly behind sb; **wir gingen ~ mit der ganzen Klasse ins Kino** the whole class went to the cinema en masse *or* as a body; **dieses zwölfbändige Lexikon wird nur ~ abgegeben** this twelve-volume encyclopaedia is only sold as a complete set; **dieser Vokal wird ~ ausgesprochen** this vowel has closed articulation.

Geschlossenheit *f* unity.

Geschluchz(e) *nt* **-es,** *no pl* sobbing.

geschlungen *ptp of* **schlingen¹** *and* **schlingen²**.

Geschlürfe *nt* **-s,** *no pl* (*inf*) slurping.

Geschmack *m* **-(e)s, ¨e** *or* (*hum, inf*) **¨er** (*lit, fig*) taste; (*Aroma auch*) flavour; (*S Ger: Geruch*) smell; (*no pl: ~ssinn*) sense of taste ◆ **je nach ~** to one's own taste; **Salz (je) nach ~ hinzufügen** add salt to taste; **seinen ~ bilden** *or* **entwickeln** (*lit*) to develop one's sense of taste; (*fig*) to acquire a sense of the aesthetic; **an etw** (*dat*) **~ finden** to acquire a taste for sth; **auf den ~ kommen** to acquire a taste for it; **einen guten ~ haben** (*Essen*) to taste good; **er hat einen guten ~** (*fig*) he has good taste; **für meinen ~** for my taste; **das ist nicht mein/nach meinem ~** that's not my/to my taste; **die ¨er sind verschieden** tastes differ; **über ~ läßt sich (nicht) streiten** (*Prov*) there's no accounting for taste(s) (*prov*).

geschmäcklerisch *adj* highly elaborate; *Aufführung auch* camp.

geschmacklich *adj* (*lit, fig*) as regards taste ◆ **ausgezeichnete ~e Qualitäten** (*form*) exquisite flavour or taste.

geschmacklos *adj* (*lit, fig*) tasteless; (*taktlos auch*) in bad taste.

Geschmacklosigkeit *f* **(a)** *no pl* (*lit, fig*) tastelessness, lack of taste; (*Taktlosigkeit auch*) bad taste. **(b)** (*Beispiel der ~*) example of bad taste; (*Bemerkung*) remark in bad taste ◆ **das ist eine ~!** that is the most appalling bad taste!

Geschmacks-: g~bildend *adj* aesthetically formative; **~bildung** *f* formation of good taste; **~empfindung** *f* sense of taste; **keine ~empfindung haben** to be unable to taste anything; **~frage** *f* matter *or* question of (good) taste; **~knospen** *pl* taste buds *pl*; **~nerv** *m* tastebud; **g~neutral** *adj* tasteless; **~richtung** *f* taste; **in sieben neuen ~richtungen** in seven new flavours; **~sache** *f* matter of taste; **das ist ~sache** it's (all) a matter of taste; **~sinn** *m* sense of taste; **~verirrung** *f* **unter ~verirrung leiden** (*iro*) to have no taste; **der Hut ist eine ~verirrung** that hat is an aberration.

geschmackvoll *adj* tasteful; (*taktvoll auch*) in good taste ◆ **~e Kleider tragen, sich ~ kleiden** to dress tastefully.

Geschmatze *nt* **-s,** *no pl* (*inf*) noisy eating.

Geschmeide *nt* **-s, -** (*geh*) jewellery *no pl* ◆ **ein ~** a piece of jewellery.

geschmeidig *adj* **(a)** *Haar, Leder, Haut* supple; *Körper, Bewegung auch* lithe, lissom(e); *Fell* sleek; (*weich*) *Handtuch, Haar* soft; *Teig* workable; *Wachs* malleable; (*anschmiegsam*) soft and clinging ◆ **er hat einen ~en Gang** he moves with supple grace; **~ glitt die Katze vom Stuhl** the cat slid off the chair with feline grace.
(b) (*fig*) (*anpassungsfähig*) flexible; (*wendig*) adroit; *Zunge, Worte* glib, smooth.

Geschmeidigkeit *f, no pl siehe adj* **(a)** suppleness; litheness, lissomeness; sleekness; softness; malleability; clinging softness. **(b)** flexibility; adroitness; glibness.

Geschmeiß *nt* **-es,** *no pl* **(a)** (*old lit, fig*) vermin *pl*. **(b)** (*Hunt*) droppings *pl*.

Geschmetter *nt* **-s,** *no pl* flourish.

Geschmier(e) *nt* **-s,** *no pl* (*inf*) mess; (*Handschrift*) scrawl; (*Geschriebenes*) scribble; (*schlechtes Bild*) daub.

geschmissen *ptp of* **schmeißen.**

geschmolzen *ptp of* **schmelzen.**

Geschmorte(s) *nt decl as adj* (*Cook*) braised meat.

Geschmunzel *nt* **-s,** *no pl* smiling.

Geschmus(e) *nt* **-s,** *no pl* (*inf*) cuddling; (*von Pärchen auch*) canoodling (*inf*).

Geschnäbel *nt* **-s,** *no pl* billing; (*hum: Küsserei*) billing and cooing.

Geschnatter *nt* **-s,** *no pl* (*lit*) cackle, cackling; (*fig*) jabber, jabbering.

Geschnetzelte(s) *nt decl as adj* (*esp Sw Cook*) *meat cut into strips stewed to produce a thick sauce.*

geschniegelt *adj* (*pej*) flashy ◆ **~ und gebügelt** *or* **gestriegelt** spruced up, all dressed up with one's hair smarmed down (*pej*).

geschnitten *ptp of* **schneiden.**

geschnoben *ptp of* **schnauben.**

Geschnüffel *nt* **-s,** *no pl* sniffing; (*fig*) nosing *or* sniffing about.

geschoben *ptp of* **schieben.**

geschollen (*old*) *ptp of* **schallen.**

gescholten *ptp of* **schelten.**

Geschöpf *nt* **-(e)s, -e** (*Geschaffenes*) creation; (*Lebewesen*) creature ◆ **wir sind alle ~e Gottes** we are all God's creatures; **sie ist sein ~** (*geh*) she is his creature.

geschoren *ptp of* **scheren¹**.

⚠ **Geschoß¹** *nt* **-sses, -sse** projectile (*form*); (*Wurf~, Rakete etc auch*) missile; (*Kugel auch*) bullet; (*fig inf: scharf geschossener Ball*) shot ◆ **ferngelenktes ~** guided missile.

⚠ **Geschoß²** *nt* **-sses, sse** (*Stockwerk*) floor, storey (*Brit*), story (*US*) ◆ **im ersten ~** on the first (*Brit*) *or* second (*US*) floor; **das Haus/Geschäft hat vier ~sse** the house has four storeys/the store has four floors.

⚠ **Geschoßbahn** *f* trajectory; (*einer Rakete auch*) flight path.

geschossen *ptp of* **schießen.**

⚠ **Geschoß-: ~garbe** *f* burst of fire; **~hagel** *m* hail of bullets.

-geschossig *adj suf* -storey *attr* (*Brit*), -story *attr* (*US*), -storeyed (*Brit*), -storied (*US*) ◆ **mehr~** multistorey.

geschraubt *adj* (*pej*) *Stil, Redeweise* pretentious.

Geschrei *nt* **-s,** *no pl* shouts *pl*, shouting; (*von Kindern, Fußballfans, Streitenden auch*) yells *pl*, yelling; (*von Verletzten, Babys, Popfans*) screams *pl*, screaming; (*schrilles ~*) shrieks *pl*, shrieking; (*fig: Aufhebens*) fuss, to-do (*inf*) ◆ **viel ~ um etw machen** to kick up (*inf*) *or* make a big fuss about sth; **ein großes ~ erheben** to set up a cry *etc*; (*fig*) to raise an outcry.

Geschreibsel *nt, no pl* (*inf*) scribble; (*fig: Schreiberei*) scribblings *pl*.

geschrieben *ptp of* **schreiben.**

geschrie(e)n *ptp of* **schreien.**

geschritten *ptp of* **schreiten.**

geschunden *ptp of* **schinden.**

Geschütz *nt* **-es, -e** gun ◆ **schweres ~** heavy artillery; **eine Kanone ist ein ~** a cannon is a piece of artillery; **ein ~ auffahren** to bring up a gun; **schweres** *or* **grobes ~ auffahren** (*fig*) to bring up one's big guns.

Geschütz-: ~bedienung *f* gunnery; (*Personal*) gun-crew; **~donner** *m* roar *or* booming of (the) guns; **~feuer** *nt* shell fire; **~rohr** *nt* gun barrel; **~stand** *m*, **~stellung** *f* gun emplacement.

geschützt *adj Winkel, Ecke* sheltered; *Pflanze, Tier* protected.

Geschützturm *m* gun turret.

Geschw. *abbr of* **Geschwister.**

Geschwader *nt* **-s, -** squadron.

Geschwader-: ~kommandeur *m* (*Naut*) commodore; **~kommodore** *m* (*Aviat*) squadron-leader (*Brit*), major (*US*).

Geschwafel *nt* **-s,** *no pl* (*pej inf*) waffle (*inf*).

geschwänzt *adj Peitsche* with tails.

Geschwätz *nt* **-es,** *no pl (pej)* prattle; *(Klatsch)* tittle-tattle *(inf)*, gossip.
Geschwatze, Geschwätze *(S Ger inf) nt* **-s,** *no pl* chattering, nattering *(inf)*.
geschwätzig *adj* talkative, garrulous; *(klatschsüchtig)* gossipy.
Geschwätzigkeit *f, no pl siehe adj* talkativeness, garrulousness; gossipiness ◆ **das haben wir deiner ~ zu verdanken** we've you and your eternal chattering/gossiping to thank for that.
geschweift *adj* **(a)** curved. **(b)** *Stern* with a tail.
geschweige *conj* **~ (denn)** let *or* leave alone, never mind.
geschwiegen *ptp of* **schweigen.**
geschwind *adj (old, S Ger)* swift, quick, fast *no adv* ◆ **~!** quick(ly)!, hurry!; **~en Schrittes** *(geh)* with rapid steps; **~ wie der Wind** *(geh)* as swift as the wind.
Geschwindigkeit *f* speed; *(Schnelligkeit auch)* swiftness, quickness; *(Phys: von Masse)* velocity ◆ **mit einer ~ von ...** at a speed of ...; **mit höchster ~** at top speed; **mit rasender ~ fahren** to belt *or* tear along *(inf)*; **eine zu große ~ draufhaben** *(inf)* to be going too fast; **an ~ zunehmen** to gather *or* pick up speed; *(Phys: Masse)* to gain momentum; **die ~ steigern/verringern** to increase/decrease one's speed, to speed up/slow down.
Geschwindigkeits-: ~abfall *m (Phys)* loss of speed; **~begrenzung, ~beschränkung** *f* speed limit; **gegen die ~begrenzung verstoßen** to exceed the speed limit; **~kontrolle** *f* speed check; **~messer** *m* **-s, -** tachometer; *(Aut auch)* speedometer, speedo *(Brit inf)*; **~überschreitung, ~übertretung** *f* exceeding the speed limit, speeding; **~zunahme** *f (Phys)* increase in velocity.
Geschwirr *nt* **-s,** *no pl (von Insekten)* buzzing; *(von Pfeilen)* whizzing.
Geschwister [1] *pl* brothers and sisters *pl* ◆ **wir sind drei ~** there are three of us in my *or* our family; **haben Sie noch ~?** do you have any brothers or sisters?
[2] *nt* **-s, -** *(form)* sibling *(form)*; *(Bruder)* brother; *(Schwester)* sister.
Geschwisterchen *nt* little brother/sister.
geschwisterlich [1] *adj* brotherly/sisterly.
[2] *adv* in a brotherly/sisterly way ◆ **sie leben ~ zusammen** they live together as brother and sister.
Geschwister-: ~liebe *f* brotherly/sisterly love; *(gegenseitig)* love between a brother and a sister; **g~los** *adj* who have no brothers or sisters; **~paar** *nt* brother and sister *pl*; **die beiden sind ein reizendes ~paar** the children are a lovely pair.
geschwollen [1] *ptp of* **schwellen.**
[2] *adj (pej)* turgid, pompous, bombastic.
geschwommen *ptp of* **schwimmen.**
geschworen [1] *ptp of* **schwören.**
[2] *adj attr* sworn.
Geschworenen-: ~bank *f* jury-box; *(die Geschworenen)* jury; **~gericht** *nt siehe* **Schwurgericht**; **~liste** *f* panel.
Geschworene(r), Geschworne(r) *(Aus) mf decl as adj* juror ◆ **die ~n** the jury *sing or pl*.
Geschwulst *f* **-, ¨e** growth; *(Hirn~, Krebs~ etc auch)* tumour.
Geschwulst-: g~artig *adj* growth-like; tumorous; **~knoten** *m* growth.
geschwunden *ptp of* **schwinden.**
geschwungen [1] *ptp of* **schwingen.**
[2] *adj* curved ◆ **leicht/kühn ~e Nase** slightly curved nose/aquiline nose.
Geschwür *nt* **-s, -e** ulcer; *(Haut~ auch)* sore; *(Furunkel)* boil; *(fig)* running sore, ulcer.
geschwür|artig *adj* ulcerous ◆ **sich ~ verändern** to go ulcerous, to ulcerate.
gesegnet *adj (geh)* **mit etw ~ sein** to be blessed with sth; **~en Leibes sein** *(old, Bibl)* to be great with child *(old, Bibl)*; **~es Neues Jahr/~e Mahlzeit!** Happy New Year/for what we are about to receive may the Lord make us truly thankful; **im ~en Alter von 84 Jahren** at the age of 84; **einen ~en Schlaf/Appetit haben** to be a sound sleeper/to have a healthy appetite.
gesehen *ptp of* **sehen.**
Geseich(e) *nt* **-(e)s,** *no pl (sl) siehe* **Geseier (b).**
Geseier, Geseire *nt* **-s,** *no pl*, **Geseires** *nt* **-,** *no pl (pej inf)* **(a)** *(Gejammer)* moaning, bellyaching *(inf)*. **(b)** *(Geschwafel)* claptrap *(inf)*.
Geselchte(s) *nt decl as adj (S Ger, Aus) salted and smoked meat.*
Gesell *m* **-en, -en** *(obs)*, **Geselle** *m* **-n, -n (a)** *(Handwerks~)* journeyman. **(b)** *(old inf: Bursche)* fellow. **(c)** *(dated: Kamerad)* companion.
gesellen* *vr* **sich zu jdm ~** to join sb; **dazu gesellte sich noch, daß ...** *(geh)* in addition to this was the fact that ..., this was accompanied by the fact that ...; *siehe* **gleich.**
Gesellen-: ~brief *m* journeyman's certificate; **~jahre** *pl* years *pl* as a journeyman; **~prüfung** *f* examination to become a journeyman; **~stück** *nt* journeyman's piece; **~zeit** *f* period as a journeyman.
gesellig *adj* sociable, convivial; *Tier* gregarious; *Verkehr* social ◆ **der Mensch ist ein ~es Tier** man is a social creature *or* animal; **~es Beisammensein** social gathering, get-together *(inf)*; **sie saßen ~ bei einer Flasche Wein zusammen** they were sitting together over a friendly bottle of wine.
Geselligkeit *f* **(a)** *no pl* sociability, conviviality; *(von Tieren)* gregariousness; *(geselliges Leben)* social intercourse ◆ **die ~ lieben** to be sociable, to enjoy company. **(b)** *(Veranstaltung)* social gathering.
Gesellschaft *f* **(a)** *(Sociol, fig: Oberschicht)* society ◆ **die ~ verändern** to change society; **eine Dame der ~** a society lady; **die ~ der Stadt** the high society of the town; **jdn in die ~ einführen** to introduce sb into society.
(b) *(Vereinigung)* society; *(Comm)* company ◆ **die ~ der Freunde** the Society of Friends; **~ des bürgerlichen Rechts** private company *or* corporation *(US)*.
(c) *(Abend~)* reception, party; *(Gäste)* guests *pl*, party ◆ **geschlossene ~** private party; **eine erlesene ~ hatte sich eingefunden** a select group of people had gathered.
(d) *(in Restaurant etc)* function.
(e) *(Umgang, Begleitung)* company, society *(old, form)* ◆ **zur ~** to be sociable; **in schlechte ~ geraten** to get into bad company; **da befindest du dich in guter ~** then you're in good company; **jdm ~ leisten** to keep sb company.
(f) *(Kreis von Menschen)* group of people; *(pej)* pack, bunch, crowd *(all inf)* ◆ **diese Familie/Abteilung ist eine komische ~** that family/department are an odd lot; **wir waren eine bunte ~** we were a mixed bunch.
Gesellschafter(in f) *m* **-s, - (a)** *(Unterhalter)* companion; *(euph: Prostituierte)* escort ◆ **ein guter ~ sein** to be good company; **er ist nicht der Typ des ~s** he's not good company; **mit einem so anregenden ~ ...** with somebody who is such good company ...
(b) *(Comm) (Teilhaber)* shareholder; *(Partner)* partner ◆ **stiller ~** sleeping *(Brit) or* silent *(US)* partner.
gesellschaftlich *adj* social; *(Sociol auch)* societal ◆ **~e Produktion** production by society; **er ist ~ erledigt** he's ruined socially; **sich ~ unmöglich machen** to disgrace oneself socially.
Gesellschafts-: ~abend *m* social evening; **~anteil** *m (Comm)* share of the business; **~anzug** *m* formal dress; **~aufbau** *m* structure of society; **~bild** *nt (Sociol)* view of society; **~dame** *f (old)* (lady's) companion; **g~fähig** *adj Verhalten* socially acceptable; *Mensch, Aussehen auch* presentable; **g~feindlich** *adj* hostile to society; **~form** *f* social system; **~formation** *f (Sociol)* development of society; **~kapital** *nt (Comm)* company's capital; **~klasse** *f (Sociol)* social class; **~klatsch** *m* society gossip; **~kleidung** *f* formal dress; **~kritik** *f* social criticism, criticism of society; **~kritiker** *m* social critic; **g~kritisch** *adj* critical of society; **g~kritisch denken** to have a critical attitude towards society; **die g~kritische Funktion einer Zeitung** the function of a newspaper as a critic of society *or* social critic; **~lehre** *f (dated)* sociology; *(Sch)* social studies *pl*; **~ordnung** *f* social system; **~politik** *f* social politics; **~raum** *m* function room; **~roman** *m* social novel; **~schicht** *f* stratum of society, social stratum; **~spiel** *nt* party game, parlour game; **~struktur** *f* structure of society; *(bestimmte auch)* social structure; **~stück** *nt (Theat)* comedy of manners; *(Art)* genre painting; **~system** *nt* social system; **~tanz** *m* ballroom dance; **~veränderung** *f* social change; **~vertrag** *m (Philos)* social contract; *(Comm)* articles *pl* of partnership, partnership agreement; **~wissenschaften** *pl* social sciences *pl*; **g~wissenschaftlich** *adj* sociological.
Gesenk *nt* **-(e)s, -e (a)** *(Tech)* die. **(b)** *(Min)* blind shaft, winze.
Gesenkschmiede *f (Tech)* drop forge.
gesessen *ptp of* **sitzen.**
Gesetz *nt* **-es, -e** *(Jur, Natur~, Prinzip)* law; *(~buch)* statute book; *(Parl: Vorlage)* bill; *(Parl: nach der dritten Lesung)* act; *(Satzung, Regel)* rule ◆ **das Miet-/Copyright-~** the Rent/Copyright Act; **(zum) ~ werden** to become law, to pass into law; **auf Grund des ~es, nach dem ~** under the law *(über +acc* on); **vor dem ~** in (the eyes of the) law; **im Sinne des ~es** within the meaning of the act; **steht etwas davon im ~?** is there any law about it?; **ich kann nichts im ~ finden, wonach das verboten wäre** I can't find any law forbidding it; **das ~ der Schwerkraft** the law of gravity; **das erste** *or* **oberste ~ (der Wirtschaft** *etc*) the golden rule (of industry *etc*); **das ~ Mose** *(Bibl)* the Law of Moses, the Mosaic Law; **ein ungeschriebenes ~** an unwritten rule; **wenn uns das ~ des Handelns aufgezwungen wird** if we are forced to take the initiative *or* the first step.
Gesetz-: ~blatt *nt* law gazette; **~buch** *nt* statute book; **Bürgerliches ~buch** Civil Code; **~entwurf** *m* (draft) bill.
Gesetzes-: ~brecher(in f) *m* **-s, -** law-breaker; **~hüter** *m (iro)* guardian of the law; **~initiative** *f* legislative initiative; *(Sw: Volksbegehren)* petition for a referendum; **~kraft** *f* the force of law; **~kraft erlangen** to become law; **~kraft haben** to be law; **g~kundig** *adj* (well-)versed in the law; **~lücke** *f* legal loophole; **~novelle** *f* amendment; **~sammlung** *f* compendium of laws *(zu* on); **~tafeln** *pl (Bibl)* tablets *on which the Ten Commandments were written*; **~text** *m* wording of a/the law; **g~treu** *adj* law-abiding; **~treue** *f* law-abidingness; **~übertretung** *f* infringement of a/the law; **~vorlage** *f* (draft) bill; **~werk** *nt* corpus of laws.
Gesetz-: g~gebend *adj attr* legislative, law-making; **die g~gebende Gewalt** the legislature; **~geber** *m* legislator, law-maker; *(Versammlung)* legislature, legislative body; **g~geberisch** *adj attr* legislative.
Gesetzgebung *f* legislation *no pl*.
Gesetzgebungs-: ~hoheit *f* legislative sovereignty; **~notstand** *m* legislative state of emergency.
gesetzkundig *adj siehe* **gesetzeskundig.**
gesetzlich [1] *adj Verpflichtung, Bestimmungen, Vertreter, Zahlungsmittel* legal; *Feiertag, Rücklage, Zinsen, Reglungen* statutory; *(rechtmäßig)* lawful, legitimate ◆ **auf ~em Wege zur Macht gelangen** to come to power by legal means.
[2] *adv* legally; *(durch Gesetze auch)* by law; *(rechtmäßig)* lawfully, legitimately ◆ **~ zu etw verpflichtet sein** to be required by law *or* to be legally required to do sth; *siehe* **schützen.**
Gesetzlichkeit *f, no pl (Gesetzmäßigkeit)* legality; *(Rechtmäßigkeit)* lawfulness, legitimacy; *(Rechtsordnung)* law.
Gesetz-: g~los *adj* lawless; **~losigkeit** *f* lawlessness; **g~mäßig** *adj* **(a)** *(gesetzlich)* legal; *(rechtmäßig)* lawful, legitimate; **(b)** *(einem Natur~ folgend)* in accordance with a law (of nature); *(rare: regelmäßig)* regular; **Denkprozesse, die g~mäßig ablaufen** thought processes which are law-governed; **~mäßigkeit** *f siehe adj* legality; lawfulness, legitimacy; regularity; **unser**

Seelenleben folgt vielleicht uns unbekannten ~mäßigkeiten perhaps the life of the mind runs in accordance with laws which are unknown to us.

gesetzt [1] *adj (reif)* sedate, sober ◆ **ein Herr im ~en Alter** a man of mature years.
[2] *conj* **~ den Fall, ...** assuming (that) ...

Gesetztheit *f (Reife)* sedateness.

Gesetz-: g~widrig *adj* illegal; *(unrechtmäßig)* unlawful; **~widrigkeit** *f siehe adj* illegality; unlawfulness *no pl*.

Geseufze *nt* **-s,** *no pl* sighing.

ges. gesch. *abbr of* **gesetzlich geschützt** reg'd.

gesichert *adj Einkommen, Existenz* secure ◆ **~es Gewehr** gun with the safety catch on.

Gesicht[1] *nt* **-(e)s, -er (a)** face ◆ **ein ~ machen** *or* **ziehen** *(inf)* to make *or* pull a face; **ein intelligentes/trauriges/böses/wütendes ~ machen** to look intelligent/sad/cross/angry; **ein langes ~ machen** to make *or* pull a long face; **was machst du denn heute für ein ~?** what's up with you today?; **jdm ein ~ schneiden** *(inf)* to make *or* pull a face at sb; **jdm ins ~ spucken** to spit in sb's face; **jdm ins ~ lachen/lügen/sehen** to laugh in sb's face/to lie to sb's face/to look sb in the face; **den Tatsachen ins ~ sehen** to face facts; **jdm etw ins ~ sagen** to tell sb sth to his face; **mir schien die Sonne ins ~** the sun was (shining) in my eyes; **es stand ihm im ~ geschrieben** it was written all over his face; **jdm ins ~ springen** *(fig inf)* to go for sb; **aufs ~ fallen** to fall on one's face; *(fig inf: Brot etc)* to fall sticky side down; **sein wahres ~ zeigen** to show (oneself in) one's true colours; **neue ~er sehen** to see some new faces; **das sieht man ihm am ~ an** you can see *or* tell (that) from his face; **sich** *(dat)* **eine (Zigarette) ins ~ stecken** *(inf)* to stick a cigarette in one's mouth *or* face *(sl)*; **jdm wie aus dem ~ geschnitten sein** to be the spitting image of sb; **der Hut steht ihr gut zu ~** *(dated)* her hat is very becoming, her hat becomes her; **dieses Verhalten steht dir nicht zu ~** *(dated)* such behaviour ill becomes you, it ill becomes you to behave like that; **das/sein ~ verlieren** to lose face; **das ~ wahren** *or* **retten** to save face; *siehe* **Schlag.**
(b) *(fig) (Aussehen)* look, appearance; *(einer Stadt, Landschaft etc auch)* face; *(geh: Charakter)* character ◆ **ein anderes/freundlicheres ~ bekommen** to look quite different/more friendly; **die Sache bekommt ein anderes ~** the matter takes on a different complexion; **das gibt der Sache ein neues ~** that puts a different complexion on the matter *or* on things.
(c) *no pl (old: Sehvermögen)* sight ◆ **das Zweite ~** second sight; **jdn aus dem ~ verlieren** *(lit)* to lose sight of sb; *(fig)* to lose touch with sb; **etw aus dem ~ verlieren** *(lit, fig)* to lose sight of sth; **jdn/etw zu ~ bekommen** to set eyes on sb/sth, to see sb/sth; **jdm zu ~ kommen** *(geh)* to be seen by sb.

Gesicht[2] *nt* **-(e)s, -e: ~e haben** to have visions.

Gesichts-: ~ausdruck *m* (facial) expression; *(Mienenspiel auch)* face; **einen ängstlichen ~ausdruck haben** to look scared, to have a scared look *or* expression on one's face; **~bildung** *f (geh)* features *pl*; **~creme** *f* face cream; **~farbe** *f* complexion; **~feld** *nt* field of vision, visual field; **~hälfte** *f* side *or* half of the face; **seine linke ~hälfte** the left side *or* half of his face; **~haut** *f* facial skin; **~kontrolle** *f* face check *(carried out by bouncers)*; **~kreis** *m* **(a)** *(dated) (Umkreis)* field of vision; *(Horizont)* horizon; **jds ~kreis** *(dat)* **entschwinden** to disappear from (sb's) sight, to be lost to sight; **jdn aus dem/seinem ~kreis verlieren** to lose sight of sb; **(b)** *(fig)* horizons *pl*, outlook; **~lähmung** *f* facial paralysis; **g~los** *adj (fig)* faceless; **~maske** *f* face mask; *(eines Chirurgen)* mask; **~massage** *f* facial massage, facial; **~milch** *f* face lotion; **~muskel** *m* facial muscle; **~nerv** *m* facial nerve; **~operation** *f* operation to one's face; **sich einer ~operation unterziehen** to undergo facial surgery; **~packung** *f* face pack; **~partie** *f* part of the/one's face; **~pflege** *f* care of one's face; **~plastik** *f* facial *or* cosmetic surgery; **~puder** *m* face powder; **~punkt** *m (Betrachtungsweise)* point of view, standpoint; *(Einzelheit)* point; **unter diesem ~punkt betrachtet** looked at from this point of view *or* standpoint; **~rose** *f (Med)* facial erysipelas *(spec)*; **~schädel** *m (Anat)* facial bones *pl*; **~schnitt** *m* features *pl*; **ein ovaler/feiner ~schnitt** an oval face/delicate features *pl*; **~verlust** *m* loss of face; **~wasser** *nt* face lotion; **~winkel** *m* visual angle; *(fig)* angle, point of view; **~züge** *pl* features *pl*.

Gesims *nt* **-es, -e** ledge.

Gesinde *nt* **-s, -** *(old)* servants *pl*; *(Bauern~)* (farm)hands *pl*.

Gesindel *nt* **-s,** *no pl (pej)* riff-raff *pl*.

Gesinde-: ~ordnung *f (Hist) rules governing relations between servant and master*; **~stube** *f (old)* servants' room.

Gesinge *nt* **-s,** *no pl (inf)* singing.

gesinnt *adj usu pred* **jdm gut/günstig/übel ~ sein** to be well/favourably/ill disposed to(wards) sb; **jdm freundlich/feindlich ~ sein** to be friendly/hostile to(wards) sb; **sozial/fortschrittlich ~ sein** to be socially/progressively minded; **er ist anders ~ als wir** his views are different from ours, he holds different views from us; **die so ~en Mitglieder** the members holding *or* taking this view.

Gesinnung *f (Charakter)* cast of mind; *(Ansichten)* views *pl*, basic convictions *pl*; *(Einstellung)* fundamental attitude; *(Denkart)* way of thinking; *(einer Gruppe)* ethos ◆ **eine liberale/edle ~** liberal-/noble-mindedness; **anständige ~** decency; **seiner ~ treu bleiben** to remain loyal to one's basic convictions; **wegen seiner ~ verfolgt werden** to be persecuted because of one's views *or* basic convictions *or* way of thinking; **seine wahre ~ zeigen** to show (oneself in) one's true colours.

Gesinnungs-: ~freund, ~genosse *m* like-minded person; **Herr Klein und seine ~genossen von der Opposition** Mr. Klein and people from the Opposition who think as he does *or* who share his views; **g~los** *adj (pej)* unprincipled; **sich g~los verhalten** to behave in an unprincipled manner, to show a total lack of character; **~losigkeit** *f* lack of principle, unprincipledness; **~lump** *m (pej)* timeserver *(pej inf)*; **~schnüffelei** *f (pej)* **~schnüffelei betreiben** to snoop around and find out people's political convictions; **~täter** *m* person motivated by political/moral convictions; **g~treu** *adj* true to one's convictions; **~treue** *f* loyalty to one's convictions; **~wandel, ~wechsel** *m* conversion.

gesittet *adj* **(a)** *(wohlerzogen)* well-mannered, well-behaved ◆ **die Kinder benahmen sich sehr ~** the children were very well-behaved *or* well-mannered. **(b)** *(zivilisiert, kultiviert)* civilized.

Gesittung *f, no pl (geh) (zivilisiertes Verhalten)* civilized (mode of) behaviour; *(Gesinnung)* ethos.

Gesocks *nt* **-es,** *no pl (pej sl)* riff-raff *pl*.

Gesöff *nt* **-(e)s, -e** *(sl)* muck *(inf)*, swill *(inf)*; *(Bier)* piss *(vulg)*.

gesoffen *ptp of* **saufen.**

gesogen *ptp of* **saugen.**

gesondert *adj* separate ◆ **Ihre Frau wird ~ benachrichtigt** your wife will be informed separately.

gesonnen [1] *ptp of* **sinnen.**
[2] *adj* **(a) ~ sein, etw zu tun** to be of a mind to do sth. **(b)** *(incorrect) siehe* **gesinnt.**

gesotten [1] *ptp of* **sieden.**
[2] *adj (dial)* boiled ◆ **G~es** boiled meat.

gespalten [1] *ptp of* **spalten.**
[2] *adj Bewußtsein* split; *Lippe, Rachen* cleft; *Huf* cloven; *Zunge* forked ◆ **mit ~er Zunge reden** *(old, liter)* to talk falsely; *(esp in Indianergeschichten)* to talk with forked tongue.

Gespann *nt* **-(e)s, -e (a)** *(Zugtiere)* team; *(zwei Ochsen)* yoke. **(b)** *(Wagen und Zugtier) (Ochsen~)* oxcart, ox-drawn cart; *(Pferde~)* horse and cart; *(zur Personenbeförderung)* horse and carriage; *(fig inf: Paar)* pair ◆ **ein gutes ~ abgeben** to make a good team.

gespannt *adj* **(a)** *Seil, Schnur* taut.
(b) *(fig)* tense; *Beziehungen auch* strained ◆ **seine Nerven waren aufs äußerste ~** his nerves were at breaking point.
(c) *(neugierig)* curious; *(begierig)* eager; *Aufmerksamkeit* close ◆ **in ~er Erwartung** in eager *or* keen anticipation; **ich bin ~, wie er darauf reagiert** I wonder how he'll react to that, I'd like to see how he reacts to that; **ich bin sehr ~, was ich zu Weihnachten bekomme** I'm longing *or* dying to know what I'm getting for Christmas; **ich bin schon sehr auf diesen Film ~** I'm dying to see this film; **ich bin auf seine Reaktion sehr ~** I'm longing *or* dying to see how he reacts; **ich bin ~ wie ein Regenschirm** *(hum inf) or* **Flitzbogen** *(hum inf)* I'm dying to know/see/find out, I'm on tenterhooks; **da bin ich aber ~!** I'm looking forward to that; *(iro)* oh really?, that I'd like to see!

Gespanntheit *f, no pl siehe adj* **(a)** tension. **(b)** tension; strain. **(c)** curiosity; eagerness; closeness ◆ **es herrscht große ~** everyone is on tenterhooks.

gespaßig *adj (S Ger, Aus) siehe* **spaßig.**

Gespenst *nt* **-(e)s, -er** ghost, spectre *(liter)*; *(fig: Gefahr)* spectre ◆ **~er sehen** *(fig inf)* to imagine things; **er sieht wie ein ~ aus** *(inf)* he looks like a ghost.

Gespenster-: ~geschichte *f* ghost story; **~glaube** *m* belief in ghosts; **g~haft** *adj* ghostly *no adv*; *(fig)* eerie, eery; **er sah g~haft bleich aus** he was deadly *or* deathly pale, he looked like a ghost; **das Licht flackerte g~haft** the light flickered eerily.

gespenstern* *vi aux sein (rare) siehe* **geistern.**

Gespenster-: ~schiff *nt* phantom ship; **~stunde** *f* witching hour.

gespenstig *(rare),* **gespenstisch** *adj* **(a)** *siehe* **gespensterhaft. (b)** *(fig: bizarr, unheimlich)* eerie, eery.

gespie(e)n *ptp of* **speien.**

Gespiele *m* **-n, -n** *(old liter, hum),* **Gespielin** *f (old liter, hum)* playmate.

gespielt *adj* feigned ◆ **mit ~em Interesse** with a pretence of being interested.

gespiesen *(hum) ptp of* **speisen.**

Gespinst *nt* **-(e)s, -e (a)** *(Tex)* weave; *(gedrehtes Garn)* thread, spun yarn; *(von Spinne)* gossamer; *(von Raupe)* cocoon. **(b)** *(fig geh)* web; *(von Lügen auch)* tissue; *(der Phantasie)* product, fabrication.

Gespinstfaser *f (Tex)* spinning fibre.

gesplissen *ptp of* **spleißen.**

gesponnen *ptp of* **spinnen.**

Gespons *m* **-es, -e** *(old, hum)* spouse *(hum, form)*.

gespornt *adj siehe* **gestiefelt.**

Gespött *nt* **-(e)s,** *no pl* mockery; *(höhnisch auch)* derision, ridicule; *(Gegenstand des Spotts)* laughing-stock ◆ **jdn/sich zum ~ der Leute machen** to make sb/oneself a laughing stock *or* an object of ridicule; **zum ~ werden** to become a laughing stock; **zum ~ der ganzen Welt werden** to become the laughing stock of the whole world; **mit jdm sein ~ treiben** to poke fun at sb.

▼ **Gespräch** *nt* **-(e)s, -e (a)** *(Unterhaltung)* conversation; *(Diskussion)* discussion; *(Dialog)* dialogue ◆ **~e** *(Pol)* talks; **ich habe ein sehr interessantes ~ mit ihm geführt** I had a very interesting conversation *or* talk with him; **ein ~ unter vier Augen** a confidential *or* private talk; **mit jdm ein ~ anknüpfen** to start a *or* get into conversation with sb; **das ~ auf etw** *(acc)* **bringen** to bring *or* steer the conversation *etc* round to sth; **im ~ sein** *(lit)* to be being discussed, to be being talked about; *(in der Schwebe)* to be under discussion; **mit jdm ins ~ kommen** to get into conversation with sb; *(fig)* to establish a dialogue with sb.
(b) *(~sstoff)* **das ~ des Tages** the topic of the hour; **das ~ der Stadt** the talk

of the town; **zum ~ werden** to become a talking-point.
▼ **(c)** (*Telec: Anruf*) (telephone) call ◆ **wir haben in unserem gestrigen ~ vereinbart, daß** ... we agreed in our telephone conversation yesterday that ...; **ein ~ für dich** a call for you; **stundenlange ~e führen** to be on the telephone for hours.

gesprächig *adj* talkative, chatty (*inf*); (*mitteilsam*) communicative ◆ **~ von etw erzählen** to talk volubly about sth; **jdn ~ machen** to make sb talk, to loosen sb's tongue.

Gesprächigkeit *f, no pl* talkativeness, chattiness (*inf*); (*Mitteilsamkeit*) communicativeness ◆ **von unglaublicher ~ sein** to be incredibly talkative *or* chatty (*inf*)/communicative.

Gesprächs-: g~bereit *adj* (*esp Pol*) ready to talk; **~bereitschaft** *f* (*esp Pol*) readiness to talk; **~dauer** *f* **(a)** (*Telec*) call time; **(b) nach vierstündiger ~dauer** after four hours of talks; **~einheit** *f* (*Telec*) unit; **~faden** *m* line of communication (*zu* with); **den ~faden weiterspinnen** to pursue the line of conversation; **~fetzen** *m* scrap *or* snippet of conversation; **~form** *f* **in ~form** in dialogue form; **~gebühr** *f* (*Telec*) charge for a/the call; **~gegenstand** *m* topic; **der Skandal ist ~gegenstand Nummer eins** the scandal is the number one topic; **damit die Leute endlich einen ~gegenstand haben** so that people at last have something to talk about; **~partner** *m* interlocutor (*form*); **~partner bei der Diskussion sind die Herren X, Y und Z** taking part in the discussion are Mr X, Mr Y and Mr Z; **mein ~partner bei den Verhandlungen** my opposite number at the talks; **er ist nicht gerade ein anregender ~partner** he's not exactly an exciting conversationalist; **wer war dein ~partner?** who did you talk with?; **mein ~partner heute abend ist** ... with me this evening is ...; **~pause** *f* break in a/the conversation/talks; **eine ~pause einlegen** to have a break, to break off (for a while); **~stoff** *m* topics *pl*; (*Diskussionsstoff*) topics to discuss; **~teilnehmer** *m* somebody taking part in (the) talks; participant in a/the discussion; (*bei Fernsehserien etc*) panellist; **~thema** *nt siehe* **~gegenstand; g~weise** *adv* in conversation.

gespreizt *adj* (*fig*) affected, unnatural.

Gespreiztheit *f* affectation, unnaturalness ◆ **von unerträglicher ~** unbearably affected.

gesprenkelt *adj* speckled.

Gespritzte(r) *m decl as adj* (*S Ger, Aus*) spritzer, wine with soda water.

gesprochen *ptp of* **sprechen.**

gesprossen *ptp of* **sprießen, sprossen.**

gesprungen *ptp of* **springen.**

Gespür *nt* **-s,** *no pl* feel(ing).

gest. *abbr of* **gestorben.**

Gestade *nt* **-s, -** (*liter*) strand (*poet*).

Gestagen [gɛsta'ge:n] *nt* **-s, -e** (*Med*) gestagen.

Gestalt *f* **-, -en (a)** (*lit, fig*) form; (*Umriß auch*) shape ◆ **in ~ von** (*fig*) in the form of; **(feste) ~ annehmen** *or* **gewinnen** to take shape; **einer Sache** (*dat*) **~ geben** *or* **verleihen** to shape sth; **das Abendmahl in beiderlei ~** (*Eccl*) Communion under both kinds; **sich in seiner wahren ~ zeigen** (*fig*) to show (oneself in) one's true colours; **~ geworden** (*liter*) made flesh *pred*; *siehe* **Ritter.**
(b) (*Wuchs*) build.
(c) (*Person, Persönlichkeit, Traum~*) figure; (*in Literaturwerken auch, pej: Mensch*) character.

gestalten* [1] *vt* to shape, to form, to fashion (*zu* into); *Wohnung* to lay out; *Programm, Abend* to arrange; *Schaufenster* to dress; *Freizeit* to organize, to structure ◆ **ich gestalte mein Leben so, wie ich will** I live *or* organize my life the way I want to; **etw interessanter/moderner** *etc* **~** to make sth more interesting/modern *etc*; **der Umbau wurde nach den ursprünglichen Plänen gestaltet** the conversion was carried out in accordance with the original plans; **die Gastgeber haben den Abend sehr lebendig gestaltet** our hosts laid on a very lively evening; **etw schöpferisch ~** to give artistic form to sth; **schöpferisches G~** creative expression; **einen historischen Stoff zu einem Roman ~** to fashion *or* mould a historical subject into a novel; **einen Stoff literarisch ~** to give literary form to one's material.
[2] *vr* (*werden*) to become; (*sich entwickeln*) to turn *or* develop (*zu* into) ◆ **sich zu einem Erfolg ~** to turn out to be a success.

Gestalter(in *f***)** *m* **-s, -** creator; (*Tech rare*) designer.

gestalterisch *adj* formal, structural ◆ **er hat eine große ~e Begabung** he has a great feeling for form.

Gestalt-: ~lehre *f* (*dated*) morphology; **g~los** *adj* formless, shapeless, amorphous; **~psychologie** *f* Gestalt psychology.

Gestaltung *f* **(a)** *siehe vt* shaping, forming, fashioning (*zu* into); lay-out; arrangement; dressing; structuring ◆ **wir bemühen uns um eine möglichst interessante ~ des Sprachunterrichts** we are trying to make our language-teaching as interesting as possible *or* to structure our language-teaching as interestingly as possible.
(b) (*liter: Gestaltetes*) creation.

Gestaltungs-: ~form *f* form; **~kraft** *f* creative power; **~prinzip** *nt* formal principle.

Gestammel *nt* **-s,** *no pl* stammering, stuttering.

gestand *pret of* **gestehen.**

gestanden [1] *ptp of* **stehen, gestehen.**
[2] *adj attr* **ein ~er Mann, ein ~es Mannsbild** a mature and experienced man.

geständig *adj* **~ sein** to have confessed; **ein ~er Mörder** a murderer who confesses.

Geständnis *nt* confession ◆ **ein ~ ablegen** to make a confession; **jdm ein ~ machen** to make a confession to sb; **jdn zu einem ~ zwingen** to force sb to make a confession.

Gestänge *nt* **-s, -** (*von Gerüst*) bars *pl*, struts *pl*; (*von Maschine*) linkage; (*Min: Bohr~*) drill stem.

Gestank *m* **-(e)s,** *no pl* stink, stench.

Gestänker *nt* **-s,** *no pl* (*inf*) trouble-making, stirring (*inf*).

Gestapo [ge'sta:po] *f* **-,** *no pl* Gestapo.

gestärkt *adj* strengthened.

▼ **gestatten*** *vti* to allow, to permit; (*einwilligen in*) to agree *or* consent to ◆ **jdm etw ~** to allow sb sth; **jdm ~, etw zu tun** to allow *or* permit sb to do sth; **~ Sie?(, darf ich ...), ~ Sie, daß ich ...?** may I ...?, would you mind if I ...?; **wenn Sie ~ ...** with your permission ...; **~ Sie eine Frage?** may I ask you something *or* a question?; **sich** (*dat*) **~, etw zu tun** (*geh*) to take the liberty of doing sth, to be *or* make so bold as to do sth (*dated, hum*); **sich** (*dat*) **etw ~** to permit *or* allow oneself sth; **wenn ich mir eine Frage/Bemerkung ~ darf ...** (*geh*) if I might be permitted a question/comment, if I may make *or* be so bold *or* free as to ask a question/make a remark ...; **mein Gehalt gestattet mir das nicht** (*geh*) my salary won't permit it; **wenn es die Umstände ~ ...** (*geh*) circumstances permitting ...

Geste ['gɛstə, 'ge:stə] *f* **-, -n** (*lit, fig*) gesture.

Gesteck *nt* **-(e)s, -e** flower arrangement.

gesteckt *adv* **~ voll** (*dial*) chock-a-block (*inf*).

gestehen *pret* **gestand,** *ptp* **gestanden** *vti* to confess (*jdm etw* sth to sb) ◆ **offen gestanden** to be frank, quite frankly.

Gestehungs-: ~kosten *pl*, **~preis** *m* (*Comm*) production costs *pl*.

Gestein *nt* **-(e)s, -e** rock(s); (*Schicht*) rock stratum.

Gesteins-: ~ader *f* vein of rock; **~art** *f* type of rock; **~bohrer** *m*, **~bohrmaschine** *f* rock drill; **~brocken** *m* rock; **~kunde** *f* petrography; **~masse** *f* mass of rock; **~probe** *f* rock sample; **~schicht** *f* rock layer *or* stratum.

Gestell *nt* **-(e)s, -e (a)** stand; (*Regal*) shelf; (*Ablage*) rack; (*Rahmen, Bett~, Brillen~, Tisch~*) frame; (*auf Böcken*) trestle; (*Wäsche~*) clothes dryer; (*Wäsche~ aus Holz*) clothes horse; (*Fahr~*) chassis; (*Flugzeug~*) undercarriage, landing gear; (*Tech: von Hochofen*) hearth.
(b) (*fig inf*) (*Beine*) pins (*inf*) *pl* ◆ **langes ~** beanpole (*inf*).

gestellt *adj* posed.

Gestellung *f* **(a)** (*old Mil*) muster. **(b)** (*form*) furnishing (*form*), making available ◆ **ich bitte um ~ von zwei Lastwagen** I request that two lorries be made available.

Gestellungsbefehl *m* (*Mil*) call-up, draft papers *pl* (*US*).

gestelzt *adj* stilted.

Gestelztheit *f* stiltedness.

gestern *adv* yesterday ◆ **~ abend** (*früh*) yesterday evening; (*spät*) last night; **die Zeitung von ~** yesterday's paper; **Ansichten von ~** outdated views, opinions of yesteryear (*liter*); **er ist nicht von ~** (*inf*) he wasn't born yesterday; **~ vor acht Tagen** a week (ago) yesterday, yesterday week; **~ in acht Tagen** a week (from) yesterday.

Gestern *nt* **-,** *no pl* yesterday ◆ **das ~** yesterday, yesteryear (*liter*); **im ~** in the past.

Gestichel *nt* **-s,** *no pl* snide remarks *pl*.

gestiefelt *adj* **(a)** wearing *or* in boots ◆ **der G~e Kater** Puss-in-Boots. **(b) ~ und gespornt** (*fig inf*) ready and waiting, ready for the off (*inf*).

gestiegen *ptp of* **steigen.**

gestielt *adj* stemmed (*auch Bot*).

Gestik ['gɛstɪk] *f* **-,** *no pl* gestures *pl*.

Gestikulation [gɛstikula'tsio:n] *f* gesticulation(s).

gestikulieren* [gɛstiku'li:rən] *vi* to gesticulate.

Gestikulieren *nt* **-s,** *no pl* gesticulation(s), gesticulating.

gestimmt *adj* **froh/düster ~** in a cheerful/sombre mood.

Gestimmtheit *f siehe* **Stimmung.**

Gestirn *nt* **-(e)s, -e** star, heavenly body.

gestirnt *adj attr* (*geh*) starry, star-studded (*liter*).

gestisch ['gɛstɪʃ] *adj* gestural ◆ **all seine Worte waren ~ untermalt** everything he said was underlined by gesture.

gestoben *ptp of* **stieben.**

Gestöber *nt* **-s, -** *siehe* **Schneegestöber.**

gestochen [1] *ptp of* **stechen.**
[2] *adj Handschrift* clear, neat ◆ **~ scharfe Fotos** needle-sharp photographs.

gestockt *adj* (*S Ger*) *Milch* soured.

gestohlen [1] *ptp of* **stehlen.**
[2] *adj* **der/das kann mir ~ bleiben** (*inf*) he/it can go hang (*inf*).

Gestöhn(e) *nt* **-s,** *no pl* moaning, groaning.

gestopft *adv* **~ voll** (*inf*) jam-packed (*inf*).

gestorben *ptp of* **sterben.**

gestört *adj* disturbed; *Schlaf auch* broken; *Verhältnis auch* troubled; *Rundfunkempfang* poor, with a lot of interference; *Einverständnis* troubled, disrupted ◆ **seelisch/geistig ~ sein** to be (psychologically/mentally) unbalanced *or* disturbed; **~er Kreislauf** circulation problems; **Kinder aus ~en Familien** children from problem families.

gestoßen *ptp of* **stoßen.**

Gestotter *nt* **-s,** *no pl* stuttering, stammering.

Gestrampel *nt* **-s,** *no pl* kicking about; (*beim Radfahren*) pedalling.

Gesträuch *nt* **-(e)s, -e** shrubbery, bushes *pl*; (*Dickicht*) thicket.

gestreckt *adj Galopp* full; *Winkel, Flugbahn* elongated.

gestreift *adj* striped ◆ **eine rot-grün ~e Bluse** a red and green striped blouse.

Gestreite *nt* **-s,** *no pl* (*inf*) bickering (*inf*), quarrelling.

gestreng *adj (old)* strict, stern ◆ **~er Herr!** gracious master *or* Lord; **die G~en Herren** *siehe* **Eisheiligen.**

gestrichen [1] *ptp of* **streichen.**
[2] *adj* (a) painted; *Papier* coated ◆ **frisch ~!** wet paint.
(b) *(genau voll)* **ein ~es Maß** a level measure; **~ voll** level; *(sehr voll)* full to the brim; **ein ~er Teelöffel voll** a level teaspoon(ful); **er hat die Hosen ~ voll** *(sl)* he's wetting *(inf)* or shitting *(vulg)* himself; **ich habe die Nase ~ voll** *(sl)* I'm fed up to the back teeth with it *(inf)*.
(c) *Wort, Satz* deleted.

gestriegelt *adj:* **~ und gebügelt** dressed up to the nines.

gestrig *adj attr* yesterday's ◆ **unser ~es Gespräch/Schreiben** our conversation (of) yesterday/our letter of yesterday; **am ~en Abend** *(geh) (früh)* yesterday evening; *(spät)* last night; **am ~en Tage** *(geh)* yesterday; **die ewig G~en** the stick-in-the-muds.

gestritten *ptp of* **streiten.**

Gestrüpp *nt* **-(e)s, -e** undergrowth, brushwood; *(fig)* jungle.

gestuft *adj (in Stufen)* terraced; *(fig) (abgestuft)* graded; *(zeitlich)* staggered.

Gestühl *nt* **-(e)s, -e** seating.

Gestümper *nt* **-s,** *no pl (pej inf)* bungling ◆ **sein erbärmliches ~ auf dem Klavier** his pathetic plonking away on the piano *(inf)*.

gestunken *ptp of* **stinken.**

Gestus ['gɛstʊs] *m* **-,** *no pl (geh)* (a) *siehe* **Gestik.** (b) *(fig: Ausdruck)* air.

Gestüt *nt* **-(e)s, -e** stud; *(Anlage auch)* stud farm.

Gestütbuch *nt* stud book.

Gestüts-: ~brand *m* stud brand; **~hengst** *m* stud (horse); **~pferd** *nt* horse at stud; **~zeichen** *nt siehe* **~brand.**

Gesuch *nt* **-(e)s, -e** petition *(auf +acc, um* for); *(Antrag)* application *(auf +acc, um* for) ◆ **ein ~ einreichen** *or* **stellen** to make *or* lodge a petition/an application.

Gesuchsteller(in *f)* *m* **-s, -** *(dated)* petitioner; *(Antragsteller)* applicant.

gesucht *adj (begehrt)* sought after ◆ **sehr ~** (very) much sought after; **Ingenieure sind ~e Arbeitskräfte** engineers are much sought after.

Gesudel *nt* **-s,** *no pl (pej) siehe* **Sudelei.**

Gesülze *nt* **-s,** *no pl (sl)* claptrap *(inf)*.

Gesumm *nt* **-(e)s,** *no pl* humming, droning.

Gesums *nt* **-es,** *no pl (inf)* fuss.

gesund *adj, comp* **¨er** *or* **-er,** *superl* **¨este(r, s)** *or* **-este(r, s)** *or adv* **am ¨esten** *or* **-esten** *(allgemein)* healthy; *(arbeits-, leistungsfähig)* fit; *Unternehmen, Politik auch* sound; *(heilsam) Lehre* salutary ◆ **frisch und ~, ~ und munter, ~ wie ein Fisch** in the pink, hale and hearty, (as) sound as a bell; **ich fühle mich nicht ganz ~** I don't feel very *or* too well; **jdn ~ schreiben** to certify sb (as) fit; **sonst bist du ~?** *(iro inf)* are you feeling all right? *(iro)*, you need your head examined *(inf)*; **jdn ~ pflegen** to nurse sb back to health; **wieder ~ werden** to get better, to get well again, to recover; **Äpfel sind ~** apples are healthy *or* good for you *or* good for your health; **bleib (schön) ~!** look after yourself.

Gesund-: g~beten *vt sep* to heal through prayer; **~beten** *nt* faith-healing; **~beter** *m* faith-healer; **~beterei** *f (pej inf)* praying; **~brunnen** *m (fig)* **das ist ein wahrer ~brunnen** it's like a fountain of youth.

gesunden* *vi aux sein* to recover *(auch fig)*, to regain one's health.

Gesunde(r) *mf decl as adj* healthy person.

Gesundheit *f* **-,** *no pl (seelisches, körperliches Wohlbefinden)* health; *(Sportlichkeit)* healthiness; *(Arbeits~, Leistungsfähigkeit)* fitness; *(von Unternehmen, Politik)* healthiness, soundness; *(von Klima, Lebensweise etc)* healthiness ◆ **bei guter ~** in good health; **bei bester ~** in the best of health; **mit meiner ~ steht es nicht zum besten** I'm not in the best of health, my health is not all (that) it might be; **~!** bless you; **auf Ihre ~!** your (very good) health; **eine robuste/eiserne/zarte ~ haben** to have a robust/an iron/a delicate constitution.

gesundheitlich *adj* **~ geht es mir nicht besonders** my health is not particularly good; **sein ~er Zustand** (the state of) his health; **aus ~en Gründen** for health reasons; **wie geht es Ihnen ~?** how is your health?

Gesundheits-: ~amt *nt* public health department; **~apostel** *m (iro)* health nut *(inf)* or freak *(inf)*; **~attest** *nt* health certificate; **~behörde** *f* health authorities *pl*; **~dienst** *m siehe* **~wesen; ~fanatiker** *m siehe* **~apostel; g~fördernd** *adj* healthy, good for the health; **~fürsorge** *f* health care; **g~halber** *adv* for health reasons; **~pflege** *f* hygiene; **Ratschläge zur ~pflege** health advice; **öffentliche ~pflege** public health (care); **~schaden** *m* health defect; **~schäden** damage to one's health; **viele Arbeiter haben dabei einen ~schaden davongetragen** the health of many workers has suffered as a result; **g~schädigend, g~schädlich** *adj* unhealthy, damaging to (one's) health; **~tee** *m* herbal tea; **~wesen** *nt* health service; **~zeugnis** *nt* certificate of health, health certificate; **~zustand** *m, no pl* state of health.

gesund-: ~machen *vr sep (fig inf)* to grow fat *(an +dat* on); **~schrumpfen** *sep* [1] *vt (fig)* to trim down, to streamline; [2] *vr* to be trimmed down *or* streamlined; **G~schrumpfung** *f* trimming down, streamlining; **~stoßen** *vr sep irreg (sl)* to line one's pockets *(inf)*.

Gesundung *f, no pl (lit, fig)* recovery; *(Genesung)* convalescence, recuperation ◆ **seine ~ macht Fortschritte** he's progressing well.

gesungen *ptp of* **singen.**

gesunken *ptp of* **sinken.**

Gesurr(e) *nt* **-s,** *no pl* humming.

Getäfel, Getäfer *(Sw) nt* **-s,** *no pl* panelling.

getan *ptp of* **tun** ◆ **nach ~er Arbeit** when the day's work is done.

Getändel *nt* **-s,** *no pl (dated, geh)* dalliance *(old, liter)*.

Getier *nt* **-s,** *no pl* (a) *(Tiere, esp Insekten)* creatures *pl.* (b) *(einzelnes)* creature.

getigert *adj (mit Streifen)* striped; *(mit Flecken)* piebald.

Getobe *nt* **-s,** *no pl (inf)* chasing about.

Getose *nt* **-s,** *no pl* raging.

Getöse *nt* **-s,** *no pl* din, racket, row; *(von Auto, Beifall etc)* roar ◆ **mit ~** with a din *etc.*

getragen [1] *ptp of* **tragen.**
[2] *adj* (a) *Kleidung, Schuhe* second-hand. (b) *(fig) Melodie, Tempo etc* stately *no adv.*

Getragenheit *f* stateliness.

Geträller *nt* **-s,** *no pl* trilling.

Getrampel *nt* **-s,** *no pl* trampling; *(Beifalls~, Protest~)* stamping.

Getränk *nt* **-(e)s, -e** drink, beverage *(form)* ◆ **er gibt viel für ~e aus** he spends a lot on drink.

Getränke-: ~automat *m* drinks machine *or* dispenser; **~dose** *f* drinks can; **~karte** *f (in Café)* list of beverages; *(in Restaurant)* wine list; **~kiosk** *m* drinks stand; **~markt** *m* drinks cash-and-carry; **~stand** *m siehe* **~kiosk; ~steuer** *f* alcohol tax.

Getrappel *nt* **-s,** *no pl* patter; *(Huf~)* clop.

Getratsch(e) *nt* **-(e)s,** *no pl (pej)* gossip, gossiping.

getrauen* *vr* to dare ◆ **getraust du dich** *or* **dir** *(inf)* **das?** do you dare do that?; **ich getraue mich nicht dorthin** I don't dare (to) *or* daren't go there; **ich getraue mich zu behaupten, daß ...** *(geh)*, **ich getraue mir die Behauptung, daß ...** *(geh)* I would venture to say that ...

Getreide *nt* **-s,** *(form)* - grain, cereal ◆ **in diesem Klima wächst kein ~** grain doesn't *or* cereals don't grow in this climate; **das ~ steht gut** the grain *or* cereal crop is doing well.

Getreide-: ~(an)bau *m* cultivation of grain *or* cereals; **~art** *f* cereal; **~börse** *f* grain *or* corn *(Brit)* exchange; **~ernte** *f* grain harvest; **~feld** *nt* grain field, cornfield *(Brit)*; **~garbe** *f* sheaf of grain; **~handel** *m* grain trade; **~händler** *m* grain *or* corn *(Brit)* merchant; **~kammer** *f siehe* **Kornkammer; ~korn** *nt* grain; **~land** *nt* (a) grain-growing land, cornland *(Brit)*; (b) *no pl (~felder)* grain fields *pl*, cornfields *pl (Brit)*; **~pflanze** *f* cereal (plant); **~produkt** *nt* cereal product; **~silo** *nt or m,* **~speicher** *m* silo; **~wirtschaft** *f* grain cultivation; **Indiens ~wirtschaft ist fast autark** India is almost self-supporting in terms of grain cultivation.

getrennt *adj* separate ◆ **~ leben** to be separated, to live apart; **sie führten ~e Kasse** they each paid for themselves; **~ schlafen** not to sleep together, to sleep in different rooms; *siehe* **Tisch.**

Getrenntschreibung *f* writing as two/three *etc* words ◆ **zu beachten ist die ~ von „zu Hause"** remember that "zu Hause" is written as two (separate) words.

getreten *ptp of* **treten.**

getreu *adj* (a) *(genau, entsprechend)* faithful, true *no adv.* (b) *pred +dat* true to. (c) *(liter, dated)* faithful, loyal, trusty *(old)*.

Getreue(r) *mf decl as adj* (faithful *or* trusty) follower.

getreulich *adj siehe* **getreu (a).**

Getriebe *nt* **-s, -** (a) *(Tech)* gears *pl*; *(~kasten)* gearbox; *(Antrieb)* drive; *(von Uhr)* movement, works *pl*; *siehe* **Sand.** (b) *(lebhaftes Treiben)* bustle, hurly-burly.

Getriebe- *in cpds (Tech)* gear.

getrieben *ptp of* **treiben.**

Getriebe-: ~öl *nt* gear(box) oil; **~schaden** *m* gearbox trouble *no indef art.*

Getriller *nt* **-s,** *no pl* warbling.

Getrippel *nt* **-s,** *no pl* tripping along; *(affektiert)* mincing.

getroffen *ptp of* **treffen.**

getrogen *ptp of* **trügen.**

Getrommel *nt* **-s,** *no pl* drumming.

getrost [1] *adj* confident ◆ **du kannst ~ sein, sei ~** rest assured, never fear; **er war ~en Mutes** *(old)* his mind was reassured.
[2] *adv* (a) *(vertrauensvoll)* confidently ◆ **~ sterben** *(geh)* to die in peace.
(b) *(bedenkenlos)* **wenn er ungezogen ist, darfst du ihm ~ eine runterhauen** if he's cheeky, feel free to *or* don't hesitate to clout him (one) *(inf)*; **du kannst dich ~ auf ihn verlassen** you need have no fears about relying on him; **man kann ~ behaupten/annehmen, daß ...** one need have no hesitation in *or* about asserting/assuming that ...

getrübt *adj (lit)* cloudy ◆ **ein ~es Verhältnis zu jdm haben** to have an unhappy relationship with sb; **er hat ein ~es Verhältnis zum Abwaschen** he's not very keen on washing up; *siehe* **trüben.**

getrunken *ptp of* **trinken.**

Getto *nt* **-s, -s** ghetto.

gettoisieren* *vt* to ghettoize.

Getue [gə'tu:ə] *nt* **-s,** *no pl (pej)* to-do *(inf)*, fuss; *(geheuchelte Höflichkeit)* affectation ◆ **ein ~ machen** to make a to-do *(inf)* or fuss; *(überhöflich sein, sich wichtig machen)* to put on airs.

Getümmel *nt* **-s,** *no pl* turmoil ◆ **das ~ des Kampfes** the tumult of battle; **sich ins ~ stürzen** to plunge into the tumult *or* hurly-burly.

Getuschel *nt* **-s,** *no pl* whispering.

ge|übt *adj Auge, Ohr, Griff* practised; *Fahrer, Segler etc* proficient ◆ **im Schreiben/Reden ~ sein** to be a proficient writer/talker.

Gevatter *m* **-s,** *or* **-n, -n** *(obs) (Pate)* godfather; *(fig)* brother ◆ **~ Tod** (Death) the Reaper *(liter)*.

Gevatterin *f (obs)* godmother; *(fig)* sister *(old)*.

Geviert [gə'fi:ɐt] *nt* **-s, -e** *(old: Quadrat)* square; *(Min)* crib; *(Typ)* quad(rat) ◆ **5 Meter im ~** *(old)* 5 metres square.

Gevögel *nt* **-s,** *no pl* **(a)** (*obs: Vögel*) birds *pl*. **(b)** (*vulg: Koitieren*) screwing (*vulg*).

GEW [ge:|e:'ve:] *abbr of* **Gewerkschaft Erziehung und Wissenschaft** ≃ NUT.

Gewächs *nt* **-es, -e (a)** (*Pflanze*) plant ◆ **er ist ein seltsames ~** (*dated*) he is an odd specimen (*inf*). **(b)** (*Weinjahrgang*) wine. **(c)** (*Med*) growth.

gewachsen [1] *ptp of* **wachsen**[1].
[2] *adj* **(a)** (*von allein entstanden*) evolved ◆ **diese in Jahrtausenden ~en Traditionen** these traditions which have evolved over the millennia.
(b) jdm/einer Sache ~ sein to be a match for sb/to be up to sth; **er ist seinem Bruder (an Stärke/Intelligenz) durchaus ~** he is his brother's equal in strength/intelligence.

Gewächshaus *nt* greenhouse; (*Treibhaus*) hothouse.

Gewackel *nt* **-s,** *no pl* (*inf*) (*von Tisch, Stuhl etc*) wobbling ◆ **~ mit den Hüften/dem Schwanz** waggling one's hips/wagging its tail.

gewagt *adj* **(a)** (*kühn*) daring; (*gefährlich*) risky. **(b)** (*moralisch bedenklich*) risqué.

Gewagtheit *f* **(a)** *no pl siehe adj* daring; riskiness; risqué nature. **(b)** (*gewagte Äußerung*) daring remark.

gewählt *adj Sprache* refined *no adv*, elegant.

Gewähltheit *f* elegance.

gewahr *adj pred* **~ werden** *+gen* (*geh*) *siehe* **gewahren**.

Gewähr *f* **-,** *no pl* guarantee ◆ **jdm ~ dafür geben, daß** ... to guarantee (sb *or* to sb) that ...; **dadurch ist die ~ gegeben, daß** ... that guarantees that ...; **die ~ für jds Zahlungsfähigkeit übernehmen** to guarantee sb's ability to pay; **die Angabe erfolgt ohne ~** this information is supplied without liability; **„ohne ~"** (*auf Fahrplan, Preisliste*) "subject to change"; (*bei Lottozahlen, statistischen Angaben*) "no liability assumed"; **für etw ~ leisten** to guarantee sth.

gewahren* *vt* (*liter*) to become aware of.

gewähren* *vt* to grant; *Rabatt, Vorteile* to give; *Sicherheit, Trost, Schutz* to afford, to give ◆ **jdm Unterstützung ~** to provide sb with support, to support sb; **jdn ~ lassen** (*geh*) not to stop sb.

gewährleisten* *vt insep* (*sicherstellen*) to ensure (*jdm etw* sb sth); (*garantieren*) to guarantee (*jdm etw* sb sth).

Gewährleistung *f* guarantee ◆ **zur ~ der Sicherheit** to ensure safety.

Gewahrsam *m* **-s,** *no pl* **(a)** (*Verwahrung*) safekeeping ◆ **etw in ~ nehmen/haben** to take sth into/have sth in safekeeping; **etw (bei jdm) in ~ geben** to hand sth over (to sb) for safekeeping.
(b) (*Haft*) custody ◆ **jdn in ~ nehmen** to take sb into custody; **in ~ sein, sich in ~ befinden** to be in custody.

Gewährs-: ~mann *m, pl* **-männer** *or* **-leute** source; **~träger** *m* (*Fin*) guarantor.

Gewährung *f* **-,** *no pl siehe vt* granting; giving; affording.

Gewalt *f* **-, -en (a)** (*Machtbefugnis, Macht, Herrschaft*) power ◆ **die drei ~en** (*Pol*) the three powers; **die ausübende** *or* **vollziehende/gesetzgebende/richterliche ~** the executive/legislature/judiciary; **elterliche ~** parental authority; **jdn in seiner ~ haben** to have sb in one's power; **~ über jdn haben** *or* **besitzen** to have power over sb; **etw in der ~ haben** (*übersehen*) to have control of sth; (*steuern können*) to have sth under control; (*entscheiden können*) to have sth in one's power; **sich in der ~ haben** to have oneself under control; **in/unter jds ~** (*dat*) **sein** *or* **stehen** to be in sb's power/under sb's control; **die ~ über etw** (*acc*) **verlieren** to lose control of sth; **~ über Leben und Tod (haben)** (to have) power over life and death.
(b) *no pl* (*Zwang*) force; (*~tätigkeit*) violence ◆ **~ anwenden** to use force; **höhere ~** acts/an act of God; **nackte ~** brute force; **mit ~** by force; **mit aller ~** (*inf*) for all one is worth; **jdm/einer Sache ~ antun** to do violence to sb/sth; **einer Frau ~ antun** to violate a woman; **sich** (*dat*) **~ antun** (*fig: sich überwinden*) to force oneself; **~ geht vor Recht** (*Prov*) might is right (*Prov*).
(c) *no pl* (*Heftigkeit, Wucht*) force; (*elementare Kraft auch*) power ◆ **die ~ der Explosion/des Sturmes** the force of the explosion/storm; **er warf sich mit ~ gegen die Tür** he hurled himself violently against the door.

Gewalt-: ~akt *m* act of violence; **~androhung** *f* threat of violence; **unter ~androhung** under threat of violence; **~anwendung** *f* use of force *or* violence; ⚠**g~bejahend** *adj* condoning violence; **~bereitschaft** *f* propensity to violence; **~einwirkung** *f* violence.

Gewalten-: ~teilung, ~trennung *f* separation of powers.

Gewalt-: g~frei *adj siehe* **g~los**; **~freiheit** *f siehe* **~losigkeit**; **~friede(n)** *m* dictated peace; **~haber** *m* **-s, -** holder of power; **die ~haber** those in power; **~herrschaft** *f, no pl* tyranny; **~herrscher** *m* tyrant.

gewaltig *adj* **(a)** (*heftig*) *Sturm etc* violent.
(b) (*groß, riesig*) colossal, immense; (*wuchtig auch*) massive; *Anblick* tremendous; *Stimme, Töne* powerful; (*inf: sehr groß*) *Unterschied, Hitze etc* tremendous, colossal (*inf*) ◆ **sich ~ irren** to be very much mistaken *or* very wrong, to be way out (*inf*); **du mußt dich ~ ändern** you'll have to change one hell of a lot (*inf*); **er hat sich ~ in meine Schwester verknallt** (*inf*) he's really got it bad for my sister (*inf*).
(c) (*geh: mächtig*) powerful ◆ **die G~en der Erde** the mighty rulers of the world.

Gewaltigkeit *f, no pl siehe adj* **(a)** violence. **(b)** colossalness, immenseness; massiveness; tremendousness. **(c)** powerfulness.

Gewalt-: ~kur *f* drastic measures *pl*; (*Hungerdiät*) crash diet; **~leistung** *f* feat of strength, tour de force; **g~los** [1] *adj* non-violent; [2] *adv* without force/violence; **~losigkeit** *f, no pl* non-violence; **~marsch** *m* forced march; **im ~marsch** at a cracking pace (*inf*); **~maßnahme** *f* (*fig*) drastic measure; **jdm mit ~maßnahmen drohen** to threaten to use force against sb; (*fig*) to threaten sb with drastic action; **~mensch** *m* pusher (*inf*); (*brutaler Mensch*) brute; **~monopol** *nt* monopoly on the use of force; **g~sam** [1] *adj* forcible; *Tod* violent; [2] *adv* forcibly, by force; **~streich** *m* (*Mil*) storm; (*fig*) coup (de force); **~tat** *f* act of violence; **~täter** *m* violent criminal; **g~tätig** *adj* violent; **~tätigkeit** *f* (*no pl: Brutalität*) violence; (*Handlung*) act of violence; **~verbrechen** *nt* crime of violence; **~verbrecher** *m* violent criminal; **~verzicht** *m* non-aggression; **~verzichtsabkommen** *nt* non-aggression treaty.

Gewand *nt* **-(e)s, ¨er** (*geh: Kleidungsstück*) garment; (*weites, langes*) robe, gown; (*Eccl*) vestment, robe; (*old: Kleidung*) garb, garments *pl*, apparel (*old*); (*fig: Maske*) guise ◆ **ein altes Buch in neuem ~** an old book with a new look *or* appearance *or* livery, an old book dressed up.

gewandet *adj* (*old, hum*) clad, apparelled (*old*) ◆ **blau-/gelb-** *etc* **~** clad in blue/yellow *etc*.

gewandt [1] *ptp of* **wenden**.
[2] *adj* skilful; (*körperlich*) nimble; (*geschickt*) deft, dexterous; *Auftreten, Redner, Stil* elegant.

Gewandtheit *f, no pl siehe adj* skilfulness; nimbleness; deftness, dexterity; elegance.

gewann *pret of* **gewinnen**.

gewärtig *adj pred* (*geh*) prepared (*gen* for) ◆ **~ sein, daß** ... to be prepared for the possibility that ...

gewärtigen* *vtr* (*geh*) to expect; (*sich einstellen auf auch*) to be prepared for ◆ **~, daß** ... to expect that .../to be prepared for the possibility that ...; **etw ~ müssen** to have to be prepared for sth, to have to expect sth.

Gewäsch *nt* **-(e)s,** *no pl* (*pej inf*) twaddle (*inf*), claptrap (*inf*).

gewaschen *ptp of* **waschen**.

Gewässer *nt* **-s, -** stretch of water ◆ **~** *pl* inshore waters *pl*, lakes, rivers and canals *pl*; **ein fließendes/stehendes ~** a stretch of running/standing water.

Gewässer-: ~kunde *f* hydrography; **~schutz** *m* prevention of water pollution.

Gewebe *nt* **-s, -** (*Stoff*) fabric, material; (*~art*) weave; (*Biol*) tissue; (*fig*) web.

Gewebe- *in cpds siehe auch* **Gewebs-**; **~probe** *f* (*Med*) tissue sample; **g~schonend** *adj* (*Comm*) kind to fabrics.

Gewebs-: ~flüssigkeit *f* (*Med*) lymph; **~transplantation** *f* (*Med*) tissue graft.

Gewehr *nt* **-(e)s, -e** (*Flinte*) rifle; (*Schrotbüchse*) shotgun ◆ **~ ab!** (*Mil*) order arms!; **das ~ über!** (*Mil*) shoulder arms!; **an die ~e!** (*Mil*) to arms!; (*dated inf*) let's get cracking (*dated inf*) *or* started; **präsentiert das ~!** (*Mil*) present arms!; **das** *or* **mit dem ~ (auf jdn) anlegen** to aim (at sb); (*Mil*) to train a gun (on sb); **~ bei Fuß stehen** (*Mil*) to stand at order arms; (*fig inf*) to be at the ready.

Gewehr-: ~griff *m* rifle position; **~griffe üben** to do rifle drill; **~kolben** *m* rifle butt/butt of a shotgun; **~kugel** *f* rifle bullet; **~lauf** *m* rifle barrel/barrel of a shotgun; **~mündung** *f* muzzle (of a rifle/shotgun); **~riemen** *m* rifle sling/gunsling.

Geweih *nt* **-(e)s, -e** (set of *sing*) antlers *pl* ◆ **das/ein ~** the antlers/a set of antlers.

Geweih-: ~ende *nt* point *or* tine (*spec*) of an antler; **~schaufel** *f* palm (of an antler).

Geweine *nt* **-s,** *no pl* (*inf*) crying.

Gewerbe *nt* **-s, - (a)** trade ◆ **Handel und ~** trade and industry; **das älteste ~ der Welt** (*hum*) the oldest profession in the world (*hum*); **ein dunkles ~** a shady business; **einem dunklen/seinem ~ nachgehen** to be in a shady trade *or* have a shady occupation/to carry on *or* practise one's trade; **ein ~ (be)treiben** *or* **ausüben** to follow a *or* carry on a trade. **(b)** (*Sw: Bauerngehöft*) farm.

Gewerbe-: ~amt *nt siehe* **~aufsichtsamt**; **~aufsicht** *f* ≃ factory safety and health control; **~aufsichtsamt** *nt* ≃ factory inspectorate; **~betrieb** *m* commercial enterprise; **~freiheit** *f* freedom of trade; **~gebiet** *nt* industrial area; (*eigens angelegt*) trading estate; **~lehrer** *m* teacher in a trade school; **~ordnung** *f* trading regulations *pl*; **~schein** *m* trading licence; **~schule** *f* trade school; **~steuer** *f* trade tax; **~tätigkeit** *f* commercial activity; **~treibende(r)** *mf decl as adj* trader; **~verein** *m* (*old*) trade association; **~zweig** *m* branch of a/the trade.

gewerblich *adj* commercial; *Lehrling, Genossenschaft* trade *attr*; (*industriell*) industrial ◆ **~e Arbeiter** industrial workers; **die ~e Wirtschaft** industry; **~er Rechtsschutz** legal protection of industrial property; **die ~en Berufe** the trades; **diese Räume dürfen nicht ~ genutzt werden** these rooms are not to be used for commercial purposes.

gewerbsmäßig [1] *adj* professional ◆ **~e Unzucht** (*form*) prostitution.
[2] *adv* professionally, for gain.

Gewerkschaft *f* (trade *or* trades *or* labor *US*) union.

Gewerkschaft(l)er(in *f*) *m* **-s, -** trade *or* labor (*US*) unionist.

gewerkschaftlich *adj* (trade *or* labor *US*) union *attr* ◆ **~er Vertrauensmann** (*im Betrieb*) shop steward; **wir haben uns ~ organisiert** we organized ourselves into a union; **~ organisierter Arbeiter** unionized *or* organized worker; **~ engagiert** involved in the (trade *or* labor) union movement.

Gewerkschafts- *in cpds* (trade/labor) union; **~bank** *f* trade union bank/labor bank; **~bewegung** *f* (trade/labor) union movement; ⚠**~boß** *m* (*usu pej*) (trade/labor) union boss; **~bund** *m* federation of trade/labor unions, ≃ Trades Union Congress (*Brit*), ≃ Federation of Labor (*US*); **g~eigen** *adj* owned by a (trade/labor) union; **~führer** *m* trade union leader; ⚠**~kongreß** *m siehe* **~tag**; **~mitglied** *nt* member of a/the (trade/labor) union; **~tag** *m* trade/labor union conference; **~verband** *m* federation of trade/labor unions; **~vorsitzende(r)** *mf* (trade/labor) union president; **~wesen** *nt* (trade/labor) union movement.

gewesen [1] *ptp of* **sein**[1].
[2] *adj attr* former.
gewichen *ptp of* **weichen**[2].
gewichst [gə'vɪkst] *adj (inf)* fly *(inf)*, crafty.
Gewicht *nt* **-(e)s, -e (a)** *no pl (lit, fig)* weight ♦ **dieser Stein hat ein großes ~/ ein ~ von 100 kg** this rock is very heavy/weighs 100 kg; **er hat sein ~ gehalten** he has stayed the same weight; **er brachte zuviel ~ auf die Waage** he weighed in too heavy; **spezifisches ~** specific gravity; **das hat ein ~!** *(inf)* it isn't half heavy! *(inf)*; **etw nach ~ verkaufen** to sell sth by weight; **~ haben** *(lit)* to be heavy; *(fig)* to carry weight; **ins ~ fallen** to be crucial; **nicht ins ~ fallen** to be of no consequence; **auf etw** *(acc)* **~ legen, einer Sache** *(dat)* **~ beilegen** *or* **beimessen** to set (great) store by sth, to lay stress on sth.
(b) *(Metallstück zum Beschweren etc, Sport)* weight.
gewichten* *vt (Statistik)* to weight; *(fig)* to evaluate.
Gewicht-: ~heben *nt* **-s,** *no pl (Sport)* weight-lifting; **~heber** *m* weight-lifter.
gewichtig *adj* **(a)** *(dated: schwer)* heavy, hefty *(inf)* ♦ **eine ~e Persönlichkeit** *(hum inf)* a personage of some weight. **(b)** *(fig) (wichtig)* weighty; *(wichtigtuerisch)* self-important; *(einflußreich)* influential.
Gewichtigkeit *f, no pl (fig) siehe adj (b)* weightiness; self-importance; influence.
Gewichts-: ~abnahme *f* loss of weight; **~analyse** *f (Chem)* gravimetric analysis; **~angabe** *f* indication of weight; **die Hersteller von Konserven sind zur ~angabe verpflichtet** the manufacturers of canned food are obliged to show the weight; **~klasse** *f (Sport)* weight (category); **~kontrolle** *f* weight check; **g~los** *adj* weightless; *(fig)* lacking substance; **~satz** *m* set of weights; **~verlagerung** *f* shifting of weight; *(fig)* shift of *or* in emphasis; **~verlust** *m* loss of weight, weight loss; **~verschiebung** *f siehe* **~verlagerung; ~zunahme** *f* increase in weight.
Gewichtung *f (Statistik)* weighting; *(fig)* evaluation.
gewieft *adj (inf)* fly *(inf)*, crafty *(in +dat* at).
gewiegt *adj* shrewd, slick *(inf)*, canny *(esp Scot inf)*.
Gewieher *nt* **-s,** *no pl* whinnying; *(fig)* guffawing, braying.
gewiesen *ptp of* **weisen.**
gewillt *adj* **~ sein, etw zu tun** to be willing to do sth; *(entschlossen)* to be determined to do sth.
Gewimmel *nt* **-s,** *no pl* swarm, milling mass; *(Menge)* crush, throng.
Gewimmer *nt* **-s,** *no pl* whimpering.
Gewinde *nt* **-s, -** *(Tech)* thread.
Gewinde- *(Tech)*: **~bohrer** *m* (screw) tap; **~bolzen** *m* threaded bolt; **~fräsen** *nt* thread milling; **~gang** *m* pitch (of screw thread); **~schneiden** *nt* thread cutting; *(für Innengewinde)* tapping.
gewinkelt *adj* angled.
Gewinn *m* **-(e)s, -e (a)** *(Ertrag)* profit ♦ **~-und-Verlust-Rechnung** profit-and-loss account; **~ abwerfen** *or* **bringen** to make a profit; **~ erzielen** to make a profit; **aus etw ~ schlagen** *(inf)* to make a profit out of sth; **etw mit ~ verkaufen** to sell sth at a profit.
(b) *(Preis, Treffer)* prize; *(bei Wetten, Glücksspiel)* winnings *pl* ♦ **einen großen ~ machen** to win a lot; **jedes Los ist ein ~** every ticket a winner; **er hat im Lotto einen ~ gehabt** he had a win on the lottery.
(c) *no pl (fig: Vorteil)* gain ♦ **das ist ein großer ~ (für mich)** I have gained a lot from this, that is of great benefit (to me); **ein ~ für die Abteilung** a valuable addition to the department.
Gewinn-: ~anteil *m* **(a)** *(Comm)* dividend; **(b)** *(beim Wetten etc)* share; **~ausschüttung** *f* prize draw; **~beteiligung** *f* **(a)** *(Ind) (Prinzip)* profit-sharing; *(Summe)* (profit-sharing) bonus; **(b)** *(Dividende)* dividend; ⚠**g~bringend** *adj (lit, fig)* profitable; **~chance** *f* chance of winning; **~chancen** *(beim Wetten)* odds.
gewinnen *pret* **gewann,** *ptp* **gewonnen** [1] *vt* **(a)** *(siegen in)* to win; *(erwerben, bekommen auch)* to gain; *jds Herz* to win; *Preis* to win ♦ **jdn (für etw) ~** to win sb over (to sth); **jdn für sich ~** to win sb over (to one's side); **jdn zum Freund ~** to win sb as a friend; **es gewinnt den Anschein, als ob ...** *(form)* it would appear that ...; **das Ufer ~** *(liter)* to reach *or* gain *(liter)* the bank; **Zeit ~** to gain time; **was ist damit gewonnen?** what good is that?; **was ist damit gewonnen, wenn du das tust?** what is the good *or* use of you *or* your doing that?; **wie gewonnen, so zerronnen** *(prov)* easy come easy go *(prov)*.
(b) *(als Profit)* to make (a profit of).
(c) *(erzeugen)* to produce, to obtain; *Erze etc* to mine, to extract, to win *(liter)*; *(aus Altmaterial)* to reclaim, to recover.
[2] *vi* **(a)** to win *(bei, in +dat* at).
(b) *(profitieren)* to gain; *(sich verbessern)* to gain something ♦ **an Bedeutung ~** to gain (in) importance; **an Boden ~** *(fig)* to gain ground; **an Höhe/ Geschwindigkeit ~** to gain height/to pick up *or* gain speed; **an Klarheit ~** to gain in clarity; **sie gewinnt durch ihre neue Frisur** her new hairstyle does something for her; **sie gewinnt bei näherer Bekanntschaft** she improves on closer acquaintance; *siehe* **wagen.**
gewinnend *adj (fig)* winning, winsome.
Gewinner(in *f***)** *m* **-s, -** winner.
Gewinnerstraße *f (inf)* **auf der ~ sein** to be headed for a win, to be on the way to victory.
Gewinn-: ~erzielungsabsicht *f (Comm)* profit motive; **~gemeinschaft** *f (Comm)* profit pool; **~klasse** *f* prize category; **~liste** *f* list of winners, winners list; **~los** *nt* winning ticket; **~maximierung** *f* maximization of profit(s); **~mitnahme** *f (Fin)* profit taking; ⚠**~nummer** *f siehe* **Gewinnummer; ~satz** *m (Tennis etc)* **mit drei ~sätzen spielen** to play the best of five sets; **der dritte Satz war sein ~satz** the third set was the winning set for him; **~schuldverschreibung** *f (Fin)* income bond; **~spanne** *f* profit margin; **~streben** *nt* pursuit of profit; **~sucht** *f* profit-seeking; **aus ~sucht** for motives of (financial/material) gain; **g~süchtig** *adj* profit-seeking *attr*; **g~trächtig** *adj* profitable.
Gewinnummer *getrennt* **Gewinn-nummer, Gewinnzahl** *f* winning number.
Gewinn- und Verlustrechnung *f (Fin)* profit and loss account.
Gewinnung *f (von Kohle, Öl)* extraction; *(von Energie, Plutonium)* production.
Gewinsel *nt* **-s,** *no pl (lit, fig)* whining.
Gewinst *m* **-(e)s, -e** *(old) siehe* **Gewinn.**
Gewirbel *nt* **-s,** *no pl* whirl(ing).
Gewirr *nt* **-(e)s,** *no pl* tangle; *(fig: Durcheinander)* jumble; *(von Paragraphen, Klauseln etc)* maze, confusion; *(von Gassen)* maze; *(von Stimmen)* confusion, babble.
Gewisper *nt* **-s,** *no pl* whispering.
⚠**gewiß** [1] *adj* **(a)** *(sicher)* certain, sure *(+gen* of) ♦ **(ja) ~!** certainly, sure *(esp US)*; **ich bin dessen ~** *(geh)* I'm certain *or* sure of it; **das ist so ~, wie die Nacht dem Tag folgt** *(geh)* as sure as night follows day; **darüber weiß man noch nichts Gewisses** nothing certain is known as yet.
(b) *attr* certain ♦ **ein gewisser Herr Müller** a certain Herr Müller; **in gewissem Maße** to some *or* a certain extent; **in gewissem Sinne** in a (certain) sense; *siehe* **Etwas.**
[2] *adv (geh)* certainly ♦ **Sie denken ~, daß ...** no doubt you think that ...; **ich weiß es ganz ~** I'm certain *or* sure of it; **eins ist** *or* **weiß ich (ganz) ~** one thing is certain *or* sure, there's one thing I know for certain *or* sure; **(aber) ~ (doch)!** (but) of course; **darf ich ...? — (aber) ~ (doch)!** may I ...? — but, of course *or* by all means.
Gewissen *nt* **-s,** *no pl* conscience ♦ **ein schlechtes ~** a guilty *or* bad conscience; **jdn/etw auf dem ~ haben** to have sb/sth on one's conscience; **das hast du auf dem ~** it's your fault; **jdm ins ~ reden** to have a serious talk with sb; **jdm ins ~ reden, etw zu tun** to get *or* persuade sb to do sth; **das mußt du vor deinem ~ verantworten** you'll have to answer to your own conscience for that; **ein gutes ~ ist ein sanftes Ruhekissen** *(Prov)* I *etc* just want to have a clear conscience, I *etc* just want to be able to sleep nights *(esp US)*; *siehe* **Ehre, Wissen.**
Gewissen-: g~haft *adj* conscientious; **~haftigkeit** *f, no pl* conscientiousness; **g~los** *adj* unprincipled, without conscience, unscrupulous; *(verantwortungslos)* irresponsible; **g~los sein** to have no conscience; **wie kann man so g~los sein und ...** how could anybody be so unscrupulous/ irresponsible as to ...; **~losigkeit** *f* unscrupulousness, lack of principle; *(Verantwortungslosigkeit)* irresponsibility.
Gewissens-: ~angst *f* pangs of conscience *pl*; **~bisse** *pl* pangs of conscience *pl*; **mach dir deswegen keine ~bisse!** there's nothing for you to feel guilty about; **~bisse bekommen** to get a guilty conscience; **ohne ~bisse** without compunction *(liter)*, without feeling guilty; **~entscheidung** *f* question of conscience, matter for one's conscience to decide; **~erforschung** *f* examination of one's conscience; **~frage** *f* matter of conscience; **~freiheit** *f* freedom of conscience; **~gründe** *pl* conscientious reasons *pl*; **~konflikt** *m* moral conflict; **~not** *f* moral dilemma; **~qual** *f (geh)* pangs of conscience *pl*; **~sache** *f siehe* **~frage; ~zwang** *m, no pl* moral constraint(s *pl*); **~zweifel** *m* moral doubt.
gewissermaßen *adv (sozusagen)* so to speak, as it were; *(auf gewisse Weise)* in a way, to an extent.
⚠**Gewißheit** *f* certainty ♦ **mit ~** with certainty; *wissen* for certain *or* sure; **~ erlangen** to achieve certain knowledge; **(zur) ~ werden** to become a certainty; *siehe* **verschaffen.**
⚠**gewißlich** *adv (old, geh) siehe* **gewiß 2.**
Gewitter *nt* **-s, -** thunderstorm; *(fig)* storm.
Gewitter-: ~fliege *f* thunder fly; **~front** *f (Met)* storm front; **~himmel** *m* stormy sky, thunderclouds *pl*.
gewitt(e)rig *adj* thundery ♦ **~ schwül** thundery (and oppressive); **~e Schwüle** thundery (and oppressive) air.
Gewitterluft *f* thundery atmosphere ♦ **es ist ~** there's thunder in the air *or* about.
gewittern* *vi impers*: **es gewittert** it's thundering.
Gewitter-: ~neigung *f (Met)* likelihood of thunderstorms; **~regen, ~schauer** *m* thundery shower; **g~schwül** *adj siehe* **gewitt(e)rig; ~schwüle** *f* thundery (and oppressive) atmosphere; **~stimmung** *f (fig)* stormy atmosphere; **~sturm** *m* thunderstorm; **~wand** *f* wall *or* mass of thunderclouds; **~wolke** *f* thundercloud; *(fig inf)* storm-cloud; **Vater hatte ~wolken auf der Stirn** Father's face was as black as thunder; **~ziege** *f (pej inf)* sour old hag.
gewittrig *adj siehe* **gewitt(e)rig.**
Gewitzel *nt* **-s,** *no pl* joking, jokes *pl*.
gewitzt *adj* crafty, cunning.
Gewitztheit *f, no pl* craftiness, cunning.
gewoben *ptp of* **weben.**
Gewoge *nt* **-s,** *no pl* surging; *(von Kornfeld auch)* waving; *(hum: von Busen)* surging.
gewogen[1] *ptp of* **wägen, wiegen**[2].
gewogen[2] *adj (geh)* well-disposed, favourably disposed *(+dat* towards).
Gewogenheit *f, no pl (geh)* favourable attitude.
gewöhnen* [1] *vt* **jdn an etw** *(acc)* **~** to make sb used *or* accustomed to sth, to accustom sb to sth; **einen Hund an Sauberkeit ~** to house-train a dog; **Sie**

➤ SPRACHE AKTIV: → 43.1

werden sich noch daran ~ müssen, daß ... you'll have to get used to *or* accept the fact that ...; an jdn/etw gewöhnt sein, jdn/etw gewöhnt sein (*inf*) to be used to sb/sth; daran gewöhnt sein, etw zu tun to be used to doing sth.
[2] *vr* sich an jdn/etw ~ to get *or* become used to sb/sth, to accustom oneself to sb/sth; du mußt dich an Ordnung/Pünktlichkeit ~ you must get used to being *or* get into the habit of being orderly/punctual; sich daran ~, etw zu tun to get used *or* accustomed to doing sth; das bin ich gewöhnt I'm used to it.

Gewohnheit *f* habit ◆ aus (lauter) ~ from (sheer) force of habit; die ~ haben, etw zu tun to have a habit of doing sth; wie es seine ~ war, nach alter ~ as was his wont *or* custom; das ist ihm zur ~ geworden it's become a habit with him; sich (*dat*) etw zur ~ machen to make a habit of sth.

Gewohnheits-: **g~gemäß, g~mäßig** [1] *adj* habitual; [2] *adv* (*ohne nachzudenken*) automatically; **~mensch** *m* creature of habit; **~recht** *nt* (*Jur*) (a) (*im Einzelfall*) established *or* customary right; (b) (*als Rechtssystem*) common law; **~sache** *f* question of habit; **~tier** *nt*: der Mensch ist ein ~tier (*inf*) man is a creature of habit; **~trinker** *m* habitual drinker; **~verbrecher** *m* habitual criminal.

gewöhnlich [1] *adj* (a) *attr* (*allgemein, üblich*) usual, customary; (*normal*) normal; (*durchschnittlich*) ordinary; (*alltäglich*) everyday ◆ ein ~er Sterblicher an ordinary mortal; ~er Bruch (*Math*) vulgar fraction.
(b) (*pej: ordinär*) common ◆ sie zieht sich immer so ~ an she always wears such common clothes.
[2] *adv* normally, usually ◆ wie ~ as usual, as per usual (*inf*).

Gewöhnlichkeit *f* (*pej*) commonness.

gewohnt *adj* usual ◆ etw (*acc*) ~ sein to be used to sth; ich bin es ~, früh aufzustehen I am used to getting up early.

gewohntermaßen *adv* usually.

Gewöhnung *f, no pl* (*das Sich-Gewöhnen*) habituation (*an +acc* to); (*das Angewöhnen*) training (*an +acc* in); (*Sucht*) habit, addiction ◆ die ~ an den Kindergarten kann bei einigen Kindern ziemlich lange dauern it can take a fairly long time for some children to get used to kindergarten.

Gewölbe *nt* -s, - (*Decken~*) vault; (*Keller~ auch*) vaults *pl*.

Gewölbe-: **~bogen** *m* arch (of a vault); **~pfeiler** *m* pier (of a vault).

gewölbt *adj Stirn* domed; *Himmel, Decke* vaulted; *Brust* bulging; *Nase* aquiline.

gewölkt *adj* (*liter*) *Stirn* o'erclouded (*poet*).

Gewölle *nt* -s, - (*Zool*) cast, pellet.

gewollt *adj* forced, artificial.

gewonnen *ptp of* gewinnen.

geworben *ptp of* werben.

geworden *ptp of* werden.

geworfen *ptp of* werfen.

gewrungen *ptp of* wringen.

Gewühl *nt* -(e)s, *no pl* (a) (*pej: das Wühlen*) (*in Kisten, Schubladen etc*) rummaging around; (*im Schlamm etc*) wallowing (about); (*im Bett*) wriggling. (b) (*Gedränge*) crowd, throng; (*Verkehrs~*) chaos, snarl-up (*inf*).

gewunden [1] *ptp of* winden[1].
[2] *adj Weg, Fluß etc* winding; *Erklärung* roundabout *no adv*, tortuous.

gewunken (*dial*) *ptp of* winken.

gewürfelt *adj* check(ed).

Gewürge *nt* -s, *no pl* (*vor dem Erbrechen*) retching.

Gewürm *nt* -(e)s, *no pl* worms *pl*; (*Kriechtiere*) creeping animals *pl*, creepy-crawlies *pl* (*inf*); (*fig*) vermin.

Gewürz *nt* -es, -e spice; (*Kräutersorte*) herb; (*Pfeffer, Salz*) condiment.

Gewürz-: **~bord** *nt siehe* ~regal; **~essig** *m* spiced/herb vinegar; **~gurke** *f* pickled gherkin; **~kraut** *nt* potherb; **~mischung** *f* mixed herbs *pl*; (*~salz*) herbal salt; **~nelke** *f* clove; **~paprika** *m* paprika; **~pflanze** *f* spice plant; (*Kräuterpflanze*) herb; **~regal** *nt* spice rack; **~ständer** *m* cruet (set).

Gewusel *nt* -s, *no pl* (*dial*) *siehe* Gewimmel.

⚠ **gewußt** *ptp of* wissen.

Geysir ['gaizɪr] *m* -s, -e geyser.

gez. *abbr. of* gezeichnet.

gezackt *adj Fels* jagged; *Hahnenkamm* toothed; *Blatt* serrated, dentate (*spec*).

gezahnt, gezähnt *adj* serrated; (*Bot*) serrated, dentate (*spec*); (*Tech*) cogged; *Briefmarke* perforated.

Gezänk, Gezanke (*inf*) *nt* -s, *no pl* quarrelling.

Gezappel *nt* -s, *no pl* (*inf*) wriggling.

gezeichnet *adj* marked; (*als Straffälliger auch*) branded ◆ vom Tode ~ *or* ein vom Tode G~er sein to have the mark of death on one.

Gezeiten *pl* tides *pl*.

Gezeiten-: **~kraftwerk** *nt* tidal power plant *or* station; **~strom** *m* tidal current; **~tafel** *f* table of (the) tides; **~wechsel** *m* turn of the tide.

Gezerre *nt* -s, *no pl* tugging.

Gezeter *nt* -s, *no pl* (*inf*) (*lit*) nagging; (*fig*) clamour ◆ in ~ (*acc*) ausbrechen (*fig*) to set up *or* raise a clamour.

Geziefer *nt* -s, *no pl* (*obs*) *siehe* Ungeziefer.

geziehen *ptp of* zeihen.

gezielt *adj* purposeful; *Schuß* well-aimed; *Frage, Maßnahme, Forschung etc* specific; *Werbung* selective, targetted; *Hilfe* welldirected; *Indiskretion* deliberate ◆ ~ schießen to shoot to kill; er hat sehr ~ gefragt he was obviously getting at something specific with his questions.

geziemen* (*old, geh*) [1] *vi +dat* to befit ◆ dieses Verhalten geziemt ihm nicht such behaviour ill befits him.
[2] *vr* to be proper ◆ wie es sich geziemt as is proper; wie es sich für ein artiges Kind geziemt as befits a well-behaved child.

geziemend *adj* proper.

geziert *adj* affected.

Gezirp(e) *nt* -(e)s, *no pl* chirruping, chirping.

Gezisch(e) *nt* -es, *no pl* hiss(ing).

Gezischel *nt* -s, *no pl* (*fig: Klatsch*) gossip, tittle-tattle (*inf*).

gezogen [1] *ptp of* ziehen.
[2] *adj Gewehrlauf etc* rifled; *Soldat* conscript(ed) ◆ ein G~er (*Mil inf*) a conscript.

Gezücht *nt* -(e)s, -e (*obs*) (*pej: Brut*) brood; (*inf: Gesindel*) riff-raff *pl*, rabble *pl*.

Gezüngel *nt* -s, *no pl* (*geh*) (*von Schlange*) darting *or* flicking of its tongue; (*von Flamme*) flickering.

Gezweig *nt* -(e)s, *no pl* (*geh*) branches *pl*.

Gezwinker *nt* -s, *no pl* winking.

Gezwitscher *nt* -s, *no pl* chirruping, twitter(ing).

gezwungen [1] *ptp of* zwingen.
[2] *adj* (*nicht entspannt*) forced; *Atmosphäre* strained; *Stil, Benehmen* stiff.

gezwungenermaßen *adv* of necessity ◆ etw ~ tun to be forced to do sth, to do sth of necessity.

Gezwungenheit *f, no pl* artificiality; (*von Atmosphäre*) constraint; (*von Stil, Benehmen*) stiffness.

ggf. *abbr of* gegebenenfalls.

Ghana *nt* -s Ghana.

Ghanaer(in *f*) *m* -s, - Ghanaian.

ghanaisch *adj* Ghanaian.

Ghetto *nt* -s, -s ghetto.

Ghostwriter ['goʊstraɪtə] *m* -s, - ghostwriter ◆ er ist der ~ des Premiers he ghosts *or* ghostwrites for the PM.

gib *imper sing of* geben.

Gibbon *m* -s, -s gibbon.

Gicht *f* -, -en (a) *no pl* (*Med, Bot*) gout. (b) (*Metal*) throat (of a/the furnace).

Gicht-: **~anfall** *m* attack of gout; **~gas** *nt* (*Metal*) top gas; **~knoten** *m* gouty deposit, tophus (*form*); **g~krank** *adj* gouty; **~kranke(r)** *mf decl as adj* gout sufferer.

Gickel *m* -s, - (*dial*) *siehe* Hahn (a).

Giebel *m* -s, - gable; (*Tür~, Fenster~*) pediment.

Giebel-: **~dach** *nt* gabled roof; **~feld** *nt* tympanum (*spec*); **~fenster** *nt* gable window; **~haus** *nt* gabled house.

gieb(e)lig *adj* gabled.

Giebel-: **~seite** *f* gable end; **~wand** *f* gable end *or* wall; **~zimmer** *nt* attic room.

Gieper *m* -s, *no pl* (*dial*) craving (*auf +acc* for).

Gier *f* -, *no pl* (*nach* for) greed; (*nach Geld auch*) avarice, lust; (*nach Macht, Ruhm auch*) craving, lust; (*Lüsternheit*) lust.

gieren[1] *vi* (*pej*) to lust (*nach* for).

gieren[2] *vi* (*Naut*) to yaw.

gieren[3] *vi* (*Sw: quietschen*) (*Tür, Scharnier etc*) to creak.

gierig *adj* greedy; (*nach Geld*) avaricious; (*lüstern*) lustful ◆ ~ nach etw sein to be greedy for sth; (*nach Macht auch, sexuell*) to lust for sth; (*nach Vergnügen auch*) to crave sth; (*nach Wissen auch*) to be avid for sth; etw ~ verschlingen (*lit, fig*) to devour sth greedily.

Gießbach *m* (mountain) torrent.

gießen *pret* goß, *ptp* gegossen [1] *vt* (a) to pour; (*verschütten*) to spill; *Pflanzen, Garten etc* to water; (*liter*) *Licht* to shed ◆ gieß das Glas nicht so voll! don't fill the glass so full!
(b) *Glas* to found (*zu* (in)to); *Metall auch* to cast (*zu* into).
[2] *vi impers* to pour ◆ es gießt in Strömen *or* wie aus Eimern it's pouring down, it's chucking it down (*inf*).

Gießer *m* -s, - (a) (*Metal*) caster, founder. (b) (*an Kanne*) pourer.

Gießerei *f* (a) *no pl* (*Gießen*) casting, founding. (b) (*Werkstatt*) foundry.

Gießerei-: **~arbeiter** *m* foundry worker; **~betrieb** *m* foundry; **~technik** *f* foundry practice.

Gießerin *f siehe* Gießer (a).

Gieß-: **~form** *f siehe* Gußform; **~grube** *f* foundry pit; **~kanne** *f* watering can; **~kannenprinzip** *nt* (*inf*) principle of indiscriminate all-round distribution; **~kelle** *f*, **~löffel** *m* casting ladle; **~ofen** *m* foundry furnace; **~pfanne** *f* casting ladle.

gietzig *adj* (*Sw*) *siehe* geizig.

Gift *nt* -(e)s, -e (*lit, fig*) poison; (*Bakterien~*) toxin; (*Schlangen~, fig: Bosheit*) venom ◆ ~ nehmen to poison oneself; das ist (wie) ~ für ihn (*inf*) that is very bad for him; darauf kannst du ~ nehmen (*inf*) you can bet your bottom dollar *or* your life on that (*inf*); sein ~ verspritzen to be venomous; ~ und Galle spucken (*inf*) *or* speien to be fuming, to be in a rage.

Gift-: **~ampulle** *f* poison capsule; **~becher** *m* cup of poison; **~drüse** *f* venom gland.

giften (*inf*) [1] *vt impers* to rile.
[2] *vi* to be nasty (*gegen* about).

Gift-: **g~frei** *adj* non-toxic, non-poisonous; **~gas** *nt* poison gas; **g~grün** *adj* bilious green; **g~haltig, g~hältig** (*Aus*) *adj* containing poison, poisonous, toxic; **~hauch** *m* (*liter*) miasma (*liter*).

giftig *adj* (a) (*Gift enthaltend*) poisonous; *Stoff, Chemikalien etc auch* toxic. (b) (*fig*) (*boshaft, haßerfüllt*) venomous; (*zornig*) vitriolic; *siehe* Zunge. (c) (*grell*) bilious.

Gift-: **~küche** *f* devil's workshop; **~mischer(in** *f*) *m* -s, - preparer of poison; (*fig*) trouble-maker, stirrer (*inf*); (*hum: Apotheker*) chemist; **~mord** *m* poisoning; **~mörder** *m* poisoner; **~müll** *m* toxic waste; **~nudel** *f* (*hum inf*) **(a)** (*Zigarre, Zigarette*) cancer tube (*hum inf*); **(b)** (*gehässige Frau*) vixen, shrew; **~pfeil** *m* poisoned arrow; **~pflanze** *f* poisonous plant; **~pilz** *m* poisonous toadstool; **~schlange** *f* poisonous snake; **~schrank** *m* poison cabinet; **~stoff** *m* poisonous *or* toxic substance; **~wirkung** *f* effect of (the) poison; **die ~wirkung machte sich nach ein paar Sekunden bemerkbar** the poison took effect after a few seconds; **~zahn** *m* fang; **jdm die ~zähne ausbrechen** (*fig inf*) to draw sb's fangs; **~zwerg** *m* (*inf*) spiteful little devil (*inf*).

Gigabyte [-baɪt] *nt* (*Comput*) gigabyte.

gigampfen* *vi* (*Sw*) to swing.

Gigant *m* giant; (*Myth*) Titan; (*fig auch*) colossus.

gigantisch *adj* gigantic, colossal.

Gigantismus *m* (*Med*) gigantism; (*fig*) giantism.

Gigantomanie *f, no pl* (*geh*) love of things big.

Gigawatt *nt* (*Elec*) gigawatt.

Gigerl *m or nt* **-s, -(n)** (*Aus inf*) dandy, peacock (*inf*).

Gigolo ['ʒiːgolo, 'ʒig-] *m* **-s, -s** gigolo.

gilben *vi aux sein* (*liter*) to yellow.

Gilde *f* **-, -n** guild.

Gildehaus *nt* guildhall.

Gilet [ʒi'leː] *nt* **-s, -s** (*Aus, Sw*) waistcoat (*Brit*), vest (*US*).

gilt *3. pers present of* **gelten.**

Gimpel *m* **-s, -** (*Orn*) bullfinch; (*inf: Einfaltspinsel*) ninny (*inf*).

Gin [dʒɪn] *m* **-s, -s** gin ♦ **~ tonic** Gin and Tonic.

Gin-Fizz ['dʒɪnfɪs] *m* **-, -** gin-fizz.

ging *pret of* **gehen.**

Ginseng ['gɪnzɛŋ, 'ʒɪnzɛŋ] *m* **-s, -s** (*Bot*) ginseng.

Ginster *m* **-s, -** (*Bot*) broom; (*Stech~*) gorse.

Gipfel *m* **-s, - (a)** (*Bergspitze*) peak; (*höchster Punkt eines Berges*) summit; (*old: Baum~*) top, tip. **(b)** (*fig: Höhepunkt*) height; (*des Ruhms, der Karriere auch*) peak; (*der Vollkommenheit*) epitome ♦ **er hat den ~ seiner Wünsche/Träume erreicht** all his wishes/dreams have been fulfilled *or* have come true; **das ist der ~!** (*inf*) that's the limit, that takes the cake (*inf*). **(c)** (*~konferenz*) summit.

Gipfel-: ~gespräch *nt* (*Pol*) summit talks *pl*; **~konferenz** *f* (*Pol*) summit conference; **~kreuz** *nt* cross on the summit of a/the mountain; **~leistung** *f* crowning achievement.

gipfeln *vi* to culminate (*in +dat* in).

Gipfel-: ~punkt *m* (*lit*) zenith; (*fig*) high point; **~stürmer** *m* (*liter*) conqueror of a/the peak; **~treffen** *nt* (*Pol*) summit (meeting).

Gips *m* **-es, -e (a)** plaster; (*gebrannter ~, Art auch*) plaster of Paris; (*Chem*) gypsum. **(b)** (*~verband*) plaster ♦ **einen Arm in ~ legen** to put an arm in plaster; **er lag sechs Wochen in ~** he was in plaster for six weeks.

Gips- *in cpds* plaster; **~abdruck,** ⚠**~abguß** *m* plaster cast; **~becher** *m* plaster mixing cup; **~bein** *nt* (*inf*) leg in plaster.

gipsen *vt* to plaster; *Arm, Bein* to put in plaster.

Gipser *m* **-s, -** plasterer.

gipsern *adj attr* plaster.

Gips-: ~figur *f* plaster (of Paris) figure; **~form** *f* plaster (of Paris) mould; **~kopf** *m* (*inf*) blockhead, dimwit, num(b)skull (*all inf*); **~korsett** *nt* (*Med*) plaster jacket; **~krawatte** *f* (*Med*) plaster collar; **~verband** *m* (*Med*) plaster cast *or* bandage (*form*); **er trug den Arm im ~verband** he had his arm in plaster *or* in a plaster cast.

Giraffe *f* **-, -n** giraffe.

Giri ['ʒiːri] (*Aus*) *pl of* **Giro.**

Girl [gøːɐl, gœrl] *nt* **-s, -s** (*inf*) girl; (*Revue~ etc*) chorus girl.

Girlande *f* **-, -n** garland (*aus* of) ♦ **etw mit ~n schmücken** to garland sth, to decorate sth with garlands.

Girlitz *m* **-es, -e** (*Orn*) serin (finch).

Giro ['ʒiːro] *nt* **-s, -s** *or* (*Aus*) **Giri** ['ʒiːri] (*Fin*) (bank) giro; (*Indossament*) endorsement ♦ **durch ~** by giro.

Giro-: ~bank *f* clearing bank; **~geschäft** *nt* (bank) giro transfer; **~konto** *nt* current account; **~verkehr** *m* giro system; (*~geschäft*) giro transfer (business); **~zentrale** *f* clearing house.

girren *vi* (*lit, fig*) to coo.

Gis *nt* **-, -** (*Mus*) G sharp ♦ **~-Dur/g~-Moll** G sharp major/minor.

Gischt *m* **-(e)s, -e** *or f* **-, -en** spray.

Gitarre *f* **-, -n** guitar.

Gitarre(n)-: ~spiel *nt* guitar-playing; **~spieler** *m* guitarist, guitar-player.

Gitarrist(in *f***)** *m* guitarist.

Gitter *nt* **-s, -** bars *pl*; (*engstäbig, vor Türen, Schaufenstern*) grille; (*in Fußboden, Straßendecke*) grid, grating; (*für Gewächse etc*) lattice, trellis; (*feines Draht~*) (wire-)mesh; (*Kamin~*) fire-guard; (*Geländer*) railing *usu pl*; (*Phys, Chem: Kristall~*) lattice; (*Elec, Geog*) grid ♦ **hinter ~n** (*fig inf*) behind bars.

Gitter-: ~bett *nt* cot (*Brit*), crib (*US*); **~elektrode** *f* (*Elec*) grid (electrode); **~fenster** *nt* barred window; **~mast** *m* (*Elec*) (lattice) pylon; **~netz** *nt* (*Geog*) grid; **~rost** *m* grid, grating; **~spannung** *f* (*Elec*) grid voltage; **~stab** *m* bar; **~struktur** *f* (*Chem*) lattice structure; **~tor** *nt* (paled) gate; **~tüll** *m* latticework tulle; **~tür** *f* (paled) gate; **~verschlag** *m* crate; **~zaun** *m* paling; (*mit gekreuzten Stäben*) lattice fence.

Glace [glaːs] *f* **-, -n** (*Sw*) ice(-cream).

Glacé- [gla'seː]: **~handschuh** *m* kid glove; **jdn mit ~handschuhen anfassen** (*fig*) to handle sb with kid gloves; **~leder** *nt* glacé leather.

glacieren* [gla'siːrən] *vt* (*Cook*) to glaze.

Glacis [gla'siː] *nt* **-, -** (*Mil*) glacis.

Gladiator *m* gladiator.

Gladiole *f* **-, -n** (*Bot*) gladiolus.

Glamour ['glɛmɐ] *m or nt* **-s,** *no pl* (*Press sl*) glamour.

Glamourgirl *nt* glamour girl.

glamourös [glamu'røːs] *adj* glamorous.

Glanz *m* **-es,** *no pl* gleam; (*von Oberfläche auch*) shine; (*Funkeln*) sparkle, glitter; (*von Augen*) sparkle; (*von Haaren*) sheen, shine; (*von Seide, Perlen*) sheen, lustre; (*von Farbe*) gloss; (*blendender: von Sonne, Scheinwerfer etc*) glare; (*fig*) (*der Schönheit, Jugend*) radiance; (*von Ruhm, Erfolg*) glory; (*Gepränge, Pracht*) splendour ♦ **mit ~ und Gloria** (*iro inf*) in grand style; **eine Prüfung mit ~ bestehen** (*inf*) to pass an exam with flying colours; **den ~ verlieren** *or* **einbüßen** (*Metall, Leder, Möbel*) to lose its shine; (*Diamanten, Augen, fig*) to lose its/one's sparkle; **etw auf ~ polieren** to polish sth till it shines; **welch ~ in dieser Hütte!** (*iro*) to what do I owe the honour (of this visit)? (*iro*).

Glanz|abzug *m* (*Phot*) glossy *or* gloss print.

glänzen *vi* (*lit, fig*) to shine; (*polierte Oberfläche auch*) to gleam; (*glitzern*) to glisten; (*funkeln*) to sparkle; (*blenden*) to glare; (*Hosenboden, Ellbogen, Nase*) to be shiny ♦ **vor jdm ~ wollen** to want to shine in front of sb; **ihr Gesicht glänzte vor Freude** her face shone with *or* was radiant with joy; *siehe* **Gold.**

glänzend *adj* shining; *Haar, Seide auch* lustrous; *Metall, Leder, Holz auch* gleaming; (*strahlend*) radiant; (*blendend*) dazzling; (*glitzernd*) glistening; (*funkelnd*) sparkling, glittering; *Papier* glossy, shiny; *Stoff, Nase, Hosenboden, Ellbogen* shiny; (*fig*) brilliant; *Aussehen, Fest* dazzling; *Gesellschaft* glittering; (*erstklassig*) marvellous, splendid ♦ **~ in Form** (*inf*) in splendid form; **ein ~er Reinfall** (*iro*) a glorious failure; **wir haben uns ~ amüsiert** we had a marvellous *or* great (*inf*) time; **mir geht es ~** I'm just fine.

Glanz-: ~form *f, no pl* (*inf*) brilliant form; **~gras** *nt* canary grass; **~idee** *f* (*inf*) brilliant idea; **~kohle** *f* glance coal; **~lack** *m* gloss (paint); **~leder** *nt* patent leather; **~leinwand** *f* (*Tex*) glazed taffeta; **~leistung** *f* brilliant achievement; **eine wissenschaftliche ~leistung** a brilliant scientific achievement; **~licht** *nt* **(a)** (*Art, fig*) highlight; **(b)** (*Phys*) reflected light; **g~los** *adj* (*lit, fig*) dull; *Augen, Haar, Vorstellung auch* lacklustre; *Lack, Oberfläche* matt; **~nummer** *f* big number, pièce de résistance; **~papier** *nt* glossy paper; **~periode** *f siehe* **~zeit; ~politur** *f* gloss polish; **~punkt** *m* (*fig*) highlight, high spot; **~rolle** *f* star role; **~stück** *nt* pièce de résistance; **g~voll** *adj* (*fig*) brilliant; *Darstellung, Unterhaltung auch* sparkling; (*prachtvoll*) glittering; **~zeit** *f* heyday; **seine ~zeit ist vorüber** he has had his day.

Glarus *nt* **-** Glarus.

Glas[1] *nt* **-es, ¨er** *or* (*als Maßangabe*) **- (a)** (*Stoff, Gefäß*) glass; (*Konserven~*) jar ♦ **buntes** *or* **farbiges** *or* **gefärbtes ~** stained glass; **„Vorsicht ~!"** "glass — handle with care"; **ein ~ Milch** a glass of milk; **ein ~ Marmelade/Gurken** a pot (*Brit*) *or* jar of jam/a jar of gherkins; **zwei ~ Wein** two glasses of wine; **zu tief ins ~ gucken** (*inf*) *or* **schauen** (*inf*), **ein ~ über den Durst trinken** (*inf*) to have one too many *or* one over the eight (*inf*); **unter ~** behind glass; (*Gewächs*) under glass.

(b) (*Brillen~*) lens *sing*; (*Fern~*) binoculars *pl*, (field-)glasses *pl*; (*Opern~*) opera glasses *pl* ♦ **¨er** (*old*) (*Brille*) spectacles *pl*, glasses *pl*.

Glas[2] *nt* **-es, -en** (*Naut: halbe Stunde*) bell ♦ **es schlägt acht ~en** it's eight bells.

Glas- *in cpds* glass; **~ballon** *m* carboy; **~bau** *m, pl* **-ten** glass structure; **~baustein** *m* glass block; **g~blasen** *vi sep irreg* to blow glass; **~bläser** *m* glassblower; **~bläserei** *f* **(a)** *no pl* (*Handwerk*) glass-blowing; **(b)** (*Werkstatt*) glassworks *sing or pl*; **~bruch** *m* broken glass.

Gläschen ['glɛːsçən] *nt dim of* **Glas[1]** (*Getränk*) little drink ♦ **darauf müssen wir ein ~ trinken** we must drink to that, that calls for a little drink.

Glas-: ~container *m* bottle bank; **~dach** *nt* glass roof.

Glaser *m* **-s, -** glazier.

Glaserei *f* **(a)** *no pl* (*Handwerk*) glasswork. **(b)** (*Werkstatt*) glazier's workshop.

Glaser-: ~handwerk *nt* glazing; **~kitt** *m* glazier's putty.

Gläserklang *m* (*dated*) the clink of glasses.

Glasermeister *m* master glazier.

gläsern *adj* glass; (*liter: starr*) glassy; (*fig: durchschaubar*) transparent; *Verwaltung* open ♦ **der ~e Bürger** the citizen under the eye of Big Brother; **sich ~ anfühlen** to feel like glass.

Gläser-: ~tuch *nt* glasscloth; **g~weise** *adv* by the glassful.

Glasfabrik *f* glassworks *sing or pl*.

Glasfaser *f* glass fibre, fibreglass.

Glasfaser-: ~kabel *nt* optical fibre cable; **~optik** *f* fibre optics *sing*; **~papier** *nt* fibreglass paper; **g~verstärkt** *adj* fibreglass-reinforced.

Glas-: ~fiber *f siehe* **~faser; ~fiberstab** *m* (*Sport*) glass fibre pole; **~flügler** *m* **-s, -** (*Zool*) clearwing; **~geschirr** *nt* glassware; **~glocke** *f* glass cover *or* dome; (*als Lampenschirm*) glass ball; **~harfe** *f* musical glasses *pl*; **~harmonika** *f* musical glasses *pl*, glass harmonica; **g~hart** *adj* brittle; (*Sport sl*) cracking (*inf*); **~haus** *nt* greenhouse; (*in botanischen Gärten etc*) glasshouse; **wer (selbst) im ~haus sitzt, soll nicht mit Steinen werfen** (*Prov*) people who live in glass houses shouldn't throw stones (*Prov*); **~hütte** *f* glassworks *sing or pl*.

glasieren* *vt* to glaze; *Kuchen* to ice, to frost (*esp US*).

glasig *adj Blick* glassy; (*Cook*) *Kartoffeln* waxy; *Speck, Zwiebeln* transparent.

Glas-: ~industrie *f* glass industry; **~kasten** *m* glass case; (*in Fabrik, Büro*) glass box; (*Hort*) cold frame; **g~klar** *adj* (*lit*) clear as glass; (*fig*) crystal-clear; **~kolben** *m* glass flask; (*von Glühlampe, Radioröhre etc*) glass bulb; **~kugel** *f* glass ball; (*Murmel*) marble; **~malerei** *f* glass painting; **~masse** *f* molten glass; **~nudel** *f* fine Chinese noodle; **~papier** *nt* glasspaper; **~perle** *f* glass bead; **~platte** *f* glass top; **~röhrchen** *nt* small glass tube; **~röhre** *f* glass tube; **~scheibe** *f* sheet of glass; (*Fenster~*) pane of glass; **~scherbe** *f*

⚠: for details of spelling reform, see supplement

fragment of glass, piece of broken glass; **~scherben** broken glass; **~schleifer** *m (Opt)* glass grinder; *(Art)* glass cutter; **~schliff** *m (Opt)* glass grinding; *(Art)* glass cutting; **~schmelze** *f* glass melt; **~schneider** *m* glass cutter; **~schrank** *m* glass-fronted cupboard; **~splitter** *m* splinter of glass.

Glast *m* **-(e)s,** *no pl (poet) siehe* **Glanz.**

Glasur *f* glaze; *(Metal)* enamel; *(Zuckerguß)* icing, frosting *(esp US)*.

Glas-: ~veranda *f* glass veranda, sun parlor *(US)*; **~versicherung** *f* glass insurance; **~waren** *pl* glassware *sing*; **g~weise** *adj, adv* by the glass; **~wolle** *f* glass wool; **~zylinder** *m* glass cylinder; *(von Petroleumlampe)* (glass) chimney.

glatt [1] *adj, comp* **-er** *or* **¨er,** *superl* **-este(r, s)** *or* **¨este(r, s)** *or adv* **am -esten** *or* **¨esten (a)** *(eben)* smooth; *Meer auch* unruffled; *Haar* straight; *(Med) Bruch* clean; *Stoff (faltenlos)* uncreased; *(ungemustert)* plain; *(Aus) Mehl* finely ground.
(b) *(schlüpfrig)* slippery.
(c) *(fig) Landung, Ablauf* smooth ◆ **eine ~e Eins** *(Sch)* a straight A.
(d) *attr (inf: klar, eindeutig)* outright; *Lüge, Unsinn etc auch* downright ◆ **das kostet ~e 1.000 Mark** it costs a good 1,000 marks.
(e) *(pej: allzu gewandt)* smooth, slick.
[2] *adv* **(a)** smoothly ◆ **er hat sich ~ aus der Affäre gezogen** he wriggled neatly out of the whole affair.
(b) *(ganz, völlig)* completely; *leugnen, ablehnen* flatly; *vergessen* clean ◆ **jdm etw ~ ins Gesicht sagen** to tell sb sth to his/her face; **die Rechnung ist ~ aufgegangen** the sum works out exactly; **es kostete ~ DM 10.000** it cost a good DM 10,000.
(c) *(inf: wirklich)* really.
(d) ~ stricken to knit garter stitch.

⚠**glattbügeln** *vt sep* to iron smooth.

Glätte *f* **-,** *no pl* **(a)** *(Ebenheit)* smoothness; *(von Haar)* sleekness. **(b)** *(Schlüpfrigkeit)* slipperiness. **(c)** *(Politur)* polish. **(d)** *(fig) (des Auftretens)* smoothness, slickness; *(des Stils)* polish.

Glatt|eis *nt* ice ◆ **„Vorsicht ~!"** "danger, black ice"; **sich auf ~ begeben** *(fig)*, **aufs ~ geraten** *(fig)* to skate on thin ice; **jdn aufs ~ führen** *(fig)* to take sb for a ride.

Glatt|eisbildung *f* formation of black ice.

Glätt|eisen *nt (Sw)* iron, smoothing iron *(old)*.

Glatt|eisgefahr *f* danger of black ice.

glätten [1] *vt (glattmachen)* to smooth out; *(glattstreichen) Haar, Tuch* to smooth; *(esp Sw: bügeln)* to iron; *(fig: stilistisch ~)* to polish up.
[2] *vr* to smooth out; *(Wellen, Meer, fig)* to subside.

Glätterin *f (esp Sw)* presser.

glatt-: ⚠~gehen *vi sep irreg aux sein* to go smoothly *or* OK *(inf)*; **⚠~hobeln** *vt sep* to plane smooth; **⚠~kämmen** *vt sep* to comb straight; *(mit Haarpomade)* to sleek down; **⚠~legen** *vt sep* to fold up carefully; **⚠~machen** *vt sep* **(a)** *(~streichen)* to smooth out; *Haare* to smooth (down); *(mit Kamm)* to comb straight; **(b)** *(inf: begleichen)* to settle; **⚠~polieren*** *vt sep* to polish highly; **⚠~rasieren*** *vt sep* to shave; **⚠~rasiert** *adj Mann, Kinn* clean-shaven; *Beine* shaved; **⚠~rühren** *vt sep* to stir till smooth; **⚠~schleifen** *vt sep irreg* to rub smooth; *Linsen, Diamanten etc* to grind smooth; *Felsen etc* to wear smooth; **⚠~schneiden** *vt sep irreg* to cut straight; **⚠~streichen** *vt sep irreg* to smooth out; *Haare* to smooth (down); **⚠~walzen** *vt sep* to roll smooth; **~weg** ['glatvɛk] *adv (inf)* simply, just, just like that *(inf)*; **er hat meinen Vorschlag ~weg abgelehnt** he simply turned my suggestion down, he turned my suggestion down flat *or* just like that *(inf)*; **das ist ~weg erlogen** that's a blatant lie; **~züngig** *adj (pej geh)* glib, smooth-tongued.

Glatze *f* **-, -n** bald head; *(rare: kahle Stelle)* bald patch *or* spot ◆ **eine ~ bekommen/haben** to go/be bald; **er zeigt Ansätze zu einer ~** he shows signs of going bald; **ein Mann mit ~** a bald(-headed) man, a man with a bald head; **sich** *(dat)* **eine ~ schneiden lassen** to have one's head shaved.

Glatz-: ~kopf *m* bald head; *(inf: Mann mit Glatze)* baldie *(inf)*; **g~köpfig** *adj* bald(-headed); **~köpfigkeit** *f, no pl* baldness.

Glaube *m* **-ns,** *no pl (Vertrauen, religiöse Überzeugung, Konfession)* faith *(an +acc* in); *(Überzeugung, Meinung)* belief *(an +acc* in) ◆ **~, Liebe, Hoffnung** faith, hope and charity; **im guten** *or* **in gutem ~n** in good faith; **(bei jdm) ~n finden** to be believed (by sb); *(Bericht, Aussage etc auch)* to find credence (with sb); **den ~n an jdn/etw verlieren** to lose faith in sb/sth; **jdm ~n schenken** to believe sb, to give credence to sb; **laß ihn bei seinem ~!** let him keep his illusions; **er ist katholischen ~ns** he is of the Catholic faith; *siehe* **Treue.**

Glauben *m* **-s,** *no pl siehe* **Glaube.**

➤ **glauben** *vti (Glauben schenken, überzeugt sein, vertrauen)* to believe *(an +acc* in); *(meinen, annehmen, vermuten)* to think ◆ **jdm ~** to believe sb; **das glaube ich dir gerne/nicht** I quite/don't believe you; **glaube es mir** believe me; **diese Geschichte/das soll ich dir ~?** do you expect me to believe that story/that?; **er glaubte mir jedes Wort** he believed every word I said; **ich glaube kein Wort davon** I don't believe a word of it; **jdm (etw) aufs Wort ~** to take sb's word (for sth); **d(a)ran ~ müssen** *(inf)* to cop it *(sl)*; *(sterben auch)* to buy it *(sl)*; **das glaubst du doch selbst nicht!** you can't be serious; **das will ich ~!** *(dated) (als Antwort)* I'm sure!, I can well believe it; **jdn etw ~ machen wollen** to try to make sb believe sth; **das glaube ich nicht von ihm** I can't believe that of him; **ob du es glaubst oder nicht, ...** believe it or not ...; **wer's glaubt, wird selig** *(iro)* a likely story *(iro)*; **wer hätte das je geglaubt!** who would have thought it?; **ich glaubte ihn zu kennen, doch ...** I thought I knew him, but ...; **ich glaubte ihn tot/in Sicherheit** I thought he was *or* thought him dead/safe; **ich glaubte ihn in Berlin** I thought he was in Berlin; **er glaubte sich unbeobachtet** he thought nobody was watching him; **man glaubte ihm den Fachmann** one could well believe him to be an expert; **es ist nicht** *or* **kaum zu ~** it's incredible *or* unbelievable; **ich glaube dir jedes Wort (einzeln)** *(iro)* pull the other one *(inf)*; **ich glaube, ja** I think so; **ich glaube, nein** I don't think so, I think not.

Glaubens-: ~artikel *m* article of faith; **~bekenntnis** *nt* creed; **~bewegung** *f* religious movement; **~bruder** *m* co-religionist *(form)*, brother in faith, fellow Buddhist/Christian/Jew *etc*; **~dinge** *pl* matters of faith *pl*; **~eifer** *m* religious zeal; **~frage** *f* question of faith; **~freiheit** *f* freedom of worship, religious freedom; **~gemeinschaft** *f* religious sect; *(christliche auch)* denomination; **~genosse** *m* co-religionist *(form)*; **~kampf** *m* religious battle; **~krieg** *m* religious war; **~lehre** *f* dogmatics *sing*; *(pej: Doktrin)* doctrine, dogma; **~sache** *f* matter of faith; **~satz** *m* dogma, doctrine; **~spaltung** *f* schism; **~streit** *m* religious controversy; **g~verwandt** *adj* **jdm g~verwandt sein** to be of a similar faith to sb; **~wechsel** *m* change of faith *or* religion; **zum ~wechsel bereit sein** to be prepared to change one's faith *or* religion; **~zweifel** *m usu pl* religious doubt; **~zwist** *m* religious controversy.

Glaubersalz *nt (Chem)* Glauber('s) salt.

glaubhaft *adj* credible, believable; *(einleuchtend)* plausible ◆ **(jdm) etw (überzeugend) ~ machen** to substantiate sth (to sb), to satisfy sb of sth.

Glaubhaftigkeit *f, no pl* credibility; *(Evidenz)* plausibility.

Glaubhaftmachung *f, no pl (Jur)* substantiation.

gläubig *adj* religious; *(vertrauensvoll)* trusting ◆ **~ hörten sie meiner Geschichte zu** they listened to and believed my story.

Gläubige(r) *mf decl as adj* believer ◆ **die ~n** the faithful.

Gläubiger(in *f***)** *m* **-s, -** *(Comm)* creditor.

Gläubiger-: ~ansprüche *pl* creditors' claims *pl*; **⚠~ausschuß** *m* committee *or* board of creditors; **~bank** *f* creditor bank; **~land** *nt*, **~staat** *m* creditor nation *or* state; **~versammlung** *f* meeting of creditors.

Gläubigkeit *f, no pl siehe adj* devoutness; trust.

glaublich *adj*: **kaum ~** scarcely credible.

glaubwürdig *adj* credible ◆ **~e Quellen** reliable sources.

Glaubwürdigkeit *f, no pl* credibility.

Glaukom *nt* **-s, -e** *(Med)* glaucoma.

glazial *adj (Geol)* glacial.

Glazial *nt* **-s, -e** *(Geol)* glacial epoch *or* episode.

gleich [1] *adj (identisch, ähnlich)* same; *(mit indef art)* similar; *(~wertig, ~berechtigt, Math)* equal; *(auf ~er Höhe)* level ◆ **der/die/das ~e ... wie** the same ... as; **in ~em Abstand** at an equal distance; **wir sind in ~er Weise daran schuld** we are equally to blame; **zu ~en Teilen** in equal parts; **in ~er Weise** in the same way; **~er Lohn für ~e Arbeit** equal pay for equal work, the same pay for the same work; **mit ~er Post** with the same post; **~e Rechte, ~e Pflichten** *(prov)* equal rights, equal responsibilities; **zur ~en Zeit** at the same time; **die beiden haben ~es Gewicht** they are both the same weight, they both weigh the same; **ich habe den ~en Wagen wie Sie** I have the same car as you; **das ~e, aber nicht dasselbe Auto** a similar car, but not the same one; **das kommt** *or* **läuft aufs ~e hinaus** it comes (down) *or* amounts to the same thing; **wir wollten alle das ~e** we all wanted the same thing; **es ist genau das ~e** it's exactly the same; **es waren die ~en, die ...** it was the same ones who/which ...; **zwei mal zwei (ist) ~ vier** two twos are four, two times two equals *or* is four; **vier plus/durch/minus zwei ist ~ ...** four plus/divided by/minus two equals *or* is ...; **jdm (an etw** *dat***) ~ sein** to be sb's equal (in sth); **ihr Männer seid doch alle ~!** you men are all the same!; **alle Menschen sind ~, nur einige sind ~er** *(hum)* all men are equal, but some are more equal than others; **es ist mir (alles** *or* **ganz) ~** it's all the same to me; **ganz ~ wer/was** *etc* no matter who/what *etc*; **ein G~es tun** *(geh)* to do the same; **G~es mit G~em vergelten** to pay like with like; **mit jdm in einem Ton von ~ zu ~ reden** *(geh)* to talk to sb as an equal; **~ und ~ gesellt sich gern** *(Prov)* birds of a feather flock together *(Prov)*; *siehe* **Boot, Münze, Strang.**
[2] *adv* **(a)** *(ebenso)* equally; *(auf ~e Weise)* alike, the same ◆ **sie sind ~ groß/alt/schwer** they are the same size/age/weight; **der Lehrer behandelt alle Kinder ~** the teacher treats all the children equally *or* the same; **~ gekleidet** dressed alike *or* the same.
(b) *(räumlich)* right, immediately, just.
(c) *(zur selben Zeit)* at once; *(sofort auch)* immediately, straight *or* right away; *(bald)* in a minute ◆ **~ zu** *or* **am Anfang** right at the beginning, at the very beginning; **~ danach** immediately *or* straight *or* right after(wards); **ich komme ~** I'm just coming, I'll be right there; **ich komme ~ wieder** I'll be right back *or* back in a moment; **das mache ich ~ heute** I'll do that today; **es muß nicht ~ sein** there's no hurry, it's not urgent; **es ist ~ drei Uhr** it's almost *or* very nearly three o'clock; **ich werde ihn ~ morgen besuchen** I'll go and see him tomorrow; **~ zu Beginn der Vorstellung ...** right at the beginning of the performance ...; **du kriegst ~ eine Ohrfeige** you'll get a slap in a minute; **habe ich es nicht ~ gesagt!** what did I tell you?; **das habe ich mir ~ gedacht** I thought that straight away; **warum nicht ~ so?** why didn't you say/do that in the first place *or* straight away?; **na komm schon! — ~!** come along — I'm just coming *or* I'll be right there; **wann machst du das? — ~!** when are you going to do it? — right away *or* in just a moment; **~ als** *or* **nachdem er ...** as soon as he ...; **so wirkt das Bild ~ ganz anders** suddenly, the picture has changed completely; **wenn das stimmt, kann ich's ja ~ aufgeben** if that's true I might as well give up right now; **deswegen braucht man nicht ~ Hunderte auszugeben** you don't have to spend hundreds because of that; **er ging ~ in die Küche/vor Gericht** he went straight to the kitchen/to

court; **sie hat sich ~ zwei Hüte gekauft** she bought *two* hats; **bis ~!** see you in a while, see you later.
(d) (*in Fragesätzen*) again ◆ **wie war doch ~ die Nummer/Ihr Name?** what was the number/your name again?
[3] *prep +dat* (*liter*) like ◆ **einer Sintflut ~** like a deluge.
[4] *conj* (*old, liter*) **ob er ~ ...** although he ...; **wenn er ~ ...** even if he ...

Gleich-: g~altrig *adj* (of) the same age; **die beiden sind g~altrig** they are both the same age; **G~altrige** people/children (of) the same age; **g~armig** *adj* (*Phys*) *Hebel* equal-armed; **g~artig** [1] *adj* of the same kind (*+dat* as); (*ähnlich*) similar (*+dat* to); (*homogen*) homogeneous (*+dat* with); [2] *adv* in the same way; similarly; homogeneously; **~artigkeit** *f* similarity; (*Homogenität*) homogeneity; **g~auf** *adv* (*esp Sport*) equal; **g~auf liegen** to be lying *or* to be equal, to be level-pegging; **g~bedeutend** *adj* synonymous (*mit* with); (*so gut wie*) tantamount (*mit* to); **~behandlung** *f* equal treatment; **g~berechtigt** *adj* with equal *or* the same rights; **g~berechtigt sein** to have equal rights; **~berechtigung** *f* equal rights *sing or pl*, equality (*+gen* for); △**g~bleiben** *sep irreg aux sein* [1] *vi* to stay *or* remain the same; (*Temperaturen, Geschwindigkeit, Kurs auch*) to remain constant; [2] *vr* **sich** (*dat*) **g~bleiben** (*Mensch*) to stay *or* remain the same; **das bleibt sich g~** it doesn't matter; △**g~bleibend** *adj Temperatur, Geschwindigkeit, Kurs* constant, steady; **g~bleibend sein** to stay *or* remain the same; (*Temperatur etc auch*) to stay *or* remain steady *or* constant; **bei g~bleibendem Gehalt** when one's salary stays the same; **in g~bleibendem Abstand** always at the same distance; **unter g~bleibenden Umständen** if things remain as they are; **er ist immer g~bleibend zuvorkommend** he is always equally helpful; **g~bleibend gute Qualität** consistent(ly) good quality; △**g~denkend** *adj siehe* **g~gesinnt**.

gleichen *pret* **glich**, *ptp* **geglichen** *vi* **jdm/einer Sache ~** to be like sb/sth; **sich ~** to be alike *or* similar; **jdm an Erfahrung/Schönheit ~** to be sb's equal *or* to equal sb in experience/beauty.

gleicher-: ~gestalt (*old*), **~maßen, ~weise** *adv* equally; **~weise ... und ...** both ... and ...

Gleich-: g~falls *adv* (*ebenfalls*) likewise; (*auch*) also; (*zur gleichen Zeit*) at the same time; **danke g~falls!** thank you, (and) the same to you; **g~farbig** *adj* (of) the same colour; **g~förmig** *adj* of the same shape; (*einheitlich, fig: eintönig*) uniform (*auch Phys*); (*ähnlich*) similar; **~förmigkeit** *f siehe adj* similarity of shape; uniformity; similarity; △**g~geartet** *adj siehe* **g~artig**; **g~gelagert** *adj* parallel; **g~geschlechtig** *adj* (*Biol, Zool*) of the same sex, same-sex *attr*; (*Bot*) homogamous; **g~geschlechtlich** *adj* **(a)** homosexual; **(b)** *siehe* **g~geschlechtig**; **~geschlechtlichkeit** *f* homosexuality *no def art*; △**g~gesinnt** *adj* like-minded; **„Ehepaar sucht g~gesinntes"** "married couple seeks couple of similar interests"; △**g~gestellt** *adj* equal (*+dat* to, with), on a par (*+dat* with); **er spricht nur mit ~gestellten** he only speaks to his equals; **rechtlich g~gestellt** equal in law; △**g~gestimmt** *adj* (*Mus*) in tune (*+dat* with); (*fig*) in harmony (*+dat* with).

Gleichgewicht *nt, no pl* (*lit*) balance, equilibrium (*auch Phys, Chem*); (*fig*) (*Stabilität*) balance; (*seelisches ~*) equilibrium ◆ **im ~** (*lit*) balanced, in equilibrium; **wieder im ~ sein** (*fig*) to become more balanced again; to regain one's equilibrium; **das ~ verlieren, aus dem ~ kommen** to lose one's balance *or* equilibrium (*auch fig*); **das ~ behalten** (*lit*) to keep one's balance *or* equilibrium; (*fig*) to retain one's equilibrium; **jdn aus dem ~ bringen** to throw sb off balance; (*fig auch*) to disturb sb's equilibrium; **das ~ einer Sache wiederherstellen** to get sth back into balance *or* equilibrium; **das ~ zwischen ...** (*dat*) **und ... halten** to maintain a proper balance between ... and ...; **diese Dinge müssen sich** (*dat*) **das ~ halten** (*fig*) these things should balance each other out.

gleichgewichtig *adj* (*ausgeglichen*) *Verhältnis* balanced; (*gleich wichtig*) equal in weight ◆ **die Kommission ist nicht ~ zusammengesetzt** the commission is not properly balanced.

Gleichgewichts-: ~empfinden, ~gefühl *nt* sense of balance; **~lage** *f* (*fig*) equilibrium; **~organ** *nt* organ of equilibrium; **~sinn** *m* sense of balance; **~störung** *f* impaired balance, disturbance of the sense of balance; **~übung** *f* (*Sport*) balancing exercise; **~zustand** *m siehe* **~lage**.

gleichgültig, gleichgiltig (*old*) *adj* indifferent (*gegenüber, gegen* to, towards); (*uninteressiert*) apathetic (*gegenüber, gegen* towards); (*unwesentlich*) trivial, immaterial, unimportant ◆ **das ist mir ~** it's a matter of (complete) indifference to me; **Politik ist ihm ~** he doesn't care about politics; **~, was er tut** no matter what he does, irrespective of what he does; **es ist mir ~, was er tut** I don't care what he does; **er war ihr nicht ~ geblieben** she had not remained indifferent to him.

Gleichgültigkeit *f* indifference (*gegenüber, gegen* to, towards); (*Desinteresse*) apathy (*gegenüber, gegen* towards).

Gleichheit *f* **(a)** *no pl* (*gleiche Stellung*) equality; (*Identität*) identity; (*Übereinstimmung*) uniformity, correspondence; (*Ind*) parity. **(b)** (*Ähnlichkeit*) similarity.

Gleichheits-: ~grundsatz *m*, **~prinzip** *nt* principle of equality; **~zeichen** *nt* (*Math*) equals sign.

Gleich-: ~klang *m* (*fig*) harmony, accord; **g~kommen** *vi sep irreg aux sein +dat* **(a)** (*die gleiche Leistung etc erreichen*) to equal (*an +dat* for), to match (*an +dat* for, in); **niemand kommt ihm an Dummheit g~** no-one can equal *or* match him for stupidity; **(b)** (*g~bedeutend sein mit*) to be tantamount *or* equivalent to, to amount to; **~lauf** *m, no pl* (*Tech*) synchronization; **g~laufend** *adj* parallel (*mit* to); (*Tech*) synchronized; △**g~lautend** *adj* identical; **g~lautende Abschrift** duplicate (copy); **g~lautende Wörter** homonyms; **g~machen** *vt sep* to make the same, to level out; *siehe* **Erdboden**; **~macher** *m* (*pej*) leveller (*pej*), egalitarian; **~macherei** *f* (*pej*) levelling down (*pej*), egalitarianism; **g~macherisch** *adj* levelling (*pej*), egalitarian; **~maß** *nt, no pl* **(a)** (*Ebenmaß*) evenness; (*von Proportionen*) symmetry; **(b)** (*geh: Regelhaftigkeit*) monotony (*pej*), regularity; **g~mäßig** *adj* even, regular; *Puls auch* steady; *Abstände* regular; *Proportionen auch* symmetrical; **er ist immer g~mäßig freundlich** he is always equally friendly; **sie hat die Bonbons g~mäßig unter die Kinder verteilt** she distributed the sweets equally among the children; **die Farbe g~mäßig auftragen** apply the paint evenly; **~mäßigkeit** *f siehe adj* evenness, regularity; steadiness; regularity; stability; symmetry; **mit** *or* **in schöner ~mäßigkeit** (*iro*) with monotonous regularity; **~mut** *m* equanimity, serenity, composure; **g~mütig** *adj* serene, composed; **~mütigkeit** *f siehe* **~mut**; **g~namig** *adj* of the same name; (*Math*) with a common denominator; **Brüche g~namig machen** to reduce fractions to a common denominator.

Gleichnis *nt* **(a)** (*Liter*) simile. **(b)** (*Allegorie*) allegory; (*Bibl*) parable.

gleichnishaft *siehe n* [1] *adj* as a simile; allegorical; parabolic.
[2] *adv* in a simile; allegorically; in a parable.

Gleich-: g~rangig *adj Beamte etc* equal in rank (*mit* to); at the same level (*mit* as); *Straßen etc* of the same grade (*mit* as), similarly graded; *Probleme etc* equally important, of equal status; **g~richten** *vt sep* (*Elec*) to rectify; **~richter** *m* (*Elec*) rectifier; **~richterröhre** *f* (*Elec*) rectifier tube (*esp US*) *or* valve; **~richtung** *f* (*Elec*) rectification.

gleichsam *adv* (*geh*) as it were, so to speak ◆ **~, als ob** just as if.

Gleich-: g~schalten *sep* (*Pol: NS, pej*) [1] *vt* to bring *or* force into line; [2] *vr* to conform, to step into line; **~schaltung** *f* (*Pol: NS, pej*) bringing *or* forcing into line; (*unter Hitler auch*) gleichschaltung; **er wehrte sich gegen eine ~schaltung** he refused to be brought *or* forced into line; **g~schenk(e)lig** *adj Dreieck* isosceles; **~schritt** *m, no pl* (*Mil*) marching in step; **im ~schritt** (*lit, fig*) in step; **im ~schritt, marsch!** forward march!; **im ~schritt marschieren** to march in step; **~schritt halten** (*lit, fig*) to keep in step; **g~sehen** *vi sep irreg* **jdm/einer Sache g~sehen** to look like sb/sth; **g~seitig** *adj Dreieck* equilateral; **g~setzen** *vt sep* (*als dasselbe ansehen*) to equate (*mit* with); (*als gleichwertig ansehen*) to treat as equivalent (*mit* to); **nichts ist mit echter Wolle g~zusetzen** there's nothing to compare with pure wool; **~setzung** *f* **die ~setzung der Arbeiter mit den Angestellten** treating workers as equivalent to office employees; **g~silbig** *adj* with the same number of syllables; **~stand** *m, no pl* **(a)** (*Sport*) **den ~stand erzielen** to draw level; **beim ~stand von 1:1** with the scores level at 1 all; **(b)** (*Pol*) equal stage of development; **g~stehen** *vi sep irreg* to be equal (*+dat* to *or* with), to be on a par (*+dat* with); (*Sport auch*) to be level (*+dat* with); **er steht im Rang einem Hauptmann g~** he is equal in rank to a captain; **~stehende** equals, people on an equal footing; **g~stellen** *vt sep* **(a)** (*rechtlich etc*) to treat as equal, to give parity of treatment (to); **daß Frauen und Männer arbeitsrechtlich g~zustellen sind** that men and women should be treated as equals *or* equally *or* given parity of treatment as far as work is concerned; *siehe* **g~gestellt**; **(b)** *siehe* **g~setzen**; **~stellung** *f, no pl* **(a)** (*rechtlich etc*) equality (*+gen* of, for), equal status (*+gen* of, for), parity; **(b)** *siehe* **~setzung**; **~stellungsbeauftragte(r)** *mf decl as adj* equal rights representative; **~strom** *m* (*Elec*) direct current, DC; **~tritt** *m siehe* **~schritt**; **g~tun** *vt impers sep irreg* **es jdm g~tun** to equal *or* match sb; **es jdm im Laufen** *etc* **g~tun** to equal *or* match sb at *or* in running *etc*.

Gleichung *f* equation ◆ **eine ~ ersten/zweiten Grades** a simple *or* linear/quadratic equation, an equation of the first/second degree (*form*).

Gleich-: g~viel *adv* (*geh*) nonetheless; **g~viel ob** no matter whether; **g~viel wie** however; **g~viel wohin** no matter where; **g~wertig** *adj* of the same value; (*gleich zu bewerten*) *Leistung, Qualität* equal (*+dat* to); *Gegner* equally *or* evenly matched; (*Chem*) equivalent; **~wertigkeit** *f, no pl siehe adj* equal value; equality; equivalence, equivalency; **g~wie** *adv* (*old*) (just) as; **g~wink(e)lig** *adj* (*Geometrie*) equiangular (*form*), with (all) angles equal; **g~wohl** (*geh*) *adv* nevertheless, nonetheless; **g~zeitig** [1] *adj* simultaneous; [2] *adv* simultaneously, at the same time; (*ebenso, sowohl*) at the same time; **ihr sollt nicht alle g~zeitig reden** you mustn't all speak at the same time; **~zeitigkeit** *f* simultaneity; **g~ziehen** *vi sep irreg* (*inf*) to catch up (*mit* with).

Gleis *nt* **-es, -e** (*Rail*) line, track, rails *pl*; (*einzelne Schiene*) rail; (*Bahnsteig*) platform; (*fig*) rut ◆ **~ 6** platform *or* track (*US*) 6; **„Überschreiten der ~e verboten"** "passengers must not cross the line"; **ein totes ~** (*lit*) a siding; (*fig*) a dead end; **jdn/etw aufs tote ~ schieben** to put sb/sth on ice (*inf*); **aus dem ~ springen** to jump the rails; **aus dem ~ kommen** (*fig*) to go off the rails (*inf*); **etw ins (rechte) ~ bringen** (*fig*) to straighten *or* sort sth out; **jdn aus dem ~ bringen** (*fig*) to put sb off his stroke; **wieder im richtigen ~ sein/wieder ins richtige ~ kommen** (*fig*) to be/get back on the rails (*inf*) *or* right lines (*inf*).

Gleis-: ~anlagen *pl* railway (*Brit*) *or* railroad (*US*) lines *pl*; △**~anschluß** *m* works siding; **~arbeiten** *pl* work on the line; line *or* track repairs; **~bau** *m, no pl* railway/railroad construction; **~baustelle** *f* place where work is being done on the line; **überall auf der Strecke waren ~baustellen** work was being done all along the line; **~bett** *nt* ballast; **~bremse** *f* rail brake; **~dreieck** *nt* triangular junction.

-gleisig *adj suf* -track, -line.

Gleis-: ~kette *f* caterpillar track; **~kettenfahrzeug** *nt* caterpillar vehicle; **~körper** *m* railway embankment.

Gleisner *m* **-s, -** (*old*) hypocrite, dissembler (*liter*).

gleisnerisch *adj* (*old*) dissembling (*liter*), hypocritical.

gleißen *vi* (*liter*) to gleam, to glisten.

Gleit-: ~boot *nt* hydroplane; **~bügel** *m* (*Elec*) pantograph, current

collector.
gleiten *pret* **glitt,** *ptp* **geglitten** *vi* **(a)** *aux sein* (*Vogel, Flugzeug, Tänzer, Boot, Skier, Schlange*) to glide; (*Blick*) to pass, to range; (*Hand auch*) to slide ◆ **ein Lächeln glitt über ihr Gesicht** a smile flickered across her face; **sein Auge über etw** (*acc*) **~ lassen** to cast an eye over sth; **die Finger über etw** (*acc*) **~ lassen** to glide *or* slide one's fingers over *or* across sth.
(b) *aux sein* (*rutschen*) to slide; (*Auto*) to skid; (*ent~: Gegenstand*) to slip; (*geh: ausrutschen*) to slip ◆ **zu Boden ~** to slip to the floor/ground; **ins Wasser ~** to slide *or* slip into the water; **ins G~ kommen** to start to slide *or* slip.
(c) (*Ind inf: ~de Arbeitszeit haben*) to have flex(i)time.
gleitend *adj* **~e Löhne** *or* **Lohnskala** sliding wage scale; **~e Arbeitszeit** flexible working hours *pl*, flex(i)time.
Gleiter *m* **-s, -** (*Aviat*) glider.
Gleit-: **~flug** *m* glide; **im ~flug niedergehen** to glide *or* plane down; **~flugzeug** *nt* glider; **~klausel** *f* (*Comm*) escalator clause; **~komma** *nt* floating point; **~kufe** *f* (*Aviat*) landing skid; **~mittel** *nt* (*Med*) lubricant; **~schirm** *m* hang-glider; **~schirmfliegen** *nt* paragliding; **~schutz** *m* (*Aut*) anti-skid(ding) device; **~wachs** *nt* (*für Skier*) wax; **~winkel** *m* gliding angle; **~zeit** *f* flex(i)time.
Glencheck ['glɛntʃɛk] *m* **-(s), -s** glencheck.
Gletscher *m* **-s, -** glacier.
Gletscher-: **g~artig** *adj* glacial; **~bach** *m* glacial stream; **~brand** *m* glacial sunburn; **~brille** *f* sun glasses *pl*; **~eis** *nt* glacial ice; **~feld** *nt* glacier; **~forschung** *f* glaciology; **~kunde** *f* glaciology; **~skifahren** *nt* glacier skiing; **~spalte** *f* crevasse; **~tor** *nt* mouth (of glacier); **~wasser** *nt* glacier water.
Glibber *m* **-s,** *no pl* (*N Ger inf*) slime.
glibberig *adj* (*N Ger inf*) slimy.
glich *pret of* **gleichen.**
Glied *nt* **-(e)s, -er** **(a)** (*Körperteil*) limb, member (*form*); (*Finger~, Zehen~*) joint ◆ **seine ~er recken** to stretch (oneself); **an allen ~ern zittern** to be shaking all over; **der Schreck fuhr ihm in alle ~er** the shock made him shake all over; **der Schreck sitzt** *or* **steckt ihr noch in den ~ern** she is still shaking with the shock; **sich** (*dat*) **alle ~er brechen** to break every bone in one's body.
(b) (*Penis*) penis, organ, member (*form*).
(c) (*Ketten~, fig*) link.
(d) (*Teil*) section, part; (*von Grashalm*) segment.
(e) (*Mit~*) member; (*Mil etc*) rank; (*Bibl*) generation; (*Math*) term ◆ **aus dem ~ treten** (*Mil*) to step forward (out of the ranks); **ins ~ zurücktreten** (*Mil*) to step back into the ranks.
Glieder-: **~armband** *nt* (*von Uhr*) expanding bracelet; **~bau** *m* limb structure; (*Körperbau*) build; **~füßer** *m* **-s, -** *usu pl* (*Zool*) arthropod; **g~lahm** *adj* heavy-limbed, weary; **ich bin ganz g~lahm** my limbs are so stiff.
gliedern [1] *vt* **(a)** (*ordnen*) to structure, to order, to organize. **(b)** (*unterteilen*) to (sub)divide (*in +acc* into).
[2] *vr* (*zerfallen in*) **sich ~ in** (*+acc*) to (sub)divide into; (*bestehen aus*) to consist of.
Glieder-: **~puppe** *f* jointed doll; (*Marionette*) (string) puppet, marionette; (*Art*) lay figure; **~reißen** *nt*, **~schmerz** *m* rheumatic pains *pl*; **~satz** *m* (*Ling*) period; **~schwere** *f* heaviness in one's limbs; **~tier** *nt* articulate.
Gliederung *f* **(a)** (*das Gliedern*) structuring, organization; (*das Unterteilen*) subdivision. **(b)** (*Aufbau*) structure; (*Unterteilung, von Organisation*) subdivision. **(c)** (*Aufstellung in Reihe etc*) formation.
Glieder-: **~zucken** *nt* twitching of the limbs; **~zug** *m* articulated train.
Glied-: **~kirche** *f* member church; **~maßen** *pl* limbs *pl*; **~satz** *m* (*Ling*) subordinate clause; **~staat** *m* member *or* constituent state; **g~weise** *adv* (*Mil*) in ranks.
glimmen *pret* **glomm** *or* (*rare*) **glimmte,** *ptp* **geglommen** *or* (*rare*) **geglimmt** *vi* to glow; (*Feuer, Asche auch*) to smoulder ◆ **~der Haß** (*geh*) smouldering hatred; **noch glomm ein Funken Hoffnung in ihm** (*geh*) a ray of hope still glimmered within him.
Glimmer *m* **-s, -** **(a)** (*Min*) mica. **(b)** (*rare: Schimmer*) gleam, glint.
glimmern *vi* to glimmer.
Glimmerschiefer *m* (*Min*) mica schist.
Glimm-: **~lampe** *f* glow lamp; ⚠**~stengel** *m* (*hum inf*) fag (*esp Brit inf*), cigarette, butt (*US inf*).
glimpflich *adj* (*mild*) mild, light, lenient ◆ **wegen des ~en Ausgangs des Unfalls** because the accident wasn't too serious; **~ davonkommen** to get off lightly; **mit jdm ~ umgehen** *or* **verfahren** to treat sb mildly *or* leniently; **~ abgehen** *or* **ablaufen** *or* **verlaufen, einen ~en Ausgang nehmen** to pass off without serious consequences; **die Sache ist für sie ~ abgegangen** *or* **verlaufen** they got off lightly.
Glitschbahn *f* (*dial*) slide.
glitschen *vi aux sein* (*inf*) to slip (*aus* out of).
glitschig *adj* (*inf*) slippery, slippy (*inf*).
glitt *pret of* **gleiten.**
glitzern *vi* to glitter; (*Stern auch*) to twinkle.
global *adj* **(a)** (*weltweit*) global, worldwide ◆ **~ verbreitet** global, worldwide. **(b)** (*ungefähr, pauschal*) general. **~ gerechnet** in round figures.
Globen *pl of* **Globus.**
Globalisierung *f* **-** *no pl* globalization ◆ **die ~ der Märkte** the globalization of markets.
Global-: **~steuerung** *f* overall control; **~strategie** *f* (*Pol*) global *or* worldwide strategy.

Globetrotter ['glo:bətrɔtɐ, 'glo:ptrɔtɐ] *m* **-s, -** globetrotter.
Globus *m* **-** *or* **-ses, Globen** *or* **-se** globe; (*inf: Kopf*) nut (*inf*).
Glöckchen *nt* (little) bell.
Glocke *f* **-, -n** (*auch Blüte*) bell; (*Käse~ etc*) cover; (*Florett~*) coquille; (*in Labor*) bell jar; (*Taucher~*) (diving) bell; (*Damenhut*) cloche; (*inf: Herrenhut*) bowler ◆ **nach den ~n von Big Ben** after the chimes from Big Ben, after Big Ben strikes; **etw an die große ~ hängen** (*inf*) to shout sth from the rooftops, to bandy sth about; **wissen, was die ~ geschlagen hat** (*inf*) to know what one is in for (*inf*) *or* what's in store for one; **über der Stadt wölbte sich eine dichte ~ von Rauch** a thick pall of smoke hung over the city.
Glocken-: **~balken** *m* (bell) yoke; **~blume** *f* bellflower, campanula; **~bronze** *f* bell metal; **g~förmig** *adj* bell-shaped; **~geläut(e)** *nt* (peal of) bells; **~gießer** *m* bell-founder; **~gießerei** *f* bell-foundry; ⚠**~guß** *m* bell-founding; **g~hell** *adj* (*geh*) bell-like; *Stimme auch* as clear as a bell; **~helm** *m* top of a/the bell; **~klang** *m* ringing *or* (*esp hell auch*) pealing (of bells); **~klöppel** *m* clapper, tongue (of a/the bell); **~läuten** *nt siehe* **~geläut(e)**; **~mantel** *m* cope (*for founding bell*); **g~rein** *adj* (*geh*) bell-like; *Stimme auch* as clear as a bell; **~rock** *m* flared skirt; **~schlag** *m* stroke (of a/the bell); (*von Uhr auch*) chime; **es ist mit dem ~schlag 6 Uhr** on the stroke it will be 6 o'clock; **auf den** *or* **mit dem ~schlag** on the stroke of eight/nine *etc*; (*genau pünktlich*) on the dot; **~speise** *f* bell metal; **~spiel** *nt* (*in Turm*) carillon; (*automatisch auch*) chimes *pl*; (*Instrument*) glockenspiel; **~strang** *m* bell rope; **~stube** *f* belfry; **~stuhl** *m* bell cage; **~ton** *m* sound of a/the bell; **~turm** *m* belltower, belfry; **~weihe** *f* consecration of a/the bell; **~zeichen** *nt* ring of a/the bell; **auf ein ~zeichen erschien der Butler** a ring on the bell summoned the butler; **~zug** *m* (*~strang*) bell rope; (*Klingelschnur*) bellpull, bell cord.
glockig *adj* bell-shaped.
Glöckner *m* **-s, -** bellringer ◆ **„Der ~ von Notre-Dame"** "The Hunchback of Notre Dame".
glomm *pret of* **glimmen.**
Gloria[1] *nt* **-s, -s** (*Eccl*) gloria, Gloria; *siehe* **Glanz.**
Gloria[2] *f* **-** *or nt* **-s,** *no pl* (*usu iro*) glory.
Glorie [-iə] *f* **(a)** *no pl* (*Ruhm*) glory, splendour. **(b)** (*Heiligenschein*) halo.
Glorienschein [-iən-] *m* halo; (*fig*) aura.
glorifizieren* *vt* to glorify.
Glorifizierung *f* glorification.
Gloriole *f* **-, -n** halo; (*fig*) aura.
glorios *adj* (*oft iro*) glorious, magnificent.
glorreich *adj* glorious ◆ **seine Laufbahn ~ beenden** to bring one's career to a glorious conclusion; **der ~e Rosenkranz** (*Eccl*) the Glorious Mysteries *pl*.
Glossar *nt* **-s, -e** glossary.
Glosse *f* **-, -n** **(a)** (*Liter*) gloss (*zu* on). **(b)** (*Press, Rad etc*) commentary. **(c)** **~n** *pl* (*inf*) snide *or* sneering comments; **seine ~n über jdn/etw machen** (*inf*) to make snide comments about sb/sth.
Glossenschreiber *m* (*Press*) commentator.
glossieren* *vt* **(a)** (*Liter*) to gloss, to write a gloss/glosses on. **(b)** (*bespötteln*) to sneer at. **(c)** (*Press, Rad etc*) to do a commentary on, to commentate on.
Glotz-: **~auge** *nt* **(a)** (*usu pl: inf*) staring *or* goggle (*inf*) eye; **~augen machen** to stare (goggle-eyed), to gawp; **(b)** (*Med*) exophthalmia (*spec*); **g~äugig** *adj, adv* (*inf*) goggle-eyed (*inf*).
Glotze *f* **-, -n** (*sl*) goggle-box (*inf*), one-eyed monster (*pej inf*), boob tube (*US inf*).
glotzen *vi* (*pej inf*) (*auf, in +acc* at) to stare, to gawp, to gape.
Glotzkasten *m* (*sl*), **Glotzkiste** *f* (*sl*), ⚠**Glotzophon** *nt* **-s, -e** (*pej inf*) goggle-box (*inf*), one-eyed monster (*pej inf*), boob tube (*US inf*).
Gloxinie [-iə] *f* (*Bot*) gloxinia.
Glubsch|auge *nt* (*inf*) *siehe* **Glotzauge (a).**
gluck *interj* **(a)** (*von Huhn*) cluck. **(b)** (*von Flüssigkeit*) glug ◆ **~ ~, weg war er** (*inf*) glug glug, and he'd gone.
▼ **Glück** *nt* **-(e)s,** (*rare*) **-e** **(a)** luck ◆ **ein seltenes ~** a funny stroke *or* piece of luck; **ein ~!** how lucky!, what a stroke *or* piece of luck!; **~/kein ~ haben** to be lucky/unlucky; **er hat das ~ gehabt, zu ...** he was lucky enough to ..., he had the good fortune to ...; **~ gehabt!** that was lucky; **auf gut ~** (*aufs Geratewohl*) on the off-chance; (*unvorbereitet*) trusting to luck; (*wahllos*) at random; **es ist ein wahres ~, daß ...** it's really lucky that ...; **du hast ~ im Unglück gehabt** it could have been a great deal worse (for you); **in ~ und Unglück** in good times and in bad, through thick and thin; **viel ~ (bei ...)!** good luck *or* the best of luck (with ...)!; **~ bei Frauen haben** to be successful with women; **jdm ~ für etw wünschen** to wish sb luck for sth; **jdm ~ wünschen zu ...** to congratulate sb on ...; **er wünscht/ich wünsche dir ~ bei deiner Prüfung** he wishes you (good) luck in your exam/good luck in your exam; **jdm zum Neuen Jahr/zum Geburtstag ~ wünschen** to wish sb (a) Happy New Year/happy birthday; **zum ~** luckily, fortunately; **zu seinem ~** luckily *or* fortunately for him; **das ist dein ~!** that's lucky for you!; **~ auf!** (*Min*) good luck!; **mehr ~ als Verstand haben** to have more luck than brains; **sie weiß noch nichts von ihrem ~** (*iro*) she doesn't know anything about it yet; **damit wirst du bei ihr kein ~ haben** you won't have any joy with her (with that) (*inf*), that won't work with her; **sein ~ machen** to make one's fortune; **sein ~ probieren** *or* **versuchen** to try one's luck; **er kann von ~ reden** *or* **sagen, daß ...** he can count himself lucky that ..., he can thank his lucky stars that ... (*inf*); **sein ~ mit Füßen treten** to turn one's back on fortune; **~ muß der Mensch haben** (*inf*) my/your *etc* luck is/was in; **das war das ~ des Tüchtigen** (*prov*) he/she deserved the break (*inf*) *or* his/her good luck; **das hat mir gerade noch zu meinem ~ gefehlt!** (*iro*) that was all I wanted; **man kann**

niemanden zu seinem ~ zwingen (*prov*) you can lead a horse to water but you can't make him drink (*Prov*); **ein Kind/Stiefkind des ~s sein** (*geh*) to have been born under a lucky star/to be a born loser; **jeder ist seines ~es Schmied** (*Prov*) life is what you make it (*prov*), everyone is the architect of his own future.
(b) (*Freude*) happiness ◆ **eheliches ~** wedded *or* marital bliss; **er ist ihr ganzes ~** he is her whole life; **das Streben nach ~** the pursuit of happiness; **~ und Glas, wie leicht bricht das!** (*prov*) happiness is such a fragile thing.

Glück-: ~auf *nt* **-s,** *no pl* (cry of) "good luck"; ⚠**g~bringend** *adj* lucky, propitious (*form*).

Glucke *f* **-, -n** (*Bruthenne*) broody *or* sitting hen; (*mit Jungen*) mother hen ◆ **wie eine ~ ist sie ständig um ihre Kinder herum** she fusses round her children like a mother hen.

glucken *vi* **(a)** (*brüten*) to brood; (*brüten wollen*) to go broody; (*fig inf*) to sit around. **(b)** (*Küken rufen*) to cluck.

glücken *vi aux sein* to be a success, to be successful ◆ **nicht ~** to be a failure, not to be a success; (*Plan auch*) to miscarry; **ihm glückt alles/nichts** everything/nothing he does is a success, he succeeds/fails at whatever he does; **dieses Bild/die Torte ist dir gut geglückt** your picture/cake has turned out very well; **endlich ist es ihm geglückt** at last he managed it; **es wollte nicht ~** it wouldn't go right.

gluckern *vi* to glug.

glückhaft *adj* (*geh*) happy.

Gluckhenne *f siehe* **Glucke.**

▼ **glücklich** 1 *adj* **(a)** (*erfolgreich, vom Glück begünstigt*) lucky, fortunate; (*vorteilhaft, treffend, erfreulich*) happy ◆ **~e Reise!** bon voyage!, pleasant journey!; **er kann sich ~ schätzen(, daß)** he can count *or* consider himself lucky (that); **wer ist der/die G~e?** who is the lucky man/woman/girl *etc*?
▼ **(b)** (*froh, selig*) happy ◆ **ein ~es Ende, ein ~er Ausgang** a happy ending; **~ machen** to bring happiness; **jdn ~ machen** to make sb happy, to bring sb happiness.
2 *adv* **(a)** (*mit Glück*) by *or* through luck; (*vorteilhaft, treffend, erfreulich*) happily ◆ **~ zurückkommen** (*in Sicherheit*) to come back safely.
(b) (*froh, selig*) happily ◆ **die ~-heiteren Tage der Kindheit** the bright and happy days of childhood.

glücklicherweise *adv* luckily, fortunately.

Glück-: g~los *adj* hapless, luckless; **~sache** *f siehe* **Glückssache.**

Glücks-: ~automat *m* (*fig*) gaming machine; **~bote** *m* bearer of (the) glad *or* good tidings; **~botschaft** *f* glad *or* good tidings *pl*; **~bringer** *m* **-s, -** bearer of (the) glad tidings; (*Talisman*) lucky charm; **~bude** *f* try-your-luck stall.

glückselig *adj* blissfully happy, blissful; *Lächeln, Gesichtsausdruck auch* rapturous.

Glückseligkeit *f* bliss, rapture.

glucksen *vi* **(a)** (*lachen*) (*Kleinkind*) to gurgle; (*Erwachsener*) to chortle. **(b)** *siehe* **gluckern.**

Glücks-: ~fall *m* piece *or* stroke of luck; **durch einen ~fall** by a lucky chance; **im ~fall kannst du mit einer Geldstrafe rechnen** if you're lucky you'll get away with a fine; **~gefühl** *nt* feeling of happiness; **~göttin** *f* goddess of luck; **die ~göttin ist mir nicht hold** (*hum, geh*) (Dame) Fortune has deserted me; **~hafen** *m* (*S Ger, Aus*) *siehe* **~bude; ~kind** *nt* child of Fortune; **~klee** *m* four-leaf(ed) clover; **~linie** *f* line of fortune *or* luck; **~pfennig** *m* lucky penny, *a new, shiny pfennig piece supposed to bring luck*; **~pilz** *m* lucky beggar (*inf*) *or* devil (*inf*); **~rad** *nt* wheel of fortune; **~ritter** *m* adventurer; **~sache** *f* **das ist ~sache** it's a matter of luck; **ich hab gedacht ... — Denken ist ~sache** (*inf*) I thought ... — you thought?; **~schwein(chen)** *nt pig as a symbol of good luck*; **~spiel** *nt* game of chance; **~spieler** *m* gambler; **~stern** *m* lucky star; **~strähne** *f* lucky streak; **eine ~strähne haben** to be on a lucky streak; **~tag** *m* lucky day.

glückstrahlend *adj* beaming *or Kind, Frau auch* radiant (with happiness).

Glücks-: ~treffer *m* stroke of luck; (*beim Schießen, Ftbl*) lucky shot, fluke (*inf*); **~umstand** *m* fortunate circumstance; **~zahl** *f* lucky number.

⚠**glückverheißend** *adj* (*liter*) *Religion, Gesichtsausdruck* which holds out a promise of happiness; *Zeichen etc* propitious (*form*), auspicious.

▼ **Glückwunsch** *m* congratulations *pl* (*zu* on) ◆ **herzlichen ~** congratulations; **herzlichen ~ zum Geburtstag!** happy birthday, many happy returns of the day; **~̈e zur Verlobung/zur bestandenen Prüfung** congratulations on your engagement/on passing your examination.

Glückwunsch-: ~adresse *f* message of congratulations, congratulatory message; **~karte** *f* greetings card; **~schreiben** *nt* letter of congratulations; **~telegramm** *nt* greetings telegram.

Glüh- (*Elec*): **~birne** *f* (electric) light bulb; **~draht** *m* filament.

glühen 1 *vi* to glow; (*fig auch*) to be aglow ◆ **der Ofen/die Sonne glüht, daß man es nicht aushalten kann** the fire/sun is too hot to bear; **vor Fieber/Scham ~** to be flushed with fever/shame; **vor Verlangen** *etc* **~** (*liter*) to burn with desire *etc*.
2 *vt* to heat until red-hot.

glühend *adj* glowing; (*heiß~*) *Metall* red-hot; *Hitze* blazing; (*fig: leidenschaftlich*) ardent; *Haß* burning; *Wangen* flushed, burning ◆ **~ heiß** scorching; *Sonne auch* blazing hot.

Glüh-: ~faden *m* (*Elec*) filament; **~kerze** *f* (*Aut*) heater *or* incandescent plug; **~lampe** *f* (*form*) electric light bulb; **~ofen** *m* (*Metal*) annealing furnace; **~strumpf** *m* (gas) mantle; **~wein** *m* glühwein, mulled wine, glogg (*US*); **~würmchen** *nt* glow-worm; (*fliegend*) firefly.

Glukose *f* **-, -n** glucose.

Glupsch|auge *nt* (*N Ger inf*) *siehe* **Glotzauge (a).**

glupschen *vi* (*N Ger inf*) *siehe* **glotzen.**

Glut *f* **-, -en (a)** (*glühende Masse, Kohle*) embers *pl*; (*Tabaks~*) burning ash; (*Hitze*) heat. **(b)** (*fig liter*) (*glühende Farbe, Hitze*) glow; (*auf Gesicht*) flush, redness; (*Leidenschaft*) ardour.

Glutamat *nt* glutamate.

Glutamin *nt* **-s, -e** glutamine.

Glutaminsäure *f* glutamic acid.

Glut-: g~äugig *adj* (*geh*) with smouldering eyes; **~ball** *m* (*poet*) fiery orb (*poet*); **~hauch** *m* (*liter*) torrid *or* sweltering heat; **g~heiß** *adj* (*geh*) swelteringly hot; **~hitze** *f* sweltering heat; **g~rot** *adj* (*liter*) fiery red; **~röte** *f* (*liter*) fiery red; **g~voll** *adj* passionate; **~wind** *m* (*liter*) torrid wind.

Glykol *nt* **-s, -e** glycol.

Glyzerin *nt* **-s,** *no pl* (*Chem*) glycerin(e).

Glyzinie *f* wisteria.

GmbH [geːǀɛmbeːˈhaː] *f* **-, -s** *abbr of* **Gesellschaft mit beschränkter Haftung** limited company, Ltd.

Gnade *f* **-, -n** (*Barmherzigkeit*) mercy; (*heiligmachende ~*) grace; (*Gunst*) favour; (*Verzeihung*) pardon ◆ **um ~ bitten** to ask for *or* crave (*liter*) mercy; **jdn um ~ für seine Sünden bitten** to ask sb to pardon (one for) one's sins; **jds ~ finden, bei jdm** *or* **vor jdm** *or* **vor jds Augen** (*dat*) **~ finden** to find favour with sb *or* in sb's eyes; **~ vor** *or* **für Recht ergehen lassen** to temper justice with mercy; **etw aus ~ und Barmherzigkeit tun** to do sth out of the kindness of one's heart; **ohne ~** without mercy; **~!** mercy!; **bei jdm in (hohen) ~n stehen** (*old*) to stand high in sb's favour; **von jds ~n** by the grace of sb; **Fürst von Gottes ~n** (*Hist*) by the Grace of God, Prince; **jdn in ~n entlassen** to allow sb to go unpunished; **jdn in ~n wieder aufnehmen** to restore sb to favour; **sich** (*dat*) **eine ~ erbitten** (*geh*) to ask *or* crave (*liter*) a favour; **jdm eine ~ gewähren** (*geh*) to grant sb a favour; **Euer ~n!** (*Hist*) Your Grace; **die Jungfrau der ~n** (*Eccl*) Our Lady of Mercy; **die ~ haben, etw zu tun** (*iro*) to graciously consent to do sth.

gnaden *vi*: **(dann) gnade dir Gott!** (then) God help you *or* heaven have mercy on you.

Gnaden-: ~akt *m* act of mercy; **~bild** *nt* (*Eccl*) picture/statue with miraculous powers; **~brot** *nt, no pl* **jdm/einem Tier das ~brot geben** to keep sb/an animal in his/her/its old age; **einem Pferd das ~brot geben** to put a horse out to grass; **das ~brot bei jdm essen** to be provided for by sb (in one's old age); ⚠**~erlaß** *m* (*Jur*) general pardon; **~frist** *f* (temporary) reprieve; **eine ~frist von 24 Stunden** a 24 hour(s') reprieve, 24 hours' grace; **~gesuch** *nt* plea for clemency; **~kraut** *nt* hedge-hyssop; **g~los** *adj* merciless; **~losigkeit** *f* mercilessness; **~mittel** *pl* (*Eccl*) means *pl* of grace; **g~reich** *adj* (*old, Eccl*) gracious; **Maria, die ~reiche** Our Gracious Lady; ⚠**~schuß** *m* coup de grâce (*by shooting*); **~stoß** *m* coup de grâce (*with sword etc, fig*); **~tod** *m* (*geh*) mercy killing, euthanasia; **~verheißung** *f* promise of grace; **g~voll** *adj siehe* **g~reich; ~weg** *m* **auf dem ~weg** by a pardon; **jedem Häftling steht der ~weg offen** every prisoner is at liberty to ask for a pardon.

gnädig *adj* (*barmherzig*) merciful; (*gunstvoll, herablassend*) gracious; *Strafe* lenient; (*freundlich*) kind ◆ **das ~e Fräulein** (*form*) the young lady; **die ~e Frau** (*form*) the mistress, madam; **der ~e Herr** (*old*) the master; **darf ich das ~e Fräulein zum Tanz bitten?** (*dated*) may I have the pleasure of this dance? (*form*); **~es Fräulein** (*dated*) madam; (*jüngere Dame*) miss; **~e Frau** (*form*) madam, ma'am; **~er Herr** (*old*) sir; **meine G~e** (*dated*) *or* **G~ste** (*dated*) my dear madam; **~er Gott!** (*inf*) merciful heavens! (*inf*); **Gott sei uns ~!** (*geh*) (may the good) Lord preserve us; **sei doch so ~, und mach mal Platz!** (*iro*) would you be so good as to make some room?; **~ davonkommen** to get off lightly; **es ~ machen** to be lenient, to show leniency.

gnatzig *adj* (*dial*) bearish (*inf*), bad-tempered.

Gneis *m* **-es, -e** (*Geol*) gneiss.

Gnom *m* **-en, -en** gnome.

gnomenhaft *adj* gnomish.

Gnosis *f* **-,** *no pl* (*Rel*) gnosis.

Gnostik *f* **-,** *no pl* (*Rel*) gnosticism.

Gnostiker(in *f*) *m* **-s, -** (*Rel*) gnostic.

gnostisch *adj* (*Rel*) gnostic.

Gnostizismus *m* **-,** *no pl* (*Rel*) Gnosticism.

Gnu *nt* **-s, -s** (*Zool*) gnu, wildebeest.

Go *nt* **-,** *no pl* go (*Japanese board game*).

Goal [goːl] *nt* **-s, -s** (*Aus, Sw Sport*) goal.

Goal- [ˈgoːl-] (*Aus, Sw*): **~getter** *m* **-s, -** scorer; **~keeper** *m* **-s, -, ~mann** *m, pl* **-männer** goalkeeper, goalie (*inf*); **~stange** *f* crossbar.

Gobelin [gobəˈlɛ̃ː] *m* **-s, -s** tapestry, Gobelin; (*Webart*) tapestry weave.

Gockel *m* **-s, -** (*esp S Ger, baby-talk*) cock; (*fig*) old goat (*inf*).

Godemiché [goːdmiˈʃeː] *m* **-, -s** dildo.

Goderl *nt* **-s, -n: jdm das ~ kratzen** (*Aus inf*) to butter sb up (*inf*).

Goethe [ˈgøːtə] *m* **-s** Goethe.

goethesch, goethisch *adj* Goethean.

Go-go-Girl [ˈgoːgogøːɐl] *nt* go-go dancer *or* girl.

Goi [ˈgoːi] *m* **-(s), Gojim** goy, Gentile.

Go-in [goːˈǀɪn] *nt* **-s, -s die Versammlung wurde durch ein ~ gestört** the meeting was disrupted (by demonstrators); **ein ~ veranstalten** to disrupt a/the meeting.

Go-Kart *m* **-(s), -s** kart, go-cart.

Gold *nt* **-(e)s,** *no pl* (*abbr* **Au**) (*lit, fig*) gold ◆ **nicht mit ~ zu bezahlen** *or* **aufzuwiegen sein** to be worth one's weight in gold; **nicht für alles ~ der Welt**

➤ SPRACHE AKTIV: **glücklich: 1b** → 41, 50.2 **Glückwunsch** → 50.6, 51.1, 51.2, 51.3

(*liter*) not for all the money in the world; **er hat ein Herz aus ~** he has a heart of gold; **er hat ~ in der Kehle** he has a golden voice; **zehnmal olympisches ~ holen** to win ten golds in the Olympics; **es ist nicht alles ~, was glänzt** (*Prov*) all that glitters *or* glisters is not gold (*Prov*); *siehe* **Morgenstunde, treu.**

Gọld- *in cpds* gold; (*von Farbe, Zool*) golden; **~ader** *f* vein of gold; **~ammer** *f* yellowhammer; **~amsel** *f* golden oriole; **~arbeit** *f* goldwork; **~barren** *m* gold ingot; **~barsch** *m* (*Rotbarsch*) redfish; (*Kaulbarsch*) ruff; **~basis** *f* gold basis; **eine Währung auf ~basis** a gold-based currency; **g~bestickt** *adj* embroidered with gold (thread); ⚠**g~betreßt** *adj* trimmed with gold braid; **~blech** *nt* gold foil; **g~blond** *adj* golden blond; **~borte** *f* gold edging *no pl*; **~broiler** *m* **-s, -** (*DDR Cook*) roast chicken; **~deckung** *f* (*Fin*) gold backing; ⚠**~doublé, ~dublée** *nt* gold-plated metal; **~druck** *m* gold print; (*Schrift*) gold lettering; **g~durchwirkt** *adj* shot with gold thread.

gọlden [1] *adj attr* (*lit, fig*) golden; (*aus Gold*) gold, golden (*liter*) ◆ **~e Schallplatte** gold disc; **~er Humor** irrepressible sense of humour; **~e Worte** wise words, words of wisdom; **ein ~es Herz haben** to have a heart of gold; **~e Berge versprechen** to promise the moon (and the stars); **die ~e Mitte** *or* **den ~en Mittelweg wählen** to strike a happy medium; **~e Hochzeit** golden wedding (anniversary); **G~er Schnitt** (*Math, Art*) golden section; **das G~e Buch** the visitors' book; **die G~e Stadt** (*geh*) Prague; **das G~e Horn** (*Geog*) the Golden Horn; **die G~e Horde** (*Hist*) the Golden Horde; **das G~e Zeitalter** (*Myth, fig*) the golden age; **das G~e Vlies** (*Myth*) the Golden Fleece; **das G~e Kalb** (*Bibl*) the golden calf; **der Tanz ums G~e Kalb** (*fig*) the worship of Mammon (*fig*); *siehe* **Brücke.**

[2] *adv* like gold ◆ **~ schimmern** to shimmer like gold.

Gọld-: ~esel *m* (*Liter*) ass which rained gold coins; **leider habe ich keinen ~esel** (*fig*) money doesn't grow on trees, I'm afraid; **~faden** *m* gold thread; **g~farben, g~farbig** *adj* golden, gold-coloured; **~feder** *f* gold nib; **~fieber** *nt* (*fig*) gold fever; **~fisch** *m* goldfish; **sich** (*dat*) **einen ~fisch angeln** (*hum inf*) to make a rich catch, to marry money; **~fuchs** *m* **(a)** (*Pferd*) golden chestnut (horse); **(b)** (*old inf*) gold piece; ⚠**g~gefaßt** *adj Brille* gold-rimmed; **g~gelb** *adj* golden brown, old gold; **g~gelockt** *adj* (*dated*) with golden locks; **g~gerändert** *adj* edged with gold; *Brille* gold-rimmed; **~gewicht** *nt* gold weight; ≃ troy weight; **~glanz** *m* (*liter*) golden gleam; **g~glänzend** *adj* (*liter*) gleaming gold; **~gräber(in** *f*) *m* gold-digger; **~grube** *f* (*lit, fig*) goldmine; **~grund** *m, no pl* (*Art*) gold ground; **g~haltig, g~hältig** (*Aus*) *adj* gold-bearing, auriferous (*spec*); **~hamster** *m* (golden) hamster.

gọldig *adj* **(a)** (*fig inf: allerliebst*) sweet, cute ◆ **du bist vielleicht ~!** (*iro*) the ideas you get! **(b)** (*poet: golden*) golden.

Gọld-: ~junge *m* (*inf*) blue-eyed boy (*inf*), golden boy (*inf*); (*Sport*) gold medallist; **~käfer** *m* (*inf: reiches Mädchen*) rich girl; **~kehlchen** *nt* (*inf*) singer with a/the golden voice; **~kind** *nt* (*inf*) little treasure (*inf*), dear child; **mein ~kind** (*als Anrede*) (my) pet *or* precious; **~klumpen** *m* gold nugget; **~küste** *f* (*Geog*) Gold Coast; **~lack** *m* **(a)** (*Bot*) wallflower; **(b)** (*Glanzlack*) gold lacquer; **~mädchen** *nt* (*inf*) blue-eyed girl (*inf*), golden girl (*inf*); (*Sport*) gold medallist; **~mark** *f* (*Hist*) gold mark.

Gọldmedaille *f* gold medal.

Gọldmedaillen-: ~gewinner, ~träger *m* gold medallist.

Gọld-: ~mine *f* gold mine; **~mundstück** *nt* gold tip; **~papier** *nt* gold foil; **~parität** *f* (*Fin*) gold parity; **~probe** *f* assay (for gold); **~rahmen** *m* gilt frame; **~rand** *m* gold edge; **mit ~rand** with a gold edge; **~rausch** *m* gold fever; **~regen** *m* (*Bot*) laburnum; (*Feuerwerkskörper*) Roman candle; (*fig*) riches *pl*; **g~reich** *adj* rich in gold; **~reif** *m* (*geh*) circlet of gold; (*Ring*) gold ring; (*Armband*) gold bracelet; **~reserve** *f* (*Fin*) gold reserves *pl*; **g~rịchtig** *adj* (*inf*) absolutely *or* dead (*inf*) right; *Mensch* all right (*inf*); **~schatz** *m* golden treasure; (*von Geld*) hoard of gold; (*Kosewort*) treasure.

Gọldschmied *m* goldsmith.

Gọldschmiede-: ~arbeit *f* (*Handwerk*) gold work; (*Gegenstand*) worked gold article; **~handwerk** *nt*, **~kunst** *f* gold work.

Gọld-: ~schnitt *m, no pl* gilt edging; **~schnittausgabe** *f* gilt-edged edition; **~schrift** *f* gold lettering; **~stück** *nt* piece of gold; (*Münze*) gold coin *or* piece, piece of gold (*old*); (*fig inf*) jewel, treasure; **~suche** *f* search for gold; **~sucher(in** *f*) *m* gold-hunter; **~ton** *m* golden colour; **~topas** *m* yellow topaz; **~tresse** *f* gold braid; **~überzug** *m* layer of gold plate; **~uhr** *f* gold watch; **g~umrändert, g~umrandet** *adj siehe* **g~gerändert**; **~vorkommen** *nt* gold deposit; **~waage** *f* gold *or* bullion balance; **jedes Wort** *or* **alles auf die ~waage legen** (*sich vorsichtig ausdrücken*) to weigh one's words; (*überempfindlich sein*) to be hypersensitive; **~währung** *f* gold standard; **eine ~währung** a currency on the gold standard; **~waren** *pl* gold articles *pl*; **~wäscher** *m* gold panner; **~wert** *m, no pl* value in gold; (*Wert des ~es*) value of gold; **~zahn** *m* gold tooth.

Golem *m* **-s,** *no pl* golem.

Gọlf[1] *m* **-(e)s, -e** (*Meerbusen*) gulf ◆ **der ~ von Biskaya** the Bay of Biscay; **der (Persische) ~** the (Persian) Gulf.

Gọlf[2] *nt* **-s,** *no pl* (*Sport*) golf.

Gọlfer(in *f*) *m* **-s, -** (*inf*) golfer.

Gọlf- *in cpds* (*Sport*) golf; **~krieg** *m* Gulf War; **~platz** *m* golf course; **~rat** *m* (*Pol*) Gulf Council; **~schläger** *m* golf club; **~spiel** *nt* **das ~spiel** golf; **~spieler** *m* golfer; **~staaten** *pl* **die ~staaten** the Gulf States *pl*; **~strom** *m* (*Geog*) Gulf Stream; **~tasche** *f* golf bag, caddie; **~wagen** *m* (*Golf*) caddie cart.

Golgatha ['gɔlgata] *nt* **-s** (*Bibl*) Golgotha.

Goliath ['go:liat] *m* **-s, -s** (*Bibl, fig*) Goliath.

Gonade *f* (*Biol*) gonad.

Gọndel *f* **-, -n** gondola; (*von Sessellift etc auch*) (cable-)car.

Gọndel-: ~bahn *f* cable railway; **~fahrt** *f* trip in a gondola; **~führer** *m* gondolier.

gọndeln *vi aux sein* to travel by gondola; (*Gondelführer*) to punt; (*inf*) (*reisen*) to travel around; (*herumfahren*) to drive around ◆ **durch die Welt ~** to go globetrotting (*inf*).

Gondoliere [gɔndo'lie:rə] *m* **-, Gondolieri** gondolier.

Gọng *m* **-s, -s** gong; (*bei Boxkampf etc*) bell ◆ **der ~ zur dritten Runde** the bell for the third round.

gọngen [1] *vi impers* **es hat gegongt** the gong has gone *or* sounded; **es gongte zum Essen** the gong went *or* sounded for dinner *etc.*

[2] *vi* to ring *or* sound a/the gong.

Gọngschlag *m* stroke of the gong.

gọnnen *vt* **jdm etw ~** not to (be)grudge sb sth; (*zuteil werden lassen*) to grant *or* allow sb sth; **jdm etw nicht ~** to (be)grudge sb sth, not to grant *or* allow sb sth; **sich** (*dat*) **etw ~** to allow oneself sth; **jdm ~, daß ...** not to (be)grudge sb the fact that ...; **er gönnte mir keinen Blick** he didn't spare me a single glance; **er gönnt ihr nicht die Luft zum Atmen** he (be)grudges her the very air she breathes; **ich gönne ihm diesen Erfolg/seine Frau von ganzem Herzen** I'm delighted for him that he's had this success/that he has such a nice wife; **das sei ihm gegönnt** I don't (be)grudge him that.

Gọnner(in *f*) *m* **-s, -** patron.

Gọnner-: g~haft *adj* (*pej*) patronizing; **g~haft tun** to play the big benefactor; **~haftigkeit** *f* (*pej*) patronizingness; **seine ~haftigkeit** his patronizing(ness); **~miene** *f* (*pej*) patronizing air; **~schaft** *f* (*Förderung*) patronage.

Gonokọkkus *m* **-, Gonokọkken** (*usu pl*) (*Med*) gonococcus.

⚠**Gonorrhö(e)** [gɔnɔ'rø:] *f* **-, -en** (*Med*) gonorrhoea ◆ **er hat die ~** he has gonorrhoea.

Goodwill ['gʊd'wɪl] *m* **-s,** *no pl* (*auch Econ*) goodwill, good will.

Goodwill-: ~reise, ~tour *f* goodwill journey *or* trip.

gor *pret of* **gären.**

Gör *nt* **-(e)s, -en** (*N Ger inf*) **(a)** (*kleines Kind*) brat (*pej inf*), kid (*inf*). **(b)** *siehe* **Göre.**

gọrdisch *adj* **der G~e Knoten** (*Myth*) the Gordian knot; **ein ~er Knoten** (*fig*) a Gordian knot.

Göre *f* **-, -n** (*N Ger inf*) **(a)** (*kleines Mädchen*) (cheeky *or* saucy) little miss. **(b)** *siehe* **Gör (a).**

Gorịlla *m* **-s, -s** gorilla; (*sl: Leibwächter auch*) heavy (*sl*).

Gọsche *f* **-, -n, Gọschen** *f* **-, -** (*S Ger, Aus: pej*) gob (*sl*), mouth ◆ **eine freche ~ haben** to have the cheek of the devil (*inf*); **halt die ~!** shut your mouth *or* gob (*sl*) *or* trap (*inf*).

Gospel ['gɔspl] *nt or m* **-s, -s, Gọspelsong** *m* gospel song.

⚠**gọß** *pret of* **gießen.**

Gọsse *f* **-, -n (a)** (*Rinnstein*) gutter; (*rare: Abfluß, Gully*) drain. **(b)** (*fig*) gutter ◆ **in der ~ enden** *or* **landen** to end up in the gutter; **jdn aus der ~ holen** *or* **ziehen** to take sb from *or* pull sb out of the gutter; **jdn** *or* **jds Namen durch die ~ ziehen** *or* **schleifen** to drag sb's name through the mud.

Gọssen-: ~ausdruck *m* vulgarity; **~jargon** *m*, **~sprache** *f* gutter language, language of the gutter.

Gote *m* **-n, -n** Goth.

Göteborg *nt* **-s** Gothenburg.

Gotha *m* **-s, -s** *directory of the German nobility*, ≃ Debrett's (Peerage) (*Brit*).

Gotik *f* **-,** *no pl* (*Art*) Gothic (style); (*gotische Epoche*) Gothic period ◆ **ein Meisterwerk der ~** a masterpiece of Gothic architecture *etc*; **typisch für die ~** typical of Gothic.

Gotin *f* Goth.

gotisch *adj* Gothic ◆ **~e Schrift** (*Typ*) Gothic (script).

Gọtt *m* **-es, ¨er (a)** god; (*als Name*) God ◆ **~ der Herr** the Lord God; **~ (der) Vater** God the Father; **~ der Allmächtige** Almighty God, God (the) Almighty; **der liebe ~** (*dated*) the good *or* dear Lord; **an ~ glauben** to believe in God; **zu ~ beten** *or* **flehen** (*liter*) to pray to God; **er ist ihr ~** she worships him like a god; **bei ~ schwören** to swear by Almighty God.

(b) in ~ entschlafen (*liter*) to pass away *or* on; **dein Schicksal liegt in ~es Hand** you are *or* your fate is in God's hands; **dich hat ~ im Zorn erschaffen!** God left something out when he put you together! (*hum*); **dem lieben ~ den Tag stehlen** to laze the day(s) away; **den lieben ~ einen guten** *or* **frommen Mann sein lassen** (*inf*) to take things as they come; **er ist wohl (ganz und gar) von ~** *or* **den ¨ern verlassen** (*inf*) he's (quite) taken leave of his senses; **~ ist mein Zeuge** (*liter*) as God is my witness; **wie ~ ihn geschaffen hat** (*hum inf*) as naked as the day (that) he was born; **ein Anblick** *or* **Bild für die ¨er** (*hum inf*) a sight for sore eyes; **das wissen die ¨er** (*inf*) heaven *or* God (only) knows; **~ weiß** (*inf*) heaven knows (*inf*), God knows (*inf*); **er hat ~ weiß was erzählt** (*inf*) he said God knows what (*inf*); **ich bin weiß ~ nicht prüde, aber ...** heaven *or* God knows I'm no prude but ...; **so ~ will** (*geh*) God willing, D.V.; **vor ~ und der Welt** before the whole world; **~ und die Welt** (*fig*) everybody; **über ~ und die Welt reden** (*fig*) to talk about everything under the sun *or* anything and everything; **im Namen ~es** in the name of God; **leider ~es** unfortunately, alas; **was ~ tut, das ist wohlgetan** God does all things well; **~es Mühlen mahlen langsam** (*hum*) the mills of God grind slowly (but they grind exceeding fine); **ein Leben wie ~ in Frankreich führen, wie ~ in Frankreich leben** (*inf*) to be in clover *or* the lap of luxury, to live the life of Riley (*inf*); **was ~ zusammengefügt hat, soll der Mensch nicht scheiden** (*prov*) what God has joined together let no man put asunder.

(c) grüß ~! (*esp S Ger, Aus*) hello, good morning/afternoon/evening; **~ zum Gruß!** (*old*) God be with you (*old*); **~ sei mit dir!** (*old*) God be with you (*old*); **~ mit dir!** (*old*) God bless you; **vergelt's ~!** (*dated*) God bless you, may you be rewarded; **wollte** *or* **gebe ~, daß ...** (*old*) (may) God grant that ...; **~ soll mich strafen, wenn ...** (*old*) may God strike me dumb if ...; **~ steh' mir bei!** God help me!; **~ hab' ihn selig!** God have mercy on his soul; **in ~es Namen!** for heaven's *or* goodness sake!; **ach (du lieber) ~!** (*inf*) oh Lord! (*inf*), oh heavens! (*inf*); **mein ~!, ach ~!** (my) God!; (*als Leerformel in Antworten*) (oh) well, (oh) you know; **großer ~!** good Lord *or* God!; **~ im Himmel!** (*dated*) heavens above!; **bei ~!** by God!; **~ behüte** *or* **bewahre!, da sei ~ vor!** God *or* Heaven forbid!; **um ~es willen!** for heaven's *or* God's sake!; **~ sei Dank!** thank God!

Gott-: g~ähnlich [1] *adj* godlike; [2] *adv verehren* as a god; **g~begnadet** *adj* divinely gifted; **g~behüte** (*esp Aus*), **g~bewahre** *adv* heaven *or* God forbid.

Gottchen *nt* **(ach) ~!** (*inf*) gosh! (*inf*), golly! (*inf*).

Gott|erbarmen *nt* **zum ~** (*inf*) pitiful(ly), pathetic(ally) (*inf*).

Götter-: ~bild *nt* idol; **~bote** *m* (*Myth*) messenger of the gods; **~dämmerung** *f* götterdämmerung, twilight of the gods; **~epos** *nt* epic of the gods; **~gatte** *m* (*dated hum*) lord and master (*hum*), better half (*inf*).

Gott-: g~ergeben *adj* (*demütig*) meek; (*fromm*) pious; **~ergebenheit** *f* meekness.

Götter-: ~gestalt *f* god; **g~gleich** *adj* godlike; **~sage** *f* myth about the gods/a god; (*als Literaturform*) mythology of the gods; **~speise** *f* (*Myth*) food of the gods; (*Cook*) jelly (*Brit*), jello (*US*); **~trank** *m* (*Myth*) drink of the gods; **~vater** *m* (*Myth*) father of the gods.

Gottes-: ~acker *m* (*old*) God's acre; **~anbeterin** *f* (*Zool*) praying mantis; **~begriff** *m* conception of God; **~beweis** *m* proof of the existence of God; **der ontologische** *etc* **~beweis** the ontological *etc* argument.

Gottesdienst *m* **(a)** (*Gottesverehrung*) worship. **(b)** (*Eccl*) service ◆ **zum ~ gehen** to go to church; **dem ~ beiwohnen** (*form*) to attend church.

Gottesdienstbesuch *m* church attendance.

Gottes-: ~friede *m* (*Hist*) (*Pax Dei*) Peace of God; (*Treuga Dei*) Truce of God; **~furcht** *f* (*geh*) fear of God; **jdn zur ~furcht erziehen** to teach sb to fear God; **g~fürchtig** *adj* godfearing; **~gabe** *f* gift of *or* from God; **~gericht** *nt* **(a)** punishment of God; **(b)** (*Hist*) *siehe* **~urteil**; **~geschenk** *nt siehe* **~gabe**; **~gnadentum** *nt, no pl* (*Hist*) doctrine of divine right; **~haus** *nt* place of worship; **~lamm** *nt* (*Rel*) Lamb of God; **~lästerer** *m* blasphemer; **g~lästerlich** *adj* blasphemous; **~lästerung** *f* blasphemy; **~leugner** *m* (*dated*) unbeliever; **~lohn** *m, no pl* (*old*) reward from God; **etw für einen ~lohn tun** to do sth for love; **~mann** *m, pl* **-männer** (*old, iro*) man of God; **~mutter** *f* (*Rel*) Mother of God; **Maria, die ~mutter** Mary (the) Mother of God; **~sohn** *m* (*Rel*) Son of God; **~staat** *m* theocracy; **Augustins „~staat"** Augustine's "City of God"; **~urteil** *nt* (*Hist*) trial by ordeal.

Gott-: g~froh *adj* (*esp Sw*) *siehe* **heilfroh**; **g~gefällig** *adj* (*old*) godly *no adv*, pleasing in the sight of God (*form*); **g~gefällig leben** to live in a manner pleasing in the sight of God **g~gegeben** *adj* god-given; **g~gesandt** *adj* (*old, liter*) sent from God; **g~geweiht** *adj* (*liter*) dedicated to God; **g~gewollt** *adj* willed by God; **g~gläubig** *adj* religious; (*NS*) non-denominational.

Gotthardchinese *m* (*Sw pej*) eyetie (*pej sl*), Italian.

Gottheit *f* **(a)** *no pl* (*Göttlichkeit*) divinity, godhood, godship ◆ **die ~** (*Gott*) the Godhead. **(b)** (*esp heidnische Göttergestalt*) deity ◆ **jdn wie eine ~ verehren** to worship sb like a god.

Göttin *f* goddess.

göttlich *adj* (*lit, fig*) divine ◆ **wir haben uns ~ amüsiert** (*lustig gemacht*) we were terribly amused; (*gut unterhalten*) we had a wonderful time; **du bist ja ~!** (*dated*) you (really) are a one (*dated inf*); **das G~e im Menschen** the divine in Man.

Göttlichkeit *f, no pl* divinity.

Gott-: g~lob *interj* thank God *or* heavens *or* goodness; **er ist g~lob wieder gesund** he has recovered now thank God *or* heavens *or* goodness; **g~los** *adj* godless; (*verwerflich*) ungodly; **~losigkeit** *f, no pl* godlessness; **~seibeiuns** *m* (*euph*) **der ~seibeiuns** the Evil One, the Tempter.

Gotts-: g~erbärmlich *adj* (*inf*) dreadful, godawful (*sl*); **~öberste(r)** *m decl as adj* (*Aus iro*) his lordship (*iro*), my noble lord (*iro*); **die ~öbersten** the noble lords.

Gott-: ~sucher *m* seeker after God; **~vater** *m, no pl* God the Father; **g~verdammich** *interj* (*sl*) bloody hell (*Brit sl*), God Almighty (*sl*); **g~verdammt, g~verflucht** *adj attr* (*sl*) goddamn(ed) (*sl*), damn(ed) (*inf*), bloody (*Brit sl*); **g~vergessen** *adj* **(a)** godless; **(b)** *siehe* **g~verlassen**; **g~verlassen** *adj* godforsaken; **g~verlassen allein** utterly alone; **~vertrauen** *nt* trust *or* faith in God; **dein ~vertrauen möchte ich haben!** I wish I had your faith; **g~voll** *adj* (*fig inf*) divine; **du bist ja g~voll!** you (really) are a one! (*inf*); **~wesen** *nt* (*liter*) god(head).

Götze *m* **-n, -n** (*lit, fig*) idol.

Götzen-: ~anbeter *m siehe* **~diener**; **~bild** *nt* idol, graven image (*Bibl*); **~diener** *m* idolater; (*fig*) worshipper; **~dienerin** *f* idolatress; (*fig*) worshipper; **~dienst, ~glaube** *m*, **~verehrung** *f* idolatry.

Götz von Berlichingen *m* (*euph*) **er beschimpfte ihn mit ~ ~ ~** he used a few four-letter words to him.

Götzzitat *nt* **das ~** ≃ the V-sign (*Brit*), the finger (*US*).

Gouache [gua(:)ʃ] *f* **-, -n** (*Art*) gouache.

Goulasch ['gʊlaʃ] *m or nt siehe* **Gulasch**.

Gourmand [gʊr'mã:] *m* **-s, -s** glutton, gourmand.

Gourmet [gʊr'mɛ, -'me:] *m* **-s, -s** gourmet.

goutieren* [gu'ti:rən] *vt* (*geh*) **(a)** (*fig*) (*Gefallen finden an*) to appreciate; (*gutheißen*) to approve (of). **(b)** (*rare: kosten, genießen*) to taste, to partake of (*liter*).

Gouvernante [guvɛr'nantə] *f* **-, -n** governess; (*pej*) schoolmarm.

gouvernantenhaft [guvɛr'nantən-] *adj* schoolmarmish.

Gouvernement [guvɛrnə'mã:] *nt* **-s, -s (a)** (*Hist*) (*Regierung*) government; (*Verwaltung*) administration. **(b)** province.

Gouverneur(in *f*) [guvɛr'nø:ɐ, -'nø:rɪn] *m* governor.

Grab *nt* **-(e)s, ¨er** grave; (*Gruft*) tomb, sepulchre; (*fig: Untergang*) end, ruination ◆ **das Heilige ~** the Holy Sepulchre; **jdn zu ~e tragen** to bear sb to his grave; **ins ~ sinken** (*old liter*) to be laid in the earth (*liter*); **ein frühes ~ finden** (*geh*) to go to an early grave; **ein ~ in fremder Erde finden** (*geh*) to be buried in foreign soil; **ein feuchtes** *or* **nasses ~ finden, sein ~ in den Wellen finden** (*liter*) to go to a watery grave, to meet a watery end; **ein Geheimnis mit ins ~ nehmen** to take a secret with one to the grave; **treu bis ans ~** faithful to the end, faithful unto death (*liter*); **(bis) über das ~ hinaus** in death, beyond the grave; **verschwiegen wie ein** *or* **das ~** (as) silent as the grave; **er würde sich im ~e umdrehen, wenn ...** he would turn in his grave if ...; **du bringst mich noch ins ~** *or* **an den Rand des ~es!** you'll be the death of me yet (*inf*), you'll send me to an early grave; **mit einem Bein** *or* **Fuß im ~e stehen** (*fig*) to have one foot in the grave; **sich** (*dat*) **selbst sein** *or* **sich** (*dat*) **sein eigenes ~ graben** *or* **schaufeln** (*fig*) to dig one's own grave; **seine Hoffnungen** *etc* **zu ~e tragen** (*geh*) to abandon *or* bury one's hopes *etc*; *siehe* **~mal**.

Grabbeigabe *f* (*Archeol*) burial object.

Grabbelei *f* (*inf*) groping *or* rummaging (about) (*inf*).

grabbeln *vi* (*inf*) to grope about, to rummage (about).

Grabbeltisch *m* (*inf*) cheap goods table *or* counter.

Gräbchen *nt dim of* **Grab**.

Grabdenkmal *nt siehe* **Grabmal**.

graben *pret* **grub**, *ptp* **gegraben** [1] *vti* **(a)** to dig; *Torf* to cut; *Kohle etc* to mine ◆ **seine Zähne in etw** (*acc*) **~** to sink *or* bury one's teeth into sth; **nach Gold/Erz ~** to dig for gold/ore.
(b) (*geh: gravieren, einkerben*) to engrave.
[2] *vr* **sich in etw** (*acc*) **~** (*Zähnen, Krallen*) to sink into sth; **das hat sich mir tief ins Gedächtnis gegraben** (*geh*) it has imprinted itself firmly on my memory; *siehe* **Grube**.

Graben *m* **-s, ¨** ditch; (*trockener ~, Mil*) trench; (*Sport*) ditch; (*Sport: Wasser~*) water-jump; (*Burg~*) moat; (*Geol*) rift (valley), graben (*spec*) ◆ **im ~ liegen** (*Mil*) to be in the trenches.

Graben-: ~kampf, ~krieg *m* (*Mil*) trench warfare *no pl, no indef art*; **~senke** *f* (rift) valley, graben (*spec*).

Gräber *pl of* **Grab**.

Gräber-: ~feld *nt* cemetery, burial ground; **~fund** *m* grave find.

Grabes- (*liter*): **~dunkel** *nt* sepulchral darkness; **~kälte** *f* grave-like cold; **~luft** *f* grave-like air; **~rand** *m*: **am ~rand** on the very brink of the grave; **~ruhe, ~stille** *f* deathly hush *or* silence; **~stimme** *f* sepulchral voice.

Grab-: ~fund *m siehe* **Gräberfund**; **~geläute** *nt* **(a)** (death) knell; **(b)** *siehe* **~gesang (b)**; **~geleit** *nt* (*geh*) **jdm das ~geleit geben** to accompany *or* follow sb's coffin; **~gesang** *m* **(a)** funeral hymn, dirge; **(b)** (*fig*) **der ~gesang einer Sache** (*gen*) **sein** to sound the death knell for sth; **~gewölbe** *nt* vault; (*von Kirche, Dom*) crypt; **~hügel** *m* mound (*over a grave*); (*Archeol*) barrow, tumulus (*form*); **~inschrift** *f* epitaph, inscription (*on gravestone etc*); **~kammer** *f* burial chamber; **~kreuz** *nt* (cross-shaped) gravestone, cross; **~legung** *f* burial, interment.

Gräblein *nt dim of* **Grab**.

Grab-: ~licht *nt* candle (on a grave); **~mal** *nt* **-s, -mäler** *or* (*geh*) **-e** monument; (*~stein*) gravestone; **das ~(mal) des Unbekannten Soldaten** the tomb of the Unknown Warrior *or* Soldier; **~nische** *f* burial niche; **~pflege** *f* care of the grave(s)/of graves; **~platte** *f* memorial slab; **~rede** *f* funeral oration; **~schänder(in *f*)** *m* **-s, -** defiler of the grave(s)/of graves; **~schändung** *f* defilement of graves.

grabschen *vti siehe* **grapschen**.

Grab-: ~schmuck *m* flowers/wreaths *pl etc* (*on a grave*); **~schrift** *f siehe* **~inschrift**; **~spruch** *m* epitaph, inscription (*on a grave*); **~stätte** *f* grave; (*Gruft*) tomb, sepulchre; **~stein** *m* gravestone, tombstone; **~stelle** *f* (burial) plot; **~stichel** *m* (*Art*) burin.

Grabung *f* (*Archeol*) excavation.

Grabungsfund *m* (*Archeol*) (archeological) find.

Grab-: ~urne *f* funeral urn; **~werkzeug** *nt* (*Zool*) claw.

Gracchen ['graxn] *pl* **die ~** (*Hist*) the Gracchi.

Gracht *f* **-, -en** canal.

Grad *m* **-(e)s, -e** (*Sci, Univ, fig*) degree; (*Mil*) rank; (*Typ: Schrift~*) size ◆ **ein Winkel von 45 ~** an angle of 45 degrees, a 45-degree angle; **unterm 32. ~ nördlicher Breite** latitude 32 degrees north; **4 ~ Kälte** 4 degrees below zero *or* freezing point, 4 degrees below; **4 ~ Wärme** 4 degrees above zero *or* freezing point; **20°** (*gesprochen: ~*) **Fahrenheit/Celsius** 20 (degrees) Fahrenheit/Centigrade; **um 5 ~ wärmer sein** to be 5 degrees warmer; **null ~** zero; **Wasser auf 80 ~ erhitzen** to heat water to 80 degrees; **es kocht bei 100 ~** boiling occurs at 100 degrees; **in ~e einteilen** to calibrate, to graduate; **Verwandte zweiten/dritten ~es** a relative once/twice removed; **Vetter zweiten ~es** second cousin; **Verbrennungen ersten ~es** (*Med*) first-degree burns; **in** *or* **bis zu einem gewissen ~e** up to a certain point, to a certain degree; **in hohem ~(e)** to a great *or* large extent; **im höchsten ~(e)** extremely; *siehe* **Gleichung**.

grad- *siehe* **gerade-**.

Gradation *f* gradation.
grad(e) *adj (inf) siehe* **gerade.**
Grad-: ~bogen *m (Surv, Mil)* quadrant; **~einteilung** *f* calibration, graduation.
Gradient [gra'diεnt] *m (Sci)* gradient.
gradieren* *vt* **(a)** *(in Grade einteilen)* to calibrate, to graduate. **(b)** *(abstufen)* to grade.
Grad-: ~kreis *m (Math)* graduated circle; **g~mäßig** *adj siehe* **graduell**; **~messer** *m* **-s, -** *(fig)* gauge *(gen, für* of); **~netz** *nt (Geog)* latitude and longitude grid; **~skala** *f* scale (of degrees).
graduell *adj (allmählich)* gradual; *(gering)* slight.
graduieren* [1] *vt* **(a)** *(in Grade einteilen)* to calibrate, to graduate. **(b)** *(Univ)* to confer a degree upon, to graduate ◆ **graduierter Ingenieur** *engineer with the diploma of a School of Engineering,* engineering graduate.
[2] *vi (Univ)* to graduate.
Graduierte(r) *mf decl as adj* graduate.
Graduierung *f (Univ)* graduation.
Grad-: ~unterschied *m* difference of degree; **g~weise** *adj* by degrees.
Graecum ['grε:kʊm] *nt* **-s,** *no pl (Univ, Sch)* examination in Greek.
Graf *m* **-en, -en** count; *(als Titel)* Count; *(britischer ~)* earl; *(als Titel)* Earl ◆ **~ Koks** *or* **Rotz** *(inf)* Lord Muck *(hum inf).*
Grafen-: ~familie *f,* **~geschlecht** *nt* family of counts/earls; **~krone** *f* (count's/earl's) coronet; **~stand** *m (Hist) (Rang)* rank of count; earldom; *(Gesamtheit der ~)* counts/earls *pl;* **jdn in den ~stand erheben** to confer the rank of count/earl upon sb, to make sb a count/bestow an earldom upon sb.
Graffel *nt* **-s,** *no pl (Aus inf) siehe* **Gerümpel.**
Graffiti *nt* **-s, -s** graffiti.
Graffito *m or nt* **-(s), Graffiti** *(Art)* graffito.
Grafik *f* **(a)** *no pl (Art)* graphic arts *pl;* *(Technik)* graphics *sing;* *(Entwurf)* design. **(b)** *(Art: Darstellung)* graphic; *(Druck)* print; *(Schaubild)* illustration; *(technisches Schaubild)* diagram.
Grafik-: ~bildschirm *m (Comput)* graphics screen; **~drucker** *m* graphics printer.
Grafiker(in *f***)** *m* **-s, -** graphic artist; *(Illustrator)* illustrator; *(Gestalter)* (graphic) designer.
Grafik- *(Comput)*: **g~fähig** *adj* **g~fähig sein** to be able to do graphics; **~karte** *f* graphics card; **~modus** *m* graphics mode; **~möglichkeit** *f* graphics *pl;* **g~orientiert** *adj* graphics-orientated; **~programm** *nt* graphics program.
Gräfin *f* countess.
grafisch *adj* graphic; *(schematisch)* diagrammatic, schematic ◆ **~es Gewerbe** graphic trades *pl.*
gräflich *adj* count's/earl's ◆ **das ~e Schloß** the count's/earl's castle; **ein ~er Diener** one of the count's/earl's servants.
Grafo- *siehe* **Grapho-.**
Grafschaft *f* land of a count; earldom; *(Admin)* county.
Grahambrot *nt* (type of) wholemeal bread.
gräko- *pref* graeco-.
Gral *m* **-s,** *no pl (Liter)* **der (Heilige) ~** the (Holy) Grail.
Grals- *in cpds* of the (Holy) Grail; **~hüter** *m (lit)* keeper of the (Holy) Grail; *(fig)* guardian; **~suche** *f* quest for the (Holy) Grail.
Gram *m* **-(e)s,** *no pl (geh)* grief, sorrow ◆ **vom** *or* **von ~ gebeugt** bowed down with grief *or* sorrow.
gram *adj pred (geh)* **jdm ~ sein** to bear sb ill-will.
grämen [1] *vr* **sich über jdn/etw ~** to grieve over sb/sth; **sich zu Tode ~** to die of grief *or* sorrow.
[2] *vt* to grieve.
gram|erfüllt *adj (geh)* grief-stricken, woebegone.
Gram-Färbung *f (Med)* Gram's method.
gramgebeugt *adj (geh)* bowed down with grief *or* sorrow.
grämlich *adj* morose, sullen; *Gedanken* morose.
Gramm *nt* **-s, -e** *or (nach Zahlenangabe)* **-** gram(me) ◆ **100 ~ Mehl** 100 gram(me)s of flour.
Grammatik *f* grammar; *(~buch)* grammar (book).
grammatikalisch *adj* grammatical.
Grammatiker(in *f***)** *m* **-s, -** grammarian.
Grammatikregel *f* grammatical rule.
grammatisch *adj* grammatical.
Gramm|atom *nt* gram(me) atom.
Grammel *f* **-, -n** *(S Ger, Aus: Cook) siehe* **Griebe.**
⚠ **Grammolekül** *nt getrennt:* **Gramm-molekül** gram(me) molecule.
⚠ **Grammophon** ® [gramo'fo:n] *nt* **-s, -e** *(dated)* gramophone *(dated),* phonograph.
gram- *(Med)*: **~negativ** *adj* Gram-negative; **~positiv** *adj* Gram-positive.
gramvoll *adj* grief-stricken, sorrowful.
Gran *nt* **-(e)s, -e** *or (nach Zahlenangabe)* **-** *(old)* **(a)** *(Apothekergewicht)* grain. **(b)** *(auch Grän: Edelmetallgewicht)* grain.
Granat *m* **-(e)s, -e** *or (Aus)* **-en (a)** *(Miner)* garnet. **(b)** *(N Ger: Garnele)* shrimp.
Granatapfel *m* pomegranate.
Granate *f* **-, -n** *(Mil) (Geschoß)* shell; *(Hand~)* grenade; *(Ftbl sl: Schuß aufs Tor)* cannonball *(inf)* ◆ **voll wie eine ~** *(sl)* absolutely plastered *(sl),* smashed out of one's mind *(sl).*
Granat-: ~feuer *nt* shelling, shellfire; **unter heftigem ~feuer liegen** to be under heavy shellfire *or* shelling; **~splitter** *m* shell/grenade splinter; **~trichter** *m* shell crater; **~werfer** *m* mortar.
Grand [grã:] *m* **-s, -s** *(Cards)* grand ◆ **~ ouvert** open grand; **~ Hand** grand solo.
Grande *m* **-n, -n** grandee.
Grandeur [grã'dø:ɐ] *f* **-,** *no pl (geh)* grandeur.
Grandezza *f* **-,** *no pl* grandeur.
Grand Hotel, Grandhotel ['grã:hotεl] *nt* luxury hotel.
grandios *adj* magnificent, superb; *(hum)* fantastic *(inf),* terrific *(inf).*
Grandiosität *f* magnificence.
Grand Prix [grã'pri:] *m* **- -, - -** Grand Prix.
Grandseigneur [grãsεn'jø:ɐ] *m* **-s, -s** *or* **-e** *(geh)* nobleman.
Grand-Tourisme-Wagen [grãtu'rism-], **GT-Wagen** [ge:'te:-] *m (Aut)* GT(-model).
Granit *m* **-s, -e** granite ◆ **auf ~ beißen (bei ...)** to bang one's head against a brick wall (with ...).
graniten *adj attr* granite, granitic *(spec); (fig)* rigid.
Granne *f* **-, -n (a)** *(Ährenborste)* awn, beard. **(b)** *(bei Tieren)* long coarse hair.
Grant *m* **-s,** *no pl (inf: S Ger, Aus)* **einen ~ haben** to be mad *(inf) or* cross *(wegen* about, *auf jdn* at sb).
grantig *adj (inf)* grumpy.
Granulat *nt* granules *pl.*
granulieren* *vti* to granulate.
Grapefruit ['gre:pfru:t] *f* **-, -s** grapefruit.
⚠ **Graph**[1] *m* **-en, -en** *(Sci)* graph.
⚠ **Graph**[2] *nt* **-s, -e** *(Ling)* graph.
⚠ **Graphem** *nt* **-s, -e** *(Ling)* grapheme.
⚠ **Graphie** *f (Ling)* written form.
⚠ **Graphik** *siehe* **Grafik.**
⚠ **graphisch** *siehe* **grafisch.**
⚠ **Graphit** *m* **-s, -e** graphite.
⚠ **Graphit-: g~grau** *adj* dark grey; **~stift** *m* lead pencil.
⚠ **Grapho-: ~loge** *m,* **~login** *f* graphologist; **~logie** *f* graphology.
grapschen, grapsen *(inf)* [1] *vt* **(sich** *dat***) etw ~** to grab sth; *(S Ger, Aus hum: stehlen)* to pinch *(inf) or* swipe *(inf)* sth.
[2] *vi* **nach etw ~** to make a grab at sth.
Gras *nt* **-es, ¨er** grass ◆ **ins ~ beißen** *(inf)* to bite the dust *(inf);* **das ~ wachsen hören** to be highly perceptive, to have a sixth sense; *(zuviel hineindeuten)* to read too much into things; **über etw** *(acc)* **~ wachsen lassen** *(fig)* to let the dust settle on sth; **darüber ist viel ~ gewachsen** *(fig)* that's dead and buried; **wo er zuschlägt, wächst kein ~ mehr** *(inf)* he packs quite a punch; **wo er hinlangt, da wächst kein ~ mehr** once he gets his hands on something you'll never recognize it any more.
Gras- *in cpds* grass; **g~bedeckt, g~bewachsen** *adj* grassy, grass-covered; **~büschel** *nt* tuft of grass.
Gräschen ['grε:sçən] *nt dim of* **Gras.**
grasen *vi* to graze.
Gras-: ~fläche *f* grassland; *(Rasen)* piece *or* patch of grass; **~fleck** *m* **(a)** grassy spot; **(b)** *(auf Kleidern etc)* grass stain; **~fresser** *m* herbivore; **~frosch** *m* grass frog; **g~grün** *adj* grass-green; **~halm** *m* blade of grass; **~hüpfer** *m* **-s, -** *(inf)* grasshopper.
grasig *adj* grassy.
Gras-: ~land *nt, no pl* grassland; **~mähmaschine** *f* mower; **~mücke** *f* *(Orn)* warbler; **~narbe** *f* turf; **~nelke** *f (Bot)* thrift; **~pflanze** *f* grass *or* graminaceous *(form)* plant.
Grass *nt* **-,** *no pl (sl)* grass *(sl).*
Grassamen *m* grass seed.
grassieren* *vi* to be rife; *(Krankheit auch)* to be rampant, to rage.
⚠ **gräßlich** *adj* **(a)** hideous, horrible; *Verbrechen auch* heinous, abominable. **(b)** *(intensiv, unangenehm)* terrible, dreadful, awful; *Mensch* horrible, awful ◆ **~ müde** terribly *or* dreadfully *or* awfully tired.
⚠ **Gräßlichkeit** *f* **(a)** *siehe adj (a)* hideousness, horribleness; heinousness. **(b)** *(gräßliche Tat etc)* atrocity.
Gras-: ~steppe *f* savanna(h); **~streifen** *m* strip of grass, grassy strip; **~teppich** *m (geh)* sward *no indef art, no pl (liter);* **~wuchs** *m* grass; **g~überwachsen, g~überwuchert** *adj* overgrown with grass.
Grat *m* **-(e)s, -e** *(Berg~)* ridge; *(Tech)* burr; *(Archit)* hip *(of roof); (fig)* (dividing) line, border.
Gräte *f* **-, -n** (fish-)bone ◆ **sich** *(dat)* **die ~n brechen** *(sl)* to get (badly) smashed up *(inf);* **ich brech' dir alle ~n einzeln!** *(sl)* I'll break every bone in your body.
Gratifikation *f* bonus.
gratinieren* *vt (Cook)* to brown (the top of) ◆ **gratinierte Zwiebelsuppe** onion soup au gratin.
gratis *adv* free; *(Comm)* free (of charge) ◆ **~ und franko** *(dated)* free of charge.
Gratis- *in cpds* free; **~aktie** *f* bonus share; **~probe** *f* free sample.
Grätsche *f* **-, -n** *(Sport)* straddle.
grätschen [1] *vi aux sein* to do a straddle (vault).
[2] *vt Beine* to straddle, to put apart.
Grätsch-: ~sitz *m* straddle position; **~sprung** *m* straddle vault; **~stellung** *f* straddle (position); **in ~stellung gehen** to take up a straddle position.
Gratulant(in *f***)** *m* well-wisher ◆ **er war der erste ~** he was the first to offer his congratulations.
Gratulation *f* congratulations *pl* ◆ **zur ~ bei jdm erscheinen** to call on sb to congratulate him/her.

⚠: Informationen zur Rechtschreibreform im Anhang

Gratulations-: ~besuch *m* congratulatory visit; **~cour** [-kuːɐ] *f* congratulatory reception; **~karte** *f* congratulations card; **~schreiben** *nt* letter of congratulation.

▼ **gratulieren*** *vi* **jdm (zu einer Sache) ~** to congratulate sb (on sth); **jdm zum Geburtstag ~** to wish sb many happy returns (of the day); **(ich) gratuliere!** congratulations!; **Sie können sich** (*dat*) **~, daß alles gutgegangen ist** you can count yourself lucky that everything went off all right.

Gratwanderung *f* (*lit*) ridge walk; (*fig*) tightrope walk.

grau *adj* grey, gray (*esp US*); *Gesicht(sfarbe) auch* ashen; (*trostlos*) gloomy, dark, bleak ◆ **~e Haare bekommen, ~ werden** (*inf*) to go grey; **der Himmel** *or* **es sieht ~ in ~ aus** the sky *or* it is looking very grey; **er malte die Lage ~ in ~** (*fig*) he painted a gloomy *or* dark *or* bleak picture of the situation; **~e Eminenz** éminence grise; **der ~e Markt** (*Comm*) the grey market; **die (kleinen) ~en Zellen** (*hum*) the little grey cells; **die ~e Substanz** (*Anat*) the grey matter; **der ~e Alltag** dull *or* drab reality, the daily round *or* grind; **in ~er Vorzeit** (*fig*) in the dim and distant *or* the misty past; **das liegt in ~er Ferne** (*fig*) it's in the dim and distant future; **~ ist alle Theorie** (*prov*) theory is no use without practice; **das ist bloß ~e Theorie** that's all very well in theory; **G~e Panther** Gray Panthers (*US*), old people's action group.

Grau *nt* **-s, -(s)** grey; (*fig*) dullness, drabness.

Grau-: g~äugig *adj* grey-eyed; **g~blau** *adj* grey-blue; **g~braun** *adj* greyish brown; **~brot** *nt siehe* **Mischbrot.**

Graubünden *nt* **-s** (*Geog*) the Grisons.

Graubündner(in *f*) *m* **-s, -** inhabitant of the Grisons.

grauen[1] *vi* (*geh: Tag*) to dawn ◆ **es begann zu ~** dawn began to break.

grauen[2] *vi impers* **mir graut vor** *or* **es graut mir vor etw** (*dat*) I dread sth; **mir graut vor ihm** I'm terrified of him.

Grauen *nt* **-s,** *no pl* **(a)** horror (*vor* of) ◆ **mich überlief ein ~** I shuddered with horror. **(b)** (*grauenhaftes Ereignis*) horror.

grauen-: ⚠**~erregend, ~haft, ~voll** *adj* terrible, atrocious; *Schmerz auch* gruesome.

Grau-: ~fuchs *m* grey fox; **~gans** *f* grey(lag) goose; ⚠**g~gestreift** *adj* grey striped; **g~grün** *adj* grey-green; ⚠**~guß** *m* (*Tech*) grey iron; **g~haarig** *adj* grey-haired; **~hörnchen** *nt* (*Zool*) grey squirrel; **~kopf** *m* (*fig*) grey-haired man/woman; **g~köpfig** *adj* grey-haired.

graulen (*inf*) [1] *vi impers* **davor grault mir** I dread it; **mir grault vor ihm** I'm scared *or* frightened of him.

[2] *vr* **sich vor jdm/etw ~** to be scared *or* frightened of sb/sth.

[3] *vt* to drive out (*aus* of).

graulich, gräulich *adj* greyish.

⚠**graumeliert** *adj attr* flecked with grey; *Haar auch* greying.

Graupe *f* **-, -n** grain of pearl barley ◆ **~n** pearl barley *sing.*

Graupel *f* **-, -n** (small) hailstone ◆ **~n** soft hail *sing*, graupel *sing* (*spec*).

graup(e)lig *adj Schauer* of soft hail ◆ **~er Schnee** snow mixed with fine hail; **~er Hagel** soft hail.

graupeln *vi impers* **es graupelt** a soft hail is falling.

Graupel-: ~regen *m*, **~schauer** *m* sleet; **~wetter** *nt* soft hail.

Graupensuppe *f* barley broth *or* soup.

grauplig *adj siehe* **graup(e)lig.**

graus *adj* (*old*) afeared (*old, liter*).

Graus *m* **-es,** *no pl* (*old*) horror ◆ **es war ein ~ zu sehen, wie ...** it was terrible to see how ...; **es ist ein ~ mit ihm** he's impossible *or* the limit, will he never learn!; **o ~!** (*old, hum*) oh horror! (*old, hum*), (alack and) alas! (*old, iro*).

grausam *adj* **(a)** (*gefühllos, roh*) cruel (*gegen, zu* to) ◆ **~ ums Leben kommen** to die a cruel death; **sich ~ für etw rächen** to take (a) cruel revenge for sth. **(b)** (*inf*) terrible, awful, dreadful.

Grausamkeit *f* **(a)** *no pl* cruelty. **(b)** (*grausame Tat*) (act of) cruelty; (*stärker*) atrocity.

Grau-: ~schimmel *m* **(a)** (*Pferd*) grey (horse); **(b)** (*Pilz*) grey mould; **~schleier** *m* (*von Wäsche*) grey(ness); (*fig*) veil; **g~schwarz** *adj* greyish black.

grausen *vi impers siehe* **grauen**[2].

Grausen *nt* **-s,** *no pl* **(a)** *siehe* **Grauen (a). (b)** (*inf*) **da kann man das große** *or* **kalte ~ kriegen** it's enough to give you the creeps (*inf*) *or* willies (*sl*).

grausig *adj siehe* **grauenhaft.**

grauslich *adj* (*dial*) *siehe* **gräßlich.**

Grau-: ~specht *m* grey-headed woodpecker; **~stufe** *f* shade of grey; **~tier** *nt* (*hum inf*) (jack)ass, donkey, mule; **~ton** *m* grey colour; **~wal** *m* grey whale; **g~weiß** *adj* greyish white; **~zone** *f* (*fig*) grey area.

Graveur(in *f*) [gra'vøːɐ, -øːrɪn] *m* engraver.

Gravier- [gra'viːɐ-]: **~anstalt** *f* engraving establishment; **~arbeit** *f* engraving.

gravieren* [gra'viːrən] *vt* to engrave.

gravierend [gra'viːrənt] *adj* serious, grave.

Gravier- [gra'viːɐ-]: **~maschine** *f* engraving machine; **~nadel** *f* graver, burin.

Gravierung [gra'viːrʊŋ] *f* engraving.

Gravimetrie [gravime'triː] *f* gravimetry.

gravimetrisch [gravi-] *adj* gravimetric.

Gravis ['graːvɪs] *m* **-, -** (*Gram*) grave accent.

Gravitation [gravita'tsioːn] *f* gravitation, gravitational pull.

Gravitations-: ~feld *nt* gravitational field; **~gesetz** *nt* law of gravitation/gravity; **~kraft** *f* gravitational force.

gravitätisch [gravi'tɛːtɪʃ] *adj* grave, solemn.

gravitieren* [gravi'tiːrən] *vi* (*Phys, fig*) to gravitate (*zu* towards).

Gravur [gra'vuːɐ], **Gravüre** [gra'vyːrə] *f* engraving.

Grazie [-iə] *f* **(a)** (*Myth*) Grace; (*hum*) beauty, belle. **(b)** *no pl* (*Liebreiz*) grace(fulness).

grazil *adj* (delicately) slender, gracile (*liter*); (*rare: geschmeidig*) nimble ◆ **~ gebaut sein** to have a delicate figure.

graziös *adj* graceful; (*lieblich*) charming.

Gräzismus *m* (*Ling*) Graecism.

Gräzist(in *f*) *m* Greek scholar, Hellenist.

Gräzistik *f* Greek studies *pl.*

Greenhorn ['griːnhɔːn] *nt* **-s, -s** (*inf*) greenhorn (*inf*).

Greenpeace ['griːnpiːs] *no art* Greenpeace.

Greenpeacer(in *f*) ['griːnpiːsɐ, -ərɪn] *m* **-s, -** (*inf*) member of Greenpeace.

Greenwich-Zeit ['grɪnɪdʒ-, -ɪtʃ-], **Greenwicher Zeit** ['grɪnɪdʒɐ-] *f* **(die) ~** GMT, Greenwich Mean Time.

Gregor *m* **-s** Gregory.

Gregorianik *f* Gregorian music.

gregorianisch *adj* Gregorian ◆ **G~er Gesang** Gregorian chant, plainsong.

Greif *m* **-(e)s,** *or* **-en, -e(n)** (*Myth*) **(Vogel) ~** griffin, griffon, gryphon.

Greif-: ~arm *m* claw arm; **~bagger** *m* grab dredger; **g~bar** *adj* (*konkret*) tangible, concrete; (*erreichbar*) available; *Ware* available, in stock *pred*; **g~bare Gestalt** *or* **g~bare Formen annehmen** to take on (a) concrete *or* tangible form; **g~bar nahe, in g~barer Nähe** within reach; **~bewegung** *f* grasping movement.

greifen *pret* **griff,** *ptp* **gegriffen** [1] *vt* **(a)** (*nehmen, packen*) to take hold of, to grasp; (*grapschen*) to seize, to grab; *Saite* to stop, to hold down; *Akkord* to strike ◆ **eine Oktave ~** to stretch *or* reach an octave; **diese Zahl ist zu hoch/zu niedrig gegriffen** (*fig*) this figure is too high/low; **zum G~ nahe sein** (*Sieg*) to be within reach; (*Folgerung*) to be obvious (to anyone); **die Gipfel waren zum G~ nahe** you could almost touch the peaks; **aus dem Leben gegriffen** taken from life.

(b) (*fangen*) to catch ◆ **G~ spielen** to play catch *or* tag; **sich** (*dat*) **jdn/etw ~** to grab sb/sth; **den werde ich mir mal ~** (*inf*) I'm going to tell him a thing or two (*inf*) *or* a few home truths.

[2] *vi* **(a) hinter sich** (*acc*) **~** to reach behind one; **um sich ~** (*fig*) to spread, to gain ground; **unter etw** (*acc*) **~** to reach under sth; **in etw** (*acc*) **~** to put one's hand into sth, to reach into sth; **nach einer Sache ~** to reach for sth; (*um zu halten*) to clutch *or* (*hastig*) grab at sth; **an etw** (*acc*) **~** (*fassen*) to take hold of sth, to grasp sth; (*berühren*) to touch sth; **zu etw ~** (*zu Pistole*) to reach for sth; (*fig: zu Methoden, Mitteln*) to turn *or* resort to sth; **zur Flasche ~** to take *or* turn to the bottle; **er greift gern nach einem guten Buch** he likes to settle down with a good book; **tief in die Tasche ~** (*fig*) to dig deep in one's pocket(s); **in die Saiten/Tasten ~** to strike up a tune; **nach den Sternen ~** to reach for the stars; **nach dem rettenden Strohhalm ~** to clutch at a straw; **zu den Waffen ~** to take up arms; **zum Äußersten ~** to resort to extremes; **nach der Macht ~** to try to seize power; **die Geschichte greift ans Herz** the story really tears *or* tugs at one's heartstrings.

(b) (*nicht rutschen, einrasten*) to grip; (*fig: wirksam werden*) to take effect; (*zum Ziel/Erfolg führen*) to achieve its ends; (*zutreffen*) (*Gesetz, Vorschrift*) to apply; (*Vergleich, Unterscheidung auch*) to hold ◆ **zu kurz ~** to fall short.

Greifer *m* **-s, -** (*Tech*) grab.

Greif-: ~fuß *m* prehensile foot; **~reflex** *m* gripping reflex *or* response; **~trupp** *m* riot squad; **~vogel** *m* bird of prey, raptor (*spec*); **~werkzeug** *nt* prehensile organ; **~zirkel** *m* (outside) callipers *pl.*

greinen *vi* (*pej*) to whine, to whimper.

Greis *m* **-es, -e** old man ◆ **ein neunzigjähriger ~** an old man of ninety, a ninety-year-old man.

greis *adj* aged; (*ehrwürdig*) venerable; (*altersgrau*) grey, hoary (*liter, hum*) ◆ **sein ~es Haupt schütteln** (*usu iro*) to shake one's wise old head.

Greisen-: ~alter *nt* extreme old age; **g~haft** *adj* very old, aged *attr*; (*von jüngerem Menschen*) like an old man/woman; **~haftigkeit** *f* extreme old age; **~haupt** *nt* (*geh*) hoary head; (*iro*) wise old head.

Greisin *f* old lady ◆ **eine neunzigjährige ~** an old lady of ninety, a ninety-year-old lady.

grell *adj Stimme, Schrei, Ton* shrill, piercing; *Licht, Sonne* glaring, dazzling; *Farbe* garish, gaudy, loud; *Kleidung, Mode* loud, flashy; *Gegensatz* sharp; (*stärker*) glaring; (*fig*) *Inszenierung, Szene* lurid ◆ **~ gegen etw** (*acc*) **abstechen** to contrast very sharply with sth.

grell-: ~beleuchtet, ~erleuchtet *adj attr* dazzlingly bright; **~bunt** *adj* gaudily coloured.

Grelle - *no pl*, **Grellheit** *f siehe adj* shrillness; glare, dazzling brightness; garishness, gaudiness; loudness, flashiness.

grellrot *adj* garish *or* gaudy red ◆ **~ geschminkt** painted a garish *or* gaudy red.

Gremium *nt* body; (*Ausschuß*) committee.

Grenadier *m* **-s, -e** (*Mil*) **(a)** (*Hist*) grenadier. **(b)** (*Infanterist*) infantryman.

Grenz- *in cpds* border, frontier; **~abfertigung** *f* border *or* frontier clearance; **~baum** *m* (*Schlagbaum*) frontier barrier; **~begradigung** *f* straightening of the border/a border/borders; **~bereich** *m* frontier *or* border zone *or* area; (*fig*) limits *pl*; **im ~bereich liegen** (*fig*) to lie at the limits; **~bevölkerung** *f* inhabitants *pl* of the/a border zone; (*esp in unwegsamen Gebieten*) frontiersmen *pl*; **~bewohner** *m* inhabitant of the/a border zone; (*esp in unwegsamen Gebieten*) frontiersman/-woman; **~durchbruch** *m* breaking through the/a border *or* frontier.

Grenze *f* **-, -n** border; (*Landes~ auch*) frontier; (*Stadt~, zwischen Grundstücken*) boundary; (*fig: zwischen Begriffen*) dividing line, boundary; (*fig: äußerstes*

Maß, Schranke) limits *pl*, bounds *pl* ◆ **die ~ zwischen Spanien und Frankreich** the Spanish-French border *or* frontier; **die ~ zu Österreich** the border with Austria, the Austrian border; **über die ~ gehen/fahren** to cross the border; **(bis) zur äußersten ~ gehen** *(fig)* to go as far as one can; **jdm ~n setzen** to lay down limits for sb; **einer Sache** *(dat)* **~n setzen** *or* **stecken** to set a limit *or* limits to sth; **keine ~n kennen** *(fig)* to know no bounds; **seine ~n kennen** to know one's limitations; **seiner Großzügigkeit sind keine ~n gesetzt** there is no limit to his generosity; **hart an der ~ des Erlaubten** bordering *or* verging on the limits of what is possible; **innerhalb seiner ~n bleiben** *(fig)* to stay within one's limits; *(finanziell)* to live within one's means; **jdn in seine ~n verweisen** *(fig)* to put sb in his place; **die ~n einhalten** to stay within the limits; **sich in ~n halten** *(fig)* to be limited; **die ~n des Möglichen** the bounds of possibility; **die oberste/unterste ~** *(fig)* the upper/lower limit; **die ~n seines Amtes überschreiten** to exceed one's office; **über die ~(n)** *(+gen)* **... hinaus** *(fig)* beyond the bounds of ...; **an ~n stoßen** *(fig)* to come up against limiting factors; **alles hat seine ~n** there is a limit *or* there are limits to everything.

grenzen *vi* **an etw** *(acc)* **~** *(lit)* to border (on) sth; *(fig)* to border *or* verge on sth.

Grenzen-: g~los [1] *adj (lit, fig)* boundless; **sich ins ~lose verlieren** to disappear into the distance; *(fig)* to go too far; [2] *adv* boundlessly; *(fig)* immensely; **~losigkeit** *f* boundlessness; *(fig)* immensity.

Grenzer *m* **-s, -** *(inf) (Zöllner)* customs man; *(Grenzsoldat)* border *or* frontier guard; *siehe auch* **Grenzbewohner.**

Grenz- *in cpds* border, frontier; **~fall** *m* borderline case; ⚠**~fluß** *m* river forming a/the border *or* frontier; **~gänger** *m* **-s, -** *(Arbeiter)* international commuter *(across a local border)*; *(heimlicher ~)* illegal border *or* frontier crosser; *(Schmuggler)* smuggler; **~gebiet** *nt* border *or* frontier area *or* zone; *(fig)* border(ing) area; **~konflikt** *m* border *or* frontier dispute; **~kontrolle** *f* border *or* frontier control; **~land** *nt* border *or* frontier area *or* zone.

Grenzler(in *f***)** *m* **-s, -** *(inf) siehe* **Grenzbewohner.**

Grenz-: ~linie *f* border; *(Sport)* line; **~mark** *f (Hist)* border *or* frontier area *or* zone; **g~nah** *adj* close to the border *or* frontier; **~nutzen** *m (Econ)* marginal utility; **~pfahl** *m* boundary post; **~posten** *m* border guard; **~schutz** *m* **(a)** *no pl* protection of the border(s) *or* frontier(s); **(b)** *(Truppen)* border *or* frontier guard(s); **~sicherungsanlagen** *pl (esp DDR)* border *or* frontier protection *sing*; **~situation** *f* borderline situation; **~soldat** *m* border *or* frontier guard; **~sperre** *f* border *or* frontier barrier; *(fig: des Grenzverkehrs)* ban on border traffic; **~stadt** *f* border town; **~stein** *m* boundary stone; **~streitigkeit** *f* boundary dispute; *(Pol)* border *or* frontier dispute; **~übergang** *m* **(a)** border *or* frontier crossing(-point); **(b)** *siehe* **~übertritt; g~überschreitend** *adj attr (Comm, Jur)* across a/the border *or* frontier/(the) borders *or* frontiers, cross-border; **~übertritt** *m* crossing of the border; **~verkehr** *m* border *or* frontier traffic; **kleiner ~verkehr** regular border traffic; **~verlauf** *m* boundary line *(between countries)*; **~verletzer** *m* **-s, -** *(esp DDR)* border *or* frontier violator; **~verletzung** *f* violation of the/a border *or* frontier; **~wache** *f siehe* **~posten; ~wacht** *f (Sw)* border *or* frontier guard; **~wall** *m* border rampart; **~wert** *m* limit; **~zeichen** *nt* boundary marker; **~ziehung** *f* drawing up of the/a border *or* frontier; **~zwischenfall** *m* border incident *or* clash.

Gretchenfrage *f (fig)* crunch question *(inf)*, sixty-four-thousand-dollar-question *(inf)*.

⚠**Greuel** *m* **-s, - (a)** *no pl (Grauen, Abscheu)* horror ◆ **~ vor etw haben** to have a horror of sth.
(b) *(~tat)* atrocity.
(c) *(Gegenstand des Abscheus)* abomination ◆ **sie/er/es ist mir ein ~** I loathe *or* detest her/him/it; **die Prüfung ist mir ein ~** I'm really dreading the exam; **es ist mir ein ~, das zu tun** I loathe *or* detest *or* cannot bear doing that.

⚠**Greuel-: ~geschichte** *f*, **~märchen** *nt* horror story; **~meldung, ~nachricht** *f* report of an atrocity/atrocities; **~propaganda** *f* atrocity propaganda, horror stories *pl*; **~tat** *f* atrocity.

⚠**greulich** *adj siehe* **gräßlich.**

Greyerzer ['graiɐtsɐ] *m* **-s, - ~ (Käse)** Gruyère.

Griebe *f* **-, -n** ≃ crackling *no indef art, no pl*, greaves *pl*.

Griebenschmalz *nt* dripping with greaves *or* crackling.

Griebs(ch) *m* **-es, -e** *(dial)* **(a)** *(Apfel~, Birnen~)* core. **(b)** *(Gurgel)* throat, gullet.

Grieche *m* **-n, -n** Greek.

Griechenland *nt* **-s** Greece.

Griechentum *nt* **das ~ (a)** *(Volkstum)* Greekness, Hellenism. **(b)** *(Zivilisation)* Hellenism, (the) Greek civilization; *(Kultur)* Greek culture, things *pl* Greek. **(c)** *(Gesamtheit der Griechen)* the Greeks *pl*.

Griechin *f* Greek (woman/girl).

griechisch *adj* Greek; *Kleidung, Architektur, Vase, Stil, Profil auch* Grecian ◆ **die ~e Tragödie** Greek tragedy; **~-orthodox** Greek Orthodox; **~-römisch** Graeco-Roman.

Griechisch(e) *nt* Greek; *siehe auch* **Deutsch(e).**

grienen *vi (N Ger inf)* to smirk *(inf)*.

Griesgram *m* **-(e)s, -e** grouch *(inf)*, misery.

griesgrämig *adj* grumpy, grouchy *(inf)*.

Grieß *m* **-es, -e (a)** semolina; *(Reis~)* ground rice. **(b)** *(Kies)* gravel *(auch Med)*; *(Sand)* grit.

Grieß-: ~brei *m* semolina; **~kloß** *m*, **~klößchen** *nt* semolina dumpling; **~pudding** *m* semolina pudding.

Griff *m* **-(e)s, -e (a)** *(das Greifen)* **der ~ an etw** *(acc)* taking hold of sth, grasping sth; *(Berührung)* touching sth; **der ~ nach etw** reaching for sth; **einen ~ in die Kasse tun** to put one's hand in the till; **einen tiefen ~ in den Geldbeutel tun** *(fig)* to dig deep in one's pocket; **der ~ nach der Droge/der Flasche** turning *or* taking to drugs/the bottle; **der ~ nach der Macht** the bid for power; **das ist ein ~ nach den Sternen** that's just reaching for the stars.
(b) *(Handgriff)* grip, grasp; *(beim Ringen, Judo, Bergsteigen)* hold; *(beim Turnen)* grip; *(Mus: Fingerstellung)* fingering; *(inf: Akkord)* chord; *(vom Tuch: Anfühlen)* feel, texture ◆ **mit festem ~** firmly; **einen ~ ansetzen** *(Ringen)* to put on *or* apply a hold; **jdn/etw im ~ haben** *(fig)* to have sb/sth under control, to have the upper hand of sb/sth; *(geistig)* to have a good grasp of sth; **ein falscher ~** *(fig)* a false move; **jdn/etw in den ~ bekommen** *(fig)* to get the upper hand of sb/sth, to gain control of sb/sth; *(geistig)* to get a grasp of sth; **(mit jdm/etw) einen guten** *or* **glücklichen ~ tun** to make a wise choice (with sb/sth), to get on to a good thing (with sb/sth) *(inf)*; **etw mit einem ~ tun** *(fig)* to do sth in the twinkling of an eye *or* in a flash.
(c) *(Stiel, Knauf)* handle; *(Pistolen~)* butt; *(Schwert~)* hilt; *(an Saiteninstrumenten)* neck.
(d) *usu pl (Hunt: Kralle)* talon.
(e) ~e *pl (Mil)* rifle positions *pl* ◆ **~e üben** *or* **kloppen** *(inf)* to do rifle drill.

griff *pret of* **greifen.**

Griff-: g~bereit *adj* ready to hand, handy; **etw g~bereit halten** to keep sth handy *or* ready to hand; **~brett** *nt (Mus)* fingerboard.

Griffel *m* **-s, -** slate pencil; *(Bot)* style.

Griffelkasten *m* pencil case *or* box.

griffig *adj Boden, Fahrbahn etc* that has a good grip; *Rad, Maschine auch* that grips well; *Gewebe* firm; *(fig) Ausdruck* useful, handy; *Slogan auch* pithy, terse; *(Aus) Mehl* coarse-grained.

Griffigkeit *f* **-,** *no pl* grip; *(von Slogan)* pithiness, terseness.

Griffloch *nt* finger hole.

Grill *m* **-s, -s** grill; *(Aut: Kühler~)* grille.

Grillade [gri'ja:də] *f (Cook)* grill.

Grille *f* **-, -n (a)** *(Zool)* cricket. **(b)** *(dated inf: Laune)* silly notion *or* idea ◆ **~n im Kopf haben** to be full of big ideas; **~n fangen** to be moody.

grillen [1] *vt* to grill.
[2] *vr* **sich ~ (lassen)** *(inf)* to roast *(inf)*.

grillenhaft *adj (dated) (trübsinnig)* moody; *(sonderbar)* strange, extraordinary.

Grill- *(Cook)*: **~fest** *nt* barbecue party; **~gericht** *nt* grill; **~restaurant** *nt*, **~room** [-ru:m] *m* **-s, -s, ~stube** *f* grillroom, grill and griddle.

Grimasse *f* **-, -n** grimace ◆ **~n schneiden** *or* **ziehen** *or* **machen** to grimace, to make *or* pull faces; **sein Gesicht zu einer ~ verziehen** to twist one's face into a grimace.

Grimassenschneider(in *f***)** *m* face-puller.

Grimm *m* **-(e)s,** *no pl (old)* fury, wrath *(old, liter)*, ire *(old, liter) (auf +acc* against).

grimm *adj (old) siehe* **grimmig.**

Grimmdarm *m* colon.

Grimmen *nt* **-s,** *no pl (S Ger)* griping pains *pl*.

grimmig *adj* **(a)** *(zornig)* furious, wrathful *(liter)* ◆ **~ lächeln** to smile grimly; **~er Humor** grim *or* morbid humour. **(b)** *(sehr groß, heftig) Kälte etc* severe, harsh.

Grind *m* **-(e)s, -e** scab; *(inf: Sw, S Ger: Kopf)* bonce *(inf)*.

Grindwal *m* pilot whale.

grinsen *vi* to grin; *(vor Schadenfreude, Dreistigkeit, höhnisch auch)* to smirk.

Grinsen *nt* **-s,** *no pl siehe vi* grin; smirk.

grippal *adj (Med)* influenzal ◆ **~er Infekt** influenza infection.

Grippe *f* **-, -n** 'flu, influenza; *(Erkältung)* cold.

Grippe- *in cpds* 'flu, influenza; **~(schutz)impfung** *f* influenza vaccination; **~welle** *f* wave of 'flu *or* influenza.

grippös *adj attr* influenzal.

Grips *m* **-es, -e** *(inf)* nous *(Brit inf)*, sense ◆ **nun strengt mal euren ~ an** use your nous *(inf) or* common sense; **~ zu etw haben** to have the nous *(inf) or* common sense to do sth.

Grislybär, Grizzlybär ['grɪsli-] *m* grizzly (bear).

⚠**Griß** *nt* **-sses,** *no pl (Aus inf) siehe* **G(e)riß.**

grob *adj, comp* **¨er**, *superl* **¨ste(r, s)** *or adv* **am ¨sten (a)** *(nicht fein)* coarse; *Arbeit* dirty *attr.*
(b) *(ungefähr)* rough ◆ **~ geschätzt/gemessen** at a rough estimate; **in ~en Umrissen** roughly.
(c) *(schlimm, groß)* gross *(auch Jur)* ◆ **den ¨sten Schmutz habe ich schon weggeputzt** I have already cleaned off the worst of the dirt; **ein ~er Fehler** a bad mistake, a gross error; **wir sind aus dem G¨sten heraus** we're out of the woods (now), we can see the light at the end of the tunnel (now); **~ fahrlässig handeln** to commit an act of culpable negligence.
(d) *(brutal, derb)* rough; *(fig: derb)* coarse; *Antwort* rude; *(unhöflich)* ill-mannered ◆ **~ gegen jdn werden** to become offensive (towards sb); **jdm ~ kommen** *(inf)* to get coarse with sb; **auf einen ~en Klotz gehört ein ~er Keil** *(Prov)* one must answer rudeness with rudeness; *siehe* **Geschütz.**

Grobe(s) *nt (fig)* dirty work ◆ **ein Mann fürs ~** *(inf)* a man who does the dirty work.

Grob- *in cpds* coarse; **g~fas(e)rig** *adj* coarse-fibred; ⚠**g~gemahlen** *adj attr* coarse-ground; **~heit** *f* **(a)** *no pl* coarseness; **(b)** *no pl (Brutalität)* roughness; *(fig)* coarseness; *(von Antwort)* rudeness; *(fig: Unhöflichkeit)* ill-manneredness; **(c)** *(Beschimpfung)* foul language *no pl*; **jdm ~heiten sagen** to be nasty to sb.

Grobian *m* **-(e)s, -e** brute.

grob-: ~knochig *adj* big-boned; **~körnig** *adj* coarse-grained.

gröblich *adj* **(a)** (*form: schlimm*) gross. **(b)** (*geh: heftig, derb*) gross ♦ **jdn ~ beschimpfen** to call sb rude names.

Grob-: g~maschig [1] *adj* large-meshed; (*~gestrickt*) loose-knit *attr*; [2] *adv* coarsely; **g~schlächtig** *adj* coarse; *Mensch* big-built, heavily built; (*fig auch*) unrefined; **~schlächtigkeit** *f siehe adj* coarseness; heavy *or* big build; lack of refinement; **~schnitt** *m* (*Tabak*) coarse cut; **~strick** *m* coarse knit.

Gröfaz *m* - (*iro*) **der ~** the Big Chief (*hum*), the great General (*iro*).

Grog *m* **-s, -s** grog.

groggy ['grɔgi] *adj pred* (*Boxen*) groggy; (*inf: erschöpft*) all-in (*inf*).

grölen *vti* (*pej*) to bawl ♦ **~de Stimme/Menge** raucous voice/crowd; **~d durch die Straßen ziehen** to roam rowdily through the streets.

Grölerei *f* (*pej*) bawling *no pl*.

Groll *m* **-(e)s,** *no pl* (*Zorn*) anger, wrath (*liter*); (*Erbitterung*) resentment ♦ **einen ~ gegen jdn hegen** to harbour a grudge against sb.

grollen *vi* (*geh*) **(a)** to rumble; (*Donner auch*) to roll, to peal (*liter*). **(b) (jdm) ~** (*old*) to be filled with wrath (against sb) (*liter*); **(mit) seinem Schicksal ~** to bemoan one's fate.

Grönland *nt* **-s** Greenland.

Grönländer(in *f*) *m* **-s, -** Greenlander.

grönländisch *adj* Greenland *attr*.

Grönlandwal *m* bowhead.

Gros¹ [groː] *nt* **-, -** [groːs] major *or* greater part, majority, bulk; *siehe* **en gros**.

Gros² [grɔs] *nt* **-ses, -se** *or* (*bei Zahlenangaben*) **-** gross.

Groschen *m* **-s, - (a)** (*Aus*) groschen.
(b) (*inf*) 10-pfennig piece; (*fig*) penny, cent (*US*) ♦ **seine paar ~ zusammenhalten** to scrape together a few pence *or* pennies/cents; **sich** (*dat*) **ein paar ~ verdienen** to earn (oneself) a few pence *or* pennies/cents, to earn (oneself) a bit of pocket money; **der ~ ist gefallen** (*hum inf*) the penny has dropped (*inf*); **bei ihm fällt der ~ pfennigweise** he's pretty slow on the uptake, it takes him a while to catch on.

Groschen-: ~blatt *nt* (*pej*) (cheap) rag (*inf*), sensational (news)paper; **die ~blätter** the gutter press (*pej*); **~grab** *nt* (*hum: Spielautomat*) one-armed bandit; **diese Parkuhr ist ein richtiges ~grab** this parking meter just swallows up your money; **~heft** *nt* (*pej*) pulp magazine; (*Krimi auch*) penny dreadful (*dated*); **~roman** *m* (*pej*) cheap *or* dime (*US*) novel.

groß [1] *adj, comp* **~̈er**, *superl* **~̈te(r, s) (a)** big; *Fläche, Raum, Haus, Hände auch* large; *Höhe, Breite* great; *Buchstabe* big, capital; *Größe, Tube, Dose, Packung etc* large; (*hoch, hochgewachsen*) tall ♦ **wie ~ bist du?** how tall are you?; **du bist ~ geworden** you've grown; **ein ganz ~es Haus/Buch** a great big house/book; **der ~e (Uhr)zeiger** the big *or* minute hand; **die Wiese ist 10.000 m² ~** the field measures 10,000 square metres *or* is 100 metres square; **ein 2 Hektar ~es Grundstück** a 2 hectare piece of land; **er ist 1,80 m ~** he is 1.80 metres (tall); **ein ~es Bier, ein G~es** (*inf*) ≃ a pint (of beer); **die ~e Masse** (*fig*) the vast majority; **~es Geld** notes *pl* (*Brit*), bills *pl* (*US*); **ich habe nur ~es Geld** I haven't any change on me; **im ~en und ganzen (gesehen)** (taken) by and large; **im G~en einkaufen** to buy in bulk *or* quantity.
(b) (*zeitlich*) *Pause, Verzögerung, Rede* big, long, lengthy ♦ **die ~en Ferien** the long holidays, the long vacation (*Univ*).
(c) (*älter*) *Bruder, Schwester* big ♦ **die G~en** (*Erwachsene*) the grown-ups; (*ältere Kinder*) the older children; **zu ~ für etw sein** to be too big for sth; **mit etw ~ geworden sein** to have grown up with sth; **~ und klein** young and old (alike); **unsere G~e/unser G~er** our eldest *or* oldest (daughter/son); (*von zwei*) our elder daughter/son.
(d) (*beträchtlich, heftig, wichtig*) big; *Erfolg, Interesse, Enttäuschung, Schreck, Hoffnung, Eile auch* great; *Summe auch* large; *Freude, Vergnügen, Schmerzen, Leid etc* great; (*bedeutend*) *Dichter, Werk, Erfindung, Schauspieler etc* great; *Lärm* a lot of; *Geschwindigkeit* high ♦ **die ~en Fragen unserer Zeit** the great *or* big questions of our time; **~e Worte/Gefühle** big words/strong feelings; **~e Worte machen** to use grand *or* big words; **~en Hunger haben** to be very hungry; **eine ~̈ere Summe** a biggish *or* largish *or* fair sum; **eine der ~̈eren Firmen** one of the major companies; **eine ~e Dummheit machen** to do something very stupid; **im ~̈ten Regen** in the midst of the downpour; **die ~e Nummer** (*im Zirkus*) the big number, the star turn; **ich habe ~e Lust zu etw/, etw zu tun** I would really like sth/to do sth; **ich habe keine ~e Lust** I don't particularly want to; **~e Mode sein** to be all the fashion; **er ist ein ~es Kind** he's a big *or* a great big (*inf*) baby; **er ist kein ~er Esser/Trinker** (*inf*) he's not a big eater/drinker; **ich bin kein ~er Redner/Opernfreund** (*inf*) I'm no great speaker/opera-lover; **die ~e Welt** (*die Fremde*) the big wide world; (*die oberen Zehntausend*) high society; **die G~en** the great figures; **jds ~e Stunde** sb's big moment; **einen ~en Namen haben** to be a big name; **das ~e Ganze** the broader perspective, the wider view; **im Kleinen wie im G~en** in small matters as well as in big *or* larger ones, whether the scale be large or small; **er hat G~es geleistet** he has achieved great things.
(e) (*~artig, bewundernswert*) great ♦ **das ist** *or* **finde ich ganz ~** (*inf*) that's really great (*inf*).
(f) (*in Eigennamen*) Great; (*vor Namen von Ballungsräumen*) Greater ♦ **Alfred/Friedrich der G~e** Alfred/Frederick the Great; **G~-Paris/-München** Greater Paris/Munich; **der G~e Ozean** the Pacific; **die G~en Seen** the Great Lakes.
(g) (*Mus*) **~e Terz** major third.
[2] *adv, comp* **~̈er**, *superl* **am ~̈ten jdn ~ anblicken** to give sb a hard stare; **was ist das schon ~?** (*inf*) big deal! (*inf*), so what? (*inf*); **was soll man da schon ~ machen/sagen?** (*inf*) you can't really do/say anything *or* very much(, can you?) (*inf*), what are you supposed to do/say?; **keiner hat sich ~ gefreut** (*inf*) nobody was particularly delighted, nobody was exactly overjoyed; **ich kümmere mich nicht ~ darum** (*inf*) I don't take much notice; **~ daherreden** (*inf*) to talk big (*inf*); **~ und breit** (*fig inf*) at great *or* enormous length, at tedious length (*pej*); **~ machen** (*baby-talk*) to do number two (*baby-talk*); **ein Wort ~ schreiben** to write a word with a capital *or* with a big A/B *etc*; **~ in Mode sein** to be the fashion; **ganz ~ rauskommen** (*sl*) to make the big time (*inf*).

Groß- *pref* Great; (*vor Namen von Ballungsräumen*) Greater.

Groß-: ≈abnehmer *m* (*Comm*) bulk purchaser *or* buyer; **≈admiral** *m* (*Naut Hist*) Grand Admiral, ≃ Admiral of the Fleet; **≈aktionär** *m* major *or* principal shareholder; **≈alarm** *m* red alert; **~alarm geben** to give a red alert; **⚠g≈angelegt** *adj attr* large-scale, on a large scale; **≈angriff** *m* large-scale *or* major attack; **⚠≈anlaß** *m* (*Sw*) *siehe* **~veranstaltung**; **g≈artig** *adj* wonderful, superb, splendid; (*prächtig*) *Bauwerk etc* magnificent, splendid; **er hat ~artiges geleistet** he has achieved great things; **eine g~artige Frau** a wonderful *or* fine woman; **g~artig tun** (*pej*) to show off, to give oneself airs; **≈aufnahme** *f* (*Phot, Film*) close-up; **≈bank** *f* major or big bank; **≈bauer** *m* big farmer; **g≈bäuerlich** *adj* of a big farmer/big farmers; **≈baustelle** *f* construction site; **≈beben** *nt* (*Geol*) major earthquake; **≈behälter** *m* tank; (*Container*) container; **≈betrieb** *m* large concern; (*Agr*) big farm; **≈bezüger** *m* **-s, -** (*Sw*) *siehe* **~abnehmer**; **≈bild** *nt* blow-up; **≈bildkamera** *f* plate camera; **≈bildschirm** *m* large screen; **≈bourgeoisie** *f* (*Sociol, Pol pej*) upper classes *pl*, upper bourgeoisie; **≈brand** *m* enormous blaze, major *or* big fire; **~britannien** *nt* (Great) Britain; **g~britannisch** *adj* (Great) British, Britannic (*rare*); **≈buchstabe** *m* capital (letter), upper case letter (*Typ*); **≈bürger** *m* (*Sociol*) member of the upper classes; **g≈bürgerlich** *adj* (*Sociol*) upper-class; **≈bürgertum** *nt* (*Sociol*) upper classes *pl*; **≈computer** *m siehe* **~rechner**; **≈demonstration** *f* mass demonstration; **g≈deutsch** *adj* (*Hist*) Pan-German; **das ~deutsche Reich** (*NS*) the Reich; **≈deutschland** *nt* (*NS*) Greater Germany; **≈druck** *m* large print; **ein Buch im ~druck** a large-print book.

Größe *f* **-, -n (a)** (*Format, Maßeinheit*) size ♦ **nach der ~** according to size; **er trägt** *or* **hat ~ 48** he takes *or* is size 48.
(b) *no pl* (*Höhe, Körper~*) height; (*Flächeninhalt*) size, area, dimensions *pl*; (*Dimension*) size, dimensions *pl*; (*Math, Phys*) quantity; (*Astron*) magnitude ♦ **nach der ~** according to height/size; **eine unbekannte ~** (*lit, fig*) an unknown quantity; **ein Stern erster ~** a star of the first magnitude.
(c) *no pl* (*Ausmaß*) extent; (*Bedeutsamkeit*) significance.
(d) *no pl* (*Erhabenheit*) greatness.
(e) (*bedeutender Mensch*) leading light, important figure.

Groß-: ~einkauf *m* bulk purchase, bulk purchasing *no indef art, no pl*; **~einsatz** *m* **~einsatz der Feuerwehr/Polizei** *etc* large-scale operation by the fire brigade/police *etc*; **der ~einsatz von Truppen** the large-scale use *or* deployment of troops; **g~elterlich** *adj attr* of one's grandparents; **im g~elterlichen Haus wohnen** to live in one's grandparents' house; **~eltern** *pl* grandparents *pl*; **~enkel** *m* great-grandchild; (*Junge*) great-grandson; **~enkelin** *f* great-granddaughter.

Größen-: ~klasse *f* (*Astron*) magnitude; (*Comm*) (size) class; **~ordnung** *f* scale; (*Größe*) magnitude; (*Math*) order (of magnitude); **ich denke in anderen ~ordnungen** I think on a different scale.

großenteils *adv* mostly, for the most part ♦ **er macht seine Arbeit ~ selbständig** he does his work mostly on his own, he does his work on his own for the most part.

Größen-: ~unterschied *m* (*im Format*) difference in size; (*in der Höhe, im Wuchs*) difference in height; (*in der Bedeutung*) difference in importance; **~verhältnis** *nt* proportions *pl* (*gen* between); (*Maßstab*) scale; **im ~verhältnis 1:100** on the scale 1:100; **etw im richtigen ~verhältnis sehen** to see sth in perspective; **~wahn(sinn)** *m* megalomania, delusions *pl* of grandeur; **g~wahnsinnig** *adj* megalomaniac(al); **g~wahnsinnig sein** to be a megalomaniac.

größer *comp of* **groß**.

größer(e)nteils *adv siehe* **großenteils**.

Groß-: ~fahndung *f* large-scale manhunt; **~familie** *f* extended family; **~feuer** *nt* major fire, enormous blaze; **g~flächig** *adj* extensive; *Gesicht* flat-featured; **~flughafen** *m* major airport; **~flugzeug** *nt siehe* **~raumflugzeug**; **~format** *nt* large size; (*bei Büchern, Fotos auch*) large format; **ein ... im ~format** a large-size .../large-format ...; **g~formatig** *adj* large-size; *Bücher, Fotos auch* large-format; **~foto** *nt* giant photo(graph); **~fresse** *f* (*vulg*) *siehe* **~maul**; **~fürst** *m* (*Hist*) grand prince; **~fürstentum** *nt* (*Hist*) grand principality; **~fürstin** *f* (*Hist*) grand princess; **g~füttern** *vt sep* to raise, to rear; **~garage** *f* large (underground) car park; **~gemeinde** *f* municipality with several villages or districts; **⚠g~gemustert** *adj* with a large pattern; **⚠g~gewachsen** *adj* tall; **~grundbesitz** *m* **(a)** large-scale land-holding; **(b)** (*die ~grundbesitzer*) big landowners *pl*; **~grundbesitzer** *m* big landowner.

Großhandel *m* wholesale trade, wholesaling *no art* ♦ **etw im ~ kaufen** to buy sth wholesale.

Großhandels- *in cpds* wholesale; **~kaufmann** *m* wholesaler.

Groß-: ~händler *m* wholesaler; (*inf: ~handlung*) wholesaler's; **~handlung** *f* wholesale business; **g~herzig** *adj* generous, magnanimous; **g~herzige Motive** the best of motives; **~herzigkeit** *f* generosity, magnanimity; **~herzog** *m* grand duke; **(der) ~herzog Roland** Grand Duke Roland; **~herzogin** *f* grand duchess; **g~herzoglich** *adj* grand ducal; **~herzogtum** *nt* grand duchy; **das ~herzogtum Luxemburg** the Grand Duchy of Luxembourg; **~hirn** *nt* cerebrum; **~hirnrinde** *f* cerebral cortex; **~indu-**

strie *f* major *or* big industry; **~industrielle(r)** *mf* major *or* big industrialist; **die französischen ~industriellen** the major *or* big French industrialists; **~inquisitor** *m (Hist)* Grand Inquisitor; **~integration** *f (Comput)* large-scale integration.

Grossist *m siehe* **Großhändler.**

Groß-: g~jährig *adj (dated)* of age, major *(form)*; **g~jährig werden** to come of age, to reach the age of majority; **g~kalib(e)rig** *adj* large-calibre.

Großkampf-: ~schiff *nt* capital ship; **~tag** *m (Mil)* day of a/the great battle; **Montag ist bei uns im Büro meist ~tag** *(hum)* it's usually all systems go on Monday in the office *(inf)*.

Groß-: ~kapital *nt* **das ~kapital** big business; **~kapitalist** *m* big capitalist; **was, du willst 5 Mark? ich bin doch kein ~kapitalist!** what - you want 5 marks? I'm not made of money! *(inf)*; **⚠g~kariert** *adj* large-check(ed); **~katze** *f* big cat; **~kind** *nt (Sw)* grandchild; **~kino** *nt* multiplex cinema; **~klima** *nt* macroclimate; **~knecht** *m (old)* chief (farm)hand; **~konzern** *m* big *or* large combine; **~kopfe(r)te(r)** *m decl as adj* **(a)** *(Aus, S Ger: pej)* bigwig *(inf)*, bigshot *(inf)*; **(b)** *(hum: Intellektueller)* egghead *(hum inf)*; **~kotz** *m (pej sl)* swank *(inf)*; **g~kotzig** *adj (pej sl)* swanky *(inf)*; **~kotzigkeit** *f (pej sl)* swank *(inf)*; **~kraftwerk** *nt* large power plant; **~kreuz** *nt* Grand Cross; **~küche** *f* canteen kitchen; **~kundgebung** *f* mass rally.

Großmacht *f (Pol)* big *or* great power.

Großmacht-: ~politik *f* (big-)power politics; **~stellung** *f* great- *or* big-power status.

Groß-: ~mama *f* grandmama *(dated)*, grandma; **~mannssucht** *f, no pl (pej)* craving for status; **~markt** *m* hypermarket; **g~maschig** *adj siehe* **grobmaschig**; **~mast** *m* mainmast; **~maul** *nt (pej inf)* bigmouth *(inf)*, loudmouth *(inf)*; **g~mäulig** *adj (pej inf)* big-mouthed *attr (inf)*, loudmouthed *(inf)*; **g~mäulig verkünden, daß ...** to brag that ...; **~mäuligkeit** *f, no pl (pej inf)* big mouth *(inf)*; **~meister** *m* Grand Master; **~mogul** *m (Hist)* Great Mogul; **~mufti** *m (Hist)* grand mufti; **~mut** *f* magnanimity; **g~mütig** *adj* magnanimous; **~mütigkeit** *f siehe* **~mut**; **~mutter** *f* grandmother; **das kannst du deiner ~mutter erzählen!** *(inf)* you can tell that one to the marines *(inf)*, pull the other one *(inf)*; **g~mütterlich** *adj attr* **(a)** *(von der ~mutter)* of one's grandmother; **im g~mütterlichen Haus wohnen** to live in one's grandmother's house; **das g~mütterliche Erbe** one's inheritance from one's grandmother; **(b)** *(in der Art einer ~mutter)* grandmotherly; **g~mütterlicherseits** *adv* on one's grandmother's side; **~neffe** *m* great-nephew; **~nichte** *f* great-niece; **~offensive** *f (Mil)* major offensive; **~oktav** *nt* large octavo; **~onkel** *m* great-uncle; **~papa** *m* grandpapa *(dated)*, grandpa; **⚠~photo** *nt siehe* **~foto**; **~plastik** *f* large sculpture; **g~porig** *adj* large-pored; **~produktion** *f* large-scale production; **~produzent** *m* large-scale producer; **~projekt** *nt* large-scale project; **~putz** *m siehe* **~reinemachen**; **~quart** *nt* large quarto; **~rat** *m (Sw)* member of a/the Cantonal parliament.

Großraum *m* **(a)** *(einer Stadt)* **der ~ München** the Munich area *or* conurbation, Greater Munich. **(b)** *siehe* **Großraumbüro.**

Großraum-: ~abteil *nt (Rail)* open-plan carriage; **~büro** *nt* open-plan office; **~flugzeug** *nt* large-capacity aircraft.

Groß-: g~räumig *adj* **(a)** *(mit g~en Räumen)* with large rooms; **g~räumig sein** to have large rooms; **(b)** *(mit viel Platz, geräumig)* roomy, spacious; **(c)** *(über g~e Flächen)* extensive; **(d)** *(im g~en Umkreis)* **g~räumiges Umfahren eines Gebietes** making a large detour around an area; **~raumwagen** *m (von Straßenbahn)* articulated tram *(Brit) or* streetcar *(US)*; *(Rail)* open-plan carriage *(Brit) or* car *(US)*; **~razzia** *f* large-scale raid; **~rechner** *m* mainframe (computer); **~reinemachen** *nt* thorough cleaning, ≃ spring-cleaning; **~schiffahrtsweg** *m* major waterway *(for seagoing ships)*; **~schnauze** *f (pej sl) siehe* **~maul**; **g~schnäuzig** *adj (pej sl) siehe* **g~mäulig**; **g~schreiben** *vt sep irreg* **g~geschrieben werden** *(fig inf)* to be stressed, to be given pride of place, to be writ large; **~schreibung** *f* capitalization; **~segel** *nt (Naut)* mainsail; **g~sprecherisch** *adj (pej)* boastful, boasting *attr*, bragging *attr*; **g~spurig** *adj (pej)* flashy *(inf)*, showy *(inf)*; **~spurigkeit** *f (pej)* flashiness *(inf)*, showiness *(inf)*.

Großstadt *f* city.

Großstadtbevölkerung *f* city population.

Großstädter *m* city-dweller.

großstädtisch *adj* big-city *attr* ♦ **München wirkt ~er als Bonn** Munich has more of a big-city feel to it than Bonn.

Großstadt- *in cpds* city; **~mensch** *m* city-dweller; **der ~mensch** urban man, city-dwellers *pl*.

Groß-: ~tante *f* great-aunt; **~tat** *f* great feat; **eine medizinische ~tat** a great medical feat; **g~technisch** *adj Projekt, Anlage* large-scale; **Kernkraft g~technisch erzeugen** to produce nuclear power on a large scale.

Großteil *m* large part ♦ **zum ~** in the main, for the most part; **zu einem ~** for the most part.

großteils, größtenteils *adv* in the main, for the most part.

größte(r, s) *superl of* **groß.**

Größt-: ~maß *nt (fig) siehe* **Höchstmaß**; **g~möglich** *adj attr* greatest possible.

Groß-: ≈tuer [-tu:ɐ] *m* **-s, -** *(pej)* boaster, bragger, show-off; **~tuerei** [-tu:əˈrai] *f (pej)* **(a)** *no pl* boasting, bragging, showing off; **(b)** *(g~tuerische Äußerung etc)* boast; **g≈tuerisch** [-tu:ərɪʃ] *adj (pej)* boastful, bragging; **g≈tun** *sep irreg (pej)* **1** *vi* to boast, to brag, to show off; **2** *vr* **sich mit etw g~tun** to show off *or* boast *or* brag about sth; **≈unternehmen** *nt siehe* **~betrieb**; **≈unternehmer** *m* big businessman *or* entrepreneur.

Großvater *m* grandfather.

großväterlich *adj* **(a)** *(vom Großvater)* of one's grandfather ♦ **er hat den ~en Betrieb übernommen** he has taken over his grandfather's business; **das ~e Erbe** one's inheritance from one's grandfather. **(b)** *(in der Art eines Großvaters)* grandfatherly.

großväterlicherseits *adv* on one's grandfather's side.

Großvater-: ~sessel, ~stuhl *m (inf)* fireside armchair; **~uhr** *f (inf)* grandfather clock.

Groß-: ~veranstaltung *f* big event; *(~kundgebung)* mass rally; **eine sportliche ~veranstaltung** a big sporting event; **~verbraucher** *m* large consumer; **~verdiener** *m* big earner; **~versuch** *m (esp Psych)* large-scale experiment; **~vieh** *nt* cattle and horses *pl*; **~wesir** *m (Hist)* grand vizier; **~wetterlage** *f* general weather situation; **die politische ~wetterlage** the general political climate.

Großwild *nt* big game.

Großwild-: ~jagd *f* big-game hunting; **eine ~jagd** a big-game hunt; **auf ~jagd gehen** to go big-game hunting; **~jäger** *m* big-game hunter.

Groß-: ~wörterbuch *nt* large *or* comprehensive dictionary; **g~wüchsig** *adj (form) siehe* **g~gewachsen**; **g~ziehen** *vt sep irreg* to raise; *Tier* to rear; **g~zügig** *adj* generous; *(weiträumig)* spacious; *Plan* large-scale, ambitious; *(inf: ungenau)* generous, liberal; **~zügigkeit** *f siehe adj* generosity; spaciousness; (large) scale, ambitiousness; generousness, liberality.

grotesk *adj* grotesque.

Grotesk *f* **-**, *no pl (Typ)* grotesque, sans serif.

Groteske *f* **-, -n** *(Art)* grotesque(rie); *(Liter)* grotesquerie.

groteskerweise *adv* ironically enough.

Grotte *f* **-, -n** grotto.

Grotten|olm *m (Zool)* olm *(spec)*.

Groupie [ˈgru:pi] *nt* **-s, -s** groupie.

grub *pret of* **graben.**

Grubber *m* **-s, -** *(Agr)* grubber.

Grübchen *nt* dimple.

Grube *f* **-, -n** pit; *(kleine)* hole, hollow; *(Min auch)* mine; *(dated: Gruft, Grab)* grave ♦ **wer andern eine ~ gräbt(, fällt selbst hinein)** *(Prov)* you can easily fall into your own trap; **in die ~ (ein)fahren** to go down the pit; **in die** *or* **zur ~ fahren** *(old)* to give up the ghost.

Grübelei *f* brooding *no pl*.

grübeln *vi* to brood *(über +acc* about, over).

Gruben- *in cpds* pit; **~arbeiter** *m* pitman; **~gas** *nt* firedamp; **~wagen** *m* mine car.

Grübler(in *f)* *m* **-s, -** brooder, brooding type.

grüblerisch *adj* pensive, brooding.

grüezi [ˈgry:ɛtsi] *interj (Sw)* hello, hi *(inf)*, good morning/afternoon/evening.

Gruft *f* **-, ¨e** tomb, vault; *(in Kirchen)* crypt; *(offenes Grab)* grave.

Grufti *m* **-s, -s** *(sl)* **(a)** *(älterer Mensch)* old fogey *(inf)*. **(b)** *(Okkultist)* ≈ gothic.

gruftig *adj (sl: altmodisch) Musik, Mode* square *(inf)*, old hat *(inf)*; *(moderig) Keller etc* musty.

grummeln *vi* to rumble; *(inf: brummeln)* to mumble.

Grum(me)t *nt* **-s**, *no pl (Agr)* aftermath, rowen *(dial, US)*.

grün *adj (alle Bedeutungen)* green; *(Pol auch)* ecologist ♦ **~e Heringe** fresh herrings; **Aal ~** *(Cook)* (dish of) fresh eel *(with parsley sauce)*; **~er Salat** lettuce; **die G~e Insel** the Emerald Isle; **ein ~er Junge** *(inf)* a greenhorn *(inf)*; **~es Licht (für etw) geben/haben** *(fig)* to give/have got the go-ahead *or* green light (for sth); **komm an meine ~e Seite!** *(inf)* come and sit up close to me; **am ~en Tisch, vom ~en Tisch aus** from a bureaucratic ivory tower; **über die ~e Grenze fahren/kommen** *(inf)* to cross the border illegally *(in a wood etc)*; **die ~e Hölle** *(fig)* the green hell of the jungle; **die ~en Lungen der Großstadt** *(fig)* the breathing spaces of the city; **~e Minna** *(inf)* Black Maria *(Brit inf)*, paddy wagon *(US inf)*; **der G~e Plan** *(Pol)* Agricultural Aid Plan; **sich ~ und blau** *or* **gelb ärgern** *(inf)* to be furious; **jdn ~ und blau** *or* **gelb schlagen** *(inf)* to beat sb black and blue; **wir haben ~e Weihnachten gehabt** we didn't have a white Christmas; **~e Welle** phased traffic lights; **~e Welle bei 60 km/h** traffic lights phased for 60 kmph; **~ im Gesicht werden** to go green (about the gills *inf*); **~e Witwe** *(inf)* lonely suburban housewife; **auf keinen ~en Zweig kommen** *(fig inf)* to get nowhere; **die beiden sind sich gar nicht ~** *(inf)* there's no love lost between them; **er ist dir nicht ~** *(inf)* you're not in his good books *(inf)*.

Grün *nt* **-s, -** *or (inf)* **-s** green; *(~flächen)* green spaces *pl*; *(Golf)* green; *(Cards: Pik)* spades *pl* ♦ **die Ampel steht auf ~** the light is at green; **das ist dasselbe in ~** *(inf)* it's (one and) the same (thing).

Grün- *in cpds* green; **~alge** *f* green alga; **g~alternativ** *adj (Pol)* green alternative; **~anlage** *f* green space *or* area; **g~äugig** *adj* green-eyed; **g~blau** *adj* greenish blue, greeny blue; **g~blind** *adj* suffering from red-green colour-blindness.

▼ **Grund** *m* **-(e)s, ¨e** **(a)** *no pl (Erdboden)* ground; *(old, dial: Erdreich auch)* soil ♦ **~ und Boden** land; **in ~ und Boden** *(fig) sich blamieren, schämen* utterly; *verdammen* outright; **jdn in ~ und Boden reden** not to leave sb a leg to stand on, to shoot sb's arguments to pieces; **bis auf den ~ zerstören/abtragen** to raze to the ground.

(b) *(Aus) (Bauplatz)* (building) plot; *(~stück)* grounds *pl*, land *no indef art, no pl*.

(c) *no pl (esp Art)* ground; *(Her)* field.

(d) *no pl (von Gefäßen, Becken etc)* bottom; *(Meeres~ auch)* (sea)bed; *(liter: Tal~)* bottom of the/a valley ♦ **~ suchen** *(im Wasser)* to look for a foothold, to try to find the bottom; **auf ~ stoßen** *(Naut)* to (run to) ground; **ein Schiff auf ~ setzen** to scuttle a ship; **das Glas/den Becher bis auf den ~ leeren** to drain the glass/tumbler.

(e) *no pl* (*lit, fig: Fundament*) foundation(s *pl*); (*das Innerste*) depths *pl* ◆ **von ~ auf** *or* **aus** entirely, completely; **etw von ~ auf ändern** to change sth fundamentally *or* from top to bottom; **von ~ auf neu gebaut/geplant** rebuilt/re-planned from scratch; **ein von ~ auf aufrechter Mensch** a thoroughly honest fellow; **den ~ zu etw legen** (*lit, fig*) to lay the foundations of *or* for sth; **einer Sache** (*dat*) **auf den ~ gehen** (*fig*) to get to the bottom of sth; **auf ~ von** *or* (*+gen*) on the basis of; **im ~e seines Herzens** in one's heart of hearts; **im ~e (genommen)** basically, fundamentally.

(f) (*Ursache, Veranlassung, Ausrede*) reason; (*Beweg~ auch*) grounds *pl* ◆ **aus gesundheitlichen** *etc* **~̈en** for health *etc* reasons, on health *etc* grounds; **aus dem einfachen ~e, daß** ... for the simple reason that ...; **ohne ~** without reason; **auf ~ von Zeugenaussagen** on the basis *or* strength of the witnesses' testimonies; **auf ~ einer Verwechslung/seiner Eifersucht** owing to *or* because of a mistake/his jealousy; **ich habe ~ zu der Annahme, daß** ... I have reason to believe *or* grounds for believing that ...; **~̈e und Gegengründe** pros and cons, arguments for and against; **einen ~ zum Feiern haben** to have good cause for (a) celebration; **es besteht kein** *or* **du hast keinen ~ zum Klagen** you have no cause to complain *or* for complaint; **die ~̈e für und wider** the cases for and against; **jdm ~ (zu etw) geben** to give sb good reason *or* cause (for sth); **jdm allen ~ geben, etw zu glauben** *etc* to give sb every reason to believe *etc* sth; **aus diesem ~** for this reason; **aus guten ~̈en, mit gutem ~** with good reason; **aus welchem ~(e)?** for what reason?; **aus ~̈en** (*+gen*) for reasons (of).

Grund- *in cpds* basic; **~akkord** *m* (*Mus*) chord in root position; **~anschauung, ~ansicht** *f* fundamental philosophy; **g~anständig** *adj* thoroughly decent; **~anstrich** *m* first coat; (*erstes Anstreichen*) application of the first coat; **~bau** *m* **(a)** (*Archit*) foundation(s *pl*); **(b)** *no pl* (*~arbeiten*) laying of the foundations; **(c)** (*Univ: Fach*) civil engineering; **~begriff** *m* basic concept; **~besitz** *m* land, property; (*das Besitzen*) ownership of land *or* property; **~besitzer** *m* landowner; **~buch** *nt* land register; **~buchamt** *nt* land registry *or* office; **g~ehrlich** *adj* thoroughly honest; **~eigentum** *nt siehe* **~besitz**; **~eigentümer** *m* landowner; **~einstellung** *f* fundamental philosophy; **~eis** *nt* ground ice, anchor-ice; *siehe* **Arsch**.

gründen [1] *vt* to found; *Argument etc* to base (*auf +acc* on); *Heim, Geschäft* to set up ◆ **gegründet 1857** established *or* founded in 1857; **eine Familie ~** to get married (and have a family).

[2] *vi* to be based *or* founded (*in +dat* on).

[3] *vr* **sich auf etw** (*acc*) **~** to be based *or* founded on sth.

Gründer *m* **-s, -** founder.

Gründerfigur *f* founder.

Gründerin *f siehe* **Gründer**.

Gründerjahre *pl* **(a)** (*Hist*) *years of rapid industrial expansion in Germany (from 1871)*. **(b)** (*fig: von Atomzeitalter etc*) early days *pl*.

Grund-: ~erwerb *m* acquisition of land; **~erwerbssteuer** *f* tax on land acquisition, land transfer tax.

Gründerzeit *f* (*Hist*) *siehe* **Gründerjahre**.

Grund-: g~falsch *adj* utterly wrong; **~farbe** *f* primary colour; (*Grundierfarbe*) ground colour; **~festen** *pl* (*fig*) foundations *pl*; **etw bis in die** *or* **in seinen ~festen erschüttern** to shake sth to the *or* its very foundations; **an den ~festen von etw rütteln** to shake the (very) foundations of sth; **~fläche** *f* (*Math*) base; **~form** *f* basic form (*auch Gram*); **~freibetrag** *m* tax-free allowance; **~gebühr** *f* basic *or* standing charge; **~gedanke** *m* basic idea; **g~gescheit** *adj* extremely bright.

Grundgesetz *nt* **(a)** (*Grundprinzip*) basic law. **(b)** (*BRD*) **das ~** the (German) Constitution.

Grundgesetz-: ~änderung *f* amendment of the (German) Constitution; **g~widrig** *adj* unconstitutional.

Grund-: ~haltung *f* basic position; ⚠**g~häßlich** *adj* extremely *or* dreadfully ugly; **~herr** *m* (*Hist*) lord of the manor; **~herrschaft** *f* (*Hist*) manorial system; **~idee** *f siehe* **~gedanke**.

grundieren* *vt* to undercoat; (*Art*) to ground.

Grundier-: ~farbe, ~schicht *f* undercoat.

Grundierung *f* **(a)** *no pl* (*das Grundieren*) undercoating; (*Art*) grounding. **(b)** (*Farbe, Fläche*) undercoat; (*Art*) ground.

Grund-: ~irrtum *m* fundamental error; **~kapital** *nt* share capital; (*Anfangskapital*) initial capital; **~kurs** *m* (*Sch, Univ*) basic *or* base course; **~lage** *f* basis; (*Mus*) root position; **als ~lage für etw dienen** to serve as a basis for sth; **auf der ~lage** *+gen or* **von** on the basis of; **die ~lagen einer Wissenschaft/eines Lehrfachs** the fundamental principles of a science/the rudiments of a subject; **etw auf eine neue ~lage stellen** *Beziehungen* to put sth on a different footing *or* basis; *Organisation etc* to change the basic structure(s) of sth; **jeder ~lage entbehren** to be completely unfounded *or* without foundation; **~lagenforschung** *f* pure research; **~last** *f* (*Tech*) constant load; **~lastkapazität** *f* (*Tech*) constant load capacity; **g~legend** *adj* fundamental, basic (*für* to); *Werk, Textbuch* standard; **sich zu etw g~legend äußern** to make a statement of fundamental importance on sth; **~legung** *f* (*lit, fig*) laying of the foundations; (*fig: ~riß*) outline.

gründlich [1] *adj* thorough; *Arbeit* painstaking, careful; *Vorbereitung auch* careful.

[2] *adv* thoroughly; (*inf: sehr auch*) really ◆ **jdm ~ die Meinung sagen** to give sb a real piece of one's mind; **da haben Sie sich ~ getäuscht** you're completely mistaken there.

Gründlichkeit *f, no pl siehe adj* thoroughness; carefulness.

Grund-: ~linie *f* (*Math, Sport*) baseline; **~linienspiel** *nt* baseline game; **~lohn** *m* basic pay *or* wage(s); **g~los** [1] *adj* **(a)** *Tiefe etc* bottomless; **(b)** (*fig: unbegründet*) groundless, unfounded; **g~loses Lachen** laughter for no reason (at all); [2] *adv* (*fig*) without reason, for no reason (at all); **~mauer** *f* foundation wall; **bis auf die ~mauern niederbrennen** to be gutted; **~menge** *f* (*Math*) fundamental *or* universal set; **~moräne** *f* (*Geol*) ground moraine; **~nahrungsmittel** *nt* basic food(stuff).

Gründonnerstag [gry:n-] *m* Maundy Thursday.

Grund-: ~ordnung *f* basic order; **~pfandrecht** *nt* encumbrance on property; **~pfeiler** *m* (*Archit*) supporting pier; (*fig*) cornerstone, keystone; **~rechenart, ~rechnungsart** *f* basic arithmetical operation; **~recht** *nt* basic *or* fundamental right; **~rente** *f* (*Econ*) ground rent; (*Insur*) basic pension; ⚠**~riß** *m* (*von Gebäude*) ground plan; (*Math*) base; (*Abriß*) outline, sketch; **„~riß der chinesischen Grammatik"** "Outline of Chinese Grammar".

Grundsatz *m* principle ◆ **aus ~** on principle; **ein Mann mit** *or* **von Grundsätzen** a man of principle; **an seinen Grundsätzen festhalten** *or* **bei seinen Grundsätzen bleiben** to stand by *or* keep to one's principles; **es sich** (*dat*) **zum ~ machen, etw zu tun** to make a principle of doing sth, to make it a matter of principle to do sth.

Grundsatz-: ~debatte, ~diskussion *f* debate on (general) principles; **~entscheidung** *f* decision of general principle; **~erklärung** *f* declaration of principle.

grundsätzlich [1] *adj* fundamental; *Frage* of principle.

[2] *adv* (*allgemein, im Prinzip*) in principle; (*aus Prinzip*) on principle; (*immer*) always; (*völlig*) absolutely ◆ **sich zu etw ~ äußern** to make a statement of principle on sth; **er ist ~ anderer Meinung als sie** he always disagrees with her, he disagrees with her on principle; **ihre Meinungen sind ~ verschieden** their views are fundamentally different; **das erlaube ich Ihnen ~ nicht** I will most definitely not permit that; **das ist ~ verboten** it is absolutely forbidden; **er hat ~ kein Interesse für so etwas** he has absolutely no interest in that sort of thing.

Grundsätzlichkeit *f* fundamental nature.

Grundsatz-: ~papier *nt* (*Pol*) (written) statement of principles; **~referat** *nt* speech/paper setting out a basic principle; **~urteil** *nt* judgement that establishes a principle.

Grund-: g~schlecht *adj* thoroughly bad; **~schrift** *f* (*Typ*) base type; **~schuld** *f* mortgage; **~schule** *f* primary (*Brit*) *or* elementary school; **~schüler** *m* primary/elementary(-school) pupil; **~schullehrer** *m* primary/elementary(-school) teacher; **g~solide** *adj* very respectable; **g~ständig** *adj* (*Bot*) basal, basilar; **~stein** *m* (*lit, fig*) foundation stone; **der ~stein zu etw sein** to form the foundation(s) of *or* for sth; **den ~stein zu etw legen** (*lit*) to lay the foundation stone of sth; (*fig*) to lay the foundations of *or* for sth; **~steinlegung** *f* laying of the foundation stone; **~stellung** *f* (*Turnen*) starting position; (*Boxen*) on-guard position; (*Chess*) initial *or* starting position; (*Mus*) root position; **~steuer** *f* (local) property tax, ≃ rates *pl* (*Brit*); **~stimme** *f* bass; **~stimmung** *f* prevailing mood; **~stock** *m* basis, foundation; **~stoff** *m* basic material; (*Rohstoff*) raw material; (*Chem*) element; **~stoffindustrie** *f* primary industry.

Grundstück *nt* plot (of land); (*Anwesen*) estate; (*Bau~ auch*) site; (*bebaut*) property ◆ **in ~en spekulieren** to speculate in property *or* in real estate.

Grundstücks-: ~haftung *f* real estate collateral; **~makler** *m* estate agent (*Brit*), real estate agent, realtor (*US*); **~preis** *m* land price; **~spekulant** *m* property speculator; **~spekulation** *f* property speculation.

Grund-: ~studium *nt* (*Univ*) basic course; **~stufe** *f* **(a)** first stage; (*Sch*) ≃ junior (*Brit*) *or* grade (*US*) school; **(b)** (*Gram*) positive (degree); **~tendenz** *f*, **~tenor** *m* basic trend; (*verborgen*) underlying trend; **~ton** *m* (*Mus*) (*eines Akkords*) root; (*einer Tonleiter*) tonic keynote; (*~farbe*) ground colour; **~übel** *nt* basic *or* fundamental evil; (*Nachteil*) basic problem; **~umsatz** *m* (*Physiol*) basal metabolism.

Gründung *f* founding, foundation; (*Archit: Fundament*) foundation(s *pl*); (*das Anlegen des Fundaments*) laying of the foundations; (*von Heim, Geschäft*) setting up ◆ **die ~ einer Familie** getting married (and having a family).

Gründungs-: ~jahr *nt* year of the foundation; **~kapital** *nt* initial capital; **~rektor** *m* (*Univ*) first vice-chancellor; **~versammlung** *f* inaugural meeting (*of a new company*).

Gründüngung *f* (*Agr*) green manuring.

Grund-: g~verkehrt *adj* completely wrong; **~vermögen** *nt* landed property, real estate; **g~verschieden** *adj* totally *or* entirely different; **~wasser** *nt* ground water; **~wasserspiegel** *m* water table, ground-water level; **~wehrdienst** *m* national (*Brit*) *or* selective (*US*) service; **den ~wehrdienst absolvieren** *or* **leisten** to do one's national/selective service; **~wert** *m* (*Philos*) fundamental value; **~wertekatalog** *m* (*Philos*) index of fundamental values; **~wort** *nt, pl* **~wörter** (*Gram*) root; **~zahl** *f* (*Math*) base (number); (*Kardinalzahl*) cardinal number; **~zins** *m* (*Hist*) feudal dues *pl* (*Hist*); **~zug** *m* essential feature *or* trait; **„~züge der Geometrie"** "Basic Geometry", "(The) Rudiments of Geometry"; **etw in seinen ~zügen darstellen** to outline (the essentials of) sth; **dieses Werk entstand in seinen ~zügen schon** ... the essential features *or* the essentials of this work appeared as early as ...

grünen *vi* (*geh*) to turn green; (*fig: Liebe, Hoffnung*) to blossom (forth).

Grünen-: ~-Abgeordnete(r) *mf decl as adj* Green MP; **~-Fraktion** *f* Green Party (*in Parliament/on council*).

Grüne(r) *mf decl as adj* **(a)** (*Pol*) Green. **(b)** (*dated inf: Polizist*) cop (*inf*), copper (*Brit inf*), bluebottle (*dated Brit inf*).

Grüne(s) *nt decl as adj* (*Farbe*) green; (*als Ausschmückung*) greenery; (*Gemüse*)

greens *pl*, green vegetables *pl*; (*Grünfutter*) green stuff ◆ **ins ~ fahren** to go to the country; **wir essen viel ~s** (*inf*) we eat a lot of greens; **~s in die Suppe tun** (*inf*) to put green vegetables in the soup.
Grün-: **~fink** *m* greenfinch; **~fläche** *f* green space *or* area; **~futter** *nt* green fodder, greenstuff; (*inf: Salat*) salad; (*inf: Gemüse*) green vegetables *pl*; **g~gelb** *adj* greenish yellow, greeny-yellow; **~gürtel** *m* green belt; **~kohl** *m* (curly) kale; **~land** *nt, no pl* meadowland *no indef art*, grassland *no indef art*; **g~lich** *adj* greenish; **~pflanze** *f* non-flowering *or* foliage plant; **~rock** *m* (*hum*) gamekeeper; (*Jäger*) huntsman; **~schnabel** *m* (*inf*) (little) whippersnapper (*inf*); (*Neuling*) greenhorn (*inf*); **sei still, du ~schnabel!** be quiet you little know-all! (*inf*); **~span** *m, no pl* verdigris; **~span ansetzen** *or* **bilden** to form verdigris; (*fig*) to grow hoary; **~specht** *m* green woodpecker; **~stich** *m* (*Phot*) green cast; **g~stichig** *adj* with a green cast; **~streifen** *m* central reservation (*Brit*), median (strip) (*US, Austral*); (*am Straßenrand*) grass verge.
grunzen *vti* to grunt.
Grünzeug *nt* greens *pl*, green vegetables *pl*; (*Kräuter*) herbs *pl*.
Grunzlaut *m* grunt.
Grüppchen *nt* (*usu pej*) little group.
Gruppe *f* **-, -n** group (*auch Math*); (*von Mitarbeitern auch*) team; (*Mil*) ≃ squad; (*Aviat*) ≃ squadron (*Brit*), group (*US*); (*von Pfadfindern*) section; (*Klasse, Kategorie auch*) class ◆ **eine ~ Zuschauer** *or* **von Zuschauern** a group of onlookers; **eine ~ von Beispielen** a list *or* series of examples; **~n (zu je fünf/sechs) bilden** to form (into) *or* to make groups (of five/six).
Gruppen- *in cpds* group; **~arbeit** *f* teamwork; **~bild** *nt* group portrait; **~bildung** *f* group formation, formation of groups; **~dynamik** *f* (*Psych*) group dynamics; **g~dynamisch** *adj* (*Psych*) group-dynamic; **~egoismus** *m* self-interest of the/a group; **~führer** *m* group leader; (*Mil*) squad leader; **~leben** *nt* group living; **~mitglied** *nt* member of a/the group, group member; **~pädagogik** *f* group teaching; **~psychologie** *f* group psychology; **~reise** *f* group travel *no pl*; **~sex** *m* group sex; **~sieg** *m* (*Sport*) **den ~sieg erringen** to win in one's group; **~sieger** *m* (*Sport*) group winner, winner in *or* of a/the group; **g~spezifisch** *adj* group-specific; **~status** *m* (*Pol*) interest-group status; **~therapie** *f* group therapy; **~unterricht** *m* group learning; **~vergewaltigung** *f* multiple rape, gang bang (*inf*); **g~weise** *adv* in groups; (*Ind, Comm, Sport auch*) in teams; (*Mil*) in squads; (*Aviat*) in squadrons.
gruppieren* [1] *vt* to group.
[2] *vr* to form a group/groups, to group.
Gruppierung *f* **(a)** *no pl* grouping. **(b)** (*Konstellation*) grouping; (*Gruppe*) group; (*Pol auch*) faction.
Grus *m* **-es, -e** (*Gesteinsschutt*) rubble; (*Kohlen~*) slack.
Grusel-: **~effekt** *m* horror effect; **~film** *m* horror *or* gothic film; **~geschichte** *f* tale of horror, horror *or* gothic story.
grus(e)lig *adj* horrifying, gruesome.
Gruselmärchen *nt siehe* **Gruselgeschichte**.
gruseln [1] *vti impers* **mich** *or* **mir gruselt auf Friedhöfen** cemeteries give me an eery feeling *or* give me the creeps; **ich kehre um, mir gruselt** I'm going back, I'm getting the creeps; **hier kann man das G~ lernen** this will teach you the meaning of fear.
[2] *vr* **hier würde ich mich ~** a place like this would give me the creeps; **sie gruselt sich vor Schlangen** snakes give her the creeps.
Grusical ['gru:zikl] *nt* **-s, -s** (*hum*) comic horror *or* gothic film/play.
gruslig *adj siehe* **grus(e)lig**.
▼ **Gruß** *m* **-es, ¨-e (a)** greeting; (*~geste, Mil*) salute ◆ **zum ~** in greeting; **der Deutsche ~** (*NS*) the Nazi salute; **er ging ohne ~ an mir vorbei** he walked past me without saying hello.
▼ **(b)** (*als Zeichen der Verbundenheit*) **viele ¨~e** best wishes (*an +acc* to); **bestell Renate bitte viele ¨~e von mir** please give Renate my best wishes *or* my regards, remember me to Renate; **schick mir einen ~ aus Paris** drop me a line from Paris; **sag ihm einen schönen ~** say hello to him (from me); **einen (schönen) ~ an Ihre Gattin!** my regards to your wife.
(c) (*als Briefformel*) **mit bestem ~** *or* **besten ¨~en** yours; **mit brüderlichem/sozialistischem ~** (*Pol*) yours fraternally; **mit freundlichen ¨~en** *or* **freundlichem ~** (*bei Anrede Mr/Mrs/Miss X*) Yours sincerely, Yours truly (*esp US*); (*bei Anrede Sir(s)/Madam*) Yours faithfully, Yours truly (*esp US*).
Gruß- (*Pol*): **~adresse, ~ansprache, ~botschaft** *f* message of greeting.
▼ **grüßen** [1] *vt* **(a)** to greet; (*Mil*) to salute ◆ **grüßt er dich auch nicht?** doesn't he say hello to you either?; **sei gegrüßt** (*old, geh, iro*) greetings; **grüß dich!** (*inf*) hello there!, hi! (*inf*).
▼ **(b)** (*Grüße übermitteln*) **Otto läßt dich (schön) ~** Otto sends his regards *or* best wishes *or* asked to be remembered to you; **ich soll Sie von ihm ~** he sends his regards *etc*; **grüß mir deine Mutter!, grüß deine Mutter von mir!** remember me to your mother, give my regards to your mother; **und grüß mir Wien/den Goldenen Löwen** and say hello to Vienna/the Golden Lion for me; **grüß Gott!** (*S Ger, Aus*) hello.
[2] *vi* to say hello, to give a greeting (*form*); (*Mil*) to salute ◆ **Otto läßt ~** Otto sends his regards; **die Berge grüßten aus der Ferne** (*liter*) the mountains greeted us in the distance.
[3] *vr* **ich grüße mich nicht mehr mit ihm** I don't say hello to him any more.
Grußformel *f* form of greeting; (*am Briefanfang*) salutation; (*am Briefende*) complimentary close, ending.
Gruß-: **g~los** *adv* without a word of greeting/farewell, without saying hello/goodbye; **~ordnung** *f* (*Mil*) saluting hierarchy; **~pflicht** *f* (*Mil*) obligation to salute; **~schreiben** *nt* greeting; (*Pol*) letter of greeting; **~telegramm** *nt* greetings telegram; (*Pol*) goodwill telegram; **~wort** *nt* greeting.
Grütz-: **~beutel** *m* (*Med*) wen; **~brei** *m* gruel.
Grütze *f* **-, -n (a)** groats *pl*; (*Brei*) gruel ◆ **rote ~** (type of) red fruit jelly. **(b)** *no pl* (*inf: Verstand*) brains (*inf*) ◆ **der hat ~ im Kopf** (*inf*) he's got brains (*inf*).
Grützkopf *m* (*inf*) **(a)** (*Dummkopf*) thickhead (*inf*), thickie (*inf*). **(b)** (*Verstand*) thick head.
Gschaftlhuber *m* **-s, -** (*S Ger, Aus inf*) busybody.
gschamig *adj* (*Aus inf*) bashful.
Gscherte(r) *mf decl as adj* (*Aus inf*) idiot.
Gschnas *nt* **-**, *no pl* (*Aus inf*) fancy-dress party.
G7 [ge:'zi:bn] *f* **-** G7.
G7-Staat *m* G7 nation.
Gspusi *nt* **-s, -s** (*S Ger, Aus inf*) **(a)** (*Liebschaft*) affair, carry-on (*inf*). **(b)** (*Liebste(r)*) darling, sweetheart.
Gstätten *f* **-, -** (*Aus inf*) grassy patch of land on a hillside.
GTI-Modell [ge:te:'|i:-] *nt* (*Aut*) GTI model.
Guatemala *nt* **-s** Guatemala.
Guatemalteke *m* **-n, -n, Guatemaltekin** *f* Guatemalan.
guatemaltekisch *adj* Guatemalan.
Guayana [gua'ja:na] *nt* **-s** Guiana; (*ehem. Brit.-~*) Guyana.
Gu(a)yaner(in *f*) [gua'ja:nɐ, -ərɪn] *m* **-s, -** Guianese; Guyanese.
gu(a)yanisch *adj* Guianese; Guyanese.
gucken ['gʊkn, (*N Ger*) 'kʊkn] [1] *vi* (*sehen*) to look (*zu* at); (*heimlich auch*) to peep, to peek; (*hervorschauen*) to peep (*aus* out of) ◆ **laß mal ~!** let's have a look, give us a look (*inf*); **jdm in die Karten ~** to look *or* have a look at sb's cards.
[2] *vt* (*inf*) **Fernsehen ~** to watch television *or* telly (*Brit inf*).
Gucker *m* **-s, -** (*inf*) **(a)** (*Fernglas*) telescope; (*Opernglas*) opera glass(es). **(b)** *pl* (*Augen*) peepers (*inf*), eyes *pl*.
Guckfenster *nt* small window; (*in Tür*) judas window.
Guck-: **~indieluft** *m siehe* **Hans**; **~kasten** *m* (*inf: Fernseher*) telly (*Brit inf*), gogglebox (*Brit inf*), tube (*US inf*); **~kastenbühne** *f* proscenium *or* fourth-wall stage; **~loch** *nt* peephole.
Guerilla[1] [ge'rɪlja, ge'rɪla] *f* **-, -s (a)** (*~krieg*) guerilla war/warfare. **(b)** (*~einheit*) guerilla unit.
Guerilla[2] [ge'rɪlja] *m* **-(s), -s** (*~kämpfer*) guerilla.
Guerilla- [ge'rɪlja-] *in cpds* guerilla.
Guerillero [gerɪl'je:ro] *m* **-s, -s** guerilla fighter.
Guernsey ['gə:nzi] *nt* **-s** Guernsey.
Gugel-: **~hupf** (*S Ger, Aus*), **~hopf** (*Sw*) *m* **-s, -e** (*Cook*) gugelhupf.
Güggeli *nt* **-s, -** (*Sw Cook*) roast chicken.
Guillotine [gɪljo'ti:nə, (*Aus*) gijo'ti:nə] *f* guillotine.
guillotinieren* [gɪljoti'ni:rən] *vt* to guillotine.
Guinea [gi'ne:a] *nt* **-s** (*Geog*) Guinea.
Guineer(in *f*) [gi'ne:ɐ, -ərɪn] *m* **-s, -** Guinean.
guineisch [gi'ne:ɪʃ] *adj* Guinean.
Gulasch *nt or m* **-(e)s, -e** *or* **-s** goulash ◆ **ich mache aus dir ~!** (*inf*) I'll beat the living daylights out of you (*inf*).
Gulasch-: **~kanone** *f* (*Mil sl*) field kitchen; **~kommunismus** *m* (*pej*) *communism which is concerned only with material well-being*; **~suppe** *f* goulash soup.
Gulden *m* **-s, -** (*Hist*) florin; (*niederländischer ~*) g(u)ilder, gulden.
gülden *adj* (*poet*) golden.
Gülle *f* **-**, *no pl* (*S Ger, Sw*) *siehe* **Jauche**.
Gully ['gʊli] *m or nt* **-s, -s** drain.
gültig *adj* valid ◆ **nach den ~en Bestimmungen** according to current regulations; **nach dem bis Mai noch ~en Gesetz** according to the law in force until May; **ab wann ist der Fahrplan ~?** when does the timetable come into effect *or* force?; **~ für zehn Fahrten** valid *or* good for ten trips; **~ werden** to become valid; (*Gesetz, Vertrag*) to come into force *or* effect; (*Münze*) to become legal tender.
Gültigkeit *f, no pl* validity; (*von Gesetz*) legal force ◆ **das Fünfmarkstück verliert im Herbst seine ~** the five-mark piece ceases to be legal tender in the autumn.
Gültigkeitsdauer *f* period of validity; (*eines Gesetzes*) period in force.
Gulyas ['gu:laʃ, 'gʊlaʃ] *nt* **-s, -e** *siehe* **Gulasch**.
Gummi *nt or m* **-s, -s** (*Material*) rubber; (*~arabikum*) gum; (*Radier~*) rubber (*Brit*), eraser; (*~band*) rubber *or* elastic band; (*in Kleidung etc*) elastic; (*inf: Kondom*) rubber (*sl*), Durex ®.
Gummi- *in cpds* rubber; **~anzug** *m* wetsuit; **~arabikum** *nt* **-s**, *no pl* gum arabic; **g~artig** [1] *adj* rubbery; [2] *adv* like rubber; **~band** *nt* rubber *or* elastic band; (*in Kleidung*) elastic; **~bär(chen** *nt*) *m* jellybaby; **~baum** *m* rubber plant; **~begriff** *m* (*inf*) elastic concept; **~boot** *nt* inflatable boat, rubber dinghy.
gummieren* *vt* to gum.
Gummierung *f* **(a)** (*Verfahren*) gumming. **(b)** (*gummierte Fläche*) gum.
Gummi-: **~harz** *nt* gum resin; **~hose** *f*, **~höschen** *nt* plastic pants *pl*; **~kissen** *nt* inflatable rubber cushion; **~knüppel** *m* rubber truncheon; **~linse** *f* (*Phot*) zoom lens; **~löwe** *m* (*hum*) paper tiger; **~mantel** *m* plastic raincoat *or* mac (*Brit*); **~muffe** *f* (*Comput: für Akustikkoppler*) rubber cups *pl*; ⚠**~paragraph** *m* (*inf*) ambiguous clause; **~reifen** *m* rubber tyre; **~sauger** *m* rubber teat (*Brit*) *or* nipple (*US*); **~schlauch** *m* rubber hose; (*bei Fahrrad etc*) inner tube; **~schutz** *m* (*dated*) sheath; **~stiefel** *m* rubber boot, gumboot, wellington (boot) (*Brit*), wellie (*Brit inf*); (*bis zu den Oberschenkeln*)

wader; **~strumpf** *m* rubber *or* elastic stocking; **~tier** *nt* rubber animal; (*aufblasbar*) inflatable animal; **~unterlage** *f* rubber sheet; **~waren** *pl* rubber goods *pl*; ⚠**~(wucht)geschoß** *nt* rubber bullet; **~zelle** *f* padded cell; **~zug** *m* (piece of) elastic.

Gunst *f* **-**, *no pl* favour; (*Wohlwollen auch*) goodwill; (*Gönnerschaft auch*) patronage; (*des Schicksals etc*) benevolence ◆ **zu meinen/deinen ~en** in my/your favour; **jdm eine ~ erweisen** (*geh*) to do sb a kindness; **jdm die ~ erweisen, etw zu tun** (*geh*) to be so gracious as to do sth for sb; **jds ~ besitzen** *or* **genießen, in jds ~** (*dat*) **stehen** to have *or* enjoy sb's favour, to be in favour with sb.

Gunst-: ~beweis *m*, **~bezeigung** *f* mark of favour; **~gewerbe** *nt* (*hum*) the oldest profession in the world (*hum*), prostitution; **~gewerblerin** *f* (*hum*) lady of easy virtue, prostitute.

günstig *adj* favourable; (*zeitlich, bei Reisen etc*) convenient; *Angebot, Preis etc* reasonable, good ◆ **jdm/einer Sache ~ gesinnt sein** (*geh*) to be favourably disposed towards sb/sth; **es trifft sich ~, daß ...** it's very lucky that ...; **~ bei etw abschneiden** to do well in sth, to come out of sth very well; **bei ~er Witterung** weather permitting; **die Stadt liegt ~ (für)** the town is well situated (for); **wie komme ich am ~sten nach ...?** what's the best *or* easiest way to get to ...?; **die Fähre um 3 Uhr ist ~er** the 3 o'clock ferry is more convenient *or* better; **im ~sten Fall(e)** with luck; **im ~sten Licht** (*lit, fig*) in the most favourable light; **etw ~ kaufen/verkaufen** to buy/sell sth for a good price; **„Kinderwagen ~ abzugeben"** "pram for sale: bargain price"; **mit Geschäften und Erholungsmöglichkeiten in ~er Lage** convenient for shops and recreational facilities.

günstigstenfalls *adv* at the very best.

Günstling *m* (*pej*) favourite.

Günstlingswirtschaft *f* (*pej*) (system of) favouritism.

Gupf *m* **-(e)s, -e** (*Aus*) head.

Guppy ['gʊpi] *m* **-s, -s** (*Zool*) guppy.

Gurgel *f* **-, -n** throat; (*Schlund*) gullet ◆ **jdm die ~ zudrücken** *or* **abdrücken** *or* **abschnüren** *or* **zuschnüren** (*lit, fig*) to strangle sb; **dann springt sie mir an die ~!** (*inf*) she'll kill me (*inf*); **sein Geld durch die ~ jagen** (*inf*) to pour all one's money down one's throat *or* gullet (*inf*); **sich** (*dat*) **die ~ schmieren** (*hum*) to oil one's throat *or* gullet (*inf*).

gurgeln *vi* **(a)** (*den Rachen spülen*) to gargle. **(b)** (*Wasser, Laut*) to gurgle.

Gurgel-: ~mittel, ~wasser *nt* gargle.

Gürkchen *nt* midget gherkin.

Gurke *f* **-, -n (a)** cucumber; (*Essig~*) gherkin ◆ **saure ~n** pickled gherkins. **(b)** (*hum inf: Nase*) hooter (*inf*), conk (*Brit inf*), nose.

gurken *vi aux sein* (*sl*) to drive.

Gurken-: ~hobel *m* slicer; **~salat** *m* cucumber salad.

gurren *vi* (*lit, fig*) to coo.

Gurt *m* **-(e)s, -e** (*Gürtel, Sicherheits~, Ladestreifen*) belt; (*Riemen*) strap; (*Sattel~*) girth; (*Archit*) girder.

Gurtband *nt* waistband.

Gürtel *m* **-s, -** (*Gurt, Zone*) belt; (*Absperrkette*) cordon ◆ **den ~ enger schnallen** (*lit, fig*) to tighten one's belt.

Gürtel-: ~linie *f* waist; **ein Schlag unter die ~linie** (*lit*) a punch/blow *etc* below the belt; **das war ein Schlag unter die ~linie** (*fig*) that really was (hitting) below the belt; **~reifen** *m* radial (tyre); **~rose** *f* (*Med*) shingles *sing or pl*; **~schnalle** *f* belt buckle; **~tier** *nt* armadillo.

gürten (*geh*) **1** *vt* to gird (*old*); *Pferd* to girth.
2 *vr* to gird oneself.

Gurt-: ~muffel *m* (*inf*) person who refuses to wear a seatbelt; **~pflicht** *f* **es besteht ~pflicht** the wearing of seatbelts is compulsory; **~straffer** *m* **-s, -** (*Aut*) seat belt tensioner.

Guru *m* **-s, -s** (*lit, fig*) guru.

GUS [geːǀuːˈǀɛs] *f* - *abbr of* **Gemeinschaft Unabhängiger Staaten** CIS.

Gusche *f* **-, -n** (*dial*) *siehe* **Gosche.**

⚠**Guß** *m* **Gusses, Güsse (a)** (*Metal*) (*no pl: das Gießen*) casting, founding; (*~stück*) cast ◆ **(wie) aus einem ~** (*fig*) a unified whole.
(b) (*Strahl*) stream, gush; (*inf: Regen~*) cloudburst, downpour ◆ **kalte Güsse** (*Med*) cold affusions.
(c) (*Zucker~*) icing, frosting (*esp US*); (*durchsichtig*) glaze ◆ **einen Kuchen mit einem ~ überziehen** to ice a cake.

⚠**Guß-: ~asphalt** *m* poured asphalt; **~beton** *m* cast concrete; **~eisen** *nt* cast iron; **g~eisern** *adj* cast-iron; **~form** *f* mould; **~naht** *f* seam.

GUS-Staat *m* CIS state.

⚠**Gußstahl** *m* cast steel.

gustieren* *vt* **(a)** *siehe* **goutieren. (b)** (*Aus*) to taste, to try.

gustiös *adj* (*Aus*) appetizing.

Gusto *m* **-s,** (*rare*) **-s** (*geh, Aus*) **(a)** (*Appetit*) **~ auf etw** (*acc*) **haben** to feel like sth. **(b)** (*fig: Geschmack*) taste ◆ **nach jds ~** to sb's taste; **mit ~** with gusto; **nach eignem ~** ad lib, just as one/he *etc* likes.

Gustostückerl *nt* **-s, -(n)** (*Aus inf*) delicacy.

gut 1 *adj, comp* **besser,** *superl* **beste(r, s)** good ◆ **probieren Sie unsere ~en Weine/Speisen!** try our fine wines/food; **er ist in der Schule/in Spanisch sehr ~** he's very good at school/Spanish; **~e Frau!** (*dated*) my dear lady; **er macht sich** (*dat*) **einen ~en Tag** (*faulenzt*) he's taking things easy for a day; (*amüsiert sich*) he's having a good day of it; **die ~e Stube** the best *or* good room; **das ist ~ gegen** *or* **für** (*inf*) **Husten** it's good for coughs; **wozu ist das ~?** (*inf*) what's that for?; **er ist immer für eine Überraschung ~** (*inf*) he's always good for a surprise; **schon war er wieder für Geschäfte ~** he was already back in business; **das war Pech, aber wer weiß, wozu es ~ ist** it was bad luck, but it's an ill wind ...; **sei so ~ (und) gib mir das** would you mind giving me that; **würden Sie so ~ sein und ...** would you be good enough to ...; **jdm ~ sein** (*old*) to love sb; **sie ist ihm von Herzen ~** (*old*) her heart is his (*liter*); **bist du mir wieder ~?** (*dated*) are you friends with me again?; **dafür ist er sich zu ~** he wouldn't stoop to that sort of thing; **sind die Bilder/die Plätzchen ~ geworden?** did the pictures/biscuits turn out all right?; **ist dein Magen wieder ~?** is your stomach better *or* all right again?; **es wird alles wieder ~!** everything will be all right; **es ist ganz ~, daß ...** it's good that ...; **wie ~, daß ...** it's good that ..., how fortunate that ...; **~, daß du das endlich einsiehst** it's a good thing *or* job (that) you realize it at last; **so was ist immer ~** that's always useful; **ich will es damit ~ sein lassen** I'll leave it at that; **laß das ~ sein!** don't worry; **laß mal ~ sein!** that's enough, that'll do; **jetzt ist aber ~!** (*inf*) that's enough; **das ist ja alles ~ und schön, aber ...** that's all very well but ... *or* all well and good but ...; **ein ~es Stück Weg(s)** (*dated*) a good way; **ein ~es Pfund Reis** a good pound of rice; **~e Besserung!** get well soon; **auf ~e Freundschaft!** here's to us!; **auf ~es Gelingen!** here's to success!; **~!** good; (*in Ordnung*) (all) right, OK; **schon ~!** (it's) all right *or* OK; **~, ~!** all right; **also ~!** all right *or* OK then; **nun ~!** fair enough, all right then; **~ und schön** (*inf*) fair enough, that's all well and good; **du bist ~!** (*inf*) you're a fine one!
2 *adv, comp* **besser,** *superl* **am besten** well ◆ **~ schmecken/riechen** to taste/smell good; **sie spricht ~ Schwedisch** she speaks Swedish well, she speaks good Swedish; **es ~ haben** to have a good time of it; **unser Volk hat es noch nie so ~ gehabt** our people have never had it so good; **er hat es in seiner Jugend nicht ~ gehabt** he had a hard time (of it) when he was young; **du hast es ~!** you've got it made; **~ wohnen** to have a nice home; **das kann ~ sein** that may well be; **so ~ wie nichts** next to nothing; **so ~ wie nicht** hardly, scarcely; **so ~ wie verloren** as good as lost; **so ~ ich kann** as best I can, as well as I can; **es dauert ~(e) drei Stunden** it lasts a good three hours; **nehmen Sie ~ ein Pfund Mehl** take a good pound of flour; **das ist aber ~ gewogen/eingeschenkt!** that's a generous measure; **~ und gern** easily; **das läßt sich nicht ~ machen** that wouldn't be easy; **(das hast du) ~ gemacht!** well done!; **darauf kann man ~ verzichten** you can easily *or* well do without that; **mach's ~!** (*inf*) cheers, cheerio!, bye!; (*stärker*) look after yourself, take care; **paß ~ auf!** be very careful; **ich kann ihn jetzt nicht ~ im Stich lassen** I can't very well let him down now; *siehe* **Gute(s).**

Gut *nt* **-(e)s, ¨er (a)** (*Eigentum*) property; (*lit, fig: Besitztum*) possession ◆ **irdische ¨er** worldly goods; **geistige ¨er** intellectual wealth; **nicht um alle ¨er der Welt** (*geh*) not for all the world; **bewegliche/unbewegliche ¨er** movables/immovables.
(b) *no pl* (*das Gute*) good, Good ◆ **~ und Böse** good and evil, Good and Evil; **das höchste ~** (*Philos*) the greatest good; (*Gesundheit etc*) one's most valuable possession.
(c) (*Ware, Fracht~*) item ◆ **¨er** goods; (*Fracht~*) freight *sing*, goods (*esp Brit*).
(d) *no pl* (*dated: Material*) material (to be treated).
(e) (*Land~*) estate.
(f) *no pl* (*Naut*) rigging, gear ◆ **laufendes/stehendes ~** running/standing rigging *or* gear.

-gut *nt suf in cpds* **(a)** *denotes material intended for or having undergone a process e.g.* **Saat~** seed; **Mahl~** substance(s) to be ground/ground substance(s).
(b) (*often not translated in English*) *denotes the totality of an abstract possession e.g.* **das deutsche Musik~/Gedanken~** (the body of) German music/thought.

Gut-: g~achten* *vi insep* (*usu infin, auch prp*) (*esp Jur*) to act as an expert witness; **~achten** *nt* **-s, -** report; **~achter(in** *f*) *m* **-s, -** expert; (*Schätzer auch*) valuator; (*Jur: Prozeß*) expert witness; **g~achtlich** *adj* (*form*) expert; **etw g~achtlich feststellen** to ascertain in an expert's report; **g~artig** *adj Kind, Hund etc* good-natured; *Geschwulst, Geschwür* benign; **~artigkeit** *f* (*von Kind etc*) good nature, good-naturedness; (*von Geschwulst*) benignity; ⚠**g~aussehend** *adj* good-looking; ⚠**g~betucht** *adj attr* (*inf*) well-heeled (*inf*); ⚠**g~bezahlt** *adj attr* highly-paid; **g~bürgerlich** *adj* solid middle-class; *Küche* homely, good plain; ⚠**g~dotiert** *adj attr* well-paid; **~dünken** *nt* **-s,** *no pl* discretion; **nach (eigenem) ~dünken** at one's own discretion, as one sees fit, as one thinks fit *or* best.

Güte *f* **-,** *no pl* **(a)** (*Herzens~, Freundlichkeit*) goodness, kindness; (*Gottes auch*) loving-kindness ◆ **würden Sie die ~ haben, zu ...** (*form*) would you have the goodness *or* kindness to ... (*form*); **ein Vorschlag zur ~** a suggestion; **in ~** amicably; **meine ~, ist der dumm!** (*inf*) my God, is he stupid! (*inf*); **ach du liebe** *or* **meine ~!** (*inf*) oh my goodness!, goodness me!
(b) (*einer Ware*) quality ◆ **ein Reinfall erster ~** (*inf*) a first-class flop, a flop of the first order *or* water (*inf*).

Güte-: ~grad *m*, **~klasse** *f* (*Comm*) grade.

Gutenacht-: ~geschichte *f* bedtime story; ⚠**~kuß** *m* goodnight kiss.

Gute(r) *mf decl as adj* **mein ~r** (*old*) my dear friend/husband; **meine ~e** (*old*) my dear; **der/die ~** the dear kind soul; (*mitleidig*) the poor soul; **die ~n und die Bösen** the good and the bad; (*inf: in Westernfilmen etc*) the goodies and the baddies (*inf*).

Güter-: ~abfertigung *f* **(a)** *no pl* dispatch of freight *or* goods (*esp Brit*); **(b)** (*Abfertigungsstelle*) freight *or* goods (*esp Brit*) office; **~abwägung** *f* choice between conflicting rights; **~angebot** *nt siehe* **Warenangebot**; **~bahnhof** *m* freight *or* goods (*esp Brit*) depot; **~fernverkehr** *m* long-distance haulage; **~gemeinschaft** *f* (*Jur*) community of property; **in ~gemeinschaft leben** to have community of property; **~nahverkehr** *m* short-distance haulage (*up to 50 km*); **~schuppen** *m* freight depot, goods shed (*Brit*); **~trennung** *f* (*Jur*) separation of property; **in ~trennung leben** to have separation of property; **~verkehr** *m* freight *or* goods (*esp Brit*) traffic; **~wagen** *m* (*Rail*) freight car (*US*), goods truck (*Brit*); **~zug** *m* freight *or* goods (*esp Brit*) train.

Gute(s) *nt decl as adj* **~s tun** to do good; **es hat alles sein ~s** (*prov*) every cloud has a silver lining (*Prov*), it's an ill wind (that blows no good) (*Prov*); **alles ~!** all the best!, good luck!; **man hört über sie nur ~s** you hear so many good things about her; **das führt zu nichts ~m** it'll lead to no good; **jdm (viel) ~s tun** to be (very) good to sb; **des ~n zuviel tun** to overdo things; **das ist des ~n zuviel** that is too much of a good thing; **das ~ daran** the good thing about it; **das ~ siegt** Good *or* good shall triumph; **das ~ im Menschen** the good in man; **im g~n wie im bösen** for better or for worse; **im g~n** *sich trennen* amicably; **ich sage es dir im g~n** I want to give you a friendly piece of advice.

Güte-: ~siegel *nt* (*Comm*) stamp of quality; **~termin** *m*, **~verhandlung** *f* (*Jur*) conciliation proceedings *pl*; **~zeichen** *nt* mark of quality; (*fig auch*) hallmark.

Gut-: ⚠g~gehen *sep irreg aux sein* [1] *vi impers* **es geht ihm g~** he is doing well *or* nicely; (*er ist gesund*) he is well; **sonst geht's dir g~!** (*iro*) are you feeling all right?, are you in your right mind?; [2] *vi* to go (off) well; **das ist noch einmal g~gegangen** it turned out all right; **wenn es g~geht** with luck; **das konnte ja nicht g~gehen** it was bound to go wrong; **wenn das man g~geht!** (*N Ger*) that's asking for trouble; **hoffentlich geht es mit den beiden g~!** (*inf*) I hope things will work out for the two of them; **⚠g~gehend** *adj attr* flourishing, thriving; **⚠g~gelaunt** *adj* cheerful, in a good mood; **⚠g~gelungen** *adj attr* very successful; *Überraschung* wonderful; **⚠g~gemeint** *adj attr* well-meaning, well-meant; **⚠g~gesinnt** *adj* well-disposed (*+dat* towards); (*von edler Gesinnung*) right-thinking; **g~gläubig** *adj* trusting; (*vertrauensselig auch*) credulous; **~gläubigkeit** *f siehe adj* trusting nature, trustingness; credulity.

Guth. *abbr of* **Guthaben.**

Gut-: g~haben *vt sep irreg* **etw g~haben** to be owed with (*bei* by), to have sth coming (to one) (*bei* from) (*inf*); **~haben** *nt* **-s, -** (*Fin, Bank~*) credit; **auf meinem Konto ist** *or* **habe ich ein ~haben von DM 500** my account is DM 500 in credit; **g~heißen** *vt sep irreg* to approve of; (*genehmigen*) to approve; **~heißung** *f* approval; **g~herzig** *adj* kind-hearted, kindly; **~herzigkeit** *f* kind-heartedness, kind(li)ness.

gütig *adj* kind; (*edelmütig*) generous, gracious ◆ **mit Ihrer ~en Erlaubnis** (*dated form*) with your kind permission; **würden Sie so ~ sein, zu ...** (*dated form*) would you be so kind as to ...

gütlich *adj* amicable ◆ **sich an etw** (*dat*) **~ tun** to make free with sth.

Gut-: g~machen *vt sep* **(a)** (*in Ordnung bringen*) *Fehler* to put right, to correct; *Schaden* to make good; **das kann ich ja gar nicht wieder g~machen!** (*fig*) how on earth can I ever repay you!; **du hast viel an ihm g~zumachen** you've a lot to make up to him (for); **(b)** (*gewinnen*) to make (*bei* out of, on); **g~mütig** *adj* good-natured; **~mütigkeit** *f* good-naturedness; **g~nachbarlich** [1] *adj* neighbourly; [2] *adv* in a neighbourly fashion, as good neighbours; **g~sagen** *vi sep* (*dated*) to vouch (*für* for).

Gutsbesitzer(in *f*) *m* lord of the manor; (*als Klasse*) landowner.

Gut-: ~schein *m* voucher, coupon; (*für Umtausch*) credit note; **g~schreiben** *vt sep irreg* to credit (*dat* to); **~schrift** *f* **(a)** *no pl* (*Vorgang*) crediting; **(b)** (*Bescheinigung*) credit note; (*Betrag*) credit (item).

Gutsel(e) *nt* **-s, -** (*S Ger*) (*Bonbon*) candy (*esp US*), sweet (*Brit*); (*Keks*) biscuit (*Brit*), cookie (*US*).

Guts-: ~haus *nt* manor (house); **~herr** *m* squire, lord of the manor; **~herrin** *f* lady of the manor; **~herrschaft** *f* squire and his family; **~hof** *m* estate.

⚠gut-: ~situiert *adj attr* well-off; **~sitzend** *adj attr* well-fitting.

Gutsverwalter(in *f*) *m* steward.

Gut-: ~templer(in *f*) *m* **-s, -** Good Templar; **⚠g~tun** *vi sep irreg* **jdm g~tun** to do sb good; **das tut g~** that's good; **o, wie g~ das tut!** oh, that's good.

guttural *adj* guttural.

Guttural -s, -e, Gutturallaut *m* (*Ling*) guttural (sound).

Gut-: ⚠g~unterrichtet *adj attr* well-informed; **wie aus g~unterrichteten Kreisen verlautet, ...** according to well-informed sources, ...; **⚠g~verdienend** *adj attr* with a good salary, high-income; **g~willig** *adj* willing; (*entgegenkommend*) obliging; (*nicht böswillig*) well-meaning; **~willigkeit** *f siehe adj* willingness; obligingness; well-meaningness.

gymnasial *adj attr* ≃ at grammar schools (*Brit*), at high schools (*US*) ◆ **die ~e Oberstufe** ≃ the sixth form (*Brit*).

Gymnasial-: ~bildung *f* ≃ grammar school education (*Brit*), high school education (*US*); **~lehrer, ~professor** *m* (*Aus*) ≃ grammar school teacher (*Brit*), high school teacher (*US*).

Gymnasiast(in *f*) *m* **-en, -en** ≃ grammar school pupil (*Brit*), high school student (*US*).

Gymnasium *nt* **(a)** (*Sch*) ≃ grammar school (*Brit*), high school (*US*). **(b)** (*Hist*) gymnasium.

Gymnastik *f* keep-fit exercises *pl*; (*Turnen*) gymnastics *sing* ◆ **~ machen** to do keep-fit (exercises)/gymnastics.

Gymnastikanzug *m* leotard.

Gymnastiker(in *f*) *m* **-s, -** gymnast.

Gymnastik-: ~saal *m* gymnasium; **~unterricht** *m* gymnastics *sing*.

gymnastisch *adj* gymnastic.

Gynäkologe *m*, **Gynäkologin** *f* gynaecologist.

Gynäkologie *f* gynaecology.

gynäkologisch *adj* gynaecological.

Gyros ['giros] *nt* -, *no pl* ≃ doner kebab.

Gyroskop [gyro'sko:p] *nt* **-s, -e** gyroscope.

H

H, h [haː] *nt* -, - H, h; (*Mus*) B.

h *abbr of* **hora(e)** (*Stunde*) hr ◆ **Abfahrt 8h/13h** (*spoken: acht/dreizehn Uhr*) departure 8 a.m./1 p.m. *or* 8⁰⁰/13⁰⁰ hours (*spoken*: eight/thirteen hundred hours); **120 km/h** (*spoken: Kilometer pro Stunde*) 120 km/h *or* kmph.

ha[1] *abbr of* **Hektar** hectare.

ha[2] *interj* ha; (*triumphierend*) aha; (*überrascht, erstaunt, verärgert*) oh; (*verächtlich*) huh ◆ **~ no** (*S Ger inf*) (*Selbstverständliches betonend*) why not; (*ungläubig*) well, well; (*aufmunternd*) come on; (*resignierend*) oh well.

hä *interj* what.

Haag *m* **-s: der ~, Den ~** The Hague; **in** *or* **im ~, in Den ~** in The Hague.

Haager *adj attr* Hague ◆ **~ Konventionen** Hague Conventions; **~ Schiedshof** International Court of Justice in The Hague.

Haar *nt* **-(e)s, -e (a)** (*Menschen~*) hair ◆ **sie hat schönes ~** *or* **schöne ~e** she has nice hair; **sich** (*dat*) **die ~e** *or* **das ~ schneiden lassen** to have *or* get one's hair cut, to have a haircut.
(b) (*Bot, Zool, Material*) hair.
(c) (*in Wendungen*) **~e auf den Zähnen haben** to be a tough customer (*Brit*) *or* cookie (*US*); **~e lassen (müssen)** to suffer badly, to come off badly; **jdm kein ~ krümmen** not to harm a hair of sb's head; **darüber laß dir keine grauen ~e wachsen** don't worry your head about it, don't lose any sleep over it; **er findet immer ein ~ in der Suppe** he always finds something to quibble about; **jdm aufs ~ gleichen** to be the spitting image of sb; **sie gleichen sich aufs ~** they are the spitting image of each other, they're as alike as two peas in a pod; **das ist an den ~en herbeigezogen** that's rather far-fetched; **sich** (*dat*) **die ~e raufen** to tear one's hair out; **sich** (*dat*) **durch die ~e fahren** to run one's fingers through one's hair; **an jdm/etw kein** *or* **nicht ein gutes ~ lassen** to pick *or* pull sb/sth to pieces; **sich** (*dat*) **in die ~e geraten** *or* **kriegen** (*inf*) to quarrel *or* squabble; **sich** (*dat*) **in den ~en liegen** to be at loggerheads; **jdm die ~e vom Kopf fressen** (*inf*) to eat sb out of house and home; **er hat mehr Schulden als ~e auf dem Kopf** he's up to his ears in debt; **um kein ~ besser** no better, not a bit *or* whit better; **um ein** *or* **ums ~** very nearly, almost; **er hat mich um ein ~ getroffen** he just missed (hitting) me by a hair's breadth; *siehe* **Berg**.

Haar-: ~ansatz *m* hairline; **~ausfall** *m* hair loss; **~balg** *m* (*Anat*) hair follicle; **~band** *nt* hairband; (*Schleife*) hair ribbon; **~boden** *m* scalp; **~breit** *nt*: **nicht ein** *or* **um kein ~breit** not an inch; **~bürste** *f* hairbrush; **~büschel** *nt* tuft of hair.

haaren [1] *vi* (*Tier*) to moult, to lose its coat *or* hair; (*Pelz etc*) to shed (hair); (*Teppich*) to shed.
[2] *vr* (*Tier*) to moult.

Haar-: ~entferner *m* **-s, -, ~entfernungsmittel** *nt* hair remover, depilatory; **~ersatz** *m* (*form*) hairpiece; (*Perücke*) wig; (*Toupet*) toupet.

Haaresbreite *f inv* **(nur) um ~** almost, very nearly; *verfehlen* by a hair's breadth; **er wich nicht um ~ von seiner Meinung ab** he did not change his opinion one iota.

Haar-: ~farbe *f* hair colour; **~festiger** *m* **-s, -** (hair) setting lotion; **~flechte** *f* (*old, geh*) plait, braid (*dated*); **~garn** *nt* yarn made from hair; **~gefäß** *nt* (*Anat*) capillary; **h~genau** *adj* exact; *Übereinstimmung* total; **die Beschreibung trifft h~genau auf ihn zu** the description fits him exactly *or* to a T (*inf*); **jdm etw h~genau erklären** to explain sth to sb in great detail; **das trifft h~genau zu** that is absolutely right.

haarig *adj* hairy; (*inf*) (*heikel, gefährlich*) hairy (*inf*); (*schwierig*) nasty.

Haar-: ~klammer *f* (*Klemme*) hairgrip; (*Spange*) hair slide, barrette (*US*); **~kleid** *nt* (*geh*) coat; **h~klein** [1] *adj* (*inf*) *Beschreibung* detailed; [2] *adv* in great *or* minute detail; **er hat mir alles h~klein berechnet** he charged me for absolutely everything; **~klemme** *f* hairgrip; **~kranz** *m* (*von Männern*) fringe (of hair); (*Frauenfrisur*) *plaits fixed around one's head;* **~künstler** *m* (*usu hum*) hair artiste; **~lack** *m* hair lacquer; **h~los** *adj* hairless; (*glatzköpfig*) bald; **~mode** *f* hairstyle; **~nadel** *f* hairpin; **~nadelkurve** *f* hairpin bend; **~netz** *nt* hairnet; **~öl** *nt* hair oil; **~pflege** *f* hair care; **zur ~pflege** (for caring) for one's hair; **~pracht** *f* superb head of hair; ⚠**~riß** *m* (*Tech*) (*in Metall, Pflaster etc*) hairline crack; **h~scharf** *adj Beschreibung, Wiedergabe* exact; *Gedächtnis* very sharp, very clear; *Unterschied* very fine; *Beobachtung* very close; **die Kugel ging h~scharf daneben** the bullet missed by a hair's breadth; **h~scharf an jdm vorbeizielen/vorbeischießen** to aim to just miss sb/to shoot just past sb; **der Glassplitter traf ihn h~scharf über dem Auge** the splinter of glass only just missed his eye; **~schleife** *f* hair ribbon; **~schmuck** *m* ornaments *pl* for one's hair; **~schneider** *m* **-s, - (a)** (*Gerät*) electric clippers *pl*; **(b)** (*inf: Friseur*) barber; **~schnitt** *m* **(a)** (*Frisur*) haircut, hairstyle; **(b)** (*das ~schneiden*) haircut; **~schopf** *m* mop *or* shock of hair; **ihr roter ~schopf** her mop *or* shock of red hair; **~seite** *f* (*von Fell*) fleece side; (*von Pelz*) fur side; (*von Teppich*) pile side; **~sieb** *nt* fine sieve; **~spalter(in** *f*) *m* **-s, -** pedant, hairsplitter; **~spalterei** *f* splitting hairs *no indef art, no pl*; **eine solche ~spalterei** hairsplitting like that; **h~spalterisch** *adj* hairsplitting; *Unterschied* minute; **~spange** *f* hair slide, barrette (*US*); **~spitze** *f* end (of a hair); **gespaltene ~spitzen** split ends; **~spray** *nt or m* hairspray; **~strähne** *f* strand *or* (*dünner*) wisp of hair; **h~sträubend** *adj* hair-raising; (*empörend*) shocking, terrible; (*unglaublich*) *Frechheit* incredible; **~strich** *m* (*dünner Strich*) hairline, hairstroke; (*von Tierfell*) growth of the hair; **~teil** *nt* hairpiece; **~tolle** *f* quiff; (*Hahnenkamm*) cockscomb; **~töner** *m* **-s, -** hair-tinting lotion; **~tönung** *f* tinting; **~tracht** *f* (*dated, geh: Frisur*) hairstyle; **~transplantation** *f* hair transplant; (*Vorgang*) hair transplantation; **~trockner** *m* **-s, -** hair dryer; **~wäsche** *f* washing one's hair *no art*; **eine regelmäßige ~wäsche** washing one's hair regularly; **~waschmittel** *nt* shampoo; **~wasser** *nt* hair lotion; **~wechsel** *m* change of coat; **~wild** *nt* (*Hunt*) game animals *pl*; **~wirbel** *m* cowlick; (*am Hinterkopf*) crown; **~wuchs** *m* growth of hair; **einen kräftigen/spärlichen ~wuchs haben** to have a lot of hair *or* a thick head of hair/thin hair *or* a thin head of hair; **~wuchsmittel** *nt* hair restorer; **~wurzel** *f* root of a/the hair.

Hab *nt*: **~ und Gut** *sing vb* possessions, belongings, worldly goods *all pl*.

Habe *f* **-,** *no pl* (*geh*) possessions *pl*, belongings *pl*.

Habeaskorpus|akte *f* (*Jur*) Act of Habeas Corpus.

Habedank *nt* **-s,** *no pl* (*poet*) thanks *pl* ◆ **ein herzliches ~** heartfelt thanks.

Habe die Ehre *interj* (*Aus*) (*Gruß*) hello; goodbye; (*Ausdruck des Erstaunens, der Entrüstung*) good heavens.

haben *pret* **hatte,** *ptp* **gehabt** [1] *vt* **(a)** to have, to have got (*esp Brit*) ◆ **ein Meter hat 100 cm** there are 100 cm in a metre; **da hast du 10 Mark/das Buch** there's 10 marks/the book; **was man hat, das hat man** (*inf*), **wer hat, der hat** (*inf*) I/she *etc* might as well have it as not; (*in bezug auf Arbeit*) once it's done it's done; **die ~'s (ja)** (*inf*) they can afford it; **wie hätten Sie es gern?** how would you like it?; **man hat wieder lange Haare** long hair is in (fashion) again; **ich kann das nicht ~** (*inf*) I can't stand it; **sie hat heute Geburtstag** it's her birthday today; **Ferien ~** to be on holiday; **er wollte sie zur Frau ~** he wanted to make her his wife.
(b) (*über etw verfügen*) *Zeit, Geld, Beziehungen* to have; (*vorrätig ~, führen auch*) to have got (*esp Brit*) ◆ **damit hat es noch Zeit** *or* **eine gute Weile** (*geh*), **die Sache hat Zeit** it's not urgent, it can wait; **Zeit ~, etw zu tun** to have the time to do sth.
(c) (*Schülersprache*) *Lehrer, Unterricht, Schule* to have; *Note* to get; (*studieren*) *Fach* to do ◆ **in der ersten Stunde ~ wir Mathe** we have maths first lesson; **was hast du diesmal in Englisch?** what did you get in English this time?
(d) (*von etw ergriffen, erfüllt, bedrückt sein*) *Zweifel, Hoffnung, Wunsch* to have ◆ **Hunger/Durst/Angst/Sorgen ~** to be hungry/thirsty/afraid/worried; **eine Krankheit ~** to have (got) an illness; **Fieber ~** to have (got) a temperature; **was hat er denn?** what's the matter with him?, what's wrong with him?; **hast du was?** are you all right?, is (there) something the matter with you?; **ich habe nichts** there's nothing wrong *or* the matter with me; **gute/schlechte Laune ~** to be in a good/bad mood.
(e) (*vorhanden sein, herrschen*) *gutes, schlechtes Wetter* to have ◆ **morgen werden wir Nebel ~** we'll have fog tomorrow; **was ~ wir heute für ein Wetter?** what's the weather like today?; **wieviel Uhr ~ wir?** what's the time?; **heute ~ wir 10°** it's 10° today; **in Australien ~ sie jetzt Winter** it's winter in Australia now; **was für ein Datum ~ wir heute?, den wievielten ~ wir heute?** what's the date today?, what's today's date?
(f) (*mit adj*) **es gut/schön/bequem ~** to have it good/nice/easy; **sie hat es warm in ihrem Zimmer** it's warm in her room; **wir ~ es noch weit bis nach Hause** it's a long way home; **es schlecht ~** to have a bad time (of it); **er hat es nicht leicht mit ihr** he has a hard time (of it) with her.
(g) (*in Infinitivkonstruktion mit zu*) **ich habe nichts zu sagen/tun** I have nothing to say/do; **nichts vom Leben zu erwarten ~** to have no expectations in life; **du hast zu gehorchen** (*müssen*) you must *or* you have to obey; **ich habe nicht zu fragen** I'm not to ask questions; (*steht mir nicht zu*) it's not up to me to

⚠: for details of spelling reform, see supplement

ask questions; **ich habe zu tun** I'm busy.
(h) (*in Infinitivkonstruktion mit Raumangabe*) **etw auf dem Boden liegen/an der Wand hängen ~** to have sth lying on the floor/hanging on the wall; **viele Bücher im Schrank stehen ~** to have a lot of books in the cupboard.
(i) (*in Infinitivkonstruktion mit sein*) **jd/etw ist zu ~** (*erhältlich*) sb/sth is to be had; (*nicht verheiratet*) sb is single; (*sexuell*) sb is available; **für etw zu ~ sein** to be keen on sth; **für ein gutes Essen ist er immer zu ~** he's always willing to have a good meal; **der ist doch für jeden Ulk zu ~** he's always one for a joke; **für gefährliche Sachen ist er immer zu ~** he's always game for anything dangerous; **er ist nicht dafür zu ~** (*nicht interessiert*) he's not keen on that; (*möchte nicht beteiligt sein*) he won't have anything to do with it.
(j) (*dial*) **es hat** (*es gibt*) there is/are.
(k) (*inf: leiden*) **es am Herzen/Magen/an der Leber ~** to have heart/stomach/liver trouble *or* trouble with one's heart/stomach/liver; **es in den Beinen ~** to have trouble with one's legs.
(l) (*Redewendungen*) **ich hab's** (*inf*) I've got it, I know; **du kannst mich gern ~** (*inf*) I don't give a damn (*inf*); **da hast du's/~ wir's!** (*inf*) there you/we are; **woher hast du denn das?** where did you get that from?; **wie gehabt!** some things don't change.
(m) *in Verbindung mit Präpositionen siehe auch dort* **jd/etw hat eine nette Art/etwas Freundliches** *etc* **an sich** (*dat*) there is something nice/friendly *etc* about sb/sth; **sie werden schon merken, was sie an ihm ~** they'll see how valuable he is; **sie hat eine große Hilfe an ihren Kindern** her children are a great help to her; **das hat er/sie/es so an sich** (*dat*) that's just the way he/she/it is; **das hat es in sich** (*inf*) (*schwierig*) that's tough, that's a tough one; (*alkoholreich*) that's strong; (*reichhaltig*) that's rich; **das hat etwas für sich** there's something to be said for that; **was hat es damit auf sich?** what is all this about, what is all this supposed to mean?; **er hat es mit dem Malen/Bergsteigen** (*inf*) he has a thing about painting/mountaineering (*inf*); **man muß immer wissen, wen man vor sich hat** one must always know who one is talking to; **etwas mit jdm ~** (*euph*) to have a thing with sb (*inf*); **etwas von etw ~** (*inf*) to get something out of sth; **das hast du jetzt davon** now see what's happened *or* what's come of it; **das hat er von seinem Leichtsinn** that's what comes of his being frivolous; **nichts/mehr/weniger von etw ~** (*inf*) to get nothing/more/less out of *or* from sth; **da habe ich dann mehr davon** that way I get more out of it; **nichts davon/von etw ~** to get nothing out of it/sth *or* no benefit from it/sth; **viel/wenig von jdm ~** to take after/not to take after sb; **die blonden Haare hat sie von ihrem Vater** she gets her blonde hair from her father; **er hat etwas von einem Erpresser (an sich** *dat***)** he's a bit of a blackmailer; **dieses Werk von Braque hat viel von Picasso** this work by Braque owes much to Picasso; **etw gegen jdn/etw ~** to have sth against sb/sth; **jd hat jdn/etw gegen sich** sb has sb/sth against him.
[2] *vr* (*inf: sich anstellen*) to make a fuss ◆ **was hast du dich denn so?** what are you making such a fuss about?; **hab dich nicht so** stop making such a fuss.
[3] *vr impers* (*inf*) **und damit hat es sich** and that's that; **die Sache hat sich** (*ist erledigt*) that's done; **es hat sich was mit der Liebe/Hoffnung** love/hope is a strange thing; **hat sich was!** (*inf*) some hopes!
[4] *v aux* **ich habe/hatte gerufen** I have/had called, I've/I'd called; **du hättest den Brief früher schreiben können** you could have written the letter earlier; **er will ihn gesehen ~** he says (that) he saw him.

Haben *nt* **-s,** *no pl* credit ◆ **im ~ stehen** to be on the credit side.
Habenichts *m* **-(es), -e** have-not.
Haben-: ~seite *f* credit side; **~zinsen** *pl* interest on credit *sing*.
Haberer *m* **-s, -** (*Aus inf*) bloke (*inf*), chap (*inf*).
Habersack *m* (*old*) knapsack, haversack.
Hab-: ~gier *f* greed, acquisitiveness; **h~gierig** *adj* greedy, acquisitive; **h~haft** *adj* **jds/einer Sache h~haft werden** (*geh*) to get hold of sb/sth.
Habicht *m* **-s, -e** hawk; (*Hühner~*) goshawk.
Habichtsnase *f* hooked nose.
habil *adj* (*dated, geh*) skilful, clever.
habil. *abbr of* **habilitatus Dr. ~** *doctor with postdoctoral university teaching qualification.*
Habilitand(in *f***)** *m* **-en, -en** *person writing postdoctoral thesis to qualify as a university lecturer.*
Habilitation *f* **(a)** (*Festakt*) *ceremony at which sb receives his/her qualification as university lecturer.* **(b)** (*Lehrberechtigung*) postdoctoral lecturing qualification.
Habilitationsschrift *f postdoctoral thesis required for qualification as a university lecturer.*
habilitieren* [1] *vr* to qualify as a university lecturer.
[2] *vt* to confer qualification as a university lecturer on.
habilitiert *adj* qualified as a university lecturer.
Habit[1] [ha'bi:t, ha'bɪt] *nt or m* **-s, -e** (*Ordenskleid*) habit; (*geh: Aufzug*) attire.
Habit[2] ['hæbɪt] *nt or m* **-s, -s** (*Psych*) habit.
Habitat *nt* (*Zool*) habitat.
habituell *adj* (*geh*) habitual.
Habitus *m* **-,** *no pl* (*geh, Med*) disposition.
Habsburg *nt* **-s** Hapsburg, Habsburg.
Habsburger(in *f***)** *m* **-s, -** Hapsburg, Habsburg.
Habsburger *adj attr*, **habsburgisch** *adj* Hapsburg *attr*, Habsburg *attr*, of the Hapsburgs *or* Habsburgs.
Hab-: ~schaft *f*, **~seligkeiten** *pl* possessions, belongings, effects (*form*) *all pl*; **~sucht** *f siehe* **~gier; h~süchtig** *adj siehe* **h~gierig.**
Habt|achtstellung *f* (*Mil, fig*) attention ◆ **in ~ stehen** *or* **sein** to stand to *or* be at attention.
hach *interj* oh; (*verächtlich*) huh.
Haché [ha'ʃe:] *nt* **-s, -s** *siehe* **Haschee.**
Hachel *f* **-, -n** (*Aus*) slicer.
hacheln *vti* (*Aus*) to chop, to slice.
Hachse ['haksə] *f* **-, -n** (*dial*) *siehe* **Haxe.**
Hack-: ~bank *f* butcher's chopping board; **~bau** *m* (*Agr*) hoe-farming; **~beil** *nt* chopper, cleaver; **~block** *m siehe* **~klotz; ~braten** *m* meat loaf; **~brett** *nt* **(a)** chopping board; **(b)** (*Mus*) dulcimer.
Hacke[1] *f* **-, -n (a)** (*dial: Ferse, am Strumpf*) heel. **(b)** (*dial, Mil: Absatz*) heel ◆ **die ~n zusammenschlagen** *or* **-klappen** (*Mil*) to click one's heels; **einen im** *or* **am ~n haben** (*N Ger inf*) to be pickled (*inf*); *siehe* **ablaufen.**
Hacke[2] *f* **-, -n (a)** (*Pickel*) pickaxe, pick; (*Garten~*) hoe. **(b)** (*Aus*) hatchet, axe.
Hackebeil *nt siehe* **Hackbeil.**
hacken [1] *vt* **(a)** (*zerkleinern*) to chop; (*im Fleischwolf*) to mince (*Brit*), to grind (*US*).
(b) *Garten, Erdreich* to hoe.
(c) (*mit spitzem Gegenstand*) *Loch* to hack, to chop; (*Vogel*) to peck.
[2] *vi* **(a)** (*mit dem Schnabel*) to peck; (*mit spitzem Gegenstand*) to hack, to chop ◆ **nach jdm/etw ~** to peck at sth/sb.
(b) (*im Garten etc*) to hoe.
(c) (*Comput*) to hack (*in +acc* into).
[3] *vr* (*sich verletzen*) to cut (oneself) ◆ **ich habe mich** *or* **mir in den Finger gehackt** I've cut my finger.
Hacken *m* **-s, -** *siehe* **Hacke[1] (a).**
Hackentrick *m* (*Sport*) backheel.
Hackepeter *m* **-s, - (a)** (*N Ger*) mince (*Brit*), minced (*Brit*) *or* ground (*US*) meat. **(b)** (*S Ger*) seasoned raw meat loaf.
Hacker(in *f***)** *m* **-s, -** (*Comput*) hacker.
Hack-: ~fleisch *nt* mince (*Brit*), minced (*Brit*) *or* ground (*US*) meat; **jdn zu** *or* **aus jdm ~fleisch machen** (*sl*) to make mincemeat of sb (*inf*); (*verprügeln*) to beat sb up; **~frucht** *f* root crop; **~klotz** *m* chopping block; **~ordnung** *f* (*lit, fig*) pecking order.
Häcksel *nt or m* **-s,** *no pl* chaff.
Häckselmaschine *f* chaffcutter.
Hack-: ~steak *nt* hamburger; **~stock** *m* (*Aus*) *siehe* **~klotz.**
Hader *m* **-s,** *no pl* (*geh*) (*Zwist*) discord; (*Unzufriedenheit*) discontentment ◆ **in ~ mit sich und der Welt leben** to be at odds with oneself and the world.
Haderer *m* **-s, -** (*geh: unzufriedener Mensch*) grumbler.
Haderlump *m* (*Aus, S Ger*) good-for-nothing.
Hadern *pl* rags *pl* (*for making paper*).
hadern *vi* (*dated, geh*) (*streiten*) to quarrel, to wrangle (*mit* with); (*unzufrieden sein*) to be at odds (*mit* with) ◆ **hadere nicht mit deinem Schicksal** you must accept your fate.
Hadernpapier *nt* rag paper.
Hades *m* **-,** *no pl* (*Myth*) Hades.
Hadrian [(*S Ger, Aus*) 'ha:dria:n] *m* **-s** Hadrian.
Hadschi *m* **-s, -s** hajji.
Hafen[1] *m* **-s, ¨ (a)** harbour (*Brit*), harbor (*US*); (*Handels~, für große Schiffe*) port; (*Jacht~*) marina; (*~anlagen*) docks *pl* ◆ **in den ~ einlaufen** to put into harbour/port. **(b)** (*fig*) haven ◆ **im ~ der Ehe landen** to get married; **in den ~ der Ehe einlaufen** to enter the state of matrimony.
Hafen[2] *m* **-s, ¨** *or* **-** (*dial*) **(a)** (*Kochtopf*) pot, pan; (*Schüssel*) dish, bowl; (*Krug*) jug. **(b)** (*Nachttopf*) chamber-pot.
Häfen *m* **-s, -** (*Aus*) **(a)** (sauce)pan. **(b)** (*inf: Gefängnis*) jug (*inf*), clink (*inf*).
Hafen- *in cpds* harbour (*Brit*), harbor (*US*); port; **~amt** *nt* harbour/port authority; **~anlagen** *pl* docks *pl*; **~arbeiter** *m* dockworker, docker; **~arzt** *m* port doctor; **~behörden** *pl* harbour/port authorities *pl*; **~blockade** *f* blockade of a harbour/port.
Häfenbruder *m* (*Aus inf*) jailbird (*inf*).
Hafen-: ~einfahrt *f* harbour entrance; **die ~einfahrt von Dover** the entrance to Dover Harbour; **~gebühr** *f usu pl* harbour/port dues *pl*; **~kneipe** *f* (*inf*) dockland pub (*Brit*) *or* bar; **~meister** *m* harbourmaster; **~polizei** *f* port *or* dock police; **~rundfahrt** *f* (boat-)trip round the harbour; **~stadt** *f* port; (*am Meer auch*) seaport; **~viertel** *nt* dock area.
Hafer *m* **-s, -** oats *pl* ◆ **ihn sticht der ~** (*inf*) he's feeling his oats (*inf*).
Hafer-: ~brei *m* porridge; **~flocken** *pl* rolled oats *pl*; **~grütze** *f* porridge; **~korn** *nt* (oat) grain.
Haferlschuh *m type of brogue.*
Hafer-: ~mehl *nt* oatmeal; **~sack** *m* fodder bag; **~schleim** *m* gruel.
Haff *nt* **-(e)s, -s** *or* **-e** lagoon.
Haflinger *m* **-s, -** Haflinger (horse).
Hafner, Häfner *m* **-s, -** (*S Ger*) (*Töpfer*) potter; (*Ofensetzer*) stove-fitter.
Hafnerei *f* (*S Ger*) (*Töpferei*) pottery; (*Ofensetzerbetrieb*) stove-fitter's works *sing or pl.*
Hafnium *nt, no pl* (*abbr* **Hf**) hafnium.
Haft *f* **-,** *no pl* (*vor dem Prozeß*) custody; (*~strafe*) imprisonment; (*~zeit*) prison sentence, term of imprisonment; (*politisch*) detention ◆ **sich in ~ befinden** to be in custody/prison/detention; **eine schwere/leichte ~ verhängen** to impose a long/short term of imprisonment; **jdn aus der ~ entlassen** to release sb from custody/prison/detention; **eine ~ absitzen** (*inf*) to do time (*inf*); **in ~ sitzen** to be held in custody/prison/detention; **in ~ nehmen** to take into custody, to detain.
-haft *adj suf* **(a)** (*-artig*) -like; -ish; -ly ◆ **kind~** childlike; **jungen~** boyish; **frauen~** womanly; **riesen~** gigantic. **(b)** (*auf Eigenschaft bezüglich*) -ly; -ive ◆ **leb~** lively; **schwatz~** talkative. **(c)** (*in Verbableitungen*) -ing ◆ **wohn~** re-

siding, resident. **(d)** *(Möglichkeit bezeichnend)* -ible, -able ◆ **glaub~** credible, believable.

Haft-: ~anstalt *f* detention centre; **~ausschließungsgrund** *m* grounds *pl* for not imposing a prison sentence; **~aussetzung** *f* suspended prison sentence; *(Unterbrechung)* parole; **h~bar** *adj (für jdn)* legally responsible; *(für etw)* (legally) liable; **~barkeit** *f siehe adj* (legal) responsibility; (legal) liability; **~befehl** *m* warrant; **einen ~befehl gegen jdn ausstellen** to issue a warrant for sb's arrest; **~beschwerde** *f* appeal against a remand in custody; **~dauer** *f* term of imprisonment.

Haftel *nt* **-s, -** *(Aus)* hook and eye *sing*.

Haftelmacher *m (Aus)* **aufpassen wie ein ~** to watch like a hawk.

haften[1] *vi (Jur)* **für jdn ~** to be (legally) responsible for sb; **für etw ~** to be (legally) liable for sth; **(jdm) für jdn/etw ~** *(verantwortlich sein)* to be responsible (to sb) for sb/sth; **die Versicherung hat für den Schaden nicht gehaftet** the insurance company did not accept liability (for the damage); **für Garderobe kann nicht gehaftet werden** the management can accept no responsibility for articles deposited, all articles are left at owner's risk.

haften[2] *vi* **(a)** *(kleben)* to stick *(an +dat* to); *(Klebstoff auch, Reifen, Phys)* to adhere; *(sich festsetzen: Rauch, Schmutz, Geruch)* to cling *(an +dat* to) ◆ **an jdm ~** *(fig: Makel etc)* to hang over sb, to stick to sb.
(b) *(Eindruck, Erinnerung)* to stick (in one's mind); *(Blick)* to become fixed ◆ **an etw** *(dat)* **~** *(hängen)* to be fixed on sth; **bei den Schülern haftet nichts** nothing sinks in with these pupils; **~de Eindrücke** lasting impressions.

⚠ **haftenbleiben** *vi sep irreg aux sein* to stick *(an or auf +dat* to); *(sich festsetzen: Rauch, Schmutz, Geruch)* to cling; *(Klebstoff auch, Phys)* to adhere; *(Eindruck, Gelerntes)* to stick.

Haft-: ~entlassung *f* release from custody/prison/detention; **~entschädigung** *f* compensation for wrongful imprisonment; **~etikett** *nt* adhesive label; **h~fähig** *adj* **(a)** *Material* adhesive; *Reifen* with good road-holding; **auf etw** *(dat)* **h~fähig sein** to stick to sth; **(b)** *(Jur)* fit to be kept in prison; **~fähigkeit** *f* **(a)** *(von Material)* adhesiveness, adhesive strength; *(von Reifen)* road-holding; **(b)** *(Jur)* fitness to be kept in prison; **~grund** *m* **(a)** *(Jur)* grounds *pl* for detaining sb (in custody); **(b)** *(Tech)* base.

Häftling *m* prisoner; *(politisch auch)* detainee.

Haft-: ~notiz *f* self-stick note; **~organ** *nt* suction pad; **~pflicht** *f* **(a)** *(Schadenersatzpflicht)* (legal) liability; *(für Personen)* (legal) responsibility; **die ~pflicht der Versicherung erstreckt sich nicht auf Glas und Silber** the insurance does not cover glass and silver; **(b)** *(inf: ~pflichtversicherung)* personal *or* public *(US)* liability insurance; *(für Auto)* ≃ third party insurance; **ich bin in keiner ~pflicht** I don't have any personal *etc* liability insurance; **h~pflichtig** *adj* liable; **h~pflichtversichert** *adj* **h~pflichtversichert sein** to have personal liability insurance; *(Autofahrer)* ≃ to have third-party insurance; **~pflichtversicherung** *f* personal *or* public *(US)* liability insurance *no indef art*; *(von Autofahrer)* ≃ third-party insurance; **~prüfung** *f* review of remand in custody; **~psychose** *f* prison psychosis *no indef art*; **~pulver** *nt (für Gebiß)* denture fixative; **~reibung** *f (Phys)* static friction; **~richter** *m* magistrate; **~schalen** *pl* contact lenses *pl*; **~strafe** *f* prison sentence; **h~unfähig** *adj (Jur)* unfit to be kept in prison.

Haftung *f* **(a)** *(Jur)* (legal) liability; *(für Personen)* (legal) responsibility ◆ **für Ihre Garderobe übernehmen wir keine ~** articles are left at owner's risk, the management accepts no responsibility for articles deposited. **(b)** *(Tech, Phys, von Reifen)* adhesion.

Haftungs- *(Jur)*: **~beschränkung** *f* limitation of liability; **~klage** *f* action to establish liability.

Haft-: ~urlaub *m* parole; **~verkürzung** *f* shortened sentence; **~verschonung** *f* exemption from imprisonment; **~zeit** *f* prison sentence.

Hag *m* **-(e)s, -e** *(poet, old) (Hain)* grove; *(Hecke)* hedge.

Hage-: ~buche *f siehe* **Hainbuche**; **~butte** *f* **-, -n** rose hip; *(inf: Heckenrose)* dogrose; **~buttentee** *m* rose-hip tea; **~dorn** *m* hawthorn.

Hagel *m* **-s,** *no pl* **(a)** hail; *(~schauer)* hailstorm. **(b)** *(große Menge) (von Steinen, Geschossen)* hail; *(von Vorwürfen, Drohungen, Anschuldigungen)* stream; *(von Schimpfworten)* stream, torrent.

Hagelkorn *nt* hailstone.

hageln [1] *vi impers* **es hagelt** it's hailing.
[2] *vi* **etw hagelt auf jdn/etw** *(Schläge, Geschosse, Steine)* sth rains down on sb/sth; *(Vorwürfe, Schimpfworte)* sb is showered with sth.
[3] *vt impers (lit)* to hail (down) ◆ **es hagelte etw** *(fig)* sth rained down; *Vorwürfe, Schimpfworte* there was a shower of sth.

Hagel-: ~schaden *m* damage caused by hail; **~schauer** *m* (short) hailstorm; **~schlag** *m* **(a)** *(Met)* hail; *(~schauer)* hailstorm; **(b)** *(Cook)* sugar crystals *pl*; **~schloße** *f (dial) siehe* **~korn**; **~sturm** *m* hailstorm; **~wetter** *nt (lit)* hailstorm.

hager *adj* gaunt, thin; *Mensch auch* lean.

Hagestolz *m* **-es, -e** *(old, hum)* confirmed bachelor.

⚠ **Hagio-: ~graph** *m (form)* hagiographer; **~graphen** *pl (Bibl)* Hagiographa; **~graphie** *f (form)* hagiography.

haha, hahaha *interj* haha, ha, ha, ha.

Häher *m* **-s, -** jay.

Hahn *m* **-(e)s, ¨e** **(a)** *(männlicher Vogel)* cock; *(männliches Haushuhn auch)* rooster; *(jünger)* cockerel; *(Wetter~)* weathercock ◆ **der gallische ~** the French cockerel; **~ im Korb sein** *(Mann unter Frauen)* to be cock of the walk; **danach kräht kein ~ mehr** *(inf)* no one cares two hoots about that any more *(inf)*; **jdm den (roten) ~ aufs Dach setzen** to set sb's house on fire.
(b) *pl auch* **-en** *(Tech)* tap, faucet *(US)*; *(Zapf~ auch)* spigot; *(Schwimmer~)* ballcock.
(c) *(Abzug)* trigger.

Hähnchen *nt* chicken; *(junger Hahn)* cockerel.

Hahnen-: ~balken *m (Build)* ridge beam; **~feder** *f* cock's plume; **~fuß** *m (Bot)* buttercup; **~fußgewächs** *nt* buttercup; **~kamm** *m (auch Frisur)* cockscomb; **~kampf** *m* **(a)** cockfight; *(Sport)* cockfighting; **(b)** *(Spiel) children's hopping game*; **~schrei** *m* cockcrow; **beim ersten ~schrei** *(fig)* at cockcrow; **~sporn** *m* cock's spur; **~tritt(muster** *nt***)** *m* dogtooth check.

Hahnium *nt, no pl (abbr* **Ha***)* hahnium.

Hahnrei *m* **-s, -e** *(dated)* cuckold ◆ **jdn zum ~ machen** to cuckold sb.

Hai *m* **-(e)s, -e, Haifisch** *m (lit, fig)* shark.

Haifischflossensuppe *f* shark-fin soup.

Hain *m* **-(e)s, -e** *(poet, geh)* grove.

Hainbuche *f* hornbeam.

Haiti [ha'i:ti] *nt* **-s** Haiti.

Haitianer(in *f***)** [hai'tia:nɐ, -ərɪn], **Haitier(in** *f***)** [ha'i:tiɐ, -iərɪn] *m* **-s, -** Haitian.

haitianisch [hai'ti-], **haitisch** *adj* Haitian.

Häkchen *nt* **(a)** *(Sew)* (small) hook ◆ **was ein ~ werden will, krümmt sich beizeiten** *(Prov)* there's nothing like starting young. **(b)** *(Zeichen)* tick, check *(US)*; *(auf Buchstaben)* diacritic *(spec)*, accent. **(c)** *(Instrument)* dental probe.

Häkel|arbeit *f* crochet (work) *no indef art*; *(das Häkeln auch)* crocheting; *(Gegenstand)* piece of crochet (work).

Häkelei *f* crocheting, crochet work.

Häkelgarn *nt* crochet thread.

hakeln [1] *vi (Fingerhakeln machen)* to finger-wrestle.
[2] *vti* **(a)** *(Ftbl, Hockey etc) siehe* **haken 3.** **(b)** *(Rugby)* to heel. **(c)** *(beim Ringen) Gegner* to get in a foot-lock.

häkeln *vti* to crochet.

Häkelnadel *f* crochet hook.

haken [1] *vi (klemmen)* to stick ◆ **es hakt** *(fig)* there's some delay, there are sticking points; **es hakt (bei jdm)** *(inf: nicht verstehen)* sb is stuck.
[2] *vt* **(a)** *(befestigen)* to hook *(an +acc* to).
(b) *(einhängen, um etw legen)* to hook *(in +acc* in, *um* around).
[3] *vti (Sport)* to trip up.

Haken *m* **-s, -** **(a)** hook; *(aus Holz auch)* peg ◆ **~ und Öse** hook and eye; **mit ~ und Ösen spielen** *(Ftbl inf)* to foul.
(b) *(inf: Schwierigkeit)* snag, catch ◆ **die Sache hat einen ~** there's a snag *or* a catch; **die Sache ist ganz ohne ~ und Ösen** there's no catch; **ein Angebot ohne ~ und Ösen** an offer with no strings attached.
(c) *(plötzlicher Richtungswechsel)* **einen ~ schlagen** to dart sideways; **~ *pl* schlagen** to dart from side to side.
(d) *(Boxen)* hook.
(e) *siehe* **Häkchen (b).**

Haken-: h~förmig *adj* hooked, hook-shaped; **~kreuz** *nt* swastika; **~nase** *f* hooked nose, hooknose.

hakig *adj siehe* **hakenförmig.**

Halali *nt* **-s, -(s)** *(Hunt)* mort.

halb [1] *adj* **(a)** *(Bruchteil)* half; *Lehrauftrag etc* part-time ◆ **ein ~er Kuchen/Meter** *etc* half a cake/metre *etc*; **der ~e Kuchen/Tag** *etc* half the cake/day *etc*; **eine ~e Stunde** half an hour; **alle ~e Stunde** every half hour; **ein ~es Jahr** six months *pl*, half a year; **ein ~es Dutzend** half a dozen; **auf ~er Höhe** at half the normal height; *(zum Gipfel)* halfway up; **auf ~em Wege** *or* **~er Strecke** *(lit)* halfway; *(fig)* halfway through; **jdm auf ~em Weg entgegenkommen** *(fig)* to meet sb halfway; **das ~e Hundert** fifty, half a hundred *(old)*; **zum ~en Preis** (at) half price; **den Apfel nur ~ essen** to eat only half the apple; **Kleid mit ~em Arm** dress with half-length sleeves.
(b) *(Mus)* **eine ~e Note** a minim *(Brit)*, a half-note *(US)*; **ein ~er Ton** a semitone; **~e Pause** minim/half-note rest.
(c) *inv (Uhrzeit)* **~ zehn** half past nine; **fünf Minuten vor/nach ~ zwei** twenty-five (minutes) past one/to two; **es schlägt ~** it's striking the half hour; **um drei/fünf Minuten nach ~** at three minutes past the half hour/at twenty-five to.
(d) *inv, no art (bei geographischen Namen)* **~ Deutschland/London** half of Germany/London.
(e) *(teilweise, stückhaft) Maßnahmen* half; *Reformen* partial; *(vermindert) Tempo* half; *Lächeln* slight; *Licht* poor ◆ **~e Arbeit leisten** to do a bad job; **die ~e Freude** half the pleasure; **die ~e Wahrheit** half of *or* part of the truth; **nichts H~es und nichts Ganzes** neither one thing nor the other; **mit ~em Ohr** with half an ear; **ein ~er Mensch/eine ~e Frau sein, sich nur wie ein ~er Mensch fühlen** not to feel a complete person/woman; *(energielos)* to feel half dead; **eine ~e Sache machen** not to do it properly; **keine ~en Sachen machen** not to do things by halves.
(f) *(inf) (große Anzahl, großer Teil)* **die ~e Stadt/Welt/Arbeit** half the town/world/work; **sie ist schon eine ~e Schottin** she is already half Scottish; **ein ~er Elektriker/Mechaniker** something of an electrician/mechanic; **(noch) ein ~es Kind sein** to be hardly *or* scarcely more than a child.
[2] *adv* **(a)** *(zur Hälfte)* half ◆ **~ rechts/links abzweigen** *(Straße, Fahrer)* to fork (off) to the right/left, to turn half right/left; **die Zeit ist ~ vorbei** half the time has already gone.
(b) *(nicht ganz, teilweise)* half ◆ **~ so gut** half as good; **etw nur ~ verstehen** to only half understand something; **ich hörte nur ~ zu** I was only half listening; **das ist ~ so schlimm** it's not as bad as all that; *(Zukünftiges)* that won't be too bad; **er weiß alles nur ~** he only knows about things superficially; **etw nur ~ machen** to only half-do sth *(inf)*.

(c) (*fast vollständig*) almost, nearly; *blind, roh* half ◆ **ich war schon ~ fertig** I was almost *or* nearly finished; **wir haben uns ~ totgelacht** we almost died laughing; **ich hätte mich ~ totärgern können** I could have kicked myself (*inf*).
(d) **~ lachend, ~ weinend** half laughing, half crying; **~ Mensch, ~ Pferd** half *or* part man, half *or* part horse; **Wein oder Sprudel? — ~ und ~** wine or mineral water? — half and half.
(e) **mit jdm ~e-~e machen** (*inf*) to go halves with sb; **~ und ~** (*inf: beinahe*) more or less; **gefällt es dir? — ~ und ~** do you like it? — sort of (*inf*) *or* so-so.

halb- *pref* (a) half ◆ **~voll/~leer** half-full/-empty. (b) (*Tech*) semi-.

Halb-: **~affe** *m* prosimian; **h~amtlich** *adj* semi-official; **~automatisch** *adj* semi-automatic; **~band** *m* half-binding; **~bildung** *f* smattering of knowledge *or* (*Ausbildung*) education; **h~bitter** *adj Schokolade* semi-sweet; **~blut** *nt* **-(e)s,** *no pl* (a) (*Mensch*) half-caste; (b) (*Tier*) crossbreed; **~blüter** *m* **-s, -** crossbreed; **~blütige(r)** *mf decl as adj* half-caste; **~bruder** *m* half-brother; **~deckung** *f* (*Fin*) partial cover; **h~dunkel** *adj* half-dark, dim; **~dunkel** *nt* semi-darkness, half-dark; (*Dämmerung*) dusk, twilight.

Halbe *f decl as adj* (*esp S Ger*) *siehe* **Halbe(r)**.

Halb|edelstein *m* semi-precious stone.

Halbe(r) *m decl as adj* half a litre (of beer) ◆ **trinken Sie noch einen ~n!** ≃ have another pint!

halber[1] *prep +gen* (*nachgestellt*) (*dated, geh*) (*wegen*) on account of; (*um ...willen*) for the sake of.

halber[2] *adj, adv* (*S Ger*) *siehe* **halb 1 (c), 2 (b, c)**.

-halber *adv suf* (*wegen*) on account of; (*um ...willen*) for the sake of ◆ **gesundheits~** for reasons of health, for medical reasons; **vorsichts~** to be on the safe side, as a precaution; **sicherheits~** (*aus Sicherheitsgründen*) for safety reasons; (*um sicher zu sein*) to be on the safe side.

Halb-: **h~erwachsen** *adj attr* half grown (up); **~erzeugnis** *nt* (*Comm*) semi-finished product.

Halbe(s) *nt decl as adj siehe* **Halbe(r)**.

Halb-: **~fabrikat** *nt siehe* **~erzeugnis**; ⚠**h~fertig** *adj attr* half-finished; (*fig*) immature; **h~fest** *adj attr Zustand, Materie* semi-solid; *Gelee* half-set; **h~fett** [1] *adj* (a) (*Typ*) secondary bold; (b) *Lebensmittel* medium-fat; [2] *adv* in secondary bold; **~finale** *nt* semi-final; **~fingerhandschuh** *m* fingerless glove; ⚠**h~gar** *adj attr* half-cooked, half-done; **h~gebildet** *adj attr* half-educated; ⚠**~geschoß** *nt* (*Archit*) mezzanine floor; **~geschwister** *pl* half brothers and sisters *pl*; **~gott** *m* (*Myth, fig*) demigod; **~götter in Weiß** (*iro*) doctors.

Halbheit *f* (*pej*) half-measure ◆ **er ist nicht für ~en** he is not one for half-measures, he doesn't do things by halves; **mach keine ~en** (*inf*) don't do things by halves.

Halb-: **h~herzig** *adj* half-hearted; **~herzigkeit** *f* half-heartedness; **h~hoch** *adj Baum* half-grown; **den Ball h~hoch abspielen** to pass the ball at shoulder height; **h~hoch fliegen** to fly at half (its/one's *etc* normal) height.

halbieren* *vt* to halve, to divide in half *or* two; (*Geometrie*) to bisect; (*in zwei schneiden*) to cut in half ◆ **eine Zahl ~** to divide a number by two.

Halbierung *f* halving, dividing in half *or* two; (*Geometrie*) bisection.

Halb-: **~insel** *f* peninsula; **~invalide** *m* semi-invalid.

Halbjahr *nt* half-year (*auch Comm*), six months ◆ **im ersten/zweiten ~** in the first/last six months of the year.

Halbjahres-: **~bericht** *m* half-yearly report; **~bilanz** *f* half-yearly figures *pl*; **~kurs** *m* six-month course; **~zeugnis** *nt* (*Sch*) half-yearly report.

Halb-: **h~jährig** *adj attr Kind* six-month-old; *Lehrgang etc* six-month; *Kündigung* six months; **h~jährlich** [1] *adj* half-yearly (*auch Comm*), six-monthly; **in h~jährlichem Wechsel** changing every six months; [2] *adv* every six months, twice a year, twice yearly; **~jahrsausweis** *m* (*Aus Sch*) half-yearly report; **~jahrskurs** *m siehe* **~jahreskurs**; **~jude** *m* half Jew; **~jude sein** to be half Jewish; **~kanton** *m* sub-canton; **~konsonant** *m* semi-consonant; **~kreis** *m* semicircle; **h~kreisförmig** [1] *adj* semicircular; [2] *adv* in a semicircle; **~kugel** *f* hemisphere; **nördliche/südliche ~kugel** northern/southern hemisphere; **h~kugelförmig** *adj* hemispherical; **h~lang** *adj Kleid, Rock* mid-calf length; *Haar* chin-length; **(nun) mach mal h~lang!** (*inf*) now wait a minute!; **h~laut** [1] *adj* low; [2] *adv* in a low voice, in an undertone; **~leder** *nt* (*Verfahren*) half-binding; **in ~leder binden** to bind in half-leather, to half-bind; **~lederband** *m* (*Buch*) half-bound volume; (*Ausgabe*) half-bound edition; **h~leinen** *adj attr Stoff* made of a fifty per cent linen mixture; *Bucheinband* half-cloth; **~leinen** *nt* (*Stoff*) fifty per cent linen material; (*Bucheinband*) half-cloth; **~leinenband** *m* (*Buch*) volume bound in half-cloth; (*Ausgabe*) edition bound in half-cloth; **~leiter** *m* (*Phys*) semiconductor; **h~linke(r, s)** *adj attr* (*Sport*) inside left; **die h~linke Abzweigung/Straße** the left fork; **~linke(r)** *m decl as adj*, **~links** *m* **-, -** (*Sport*) inside left; ⚠**h~links** *adv* (*Sport*) *spielen* (at) inside left; (*im Theater*) *sitzen* left of centre; **h~links abbiegen** to fork left; **die Straße h~links** the left fork; **das Auto kam von h~links** the car approached sharp left; **h~mast** *adv* (a) at half-mast; **(eine Flagge) h~mast hissen** to hoist a flag to half-mast; **h~mast flaggen** to fly a flag/flags at half-mast; **auf h~mast stehen** to fly *or* be at half-mast; (b) (*hum: verrutschte Socken etc*) at half-mast; **h~matt** *adj* (*Phot*) semimatt; **~messer** *m siehe* **Radius**; **~metall** *nt* semi-metal; **~monatsschrift** *f* fortnightly periodical; **~mond** *m* (*Astron*) half-moon; (*Symbol*) crescent; (*an Fingernägeln*) half-moon; **bei ~mond** when there is a half-moon; **wir haben ~mond** there's a half-moon; **h~mondförmig** *adj* crescent-shaped; ⚠**h~nackt** *adj attr* half-naked; *Arm* half-covered; ⚠**h~offen** *adj attr* half-open; *Gefängnis* open; **h~part** *adv*: **h~part machen** (*bei einer Unternehmung*) to go halves; (*bei Gewinn*) to split it fifty-fifty; **~pension** *f* half-board; **in ~pension wohnen** to have half-board; **~produkt** *nt siehe* **~erzeugnis**; **h~rechte(r, s)** *adj* (*Sport*) inside right; **die h~rechte Abzweigung/Straße** the right fork; **~rechte(r)** *m decl as adj*, **~rechts** *m* **-, -** (*Sport*) inside right; ⚠**h~rechts** *adv* (*Sport*) *spielen* (at) inside right; (*im Theater*) *sitzen* right of centre; **h~rechts abbiegen** to fork right; **die Straße h~rechts** the right fork; **das Auto kam von h~rechts** the car approached sharp right; **h~reif** *adj attr* half-ripe; **~relief** *nt* half-relief, mezzo relievo; **h~rund** *adj attr Tisch etc* semicircular; *Ecke* half-rounded; **~rund** *nt* semicircle, half circle; **im ~rund** in a semicircle; **~schatten** *m* half shadow; (*Astron*) penumbra; **~schlaf** *m* light sleep, doze; **im ~schlaf sein** to be half asleep; **~schritt-Taste** *f* condensed key, half-space key; **~schuh** *m* shoe; **~schwergewicht** *nt* (a) *no pl* (*Klasse*) light-heavyweight division; **ein Boxkampf im ~schwergewicht** a light-heavyweight contest; (b) (*Boxer*) light-heavyweight; **~schwergewichtler** *m* light-heavyweight; **~schwester** *f* half-sister; **~seide** *f* fifty per cent silk mixture; **h~seiden** *adj* (*lit*) fifty per cent silk; (*fig*) *Dame* fast; *Aussehen* flashy; (*schwul*) gay; **h~seidenes Milieu, h~seidene Kreise** the demimonde; **h~seitig** *adj Anzeige etc* half-page; (*Med*) *Kopfschmerzen* in one side of one's head; **h~seitige Lähmung** hemiplegia; **h~seitig gelähmt** hemiplegic; **h~staatlich** *adj attr* partly state-run *or* state-controlled; **h~stark** *adj attr Sprache, Manieren, Jugendliche* rowdy; **~starke(r)** *m decl as adj* young hooligan *or* rowdy, ≃ teddy boy (*Brit*); **h~stündig** *adj attr* half-hour *attr*, lasting half an hour; **h~stündlich** [1] *adj* half-hourly; [2] *adv* every half an hour, half-hourly; **~stürmer** *m* (*Ftbl*) half-back; **h~tags** *adv* in the mornings/afternoons; (*in bezug auf Angestellte auch*) part-time.

Halbtags-: **~arbeit** *f* (a) (*Arbeitsverhältnis*) half-day *or* morning/afternoon job; (*von Angestellten auch*) part-time job; (b) (*Arbeitszeit*) half-time/part-time working; **~beschäftigung** *f* half-day *or* part-time *or* morning/afternoon job; **~kraft** *f* worker employed for half-days *or* mornings/afternoons only; **~schule** *f* half-day school.

Halb-: **~ton** *m* (*Mus*) semitone; (*Art, Phot*) half-tone; **~tonschritt** *m* semitone; ⚠**h~tot** *adj attr* (*lit*) half dead; **~totale** *f* (*Film*) medium shot; **~trauer** *f* half-mourning; **h~trocken** *adj Wein* medium-dry; ⚠**h~verdaut** *adj attr* (*lit, fig*) half-digested; **~vers** *m* half-line, hemistich; **~vokal** *m* semivowel; ⚠**h~voll** *adj attr* half-filled; *Behälter auch* half-full; ⚠**h~wach** *adj attr* half awake; **in h~wachem Zustand** half awake; **~wahrheit** *f* half-truth; **~waise** *f person who has lost one parent*; **er/sie ist ~waise** he/she has lost one of his/her parents; **h~wegs** *adv* (a) partly; *gut, adäquat* reasonably; *annehmbar* halfway; **wenn es dir wieder h~wegs besser geht** when you're feeling a bit better; **wenn Sie h~wegs eine Vorstellung haben, ...** if you have the least idea; (b) (*dated: auf halber Strecke*) halfway; **~welt** *f* demimonde; **~weltdame** *f* demimondaine; **~weltergewicht** *nt* (*Klasse*) light-welterweight *no def art*; (*Sportler*) light-welterweight; **~wert(s)zeit** *f* (*Phys*) half-life; **h~wild** *adj attr Mensch* uncivilized; *Tier* half wild; **wie die ~wilden** (*inf*) like (a bunch of) savages; **~wissen** *nt* (*pej*) superficial knowledge; **h~wöchentlich** [1] *adj* twice-weekly; [2] *adv* twice weekly; **h~wüchsig** *adj* adolescent; **~wüchsige(r)** *mf decl as adj* adolescent; **~zeile** *f* (*Poet*) half line; **~zeit** *f* (*Sport*) (*Hälfte*) half; (*Pause*) half-time; **~zeitpfiff** *m* half-time whistle; **h~zivilisiert** *adj attr* half-civilized.

Halde *f* **-, -n** (a) (*Abfall~*) mound, heap; (*Min*) (*Abbau~*) slagheap ◆ **etw auf ~ legen** *Ware, Vorräte* to stockpile sth; *Pläne etc* to shelve sth. (b) (*geh: Abhang*) slope.

half *pret of* **helfen**.

Half-Back ['ha:fbɛk] *m* **-s, -s** (*Sw*) half-back.

Hälfte *f* **-, -n** (a) half ◆ **die ~ der Kinder war abwesend** half the children were absent; **die ~ einer Sache** (*gen*) *or* **von etw** half (of) sth; **eine/die ~ des Apfels** half of/half (of) the apple; **wir haben schon die ~ (des Vorrats) verbraucht** we have already used up half (the stocks); **die ~ ist gelogen** half of it is lies; **Rentner zahlen die ~** pensioners pay half price; **um die ~ mehr/zuviel** half as much again/too much by half; **um die ~ steigen** to increase by half *or* fifty per cent; **um die ~ kleiner/größer** half as small *or* big/half as big again; **es ist zur ~ fertig/voll** it is half finished/full; **die Beiträge werden je zur ~ vom Arbeitgeber und Arbeitnehmer bezahlt** the employer and employee each pay half (of) the contribution; **das werde ich zur ~ bezahlen** I will pay half (of it); **meine bessere ~** (*hum inf*) my better half (*hum inf*).
(b) (*Mitte: einer Fläche*) middle ◆ **auf der ~ des Weges** halfway.

hälften *vt* (*rare*) *siehe* **halbieren**.

Halfter[1] *m or nt* **-s, -** (*für Tiere*) halter.

Halfter[2] *f* **-, -n** *or nt* **-s, -** (*Pistolen*) holster.

halftern *vt* to halter, to put a halter on.

halkyonisch *adj* (*liter*): **~e Tage** halcyon days.

Hall *m* **-(e)s, -e** (a) reverberation, echo. (b) (*Nachhall*) echo.

Halle *f* **-, -n** hall; (*Hotel~*) lobby, vestibule; (*Werks~, Fabrik~*) shed; (*Sport~*) (sports) hall, gym(nasium); (*Tennis~*) covered tennis court(s); (*Schwimm~*) indoor swimming pool; (*Flugzeug~*) hangar ◆ **in der ~** (*im Gegensatz zu draußen*) inside, indoors; **Fußball in der ~** indoor football; **in der ~ des Postamts** in the post office; **in diesen heiligen ~n** (*iro*) in these august surroundings (*iro*).

halleluja(h) *interj* halleluja(h).

Halleluja(h) *nt* **-s, -s** (*Rel, Mus*) halleluja(h) ◆ **das ~ aus Händels „Messias"** the Hallelujah Chorus from Handel's "Messiah".

hallen *vi* to reverberate, to echo (*auch fig*), to resound.

Hallen- *in cpds* (*Sport*) indoor; **~bad** *nt* indoor swimming pool; **~fußball** *m* indoor football; **~kirche** *f* hall church; **~schwimmbad** *nt* indoor swimming pool; **~sport** *m* indoor sport(s); **~tennis** *nt* indoor tennis.

⚠: Informationen zur Rechtschreibreform im Anhang

Halleysch *adj*: **der ~e Komet** Halley's Comet.

Hallig *f* **-, -en** *a small island off Schleswig-Holstein.*

Hallimasch *m* **-(e)s, -e** *(Bot)* honey agaric.

hallo *interj* **(a)** ['halo] hello; *(zur Begrüßung auch)* hi *(inf)*. **(b)** [ha'lo:] *(überrascht)* hello.

Hallo *nt* **-s, -s** cheer *usu pl*; *(Gruß)* hello.

Hallodri *m* **-s, -(s)** *(Aus, S Ger inf)* rogue.

Hallstattzeit *f (Archeol)* Hallstatt period.

Halluzination *f* hallucination ◆ **ich leide wohl an ~en** *(fig)* I must be seeing things.

halluzinatorisch *adj* hallucinatory.

halluzinieren* *vi* to hallucinate.

halluzinogen *adj (Med)* hallucinogenic.

Halluzinogen *nt* **-s, -e** *(Med)* hallucinogen.

Halm *m* **-(e)s, -e** stalk, stem; *(Gras~)* blade of grass; *(Stroh~, zum Trinken)* straw ◆ **Getreide auf dem ~** standing grain.

Halma *nt* **-s,** *no pl* halma, Chinese chequers *sing.*

Hälmchen *nt dim of* **Halm.**

Halo *m* **-(s), -s** *or* **-nen** [-'lo:nən] *(Astron, Met)* halo; *(TV)* shadow.

halogen *adj* halogenous.

Halogen *nt* **-s, -e** halogen.

Halogen-: **~birne** *f* halogen bulb; **~(glüh)lampe** *f* halogen lamp; **~licht** *nt* halogen light; **~scheinwerfer** *m* halogen headlamp.

Hals¹ *m* **-es, ⸚e (a)** *(von außen gesehen)* neck ◆ **einen langen ~ machen, den ~ recken** to crane one's neck; **sich** *(dat)* **nach jdm/etw den ~ verrenken** *(inf)* to crane one's neck to see sb/sth; **jdm um den ~ fallen** to fling one's arms around sb's neck; **sich jdm an den ~ werfen** *(fig inf)* to throw oneself at sb; **sich** *(dat)* **den ~ brechen** *(inf)* to break one's neck; **etw kostet jdn** *or* **jdm** *or* **bricht jdm den ~** *(inf)* sth will cost sb his/her neck; **sich um den** *or* **seinen ~ reden** *(inf)* to put one's head in the noose; **~ über Kopf abreisen/den Koffer packen** to leave/pack one's case in a rush *or* hurry; **ihm steht das Wasser bis zum ~** *(fig)* he is up to his neck in it *(inf)*; **bis über den ~** *(fig inf)* up to one's ears; **jdn auf dem** *or* **am ~ haben** *(inf)* to be lumbered *or* saddled with sb *(inf)*; **jdm/sich etw auf den ~ laden** *(inf)* to lumber *or* saddle sb/oneself with sth *(inf)*; **jdn jdm auf den ~ schicken** *or* **hetzen** *(inf)* to put sb onto sb; **jdm mit etw vom ~(e) bleiben** *(inf)* not to bother sb with sth *(inf)*; **sich/jdm jdn/etw vom ~e schaffen** *(inf)* to get sb/sth off one's/sb's back *(inf)*; **sich** *(dat)* **die Pest an den ~ ärgern (können)** to be mad *or* furious with oneself *(mit* over).
(b) *(Kehle, Rachen)* throat ◆ **sie hat es am** *or* **im ~** *(inf)* she has a sore throat; **aus vollem ~(e)** at the top of one's voice; **aus vollem ~(e) lachen** to roar with laughter; **es hängt** *or* **wächst mir zum ~ heraus** *(inf)* I'm sick and tired of it, I've had it up to here *(inf)*; **sie hat es in den falschen** *or* **verkehrten ~ bekommen** *(inf) (sich verschlucken)* it went down the wrong way; *(falsch verstehen)* she took it wrongly; **etw bleibt jdm im ~ stecken** *(lit, fig)* sth sticks in sb's throat; **er kann den ~ nicht voll (genug) kriegen** *(fig inf)* he is never satisfied.
(c) *(Flaschen~, Geigen~, Säulen~)* neck; *(Noten~)* stem; *siehe* **brechen.**
(d) *(von Knochen)* neck; *(Gebärmutter~)* cervix, neck of the womb.

Hals² *m* **-es, -en** *(Naut)* tack.

Hals-: **~abschneider** *m* **-s, -** *(pej inf)* shark *(inf)*; **h~abschneiderisch** *adj (pej inf) Preise, Maßnahme* extortionate, exorbitant; *Mensch* cutthroat *(inf)*; **~ansatz** *m* base of the neck; **~ausschnitt** *m* neck(line); **~band** *nt (Hunde~)* collar; *(Schmuck)* necklace; *(eng anliegend)* choker; **h~brecherisch** *adj* dangerous, risky; *Tempo* breakneck; *Fahrt* hair-raising; *Weg* treacherous; **~bund** *m,* **~bündchen** *nt* neckband.

Hälschen ['hɛlsçən] *nt dim of* **Hals¹.**

halsen¹ *vt (rare)* to embrace.

halsen² *vi (Naut)* to wear.

Hals|entzündung *f* sore throat.

-halsig *adj suf* -necked.

Hals-: **~kette** *f (Schmuck)* necklace; *(für Hund)* chain; **~krause** *f (Fashion, Zool)* ruff; **~länge** *f* neck; **(um) eine ~länge/zwei ~längen** by a neck/half a length; **h~los** *adj* without a neck.

Hals-Nasen-Ohren-: **~-Arzt** *m* ear, nose and throat specialist; **~-Heilkunde** *f* ear, nose and throat medicine; **~-Krankheit** *f* disease of the ear, nose and throat.

Hals-: **~partie** *f* neck/throat area, area *or* region of the neck/throat; **~schlagader** *f* carotid (artery); **~schmerzen** *pl* sore throat *sing*; **~schmuck** *m* necklace; *(Sammelbegriff)* necklaces *pl*; **h~starrig** *adj* obstinate, stubborn; **~starrigkeit** *f* obstinacy, stubbornness; **~stück** *nt (Cook)* neck; **~tuch** *nt* scarf; **~- und Beinbruch** *interj* good luck; **~weh** *nt siehe* **~schmerzen;** **~weite** *f* neck size; **~wickel** *m (Med)* throat compress; **~wirbel** *m* cervical vertebra.

Halt *m* **-(e)s, -e (a)** *(für Füße, Hände, Festigkeit)* hold; *(lit, fig: Stütze)* support; *(fig: innerer ~)* security *no art* ◆ **~/einen besseren ~ haben** *(Ding)* to hold/hold better; **jdm/einer Sache ~ geben** to support sb/sth; **dem Haar ~ geben** to give hold to one's hair; **keinen ~ haben** to have no hold/support; to be insecure; **~ suchen/finden** to look for/find a hold/a support/security; **auf dem Eis den ~ verlieren** to lose one's footing on the ice; **ohne inneren ~** insecure.
(b) *(geh: Anhalten)* stop ◆ **ohne ~** non-stop, without stopping.

halt¹ *interj* stop; *(Mil)* halt.

halt² *adv (dial)* **(a)** *siehe* **eben 2 (d). (b)** *(Aus)* **und so ~** and so on *or* forth.

▼ **haltbar** *adj* **(a)** *(nicht leicht verderblich)* **~ sein** *(Lebensmittel)* to keep (well); **~e Lebensmittel** food which keeps (well); **das ist sechs Monate ~** that will keep for six months; **etw ~ machen** to preserve sth; **~ bis 6.11.** use by 6 Nov; **nur begrenzt/schlecht ~** perishable/highly perishable.
(b) *(widerstandsfähig)* durable; *Stoff, Kleider* hardwearing; *Beziehung, Ehe* long-lasting.
▼ **(c)** *Behauptung, Theorie, Annahme* tenable.
(d) *pred Festung* defensible ◆ **die Stadt ist nicht mehr ~** the town can't be held any longer.
(e) *Position, Rang, Platz* tenable; *Zustand, Lage* tolerable ◆ **diese Position ist nicht mehr ~** this position can't be maintained any longer.
(f) *(Sport) Ball, Wurf* stoppable; *Schuß auch* savable.

haltbargemacht *adj attr* artificially preserved.

Haltbarkeit *f siehe adj (a - c)* **(a)** *(von Lebensmitteln)* **eine längere ~ haben** to keep longer; **Lebensmittel von kurzer ~** perishable food; **die begrenzte ~ von Fleisch** the perishability of meat.
(b) durability; hard-wearingness; long-lastingness.
(c) tenability.

Haltbarkeits-: **~datum** *nt* eat-by date, best-before date; **~dauer** *f length of time for which food may be kept*; **eine kurze/lange ~dauer haben** to be/not to be perishable.

Halte-: **~bogen** *m (Mus)* tie; **~griff** *m* **(a)** grip, handle; *(in Bus)* strap; *(an Badewanne)* handrail; **(b)** *(Sport)* hold; **~gurt** *m* seat *or* safety belt; *(an Kinderwagen)* safety harness.

▼ **halten** *pret* **hielt,** *ptp* **gehalten** [1] *vt* **(a)** *(festhalten, in Position ~)* to hold; *(fig: behalten)* to keep; *(aufhalten, zurückhalten)* to stop ◆ **jdm etw ~** to hold sth for sb; **sich** *(dat)* **den Kopf/Bauch ~** to hold one's head/stomach; **den Schnabel** *or* **Mund ~** *(inf)* to keep one's mouth shut *(inf)*, to hold one's tongue; **jdm den Mantel ~** to hold sb's coat (for him/her); **ich konnte ihn/es gerade noch ~** I just managed to grab hold of him/it; **sie läßt sich nicht ~, sie ist nicht zu ~** *(fig)* there's no holding her; **es hält mich hier nichts mehr** there's nothing to keep me here any more; **es hält dich niemand** nobody's stopping you.
(b) *(in Position bringen)* **einen Fuß ins Wasser ~** to put one's foot into the water; **etw gegen das Licht ~** to hold sth up to the light; **den Arm in die Höhe ~** to hold one's arm up.
(c) *(tragen, stützen) Bild, Regal, Brücke* to hold up.
(d) *(zurückhalten, in sich ~, fassen)* to hold; *Tränen* to hold *or* keep back ◆ **die Wärme/Feuchtigkeit ~** to retain heat/moisture; **dieses Material hält keinen Lack** this material will not take varnish; **er kann den Urin** *or* **das Wasser nicht ~** he can't hold his water, he's incontinent.
(e) *(Sport)* to save.
(f) *(unterhalten, besitzen) Haustier* to keep; *Chauffeur, Lehrer* to employ; *Auto* to run ◆ **sich** *(dat)* **jdn/etw ~** to keep sb/sth; **jdm etw ~** to keep sth for sb; **wir können uns kein Auto ~** we can't afford to run a car.
(g) *(abonniert haben)* **(sich** *dat***) eine Zeitung** *etc* **~** to take a paper *etc.*
(h) *(behandeln)* to treat ◆ **er hält seine Kinder sehr streng** he's very strict with his children.
(i) *(behalten)* to keep; *Besitz auch* to hold on to; *Festung* to hold; *Position* to hold (on to); *Rekord (innehaben)* to hold; *(beibehalten)* to keep up.
(j) *(beibehalten, aufrechterhalten)* to keep up, to maintain; *Disziplin, Temperatur* to maintain; *Kurs* to keep to, to hold ◆ **Ruhe ~** to keep quiet; **die Balance** *or* **das Gleichgewicht ~** to keep one's balance; **den Ton ~** to stay in tune *or* in key; **die These läßt sich nicht länger/ist nicht länger zu ~** this thesis is no longer tenable; **Kontakt ~** to keep in touch, to maintain contact; **(mit jdm) Verbindung ~** to keep in touch (with sb).
(k) *(in einem Zustand, an einem Ort ~)* to keep ◆ **er hält sein Haus immer tadellos** he always keeps his house spotless; **den Abstand gleich ~** to keep the distance the same; **ein Land besetzt ~** to keep a country under occupation.
(l) *(handhaben, verfahren mit)* **es mit etw so/anders ~** to deal with *or* handle sth like this/differently; **wie hältst du's mit der Religion?** what's your attitude towards religion?; **das kannst du ~ wie du willst** that's completely up to you.
(m) *(Neigung haben für)* **es (mehr** *or* **lieber) mit jdm/etw ~** *(Neigung haben für)* to prefer sb/sth; *(einverstanden sein)* to agree with sb/sth; **er hält es mit der Bequemlichkeit/Sauberkeit** he likes things to be comfortable/clean.
(n) *(gestalten)* to do; *Aufsatz* to write; *Zimmer auch* to decorate ◆ **ein in Braun gehaltener Raum** a room decorated in brown; **das Kleid ist in dunklen Tönen gehalten** the dress is in dark colours; **das Mobiliar ist in einem hellen Holz gehalten** the furniture is made of a light wood; **etw einfach ~** to keep sth simple.
(o) *(veranstalten, abhalten)* to give; *Rede auch* to make; *Gottesdienst, Zwiesprache* to hold; *Wache* to keep ◆ **Mittagsschlaf ~** to have an afternoon nap; **Winterschlaf ~** to hibernate; **Unterricht ~** to teach; **Selbstgespräche ~** to talk to oneself.
(p) *(einhalten, erfüllen)* to keep ◆ **man muß ~, was man verspricht** a promise is a promise; **der Film hält nicht, was er/der Titel verspricht** the film doesn't live up to expectations/its title.
(q) *(einschätzen)* **jdn/etw für jdn/etw ~** to take sb/sth for *or* to be sb/sth; **ich habe ihn (irrtümlich) für seinen Bruder gehalten** I (mis)took him for his brother; **jdn für ehrlich ~** to think *or* consider sb is honest; **es für Unsinn ~** to think *or* consider sth is nonsense; **wofür ~ Sie mich?** what do you take me for?; **das halte ich nicht für möglich** I don't think that is possible.
▼ **(r)** *(denken über)* **etw von jdm/etw ~** to think sth of sb/sth; **ich halte nichts davon, das zu tun** I don't think much of doing that; **etwas/viel auf etw** *(acc)* **~** to place some/great emphasis on sth, to attach some/great importance *or* value to sth; **du solltest mehr auf dich ~** *(auf Äußeres achten)* you should

take more pride in yourself; (*selbstbewußt sein*) you should be more self-confident; **wenn man etwas auf sich** (*acc*) **hält ...** if you think you're somebody ...; **nicht viel von jdm/etw ~** not to think much of sb/sth; **nicht viel vom Beten/Sparen** *etc* **~** not to be a great one for praying/saving *etc* (*inf*).
[2] *vi* **(a)** (*festhalten, zusammenhalten, standhalten*) to hold; (*haftenbleiben auch*) to stick ◆ **kannst du mal 'n Moment ~?** can you just hold that (for) a moment?
(b) (*bestehen bleiben, haltbar sein, heil bleiben*) to last; (*Konserven auch*) to keep; (*Wetter auch, Frisur, Comm: Preise*) to hold; (*Stoff*) to wear well ◆ **dieser Stoff hält lang** this material wears well.
(c) (*stehenbleiben, anhalten*) to stop ◆ **ein ~der Wagen** a stationary car; **zum H~ bringen** to bring to a stop *or* standstill; **~ lassen** (*Mil*) to call a halt; **halt mal, ...** (*Moment mal*) hang (*inf*) *or* hold on, ...; **halt mal, stop** (*hum*) hang (*inf*) *or* hold on a minute!; *siehe* **halt**[1].
(d) (*Sport*) to make a save ◆ **unser Tormann hat heute wieder großartig gehalten** our goalkeeper made some good saves again today; **kann der denn (gut) ~?** is he a good goalkeeper?
(e) (*in einem Zustand erhalten*) **Sport hält jung** sport keeps you young; **die Plastikverpackung hält frisch** the plastic wrapping keeps things fresh.
(f) **auf etw** (*acc*) **~** (*zielen*) to aim at sth; (*steuern*) to head for sth; **etwas mehr nach links ~** to keep more to the left; (*zielen*) to aim more to the left; **nach Süden/auf Chikago ~** to head south/for Chicago.
(g) (*jdm beistehen, treu sein*) **zu jdm ~** to stand *or* stick by sb; (*favorisieren*) to support sb.
(h) (*Wert legen auf, praktizieren*) **(sehr) auf etw** (*acc*) **~** to attach (a lot of) importance to sth.
(i) (*stolz sein*) **auf sich** (*acc*) **~** (*auf Äußeres achten*) to take a pride in oneself; (*selbstbewußt sein*) to be self-confident.
(j) (*sich beherrschen*) **an sich** (*acc*) **~** to control oneself.
[3] *vr* **(a)** (*sich festhalten*) to hold on (*an +dat* -to).
(b) (*sich nicht verändern, nicht verderben*) to keep; (*Blumen auch, Wetter*) to last; (*Preise*) to hold ◆ **er hat sich gut gehalten** (*inf*) he's well-preserved.
(c) (*bleiben*) to stay ◆ **der Autofahrer hielt sich ganz rechts** the driver kept to the right; **ich halte mich an die alte Methode** I'll stick to *or* with *or* stay with the old method.
(d) (*nicht verschwinden*) to last; (*Schnee auch*) to stay; (*Geruch, Rauch*) to stay, to hang around.
(e) (*sich orientieren nach, sich richten nach*) to keep (*an +acc, nach* to) ◆ **sich an ein Versprechen ~** to keep a promise; **sich an die Tatsachen/den Text ~** to keep *or* stick to the facts/text; **sich (nach) links ~** to keep (to the) left; **sich nach Westen ~** to keep going westwards; *siehe* **Vorschrift**.
(f) (*seine Position behaupten*) to hold *or* hang on; (*haften*) to hold, to stick ◆ **sich auf den Beinen ~** to stay on one's feet.
(g) (*sich behaupten*) to bear up; (*in Kampf*) to hold out ◆ **sich gut ~** (*in Prüfung, Spiel etc*) to make a good showing, to do well.
(h) (*sich beherrschen*) to control oneself ◆ **sich nicht ~ können** to be unable to control oneself.
(i) (*eine bestimmte Haltung haben*) to carry *or* hold oneself ◆ **er hält sich sehr aufrecht/gerade** he holds *or* carries himself very erect/straight; **sich (im Gleichgewicht) ~** to keep one's balance; *siehe* **Bein**.
(j) **sich an jdn ~** (*sich wenden an*) to ask sb; (*sich richten nach*) to follow sb; (*sich gut stellen mit*) to keep in with sb; **ich halte mich lieber an den Wein** I'd rather keep *or* stick to wine.
(k) **er hält sich für einen Spezialisten/besonders klug** he thinks he's a specialist/very clever.

Halte-: ~platz *m* (*Taxi~*) taxi rank *or* stand; **~punkt** *m* (*Rail*) stop.
Halter *m* **-s, -** **(a)** (*Halterung*) holder. **(b)** (*Socken~*) garter; (*Strumpf~, Hüft~*) suspender (*Brit*) *or* garter (*US*) belt. **(c)** (*Jur*) (*Kraftfahrzeug~, Tier~*) owner. **(d)** (*rare: Griff*) handle.
Halteriemen *m* strap.
Halterung *f* mounting; (*für Regal etc*) support.
Halte-: ~schild *nt* stop *or* halt sign; **~schlaufe** *f* (*in Bus etc*) strap; **~signal** *nt* (*Rail*) stop signal; **~stelle** *f* stop; **~verbot** *nt* **(absolutes** *or* **uneingeschränktes) ~verbot** no stopping; (*Stelle*) no stopping zone; **eingeschränktes ~verbot** no waiting; (*Stelle*) no waiting zone; **hier ist ~verbot** there's no stopping here; **~verbot(s)schild** *nt* no stopping sign; **~vorrichtung** *f* *siehe* **Halterung**.
-haltig, -hältig (*Aus*) *adj suf* containing ◆ **stark alkohol~** containing a lot of alcohol, with a high alcohol content.
Halt-: h~los *adj* (*schwach*) insecure; (*hemmungslos*) unrestrained; (*unbegründet*) groundless, unfounded; **~losigkeit** *f siehe adj* lack of security; uninhibitedness; groundlessness; ⚠**h~machen** *vi sep* to stop; **vor nichts h~machen** (*fig*) to stop at nothing; **vor niemandem h~machen** (*fig*) to spare no-one; **~signal** *nt* (*Rail*) stop signal; **~taste** *f* pause button.
Haltung *f* **(a)** (*Körper~*) posture; (*Stellung*) position; (*esp Sport*) (*typische Stellung*) stance; (*bei der Ausführung*) style ◆ **~ annehmen** (*esp Mil*) to stand to attention.
(b) (*fig*) (*Auftreten*) manner; (*Einstellung*) attitude ◆ **in majestätischer/würdiger ~** with majestic/dignified bearing.
(c) *no pl* (*Beherrschtheit*) composure ◆ **~ bewahren** to keep one's composure.
(d) *no pl* (*von Tieren, Fahrzeugen*) owning.
Haltungs-: ~fehler *m* **(a)** (*Med*) bad posture *no indef art, no pl*; **(b)** (*Sport*) style fault; **~mängel** *pl* bad posture *sing*; **~schaden** *m* damaged posture *no pl*; **zu ~schäden führen** to damage one's posture.
Halt-: ~verbot *nt* (*form*) *siehe* **Halteverbot**; **~zeichen** *nt siehe* **Haltesignal**.

Halunke *m* **-n, -n** **(a)** scoundrel. **(b)** (*hum*) rascal, scamp.
Ham and eggs ['hæm ənd 'ɛgz] *pl* bacon *or* ham (*US*) and eggs *sing or pl*.
Hämatit *m* **-s, -e** haematite.
Hämatologe *m*, **Hämatologin** *f* haematologist.
Hämatologie *f* haematology.
hämatologisch *adj* haematological.
Hämatom *nt* **-s, -e** haematoma.
Hamburg *nt* **-s** Hamburg.
Hamburger[1] *m* **-s, -** (*Cook*) hamburger.
Hamburger[2] *adj attr* Hamburg.
Hamburger(in *f*) *m* **-s, -** native *or* (*Einwohner*) inhabitant of Hamburg.
Hamburgerbrötchen *nt* roll *or* bun (for hamburger).
hamburgern *vi* to speak with a Hamburg dialect.
hamburgisch *adj* Hamburg *attr*.
Häme *f* **-**, *no pl* (*rare*) malice.
hämisch *adj* malicious, spiteful ◆ **er hat sich ~ gefreut** he gloated.
Hamit(in *f*) *m* **-en, -en** Hamite.
hamitisch *adj* Hamitic.
Hammel *m* **-s, -** or (*rare*) **¨** **(a)** (*Zool*) wether, castrated ram. **(b)** *no pl* (*Cook*) mutton. **(c)** (*fig pej*) ass, donkey.
Hammel-: ~beine *pl*: **jdm die ~beine langziehen** (*hum inf*) to give sb a dressing-down; **jdn bei den ~beinen nehmen/kriegen** (*inf*) to take sb to task/get hold of sb; **~braten** *m* roast mutton; **~fleisch** *nt* mutton; **~herde** *f* herd *or* flock of wethers *or* rams; (*pej inf*) flock of sheep; **~keule** *f* (*Cook*) leg of mutton; **~sprung** *m* (*Parl*) division.
Hammer *m* **-s, ¨** **(a)** (*Werkzeug, von Auktionator*) hammer; (*Holz~*) mallet ◆ **~ und Sichel** hammer and sickle; **~ und Zirkel im Ährenkranz** *hammer and pair of compasses in a garland of corn, symbol of the GDR*; **unter den ~ kommen** to come under the hammer; **zwischen ~ und Amboß geraten** (*fig*) to come under attack from both sides; **das ist ein ~!** (*sl*) (*unerhört*) that's absurd!; (*prima*) that's fantastic! (*inf*).
(b) (*Sportgerät*) hammer.
(c) (*Anat*) hammer, malleus.
(d) (*Klavier~, Glocken~*) hammer.
(e) (*sl: schwerer Fehler*) howler (*inf*) ◆ **einen ~ haben** to be round the bend (*inf*) *or* twist (*inf*).
hämmerbar *adj* malleable.
Hämmerchen *nt dim of* **Hammer**.
Hammer-: h~förmig *adj* hammer-shaped; **~hai** *m* hammerhead (shark); **~kopf** *m* hammerhead; (*Sport: auch* **~kugel**) hammerhead.
hämmern [1] *vi* **(a)** to hammer; (*fig auch, mit den Fäusten etc*) to pound; (*inf: beim Klavierspielen etc*) to pound, to thump.
(b) (*~des Geräusch verursachen: Maschine, Motor*) to make a hammering sound.
(c) (*Puls, Herz, Blut*) to pound.
(d) (*Sport sl*) to hammer *or* slam the ball (*inf*).
[2] *vt* **(a)** to hammer; *Blech auch, Metallgefäße, Schmuck etc* to beat.
(b) (*inf*) *Melodie, Rhythmus etc* to hammer *or* pound out.
(c) (*Sport sl*) to hammer (*inf*), to slam (*inf*).
(d) (*fig inf: einprägen*) **jdm etw ins Bewußtsein** *etc* **~** to hammer *or* knock sth into sb's head (*inf*).
[3] *vi impers* **es hämmert** there's a sound of hammering.
Hammer-: ~schlag *m* **(a)** hammer blow; (*fig*) bolt from the blue; **(b)** (*Sport*) (*Boxen*) rabbit punch; (*Faustball*) smash; **(c)** (*Schmiederei*) hammer *or* mill scale; **~schmied** *m* (*old*) *person working in a hammer mill*; **~schmiede** *f* (*old*) hammer mill; **~stiel** *m* handle *or* shaft of a/the hammer; **~werfen** *nt* **-s**, *no pl* (*Sport*) hammer(-throwing); **~werfer** *m* (*Sport*) hammer thrower; **~werk** *nt* (*old*) hammer mill; **~wurf** *m* (*Sport*) **(a)** hammer throw; **(b)** *siehe* **~werfen**; **~zehe** *f* (*Med*) hammertoe.
Hammond|orgel ['hæmənd-] *f* electric organ.
Hämoglobin *nt* **-s**, *no pl* haemoglobin.
Hämophilie *f* haemophilia.
⚠**Hämorrhoiden** [hɛmɔro'iːdən] *pl* piles *pl*, haemorrhoids *pl*.
⚠**Hämorrhoidenschaukel** *f* (*hum*) boneshaker (*inf*).
Hampelei *f* (*pej inf*) (continual) fidgeting *no pl*.
Hampelmann *m*, *pl* **-männer** **(a)** jumping jack. **(b)** (*inf*) (*zappeliger Mensch*) fidget ◆ **er ist nur ein ~** he just lets people walk all over him; **jdn zu einem ~ machen** to walk all over sb.
hampeln *vi* to jump about; (*zappeln*) to fidget.
Hamster *m* **-s, -** hamster.
Hamsterbacken *pl* (*fig inf*) chubby cheeks *pl*.
Hamsterer(in *f*) *m* **-s, -** (*inf*) squirrel (*inf*).
Hamster-: ~fahrt *f* foraging trip; **auf ~fahrt gehen** to go foraging; **~kauf** *m* panic-buying *no pl*; **~käufe machen** to buy in order to hoard; (*bei Knappheit*) to panic-buy.
hamstern *vti* (*speichern*) to hoard; (*bei Hamsterfahrt*) to forage; (*Hamsterkäufe machen*) to panic-buy.
Hamster-: ~tasche *f* large shopping bag; **~ware** *f siehe* **hamstern** hoarded/foraged/panic-bought goods.
Hand *f* **-, ¨e** **(a)** hand ◆ **jdm die ~ geben** *or* **reichen** (*geh*) to give sb one's hand; **jdm die ~ drücken/schütteln/küssen** to press/shake/kiss sb's hand; **jdn an der ~ haben/an die** *or* **bei der ~ nehmen/an der ~ fassen** to have/take/grab sb by the hand; **jdm etw aus der ~ nehmen** to take sth from *or* off sb (*auch fig*), to take sth out of sb's hand; **etw in ¨en halten** (*geh*) to hold *or* have sth in one's hands; **die Arbeit seiner ¨e** his handiwork; **in die ¨e klat-**

schen to clap one's hands; **eine ~/zwei ¨~e breit** ≃ six inches/a foot wide.
(b) (*Mus*) hand ◆ **Stück für vier ¨~e** *or* **zu vier ¨~en** (piano) duet; **zu vier ¨~en spielen** to play a (piano) duet.
(c) (*Cards*) hand ◆ **auf der ~** in one's hand.
(d) *no pl* (*Sport: ~spiel*) hand-ball ◆ **~ machen** to handle the ball.
(e) (*Besitz, Obhut*) possession, hands ◆ **aus** *or* **von privater ~** privately; **etw aus der ~ geben** to let sth out of one's sight; **durch jds ¨~e** *or* **~ gehen** to pass *or* go through sb's hands; **von ~ zu ~ gehen** to pass from hand to hand; **etw geht in jds ¨~e über** sth passes to sb *or* into sb's hands; **zu jds ¨~en, zu ¨~en von jdm** for the attention of sb; *siehe* **treu.**
(f) (*nicht mit Maschine, Hilfsmittel*) **mit der ~, von ~** by hand; **von ~ geschrieben/genäht** handwritten/handsewn; **aus der ~** freehand; **Vermittlung von ~** (*Telec*) operator-connected calls *pl.*
(g) (*in Redewendungen*) **¨~e hoch** (put your) hands up; **~ aufs Herz** cross your heart, word of honour; **eine ~ wäscht die andere** if you scratch my back I'll scratch yours; **ich wasche meine ¨~e in Unschuld** I wash my hands of it *or* the matter; **er nimmt niemals ein Buch in die ~** he never picks up a book; **bei etw die** *or* **seine ~ im Spiel haben** to have a hand in sth; **er hat überall seine ~ im Spiel** he has a finger in every pie; **etw hat ~ und Fuß** sth is well done; **etw hat weder ~ noch Fuß** sth doesn't make sense; **sich mit ¨~en und Füßen gegen etw wehren** to fight sth tooth and nail; **mit ¨~en und Füßen reden** to talk *or* speak with one's hands; **man konnte die ~ nicht vor den Augen sehen** you couldn't see your hand in front of your face; **die ¨~e überm Kopf zusammenschlagen** to throw up one's hands in horror; **die** *or* **seine ¨~e über jdn halten** to protect *or* shield sb.
(h) (*in Verbindung mit Adjektiv*) **rechter/linker ~, zur rechten/linken ~** on the right-/left-hand side; **in guten/schlechten/sicheren ¨~en sein** to be in good/bad/safe hands; **eine ruhige/sichere ~** a steady hand; **eine starke** *or* **feste ~** (*fig*) a firm hand; **eine lockere** *or* **lose ~ haben** (*hum inf*) to let fly (*inf*) at the slightest provocation; **bei etw eine glückliche ~ haben** to have a lucky touch with sth; **ihm fehlt die leitende** *or* **lenkende ~** he lacks a guiding hand; **in festen ¨~en sein** to be spoken for; **mit leeren/vollen ¨~en** empty-handed/open-handedly; **mit der flachen ~** with the flat *or* palm of one's hand; *siehe* **rechte(r, s), linke(r, s)** *etc.*
(i) (*in Verbindung mit Verb*) **alle ¨~e voll zu tun haben** to have one's hands full; **jdm auf etw** (*acc*) **die ~ geben** to give sb one's hand on sth; **jdm etw in die ~ versprechen** to promise sb sth *or* sth to sb; **um jds ~ anhalten** *or* **bitten** to ask for sb's hand (in marriage); **jdm/sich** *or* **einander die ~ fürs Leben reichen** to marry sb/to tie the knot; **sich** *or* **einander** (*geh*) **die ~ reichen können** to be tarred with the same brush; **da können wir uns die ~ reichen** snap! (*inf*); **sich** (*dat*) **für jdn/etw die ~ abhacken lassen** (*inf*) to stake one's life on sb/sth; **seine** *or* **die ~ für jdn ins Feuer legen** to vouch for sb; **jdn auf ¨~en tragen** to cherish sb; **jdm aus der ~ fressen** to eat out of sb's hand; **die** *or* **seine ~ hinhalten** *or* **aufhalten** (*fig inf*) to hold out one's hand (for money); **(bei etw) mit ~ anlegen** to lend a hand (with sth); **letzte ~ an etw** (*acc*) **legen** to put the finishing touches to sth; **die ¨~e in den Schoß legen** to sit back and do nothing; **~ an jdn legen** (*geh*) to lay a hand on sb; **~ an sich legen** (*geh*) to kill oneself; **seine** *or* **die ~ auf etw** (*acc*) **legen** (*geh*) to lay (one's) hands on sth; **die ~ auf der Tasche halten** (*inf*) to hold the purse-strings; **die ~ auf etw** (*dat*) **haben** *or* **halten** to keep a tight rein on sth; **das liegt auf der ~** (*inf*) that's obvious.
(j) (*in Verbindung mit Präpositionen*) **an ~ eines Beispiels/von Beispielen** with an example/examples; **an ~ dieses Berichts/dieser Unterlagen** from this report/these documents; **jdn an der ~ haben** to know of sb; **etw aus der ~ sagen können** to be able to say sth offhand; **etw aus erster/zweiter ~ wissen** to know sth first/second hand; **ein Auto aus erster/zweiter ~** a car which has had one previous owner/two previous owners; **etw aus der ~ essen** to eat sth out of one's hand; **etw aus der ~ legen** to put *or* lay sth aside; **etw bei der** *or* **zur ~ haben** to have sth to hand; *Ausrede, Erklärung* to have sth ready; **mit etw schnell** *or* **gleich bei der ~ sein** (*inf*) to be ready with sth; **~ in ~** hand in hand; **jdm/einer Sache in die ¨~e arbeiten** to play into sb's hands/the hands of sth; **jdm in die ~** *or* **¨~e fallen** *or* **geraten** *or* **kommen** to fall into sb's hands; **jdn/etw in die ~** *or* **¨~e kriegen** *or* **bekommen** to get one's hands on sb/sth; **jdn (fest) in der ~ haben** to have sb (well) in hand; **von der ~ in den Mund leben** to live from hand to mouth; **etw in der ~ haben** to have sth; **ich habe diese Entscheidung nicht in der ~** it's not in my hands; **etw gegen jdn in der ~ haben** to have something *or* some hold on sb; **sich in der ~ haben** to have oneself under control; **etw in jds ~** *or* **¨~e legen** to put sth in sb's hands; **etw liegt** *or* **ist in jds ~** sth is in sb's hands; **in jds ~ sein** to be in sb's hands; **etw in die ~ nehmen** to pick sth up; (*fig*) to take sth in hand; **jdm etw in die ~** *or* **¨~e spielen** to pass sth on to sb; **hinter vorgehaltener ~** on the quiet; **das ist mit ¨~en zu greifen** that's as plain as a pikestaff *or* the nose on your face; **etw zerrinnt** *or* **schmilzt jdm unter den ¨~en** sb goes through sth like water *or* like nobody's business (*inf*); **unter jds ¨~en/jdm unter der ~** *or* **den ¨~en wegsterben** to die while under sb's care; **von jds ~ sterben** to die at sb's hand; **etw geht jdm flott** *or* **schnell/leicht von der ~** sb does sth quickly/finds sth easy; **etw läßt sich nicht von der ~ weisen, etw ist nicht von der ~ zu weisen** sth cannot be denied *or* gainsaid (*form*); **zur ~ sein** to be at hand; **etw zur ~ nehmen** to pick sth up; **jdm zur** *or* **an die ~ gehen** to lend sb a helping hand.

Hand-: ~abwehr *f* (*Sport*) save; **durch ~abwehr klären** to save, to clear; **~abzug** *m* (*Typ*) proof pulled by hand; (*Phot*) print made by hand; **~antrieb** *m* hand-driven mechanism; **mit ~antrieb** hand-driven; **~apparat** *m* **(a)** reference books (*on open shelves*) *pl*; **(b)** (*Telec*) handset.

Hand|arbeit *f* **(a)** work done by hand; (*Gegenstand*) article made by hand, handmade article ◆ **etw in ~ herstellen** to produce *or* make sth by hand; **der Tisch ist ~** the table is handmade *or* made by hand.
(b) (*körperliche Arbeit*) manual work.
(c) (*Nähen, Sticken etc, als Schulfach*) needlework *no pl*; (*Stricken*) knitting *no pl*; (*Häkeln*) crochet(ing) *no pl* ◆ **diese Tischdecke ist ~** this tablecloth is handmade; **eine ~ aus dem 18. Jahrhundert** a piece of needlework *etc* from the 18th century.
(d) (*kunsthandwerklich*) handicraft *no pl* ◆ **eine ~** a piece of handicraft work.

Hand|arbeiten *nt* **-s,** *no pl* (*Sch*) needlework.

hand|arbeiten *vi insep* to do needlework/knitting/crocheting.

Hand|arbeiter *m* manual worker.

Hand|arbeits-: ~geschäft *nt* needlework and wool shop; **~heft** *nt* sewing, knitting and crocheting manual; **~korb** *m* workbasket.

Hand-: ~aufheben *nt* **-s,** *no pl* (*bei Wahl*) show of hands; **sich durch ~aufheben zu Wort melden** to ask leave to speak by raising one's hand; **~auflegen** *nt* **-s,** *no pl*, **~auflegung** *f* laying on of hands; **~ausgabe** *f* (*Buch*) concise edition; **~ball** *m* **(a)** (*Ball*) handball; **(b)** *no pl* (*inf auch nt*) (*Spiel*) handball; **~ballen** *m* (*Anat*) ball of the thumb; **~baller(in** *f*) *m* **-s, -** (*inf*) *siehe* **~ballspieler; ~ballspiel** *nt* **(a)** (*Spiel*) game of handball; **(b)** (*Disziplin*) handball *no def art*; **~ballspieler** *m* handball player; **h~bedient** *adj* manually operated, hand-operated; **~bedienung** *f* hand *or* manual operation *or* control; **mit** *or* **für ~bedienung** hand-operated; **~beil** *nt* hatchet; **~besen** *m* hand brush; **~betrieb** *m* hand *or* manual operation; **für** *or* **mit ~betrieb** hand-operated; **h~betrieben** *adj* hand-operated; **~bewegung** *f* sweep of the hand; (*Geste, Zeichen*) gesture; **~bibliothek** *f* reference library *or* books *pl* (*on open shelves*); **~bohrer** *m* gimlet, auger; **~bohrmaschine** *f* (hand) drill; **~brause** *f siehe* **~dusche; h~breit** [1] *adj* ≃ six-inch wide *attr*, six inches wide *pred*; [2] *adv* ≃ six inches; **~breit** *f* **-, -** ≃ six inches; **~bremse** *f* handbrake (*Brit*), parking brake (*US*); **~buch** *nt* handbook; (*technisch*) manual; **~bücherei** *f siehe* **~bibliothek.**

Händchen *nt dim of* **Hand** little hand ◆ **~ halten** (*inf*) to hold hands; **für etw ein ~ haben** (*inf*) to have a knack for sth; (*gut können*) to be good at sth; **~ geben** to shake hands.

Händchen-: ~halten *nt* **-s,** *no pl* holding hands *no def art*; ⚠**h~haltend** *adj* holding hands.

Hand-: ~creme *f* hand cream; **~deutung** *f* palmistry; **~druck** *m* (*Typ, Tex*) block print; (*Verfahren*) block printing; **~dusche** *f* shower attachment.

Hände-: ~druck *m* handshake; **~handtuch** *nt* hand towel.

Hand|einstellung *f* (*Tech*) manual *or* hand-operated setting.

Händeklatschen *nt* applause *no pl.*

Handel[1] *m* **-s,** *no pl* **(a)** (*das Handeln*) trade; (*esp mit illegaler Ware*) traffic ◆ **~ mit etw/einem Land** trade in sth/with a country.
(b) (*Warenverkehr*) trade; (*Warenmarkt*) market ◆ **im ~ sein** to be on the market; **etw in den ~ bringen/aus dem ~ ziehen** to put sth on/take sth off the market; **(mit jdm) ~ (be)treiben** to trade (with sb); **~ und Wandel** (*dated*) doings and dealings *pl.*
(c) (*Abmachung, Geschäft*) deal, transaction; (*inf*) deal ◆ **mit jdm in den ~ kommen** to do business with sb.
(d) (*Wirtschaftszweig*) commerce, trade; (*die Handeltreibenden*) trade.
(e) (*dial: Handelsunternehmen*) business ◆ **er betreibt/hat einen ~ in** *or* **mit Kohlen und Heizöl** he runs/has a coal and fuel oil business.

Handel[2] *m* **-s, ¨** *usu pl* quarrel, argument.

Hand|elfmeter *m* penalty for a hand-ball.

handeln [1] *vi* **(a)** (*Handel treiben*) to trade ◆ **er handelt mit Gemüse** he trades *or* deals in vegetables, he's in the vegetable trade; **er handelt mit Drogen** he traffics in drugs; **er handelt in Gebrauchtwagen** he's in the second-hand car trade; he sells second-hand cars.
(b) (*feilschen*) to bargain, to haggle (*um* about, over); (*fig: verhandeln*) to negotiate (*um* about) ◆ **ich lasse schon mit mir ~** I'm open to persuasion; (*in bezug auf Preis*) I'm open to offers.
(c) (*tätig werden, agieren*) to act ◆ **er ist ein schnell ~der Mensch** he's a quick-acting person.
(d) (*sich verhalten*) to act, to behave ◆ **gegen jdn** *or* **an jdm gut/als Freund ~** (*geh*) to act *or* behave well/as *or* like a friend towards sb.
(e) (*sprechen*) **von etw** *or* **über etw** (*acc*) **~** to deal with sth; (*Aufsatz etc auch*) to be about sth.
[2] *vr impers* **(a) es handelt sich bei diesen sogenannten UFOs um optische Täuschungen** these so-called UFO's are optical illusions; **es handelt sich hier/dabei um ein Verbrechen** it's a crime we are dealing with here/there; **bei dem Festgenommenen handelt es sich um X** the person arrested is X.
(b) (*betreffen*) **sich um etw ~** to be about sth, to concern sth; **worum handelt es sich, bitte?** what's it about, please?; **es handelt sich darum, daß ich einen Kredit beantragen möchte** it is about *or* concerns a loan which I wish to apply for.
(c) (*um etwas gehen, auf etw ankommen*) **sich um etw ~** to be a question *or* matter of sth; **es handelt sich nur ums Überleben** it's simply a question of survival.
[3] *vt* **(a)** to sell (*für* at, for); (*an der Börse*) to quote (*mit* at); *Drogen etc* to traffic in.
(b) *Preis etc* (*hinauf~*) to push up, to raise; (*herunter~*) to bring down.

Handeln *nt* **-s,** *no pl* **(a)** (*Feilschen*) bargaining, haggling. **(b)** (*das Handeltreiben*) trading ◆ **das ~ mit Schmuck** trading *or* dealing in jewellery. **(c)** (*Verhalten*) behaviour. **(d)** (*das Tätigwerden*) action.

handelnd *adj* **die ~en Personen in einem Drama** the characters in a drama, the dramatis personae *pl*; **das ~e Subjekt** the active subject.

⚠: for details of spelling reform, see supplement

Handels-: ~abkommen *nt* trade agreement; **~akademie** *f (Aus)* commercial college; **~akademiker** *m (Aus)* graduate of a commercial college; **~artikel** *m* commodity; **~attaché** *m* commercial attaché; **~bank** *f* merchant bank; **~beschränkung** *f* trading restriction, restriction on trade; **~betrieb** *m* trading *or* business concern; **~bezeichnung** *f* trade name; **~beziehungen** *pl* trade relations *pl*; **~bilanz** *f* balance of trade; **aktive/passive ~bilanz** balance of trade surplus/deficit; **~brauch** *m* trade *or* commercial practice; **~defizit** *nt* trade deficit; **h~einig, h~eins** *adj pred* **h~einig werden/sein** to agree terms, to come to an agreement; **h~fähig** *adj Güter etc* marketable, merchantable; **~firma** *f* (commercial *or* business) firm; **~flagge** *f (Naut)* merchant flag; **~flotte** *f* merchant fleet; **~freiheit** *f* **(a)** *(Comm)* freedom of trade *no pl*; **(b)** *siehe* **Handlungsfreiheit**; **~gesellschaft** *f* commercial company; **~gesetz** *nt* commercial law; **~gesetzbuch** *nt* code of commercial law; **~gewerbe** *nt* commerce *no art*; **~gut** *nt siehe* **~ware**; **~hafen** *m* trading port; **~haus** *nt* business house, firm; **~kammer** *f* chamber of commerce; **~kette** *f* **(a)** chain of retail shops; **(b)** *(Weg der Ware)* sales route *(from manufacturer to buyer)*; **~klasse** *f* grade; **Heringe der ~klasse 1** grade 1 herring; **~krieg** *m* trade war; **~krise** *f* commercial crisis; **~lehrer(in** *f) m* teacher of commercial subjects; **~macht** *f* trading nation *or* power; **~makler** *m* broker; **~marine** *f* merchant navy, mercantile marine *(form)*; **~marke** *f* trade name; **~metropole** *f* commercial metropolis; **~minister** *m* ≃ Trade Secretary *(Brit)*, Secretary of Commerce *(US)*; **~ministerium** *nt* ≃ Board of Trade *(Brit)*, Department of Commerce *(US)*; **~mission** *f* trade mission; **~name** *m siehe* **~bezeichnung**; **~nation** *f* trading nation; **~niederlassung** *f* branch (of a trading organization); **~objekt** *nt* commodity; **~organisation** *f* **(a)** *(allgemein)* trading organization; **(b)** *(DDR) state-owned commercial concern which runs stores, hotels etc*; **~partner** *m* trading partner; **~platz** *m* trading centre; **~politik** *f* trade *or* commercial policy; **h~politisch** [1] *adj* relating to trade *or* commercial policy; [2] *adv* as far as trade *or* commercial policy is concerned; **~realschule** *f (esp Sw) siehe* **~schule**; **~recht** *nt* commercial law *no def art, no pl*; **h~rechtlich** [1] *adj* of/about commercial law; [2] *adv* according to commercial law; **~register** *nt* register of companies; **~reisende(r)** *m decl as adj siehe* **~vertreter**; **~schiff** *nt* trading ship *or* vessel, merchantman *(old)*; **~schiffahrt** *f* merchant shipping *no def art*; **~schranke** *f usu pl* trade barrier; **~schule** *f* commercial school *or* college; **~schüler** *m* student at a commercial school *or* college; **~spanne** *f* profit margin; **~sperre** *f* trade embargo *(gegen* on); **~sprache** *f* commercial language; **~stadt** *f* trading city *or* centre; **~stand** *m (Sociol)* merchant class; **~straße** *f (Hist)* trade route; **h~üblich** *adj* usual *or* customary (in the trade *or* in commerce); **etw zu den h~üblichen Preisen kaufen** to buy sth at normal (trade) prices.

handelsüchtig *adj* quarrelsome.

Handels-: ~unternehmen *nt* commercial enterprise; **~verkehr** *m* trade; **~vertrag** *m* trade agreement; **~vertreter** *m* commercial traveller *or* representative; **~vertretung** *f* trade mission; **~volk** *nt* trading nation; **~ware** *f* commodity; **keine ~ware** no commercial value; **~waren** *pl* commodities *pl*, merchandise *sing*; **~weg** *m* **(a)** sales route; **(b)** *siehe* **~straße**; **~wert** *m* market value; **~wesen** *nt* commerce, trade *no def art*; **~zentrum** *nt* trading *or* commercial centre; **~zweig** *m* branch.

⚠ **handeltreibend** *adj attr* trading.

Handeltreibende(r) *mf decl as adj* trader, tradesman/-woman.

Hände-: ~ringen *nt* **-s,** *no pl (fig)* wringing of one's hands; **h~ringend** *adv* wringing one's hands; *(fig)* imploringly; **~schütteln** *nt* **-s,** *no pl* handshaking; **~trockner** *m* hand drier; **~waschen** *nt* **-s,** *no pl* washing one's hands; **jdn zum ~waschen schicken** to send sb to wash his/her hands; **das ~waschen kostet ...** it costs ... to wash your hands.

Hand-: ~feger *m* hand brush; **wie ein wild gewordener ~feger** *(inf)* like a wild thing; **~fertigkeit** *f* dexterity; **~fessel** *f* **(a)** manacle; **etw als ~fessel benutzen** to tie sb's hands together with sth; **(b)** *(Handschelle)* handcuff; **h~fest** *adj* **(a)** *(kräftig) Mensch* sturdy, robust; *Essen* solid, substantial; **(b)** *(fig) Schlägerei* violent; *Skandal* huge; *Vorschlag, Argument* well-founded, solid; *Beweis* solid, tangible; *Lüge, Betrug* flagrant, blatant; **~feuerlöscher** *m* hand fire extinguisher; **~feuerwaffe** *f* hand gun; **~fläche** *f* palm *or* flat (of the/one's hand); **~funkgerät** *nt* walkie-talkie; **~gas** *nt (Aut: Vorrichtung)* hand throttle; **~gas haben/geben** to have a/pull out the hand throttle; **mit ~gas fahren** to use the hand throttle; **h~gearbeitet** *adj* handmade; *Stickerei etc* handworked; **h~gebunden** *adj* hand-bound; **h~gefertigt** *adj siehe* **h~gearbeitet**; **h~geknüpft** *adj* handwoven; **~geld** *nt (Sport)* transfer fee; *(Hist)* earnest money; *(Mil Hist)* bounty; **~gelenk** *nt* wrist; **aus dem ~gelenk** *(fig inf) (ohne Mühe)* with the greatest of ease, effortlessly; *(improvisiert)* off the cuff; **etw aus dem ~gelenk schütteln** *(fig inf)* to do sth effortlessly *or* with no trouble at all; **ein lockeres** *or* **loses ~gelenk haben** *(inf)* to let fly at the slightest provocation; **h~gemacht** *adj* handmade; **h~gemalt** *adj* hand-painted; **h~gemein** *adj* **(mit jdm) h~gemein werden** to come to blows (with sb); **~gemenge** *nt* scuffle, fight; **h~genäht** *adj* hand-sewn; **~gepäck** *nt* hand luggage *no pl or* baggage *no pl*; **~gerät** *nt (Sport)* hand apparatus; **h~gerecht** *adj, adv* handy; **h~geschliffen** *adj* hand-ground; **h~geschmiedet** *adj* hand-forged; **h~geschöpft** *adj Papier* handmade; **h~geschrieben** *adj* handwritten; **h~gesetzt** *adj (Typ)* hand-set, set by hand; **h~gesponnen** *adj* hand-spun; **h~gesteuert** *adj (Tech)* hand-operated; **h~gestrickt** *adj* hand-knitted; *(fig)* homespun; *Lösung* homegrown; **~gestrickte(s)** *nt decl as adj* hand-knitted goods *pl*; **h~gewebt** *adj* handwoven; **~granate** *f* hand grenade; **h~greiflich** *adj* **(a)** *Streit, Auseinandersetzung* violent; **h~greiflich werden** to become violent; **(b)** *(fig: offensichtlich)* clear; *Erfolg auch* visible; *Lüge* blatant, flagrant; **etw h~greiflich vor Augen führen** to demonstrate sth clearly; **~greiflichkeit** *f siehe adj* **(a)** *usu pl* violence *no pl*; **(b)** clarity; blatancy, flagrance; **~griff** *m* **(a)** *(Bewegung)* movement; *(im Haushalt)* chore; **keinen ~griff tun** not to lift a finger; **mit einem ~griff** *öffnen* with one flick of the wrist; *(schnell)* in no time; **mit ein paar ~griffen** in next to no time; **(b)** *(Gegenstand)* handle; **h~groß** *adj* hand-sized; **h~habbar** *adj* manageable; **leicht/schwer h~habbar** easy/difficult to manage; **~habe** *f (fig)* **ich habe gegen ihn keine ~habe** I have no hold on him; **etw als ~habe (gegen jdn) benutzen** to use sth as a lever (against sb); **h~haben** *vt insep* to handle; *Maschine auch* to operate, to work; *Gesetz* to implement, to administer; **~habung** *f siehe vt* handling; operation, working; implementation, administration; **~harmonika** *f* concertina; **~hebel** *m* hand-operated *or* manually operated lever.

-händig *adj suf* -handed.

Handikap ['hɛndikɛp] *nt* **-s, -s** *(Sport, fig)* handicap.

handikapen ['hɛndikɛpn] *vt insep* to handicap.

Handikap-: ~rennen *nt* handicap (race); **~spiel** *nt* handicap game.

Hand-in-Hand-Arbeiten *nt* **-s,** *no pl* cooperation.

händisch *adj (Aus)* manual.

Hand-: ~kamera *f* hand-held camera; **~kante** *f* side of the/one's hand; **~kantenschlag** *m* karate chop; **~karren** *m* handcart; **~käse** *m strong-smelling round German cheese*; **~katalog** *m* ready-reference catalogue; **~koffer** *m* (small) suitcase; **h~koloriert** *adj* hand-painted; **~korb** *m* (small) basket; **~kreissäge** *f* hand-held circular saw; **~kurbel** *f* hand crank; *(Aut)* starting handle; ⚠**~kuß** *m* kiss on the hand; *(Eccl)* kiss *(on the ring of a bishop etc)*; **mit ~kuß** *(fig inf)* with pleasure, gladly; **zum ~kuß kommen** *(Aus fig)* to come off worse; **~lampe** *f siehe* **~leuchte**; **~langer** *m* **-s, -** odd-job man, handyman; *(fig: Untergeordneter)* dogsbody *(inf)*; *(fig pej: Gehilfe)* henchman; **~langerarbeit** *f (pej)* donkey work *no pl*; **~langerdienst** *m* dirty work *no pl*; **~lauf** *m (an Treppen)* handrail.

Händler(in *f) m* **-s, -** trader, dealer; *(Auto~)* dealer; *(Ladenbesitzer)* shopkeeper *(Brit)*, store owner *(US)*; *(Fisch~)* fishmonger; *(Fleisch~)* butcher; *(Gemüse~)* greengrocer ◆ **ambulanter** *or* **fliegender ~** street trader.

Händler-: ~preis *m* trade price; **~rabatt** *m* trade discount.

Hand-: ~lesekunst *f* **(die) ~lesekunst** palmistry, (the art of) reading palms; **~leser** *m* palm reader, palmist; **~leuchte** *f* inspection lamp.

handlich *adj* **(a)** *Gerät, Format, Form* handy; *Gepäckstück* manageable, easy to manage; *Auto* manoeuvrable.
(b) *(Sw: behende)* handy, dexterous.
(c) *(Sw: mit der Hand)* with one's hand(s).

Handlichkeit *f, no pl siehe adj (a)* handiness; manageability; manoeuvrability.

Hand-: ~linie *f* line (in the palm of the hand); **~liniendeutung** *f* **(die) ~liniendeutung** palmistry.

Handlung *f* **(a)** *(Vorgehen, Handeln)* action, deed; *(Tat, Akt)* act.
(b) *(Geschehen)* action; *(~sablauf)* plot ◆ **der Ort der ~** the scene of the action.
(c) *(dated) (mit Waren)* business; *(Laden)* shop.

Handlungs-: ~ablauf *m* plot; **h~arm** *adj* thin on plot; **~armut** *f* lack of plot *or* action; **~bedarf** *m* need for action; **~bevollmächtigte(r)** *mf* authorized agent, proxy; **h~fähig** *adj Regierung* capable of acting, able to act; *(Jur)* empowered *or* authorized to act; **eine h~fähige Mehrheit** a working majority; **~fähigkeit** *f (von Regierung)* ability to act; *(Jur)* power to act; **~freiheit** *f* freedom of action; **~gerüst** *nt (Liter)* framework; **h~reich** *adj* action-packed, full of action; **~reichtum** *m* abundance of action; **~reisende(r)** *m (Comm)* commercial traveller, rep(resentative); **~spielraum** *m* scope (of action); **~theorie** *f (Sociol)* theory of action; **h~unfähig** *adj Regierung* incapable of acting, unable to act; *(Jur)* without power to act; **~unfähigkeit** *f (von Regierung)* inability to act; *(Jur)* lack of power to act; **~verb** *nt* transitive verb; **~verlauf** *m siehe* **~ablauf**; **~vollmacht** *f* proxy; **~weise** *f* way of behaving, behaviour *no pl*, conduct *no pl*; **eine selbstlose/edelmütige ~weise** unselfish *or* conduct/noble conduct.

Hand-: ~mehr *nt* **-s,** *no pl (Sw)* show of hands; **~mühle** *f* hand-mill; **~pflege** *f* care of one's hands; **~presse** *f (Typ)* hand-press; **~pumpe** *f* hand-pump; **~puppe** *f* glove puppet; **~puppenspiel** *nt (Technik)* glove puppetry; *(Stück)* glove puppet show; **~reichung** *f* **(a)** helping hand *no pl*; **(b)** *(Instruktion, Empfehlung)* recommendation; **~rücken** *m* back of the/one's hand; **auf beiden ~rücken** on the back of both hands; **~säge** *f* hand-saw; **~satz** *m (Typ)* hand-setting, hand-composition; **~schalter** *m* manual switch; **~schaltung** *f (Aut)* manual controls *pl*; **~schelle** *f usu pl* handcuff; **jdm ~schellen anlegen** to handcuff sb, to put handcuffs on sb; **in ~schellen** in handcuffs, handcuffed; **~schlag** *m* **(a)** *(Händedruck)* handshake; **mit** *or* **durch** *or* **per ~schlag** with a handshake; **ein Geschäft durch ~schlag abschließen** to shake on a deal; **(b) keinen ~schlag tun** not to do a stroke (of work); **~schreiben** *nt* handwritten letter; **~schrift** *f* **(a)** handwriting; *(fig)* (trade)mark; **er hat eine gute/leserliche ~schrift** he has a good/legible hand, he has good/legible handwriting; **etw trägt/verrät jds ~schrift** *(fig)* sth bears *or* has sb's (trade)mark; *(Kunstwerk auch)* sth shows the hand of sb; **eine kräftige/gute ~schrift haben** *or* **schreiben** *(fig inf)* to be a hard/good hitter; **(b)** *(Text)* manuscript; **~schriftendeutung** *f* **(die) ~schriftendeutung** the study of handwriting, graphology; **h~schriftlich** [1] *adj* handwritten; [2] *adv korrigieren, einfügen* by hand; *sich bewerben* in writing; **einen Brief h~schriftlich beantworten/schreiben** to answer a letter in writing *or* by hand/to write a letter.

⚠: Informationen zur Rechtschreibreform im Anhang

Handschuh *m (Finger~)* glove; *(Faust~)* mitten, mitt *(inf)*.

Handschuh-: ~fach *nt*, **~kasten** *m (Aut)* glove compartment; **~macher** *m* glove maker.

Hand-: ~schutz *m* protection *no pl* for the hands; *(Handschuhe)* hand protection *no pl*; *(an Maschine)* hand guard; **~setzer** *m (Typ)* hand compositor; **h~signiert** *adj* signed, autographed; **~skizze** *f* rough sketch; **~spiegel** *m* hand mirror *or* glass; **~spiel** *nt, no pl* **(a)** *(Sport)* handball; **(b)** *(Cards)* (finishing a game by) playing all one's hand at once; **~stand** *m (Sport)* handstand; **~standüberschlag** *m (Sport)* handspring; **~steuerung** *f* manual control; **~streich** *m* **in** *or* **durch einen ~streich** in a surprise coup; *(Mil)* by surprise; **in einem** *or* **durch einen kühnen/detailliert geplanten ~streich** in a bold/minutely planned coup; **~tasche** *f* handbag *(Brit)*, purse *(US)*; **~taschenraub** *m* bag-snatching; **~teller** *m* palm (of the/one's hand); **~trommel** *f* hand drum.

Handtuch *nt* towel; *(Geschirr~)* tea towel, teacloth; *(Papier~)* paper towel ◆ **das ~ werfen** *or* **schmeißen** *(inf) (lit)* to throw in the towel; *(fig)* to throw in the sponge *or* towel.

Handtuch- *in cpds* towel; **~halter** *m* towel-rail; **~spender** *m* towel dispenser.

Hand-: ~umdrehen *nt (fig)*: **im ~umdrehen** in the twinkling of an eye; **h~verlesen** *adj Obst etc* hand-graded; *(fig) Gesellschaft etc* hand-picked; **h~vermittelt** *adj Telefongespräch* connected through *or* by the operator; **~vermittlung** *f* connection by the operator; **eine durch ~vermittlung hergestellte Telefonverbindung** a call connected through *or* by the operator; ⚠**~voll** *f* -, - *(lit, fig)* handful; **~waffe** *f* hand weapon; **~wagen** *m* hand-cart; **h~warm** *adj* hand-hot; **etw h~warm waschen** to wash sth in hand-hot water; **~wäsche** *f* washing by hand; *(Wäschestücke)* hand wash; **~webstuhl** *m* hand-loom.

Handwerk *nt* **(a)** *(Beruf)* trade; *(Kunst~)* craft; *(fig: Tätigkeit)* business ◆ **das lederverarbeitende ~** the leather worker's trade; **das ~ des Bäckers** the baking trade; **das ~ des Schneiders/Schreiners** the trade of tailor/joiner; **das ~ des Töpfers** the potter's craft; **der Krieg ist das einzige ~, das er versteht** *or* **beherrscht** war is the only business he knows anything about; **sein ~ verstehen** *or* **beherrschen** *(fig)* to know one's job; **jdm ins ~ pfuschen** *(fig)* to tread on sb's toes; **jdm das ~ legen** *(fig)* to put a stop to sb's game *(inf) or* to sb.
(b) *no pl (Wirtschaftsbereich)* trade.

handwerkeln *vi insep (hum)* to potter about (making things).

Handwerker *m* **-s, -** (skilled) manual worker; *(Kunst~)* craftsman ◆ **wir haben seit Wochen die ~ im Haus** we've had workmen *or* tradesmen in the house for weeks.

Handwerkerin *f* (skilled) manual worker; *(Kunst~)* craftswoman.

Handwerkerschaft *f* trade *sing or pl*.

handwerklich *adj Ausbildung* as a manual worker/craftsman; *(fig)* technical ◆ **~er Beruf** skilled trade; **die ~e Ausführung des Möbelstücks** the workmanship *or* craftsmanship of the piece of furniture; **~es Können** craftsmanship; **~e Fähigkeiten** manual skills; **~ ist der Fotograf perfekt** technically the photographer is perfect.

Handwerks-: ~beruf *m* skilled trade; **~betrieb** *m* workshop; **~bursche** *m (old)* travelling journeyman; **~kammer** *f* trade corporation; **~mann** *m, pl* **-leute** *(obs) siehe* **Handwerker**; **~zeug** *nt, no pl* tools *pl*; *(fig)* tools of the trade *pl*, equipment.

Hand-: ~werkzeug *nt* hand tools *pl*; **~winde** *f* hand-winch; **~wörterbuch** *nt* concise dictionary; **~wurzel** *f (Anat)* carpus; **~wurzelknochen** *m (Anat)* carpal bone.

Handy ['hɛndi] *nt* **-s, -s** *(Telec)* mobile (phone).

Hand-: ~zeichen *nt* signal; *(Geste auch)* sign; *(bei Abstimmung)* show of hands; **durch ~zeichen** by a show of hands; **er gab mir durch ein ~zeichen zu verstehen, daß ich still sein sollte** he signalled to me to be quiet, he gave me a sign to be quiet; **~zeichnung** *f* **(a)** *(Skizze)* sketch; **(b)** *(Art)* drawing; **~zettel** *m* handout, leaflet, handbill.

hanebüchen *adj (dated, geh)* outrageous, scandalous.

Hanf *m* **-(e)s,** *no pl (Pflanze, Faser)* hemp; *(Samen)* hempseed.

Hänfling *m (Orn)* linnet.

Hanf- *in cpds* hemp-; **~seil** *nt*, **~strick** *m* hemp-rope.

Hang *m* **-(e)s, ⸚e** **(a)** *(Abhang)* slope. **(b)** *no pl (Neigung)* tendency ◆ **er hat einen (deutlichen) ~ zur Kriminalität** he has a (marked) tendency towards criminality.

Hangar ['haŋgaːɐ, haŋ'gaːɐ] *m* **-s, -s** hangar, shed.

Hänge-: ~backen *pl* flabby cheeks *pl*; **~bauch** *m* drooping belly *(inf)*; **~brücke** *f* suspension bridge; **~brust** *f*, **~busen** *m (pej)* sagging *or* droopy *(inf)* breasts *pl or* bosom *no pl*; **~dach** *nt* suspended roof; **~gleiter** *m (Sport)* hang-glider; **~kleid** *nt* loose dress, smock; **~lampe** *f* drop-light.

hangeln *vir (vi: aux sein or haben)* **er hangelte (sich) an einem Tau über den Fluß** he moved hand over hand along a rope over the river; **er hangelte sich am Fels hinunter/über den Abgrund** he let himself down the cliff hand over hand/he crossed the chasm hand over hand.

Hänge-: ~mappe *f* suspension file; **~matte** *f* hammock.

hangen *vi (obs, dial) (dial: aux sein) siehe* **hängen 1**.

Hangen *nt*: **mit ~ und Bangen** with fear and trembling.

Hängen *nt* **-s,** *no pl* **(a) Tod durch ~** death by hanging. **(b) mit ~ und Würgen** *(inf)* by the skin of one's teeth.

hängen [1] *vi pret* **hing,** *ptp* **gehangen** **(a)** to hang ◆ **die Gardinen ~ schon** the curtains are already up; **die Tür hängt in den Angeln** the door hangs on its hinges.
(b) *(gehenkt werden)* to hang.
(c) *(herunter~)* to hang ◆ **mit ~den Schultern** with drooping shoulders; **die Blumen ließen die Köpfe ~** the flowers hung their heads; **den Kopf ~ lassen** *(fig)* to be downcast *or* crestfallen; **das Kleid hing ihr am Leib** the dress hung on her.
(d) *(sich neigen)* to lean ◆ **der Wagen hängt (stark) nach rechts** the car leans (badly) to the right.
(e) *(inf: lässig sitzen)* to slouch ◆ **in der Kurve ~** *(Motorradfahrer)* to lean into the bend.
(f) *(befestigt sein)* to hang; *(Wohnwagen etc)* to be on *(an etw (dat)* sth); *(sich festhalten)* to hang on *(an +dat* to) ◆ **das Bild hängt an der Wand/am Nagel/an einem Aufhänger** the picture is hanging on the wall/on the nail/by a loop; **sie hing ihm am Hals/an der Schulter** she hung around his neck/clung to his shoulder; **das Kalb hängt am Euter der Mutter** the calf hangs on to its mother's udder; **der Knopf hängt nur noch an einem Faden** the button is only hanging (on) by a thread.
(g) *(angeschlossen, verbunden sein: Lautsprecher, Telefonapparat etc)* to be connected (up) *(an +dat* to) ◆ **der Patient hängt an der künstlichen Niere/am Tropf** the patient is on the kidney machine/connected (up) to the drip.
(h) *(inf: abhängen von)* **an jdm ~** to depend on sb.
(i) *(inf: dazugehören)* to be involved *(an +dat* in) ◆ **daran hängt viel Arbeit** there's a lot of work involved in that.
(j) *(behangen sein, vollgehängt sein)* to be full ◆ **der Schrank hängt voll(er) Kleider** the cupboard is full of clothes; **der Baum hängt voller Früchte** the tree is laden with fruit.
(k) *(kleben)* to be stuck *(an +dat* on) ◆ **ihre Blicke** *or* **Augen hingen an dem Sänger** her eyes were fixed on the singer; **sie hing am Mund** *or* **an den Lippen des Redners** she hung on the speaker's every word.
(l) *(festhängen)* to be caught *(mit* by).
(m) *(schweben, im Raum stehen)* to hang ◆ **eine Wolke hing im Tal** a cloud hung over the valley; **eine unerträgliche Spannung hing im Raum** there was an unbearable tension in the room; **eine Gefahr/ein Fluch hängt über uns** danger/a curse is hanging over us; *siehe* **Luft**.
(n) *(inf: sich aufhalten)* to hang about *or* around *(inf)* ◆ **er hängt den ganzen Tag vorm Fernseher/am Telefon** he spends all day in front of the telly/on the phone *(inf)*; **wo hängt bloß der Jürgen schon wieder?** where on earth has Jürgen got to now?
(o) *(nicht vorankommen)* to hang fire; *(inf: vergeblich warten)* to hang about *(inf)*; *(Sch inf, Sports sl)* to be behind ◆ **die Partie hängt** *(Chess)* the game is held over *or* adjourned.
(p) *(Chess: Figur)* to be vulnerable ◆ **der Springer hängt** the knight is vulnerable.
(q) *(nicht verzichten mögen auf, lieben)* **an jdm/etw ~** to be very attached to *or* fond of sb/sth; **er hängt am Leben** he clings to life.

[2] *vt pret* **hängte,** *ptp* **gehängt,** *(dial auch) pret* **hing,** *ptp* **gehangen** **(a)** *(aufhängen, henken)* to hang ◆ **wir müssen noch die Gardinen ~** we still have to put up *or* hang the curtains; **er hängt sich all sein Geld** *or* **alles auf den Leib** *(inf)* he spends all his money on clothes; *siehe* **Nagel, Brotkorb, Glocke**.
(b) *(vollhängen, behängen mit)* to fill ◆ **er hängte die Wand voll Bilder** he hung pictures all over the wall, he filled the wall with pictures.
(c) *(einhängen)* **er hängte den Telefonhörer in die Gabel** he hung up *or* rang off, he put *or* placed the receiver back on the hook.
(d) *(hängenlassen, beugen)* to hang ◆ **der Elefant hängte seinen Rüssel ins Wasser** the elephant dangled his trunk in the water; **seine Nase in etw** *(acc)* **~** *(inf: riechen)* to stick one's nose into sth *(inf)*.
(e) *(an +acc* to) *(anschließen)* to connect; *(befestigen) Wohnwagen etc* to hitch up.

[3] *vr pret* **hängte,** *ptp* **gehängt,** *(dial auch) pret* **hing,** *ptp* **gehangen** **(a)** **sich an etw** *(acc)* **~** to hang on to sth; **er hängte sich ihr an den Hals/Arm/Rockzipfel** he hung on to *or* clung to her neck/arm/apron-strings; **sich von etw/über etw** *(acc)* **~** to suspend oneself from/over sth; **sich unter etw** *(acc)* **~** to hang onto the underside of sth; **sich ins Seil/in die Seile ~** *(Bergsteiger, Ringer)* to lean against the rope/ropes; **er hängte sich ans Telefon** *or* **an die Strippe** *(inf)* he got on the phone; **sich an die Flasche/an den Wasserhahn ~** *(inf)* to have a good long drink.
(b) **sich an etw** *(acc)* **~** *(sich festsetzen)* to cling *or* stick to sth; **sich an jdn ~** *(sich anschließen)* to latch on to sb *(inf)*.
(c) **sich an jdn/etw ~** *(gefühlsmäßig binden)* to become attached to sb/sth.
(d) *(verfolgen)* **sich an jdn/an ein Fahrzeug ~** to set off in (hot) pursuit of sb/a vehicle.
(e) **sich in etw** *(acc)* **~** *(sl) (sich engagieren)* to get involved in sth; *(sich einmischen)* to meddle in sth.

⚠**hängenbleiben** *vi sep irreg aux sein* **(a)** to get caught *(an +dat* on).
(b) *(Sport) (zurückbleiben)* to get left behind; *(nicht durch-, weiterkommen)* not to get through ◆ **der Aufschlag blieb im Netz hängen** the ball didn't get past the net; **der Angriff blieb vor dem Strafraum hängen** the attack didn't get past the front of the penalty area; **die Mannschaft blieb schon in der ersten Runde hängen** the team didn't get past *or* through the first round.
(c) *(Sch inf: nicht versetzt werden)* to stay down.
(d) *(sich aufhalten)* to stay on ◆ **bei einer Nebensächlichkeit ~** to get bogged down with a secondary issue, to get sidetracked.
(e) *(sich festsetzen, haftenbleiben)* to get stuck *or* caught *(in, an +dat* on); *(Blick, Augen)* to rest *(an +dat* on) ◆ **es bleibt ja doch alles an mir hängen** *(fig inf)* in the end it's all down to me anyhow *(inf)*; **der Verdacht ist an ihm hängengeblieben** suspicion rested on him; **vom Lateinunterricht ist bei ihm nicht viel**

hängengeblieben (*fig inf*) not much of his Latin stuck (*inf*).

hängend [1] *prp of* **hängen.**
[2] *adj* hanging ◆ **~e Gärten** hanging gardens; **mit ~er Zunge kam er angelaufen** (*fig*) he came running up panting; **mit ~em Kopf** (*fig*) in low spirits, crestfallen; **~ befestigt sein** to be hung up; **~e Ventile** (*Tech*) overhead valves.

⚠ **hängenlassen** *sep irreg, ptp* **hängen(ge)lassen** [1] *vt* **(a)** (*vergessen*) to leave behind. **(b)** (*inf: im Stich lassen*) to let down. **(c)** (*Sch: nicht versetzen*) to keep down.
[2] *vr* to let oneself go ◆ **laß dich nicht so hängen!** don't let yourself go like this!, pull yourself together!; **er läßt sich furchtbar hängen** he has really let himself go.

Hänge-: ~ohr *nt* lop ear; **~partie** *f* (*Chess*) adjourned game; (*fig*) stalemate; **~pflanze** *f* trailing plant.

Hänger *m* **-s, -** **(a)** *siehe* **Anhänger. (b)** *siehe* **Hängekleid. (c)** (*Mantel*) loose (-fitting) coat. **(d)** (*sl: fauler Mensch*) layabout.

Hangerl *nt* **-s, -(n)** (*Aus*) **(a)** *siehe* **Lätzchen. (b)** *siehe* **Geschirrhandtuch.**

Hänge-: ⚠**~schloß** *nt siehe* **Vorhängeschloß; ~schrank** *m* wall-cupboard; **~schultern** *pl* drooping shoulders *pl.*

hängig *adj* **(a)** (*Sw Jur*) *siehe* **anhängig. (b)** (*form*) sloping, inclined.

Hanglage *f* sloping site ◆ **in ~** situated on a slope.

Hang-: ~segeln *nt* (*Sport*) hang-gliding; **~täter** *m* (*Jur*) *person with criminal tendencies.*

Hannemann *m*: **~ geh du voran** (*inf*) you go first.

Hannibal *m* **-s** Hannibal.

Hannover [ha'no:fɐ] *nt* **-s** Hanover.

Hannoveraner [hanova'ra:nɐ] *m* **-s, -** Hanoverian (horse).

Hannoveraner(in *f*) *m* **-s, -** Hanoverian.

hannoverisch [ha'no:fərɪʃ] (*rare*), **hannoversch** [ha'no:fɐʃ], **hannöversch** [ha'nø:fɐʃ] (*old*) *adj* Hanoverian.

Hans *m* **-'** *or* **-ens: ~ Guckindieluft** Johnny Head-in-the-Air; **~ im Glück** (*fig*) lucky dog (*inf*) *or* devil (*inf*).

Hansa *f* **-,** *no pl* (*Hist*) *siehe* **Hanse.**

Hansaplast ® *nt* **-(e)s,** *no pl* Elastoplast ®.

Hänschen ['hɛnsçən] *nt* **-s** *dim of* **Hans; was ~ nicht lernt, lernt Hans nimmermehr** (*Prov*) ≃ you can't teach an old dog new tricks (*Prov*).

Hansdampf *m* **-(e)s, -e** Jack-of-all-trades (and master of none) ◆ **er ist ein ~ in allen Gassen** he knows everybody and everything.

Hanse *f* **-,** *no pl* (*Hist*) Hanseatic League, Hansa, Hanse.

Hanseat(in *f*) *m* **-en, -en** citizen of a Hansa town; (*Hist*) Hanseatic merchant, merchant belonging to the Hanseatic League.

Hanseatengeist *m* Hanseatic spirit.

hanseatisch *adj* **(a)** (*Hist*) Hanseatic. **(b)** (*hansestädtisch*) Hanseatic. **(c)** (*fig: ~ vornehm*) cool and reserved.

Hansebund *m* (*Hist*) Hanseatic League.

Hansel, Hänsel *m* **-s** *dim of* **Hans** (*dial: Trottel*) dolt, ninny (*inf*) ◆ **~ und Gretel** Hansel and Gretel; **ein paar ~** (*dial: wenige*) a few.

Hänselei *f* teasing *no pl.*

hänseln *vt* to tease.

Hanse-: ~stadt *f* Hansa *or* Hanseatic *or* Hanse town; **h~städtisch** *adj* Hanseatic.

hansisch *adj* (*Hist*) Hanseatic.

Hans-: ~wurst *m* **-(e)s, -e** *or* (*hum*) **¨e (a)** buffoon, clown; **(b)** (*Theat*) fool, clown; **~wurstiade** *f* **(a)** (*auch* **~wursterei**) clowning, buffoonery; **(b)** (*Theat*) ≃ harlequinade.

Hantel *f* **-, -n** (*Sport*) dumb-bell.

hanteln *vi* (*Sport*) to exercise with dumb-bells.

hantieren* *vi* **(a)** (*arbeiten*) to be busy. **(b)** (*umgehen mit*) **mit etw ~** to handle sth; **seine Geschicklichkeit im H~ mit Begriffen** (*fig*) his skill in handling ideas. **(c)** (*herum~*) to tinker *or* fiddle about (*an +dat* with, on).

hantig *adj* (*Aus, S Ger*) **(a)** (*bitter*) bitter. **(b)** (*barsch*) brusque, abrupt.

haperig *adj* (*N Ger*) *siehe* **stockend.**

hapern *vi impers* (*inf*) **es hapert an etw** (*dat*) (*fehlt*) there is a shortage *or* lack of sth; **es hapert bei jdm mit etw** (*fehlt*) sb is short of sth, sb is badly off for sth; **es hapert (bei jdm) mit etw** (*klappt nicht*) sb has a problem with sth; **mit der Grammatik hapert es bei ihm** he's weak in *or* poor at grammar.

Häppchen *nt dim of* **Happen** morsel, bit; (*Appetithappen*) titbit.

häppchenweise *adv* (*inf: lit, fig*) bit by bit.

Happen *m* **-s, -** (*inf*) mouthful, morsel; (*kleine Mahlzeit*) bite, snack ◆ **ein fetter ~** (*fig*) a good catch; **nach dem Theater aßen wir noch einen ~** after the theatre we had a bite to eat (*inf*) *or* a snack; **ich habe heute noch keinen ~ gegessen** I haven't had a bite to eat all day.

Happening ['hɛpənɪŋ] *nt* **-s, -s** (*Theat*) happening; (*Art*) action painting.

happig *adj* (*inf*) steep (*inf*).

Happy-End, Happyend (*Aus*) ['hɛpɪ'|ɛnt] *nt* **-s, -s** happy ending ◆ **ein Film/Buch/eine Geschichte mit ~** a film/book/story with a happy ending.

Harakiri *nt* **-(s), -s** harakiri.

Harald *m* **-s** Harold.

Härchen *nt dim of* **Haar** little *or* tiny hair.

Hard- ['ha:d-]: **~liner** [-laɪnɐ] *m* **-s, -** (*Pol*) hardliner; **~rock** *m* **-(s),** *no pl* hard rock

Hardtop [-tɔp] *nt* **-s, -s** (*Aut: Dach, Wagen*) hardtop; **ein Cabrio mit ~top** a cabriolet with a hardtop.

Hardthöhe *f* Hardthöhe (*seat of the* (*West*) *German Ministry of Defence*).

Hardware ['ha:dwɛə] *f* **-, -s** (*Comput*) hardware.

Harem *m* **-s, -s** (*auch hum inf*) harem.

Harems-: ~dame *f* lady of the/a harem; **~wächter** *m* harem guard.

hären *adj* (*rare*) **~es Gewand** hairshirt.

Häresie *f* (*lit, fig*) heresy.

Häretiker(in *f*) *m* **-s, -** (*lit, fig*) heretic.

häretisch *adj* (*lit, fig*) heretical.

Harfe *f* **-, -n** harp.

Harfenist(in *f*) *m* harpist.

Harfen-: ~klang *m* sound of the/a harp; **~spiel** *nt no pl* harp-playing; **~spieler** *m* harp-player, harpist.

Harfner(in *f*) *m* **-s, -** (*obs*) harp-player, harpist.

Harke *f* **-, -n** (*esp N Ger*) rake ◆ **jdm zeigen, was eine ~ ist** (*fig inf*) to show sb what's what (*inf*).

harken *vti* (*esp N Ger*) to rake.

Harlekin ['harleki:n] *m* **-s, -e** Harlequin.

Harlekinade *f siehe* **Hanswurstiade.**

Harm *m* **-(e)s,** *no pl* (*poet, obs*) sore affliction (*liter*), grief.

härmen *vtr* (*old*) *siehe* **grämen.**

harmlos *adj* **(a)** (*ungefährlich*) harmless; *Berg, Piste, Kurve* easy; *Schnupfen, Entzündung etc* slight, mild ◆ **eine ~e Grippe** a mild bout of flu. **(b)** (*unschuldig, gutartig, naiv*) innocent; (*unbedenklich*) harmless, innocuous ◆ **er ist ein ~er Mensch** he's harmless (enough), he's an innocuous type.

Harmlosigkeit *f, no pl siehe adj* **(a)** harmlessness; easiness; slightness, mildness. **(b)** innocence; harmlessness, innocuousness ◆ **in aller ~** in all innocence.

Harmonie *f* (*Mus, fig*) harmony.

Harmonie-: ~gesetz *nt usu pl* rule of harmony; **~lehre** *f* (*Gebiet*) harmony; (*Theorie*) harmonic theory; **~musik** *f* music for wind instruments.

harmonieren* *vi* (*Mus, fig*) to harmonize; (*farblich auch*) to go together, to match.

Harmonik *f, no pl* harmony.

Harmonika *f* **-, -s** *or* **Harmoniken** harmonica; (*Mund~ auch*) mouth organ; (*Zieh~*) accordion.

Harmonikatür *f* folding *or* accordion door.

harmonisch *adj* (*Mus, Math*) harmonic; (*wohlklingend, fig*) harmonious ◆ **das klingt nicht sehr ~** that's not a very harmonious sound; **sie leben ~ zusammen** they live together in harmony.

harmonisieren* *vt Musik, Steuern* to harmonize; (*fig*) to coordinate.

Harmonisierung *f* (*von Musik, Steuern*) harmonization; (*fig*) coordination.

Harmonium *nt* harmonium.

Harn *m* **-(e)s, -e** urine ◆ **~ lassen** to pass water, to urinate.

Harn-: ~blase *f* bladder; **~blasenentzündung** *f siehe* **Blasenentzündung; ~drang** *m* (*form*) urge *or* need to pass water *or* to urinate.

harnen *vi* (*form*) to urinate, to pass water, to micturate (*form*).

Harn-: ~entleerung *f* urination, passing of water, micturition (*form*); **~flasche** *f* urinal.

Harnisch *m* **-(e)s, -e** armour ◆ **in ~ sein** (*fig*) to be up in arms, to have one's hackles up; **jdn in ~ bringen** (*fig*) to get sb up in arms, to get sb's hackles up.

Harn-: ~lassen *nt* **-s,** *no pl* (*form*) urination, passing of water, micturition (*form*); **~leiter** *m* ureter; **~organ** *nt* urinary organ; **~probe** *f* urine sample *or* specimen; **~röhre** *f* urethra; **~säure** *f* (*Chem*) uric acid; **~stein** *m* (*Med*) urinary calculus; **~stoff** *m* (*Chem*) urea, carbamide; **h~treibend** *adj* (*form*) diuretic; **~untersuchung** *f* urine analysis, urinalysis; **~vergiftung** *f* uraemia; **~wege** *pl* (*Anat*) urinary tract *sing*; **~zucker** *m* sugar in the urine.

Harpsichord [harpsi'kɔrt] *nt* **-(e)s, -e** (*old*) *siehe* **Cembalo.**

Harpune *f* **-, -n** harpoon.

Harpunen-: ~geschütz *nt*, **~kanone** *f*, **~werfer** *m* harpoon-gun.

Harpunier *m* **-s, -e** harpooner.

harpunieren* *vti* to harpoon.

Harpyie [har'py:jə] *f usu pl* (*Myth*) Harpy.

harren *vi* (*geh*) **jds/einer Sache ~, auf jdn/etw ~** to await sb/sth, to wait for sb/sth; *siehe* **Ding**[1].

Harsch *m* **-(e)s,** *no pl* frozen snow.

harsch *adj* **(a)** harsh. **(b)** (*verharscht*) *Schnee* frozen.

harschen *vi* to freeze over.

harschig *adj Schnee* frozen.

Harschschnee *m* frozen snow.

hart [1] *adj, comp* **¨er,** *superl* **¨este(r, s) (a)** (*nicht weich, nicht sanft*) hard; *Matratze, Bett, Federung, Apfelschale auch* firm; *Aufprall, Ruck auch* violent; *Wind* strong; *Ei* hard-boiled ◆ **~ werden** to get hard, to harden; **Eier ~ kochen** to hard-boil eggs; **der Boden ist ~ gefroren** the ground is frozen hard *or* solid; **er hat einen ~en Leib** (*Med old*) he is constipated; **er hat einen ~en Schädel** *or* **Kopf** (*fig*) he's pig-headed *or* obstinate; **ein ~es Herz haben** (*fig*) to have a hard heart, to be hard-hearted; **~ wie Stahl/Stein** as hard as steel/stone.
(b) (*scharf*) *Konturen, Kontrast, Formen,* (*Phot*) *Negativ* sharp; (*Gesichts*)*züge, Konsonant* hard; *Licht* harsh, hard; *Klang, Ton, Aussprache, Akzent* harsh.
(c) (*rauh*) *Spiel, Gegner* rough; (*fig*) *Getränke* strong; *Droge* hard; *Porno* hard-core; *Kriminalfilm etc, Western* tough.
(d) (*widerstandsfähig, robust*) tough ◆ **gelobt sei, was ~ macht** (*prov, usu iro*) anything for toughness!; treat 'em rough, make 'em tough! (*inf*); **er ist ~ im Nehmen** he's tough.
(e) (*stabil, sicher*) *Währung, Devisen* stable ◆ **in ~en Dollars** in hard dollars.
(f) (*streng, gnadenlos, kompromißlos*) *Mensch, Kampf* hard; *Wort auch* strong,

⚠: Informationen zur Rechtschreibreform im Anhang

harsh; *Winter, Frost, Vertragsbedingung auch* severe; *Strafe, Urteil, Kritik* severe, harsh; *Maßnahmen, Gesetze, Politik, Kurs* tough; *Auseinandersetzung* violent ◆ **der ~e Kern einer Vereinigung** the hard core of an organization; **er ist durch eine ~e Schule gegangen** (*fig*) he has been through a hard school; **~ bleiben** to stand *or* remain firm; **~ mit jdm sein** to be hard on sb, to be harsh with sb; **es fielen ~e Worte** hard *or* strong *or* harsh words were used; **es geht ~ auf ~** it's a tough fight *or* real battle.

(g) (*schwer zu ertragen*) *Los, Schicksal, Tatsache* hard, cruel; *Verlust* cruel; *Wirklichkeit, Wahrheit* harsh ◆ **es war sehr ~ für ihn, daß er ...** it was very hard for him to ...; **oh, das war ~!** (*inf: Witz etc*) oh, that was painful!

(h) (*mühevoll, anstrengend*) *Arbeit, Leben, Zeiten* hard, tough.

(i) (*Phys*) *Strahlen* hard.

2 *adv, comp* **¨er**, *superl* **am ¨esten (a)** hard ◆ **er schläft gerne ~** he likes sleeping on a hard surface/bed.

(b) (*scharf*) *kontrastiert* sharply ◆ **~ klingen** to sound harsh; **er spricht manche Laute zu ~ aus** he makes some sounds too hard.

(c) (*heftig, rauh*) roughly; *fallen, aufprallen* hard ◆ **er läßt die Kupplung immer so ~ kommen** he always lets the clutch in so roughly *or* violently; **~ aneinandergeraten** (*sich prügeln*) to come to blows, to have a (real) set-to (*inf*); (*sich streiten*) to get into a fierce argument, to have a (real) set-to (*inf*); **~ einsteigen** (*Sport*) to go hard at it; **jdn ~ anfahren** to bite sb's head off (*inf*); **jdm ~ zusetzen** to press sb hard; **etw trifft jdn ~** (*lit, fig*) sth hits sb hard; **~ diskutieren** to have a vigorous discussion; **~ spielen** (*Sport*) to play rough.

(d) (*streng*) severely, harshly ◆ **~ durchgreifen** to take tough *or* rigorous action; **jdn ~ anfassen** to be hard on sb, to treat sb harshly.

(e) (*mühevoll*) hard ◆ **~ arbeiten** to work hard; **es kommt mich ~ an** (*geh*) I find it hard.

(f) (*nahe*) close (*an +dat* to) ◆ **das ist ~ an der Grenze der Legalität/des Zumutbaren** that's pushing legality/reasonableness to its (very) limit(s), that's on the very limits of legality/of what's reasonable; **das ist ~ an der Grenze zum Kriminellen/zum Kitsch** that's very close to being criminal/kitsch; **wir fuhren ~ am Abgrund vorbei** (*fig*) we were (very) close to *or* on the (very) brink of disaster; **~ am Wind (segeln)** (*Naut*) (to sail) close to the wind; **~ auf ein Ziel zuhalten** (*Naut*) to head straight for a destination.

Hart-: ~bahn *f* (*Sport*) hard track; **h~bedrängt** *adj attr* hard-pressed; **~beton** *m* (especially) hard concrete; **h~blätt(e)rig** *adj* (*Bot*) hard-leaved.

Härte *f* **-, -n** *siehe adj* **(a)** hardness; firmness; violence; (*Härtegrad*) degree *or* grade (of hardness) ◆ **die ~, mit der er bremste** the violence with which he braked.

(b) *no pl* (*Schärfe*) sharpness; hardness; harshness.

(c) (*Rauheit*) roughness *no pl* ◆ **sie spielten mit größter ~** they played very rough.

(d) *no pl* (*Robustheit*) toughness.

(e) *no pl* (*Stabilität*) stability.

(f) *no pl* (*Strenge*) hardness; harshness; severity; toughness; violence ◆ **eine Auseinandersetzung in großer ~ führen** to have a violent argument; **mit großer ~ diskutieren** to have a very heated discussion.

(g) (*schwere Erträglichkeit*) cruelty, harshness ◆ **der Schicksalsschlag traf ihn in seiner ganzen ~** this blow of fate struck him with all its force *or* cruelty; **soziale ~n** social hardships; (*Fälle*) cases of social hardship.

(h) (*Phys*) degree of penetration.

Härte-: ~ausgleich *m* (*Admin*) compensation for (social) hardship; **~fall** *m* case of hardship; (*inf: Mensch*) hardship case; **~fonds** *m* hardship fund; **~grad** *m* degree *or* grade of hardness; **~klausel** *f* hardship clause; **~mittel** *nt* (*Metal*) hardening agent.

härten **1** *vt* to harden; *Stahl auch* to temper.

2 *vi* to harden.

3 *vr* (*Stoff*) to harden; (*rare: Mensch*) to toughen oneself up.

Härte-: ~ofen *m* (*Metal*) tempering oven *or* furnace; ⚠**~paragraph** *m* paragraph dealing with cases of hardship.

härter *comp of* **hart.**

Härter *m* **-s, -** (*Tech*) hardener, hardening agent.

Härteskala *f* scale of hardness, Mohs scale.

härteste(r, s) *superl of* **hart.**

Härte-: ~test *m* endurance test; (*fig*) acid test; **~zustand** *m* hard state; **im ~zustand läßt sich das Material wie Metall bearbeiten** in the hard state *or* when it is hard this material can be worked like metal.

Hart-: ~faserplatte *f* hardboard, fiberboard (*US*); ⚠**h~gebrannt** *adj attr Ziegel, Keramik* hard-baked; ⚠**h~gefroren** *adj attr* frozen, frozen stiff *pred*, frozen hard *pred*; ⚠**h~gekocht** *adj attr Ei* hard-boiled; (*fig*) *Mensch auch* hard-baked (*inf*); **~geld** *nt* hard cash; **h~gesotten** *adj* **(a)** (*fig*) hard-baked (*inf*), hard-boiled; **(b)** (*Aus*) *siehe* **h~gekocht**; **h~geworden** *adj attr* hard; **~gummi** *nt* hard rubber; **h~herzig** *adj* hard-hearted; **~herzigkeit** *f* hard-heartedness; **~holz** *nt* hardwood; **~käse** *m* hard cheese; **~laubgewächs** *nt* (*Bot*) sclerophyllous evergreen (*spec*); **h~leibig** *adj* (*Med old*) constipated; **~leibigkeit** *f* (*Med old*) constipation; **h~löten** *vti sep* to hard-solder; **~metall** *nt* hard metal; **h~näckig** *adj* (*stur*) *Mensch, Haltung* obstinate, stubborn; (*ausdauernd*) *Widerstand* stubborn; *Lügner* persistent; *Beharrlichkeit* dogged, persistent; (*langwierig*) *Krankheit, Fleck* stubborn; **~näckigkeit** *f siehe adj* obstinacy, stubbornness; persistence; doggedness; stubbornness; **~packung** *f* hard pack; **~pappe** *f* cardboard; **~platz** *m* (*Sport*) hard sports area; (*für Ballspiele*) hard pitch; (*Tennis*) hard court; **~schalenkoffer** *m* hard-top case; **h~schalig** *adj Frucht* hard-shelled, testaceous (*spec*); *Apfel, Traube* having a tough skin, tough-skinned; **~spiritus** *m* methylated spirits in solid form.

Hartung *m* **-s, -e** (*obs*) January.

Härtung *f* (*Tech*) hardening; (*von Stahl auch*) tempering.

Hart-: ~ware *f* hardware *no pl*; **~weizengrieß** *m* semolina; **~wurst** *f* salami-type sausage.

Harz¹ *nt* **-es, -e** resin.

Harz² *m* **-es** (*Geog*) Harz Mountains *pl.*

harz|artig *adj* resin-like, resinous, resinoid.

harzen **1** *vt Wein* to treat with resin, to resinate.

2 *vi* (*Baum, Holz*) to secrete *or* exude resin.

Harzer¹ *m* **-s, -** (*Cook*) Harz cheese.

Harzer² *adj* (*Geog*) Harz ◆ **~ Roller** (*Zool*) roller canary; (*Cook*) (roll-shaped) Harz cheese; **~ Käse** Harz cheese.

Harzer(in *f*) *m* **-s, -** native *or* (*Einwohner*) inhabitant of the Harz Mountains.

harzhaltig *adj Holz* resinous, containing resin.

harzig *adj* **(a)** *Holz, Geruch, Geschmack, Wein* resinous, resiny. **(b)** (*Sw fig: zähflüssig*) slow-moving.

Hasard [ha'zart] *nt* **-s,** *no pl siehe* **Hasardspiel, (mit etw) ~ spielen** (*fig geh*) to gamble (with sth).

Hasardeur [hazar'døːɐ] *m* (*geh*) gambler.

Hasardspiel [ha'zart-] *nt* game of chance; (*fig geh*) gamble ◆ **glatte Fahrbahnen machen das Autofahren zum ~** slippy roads make driving a treacherous business.

Hasch *nt* **-(s),** *no pl* (*inf*) hash (*inf*).

Haschee *nt* **-s, -s** (*Cook*) hash.

Haschen *nt* **-s,** *no pl* catch, tag.

haschen¹ (*dated, geh*) **1** *vt* to catch ◆ **hasch mich, ich bin der Frühling** (*hum inf*) come and get me boys! (*hum*).

2 *vi* **nach etw ~** to make a grab at sth; **nach Beifall/Lob** *etc* **~** to fish *or* angle for applause/praise *etc.*

haschen² *vi* (*inf*) to smoke (hash) (*inf*).

Häschen ['hɛsçən] *nt* **(a)** *dim of* **Hase** young hare, leveret. **(b)** (*inf: Kaninchen, Playboy~*) bunny (*inf*). **(c)** (*Kosename*) sweetheart, sweetie(pie).

Hascher(in *f*) *m* **-s, -** (*inf*) hash smoker.

Häscher *m* **-s, -** (*old, geh*) henchman.

Hascherl *nt* **-s, -(n)** (*Aus inf*) poor soul *or* thing *or* creature.

haschieren* *vt* (*Cook*) *Fleisch* to mince (*Brit*), to grind (*US*).

Haschisch *nt or m* **-(s),** *no pl* hashish.

Haschischrausch *m* state of euphoria produced by hashish ◆ **im ~** under the effects of hashish.

Haschmich *m* **-s,** *no pl* (*inf*) **einen ~ haben** to have a screw loose (*inf*), to be off one's rocker (*inf*).

Hase *m* **-n, -n** hare; (*männlicher ~ auch*) buck; (*dial: Kaninchen, Oster~, in Märchen*) rabbit ◆ **falscher ~** (*Cook*) meat loaf; **wissen/sehen, wie der ~ läuft** (*fig inf*) to know/see which way the wind blows; **alter ~** (*fig inf*) old hand; **da liegt der ~ im Pfeffer** (*inf*) that's the crux of the matter; **mein Name ist ~ (, ich weiß von nichts)** I don't know anything about anything.

Hasel *f* **-, -n** (*Bot*) hazel.

Hasel-: ~huhn *nt* hazel grouse; **~kätzchen** *nt* (*Bot*) (hazel) catkin, lamb's tail (*inf*); **~maus** *f* dormouse; ⚠**~nuß** *f* hazelnut, cob-nut; **~rute** *f* hazel rod *or* switch; **~strauch** *m* hazel-bush.

Hasen-: ~braten *m* roast hare; **~brot** *nt* (*inf*) left-over sandwich; **~fuß** *m* **(a)** hare's foot; **(b)** (*dated inf*) milksop (*dated*); **h~füßig** *adj* (*dated inf*) chicken-hearted (*inf*), lily-livered (*inf*); **~herz** *nt* **(a)** hare's heart; **(b)** (*dated inf*) *siehe* **~fuß (b)**; **~jagd** *f* hare-hunt; **auf (die) ~jagd gehen** to go hunting hares *or* on a hare-hunt; **~klein** *nt* **-s,** *no pl* (*Cook*) jointed hare; **~panier** *nt* **das ~panier ergreifen** (*dated inf*) to turn tail (and run); **~pfeffer** *m* (*Cook*) ≃ jugged hare; **h~rein** *adj* (*Hunt*) *Hund* trained to chase hares only on command; **jd/etw ist nicht (ganz) h~rein** (*inf*) sb/sth is not (quite) above board, there's something fishy about sb/sth (*inf*); **~scharte** *f* (*Med*) hare-lip.

Häsin *f* doe, female hare.

Haspel *f* **-, -n (a)** (*Förderwinde*) windlass. **(b)** (*Garn~*) reel.

haspeln *vti* **(a)** (*inf: hastig sprechen*) to splutter, to sputter; *Gebete, Entschuldigung* to sp(l)utter out. **(b)** (*wickeln*) to wind up, to reel up; (*abwickeln*) to unwind, to reel off.

⚠ **Haß** *m* **Hasses,** *no pl* **(a)** hatred, hate (*auf +acc, gegen* of) ◆ **Liebe und ~** love and hate *or* hatred; **sich** (*dat*) **jds ~ zuziehen, jds ~ auf sich** (*acc*) **ziehen** to incur sb's hatred.

(b) (*inf: Wut, Ärger*) **wenn ich so etwas sehe, könnt' ich einen ~ kriegen** (*inf*) when I see something like that I could get really angry; **einen ~ (auf jdn) schieben** (*sl*) *or* **haben** (*inf*) to be really sore (with sb) (*inf*).

⚠ **Haß|ausbruch** *m* burst of hatred.

▼ **hassen** *vti* to hate, to detest, to loathe ◆ **etw ~ wie die Pest** (*inf*) to detest sth.

hassenswert *adj* hateful, odious, detestable.

⚠ **Haß-: h~erfüllt** *adj* full of hate *or* hatred; **~gefühl** *nt* feeling of hatred.

⚠ **häßlich** *adj* **(a)** ugly ◆ **~ wie die Nacht** *or* **die Sünde** (as) ugly as sin. **(b)** (*gemein*) nasty, mean. **das war ~ von ihm** that was nasty *or* mean of him; **~ über jdn sprechen** to be nasty *or* mean about sb. **(c)** (*unerfreulich*) nasty; *Vorfall, Streit auch* ugly.

⚠ **Häßlichkeit** *f siehe adj* **(a)** ugliness *no pl.* **(b)** nastiness *no pl*, meanness *no pl*; (*Bemerkung*) nasty *or* mean remark. **(c)** nastiness; ugliness.

⚠ **Haß-: ~liebe** *f* love-hate relationship (*für* with); **~liebe für jdn empfinden** to have a love-hate relationship with sb; **~tirade** *f* tirade of hatred; **h~verzerrt** *adj Gesicht* twisted (up) with hatred.

hast *2. pers sing present of* **haben.**
Hast *f -, no pl* haste ◆ **voller ~** in great haste, in a great hurry *or* rush; **ohne ~** without haste, without hurrying *or* rushing; **mit fliegender/rasender ~** in a tearing/frantic hurry; **mit einer solchen ~** in such a hurry *or* rush, in such haste; **nur keine (jüdische) ~!** not so fast!, hold your horses! *(inf)*.
haste *(inf) contr of* **hast du; (was) ~ was kannste** as quick *or* fast as possible; **~ was, biste was** *(prov)* money brings status.
hasten *vi aux sein (geh)* to hasten *(form)*, to hurry.
hastig *adj* hasty; *Essen auch, Worte* hurried, rushed ◆ **nicht so ~!** not so fast!; **er schlang sein Essen ~ hinunter** he gobbled down his food; **sein ~es Rauchen** his hasty way of smoking.
Hastigkeit *f* hurriedness ◆ **sie ißt/schwimmt** *etc* **mit einer solchen ~** she eats/swims *etc* in such a hasty manner.
hat *3. pers sing present of* **haben.**
Hätschelei *f (pej)* pampering, mollycoddling.
Hätschelkind *nt (pej) (Kind)* pampered child; *(fig: Liebling)* blue-eyed boy/girl *(inf)*, darling.
hätscheln *vt (liebkosen)* to pet, to fondle; *(zu weich behandeln)* to pamper, to mollycoddle; *(bevorzugen)* to pamper, to indulge; *(hängen an) Plan, Idee* to cherish, to nurse; *Schmerz* to nurse, to indulge.
hatschen *vi aux sein (Aus, S Ger inf) (schlendern)* to amble along; *(mühsam gehen)* to trudge along; *(hinken)* to hobble ◆ **durch die Berge ~** to trudge through the mountains.
hatschert *adj (Aus inf)* hobbling ◆ **er geht ~** he hobbles (along).
hatschi *interj* atishoo ◆ **~ machen** *(baby-talk)* to sneeze.
hatte *pret of* **haben.**
Hat-Trick, Hattrick ['hættrɪk] *m -s, -s (Sport)* hat-trick; *(fig)* masterstroke.
Hatz *f -, -en* **(a)** *(Hunt, fig)* hunt. **(b)** *(fig: esp S Ger, Aus)* rush.
Hau *m -s, -e (inf)* bash *(inf)*, clout *(inf)* ◆ **einen ~ haben** to be thick *(inf)*.
Häubchen *nt dim of* **Haube.**
Haube *f -, -n* **(a)** bonnet; *(Aus, S Ger: Mütze)* (woollen) cap; *(von Krankenschwester etc)* cap ◆ **jdn unter die ~ bringen** *(hum)* to marry sb off; **unter der ~ sein/unter die ~ kommen** *(hum)* to be/get married.
(b) *(bei Vögeln)* crest.
(c) *(allgemein: Bedeckung)* cover; *(Trocken~)* (hair) dryer, drying hood *(US)*; *(für Kaffee-, Teekanne)* cosy; *(Motor~)* bonnet, hood *(US)* ◆ **der hat einiges unter der ~** *(inf)* it's got quite some engine *(inf)*.
Hauben-: ~lerche *f* crested lark; **~meise** *f* crested tit; **~taucher** *m (Zool)* great crested grebe.
Haubitze *f -, -n* howitzer.
Hauch *m -(e)s, -e (geh, poet)* **(a)** *(Atem)* breath; *(Luftzug)* breath of air, breeze. **(b)** *(Duft)* smell; *(von Parfüm auch)* waft ◆ **ein ~ von Frühling/Harz** a breath of spring/a delicate smell of resin. **(c)** *(Flair)* aura, air ◆ **ihr Haus hat den ~ des Exotischen** their house has an exotic air (about it) *or* an aura of exoticism. **(d)** *(Andeutung, Anflug, Schicht)* hint, touch; *(von Lächeln)* hint, ghost.
hauchdünn *adj* extremely thin; *Scheiben, Schokoladentäfelchen* wafer-thin; *Strümpfe, Strumpfhose* sheer; *(fig) Mehrheit* extremely narrow; *Sieg* extremely close.
hauchen [1] *vi* to breathe ◆ **gegen/auf etw** *(acc)* **~** to breathe on sth.
[2] *vt (lit, fig, liter: flüstern)* to breathe ◆ **jdn einen Kuß auf die Wange ~** *(liter)* to brush sb's cheek with one's lips; **das Jawort ~** *(liter)* to breathe "I will"; **jdm etw** *(acc)* **ins Ohr ~** *(liter)* to whisper sth in sb's ear; **er hauchte mir den Zigarettenrauch ins Gesicht** he blew the cigarette smoke in(to) my face.
Hauch-: h~fein *adj* extremely fine; **~laut** *m (Phon)* aspirate; **h~zart** *adj* very delicate; *Schokoladentäfelchen* wafer-thin.
Haudegen *m (fig)* old campaigner, (old) warhorse.
Haue *f -, -n* **(a)** *(S Ger, Sw, Aus) siehe* **Hacke²** **(a)**. **(b)** *no pl (inf: Prügel)* (good) hiding *(inf) or* spanking ◆ **~ kriegen** to get a good hiding *(inf) or* spanking.
hauen *pret* **haute,** *ptp* **gehauen** *or (dial)* **gehaut** [1] *vt* **(a)** *pret auch* **hieb** *(inf: schlagen)* to hit, to clout *(inf)*, to clobber *(inf)* ◆ **er haute den Stein in zwei Teile** he smashed the stone in two; **er haute ihr das Heft um die Ohren** he hit *or* clouted *(inf) or* clobbered *(inf)* her round the head with the exercise book.
(b) *(inf: verprügeln)* to hit, to belt *(sl)*, to thump *(inf)* ◆ **hau(t) ihn!** let him have it! *(inf)*, belt *or* thump him (one) *(sl)*.
(c) *(meißeln) Statue, Figur* to carve; *Stufen* to cut, to hew *(form)*; *Loch* to cut, to knock.
(d) *pret* **hieb** *(geh: mit Waffe schlagen)* to make a thrust at sb ◆ **jdn aus dem Sattel/vom Pferd ~** to knock sb out of the saddle/from his horse.
(e) *(inf: stoßen) jdn, Gegenstand* to shove *(inf)*; *Körperteil* to bang, to knock *(an +acc* on, against) ◆ **das haut einen vom Stuhl** *or* **aus den Latschen** *or* **aus dem Anzug** *or* **den stärksten Mann aus dem Anzug** it really knocks you sideways *(inf)*.
(f) *(inf) (werfen)* to chuck *(inf)*, to fling; *Farbe* to slap *(inf) (auf +acc* on) ◆ **er hat ihm eine 6 ins Zeugnis gehauen** he slammed a 6 on his report *(inf)*.
(g) *(dial) (fällen) Baum* to chop (down), to hew (down); *(mähen) Gras* to cut; *(zerhacken) Holz, Fleisch* to chop (up).
(h) *(Min) Erz* to cut; *Kohle* to break.
[2] *vi* **(a)** *pret auch* **hieb** *(inf: schlagen)* to hit ◆ **jdm ins Gesicht ~** to hit *or* clout *(inf) or* clobber *(inf)* sb in the face; **jdm auf die Schulter ~** to clap *or* slap sb on the shoulder; **hau doch nicht so (auf die Tasten)** don't thump like that; **er haute und haute** he banged *or* thumped away.
(b) *(inf: prügeln)* **nicht ~, Papi!** don't hit *or* thump *(inf)* me, daddy!; **er haut immer gleich** he's quick to hit out.
(c) *pret* **hieb** *(geh: mit Waffe)* to lash out ◆ **er hieb mit dem Degen (auf seinen Gegner)** he made a thrust (at his opponent) with his dagger; **es geht auf H~ und Stechen** *(fig)* there's a tough battle.
(d) *aux sein (inf: stoßen)* to bang, to hit ◆ **er ist mit dem Fuß gegen einen spitzen Stein gehauen** he banged *or* hit his foot against a sharp stone; **das Boot ist (mit dem Kiel) auf eine Sandbank gehauen** the boat('s keel) hit *or* struck a sandbank.
[3] *vr (inf)* **(a)** *(sich prügeln)* to scrap, to fight ◆ **sich mit jdm ~** to scrap *or* fight with sb.
(b) *(sich setzen, legen)* to fling oneself.
Hauer *m -s, -* **(a)** *(Min)* face-worker. **(b)** *(Aus) siehe* **Winzer(in).** **(c)** *(Zool)* tusk; *(hum: großer Zahn)* fang.
Häuer *m -s, - (Aus) siehe* **Hauer (a).**
Hauerei *f (inf)* scrap, fight.
Häufchen *nt dim of* **Haufen** small heap *or* pile ◆ **ein ~ Unglück** a picture of misery; *siehe* **Elend.**
Haufe *m -ns, -n (rare) siehe* **Haufen.**
häufeln *vt* **(a)** *Kartoffeln, Spargel* to hill up. **(b)** *(Haufen machen aus)* to heap *or* pile up.
Haufen *m -s, -* **(a)** heap, pile ◆ **jdn/ein Tier über den ~ rennen/fahren** *etc (inf)* to knock *or* run sb/an animal down, to run over sb/an animal; **jdn/ein Tier über den ~ schießen** *(inf) or* **knallen** *(inf)* to shoot sb/an animal down; **etw** *(acc)* **über den ~ werfen** *(inf) or* **schmeißen** *(inf) (verwerfen)* to throw *or* chuck *(inf)* sth out; *(durchkreuzen)* to mess sth up *(inf)*; **der Hund hat da einen ~ gemacht** the dog has made a mess there *(inf)*; **so viele Dummköpfe/soviel Idiotie/soviel Geld habe ich noch nie auf einem ~ gesehen** *(inf)* I've never seen so many fools/so much idiocy/money in one place before.
(b) *(inf: große Menge)* load *(inf)*, heap *(inf)* ◆ **ein ~ Arbeit/Geld/Bücher** a load *or* heap of work/money/books *(all inf)*, piles *or* loads *or* heaps of work/money/books *(all inf)*; **ein ~ Unsinn** a load of (old) rubbish *(inf)*, a load of nonsense *(inf)*; **ein ~ Zeit** loads *or* heaps of time *(inf)*; **ich hab noch einen ~ zu tun** I still have loads *or* piles *or* heaps *or* a load to do *(all inf)*; **in ~** by the ton *(inf)*; **er hat einen ganzen ~ Freunde** he has a whole load of friends *(inf)*, he has loads *or* heaps of friends *(inf)*.
(c) *(Schar)* crowd; *(von Vögeln)* flock; *(Sternen~)* cluster of stars ◆ **ein ~ Schaulustige(r)** a crowd of onlookers; **dichte ~ von Reisenden** dense crowds of travellers; **dem ~ folgen** *(pej)* to follow the crowd; **der große ~** *(pej)* the common herd, the masses *pl*.
(d) *(Gruppe, Gemeinschaft)* crowd *(inf)*, bunch *(inf)*; *(Mil)* troop.
häufen [1] *vt* to pile up, to heap up; *(sammeln)* to accumulate ◆ **Bücher auf den Tisch ~** to pile books onto the table; **ein gehäufter Teelöffel Salz** a heaped teaspoonful of salt; **Lob auf jdn ~** *(fig)* to heap praise(s) (up)on sb.
[2] *vr (lit, fig: sich ansammeln)* to mount up; *(zahlreicher werden: Unfälle, Fehler, Fachausdrücke etc)* to occur increasingly often ◆ **dieser Fehler tritt allerdings gehäuft auf** indeed this error occurs increasingly *or* occurs more and more frequently; **das kann schon mal vorkommen, es darf sich nur nicht ~** these things happen, just as long as they don't happen too often.
Haufen-: ~dorf *nt* scattered village; **h~weise** *adv* **(a)** *(in Haufen)* in heaps *or* piles; **(b)** *(inf: in großer Zahl, Menge)* piles *or* heaps *or* loads of *(all inf)*; **etw h~weise haben** to have piles *or* heaps *or* loads of sth *(all inf)*; **~wolke** *f siehe* **Kumuluswolke.**
häufig [1] *adj* frequent; *(weit verbreitet auch)* common, widespread ◆ **seine Anfälle werden ~er** his attacks are becoming more frequent.
[2] *adv* often, frequently.
Häufigkeit *f* frequency; *(räumliche Verbreitung)* commonness.
Häufigkeits- *in cpds* frequency-; **~grad** *m* frequency rank; **~zahl, ~ziffer** *f* frequency.
Häufung *f* **(a)** *(fig: das Anhäufen)* accumulation, amassment. **(b)** *(das Sich-Häufen)* increasing number ◆ **in ähnlicher** *etc* **~** in similar *etc* numbers *pl*.
Haupt *nt -(e)s, Häupter* **(a)** *(geh: Kopf)* head ◆ **entblößten ~es** bareheaded; **gesenkten/erhobenen ~es** with one's head bowed/raised; **zu jds Häupten** at sb's head; **jdn aufs ~ schlagen** *(fig: besiegen)* to vanquish; **eine Reform an ~ und Gliedern** a total *or* wide-reaching reform. **(b)** *(zentrale Figur)* head. **(c)** *(poet: von Berg)* peak.
Haupt- *in cpds* main, principal, chief; **~achse** *f* main *or* principal axis; *(von Fahrzeug)* main axle; **~akteur** *m (lit, fig)* leading light; *(pej)* kingpin; **~aktion** *f siehe* **Haupt- und Staatsaktion; ~aktionär** *m* principal *or* main shareholder; **~akzent** *m* **(a)** *(Ling)* main *or* primary accent *or* stress; **(b)** *(fig)* main emphasis; **auf etw** *(acc)* **den ~akzent legen** to put *or* place the main emphasis on sth; **~altar** *m* high altar; **h~amtlich** [1] *adj* full-time; **h~amtliche Tätigkeit** full-time office; [2] *adv* (on a) full-time (basis); **h~amtlich tätig sein** to work full-time; **~angeklagte(r)** *mf* main *or* principal defendant; ⚠**~anschluß** *m (Telec)* main extension; **nur einen ~anschluß haben** to have a phone without extensions; **~anteil** *m* main *or* principal part *or* share; **~arbeit** *f* main (part of the) work; **~ausgang** *m* main exit; **~bahnhof** *m* main *or* central station; **~belastungszeuge** *m* main *or* principal *or* chief witness for the prosecution; **~beruf** *m* chief *or* main occupation *or* profession; **er ist Lehrer im ~beruf** his main *or* chief occupation *or* profession is that of teacher; **h~beruflich** [1] *adj Lehrer, Gärtner etc* full-time; **h~berufliche Tätigkeit** main *or* chief occupation; [2] *adv* full-time; **h~beruflich tätig sein** to be employed full-time, to be in full-time employment; **er ist h~beruflich bei dieser Firma tätig** *(voll angestellt)* he is employed full-time by this firm; *(im Gegensatz zu Nebenerwerb)* his main employment is at this firm; **~beschäftigung** *f* **(a)** main *or* chief occupation *or* pursuit; **(b)** *(Hauptberuf)* main *or* chief occupation *or* job; **~betrieb**

m **(a)** (*Zentralbetrieb*) headquarters *sing or pl*; **(b)** (*geschäftigste Zeit*) peak period; (*Hauptverkehrszeit auch*) rush hour; **~buch** *nt* (*Comm*) ledger; **~büro** *nt* head office; **~darsteller(in** *f*) *m* principal actor/actress, leading man/lady; **~daten** *pl* main facts *pl*; **~deck** *nt* main deck; **~eingang** *m* main entrance; **~einnahmequelle** *f* main *or* chief source of income; **~einwand** *m* main *or* chief *or* principal objection (*gegen* to).

Häuptel *nt* **-s, -** (*Aus*) head (of lettuce *etc*).

Häuptelsalat *m* (*Aus*) lettuce.

Haupt-: ~entlastungszeuge *m* main *or* principal witness for the defence; **~erbe[1]** *m* principal heir; **~erbe[2]** *nt* principal inheritance; **~ereignis** *nt* main *or* principal event.

Haupteslänge *f* **jdn um ~ überragen** (*lit, fig*) to be head and shoulders above sb.

Haupt-: ~fach *nt* (*Sch, Univ*) main *or* principal subject, major (*US*); **etw im ~fach studieren** to study sth as one's main *or* principal subject, to major in sth (*US*); **~fehler** *m* main *or* chief *or* principal fault; **~feind** *m* main *or* chief enemy; **~feld** (*sl*), **~feldwebel** *m* (company) sergeant major; **~figur** *f* (*Liter*) central *or* main *or* principal character *or* figure; (*fig*) leading *or* central figure; **~film** *m* main film; **~forderung** *f* main *or* chief *or* principal demand; **~frage** *f* main *or* principal question *or* issue; **~gang** *m* **(a)** (*Archit etc*) main corridor; (*in Kirche, Theater, Kino*) central aisle; **(b)** (*Cook*) main course; **~gebäude** *nt* main building; **~gedanke** *m* main idea; **~gefreite(r)** *m* ≃ lance corporal (*Brit*), private first class (*US*); **~gegenstand** *m* **(a)** main *or* chief topic, main subject; **(b)** (*Aus Sch*) *siehe* **~fach; ~gericht** *nt* main course.

Hauptgeschäft *nt* **(a)** (*Zentrale*) head office, headquarters *sing or pl*. **(b)** (*Hauptverdienst*) main business, major part of one's business.

Hauptgeschäfts-: ~stelle *f* head office, headquarters *sing or pl*; **~straße** *f* main shopping street; **~zeit** *f* peak (shopping) period *or* hours *pl*.

Haupt-: ~gesichtspunkt *m* main *or* major consideration; **~gewicht** *nt* (*lit*) major part of the weight, bulk of the weight; (*fig*) main emphasis; **~gewinn** *m* first prize; **~grund** *m* main *or* principal *or* chief reason; **~haar** *nt* (*geh*) hair (of the/one's head); **~hahn** *m* mains cock *or* tap (*Brit*); **~handlung** *f* (*Liter etc*) main plot; **~interesse** *nt* main *or* chief interest; **~kampflinie** *f* main front; **~kennzeichen** *nt siehe* **~merkmal; ~kläger** *m* principal plaintiff; **~last** *f* main load, major part of the load; (*fig*) main *or* major burden; **~leitung** *f* mains *pl*; **~leute** *pl of* **~mann (a); ~lieferant** *m* main *or* principal *or* chief supplier.

Häuptling *m* chief(tain); (*esp von Dorf*) headman.

häuptlings *adv* (*old, geh*) *siehe* **kopfüber.**

Haupt-: ~macht *f* (*Mil*) bulk *or* main body of its/the forces; **~mahlzeit** *f* main meal; **~mangel** *m* main deficiency, main *or* principal defect; **~mann** *m, pl* **-leute (a)** (*Mil*) captain; **(b)** (*Hist: Führer*) leader; **~masse** *f* bulk, main body; **~menü** *nt* (*Comput*) main menu; **~merkmal** *nt* main feature, chief *or* principal characteristic; **~mieter** *m* main tenant; **~motiv** *nt* **(a)** (*Beweggrund*) primary *or* main motive; **(b)** (*Art, Liter, Mus*) main *or* principal motif; **~nahrungsmittel** *nt* staple *or* principal food; **~nenner** *m* (*Math, fig*) common denominator; **~niederlassung** *f* head office, headquarters *sing or pl*; **~person** *f* (*lit, fig*) central figure; **~platine** *f* (*Comput*) motherboard; **~portal** *nt* main portal *or* doorway; **~post** *f* (*inf*), **~postamt** *nt* main post office; **~probe** *f* final rehearsal; (*Kostümprobe*) dress rehearsal; **~problem** *nt* main *or* chief *or* principal problem; **~produkt** *nt* main product; (*esp im Gegensatz zu Nebenprodukt*) primary product; **~prozessor** *m* (*Comput*) main processor; **~quartier** *nt* (*Mil, fig*) headquarters *sing or pl*; **~quelle** *f* (*lit, fig*) main *or* primary source; **~rechnungsart** *f* (*Math*) basic arithmetical operation; **~redner** *m* main *or* principal speaker; **~reisezeit** *f* peak travelling time(s *pl*); **~revier** *nt siehe* **~wache; ~rohr** *nt* main pipe; (*von Gas-/Wasserleitung*) main, mains pipe; **~rolle** *f* (*Film, Theat*) leading *or* main role *or* part, lead; **die ~rolle spielen** (*fig*) to be all-important; (*wichtigste Person sein*) to play the main role *or* part; **~runde** *f* (*Sport*) main round; **~sache** *f* main thing; (*in Brief, Rede etc*) main point; **in der ~sache** in the main, mainly; **~sache, es klappt/du bist glücklich** the main thing is that it comes off/you're happy; **h~sächlich** [1] *adv* mainly, chiefly, principally; [2] *adj* main, chief, principal; **~saison** *f* peak *or* high season; **~saison haben** to have its/their peak season; **~satz** *m* **(a)** (*Gram*) (*übergeordnet*) main clause; (*alleinstehend*) sentence; **(b)** (*Mus*) first *or* main subject; **(c)** (*Philos*) main proposition; **~schalter** *m* (*Elec*) main *or* master switch; **~schiff** *nt* (*Archit*) nave; **~schlagader** *f* aorta; **~schlüssel** *m* master key; ⚠**~schulabschluß** *m* **den ~schulabschluß haben** ≃ to have completed secondary modern school (*Brit*) *or* junior high (school) (*US*); **~schuld** *f* main blame, principal fault (*esp Jur*); **~schuldige(r)** *mf* person mainly to blame *or* at fault, main offender (*esp Jur*); **er ist der ~schuldige** he is mainly to blame *or* at fault/he is the main offender; **~schule** *f* ≃ secondary modern (school) (*Brit*), junior high (school) (*US*); **~schüler** *m* ≃ secondary modern/junior high (school) pupil; **~schullehrer** *m* ≃ secondary modern/junior high (school) teacher; **~schwierigkeit** *f* main *or* chief *or* principal difficulty; **~segel** *nt* main sail; **~seminar** *nt* (*Univ*) seminar for advanced students; **~sicherung** *f* (*Elec*) main fuse; **~sitz** *m* head office, headquarters *sing or pl*; **~sorge** *f* main *or* chief worry; **~speicher** *m* (*Comput*) main memory; **~stadt** *f* capital (city); **~städter** *m* citizen of the capital, metropolitan; **h~städtisch** *adj* metropolitan, of the capital (city); **~stoßrichtung** *f* (*Mil, fig*) main object of one's/the attack (*gegen* on); **~straße** *f* (*Durchgangsstraße*) main *or* major road; (*im Stadtzentrum etc*) main street; **~strecke** *f* (*Rail*) main line; (*Straße*) main *or* primary (*Admin*) route; **~strömung** *f* (*lit, fig*) main current; **~stütze** *f* (*fig*) mainstay, main support *or* prop; **~sünde** *f* (*Rel*) cardinal sin; **~täter** *m* main *or* chief *or* principal culprit; **~tätigkeit** *f* main *or* principal *or* chief activity; (*beruflich*) main occupation; **~teil** *m* main part; (*größter Teil auch*) major part; **~thema** *nt* main *or* principal topic; (*Mus, Liter*) main *or* principal theme; **~ton** *m* (*Ling*) main *or* primary stress; (*Mus*) principal note; **~treffer** *m* top prize, jackpot (*inf*); **den ~treffer machen** (*inf*) to win the top prize, to hit the jackpot (*inf*); **~treppe** *f* main staircase *or* stairs *pl*; **~tribüne** *f* main stand; (*Sport auch*) grandstand; **~- und Staatsaktion** *f* **aus etw eine ~- und Staatsaktion machen** to make a great issue of sth, to make a song and dance about sth (*inf*), to make a Federal case out of sth (*US inf*); **~unterschied** *m* main *or* principal difference; **~ursache** *f* main *or* chief *or* principal cause; **~verantwortliche(r)** *mf* person mainly *or* chiefly responsible; **~verantwortung** *f* main responsibility; **~verdiener** *m* main *or* principal earner; **~verdienst[1]** *m* main income; **~verdienst[2]** *nt* chief merit; **~verfahren** *nt* (*Jur*) main proceedings *pl*; **~verhandlung** *f* (*Jur*) main hearing.

Hauptverkehr *m* peak(-hour) traffic; (*Verkehrsteilnehmer*) main traffic, bulk of the traffic.

Hauptverkehrs-: ~ader *f* main highway, arterial route; **~straße** *f* (*in Stadt*) main street; (*Durchgangsstraße*) main thoroughfare; (*zwischen Städten*) main highway, trunk road (*Brit*); **~zeit** *f* peak traffic times *pl*; (*in Stadt, bei Pendlern auch*) rush hour.

Haupt-: ~verlesen *nt* (*Sw Mil*) roll call; **~versammlung** *f* general meeting; **~wache** *f* main police station; **~wäsche** *f*, **~waschgang** *m* main wash; **~werk** *nt* **(a)** (*Art etc*) main *or* principal work; **(b)** (*Fabrik*) main factory *or* works *sing or pl*; **~wohnsitz** *m* main place of residence, main domicile (*form*); **~wort** *nt* (*Gram*) noun; **h~wörtlich** *adj* (*Gram*) nominal; **~zeit** *f* (*~saison*) peak times *pl*; (*in bezug auf Obst etc*) main season; **~zeuge** *m* principal *or* main *or* chief witness; **~ziel** *nt* main *or* principal aim *or* goal; **~zollamt** *nt* main customs office; **~zug** *m* **(a)** (*Rail*) scheduled train; **(b)** *usu pl* (*Charakteristikum*) main *or* principal feature, chief characteristic; **~zweck** *m* main *or* chief purpose *or* object.

hau ruck *interj* heave-ho.

Hauruck *nt* **-s, -s** heave.

Haus *nt* **-es, Häuser (a)** (*Gebäude*) (*esp Wohn~*) house; (*Firmengebäude*) building, premises *pl* (*form*) ◆ **er war nicht im ~, sondern im Garten** he wasn't in the house *or* indoors but in the garden; **laß uns ins ~ gehen** let's go in(doors) *or* inside *or* into the house; **Tomaten kann man im ~ ziehen** tomatoes can be grown indoors *or* inside *or* in the house; **der Klavierlehrer kommt ins ~** the piano teacher comes to the house; **er ist nicht im ~e** (*in der Firma*) he's not in the building *or* on the premises, he's not in; **aus dem ~ gehen** to leave the house; **mit jdm ~ an ~ wohnen** to live next door to sb; **wir wohnen ~ an ~** we live next door to each other, we are next-door neighbours; **von ~ zu ~ gehen** to go from door to door *or* from house to house; **das ~ Gottes** *or* **des Herrn** (*geh*) the House of God *or* of the Lord; **~ der Jugend** youth centre.

(b) (*Zuhause, Heim*) home ◆ **~ und Hof** (*fig*) house and home; **~ und Herd verlassen** to leave house and home, to leave one's home (behind); **etw ins/frei ~ liefern** (*Comm*) to deliver sth to the door/to deliver sth free *or* carriage paid; **wir liefern frei ~** we offer free delivery; **ein großes ~ führen** (*fig*) to entertain lavishly *or* in style; **jdm das ~ führen** to keep house for sb; **jdm das ~ verbieten** not to allow sb in the house, to forbid sb (to enter) the house; **aus dem ~ sein** to be away from home; **außer ~ essen** to eat out; **im ~e meiner Schwester** at my sister's (house); **er hat nichts zu essen im ~** he has nothing in the house; **jdn ins ~ nehmen** to take sb in(to one's home); **ein Fernsehgerät kommt mir nicht ins ~!** I won't have a television set in the house!; **ins ~ stehen** (*fig*) to be on the way; **jdm steht etw ins ~** (*fig*) sb is facing sth; **nach ~e** (*lit, fig*) home; **jdn nach ~e bringen** to take *or* see sb home; **komm mir bloß nicht damit nach ~e!** (*fig inf*) don't you (dare) come that one with me (*inf*)!; **jdn nach ~e schicken** (*fig inf*) to send sb packing (*inf*); **Grüße von ~ zu ~** (*form*) regards from ourselves to you all; **zu ~e** at home (*auch Sport*); **bei jdm zu ~e** at sb's (place), in sb's house *or* home; **bei uns zu ~e** at home; **wie geht's zu ~e?** how are they (all) at home?, how are the folks? (*inf*); **von zu ~e aus** from home; **für jdn/niemanden zu ~e sein** to be at home to sb/nobody; **irgendwo zu ~e sein** (*Mensch, Tier*) to live somewhere; (*sich heimisch fühlen*) to be at home somewhere; (*Brauch*) to be customary *or* practised somewhere; **in etw** (*dat*) **zu ~e sein** (*fig*) to be at home in sth; **sich wie zu ~e fühlen** to feel at home; **fühl dich wie zu ~e!** make yourself at home!; **damit kannst du zu ~e bleiben, bleib doch damit zu ~e** (*fig inf*) you can keep it/them *etc* (*inf*).

(c) (*Bewohnerschaft eines ~es*) household ◆ **ein Freund des ~es** a friend of the family; **die Dame/Tochter** *etc* **des ~es** (*form*) the lady/daughter *etc* of the house; **der Herr des ~es** (*form*) the master of the house.

(d) (*geh: Herkunft*) **aus gutem/bürgerlichem ~(e)** from a good/middle-class family; **aus adligem ~(e)** of noble birth, of *or* from a noble house (*form*); **von ~e aus** (*ursprünglich*) originally; (*von Natur aus*) naturally.

(e) (*Dynastie*) House ◆ **das ~ Habsburg** the House of the Hapsburgs, the Hapsburg dynasty; **das ~ Windsor** the House of Windsor; **aus dem ~ Davids** of the House of David.

(f) (*geh: Unternehmen*) House (*form*) ◆ **das ~ Siemens** the House of Siemens; **„~ Talblick"** (*Name*) "Talblick (House)"; **das erste ~ am Platze** (*Hotel*) the finest *or* best hotel in town; (*Kaufhaus*) the top *or* best store in town; **ein gepflegtes** *or* **gut geführtes ~** (*Restaurant*) a well-run house.

(g) (*Theater*) theatre; (*Saal, Publikum*) house ◆ **vor vollem ~ spielen** to play to

⚠: for details of spelling reform, see supplement

a full house; **das große/kleine ~** the large *or* main/small theatre.
(h) *(Parl)* House ◆ **Hohes ~!** *(form)* ≃ honourable members (of the House)!; **dieses hohe ~** ... the *or* this House ...
(i) *(von Schnecke)* shell, house *(inf)*.
(j) *(Astrol)* house.
(k) *(dated inf: Kerl)* chap *(Brit inf)*, fellow ◆ **grüß dich Hans, (du) altes ~!** *(inf)* hallo Hans, old chap *(inf)* *or* chum *(dated inf)*.

Haus-: **~altar** *m* family *or* house altar; **~andacht** *f* family worship; **~angestellte(r)** *mf* domestic servant; *(esp Frau)* domestic; **~antenne** *f* roof aerial; **~anzug** *m* leisure suit; **~apotheke** *f* medicine cupboard *or* chest; **~arbeit** *f* **(a)** housework *no pl*; **(b)** *(Sch)* homework *no indef art, no pl*, piece of homework, assignment *(esp US)*; **~arrest** *m (im Internat)* detention; *(Jur)* house arrest; **~arrest haben** to be in detention/under house arrest; **Fritz kann nicht zum Spielen rauskommen, er hat ~arrest** Fritz can't come out to play — he's being kept in; **~arzt** *m* family doctor, GP; *(von Heim, Anstalt)* resident doctor; **~aufgabe** *f (Sch)* homework *no indef art, no pl*, piece of homework, assignment *(esp US)*; **~aufgaben** *pl* homework *sing, no indef art*; **seine ~aufgaben machen** *(auch fig)* to do one's homework; **~aufgabenüberwachung** *f (Sch)* homework supervision; **~aufsatz** *m (Sch)* homework essay, essay for homework; **h~backen** *adj (fig)* homespun, drab, homely *(US)*; *Kleidung* unadventurous; **~ball** *m* (private) ball *or* dance; **~bank** *f* bank; **~bar** *f* home bar; *(Möbelstück)* cocktail *or* drinks cabinet; **~bau** *m* house building *or* construction; *(das Bauen)* building of a/the house; **~besetzer** *m* occupier of a/the house; *(esp um dort zu wohnen)* squatter; **~besetzung** *f siehe* **~besetzer** house occupation; squat(ting action); **~besitz** *m* house ownership; **~besitz haben** to own a house/houses; **~besitzer** *m* home-owner, house-owner; *(~wirt)* landlord; **~besorger** *m (Aus) siehe* **~meister**; **~besuch** *m* home visit; **~bewohner** *m* (house) occupant *or* occupier; **~bibliothek** *f* library; **~bock** *m (Zool)* house longhorn; **~boot** *nt* houseboat; **~brand** *m* **(a)** house fire; **(b)** *(Brennstoff)* domestic *or* heating fuel; **~briefkasten** *m* letter box *(Brit)*, mailbox *(US)*; **~bursche** *m* pageboy, bellboy *(US)*, bellhop *(US)*.

Häuschen ['hɔysçən] *nt* **(a)** *dim of* **Haus**.
(b) *(fig inf)* **ganz aus dem ~ sein** to be out of one's mind with joy/excitement/fear *etc (inf)*; **ganz aus dem ~ geraten** to go berserk *(inf)*; **jdn (ganz) aus dem ~ bringen** to make sb go berserk *(inf)*.
(c) *(inf: Karo)* square, block.
(d) *(euph inf: Toilette)* loo *(Brit inf)*, bathroom *(US)*, smallest room *(hum inf)*; *(außerhalb des Gebäudes)* privy, outside loo *(Brit inf)*.

Haus-: **~dame** *f* housekeeper; **~detektiv** *m* house detective; *(von Kaufhaus)* store detective; **~diener** *m* **(a)** *(in Privathaushalt)* manservant; **(b)** *(in Hotel)* hotel servant; *(Gepäckträger)* (hotel) porter; **~drachen** *m (inf)* dragon *(inf)*, battle-axe *(inf)*; **~durchsuchung** *f (Aus) siehe* **~suchung**; **h~eigen** *adj* belonging to a/the hotel/firm *etc*; **~eigentümer** *m* home owner; **~einfahrt** *f (Aus)*, **~eingang** *m* (house) entrance.

Häusel *nt* **-s, -** *(Aus, dial) siehe* **Häuschen (a, d)**.

Hausen *m* **-s, -** *(Zool)* sturgeon.

hausen *vi* **(a)** *(wohnen)* to live. **(b)** *(wüten)* **(übel** *or* **schlimm) ~** to wreak *or* create havoc; **schrecklich ~** to wreak the most dreadful havoc; **wie die Wandalen ~** to act like vandals. **(c)** *(Sw, S Ger: sparsam sein)* to be economical.

Häuser-: **~block** *m* block (of houses); **~flucht** *f siehe* **~reihe**; **~front** *f* front of a terrace *or* row of houses.

Häuserin *f (Aus, S Ger) siehe* **Haushälterin**.

Häuser-: **~kampf** *m (Mil)* house-to-house fighting; *(Pol)* squatting actions *pl*; *(einzelner Fall)* squat(ting action); **~makler** *m* estate agent, realtor *(US)*; **~meer** *nt* mass of houses; **~reihe, ~zeile** *f* row of houses; *(aneinandergebaut)* terrace.

Haus-: **~flagge** *f (Naut)* house flag; **~flur** *m* (entrance) hall, hallway.

Hausfrau *f* **(a)** housewife; *(Gastgeberin)* hostess. **(b)** *(Aus, S Ger) siehe* **Hauswirtin**.

Hausfrauen-: **~art** *f* **Wurst** *etc* **nach ~art** home-made-style sausage *etc*; **~brigade** *f (DDR)* housewives' brigade; **~pflicht** *f* housewifely duty.

Haus-: **h~fraulich** *adj* housewifely; **~freund** *m* **(a)** *(Freund der Familie)* friend of the family; **(b)** *(euph inf)* man friend; **~friede(n)** *m* domestic peace; **~friedensbruch** *m (Jur)* trespass *(in sb's house)*; **~gans** *f* (domestic) goose; **~gast** *m (von Pension etc)* resident, guest; **~gebrauch** *m* **für den ~gebrauch** *(Gerät)* for domestic *or* household use; *(Obst-, Gemüsenbau)* for one's own consumption; **sein Französisch reicht für den ~gebrauch** *(inf)* his French is (good) enough to get by (on); **~geburt** *f* home birth; **~gehilfin** *f* home help; **~geist** *m* **(a)** household spirit; *(Gespenst)* household ghost; **(b)** *(hum: ~angestellter)* faithful retainer *(old, hum)*; **h~gemacht** *adj* home-made; *(fig) Problem etc* of one's own making; **~gemeinschaft** *f* household (community); **mit jdm in ~gemeinschaft leben** to live together with sb (in the same household); **~genosse** *m* fellow tenant/lodger; **~götter** *pl (Myth)* household gods *pl*.

Haushalt *m* **-(e)s, -e (a)** *(Hausgemeinschaft)* household; *(~sführung)* housekeeping ◆ **Geräte für den ~** household utensils; **den ~ führen** to run the household; **jdm den ~ führen** to keep house for sb. **(b)** *(fig: Biol etc)* balance. **(c)** *(Etat)* budget.

Haushalt- *in cpds siehe* **Haushalts-**.

⚠**haushalten** *vi sep irreg* **(a)** *(sparsam wirtschaften)* to be economical ◆ **mit etw ~** *mit Geld, Zeit* to be economical with sth, to use sth economically; *mit Kräften, Vorräten auch* to conserve sth. **(b)** *(den Haushalt führen)* to keep house.

Haushälter(in *f*), Haushalter(in *f*) *(rare)* *m* **-s, -** housekeeper.

haushälterisch *adj* thrifty, economical ◆ **mit etw ~ umgehen** *siehe* **haushalten (a)**.

Haushalts- *in cpds* household; *(Pol)* budget; **~artikel** *m* household item *or* article; **~buch** *nt* housekeeping book; **(ein) ~buch führen** to keep a housekeeping book; **~debatte** *f (Parl)* budget debate; **~defizit** *nt (Pol)* budget deficit; **~fragen** *pl (Pol)* budgetary questions *pl*; **~führung** *f* housekeeping; **doppelte ~führung** running two homes; **~geld** *nt* housekeeping money; **~gerät** *nt* household appliance; **~hilfe** *f* domestic *or* home help; **~jahr** *nt (Pol, Econ)* financial *or* fiscal year; **~kasse** *f* household *or* family budget; **~loch** *nt* budget deficit; **das ~loch stopfen** to cure the budget deficit; **~mittel** *pl (Pol)* budgetary funds *pl*; **~packung** *f* family pack; **~plan** *m (Pol)* budget; **~planung** *f (Pol)* budgetary planning, planning of a budget; **~politik** *f (Pol)* budgetary policy; **h~politisch** *adj* concerning budgetary policy; **die Regierung hat h~politisch versagt** the government has failed in its budgetary policy; **~waage** *f* kitchen scales *pl*; **~waren** *pl* household goods *pl*.

Haushaltung *f* **(a)** *(das Haushaltführen)* housekeeping, household management; *(das Sparsamsein)* economizing *(mit* with). **(b)** *(form) siehe* **Haushalt (a)**.

Haushaltungs-: **~buch** *nt* housekeeping book; **~kosten** *pl* household *or* housekeeping expenses; **~vorstand** *m (form)* head of the household.

Haus-: **~herr** *m* **(a)** head of the household; *(Gastgeber, Sport)* host; **(b)** *(Jur)* householder; **(c)** *(Aus, S Ger) siehe* **~besitzer(in)**; **~herrin** *f* **(a)** lady of the house; *(Gastgeberin)* hostess; **(b)** *(Aus, S Ger) siehe* **~besitzer(in)**; **h~hoch** **[1]** *adj* (as) high as a house/houses; *(fig) Sieg* crushing; **der h~hohe Favorit** the hot favourite *(inf)*; **[2]** *adv* high (in the sky); **jdn h~hoch schlagen** to give sb a hammering *(inf)* *or* thrashing *(inf)*; **h~hoch gewinnen** to win hands down *or* by miles *(inf)*; **jdm h~hoch überlegen sein** to be head and shoulders above sb; **~huhn** *nt* domestic fowl.

hausieren* *vi* to hawk, to peddle *(mit etw* sth) ◆ **mit etw ~ gehen** *(fig) mit Plänen etc* to hawk sth about; *mit Gerüchten* to peddle sth; **„H~ verboten"** "no hawkers *or* peddlers".

Hausierer(in *f*) *m* **-s, -** hawker, peddler, pedlar.

Haus-: **h~intern** *adj siehe* **firmenintern**; **~jacke** *f* house jacket; **~jurist** *m* company lawyer; **~kaninchen** *nt* domestic rabbit; **~kapelle** *f* **(a)** *(Rel)* private chapel; **(b)** *(Musikkapelle)* resident band; *(an Fürstenhof)* resident *or* private orchestra; **~katze** *f* domestic cat; **~kauf** *m* house-buying *no art*, house purchase; **~kleid** *nt* housecoat; **~konzert** *nt* family concert; **~korrektur** *f (Typ)* proofreading *(carried out by the publishers)*; **~lehrer(in *f*)** *m* (private) tutor; **~leute** *pl (dial, inf) siehe* **Wirtsleute**; *(Sw)* tenants *pl*.

häuslich *adj Angelegenheiten, Pflichten, Friede etc* domestic; *(der Familie gehörend)* family *attr*; *(an ~en Dingen interessiert)* domesticated; *(das Zuhause liebend)* home-loving ◆ **der ~e Herd** the family home; **sich ~ niederlassen** to make oneself at home; **sich ~ einrichten** to settle in.

Häuslichkeit *f* domesticity.

Hausmacher-: **~art** *f* **Wurst** *etc* **nach ~art** home-made-style sausage *etc*; **~kost** *f* home cooking; **~wurst** *f* home-made sausage.

Haus-: **~macht** *f (Hist)* allodium; *(fig)* power base; **~mädchen** *nt* (house)maid; **~mann** *m, pl* **~männer** *(den Haushalt versorgender Mann)* househusband; **~mannskost** *f* plain cooking *or* fare; **~mantel** *m* housecoat; **~märchen** *nt* folk tale; **„~- und Kindermärchen"** "Fairy Tales"; **~marke** *f (eigene Marke)* own brand *or* label; *(bevorzugte Marke)* favourite brand; **~maus** *f* house mouse; **~meister** *m* **(a)** caretaker, janitor; **(b)** *(Sw) siehe* **~besitzer**; **~mitteilung** *f* internal memo; **~mittel** *nt* household remedy; **~müll** *m* domestic rubbish *(Brit)* *or* garbage *(US)*, domestic refuse; **~musik** *f* music at home, family music; **~mutter** *f (von Herberge etc)* housemother; **~mütterchen** *nt (hum)* little mother; *(pej)* housewife, wife and mother; **~nummer** *f* street *or* house number; **~ordnung** *f* house rules *pl* *or* regulations *pl*; **~partei** *f* tenant; *(Aus)* household; **~postille** *f (old)* collection of instructional reading for the family; *(fig)* manual; **~putz** *m* house cleaning; **~rat** *m* **-(e)s,** *no pl* household equipment *or* goods *pl*; **~ratversicherung** *f* (household) contents insurance; **~recht** *nt* right(s *pl*) as a householder *(to forbid sb entrance)*; **von seinem ~recht Gebrauch machen** to show sb the door, to tell sb to leave; **~rind** *nt* domestic cattle *pl*; **~sammlung** *f* house-to-house *or* door-to-door collection; **~schlachten** *nt*, **~schlachtung** *f* home slaughtering; **~schlüssel** *m* front-door key, house key; **~schuh** *m* slipper; **~schwamm** *m* dry rot; **~schwein** *nt* domestic pig.

Hausse ['hoːs(ə)] *f* **-, -n** *(Econ: Aufschwung)* boom *(an +dat* in); *(St Ex: Kurssteigerung)* bull market ◆ **~ haben** *(St Ex)* to rise on the Stock Exchange; **wenn man ~ hat, ...** *(St Ex)* when there's a bull market ...; **auf ~ spekulieren** *(St Ex)* to bull.

Haussegen *m* house blessing *or* benediction ◆ **bei ihnen hängt der ~ schief** *(hum)* they're a bit short on domestic bliss *(inf)*.

Haussespekulation ['hoːsə-] *f (St Ex)* bull speculation.

Haussier [(h)o'sieː] *m* **-s, -s** *(St Ex)* bull.

Haus-: **~stand** *m* household, home; **einen ~stand gründen** to set up house *or* home; **~suchung** *f (in einem Haus)* house search; *(in mehreren Häusern)* house-to-house search; **~suchungsbefehl** *m* search-warrant; **~telefon** *nt* internal telephone; **~tier** *nt* domestic animal; *(aus Liebhaberei gehalten)* pet; **~tochter** *f* lady's help; **~trauung** *f* wedding at home; **~tür** *f* front door; **gleich vor der ~tür** *(fig inf)* on one's doorstep; **~türgeschäft** *nt* door-to-door sales *pl*; **~tyrann** *m (inf)* domestic *or* household tyrant; **~vater** *m (von Heim etc)* housefather; **~verbot** *nt* ban on entering the house/a place; **jdm ~verbot erteilen** to bar *or* ban sb from the house, to forbid sb to enter the house; **in einem Lokal/bei jdm ~verbot haben** to be barred *or* banned from a pub (*Brit*) *or* bar/sb's house/a building; **~versammlung** *f* house meeting; **~verwalter** *m* (house) supervisor; **~verwaltung** *f* property *or* house management; **~wappen** *nt* family coat of arms; **~wart** *m siehe* **~meister**; **~wirt** *m* landlord; **~wirtin** *f* landlady.

Hauswirtschaft *f* **(a)** (*Haushaltsführung*) housekeeping; (*finanziell auch*) home economics *sing*. **(b)** (*Sch*) home economics *sing*, domestic science.

hauswirtschaftlich *adj* domestic ◆ **ein ~er Kurs** a course on home economics *or* domestic science; **~ interessiert** interested in domestic matters.

Hauswirtschafts-: ~lehre *f* (*Sch*) home economics *sing*, domestic science; **~lehrer** *m* home economics *or* domestic science teacher; **~schule** *f* school of home economics *or* domestic science.

Haus-: ~wurfsendung *f* (house-to-house) circular; **~zeitschrift, ~zeitung** *f* company magazine; **~zelt** *nt* frame tent; **~zentrale** *f* (*Telec*) (internal) switchboard.

Haus-zu-Haus-: ~-Transport *m* (*Rail etc*) door-to-door service; **~-Verkehr** *m* (*Rail etc*) door-to-door service.

Haut *f* **-, Häute** skin; (*dick, esp von größerem Tier*) hide; (*geschälte Schale von Obst etc*) peel; (*inf: Mensch*) sort (*inf*) ◆ **naß bis auf die ~** soaked to the skin; **nur ~ und Knochen sein** to be only *or* nothing but skin and bones; **viel ~ zeigen** (*hum*) to show all one's got (*hum*), to show a lot (of bare skin); **mit ~ und Haar(en)** (*inf*) completely, totally; **er ist ihr mit ~ und Haar(en) verfallen** (*inf*) he's head over heels in love with her, he's fallen for her hook, line and sinker (*inf*); **das geht** *or* **dringt unter die ~** that gets under one's skin; **in seiner ~ möchte ich nicht stecken** I wouldn't like to be in his shoes; **er fühlt sich nicht wohl in seiner ~** (*inf*), **ihm ist nicht wohl in seiner ~** (*inf*) (*unglücklich, unzufrieden*) he's (feeling) rather unsettled; (*unbehaglich*) he feels uneasy *or* uncomfortable; **er kann nicht aus seiner ~ heraus** (*inf*) he can't change the way he is, a leopard can't change its spots (*prov*); **aus der ~ fahren** (*inf*) (*aus Ungeduld*) to work oneself up into a sweat (*inf*); (*aus Wut*) to go through the roof (*inf*), to hit the ceiling (*inf*); **das ist zum Aus-der-~-Fahren!** it's enough to drive you up the wall (*inf*) *or* round the bend (*inf*); **auf der faulen ~ liegen** (*inf*), **sich auf die faule ~ legen** (*inf*) to sit back and do nothing, not to lift a finger (*inf*); **seine ~ zu Markte tragen** (*sich in Gefahr begeben*) to risk one's neck *or* hide (*inf*); (*euph: Frau*) to sell one's charms; **seine eigene ~ retten** to save one's (own) skin; (*esp vor Prügel*) to save one's (own) hide (*inf*); **sich seiner ~ wehren** to defend oneself vigorously; **seine ~ so teuer wie möglich verkaufen** (*inf*) to sell oneself as dearly as possible; *siehe* **ehrlich**.

Haut- *in cpds* skin; **~abschürfung** *f* graze; **~arzt** *m* skin specialist, dermatologist; **~atmung** *f* cutaneous respiration; **die ~atmung verhindern** to stop the skin from breathing; **~ausschlag** *m* (skin) rash *or* eruption (*form*).

Häutchen *nt* **-s, -** *dim of* **Haut** (*auf Flüssigkeit*) skin; (*Anat, Bot*) membrane; (*an Fingernägeln*) cuticle.

haute *pret of* **hauen**.

Haute Couture [(h)oːtkuˈtyːʁ] *f* **- -,** *no pl* haute couture.

häuten [1] *vt Tiere* to skin.
[2] *vr* (*Tier*) to shed its skin; (*Schlange auch*) to slough (its skin); (*hum: Mensch*) to peel.

haut|eng *adj* skintight.

Hautevolee [(h)oːtvoˈleː] *f* **-,** *no pl* upper crust.

Haut-: ~falte *f* skin fold; **~farbe** *f* skin colour; **nur, weil er eine andere ~farbe hat** just because his skin is a different colour; **h~farben** *adj* flesh-coloured; **~flügler** *m* **-s, -** hymenopter(on); **h~freundlich** *adj Stoff* kind to one's *or* the skin; **h~freundliches Heftpflaster** micropore tape.

-häutig *adj suf* -skinned.

Haut-: ~jucken *nt* **-s,** *no pl* itching; **eine Creme gegen ~jucken** a cream for skin irritations; **~klinik** *f* dermatology clinic, skin clinic; **h~nah** *adj* **(a)** (*Anat*) close to the skin; **(b)** (*sehr eng, Sport*) (very) close; **h~nah tanzen** to dance very close(ly); **(c)** (*fig inf: wirklichkeitsnah*) *Kontakt* (very) close; *Problem* that affects us/him *etc* directly; *Darstellung, Schilderung* deeply affective; **h~nah in Kontakt mit etw kommen** to come into (very) close contact with sth; **~pflege** *f* skin care; **~pilz** *m* (*Med*) fungal skin infection, dermatophyte (*spec*); **h~schonend** *adj* kind to the skin; *Spülmittel auch* kind to the hands; **~spezialist** *m* skin specialist, dermatologist; **~transplantation** *f* (*Operation*) skin graft; (*Verfahren*) skin grafting.

Häutung *f* skinning; (*von Schlange*) sloughing ◆ **verschiedene ~en durchmachen** to slough several skins.

Hautwunde *f* superficial *or* skin wound.

Havanna(zigarre) [haˈvana-] *f* **-, -s** Havana (cigar).

Havarie [havaˈriː] *f* **(a)** (*Naut, Aviat*) (*Unfall*) accident; (*Schaden*) average (*spec*), damage *no indef art, no pl*. **(b)** (*Aus*) (*Kraftfahrzeugunfall*) accident; (*Kraftfahrzeugschaden*) damage *no indef art, no pl*.

havarieren* [havaˈriːrən] *vi* **(a)** to be damaged. **(b)** (*Aus: Fahrzeug*) to crash.

havariert [havaˈriːɐt] *adj* damaged.

Havarist [havaˈrɪst] *m* (*Reeder*) owner of a/the damaged ship; (*Schiff*) damaged ship.

Hawaianer(in *f*) [havaiˈaːnɐ, -ərɪn] *m* **-s, -** Hawaiian.

hawaianisch *adj* Hawaiian.

Hawaii [haˈvaii] *nt* **-s** Hawaii.

Hawaiigitarre *f* Hawaiian guitar.

hawaiisch [haˈvaiɪʃ] *adj* Hawaiian.

Haxe *f* **-, -n** (*Cook*) leg (joint); (*S Ger inf*) (*Fuß*) foot, plate of meat (*Brit sl*); (*Bein*) leg ◆ **„~n abkratzen!"** "wipe your feet!".

Hbf *abbr of* **Hauptbahnhof**.

H-Bombe [ˈhaː-] *f* H-bomb.

h.c. [haːˈtseː] *abbr of* **honoris causa**.

HD [haːˈdeː] *f* **-,** *no pl* (*Sw*) *abbr of* **Hilfsdienst**.

HD-Diskette [haːˈdeː-] *f* (*Comput*) HD diskette.

he *interj* hey; (*fragend*) eh.

Headhunter(in *f*) [ˈhɛdhʌntɐ, -ərɪn] *m* **-s, -** headhunter.

Hearing [ˈhɪərɪŋ] *nt* **-(s), -s** hearing.

heavy [ˈhɛvi] *adj pred* (*sl: schwerfällig*) heavy, cumbersome ◆ **das war einfach zu heavy für sie** (*Erlebnis etc*) it was simply too much for her to take.

Heavy Metal [ˈhɛviˈmɛtl] *nt* **-,** *no pl* (*Mus*) heavy metal.

Hebamme *f* **-, -n** midwife.

Hebe-: ~balken, ~baum *m* lever; **~bock** *m* (hydraulic) jack; **~bühne** *f* hydraulic ramp.

Hebel *m* **-s, - (a)** (*Phys, Griff*) lever; (*an Maschinen auch*) handle; (*fig*) leverage ◆ **den ~ ansetzen** to position the lever; (*fig*) to tackle it, to set about it; **den ~ an der richtigen Stelle ansetzen** (*fig*) to set about *or* tackle it in the right way; **alle ~ in Bewegung setzen** (*inf*) to move heaven and earth; **am längeren ~ sitzen** (*inf*) to have the whip hand.
(b) (*Sport*) *siehe* **Hebelgriff**.

Hebel-: ~arm *m* (lever) arm; **~griff** *m* (*Sport*) lever hold; **~kraft** *f* leverage; **~wirkung** *f* leverage.

heben *pret* **hob**, *ptp* **gehoben** [1] *vt* **(a)** (*nach oben bewegen*) to lift, to raise; *Augenbraue* to raise; *Kamera, Fernglas* to raise ◆ **die Stimme ~** (*lauter sprechen*) to raise one's voice, to speak up; (*höher sprechen*) to raise one's/the pitch; **die Hand/Faust gegen jdn ~** (*geh*) to raise one's hand against sb/to shake one's fist at sb; **einen ~ gehen** (*inf*) to go for a drink; **er hebt gern einen** (*inf*) he likes *or* enjoys a drink; *siehe* **gehoben**.
(b) (*nach oben befördern, hochheben*) to lift; *Wrack* to raise, to bring up; *Schatz* to dig up; (*Sport*) *Gewicht* to lift ◆ **er hob das Kind auf die Mauer/vom Baum** he lifted the child (up) onto the wall/(down) from the tree; **jdn auf die Schultern ~** to hoist *or* lift sb onto one's shoulders *or* shoulder-high; **den Ball in den Strafraum/ins Tor ~** to lob the ball into the penalty area/goal; **heb deine Füße!** pick your feet up!
(c) (*verbessern*) *Farbe* to bring out, to enhance; *Selbstbewußtsein, Effekt* to heighten; *Ertrag* to increase; *Geschäft* to increase, to boost; *Stimmung, Wohlstand* to improve; *Niveau* to raise, to increase; *jds Ansehen* to boost, to enhance ◆ **jds Stimmung ~** to cheer sb up; **das hebt den Mut** that boosts *or* raises one's morale.
(d) (*S Ger: halten*) to hold.
[2] *vr* **(a)** (*sich nach oben bewegen*) to rise; (*Vorhang auch*) to go up; (*Nebel, Deckel*) to lift ◆ **sich ~ und senken** (*Schiff*) to rise and fall; (*Busen*) to heave.
(b) (*geh: emporragen*) to tower up, to rise up.
(c) (*verbessern*) (*Stimmung, Konjunktur, Handel*) to improve ◆ **da hob sich seine Stimmung** that cheered him up.
(d) (*S Ger: sich halten*) to hold on (*an +dat* to).
[3] *vt impers* **es hebt jdm den Magen** *or* **jdn** (*inf*) sb feels sick; **es hebt mir den Magen** *or* **mich, wenn ich das sehe** (*inf*) seeing that makes me feel sick *or* turns my stomach (*inf*).
[4] *vi* **(a)** (*Sport*) to do weight-lifting.
(b) (*S Ger: haltbar sein*) to hold; (*Nahrungsmittel*) to keep.

Heber *m* **-s, - (a)** (*Chem*) pipette. **(b)** (*Tech*) (hydraulic) jack. **(c)** (*Sport: Gewicht~*) weight-lifter.

Hebesatz *m* (*Fin*) rate of assessment.

-hebig *adj suf* (*Poet*) -footed.

Hebräer(in *f*) *m* **-s, -** Hebrew.

hebräisch *adj* Hebrew.

Hebräisch(e) *nt decl as adj* Hebrew; *siehe auch* **Deutsch(e)**.

Hebung *f* **(a)** (*von Schatz, Wrack etc*) recovery, raising.
(b) (*Geol*) elevation, rise (in the ground).
(c) *no pl* (*fig: Verbesserung*) improvement; (*von Effekt, Selbstbewußtsein*) heightening; (*von Lebensstandard, Niveau*) rise ◆ **seine Fröhlichkeit trug zur ~ der gedrückten Stimmung bei** his cheerfulness helped to relieve the subdued mood.
(d) (*Poet*) stressed *or* accented syllable.

hecheln [1] *vt Flachs, Hanf* to hatchel, to heckle.
[2] *vi* **(a)** (*inf: lästern*) to gossip. **(b)** (*keuchen*) to pant.

Hecht *m* **-(e)s, -e** (*Zool*) pike; (*inf: Bursche*) chap (*inf*), bloke (*Brit inf*), guy (*inf*) ◆ **das ist ein ~** (*inf*) he's some guy (*inf*) *or* quite a guy (*inf*); **er ist (wie) ein ~ im Karpfenteich** (*fig*) (*sehr aktiv*) he certainly shakes people up; (*sorgt für Unruhe*) he's a stirrer (*inf*).

hechten *vi aux sein* (*inf*) to dive, to make a (headlong) dive; (*beim Schwimmen*) to do a racing dive; (*beim Geräteturnen*) to do a forward dive.

Hecht-: ~rolle *f* (*Sport*) dive roll; **~sprung** *m* (*beim Schwimmen*) racing dive; (*beim Turnen*) forward dive; (*Ftbl inf*) (headlong *or* full-length) dive; **~suppe** *f*: **es zieht wie ~suppe** (*inf*) it's blowing a gale (in here) (*inf*), there's a terrible draught.

Heck *nt* **-(e)s, -e (a)** *pl auch* **-s** (*Naut*) stern; (*Aviat*) tail, rear; (*Aut*) rear, back.
(b) (*N Ger: Gatter*) gate.

Heck|antrieb *m* (*Aut*) rear-wheel drive.

Hecke *f* **-, -n** hedge; (*am Wegrand*) hedgerow.

Hecken-: ~rose *f* dogrose, wild rose; **~schere** *f* hedge-clippers *pl*; **~schütze** *m* sniper.

Heck-: ~fenster *nt* (*Aut*) rear window *or* windscreen; **~flosse** *f* (*Aut*) tail fin; **~klappe** *f* (*Aut*) tailgate; **h~lastig** *adj* tail-heavy; **~licht** *nt* (*Aviat*) tail-light.

Heckmeck *m* **-s,** *no pl* (*inf*) (*dummes Gerede*) nonsense, rubbish; (*dumme*

Streiche) stupid *or* daft *(inf)* things *pl*; *(Umstände)* fuss, palaver *(inf)*; *(unnötiges Zeug)* rubbish ◆ **mach doch keinen ~** don't be so stupid *or* daft *(inf)*.
Heckmotor *m (Aut)* rear engine ◆ **mit ~** rear-engined.
Heckscheibe *f (Aut)* rear window.
Heckscheiben-: ~heizung *f* rear windscreen *(Brit) or* windshield *(US)* heater; **~wischer** *m* rear windscreen *(Brit) or* windshield *(US)* wiper.
Heck-: ~schütze *m* rear gunner; **~spoiler** *m* rear spoiler; **~tür** *f (Aut)* tailgate; *(von Lieferwagen)* rear doors *pl*; **~türmodell** *nt* hatchback (car); **~welle** *f (Naut)* wash *no pl*.
heda *interj* hey there.
Hederich *m* **-s,** *no pl (Bot)* wild radish.
Hedonismus *m* hedonism.
hedonistisch *adj* hedonistic.
Heer *nt* **-(e)s, -e** *(lit, fig)* army ◆ **beim ~** in the army; **in das ~ eintreten** to join the army, to enlist in the army; *siehe* **wild.**
Heerbann *m (Hist)* levy.
Heeres-: ~bericht *m* military communiqué *or* despatch; **~bestände** *pl* army stores *pl or* supplies *pl*; **~dienst** *m, no pl (Hist)* military service; **~dienstvorschrift** *f* army regulations *pl*; **~gruppe** *f* army group; **~leitung** *f* command.
Heer(es)zug *m (Hist)* campaign.
Heer-: ~führer *m (Hist)* army commander; **~lager** *nt* army camp; **der Flughafen glich einem ~lager** the airport was like a refugee camp; **~schar** *f (liter)* legion, troop; *(fig: große Menge)* host; **die himmlischen ~scharen** the heavenly hosts; **~schau** *f (old)* military parade; **~straße** *f* military road; **~wesen** *nt* army.
Hefe *f* **-, -n** yeast ◆ **die ~ des Volkes** *(geh: treibende Kraft)* the (driving) force behind the people; *(pej: Abschaum)* the scum of the earth.
Hefe(n)-: ~gebäck *nt* yeast-risen pastry; **~kranz** *m* ≃ savarin; **~kuchen** *m* yeast cake; **~pilz** *m* yeast plant; **~stück(chen)** *nt* yeast pastry, ≃ Danish pastry; **~teig** *m* yeast dough; **wie ein ~teig auseinandergehen** *(fig inf)* to put on mounds of fat.
Heft[1] *nt* **-(e)s, -e** *(von Werkzeug, Messer)* handle; *(von Säge, Feile auch)* grip; *(von Dolch, Schwert)* hilt ◆ **das ~ in der Hand haben** *(fig)* to hold the reins, to be at the helm; **das ~ in der Hand behalten** *(fig)* to remain in control *or* at the helm; **das ~ aus der Hand geben** *(fig)* to hand over control *or* the reins; **jdm das ~ aus der Hand nehmen** *(fig)* to seize control/power from sb; **ich lasse mir nicht das ~ aus der Hand nehmen** nobody's going to take over from me.
Heft[2] *nt* **-(e)s, -e (a)** *(Schreib~)* exercise book. **(b)** *(Zeitschrift)* magazine; *(Comic~)* comic; *(Nummer)* number, issue ◆ **„National Geographic 1998, ~ 3"** "National Geographic 1998, No. 3". **(c)** *(geheftetes Büchlein)* booklet.
Heftchen *nt* **(a)** *dim of* **Heft**[2]. **(b)** *(pej) (billiger Roman)* rubbishy *or* cheap *or* pulp novel *(pej)*; *(schlechte Zeitschrift, Comic~)* rag *(pej inf)*. **(c)** *(Fahrkarten~, Eintrittskarten~)* book(let) of tickets; *(Briefmarken~)* book of stamps.
heften [1] *vt* **(a)** *(nähen) Saum, Naht* to tack (up), to baste; *Buch* to sew, to stitch; *(klammern)* to clip *(an +acc* to); *(mit Heftmaschine auch)* to staple *(an +acc* to).
(b) *(befestigen)* to pin, to fix ◆ **er heftete mit Reißzwecken eine Landkarte an die Wand** he pinned a map on the wall; **jdm ein Abzeichen an die Brust ~** to pin a decoration to sb's chest; **den Blick** *or* **die Augen auf jdn/etw ~** to gaze at *or* fix one's eyes on sb/sth, to stare fixedly at sb/sth.
[2] *vr* **(a)** *(Blick, Augen)* **sich auf jdn/etw ~** to fix onto sb/sth.
(b) sich an jdn ~ to latch on to sb; **sich an jds Spur** *or* **Fährte ~** to follow sb's trail; **sich an jds Fersen** *or* **Sohlen ~** *(fig) (jdn verfolgen)* to dog sb's heels; *(bei Rennen etc)* to stick to sb's heels.
Hefter *m* **-s, - (a)** (loose-leaf) file. **(b)** *(Heftapparat)* stapler.
Heft-: ~faden *m*, **~garn** *nt* tacking thread.
heftig *adj* **(a)** *(stark, gewaltig)* violent; *Kopfschmerzen auch* severe, acute; *Schmerz* intense, acute; *Erkältung* severe; *Fieber* raging, severe; *Zorn, Ärger, Haß* violent, burning *no adv*, intense; *Liebe, Sehnsucht* ardent, burning *no adv*, intense; *Leidenschaft* violent, fierce; *Abneigung auch* intense; *Widerstand* vehement; *Weinen* bitter; *Lachen* uproarious; *Atmen* heavy; *Kontroverse, Kampf, Wind* fierce; *Regen* lashing *no adv*, driving *no adv*, heavy; *Frost* severe, heavy ◆ **ein ~er Regenguß** a downpour; **der Regen schlug ~ gegen die Scheiben** the rain pounded *or* beat against the windows; **er hat sich ~ in sie verliebt** he has fallen violently *or* madly *(inf)* in love with her; **~ nicken/rühren** to nod/stir *or* beat vigorously; **sie knallte die Tür ~ ins Schloß** she slammed *or* banged the door (shut); **er hat ~ dagegen gewettert** he raged vehemently against it.
(b) *(jähzornig, ungehalten) Mensch, Art* violent(-tempered); *Ton* fierce, vehement; *Worte* violent ◆ **~ werden** to fly into a passion.
Heftigkeit *f* **-,** *no pl siehe adj* **(a)** violence; severity, acuteness; intensity, acuteness; severity; fierceness; vehemence; intensity; bitterness; uproariousness; heaviness; ferocity, fierceness; heaviness; severity, heaviness. **(b)** violent temper, violence; fierceness, vehemence; violence.
Heft-: ~klammer *f* staple; **~maschine** *f* stapler; **~naht** *f (Sew)* basted *or* tacked seam; *(Tech)* tack weld; **~pflaster** *nt* (sticking) plaster, adhesive tape *(US)*; **~roman** *m* cheap paperback novel, dime novel *(US)*; **~stich** *m* tacking-stitch; **~zwecke** *f* drawing-pin *(Brit)*, thumb-tack *(US)*.
Hegelianer *m* **-s, -** Hegelian.
hegelianisch, hegel(i)sch *adj* Hegelian.
Hegemonie *f* hegemony.
hegen *vt* **(a)** *(pflegen) Wild, Pflanzen* to care for, to tend; *(geh: umsorgen) jdn* to care for, to look after ◆ **jdn ~ und pflegen** to lavish care and attention on sb.
(b) *(empfinden, haben) Haß, Groll, Verdacht* to harbour; *Mißtrauen, Achtung, Abneigung* to feel; *Zweifel* to entertain; *Hoffnung, Wunsch* to cherish; *Plan, Unternehmen* to foster ◆ **ich hege den starken Verdacht, daß ...** I have a strong suspicion that ...; **ich hege schon lange den Plan auszuwandern** for a long time I've been contemplating emigrating.
Heger *m* **-s, -** gamekeeper.
Hehl *nt or m* **kein** *or* **keinen ~ aus etw machen** to make no secret of sth.
Hehler(in *f***)** *m* **-s, -** receiver (of stolen goods), fence *(inf)* ◆ **der ~ ist schlimmer als der Stehler** *(Prov)* it is worse to condone a crime than to commit it.
Hehlerei *f* **-,** *no pl* receiving (stolen goods).
hehr *adj (liter)* noble, sublime.
hei *interj* wow.
Heia *f* **-,** *no pl (baby-talk)* bye-byes *(baby-talk)*, beddy-byes *(baby-talk)* ◆ **ab in die ~** off to bye-byes *etc*; **in die ~ gehen** to go bye-byes *etc*; **h~ machen** to have a little nap *or* sleep.
Heiabett *nt (baby-talk)* beddy-byes *(baby-talk)*.
Heide[1] *m* **-n, -n, Heidin** *f* heathen, pagan; *(Nichtjude)* Gentile.
Heide[2] *f* **-, -n (a)** moor, heath; *(~land)* moorland, heathland. **(b)** *(~kraut)* heather.
Heide-: ~kraut *nt* heather; **~land** *nt* moorland, heathland.
Heidelbeere *f* bilberry, blueberry *(esp US, Scot)*.
Heidelbeer-: ~kraut *nt*, **~strauch** *m* bilberry *or* blueberry bush.
Heiden-: ~angst *f* **eine ~angst vor etw** *(dat)* **haben** *(inf)* to be scared stiff of sth *(inf)*; **~arbeit** *f (inf)* real slog *(inf)*; **~geld** *nt (inf)* packet *(inf)*; **~krach, ~lärm** *m (inf)* unholy din *(inf)*; **h~mäßig** *(inf)* [1] *adj* huge, massive; [2] *adv* incredibly; **h~mäßig Geld verdienen** to earn a (real) packet *(inf)*; **~mission** *f* missionary work among the heathen; **~respekt** *m (inf)* healthy respect; **~spaß** *m (inf)* terrific fun; **einen ~spaß haben** to have a whale of a time *(inf)*; **das macht ihm einen ~spaß** he finds it terrific fun; **~spektakel** *m (inf)* awful row; *(Schimpfen)* awful fuss.
Heidentum *nt, no pl* heathenism, heathendom, paganism ◆ **das ~** *(Menschen)* the heathen *pl*, the pagans *pl*.
heidi *interj*: **~ ging es den Berg hinab** down the hill they/we *etc* went; **~ (, dann geht's los)** here they/we *etc* go.
Heidin *f siehe* **Heide**[1].
heidnisch *adj* heathen; *(auf Götterkult bezüglich)* pagan ◆ **~ leben** to live a heathen *or* pagan life.
Heidschnucke *f* **-, -n** *German moorland sheep*.
heikel *adj* **(a)** *(schwierig, gefährlich) Angelegenheit, Situation, Thema* tricky, delicate; *Frage* awkward, tricky.
(b) *(dial) Mensch* particular, pernickety *(inf) (in bezug auf +acc* about); *(wählerisch auch)* fussy; *(in bezug aufs Essen auch)* fussy, choosy.
(c) *(dial) Stoff, Farbe* difficult ◆ **die Farbe/der Stoff ist mir zu ~** that colour/material is too much of a nuisance.
heil *adj* **(a)** *(unverletzt) Mensch* unhurt, uninjured; *Glieder* unbroken; *Haut* undamaged ◆ **wieder ~ sein/werden** *(wieder gesund)* to be/get better again; *(Wunde)* to have healed/to heal up; *(Knochen)* to have mended/to mend; **~ nach Hause kommen** to get home safe and sound; **~ machen** *(inf) (heilen)* to make better; *(reparieren)* to fix, to mend; **etw ~ überstehen** *Unfall* to come through sth without a scratch; *Prüfung* to get through sth; **Gott sei Dank sind die Glieder noch ~** thank goodness there are no broken bones; **mit ~en Gliedern** *or* **~ am Ziel ankommen** to reach the finish without breaking any bones; **mit ~er Haut davonkommen** to escape unscathed *or (lit auch)* in one piece.
(b) *(inf: ganz)* intact; *Kleidungsstück* decent *(inf)* ◆ **die ~e Welt** an ideal world *(without problems, uncertainties etc)*.
Heil [1] *nt* **-s,** *no pl* **(a)** *(Wohlergehen)* well-being, good ◆ **sein ~ bei jdm versuchen** *(inf)* to try one's luck with sb; **jdm ~ und Segen wünschen** to wish sb every blessing.
(b) *(Eccl, fig)* salvation ◆ **sein ~ in etw** *(dat)* **suchen** to seek one's salvation in sth; **sein ~ in der Flucht suchen** to flee for one's life; **zu jds ~(e) gereichen** *(geh)* to be sb's salvation; **im Jahr des ~s 1848** *(old)* in the year of grace 1848 *(old)*.
[2] *interj*: **~!** hail! *(old)*; **~ dem König!** long live *or* God save the King!; **~ Hitler!** heil Hitler!; **Berg/Ski/Petri ~!** good climbing/skiing/fishing!
Heiland *m* **-(e)s, -e** *(Rel)* Saviour, Redeemer; *(fig geh: Retter)* saviour.
Heil-: ~anstalt *f* nursing home; *(für Sucht- oder Geisteskranke)* home; **~anstalt für Geisteskranke** mental home; **~bad** *nt (Bad)* medicinal bath; *(Ort)* spa, watering-place *(old)*; **h~bar** *adj* curable; **~barkeit** *f* **-,** *no pl* curability; **h~bringend** *adj (Rel)* redeeming; *Wirkung, Kur* beneficial; *Kräuter* medicinal; **sie warteten auf den h~bringenden Regen** they were waiting for the vitally needed rain; **~butt** *m* halibut.
heilen [1] *vi aux sein (Wunde, Bruch)* to heal (up); *(Entzündung)* to clear up.
[2] *vt Kranke, Krankheiten* to cure; *Wunde* to heal; *(Rel)* to heal ◆ **als geheilt entlassen werden** to be discharged with a clean bill of health; **Jesus heilt uns von unseren Sünden** Jesus redeems us from our sins; **jdn von etw ~** *(lit, fig)* to cure sb of sth; **von jdm/etw geheilt sein** *(fig)* to have got over sb/sth; **die Zeit heilt (alle) Wunden** time heals all wounds.
heilend *adj* healing.
Heiler *m* **-s, -** *(geh)* healer.
Heil-: ~erde *f* healing earth; **~erfolg** *m* success; **zum ~erfolg führen** to lead to a successful cure; **~fasten** *nt* **-s** *no pl* remedial fasting; **~fleisch** *nt* **ich habe gutes ~fleisch** I heal quickly *or* easily; **h~froh** *adj pred (inf)* jolly glad

(*inf*); **~gymnastik** *f etc siehe* **Krankengymnastik** *etc.*

heilig *adj* **(a)** holy; (*geweiht, geheiligt auch*) sacred; (*bei Namen von Heiligen*) Saint; (*old: fromm auch*) devout, saintly; (*pej*) holier-than-thou ♦ **jdm ~ sein** (*lit, fig*) to be sacred to sb; **bei allem, was ~ ist** by all that is *or* I hold sacred; **die ~e Veronika/der ~e Augustinus** Saint Veronica/Augustine; **H~er Abend** Christmas Eve; **das ~e Abendmahl/die ~e Kommunion** Holy Communion; **die H~e Dreifaltigkeit/Familie/Stadt** the Holy Trinity/Family/City; **die H~e Jungfrau** the Blessed Virgin; **H~e Maria** Holy Mary; **der H~e Geist/Vater/Stuhl** the Holy Spirit/Father/See; **die H~en Drei Könige** the Three Kings *or* Wise Men, the Magi; **das H~e Land** the Holy Land; **die H~e Schrift** the Holy Scriptures *pl*; **das H~e Römische Reich** the Holy Roman Empire; **die H~e Allianz** the Holy Alliance; **das H~ste** (*lit, fig*) the holy of holies.

(b) (*fig: ernst*) *Eid, Pflicht* sacred, solemn; *Recht* sacred; *Eifer, Zorn* righteous; (*von Ehrfurcht erfüllt*) *Stille, Schauer* awed; (*unantastbar*) *Würde, Gefühl, Gewohnheit* sacred ♦ **es ist mein ~er Ernst** I am deadly serious *or* in dead earnest.

(c) (*inf: groß*) incredible (*inf*); *Respekt auch* healthy ♦ **mit jdm/etw seine ~e Not haben** to have a hard time with sb/sth; **von einer ~en Angst gepackt werden** to be scared out of one's wits.

(d) (*inf: in Ausrufen*) **(ach du) ~er Bimbam** *or* **Strohsack, ~es Kanonenrohr!** holy smoke! (*inf*).

Heilig|abend *m* Christmas Eve.

heiligen *vt* (*weihen*) to hallow, to sanctify; (*heilighalten*) to hallow, to keep holy; *Sonntag etc* to keep holy, to observe ♦ **der Zweck heiligt die Mittel** the end justifies the means; **durch die Zeit geheiligt** time-honoured; *siehe* **geheiligt.**

Heiligen-: ~bild *nt* holy picture; **~legende** *f* life *or* story of the saints; **~schein** *m* halo; **jdn mit einem ~schein umgeben** (*fig*) to put sb on a pedestal; **sich mit einem ~schein umgeben** (*fig*) to be holier-than-thou; **~verehrung** *f* veneration of the saints.

Heilige(r) *mf decl as adj* (*lit, fig*) saint ♦ **ein sonderbarer** *or* **wunderlicher ~r** (*inf*) a queer fish (*inf*).

Heilig-: ⚠h~halten *vt sep irreg* to keep holy *or Andenken auch* sacred; *Sonntag auch* to observe; **~keit** *f* holiness; (*Geweihtheit, Geheiligtheit auch, von Eigentum*) sacredness; (*von Zorn*) righteousness; **Eure/Seine ~keit** your/his Holiness; **im Geruch der ~keit stehen** to be surrounded by an aura of sanctity; **⚠h~sprechen** *vt sep irreg* to canonize; **~sprechung** *f* canonization; **~tum** *nt* (*Stätte*) shrine; (*Gegenstand*) (holy) relic; **Schändung eines ~tums** sacrilege; **jds ~tum sein** (*inf*) (*Zimmer*) to be sb's sanctum; (*Gegenstand etc*) to be sacrosanct (to sb).

Heiligung *f* **die ~ des Sonntags** Sunday *or* Lord's day observance; **die ~ des Sabbats** the observance of the Sabbath.

Heil-: ~klima *nt* healthy climate; **~kraft** *f* healing power; **h~kräftig** *adj Pflanze, Tee* medicinal; *Wirkung* curative; **ein h~kräftiges Mittel** a curative; **~kraut** *nt usu pl* medicinal herb; **~kunde** *f* medicine; **h~kundig** *adj* skilled in medicine *or* the art of healing; **~kundige(r)** *mf decl as adj* person skilled in medicine *or* the art of healing, healer; **h~los** *adj* unholy (*inf*); *Durcheinander, Verwirrung auch* hopeless; *Schreck* terrible, frightful; **sich h~los verirren** to get hopelessly lost; **h~los verschuldet sein** to be up to one's ears in debt; **~methode** *f* cure; **~mittel** *nt* (*lit, fig*) remedy, cure; (*Medikament*) medicine; **~pädagogik** *f* remedial education; **~pflanze** *f* medicinal plant; **~praktiker** *m* non-medical practitioner; **~quelle** *f* medicinal spring; **~salbe** *f* (medicated) ointment; **h~sam** *adj* **(a)** (*dated: heilend*) *Wirkung* healing; *Arznei auch* curative; *Klima* salutary, beneficial; **(b)** (*fig: förderlich*) *Erfahrung, Strafe* salutary.

Heils-: ~armee *f* Salvation Army; **~botschaft** *f* message of salvation, gospel.

Heilschlaf *m* healing sleep (*induced for therapeutic ends*).

Heils-: ~geschichte *f* heilsgeschichte, *interpretation of history stressing God's saving grace;* **~lehre** *f* (*Rel, fig*) doctrine of salvation; **~ordnung** *f* order of salvation.

Heilstätte *f* (*form*) sanatorium (*Brit*), sanitarium (*US*), clinic.

Heilung *f* (*das Heilen*) (*von Wunde*) healing; (*von Krankheit, Kranken*) curing; (*Rel*) healing; (*das Gesundwerden*) cure ♦ **~ in etw** (*dat*) **finden** to find relief in sth.

⚠Heilungsprozeß *m* healing process.

Heil-: ~verfahren *nt* (course of) treatment; **~zweck** *m*: **zu ~zwecken** for medicinal purposes.

heim *adv* home ♦ **~, bitte** let's go home; **~ ins Reich** (*NS*) back to the Reich (*referring to formerly German areas and their inhabitants*).

Heim *nt* **-(e)s, -e** (*Zuhause, Anstalt*) home; (*Obdachlosen~, für Lehrlinge*) hostel; (*Studentenwohn~*) hall of residence, hostel; (*von Sportverein*) clubhouse; (*Freizeit~*) recreation centre ♦ **~ und Herd** (*liter*) house and home.

Heim- *in cpds* home; **~abend** *m* social evening; **~arbeit** *f* (*Ind*) homework, outwork *both no indef art*; **etw in ~arbeit herstellen lassen** to have sth produced by homeworkers; **~arbeiter** *m* (*Ind*) homeworker; **~arbeitsplatz** *m* **die Zahl der ~arbeitsplätze nimmt zu** more and more people work from home.

Heimat *f* **-, -en** home; (*~ort auch*) home town; (*~land auch*) native country; (*Bot, Zool auch*) natural habitat ♦ **die ~ verlassen** to leave one's home; **jdm zur ~ werden** to become sb's home.

Heimat- *in cpds* home; **~anschrift** *f* home address; **~dichter** *m* regional writer; **~dichtung** *f* regional literature; **~erde** *f* native soil; **~film** *m sentimental film in idealized regional setting;* **~forschung** *f* research into local history; **~hafen** *m* home port; **~kunde** *f* (*Sch*) local history; **h~kundlich** *adj* local history *attr*; **er hat h~kundliche Interessen** he is interested in local history; **~kunst** *f* regional art; **~land** *nt* native country *or* land; **h~lich** *adj* (*zur Heimat gehörend*) native; *Bräuche, Dialekt* local; (*an die Heimat erinnernd*) *Gefühle, Wehmut* nostalgic; *Klänge* of home; **die h~lichen Berge** the mountains of (one's) home; **das mutet mich h~lich an, das kommt mir h~lich vor** that reminds me of home; **h~licher Boden** native soil; **~liebe** *f* love of one's native country *or* land; **h~los** *adj* homeless; **~lose(r)** *mf decl as adj* homeless person; **die ~losen** the homeless; **~losigkeit** *f* homelessness; **~museum** *nt* museum of local history; **~ort** *m* **(a)** home town/village; **(b)** *siehe* **~hafen**; **~recht** *nt* right of domicile; **~schriftsteller** *m* regional writer; **~sprache** *f* native dialect; (*Baskisch etc*) native language; **h~vertrieben** *adj* displaced; **~vertriebene(r)** *mf decl as adj* displaced person, expellee (*esp from former Eastern German province*).

Heim-: h~begeben* *vr sep irreg* to make one's way home; **h~begleiten*** *vt sep* **jdn h~begleiten** to take *or* see sb home; **h~bringen** *vt sep irreg* (*nach Hause bringen*) to bring home; (*h~begleiten*) to take *or* see home; **~bügler** *m* rotary iron.

Heimchen *nt* (*Zool*) house cricket ♦ **~ (am Herd)** (*pej: Frau*) housewife.

Heim-: ~computer *m* home computer; **h~dürfen** *vi sep irreg* **darf ich/sie heim?** may I/she go home?; **h~eilen** *vi sep aux sein* to hurry home.

heimelig *adj* cosy, homely.

Heim-: h~fahren *vti sep irreg* (*vi: aux sein*) to drive home; **~fahrt** *f* journey home, return journey; (*Naut*) return voyage, voyage home; **h~finden** *vi sep irreg* to find one's way home; **h~führen** *vt sep* to take home; **ein Mädchen h~führen** (*dated*) to take a girl as one's wife (*dated*); **~gang** *m* (*euph geh: Tod*) passing away; **beim ~gang meiner Mutter** when my mother was called to her Lord *or* Maker (*euph*); **~gegangene(r)** *mf decl as adj* (*euph geh*) deceased; **unser lieber ~gegangener** our dear departed friend/father *etc*; **h~gehen** *sep irreg aux sein* **1** *vi* to go home; (*euph geh*) to pass away *or* on; **2** *vi impers* **es geht h~** we're going home; **h~holen** *vt sep* to fetch home; **Gott hat ihn h~geholt** he has been called to his Maker; **~industrie** *f* cottage industry.

heimisch *adj* **(a)** (*einheimisch*) (*Zool, Bot*) indigenous, native (*in +dat* to); (*national*) home; (*ortsansässig*) local; (*regional*) regional; *Gewässer* home ♦ **etw ~ machen** to introduce sth (*in +dat* to).

(b) (*vertraut*) familiar ♦ **an einem Ort ~ sein** to feel at home in a place; **sich ~ fühlen** to feel at home; **vom ~en Herd weg sein** to be away from house and home; **in einer Sprache** *etc* **~ sein** to be *or* feel at home in a language *etc*; **sich ~ machen** to make oneself at home; **~ werden** to become acclimatized (*an, in +dat* to), to settle in (*an, in +dat* to).

Heim-: ~kampf *m* (*Sport*) home match *or* game *or* (*Boxen*) fight; **~kehr** *f* **-,** *no pl* homecoming, return; **h~kehren** *vi sep aux sein* to return home (*aus* from); **~kehrer** *m* **-s, -** homecomer; **~kind** *nt* institution child, child brought up in a home; **~kino** *nt* home movies *pl*; (*Ausrüstung*) home movie kit; (*inf: TV*) goggle-box (*Brit inf*), tube (*US inf*); **h~kommen** *vi sep irreg aux sein* to come *or* return home; **h~können** *vi sep irreg* to be able to go home; **~kunft** *f* **-,** *no pl* (*geh*) *siehe* **~kehr**; **~leiter** *m* head *or* warden of a/the home/hostel; **~leitung** *f* person(s) in charge of a/the home/hostel; **ihr wurde die ~leitung übertragen** she was put in charge of the home *etc*; **h~leuchten** *vi sep* (*fig inf*) **jdm h~leuchten** to give sb a piece of one's mind.

heimlich **1** *adj* (*geheim, verborgen*) secret; *Treffen auch* clandestine; *Benehmen* secretive; *Bewegungen* furtive.

2 *adv* secretly; *treffen, tun auch* in secret; *lachen* inwardly ♦ **er blickte sie ~ an** he stole a glance at her; **sich ~ entfernen** to steal *or* sneak away; **~, still und leise** (*inf*) quietly, on the quiet.

Heimlichkeit *f siehe adj* secrecy; clandestineness; secretiveness; furtiveness; (*Geheimnis*) secret ♦ **in aller ~** secretly, in secret; **nur keine ~en!** (*inf*) stop being (so) secretive, no secrets now!

Heimlich-: ~tuer(in *f*) *m* **-s, -** secretive person; **~tuerei** *f* secrecy, secretiveness; **h~tun** *vi sep irreg* to be secretive (*mit* about).

Heim-: h~müssen *vi sep irreg* to have to go home; **~mutter** *f* mother of a/the home; (*von Jugendherberge*) warden; **~ordnung** *f* rules and regulations of a/the home/hostel; **~reise** *f* journey home, homeward journey; (*Naut*) voyage home, homeward voyage; **h~reisen** *vi sep aux sein* to travel home; **~sauna** *f* home sauna; **h~schicken** *vt sep* to send home; **~spiel** *nt* (*Sport*) home match *or* game; **~statt** *f* (*liter*) home; **ohne ~statt** without a home; **~stätte** *f* **(a)** (*Zuhause*) home; **(b)** (*Jur*) homestead.

heimsuchen *vt sep* to strike; (*für längere Zeit*) to plague; (*Feind auch*) to attack; (*Gespenst*) to haunt; (*Krankheit auch*) to afflict; (*Alpträume, Vorstellungen*) to afflict, to haunt; (*Schicksal*) to overtake, to afflict; (*inf: besuchen*) to descend on (*inf*) ♦ **von Dürre/Krieg/vom Streik heimgesucht** drought-stricken/war-torn *or* -ravaged/strike-torn; **Gott suchte die Ägypter mit schweren Plagen heim** God visited terrible plagues on the Egyptians.

Heimsuchung *f* **(a)** (*Schicksalsschlag*) affliction; (*Katastrophe*) disaster; (*Plage*) plague. **(b) Mariä ~** the visitation of Mary.

Heimtrainer *m* **(a)** (*Person*) personal trainer. **(b)** (*Gerät*) exercise machine; (*Trimmrad*) exercise bike.

heimtrauen *vr sep* to dare to go home.

Heimtücke *f, no pl siehe adj* insidiousness; maliciousness; insidiousness; treacherousness.

heimtückisch *adj* (*hinterlistig*) insidious; (*boshaft*) malicious; *Krankheit* insidious; (*gefährlich*) *Glatteis, Maschine* treacherous.

Heim-: ~vorteil *m* (*Sport, fig*) home advantage; **h~wärts** *adv* (*nach Hause zu*) home; (*auf dem ~weg*) on the way home; **h~wärts ziehen/gehen** to go homewards; **~weg** *m* way home; **sich auf den ~weg machen** to set out *or* head for home; **~weh** *nt* homesickness *no art*; **~weh haben/bekommen** to be/become homesick (*nach* for); **krank vor ~weh sein** to be pining for home, to be very homesick; **h~wehkrank** *adj* homesick; **~werker** *m* handyman; **h~wollen** *vi sep* to want to go home; **h~zahlen** *vt sep* **jdm etw h~zahlen** to pay sb back for sth; **h~ziehen** *sep irreg* [1] *vi aux sein* to return home; [2] *vt impers* **es zog ihn h~** he felt he wanted to go home.

Hein *m*: **Freund ~** (*old*) Death.

Heini *m* **-s, -s** (*inf*) bloke (*Brit inf*), guy (*inf*); (*Dummkopf*) idiot, fool.

Heinzelmännchen *nt* brownie.

Heirat *f* **-, -en** marriage; (*Feier*) wedding; (*Partie*) match.

Heiraten *nt* **-s,** *no pl* marriage, getting married *no def art.*

▼ **heiraten** [1] *vt* to marry.
[2] *vr* to get married.
▼[3] *vi* to get married, to marry ◆ **aufs Land/in die Stadt/nach Berlin ~** to marry *or* get married and settle in the country/in town/in Berlin; **in eine reiche/alte Familie ~** to marry into a rich/old family; **~ müssen** (*euph*) to have to get married; **„wir ~"** "we are getting married"; **„geheiratet haben ..."** ≃ "marriages", "marriage announcements".

Heirats-: ~absichten *pl* marriage plans *pl*; **~alter** *nt* marriageable *or* marrying age; (*Jur*) *minimum legal age for marriage*; **~annonce** *f siehe* **~anzeige (b)**; **~antrag** *m* proposal (of marriage); **jdm einen ~antrag machen** to propose to sb; **~anzeige** *f* **(a)** (*Bekanntgabe*) announcement of a forthcoming marriage; **(b)** (*Annonce für Partnersuche*) advertisement for a marriage partner; **~büro** *nt* marriage bureau; **~erlaubnis** *f* consent (to a marriage); **h~fähig** *adj* marriageable; **~kandidat** *m* (*Bräutigam*) husband-to-be; (*ehewilliger Junggeselle*) eligible bachelor, *person on the lookout for a wife*; **~institut** *nt* marriage bureau; **h~lustig** *adj* eager to get married; **~schwindel** *m* marriage proposal made under false pretences; **~schwindler** *m* person who makes a marriage proposal under false pretences; **~urkunde** *f* marriage certificate; **~urlaub** *m* leave to get married; **~vermittler** *m* marriage broker; **~vermittlung** *f* (*Büro*) marriage bureau; **diskrete ~vermittlung** marriages arranged discreetly; **~versprechen** *nt* (*Jur*) promise of marriage; **Bruch des ~versprechens** breach of promise (of marriage).

heisa *interj* hey.

heischen *vt* (*geh*) **(a)** *Beifall, Hochachtung, Aufmerksamkeit etc* to demand. **(b)** (*dated: erbitten*) to beg *or* ask for.

heiser *adj* hoarse; (*dunkel klingend*) husky; *Laut* croaky ◆ **~ reden** to talk hoarsely *or* in a hoarse voice; **sich ~ schreien/reden** (*lit, fig*) to shout/talk oneself hoarse.

Heiserkeit *f siehe adj* hoarseness; huskiness.

heiß *adj* **(a)** hot; *Zone* torrid ◆ **brennend/siedend/glühend ~** burning/boiling/scorching hot; **drückend ~** oppressively hot; **jdm ist/wird ~** sb is/is getting hot; **sie hat einen ~en Kopf** (*wegen Fieber*) she has a burning forehead; (*vom Denken*) her head is spinning; **etw ~ machen** to heat sth up; **es überläuft mich ~ und kalt** I feel hot and cold all over; **~e Tränen weinen** to cry one's heart out; **mit der ~en Nadel genäht** thrown together; **es wird nichts so ~ gegessen, wie es gekocht wird** (*prov*) things are never as bad as they seem; **eine/ein Paar H~e** (*dial*) a hot sausage/a couple of hot sausages; **~!** (*inf: fast gefunden*) you're hot; *siehe* **baden.**
(b) (*heftig*) *Diskussion, Kampf, Auseinandersetzung* heated, fierce; *Zorn* impassioned; *Begierde* passionate, burning; (*innig*) *Liebe, Wunsch* burning, fervent ◆ **es ging ~ her** things got heated; **das Gebiet/die Stadt ist ~ umkämpft** the area/town is being hotly *or* fiercely fought over; **jdn/etw ~ und innig lieben** to love sb/sth madly; **sich die Köpfe ~ reden, sich ~ reden** *or* **diskutieren** to talk till one is blue in the face; **~en Dank** very many thanks.
(c) (*aufreizend*) *Musik, Sachen, Bilder* hot; (*inf: sexuell erregt auch*) randy (*Brit inf*), horny (*inf*) ◆ **~e Höschen** hot pants; **jdn ~ machen** (*inf*) to turn sb on (*inf*).
(d) (*gefährlich*) *Ware, Geld,* (*radioaktiv*) *Teilchen etc* hot; *Gegend, Thema* hotly-disputed ◆ **das wird ein ~er Winter** things are going to be pretty hot this winter (*inf*); **ein ~es Eisen** a hot potato; **ein ~es Eisen anfassen** (*inf*) to grasp the nettle.
(e) *attr* (*inf*) *Favorit, Tip, Maschine* hot ◆ **ein ~er Ofen** a motorbike; **~er Draht** hotline; **~e Spur** firm lead.
(f) *pred* (*inf: brünstig*) **~ sein** to be on heat.

heißa *interj* hey.

heißblütig *adj* (*erregbar*) hot-tempered; (*leidenschaftlich*) hot-blooded.

heißen *pret* **hieß,** *ptp* **geheißen** [1] *vt* **(a)** (*nennen*) to call; (*old: Namen geben*) *jdn, Ort* to name ◆ **das heiße ich klug vorgehen!** that's what I call being clever; **jdn einen Lügner** *etc* **~** to call sb a liar *etc*; **oder wie heißt man das?** (*inf*) ... or what do you call it?; **... oder wie man das heißt** ... or whatever it's called.
(b) (*geh: auffordern*) to tell, to bid (*form*) ◆ **jdn etw tun ~** to tell sb to do sth, to bid sb do sth; **jdn willkommen ~** to bid sb welcome.
[2] *vi* **(a)** (*den Namen haben, bezeichnet werden*) to be called (*Brit*) *or* named; (*als Titel haben auch*) to be titled ◆ **wie ~ Sie/heißt die Straße?** what are you/is the street called?, what's your name/the name of the street?; **ich heiße Müller** I'm called *or* my name is Müller; **sie heißt jetzt anders** her name is different now, she has changed her name; **nach jdm ~** to be called after (*Brit*) *or* for (*US*) sb; **wie kann man nur Gotthelf/so ~?** how can anyone have a name like Gotthelf/like that?; **wie heißt das?** what is that called?; **eigentlich heißt es richtig X** actually the correct word is X; **... und wie sie alle ~** ... and the rest of them; **... so wahr ich Franz-Josef heiße** (*als Bekräftigung*) ... as sure as I'm standing here; **... dann will ich Fridolin ~** ... then I'm a Dutchman.
(b) (*bestimmte Bedeutung haben*) to mean ◆ **was heißt „gut" auf englisch?** what is the English (word) for "gut"?; **„gut" heißt auf englisch „good"** the English (word) for "gut" is "good"; **soll/will ~** (*am Satzanfang*) in other words; **ich weiß, was es heißt, allein zu sein** I know what it means to be alone.
(c) (*lauten*) to be; (*Spruch, Gedicht etc*) to go.
(d) das heißt that is; (*in anderen Worten*) that is to say.
[3] *vi impers* **(a) es heißt, daß ...** (*es geht die Rede*) they say that ...; **es soll nicht ~, daß ...** never let it be said that ...
(b) (*zu lesen sein*) **in der Bibel/im Gesetz/in seinem Brief heißt es, daß ...** the Bible/the law/his letter says that ..., in the Bible *etc* it says that ...; **bei Hegel/Goethe** *etc* **heißt es ...** Hegel/Goethe says ...; **es heißt hier ...** it says here ...
(c) (*es ist nötig*) **es heißt, etw zu tun** you/we/he *etc* must do sth; **nun heißt es handeln** now it's time to act; **da heißt es aufgepaßt** *or* **aufpassen** you'd better watch out.

Heiß-: ⚠h~ersehnt *adj attr* much longed for; **⚠h~geliebt** *adj* dearly beloved; **~hunger** *m* ravenous *or* voracious appetite; **etw mit ~hunger essen** to eat sth ravenously *or* voraciously; **etw mit wahrem ~hunger verschlingen** (*fig*) to really devour sth; **h~hungrig** *adj* ravenous, voracious; **h~laufen** *vi sep irreg aux sein* (*Motor, Auto, Maschinenteil*) to overheat; (*Diskussionsteilnehmer etc*) to become heated; (*Telefonleitungen, -drähte*) to buzz.

Heißluft *f* hot air ◆ **Kochen mit ~** fan-assisted cooking.

Heißluft-: ~heizung *f* hot-air heating; **~herd** *m* fan-assisted oven; **~motor** *m* hot-air *or* Stirling ® engine; **~trockner** *m* hot-air dryer.

Heiß-: ~mangel *f* (*Gerät*) rotary iron; (*Ort*) *laundry specializing in ironing sheets etc*; **~sporn** *m* hothead; **⚠h~umkämpft** *adj attr* hotly disputed; **⚠h~umstritten** *adj attr* hotly debated; **~wasserbereiter** *m* **-s, -** geyser, water heater; **~wasserspeicher** *m* hot (water) tank.

heiter *adj* (*fröhlich*) cheerful; *Mensch, Wesen auch* happy; (*ausgeglichen*) serene; (*amüsant*) *Geschichte* amusing, funny; (*leicht betrunken*) merry; (*hell, klar*) *Farbe, Raum* bright; *Himmel, Tag* bright, clear; *Wetter* clear, fine; (*Met*) fair ◆ **~ werden** to become cheerful; (*Gesicht*) to brighten; (*Wetter*) to brighten *or* clear up; **~er werden** to cheer up; (*Wetter*) to brighten up, to become brighter; **das kann ja ~ werden!** (*iro*) that sounds great (*iro*); **aus ~em Himmel** (*fig*) out of the blue.

Heiterkeit *f, no pl siehe adj* cheerfulness; happiness; serenity; amusingness, funniness; merriness; brightness; clearness; fineness; (*heitere Stimmung*) merriment; (*Belustigung*) amusement.

Heiterkeits-: ~ausbruch *m* fit of merriment; **~erfolg** *m* **einen ~erfolg haben** to raise a laugh.

Heiz-: ~anlage *f* heating system; **~apparat** *m siehe* **~gerät**; **h~bar** *adj Heckscheibe etc* heated; *Zimmer auch* with heating; **der Saal ist schwer h~bar** the hall is difficult to heat; *siehe auch* **beheizbar**; **~(bett)decke** *f* electric blanket; **~element** *nt* heating element.

heizen [1] *vi* (*die Heizung anhaben*) to have the/one's heating on; (*Wärme abgeben*) to give off heat ◆ **der Ofen heizt gut** the stove gives (off) a good heat; **mit Holz/Strom** *etc* **~** to use wood/electricity *etc* for heating; **ab November wird geheizt** the heating is put on in November.
[2] *vt* (*warm machen*) to heat; (*verbrennen*) to burn; (*be~*) *Lokomotive* to stoke ◆ **den Ofen heize ich nur mit Holz** I only burn wood in the stove.
[3] *vr* **sich gut/schlecht ~** to be easily heated *or* easy to heat/not easily heated *or* hard to heat.

Heizer *m* **-s, -** boilerman; (*von Lokomotive, Schiff*) stoker.

Heiz-: ~fläche *f* heating surface; **~gas** *nt* fuel gas; **~gerät** *nt* heater; **~kessel** *m* boiler; **~kissen** *nt* electric heat pad; **~körper** *m* (*Gerät*) heater; (*von Zentralheizung*) radiator; (*Element*) heating element; **~körperverkleidung** *f* radiator cover; **~kosten** *pl* heating costs *pl*; **~kostenpauschale** *f* fixed heating cost; **~kraft** *f* calorific *or* heating power; **~kraftwerk** *nt* thermal power station; **~lüfter** *m* fan heater; **~material** *nt* fuel (*for heating*); **~ofen** *m siehe* **~gerät**; **~öl** *nt* heating *or* fuel oil; **~platte** *f* hotplate; **~sonne** *f* electric fire; **~strahler** *m* electric (wall) heater.

Heizung *f* heating; (*Heizkörper*) heater; (*von Zentralheizung*) radiator.

Heizungs-: ~anlage *f* heating system; **~keller** *m* boiler room; **~monteur** *m* heating engineer; **~rohr** *nt* heating pipe; **~technik** *f* heating engineering.

Heizwert *m* calorific value.

Hektar *nt or m* **-s, -e** hectare.

Hektik *f* **-,** *no pl* (*Hast*) hectic rush; (*von Großstadt etc*) hustle and bustle; (*von Leben etc*) hectic pace ◆ **sie ißt/arbeitet mit einer solchen ~** she eats/works at such a hectic pace; **nur keine ~** take it easy.

hektisch *adj* (*auch dated Med*) hectic; *Mensch auch* frantic; *Arbeiten* frantic, furious ◆ **es geht ~ zu** things are hectic; **ich lebe zur Zeit ~** my life is very hectic just now; **nur mal nicht so ~** take it easy.

Hekto-: ⚠~graphie *f* (*Verfahren*) hectography; (*Abzug*) hectograph (copy); **⚠h~graphieren*** *vt insep* to hectograph, to copy; **~liter** *m or nt* hectolitre; **~watt** *nt* hectowatt.

Helanca ® *nt* **-,** *no pl* stretch fabric.

helau *interj greeting used at Carnival time.*

Held *m* **-en, -en** hero ◆ **der ~ des Tages** the hero of the hour; **kein ~ in etw** (*dat*) **sein** not to be very brave about sth; (*in Schulfach etc*) to be no great shakes at sth (*inf*); **du bist mir ein rechter** *or* **schöner ~!** (*iro*) some hero you are!; **den ~en spielen** (*inf*) to come *or* play the (great) hero.

Helden-: ~brust *f* (*hum*) manly chest; **~darsteller** *m* (*Theat*) heroic leading man; **~dichtung** *f* epic *or* heroic poetry; **~epos** *nt* heroic epic; **~friedhof** *m* military cemetery; **~gedenktag** *m* (*old*) ≃ Remembrance

➤ SPRACHE AKTIV: **heiraten: 3** → 51.3

Day, Memorial Day (*US*); **~gestalt** *f* hero; **h~haft** *adj* heroic, valiant; **~lied** *nt* (*Liter*) epic song *or* lay; **~mut** *m* heroic courage; **h~mütig** *adj siehe* **h~haft**; **~pose** *f* heroic pose; **~rolle** *f* (*Theat*) hero's part *or* rôle; **~sage** *f* heroic saga; **~stück** *nt*: **das war kein ~stück** (*inf*) that didn't exactly cover you/him *etc* in glory; **~tat** *f* heroic deed *or* feat; **~tenor** *m* heroic tenor; **~tod** *m* heroic death, hero's death; **den ~tod sterben** to die a hero's death; (*Mil*) to be killed in action; **~tum** *nt, no pl* heroism.

Heldin *f* heroine.

helfen *pret* **half**, *ptp* **geholfen** *vi* **(a)** to help (*jdm* sb); (*mit anfassen auch*) to lend a hand ◆ **jdm bei etw ~** to help sb with sth, to lend sb a hand with sth; **jdm etw tun ~** to help sb do sth; **er half ihr aus dem Mantel/einer Verlegenheit** he helped her out of her coat *or* off with her coat/out of a difficulty; **ihm/dir ist nicht zu ~** (*fig*) he is/you are beyond help; **dem Kranken ist nicht mehr zu ~** the patient is beyond help; **ich kann mir nicht ~** I can't help it; **ich kann mir nicht ~, ich muß es tun** I can't help doing it; **ich werd' dir/ihm (schon) ~!** I'll give you/him what for (*inf*); **ich werde dir ~, die Tapeten zu beschmieren** I'll teach you to mess up the wallpaper (*inf*); **er weiß sich** (*dat*) **zu ~** he is very resourceful; **man muß sich** (*dat*) **nur zu ~ wissen** (*prov*) you just have to use your head; **er weiß sich** (*dat*) **nicht mehr zu ~** he is at his wits' end; **hilf dir selbst, dann** *or* **so hilft dir Gott** (*Prov*) God helps those who help themselves (*Prov*).
(b) *auch vi impers* (*dienen, nützen*) to help ◆ **es hilft nichts** it's no use *or* no good; **da ist nicht zu ~** there's no help for it; **da hilft alles nichts ...** there's nothing for it ...; **da hilft kein Jammern und kein Klagen** it's no use moaning; **es hilft ihm nichts, daß ...** it's no use to him that ...; **das hilft mir wenig, damit ist mir nicht geholfen** that's not much help to me; **das hat mir schon viel geholfen** that has been a great help to me; **was hilft's?** what's the use?; **was hülfe es dem Menschen, wenn ...** (*Bibl*) what does it profit a man if ... (*Bibl*).
(c) (*heilsam sein*) to help; (*heilen auch: Arzt*) to cure ◆ **diese Arznei hilft gegen** *or* **bei Kopfweh** this medicine is good for headaches *or* helps to relieve headaches; **jetzt kann nur noch eine Operation ~** only an operation will help now *or* do any good now.

Helfer *m* **-s, -** helper; (*Mitarbeiter*) assistant; (*von Verbrecher*) accomplice; (*inf: Gerät*) help ◆ **~ in Steuersachen** tax adviser; **ein ~ in der Not** a friend in need.

Helferin *f siehe* **Helfer**.

Helfershelfer *m* accomplice; (*Jur: vor/nach begangener Tat*) accessory before/after the fact.

Helferzelle *f* (*Med*) helper cell.

Helgoland *nt* **-s** Heligoland.

Helikopter *m* **-s, -** helicopter.

Helium *nt, no pl* (*abbr* **He**) helium.

hell *adj* **(a)** (*optisch*) light; *Licht, Beleuchtung, Himmel* bright; *Farbe auch* pale; *Kleidungsstück auch* light-coloured; *Haar, Teint* fair; *Hautfarbe* (*von Rasse*) fair, pale; (*fig*) *Zukunft* bright ◆ **es wird ~** it's getting light; **~ bleiben** to stay light; **am ~en Tage** in broad daylight; **bis in den ~en Morgen schlafen** to sleep late; **in ~en Flammen** in flames, ablaze; **~es Bier** ≃ lager.
(b) (*akustisch*) *Laut, Ton, Stimme* high(-pitched); *Gelächter* ringing.
(c) (*inf: klug*) *Junge* bright, intelligent; (*geistig klar*) *Augenblicke* lucid ◆ **er ist ein ~er Kopf, er hat einen ~en Kopf** he has brains; *siehe* **helle**.
(d) *attr* (*stark, groß*) great; *Verwunderung etc* utter; *Verzweiflung, Unsinn* sheer, utter; *Neid* pure ◆ **von etw ~ begeistert/entzückt sein** to be very enthusiastic/quite delighted about sth; **in ~en Scharen** in great numbers; **seine ~e Freude an etw** (*dat*) **haben** to find great joy *or* pleasure in sth.

Hellas *nt* **-'** Hellas.

hell- *in cpds* (*esp auf Farben bezüglich*) light; **~auf** *adv* completely, utterly; **~auf lachen** to laugh out loud; **~blau** *adj* light blue; **~blond** *adj* very fair, blonde; **~braun** *adj* light brown; **H~dunkel** *nt* (*Art*) chiaroscuro.

Helle *f* **-**, *no pl siehe* **Helligkeit**.

helle *adj pred* (*inf*) bright, clever ◆ **Mensch, sei ~!** use your loaf, mate! (*inf*).

Hellebarde *f* **-, -n** (*Hist*) halberd.

Hellene *m* **-n, -n** (ancient) Greek, Hellene.

hellenisch *adj* Hellenic.

hellenisieren* *vt* to hellenize.

Hellenismus *m* Hellenism.

Hellenist(in *f*) *m* Hellenist.

Hellenistik *f* classical Greek studies *pl*.

hellenistisch *adj* Hellenistic ◆ **die ~e Staatenwelt** the Empire of Ancient Greece.

Heller *m* **-s, -** (*Hist*) heller ◆ **das ist keinen (roten** *or* **lumpigen)** *or* **nicht einen ~ wert** that isn't worth a brass farthing; **er besitzt keinen (roten** *or* **lumpigen) ~** he doesn't have a penny to his name, he doesn't have two pennies to rub together; **darauf geb ich keinen (roten) ~** I wouldn't give you tuppence for it; **auf ~ und Pfennig** *or* **bis auf den letzten ~** (down) to the last farthing *or* penny; *stimmen* down to the last detail.

Helle(s) *nt decl as adj* ≃ lager.

⚠ **helleuchtend** *adj attr getrennt* **hell-leuchtend** brightly shining; *Farbe* bright; *Kleid* brightly coloured.

hell-: **~haarig** *adj* fair-haired; **~häutig** *adj* fair-skinned; (*von Rasse auch*) pale-skinned; **~hörig** *adj* keen of hearing; (*Archit*) poorly soundproofed; **~hörig sein** (*fig: Mensch*) to have sharp ears; **als er das sagte, wurde ich ~hörig** when he said that I pricked up my ears; **jdn ~hörig machen** to make sb prick up their ears.

⚠ **hellicht** *adj getrennt* **hell-licht**: **am ~en Tage** in broad daylight; **es ist ~er Tag** it is broad daylight.

Helligkeit *f, no pl siehe* **hell (a)** lightness; brightness; paleness; fairness; paleness; brightness; (*helles Licht*) light; (*Phys, Astron*) luminosity.

Helligkeitsregler *m* brightness control.

Helling *f* **-, -en** *or* **Helligen** *or m* **-s, -e** (*Naut*) slipway.

⚠ **hellodernd** *adj attr getrennt* **hell-lodernd** blazing.

Hell-: **h~rot** *adj* bright red; **h~sehen** *vi infin only* **h~sehen können** to have second sight, to be clairvoyant; **du kannst wohl h~sehen!** you must have second sight *or* be clairvoyant; **~sehen** *nt* clairvoyance; **~seher(in** *f*) *m* (*lit, fig*) clairvoyant; **h~seherisch** *adj attr* clairvoyant; **h~sichtig** *adj* shrewd; ⚠**h~strahlend** *adj attr* brilliant, brightly shining; **h~wach** *adj* (*lit*) wide-awake; (*fig*) alert; **~werden** *nt* **-s**, *no pl* daybreak.

Helm *m* **-(e)s, -e** helmet; (*Archit*) helm roof.

Helm-: **~busch** *m* plume; **~pflicht** *f* **es besteht ~pflicht** the wearing of crash helmets is compulsory; **~schmuck** *m* crest.

Helot *m* **-en, -en** Helot.

Helotentum *nt, no pl* (*Sklaverei*) helotism, helotage; (*alle Heloten*) helotry.

Helsinki *nt* **-s** Helsinki.

hem [həm, hm] *interj* hem.

Hemd *nt* **-(e)s, -en** (*Ober~*) shirt; (*Unter~*) vest (*Brit*), undershirt (*US*) ◆ **etw wie das** *or* **sein ~ wechseln** (*fig*) to change sth with monotonous regularity; **für dich gebe ich auch das letzte** *or* **mein letztes ~ her** (*inf*) I'd give you the shirt off my back (*inf*); **naß bis aufs ~** wet through, soaked to the skin; **jdn bis aufs ~ ausziehen** (*fig inf*) to have the shirt off sb's back (*inf*), to fleece sb (*inf*); **das ~ ist mir näher als der Rock** (*Prov*) charity begins at home (*Prov*).

Hemd-: **~ärmel** *m siehe* **Hemdsärmel**; **~bluse** *f* shirt(-blouse), shirtwaist (*US*); **~blusenkleid** *nt* shirtwaister (dress); **~brust** *f* dickey.

Hemden-: **~matz** *m* (*inf*) *small child dressed only in a vest*, ≃ Wee Willie Winkie; **~stoff** *m* shirting.

Hemd-: **~hose** *f* combinations *pl*, coms *pl* (*inf*); **~knopf** *m* shirt button; **~kragen** *m* shirt collar.

Hemds-: **~ärmel** *m* shirt sleeve; **in ~ärmeln** in one's shirt sleeves; **h~ärmelig** *adj* shirt-sleeved; (*fig inf*) down-to-earth; *Ausdrucksweise, Empfang, Einstellung* casual.

Hemisphäre *f* **-, -n** hemisphere.

hemisphärisch *adj* hemispheric(al).

hemmen *vt Entwicklung, Fortschritt* to hinder, to hamper; *Lauf der Geschehnisse etc* to check; (*verlangsamen*) to slow down; *Maschine, Rad* to check; *Wasserlauf* to stem; (*Med*) *Blut* to staunch; (*Psych*) to inhibit; *Leidenschaften* to restrain, to check ◆ **jdn in seiner Entwicklung ~** to hinder *or* hamper sb's development; *siehe* **gehemmt**.

Hemmnis *nt* hindrance, impediment (*für* to).

Hemm-: **~rad** *nt* (*von Uhr*) escapement; **~schuh** *m* brake shoe; (*fig*) hindrance, impediment (*für* to); **jdm einen ~schuh in den Weg legen** (*fig*) to obstruct sb; **~schwelle** *f* inhibition level; **~stoff** *m* (*Chem*) inhibitor.

Hemmung *f* **(a)** (*Psych*) inhibition; (*Bedenken*) scruple ◆ **da habe ich ~en** I've got scruples about that; **an ~en leiden** to suffer from inhibitions; **keine ~en kennen** to have no inhibitions, not to feel inhibited; **nur keine ~en** don't feel inhibited.
(b) *siehe vt* hindering, hampering; check (*gen* to); slowing down; checking; stemming; staunching.
(c) (*von Gewehr*) *siehe* **Ladehemmung**.
(d) (*von Uhr*) escapement.

Hemmungs-: **h~los** *adj* (*rückhaltlos*) unrestrained; (*skrupellos*) unscrupulous; **~losigkeit** *f siehe adj* lack of restraint; unscrupulousness; **~nerv** *m* inhibitor (nerve).

Hendl *nt* **-s, -(n)** (*Aus*) chicken.

Hengst *m* **-(e)s, -e** stallion; (*Kamel~, Esel~*) male; (*sl: Mann*) stud (*sl*).

Hengst-: **~fohlen, ~füllen** *nt* (male) foal, colt.

Henkel *m* **-s, -** handle.

Henkel-: **~glas** *nt* glass with a handle; **~korb** *m* basket with a handle; **~krug** *m* jug (with a handle); **~mann** *m, pl* **-männer** (*inf*) canteen; **~ohren** *pl* (*inf*) big, sticking-out ears (*inf*); **~topf** *m* pot *or* pan with a handle/handles.

henken *vt* (*old*) to hang.

Henker *m* **-s, -** hangman; (*Scharfrichter*) executioner ◆ **zum ~** (*old inf*) hang it all (*inf*), zounds (*obs inf*); **was zum ~!** (*old inf*) what the devil (*inf*); **hol's der ~!** (*old inf*) the devil take it! (*old inf*); **hol mich der ~** (*old inf*) zounds (*obs inf*); **scher dich** *or* **geh zum ~!** (*old inf*) go to the devil! (*inf*).

Henker(s)beil *nt* executioner's axe.

Henkers-: **~hand** *f* **durch** *or* **von ~hand sterben** to be executed; **~knecht** *m* (*Hist*) hangman's *or* (*von Scharfrichter*) executioner's assistant; (*fig*) torturer; (*Handlanger*) henchman; **~mahl(zeit** *f*) *nt* last meal before execution; (*hum inf*) last slap-up meal (*before examination etc*).

Henna *f* **-** *or nt* **-(s)**, *no pl* henna ◆ **mit ~ färben** to dye with henna, to henna.

Henne *f* **-, -n** hen.

Hepatitis *f* **-, Hepatitiden** hepatitis.

her *adv siehe auch* **herkommen, hermüssen, hersein** *etc* **(a)** (*räumlich*) **von der Kirche/Frankreich/dem Meer ~** from the church/France/the sea; **er winkte vom Nachbarhaus ~** he waved from the house next door; **~ zu mir!** come here (to me); **um mich ~** (all) around me; **von weit ~** from a long way off *or* away, from afar (*liter*); *siehe auch* **hin**.
(b) (*in Aufforderung*) **Bier/Essen ~!** bring (me/us) some beer/food (here); **~ mit der Brieftasche!** hand over the briefcase, give me the briefcase; **(wieder) ~ mit den alten Bräuchen** give me/us the old way of doing things, bring

⚠: for details of spelling reform, see supplement

back the old customs I say; **~ damit!** give me that, give that here (*inf*); **immer ~ damit!** let's have it/them (then).
(c) (*von etwas aus gesehen*) **von der Idee/Form/Farbe ~** as for the idea/form/colour, as far as the idea/form/colour is concerned *or* goes; **vom finanziellen Standpunkt ~** from the financial point of view; **von den Eltern ~ gute Anlagen haben** to have inherited good qualities from one's parents.
(d) (*zeitlich*) **ich kenne ihn von früher ~** I know him from before *or* from earlier times, I used to know him (before); **von der Schule/meiner Kindheit ~** since school/my childhood; **von der letzten Saison ~** from last season; *siehe* **hersein**.

herạb *adv* down ◆ **den Hügel/die Treppe ~** down the hill/stairs; **von oben ~** (down) from above; *siehe* **oben**.

herạb- *pref siehe auch* **herunter-**, **runter-** down; **~blicken** *vi sep siehe* **~sehen**; **~flehen** *vt sep* (*liter*) to call down; **~fließen** *vi sep irreg aux sein* to flow down; **~hängen** *vi sep irreg* to hang down; **langes ~hängendes Haar** long, flowing hair; **~kommen** *vi sep irreg aux sein* (*geh*) to come down, to descend (*liter, form*); **~lassen** *sep irreg* [1] *vt* to let down, to lower; [2] *vr* (a) (*lit*) to let oneself down, to lower oneself; (b) (*fig*) to lower oneself; **sich zu etw ~lassen** to condescend *or* deign to do sth; **sich auf jds Ebene** (*acc*) **~lassen** to descend to sb's level; **wenn du dich ~lassen könntest, mir dabei zu helfen** if you would condescend *or* deign to help me with it; **~lassend** *adj* condescending; **H~lassung** *f* condescension; **~mindern** *vt sep* (*schlechtmachen*) *Leistung, Qualitäten* to belittle, to disparage; (*bagatellisieren*) *Gefahr, Problem* to minimize, to make little of; (*reduzieren*) *Geschwindigkeit, Länge, Niveau* to reduce; **~rieseln** *vi sep aux sein* to trickle down; (*Schneeflocken, Staub, Musik*) to float *or* waft down; **~sehen** *vi sep irreg* (*lit, fig*) to look down (*auf +acc* on); **~senken** *vr sep* (*geh: Nebel, Dunkelheit, Abend*) to fall; **~setzen** *vt sep Ware* to reduce; *Preise, Kosten auch* to lower; *Geschwindigkeit auch* to slacken off; *Niveau* to lower, to debase; (*schlechtmachen*) *Leistungen, Fähigkeiten, jdn* to belittle, to disparage; **zu stark ~gesetzten Preisen** at greatly reduced prices; **H~setzung** *f siehe vt* reduction; lowering; slackening off; debasement, lowering; belittling, disparagement; (*Kränkung*) slight, snub; **~sinken** *vi sep irreg aux sein* to sink (down); (*liter: Nacht*) to fall, to descend (*liter*); **~steigen** *vi sep irreg aux sein* to get down, to descend; (*von Pferd*) to dismount; (*von Berg*) to climb down, to descend; **~stoßen** *vi sep irreg aux sein* to swoop (down); **~stürzen** *sep* [1] *vt* to push off (*von etw* sth); [2] *vi aux sein* to fall off (*von etw* sth); (*Felsbrocken*) to fall down (*von* from); (*geh: Wasserfall*) to cascade *or* plunge down, to come rushing down; [3] *vr* to jump off (*von etw* sth); **er stürzte sich vom Turm ~** he threw himself *or* jumped off *or* from the tower; **~würdigen** *sep* [1] *vt* to belittle, to disparage; [2] *vr* to degrade *or* lower oneself; **H~würdigung** *f* belittling, disparagement; **~ziehen** *vt sep irreg* (*lit*) to pull down; *Mundwinkel* to turn down; (*fig*) *jdn* to drag down.

Herạldik *f, no pl* heraldry.

herạldisch *adj* heraldic.

herạn *adv* **rechts/links ~!** over to the right/left; **immer** *or* **nur ~!** come on *or* along (then)!; **bis an etw** (*acc*) **~** close *or* near to sth, right by *or* beside sth; (*mit Bewegungsverb*) right up to sth.

▼ **herạn-** *pref siehe auch* **ran-**; **~arbeiten** *vr sep* (*sich nähern*) to work one's way along; **sich an jdn/etw ~arbeiten** to work one's way (along *or* over) towards sb/sth; **~bilden** *vt sep* to train (up); (*in der Schule*) to educate; **~bringen** *vt sep irreg* (*herbringen*) to bring over; **sein Spurt brachte ihn näher an den führenden Läufer ~** his spurt brought him up towards *or* nearer to the leader; **die Schüler bedächtig an diese schwierigen Probleme ~bringen** to introduce the pupils slowly to these difficult problems; **~eilen** *vi sep aux sein* to rush *or* hurry over; **~fahren** *vti sep irreg aux sein* to drive *or* (*mit Fahrrad*) ride up (*an +acc* to); **~führen** *sep* [1] *vt jdn* to lead up; *Truppen* to bring up; **jdn an etw** (*acc*) **~führen** (*lit*) to lead/bring sb up to sth; (*fig*) (*Frage, Problem*) to lead *or* bring sb to sth; (*Lehrer etc*) to introduce sb to sth; [2] *vi* **an etw** (*acc*) **~führen** (*lit, fig*) to lead to sth; **~gehen** *vi sep irreg aux sein* to go up (*an +acc* to); **ich würde nicht näher ~gehen** I wouldn't go any nearer *or* closer; **an jdn/etw ~gehen** (*lit*) to go up to sb/sth; (*fig: angreifen*) *an Problem, Aufgabe* to tackle *or* approach sth; *an Gegner* to set about sb; **~kommen** *vi sep irreg aux sein* (a) (*räumlich*) to come *or* draw near (*an +acc* to), to approach (*an etw* (*acc*) sth); (*zeitlich*) to draw near (*an +acc* to), to approach (*an etw* (*acc*) sth); **das lasse ich mal an mich ~kommen** (*fig inf*) I'll cross that bridge when I come to it (*prov*); **die Verfolger kamen dicht an den führenden Läufer ~** those behind were almost catching up with the leader; **die Verfolger kamen immer näher ~** our pursuers were gaining on us; **auf 1:3 ~kommen** to pull up *or* back to 1-3; **er läßt alle Probleme an sich ~kommen** he always adopts a wait-and-see attitude; (b) (*erreichen, bekommen*) **an den Chef/Motor kommt man nicht ~** you can't get hold of the boss/get at *or* to the engine; **wie komme ich nur an das Kapital ~?** how do I get hold of *or* (*wenn festgelegt*) get at the capital?; (c) (*sich messen können mit*) **an jdn ~kommen** to be up to the standard of sb; **an etw** (*acc*) **~kommen** to be up to (the standard of) sth; **an diesen Wissenschaftler kommt keiner ~** there's no-one who is a patch on this scientist; **er kommt nicht an seinen Vater ~** he's not a patch on his father; (d) **an etw** (*acc*) **~kommen** (*grenzen an*) to verge on sth; **~machen** *vr sep* (*inf*) **sich an etw** (*acc*) **~machen** to get down to sth, to get going on sth (*inf*); **sich an jdn ~machen** to approach sb, to have a go at sb (*inf*); *an Mädchen* to make up to sb, to chat sb up (*inf*); **~nahen** *vi sep aux sein* (*geh*) to
▼ approach; (*Katastrophe, Unwetter auch*) to be imminent; **~reichen** *vi sep* **an jdn/etw ~reichen** (*lit*) (*Mensch*) to reach sb/sth; (*Weg, Gelände etc*) to reach (up to) sth; (*fig: sich messen können mit*) to come up to (the standard of) sb/sth, to come near sb/sth; **er reicht nicht an mich ~** (*fig*) he doesn't come up to my standard *or* come near me, he can't touch me (*inf*); **~reifen** *vi sep aux sein* (*geh*) (*Obst*) to ripen; (*fig*) (*Jugendliche*) to mature; (*Plan, Entschluß, Idee*) to mature, to ripen; **zur Frau/zum Mann/zum Erwachsenen ~reifen** to mature into a woman/man/adult; **~rücken** *sep* [1] *vi aux sein* (*sich nähern*) to approach (*an etw* (*acc*) sth); (*Truppen auch*) to advance (*an +acc* upon, towards); (*dicht aufrücken*) to come/go nearer *or* closer (*an +acc* to); **er rückte mit seinem Stuhl ~** he brought *or* drew his chair up *or* nearer; [2] *vt* to pull/push over *or* up (*an +acc* to); **rück deinen Stuhl ~** bring *or* draw up your chair; **~schaffen** *vt sep* to bring (along); **~schleichen** *vir sep irreg* (*vi: aux sein*) to creep up (*an etw* (*acc*) to sth, *an jdn* on sb); **~tasten** *vr sep* (*lit*) to feel *or* grope one's way over (*an +acc* to); (*fig*) to feel one's way; **sich an eine Frage ~tasten** to approach a matter cautiously; **~tragen** *vt sep irreg* to bring (over), to carry over; **etw an jdn ~tragen** (*fig*) to take/bring sth to sb, to go to sb with sth; **~treten** *vi sep irreg aux sein* (*lit*) to come/go up (*an +acc* to); **näher ~treten** to come/go nearer; **bitte treten Sie näher ~!** this way!, come along!; **an jdn ~treten** (*fig*) (*konfrontieren: Probleme, Zweifel, Versuchung*) to confront *or* face sb; **mit etw an jdn ~treten** (*sich wenden an*) to go to *or* approach sb with sth; **~wachsen** *vi sep irreg aux sein* (*geh*) to grow; (*Kind*) to grow up; (*fig: Probleme, Konkurrenz*) to grow up (*jdm* around sb); **zu einer schönen jungen Frau ~wachsen** to grow (up) into *or* to be a lovely young woman; **die ~wachsende Generation** the rising generation, the up and coming generation; **H~wachsende** *pl* (*Jur*) adolescents *pl*; **~wagen** *vr sep* to venture near, to dare to come/go near; **sich an etw** (*acc*) **~wagen** (*lit*) to venture near sth, to dare to come/go near sth; (*fig*) to venture to tackle sth; **er wagte sich nicht an sie ~** he did not dare to approach her; **~winken** *vt sep* to beckon *or* wave over; *Taxi* to hail; **einen Polizisten ~winken** to call a policeman over; **~ziehen** *sep irreg* [1] *vt* (a) (*näher bringen*) to pull over, to draw near (*an +acc* to); (b) (*zu Hilfe holen*) to call in; *Literatur* to consult; **jdn zur Hilfe/Unterstützung ~ziehen** to enlist sb's aid *or* help/support; (c) (*einsetzen*) *Arbeitskräfte, Kapital* to bring in; **jdn zu einer Aufgabe ~ziehen** to enlist sb to do a task; (d) (*geltend machen*) *Recht, Paragraphen, Quelle, Zitat* to call *or* bring into play; **etw zum Vergleich ~ziehen** to use sth by way of comparison; (e) (*aufziehen*) *Tier, Kind* to raise; *Pflanze auch* to cultivate; **jdn zu etw ~ziehen** to bring sb up to be sth; **sich** (*dat*) **Revolutionäre/Jasager ~ziehen** (*pej*) to make revolutionaries/yes-men for oneself; [2] *vi aux sein* to approach; (*Mil*) to advance.

Herạnziehungsbescheid *m* (*Admin*) final notice.

herauf [1] *adv* up ◆ **vom Tal ~** up from the valley; **von unten ~** up from below; **vom Süden ~** (*inf*) up from the south.
[2] *prep +acc* up ◆ **den Fluß/Berg/die Treppe ~** up the river/mountain/stairs.

herạuf- *pref siehe auch* **rauf-** up; **~arbeiten** *vr sep* (*lit, fig*) to work one's way up; **~bemühen*** *sep* [1] *vt* to trouble to come up, to ask (to come) up; [2] *vr* to take the trouble to come up; **~beschwören*** *vt sep irreg* (a) (*wachrufen*) *Erinnerung, Vergangenheit* to evoke; (b) (*herbeiführen*) *Unglück, Streit, Krise* to cause, to give rise to; **~bitten** *vt sep irreg* to ask (to come) up; **~bringen** *vt sep irreg* to bring up; **~dämmern** *vi sep aux sein* (*liter*) to dawn; **~dringen** *vi sep irreg aux sein* to rise (up) from below; (*Geruch*) to waft up; **ein Geräusch drang zu ihm ~** a noise from below reached him *or* his ears; **~dürfen** *vi sep irreg* (*inf*) to be allowed up; **~führen** *sep* [1] *vt Pferd etc* to lead up; *jdn* to show up; [2] *vi* (*Weg etc*) to lead up; **~kommen** *vi sep irreg aux sein* to come up; (*in oberes Stockwerk*) to come up(stairs); (*auf Boot, Kutsche*) to climb *or* come *or* get aboard; (*Mond, Geräusch, Nebel, Wolke auch*) to rise; (*Gewitter*) to approach; **~lassen** *vt sep irreg* to allow (to come) up; **er wollte mich nicht in den 2. Stock ~lassen** he wouldn't let me come up to the 2nd floor; **~reichen** *sep* [1] *vt* to hand *or* pass up; [2] *vi* to reach; **der Baum reicht bis zum Fenster ~** the tree reaches (up to) *or* comes up to the window; **~setzen** *sep* [1] *vt Preise etc* to increase, to raise; [2] *vr* **komm setz dich zu mir ~** come up here and sit with me, come and sit up here with me; **~steigen** *vi sep irreg aux sein* (a) to climb up; (*Dampf, Rauch*) to rise; (*Erinnerungen*) to well up (*in jdm* in sb); (b) (*liter: anbrechen*) (*Tag, neue Zeit*) to dawn; (*Dämmerung*) to break; **~ziehen** *sep irreg* [1] *vt* to pull up; **er zog ihn zu sich ~** (*lit*) he pulled him up to him; (*fig*) he raised him to his own level; [2] *vi aux sein* (a) (*Gewitter, Unheil etc*) to approach; (*liter: Nacht, Tag, Zeitalter auch*) to draw nigh (*liter*) *or* near; (b) (*nach oben umziehen*) to move up.

heraus *adv siehe auch* **herauskommen, heraussein** *etc* out ◆ **~ da!** (*inf*) get *or* come out of there!; **da ~?** out of there?; **~ aus den Federn!** (*inf*) rise and shine! (*inf*); **~ mit ihm** (*inf*) get him out!; **~ damit!** (*inf*) (*gib her*) hand it over!; **~ mit der Sprache** *or* **damit!** (*inf*) out with it! (*inf*); **zum Fenster ~** out of the window; **nach vorn ~ wohnen** to live facing *or* at the front; **von innen ~** to the core, through and through; **das rostet von innen ~ durch** it's rusting through from the inside; **mir ist von innen ~ kalt** I'm cold inside; **etw von innen ~ heilen** to cure sth from inside; **aus einem Gefühl der Verlassenheit/dem Wunsch ~** out of a feeling of forlornness/the desire; *siehe* **freiheraus**.

heraus- *pref siehe auch* **raus-** out; **~arbeiten** *sep* [1] *vt* (*aus Stein, Holz*) to carve (*aus* out of); (*fig*) to bring out; [2] *vr* to work one's way out (*aus* of); **~bekommen*** *vt sep irreg* (a) *Fleck, Nagel etc* to get out (*aus* of); (b) (*ermitteln, ~finden*) *Täter, Ursache, Geheimnis* to find out (*aus jdm* from sb); *Lösung, Aufgabe* to work *or* figure out; (c) *Wechselgeld* to get back; **Sie bekommen noch 1 Mark ~** you still have 1 mark change to come; **~bilden** *vr sep* to form, to develop (*aus* out of); **~boxen** *vt sep* (*aus* of) *Ball* to punch out; (*inf*) *jdn* to bail out (*inf*); **~bringen** *vt sep irreg* (a) (*lit*) to bring out (*aus* of); (b) (*inf: entfernen, ermitteln*) *siehe* **~bekommen (a, b)**; (c) (*auf den Markt bringen*) to bring out; *neues Modell auch* to launch; **jdn/etw ganz groß ~bringen** to launch sb/sth in a big way, to give sb/sth a big build-up; **die Affäre wurde in allen Zeitungen groß ~gebracht** the affair made a big splash *or* they made a big splash of the affair in the papers; **(d)** *(hervorbringen) Worte* to utter, to say; **er brachte kein Wort/keinen Ton ~** he couldn't utter a word/sound; **aus ihm war kein Wort ~zubringen** they couldn't get a (single) word out of him; **~drehen** *vt sep Birne, Schraube* to unscrew *(aus* from); **~dringen** *vi sep irreg aux sein* to come out *(aus* of); *(Wasser, Information auch)* to leak out *(aus* from); **~drücken** *vt sep* to squeeze out *(aus* of); **die Brust ~drücken** to stick one's chest out; **~fahren** *sep irreg* [1] *vi aux sein* **(a)** *(aus* of) to come out; *(Auto, Fahrer auch)* to drive out; *(Zug auch)* to pull *or* draw out; *(Radfahrer auch)* to ride out; **aufs Land/zu Besuch ~gefahren kommen** to drive *or* come out to the country/for a visit; **(b)** *(schnell herauskommen)* to leap out; *(entweichen)* to come out; *(Wort etc)* to slip out, to come out; **das Wort ist mir nur so ~gefahren** that word just came *or* slipped out somehow; [2] *vt* **(a)** *(aus* of) *Zug, Auto* to drive out; *Fahrrad* to ride out; **(b)** *(Sport)* **eine gute** *or* **schnelle Zeit/den Vorsprung ~fahren** to make good time/the lead; **einen Sieg ~fahren** to drive/ride to victory; **verlorene Minuten ~fahren** to make up for lost time; **~filtern** *vt sep (aus* of) to filter out; *(fig auch)* to sift out; **~finden** *sep irreg* [1] *vt Fehler, Fakten, Täter etc* to find out; *(~lesen) Gesuchtes* to pick out *(aus* from among, from), to find *(aus* (from) among); **er hat ~gefunden, daß** ... he has found out *or* discovered that ...; *(erkannt)* he has found *or* discovered that ...; [2] *vr* to find one's way out *(aus* of); **~fischen** *vt sep (inf)* to fish out *(inf) (aus* of); **sich** *(dat)* **etw ~fischen** to pick sth out (for oneself); **sich immer das Beste aus allem ~fischen** always to take the best of everything; **~fliegen** *sep irreg* [1] *vi aux sein (aus* of) *(lit)* to fly out; *(inf: ~fallen)* to come flying out; [2] *vt* to fly out *(aus* of).

Herausforderer *m* **-s, -** challenger.

herausfordern *sep* [1] *vt (esp Sport)* to challenge *(zu* to); *(provozieren)* to provoke *(zu etw* to do sth); *Kritik, Protest* to invite; *(heraufbeschwören) Gefahr* to court; *Unglück* to court, to invite ♦ **das Schicksal ~** to tempt fate *or* providence.
[2] *vi* **zu etw ~** *(provozieren)* to invite sth.

herausfordernd *adj* provocative; *(lockend auch)* inviting; *Blick auch* come-hither *attr*; *(Auseinandersetzung suchend) Reden, Haltung, Blick* challenging.

Herausforderung *f* challenge; *(Provokation)* provocation.

heraus-: ~fühlen *vt sep (fig)* to sense *(aus* from); **~führen** *vti sep (lit, fig)* to lead out *(aus* of).

Herausgabe *f* **(a)** *(Rückgabe)* return, handing back; *(von Personen)* handing over, surrender, delivery ♦ **Klage auf ~** action for restitution *or* return *(für* of). **(b)** *(von Buch etc)* publication.

herausgeben *sep irreg* [1] *vt* **(a)** *(zurückgeben)* to return, to hand *or* give back; *Gefangene etc* to hand over, to surrender, to deliver.
(b) *(veröffentlichen, erlassen)* to issue; *Buch, Zeitung* to publish; *(bearbeiten)* to edit.
(c) *(Wechselgeld geben) Betrag* to give in *or* as change ♦ **wieviel hat er dir herausgegeben?** how much change *or* what change did he give you (back)?; **2 DM/zu wenig ~** to give 2 marks change/too little change.
(d) *(herausreichen)* to hand *or* pass out *(aus* of).
[2] *vi (Wechselgeld geben)* to give change *(auf +acc* for) ♦ **er hat vergessen, mir herauszugeben** he's forgotten to give me my change; **können Sie (mir) ~?** can you give me change?, have you got the *or* enough change?; **falsch ~** to give the wrong change.

Herausgeber(in *f***)** *m (Verleger)* publisher; *(Redakteur)* editor.

heraus-: ~gehen *vi sep irreg aux sein (aus* of) to go out; *(Fleck, Korken etc)* to come out; **aus sich ~gehen** *(fig)* to come out of one's shell *(fig)*; **~greifen** *vt sep irreg* to pick *or* single out *(aus* of); *Beispiel* to take; **sich** *(dat)* **einzelne Demonstranten ~greifen** to pick on *or* single out individual demonstrators; **~haben** *vt sep irreg (inf)* **(a)** *(entfernt haben)* to have got out *(aus* of); **ich will ihn aus der Firma ~haben** I want him out of the firm; **(b)** *(begriffen haben)* to have got *(inf)*; *(gelöst haben) Problem, Rätsel, Aufgabe* to have solved; *Geheimnis* to have found out; **ich habe es jetzt ~, wie man das am besten macht** I've got it - I know the best way to do it now; **jetzt hat er die Handhabung der Maschine ~** he's got the knack *or* hang of the machine now *(inf)*; *siehe* **Dreh** *etc*; **(c)** *(zurückbekommen haben)* to have got back; **~halten** *sep irreg* [1] *vt* **(a)** *(lit) Hand, Gegenstand* to put *or* stick out *(aus* of); **(b)** *(fernhalten) Tiere, Eindringlinge* to keep out *(aus* of); **(c)** *(fig: nicht verwickeln)* to keep out *(aus* of); [2] *vr* to keep out of it; **sich aus etw ~halten** to keep out of sth; **halt du dich mal ~!** you keep *or* stay out of it *or* this; **~hängen** *sep* [1] *vt* to hang out *(aus* of); **den Intellektuellen ~hängen** *(inf)* to show off about being an intellectual *(inf)*; [2] *vi irreg* to hang out *(aus* of); **~hauen** *vt sep irreg* **(a)** *Bäume* to cut *or* chop down, to remove; *(aus Stein) Stufe, Figur, Relief* to carve, to cut *(aus* out of); **(b)** *(inf: erlangen) bessere Löhne, Bedingungen, Vorteile* to get; **~heben** *sep irreg* [1] *vt* to lift out *(aus* of); *(fig: betonen)* to bring out; [2] *vr* to stand out; **er hebt sich durch seine Begabung ~** he stands out on account of his talent; **~helfen** *vi sep irreg* **jdm ~helfen** *(lit, fig)* to help sb out *(aus* of); **jdm aus dem Zug ~helfen** to help sb off the train; **~holen** *vt sep* **(a)** *(lit) (aus* of) to get out; *(~bringen)* to bring *or* fetch out; **(b)** *(fig) Antwort, Geheimnis* to get out *(aus* of), to extract *(form) (aus* from); *Vorteil* to gain *(aus* from); *Zeit* to make up; *Ergebnis* to get, to achieve; *Sieg* to win, to gain; **er hat bei diesem Geschäft ganz schön viel (Geld) ~geholt** he has made *or* got a lot of money out of this deal; **~hören** *vt sep (wahrnehmen)* to hear; *(fühlen)* to detect, to sense *(aus* in); **~kehren** *vt sep (lit)* to sweep out *(aus* of); *(fig: betonen) Bildung, Überlegenheit* to parade; **Strenge ~kehren** to show one's sterner *or* stricter side; **den reichen Mann/Vorgesetzten ~kehren** to parade the fact that one is rich/the boss; **~klingen** *vi sep irreg* to ring out *(aus* from); *(zum Ausdruck kommen)* to ring through *(aus etw* sth).

herauskommen *vi sep irreg aux sein* **(a)** to come out *(aus* of) ♦ **ich bin schon seit Tagen aus den Kleidern/dem Haus nicht herausgekommen** I haven't had these clothes off/I haven't been out of the house in days; **er ist nie aus seinem Land/Dorf herausgekommen** he has never been out of *or* has never left his country/village; **sie kommt zu wenig heraus** *(inf)* she doesn't go *or* get out enough; **aus sich ~** to come out of one's shell; **er kam aus dem Staunen/der Verwunderung nicht heraus** he couldn't get over his astonishment/amazement; **er kam aus dem Lachen nicht heraus** he couldn't stop laughing; **wie kommen wir bloß hier heraus?** how do *or* shall we get out of here?
(b) *(inf: aus bestimmter Lage)* to get out *(aus* of) ♦ **aus seinen Schwierigkeiten/Sorgen ~** to get over one's difficulties/worries; **aus den Schulden ~** to get out of debt; **mit einem Gewinn ~** to get *or* win a prize.
(c) *(auf den Markt kommen)* to come out; *(neues Modell auch)* to be launched ♦ **mit einem neuen Modell ~** to bring out a new model, to come out with a new model.
(d) *(bekanntgegeben werden)* to come out; *(Börsenkurse auch)* to be published; *(Gesetz)* to come into force; *(bekanntwerden: Schwindel, Betrug etc auch)* to come to light ♦ **es wird bald ~, daß du das Auto gestohlen hast** they'll soon find out *or* it will soon come out that you stole the car.
(e) *(sichtbar werden)* to come out; *(Fleck)* to appear; *(zur Geltung kommen, hörbar werden)* to come over ♦ **ganz groß ~** *(inf)* to make a big splash *(inf)*, to have a big impact.
(f) *(geäußert werden)* to come out ♦ **mit etw ~** to come out with sth; **mit der Sprache ~** to come out with it *(inf)*.
(g) *(Resultat haben)* **bei etw ~** to come of sth, to emerge from sth; **und was soll dabei ~?** and what is that supposed to achieve?, and where is that supposed to get us?; **bei dieser Rechenaufgabe kommt 10 heraus** this sum comes to 10, the answer to this sum is 10; **es kommt nichts dabei heraus, da kommt nichts bei heraus** *(N Ger)* it doesn't lead anywhere *or* get us anywhere *or* achieve anything; **dabei wird nichts Gutes ~** no good will come of it; **es kommt auf eins** *or* **auf dasselbe** *or* **aufs gleiche heraus** it comes (down) to *or* boils down to the same thing.
(h) *(Sw: ausgehen)* to turn out.
(i) *(inf: aus der Übung kommen)* to get out of practice.
(j) *(Cards)* to lead ♦ **wer kommt heraus?** whose lead is it?, who leads?

heraus-: ~kriegen *vt sep (inf) siehe* **~bekommen, rauskriegen**; **~kristallisieren*** *sep* [1] *vt (Chem)* to crystallize *(aus* out of); *(fig) Fakten, Essenz, Punkte* to extract *(aus* from); [2] *vr (Chem)* to crystallize (out); *(fig)* to crystallize, to take shape; **~lassen** *vt sep irreg* to let out *(aus* of); **~laufen** *sep irreg* [1] *vi aux sein* to run out *(aus* of); [2] *vt (Sport) Vorsprung, Zeit, Sekunden* to gain; *Sieg, zweiten Platz auch* to win; **~lesen** *vt sep irreg (erkennen)* to gather *(aus* from); **aus seinem Brief/seiner Miene las ich Kummer ~** from his letter/expression I could tell *or* I gathered that he was worried; **was die Kritiker aus seinem Roman alles ~lesen wollen** the things the critics try to read into his novel; **~locken** *vt sep (aus* of) to entice out; *Gegner, Tier auch* to lure out; **etw aus jdm ~locken** *(ablisten)* to get *or* worm *(inf)* sth out of sb; **jdn aus seiner Reserve ~locken** to draw sb out of his shell; **~lügen** *vr sep irreg* to lie one's way out of it; **sich aus etw ~lügen** to lie one's way out of sth; **~machen** *sep (inf)* [1] *vt (aus* of) to take out; *Fleck* to get out; [2] *vr (sich gut entwickeln)* to come on (well); *(finanziell)* to do well; *(nach Krankheit)* to pick up; **sie hat sich prächtig ~gemacht** she has really blossomed *or* bloomed; **~müssen** *vi sep irreg (inf)* **(a)** *(entfernt werden müssen)* to have to come out; **(b)** *(aufstehen müssen)* to have to get up; **(c)** *(gesagt werden müssen)* to have to come out; **~nehmbar** *adj* removable; **~nehmen** *vt sep irreg* **(a)** to take out *(aus* of); *(inf) Zahn auch* to pull out; *Kind (aus der Schule etc)* to take away, to remove *(aus* from); **sich** *(dat)* **die Mandeln ~nehmen lassen** to have one's tonsils out; **den Gang ~nehmen** *(Aut)* to put the car into neutral; **(b)** *(inf: sich erlauben)* **es sich** *(dat)* **~nehmen, etw zu tun** to have the nerve to do sth *(inf)*; **sich** *(dat)* **Freiheiten ~nehmen** to take liberties; **Sie nehmen sich zuviel ~** you're going too far; **~pauken** *vt sep (inf)* **jdn (aus etw) ~pauken** to get sb off the hook *(inf)*, to bail sb out (of sth) *(inf)*; **~picken** *vt sep (aus* of) *(Vögel)* to peck out; *(fig) das Beste* to pick out; **~platzen** *vi sep aux sein (inf) (spontan sagen)* to blurt it out; *(lachen)* to burst out laughing; **mit etw ~platzen** to blurt sth out; **~pressen** *vt sep (aus* of) to squeeze out; *Saft etc auch* to press out; *Geld, Geständnis auch* to wring out; **~putzen** *vt sep jdn* to dress up; *(schmücken) Stadt, Weihnachtsbaum, Wohnung etc* to deck out; **sich prächtig ~putzen** to get dressed up, to do oneself up *(inf)*; *(Stadt)* to be decked out magnificently; **~ragen** *vi sep siehe* **hervorragen**; **~reden** *vr sep* to talk one's way out of it *(inf)*; **~reißen** *vt sep irreg* **(a)** *(lit) (aus* of) to tear *or* rip out; *Zahn, Baum* to pull out; **(b) jdn aus etw ~reißen** *(aus Umgebung)* to tear sb away from sth; *(aus Arbeit, Spiel, Unterhaltung)* to drag sb away from sth; *(aus Schlaf, Träumerei)* to startle sb out of sth; *(aus Lethargie, Sorgen)* to shake sb out of sth; **jdn aus seinem Kummer ~reißen** to take sb out of himself; **(c)** *(inf: aus Schwierigkeiten)* **jdn ~reißen** to get sb out of it *(inf)*; **(d)** *(inf: wiedergutmachen)* to save; **~rücken** *sep* [1] *vt* to push out *(aus* of); *(inf: hergeben) Geld* to cough up *(inf)*; *Beute, Gegenstand* to hand over; [2] *vi aux sein* **(a)** *(lit)* to move out; **(b)** *(inf: hergeben)* **mit etw ~rücken** *(mit Geld)* to cough sth up *(inf)*; *(mit Beute)* to hand sth over; **(c)** *(inf: aussprechen)* **mit etw ~rücken** to come out with sth; **rück schon mit deinem Problem ~!** come on (now), out with it, out with it now, what's the problem?; **mit der Sprache ~rücken** to come out with it; **~rufen** *sep irreg* [1] *vt* to call *or* shout out *(aus* of); **das Publikum rief den Schauspieler noch dreimal ~** the audience called the actor back another three times; [2] *vi* to call *or* shout out *(aus* of); **~rutschen** *vi sep aux sein (lit)* to slip out *(aus* of); *(fig inf: Bemerkung)* to slip out; **das ist mir nur so ~gerutscht** it just slipped out somehow, I just let it slip (out) somehow; **~saugen** *vt sep* to suck out (*aus* of); **~schälen** *sep* [1] *vt das Eßbare etc* (*aus* of) to get out, to dig out (*inf*); (*ausschneiden*) *schlechte Stelle auch* to scrape out; (*fig: absondern*) *Fakten, Elemente* to single out; **sich aus seinen Sachen ~schälen** (*inf*) to peel off one's clothes; [2] *vr* (*fig: deutlich werden*) to become evident *or* apparent; **~schauen** *vi sep* (*dial*) **(a)** (*Mensch*) to look out (*aus, zu* of); **(b)** (*zu sehen sein*) to show; **(c)** (*inf*) *siehe* **~springen (c)**; **~schießen** *sep irreg* [1] *vi* **(a)** (*lit*) **aus einem Gebäude ~schießen** to shoot from a building; **(b)** *aux sein* (*auch* **~geschossen kommen**) (*aus* of) to shoot out; [2] *vt* to shoot out; **~schinden** *vt sep irreg* (*inf*) *siehe* **~schlagen 1(b)**; **~schlagen** *sep irreg* [1] *vt* **(a)** (*lit*) to knock out (*aus* of); **aus einem Stein Funken ~schlagen** to strike sparks from *or* off a stone; **(b)** (*inf: erreichen*) *Geld* to make; *Erlaubnis, Verzögerung, Gewinn, Vorteil* to get; *Zeit* to gain; **seine Kosten ~schlagen** to cover one's costs; [2] *vi aux sein* (*Flammen*) to leap *or* shoot out; **die Flammen schlugen zum Dach ~** the flames were leaping through the roof; **~schleudern** *vt sep* (*werfen*) to hurl out (*aus* of); *Piloten* to eject; (*fig*) *Fragen, Vorwürfe, wütende Worte* to burst out with; **~schlüpfen** *vi sep aux sein* (*lit, fig*) to slip out (*aus* of); **~schmecken** *sep* [1] *vt* to taste; [2] *vi* to be prominent (over the other flavours); **~schmeißen** *vt sep irreg* (*inf: lit, fig*) to throw *or* chuck (*inf*) *or* sling (*inf*) out (*aus* of); **~schneiden** *vt sep irreg* to cut out (*aus* of); **~schreiben** *vt sep irreg Stellen, Zitat etc* to copy out (*aus* of); **~schreien** *vt sep irreg Haß, Gefühle* to shout out.

⚠**heraussein** *vi sep irreg aux sein* (*Zusammenschreibung nur bei infin und ptp*) (*inf*)
(a) (*entfernt sein*) to be out; (*Blinddarm etc auch*) to have been taken out.
(b) (*hervorgekommen sein: Sterne, Blumen etc*) to be out.
(c) (*herausgekommen sein*) (*Buch, Programm etc*) to be out; (*Gesetz*) to be in force.
(d) (*bekannt sein*) to be known; (*entschieden sein*) to have been *or* to be settled *or* decided.
(e) (*hinter sich haben*) (*aus* of) to be out, to have got out ♦ **aus der Schule ~** to have left school; **aus dem Gröbsten** *or* **Ärgsten** *or* **Schlimmsten ~** to have got past the worst (part); (*bei Krise, Krankheit*) to be over the worst; **wenn ich nur erst aus dieser Stadt heraus wäre** if only I were out of this town; *siehe* **fein**.
(f) (*gesagt worden sein*) (*Wahrheit*) to be out; (*Worte*) to have come out.

heraußen *adv* (*S Ger, Aus*) out here.

heraus-: ~springen *vi sep irreg aux sein* (*aus* of) **(a)** (*lit*) to jump *or* leap out; **(b)** (*sich lösen*) to come out; **aus dem Gleis ~springen** to jump the rails; **(c)** (*inf*) **dabei springt ein fetter Gewinn ~** there is a handsome profit in it; **dabei springt nichts ~** there's nothing to be got out of it; **was springt für mich dabei ~?** what's in it for me?; **~sprudeln** *sep* [1] *vi aux sein* to bubble out (*aus* of); [2] *vt Worte, Sätze* to come gushing out with; **~stehen** *vi sep irreg* (*S Ger: aux sein*) to stand *or* stick out, to protrude; **~stellen** *sep* [1] *vt* **(a)** (*lit*) to put outside; (*Sport*) to send off; **(b)** (*fig: hervorheben*) to emphasize, to underline; *jdn* to give prominence to; [2] *vr* (*Unschuld, Wahrheit*) to come to light; **sich als falsch/wahr/richtig/begründet ~stellen** to show itself to be *or* to prove (to be) wrong/true/correct/well-founded; **es stellte sich ~, daß ...** it turned out *or* emerged that ...; **es wird sich ~stellen, wer recht hat/was getan werden muß** we shall see who is right/what must be done; **das muß sich erst ~stellen** that remains to be seen; **~strecken** *vt sep* to stick out (*zu, aus* of); **~streichen** *vt sep irreg* **(a)** *Fehler etc* to cross out, to delete (*aus* in); **(b)** (*betonen*) *Verdienste etc* to stress, to lay great stress upon; **~strömen** *vi sep aux sein* (*aus* of) (*Flüssigkeit*) to stream *or* pour out; (*Gas*) to come out; (*Menschenmenge*) to pour out; **~stürzen** *vi sep aux sein* **(a)** (*auch* **~gestürzt kommen**) (*eilen*) to rush out (*aus* of); **(b)** (*fallen*) to fall out; **zum Fenster ~stürzen** to fall out of the window; **~suchen** *vt sep* to pick out; **~treten** *vi sep irreg aux sein* to step *or* come out (*aus* of), to emerge (*aus* from); (*Adern etc*) to stand out, to protrude; **~trommeln** *vt sep* (*inf*) to get out; **~wachsen** *vi sep irreg aux sein* to grow out (*aus* of); **~wagen** *vr sep* to dare to come out (*aus* of); to venture out (*aus* of) *or* forth (*liter*) (*aus* from); **~winden** *vr sep irreg* (*fig*) to wriggle out of it; **sich aus etw ~winden** to wriggle out of sth; **~wirtschaften** *vt sep* to make (*aus* out of); **~wollen** *vi sep* to want to get out (*aus* of); **nicht mit etw ~wollen** (*inf: sagen wollen*) not to want to come out with sth (*inf*); **er wollte nicht mit der Sprache ~** (*inf*) he didn't want to come out with it (*inf*); **~ziehen** *sep irreg* [1] *vt* to pull out (*aus* of); (*~schleppen*) to drag out (*aus* of); (*Chem, Med*) to extract (*aus* from); *Truppen auch* to withdraw (*aus* from); **die Essenz aus einem Buch ~ziehen** to extract the main substance from a book; **muß ich dir die Antworten einzeln ~ziehen?** (*inf*) do I have to drag answers out of you bit by bit?; [2] *vr* to pull oneself out (*aus* of).

herb *adj* **(a)** *Geruch* sharp; *Geschmack auch, Parfüm* tangy; *Wein* dry. **(b)** *Enttäuschung, Verlust* bitter; *Erwachen* rude; *Erkenntnis, Wahrheit* cruel. **(c)** (*streng*) *Züge, Gesicht* severe, harsh; *Art, Wesen, Charakter, Mensch* dour; *Schönheit* severe, austere. **(d)** (*unfreundlich*) *Worte, Kritik* harsh.

Herbarium *nt* herbarium, herbary.

herbei *adv* (*geh*) come (here) ♦ **(alle Mann) ~!** come here (everybody)!

herbei-: ~bringen *vt sep irreg jdn, Gegenstand* to bring over; *Indizien, Beweise* to provide; *Sachverständige* to bring in; **~eilen** *vi sep aux sein* to hurry *or* rush over; **~führen** *vt sep* **(a)** (*bewirken*) *Entscheidung, Konfrontation etc* to bring about; (*verursachen auch*) to cause; **den Tod** *etc* **~führen** (*Med*) to cause death *etc* (*form*); **(b)** (*an einen Ort*) to bring; *Schaulustige* to draw; **~holen** *vt sep* to bring; *Verstärkung* to bring in; *Arzt, Taxi, Polizisten* to fetch; **einen Arzt ~holen lassen** to send for a doctor; **~kommen** *vi sep irreg aux sein siehe* **herankommen**; **~lassen** *vr sep irreg* **sich zu etw ~lassen, sich ~lassen, etw zu tun** to condescend *or* deign to do sth; **~laufen** *vi sep irreg aux sein* to come running up; **~rufen** *vt sep irreg* to call over; *Verstärkung* to call in; *Arzt, Polizei, Taxi* to call; **~schaffen** *vt sep* to bring; *Geld* to get, to get hold of (*inf*); *Beweise* to produce; **~sehnen** *vt sep* to long for; **~strömen** *vi sep aux sein* to come flocking, to come in (their) crowds; **~winken** *vt sep siehe* **heranwinken**; **~ziehen** *sep irreg* [1] *vt siehe* **Haar**; [2] *vi aux sein siehe* **heranziehen 2**; **~zitieren*** *vt sep* (*inf*) to send for.

her-: ~bekommen* *vt sep irreg* (*inf*) to get; **~bemühen*** *sep* (*geh*) [1] *vt* **jdn ~bemühen** to trouble sb to come here; [2] *vr* to take the trouble to come here; **~beordern*** *vt sep* to summon, to send for.

Herberge *f* **-, -n (a)** *no pl* (*Unterkunft*) lodging, accommodation *both no indef art*; (*fig*) refuge. **(b)** (*old, Gasthaus*) inn; (*Jugend~*) (youth) hostel.

Herbergs-: ~mutter *f* (youth hostel) warden; **~vater** *m* (youth hostel) warden.

her-: ~bestellen* *vt sep* to ask to come; **~beten** *vt sep* (*pej*) to rattle off.

Herbheit *f, no pl siehe adj* **(a)** sharpness; tanginess; dryness. **(b)** bitterness; rudeness; cruelness. **(c)** severity, harshness; dourness; severity, austerity. **(d)** harshness.

herbitten *vt sep irreg* to ask to come.

Herbizid *nt* **-(e)s, -e** herbicide.

herbringen *vt sep irreg* to bring (here); **bring mir das Buch her** bring me the book (over); *siehe* **hergebracht**.

Herbst *m* **-(e)s, -e** autumn, fall (*US*) ♦ **im ~** in autumn, in the fall (*US*); **der ~ des Lebens** (*liter*) the autumn of (one's) life (*liter*); **auch der ~ hat noch schöne Tage** (*prov*) you're never too old.

Herbst- *in cpds* autumn, fall (*US*); **~anfang** *m* beginning of autumn; **~aster** *f* Michaelmas daisy.

herbsten [1] *vi impers*: **es herbstet** (*liter*) autumn is nigh (*liter*).
[2] *vt* (*dial*) *Wein* to harvest.

Herbstes- (*poet*) *in cpds siehe* **Herbst-**.

Herbst-: ~farben *pl* autumn *or* autumnal colours *pl*; **~ferien** *pl* autumn *or* fall (*US*) holiday(s); (*Sch*) half-term holiday(s) (*in the autumn term*); **h~lich** *adj* autumn *attr*; (*wie im Herbst auch*) autumnal; **das Wetter wird schon h~lich** autumn is in the air; **das Wetter ist schon h~lich** it's already autumn weather; **h~lich kühles Wetter** cool autumn weather; **sich ~lich kleiden** to dress for the autumn; **~monat** *m* autumn month; **der ~monat** (*old*) September; **~-Tagundnachtgleiche** *f* autumnal equinox; **~zeitlose** *f* **-n, -n** meadow saffron.

Herd *m* **-(e)s, -e (a)** (*Küchen~*) cooker, stove; (*Kohle~*) range; (*fig: Heim*) home ♦ **eigener ~ ist Goldes wert** (*Prov*) there's no place like home (*Prov*); **den ganzen Tag am ~ stehen** (*fig*) to slave over a hot stove all day.
(b) (*Med: Krankheits~*) focus; (*Geol: von Erdbeben*) epicentre; (*fig: von Rebellion etc*) seat.
(c) (*Tech*) hearth.

Herd|abdeckplatte *f* electric ring cover.

Herde *f* **-, -n** (*lit*) herd; (*von Schafen, fig geh: Gemeinde*) flock ♦ **mit der ~ laufen, der ~ folgen** (*pej*) to follow the herd.

Herden-: ~instinkt *m* (*lit, fig pej*) herd instinct; **~tier** *nt* gregarious animal; **~trieb** *m* (*lit, fig pej*) herd instinct; **h~weise** *adv* in herds; (*Schafe*) in flocks; (*fig auch*) in crowds.

Herdplatte *f* (*von Kohleherd*) (top) plate; (*von Elektroherd*) hotplate.

herein *adv* in ♦ **~!** come in!, come! (*form*); **nur ~!** do come in!; **immer ~!** come along in!; **hier ~!** in here!; **von (dr)außen ~** from outside; **auf dem Wege von draußen ~** on the way in.

herein- *pref siehe auch* **rein-** in; **~bekommen** *vt sep irreg* (*inf*) *Waren* to get in; *Radiosender* to get; *Unkosten etc* to recover; **~bemühen*** *sep* (*geh*) [1] *vt* to trouble to come in; [2] *vr* to take the trouble to come in; **~bitten** *vt sep irreg* to ask (to come) in; **~brechen** *vi sep irreg aux sein* **(a)** (*eindringen: Wasser, Flut, Wellen*) to gush in; **über jdn/etw ~brechen** (*lit, fig*) to descend upon sb/sth; **(b)** (*Gewitter*) to break; (*Krieg, Pest*) to break out; **das Unglück brach über ihn ~** misfortune overtook him; **(c)** (*liter: anbrechen*) (*Nacht, Abend*) to fall, to close in; (*Winter*) to set in; **(d)** (*lit: nach innen stürzen*) to fall in; **~bringen** *vt sep irreg* **(a)** to bring in; **(b)** (*inf: wettmachen*) *Geldverlust* to make good; *Zeit-, Produktionsverluste* to make up for; *Unkosten* to get back; **~drängen** *vir sep* to push one's way in; **~dringen** *vi sep irreg aux sein* (*Licht, Wasser*) to come in (*in +acc* -to); **ein Geräusch/Geruch drang** *or* **es drang ein Geräusch/Geruch ins Zimmer ~** a sound/smell reached the room; **~dürfen** *vi sep irreg* (*inf*) to be allowed in; **darf ich ~?** may *or* can I come in?; **~fahren** *vti sep irreg* (*vi: aux sein*) to drive in; (*mit Fahrrad*) to ride in; **~fallen** *vi sep irreg aux sein* **(a)** to fall in (*in +acc* -to); **(b)** (*inf*) to fall for it (*inf*); (*betrogen werden*) to be had (*inf*); **auf jdn/etw ~fallen** to be taken in by sb/sth, to be taken for a ride (by sb) (*inf*)/to fall for sth; **mit jdm/etw ~fallen** to have a bad deal with sb/sth; **~führen** *vt sep* to show in; **~holen** *vt sep* to bring in (*in +acc* -to); **~kommen** *vi sep irreg aux sein* to come in (*in +acc* -to); **wie ist er ~gekommen?** how did he get in?; **ins Haus ~kommen** to come in *or* inside; **~kriegen** *vt sep* (*inf*) *siehe* **~bekommen, reinkriegen**; **~lassen** *vt sep irreg* to let in (*in +acc* -to); **~legen** *vt sep* **(a)** to lay (down); **(b)** (*inf*) **jdn ~legen** (*betrügen*) to take sb for a ride (*inf*); (*anführen*) to take sb in; **~nehmen** *vt sep irreg* to bring in (*in +acc* -to); (*in Liste, Kollektion etc aufnehmen*) to put in, to include; (*Comm*) *Aufträge* to accept; **~nötigen** *vt sep* to urge to come in; **sie hat mich förmlich ~genötigt** she insisted that I come in; **~platzen** *vi sep aux sein* (*inf*) to burst *or* come bursting in (*in +acc* -to); **bei jdm ~platzen** to burst in on sb; **~regnen** *vi impers sep* **es regnet ~** the rain is coming in; **~reiten** *sep irreg* [1] *vti* (*vi: aux sein*) to ride in (*in +acc* -to); [2] *vr* (*inf*) to land oneself in it *or* in the soup (*inf*); **~rufen** *vt sep irreg* to call in; **~schauen** *vi sep* (*dial*) to look in (*in +acc* -to); **(bei jdm) ~schauen** (*inf*) to look in on sb (*inf*), to look sb up (*inf*); **~schleichen** *vir sep irreg* (*vi: aux sein*) (*in +acc* to) to creep *or* slip in; (*heimlich*) to sneak in; **~schneien** *sep* [1] *vi impers* **es schneit ~** the snow's coming in; [2] *vi aux sein* (*inf*) to drop in (*inf*); **~sehen** *vi sep irreg* to see/look in (*in +acc* -to); **~spazieren*** *vi sep aux sein* to breeze in (*in +acc* -to); **~spaziert!** come right in!; **~stecken** *vt sep* (*in +acc* -to) to put in; *Kopf, Hand auch* to stick in; **~strömen** *vi sep aux sein* (*in +acc* -to) to stream *or* pour in; **~stürmen** *vi sep aux sein* to storm *or* come storming in (*in +acc* -to); **~stürzen** *vi sep aux sein* to rush in (*in +acc* -to); **~wagen** *vr sep* (*in +acc* -to) to dare to come in, to venture in; **~wollen** *vi sep* (*inf*) to want to come in.

Her-: h~fahren *sep irreg* [1] *vi aux sein* to come *or* get here; **hinter/vor jdm/etw h~fahren** to drive *or* (*mit Rad*) ride (along) behind/in front of *or* ahead of sb/sth; **der Detektiv fuhr hinter dem Auto h~** the detective followed *or* trailed the car; [2] *vt* to drive *or* bring here; **~fahrt** *f* journey here; **auf der ~fahrt** on the journey *or* way here; **h~fallen** *vi sep irreg aux sein* **über jdn h~fallen** to attack sb, to fall upon sb; (*mit Fragen*) to attack sb, to pitch into sb; (*kritisieren*) to pull sb to pieces; **über etw** (*acc*) **h~fallen** to descend upon sth; *über Geschenke, Eßbares etc* to pounce upon sth; **h~finden** *vi sep irreg* to find one's way here.

herg. *abbr of* **hergestellt** manufactured, mfd.

Hergang *m* **-(e)s,** *no pl* (*von Schlacht*) course ◆ **schildern Sie mir genau den ~ dieses Vorfalls** tell me exactly what happened; **der ~ des Unfalls** the way the accident happened, the details of the accident.

her-: ~geben *sep irreg* [1] *vt* (*weggeben*) to give away; (*überreichen, aushändigen*) to hand over; (*zurückgeben*) to give back; **gib das ~!** give me that, let me have that; **viel/einiges/wenig ~geben** (*inf: erbringen*) to be a lot of use/of some use/not to be much use; **das Buch gibt nicht viel ~** the book doesn't tell me/you (very) much; **das Thema gibt viel/nichts ~** there's a lot/nothing to this topic; **ein Essen, das was ~gibt** a fine spread; **was die Beine ~gaben** as fast as one's legs would carry one; **was die Lunge/Stimme ~gab** at the top of one's voice; **seinen Namen für etw ~geben** to lend one's name to sth; [2] *vr* **sich zu** *or* **für etw ~geben** to be (a) party to sth; **dazu gebe ich mich nicht ~** I won't have anything to do with it; **eine Schauspielerin, die sich für solche Filme ~gibt** an actress who allows herself to be involved in such films; **~gebracht** [1] *ptp of* **~bringen**; [2] *adj* (*traditionell*) **in ~gebrachter Weise** as is/was traditional; **~gehen** *sep irreg aux sein* [1] *vi* **(a) hinter/vor/neben jdm ~gehen** to walk (along) behind/in front of *or* ahead of/beside sb; **(b)** (*S Ger, Aus*) *siehe* **~kommen**; **(c) ~gehen und etw tun** (*einfach tun*) just *or* simply to (go and) do sth; [2] *vi impers* (*inf*) (*zugehen*) **so geht es ~** that's the way it goes *or* is; **es ging heiß ~** things got heated (*inf*), (the) sparks flew; **hier geht es hoch ~** there's plenty going on here; **~gehören*** *vi sep* to belong here; (*fig auch*) to be relevant; **~gelaufen** [1] *ptp of* **~laufen**; [2] *adj attr* (*pej*) *siehe* **dahergelaufen**; **~haben** *vt sep irreg* (*inf*) **wo hat er das ~?** where did he get that from?; **~halten** *sep irreg* [1] *vt* to hold out; [2] *vi* to suffer (for it), to pay for it; **für etw ~halten** to pay for sth; **er muß als Sündenbock ~halten** he is the scapegoat; **als Entschuldigung für etw ~halten** to serve *or* be used as an excuse for sth; **~holen** *vt sep* (*inf*) to fetch; **~holen lassen** to send for; **weit ~geholt sein** (*fig*) to be far-fetched; **~hören** *vi sep* (*inf*) to listen; **alle** *or* **alles mal ~hören!** listen (to me) *or* listen here (*inf*) *or* pay attention everybody, everybody listen (to me).

Hering *m* **-s, -e (a)** herring ◆ **ein gedörrter ~** a kipper; **wie die ~e zusammengedrängt** packed in like sardines (in a tin); **dünn wie ein ~** as thin as a rake.
(b) (*Zeltpflock*) (tent) peg.
(c) (*fig inf: schwächlicher Mensch*) weakling.

Heringstopf *m* pickled herring with sour cream.

herinnen *adv* (*S Ger, Aus*) *siehe* **drinnen, innen.**

her-: ~jagen *sep* [1] *vt* (*auf jdn zu*) to drive *or* chase over *or* across; **jdn vor sich** (*dat*) **~jagen** to chase sb along in front of one; [2] *vi aux sein* **hinter jdm ~jagen** to chase after sb; **hinter etw** (*dat*) **~jagen** to be after sth; **~kommen** *vi sep irreg aux sein* to come here; (*sich nähern*) to come, to approach; (*~stammen*) to come from; **komm ~!** come here!; **von jdm/etw ~kommen** (*stammen*) to come from sb/sth; **ich weiß nicht, wo das ~kommt** (*was der Grund ist*) I don't know why it is *or* what the reason is; **~kömmlich** *adj* conventional; **nach ~kömmlichem Brauch** according to convention; **~kriegen** *vt sep* (*inf*) to get; **ich kriege ihn einfach nicht ~** I simply can't get him to come (here).

Herkules *m* **-, -se** (*Myth, fig*) Hercules.

Herkules|arbeit *f* (*fig*) Herculean task.

herkulisch *adj* Herculean.

Herkunft *f* **-,** *no pl* origin; (*soziale*) background, origins *pl* ◆ **er ist britischer** (*gen*) **~, er ist seiner ~ nach Brite** he is of British extraction *or* descent *or* origin; **er ist aristokratischer** (*gen*) **~** he comes from an aristocratic family, he is of aristocratic descent.

Herkunfts-: ~bezeichnung *f* (*Comm*) designation of origin; **~land** *nt* (*Comm*) country of origin; **~ort** *m* place of origin.

her-: ~laufen *vi sep irreg aux sein* to come running; **lauf doch mal ~ zu mir!** come over here to me; **hinter** (*lit, fig*)/**vor/neben jdm ~laufen** to run after/ahead of/beside sb; **~leiern** *vt sep* (*inf*) to spout (*inf*); **~leihen** *vt sep irreg* (*Aus, S Ger*) to lend (out); **~leiten** *sep* [1] *vt* **(a)** (*ableiten, folgern*) to derive (*aus* from); **(b)** (*an bestimmten Ort leiten*) to bring; [2] *vr* **sich von etw ~leiten** to come from sth, to be derived from sth; **~locken** *vt sep* to entice, to lure; **~machen** *sep* (*inf*) [1] *vr* **sich über etw** (*acc*) **~machen** (*in Angriff nehmen*) *Arbeit, Buch, Essen* to get stuck into sth (*inf*); (*Besitz ergreifen*) *Eigentum, Gegenstände* to pounce (up)on sth; **sich über jdn ~machen** to lay into sb (*inf*); [2] *vt* **viel ~machen** to look impressive; **wenig ~machen** not to look very impressive; **nichts ~machen** not to be up to much (*inf*); **von jdm/etw viel ~machen** to crack sb/sth up to be quite fantastic (*inf*), to make a big thing of sb/sth (*inf*); **von jdm/etw wenig/nichts ~machen** not to make a big thing of sb/sth (*inf*); **viel von sich ~machen** to be full of oneself; **er macht wenig** *or* **nicht viel von sich ~** he's pretty modest.

Hermaphrodit *m* **-en, -en** hermaphrodite.

Hermelin[1] *nt* **-s, -e** (*Zool*) ermine.

Hermelin[2] *m* **-s, -e** (*Pelz*) ermine.

Hermeneutik *f, no pl* hermeneutics *sing.*

hermeneutisch *adj* hermeneutic(al).

Hermes-Bürgschaft *f* government export credit guarantee.

hermetisch *adj* hermetic ◆ **die Häftlinge sind ~ von der Außenwelt abgeschlossen** the prisoners are completely shut off from the outside world; **~ abgeriegelt** completely sealed off.

hermüssen *vi sep irreg* (*inf*) **(a) das muß her** I/we have to have it. **(b)** (*kommen müssen*) to have to come (here) ◆ **hinter jdm ~** to have to go after sb.

hernach *adv* (*dated, dial*) afterwards.

hernehmen *vt sep irreg* **(a)** (*beschaffen*) to get, to find ◆ **wo soll ich das ~?** where am I supposed to get that from?
(b) (*dial inf*) **jdn ~** (*stark fordern, belasten*) to make sb sweat (*inf*); (*mitnehmen: Krankheit, Schock, Nachricht, Anstrengung*) to take it out of sb (*inf*).
(c) (sich *dat***) jdn ~** (*dial: tadeln, verprügeln*) to give it to sb (*inf*), to let sb have it (*inf*).
(d) (*dial: nehmen*) to take.

hernieder *adv* (*liter*) down.

heroben *adv* (*Aus, S Ger*) up here.

Heroe [he'ro:ə] *m* **-n, -n** (*geh*) *siehe* **Heros.**

Heroenkult(us) [he'ro:ən-] *m* (*geh*) hero-worship.

Heroin [hero'i:n] *nt* **-s,** *no pl* heroin.

Heroine [hero'i:nə] *f* (*dated Theat*) heroine.

heroisch [he'ro:ɪʃ] *adj* (*geh*) heroic.

heroisieren* [heroi'zi:rən] *vt jdn* to make a hero of; *Tat* to glorify.

Heroismus [hero'ɪsmʊs] *m, no pl* (*geh*) heroism.

Herold *m* **-(e)s, -e** (*Hist: Bote*) herald; (*fig: Vorbote auch*) harbinger.

Heros *m* **-, Heroen** hero.

Herpes *m* **-,** *no pl* (*Med*) herpes.

Herpes-Virus *nt* herpes virus.

herplappern *vt sep* (*inf*) to reel off ◆ **was sie immer so herplappert** the things she's always talking about.

Herr *m* **-(e)n, -en (a)** (*Gebieter*) lord, master; (*Herrscher*) lord, ruler (*über +acc* of); (*von Hund*) master ◆ **mein ~ und Gebieter** my lord and master; **der junge ~** (*form*) the young master; **die ~en der Schöpfung** (*hum: Männer*) the gentlemen; **sein eigener ~ sein** to be one's own master *or* boss; **~ im eigenen Haus sein** to be master in one's own house; **~ einer Sache** (*gen*) **sein/werden** (*in der Hand haben*) to have/get sth under control; **~ der Lage** *or* **Situation sein/bleiben** to be/remain master of the situation, to have/keep the situation under control; **nicht mehr ~ seiner Sinne sein** not to be in control of oneself any more; **~ über Leben und Tod sein** to have the power of life and death (*gen* over); **über jdn/etw ~ werden** to master sb/sth; **man kann nicht** *or* **niemand kann zwei ~en dienen** (*prov*) no man can serve two masters (*prov*); **wie der ~, so's Gescherr!** (*prov*) like master, like man! (*prov*); *siehe* **Land.**
(b) (*Gott, Christus*) Lord ◆ **Gott, der ~** the Lord God; **der ~ Jesus** the Lord Jesus; **der ~ der Heerscharen** the Lord of Hosts; **~, du meine Güte!** good(ness) gracious (me)!; **~ des Himmels!** good Lord!; **er ist ein großer Schwindler/Esser** *etc* **vor dem ~n** (*hum inf*) what a great fibber/eater *etc* he is.
(c) (*feiner ~, Mann*) gentleman ◆ **ein geistlicher/adliger ~** *or* **~ von Adel** a clergyman/nobleman; **„~en"** (*Toilette*) "gentlemen", "gents", "men"; **den (großen) ~n spielen** *or* **markieren** (*inf*) to give oneself airs; *siehe* **alt.**
(d) (*vor Eigennamen*) Mr; (*vor Titeln*) *usu not translated*; (*in Anrede ohne Namen*) sir ◆ **(mein) ~!** sir!; **bitte, der ~** (*beim Servieren*) there you are, sir; **der ~ wünscht?** what can I do for you, sir?; **Ihr ~ Vater** (*form*) your father; **~ Nachbar** (*form*) excuse me, sir; **~ Dr./Doktor/Professor Schmidt** Dr/Doctor/Professor Schmidt; **~ Doktor/Professor** doctor/professor; **~ Präsident/Vorsitzender** Mr President/Chairman; **der ~ Präsident/Vorsitzende** the President/Chairman; **lieber** *or* **werter** (*dated*) *or* **sehr geehrter** *or* **sehr verehrter** (*form*) **~ A** (*in Brief*) Dear Mr A; **an den ~n Abgeordneten C. Schmidt** C. Schmidt, MP; **werte** *or* **sehr geehrte ~en** (*in Brief*) Dear Sirs.
(e) (*allgemein gesehen: Tanzpartner, Begleiter*) gentleman; (*auf eine bestimmte Dame bezogen*) partner; (*bei Cocktailparty, Theaterbesuch etc*) (gentleman) companion.
(f) (*Sport*) **Vierhundert-Meter-Staffel der ~en** men's hundred metres relay.

Herrchen *nt* (*inf: von Hund*) master.

Her-: h~reichen *vt sep* to hand , to pass; **~reise** *f* journey here; **auf der ~reise von X** on the journey from X.

Herren- *in cpds* men's; (*auf Kleidung bezüglich auch*) gents' (*dated*); (*auf einzelnes Exemplar bezüglich*) man's; gent's; **~abend** *m* stag night; **seinen ~abend haben** to have a night out with the boys (*inf*); **~artikel** *pl* gentlemen's requisites *pl* (*dated*); **~ausstatter** *m* **-s, -** gents' *or* men's outfitter; **~begleitung** *f* **~begleitung erwünscht** please bring a gentleman *or* (*bei Ball*) partner; **in ~begleitung** in the company of a gentleman; **~bekanntschaft** *f* gentleman acquaintance; **eine ~bekanntschaft machen** to make the acquaintance of a gentleman; **~bekleidung** *f* menswear; **~besuch** *m* (gentle)man visitor/visitors; **~doppel** *nt* (*Tennis etc*) men's doubles *sing*; **~einzel** *nt* (*Tennis etc*) men's singles *sing*; **~(fahr)rad** *nt* man's bicycle *or* bike (*inf*); **~friseur** *m* men's hairdresser, barber; **~gesellschaft** *f* **(a)**

(*gesellige Runde*) stag party; **(b)** *no pl* (*Begleitung von Herrn*) **in ~gesellschaft sein** to be in the company of gentlemen/a gentleman; **~haus** *nt* **(a)** manor house; **(b)** (*Hist*) upper chamber; **~jahre** *pl siehe* **Lehrjahr**; **~konfektion** *f* men's ready-to-wear clothes *pl*; (*Abteilung*) menswear department; **~leben** *nt* life of luxury and ease; **h~los** *adj* abandoned; *Hund etc* stray; **~mangel** *m* shortage of men; **~mensch** *m* member of the master race; **~mode** *f* men's fashion; **~partie** *f* (*Ausflug*) men-only outing; (*Gesellschaft*) stag party; **~rasse** *f* master race; **~reiten** *nt* amateur racing; **~reiter** *m* **(a)** (*Sport*) amateur jockey; **(b)** (*iro*) stuffed shirt (*inf*); **~salon** *m* barber's; **~sattel** *m* (man's) saddle; **im ~sattel reiten** to ride astride; **~sauna** *m* (*euph*) massage parlour; **~schneider** *m* gentlemen's tailor; **~schnitt** *m* (*Frisur*) haircut like a man's; **~sitz** *m* **(a)** (*Gutshof*) manor house; **(b) im ~sitz reiten** to ride astride; **~tiere** *pl siehe* **Primat**[2]; **~toilette** *f* men's toilet *or* restroom (*US*), gents *sing*; **~volk** *nt* master race; **~welt** *f* (*dated hum*) gentlemen *pl*; **~winker** *m* (*hum*) kiss-curl; **~witz** *m* dirty joke; **~zimmer** *nt* study; (*Rauchzimmer*) smoking room.

Herrgott *m* (*dated inf*) (*Anrede*) God, Lord ◆ **der ~** God, the Lord (God); (*S Ger, Aus: Figur*) figure of the Lord; **~ (Sakrament)!** (*inf*) good God *or* Lord!; **~ noch mal!** (*inf*) damn it all! (*inf*).

Herrgotts-: ~früh(e) *f*: **in aller ~früh(e)** (*inf*) at the crack of dawn; **~schnitzer** *m* (*S Ger, Aus*) carver of crucifixes; **~winkel** *m* (*S Ger, Aus*) *corner of a room with a crucifix*.

herrichten *sep* [1] *vt* **(a)** (*vorbereiten*) to get ready (*dat, für* for); *Bett* to make; *Tisch* to set. **(b)** (*instand setzen, ausbessern*) to do up (*inf*).
[2] *vr* (*dial*) to get dressed up.

Herrin *f* (*Hist: Herrscherin*) female ruler; (*von Hund, old: Haus~*) mistress ◆ **die ~** (*Anrede*) my lady.

herrisch *adj* overbearing, imperious; *Ton auch* peremptory.

herrje(h), herrjemine *interj* goodness gracious.

herrlich *adj* marvellous; *Anblick, Tag, Wetter auch* magnificent, glorious, lovely; *Kleid* gorgeous, lovely; *Essen, Witz, Geschichte auch* wonderful, lovely ◆ **das ist ja ~** (*iro*) that's great; **du bist so ~ doof/naiv** (*iro*) you are so wonderfully stupid/naïve; **wir haben uns ~ amüsiert** we had marvellous fun.

Herrlichkeit *f* **(a)** *no pl* (*Schönheit, Pracht*) glory, magnificence, splendour ◆ **die ~ Gottes** the glory of God; **Pracht und ~** pomp and circumstance; (*von Natur*) glory; **die ~ wird nicht lange dauern** (*iro inf*) this is too good to last; **ist das die ganze ~?** is that all there is to it?; **aus und vorbei mit der ~** here we go again. **(b)** *usu pl* (*prächtiger Gegenstand*) treasure. **(c)** (*obs: Anrede*) lordship.

Herrschaft *f* **(a)** (*Macht*) power; (*Staatsgewalt*) rule ◆ **zur ~ gelangen** *or* **kommen** to come to power; **sich der ~ bemächtigen** to seize power; **unter der ~** under the rule (*gen, von* of); **unter jds ~ (*acc*) fallen** to come under sb's rule; **während der ~** (*+gen*) in the reign of.
(b) (*Gewalt, Kontrolle*) control ◆ **er verlor die ~ über sich** he lost his self-control; **er verlor die ~ über sein Auto** he lost control of his car, his car went out of control.
(c) (*old: Dienst~*) master and mistress *pl* ◆ **die ~en** (*Damen und Herren*) the ladies and gentlemen; **hohe ~en** (*dated*) persons of high rank *or* standing; **würden die ~en bitte ...** would sir and madam please .../ladies and gentlemen, would you please .../ladies, would you please .../gentlemen, would you please ...; **was wünschen die ~en?** what can I get you?; (*von Butler*) you rang?; **(meine) ~en!** ladies and gentlemen.
(d) (*inf: Ausruf*) **~ (noch mal)** hang it (all) (*inf*).
(e) (*Hist: Landgut*) domain, estate, lands *pl*.

herrschaftlich *adj* of a person of high standing; (*vornehm*) grand ◆ **die ~e Kutsche** his lordship's coach.

Herrschafts-: ~anspruch *m* claim to power; (*von Thronfolger*) claim to the throne; **~bereich** *m* territory; **~form** *f* form *or* type of rule; **~gewalt** *f* authority, power; **h~los** *adj* without rule *or* government; **~losigkeit** *f* state of being without rule *or* government; **~system** *nt* system of rule.

herrschen [1] *vi* **(a)** (*Macht, Gewalt haben*) to rule; (*König*) to reign; (*fig*) (*Mensch*) to dominate; (*Geld*) to hold sway; (*Tod, Terror*) to rule, to hold sway.
(b) (*vor~*) (*Angst, Ungewißheit, Zweifel*) to prevail; (*Verkehr, Ruhe, Betriebsamkeit*) to be prevalent; (*Nebel, Regen, Kälte*) to be predominant; (*Krankheit, Not*) to be rampant, to rage; (*Meinung, Ansicht*) to predominate ◆ **überall herrschte Freude/Terror** there was joy/terror everywhere; **im Zimmer herrschte bedrückende Stille** it was oppressively quiet in the room; **hier herrscht Ordnung** things are orderly round here; **hier herrscht ein anderer Ton** the atmosphere is different here; **hier ~ ja Zustände!** things are in a pretty state round here!
(c) (*in herrischem Ton reden*) to snap, to bark.
[2] *vi impers* **es herrscht schlechtes Wetter** the weather is bad, we're having bad weather; **es herrschte Schweigen** silence reigned; **es herrscht Ungewißheit darüber, ob ...** there is uncertainty about whether ...

herrschend *adj Partei, Klasse* ruling; *König* reigning; *Bedingungen, Verhältnisse, Meinungen* prevailing; *Mode* current ◆ **die H~en** the rulers, those in power.

Herrscher(in *f*) *m* **-s, -** (*über +acc* of) ruler; (*König auch*) sovereign.

Herrscher-: ~blick *m* imperious look; **mit ~blick** with an imperious look; **~familie** *f* ruling family; **~geschlecht** *nt* ruling dynasty; **~haus** *nt* ruling house *or* dynasty; **~natur** *f* **(a)** (*Mensch*) domineering person; **(b)** (*Wesensart*) domineering character.

Herrschsucht *f* domineeringness.

herrschsüchtig *adj* domineering.

her-: ~rücken *sep* [1] *vt* to move nearer *or* closer; [2] *vi aux sein* to move *or* come nearer *or* closer; **~rufen** *vt sep irreg* to call (over); *Tier* to call; **~rühren** *vi sep* **von etw ~rühren** to be due to sth, to stem from sth; **~sagen** *vt sep* to recite; **~schaffen** *vt sep* (*inf*) *siehe* **herbeischaffen**; **~schauen** *vi sep* (*dial*) to look here *or* this way; **zu jdm ~schauen** to look in sb's direction; **da schau ~!** (*Aus inf*) well, I never! (*inf*); **~schenken** *vt sep* (*inf*) *siehe* **verschenken**; **~schicken** *vt sep* to send; **jdn hinter jdm ~schicken** to send sb after sb; **~schleichen** *vir sep irreg* (*vi: aux sein*) **(a)** to creep up; **(b) (sich) hinter jdm ~schleichen** to creep along behind sb; **~sehen** *vi sep irreg* **(a)** to look here *or* this way; **zu jdm ~sehen** to look in sb's direction; **(b) hinter jdm/etw ~sehen** to follow sb with one's eyes; ⚠**~sein** *vi sep irreg aux sein* (*Zusammenschreibung nur bei infin und ptp*) **(a)** (*zeitlich*) **das ist schon 5 Jahre ~** that was 5 years ago; **es ist schon 5 Jahre ~, daß ...** it was 5 years ago that ...; **es ist kaum ein Jahr ~, daß ...** it's hardly a year since ...; **wie lange ist es ~?** how long ago was it?; **(b)** (*~stammen*) to come from; **mit jdm/etw ist es nicht weit ~** (*inf*) sb/sth is not up to much (*inf*); **(c) hinter jdm/etw ~sein** to be after sb/sth; **dahinter ~sein, daß jd etw tut** to be on to sb to do sth; **~spionieren*** *vi sep* **hinter jdm ~spionieren** to spy on sb; **~stammen** *vi sep* **(a)** (*abstammen*) to come from; **wo stammst du ~?** where do you come from originally?; **(b)** (*~rühren*) **von etw ~stammen** to stem from sth; **(c)** (*~kommen*) **von jdm/etw ~stammen** to come from sb/sth.

herstellbar *adj* capable of being produced *or* manufactured ◆ **schwer ~e Waren** goods which are difficult to produce *or* manufacture.

herstellen *vt sep* **(a)** (*erzeugen*) to produce; (*industriell auch*) to manufacture ◆ **von Hand ~** to make *or* produce sth by hand; **in Deutschland hergestellt** made in Germany.
(b) (*zustande bringen*) to establish; *Kontakt auch, (Telec) Verbindung* to make; *Stromkreis* to complete.
(c) (*gesundheitlich*) *jdn* to restore to health; *Gesundheit* to restore ◆ **er ist wieder ganz hergestellt** he has quite recovered.
(d) (*an bestimmten Platz*) to put *or* place here ◆ **sich (zu jdm) ~** to come over (to sb); **etw zu jdm ~** to put sth by sb.

Hersteller *m* **-s, -** (*Produzent*) manufacturer; (*im Verlag*) production manager.

Hersteller-: ~betrieb *m*, **~firma** *f* manufacturing firm, manufacturer.

Herstellung *f, no pl* **(a)** *siehe vt (a)* production; manufacture. **(b)** *siehe vt (b)* establishment; making; completion. **(c)** (*von Gesundheit*) restoration. **(d)** (*Abteilung im Verlag*) production department.

Herstellungs-: ~fehler *m* manufacturing defect *or* fault; **~kosten** *pl* manufacturing *or* production costs *pl*; **~land** *nt* country of manufacture; **~preis** *m* cost of manufacture; **~verfahren** *nt* manufacturing *or* production method.

her-: ~stürzen *sep* [1] *vi aux sein* **(a)** (*auch* **~gestürzt kommen**) to come rushing up; **(b) hinter jdm/etw ~stürzen** to rush after sb/sth; [2] *vr* **sich hinter jdm ~stürzen** to throw oneself after sb; **~tragen** *vt sep irreg* **(a)** (*an bestimmten Ort*) to carry here; **(b) etw vor/hinter jdm/etw ~tragen** to carry sth in front of/behind sb/sth; **~trauen** *vr sep* to dare to come here; **~treiben** *sep irreg* [1] *vt* **(a)** (*an bestimmten Ort*) to drive here; (*Wind*) to blow here; (*Strömung*) to wash here; **etw zu uns ~treiben** to drive/blow/wash sth over to us; **(b) jdn/etw vor jdm/etw ~treiben** to drive *or* (*Wind*) blow sb/sth in front of *or* before sb/sth; **jdn/etw hinter jdm/etw ~treiben** to drive *or* (*Wind*) blow sb/sth behind sb/sth; **was treibt dich ~?** what brings you here?; [2] *vi aux sein* to be driven (*vor +dat* in front of, before); (*Wolken*) to blow; (*in der Strömung*) to be washed; **~treten** *vi sep irreg aux sein* to step up.

Hertz *nt* **-, -** (*Phys, Rad*) hertz.

herüben *adv* (*S Ger, Aus*) over here.

herüber *adv* over here; (*über Fluß, Straße, Grenze etc*) across ◆ **~ und hinüber** to and fro, back and forth; **~ ist es nicht weiter als hinüber** (*prov*) coming or going, the distance is the same; **da ~** over/across there; *siehe* **herübersein**.

herüber- *pref siehe auch* **rüber-** over; (*über Straße, Fluß, Grenze etc*) across; **~bitten** *vt sep irreg* to ask (to come) over; **~bringen** *vt sep irreg* to bring over/across (*über etw (acc)* sth); **~dürfen** *vi sep irreg* to be allowed (to come) over/across; **~fahren** *sep irreg* [1] *vi aux sein* to come *or* (*mit Auto etc*) drive over/across (*über etw (acc)* sth); [2] *vt* (*über etw (acc)* sth) *Auto etc* to drive over/across; *Fahrgast, Güter* to take over/across; **~fliegen** *vti sep irreg* (*vi: aux sein*) to fly over/across (*über etw (acc)* sth); **~geben** *vt sep irreg* to pass (*über +acc* over); **~grüßen** *vi sep* **(zu jdm) ~grüßen** to nod/call *etc* across to sb in greeting; **~holen** *vt sep* to fetch; *jdn* to fetch over; **~kommen** *vi sep irreg aux sein* to come over/across (*über etw (acc)* sth); (*inf: zu Nachbarn*) to pop round (*inf*); **wie sind die Leute (über die Mauer/den Fluß) ~gekommen?** how did the people get over (the wall)/across (the river)?; **~lassen** *vt sep irreg* to allow (to come) over/across (*über etw (acc)* sth); (*aus Land*) to allow (to come) out; **~laufen** *vi sep irreg aux sein* to run over/across (*über etw (acc)* sth); **~reichen** *sep* [1] *vt siehe* **~geben**; [2] *vi* to reach across (*über etw (acc)* sth); **~retten** *vt sep* **etw in die Gegenwart ~retten** to preserve sth; **~schicken** *vt sep* to send over/across; **~schwimmen** *vi sep irreg aux sein* to swim across (*über etw (acc)* sth); **~sehen** *vi sep irreg* to look over (*über etw (acc)* sth); **zu jdm ~sehen** to look over/across to sb; **~wechseln** *vi sep aux sein or haben* (*Tiere*) to cross (*über etw (acc)* sth); **in unsere Partei/unseren Verein ~wechseln** to join our party/club, to swap parties/clubs (and join ours); **~wehen** *sep* (*über etw (acc)* sth) [1] *vi* **(a)** (*Wind*) to blow over/across; **(b)** *aux sein* (*Klang*) to be blown over/across; (*Duft*) to waft over/across; [2] *vt* to blow over/across; **~werfen** *vt sep irreg* to throw over/across (*über etw (acc)* sth); **~wollen** *vi sep* to want to come over/across (*über etw (acc)* sth); **~ziehen** *sep irreg* (*über etw (acc)* sth) [1] *vt* to pull over/across; (*fig*) to win over; [2] *vi aux sein* (*Truppen, Wolken*) to move over/across; (*umziehen*) to move.

herum *adv* **(a)** (*örtlich richtungsangebend*) **um ... ~** (a)round; **links/rechts ~**

(a)round to the left/right; **hier/dort ~** (a)round here/there; **oben ~** (*über Gegenstand, Berg*) over the top; (*in bezug auf Körper*) round the top; **sie ist oben ~ ziemlich füllig** she's quite well endowed (*hum*); **unten ~** (*unter Gegenstand*) underneath; (*um Berg, in bezug auf Körper*) around the bottom; **oben/unten ~ fahren** to take the top/lower road; **wasch dich auch unten ~** (*euph*) don't forget to wash down below; **verkehrt ~** the wrong way round; (*hinten nach vorn*) back to front; (*links nach außen*) inside out; (*oben nach unten*) upside down; **immer um etw ~** round and round sth.

(b) (*kreisförmig angeordnet, in der Nähe*) **um ... ~** around; **hier ~** (a)round here; (*in der Nähe auch*) hereabouts; **alle um mich ~ wußten, daß ...** everyone around *or* round me knew that ...

(c) um ... ~ (*ungefähre Mengenangabe*) about, around; (*Zeitangabe*) (at) about *or* around; *siehe auch* **herumsein.**

herum- *pref siehe auch* **umher-, rum-** (a)round; **~albern** *vi sep* (*inf*) to fool *or* lark (*inf*) around; **~ärgern** *vr sep* (*inf*) **sich mit jdm/etw ~ärgern** to keep struggling with sb/sth; **~balgen** *vr sep* (*inf*) to romp about; **~basteln** *vi sep* (*inf*) to tinker *or* mess (*inf*) about (*an +dat* with); **~bekommen** *vt sep irreg* (*inf*) *jdn* to talk round; **etw ~bekommen** to (manage to) get sth round (*um etw* sth); **~bessern** *vi sep* **an etw** (*dat*) **~bessern** to fiddle around correcting sth; **~blättern** *vi sep* **(in einem Buch) ~blättern** to leaf *or* browse through a book; **~bohren** *vi sep* (*mit Stock, Finger etc*) to poke around; (*mit Bohrer*) to drill; **sich** (*dat*) **in der Nase ~bohren** to pick one's nose; **~bringen** *vt sep irreg* (*inf*) **(a)** *siehe* **~bekommen; (b)** *Zeit* to get through; **~brüllen** *vi sep* to yell; **~bummeln** *vi sep* (*inf*) **(a)** (*trödeln*) to mess about (*inf*); **(b)** *aux sein* (*spazieren*) to stroll (a)round (*in etw* (*dat*) sth); **~doktern** *vi sep* (*inf*) **an jdm/einer Krankheit/einer Wunde ~doktern** to try to cure sb/an illness/heal a wound (*unsuccessfully, using many different remedies*); **an etw** (*dat*) **~doktern** (*fig*) to fiddle *or* tinker about with sth; **~drehen** *sep* [1] *vt Schlüssel* to turn; (*wenden*) *Decke, Tuch, Braten etc* to turn (over); **jdm das Wort im Mund ~drehen** to twist sb's words; [2] *vr* to turn (a)round; (*im Liegen*) to turn over; [3] *vi* (*inf*) **an etw** (*dat*) **~drehen** to fiddle *or* tinker about with sth; **~drücken** *sep* [1] *vr* (*inf*) **(a)** (*sich aufhalten*) to hang (a)round (*um etw* sth); **(b)** (*vermeiden*) **sich um etw ~drücken** to dodge sth; [2] *vi* **an etw** (*dat*) **~drücken** to squeeze sth; [3] *vt Hebel* to turn; **~drucksen** *vi sep* (*inf*) to hum and haw (*inf*); **~erzählen*** *vt sep* **etw bei jdm ~erzählen** to tell sb about sth; **erzähl das nicht ~** don't spread that around; **~experimentieren*** *vi sep* to experiment; **~fahren** *sep irreg* [1] *vi aux sein* **(a)** (*umherfahren*) to go *or* travel *or* (*mit Auto*) drive around; **in der Stadt ~fahren** to go/drive (a)round the town; **(b)** (*um etw ~fahren*) to go *or* (*mit Auto*) drive or (*mit Schiff*) sail (a)round; **(c)** (*sich rasch umdrehen*) to turn round quickly, to spin (a)round; **(d)** *auch aux haben* **sich** (*dat*) **(mit den Händen) in den Haaren/im Gesicht ~fahren** to run one's fingers through one's hair/to wipe one's face; [2] *vt* to drive (a)round; **~fingern** *vi sep* (*inf*) **an etw** (*dat*) **~fingern** to fiddle about with sth; (*an Körperteil*) to finger sth; **~flattern** *vi sep aux sein* (*umherflattern*) to flutter about; **um etw ~flattern** to flutter around sth; **~flegeln** *vi sep* to loll about *or* around; **~fliegen** *sep irreg* [1] *vi aux sein* to fly around (*um jdn/etw* sb/sth); (*inf: ~liegen*) to be kicking around (*inf*); [2] *vt jdn* to fly about *or* around; **~fragen** *vi sep* (*inf*) to ask around (*bei* among); **~fuchteln** *vi sep* (*inf*) **(mit den Händen) ~fuchteln** to wave one's hands about *or* around; **mit einer Pistole ~fuchteln** to wave a pistol around, to brandish a pistol; **~führen** *sep* [1] *vt* **(a)** *jdn, Tier* to lead around (*um etw* sth); (*bei Besichtigung*) to take *or* show (a)round; **jdn in einer Stadt/im Haus ~führen** to take *or* show sb (a)round a town/the house; **jdn an der Nase ~führen** to lead sb up the garden path; **(b)** (*leiten, dirigieren*) **jdn/etw um etw ~führen** to direct sb/sth around sth; **(c)** (*bauen*) **etw um etw ~führen** to build *or* take sth (a)round sth; [2] *vi* **um etw ~führen** to go (a)round sth; **~fuhrwerken** *vi sep* (*inf*) to bustle about, to busy oneself; **~fummeln** *vi sep* (*inf*) (*an +dat* with) to fiddle *or* fumble about; (*an Auto*) to mess about; (*basteln*) to tinker (about); **~geben** *vt sep irreg* to hand *or* pass (a)round; **~gehen** *vi sep irreg aux sein* (*inf*) **(a)** (*um etw ~gehen*) to walk *or* go (a)round (*um etw* sth); **(b)** (*ziellos umhergehen*) to go *or* wander (a)round (*in etw* (*dat*) sth); **es ging ihm im Kopf ~** it went round and round in his head; **(c)** (*von einem zum andern gehen: Mensch*) to go (a)round; (*~gereicht werden*) to be passed *or* handed (a)round; (*weitererzählt werden*) to go around (*in etw* (*dat*) sth); **etw ~gehen lassen** to circulate sth; **(d)** (*zeitlich: vorbeigehen*) to pass; **~geistern** *vi sep aux sein* (*inf*) (*Gespenster etc*) to haunt (*in etw* (*dat*) sth); (*Mensch*) to wander (a)round; **in jds Kopf ~geistern** (*Idee*) to possess sb; **~gondeln** *vi sep aux sein* (*inf*) to drive around; **~haben** *vt sep irreg* (*inf*) **(a)** *Zeit* to have finished; **(b)** (*überredet haben*) to have talked round; **~hacken** *vi sep* (*fig inf*) **auf jdm ~hacken** to pick on sb (*inf*); **~hängen** *vi sep irreg* **(a)** (*inf: unordentlich aufgehängt sein*) to hang around; **(b)** (*inf: sich lümmeln*) to loll about; **(c)** (*sl: ständig zu finden sein*) to hang out (*inf*); **~hantieren*** *vi sep* (*inf*) to fiddle (about) (*an +dat* with); **~hetzen** *vi sep aux sein* to rush around; **~horchen** *vi sep* (*inf*) to keep one's ears open; **~huren** *vi sep* (*sl*) to whore around (*sl*); **~irren** *vi sep aux sein* to wander around; **~knobeln** *vi sep* (*inf*) **an etw** (*dat*) **~knobeln** to rack one's brains about sth; **~kommandieren*** *sep* (*inf*) [1] *vt* to order about, to boss around *or* about (*inf*); [2] *vi* to give orders; **~kommen** *vi sep irreg aux sein* (*inf*) **(a)** (*um eine Ecke etc*) to come round (*um etw* sth); **(b)** (*~gehen, ~fahren etc können*) to get round (*um etw* sth); **(c)** (*vermeiden können*) **um etw ~kommen** to get out of *or* avoid sth; **darum ~kommen, etw zu machen** to get out of *or* avoid doing sth; **mit den Armen um etw ~kommen** to be able to get one's arms (a)round sth; **wir kommen um die Tatsache nicht ~, daß ...** we cannot get away from *or* overlook the fact that ...; **(d)** (*reisen*) to get about *or* around (*in etw* (*dat*) sth); **er ist viel** *or* **weit ~gekommen** he has got around a great deal, he has seen a lot of the world; **~krabbeln** *vi sep aux sein* (*inf*) to crawl around *or* about; **~kramen** *vi sep* (*inf*) to rummage about *or* around; **~krebsen** *vi sep* (*inf*) **(a)** (*sich verzweifelt bemühen*) to struggle; **(b)** (*sich unwohl fühlen*) to drag oneself around *or* about (*inf*); **(c)** *aux sein* (*langsam or schwerfällig gehen*) to trudge (a)round; **~kriechen** *vi sep irreg aux sein* (*inf*) to crawl about *or* around (*um etw* sth); **~kriegen** *vt sep* (*inf*) *siehe* **~bekommen; ~kritisieren*, ~kritteln** *vi sep* to find fault (*an +dat* with), to pick holes (*an +dat* in); **~kurieren*** *vi sep siehe* **~doktern; ~kutschieren*** *vti sep* (*vi: aux sein*) to drive (a)round; **~laborieren*** *vi sep* (*inf*) **an etw** (*dat*) **~laborieren** to try to get rid of sth; **~laufen** *vi sep irreg aux sein* (*inf*) (*um etw ~laufen*) to run round (*um etw* sth); (*umherlaufen*) to run *or* go about *or* around; **so kannst du doch nicht ~laufen** (*fig inf*) you can't run *or* go around (looking) like that; **~liegen** *vi sep irreg* (*inf*) to lie around *or* about (*um etw* sth); **~lümmeln** *vir sep* (*inf*) to loll around; **~lungern** *vi sep* (*inf*) to hang about *or* around; **~machen** *sep* (*inf*) [1] *vi* **(a)** (*sich überlegen*) to think about; **da braucht man doch nicht so lange ~zumachen** you don't need to think about it for so long; **(b)** (*sich beschäftigen*) **an jdm/etw ~machen** to fuss about sb/sth; **(c)** (*~fingern*) **an etw** (*dat*) **~machen** to pick at sth; (*an den Haaren*) to fiddle with sth; **(d)** (*~nörgeln*) **an jdm/etw ~machen** to go on at sb/about sth (*inf*); [2] *vt* to put (a)round (*um etw* sth); **~mäkeln** *vi sep siehe* **~kritteln; ~nörgeln** *vi sep* **an jdm/etw ~nörgeln** to find fault with sb/sth; **~pfuschen** *vi sep* (*inf*) to mess about (*inf*) (*an +dat* with); **~pusseln** *vi sep* (*inf*) to fiddle about (*an +dat* with); **~quälen** *vr sep* (*inf*) to struggle; (*mit Problemen*) to worry oneself sick (*mit* over) (*inf*); **sich mit Rheuma ~quälen** to be plagued by rheumatism; **~raten** *vi sep irreg* (*inf*) to guess; **~rätseln** *vi sep* **(an etw** *dat*) **~rätseln** to (try to) figure sth out; **~reden** *vi sep* (*inf*) (*belangloses Zeug reden*) to talk *or* chat away; **um etw ~reden** (*ausweichend*) to talk (a)round sth; **~reichen** *vt sep* **(a)** (*~geben*) to pass round; (*fig inf*) *Besucher* to show off; **(b)** (*lang genug sein*) to reach (a)round (*um etw* sth); **~reisen** *vi sep aux sein* to travel about; **~reißen** *vt sep irreg* to pull *or* swing round (hard); **das Steuer ~reißen** (*fig*) to change *or* alter course; **~reiten** *vi sep irreg* **(a)** *aux sein* (*umherreiten*) to ride around *or* about; (*um etw ~reiten*) to ride (a)round (*um etw* sth); **(b)** (*fig inf*) **auf jdm/etw ~reiten** to keep on at sb/about sth; **~rennen** *vi sep irreg aux sein* (*inf*) (*um etw ~rennen*) to run round (*um etw* sth); (*umherrennen*) to run about *or* around; **~rutschen** *vi sep aux sein* (*inf*) to fidget about; **~scharwenzeln*** *vi sep aux sein* (*inf*) to dance attendance (*um* on); **~schicken** *vt sep* (*inf*) *jdn* to send round (*bei* to); *Brief etc* to circulate; **~schlagen** *sep irreg* [1] *vt Papier, Tuch etc* to wrap round (*um etw* sth); [2] *vr* (*inf*) **sich mit jdm ~schlagen** (*lit*) to fight *or* scuffle with sb; (*fig*) to fight a running battle with sb; **sich mit etw ~schlagen** (*fig*) to keep struggling with sth; **~schleichen** *vi sep irreg aux sein* to creep (a)round (*um etw* sth); **~schleifen** *vt sep* (*dial inf*) to drag around; **~schlendern** *vi sep aux sein* to stroll *or* saunter about (*in der Stadt* (in) the town); **~schleppen** *vt sep* (*inf*) *Sachen* to lug around (*inf*); *jdn* to drag around; **etw mit sich ~schleppen** *Kummer, Sorge, Problem* to be troubled *or* worried by sth; *Krankheit, Infektion* to be going around with sth; **~schnüffeln** *vi sep* (*inf*) to sniff around (*in etw* (*dat*) sth); (*fig*) to snoop around (*in +dat* in); **~schreien** *vi sep irreg* (*inf*) to shout out loud; **~schwänzeln** *vi sep aux sein* (*inf*) *siehe* **~scharwenzeln; ~schwirren** *vi sep aux sein* (*inf*) **sie muß hier irgendwo ~schwirren** she must be floating around here somewhere (*inf*); ⚠**~sein** *vi sep irreg aux sein* (*inf*) (*Zusammenschreibung nur bei infin und ptp*) **(a)** (*vorüber sein*) to be past *or* over; **(b)** (*verbreitet worden sein: Gerücht, Neuigkeit, Nachricht*) to have got (a)round; **(c)** (*in jds Nähe sein*) **um jdn ~sein** to be (a)round sb; **(d)** (*um etw gelaufen, gefahren sein*) to be round (*um etw* sth); **~sitzen** *vi sep irreg aux haben or sein* to sit round (*um jdn/etw* sb/sth); **~spielen** *vi sep* (*inf*) **mit etw ~spielen** to play about *or* around with sth; **an etw** (*dat*) **~spielen** to fiddle about *or* around with sth; **auf etw** (*dat*) **~spielen** to play around on sth; **~sprechen** *vr sep irreg* to get about; **es dürfte sich ~gesprochen haben, daß ...** it has probably got about that ...; **~spuken** *vi sep* to haunt; **die Idee spukt jdm im Kopf** *or* **in jds Kopf ~** sb has the idea; **~stänkern** *vi sep* (*inf*) to moan, to gripe (*inf*), to bellyache (*inf*); **~stehen** *vi sep irreg aux haben or sein* **(a)** (*Sachen*) to be lying around; **der Sessel steht blöd ~** the chair is in a stupid place; **(b)** (*Menschen*) to stand (a)round (*um jdn/etw* sb/sth); **~stöbern** *vi sep* (*inf*) **(a)** (*suchen*) to rummage around *or* about; **(b)** (*~schnüffeln*) to snoop around; **~stochern** *vi sep* (*inf*) to poke about; **im Essen ~stochern** to pick at one's food; **in den Zähnen ~stochern** to pick one's teeth; **~stoßen** *vt sep irreg jdn* to shove around; **~streichen** *vi sep irreg aux sein* (*um jdn/etw* sb/sth) to creep around; (*Verbrecher, Katze*) to prowl around; **~streifen** *vi sep aux sein* to roam around; **~streiten** *vr sep irreg* to squabble; **~streunen, ~strolchen** *vi sep aux sein* (*inf*) to prowl around; **~stromern** *vi sep aux sein* (*inf*) to wander *or* roam about *or* around; **~tanzen** *vi sep aux sein* (*inf*) (*umhertanzen*) to dance around; **um jdn/etw ~tanzen** to dance (a)round sb/sth; **sie tanzt ihm auf der Nase ~** she does as she pleases *or* likes with him; **~tappen** *vi sep aux sein* (*inf*) to grope around *or* about; **~tasten** *vi sep* **(a)** (*tastend fühlen*) to grope around *or* about; **(b)** *aux sein* (*inf: tastend gehen*) to grope around *or* about; **~toben** *vi sep* (*inf*) **(a)** *auch aux sein* (*umherlaufen*) to romp around *or* about; **(b)** (*schimpfen*) to shout and scream; **~tollen** *vi sep aux sein* (*inf*) to romp about *or* around; **~tragen** *vt sep irreg* (*inf*) **(a)** to carry about *or* (a)round; **um etw ~tragen** to carry (a)round sth; **Sorgen mit sich ~tragen** to have worries; **eine Idee mit sich ~tragen** to be contemplating an idea, to be thinking about an idea; **(b)** (*weitererzählen*) to spread around; **~trampeln** *vi sep aux sein* (*inf*) to trample (*auf +dat* on); **jdm auf den Nerven** *or* **auf jds Nerven ~trampeln** to get on sb's nerves; **auf jdm ~trampeln** (*fig*) to get at sb; **~treiben** *vr sep irreg* (*inf*) (*~ziehen in*) to hang around *or* about (*in +dat* in) (*inf*); (*liederlich leben*) to hang around *or* about in bad places/

company; **die treibt sich mal wieder irgendwo in Spanien ~** she's off gadding about in Spain again (*inf*); **sich mit jdm ~treiben** to hang *or* knock around with sb (*inf*).

Herumtreiber(in *f*) *m* **-s, -** (*pej*) **(a)** (*Mensch ohne feste Arbeit, Wohnsitz*) tramp. **(b)** (*inf*) (*Streuner*) vagabond; (*liederlich*) good-for-nothing; (*Frau*) tramp (*inf*).

herum-: ~treten *vi sep irreg* (*inf*) *siehe* **~trampeln**; **~trödeln** *vi sep* (*inf*) to dawdle (*mit* over); **~turnen** *vi sep aux sein* (*inf*) to clamber *or* scramble about; **~vagabundieren*** *vi sep aux sein* (*pej*) to roam about; **~wälzen** *sep* **1** *vt Stein* to turn over; **2** *vr* to roll around; **sich (schlaflos) im Bett ~wälzen** to toss and turn in bed; **~wandern** *vi sep aux sein* (*umhergehen*) to wander about; **um etw ~wandern** to wander (a)round sth; **~werfen** *sep irreg* **1** *vt* **(a)** (*achtlos werfen*) to throw around (*in etw* (*dat*) sth); **(b)** (*heftig bewegen*) *Kopf* to turn (quickly); *Steuer, Hebel* to throw around; **2** *vr* to roll over; **sich (im Bett) ~werfen** to toss and turn (in bed); **3** *vi* (*inf*) **mit Bemerkungen/Geld** *etc* **~werfen** to fling *or* throw remarks/one's money *etc* around; **~wickeln** *vt sep* (*um etw* sth) to wrap (a)round; *Schnur, Faden etc* to wind (a)round; **~wirbeln** *vti sep* (*vi: aux sein*) **jdn** *or* **mit jdm ~wirbeln** to whirl *or* spin sb (a)round; **~wirtschaften** *vi sep* (*inf*) to potter about; **~wühlen** *vi sep* (*inf*) to rummage about *or* around; (*Schwein*) to root around; (*~schnüffeln*) to nose *or* snoop about *or* around; **~wursteln** *vi sep* (*inf*) to fiddle *or* mess (*inf*) around *or* about (*an +dat* with); **~zanken** *vr sep* to squabble; **~zeigen** *vt sep* to show around; **~ziehen** *sep irreg* **1** *vi aux sein* **(a)** (*von Ort zu Ort ziehen*) to move around; (*inf: sich ~treiben in*) to go around (*in etw* (*dat*) sth); **in der Welt ~ziehen** to roam the world; **mit jdm ~ziehen** (*inf*) to go *or* hang around with sb; **(b)** (*um etw ~*) to move around (*um etw* sth); **2** *vt* **etw mit sich ~ziehen** to take sth (around) with one; **3** *vr* **sich um etw ~ziehen** (*Hecke etc*) to run (a)round sth; **~ziehend** *adj attr Händler* itinerant; *Musikant, Schauspieler* wandering, strolling; **~zigeunern*** *vi sep aux sein* (*pej*) to roam *or* wander (a)round (*in etw* (*dat*) sth).

herunten *adv* (*S Ger, Aus*) down here; *siehe* **herunterhaben, heruntersein.**

herunter **1** *adv* down ◆ **~!** get down!; **~ mit euch** get/come down; **~ mit ihm** get him down; **~ damit** get *or* bring it down; (*in bezug auf Kleider*) get *or* take it off; **da/hier ~** down there/here; **den Hut ~, ~ mit dem Hut** get *or* take your hat off; **vom Berg ~** down the mountain; **vom Himmel ~** down from heaven; **bis ins Tal ~** down into the valley; *siehe auch* **herunterhaben, heruntersein** *etc*.
2 *prep +acc* (*nachgestellt*) down.

herunter- *pref siehe auch* **runter-, herab-** down; **~bekommen** *vt sep irreg siehe* **~kriegen**; **~bemühen*** *sep* **1** *vt* **jdn ~bemühen** to ask sb to come down; **2** *vr* to come down; **~bitten** *vt sep irreg* **jdn ~bitten** to ask sb to come down; **~brennen** *vi sep irreg* **(a)** (*Sonne*) to burn *or* scorch down; **(b)** *aux sein* (*Haus, Feuer etc*) to burn down; **~bringen** *vt sep irreg* **(a)** to bring down; **(b)** (*zugrunde richten*) to ruin; **(c)** (*inf*) *siehe* **~kriegen**; **~drücken** *vt sep Hebel, Pedal* to press down; *Preise* to force *or* bring down; *Niveau* to lower; **~fahren** *sep irreg* **1** *vi aux sein* to go down; **~gefahren kommen** to come down; **2** *vt* to bring down; **~fallen** *vi sep irreg aux sein* to fall down; **von etw ~fallen** to fall off sth; **ihm fiel die Kinnlade ~** his jaw dropped; **~fliegen** *vi sep irreg aux sein* to fly down; (*inf*) to fall down; **~geben** *vt sep irreg* to hand down; **~gehen** *vi sep irreg aux sein* to go down; (*Fieber, Temperatur auch*) to drop; (*Preise auch*) to come down, to drop; (*Flugzeug*) to descend; **von etw ~gehen** (*inf*) to get down from *or* get off sth; **auf etw** (*acc*) **~gehen** (*Preise*) to go down to sth; (*Geschwindigkeit*) to slow down to sth; **mit den Preisen ~gehen** to lower *or* cut one's prices; **~gekommen** **1** *ptp of* **~kommen**; **2** *adj Haus* dilapidated; *Stadt* run-down; *Mensch* down-at-heel; **~haben** *vt sep irreg* (*inf*) (*~geholt haben*) to have got down; (*abgenommen haben*) to have lost; **~handeln** *vt sep* (*inf*) *Preis* to beat down; **etw um 20 Mark ~handeln** to get 20 marks knocked off sth; **~hängen** *vi sep irreg* to hang down; (*Haare*) to hang; **~hauen** *vt sep irreg* (*inf*) **(a)** **jdm eine ~hauen** to give sb a clip round the ear (*inf*); **(b)** (*schnell machen*) to dash *or* knock off (*inf*); **~heben** *vt sep irreg* to lift down; **~helfen** *vi sep irreg* **jdm ~helfen** to help sb down; **~holen** *vt sep* to fetch down; (*inf*) *Vogel* to bring down, to bag; *Flugzeug* to bring down; **~klappen** *vt sep* to turn down; *Sitz* to fold down; *Deckel* to close; **~klettern** *vi sep aux sein* to climb down; **~kommen** *vi sep irreg aux sein* **(a)** (*nach unten kommen*) to come down; (*inf: ~können*) to get down; **(b)** (*fig inf: verfallen*) (*Stadt, Firma*) to go downhill; (*Wirtschaft*) to go to rack and ruin; (*gesundheitlich*) to become run-down; **er ist so weit ~gekommen, daß ...** (*sittlich*) he has sunk so low that ...; *siehe* **~gekommen**; **(c)** (*fig inf: von etw wegkommen*) (*von schlechten Noten*) to get over (*von etw* sth); **von Drogen/Alkohol ~kommen** to kick the habit (*sl*); **~können** *vi sep irreg* to be able to get down; **~kriegen** *vt sep* (*inf*) **(a)** (*~holen, schlucken können*) to get down; (*abmachen können*) to get off; **(b)** (*abnehmen*) to lose; **~kurbeln** *vt sep Fensterscheibe* to wind down; **~laden** *vt sep irreg* (*Comput*) to download (*auf +acc* into); **~lassen** *sep irreg* **1** *vt* (*abseilen*) *Gegenstand* to let down, to lower; *Hose* to take down; *jdn* to lower; **sie läßt mich nicht ~** (*inf*) she won't let me down; **2** *vr* (*am Seil*) to lower oneself; **~leiern** *vt sep* (*inf*) to reel off; **~lesen** *vt sep irreg* (*pej*) to read off; **~machen** *vt sep* (*inf*) **(a)** (*schlechtmachen*) to run down, to knock (*inf*); **(b)** (*zurechtweisen*) to tell off; **(c)** (*abmachen*) to take down; *Schminke, Farbe, Dreck* to take off; **~nehmen** *vt sep irreg* to take down; (*inf: von Schule*) to take away; **etw vom Tisch** *etc* **~nehmen** to take sth off the table *etc*; **~putzen** *vt sep* (*inf*) **jdn ~putzen** to tear sb off a strip (*inf*); **~rasseln** *vt sep* (*inf*) to rattle *or* reel off; **~reichen** *sep* **1** *vt* to pass *or* hand down; **2** *vi* to reach down; **~reißen** *vt sep irreg* (*inf*) **(a)** (*von oben nach unten*) to pull *or* tear down; **(b)** (*abreißen*) *Pflaster, Tapete etc* to pull off; **(c)** (*sl*) *Zeit* to get through; **~rutschen** *vi sep aux sein* to slide down; *siehe* **Buckel**;

~schalten *vi sep* (*Aut*) to change *or* shift (*US*) down (*in +acc* into); **~schießen** *sep irreg* **1** *vti* (*mit Geschoß*) to shoot down; **2** *vi aux sein* (*inf: sich schnell bewegen*) to shoot down; **~schlagen** *vt sep irreg* **(a)** **jdm den Hut** *etc* **~schlagen** to knock sb's hat *etc* off; **etw vom Baum ~schlagen** to knock sth off the tree; **(b)** *Kragen, Hutkrempe* to turn down; **~schlucken** *vt sep* to swallow; **~schrauben** *vt sep* (*lit*) *Deckel etc* to screw off; *Petroleumlampe* to turn down; (*fig*) *Ansprüche, Niveau* to lower; **~sehen** *vi sep irreg* **(a)** (*von oben*) to look down; **(b)** (*fig: mustern*) **an jdm ~sehen** to look sb up and down; **(c)** (*fig: geringschätzig behandeln*) **auf jdn ~sehen** to look down on sb; **⚠~sein** *vi sep irreg aux sein* (*inf*) (*Zusammenschreibung nur bei infin und ptp*) **(a)** (*von oben*) to be down; **(b)** (*~gelassen sein*) to be down; **(c)** (*abgeschnitten sein*) to be (cut) off; **(d)** (*Fieber, Preise*) to be lower *or* down; **wenn die 5 Kilo Übergewicht ~ sind** when I/you *etc* have lost those 5 kilos excess weight; **(e)** (*inf*) **mit den Nerven/der Gesundheit ~sein** to be at the end of one's tether/to be run-down; **(f)** (*abgewirtschaftet haben*) to be in a bad way; **~setzen** *vt sep* (*inf*) *siehe* **herabsetzen**; **~spielen** *vt sep* (*inf*) *Stück* to run through; (*verharmlosen*) *Problem, Vorfall* to play down; **~steigen** *vi sep irreg aux sein* to climb down; **~stürzen** *sep* **1** *vi aux sein* (*~fallen*) to fall *or* tumble down; (*inf: ~eilen*) to rush down; **2** *vt* **(a)** **jdn ~stürzen** to throw/push sb down; **(b)** (*inf: schnell trinken*) to gulp down; **3** *vr* to throw oneself down; **~werfen** *vt sep irreg* to throw down; (*unabsichtlich*) to drop; **~wirtschaften** *vt sep* (*inf*) to bring to the brink of ruin; **~wollen** *vi sep* (*inf*) to want to get down; **~ziehen** *sep irreg* **1** *vt* **(a)** to pull down; *Pullover etc* to pull off; **etw von etw ~ziehen** to pull sth off sth; **(b)** (*fig*) **jdn auf sein Niveau/seine Ebene/zu sich ~ziehen** to pull sb down to one's own level; **2** *vi aux sein* to go *or* move down; (*umziehen*) to move down; **3** *vr* to go down.

hervor *adv* **aus etw ~** out of sth; **hinter dem Tisch ~** out from behind the table; **~ mit euch** (*geh*) out you come.

▼ **hervor-: ~brechen** *vi sep irreg aux sein* (*geh*) to burst *or* break out; (*Sonne, fig: Gefühl*) to break through; (*Quelle, Flüssigkeit*) to gush out *or* forth (*liter*); **~bringen** *vt sep irreg* **(a)** to produce; *Blüten, Früchte, Pflanzen auch* to bring forth; *Worte* to utter; **(b)** (*verursachen*) *Unheil, Böses* to create; **~dringen** *vi sep irreg aux sein* (*geh*) to issue forth (*liter*); **~gehen** *vi sep irreg aux sein* **(a)** (*geh: entstammen*) to come (*aus* from); **aus der Ehe gingen zwei Kinder ~** the ▼ marriage produced two children; **(b)** (*sich ergeben, zu folgern sein*) to follow; **daraus geht ~, daß ...** from this it follows that ...; **(c)** (*etwas überstehen*) to emerge; **als Sieger ~gehen** to emerge victorious; **aus etw ~gehen** to come out of sth; **~gucken** *vi sep* (*inf*) to peep out (*unter +dat* (from) under); **~heben** *vt sep irreg* to emphasize, to stress; **~holen** *vt sep* to bring out; **~kehren** *vt sep* (*geh*) to emphasize; **er kehrt immer den feinen Mann ~** he always emphasizes what a gentleman he is; **~kommen** *vi sep irreg aux sein* to come out (*hinter +dat* from behind); **~locken** *vt sep* to entice *or* lure out (*aus* from, *hinter +dat* from behind); **dein Gejammer lockt bei mir keine Träne ~** your moaning is not going to move me; **~quellen** *vi sep irreg aux sein* (*Wasser*) to gush forth (*aus* from) (*liter*); (*Tränen*) to well up (*aus* in); (*Blut*) to spurt out (*aus* of); (*Körperfülle*) to bulge *or* protrude (*aus* from, *unter +dat* from under); **~ragen** *vi sep* **(a)** (*Felsen, Stein etc*) to jut out, to project; (*Nase*) to protrude; **(b)** (*fig: sich auszeichnen*) to stand out; **er ragt unter den anderen/durch seine Intelligenz ~** he stands out from the others/because of his intelligence; **~ragend** *adj* **(a)** (*lit: vorstehend*) projecting; *esp Körperteil* protruding; **(b)** (*fig: ausgezeichnet*) excellent; *Mensch, Leistung etc auch* outstanding; **er hat H~ragendes geleistet** his achievement was outstanding; **~rufen** *vt sep irreg* **(a)** (*rufen*) **jdn ~rufen** to call (to) sb to come out; (*Theat* ▼ *etc*) to call for sb; **(b)** (*bewirken*) to cause, to give rise to; *Bewunderung* to arouse; *Reaktion, Krankheit* to cause; *Eindruck* to create; **~sehen** *vi sep irreg* (*Unterrock*) to show; (*Mensch*) to look out; **hinter etw** (*dat*) **~sehen** (*Mensch*) to look out from behind sth; (*Mond, Sterne*) to shine out from behind sth; **~springen** *vi sep irreg aux sein* **(a)** to jump *or* leap out (*hinter +dat* from behind); **(b)** (*Felsen*) to project, to jut out; (*Nase*) to protrude, to stick out; **~sprudeln** *vi sep aux sein* to bubble *or* gush out; (*Worte*) to gush (out); **~stechen** *vi sep irreg aux sein* (*lit, fig*) to stand out; **~stechend** *adj* striking; **~stehen** *vi sep irreg aux sein* (*Spitze*) to project, to jut out; (*Nase, Ohren etc*) to stick out; **~stoßen** *vt sep irreg* (*fig*) *Worte* to gasp (out); **~stürzen** *vi sep aux sein* to rush *or* hurtle out (*hinter +dat* from behind); **~suchen** *vt sep* (*heraussuchen*) to look out; **~trauen** *vr sep* (*inf*) *siehe* **~wagen**; **~treten** *vi sep irreg aux sein* **(a)** (*heraustreten*) to step out, to emerge (*hinter +dat* from behind); (*Backenknochen*) to protrude; (*Adern*) to bulge; (*Sonne, Mond*) to emerge (*hinter +dat, aus* from behind); **(b)** (*sichtbar werden*) to stand out; (*fig auch*) to become evident; **(c)** (*an die Öffentlichkeit treten*) to come to the fore; **~tun** *vr sep irreg* to distinguish oneself; (*inf: sich wichtig tun*) to show off (*mit etw* sth); **~wagen** *vr sep* to dare to come out; **~zaubern** *vt sep* (*lit, fig*) to conjure up; **~ziehen** *vt sep irreg* to pull out (*unter +dat* from under); **etw aus/zwischen etw** (*dat*) **~ziehen** to pull sth out of/from among sth.

Her-: h~wagen *vr sep* to dare to come; **h~wärts** *adv* on the way here; **~weg** *m* way here; **auf dem ~weg** on the way here.

Herz *nt* **-ens, -en** **(a)** (*Organ, herzförmiges, Cook*) heart ◆ **mir schlug das ~ bis zum Hals** my heart was thumping *or* pounding, my heart was in my mouth; **sein ~ schlug höher** his heart leapt; **die ~en höher schlagen lassen** to make people's hearts beat faster; **er drückte sie an sein ~** he clasped her to his breast; **komm an mein ~** come into my arms.
(b) (*Gemüt, Gefühl*) heart ◆ **ein goldenes ~** a heart of gold; **ein gutes ~ haben** to be good-hearted, to have a good heart; **leichten/schweren/traurigen ~ens** light-heartedly *or* with a light heart/with a heavy/sad heart; **der Anblick rührte ihr das ~** the sight touched her heart; **es gab mir einen Stich ins ~** it hurt me; (*traurig stimmen*) it saddened me; **es ging mir bis ins ~** it cut me

to the quick; (*traurig stimmen*) it saddened me very much; **seinem ~en Luft machen** to give vent to one's feelings; **sich** (*dat*) **etw vom ~en reden** to get sth off one's chest; **den Weg in die** *or* **zu den ~en finden** to find one's way into people's hearts; **alle ~en im Sturm erobern** to capture people's hearts; **du sprichst mir aus dem ~en** that's just what I feel; **jdm das ~ schwer machen** to sadden *or* grieve sb; **mir ist das ~ schwer** I have a heavy heart; **haben Sie doch ein ~!** have a heart!; **im Grund seines ~ens** in his heart of hearts; **aus tiefstem ~en** from the bottom of one's heart; **mit ganzem ~en** wholeheartedly; **er ist mit ganzem ~en bei der Arbeit** he is putting himself heart and soul into his work; **ein Mann nach meinem ~en** a man after my own heart; **ohne ~** heartless; **ich weiß, wie es dir ums ~ ist** I know how you feel; **es wurde ihr leichter ums ~** she felt easier *or* relieved; **es ging mir zu ~en** it touched me deeply.

(c) (*Liebe*) heart ◆ **mein ~ gehört dir/der Musik** my heart belongs to you/to music; **jdm sein ~ schenken** to give sb one's heart; **dieser Hund ist mir ans ~ gewachsen** I have grown fond of *or* become attached to this dog; **ein ~ für jdn/etw haben** to be fond of sb/sth; **habt ein ~ für die Armen** spare a thought for the poor; **sein ~ für etw entdecken** to start liking sth; **er hat sie in sein ~ geschlossen** he has grown fond of her; **sein ~ an jdn/etw hängen** to commit oneself heart and soul to sb/sth; **jds ~ hängt an jdm/etw** sb is committed heart and soul to sb/sth; (*an Geld*) sb is preoccupied with sth; **die Dame seines ~ens** the lady of his dreams.

(d) (*liter: Mut*) heart, courage ◆ **sich** (*dat*) **ein ~ fassen** *or* **nehmen** to take heart; **sein ~ in beide Hände nehmen** to take one's courage in both hands; **ihm rutschte** *or* **fällt das ~ in die Hose(ntasche)** (*inf*) his heart sank.

(e) (*Inneres: von Salat, Stadt, Land*) heart.

(f) *pl* - (*Cards*) (*no pl: Farbe*) hearts *pl*; (*~karte*) heart.

(g) (*old: Kosewort*) dear (heart).

(h) (*Redewendungen*) **ein ~ und eine Seele sein** to be the best of friends; **alles, was das ~ begehrt** everything one's heart desires; **mir blutet das ~, mein ~ blutet** my heart bleeds (*auch iro*); **es zerreißt mir das ~** it breaks my heart; **jds ~ brechen/gewinnen/stehlen** to break/win/steal sb's heart; **gib deinem ~en einen Stoß!** go on!; **er hat das ~ auf dem** *or* **am rechten Fleck** his heart is in the right place; **mir lacht das ~ im Leibe** my heart leaps with joy; **das ~ auf der Zunge tragen** to speak one's mind; **jdm dreht sich das ~ im Leib um/jdm tut das ~ im Leibe weh** sb feels sick at heart; **es liegt mir am ~en** I am very concerned about it; **jdm etw ans ~ legen** to entrust sth to sb; **ich lege es dir ans ~, das zu tun** I (would) ask you particularly to do that; **etw auf dem ~en haben** to have sth on one's mind; **jdn/etw auf ~ und Nieren prüfen** to examine sb/sth very thoroughly; **ein Kind unter dem ~en tragen** (*Bibl, old*) to be with child (*old*); **eine schwere Last** *or* **eine Zentnerlast fiel ihr vom ~en** a heavy load was lifted from her mind; **von ~en** with all one's heart; **etw von ~en gern tun** to love doing sth; **jdn von ~en gern haben** to love sb dearly; **jdm von ganzem ~en danken** to thank sb with all one's heart; **von ~en kommend** heartfelt; **sich** (*dat*) **etw zu ~en nehmen** to take sth to heart.

herzählen *vt sep* to count.

Herz- *in cpds* (*Anat, Med*) cardiac; **h~allerliebst** *adj* (*old, hum*) most charming; **~allerliebste(r)** *mf decl as adj* (*old, hum*) darling, dearest; **~anfall** *m* heart attack; **~as** *nt* ace of hearts; **~attacke** *f* heart attack.

herzaubern *vt sep* to produce out of thin air.

Herz-: h~beklemmend *adj* oppressive; **~beklemmung** *f* **~beklemmungen bekommen** to feel as if one cannot breathe; **~beschwerden** *pl* heart trouble *sing*; **~beutel** *m* pericardium; **~beutelentzündung** *f* pericarditis; **h~bewegend** *adj* heart-rending; **~blatt** *nt* **(a)** (*Bot*) grass of Parnassus; **(b)** (*dated inf*) darling; **h~blättrig** *adj* heart-shaped; **~blut** *nt* (*poet*) lifeblood; **~bube** *m* jack *or* knave of hearts.

Herzchen *nt* little heart; (*inf: Kosewort*) (little) darling.

Herz-: ~chirurg *m* heart *or* cardiac surgeon; **~chirurgie** *f* heart *or* cardiac surgery; **~dame** *f* **(a)** (*Cards*) queen of hearts; **(b)** (*old, hum: Angebetete*) beloved.

herzeigen *vt sep* to show ◆ **zeig (mal) her!** let me see, let's see; **das kann man ~** that's worth showing off.

Herzeleid *nt* (*old*) heartache.

herzen *vt* (*dated*) to hug.

Herzens-: ~angelegenheit *f* (*dated*) affair of the heart, affaire de cœur; **~bedürfnis** *nt* (*dated*) **es ist mir ein ~bedürfnis** it is a matter dear to my heart; **~bildung** *f* (*geh*) nobleness of heart; **~brecher** *m* **-s, -** (*fig inf*) heart-breaker; **~ergießung** *f*, ⚠**~erguß** *m* (*dated, hum*) emotional outpourings *pl*; **~freude** *f* (*dated*) **es ist mir eine ~freude** it warms my heart; **~grund** *m* (*dated*) **aus tiefstem ~grund** from the very bottom of one's heart; **h~gut** *adj* good-hearted; **~güte** *f* good-heartedness; **~lust** *f* **nach ~lust** to one's heart's content; **~qual** *f* (*old*) *usu pl* great emotional torment *pl rare*; **~wunsch** *m* dearest wish.

Herz-: h~erfreuend *adj* heart-warming; **h~erfrischend** *adj* refreshing; **h~ergreifend** *adj* heart-rending; **h~erquickend** *adj* refreshing; **h~erwärmend** *adj* heart-warming; **h~erweichend** *adj* heart-rending; **~erweiterung** *f* cardiectasis (*spec*), dilation of the heart; **~fehler** *m* cardiac *or* heart defect; **~flattern** *nt* **-s,** *no pl* palpitations *pl* (of the heart); **~flimmern** *nt* **-s,** *no pl* heart flutter; (*Kammerflimmern*) (ventricular) fibrillation; **~flimmern haben** to have a heart flutter/to be in fibrillation; **ich habe ~flimmern** (*fig*) my heart misses *or* skips a beat; **h~förmig** *adj* heart-shaped; **~gegend** *f*, *no pl* cardiac region, area of the heart (*auch fig*); **~geräusche** *pl* heartbeats *pl*; **h~haft** *adj* **(a)** (*dated: mutig*) brave; **(b)** (*kräftig*) hearty; *Händedruck, Griff* firm; *Geschmack* strong; **h~haft gähnen** to yawn widely; **alle packten h~haft zu** everyone got stuck in (*inf*); **das schmeckt h~haft** that's tasty; **(c)** (*nahrhaft*) *Essen* substantial.

herziehen *sep irreg* 1 *vt* to draw *or* pull closer *or* nearer ◆ **jdn/etw hinter sich** (*dat*) **~** to pull *or* drag sb/sth (along) behind one.

2 *vi* **(a)** *aux sein* (*herankommen*) to approach ◆ **hinter/neben/vor jdm ~** to march along behind/beside/in front of sb.

(b) *aux sein* (*umziehen*) to move here.

(c) *aux sein* **über jdn/etw ~** (*inf*) to knock sb/sth (*inf*), to pull sb/sth to pieces (*inf*).

herzig *adj* delightful, sweet.

Herz-: ~infarkt *m* heart attack, cardiac infarction (*spec*); **~insuffizienz** *f* cardiac insufficiency; **~-Jesu-Bild** *nt* Sacred Heart painting; **~kammer** *f* ventricle; **~kirsche** *f* (bigarreau) cherry; **~klappe** *f* cardiac *or* heart valve; **~klappenentzündung** *f* endocarditis; **~klappenfehler** *m* valvular heart defect; **~klopfen** *nt* **-s,** *no pl* **ich hatte/bekam ~klopfen** my heart was/started pounding; (*durch Kaffee*) I had/got palpitations; **mit ~klopfen** with a pounding heart, with one's heart in one's mouth; **~krampf** *m* heart spasm; **h~krank** *adj* suffering from a heart condition; **h~krank sein/werden** to have/get a heart condition; **~krankheit** *f* heart condition; **~kranzgefäß** *nt usu pl* coronary (blood) vessel; **~leiden** *nt siehe* **~krankheit**; **h~leidend** *adj* with a heart condition.

➤ **herzlich** *adj Empfang, Freundschaft* warm; *Wesen, Mensch* warm(-hearted); *Lachen* hearty; *Bitte* sincere ◆ **~e Grüße an Ihre Frau Gemahlin** kind(est) regards *or* remember me to your wife; **mit ~en Grüßen** kind regards; **~en Dank!** many thanks, thank you very much indeed; **~es Beileid!** you have my sincere *or* heartfelt sympathy *or* condolences *pl*; **zu jdm ~ sein** to be kind to sb; **eine ~e Bitte an jdn richten** to make a cordial request to sb; **~ gern!** with the greatest of pleasure!; **ich würde ~ gern einmal wieder die Stätten meiner Kindheit besuchen** I should so much like to visit my childhood haunts again; **~ schlecht** pretty awful; **~ wenig** precious little; **ich habe es ~ satt** I am thoroughly *or* utterly sick of it, I'm sick and tired of it.

Herzlichkeit *f siehe adj* warmth; warm(-hearted)ness; heartiness; sincerity.

Herz-: ~liebchen *nt* (*old*) sweetheart, dearest; **~liebste(r)** *mf* (*old*) *siehe* **~allerliebste(r)**; **~linie** *f* heart line; **h~los** *adj* heartless, unfeeling; **~losigkeit** *f* heartlessness *no pl*; **~-Lungen-Maschine** *f* heart-lung machine; **~massage** *f* heart massage; **~mittel** *nt* cardiac drug; **~muschel** *f* (*Zool*) cockle; **~muskel** *m* heart *or* cardiac muscle.

Herzog ['hɛrtso:k] *m* **-s, ¨e** *or* (*rare*) **-e** duke ◆ **Otto ~ von Stein** Otto Duke of Stein, Duke Otto of Stein.

Herzogin ['hɛrtso:gɪn] *f* duchess.

herzoglich ['hɛrtso:klɪç] *adj attr* ducal.

Herzogswürde *f* (*Rang*) dignity *or* rank of a duke; (*Titel*) dukedom ◆ **der König verlieh ihm die ~** the king bestowed a dukedom *or* the rank of duke upon him.

Herzogtum *nt* dukedom, duchy.

Herz-: ~patient *m* heart *or* cardiac patient; **~rhythmus** *m* heart *or* cardiac rhythm; **~rhythmusstörung** *f* palpitations *pl*, cardiac disrhythmia (*spec*); **~schlag** *m* **(a)** (*einzelner*) heartbeat; **einen ~schlag lang** (*liter*) for one fleeting second; **mit jedem ~schlag** (*liter*) with every beat of my/his *etc* heart; **(b)** (*~tätigkeit*) heart *or* pulse rate; (*fig liter*) throbbing *or* pulsating life; **(c)** (*~stillstand*) heart attack, heart failure *no indef art, no pl*; **~schmerz** *m* stabbing pain in the chest; **~schrittmacher** *m* pacemaker; **~schwäche** *f* a weak heart; **wegen einer vorübergehenden ~schwäche** because my/his *etc* heart faltered for a moment; **an ~schwäche leiden** to have a weak heart; **h~stärkend** *adj* cardiotonic (*spec*); **h~stärkend wirken** to stimulate the heart; **ein h~stärkendes Mittel** a cardiac stimulant, a cardiotonic (*spec*); **~stich** *m usu pl* stabbing pain in the chest; **~stillstand** *m* cardiac arrest; **~stolpern** *nt* irregular heartbeat; **~stück** *nt* (*fig geh*) heart, core; **~tätigkeit** *f* heart *or* cardiac activity; **~tod** *m* death from heart disease.

herzu- *siehe* **herbei-**.

Herzug *m* (*inf*) **(a)** (*Rail*) downtrain. **(b)** (*Umzug*) **seit meinem ~** since I came here, since coming here.

Herz-: ~verfettung *f* fatty degeneration of the heart; **h~zerreißend** *adj* heartbreaking, heart-rending; **h~zerreißend weinen** to weep distressingly.

Hesekiel [he'ze:kie:l, -iɛl] *m* - Ezekiel.

Hesse *m* **-n, -n, Hessin** *f* Hessian.

Hessen *nt* **-s** Hesse.

hessisch *adj* Hessian.

Hetäre *f* **-, -n** (*Hist*) hetaira; (*fig geh: Dirne*) courtesan.

hetero *adj pred* (*inf*) hetero (*inf*), straight (*sl*).

Hetero *m* **-s, -s** (*inf*) hetero (*inf*).

Hetero-: h~dox *adj* heterodox; **~doxie** *f* heterodoxy; **h~gen** *adj* (*geh*) heterogeneous; **~genität** *f* (*geh*) heterogeneity; **h~nom** *adj* (*geh*) heteronomous; **~nomie** *f* (*geh*) heteronomy; **~sexualität** *f* heterosexuality; **h~sexuell** *adj* heterosexual; **~sexuelle(r)** *mf decl as adj* heterosexual.

Hethiter(in *f*) *m* **-s, -** Hittite.

hethitisch *adj* Hittite.

Hetz *f* **-,** (*rare*) **-en** (*Aus inf*) laugh (*inf*) ◆ **aus** *or* **zur ~** for a laugh.

Hetz- (*pej*) *in cpds* rabble-rousing (*pej*).

Hetze *f* **-, -n (a)** (*Hunt*) *siehe* **Hetzjagd**. **(b)** *no pl* (*Hast*) (mad) rush, hurry; (*Getriebensein*) hustle and bustle, (mad) rush. **(c)** *no pl* (*pej*) (*Aufreizung*) rabble-rousing propaganda.

hetzen 1 *vt* **(a)** (*lit, fig: jagen*) to hound ◆ **die Hunde auf jdn/etw ~** to set the dogs on(to) sb/sth; *siehe* **Hund, gehetzt**.

(b) (*inf: antreiben*) to rush, to hurry.

⚠: for details of spelling reform, see supplement

➤ SPRACHE AKTIV: **herzlich** → 48.2, 49, 50.6, 51.1, 51.2, 51.3, 52.1, 52.2, 52.3

[2] *vr* to hurry oneself, to rush oneself.
[3] *vi* **(a)** (*sich beeilen*) to rush ◆ **hetz nicht so** don't be in such a rush.
(b) *aux sein* (*eilen*) to tear, to race, to dash ◆ **ich bin ganz schön gehetzt, um ...** I rushed like mad to ... (*inf*), I had an awful rush to ...; **hetz nicht so** don't go so fast.
(c) (*pej: Haß schüren*) to agitate, to stir up hatred; (*inf: lästern*) to say malicious things ◆ **gegen jdn/etw ~** to agitate against *or* stir up hatred against sb/sth; **er hetzt immer gegen seinen Onkel** he's always running his uncle down *or* saying malicious things about his uncle; **sie hat so lange gehetzt, bis er ...** she kept on being nasty until he finally ...; **zum Krieg ~** to agitate for war; **gegen Minderheiten ~** to stir up hatred against minorities; **bei jdm gegen jdn ~** to try to turn *or* set sb against sb.
Hetzer(in *f*) *m* **-s, -** rabble-rouser, malicious agitator.
Hetzerei *f* **(a)** *no pl* (*Hast*) *siehe* **Hetze (b)**. **(b)** (*das Haßschüren*) rabble-rousing, malicious agitation, mischief-making ◆ **~ zum Krieg** warmongering. **(c)** (*hetzerische Äußerung*) rabble-rousing attack (*gegen* on).
hetzerisch *adj* rabble-rousing *attr*, virulent.
Hetz-: h~halber *adv* (*Aus inf*) for a laugh (*inf*); **~hund** *m* hound, hunting dog; **~jagd** *f* **(a)** (*lit, fig*) hounding (*auf +acc* of); **(b)** (*fig: Hast*) rush, hurry; **es war die reinste ~jagd** it was one mad rush; **die ~jagd der Kinder durch den Garten** the children tearing *or* racing through the garden.
Hetzkampagne *f* malicious campaign.
Heu *nt* **-(e)s,** *no pl* hay ◆ **Geld wie ~ haben** (*inf*) to have pots *or* oodles of money (*inf*).
Heu-: ~boden *m*, **~bühne** (*Sw*) *f* hayloft; **~bündel** *nt* bundle *or* bale of hay.
Heuchelei *f* hypocrisy ◆ **spar dir deine ~en** cut out the hypocrisy *or* cant.
heucheln [1] *vi* to be a hypocrite.
[2] *vt Zuneigung, Mitleid etc* to feign, to simulate.
Heuchler(in *f*) *m* **-s, -** hypocrite.
heuchlerisch *adj* hypocritical ◆ **~es Gerede** hypocritical talk, cant.
heuen *vi* (*dial*) to make hay ◆ **das H~** haymaking.
heuer *adv* (*S Ger, Aus, Sw*) this year.
Heuer *f* **-, -n** (*Naut*) pay.
Heuer-: ~büro *nt* (seamen's) employment office; **~lohn** *m siehe* **Heuer**.
heuern *vt* to sign on, to engage, to hire.
Heu|ernte *f* hay harvest; (*Ertrag*) hay crop.
Heuervertrag *m* contract of employment (*of seaman*).
Heu-: ~forke (*N Ger*), **~gabel** *f* pitchfork, hayfork; **~haufen** *m* haystack, hayrick.
Heulboje *f* (*Naut*) whistling buoy; (*pej inf: Popsinger*) groaner (*inf*); (*Kind*) wailing Willie (*sl*).
heulen *vi* **(a)** (*inf: weinen*) to howl, to bawl (*inf*), to wail; (*vor Schmerz*) to scream; (*vor Wut*) to howl ◆ **ich hätte ~ können** I could have cried; **es ist einfach zum H~** it's enough to make you weep; *siehe* **Elend**. **(b)** (*Meer, Flugzeug, Motor*) to roar; (*Wind auch, Tiere*) to howl; (*Sirene*) to wail.
Heulen *nt* **-s,** *no pl siehe vi* **(a)** howling, bawling, wailing ◆ **~ und Zähneklappern** (*Bibl*) wailing and gnashing of teeth. **(b)** roaring; howling; wailing.
Heuler *m* **-s, - (a)** (*von Motor*) roar. **(b)** (*Feuerwerkskörper*) screamer. **(c)** (*sl*) **das ist ja der letzte ~** that's bloody incredible (*sl*).
Heulerei *f* (*inf*) constant bawling (*inf*).
Heul-: ~krampf *m* (*inf*) fit of blubbering (*inf*); **~peter** *m*, **~suse** *f* cry-baby (*inf*); **~ton** *m* (*von Sirene*) wail.
Heu-: ~machen *nt* **-s,** *no pl*, **~mahd** *f* haymaking; **~mond** (*old liter*), **~monat** (*old*) *m* July; **~reiter, ~reuter** *m* rickstand.
heurig *adj attr* (*S Ger, Aus*) this year's ◆ **der ~e Wein** this year's wine.
Heurige *pl decl as adj* (*esp Aus*) early potatoes *pl*.
Heurige(r) *m decl as adj* (*esp Aus*) new wine.
Heuristik *f* (*Philos*) heuristics *sing*.
heuristisch *adj* (*Philos*) heuristic.
Heu-: ~schnupfen *m* hay fever; **~schober** *m* barn; **~schrecke** *f* **-, -n** grasshopper; (*in heißen Ländern*) locust; **~speicher, ~stadel** *m* (*S Ger, Aus, Sw*) barn.
heute, heut (*inf*) *adv* **(a)** (*an diesem Tag*) today ◆ **~ morgen/abend** this morning/this evening *or* tonight; **~ früh** this morning; **~ nacht** tonight; **„~ geschlossen"** "closed today"; **~ noch** (*heutzutage*) still ... today, even today; **ich muß ~ noch zur Bank** I must go to the bank today; **bis ~** (*bisher, heute immer noch*) to this day; **bis ~ nicht** (*noch nicht*) not ... to this day; **von ~ ab** *or* **an, ab ~** from today (on), from this day (forth) (*liter*); **~ in einer Woche** a week today *or* from now, today week; **~ vor acht Tagen** a week ago today; **~ in einem Jahr** a year from today *or* now, a year hence (*geh*); **Milch/die Zeitung von ~** today's milk/paper; **~ mir, morgen dir** (*Prov*) (it's my turn today,) your turn may come tomorrow; **lieber ~ als morgen** the sooner the better; **etw von ~ auf morgen verschieben** to put sth off until tomorrow; **von ~ auf morgen** (*fig: rasch, plötzlich*) overnight, from one day to the next.
(b) (*in der gegenwärtigen Zeit*) nowadays, these days, today ◆ **das H~** the present, today; **das Italien/der Mensch von ~** present-day *or* contemporary *or* modern Italy/man; **der Bauer/die Frau/die Stadt von ~** the farmer/woman/town of today, today's farmers/women/towns; **die Jugend von ~** the young people of today, modern youth.
heutig *adj attr* today's; (*von heute auch*) the day's; (*gegenwärtig*) modern, contemporary ◆ **der ~e Tag** today; **am ~en Abend** this evening; **anläßlich Ihres ~en Geburtstags** to mark your birthday today; **unser ~es Schreiben** (*Comm*) our letter of today('s date); **die ~e Zeitung** today's paper; **bis zum ~en Tage** to date, to this day; **aus ~er Sicht** from today's standpoint, from a modern *or* contemporary point of view; **wir H~en** (*geh*) we people of today, we modern men and women.
heutigentags *adv* (*dated*) *siehe* **heute (b)**.
heutzutage *adv* nowadays, these days, today.
Heu-: ~wagen *m* haycart, haywagon; **~wender** *m* **-s, -** tedder.
Hexa- [hɛksa-] *in cpds* hexa-; **h~dezimal** *adj* (*Comput*) hexadecimal, hex; **~eder** *nt* **-s, -** hexahedron; **~gon** *nt* **-s, -e** hexagon; **h~gonal** *adj* hexagonal; **~gramm** *nt* hexagram; **~meter** [hɛ'ksa:metɐ] *m* hexameter.
Hexe *f* **-, -n** witch; (*inf: altes Weib*) old hag *or* crone ◆ **diese kleine ~!** that little minx *or* hussy!
hexen [1] *vi* to practise witchcraft ◆ **er kann ~** he knows (how to work) black magic; **ich kann doch nicht ~** (*inf*) I can't work miracles, I'm not a magician.
[2] *vt* to conjure up ◆ **~, daß ...** to cast a (magic) spell so that ...
Hexen-: ~einmaleins *nt* magic square; **~glaube** *m* belief in witches; **~haus** *nt* enchanted house; **~häuschen** *nt* gingerbread house; **~jagd** *f* witch-hunt; **~kessel** *m* (*fig*) pandemonium *no art*, bedlam *no art*; **ein wahrer ~kessel** absolute pandemonium *or* bedlam; **~kunst** *f* witchcraft, sorcery, witchery; **~meister** *m* sorcerer; **~probe** *f* (*Hist*) witches' ordeal; ⚠**~prozeß** *m* witch trial; **~ring** *m* fairy ring; **~sabbat** *m* witches' sabbath; (*fig*) bedlam *no art*, pandemonium *no art*; ⚠**~schuß** *m* (*Med*) lumbago; **~verbrennung** *f* burning of a witch/witches; **~verfolgung** *f* witch-hunt; **~wahn** *m* obsessive belief in witches; **~werk** *nt* sorcery, witchcraft, witchery.
Hexer *m* **-s, -** sorcerer.
Hexerei *f* witchcraft *no pl*, sorcery, witchery *no pl*; (*von Zaubertricks*) magic *no pl*.
HG *abbr of* **Handelsgesellschaft**.
hg. *abbr of* **herausgegeben** ed.
Hiatus *m* **-, -** hiatus.
hibbelig *adj* (*dial*) jittery.
Hibiskus *m* **-, Hibisken** hibiscus.
hick *interj* hic.
Hickhack *m or nt* **-s, -s** squabbling *no pl*.
hie *adv* (*old*) here ◆ **~ und da** (*manchmal*) (every) now and then, every so often, (every) once in a while; (*stellenweise*) here and there; **~ ... ~** *or* **da** on the one side ... on the other (side).
hieb (*geh*) *pret of* **hauen**.
Hieb *m* **-(e)s, -e (a)** (*Schlag*) stroke, blow; (*Faust~*) blow; (*Peitschen~*) lash, crack; (*Fechten*) cut ◆ **auf den ersten ~ fällt kein Baum** (*prov*) Rome wasn't built in a day (*Prov*); **auf einen ~** (*inf*) in one go; **ein Glas auf einen ~ leer trinken** (*inf*) to down a glass in one (*inf*).
(b) (*~wunde*) gash, slash.
(c) ~e *pl* (*dated: Prügel*) hiding, thrashing, beating ◆ **~e bekommen** to get a hiding *or* thrashing *or* beating; **gleich gibt es** *or* **setzt es ~e!** you'll get a (good) hiding in a minute.
(d) (*fig*) dig, cutting remark ◆ **der ~ saß** that (dig) went *or* struck home; **~e bekommen** to be on the receiving end of some cutting remarks.
Hieb-: h~fest *adj*: **hieb- und stichfest** (*fig*) watertight; **~waffe** *f* cutting weapon; **~wunde** *f* gash, slash.
hielt *pret of* **halten**.
hienieden *adv* (*old liter*) here below.
hier *adv* **(a)** (*räumlich*) here; (*in diesem Land auch*) (here) in this country; (*~ am Ort auch*) locally ◆ **das Haus ~** this house; **dieser ~** this one (here); **~!** (*beim Appell*) present!, here!; **~ und da** here and there; **Herr Direktor ~, Herr Direktor da** (*iro*) yes sir, yes sir, three bags full sir; **~ draußen/drinnen** out/in here; **~ entlang** along here; **~ herum** hereabouts, around here; **~ hinein** in here; **~ oben/unten** up/down here; **~ vorn/hinten** in front/at the back here, here in front/at the back; **er ist von ~** he's a local (man), he comes from (a)round here; **er ist nicht von ~** he's a stranger here, he's not a local; **Tag Klaus, ~ (spricht) Hans** (*Telec*) hello Klaus, Hans here; **~ spricht Dr. Müller** (*Telec*) this is Dr Müller (speaking); **von ~ ab** from here (on *or* onwards); **von ~ aus** from here; **~ sehen Sie ...** here you (can) see ...; **~ und heute** (*geh*) here and now; **das H~ und Heute** (*geh*) the here and now; **er ist ein bißchen ~** (*sl*) he's got a screw loose (*inf*).
(b) (*zeitlich*) now ◆ **~ und da** (every) now and then, every so often; **von ~ ab** *or* **an** from now on, henceforth (*form*).
(c) (*fig*) here ◆ **das steht mir bis ~** (*sl*) I'm fed up to here (*inf*) *or* to the back teeth (*inf*) (with it), I've had it up to here (*inf*); **~ versagte ihm die Stimme** here *or* at this point *or* at this juncture his voice failed him.
hieran *adv* **(a)** (*lit*) here. **(b)** (*fig*) **wenn ich ~ denke** when I think of *or* about this; **er erinnert sich ~** he remembers this; **~ erkenne ich es** I recognize it by this; **~ kann es keinen Zweifel geben** there can be no doubt about that.
Hierarchie *f* hierarchy.
hierarchisch *adj* hierarchic(al).
hier-: ~auf *adv* **(a)** (*lit*) (on) here, on this; **(b)** (*fig*) on this; (*daraufhin*) hereupon; **er setzte sich, und ~auf ...** he sat down and then ...; **~aufhin** *adv* hereupon; **und ~aufhin ...** and then ...; **~aus** *adv* **(a)** (*lit*) out of/from this, from here; **~aus ist das Geld gestohlen worden** the money was stolen from here; **(b)** (*fig*) from this; **~aus folgt/geht hervor, daß ...** from this it follows that ..., hence (it follows that) ...; ⚠**~behalten** *vt sep irreg* **jdn/etw ~behalten** to keep sb/sth here; **~bei** *adv* **(a)** (*lit*) (*währenddessen*) doing this; **(b)** (*fig*) (*bei dieser Gelegenheit*) on this occasion; (*in diesem Zusammenhang*) in this connection; ⚠**~bleiben** *vi sep irreg aux sein* to stay here; **~geblieben!** stop!; **~durch** *adv* **(a)** (*lit*) through here; **(b)** (*fig*) through this; **ich lasse**

mich ~durch nicht ärgern I shan't let this annoy me; ~durch teilen wir Ihnen mit, daß ... we hereby inform you that ...; ~ein *adv* (a) (*lit*) in(to) this, in here; (b) (*fig*) in/to this; ~ein mußt du dich fügen you will just have to get used to the idea; ~für *adv* for this; ~gegen *adv* (*lit, fig*) against this; ~her *adv* here; (komm) ~her! come here *or* hither (*liter, old*); bis ~her (*örtlich*) up to here; (*zeitlich*) up to now, so far; mir steht's bis ~her (*sl*) I'm fed up to here *or* to the back teeth (*inf*); *siehe* bis²; ~herauf *adv* up here; bis ~herauf up to here.

⚠**hierher-:** ~bemühen* *sep* [1] *vt jdn* to ask *or* trouble to come (here); [2] *vr* to take the trouble to come (here); ~bitten *vt sep irreg* to ask to come (here); ~blicken *vi sep* to look this way *or* over here; ~bringen *vt sep irreg* to bring (over) here; ~fahren *sep irreg* [1] *vi aux sein* to come here; [2] *vt etw* to drive here; *jdn* to drive (here), to give a lift *or* ride (here); ~führen *sep* [1] *vt* to lead here; [2] *vi* (*Weg etc*) to lead here, to come this way; ~gehören* *vi sep* to belong here; (*fig: relevant sein*) to be relevant; nicht ~gehörende Bemerkungen irrelevant remarks; ~holen *vt sep* to bring here; ~kommen *vi sep irreg aux sein* to come here; ~laufen *vi sep irreg aux sein* to run here; ~gelaufen kommen to come running up; ~legen *sep* [1] *vt* to lay (down) here; [2] *vr* to lie (down) here, to lay oneself (down) here; ~locken *vt sep* to entice *or* lure here; ~schaffen *vt sep* to bring here; ~schicken *vt sep* to send here; ~setzen *sep* [1] *vt* to put here; [2] *vr* to sit (down) here; ~stellen *sep* [1] *vt* to put here; [2] *vr* to stand here; ~tragen *vt sep irreg* to carry here.

hierherum *adv* around *or* round (*esp Brit*) here; (*in diese Richtung*) this way around; (*inf: ungefähr hier*) hereabouts, around here (somewhere).

⚠**hierher-:** ~wagen *vr sep* to dare to come here; ~ziehen *sep irreg* [1] *vt* (*fig*) to bring here; [2] *vi aux sein* to come here.

hier-: ~hin *adv* here; ~hin und dorthin here and there, hither and thither (*liter*); bis ~hin up to here; ~hinab *adv* down here; ~hinauf *adv* up here; ~hinaus *adv* out here; ~hinein *adv* in here; ~hinter *adv* behind here; ~hinunter *adv* down here; ~in *adv* (*lit, fig*) in this; ⚠~lassen *vt sep irreg* to leave here; ~mit *adv* with this, herewith (*obs, form*); ~mit ist der Fall erledigt this settles the matter; ~mit bin ich einverstanden I agree to this; ~mit erkläre ich ... (*form*) I hereby declare ... (*form*); ~mit bestätigen wir den Eingang Ihres Briefes we herewith *or* hereby acknowledge receipt of your letter; ~mit wird bescheinigt, daß ... this is to certify that ...; ~nach *adv* after this, afterwards; (*daraus folgend*) according to this; ~neben *adv* beside this, next to this.

Hieroglyphe [hiero'gly:fə] *f* -, -n hieroglyph(ic); (*fig hum*) hieroglyphic.

hier-: ~orts *adv* (*geh*) here; ⚠~sein *vi sep irreg aux sein* (*Zusammenschreibung nur bei infin und ptp*) to be here; während meines H~seins during my stay; was ist der Zweck seines H~seins? what is the purpose of his being here *or* his presence?; ~selbst *adv* (*old*) in this very place, even here (*old*); ~über *adv* (a) (*lit*) over this *or* here; (*oberhalb dieser Stelle*) over it; (b) (*fig*) about this; (*geh: währenddessen*) in the midst of it; ~über ärgere ich mich this makes me angry; ~um *adv* (a) (*lit*) (a)round this *or* here; (b) (*fig*) about *or* concerning this; ~um handelt es sich nicht this isn't the issue; ~unter *adv* (a) (*lit*) under *or* beneath this *or* here; (b) (*fig*) by this *or* that; (*in dieser Kategorie*) among these; ~unter fallen auch die Sonntage this includes Sundays; ~von *adv* (a) (*lit*) (*örtlich*) from here *or* this; (*von diesem etc*) from this; (*aus diesem Material*) out of this; (b) ~von habe ich nichts gewußt I knew nothing of *or* about this; ~von abgesehen apart from this; ~von kannst du nichts haben you can't have any of this; ~vor *adv* (a) (*lit*) in front of this *or* here; (b) (*fig*) ~vor ekele/fürchte ich mich it revolts/frightens me; ~vor möge uns Gott bewahren may God preserve us from this; ~vor hat er großen Respekt he has a great respect for this; ~zu *adv* (a) (*dafür*) for this; (*dazu*) with this; (b) (*außerdem*) in addition to this, moreover; (c) (*zu diesem Punkt*) about this; ~zu gehören auch die Katzen this also includes the cats; ~zu habe ich etwas Wichtiges zu sagen I have something important to say on *or* about *or* to this; ~zu wünsche ich Ihnen viel Glück I wish you luck in this; vgl ~zu S. 370 cf p 370; ⚠~zulande *adv* in these parts; ~zwischen *adv* between these.

hiesig *adj attr* local ♦ die ~en Verhältnisse local conditions, conditions here; meine ~en Verwandten my relatives here; er ist kein H~er he is not a local (man), he's not from these parts.

hieß *pret of* heißen.

hieven ['hi:fn, 'hi:vn] *vt* (*esp Naut*) to heave.

Hi-Fi-Anlage ['haifi-] *f* hi-fi set *or* system.

Hifthorn *nt* (*Hunt*) hunting horn.

high [haɪ] *adj pred* (*sl*) high (*sl*).

highjacken ['haidʒɛkn] *vt insep* (*inf*) to hi(gh)jack.

Highjacker ['haidʒɛkɐ] *m* -s, - *siehe* Hijacker.

Highlife ['hailaif] *nt* -s, *no pl* high life ♦ ~ machen (*inf*) to live it up (*inf*).

High Tech [haɪ'tek] *nt* - -, *no pl* high tech, hi tech.

High-Tech- *in cpds* high-tech.

hihi *interj* heehee, teehee.

Hijacker ['haidʒɛkɐ] *m* -s, - hi(gh)jacker.

hilb *adj* (*Sw*) sheltered, protected from the wind.

Hildebrandslied *nt* (*Liter*) Lay of Hildebrand.

hilf *imper sing of* helfen.

Hilfe *f* -, -n (a) *no pl* help; (*finanzielle*) aid, assistance, help; (*für Notleidende*) aid, relief ♦ zu ~! help!; um ~ rufen/schreien to call/shout for help; jdm zu ~ kommen to come to sb's aid *or* assistance *or* rescue; jdn um ~ bitten to ask sb for help *or* assistance; jdm ~ leisten to help sb; bei jdm ~ suchen to seek sb's help *or* assistance; mit ~ with the help *or* aid (*gen* of); ohne ~ without help *or* assistance; (*selbständig*) unaided; etw zu ~ nehmen to use sth; ohne fremde ~ gehen to walk unaided; jds Gedächtnis (*dat*) zu ~ kommen to jog sb's memory; *siehe* erste(r, s).
(b) (*Hilfsmittel, ~stellung*) aid; (*Haushalts~*) (domestic) help ♦ ~n geben (*beim Turnen*) to give support; (*beim Reiten*) to give aids; du bist mir eine schöne ~! (*iro*) a fine help *you* are (to me)! (*iro*).

Hilfe-: h~flehend *adj* imploring, beseeching; ~leistung *f* aid, assistance; unterlassene ~leistung (*Jur*) denial of assistance; ~ruf *m* call for help; ~schrei *m* cry *or* shout for help, cry of "help"; ~stellung *f* (*Sport, fig*) support; jdm ~stellung geben to give sb support; (*fig auch*) to back sb up; ⚠h~suchend *adj Mensch* seeking help; *Blick* imploring, beseeching; täglich wenden sich Hunderte h~suchend an diese Organisation hundreds turn every day to this charity seeking help; die ~suchenden those seeking help.

Hilf-: h~los *adj* helpless; (*schutzlos auch*) defenceless; (*ratlos auch*) clueless (*inf*); ~losigkeit *f siehe adj* helplessness; defenceless; cluelessness (*inf*); h~reich *adj* helpful; (*nützlich auch*) useful; eine h~reiche Hand a helping hand; er reichte ihr h~reich seine Hand he held out a helping hand to her.

Hilfs-: ~aktion *f* relief action; ~arbeiter *m* labourer; (*in Fabrik*) unskilled worker; ~assistent *m* (*Univ*) ≃ tutorial assistant; h~bedürftig *adj* in need of help; (*notleidend*) needy, in need *pred*; die ~bedürftigen the needy, those in need; ~bedürftigkeit *f* need(iness); h~bereit *adj* helpful, ready to help *pred*; ~bereitschaft *f* helpfulness, readiness to help; ~dienst *m* emergency service; (*bei Katastrophenfall*) (emergency) relief service; (*Kfz-~*) emergency *or* (emergency) breakdown service; ~feuerwehr *f* auxiliary fire service; ~fonds *m* relief fund; ~geistliche(r) *m* curate; ~gelder *pl* back-up funds *pl*; ~komitee *nt* relief action committee; ~konstruktion *f* (*Math*) rough diagram; (*fig*) temporary measure; ~kraft *f* assistant, helper; (*Aushilfe*) temporary worker; wissenschaftliche/fachliche ~kraft research/technical assistant; ~lehrer *m* supply teacher; ~linie *f* (*Math*) auxiliary line; ~maßnahme *f* relief action *no pl*; (*zur Rettung*) rescue action *no pl*; ~mittel *nt* aid; ~motor *m* (*Aut*) auxiliary engine; Fahrrad mit ~motor moped, motor-assisted bicycle; ~organisation *f* relief organization; ~personal *nt* auxiliary staff; (*Aushilfspersonal*) temporary staff *or* help; ~polizei *f* auxiliary police; ~polizist *m* auxiliary policeman; ~prediger, ~priester *m* curate; ~programm *nt* relief *or* aid programme; ~quelle *f* (a) (*Geldquelle*) source of money, pecuniary *or* financial (re)sources *pl*; (b) (*für wissenschaftliche Arbeit*) source; ~ruder *nt* (*Aviat*) auxiliary rudder; ~schiff *nt* auxiliary vessel; ~schule *f* (*dated*) school for backward children; ~schüler *m* (*dated*) pupil at/from a school for backward children; ~schullehrer *m* (*dated*) teacher at a school for backward children; ~schwester *f* auxiliary (nurse); ~sheriff *m* assistant *or* deputy sheriff; ~sprache *f* auxiliary language; ~triebwerk *nt* auxiliary engine; ~trupp *m* group of helpers; ~truppe *f* (*Mil*) auxiliary troops *pl*; (*Verstärkung*) reinforcements *pl*; (*Pol pej*) back-up army *or* boys *pl*; ~verb *nt* auxiliary verb; ~werk *nt* relief organization; h~willig *adj* willing to help *pred*; ~willige(r) *mf decl as adj* voluntary helper; ~wissenschaft *f* (*gen* to) complementary science; (*Geisteswissenschaft*) complementary subject; ~zeitwort *nt siehe* ~verb.

Himalaja *m* -(s) der ~ the Himalayas *pl*.

Himbeere *f* raspberry.

Himbeer-: ~eis *nt* raspberry ice(-cream); ~geist *m, no pl* (white) raspberry brandy; h~rot *adj* raspberry-coloured; ~saft *m* raspberry juice; ~strauch *m* raspberry bush.

Himmel *m* -s, (*poet*) - (a) sky ♦ am ~ in the sky; unter dem ~ Spaniens, unter spanischem ~ under *or* beneath a Spanish sky; zwischen ~ und Erde in midair; in den ~ ragen to tower (up) into the sky; jdn/etw in den ~ (er)heben *or* loben *or* rühmen to praise sb/sth to the skies; jdm hängt der ~ voller Geigen everything in the garden is lovely for sb; gute Lehrer fallen nicht vom ~ good teachers don't grow on trees; der Frieden fällt nicht einfach vom ~, sondern ... peace doesn't just fall out of the blue, but ...; eher stürzt der ~ ein, als daß ... (*geh*) the skies will fall before ... (*liter*).
(b) (*Rel: ~reich*) heaven ♦ im ~ in heaven; den Blick gen ~ richten (*liter*) to look heavenward(s), to raise one's eyes towards heaven; in den ~ kommen to go to heaven; zum *or* in den ~ auffahren, gen ~ fahren to ascend into heaven; der Sohn des ~s (*Kaiser von China*) the Celestial Emperor; der ~ auf Erden heaven on earth; dem ~ sei Dank (*old*) thank God *or* Heaven(s); der ~ ist *or* sei mein Zeuge (*old*) as Heaven *or* God is my witness; (das) weiß der ~! (*inf*) God *or* Heaven (only) knows; der ~ bewahre mich davor! (*old*) may Heaven (*or* God) preserve me; das schreit zum ~ it's a scandal; es stinkt zum ~ (*inf*) it stinks to high heaven (*inf*); der ~ verhüte (*old*) Heaven *or* God forbid; Gott im ~! good Heavens!; (ach) du lieber ~! (*inf*) good Heavens!, good(ness) gracious!; ~ (noch mal)! (*inf*) good God!, hang it all! (*inf*); um(s) ~s willen (*inf*) for Heaven's *or* goodness sake (*inf*); ~, Arsch und Zwirn (*sl*) *or* Wolkenbruch (*sl*) bloody hell! (*Brit sl*), Christ Almighty! (*sl*).
(c) (*Bett~ etc*) canopy; (*im Auto*) roof.

Himmel-: h~an *adv* (*poet*) heavenward(s); h~angst *adj pred* mir wurde h~angst I was scared to death; ~bett *nt* four-poster (bed); h~blau *adj* sky-blue, azure (*liter*); ~donnerwetter *interj* (*sl*) damn it (*sl*); ~donnerwetter noch (ein)mal! damn and blast it! (*sl*).

Himmelfahrt *f* (a) (*Rel*) Christi ~ the Ascension of Christ; Mariä ~ the Assumption of the Virgin Mary. (b) (*no art: Feiertag*) Ascension Day.

Himmelfahrts-: ~kommando *nt* (*Mil inf*) suicide squad *or* (*Unternehmen*) mission; ~nase *f* (*hum inf*) turned-up *or* snub nose; ~tag *m* der/am ~tag Ascension Day/on Ascension Day.

Himmel-: ~herrgott *interj* (*sl*) damn (it) (*sl*), bloody hell (*Brit sl*); ~herrgott

⚠: for details of spelling reform, see supplement

noch (ein)mal! damn and blast! (*sl*); **~herrgottsakra** *interj* (*S Ger, Aus*) damn (it) (*sl*), bloody hell (*Brit sl*); **h~hoch** [1] *adj* sky-high; [2] *adv* high into the sky; **h~hoch jauchzend, zu Tode betrübt** up one minute and down the next; **~hund** *m* (*pej*) scoundrel, cur (*pej*); (*inf: Draufgänger*) clever bastard (*sl*); **~reich** *nt, no pl* (*Rel*) Kingdom of Heaven; **ins ~reich eingehen** *or* **kommen** to enter the Kingdom of Heaven; **ein ~reich für ...** I'd give anything *or* my right arm for ...

Himmels-: ~achse *f* celestial axis; **~äquator** *m* celestial equator, equinoctial line *or* circle; **~bahn** *f* (*liter*) celestial path *or* orbit; **~braut** *f* (*liter*) bride of Christ (*liter*).

Himmel-: ~schlüssel *m or nt siehe* **Himmelsschlüssel**; **h~schreiend** *adj Unrecht* outrageous, scandalous; *Unkenntnis, Verhältnisse* appalling; *Unsinn* utter *attr*; *Schande* crying *attr.*

Himmels-: ~erscheinung *f* celestial phenomenon; **~feste** *f* (*liter*) firmament (*liter*); **~fürst** *m* (*Rel, liter*) King of Heaven; **~gabe** *f* (*geh*) gift from heaven; **~gewölbe** *nt* (*liter*) vault of heaven (*liter*), firmament (*liter*); **~karte** *f* star map *or* chart; **~königin** *f* (*Rel*) Queen of Heaven; **~körper** *m* heavenly *or* celestial body; **~kugel** *f* (*liter*) celestial globe (*liter*) *or* sphere (*liter*); **~kunde** *f* astronomy; **~kuppel** *f* (*liter*) *siehe* **~gewölbe**; **~leiter** *f* (*Bot*) Jacob's Ladder; **~macht** *f*: **die Liebe ist eine ~macht** love is a power of heaven; **~pforte** *f* (*liter*) gate of heaven; **~pol** *m* celestial pole; **~richtung** *f* direction; **die vier ~richtungen** the four points of the compass; **~schlüssel** *m or nt* (*Bot*) cowslip; **~schrift** *f* skywriting; **~spion** *m* (*inf*) spy satellite; **~stürmer** *m* (*liter*) (romantic) idealist; **~tor** *nt*, **~tür** *f* (*geh*) *siehe* **~pforte**.

himmelstürmend *adj attr* (*liter*) boundless.

Himmels-: ~wagen *m* (*Astron*) Great Bear; **~zelt** *nt* (*poet*) canopy of heaven (*poet*), firmament (*liter*).

himmel-: ~wärts *adv* (*liter*) heavenward(s); **~weit** *adj* (*fig inf*) tremendous, fantastic (*inf*); **zwischen uns besteht ein ~weiter Unterschied** there's a world of difference between us; **~weit voneinander entfernt, ~weit verschieden** (*fig*) poles apart; **wir sind noch ~weit davon entfernt** we're still nowhere near it.

himmlisch *adj* **(a)** *attr* (*göttlich*) heavenly, celestial (*liter*) ◆ **eine ~e Fügung** divine providence; **der ~e Vater** our Heavenly Father; **die H~en** (*old poet*) the gods; **das ~e Jerusalem** the new Jerusalem.

(b) (*fig*) (*wunderbar*) heavenly, divine; (*unerschöpflich*) *Geduld* infinite ◆ **~ bequem** beautifully *or* wonderfully comfortable.

hin *adv* **(a)** (*räumlich*) **bis zum Haus ~** up to the house, as far as the house; **geh doch ~ zu ihr!** go to her; (*besuche sie auch*) go and see her; **nach Süden/Stuttgart ~** towards the south/Stuttgart; **über die ganze Welt ~** all over the world, throughout the world; **die Wüste erstreckt sich über 2000 km ~** the desert stretches for 2000 km; **nach außen ~** (*fig*) outwardly; **das Boot glitt über die Wellen ~** the boat glided along over the waves; **~ fahre ich mit dem Zug, zurück ...** on the way out I'll take the train, coming back ...; **die Fähre geht heute abend nur noch (zur Insel) ~** the ferry's only making the outward trip *or* is only going out (to the island) this evening; **zur anderen Seite ~ sind es 2 km** it's 2 kms to the other side; **bis zu diesem Punkt ~** up to this point; **die Straße verläuft nach rechts ~** the road goes off to the right; **dreht euch/seht mal alle zur Tafel ~** face the/look at the blackboard.

(b) (*als Teil eines Wortpaares*) **~ und her** (*räumlich*) to and fro, back and forth; (*~ und zurück*) there and back; **etw ~ und her überlegen/diskutieren** to think about sth a lot/to discuss sth over and over *or* a lot; **das H~ und Her** the comings and goings *or* to-ings and fro-ings *pl*; **nach langem H~ und Her** eventually; **das reicht nicht ~ und nicht her** (*inf*) that won't go very far at all, that's nothing like enough (*inf*); **Regen/Feiertag ~, Regen/Feiertag her** rain/holiday or no rain/holiday, whether it rains/whether it's a holiday or not; **Mörder/Sohn ~, Mörder/Sohn her** murderer/son or not, I don't care whether he *is* a murderer/his *etc* son; **~ und zurück** there and back; **eine Fahrkarte/einmal London ~ und zurück** a return (ticket), a round trip (*esp US*)/a return *or* round trip (*esp US*) to London; **~ und zurück? — nein, nur ~ bitte** return *or* round trip? — no, just a single please; **der Flug von X nach Y ~ und zurück kostet** ... the return flight *or* round trip from X to Y costs ...; **~ und wieder** (every) now and then, (every) now and again.

(c) (*zeitlich*) **es sind nur noch drei Tage ~** it's only three days (from) now; **bis zu den Ferien sind noch drei Wochen ~** it's (still) three weeks till *or* until the holidays; **noch weit ~** a long way off *or* away; **lange Zeit ~** for a long time, over a long period; **zum Sommer ~** towards summer, as summer draws nearer *or* approaches; **gegen Mittag ~** towards midday; **über die Jahre ~** over the years, as (the) years go by; **die Kälte zog sich bis in den Juni ~** the cold lasted up until (and during) June.

(d) (*fig*) **auf meine Bitte/meinen Vorschlag ~** at my request/suggestion; **auf meinen Brief/Anruf ~** on account of my letter/phone-call; **auf die Gefahr ~, ... zu werden** at the risk of being ...; **auf sein Versprechen/seinen Rat ~** on the basis of his promise/(up)on his advice; **etw auf etw** (*acc*) **~ untersuchen/prüfen** to inspect/check sth for sth; **etw auf etw** (*acc*) **~ planen/anlegen** to plan/design sth with sth in mind; **vor sich ~ sprechen** *etc* to talk *etc* to oneself; **vor sich ~ stieren** to stare straight ahead *or* into space; **vor sich ~ dösen** to doze.

(e) (*inf: als trennbarer Bestandteil von Adverbien*) **da will ich nicht ~** I don't want to go (there); **wo geht ihr ~?** where are you going?

(f) (*elliptisch*) **nichts wie ~** (*inf*) let's go (then)!, what are we waiting for? (*inf*); **wo ist es/sie ~?** where has it/she gone?; **ist es weit bis ~?** (*inf*) is it far?; *siehe* **hinsein, nach, zu** *etc.*

hinab *adv, pref siehe* **hinunter**.

hinan *adv* (*liter*) upwards.

hinan- *pref siehe* **hinauf-**.

hin|arbeiten *vi sep*: **auf etw** (*acc*) **~** *auf ein Ziel* to work towards sth, to aim at sth; *auf eine Prüfung* to work for sth.

hinauf *adv* up ◆ **den Berg/die Straße ~** up the mountain/street; **den Fluß ~** up the river; **die Treppe ~** up the stairs, upstairs; **dort ~** up there; **bis ~ zu** up to.

hinauf- *pref siehe auch* **herauf-, rauf-** up; **~arbeiten** *vr sep* (*lit, fig*) to work one's way up; **~begeben*** *vr sep irreg* to go up(stairs); **~begleiten*** *vt sep* to take up(stairs); **~bemühen*** *sep* [1] *vt* to trouble to go/come up(stairs); [2] *vr* to be so kind as to go/come up(stairs); **~bitten** *vt sep irreg* to ask to go/come up(stairs); **~blicken** *vi sep* to look up; **~bringen** *vt sep irreg* to bring/take up; **~fahren** *sep irreg* [1] *vi aux sein* to go up; (*in Auto auch*) to drive up; [2] *vt jdn* to take up; (*in Auto auch*) to drive up; *Aufzug* to take up; **~fallen** *vi sep irreg aux sein*: **die Treppe ~fallen** (*hum*) to fall up the stairs; **~führen** *vti sep* to lead up; **~gehen** *vi sep irreg aux sein* to go up; (*Preise, Fieber auch*) to rise; **die Treppe ~gehen** to go *or* walk up the stairs; **einen Berg ~gehen** to climb *or* go up a mountain; **mit dem Preis ~gehen** to put up the price; **~gelangen*** *vi sep aux sein* (*geh*) to (manage to) get up; **~klettern** *vi sep aux sein* to climb up; **auf einen Baum ~klettern** to climb up a tree; **~kommen** *vi sep irreg aux sein* to come up; (*schaffen*) to (manage to) get up; **~laufen** *vi sep irreg aux sein* to run up; **die Treppe ~laufen** to run up the stairs; (*im Haus auch*) to run upstairs; **~reichen** *sep* [1] *vi* to reach up; [2] *vt* to hand *or* pass up; **~schauen** *vi sep* to look up; **~schicken** *vt sep* to send up; **~schieben** *vt sep irreg* to push up; **~schrauben** *vt sep* to screw up; (*fig*) *Preise* to put up; *Produktion, Forderungen* to step up; **~sehen** *vi sep irreg* to look up; **~setzen** *vt sep* (*fig*) *Preis etc* to raise, to increase, to put up; **~steigen** *vi sep irreg aux sein* to climb up; **~tragen** *vt sep irreg* to carry *or* take up; **~ziehen** *sep irreg* [1] *vt* to pull up; [2] *vi aux sein* to move up; [3] *vr* to pull oneself up; **sich an einem Seil ~ziehen** to pull oneself up with a rope.

hinaus *adv* **(a)** (*räumlich*) out ◆ **~ (mit dir)!** (get) out!, out you go!; **über** (*+acc*) **~** beyond, over; **aus dem** *or* **zum Fenster ~** out of the window; **hier/dort ~** this/that way out; **hinten/vorn ~** at the back *or* rear/front; **nach hinten/vorn ~ wohnen** to live towards *or* facing the back/the front; **zur Straße ~** facing the street; **durch die Tür ~** out of *or* out through the door.

(b) (*zeitlich*) **auf Jahre/Monate ~** for years/months to come; **bis weit über die Siebzig ~** until well over *or* after *or* past seventy; **wir werden damit über Mittwoch ~ beschäftigt sein** we'll be busy with that until after Wednesday.

(c) (*fig*) **über** (*+acc*) **~** over and above; (*über Gehalt, Summe auch*) on top of; **über das Grab ~** beyond the grave; **darüber ~** over and above this, on top of this, in addition to this; *siehe* **hinaussein, hinauswollen** *etc.*

hinaus- *pref siehe auch* **heraus-, raus-**; **~befördern*** *vt sep* (*inf*) *jdn* to kick out (*inf*), to chuck out (*inf*) (*aus* of); **~begeben*** *vr sep irreg* (*geh*) to go out (*aus* of); **~begleiten*** *vt sep* to see out (*aus* of); **~beugen** *vr sep* to lean out (*aus* of); **sich zum Fenster ~beugen** to lean out of the window; **~blicken** *vi sep* to look out (*aus* of); **zum Fenster ~blicken** to look out of the window; **~bringen** *vt sep irreg* (*aus* of) *etw* to take/bring out; *jdn* to take out; **~bugsieren*** *vt sep* (*inf*) *jdn* to steer *or* hustle out (*aus* of); **~drängen** *sep* [1] *vt* to force out (*aus* of); (*eilig*) to hustle out (*aus* of); (*fig*) to oust (*aus* from), to force out (*aus* of); [2] *vi aux sein* to push *or* force one's way out (*aus* of); **~dürfen** *vi sep irreg* to be allowed (to go) out (*aus* of); **darf ich ~?** may I go out?; **über einen Punkt nicht ~dürfen** not to be allowed (to go) beyond a point; **~eilen** *vi sep aux sein* (*geh*) to hurry out (*aus* of); **~ekeln** *vt sep* (*inf*) to drive out (*aus* of); **~fahren** *sep irreg* [1] *vi aux sein* **(a) aus etw ~fahren** to go out of sth, to leave sth; (*in Fahrzeug auch*) to drive out of sth; **(b)** (*reisen*) to go out; **aufs Meer ~fahren** to sail out across the sea; **(c) über etw** (*acc*) **~fahren** to go beyond sth; [2] *vt Wagen* to drive out (*aus* of); **~fallen** *vi sep irreg aux sein* (*aus* of) to fall out; (*Licht*) to come out; **~finden** *vi sep irreg* to find one's *or* the way out (*aus* of); **ich finde schon allein ~** I can find my own way out, I can see myself out; **~fliegen** *sep irreg* [1] *vi aux sein* (*aus* of) **(a)** to fly out; (*inf: ~fallen*) to go flying out (*inf*); **über ein Ziel ~fliegen** to fly past *or* go flying past a target destination; **(b)** (*inf: ~geworfen werden*) to get kicked *or* chucked out (*inf*); [2] *vt* to fly out (*aus* of); **~führen** *sep* [1] *vi* **(a)** (*nach draußen führen*) to lead out (*aus* of); **(b)** (*weiter führen als*) **über etw** (*acc*) **~führen** (*lit, fig*) to go beyond sth; [2] *vt* to lead out (*aus* of); (*Weg, Reise*) to take (*über +acc* beyond); **~gehen** *sep irreg aux sein* [1] *vi* **(a)** (*nach draußen gehen*) to go out(side); **aus dem Zimmer/auf die Straße ~gehen** to go *or* walk out of the room/out onto the street; **(b)** (*gesandt werden*) to go (out), to be sent out; **(c) auf etw** (*acc*) **~gehen** (*Tür, Zimmer*) to open onto sth; (*Fenster*) to look (out) onto *or* open onto sth; **das Fenster geht nach Osten ~** the window looks *or* faces east; **zu** *or* **nach etw ~gehen** (*Straße, Weg*) to go out to; **(d)** (*fig: überschreiten*) **über etw** (*acc*) **~gehen** to go beyond sth; **das geht über meine Kräfte ~** it's too much for me to bear, I (just) can't take any more; **über seine Befugnisse ~gehen** to overstep one's authority, to exceed one's powers; **das geht über meine Geduld ~** that's more than my patience can stand; [2] *vi impers* **wo geht es ~?** where's the way out?; **~gelangen*** *vi sep aux sein* (*lit geh*) to get out; **über etw** (*acc*) **~gelangen** (*fig*) to get beyond sth; **~geleiten*** *vt sep* (*geh*) to show out (*aus* of); **~graulen** *vt sep* (*inf*) to drive out (*aus* of); **~greifen** *vt sep irreg* (*fig*) **über etw** (*acc*) **~greifen** to reach beyond sth; **~gucken** *vi sep* to look out (*aus* of); **~halten** *vt sep irreg* to hold out; **den Kopf zum Fenster ~halten** to stick *or* put one's head out of the window; **~hängen** *vti sep irreg* to hang out; **eine Fahne zum Fenster ~hängen** to hang a flag out of the window; **~heben** *vt sep irreg* **etw über etw** (*acc*) **~heben** to raise *or* lift sth above sth, to put sth on a higher *or* different level to sth; **~jagen** *sep* (*aus* of) [1] *vt* (*lit: aus dem Zimmer, nach* *draußen)* to drive *or* chase out; *(fig: aus dem Haus)* to turn *or* drive out; [2] *vi aux sein* to bolt *or* dive out; **~katapultieren*** *vt sep (Pol sl)* to throw out, to chuck out *(inf) (aus* of); **~klettern** *vi sep aux sein* to climb out *(aus* of); **~kommen** *vi sep irreg aux sein* **(a)** to come out(side); **ich bin den ganzen Tag noch nicht ~gekommen** I haven't been *or* got out(side) yet today; **zu jdm aufs Land ~kommen** to come out to see sb in the country; **(b) über etw** *(acc)* **~kommen** to go beyond sth; *(fig)* to get beyond sth; **(c)** *(fig: ~laufen)* **das kommt auf dasselbe** *or* **auf eins** *or* **aufs gleiche ~** it boils *or* comes down to the same thing, it amounts *or* comes to the same thing; **~komplimentieren*** *vt sep (hum)* to usher out *(aus* of); **~lassen** *vt sep irreg (aus* of) to leave out; *(~begleiten)* to show out; **~laufen** *vi sep irreg aux sein (aus* of) **(a)** *(lit)* to run out; **(b)** *(fig)* **auf etw** *(acc)* **~laufen** to amount to sth; **es läuft auf dasselbe** *or* **auf eins** *or* **aufs gleiche ~** it boils *or* comes down to the same thing, it amounts *or* comes to the same thing; **wo(rauf) soll das ~laufen?** how's it all going to end?, what are things coming to?; **~lehnen** *vr sep* to lean out *(aus* of); **sich zum Fenster ~lehnen** to lean out of the window; **~manövrieren*** *vt sep* **sich/jdn aus etw ~manövrieren** to manoeuvre oneself/sb out of sth; **~müssen** *vi sep irreg* to have to go out *(aus* of); **~nehmen** *vt sep irreg* to take out *(aus* of); **~posaunen*** *vt sep (inf) siehe* **ausposaunen; ~ragen** *vi sep aux sein* **(a)** *(horizontal)* to project, to jut out *(über +acc* beyond); *(vertikal)* to tower up *(über +acc* above, over); **(b)** *(fig)* **über jdn/etw ~ragen** to tower above sb/sth; **~reden** *vr sep (dial) siehe* **herausreden; ~reichen** *sep* [1] *vt* to hand *or* pass out *(aus* of); **jdm etw zum Fenster ~reichen** to hand *or* pass sb sth out of the window; [2] *vi* **(a)** *(bis nach draußen reichen)* to reach, to stretch *(bis* as far as); **(b) über etw** *(acc)* **~reichen** *(lit)* to stretch beyond sth; *(fig)* to go beyond sth; **~rennen** *vi sep irreg aux sein* to run out *(aus* of); **~rücken** *vi sep aux sein (lit)* to move out *(aus* of); **die Soldaten rückten zur Stadt ~** the soldiers marched *or* moved out of (the) town; **~schaffen** *vt sep* to take out *(aus* of); **~schauen** *vi sep siehe* **~blicken; ~scheren** *vr sep* to get out *(aus* of); **~schicken** *vt sep* to send out *(aus* of); **~schieben** *vt sep irreg* **(a)** *Gegenstand* to push out *(aus* of); **(b)** *(fig)* to put off, to postpone; **~schießen** *vi sep irreg* **(a) er hat zum Fenster ~geschossen** he fired out of the window; **(b)** *aux sein (~rennen)* to shoot *or* dart out *(aus* of); **über das Ziel ~schießen** *(fig)* to go too far, to overshoot the mark; **~schmeißen** *vt sep irreg (inf)* to kick *or* chuck out *(inf) (aus* of); ⚠**H~schmiß** *m* **-sses, -sse** *(inf)* **man drohte ihm mit H~schmiß (aus der Kneipe)** they threatened to kick *or* chuck him out (of the pub) *(inf)*; **das war ein regelrechter H~schmiß** he was simply kicked *or* chucked out *(inf)*; **~schmuggeln** *vt sep* to smuggle out *(aus* of); **~schreien** *sep irreg* [1] *vi* to shout out *(aus* of); **zum Fenster ~schreien** to shout out of the window; [2] *vt (geh) Schmerz, Haß* to proclaim *(geh)*; **~schwimmen** *vi sep irreg aux sein (aus* of, *über +acc* beyond, past) to swim out; *(Gegenstände)* to float out; **~sehen** *vi sep irreg siehe* **~blicken;** ⚠**~sein** *vi sep irreg aux sein (Zusammenschreibung nur bei infin und ptp)* **(a)** *(lit inf: ~gegangen sein)* to be out, to have gone out; **(b)** *(fig: hinter sich haben)* **über etw** *(acc)* **~sein** *über Kindereien, Dummheiten* to be past *or* beyond sth; *über ein Alter* to be past sth; **~setzen** *sep* [1] *vt* to put out(side); **jdn ~setzen** *(inf)* to chuck *or* kick sb out *(inf)*; [2] *vr* to (go and) sit outside; **~stehlen** *vr sep irreg (geh)* to steal out *(geh) (aus* of); **~steigen** *vi sep irreg aux sein* to climb out *(aus* of); **zum Fenster ~steigen** to climb out of the window; **~stellen** *vt sep* to put *or* take out(side); *Sportler* to send off; **~strecken** *vt sep* to stick *or* put out *(aus* of); **~strömen** *vi sep aux sein* to pour out, to come milling out *(aus* of); **~stürmen** *vi sep aux sein* to storm out *(aus* of); **~stürzen** *sep (aus* of) [1] *vi aux sein* **(a)** *(~ fallen)* to fall out; **(b)** *(~eilen)* to rush *or* dash out; [2] *vr* to throw oneself *or* dive out; [3] *vt* to throw out; **~tragen** *vt sep irreg* **(a)** to carry out *(aus* of); **(b)** *(geh)* **etw in alle Welt ~tragen** to spread sth abroad; **(c)** *(weiter tragen als)* **über etw** *(acc)* **~tragen** to carry sth over *or* beyond sth; **~treiben** *vt sep irreg* to drive out *(aus* of); **~treten** *vi sep irreg aux sein* to step out(side); **ins Leben ~treten** *(geh)* to go out into the world; **~trompeten*** *vt sep (inf) siehe* **ausposaunen; ~wachsen** *vi sep irreg aux sein* **über etw** *(acc)* **~wachsen** *(lit)* to grow taller than sth; *(fig: durch Reifer werden, Fortschritte etc)* to outgrow sth; **er wuchs über sich selbst ~** he surpassed himself; **~wagen** *vr sep* to venture out *(aus* of); **~weisen** *sep irreg* [1] *vt* **jdn ~weisen** to show sb the door, to ask sb to leave; [2] *vi* to point out(wards); **über eine Frage/Sache ~weisen** *(fig)* to reach *or* point beyond a question/ matter; **~werfen** *vt sep irreg (aus* of) **(a)** to throw *or* cast *(liter)* out; **einen Blick ~werfen** to glance *or* look out(side), to take a glance *or* look out(side); **das ist ~geworfenes Geld** it's money down the drain; **Geld zum Fenster ~werfen** to throw money out of the window *or* down the drain; **(b)** *(inf) (entfernen)* to chuck *or* kick out *(inf)*; **~wollen** *vi sep* to want to go *or* get out *(aus* of); **worauf willst du ~?** *(fig)* what are you getting *or* driving at?; **hoch ~wollen** to aim high, to set one's sights high; **~ziehen** *sep irreg* [1] *vt* **(a)** *(nach draußen ziehen)* to pull out *(aus* of); **(b)** *(fig) Verhandlungen etc* to protract, to drag out; *Urlaub etc* to prolong; [2] *vi aux sein* to go out *(aus* of); **in die Welt ~ziehen** to go out into the world; **aufs Land/vor die Stadt ~ziehen** to move out into the country/out of town; **den Dampf/Rauch ~ziehen lassen** to let the steam/smoke out; [3] *vr (Verhandlungen etc)* to drag on; *(Abfahrt etc)* to be delayed, to be put off; [4] *vt impers* **es zog ihn ~ in die weite Welt** he felt the urge to be off into the big wide world; **mich zieht's wieder ~ in die Ferne** I've an urge to be off and away; **bei diesem schönen Wetter zieht's mich ~** I want to be out-of-doors with the weather like this; **~zögern** *sep* [1] *vt* to delay, to put off; [2] *vr* to be delayed, to be put off.

hin-: ~begeben* *vr sep irreg* **sich zu jdm ~begeben** *(form)* to go to sb, to betake oneself to sb *(old, form)*; **~bekommen*** *vt sep irreg (inf) siehe* **~kriegen; ~bemühen*** *sep* [1] *vt* **jdn ~bemühen** to trouble sb to go, to give sb the trouble of going; [2] *vr* to take the trouble to go; **~beordern*** *vt sep* to summon, to send for; **~bestellen*** *vt sep* to tell to go/come; **~biegen** *vt sep irreg (fig inf)* **(a)** *etw* to arrange, to sort out; **das** *or* **die Sache werden wir schon ~biegen** we'll sort it out *or* arrange matters somehow; **(b)** *jdn* to lick into shape *(inf)*; **~blättern** *vt sep (inf)* to fork *or* shell out *(inf)*, to cough up *(inf)*; **H~blick** *m*: **im** *or* **in H~blick auf** *(+acc) (angesichts)* in view of; *(mit Bezug auf)* with regard to; **im H~blick darauf, daß ...** in view of the fact that ...; **~blicken** *vi sep* to look *or* glance *(auf +acc, nach* at, towards); **~bringen** *vt sep irreg* **(a)** *etw* to take there; *(begleiten) jdn* to take there; *(in Auto auch)* to drive there; **(b)** *(fig) Zeit* to spend, to pass; *(in Muße)* to idle *or* while away; **sein Leben kümmerlich ~bringen** to eke out an existence; **(c)** *siehe* **~kriegen; ~deichseln** *vt sep (inf) etw* to arrange, to sort out; **~denken** *vi sep irreg* **wo denkst du ~?** whatever are you thinking of!

hinderlich *adj* **~ sein** to be in the way, to be a nuisance; *(Kleidungsstück auch)* to be restricting; **ein ~er Gipsverband** a restricting plaster cast, a plaster cast that gets in the way *or* is a nuisance; **jds Fortkommen** *(dat)* **~ sein** *(Gebrechen, Vorurteil etc)* to be a hindrance *or* obstacle to sb's advancement, to get in the way of sb's advancement; **eher ~ als nützlich sein** to be more of a hindrance than a help; **sich ~ auswirken** to prove to be a hindrance; **jdm ~ sein** to get in sb's way.

hindern [1] *vt* **(a)** *Fortschritte, Wachstum* to impede, to hamper; *jdn* to hinder *(bei* in).

(b) *(abhalten von)* to prevent *(an +dat* from), to stop ♦ **ja bitte, ich will Sie nicht ~** please do, I shan't stand in your way; **machen Sie, was Sie wollen, ich kann Sie nicht ~** do what you like, I can't stop *or* prevent you; **was hindert dich, hinzugehen?** what prevents *or* keeps you from going (there)?, what stops you going (there)?

[2] *vi (stören)* to be a hindrance *(bei* to).

Hindernis *nt* **(a)** *(lit, fig)* obstacle; *(Erschwernis, Behinderung)* hindrance; *(beim Sprechen)* handicap, impediment ♦ **sie empfand das Kind als ~/als ~ für ihre Karriere** she saw the child as a hindrance/as a hindrance to *or* an obstacle for her career; **gesetzliches ~** *(form)* legal impediment *or* obstacle; **jdm ~se in den Weg legen** *(fig)* to put obstacles in sb's path *or* way; **eine Reise mit ~sen** a journey full of hitches.

(b) *(Sport) (beim ~lauf, auf Parcours)* jump; *(Hürde auch)* hurdle; *(beim Pferderennen auch)* fence; *(Golf)* hazard.

Hindernis-: ~lauf *m* steeplechase *(in athletics)*; **~läufer** *m* steeplechaser *(in athletics)*; **~rennen** *nt* steeplechase.

Hinderung *f* **(a)** *siehe* **Behinderung ♦ ohne ~** without let or hindrance *(Jur)*. **(b)** *(Störung)* obstruction.

Hinderungsgrund *m* obstacle ♦ **etw als ~ angeben** to give sth as an excuse.

hindeuten *vi sep* to point *(auf +acc, zu* at) ♦ **es deutet alles darauf hin, daß ...** everything indicates that *or* points to the fact that ...

Hindi *nt* - Hindi.

Hindin *f (old, liter)* hind.

hin-: ~drängen *sep* [1] *vt* **jdn zum Ausgang** *etc* **~drängen** to push sb towards the exit *etc*; [2] *vr* **sich zu etw ~drängen** to push one's way towards sth; [3] *vi* **zum Ausgang ~drängen** to push one's way towards the exit *etc*; **auf eine Änderung ~drängen** to agitate for a change; **alles in ihrem Innern drängte zum Künstlerberuf ~** everything within her urged her towards an artistic profession; **~drehen** *vt sep (fig inf) siehe* **~deichseln.**

Hindu *m* **-(s), -(s)** Hindu.

Hinduismus *m* Hinduism.

hinduistisch *adj* Hindu.

hindurch *adv* **(a)** *(räumlich)* through ♦ **dort ~** through there; **mitten ~** straight through; **quer ~** straight across; **durch den Wald ~** through the wood.

(b) *(zeitlich)* through(out) ♦ **das ganze Jahr ~** throughout the year, all (the) year round; **die ganze Nacht ~** all (through the) night, throughout the night, all night long; **die ganze Zeit ~** all the time; **Jahre ~** for years (and years); **den ganzen Tag ~** all day (long); **durch etw ~** through sth.

hindurchgehen *vi sep irreg aux sein (lit, fig)* to go through *(durch etw* sth).

hindürfen *vi sep irreg* to be allowed to go *(zu* to) ♦ **da darfst du nicht mehr hin** you are not to *or* you mustn't go there any more.

Hindustan *nt* **-s** Hindustan.

Hindustani *m* **-(s), -(s)** Hindustani.

hin|eilen *vi sep aux sein* to rush *or* hurry *(zu* to) ♦ **ich eilte sofort hin** I rushed there at once.

hinein *adv* **(a)** *(räumlich)* in ♦ **da ~** in there; **nur ~!** *(inf)* go right in!; **~ mit dir!** *(inf)* in you go!; **in etw** *(acc)* **~** into sth; **bis in etw** *(acc)* **~** right inside sth; **mitten ~ in etw** *(acc)* right into *or* right in the middle of sth; **leg es oben/ unten ~** put it in the top/bottom; *siehe* **Blaue[2]**.

(b) *(zeitlich)* into ♦ **bis tief in die Nacht ~** well *or* far into the night.

hinein- *pref siehe auch* **ein-, herein-, rein-** in; **~begeben*** *vr sep irreg* to enter *(in etw (acc)* sth); **~bekommen*** *vt sep irreg (inf)* to get in *(in +acc* -to); **~bemühen*** *sep* [1] *vt* to trouble to go in; [2] *vr* to be so kind as to go in *(in +acc* -to); **~blicken** *vi sep* to look in *(in +acc* -to); **ins Fenster ~blicken** to look in at the window; **~bohren** *sep (in +acc* -to) [1] *vt* to dig in; [2] *vr* to bore one's way in; **~bringen** *vt sep irreg* **(a)** *(~tragen)* to bring/take in *(in +acc* -to); **(b)** *siehe* **~bekommen; ~bugsieren*** *vt sep (inf)* to manoeuvre in *(in +acc* -to); **~denken** *vr sep irreg* **sich in ein Problem ~denken** to think oneself into a problem; **sich in jdn ~denken** to put oneself in sb's position; **~deuten** *vt sep* **etw in einen Satz ~deuten** to read sth into a sentence; **etw in die Natur ~deuten** to attribute nature with sth; **~drängen** *sep (in +acc* -to) [1] *vt* to push in; [2] *vir (vi: aux sein)* to push one's way in; **~fallen** *vi sep* *irreg aux sein* to fall in (*in +acc* -to); **~finden** *vr sep irreg* (*fig*) (*sich vertraut machen*) to find one's feet; (*sich abfinden*) to come to terms with it; **sich ~finden in etw** (*acc*) to get familiar with sth; to come to terms with sth; **~fressen** *vt sep irreg* (*inf*) **etw in sich** (*acc*) **~fressen** (*lit*) to wolf sth (down) (*inf*), to gobble sth down *or* up; (*fig*) *Kummer etc* to suppress sth; **~geheimnissen*** *vt sep* (*inf*) **etw in etw** (*acc*) **~geheimnissen** to read sth into sth; **~gehen** *vi sep irreg aux sein* **(a)** to go in; **in etw** (*acc*) **~gehen** to go into sth, to enter sth; **(b)** (*~passen*) to go in (*in +acc* -to); **in den Bus gehen 50 Leute ~** the bus holds 50 people, there is room for 50 people in the bus; **~gelangen*** *vi sep aux sein* (*geh*) to get in (*in +acc* -to); **~geraten*** *vi sep irreg aux sein* **in etw** (*acc*) **~geraten** to get involved in sth, to get into sth; **in ein Unwetter ~geraten** to get into a thunderstorm; **in eine Schlägerei ~geraten** to get into *or* get involved in a brawl; **~gießen** *vt sep irreg* to pour in (*in +acc* -to); **etw in sich ~gießen** (*inf*) to pour sth down one's throat (*inf*), to down sth; **~greifen** *vi sep irreg* to reach inside; **in etw** (*acc*) **~greifen** to reach into sth; **~gucken** *vi sep* (*inf*) (*in Zimmer, Kiste*) to look *or* take a look in (*in +acc* -to); (*in Buch*) to take a look in (*in etw* (*acc*) sth); **~halten** *sep irreg* [1] *vt* to put in (*in etw* (*acc*) sth); [2] *vi* (*inf*) (*mit Gewehr etc*) to aim (*in +acc* at); **mitten in die Menge ~halten** to aim into the crowd; **~heiraten** *vi sep siehe* **einheiraten**; **~interpretieren*** *vt sep siehe* **~deuten**; **~klettern** *vi sep aux sein* to climb in (*in +acc* -to); **~knien** *vr sep* (*fig inf*) **sich in etw** (*acc*) **~knien** to get into sth (*inf*); **~kommen** *vi sep irreg aux sein* (*in +acc* -to) **(a)** to come in; **(b)** (*lit, fig: ~gelangen können*) to get in; **nach 21 Uhr kommt man nicht (mehr) ~** you can't get in after 9 o'clock; **(c)** *siehe* **~geraten**; **~komplimentieren*** *vt sep* to usher in (*in +acc* -to); **~kriechen** *vi sep irreg aux sein* to creep *or* slip in (*in +acc* -to); *siehe* **reinkriechen**; **~kriegen** *vt sep* (*inf*) *siehe* **~bekommen**; **~lachen** *vi sep* **in sich ~lachen** to laugh to oneself; **~lassen** *vt sep irreg* to let in (*in +acc* -to); **~laufen** *vi sep irreg aux sein* to run in (*in +acc* -to); **in sein eigenes Unglück ~laufen** to be heading for misfortune; **etw in sich ~laufen lassen** (*inf*) to knock sth back (*inf*); **~legen** *vt sep* **(a)** (*lit, fig*) *Gefühl etc* to put in (*in +acc* -to); **(b)** (*~deuten*) **etw in jds Worte ~legen** to put sth in sb's mouth; **~lesen** *vt sep irreg* **etw in etw** (*acc*) **~lesen** to read sth into sth; **~leuchten** *vi sep* to shine in (*in +acc* -to); **mit einer Lampe in eine Höhle ~leuchten** to shine a light into a cave; **~manövrieren*** *vt sep* to manoeuvre in (*in +acc* -to); **~passen** *sep* [1] *vi* **in etw** (*acc*) **~passen** to fit into sth; (*fig*) to fit in with sth; [2] *vt siehe* **einpassen**; **~pfuschen** *vi sep* (*inf*) **jdm in seine Arbeit/Angelegenheiten ~pfuschen** to meddle *or* interfere in sb's work/affairs; **~platzen** *vi sep aux sein* (*fig inf*) to burst in (*in +acc* -to); **~pressen** *vt sep* **(a)** to press in (*in +acc* -to); **(b)** (*fig*) **etw in ein Schema ~pressen** to force sth into a mould; **er läßt sich in kein Schema ~pressen** he won't be pigeon-holed (*inf*); **~projizieren*** *vt sep* to project (*in +acc* into); **sich in jdn ~projizieren** to project one's ideas/feelings *etc* into *or* onto sb; **~pumpen** *vt sep* to pump in (*in +acc* -to); *Geld auch* to pour in; **~ragen** *vi sep aux sein* (*lit, fig*) to project (*in +acc* into); **~reden** *vi sep* **(a)** (*lit: unterbrechen*) to interrupt (*jdm* sb); **jdm ~reden** (*fig: sich einmischen*) to meddle *or* interfere in sb's affairs; **jdm in seine Angelegenheiten/Entscheidungen/in alles ~reden** to meddle *or* interfere in sb's affairs/decision-making/in all sb's affairs; **(b) ins Leere ~reden** to talk into a vacuum, to talk to oneself; **sich in (seine) Wut ~reden** to talk oneself into *or* work oneself up into a rage; **~regnen** *vi impers sep* **es regnet (ins Zimmer) ~** (the) rain is coming in(to) the room; **~reichen** *sep* [1] *vt* to hand *or* pass in; **(jdm) etw zum** *or* **durchs Fenster ~reichen** to hand *or* pass sth in (to sb) through the window; [2] *vi* (*lang genug sein*) to reach in (*in +acc* -to); (*sich erstrecken*) to extend (*in +acc* as far as); **in etw** (*acc*) **~reichen** (*zeitlich*) to go over into sth; **Bräuche, die bis ins 20. Jahrhundert ~reichen** customs that hang *or* come over into the 20th century; **~reißen** *vt sep irreg* (*fig inf*) to drag in (*in +acc* -to); **~reiten** *sep irreg* [1] *vi aux sein* to ride in (*in +acc* -to); [2] *vt* (*inf*) *siehe* **reinreiten**; **~rennen** *vi sep irreg aux sein* to run in (*in +acc* -to); **in sein Unglück/Verderben ~rennen** to be heading for misfortune/disaster; **~rufen** *vt sep irreg* to call *or* shout in (*in +acc* -to); **~schaffen** *vt sep siehe* **~bringen**; **~schauen** *vi sep* to look in; **ins Zimmer/Fenster ~schauen** to look into the room/in at the window; **eben mal ~schauen** (*inf*) to look *or* pop in (*inf*); **sich** (*dat*) **in etw nicht ~schauen lassen** to keep sth to oneself; **~schaufeln** *vt sep* to shovel in (*in +acc* -to); **Essen in sich ~schaufeln** (*inf*) to shovel food into oneself *or* down one's gullet (*inf*); **~schießen** *vi sep irreg* **(a)** *aux sein* (*inf: Wasser etc*) to rush *or* gush in (*in +acc* -to); **~geschossen kommen** (*Wasser*) to come gushing *or* rushing in; (*inf: Mensch*) to shoot in (*inf*), to come shooting in (*inf*); **(b) in eine Menschenmenge ~schießen** to shoot into a crowd; **~schlagen** *vt sep irreg* (*in +acc* -to) *Nagel* to knock in; *Eier* to break in; *Krallen* to sink in; **ein Loch ins Eis ~schlagen** to knock a hole in the ice; **~schleichen** *vir sep irreg* (*vi: aux sein*) to creep *or* sneak in (*in +acc* -to); **~schliddern, ~schlittern** *vi sep aux sein* (*inf*) **in etw** (*acc*) **~schliddern** *or* **~schlittern** to get involved in *or* mixed up with sth; **~schlingen** *vt sep irreg* **etw (gierig) in sich ~schlingen** to devour sth (greedily); **~schlüpfen** *vi sep aux sein* to slip in (*in +acc* -to); **~schmuggeln** *vt sep* to smuggle in (*in +acc* -to); **~schneien** *sep* [1] *vi impers* **es schneit (ins Zimmer) ~** the snow is coming in(to the room); [2] *vi aux sein siehe* **hereinschneien**; **~schreiben** *vt sep irreg* to write in (*in etw* (*acc*) sth); **~schütten** *vt sep* to pour in (*in +acc* -to); **etw in sich ~schütten** (*inf*) to knock sth back (*inf*); **~sehen** *vi sep irreg siehe* **~blicken**; **~setzen** *sep* [1] *vt* to put in (*in +acc* -to); [2] *vr* (*in Fahrzeug*) to get into (*in etw* (*acc*) sth); (*in Sessel*) to sit (oneself) down (*in +acc* in(to)); (*in Sessellift, Kettenkarussell etc*) to sit oneself in (*in etw* (*acc*) sth); **sich wieder ~setzen/ins Zimmer ~setzen** to go back and sit inside/in the room; **~spazieren*** *vi sep aux sein* to walk in (*in +acc* -to); **nur ~spaziert!** please go in; **~spielen** *sep* [1] *vi* (*beeinflussen*) to have a part to play (*in +acc* in); **in etw** (*acc*) **~spielen** (*grenzen an*) to verge on sth; **da spielen noch andere Gesichtspunkte ~** other factors have a part to play (in it) *or* enter into it; [2] *vt* (*Sport*) **den Ball in den Strafraum** *etc* **~spielen** to play the ball into the penalty area *etc*; **~sprechen** *vi sep irreg* **ins Mikrophon ~sprechen** to speak *or* talk into the microphone; **~springen** *vi sep irreg aux sein* (*in +acc* -to) **(a)** to jump *or* leap *or* spring in; **(b)** (*inf: ~laufen*) to pop in (*inf*); **~stecken** *vt sep* (*in +acc* -to) to put in; *Nadel etc auch* to stick in; **den Kopf zum Fenster ~stecken** to put *or* stick one's head in at *or* in through the window; **Geld/Arbeit** *etc* **in etw** (*acc*) **~stecken** to put money/some work *etc* into sth; **viel Mühe in etw** (*acc*) **~stecken** to put a lot of effort into sth; **~steigern** *vr sep* to get into *or* work oneself up into a state, to get worked up; **sich in seine Wut/Hysterie/seinen Ärger ~steigern** to work oneself up into a rage/hysterics/a temper; **sich in seinen Kummer/Schmerz ~steigern** to let oneself be completely taken up with one's worries/to let the pain take one over completely; **sie hat sich in die Vorstellung ~gesteigert, daß ...** she has managed to convince herself that ..., she has talked herself into believing that ...; **sich in eine Rolle ~steigern** to become completely caught up in a role; **~stopfen** *vt sep* to stuff *or* cram in (*in +acc* -to); **Essen in sich** (*acc*) **~stopfen** to stuff *or* cram oneself with food; **~stoßen** *sep irreg* [1] *vt* *Schwert etc* to thrust in (*in +acc* -to); **jdn in etw ~stoßen** (*lit*) to push sb into sth; (*fig*) to plunge sb into sth; [2] *vi aux sein* **in eine Lücke ~stoßen** to steer into a space; **in ein Gebiet ~stoßen** to enter a district; **~strömen** *vi sep aux sein* to stream *or* flood in (*in +acc* -to); **~stürzen** *sep* [1] *vi aux sein* to plunge in (*in +acc* -to); (*~eilen*) to rush in (*in +acc* -to); **zur Tür ~stürzen** to rush in through the door; [2] *vt* to throw *or* hurl in (*in +acc* -to); **jdn ins Elend ~stürzen** to plunge sb into misery; [3] *vr* (*in +acc* -to) to throw *or* hurl oneself in, to plunge in; **sich in die Arbeit/in Schulden ~stürzen** to throw oneself into one's work/to plunge oneself into debt; **sich ins Vergnügen ~stürzen** to plunge in and start enjoying oneself, to let it all hang out (*sl*); **~tappen** *vi sep aux sein* (*fig inf*) to walk right into it (*inf*); **in eine Falle ~tappen** to walk into a trap; **~tragen** *vt sep irreg* (*in +acc* -to) to carry in; (*fig*) to bring in; **~treiben** *vt sep irreg* to drive in (*in +acc* -to); **jdn in etw** (*acc*) **~treiben** (*fig*) to force sb into sth; **~tun** *vt sep irreg* to put in (*in +acc* -to); **einen Blick in etw** (*acc*) **~tun** to take a look in sth; *ins Buch etc* to take a look at sth; **~versetzen*** *vr sep* **sich in jdn** *or* **in jds Lage ~versetzen** to put oneself in sb's position; **sich in etw** (*acc*) **~versetzt fühlen** to imagine oneself in sth; **sich in eine Rolle ~versetzen** to empathize with a part; **~wachsen** *vi sep irreg aux sein* **in etw** (*acc*) **~wachsen** (*lit, fig*) to grow into sth; **~wagen** *vr sep* to venture in (*in +acc* -to); **~werfen** *vt sep irreg* (*in +acc* -to) to throw in; *Truppen* to send in; **den Ball durchs Fenster ~werfen** to throw the ball in at *or* through the window; **~wollen** *vi sep* (*inf*) to want to go *or* get in (*in +acc* -to); **das will mir nicht in den Kopf ~** I just can't understand it; **~zerren** *vt sep* (*lit, fig*) to drag in (*in +acc* -to); **~ziehen** *sep irreg* [1] *vt* to pull *or* drag in (*in +acc* -to); **jdn in eine Angelegenheit/einen Streit ~ziehen** to drag sb into an affair/a quarrel; [2] *vi aux sein* (*in +acc* -to) to go in; (*in ein Haus*) to move in; **~zwängen** *sep* (*in +acc* -to) [1] *vt* to force *or* squeeze in; [2] *vr* to squeeze (oneself) in; **~zwingen** *vt sep irreg* to force in (*in +acc* -to).

hin-: ~fahren *sep irreg* [1] *vi aux sein* to go there; (*mit Fahrzeug auch*) to drive there; (*mit Schiff auch*) to sail there; **mit der Hand über etw** (*acc*) **~fahren** (*fig*) to run one's hand over sth; **fahre ~!** (*old, poet*) farewell! (*old*), fare-thee-well! (*old, poet*); [2] *vt* to drive *or* take there; **H~fahrt** *f* journey there; (*Naut*) voyage out; (*Rail*) outward journey; **auf der H~fahrt** on the journey *or* way there *etc*; **~fallen** *vi sep irreg aux sein* to fall (down).

hinfällig *adj* **(a)** frail. **(b)** (*fig: ungültig*) invalid; *Argument auch* untenable ◆ **etw ~ machen** to render sth invalid, to invalidate sth.

Hinfälligkeit *f, no pl* frailness; (*von Argument*) invalidity.

hin-: ~finden *vir sep irreg* (*inf*) to find one's way there; **~fläzen, ~flegeln** *vr sep* (*inf*) to loll about *or* around; **~fliegen** *vi sep irreg aux sein* to fly there; (*inf: ~fallen*) to come a cropper (*inf*); **der Ball flog über die Köpfe ~** the ball flew over their heads; **H~flug** *m* outward flight.

hinfort *adv* (*old*) henceforth (*old*).

hinführen *sep* [1] *vt* to lead there ◆ **jdn zu etw ~** (*fig*) to lead sb to sth.
[2] *vi* to lead *or* go there ◆ **zu/zwischen etw** (*dat*) **~** to lead to/between sth; **wo soll das ~?** (*fig*) where is this leading to?

hing *pret of* **hängen**.

Hingabe *f -, no pl* (*fig*) (*Begeisterung*) dedication; (*Selbstlosigkeit*) devotion; (*völliges Aufgehen*) (self-)abandon ◆ **mit ~ tanzen/singen** *etc* to dance/sing *etc* with abandon; **unter ~ seines Lebens** (*geh*) by laying down one's life.

hingabefähig *adj siehe n* capable of dedication/devotion/(self-)abandon.

Hingang *m -s, no pl* (*old, form*) decease, demise (*form*).

hingeben *sep irreg* [1] *vt* to give up; *Ruf, Zeit, Geld auch* to sacrifice; *Leben* to lay down, to sacrifice.
[2] *vr* **(a) sich einer Sache** (*dat*) **~** *der Arbeit* to devote *or* dedicate oneself to sth; *dem Laster, Genuß, der Verzweiflung* to abandon oneself to sth; **sich Hoffnungen/einer Illusion ~** to cherish hopes/to labour under an illusion.
(b) sie gab sich ihm hin she gave herself *or* surrendered to him; **sich Gott ~** to give oneself to God.

hingebend *adj* devoted.

Hingebung *f, no pl siehe* **Hingabe**.

hingebungsvoll [1] *adj* (*selbstlos*) devoted; (*begeistert*) abandoned.
[2] *adv* devotedly; with abandon; *lauschen* raptly.

hingegen *conj* (*geh*) however; (*andererseits auch*) on the other hand.

hin-: ~gegossen *adj* (*fig inf*) **sie lag/saß wie ~gegossen auf dem Bett** she had draped herself artistically on the bed; **~gehen** *vi sep irreg aux sein* **(a)** (*dorthin gehen*) to go (there); **gehst du auch ~?** are you going too?; **wo gehst du ~?** where are you going?; **wo geht es hier ~?** where does this go?; **(b)** (*Zeit*) to pass, to go by; (c) (*fig: tragbar sein*) das geht gerade noch ~ that will just about do *or* pass; diesmal mag es noch ~gehen I'll let it go *or* pass this once; (jdm) etw ~gehen lassen to let sth pass, to let sb get away with sth; **~gehören*** *vi sep* to belong; wo gehört das ~? where does this belong *or* go?; wo gehören die Gabeln ~? where do the forks live? (*inf*); **~gelangen*** *vi sep aux sein* (*geh*) to get there; **~geraten*** *vi sep irreg aux sein* irgendwo ~geraten to get somewhere; wo bin ich denn hier ~geraten? (*inf*) what kind of place is this then?; **~gerissen** [1] *ptp of* ~reißen; [2] *adj* enraptured, enchanted; ~gerissen lauschen to listen with rapt attention; ich bin ganz ~- und hergerissen (*iro*) absolutely great *or* fantastic! (*iro*); **~gleiten** *vi sep irreg aux sein* to glide; (*geh: Zeit*) to slip away; **~haben** *vt sep irreg* (*inf*) wo willst du dies ~haben? where do you want this (to go)?; **~halten** *vt sep irreg* (a) (*entgegenstrecken*) to hold out (*jdm* to sb); (b) (*fig*) *jdn* to put off, to stall; (*Mil*) to stave off.

Hinhalte-: ~politik *f* stalling *or* delaying policy; **~taktik** *f* stalling *or* delaying tactics.

hinhauen *sep irreg* (*inf*) [1] *vt* (a) (*nachlässig machen*) to knock off (*inf*). (b) (*hinwerfen*) to slam *or* plonk (*inf*) *or* bang down.
[2] *vi* (a) (*zuschlagen*) to hit hard ♦ (mit der Faust) ~ to thump *or* clobber (*inf*) it/sth (with one's fist). (b) (*gutgehen*) es hat hingehauen I/we *etc* just managed it; das wird schon ~ it will be OK (*inf*) or all right. (c) (*klappen, in Ordnung sein*) to work. ich habe das so lange geübt, bis es hinhaute I practised it till I could do it.
[3] *vr* (*sl*) (*sich hinflegeln, hinlegen*) to flop down (*inf*); (*sich schlafen legen*) to crash out (*inf*).
[4] *vt impers* es hat ihn hingehauen he fell over.

hin-: ~hören *vi sep* to listen; **~kauern** *vr sep* to cower (down).

Hinkebein *nt*, **Hinkefuß** *m* (*inf*) (*verletztes Bein*) gammy leg (*inf*) ♦ das alte/du Hinkebein the old man with his/you with your gammy leg.

Hinkelstein *m* (*inf*) menhir.

hinken *vi* (a) (*gehbehindert sein*) to limp, to walk with a limp ♦ mit *or* auf dem rechten Bein ~ to have a limp in one's right leg. (b) *aux sein* (*sich fortbewegen*) to limp. (c) (*fig*) (*Beispiel, Vergleich, Bild*) to be inappropriate; (*Formulierung auch*) to be inapt; (*Vers, Reim*) to be clumsy.

hin-: ~knallen *sep* (*inf*) [1] *vt* to slam *or* bang down; [2] *vi aux sein* to fall flat; **~knien** *vir sep* (*vi: aux sein*) to kneel (down); **~kommen** *vi sep irreg aux sein* (a) (*an einen Ort* ~) (da) ~kommen to get there; nach X ~kommen to get to X; kommst du mit ~? are you coming too?; wie komme ich zu dir ~? how do I get to your place?; könnt ihr alle zu ihm ~kommen? can you all go to his place?; (b) (*an bestimmten Platz gehören*) to go; wo ist das Buch ~gekommen? where has the book got to?; wo kämen wir denn ~, wenn ... (*inf*) where would we be if ...; wo kämen wir denn da ~? (*inf*) where would we be then?; (c) (*inf: in Ordnung kommen*) das kommt schon noch ~ that will turn out OK (*inf*); (d) (*inf: auskommen*) to manage; wir kommen (damit) ~ we will manage; (e) (*inf: ausreichen, stimmen*) to be right; **~kriegen** *vt sep* (*inf*) (a) (*fertigbringen*) to do, to manage; wie er es nur immer ~kriegt, daß die anderen alles für ihn machen I don't know how he manages to get the others to do everything for him; das hast du gut ~gekriegt you've made a nice job of it; wie kriegt sie das bloß immer ~? I don't know how she does it; (b) (*in Ordnung bringen*) to mend, to fix; (*gesundheitlich*) to cure; **H~kunft** *f* (*Aus*): in H~kunft in future; **~künftig** (*Aus*) [1] *adj* future; [2] *adv* in future; **~langen** *vi sep* (*inf*) (a) (*zupacken*) to grab him/her/it *etc*; (*ziehen/schieben*) to pull/push hard; (*dial: anfassen*) to touch; (*zuschlagen*) to take a (good) swipe (*inf*); (*foulen*) to play rough; *siehe* Gras; (b) (*sich bedienen*) to help oneself to a lot; (*viel Geld verlangen*) to overcharge; (c) (*ausreichen*) to do; (*Geld*) to stretch; mein Geld langt dafür nicht ~ my money won't stretch to that; (d) (*auskommen*) to manage; **~länglich** [1] *adj* (*ausreichend*) adequate; keine ~längliche Anzahl an insufficient number; [2] *adv* (*ausreichend*) adequately; (*zu Genüge*) sufficiently; **~lassen** *vt sep irreg* jdn (da) ~lassen to let sb go (there); **~laufen** *vi sep irreg aux sein* (a) (*zu bestimmter Stelle laufen*) to run there; (*vorbei-, entlang-, dahinlaufen*) to run; (*inf: zu Veranstaltung, Amt, Rechtsanwalt etc*) to rush; (b) (*dial inf: nicht fahren*) to walk; (c) (*verlaufen: mit Ortsangabe, in bestimmte Richtung*) to run; **~legen** *sep* [1] *vt* (a) to put down; *Zettel* to leave (*jdm* for sb); (*flach legen*) *Verletzten etc* to lay down; (*ins Bett, zum Schlafen*) to put to bed; (*inf: bezahlen müssen*) to fork out (*inf*); (b) (*inf: glänzend darbieten*) to perform *or Rede, Vortrag* give effortlessly and brilliantly; er hat einen tollen Steptanz ~gelegt he did a neat bit of tap-dancing; [2] *vr* to lie down; ~legen! (*Mil*) down!; sich lang *or* der Länge nach ~legen (*inf*) to fall flat; da legst du dich (lang) ~! (*inf*) it's unbelievable; **~lenken** *vt sep* etw (auf etw *acc*) ~lenken *Fahrzeug, Pferd* to steer sth (towards sth); *Fluß, Wasser, Blicke, jds Aufmerksamkeit* to direct sth to sth; *Schritte, Gespräch* to turn sth to sth; **~lümmeln** *vr sep* (*inf*) to loll *or* lounge about *or* around (*auf +acc* on).

hinmachen *sep* [1] *vt* (*inf*) (a) (*anbringen*) to put on; *Bild* to put up. (b) (*kaputtmachen*) to wreck, to ruin; (*sl: umbringen*) to bump off (*inf*), to do in (*inf*).
[2] *vi* (a) (*inf: Notdurft verrichten*) to do one's/its *etc* business (*euph*). (b) (*dial: sich beeilen*) to get a move on (*inf*). (c) *aux sein* (*dial inf: an bestimmten Ort gehen*) to go there.

Hin-: ~marsch *m* way *or* (*Mil*) march there; **h~morden** *vt sep* (*geh*) to massacre; **h~murmeln** *vti sep* to murmur; **h~müssen** *vi sep irreg* to have to go; **~nahme** *f -, no pl* acceptance; **h~nehmen** *vt sep irreg* (a) (*ertragen*) to take, to accept; *Beleidigung* to swallow; etw als selbstverständlich h~nehmen to take sth for granted; (b) (*inf: mitnehmen*) to take; **h~neigen** *sep* [1] *vt Kopf, Körper* to incline; [2] *vr* (*zu* towards) (*Mensch*) to lean; (*fig*) to incline *or* have leanings; (*Zweige, Baum*) to lean; (*Landschaft*) to incline; [3] *vi* (*fig*) zu etw h~neigen to incline towards sth; *zu Vorbild* to tend to follow.

hinnen *adv* (*old, liter*) von ~ hence; von ~ gehen *or* scheiden (*fig*) to depart this life, to pass on.

hin-: ~passen *vi sep* (*Platz haben*) to fit (in); (*gut aussehen*) to go (well); (*Mensch: am Platz sein*) to fit in; **~pfeffern** *vt sep* (*inf*) *Gegenstand* to bang *or* slam down (*inf*); (*fig*) *Antwort, Kritik* (*mündlich*) to rap out; (*schriftlich*) to scribble down; **~pfuschen** *vt sep* (*inf*) to dash off; **~plappern** *vt sep* to say; *Unsinn* to talk; das hat sie nur so ~geplappert she said that without thinking; **~plumpsen** *vi sep aux sein* (*inf*) to fall down (with a thud); etw ~plumpsen lassen to dump *or* plump (*inf*) sth down; sich ~plumpsen lassen to plump oneself down (*inf*), to flop down; **~raffen** *vt sep siehe* dahinraffen; **~reichen** *sep* [1] *vt* jdm etw ~reichen to hand *or* pass sb sth *or* sth to sb; *Hand* to hold out sth to sb; [2] *vi* (a) (*ausreichen*) to be enough, to suffice (*form*); (b) (*sich erstrecken*) bis zu etw ~reichen to stretch to sth; **~reichend** *adj* (*ausreichend*) adequate; (*genug*) sufficient; (*reichlich*) ample; keine ~reichenden Beweise insufficient evidence; es ist noch ~reichend Zeit there is ample time; **H~reise** *f* journey there *or* out, outward journey; (*mit Schiff*) voyage out, outward voyage; H~- und Rückreise journey there and back; die H~reise nach London the journey to London; auf der H~reise on the way there; **~reißen** *vt sep irreg* (*fig*) (a) (*begeistern*) to thrill, to enrapture; *siehe* ~gerissen; (b) (*überwältigen*) jdn zu etw ~reißen to force sb into sth; die Zuschauer zu Beifallsstürmen ~reißen to elicit thunderous applause from the audience; sich ~reißen lassen to let oneself be *or* get carried away; sich zu einer Entscheidung ~reißen lassen to let oneself be carried away into making a decision; **~reißend** *adj* fantastic; *Landschaft, Anblick* enchanting; *Schönheit, Mensch* captivating; *Redner auch* thrilling; ~reißend schön aussehen to look quite enchanting; ~reißend schön Klavier spielen to play the piano quite enchantingly *or* delightfully; **~rennen** *vi sep irreg aux sein siehe* ~laufen (a); **~richten** *vt sep* to execute; jdn durch den Strang/elektrischen Stuhl ~richten to hang sb/to send sb to the electric chair.

Hinrichtung *f* execution.

Hinrichtungs-: ~kommando *nt* execution *or* (*bei Erschießen*) firing squad; **~stätte** *f* place of execution.

hin-: ~rücken *vt sep Gegenstand* to push over; **~sagen** *vt sep* to say without thinking; **~schaffen** *vt sep* to get there; **~schauen** *vi sep* (*dial*) *siehe* ~sehen; **~schaukeln** *vt sep* (*sl*) to fix (*inf*), to manage; **~scheiden** *vi sep irreg aux sein* (*liter*) to pass away, to depart this life (*form*); der H~geschiedene the deceased, the (dear) departed; **H~scheiden** *nt* (*liter*) demise; **~scheißen** *vi sep irreg* (*vulg*) to crap (*vulg*); **~schicken** *vt sep* to send; **~schieben** *vt sep irreg* to push over; **H~schied** *m -(e)s, no pl* (*Sw*) *siehe* H~scheiden; **~schielen** *vi sep* to glance (*zu* at); **~schlachten** *vt sep* to slaughter, to butcher; **~schlagen** *vi sep irreg* (a) to strike *or* hit; (b) *aux sein* (*~fallen*) to fall over; der Länge nach *or* längelang *or* lang ~schlagen (*inf*) to fall flat (on one's face); **~schleichen** *vir sep irreg* (*vi: aux sein*) to creep *or* steal *or* sneak up; **~schleppen** *sep* [1] *vt* to carry, to lug (*inf*); (*inf: mitnehmen*) to drag along; [2] *vr* (*Mensch*) to drag oneself along; (*fig*) to drag on; **~schludern** *vt sep* (*inf*) *Arbeit* to dash off; **~schmeißen** *vt sep irreg* (*inf*) (*hinwerfen*) to fling *or* chuck down (*inf*); (*fig: aufgeben*) *Arbeit etc* to chuck *or* pack in (*inf*); **~schmelzen** *vi sep irreg aux sein* (*hum, inf*) (*Mensch*) to swoon; (*Wut*) to melt away; **~schmieren** *vt sep* (*inf*) *Schmutz* to spread, to smear; (*pej*) (*malen*) to daub; (*flüchtig schreiben*) to scribble; **~schreiben** *sep irreg* [1] *vt* to write; (*flüchtig niederschreiben*) to bung down (*inf*); *Aufsatz* to dash off; [2] *vi* (*inf*) to write (there); **~schwinden** *vi sep irreg aux sein siehe* dahinschwinden; **~sehen** *vi sep irreg* to look; ich kann (gar) nicht ~sehen I can't bear to look; ohne ~zusehen without looking; bei genauerem H~sehen on looking more carefully; vor sich ~sehen to look *or* stare straight ahead.

⚠**hinsein** *vi sep irreg aux sein* (*Zusammenschreibung nur bei infin und ptp*) (*inf*) (a) (*kaputt sein*) to have had it ♦ hin ist hin what's done is done.
(b) (*erschöpft sein*) to be shattered (*inf*).
(c) (*verloren sein*) to be lost; (*Ruhe*) to have disappeared; (*ruiniert sein*) to be in ruins.
(d) (*sl: tot sein*) to have kicked the bucket (*sl*).
(e) (*begeistert sein*) (von etw) ~ to be mad about sth.
(f) bis dahin ist es noch lange hin it's a long time till then.

hinsetzen *sep* [1] *vt* to put *or* set down; *jdn* to seat, to put; *Kind* to sit down.
[2] *vr* (a) (*lit*) to sit down ♦ sich gerade ~ to sit up straight. (b) (*inf: sich bemühen*) to buckle down to it, to set to.

▼ **Hinsicht** *f -, no pl* in dieser ~ in this respect *or* regard; in mancher *or* gewisser ~ in some *or* many respects *or* ways; in jeder ~ in every respect; in finanzieller/wirtschaftlicher ~ financially/economically; in beruflicher ~ with regard to my/his job; in ~ auf (*+acc*) *siehe* hinsichtlich.

hinsichtlich *prep +gen* (*bezüglich*) with regard to; (*in Anbetracht*) in view of.

hin-: ~siechen *vi sep aux sein* (*geh*) *siehe* dahinsiechen; **~sinken** *vi sep irreg aux sein* (*geh*) to sink (down); (*ohnmächtig werden*) to faint, to swoon; (*tot*) to drop down dead; **~sollen** *vi sep* (*inf*) wo soll ich/das Buch ~? where do I/does the book go?; wo soll ich mit dem Paket ~? what should I do with this parcel?; eigentlich sollte ich ja zu der Party ~ I really ought to go to the party; **H~spiel** *nt* (*Sport*) first leg; **~starren** *vi sep* to stare; **~stellen** *sep* [1] *vt* (a) (*niederstellen*) to put down; (*an bestimmte Stelle*) to put; (*inf*) *Gebäude* to put up; (*abstellen*) *Fahrzeug* to put, to park; er tut seine Pflicht, wo man ihn auch ~stellt he does his duty wherever he is; (b) (*auslegen*) *Vorfall, Angelegenheit, Sachlage* to describe; jdn/etw als jdn/etw ~stellen (*bezeichnen*) to make sb/sth out to be sb/sth; [2] *vr* to stand; (*Fahrer*) to park; sich gerade ~stellen to stand up straight; sich vor jdn *or* jdm ~stellen to stand in front of sb; sie

➤ SPRACHE AKTIV: Hinsicht → 32.3

hat sich vor mich/ihn ~gestellt she came and stood in front of me/went and stood in front of him; **sich als etw ~stellen** (*fig*) to make oneself out to be sth; **~steuern** *sep* [1] *vi* (a) *aux sein* to steer; **wo steuert sie ~?** where is she going?; (b) (*fig*) **in der Diskussion auf etw** (*acc*) **~steuern** to steer the discussion towards sth; **auf ein Ziel ~steuern** (*fig*) to aim at a goal; [2] *vt* to steer; **~strecken** *sep* [1] *vt* (a) *Hand, Gegenstand* to hold out; (b) (*liter*) *jdn* to fell; [2] *vr* to stretch (oneself) out, to lie down; **~strömen** *vi sep aux sein* (*Fluß, Wasser*) to flow; (*Menschen*) to flock there; **sie strömten zur Ausstellung ~** they flocked to the exhibition; **~stürzen** *vi sep aux sein* (a) (*~fallen*) to fall down heavily; (b) (*~eilen*) **nach** *or* **zu jdm/etw ~stürzen** to rush *or* dash towards sb/sth.

Hint|an-: h~setzen *vt sep* (*zurückstellen*) to put last; (*vernachlässigen*) to neglect; **~setzung** *f* disregard; (*Vernachlässigung*) neglect; **unter ~setzung einer Sache** (*gen*) (*form*) regardless of *or* without regard for sth; **h~stellen** *vt sep siehe* **h~setzen.**

hinten *adv* (a) behind ♦ **von ~** from the back; (*bei Menschen auch*) from behind; **nach ~** to the back; **von weit ~** from the very back; **~ im Buch/in der Schlange/auf der Liste** at the back of the book/queue/at the end of the list; **sich ~ anstellen** to join the end of the queue (*Brit*) *or* line (*US*); **~ im Bild** in the back of the picture; **nach ~ abgehen** (*Theat*) to exit at the back of the stage; **nach ~ laufen** to run to the back; **von ~ anfangen** to begin from the end; **das Alphabet von ~ aufsagen** to say the alphabet backwards; **etw ~ anfügen** to add sth at the end; **~ bleiben** (*lit*) to stay behind *or* at the back; (*fig*) to lag behind.
(b) (*am rückwärtigen Ende*) at the back; (*Naut*) aft; (*am Gesäß*) on one's behind ♦ **von ~** from behind; *jdn erkennen auch* from the back; **~ im Auto/Bus** in the back of the car/bus; **der Blinker ~** the rear indicator; **~ und vorn nichts haben** (*inf*) to be as flat as a pancake (*inf*); **nach ~** to the back; *fallen, ziehen* backwards; **jdn am liebsten von ~ sehen** (*inf*) to be glad to see the back of sb; **nach ~ ausschlagen** (*Pferd*) to kick out; **jdm ~ hinein-** *or* **reinkriechen** (*inf*) to lick sb's boots; *siehe* **Auge.**
(c) (*auf der Rückseite*) at the back; (*von Gebäude auch*) at the rear ♦ **das Buch ist ~ schmutzig** the back (cover) of the book is dirty; **~ auf der Medaille** on the back *or* the reverse side of the medal; **ein nach ~ gelegenes Zimmer** a room facing the back; **ein Blick nach ~** a look behind; **etw von ~ und vorn betrachten** (*fig*) to consider sth from all angles.
(d) (*weit entfernt*) **das Auto da ~** the car back there; **sie waren ziemlich weit ~** they were quite far back; **~ im Walde** deep in the forest; **~ in der Mongolei** far away in Mongolia.
(e) (*fig*) **~ und vorn** *betrügen* left, right and centre; *bedienen* hand and foot; *verwöhnen* rotten (*inf*); *egal sein* absolutely, utterly; **das stimmt ~ und vorn nicht** *or* **weder ~ noch vorn** that is absolutely untrue; **das reicht** *or* **langt ~ und vorn nicht** *or* **weder ~ noch vorn** that's nowhere near enough; **dann heißt es Frau Schmidt ~ und Frau Schmidt vorn** then it's Mrs Smith this and Mrs Smith that; **ich weiß nicht mehr, wo ~ und vorn ist** I don't know whether I'm coming or going.

hinten-: ~dran *adv* (*inf*) (*am hinteren Ende*) at the back; (*fig: im Hintertreffen*) behind; **~drauf** *adv* (*inf*) on the back; (*von LKW*) in the back; (*auf Gesäß*) on one's behind; **~drein** *adv siehe* **hinterher**; **~herum** *adv* (a) (*von der hinteren Seite*) from the back; **kommen Sie ~herum** come round the back; (b) (*fig inf*) (*auf Umwegen*) in a roundabout way; (*illegal*) under the counter; **er hat mir ~herum erzählt, daß sie ...** he told me behind her back that she ...; **~nach** *adv* (*Aus, S Ger*) *siehe* **hinterher**; **~rum** *adv* (*inf*) *siehe* **~herum**; **~über** *adv* backwards; **er fiel/kippte ~über** he fell over backwards.

hinter *prep +dat or* (*mit Bewegungsverben*) *+acc* (a) (*räumlich*) behind ♦ **~ dem Haus** behind *or* at the back *or* rear of the house; **~ jdm/etw her** behind sb/sth; **~ etw** (*acc*) **kommen** (*fig: herausfinden*) to get to the bottom of sth; **~ die Wahrheit kommen** to get to the truth; **sich ~ jdn stellen** (*lit*) to stand behind sb; (*fig*) to support sb, to get behind sb; **~ jdm/etw stehen** (*lit, fig*) to be behind sb/sth; **jdn ~ sich** (*dat*) **haben** (*lit, fig*) to have sb behind one; **~ dem Hügel/der Tür hervor** (out) from behind the hill/door; **jdn weit ~ sich** (*dat*) **lassen** to leave sb far behind; (*im Rennen auch*) to outdistance sb; **~ etw** (*dat*) **stecken, sich ~ etw** (*dat*) **verbergen** to be *or* lie behind sth; **~ seinen Reden steckt nicht viel** there's not much in his speeches.
(b) *+dat* (*nach*) after ♦ **vier Kilometer ~ Glasgow/~ der Grenze** four kilometres outside Glasgow/beyond the border; **~ diesem Satz steht ein Fragezeichen** there is a question-mark at the end of this sentence; **er ist ~ mir dran** it's his turn after me.
(c) *+dat* (*in Rangfolge*) after; (*in Bedeutung*) behind ♦ **an Talent nicht ~ jdm zurückstehen** to be just as talented as sb; **sie stand nicht ~ ihm zurück** she did not lag behind him; **ich stelle das Privatleben ~ der Arbeit zurück** I put my work before my private life.
(d) **etw ~ sich** (*dat*) **haben** (*zurückgelegt haben*) to have got through sth; *Strecke* to have covered sth; *Land* to have left sth; (*überstanden haben*) to have got sth over (and done) with; *Krankheit, Zeit* to have been through sth; *anstrengende Tage* to have had sth; *Studium* to have completed *or* finished sth; **sie hat viel ~ sich** she has been through a lot; **das Schlimmste haben wir ~ uns** we're past *or* we've got over the worst; **etw ~ sich** (*acc*) **bringen** to get sth over (and done) with; *Strecke* to cover sth; *Arbeit* to get sth done; **das liegt ~ ihr** that is behind her; **sich ~ etw** (*acc*) **machen** to get down to sth; *siehe* **hersein.**
(e) (*inf*) *siehe* **dahinter.**

Hinter-: ~achse *f* rear *or* back axle; **~ansicht** *f* rear *or* back view; **~ausgang** *m* back *or* rear exit; **~backe** *f usu pl* buttock; (*von Tier*) hindquarter; **sich auf die ~backen setzen** (*fig inf*) to get down to it; **~bänkler** *m* **-s, -** (*Pol pej*) backbencher; **~bein** *nt* hind leg; **sich auf die ~beine stellen** *or* **setzen** (*lit*) to rear up (on one's hind legs); (*fig inf*) (*sich widersetzen*) to kick up a fuss (*inf*); (*sich anstrengen*) to pull one's socks up (*inf*).

Hinterbliebenen-: ~fürsorge *f welfare service for surviving dependents*; **~rente** *f* surviving dependents' pension.

Hinterbliebene(r) *mf decl as adj* surviving dependent ♦ **die ~n** the bereaved family.

hinter-: ~bringen* *vt insep irreg* **jdm etw ~bringen** to mention sth to sb; **H~deck** *nt* (*Naut*) afterdeck; **~drein** *adv siehe* **~her.**

hintere *adj siehe* **hintere(r, s).**

hinter|einander *adv* (*räumlich*) one behind the other, behind each other; (*in einer Reihe nebeneinander*) next to one another; (*in Reihenfolge, nicht gleichzeitig, ohne Unterbrechung*) one after the other ♦ **~ hereinkommen** to come in one by one *or* one at a time; **dicht ~** (*räumlich*) close behind one another; (*zeitlich*) close on one another; **zwei Tage ~** two days running; **dreimal ~** three times in a row; **es hat monatelang ~ geregnet** it has rained for months on end; **etw ~ tun** (*nicht gleichzeitig*)to do sth one after the other; (*der Reihe nach*) to do sth in turn; (*ohne Unterbrechung*) to do sth in one go *or* all at once.

hinter|einander-: ⚠**~fahren** *vi sep irreg aux sein* (*mit Auto/Fahrrad*) to drive/ride behind one another *or* one behind the other; ⚠**~gehen** *vi sep irreg aux sein* to walk behind one another *or* one behind the other; **~her** *adv* behind one another; ⚠**~schalten** *vt sep* (*Elec*) to connect in series; **H~schaltung** *f* (*Elec*) series connection; ⚠**~stehen** *vi sep irreg aux haben or* (*S Ger*) *sein* to stand behind one another *or* one behind the other; **~weg** *adv* (*zeitlich*) running, in a row; (*nacheinander*) one after the other.

Hinter|eingang *m* rear entrance.

Hintere(r) *m decl as adj* (*inf*) *siehe* **Hintern.**

hintere(r, s) *adj* back; (*von Tier, Gebäude, Zug auch*) rear ♦ **der/die/das H~** the one at the back; **das ~ Ende des Saals** the back *or* rear of the room; **die H~n** those at the back, those behind; **am ~n Ende** at the far end; *siehe* **hinterste(r, s).**

Hinter-: h~fotzig *adj* (*dial inf*) underhand(ed); **~fotzigkeit** *f* (*dial inf*) underhandedness; (*Bemerkung*) underhand(ed) remark; **h~fragen*** *vt insep* to analyze; *Brauch, Recht etc* to question; **~fuß** *m* hind foot; **~gaumenlaut** *m* velar (sound); **~gebäude** *nt siehe* **~haus**; **~gedanke** *m* ulterior motive; **ohne ~gedanken** without any ulterior motive(s); **h~gehen¹*** *vt insep irreg* (*betrügen*) to deceive; *Ehepartner etc auch* to be unfaithful to; (*umgehen*) *Verordnung, Gesetze, Prinzip* to circumvent; **h~gehen²** *vi sep irreg aux sein* (*dial inf*) to go to the back *or* rear (*in +acc* of); **~gestell** *nt* (*hum inf*) (*Beine*) hind legs *pl* (*inf*), pins *pl* (*inf*); (*Po*) rump (*inf*), backside (*inf*); **~glasmalerei** *f* (*Bild*) verre églomisé picture; (*Technik*) verre églomisé technique.

Hintergrund *m* (*von Bild, Raum*) background; (*von Bühne, Saal*) back; (*Theat: Kulisse*) backdrop, backcloth; (*fig: verborgene Zusammenhänge*) background *no pl* (*gen* to) ♦ **im ~** in the background; **im ~ der Bühne** at the back of the stage; **vor dem ~** (*lit, fig*) against the background; **der musikalische/akustische ~** the background music/sounds *pl*; **im ~ bleiben/stehen** (*lit, fig*) to stay/be in the background; **in den ~ treten** *or* **rücken** (*fig*) to be pushed into the background.

Hinter-: ~grundgespräch *nt* (*Pol*) briefing; **h~gründig** *adj* cryptic, enigmatic; **~gründigkeit** *f* crypticness, enigmaticness; (*Bemerkung*) cryptic *or* enigmatic remark; **~grundprogramm** *nt* (*Comput*) background program; **h~haken** *vi sep* (*inf*) to follow that/it *etc* up; **~halt** *m* (a) ambush; **jdn aus dem ~halt überfallen** to ambush *or* waylay sb; **jdn/etw aus dem ~halt angreifen** (*esp Mil*) to ambush sb/sth; (*Sport, fig*) to make a surprise attack on sb/sth; **im ~halt lauern** *or* **liegen** to lie in wait *or* (*esp Mil*) ambush; (b) (*inf*) **etw im ~halt haben** to have sth in reserve; **ohne ~halt** unreservedly; **h~hältig** *adj* underhand(ed); **~hältigkeit** *f* underhandedness; (*Handlung*) underhand(ed) act; **~hand** *f* (*von Pferd, Hund*) hindquarters *pl*; **etw in der ~hand haben** (*fig: in Reserve*) to have sth up one's sleeve; **~haupt** *nt* back of one's/the head; **~haus** *nt part of a tenement house accessible only through a courtyard and thus considered inferior.*

hinterher *adv* (*räumlich*) behind, after; (*zeitlich*) afterwards.

hinterher-: ~fahren *vi sep irreg aux sein* to drive behind (*jdm* sb); **~hinken** *vi sep aux sein* to limp behind (*jdm* sb); (*fig*) to lag behind (*hinter etw* (*dat*) sth, *mit* with, in); **~kommen** *vi sep irreg aux sein* (a) (*danach kommen*) (*räumlich*) to follow (behind *or* after); (*zeitlich*) to come after; (b) (*als letzter kommen*) to bring up the rear; **~laufen** *vi sep irreg aux sein* to run behind (*jdm* sb); **jdm ~laufen** (*fig inf: sich bemühen um*) to run (around) after sb; **einem Mädchen ~laufen** (*inf*) to run after a girl; **~schicken** *vt sep* to send on (*jdm* to sb); *jdn* to send after (*jdm* sb); ⚠**~sein** *vi sep irreg aux sein* (*Zusammenschreibung nur bei infin und ptp*) (*inf*) (*lit: verfolgen*) to be after (*jdm* sb); (*fig*) (*zurückgeblieben sein*) to lag behind; **~sein, daß ...** to see to it that ...

Hinter-: ~hof *m* backyard; (*zwischen Vorder- und Hinterhaus*) courtyard; **~indien** *nt* South-East Asia; **~kopf** *m* back of one's head; **etw im ~kopf haben/behalten** (*inf*) to have/keep sth in the back of one's mind; **~lader** *m* **-s, -** breech-loader; (*inf: Homosexueller*) fag (*pej*); **~lage** *f* (*Sw*) security; **~land** *nt* hinterland; (*Ind*) back-up area; **h~lassen¹*** *vt insep irreg* to leave; (*testamentarisch auch*) to bequeath (*jdm etw* sb sth, sth to sb); **h~lassene Werke/Schriften** posthumous works; **h~lassen²** *vt sep irreg* (*dial inf*) **jdn h~lassen** to let sb go behind, to allow sb to go behind; **~lassenschaft** *f* estate; (*literarisch, fig*) legacy; **die ~lassenschaft seines Vorgängers aufarbeiten** to finish (off) sb else's (unfinished) work; **jds ~lassenschaft antreten** (*beerben*) to inherit sb's estate; (*jdm nachfolgen*) to follow sb; **~lassung** *f* (*form*) **unter ~lassung von Schulden** leaving (unsettled *or* unpaid) debts;

h~lastig adj (Aviat) tail-heavy; (Naut) stern-heavy; **~lauf** m (Hunt) hind leg; **h~legen*** vt insep (a) (verwahren lassen) to deposit; (b) (als Pfand h~legen) to leave.

Hinterlegung f deposit.

Hinterlegungs-: ~schein m deposit receipt; **~summe** f sum deposited.

hinterleuchtet adj (Comput) Bildschirm backlit.

Hinterlist f -, no pl (a) siehe adj craftiness, cunning; treachery; deceitfulness. (b) (Trick, List) ruse, trick.

hinterlistig adj (tückisch) crafty, cunning; (verräterisch) treacherous; (betrügerisch) deceitful.

hinterm = hinter dem.

Hintermann m, pl ¨er (a) person/car behind (one) ◆ mein ~ the person/car behind me. (b) (inf) (Gewährsmann) contact ◆ die ¨er des Skandals the men behind the scandal. (c) (Fin: von Wechsel) subsequent endorser.

Hintermannschaft f (Sport) defence.

hintern = hinter den.

Hintern m -s, - (inf) bottom (inf), backside (inf), behind ◆ ein Tritt in den ~ a kick in the pants or up the backside (inf); jdm den ~ versohlen to tan sb's hide; ein paar auf den ~ or den ~ voll bekommen to get one's bottom smacked (inf); sich auf den ~ setzen (hinfallen) to fall on one's bottom etc; (eifrig arbeiten) to buckle down to work; jdm in den ~ kriechen to lick sb's boots, to suck up to sb; mit dem Zeugnis kann er sich (dat) den ~ wischen he might as well use that certificate for toilet paper.

Hinter-: ~pfote f hind paw; **~pfuiteufel** nt -s, no pl (pej inf) siehe ~tupfing(en); **~rad** nt rear or back wheel; **~radantrieb** m rear wheel drive; **h~rücks** adv from behind; (fig: heimtückisch) behind sb's back.

hinters = hinter das.

Hinter-: ~schiff nt stern; **~seite** f back; (von Münze) reverse side; (inf: Hintern) backside (inf); **~sinn** m underlying or deeper meaning (gen behind); **h~sinnig** adj cryptic.

hinterste(r, s) adj superl of hintere(r, s) very back, backmost; (entlegenste) remotest ◆ die H~n those at the very back; das ~ Ende the very end or (von Saal) back; in der ~n Reihe in the very back row; das H~ zuvorderst kehren (inf) to turn everything upside down.

Hinterste(r) m decl as adj (inf) siehe Hintern.

Hinter-: ~steven m (Naut) stern-post; (hum inf: Gesäß) backside (inf); **~teil** nt (a) (inf) backside (inf); (von Tier) hindquarters pl; (b) auch m back or rear part; **~treffen** nt im ~treffen sein to be at a disadvantage; ins ~treffen geraten or kommen to fall behind; **h~treiben*** vt insep irreg (fig) to foil, to thwart; Gesetz to block; **~treibung** f siehe vt foiling, thwarting; blocking; **~treppe** f back stairs pl; **~treppenroman** m (pej) cheap or trashy novel, penny dreadful (dated Brit), dime novel (US); **~tupfing(en)** nt -s, no pl (inf) the back of beyond; **~tür** f, (Aus) **~türl** nt -s, -(n) back door; (fig inf: Ausweg, Umweg) loophole; durch die ~tür (fig) through the back door; sich (dat) eine ~tür or ein ~türchen offenhalten or offenlassen (fig) to leave oneself a loophole or a way out; **~wäldler** m -s, - (inf) backwoodsman, hillbilly (esp US); **h~wäldlerisch** adj (inf) backwoods attr; Ansichten, Benehmen, Methoden auch hick attr; ein h~wäldlerischer Mensch a backwoodsman, a hillbilly (esp US); **h~ziehen*** vt insep irreg Steuern to evade; Material to appropriate; **~ziehung** f siehe vt evasion; appropriation; **~zimmer** nt back room.

hin-: ~tragen vt sep irreg to take or carry there; **~treiben** sep irreg [1] vt (Wind) to blow; (Strömung) to wash; [2] vt impers es trieb ihn immer wieder ~ something always drove him back there; **~treten** vi sep irreg (a) aux sein vor jdn ~treten to go up to sb; vor Gott to step before sb; zu jdm/etw ~treten to step over to sb/sth; (b) (mit Fuß stoßen) to kick (sth); **~tun** vt sep irreg (inf) to put; ich weiß nicht, wo ich ihn ~tun soll (fig) I can't (quite) place him.

hinüber adv over; (über Grenze, Straße, Fluß auch) across ◆ da ~ over there; ~ und herüber back and forth; quer ~ right across; bis zum anderen Ufer ~ over or across to the other bank; siehe ~sein.

hinüber- pref siehe auch herüber-, rüber-; **~befördern*** vt sep to transport across (über etw (acc) sth); **~blicken** vi sep to look across (zu jdm to sb); **~bringen** vt sep irreg to take across (über etw (acc) sth); **~dämmern** vi sep aux sein (einschlafen) to doze off; (sterben) to pass away in one's sleep; **~fahren** sep irreg [1] vt (über etw (acc) sth) jdn to take across; Gepäck etc auch to carry across; Auto to drive across; [2] vi aux sein to travel or go across; nach Frankreich ~fahren to cross or go across to France; über den Fluß ~fahren to cross the river; **~führen** sep [1] vt jdn (über die Straße/dort/in das andere Zimmer) ~führen to take sb across (the street)/over (there)/over (into the other room); [2] vi (verlaufen: Straße, Brücke) to go across (über etw (acc) sth); **~gehen** vi sep irreg aux sein (a) to go or walk across; (über Brücke auch, zu anderem Haus, zu jdm) to go or walk over (über etw (acc) sth); (b) (euph: sterben) to pass away; **~gelangen*** vi sep aux sein to get across (über etw (acc) sth); **~helfen** vi sep irreg jdm ~helfen to help sb across (über etw (acc) sth); (fig: über Schwierigkeiten) to help sb out (über +acc of); jdm (ins Jenseits) ~helfen (leichten Tod verschaffen) to help sb to die; (töten) to bump sb off (inf); **~kommen** vi sep irreg aux sein (über etw (acc) sth) to come across; (über Brücke, Fluß auch, über Hindernis, zu Besuch) to come over; (~können) to get across/over; **~lassen** vt sep irreg to let or allow across; (über Kreuzung, Brücke auch, zu Besuch) to let or allow over (über etw (acc) sth); **~reichen** sep [1] vt to pass across; (über Zaun etc) to pass over (jdm to sb, über etw (acc) sth); [2] vi to reach across (über etw (acc) sth); (fig) to extend (in +acc into); **~retten** sep [1] vt to bring to safety; (fig) Humor, Tradition to keep alive; etw in die Gegenwart ~retten to keep sth alive; [2] vr (über Grenze) to reach safety; (fig: Brauch) to be kept alive; **~rufen** sep irreg [1] vt to call out; [2] vi to call over (über etw (acc) sth); **~schaffen** vt sep to get across (über etw (acc) sth); **~schicken** vt sep to send across or (zu Besuch) over (über etw (acc) sth); **~schlummern** vi sep aux sein (euph: sterben) to pass away; **~schwimmen** vi sep irreg aux sein to swim across (über etw (acc) sth); ⚠**~sein** vi sep irreg aux sein (Zusammenschreibung nur bei infin und ptp) (inf) (a) (verdorben sein) to be off or bad; (kaputt, unbrauchbar, tot sein) to have had it (inf); (ruiniert sein: Firma, Politiker) to be done for; (b) (betrunken sein) to be well away (inf); (betäubt sein) to be (knocked) out (inf); **~spielen** sep [1] vi (geh) dieses Rot spielt leicht ins Violett ~ this red has a slight purple tinge or tinge of purple; [2] vt Ball to pass (jdm to sb); **~steigen** vi sep irreg aux sein to climb over (über etw (acc) sth); **~tragen** vt sep irreg to carry across (über etw (acc) sth); **~wechseln** vi sep aux haben or sein to change over (zu, in +acc to); zu einer anderen Partei ~wechseln to go over to another party; **~werfen** vt sep irreg to throw over (über etw (acc) sth); einen Blick ~werfen to glance over; **~ziehen** sep irreg [1] vt to pull across (über etw (acc) sth); (fig: umstimmen) to win over (auf +acc to); [2] vi aux sein (a) (marschieren) to move or march across; (b) (sich bewegen: Rauch, Wolken) to move across (über etw (acc) sth); [3] vr (sich erstrecken) to stretch over (nach, zu to).

hin- und her-: ~bewegen* vtr sep to move to and fro; **~fahren** sep irreg [1] vi aux sein to travel to and fro or back and forth; [2] vt to drive to and fro or back and forth.

Hin|undhergerede, Hin-und-Her-Gerede nt (inf) das ewige ~ this continual argy-bargy (inf) or carrying-on (inf).

Hin- und Rück-: ~fahrt f return journey, round trip (US); **~flug** m return flight; **~weg** m round trip.

hinunter [1] adv down ◆ bis ~ zu down to; ins Tal ~ down into the valley; am Hügel ~ down the hill; dort or da ~ down there; ~ mit ihm! down with him; ~ mit der Arznei get this medicine down.
[2] prep +acc (nachgestellt) down.

hinunter- pref siehe auch herunter-, runter- down; **~blicken** vi sep to look down; **~bringen** vt sep irreg to take down; (inf: schlucken können) to be able to get down; **~fahren** sep irreg [1] vi aux sein to go down; (Fahrstuhl, Bergbahn auch) to descend; in etw (acc)/nach etw ~fahren to go down into sth/to sth; [2] vt Passagier to take down; Fahrzeug to drive down; **~fallen** vi sep irreg aux sein to fall down; **~fließen** vi sep irreg aux sein to flow down; **~gehen** vi sep irreg aux sein to go down; (zu Fuß auch) to walk down; (Flugzeug) to descend (auf +acc to); **~gießen** vt sep irreg to pour down; Getränke to knock back (inf); **~kippen** vt sep to tip down; (inf) Getränke to knock back (inf); **~klettern** vi sep aux sein to climb down; **~lassen** vt sep irreg to lower, to let down; er läßt mich nicht ~ (inf) he won't let me get down; **~laufen** vi sep irreg aux sein to run down; es lief ihm eiskalt den Rücken ~ a shiver ran down his spine; **~reichen** sep [1] vt to hand or pass down; [2] vi to reach down; (fig: in Rangfolge) to apply (bis zu down to); **~reißen** vt sep irreg to pull or drag down; **~schalten** vi sep (Aut) to change or shift (US) down; **~schauen** vi sep (dial) to look down; **~schlingen** vt sep irreg (inf) to gulp down; Essen to gobble down; **~schlucken** vt sep to swallow (down); (fig) Beleidigung to swallow; Kritik to take; Ärger, Tränen to choke back; **~schmeißen** vt sep irreg (inf) to throw or chuck (inf) down; **~schütten** vt sep siehe ~gießen; **~sehen** vi sep irreg to look down; **~spülen** vt sep (a) (in Toilette, Ausguß) to flush away; etw die Toilette/den Ausguß ~spülen to flush sth down the toilet/drain; (b) Essen, Tablette to wash down; (fig) Ärger to soothe; **~stürzen** sep [1] vi aux sein (a) (~fallen) to tumble or fall down; (b) (eilig ~laufen) to rush or dash down; [2] vt jdn to throw or hurl down; Getränk to gulp down; [3] vr to throw or fling oneself down; **~werfen** vt sep irreg to throw down; (inf: fallen lassen) to drop; einen Blick ~werfen to glance down; **~würgen** vt sep Essen etc to choke down; (fig) Wut, Tränen to choke back; **~ziehen** sep irreg [1] vt to pull down; [2] vi aux sein to move down; [3] vr to run down.

Hin-: h~wagen vr sep to dare to go there; **h~wärts** adv on the way there; die Strecke h~wärts the way there; **~weg** m way there; auf dem ~weg on the way there.

hinweg adv (a) (old: fort) away ◆ ~ mit der Unterdrückung down with oppression.
(b) über jdn/etw ~ over sb or sb's head/sth; über alle Hindernisse etc ~ (fig) despite all the difficulties etc.
(c) (zeitlich) über eine Zeit/zwei Jahre ~ over a period of time/over (a period of) two years.

hinweg- pref siehe auch weg- away; **~bringen** vt sep irreg (fig) jdn über etw (acc) ~bringen to help sb to get over sth; **~gehen** vi sep irreg aux sein über etw (acc) ~gehen to pass over or across sth; (nicht beachten) to pass over or disregard sth; **~helfen** vi sep irreg (fig) jdm über etw (acc) ~helfen to help sb get over sth; **~kommen** vi sep irreg aux sein (fig) über etw (acc) ~kommen (überstehen, verwinden) to get over sth; (sich ~setzen können) to dismiss sth; ich komme nicht darüber ~, daß ... (inf) I can't get over the fact that ...; **~raffen** vt sep (geh) to carry off; **~sehen** vi sep irreg über jdn/etw ~sehen (lit) to see over sb or sb's head/sth; (fig) (ignorieren) to ignore sb/sth; (unbeachtet lassen) to overlook sb/sth; darüber ~sehen, daß ... to overlook the fact that ...; **~setzen** sep [1] vi aux haben or sein über etw (acc) ~setzen to jump or leap over sth; [2] vr (fig) sich über etw (acc) ~setzen (nicht beachten) to disregard or dismiss sth; (überwinden) to overcome sth; **~täuschen** vt sep jdn über etw (acc) ~täuschen to mislead or deceive sb about sth; darüber ~täuschen, daß ... to hide the fact that ...; sich nicht darüber ~täuschen lassen, daß ... not to blind oneself to the fact that ...; **~trösten** vt sep jdn über etw (acc) ~trösten to console sb about sth; deine Entschuldigung tröstet mich nicht darüber ~, daß ... your apology does not make up for the fact that ...

Hinweis m -es, -e (a) (Rat) tip, piece of advice; (Bemerkung) comment;

(*amtlich*) notice ◆ **darf ich mir den ~ erlauben, daß** ... may I point out *or* draw your attention to the fact that ...; **~e für den Benutzer** notes for the user.
(b) (*Verweisung*) reference ◆ **unter ~ auf** (+*acc*) with reference to.
(c) (*Anhaltspunkt, Anzeichen*) indication; (*esp von Polizei*) clue.
(d) (*Anspielung*) allusion (*auf* +*acc* to).

hinweisen *sep irreg* **1** *vt* **jdn auf etw** (*acc*) ~ to point sth out to sb. **2** *vi* **auf jdn/etw ~** to point to sb/sth; (*verweisen*) to refer to sb/sth; **darauf ~, daß** ... to point out that ...; (*nachdrücklich*) to stress *or* emphasize that ...; (*anzeigen*) to indicate that ...

hinweisend *adj* (*Gram*) demonstrative.

Hinweis-: ~schild *nt*, **~tafel** *f* sign.

hin-: ~wenden *sep irreg* **1** *vt* to turn (*zu, nach* towards); **2** *vr* (*lit*) to turn (*zu, nach* towards, to); (*fig: Mensch*) to turn (*zu* to); **H~wendung** *f* (*fig*) turning (*zu* to); **eine H~wendung zum Besseren** a turn for the better; **~werfen** *sep irreg* **1** *vt* **(a)** (*wegwerfen, zu Boden werfen*) to throw down; (*fallen lassen*) to drop; **jdm etw ~werfen** to throw sth to sb; **(b)** (*flüchtig machen*) *Bemerkung* to drop casually; *Wort* to say casually; *Zeilen, Roman, Zeichnung* to dash off; **einen Blick ~werfen** to glance at it/them; **eine ~geworfene Bemerkung** a casual remark; **(c)** (*inf: aufgeben*) *Arbeit, Stelle* to give up, to chuck (in) (*inf*); **2** *vr* to throw *or* fling oneself down; (*auf die Knie*) to go down *or* throw oneself down on one's knees.

hinwieder, hinwiederum (*old*) *adv* (*dagegen*) on the other hand; (*dann wieder*) in turn.

hin-: ~wirken *vi sep* **auf etw** (*acc*) **~wirken** to work towards sth; **kannst du (nicht) (bei ihm) darauf ~wirken, daß er mich empfängt?** couldn't you use your influence to get him to *or* make him see me?; **~wollen** *vi sep* (*inf*) to want to go.

Hinz *m*: **~ und Kunz** (*inf*) every Tom, Dick and Harry; **von ~ zu Kunz** from pillar to post.

hin-: ~zählen *vt sep* to count out (*jdm* to sb); **~zaubern** *vt sep* (*fig*) to rustle *or* whip up (*inf*); **~ziehen** *sep irreg* **1** *vt* **(a)** (*zu sich ziehen*) to draw *or* pull (*zu* towards); (*fig: anziehen*) to attract (*zu* to); **es zieht sie zur Kunst ~** she feels attracted to art; **(b)** (*fig: in die Länge ziehen*) to draw *or* drag out; **2** *vi aux sein* **(a)** (*sich in bestimmte Richtung bewegen*) to move (*über* +*acc* across, *zu* towards); (*weggehen, -marschieren*) to move *or* go away; **(b)** (*liter: Wolken, Rauch etc*) to drift, to move (*an* +*dat* across); **(c)** (*umziehen*) to move there; **3** *vr* **(a)** (*lange dauern, sich verzögern*) to drag on; (*sich verzögern*) to be delayed; **(b)** (*sich erstrecken*) to stretch, to extend; **~zielen** *vi sep* **auf etw** (*acc*) **~zielen** to aim at sth; (*Pläne etc*) to be aimed at sth; (*Bemerkung*) to refer to sth.

hinzu *adv* (*räumlich*) there, thither (*obs*); (*überdies, obendrein*) besides, in addition ◆ **~ kommt noch, daß ich** ... moreover I ...

hinzu-: ~bekommen* *vt sep irreg* to get *or Kind* have in addition; **~denken** *vt sep irreg* to add in one's mind *or* imagination; **~erfinden*** *vt sep irreg* **etw ~erfinden** to make up and add sth; **~fügen** *vt sep* to add (*dat* to); (*beilegen*) to enclose; **H~fügung** *f* addition; **unter H~fügung von etw** (*form*) by adding sth; (*als Beilage*) enclosing sth; **~gesellen*** *vr sep* to join (*jdm* sb); **~gewinnen*** *vt sep irreg* to get in addition; *neue Mitglieder* to gain; **~kommen** *vi sep irreg aux sein* **(a)** (*hinkommen, eintreffen*) to arrive; **sie kam gerade ~, als** ... she happened to come on the scene when ...; **es werden später noch mehrere ~kommen** more people will join us *or* come along later; **(zu etw) ~kommen** (*sich anschließen*) to join sth; **(b)** (*zusätzlich eintreten*) to supervene, to ensue; (*beigefügt werden*) to be added; **zu etw ~kommen** to be added to sth; **es kommt noch ~, daß** ... there is also the fact that ...; **kommt sonst noch etwas ~?** will there be anything else?; **~nehmen** *vt sep irreg* to include; **etw zu etw ~nehmen** to add sth to sth; **~rechnen** *vt sep* to add on; **~setzen** *vt sep* to add; **~treten** *vi sep irreg aux sein* **(a)** (*herantreten*) to come up; **zu den anderen ~treten** to join the others; **(b)** (*zusätzlich*) *siehe* **~kommen (b)**; **~tun** *vt sep irreg* (*inf*) to add; **H~tun** *nt siehe* **Dazutun**; **~zählen** *vt sep* to add; **~ziehen** *vt sep irreg* to consult; **H~ziehung** *f, no pl* consultation (*gen* with); **unter H~ziehung eines Lexikons** by consulting a dictionary.

Hiob *m* **-s** Job ◆ **das Buch ~** the Book of Job.

Hiobsbotschaft, Hiobspost (*old*) *f* bad news *no pl or* tidings *pl*.

Hip-Hop, Hiphop *m* **-(s)** *no pl* (*Mus*) hiphop.

hip(p) *adj* (*sl*) hip (*sl*).

Hippe *f* **-, -n** (*Messer*) pruning knife; (*Sense des Todes*) scythe.

hipp, hipp, hurra *interj* hip, hip, hurrah *or* hurray.

Hipphipphurra *nt* **-s, -s** cheer ◆ **ein dreifaches ~** three cheers.

Hippie ['hɪpi] *m* **-s, -s** hippie.

Hippodrom *nt or m* **-s, -e** hippodrome.

hippokratisch *adj* Hippocratic ◆ **~er Eid** Hippocratic oath.

Hirn *nt* **-(e)s, -e (a)** (*Anat*) brain.
(b) (*inf*) (*Kopf*) head; (*Verstand*) brains *pl*, mind ◆ **sich** (*dat*) **das ~ zermartern** to rack one's brain(s); **diese Idee ist doch nicht deinem ~ entsprungen?** that's not your own idea *or* brainwave, is it?
(c) (*Cook*) brains *pl*.

Hirn- *siehe auch* **Gehirn-**; **~anhang** *m*, **~anhangsdrüse** *f* (*Anat*) pituitary gland; **~gespinst** *nt* fantasy; **~haut** *f* (*Anat*) meninges *pl*; **~hautentzündung** *f* (*Med*) meningitis; **h~los** *adj* brainless; **~rinde** *f* (*Anat*) cerebral cortex; **h~rissig** *adj* hare-brained; **~stamm** *m* brainstorm; **~tod** *m* (*Med*) brain death; **h~tot** *adj* brain dead; **~tumor** *m* brain tumour; **h~verbrannt** *adj* hare-brained; **~windung** *f* (*Anat*) convolution of the brain; **~zentrum** *nt* brain centre.

Hirsch *m* **-es, -e (a)** (*Paarhufer*) deer; (*Rot~*) red deer; (*männlicher Rot~*) stag; (*Cook*) venison. **(b)** (*inf: Schimpfwort*) clot (*inf*).

Hirsch-: ~art *f* kind *or* species *sing* of deer; **~bock** *m* stag; **~braten** *m* (*Cook*) roast of venison; (*Gericht*) roast venison; **~brunft, ~brunst** *f* rut; **zur Zeit der ~brunft** during the rutting season; **~fänger** *m* hunting knife; **~geweih** *nt* antlers *pl*.

Hirschhorn *nt* horn.

Hirschhorn-: ~knopf *m* horn button; **~salz** *nt* (*Chem*) ammonium carbonate.

Hirsch-: ~jagd *f* stag-hunt/-hunting; **~käfer** *m* stag-beetle; **~kalb** *nt* (male) fawn, (male) deer calf; **~keule** *f* haunch of venison; **~kuh** *f* hind; **~leder** *nt* buckskin, deerskin; **h~ledern** *adj* buckskin, deerskin; **~lederne** *f decl as adj* (*esp Aus*) buckskin breeches *pl*, buckskins *pl* (*US*).

Hirse *f* **-, -n** millet.

Hirse-: ~brei *m* millet gruel; **~korn** *nt* millet seed.

Hirt *m* **-en, -en** herdsman; (*Schaf~*) shepherd ◆ **wie der ~, so die Herde** (*Prov*) like master, like man (*prov*).

-hirt *m in cpds* -herd.

Hirte *m* **-n, -n (a)** (*liter*) *siehe* **Hirt. (b)** (*Eccl: Seelsorger*) shepherd ◆ **der Gute ~** the Good Shepherd.

hirten *vi* (*Sw*) to tend one's herd/sheep *etc*.

Hirten-: ~amt *nt* (*Eccl*) pastorate, pastorship; **~brief** *m* (*Eccl*) pastoral; **~dichtung** *f siehe* **Schäferdichtung**; **~flöte** *f* shepherd's pipe; **~gedicht** *nt* pastoral; **~gott** *m* god of shepherds; **~hund** *m* sheepdog; **~junge, ~knabe** (*liter*) *m* shepherd boy; **~lied** *nt* shepherd's song; **h~los** *adj* (*lit, fig*) shepherdless; **~mädchen** *nt* young shepherdess; **~spiel** *nt* pastoral (play); **~stab** *m* shepherd's crook; (*Eccl*) crosier; **~täschel(kraut)** *nt* **-s, -** shepherd's-purse; **~volk** *nt* pastoral people.

Hirtin *f* herdswoman; (*Schaf~*) shepherdess.

His, his *nt* **-, -** (*Mus*) B sharp.

Hisb Allah, Hisbollah *f* **-** *no pl* Hizbollah.

Hispanismus *m* (*Ling*) Hispanicism.

Hispanist(in *f*) *m* Spanish specialist, Hispanist; (*Student*) Spanish student; (*Professor etc*) Spanish lecturer/professor.

Hispanistik *f* Spanish (language and literature).

hissen *vt* to hoist.

Histamin *nt* **-s,** *no pl* histamine.

Histologe *m*, **Histologin** *f* histologist.

Histologie *f* histology.

histologisch *adj* histological.

Histörchen *nt* anecdote; (*Klatschgeschichte*) little tale *or* story.

Historie [-iə] *f* (*old*) **(a)** (*Weltgeschichte*) history. **(b)** (*Erzählung*) story, tale.

Historien [-iən] *pl* **Shakespeares ~** Shakespeare's history plays *or* histories.

Historien-: ~maler *m* historical painter; **~malerei** *f* historical painting.

Historik *f* history.

Historiker(in *f*) *m* **-s, -** historian.

⚠ **Historiograph** *m* historiographer.

historisch *adj* historical; *Verständnis, Kenntnisse auch* of history; (*geschichtlich bedeutsam*) *Gestalt, Ereignis, Gebäude* historic ◆ **das ist ~ belegt** there is historical evidence for this; **~ denken** to think in historical terms; **~ betrachtet** seen in the light of history.

historisch-kritisch *adj Ausgabe* historico-critical.

Historismus *m, no pl* historicism.

Hit *m* **-s, -s** (*Mus, fig inf*) hit.

Hitler *m* **-s** Hitler.

Hitler-: ~gruß *m* Hitler salute; **~jugend** *f* Hitler Youth (organization); **~junge** *m* member of the Hitler Youth; **~reich** *nt* (Third) Reich; **~zeit** *f* Hitler era.

Hit-: ~liste *f* charts *pl*; **~parade** *f* hit parade.

Hitze *f* **-, -n (a)** heat; (*~welle*) heat wave ◆ **vor ~ umkommen** to be sweltering (in the heat); **eine ~ ist das!** the heat (is incredible)!; **die fliegende ~ bekommen** (*Med*) to get hot flushes; (*inf*) to get all hot and bothered; **bei starker/mittlerer/mäßiger ~ backen** (*Cook*) bake in a hot/medium/moderate oven.
(b) (*fig*) passion ◆ **in ~/leicht in ~ geraten** to get heated/to get worked up easily; **jdn in ~ bringen/sich in ~ reden** to get sb/oneself all worked up; **in der ~ des Gefecht(e)s** (*fig*) in the heat of the moment.
(c) (*Zool*) heat.

Hitze-: h~abweisend *adj* heat-repellant; **~ausschlag** *m* heat rash, prickly heat *no art*; **h~beständig** *adj* heat-resistant; **~beständigkeit** *f* heat resistance; **~bläschen** *nt* heat-spot; **h~empfindlich** *adj* sensitive to heat; **~ferien** *pl* (*Sch*) *time off from school on account of excessively hot weather*; **h~frei** *adj* **h~frei haben** *to have time off from school/work on account of excessively hot weather*; **~pickel** *m* (*inf*) *siehe* **~bläschen**; **~(schutz)schild** *m* heat shield; **~wallung** *f usu pl* (*Med*) hot flush; **~welle** *f* heat wave.

hitzig *adj* **(a)** (*aufbrausend*) *Mensch* hot-headed; *Antwort, Reaktion, Debatte* heated; (*leidenschaftlich*) *Temperament, Typ, Diskussionsteilnehmer* passionate; *Blut* hot ◆ **~ werden** (*Mensch*) to flare up; (*Debatte*) to grow heated; **nicht so ~!** don't get so excited!, hold your horses!; **ein ~er Kopf** (*geh*) a hothead.
(b) (*dated Med: fiebrig*) *Kopf, Gesichtsfarbe* fevered; *Fieber* high.
(c) (*Zool*) on heat.

Hitzigkeit *f siehe adj (a)* hot-headedness; heatedness; passionateness.

Hitz-: ~kopf *m* hothead; **h~köpfig** *adj* hot-headed; **~schlag** *m* (*Med*) heat-stroke.

HIV [ha:|i:'fau] *abbr of* **Human Immunodeficiency Virus** HIV.

HIV- [ha:|i:'fau-] *in cpds* HIV-; **~-infiziert** *adj* HIV-infected; **~-negativ** *adj* HIV-negative; **~-Negative(r)** *mf decl as adj* HIV-negative person;

~-positiv *adj* HIV-positive; **~-Positive(r)** *mf decl as adj* HIV-positive person; **~-Virus** *nt* HIV-virus.

Hiwi *m* **-s, -s (a)** *abbr of* **Hilfswillige(r)**. **(b)** *(Univ sl)* helper. **(c)** *(pej inf: Hilfskraft)* dogsbody *(inf)*.

hj. *abbr of* **halbjährlich.**

Hj. *abbr of* **Halbjahr.**

hl. *abbr of* **heilig.**

Hl. *abbr of* **Heilige(r)** St.

hm *interj* hm.

H-Milch ['ha:-] *f* long-life milk.

h-Moll ['ha:-] *nt* **-,** *no pl* B-minor.

HNO-Arzt [ha:|ɛn'|o:-] *m* ENT specialist.

hob *pret of* **heben.**

Hobby *nt* **-s, -s** hobby.

Hobby-: ~computer *m* games computer; home computer; **~ferien** *pl* activity holiday *sing*; **~fotograf** *m* amateur photographer; **~koch** *m* **er ist ~koch** cooking is his hobby; **~raum** *m* hobby-room, workroom.

Hobel *m* **-s, -** *(Tech)* plane; *(Cook)* slicer.

Hobel-: ~bank *f* carpenter's *or* joiner's bench; **~eisen** *nt* plane -iron; **~maschine** *f* planer, planing machine; **~messer** *nt siehe* **~eisen.**

hobeln *vt* **(a)** *auch vi (Tech)* to plane *(an etw (dat)* sth); *(glätten) Brett* to plane down ◆ **wo gehobelt wird, da fallen Späne** *(Prov)* you can't make an omelette without breaking eggs *(Prov)*. **(b)** *(Cook)* to slice.

Hobelspan *m*, **Hobelscha(r)te** *f (Aus)* shaving.

Hoboe [-'bo:ə] *f* **-, -n** *(old) siehe* **Oboe.**

Hoch *nt* **-s, -s (a)** *(Ruf)* **ein (dreifaches) ~ für** *or* **auf jdn ausbringen** to give three cheers for sb; **ein ~ dem Brautpaar** a toast to the bride and groom.
(b) *(Met, fig)* high.

hoch [1] *adj, attr* **hohe(r, s)** *comp* **höher,** *superl* **¨ste(r, s) (a)** *(räumliche Ausdehnung)* high; *Wuchs, Zimmer, Baum, Mast* tall; *Leiter* tall, long; *Schnee, Wasser* deep ◆ **10 cm ~** 10 cm high; **auf dem hohen Roß sitzen** *(fig)* to be on one's high horse.
(b) *(mengenmäßig, Ausmaß bezeichnend) Preis, Verdienst, Temperatur, Druck etc* high; *Betrag, Summe* large; *Strafe, Gewicht* heavy; *Profit auch, Lotteriegewinn* big; *Verlust auch* big, severe; *Schaden* extensive ◆ **mit hoher Wahrscheinlichkeit** in all probability; **in hohem Maße** in *or* to a high degree.
(c) *(in bezug auf Rang, Ansehen, Bedeutung) Stellung, Position, Amt, Adel, Meinung* high; *Geburt auch* noble; *Rang auch* superior; *Persönlichkeit* distinguished; *Ehre* great; *Fest auch, Besuch, Feiertag, Jubiläum* important; *Offizier* high-ranking; *Favorit* hot; *(Jur, Pol)* high ◆ **das Hohe Haus** *(Parl)* the House; **ein hohes Tier** *(inf)* a big fish *(inf)*; **hohe Herrschaften** *(form)* ladies and gentlemen; **ein Mann von hohem Ansehen/hoher Bildung** a man of high standing/of culture; *siehe* **Gewalt.**
(d) *(qualitativ, sehr groß) Lebensstandard, Ansprüche* high; *Bedeutung, Genuß, Gut, Glück* great.
(e) *(esp Mus)* high ◆ **das hohe C** top C.
(f) *Alter* great, advanced ◆ **ein hohes Alter erreichen** to live to a ripe old age; **er ist ein hoher Siebziger** he is well into his seventies; **im hohen Mittelalter** at the height of the Middle Ages.
(g) *(in Wendungen)* **das ist mir zu ~** *(inf)* that's (well) above my head; **in hoher Blüte stehen** to be in full bloom; *(fig) (Mensch)* to be in one's prime; *(Kultur)* to be at its zenith; *(Wohlstand)* to flourish, to be flourishing; **hohe Flut** spring tide; **die hohe Jagd** deer hunt(ing); **das Hohe Lied** *(Bibl)* the Song of Songs; **ein hohes Lied auf jdn/etw singen** to sing sb's/sth's praises; **die Hohe Schule** *(beim Reiten)* haute école; *(old geh: Hochschule)* university, college; **die Hohe Schule des Lebens/der Menschenkenntnis** the school of life; **es ist hohe Zeit** *(geh)* it's high time; **der hohe Norden** the far North; *siehe* **höchste(r, s), bestimmen.**
[2] *adv, comp* **höher,** *superl* **am ¨sten (a)** *(nach oben)* up ◆ **er sah zu uns ~** *(inf)* he looked up to us; **~ emporragend** towering (up); **ein ~ aufgeschossener Mann** a very tall man; **den Kopf ~ tragen** to hold one's head high; **die Nase ~ tragen** *(inf)* to be stuck up *or* toffee-nosed, to go around with one's nose in the air *(all inf)*; **zwei Treppen ~ wohnen** to live two floors up; **nach Hamburg ~** up to Hamburg; **er krempelte sich die Hosenbeine so ~, daß ...** he rolled up his trouser-legs so far that ...
(b) *(in einiger Höhe)* high ◆ **~ oben** high up; **~ am Himmel** high (up) in the sky; **die Sonne steht ~** the sun is high in the sky; **~ zu Roß** on horseback; **~ werfen/sitzen/wachsen** to throw high/sit up high/grow tall; **4.000 m ~ fliegen** to fly at a height of 4,000 metres.
(c) *(Bedeutung, Ansehen, Qualität bezeichnend) verehren, schätzen, qualifiziert* highly ◆ **das rechne ich ihm ~ an** (I think) that is very much to his credit; **~ hinauswollen** to aim high, to be ambitious; **in der Rangordnung sehr ~ stehen** to be very high up in the hierarchy.
(d) *(Ausmaß, Menge bezeichnend) bezahlen, versichern, willkommen, begabt* highly; *besteuern, verlieren* heavily; *gewinnen* handsomely; *verschuldet* heavily, deeply; *zufrieden, beglückt, erfreut etc* very ◆ **drei Mann ~** *(inf)* three of them; **~ (ein)schätzen/zu ~ (ein)schätzen** to estimate generously/to overestimate; **wie ~ kalkulieren Sie den Bedarf?** how high would you put the requirements?; **wenn es ~ kommt** *(inf)* at (the) most, at the outside; **~ setzen** *or* **spielen** *(im Spiel)* to play for high stakes; **~ favorisiert sein** to be the hot favourite; **wie ~ kommt das?** how much is that?; **~ wetten** to place high bets; **~ zu stehen kommen** *(lit, fig)* to cost dearly; **der Alkoholgehalt liegt sehr ~** the alcohol level is very high; **er ist ~ an Jahren/betagt** he has reached a ripe old age; **~ in den Siebzigern** well into his *etc* seventies; **bis ~ ins 13. Jahrhundert** until well into the 13th century; **wie ~ steht das Thermometer?** how high is the temperature?
(e) *(Math)* **7 ~ 3** 7 to the power of 3, 7 to the 3rd.
(f) *(Mus)* high.
(g) *(in Wendungen)* **es ging ~ her** *(inf)* there were lively goings-on *(inf)*; **die See geht ~** the sea is running high; **~ lebe der König!** long live the King!; **~ und heilig versprechen** to promise faithfully; **~ und heilig schwören** *(inf)* to swear blind *(inf)*; **~!** cheers!; **die Menge rief ~!** the crowd cheered; *siehe* **hochleben.**

hoch- *pref (in Verbindung mit Bewegungsverb)* up; *(in Verbindung mit adj) bezahlt, qualifiziert, versichert, begabt etc* highly; *zufrieden, beglückt, erfreut, elegant etc* very; *besteuert* heavily; *verschuldet* deeply.

Hoch-: h~achtbar *adj attr (dated)* highly respectable; ⚠**h~achten** *vt sep* to respect highly; **~achtung** *f* deep respect; **jdm seine ~achtung für seine Leistung zollen** to be full of admiration for sb's achievement; **bei aller ~achtung vor jdm/etw** with (the greatest) respect for sb/sth; **meine ~achtung!** well done!; **mit vorzüglicher ~achtung** *(form: Briefschluß)* yours faithfully; **h~achtungsvoll** *adv (Briefschluß) (bei Anrede mit Sir/Madam)* yours faithfully; *(bei Anrede mit Namen)* yours sincerely; **~adel** *m* high nobility; **h~aktiv** *adj (Atommüll etc)* high-level; **h~aktuell** *adj* highly topical; **h~alpin** *adj* (high) alpine; **~altar** *m* high altar; **~amt** *nt (Eccl)* High Mass; **h~angesehen** *adj attr* highly regarded/esteemed; **h~anständig** *adj* very decent; **~antenne** *f* roof aerial *(Brit) or* antenna *(US)*; **h~arbeiten** *vr sep* to work one's way up; **h~auflösend** *adj (Comput, TV)* high-resolution; **~bahn** *f* elevated railway *or* railroad *(US)*, el *(US inf)*; **~barock** *m or nt* high baroque; **~bau** *m, no pl* structural engineering; *siehe* **~-und-Tiefbau**; **h~bäumen** *vr sep siehe* **aufbäumen**; **h~beansprucht** *adj attr (Tech)* highly stressed; ⚠**h~begabt** *adj attr* highly gifted *or* talented; **~begabte(r)** *mf decl as adj* gifted person *or* child; **~begabtenförderung** *f* bursary for gifted students; **h~beglückt** *adj attr* supremely *or* blissfully happy; **h~beinig** *adj* long-legged; *Auto* high on the road; **h~bekommen*** *vt sep irreg Stein, Motorhaube etc* to (manage to) lift *or* get up; *Reißverschluß* to (manage to) get *or* do up; **h~beladen** *adj attr* with a high load; **h~berühmt** *adj* very famous; **h~betagt** *adj* aged *attr*, advanced in years; **~betrieb** *m (in Geschäft, Fabrik etc)* peak period; *(im Verkehr)* rush hour; *(Hochsaison)* high season; **~betrieb haben** to be at one's/its busiest; **h~biegen** *vtr sep irreg* to bend up *or* upward(s); **h~binden** *vt sep irreg Haare, Pflanze* to tie up; **h~blicken** *vi sep siehe* **h~sehen**; **~blüte** *f (fig) (von Geschichte, Literatur)* golden age; **seine ~blüte haben** to be at its zenith; **h~bocken** *vt sep* to jack up; **h~bringen** *vt sep irreg (inf)* **(a)** *(nach oben bringen)* to bring *or* take up; **(b)** *(inf: h~heben, h~drücken können)* to (manage to) get up; **einen/keinen h~bringen** *(sl)* to be able/not to be able to get it up *(sl)*; **(c)** *(fig) (leistungsfähig machen)* to get going; *Kranken* to get back on his *etc* feet; *Schüler* to get up to scratch; **(d)** *(fig inf: ärgern)* **jdn h~bringen** to get sb's back up *(inf)*; **~burg** *f (fig)* stronghold; **~decker** *m* **-s, -** *(Aviat)* high-wing monoplane; **h~deutsch** *adj* standard *or* High German; **die h~deutsche Lautverschiebung** the High German sound shift; **~deutsch(e)** *nt* standard *or* High German, the standard *or* High German language; **h~dienen** *vr sep* to work one's way up; ⚠**h~dotiert** *adj attr Mensch* highly remunerated; *Arbeit* highly remunerative; **h~drehen** *vt sep Fenster* to wind up; *Motor* to rev.

Hochdruck *m* **(a)** *(Met)* high pressure. **(b)** *(Typ) (no pl: Verfahren)* surface *or* relief printing; *(Gedrucktes)* relief print. **(c)** *(Phys)* high pressure. **(d)** *(Med: Blutdruck)* high blood pressure. **(e)** *(fig)* **mit ~ arbeiten** to work at full stretch.

Hochdruck-: ~gebiet *nt (Met)* high-pressure area, anticyclone; **~verfahren** *nt (Typ)* relief printing method.

Hoch-: ~ebene *f* plateau; ⚠**h~empfindlich** *adj (Tech) Stoff, Material, Gerät, Instrumente* highly sensitive; *Film* fast; *Stoff* very delicate; **diese Farbe/dieser Teppich ist h~empfindlich** this colour/carpet shows up everything; **~energie-Laser** *m* high-energy laser; ⚠**h~entwickelt** *adj attr Kultur, Volk, Land* highly developed; *(verfeinert) Geräte, Maschinen, Methoden* sophisticated; **h~erhoben** *adj attr* raised high; **h~erhobenen Hauptes** *(fig)* with head held high; **h~explosiv** *adj (lit, fig)* highly explosive; **h~fahren** *sep irreg* [1] *vi aux sein* **(a)** *(nach oben fahren)* to go up; *(in Auto auch)* to drive up; **(b)** *(erschreckt)* to start (up); **aus dem Schlaf h~fahren** to wake up with a start; **(c)** *(aufbrausen)* to flare up; [2] *vt* to take up; *(in Auto auch)* to drive up; **h~fahrend** *adj* **(a)** *(überheblich)* arrogant; **(b)** *siehe* **h~fliegend**; **h~fein** *adj (von Qualität)* high quality; **h~fest** *adj Kunststoff* reinforced; **~finanz** *f* high finance; **~fläche** *f siehe* **~ebene**; **h~fliegen** *vi sep irreg aux sein* to fly up; *(Vogel auch)* to soar; *(in die Luft geschleudert werden)* to be thrown up; **h~fliegend** *adj* ambitious; *(übertrieben)* high-flown; **h~florig** *adj Samt, Teppich* deep-pile *attr*; **~form** *f* top form; **~format** *nt* vertical format; **h~frequent** *adj* high frequency.

Hochfrequenz *f (Elec)* high frequency.

Hochfrequenz-: ~kamera *f* high-speed camera; **~strom** *m* high-frequency current; **~technik** *f* high-frequency engineering.

Hoch-: ~frisur *f* upswept hairstyle; **sie hat eine ~frisur** she wears her hair up; **~garage** *f* multi-storey car park; **h~gebenedeit** *adj (old, Eccl)* most blessed; **~gebirge** *nt* high mountains *pl*, high mountain region *or* area; **~gebirgspflanze** *f* alpine plant; **h~geboren** *adj (dated)* high-born; **(Eure** *or* **Euer) ~geboren** *(Anrede)* your Honour; **seine ~geboren** his Honour; ⚠**h~geehrt** *adj attr* highly honoured; **h~geehrter Herr** *(old: im Brief)* esteemed Sir *(old)*; **~gefühl** *nt* elation; **ein ~gefühl haben** to have a feeling of elation, to feel elated; **im ~gefühl des Sieges** elated by the victory; **h~gehen** *vi sep irreg aux sein* **(a)** *(sich nach oben bewegen)* to rise; *(Preise auch)* to go up, to climb; (*Ballon auch*) to ascend; (*Wellen*) to surge; **(b)** (*inf: hinaufgehen*) to go up; **(c)** (*inf: explodieren*) to blow up; (*Bombe*) to go off; **etw h~gehen lassen** to blow sth up; **(d)** (*inf: wütend werden*) to go through the roof; **da geht einem der Hut h~** (*fig inf*) it's enough to make you blow your top (*inf*); **(e)** (*inf: gefaßt werden*) (*einzelner Verbrecher*) to get nabbed (*inf*); (*Bande auch*) to be blown sky-high (*inf*); **jdn h~gehen lassen** to bust sb (*inf*); **h~geistig** *adj* highly intellectual; *Lektüre, Mensch auch* highbrow *no adv*; **h~gelegen** *adj attr* high-altitude, high-lying; **ein h~gelegener Ort in den Alpen** a place situated high up in the Alps; **h~gelehrt** *adj* erudite, very learned; **h~gemut** *adj* (*geh*) cheerful, in good spirits; ⚠**~genuß** *m* great *or* special treat; (*großes Vergnügen*) great pleasure; **jdm ein ~genuß sein** to be a real treat for sb; **~gericht** *nt* (*Hist*) (*Gericht*) criminal court; (*Richtstätte*) scaffold; **h~gerüstet** *adj Land* with a full military arsenal; *Technik, System* highly sophisticated; **eine h~gerüstete Supermacht** a military superpower; ⚠**h~geschätzt** *adj attr Mensch* highly esteemed; *Sache* greatly valued, much treasured; **h~geschlossen** *adj Kleid etc* high-necked.

Hochgeschwindigkeits-: ~-Computer *m* high-speed computer; **~zug** *m* high-speed train.

hoch-: ~gespannt *adj* (*fig*) *Erwartungen* extreme; **~gesteckt** *adj* (*fig*) *Ziele* ambitious; ⚠**~gestellt** *adj attr* (*fig*) *Persönlichkeit* high-ranking, important; **~gestochen** *adj* (*pej inf*) highbrow; *Reden* high-faluting; *Stil* pompous; (*eingebildet*) stuck-up; ⚠**~gewachsen** *adj* tall; **~gezüchtet** *adj* (*usu pej*) *Motor* souped-up (*sl*); *Geräte* fancy (*inf*); *Tiere, Pflanzen* overbred.

Hochglanz *m* high polish *or* shine; (*Phot*) gloss ◆ **etw auf ~ polieren** *or* **bringen** to polish sth until it gleams, to make sth shine like a new pin; (*fig*) to make sth spick and span.

Hochglanz|abzug *m* (*Phot*) glossy print.

hochglänzend *adj Stoff, Oberfläche* very shiny; *Papier, Fotoabzug* very glossy; *Möbel* highly polished.

Hochglanz-: ~papier *nt* high gloss paper; **~politur** *f* (*Oberfläche*) mirror polish *or* finish; (*Poliermittel*) (furniture) polish.

Hoch-: ~gotik *f* high gothic period; **h~gradig** *adj no pred* extreme; (*inf*) *Unsinn etc* absolute, utter; **h~gucken** *vi sep siehe* **h~sehen**; **h~hackig** *adj Schuhe* high-heeled; **h~halten** *vt sep irreg* **(a)** (*in die Höhe halten*) to hold up; **(b)** (*in Ehren halten*) to uphold; **~haus** *nt* high-rise *or* multi-storey building; (*Wolkenkratzer*) sky-scraper; **h~heben** *vt sep irreg Hand, Arm* to lift, to raise, to hold up; *Kind, Last* to lift up; **durch ~heben der Hände abstimmen** to vote by (a) show of hands; **h~herrschaftlich** *adj* very elegant *or* grand; *Wohnung auch* palatial; **h~herzig** *adj* generous, magnanimous; *Mensch auch* big-hearted; **~herzigkeit** *f* generosity, magnanimity; (*von Mensch auch*) big-heartedness; ⚠**h~industrialisiert** *adj attr* highly industrialized; **h~intelligent** *adj* highly intelligent; **h~interessant** *adj* most interesting; **h~jagen** *vt sep* (*inf*) **(a)** (*aufscheuchen*) *Vögel* to scare up; *Menschen* to get up; **(b)** (*sprengen*) to blow up; **(c)** *Motor* to rev up; **h~jubeln** *vt sep* (*inf*) *Künstler, Film, Politiker etc* to build up, to hype (*inf*); **h~kämmen** *vt sep Haar* to put up; **h~kant** *adv* **(a)** (*lit*) on end; **h~kant stellen** to up-end, to put on end; **(b)** (*fig inf: auch* **h~kantig**) **h~kant hinauswerfen/hinausfliegen** to chuck/be chucked out (*inf*); **h~karätig** *adj* **(a)** *Diamanten, Gold* high-carat; **(b)** (*fig*) top-class; **~kirche** *f* High Church; **h~klappbar** *adj Tisch, Stuhl* folding; *Sitz* tip-up; **h~klappen** *sep* [1] *vt Tisch, Stuhl* to fold up; *Sitz* to tip up; *Kühlerhaube, Deckel* to raise, to lift up; *Mantelkragen* to turn up; [2] *vi aux sein* (*Tisch, Stuhl*) to fold up; (*Sitz*) to tip up; **h~klettern** *vi sep aux sein* (*lit, fig*) to climb up; **h~kommen** *vi sep irreg aux sein* **(a)** (*inf: hinauf-, heraufkommen*) to come up; **(b)** (*inf*) **das Essen ist ihm h~gekommen** he threw up (his meal) (*inf*); **es kommt mir h~** it makes me sick; **(c)** (*aufstehen können*) to (manage to) get up; (*fig: sich aufraffen, gesund werden*) to get back on one's feet; **(d)** (*inf: beruflich, gesellschaftlich*) to come up in the world; **niemanden (neben sich** *dat*) **h~kommen lassen** not to tolerate competition; **~konjunktur** *f* boom; **h~können** *vi sep irreg* (*inf*) (*aufstehen können*) to be able to get up; (*hinaufsteigen können*) to be able to get up (*auf etw* (*acc*) onto sth, *auf Berg* the mountain); **hinten nicht mehr h~können** (*inf*) to be more dead than alive; **h~konzentriert** *adj* highly concentrated; **h~krempeln** *vt sep Ärmel, Hosenbeine* to roll up; **h~kriegen** *vt sep* (*inf*) *siehe* **h~bekommen**; **er kann keinen h~kriegen** (*sl*) he can't get it up (*sl*); **h~kultiviert** *adj* highly sophisticated; *Lebensart* highly civilized; **~kultur** *f* (very) advanced civilization; **h~kurbeln** *vt sep Fenster* to wind up; **h~laden** *vt sep irreg* (*Comput*) to upload; **~land** *nt* highland; **das schottische ~land** the Scottish Highlands *pl*; **~länder(in** *f*) *m* **-s, -** highlander; **~landkaffee** *m* high-grown coffee; **~lautung** *f* (*Ling*) Standard German pronunciation; **h~leben** *vi sep* **jdn h~leben lassen** to give three cheers for sb; **er lebe h~!** three cheers (for him)!; **h~ lebe der König!** long live the King!; **h~legen** *vt sep* **(a)** *Beine etc* to put up; **(b)** (*inf: nach oben legen*) to put high up.

Hochleistung *f* first-class performance.

Hochleistungs- *in cpds* high-performance; **~motor** *m* high-performance engine; **~öl** *nt* heavy-duty oil; **~sorte** *f* (*Agr*) high-yield variety; **~sport** *m* top-class sport; **~sportler** *m* top athlete; **~training** *nt* intensive training.

höchlich(st) *adv* (*dated*) highly, greatly, most.

Hoch-: h~löblich *adj* (*dated*) very *or* highly praiseworthy; (*iro*) most appreciated; **~lohnland** *nt* country with high wage costs; **~mittelalter** *nt* high Middle Ages *pl*; **h~modern** *adj* very modern, ultra-modern; **~moor** *nt* moor; **~mut** *m* arrogance; **~mut kommt vor dem Fall** (*Prov*) pride comes before a fall (*Prov*); **h~mütig** *adj* arrogant; **~mütigkeit** *f* arrogance; **h~näsig** *adj* (*inf*) snooty (*inf*); **~näsigkeit** *f* (*inf*) snootiness (*inf*); **~nebel** *m* (low) stratus; **h~nehmen** *vt sep irreg* **(a)** (*heben*) to lift; *Kind, Hund* to pick *or* lift up; **(b)** (*dial: in oberes Stockwerk*) to take up; **(c)** (*inf: necken*) **jdn h~nehmen** to pull sb's leg; **(d)** (*inf: schröpfen*) **jdn h~nehmen** to fleece sb (*inf*); **(e)** (*inf: verhaften*) to pick up (*inf*); **~ofen** *m* blast furnace; **h~päppeln** *vt sep* (*inf*) *Tier, Kind, Kranken* to feed up; (*fig*) to nurse back to health; **~parterre** *nt* raised ground floor; **~plateau** *nt* plateau; **h~polymer** *adj* (*Chem*) high-polymeric; **h~prozentig** *adj alkoholische Getränke* high-proof; *Lösung* highly concentrated; ⚠**h~qualifiziert** *adj attr* highly qualified; **~rad** *nt* penny-farthing (bicycle); **h~rädrig** *adj* with high wheels; **h~ragen** *vi sep aux sein or haben* (*Bäume*) to rise (up); (*Berge, Türme, Häuser*) to tower (up), to rise up; **h~ranken** *vir sep* (*vi: aux sein*) to creep (up), to climb (up); **h~rechnen** *sep* [1] *vt* to project; [2] *vi* to make a projection; **~rechnung** *f* projection; **~reck** *nt* high *or* horizontal bar; **h~recken** *sep* [1] *vt Arme, Hände* to raise *or* stretch up; **den Hals** *or* **Kopf h~recken** to crane one's neck; [2] *vr* to draw oneself up; **h~reißen** *vt sep irreg Arme* to bring up; *Kamera, Waffe* to lift quickly; (*Aviat*) to put into a steep climb, to hoick (*spec*); **~relief** *nt* high relief; **~renaissance** *f* high renaissance; **h~rot** *adj* bright red; **mit h~rotem Gesicht** with one's face as red as a beetroot; **~ruf** *m* cheer; **h~rüsten** *vt sep* **ein Land h~rüsten** to increase the weaponry of a country; **~rüstung** *f, no pl* arms build-up; **h~rutschen** *vi sep aux sein* (*Kleidungsstück*) to ride up; (*inf: aufrücken*) to move up; **~saison** *f* high season; ⚠**h~schätzen** *vt sep siehe* **h~achten**; **h~schaukeln** *sep* [1] *vt Problem, Angelegenheit* to blow up; [2] *vr* to work oneself up; **h~scheuchen** *vt sep* (*inf*) *siehe* **aufscheuchen**; **h~schießen** *sep irreg* [1] *vi aux sein* to shoot up; [2] *vt Feuerwerksrakete, Leuchtkugel* to send up; **h~schlagen** *sep irreg* [1] *vt Kragen* to turn up; [2] *vi aux sein* (*Wellen*) to surge up; (*Flammen*) to leap up; **h~schnellen** *vi sep aux sein* (*Lachse*) to leap up; (*Feder, Mensch, Preise auch*) to shoot up; ⚠**h~schrauben** *vt sep* (*lit*) to raise; (*fig*) *Preise* to force up; *Erwartungen* to raise; *Forderungen, Ansprüche* to increase; **h~schrecken** *vti sep* (*vi: irreg aux sein*) *siehe* **aufschrecken**.

Hochschul-: ⚠~abschluß *m* degree; **mit ~abschluß** with a degree; **~absolvent** *m* graduate; **~(aus)bildung** *f* (*Ausbildung*) college/university training; (*Bildung*) university education.

Hochschule *f* college; (*Universität*) university ◆ **Technische ~** technical college, college of technology.

Hochschüler(in *f*) *m* student; (*Universitäts~ auch*) undergraduate.

Hochschul-: ~lehrer *m* college/university teacher, lecturer (*Brit*); **~politik** *f* higher education policy; **~reform** *f* university reform; **~reife** *f academic standard required for university entrance*; **er hat (die) ~reife** ≃ he's got his A-levels (*Brit*), he's graduated from high school (*US*); **~studium** *nt* higher education, university education; **~wesen** *nt* system of higher education, university system; **~zugang** *m* university entrance *or* admission.

hochschwanger *adj* well advanced in pregnancy, very pregnant (*inf*).

Hochsee *f* high sea ◆ **auf ~** on the high seas *or* open sea.

Hochsee-: ~fischerei *f* deep-sea fishing; **~kutter** *m* deep-sea cutter; **~schiffahrt** *f* deep-sea shipping; **h~tüchtig** *adj* oceangoing.

Hoch-: h~sehen *vi sep irreg* to look up; **~seil** *nt* high wire, tightrope; **~seilakt** *m* (*von Artisten*) high-wire *or* tightrope act; (*fig*) tightrope walk; **h~sensibel** *adj Apparat, Angelegenheit* highly sensitive; **~sicherheitstrakt** *m* high-security wing; **~sitz** *m* (*Hunt*) (raised) hide; **~sommer** *m* height of the summer; (*Zeitabschnitt*) midsummer *no art*; **h~sommerlich** *adj* very summery.

Hochspannung *f* (*Elec*) high voltage, high tension; (*fig*) high tension ◆ **„Vorsicht ~"** "danger — high voltage".

Hochspannungs-: ~leitung *f* high tension line, power line; **~mast** *m* pylon; **~technik** *f* high-voltage engineering.

Hoch-: h~spielen *vt sep* (*fig*) to blow up, to play up; **etw (künstlich) h~spielen** to blow sth up out of all proportion; **~sprache** *f* standard language; **h~sprachlich** *adj* standard; **h~sprachlich heißt es ...** in standard German/English *etc* that's ...; **h~springen** *vi sep irreg aux sein* **(a)** (*inf: aufspringen*) to jump up (*an jdm* on sb); **auf etw** (*acc*) **h~springen** to jump (up) on sth; **(b)** (*inf: schnell hinauflaufen*) to run up; **(c)** *infin, ptp only* (*Sport*) to do the high jump; **~springer** *m* high jumper; **~sprung** *m* (*Disziplin*) high jump; (*Sprung*) jump.

höchst [1] *adj siehe* **höchste(r, s)**.
[2] *adv* (*überaus*) highly, extremely, most.

Höchst- *in cpds* (*obere Grenze angebend*) (*mit n*) maximum; (*mit adj*) *siehe* **Hoch-**; (*mit adj: Intensität ausdrückend*) extremely, most; **~alter** *nt* maximum age.

Hoch-: h≈stämmig *adj Baum* tall; *Rosen* long-stemmed; **≈stand** *m* (*Hunt*) *siehe* **~sitz**; **~stapelei** *f* (*Jur*) fraud; (*einzelner Fall*) swindle, con trick; (*fig: Aufschneiderei*) boasting *no pl*; **h≈stapeln** *vi sep* to be fraudulent, to practise fraud (*form*); (*fig*) to put one over (*inf*); **≈stapler** *m* **-s, -** confidence trickster, con man (*inf*); (*fig*) fraud; **≈start** *m* (*Sport*) standing start.

Höchst-: ~betrag *m* maximum amount; **~bietende(r)** *mf decl as adj* highest bidder.

höchste *adj siehe* **höchste(r, s)**.

Höchste *siehe* **Höchste(r), Höchste(s)**.

hoch-: ~stecken *vt sep* to pin up; *Haare auch* to put up; **~stehend** *adj* **(a)** (*gesellschaftlich*) of high standing; (*kulturell*) advanced; (*geistig*) highly intellectual; **(b)** (*entwicklungsmäßig, qualitativ*) superior; **(c)** *Kragen* turned-up; **~steigen** *vi sep irreg aux sein siehe* **hinauf-/heraufsteigen, aufsteigen**.

höchst-: ~eigen *adj, adv* **~eigen, in ~eigener Person** (*dated, hum*) in person.

hoch-: ~stellen *vt sep* **(a)** (*an höhere Stelle*) *Stühle etc* to put up; (*außer Reichweite*) to put *or* place high up; **~gestellte Zahlen** superior numbers; **(b)** (*inf: höher einstellen*) *Heizung, Ventilator etc* to turn up; **(c)** *Kragen* to turn up; **H~stelltaste** *f* (*Comput*) shift key; **~stemmen** *sep* [1] *vt* to lift *or* raise up (with great effort); [2] *vr* to raise oneself up.

höchstenfalls *adv* at (the) most, at the outside.

höchstens *adv* **(a)** (*nicht mehr, länger als*) not more than; (*bestenfalls*) at the most, at best. **(b)** (*außer*) except.

Höchste(r) *m decl as adj* **der ~** the Lord, the Supreme Being.

höchste(r, s) [1] *adj, superl of* **hoch (a)** (*räumliche Ausdehnung*) highest; *Wuchs, Zimmer, Baum, Mast* tallest; *Leiter* tallest, longest.
(b) *Preis, Verdienst, Temperatur, Druck etc* highest; *Betrag, Summe* largest; *Strafe, Gewicht* heaviest; *Profit auch, Lotteriegewinn* biggest; *Verlust* most severe; *Schaden* most expensive; (*maximal*) *Verdienst, Temperatur, Geschwindigkeit etc* maximum *attr* ◆ **im ~n Grade/Maße** extremely; **im ~n Fall(e)** at the most.
(c) (*im Rang*) highest; *Ehre* greatest; *Fest* most important; *Offizier* highest-ranking ◆ **das ~ Wesen** the Supreme Being; **die ~ Instanz** the supreme court of appeal; **sich an ~r Stelle beschweren** to complain to the highest authority.
(d) *attr* (*qualitativ, äußerst*) *Lebensstandard, Ansprüche* highest; *Bedeutung, Genuß, Glück* greatest, supreme; *Gut* greatest; *Not, Gefahr, Wichtigkeit* utmost, greatest; *Freude* greatest; *Konzentration* extreme ◆ **zu meiner ~n Zufriedenheit** to my great satisfaction.
(e) *Alter* greatest; (*Mus*) highest.
(f) (*in Wendungen*) **~ Zeit** *or* **Eisenbahn** (*inf*) high time; **der ~ Norden** the extreme North; **das ist das ~ der Gefühle** that is the highest *or* most sublime feeling *or* of feelings; **aufs ~ erfreut** *etc* highly *or* greatly *or* tremendously (*inf*) pleased *etc*; **das ist das ~, was ich bezahlen/tun kann** that is the most I can do/pay.
[2] *adv* **am ~n (a)** (*in größter Höhe*) highest ◆ **mittags steht die Sonne am ~n** the sun is highest at noon.
(b) (*in größtem Ausmaß*) *verehren, schätzen* most (of all); *versichern, begabt* most; *besteuert, verlieren* (the) most heavily; *verschuldet* (the) most deeply ◆ **in der Rangordnung am ~n stehen** to be the highest up in the hierarchy; **er ist am ~n qualifiziert** he is the most (highly) qualified; **am ~n stehen** (*Kurse, Temperatur*) to be at its highest.

Höchste(s) *nt decl as adj* (*fig*) highest good ◆ **nach dem ~n streben** to aspire to the ideal *or* to perfection.

Höchst-: ~fall *m* **im ~fall** *siehe* **höchstens (a)**; **~form** *f* (*Sport*) top form; **~frequenzwelle** *f* microwave; **~gebot** *nt* highest bid; **~geschwindigkeit** *f* top *or* maximum speed; **zulässige ~geschwindigkeit** speed limit; **~grenze** *f* upper limit.

Hoch-: h~stielig *adj* long-stemmed; **h~stilisieren*** *vt sep* to build up (*zu* into); **~stimmung** *f* high spirits *pl*.

Höchst-: ~leistung *f* best performance; (*bei Produktion*) maximum output; **~maß** *nt* maximum amount (*an +dat* of); **h~persönlich** *adv* personally; **es ist der Prinz h~persönlich** it's the prince in person; **~preis** *m* top *or* maximum price.

Hoch-: ~straße *f* fly-over; **h~streben** *vi sep aux sein* **(a)** *siehe* **aufstreben**; **(b)** (*fig: nach Höherem streben*) to aspire (*nach* to, after); **h~streifen** *vt sep Ärmel* to push up.

▼ **Höchst-: h~richterlich** *adj* of the supreme court; **~satz** *m* (*beim Glücksspiel*) maximum stake; (*bei Versicherungen*) maximum rate; **~stand** *m* highest level; **~strafe** *f* maximum penalty; **h~wahrscheinlich** *adv* in all probability, most probably *or* likely; **~wert** *m* maximum value.

hochstylen [-stailən] *vt sep* to give style to; (*pej*) *Person* to hype (*inf*); *Auto* to soup up (*inf*); *Laden etc* to tart up (*inf*) ◆ **ein hochgestyltes Produkt** a stylish product.

höchstzulässig *adj attr* maximum (permissible).

Hoch-: ~tal *nt* high-lying valley; **~technologie** *f* high technology; **~temperaturreaktor** *m* high temperature reactor; **h~tönend** *adj* high-sounding; **~tour** *f* **auf ~touren laufen/arbeiten** (*Maschinen*) to run at full speed; (*fig: Mensch, Fabrik etc*) to run/work etc at full steam; **etw auf ~touren bringen** *Motor* to rev sth up to full speed; *Maschine, Produktion, Kampagne* to get sth into full swing; **jdn auf ~touren bringen** (*inf*) to get sb really going (*inf*); **h~tourig** *adj Motor* high-revving; **h~tourig fahren** to drive at high revs; **h~trabend** *adj* (*pej*) pompous, turgid; **h~treiben** *vt sep irreg* **(a)** (*hinauftreiben*) to drive up; **(b)** (*fig*) *Preise, Löhne, Kosten* to force up; **~- und Tiefbau** *m* structural and civil engineering; **h~verdient** *adj attr Mensch* of great merit; *Lob* much-deserved; **h~verehrt** *adj attr* highly respected *or* esteemed; (*in Brief*) esteemed (*old*); **h~verehrter Herr Vorsitzender** ... Mr Chairman ...; **h~verehrter Herr Präsident!** Mr President, Sir!; (*in Brief*) Dear Sir; **~verrat** *m* high treason; **~verräter** *m* person guilty of high treason, traitor; **h~verräterisch** *adj* treasonable; **h~verschuldet** *adj attr* deep in debt; **h~verzinslich** *adj* bearing *or* yielding a high rate/high rates of interest; **~wald** *m* timber forest.

Hochwasser *nt* **(a)** (*Höchststand von Flut*) high tide. **(b)** (*überhoher Wasserstand in Flüssen, Seen*) high water; (*Überschwemmung*) flood ◆ **~ haben** (*Fluß*) to be in flood; **er hat ~** (*hum inf*) his trousers are at half-mast (*inf*).

Hochwasser-: ~gefahr *f* danger of flooding; **~hosen** *pl* (*hum inf*) trousers at half-mast (*inf*); **~katastrophe** *f* flood disaster; **~schaden** *m* flood damage; **~stand** *m* high-water level.

Hoch-: h~werfen *vt sep irreg* to throw up; **h~wertig** *adj* high-quality *attr*, of high quality; *Nahrungsmittel* highly nutritious; *Stahl* high-grade; (*Chem*) high-valency *attr*, of high valency; **~wild** *nt* big game (*including bigger game birds*); **h~willkommen** *adj attr* most *or* very welcome; **h~wohlgeboren** *adj* (*obs*) honourable; **(Euer) ~wohlgeboren** Your Honour; **h~wölben** *sep* [1] *vt* **etw h~wölben** to make sth bulge up; [2] *vr* to bulge up; **h~wollen** *vi sep* (*inf*) to want to get up (*inf*); (*aufstehen wollen auch*) to want to get up; (*in die Höhe wollen auch, nach Norden wollen*) to want to go up; **~würden** *m* **-s**, *no pl* (*dated: Anrede*) Reverend Father; **h~würdig** *adj* (*dated*) Reverend; **~zahl** *f* exponent.

▼ **Hochzeit¹** *f* **-, -en** wedding; (*Eheschließung auch*) marriage ◆ **~ machen/haben** to get married; **~ halten/feiern** to have a wedding; **etw zur ~ geschenkt bekommen/schenken** to get/give sth as a wedding present; **grüne ~** wedding day; **silberne/goldene/diamantene ~** silver/golden/diamond wedding (anniversary); **man kann nicht auf zwei ~en tanzen** (*prov*) you can't have your cake and eat it (*prov*).

Hochzeit² *f* **-, -en** (*liter: Blütezeit*) golden age.

hochzeiten *vi insep* (*dated, Aus, S Ger*) to marry.

Hochzeiter *m* **-s, -** (*dated, Aus, Sw, S Ger*) bridegroom ◆ **die ~** the bride and groom.

hochzeitlich *adj* bridal *attr*, wedding *attr* ◆ **die Braut/der Bräutigam war ~ gekleidet** the bride was in her wedding dress/the groom was in his wedding attire; **~ geschmückt** decorated for the wedding.

Hochzeits- *in cpds* wedding; **~anzeige** *f* wedding announcement; **~feier** *f* wedding celebration; (*Empfang*) reception, wedding breakfast; **~fest** *nt* wedding celebration; **~flug** *m* (*Zool*) nuptial flight; **~gast** *m* wedding guest; **~kleid** *nt* wedding dress, bridal dress *or* gown; **~nacht** *f* wedding night; **~reise** *f* honeymoon; **wohin geht die ~reise?** where are you going on (your) honeymoon?; **~reisende** *pl* honeymoon couple, honeymooners *pl*; **~tag** *m* wedding day; (*Jahrestag*) wedding anniversary; **~zug** *m* wedding procession.

Hoch-: h~ziehen *sep irreg* [1] *vt* **(a)** to pull up; *Hosen etc auch* to hitch up; *Fahne* to run up; *Augenbrauen* to raise, to lift; **die Maschine h~ziehen** (*Aviat*) to put the aircraft into a steep climb; **(b)** (*inf: bauen*) to throw up (*inf*); [2] *vr* to pull oneself up; **sich an etw** (*dat*) **h~ziehen** to climb up sth; (*fig inf*) to get a kick out of sth (*inf*); **~ziel** *nt* (*geh*) ultimate goal; **~zinspolitik** *f* (*Econ*) high interest rate policy.

Hock *m* **-s, ¨-e** (*Sw, dial*) get-together.

Hocke¹ *f* **-, -n** squatting position; (*Übung*) squat; (*beim Turnen*) squat vault; (*beim Skilaufen*) crouch; (*beim Ringen*) mat position ◆ **in die ~ gehen/in der ~ sitzen** to squat.

Hocke² *f* **-, -n** stook, shock.

hocken [1] *vi* (*S Ger: aux sein*) **(a)** (*in der Hocke sitzen*) to squat, to crouch. **(b)** (*inf: sitzen*) to sit; (*auf Hocker*) to perch. **(c)** (*pej inf*) to sit around. **(d)** (*Sport*) **übers Pferd ~** to squat-vault over the horse.
[2] *vr* **(a)** (*in Hockstellung gehen*) to squat. **(b)** (*inf: sich setzen*) to sit down, to plonk oneself down (*inf*).

⚠ **hockenbleiben** *vi sep irreg aux sein* (*dial inf*) *siehe* **sitzenbleiben**.

Hocker *m* **-s, - (a)** (*Stuhl*) stool. **(b)** (*Archeol*) seated burial.

Höcker *m* **-s, - (a)** (*von Kamel, inf: Buckel*) hump; (*auf Schnabel*) knob. **(b)** (*Erhebung*) bump; (*in Gelände*) hump; (*kleiner Hügel*) hummock, hump.

Hockergrab *nt* seated burial.

höck(e)rig *adj* (*uneben*) bumpy; (*buckelig*) hunch-backed; *Nase* with a bump; *Schnabel* with a knob.

Hockey ['hɔki, 'hɔke] *nt* **-s**, *no pl* hockey (*Brit*), field hockey (*US*).

Hockey-: ~ball *m* hockey ball; **~schläger** *m* hockey stick; **~spieler** *m* hockey player; **~stock** *m siehe* **~schläger**.

höckrig *adj siehe* **höck(e)rig**.

Hock-: ~sitz *m* squat; **~sprung** *m* (*Sport*) (*über Gerät*) squat vault; (*beim Bodenturnen*) crouch jump; **~stellung** *f* crouched *or* squatting position; (*Archeol*) seated position.

Hode *m* **-n, -n**, *f* **-, -n**, **Hoden** *m* **-s, -** testicle.

Hoden-: ~bruch *m* scrotal hernia; **~entzündung** *f* inflammation of the testicles, orchitis (*spec*); **~sack** *m* scrotum.

Hof *m* **-(e)s, ¨-e (a)** (*Platz*) yard; (*Innen~*) courtyard; (*Schul~*) schoolyard, playground; (*Kasernen~*) square.
(b) (*Bauern~*) farm; (*Gebäudekomplex auch*) farmyard.
(c) (*Fürsten~*) court ◆ **bei** *or* **am ~e** at court; **am ~e Ludwig XIV** at the court of Louis XIV.
(d) einem Mädchen den ~ machen (*dated, hum*) to court a girl (*dated*), to pay court to a girl (*form*).
(e) (*um Sonne, Mond*) halo.
(f) (*in Namen: Gasthof, Hotel*) hotel, inn.

Hof-: ~amt *nt* court appointment; **~arzt** *m* court physician; **~ball** *m* court ball; **~dame** *f* lady-in-waiting; **~dichter** *m* court poet; (*in GB*) poet laureate.

höfeln *vi* (*Sw*) to flatter (*jdm* sb).

Hof-: ~erbe *m* heir to a/the farm; **~etikette** *f* court etiquette; **h~fähig** *adj* acceptable at court; (*gesellschaftsfähig*) presentable; **~fähigkeit** *f* right/privilege to be present at court.

Hoffart *f* **-**, *no pl* (*dated*) pride, arrogance, haughtiness.

hoffärtig *adj* (*dated*) proud, arrogant, haughty.

▼ **hoffen** [1] *vi* **(a)** (*von Hoffnung erfüllt sein*) to hope ◆ **auf Gott ~** to trust in God; **auf jdn ~** to set one's hopes on sb; **auf etw ~** (*acc*) to hope for sth; **da bleibt nur zu ~** one can only hope; **sie hofften auf ihre Verbündeten** (*auf Erscheinen*) they were waiting for their allies; (*auf Hilfe*) they set their hopes on their allies; **der Mensch hofft, solange er lebt** (*Prov*) hope springs eternal (*prov*); **H~ und Harren macht manchen zum Narren** (*Prov*) some people never give up hoping, pigs might fly (*inf*).
▼ **(b)** (*wünschen und erwarten*) to hope ◆ **~, daß ...** to hope that ...; **ich will nicht ~, daß er das macht** I hope he doesn't do that; **ich will/wir wollen ~, daß ...** I/we can only hope that ..., it is to be hoped that ...

[2] *vt* to hope for ◆ **~ wir das Beste!** let's hope for the best!; **es ist zu ~** it is to be hoped; **ich hoffe es** I hope so; **das will ich (doch wohl) ~** I should (jolly well *Brit inf*) hope so; **das wollen wir ~** let's hope so; **ich will es nicht ~** I hope not; **sie hatten nichts mehr zu ~** they had nothing left to hope for.

hoffentlich *adv* hopefully ◆ **~!** I hope so, let us hope so; **~ nicht** I/we hope not; **~ ist das bald vorbei** I/we *etc* hope that it will be over soon, hopefully it will be over soon; **du bist mir doch ~ nicht böse** I (do) hope (that) you're not angry with me.

-höffig *adj suf (Min)* promising a rich yield of.

höfflich *adj (Min)* promising a rich yield.

Hoffnung *f* hope; (*auf Gott*) trust (*auf +acc* in) ◆ **sich** (*dat*) **~en machen** to have hopes; **sich** (*dat*) **keine ~en machen** not to hold out any hopes; **er macht sich ~en bei ihr** (*inf*) he fancies his chances with her (*inf*); **mach dir keine ~(en)!** I wouldn't even think about it; **jdm ~en machen** to raise sb's hopes; **jdm ~en machen, daß ...** to lead sb to hope that ...; **jdm auf etw** (*acc*) **~en machen** to lead sb to expect sth; **jdm keine ~en machen** not to hold out any hopes for sb; **seine ~en auf jdn/etw setzen** to place one's hopes in *or* pin one's hopes on sb/sth; **die ~ aufgeben/verlieren** to abandon/lose hope; **eine ~ begraben** *or* **zu Grabe tragen** to abandon a hope; **eine ~ zerstören/enttäuschen** to dash/disappoint sb's hopes; **in der ~, bald von Ihnen zu hören** hoping to hear *or* in the hope of hearing from you soon; **sich einer ~/unbegründeten/falschen ~en hingeben** to cherish hopes/unfounded/false hopes; **zu schönen** *or* **zu den schönsten ~en berechtigen** to give rise to great hopes; **~ auf etw** (*acc*) **haben** to have hopes of getting sth; **guter ~ sein** (*euph: schwanger*) to be expecting.

Hoffnungs-: **h~freudig, h~froh** [1] *adj* hopeful; [2] *adv* in happy anticipation; **~funke(n)** *m* glimmer of hope; **~lauf** *m* (*Sport*) repechage; **h~los** *adj* hopeless; **~losigkeit** *f, no pl* hopelessness; (*Verzweiflung*) despair; **~schimmer** *m* glimmer of hope; **~strahl** *m* ray of hope; **~träger** *m* person on whom hopes are pinned; **er war der ~träger der Partei** he carried the hopes of the party; **h~voll** [1] *adj* hopeful; (*vielversprechend*) promising; [2] *adv* full of hope.

Hof-: **~gang** *m* yard exercise; **~geistliche(r)** *m* court chaplain; **~gesellschaft** *f* court society; **~gesinde** *nt* **(a)** (*auf Bauernhof*) farm workers *pl*; **(b)** (*am Fürstenhof*) servants *pl* at (the/a) court; ⚠**h~halten** *vi sep irreg* (*lit, fig*) to hold court; **~haltung** *f* (holding of) court; **~herr** *m* (*Gutsherr*) estate owner; (*in England*) squire; **~hund** *m* watchdog.

hofieren* *vt* (*dated*) to court.

höfisch *adj* **(a)** (*eines Fürstenhofs*) *Leben, Sitten, Vergnügen* courtly *no adv.* **(b)** (*Liter*) *Dichtung etc* courtly *no adv.* **(c)** (*old: kultiviert*) *Benehmen, Kleidung* sophisticated.

Hof-: **~kapelle** *f* **(a)** (*Kirche am Hof*) court chapel; **(b)** (*Mus*) court orchestra; **~knicks** *m* court *or* formal curtsey; **~lager** *nt* temporary residence; **~lager halten** to hold court; **~leben** *nt* court life.

höflich *adj* polite; (*zuvorkommend*) courteous ◆ **ich bitte Sie ~** I (would) respectfully ask you; **wir teilen Ihnen ~(st) mit** we beg to inform you.

Höflichkeit *f* **(a)** *no pl siehe adj* politeness; courteousness ◆ **jdm etw mit aller ~ sagen** to tell sb sth very politely *or* with the utmost politeness. **(b)** (*höfliche Bemerkung*) compliment ◆ **jdm ~en sagen** to compliment sb.

Höflichkeits-: **~besuch** *m* courtesy visit; **~bezeigung** *f* act *or* mark of courtesy; **~floskel** (*pej*), **~formel** *f* polite phrase; **h~halber** *adv* out of courtesy.

Hoflieferant *m* purveyor to the court.

Höfling *m* courtier; (*pej: Schmeichler*) sycophant.

Hof-: **~marschall** *m* (*Hist*) major-domo; (*in GB*) Lord Chamberlain; **~meister** *m* (*Hist*) **(a)** (*Gutsverwalter*) steward, bailiff; **(b)** (*Erzieher*) (private) tutor; **~narr** *m* (*Hist*) court jester; **~prediger** *m* (*Hist*) court chaplain; **~rat** *m* **(a)** (*Hist*) Court Counsellor; (*in GB*) Privy Counsellor; **(b)** (*Aus: Ehrentitel*) Hofrat, ≃ Counsellor; **~sänger** *m* (*Hist*) minstrel; **~schranze** *f or* (*rare*) *m* (*Hist pej*) fawning courtier; **~seite** *f* courtyard side (*of building*); **~staat** *m* (*Hist*) (royal *etc*) household; **~statt** *f* -, **-en** *or* **¨-en** farmstead; **~theater** *nt* (*Hist*) court *or* royal theatre; **~tor** *nt* yard gate; **~trauer** *f* court mourning; **~tür** *f* yard gate.

HO-Geschäft ['ha:|'o:-] *nt* (*DDR*) state retail shop.

hohe *adj siehe* **hoch**.

Höhe *f* -, **-n** **(a)** (*Ausdehnung nach oben*) height; (*Flug~, Berg~, ~ über Meeresspiegel auch, Astron, Math*) altitude; (*von Schnee, Wasser*) depth ◆ **in die/der ~** (up) into/in the air; **aus der ~** from above; **Ehre sei Gott in der ~** glory to God in the highest *or* on high; **an ~ gewinnen** (*Aviat*) to gain height, to climb; **in einer ~ von** at a height/an altitude of; **in die ~ gehen/treiben** (*fig: Preise etc*) to go up/force up; **einen Betrieb wieder in die ~ bringen** to put a business back on its feet again; **in die ~ gehen** (*fig inf*) to hit the roof (*inf*).

(b) (*An~*) hill; (*Gipfel*) top, summit; (*fig: ~punkt, Blütezeit etc*) height ◆ **auf der ~ sein** (*fig inf*) (*leistungsfähig*) to be at one's best; (*gesund*) to be fighting fit (*inf*); **die sanften ~n** the gentle slopes; **sich nicht auf der ~ fühlen, nicht auf der ~ sein** (*leistungsfähig*) to feel below par; (*gesundheitlich*) not to be up to scratch; **auf der ~ des Lebens** in the prime of (one's) life; **die ~n und Tiefen des Lebens** the ups and downs of life; **auf der ~ der Zeit** up-to-date; **das ist doch die ~!** (*fig inf*) that's the limit!

(c) (*Ausmaß, Größe*) (*von Mieten, Preisen, Unkosten, Temperatur, Geschwindigkeit, Strafe, Phys: Stromspannung*) level; (*von Summe, Gewinn, Verlust, Gewicht, Geldstrafe*) size, amount; (*von Wert, Druck*) amount; (*von Einkommen*) size; (*von Schaden*) extent ◆ **ein Zuwachs/Betrag in ~ von** an increase/amount of; **Zinsen in ~ von** interest at the rate of; **bis zu einer ~ von** up to a maximum of.

(d) (*fig: Größe*) (*von Lebensstandard, Ansprüchen etc*) level.

(e) (*Mus: Ton~, von Stimme*) pitch; (*Rad: Ton~*) treble *no pl.*

(f) (*Naut, Geog: Breitenlage*) latitude ◆ **auf der ~ von** at the level of; **auf der ~ von Dover** (*Naut*) off Dover; **auf gleicher ~** level with each other.

Hoheit *f* **(a)** *no pl* (*Staats~*) sovereignty (*über +acc* over). **(b)** (*Mitglied einer fürstlichen Familie*) member of a/the royal family; (*als Anrede*) Highness ◆ **Seine/Ihre Königliche ~** His/Her Royal Highness. **(c)** *siehe* **Erhabenheit**.

hoheitlich *adj* (*von Staatsgewalt ausgehend*) *Befehl, Handlung* sovereign; (*von einem Fürsten*) *Gemächer* royal; *Auftreten, Geste* majestic.

Hoheits-: **~abzeichen** *nt* nationality marking; **~akt** *m* act of sovereignty; **~bereich** *m* **(a)** *siehe* **~gebiet**; **(b)** (*Rechtsbereich*) jurisdiction; **~gebiet** *nt* sovereign territory; **~gewalt** *f* (national) jurisdiction; **~gewässer** *pl* territorial waters *pl*; **~recht** *nt usu pl* sovereign jurisdiction *or* rights *pl*; **h~voll** *adj* majestic; **~zeichen** *nt* national emblem.

Hohelied *nt* **Hohenlied(e)s**, *no pl* Song of Songs; (*fig geh*) song.

Höhen-: **~angabe** *f* altitude reading; (*auf Karte*) altitude mark; **~angst** *f* fear of heights; **~flosse** *f* (*Aviat*) tailplane; **~flug** *m* high-altitude flight; **geistiger/künstlerischer ~flug** intellectual/artistic flight (of fancy); **h~gleich** [1] *adj* level; [2] *adv* on a level; **~klima** *nt* mountain climate; **~krankheit** *f* (*Med*) altitude sickness; (*im Gebirge auch*) mountain sickness; (*beim Fliegen auch*) aeroembolism (*spec*); **~kurort** *m* mountain (health) resort; **~lage** *f* altitude; **~leitwerk** *nt* (*Aviat*) elevators *pl*; **~linie** *f* contour (line); **~luft** *f* mountain air; **~marke** *f* bench mark; **~messer** *m* **-s, -** (*Aviat*) altimeter, altitude meter; **~messung** *f* **(a)** (*Aviat*) measuring altitude; **(b)** (*Tech*) levelling; **~rekord** *m* (*Aviat*) altitude record; **~rücken** *m* (mountain) crest *or* ridge; **~ruder** *nt* (*Aviat*) elevator; **~schicht** *f* contour level; **~schreiber** *m* (*Aviat*) altigraph; **~sonne** *f* (*im Gebirge*) mountain sun; (*Lampe: auch* **künstliche ~sonne**) sunray lamp; (*Behandlung*) sunray treatment; **~steuer** *nt siehe* **~ruder**; **~strahlung** *f* cosmic radiation; **~training** *nt* (*Sport*) (high-)altitude training; **~unterschied** *m* difference in altitude; **~verlust** *m* loss of height *or* altitude; **h~verstellbar** *adj* (*Tech*) *Sitz* height-adjustable; **~wind** *m* high-altitude wind; **~zahl** *f* (*auf Landkarten*) height above sea level; **~zug** *m* range of hills, mountain range.

Hohepriester *m* **Hohenpriesters**, - high priest.

hohepriesterlich *adj Gewänder, Amt* high priest's *attr.*

Höhepunkt *m* highest point; (*des Abends, des Tages, des Lebens*) high point, high spot; (*einer Veranstaltung*) high spot, highlight; (*einer Karriere, des Ruhms, der Macht*) pinnacle, peak, height; (*des Glücks etc*) height, peak; (*einer Entwicklung*) peak, summit, apex; (*einer Kurve*) vertex; (*eines Stücks, Orgasmus*) climax ◆ **auf den ~ bringen** to bring to a climax; **den ~ erreichen** to reach a *or* its/one's climax; (*Krankheit*) to reach *or* come to a crisis; **den ~ überschreiten** to pass the peak.

hohe(r, s) *adj siehe* **hoch**.

höher *adj comp of* **hoch** (*lit, fig*) higher; *Macht* superior; *Klasse* upper; *Auflage* bigger; (*Comput*) *Programmiersprache* high-level ◆ **~e Berufsstände** the professions; **~e Bildung** higher education; **~es Lehramt** ≃ graduate teachership; **~e Schule** secondary school, high school (*esp US*); **~e Töchterschule** (*old, hum*) school for young ladies; **~e Tochter** (*dated, hum*) young lady; **~e Gewalt** an act of God; **in ~em Maße** to a greater extent; **~er Blödsinn** (*iro*) utter nonsense; **in ~en Regionen** *or* **Sphären schweben** to have one's head in the clouds; **ihre Herzen schlugen ~** their hearts beat faster; **etw ~ bewerten** to rate sth higher *or* more highly; **sich ~ versichern** to increase one's insurance (premium); **sich zu H~em berufen fühlen** to feel (oneself) called to higher things *or* to greater things.

höher-: ⚠**~gestellt** *adj attr* higher, more senior; ⚠**~liegend** *adj attr* higher; ⚠**~schrauben** *vt sep* (*fig*) *Anforderungen* to increase, to step up; *Ansprüche* to increase; *Preise* to force *or* push up; ⚠**~stehend** *adj attr* higher; ⚠**~stufen** *vt sep Person* to upgrade; **~wertig** *adj* (*Chem*) of higher valency.

hohl *adj* **(a)** (*lit, fig: leer*) hollow; *Geschwätz etc* empty, shallow; *Blick* empty, vacant.

(b) (*konkav*) hollow; *Wangen auch* sunken; *Augen auch* deep-set ◆ **ein ~es Kreuz** a hollow back; **in der ~en Hand** in the hollow of one's hand; **aus der ~en Hand trinken** to drink with cupped hands; **eine ~e Hand machen** (*lit*) to cup one's hand; (*fig inf*) to hold one's hand out (*for money, a tip etc*); **~e Gasse** narrow pass *or* defile.

(c) *Klang, Stimme, Husten* hollow.

Hohl-: **h~äugig** *adj* hollow- *or* sunken-eyed; **~block(stein), ~blockziegel** *m* cavity block.

Höhle *f* -, **-n** cave, cavern; (*in Baum*) hole, hollow bit; (*Tierbehausung*) cave, den; (*Augen~*) socket; (*fig: schlechte Wohnung*) hovel, hole (*inf*).

Höhlen- *in cpds* cave; **~bär** *m* cave-bear; **~bewohner** *m* cave dweller, caveman, troglodyte; **~forscher** *m* cave explorer; (*unter der Erde auch*) potholer; **~forschung, ~kunde** *f* speleology; **~gleichnis** *nt* (*Philos*) Allegory of the Cave; **~malerei** *f* cave painting; **~mensch** *m* caveman; **~tier** *m* cave-animal.

Hohl-: **~heit** *f, no pl* (*fig*) *siehe adj* hollowness; emptiness, shallowness; **~kopf** *m* (*pej*) blockhead (*inf*), numskull (*inf*), dunce; **h~köpfig** *adj* (*pej*) empty-headed, brainless, foolish; **~körper** *m* hollow body; **~kreuz** *nt* (*Med*) hollow back; **~kugel** *f* hollow sphere; **~maß** *nt* measure of capacity; (*für Getreide etc auch*) dry measure; **~nadel** *f* (*Med*) cannula.

Hohlraum *m* hollow space; (*Build auch*) cavity.

Hohlraum-: **~versiegelung** *f* (*Aut*) cavity seal; **~ziegel** *m* cavity block.

Hohl-: **~saum** *m* (*Sew*) hemstitch; **~saumarbeit** *f* drawn-thread work; **~schliff** *m* hollow grinding; **ein Messer mit ~schliff** a hollow-ground knife; **~spiegel** *m* concave mirror; **~tiere** *pl* coelenterata (*spec*).

Höhlung *f* hollow.

Hohl-: h~wangig *adj* hollow-cheeked; **~weg** *m* narrow pass *or* defile; **~würmer** *pl* aschelminthes *pl* (*spec*); **~ziegel** *m* **(a)** (*Hohlstein*) cavity brick; **(b)** (*Dachziegel*) hollow tile.

Hohn *m* **-(e)s,** *no pl* scorn, derision, mockery ◆ **jdn mit ~ und Spott überschütten** to heap *or* pour scorn on sb; **nur ~ und Spott ernten** to get nothing but scorn and derision; **das hat er mir zum ~ getan** he did it just to show his contempt for me; **ein ~ auf etw** (*acc*) a mockery of sth; **das ist der reine** *or* **reinste ~** it's a sheer *or* utter mockery; **der Tatsache** (*dat*) **zum ~** in defiance of the fact(s).

höhnen [1] *vt* (*geh*) *jdn* to mock.
[2] *vi* to jeer, to scoff, to sneer (*über +acc* at).

Hohngelächter *nt* scornful *or* derisive *or* sneering laughter.

höhnisch *adj* scornful, mocking, sneering.

Hohn-: ~lachen *nt siehe* **~gelächter**; ⚠**h~lachen** *vi sep* to laugh scornfully *or* derisively; **ich höre ihn schon h~lachen** I can hear his sneers already; ⚠**h~sprechen** *vi sep irreg* to make a mockery (*dat* of); **jdm h~sprechen** to mock at *or* deride sb; **das spricht jeder Vernunft h~** that flies right in the face of all reason.

hoho *interj* oho.

Höker(in *f*) *m* **-s, -** (*old*) street trader *or* pedlar.

Hökerfrau *f* (*old*), **Hökerweib** *nt* (*old, pej*) *siehe* **Höker(in).**

hökern *vi* (*old*) to peddle ◆ **mit etw ~** to peddle sth.

Hokuspokus *m* **-,** *no pl* (*Zauberformel*) hey presto; (*Zauberstück*) (conjuring) trick(s); (*fig*) (*Täuschung*) hocus-pocus (*inf*), jiggery-pokery (*inf*); (*Drumherum*) palaver (*inf*), fuss ◆ **die veranstalten immer einen ~, wenn Besuch kommt** they always make such a palaver (*inf*) *or* fuss when they have visitors.

hold *adj* **(a)** (*poet, dated*) fair, sweet; (*hum*) dear, beloved, fair ◆ **~er Friede** sweet *or* blessed peace; **die ~e Weiblichkeit** (*hum*) the fair sex; **mein ~er Gatte** (*hum*) my dear *or* beloved husband (*hum*); **meine H~e** my sweet.
(b) *pred* (*geh: gewogen*) **jdm ~ sein** to be fond of *or* well-disposed to(wards) sb; **das Glück war ihm ~** fortune smiled upon him.

Holder *m* **-s, -** (*dial*) *siehe* **Holunder.**

Holdinggesellschaft *f* (*Comm*) holding company.

Holdrio *nt* **-s, -s** (shout of) halloo.

holdselig *adj* (*liter*) sweet, lovely, fair.

holen *vt* **(a)** to fetch, to get; (*herunternehmen*) to get *or* take *or* fetch down; (*herausnehmen*) to get *or* take out ◆ **Luft/Atem ~** to draw breath, to catch one's breath; **jdn aus dem Bett ~** to get *or* drag (*inf*) sb out of bed; **das Kind mußte geholt werden** the baby had to be pulled out; *siehe* **Teufel.**
(b) (*abholen*) to fetch, to pick up; *Verbrecher, Patienten* to take away.
(c) (*kaufen*) to get, to pick up (*inf*).
(d) (*herbeirufen, ~ lassen*) *Polizei, Hilfe* to fetch, to get ◆ **jdn ~ lassen** to send for sb; **einen Moment, ich lasse ihn schnell ans Telefon ~** just a moment, I'll have someone fetch *or* get him to the phone; **der Professor hat seinen Assistenten an die neue Uni geholt** the professor brought his assistant to the new university.
(e) (*erringen, gewinnen*) *Sieg, Preis* to win, to get.
(f) (*sich zuziehen*) *Krankheit* to catch, to get; *elektrischen Schlag* to get ◆ **sich** (*dat*) **Schläge ~** to get a beating; **sonst wirst du dir etwas ~** or you'll catch something; **sich** (*dat*) **eine Erkältung/den Tod** (*inf*) **~** to catch a cold/one's death (*inf*).
(g) (*bekommen, erwerben*) to get ◆ **sich** (*dat*) **etw ~** to get (oneself) sth; **dabei ist nichts zu ~** (*inf*) there's nothing in it; **bei ihm ist nichts zu ~** (*inf*) you *etc* won't get anything out of him.
(h) (*Naut*) *Anker* to raise, to hoist; *Segel, Taue* to take in.

holla *interj* hullo, hallo, hello, hey; (*überrascht*) hey; (*hoppla*) whoops.

Holland *nt* **-s** Holland, the Netherlands *pl.*

Holländer[1] *m* **-s, -** Dutchman ◆ **die ~** the Dutch (people); **er ist ~** he is Dutch *or* a Dutchman; *siehe* **fliegend.**

Holländer[2] *m* **-s,** *no pl* Dutch cheese.

Holländer[3] *m* **-s, -** (*bei Papierherstellung*) hollander.

Holländerin *f* Dutchwoman, Dutch girl.

holländisch *adj* Dutch.

Holländisch(e) *nt decl as adj* Dutch, the Dutch language; *siehe auch* **Deutsch(e).**

Holle *f*: **Frau ~ schüttelt die Betten aus** it is snowing.

Hölle *f* **-,** (*rare*) **-n** hell ◆ **in der ~** in hell; **die ~ auf Erden** hell on earth; **fahr zur ~!** (*liter*) go to the devil!; **in die ~ kommen** to go to hell; **ich werde ihm die ~ heiß machen** (*inf*) I'll give him hell (*inf*); **sie machte ihm das Leben zur ~** she made his life (a) hell (*inf*); **es war die (reinste) ~** (*inf*) it was (pure) hell (*inf*); **die ~ ist los** (*inf*) all hell has broken loose (*inf*).

Höllen- *in cpds* (*der Hölle*) of hell, infernal; (*inf: groß*) hellish (*inf*), infernal (*inf*); **~angst** *f* terrible fear; **eine ~angst haben** to be scared stiff (*inf*); **~brand** *m* (*liter*) hellfire; **~brut** *f* (*pej liter*) diabolical *or* fiendish mob *or* rabble; **~fahrt** *f* Descent into Hell; **~fürst** *m* (*liter*) Prince of Darkness; **~hund** *m* (*Myth*) hound of hell, hell-hound; **~lärm** *m* hellish (*inf*) *or* infernal (*inf*) noise; **~mächte** *pl* (*liter*) powers of darkness *pl*; **~maschine** *f* (*dated*) infernal machine (*dated*), time bomb; **~pein, ~qual** *f* (*liter*) torments *pl* of hell; (*fig inf*) agony; **eine ~qual/~qualen ausstehen** to suffer agony; **~rachen, ~schlund** *m* (*liter*) jaws *pl* of hell; **~spektakel** *m* (*inf*) *siehe* **~lärm**; **~stein** *m* (*Chem*) silver nitrate, lunar caustic.

Holler *m* **-s, -** (*dial*) *siehe* **Holunder.**

Hollerithmaschine *f* Hollerith machine.

höllisch *adj* **(a)** *attr* (*die Hölle betreffend*) infernal, of hell.
(b) (*inf: außerordentlich*) dreadful, frightful, hellish (*inf*) ◆ **eine ~e Angst haben** to be scared stiff (*inf*); **~ fluchen** to swear like a trooper; **es tut ~ weh** it hurts like hell (*inf*), it's hellish(ly) painful (*inf*); **die Prüfung war ~ schwer** the exam was hellish(ly) difficult (*inf*).

Hollywoodschaukel *f* ['hɔlɪwʊd-] swing hammock.

Holm[1] *m* **-(e)s, -e (a)** (*von Barren*) bar; (*von Geländer*) rail; (*von Leiter*) side rail. **(b)** (*Aviat*) (*längs*) longeron; (*quer*) spar. **(c)** (*Stiel, Griff*) (*Axt~*) shaft, handle; (*Ruder~*) shaft.

Holm[2] *m* **-(e)s, -e** islet, small island.

Holmium *nt, no pl* (*abbr* **Ho**) holmium.

Holocaust ['hɔləkɔːst] *m* **-(s), -(s)** holocaust.

Holocaust- *in cpds* holocaust; **~-Gedenkstätte** *f* holocaust memorial.

Holo-: ~gramm *nt* hologram; ⚠**~graphie** *f* holography.

holp(e)rig *adj* **(a)** *Weg, Pflaster* bumpy. **(b)** (*schwerfällig*) *Rede, Verse* clumsy, jerky ◆ **~ lesen** to read jerkily *or* haltingly.

holpern *vi* to bump, to jolt ◆ **beim Lesen holpert er noch** he still stumbles (over his words) when reading, he still reads haltingly; **~de Verse** rough *or* stumbling *or* halting verse.

Holschuld *f* (*Comm*) *debt to be collected from the debtor at his residence.*

holterdiepolter *adv* helter-skelter ◆ **der Wagen fuhr ~ den Berg hinunter** the cart went careering down the mountainside; **die Blechdose fiel ~ die Treppe hinunter** the tin went crash bang wallop down the stairs (*inf*).

hol|über *interj* (*old*) **Fährmann ~!** ahoy there, ferryman *or* boatman!

Holunder *m* **-s, -** elder; (*Früchte*) elderberries *pl* ◆ **spanischer** *or* **blauer ~** lilac.

Holunder- *in cpds* elder; **~beere** *f* elderberry; **~busch, ~strauch** *m* elder bush; **~wein** *m* elderberry wine.

Holz *nt* **-es, ¨er (a)** wood; (*zum Bauen, Schreinern auch*) timber, lumber (*US*); (*Streich~*) match ◆ **ein ~** a piece of wood *or* timber; (*~art*) a wood; **lange ¨er** long, untrimmed logs *or* timbers; **runde ¨er** short, untrimmed logs *or* timbers; **flüssiges ~** (*Tech*) plastic wood; **aus ~** made of wood, wooden; **~ fällen** to fell *or* cut down trees; **~ sägen** (*lit*) to saw wood; (*inf: schnarchen*) to snore, to saw wood (*US inf*); **aus einem anderen ~ (geschnitzt) sein** (*fig*) to be cast in a different mould; **aus grobem ~ geschnitzt sein** (*fig*) to be insensitive; **aus hartem** *or* **härterem ~ geschnitzt sein** (*fig*) to be made of stern *or* sterner stuff; **aus demselben ~ geschnitzt sein** (*fig*) to be cast in the same mould; **er saß da wie ein Stück ~** he sat there like a lump of wood *or* lead; **ich bin nicht aus ~!** I'm not made of stone, I am made of flesh and blood; **~ vor der Hütte** *or* **Tür haben** (*inf*) to be well-endowed *or* well-stacked (*inf*), to have big boobs (*inf*); **~!** (*Tennis etc*) wood!; **Dummheit und Stolz wachsen auf einem ~** (*Prov*) stupidity and pride grow on the same tree.
(b) (*Kegel*) skittle, ninepin ◆ **~ schieben** to play skittles *or* ninepins; **gut ~!** have a good game!
(c) (*dated: Wald, Gehölz*) wood, woods *pl.*

Holz- *in cpds* wood; (*aus ~ auch*) wooden; (*Build, Comm etc*) timber; **~apfel** *m* crab apple; **~arbeiter** *m* woodworker; (*im Wald*) woodcutter, woodman, lumberjack; **h~arm** *adj Gegend* sparsely wooded *or* timbered; *Papier* with (a) low wood content; **~art** *f* kind of wood *or* timber; **h~artig** *adj* woody, wood-like; **~asche** *f* wood-ashes *pl*; **~auge** *nt*: **~auge, sei wachsam** (*inf*) be careful; **~bau** *m* **-s (a)** *no pl* wood- *or* timber-frame construction; **(b)** *pl* **-ten** wooden building; **~bearbeitung** *f* woodworking; (*im Sägewerk*) timber processing; **~bein** *nt* wooden leg; **~bestand** *m* stock of wood *or* timber, wood *or* timber stock; (*im Wald*) stand of timber; **~bildhauer** *m* wood carver; **~bläser** *m* woodwind player; **wo sitzen die ~bläser?** where do the woodwind sit *or* does the woodwind section sit?; **~blasinstrument** *nt* woodwind instrument; **~block** *m* block of wood; **~bock** *m* **(a)** (*Stützgestell*) wooden stand *or* trestle; **(b)** (*Insekt*) wood tick, dog tick; **~boden** *m* **(a)** (*Fußboden*) wooden floor; **(b)** (*für Holz*) wood- *or* timber-loft; **(c)** (*von Truhe etc*) wooden bottom; **(d)** (*Forstwesen*) wooded *or* timbered ground; **~bohrer** *m* **(a)** (*Tech*) wood drill; **(b)** (*Zool*) goat moth, leopard moth; **~brandmalerei** *f* (*Art*) poker-work, pyrography (*form*); **~brei** *m* wood pulp; **~bündel** *nt* bundle of wood, faggot.

Hölzchen *nt* small piece of wood; (*Streichholz*) match.

Holzdruck *m* (*Art*) wood engraving.

holzen [1] *vi* **(a)** (*Bäume fällen*) to cut down *or* fell timber, to lumber. **(b)** (*esp Ftbl*) to hack; (*Mus*) to play badly.
[2] *vt* (*rare*) *Wald* to clear.

Holzer *m* **-s, -** (*pej inf*) hacker, rough player.

Holzerei *f* (*inf*) (*Rauferei*) roughhouse (*inf*); (*Ftbl auch*) rough game *or* match; (*Mus*) third- *or* fourth-rate playing.

hölzern *adj* (*lit, fig*) wooden ◆ **so ein ~er Kerl** such a wooden sort of chap.

Holz-: ~fällen *nt* **-s,** *no pl* tree-felling, lumbering; **~fäller** *m* **-s, -** woodcutter, woodsman, lumberjack; **~faser** *f* wood fibre; **~faserplatte** *f* (wood) fibreboard; **~fäule** *f* wood *or* dry/wet rot; **h~frei** *adj Papier* wood-free; **~frevel** *m* (*Jur*) offence against forest laws, infringement of forest regulations; **~hacken** *nt* **-s,** *no pl* cutting *or* chopping wood; **~hacker** *m* **-s, -** (*Aus, old*) **(a)** woodcutter; **(b)** *siehe* **~fäller**; **h~haltig** *adj Papier* woody; **~hammer** *m* mallet; **jdm etw mit dem ~hammer beibringen** to hammer sth into sb (*inf*); **~hammermethode** *f* (*inf*) sledgehammer method (*inf*); **~handel** *m* timber trade; **~haufen** *m* woodpile, pile *or* stack of wood; **~haus** *nt* wooden *or* timber house.

holzig *adj* woody; *Spargel, Rettich auch* stringy, tough.

Holz-: ~kitt *m* plastic wood; **~klotz** *m* wood block, block of wood, log; (*Spielzeug*) wooden brick; **er saß da wie ein ~klotz** (*inf*) he sat there like a block *or* lump of wood; **~kohle** *f* charcoal; **~kopf** *m* (*fig inf*) blockhead (*inf*); **~lager** *nt* timberyard; **~nagel** *m* wooden nail *or* peg; **~ofen** *m* wood-burning oven; **~pantine** *f*, **~pantoffel** *m* clog; **~pflaster** *nt* wood-block paving; **~pflock** *m* (wooden) peg; **h~reich** *adj* well-timbered *or* -wooded; **ein h~reiches Land** a country rich in timber; **~schädling** *m* wood pest; **~scheit** *nt* piece of (fire)wood, log; **~schlag** *m* (*Vorgang*) tree-felling, lumbering; (*Ort*) felling *or* lumbering area; **~schliff** *m* mechanical wood pulp; **~schneider** *m* wood engraver; **~schnitt** *m* (*Art*) **(a)** *no pl* (*Kunst*) (art of) wood engraving; **(b)** (*Gegenstand*) wood engraving, woodcut; **h~schnittartig** *adj* (*fig*) simplistic; **~schnitzer** *m* wood carver; **~schnitzerei** *f* (art *or* craft of) wood carving; **~schuh** *m* wooden shoe, clog, sabot; **~schuhtanz** *m* clog dance; **~schutzmittel** *nt* wood preservative; **~schwamm** *m* wood fungus, dry rot; **~span** *m* chip (of wood); (*beim Hobeln*) wood shaving; **~splitter** *m* splinter *or* sliver of wood; **~stich** *m* wood engraving; **~stift** *m* small wooden nail *or* pin; **~stock** *m* (engraved) wood block; **~stoß** *m* pile of wood; **~tafel** *f* wooden panel; (*Sch*) wooden blackboard; **~täfelung** *f* wood(en) panelling; **~taube** *f* woodpigeon; **⚠h~verarbeitend** *adj attr* wood-processing; **~verarbeitung** *f* wood-processing; **~verkohlung** *f* carbonization, wood distillation; **~verschlag** *m* **(a)** (*Schuppen*) wooden shed; **(b)** (*Verpackung*) wooden crate; **~waren** *pl* wooden articles, articles made of wood; **~weg** *m* logging-path; **auf dem ~weg sein** (*fig inf*) to be on the wrong track (*inf*); **wenn du meinst, ich gebe dir das, dann bist du auf dem ~weg** if you think I'm going to give it to you, you've got another think coming (*inf*); **~wirtschaft** *f* timber industry; **~wolle** *f* wood-wool; **~wurm** *m* woodworm.

Homebanking, Home-Banking ['həumbɛŋkɪŋ] *nt - no pl* home banking.

Homepage ['həumpeɪdʒ] *f* **-, -s** (*Comput: im Internet*) home page.

homerisch *adj* Homeric.

Hometrainer ['həumtreːnɐ] *m* home exercise machine.

Hommage [ɔ'maːʒ] *f* **-, -n** homage.

Homo *m* **-s, -s** (*dated inf*) homo (*dated inf*), queer (*inf*).

Homo- *in cpds* homo; **h~gen** *adj* homogeneous; **h~genisieren*** *vt* to homogenize; **~genität** *f* homogeneity; **~nym** *nt* **-(e)s, -e** homonym; **h~nym** *adj* homonymous; **~nymie** *f* homonymy.

Homöopath *m* **-en, -en** homoeopath.

Homöopathie *f*, *no pl* homoeopathy.

homöopathisch *adj* homoeopathic.

Homo-: ⚠h~phon *adj* (*Mus*) homophonic; (*Ling*) homophonous; **~sexualität** *f* homosexuality; **h~sexuell** *adj* homosexual; **~sexuelle(r)** *mf decl as adj* homosexual.

Homunkulus *m* **-, -sse** *or* **Homunkuli** homunculus.

honett *adj* (*dated, geh*) honest, upright, respectable.

Hongkong *nt* **-s** Hong Kong.

Honig *m* **-s,** *no pl* honey ◆ **türkischer ~** halva(h), ≃ nougat; **sie schmierte ihm ~ ums Maul** *or* **um den Bart** *or* **Mund** (*inf*) she buttered him up (*inf*).

Honig-: ~biene *f* honey-bee; **~brot** *nt* **(a)** *siehe* **~kuchen**; **(b)** bread and honey; **h~farben** *adj* honey-coloured; **h~gelb** *adj* honey-yellow; **~klee** *m* (*Bot*) melitot; **~kuchen** *m* honeycake; **~kuchenpferd** *nt* (*fig inf*) simpleton; **grinsen wie ein ~kuchenpferd** to grin like a Cheshire cat; **~lecken** *nt* (*fig*) **das ist kein ~lecken** it's no picnic; **~melone** *f* honeydew melon; **~mond** *m* (*rare*) honeymoon; **~schlecken** *nt siehe* **~lecken**; **~schleuder** *f* honey extractor; **h~süß** *adj* as sweet as honey; (*fig*) *Worte, Ton* honeyed; *Lächeln* sickly sweet; **er lächelte h~süß** he smiled a sickly sweet smile; **~tau** *m* (*pflanzlich, tierisch*) honeydew; **~wabe** *f* honeycomb; **~wein** *m siehe* **Met**; **~zelle** *f* honeycomb cell.

Honneurs [(h)ɔ'nøːɐs] *pl*: **die ~ machen** (*geh, iro*) to do the honours, to welcome the guests.

Honorar *nt* **-s, -e** fee; (*Autoren~*) royalty.

Honorar-: ~abrechnung *f* statement of account; (*von Schriftsteller*) royalties account; **h~frei** *adj* free of charge; **~professor** *m* honorary professor (*with no say in faculty matters*).

Honoratioren [honora'tsioːrən] *pl* dignitaries *pl*, notabilities *pl*.

honorieren* *vt* (*Comm*) *Wechsel, Scheck* to honour, to meet; (*fig: anerkennen*) to reward ◆ **jdm etw ~** to pay sb (a fee) for sth, to remunerate sb for sth; **meine Arbeit wird schlecht honoriert** my work is poorly remunerated.

Honorierung *f* (*einer Rechnung*) payment (of a fee); (*Bezahlung*) remuneration; (*Comm: von Wechsel, Scheck*) acceptance.

honorig *adj* (*dated*) (*ehrenhaft*) respectable, honourable; (*anständig*) decent.

honoris causa *adv* **Dr. ~ ~** honorary doctor.

hopfen *vt Bier* to hop.

Hopfen *m* **-s, -** (*Bot*) hop; (*beim Brauen*) hops *pl* ◆ **bei** *or* **an ihm ist ~ und Malz verloren** (*inf*) he's a hopeless case, he's a dead loss (*inf*).

Hopfen- *in cpds* hop; **~(an)bau** *m* hop cultivation, hop-growing; **~darre** *f* hop drier *or* kiln; **~stange** *f* hop-pole.

Hoplit *m* **-en, -en** (*Hist*) hoplite.

hopp *interj* quick ◆ **bei ihr muß alles ~ ~ gehen** she insists on doing everything chop-chop *or* at the double *or* double-quick (*all inf*); **mach mal ein bißchen ~!** (*inf*) chop, chop! (*inf*); **~e ~e Reiter machen** (*baby-talk*) to ride a cock-horse (*on sb's knee*).

hoppeln *vi aux sein* (*Hase*) to lollop.

Hoppelpoppel *nt* **-s, -** (*dial*) **(a)** *breakfast made from scrambled egg with ham and fried potatoes*. **(b)** (*Getränk*) eggnog.

hoppla *interj* (*beim Stolpern, Zusammenstoßen, Fangen etc*) whoops, oops; (*beim Zuwerfen*) catch ◆ **~, jetzt habe ich die richtige Idee!** aha *or* Eureka, now I've got it!; **~, wer kommt denn da?** hullo, who's that coming there?; **~, jetzt komm' ich!** look out, here I come!

hoppnehmen *vt sep* (*inf: verhaften*) to catch, to nick (*inf*).

Hops *m* **-es, -e** (*inf*) hop, jump ◆ **einen ~ über etw** (*acc*) **machen** to hop *or* jump over sth.

hops[1] *interj* jump ◆ **~ waren sie über den Graben weg** with a jump they were over the ditch.

hops[2] *adj pred* **~ sein** (*inf: verloren*) to be lost; (*Geld*) to be down the drain (*inf*); (*inf: entzwei*) to be broken *or* kaputt (*inf*); **~ gehen** (*inf: verlorengehen*) to get lost; (*inf: entzweigehen*) to get broken; (*sl: verhaftet werden*) to get nabbed (*inf*); (*sl: sterben*) to kick the bucket (*sl*), to croak (*sl*); **etw ~ gehen lassen** (*inf: stehlen*) to pinch sth (*inf*); **jdn ~ nehmen** (*sl: verhaften*) to nab sb (*inf*).

hopsa *interj siehe* **hoppla**.

hopsala *interj* upsadaisy.

hopsasa *interj* up we go.

hopsen *vi aux sein* (*inf*) to hop, to skip, to jump.

Hopser *m* **-s, -** **(a)** (*inf: kleiner Sprung*) (little) jump *or* leap ◆ **sein Herz tat vor Freude einen ~** his heart gave a little leap for joy. **(b)** (*Tanz*) ecossaise.

Hopserei *f* (*inf*) (*Hüpferei*) jumping about *or* up and down; (*pej: Tanzen*) hopping about.

Hör-: ~apparat *m* hearing aid; **h~bar** *adj* audible; **sich h~bar machen** (*inf*) to speak up; **~bereich** *m* (*des Ohrs*) hearing range; (*eines Senders*) transmission area; **~bild** *nt* (*Rad*) feature broadcast, radio feature; **~brille** *f* hearing-aid glasses *pl or* spectacles *pl*; **~buch** *nt* talking book.

horchen *vi* to listen (*dat, auf +acc* to); (*heimlich*) to eavesdrop ◆ **horch!** (*liter*) hark! (*old, liter*).

Horcher *m* **-s, -** eavesdropper ◆ **der ~ an der Wand hört seine eigne Schand'** (*Prov*) eavesdroppers never hear any good of themselves.

Horch-: ~gerät *nt* (*Mil*) sound detector *or* locator; (*Naut*) hydrophone; **~posten** *m* (*Mil*) listening post; **auf ~posten sein** to be listening out for sth.

Horde[1] *f* **-, -n** (*lit, fig*) horde.

Horde[2] *f* **-, -n** rack.

hordenweise *adv* in hordes.

hören *vti* **(a)** to hear ◆ **ich höre dich nicht** I can't hear you; **ich hörte ihn kommen** I heard him coming; **sei mal still, ich will das ~** be quiet, I want to hear this *or* listen to this; **er hat an der Wand gehört** he was listening at the wall; **gut/schlecht ~** to have good/bad hearing, to hear well; **schwer ~** to be hard of hearing; **du hörst wohl schwer** *or* **schlecht!** (*inf*) you must be deaf!, are you hard of hearing?; **hört, hört!** (*Zustimmung*) hear! hear!; (*Mißfallen*) come, come!; **etw an etw** (*dat*) **~** to hear sth from sth; **das läßt sich ~** (*fig*) that doesn't sound bad; **das läßt sich schon eher ~** (*inf*) that sounds (a bit) more like it; **das werde ich noch lange ~ müssen** *or* **zu ~ bekommen** I shall never hear the end *or* last of it; **ich will gar nichts ~!** I don't want to hear it; **ich habe sagen ~** I've heard said *or* tell; **ich habe es sagen ~** I've heard it said; **er hört sich gern reden** he likes the sound of his own voice; **hör mal!, ~ Sie mal!** listen; **na hör mal!, na ~ Sie mal!** wait a minute!, look here!, listen here!

(b) (*anhören*) *Hörspiel, Vortrag, Radio* to listen to; *Berichte, Sänger* to hear; (*zu Wort kommen lassen*) to listen to, to hear; (*Rad: empfangen*) to get ◆ **ich will auch gehört werden** I want to be heard too; **bei wem ~ Sie in diesem Semester?** whose lectures are you going to this term?; **eine französische Vorlesung bei Professor X ~** to go to a French lecture by Professor X.

(c) (*sich nach etw richten*) to listen, to pay attention; (*dial: gehorchen*) to obey, to listen ◆ **auf jdn/etw ~** to listen to *or* heed sb/sth; **wer nicht ~ will, muß fühlen** (*Prov*) what did I tell you?; **der Hund hört auf den Namen Tobias** the dog answers to the name of Tobias.

(d) (*erfahren*) to hear ◆ **von etw ~** to hear about *or* of sth; **von jdm gehört haben** to have heard of sb; **von jdm ~** (*Nachricht bekommen*) to hear from sb; **Sie werden noch von mir ~** *or* **zu ~ kriegen** (*inf*) (*Drohung*) you'll be hearing from me, you haven't heard the last of this; **man hörte nie mehr etwas von ihm** he was never heard of again; **nie gehört!** (*inf*) never heard of him/it; **etwas/nichts von sich ~ lassen** to get/not to get in touch; **lassen Sie von sich ~** keep in touch; **ich lasse von mir ~** I'll be in touch; **er ließ nichts von sich ~** I *etc* haven't heard from him; **nach allem, was ich (über ihn/darüber) höre** from what I've heard *or* I hear (about him/it); **soviel man hört** from what I hear/one hears; **er kommt, wie ich höre** I hear he's coming; **man höre und staune!** would you believe it!; **das** *or* **so etwas habe ich ja noch nie gehört!** I've never heard anything like it (in all my life)!; **er wollte nichts** *or* **von nichts gehört haben** he pretended not to have heard anything about it; **ich will davon** *or* **von der Sache nichts gehört haben** I don't want to know anything about it; **ich will mal nichts gehört haben** (*inf*) I haven't heard a thing, right? (*inf*).

Hören *nt* **-s,** *no pl* hearing; (*Radio~*) listening ◆ **das ~ von Musik** listening to music; **es verging ihm ~ und Sehen** he didn't know whether he was coming or going (*inf*); **er fuhr so schnell, daß mir ~ und Sehen verging** he drove so fast I almost passed out.

Hörensagen *nt*: **vom ~** from *or* by hearsay.

hörenswert *adj* worth hearing *or* listening to.

Hörer *m* **-s, -** **(a)** (*Rad*) listener; (*Univ*) student/person (attending lectures) ◆ **sich als ~ einschreiben** to enrol for a lecture course. **(b)** (*Telec*) receiver; (*Kopf~*) head- *or* earphone.

Hörerbrief *m* listener's letter.

Hörerin *f siehe* **Hörer (a)**.

Hörerschaft *f* (*Rad*) listeners *pl*, audience; (*Univ*) number of students/people (attending a lecture).

Hör-: ~fehler *m* (*Med*) hearing defect; **diese falsche Information beruht auf einem ~fehler** the information was got wrong because something was misheard; **das war ein ~fehler** I/he *etc* misheard it; **~folge** *f (Rad)* radio series; *(Geschichte in Fortsetzungen)* radio serial; **~funk** *m* sound radio; **~gerät** *nt*, **~hilfe** *f* hearing aid; **~grenze** *f* auditory threshold, limit of hearing.

hörig *adj* enslaved; *(Hist)* in bondage ◆ **jdm (sexuell) ~ sein** to be (sexually) dependent on sb, to be in sb's thrall *(liter)*; **sich** *(dat)* **jdn ~ machen** to make sb sexually dependent on one; **er ist ihr ~** she has sexual power over him.

Hörige(r) *mf decl as adj (Hist)* bondsman, bondswoman, serf; *(fig: sexuell ~)* person who is sexually dependent on sb.

Hörigkeit *f (Hist)* bondage, serfdom; *(sexuell)* sexual dependence.

Horizont *m* **-(e)s, -e** *(lit, fig)* horizon; *(Geol auch)* zone ◆ **am ~** on the horizon; **das geht über meinen ~** *(fig)* that is beyond me *or* my comprehension; **er hat einen begrenzten** *or* **beschränkten ~** he has limited horizons.

horizontal *adj* horizontal ◆ **das ~e Gewerbe** *(inf)* the oldest profession in the world *(inf)*.

Horizontale *f* **-, -(n)** *(Math)* horizontal (line) ◆ **er befindet sich in der ~n** *(inf)* he is lying down (in bed); **sich in die ~ begeben** *(inf)* to adopt the horizontal *(hum)*.

Hormon *nt* **-s, -e** hormone.

hormonal, hormonell *adj* hormone *attr*, hormonal ◆ **jdn/etw ~ behandeln** to treat sb/sth with hormones, to give sb hormone treatment.

Hormon-: ~behandlung *f* hormone treatment; **~drüse** *f* endocrine gland; **~haushalt** *m* hormone *or* hormonal balance; **~präparat** *nt* hormone preparation; **~spiegel** *m* hormone level.

Hörmuschel *f* **-, -n** *(Telec)* earpiece.

Horn *nt* **-(e)s, ¨er (a)** *(von Tieren, Trink~)* horn; *(fig inf: Beule)* bump, lump ◆ **jdn mit den ¨ern aufspießen** to gore sb; **sich** *(dat)* **die ¨er ablaufen** *or* **abstoßen** *(inf)* to sow one's wild oats; **den Stier an** *or* **bei den ¨ern packen** *or* **fassen** *(fig)* to take the bull by the horns; **jdm ¨er aufsetzen** *(inf)* to cuckold sb, to give sb horns *(old)*; **¨er tragen** *(fig)* to be a cuckold.
(b) *(Mus)* horn; *(Mil)* bugle; *(von Auto etc)* horn, hooter ◆ **die ¨er** *(im Orchester)* the horns *pl*, the horn section; **ins ~ stoßen** to blow *or* sound the horn; **ins gleiche/in jds ~ blasen** *or* **stoßen** *or* **tuten** to chime in.
(c) *(bei Schnecke)* horn, feeler.

Horn-: h~artig *adj* horn-like; **~berger Schießen** *nt*: **wie das ~berger Schießen ausgehen** *or* **enden** to come to nothing; **~bläser** *m (Mus)* horn player; **~blende** *f (Geol)* hornblende; **~brille** *f* horn-rimmed glasses *pl or* spectacles *pl*.

Hörnchen *nt* **-s, - (a)** *(kleines Horn)* little horn. **(b)** *(Gebäck)* croissant. **(c)** *(Zool)* squirrel; *(Backen~)* chipmunk, ground squirrel; *(Flug~)* flying squirrel.

Hörnerklang *m* sound of horns *or* bugles.

hörnern *adj* (made of) horn.

Hörnerv *m* auditory nerve.

Horn-: h~förmig *adj* horn-shaped; **~gestell** *nt* **eine Brille mit ~gestell** horn-rimmed glasses *pl*; **~haut** *f* (patch of) hard *or* horn skin, callous; *(des Auges)* cornea; **~hautentzündung** *f (Med)* inflammation of the cornea, keratitis *(spec)*; **~hauttrübung** *f (Med)* corneal opacity.

hornig *adj* horny, like horn.

Hornisse *f* **-, -n** hornet.

Hornissennest *nt* hornet's nest.

Hornist *m* horn player; *(Mil)* bugler.

Horn-: ~kamm *m* horn comb; **~ochs(e)** *m (fig inf)* blockhead *(inf)*, idiot; **~signal** *nt (Mil)* bugle call; *(Rail)* horn signal; *(Auto)* honk, hoot.

Hornung *m* **-s, -e** *(obs)* February.

Hornvieh *nt* horned cattle *pl*; *(fig) siehe* **Hornochs(e)**.

Hör|organ *nt* organ of hearing.

Horoskop *nt* **-s, -e** horoscope ◆ **jdm das ~ stellen** to cast sb's horoscope.

Hörprobe *f* **jetzt eine ~ aus seiner letzten Platte** now here's a sample from his latest record.

horrend *adj* horrendous.

horribile dictu *adv (geh)* terrible to relate.

horrido *interj (Hunt)* halloo.

Horrido *nt* **-s, -s** halloo(ing).

Hörrohr *nt* **(a)** ear trumpet. **(b)** *(Med)* stethoscope.

Horror *m* **-s,** *no pl* horror *(vor +dat* of) ◆ **ein unbeschreiblicher ~ überfiel mich** I was seized by an indescribable feeling of horror.

Horror- *in cpds* horror; **~film** *m* horror film; **~schocker** *m (Press sl)* horror film/novel/book; **~szene** *f* scene of horror, horrific scene; **~trip** *m (inf)* horror trip *(sl)*.

Hör-: ~saal *m (Univ)* lecture room *or* hall *or* theatre; **~schwelle** *f* auditory threshold.

Horsd'œuvre [(h)ɔr'dø:vʀ, (h)o:ʀ'dø:vʀ] *nt* **-s, -s** hors d'œuvre.

Hörspiel *nt (Rad)* radio play.

Horst *m* **-(e)s, -e (a)** *(Nest)* nest; *(Adler~)* eyrie. **(b)** *(Gehölz)* thicket, shrubbery. **(c)** *(Bot) (von Blumen)* cluster; *(von Bambus, Gras)* tuft. **(d)** *(Geol)* horst. **(e)** *siehe* **Fliegerhorst**.

Hörsturz *m* hearing loss.

Hort *m* **-(e)s, -e (a)** *(old, poet: Schatz)* hoard, treasure. **(b)** *(geh: Zufluchtsstätte)* refuge, shelter ◆ **ein ~ der Freiheit** a stronghold of liberty; **der Herr sei mein ~** *(Bibl)* the Lord be my refuge *(Bibl)*. **(c)** *(Kinder~) day-home for schoolchildren in the afternoon.*

horten *vt Geld, Vorräte etc* to hoard; *Rohstoffe etc* to stockpile.

Hortensie [-iə] *f* hydrangea.

Hortung *f, no pl siehe vt* hoarding; stockpiling.

Hör-: ~weite *f* hearing range; **in/außer ~weite** within/out of hearing *or* earshot; **~zentrum** *nt (Anat)* auditory *or* acoustic centre.

Höschen ['hø:sçən] *nt* **(a)** *(Kinderhose)* (pair of) trousers *or* pants; *(Strampel~)* (pair of) rompers *pl* ◆ **kurze(s) ~** (pair of) shorts *pl*. **(b)** *(Unterhose)* (pair of) panties *pl or* knickers *pl*; *(für Kinder)* (pair of) underpants *pl or* pants *pl (Brit)*. **(c)** *(Zool: einer Biene)* pollen load *or* pellet.

Höschenwindel *f* disposable nappy *(Brit) or* diaper *(US)*.

Hose *f* **-, -n** trousers *pl*, pants *pl*; *(Damen~ auch)* slacks *pl*; *(Bund~)* breeches *pl*; *(Reit~)* jodhpurs *pl*, (riding) breeches *pl*; *(Bade~)* swimming trunks *pl*; *(Unter~)* underpants *pl*, pants *pl (Brit)*; *(von Vogel)* leg feathers *pl* ◆ **ich brauche eine neue ~** I need a new pair of trousers *or* pants, I need some new trousers *or* pants; **zwei ~n** two pairs of trousers *or* pants; **die ~n anhaben** *(fig inf)* to wear the trousers *or* pants *(inf)*; **das Herz fiel** *or* **rutschte ihm in die ~** *(inf)* his heart was in his mouth; **die ~n voll haben** *(lit)* to have dirtied oneself, to have made a mess in one's pants; *(fig inf)* to be scared shitless *(vulg)*, to be wetting oneself *(inf)*; **sich** *(dat)* **in die ~n machen** *(lit)* to dirty oneself, to make a mess in one's pants; *(fig inf)* to shit *(vulg) or* wet *(inf)* oneself; **in die ~ gehen** *(sl: Witz, Prüfung)* to be a complete wash-out *(inf) or* flop *(inf)*; **tote ~** *(sl)* nothing doing *(sl)*; **der Film war tote ~** the film was a dead loss *(inf)*.

Hosen-: ~anzug *m* trouser suit *(Brit)*, pantsuit *(US)*; **~aufschlag** *m* turn-up *(Brit)*, cuff *(US)*; **~band** *nt* knee-band; **~bandorden** *m* Order of the Garter; **~bein** *nt* trouser leg; **~boden** *m* seat (of trousers); **den ~boden vollkriegen** *(inf)* to get a smacked bottom; **sich auf den ~boden setzen** *(inf) (arbeiten)* to get stuck in *(inf)*, to knuckle down; *(stillsitzen)* to sit down and stay sitting down; **~boje** *f (Naut)* breeches buoy; **~bügel** *m* trouser hanger; **~bund** *m* waistband; **~klammer** *f* trouser clip, cycle clip; **~klappe** *f* flap; **~knopf** *m* trouser button; **~latz** *m (Verschluß)* flies *pl*, fly; *(von Latzhose)* bib; **~matz** *m (inf) (kleines Kind)* **du (kleiner) ~matz** my little darling *or* chap *or* fellow; **~naht** *f* trouser seam; **mit den Händen an der ~naht** *(Mil)* (stand to attention,) thumbs on (your) trouser seams; **~rock** *m* divided skirt, culottes *pl*, pantskirt; **~scheißer** *m* **(a)** *(inf: Kind)* mucky pup *(inf)*; **du kleiner ~scheißer** you mucky little pup; **(b)** *(sl: Feigling)* chicken *(inf)*; *(Junge)* scaredy-pants *(inf)*; **~schlitz** *m* flies *pl*, fly; **~spanner** *m* trouser hanger; **~stall** *m (inf) (Schlitz)* flies *pl*, fly; **~tasche** *f* trouser pocket, pants *or* trousers pocket *(US)*; **~träger** *pl* (a pair of) braces *pl (Brit) or* suspenders *pl (US)*.

hosianna *interj* hosanna.

Hosianna *nt* **-s, -s** hosanna.

Hospital *nt* **-s, -e** *or* **Hospitäler** *(dated)* **(a)** *(Krankenhaus)* hospital. **(b)** *(Pflegeheim)* (old people's) home.

Hospitalismus *m (Med)* hospitalism.

Hospitant *m (Sch, Univ)* someone sitting in on lectures/classes.

Hospitation *f (Sch, Univ)* sitting in on lectures/classes *(bei jdm* with sb).

hospitieren* *vi (Sch, Univ)* to sit in on lectures/classes *(bei jdm* with sb).

Hospiz *nt* **-es, -e** hospice; *(christliches ~) private hotel under religious management.*

Host *m* **-s, -s** *(Comput)* host.

Hostess, ⚠Hosteß *f* **-, Hostessen** hostess.

Hostie ['hɔstiə] *f (Eccl)* host, consecrated wafer.

Hostien- [-iən]: **~gefäß** *nt* pyx, ciborium; **~kelch** *m* chalice; **~schachtel** *f* box for communion wafers; **~schrein** *m* tabernacle; **~teller** *m* paten.

Hot dog *nt or m* **-s, -s** *(Cook)* hot dog.

Hotel *nt* **-s, -s** hotel.

Hotelboy *m* page (boy), bellboy *(US)*, bellhop *(US)*.

Hotelfach *nt, no pl* hotel management.

Hotelfach-: ~frau *f* hotel manageress; **~mann** *m* hotel manager; **~schule** *f* college of hotel management.

Hotelführer *m* hotel guide.

Hotel garni *nt* bed and breakfast hotel.

Hotel-: ~gewerbe *nt* hotel business; **~halle** *f* (hotel) lobby.

Hotellerie *f (Sw)* hotel business.

Hotelier [-'lie:] *m* **-s, -s** hotelier.

Hotel-: ~nachweis *m siehe* **~verzeichnis**; **~page** *m siehe* **~boy**; **~portier** *m* hotel *or* hall porter; **~silber** *nt* hotel cutlery; **~- und Gaststättengewerbe** *nt* hotel and restaurant trade, catering industry; **~verzeichnis** *nt* hotel register.

Hotline ['hɔtlaın] *f* **-, -s** *(Telec: Informationsdienst, Sorgentelefon)* hot line ◆ **eine ~ einrichten** to set up a hot line.

hott *interj (vorwärts)* gee up; *(nach rechts)* gee.

Hottentotte *m* **-n, -n** Hottentot ◆ **sie benehmen sich wie die ~n** *(inf)* they behave like savages.

hpts. *abbr of* **hauptsächlich**.

Hptst. *abbr of* **Hauptstadt**.

Hr. *abbr of* **Herr** Mr.

Hrn. *abbr of* **Herrn**.

hrsg. *abbr of* **herausgegeben** edited, ed.

Hrsg. *abbr of* **Herausgeber** ed.

HTLV III [ha:te:|ɛlfaʊ'drai] *siehe* **HIV**.

hu *interj (Schaudern)* ugh; *(Schrecken, Kälte etc)* whew.

hü *interj (vorwärts)* gee up; *(nach links)* wo hi ◆ **einmal sagt er ~, einmal hott** *(inf)* first he says one thing and then another, he's always chopping and changing.

Hub *m* **-(e)s, ¨e** *(Tech)* **(a)** *(bei Maschinen: Kolben~)* (piston) stroke. **(b)** *(bei Kränen: Leistung)* lifting *or* hoisting capacity, lift.

Hub(b)el *m* **-s, -** *(inf)* bump.

hubb(e)lig *adj (inf)* bumpy.
Hubble-Teleskop ['hʌbl-] *nt* Hubble telescope.
Hubbrücke *f* lift bridge.
hüben *adv* over here, (on) this side ◆ **~ und** *or* **wie drüben** on both sides.
Hubertusjagd *f* St Hubert's Day hunt.
Hub-: ~insel *f* drilling rig *or* platform; **~karren** *m* lift(ing) truck; **~kraft** *f* lifting *or* hoisting capacity; **~magnet** *m* solenoid; **~raum** *m (Aut)* cubic capacity.
hübsch *adj* **(a)** *(gutaussehend)* pretty; *(reizvoll) Ausflug, Geschenk* lovely, delightful, nice; *(inf: nett)* lovely, nice ◆ **sich ~ machen** to make oneself look pretty; **er macht das schon ganz ~** he's doing it very nicely; **das wäre doch ~, wenn ...** it would be lovely if ...; **ihr (beiden) H~en** *(inf)* you two.
(b) *(iro inf: unangenehm)* fine, pretty, nice ◆ **eine ~e Geschichte/Bescherung** a pretty kettle of fish, a fine how-d'ye-do; **das kann ja ~ werden** that'll be just great; **da hast du dir etwas H~es eingebrockt!** now you've got yourself into a fine *or* pretty mess!
(c) *(inf: beträchtlich)* tidy, pretty, nice ◆ **ein ~es Vermögen/ein ~es Sümmchen** a pretty penny *(inf)*, a tidy sum.
(d) *nur adv (ziemlich)* pretty ◆ **da mußte ich aber ganz ~ arbeiten** I really had to work pretty hard; **ganz ~ viel bezahlen** to pay quite a bit.
(e) *nur adv (inf: wie es sein soll)* **das werde ich ~ bleiben lassen** I'm going to leave well alone; **das wirst du ~ sein lassen** you're going to do nothing of the kind; **sei ~ artig!** be a good boy/girl; **immer ~ langsam!** nice and easy does it, (take it) nice and slowly.
Hubschrauber *m* **-s, -** helicopter.
Hubschrauber-: ~dienst *m* helicopter service; **~flugplatz, ~landeplatz** *m* heliport; **~träger** *m (Naut)* helicopter-carrier.
Hubvolumen *nt (Tech) siehe* **Hubraum**.
huch *interj* ooh.
Hucke *f* **-, -n** *(obs) (Last)* load; *(Korb)* pannier ◆ **jdm die ~ vollhauen** *(inf)* to give sb a good thrashing *(inf) or* hiding; **die ~ vollkriegen** *(inf)* to get a thrashing *(inf) or* hiding; **jdm die ~ vollügen** *(inf)* to tell sb a pack of lies; **sich** *(dat)* **die ~ vollsaufen** *(sl)* to have a skinful *(sl)*.
huckepack *adv* piggy-back *(auch Comput)*, pick-a-back ◆ **ein Kind ~ nehmen/tragen** to give a child a piggy-back (ride), to carry a child piggy-back *or* pick-a-back.
Huckepack-: ~verfahren *nt (Space, Rail)* piggy-back system; *(Chem)* piggy-back process; **~verkehr** *m (Rail)* piggy-back transport *(US)*, motorail service; **im ~verkehr** by motorail *or* rail.
Hudelei *f (esp S Ger, Aus inf)* slipshod *or* sloppy *(inf)* work.
hudeln *vi (esp S Ger, Aus inf)* to work sloppily, to do slipshod work.
Hudler *m* **-s, -** *(esp S Ger, Aus inf)* slipshod *or* sloppy worker, bungler *(inf)*.
hudlig *adj (esp S Ger, Aus inf)* slipshod, sloppy *(inf)* ◆ **~ arbeiten** to work sloppily, to do sloppy *or* slipshod work.
Huf *m* **-(e)s, -e** hoof ◆ **einem Pferd die ~e beschlagen** to shoe a horse.
Hufbeschlag *m* (horse)shoeing.
Huf|eisen *nt* horseshoe.
Huf|eisen-: h~förmig *adj* horseshoe-shaped, (in) the shape of a horseshoe; **~magnet** *m* horseshoe magnet.
Hufendorf *nt village arranged in a straight line with strips of farmland extending behind each house.*
Huf-: ~lattich *m (Bot)* coltsfoot; **~nagel** *m* horseshoe-nail; **~schlag** *m (Getrappel)* hoofbeats *pl*; *(Stoß)* kick (from a horse); **dabei hat er einen ~schlag abbekommen** the horse kicked him; **~schmied** *m* blacksmith, farrier; **~schmiede** *f* smithy, blacksmith's *or* farrier's (workshop).
Hüft-: ~bein *nt* hip-bone; **~bruch** *m* fractured hip, hip fracture.
Hüfte *f* **-, -n** hip; *(von Tieren)* haunch ◆ **bis an die ~n reichen** to come up to the waist; **wir standen bis an die ~n in Brennesseln/im Wasser** we stood waist-high *or* up to the waist in stinging nettles/waist-deep *or* up to the waist in water; **aus der ~ schießen** to shoot from the hip; **mit wiegenden ~n** with hips swaying; **die Arme in die ~n stützen** to put/have one's hands on one's hips; **er stand mit den Armen in die ~n gestützt da** he stood there hands on hips *or* with arms akimbo.
Hüft-: ~gegend *f* hip region; **~gelenk** *nt* hip joint; **~gürtel, ~halter** *m* girdle; **h~hoch** *adj Pflanzen etc* waist-high; *Wasser etc* waist-deep; **wir standen h~hoch im Farnkraut/Schlamm** we stood waist-high in ferns/waist-deep in mud; **h~hohe Gummistiefel** rubber waders.
Huftier *nt* hoofed animal, ungulate *(form)*.
Hüft-: ~knochen *m siehe* **~bein**; **~leiden** *nt* hip trouble; **~schmerz** *m* pain in the hip; **~verrenkung** *f* dislocation of the hip.
Hügel *m* **-s, -** hill; *(Grab-, Erdhaufen)* mound ◆ **ein kleiner ~** a hillock.
Hügel-: h~ab *adv* downhill; **h~an, h~auf** *adv* uphill; **~beet** *nt* raised bed; **~grab** *nt (Archeol)* barrow, tumulus.
hüg(e)lig *adj* hilly, undulating, rolling *attr.*
Hügel-: ~kette *f* range *or* chain of hills; **~land** *nt* hilly country.
Hugenotte *m* **-n, -n, Hugenottin** *f* Huguenot.
hüglig *adj siehe* **hüg(e)lig**.
hüh *interj siehe* **hü**.
huh *interj siehe* **hu**.
Huhn *nt* **-(e)s, ¨er (a)** chicken *(auch Cook)*; *(Henne auch)* hen; *(Gattung)* fowl, gallinaceous bird *(form)* ◆ **mit den ¨ern aufstehen** *(inf)* to get up with the lark; **mit den ¨ern zu Bett gehen** *(inf)* to go to bed early; **da lachen ja die ¨er** *(inf)* what a joke, it's enough to make a cat laugh *(inf)*; **ich sehe aus wie ein gerupftes ~** *(inf)* my hair looks like a haystack *(inf)*.
(b) *(fig inf)* **du krankes ~** you poor old thing; **ein verrücktes** *or* **komisches** *or* **ulkiges ~** a queer bird *(inf) or* fish *(inf)*; **ein dummes ~** a silly goose; **ein versoffenes ~** a tippler.
Hühnchen *nt* (young) chicken, pullet; *(Brat~)* (roast) chicken ◆ **mit jdm ein ~ zu rupfen haben** *(inf)* to have a bone to pick with sb *(inf)*.
Hühner-: ~auge *nt (Med)* corn; **jdm auf die ~augen treten** *(hum)* to tread on sb's corns *(inf)*; **~augenpflaster** *nt* corn plaster; **~bouillon, ~brühe** *f* (clear) chicken broth; **~brust** *f (Cook)* chicken breast; *(Med, fig)* pigeon-breast, chicken-breast *(US)*; **~dieb** *m* chicken thief; **er mußte sich wie ein ~dieb wegschleichen** he had to slink off with his tail between his legs; **~draht** *m* chicken wire; **~ei** *nt* hen's egg; **~farm** *f* chicken farm; **~frikassee** *nt* chicken fricassee; **~futter** *nt* chicken feed; **~habicht** *m* goshawk; **~haus** *nt* henhouse, chicken-coop; **~gott** *m (Miner)* holy-stone; **~hof** *m* chicken run; **~hund** *m* pointer; **~klein** *nt* **-s,** *no pl (Cook)* chicken trimmings *pl*; **~leiter** *f* chicken ladder; **~mist** *m* chicken droppings *pl*; *(zum Düngen)* chicken manure; **~pastete** *f* chicken pie; **~pest** *f (Vet)* fowl pest; **~stall** *m* henhouse, chicken-coop; **~stange** *f* perch, (chicken) roost; **~suppe** *f* chicken soup; **~vögel** *pl (Orn)* gallinaceans *pl (form)*, gallinaceous birds *pl (form)*; **~zucht** *f* chicken breeding *or* farming.
hui [hui] *interj* whoosh ◆ **~, das war aber schnell!** wow, that was quick!; **außen ~, innen pfui, oben ~, unten pfui** *(prov inf)* the outside's fine but underneath he/she *etc* is filthy.
Huld *f* **-,** *no pl (old liter) (Güte)* grace, graciousness; *(Gunst)* favour ◆ **jdm seine ~ schenken** to bestow one's favour upon sb *(liter)*; **sie stand in seiner ~** she was in his good graces.
huldigen *vi +dat (liter)* **(a)** *einem König, Papst etc* to render *or* do *or* pay homage to; *einem Künstler, Lehrmeister etc* to pay homage to; *einer Dame* to pay one's attentions *or* addresses to *(liter)*. **(b)** *einer Ansicht* to subscribe to; *einer Sitte, einem Glauben etc* to embrace; *einem Laster* to indulge in.
Huldigung *f (old, liter)* **(a)** *(Hist: Treueid)* homage, oath of allegiance. **(b)** *(Verehrung)* homage; *(einer Dame)* attentions *pl (liter)*, addresses *pl (liter)*; *(Beifall)* homage ◆ **jdm seine ~ darbringen** to pay homage to sb.
huldreich, huldvoll *adj (old, liter)* gracious.
Hülfe *f* **-, -n** *(obs) siehe* **Hilfe**.
Hülle *f* **-, -n (a)** cover; *(Schallplatten ~ auch)* sleeve; *(für Ausweiskarten etc auch)* holder, case; *(Cellophan~)* wrapping; *(liter, hum: Kleidung)* clothes *pl*, piece of clothing; *(liter: eines Menschen)* exterior; *(abgestreifte Schlangenhaut)* skin ◆ **die ~ fallen lassen** to peel *or* strip off; **die letzten ~n fallen lassen** to shed the last layer; **der Körper als ~ der Seele** the body as the temple of the soul; **die sterbliche ~** the mortal remains *pl*.
(b) *(Anat)* integument.
(c) *(Bot)* involucre.
(d) *(Phys: Atom~)* shell.
(e) in ~ und Fülle in abundance; **Äpfel/Whisky/Frauen/Sorgen** *etc* **in ~ und Fülle** apples/whisky/women/worries galore; **es gab alles in ~ und Fülle** there was an abundance *or* plenty of everything.
hüllen *vt (geh)* to wrap ◆ **in Dunkel gehüllt** shrouded in darkness; **in Flammen gehüllt** enveloped in flames; **in Wolken gehüllt** covered *or* enveloped *or* veiled *(liter)* in clouds; **sich fest in seinen Mantel ~** to wrap oneself up tight in one's coat; **sich (über etw** *acc*) **in Schweigen ~** to remain silent (on *or* about sth).
hüllenlos *adj* unclothed.
Hüllwort *nt (Ling)* euphemism.
Hülse *f* **-, -n (a)** *(Schale)* hull, husk; *(Schote)* pod; *(Bot: Frucht)* involucre *(form)*. **(b)** *(Etui, Kapsel)* case; *(für Film)* cartridge; *(Phys: für gefährliche Stoffe)* capsule; *(von Geschoß)* case; *(von Patronen)* (cartridge) case ◆ **er ist nur noch eine leere ~** he is now just an empty shell.
Hülsenfrucht *f usu pl* peas and beans *pl*, pulse *(form)*.
human *adj* humane; *(verständnisvoll auch)* considerate.
Human-: ~genetik *f* human genetics *sing*; **~genetiker(in** *f*) *m* human geneticist.
Humanisierung *f* humanization.
Humanismus *m* humanism; *(Hist)* Humanism.
Humanist(in *f*) *m* humanist; *(Hist)* Humanist; *(Altsprachler)* classicist.
humanistisch *adj siehe n* humanist(ic); Humanist; classical ◆ **~ gebildet** educated in the classics *or* humanities; **~e Bildung** classical education, education in the classics *or* the humanities; **~es Gymnasium** *secondary school with bias on Latin and Greek*; ≃ grammar school *(Brit)*.
humanitär *adj* humanitarian.
Humanität *f, no pl* humaneness, humanity; *(als Bildungsideal)* humanitarianism.
Humanitätsduselei *f (pej)* sentimental humanitarianism.
Human-: ~medizin *f* (human) medicine; **~mediziner** *m* medic *(inf)*; medical student; doctor of medicine.
Humbug *m* **-s,** *no pl (inf) (Schwindel)* humbug *(inf)*; *(Unsinn auch)* stuff and nonsense *(inf)*.
Hummel *f* **-, -n** bumble-bee ◆ **~n im** *or* **unterm Hintern haben** *(dated inf)* to have ants in one's pants *(inf)*.
Hummer *m* **-s, -** lobster.
Hummer-: ~cocktail *m* lobster cocktail; **~krabben** *pl* king prawns; **~reuse** *f* lobster pot; **~schere** *f* lobster claw.
Humor *m* **-s,** *(rare)* **-e** humour; *(Sinn für ~)* sense of humour ◆ **er hat keinen (Sinn für) ~** he has no sense of humour; **etw mit ~ nehmen/tragen** to take/bear sth with a sense of humour *or* cheerfully; **er nahm die Bemerkung mit ~ auf** he took the remark good-humouredly *or* in good humour; **er hat einen eigenartigen ~** he has a strange sense of humour; **er verliert nie den ~**

he never loses his sense of humour; **langsam verliere ich den ~** it's getting beyond a joke; **da hat selbst er den ~ verloren** it was going too far even for him, even he didn't think it funny any more; **~ ist, wenn man trotzdem lacht** (*prov*) having a sense of humour means looking on the bright side.

Humoreske *f* **-, -n** (*liter*) humorous story/sketch; (*Mus*) humoresque.

humorig *adj* (*geh*) humorous, genial.

Humorist(in *f*) *m* humorist; (*Komiker*) comedian.

humoristisch *adj* humorous ◆ **er ist/hat ein großes ~es Talent** he is a very funny *or* amusing person.

Humor-: h~los *adj* humourless; *Buch etc auch* lacking in *or* devoid of humour; *Mensch auch* lacking (a sense of) humour *or* in humour; **er hat recht h~los auf unsere Scherze reagiert** he didn't find our jokes funny at all; **~losigkeit** *f siehe adj* humourlessness; lack of (a sense of) humour; **mit der für ihn typischen ~losigkeit** with his usual lack of humour; **h~voll** *adj* humorous, amusing; **er kann sehr h~voll erzählen** he is a very amusing *or* humorous talker.

humos *adj Boden* humus *attr*.

Humpelei *f, no pl* (*inf*) hobbling.

humpeln *vi* **(a)** *aux sein* to hobble. **(b)** (*inf: ständig hinken*) to limp, to walk with *or* have a limp.

Humpen *m* **-s, -** tankard, mug; (*aus Ton*) stein.

Humus *m* **-,** *no pl* humus.

Humus-: ~boden *m*, **~erde** *f* humus soil.

Hund *m* **-(e)s, -e (a)** dog; (*Jagd~ auch*) hound; (*sl: Schurke*) swine (*sl*), bastard (*sl*) ◆ **der Große/Kleine ~** (*Astron*) Great(er) Dog/Little *or* Lesser Dog; **junger ~** puppy, pup; **die Familie der ~e** the dog *or* canine family; **~e, die (viel) bellen, beißen nicht** empty vessels make most noise (*Prov*); **getroffene ~e bellen** (*inf*) if the cap fits, wear it; **viele ~e sind des Hasen Tod** (*Prov*) there is not much one person can do against many; **wie ~ und Katze leben** to live like cat and dog, to lead a cat-and-dog life; **ich würde bei diesem Wetter keinen ~ auf die Straße jagen** I wouldn't send a dog out in this weather; **damit kann man keinen ~ hinterm Ofen hervorlocken** (*inf*) that's not going to tempt anybody; **müde wie ein ~ sein** (*inf*) to be dog-tired; **er ist bekannt wie ein bunter ~** (*inf*) everybody knows him; **kein ~ nimmt ein Stück Brot von ihm** everyone avoids him like the plague; **das ist (ja) zum Junge-~e-Kriegen** (*inf*) it's enough to give you kittens; **da wird der ~ in der Pfanne verrückt** (*inf*) it's enough to drive you round the twist (*inf*); **da liegt der ~ begraben** (*inf*) (so) that's what is/was behind it all; (*Haken, Problem etc*) that's the problem; **er ist mit allen ~en gehetzt** (*inf*) he knows all the tricks, there are no flies on him (*inf*); **er ist ein armer ~** he's a poor soul *or* devil (*inf*); **er ist völlig auf dem ~** (*inf*) he's really gone to the dogs (*inf*); **auf den ~ kommen** (*inf*) to go to the dogs (*inf*); **jdn auf den ~ bringen** (*inf*) to ruin sb; (*gesundheitlich*) to ruin sb's health; **die Weiber haben/der Suff hat ihn auf den ~ gebracht** (*inf*) women have/drink has been his ruin *or* downfall; **vor die ~e gehen** (*sl*) to go to the dogs (*inf*); (*sterben*) to die, to perish; (*getötet werden*) to cop it (*inf*), to be killed; **du blöder ~** (*sl*) you silly *or* stupid bastard (*sl*); **du gemeiner ~** (*sl*) you rotten bastard (*sl*); **du schlauer** *or* **gerissener ~** (*sl*) you sly *or* crafty devil *or* old fox; **kein ~** (*inf*) not a (damn *inf*) soul.
(b) (*Min: Förderwagen*) truck, tub.

Hündchen *nt dim of* **Hund** doggy (*inf*), little dog; (*kleiner Hund*) small *or* little dog; (*junger Hund*) puppy, pup, puppy-dog (*baby-talk*).

Hunde-: ~arbeit *f* (*fig inf*): **eine ~arbeit** an awful job, the devil's own job (*inf*); **~art** *f siehe* **~rasse**; ⚠**~biß** *m* dog bite; **er hat einen ~biß abbekommen** he was/has been bitten by a dog; **~dreck** *m* dog's muck; **h~elend** *adj* (*inf*) **mir ist h~elend** I feel lousy (*inf*); **~fänger** *m* dog-catcher; **~floh** *m* dog flea; **~fraß** *m* (*pej sl*) (pig-)swill (*pej inf*); **~futter** *nt* dog food; **~gebell** *nt* barking (of dogs); **~gekläff** *nt* (*pej*) yapping (of dogs); **~gespann** *nt* team of dogs; **~halsband** *nt* dog collar; **~halter(in** *f*) *m* (*form*) dog owner; **~haltung** *f* owning dogs; **~hütte** *f* (*lit, fig*) (dog) kennel; **h~kalt** *adj* (*inf*) freezing cold; **~kälte** *f* (*inf*) freezing cold; **~kot** *m* dog dirt; **~köttel** *m* **-s, -** (*inf*) dog dirt *or* droppings *pl*; **~kuchen** *m* dog-biscuit; **~leben** *nt* (*inf*) dog's life (*inf*); **~leine** *f* dog lead *or* leash; **~liebhaber** *m* dog-lover; **~lohn** *m* (*pej inf*) miserable *or* rotten (*inf*) wage(s); **~marke** *f* dog licence disc, dog tag (*US*); (*hum inf: Erkennungsmarke*) identity disc, dog-tag (*US inf*); **h~müde** *adj pred, adv* (*inf*) dog-tired; **~narr** *m* (*inf*) fanatical dog lover, dog-freak (*inf*); **~rasse** *f* breed (of dog); **~rennen** *nt* greyhound *or* dog racing *no art*, dogs (*inf*); (*Wettkampf*) greyhound race.

hundert *num* a *or* one hundred ◆ **einige ~ Menschen** a few hundred people; **einer unter ~** one in a hundred; **in ~ Jahren** in a hundred years (from now); **ich wette ~ gegen eins** (*inf*) I'll bet *or* lay a hundred to one, I'll bet you anything (*inf*).

Hundert[1] *f* **-, -en** (*Zahl*) hundred.

Hundert[2] *nt* **-s, -e** hundred ◆ **es geht in die ~e** it runs into the hundreds; **~e von Menschen** hundreds of people; **einer unter ~en** one out of hundreds; **zehn vom ~** ten per cent; **zu ~en** by the hundred, in (their) hundreds; **einige ~ (Stecknadeln)** a few hundred (pins).

hundert|eins *num* a hundred and one.

Hunderter *m* **-s, - (a)** (*von Zahl*) (the) hundred. **(b)** (*Geldschein*) hundred(-pound/-dollar *etc* note).

hunderterlei *adj inv* a hundred and one.

Hundert-: h~fach, h~fältig (*geh*) [1] *adj* hundredfold; **die h~fache Menge** a hundred times the amount; [2] *adv* a hundred times; **jdm etw h~fach zurückgeben/vergelten** (*fig*) to repay sb a hundredfold *or* a hundred times over for sth; **h~fünfzigprozentig** *adj* (*iro*) fanatical; **er ist ein ~fünfzigprozentiger** he's a fanatic; **~jahrfeier** *f* centenary, centennial (*US*); (*Festlichkeiten auch*) centenary *or* centennial celebrations *pl*; **h~jährig** *adj attr* (one-)hundred-year-old; **der ~jährige Kalender** the Hundred Years' Calendar (*for weather prediction*); **der ~jährige Krieg** (*Hist*) the Hundred Years' War; **das Ergebnis einer h~jährigen Entwicklung/Arbeit** the result of a hundred years of development/work; **~jährige(r)** *mf decl as adj* centenarian; **h~jährlich** *adj* every hundred years; **h~mal** *adv* a hundred times; **ich hab' dir schon h~mal gesagt ...** if I've told you once I've told you a hundred times ...; **~meterlauf** *m* (*Sport*) **der/ein ~meterlauf** the/a 100 metres *sing*; **h~prozentig** *adj* (a *or* one) hundred per cent; *Alkohol* pure; **ein h~prozentiger Konservativer** *etc* an out-and-out conservative *etc*; **er ist h~prozentig Amerikaner** *etc* he's one hundred per cent American *etc*; **Sie haben h~prozentig recht** you're absolutely right; **ich bin mir h~prozentig sicher** I'm a hundred per cent sure; **das weiß ich h~prozentig** that's a fact; **ich bin mit ihm h~prozentig einer Meinung** I agree with him one hundred per cent; **ich werde ihn h~prozentig im Krankenhaus besuchen** I'll definitely visit him in hospital; **h~prozentig?** (*inf*) are you absolutely sure?; **~satz** *m* (*form*) percentage; **~schaft** *f* (*Mil*) group of a *or* one hundred; (*Hist: bei den Römern*) century.

Hundertstel *nt* **-s, -** hundredth.

hundertste(r, s) *adj* hundredth ◆ **vom H~n ins Tausendste kommen** (*fig*) to get carried away.

Hundert-: h~tausend *num* a *or* one hundred thousand; **~tausende von Menschen** hundreds of thousands of people; **~tausendstel** *nt* **-s, -** hundred thousandth; **h~undeins** *num* a *or* one hundred and one.

hundertweise *adv* by the hundred, in hundreds.

Hunde-: ~salon *m* dog parlour; **~scheiße** *f* (*sl*) dogshit (*vulg*), dog mess (*inf*); **~schlitten** *m* dog sled(ge) *or* sleigh; **~schnauze** *f* nose, snout; **kalt wie eine ~schnauze sein** (*inf*) to be ice-cold *or* as cold as ice; **~sohn** *m* (*pej liter*) cur; **~sperre** *f* ban on (bringing in) dogs; **~staffel** *f* dog branch; **~staupe** *f* (*Vet*) distemper; **~steuer** *f* dog licence fee; **~wache** *f* (*Naut*) middle watch; **~wetter** *nt* (*inf*) foul *or* filthy weather; **~zucht** *f* dog breeding; **~züchter** *m* dog breeder; **~zwinger** *m* (dog) compound; (*städtisch*) dog pound.

Hündin *f* bitch.

hündisch *adj* (*fig*) fawning *attr*, sycophantic ◆ **~e Ergebenheit** dog-like devotion.

Hündlein *nt dim of* **Hund** doggy (*inf*), little dog; (*kleiner Hund*) little *or* small dog.

Hunds-: ~fott *m* **-s, ¨er** (*obs, dial*) (miserable) cur; **h~föttisch** *adj* (*obs, dial*) dastardly (*old*); **h~gemein** *adj* (*inf*) shabby, mean; (*schwierig*) fiendishly difficult; *Schmerz etc* terrible; **es tut h~gemein weh** it hurts like hell (*inf*); **er kann h~gemein werden** he can get really nasty; **h~miserabel** *adj* (*inf*) abominable, abysmal (*inf*), lousy (*inf*); **mir geht es** *or* **ich fühle mich h~miserabel** I feel rotten (*inf*) *or* lousy (*inf*); **~stern** *m* Dog Star; **~tage** *pl* dog days *pl*; **~veilchen** *nt* (heath) dog violet.

Hüne *m* **-n, -n** giant, colossus ◆ **ein ~ von Mensch** (*geh*) a giant of a man.

Hünen-: ~gestalt *f* (*geh*) Titanic *or* colossal figure *or* frame; **~grab** *nt* megalithic grave; **h~haft** *adj* (*geh*) gigantic, colossal.

Hunger *m* **-s,** *no pl* (*lit, fig*) hunger (*nach* for); (*Hungersnot*) famine; (*nach Bildung auch*) thirst; (*nach fernen Ländern, Sonne etc*) yearning; (*nach Literatur*) appetite ◆ **~ bekommen/haben** to get/be hungry; **ich habe keinen richtigen ~** I'm not really hungry; **~ auf etw** (*acc*) **haben** to feel like (eating) sth; **den ~ bekämpfen** to combat hunger; **~ leiden** (*geh*) to go hungry, to starve; **ich habe ~ wie ein Wolf** *or* **Bär** (*inf*) I could eat a horse (*inf*); **~s** (*liter*) *or* **vor ~ sterben** to die of hunger *or* starvation, to starve to death; **ich sterbe vor ~** (*inf*) I'm starving (*inf*), I'm dying of hunger (*inf*); **~ ist der beste Koch** (*Prov*) hunger is the best sauce (*Prov*).

Hunger-: ~blockade *f* hunger *or* starvation blockade; **~dasein** *nt* existence at starvation level; **~gefühl** *nt* hungry feeling; **~jahr** *nt* hungry year, year of hunger; **~künstler** *m* (professional) faster, *person who, for pay, goes without nourishment for prolonged periods*; **ich bin doch kein ~künstler** I'm not on a starvation diet; **~kur** *f* starvation diet; **~land** *nt* famine-stricken country; **~leben** *nt siehe* **~dasein**; **~leider** *m* **-s, -** (*dated*) starving wretch, starveling; **~lohn** *m* (*fig*) pittance.

hungern [1] *vi* **(a)** (*Hunger leiden*) to go hungry, to starve ◆ **jdn ~ lassen** to let sb go hungry; (*zur Strafe auch*) to make sb starve; **ich hungere schon seit fünf Tagen** I haven't eaten a thing for five days.
(b) (*fasten*) to go without food.
(c) (*fig geh: verlangen*) to hunger (*nach* for).
[2] *vt impers* (*geh*) **mich hungert** I am *or* feel hungry; **ihn hungert nach Macht** he hungers *or* is hungry for power.
[3] *vr* **sich zu Tode ~** to starve oneself to death; **sich schlank ~** to go on a starvation diet; **er hat sich durch die Studentenzeit gehungert** he starved his way through university.

hungernd *adj, no comp* hungry, starving.

Hunger|ödem *nt* (*Med*) famine oedema (*spec*).

Hungersnot *f* famine.

Hunger-: ~streik *m* hunger strike; **~tag** *m* (*inf*) fast day; **~tod** *m* death from starvation; **den ~tod erleiden** *or* **sterben** to die of hunger *or* starvation; **~tuch** *nt* (*Eccl*) Lenten veil; **am ~tuch nagen** (*fig*) to be starving, to be on the breadline (*inf*); **~turm** *m* (*Hist*) dungeon, oubliette.

hungrig *adj* (*lit, fig*) hungry (*nach* for) ◆ **Arbeit macht ~** work makes you hungry *or* gives you an appetite; **Gartenarbeit macht ~** gardening is hungry work; **~ nach** *or* **auf** (*acc*) **etw sein** to feel like (eating) sth; **~ nach Luft/Literatur** gasping for air/thirsting for good literature.

Hunne *m* **-n -n, Hunnin** *f* (*Hist*) Hun.
Hupe *f* **-, -n** horn ◆ **auf die ~ drücken** to press/sound the horn.
hupen *vi* to sound *or* hoot *or* honk (*Aut inf*) the horn, to hoot ◆ „~" "sound your horn".
Hüpfburg *f* bouncy castle.
hupfen *vi* (*esp S Ger*) *aux sein siehe* **hüpfen** ◆ **das ist gehupft wie gesprungen** (*inf*) it doesn't make any difference, it's six of one and half a dozen of the other (*inf*).
hüpfen *vi aux sein* to hop; (*Lämmer, Zicklein etc*) to frisk, to gambol; (*Ball*) to bounce ◆ **vor Freude ~** to jump for joy; **die Kinder hüpften vor Freude im Zimmer herum** the children went skipping round the room in sheer delight; **sein Herz hüpfte vor Freude** his heart leapt for joy; **H~ spielen** to play (at) hopscotch.
Hüpfer, Hupfer (*esp S Ger*) *m* **-s, -** hop, skip, bounce ◆ **mein Herz machte einen ~** my heart leapt.
Hüpfspiel *nt* hopscotch.
Hup-: ~konzert *nt* (*inf*) chorus of hooting *or* horns; **~signal** *nt* (*Aut*) hoot; *siehe* **~zeichen**; **~ton** *m* sound of a horn/hooter/whistle; **~zeichen** *nt* (*Aut*) hoot; „**~zeichen geben**" "sound your horn".
Hürde *f* **-, -n (a)** (*Sport, fig*) hurdle ◆ **eine ~ nehmen** to take *or* clear a hurdle. **(b)** (*Viehzaun*) fold, pen.
Hürden-: ~lauf *m* (*Sportart*) hurdling; (*Wettkampf*) hurdles *pl or sing*; **~läufer** *m* hurdler; **~rennen** *nt* (*Horseracing*) steeplechase.
Hure *f* **-, -n** whore.
huren *vi* (*inf*) to whore, to go whoring.
Huren-: ~bock *m* (*pej sl*) whoremonger; **h~haft** *adj* (*pej*) whorish; **~haus** *nt* (*dated*) whorehouse (*sl*), brothel; **~kind** *nt* (*old*) child of a whore; whoreson (*obs*); (*Typ*) widow; **~sohn** *m* (*pej sl*) bastard (*sl*), son of a bitch (*esp US sl*).
Hurerei *f* whoring.
hurra [hʊ'ra:, 'hʊra] *interj* hurray, hurrah.
Hurra *nt* **-s, -s** cheers *pl* ◆ **ein dreifaches ~** three cheers.
Hurra-: ~geschrei *nt* cheering; **~patriot** *m* flag-waving patriot, jingoist, chauvinist; **~patriotismus** *m* flag-waving, jingoism, chauvinism; **~ruf** *m* cheer.
Hurrikan *m* **-s, -e** *or* (*bei engl. Aussprache*) **-s** hurricane.
hurtig *adj* (*old, dial*) nimble; (*schnell*) quick.
Hurtigkeit *f, no pl* (*old, dial*) *siehe adj* nimbleness; quickness, speed.
Husar *m* **-en, -en** (*Hist*) hussar.
Husaren-: ~streich *m*, **~stück** *nt* (*fig*) (daring) escapade *or* exploit.
husch *interj* **(a)** (*aufscheuchend*) shoo. **(b)** (*antreibend*) come on. **(c)** (*schnell*) quick, quickly now ◆ **er macht seine Arbeit immer ~ ~** (*inf*) he always whizzes through his work (*inf*); **und ~, weg war er** and whoosh! he was gone.
Husch *m* **-(e)s, -e** (*inf*) **im ~** in a flash (*inf*) *or* jiffy (*inf*); **er kam auf einen ~ vorbei** he dropped in on me *or* by for a minute.
huschen *vi aux sein* to dart, to flit; (*Mäuse etc auch*) to scurry; (*Lächeln*) to flash, to flit; (*Licht*) to flash.
Husky ['haski] *m* **-s, -s** husky.
hussa(sa) *interj* (*old, liter*) tally-ho; (*hü*) gee-up.
hüsteln *vi* to give a slight cough, to cough slightly ◆ **er hüstelt noch** he still has a slight cough; **anstatt zu antworten, hüstelte er nur spöttisch** instead of answering he just cleared his throat sarcastically.
husten [1] *vi* to cough ◆ **auf etw** (*acc*) **~** (*inf*) not to give a damn for sth (*inf*); **der Motor hustet** (*inf*) the engine is coughing (and spluttering).
[2] *vt* to cough; *Blut* to cough (up) ◆ **denen werde ich was ~** (*inf*) I'll tell them where they can get off (*inf*).
Husten *m* **-s,** *no pl* cough ◆ **~ haben** to have a cough.
Husten-: ~anfall *m* coughing fit; **~bonbon** *m or nt* cough drop *or* sweet; **~mittel** *nt* cough medicine/drop *or* sweet; **~reiz** *m* tickle in *or* irritation of the throat; **seinen ~reiz unterdrücken** to suppress the need *or* urge to cough; **~saft** *m* cough syrup *or* mixture; ⚠**h~stillend** *adj* cough-relieving; **das wirkt h~stillend** it relieves coughing *or* one's cough; **~tee** *m tea which is good for coughs*; **~tropfen** *pl* cough drops *pl*.
Hut[1] *m* **-(e)s, ¨e** hat; (*von Pilz*) cap ◆ **den ~ aufsetzen/abnehmen/lüften** (*geh*) to put on/take off/raise one's hat; **den** *or* **mit dem ~ in der Hand** with his hat in his hand; **vor jdm den ~ abnehmen** *or* **ziehen** (*fig*) to take off one's hat to sb; **vor etw** (*dat*) **den ~ ziehen** (*fig*) to take off one's hat to sth; **~ ab!** I take my hat off to him/you *etc*; **~ ab vor solcher Leistung!** I take my hat off to you/that; **mit dem ~e in der Hand kommt man durch das ganze Land** (*Prov*) politeness will serve you well in life; **das kannst du dir an den ~ stecken!** (*inf*) you can stick (*sl*) *or* keep (*inf*) it; **unter einen ~ bringen** *or* **kriegen** (*inf*) to reconcile, to accommodate, to cater for; *Verpflichtungen, Termine* to fit in; **da geht einem der ~ hoch** (*inf*) (*vor Zorn*) it's enough to make you blow your top (*inf*); (*vor Spaß, Überraschung*) it is amazing, it beats everything; **da geht euch der ~ hoch** (*inf*) you'll have a whale of a time (*inf*); **den** *or* **seinen ~ nehmen (müssen)** (*inf*) to (have to) go, to (have to) pack one's bags (*inf*); **das ist doch ein alter ~!** (*inf*) that's old hat! (*inf*); **jdm eine auf den ~ geben** (*inf*) to give sb a rocket (*inf*) *or* wigging (*inf*); **eins auf den ~ kriegen** (*inf*) to get a rocket (*inf*) *or* wigging (*inf*); **damit/mit ihm habe ich nichts am ~** (*inf*) I don't want to have anything to do with that/him.
Hut[2] *f* **-,** *no pl* **(a)** (*geh*) protection, keeping ◆ **unter** *or* **in meiner ~** in my keeping; (*Kinder*) in my care; **in guter** *or* **sicherer ~** in safe keeping, in good *or* safe hands.
(b) auf der ~ sein to be on one's guard (*vor +dat* against).
Hut-: ~ablage *f* hat rack; **~band** *nt* hatband; (*von Damenhut*) hat ribbon.
Hütchen *nt dim of* **Hut**[1] little hat.
Hütejunge *m* (*liter*) shepherd boy.
▼ **hüten** [1] *vt* to look after, to mind; *Vieh etc auch* to tend, to keep watch over (*liter*); (*geh*) *Geheimnisse* to guard, to keep; (*geh*) *Briefe* to keep ◆ **das Bett/Haus ~** to stay in bed/indoors; **hüte deine Zunge!** (*liter*) guard your tongue! (*liter*).
▼ [2] *vr* to guard *or* be on one's guard (*vor +dat* against), to beware (*vor +dat* of) ◆ **ich werde mich ~!** no fear!, not likely!, I'll do nothing of the kind!; **du wirst dich schwer ~!** you'll do nothing of the kind!; **ich werde mich ~, ihm das zu erzählen** there's no chance of me telling him that; **sich ~, etw zu tun** to take care not to do sth; **hüte dich, etwas zu verraten** take care not to give anything away, mind you don't give anything away; **~ Sie sich vor ihm** be on your guard against him.
Hüter(in *f***)** *m* **-s, -** guardian, keeper, custodian; (*Vieh~*) herdsman ◆ **die ~ der Ordnung** (*hum*) the custodians of the law; **soll ich meines Bruders ~ sein?** (*Bibl*) am I my brother's keeper?
Hut-: ~feder *f* (hat) feather; (*größere, bei Tracht*) plume; **~filz** *m* (hat) felt; **~geschäft** *nt* hat shop, hatter's (shop); (*für Damen auch*) milliner's (shop); **~größe** *f* hat size, size of hat; **~krempe** *f* brim (of a hat); **~laden** *m siehe* **~geschäft**; **~macher** *m* hatter, hat maker; (*für Damen auch*) milliner; **~macherin** *f* milliner; **~nadel** *f* hat pin; **~schachtel** *f* hatbox.
Hutsche(n) *f* **-, -n** (*Aus*) *siehe* **Schaukel**.
hutschen (*Aus*) [1] *vi siehe* **schaukeln**.
[2] *vr* (*inf*) to go away.
Hut-: ~schleife *f* hat bow; **~schnur** *f* hat string *or* cord; **das geht mir über die ~schnur** (*inf*) that's going too far.
Hutschpferd *nt* (*Aus*) *siehe* **Schaukelpferd**.
Hutständer *m* hatstand.
Hütte *f* **-, -n (a)** hut; (*schäbiges Häuschen auch*) shack; (*hum: Haus*) humble abode; (*Jagd~*) (hunting) lodge; (*Holz~, Block~*) cabin; (*Wochenendhäuschen*) cottage; (*Schutz~*) hut, bothy (*Scot*); (*Hunde~*) kennel; (*Bibl*) Tabernacle; (*Naut*) poop ◆ **hier laßt uns eine ~ bauen** let's stay here; *siehe* **Glanz**.
(b) (*Tech: Hüttenwerk*) iron and steel works *pl or sing*; (*Glas~*) glassworks *pl or sing*; (*Ziegel~*) brickworks *pl or sing*.
Hütten-: ~arbeiter *m* worker in an iron and steel works; **~industrie** *f* iron and steel industry; **~käse** *m* cottage cheese; **~kombinat** *nt* (*DDR*) iron and steel combine; **~kunde** *f* metallurgy; **~rauch** *m* (*Chem*) flaky arsenic; (*Metal*) waste gases *pl*; **~ruhe** *f* **um zehn ist ~ruhe** lights out at ten; **~schuh** *m* slipper-sock; **~technik** *f* metallurgical engineering; **~werk** *nt siehe* **Hütte (b)**; **~wesen** *nt siehe* **~industrie**; **~zauber** *m* après-ski party.
Hutzel *f* **-, -n** (*S Ger*) **(a)** dried pear. **(b)** (*inf*) wizened *or* wrinkled old woman.
Hutzelbrot *nt* (*S Ger*) fruit bread ◆ **ein ~** a fruit loaf.
hutz(e)lig *adj Obst* dried; *Mensch* wizened.
Hutzel-: ~männchen, ~männlein *nt* gnome; **~weiblein** *nt siehe* **Hutzel (b)**.
hutzlig *adj siehe* **hutz(e)lig**.
HwG [ha:ve:'ge:] (*Admin sl*) *abbr of* **häufig wechselnder Geschlechtsverkehr** frequent changing of sexual partners.
HwG-Mädchen *nt* (*Admin sl*) *girl listed by police or medical authorities as being promiscuous*.
Hyäne *f* **-, -n** hyena; (*fig*) wildcat.
Hyazinthe [hya'tsɪntə] *f* **-, -n** hyacinth.
hybrid *adj* **(a)** (*Biol, Ling*) hybrid. **(b)** (*liter: hochmütig*) arrogant, hubristic (*liter*).
Hybride *f* **-, -n** *or m* **-n, -n** (*Biol*) hybrid.
Hybris ['hy:brɪs] *f* **-,** *no pl* (*liter*) hubris (*liter*).
Hydra *f* **-** (*Zool, Myth, fig liter*) hydra.
Hydrant *m* hydrant.
Hydrat *nt* hydrate.
Hydraulik *f* hydraulics *sing*; (*Antrieb, Anlage*) hydraulic system, hydraulics *pl*.
hydraulisch *adj* hydraulic.
Hydrid *nt* **-(e)s, -e** hydride.
hydrieren* *vt* (*Chem*) to hydrogenate.
Hydro- [hydro-]: **~biologie** *f* hydrobiology; **~dynamik** *f* hydrodynamics *sing*; ⚠**~graphie** *f* hydrography; ⚠**h~graphisch** *adj* hydrographic(al); **~kultur** *f* (*Bot*) hydroculture; **~lyse** *f* **-, -n** (*Chem*) hydrolysis; **h~phil** *adj* hydrophilic; **h~phob** *adj* hydrophobic; **~statik** *f* (*Phys*) hydrostatics *sing*; **~therapie** *f* (*Med*) hydrotherapy.
Hygiene [hy'gie:nə] *f* **-,** *no pl* hygiene ◆ **politische ~** political expediency.
Hygienepapier *nt* (toilet) tissue.
hygienisch [hy'gie:nɪʃ] *adj* hygienic.
Hygro-: ~meter *nt* (*Met*) hygrometer; **~skop** *nt* **-s, -e** (*Met*) hygroscope.
Hymen ['hy:mən] *nt* **-s, -** (*Anat*) hymen, maidenhead.
Hymne ['hʏmnə] *f* **-, -n** hymn; (*National~*) (national) anthem.
hymnisch *adj* hymnal ◆ **~e Worte** (*liter*) paean (*liter*); **jdn/etw in ~en Worten loben** (*liter*) to sing paeans to sb/sth (*liter*).
Hymnus *m* **-, Hymnen** (*liter*) *siehe* **Hymne**.
Hyperbel *f* **-, -n** (*Math*) hyperbola; (*Rhetorik*) hyperbole.
hyperbolisch *adj* hyperbolic.
hyper-: ~korrekt *adj* hypercorrect; **~kritisch** *adj* hypercritical; **H~link -s, -s** (*Comput*) hyperlink; **~modern** *adj* (*inf*) ultramodern; **~sensibel** *adj* hypersensitive; **~sensibilisieren*** *vt insep* (*esp Phot*) to hypersensitize.
Hyper-: ~tonie *f* (*Med*) hypertonia; **h~troph** *adj* (*Med*) hypertrophic; (*fig liter*) hypertrophied (*liter*); **~trophie** *f* (*Med*) hypertrophy.

➤ SPRACHE AKTIV: **hüten: 2 → 28.1, 29.2**

Hypnose *f* -, -n hypnosis ◆ **unter ~ stehen** to be under hypnosis; **jdn in ~ versetzen** to put sb under hypnosis.
Hypnosebehandlung *f* hypnotherapy.
Hypnotikum *nt* -s, **Hypnotika** (*Pharm*) hypnotic.
hypnotisch *adj* hypnotic.
Hypnotiseur [hypnoti'zøːɐ] *m* hypnotist.
hypnotisierbar *adj* hypnotizable.
hypnotisieren* *vt* to hypnotize.
Hypnotismus *m* hypnotism.
Hypochonder [hypo'xɔndɐ] *m* -s, - hypochondriac.
Hypochondrie [hypoxɔn'driː] *f* hypochondria.
hypochondrisch *adj* hypochondriac(al).
Hypokrit [hypo'kriːt] *m* -en, -en (*liter*) hypocrite.
hypokritisch *adj* (*liter*) hypocritical.
Hypophyse *f* -, -n (*Anat*) hypophysis (*spec*), pituitary gland.
Hypostase [hypo'staːzə] *f* -, -n (*liter, Philos*) hypostasis.
hypostasieren* *vti* (*liter, Philos*) to hypostatize.
Hypostasierung *f* (*liter, Philos*) hypostatization.
hypotaktisch *adj* (*Gram*) hypotactic.
Hypotaxe *f* -, -n (*Gram*) hypotaxis.
Hypotenuse *f* -, -n (*Math*) hypotenuse.
Hypothek *f* -, -en mortgage; (*fig*) (*Belastung*) burden of guilt; (*Handikap*) handicap ◆ **eine ~ aufnehmen** to raise a mortgage; **etw mit einer ~ belasten** to mortgage sth.
hypothekarisch *adj* **das Haus ist ~ belastet** the house is mortgaged; **~er Gläubiger** mortgagee; **~er Kredit** mortgage credit; **~e Sicherheit** mortgage security.
Hypotheken-: ~bank *f bank specializing in mortgages*; **~brief** *m* mortgage deed *or* certificate; **~darlehen** *nt* mortgage (loan); **h~frei** *adj* unmortgaged; **~gläubiger** *m* mortgagee; **~pfandbrief** *m* mortgage bond; **~schuld** *f* mortgage debt; **~schuldner** *m* mortgagor, mortgager; **~urkunde** *f siehe* **~brief**; **~zinsen** *pl* mortgage interest.
Hypothese *f* -, -n hypothesis.
hypothetisch *adj* hypothetical.
Hysterektomie *f* hysterectomy.
Hysterie *f* hysteria.
Hysteriker(in *f*) *m* -s, - hysteric, hysterical person.
hysterisch *adj* hysterical ◆ **einen ~en Anfall bekommen** (*fig*) to go into *or* have hysterics.

I

I, i [iː] *nt* I, i ◆ **der Punkt** *or* **das Tüpfelchen auf dem ~** (*lit*) the dot on the i; (*fig*) the final touch.
i [iː] *interj* (*inf*) ugh (*inf*) ◆ **~ bewahre!** (*dated*) not on your life! (*inf*); **~ wo!** not a bit of it! (*inf*), (good) heavens no!; **~ gitt (~ gitt)!** ugh! (*inf*).
i.A. *abbr of* **im Auftrag** pp.
IAEA [iː|aː|eː'|aː] *f - abbr of* **Internationale Atomenergie-Agentur** IAEA.
iah ['iː'aː, i'aː] *interj* hee-haw.
iahen* ['iː'aːən, i'aːən] *vi* to hee-haw (*inf*), to bray.
i. allg. *abbr of* **im allgemeinen.**
Iambus ['iambʊs] *m -,* **Iamben** *siehe* **Jambus.**
Iberer(in *f*) *m* **-s,** - Iberian.
iberisch *adj* Iberian ◆ **die I~e Halbinsel** the Iberian Peninsula.
Ibero|amerika *nt* Ibero-America.
ibero|amerikanisch *adj* Ibero-American.
IBFG [iːbeː|ɛf'geː] *m abbr of* **Internationaler Bund Freier Gewerkschaften** ICFTU.
ibid(em) *adv* ibid.
IC [iː'tseː] *m* **-(s), -s** *abbr of* **Intercity-Zug.**
IC- *in cpds* intercity; **~-Betreuer** *m* intercity steward.
ICE [iːtseː'|eː] *m* **-(s), -s** *abbr of* **Intercity-Express.**
ich *pers pron gen* **meiner,** *dat* **mir,** *acc* **mich** I ◆ **immer ~!** (it's) always me!; **immer ~ soll an allem schuld sein** it's always my fault; **~ Idiot!** what an idiot I am!; **und ~ Idiot habe es gemacht** and I, like a fool, did it, and idiot that I am, I did it; **~ nicht!** not me!, not I!; **ihr könnt ja hingehen, aber ~ nicht!** you're welcome to go, but I won't; **wer hat den Schlüssel? — ~ nicht!** who's got the key? — not me, I haven't!; **~ selbst** I myself; **könnte ~ bitte den Chef sprechen? — das bin ~ (selbst)** could I speak to the boss? — I am the boss *or* that's me; **~ (selbst) war es** it was me *or* I (*form*); **wer hat gerufen? — ~!** who called? — (it was) me, I did!; **kennst du mich nicht mehr? — ~ bin's!** don't you remember me? it's me!; **~, der immer so gutmütig ist** *or* **der ~ immer so gutmütig bin** I, who am always so good-natured.
Ich *nt* **-(s), -(s)** self; (*Pysch*) ego ◆ **das eigene ~** one's (own) self/ego; **das eigene ~ verleugnen** to deny the self; **mein anderes** *or* **zweites ~** (*selbst*) my other self; (*andere Person*) my alter ego.
Ich-: ⚠**~bewußtsein** *nt* awareness of the self; **i~bezogen** *adj* self-centred, egocentric; **~erzähler** *m* first-person narrator; **~erzählung** *f* story in the first person, first-person narrative; **~form** *f* first person; **~-Laut** *m* (*Phon*) *ch sound as in ich,* palatal fricative; ⚠**~-Roman** *m* novel in the first person, first-person novel; **~stärke** *f* (*Pysch*) ego strength; **~sucht** *f* egoism; **i~süchtig** *adj* egoistic(al).
IC-Zuschlag *m* intercity supplement.
ideal *adj* ideal.
Ideal *nt* **-s, -e** ideal ◆ **sie ist das ~ einer Lehrerin** she's the ideal *or* perfect teacher.
Ideal- *in cpds* ideal; **~bild** *nt* ideal; **~fall** *m* ideal case; **im ~fall** ideally; **~figur** *f* ideal figure; **~gewicht** *nt* ideal *or* optimum weight.
idealisieren* *vt* to idealize.
Idealisierung *f* idealization.
Idealismus *m* idealism.
Idealist *m* idealist.
idealistisch *adj* idealistic.
Ideal-: **~konkurrenz** *f* (*Jur*) *commission of two or more crimes in one and the same act;* **~typus** *m* (*Sociol*) ideal type; **~vorstellung** *f* ideal; **~zustand** *m* ideal state of affairs.
▼ **Idee** *f* **-, -n** [i'deːən] **(a)** (*Einfall, Philos*) idea ◆ **die ~ zu etw** the idea for sth; **überhaupt keine ~n haben** to have not a single idea in one's head, to have no ideas at all; **wie kommst du denn auf** ***die*** **~?** whatever gave you that idea?; **ich kam auf die ~, sie zu fragen** I hit on the idea of asking her; **jdn auf die ~ bringen, etw zu tun** to give sb the idea of doing sth; **jdn auf andere ~n bringen** to make sb think about something else; **~n müßte man haben!** what it is to have ideas!
(b) (*ein wenig*) shade, trifle ◆ **eine ~ Salz** a touch *or* hint of salt; **keine ~ besser** not a whit better.
ideell *adj* ideational (*form, Philos*); *Wert, Gesichtspunkt, Ziele* non-material; *Bedürfnisse, Unterstützung* spiritual.
Ideen- [i'deːən-]: **i~arm** *adj* (*einfallsarm*) lacking in ideas; (*phantasiearm*) unimaginative, lacking in imagination; **~armut** *f* lack of ideas; unimaginativeness, lack of imagination; **~austausch** *m* exchange of ideas; **~gut** *nt* ideas *pl*, intellectual goods *pl*; **i~los** *adj* (*einfallslos*) devoid of ideas; (*phantasielos*) unimaginative, devoid of imagination; **~losigkeit** *f* lack of ideas; unimaginativeness, lack of imagination; **i~reich** *adj* (*einfallsreich*) full of ideas; (*phantasiereich*) imaginative, full of imagination; **~reichtum** *m* inventiveness; imaginativeness; **~welt** *f* world of ideas *or* forms.
Iden *pl* **die ~ des März** the Ides of March.
Identifikation *f* identification.
Identifikationsfigur *f* role model.
identifizieren* **1** *vt* to identify.
2 *vr* **sich ~ mit** to identify (oneself) with.
Identifizierung *f* identification.
identisch *adj* identical (*mit* with).
Identität *f* identity.
Identitäts-: **~krise** *f* identity crisis; **~nachweis** *m* proof of identity.
Ideogramm *nt* **-(e)s, -e** (*Ling*) ideogram.
Ideologe *m,* **Ideologin** *f* ideologist.
Ideologie *f* ideology.
ideologisch *adj* ideological.
ideologisieren* *vt* to ideologize.
Ideologisierung *f* ideologization.
Idiom *nt* **-s, -e** idiom.
Idiomatik *f* idiomaticity; (*Redewendungen*) idioms *pl*.
idiomatisch *adj* idiomatic.
Idioplasma *nt* (*Biol*) germ plasm, idioplasm.
Idiot *m* **-en, -en** idiot; (*auch inf*) fool.
Idioten-: **~hügel** *m* (*hum inf*) nursery *or* beginners' slope; **i~sicher** *adj* (*inf*) foolproof *no adv*; **etw i~sicher erklären** to explain sth so that even a fool *or* an idiot could understand it.
Idiotie *f* idiocy; (*inf*) lunacy, madness, craziness.
Idiotin *f* idiot; (*auch inf*) fool.
idiotisch *adj* idiotic.
Idiotismus *m* idiotism; (*inf*) lunacy, madness, craziness.
Idol *nt* **-s, -e** idol.
Idyll *nt* **-s, -e** idyll; (*Gegend*) idyllic place *or* spot.
Idylle *f* **-, -n** idyll.
idyllisch *adj* idyllic.
IG [iː'geː] *f* **-, -s** *abbr of* **Industriegewerkschaft** ≃ TU.
Igel *m* **-s, - (a)** (*Zool*) hedgehog; (*Blumen~*) pin-holder. **(b)** (*Mil: ~stellung*) position of all-round defence.
Iglu ['iːglu] *m or nt* **-s, -s** igloo.
Ignorant *m* ignoramus.
Ignoranz *f* ignorance.
ignorieren* *vt* to ignore.
IHK [iːhaː'kaː] *f abbr of* **Industrie- und Handelskammer.**
ihm *pers pron dat of* **er, es**[1] (*bei Personen*) to him; (*bei Tieren und Dingen*) to it; (*nach Präpositionen*) him/it ◆ **ich gab es ~** I gave it (to) him/it; **ich gab ~ den Brief** I gave him the letter, I gave the letter to him; **ich sagte ~, daß ...** I told him that ..., I said to him that ...; **ich werde es ~ sagen** I'll tell him; **es war ~, als ob er träumte** he felt as though he were dreaming; **es ist ~ nicht gut** he doesn't feel well; **sie schnitt ~ die Haare** she cut his hair (for him); **ein Freund von ~** a friend of his, one of his friends; **wir gingen zu ~** (*haben ihn aufgesucht*) we went to see him; (*mit zu ihm nach Hause*) we went to his place; **ich habe ~ das gemacht** I did it for him; **sie hat ~ einen Pulli gestrickt** she knitted him a sweater, she knitted a sweater for him.
ihn *pers pron acc of* **er** him; (*bei Tieren und Dingen*) it.
ihnen *pers pron dat of* **sie** *pl* to them; (*nach Präpositionen*) them; *siehe* **ihm.**
Ihnen *pers pron dat of* **Sie** to you; (*nach Präpositionen*) you; *siehe* **ihm.**
ihr **1** *pers pron* **(a)** *gen* **euer,** *dat* **euch,** *acc* **euch** *2. pers pl nom* you ◆ **I~** (*in Briefen*) you; (*obs, dial: als Anrede eines Erwachsenen*) thou (*obs, dial*).
(b) *dat of* **sie** *sing* (*bei Personen*) to her; (*bei Tieren und Dingen*) to it; (*nach Präpositionen*) her/it ◆ **I~** (*obs: in der Anrede als eines weiblichen Wesens*) (to) thee (*obs, dial*); *siehe* **ihm.**
2 *poss pron* **(a)** (*einer Person*) her; (*eines Tiers, Dings, Abstraktum*) its.

➤ SPRACHE AKTIV: **Idee: a** → 38.1, 38.2, 40.3, 53.1, 53.3

⚠: Informationen zur Rechtschreibreform im Anhang

(b) (*von mehreren*) their.
Ihr [1] *pers pron siehe* **ihr 1 (a, b).**
[2] *poss pron sing and pl* your ◆ **~ Franz Müller** (*Briefschluß*) yours, Franz Müller.
ihrer *pers pron* **(a)** *gen of* **sie** *sing* (*bei Personen*) of her ◆ **wir werden ~ gedenken** we will remember her. **(b)** *gen of* **sie** *pl* of them ◆ **es waren ~ zehn** there were ten of them, they were ten; **wir werden ~ gedenken** we will remember them.
Ihrer *pers pron gen of* **Sie** of you ◆ **wir werden ~ gedenken** we will remember you.
ihre(r, s) *poss pron* (*substantivisch*) **(a)** (*einer Person*) hers; (*eines Tiers*) its ◆ **der/die/das ~** (*geh*) hers/its; **sie tat das ~** (*geh*) she did her part; **I~ Majestät** Her Majesty; **sie und die I~n** (*geh: Familie*) she and hers; **das I~** (*geh: Besitz*) what is hers.
(b) (*von mehreren*) theirs ◆ **der/die/das ~** (*geh*) theirs; **sie taten das ~** (*geh*) they did their bit.
Ihre(r, s) *poss pron sing and pl* (*substantivisch*) yours ◆ **der/die/das ~** (*geh*) yours; **stets** *or* **ganz der ~** (*old*) yours ever; **schöne Grüße an Sie und die ~n** (*geh*) best wishes to you and your family; **tun Sie das ~** (*geh*) you do your bit.
ihrerseits *adv* (*bei einer Person*) for her part; (*bei mehreren*) for their part; (*von ihrer Seite*) on her/their part.
Ihrerseits *adv* for your part; (*von Ihrer Seite*) on your part.
ihresgleichen *pron inv* (*von einer Person*) people like her; (*von mehreren*) people like them; (*von Dingen*) others like it, similar ones; (*pej auch*) her/their sort, the likes of her/them ◆ **sie fühlt/fühlen sich am wohlsten unter ~** she feels/they feel most at home among her/their own kind *or* among people like her(self)/them(selves); **eine Frechheit, die ~ sucht!** an incredible cheek!
Ihresgleichen *pron inv* people like you; (*pej auch*) your sort, the likes of you ◆ **Sie sollten Kontakt mit ~ pflegen** you should keep in contact with your own kind (of people) *or* with people like yourself *or* you.
ihret-: ~halben (*dated*), **~wegen, ~willen** *adv* (*bei Personen*) (*wegen ihr/ihnen*) (*sing*) because of her; (*pl*) because of them; (*ihr/ihnen zuliebe auch*) for her sake/their sake(s); (*um sie*) about her/them; (*für sie*) on her/their behalf; (*bei Dingen und Tieren*) (*sing*) because of it; (*pl*) because of them; **sie sagte, ~wegen könnten wir gehen** she said that, as far as she was concerned, we could go.
Ihret-: ~halben (*dated*), **~wegen, ~willen** *adv* because of you; (*Ihnen zuliebe*) (*sing auch*) for your sake; (*pl auch*) for your sake(s); (*um Sie*) about you; (*für Sie*) on your behalf.
ihrige *poss pron* (*old, geh*) **der/die/das ~** (*von einer Person*) hers; (*von mehreren*) theirs; *siehe auch* **ihre(r, s).**
Ihrige *poss pron* **der/die/das ~** yours; *siehe auch* **Ihre(r, s).**
Ihro *poss pron* (*obs*) your.
i. J. *abbr of* **im Jahre.**
Ikon *nt* **-s, -e** (*Comput*) icon.
Ikone *f* **-, -n** icon.
Ilex *f or m* **-,** *no pl* holly.
Ilias *f* **-** Iliad.
ill. *abbr of* **illustriert.**
illegal *adj* illegal.
Illegalität *f* illegality.
illegitim *adj* illegitimate.
illiquid *adj* illiquid.
illoyal *adj* disloyal.
Illoyalität *f* disloyalty.
Illumination *f* illumination.
illuminieren* *vt* to illuminate.
Illusion *f* illusion ◆ **jdm alle ~en nehmen** *or* **rauben** to rob sb of all his/her *etc* illusions; **sich** (*dat*) **~en machen** to delude oneself; **darüber macht er sich keine ~en** he doesn't have any illusions about it; **sich der ~ hingeben, daß** ... to be under the illusion that ..., to labour under the misapprehension that ...
illusionär *adj* illusionary.
Illusionismus *m* illusionism.
Illusionist *m* illusionist.
illusionistisch *adj* (*Art*) illusionistic.
illusionslos *adj* **ein ~er Mensch** a person with no illusions; **~ sein** to have no illusions; **~ werden** to lose one's illusions.
illusorisch *adj* illusory ◆ **es ist völlig ~, zu glauben** ... it's a complete illusion to believe ...
illuster *adj* (*geh*) illustrious.
Illustration *f* illustration ◆ **zur ~ von etw** to illustrate sth, as an illustration of sth.
illustrativ *adj* **(a)** (*mit Anschauungsmaterial*) illustrated ◆ **etw ~ aufzeigen** to show sth with illustrations. **(b)** (*anschaulich*) illustrative ◆ **er hat sehr ~ geschildert, wie** ... he described very vividly how ...
Illustrator *m* illustrator.
illustrieren* *vt* to illustrate (*jdm etw* sth for sb).
Illustrierte *f* **-n, -n** magazine, mag (*inf*).
Illustrierung *f* illustration.
Iltis *m* **-ses, -se** polecat.
im *prep contr of* **in dem (a)** (*räumlich*) in the ◆ **~ zweiten Stock** on the second floor; **~ Kino/Theater** at the cinema/theatre; **die Beleuchtung ~ Kino/Theater** the lighting in the cinema/theatre; **Freiburg ~ Breisgau** Freiburg in Breisgau; **~ Bett** in bed; **~ „Faust"** in "Faust".
(b) (*zeitlich*) in the ◆ **~ Mai** in May; **~ Jahre 1866** in (the year) 1866; **~ Alter von 91 Jahren** at the age of 91; **~ letzten/nächsten Jahr** last/next year; **~ letzten Jahr des Krieges** in the last year of the war; **~ nächsten Jahr ging er** (in) the next year he went.
(c) *+superl* **nicht ~ geringsten** not in the slightest.
(d) (*als Verlaufsform*) **~ Kommen/Gehen** *etc* **sein** to be coming/going *etc*; **etw ~ Liegen/Stehen** *etc* **tun** to do sth lying down/standing up *etc*.
(e) ~ Trab/Laufschritt *etc* at a trot/run *etc*.
Image ['ɪmɪtʃ] *nt* **-(s), -s** image.
Image-: i~bildend *adj* image-building; **~pflege** *f* image-building; **~verfall** *m* loss of prestige; **~verlust** *m* damage to one's image; **~werbung** *f* image promotion ◆ **~werbung betreiben** to promote one's image.
imaginär *adj* imaginary.
Imagination *f* (*geh*) imagination.
Imago *f* **-, Imagines** [i'ma:gine:s] (*Biol, Psych*) imago; (*Art*) image.
Imam *m* **-s, -s** *or* **-e** imam.
⚠**Imbiß** *m* **-sses, -sse** snack.
⚠**Imbiß-: ~halle** *f* snack bar; **~stand** *m* ≃ hot-dog stall *or* stand; **~stube** *f* cafe; (*in Kaufhaus etc*) cafeteria.
Imitation *f* imitation.
Imitator *m*, **Imitatorin** *f* imitator; (*von Schmuck, einem Bild*) copyist.
imitieren* *vt* to imitate ◆ **imitierter Schmuck** imitation jewellery.
Imker *m* **-s, -** beekeeper, apiarist (*form*).
Imkerei *f* beekeeping, apiculture (*form*).
imkern *vi* to keep bees.
immanent *adj* inherent, intrinsic; *Kriterien* internal; (*Philos*) immanent ◆ **einer Sache** (*dat*) **~ sein** to be inherent in sth; **~e Wiederholung** incorporative repetition.
Immanenz *f* (*Philos*) immanence.
immateriell *adj* incorporeal, immaterial.
Immatrikulation *f* matriculation (*form*), registration (*at university*).
immatrikulieren* [1] *vt* to register (*at university*) (*an +dat* at).
[2] *vr* to matriculate (*form*), to register (*at university*).
Imme *f* **-, -n** (*poet*) bee.
immens *adj* immense, huge, enormous.
immer *adv* **(a)** (*häufig, ständig*) always ◆ **schon ~** always; **auf** *or* **für ~** for ever, for always; **~ diese Aufregung/Nörgelei** this continual *or* there's always this excitement/niggling; **~ diese Probleme!** all these problems!; **~ diese Studenten/das Telefon** these wretched students/that wretched phone; **~, wenn** ... whenever ..., every time that ...; **~ mal** (*inf*) from time to time, now and again; **~ geradeaus gehen** to keep going straight on; **~ und ewig** (*liter*) for ever and ever; **~ langsam voran!** (*inf*), **(nur) ~ schön langsam!** (*inf*) take your time (about it), take it slowly; **~ (schön) mit der Ruhe** (*inf*) take it easy; **(nur) ~ her damit!** (*inf*) (just) hand it over!; **noch ~, ~ noch** still; **~ noch nicht** still not (yet); **bist du denn ~ noch nicht fertig?** are you still not ready?, aren't you ready yet?; **nur ~ zu!** keep it up!, keep up the good work!; **~ wieder** again and again, time after time, time and (time) again; **etw ~ wieder tun** to keep on doing sth; **wie ~** as usual, as always.
(b) *+comp* **~ besser** better and better; **~ häufiger** more and more often; **~ mehr** more and more; **es nimmt ~ mehr zu** it increases all the time *or* continually, it keeps on increasing; **~ größer werdende Schulden** constantly increasing debts; **sein Benehmen wird ~ schlechter** his behaviour gets worse and worse *or* goes from bad to worse.
(c) wer/wie/wann/wo/was (auch) ~ whoever/however/whenever/wherever/whatever.
(d) (*inf: jeweils*) **gib mir ~ drei Bücher auf einmal** give me three books at a time; **stellt euch in einer Reihe auf, ~ zwei zusammen** line up in twos; **~ am dritten Tag** every third day.
immer-: ~dar *adv* (*liter*) forever, evermore; **~fort** *adv* all the time, the whole time, constantly; **~grün** *adj attr* (*lit, fig*) evergreen; **I~grün** *nt* evergreen; **~hin** *adv* all the same, anyhow, at any rate; (*wenigstens*) at least; (*schließlich*) after all; ⚠**~während** *adj attr* perpetual, eternal; *Kalender* perpetual; **~zu** *adv siehe* **~fort.**
Immigrant(in *f*) *m* immigrant.
Immigration *f* immigration.
immigrieren* *vi aux sein* to immigrate.
Immission *f* (*Jur*) *effect on neighbouring property of gases, smoke, noise, smells etc.*
Immissions-: ~schaden *m* pollution damage; **~schutz** *m* air pollution control; **~schutzgesetz** *nt* air pollution laws *pl*.
immobil *adj* immobile, immoveable; *Vermögen, Besitz* real, immoveable.
Immobilien [-'bi:liən] *pl* real estate *sing*, real *or* immoveable property *sing* (*form*), immoveables *pl* (*form*); (*in Zeitungsannoncen*) property *sing*.
Immobilien-: ~fonds *m* (*Fin*) real estate fund; **~händler, ~makler** *m* (real) estate agent (*Brit*), realtor (*US*).
Immoralität *f* immorality.
Immortalität *f* immortality.
Immortelle *f* (*Bot*) everlasting (flower), immortelle.
immun *adj* immune (*gegen* to).
Immun|abwehr *f* (*Med*) immune defence.
immunisieren* *vt* (*form*) to immunize (*gegen* against).
Immunisierung *f* (*form*) immunization (*gegen* against).
Immunität *f* immunity.

Immunologe *m*, **Immunologin** *f* immunologist.
Immunologie *f* immunology.
immunologisch *adj* immunological.
Immun- *in cpds* (*Med*) immune; **~schwäche** *f* immunodeficiency; **~schwächekrankheit** *f* immune deficiency syndrome; **~system** *nt* immune system.
Imperativ *m* (*Gram*) imperative (form); (*Philos*) imperative.
imperativisch [-'ti:vɪʃ] *adj* (*Gram*) imperative.
Imperator *m* (*Hist*) emperor; (*Mil*) general.
imperatorisch *adj* imperial; (*fig*) imperious.
Imperfekt *nt* **-s, -e, Imperfektum** *nt* **-s, Imperfekta** (*Gram*) imperfect (tense).
Imperialismus *m* imperialism.
Imperialist *m* imperialist.
imperialistisch *adj* imperialistic.
Imperium *nt* (*Gebiet*) empire; (*Herrschaft*) imperium.
impertinent *adj* (*geh*) impertinent, impudent.
Impertinenz *f* (*geh*) impertinence, impudence.
Impetus *m* **-,** *no pl* (*geh*) impetus, momentum; (*Tatkraft*) drive.
Impf-: **~aktion** *f* vaccination *or* inoculation programme; **~arzt** *m* vaccinator, inoculator.
impfen *vt* to vaccinate, to inoculate.
Impfling *m person who has just been or is to be vaccinated.*
Impf-: ⚠**~paß** *m* vaccination card, *record of the vaccinations one has been given*; of the vaccinations one has been given; **~pflicht** *f* compulsory vaccination *or* inoculation, requirement to be vaccinated *or* inoculated; **~pistole** *f* vaccination gun; **~schaden** *m* vaccine damage; **~schein** *m* certificate of vaccination *or* inoculation; **~schutz** *m* protection given by vaccination; **~stoff** *m* vaccine, serum.
Impfung *f* vaccination, inoculation.
Impfzwang *m siehe* **Impfpflicht.**
Implantat *nt* implant.
Implantation *f* (*Med*) implantation.
implementieren* *vt* to implement.
implizieren* *vt* to imply.
implizit, implizite (*geh*) *adv* by implication, implicitly ◆ **etw ~ sagen** to imply sth, to say sth by implication.
implodieren* *vi aux sein* to implode.
Implosion *f* implosion.
Imponderabilien [-'bi:liən] *pl* (*geh*) imponderables *pl.*
imponieren* *vi* to make an impression (*jdm* on sb), to impress (*jdm* sb) ◆ **dadurch hat er imponiert** he made an impression by that; **es imponiert mir, wie sie das schafft** it impresses me how she manages it, I'm impressed by the way she manages it.
imponierend *adj* impressive; *Gebäude auch* imposing.
Imponiergehabe *nt* (*Zool*) display pattern; (*fig pej*) exhibitionism.
Import *m* **-(e)s, -e** **(a)** (*Handel*) import ◆ **der ~ sollte den Export nicht übersteigen** imports should not exceed exports; **der ~ von Obst und Gemüse ist gestiegen** the import *or* importation of fruit and vegetables has increased, fruit and vegetable imports have increased.
(b) (*~ware*) import ◆ **der Salat ist holländischer ~** the lettuce was imported from Holland *or* is a Dutch import.
Importe *f* **-, -n** *usu pl* imported cigar.
Importeur(in *f*) [ɪmpɔr'tøːɐ, -'tøːrɪn] *m* importer.
Import- *in cpds* import; **~geschäft** *nt* (*Handel*) import trade; (*Firma*) import business.
importieren* *vt* (*auch Comput*) to import.
Importland *nt* importing country.
imposant *adj Gebäude, Kunstwerk, Figur* imposing; *Leistung* impressive; *Stimme* commanding.
impotent *adj* impotent.
Impotenz *f* impotence.
imprägnieren* *vt* to impregnate; (*wasserdicht machen*) to (water)proof.
Imprägnierung *f* impregnation; (*von Geweben*) (water)proofing; (*nach der Reinigung*) reproofing.
impraktikabel *adj* impracticable.
Impresario *m* **-s, -s** *or* **Impresarii** impresario.
Impression *f* impression (*über +acc* of).
Impressionismus *m* impressionism.
Impressionist *m* impressionist.
impressionistisch *adj* impressionistic.
Impressum *nt* **-s, Impressen** imprint; (*von Zeitung*) masthead.
Imprimatur *nt* (*Typ*) imprimatur.
Improvisation [ɪmproviza'tsio:n] *f* improvization; (*von Rede, Gedicht, Musik auch*) extemporization.
Improvisationstalent *nt* talent for improvization; (*Mensch*) (great) improvizer.
improvisieren* [-vi'zi:rən] *vti* to improvize; (*Mus auch*) to extemporize; *eine Rede auch* to ad-lib (*inf*), to extemporize.
Impuls *m* **-es, -e** impulse ◆ **etw aus einem ~ heraus tun** to do sth on the spur of the moment *or* on impulse; **einer Sache** (*dat*) **neue ~e geben** to give sth new impetus *or* momentum; **äußere ~e veranlaßten ihn dazu** external factors made him do it.
impulsiv *adj* impulsive ◆ **~e Äußerungen/Entschlüsse** spur of the moment *or* impulsive remarks/decisions; **~ handeln** to act impulsively *or* on impulse.
Impulsivität *f* impulsiveness.
⚠**imstande** *adj pred* **~ sein, etw zu tun** (*fähig*) to be able to do sth, to be capable of doing sth; (*in der Lage*) to be in a position to do sth; **er ist zu allem ~** he's capable of anything; **er ist ~ und erzählt es meiner Mutter** he's (quite) capable of telling my mother.
in [1] *prep siehe auch* **im, ins** **(a)** (*räumlich*) (*wo? +dat*) in; (*innen auch*) inside; (*bei kleineren Orten auch*) at; (*wohin? +acc*) in, into ◆ **sind Sie schon ~ Deutschland gewesen?** have you ever been to Germany?; **~ der Schweiz** in Switzerland; **~ die Schweiz** to Switzerland; **er ist Professor ~ London** he is a professor at London (University); **~ die Schule/Kirche gehen** to go to school/church; **er ist ~ der Schule/Kirche** he's at *or* in school/church; **die Heizung ~ der Schule/Kirche** the heating in the school/church; **er ging ~s Theater/Kino** he went to the theatre/cinema.
(b) (*zeitlich*) (*wann? +dat*) in; (*bis +acc*) into ◆ **~ diesem Jahr** (*laufendes Jahr*) this year; (*jenes Jahr*) (in) that year; **heute/morgen ~ acht Tagen/zwei Wochen** a week/two weeks today/tomorrow; **bis ~s 18. Jahrhundert** into *or* up to the 18th century; **vom 16. bis ~s 18. Jahrhundert** from the 16th to the 18th century; **bis ~s 18. Jahrhundert zurück** back to the 18th century.
(c) **~ Englisch steht er sehr schwach** he's very weak in *or* at English; **das ist ~ Englisch** it's in English; **~s Englische übersetzen** to translate into English; **~ Mathe haben wir einen neuen Lehrer** we've a new teacher in *or* for maths; **~ die Hunderte gehen** to run into (the) hundreds; **sie hat es ~ sich** (*dat*) (*inf*) she's quite a girl; **der Text/die Rechenarbeit hat es ~ sich** (*dat*) (*inf*) the text/the arithmetic test is a tough one; **dieser Whisky hat es ~ sich** (*dat*) (*inf*) this whisky packs quite a punch *or* has quite a kick (*inf*); **er macht jetzt ~ Gebrauchtwagen** (*inf*) he's in the second-hand car business.
[2] *adj pred* (*sl*) **~ sein** to be in (*inf*).
in|adäquat *adj* inadequate.
in|akkurat *adj* inaccurate.
in|aktiv *adj* inactive; *Mitglied* non-active; (*Mil*) inactive, on the reserve list.
in|akzeptabel *adj* un- *or* inacceptable.
In|angriffnahme *f* **-,** *no pl* (*form*) starting, commencement (*form*).
In|anspruchnahme *f* **-,** *no pl* (*form*) **(a)** (*Beanspruchung*) demands *pl*, claims *pl* (*gen* on) ◆ **seine ~ durch diese Nebenbeschäftigung** the demands *or* claims made on him by this second job; **im Falle einer ~ der Arbeitslosenunterstützung** where unemployment benefit has been sought (*form*); **bei ~ des Versicherungsschutzes entfällt der Rabatt** the discount is forfeited should an insurance claim be submitted.
(b) (*Auslastung: von Einrichtungen, Verkehrsystem etc*) utilization ◆ **wegen zu geringer ~ des Freizeitzentrums** as a result of under-utilization of the leisure centre, because too few people have been availing themselves of the leisure centre.
in|artikuliert *adj* inarticulate.
In|augenscheinnahme *f* **-,** *no pl* (*form*) inspection.
inbegr. *abbr of* **inbegriffen.**
Inbegriff *m* **-(e)s,** *no pl* perfect example; (*der Schönheit, Güte, des Bösen etc*) epitome, embodiment ◆ **sie war der ~ der Schönheit/Tugend** she was beauty/virtue personified *or* incarnate; **diese neue Kirche ist der ~ der modernen Architektur** this new church epitomizes modern architecture.
inbegriffen *adj pred* included ◆ **die Mehrwertsteuer ist im Preis ~** the price includes VAT *or* is inclusive of VAT, VAT is included in the price.
Inbesitznahme *f* **-, -n** (*form*) taking possession.
Inbetriebnahme *f* **-, -n** commissioning; (*von Gebäude, U-Bahn etc*) inauguration ◆ **die ~ des Geräts erfolgt in zwei Wochen** the appliance will be put into operation in two weeks.
Inbrunst *f* **-,** *no pl* fervour, fervency, ardour.
inbrünstig *adj* fervent, ardent.
Inbusschlüssel ® *m* (*Tech*) Allen key ®.
Indanthren ® *nt* **-s, -e** *colour-fast dye.*
Indefinitpronomen *nt* indefinite pronoun.
indem [1] *conj* **(a)** (*während der ganzen Zeit*) while, whilst (*liter*); (*in dem Augenblick*) as ◆ **~ er sich hinsetzte, sagte er ...** sitting down, he said ..., as he sat down he said ... **(b)** (*dadurch, daß*) **~ man etw macht** by doing sth.
[2] *adv* (*old*) meanwhile, (in the) meantime.
Inder(in *f*) *m* **-s, -** Indian.
indes (*rare*), **indessen** [1] *adv* **(a)** (*zeitlich*) meanwhile, (in the) meantime. **(b)** (*adversativ*) however.
[2] *conj* **(a)** (*geh*) (*zeitlich*) while. **(b)** (*adversativ*) **indes** (*liter*) however; (*andererseits*) whereas.
Index *m* **-(es), -e** index (*auch Comput*); (*Eccl*) Index.
Index|anleihe *f* (*Fin*) index-linked loan, index loan.
indexieren* *vti* (*Comput*) to index.
Indianer(in *f*) *m* **-s, -** (Red *or* American) Indian.
indianisch *adj* (Red *or* American) Indian.
Indianistik *f* American Indian studies *pl.*
Indien ['ɪndiən] *nt* **-s** India.
indifferent *adj* **(a)** (*geh*) indifferent (*gegenüber* to). **(b)** (*Chem, Phys*) inert; *Gas auch* rare, inactive.
Indifferenz *f* (*geh*) indifference (*gegenüber* to, towards).
Indignation *f* (*geh*) indignation (*über +acc* at).
indigniert *adj* (*geh*) indignant.
Indignität *f* (*Jur*) incapability of inheriting.
Indigo *nt or m* **-s, -s** indigo.
indigoblau *adj* indigo blue.

Indikation *f (Med)* indication ◆ **ethische/eugenische/medizinische/soziale ~** ethical/eugenic/medical/social grounds for the termination of pregnancy.
Indikativ *m (Gram)* indicative.
indikativisch ['ɪndikati:vɪʃ] *adj (Gram)* indicative.
Indikator *m* indicator.
Indio *m* **-s, -s** (Central/South American) Indian.
indirekt *adj* indirect ◆ **~e Rede** indirect *or* reported speech.
indisch *adj* Indian.
indiskret *adj* indiscreet.
Indiskretion *f* indiscretion.
indiskutabel *adj* out of the question.
indisponiert *adj (geh)* indisposed.
Indisposition *f (geh)* indisposition.
Indium *nt, no pl (abbr* **In***)* indium.
individualisieren* [ɪndividuali'zi:rən] *vt* to individualize.
Individualisierung [ɪndividuali'zi:rʊŋ] *f* individualization.
Individualismus [ɪndividua'lɪsmʊs] *m* individualism.
Individualist [ɪndividua'lɪst] *m* individualist.
individualistisch [ɪndividua'lɪstɪʃ] *adj* individualistic.
Individualität [ɪndividuali'tɛ:t] *f* **(a)** *no pl* individuality. **(b)** *(Charakterzüge)* individual characteristic.
Individualverkehr *m (Mot)* private transport.
individuell [ɪndivi'duɛl] *adj* individual ◆ **etw ~ gestalten** to give sth a personal note; **es ist ~ verschieden** it differs from person to person *or* case to case, it's different for each person.
Individuum [ɪndi'vi:duʊm] *nt* **-s, Individuen** [ɪndi'vi:duən] individual.
Indiz *nt* **-es, -ien** [-iən] **(a)** *(Jur)* clue; *(als Beweismittel)* piece of circumstantial evidence ◆ **alles beruht nur auf ~ien** everything rests only on circumstantial evidence. **(b)** *(Anzeichen)* sign, indication *(für* of*)*.
Indizes *pl of* **Index.**
Indizienbeweis *m* circumstantial evidence *no pl*; piece of circumstantial evidence.
indizieren* *vt (Med)* to indicate; *(Eccl)* to put on the Index; *(Comput)* to index.
Indochina *nt* Indochina.
indogermanisch *adj* Indo-Germanic, Indo-European.
Indoktrination *f* indoctrination.
indoktrinieren* *vt* to indoctrinate.
Indonesien [-iən] *nt* **-s** Indonesia.
Indonesier(in *f***)** [-iɐ, -iərɪn] *m* **-s, -** Indonesian.
indonesisch *adj* Indonesian.
Indossament *nt (Comm)* endorsement.
Indossant *m (Comm)* endorser.
Indossat *m* **-en, -en** *(Comm)* endorsee.
indossieren* *vt (Comm)* to endorse.
Induktion *f* induction.
Induktions-: i~gehärtet *adj* induction hardened; **~schleife** *f* induction loop; **~strom** *m* induced current.
induktiv *adj* inductive.
industrialisieren* *vt* to industrialize.
Industrialisierung *f* industrialization.
Industrie *f* industry ◆ **in der ~ arbeiten** to be *or* work in industry.
Industrie- *in cpds* industrial; **~abfälle** *pl* industrial waste; **~anlage** *f* industrial plant *or* works *pl*; **~betrieb** *m* industrial firm *or* company; **~erzeugnis** *nt* industrial product; **~gebiet** *nt* industrial area; **~gewerkschaft** *f* industrial (trade) union; **~gewerkschaft Druck und Papier** printers' union; **~kapitän** *m (inf)* captain of industry; **~kaufladen** *m (DDR)* factory shop; **~kaufmann** *m* industrial manager; **~kombinat** *nt (DDR)* industrial combine; **~land** *nt* industrialized country; **~landschaft** *f* industrial landscape.
industriell *adj* industrial.
Industrielle(r) *m decl as adj* industrialist.
Industrie-: ~müll *m* industrial waste; **~nation** *f siehe* **~staat**; **~park** *m* industrial estate; **~roboter** *m* industrial robot; **~staat** *m* industrial nation; **~stadt** *f* industrial town; **~- und Handelskammer** *f* chamber of commerce; **~zweig** *m* branch of industry.
induzieren* *vt (Phys)* to induce.
in|effektiv *adj* ineffective, ineffectual; *(unproduktiv auch)* inefficient.
in|einander *adv sein, liegen etc* in(side) one another *or* each other; *legen, hängen etc* into one another *or* each other ◆ **~ übergehen** to merge (into one another *or* each other); **die Fäden haben sich alle ~ verwickelt** the threads have got all tangled up in each other *or* in one another; **sich ~ verlieben** to fall in love with each other.
⚠**in|einander-: ~fließen** *vi sep irreg aux sein* to merge; *(Farben, Flüsse auch)* to flow into each other *or* one another; **~fügen** *vt sep* to fit into each other *or* one another; **~greifen** *vi sep irreg (lit)* to interlock; *(Zahnräder, Zinken auch)* to mesh *or* engage (with each other *or* one another); *(fig: Ereignisse, Ressorts etc)* to overlap; **~passen** *vi sep* to fit into each other *or* one another, to fit together; **~schieben** *vtr sep irreg* to telescope; **sich ~schieben lassen** to be telescopic.
infam *adj* infamous.
Infamie *f* infamy ◆ **das ist eine ~** that's infamous *or* outrageous.
Infanterie *f* infantry.
Infanterieregiment *nt* infantry *or* foot regiment.
Infanterist *m* infantryman, foot soldier.

infantil *adj* infantile.
Infantilismus *m* infantilism.
Infantilität *f* childishness, puerility *(pej)*.
Infarkt *m* **-(e)s, -e** *(Med)* infarct *(spec)*; *(Herz~)* coronary (thrombosis).
Infekt *m* **-(e)s, -e, Infektion** *f* infection.
Infektions-: ~gefahr *f* danger of infection; **~herd** *m* focus of infection; **~kette** *f* chain of infection; **~krankheit** *f* infectious disease.
infektiös [ɪnfɛk'tsiø:s] *adj* infectious.
infernalisch *adj (geh)* infernal.
Inferno *nt* **-s,** *no pl (lit, fig)* inferno.
Infiltration *f* infiltration.
infiltrieren* *vt* to infiltrate.
infinit *adj (Gram)* non-finite.
infinitesimal *adj (Math)* infinitesimal.
Infinitiv *m* infinitive.
Infinitiv-: ~konstruktion *f* infinitive construction; **~satz** *m* infinitive clause.
infizieren* 1 *vt* to infect.
2 *vr* to be *or* get infected *(bei* by*)*.
in flagranti *adv* in the act, red-handed, in flagrante delicto *(form)*.
Inflation *f* inflation.
inflationär [ɪnflatsio'nɛ:ɐ] *adj* inflationary ◆ **sich ~ entwickeln** to develop in an inflationary way.
inflationistisch [ɪnflatsio'nɪstɪʃ] *adj* inflationary.
Inflations-: ~angst *f* fear of inflation; **i~hemmend** *adj* anti-inflationary; **~rate** *f* rate of inflation; **i~sicher** *adj* inflation-proof.
inflatorisch *adj* inflationary.
inflexibel *adj (lit, fig)* inflexible.
Inflexibilität *f (lit, fig)* inflexibility.
Influenz *f (Phys)* electrostatic induction.
Info *nt* **-, -s** *(inf)* info *(inf)*.
➤ **infolge** *prep +gen or von* as a result of, owing to, because of.
infolgedessen *adv* consequently, as a result (of that), because of that.
Informatik *f* information technology, informatics *sing*.
Informatiker(in *f***)** *m* **-s, -** computer *or* information scientist.
➤ **Information** *f* information *no pl (über +acc* about, on*)* ◆ **eine ~** (a piece of) information; **~en weitergeben** to pass on information; **zu Ihrer ~** for your information; **wo ist die ~?** where is information *or* the information desk?
informationell [ɪnfɔrmatsio'nɛl] *adj* informational ◆ **~e Selbstbestimmung** (right of) access to personal files.
Informations-: ~austausch *m* exchange of information; **~büro** *nt* information bureau; **~defizit** *nt* information lag, lack of information; ⚠**~fluß** *m* flow of information; **~gesellschaft** *f* information society; **~gewinnung** *f* information gathering; **~material** *nt* information; **~quelle** *f* source of information; **~stand** *m* **(a)** information stand; **(b)** *no pl (Wissensstand)* level of information; **~technik** *f* information technology; **~theorie** *f* information theory; **~verarbeitung** *f* information processing; **~vorsprung** *m* **einen ~vorsprung haben** to be better informed.
informativ *adj* informative.
informatorisch *adj* informational.
informell *adj* informal.
informieren* 1 *vt* to inform *(über +acc, von* about, of*)* ◆ **da bist du falsch** *or* **nicht richtig informiert** you've been misinformed, you've been wrongly informed; **jdn nur unvollständig/einseitig ~** to give sb only part/one side of the information; **informierte Kreise** informed circles.
2 *vr* to find out, to inform oneself *(über +acc* about*)* ◆ **sich ständig über den neuesten Stand der Medizin ~** to keep oneself informed about the latest developments in medicine.
Informiertheit *f* knowledge ◆ **wegen der zunehmenden ~ der Jugendlichen** since young people are becoming increasingly well-informed; **die mangelnde ~ der Bevölkerung** the population's lack of information *or* lack of knowledge of the facts.
Infostand *m (inf)* information stand.
Infotainment [info'teɪnmənt] *nt* **-s** *no pl* infotainment.
Infra-: i~rot *adj* infra-red; **~rotstrahler** *m* **-s, -** infra-red lamp; **~schall** *m* infrasonic *or* subsonic waves *pl*; **~struktur** *f* infrastructure.
Infusion *f* infusion.
Ing. *abbr of* **Ingenieur.**
Ingenieur(in *f***)** [ɪnʒe'niø:ɐ, -iø:rɪn] *m* engineer.
Ingenieur-: ~büro *nt* engineer's office; **~schule** *f* school of engineering.
Ingrimm *m* **-(e)s,** *no pl (liter)* wrath, ire *(liter)*.
ingrimmig *adj (liter)* wrathful *(liter)*, ireful *(liter)*.
Ingwer *m* **-s,** *no pl* ginger.
Inh. *abbr of* **Inhaber** prop.; **Inhalt.**
Inhaber(in *f***)** *m* **-s, -** *(von Geschäft, Firma)* owner; *(von Hotel, Restaurant auch)* proprietor/proprietress; *(von Konto, Aktie, Lizenz, Patent, Rekord, Orden)* holder; *(von Scheck, Paß)* bearer.
Inhaberpapier *nt (Fin)* bearer security.
inhaftieren* *vt insep* to take into custody.
Inhaftierung *f (das Inhaftieren)* arrest; *(Haft)* imprisonment.
Inhalation *f (Med)* inhalation.
inhalieren* *vti insep (Med, inf)* to inhale.
Inhalt *m* **-(e)s, -e (a)** *(von Behälter, Paket)* contents *pl*.
(b) *(von Buch, Brief, Begriff)* content, contents *pl*; *(des Lebens)* meaning ◆ **welchen ~ hatte der Film/das Gespräch?, was hatte der Film/das Gespräch zum**

➤ SPRACHE AKTIV: **infolge** → 44.1 **Information** → 46.1, 46.4, 47.1, 48.3

~? what was the subject matter *or* content of the film/discussion?; **über ~e diskutieren** to discuss the real issues; **ein Brief des ~s, daß ...** (*form*) a letter to the effect that ...
(**c**) (*Math*) (*Flächen~*) area; (*Raum~*) volume ◆ **der ~ der Flasche beträgt zwei Liter** the bottle has a volume of two litres, the bottle holds two litres.

inhaltlich *adj* as regards content.

Inhalts-: **~angabe** *f* summary, précis (*esp Sch*); **i~arm, i~leer** *adj* (*geh*) lacking (in) content; *Leben* meaningless; **i~los** *adj* empty; *Leben auch* meaningless; *Buch, Vortrag* lacking in content; **i~reich** *adj* full; **i~schwer** *adj* (*geh: bedeutungsvoll*) significant, of consequence; **~übersicht** *f* summary of the contents; **~verzeichnis** *nt* list *or* table of contents; (*Comput*) directory; **„~verzeichnis"** "contents".

inhärent *adj* (*geh*) inherent.

inhuman *adj* (*unmenschlich, brutal*) inhuman; (*unbarmherzig*) inhumane.

Inhumanität *f* inhumanity.

Initiale [ini'tsia:lə] *f* **-, -n** (*geh*) initial.

initialisieren* [initsiali'zi:rən] *vt* (*Comput*) to initialize.

Initialisierung [initsiali'zi:rʊŋ] *f* (*Comput*) initialization.

Initiation [initsia'tsio:n] *f* initiation.

Initiationsritus *m* initiation rite.

initiativ [initsia'ti:f] *adj* **~ werden** to take the initiative.

Initiative [initsia'ti:və] *f* (**a**) *no pl* initiative ◆ **aus eigener ~** on one's own initiative; **die ~ ergreifen** to take the initiative. (**b**) (*Anstoß*) initiative. **auf jds ~** (*acc*) **hin** on sb's initiative; (*Sw Pol*) *siehe* **Volksbegehren.**

Initiator(in *f*) [ini'tsia:tɔr, -'to:rɪn] *m* (*geh*) initiator.

initiieren* [initsi'i:rən] *vt* (*geh*) initiate.

Injektion *f* injection.

Injektionsspritze *f* hypodermic (syringe).

injizieren* [ɪnji'tsi:rən] *vt* (*form*) to inject (*jdm etw* sb with sth).

Inka *m* **-(s), -s** Inca.

Inkarnation *f* incarnation.

Inkasso *nt* **-s, -s** *or* (*Aus*) **Inkassi** (*Fin*) collection.

Inkassobüro *nt*, **Inkassofirma** *f* (*Fin*) collection agency.

Inkassostelle *f* (*Fin*) collection point.

Inkaufnahme *f* **-**, *no pl* (*form*) acceptance ◆ **unter ~ finanzieller Verluste** accepting the inevitable financial losses.

inkl. *abbr of* **inklusive.**

inklusive [-'zi:və] [1] *prep +gen* inclusive of ◆ **~ Heizung** heating included, inclusive of *or* including heating.
[2] *adv* inclusive.

Inkognito *nt* **-s, -s** incognito.

inkognito *adv* incognito.

inkompatibel *adj* incompatible.

Inkompatibilität *f* incompatibility.

inkompetent *adj* incompetent.

Inkompetenz *f* incompetence.

inkongruent *adj* (*Math*) non-congruent.

Inkongruenz *f* (*Math*) non-congruence.

inkonsequent *adj* inconsistent.

Inkonsequenz *f* inconsistency.

inkonstant *adj* inconstant.

Inkonstanz *f* inconstancy.

Inkorporation *f* (*geh*) incorporation.

inkorporieren* *vt* to incorporate (*in +acc* in, into).

inkorrekt *adj* incorrect.

Inkorrektheit *f* (**a**) *no pl* (*des Benehmens*) incorrectness, impropriety; (*der Arbeit etc*) incorrectness, inaccuracy. (**b**) (*Formfehler*) impropriety, breach of propriety; (*Ungenauigkeit*) inaccuracy.

Inkrafttreten *nt* **-s**, *no pl* coming into effect *or* force ◆ **das ~ von etw verhindern** to prevent sth from coming into effect *or* force; **bei ~ von etw** when sth comes/came *etc* into effect *or* force.

inkriminieren* *vt* to incriminate.

Inkubation *f* incubation.

Inkubationszeit *f* incubation period.

Inkubator *m* incubator.

Inkubus ['ɪnkubʊs] *m* **-, Inkuben** incubus.

Inkulanz *f* disobligingness.

Inkunabel *f* **-, -n** incunabulum.

Inland *nt* **-(e)s**, *no pl* (**a**) (*als Staatsgebiet*) home ◆ **im ~ hergestellte Waren** home-produced goods, goods produced at home; **im In- und Ausland** at home and abroad; **die Gebühren für einen Brief im ~** inland *or* domestic letter rates. (**b**) (*Inneres eines Landes*) inland ◆ **im ~** inland; **ins ~ ziehen** to move inland.

Inland- *in cpds* (*Comm*) home, domestic; (*Geog*) inland; **~bedarf** *m* home *or* domestic requirements *pl*; **~eis** *nt* ice sheet; **~flug** *m* domestic *or* internal flight.

inländisch *adj* home *attr*, domestic; (*Geog*) inland.

Inlands-: **~gespräch** *nt* (*Telec*) inland call; **~markt** *m* home *or* domestic market; **~porto** *nt* inland postage; **~verkehr** *m* domestic traffic; (*Handel*) home trade; **Briefe im ~verkehr** letters within the country, inland *or* domestic letters; **er ist Fernfahrer, aber nur im ~verkehr** he's a long-distance driver, but only on inland *or* domestic routes.

Inlaut *m* **im ~ vorkommen** to occur (word) medially *or* in (word) medial position.

Inlett *nt* **-(e)s, -e** (*Hülle*) cambric case; (*~stoff*) cambric.

inliegend *adj* (*form, Aus*) enclosed.

Inliner ['ɪnlaɪnɐ] *m* **-s, -** (*Rollschuh*) rollerblade.

Inline-Skater ['ɪnlaɪnske:tɐ] *m* **-s, -** (**a**) (*Rollschuh*) rollerblade. (**b**) (*Person*) rollerblader.

Inline-Skates ['ɪnlaɪnske:ts] *pl* rollerblades *pl*.

inmitten [1] *prep +gen* in the middle *or* midst of.
[2] *adv* **~ von** amongst, surrounded by.

innehaben *vt sep irreg* (*form*) to hold.

innehalten *sep irreg* [1] *vi* to pause, to stop ◆ **er hielt im Satz/Sprechen inne** he paused in mid-sentence/he stopped speaking; **mit der Rede ~** to pause, to stop speaking; **mit der Rede ~, um Luft zu holen** to pause for breath.
[2] *vt* (*old*) *siehe* **einhalten.**

innen *adv* (**a**) inside; (*auf der Innenseite*) on the inside; (*im Haus*) indoors, inside ◆ **~ und außen** inside and out(side); **der Mantel hat ~ Pelz und außen Leder** the coat has fur (on the) inside and leather (on the) outside; **nach ~** inwards; **tief ~ tut es doch weh** deep down inside it really hurts; **die Tür geht nach ~ auf** the door opens inwards; **die Truppen drangen nach ~ vor** the troops pushed inland; **die Haare nach ~ tragen** to have one's hair curled under; **nach ~ laufen** to be pigeon-toed; **von ~** from (the) inside; **wie sieht das Haus von ~ aus?** what does the house look like from the inside?, what does the inside of the house look like?; **sich von ~ her aufwärmen** to warm oneself from (the) inside, to get warm inside.
(**b**) (*esp Aus*) *siehe* **drinnen.**

Innen-: **~antenne** *f* indoor aerial (*Brit*) *or* antenna (*US*); **~arbeiten** *pl* work on the interior; **~architekt** *m* interior designer; **~architektur** *f* interior design; **~aufnahme** *f* indoor photo(graph); (*Film*) indoor shot *or* take; **~ausstattung** *f* interior décor *no pl*; (*das Ausstatten*) interior decoration and furnishing; (*von Auto*) interior fittings *pl*; **~bahn** *f* (*Sport*) inside lane; **~beleuchtung** *f* interior lighting; **~dekoration** *f* interior decoration; **~dienst** *m* office duty; **im ~dienst sein** to work in the office; **~dienst machen** *or* **haben** to work in the office, to be on office duty; **i~drin** *adv* (*inf*) inside; **~einrichtung** *f* (interior) furnishings *pl*; (*das Einrichten*) interior furnishing *no pl*; **~fläche** *f* (**a**) (*innere Fläche*) inside, inside *or* interior surface; (*der Hand*) palm; (**b**) (*Flächeninhalt*) internal surface area; **~hof** *m* inner courtyard; (*bei Universitäten, Klöstern*) quadrangle, quad (*inf*); **~kurve** *f* inside bend; **~leben** *nt*, *no pl* (**a**) (*inf: seelisch*) inner *or* emotional life; **sein ~leben offenbaren** to reveal one's innermost thoughts *or* feelings; (**b**) (*inf: körperlich*) insides *pl*; **~leuchte** *f* (*Aut*) courtesy *or* interior light; **~minister** *m* minister of the interior; (*in GB*) Home Secretary; (*in den USA*) Secretary of the Interior; **~ministerium** *nt* ministry of the interior; (*in GB*) Home Office; (*in den USA*) Department of the Interior; **~politik** *f* domestic policy/policies *pl*; (*innere Angelegenheiten*) home *or* domestic affairs *pl*; **~politiker** *m* domestic politician; **i~politisch** *adj* domestic, internal, home *attr*; **auf i~politischem Gebiet** in the field of home affairs; **i~politisch gesehen, aus i~politischer Sicht** (seen) from the point of view of domestic policy; **i~politisch hat die Regierung versagt** the government has failed with its domestic policy/policies; **~raum** *m* (**a**) **~räume** inner rooms *pl*; **die prächtigen ~räume des alten Schlosses** the magnificent interior *or* rooms of the old castle; (**b**) *no pl* room inside; (*von Wagen auch*) interior; **einen kleinen ~raum haben** to be small inside, not to have much room inside; (*von Wagen auch*) to have a small interior; **mit großen ~raum** with a lot of room inside; (*von Wagen auch*) with a large interior; **~rolle** *f*, *no pl* **eine ~rolle tragen** to have one's hair turned *or* curled under at the ends; **~seite** *f* inside; **die ~seite von etw nach außen kehren** to turn sth inside out; **~spiegel** *m* (*Aut*) interior mirror; **~stadt** *f* town centre, centre of the town; (*einer Großstadt*) city centre, centre of the city; **~tasche** *f* inside pocket; **~temperatur** *f* inside temperature; (*in einem Gebäude*) indoor temperature; **wir haben 20° ~temperatur** the temperature indoors is 20°; **bei 20° ~temperatur** when the temperature indoors *or* the indoor temperature is 20°, when it's 20° indoors; **~toilette** *f* inside toilet; **~welt** *f* inner world; **er hat sich völlig in seine ~welt zurückgezogen** he has withdrawn completely into his own private world; **~winkel** *m* (*Math*) interior angle.

inner-: **~betrieblich** *adj* in-house; **das wird ~betrieblich geregelt werden** that will be settled in-house; **~deutsch** *adj* intra-German; **~deutscher Handel** trade between the two Germanies.

Innereien *pl* innards *pl*; (*von Geflügel auch*) giblets *pl*.

innere(r, s) *adj* (**a**) (*örtlich*) inner; (*im Körper befindlich, inländisch*) internal ◆ **Facharzt für ~ Krankheiten** internist; **das ~ Ohr** the inner ear; **die ~n Angelegenheiten eines Landes** the internal *or* home *or* domestic affairs of a country; **der Whisky sorgte für die ~ Wärme** (*inf*) the whisky warmed our/their *etc* insides (*inf*); **I~ Mission** Home Mission; **~r Monolog** (*Liter*) interior monologue; **im innersten Herzen** deep in one's heart, in one's heart of hearts; **eine ~ Uhr** (*inf*) an internal *or* a biological clock; **~ Emigration** inner emigration, *withdrawal into private life of artists and intellectuals who remained in Germany through the Nazi period but did not support the Third Reich; any similar withdrawal.*
(**b**) (*geistig, seelisch*) inner ◆ **~ Werte** *pl* inner worth *no pl*; **eine ~ Stimme** an inner voice, a voice within; **vor meinem ~n Auge** in my mind's eye; **~ Führung** (*Mil*) moral leadership.

Innere(s) *nt decl as adj* (**a**) inside; (*von Kirche, Wagen, Schloß auch*) interior; (*Mitte*) middle, centre ◆ **Minister des Inner(e)n** minister of the interior; (*in GB*) Home Secretary; (*in den USA*) Secretary of the Interior; **das ~ nach außen kehren** to turn something inside out; **ins ~ des Landes** into the heart of the country.
(**b**) (*fig: Gemüt, Geist*) heart ◆ **ich wußte, was in seinem ~n vorging** I knew

what was going on inside him; **sein ~s rebellierte dagegen** his inner self rebelled against it; **im tiefsten ~n** (deep) in one's heart, in one's heart of hearts.

innerhalb [1] *prep +gen* **(a)** *(örtlich)* inside, within ◆ **~ dieser Regelung** within this ruling. **(b)** *(zeitlich)* within ◆ **~ (von) zehn Minuten** within ten minutes, in ten minutes, inside (of) ten minutes.
[2] *adv* inside; *(eines Landes)* inland ◆ **weiter ~** further in; **weiter ~ im Lande** further inland.

innerlich *adj* **(a)** *(körperlich)* internal ◆ **dieses Medikament ist ~ anzuwenden** this medicament is to be taken internally.
(b) *(geistig, seelisch)* inward, inner *no adv*; *Gedicht, Mensch* inward; *Hemmung* inner ◆ **ein ~ gefestigter Mensch** a person of inner strength; **~ schäumte er vor Wut** inwardly *or* inside he was boiling with rage; **~ lachen** to laugh inwardly *or* to oneself.

Innerlichkeit *f (liter)* inwardness.

inner-: ~parteilich *adj* within the party; **~parteiliche Schwierigkeiten** internal difficulties in the party, difficulties within the party; **eine ~parteiliche Diskussion** a party discussion; **~parteiliche Demokratie** democracy (with)in the party structure; **~staatlich** *adj* domestic, internal.

innerste(r, s) *adj superl of* **innere(r, s)** innermost, inmost; *(fig auch)* deepest.

Innerste(s) *nt decl as adj (lit)* innermost part, heart; *(fig)* heart ◆ **tief im ~n liebte sie ihn** in her heart of hearts *or* deep in her heart she loved him; **bis ins ~ getroffen** hurt to the quick, deeply *or* profoundly hurt.

innert *prep +gen or dat (Aus, Sw)* within, in, inside (of).

innewerden *vi sep irreg aux sein* **(sich** *dat***) einer Sache** *(gen)* **~** to become aware *or* cognizant *(form)* of sth.

innewohnen *vi sep +dat* to be inherent in.

innig *adj Glückwünsche, Grüße* heartfelt *no adv*, hearty; *Beileid* heartfelt, deep, profound; *Vergnügen* deep, profound; *Freundschaft, Beziehung* intimate *(auch Chem)* ◆ **etw aufs ~ste erhoffen/wünschen** to hope/wish for sth most fervently *or* ardently; **mein ~ster Wunsch** my dearest wish; **jdn ~ lieben** to love sb dearly *or* deeply *or* with all one's heart.

Innigkeit *f (von Glückwünschen, Grüßen)* warmth, sincerity; *(von Empfindung)* depth; *(von Liebe)* intensity; *(von Freundschaft, Beziehung)* intimacy ◆ **mit ~ beten/hoffen** to pray/hope fervently *or* ardently.

inniglich *adv (poet) (herzlich)* sincerely, warmly; *(tief)* deeply, profoundly; *lieben* deeply, dearly; *(eng)* intimately, closely.

Innovation *f* innovation.

innovativ *adj* innovative ◆ **~ tätig sein** to do innovative work.

Innung *f* (trade) guild ◆ **du blamierst die ganze ~** *(hum inf)* you're letting the (whole) side down *(inf)*.

in|offiziell *adj* unofficial ◆ **jdm etw ~ mitteilen** to tell sb sth unofficially *or* off the record.

Inokulation *f* inoculation.

inokulieren* *vt* to inoculate.

in|operabel *adj (Med)* inoperable.

in|opportun *adj* inopportune.

in petto *siehe* **petto**.

in puncto *siehe* **puncto**.

Input ['ɪnpʊt] *m or nt* **-s, -s** input.

Inquisition *f* Inquisition.

Inquisitions-: ~gericht *nt* Court of the Inquisition, inquisitional court; **~methode** *f* inquisitional method.

Inquisitor *m* inquisitor.

inquisitorisch *adj* inquisitorial.

ins *contr of* **in das** ◆ **~ Rollen/Rutschen geraten** *or* **kommen** to start rolling/sliding.

Insasse *m* **-n, -n, Insassin** *f (eines Fahrzeuges)* passenger; *(eines Autos auch)* occupant; *(einer Anstalt)* inmate.

Insassenversicherung *f* passenger insurance.

insbesondere *adv* particularly, (e)specially, in particular.

Inschrift *f* inscription, legend *(form)*.

Insekt *nt* **-(e)s, -en** insect.

Insekten-: ~bekämpfung *f* insect control; **~bekämpfungsmittel** *nt* insecticide; **⚠i~fressend** *adj attr* insect-eating, insectivorous *(form)*; **~fresser** *m* insect-eater, insectivore *(form)*; **~gift** *nt* insecticide; **~kunde** *f* entomology; **~plage** *f* plague of insects; **~pulver** *nt* insect powder, (powder) insecticide; **~schutzmittel** *nt* insect-repellent; **~stich** *m (von Ameisen, Mücken, Flöhen)* insect bite; *(von Bienen, Wespen)* (insect) sting; **~vertilgungsmittel** *nt* insecticide.

Insektizid *nt* **-s, -e** *(form)* insecticide.

Insel *f* **-, -n** *(lit, fig)* island, isle *(poet)* ◆ **die Britischen ~n** the British Isles; **die ~ Man** the Isle of Man.

Inselbewohner *m* islander, inhabitant of an/the island.

Inselchen *nt* little island, islet *(poet)*.

Insel-: ~gruppe *f* archipelago, group of islands; **~lage** *f* island position; **Großbritannien, infolge seiner ~lage ...** Great Britain, because it is an island ...; **~mentalität** *f* insular mentality; **i~reich** *adj* with a lot of islands; **~reich** *nt* island kingdom; **~staat** *m* island state; **~volk** *nt* island nation *or* race *or* people; **~welt** *f* island world; **die ~welt Mittelamerikas** the world of the Central American islands.

Inserat *nt* advert *(Brit inf)*, ad *(inf)*, advertisement.

Inseratenteil *m* advertisement section, adverts *pl (Brit inf)*, ads *pl (inf)*.

Inserent *m* advertiser.

inserieren* *vti* to advertise ◆ **etw in der Zeitung ~** to advertise sth in the paper, to insert *or* put an advertisement in the paper for sth.

insgeheim *adv* secretly, in secret.

insgemein *adv (old)* in general, on the whole, by and large.

insgesamt *adv (alles zusammen)* altogether; *(im großen und ganzen)* all in all, on the whole, by and large ◆ **die Kosten belaufen sich auf ~ 1.000 DM** the costs amount to a total of DM 1,000; **ein Verdienst von ~ 2.000 DM** earnings totalling DM 2,000.

Insider ['ɪnsaɪdə] *m* **-s, -** insider ◆ **der Witz war nur für ~ verständlich** that was an in-joke, that joke was just for the in-crowd; **~ der Jazz-Scene** those in on the jazz scene, those in the know about the jazz scene.

Insider-: ~geschäft *nt* insider deal; **~handel** *m* insider trading *or* dealing.

Insignien [ɪn'zɪgniən] *pl* insignia *pl*.

insignifikant ['ɪnzɪgnifikant] *adj (geh)* insignificant, of no consequence.

insistieren* [ɪnzɪs'tiːrən] *vi (geh)* to insist *(auf +dat* on).

Inskription *f* inscription.

insofern [1] *adv* in this respect ◆ **~ ... als** in so far as, inasmuch as, in that; **er hat ~ recht, als ...** he's right in so far as *or* inasmuch as *or* in that ...
[2] [ɪnzo'fɛrn] *conj (wenn)* if.

insolvent ['ɪnzɔlvɛnt] *adj (Comm)* insolvent.

Insolvenz ['ɪnzɔlvɛnts] *f (Comm)* insolvency.

insoweit [ɪn'zoːvait] *adv*, [ɪnzo'vait] *conj siehe* **insofern**.

Insp. *abbr of* **Inspektor**.

in spe [ɪn'speː] *adj (inf)* to be, future ◆ **unser Schwiegersohn ~ ~** our son-in-law to be, our future son-in-law.

Inspekteur [ɪnspɛk'tøːɐ] *m (Mil)* Chief of Staff.

Inspektion *f* **(a)** inspection; *(Aut)* service ◆ **ich habe mein Auto zur ~ gebracht** I've taken my car in for a service *or* to be serviced. **(b)** *(Behörde)* inspectorate.

Inspektionsreise *f* tour of inspection.

Inspektor(in *f***)** [ɪn'spɛktɔr, -'toːrɪn] *m* inspector; *(Verwalter, Aufseher)* superintendent.

Inspiration [ɪnspira'tsioːn] *f* inspiration.

inspirieren* [ɪnspi'riːrən] *vt* to inspire ◆ **sich von etw ~ lassen** to get one's inspiration from sth.

Inspizient(in *f***)** [ɪnspi'tsiɛnt, -ɪn] *m (Theat)* stage-manager; *(Aufseher)* inspector.

inspizieren* [ɪnspi'tsiːrən] *vt* to inspect.

Inspizierung *f* inspection.

instabil ['ɪnstabiːl] *adj* unstable.

Instabilität *f* instability.

Installateur [ɪnstala'tøːɐ] *m* plumber; *(Elektro~)* electrician, electrical fitter; *(Gas~)* gas-fitter.

Installation [ɪnstala'tsioːn] *f* **(a)** *(no pl: das Installieren)* installation; *(Tech auch)* fitting. **(b)** *(Anlage)* installation; *(in Bauten)* fittings *pl*, installations *pl*; *(Wasser~)* plumbing *no pl*. **(c)** *(old, Sw: Amtseinsetzung)* installation.

installieren* [ɪnsta'liːrən] [1] *vt* to install *(auch fig, Comput)*, to put in.
[2] *vr* to install oneself.

instand *adj* in good condition *or* repair; *(funktionsfähig)* in working order, working ◆ **etw ~ halten** to maintain sth, to keep sth in good condition *or* repair/in working order; **etw ~ setzen** to get sth into good condition *or* repair/into working order; *(reparieren auch)* to repair sth.

Instand-: ⚠i~besetzen* *vt sep (sl)* **ein Haus i~besetzen** to squat in a house *(and do it up)*; **~haltung** *f (von Gerät)* maintenance, servicing; *(von Gebäude)* maintenance, upkeep; **~haltungskosten** *pl* maintenance costs *pl*; *(von Gebäude auch)* upkeep costs *pl*.

inständig *adj* urgent ◆ **~ bitten** to beg, to implore, to beseech; **~ hoffen** to hope fervently.

Instand-: ~setzung *f (von Gerät)* overhaul; *(von Gebäude)* restoration; *(Reparatur auch)* repair; **~setzungsarbeiten** *pl* repairs *pl*, repair work.

Instanz [ɪn'stants] *f* **(a)** *(Behörde)* authority ◆ **er ging von einer ~ zur nächsten** he went from one office *or* department to the next.
(b) *(Jur)* court; *(Verhandlungsstadium)* (court-)case; *(strafrechtlich auch)* trial ◆ **Verhandlung in erster/zweiter ~** first/second court-case, hearing at the court of second instance *(form)*; **Berufung in erster/zweiter ~** first/second appeal; **ein Urteil letzter ~** *(lit, fig)* a final judgement; **er ging von einer ~ zur anderen** he went through all the courts.

Instanzen-: ~weg, ~zug *(Aus) m* official *or* prescribed channels *pl*, channels *pl (US)*; *(Jur)* stages *pl* of appeal; **auf dem ~weg** through (the official *or* prescribed) channels/the various stages of appeal.

Instinkt [ɪn'stɪŋkt] *m* **-(e)s, -e** *(lit, fig)* instinct ◆ **aus ~** instinctively, by instinct.

instinkthaft *adj* instinctive.

Instinkthandlung *f* instinctive act ◆ **das ist eine reine ~** it's purely instinctive (behaviour).

instinktiv [ɪnstɪŋk'tiːf] *adj* instinctive.

instinktmäßig [1] *adj* instinctive.
[2] *adv* instinctively, by instinct; *(Instinkte betreffend)* as far as instinct is concerned.

Institut [ɪnsti'tuːt] *nt* **-(e)s, -e** institute; *(Jur: Institution)* institution.

Institution [ɪnstitu'tsioːn] *f* institution.

institutionalisieren* [ɪnstitutsio-] *vt* to institutionalize.

institutionell [ɪnstitutsio'nɛl] *adj* institutional.

Institutsleiter *m* director of an/the institute.

instruieren* [ɪnstru'iːrən] *vt* to instruct; *(über Unternehmen, Plan etc)* to brief; *Anwalt* to brief.

Instrukteur [ɪnstrʊk'tøːɐ] *m* instructor.
Instruktion [ɪnstrʊk'tsioːn] *f* instruction ◆ **laut ~** according to instructions.
instruktiv [ɪnstrʊk'tiːf] *adj* instructive.
Instrument [ɪnstru'mɛnt] *nt* instrument; (*Hammer etc auch*) tool, implement ◆ **er ist ~ des** ... he is the instrument of ...
instrumental [ɪnstrumɛn'taːl] *adj* (*Mus*) instrumental.
Instrumental- *in cpds* instrumental; **~begleitung** *f* instrumental accompaniment; **ohne ~begleitung singen** to sing unaccompanied.
instrumentalisieren* *vt* **(a)** (*Mus*) to arrange for instruments. **(b)** *Theorie, Plan etc* to harness; (*ausnutzen*) to exploit.
Instrumental-: ~satz *m* (*Gram*) instrumental clause; (*Mus*) (*Bearbeitung*) instrumental version; (*Teilstück*) instrumental section; **~stück** *nt* instrumental piece.
Instrumentarium [ɪnstrumɛn'taːriʊm] *nt* (*lit*) equipment, instruments *pl*; (*Mus*) instruments *pl*; (*fig*) apparatus.
instrumentell [ɪnstrumɛn'tɛl] *adj* with instruments.
Instrumenten-: ~brett *nt* instrument panel; **~flug** *m* instrument flight; (*das Fliegen auch*) instrument flying, flying on instruments; **~tafel** *f* control *or* instrument panel.
instrumentieren* [ɪnstrʊmɛn'tiːrən] *vt* (*Mus*) to arrange for instruments; (*für Orchester*) to orchestrate; (*Tech*) to fit out *or* equip with instruments.
Instrumentierung *f* instrumentation.
Insuffizienz ['ɪnzʊfitsiɛnts] *f* (*Med, geh*) insufficiency.
Insulaner(in *f***)** *m* **-s, -** (*usu hum*) islander.
insular *adj* insular.
Insulin *nt* **-s,** *no pl* insulin.
Insulin- *in cpds* insulin; **~schock** *m* insulin *or* hypoglycaemic (*spec*) shock; **~stoß** *m* insulin boost.
Inszenator *m* (*Theat*) director; (*fig*) stage-manager.
inszenatorisch *adj* directing *attr* ◆ **eine ~e Glanzleistung** a brilliant piece of directing *or* (*fig*) stage-management.
inszenieren* *vt* **(a)** (*Theat*) to direct; (*Rad, TV*) to produce. **(b)** (*fig*) to stage-manage. **einen Streit ~** to start an argument; **ein Theater ~** to kick up a fuss (*inf*).
Inszenierung *f* production ◆ **ein Stück in neuer ~ aufführen** to put on a new production of a play.
intakt *adj* intact ◆ **ich bin nach meiner Grippe noch nicht ganz ~** (*inf*) I'm still feeling a bit fragile after my flu.
Intarsia *f* **-, Intarsien** [-iən], **Intarsie** [ɪn'tarziə] *f usu pl* marquetry *no pl*, inlay, inlaid work *no pl*.
integer *adj* (*geh*) **~ sein** to be full of integrity; **ein integrer Mensch** a person of integrity; **sich ~ verhalten** to behave with integrity.
integral *adj attr* integral.
Integral *nt* **-s, -e** integral.
Integral-: ~helm *m* full-face helmet; **~rechnung** *f* integral calculus.
Integration *f* integration.
Integrations-: ~figur *f* unifying figure; **~klasse** *f* (*Sch*) integrated class; **~kraft** *f* unifying force.
integrativ *adj Erziehung, Zusammenarbeit etc* integrated; *Weltanschauung etc* holistic.
integrierbar *adj* capable of being integrated, assimilable; (*Math*) integrable.
integrieren* *vt* to integrate (*auch Math*).
integriert *adj* integrated; *Sicherheitsvorrichtung auch* integral, in-built ◆ **~e Schaltung** integrated circuit; **~e Gesamtschule** comprehensive (school) (*Brit*).
Integrierung *f* integration *no pl*.
Integrität *f* integrity.
Intellekt *m* **-(e)s,** *no pl* intellect.
Intellektualismus *m* intellectualism.
intellektuell *adj* intellectual.
Intellektuelle(r) *mf decl as adj* intellectual.
Intellelle(r) *mf decl as adj* (*hum inf*) intellectual, egghead (*inf*).
intelligent *adj* intelligent.
Intelligenz *f* intelligence; (*Personengruppe*) intelligentsia *pl* ◆ **Elefanten haben eine hochentwickelte ~** elephants are highly intelligent *or* have a great deal of intelligence; **künstliche ~** artificial intelligence.
Intelligenzbestie *f* (*pej inf*) egghead (*inf*).
Intelligenzija [-tsija] *f* **-,** *no pl* intelligentsia *pl*.
Intelligenzleistung *f* display of intelligence ◆ **eine ~ von jdm** a display of sb's intelligence; **das war wieder eine ~ von dir!** (*iro*) that was intelligent *or* bright of you (*iro*).
Intelligenzler *m* **-s, -** (*inf*) egghead (*inf*).
Intelligenz-: ~quotient *m* intelligence quotient, IQ; **~test** *m* intelligence test; **einen ~test mit jdm machen** to give sb an intelligence test, to test sb's IQ.
Intendant *m* director; theatre-manager.
Intendantur *f* (*Amtszeit*) period of directorship; (*Amtssitz*) director's office; theatre-manager's office ◆ **während seiner ~** while he was director/theatre-manager, during his directorship *or* the period of his directorship.
Intendanz *f* (*Amt*) directorship; (*Büro*) director's/theatre-manager's office.
intendieren* *vt* (*geh*) to intend ◆ **eine Beleidigung hatte ich damit nicht intendiert** I didn't intend that as an insult.
Intensität *f* intensity.
intensiv *adj Arbeit, Forschung, Landwirtschaft* intensive; *Farbe, Gefühl* intense; *Geruch* powerful, strong; *Blick* intent, intense ◆ **jdn ~ beobachten** to watch sb intently.
intensivieren* [-'viːrən] *vt* to intensify.
Intensivierung *f* intensification.
Intensiv-: ~kurs *m* intensive course; **~station** *f* intensive care unit.
Intention *f* (*geh*) intention, intent.
intentional [ɪntɛntsio'naːl] *adj* (*Philos*) intentional.
Inter- *in cpds* inter-; **~aktion** *f* interaction; **i~aktiv** *adj* interactive; **~city** *m* **-(s), -s** inter-city (train) (*Brit*); **~city-Expreß** *m* high-speed inter-city (train) (*Brit*); **~city-Verkehr** *m* (*Rail*) inter-city traffic (*Brit*), express traffic; **~city-Zug** *m* inter-city (train) (*Brit*); **i~dependent** *adj* interdependent; **~dependenz** *f* interdependence.
interdisziplinär *adj* interdisciplinary.
interessant *adj* interesting ◆ **zu diesem Preis ist das nicht ~ für uns** (*Comm*) we are not interested at that price; **das ist ja ~!** (that's) very interesting!; **sich ~ machen** to attract attention (to oneself); **sich bei jdm ~ machen** to attract sb's attention.
interessanterweise *adv* interestingly enough.
Interesse *nt* **-s, -n** interest ◆ **~ an jdm/etw** *or* **für jdn/etw haben** to be interested in sb/sth; **aus ~** out of interest, for interest; **es liegt in Ihrem eigenen ~** it's in your own interest(s); **die ~n eines Staates wahrnehmen** to look after the interests of a state; **sein ~ gilt** ... his interest is *or* lies in ..., he's interested in ...; **das ist für uns nicht von ~** that's of no interest to us, we're not interested in that; **er tat es** *or* **handelte in meinem ~** he did it for my good *or* in my interest.
Interesse-: i~halber *adv* for *or* out of interest; **i~los** *adj* indifferent; **~losigkeit** *f* indifference.
Interessen-: ~bereich *m*, **~gebiet** *nt* field of interest; **das gehört nicht zu meinem ~bereich** that isn't one of my interests, that's outside my field of interests; **~gegensatz** *m* clash of interests; **~gemeinschaft** *f* **(a)** community of interests; (*Menschen*) group of people sharing interests; **(b)** (*Econ*) syndicate; **~gruppe** *f* interest group; (*Lobby*) lobby; **~kollision** *f* conflict of interests; **~sphäre** *f* (*Pol*) sphere of influence.
Interessent(in *f***)** *m* interested person *or* party (*form*); (*Bewerber auch*) applicant; (*Comm: Kauflustiger auch*) prospective customer ◆ **~en werden gebeten** ... those interested are requested ...; **es haben sich mehrere ~en gemeldet** several people have shown interest.
Interessentenkreis *m* market.
Interessen-: ~verband *m* syndicate; (*Lobby*) lobby; **~vertretung** *f* representation of interests; (*Personen*) group representing one's interests.
interessieren* **1** *vt* to interest (*für, an +dat* in) ◆ **es würde mich doch sehr ~, was du damit machen willst** it would interest me very much to know *or* I'd be very interested to know what you want to do with it; **das interessiert mich (gar) nicht!** I'm not (the least *or* slightest bit) interested; **ich liege hier im Sterben, aber das interessiert dich gar nicht** here I am on my death-bed, but you don't care; **das hat dich nicht zu ~!** that's none of your business!, don't be so nosey! (*inf*).
2 *vr* to be interested (*für* in); (*mit Interesse verfolgen auch*) to take an interest (*für* in) ◆ **er begann schon mit acht Jahren, sich für Musik zu ~** he started to be interested *or* to take *or* show an interest in music when he was eight.
interessiert *adj* interested (*an +dat* in) ◆ **~ zuhören** *etc* to listen *etc* with interest; **vielseitig ~ sein** to have a wide range of interests; **politisch ~** interested in politics; **ein ~er Mensch** a person with a number of interests.
Interface ['ɪntɐfeːs] *nt* **-, -s** (*Comput*) interface.
Interferenz *f* (*Phys, Ling*) interference *no pl*.
Interferon *nt* **-s, -e** interferon.
Interhotel *nt* (*DDR*) international hotel.
Interieur [ɛ̃te'riøːɐ] *nt* **-s, -s** *or* **-e** interior.
Interim *nt* **-s, -s** interim.
Interims- *in cpds* interim; **~abkommen** *nt* interim agreement; **~regierung** *f* caretaker *or* provisional government; **~schein** *m* (*Fin*) scrip.
Interjektion *f* interjection.
Inter-: i~konfessionell *adj* interdenominational; **i~kontinental** *adj* intercontinental; **~kontinentalrakete** *f* intercontinental missile; **~leukin** *nt* **-s, -e** interleukin; **i~linear** *adj* interlinear.
Intermezzo [-'mɛtso] *nt* **-s, -s** *or* **Intermezzi** (*Mus*) intermezzo; (*fig auch*) interlude; (*ärgerlich*) contretemps *sing*.
intermittierend *adj* intermittent.
intern *adj* internal ◆ **~er Schüler** boarder; **diese Maßnahmen müssen vorläufig ~ bleiben** for the time being these measures must be kept private; **die ~en Schwierigkeiten des Landes** the country's internal *or* domestic difficulties.
-intern *adj suf* **schul-/ausschuß~e Angelegenheiten** internal school/committee matters; **etw schul~ regeln** to settle sth internally within the school(s).
internalisieren* *vt* (*spec*) to internalize.
Internat *nt* boarding school.
international [ɪntɐnatsio'naːl] *adj* international.
Internationale [ɪntɐnatsio'naːlə] *f* **-, -n** Internationale.
internationalisieren* [ɪntɐnatsio-] *vt* to make international.
Internationalismus *m* internationalism.
Internatsschüler *m* boarder, boarding (school) pupil.
Internet *nt* **-** *no pl* (*Comput*) internet ◆ **Anschluß ans ~ haben** to be connected to the internet; **im ~ surfen** to surf the internet.
Internet-Café *nt* internet café.
Internet-Knoten *m* point of presence, POP.

internieren* *vt* to intern.
Internierte(r) *mf decl as adj* internee.
Internierung *f* internment.
Internierungslager *nt* internment camp.
Internist *m* internist.
Internspeicher *m (Comput)* memory.
Internum *nt* **-s, Interna** *usu pl* internal matter; *(geheim)* restricted information.
interparlamentarisch *adj* interparliamentary.
Interpellation *f* (parliamentary) question.
interpellieren* *vi* to ask a (parliamentary) question.
interplanetar(isch) *adj* interplanetary *no adv.*
Interpol *f* - Interpol.
Interpolation *f* interpolation.
interpolieren* *vt* to interpolate.
Interpret *m* **-en, -en** interpreter *(of music, art etc)* ♦ **Lieder verschiedener ~en** songs by various singers.
Interpretation *f* interpretation; *(eines Liedes auch)* version.
Interpreter [ɪn'tɜːprɛtɐ] *m (Comput)* interpreter.
interpretieren* *vt* to interpret ♦ **etw falsch ~** to misinterpret sth.
Interpretin *f siehe* **Interpret.**
interpunktieren* *vt* to punctuate.
Interpunktion *f* punctuation.
Interpunktions-: ~regel *f* rule of punctuation, punctuation rule; **~zeichen** *nt* punctuation mark.
Interrail-Karte ['ɪntɐˌreːl-] *f* inter-rail ticket.
Interregio *m* **-s, -s, Interregio-Zug** *m fast train running at regular intervals.*
Interregnum *nt* **-s, Interregnen** *or* **Interregna** interregnum.
interrogativ *adj* interrogative.
Interrogativ-: ~pronomen *nt* interrogative pronoun; **~satz** *m* interrogative clause.
Interruptus *m* **-,** *no pl (inf)* coitus interruptus.
Intershop ['ɪntɐʃɔp] *m* **-s, -s** *(DDR)* international shop.
interstellar [-ste'laːɐ] *adj* interstellar.
Intervall [-'val] *nt* **-s, -e** interval *(auch Mus)* ♦ **sich in längeren ~en sehen** to see each other at infrequent intervals.
Intervall-: ~schaltung *f* interval switch; **~training** *nt* interval training.
intervenieren* [-ve'niːrən] *vi* to intervene.
Intervention [-vɛn'tsioːn] *f* intervention.
Interview ['ɪntɐvjuː] *nt* **-s, -s** interview.
interviewen* [-'vjuːən] *vt* to interview *(jdn zu etw* sb on *or* about sth).
Interviewer(in *f*) [-'vjuːɐ, -'vjuːərɪn] *m* **-s, -** interviewer.
Intervision [-vi'zioːn] *f* Intervision.
Interzonen- *in cpds* interzonal; **~zug** *m train for traffic between West Germany and the GDR.*
Inthronisation *f* enthronement.
inthronisieren* *vt* to enthrone.
Intifada *f* - *no pl* intifada.
intim *adj* intimate ♦ **ein ~er Kenner von etw sein** to have an intimate knowledge of sth; **etw im ~en Kreis feiern** to celebrate sth with one's closest *or* most intimate friends; **meine ~en Angelegenheiten** my intimate personal affairs.
Intim-: ~bereich *m* **(a)** *(Anat)* genital area; **(b)** *(fig) siehe* **~sphäre**; **~feind** *m* favourite enemy; **~hygiene** *f* personal hygiene.
Intimität *f* **(a)** *no pl (Gemütlichkeit, Vertraulichkeit)* intimacy.
(b) *(private Angelegenheit)* intimacy ♦ **jdm allerlei ~en erzählen** to tell sb all kinds of intimate details *or* intimacies; **bitte keine ~en!** please don't go into intimate details.
(c) *(sexuell)* intimacy ♦ **zwischen den beiden kam es zu ~en** they became intimate with each other; **~en austauschen** to kiss and pet; **bitte keine ~en in meinem Haus!** I'll have none of that sort of thing going on in my house!; **er hat sich einige ~en erlaubt** he became rather familiar.
Intim-: ~kontakt *m (form)* intimate contact; **~lotion** *f* vaginal lotion; **~partner** *m (form)* sexual partner; **~sphäre** *f* private life; **jds ~sphäre verletzen** to invade sb's privacy; **diese Frage greift in die ~sphäre ein** that question is an invasion of my/your *etc* privacy; **~spray** *nt* intimate deodorant spray.
Intimus *m* **-, Intimi** *(hum)* confidant.
Intimverkehr *m* intimacy ♦ **~ mit jdm haben** to be intimate with sb.
intolerant *adj* intolerant *(einer Sache gegenüber* of sth, *jdm gegenüber* of *or* towards sb).
Intoleranz *f* intolerance.
Intonation *f* intonation.
intonieren* *vt* **(a) einen Satz falsch/anders ~** to give a sentence the wrong/a different intonation. **(b)** *(Mus) Melodie* to sing; *(Kapelle)* to play; *Ton* to give ♦ **wer kann das Lied ~?** who can start the song off?, who can show us how the song goes?
intransigent *adj (liter)* intransigent.
intransitiv *adj* intransitive.
intravenös [-ve'nøːs] *adj* intravenous.
intrigant *adj (geh)* scheming, designing.
Intrigant(in *f*) *m* schemer, intriguer.
Intrige *f* **-, -n** intrigue, conspiracy, scheme.
Intrigen-: ~spiel *nt* intriguing, plotting; **~wirtschaft** *f* hive of intrigue.
intrigieren* *vi* to intrigue, to scheme, to plot.
Introitus [ɪn'troːitʊs] *m* **-, -** *(Gesang)* introit; *(Anat)* introitus.
introvertiert [-vɛr'tiːɐt] *adj* introverted.
Introvertiertheit *f* introversion.
Intuition [ɪntui'tsioːn] *f* intuition.
intuitiv [ɪntui'tiːf] *adj* intuitive.
intus *adj (inf)* **etw ~ haben** *(wissen)* to have got sth into one's head *(inf)*; *Essen, Alkohol* to have sth down *(inf) or* inside one *(inf)*; **er hat schon etwas** *or* **einiges ~** he's had a few.
invalid(e) [ɪnva'liːt, -'liːdə] *adj (rare)* disabled, invalid *attr.*
Invalide [ɪnva'liːdə] *m* **-n, -n** disabled person, invalid ♦ **er ist ~** he's disabled *or* an invalid; **der Krieg hat ihn zum ~n gemacht** he was disabled in the war; **ich mache dich zum ~n!** *(inf)* I'll cripple you! *(inf)*.
Invaliden-: ~heim *nt* home for disabled persons *or* people, home for the disabled; **~rente** *f* disability pension; **~versicherung** *f* disability insurance.
Invalidität [ɪnvalidi'tɛːt] *f* disability.
invariabel [ɪnvaːria:bl] *adj* invariable.
invariant [ɪnvaːriant] *adj* invariant.
Invariante [-va-] *f* **-, -n** *(Math)* invariant, invariable.
Invasion [ɪnvaː'zioːn] *f (lit, fig)* invasion.
Invasor [ɪn'vaːzɔr] *m usu pl* invader.
Invektive [ɪnvɛk'tiːvə] *f (geh)* invective *no pl.*
Inventar [ɪnvɛn'taːɐ] *nt* **-s, -e (a)** *(Verzeichnis)* inventory; *(Comm)* assets and liabilities *pl* ♦ **das ~ aufnehmen** to do the inventory; **etw ins ~ aufnehmen** to put sth on the inventory.
(b) *(Einrichtung)* fittings *pl*; *(Maschinen)* equipment *no pl*, plant *no pl* ♦ **lebendes ~** livestock; **totes ~** fixtures and fittings *pl*; **er gehört schon zum ~** *(fig)* he's part of the furniture.
Inventarisation [ɪnvɛnt-] *f* compilation of an inventory.
inventarisieren* [-vɛn-] *vt* to take *or* make an inventory of.
Inventarisierung *f siehe* **Inventarisation.**
Inventur [ɪnvɛn'tuːɐ] *f* stocktaking ♦ **~ machen** to stocktake.
Inversion [ɪnvɛr'zioːn] *f (Gram)* inversion.
Inversions-: ~temperatur *f* temperature inversion; **~wetterlage** *f* inverted atmospheric conditions *pl.*
invertiert [ɪnvɛr'tiːɐt] *adj* inverted.
Invest- [ɪn'vɛst-] *in cpds (DDR)* investment.
investieren* [ɪnvɛs'tiːrən] *vti (Comm)* to invest; *(fig auch)* to put ♦ **Geld in seine Freundin ~** *(inf)* to invest money in one's girlfriend *(hum)*; **Gefühle in jdn ~** *(inf)* to become (emotionally) involved with sb.
Investierung, Investition [ɪnvɛst-] *f* investment.
Investitions- *in cpds* investment; **~anreiz** *m* investment incentive; **~gut** *nt usu pl* item of capital expenditure; **~hilfe** *f* investment aid.
Investitur [ɪnvɛsti'tuːɐ] *f (Eccl)* investiture.
Investment [ɪn'vɛstmənt] *nt* **-s, -s** investment.
Investment-: ~fonds *m* investment fund; **~gesellschaft** *f* investment trust; **~papier, ~zertifikat** *nt* investment fund certificate.
In-vitro-Fertilisation *f* in vitro fertilization.
inwärts *adv siehe* **einwärts.**
inwendig *adj* **(a)** *(rare)* inside. **(b)** *(inf)* **jdn/etw in- und auswendig kennen** to know sb/sth inside out.
inwiefern, inwieweit *adv (im Satz)* to what extent, how far; *(alleinstehend)* in what way.
Inzahlungnahme *f* **-, -n** *(Comm)* **die ~ von etw** the acceptance of sth in part payment *or* as a trade-in; **bei ~ des alten Wagens** when the old car is traded in *or* is taken as a trade-in.
Inzest *m* **-(e)s, -e** incest *no pl.*
inzestuös *adj* incestuous.
Inzucht *f* inbreeding ♦ **verfluchte ~!** *(sl)* bugger! *(sl)*.
inzw. *abbr of* **inzwischen.**
inzwischen *adv* (in the) meantime, meanwhile ♦ **ich gehe ~ auf die Post** I'll go to the post in the meantime; **sie hatte ~ davon erfahren** meanwhile *or* in the meantime she'd learnt of this; **er hat sich ~ verändert** he's changed since (then); **er ist ~ 18 geworden** he's now 18.
IOK [iːoː'kaː] *nt* **-s** *abbr of* **Internationales Olympisches Komitee** IOC.
Ion [ioːn, 'iːɔn] *nt* **-s, -en** ion.
Ionen(aus)tauscher ['ioːnən-] *m* ion exchanger.
Ionisation [ioniza'tsioːn] *f* ionization.
ionisch ['ioːnɪʃ] *adj (Archit, Poet)* ionic; *(Mus)* ionian ♦ **I~es Meer** Ionian Sea.
ionisieren* [ioni'ziːrən] *vt* to ionize.
Ionosphäre [iono'sfɛːrə] *f* ionosphere.
⚠ **I-Punkt** ['iːpʊŋkt] *m* dot on the i ♦ **~e setzen** *or* **machen** to dot one's *or* the i's, to put the dots on the i's.
IQ *abbr of* **Intelligenzquotient** IQ.
i.R. [iː'|ɛr] *abbr of* **im Ruhestand** retd.
Irak [i'raːk, 'iːrak] *m* **-s (der) ~** Iraq.
Iraker(in *f*) *m* **-s, -** Iraqi.
irakisch *adj* Iraqi.
Iran *m* **-s (der) ~** Iran.
Iraner(in *f*) *m* **-s, -** Iranian.
iranisch *adj* Iranian.
irden *adj* earthenware, earthen ♦ **~e Waren** earthenware.
irdisch *adj* earthly *no adv* ♦ **den Weg alles I~en gehen** to go the way of all flesh.

Ire *m* **-n, -n** Irishman; Irish boy ◆ **die ~n** the Irish; **er ist ~** he is Irish.

irgend [1] *adv* at all ◆ **wenn ~ möglich, wenn es ~ geht** if it's at all possible; **was ich ~ kann ...** whatever I can ...; **wer (es) ~ kann, wer ~ es kann** whoever can; **so sanft wie ~ möglich** as gently as possible *or* as I/you *etc* possibly can; **so lange ich ~ kann** as long as I possibly can; **wo es ~ geht, wo ~ es geht** where it's at all possible, wherever (it's) possible.
[2] *mit indef pron* **~ jemand** somebody; (*fragend, verneinend, bedingend*) anybody; **ich bin nicht ~ jemand** I'm not just anybody; **~ etwas** something; (*fragend, verneinend, bedingend*) anything; **was zieh' ich an? — ~ etwas** what shall I wear? — anything, any old thing (*inf*); **~ so ein Tier** some animal; **ein Fuchs oder ~ so ein Tier** a fox or some such animal.

irgend|ein *indef pron* some; (*fragend, verneinend, bedingend*) any ◆ **er hat so ~ Schimpfwort verwendet** he used some swearword or other; **ich will nicht ~ Buch** I don't want just any (old *inf*) book; **haben Sie noch ~en Wunsch?** is there anything else you would like?; **das kann ~ anderer machen** somebody *or* someone else can do it.

irgend|eine(r, s) *indef pron* (*nominal*) (*bei Personen*) somebody, someone; (*bei Dingen*) something; (*fragend, verneinend, bedingend*) anybody, anyone/anything ◆ **welchen wollen Sie? — ~n** which one do you want? — any one, any old one (*inf*).

irgend|einmal *adv* some time or other, sometime; (*fragend, bedingend*) ever.

irgendwann *adv* sometime ◆ **~ werde ich wohl kommen** I'll come some time or other *or* sometime; **~ einmal** some time; (*fragend, bedingend*) ever.

irgendwas *indef pron* (*inf*) something; (*fragend, verneinend, bedingend*) anything ◆ **er murmelte so ~** he murmured something or other; **was soll ich sagen? — ~** what shall I say? — anything *or* any old thing (*inf*).

irgendwelche(r, s) *indef pron* some; (*fragend, verneinend, bedingend, jede beliebige*) any ◆ **sind noch ~ Reste da?** is there still something left?, is there anything left?

irgendwer *indef pron* (*inf*) *siehe* **irgend 2.**

irgendwie *adv* somehow (or other) ◆ **ist es ~ möglich?** is it at all possible?; **kannst du dir das ~ vorstellen?** can you possibly imagine it?; **ich hab' das ~ schon mal gesehen** I've just got a feeling I've seen it before; **das macht man nicht ~** you shouldn't do that just anyhow *or* any old how (*inf*).

irgendwo *adv* somewhere (or other), someplace (*esp US inf*); (*fragend, verneinend, bedingend*) anywhere, any place (*esp US inf*).

irgendwoher *adv* from somewhere (or other), from someplace (*esp US inf*); (*fragend, verneinend, bedingend*) from anywhere *or* any place (*esp US inf*).

irgendwohin *adv* somewhere (or other), someplace (*esp US inf*); (*fragend, verneinend, bedingend*) anywhere, any place (*esp US inf*).

Iridium *nt, no pl* (*abbr* **Ir**) iridium.

Irin *f* Irishwoman; Irish girl ◆ **sie ist ~** she is Irish.

Iris *f* **-, -** *or* (*Opt auch*) **Iriden** iris.

irisch *adj* Irish ◆ **~-römisches Bad** Turkish bath; **I~e See** Irish Sea.

Iris-: ~diagnostik *f* iridology; **~diagnostiker** *m* iridologist.

irisieren* *vi* to iridesce ◆ **~d** iridescent.

Irland *nt* **-s** Ireland; (*Republik* ~) Eire.

irländisch *adj* Irish ◆ **I~es Moos** Irish moss.

Ironie *f* irony.

ironisch *adj* ironic, ironical.

ironisieren* *vt* to treat ironically.

irr *adj siehe* **irr(e).**

irrational ['ɪratsiona:l] *adj* irrational (*auch Math*).

Irrationalismus *m* irrationalism.

irr(e) [1] *adj* **(a)** (*geistesgestört*) mad, crazy, insane; *Blick auch* crazed, demented, wild ◆ **das macht mich ganz ~** it's driving me mad *or* crazy *or* insane; **jdn für ~ halten** (*inf*)/**erklären** (*inf*) to think sb is mad/to tell sb he/she *etc* is mad; **wie ~** (*fig inf*) like mad (*inf*) *or* crazy (*inf*); **~es Zeug reden** (*fig*) to say crazy things, to babble away.
(b) *pred* (*verwirrt, unsicher*) muddled, confused ◆ **an jdm/etw ~ werden** (*liter*) to lose (one's) faith in sb/sth.
(c) (*inf*) *Party, Hut* wild (*inf*), crazy (*inf*) ◆ **er war ~ angezogen** he was wearing outrageous clothes.
[2] *adv* **(a)** (*verrückt*) insanely, in a mad *or* insane way.
(b) (*sl: sehr*) incredibly (*inf*) ◆ **~ gut/hübsch** (*sl*) brilliant (*inf*)/real pretty (*inf*).

Irre *f* **-,** *no pl*: **jdn in die ~ führen** (*lit, fig*) to lead sb astray; **sich in die ~ führen lassen** (*lit, fig*) to be led astray, to be misled.

irreal *adj* unreal.

Irre-: i~führen *vt sep* to mislead; (*lit auch*) to lead astray; **sich i~führen lassen** to be misled *or* led astray; **i~führend** *adj* misleading; **~führung** *f* misleading; **durch bewußte ~führung der Öffentlichkeit** by deliberately misleading the public; **i~gehen** *vi sep irreg aux sein* **(a)** (*lit geh*) (*sich verirren*) to go astray, to lose one's way; (*umherirren*) to wander astray; **(b)** (*fig*) to be mistaken.

irregulär *adj* irregular.

Irregularität *f* irregularity.

irreleiten *vt sep* to mislead, to lead astray ◆ **irregeleitete Jugendliche** misguided youth; **~de Informationen** misleading information.

irrelevant ['ɪrelevant] *adj* irrelevant (*für* for, to).

Irrelevanz *f* irrelevance (*für* for, to).

irreligiös *adj* irreligious.

Irreligiosität *f* irreligion.

irremachen *vt sep* to confuse, to muddle.

▼ **irren** [1] *vi* **(a)** *aux sein* (*ziellos umherschweifen*) to wander, to stray, to roam.
(b) (*sich täuschen*) to be mistaken *or* wrong ◆ **I~ ist menschlich** (*Prov*) to err is human (*Prov*).

▼ [2] *vr* to be mistaken *or* wrong ◆ **jeder kann sich mal ~** anyone can make a mistake, everyone makes mistakes; **sich in jdm/etw ~** to be mistaken in *or* about sb/about sth, to be wrong about sb/sth; **wenn ich mich nicht irre ...** if I'm not mistaken ..., unless I'm very much mistaken ...; **ich irre mich nie!** I'm never wrong *or* mistaken!, I never make mistakes!

Irren-: ~anstalt *f* (*dated*) lunatic asylum (*dated*), loony-bin (*inf*); **~arzt** *m* (*old, pej*) psychiatrist; **~haus** *nt* (*dated, pej*) lunatic asylum (*dated*), loony-bin (*inf*); **hier geht es zu wie im ~haus** (*inf*) this place is an absolute madhouse; **i~hausreif** *adj* (*inf*) **i~hausreif sein** to be cracking up (*inf*).

irreparabel *adj* irreparable.

Irre(r) *mf decl as adj* lunatic; (*fig auch*) madman ◆ **ein armer ~r** (*hum inf*) a poor fool *or* idiot.

irrereden *vi sep* to rave, to rant, to talk dementedly.

Irr(e)sein *nt* insanity ◆ **manisch-depressives ~** manic depression, manic-depressive psychosis.

irreversibel ['ɪreverzi:bl] *adj* (*Phys, Biol*) irreversible.

Irr-: ~fahrt *f* wandering, odyssey (*liter*); **nach langer ~fahrt** after a long period of wandering (*auch fig*); **~gang** *m* (*lit*) blind alley (*in maze, pyramid*); (*fig, usu pl*) maze, labyrinth; **die ~gänge des Gebäudes** the maze *or* labyrinth of corridors in the building; **~garten** *m* maze, labyrinth; **~glaube(n)** *m* (*Rel*) heretical belief, heresy (*auch fig*); (*irrige Ansicht*) mistaken belief; **i~gläubig** *adj* heretical; **die ~gläubigen** the heretics.

irrig *adj* incorrect, wrong, false.

irrigerweise *adv* wrongly, incorrectly ◆ **etw ~ glauben** to believe sth mistakenly *or* wrongly.

irritieren* *vt* (*verwirren*) to confuse, to muddle; (*ärgern*) to irritate.

Irr-: ~läufer *m* **(a)** *stray letter, document etc delivered to the wrong address*; **(b)** (*Mil*) stray bullet/grenade *etc*; **~lehre** *f* heresy, heretical *or* false doctrine; **~licht** *nt* jack o'lantern, will-o'-the-wisp; **i~lichtern** *vi insep* to flit about; **der i~lichternde Künstler** the erratic artist.

Irrsinn *m, no pl* madness, insanity ◆ **das ist ja ~!** (*inf*) that's (sheer *or* absolute) madness *or* lunacy!; **auf den ~ verfallen, etw zu tun** to have the mad *or* crazy idea of doing sth.

irrsinnig *adj* mad, crazy, insane; (*inf: stark*) terrific, tremendous ◆ **wie ein I~er** like a madman; **das Kind schrie wie ~** the child yelled like mad (*inf*) *or* like crazy (*inf*); **ein ~er Verkehr** (*inf*) a terrific *or* a crazy (*inf*) amount of traffic; **~ viele Leute** (*inf*) a tremendous *or* terrific number of people.

Irrsinnigkeit *f* madness, craziness, insanity.

Irrsinns- *in cpds* (*inf*) terrific, tremendous; **~hitze** *f* (*inf*) **da ist eine ~hitze** the heat there is absolutely incredible; **~verkehr** *m* (*inf*) **da ist ein ~verkehr** there's a crazy (*inf*) *or* terrific amount of traffic there; **~tat** *f* insanity.

Irrtum *m* mistake, error ◆ **ein ~ von ihm** a mistake on his part; **im ~ sein, sich im ~ befinden** to be wrong *or* mistaken, to be in error; **~!** wrong!, you're wrong there!; **~, ich war es gar nicht!** that's where you're wrong *or* you're wrong there, it wasn't me!; **~ vorbehalten!** (*Comm*) errors excepted; **einen ~ zugeben** to admit to (having made) a mistake *or* an error; **jdm einen ~ nachweisen** to show that sb has made a mistake.

irrtümlich [1] *adj attr* mistaken, erroneous.
[2] *adv* mistakenly, erroneously; (*aus Versehen*) by mistake.

irrtümlicherweise *adv* mistakenly, erroneously; (*aus Versehen*) by mistake.

Irrung *f* (*liter*) **die ~en und Wirrungen meines Lebens** the aberrations of my life; *siehe* **Irrtum.**

Irr-: ~weg *m* **(a)** wandering *or* tortuous path; (*~fahrt*) wandering; **(b)** (*fig*) **auf dem ~weg sein** to be on the wrong track; **zu studieren erwies sich für ihn als ~weg** going to university turned out to be a mistake for him; **auf ~wege geraten** to go astray, to leave the straight and narrow; **~wisch** *m* **-es, -e** **(a)** *siehe* **Irrlicht**; **(b)** (*lebhafter Mensch*) imp.

-is *adj suf* (*Mus*) sharp.

ISBN [i:|ɛsbe:'|ɛn] *f abbr of* **Internationale Standard-Buchnummer** ISBN.

Ischias *m or nt* **-,** *no pl* sciatica.

Ischiasnerv *m* sciatic nerve.

ISDN [i:|ɛsde:'|ɛn] *abbr of* **Integrated Services Digital Network** (*Telec*) ISDN.

ISDN-Netz *nt* ISDN network.

Isegrim *m* **-s, -e** (*Liter*) the big bad wolf.

Islam *m* **-s,** *no pl* Islam.

islamisch *adj* Islamic.

Islamisierung *f, no pl* Islamization.

Island *nt* **-s** Iceland.

Isländer(in *f***)** *m* **-s, -** Icelander.

isländisch *adj* Icelandic ◆ **I~es Moos** Iceland moss.

Isländisch(e) *nt* Icelandic; *siehe auch* **Deutsch(e).**

Ismus *m* **-, Ismen** (*pej*) ism.

Isobare *f* **-, -n** isobar.

isochron [izo'kro:n] *adj* isochronal, isochronous.

Isochronismus [izokro'nɪsmʊs] *m* isochronism.

Iso-Drink *m* **-s, -s** isotonic drink.

Isolation *f* **(a)** (*das Absondern, Isolieren*) isolation (*auch Med, Biol*); (*von Häftlingen auch*) putting in solitary confinement; (*das Isoliertsein*) isolation (*auch Med, Biol*); (*von Häftlingen*) solitary confinement ◆ **die Studenten protestierten gegen die ~ politischer Häftlinge** the students protested against political prisoners' being put in solitary confinement.
(b) (*Elec, gegen Lärm, Kälte etc*) insulation; (*von Wasserleitung, Boiler, Speicher auch*) lagging.

➤ SPRACHE AKTIV: **irren: 2 → 39.1**

Isolationismus *m* isolationism.
Isolations-: ~folter *(pej)*, **~haft** *f* solitary confinement.
Isolator *m* insulator.
Isolierband *nt* insulating tape *(Brit)*, friction tape *(US)*.
isolierbar *adj* isolable; *(Tech)* insulable.
Isolierbox *f (für Getränke etc)* cooler box.
isolieren* [1] *vt* **(a)** *(absondern)* to isolate *(auch Med, Biol)*; *Häftlinge auch* to put in(to) solitary confinement ◆ **jdn isoliert halten** to keep sb in isolation *or* isolated/in solitary confinement; **völlig isoliert leben** to live in complete isolation, to live isolated from the world; **ein Problem isoliert betrachten** to look at a problem in isolation. **(b)** *elektrische Leitungen, Häuser, Fenster* to insulate; *Wasserleitungen, Speicher auch* to lag.
[2] *vr* to isolate oneself *or* cut oneself off (from the world).
Isolier-: ~fenster *nt* double-glazed window; **~haft** *f siehe* **Isolationshaft**; **~kanne** *f* thermos ® flask, vacuum flask; **~material** *nt* insulating material; *(für Wasserleitungen, Speicher auch)* lagging; **~schicht** *f* insulating layer; **~station** *f* isolation ward.
Isoliertheit *f* isolatedness.
Isolierung *f siehe* **Isolation.**
Iso-Matte *f* foam mattress, Karrimat ®.
Isomerie *f* isomerism.
Isometrie *f* isometry.
isometrisch *adj* isometric.
isomorph *adj* isomorphic; *Kristalle auch* isomorphous.
Isotherme *f* **-, -n** isotherm.
isotonisch *adj* isotonic ◆ **~ Getränke** isotonic drinks.
Isotop *nt* **-s, -e** isotope.

Israel ['ɪsraɛl] *nt* **-s** Israel ◆ **das Volk ~** the people of Israel.
Israeli[1] *m* **-(s), -(s)** Israeli.
Israeli[2] **-, -(s), Israelin** *f* Israeli.
israelisch *adj* Israeli.
Israelit *m* **-en, -en** Israelite.
israelitisch *adj* Israelite.
⚠ **iß** *imper sing of* **essen.**
ist *3. pers sing present of* **sein**[1].
Istanbul *nt* **-s** Istanbul.
⚠ **Ist-Bestand** *m (Geld)* cash in hand; *(Waren)* actual stock.
Isthmus *m* **-, Isthmen** isthmus.
Ist-: ~stärke *f (Mil)* actual *or* effective strength; **~wert** *m* actual value.
Itaker *m* **-s, -** *(pej)* dago *(pej)*, Eyetie *(pej)*.
Italien [-iən] *nt* **-s** Italy.
Italiener(in *f*) [-'lieːnɐ, -ərɪn] *m* **-s, -** Italian.
italienisch [-'lieːnɪʃ] *adj* Italian ◆ **die ~e Schweiz** Italian-speaking Switzerland.
Italienisch(e) [-'lieːnɪʃ(ə)] *nt* Italian; *siehe auch* **Deutsch(e).**
Italowestern *m* spaghetti western.
iterativ *adj (Gram)* iterative.
⚠ **I-Tüpfelchen** *nt* dot (on the/an i) ◆ **bis aufs ~** *(fig)* (right) down to the last (little) detail.
Itzig *m* **-(e)s, -e** *(dated pej)* Yid *(pej)*, Jewboy *(pej)*.
i.V. [iː'fau] *abbr of* **in Vertretung; im Vorjahre; in Vorbereitung.**
Iwan *m* **-s,** *no pl (inf)* **der ~** *(Volk)* the Russkies *(inf) pl*; *(Mensch)* the Russky *(inf)*.
IWF [iːveː'|ɛf] *m* **-** *abbr of* **Internationaler Währungsfonds** IMF.

J

J, j [jɔt, (*Aus*) jeː] *nt* J, j.

ja *adv* **(a)** (*zustimmend*) yes, yeah (*inf*); aye (*dial, Scot, Parl*); yea (*US Parl*); (*bei Trauung*) I do ◆ **kommst du morgen?** — **~** are you coming tomorrow? — yes(, I am); **haben Sie das gesehen?** — **~** did you see it? — yes(, I did); **ich glaube ~** (yes) I think so; **sagen Sie doch ~** please say yes; **zu etw ~ sagen** to say yes to sth; **~ und amen zu etw sagen** (*inf*) to agree (slavishly) with sth; **wenn ~** if so; **~! ~!, riefen die Zuschauer** go on! go on!, shouted the crowd.
(b) (*fragend*) really? **er war gestern da — ~?** he was there yesterday — really?, was he?; **ich habe gekündigt — ~?** I've quit — have you?, really?; **~, bitte?** yes?, hello?
(c) (*feststellend*) **aber ~!** yes, of course, but of course; **ach ~!** oh yes; **nun ~** oh well; **kann ich reinkommen? — ~ bitte** can I come in? — Yes, do; **~ doch** *or* **freilich** *or* **gewiß** yes, of course; **~ so!** I see.
(d) (*zweifelnd, ungläubig*) really? **ich esse gern rohen Fisch — ~?** I like raw fish — really?, do you?; **er braucht keinen Urlaub, er arbeitet lieber — ~?** he doesn't need any holiday, he'd rather work — really?, would he?
(e) (*unbedingt*) **komm ~ pünktlich!** be punctual; **sei ~ vorsichtig!** be careful; **vergessen Sie es *ja* nicht!** don't forget, whatever you do!; **tu das *ja* nicht, ich warne dich!** just don't do that, I'm warning you.
(f) (*einräumend, schließlich*) **es ist ~ noch früh** it's still early (after all); **sie ist ~ erst fünf** (after all) she's only five; **es ist ~ nicht so schlimm** it's not really as bad as all that, (after all) it's not that bad; **das ist ~ richtig, aber ...** that's (certainly) right, but ...; **ich kann es ~ mal versuchen, aber ...** I could always try it, but ...
(g) (*als Steigerung*) even, nay (*liter*) ◆ **das ist gut, ~ sogar sehr gut** it's good, in fact it's even very good.
(h) (*feststellend*) **da hat man's ~, da haben wir's ~** there you are (then); **da kommt er ~** there *or* here he is; **das ist es ~** that's just it; **hier *ist* ~ Herr Meier** here's Mr Meier himself; **~, was haben wir denn hier?** well, what have we here?; **das sag' ich ~!** that's just what I say; **das wissen wir ~ alle** we all know that (anyway); **Sie wissen ~, daß ...** you (already) know that ..., as you know ...; **Sie wissen ~, wie das so ist** you know how it is, (don't you?).
(i) (*verstärkend, wirklich*) just ◆ **das ist ~ fürchterlich** that's (just) terrible, terrible, that's what it is!; **das weiß man ~ eben nie vorher** you just never know in advance.
(j) (*aber*) **~, sagen Sie mal** now look here; **~, was du nicht sagst!** you don't say!
(k) (*vergewissernd*) right?, OK? ◆ **du kommst doch morgen, ~?** you're coming tomorrow, right *or* aren't you?; **du rufst mich doch an, ~?** you'll give me a call, right *or* OK *or* won't you?; **das ist also abgemacht, ~?** that's agreed then, right *or* OK?

Ja *nt* **-s, -(s)** yes; aye (*dial, Scot, Parl*); yea (*US Parl*) ◆ **mit ~ antworten/stimmen** to answer/vote yes; **ein ~ zum Kind/Frieden** a vote in favour of children/peace; **das ~ vor dem Traualtar sprechen** to say "I do" at the altar.

Jabo *m* **-s, -s** *abbr of* **Jagdbomber.**

Jacht *f* **-, -en** yacht.

Jacht-: ~klub *m* yacht club; **~sport** *m* yachting, sailing.

jäck *adj* (*dial*) crazy.

Jäckchen *nt* **(a)** *dim of* **Jacke** little jacket. **(b)** (*Baby~*) matinée jacket.

Jacke *f* **-, -n** jacket, coat (*esp US*); (*Woll~*) cardigan; (*Comm: Unterhemd*) vest (*Brit*), undershirt (*US*) ◆ **das ist ~ wie Hose** (*inf*) it doesn't make any difference (either way), it's six of one and half a dozen of the other (*inf*); **jdm die ~ vollhauen** (*inf*) to give sb a thrashing; **sich** (*dat*) **die/eine ~ anziehen** (*fig inf*) to take sth personally; **wem die ~ paßt ...** (*fig inf*) if the cap fits ...

Jacken-: ~kleid *nt* (*Kostüm*) costume, suit, two-piece; (*Kleid und Jacke*) two-piece; **~tasche** *f* jacket *or* coat (*esp US*) pocket.

Jacketkrone [ˈdʒɛkɪt-] *f* (*Zahnheilkunde*) jacket crown.

Jackett [ʒaˈkɛt] *nt* **-s, -s** jacket, coat (*esp US*).

⚠ **Jackettasche** *f getrennt:* **Jackett-tasche** jacket *or* coat (*esp US*) pocket.

Jackpot [ˈdʒɛkpɔt] *m* **-s, -s** (*im Lotto etc*) rollover jackpot; **den ~ knacken** to hit the jackpot.

Jacquardmuster [ʒaˈkaːr-] *nt* Jacquard weave.

Jade *m or f* **-,** *no pl* jade.

jadegrün *adj* jade green.

Jagd *f* **-, -en (a)** hunt; (*Ausführung der ~*) hunting; (*mit dem Gewehr auch*) shoot, shooting; (*fig: Verfolgung*) hunt (*nach* for), chase (*nach* after); (*Wettlauf*) race ◆ **die ~ auf Rotwild/Fasanen** deer-/pheasant-hunting; **hohe/niedere ~** big/small game-hunting; **auf der ~ sein/auf die ~ (nach etw) gehen** (*lit, fig*) to be/to go hunting (for sth), to be on the hunt (for sth); **auf jdn/etw ~ machen** (*lit, fig*) to hunt for sb/sth; **von der ~ leben** to live by hunting; **ein Buch über die ~** a book about hunting; **die ~ nach Geld/Glück** *etc* the pursuit of *or* quest for money/fortune *etc*; **in wilder ~ sprengten sie über die Brücke** in their wild chase they charged over the bridge.
(b) (*~revier*) preserve, shoot.
(c) (*Wildbestand*) game.
(d) (*~gesellschaft*) hunt, hunting *or* shooting party.

Jagd-: ~aufseher *m* (*Angestellter*) gamekeeper; (*Beamter*) game warden; **j~bar** *adj* ... **sind j~bar** ... may be hunted, ... are fair game; **~beute** *f* bag; **~bomber** *m* (*Mil*) fighter-bomber; **~flieger** *m* (*Mil*) fighter pilot; **~flinte** *f* hunting rifle, sporting gun *or* rifle, shotgun; **~flugzeug** *nt* (*Mil*) fighter plane *or* aircraft; **~frevel** *m* (*form*) poaching; **~frevler** *m* (*form*) poacher; **~gebiet** *nt* hunting ground; **~geschwader** *nt* (*Mil*) fighter squadron; **~gesellschaft** *f* hunt, hunting *or* shooting party; **~gewehr** *nt* hunting rifle, sporting gun *or* rifle, shotgun; **~glück** *nt* good luck *or* fortune in hunting; **wir hatten kein ~glück** we didn't bag anything; **~göttin** *f* goddess of hunting *or* the hunt *or* the chase (*liter*); **~gründe** *pl*: **in die ewigen ~gründe eingehen** to go to the happy hunting-grounds; **~haus** *nt* hunting lodge; **~herr** *m* owner of a/the hunting ground; **~horn** *nt* hunting horn; **~hund** *m* hunting dog; **~hütte** *f siehe* **~haus**; **~messer** *nt* hunting knife; **~pächter** *m* game tenant; **~recht** *nt* **(a)** hunting *or* shooting rights *pl*; **(b)** (*~bestimmungen*) game laws *pl*; **~rennen** *nt* steeplechase; **~revier** *nt* shoot; (*von Indianern etc*) preserve; **~schaden** *m* damage caused by hunting; **~schein** *m* hunting/shooting licence; **einen ~schein haben** (*hum sl*) to be certified (*inf*); ⚠**~schloß** *nt* hunting lodge; **~schutz** *m* **(a)** (*Hunt*) game protection; **(b)** (*Mil*) fighter cover; **~staffel** *f* (*Mil*) fighter flight; **~tasche** *f* game bag; **~verbot** *nt* ban on hunting; (*als Strafe*) ban from hunting; **~wesen** *nt* hunting; **~wild** *nt* game; **~wurst** *f* smoked sausage; **~zeit** *f* hunting/shooting season.

jagen [1] *vt* **(a)** *Tier, Menschen* to hunt.
(b) (*hetzen*) to chase, to drive; (*treiben*) *Wild* to drive ◆ **jdn in die Flucht ~** to put sb to flight; **jdn zu Tode ~** to hound sb to death; **jdn aus dem Bett ~** (*inf*) to chase sb out of bed; **jdn aus dem Haus ~** to drive *or* chase sb out of the house; **jdm eine Spritze in den Arm ~** (*inf*) to stick a needle in sb's arm; **ein Unglück jagte das andere** one misfortune followed hard on (the heels of) the other; **Geld/Benzin durch den Auspuff ~** (*inf*) to burn money/a lot of juice (*inf*); **sein ganzes Geld durch die Kehle ~** to booze all one's money away (*inf*); **mit diesem Essen kannst du mich ~** (*inf*) I wouldn't eat this if you paid me.
(c) (*erlegen*) to bag.
[2] *vi* **(a)** (*auf die Jagd gehen*) to hunt, to go hunting; (*mit dem Gewehr auch*) to shoot, to go shooting.
(b) *aux sein* (*rasen*) to race ◆ **nach etw ~** to chase after sth; **in ~der Eile** in great haste.
[3] *vr* (*Geschehnisse etc*) to follow one on the heels of the other.

Jäger *m* **-s, - (a)** hunter, huntsman ◆ **~ und Sammler** hunters and gatherers. **(b)** (*Mil*) (*Gebirgs~*) rifleman; (*Jagdflieger*) fighter pilot; (*Sportflugzeug*) fighter (plane).

Jägerbataillon *nt* rifle battalion.

Jägerei *f, no pl* hunting; (*mit dem Gewehr auch*) shooting.

Jägerhut *m* Tyrolean hat.

Jägerin *f* huntress, huntswoman.

Jäger-: ~latein *nt* (*inf*) hunters' yarns *pl*; **jdm ~latein auftischen** to tell sb tall stories about one's hunting exploits; **~schnitzel** *nt* veal/pork with mushrooms and peppers.

Jägersmann *m, pl* **-leute** (*dated, liter*) hunter, huntsman.

Jäger-: ~sprache *f* hunter's jargon; **~zaun** *m* rustic fence.

Jaguar *m* **-s, -e** jaguar.

jäh(e) *adj* (*geh*) **(a)** (*plötzlich*) sudden; *Schmerz auch* sharp; (*unvermittelt*) *Wechsel, Ende, Bewegung auch* abrupt; *Flucht auch* headlong, precipitous. **(b)** (*steil*) sheer ◆ **der Abhang steigt ~ an/fällt ~ herab** the slope rises/falls sharply *or* steeply *or* plunges *or* plummets down.

jählings *adv* (*liter*) **(a)** (*plötzlich*) suddenly; *aufhören, abbrechen auch* abruptly;

(*fliehen*) headlong. **(b)** (*steil*) steeply, precipitously; (*hinabfallen*) headlong.

Jahr *nt* **-(e)s, -e** **(a)** year ◆ **ein halbes ~** six months *sing or pl*; **ein dreiviertel ~** nine months *sing or pl*; **anderthalb ~e** one and a half years *sing*, eighteen months *sing or pl*; **zwei ~e Garantie** a two-year guarantee; **im ~(e) 1066** in (the year) 1066; **die sechziger ~e** the sixties *sing or pl*; **alle ~e** every year; **alle zehn ~e** every ten years; **ein ~ ums andere** year after year; **auf ~e hinaus** for years ahead; **auf ~ und Tag** to the very day; **einmal im ~(e)** once a year; **das ganze ~ über** all year (round *or* through); **pro ~** a year, per annum; **das Buch des ~es** the book of the year; **noch nach ~en** years later; **nach ~ und Tag** after (many) years; **vor ~ und Tag** (many) years ago; **seit ~ und Tag** for years; **mit den ~en** as (the) years go by, over the years; **zwischen den ~en** (*inf*) between Christmas and New Year.

(b) (*Alter, Lebens~*) **er ist zehn ~e (alt)** he is ten years old; **mit dreißig ~en, in seinem dreißigsten ~** (*liter*) at the age of thirty, in his thirtieth year (*liter*); **Personen über 18 ~e/unter 18 ~en** people over/under (the age of) 18; **in die ~e kommen** (*inf*) to be getting on (in years); **man sieht ihm seine ~e nicht an** his age doesn't *or* his years don't show; **in den besten ~en sein** *or* **stehen** to be in the prime of one's life; **mit den ~en** as one gets older.

jahr|aus *adv*: **~, jahrein** year in, year out.

Jahrbuch *nt* yearbook; (*Ausgabe einer Sammlung etc*) annual; (*Kalender*) almanac.

Jährchen *nt* (*hum inf*) year.

jahrelang [1] *adj attr* lasting for years ◆ **~es Warten/~e Planungen/ Forschungen** years of waiting/planning/research.

[2] *adv* for years ◆ **und dann dauerte es noch ~, bevor ...** and then it took years until ...; **schon ~ verspricht man uns ...** they've been promising us ... for years.

jähren *vr* **heute jährt sich der Tag, daß ...** *or* **an dem ...** it's a year ago today that ...; **der Tag jährt sich zum dritten Mal, daß ...** *or* **an dem ...** it's three years ago that ...

Jahres- *in cpds* annual, yearly; ⚠**~abschluß** *m* **(a)** (*Comm*) annual accounts *pl*; **(b)** (*~ende*) end of the year; **~anfang** *m siehe* **~beginn**; **~ausgleich** *m* (*Fin*) *siehe* **Lohnsteuerjahresausgleich**; **~ausklang** *m* (*geh*) **zum ~ausklang** to see the old year out; **~beginn** *m* beginning of a/the new year; **~beitrag** *m* annual *or* yearly subscription; **~bericht** *m* annual *or* yearly report; **~bestzeit** *f* (*Sport*) best time of the year; **~bilanz** *f* (*Comm*) annual balance sheet; **~einkommen** *nt* annual income; **~ende** *nt* end of the year; **~feier** *f* anniversary; (*Feierlichkeiten*) anniversary celebrations *pl*; **~frist** *f*: **binnen/ nach ~frist** within/after (a period of) one year; **~gehalt** *nt* annual salary; **~hauptversammlung** *f* (*Comm*) annual general meeting, AGM; **~karte** *f* annual season ticket; **~mitte** *f* middle of the year; **~mittel** *nt* (*Met*) average annual temperature; **~netzkarte** *f ticket giving one year's unlimited travel*; **~ring** *m* (*eines Baumes*) annual ring; **~tag** *m* anniversary; **~umsatz** *m* (*Comm*) annual *or* yearly turnover; **~urlaub** *m* annual holiday *or* leave; **~wagen** *m* one-year-old car; **~wechsel** *m*, **~wende** *f* new year; **jdm zum ~wechsel Glück wünschen** to wish sb a happy New Year; **~zahl** *f* date, year; **~zeit** *f* season; **für die ~zeit zu kalt** cold for the time of year.

Jahr-: ~fünft *nt* **-(e)s, -e** five years *pl*, quinquennium (*form*); **~gang** *m* **(a)** (*Sch, Univ*) year; **er ist ~gang 1970** he was born in 1970; **die ~gänge 1970-73** the 1970-73 age-group; **er ist mein/wir sind ein ~gang** we were born in the same year; (*als Schulabgänger etc*) we were in the same year; **(b)** (*alle Zeitschriften etc von einem Jahr*) year's issues *pl*; (*einer Fachzeitschrift*) volume; **Nr. 20, ~gang 31** No. 20, 31st year; **Spiegel, ~gang 1980** Spiegel of the year *or* for 1980; **(c)** (*von Wein*) vintage, year; **~hundert** *nt* **-s, -e** century; **das ~hundert der Aufklärung** the Age of Enlightenment; **~hunderte haben die Menschen ...** for centuries men have ...

jahrhunderte-: ~alt *adj* centuries-old; **~lang** [1] *adj* lasting for centuries; **eine ~lange Entwicklung** centuries of development; [2] *adv* for centuries.

Jahrhundert-: ~feier *f* centenary; (*Feierlichkeiten*) centenary celebrations *pl*; **~wende** *f* turn of the century.

-jährig *adj suf* **(a)** (*... Jahre alt*) -year-old ◆ **ein Fünf~er** a five-year-old.

(b) (*Jahre dauernd*) years of ◆ **nach elf~en Verhandlungen** after eleven years of negotiations; **nach drei~er Verspätung** after a three-year delay.

(c) (*Ordinalzahl*) anniversary of ◆ **der 70~e Gründungstag** the 70th anniversary (of the foundation).

jährlich [1] *adj* annual, yearly.

[2] *adv* every year, annually, yearly; (*Comm*) per annum ◆ **einmal/zweimal ~** once/twice a year *or* yearly.

Jährling *m* yearling.

Jahrmarkt *m* (fun-)fair ◆ **~ der Eitelkeiten** (*liter*) vanity fair.

Jahrmarkts-: ~bude *f* booth *or* stall (at a fairground); (*Schaubude*) sideshow; **~künstler** *m* fair-ground artiste.

Jahr-: ~millionen *pl* millions of years; **j~millionenlang** [1] *adj* millions of years of; [2] *adv* for millions of years; **~tausend** *nt* **-s, -e** millennium, a thousand years; **in unserem ~tausend** in our millennium; **~tausende** thousands of years; **j~tausendelang** [1] *adj* thousands of years of; [2] *adv* for millennia *or* thousands of years; **~tausendfeier** *f* millennium; (*Feierlichkeiten*) millennium celebrations *pl*; **~zehnt** *nt* **-(e)s, -e** decade; **j~zehntelang** [1] *adj* decades of; [2] *adv* for decades.

Jahve, Jahwe ['ja:va] *m* **-s** Jehovah, Yahweh (*rare*).

Jähzorn *m* violent temper; (*plötzlicher Ausbruch*) outburst of temper, violent outburst ◆ **im ~** in a violent temper *or* rage; **zum ~ neigen** to be prone to violent outbursts (of temper).

jähzornig *adj* violent-tempered, irascible; (*~ erregt*) furious, in a violent temper ◆ **er ist manchmal so ~, daß ...** he sometimes becomes so furious *or* gets into such a violent temper that ...

Jakob *m* **-s** James; (*Bibl*) Jacob; *siehe* **wahr**.

Jakobiner(in *f*) *m* **-s, -** (*Hist*) Jacobin; (*Rel auch*) Dominican.

Jakobinermütze *f* liberty cap.

Jakobsleiter *f* (*Bibl, Bot*) Jacob's ladder; (*Naut auch*) rope ladder.

Jakobus *m* **-** James.

Jalousie [ʒalu'zi:] *f* venetian blind.

Jamaika *nt* **-s** Jamaica.

Jamaikaner(in *f*) *m* **-s, -** Jamaican.

jamaikanisch *adj* Jamaican.

Jambendichtung *f* iambic poetry.

Jambus *m* **-, Jamben** (*Poet*) iamb(us), iambic foot.

jambisch *adj* (*Poet*) iambic.

Jammer *m* **-s,** *no pl* **(a)** (*Elend*) misery, wretchedness ◆ **ein Bild des ~s bieten** *or* **sein** to be the picture of misery; **der ~ überkam ihn** a feeling of misery came over him; **es ist ein ~, diesen Verfall mit ansehen zu müssen** it is a wretched thing *or* heart-breaking to have to watch this decay; **es wäre ein ~, wenn ...** (*inf*) it would be a crying shame if ... (*inf*).

(b) (*Klage*) wailing, lamentation.

Jammer-: ~bild *nt* (*geh*) picture of misery, piteous *or* wretched sight; **~geschrei** *nt* (*inf*) *siehe* **Jammer (b)**; **~gestalt** *f* wretched figure; **~lappen** *m* (*sl*) wet (*sl*), sissy (*inf*).

jämmerlich [1] *adj* wretched, pitiful; (*beklagenswert auch*) *Zustand* lamentable, deplorable; (*inf*) *Erklärung, Bericht, Entschuldigung etc* pitiful, pathetic (*inf*).

[2] *adv* (*inf: sehr*) terribly (*inf*).

Jämmerlichkeit *f* wretchedness.

jammern [1] *vi* to wail (*über +acc* over); (*sich beklagen auch*) to moan, to yammer (*inf*) ◆ **nach jdm/etw ~** to whine *or* yammer (*inf*) for sb/sth; **der Gefangene jammerte um Wasser** the prisoner begged pitifully *or* moaned for water.

[2] *vt* (*old*) to move to pity ◆ **er jammert mich** I feel sorry for him, I pity him.

Jammer-: j~schade *adj* **es ist j~schade** (*inf*) it's a terrible pity *or* a crying shame (*inf*); **~tal** *nt* (*Bibl, liter*) vale of tears (*liter*); **j~voll** *adj siehe* **jämmerlich**.

Janker *m* **-s, -** (*S Ger, Aus*) Tyrolean jacket; (*Strickjacke*) cardigan.

Jänner *m* **-s, -** (*Aus, Sw, S Ger*) January.

Januar *m* **-(s), -e** January; *siehe* **März**.

Janus- (*Myth, liter*): **~gesicht** *nt*, **~kopf** *m* Janus face; **j~gesichtig, j~köpfig** *adj* Janus-faced.

Japan *nt* **-s** Japan.

Japaner(in *f*) *m* **-s, -** Japanese.

japanisch *adj* Japanese.

Japanisch(e) *nt* Japanese; *siehe auch* **Deutsch(e)**.

Japanologe *m*, **Japanologin** *f* Japanese specialist; (*Student*) student of Japanese (studies).

Japanologie *f* Japanese studies.

jappen (*N Ger*), **japsen** *vi* (*inf*) to pant.

Jargon [ʒar'gõ:] *m* **-s, -s** jargon, slang, lingo (*inf*).

Jasager *m* **-s, -** yes-man.

Jasmin *m* **-s, -e** jasmine.

Jaspis *m* **-(ses), -se** jasper.

Jastimme *f* vote in favour (of), vote for; (*Parl auch*) aye (*Brit*), yea (*US*).

jäten *vti* to weed.

Jauche *f* **-,** *no pl* liquid manure; (*Med*) sanies (*form*), ichor (*form*); (*pej sl*) (*Getränk*) (pig-)swill, piss (*vulg*); (*Abwasser*) sewage ◆ **das stinkt wie ~** it stinks like nobody's business (*inf*), it stinks to high heaven.

Jauche(n)grube *f* cesspool, cesspit; (*Agr*) liquid manure pit.

jauchen *vti* to manure; (*Med*) to discharge (sanies *or* ichor).

Jauchewagen *m* liquid manure transporter *or* (*Karren*) cart.

jauchzen *vi* (*geh*) to rejoice (*liter*), to exult (*liter*); (*Publikum*) to cheer; (*Kinder*) to shout and cheer; (*Säugling*) to chuckle, to laugh.

Jauchzer *m* **-s, -** jubilant cheer *or* shout ◆ **sie stieß einen lauten, begeisterten ~ aus** she gave a loud yippee (*inf*), she cheered.

jaulen *vi* (*lit, fig*) to howl; (*lit*) to yowl.

Jause *f* **-, -n** (*Aus*) break (for a snack); (*Proviant*) snack ◆ **eine ~ halten** *or* **machen** to stop for a snack.

jausen *vi* (*Aus*) to stop for a snack; (*in der Arbeitspause*) to have a tea break.

Jausenstation *f* (*Aus*) snack-bar.

Java ['ja:va] *nt* **-s** Java.

Javaner(in *f*) [ja'va:nɐ, -ərɪn] *m* **-s, -** Javanese.

javanisch [ja'va:nɪʃ] *adj* Javanese.

jawohl, jawoll (*hum, inf*) *adv* yes; (*Mil*) yes, sir; (*Naut*) aye, aye, sir ◆ **stimmt das wirklich? — ~** is that really right? — yes, it is, yes, indeed; **haben Sie 50 DM gesagt? — ~** did you say 50 marks? — right *or* correct *or* I did *or* I did indeed.

Jawort *nt* **jdm das ~ geben** to consent to marry sb, to say yes to sb; (*bei Trauung*) to say "I do"; **sich** *or* **einander das ~ geben** to get married.

Jazz [dʒæz, dʒɛs, jats] *m* **-,** *no pl* jazz.

Jazz- *in cpds* jazz.

Jazzer ['dʒɛsɐ, 'jatsɐ] *m* **-s, -** (*inf*) jazz-man (*inf*).

Jazzkeller *m* jazz club.

je[1] [1] *adv* **(a)** (*jemals*) ever.

(b) (*jeweils*) every, each ◆ **für ~ drei Stück zahlst du eine Mark** you pay one mark for (every) three; **~ zwei Schüler aus jeder Klasse** two children from each class; **ich gebe euch ~ zwei Äpfel** I'll give you two apples each *or* each

⚠: for details of spelling reform, see supplement

of you two apples; **sie zahlten ~ eine Mark** they paid one mark each, each (of them) paid one mark.
[2] *prep +acc* (*pro*) per ◆ **~ Person zwei Stück** two per person; **~ zehn Exemplare ein Freiexemplar** one free copy for every ten copies.
[3] *conj* **(a) ~ eher, desto** *or* **um so besser** the sooner the better; **~ länger, ~ lieber** the longer the better.
(b) ~ nach according to, depending on; **~ nach Wunsch** just as one wishes; **~ nachdem** it all depends; **~ nachdem, wie gut man arbeitet ...** depending on how well you work ...

je[2] *interj* **ach** *or* **o ~!** oh dear!; **o ~!** (*old*) alas! (*old, Bibl, liter*); **~ nun** (*dated*) oh, well.

Jeans [dʒi:nz] *pl* jeans *pl*.

Jeans- *in cpds* denim; **~anzug** *m* denim suit; **~stoff** *m* denim.

Jeck *m* **-en, -en** (*dial*) *siehe* **Narr.**

jedenfalls *adv* anyhow, in any case; (*zumindest*) at least, at any rate ◆ **~ ist es schon zu spät** it's too late now anyhow *or* in any case; **er ist nicht gekommen, aber er hat sich ~ entschuldigt** he didn't come but at least *or* at any rate he apologized *or* he did at least *or* at any rate apologize; **ob er krank ist, weiß ich nicht, ~ ist er nicht gekommen** I don't know whether he's ill or not, at any rate *or* in any case *or* anyhow he didn't come; **er sagte nichts über den Mord, ~ nichts Neues** he said nothing about the murder, or at any rate *or* at least nothing new; **er ist nicht reif zum Studieren, ~ jetzt noch nicht** he's not mature enough to study, at least *or* at any rate not yet; **ich weiß nicht, ob das nötig ist, ~ ist es hier so üblich** I don't know if it's necessary, but it's what we do here (anyhow *or* at any rate).

jede(r, s) *indef pron* **(a)** (*adjektivisch*) (*einzeln*) each; (*von zweien auch*) either; (*~ von allen*) every; (*~r beliebige*) any ◆ **~ von beiden kann sich verspäten** either of them could be late; **das weiß doch ~s Kind** any *or* a child knows that, any *or* a child could tell you that; **ohne ~ Anstrengung/Vorstellung** *etc* without any effort/idea, with no effort/idea *etc*; **zu ~r Stunde** at all times; **es kann ~n Augenblick passieren** it might happen any minute *or* at any moment; **fern von ~r Kultur** far from all civilization.
(b) (*substantivisch*) (*einzeln*) each (one); (*~ von allen*) everyone, everybody; (*~ beliebige*) anyone, anybody ◆ **~r von uns** each (one)/every one/any one of us; **ein ~r** (*liter*) each (one); **~r von uns beiden** each (one) of us; **er gab ~m von beiden ein Buch** he gave each *or* both of them a book; **~r zweite** every other *or* second one; **~r für sich** everyone for himself; **~r/~/~s für sich ist ganz nett, aber beide zusammen ...** each one by himself/herself/itself *or* each one alone is quite nice, but together ...; **geht jetzt ~r in sein Bett!** go to bed now, both/all of you; **das kann ~r/nicht ~r** anyone *or* anybody can do that/not everyone *or* everybody can do that; **er spricht nicht mit ~m** he doesn't speak to just anybody *or* anyone.

jedermann *indef pron* everyone, everybody; (*jeder, beliebige auch*) anyone, anybody ◆ **J~** (*Theat*) Everyman; **das ist nicht ~s Sache** it's not everyone's cup of tea (*inf*); **Herr/Frau J~** Mr/Mrs Average (Citizen).

jederzeit *adv* at any time ◆ **du kannst ~ kommen** you can come any time (you like); **ja, ~** sure, any time.

jedesmal *adv* every *or* each time ◆ **~, wenn sie ...** each *or* every time she ..., whenever she ...; **~ ist es so(, daß ...)** it happens every *or* each time (that ...).

jedoch *conj, adv* however ◆ **er verlor ~ die Nerven** he lost his nerve however *or* though.

jedwede(r, s) *indef pron* (*old*) *siehe* **jede(r, s).**

Jeep ® [dʒi:p] *m* **-s, -s** jeep.

jegliche(r, s) *indef pron* (*adjektivisch*) any; (*substantivisch*) (*old, liter: auch* **ein ~r**) each (one).

jeher ['je:he:ɐ] *adv*: **von** *or* **seit ~** always; **das ist schon seit ~ so** it has always been like that.

Jehova [je'ho:va] *m* **-s** Jehovah ◆ **die Zeugen ~s** Jehovah's witnesses.

jein *adv* (*hum*) yes and no.

Jelängerjelieber *nt* **-s, -** honeysuckle.

jemals *adv* ever.

jemand *indef pron* somebody, someone; (*bei Fragen, bedingenden Sätzen auch, Negation*) anybody, anyone ◆ **ist da ~?** is anybody *or* somebody there?; **du lachst so, hat dir ~ ein Kompliment gemacht?** why are you smiling? has somebody *or* someone paid you a compliment?; **ohne ~en zu fragen** without asking anybody *or* anyone; **ich brauche ~en, der mir den Fernseher repariert** I need somebody *or* someone to repair my television set; **~ Fremdes/Neues** a stranger/somebody *or* someone new.

jemine ['je:mine] *interj* (*old*) *siehe* **ojemine, herrjemine.**

Jenaer Glas ® ['je:naɐ-] *nt* Pyrex ®, heatproof glass.

jene(r, s) *dem pron* (*geh*) **(a)** (*adjektivisch*) that; *pl* those; (*der Vorherige, die Vorherigen*) the former ◆ **in ~m Leben** *or* **~r Welt** in the next life *or* world; **in ~n Tagen** in those days; (*zukünftig*) in those days ahead, in those days to come; **in ~r Zeit** at that time, in those times.
(b) (*substantivisch*) that one; *pl* those (ones); (*der Vorherige, die Vorherigen*) the former ◆ **bald dieser, bald ~r** first one then the other; **von diesem und ~m sprechen** to talk about this and that.

jenseitig *adj attr* opposite, other ◆ **die ~en Vororte** the suburbs on the other side; **das ~e Leben** the life hereafter, the life after death.

jenseits [1] *prep +gen* on the other side of ◆ **2 km ~ der Grenze** 2 kms beyond the border *or* the other side of the border.
[2] *adv* **~ von** on the other side of; **~ von Gut und Böse** beyond good and evil, over and above good and evil; (*hum inf*) past it (*inf*).

Jenseits *nt* **-, no pl** hereafter, next world ◆ **jdn ins ~ befördern** (*inf*) to send sb to kingdom come (*inf*).

Jeremias *m* **-** (*Bibl*) Jeremiah.

Jersey ['dʒø:ɐzi] *nt* **-** (*Geog*) Jersey.

Jesaja *m* **-s** (*Bibl*) Isaiah.

Jesses *interj* (*inf*) Jesus (*inf*).

Jesuit *m* **-en, -en** Jesuit.

Jesuiten-: ~orden *m* Jesuit Order; **~schule** *f* Jesuit school.

jesuitisch *adj* Jesuit.

Jesus *m gen* **Jesu,** *dat* **-** *or* **Jesu,** *acc* **-** *or* **Jesum** Jesus ◆ **~ Christus** Jesus Christ; **~, Maria (und Josef)!** (*dial inf*) holy Mary mother of God! (*dial inf*).

Jesus-: ~kind *nt*: **das ~kind** the Infant Jesus, the Christ Child; **~latschen** *pl* (*inf*) Jesus sandals *pl*.

Jet [dʒɛt] *m* **-(s), -s** (*inf*) jet.

Jetlag, Jet-lag ['dʒɛtlɛg] *m* jetlag ◆ **unter ~ leiden** to suffer from jetlag, to be jetlagged.

Jeton [ʒə'tõ:] *m* **-s, -s** chip.

Jet-set ['dʒɛtsɛt] *m* **-s,** (*rare*) **-s** (*inf*) jet-set.

jetten ['dʒɛtn] *vi aux sein* (*inf*) to jet (*inf*), to fly.

Jet-Zeit|alter *nt* (*inf*) jet age.

jetzig *adj attr* present *attr*, current ◆ **in der ~en Zeit** in our *or* present times; **im ~en Augenblick** at the present moment (in time).

jetzo *adv* (*obs*) *siehe* **jetzt.**

jetzt *adv* now; (*heutzutage auch*) nowadays ◆ **sie ist ~ in der Schweiz** she's in Switzerland now, she's now in Switzerland; **bis ~** so far; **ich bin ~ (schon) fünf Tage hier** I have been here five days now; **für ~** for now, for the present; **gleich ~, ~ gleich** right now, straight away; **schon ~** already; **~ schon?** already?; **~ noch?** (what) now?; **das ist noch ~ der Fall** it's still the case today; **~ oder nie!** (it's) now or never!; **habe ich ~ den Brief eingeworfen?** now did I post that letter?, did I post that letter now?

Jetzt *nt* **-, no pl** (*geh*) present.

Jetztzeit *f, no pl* (*geh*) present (time), modern times *pl* *or* age.

jew. *abbr of* **jeweils.**

jeweilig *adj attr* respective; (*vorherrschend*) *Verhältnisse, Bedingungen* prevailing ◆ **die ~e Regierung** the government of the day.

jeweils *adv* at a *or* any one time; (*jedesmal*) each time; (*jeder einzelne*) each ◆ **~ am Monatsletzten** on the last day of each month; **die ~ betroffenen Landesregierungen müssen ...** each of the governments concerned must ...; **die ~ durch Schiebetüren abgetrennten Räume** the rooms, each (of which are) separated (off) by sliding doors; **die ~ größten aus einer Gruppe** the biggest from each group.

Jg. *abbr of* **Jahrgang.**

Jh. *abbr of* **Jahrhundert.**

JH *abbr of* **Jugendherberge** YH.

jhrl. *abbr of* **jährlich.**

jiddisch *adj* Yiddish.

Jiddisch(e) *nt decl as adj* Yiddish; *siehe* **Deutsch(e).**

Jiu-Jitsu ['dʒi:u'dʒɪtsu] *nt* **-s,** *no pl* j(i)u-jitsu.

Job [dʒɔp] *m* **-s, -s** (*inf, Comput*) job.

jobben ['dʒɔbn] *vi* (*inf*) to work, to have a job.

Jobber ['dʒɔbɐ] *m* **-s, -** (*inf*) casual worker; (*Börsen~*) jobber.

Jobkiller *m* **-s, -** (*inf*) job killer.

Job-sharing [-ʃɛarɪŋ] *nt* **-s,** *no pl* job sharing.

Joch *nt* **-(e)s, -e (a)** (*lit, fig*) yoke ◆ **Ochsen ins ~ spannen** to yoke *or* harness oxen; **sich einem ~** *or* **unter ein ~ beugen** (*fig*) to submit to *or* bend under the yoke; **das ~ abwerfen** *or* **abschütteln** (*fig*) to shake *or* throw off the yoke.
(b) (*dated: Gespann Ochsen*) yoke.
(c) (*Archit*) truss; (*Kirchen~*) bay; (*Brücken~*) span.
(d) (*Berg~*) ridge.
(e) (*old: Feldmaß*) acre.

Joch-: ~bein *nt* cheek-bone, malar bone (*form*); **~bogen** *m* **(a)** (*Anat*) zygomatic arch (*spec*), zygoma (*spec*); **(b)** (*Archit*) bay.

Jockei ['dʒɔke], **Jockey** ['dʒɔki] *m* **-s, -s** jockey.

Jockeymütze *f* jockey cap.

Jod *nt* **-s,** *no pl* (*abbr* **J**) iodine.

jodeln *vti* to yodel.

jodhaltig *adj* containing iodine, iodic (*form*).

Jodler *m* **-s, -** (*Ruf*) yodel.

Jodler(in *f*) *m* **-s, -** (*Mensch*) yodeller.

Jod-: ~präparat *nt* iodine preparation: **~quelle** *f* iodine(-containing) spring; **~salbe** *f* iodine ointment; **~tinktur** *f* iodine tincture.

Joga *m* **-(s),** *no pl* yoga.

Jogasitz *m, no pl* lotus position.

joggen ['dʒɔgn] *vi* to jog.

Jogger(in *f*) ['dʒɔgɐ, -ərɪn] *m* jogger.

Jogging ['dʒɔgɪŋ] *nt* **-,** *no pl* jogging.

Jogging- *in cpds* jogging; **~anzug** *m* jogging suit, tracksuit.

⚠ **Joghurt** *m or nt* **-(s), -(s)** yoghurt, yoghourt.

⚠ **Joghurtbereiter** *m* **-s, -s** yoghurt maker.

Jogi *m* **-s, -s** yogi.

Johann *m* **-** *siehe* **Johannes.**

Johanna *f* **-** Joanna ◆ **(die heilige) ~ von Orléans** (Saint) Joan of Arc.

Johannes *m* **-** *or* (*ohne Artikel*) **Johannis** (*Bibl*) John.

Johannes|evangelium *nt* St John's Gospel, Gospel according to St John.

Johanni(s) *nt siehe* **Johannistag.**

Johannis-: ~beere *f* **rote/schwarze ~beere** redcurrant/blackcurrant;

~beerstrauch *m* redcurrant/blackcurrant bush; **~brot** *nt* (*Bot*) carob; **~fest** *nt* Midsummer's Day; **~feuer** *nt* Midsummer's Eve bonfire; **~käfer** *m* (*Glühwürmchen*) glow-worm; (*Junikäfer*) summer chafer; **~kraut** *nt, no pl* rose of Sharon; **~nacht** *f* Midsummer's Eve; **~tag** *m* Midsummer's Day; **~trieb** *m* (*Bot*) lammas shoot; (*fig*) late romantic stirrings *pl*; **~würmchen** *nt siehe* **~käfer**.

Johanniter *m* **-s, -** Knight of St John of Jerusalem ◆ **~ Unfallhilfe** St John's Ambulance (Brigade).

Johanniter|orden *m* Order of St John of Jerusalem.

johlen *vi* to howl.

Joint [dʒɔɪnt] *m* **-s, -s** (*inf*) joint (*inf*).

Joint Venture [-'ventʃəʳ] *nt* **- -s, - -s** (*Comm*) joint venture.

Jojo *nt* **-s, -s** yo-yo.

Joker ['jo:kɐ, 'dʒɔ:kɐ] *m* **-s, -** (*Cards*) joker.

Jokus *m* **-, -se** (*dated, inf*) jape (*dated*), joke, prank ◆ **da hat sich jemand einen ~ gemacht** someone's been playing a prank.

Jolle *f* **-, -n** (*Naut*) jolly-boat, dinghy.

Jollenkreuzer *m* cabin yacht.

Jona *m* **-, Jonas** *m* **-** (*Bibl*) Jonah.

Jongleur [ʒõ'glø:ɐ] *m* juggler.

jonglieren* [ʒõ'gli:rən] *vi* (*lit, fig*) to juggle.

Joppe *f* **-, -n** (*dial*) jacket.

Jordan *m* **-s** Jordan ◆ **über den ~ gehen** (*inf*) to cross the great divide (*inf*).

Jordanien [-iən] *nt* **-s** Jordan.

Jordanier(in *f*) [-iɐ, -iərɪn] *m* **-s, -** Jordanian.

jordanisch *adj* Jordanian.

Josef, Joseph *m* **-s** Joseph.

Jot *nt* **-, -** (the letter) J/j.

Jota *nt* **-(s), -s** iota ◆ **kein** *or* **nicht ein ~** not a jot *or* one iota.

Joule [dʒu:l] *nt* **-(s), -** (*abbr* **J**) joule.

Journaille [ʒʊr'naljə] *f* **-,** *no pl* (*pej*) yellow press; (*Presse im allgemeinen*) press; (*Journalisten*) hacks *pl* (*pej*).

Journal [ʒʊr'na:l] *nt* **-s, -e (a)** (*dated: Tagebuch*) journal (*old*), diary; (*Comm*) daybook; (*Naut*) log(-book). **(b)** (*dated: Zeitschrift*) magazine, periodical; (*old: Zeitung*) journal (*old*); (*Fach~*) journal.

Journaldienst *m* (*Aus*) *siehe* **Bereitschaftsdienst.**

Journalismus [ʒʊrna'lɪsmʊs] *m, no pl* journalism.

Journalist(in *f*) [ʒʊrna'lɪst, -ɪstɪn] *m* journalist.

Journalistik [ʒʊrna'lɪstɪk] *f, no pl* journalism.

journalistisch [ʒʊrna'lɪstɪʃ] *adj* journalistic.

jovial [jo'via:l] *adj* jovial.

Jovialität [joviali'tɛ:t] *f, no pl* joviality.

Joystick ['dʒɔɪstɪk] *m* **-s, -s** (*Comput*) joystick.

jr. *abbr of* **junior** jnr., jr.

Jubel *m* **-s,** *no pl* (*von Volk, Menge etc*) jubilation; (*~rufe auch*) cheering ◆ **~, Trubel, Heiterkeit** laughter and merriment.

Jubel-: ~feier *f*, **~fest** *nt* jubilee; (*Feierlichkeiten*) jubilee celebration; **~geschrei** *nt* (*pej*) shouting and cheering; **~greis** *m old person celebrating a jubilee or anniversary*; (*fig inf*) gay old spark (*inf*); **~hochzeit** *f* special wedding anniversary (*silver, golden etc anniversary*); **~jahr** *nt* jubilee year; **nur alle ~jahre (einmal)** (*inf*) once in a blue moon (*inf*).

jubeln *vi* to cheer, to shout with joy, to rejoice (*liter*) ◆ **jubelt nicht zu früh** don't start celebrating too early.

Jubel-: ~paar *nt* happy couple (*celebrating a special, e.g. silver or golden, wedding anniversary*); **~ruf** *m* (triumphant) cheer; **~tag** *m* (silver, golden *etc*) wedding anniversary.

Jubilar(in *f*) *m person celebrating an anniversary.*

Jubilate *no art* (*Eccl*) Jubilate (Sunday).

Jubiläum *nt* **-s, Jubiläen** jubilee; (*Jahrstag*) anniversary.

Jubiläums- *in cpds* jubilee.

jubilieren* *vi* (*liter*) to rejoice (*liter*); (*Vögel*) to sing joyfully; *siehe* **jubeln.**

juchhe(i), juchheißa, juchhu (*inf*) *interj* hurrah, hooray.

Juchten *nt or m* **-s,** *no pl* **(a)** (*~leder*) Russia leather *or* calf, Russia. **(b)** (*Parfüm*) Russian leather.

Juchtenleder *nt* Russia leather *or* calf, Russia.

juchzen *vi* to shriek with delight.

juckeln *vi aux sein* (*inf: Auto, Zug*) to jog *or* chug along ◆ **er ist durch die Stadt/über Land gejuckelt** he's been jogging around town/across country.

jucken [1] *vti* to itch ◆ **es juckt mich am Rücken, der Rücken juckt mir** *or* **mich** my back itches; **der Stoff juckt mich** this material makes me itch; **es juckt mich, das zu tun** (*inf*) I'm itching to do it (*inf*); **ihn juckt das Geld dabei** (*inf*) he finds the money attractive; **das juckt mich doch nicht** (*inf*) I don't care; **ihn** *or* **ihm juckt das Fell** (*inf*) *or* **der Buckel** (*inf*) he's asking for a good hiding; **wen's juckt, der kratze sich** (*prov*) if you don't like it you know what you can do (*inf*).

[2] *vt* (*kratzen*) to scratch.

Juck-: ~pulver *nt* itching powder; **~reiz** *m* itching; **einen ~reiz in der Nase haben** to have an itch in one's nose.

Judäa *nt* **-s** Jud(a)ea.

Judaismus *m* Judaism.

Judas[1] *m* **-** (*Bibl*) Judas.

Judas[2] *m* **-, -se** (*fig liter*) Judas.

Judas-: ⚠~kuß *m* (*liter*) Judas kiss; **der ~kuß** (*Bibl*) the Betrayal; **~lohn** *m* (*liter*) blood money, thirty pieces of silver *pl*.

Jude *m* **-n, -n** Jew ◆ **er ist ~** he is a Jew; *siehe* **ewig.**

⚠: for details of spelling reform, see supplement

Juden-: ~christ *m* Judaist, Judaeo-Christian; **~feind, ~gegner** *m* anti-Semite; **j~feindlich** *adj* anti-Semitic; **⚠~haß** *m* anti-Semitism; **~heit** *f* Jewry; **~stern** *m* star of David; **~tum** *nt* **(a)** (*Judaismus*) Judaism; **(b)** (*Gesamtheit der ~*) Jews *pl*, Jewry; **(c)** (*jüdisches Wesen*) Jewishness; **~verfolgung** *f* persecution of (the) Jews; **~viertel** *nt* Jewish quarter.

Jüdin *f* Jew, Jewish woman.

jüdisch *adj* Jewish.

judizieren* *vi* (*old, Jur*) *siehe* **urteilen.**

Judo[1] *m* **-s, -s** (*Pol inf*) Young Democrat.

Judo[2] *nt* **-s,** *no pl* judo.

Judoka *m* **-s, -s** judoka.

Jugend *f* **-,** *no pl* **(a)** (*~zeit*) youth; (*Jungsein, Jugendlichkeit auch*) youthfulness ◆ **frühe ~** early youth, adolescence; **in ihrer ~ waren sie** ... in their youth they were ...; **von ~ an** *or* **auf** from one's youth.

(b) (*junge Menschen*) youth, young people *pl* ◆ **die heutige ~** young people *or* the youth of today, modern youth; **die weibliche/männliche ~** young women/men; **~ hat keine Tugend** (*Prov*) young people are all the same; **Haus der ~** (*BRD*) youth centre.

(c) (*Sport*) youth team.

Jugend-: ~alter *nt* adolescence; **~amt** *nt* youth welfare department; **~arbeit** *f, no pl* **(a)** (*Arbeit Jugendlicher*) youth employment; **(b)** (*~fürsorge*) youth work; **~arbeitslosigkeit** *f* youth unemployment; **~arrest** *m* (*Jur*) detention, borstal (*Brit*); **~bekanntschaft** *f* friend of one's youth; **~bewegung** *f* **(a)** youth movement; **(b)** (*Hist*) German Youth Movement (*of the early 1920's*); **~bild** *nt* picture *or* photo taken when one was young; **~bilder Churchills** pictures of the young Churchill; **~bildnis** *nt* (*Art, fig*) **~bildnis von X** portrait of X as a young man/woman; **~brigade** *f* (*DDR*) youth brigade (*work team consisting of young people*); **~buch** *nt* book for the younger reader *or* young people; **~bücherei** *f* library for the younger reader; **~buchverlag** *m* publishing house specializing in literature for young people; **~elf** *f* youth team; **~erinnerung** *f* youthful memory; **meine ~erinnerungen** memories of my youth; **j~frei** *adj Film* U(-certificate), G (*US*); **~freund** *m* friend of one's youth; **~funk** *m* (*Rad*) broadcasting *or* radio for young people; (*Sendung*) broadcast *or* programme for young people; **~fürsorge** *f* youth welfare; (*für Schulkinder*) child guidance; **~gedicht** *nt* youthful poem; **j~gefährdend** *adj* liable to corrupt the young; **~gericht** *nt* juvenile court; **~gespiele** *m*, **~gespielin** *f* (*hum*) young playmate; **~gruppe** *f* youth group; **~heim** *nt* **(a)** youth club; **(b)** (*Wohnheim*) young people's home.

Jugendherberge *f* youth hostel.

Jugendherbergs-: ~ausweis *m* youth hostelling card, YHA card; **~mutter** *f*, **~vater** *m* youth hostel warden; **~verband** *m* Youth Hostel Association.

Jugend-: ~hilfe *f* (*Admin*) help for young people; **~irresein** *nt* (*Med*) juvenile schizophrenia; **~jahre** *pl* days of one's youth *pl*; **~kriminalität** *f* juvenile delinquency.

jugendlich *adj* (*jung*) young; (*von Jugend, jung wirkend*) youthful ◆ **er kleidet sich immer sehr ~** he always wears very youthful *or* young-looking clothes; **eine ~e Erscheinung** a young- *or* youthful-looking person; **~e Banden** gangs of youths; **ein ~er Täter** a young offender, a juvenile delinquent; **~er Leichtsinn** youthful frivolity; **das sagst du so in deinem ~en Leichtsinn** (*hum*) I admire your confidence.

Jugendliche(r) *mf decl as adj* young person; (*männlicher ~ auch*) youth.

Jugendlichkeit *f* youthfulness.

Jugend-: ~liebe *f* **(a)** young love; **(b)** (*Geliebter*) love *or* sweetheart of one's youth; **~literatur** *f* literature for younger readers *or* young people; **~mannschaft** *f* youth team; **~organisation** *f* youth organization; **~pflege** *f* youth welfare; **~pfleger** *m* youth (welfare) worker; **~psychologie** *f* adolescent psychology; **~recht** *nt* law relating to young persons; **~richter** *m* (*Jur*) *magistrate in a juvenile court*; **~schriften** *pl* publications for young people; (*eines Autors*) youthful writings; **~schriftsteller** *m* writer of books for young people; **~schutz** *m* protection of children and young people; **~sekte** *f* youth sect; **~sendung** *f* (*Rad*) programme for younger listeners *or* (*TV*) younger viewers; **~spiele** *pl* youth games *pl*; **~stil** *m* (*Art*) Art Nouveau; **~strafanstalt** *f* (*form*) reform school, approved school (*Brit*), borstal (*Brit*); **~strafe** *f* detention *no art* in a reform school *etc*; **~streich** *m* youthful exploit *or* escapade; **~sünde** *f* youthful misdeed; **~theater** *nt* youth theatre; **~torheit** *f* youthful folly, folly of one's youth; **~traum** *m* youthful dream; **~verband** *m* youth organization; **~verbot** *nt* **für einen Film ~verbot aussprechen** to ban a film for young people; **~vertretung** *f* youth representatives *pl*; **~vorstellung** *f* performance for young people; **~weihe** *f* (*Rel*) initiation; (*DDR*) *ceremony in which 14-year-olds are given adult social status*; **~zeit** *f* youth, younger days *pl*; **~zentrum** *nt* youth centre.

Jugoslawe *m* **-n, -n** Yugoslav.

Jugoslawien [-iən] *nt* **-s** Yugoslavia.

Jugoslawin *f* Yugoslav.

jugoslawisch *adj* Yugoslav(ian).

Julei *m* **-s, -s** (*esp Comm*) *siehe* **Juli.**

Juli *m* **-(s), -s (a)** July; *siehe* **März. (b)** (*Pol inf*) Young Liberal.

julianisch *adj* **der J~e Kalender** the Julian Calendar.

Jumbo(-Jet) ['jʊmbo(dʒɛt)] *m* **-s, -s** Jumbo (jet).

Jumper ['jʊmpɐ, 'dʒampɐ] *m* **-s, -** jumper (*Brit*), sweater.

jun. *abbr of* **junior** jun.

jung *adj, comp* **¨er**, *superl* **¨ste(r, s)** *or adv* **am ¨sten** (*lit, fig*) young; *Aktien* new ◆ ~ **und alt** (both) young and old; **von ~ auf** from one's youth; **der ~e Meyer** young Meyer; (*Sohn*) Meyer junior; **sie ist 18 Jahre ~** (*hum*) she's 18 years young (*hum*); **~ heiraten/sterben** to marry/die young; **sich** (*dat*) **ein ~es Herz bewahren** to stay young at heart; **~ gefreit, nie gereut** (*Prov*) if you marry young you won't regret it; **so ~ kommen wir nicht mehr zusammen** (*hum*) you're only young once; *siehe* **jünger, jüngste(r, s)**.

Jụng-: ~akademiker *m* graduate; **~arbeiter** *m* juvenile employee *or* worker; **~bauer** *m* young farmer; **~brunnen** *m* fountain of youth; **~bürger** *m* junior citizen.

Jụngchen *nt* (*inf*) lad(die) (*inf*).

Jụngdemokrat(in *f*) *m* (*BRD*) Young Democrat.

Jụnge[1] *m* **-n, -n** *or* (*dated inf*) **-ns** *or* (*inf*) **Jungs** boy; (*Lauf~*) errand-boy; (*Cards*) jack, knave ◆ **~, ~!** (*inf*) boy oh boy (*inf*); **sie ist ein richtiger ~** she's a real tomboy; **alter ~** (*inf*) my old mate (*inf*) *or* pal (*inf*); **mein lieber ~!** my dear boy; (*in Brief*) my dear son; **ein schwerer ~** (*inf*) a (big-time) crook; **unsere Jungs haben gewonnen** our boys *or* lads won.

Jụnge[2] *mf* **-n**, *no pl* (*inf*) **der/die ~** Mr/Miss X junior, the young Mr/Miss X.

Jụ̈ngelchen *nt* (*pej*) young lad.

jụngen *vi* to have young; (*Hündin auch*) to have pups; (*Katze auch*) to have kittens.

Jụngen-: ~gesicht *nt* boy's *or* boyish face; **j~haft** *adj* boyish; **sie ist ein j~haftes Mädchen** she's a bit of a tomboy; **~klasse** *f* (*Sch*) boys' class; **~schule** *f* boys' school; **~streich** *m* boyish prank *or* trick.

jụ̈nger *adj* **(a)** *comp of* **jung** younger ◆ **sie sieht ~ aus, als sie ist** she looks younger than she is, she doesn't look her age; **Holbein der J~e** Holbein the Younger, the younger Holbein. **(b)** *Geschichte, Entwicklung etc* recent ◆ **die ~e Steinzeit** the later *or* New Stone Age.

Jụ̈nger *m* **-s, -** (*Bibl, fig*) disciple.

Jụ̈ngerin *f* (*fig*) disciple.

Jụ̈ngerschaft *f* disciples *pl*; (*Jüngertum*) discipleship.

Jụnge(s) *nt decl as adj* (*Zool*) young one; (*von Hund*) pup(py); (*von Katze*) kitten; (*von Wolf, Löwe, Bär*) cub; (*von Vogel*) young bird, nestling ◆ **die ~n** the young.

Jụngfer *f* **-, -n (a)** (*old, hum*) (*ledige Frau*) spinster ◆ **eine alte ~** an old maid. **(b)** (*old: Jungfrau*) virgin, maiden (*old*); (*als Anrede*) mistress (*old*). **(c)** (*Kammer~*) maid.

jụ̈ngferlich *adj* old-maidish.

Jụngfern-: ~fahrt *f* maiden voyage; **~flug** *m* maiden flight; **~häutchen** *nt* (*Anat*) hymen (*Anat*), maidenhead; **~inseln** *pl* Virgin Islands *pl*; **~kranz** *m* (*old*) (bridal) bouquet; **~rede** *f* (*Parl*) maiden speech; **~reise** *f siehe* **~fahrt**; **~schaft** *f, no pl siehe* **Jungfräulichkeit**; **~stand** *m* (*old*) spinsterhood; **~zeugung** *f* (*Biol*) parthenogenesis.

Jụngfilmer *m* young film maker ◆ **die deutschen ~** the young German film makers.

Jụngfrau *f* virgin; (*Astron, Astrol*) Virgo *no art* ◆ **ich bin ~** I am a virgin; I am (a) Virgo; **die ~ Maria** the Virgin Mary; **die heilige ~** the Blessed *or* Holy Virgin; **die ~ von Orléans** Joan of Arc, the Maid of Orleans; **dazu bin ich gekommen wie die ~ zum Kind(e)** it just fell into my hands; *siehe* **eisern**.

jụngfräulich *adj Mädchen, Schnee* virgin; (*liter*) *Seele* pure, innocent.

Jụngfräulichkeit *f siehe adj* virginity; purity, innocence.

Jụnggeselle *m* bachelor.

Jụnggesellen-: ~bude *f* (*inf*) bachelor pad (*inf*); **~dasein, ~leben** *nt* bachelor's life; **~tum** *nt* bachelorhood, bachelordom; **~wirtschaft** *f* (*inf*) bachelor squalor; **~wohnung** *f* bachelor flat; **~zeit** *f* bachelor days *pl*.

Jụnggesellin *f* single woman.

Jụnglehrer *m* student teacher.

Jụ̈ngling *m* (*liter, hum*) youth.

Jụ̈nglings-: ~alter *nt* (*liter*) youth; **j~haft** *adj* (*geh*) youthful, boyish.

Jụng-: ~mädel *nt* (*dated*) young girl; **~mann** *m, pl* **~männer** (*dated*) young man; **~sozialist** *m* (*BRD*) Young Socialist.

jụ̈ngst *adv* (*geh*) recently, lately ◆ **der ~ verstorbene** ... the late ...; **der ~ erlassene Befehl** the recent decree.

Jụngsteinzeit *f* Neolithic age, New Stone Age.

jụ̈ngstens *adv* (*old, liter*) *siehe* **jüngst**.

jụ̈ngste(r, s) *adj* **(a)** *superl of* **jung** youngest. **(b)** *Werk, Schöpfung, Ereignis* latest, (most) recent; *Zeit, Vergangenheit* recent ◆ **in der ~n Zeit** recently; **ein Ausdruck aus der ~n Zeit** a recent expression; **das J~ Gericht** the Last Judgement; **der J~ Tag** Doomsday, the Day of Judgement; **man merkt, daß er/sie nicht mehr der/die J~ ist** you can tell that he/she is not as young as he/she used to be; **sie ist auch nicht mehr die J~** she's no chicken (*inf*).

Jụng-: ~stier *m* young steer; **~tier** *nt* young animal; **~verheiratete(r)** *mf decl as adj* newly-wed; **j~vermählt** *adj* (*geh*) newly-wed, recently married; **die ~vermählten** the newly-weds; **~vieh** *nt* young cattle *pl*; **~wähler** *m* young voter; **~wild** *nt* young game.

Juni *m* **-(s), -s** June; *siehe* **März**.

Junikäfer *m* chafer.

junior *adj* **Franz Schulz ~** Franz Schulz, Junior.

Junior *m* **(a)** (*usu hum: Sohn*) junior ◆ **wie geht's dem ~?** how's junior? **(b)** (*auch* **~chef**) son of the chairman/boss ◆ **kann ich mal den ~(chef) sprechen?** can I speak to Mr X junior? **(c)** *usu pl* (*Sport*) junior.

Juniorin *f siehe* **Junior (c)**.

Junior-: ~partner *m* junior partner; ⚠**~paß** *m* (*Rail*) ≃ young persons' railcard.

Junk-Bond [ˈdʒaŋkbɔnd] *m* **-s, -s** (*Fin*) junk bond.

Jụnker *m* **-s, -** (*Hist*) squire; (*preußisch*) Junker.

Jụnkertum *nt, no pl* squirarchy; (*in Preußen*) Junkerdom.

Junkfood, Junk food [ˈdʒaŋkfuːd] *nt* **-s, -s** (*inf*) junk food.

Junkie [ˈdʒaŋki] *m* **-s, -s** (*inf*) junkie (*inf*).

Jụnktim *nt* **-s, -s** (*Pol: Paket*) package (deal) ◆ **zwischen X und Y besteht ein ~** X is dependent on Y.

Juno *m* **-s, -s** (*esp Comm*) June.

Junta [ˈxʊnta, ˈjʊnta] *f* **-, Junten** (*Pol*) junta.

Jupe [ʒyp] *m* **-s, -s** (*Sw*) skirt.

Jupiter *m* **-s** Jupiter.

Jupiterlampe ® *f* klieg light.

jur. *abbr of* **juristisch**.

Jura[1] *m* **-s**, *no pl* (*Geol, Geog*) Jura (Mountains) *pl*; (*Kanton*) the Canton of Jura.

Jura[2] *no art* (*Univ*) law.

Jurạssier(in *f*) [-iɐ, -iərɪn] *m* **-s, -** person from the Canton of Jura.

jurạssisch *adj* (*Geol*) Jurassic; (*aus Kanton Jura*) of the Canton of Jura.

Jurastudium *nt* study of law ◆ **das ~ dauert acht Semester** the law degree (course) takes four years.

juridisch *adj* (*old, Aus*) *siehe* **juristisch**.

Jurisdiktion *f* (*geh*) administration of justice; (*rare: Gerichtshoheit*) jurisdiction.

Jurisprudẹnz *f* (*geh*) jurisprudence.

Jurịst *m* jurist, legal eagle (*hum inf*); (*Student*) law student.

Jurịsten-: ~deutsch *nt*, **~sprache** *f, no pl* legalese (*pej*), legal jargon *or* language.

Juristerei *f, no pl* (*inf*) law.

Jurịstin *f* jurist; law student.

jurịstisch *adj* legal; *Problem etc auch* juridical (*form*); *Studium auch* law *attr* ◆ **die J~e Fakultät** the Faculty of Law; **eine ~e Person** a legal entity, a corporation, a corporate body.

Juror(in *f*) [ˈjuːrɔr, -ˈroːrɪn] *m* juror, member of the jury; (*bei Wettbewerb*) member of the jury, judge, adjudicator.

Jụrte *f* **-, -n** jurt.

Jury [ʒyˈriː, ˈʒyːri:] *f* **-, -s** jury *sing or pl*; (*bei Wettbewerb auch*) judges *pl*, adjudicators *pl*.

Jus [ʒyː] *f or m or nt* **-**, *no pl* **(a)** (*Bratensaft*) gravy; (*geliert*) dripping. **(b)** (*Sw: Fruchtsaft*) juice.

Juso *m* **-s, -s** (*BRD*) *abbr of* **Jungsozialist** Young Socialist.

jụst *adv* (*old*) precisely, exactly, just ◆ **~ gekommen** just come.

justieren* *vt* to adjust; *Gewehr, Zielfernrohr etc auch* to collimate (*form*); *Münzen auch* to weight; (*Typ, Comput*) to justify.

Justierschraube *f* (*Tech*) adjusting screw.

Justierung *f siehe vt* adjustment; collimation (*form*); weighting; justification.

Justierwaage *f* adjusting balance.

Justitia [jʊsˈtiːtsia] *f* **-s** Justice; (*fig*) the law.

⚠**justitiabel** [jʊstiˈtsiaːbl] *adj* (*geh*) litigable.

⚠**Justitiar** [jʊstiˈtsiaːɐ] *m* lawyer, legal adviser.

Justiz [jʊsˈtiːts] *f* **-**, *no pl* (*als Prinzip*) justice; (*als Institution*) judiciary; (*die Gerichte*) courts *pl*.

Justiz-: ~beamte(r) *m* judicial officer; **~behörde** *f* legal *or* judicial authority; **~hoheit** *f* legal sovereignty; **~irrtum** *m* miscarriage of justice; **~minister** *m* minister of justice, justice minister, ≃ Attorney General (*US*), ≃ Lord (High) Chancellor (*Brit*); **~ministerium** *nt* ministry of justice, ≃ Department of Justice (*US*); **~mord** *m* judicial murder; **~palast** *m* palace of justice; **~verwaltung** *f* administration of justice; **~vollzugsanstalt** *f* (*form*) place of detention.

Jute *f* **-**, *no pl* jute.

Jütland *nt* **-s** (*Geog*) Jutland.

juvenil [juveˈniːl] *adj* (*geh*) juvenile.

Juwel[1] [juˈveːl] *m or nt* **-s, -en** jewel, gem ◆ **~en** (*Schmuck*) jewellery, jewelry.

Juwel[2] *nt* **-s, -e** (*fig*) jewel, gem.

Juwelier *m* **-s, -e** jeweller; (*Geschäft*) jeweller's (shop).

Juwelier-: ~geschäft *nt* jeweller's (shop); **~waren** *pl* jewel(le)ry.

Jụx *m* **-es, -e** (*inf*) **etw aus ~ tun/sagen** to do/say sth as a joke *or* in fun; **etw aus lauter ~ und Tollerei tun** to do sth out of sheer high spirits; **sich** (*dat*) **einen ~ aus etw machen** to make a joke (out) of sth.

jụxen *vi* (*inf*) to joke.

jụxig *adj* (*inf*) funny.

jwd [jɔtveːˈdeː] *adv* (*hum*) in the back of beyond; (*weit entfernt*) miles out (*inf*).

K

K, k [ka:] *nt* **-, -** K, k.
Kaaba *f* **-,** *no pl* Kaaba, Caaba.
Kabale *f* **-, -n** (*old*) cabal (*old*).
Kabarett *nt* **-s, -e** *or* **-s (a)** cabaret; (*Darbietung auch*) cabaret show; (*in Bar etc auch*) floor show ◆ **ein politisches ~** a satirical political revue, a political satire. **(b)** (*Servierplatte*) serving dish (*divided into sections*).
Kabarettist(in *f*) *m* cabaret artist.
kabarettistisch *adj Darbietung* cabaret; *Stil* revue *attr*; *Eskapaden* farcical.
Kabäuschen [ka'bɔysçən] *nt* (*inf*) (*Zimmer*) cubbyhole (*inf*); (*Laube*) hut, cabin.
Kabbala *f* **-** (*Rel*) cabbala.
Kabbelei *f* (*inf*) bickering, squabbling.
kabbelig *adj Meer* choppy.
kabbeln *vir* (*inf*) to bicker, to squabble.
Kabel *nt* **-s, - (a)** (*Elec*) wire; (*von Elektrogeräten auch*) flex; (*Telefon~*) flex, cord; (*Strom- oder Telegraphenleitung*) cable. **(b)** (*old Naut: Tau*) rope; (*Drahtseil*) cable. **(c)** (*Telegramm*) cable(gram).
Kabel-: ⚠~anschluß *m* (*TV*) cable connection; **~anschluß haben** to get cable (TV); **~baum** *m* (*Elec*) harness; **~bericht** *m* cabled report; **~fernsehen** *nt* cable television.
Kabeljau *m* **-s, -e** *or* **-s** cod.
Kabel-: ~länge *f* (*Naut*) cable, cable's length; **~leger** *m* **-s, -** (*Naut*) cable layer; **~mantel** *m* cable covering.
kabeln *vti* to cable.
Kabel-: ~netz *nt* (*TV*) cable network; **~trommel** *f* cable drum *or* reel.
Kabine *f* (*Umkleide~, Anprobier~, Dusch~*) cubicle; (*Naut, Aviat, von Kran*) cabin; (*Telec, zum Plattenhören auch*) booth; (*Vorführ~*) projection room; (*Seilbahn~*) car.
Kabinen-: ~bahn *f* cable railway; **~koffer** *m* cabin trunk; **~roller** *m* bubble-car.
Kabinett[1] *nt* **-s, -e (a)** (*Pol*) cabinet. **(b)** (*für Kunstsammlungen*) (*Raum*) gallery; (*Schrank*) cabinet. **(c)** (*Zimmer*) (*Aus: kleines Zimmer*) closet; (*old: Arbeitszimmer*) cabinet.
Kabinett[2] *m* **-s, -e** *m siehe* **~wein.**
Kabinetts-: ⚠~beschluß *m* cabinet decision; **~frage** *f* (*rare*) *siehe* **Vertrauensfrage; ~justiz** *f interference in the course of justice by a sovereign*; **~mitglied** *nt* cabinet member, member of the cabinet.
Kabinettstück *nt* **(a)** (*old: einer Sammlung*) showpiece, pièce de résistance. **(b)** (*fig*) masterstroke.
Kabinetts|umbildung *f* cabinet reshuffle.
Kabinettwein *m high quality German white wine.*
Kabrio *nt* **-(s), -s** (*inf*) convertible.
Kabriolett [kabrio'let, (*Aus, S Ger*) kabrio'le:] *nt* **-s, -s (a)** (*Aut*) convertible. **(b)** (*Hist*) cabriolet.
Kabuff *nt* **-s, -e** *or* **-s** (*inf*) (poky) little corner.
Kachel *f* **-, -n** (glazed) tile ◆ **etw mit ~n auslegen** to tile sth, to cover sth with *or* in tiles.
kacheln *vt* to tile.
Kachel|ofen *m* tiled stove.
Kacke *f* **-,** *no pl* (*vulg*) crap (*vulg*), shit (*vulg*) ◆ **dann ist aber die ~ am Dampfen** then the shit will really hit the fan (*vulg*).
kacken *vi* (*vulg*) to crap (*vulg*), to shit (*vulg*).
Kadaver [ka'da:vɐ] *m* **-s, -** carcass.
Kadavergehorsam *m* (*pej*) blind *or* slavish obedience.
Kadenz *f* cadence; (*Improvisation*) cadenza.
Kader *m* **-s, -** (*Mil, Pol*) cadre; (*Sport*) squad; (*DDR, Sw*) (*Fachleute*) group of specialists; (*Fachmann*) specialist; (*Sw: Vorgesetzte*) management.
Kader-: ~leiter *m* (*DDR*) personnel officer; **~schmiede** *f* **-,** *no pl* (*pej*) élite school.
Kadett *m* **-en, -en** (*Mil*) cadet.
Kadetten-: ~anstalt *f* cadet school; **~schulschiff** *nt* naval (cadet) training ship.
Kadi *m* **-s, -s** (*dated inf*) beak (*inf*) ◆ **jdn vor den ~ schleppen** to take sb to court; **zum ~ laufen** to go to court.
Kadmium *nt* **-s** cadmium.
Käfer *m* **-s, - (a)** beetle (*auch inf: VW*). **(b)** (*sl: Mädchen*) bird (*esp Brit inf*), chick (*esp US inf*) ◆ **ein flotter ~** (*dated inf*) a nice bit of skirt (*Brit inf*).
Kaff *nt* **-s, -s** *or* **-e** (*inf*) dump (*inf*), hole (*inf*).
Kaffee[1] [*or* ka'fe:] *m* **-s, -s (a)** coffee ◆ **zwei ~, bitte!** two coffees please; **~ mit Milch** white coffee (*Brit*), coffee with milk; **~ verkehrt** (*dated*) white coffee (*made with hot milk*) (*Brit*), coffee with hot milk; **~ kochen** to make coffee; **das ist kalter ~** (*inf*) that's old hat (*inf*); **da kommt einem der ~ hoch** (*sl*) it makes you sick (*inf*); **dir haben sie wohl was in den ~ getan!** (*inf*) you must be joking *or* kidding (*inf*).
(b) *no pl* (*Nachmittags~*) ≃ (afternoon) tea ◆ **~ und Kuchen** coffee and cakes, ≃ afternoon tea; **jdn zu ~ und Kuchen einladen** to invite sb for *or* to (afternoon) tea.
Kaffee[2] *nt* **-s, -s** (*old*) *siehe* **Café.**
Kaffee-: ~bohne *f* coffee bean; **k~braun** *adj* coffee-coloured; **⚠~-Ersatz** *m* coffee substitute; **⚠~-Extrakt** *m* coffee essence; **~fahrt** *f* day trip; (*Verkaufsfahrt*) promotional trip (*during which passengers are served coffee and offered goods to buy*); **~filter** *m* coffee filter; (*inf: Filterpapier*) filter (paper); **~geschirr** *nt* coffee set; **~haus** *nt* café; **~hausmusik** *f* (*pej*) palm court music; **~kanne** *f* coffeepot; **~klatsch** (*inf*) *m* **-s,** *no pl*, **~kränzchen** *nt* coffee klatsch (*US*), hen party (*inf*), ≃ coffee morning; **ich treffe mich mit meinen Freundinnen zu einem ~klatsch** I'm meeting some friends for a chat over (a cup of) coffee *or* tea; **~löffel** *m* coffee spoon; **~maschine** *f* coffee machine; **~mischung** *f* blended coffee; **~mühle** *f* coffee grinder; **~mütze** *f siehe* **~wärmer; ~pause** *f* coffee break; **~satz** *m* coffee grounds *pl*; **aus dem ~satz wahrsagen** *or* **lesen** to read (the) tea leaves; **~service** *nt* coffee set; **~sorte** *f* type *or* sort of coffee; **~strauch** *m* coffee tree; **~stube** *f* coffee shop; **~tante** *f* (*hum*) coffee addict; (*in Café*) old biddy; **~tasse** *f* coffee cup; **~tisch** *m* (*Frühstückstisch*) breakfast table; (*nachmittags*) (afternoon) tea table; **~wärmer** *m* **-s, -** cosy (for coffee pot); **~wasser** *nt* water for coffee, coffee water; **ich habe das ~wasser schon aufgesetzt** I've just put the kettle on.
Kaffer *m* **(a) -n, -n** kaffir; (*pej inf*) nigger. **(b) -s, -** (*pej inf: dummer Kerl*) thickhead (*inf*), duffer (*inf*).
Käfig *m* **-s, -e** cage ◆ **sie sitzt in einem goldenen ~** (*fig*) she is just a bird in a gilded cage.
Käfig-: ~haltung *f* caging; **~vogel** *m* cage bird.
Kafiller *m* **-s, -** (*dial*) knacker.
kafkaesk *adj* Kafkaesque.
Kaftan *m* **-s, -e** caftan.
kahl *adj Mensch, Kopf* bald; (*~geschoren*) shaved, shorn; *Vogel* bald, featherless; *Wand, Raum* bare; *Pflanze, Baum* bare, leafless; *Landschaft, Berge* barren, bleak ◆ **eine ~e Stelle** a bald patch; **~ werden** (*Mensch*) to go bald; (*Baum*) to lose its leaves.
Kahl-: ~fraß *m* defoliation; **⚠k~fressen** *vt sep irreg* to strip bare; *Ernte* to destroy completely; **~frost** *m* black frost; **⚠k~geschoren** *adj Kopf* shaven, shorn; **~heit** *f siehe adj* baldness; featherlessness; bareness, leaflessness; barrenness; **~kopf** *m* bald head; (*Mensch*) bald person; **ein ~kopf sein** to be bald; **k~köpfig** *adj* bald(-headed); **~köpfigkeit** *f* baldness, bald-headedness; **⚠k~scheren** *vt sep irreg Schafe* to shear; *Hecken* to cut right back; **jdn k~scheren** to shave sb's head; **~schlag** *m* **(a)** (*abgeholzte Fläche*) clearing; **(b)** (*Tätigkeit*) deforestation; **(c)** (*inf*) **(Aktion) ~schlag** (*Entlassungen*) axing; (*Abriß*) demolition; **⚠k~schlagen** *vt sep irreg* to deforest, to clear; **~wild** *nt* (*geweihlose, weibliche Tiere*) does *pl*; (*geweihlose Kälber*) fawns *pl*.
Kahm *m* **-(e)s,** *no pl* mould.
kahmig *adj* mouldy.
Kahn *m* **-(e)s, ⸚e (a)** (small) boat; (*Stech~*) punt ◆ **~ fahren** to go boating/punting. **(b)** (*Lastschiff*) barge ◆ **ein alter ~** (*inf*) an old tub (*inf*). **(c)** (*inf*) (*Bett*) bed, pit (*inf*); (*dated: Gefängnis*) jug (*dated inf*); (*Ftbl: Tor*) net ◆ **⸚e** (*große Schuhe*) clodhoppers (*inf*).
Kahnfahrt *f* row; (*in Stechkahn*) punt.
Kai *m* **-s, -e** *or* **-s** quay; (*Uferdamm auch*) waterfront.
Kai|anlage *f* quayside.
Kaiman *m* **-s, -e** (*Zool*) cayman.
Kaimauer *f* quay wall.
Kainsmal, Kainszeichen *nt* (*Stigma*) mark of Cain.
Kairo *nt* **-s** Cairo.

⚠: for details of spelling reform, see supplement

Kaiser *m* **-s, -** emperor ◆ **der deutsche ~** the German Emperor, the Kaiser; **wo nichts ist, hat der ~ sein Recht verloren** *(Prov)* you can't get blood from a stone; **gebt dem ~, was des ~s ist!** *(Bibl)* render unto Caesar the things which are Caesar's; **(da,) wo selbst der ~ zu Fuß hingeht** *(dated hum)* the smallest room (in the house) *(hum)*; **das ist ein Streit um des ~s Bart** that's just splitting hairs; **er kommt sich vor wie der ~ von China** *(inf)* he thinks he's the king of the castle *or* God.
Kaiser-: ~adler *m* imperial eagle; **~haus** *nt* imperial family.
Kaiserin *f* empress.
Kaiserinmutter *f* dowager empress.
Kaiserkrone *f* **(a)** imperial crown. **(b)** *(Bot)* crown imperial.
kaiserlich *adj* imperial ◆ **diese Besitzungen waren früher ~** these possessions used to belong to the Emperor; **Seine K~e Majestät** His Imperial Majesty; **~ gesinnt** monarchistic, imperialistic.
Kaiserliche(r) *m decl as adj* Imperialist.
kaiserlich-königlich *adj* imperial and royal *(pertaining to the Dual Monarchy of Austro-Hungary)*.
Kaiser-: ~pfalz *f* imperial palace; **~reich** *nt* empire; **~schmarr(e)n** *m* **-s, -** *(Aus) sugared, cut-up pancake with raisins*; **~schnitt** *m* Caesarean (section); **~stadt** *f* imperial city.
Kaisertum *nt* **(a)** Empire. **(b)** *siehe* **Kaiserwürde (b)**.
Kaiser-: ~wetter *nt (dated)* magnificent sunshine; **~würde** *f* **(a)** *(Ehre)* honour *or* dignity of an emperor; **(b)** *(Amt)* emperorship.
Kajak *m or nt* **-s, -s** kayak.
Kajal *m - no pl* kohl.
Kajalstift *m* kohl eye pencil.
Kaje *f* **-, -n** *(N Ger) siehe* **Kai**.
Kajütboot *nt* cabin boat.
Kajüte *f* **-, -n** cabin; *(größer auch)* stateroom.
Kakadu *m* **-s, -s** cockatoo.
Kakao [*auch* ka'kau] *m* **-s, -s** cocoa ◆ **jdn durch den ~ ziehen** *(inf) (veralbern)* to make fun of sb, to take the mickey out of sb *(inf)*; *(boshaft reden)* to run *or* do sb down.
Kakao-: ~bohne *f* cocoa bean; **~pulver** *nt* cocoa powder; **~strauch** *m* cacao palm.
kakeln *vi (inf)* to chat, to blether *(inf)*.
Kakerlak *m* **-s** *or* **-en, -en** cockroach.
Kaki *f* **-, -s** *(Frucht)* kaki; *(Baum auch)* Japanese persimmon.
⚠ **Kakophonie** *f (geh)* cacophony.
Kaktee *f* **-, -n** [-e:ən], **Kaktus** *m* **-, Kakteen** [-e:ən] *or (inf)* **-se** cactus.
Kalabreser *m* **-s, -** slouch hat.
Kalabrien [-iən] *nt* **-s** Calabria.
Kalamität *f (geh)* calamity; *(heikle Lage)* predicament.
Kalander *m* **-s, -** *(Tech)* calender.
kalandern* *vt (Tech)* to calender.
Kalaschnikow *f* **-, -s** kalashnikov.
Kalauer *m* **-s, -** corny joke; *(Wortspiel)* corny pun; *(alter Witz)* old chestnut.
kalauern *vi (inf)* to joke; to pun.
Kalb *nt* **-(e)s, ¨er (a)** calf; *(von Rehwild auch)* fawn; *siehe* **golden, stechen. (b)** *(inf: Mädchen)* silly young girl *or* thing.
Kälbchen *nt dim of* **Kalb**.
kalben *vi (Kuh, Gletscher)* to calve.
kälbern, kalbern *vi (inf)* to fool *or* mess about *or* around *(inf)*.
Kälberne(s) *nt decl as adj (S Ger, Aus)* veal.
Kalb-: ~fell *nt siehe* **Kalbsfell**; **~fleisch** *nt* veal; **~leder** *nt siehe* **~sleder**.
Kälblein *nt dim of* **Kalb**.
Kalbs-: ~braten *m* roast veal; **~fell** *nt* **(a)** *(Fell)* calfskin; **(b)** *(old: Trommel)* drum; **~hachse, ~haxe** *f (Cook)* knuckle of veal; **~keule** *f* leg of veal; **~leber** *f* calves' liver; **~leder** *nt* calfskin; **~schnitzel** *nt* veal cutlet.
Kaldaune *f* **-, -n** entrails *pl*.
Kalebasse *f* **-, -n** calabash.
Kaledonien [-iən] *nt* **-s** *(liter)* Caledonia.
Kaleidoskop *nt* **-s, -e** kaleidoscope.
kaleidoskopisch *adj* kaleidoscopic.
kalendarisch *adj* calendrical.
Kalendarium *nt (geh, Eccl)* calendar.
Kalender *m* **-s, -** calendar; *(Taschen~)* diary ◆ **etw im ~ rot anstreichen** to make sth a red-letter day.
Kalender-: ~blatt *nt* page of a/the calendar; **~block** *m* day-by-day calendar; **~jahr** *nt* calendar year; **~monat** *m* calendar month; **~spruch** *m* calendar motto.
Kalesche *f* **-, -n** *(Hist)* barouche.
Kalfakter *m* **-s, -, Kalfaktor** *m* **(a)** *(old: Heizer)* boilerman, stoker. **(b)** *(allgemeiner Gehilfe)* odd-job man.
kalfatern* *vti (Naut)* to caulk.
Kali *nt* **-s, -s** potash.
Kaliber *nt* **-s, -** *(lit, fig)* calibre; *(zum Messen)* calibrator.
Kali-: ~bergwerk *nt* potash mine; **~dünger** *m* potash fertilizer.
Kalif *m* **-en, -en** caliph.
Kalifat *nt* caliphate.
Kalifornien [-iən] *nt* **-s** California.
kalifornisch *adj* Californian.
kalihaltig *adj* containing potassium.
Kaliko *m* **-s, -s** calico; *(für Buchbinderei)* cloth.
Kali-: ~salpeter *m* saltpetre; **~salz** *nt* potassium salt.
Kalium *nt* **-s**, *no pl (abbr* **K**) potassium.
Kalk *m* **-(e)s, -e** lime; *(zum Tünchen)* whitewash; *(Anat)* calcium ◆ **gebrannter/gelöschter ~** quicklime/slaked lime; **Wände/Decken mit ~ bewerfen** to whitewash walls/ceilings; **bei ihm rieselt schon der ~** *(inf)* he's going a bit gaga *(inf) or* losing his marbles *(inf)*.
Kalk-: k~artig *adj* chalky, calcareous *(form)*; **~boden** *m* chalky soil; **~brennerei** *f* lime works *sing or pl*.
kalken *vt* **(a)** *(tünchen)* to whitewash. **(b)** *(Agr)* to lime.
Kalk-: ~erde *f* chalky soil; **~grube** *f* lime pit; **k~haltig** *adj Boden* chalky; *Wasser* hard; **~mangel** *m (Med)* calcium deficiency; *(von Boden)* lime deficiency; **~ofen** *m* lime kiln; **~schiefer** *m* calcareous slate; *(Typ)* lithostone; **~stein** *m* limestone; **~steinbruch** *m* limestone quarry.
Kalkül *m or nt* **-s, -e (a)** calculation *usu pl*. **(b)** *(Math)* calculus.
Kalkulation *f* calculation; *(Kostenberechnung)* costing.
Kalkulator *m* **-s, -en (a)** *(als Beruf)* cost estimator. **(b)** *(berechnender Mensch)* cool calculating type *(inf)*.
kalkulatorisch *adj* arithmetical ◆ **~e Methoden** methods of calculation; **das ist ~ einwandfrei, aber** ... the figures are perfect, but ...
kalkulierbar *adj* calculable.
kalkulieren* *vt* to calculate.
Kalkutta *nt* **-s** Calcutta.
⚠ **Kalligraphie** *f* calligraphy.
kallös *adj (Med)* callous.
Kallus *m* **-, -se** *(Biol, Med)* callus.
Kalme *f* **-, -n** *(Naut)* calm.
Kalmen-: ~gürtel *m*, **~zone** *f* calm belt *or* zones *pl*.
Kalmück(e) *m* **-en, -en** Kalmu(c)k *(member of Mongol tribe)*.
Kalorie *f* calorie.
Kalorien- [-iən]: **k~arm** *adj* low-calorie; **~bombe** *f (inf)* **das ist eine echte ~bombe** it's got about sixty million calories *(inf)*; **~gehalt** *m* calorie content; **k~reduziert** *adj (Kost, Mahlzeit)* reduced calorie; **k~reduzierte Kost** reduced calorie food; **k~reich** *adj* high-calorie.
Kalorimeter *m* **-s, -** calorimeter.
kalt *adj, comp* **¨er**, *superl* **¨este(r, s)** *or (adv)* **am ¨esten** cold ◆ **mir ist/wird ~** I am/I'm getting cold; **im K~en** in the cold; **~ schlafen** to sleep in an unheated room; **~e Platte** cold meal; **abends essen wir ~** we eat a cold meal in the evening; **etw ~ stellen** to put sth to chill; **etw ~ bearbeiten** *(Tech)* to work sth cold; **die Wohnung kostet ~ 480 DM** the flat costs 480 DM without heating; **~ rauchen** *(hum)* to have an unlit cigarette in one's mouth; **jdm die ~e Schulter zeigen** to give sb the cold shoulder, to cold-shoulder sb; **da kann ich nur ~ lächeln** *(inf)* that makes me laugh; **~es Grausen** *or* **Entsetzen überkam mich** my blood ran cold; **es überlief ihn ~** cold shivers ran through him; **der ~e** *or* **K~e Krieg** the Cold War; **~er Krieger** cold warrior; **ein ~er Staatsstreich** a bloodless coup.
Kalt-: ⚠**k~bleiben** *vi sep irreg aux sein (fig)* to remain unmoved *or* impassive; **~blut** *nt* carthorse; **~blüter** *m* **-s, -** *(Zool)* cold-blooded animal; **k~blütig** *adj* **(a)** *(fig) Mensch, Mord* cold-blooded; *(gelassen) Handlung* cool; *Mensch* cool, cold-headed, calm; **(b)** *(Zool)* cold-blooded; **~blütigkeit** *f siehe adj* cold-bloodedness; cool(ness); cool-headedness.
Kälte *f* **-**, *no pl* **(a)** *(von Wetter, Material etc)* cold; *(~periode)* cold spell ◆ **die ~ des Stahls/Steins** *etc* the coldness *or* cold of the steel/stone *etc*; **fünf Grad ~** five degrees of frost *or* below freezing; **vor ~ zittern** to shiver with cold; **bei dieser ~** in this cold; **hier ist eine solche ~, daß** ... it is so cold here that ... **(b)** *(fig)* coldness, coolness.
Kälte-: ~anlage *f* refrigeration plant; **k~beständig, k~fest** *adj* cold-resistant; **~brücke** *f (Build)* transmitter of cold; **die Fugen wirken als ~brücken** the gaps introduce cold air; **~einbruch** *m* cold spell; **k~empfindlich** *adj* sensitive to cold; *Mensch auch* chilly; **~erzeugung** *f* refrigeration; **k~fest** *adj siehe* **k~beständig**; **~gefühl** *nt* feeling of cold(ness); **~grad** *m* degree of frost; **~maschine** *f* refrigeration machine; **~pol** *m (Geog)* cold pole, pole of cold; **~resistenz** *f* cold-resistance, resistance to cold; **~sturz** *m siehe* **~einbruch**; **~technik** *f* refrigeration technology; **~tod** *m* **den ~tod sterben** to freeze to death, to die of exposure; *(Erde)* to freeze over completely; **~welle** *f* cold spell.
Kalt-: ~front *f siehe* **~(luft)front**; ⚠**k~gepreßt** *adj Öl* cold-pressed; **~haus** *nt* refrigerated glasshouse; **k~herzig** *adj* cold-hearted; ⚠**k~lächelnd** *adv (iro)* cool as you please; ⚠**k~lassen** *vt sep irreg (fig)* **jdn k~lassen** to leave sb cold; **~leim** *m* wood glue; **~luft** *f (Met)* cold air; **~(luft)front** *f (Met)* cold front; **k~machen** *vt sep (sl)* to do in *(inf)*; **~miete** *f* rent exclusive of heating; **~schale** *f (Cook) cold sweet soup*; **k~schnäuzig** *adj (inf) (gefühllos)* cold, unfeeling, callous; *(unverschämt)* insolent; *Kritiker* sarky *(inf)*, sarcastic; **k~schnäuzig sagte sie** ... as cool as you please she said ...; **~schnäuzigkeit** *f (inf) siehe adj* coldness, unfeelingness, callousness; insolence; sarcasm; **~schweißen** *nt* cold weld; **~start** *m* cold start; **~startautomatik** *f* automatic choke; **k~stellen** *vt sep (inf) jdn* to demote, to put out of harm's way *(inf)*; **~wasserkur** *f siehe* **Kneippkur**; **~welle** *f (Frisur)* cold perm *or* wave.
Kalvarienberg [kal'va:riən-] *m* Calvary.
kalvinisch [kal'vi:nɪʃ] *adj* calvinistic.
Kalvinismus [kalvi'nɪsmʊs] *m* Calvinism.
Kalvinist(in *f*) [kalvi'nɪst(ɪn)] *m* Calvinist.
kalvinistisch [kalvi'nɪstɪʃ] *adj* calvinist(ic).
Kalzium ['kaltsiʊm] *nt, no pl (abbr* **Ca**) calcium.
kam *pret of* **kommen**.
Kamarilla [kama'rɪlja, kama'rɪla] *f* **-, Kamarillen** *(geh)* political clique.
Kamee *f* **-, -n** [-e:ən] cameo.

Kamel *nt* **-(e)s, -e** (a) camel ♦ **eher geht ein ~ durchs Nadelöhr ...** it is easier for a camel to go through the eye of a needle ... (b) (*inf*) clot (*Brit inf*), clown (*inf*) ♦ **ich ~!** silly *or* stupid me!
Kamel-: ~fohlen, ~füllen *nt* camel foal; **~haar** *nt* (*Tex*) camel hair.
Kamelie [-iə] *f* camellia.
Kamelle *f usu pl* (*inf*) **das sind doch alte** *or* **olle ~n** that's old hat (*inf*); **er hat nichts als alte** *or* **olle ~n erzählt** he just said the same old things.
Kameltreiber *m* camel driver, cameleer; (*pej: Orientale*) wog (*pej*).
Kamera *f* **-, -s** camera.
Kamerad *m* **-en, -en** (*Mil etc*) comrade; (*Gefährte, Lebens~*) companion, friend; (*dated: Arbeits~*) workmate; (*dated: Freund*) friend, buddy (*inf*), chum (*inf*).
Kameraderie *f* (*pej*) bonhomie.
Kameradschaft *f* comradeship, camaraderie.
kameradschaftlich *adj* comradely ♦ **eine ~e Ehe** a companionate marriage.
Kameradschaftlichkeit *f* comradeship, comradeliness.
Kameradschafts-: ~abend *m* reunion; **~ehe** *f* companionate marriage; **~geist** *m* spirit of comradeship, esprit de corps.
Kamera-: ~einstellung *f* shot; **~fahrt** *f* camera movement; **~frau** *f* camerawoman; **~führung** *f* camera work.
Kameralistik *f* (*old*) finance.
Kamera-: ~mann *m, pl* **~männer** cameraman; **k~scheu** *adj* camera-shy; **~schwenk** *m* pan.
Kamerun *nt* **-s** the Cameroons *pl*.
Kamikaze *m* **-, -** Kamikaze.
Kamikaze-: ~-Angriff *m* Kamikaze attack; **~-Flieger** *m* Kamikaze pilot.
Kamille *f* **-, -n** camomile.
Kamillentee *m* camomile tea.
Kamin *m or* (*dial*) *nt* **-s, -e** (a) (*Schornstein*) chimney; (*Abzugsschacht*) flue ♦ **etw in den ~ schreiben** to write sth off. (b) (*offene Feuerstelle*) fireplace ♦ **eine Plauderei am ~** a fireside chat; **wir saßen am** *or* **vor dem ~** we sat by *or* in front of the fire *or* round the hearth. (c) (*Geol: Fels~*) chimney.
Kamin-: ~besteck *nt siehe* **~garnitur**; **~feuer** *nt* open fire, fire in the grate; **~garnitur** *f* fireside companion set; **~kehrer** *m* **-s, -** (*dial*) *siehe* **Schornsteinfeger**; **~sims** *m or nt* mantelpiece.
Kamm *m* **-(e)s, ¨-e** (a) (*für Haar, Webe~*) comb ♦ **sich** (*dat*) **mit dem ~ durch die Haare fahren** to run a comb through one's hair; **alle/alles über einen ~ scheren** (*fig*) to lump everyone/everything together.
(b) (*von Vogel, Eidechse etc*) comb; *siehe* **schwellen.**
(c) (*von Pferd*) crest.
(d) (*Cook*) (*Hammelfleisch*) (middle) neck; (*Schweinefleisch*) spare rib; (*Rindfleisch*) neck.
(e) (*von Trauben*) stalk.
(f) (*Gebirgs~*) crest, ridge; (*Wellen~*) crest.
kämmen [1] *vt Haar, Baumwolle* to comb; *Wolle auch* to card, to tease ♦ **sie kämmte ihm die Haare** she combed his hair.
[2] *vr* to comb one's hair.
Kammer *f* **-, -n** (a) (*allgemein*) chamber; (*Parl auch*) house; (*Ärzte~, Anwalts~*) professional association; (*Herz~*) ventricle; (*Mil*) store *usu pl* ♦ **Erste/Zweite ~** Upper/Lower House. (b) (*Zimmer*) (small) room, box room; (*dial: Schlafzimmer*) bedroom.
Kammer-: ~bulle *m* (*Mil sl*) quartermaster; **~diener** *m* valet.
Kämmerei *f* (a) (*Hist: Finanzverwaltung*) treasury (*old*); finance department. (b) (*Tex*) combing works *sing or pl*.
Kämmerer *m* **-s, -** (a) (*Beamter*) finance officer. (b) (*Hist, Eccl*) chamberlain.
Kammer-: ~frau *f* (*Hist*) lady-in-waiting; **~gericht** *nt* ≃ Supreme Court; **~herr** *m* (*Hist*) chamberlain; **~jäger** *m* (*Schädlingsbekämpfer*) pest controller; (*Leibjäger*) (head) gamekeeper; **~jungfer** *f* lady-in-waiting; **~konzert** *nt* chamber concert.
Kämmerlein *nt* chamber ♦ **im stillen ~** in private.
Kammer-: ~mädchen *nt siehe* **~jungfer**; **~musik** *f* chamber music; **~orchester** *nt* chamber orchestra; **~sänger** *m*, **~schauspieler** *m* (*Titel*) *title formerly given by Duke etc, now by authorities, to singer/actor for excellence*; **~spiel** *nt* (a) (*Schauspiel*) play for a studio theatre; (b) (*Theater*) studio theatre; **~ton** *m* concert pitch; **~zofe** *f* chambermaid.
Kamm-: ~garn *nt* worsted; **~muschel** *f siehe* **Kammuschel**; **~rad** *nt* cogwheel; **~stück** *nt* (*Cook*) shoulder.
⚠ **Kammuschel** *nt getrennt* **Kamm-muschel** scallop.
Kamp *m* **-(e)s, ¨-e** (*N Ger*) plot (of land), field.
Kampagne [kam'panjə] *f* **-, -n** (a) campaign. (b) (*bei Ausgrabungen*) stage.
Kämpe *m* **-n, -n** (*obs, iro*) (old) campaigner *or* soldier.
Kampf *m* **-(e)s, ¨-e** fight, struggle (*um* for); (*Mil auch*) combat; (*Mil: Gefecht*) battle; (*Feindbegegnung*) engagement, encounter; (*Box~*) fight, bout, contest ♦ **jdm/einer Sache den ~ ansagen** (*fig*) to declare war on sb/sth; **den ~/die ¨-e einstellen** to stop fighting; **den ~ um etw verloren geben** to abandon the struggle for sth; **den ~ aufgeben** to give up the struggle; **den ~ abbrechen** (*Sport*) to stop the fight; **es kam zum ~** clashes occurred, fighting broke out; **auf in den ~!** (*hum*) once more unto the breach! (*hum*); **er ist im ~ gefallen** he fell in action *or* battle; **im ~ für die Freiheit/Frankreich** in the struggle for freedom/the battle for France; **der ~ ums Dasein** the struggle for existence; **der ~ der Geschlechter** *or* **zwischen den Geschlechtern** the battle of the sexes; **der ~ um die Macht** the battle *or* struggle for power; **ein ~ auf Leben und Tod** a fight to the death; **~ dem Atomtod!** fight the nuclear menace!; **innere ¨-e** inner conflicts.

Kampf-: ~abschnitt *m* combat zone *or* sector; **~abstimmung** *f* vote; **es kam zur ~abstimmung** they put it to the vote; **~abzeichen** *nt* campaign medal; **~ansage** *f* declaration of war; (*Sport*) announcement; **~bahn** *f* sports stadium, arena; **~begier(de)** *f* (*liter*) bellicosity (*liter*); **k~bereit** *adj* ready for battle; **~bomber** *m* fighter bomber; **~einsatz** *m* combat mission.
kämpfen [1] *vi* to fight, to struggle (*um, für* for); (*Sport: angreifen*) to attack ♦ **gegen etw ~** to fight (against) sth; **die Rangers-Elf kämpft morgen gegen Celtic** Rangers are playing (against) Celtic tomorrow; **mit dem Tode ~** to fight for one's life; **mit den Tränen ~** to fight back one's tears; **gegen die Wellen ~** to battle against the waves; **ich hatte mit schweren Problemen zu ~** I had difficult problems to contend with; **ich habe lange mit mir ~ müssen, ehe ...** I had a long battle with myself before ...
[2] *vt* (*usu fig*) *Kampf* to fight.
Kampfer *m* **-s,** *no pl* camphor.
Kämpfer *m* **-s, -** (*Archit*) impost.
Kämpfer(in *f*) *m* **-s, -** fighter; (*Krieger auch*) warrior.
kämpferisch *adj* aggressive; *Spiel auch* attacking.
kampf|erprobt *adj* battle-tried.
Kampfeslust *f* pugnacity.
Kampf-: k~fähig *adj* (*Mil*) fit for action; *Boxer* fit to fight; **~flugzeug** *nt* fighter (plane); **~gas** *nt* poison gas; **~geist** *m* fighting spirit; **~gemeinschaft** *f* (*Pol*) action group; **~gruppe** *f* task force; (*Mil auch*) combat group; **~hahn** *m* (*lit, fig*) fighting cock; **~handlung** *f usu pl* clash *usu pl*; **~hubschrauber** *m* helicopter gunship; **~hund** *m* fighting dog; **~kraft** *f* fighting strength; **k~los** *adj* peaceful; **sich k~los ergeben, k~los aufgeben** to surrender without a fight; **k~lustig** *adj* belligerent, pugnacious; **~maßnahme** *f* offensive measure; **~maßnahmen ergreifen** to go onto the offensive; **~panzer** *m* combat tank; **~platz** *m* battlefield; (*Sport*) arena, stadium; **~preis** *m* (a) (*in Wett~*) prize; (b) (*Comm*) cut-throat price; **~richter** *m* (*Sport*) referee; (*Tennis*) umpire; (*Schwimmen, Skilaufen*) judge; **~schrift** *f* broadsheet; **~sport** *m* martial art; **~stärke** *f* (*Mil*) combat strength; **~stoff** *m* weapon, warfare agent; **~tag** *m* **~tag der Arbeiterklasse** (*DDR*) May Day; **k~unfähig** *adj* (*Mil*) unfit for fighting *or* battle; (*Sport*) unfit; **einen Panzer/ein Schiff k~unfähig machen** to put a tank/ship out of action, to cripple a tank/ship; **k~unfähig schlagen** (*Boxen*) to put out of the fight; **~wagen** *m* chariot.
kampieren* *vi* to camp (out) ♦ **im Wohnzimmer ~** (*inf*) to doss down in the sitting room (*inf*).
Kanaan ['ka:naan] *nt* **-s** (*Bibl*) Canaan.
Kanada *nt* **-s** Canada.
Kanadier [-iɐ] *m* **-s, -** Canadian; (*Sport*) Canadian canoe.
Kanadierin [-iərin] *f* Canadian (woman/girl).
kanadisch *adj* Canadian.
Kanaille [ka'naljə] *f* **-, -n** (*dated pej*) (*gemeiner Mensch*) scoundrel, rascal; (*Pöbel, Mob*) rabble, canaille.
Kanake *m* **-n, -n** (*Südseeinsulaner*) Kanaka; (*pej: Ausländer, Südländer*) wop (*pej*), dago (*pej*).
Kanal *m* **-s, Kanäle** (a) (*Schiffahrtsweg*) canal; (*Wasserlauf*) channel; (*zur Bewässerung auch*) ditch; (*zur Entwässerung*) drain; (*für Abwässer*) sewer ♦ **der (Ärmel)k~** the (English) Channel; **sich** (*dat*) **den ~ vollaufen lassen** (*sl*) to get canned (*sl*); **den ~ voll haben** (*sl*) (*betrunken sein*) to be canned (*sl*); (*es satt haben*) to have had a bellyful (*sl*).
(b) (*Radio, TV, fig: Weg*) channel ♦ **etw durch die richtigen Kanäle weiterleiten** to pass sth on through the proper channels; **dunkle Kanäle** dubious channels.
Kanal-: ~arbeiter *m* (a) sewerage worker; (b) *pl* (*fig Pol*) pressure group; **~bau** *m* canal building *or* construction; **~deckel** *m* drain cover.
Kanalisation *f* (a) (*für Abwässer*) sewerage system, sewers *pl*; (*das Kanalisieren*) sewerage installation. (b) (*Begradigung eines Flußlaufes*) canalization.
kanalisieren* [1] *vt Fluß* to canalize; (*fig*) *Energie, Emotionen etc* to channel.
[2] *vti* to install *or* lay sewers (in).
Kanal-: ~tunnel *m* channel tunnel; **~zone** *f* canal zone.
Kanapee *nt* **-s, -s** (*old, hum*) sofa, couch, settee.
Kanaren *pl* (*form*) Canary Islands *pl*.
Kanarienvogel [-iən-] *m* canary.
Kanarische Inseln *pl* Canaries *pl*, Canary Islands *pl*.
Kandare *f* **-, -n** (curb) bit ♦ **jdn an die ~ nehmen** (*fig*) to take sb in hand.
Kandelaber *m* **-s, -** candelabra.
Kandidat *m* **-en, -en** candidate; (*bei Bewerbung auch*) applicant ♦ **jdn als ~en aufstellen** to nominate sb, to put sb forward as a candidate.
Kandidatenliste *f* list of candidates.
Kandidatin *f* candidate; (*bei Bewerbung auch*) applicant.
Kandidatur *f* candidature, candidacy.
kandidieren* *vi* (*Pol*) to stand, to run (*für* for) ♦ **für das Amt des Präsidenten ~** to stand *or* run for president.
kandiert *adj Frucht* candied.
Kandis(zucker) *m* **-** rock candy.
⚠ **Känguruh** ['kɛŋguru] *nt* **-s, -s** kangaroo.
Kanin *nt* **-s, -e** rabbit (fur).
Kaninchen *nt* rabbit ♦ **sich wie ~ vermehren** (*inf*) to breed like rabbits.
Kaninchen-: ~bau *m* rabbit warren; **~stall** *m* rabbit hutch.
Kanister *m* **-s, -** can; (*Blech~*) jerry can.
⚠ **Kann-Bestimmung** *f* (*Jur*) discretionary provision.
Kännchen *nt* (*für Milch*) jug; (*für Kaffee*) pot ♦ **ein ~ Kaffee** a pot of coffee.

⚠: for details of spelling reform, see supplement

Kanne *f* **-, -n** can; (*Tee~, Kaffee~*) pot; (*Milch~*) churn; (*Öl~*) can, tin; (*Wein~*) ≃ tankard; (*Gieß~*) watering can.
kanneliert *adj* (*Archit*) fluted.
Kannibale *m* **-n, -n, Kannibalin** *f* cannibal.
kannibalisch *adj* cannibalistic; (*brutal*) rough ♦ **ich habe ~en Hunger** (*hum inf*) I could eat a horse (*inf*).
Kannibalismus *m* cannibalism.
kannte *pret of* **kennen.**
Kanon *m* **-s, -s** (*alle Bedeutungen*) canon.
Kanonade *f* (*Mil*) barrage; (*fig auch*) tirade.
Kanone *f* **-, -n (a)** gun; (*Hist*) cannon; (*sl: Pistole*) rod (*US sl*), gat (*sl*), shooter (*sl*) ♦ **~n auffahren** (*lit, fig*) to bring up the big guns; **mit ~n auf Spatzen schießen** (*inf*) to take a sledgehammer to crack a nut. **(b)** (*fig inf: Könner*) ace (*inf*). **(c)** (*inf*) **das ist unter aller ~** that defies description.
Kanonen-: ~boot *nt* gunboat; **~bootdiplomatie, ~bootpolitik** *f* gunboat diplomacy; **~donner** *m* rumbling of guns; **~futter** *nt* (*inf*) cannon fodder; **~kugel** *f* cannon ball; **~ofen** *m* cylindrical iron stove; **~rohr** *nt* gun barrel; **heiliges ~rohr!** (*inf*) good grief (*inf*); **~schlag** *m* (*Feuerwerkskörper*) (fire)cracker.
Kanonier *m* **-s, -e** (*Mil*) gunner, artilleryman.
Kanoniker *m* **-s, -, Kanonikus** *m* **-, Kanonizi** (*Eccl*) canon.
Kanonisation *f* (*Eccl*) canonization.
kanonisch *adj* (*Eccl*) canonical ♦ **~es Recht** canon law.
kanonisieren* *vt* (*Eccl*) to canonize.
Kanonisse *f* **-, -n, Kanonissin** *f* canoness.
Kanossa *nt* **-s** (*fig*) humiliation.
Kanossagang *m*: **einen ~ machen** *or* **antreten müssen** to eat humble pie.
Kantate[1] *f* **-, -n** (*Mus*) cantata.
Kantate[2] *no art* (*Eccl*) *fourth Sunday after Easter.*
Kante *f* **-, -n** (*eines Gegenstandes, einer Fläche*) edge; (*Rand, Borte*) border; (*Web~*) selvedge ♦ **wir legten die Steine ~ an ~** we laid the stones end to end; **etw auf ~ kleben** to stick sth with the edges flush; **Geld auf die hohe ~ legen** (*inf*) to put money by (*inf*) *or* away; **Geld auf der hohen ~ haben** (*inf*) to have (some) money put by (*inf*) *or* away; *siehe* **abstoßen, fehlen.**
Kanten *m* **-s, -** (*N Ger*) crust, heel (*dial*).
kanten *vt* **(a)** to tilt ♦ **nicht ~!** (*bei Kisten etc*) do not tilt!, this way up! **(b)** (*mit Kanten versehen*) to trim, to edge. **(c)** *auch vi* (*Ski*) to edge.
Kanter *m* **-s, -** canter.
Kant-: ~haken *m*: **jdn beim ~haken nehmen** (*inf*) *or* **zu fassen kriegen** (*inf*) to haul sb over the coals (*inf*); **~holz** *nt* (piece of) squared timber.
kantig *adj Holz* edged, squared; *Gesicht* angular.
-kantig *adj suf* -edged.
Kantilene *f* **-, -n** (*Mus*) cantilena.
Kantine *f* canteen.
Kantisch, kantisch *adj* Kantian.
Kanton *m* **-s, -e** canton.
Kantonist *m*: **ein unsicherer ~ sein** to be unreliable.
Kantor *m* choirmaster; (*in Synagoge*) cantor.
Kantorei *f* (church) choir.
Kantorin *f* choirmistress.
Kanu *nt* **-s, -s** canoe.
Kanüle *f* **-, -n** (*Med*) cannula.
Kanute *m* **-n, -n** canoeist.
Kanzel *f* **-, -n (a)** pulpit ♦ **auf der ~** in the pulpit; **die ~ besteigen** to get into the pulpit; **von der ~ herab** from the pulpit. **(b)** (*Aviat*) cockpit. **(c)** (*eines Berges*) promontory, spur. **(d)** (*Hunt*) (look-out) platform.
Kanzel-: ~dach *m* canopy; **~redner** *m* orator.
Kanzlei *f* **(a)** (*Dienststelle*) office; (*Büro eines Rechtsanwalts, Notars etc*) chambers *pl.* **(b)** (*Hist, Pol*) chancellery.
Kanzlei-: ~sprache *f* official language; **~stil** *m* (*pej*) officialese.
Kanzler *m* **-s, - (a)** (*Regierungschef*) chancellor; *siehe* **Bundes~, Reichs~. (b)** (*diplomatischer Beamter*) chancellor, chief secretary. **(c)** (*Univ*) vice-chancellor.
Kanzler-: ~amt *nt* (*Gebäude*) chancellory; (*Posten*) chancellorship; **~amtschef** *m* head of the chancellory; **~berater** *m* adviser to the chancellor; **~bonus** *m* advantage of being the chancellor in power; **~kandidat** *m* candidate for the post of chancellor.
Kanzlist *m* (*old*) clerk.
Kaolin *m or nt* **-s, -e** kaolin.
Kap *nt* **-s, -s** cape, headland ♦ **~ der Guten Hoffnung** Cape of Good Hope; **~ Hoorn** Cape Horn.
Kapaun *m* **-s, -e** capon.
Kapazität *f* capacity; (*fig: Experte*) expert, authority.
Kapee *nt*: **schwer von ~ sein** (*inf*) to be slow on the uptake (*inf*).
Kapelle *f* **(a)** (*kleine Kirche etc*) chapel. **(b)** (*Mus*) band, orchestra.
Kapellmeister *m* (*Mus*) director of music; (*Mil, von Tanzkapelle etc*) bandmaster, bandleader.
Kaper[1] *f* **-, -n** (*Bot, Cook*) caper.
Kaper[2] *m* **-s, -** (*Naut*) privateer.
Kaperbrief *m* letter of marque.
kapern *vt* (*Naut*) *Schiff* to seize, to capture; (*fig inf*) *Ding* to commandeer (*inf*), to grab; *jdn* to grab; (*mit Beschlag belegen*) to buttonhole, to collar (*inf*).
Kaperschiff *nt* privateer.
kapieren* *vti* (*inf*) to get (*inf*), to understand ♦ **kapiert?** got it? (*inf*); **kapierst du (denn) jetzt?** do you get it now? (*inf*); **er hat schnell kapiert** he caught on quick (*inf*).
Kapillargefäß *nt* (*Anat*) capillary.
kapital *adj* **(a)** (*Hunt*) *Hirsch* royal ♦ **einen ~en Bock schießen** (*fig*) to make a real bloomer (*inf*). **(b)** (*grundlegend*) *Mißverständnis etc* major.
Kapital *nt* **-s, -e** *or* **-ien** [-iən] **(a)** (*Fin*) capital *no pl*; (*pl: angelegtes ~*) capital investments *pl* ♦ **flüssiges** *or* **verfügbares ~** ready *or* available capital; **er ist mit 35% am ~ dieser Firma beteiligt** he has a 35% stake in this firm. **(b)** (*fig*) asset. **aus etw ~ schlagen** (*pej*) (*lit, fig*) to make capital out of sth; (*fig auch*) to capitalize on sth.
Kapital-: ⚠**~abfluß** *m, no pl* capital outflow; **~abwanderung** *f* exodus of capital; **~anlage** *f* capital investment, investment of capital; **~anlagegesellschaft** *f* investment fund; **~beteiligungsgesellschaft** *f* capital investment company; **~decke** *f* capital resources *pl*; **~einlage** *f* capital contribution; **~erhöhung** *f* capital increase; **~ertragssteuer** *f* capital gains tax; **~flucht** *f* flight of capital; **~gesellschaft** *f* (*Comm*) joint-stock company; **k~intensiv** *adj* capital-intensive.
kapitalisieren* *vt* to capitalize.
Kapitalismus *m* capitalism.
Kapitalist(in *f*) *m* capitalist.
kapitalistisch *adj* capitalist.
Kapital-: ~lebensversicherung *f* capital sum life insurance, endowment insurance; **~markt** *m* money market; **~sammelstelle** *f* institutional investor; **~stückkosten** *pl* (*Econ*) unit production costs *pl*; **~verbrechen** *nt* serious crime; (*mit Todesstrafe*) capital crime *or* offence; **~versicherung** *f* (*Insur*) capital insurance.
Kapitän *m* **-s, -e (a)** (*Naut, Mil*) captain; (*esp auf kleinerem Schiff auch*) skipper (*inf*); (*auf Handelsschiff auch*) master ♦ **~ zur See** (*Mil*) captain. **(b)** (*Sport*) captain. **(c)** (*Aviat*) captain.
Kapitänleutnant *m* lieutenant-commander.
Kapitänspatent *nt* master's certificate.
Kapitel *nt* **-s, - (a)** chapter; (*fig auch*) period; (*Angelegenheit*) chapter of events, story ♦ **ein dunkles ~ in seinem Leben** a dark chapter in his life; **das ist ein anderes ~** that's another story; **das ist ein ~ für sich** that's a story all to itself; **für mich ist dieses ~ erledigt** as far as I'm concerned the matter is closed. **(b)** (*Eccl: Dom~*) chapter.
Kapitell *nt* **-s, -e** capital.
Kapitulation *f* (*von Armee, Land*) surrender, capitulation (*auch fig*) (*vor +dat* to, in the face of) ♦ **bedingungslose ~** unconditional surrender; **das ist eine ~ vor deinen Pflichten/Kindern** that's refusing to face up to your responsibilities/that's capitulating to your children.
kapitulieren* *vi* (*sich ergeben*) to surrender, to capitulate; (*fig: aufgeben*) to give up, to capitulate (*vor +dat* in the face of).
Kaplan *m* **-s, Kapläne** (*in Pfarrei*) curate; (*mit besonderen Aufgaben*) chaplain.
Kapo *m* **-s, -s (a)** (*Aufseher*) overseer; (*S Ger inf: Vorarbeiter*) gaffer (*inf*). **(b)** (*Mil sl: Unteroffizier*) NCO; (*Feldwebel*) sarge (*sl*); (*Obergefreiter*) corp (*sl*).
Kapodaster *m* **-s, -** capo.
Kapok *m* **-s,** *no pl* (*Tex*) kapok.
Kaposi *nt* **-(s), -s, Kaposi-Sarkom** *nt* **-s, -e** (*Med*) Kaposi's sarcoma.
Kappe *f* **-, -n** cap; (*Flieger~, Motorradmütze*) helmet; (*Narrenmütze*) jester's cap; carnival *or* fancy-dress hat; (*von Jude*) skullcap; (*von Füllfederhalter, Saftflaschen auch*) top; (*Schuh~*) (*vorne*) toe(cap); (*hinten*) heelpiece; (*Archit*) coping ♦ **eine ~ aus Schnee** a snowcap; **das nehme ich auf meine ~** (*fig inf*) I'll take the responsibility for that, on my head be it; **das geht auf meine ~** (*inf: ich bezahle*) that's on me.
kappen *vt* **(a)** (*Naut*) *Tau, Leine* to cut; *Ast* to cut back, to trim; (*Med*) *Mandeln* to clip (off); (*fig inf*) *Finanzmittel* to cut (back). **(b)** (*kastrieren*) *Hähne* to caponize.
Kappen|abend *m carnival fancy-dress party where fancy-dress hats are worn.*
Kappes *m* **-, -** (*dial: Kohl*) cabbage ♦ **~ reden** (*sl*) to talk (a load of) rubbish *or* baloney (*sl*).
Käppi *nt* **-s, -s** cap.
Kappnaht *f* French seam.
Kaprice [ka'priːsə] *f* **-, -n** caprice.
Kapriole *f* **-, -n** capriole; (*fig*) caper ♦ **~n machen** to cut capers.
Kaprize (*Aus*) *f* **-, -n** *siehe* **Kaprice.**
kaprizieren* *vr* (*geh*) to insist (*auf +acc* on).
kapriziös *adj* (*geh*) capricious.
Kapsel *f* **-, -n** (*Etui*) container; (*Anat, Bot, Pharm, Space etc*) capsule; (*an einer Flasche*) cap, top; (*Spreng~*) detonator.
kaputt *adj* (*inf*) broken; *esp Maschine, Glühbirne etc* kaput (*sl*); (*erschöpft*) *Mensch* shattered (*inf*), done in (*inf*), knackered (*Brit sl*); *Ehe* broken; *Beziehungen, Gesundheit* ruined; *Nerven* shattered; *Firma* bust *pred* (*inf*) ♦ **das alte Auto/das Dach/ihre Ehe ist ~** (*irreparabel*) (*inf*) the old car/the roof/her marriage has had it (*inf*); **irgend etwas muß an deinem Auto ~ sein** something must be wrong with your car; **der Fernseher ist ~** (*vorläufig*) the TV is on the blink (*inf*); **mein ~es Bein** my gammy (*inf*) *or* bad leg; (*gebrochen*) my broken leg; **mein ~es Auge** my dud eye (*inf*); **meine Hose ist ~** (*nicht mehr tragbar*) my trousers have had it (*inf*); (*zerrissen*) my trousers are torn *or* ripped; (*am Saum*) my trousers are coming apart; **das ~e Deutschland** the (war-)shattered Germany; **die ~e Welt** this mess of a world; **ein ~er Typ** (*inf*) a wreck (*inf*).
kaputt-: ~fahren *vt sep irreg* (*inf*) (*überfahren*) to run over; *Auto* to drive *or* run into the ground, to knacker (*Brit sl*); (*durch Unfall*) to smash (up), to write off; **~gehen** *vi sep irreg aux sein* (*inf*) to break; (*esp Maschine*) to go kaput (*sl*); (*esp Glühbirne, Elektronenröhre etc*) to go kaput (*sl*), to go phut (*inf*);

(*Ehe*) to break up, to go on the rocks (*inf*) (*an +dat* because of); (*Beziehungen, Gesundheit, Nerven*) to be ruined, to go to pot (*inf*); (*Firma*) to go bust (*inf*), to fold up; (*Waschmaschine, Auto*) to break down, to pack up (*Brit inf*); (*Kleidung*) to come to pieces; (*zerrissen werden*) to tear; (*sl: sterben*) to kick the bucket (*inf*), to croak (*sl*); (*Blumen*) to die off; **der Fernseher ist schon wieder ~gegangen** (*vorläufig*) the TV has gone on the blink again (*inf*); **in dem Büro/an diesem Job gehe ich noch ~** this office/job will be the death of me (*inf*); **~kriegen** *vt sep* (*inf*) *Zerbrechliches* to break; *Auto* to ruin; *jdn* to wear out; **das Auto/der Hans ist nicht ~zukriegen** this car/Hans just goes on for ever; **~lachen** *vr sep* (*inf*) to die laughing (*inf*); **ich lach' mich ~!** what a laugh!; **ich hätte mich ~lachen können** I nearly killed myself (*sl*); **~machen** *sep* (*inf*) [1] *vt* to ruin; *Zerbrechliches* to break, to smash; *Brücke, Sandburg* to knock down; (*erschöpfen*) *jdn* to wear out, to knacker (*Brit sl*); **diese ewigen Sorgen/die Kinder machen mich ~** these never-ending worries/the children will be the death of me (*inf*); [2] *vr* (*sich überanstrengen*) to wear oneself out, to slog oneself into the ground (*inf*), to knacker oneself (*Brit sl*); **~schlagen** *vt sep irreg* (*inf*) to break, to smash.

Kapuze *f -, -n* hood; (*Mönchs~*) cowl.

Kapuziner *m -s, -* (*Eccl*) Capucin (monk); (*Bot: auch* **~kresse** *f*) nasturtium.

Kar *nt -(e)s, -e* corrie, cwm, cirque.

Karabiner *m -s, -* **(a)** (*Gewehr*) carbine. **(b)** (*auch* **~haken**) karabiner, snap link, crab (*inf*).

Karacho *nt -s, no pl*: **mit** *or* **im ~** (*inf*) at full tilt, hell for leather (*inf*); **er rannte/fuhr mit ~ gegen die Wand** he ran/drove smack into the wall.

Karaffe *f -, -n* carafe; (*mit Stöpsel*) decanter.

Karambolage [karambo'la:ʒə] *f -, -n* (*Aut*) collision, crash; (*Billard*) cannon.

Karambole *f -, -n* (*beim Billardspiel*) red (ball).

karambolieren* *vi aux sein* (*beim Billard*) to cannon; (*Autos*) to crash (*mit* into), to collide (*mit* with).

Karamel *m -s, no pl* caramel *no pl*.

Karamelle *f* caramel (toffee).

Karaoke *nt - no pl* karoake.

Karat *nt -(e)s, -e or* (*bei Zahlenangabe*) *-* (*Measure*) carat ◆ **das Gold dieses Ringes hat 9 ~** this ring is made of 9-carat gold.

Karate *nt -(s), no pl* karate.

Karatehieb *m* karate chop.

-karäter *m in cpds* **-s, - Zehn~** ten-carat diamond/stone.

-karätig *adj suf* carat.

Karavelle [kara'vɛlə] *f* caravel.

Karawane *f -, -n* caravan.

Karawanenstraße *f* caravan route.

Karbid *nt -(e)s, -e* carbide.

Karbidlampe *f* davy lamp.

Karbol *nt -s, no pl*, **Karbolsäure** *f* carbolic acid.

Karbonat *nt* carbonate.

karbonisieren* *vt* to carbonize; *Getränke* to carbonate.

Karbunkel *m -s, -* (*Med*) carbuncle.

Kardamom *m -s, no pl* cardamom.

Kardan-: ~gelenk *nt* universal joint; **~tunnel** *m* transmission tunnel; **~welle** *f* prop(eller) shaft.

Kardinal *m -s,* **Kardinäle (a)** (*Eccl*) cardinal. **(b)** (*Orn*) cardinal (bird).

Kardinal-: ~fehler *m* cardinal error; **~tugend** *f* (*Philos, Rel*) cardinal virtue; **~zahl** *f* cardinal (number).

Kardio-: ~gramm *nt* cardiogram; **~logie** *f* cardiology; **k~logisch** *adj* cardiological.

Karenz-: ~tag *m* unpaid day of sick leave; **~zeit** *f* waiting period.

Karfiol *m -s, no pl* (*Aus*) cauliflower ◆ **zwei (Rosen) ~** two cauliflowers.

Karfreitag *m* Good Friday.

Karfunkel *m -s, -* **(a)** *siehe* **Karbunkel. (b)** *siehe* **Karfunkelstein.**

Karfunkelstein *m red precious stone such as ruby or garnet*, carbuncle (stone).

karg *adj* **(a)** (*spärlich*) *Vorrat* meagre, sparse; (*unfruchtbar*) *Boden* barren; (*dürftig*) *Gehalt, Einkommen* meagre ◆ **~ möbliert** sparsely furnished; **~ leben** to lead a meagre existence.
(b) (*geizig*) mean, sparing ◆ **etw ~ bemessen** to be mean *or* stingy (*inf*) with sth; **die Portionen sind sehr ~ bemessen** they are very mean *or* stingy (*inf*) with the helpings.

kargen *vi* (*sparsam sein*) to stint (*mit* on), to scrimp and save (*mit* with); (*knausern*) to be mean *or* stingy (*inf*) (*mit* with); (*mit Lob*) to be grudging.

Kargheit *f siehe adj* (*a*) meagreness, sparseness; barrenness.

kärglich *adj Vorrat* meagre, sparse; *Mahl* frugal; (*dürftig*) *Gehalt, Einkommen* meagre ◆ **unter ~en Bedingungen leben** to live in impoverished conditions; **sie leben ~** they lead a meagre existence.

Kärglichkeit *f siehe adj* meagreness, sparseness; frugality.

Kargo *m -s, -s* cargo.

Karibe *m -n, -n* Carib.

Karibik *f - die ~* the Caribbean.

Karibin *f* Carib.

karibisch *adj* Caribbean ◆ **das K~e Meer** the Caribbean Sea; **die K~en Inseln** the Caribbean Islands.

kariert *adj Stoff, Muster* checked, checkered (*esp US*); *Papier* squared ◆ **red' nicht so ~!** (*inf*) don't talk such rubbish; **~ gucken** (*inf*) to look puzzled.

Karies ['ka:riɛs] *f -, no pl* caries.

Karikatur *f* caricature ◆ **eine ~ von jdm/etw zeichnen** (*lit*) to draw a caricature of sb/sth; (*lit, fig*) to caricature sb/sth.

Karikaturist(in *f*) *m* cartoonist; (*Personenzeichner auch*) caricaturist.

karikaturistisch *adj* caricatural (*form*), caricature ◆ **dieser Artikel ist ~** this article is a caricature.

karikieren* *vt* to caricature.

kariös *adj Zahn* carious, decayed.

Karitas *f -, no pl* (*Nächstenliebe*) charity; (*Verband auch*) charitable organization.

karitativ *adj* charitable.

Karkasse *f -, -n* **(a)** (*Cook*) carcass. **(b)** (*Aut: von Reifen*) casing.

Karl *m -s* Charles ◆ **~ der Große** Charlemagne.

Karma *nt -s, no pl* karma.

Karmeliter(in *f*) *m -s, -* Carmelite.

Karmesin *nt -s, no pl* crimson.

karmesin(rot) *adj* crimson.

karmin(rot) *adj* carmine (red).

Karneval ['karnəval] *m -s, -e or -s* carnival.

Karnevalszug *m* carnival procession.

Karnickel *nt -s, -* (*inf*) **(a)** bunny (rabbit) (*inf*), rabbit. **(b)** (*hum: Schuldiger*) scapegoat.

Karnickel-: ~bock *m* buck rabbit; **~stall** *m* rabbit hutch.

karnivor [karni'vo:ɐ] *adj* (*Biol*) carnivorous.

Kärnten *nt -s* Carinthia.

Karo *nt -s, -s* (*Quadrat*) square; (*auf der Spitze stehend*) diamond, lozenge; (*Muster*) check; (*diagonal*) diamond; (*Cards*) diamonds *pl*.

Karo- *in cpds* (*Cards*) of diamonds.

Karolinger *m -s, -* Carolingian.

karolingisch *adj* Carolingian ◆ **K~e Minuskeln** Caroline minuscule.

Karomuster *nt* checked *or* chequered (*esp US*) pattern.

Karosse *f -, -n* (*Prachtkutsche*) (state) coach; (*fig: großes Auto*) limousine.

Karosserie *f* bodywork.

Karosserie-: ~bauer *m* coachbuilder; **~schaden** *m* damage to the bodywork; **~schlosser** *m* panelbeater; **~werkstatt** *f* body (repair) shop.

Karotin *nt -s, -e* carotene, carotin.

Karotte *f -, -n* (small) carrot.

Karpaten *pl* Carpathian Mountains *pl*, Carpathians *pl*.

Karpell *nt -s, -e or -a* (*Bot*) carpel.

Karpfen *m -s, -* carp.

Karpfen-: k~artig *adj* (*lit*) carp-like; (*fig*) *Gesicht, Aussehen* fish-like; **~teich** *m* carp pond; *siehe* **Hecht.**

Karre *f -, -n* **(a)** *siehe* **Karren. (b)** (*inf: klappriges Auto*) (old) crate (*inf*) *or* heap (*inf*).

Karree *nt -s, -s* **(a)** (*Viereck*) rectangle; (*Rhombus*) rhombus; (*Quadrat*) square; (*Formation: esp Mil*) square. **(b)** (*Häuserblock*) block ◆ **einmal ums ~ gehen** to walk round the block. **(c)** (*esp Aus: Cook*) loin.

Karren *m -s, -* **(a)** (*Wagen*) cart; (*esp für Garten, Baustelle*) (wheel)barrow; (*für Gepäck etc*) trolley ◆ **ein ~ voll Obst** a cartload of fruit.
(b) (*fig inf*) **jdm an den ~ fahren** to take sb to task; **den ~ einfach laufen lassen** to let things go *or* slide; **den ~ in den Dreck fahren** to ruin things, to get things in a mess; **der ~ ist hoffnungslos verfahren, der ~ steckt im Dreck** we/they *etc* are really in a mess; **den ~ aus dem Dreck ziehen** *or* **wieder flottmachen** to put things back on the rails, to get things sorted out.

karren [1] *vt* to cart ◆ **jdn ~** (*inf: mit Auto*) to give sb a lift, to drive sb.
[2] *vi aux sein* (*inf: mit dem Auto*) to drive (around).

Karrengaul *m* (*pej*) (old) nag.

Karrette *f* (*Sw*) (*Schubkarre*) (hand)cart, trolley.

Karriere [ka'rie:rə, -iɛ:rə] *f -, -n* **(a)** (*Laufbahn*) career ◆ **~ machen** to make a career for oneself. **(b)** (*voller Galopp*) (full) gallop ◆ **~ reiten** to gallop, to ride at a gallop.

Karriere-: k~dienlich *adj* career-enhancing; **~frau** *f* career woman; **~knick** *m* **es kam zu einem ~knick** his/her career took a downturn; **~macher** *m* careerist.

Karrierist(in *f*) *m* careerist.

karriolen* *vi aux sein* (*dated inf*) to gallivant (around).

Kärrner *m -s, -* (*Fuhrmann*) carter.

Kärrner|arbeit *f* hard labour *or* toil.

Karsamstag *m* Easter Saturday, Holy Saturday.

Karst[1] *m -(e)s, -e* (*Hacke*) two-pronged mattock *or* hoe.

Karst[2] *m -(e)s, -e* (*Geog, Geol*) karst.

karstig *adj* karstic.

Kartätsche *f -, -n* **(a)** (*Mil*) case shot. **(b)** (*Build*) plasterer's float, darby.

Kartause *f -, -n* chartreuse, Carthusian monastery.

Kartäuser *m -s, -* **(a)** Carthusian (monk). **(b)** (*Likör*) chartreuse.

Karte *f -, -n* **(a)** (*Post~, Kartei~, Loch~, Visiten~ etc, auch Comput*) card.
(b) (*Fahr~, Eintritts~*) ticket; (*Einladungs~*) invitation (card); (*Bezugsschein*) coupon; (*Essens~*) luncheon voucher, meal ticket (*US*); (*Mitglieds~*) (membership) card ◆ **die ~n, bitte!** tickets, please!
(c) (*Land~*) map; (*See~*) chart ◆ **~n lesen** to map-read.
(d) (*Speise~*) menu; (*Wein~*) wine list ◆ **nach der ~** à la carte.
(e) (*Spiel~*) (playing) card ◆ **jdm die ~ lesen** to tell sb's fortune from the cards; **mit offenen ~n spielen** (*lit*) to play with one's cards on the table; (*fig*) to put one's cards on the table; **er spielt mit verdeckten ~n** (*fig*) he's playing his cards *or* it very close to his chest; **du solltest deine ~n aufdecken** (*fig*) you ought to show your hand *or* put your cards on the table; **alle ~n in der Hand halten** (*fig*) to hold all the cards; **er läßt sich nicht in die ~n sehen** *or* **gucken** (*fig*) he's playing it close to his chest; **jdm in die ~n sehen** (*lit*) to

look *or* take a look at sb's cards; **alles auf eine ~ setzen** (*lit*) to stake everything on one card; (*fig*) to stake everything on one chance; (*andere Möglichkeiten ausschließen*) to put all one's eggs in one basket (*prov*); **du hast auf die falsche ~ gesetzt** (*fig*) you backed the wrong horse; **schlechte/gute ~n haben** to have a bad/good hand; (*fig*) to be in a difficult/strong position.

Kartei *f* card file, card index.

Kartei-: ~karte *f* file *or* index card; **~kasten** *m* file-card box; **~leiche** *f* (*inf*) sleeping *or* non-active member; **die meisten Mitglieder sind bloß ~leichen** most of the members are just names on the files; **~schrank** *m* filing cabinet.

Kartell *nt* **-s, -e (a)** (*Comm*) cartel. **(b)** (*Interessenvereinigung*) alliance; (*pej*) cartel.

Kartell-: ~amt *nt*, **~behörde** *f* monopolies *or* anti-trust commission; **~gesetz** *nt* monopolies *or* anti-trust law; **~gesetzgebung** *f* anti-trust legislation.

Karten-: ~blatt *nt* map, (map)sheet; **~haus** *nt* **(a)** house of cards; **wie ein ~haus zusammenstürzen** *or* **in sich zusammenfallen** to collapse like a house of cards; **(b)** (*Naut*) chart room; **~kunststück** *nt* card trick; **~legen** *nt* **-s (a)** *siehe* **~lesen (b)**; **(b)** (*Patience*) patience; **~leger(in** *f*) *m* **-s, -** fortune-teller (*who reads cards*); **~leselampe** *f* (*Aut*) mapreading lamp; **~lesen** *nt* **(a)** (*von Landkarten etc*) map-reading; **(b)** (*Wahrsagen*) fortune-telling (*using cards*), reading the cards, cartomancy (*form*); **~leser** *m* (*von Landkarten*) map-reader; **~organisation** *f siehe* **Kreditkartenorganisation**; **~spiel** *nt* **(a)** (*das Spielen*) card-playing; (*ein Spiel*) card game; **beim ~spiel** when playing cards; **(b)** (*Karten*) pack *or* deck (of cards); **~telefon** *nt* cardphone; **~vorverkauf** *m* advance sale of tickets; advance booking office; **~werk** *nt* map book, book of maps; **~zeichen** *nt* (map) symbol; **~zeichner** *m* cartographer, mapmaker.

kartesianisch, kartesisch *adj* Cartesian.

Karthager(in *f*) *m* **-s, -** Carthaginian.

Karthago *nt* **-s** Carthage.

kartieren* *vt Gebiet* to map out; (*in Kartei einordnen*) to file.

Kartoffel *f* **-, -n (a)** potato ◆ **rin in die ~n, raus aus die ~n** (*sl*) first it's one thing, then (it's) another, you're/he's *etc* always chopping and changing; **etw/jdn fallen lassen wie eine heiße ~** (*inf*) to drop sth/sb like a hot potato; *siehe* **Bauer**[1]. **(b)** (*inf*) (*Nase*) hooter (*Brit inf*), conk (*inf*); (*Loch*) (gaping) hole.

Kartoffel- *in cpds* potato; **~brei** *m* mashed potatoes *pl*; **~chips** *pl* potato crisps *pl* (*Brit*), potato chips *pl* (*US*); **~ferien** *pl* (*inf*) autumn holiday(s); **~feuer** *nt fire made from dried potato leaves etc with general celebration after potato harvest*; **~käfer** *m* Colorado beetle; **~kraut** *nt* potato foliage *or* leaves; **~mehl** *nt* potato flour; **~miete** *f* (*Agr*) potato clamp; **~puffer** *m* potato fritter; **~püree** *nt* mashed potatoes *pl*; **~salat** *m* potato salad; **~schalen** *pl* potato-skin; (*abgeschält*) potato peel(ings); **~schäler** *m* potato peeler; **~stampfer** *m* potato masher.

⚠ **Kartograph(in** *f*) *m* cartographer.

⚠ **Kartographie** *f* cartography.

⚠ **kartographisch** *adj* cartographical.

Karton [kar'tɔŋ, kar'tõ:, kar'to:n] *m* **-s, -s (a)** (*steifes Papier, Pappe*) card, cardboard ◆ **ein ~** a piece of card *or* cardboard. **(b)** (*Schachtel*) cardboard box. **(c)** (*Art*) cartoon. **(d)** (*Leerblatt*) blank page for one's own notes.

Kartonage [karto'na:ʒə] *f* **-, -n** (*Verpackung*) cardboard packaging.

kartonieren* *vt Bücher* to bind in board ◆ **kartoniert** paperback.

Kartothek *f* **-, -en** card file, card index.

Kartusche *f* **-, -n (a)** (*Archit, Her*) cartouche. **(b)** cartridge; (*Hist Mil: Patronentasche*) ammunition pouch.

Karussell *nt* **-s, -s** *or* **-e** merry-go-round, roundabout (*Brit*), carousel ◆ **~ fahren** to have a ride on the merry-go-round *etc*.

Karwoche *f* (*Eccl*) Holy Week.

Karyatide *f* **-, -n** (*Archit*) caryatid.

Karzer *m* **-s, -** (*Hist*) **(a)** (*Zelle*) detention cell (*in school or university*). **(b)** (*Strafe*) detention.

Karzinogen *nt* **-s, -e** carcinogen.

karzinogen *adj* (*Med*) carcinogenic.

Karzinologie *f* (*Med*) oncology.

Karzinom *nt* **-s, -e** (*Med*) carcinoma, malignant growth.

Kasack *m* **-s, -s** tunic.

Kaschemme *f* **-, -n** low dive.

kaschen *vt* (*inf*) to catch; (*verhaften*) to nab (*inf*).

kaschieren* *vt* **(a)** (*fig: überdecken*) to conceal. **(b)** *Bucheinband* to laminate.

Kaschmir[1] *nt* **-s** (*Geog*) Kashmir.

Kaschmir[2] *m* **-s, -e** (*Tex*) cashmere.

Kaschube *m* **-n, -n, Kaschubin** *f* Kashub(e).

Käse *m* **-s, - (a)** cheese ◆ **weißer ~** curd cheese; **~ schließt den Magen** cheese rounds off a meal nicely. **(b)** (*inf: Unsinn*) rubbish, twaddle (*inf*).

Käse- *in cpds* cheese; **~blatt, ~blättchen** *nt* (*inf*) local rag (*inf*); **~brot** *nt* bread and cheese; **~brötchen** *nt* cheese roll; **~gebäck** *nt* cheese savouries *pl*; **~glocke** *f* cheese cover; (*fig*) dome; **~hobel** *m* cheese slice.

Kasein *nt* **-s, -e** casein.

Käsekuchen *m* cheesecake.

Kasel *f* **-, -n** (*Eccl*) chasuble.

Kasematte *f* **-, -n** casemate.

käsen *vi* (*rare*) to make cheese.

Käseplatte *f* cheese board.

Käserei *f* **(a)** (*~betrieb*) cheese dairy. **(b)** (*Käseherstellung*) cheese-making.

Kaserne *f* **-, -n** barracks *pl*.

Kasernen-: ~arrest *m* confinement to barracks; **~hof** *m* barrack square; **~hofton** *m*: **es herrscht ein richtiger ~hofton** it's like being on the parade ground.

kasernieren* *vt Truppen* to quarter in barracks; *Flüchtlinge, Obdachlose etc* to quarter, to billet.

Käse-: ~stange *f* cheese straw; **~torte** *f* cheesecake; **k~weiß** *adj* (*inf*) white *or* pale (as a ghost).

käsig *adj* **(a)** (*fig inf*) *Gesicht, Haut* pasty, pale; (*vor Schreck*) white, pale. **(b)** (*lit*) cheesy.

Kasino *nt* **-s, -s (a)** (*Spielbank*) casino. **(b)** (*Offiziers~*) (officers') mess *or* club; (*Speiseraum*) dining room, cafeteria.

Kaskade *f* **(a)** (*Wasserfall*) waterfall, cascade (*poet*); (*in Feuerwerk*) cascade ◆ **die Wasser stürzen in ~n hinab** the waters cascade down. **(b)** (*Zirkussprung*) acrobatic leap.

Kaskoversicherung *f* (*Aut*) (*Teil~*) ≃ third party, fire and theft insurance; (*Voll~*) fully comprehensive insurance; (*Naut*) hull insurance.

Kasper *m* **-s, -, Kasperl** *m or nt* **-s, -(n)** (*Aus, S Ger*), **Kasperle** *m or nt* **-s, -** (*S Ger*) **(a)** (*im Puppenspiel*) Punch. **(b)** (*inf*) clown (*inf*), fool.

Kasperle-: ~figur *f* glove puppet; **~theater** *nt* Punch and Judy (show); (*Gestell*) Punch and Judy theatre.

kaspern *vi* (*inf*) to clown (*inf*) *or* fool around.

Kaspisches Meer *nt* Caspian Sea.

Kassa *f* **-, Kassen** (*esp Aus*) *siehe* **Kasse (a)**.

Kassa-: ~geschäft *nt* (*Comm*) cash transaction; (*St Ex*) spot transaction; **~kurs** *m* spot rate; **~markt** *m* spot market.

Kassandraruf *m* prophecy of doom, gloomy prediction.

Kassation *f* (*Jur*) quashing, reversal; (*von Urkunde*) annulment.

Kasse *f* **-, -n (a)** (*Zahlstelle*) cashdesk, till, cash point; (*Zahlraum*) cashier's office; (*Theat etc*) box office; (*in Bank*) cash point, cashdesk; (*in Supermarkt*) check-out ◆ **an der ~** (*in Geschäft*) at the desk.

(b) (*Geldkasten*) cashbox; (*in Läden*) cash register, till; (*Geldmittel*) coffers *pl*; (*bei Spielen*) kitty; (*in einer Spielbank*) bank ◆ **in die ~ greifen** (*inf*) to dip into the till *or* cashbox; **der Film hat volle ~n gemacht** the film was a big box-office success; **die ~n klingeln** the tills are ringing, the money is really rolling in.

(c) (*Bargeld*) cash ◆ **ein Verkauf per ~** (*form*) a cash sale; **bei ~ sein** (*inf*) to be flush (*inf*) *or* in the money (*inf*); **knapp/gut/schlecht bei ~ sein** (*inf*) to be short of cash *or* out of pocket/well-off/badly-off; **~ machen** to check one's finances; (*in Geschäft*) to cash up; (*sl: gut verdienen*) to be raking it in (*inf*), to make a bomb (*sl*); **die ~ führen** to be in charge of the money; **die ~ stimmt!** (*inf*) the money's OK (*inf*); **ein Loch in die ~ reißen** (*fig*) to make a dent *or* hole in one's finances; **zur ~ bitten** to ask for money; **jdn zur ~ bitten** to ask sb to pay up.

(d) (*inf: Spar~*) (savings) bank.

(e) *siehe* **Krankenkasse**.

Kasseler *nt* **-s, -** *lightly smoked pork loin*.

Kassen-: ⚠**~abschluß** *m* cashing-up; **~abschluß machen** to cash up; **~arzt** *m doctor who treats members of sickness insurance schemes*; ≃ National Health general practitioner (*Brit*); **~automat** *m* cash dispenser (*Brit*), automatic teller; **~beleg** *m* sales receipt *or* check (*US*); **~bericht** *m* financial report; (*in Verein etc auch*) treasurer's report; **~bestand** *m* cash balance, cash in hand; **~bon** *m* sales slip *or* receipt; **~buch** *nt* cashbook; **~erfolg** *m* (*Theat etc*) box-office hit; **~führer** *m* treasurer; **~füller** *m* box-office hit; **~obligation** *f* (*St Ex*) medium-term bond; **~patient** *m patient belonging to medical insurance scheme*; ≃ National Health patient (*Brit*); **~preis** *m* cash price; **~prüfung** *f* audit; **~rekord** *m* record takings *pl*; **~schalter** *m siehe* **Kasse (a)**; **~schlager** *m* (*inf*) (*Theat etc*) box-office hit; (*Ware*) big seller; **~stand** *m* (*Comm*) cash in till; **~stunden** *pl* hours of business (of cashier's office *etc*); **~sturz** *m* (*Comm*) cashing-up; **~sturz machen** to check one's finances; (*Comm*) to cash up; **~wart** *m* **-s, -e** treasurer; **~zettel** *m* sales slip.

Kasserolle *f* **-, -n** saucepan; (*mit Henkeln*) casserole.

Kassette *f* **(a)** (*Kästchen*) case, box.

(b) (*für Bücher*) slipcase; (*Bücher in ~*) set, pack (*Comm*); (*Geschenk~*) gift case/set; (*für Schallplatten*) box; set; (*Tonband ~, Filmbehälter*) cassette; (*Aufbewahrungs~*) container; (*für Bücher*) library case; (*für Film*) can.

(c) (*Archit*) coffer.

Kassetten-: ~deck *nt* cassette deck; **~decke** *f* coffered ceiling; **~film** *m* (*Phot*) cartridge film; **~recorder** *m* cassette recorder.

Kassiber *m* **-s, -** secret message, stiff (*US sl*).

Kassier *m* **-s, -e** (*S Ger, Aus, Sw*) *siehe* **Kassierer(in)**.

kassieren* [1] *vt* **(a)** *Gelder etc* to collect (up), to take in; (*inf*) *Abfindung, Finderlohn* to pick up (*inf*) ◆ **nach seinem Tode kassierte sie 50.000 Mark** (*inf*) after his death she collected 50,000 marks; **bei jedem Verkauf kassiert er eine Menge Geld** (*inf*) he makes a packet on every sale (*inf*).

(b) (*inf: wegnehmen*) to take away, to confiscate.

(c) (*inf: verhaften*) to nab (*inf*).

(d) (*Jur*) *Urteil* to quash.

[2] *vi* **(a)** (*abrechnen*) to take the money ◆ **bei jdm ~** to collect *or* get money from sb; **Sie haben bei mir schon kassiert** I've paid already; **darf ich ~, bitte?** would you like to pay now?

(b) (*sl: Geld einnehmen*) to take the money; (*verdienen*) to make money ◆ **seit Willi seine Würstchenbude hat, kassiert er ganz schön** since Willi has had his sausage stall, he's really been raking it in (*inf*) *or* making a bomb (*sl*); **bei diesem Geschäft hat er ganz schön kassiert** he cleaned up very nicely on this

deal (*inf*).
Kassierer(in *f*) *m* **-s,** - cashier; (*Bank~*) clerk, teller; (*Einnehmer*) collector; (*eines Klubs*) treasurer.
Kastagnette [kastan'jɛtə] *f* castanet.
Kastanie [-iə] *f* chestnut; (*Roß~*) (horse)chestnut; (*Edel~*) (sweet) chestnut ◆ **glasierte ~n** marrons glacés; **für jdn die ~n aus dem Feuer holen** (*fig*) to pull sb's chestnuts out of the fire.
Kastanien- [-iən]: **~baum** *m* chestnut tree; **k~braun** *adj* maroon; *Pferd, Haar* chestnut; **~holz** *nt* chestnut (wood).
Kästchen *nt* **(a)** (*kleiner Kasten*) small box; (*für Schmuck*) case, casket. **(b)** (*auf kariertem Papier*) square.
Kaste *f* **-, -n** caste.
kasteien* *vr* (*als Bußübung*) to castigate *or* chastise oneself, to mortify the flesh (*liter*); (*sich Entbehrungen auferlegen*) to deny oneself.
Kasteiung *f* castigation, mortification of the flesh; self-denial.
Kastell *nt* **-s, -e** (small) fort; (*Naut, Hist*) castle.
Kastellan *m* **-s, -e** (*Aufsichtsbeamter, Hausmeister*) steward; (*old dial: in Schulen etc*) janitor, caretaker; (*Hist: Schloßvogt*) castellan.
Kasten *m* **-s, ̈** **(a)** box; (*Kiste*) crate, case; (*Truhe*) chest; (*Aus: Schrank*) cupboard; (*N Ger: Schublade*) drawer; (*Brief~*) postbox, letterbox; (*Schau~*) showcase, display case; (*Brot~*) breadbin; (*Sport: Gerät*) box.
(b) (*inf*) (*altes Schiff*) tub (*inf*); (*alter Wagen, Flugzeug*) crate (*inf*); (*altes großes Haus*) barrack(s) *or* barn (of a place) (*inf*); (*Radio, Fernsehapparat etc*) box (*inf*).
(c) (*inf: großer, breiter Mann*) heavyweight (*inf*), big bloke (*Brit inf*).
(d) (*inf*) **er hat viel auf dem ~** he's brainy (*inf*).
(e) (*inf: Fußballtor*) goal ◆ **sie müssen noch ein Tor in den ~ bringen** they need to put another one in the back of the net; **wer geht in den ~?** who's going in goal?
Kasten-: **~form** *f* (*Cook*) (square) baking tin; **~geist** *m* (*Sociol, Rel*) caste spirit; (*von Cliquen*) clannishness, cliquishness; (*Klassenbewußtsein*) class spirit *or* outlook; **~wagen** *m* (*Aut*) van, truck, panel truck (*US*); (*auf Bauernhof*) box cart; **~wesen** *nt* caste system.
Kastilien [-iən] *nt* **-s** Castille.
Kastrat *m* **-en, -en** eunuch; (*Mus Hist*) castrato.
Kastration *f* castration.
Kastrations-: **~angst** *f* fear of castration; **~komplex** *m* castration complex.
kastrieren* *vt* (*lit, fig*) to castrate; *Tiere auch* to geld.
Kasuistik *f* casuistry.
kasuistisch *adj* casuistic.
Kasus *m* **-, -** (*Gram*) case.
Kasus-: **~bildung** *f* case formation, declension; **~endung** *f* (case) ending.
Kat *m* **-s, -s** *abbr of* **Katalysator.**
Kata- *in cpds* cata-; **~falk** *m* **-s, -e** catafalque; **~kombe** *f* **-, -n** catacomb.
Katalane *m* **-n, -n, Katalanin** *f* Catalan.
Katalanien [-iən] *nt* **-s** Catalonia.
Katalanisch(e) *nt* Catalan; *siehe auch* **Deutsch(e).**
Katalog *m* **-(e)s, -e** catalogue.
katalogisieren* *vt* to catalogue.
Katalogisierung *f* cataloguing.
katalogmäßig *adj Liste* catalogued ◆ **er erfaßte seine Funde ~** he made a catalogue of *or* catalogued his finds.
Katalonien [-iən] *nt* **-s** Catalonia.
Katalysator *m* (*lit, fig*) catalyst; (*Aut*) catalytic converter.
Katalysator-: **~auto** *nt* car fitted with a catalytic converter; **~-Modell** *nt* model with a catalytic converter.
Katalyse *f* **-, -n** (*Chem*) catalysis.
katalytisch *adj* catalytic.
Katamaran *m* **-s, -e** catamaran.
Katapult *nt or m* **-(e)s, -e** catapult.
katapultieren* [1] *vt* to catapult.
[2] *vr* to catapult oneself; (*Pilot*) to eject.
Katapultsitz *m* ejector *or* ejection seat.
Katarakt *m* **-(e)s, -e** cataract.
⚠ **Katarrh** *m* **-s, -e** catarrh.
Kataster *m or nt* **-s, -** land register, cadaster (*spec*).
Katasteramt *nt* land registry.
katastrieren* *vt Grundstücke* to register, to enter in the land register.
katastrophal *adj* disastrous; *Auswirkungen etc auch* catastrophic; (*haarsträubend schlecht auch*) atrocious ◆ **der Mangel an Brot ist ~ geworden** the bread shortage has become catastrophic; **das Zimmer sieht ja ~ aus** the room looks absolutely disastrous.
Katastrophe *f* **-, -n** disaster, catastrophe; (*Theat, Liter*) catastrophe, (tragic) dénouement ◆ **der ist eine ~** (*inf*) he's a real disaster (area) (*inf*) *or* catastrophe (*inf*).
Katastrophen-: **~abwehr** *f* disaster prevention; **~alarm** *m* emergency alert; **~dienst** *m* emergency service; **~einsatz** *m* duty *or* use in case of disaster; **für den ~einsatz** for use in case of disaster; **~gebiet** *nt* disaster area; **~opfer** *nt* disaster victim; **~schutz** *m* disaster control; (*im voraus*) disaster prevention.
Katatonie *f* (*Psych*) catatonia.
Kate *f* **-, -n** (*N Ger*) cottage, croft (*Scot*).
Katechese *f* **-, -n** catechesis.
Katechet(in *f*) *m* **-en, -en** catechist.
Katechismus *m* catechism.
Katechist(in *f*) *m* catechist.
kategorial *adj* categorical.
Kategorie *f* category ◆ **er gehört auch zur ~ derer, die ...** he's one of those *or* of that sort who ...
kategorisch *adj* categorical, absolute; *Ablehnung auch* flat ◆ **der K~e Imperativ** the categorical imperative; **ich weigerte mich ~** I refused outright, I absolutely refused; **er lehnte ~ ab** he categorically refused; **... erklärte er ~ ...** he declared emphatically.
kategorisieren* *vt* to categorize.
Kater *m* **-s, -** **(a)** tom(cat) ◆ **wie ein verliebter ~** like an amorous tomcat; *siehe* **gestiefelt. (b)** (*Katzenjammer*) hangover.
Kater-: **~frühstück** *nt breakfast (of pickled herring etc) to cure a hangover;* **~stimmung** *f* depression, the blues *pl* (*inf*).
katexochen [kat|ɛksɔ'xe:n] *adv* (*liter*) **Demokratie ~** the epitome of democracy.
kath. *abbr of* **katholisch.**
Katharsis *f* **-,** *no pl* (*Liter, fig*) catharsis.
kathartisch *adj* (*Liter, fig*) cathartic.
Katheder *m or nt* **-s, -** (*in Schule*) teacher's desk; (*in Universität*) lectern ◆ **etw vom ~ herab erklären** to declare sth ex cathedra (*hum, form*).
Kathedrale *f* **-, -n** cathedral.
Katheter *m* **-s, -** (*Med*) catheter.
Kathode *f* **-, -n** (*Phys*) cathode.
Kathoden-: **~strahlen** *pl* (*Phys*) cathode rays *pl*; **~strahlröhre** *f* (*TV etc*) cathode ray tube.
Kathole *m* **-n, -n** (*inf*) Catholic, Papist (*pej*).
Katholik(in *f*) *m* **-en, -en** (Roman) Catholic.
katholisch *adj* (Roman) Catholic ◆ **sie ist streng ~** she's a strict Catholic; **jdn ~ erziehen** to bring sb up (as) a Catholic.
Katholizismus *m* (Roman) Catholicism.
Kat-Modell *nt* (*Aut*) *abbr of* **Katalysator-Modell.**
katschen, kätschen *vi* (*S Ger, Sw*) to chomp (*inf*).
Kattanker *m* (*Naut*) kedge.
Kattegatt *nt* **-s** Kattegat.
Kattun *m* **-s, -e** (*old*) cotton, calico.
katzbalgen *vr* to romp around.
Katzbalgerei *f* romping.
katzbuckeln *vi* (*pej inf*) to bow and scrape, to grovel.
Kätzchen *nt* **(a)** (*junge Katze, inf: Mädchen*) kitten; (*Katze*) pussy (*inf*). **(b)** (*Bot*) catkin.
Katze *f* **-, -n** cat ◆ **meine Arbeit war für die Katz** (*fig*) my work was a waste of time; **das hat die ~ gefressen** (*fig*) the fairies took it (*hum inf*); **Katz und Maus mit jdm spielen** to play cat and mouse with sb; **wie die ~ um den heißen Brei herumschleichen** to beat about the bush; **die ~ aus dem Sack lassen** (*inf*) to let the cat out of the bag; **die ~ im Sack kaufen** to buy a pig in a poke (*prov*); **die ~ läßt das Mausen nicht** (*Prov*) the leopard cannot change its spots (*Prov*); **bei Nacht sind alle ~n grau** all cats are grey at night; **wenn die ~ aus dem Haus ist, tanzen die Mäuse (auf dem Tisch)** (*Prov*) when the cat's away the mice will play (*Prov*).
Katzelmacher *m* (*S Ger, Aus: pej: Italiener*) Eyetie (*pej*).
Katzen-: **~auge** *nt* **(a)** (*Straßenmarkierung*) cat's-eye; (*Rückstrahler*) reflector; **(b)** (*Min*) cat's-eye; **~buckel** *m* arched back (of a cat); **einen ~buckel machen** to arch one's back; **k~freundlich** *adj* (*pej*) overfriendly; **k~haft** *adj* cat-like, feline; **~hai** *m* dogfish; **~jammer** *m* (*inf*) **(a)** (*Kater*) hangover; **(b)** (*jämmerliche Stimmung*) depression, the blues *pl* (*inf*); **ich habe ~jammer** I feel down (in the dumps) (*inf*), I've got the blues (*inf*); **~kopf** *m* (*fig*) **(a)** (*Kopfstein*) cobble(stone); **(b)** (*Sch: Schlag*) cuff (on the head), box round the ears; **~kraut** *nt* catnip; **~musik** *f* (*fig*) caterwauling, din, racket (*inf*); **~sprung** *m* (*inf*) stone's throw; **~streu** *f* cat litter; **~tisch** *m* (*hum*) children's table; **die Kinder essen am ~tisch** the children are eating at their own table; **~wäsche** *f* (*hum inf*) a lick and a promise (*inf*), a cat's lick (*inf*); **~wäsche machen** to give oneself a lick and a promise; **~zunge** *f* (*Schokolade*) langue de chat.
Katz-und-Maus-Spiel *nt* cat-and-mouse game.
Kau-: **~apparat** *m* masticatory apparatus; **~bewegung** *f* chewing movement.
Kauderwelsch *nt* **-(s),** *no pl* (*pej*) (*Fach- oder Geheimsprache*) lingo (*inf*), jargon; (*Gemisch aus mehreren Sprachen/Dialekten*) hotchpotch *or* mishmash (of different languages/dialects); (*unverständliche Sprache*) double dutch, gibberish.
kauderwelschen *vi siehe n* to talk jargon; to talk a hotchpotch *or* mishmash (of different languages/dialects); to talk double dutch *or* gibberish.
kauen [1] *vt* to chew; (*Med, form*) to masticate; *Nägel* to bite, to chew; *Wein* to taste.
[2] *vi* to chew ◆ **an etw** (*dat*) **~** to chew (on) sth; **an den Nägeln ~** to bite *or* chew one's nails; **daran hatte ich lange zu ~** (*fig*) it took me a long time to get over it; **daran wird er zu ~ haben** (*fig*) that will really give him food for thought *or* something to think about; **gut gekaut ist halb verdaut** (*Prov*) you should chew your food properly; **das K~** chewing; (*Med, form*) mastication.
kauern *vir* (*vi auch aux sein*) to crouch (down); (*ängstlich*) to cower; (*schutzsuchend*) to be huddled (up).
Kauf *m* **-(e)s, Käufe** (*das Kaufen*) buying *no pl*, purchase (*esp form*), purchasing *no pl* (*esp form*); (*das Gekaufte*) purchase (*esp form*), buy ◆ **das war ein günstiger ~** that was a good buy; **diese Käufe haben sich gelohnt** it was worth buying these; **mit diesem Anzug machen Sie bestimmt einen guten ~** this

⚠: for details of spelling reform, see supplement

suit is definitely a good buy; **ein ~ auf Kredit** a credit purchase; **etw zum ~ anbieten** to offer sth for sale; **einen ~ abschließen** *or* **tätigen** (*form*) to complete a purchase; **etw durch ~ erwerben** (*form*) to purchase sth; **etw in ~ nehmen** (*fig*) to accept sth.

Kauf-: ~absicht *f* intention to buy; **~auftrag** *m* purchasing *or* buying order; **~bereitschaft** *f* willingness to buy; **~brief** *m* deed of purchase; (*esp für Grundstücke*) title deed.

kaufen 1 *vt* (a) (*auch* **sich** (*dat*) ~) to buy, to purchase (*esp form*) ◆ **ich kauf' dir ein Geschenk** I'll buy you a present *or* a present for you; **ich habe (mir) einen neuen Anzug gekauft** I bought (myself) a new suit; **diese Zigaretten werden viel/nicht gekauft** we sell a lot of these cigarettes/nobody buys these cigarettes; **jetzt wird nicht schon wieder eine neue Hose gekauft!** you're not going to buy another pair of trousers!; **dafür kann ich mir nichts ~** (*iro*), **was kann man sich** (*dat*) **dafür (schon) ~** (*iro*) what use is that to me!, that's a fat lot of use! (*inf*).
(b) (*bestechen*) *jdn* to bribe, to buy off; *Spiel* to fix; *Stimmen* to buy ◆ **der Sieg war gekauft** it was fixed.
(c) **sich** (*dat*) **jdn ~** (*inf*) to give sb a piece of one's mind (*inf*); (*tätlich*) to fix sb (*inf*).
(d) *auch vi* (*Cards*) to buy.
2 *vi* to buy; (*Einkäufe machen*) to shop ◆ **auf dem Markt kauft man billiger** it is cheaper to shop *or* you can buy things cheaper at the market; **das K~** buying, purchasing (*esp form*).

Käufer(in f) *m* **-s, -** buyer, purchaser (*esp form*); (*Kunde*) customer, shopper.

Kauf-: ~fahrer *m* (*old*) merchant ship, merchantman; **~frau** *f* businesswoman; **~halle** *f*, **~haus** *nt* department store; **~hausdetektiv** *m* store detective; **~kraft** *f* (*von Geld*) buying *or* purchasing power; (*vom Käufer*) spending power; **Kunden mit ~kraft** customers with money to spend; **k~kräftig** *adj* **eine k~kräftige Währung** a currency with good purchasing power; **k~kräftige Kunden** customers with money to spend.

Kaufkraft-: ~lenkung *f* control of (consumer) spending; **~schwund** *m* drop in purchasing power; **~überhang** *m* excess *or* surplus (consumer) spending power; **~verlust** *m* loss of purchasing power.

Kauf-: ~laden *m* (a) (*rare: Ladengeschäft*) (small) shop; (b) (*Spielzeug*) toy shop; **~leute** *pl of* **~mann.**

käuflich *adj* (a) (*zu kaufen*) for sale, purchasable (*form*) ◆ **etwas, was nicht ~ ist** something which cannot be bought; **etw ~ erwerben** (*form*) to purchase sth.
(b) (*fig*) venal ◆ **~e Liebe** (*geh*) prostitution; **ein ~es Mädchen** (*geh*) a woman of easy virtue; **Freundschaft ist nicht ~** friendship cannot be bought.
(c) (*fig: bestechlich*) venal ◆ **~ sein** to be easily bought; **ich bin nicht ~** you cannot buy me!

Käuflichkeit *f* (a) purchasability (*form*) ◆ **Kennzeichen des Kapitalismus ist die ~ aller Dinge** it is a characteristic of capitalism that everything can be bought *or* is for sale. (b) (*fig*) (*Bestechlichkeit*) corruptibility, venality.

Kauf-: ~lust *f* desire to buy (things); (*St Ex*) buying; **die ~lust hat plötzlich zugenommen** people have suddenly gone on a spending spree; **k~lustig** *adj* inclined to buy, in a buying mood; **in den Straßen drängten sich die ~lustigen** the streets were thronged with shoppers.

Kaufmann *m, pl* **-leute** (a) (*Geschäftsmann*) businessman; (*Händler*) trader; (*Tabak~, Gewürz~, Woll~ etc*) merchant ◆ **gelernter ~** person with qualifications in business *or* commerce; **jeder ~ lobt seine Ware** (*Prov*) a salesman will always praise his own wares.
(b) (*Einzelhandels~*) small shopkeeper, grocer ◆ **zum ~ gehen** to go to the grocer's.

kaufmännisch *adj* commercial, business *attr* ◆ **~er Angestellter** office worker; **er wollte einen ~en Beruf ergreifen** he wanted to make a career in business *or* commerce; **er übt einen ~en Beruf aus** he is in business *or* commerce; **Fachschule für ~e Berufe** commercial college, business school; **~ denken** to think in commercial *or* business terms; **alles K~e** everything commercial, everything to do with business; **alles K~e macht seine Frau für ihn** his wife looks after the business side of things for him; **sie ist ~ tätig** she is in business *or* is a businesswoman.

Kaufmannschaft *f* (*geh*) merchants *pl*.

Kaufmanns-: ~gehilfe *m* assistant, clerk; (*im Laden*) sales assistant, clerk (*US*); **~laden** *m* (a) (*dated*) grocer's; (*Gemischtwarenhandlung*) general store; (b) (*Spielzeug*) toy grocer's shop; **~lehrling** *m* management trainee; **~stand** *m* merchant class.

Kauf-: ~option *f* (*St Ex*) call option; (*Comm*) option to buy; **~preis** *m* purchase price; **~rausch** *m* spending spree; **im ~rausch sein** to be on a spending spree; **~summe** *f* money; **~unlust** *f* consumer resistance; **~vertrag** *m* bill of sale; **~wert** *m* market value; **~zwang** *m* obligation to buy; **kein/ohne ~zwang** no/without obligation.

Kaugummi *m* chewing gum.

Kaukasien [-iən] *nt* **-s** Caucasia.

Kaukasier(in f) [-iɐ, -iərın] *m* **-s, -** Caucasian.

kaukasisch *adj* Caucasian.

Kaukasus *m* **-: der ~** (the) Caucasus.

Kaulquappe *f* tadpole.

kaum 1 *adv* (a) (*noch nicht einmal*) hardly, scarcely, barely ◆ **er verdient ~ 200 Mark/ich habe ~ noch 10 Liter** he earns hardly *etc* 200 marks/I've hardly *etc* 10 litres left; **das kostet ~ 200 Mark/man braucht ~ 10 Liter** it doesn't even cost 200 marks/you'll need less than 10 litres; **sie war ~ hereingekommen, als ...** hardly *or* scarcely *or* no sooner had she come in when ..., she had hardly *etc* come in when ...; **~ jemand/jemals** hardly *or* scarcely anyone/ever; **es ist ~ möglich, daß ...** it is hardly *or* scarcely possible that ...; **es ist ~ zu glauben, wie ...** it's hardly *or* scarcely believable *or* to be believed how ...; **wir hatten ~ noch Benzin** we had hardly *or* scarcely any petrol left, we hardly *etc* had any petrol left; **er kann ~ noch sprechen/laufen** he can hardly *etc* speak/walk any more; **ich hatte ~ noch damit gerechnet, daß ...** I hardly *or* scarcely thought that ... any more.
(b) (*wahrscheinlich nicht*) hardly, scarcely ◆ **~!** hardly, scarcely; **wohl ~/ich glaube ~** I hardly *or* scarcely think so; **ich glaube ~, daß ...** I hardly *or* scarcely think that ...; **das wird wohl ~ stimmen** that can hardly *or* scarcely be right/true, surely that can't be right/true; **das wird ~ passieren** that's hardly *or* scarcely likely to happen.
2 *conj* hardly, scarcely ◆ **~ daß wir das Meer erreicht hatten ...** hardly *etc* had we reached the sea when ..., no sooner had we reached the sea than ...; **~ gerufen, eilte der Diener herbei** no sooner summoned, the servant hurried in; **er verdient äußerst wenig, ~ daß er davon satt wird** he earns extremely little and can hardly even buy enough to eat.

Kaumuskel *m* jaw muscle, masseter (*spec*).

Kaurimuschel *f* cowrie shell.

kausal *adj* causal.

Kausalgesetz *nt* law of causality.

Kausalität *f* causality.

Kausalitätsprinzip *nt* principle of causality.

Kausal-: ~kette *f* causal chain, chain of cause and effect; **~nexus** *m* (*geh*) causal connection; **~satz** *m* causal clause; **~zusammenhang** *m* causal connection.

Kausativ *nt* (*Gram*) causative.

kausativ *adj* (*Gram*) causative.

kaustisch *adj* (*Chem, fig*) caustic.

Kautabak *m* chewing tobacco.

Kautel *f* **-, -en** (*geh*) proviso.

Kaution *f* (a) (*Jur*) bail ◆ **~ stellen** to stand bail; **er stellte 1000 Mark ~** he put up 1000 marks (as) bail; **gegen ~** on bail; **jdn gegen ~ freibekommen** to bail sb out. (b) (*Comm*) security. (c) (*für Miete*) deposit.

Kautschuk *m* **-s, -e** (india)rubber.

Kautschukmilch *f* latex.

Kauwerkzeuge *pl* masticatory organs *pl*.

Kauz *m* **-es, Käuze** (a) screech owl. (b) (*Sonderling*) odd *or* strange fellow, oddball (*inf*) ◆ **ein komischer ~** an odd bird; **ein wunderlicher alter ~** a strange old bird.

Käuzchen *nt dim of* **Kauz (a).**

kauzig *adj* odd, cranky.

Kauzigkeit *f* crankiness.

Kavalier [kava'liːɐ] *m* **-s, -e** (a) (*galanter Mann*) gentleman ◆ **er ist immer ~** he's always a gentleman *or* always chivalrous; **der ~ genießt und schweigt** one does not boast about one's conquests. (b) (*dated: Begleiter einer Dame*) beau (*old*), young man (*dated*).

Kavaliersdelikt *nt* trivial offence, (mere) peccadillo.

Kavalier(s)-: ~start *m* (*Aut*) racing start; **~tuch** *nt* (*dated*) handkerchief in one's top pocket.

Kavalkade [kaval'kaːdə] *f* cavalcade.

Kavallerie [kavalə'riː] *f* (*Mil*) cavalry.

Kavalleriepferd *nt* cavalry horse.

Kavallerist [kavalə'rıst] *m* (*Mil Hist*) cavalryman.

Kaventsmann [ka'vɛntsman] *m, pl* **-männer** (*N Ger inf*) whopper (*inf*).

Kaverne *f* cavern.

Kaviar ['kaːviar] *m* **-s, -e** caviar.

Kaviarbrot *nt* French loaf.

KB [kaː'beː], **KByte** ['kaːbait] *nt* **-(s), -(s)** *abbr of* **Kilobyte** k, kbyte.

Kcal *abbr of* **Kilokalorie.**

Kebab *m* **-(s), -s** kebab.

Kebse *f* **-, -n, Kebsweib** *nt* (*old, Bibl*) concubine.

keck *adj* (a) (*dated: frech*) cheeky, saucy. (b) (*dated: flott*) *Mädchen* pert; *Hut auch* cheeky, saucy ◆ **sie trug den Hut ~ auf einem Ohr** she wore her hat at a jaunty *or* saucy angle over one ear. (c) (*old: tapfer*) bold.

keckern *vi* to snarl, to growl.

Keckheit *f siehe adj* (a) cheekiness, sauciness. (b) pertness; cheekiness, sauciness. (c) boldness.

Keeper ['kiːpɐ] *m* **-s, -** (*Aus Sport*) (goal)keeper.

Keep-Smiling ['kiːp'smaılıŋ] *nt* **- -s,** *no pl* fixed smile.

Kefir *m* **-s,** *no pl* kefir (*a milk product similar to yoghurt, of Turkish origin*).

Kegel *m* **-s, -** (a) (*Spielfigur*) skittle, ninepin; (*bei Bowling*) pin ◆ **wir schieben ~** (*inf*) we play skittles *or* ninepins; we go bowling; **~ aufsetzen** to set the skittles/pins up; *siehe* **Kind.** (b) (*Geometrie*) cone; (*Berg~*) peak. (c) (*Licht~, Scheinwerfer~*) beam (of light). (d) (*Typ*) body, shank.

Kegel-: ~bahn *f* (bowling) lane; (*Anlage*) skittle-alley; (*automatisch*) bowling alley; **~bruder** *m* (*inf*) member of a skittle/bowling club; **k~förmig** *adj* conical; **~kugel** *f* bowl; **~mantel** *m* surface of a cone.

kegeln *vi* to play skittles *or* ninepins; (*bei Bowling*) to play bowls ◆ **~ gehen** to play skittles; to go bowling.

Kegel-: ~rad *nt* (*Tech*) bevelled *or* mitre wheel; ⚠**k~scheiben** (*Aus*), ⚠**k~schieben** *vi sep irreg siehe* **Kegel (a)**; **~schnitt** *m* conic section; **~schwester** *f* (*inf*) member of a skittle/bowling club; **~sport** *m* bowling; **~stumpf** *m* frustum.

Kegler(in f) *m* **-s, -** skittle-player; (*bei Bowling*) bowler.

Kehle *f* **-, -n (a)** (*Gurgel*) throat ◆ **(sich *dat*) die ~ schmieren** (*inf*) *or* **anfeuchten** (*inf*) to wet one's whistle (*inf*); **das ist ihm in die falsche ~ gekommen, er hat das in die falsche ~ bekommen** (*lit*) it went down the wrong way *or* got stuck in his throat; (*fig*) he took it the wrong way; **eine rauhe ~ haben** to be hoarse; **er hat Gold in der ~** (*inf*) his voice is/could be a real gold-mine; **aus voller ~** at the top of one's voice *or* lungs.
(b) (*ausgerundeter Winkel*) moulding; (*Rille*) groove.

kehlig *adj Sprechweise* guttural; *Lachen, Alt* throaty.

Kehlkopf *m* larynx.

Kehlkopf-: ~entzündung *f*, ⚠**~katarrh** *m* laryngitis; **~krebs** *m* cancer of the throat; ⚠**~mikrophon** *nt* throat microphone; **~spiegel** *m* laryngoscope.

Kehllaut *m* guttural (sound).

Kehlung *f* (*Archit*) groove, flute.

Kehlverschlußlaut *m* (*Phon*) glottal stop.

Kehr-: ~aus *m* **-,** *no pl* last dance; (*fig: Abschiedsfeier*) farewell celebration; **den ~aus machen** (*fig*) to have a farewell celebration; **~besen** *m* broom; **~blech** *nt* (*S Ger*) shovel.

Kehre *f* **-, -n (a)** (sharp) turn *or* bend; (*Haarnadelkurve*) hairpin bend. **(b)** (*Turnübung*) rear *or* back vault.

kehren[1] [1] *vt* **(a)** to turn ◆ **die Augen** *or* **den Blick zum Himmel/zu Boden ~** (*liter*) to turn one's eyes *or* gaze heavenwards/to cast one's eyes to the ground (*liter*); **in sich** (*acc*) **gekehrt** (*versunken*) pensive, wrapped in thought; (*verschlossen*) introspective, introverted; *siehe* **Rücken**.
(b) (*kümmern*) to bother ◆ **was kehrt mich das?** what do I care about that?
[2] *vr* **(a)** to turn ◆ **eines Tages wird sich sein Hochmut gegen ihn ~** one day his arrogance will rebound against him.
(b) er kehrt sich nicht daran, was die Leute sagen he doesn't mind *or* care what people say.
[3] *vi* to turn (round); (*Wind*) to turn.

kehren[2] *vti* (*esp S Ger: fegen*) to sweep ◆ **ich muß noch ~** I've still got to do the sweeping; **jeder kehre vor seiner Tür!** (*Prov*) everyone should first put his own house in order; *siehe* **Besen**.

Kehricht *m or nt* **-s,** *no pl* (*old, form*) sweepings *pl* ◆ **den ~ zusammenfegen** to sweep up the rubbish; *siehe* **feucht**.

Kehr-: ~maschine *f* (*Straßen~*) road-sweeper, road sweeping machine; (*Teppich~*) carpet-sweeper; **~platz** *m* (*Sw*) turning area; **~reim** *m* chorus, refrain; **~schaufel** *f* shovel; **~seite** *f* **(a)** (*von Münze*) reverse; **(b)** (*inf: Rücken*) back; (*hum: Gesäß*) backside (*inf*), behind; (*fig: Nachteil*) drawback; **jdm seine ~seite zuwenden** to turn one's back on sb; **(c)** (*fig: Schattenseite*) other side; **die ~seite der Medaille** the other side of the coin.

kehrt *interj* (*Mil*) **ganze Abteilung ~!** company, about turn!

Kehrt-: k~machen *vi sep* to turn round, to do an about-turn; (*zurückgehen*) to turn back; (*Mil*) to about-turn; **~wendung** *f* about-turn; **diese plötzliche ~wendung wurde scharf kritisiert** this sudden about-turn *or* volte-face was sharply criticized.

Kehr-: ~wert *m* reciprocal value; **~woche** *f* (*S Ger*) *week when a resident has to take his/her turn to clean the communal areas of flats etc*, cleaning week.

keifen *vi* to bicker.

Keiferei *f* (*inf*) bickering.

Keil *m* **-(e)s, -e** wedge (*auch Mil*); (*als Hemmvorrichtung auch*) chock; (*Faust~*) hand-axe; (*Sew: Zwickel*) gusset; (*Kopf~*) headrest ◆ **einen ~ in etw** (*acc*) **treiben** to put a wedge in sth; (*zum Befestigen auch*) to wedge sth; **einen ~ zwischen zwei Freunde treiben** (*fig*) to drive a wedge between two friends; *siehe* **grob**.

Keil-: ~absatz *m* wedge heel, wedge; **~bein** *nt* sphenoid (bone).

Keile *pl* (*inf*) thrashing, hiding ◆ **~ bekommen** *or* **kriegen** *or* **beziehen** to get *or* be given a thrashing *or* hiding; **dahinten gibt's gleich ~** there's going to be a fight over there.

keilen [1] *vt* **(a)** (*mit Keil*) to wedge. **(b)** (*sl: anwerben*) *Mitglieder* to rope in (*inf*).
[2] *vr* (*dial inf: sich prügeln*) to fight.

Keiler *m* **-s, -** wild boar.

Keilerei *f* (*inf*) punch-up (*inf*), brawl, fight.

Keil-: k~förmig *adj* wedge-shaped; **~haue** *f* (*Min*) pick(axe); **~hose** *f*, **~hosen** *pl* slacks *pl*, ski pants *pl*; **~kissen, ~polster** (*Aus*) *nt* wedge-shaped pillow (*used as a headrest*); **~rahmen** *m* stretcher (*for artist's canvas*); **~riemen** *m* drive-belt; (*Aut*) fan-belt; **~schrift** *f* cuneiform script.

Keim *m* **-(e)s, -e (a)** (*kleiner Trieb*) shoot, sprout ◆ **die ersten ~e ihrer jungen Liebe** (*liter*) the first blossomings *or* burgeoning of their young love (*liter*).
(b) (*Embryo, fig*) embryo, germ; (*Krankheits~*) germ ◆ **im ~e** (*fig*) in embryo, in embryonic form; **etw im ~ ersticken** to nip sth in the bud.
(c) (*fig: des Hasses, der Liebe etc*) seed *usu pl* ◆ **den ~ zu etw legen** to sow the seeds of sth.

Keim-: ~blatt *nt* **(a)** (*Bot*) cotyledon; **(b)** (*Zool*) blastema; **~drüse** *f* gonad; **~drüsenhormon** *nt* sex hormone.

keimen *vi* **(a)** to germinate; (*Pflanzen*) to put out shoots, to shoot; (*Knollen*) to sprout. **(b)** (*Verdacht*) to be aroused; (*Hoffnung auch*) to stir (in one's breast *liter*) ◆ **das ~de Leben** (*geh*) the seeds of a new life.

Keim-: k~frei *adj* germ-free, free of germs *pred*; (*Med auch, fig*) sterile, **k~frei machen** to sterilize; **k~haft** *adj* (*geh*) embryonic, seminal; **k~haft vorhanden sein** to be present in embryo *or* in embryonic *or* seminal form; **~ling** *m* **(a)** (*Embryo*) embryo; **(b)** (*~pflanze*) sprout, shoot; **~plasma** *nt* germ plasm; **k~tötend** *adj* germicidal; **k~tötendes Mittel** germicide; **~träger** *m* carrier.

Keimung *f* germination.

Keimzelle *f* germ cell; (*fig*) nucleus.

kein, keine, kein *indef pron* **(a)** (*adjektivisch*) no; (*mit sing n auch*) not a; (*mit pl n, bei Sammelbegriffen, bei Abstrakten auch*) not any ◆ **~ Mann/~e Häuser/~ Whisky ...** no man/houses/whisky ...; **hast du ~ Herz?** have you no heart?; **hast du ~ Gefühl?** have you no *or* haven't you got any feeling?; **hast du ~en Bleistift?** haven't you got a *or* have you no pencil?; **hast du ~e Vorschläge/Geschwister?** haven't you got any *or* have you no suggestions/brothers and sisters?; **ich sehe da ~en Unterschied** I see no difference, I don't see any *or* a difference; **da sind ~e Häuser** there are no *or* there aren't any houses there; **er hatte ~e Chance** he had no *or* he didn't have a *or* any chance; **er ist ~ echter Schotte** he is no *or* not a true Scot; **er ist ~ Lehrer** he is not a teacher; (*~ guter auch*) he's no teacher; **~e Widerrede/Ahnung!** no arguing/idea!; **~e schlechte Idee** not a bad idea; **~e Lust/Angst!** don't want to/don't worry; **das ist ~e Antwort auf unsere Frage** that's not an *or* the answer to our question; **er ist noch ~ erfahrener Lehrer** he is not yet an experienced teacher; **~ bißchen** not a bit; **ich habe ~ bißchen Lust/Zeit** I've absolutely no desire to/time; **ich bin doch ~ Kind mehr!** I am not a child any longer *or* no longer a child; **~ anderer als er ...** only he ..., no-one else but he ...; **das habe ich ~em anderen als dir gesagt** I have told nobody else *or* haven't told anybody else apart from you; **~ einziger** (*niemand*) not a single one *or* person; **~ einziges Mal** not a single time; **in ~ster Weise** (*incorrect*) not in the least.
(b) (*nicht einmal*) less than ◆ **~e Stunde/drei Monate** less than an hour/three months; **~e 5 Mark** under 5 marks.

keine(r, s) *indef pron* (*substantivisch*) (*niemand*) nobody (*auch subj*), no-one (*auch subj*), not anybody, not anyone; (*von Gegenstand*) not one, none; (*bei Abstraktum*) none; (*obj*) not any, none; (*von Gegenständen, bei Abstrakta*) none; (*obj*) not any, none ◆ **~r liebt mich** nobody *or* no-one loves me; **es war ~r da** there was nobody *etc* there, there wasn't anybody *etc* there; (*Gegenstand*) there wasn't one there; **es waren ~ da** there wasn't anybody *etc* there; (*Gegenstände*) there weren't any *or* there were none there; **ich habe ~s** I haven't got one; **von diesen Platten ist ~ ...** none *or* not one of these records is ...; **haben Sie Äpfel? — nein, leider haben wir ~** have you any apples? — no, I'm afraid we haven't (any); **hast du schon ein Glas? — nein, ich habe ~s** have you a glass? — no, I haven't (got one) *or* no, I don't (*US*); **~r von uns/von uns (beiden)** none/neither of us; (*betont*) not one of us; **er hat ~n von beiden angetroffen** he didn't meet either *or* he met neither of them; **~s der (beiden) Kinder/Bücher** neither of the children/books; **~s der sechs Kinder/Bücher** none of the six children/books; (*betont*) not one of the six children/books; **er kannte ~s der (fünf) Kinder** he didn't know any of *or* he knew none of the (five) children; **ist Bier da? — nein, ich habe ~s gekauft** is there any beer? — no, I didn't buy any.

keinerlei *adj attr inv* no ... what(so)ever *or* at all.

keinerseits *adv* **sein Vorschlag fand ~ Zustimmung** his suggestion met with no support anywhere *or* from any side; **ich möchte mich ~ festlegen** I wouldn't like to commit myself in any direction.

keinesfalls *adv* under no circumstances, not ... under any circumstances ◆ **~ darfst du ...** under no circumstances *or* on no account must you ...; **aber er ist ~ dümmer als sein Bruder** he is at least as intelligent as his brother.

keineswegs *adv* not at all, by no means; (*als Antwort*) not in the least, not at all ◆ **ich fühle mich ~ schuldig** I do not feel in the least *or* in any way guilty.

keinmal *adv* never once, not once ◆ **er war noch ~ im Kino** he has never *or* not once been to the cinema, never *or* not once has he been to the cinema; *siehe* **einmal**.

keins = **keines**, *siehe* **keine(r, s)**.

Keks *m* **-es, -e** *or* (*Aus*) *nt* **-, -** biscuit (*Brit*), cookie (*US*) ◆ **jdm auf den ~ gehen** (*inf*) to get on sb's nerves.

Kelch *m* **-(e)s, -e (a)** (*Trinkglas*) goblet; (*Eccl*) chalice, communion cup ◆ **den (bitteren) ~ (des Leidens) bis zur Neige leeren** (*fig*) to drain the (bitter) cup of sorrow (to the last); **möge dieser ~ an mir vorübergehen** (*Bibl*) let this cup pass from me; **dieser ~ ist noch einmal an mir vorübergegangen** I have been spared again, the Good Lord has spared me again.
(b) (*Bot*) calyx; (*liter*) cup, bell, chalice (*poet*).

Kelchblatt *nt* sepal.

Kelch-: k~förmig *adj* cup-shaped, bell-shaped; **die k~förmig geöffnete Blüte** the cup-shaped *or* bell-shaped blossom; **~glas** *nt* goblet, goblet-shaped glass.

Kelim *m* **-(s), -(s)** kilim (*Eastern carpet*).

Kelle *f* **-, -n (a)** (*Suppen~ etc*) ladle; (*Schaumlöffel*) strainer, straining spoon. **(b)** (*Maurer~*) trowel. **(c)** (*Signalstab*) signalling disc.

Keller *m* **-s, -** cellar; (*Geschoß*) basement; (*Gaststätte*) (cellar) restaurant/bar ◆ **im ~ sitzen** (*inf: beim Kartenspiel*) to have minus points.

Keller- *in cpds* cellar; basement; **~assel** *f* wood-louse.

Kellerei *f* wine/champagne/fruit-juice producer's; (*Lagerraum*) cellar(s) ◆ **Wein direkt von der ~ kaufen** to buy wine direct from the producer's.

Keller-: ⚠**~geschoß** *nt* basement; **~gewölbe** *nt* vaulted cellar roof; (*Keller*) cellars *pl*; (*Verlies*) dungeon; **~kind** *nt* unhealthy slum kid; **~kneipe** *f* (*inf*), **~lokal** *nt* cellar bar; **~meister** *m* vintner; (*in Kloster*) cellarer; **~wohnung** *f* basement flat.

Kellner *m* **-s, -** waiter.

Kellnerin *f* waitress.

kellnern *vi* (*inf*) to work as a waiter/waitress, to wait on tables (*US*).

Kelte *m* **-n, -n, Keltin** *f* Celt.

Kelter *f* **-, -n** winepress; (*Obst~*) press.

⚠: for details of spelling reform, see supplement

keltern *vt Trauben, Wein* to press.
Kelvin *nt* **-s,** *no pl* (*Phys*) Kelvin.
Kemenate *f* **-, -n** lady's heated apartment(s) (*in a castle*); (*fig*) boudoir.
Kenia *nt* **-s** Kenya.
Kenianer(in *f*) *m* **-s, -** Kenyan.
kenianisch *adj* Kenyan.
kennen *pret* **kannte**, *ptp* **gekannt** *vt* to know; (*~gelernt haben auch*) to be acquainted with; (*geh: er~*) to recognize ◆ **er kennt das Leben** he knows the ways of the world, he knows about life; **er kennt den Hunger nicht** he has never known hunger, he doesn't know what hunger is; **er kennt keine Müdigkeit** he never gets tired, he doesn't know what tiredness means; **kein Erbarmen/Mitleid** *etc* ~ to know no mercy/pity *etc*; **ich habe mich nicht mehr gekannt vor Wut** I was beside myself with anger; **so was ~ wir hier nicht!** we don't have that sort of thing here; **jdn als etw ~** to know sb to be sth; **~ Sie sich schon?** do you know each other (already)?; **~ Sie den (schon)?** (*Witz*) have you heard this one?; **das ~ wir (schon)** (*iro*) we know all about that; **kennst du mich noch?** do you remember me?; **wie ich ihn kenne ...** if I know him (at all) ...; **du kennst dich doch!** you know what you're like; **so kenne ich dich ja (noch) gar nicht!** I've never known you like this before; **da kennst du mich aber schlecht** you don't know me, that just shows how little you know me.
kennenlernen *vt sep* to get to know, to become acquainted with (*form*); (*zum ersten Mal treffen*) to meet ◆ **sich ~** to get to know each other; to meet each other; **jdn näher ~** to get to know sb better, to become better acquainted with sb; **ich freue mich, Sie kennenzulernen** (*form*) (I am) pleased to meet you *or* to make your acquaintance (*form*); **der soll** *or* **wird mich noch ~** (*inf*) he'll have me to reckon with (*inf*); **bei näherem K~ erwies er sich als ...** on closer acquaintance he proved to be ...
Kenner(in *f*) *m* **-s, - (a)** (*Sachverständiger*) expert (*von or gen* on/in), authority (*von or gen* on) ◆ **~ der internen Vorgänge** those who know about the internal procedures; **da zeigt sich der ~, da merkt man den ~** there you (can) see the (touch of the) expert. **(b)** (*Wein~ etc*) connoisseur, co(g)noscente (*esp Art*).
Kennerblick *m* expert's eye.
kennerhaft, kennerisch *adj* like a connoisseur ◆ **mit ~em Blick/Griff** with the eye/touch of an expert.
Kenner-: ~miene *f* connoisseur's expression; **mit ~miene betrachtete er ...** he looked at ... like a connoisseur; **er versuchte, eine ~miene aufzusetzen** he tried to look like a connoisseur; (*bei Erklärung etc*) he tried to look knowledgeable; **~schaft** *f* connoisseurship (*rare*); (*Fachkenntnis*) expertise.
Kennkarte *f* (*dated*) identity card.
kenntlich *adj* (*zu erkennen*) recognizable, distinguishable (*an +dat* by); (*deutlich*) clear ◆ **etw ~ machen** to identify *or* indicate sth (clearly); **etw für jdn ~ machen** to make sth clear to sb, to indicate sth to sb; **etw gut ~ anbringen** to display sth clearly *or* prominently *or* visibly (*an +dat* on); **bei Dunkelheit gut ~ sein** to be easily visible *or* distinguishable in the dark.
➤ **Kenntnis** *f* **(a)** (*Wissen*) knowledge *no pl* ◆ **über ~se von etw verfügen** to be knowledgeable about sth, to know about sth; **gute ~se in Mathematik haben** to have a good knowledge of mathematics; **ohne ~ des Englischen** without any *or* a knowledge of English, without knowing English.
(b) *no pl* (*form*) **etw zur ~ nehmen** to note sth, to take note of sth; **ich nehme zur ~, daß ...** I note that ...; **jdn von etw in ~ setzen** to inform *or* advise (*Comm, form*) sb about sth; **von etw ~ erhalten** to learn *or* hear about sth; **das entzieht sich meiner ~** I have no knowledge of it; **bei voller ~ der Sachlage** in full knowledge of the situation; **ohne ~ der Umstände** without any knowledge of the circumstances.
Kenntnis-: ~nahme *f* **-,** *no pl* (*form*) **zur ~nahme an ...** for the attention of ...; **nach ~nahme** after perusal (*form*); **k~reich** *adj* (*geh*) learned, knowledgeable.
-kenntnisse *pl in cpds* knowledge of ...
Kenntnisstand *m* **-(e)s,** *no pl* **nach dem neuesten ~** according to the latest information.
Kennung *f* (*Telec*) call sign; (*von Leuchtfeuern*) signal; (*Comput*) password.
Kenn-: ~wort *nt, pl* **~wörter** (*Chiffre*) code name; (*Losungswort*) password, code word; (*Comm*) reference; **~zahl** *f* code *or* identification number; (*Telec auch*) code; **~zeichen** *nt* **(a)** (*Aut*) number plate (*Brit*), license plate (*US*); (*Aviat*) markings *pl*; **amtliches/polizeiliches ~zeichen** registration number (*Brit*), license number (*US*); **(b)** (*Markierung*) mark, sign; (*bei Tier*) marking(s); (*in Personenbeschreibung*) **unveränderliche ~zeichen** distinguishing marks *or* features; **besondere ~zeichen** particular characteristics; **(c)** (*Eigenart, Charakteristikum*) (typical) characteristic (*für, gen* of); (*für Qualität*) hallmark; (*Erkennungszeichen*) mark, sign; **ein typisches ~zeichen des Intellektuellen** a typical mark *or* sign of the intellectual; **als ~zeichen eine Nelke im Knopfloch vereinbaren** to agree on a carnation in one's buttonhole as a means of identification; **ein ~zeichen des Genies** a mark *or* sign *or* hallmark of genius; **(d)** (*Anzeichen*) symptom (*für* of); **k~zeichnen** *insep* [1] *vt* **(a)** to mark, to indicate; (*durch Etikett auch*) to label; *Weg etc* to mark, to signpost; (*Logik*) to denote; **etw als zerbrechlich k~zeichnen** to mark *or* label sth fragile; **(b)** (*charakterisieren*) to characterize; **jdn als etw k~zeichnen** to show sb to be sth, to mark sb out as sth; [2] *vr* to be characterized; **k~zeichnend** *adj* (*charakteristisch*) typical, characteristic (*für* of); **~ziffer** *f* (code) number; (*Math*) characteristic; (*Comm*) reference number; (*bei Zeitungsinserat*) box number; (*DDR*) reference number (for production planning).
Kenotaph *nt* **-s, -e** cenotaph.
Kentaur *m* **-en, -en** centaur.
kentern *vi aux sein* **(a)** (*Schiff*) to capsize. **(b) die Ebbe/Flut kentert** the tide is turning.
Keplersche Gesetze *pl* Kepler's laws *pl*.
keppeln *vi* (*Aus inf*) *siehe* **keifen.**
Keramik *f* **(a)** *no pl* (*Art*) ceramics *pl*; (*als Gebrauchsgegenstände auch*) pottery; (*Arbeitszweig*) ceramics *sing*. **(b)** (*Kunstgegenstand*) ceramic; (*Gebrauchsgegenstand auch*) piece of pottery ◆ **~en** ceramics/pottery.
keramisch *adj* ceramic; *Gebrauchsgegenstand auch* pottery.
Kerbe *f* **-, -n** notch; (*kleiner*) nick ◆ **in die gleiche** *or* **dieselbe ~ hauen** *or* **schlagen** (*fig inf*) to take the same line.
Kerbel *m* **-s,** *no pl* chervil.
kerben *vt Holz* to cut *or* carve a notch/notches in, to notch; *Inschrift, Namen* to carve.
Kerbholz *nt* (*fig inf*) **etwas auf dem ~ haben** to have done something wrong *or* bad; **er hat so manches auf dem ~** he has quite a record; **es gab fast keinen, der nichts auf dem ~ hatte** there was hardly anybody who had a completely clean record.
Kerbtier *nt* insect.
Kerbung *f* (*das Kerben*) notching; (*die Kerben*) notches *pl*; (*kleiner*) nicks *pl*.
Kerker *m* **-s, - (a)** (*Hist, geh*) dungeon (*esp Hist*), prison; (*Strafe*) imprisonment. **(b)** (*Aus*) *siehe* **Zuchthaus.**
Kerker-: ~meister *m* (*Hist, geh*) gaoler, jailer; **~strafe** *f* **(a)** (*Hist*) imprisonment in the dungeons; **(b)** (*Aus*) *siehe* **Zuchthausstrafe.**
Kerl *m* **-s, -e** *or* **-s** (*inf*) chap, fellow, guy, bloke (*Brit*) (*all inf*); (*pej*) character; (*Mädchen*) girl, lass (*inf*) ◆ **du gemeiner ~!** you mean thing (*inf*) *or* swine (*inf*); **ein ganzer/richtiger ~** a real man; **sie hat schon wieder einen neuen ~** she's got another guy *or* bloke; **die langen ~s** (*Hist*) (soldiers of) the bodyguard of the King of Prussia.
Kern *m* **-(e)s, -e** (*von Obst*) pip, seed; (*von Steinobst*) stone; (*Nuß~*) kernel; (*Phys, Biol*) nucleus; (*Holz~*) heartwood; (*fig*) (*von Problem, Sache*) heart, crux, core; (*von Stadt*) centre; (*von Gruppe*) core ◆ **jede Legende hat einen wahren ~** at the heart of every legend there is a core of truth; **in ihr steckt ein guter ~** there's some good in her somewhere; **bis zum ~ einer Sache vordringen** to get to the heart *or* the bottom of a matter; **der harte ~** (*fig*) the hard core.
Kern- *in cpds* (*Nuklear-*) nuclear; **~arbeitszeit** *f* core time; **~beißer** *m* **-s, -** (*Orn*) hawfinch; **~brennstoff** *m* nuclear fuel; **~chemie** *f* nuclear chemistry; **~energie** *f* nuclear energy; **~energiegegner** *m* opponent of nuclear energy; **~explosion** *f* nuclear explosion; **~fach** *nt* (*Sch*) core subject; **~familie** *f* (*Sociol*) nuclear family; **~forscher** *m* nuclear scientist *or* researcher; **~forschung** *f* nuclear research; **~forschungszentrum** *nt* nuclear research centre; **~frage** *f* central issue, central question; **~frucht** *f* malaceous fruit (*form*), pome (*form*); **~fusion** *f* nuclear fusion; **~gebiet** *nt* heartland; **~gedanke** *m* central idea; **~gehäuse** *nt* core; **k~gesund** *adj* as fit as a fiddle, completely fit; **~gruppe** *f* nucleus; **~holz** *nt* heartwood.
kernig *adj* full of pips; (*fig*) *Ausspruch* pithy; (*urwüchsig*) earthy; (*kraftvoll*) robust, powerful; (*sl: gut*) great (*inf*).
Kernkettenreaktion *f* nuclear chain reaction.
Kernkraft *f* **-,** *no pl* nuclear power.
Kernkraft- *in cpds* nuclear power; **~befürworter** *m* supporter of nuclear power.
Kernkräfte *pl* forces in the nucleus *pl*, nuclear forces *pl*.
Kernkraft-: ~gegner *m* opponent of nuclear power; **~werk** *nt* nuclear power station, nuke (*US sl*).
Kern-: ~ladungszahl *f* atomic number; **~land** *nt* heartland; **k~los** *adj* seedless, pipless; **~mannschaft** *f* (*Sport, fig*) core *or* nucleus of a/the team; (*von Partei*) central caucus; (*von Regierung*) inner cabinet; **~modell** *nt* model of the nucleus; **~obst** *nt* malaceous fruit (*form*), pome (*form*); **~physik** *f* nuclear physics; **~physiker** *m* nuclear physicist; **~plasma** *nt* nucleoplasm; **~problem** *nt* central problem; **~punkt** *m* central point, crux; **~reaktion** *f* nuclear reaction; **~reaktor** *m* nuclear reactor; **~satz** *m* **(a)** key sentence, key phrase; **(b)** (*Ling*) kernel sentence; (*Satzform*) simple sentence; **~schatten** *m* complete shadow; (*Astron*) umbra; **~schmelze** *f* meltdown; **~seife** *f* washing soap; **~spaltung** *f* nuclear fission; **die erste ~spaltung** the first splitting of the atom; **~speicher** *m* core memory; ⚠**~spin-Tomograph** *m* MRI scanner; ⚠**~spin-Tomographie** *f* magnetic resonance imaging; **~sprengkopf** *m* nuclear warhead; **~spruch** *m* pithy saying; **~stück** *nt* (*fig*) main item, centrepiece; (*von Theorie etc*) crucial *or* central element *or* part, core; (*von Roman etc*) crucial *or* key passage; **~technik** *f* nuclear technology, nucleonics; **k~technisch** *adj* **k~technische Anlage** nuclear plant; **k~technische Entwicklung** development of nuclear technology; **~teilchen** *nt* nuclear particle; **~teilung** *f* (*Biol*) nuclear division; **~truppe** *f* (*Mil*) core unit *or* division; (*fig*) core team; **~unterricht** *m* (*Sch*) core curriculum; **~verschmelzung** *f* **(a)** (*Phys*) *siehe* **~fusion**; **(b)** (*Biol*) cell union.
Kernwaffe *f* nuclear weapon.
Kernwaffen-: k~frei *adj* nuclearfree; **~sperrvertrag** *m* Nuclear Non-proliferation Treaty; **~versuch** *m* nuclear (weapons) test.
Kernzeit *f* core time.
Kerosin *nt* **-s, -e** kerosene.
Kerub *m* **-s, -im** *or* **-e** *siehe* **Cherub.**
Kerze *f* **-, -n (a)** (*Wachs~*) candle; (*Blüte der Kastanie*) candle, thyrus (*form*). **(b)** (*Aut*) plug. **(c)** (*Turnen*) shoulder-stand. **(d)** (*Ftbl*) skyer.
Kerzen-: ~beleuchtung *f* candlelight; **~birne** *f* (*Elec*) candle bulb; **~docht** *m* candle wick; **~form** *f* (*einer Glühbirne*) candle-shape; **k~förmig** *adj* candle-shaped; **k~gerade** *adj* (as) straight as a die, erect; **~gesicht** *nt*

➤ SPRACHE AKTIV: **Kenntnis: a** → 46.2, 46.3

⚠: Informationen zur Rechtschreibreform im Anhang

(*Tech*) appearance *or* look of a/the (spark) plug; **~halter** *m* candlestick; (*am Weihnachtsbaum, auf Kuchen etc*) candle holder; **~leuchter** *m* candlestick; **~licht** *nt, no pl* candlelight; **~schein** *m* candlelight; **im ~schein des Weihnachtsbaumes** in the light of the Christmas-tree candles, in the candle-lit glow of the Christmas-tree; **~schlüssel** *m* (spark) plug spanner; **~stummel, ~stumpf** *m* candle stump.

Kescher *m* **-s, -** fishing-net; (*Hamen*) landing-net.

⚠ **keß** *adj* (*flott*) saucy; *Kleid, Hut etc* jaunty; (*vorwitzig*) cheeky;(*frech*) fresh.

Kessel *m* **-s, - (a)** (*Tee~*) kettle; (*Wasch~*) copper; (*Koch~*) pot; (*für offenes Feuer*) cauldron; (*esp in Brauerei*) vat; (*Dampf~*) boiler; (*Behälter für Flüssigkeiten etc*) tank.
(b) (*Mulde*) basin, basin-shaped valley; (*Hunt*) semi-circular ring of hunters; (*Mil*) encircled area.

Kessel-: ~flicker *m* **-s, -** tinker; **~haus** *nt* boiler house; **~jagd** *f siehe* **~treiben**; **~pauke** *f* kettle drum; **~raum** *m* boiler room; **~schlacht** *f* (*Mil*) battle of encirclement; **~stein** *m* scale, fur; **~treiben** *nt* (*Hunt*) hunt using a circle of beaters; (*fig: in Zeitung etc*) witchhunt; **~wagen** *m* (*Rail*) tank wagon *or* car.

⚠ **Keßheit** *f siehe adj* sauciness; jauntiness; cheekiness.

⚠ **Ketchup** ['kɛtʃap] *m or nt* **-(s), -s** ketchup.

Ketsch *f* **-, -en** (*Naut*) ketch.

ketschen *vti siehe* **catchen**.

Kette *f* **-, -n (a)** chain; (*von Kettenfahrzeug*) chain track ◆ **einen Hund an die ~ legen** to put a dog on the chain, to chain up a dog; **in ~n liegen** (*fig geh*) to be in chains *or* bondage; **in ~n schlagen** (*liter*) to put in chains; **seine ~n zerreißen** *or* **sprengen** (*fig geh*) to throw off one's chains *or* shackles *or* fetters.
(b) (*fig: ununterbrochene Reihe*) chain; (*von Menschen auch*) line; (*von Fahrzeugen*) line, string; (*von Unfällen, Erfahrungen etc*) series, string ◆ **eine ~ von Ereignissen** a chain of events.
(c) (*Berg~, Seen~*) chain.
(d) (*Hunt*) (*von Rebhühnern*) covey; (*von Wildenten*) skein.
(e) (*Aviat, Mil*) flight.
(f) (*Comm: von Läden*) chain.
(g) (*Tex*) warp.

Kettel *m* **-s, -** *or f* **-, -n** (*dial*) *siehe* **Krampe**.

ketten *vt* to chain (*an +acc* to) ◆ **jdn an sich ~** (*fig*) to bind sb to oneself; **sich an jdn/etw ~** (*fig*) to tie *or* bind oneself to sb/sth.

Ketten-: ~antrieb *m* chain drive; **mit ~antrieb** chain-driven; **~armband** *nt* chain bracelet; **~brief** *m* chain letter; **~brücke** *f* chain bridge; **~fahrzeug** *nt* tracked vehicle, track-laying vehicle; **~gebirge** *nt* mountain chain; **~glied** *nt* (chain-)link; **~hemd** *nt* (*Hist*) coat of (chain-) mail; **~hund** *m* guard-dog, watchdog; **~karussell** *nt* merry-go-round (*with gondolas suspended on chains*); **~rad** *nt* sprocket(-wheel); **~rauchen** *nt* chain-smoking; **~raucher** *m* chain-smoker; **~reaktion** *f* chain reaction; **~reim** *m* (*Poet*) interlaced rhyme; **~säge** *f* chainsaw; **~schaltung** *f* dérailleur gear; ⚠**~schluß** *m* (*Logik*) sorites; **~schutz** *m* chain guard; **~spanner** *m* (*bei Fahrrad etc*) chain adjuster; **~stich** *m* (*Sew*) chain stitch.

Ketzer *m* **-s, -** (*Eccl, fig*) heretic.

Ketzerei *f* heresy.

Ketzergericht *nt* (*Hist*) (court of) inquisition.

Ketzerin *f siehe* **Ketzer**.

ketzerisch *adj* (*Eccl, fig*) heretical.

Ketzertaufe *f* (*Hist*) heretical baptism.

keuchen *vi* **(a)** (*schwer atmen*) to pant, to puff, to gasp (for breath); (*Asthmatiker etc*) to wheeze ◆ **mit ~dem Atem** panting, puffing; wheezing.
(b) *aux sein* (*sich schwer atmend fortbewegen*) to pant, to puff; (*Zug*) to puff, to chug.

Keuchhusten *m* whooping cough.

Keule *f* **-, -n (a)** club, cudgel; (*Sport*) (Indian) club. **(b)** (*Cook*) leg; (*von Wild auch*) haunch. **(c) chemische ~** Chemical Mace ®.

Keulen-: ~hieb, ~schlag *m* blow with a club *or* cudgel; **er bekam einen ~hieb auf den Kopf** he was hit on the head with a club *or* cudgel; **es traf ihn wie ein ~schlag** (*fig*) it hit him like a thunderbolt; **~schwingen** *nt* **-s,** *no pl* (*Sport*) (Indian) club swinging.

keusch *adj* (*lit, fig*) chaste ◆ **~ und züchtig** pure and chaste.

Keusche *f* **-, -n** (*Aus inf*) cottage; (*pej: baufälliges Haus*) hovel.

Keuschheit *f* chasteness; (*Unberührtheit auch*) chastity.

Keuschheits-: ~gelübde *nt* vow of chastity; **~gürtel** *m* chastity belt.

Keyboard ['ki:bɔrt] (*Comput, Mus*) keyboard ◆ **sie spielt ~** she plays keyboards.

Keyboardspieler ['ki:bɔrt-] *m* (*Mus*) keyboards player.

kfm *abbr of* **kaufmännisch**.

Kfz [ka|ɛf'tsɛt] *nt* **-(s), -(s)** (*form*) *abbr of* **Kraftfahrzeug** motor vehicle.

Kfz- *in cpds* motor vehicle; **~-Zulassung, ~-Zulassungsstelle** *f* motor vehicle licensing centre.

kg *abbr of* **Kilogramm** kg.

KG [ka'ge:] *f* **-, -s** *abbr of* **Kommanditgesellschaft** limited partnership.

KGB [ka:ge:'be:] *m* **-(s),** *no pl* KGB.

KGB-Chef *m* head of the KGB.

kgl *abbr of* **königlich** royal.

K-Gruppe ['ka:-] *f* (*BRD Pol*) Communist splinter group.

k.g.V., kgV *abbr of* **kleinstes gemeinsames Vielfaches** lowest common multiple, lcm.

Khaki[1] *m* **-s,** *no pl* (*Stoff*) khaki.

Khaki[2] *nt* **-s,** *no pl* (*Farbe*) khaki.

khaki *adj pred* khaki.

khakifarben *adj* khaki(-coloured).

Khartum *nt* **-s** Khartoum.

KHz, kHz *abbr of* **Kilohertz** kHz.

kibbeln *vir* (*dial*) *siehe* **kabbeln**.

Kibbuz *m* **-, Kibbuzim** *or* **-e** kibbutz.

Kicherei *f* giggling.

Kicher|erbse *f* chick-pea.

kichern *vi* to giggle.

Kick *m* **-(s), -s** (*inf: Stoß*) kick; (*sl: Spiel*) kick-about, kick-around.

Kickboxen *nt* kick boxing.

Kickboxer *m* kick boxer.

Kickdown [kɪk'daun] *nt* **-s,** *no pl* (*Aut*) kickdown.

kicken (*Ftbl inf*) **1** *vt* to kick, to boot (*inf*).
2 *vi* to play football; (*den Ball ~*) to kick ◆ **für eine Mannschaft ~** to play for a team.

Kicker *m* **-s, -** (*Ftbl inf*) player.

Kick-off *m* **-s, -s** (*Ftbl: esp Sw*) kick-off.

Kickstarter *m* (*bei Motorrad*) kick-starter.

Kid *nt* **-s, -s (a)** *usu pl* (*inf: Jugendlicher*) kid (*inf*). **(b)** (*Leder*) kid (leather). **(c)** *usu pl* (*Handschuh*) kid glove.

kidnappen ['kɪtnɛpn] *vt insep* to kidnap.

Kidnapper(in *f*) ['kɪtnɛpɐ, -ərɪn] *m* **-s, -** kidnapper.

Kidnapping ['kɪtnɛpɪŋ] *nt* **-s, -s** kidnapping.

kiebig *adj* (*inf*) cheeky, saucy, fresh (*inf*).

Kiebitz *m* **-es, -e** (*Orn*) lapwing, peewit, green plover; (*Cards inf*) kibitzer.

kiebitzen *vi* (*inf*) to spy; (*Cards*) to kibitz.

Kiefer[1] *f* **-, -n** pine (tree); (*Holz*) pine(wood).

Kiefer[2] *m* **-s, -** jaw; (*~knochen*) jawbone.

Kiefer-: ~anomalie *f* malformation of the jaw; **~bruch** *m* broken *or* fractured jaw; **~chirurg** *m* oral surgeon; **~chirurgie** *f* oral surgery.

Kieferhöhle *f* (*Anat*) maxillary sinus.

Kieferhöhlen-: ~entzündung *f* sinusitis; **~vereiterung** *f* sinus infection.

Kiefern-: ~holz *nt* pine(wood); **~nadel** *f* pine needle; **~schonung** *f* pinery, pine plantation; **~wald** *m* pine wood; (*größer*) pine forest; **~zapfen** *m* pinecone.

Kiefer-: ~orthopäde *m* orthodontist; **~orthopädie** *f* orthodontics; **k~orthopädisch** *adj* orthodontic.

kieken *vi* (*dial*) *siehe* **gucken**.

Kieker *m* **-s, - (a)** (*N Ger inf*) binoculars *pl*. **(b) jdn auf dem ~ haben** (*inf*) to have it in for sb (*inf*).

Kiel *m* **-(e)s, -e (a)** (*Schiffs~*) keel ◆ **ein Schiff auf ~ legen** to lay down a ship. **(b)** (*Feder~*) quill.

Kiel-: ~boot *nt* keel boat; **~feder** *f* quill pen; **k~holen** *vt insep* (*Naut*) **(a)** *Schiff* to careen; **(b)** *Matrosen* to keelhaul; **~linie** *f* line ahead; **k~oben** *adv* bottom up; **~raum** *m* bilge; **~wasser** *nt* wake, wash; **in jds ~wasser** (*dat*) **segeln** *or* **schwimmen** (*fig*) to follow in sb's wake.

Kieme *f* **-, -n** gill.

Kiemen- (*Zool*): **~atmer** *m* **-s, -** gill-breather; **~atmung** *f* gill-breathing.

Kien *m* **-(e)s,** *no pl* pine.

Kien-: ~apfel *m siehe* **Kiefernzapfen**; **~fackel** *f* pinewood torch; **~holz** *nt* pine; **~span** *m* pinewood spill; **~zapfen** *m siehe* **Kiefernzapfen**.

Kiepe *f* **-, -n** (*dial*) pannier, dosser.

Kiepenhut *m* poke-bonnet.

Kies *m* **-es, -e (a)** gravel; (*am Strand*) shingle. **(b)** *no pl* (*inf: Geld*) dough (*inf*), lolly (*inf*).

Kiesel *m* **-s, -** pebble.

Kiesel|erde *f* silica.

kieseln *vt* (*dial*): **es kieselt** it's hailing.

Kiesel-: ~säure *f* (*Chem*) **(a)** silicic acid; **(b)** (*Siliziumdioxyd*) silica; **~stein** *m* pebble; **~strand** *m* pebble beach, shingle beach.

Kiesgrube *f* gravel pit.

kiesig *adj* gravelly; *Strand* shingly.

Kiesweg *m* gravel(led) path.

Kie(t)z *m* **-es, -e** (*dial*) **(a)** (*Stadtgegend*) district, area. **(b)** (*sl: Bordellgegend*) red-light district.

kiffen *vi* (*sl*) to smoke pot (*sl*) *or* grass (*sl*), to smoke (*sl*).

Kiffer(in *f*) *m* **-s, -** (*sl*) pot-smoker (*sl*).

kikeriki *interj* cock-a-doodle-doo.

Kikeriki *nt* **-s, -s** (*Hahnenschrei*) cock-a-doodle-doo.

Kilbi *f* **-, Kilbenen** (*Sw*) *siehe* **Kirchweih**.

killekille *interj* (*baby-talk*) tickle, tickle, kitchie, kitchie ◆ **(bei jdm) ~ machen** to tickle sb.

killen[1] (*sl*) **1** *vt* to bump off (*inf*), to do in (*inf*), to kill; (*esp mit Auftrag*) to hit (*sl*).
2 *vi* to kill, to murder.

killen[2] *vi* (*Naut*) to shake, to shiver.

Killer(in *f*) *m* **-s, -** (*sl*) killer, murderer; (*gedungener*) hit-man.

Killerinstinkt *m* (*inf*) killer instinct.

Killerzelle *f* (*Physiol*) killer cell.

Kilo *nt* **-s, -(s)** kilo.

Kilo- *in cpds* kilo-; **~byte** *nt* kilobyte; **~gramm** *nt* kilogram(me); **~hertz** *nt* kilocycle; **~joule** *nt* kilojoule; **~kalorie** *f* kilocalorie.

⚠: for details of spelling reform, see supplement

Kilometer *m* kilometre; (*inf: Stundenkilometer*) k (*inf*) ◆ **bei ~ 547** (*~stein*) at kilometre 547; **wir konnten nur 80 ~ fahren** we could only do 80.

Kilometer-: ~fresser *m* (*inf*) long-haul driver; **er ist ein richtiger ~fresser** he really eats up the miles (*inf*); **~geld** *nt* mileage (allowance); **k~lang** [1] *adj* miles long; **k~lange Strände** miles and miles of beaches; **ein k~langer Stau** a tailback several miles/kilometres long; [2] *adv* for miles (and miles), for miles on end; **~pauschale** *f* mileage allowance (against tax); **~stand** *m* mileage; **der ~stand des Autos ist ...** the car has done ..., the car has ... on the clock (*inf*), the mileage on the car is ...; **~stein** *m* milestone; **k~weit** [1] *adj* miles long; **ein k~weiter Blick** a view for miles; **in k~weiter Entfernung** miles away in the distance; **ein k~weiter Marsch** a march of several miles/ kilometres; [2] *adv* for miles (and miles); **~zähler** *m* mileage indicator *or* counter, mileometer, odometer.

Kilo-: ~watt *nt* kilowatt; **~wattstunde** *f* kilowatt hour.

Kimbern *pl* (*Hist*) Cimbri *pl.*

Kimm *f* **-,** *no pl* (*Naut*) **(a)** (*Horizont*) apparent *or* visual horizon. **(b)** (*am Schiffskörper*) bilge.

Kimme *f* **-, -n (a)** (*von Gewehr*) back sight. **(b)** (*inf: Gesäßfalte*) cleft between the buttocks, great divide (*hum*). **(c)** (*rare*) *siehe* **Kerbe**[1].

Kimmung *f* (*Naut*) **(a)** (*Horizont*) visual horizon. **(b)** (*Luftspiegelung*) mirage.

Kimono *m* **-s, -s** kimono.

Kind *nt* **-(e)s, -er** child, kid (*inf*); (*Kleinkind*) baby; (*esp Psych, Med*) infant ◆ **ein ~ erwarten/bekommen** *or* **kriegen** to be expecting a baby/to have a baby *or* child; **von ~ auf** *or* **an** since he/we *etc* was/were a child/children, from childhood; **einem Mädchen ein ~ machen** (*sl*) to knock a girl up (*sl*), to put a girl in the club (*inf*); **sie kriegt ein ~** she's going to have a baby *or* child; **aber ~!** child, child; **schönes ~!** (*old: als Anrede*) my pretty maid (*old*); **die ~er Gottes** (*geh*) the children of the Lord; **ein echtes Wiener ~** (*dated*) a true son/daughter of Vienna; **ein ~ seiner Zeit sein** to be a child of one's times; **sie ist kein ~ von Traurigkeit** (*hum*) she enjoys life; **er ist ein großes ~** he's a big baby; **sich freuen wie ein ~** to be as pleased as Punch; **er kann sich wie ein ~ freuen** he takes a childlike pleasure in (simple) things; **das weiß doch jedes ~!** any five-year-old would tell you that!; **du bist aber ein kluges ~!** (*iro*) clever kid!; **er ist redlicher/armer Leute ~** (*dated*) he was the child of upright/poor parents; **da kommt das ~ im Manne durch** all men are boys at heart; **wie sag' ich's meinem ~e?** (*hum*) I don't know how to put it; (*bei Aufklärung*) what to tell your children; **das ist nichts für kleine ~er** (*fig inf*) that's not for your innocent *or* your young ears/eyes; **aus ~ern werden Leute** (*Prov*) children grow up quickly, don't they?; **~er und Narren** *or* **Betrunkene sagen die Wahrheit** (*fig*) children and fools speak the truth; **ein ~ des Todes sein** (*dated*) to be a goner (*inf*); **mit ~ und Kegel** (*hum inf*) with the whole family; **das ~ muß einen Namen haben** (*fig*) you/we *etc* have to call it something; **das ~ mit dem Bade ausschütten** to throw out the baby with the bathwater (*prov*); **wir werden das ~ schon schaukeln** (*inf*) we'll soon have that *or* everything sorted out; **los, ~er/hört mal alle her, ~er!** let's go, kids/ listen, kids; **~er, ~er!** dear, dear!, goodness me!, good heavens!.

Kind-: ~bett *nt* (*old*) childbed (*old*); **im ~bett** in confinement; **~bettfieber** *nt* childbed fever.

Kindchen *nt dim of* **Kind** child; (*zu Erwachsenen*) kid(do) (*inf*).

Kindel *nt* **-s, -(n)** (*dial*) *dim of* **Kind** kiddy.

Kinder-: ~arbeit *f* child labour; **k~arm** *adj* with few children; *Familie* small; **ein k~armes Land** a country with a low birth rate; **~art** *f* the way children are; **~arzt** *m* paediatrician; **~augen** *pl* children's eyes *pl*; **etw mit ~augen anschauen** to gaze wide-eyed at sth; **vor Erstaunen ~augen machen/bekommen** to be wide-eyed with astonishment; **~beihilfe** *f* (*Aus*) *siehe* **~geld**; **~beilage** *f* children's supplement, children's page; **~bekleidung** *f* children's wear; **~besteck** *nt* child's cutlery; **~bett** *nt* cot; **~bild** *nt* childhood photograph; **das ist ein ~bild (von) meiner Mutter** that's a photograph of my mother as a child *or* when she was a child; **~buch** *nt* children's book; **~büro** *nt* local childrens' bureau (*for complaints, suggestions etc*).

Kinderchen *pl* children *pl.*

Kinder-: ~chor *m* children's choir; **~dorf** *nt* children's village.

Kinderei *f* childishness *no pl* ◆ **~en** childishness, childish nonsense.

Kinder-: ~erziehung *f* bringing up of children; (*durch Schule*) education of children; **sie versteht nichts von ~erziehung** she knows nothing about bringing up/educating children; **~fahrkarte** *f* child's ticket; **~fahrrad** *nt* child's *or* children's bicycle; **~feind** *m* child-hater; **k~feindlich** [1] *adj* hostile to children, anti-children; *Architektur, Planung* not catering for children; **k~feindliche Steuerpolitik** tax policies which penalize having children; [2] *adv* without regard to children; **~feindlichkeit** *f* hostility to children, anti-children attitude; (*von Architektur*) failure to cater for children; **~fernsehen** *nt* children's television; **~fest** *nt* children's party *or* (*von Stadt etc*) fête; **~film** *m* children's film; **~frau** *f*, **~fräulein** *nt* (*dated*) nanny, children's nurse; **~freibetrag** *m* child allowance; **~freund** *m* **~freund sein** to be fond of children; **k~freundlich** [1] *adj Mensch* fond of children; *Gesellschaft* child-orientated, child-friendly; *Möbel, Architektur etc* child-friendly; **eine k~freundliche Steuerpolitik** a tax policy which encourages one to have children; [2] *adv* with children in mind; **~freundlichkeit** *f siehe adj* fondness for children; child-orientation; child-friendliness; **~freundschaft** *f* friendship between children; **~funk** *m* children's radio *or* programmes *pl*; **~garten** *m* nursery school, kindergarten; **~gärtner(in** *f*) *m* nursery-school teacher; **~geburtstag** *m* (*Feier*) children's birthday party; **~geld** *nt* child benefit *or* allowance; **~geschrei** *nt* screams *pl* of children; **er kann ~geschrei nicht vertragen** he can't stand children screaming; **dieses ~geschrei ...!** these children *or* kids (*inf*) screaming ...!; **~gesicht** *nt* baby face; **~glaube** *m* childlike faith; **~gottesdienst** *m* children's service; **~heilkunde** *f* paediatrics; **Facharzt für ~heilkunde** paediatrician; **~heim** *nt* children's home; **~hort** *m* day-nursery, crèche; **~jahre** *pl* childhood years *pl*; **~kleidung** *f* children's clothes *pl*; **~klinik** *f* children's clinic, paediatric clinic; **~korb** *m* baby-carrier; **~kram** *m* (*inf*) kids' stuff (*inf*); **~krankenhaus** *nt* children's hospital; **~krankheit** *f* (*allgemein*) children's illness *or* disease; (*eines bestimmten Menschen*) childhood illness *or* disease; (*fig*) teething troubles *pl*; **~kreuzzug** *m* (*Eccl Hist*) Children's Crusade; **~kriegen** *nt* **-s,** *no pl* **sie hat keine Lust zum ~kriegen** she doesn't want to have children; **~krippe** *f* day-nursery, crèche; **~laden** *m* (left-wing) play-group; **~lähmung** *f* poliomyelitis, polio; **~lähmungsimpfung** *f* polio vaccination *or* inoculation; **k~leicht** *adj* childishly simple, dead easy (*inf*); **es ist k~leicht** it's child's play *or* kid's stuff (*inf*).

Kinderlein *pl* children *pl.*

Kinder-: k~lieb *adj* fond of children; **~liebe** *f* (*Liebe zwischen ~n*) children's love, children's affection; (*Liebe zu ~n*) love of *or* for children; **~lied** *nt* ≃ nursery rhyme; **k~los** *adj* childless; **~losigkeit** *f* childlessness; **~mädchen** *f* nanny; **~märchen** *nt* (children's) fairy tale, fairy story; **~moden** *pl* children's fashions *pl*; **~mord** *m* child murder; (*Jur*) infanticide; **der bethlehemitische ~mord, der ~mord zu Bethlehem** (*Bibl*) the massacre of the innocents; **~mörder** *m* child-murderer; **~mund** *m* (*fig*) children's talk, child's way of talking; **das wirkt spaßig, weil es aus ~mund kommt** that sounds funny coming from a child; **~mund tut Wahrheit kund** (*Prov*) out of the mouths of babes and sucklings (*prov*); **~narr** *m* great lover of children; **er ist ein ~narr** he adores children; **~paradies** *nt* children's paradise; **~pflegerin** *f* children's nurse; (*~mädchen*) nanny; **~popo** *m* (*inf*) baby's bottom (*inf*); **glatt wie ein ~popo** smooth as a baby's bottom (*inf*); **~pornographie** *f* child pornography; **~prostitution** *f* child prostitution; **~psychologie** *f* child psychology; **~raub** *m* baby-snatching; (*Entführung*) kidnapping (of a child/children); **k~reich** *adj* with many children; *Familie* large; **~reichtum** *m* an abundance of children; **der ~reichtum Kenias** the abundance of children in Kenya; **~reim** *m* nursery rhyme; **~reisebett** *nt* travel cot; **~sachen** *pl* (*Kleidung*) children's clothes *pl*; (*Gegenstände*) children's things *pl*; (*Spielsachen*) toys *pl*; **~schänder** *m* **-s, -** child molester; **~schar** *f* swarm of children; **~schreck** *m* bog(e)yman; **~schuh** *m* child's shoe; **~schuhe sind teuer** children's shoes are dear; **etw steckt noch in den ~schuhen** (*fig*) sth is still in its infancy; **~schutz** *m* protection of children; **~schutzbund** *m* ≃ NSPCC; **~schwester** *f siehe* **~pflegerin**; **~segen** *m* (*dated*) children *pl*; **es war ihnen kein ~segen beschert** they were not blessed with children; **k~sicher** *adj* childproof; **~sicherung** *f* (*Aut*) childproof safety catch; **~sitz** *m* child's seat; (*im Auto*) child's safety seat; **~spiel** *nt* children's game; (*fig*) child's play *no art*; **~spielplatz** *m* children's playground; **~spielzeug** *nt* (children's) toys *pl*; **~sprache** *f* (*von Kindern*) children's language; (*verniedlichend von Erwachsenen*) baby talk *no art*; **~station** *f* children's ward; **~sterblichkeit** *f* infant mortality; **~stimme** *f* child's voice; **~streich** *m* childish prank; **~stube** *f* (*fig*) upbringing; **~stuhl** *m* child's chair; (*Hochstuhl*) high chair; **~stunde** *f* children's hour; **~tagesheim** *nt*, **~tagesstätte** *f* day nursery, crèche; **~taufe** *f* infant baptism; **~teller** *m* (*in Restaurant*) children's portion; **~theater** *nt* children's theatre; (*Jugendtheater*) youth theatre; **~trommel** *f* toy drum; **~vers** *m* nursery rhyme; **~wagen** *m* pram (*Brit*), baby carriage (*US*), perambulator (*form*); (*Sportwagen*) pushchair (*Brit*), baby-stroller (*US*); **~welt** *f* world of children; **~zahl** *f* number of children; **~zimmer** *nt* child's/children's room; (*esp für Kleinkinder*) nursery; **~zulage** *f*, **~zuschlag** *m* child benefit.

Kindes-: ~abtreibung *f* abortion; **~alter** *nt* childhood; **im ~alter** at an early age; **~aussetzung** *f* abandoning of children; **~aussetzungen** cases of children being abandoned; **~beine** *pl*: **von ~beinen an** from childhood, from an early age; **~entführung** *f* kidnapping (of a child/children); **~entziehung** *f* (*Jur*) child abduction; **~kind** *nt* grandchild; **~liebe** *f* child's/children's love; ⚠**~mißhandlung** *f* child abuse; **~mord** *m* child-murder, murder of a child; **~mörder** *m* child-murderer; **~nöte** *pl* (*old*) travail (*old*); **~raub** *m siehe* **Kinderraub**; **~tötung** *f* (*Jur: von eigenem Säugling*) infanticide; **~verwechs(e)lung** *f* confusion of children's identity.

Kind-: ~frau *f* Lolita; **k~gemäß** *adj* suitable for a child/children; **k~haft** *adj* childlike; **~heit** *f* childhood; (*früheste ~heit*) infancy.

Kindheits-: ~erinnerung *f* childhood memory; **~traum** *m* childhood dream.

kindisch *adj* (*pej*) childish ◆ **sich ~ über etw** (*acc*) **freuen** to be as pleased as Punch about sth; **er kann sich ~ freuen** he takes a childlike pleasure in (simple) things.

Kindl *nt* **-s, -(n)** (*dial*) *dim of* **Kind.**

kindlich [1] *adj* childlike; (*pej*) childish.
[2] *adv* like a child.

Kindlichkeit *f* childlikeness; (*pej*) childishness.

Kinds- *in cpds siehe* **Kindes-**; **~bewegungen** *pl* (*Med*) foetal movements *pl*; **~kopf** *m* (*inf*) big kid (*inf*); **sei kein ~kopf** don't be so childish; **~lage** *f* (*Med*) presentation of the foetus; **~tod** *m* **plötzlicher ~tod** cot death.

Kindtaufe *f* (*old*) christening.

Kinemathek *f* **-, -en** film library *or* archive.

⚠ **Kinematographie** *f* cinematography.

Kinetik *f* kinetics *sing.*

⚠: Informationen zur Rechtschreibreform im Anhang

kinetisch *adj* kinetic.
Kinigelhase *m (Aus, dial) siehe* **Kaninchen.**
Kinkerlitzchen *pl (inf)* knicknacks *pl (inf)*; *(dumme Streiche)* tomfoolery *sing (inf)*.
Kinn *nt* **-(e)s, -e** chin.
Kinn-: ~bart *m* goatee (beard); **~haken** *m* hook to the chin; **~lade** *f* jaw (-bone); **~riemen** *m (am Helm)* chinstrap; **~schutz** *m (Hockey)* chin-guard.
Kino *nt* **-s, -s** cinema; *(Gebäude auch)* movie theater *(US)* ♦ **ins ~ gehen** to go to the cinema *or* pictures *(Brit) or* movies *(esp US)*.
Kino- *in cpds* cinema, movie *(esp US)*; **~besuch** *m* visit to the cinema; *(Besucherrate)* cinema attendances *pl*; **~besucher** *m* cinemagoer; **~center** *nt* cinema complex, multi-screen cinema; **~film** *m* cinema film; **~freudig** *adj* cinema-loving; **~gänger(in** *f***)** *m* **-s, -** cinemagoer; **~hit** *m* blockbuster; **~karte** *f* cinema ticket; **~kasse** *f* cinema box office; **~programm** *nt* film programme; *(Übersicht)* film guide; **~reklame** *f* **(a)** cinema advertisement; **(b)** *siehe* **~werbung**; **~vorstellung** *f* performance, programme; **~werbung** *f* cinema advertising.
Kintopp *m or nt* **-s, -s** *or* **⸗e** *(dated)* **(a)** pictures *pl (Brit)*, movies *pl (US)* ♦ **im ~ sein** to be at the pictures/movies. **(b)** *(als Kulturphänomen)* cinema.
Kiosk *m* **-(e)s, -e** kiosk.
Kipf *m* **-(e)s, -e** *(S Ger)* (stick) loaf.
Kipfe(r)l *nt* **-s, -(n)** *(Aus)* croissant.
Kipfler *pl (Aus)* salad potatoes *pl*.
Kippe *f* **-, -n (a)** *(Sport)* spring.
(b) auf der ~ stehen *(Gegenstand)* to be balanced precariously; **sie steht auf der ~** *(fig)* it's touch and go with her; **es steht auf der ~, ob ...** *(fig)* it's touch and go whether ...
(c) *(inf: Zigarettenstummel)* cigarette stub, fag-end *(Brit inf)*, dog-end *(Brit inf)*; *(sl: Zigarette)* fag *(Brit inf)*, butt *(US sl)*.
(d) *(Müll~, Min)* tip.
kippelig *adj (inf) (wackelig)* wobbly; *Möbel auch* rickety; *Angelegenheit* shaky ♦ **sie steht ~ in der Schule** she's a bit shaky at school.
kippeln *vi (inf)* to wobble, to be wobbly *or* rickety ♦ **(mit dem Stuhl) ~** to tilt (on one's chair).
kippen [1] *vt* **(a)** *Behälter, Fenster* to tilt; *Ladefläche, Tisch* to tip *or* tilt (up); *(fig: umstoßen) Urteil* to overturn; *Regierung, Minister* to topple ♦ **etw aus dem Gleichgewicht ~** to tilt sth; **„bitte nicht ~"** "please do not tilt"; **einen/ein paar ~** *(inf: trinken)* to have a drink/to down a few *(inf)*.
(b) *(mit Ortsangabe: schütten)* to tip.
[2] *vi aux sein* to tip over; *(esp höhere Gegenstände)* to topple (over); *(Fahrzeug, Schiff)* to overturn; *(Mensch)* to topple, to fall; *(Wechselkurse, Gewinne)* to plummet ♦ **aus den Latschen** *or* **Pantinen ~** *(fig inf) (überrascht sein)* to fall through the floor *(inf)*; *(ohnmächtig werden)* to pass out.
Kipper *m* **-s, -** *(Aut)* tipper, dump(er) truck; *(Rail)* (tipper) wagon.
Kippfenster *nt* tilt window.
kipplig *adj siehe* **kippelig.**
Kipp-: ~lore *f* tipper wagon; **~schalter** *m* toggle switch; **~wagen** *m siehe* **Kipper.**
Kir *m* **-, -** kir.
Kirche *f* **-, -n** *(Gebäude, Organisation)* church; *(bestimmte Glaubensgemeinschaft)* Church; *(Gottesdienst)* church *no art* ♦ **zur ~ gehen** to go to church; **die ~ im Dorf lassen** *(fig)* not to get carried away.
Kirchen- *in cpds* church; **~älteste(r)** *mf decl as adj* church elder; **~amt** *nt* **(a)** ecclesiastical office; **(b)** *(Verwaltungsstelle)* church offices *pl*; **~austritt** *m* leaving the Church *no art*; ~austritte (cases of) people leaving the Church; **~bank** *f* (church) pew; **~bann** *m* anathema; *(Interdikt)* interdict; **den ~bann über jdn verhängen** to excommunicate/interdict sb; **~besuch** *m* church-going; **~blatt** *nt* parish magazine; **~buch** *nt* church register; **~chor** *m* church choir; **~diebstahl** *m* theft from a/the church; **~diener** *m* sexton; **k~feindlich** *adj* anticlerical; **~fenster** *nt* church window; **~fest** *nt* religious *or* church festival; **~fürst** *m* high dignitary of the Church; *(katholisch)* prince of the Church; **~gemeinde** *f* parish; **~geschichte** *f* church *or* ecclesiastical history; **~glocke** *f* church bell; **~gut** *nt* church property; **~jahr** *nt* church *or* ecclesiastical year; **~kampf** *m* struggle between Church and state; **~lehrer** *m* Doctor of the Church; **~leitung** *f* government of the Church; *(Gremium)* governing body of the Church; **~licht** *nt*: **kein (großes) ~licht sein** *(fig inf)* to be not very bright; **~lied** *nt* hymn; **~mann** *m, pl* **~männer** churchman; **~maus** *f*: **arm wie eine ~maus** poor as a church mouse; **~musik** *f* church *or* sacred music; **~politik** *f* church policy; **k~politisch** [1] *adj* relating to church policy; [2] *adv* in relation to church policy; **~rat** *m (Person)* member of the Church Council; *(Gremium)* Church Council; **~raub** *m* theft from a/the church; *(von geweihtem Gegenstand)* sacrilege; **~räuber** *m* church-robber; **~recht** *nt* canon law; **k~rechtlich** *adj* canonical; **~schänder** *m* **-s, -** desecrator, profaner; **~schiff** *nt (Längsschiff)* nave; *(Querschiff)* transept; **~spaltung** *f* schism; **~staat** *m (Hist)* Papal States *pl*; *(Vatikanstaat)* Vatican City; **~steuer** *f* church tax; **~strafe** *f* ecclesiastical punishment; **~tag** *m* Church congress; **~tonart** *f* church *or* ecclesiastical mode; **~vater** *m* Father of the Church, Church Father; **~verfolgung** *f* persecution of the Church; **~vorstand** *m* parish council.
Kirch-: ~gang *m* going to church *no art*; **der sonntägliche ~gang** going to church on Sunday; **~gänger(in** *f***)** *m* **-s, -** churchgoer; **~hof** *m* churchyard; *(Friedhof)* graveyard.
kirchlich *adj* church *attr*; *Zustimmung, Mißbilligung* by the church; *Amt auch, Gebot, Gericht* ecclesiastical; *Musik auch* sacred, religious; *Feiertag auch* religious; *Land, Mensch* religious, devout; *Recht* canon ♦ **sich ~ trauen lassen** to get married in church, to have a church wedding; **~ bestattet werden** to have a religious funeral.
Kirch-: ~spiel *nt*, **~sprengel** *m* parish; **~tag** *m (Aus, S Ger) siehe* **~weih.**
Kirchturm *m* church steeple.
Kirchturmspitze *f* church spire.
Kirch-: ~weih *f* **-, -en** fair, kermis *(US)*; **~weihe** *f* consecration of a/the church.
Kirmes *f* **-, -sen** *(dial) siehe* **Kirchweih.**
kirre *adj pred (inf) Tier* tame; *Mensch* compliant ♦ **jdn ~ machen** to soften sb up *(inf)*.
Kirsch *m* **-(e)s, -** *siehe* **Kirschwasser.**
Kirsch- *in cpds* cherry; **~baum** *m* cherry tree; *(Holz)* cherry (wood); **~blüte** *f* cherry blossom; *(Zeit)* cherry blossom time.
Kirsche *f* **-, -n** cherry ♦ **mit ihm ist nicht gut ~n essen** *(fig)* it's best not to tangle with him.
Kirschenmund *m (poet)* cherry (red) lips *pl*.
Kirsch-: ~entkerner, ~entsteiner *m* **-s, -** cherry-stoner; **~kern** *m* cherry stone; **~likör** *m* cherry brandy; **k~rot** *adj* cherry(-red); **~stein** *m* cherry stone; **~torte** *f* cherry gateau; **Schwarzwälder ~torte** Black Forest gateau; **~wasser** *nt* kirsch.
Kissen *nt* **-s, -** cushion; *(Kopf~)* pillow; *(Stempel~, an Heftpflaster)* pad; *(Duft~, Haarshampoo~)* sachet.
Kissen-: ~bezug *m* cushion cover; *(Kopf~)* pillow case; **~schlacht** *f* pillow fight.
Kiste *f* **-, -n (a)** *(Behälter)* box; *(für Obst auch, für Wein etc)* case; *(Latten~)* crate; *(Truhe)* chest; *(sl: Bett)* sack *(sl)* ♦ **eine ~ Wein/Zigarren** a case of wine/box of cigars; **in die ~ springen** *(sl)* to kick the bucket *(inf)*.
(b) *(inf) (Auto, Flugzeug)* crate *(inf)*; *(Schiff)* tub *(inf)*; *(Fernsehen)* box *(inf)*.
(c) *(inf) (Angelegenheit)* affair; *(Beziehungs~)* relationship ♦ **fertig ist die ~!** that's that (done)!; **das ist eine faule ~!** that's a fishy business! *(inf)*; **immer dieselbe ~** always the same old thing; **eine schwere ~** a big problem; **eine alte ~** an old chestnut.
kistenweise *adv* by the box/case *etc*.
Kitsch *m* **-es,** *no pl* kitsch.
kitschig *adj* kitschy.
Kitt *m* **-(e)s, -e** *(Fenster~)* putty; *(für Porzellan, Stein etc)* cement; *(fig)* bond ♦ **der ganze ~** *(inf)* the whole caboodle *(inf)*.
Kittchen *nt (inf)* clink *(inf)*.
Kittel *m* **-s, - (a)** *(Arbeits~)* overall; *(von Arzt, Laborant etc)* (white) coat. **(b)** *(blusenartiges Kleidungsstück)* smock. **(c)** *(Aus: Damenrock)* skirt.
Kittel-: ~kleid *nt* frock; **~schürze** *f* overall.
kitten *vt* to cement, to stick together with cement; *Fenster* to putty; *(füllen)* to fill; *(fig)* to patch up.
Kitz *nt* **-es, -e** *(Reh~)* fawn; *(Ziegen~, Gemsen~)* kid.
Kitzel *m* **-s, -** tickle; *(~gefühl)* tickling feeling; *(fig)* thrill.
Kitzelgefühl *nt* tickling feeling.
kitz(e)lig *adj (lit, fig)* ticklish.
Kitzeligkeit *f (lit, fig)* ticklishness.
kitzeln [1] *vt (lit, fig)* to tickle ♦ **jdn unter den Armen/am Bauch ~** to tickle sb under the arms/sb's stomach; **jdm das Zwerchfell ~** *(fig)* to make sb laugh.
[2] *vi* to tickle.
[3] *vt impers* **es kitzelt mich** I've got a tickle; **es kitzelt mich, das zu tun** I'm itching to do it.
Kitzeln *nt* **-s,** *no pl* tickling ♦ **er findet das ~ angenehm** he likes being tickled; **ein angenehmes ~** a nice tickle.
Kitzler *m* **-s, -** *(Anat)* clitoris.
kitzlig *adj siehe* **kitz(e)lig.**
Kiwi[1] *f* **-, -s** *(Frucht)* kiwi.
Kiwi[2] *m* **-s, -s** *(Orn)* kiwi; *(inf: Neuseeländer)* Kiwi.
KKW [ka:ka:'ve:] *nt* **-s, -s** *abbr of* **Kernkraftwerk.**
klabastern* *vi aux sein (N Ger)* to plod, to clump, to stump.
Klabautermann *m, pl* **-männer** *(Naut)* ship's kobold.
klack *interj* click; *(platschend)* splosh.
klacken *vi (inf)* to click; *(bei Aufprall)* to crash; *(klappern)* to rattle.
klackern *vti (dial) siehe* **kleckern.**
klacks *interj* splosh.
Klacks *m* **-es, -e** *(inf)* **(a)** *(Geräusch)* splosh.
(b) *(von Kartoffelbrei, Sahne etc)* dollop *(inf)*; *(von Senf, Farbe etc auch)* blob *(inf)*.
(c) *(fig)* **das ist ein ~** *(einfach)* that's a piece of cake *(inf)*; *(wenig)* that's nothing *(inf)*; **die 500 Mark sind für ihn ein ~** the 500 marks are peanuts *or* chickenfeed to him *(inf)*.
klacksen *(inf)* [1] *vt Sahne, Kartoffelbrei etc* to dollop *(inf)*; *Farbe* to splash ♦ **die Sahne/den Kartoffelbrei** *etc* **auf etw** *(acc)* **~** to put a dollop of cream/mashed potato on sth *(inf)*.
[2] *vi (Brei, Sahne)* to go smack; *(Farbe)* to splash.
Kladde *f* **-, -n** *(Sch)* rough book; *(Notizbuch)* notebook; *(Block)* scribbling pad ♦ **in ~** *(inf)* in rough; **~ führen** to take notes.
kladderadatsch *interj* crash-bang-wallop.
Kladderadatsch *m* **-(e)s, -e** *(inf)* **(a)** *(Geräusch)* crash-bang-wallop *(inf)*. **(b)** *(fig) (Kram, Durcheinander)* mess; *(Streit)* bust-up *(inf)*; *(Skandal)* scandal ♦ **da haben wir den ~!** what a mess!
klaffen *vi* to gape; *(Spalte, Abgrund auch)* to yawn ♦ **da klafft eine Wunde/ein Loch** there is a gaping wound/a gaping hole; **zwischen uns beiden klafft ein Abgrund** *(fig)* we are poles apart.

kläffen *vi (pej, fig)* to yap.
klaffend *adj* gaping; *Spalte, Abgrund auch* yawning; *(fig)* irreconcilable; *Widerspruch* blatant.
Kläffer *m* **-s, -** *(lit, fig: pej)* yapper.
Klafter *m or nt* **-s, -** *or (rare) f* **-, -n** fathom.
klafterweise *adv (fig)* by the ton.
klagbar *adj (Jur) Sache* actionable; *Anspruch, Forderung* enforceable.
Klage *f* **-, -n (a)** *(Beschwerde)* complaint ◆ **(bei jdm) über jdn/etw ~ führen** to lodge a complaint (with sb) about sb/sth; **~n (über jdn/etw) vorbringen** to make complaints (about sb/sth); **Grund zu ~n/zur ~** reason for complaint *or* to complain; **daß mir keine ~n kommen!** *(inf)* don't let me hear any complaints.
(b) *(Äußerung von Schmerz)* complaint; *(Äußerung von Trauer)* lament(ation) *(um, über +acc* for); *(~laut)* plaintive cry.
(c) *(Jur) (im Zivilrecht)* action, suit; *(im Strafrecht auch)* charge; *(Scheidungs~ auch)* petition; *(~schrift, Wortlaut) (im Strafrecht)* charge; *(im Zivilrecht)* charge, plaint ◆ **eine ~ gegen jdn einreichen/erheben** to institute proceedings against sb; **eine ~ auf etw** *(acc)* an action for sth; **öffentliche ~** criminal charge.
Klage-: ~abweisung *f (Jur)* dismissal of an action; **~erhebung** *f (Jur)* institution of proceedings; **~frist** *f (Jur)* period for instituting proceedings; **k~führend** *adj (Jur)* suing; **die k~führende Partei** the plaintiff; **~gesang** *m* lament; **~geschrei** *nt* wailing; **~grund** *m (Jur)* cause of action; **~laut** *m* plaintive cry; *(schmerzerfüllt)* cry of pain; **~lied** *nt* lament; **ein ~lied über jdn/etw anstimmen** *(fig)* to complain about sb/sth; **~mauer** *f* **die ~mauer** The Wailing Wall.
klagen [1] *vi* **(a)** *(jammern)* to moan, to wail; *(Tiere)* to cry.
(b) *(trauern, Trauer äußern)* to lament *(um jdn/etw* sb/sth), to wail.
(c) *(sich beklagen)* to complain ◆ **über etw** *(acc)* **~** to complain about sth; **über Rückenschmerzen/Schlaflosigkeit ~** to complain of backache/insomnia; **ohne zu ~** without complaining; **ich kann nicht ~** *(inf)* mustn't grumble *(inf)*.
(d) *(Jur)* to sue *(auf +acc* for).
[2] *vt* **(a) jdm sein Leid/seine Not/seinen Kummer ~** to pour out one's sorrow/distress/grief to sb; **dem Himmel** *or* **Gott sei's geklagt** alas, alack.
(b) *(Aus) siehe* **verklagen**.
klagend *adj (trauererfüllt) Mensch* lamenting; *Blick, Ton, Schrei* plaintive; *Gesicht* sorrowful; *(schmerzerfüllt)* pained; *(jammernd, sich beklagend)* complaining ◆ **der ~e Teil/die ~e Partei** the plaintiff.
Klage-: ~partei *f (Jur)* plaintiff; **~punkt** *m usu pl* particular of a charge/plaint/petition.
Kläger(in *f*) *m* **-s, -** *(Jur) (im Zivilrecht)* plaintiff; *(in Scheidungssachen)* petitioner; *(im Strafrecht auch)* prosecuting party ◆ **wo kein ~ ist, ist auch kein Richter** *(Prov)* well, if no-one complains ...
Klage-: ~ruf *m* plaintive cry; *(Schmerzensschrei)* cry of pain; **~schrift** *f (Jur)* charge; *(bei Scheidung)* petition; **~ton** *m* plaintive sound; *(pej)* whine; **~weg** *m (Jur)* **auf dem** *or* **im ~weg(e)** by (taking *or* bringing) legal action; **den ~weg beschreiten** to take legal action; **~weib** *nt* wailer, mourner.
kläglich [1] *adj* pitiful; *Ende auch* wretched; *Leistung auch* pathetic; *Rest* miserable; *Niederlage, Verhalten* despicable; *(pej: dürftig)* pathetic.
[2] *adv (in beschämender Weise)* miserably.
Kläglichkeit *f siehe adj* pitifulness; wretchedness; miserableness; despicableness ◆ **die ~ des Angebots** the pathetic choice.
klaglos [1] *adj (Jur) Schuld, Forderung* non-actionable.
[2] *adv (ohne Klagen)* uncomplainingly.
Klamauk *m* **-s,** *no pl (inf) (Alberei)* tomfoolery; *(im Theater etc)* slapstick; *(Lärm)* racket *(inf)*; *(Reklamewirbel)* hullabaloo; *(Aufheben)* fuss, to-do ◆ **~ machen** *(albern)* to fool about; **laß den ~** stop fooling about/making this racket/making such a fuss.
klamm *adj* **(a)** *(steif vor Kälte)* numb. **(b)** *(naß und kalt)* clammy; *Wäsche* cold and damp ◆ **~ sein** *(fig inf)* to be hard up *(inf)*.
Klamm *f* **-, -en** gorge.
Klammer *f* **-, -n (a)** *(Wäsche~)* peg; *(Hosen~)* clip; *(Büro~)* paperclip; *(Heft~)* staple.
(b) *(Haar~)* (hair)grip.
(c) *(Med: Wund~)* clip; *(für Zähne)* brace.
(d) *(in Text, Math, ~ausdruck)* bracket; *(Mus)* brace ◆ **~ auf/zu** open/close brackets; **in ~n** in brackets; **runde/eckige/spitze ~** round/square/pointed brackets; **geschweifte ~n** braces.
(e) *(Bau~)* clamp, cramp; *(zur Verpackung)* cramp.
Klammer-: ~affe *m (Zool)* spider monkey; **er ist ein richtiger ~affe** *(fig inf)* he's always clinging on to you; **sie saß wie ein ~affe auf dem Motorrad** *(inf)* she sat on the motorcycle clinging on for dear life; **~beutel** *m* peg bag; **~hefter** *m* **-s, -** stapler.
klammern [1] *vt (an +acc* to) *Wäsche* to peg; *Papier etc* to staple; *(Tech)* to clamp; *(Med) Wunde* to clip; *Zähne* to brace.
[2] *vr* **sich an jdn/etw ~** *(lit, fig)* to cling to sb/sth.
[3] *vi (Sport)* to clinch.
klammheimlich *(inf)* [1] *adj* clandestine, on the quiet.
[2] *adv* on the quiet ◆ **~ aus dem Haus gehen** to sneak out of the house.
Klamotte *f* **-, -n (a) ~n** *pl (inf) (Kleider, Siebensachen)* gear *sing (inf)*; *(Zeug)* stuff *no pl.* **(b)** *(sl) (großes Geschoß)* great big thing; *(Steinbrocken)* great big rock. **(c)** *(pej: Theaterstück, Film)* rubbishy old play/film *etc* ◆ **das ist doch eine alte ~, das sind doch alte ~n** *(inf)* that's old hat *(inf)*.
Klamottenkiste *f*: **aus der ~ hervorholen** *(pej inf)* to dig up again.

Klampfe *f* **-, -n** *(inf)* guitar.
klamüsern* *vt (N Ger inf)* to puzzle over.
Klan *m* **-s, -e** *siehe* **Clan**.
klang *pret of* **klingen**.
Klang *m* **-(e)s, ¨-e** sound; *(Tonqualität)* tone ◆ **der ~ von Glocken/Glöckchen/Gläsern** the chiming of bells/tinkling of small bells/clinking of glasses; **¨-e** *(Musik)* sounds, tones; **der Name hat einen guten ~** the name has a good ring to it; *(guten Ruf)* the name has a good reputation; *siehe* **Sang**.
Klang-: ~bild *nt* sound; *(Phys)* sound pattern; **~boden** *m siehe* **Resonanzboden**; **~effekt** *m* sound effect; **~farbe** *f* tone colour; **~folge** *f* tonal sequence; **~fülle** *f* richness of tone; *(von Stimme, Gedicht)* sonority; **~körper** *m (von Musikinstrument)* body; *(Orchester)* orchestra; *(~bild)* body of sound; **k~lich** [1] *adj Qualität* tonal; **k~liche Unterschiede** differences in sound; *(von Tonqualität)* tonal difference; [2] *adv* **k~lich gut sein** *(Musik, Lied, Gedicht, Stimme)* to sound good; *(Instrument, Gerät)* to have a good tone *or* sound; **k~los** *adj* toneless; *siehe* **sang- und klanglos**; **~regler** *m (Rad etc)* tone control; **k~rein** *adj* pure; **k~rein sein** to have a pure tone *or* sound; **~reinheit** *f* purity of tone *or* sound; **k~schön** *adj* beautiful sounding; **k~treu** *adj Wiedergabe* faithful; *Empfänger* high-fidelity; *Ton* true; **k~treu sein** to have high fidelity; **~treue** *f* fidelity; **k~voll** *adj Stimme, Sprache* sonorous, euphonic *(liter)*; *Wiedergabe* full; *Melodie* tuneful; *(fig) Titel, Name* fine-sounding; **~wort** *nt* onomatopoeia.
klapp *interj* snap; *(beim Türschließen)* click; *siehe* **klipp**.
Klapp-: ~bett *nt* folding bed; **~brücke** *f* bascule bridge; **~deckel** *m* hinged lid.
Klappe *f* **-, -n (a)** flap; *(an Lastwagen)* tailgate; *(seitlich)* side-gate; *(an Kombiwagen)* back; *(von Tisch)* leaf; *(von Ofen)* shutter, flap; *(Klappdeckel)* (hinged) lid; *(an Oboe etc)* key; *(Falltür)* trapdoor; *(Film)* clapperboard.
(b) *(Schulter~)* strap; *(Hosen~, an Tasche)* flap; *(Augen~)* patch; *(von Visier)* shutter.
(c) *(Fliegen~)* (fly) swat.
(d) *(Herz~)* valve.
(e) *(inf: Mund)* trap *(inf)* ◆ **die ~ halten** to shut one's trap *(inf)*; **die ~ aufreißen, eine große ~ haben, die große ~ schwingen** to have a big mouth *(inf)*.
(f) *(inf: Bett)* pit *(inf)* ◆ **sich in die ~ hauen** *(inf)* to hit the hay *(inf) or* sack *(inf)*.
(g) *(Aus Telec)* extension.
(h) *(sl: von Homosexuellen)* pick-up spot, cottage *(sl)*.
klappen [1] *vt* **etw nach oben/unten ~** *Sitz, Bett* to fold sth up/down; *Kragen* to turn sth up/down; *Deckel* to lift sth up, to raise sth/to lower sth, to put sth down; **etw nach vorn/hinten ~** *Sitz* to tip sth forward/back; *Deckel* to lift sth forward/back.
[2] *vi* **(a)** to bang.
(b) *(fig inf)* to work; *(gutgehen auch)* to work out; *(reibungslos stattfinden: Aufführung, Abend)* to go smoothly ◆ **wenn das mal klappt** if that works out; **hat es mit den Karten/dem Job geklappt?** did you get the tickets/job all right *or* OK *(inf)*?; **mit dem Flug hat alles geklappt** the flight went all right, there was no problem with the flight.
Klappen-: ~fehler *m (Med)* valvular defect; **~text** *m (Typ)* blurb.
Klapper *f* **-, -n** rattle.
Klapper-: k~dürr *adj (inf)* thin as a rake; **~gestell** *nt (hum inf) (Mensch)* bag of bones; *(Fahrzeug)* boneshaker *(inf)*.
klapp(e)rig *adj siehe* **klapprig**.
Klapperkasten *m*, **Klapperkiste** *f (pej)* boneshaker *(inf)*.
klappern *vi* **(a)** to clatter; *(Klapperschlange, Fenster, Baby)* to rattle; *(Lider)* to bat; *(Mühle)* to clack; *(auf der Schreibmaschine)* to clatter away; *(mit Stricknadeln)* to click ◆ **er klapperte vor Kälte/Angst mit den Zähnen** his teeth were chattering with cold/fear; **K~ gehört zum Handwerk** *(prov)* making a big noise is part of the business.
(b) *aux sein (sich ~d fortbewegen)* to clatter along; *(Auto etc auch)* to rattle along.
Klapper-: ~schlange *f (Zool)* rattlesnake; *(fig)* rattletrap; **~storch** *m (babytalk)* stork; **er glaubt noch immer an den ~storch** he still thinks babies are found under the gooseberry bush.
Klapp-: ~fahrrad *nt* folding bicycle *or* bike; **~fenster** *nt* top-hung window; **~hut** *m* crush-hat; **~laden** *m* folding shutter; **~messer** *nt* flick knife; **~rad** *nt siehe* **~fahrrad**.
klapprig *adj* rickety, shaky; *(fig inf) Mensch* shaky, tottery.
Klapp-: ~sitz *m* folding seat; **~stuhl** *m* folding chair; **~stulle** *f (N Ger)* sandwich; **~tisch** *m* folding table; **~tür** *f* trapdoor; **~verdeck** *nt* folding *or* collapsible hood; **~zylinder** *m* opera hat.
Klaps *m* **-es, -e (a)** *(inf)* **einen ~ haben** to have a screw loose *(inf)*, to be off one's rocker *(inf)*. **(b)** *(Schlag)* smack, slap.
Klapsmühle *f (pej inf)* loony bin *(inf)*, nut house *(inf)*.
▼ **klar** *adj* clear; *(fertig)* ready ◆ **~ zum Gefecht/Einsatz** *(Mil)* ready for action; **~ zum Start** *(Sport)* ready (for the start); **~ Schiff** *(lit, fig)*/**Deck machen** *(Naut)* to clear the decks; **ein ~er Fall** *(inf)* sure thing *(inf)*; **ein ~er Fall von ...** *(inf)* a clear case of ...; **das ist doch ~!** *(inf)* of course; **na ~!** *(inf)* of course!, sure! *(inf)*; **alles ~?** everything all right *or* OK? *(inf)*; **jetzt ist** *or* **wird mir alles ~!** now I understand; **einen ~en Augenblick haben** to have a lucid moment; **bei ~em Verstand sein** to be in full possession of one's faculties; *(inf)* to be in one's right mind; **etw ~ und deutlich sagen** to spell sth out; **jdm etw ~ und deutlich sagen** to tell sb sth straight *(inf)*; **etw tritt ~ zutage** sth becomes apparent *or* obvious *or* clear; **~ wie Kloßbrühe** *or* **dicke Tinte** *(inf)* clear as

mud (*inf*); **sich** (*dat*) **über etw** (*acc*) **im ~en sein** to be aware of sth; **sich** (*dat*) **darüber im ~en sein, daß ...** to realize that ...; **ins ~e kommen** to get things straight; **mit jdm/seinem Privatleben ins ~e kommen** to straighten things out with sb/to sort out one's private life; *siehe* **klipp.**

Klar *nt* **-(e)s, -(e)** (*Aus*) *siehe* **Eiweiß.**

Klär|anlage *f* sewage plant; (*von Fabrik*) purification plant.

Klar-: ~apfel *m* early dessert apple; **~blick** *m* (*fig*) clear-sightedness; ⚠**k~blickend** *adj* clear-sighted; ⚠**k~denkend** *adj attr* clear-thinking.

klären [1] *vt* to clear; *Wasser, Luft* to purify; *Abwasser* to treat; *Bier, Wein* to fine; *Fall, Sachlage* to clarify, to clear up; *Frage* to settle.
[2] *vi* (*Sport*) to clear (the ball).
[3] *vr* (*Wasser, Himmel*) to clear; (*Wetter*) to clear up; (*Meinungen, Sachlage*) to become clear; (*Streitpunkte*) to be clarified; (*Frage*) to be settled.

Klare(r) *m decl as adj* (*inf*) schnapps.

klargehen *vi sep irreg aux sein* (*inf*) to be all right *or* OK (*inf*) ◆ **ist es mit dem Examen klargegangen?** did the exam go all right *or* OK? (*inf*).

Klärgrube *f* cesspit.

Klarheit *f* **(a)** (*fig: Deutlichkeit*) clarity; (*geistige ~*) lucidity ◆ **sich** (*dat*) **~ über etw** (*acc*) **verschaffen** to find out about sth, to get clear about sth; *über Sachlage* to clarify sth; **~ über etw** (*acc*) **haben** to be clear about sth; **jdm etw in aller ~ sagen** to tell sb sth in plain language. **(b)** (*Reinheit*) clearness.

klarieren* *vt* (*Naut*) **(a)** to make ready. **(b)** (*Zoll*) to clear (through customs).

Klarinette *f* clarinet.

Klarinettist(in *f*) *m* clarinettist.

Klarisse *f* **-, -n, Klarissin** *f* nun of the order of St Clare.

Klar-: k~kommen *vi sep irreg aux sein* (*inf*) to manage, to get by (*inf*); **mit etw k~kommen** to be able to cope with sth; **mit jdm k~kommen** to be able to deal *or* cope with sb; **k~kriegen** *vt sep* (*inf*) to sort out; **ein Problem k~kriegen** to sort out *or* crack (*inf*) a problem; **~lack** *m* clear varnish; **k~lackbehandelt** *adj* varnished; **k~legen** *vt sep* to make clear, to explain; **~luftturbulenz** *f* (*Aviat*) (pocket of) air turbulence; **k~machen** *sep* [1] *vt* to make clear, to explain; *Schiff* to make ready, to get ready; *Flugzeug* to clear; **jdm etw k~machen** to make sth clear to sb; **sich** (*dat*) **etw/die Unterschiede** *etc* **k~machen** to realize sth/get the differences *etc* clear in one's own mind; **sich** (*dat*) **ein Thema k~machen** to get a subject sorted out in one's mind; [2] *vr* (*sl: Toilette machen etc*) to get ready; [3] *vi* (*Naut*) to make ready, to get ready; **zum Gefecht k~machen** to clear the decks for action.

Klärschlamm *m* sludge.

Klarschriftleser *m* (**optischer**) ~ optical character reader.

⚠**klarsehen** *vi sep irreg* to see clearly ◆ **in etw** (*dat*) **~** to have understood sth.

Klarsicht- *in cpds* transparent; **~folie** *f* clear film; **~hülle** *f* clear plastic folder; **~packung** *f* see-through pack; **~scheibe** *f* (*Aut*) anti-mist panel.

Klar-: k~spülen *vti sep* to rinse; **k~stellen** *vt sep* (*klären*) to clear up, to clarify; (*k~machen*) to make clear; **ich möchte k~stellen, daß ...** I would like to make it clear that ...; **~stellung** *f* clarification; **~text** *m* uncoded text, text in clear; **im ~text** in clear; (*fig inf*) in plain English; **mit jdm ~text reden** (*fig inf*) to give sb a piece of one's mind.

Klärung *f* **(a)** purification. **(b)** (*fig*) clarification.

⚠**klarwerden** *sep irreg aux sein* [1] *vr* **sich** (*dat*) **(über etw** *acc*) **~** to get (sth) clear in one's mind.
[2] *vi* **jdm wird etw klar** sth becomes clear to sb; **ist dir das noch immer nicht klargeworden?** do you still not understand?

⚠**klaß** *adj* (*Aus inf*) *siehe* **klasse.**

klasse *adj inv* (*inf*) great (*inf*); *siehe* **Klasse.**

Klasse *f* **-, -n (a)** class; (*Spiel~*) league; (*Steuer~ auch*) bracket; (*Wert ~ auch*) rate; (*Güter~*) grade ◆ **ein Maler erster ~** a first-class *or* first-rate painter; **ein Fahrschein zweiter ~** a second-class ticket; **das ist (große) ~!** (*inf*) that's great *or* tremendous *or* marvellous! (*all inf*). **(b)** (*Sch*) class, form; (*Raum*) classroom.

Klasse- *in cpds* (*inf*) top-class.

Klassement [-'mã:] *nt* **-s, -s** (*Sport*) (list of) rankings *pl*.

Klassen-: ~älteste(r) *mf* oldest pupil in the class; **~arbeit** *f* (written) class test; **~aufsatz** *m* essay written in class; **~ausflug** *m* class outing; **~beste(r)** *mf* best pupil; **wer ist ~beste(r)?** who is top of the class?; ⚠**~bewußtsein** *nt* class consciousness; **~bild** *nt* class photograph; **~buch** *nt* (class-) register; **~buchführer** *m* pupil in charge of the class-register; **~dünkel** *m siehe* **Standesdünkel**; **~durchschnitt** *m* class average; **~erste(r)** *mf siehe* **~beste(r)**; **~feind** *m* (*Pol*) class enemy; **~foto** *nt* class photograph; **~frequenz** *f* size of a/the class/the classes; **~gegensatz** *m usu pl* (*Sociol*) class difference; **~geist** *m* (*Sch dated, Sociol*) class spirit; **~gesellschaft** *f* class society; ⚠**~haß** *m* (*Sociol*) class hatred; **~herrschaft** *f* class rule; **~interesse** *nt* (*Sociol*) class interest; **~justiz** *f* (*Pol*) legal system with class bias; **~kamerad** *m* classmate; **~kampf** *m* class struggle; **~keile** *f* (*Sch dated*) a thrashing from the rest of the class *or* from one's classmates; **~krieg** *m* class warfare; **~lage** *f* (*Sociol*) class position; **~lehrer, ~leiter** *m* class teacher, form teacher, form master/mistress; **~lektüre** *f* class reading; **k~los** *adj Gesellschaft* classless; *Krankenhaus* one-class; **~los** *nt draw ticket in a Klassenlotterie*; **~lotterie** *f lottery in which draws are made on a number of different days and in which tickets can be bought for each individual draw*; **~raum** *m* classroom; **~schrank** *m* classroom cupboard; **~schranke** *f* class barrier; **~spiegel** *m* (*Sch*) seating plan of the class; **~sprecher** *m* (*Sch*) class spokesman, ≃ form captain; **~staat** *m* (*Pol*) state governed by one class; **~stärke** *f* (*Sch*) size of a/the class/the classes; **~treffen** *nt* (*Sch*) class reunion; **~unterschied** *m* class difference; **~verband** *m* **im ~verband** as a class; **~vorstand** *m* (*esp Aus*) *siehe* **~lehrer**; **~wahlrecht, ~wahlsystem** *nt* electoral system based on class, class system of franchise; **k~weise** [1] *adj* by class; **k~weiser Aufbau** arrangement by class; [2] *adv sitzen, sich aufstellen* in classes; *erscheinen* as a class; **~ziel** *nt* (*Sch*) required standard; **das ~ziel nicht erreichen** not to reach the required standard; (*fig*) not to make the grade; **~zimmer** *nt* classroom.

Klassifikation *f* classification.

klassifizierbar *adj* classifiable.

klassifizieren* *vt* to classify ◆ **~d** classificatory.

Klassifizierung *f* classification.

-klassig *adj suf* -class.

Klassik *f, no pl* classical period; (*inf: klassische Musik, Literatur*) classical music/literature ◆ **die antike ~** Classical Antiquity.

Klassiker(in *f*) *m* **-s, -** classic ◆ **ein ~ des Jazz/der modernen Musik** a jazz classic/a classic of modern music; **die antiken ~** the classics.

klassisch *adj* **(a)** (*die Klassik betreffend, antik, traditionell*) classical. **(b)** (*typisch, vorbildlich, zeitlos*) classic. **(c)** (*iro inf: prächtig*) classic.

Klassizismus *m* classicism.

klassizistisch *adj* classical.

⚠**-kläßler(in** *f*) *m in cpds* **-s, -** (*Sch*) -former.

klatsch *interj* splash, splosh; (*bei Schlag, Aufprall*) smack.

Klatsch *m* **-(e)s, -e (a)** splosh, splash; (*bei Schlag, Aufprall*) smack. **(b)** *no pl* (*pej inf: Tratsch*) gossip, scandal.

Klatschbase *f* (*pej inf*) (*tratschend*) scandalmonger, gossip; (*redselig*) chatterbox (*inf*).

Klatsche *f* **-, -n** (*inf*) **(a)** *siehe* **Klatschbase. (b)** (*Sch*) (*Denunziant*) sneak, telltale (*inf*); (*Hilfsmittel*) crib (*inf*). **(c)** (*Fliegenklappe*) fly swatter.

klatschen [1] *vi* **(a)** to clap ◆ **in die Hände ~** to clap one's hands.
(b) (*einen Klaps geben*) to slap ◆ **jdm auf die Schenkel/sich** (*dat*) **gegen die Stirn ~** to slap sb's thighs/one's forehead.
(c) *aux sein* (*aufschlagen*) (*harte Gegenstände*) to go smack; (*Flüssigkeiten*) to splash ◆ **der Regen klatschte gegen die Fenster** the rain beat against the windows.
(d) (*pej inf*) (*tratschen*) to gossip; (*dial: petzen*) to sneak, to tell tales (*bei* to) ◆ **über jdn/etw ~** to gossip *or* spread gossip about sb.
[2] *vt* **(a)** to clap; *Takt* to clap out ◆ **jdm Beifall ~** to applaud *or* clap sb. **(b)** (*knallen*) to smack, to slap; (*werfen*) to throw; *Fliegen* to swat.

Klatschen *nt* **-s,** *no pl* **(a)** (*Beifall~*) applause. **(b)** (*inf: Tratschen*) gossiping.

⚠**klatschenaß** *adj* (*inf*) *siehe* **klatschnaß.**

Klatscherei *f* (*pej inf*) **(a)** (*Beifall~*) clapping. **(b)** (*Tratscherei*) gossiping, gossipmongering.

Klatscher(in *f*) *m* **-s, - (a)** *siehe* **Klatschbase. (b)** (*Beifall~*) applauder.

Klatsch-: ~geschichte *f* (*pej*) gossip *no pl*; **eine ~geschichte** a piece of gossip; **k~haft** *adj* gossipy; **~kolumnist** *m* (*inf*) gossip columnist; **~maul** *nt* (*pej inf*) **(a)** big mouth; **(b)** (*Mensch*) gossip (merchant), scandalmonger; **~mohn** *m* (corn) poppy; ⚠**k~naß** *adj* (*inf*) sopping wet (*inf*); **~spalte** *f* (*Press inf*) gossip column; **k~süchtig** *adj* extremely gossipy; **~tante** *f*, **~weib** *nt* (*pej inf*) gossip(monger), scandalmonger.

klauben *vt* **(a)** (*S Ger, Aus, Sw*) (*auflesen*) to pick up; (*auslesen*) to pick out ◆ **etw in einen Korb ~** to pick sth up and put it in a basket; **etw aus etw ~** to pick sth out from sth.
(b) (*Aus: sammeln*) to collect; *Holz, Pilze, Kräuter auch* to gather; *Beeren* to pick.
(c) (*Sw: kneifen*) to pinch ◆ **Worte ~** (*dial*) to split hairs.

Klaue *f* **-, -n** claw; (*Huf*) hoof; (*pej inf: Hand*) talons *pl* (*pej inf*); (*pej inf: Schrift*) scrawl (*pej*) ◆ **in den ~n der Verbrecher** *etc* in the clutches of the criminals *etc*; **den ~n des Todes entkommen** to escape from the jaws of death.

klauen (*inf*) [1] *vt* to nick (*Brit inf*), to pinch (*inf*) (*jdm etw* sth from sb); *Ideen auch* to crib (*jdm etw* sth from sb).
[2] *vi* to steal, to nick (*Brit inf*) *or* pinch things (*inf*).

Klauenseuche *f siehe* **Maul- und Klauenseuche.**

Klause *f* **-, -n (a)** (*von Mönch, Einsiedler*) hermitage; (*Klosterzelle*) cell; (*fig hum*) den. **(b)** (mountain) defile.

Klausel *f* **-, -n** clause; (*Vorbehalt*) proviso; (*Bedingung*) condition, stipulation.

Klausner *m* **-s, -** *siehe* **Einsiedler.**

Klaustrophobie *f* (*Psych*) claustrophobia.

klaustrophobisch *adj* (*Psych*) claustrophobic.

klausulieren* *vt siehe* **verklausulieren.**

Klausur *f* **(a)** (*Univ auch* **~arbeit**) exam, paper ◆ **~en korrigieren** to mark scripts *or* exam papers. **(b)** *no pl* (*Abgeschlossenheit*) seclusion ◆ **eine Arbeit unter** *or* **in ~ schreiben** to write an essay *etc* under examination conditions. **(c)** (*Eccl: Räume*) enclosure, cloister.

Klausurtagung *f* convention, conference.

Klaviatur [klavia'tu:ɐ] *f* keyboard.

Klavichord [klavi'kɔrt] *nt* **-(e)s, -e** clavichord.

Klavier [-'vi:ɐ] *nt* **-s, -e** piano ◆ **~ spielen** to play the piano; **er spielt ein hervorragendes ~** (*sl*) he's great on (the) piano (*inf*).

Klavier- *in cpds* piano; **~auszug** *m* piano score; **~bauer** *m* piano-maker; **~bearbeitung** *f* piano arrangement; **~begleitung** *f* piano accompaniment; **~deckel** *m* piano lid; **~hocker** *m* piano stool; **~konzert** *nt* **(a)** (*Musik*) piano concerto; **(b)** (*Vorstellung*) piano recital; **~schule** *f* (*Lehrbuch*) piano tutor; **~sonate** *f* piano sonata; **~spiel** *nt* piano playing; **~spieler** *m* pianist, piano player; **~stimmer** *m* piano-tuner; **~stück** *nt* piano piece, piece of piano-music.

Klebe-: ~band *nt* adhesive tape, sticky tape; **~bindung** *f* (*Typ*) adhesive binding; **~falz** *m* (gummed) stamp hinge *or* mount; **~folie** *f siehe* **Klebfolie**; **~mittel** *nt* adhesive.

kleben [1] *vi* **(a)** to stick ◆ **an etw** *(dat)* ~ *(lit)* to stick to sth; **an den Traditionen** ~ to cling *or* stick to tradition; **an seinen Händen klebt Blut** *(fig)* he has blood on his hands; **klebt nicht so am Text** don't stick so much *or* so close to the text.
(b) *(inf: für Sozialversicherung)* to pay stamps.
[2] *vt* to stick; *(mit Klebstoff auch)* to glue; *(mit Leim auch)* to paste; *Film, Tonband* to splice ◆ **Marken** ~ *(inf: Insur)* to pay stamps; **jdm eine** ~ *(inf)* to belt sb one *(inf)*.
klebenbleiben *vi sep irreg aux sein* to stick *(an +dat* to); *(Sch inf)* to stay down a year, to repeat a year; *(fig inf: nicht wegkommen)* to get stuck.
Klebe-: ~pflaster *nt* sticking plaster, adhesive plaster; **~presse** *f* splicer.
Kleber *m* **-s, -** **(a)** *(inf) siehe* **Klebstoff**. **(b)** *(im Mehl)* gluten.
Klebe-: ~stelle *f* join; *(an Film)* splice; **~stoff** *m siehe* **Klebstoff**; **~streifen** *m siehe* **Klebstreifen**; **~zettel** *m* gummed label.
Kleb-: ~festigkeit *f* adhesiveness; **~fläche** *f* surface to be stuck; **~folie** *f* adhesive film; *(d-c-fix ®)* fablon ®; *(für Lebensmittel)* cling film ®; **~kraft** *f* adhesive strength; **~mittel** *nt siehe* **Klebemittel**.
klebrig *adj* sticky; *Farbe* tacky; *Geldgeschäfte* shady; *(klebfähig)* adhesive.
Klebrigkeit *f siehe adj* stickiness; tackiness; adhesiveness.
Kleb-: ~stoff *m* adhesive; **~streifen** *m* adhesive tape; *(selbstklebend auch)* sticky tape; *(zum Befeuchten)* gummed tape.
Klebung *f* bond.
Kleckerei *f* mess ◆ **ohne ~ geht's nicht** you can't do it without making a mess.
kleckern [1] *vt* to spill; *Farbe auch* to splash.
[2] *vi* **(a)** to make a mess. **(b)** *(tropfen)* to spill; *(Farbe auch)* to splash. **(c)** *(inf: stückchenweise arbeiten)* to fiddle about ◆ **nicht ~, sondern klotzen** *(inf)* to do things in a big way *(inf)*, to think big *(inf)*; **gekleckert kommen** to come in dribs and drabs.
kleckerweise *adv* in dribs and drabs.
Klecks *m* **-es, -e** *(Tinten~)* (ink)blot; *(Farb~)* blob; *(Fleck)* stain.
klecksen *vi (mit Tinte)* to make blots/a blot; *(Kugelschreiber etc auch)* to blot; *(pej inf: malen)* to daub.
Kleckserei *f (pej inf)* daubing; *(von Schüler, Kugelschreiber)* making blots.
Kledage [kle'da:ʒə], **Kledasche** *f* **-,** *no pl (sl)* clobber *(sl)*, gear *(inf)*.
Klee *m* **-s,** *no pl* clover ◆ **jdn/etw über den grünen ~ loben** to praise sb/sth to the skies.
Kleeblatt *nt* cloverleaf; *(Mot)* cloverleaf (intersection); *(fig: Menschen)* threesome, trio ◆ **vierblättriges ~** four-leaf clover; **das irische ~** the (Irish) shamrock.
Kleiber *m* **-s, -** *(Orn)* nuthatch.
Kleid *nt* **-(e)s, -er** **(a)** *(Damen~)* dress ◆ **ein zweiteiliges ~** a two-piece (suit).
(b) ~er *pl (Kleidung)* clothes *pl*, clothing *sing (esp Comm)*, garments *pl (Comm)*; **warme ~er mitbringen** to bring warm clothes *or* clothing; **~er machen Leute** *(Prov)* fine feathers make fine birds *(Prov)*; **ich bin zwei Tage nicht aus den ~ern gekommen** I haven't been to bed for two days.
(c) *(old: Gewand)* garment; *(old, Sw, S Ger: Herrenanzug)* suit; *(liter: Uniform)* uniform.
(d) *(liter) (Feder~)* plumage; *(Pelz)* coat, fur; *(fig: von Natur, Bäumen etc)* mantle *(liter)*, cloak *(liter)* ◆ **der Winter hatte der Erde ein weißes ~ angezogen** winter had clad the earth in white *(liter)*.
-kleid *nt in cpds* **Sommer-/Ordens-/Herbst~** summer dress/monastic robe/autumn cloak *or* mantle *(liter)*.
Kleidchen *nt dim of* **Kleid** little dress; *(leicht)* flimsy dress.
kleiden [1] *vr* to dress; *(Kleider anziehen auch)* to dress oneself, to clothe oneself *(liter, form)* ◆ **die Natur kleidet sich in Weiß** *(liter)* nature dons a cloak *or* mantle of white *(liter)*; *siehe* **gekleidet**.
[2] *vt* **(a)** *(mit Kleidern versehen)* to clothe, to dress; *(fig) Gedanken, Ideen* to clothe, to couch ◆ **die Armen ~** to clothe the poor; **etw in schöne Worte ~** to dress sth up *or* to couch sth in fancy words.
(b) jdn ~ *(jdm stehen)* to suit sb.
Kleider-: ~ablage *f (Raum)* cloakroom; *(Garderobenablage)* coat rack; *(Ständer)* hat- *or* coat-stand; **~bügel** *m* coathanger; **~bürste** *f* clothes brush; **~haken** *m* coat hook; **~kammer** *f (Mil etc)* uniform store; **~kasten** *m (Aus, Sw) siehe* **~schrank (a)**; **~macher** *m (Aus) siehe* **Schneider**; **~ordnung** *f* dress regulations *pl*; **~sack** *m* suit bag; **~schrank** *m* **(a)** wardrobe; **(b)** *(inf: Mensch)* great hulk (of a man) *(inf)*.
kleidsam *adj* flattering.
Kleidung *f, no pl* clothes *pl*, clothing *(esp Comm)* ◆ **warme ~** warm clothing *or* clothes; **für jds (Nahrung und) ~ sorgen** to (feed and) clothe sb.
Kleidungsstück *nt* garment ◆ **~e** *pl* clothes *pl*; **ein warmes ~ mitnehmen** to bring something warm (to wear).
Kleie *f, no pl* bran.
klein *adj* **(a)** little, small; *Finger* little; *Format, Gehalt, Rente, Zahl, (Hand)schrift, Buchstabe* small; *(Mus) Terz* minor ◆ **die K~en Antillen** *etc* the lesser Antilles *etc*; **K~ Paris** *etc* little *or* miniature Paris *etc*; **der K~e Bär** *or* **Wagen** the Little Bear, Ursa Minor; **die K~e Strafkammer** *(Jur)* the lower criminal court; **haben Sie es nicht ~er?** do you not have anything smaller?; **ein ~ bißchen** *or* **wenig** a little (bit); **ein ~ bißchen** *or* **wenig Salat** a little (bit of) salad; **ein ~es Bier, ein K~es** *(inf)* a small beer, ≃ half a pint, a half; **~es Geld** small change; **K~ Roland** little Roland; **du ~er Teufel!** you little devil!; **ein süßes ~es Püppchen** a sweet little thing; **hallo, ~er Mann!** hullo, little man; **ein schönes ~es Auto** a nice little car; **er fährt ein ~es Auto** he drives a little *or* small car; **mit seiner ~en Frau** with his little wife; **ich wußte nicht, daß seine Frau so ~ ist** I didn't know his wife was so small *or* little; **eine ~e, hübsche Wohnung** a small, pretty flat; **eine hübsche ~e Wohnung** a nice little flat; **mein ~er Bruder** my little brother; **er ist ~er als sein Bruder** he's smaller than his brother; **als ich (noch) ~ war** when I was little; **~ für sein Alter** small *or* little for his age; **er schreibt sehr ~** he writes very small, his writing is very small; **sich ~ machen** to bend down low; to curl up tight; **um durch die enge Tür zu kommen, muß man sich ~ machen** to get through this narrow door you have to squeeze yourself in; **macht euch ein bißchen ~er!** squeeze up closer; **den mach' ich so ~ mit Hut!** *(hum)* I'll cut him down to size, I'll make him look *that* big; **~ aber oho** *(inf)* good things come in small packages; **ein Wort ~ drucken/schreiben** to print/write a word with small initial letters, to use small initial letters; **~ beigeben** *(inf)* to give in quietly *or* gracefully; **jdn ~ und häßlich machen** *(inf)* to make sb feel small; **ganz ~ (und häßlich) werden** *(inf)* to look humiliated *or* deflated; **im ~en** in miniature; **bis ins ~ste** in every possible *or* in minute detail, right down to the smallest detail; **von ~ an** *or* **auf** *(von Kindheit an)* from his childhood *or* early days; *(von Anfang an)* from the very beginning, from scratch; **~e Kinder ~e Sorgen, große Kinder große Sorgen** *(prov)* bigger children just mean bigger problems; **~ stellen** *or* **drehen** *(Cook)* to put sth on low *or* a low heat; **um ein ~es zu ...** *(geh)* a little *or* a trifle too ...
(b) *(kurz) Wuchs, Schritt* little, small, short; *Weile, Pause* little, short; *Vortrag* short ◆ **~en Augenblick, bitte!** just one moment, please; **einen Kopf ~er als jd sein** to be a head shorter than sb.
(c) *(geringfügig)* little, small, slight; *Betrag, Summe* little, small ◆ **beim ~sten Schreck** at the slightest *or* smallest shock; **das ~ere Übel** the lesser evil; **ein paar ~ere Fehler** a few minor mistakes; **eine ~ere Unpäßlichkeit** a minor ailment.
(d) *(unbedeutend)* petty *(pej)*; *Leute* ordinary ◆ **er ist ein ~er Geist** he is small-minded; **der ~e Mann** the ordinary citizen, the man in the street; **ein ~er Ganove** a small-time *or* petty crook; **die K~en** *or* **~en Gauner fängt man, die Großen läßt man laufen** *(prov)* it's always the big fish that get away; **sein Vater war (ein) ~er Beamter** his father was a minor civil servant; **~e Leute übersieht man** *(hum)* I'm *etc* so small and insignificant.
(e) *(armselig) Verhältnisse* humble, lowly, modest ◆ **~ anfangen** to start off in a small way.
(f) *Prüfung* intermediate.
-klein *nt in cpds* **-s,** *no pl siehe* **Gänse-, Hasen-** *etc*.
Klein-: ≂aktionär *m* small shareholder; **≂anleger** *m (Fin)* small investor; **≂anzeige** *f* classified advertisement, small ad *(inf)*; **≂arbeit** *f* detailed work; **in zäher/mühseliger ~arbeit** with rigorous/painstaking attention to detail; **~asien** *nt* Asia Minor; **≂auto** *nt siehe* **~wagen**; **≂bahn** *f* narrow-gauge railway; **≂bauer** *m* small farmer, smallholder; **k≂bekommen*** *vt sep irreg siehe* **k~kriegen**; **≂betrieb** *m* small business; **bäuerlicher/handwerklicher/industrieller ~betrieb** smallholding/(small) workshop/small factory; **≂bildkamera** *f* 35 mm camera; **≂buchstabe** *m* small letter; **≂bürger** *m* petty bourgeois; **k≂bürgerlich** *adj* lower middle-class, petty bourgeois *(pej)*; **er reagierte typisch k≂bürgerlich** his reaction was typically lower middle-class *or* petty bourgeois; **≂bürgertum** *nt (Sociol)* lower middle class, petty bourgeoisie; **≂bus** *m* minibus.
Kleineleutemilieu *nt* world of ordinary people.
Kleine(r) *mf decl as adj* **(a)** little one *or* child; little boy/girl; baby ◆ **unser ~r** *(Jüngster)* our youngest (child); **die lieben ~n** *(iro)* the dear *or* sweet little things; **eine hübsche ~** a pretty little girl *or* thing; **die Katze mit ihren ~n** the cat with its kittens *or* babies *(inf)*.
(b) *(inf: auch ~s: Schatz, Liebling)* baby *(inf)* ◆ **na ~/~r!** *(zu einem Kind)* hullo little girl/sonny Jim!; **na ~r!** *(Prostituierte zu einem Passanten)* hullo, dear *or* love.
Kleine(s) *nt decl as adj*: **etwas ~s** *(inf)* a little baby *or* stranger *(hum)*.
Klein-: ~familie *f (Sociol)* nuclear family; **~format** *nt* small format; **ein Buch/Bild im ~format** a small-format book/picture; **~garten** *m* allotment *(Brit)*, garden plot; **~gärtner** *m* allotment holder *(Brit)*, garden plot holder; **~gebäck** *nt* biscuits *(Brit) pl*, cookies *(US) pl*; **⚠k~gedruckt** *adj attr* in small print; **~gedruckte(s)** *nt* small print; **~geist** *m (pej)* small-minded person; **k~geistig** *adj (pej)* small-minded, petty; **~geld** *nt* (small) change; **das nötige ~geld haben** *(fig)* to have the necessary wherewithal *(inf)*; **⚠k~gemustert** *adj* small-patterned; **k~gewachsen** *adj* short, small; *Baum* small; **k~gläubig** *adj* **(a)** *(Rel)* doubting, sceptical; **der k~gläubige Thomas** doubting Thomas; **ihr ~gläubigen!** *(Bibl)* o ye of little faith; **(b)** *(zweiflerisch)* timid; **k~gläubig sein** to lack conviction; **sei doch nicht so k~gläubig!** don't be so timid; **~gruppe** *f (Sociol)* small group; **⚠k~hacken** *vt sep* to chop up small; **~häusler** *m* **-s, -** *(Aus)* small farmer; **~heit** *f* smallness, small size; **k~herzig** *adj* fainthearted; **~hirn** *nt (Anat)* cerebellum; **~holz** *nt, no pl* firewood, kindling; **~holz aus jdm machen** *(inf)* to make mincemeat out of sb *(inf)*.
Kleinigkeit *f* **(a)** little *or* small thing; *(Bagatelle)* small *or* trifling *or* trivial matter *or* thing, trifle; *(Einzelheit)* minor detail *or* point, small point ◆ **ich habe noch ein paar ~en in der Stadt zu erledigen** I still have a few little things to attend to in town; **es war nur eine ~ zu reparieren** there was only something minor to be repaired; **die Reparatur/Prüfung war eine ~** the repair job/exam was no trouble at all; **eine ~ essen** to have a bite to eat, to eat a little something; **jdm eine ~ schenken/bezahlen** to give/pay sb a little something; **die ~ von 1000 DM** *(iro)* the small matter of 1,000 marks; **das kostet eine ~** *(iro)* that'll cost a pretty penny; **wegen** *or* **bei jeder ~** for the slightest reason; **das war doch (nur) eine ~!** it was nothing; **das ist doch eine ~!** that isn't (asking) much; **das ist für mich keine ~** that is no small matter for me; **wir haben noch ein paar ~en geändert** we've changed one or two

details *or* made one or two small changes; **großen Wert auf ~en legen** to be a stickler for detail(s); **bis auf die letzten ~en ist alles fertig** everything is ready apart from the last-minute odds and ends; **sich nicht mit ~en abgeben** *or* **befassen** not to bother over details.
(b) (*ein bißchen*) **eine ~** a little (bit), a trifle, a shade; **eine ~ zu groß/nach rechts** a little (bit) *etc* too big/to the right; **das wird eine ~ dauern** it will take a little while.

Kleinigkeits-: ~krämer *m* (*pej*) stickler for detail, pedant; **~krämerei** *f* (*pej*) pernicketiness, pedantry.

Klein-: ~kaliber *nt* small bore; **~kalibergewehr** *nt* small-bore rifle; **k~kalibrig** *adj* small-bore *attr only*; **k~kariert** *adj* (*fig*) tuppenny-ha'penny *attr only* (*inf*), small-time (*inf*); (*lit rare*) finely checked *or* chequered; **k~kariert sein** (*fig*) to be small- *or* petty-minded; **k~kariert denken** to think small; **~kind** *nt* small child, toddler (*inf*), infant (*Psych*); **~klima** *nt* (*Met*) microclimate; **~kram** *m* (*inf*) odds and ends *pl*; (*kleinere Arbeiten*) odd jobs *pl*; (*Trivialitäten*) trivialities *pl*, trivia *pl*; **~krämer** *m* (*pej*) small-minded person; **~kredit** *m* personal loan; **~krieg** *m* (*fig*) battle; **einen ~krieg mit jdm führen** to be fighting a running battle with sb.

kleinkriegen *vt sep* **(a)** (*lit*) *Holz* to chop (up); *Nuß* to break ♦ **er kann das Fleisch mit den Zähnen nicht ~** he can't break up his meat with his teeth.
(b) (*inf: kaputtmachen*) to smash, to break.
(c) (*inf*) (*gefügig machen*) to bring into line (*inf*); (*unterkriegen, müde machen*) to get down; (*körperlich*) to tire out ♦ **er/unser altes Auto ist einfach nicht kleinzukriegen** he just won't be beaten/our old car just goes on for ever; **er ließ sich auch trotz erpresserischer Drohungen nicht ~** in spite of blackmail threats he was not to be intimidated.
(d) (*inf*) *Geld* to blow (*inf*), to get through.

Kleinkunst *f* cabaret.

Kleinkunstbühne *f* cabaret.

kleinlaut *adj* abashed, subdued, meek ♦ **dann wurde er ganz ~** it took the wind out of his sails, that made him shut up; **etw ~ zugeben** to admit sth shamefacedly; **~ um Verzeihung bitten** to apologize rather sheepishly.

kleinlich *adj* petty; (*knauserig*) mean, stingy (*inf*); (*engstirnig*) narrow-minded.

Kleinlichkeit *f siehe adj* pettiness; meanness, stinginess (*inf*); narrow-mindedness.

⚠ **kleinmachen** *vt sep* **(a)** to chop *or* cut up. **(b)** (*inf*) *Geld* (*wechseln*) to change; (*ausgeben*) to blow (*inf*). **(c)** (*inf: erniedrigen*) **jdn ~** to make sb look small.

Klein-: ~möbel *pl* smaller items of furniture; **~mut** *m* faintheartedness, timidity; **k~mütig** *adj* fainthearted, timid.

Kleinod ['klaino:t] *nt* **-(e)s, -ien** [klai'no:diən] *or* **-e** (*lit, fig*) jewel, gem ♦ **sie war sein ~** (*liter*) she was his treasure *or* his pride and joy.

Klein-: ~rentner *m person living on small pension*; ⚠**k~schneiden** *vt sep irreg* to cut up small, to cut up into small pieces; **k~schreiben** *vt sep irreg* (*fig*) to set little store by; **k~geschrieben werden** to count for (very) little; **~schreibung** *f* use of small initial letters; **~staat** *m* small state; **~stadt** *f* small town; **~städter** *m* small-town dweller, provincial (*pej*); **k~städtisch** *adj* provincial, small-town *attr.*

Kleinstbetrag *m* small sum; (*bei Wetten*) minimum stake ♦ **~̈e unter DM 1 sind unzulässig** sums below the minimum of DM 1 are not acceptable.

kleinste(r, s) *superl of* **klein.**

Kleinst-: k~möglich *adj* smallest possible; **~wohnung** *f* one-room apartment *or* flatlet (*Brit*).

Klein-: ~tier *nt* small animal; **~tierpraxis** *f* small animal (veterinary) practice; **~vieh** *nt*: **~vieh macht auch Mist** (*prov*) many a mickle makes a muckle, every little helps; **~wagen** *m* small car; **k~weis** *adv* (*Aus*) gradually; **~wohnung** *f* flatlet (*Brit*), small apartment; **k~wüchsig** *adj* (*geh*) small; *Volk auch* small in stature; **~zeug** *nt* (*inf*) small odds and ends *pl*.

Kleister *m* **-s, -** (*Klebstoff*) paste; (*pej: dicke Speise*) goo (*inf*).

kleist(e)rig *adj* (*pej inf*) gooey (*inf*).

kleistern *vti* **(a)** (*zusammenkleben*) to paste. **(b)** (*dated inf*) **jdm eine ~** to slap sb in the face *or* sb's face.

Klementine *f* clementine.

⚠ **Klemmappe** *f getrennt* **Klemm-mappe** spring folder *or* binder.

Klemmbrett *nt* clipboard.

Klemme *f* **-, -n (a)** (*Haar~, für Papiere etc*) clip; (*Elec*) crocodile clamp *or* clip; (*Med*) clamp. **(b)** (*fig inf*) **in der ~ sitzen** *or* **sein** to be in a fix *or* tight spot *or* jam (*all inf*); **jdm aus der ~ helfen** to help sb out of a fix *or* tight spot *or* jam (*all inf*).

klemmen [1] *vt* **(a)** *Draht etc* to clamp, to clip; (*in Spalt*) to stick, to wedge, to jam ♦ **sich** (*dat*) **den Finger in etw** (*dat*) **~** to catch *or* trap one's finger in sth; **sich** (*dat*) **etw unter den Arm ~** to stick *or* tuck sth under one's arm; **sich** (*dat*) **eine Zigarette zwischen die Lippen ~** (*inf*) to stick a cigarette in one's mouth.
(b) (*inf: stehlen*) to pinch (*inf*), to swipe (*inf*).
[2] *vr* to catch oneself (*in +dat* in) ♦ **sich hinter etw** (*acc*) **~** (*inf*) to get stuck into sth (*inf*); **sich hinter jdn ~** (*inf*) to get on to sb.
[3] *vi* (*Tür, Schloß etc*) to stick, to jam.

Klemmer *m* **-s, -** pince-nez.

Klempner(in *f*) *m* **-s, -** plumber.

Klempnerei *f* **(a)** *no pl* plumbing. **(b)** (*Werkstatt*) plumber's workshop.

Klempnerladen *m* plumber's (shop) ♦ **der General trägt** *or* **hat einen ganzen ~ auf der Brust** (*hum*) the general has a whole load of ironmongery on his breast (*inf*).

klempnern *vi* to do plumbing.

Kleopatra *f* **-** Cleopatra.

Klepper *m* **-s, -** nag, hack.

Klepper-®: ~boot *nt* faltboat, foldboat, folding boat; **~mantel** *m* mackintosh, mac (*inf*).

Kleptomane *m*, **Kleptomanin** *f* kleptomaniac.

Kleptomanie *f* kleptomania.

klerikal *adj* (*pej*) clerical.

Klerikalismus *m* (*pej*) clericalism.

Kleriker *m* **-s, -** cleric.

Klerus *m* **-,** *no pl* clergy.

Klettband *nt* Velcro® strip.

Klette *f* **-, -n** (*Bot*) burdock; (*Blütenkopf*) bur(r); (*pej: lästiger Mensch*) nuisance, bind (*inf*) ♦ **sich wie eine ~ an jdn hängen** to cling to sb like a limpet *or* barnacle; **wie die ~n zusammenhalten** to stick together.

Kletter-: ~affe *m* (*inf*) **er ist ein richtiger ~affe** he can climb like a monkey; **~baum** *m* climbing tree.

Kletterer *m* **-s, -** climber.

Kletter-: ~gerüst *nt* climbing frame; **~max(e)** *m* **-es, -e** (*inf*) steeplejack.

klettern *vi aux sein* to climb; (*mühsam*) to clamber ♦ **auf Bäume ~** to climb trees.

Kletter-: ~partie *f* climbing trip *or* outing; **~pflanze** *f* climbing plant, climber; **~rose** *f* climbing rose; **~stange** *f* climbing pole; **~tour** *f siehe* **~partie.**

⚠ **Klettverschluß** *m* Velcro ® fastener.

Kletze *f* **-, -n** (*S Ger, Aus*) dried pear.

Kletzenbrot *nt* (*S Ger, Aus*) fruit bread.

klicken *vi* to click.

Klicker *m* **-s, -** marble; (*Spiel*) marbles *sing.*

klickern *vi* to play marbles.

Klient [kli'ɛnt] *m* **-en, -en** client.

Klientel [kliɛn'tɛl] *f* **-, -en** clients *pl*, clientèle.

Klientin [kli'ɛntın] *f* client.

klieren *vi* (*dial*) to scrawl.

Kliff *nt* **-(e)s, -e** cliff.

Kliffküste *f* cliffs *pl.*

Klima *nt* **-s, -s** *or* **-te** [kli'ma:tə] (*lit, fig*) climate; (*fig auch*) atmosphere.

Klima-: ~änderung *f* climatic change; **~anlage** *f* air-conditioning (system); **mit ~anlage** air-conditioned; **~forscher** *m* climatologist; **~kammer** *f* climatic chamber; **~katastrophe** *f* climatic disaster; **~kollaps** *m* climatic breakdown.

Klimakterium *nt* climacteric, menopause.

Klima-: ~kunde *f siehe* **Klimatologie**; **~schwankung** *f* climatic variation.

klimatisch *adj no pred* climatic.

klimatisieren* *vt* to air-condition.

Klimatologie *f* climatology.

Klimawechsel *m* (*lit, fig*) change in the climate.

Klimazone *f* (climatic) zone.

Klimbim *m* **-s,** *no pl* (*inf*) odds and ends *pl*; (*Umstände*) fuss (and bother).

klimmen *pret* **klomm** *or* **klimmte,** *ptp* **geklommen** *or* **geklimmt** *vi aux sein* (*rare*) to clamber, to scramble.

Klimmzug *m* (*Sport*) pull-up ♦ **geistige ~̈e machen** (*fig*) to do intellectual *or* mental acrobatics.

Klimperei *f* (*inf*) tinkling; (*stümperhaft*) plonking (*inf*); (*auf Banjo etc*) twanging.

Klimperkasten *m* (*inf*) piano, joanna (*inf*).

klimpern *vi* to tinkle; (*stümperhaft ~*) to plonk away (*inf*); (*auf Banjo*) to twang ♦ **mit Geld** *etc* **~** to jingle coins; **mit den Wimpern ~** (*inf*) to flutter one's eyelashes.

kling *interj* clink, ting, ding ♦ **~ machen** (*Metall, Glas etc*) to clink; **mit K~ und Klang** (*old*) to the sound of music.

Klinge *f* **-, -n** blade; (*liter: Schwert*) sword, blade (*liter*) ♦ **eine gute ~ schlagen** (*Fencing*) to be a good swordsman; **mit blanker ~** (*liter*) with drawn sword; **er führt eine scharfe ~** (*fig*) he is a dangerous opponent; **jdn über die ~ springen lassen** (*sl*) (*umbringen*) to bump sb off (*inf*), to rub sb out (*sl*); (*opfern*) to leave sb to be killed.

Klingel *f* **-, -n** bell.

Klingel-: ~anlage *f* bell system; **~beutel** *m* collection bag; **~draht** *m* bell wire.

klingeling *interj* dingaling.

Klingelknopf *m* bell button *or* push.

klingeln *vi* to ring (*nach* for); (*Motor*) to pink, to knock ♦ **es hat schon zum ersten/zweiten/dritten Mal geklingelt** (*in Konzert, Theater*) the three-/two-/one-minute bell has already gone; **es hat schon geklingelt** (*in Schule*) the bell has already gone; **es hat geklingelt** (*Telefon*) the phone just rang; (*an Tür*) somebody just rang the doorbell; **es klingelt an der Tür** (*als Bühnenanweisung*) there is a ring at the door; **hat es jetzt endlich geklingelt?** (*fig inf*) has the penny finally dropped? (*inf*); **K~** ringing.

Klingel-: ~schnur *f* bellpull; **~zeichen** *nt* ring; **auf ein ~zeichen hin** at the ring of a bell; **auf ein besonderes ~zeichen hin** in response to a special ring; **~zug** *m* bellpull.

▼ **klingen** *pret* **klang,** *ptp* **geklungen** *vi* to sound; (*Glocke, Ohr*) to ring; (*Glas*) to clink; (*Metall*) to clang ♦ **nach etw ~** to sound like sth; **mein linkes Ohr klingt** I have a ringing (sound) in my left ear; **das klingt mir wie Musik in den Ohren** that is music to my ears; **die Gläser ~ lassen** to clink glasses; **die Glocke klingt dumpf/hell** the bell has a dull/clear ring.

klingend *adj* **mit ~em Spiel** (*old Mil*) with fife and drum; **in** *or* **mit ~er Münze**

(*old, liter*) in coin of the realm; **~e Register** (*Mus*) (sounding) stops *pl*; **~er Reim** (*Poet*) feminine rhyme.
Klinik *f* **-, -en** clinic; (*Universitäts~*) (university) hospital.
Klinika, Kliniken *pl of* **Klinikum.**
Kliniker(in *f*) *m* **-s, -** (*Med*) clinician; (*Univ*) medical student attached to a hospital.
Klinikum *nt* **-s, Klinika** *or* **Kliniken** (*Univ*) clinic.
klinisch *adj* clinical ◆ **~ tot** clinically dead; **~er Blick** cold glance.
Klinke *f* **-, -n** (*Tür~*) (door) handle; (*Sperr~*) catch, ratchet, pawl; (*Telec*) jack ◆ **~n putzen** (*inf*) to go *or* canvass/sell from door to door, to go *or* do door-to-door canvassing/selling.
Klinkenputzer *m* (*inf*) (*Hausierer*) hawker; (*Vertreter*) door-to-door salesman; (*Wahlkandidat*) door-to-door canvasser; (*Bettler*) beggar.
Klinker *m* **-s, - (a)** (*Ziegelstein*) clinker brick, (Dutch) clinker. **(b)** (*Naut*) clinker.
Klinker-: ~bau *m* clinker building; **~boot** *nt* clinker(-built) boat; **~stein** *m siehe* **Klinker (a).**
Klinomobil *nt* **-s, -e** mobile clinic.
klipp [1] *interj* **~, klapp** click, clack; (*Schuhe, Hufe*) clip, clop.
[2] *adv*: **~ und klar** clearly, plainly; (*offen*) frankly, openly.
Klipp *m* **-s, -s** clip.
Klippe *f* **-, -n** (*Fels~*) cliff; (*im Meer*) rock; (*fig*) hurdle, obstacle ◆ **~n umschiffen** (*lit, fig*) to negotiate obstacles.
Klippen-: ~küste *f* rocky coast; **k~reich** *adj* rocky.
Klipp-: ~fisch *m* dried, salted cod; **~schule** *f* (*pej*) second-rate school.
Klips *m* **-es, -e** *siehe* **Clip.**
klirren *vi* to clink; (*Glas auch*) to tinkle; (*Fensterscheiben*) to rattle; (*Waffen*) to clash; (*Ketten, Sporen*) to jangle; (*Lautsprecher, Mikrophon*) to crackle; (*Eis*) to crunch ◆ **~de Kälte** (*liter*) crisp cold; **~der Frost** sharp frost; **~de Töne** tinny sounds.
Klirrfaktor *m* distortion (factor).
Klischee *nt* **-s, -s** (*Typ*) plate, block; (*fig: Ausdruck, Phrase*) cliché.
Klischee-: ~anstalt *f* (*Typ*) plate-maker's; **k~haft** *adj* (*fig*) stereotyped, hackneyed; **~vorstellung** *f* cliché, stereotype.
klischieren* *vt* (*Typ*) to make plates for, to stereotype.
Klistier *nt* **-s, -e** enema, clyster (*spec*).
Klistierspritze *f* enema (syringe).
Klitoris *f* **-, -** *or* **Klitorides** clitoris.
klitsch *interj* **~, klatsch** slip, slop.
Klitsch *m* **-(e)s, -e** (*dial*) **(a)** (*Schlag*) slap, smack. **(b)** (*Brei*) doughy *or* soggy mass.
Klitsche *f* **-, -n** (*pej inf*) dilapidated building; (*Theat*) small-time theatre.
klitschig *adj* (*dial*) doughy, soggy.
⚠ **klitschnaß** *adj* (*inf*) drenched, soaking *or* sopping (*inf*) wet.
klittern *vt Geschichte* to concoct.
Klitterung *f siehe* **Geschichts~.**
klitzeklein *adj* (*inf*) tiny, teeny-weeny (*inf*).
Klivie ['kli:viə] *f* (*Bot*) clivia.
Klo *nt* **-s, -s** (*inf*) loo (*Brit inf*), john (*US inf*) ◆ **aufs ~ gehen** to go to the loo *or* john.
Kloake *f* **-, -n** sewer; (*fig auch*) cesspool; (*Zool*) cloaca.
Kloaken-: ~journalismus *m* gutter journalism; **~tiere** *pl* the monotremes *pl* (*form*), *eg* duck-billed platypus; porcupine; ant-eater.
Kloben *m* **-s, - (a)** (*Holzklotz*) log. **(b)** (*Eisenhaken*) hook.
klobig *adj* hefty (*inf*), bulky; *Mensch* hulking great (*inf*); *Benehmen* boorish; *Hände* massive, hefty (*inf*).
Klo-: ~bürste *f* (*inf*) toilet *or* loo (*Brit inf*) brush; **~frau** *f* (*inf*) toilet *or* loo (*Brit inf*) attendant.
klomm *pret of* **klimmen.**
Klon *m* **-s, -e** clone.
klonen *vti* to clone.
Klonen *nt* **-s,** *no pl* cloning.
klönen *vi* (*N Ger inf*) to (have a) natter (*Brit inf*).
Klönschnack *m* (*N Ger inf*) natter (*Brit inf*).
Klopapier *nt* (*inf*) toilet *or* loo (*Brit inf*) paper, bumf (*dated Brit inf*).
Klöpfel *m* **-s, - (a)** (*Holzhammer*) square mallet; (*Steinmetzwerkzeug*) stone-mason's maul. **(b)** (*old: Glocken~*) tongue, clapper.
klopfen [1] *vt* to knock; *Fleisch, Teppich* to beat; *Steine* to knock down ◆ **den Takt ~** to beat time.
[2] *vi* to knock; (*leicht auch*) to tap; (*Herz*) to beat; (*vor Aufregung, Anstrengung auch*) to pound; (*Puls, Schläfe*) to throb; (*Specht*) to tap, to hammer; (*Motor*) to knock, to pink; (*beim Kartenspiel*) to pass ◆ **klopf doch noch mal!** give another knock, knock again; **sie klopften wiederholt heftig an die Tür** they kept pounding away at the door; **es klopft** (*Theat*) there is a knock at the door; **es hat geklopft** there's someone knocking at the door; **„bitte laut ~"** "please knock loudly"; **jdm auf die Schulter/den Rücken/den Hintern ~** to tap sb on the shoulder/to pat sb on the back/the bottom; **jdm auf die Finger ~** (*lit, fig*) to give sb a rap *or* to rap sb on the knuckles; **mit ~dem Herzen** with beating *or* pounding heart; **ein ~der Schmerz** a throbbing pain; *siehe* **Busch.**
Klopfer *m* **-s, -** (*Tür~*) (door) knocker; (*Fleisch~*) (meat) mallet; (*Teppich~*) carpet beater.
Klopf-: k~fest *adj* antiknock; **~festigkeit** *f* antiknock quality; **~zeichen** *nt* knock.
Kloppe *pl*: (*dial inf*) **~ kriegen** to be given a hiding *or* thrashing.
Klöppel *m* **-s, -** (*Glocken~*) tongue, clapper; (*Spitzen~*) bobbin; (*Trommel~*) stick.
Klöppelarbeit *f* pillow lace.
Klöppelei *f* (pillow) lace making.
klöppeln *vi* to make (pillow) lace ◆ **eine Tischdecke ~** to make a lace tablecloth.
Klöppelspitze *f* pillow lace.
kloppen (*N Ger inf*) [1] *vt* to hit; *siehe* **Griff, Skat.**
[2] *vr* to fight, to scrap (*inf*), to brawl.
Klopperei *f* (*N Ger inf*) fight, brawl.
Klöppler(in *f*) *m* **-s, -** (pillow) lace maker.
Klops *m* **-es, -e** (*Cook*) meatball.
Klosett *nt* **-s, -e** *or* **-s** lavatory, toilet.
Klosett-: ~becken *nt* lavatory *or* toilet bowl, lavatory pan; **~brille** *f* toilet seat; **~bürste** *f* lavatory *or* toilet brush; **~deckel** *m* lavatory *or* toilet seat lid; **~frau** *f* lavatory attendant; **~papier** *nt* lavatory *or* toilet paper.
Kloß *m* **-es, ¨e** dumpling; (*Fleisch~*) meatball; (*Boulette*) rissole ◆ **einen ~ im Hals haben** (*fig*) to have a lump in one's throat.
Kloßbrühe *f*: **klar wie ~** as clear as day; (*iro*) as clear as mud.
Kloster *nt* **-s, ¨** cloister; (*Mönchs~ auch*) monastery; (*Nonnen~ auch*) convent, nunnery (*old*) ◆ **ins ~ gehen** to enter a monastery/convent, to become a monk/nun.
Kloster-: ~bruder *m* (*old*) monk; **~frau** *f* (*old*) nun; **~kirche** *f* monastery/convent church; **~leben** *nt* monastic/convent life.
klösterlich *adj Leben* monastic/convent; *Stille, Abgeschiedenheit* cloistered.
Klosterschule *f* monastic/convent school.
Klöten *pl* (*sl*) balls *pl* (*sl*).
Klotz *m* **-es, ¨e** (*Holz~*) block (of wood); (*pej: Beton~*) concrete block *or* monstrosity; (*inf: Person*) great lump (*inf*) *or* clod (*inf*) ◆ **sich** (*dat*) **einen ~ ans Bein binden** (*inf*) to tie a millstone around one's neck; **jdm ein ~ am Bein sein** to be a hindrance to sb, to be a millstone around sb's neck; **schlafen wie ein ~** (*inf*) to sleep like a log.
Klötzchen *nt dim of* **Klotz.**
klotzen [1] *vt* (*inf*) **Hochhäuser in die Stadt ~** to throw up skyscrapers in the town.
[2] *vi* (*sl*) (*hart arbeiten*) to slog (away) (*inf*); (*protzig auftreten*) to show off ◆ **mit Geld ~** to flash one's money around (*inf*); *siehe* **kleckern.**
klotzig *adj* (*sl*) huge, massive.
Klub *m* **-s, -s** club.
Klub-: ~abend *m* club night; **~garnitur** *f* club-style (three-piece) suite; **~haus** *nt* clubhouse; **~jacke** *f* blazer; **~leben** *nt* club life; **~lokal** *nt* club bar; **~sessel** *m* club chair.
kluckern *vi siehe* **gluckern.**
Kluft *f* **-, ¨e (a)** (*Erdspalte*) cleft; (*zwischen Felsenrändern auch*) ravine; (*in Bergen*) crevasse; (*Abgrund*) chasm.
(b) (*fig*) gulf, gap ◆ **in der Partei tat sich eine tiefe ~ auf** a deep rift opened up in the party.
(c) *no pl* (*Uniform, Kleidung*) uniform; (*inf: Kleidung*) gear (*sl*), garb (*hum*) ◆ **sich in seine gute/beste ~ werfen** to put on one's Sunday best *or* one's glad rags (*hum*).
klug *adj, comp* **¨er,** *superl* **¨ste(r, s),** *adv superl* **am ¨sten** clever, intelligent; *Augen* intelligent; *Humor* witty, sophisticated; (*vernünftig*) *Entscheidung, Rat* wise, sound; *Überlegung* prudent; (*geschickt*) *Antwort, Analyse, Geschäftsmann* shrewd, clever ◆ **es wird am ¨sten sein, wenn ...** it would be most sensible if ..., it would be the best idea if ...; **es wäre politisch/geschäftlich ~ ...** it would make good political/business sense ...; **~ geschrieben/durchdacht** cleverly *or* intelligently written/thought out; **ein ~er Philosoph** an astute philosopher; **ein ~er Kopf** a capable person; **ein ~er Kopf, der Kleine** he's a bright lad; **in ~er Voraussicht** with shrewd foresight; **ich werde daraus nicht ~, da soll einer draus ~ werden** I cannot make head or tail of it, I can't make it out; **aus ihm werde ich nicht ~** I don't know what to make of him, I can't make him out; **im nachhinein ist man immer ¨er** one learns by experience; **~ reden** *or* **tun kann jeder ...** anyone can talk ...; **~e Reden halten** *or* **führen** (*iro*) to make fine-sounding speeches; **~e Bemerkungen/Ratschläge** (*iro*) clever *or* helpful remarks/advice (*iro*); **wer war denn so ~ ...** (*iro*) who was the bright *or* clever one ...; **so ~ bin ich auch** (*iro*) you don't say!; **nun bin ich genauso ~ wie zuvor** *or* **vorher** I am still none the wiser; **der K¨ere gibt nach** (*Prov*) discretion is the better part of valour (*Prov*); **der ~e Mann baut vor** (*Prov*) the wise man takes precautions; **wer ~ ist, fährt mit der Bahn** it makes more sense to go by train; **wenn du ~ bist, haust du sofort ab** if you're smart you'll beat it (*inf*).
klügeln *vi* to puzzle (*wie/was* as to how/what) ◆ **wieder etwas zum K~ für unsere Rätselfreunde** another brain-teaser for our puzzle fans.
klugerweise *adv* (very) cleverly, (very) wisely.
Klugheit *f siehe adj* cleverness, intelligence; wisdom, soundness; prudence; shrewdness, cleverness ◆ **aus ~** (very) wisely; **die ~ eines Sokrates** the astuteness of a Socrates; **deine ~en kannst du dir sparen** (*iro*) you can save your clever remarks.
Klügler *m* **-s, -** fiddle, fiddly person.
Klug-: ⚠**k~reden** *vi sep* to talk big, to make fine-sounding speeches; **~redner** *m* know-all; **k~scheißen** *vi sep irreg* (*sl*) to shoot one's mouth off (*inf*); **~scheißer** *m* (*sl*) big mouth (*inf*), smart-aleck (*inf*), smart-ass (*sl*); **k~schnacken** *vi* (*N Ger inf*) *siehe* **k~reden**; **~schnacker** *m* **-s, -** (*N Ger inf*) *siehe* **~redner.**
Klump *no art* (*inf*) **ein Auto zu ~ fahren** to smash up a car; **jdn zu ~ hauen** to

beat sb to a pulp (*inf*).
Klumpatsch *m* **-s,** *no pl* (*inf*): **der ganze ~** the whole (kit and) caboodle (*inf*).
Klümpchen *nt dim of* **Klumpen**.
klumpen *vi* (*Sauce*) to go lumpy.
Klumpen *m* **-s, -** lump; (*Erd~ auch*) clod; (*Gold~*) nugget; (*Blut~*) clot ◆ **~ bilden** (*Mehl etc*) to go lumpy; (*Blut*) to clot; **steht doch nicht alle auf einem ~!** don't all stand in a huddle.
Klumpert *nt* **-s,** *no pl* (*Aus*) *siehe* **Klumpatsch**.
Klump-: ~fuß *m* club-foot; **k~füßig** *adj* club-footed.
klumpig *adj* lumpy.
Klüngel *m* **s, -** (*inf: Clique*) clique; (*dial: Kram*) mess.
Klüngelwirtschaft *f* (*inf*) nepotism *no pl*.
Klunker *m* **-s, - (a)** (*sl: Edelstein*) rock (*sl*). **(b)** *siehe* **Troddel**.
Kluppe *f* **-, -n** calipers *pl*; (*Schneid~*) die-stock.
Klüse *f* **-, -n** (*Naut*) hawsehole ◆ **~n** (*N Ger inf*) eyes *pl*.
Klüver ['kly:vɐ] *m* **-s, -** (*Naut*) jib.
Klüverbaum *m* (*Naut*) jib boom.
km *abbr of* **Kilometer** km.
km/h *abbr of* **Kilometer pro Stunde** kph.
kn (*Naut*) *abbr of* **Knoten** kt.
knabbern *vti* to nibble ◆ **nichts zu ~ haben** (*inf*) to have nothing to eat; **daran wirst du noch zu ~ haben** (*fig inf*) it will really give you something to think about *or* get your teeth into; **an dieser Aufgabe habe ich lange zu ~ gehabt** (*fig inf*) I spent ages puzzling over this exercise.
Knabe *m* **-n, -n** (*liter*) boy, lad ◆ **„~n"** (*old*) boys; **na alter ~!** (*inf*) well old boy (*inf*) *or* chap (*inf*).
Knaben-: ~alter *nt* boyhood; **im ~alter** in his boyhood; **~chor** *m* boys' choir; **k~haft** *adj* boyish; **~kraut** *nt* (wild) orchid; **~liebe** *f* (*liter*) paederasty, homosexual love; **~schule** *f* (*old*) boys' school; **~stimme** *f* boy's voice; (*Mus auch*) treble voice.
Knack *m* **-(e)s, -e** crack.
knack *interj* crack ◆ **~ machen** to crack, to go crack.
Knäckebrot *nt* crispbread.
knacken [1] *vt* **(a)** *Nüsse,* (*fig inf*) *Rätsel, Kode, Geldschrank* to crack; *Läuse* to squash, to crush.
(b) (*inf*) *Auto* to break into, to burgle; (*Mil sl*) *Panzer* to knock out.
[2] *vi* (*brechen*) to crack, to snap; (*Glas etc*) to crack; (*Dielen, Stuhl*) to creak; (*Holz*) (*knistern*) to crackle ◆ **mit den Fingern ~** to crack one's fingers; **es knackt im Radio** the radio is crackling; **es knackt im Gebälk** the beams are creaking; **an etw** (*dat*) **zu ~ haben** (*inf*) to have sth to think about *or* chew on (*inf*); (*darüber hinwegkommen*) to have a rough time getting over sth; **an dieser Aufgabe hatte ich ganz schön zu ~** (*inf*) I really had to sweat over this exercise.
Knacker *m* **-s, - (a)** *siehe* **Knackwurst**. **(b)** (*pej inf*) **alter ~** old fog(e)y (*inf*).
Knacki *m* **-s, -s** (*sl*) jailbird (*inf*).
knackig *adj* crisp; *Apfel auch* crunchy; (*inf*) *Mädchen* tasty (*inf*); *Figur, Rock, Hose* sexy.
Knack-: ~laut *m* glottal stop; **~mandel** almond in the shell; **~punkt** *m* (*inf*) crunch (*inf*).
Knacks *m* **-es, -e (a)** (*Sprung*) crack.
(b) (*inf: Schaden*) **das Radio/der Fernseher hat einen ~** there is something wrong with the radio/television; **die Ehe der beiden hat schon lange einen ~** their marriage has been cracking up for a long time; **er hat einen ~ (weg)bekommen** he/his health/his nerves took a knock; **er hat einen ~ weg** he's a bit screwy (*inf*); his health isn't so good.
knacks *interj* crack, crash.
Knackwurst *f type of frankfurter, the skin of which makes a cracking sound when bitten.*
Knall *m* **-(e)s, -e** bang; (*mit Peitsche*) crack; (*bei Tür*) bang, slam; (*von Korken*) pop; (*inf: Krach*) trouble ◆ **der ~ eines Schusses** a shot; **~ auf Fall** (*inf*) all of a sudden; **jdn ~ auf Fall entlassen** (*inf*) to dismiss sb completely out of the blue (*inf*); **einen ~ haben** (*inf*) to be crazy (*inf*) *or* crackers (*Brit inf*).
Knall-: ~bonbon *nt* (Christmas) cracker; **~effekt** *m* (*inf*) bombshell (*inf*); **einen ~effekt haben/ein ~effekt sein** to come as/be a real bombshell.
knallen [1] *vi* **(a)** to bang, to explode; (*Schuß*) to ring out; (*Feuerwerk*) to (go) bang; (*Pfropfen*) to (go) pop; (*Peitsche*) to crack; (*Tür etc*) to bang, to slam; (*Auspuff*) to misfire; (*aux sein: auftreffen*) to bang ◆ **mit der Peitsche ~** to crack the whip; **mit der Tür ~** to bang *or* slam the door; **mit den Absätzen ~** (*Soldaten etc*) to click one's heels; **einen Pfropfen ~ lassen** to pop a cork; **draußen knallte es** there was a shot/were shots outside; **bleib stehen, sonst knallt's** (*inf*) stand still or I'll shoot; **sei nicht so frech, sonst knallt's** (*inf*) don't be so cheeky, or there'll be trouble; **der Fahrer ist gegen die Windschutzscheibe geknallt** the driver hit the windscreen; **der Ball knallte gegen den Pfosten** (*inf*) the ball banged *or* slammed against the post.
(b) (*inf: Sonne*) to blaze *or* beat down.
[2] *vt* to bang; *Tür, Buch auch* to slam; *Ball auch* to belt (*inf*); *Schüsse* to fire (off); *Peitsche* to crack ◆ **den Hörer auf die Gabel ~** (*inf*) to slam *or* bang down the receiver; **jdm eine ~** (*inf*) to clout sb (*inf*), to belt sb (one) (*inf*); **jdm ein paar vor den Kopf/Latz ~** (*sl*) to clout sb one (*sl*), to stick one on sb (*sl*).
knallend *adj Farbe* bright, loud, gaudy.
Knall-: k~eng *adj* (*inf*) skintight; **~erbse** *f* toy torpedo.
Knallerei *f* (*inf*) (*Schießerei*) shooting; (*Feuerwerk*) banging of fireworks.
Knall-: ~frosch *m* jumping jack; **~gas** *nt* oxyhydrogen; **k~gelb** *adj* (*inf*) bright yellow; **k~grün** *adj* (*inf*) bright green; **k~hart** *adj* (*inf*) *Film* brutal; *Porno* hard-core; *Job* really tough; *Truppen, Mensch* really tough, as hard as nails; *Schuß, Schlag* really hard; **ein k~harter Schuß/Schlag** a real humdinger (of a shot/punch) (*inf*); **der Film zeigt k~hart, wie ...** the film shows brutally *or* without pulling any punches how ...; **k~heiß** *adj* (*inf*) blazing *or* boiling hot; **~hitze** *f* (*inf*) blazing heat, heatwave.
knallig *adj* (*inf*) *Farben* loud, gaudy.
Knall-: ~kopf (*inf*), **~kopp** (*inf*) *m* fathead (*inf*), blockhead (*inf*); **~körper** *m* fire-cracker; **k~rot** *adj* (*inf*) bright red, scarlet; *Gesicht* as red as a beetroot (*inf*); **~schleppe** *f* (*Aviat*) sonic boom.
knapp *adj* **(a)** (*nicht ausreichend vorhanden*) *Vorräte, Arbeitsstellen* scarce, in short supply; *Geld auch* tight; *Taschengeld* meagre; *Gehalt* low, meagre ◆ **mein Geld ist ~** I'm short of money; **mein Geld wird ~** I am running short of *or* out of money; **das Essen wird ~** we/they *etc* are running short of *or* out of food; **mein Geld/meine Zeit ist ~ bemessen** I am short of money/time; **er hat ihr das Taschengeld ~ bemessen** he was mean with her pocket money; **~ mit (dem) Geld sein** (*inf*) to be short of money.
(b) (*gerade noch ausreichend*) *Zeit, Geld, Miete* just *or* barely sufficient *or* enough; *Mehrheit* narrow, small, bare; *Sieg* narrow; *Kleidungsstück etc* (*eng*) tight; (*kurz*) short; *Bikini* scanty ◆ **wir haben ~ verloren/gewonnen** we only just lost/won; **ich verprügele dich, aber nicht zu ~** (*dated*) I'll give you a thrashing, and how!
(c) (*nicht ganz*) almost ◆ **ein ~es Pfund Mehl** just under a pound of flour; **seit einem ~en** *or* **~ einem Jahr wohne ich hier** I have been living here for almost a year.
(d) (*kurz und präzis*) *Stil, Worte* concise; *Geste* terse; (*lakonisch*) *Antwort* pithy.
(e) (*gerade so eben*) just ◆ **er ist ~ an mir vorbeigefahren** he just got *or* scraped past me; **mit ~er Not** only just, by the skin of one's teeth; **der Rock endete ~ über dem Knie** the skirt came to just above the knee.
Knappe *m* **-n, -n (a)** (*Hist: eines Ritters*) squire. **(b)** (*Min*) qualified miner.
⚠**knapphalten** *vt sep irreg*: **jdn ~** to keep sb short (*mit* of).
Knappheit *f* (*Lebensmittel~*) scarcity, shortage; (*von Zeit, Geld*) shortage; (*fig: des Ausdrucks*) conciseness, concision ◆ **wegen der ~ der uns zur Verfügung stehenden Zeit** because of the shortness of the time at our disposal.
Knappschaft *f* (*Min*) miners' guild.
knapsen *vi* (*inf*) to scrimp (*mit, an +dat* on), to be stingy (*inf*) (*mit, an +dat* with) ◆ **an etw** (*dat*) **zu ~ haben** to have a rough time getting over sth.
Knarre *f* **-, -n (a)** (*sl: Gewehr*) shooter (*sl*). **(b)** (*Rassel*) rattle.
knarren *vi* to creak ◆ **eine ~de Stimme** a rasping *or* grating voice.
Knast *m* **-(e)s,** *no pl* (*sl*) clink (*inf*), can (*US sl*) ◆ **~ schieben** (*sl*) to do bird (*Brit sl*), to do time (*inf*).
Knastbruder *m* (*sl*) jailbird (*inf*).
Knaster *m* **-s, -** (*inf*) baccy (*inf*) ◆ **was rauchst du denn für einen ~!** what's that foul-smelling stuff you're smoking!
Knasti *m* **-s, -s** (*sl*) jailbird (*inf*).
Knastologe *m* (*hum*) jailbird (*inf*).
Knatsch *m* **-es,** *no pl* (*inf*) trouble ◆ **das gibt ~** that means trouble.
knatschig *adj* (*inf*) upset, whingy (*inf*).
knattern *vi* (*Motorrad*) to roar; (*Preßlufthammer*) to hammer; (*Maschinengewehr*) to rattle, to chatter; (*Schüsse*) to rattle out; (*Fahne im Wind*) to flap.
Knäuel *m or nt* **-s, -** ball; (*wirres*) tangle; (*fig: Durcheinander*) muddle; (*von Menschen*) group, knot; (*in Problemen*) knot, tangle; (*hum: Hund*) bundle of fluff (*inf*).
Knauf *m* **-(e)s, Knäufe** (*Tür~*) knob; (*von Schwert etc*) pommel.
Knauser *m* **-s, -** (*inf*) scrooge (*inf*).
Knauserei *f* (*inf*) meanness, stinginess (*inf*).
knauserig *adj* (*inf*) mean, stingy (*inf*).
knausern *vi* (*inf*) to be mean *or* stingy (*inf*) (*mit* with).
Knaus-Ogino-Methode *f* (*Med*) rhythm method.
knautschen *vti* (*inf*) to crumple (up); *Kleid etc auch* to crease.
knautschig *adj* (*inf*) *Anzug, Kleid* crumpled-up, crumply (*inf*).
Knautsch-: ~lack *m*, **~(lack)leder** *nt* wet-look leather; **~zone** *f* (*Aut*) crumple zone.
Knebel *m* **-s, -** (*Mund~*) gag; (*Paket~*) (wooden) handle; (*an Mänteln*) toggle; (*Fenster~*) (handle of) window catch.
Knebel-: ~bart *m* Van Dyke (beard); **~knopf** *m* toggle fastening.
knebeln *vt jdn, Presse* to gag.
Kneb(e)lung *f, no pl* (*lit, fig*) gagging.
Knebelvertrag *m* oppressive contract ◆ **jdn durch einen ~ binden** to screw sb down with a tight contract (*inf*).
Knecht *m* **-(e)s, -e (a)** servant; (*beim Bauern*) (farm-)labourer *or* worker; (*Stall~*) stableboy. **(b)** (*fig: Sklave*) slave (*gen* to). **(c) ~ Ruprecht** *helper to St Nicholas (Santa Claus).*
knechten *vt* (*geh*) to subjugate, to oppress ◆ **alle unterdrückten und geknechteten Völker ...** all oppressed and enslaved peoples ...; **sie wollten sich nicht mehr von ihm ~ lassen** they refused to be his slaves any longer.
knechtisch *adj* (*geh*) *Charakter* subservient, submissive; *Unterwürfigkeit, Verhalten auch* servile, slavish ◆ **jdm/einer Sache ~ ergeben sein** to be a complete slave *or* totally enslaved to sb/sth.
Knechtschaft *f* slavery, servitude, bondage.
Knechtung *f, no pl* (*geh*) enslavement, subjugation.
kneifen *pret* **kniff**, *ptp* **gekniffen** [1] *vt* to pinch ◆ **jdn/jdn** *or* **jdm in den Arm ~** to pinch sb/sb's arm; **der Hund kniff den Schwanz zwischen die Beine** the dog put his tail between his legs.
[2] *vi* **(a)** to pinch.
(b) (*Univ sl*) *to fail to remain motionless during a student duel.*

⚠: for details of spelling reform, see supplement

(c) (*inf*) (*ausweichen*) to chicken out (*sl*), to get *or* back out (*vor +dat* of); (*vor Arbeit auch*) to duck out (*vor +dat* of); (*vor Duell*) to back out, to show the white feather.

Kneifer *m* **-s, -** **(a)** (*Brille*) pince-nez. **(b)** (*inf*) (*Feigling*) yellowbelly (*inf*), chicken (*sl*); (*Drückeberger*) skiver (*Brit inf*), shirker.

Kneifzange *f* pliers *pl*; (*kleine*) pincers *pl* ◆ **eine ~** (a pair of) pliers/(a pair of) pincers.

Kneipe *f* **-, -n** (*inf*) (*Lokal*) pub (*Brit*), bar, saloon (*US*).

Kneipen-: ~bummel *m* pub crawl (*Brit*), bar hop (*US*); **~wirt** *m* (*inf*) publican (*Brit*), pub-owner (*Brit*), (pub) landlord (*Brit*), bar-keeper, saloon-keeper (*US*).

Kneiper *m* **-s, -, Kneipier** [knai'pie:] *m* **-s, -s** (*inf*) *siehe* **Kneipenwirt.**

kneippen *vi* to undergo a Kneipp cure.

Kneippkur *f* Kneipp cure, *type of hydropathic treatment combined with diet, rest etc.*

kneisen *vt* (*Aus inf*) to notice.

Knesset(h) *f* **-,** *no pl* Knesset.

Knet *m* **-s,** *no pl* modelling clay; (*Plastilin*) plasticine ®.

knetbar *adj* workable; *Teig auch* kneadable.

Knete *f* **-,** *no pl* (*sl*) dough (*inf*).

kneten [1] *vt Teig* to knead; *Plastilin, Ton* to work; *Figuren* to model; *Muskeln, Rücken* to knead, to work; *siehe* **formen.**
[2] *vi* (*mit Plastilin spielen*) to play with plasticine ® *or* modelling clay.

Knet-: ~gummi *m or nt* plasticine ®; **~masse** *f* modelling clay.

Knick *m* **-(e)s, -e** *or* **-s** **(a)** (*leichter Sprung*) crack. **(b)** (*Kniff, Falte*) crease, crinkle; (*Eselsohr*) dog-ear; (*Biegung*) (sharp) bend; (*bei Draht, auf Oberfläche*) kink ◆ **einen ~ machen** to bend sharply; *siehe* **Optik. (c)** *pl* **-s** (*N Ger: Hecke*) hedgerow.

Knickebein *m* **-s,** *no pl* advocaat.

knicken *vti* (*vi: aux sein*) to snap; *Papier* to fold, to crease ◆ **„nicht ~!"** "do not bend *or* fold"; *siehe* **geknickt.**

Knicker *m* **-s, -** (*inf*) scrooge (*inf*).

Knickerbocker ['knɪkɐbɔkɐ] *pl* knickerbockers *pl* (*old*), plus-fours *pl*.

knick(e)rig *adj* (*inf*) stingy (*inf*), mean.

Knick(e)rigkeit *f* (*inf*) stinginess (*inf*), meanness.

knickern *vi* (*inf*) to be stingy (*inf*) (*mit* with).

Knickfuß *m* (*Med*) (type of) club-foot.

knickrig *adj* (*inf*) *siehe* **knick(e)rig.**

Knickrigkeit *f* (*inf*) *siehe* **Knick(e)rigkeit.**

Knicks *m* **-es, -e** **(a)** bob; (*tiefer*) curts(e)y ◆ **einen ~ machen** to drop a curts(e)y, to curts(e)y (*vor +dat* to). **(b)** (*heller Knacks*) crack, click.

knicksen *vi* to curts(e)y, to drop a curts(e)y (*vor +dat* to).

Knie *nt* **-s, -** **(a)** (*auch Hosen~*) knee ◆ **auf ~n** on one's knees, on bended knee; **auf die ~ fallen, in die ~ sinken** (*geh*) to fall on *or* drop to one's knees; **sich vor jdm auf die ~ werfen** to throw oneself on one's knees in front of sb; **jdn auf ~n bitten** to go down on bended knees to sb (and beg); **jdm auf ~n danken** to go down on one's knees and thank sb; **in die ~ gehen** to kneel, to fall on one's knees; (*fig*) to be brought to one's knees; **jdn übers ~ legen** (*inf*) to put sb across one's knee; **etw übers ~ brechen** (*fig*) to rush (at) sth; **die ~ beugen** to bend one's knees; (*vor dem Altar*) to bow, to genuflect (*form*); (*fig*) to give in, to bend the knee.
(b) (*Fluß~*) sharp bend; (*in Rohr*) elbow.

Knie-: ~beuge *f* (*Sport*) knee-bend; **in die ~beuge gehen** to bend one's knees; **~bundhose** *f* knee breeches; **~fall** *m* genuflection (*form*); **einen ~fall vor jdm tun** (*geh*) *or* **machen** (*lit, fig*) to kneel before sb; (*fig auch*) to bow before sb; **k~fällig** [1] *adj Verehrung* humble, lowly; [2] *adv* on one's knees, on bended knee; **k~frei** *adj Rock* above the knee; **~gelenk** *nt* knee joint; **k~hoch** *adj Schnee, Wasser* knee-deep; *Gras* knee-high; **~hose** *f* knee breeches *pl*; **~kehle** *f* back *or* hollow of the knee; **~kissen** *nt* (*Eccl*) hassock; **k~lang** *adj* knee-length.

knien [kni:n, 'kni:ən] [1] *vi* to kneel ◆ **im K~** on one's knees, kneeling.
[2] *vr* to kneel (down) ◆ **sich in die Arbeit ~** (*fig*) to get down to *or* stuck into (*inf*) one's work.

Knierohr *nt* elbow(-pipe).

Knies *m* **-,** *no pl* (*dial inf*) row, argument.

Knie-: ~scheibe *f* kneecap; **~scheibenreflex, ~sehnenreflex** *m* knee *or* patellar (*spec*) reflex; **~schnackler** *m* **-s, -** (*dial inf*) wobbly knees *pl*; **~schützer** *m* **-s, -** kneepad, kneeguard; **~strumpf** *m* knee-sock, knee-length sock; **~stück** *nt* elbow joint; **k~tief** *adj* knee-deep; **~welle** *f* knee circle.

kniff *pret of* **kneifen.**

Kniff *m* **-(e)s, -e** **(a)** (*inf*) trick ◆ **den ~ bei etw heraushaben** to have the knack of sth (*inf*); **es ist ein ~ dabei** there is a (special) knack to it (*inf*). **(b)** (*Falte*) crease, fold. **(c)** (*Kneifen*) pinch.

Kniffelei *f* (*inf*) fiddly job.

kniff(e)lig *adj* (*inf*) fiddly; (*heikel*) tricky.

Knigge *m* **-(s), -** etiquette manual.

Knilch *m* **-s, -e** (*pej inf*) twit (*Brit inf*), clown (*inf*).

knips *interj* click.

knipsen [1] *vt* **(a)** *Fahrschein* to punch, to clip. **(b)** (*Phot inf*) to snap (*inf*).
[2] *vi* **(a)** (*Phot inf*) to take pictures. **(b)** (*klicken*) to click ◆ **mit den Fingern ~** to snap one's fingers.

Knipser **-s, -** (*inf*), **Knipsschalter** *m* shutter.

Knirps *m* **-es, -e** **(a)** (*Junge*) whippersnapper; (*pej auch*) squirt. **(b)** ® folding *or* telescopic umbrella.

knirschen *vi* (*Sand, Schnee*) to crunch; (*Getriebe*) to grind ◆ **mit den Zähnen ~** to grind one's teeth; (*vor Wut auch*) to gnash one's teeth.

knistern *vi* (*Feuer*) to crackle; (*Papier, Seide*) to rustle ◆ **mit Papier** *etc* **~** to rustle paper *etc*; **es knistert im Gebälk** (*fig*) there is trouble brewing *or* afoot (*gen* in).

Knittel *m* **-s, -** (*dial*) *siehe* **Knüppel.**

Knittelvers *m* rhyming couplets (using a four-stress line).

knitter-: ~arm *adj* crease-resistant; **~frei** *adj Stoff, Kleid* non-crushable, crease-resistant.

knittern *vti* to crease, to crush.

Knobelbecher *m* **(a)** dice cup. **(b)** (*Mil sl*) army boot.

knobeln *vi* **(a)** (*würfeln*) to play dice; (*um eine Entscheidung*) to toss for it (*inf*) ◆ **sie knobelten darum, wer bezahlen sollte** they tossed (for it) to decide who should pay. **(b)** (*nachdenken*) to puzzle (*an +dat* over).

Knoblauch *m* **-(e)s,** *no pl* garlic.

Knoblauch-: ~brot *nt* garlic bread; **~geruch** *m* smell of garlic; **~presse** *f* garlic press; **~zehe** *f* clove of garlic.

Knöchel *m* **-s, -** **(a)** (*Fuß~*) ankle ◆ **bis über die ~** up to the ankles, ankle-deep. **(b)** (*Finger~*) knuckle.

Knöchel-: ~bruch *m* broken ankle; **k~lang** *adj* ankle-length; **k~tief** *adj* ankle-deep.

Knochen *m* **-s, -** **(a)** bone; (*pl sl*) arms *pl*; legs *pl*; (*Hände*) paws *pl* (*inf*) ◆ **Fleisch mit/ohne ~** meat on/off the bone; **die Wunde geht bis auf den ~** the wound has penetrated to the bone; **mir tun alle ~ weh** (*inf*) every bone in my body is aching; **er ist bis auf die ~ abgemagert** he is just (a bag of) skin and bones; **brich dir nicht die ~!** (*inf*) don't break anything *or* your neck!; **dem breche ich alle ~ einzeln** (*sl*) I'll break every bone in his body; **das geht auf die ~** (*sl*) it knackers you (*Brit sl*) *or* breaks your back; **ihm steckt** *or* **sitzt die Grippe/Angst in den ~** (*inf*) he's got flu/he's scared stiff (*inf*); **naß bis auf die ~** (*inf*) soaked to the skin; **kein Mark** *or* **keinen Mumm in den ~ haben** (*inf*) to have no guts *or* spunk (*inf*); **der Schreck fuhr ihm in die ~** he was paralyzed with shock; **sich bis auf die ~ blamieren** (*inf*) to make a proper fool of oneself (*inf*); **er ist konservativ bis in** *or* **auf die ~** (*inf*) he is conservative through and through, he is a dyed-in-the-wool conservative.
(b) (*dated sl: Kerl*) chap (*inf*), bloke (*Brit inf*) ◆ **du fauler/müder ~** you lazy/indolent so-and-so (*inf*).
(c) (*inf: großer Hausschlüssel*) large door-key.

Knochen-: ~arbeit *f* hard graft (*inf*); **~bau** *m* bone structure; **~bruch** *m* fracture; **~erweichung** *f* (*Med*) softening of the bones, osteomalacia (*spec*); **~gerüst** *nt* skeleton; **k~hart** *adj* (*inf*) rock-hard; **~haut** *f* periosteum (*spec*); **~hautentzündung** *f* periostitis (*spec*); **~leim** *m* bone glue; **~mann** *m* (*liter*) Death; **~mark** *nt* bone marrow; **~markentzündung** *f* osteomyelitis; **~mehl** *nt* bone meal; **~naht** *f* (*Anat*) bone suture; **~schinken** *m* ham on the bone; **~schwund** *m* bone atrophy, atrophy of the bone; **k~trocken** *adj* (*inf*) bone dry; (*fig*) *Humor etc* very dry; **~tuberkulose** *f* bone tuberculosis, tuberculosis of the bone.

knöch(e)rig *adj* **(a)** (*knochenartig*) bony, bone-like, osseous (*form*). **(b)** *siehe* **knöchern.**

knöchern *adj Gerät etc* bone *attr*, of bone; *Material auch* bony, osseous (*form*); (*inf: großknochig*) *Mensch, Körperbau* bony; (*pej inf: nicht anpassungsfähig*) set in one's ways.

knochig *adj* bony.

knöchrig *adj siehe* **knöch(e)rig.**

Knockdown [nɔk'daun] *m* **-(s), -s** knockdown.

Knockout [nɔk'|aut] *m* **-(s), -s** knockout.

Knödel *m* **-s, -** dumpling.

knödeln *vi* to sing in a strangled voice.

Knofel *m* **-s,** *no pl* (*inf*) *siehe* **Knoblauch.**

Knöllchen *nt* **(a)** *dim of* **Knolle. (b)** (*inf: Strafzettel*) (parking) ticket.

Knöllchenbakterien *pl* rhizobin *pl*.

Knolle *f* **-, -n** (*Bot*) nodule, tubercule; (*von Kartoffel, Dahlie*) tuber; (*Kartoffel*) potato; (*inf: Nase*) conk (*Brit inf*).

Knollen *m* **-s, -** **(a)** *siehe* **Knolle. (b)** (*Klumpen*) lump.

Knollen-: ~blätterpilz, ~blätterschwamm *m* amanita; **grüner ~blätterpilz** deadly amanita, death cup, death angel; **weißer ~blätterpilz** destroying angel; **~nase** *f* (*Med*) rhinophyma (*spec*), (nodular) swelling of the nose; (*inf*) conk (*Brit inf*).

knollig *adj Wurzel* tuberous; *Auswuchs* knobbly, knotty; *Nase* bulbous; (*inf: klumpig*) lumpy.

Knopf *m* **-(e)s, ¨e** **(a)** (*an Kleidungsstück etc*) button ◆ **etw an den ¨en abzählen** to decide sth by counting off one's buttons.
(b) (*an Gerät, elektrischer Anlage etc*) (push-) button; (*an Akkordeon*) button.
(c) (*an Tür, Stock*) knob; (*Sattel~, Degen~*) pommel.
(d) (*S Ger, Aus: Knoten*) knob.
(e) (*inf*) (*Kind*) little chap *or* fellow/little lass(ie); (*Kerl*) chap, fellow ◆ **ein fieser ~** a nasty so-and-so.

knöpfen, knöpfeln (*Aus inf*) *vt* to button (up) ◆ **einen Kragen auf ein Kleid ~** to button a collar to a dress; **ein Kleid zum K~** a dress that buttons up.

Knopf-: ~leiste *f* button tape; **~loch** *nt* buttonhole; **aus allen ~löchern platzen** (*inf*) to be bursting at the seams; **~zelle** *f* round cell battery.

Knopp *m* **-s, ¨e** (*dial*) *siehe* **Knopf.**

knorke *adj* (*dated sl*) smashing (*Brit inf*), swell (*esp US inf*).

Knorpel *m* **-s, -** (*Anat, Zool*) cartilage; (*Cook*) gristle.

knorpelig *adj* (*Anat*) cartilaginous; *Fleisch* gristly.

Knorren *m* **-s, -** (*im Holz*) knot; (*an Weide*) burl, burr; (*Baumstumpf*) (tree) stump; (*Aststumpf*) snag.

knorrig *adj Baum* gnarled; *Holz, Klotz* knotty; (*fig*) *alter Mann* rugged; (*eigenwillig*) *Mensch, Charakter* surly, gruff.

Knospe *f* -, -n bud ◆ **~n ansetzen** *or* **treiben** to bud; **die zarte ~ ihrer Liebe** (*liter*) the tender bud of their love.

knospen *vi* to bud ◆ **~d** (*lit, fig liter*) budding.

Knötchen *nt dim of* **Knoten.**

Knoten *m* **-s,** - **(a)** knot; (*Med*) (*Geschwulst*) lump; (*Gicht~*) tophus (*spec*); (*Phys, Bot, Math, Astron*) node; (*fig: Verwicklung*) plot ◆ **sich** (*dat*) **einen ~ ins Taschentuch machen** (*inf*) to tie a knot in one's handkerchief.
(b) (*Naut*) knot.
(c) (*Haar~*) bun, knot.
(d) *siehe* **Knotenpunkt.**

knoten *vt Seil etc* to (tie into a) knot, to tie a knot in.

Knoten-: ~bahnhof *m* junction; **~punkt** *m* (*Mot*) (road) junction, (road) intersection; (*Rail*) junction; (*fig*) centre; (*von Argumentation, Handlung etc*) nodal point.

Knöterich *m* knotgrass.

knotig *adj* knotty, knotted, full of knots; *Äste, Finger* gnarled; *Geschwulst* nodular.

Know-how ['nouhau] *nt* **-s,** *no pl* know-how.

Knubbel *m* **-s,** - (*inf*) lump.

Knuff *m* **-(e)s, ¨-e** (*inf*) poke; (*mit Ellbogen*) nudge.

knuffen *vti* (*inf*) to poke (*inf*); (*mit Ellbogen*) to nudge.

knülle *adj pred* (*dial inf*) tight (*inf*), stoned (*sl*).

knüllen *vti* to crumple, to crease (up).

Knüller *m* **-s,** - (*inf*) sensation; (*Press*) scoop.

knüpfen [1] *vt Knoten* to tie; *Band* to knot, to tie (up); *Teppich* to knot; *Netz* to mesh; *Freundschaft* to form, to strike up ◆ **jdn an den nächsten Baum/den Galgen ~** (*inf*) to hang sb from the nearest tree/the gallows, to string sb up (*inf*); **etw an etw** (*acc*) **~** (*lit*) to tie *or* knot sth to sth; (*fig*) *Bedingungen* to attach sth to sth; *Hoffnungen* to pin sth on sth; **große Erwartungen an etw** (*acc*) **~** to have great expectations of sth; **Freundschaftsbande enger ~** to strengthen *or* tighten the bonds of friendship; **Bande der Freundschaft ~ ihn an diese Schule** he is attached *or* linked to the school by bonds *or* ties of friendship; *siehe* **Band²**.
[2] *vr* **sich an etw** (*acc*) **~** to be linked to *or* connected with sth; **an diese Bemerkung knüpften sich einige Fragen** this remark raised several questions; **an diese Erfindung ~ sich viele technische Möglichkeiten** this discovery has many technical possibilities.

Knüppel *m* **-s,** - **(a)** stick; (*Waffe*) cudgel, club; (*Polizei~*) truncheon; (*Metal*) billet ◆ **Politik des großen ~s** big stick policy; **man sollte mit dem ~ dreinschlagen** (*fig*) someone ought to get tough *or* to wave the big stick; **jdm (einen) ~ zwischen die Beine werfen** (*fig*) to put a spoke in sb's wheel.
(b) (*Aviat*) control stick, joystick; (*Aut*) gear stick.
(c) (*dial: Brötchen*) ≃ crusty bridge roll.

Knüppel-: ~damm *m* log road; **k~dick** (*inf*) [1] *adj Steak, Schicht* very thick, good and thick *pred*; **er schmiert sich die Butter k~dick aufs Brot** he puts lashings of butter on his bread; [2] *adv* **wenn's kommt, kommt's immer gleich k~dick** it never rains but it pours (*prov*); **bei dem kam es ja wirklich k~dick** he had one problem after another; **k~dick(e) voll sein** (*Straßenbahn, Koffer etc*) to be jam-packed, to be packed solid; (*sl: betrunken*) to be absolutely plastered (*sl*); **k~hart** *adj* (*inf*) rock-hard.

knüppeln [1] *vi* to use one's truncheon; (*Sport sl*) to hack, to kick wildly.
[2] *vt* to club, to beat with a club *or* stick; (*Polizei*) to use one's truncheon on, to beat with one's truncheon.

Knüppel-: ~schaltung *f* (*Aut*) floor-mounted gear change; **k~voll** *adj* (*inf*) jam-packed, packed solid.

knurren [1] *vi* (*Hund etc*) to growl; (*wütend*) to snarl; (*Magen*) to rumble; (*fig: sich beklagen*) to moan, to groan (*über* +*acc* about).
[2] *vti* (*mürrisch sagen*) to growl.

Knurren *nt* **-s,** *no pl siehe vi* growl(ing); snarl(ing); rumble, rumbling; moan(ing).

Knurrhahn *m* gurnard.

knurrig *adj* grumpy; *Angestellte etc* disgruntled.

Knusperhäuschen *nt* gingerbread house.

knusperig *adj siehe* **knusprig.**

knuspern *vti* to crunch ◆ **etwas zum K~** something to nibble; **an etw** (*dat*) **~** to crunch away at sth.

knusprig *adj Braten* crisp; *Gebäck auch* crunchy; *Brötchen auch* crusty; (*fig*) *Mädchen* scrumptious (*inf*).

Knust *m* **-(e)s, -e** *or* **¨-e** (*N Ger*) (end) crust, heel.

Knute *f* **-, -n** (*old*) knout (*old*), lash ◆ **jds ~ zu spüren bekommen** to feel sb's lash; **unter jds ~** (*dat*) **stehen** to be completely dominated by sb; **jdn unter seine ~ bringen** to get sb in one's clutches.

knutschen (*inf*) [1] *vt* to pet *or* smooch (*inf*) *or* neck (*inf*) with.
[2] *vir* to pet, to smooch (*inf*), to neck (*inf*).

Knutscherei *f* petting, smooching (*inf*), necking (*inf*).

Knutschfleck *m* (*inf*) love bite (*inf*).

Knüttel *m* **-s,** - *siehe* **Knüppel.**

Knüttelvers *m siehe* **Knittelvers.**

k. o. [ka:'|o:] *adj pred* (*Sport*) knocked out; (*fig inf*) whacked (*inf*), all in (*inf*) ◆ **jdn ~ schlagen** to knock sb out.

K. o. [ka:'|o:] *m* **-(s), -s** knockout, K.O ◆ **Sieg durch ~** victory by a knockout.

ko|agulieren* *vti* (*Med, Chem*) to coagulate, to clot.

Koala *m* **-s, -s, Koalabär** *m* koala (bear).

ko|alieren* *vi* (*esp Pol*) to form a coalition (*mit* with).

Ko|alition *f* (*esp Pol*) coalition ◆ **kleine/große ~** little/grand coalition.

Koalitionär *m* (*Pol: Abgeordneter*) coalition member; (*Partei*) coalition party.

Ko|alitions- *in cpds* coalition; **~absprache** *f* coalition agreement; **~aussage** *f* statement of willingness to form a coalition; **k~fähig** *adj* **k~fähig sein** to be suitable as a coalition partner; **~fähigkeit** *f* suitability as a coalition partner; **~freiheit** *f* freedom to form a coalition; **~gespräch** *nt* coalition talks *pl*; **~krieg** *m* (*Hist*) coalition war; **~partner** *m* coalition partner; **~recht** *nt* right of combination; **~regierung** *f* coalition government.

ko|axial *adj* (*Tech*) co-axial.

Kobalt *nt* **-s,** *no pl* (*abbr* **Co**) cobalt.

kobaltblau *adj* cobalt blue.

Kobel *m* **-s,** - (*S Ger, Aus*), **Koben** *m* **-s,** - **(a)** *siehe* **Schuppen. (b)** *siehe* **Stall.**

Kobold *m* **-(e)s, -e** goblin, imp.

Kobolz *m*: **~ schießen** to turn *or* do somersaults.

Kobra *f* **-, -s** cobra.

Koch *m* **-s, ¨-e, Köchin** *f* **(a)** cook; (*von Restaurant etc auch*) chef ◆ **viele ¨-e verderben den Brei** (*Prov*) too many cooks spoil the broth (*Prov*). **(b)** (*Aus: Brei*) (*Apfel~ etc*) purée; (*Gries~ etc*) pudding.

Koch-: ~apfel *m* cooking apple, cooker; **k~bar** *adj* suitable for boiling, that may be boiled; **~buch** *nt* cookery book, cookbook; **k~echt** *adj* (*Tex*) *Farbe* fast at 100°, fast even in boiling water; *Wäsche etc* suitable for boiling, that may be boiled; **~ecke** *f* kitchen *or* cooking area.

Köchelverzeichnis *nt* (*Mus*) Köchel index ◆ **~ 25** Köchel *or* K. (number) 25.

kochen [1] *vi* **(a)** (*Flüssigkeit, Speise*) to boil ◆ **etw langsam** *or* **auf kleiner Flamme ~ lassen** to let sth simmer *or* to simmer sth (over a low heat); **etw zum K~ bringen** to bring sth to the boil; **jdn zum K~ bringen** (*fig inf*) to make sb's blood boil; **der Kühler/das Auto kocht** (*inf*) the cooling system/car is overheating; **er kochte vor Wut** (*inf*) he was boiling *or* seething with rage.
(b) (*Speisen zubereiten*) to cook; (*als Koch fungieren*) to do the cooking; (*als Koch arbeiten*) to work as a cook/chef ◆ **er kocht gut** he's a good cook, he is good at cooking; **er kocht scharf/pikant** his cooking is (always) highly seasoned/spiced.
[2] *vt* **(a)** *Flüssigkeit, Nahrungsmittel, Wäsche* to boil ◆ **etw langsam** *or* **auf kleiner Flamme ~** to simmer sth over a low heat.
(b) (*zubereiten*) *Essen* to cook; *Kakao* to make; (*aufgießen*) *Kaffee, Tee* to make, to brew ◆ **etw gar/weich ~** to cook sth through/until (it is) soft; **Eier weich/hart ~** to soft-boil/hard-boil eggs.
[3] *vi impers* (*fig*) to be boiling ◆ **es kocht in ihm** he is boiling *or* seething with rage; **im Stadion kochte es wie in einem Hexenkessel** the atmosphere in the stadium was electric.
[4] *vr* **sich gut/schlecht ~** to cook/not to cook well.

kochend *adj* (*lit, fig*) boiling; (*liter*) *See* raging ◆ **~ heiß sein** to be boiling hot; (*Suppe etc*) to be piping hot.

⚠ **kochendheiß** *adj attr* boiling hot; *Suppe etc* piping hot.

Kocher *m* **-s,** - (*Herd*) cooker, stove; (*Camping~*) (primus) stove; (*Kochplatte*) hotplate; (*Wasser~*) ≃ (electric) kettle.

Köcher *m* **-s,** - (*für Pfeile*) quiver; (*für Golfschläger*) golf bag; (*für Kameraobjektiv etc*) case.

Kocherei *f* (*inf*) cooking.

Koch-: ~feld *nt* ceramic hob; **k~fertig** *adj* ready-to-cook *attr*, ready to cook *pred*; **k~fest** *adj* (*Tex*) *siehe* **kochecht**; **~fleisch** *nt* stewing *or* braising meat; **~gelegenheit** *f* cooking facilities *pl*; **~geschirr** *nt* (*esp Mil*) billy(can), mess tin (*Mil*); **~herd** *m siehe* **Herd.**

Köchin *f siehe* **Koch.**

Koch-: ~käse *m* (*type of*) soft cheese; **~kunst** *f* culinary art, art of cooking; **seine ~kunst** *or* **~künste** his cooking (ability); **~künstler** *m* cookery expert, expert cook; **~kurs(us)** *m* cookery course; **~löffel** *m* cooking spoon; **~nische** *f* kitchenette; **~platte** *f* **(a)** (*Herdplatte*) hotplate; **(b)** (*Kocher*) cooker; **~rezept** *nt* recipe; **~salz** *nt* common salt; (*Chem auch*) sodium chloride; (*Cook*) cooking salt; **~salzinfusion** *f* (*Med*) saline infusion; **~schinken** *m* boiled ham; **~topf** *m* (cooking) pot; (*mit Stiel*) saucepan; **~wäsche** *f* washing that can be boiled; **~wasser** *nt* cooking water, water in which (the) vegetables have been boiled; **~zeit** *f* cooking time.

kodd(e)rig *adj* (*N Ger inf*) **(a)** (*unwohl*) sick, queasy ◆ **mir ist ganz ~** I feel sick *or* queasy.
(b) (*frech*) insolent, impudent.

Kode [ko:t, 'ko:də] *m* **-s, -s** code.

Kodein *nt* **-s,** *no pl* codeine.

Köder *m* **-s,** - bait; (*fig auch*) lure.

Köderfisch *m* bait fish.

ködern *vt* (*lit*) to lure; (*fig*) to tempt, to entice ◆ **er will dich mit diesen Versprechungen nur ~** these promises of his are only a bait (to lure you); **jdn zu ~ versuchen** to woo sb; **jdn für etw ~** to rope sb into sth (*inf*); **sich von jdm/etw nicht ~ lassen** not to be tempted by sb/sth.

Kodex *m* - *or* **-es, -e** *or* **Kodices** *or* **Kodizes** (*Gesetzbuch*) codex, code; (*Handschrift*) codex, manuscript; (*fig*) (moral) code.

kodieren* *vt* to (en)code.

Kodifikation *f* codification.

kodifizieren* *vt* to codify; (*fig geh*) to write down ◆ **kodifiziertes Recht** codified *or* statute law.

Ko|edukation *f* co-education.

⚠: for details of spelling reform, see supplement

Ko|effizient *m* coefficient.
Ko|existenz *f* coexistence.
Kofel *m* **-s, -** (*Aus, S Ger*) rounded *or* dome-shaped mountain top.
Koffein *nt* **-s,** *no pl* caffeine.
koffeinfrei *adj* decaffeinated.
Koffer *m* **-s, - (a)** (suit)case, bag; (*Übersee~, Schrank~*) trunk; (*Arzt~*) bag; (*für Schreibmaschine, Kosmetika etc*) (carrying) case ◆ **die ~** *pl* (*Gepäck*) the luggage *or* baggage *or* bags *pl*; **die ~ packen** (*lit, fig*) to pack one's bags; **aus dem ~ leben** to live out of a suitcase.
(b) (*Mil sl*) heavy shell.
Koffer|anhänger *m* luggage label *or* tag.
Köfferchen *nt dim of* **Koffer.**
Koffer-: ~gerät *nt* portable (set); **~kuli** *m* (luggage) trolley (*Brit*), cart (*US*); **~radio** *nt* portable radio; **~raum** *m* (*Aut*) boot (*Brit*), trunk (*US*); (*Volumen*) luggage space; **~schreibmaschine** *f* portable (typewriter); **~träger** *m* porter.
Kogel *m* **-s, -** (*Aus, S Ger*) *siehe* **Kofel.**
Kogge *f* **-, -n** (*Naut*) cog.
Kognak ['kɔnjak] *m* **-s, -s** *or* **-e** brandy.
Kognakschwenker *m* **-s, -** brandy glass, balloon glass.
kognitiv *adj* (*Philos, Psych*) cognitive.
Kohabitation *f* (*form*) cohabitation.
Kohäsion *f* (*Phys, geh*) cohesion.
Kohl *m* **-(e)s, -e (a)** cabbage ◆ **das macht den ~ auch nicht fett** (*inf*) that's not much help. **(b)** (*inf: Unsinn*) rubbish, nonsense ◆ **aufgewärmter ~** old stuff *or* story.
Kohldampf *m, no pl* (*inf*) **~ haben** *or* **schieben** to be starving *or* famished.
Kohle *f* **-, -n (a)** (*Brennstoff*) coal; (*Stück ~*) (lump of) coal; (*dial: Brikett*) briquette ◆ **wir haben keine ~n mehr** we have no coal left; **weiße ~** white coal, water power, hydroelectric power; **glühende ~n** (*lit*) (glowing) embers; **glühende** *or* **feurige ~n auf jds Haupt sammeln** (*geh*) to heap coals of fire on sb's head; **(wie) auf (glühenden** *or* **heißen) ~n sitzen** to be like a cat on hot bricks, to be on tenterhooks.
(b) (*Verkohltes, Holz~*) charcoal ◆ **(tierische** *or* **medizinische) ~** animal charcoal.
(c) (*Art: ~stift*) (stick of) charcoal ◆ **mit ~ zeichnen** to draw with *or* in charcoal.
(d) (*Tech*) carbon.
(e) (*inf: Geld*) dough (*inf*), cash (*inf*) ◆ **die ~n stimmen** the money's right.
Kohle-: ~filter *m* charcoal filter; **~hydrat** *nt* carbohydrate; **~hydrierung** *f* (*Tech*) hydrogenation of coal; **~kraftwerk** *nt* coal-fired power station.
kohlen¹ *vi* **(a)** (*Naut, Rail*) to take on coal. **(b)** (*verkohlen*) to char, to carbonize. **(c)** (*Ruß erzeugen*) to smoke.
kohlen² *vti* (*inf*) to talk a load of nonsense *or* rubbish (*inf*); (*lügen*) to lie, to tell lies ◆ **unglaublich, was der wieder kohlt** it's incredible the nonsense he's been talking again/the lies he's been telling again.
Kohlen- *in cpds* coal; **≈bergbau** *m* coal-mining; **≈bergwerk** *nt* coalmine, pit, colliery; **≈bunker** *m* coalbunker; **≈dioxyd** *nt* carbon dioxide; **≈gas** *nt* coal gas; **≈gebiet** *nt* coal-mining area; **≈grube** *f* coalmine, pit; **≈grus** *m* (coal) slack; **≈halde** *f* pile of coal; **≈halden** *pl* coal stocks *pl*; **≈heizung** *f* coal heating; (*Anlage*) coal heating system; **≈herd** *m* range; **≈hydrat** *nt siehe* **Kohlehydrat**; **≈industrie** *f* coal industry; **≈kasten** *m* coal-box; **≈keller** *m* coal cellar; **≈lager** *nt* **(a)** (*Vorrat*) coal depot; **(b)** (*im Stollen, Berg*) coal seam *or* bed; **~monoxyd** *nt* carbon monoxide; **≈ofen** *m* (coal-burning) stove; **≈pott** *m* (*inf*) **(a)** coal-mining area; **(b)** (*Ruhrgebiet*) *siehe* **Ruhrpott**; **≈revier** *nt siehe* **~gebiet**; **≈sack** *m* coalsack; **k≈sauer** *adj* **k~saurer Kalk/k~saures Natrium** calcium/sodium carbonate; **≈säure** *f* **(a)** (*Chem*) carbonic acid; **(b)** (*inf: in Getränken*) fizz (*inf*); **k≈säurehaltig** *adj Getränke* carbonated; **≈schaufel** *f* coal shovel; **≈staub** *m* coaldust; **≈staublunge** *f* anthracosis; **≈stoff** *m* (*abbr* **C**) carbon; **≈stoff-Datierung** *f* (radio)carbon dating; **≈trimmer** *m* **-s, -** (coal) trimmer; **≈wagen** *m* **(a)** (*Rail: Tender*) tender; (*Waggon*) coal truck; **(b)** (*LKW*) coal lorry (*Brit*) *or* truck; **≈wasserstoff** *m* hydrocarbon; **≈zange** *f* (pair of) fire *or* coal tongs; **≈zeche** *f siehe* **~bergwerk.**
Kohlepapier *nt* carbon paper.
Köhler *m* **-s, -** charcoal burner.
Köhlerei *f* charcoal burning.
Kohle-: ~stab *m* (*Tech*) carbon rod; **~stift** *m* (*Art*) piece *or* stick of charcoal; **~tablette** *f* (*Med*) charcoal tablet; **~zeichnung** *f* charcoal drawing.
Kohl-: ≈kopf *m* cabbage; **≈meise** *f* great tit; **k≈(pech)rabenschwarz** *adj* **(a)** *Haar* jet black, raven *attr*, raven-black; *Nacht* pitch-black; **(b)** (*inf: sehr schmutzig*) as black as coal; **~rabi** *m* **-(s), -(s)** kohlrabi; **≈rübe** *f* **(a)** *siehe* **Steckrübe**; **(b)** (*inf: Kopf*) bonce (*sl*), nut (*inf*); **≈salat** *m* coleslaw; **k≈schwarz** *adj Haare, Augen* jet black; *Gesicht, Hände* black as coal; **≈sprosse** *f* (*Aus*) (Brussels) sprout; **≈weißling** *m* cabbage white (butterfly).
Kohorte *f* **-, -n** (*Hist*) cohort.
koitieren* [koi'tiːrən] *vi* (*esp Med*) to engage in coitus *or* sexual intercourse.
Koitus ['koːitʊs] *m* **-, -** *or* **-se** (*esp Med*) coitus, coition.
Koje *f* **-, -n (a)** (*esp Naut*) bunk, berth; (*inf: Bett*) bed ◆ **sich in die ~ hauen** (*inf*) to hit the sack (*inf*) *or* the hay (*inf*). **(b)** (*Ausstellungs~*) stand.
Kojote *m* **-n, -n** coyote.
Koka *f* **-, -** (*Bot*) coca.
Kokain *nt* **-s,** *no pl* cocaine.
kokainsüchtig *adj* addicted to cocaine ◆ **ein K~er** a cocaine addict.
Kokarde *f* **-, -n** cockade.
kokeln *vi* (*inf*) to play with fire ◆ **mit Kerzen/Streichhölzern ~** to play with (lighted) candles/matches.
Kokerei *f* (*Tätigkeit*) coking; (*Anlage*) coking plant.
kokett *adj* coquettish, flirtatious.
Koketterie *f* **(a)** *no pl* (*Eigenschaft*) coquettishness, coquetry, flirtatiousness. **(b)** (*Bemerkung*) coquettish *or* flirtatious remark, coquetry.
kokettieren* *vi* to flirt ◆ **mit seinem Alter ~** to play up *or* upon one's age; **mit einem Gedanken/System** *etc* **~** to toy with an idea/method *etc.*
Kokolores, Kokolorus *m* **-,** *no pl* (*inf*) **(a)** (*Unsinn*) rubbish, nonsense, twaddle (*inf*). **(b)** (*Umstände*) palaver (*inf*), fuss ◆ **mach doch nicht solchen ~** don't make such a palaver *or* fuss.
Kokon [ko'kõː] *m* **-s, -s** (*Zool*) cocoon.
Kokos¹ *f* **-, -** *siehe* **Kokospalme.**
Kokos² *nt* **-,** *no pl* coconut.
Kokos- *in cpds* coconut; **~fett** *nt* coconut oil; **~flocken** *pl* desiccated coconut; **~läufer** *m* coconut matting; **~milch** *f* coconut milk; ⚠**~nuß** *f* coconut; **~öl** *nt* coconut oil; **~palme** *f* coconut palm *or* tree; **~raspeln** *pl* desiccated coconut.
Kokotte *f* **-, -n** (*old*) cocotte.
Koks¹ *m* **-es, -e** coke; (*inf: Unsinn*) rubbish, nonsense; (*Geld*) dough (*inf*), cash (*inf*).
Koks² *m or nt* **-es,** *no pl* (*sl: Kokain*) coke (*sl*).
koksen *vi* (*sl: Kokain nehmen*) to take coke (*sl*).
Kokser(in *f*) *m* **-s, -** (*sl*) cocaine *or* coke (*sl*) addict.
Kola¹ *f* **-,** *no pl siehe* **Kolanuß.**
Kola² *pl of* **Kolon.**
Kola-: ~baum *m* cola *or* kola tree; ⚠**~nuß** *f* cola *or* kola nut.
Kolben *m* **-s, - (a)** (*dickes Ende, Gewehr~*) butt; (*Tech: Motor~, Pumpen~*) piston; (*Chem: Destillier~*) retort; (*von Glühlampe*) bulb; (*von Lötapparat*) bit; (*inf: Nase*) conk (*Brit inf*), hooter (*Brit inf*), beak (*inf*); (*sl: Penis*) prick (*vulg*), cock (*vulg*), tool (*sl*). **(b)** (*Bot*) spadix; (*Mais~*) cob.
Kolben-: k~förmig *adj* club-shaped; **etw verdickt sich k~förmig** sth widens into a club shape; **~fresser** *m* **-s, -** (*inf*) piston seizure; **(den) ~fresser haben** to have piston seizure; **~halter** *m* plunger refill (fountain) pen; **~hub** *m* (*von Pumpe*) plunger stroke; (*Aut*) piston stroke; **~ring** *m* piston ring.
Kolchos *m or nt* **-, Kolchose, Kolchose** *f* **-, -n** collective farm, kolkhoz.
Kolchosbauer *m* worker on a collective farm.
Kolibakterien *pl* E. coli *pl.*
Kolibri *m* **-s, -s** humming bird, colibri (*spec*).
Kolik *f* **-, -en** colic.
kolik|artig *adj* colicky.
Kolkrabe *m* raven.
kollabieren* *vi aux sein* (*Med*) to collapse.
Kollaborateur(in *f*) [-'tøːɐ, -'tøːrɪn] *m* (*Pol*) collaborator.
Kollaboration *f* collaboration.
kollaborieren* *vi* to collaborate.
Kollage [kɔ'laːʒə] *f* **-, -n** *siehe* **Collage.**
Kollaps *m* **-es, -e** (*Med*) collapse ◆ **einen ~ erleiden** to collapse.
Kollation *f* (*Liter*) collation, comparison; (*Typ*) collation.
kollationieren* [kɔlatsio'niːrən] *vt* (*Liter*) to collate, to compare; (*Typ*) to collate.
Kolleg *nt* **-s, -s** *or* **-ien** [-iən] **(a)** (*Univ: Vorlesung*) lecture; (*Vorlesungsreihe*) (course of) lectures. **(b)** (*Sch*) college. **(c)** (*Eccl*) theological college.
Kollege *m* **-n, -n, Kollegin** *f* colleague; (*Arbeiter auch*) workmate ◆ **seine ~n vom Fach** his professional colleagues, his fellow doctors/teachers *etc*; **meine ~n** the people I work with, my colleagues; **seine ~n in der Ärzteschaft** his fellow doctors; **~ kommt gleich!** somebody will be with you right away; **Herr ~!** Mr X/Y; **der (Herr) ~ (Müller)** (*Pol*) the honourable member.
Kollegen-: ~rabatt *m* trade discount; **~schaft** *f* colleagues *pl.*
Kolleg-: ~geld *nt* lecture fee; **~heft** *nt* (student's) notebook.
kollegial *adj* cooperative ◆ **das war nicht sehr ~ von ihm** that wasn't what you would expect from a colleague; **mit ~en Grüßen** ≃ yours sincerely; **sich ~ verhalten** to act like a good colleague.
Kollegialität *f* cooperativeness.
Kollegin *siehe* **Kollege.**
Kollegium *nt* **(a)** (*Lehrer~ etc*) staff; (*Ausschuß*) working party. **(b)** *siehe* **Kolleg.**
Kollegmappe *f* document case.
Kollekte *f* **-, -n** (*Eccl*) offering, collection, offertory.
Kollektion *f* collection; (*Sortiment*) range; (*Fashion*) collection ◆ **~ (an Mustern)** (set of) samples.
kollektiv *adj* collective.
Kollektiv *nt* collective.
Kollektiv-: ~arbeit *f* (*Tätigkeit*) collective work, collaboration; (*Ergebnis*) collective piece of work; **~begriff** *m* (*Ling*) collective (term); **~geist** *m* corporate *or* collective spirit.
kollektivieren* [-'viːrən] *vt* to collectivize.
Kollektivismus [-'vɪsmʊs] *m, no pl* collectivism.
Kollektivist(in *f*) [-'vɪst(ɪn)] *m* collectivist.
Kollektiv-: ~schuld *f* collective guilt; **~strafe** *f* collective punishment.
Kollektivum [-'tiːvʊm] *nt* **-s, Kollektiva** [-'tiːva] *or* **Kollektiven** [-'tiːvən] (*Ling*) collective (noun).
Kollektiv-: ~vertrag *m* collective agreement; (*DDR Econ*) house agreement; (*Pol*) multilateral treaty; **~wirtschaft** *f* (*Econ*) collective economy.

⚠: Informationen zur Rechtschreibreform im Anhang

Kollektor *m (Elec)* collector; *(Sonnen~)* solar collector *or* panel.
Koller *m* **-s, -** **(a)** *(inf) (Anfall)* silly *or* funny mood; *(Wutanfall)* rage; *(Tropen~, Gefängnis~)* tropical/prison madness ◆ **seinen ~ bekommen/haben** to get into/to be in one of one's silly *or* funny moods; **einen ~ haben/bekommen** to be in/fly into a rage.
(b) *(Vet: bei Pferden)* staggers *sing.*
kollern [1] *vi* **(a)** *(Truthahn etc)* to gobble; *(Magen, Darm)* to rumble. **(b)** *aux sein (dial) siehe* **kullern.**
[2] *vi impers* **es kollert in seinem Bauch** his stomach is rumbling.
kollidieren* *vi (geh)* **(a)** *aux sein (Fahrzeuge)* to collide, to be in collision. **(b)** *aux sein or haben (fig)* to conflict, to be in conflict, to clash; *(Termine)* to clash ◆ **miteinander ~** to conflict, to clash, to be in conflict (with each other); **er ist mit dem Gesetz kollidiert** he has collided with the law.
Kollier [kɔ'lie:] *nt* **-s, -s** necklet, necklace.
Kollision *f (geh) (Zusammenstoß)* collision; *(Streit)* conflict, clash; *(von Terminen)* clash ◆ **mit dem Gesetz in ~ geraten** *or* **kommen** to come into conflict with *or* to collide with the law.
Kollisionskurs *m (Naut, Aviat)* collision course ◆ **auf ~ gehen, einen ~ ansteuern** *(fig)* to be heading for trouble.
Kolloid *nt* **-s, -e** *(Chem)* colloid.
Kolloquium *nt* colloquium; *(Aus Univ: Prüfung)* examination.
Köln *nt* **-s** Cologne.
Kölner *adj attr* Cologne ◆ **der ~ Dom** Cologne Cathedral.
Kölner(in *f***)** *m* **-s, -** inhabitant *or (gebürtiger)* native of Cologne ◆ **er ist ~** he lives in/comes from Cologne.
kölnisch *adj* Cologne ◆ **er spricht K~** he speaks (the) Cologne dialect.
⚠**Kölnischwasser, Kölnisch Wasser** *nt* eau de Cologne, cologne.
Kolombine *f (Theat)* Columbine.
Kolon *nt* **-s, -s** *or* **Kola** *(Typ, Anat)* colon.
Koloniakübel *m (Aus)* dustbin *(Brit)*, trash *or* garbage can *(US)*.
kolonial *adj (rare)* colonial.
Kolonial- *in cpds* colonial; **~besitz** *m* colonial possessions *pl*; **das Land ist in ~besitz** that country is a colony.
Kolonialismus *m, no pl* colonialism.
Kolonial-: ~macht *f* colonial power; **~stil** *m* Colonial (style); **~waren** *pl* groceries *pl*; *(Erzeugnisse der Kolonien)* colonial produce; **~warenhändler** *m (dated)* grocer; **~warenhandlung** *f*, **~warengeschäft** *nt (dated)* grocer's (shop); **~zeit** *f* colonial times *pl*; **ein Relikt aus der ~zeit** a relic of the colonial past *or* of colonial times.
Koloniawagen *m (Aus)* refuse lorry *(Brit) or* truck.
Kolonie *f (alle Bedeutungen)* colony; *(Ansiedlung auch)* settlement; *(Ferien~)* camp.
Kolonisation *f siehe vt* settlement; colonization.
kolonisieren* *vt* **(a)** *(erschließen) Gebiet* to settle in. **(b)** *(zur Kolonie machen) Land* to colonize.
Kolonist(in *f***)** *m* colonist; *(Siedler)* settler.
Kolonnade *f* colonnade.
Kolonne *f* **-, -n** column; *(Autoschlange, fig: Menge)* queue *(Brit)*, line; *(zur Begleitung esp Mil)* convoy; *(Arbeits~)* gang ◆ **„Achtung ~!"** "convoy"; **~ fahren** to drive in (a) convoy.
Kolonnen-: ~fahren *nt* **-s,** *no pl* driving in (a) convoy; **~springen** *nt* jumping the (traffic) queue *(Brit) or* line; **~springer** *m* queue-jumper *(Brit)*; **~verkehr** *m* a queue/queues *(Brit) or* a line/lines of traffic, a tailback.
Kolophonium *nt, no pl* rosin, resin, colophony *(spec)*.
Koloratur *f* coloratura.
kolorieren* *vt* to colour.
Kolorit *nt* **-(e)s, -e** *(Art)* colouring; *(Mus)* (tone) colour; *(Liter, fig)* atmosphere, colour.
⚠**Koloß** *m* **-sses, -sse** colossus; *(fig auch)* giant ◆ **der ~ von Rhodos** the Colossus of Rhodes.
kolossal [1] *adj* colossal, tremendous, enormous; *(inf) Dummheit auch* crass *attr.*
[2] *adv (inf)* tremendously, enormously ◆ **sich ~ verschätzen** to make a colossal mistake.
Kolossal-: ~film *m* epic film, (film) epic; **~gemälde** *nt (inf)* spectacular painting; **~schinken** *m (pej geh)* spectacular.
Kolosser(in *f***)** *m* **-s, -** **(a)** *(Hist)* Colossian. **(b)** *(Bibl) siehe* **Kolosserbrief.**
Kolosserbrief *m* Epistle to the Colossians, Colossians *sing, no def art.*
Kolosseum *nt* **-s,** *no pl* **das ~** the Colosseum.
Kolportage [kɔlpɔr'ta:ʒə] *f* **-, -n** **(a)** *(Press)* cheap sensationalism. **(b)** *(minderwertige Literatur)* trash, rubbish. **(c)** *(old: Wandergewerbe)* peddling.
Kolportage-: ~literatur *f* trashy literature; **~roman** *m* trashy novel.
kolportieren* *vt* **(a)** *Nachricht* to spread, to circulate; *Gerüchte auch* to peddle ◆ **die Zeitung kolportierte, daß ...** the paper spread the story that ... **(b)** *(old) Bücher etc* to peddle.
kölsch *adj siehe* **kölnisch.**
Kölsch *nt* **-, -** *(Bier)* ≃ (strong) lager.
Kolumbianer(in *f***)** *m* **-s, -** Colombian.
kolumbianisch *adj* Colombian.
Kolumbien [-iən] *nt* **-s** Colombia.
Kolumbier(in *f***)** [-iɐ, -iərɪn] *m* **-s, -** Colombian.
Kolumbine *f (Theat)* Columbine.
kolumbisch *adj* Colombian.
Kolumbus *m* **-** **Christoph ~** Christopher Columbus; *siehe* **Ei.**
Kolumne *f* **-, -n** *(Typ, Press)* column.

Kolumnentitel *m (Typ)* headline, running head ◆ **toter ~** folio, page number; **lebender ~** running head.
Kolumnist(in *f***)** *m* columnist.
Koma *nt* **-s, -s** *or* **-ta** *(Med)* coma.
Kombattant(in *f***)** *m (geh)* combatant.
Kombi *m* **-s, -s** *(Aut)* estate (car) *(Brit)*, station wagon *(esp US)*.
Kombikarte *f (Fahr-/Eintrittskarte)* combination ticket *(for travel and admission)*.
Kombinat *nt (Econ)* combine.
Kombination *f* **(a)** *(Verbindung, Zusammenstellung, Zahlen~)* combination; *(Sport: Zusammenspiel)* concerted move, (piece of) teamwork ◆ **alpine/nordische ~** *(Ski)* Alpine/Nordic combination.
(b) *(Schlußfolgerung)* deduction, reasoning; *(Vermutung)* conjecture.
(c) *(Kleidung)* suit, ensemble; *(Hemdhose)* combinations *pl*, combs *pl (inf)*; *(Arbeitsanzug)* overalls *pl*, boilersuit; *(Flieger~)* flying suit.
Kombinations-: ~gabe *f* powers of deduction *or* reasoning; ⚠**~schloß** *nt* combination lock.
Kombinatorik *f (Math)* combination theory, theory of combinations.
kombinatorisch *adj* **(a)** *Fähigkeiten* deductive; *Problem, Logik* combinatory. **(b)** *(Ling)* **~er Lautwandel** conditioned sound change.
kombinieren* [1] *vt* to combine; *Kleidungsstücke auch* to wear together ◆ **Möbel zum K~** unit furniture; **zum beliebigen K~** to mix and match.
[2] *vi* **(a)** *(folgern)* to deduce; *(vermuten)* to suppose ◆ **gut ~ können** to be good at deducing *or* deduction; **ich kombiniere: ...** I conclude: ...; **du hast richtig kombiniert** your conclusion is/was right, you have come to the right conclusion.
(b) *(Sport)* to make a concerted move.
Kombi-: ~wagen *m* estate (car) *(Brit)*, station wagon *(esp US)*; **~zange** *f* combination pliers *pl.*
Kombüse *f* **-, -n** *(Naut)* galley.
Komet *m* **-en, -en** comet; *(fig)* meteor.
kometen-: ~artig *adj* **(a)** *(Astron)* comet-like; **(b)** *(fig) siehe* **~haft**; **~haft** *adj (fig) Aufstieg, Karriere* meteoric; *Aufschwung* rapid.
Komfort [kɔm'fo:ɐ] *m* **-s,** *no pl (von Hotel etc)* luxury; *(von Möbel etc)* comfort; *(von Auto)* luxury features *pl*; *(von Gerät)* extras *pl*; *(von Wohnung)* amenities *pl*, mod cons *pl (inf)* ◆ **ein Auto mit allem ~** a luxury car, a car with many luxury features.
-komfort *m in cpds* comfort ◆ **Fahr~** (motoring) comfort; **ein Fernsehgerät mit großem Bedienungs~** a television set with easy-to-use controls.
komfortabel *adj (mit Komfort ausgestattet)* luxurious, luxury *attr*; *Haus, Wohnung* well-appointed; *(bequem) Sessel, Bett* comfortable; *(praktisch) Bedienung* convenient.
Komfortwohnung [kɔm'fo:ɐ-] *f* luxury flat.
Komik *f* **-,** *no pl (das Komische)* comic; *(komische Wirkung)* comic effect; *(lustiges Element: von Situation)* comic element ◆ **tragische ~** tragi-comedy; **ein Sinn für ~** a sense of the comic.
Komiker *m* **-s, -** comedian, comic; *(fig auch)* joker *(inf)* ◆ **Sie ~** you must be joking.
Kominform *nt* **-s,** *no pl (Hist)* **das ~** the Cominform.
Komintern *f* **-,** *no pl (Hist)* **die ~** the Comintern.
komisch *adj* **(a)** *(spaßhaft, ulkig)* funny, comical; *(Theat) Rolle, Person, Oper* comic ◆ **der ~e Alte** *(Theat)* the comic old man; **das K~e** *(Liter)* the comic; **das K~e daran** the funny thing about it.
(b) *(seltsam, verdächtig)* funny, strange, odd ◆ **das K~e daran ist ...** the funny *or* strange *or* odd thing about it is ...; **~, ich hab' schon wieder Hunger** funny, I'm hungry again already; **~, daß ich das übersehen habe** it's funny *or* odd that I should have missed that; **mir ist/wird so ~** *(inf)* I feel funny *or* strange *or* odd; **er war so ~ zu mir** he acted so strangely towards me.
komischerweise *adv* funnily enough.
Komitee *nt* **-s, -s** committee.
Komma *nt* **-s, -s** *or* **-ta** comma; *(Math)* decimal point ◆ **fünf/null ~ drei** five/nought point three.
Kommandant *m (Mil)* commanding officer; *(Naut)* captain; *(von Festung auch)* commander; *(von Stadt)* commandant.
Kommandantur *f (Funktion)* command; *(Gebäude auch)* headquarters *sing.*
Kommandeur [kɔman'dø:ɐ] *m* commander.
kommandieren* [1] *vt* **(a)** *(befehligen)* to command, to be in command of. **(b)** *(befehlen)* **jdn an einen Ort/zu sich ~** to order sb to a place/to appear.
[2] *vi* **(a)** *(Befehlsgewalt haben)* to be in command ◆ **~der General** commanding general.
(b) *(Befehle geben)* to command, to give (the) orders ◆ **er kommandiert gern** he likes to be the one to give (the) orders, he likes ordering people about.
Kommanditgesellschaft *f (Comm)* limited partnership.
Kommanditist(in *f***)** *m* **-en, -en** limited partner.
Kommando *nt* **-s, -s** **(a)** *(Befehl)* command, order ◆ **das ~ zum Schießen geben** to give the command *or* order to fire; **auf ~ schreit ihr alle ...** (up)on the command (you) all shout ...; **ich mache nichts auf ~** I don't do things to order *or* on command; **wie auf ~ stehenbleiben** to stand still as if by command; **der Hund gehorcht auf ~** the dog obeys on command.
(b) *(Befehlsgewalt)* command ◆ **wer hat das ~?** who is in command?; **das ~ haben** *or* **führen/übernehmen** to be in *or* have/take command *(über +acc* of).
(c) *(Mil) (Behörde)* command; *(Abteilung)* commando.
Kommando-: ~brücke *f (Naut)* bridge; **~kapsel** *f (Space)* command module; **~raum** *m* control room; **~stab** *m* command (staff); **~stand, ~turm** *m (Naut)* conning tower; **~unternehmen** *nt* commando opera-

⚠: for details of spelling reform, see supplement

tion; **~wirtschaft** *f* controlled economy.

kommen *pret* **kam**, *ptp* **gekommen** *aux sein* [1] *vi* **(a)** to come; (*ankommen auch, geboren werden*) to arrive; (*herkommen*) to come over; (*in Gang ~: Motor, Feuer*) to start; (*sl: einen Orgasmus haben*) to come (*sl*); (*Telec: sich melden*) to come in ♦ **ich komme (schon)** I'm (just) coming; **ich habe zwei Stunden gewartet, aber sie kam und kam nicht** I waited two hours but she just didn't come; **er wird gleich ~** he'll be here right away; **die Bedienung/der Nachtisch kommt gleich** we'll be served/the dessert is coming straight away; **da kommt er ja!** here he comes; **wann soll der Zug/das Baby ~?** when is the train/baby due?; **das Kind ist gestern nacht gekommen** the baby arrived last night; **bei Schmidts kommt ein Baby** the Schmidts are having *or* expecting a baby; **da kann** *or* **könnte ja jeder ~ und sagen ...** anybody *or* any Tom, Dick or Harry (*inf*) could come and say ...; **Torwart zu sein ist langweilig, wenn nie ein Ball kommt** it is boring to be a goalkeeper if the ball never comes your way; **mein Mann kommt alle drei Wochen** my husband comes home every three weeks; **nach Hause ~** to come *or* get home; **von der Arbeit ~** to come *or* get home from work; **zum Essen ~** to come home for lunch/dinner *etc*; **der Wagen kommt in 16 sec. auf 100 km/h** the car reaches 100 km/h in 16 sec.

(b) (*auffordernd*) to come on *or* along ♦ **komm, wir gehen/sag schon** come on *or* along, we're going/tell me; **komm, sei nicht so stur** come on *or* now, don't be so obstinate; **ach komm!** come on!; **komm, fang bloß nicht wieder damit an** come on, don't start that again; **komm, komm** (*beschwichtigend, zweifelnd*) come, come!; (*ermahnend*) come on; **komm, komm, wir müssen uns beeilen!** come on, we must hurry; **komm, komm, werd nicht frech!** now now, don't be cheeky.

(c) (*Reihenfolge*) to come ♦ **das Schlimmste kommt noch** the worst is yet to come; **warte, das kommt noch** wait, it's coming (later); **ich komme zuerst an die Reihe** I'm first, it's my turn first; **jetzt kommt's** here it comes, wait for it! (*inf*); **das Zitat/Lied kommt gleich/erst später** that line/song should be coming up soon/doesn't come till later; **das Lied kommt als nächstes** that song is next.

(d) (*erscheinen, auftauchen*) to come out; (*Zähne*) to come (through) ♦ **bohren, bis Öl/Grundwasser kommt** to bore until one strikes oil/finds water; **paß auf, ob hier eine Tankstelle kommt** watch out and see if there's a filling station; **jetzt muß bald die Grenze/Hannover ~** we should soon be at the border/in Hanover; **die Kreuzung/das Zitat muß noch ~** we haven't got *or* come to the crossing/that line yet; **wie sie (gerade) ~** just as they come.

(e) (*stattfinden, eintreten*) (*Gewitter, Abend, Antwort, Reue*) to come; (*Zwischenfall*) to occur; (*Not*) to arise; (*TV, Rad, Theat etc: gegeben werden*) to be on ♦ **der Mai ist gekommen** May is here *or* has come; **der Winter kommt mit großen Schritten** winter is rapidly *or* fast approaching; **ich glaube, es kommt ein Unwetter** I think there's some bad weather on the way; **was kommt diese Woche im Kino/Theater?** what's on at the cinema/theatre this week?

(f) (*geschehen, sich zutragen*) to happen ♦ **egal, was kommt, ich bleibe fröhlich** whatever happens, I shall remain cheerful; **komme, was da wolle** come what may; **seine Hochzeit kam für alle überraschend** his wedding came as a surprise for everyone; **das mußte ja so** *or* **so mußte es ja ~** it had to happen; **das hätte nicht ~ dürfen** that should never *or* shouldn't have happened; *siehe auch* **3**.

(g) (*Grund, Ursache angebend*) to come ♦ **daher kommt es, daß ...** (and) that's (the reason) why ...; **das kommt davon, daß ...** that's because ...; **das kommt davon** *or* **daher, daß es soviel geregnet hat** that comes from *or* is because of all the rain we've had; **das kommt davon, wenn man nicht zuhört** that's what happens when you don't listen, that comes of *or* that's what comes of not listening; **das kommt davon!** see what happens?

(h) (*in Verbindung mit Dativ*) *siehe auch n, adj* **ihm kamen Zweifel** he started to have doubts; **jdm kommen die Tränen** tears come to sb's eyes; **ihm kam das Grausen** terror seized him, he was terrified; **mir kommt ein Gedanke/eine Idee** I just thought of something *or* had a thought/idea, a thought/an idea occurs to me; **es kommt jdm** (*fällt ein*) it dawns on sb; (*wird klar*) it becomes clear to sb; **das Wort/sein Name kommt mir im Moment nicht** the word/his name escapes me for the moment; **es kommt ihm** (*sl: er hat eine Ejakulation*) he's coming (*sl*); **du kommst mir gerade recht** (*iro*) you're just what I need; **das kommt mir gerade recht** that's just fine; **jdm frech/dumm ~** to be cheeky to sb/to act stupid; **komm mir nur nicht so** don't you take that attitude with me!; **wie kommst du mir denn?** what kind of attitude do you call that then?; **so darfst du mir nicht ~** you'd better not take that attitude with me!

(i) *in Verbindung mit vb siehe auch dort* **angelaufen/dahermarschiert ~** to come running/marching along *or* (*auf einen zu*) up; **herbeigelaufen/heruntergeklettert ~** to come running up/climbing down; **da kommt ein Vogel geflogen** there's a bird; **ich komme dann zu dir gefahren** I'll drive over to your place then; **kommt essen!** come and eat!; **jdn besuchen ~** to come and visit sb; **auf dem Sessel/neben jdm zu sitzen ~** to end up sitting in the armchair/next to sb; **jdn ~ sehen** to see sb coming; **ich habe es ~ sehen** I saw it coming; **die Zeit für gekommen halten** to think the time has come; **jdn ~ lassen** *Arzt, Polizei* to send for sb, to call sb in; (*zu sich rufen*) *Schüler, Sekretärin* to send for sb, to summon sb (*form*); **etw ~ lassen** *Mahlzeit, Taxi* to order; *Kupplung* to let in; *Seil* to let come; *Motor* to start up.

(j) (*kosten, sich belaufen*) **das kommt zusammen auf 20 DM** that comes to *or* adds up to *or* makes DM 20; **egal, wie oft ich zähle, ich komme nur auf 99** however many times I count it up, I only get 99 *or* make it 99; **ich komme auf 2 500 Mark im Monat** I get *or* make 2,500 marks a month.

(k) (*gelangen*) to get; (*mit Hand etc erreichen können*) to reach ♦ **wie komme ich nach London?** how do I get to London?; **ich komme mit meiner Hand bis an die Decke** I can reach up to the ceiling with my hand; **ich komme zur Zeit nicht an die frische Luft/aus dem Haus/ins Theater** at the moment I never get out into the fresh air/out of the house/to the theatre; **durch den Zoll/die Prüfung ~** to get through customs/the exam; **zu einem Entschluß/einer Entscheidung/Einigung ~** to come to a conclusion/decision/an agreement; **in das Alter ~, wo ...** to reach the age when ...; **die Entwicklung kam zu ihrem Höhepunkt** developments reached their climax.

(l) (*geraten*) to get ♦ **ins Wackeln/in Bewegung/ins Erzählen ~** to start shaking *or* to shake/moving *or* to move/talking *or* to talk; **zum Blühen/Wachsen** *etc* **~** to start flowering *or* to flower/growing *or* to grow; **zum Stehen/Stillstand ~** to come to a halt *or* stop/standstill; **er schießt auf alles, was ihm vor die Flinte kommt** he shoots at everything he gets in his sights.

(m) (*hingehören*) to go, to belong ♦ **das Buch kommt ins oberste Fach** the book belongs *or* goes on the top shelf; **in die Ecke kommt noch ein Schrank** another cupboard is to go in that corner; **das kommt unter „Sonstiges"** that comes *or* goes *or* belongs under miscellaneous; **da kommt ein Deckel drauf** it has to have a lid on it.

(n) (*gebracht werden*) to go ♦ **ins Gefängnis ~** to go *or* be sent to prison; **in die** *or* **zur Schule ~** to go to *or* start school; **ins Altersheim/Krankenhaus ~** to go into an old peoples' home/into hospital; **auf die Universität ~** to go (up) to university.

(o) (*sich entwickeln*) (*Samen, Pflanzen*) to come on ♦ **langsam kam ihm das Verständnis** understanding slowly came to him.

(p) (*Redewendungen*) **komm' ich heut nicht, komm' ich morgen** (*prov*) you'll see me when you see me; **kommt Zeit, kommt Rat** (*Prov*) things have a way of working themselves out; **wer zuerst kommt, mahlt zuerst** (*Prov*) first come first served.

[2] *vi mit Präpositionen siehe auch dort* **an etw** (*acc*) **~** (*berühren*) to touch sth; (*sich verschaffen*) to get hold of sth; **auf etw** (*acc*) **~** (*sich erinnern*) to think of sth; (*sprechen über*) to come *or* get onto sth; **auf einen Gedanken/eine Idee ~** to get an idea, to have a thought/an idea; **das kommt auf die Rechnung/auf mein Konto** that goes onto the bill/into my account; **auf ihn/darauf lasse ich nichts ~** (*inf*) I won't hear *or* have a word against him/it; **auf jeden ~ fünf Mark** there are five marks (for) each; **auf jeden Haushalt ~ $1\frac{1}{2}$ m³ Wasser pro Tag** each household consumes $1\frac{1}{2}$ cu.m. of water per day; **wie kommst du darauf?** what makes you think that?; **darauf bin ich nicht gekommen** I didn't think of that; **ich komme im Moment nicht auf seinen Namen** his name escapes me *or* I can't think of his name for the moment; **hinter etw** (*acc*) **~** (*herausfinden*) to find sth out, to find out sth; **mit einer Frage/einem Anliegen ~** to have a question (to ask)/a request (to make); **komm mir nicht wieder damit!** don't start that all over again!; **komm (mir) bloß nicht mit der Entschuldigung** don't come to me with that excuse; **damit kann ich ihm nicht ~** (*mit Entschuldigung*) I can't give him that; (*mit Bitte*) I can't ask him that; **um etw ~** (*verlieren*) *um Geld, Besitz, Leben* to lose sth; *um Essen, Schlaf* to (have to) go without sth, to miss (out on) sth; (*vermeiden können*) to get out of sth; **zu etw ~** (*Zeit finden für*) to get round to sth; (*erhalten*) to come by sth, to get sth; *zu Ehre* to receive sth; (*erben*) to come into sth; (*sich verschaffen*) to get hold of sth, to get oneself sth; (*inf: haben wollen*) to want sth; **wie komme ich zu der Ehre?** to what do I owe this honour?; **hierzu kommt noch seine Kurzsichtigkeit** then there's his short-sightedness too *or* on top of that; **zu nichts/viel ~** (*zeitlich*) not to get round to anything/to get round to doing a lot; (*erreichen*) to achieve nothing/a lot; **zu sich ~** (*Bewußtsein wiedererlangen*) to come round, to come to one's senses; (*aufwachen*) to come to one's senses; (*sich fassen*) to recover, to get over it; (*sich finden*) to sort oneself out.

[3] *vi impers* **es ~ jetzt die Nachrichten/die Clowns** and now (follows/follow) the news/clowns; **es werden viele Leute ~** a lot of people will come; **es ist weit gekommen!** it has come to that!; **es kommt noch einmal so weit** *or* **dahin, daß ...** it will get to the point where ...; **so weit kommt es (noch)** that'll be the day (*inf*); **wie kommt es, daß du ...?** how is it that you ...?, how come you ...? (*inf*); **ich wußte, daß es so ~ würde** I knew (that) that would happen; **dazu kam es gar nicht mehr** it didn't come to that; **wir wollten noch ..., aber es kam nicht mehr dazu** we still wanted to ..., but we didn't get (a)round to it; **es kam zum Streit** there was a quarrel; **es kam eins zum anderen** one thing led to another; **und so kam es, daß ...** and that is how it happened that ...; **es kam, wie es ~ mußte** the inevitable happened; **es kommt immer anders, als man denkt** (*prov*) things never turn out the way one expects; **es mag ~, wie es ~ will** whatever happens, come what may; **entweder gehe ich ins Kino oder trinken — wie es (gerade) kommt** (*inf*) either I'll go to the cinema or for a drink — or whatever (*inf*).

[4] *vt* (*inf: kosten*) to cost.

Kommen *nt* **-s,** *no pl* coming ♦ **ein einziges ~ und Gehen** a constant coming and going; **etw ist im ~** sth is coming in, sth is on the way in; **jd ist im ~** sb is on his/her way up.

kommend *adj Jahr, Woche, Generation* coming; *Ereignisse, Mode* future ♦ **die nach uns K~en** (*geh*) the coming generations, generations to come; **der ~e Meister** the future champion; **(am) ~en Montag** next Monday; **~e Weihnachten** next Christmas; **in den ~en Jahren** in the coming years, in the years to come.

kommensurabel *adj* (*Math, fig geh*) commensurable.

Komment [kɔ'mã:] *m* **-s, -s** (*Univ*) code of conduct (*of student fraternity*).

Kommentar *m* (*Bemerkung, Stellungnahme*) comment; (*Press, Jur, Liter*) commentary ♦ **jeden (weiteren) ~ ablehnen** to decline to comment (further) *or* to make any (further) comment; **kein ~!** no comment; **~ überflüssig!** no comment (necessary)!; **einen ~ (zu etw) (ab)geben** to (make a)

comment on sth.
Kommentator *m*, **Kommentatorin** *f* commentator.
kommentieren* *vt* (*Press etc*) to comment on; (*Jur, Liter*) to write a commentary on ◆ **kommentierte Ausgabe** (*Liter*) annotated edition.
Kommers *m* **-es, -e** *evening meeting of student fraternity with drinking ceremony.*
kommerzialisieren* *vt* **(a)** (*vermarkten*) to commercialize. **(b)** (*Schulden umwandeln*) **eine öffentliche Schuld ~** to convert a public debt into a private loan.
Kommerzialisierung *f siehe vt* **(a)** commercialization. **(b)** conversion of a public debt into a private loan.
Kommerzialrat *m* (*Aus*) *siehe* **Kommerzienrat.**
kommerziell *adj* commercial ◆ **rein ~ denken** to think purely in commercial terms *or* purely commercially.
Kommerzienrat [-iən-] *m* (*Hist*) *title conferred on distinguished businessman.*
Kommilitone *m* **-n, -n, Kommilitonin** *f* fellow student ◆ **wir brauchen noch drei ~n, die Flugblätter verteilen** we need three more people *or* students to hand out leaflets.
⚠ **Kommiß** *m* **-sses,** *no pl* (*dated inf*) army ◆ **beim ~ sein** to be in the army; **zum ~ müssen** to have to go into the army.
Kommissar, Kommissär (*esp Aus*) *m* (*Admin*) commissioner; (*Polizei~*) inspector; (*ranghöher*) (police) superintendent.
Kommissariat *nt* **(a)** (*Admin*) (*Amt*) commissionership; (*Dienststelle, Amtsbereich*) commissioner's department. **(b)** (*Polizei*) (*Amt*) office of inspector; office of superintendent; (*Dienststelle, Amtsbereich*) superintendent's department; (*Aus: Polizeidienststelle*) police station.
kommissarisch *adj* temporary.
⚠ **Kommißbrot** *nt* rye bread; army bread.
Kommission *f* **(a)** (*Ausschuß*) committee; (*zur Untersuchung*) commission. **(b)** (*Comm*) commission ◆ **etw in ~ geben** to give goods (to a dealer) for sale on commission; **etw in ~ nehmen/haben** to take/have sth on commission.
Kommissionär *m* commission agent; (*im Verlagswesen*) wholesale bookseller, wholesaler.
kommissionieren* *vt* (*Aus*) to commission.
Kommissions-: ~buchhandel *m* wholesale book trade; **~gebühr** *f* commission; **~geschäft** *nt* commission *or* agency business.
⚠ **Kommißstiefel** *m* army boot; (*fig pej*) jackboot.
kommod *adj* (*old, dial*) comfortable.
Kommode *f* **-, -n** chest of drawers; (*hohe*) tallboy, highboy (*US*).
Kommodität *f* (*old*) comfort.
Kommodore *m* **-s, -n** *or* **-s** (*Naut*) commodore; (*Aviat*) wing commander (*Brit*), lieutenant colonel (*US*).
kommunal *adj* local; (*von Stadt auch*) municipal.
Kommunal-: ~abgaben *pl* local rates and taxes *pl*; **~anleihe** *f* municipal loan.
kommunalisieren* *vt* to put under the control of the local authorities.
Kommunal-: ~obligation *f* municipal bond; **~politik** *f* local government politics *sing or pl*; **~verwaltung** *f* local government; **~wahlen** *pl* local (government) *or* municipal elections *pl.*
Kommunarde *m* **-n, -n** **(a)** (*Hist*) Communard. **(b)** (*dated: Mitglied einer Wohngemeinschaft*) member of a commune, commune-dweller, communard ◆ **er ist ein ~** he lives in a commune.
Kommune *f* **-, -n** **(a)** local authority district. **(b)** (*Wohngemeinschaft*) commune. **(c)** (*Pariser ~*) (Paris) Commune.
Kommunikant(in *f*) *m* (*Eccl*) communicant; (*Erst~*) first communicant.
Kommunikation *f* communication ◆ **die ~ ist unmöglich geworden** communication has become impossible.
Kommunikations-: ~mittel *nt* means of communication; **~satellit** *m* communications satellite; **~schwierigkeiten** *pl* communication difficulties; **~wissenschaften** *pl* communication studies.
kommunikativ *adj* communicative; *Brief etc auch* informative.
Kommunion *f* (*Eccl*) (Holy) Communion; (*Erst~*) first Communion.
Kommunion-: ~bank *f* Communion rail; **~kind** *nt* first communicant.
⚠ **Kommuniqué** [kɔmyni'ke:] *nt* **-s, -s** communiqué.
Kommunismus *m* communism.
Kommunist(in *f*) *m* Communist.
Kommunistenfresser *m* (*pej inf*) Commie basher (*inf*).
kommunistisch *adj* communist ◆ **das K~e Manifest** the Communist Manifesto.
kommunizieren* *vi* **(a)** to communicate ◆ **~de Röhren** (*Phys*) communicating tubes. **(b)** (*Eccl*) to receive (Holy) Communion.
Komödiant *m* **(a)** (*old*) actor, player (*old*). **(b)** (*fig*) play-actor.
Komödianten-: k~haft *adj Gebaren* theatrical, histrionic; **~tum** *nt* histrionics *pl.*
Komödiantin *f* **(a)** (*old*) actress. **(b)** (*fig*) play-actor.
komödiantisch *adj* (*schauspielerisch*) acting; (*pej*) theatrical, histrionic.
Komödie [-iə] *f* comedy; (*fig*) (*heiteres Ereignis*) farce; (*Täuschung*) play-acting ◆ **die Stuttgarter ~** the Stuttgart Comedy Theatre; **~ spielen** (*fig*) to put on an act.
Kompagnon [kɔmpan'jõ:, 'kɔmpanjõ] *m* **-s, -s** (*Comm*) partner, associate; (*iro*) pal (*inf*), chum (*inf*), buddy (*inf*).
kompakt *adj* compact; *Gestein, Schicht, Brot, Masse auch* solid.
Kompakt-: ~anlage *f* (*Rad*) audio system; **~auto** *nt* compact (*US*), medium-sized family saloon; **~bauweise** *f* compact functional style; **~kamera** *f* compact camera; **~wagen** *m* (*Aut*) small family car, subcompact (*US*).
Kompanie *f* (*Mil*) company; (*old Comm*) trading company; (*Firma*) firm ◆ **damit kann man ja eine ganze ~ füttern** that's enough to feed a whole army.
Kompaniechef, Kompanieführer *m* (*Mil*) company commander.
Komparation *f* (*Gram*) comparison.
Komparatistik *f* comparative literature.
Komparativ *m* (*Gram*) comparative.
Komparse *m* **-n, -n, Komparsin** *f* (*Film*) extra; (*Theat*) supernumerary ◆ **er war nur ein ~** he only had a walk-on part.
Komparserie *f* extras *pl*; supernumeraries *pl* ◆ **die ganze ~** ... all those with walk-on parts ...
⚠ **Kompaß** *m* **-sses, -sse** compass ◆ **nach dem ~** by the compass.
⚠ **Kompaß-: ~häuschen** *nt* (*Naut*) binnacle; **~nadel** *f* compass needle.
kompatibel *adj* (*liter, Tech*) compatible.
Kompatibilität *f* (*liter, Tech*) compatibility.
Kompendium *nt* **(a)** (*Abriß*) compendium. **(b)** (*Phot*) lenshood (with bellows extension).
Kompensation *f* compensation.
Kompensationsgeschäft *nt* barter (transaction).
Kompensator *m* (*Tech*) compensator.
kompensieren* *vt* to compensate for, to offset.
kompetent *adj* competent; (*befugt auch*) authorized ◆ **für solche Fälle ist dieses Gericht nicht ~** this court has no jurisdiction in *or* is not competent to decide such cases; **der dafür ~e Kollege** the man responsible for that; **dafür bin ich nicht ~** I'm not responsible for that.
Kompetenz *f* **(a)** (area of) authority *or* competence; (*eines Gerichts*) jurisdiction, competence ◆ **da hat er ganz eindeutig seine ~en überschritten** he has quite clearly exceeded his authority *or* powers here; **er hat die alleinige ~, hierüber zu entscheiden** he alone has the authority *or* competence *or* is competent to decide on this issue; **ich will dir nicht deine ~(en) streitig machen** I don't want to infringe on your field; **das fällt in die ~ dieses Amtes** that's the responsibility of this office; **seine mangelnde ~ in dieser Frage** his lack of competence in this issue.
(b) (*Ling*) competence.
Kompetenz-: ~bereich *m* area of competence; **~gerangel** *nt* bickering over responsibilities; **~streitigkeiten** *pl* dispute over respective areas of responsibility *or* competence; (*bei Gewerkschaften, fig*) demarcation dispute; **~wirrwarr** *m* confusion *or* muddle about areas of responsibilities; demarcation confusion.
Kompilation *f* (*geh*) compilation.
kompilieren* *vt* (*geh*) to compile.
kompl. *abbr of* **komplett** complete.
Komplement *nt* (*Math*) complement.
komplementär *adj Therapie, Beweise* complementary.
Komplementär(in *f*) *m fully liable partner in a limited partnership.*
Komplementärfarbe *f* complementary colour.
Komplet[1] [kõ'ple:, kɔm'ple:] *nt* **-(s), -s** (*Fashion*) matching dress/skirt and coat.
Komplet[2] [kɔm'ple:t] *f* **-, -e** (*Eccl*) complin(e).
komplett [1] *adj* complete ◆ **ein ~es Frühstück** a full breakfast; **ein ~es Menü** a (full) three course meal.
[2] *adv* completely.
komplettieren* *vt* (*geh*) to complete.
Komplex *m* **-es, -e** complex ◆ **er steckt voller ~e** he has so many complexes *or* hang-ups (*inf*).
komplex *adj* complex ◆ **~ aufgebaut** complex in structure.
Komplexität *f* complexity.
Komplice [kɔm'pli:tsə] *m* **-n, -n** *siehe* **Komplize.**
Komplikation *f* complication.
Kompliment *nt* compliment ◆ **jdm ~e machen** to pay sb compliments, to compliment sb (*wegen* on); **mein ~!** my compliments!
Komplize *m* **-n, -n, Komplizin** *f* accomplice.
komplizieren* *vt* to complicate.
kompliziert *adj* complicated, involved; (*Med*) *Bruch* compound ◆ **sei doch nicht so ~** don't be so complicated; **sich ~ ausdrücken** to express oneself in a complicated *or* an involved way.
Kompliziertheit *f* complexity.
Komplizin *f siehe* **Komplize.**
Komplott *nt* **-(e)s, -e** plot, conspiracy ◆ **ein ~ schmieden** to hatch a plot; **ein ~ zur Ermordung** ... a plot *or* conspiracy to murder ...
Komponente *f* **-, -n** component.
komponieren* *vti* to compose; (*Liter auch*) to construct.
Komponist(in *f*) *m* composer.
Komposita *pl of* **Kompositum.**
Komposition *f* composition; (*Liter auch*) construction.
kompositorisch *adj* compositional.
Kompositum *nt* **-s, Komposita** (*Gram, Pharm*) compound.
Kompost *m* **-(e)s, -e** compost.
Kompost-: ~er *m* **-s, -** compost maker; **~erde** *f* compost; **~haufen** *m* compost heap.
Kompostieranlage *f* composting plant.
kompostieren* [1] *vt* to compost.
[2] *vi* to make compost.
Kompott *nt* **-(e)s, -e** stewed fruit, compote.

⚠ **kompreß** *adv (Typ)* solid.
Kompresse *f* compress.
Kompression *f (Tech)* compression.
Kompressions-: ~pumpe *f* pressure pump; **~verband** *m* compression *or* pressure bandage.
Kompressor *m* compressor.
komprimieren* *vt* to compress; *(fig)* to condense.
⚠ **Kompromiß** *m* **-sses, -sse** compromise ◆ **einen ~ schließen** to (make a) compromise; **sie sind zu keinem ~ bereit** they are not prepared to compromise.
⚠ **Kompromiß-: k~bereit** *adj* prepared *or* willing to compromise; **~bereitschaft** *f* willingness to compromise; **k~los** *adj* uncompromising; **~lösung** *f* compromise solution.
kompromittieren* [1] *vt* to compromise.
[2] *vr* to compromise oneself.
Komsomol *m* **-,** *no pl* Comsomol.
Komsomolze *m* **-n, -n** member of the Comsomol.
⚠ **Komteß** *f* **-** *or* **-sse, -ssen** countess.
Komtur *m* **-s, -e** commander (of a knightly order).
Kondensat *nt* condensate; *(fig)* distillation, condensation.
Kondensation *f (Chem, Phys)* condensation.
Kondensator *m (Aut, Chem)* condenser; *(Elec auch)* capacitor.
kondensieren* *vti (lit, fig)* to condense; *(fig auch)* to distil.
Kondens-: ~milch *f* evaporated milk; **~streifen** *m (Aviat)* vapour trail; **~wasser** *nt* condensation.
Kondition *f* **(a)** condition, shape, form; *(Durchhaltevermögen)* stamina ◆ **wie ist seine ~?** what sort of condition *etc* is he in?; **er hat überhaupt keine ~** he is completely unfit; *(fig)* he has absolutely no stamina; **er zeigte heute eine ausgezeichnete ~** he was in top form today. **(b)** *(Bedingung)* condition.
konditional |kɔnditsio'na:l| *adj* conditional.
Konditionalsatz *m* conditional clause.
konditionieren* |kɔnditsio'ni:rən| *vt (Biol, Psych)* to condition.
Konditions-: ~schwäche *f* lack of fitness *no pl*; **~training** *nt* fitness training.
Konditor *m*, **Konditorin** *f* pastry-cook.
Konditorei *f* cake shop; *(mit Café)* café.
Konditorwaren *pl* cakes and pastries *pl*.
Kondolenz- *in cpds* of condolence; **~besuch** *m* visit of condolence; **~buch** *nt* condolences book.
kondolieren* *vi* **(jdm) ~** to offer one's condolences (to sb), to condole with sb; **schriftlich ~** to write a letter of condolence.
Kondom *m or nt* **-s, -e** condom, contraceptive sheath.
Kondomerie *f* **-, -n** *(inf)* condom shop *(esp Brit) or* store *(US)*.
Kondominium *nt* condominium.
Kondor *m* **-s, -e** condor.
Kondukteur |kɔndʊk'tø:ɐ| *m (Aus, Sw)* conductor.
Kondukteurin |kɔndʊk'tø:rɪn| *f (Aus, Sw)* conductress.
Konen *pl of* **Konus.**
Konfekt *nt* **-(e)s, -e** confectionery.
Konfektion *f (Herstellung)* manufacture of off-the-peg *or* ready-made *or* ready-to-wear clothing; *(Industrie)* clothing industry, rag trade *(inf)*; *(Bekleidung)* off-the-peg *or* ready-made *or* ready-to-wear clothes *pl or* clothing.
Konfektionär |kɔnfɛktsio'nɛ:ɐ| *m (dated) (Unternehmer)* clothing manufacturer; *(Angestellter)* executive employee in the clothing industry.
konfektionieren* *vt Kleidung* to make.
Konfektions- *in cpds* off-the-peg, ready-made, ready-to-wear; **~anzug** *m* off-the-peg *etc* suit; **~geschäft** *nt* (off-the-peg) clothes shop *or* store; **~ware** *f* off-the-peg *etc* clothing.
Konferenz *f* conference ; *(Besprechung)* meeting; *(Ausschuß)* committee.
Konferenz- *in cpds* conference; **~schaltung** *f (Telec)* conference circuit; *(Rad, TV)* (television/radio) link-up; **~teilnehmer** *m* person attending a conference/meeting; **~zimmer** *nt* conference room.
konferieren* *vi* to confer, to have *or* hold a conference *or* discussion *(über +acc* on *or* about).
Konfession *f* (religious) denomination ◆ **welche ~ haben Sie?** what denomination are you?; **die Augsburger ~** the Augsburg Confession.
konfessionell *adj* denominational.
Konfessions-: k~los *adj* non-denominational, undenominational; **~schule** *f* denominational school.
Konfetti *nt* **-s,** *no pl* confetti.
Konfetti: ~regen *m* shower of confetti; *(in US: bei Empfängen)* shower of ticker-tape; **~schlacht** *f* confetti battle.
Konfident *m (old)* confidant; *(Aus)* police informer.
Konfiguration *f* configuration.
konfigurieren *vt Computer, Software* to configure.
Konfirmand(in *f*) *m* **-en, -en** *(Eccl)* candidate for confirmation, confirmand.
Konfirmanden|unterricht *m* confirmation classes *pl*.
Konfirmation *f (Eccl)* confirmation.
Konfirmations- *in cpds* confirmation; **~spruch** *m* confirmation text *(chosen by confirmand as motto)*.
konfirmieren* *vt (Eccl)* to confirm.
Konfiserie *f (Sw)* **(a)** *siehe* **Konditorei. (b)** *siehe* **Konfekt.**
Konfiskation *f* confiscation.
konfiszieren* *vt* to confiscate.
Konfitüre *f* **-, -n** jam.
Konflikt *m* **-s, -e** conflict ◆ **bewaffneter ~** armed conflict; **mit dem Gesetz in ~ geraten** to come into conflict with the law, to clash with the law; **kommst du da nicht mit deinem Gewissen in ~ ?** how can you reconcile that with your conscience?; **er befindet sich in einem ~** he is in a state of inner conflict.
Konflikt-: ~fall *m* conflict; **im ~fall** in case of conflict; **~feld** *nt* area of conflict; **~forscher** *m* researcher into conflict; **~forschung** *f* conflict studies, research into the subject of conflict; **k~freudig** *adj* combative; **er ist sehr k~freudig** he is very combative, he thrives on conflict; **~herd** *m (esp Pol)* centre of conflict; **~kommission** *f (DDR)* grievance committee *or* tribunal; **k~los** *adj* without conflict; **~situation** *f* conflict situation; **~stoff** *m* cause for conflict.
Konföderation *f* confederacy.
konföderieren* *vr (liter)* to confederate.
Konföderierte(r) *m decl as adj* confederate.
konform *adj Ansichten etc* concurring ◆ **mit jdm ~ gehen** to agree *or* to be in agreement with sb *(in +dat* about); **in etw** *(dat)* **~ sein** to agree in sth.
Konformismus *m* conformism.
Konformist(in *f*) *m (pej)* conformist.
konformistisch *adj* conformist, conforming.
Konformität *f* conformity.
Konfrater *m (Eccl)* fellow clergyman; fellow monk.
Konfrontation *f* confrontation.
Konfrontationskurs *m* **auf ~ gehen, ~ steuern** to be heading for a confrontation.
konfrontieren* *vt* to confront *(mit* with) ◆ **zwei Parteien ~** to bring two parties face to face, to confront two parties with one another.
Konfrontierung *f siehe* **Konfrontation.**
konfus *adj* confused, muddled.
konfuzianisch *adj* Confucian.
Konfuzius *m* **-** Confucius.
kongenial *adj (geh)* sympathetic ◆ **~e Geister** kindred *or* congenial spirits.
Konglomerat *nt* **(a)** *(Geol)* conglomerate. **(b)** *(Ansammlung)* conglomeration.
Kongo *m* **-(s)** Congo.
Kongolese *m* **-n, -n, Kongolesin** *f* Congolese.
⚠ **Kongreß** *m* **-sses, -sse (a)** *(Pol)* congress; *(fachlich)* convention, conference ◆ **der Wiener ~** the Congress of Vienna. **(b)** *(in USA)* Congress.
⚠ **Kongreß-: ~mitglied** *nt* **(a)** person attending a congress/conference *or* convention; **(b)** *(in USA)* congressman/-woman; **~teilnehmer** *m* person attending a congress/conference *or* convention; **~zentrum** *nt* congress/conference centre.
kongruent *adj (Math)* congruent; *(Gram)* concordant, congruent; *(geh) Ansichten* concurring.
Kongruenz *f (Math)* congruence; *(Gram)* concord, agreement, congruence; *(geh: von Ansichten)* concurrence.
kongruieren* *vi* to be congruent; *(geh: Ansichten)* to concur, to correspond.
K.-o.-Niederlage [ka:'|o:-] *f* KO defeat.
Konifere *f* **-, -n** conifer.
König *m* **-s, -e** king ◆ **des ~s Rock** *(old, liter)* the king's uniform; **die Heiligen Drei ~e** The Three Kings *or* Magi; **der ~ der Tiere/Lüfte** the king of the beasts/lord of the skies.
Königin *f (auch Zool)* queen ◆ **~ der Nacht** *(Bot)* queen of the night, night-flowering cereus.
Königin-: ~mutter *f* queen mother; **~pastete** *f* vol-au-vent; **~witwe** *f* dowager queen.
königlich [1] *adj* royal; *Auftreten, Stolz etc auch* regal ◆ **das ~e Spiel** chess, the royal game, the game of kings.
[2] *adv (inf) (köstlich, ungeheuer)* **sich ~ freuen** to be as pleased as Punch *(inf)*; **sich ~ amüsieren** to have the time of one's life *(inf)*.
Königreich *nt* kingdom, realm *(poet)*.
Königs-: k~blau *adj* royal blue; **~hof** *m* royal *or* king's court; **~kerze** *f (Bot)* mullein; **~kind** *nt (liter)* king's son *or* daughter; **~krone** *f* royal crown; **~mord** *m* regicide; **~paar** *nt* royal couple; **~sohn** *m (liter)* king's son, prince; **~tiger** *m* Bengal tiger; **~tochter** *f (liter)* king's daughter, princess; **k~treu** *adj* royalist; **~wasser** *nt (Chem)* aqua regia; **~weg** *m (idealer Weg)* ideal way; **~würde** *f* royal dignity.
Königtum *nt* **(a)** *no pl* kingship. **(b)** *(Reich)* kingdom.
konisch *adj* conical.
Konjektur *f (Vermutung)* conjecture; *(Liter: Lesart)* conjectured version.
Konjugation *f* conjugation.
konjugieren* *vt* to conjugate.
Konjunktion *f (Astron, Gram)* conjunction.
Konjunktionalsatz *m (Gram)* conjunctional clause.
Konjunktiv *m (Gram)* subjunctive.
konjunktivisch *adj* subjunctive.
Konjunktur *f* economic situation, economy; *(Hoch~)* boom ◆ **steigende/fallende** *or* **rückläufige ~** upward/downward economic trend, increasing/decreasing economic activity.
Konjunktur-: k~abhängig *adj* dependent on economic factors; **~abschwung** *m* economic downturn; **~aufschwung** *m* economic upturn; **k~bedingt** *adj* influenced by *or* due to economic factors; **~einbruch** *m* slump.

konjunkturell *adj* economic; *Arbeitslosigkeit* resulting from the economic situation, due to economic factors ◆ ~ **bedingt** caused by economic factors.

Konjunktur-: ~politik *f measures or policies aimed at preventing economic fluctuation*; **~rückgang** *m* slowdown in the economy; **~schwäche** *f* weakness of economic activity; **~zuschlag** *m refundable increase in taxation paid into the Bundesbank to help the national economy.*

konkav *adj* concave.

Konkavspiegel *m* concave mirror.

Konklave [kɔn'kla:və, kɔŋ-] *nt* **-s, -n** (*Eccl*) conclave.

Konklusion *f* (*geh, Philos*) conclusion.

Konkordanz *f* concordance.

Konkordat *nt* concordat.

konkret *adj* concrete ◆ **ich kann es dir noch nicht ~ sagen** I can't tell you definitely; **ich kann dir nichts K~es sagen** I can't tell you anything definite *or* concrete; **drück dich etwas ~er aus** would you put that in rather more concrete terms; **ich kann mir ~ vorstellen, wie** ... I can very clearly imagine how ...

konkretisieren* *vt* to put in concrete form *or* terms.

Konkubinat *nt* concubinage.

Konkubine *f* concubine.

Konkurrent(in *f*) *m* rival; (*Comm auch*) competitor.

Konkurrenz *f* (*Wettbewerb*) competition, rivalry; (*~betrieb*) competitors *pl*; (*Gesamtheit der Konkurrenten*) competition, competitors *pl* ◆ **die ~ in diesem Sport/auf diesem Gebiet ist größer geworden** the competition in this sport/field has increased; **jdm ~ machen** (*Comm, fig*) to compete with sb; (*Comm*) to be in/enter into competition with sb; **zur ~ (über)gehen** to go over to the competitor(s); **außer ~ sein** to have no competition.

Konkurrenz-: ~druck *m* pressure of competition; **k~fähig** *adj* competitive; **~kampf** *m* competition; (*zwischen zwei Menschen auch*) rivalry; **wir müssen mit einem sehr harten ~kampf rechnen** we have to reckon with some very tough competition; **ein ~kampf, bei dem wir uns durchgesetzt haben** a competitive situation in which we won out; **~klausel** *f* (*in Vertrag*) competition restraint clause; **k~los** *adj* without competition.

konkurrieren* *vi* to compete; (*Comm auch*) to be in/go into competition.

Konkurs *m* **-es, -e** bankruptcy ◆ **in ~ gehen** to go bankrupt, to go into receivership (*esp form*); **~ machen** (*inf*) to go bankrupt *or* bust (*inf*); *siehe* **anmelden.**

Konkurs-: ~masse *f* bankrupt's estate; **~verfahren** *nt* bankruptcy proceedings *pl*; **~verwalter** *m* receiver; (*von Gläubigern bevollmächtigt*) trustee.

▼ **können** *pret* **konnte**, *ptp* **gekonnt** *or* (*bei modal aux vb*) ~ *vti, modal aux vb* **(a)** (*vermögen*) to be able to ◆ **ich kann es machen** I can do it, I am able to do it; **ich kann es nicht machen** I cannot *or* can't do it, I am not able to do it; **man konnte ihn retten** they were able to *or* they managed to save him; **man konnte ihn nicht retten** they couldn't *or* were unable to save him; **ich konnte es nicht verstehen** I could not *or* couldn't *or* was unable to understand it; **ich habe es sehen ~** I could see it, I was able to see it; **es ist furchtbar, nicht schlafen zu ~** it's terrible not to be able to sleep; **er hat es gekonnt** he could do it, he was able to do it; **morgen kann ich nicht** I can't (manage) tomorrow; **das hättest du gleich sagen ~** you could *or* might have said that straight away; **das hätte ich dir gleich sagen ~** I could have told you that straight away; **ich kann das nicht mehr sehen** I can't stand the sight of it any more; **ich kann das nicht mehr hören** I don't want to hear that again; **ich kann nicht mehr** I can't go on; (*ertragen*) I can't take any more; (*essen*) I can't manage *or* eat any more; **kannst du noch?** can you go on?; (*essen*) can you manage some more?; **mir kann keiner!** (*inf*) I'm all right, Jack (*inf*); **ich habe das alles schriftlich, mir kann keiner!** I've got it all in writing, they can't touch me; **so schnell er konnte** as fast as he could *or* was able to; **~ vor Lachen!** (*inf*) I wish I could, chance would be a fine thing (*inf*); **man kann alles, wenn man (nur) will** (*Prov*) where there's a will there's a way (*Prov*).

(b) (*beherrschen*) *Sprache* to know, to be able to speak; *Gedicht, Lied* to know; *Schach* to be able to play; *Klavier spielen, lesen, schwimmen, Skilaufen etc* to be able to, to know how to ◆ **er kann seine Schulaufgabe wieder nicht** he can't do his homework again; (*nicht gemacht*) he hasn't done his homework again; **was ~ Sie?** what can you do?; **was du alles kannst!** the things you can do!; **er kann was** he's very capable *or* able; **unser Chef kann viel/nichts** our boss is a very capable *or* able man/our boss is incapable *or* useless; **er kann gut Englisch** he speaks English well.

▼ **(c)** (*dürfen*) to be allowed *or* permitted to ◆ **kann ich jetzt gehen?** can I go now?; **könnte ich ...?** could I ...?; **er kann sich nicht beklagen** he can't complain; **man kann wohl sagen, daß** ... one could well say that ...; **du kannst mich (gern haben)!** (*inf*) get lost! (*inf*); **er kann mich (mal)** (*sl*) he can get stuffed (*sl*), he can go to hell (*sl*); **kann ich mit?** (*inf*) can I come with you?

▼ **(d)** (*möglich sein*) **Sie könnten recht haben** you could *or* might *or* may be right; **er kann jeden Augenblick kommen** he could *or* might *or* may come any minute; **das kann nur er gewesen sein** it can only have been him; **das kann nicht sein** that can't be true; **das kann fast nicht sein** that can't be true, it's almost unbelievable; **es kann sein/es kann nicht sein, daß er dabei war** he could *or* might *or* may have been there/he couldn't *or* can't possibly have been there; **kann sein** maybe, could be.

(e) (*mit Partikel*) **für etw ~** to be responsible *or* to blame for sth; **ich kann nichts dafür** it's not my fault; **ich kann nichts dazu** I can't do anything about it; **ich könnte auf ein Bier** (*sl*) I could just do with a beer (*inf*).

Können *nt* **-s,** *no pl* ability, skill.

Könner *m* **-s, -** expert.

Konnex *m* **-es, -e** (*geh*) connection; (*Verbindung auch*) contact.

Konnossement [kɔnɔsə'mɛnt] *nt* **-s, -s** (*Comm*) bill of lading.

konnte *pret of* **können.**

Konrektor *m*, **Konrektorin** *f* (*an Schule*) deputy headteacher (*Brit*) *or* principal; (*an Universität*) deputy vice-chancellor.

Konsekration *f* (*Eccl*) consecration.

konsekrieren* *vt* (*Eccl*) to consecrate.

konsekutiv *adj* consecutive.

Konsekutivsatz *m* consecutive clause.

Konsens *m* **-es, -e** agreement, assent, consent.

konsequent *adj* consistent; (*Sport*) *Deckung* close, tight ◆ **er hat ~ „nein" gesagt** he stuck to his answer of "no"; ... **werden gebeten, die Sicherheitsmaßnahmen ~ einzuhalten** ... are required to observe the safety regulations strictly; **wir werden ~ durchgreifen** we will take rigorous action; **~e Weiterentwicklung eines Stils** logically consistent development of a style; **wenn du das ~ durchdenkst** if you follow it through to its logical conclusion; **eine Spur ~ verfolgen** to follow up a clue rigorously; **ein Ziel ~ verfolgen** to pursue an objective single-mindedly; **einen Fall ~ untersuchen** to investigate a case rigorously *or* thoroughly.

Konsequenz *f* **(a)** (*Schlußfolgerung*) consequence ◆ **die ~en tragen** to take the consequences; **(aus etw) die ~en ziehen** to come to the obvious conclusion; to take the appropriate *or* logical step; **wenn es dir hier nicht gefällt, solltest du die entsprechenden ~en ziehen und gehen** if you don't like it here, you should do something about it and go; **ich werde meine ~en ziehen** there's only one thing for me to do.

(b) *siehe adj* consistency; closeness, tightness; (*bei Maßnahmen*) rigorousness, rigour ◆ **die ~, mit der er sein Ziel verfolgte** the single-mindedness with which he pursued his aim; **die ~, mit der er seinen Malstil weiterentwickelte** the logical consistency with which he developed his painting style.

Konservatismus [-va-] *m siehe* **Konservat(iv)ismus.**

konservativ [-va-] *adj* conservative; (*Brit Pol*) Conservative, Tory.

Konservative(r) [-va-] *mf decl as adj* conservative; (*Brit Pol*) Conservative, Tory.

Konservat(iv)ismus [-vat(iv)ɪsmʊs] *m* conservatism.

Konservator [kɔnzɛr'va:tɔr] *m* curator, keeper.

Konservatorium [kɔnzɛrva'to:riʊm] *nt* conservatory.

Konserve [kɔn'zɛrvə] *f* **-, -n** preserved food; (*in Dosen*) tinned (*Brit*) *or* canned food; (*~ndose*) tin (*Brit*), can; (*Med: Blut~ etc*) stored blood *etc*; blood bottle; (*Rad, TV*) pre-recorded *or* canned (*inf*) material; (*Ton~*) recorded/taped music ◆ **sich aus** *or* **von ~n ernähren** to live out of cans.

Konserven-: ~büchse, ~dose *f* tin (*Brit*), can.

konservieren* [kɔnzɛr'vi:rən] *vt* to preserve, to conserve; *Leichen* to preserve; *Auto* to wax.

Konservierung *f* preservation, conservation; (*der Umwelt*) conservation; (*von Leichen*) preservation.

konsistent *adj Masse* solid.

Konsistenz *f* consistency; (*von Gewebe*) texture.

Konsole *f* **-, -n** (*Archit: Kragstein*) console, corbel; (*old: an Möbeln*) bracket.

konsolidieren* *vtr* to consolidate; (*Fin*) *Anleihen* to fund, to consolidate.

Konsolidierung *f* consolidation.

Konsonant *m* consonant.

konsonantisch *adj* consonant(al).

Konsonanz *f* (*Mus*) consonance.

Konsorten *pl* (*pej inf*) gang (*inf*), mob (*inf*), crowd (*inf*) ◆ **X und ~** X and his gang *etc.*

Konsortium [kɔn'zɔrtsiʊm] *nt* consortium, syndicate, group.

Konspiration [kɔnspira'tsio:n] *f* conspiracy, plot.

konspirativ [kɔnspira'ti:f] *adj* conspiratorial ◆ **~er Treff** meeting place (*for terrorists etc*), meet; **~e Wohnung** safe house.

konspirieren* [kɔnspi'ri:rən] *vi* to conspire, to plot.

konstant [kɔn'stant] *adj* constant.

Konstante [kɔn'stantə] *f* **-(n), -n** constant.

Konstantenspeicher [kɔn'stantənʃpaiçə] *m* (*Comput*) macro.

Konstantin ['kɔnstanti:n] *m* **-** Constantine.

Konstantinopel *nt* **-s** (*old*) Constantinople.

Konstanz[1] *f* (*geh*) constancy.

Konstanz[2] *nt* **-'** Constance.

konstatieren* [kɔnsta'ti:rən] *vt* to see, to notice ◆ **ich konstatiere, Sie haben schon wieder Ihre Hausaufgaben nicht gemacht** I see *or* notice you haven't done your homework once again; **in ihrer Rede konstatierte sie, daß** ... in her speech she made the point that ...

Konstellation [kɔnstɛla'tsio:n] *f* **(a)** constellation. **(b)** (*fig*) line-up; (*von Umständen, Faktoren etc*) combination ◆ **diese wirtschaftliche ~** this economic situation; **die neue ~ in der Partei** the new line-up in the party; **die ~ in dem Gremium** the make-up of the committee.

konsternieren* [kɔnstɛr'ni:rən] *vt* to scandalize.

konstituieren* [kɔnstitu'i:rən] **1** *vt* to constitute, to set up ◆ **~de Versammlung** constituent assembly.

2 *vr* to be constituted *or* set up.

Konstitution [kɔnstitu'tsio:n] *f* (*Pol, Med*) constitution; (*Phys auch*) structure.

konstitutionell [kɔnstitutsio'nɛl] *adj* constitutional.

konstitutiv [kɔnstitu'ti:f] *adj* constitutive.
konstruieren* [kɔnstru'i:rən] *vt* to construct (*auch Math*); (*Gram auch*) to construe ◆ **ein konstruierter Fall** a hypothetical case; **ein konstruiertes Wort** a made-up word; **der Satz klingt sehr konstruiert** the sentence sounds very artificial.
Konstrukt [kɔn'strʊkt] *nt* **-(e)s, -e** (*Ling*) construct.
Konstrukteur(in *f*) [kɔnstrʊk'tø:ɐ, tø:rɪn] *m* designer.
Konstruktion [kɔnstrʊk'tsio:n] *f* construction; (*Entwurf, Bauart auch*) design; (*gedanklich, philosophisch auch*) construct ◆ **erlauben Sie mir die ~ des folgenden Falles** allow me to make up *or* construct the following case; **es bieten sich folgende ~en des Handlungsvorganges an** there are several possible reconstructions of the event.
Konstruktions-: ~büro *nt* drawing office; **~fehler** *m* (*im Entwurf*) design fault; (*im Aufbau*) structural defect.
konstruktiv [kɔnstrʊk'ti:f] *adj* constructive.
Konstruktivismus [-'vɪsmʊs] *m* (*Art*) constructivism.
Konsul *m* **-s, -n** consul.
konsularisch *adj* consular.
Konsulat *nt* consulate.
Konsultation *f* (*form*) consultation ◆ **jdn zur ~ hinzuziehen** to consult sb.
konsultieren* *vt* (*form*) to consult.
Konsum *m* **-s, -s (a)** [kɔn'zu:m] *no pl* (*Verbrauch*) consumption. **(b)** ['kɔnzu:m, 'kɔnzʊm] (*Genossenschaft*) cooperative society; (*Laden*) cooperative store, co-op (*inf*).
Konsum|artikel *m* consumer item. **~** *pl* consumer goods *pl*.
Konsumation *f* (*Aus, Sw*) *food and drink consumed in a restaurant.*
Konsument *m* consumer.
Konsumentenhaltung *f* (*pej*) passive *or* non-participating attitude.
Konsum-: ~genossenschaft *f siehe* **Konsum (b)**; **~gesellschaft** *f* consumer society; **~gut** *nt usu pl* consumer item; **~güter** consumer goods *pl*; **k~hungrig** *adj* consumption-oriented; *Gesellschaft auch* consumerist.
konsumieren* *vt* to consume.
Konsumismus *m* consumerism.
Konsum-: ~tempel *m* shrine to consumerism; **~terror** *m* (*pej*) pressures *pl* of a materialistic society; **~zwang** *m* (*Sociol*) compulsion to buy.
Kontakt *m* **-(e)s, -e** contact (*auch Elec*); (*pl: Aut*) contact breakers *pl* ◆ **mit jdm in ~ kommen** to come into contact with sb; **mit jdm ~ bekommen, zu jdm ~ finden** to get to know sb; **ich bekomme mit ihm keinen ~** I don't feel I really know him; **mit jdm ~ aufnehmen** to get in contact *or* touch with sb, to contact sb; **mit jdm in ~ stehen** to be in contact *or* touch with sb; **~ herstellen** to make *or* establish contact; **den ~ unterbrechen** to break contact; **keinen ~ mehr haben, den ~ verloren haben** to have lost contact *or* touch, to be out of touch.
Kontakt-: ~abzug *m* (*Phot*) contact print; **~adresse** *f* accommodation address; **er hinterließ eine ~adresse** he left behind an address where he could be contacted; **~anzeige** *f* lonely hearts ad; **~anzeigen** *pl* personal column; **k~arm** *adj* **er ist k~arm** he finds it difficult to make friends; **~bildschirm** *m* touch-sensitive screen; **k~freudig** *adj* sociable, outgoing; **sie ist k~freudig** she makes friends easily; **~linse** *f* contact lens; **~mangel** *m* lack of contact; **~mann** *m, pl* **~männer** (*Agent*) contact; **~nahme** *f* **-, -n** (*form*) contacting; **~person** *f* contact.
Kontamination *f* (*Kerntechnik*) contamination; (*Gram*) blend(ing).
kontaminieren* *vi* to contaminate, to pollute; (*Gram*) to blend.
Kontemplation *f* contemplation.
kontemplativ *adj* contemplative.
Konten *pl of* **Konto.**
Kontenance [kõtə'nã:s] *f* **-,** *no pl* (*geh*) composure ◆ **die ~ bewahren** to keep one's composure *or* countenance.
Konter- *in cpds* (*Sport*) counter-; **~admiral** *m* rear-admiral; **~bande** *f* **-,** *no pl* contraband.
Konterfei *nt* **-s, -s** *or* **-e** (*old, hum*) likeness, portrait.
konterfeien* *vt* to portray.
konterkarieren *vt* to counteract; *Aussage* to contradict.
kontern *vti Schlag, Angriff* to counter.
Konter-: ~revolution *f* counter-revolution; **~schlag** *m* (*Sport, fig*) counter-attack; (*Boxen*) counter(-blow *or* -punch).
Kontext *m* **-(e)s, -e** context.
Konti *pl of* **Konto.**
Kontinent *m* **-(e)s, -e** continent.
kontinental *adj* continental.
Kontinental-: ~-Drift *f* continental drift; **~europa** *nt* the Continent; **~klima** *nt* continental climate; **~sockel** *m* continental shelf; **~sperre** *f* (*Hist*) Continental System.
Kontingent [kɔntɪŋ'gɛnt] *nt* **-(e)s, -e** (*Mil: Truppen~*) contingent; (*Comm*) quota, share; (*Zuteilung*) allotment, allocation.
kontingentieren* [kɔntɪŋgɛn'ti:rən] *vt* (*Comm*) to allocate, to apportion ◆ **den Import ~** to fix *or* impose import quotas.
Kontingenz [kɔntɪŋ'gɛnts] *f* (*Philos*) contingency.
Kontinua *pl of* **Kontinuum.**
kontinuierlich *adj* continuous.
Kontinuität [kɔntinu|i'tɛ:t] *f* continuity.
Kontinuum *nt* **-s, Kontinua** continuum.
Konto *nt* **-s, Konten** *or* **Konti** account ◆ **auf meinem/mein ~** in my/into my account; **das geht auf mein ~** (*inf*) (*ich bin schuldig*) I am responsible *or* to blame for this; (*ich zahle*) this is on me (*inf*).
Konto-: ~auszug *m* (bank) statement, statement (of account); **~auszugsdrucker** *m* bank statement machine; **~bewegung** *f* transaction; ⚠**k~führend** *adj Bank* where an account is held; **~führung** *f* running of an account; **~führungsgebühr** *f* bank charge; **~inhaber** *m* account holder; **~nummer** *f* account number.
Kontor *nt* **-s, -e (a)** (*Büro*) office; *siehe* **Schlag. (b)** (*Handelsniederlassung*) branch office.
Kontorist(in *f*) *m* clerk/clerkess.
Kontostand *m* balance, state of an account.
kontra *prep +acc* against; (*Jur*) versus.
Kontra *nt* **-s, -s** (*Cards*) double ◆ **jdm ~ geben** (*Cards*) to double; (*fig*) to contradict sb.
Kontra-: ⚠**~baß** *m* double-bass; **k~diktorisch** *adj* contradictory.
Kontrahent [kɔntra'hɛnt] *m* (*Vertragsschließender*) contracting party; (*Gegner*) opponent, adversary.
kontrahieren* [kɔntra'hi:rən] *vt* (*Ling, Med*) to contract.
Kontra|indikation *f* (*Med*) contra-indication.
Kontrakt *m* **-(e)s, -e** contract.
Kontraktion *f* (*Med*) contraction.
Kontra-: ~post *m* **-(e)s, -e** (*Art*) contrapposto; **k~produktiv** *adj* counter-productive. **~punkt** *m* (*Mus*) counterpoint; **k~punktisch** *adj* (*Mus*) contrapuntal.
konträr *adj* (*geh*) *Meinungen* contrary, opposite.
Kontrast *m* **-(e)s, -e** contrast.
Kontrast-: ~brei *m* (*Med*) barium meal; **~farbe** *f* contrasting colour; **~filter** *m* (*Phot*) yellow filter.
kontrastieren* *vi* to contrast.
Kontrast-: ~mittel *nt* (*Med*) contrast medium; **~programm** *nt* alternative programme; **~regelung** *f* contrast control; **~regler** *m* contrast (control); **k~reich** *adj* full of *or* rich in contrast, of many contrasts.
Kontratenor *m* counter-tenor.
Kontrazeption *f* (*form*) contraception.
kontribuieren* *vt* (*old*) to contribute.
Kontribution *f* (*old*) contribution.
Kontroll|abschnitt *m* (*Comm*) counterfoil, stub.
⚠**Kontrollampe** *f getrennt* **Kontroll-lampe** pilot lamp; (*Aut: für Ölstand*) warning light.
Kontrollbeamte(r) *m* inspector; (*an der Grenze*) frontier guard; (*zur Paßkontrolle*) passport officer; (*zur Zollkontrolle*) customs officer; (*zur Überwachung*) security officer.
Kontrolle *f* **-, -n (a)** (*Beherrschung, Regulierung*) control ◆ **über jdn/etw die ~ verlieren** to lose control of sb/sth; **jdn/etw unter ~ haben/halten** to have/keep sb/sth under control.
(b) (*Nachprüfung*) check (*gen* on); (*Aufsicht*) supervision; (*Paß~*) passport control; (*Zoll~*) customs examination ◆ **zur ~ haben wir noch einmal alles nachgerechnet** we went over all the figures again to check; **~n durchführen** to carry out *or* make checks; **der Luftverkehr ist unter ständiger ~** air traffic is kept under constant surveillance, a constant check is kept on air traffic; **nach einer sorgfältigen ~ der Waren** after a careful inspection of *or* check on *or* of the goods; **die ~ von Lebensmitteln** the inspection of foodstuffs.
(c) (*Person*) inspector; (*Paß~/Zoll~*) passport/customs officer; (*in Fabrik*) security officer; (*Polizist*) (*im Verkehr*) traffic police; (*an der Grenze*) frontier guard; (*in Bibliotheken etc*) person at the check-out desk.
(d) (*Stelle*) (*für Nach-/Überprüfung, Verkehr*) checkpoint; (*Paß~/Zoll~*) passport control/customs; (*vor Fabrik*) gatehouse; (*an der Grenze*) border post; (*in Bibliotheken etc*) check-out desk.
Kontrolleur [kɔntrɔ'lø:ɐ] *m* inspector.
Kontroll-: ~funktion *f* controlling function; **~gang** *m* (inspection) round; **~gruppe** *f* **(a)** (*Med, Psych*) control group; **(b)** (*Aufsichtsorgan*) surveillance group.
kontrollierbar *adj Behauptung* checkable, verifiable.
kontrollieren* *vt* **(a)** (*regulieren, beherrschen*) to control.
(b) (*nachprüfen, überwachen*) to check; (*Aufsicht haben über*) to supervise; *Paß, Fahrkarte etc* to inspect, to check ◆ **die Qualität der Waren muß streng kontrolliert werden** a strict check must be kept on the quality of the goods; **jdn/etw nach etw** *or* **auf etw** (*acc*) **~** to check sb/sth for sth.
Kontrolliste *f getrennt* **Kontroll-liste** check-list.
Kontroll-: ~kommission *f* control commission; **~lampe** *f siehe* **Kontrollampe**; ⚠**~liste** *f siehe* **Kontrolliste**; **~organ** *nt* monitoring body; **~punkt** *m* checkpoint; **~pflicht** *f* control; **seine ~pflicht vernachlässigen** to neglect one's supervisory responsibilities; **~rat** *m*: **Alliierter ~rat** Allied Control Council; **~stelle** *f* checkpoint; **~stempel** *m* inspection stamp; **~system** *nt* control system; **~turm** *m* control tower; **~uhr** *f* time clock; **~zentrum** *nt* control centre; (*Space also*) mission control.
kontrovers [kɔntro'vɛrs] *adj* controversial.
Kontroverse [kɔntro'vɛrzə] *f* **-, -n** controversy.
Kontur *f* **-, -en** *or* (*Art*) *m* **-s, -en** outline, contour ◆ **~en annehmen** to take shape.
Konturenstift *m* liner.
konturieren* *vt* (*lit, fig*) to outline.
Kontursitz *m* contoured seat.
Konus *m* **-, -se** *or* (*Tech*) **Konen** (*Math*) cone; (*Tech*) taper; (*Typ*) body.
Konvektor [kɔn'vɛktɔr] *m* convector (heater).
Konvenienz [kɔnve'niɛnts] *f* (*geh*) propriety; (*Bequemlichkeit*) convenience.
Konvent [kɔn'vɛnt] *m* **-(e)s, -e (a)** (*Versammlung*) convention. **(b)** (*Kloster*)

convent; (*Mönchs~*) monastery.
Konvention [kɔnvɛn'tsio:n] *f* **(a)** (*Herkommen*) convention ♦ **sich über die ~en hinwegsetzen** to sweep aside *or* ignore (social) conventions. **(b)** (*im Völkerrecht*) convention.
Konventionalstrafe [kɔnvɛntsio'na:l-] *f* penalty *or* fine (for breach of contract).
konventionell [kɔnvɛntsio'nɛl] *adj* conventional.
konvergent [kɔnvɛr'gɛnt] *adj* convergent, converging.
Konvergenz [kɔnvɛr'gɛnts] *f* convergence.
Konvergenztheorie *f* theory of convergence.
konvergieren* [kɔnvɛr'gi:rən] *vi* to converge.
Konversation [kɔnvɛrza'tsio:n] *f* conversation ♦ **~ machen** to make conversation *or* small talk (*inf*).
Konversationslexikon *nt* encyclopaedia.
Konversion [kɔnvɛr'zio:n] *f* conversion.
Konverter [kɔn'vɛrtɐ] *m* **-s, -** converter.
konvertibel [kɔnvɛr'ti:bl] *adj* (*Fin*) convertible.
Konvertibilität *f* (*Fin*) convertibility.
konvertierbar [kɔnvɛr'ti:ɐba:ɐ] *adj* (*Fin*) convertible.
Konvertierbarkeit *f* (*Fin*) convertibility.
konvertieren* [kɔnvɛr'ti:rən] [1] *vt* to convert (*in +acc* into).
[2] *vi aux haben or sein* to be converted.
Konvertit(in *f*) [kɔnvɛr'ti:t(ɪn)] *m* **-en, -en** convert.
konvex [kɔn'vɛks] *adj* convex.
Konvex-: k~konkav *adj* convexo-concave; **~linse** *f* convex lens; **~spiegel** *m* convex mirror.
Konvikt [kɔn'vɪkt] *nt* **-(e)s, -e** seminary.
Konvoi ['kɔnvɔy, -'-] *m* **-s, -s** convoy ♦ **im ~ fahren** to drive in convoy.
Konvolut [kɔnvo'lu:t] *nt* **-(e)s, -e** (*geh*) bundle (of papers).
Konvulsion [kɔnvʊl'zio:n] *f usu pl* (*Med*) convulsion.
konvulsivisch [kɔnvʊl'zi:vɪʃ] *adj* (*Med*) convulsive.
konzedieren* *vt* (*geh*) to concede, to grant (*jdm etw* sb sth).
Konzentrat *nt* concentrate; (*fig: eines Buches etc*) condensed version.
Konzentration *f* concentration (*auf +acc* on).
Konzentrations-: ~fähigkeit *f* power of concentration *usu pl*; **~lager** *nt* concentration camp; **~mangel** *m* lack of concentration; **~schwäche** *f* weak *or* poor concentration; **~vermögen** *nt siehe* **~fähigkeit.**
konzentrieren* [1] *vt* to concentrate (*auf +acc* on); *Truppen auch* to mass.
[2] *vr* to concentrate (*auf +acc* on); (*Untersuchung, Arbeit etc*) to be concentrated (*auf +acc* on).
konzentriert *adj* **(a)** (*Chem*) concentrated. **(b) mit ~er Aufmerksamkeit** with all one's concentration; **~ arbeiten/zuhören** to work/listen with concentration; **~ nachdenken** to concentrate.
konzentrisch *adj* (*Math, Mil*) concentric.
Konzept *nt* **-(e)s, -e** (*Rohentwurf*) draft, notes *pl*; (*für Aufsatz etc auch*) rough copy; (*Plan, Programm*) plan, programme; (*Begriff, Vorstellung*) concept ♦ **es ist jetzt wenigstens als** *or* **im ~ fertig** at least the draft *etc* is ready now; **jdn aus dem ~ bringen** to put sb off, to break sb's train of thought; (*inf: aus dem Gleichgewicht*) to upset sb; **aus dem ~ geraten** to lose one's thread; (*inf: aus dem Gleichgewicht*) to get upset; **das paßt mir nicht ins ~** that doesn't fit in with *or* suit my plans; (*gefällt mir nicht*) I don't like the idea; **jdm das ~ verderben** to spoil sb's plans.
Konzeption *f* **(a)** (*Med*) conception. **(b)** (*geh*) (*Gedankengang*) idea; (*Entwurf*) conception ♦ **seine ~ der Außenpolitik** his idea *or* conception of foreign policy; **ein schon in der ~ verfehltes Gedicht** a poem which in its (very) conception was a failure.
konzeptionell [kɔntsɛptsio'nɛl] *adj* (*geh*) conceptional.
Konzeptions-: ~furcht *f* (*Psych*) conception phobia, fear of conceiving; **k~los** *adj* without a definite line; *Außenpolitik etc auch* amorphous; **das Programm wirkt auf mich recht k~los** the programme strikes me as lacking any definite line; **~losigkeit** *f* lack of any definite line, amorphousness.
Konzept-: ~kunst *f* conceptual art; **~papier** *nt* rough paper.
Konzern *m* **-s, -e** combine, group (of companies) ♦ **die ~e haben zuviel Macht** the big companies have too much power.
Konzernbildung *f* formation of combines.
Konzert *nt* **-(e)s, -e** concert; (*von klassischen Solisten auch*) recital; (*Komposition*) concerto ♦ **die Kinder heulten im ~** the children cried in unison.
Konzert-: ~abend *m* concert evening; **~agentur** *f* concert artists' agency.
konzertant *adj* (*Mus*) in concerto form; *Sinfonie* concertante.
Konzert-: ~besucher *m* concert-goer; **~flügel** *m* concert grand.
konzertieren* [1] *vi* to give a concert; (*als Solist mitwirken*) to play in a concert.
[2] *vt* (*geh: abstimmen*) to concert.
konzertiert *adj* **~e Aktion** (*Fin, Pol*) concerted action.
Konzertina *f* **-, Konzertinen** concertina.
Konzert-: ~meister *m* leader, concertmaster (*US*); **~pavillon** *m* bandstand; **~pianist** *m* concert pianist; **~saal** *m* concert hall; **~sänger** *m* concert singer.
Konzession *f* **(a)** (*Gewerbeerlaubnis*) concession, licence, franchise. **(b)** (*Zugeständnis*) concession (*an +acc* to).
Konzessionär(in *f*) *m* concessionaire, licensee.
Konzessions-: k~bereit *adj* ready *or* willing to make concessions; **~bereitschaft** *f* readiness to make concessions.
konzessiv *adj* (*Gram*) concessive.
Konzessivsatz *m* (*Gram*) concessive clause.

Konzil *nt* **-s, -e** *or* **-ien** [-iən] (*Eccl, Univ*) council.
konziliant *adj* (*versöhnlich*) conciliatory; (*entgegenkommend*) generous.
Konzipient *m* (*Aus*) articled clerk.
konzipieren* [1] *vt* to conceive; (*entwerfen auch*) to design.
[2] *vi* (*Med*) to conceive.
konzis *adj* (*liter*) concise.
Koofmich *m* **-s, -s** *or* **-e** (*pej inf*) businessman type.
Koog *m* **-es, Köge** (*N Ger*) *siehe* **Polder.**
Ko|operation *f* cooperation.
ko|operativ *adj* cooperative.
Ko|operative *f* (*Econ*) cooperative.
Ko|operator *m* **(a)** (*Aus*) curate. **(b)** (*rare*) cooperator.
ko|operieren* *vi* to cooperate.
Ko|optation *f* coopting, cooption.
Ko|ordinate *f* **-, -n** (*Math*) coordinate.
Ko|ordinaten- (*Math*): **~achse** *f* coordinate axis; **~kreuz, ~system** *nt* coordinate system.
Ko|ordination *f* coordination.
Ko|ordinator *m*, **Ko|ordinatorin** *f* coordinator.
ko|ordinieren* *vt* to coordinate.
ko|ordinierend *adj* (*Gram*) coordinating.
Kopeke *f* **-, -n** copeck, kopeck.
Kopenhagen *nt* **-s** Copenhagen.
Kopenhagener *adj* Copenhagen *attr.*
Kopenhagener(in *f*) *m* person from Copenhagen.
Köpenickiade *f* hoax involving impersonation.
Köper *m* **-s,** *no pl* (*Tex*) twill.
kopernikanisch *adj* Copernican.
Kopf *m* **-(e)s, ¨e** **(a)** (*allgemein*) head; (*bei Plattenspieler*) head, pick-up; (*Pfeifen~*) bowl; (*Brief~*) (letter-)head; (*Zeitungs~*) head, heading; (*Nachrichten~*) heading; (*Spreng~, Gefechts~*) warhead ♦ **mit bloßem ~** bareheaded; **~ an ~** shoulder to shoulder; (*Pferderennen, Sport*) neck and neck; **bis über den ~** (*im Wasser*) up to one's neck *or* (*in Schulden*) ears; **~ voraus** *or* **voran** headfirst; **~ weg!** (*inf*) mind your head!; **~ hoch!** chin up!; **~ runter** *or* **ab!** off with his/her/their head(s); **auf dem ~ stehen** to stand on one's head; **sich** (*dat*) **den ~ waschen** to wash one's hair; **jdm den ~ waschen** (*inf*) to give sb a piece of one's mind (*inf*); **den ~ in den Nacken werfen** to throw one's head back; **den ~ oben behalten** to keep one's chin up; **jdm den ~ abschlagen** to behead sb, to cut sb's head off; **jdn einen ~ kürzer machen** (*sl*) to cut *or* chop sb's head off; **es werden ¨e rollen** heads will roll; **jds ~ fordern** (*lit, fig*) to demand sb's head; (*fig auch*) to cry for sb's blood; **von ~ bis Fuß** from top to toe, from head to foot; **sich** (*dat*) **an den ~ fassen** *or* **schlagen** (*fig*) to be (left) speechless; **das hältst du ja im ~ nicht aus!** (*sl*) it's absolutely incredible (*inf*); **die ¨e zusammenstecken** to go into a huddle (*inf*); **einen schweren** *or* **dicken** (*inf*) **~ haben** to have a thick head *or* a hangover; **mit besoffenem ~** (*sl*) drunk out of one's mind (*inf*); **sich den ~ zuschütten** *or* **zuziehen** to get tanked up (*inf*); **Geld** *etc* **auf den ~ hauen** (*inf*) to blow one's money *etc* (*inf*); **jdm auf den ~ spucken können** (*inf*) to tower above sb, to be head and shoulders above sb; **jdm über den ~ wachsen** (*lit*) to outgrow sb; (*fig*) (*Sorgen etc*) to be too much for sb, to be more than sb can cope with; (*Konkurrent etc*) to outstrip sb; **jdm auf dem ~ herumtrampeln** (*inf*) *or* **herumtanzen** (*inf*) to walk all over sb (*inf*); **den ~ für jdn/etw hinhalten** (*inf*) to take the blame *or* rap (*inf*) for sb/sth; **dafür halte ich meinen ~ nicht hin** (*inf*) I'm not putting my head on the chopping block for that; **etw auf den ~ stellen** (*lit, fig: durchsuchen*) to turn sth upside down; (*fig*) *Tatsachen* to stand facts on their heads; **und wenn du dich auf den ~ stellst, ...** (*inf*), **du kannst dich auf den ~ stellen, ...** (*inf*) no matter what you say/do ..., you can say/do what you like ...; **du kannst dich auf den ~ stellen, du wirst ihn nicht umstimmen** (*inf*) you can talk till you're blue in the face, you won't make him change his mind (*inf*); **jdn den ~ kosten** (*lit*) to cost sb his head; (*fig*) to cost sb his career *or* job; **das hat ihn den ~ gekostet** (*fig*) that was the end of the road for him; **~ und Kragen riskieren** *or* **wagen** (*inf*) (*körperlich*) to risk life and limb; (*beruflich etc*) to risk one's neck; **sich um seinen ~ reden** to sign one's own death warrant; **auf jds ~** (*acc*) **eine Summe/Belohnung aussetzen** to put a sum of money/reward on sb's head; **er ist nicht auf den ~ gefallen** he's no fool; **jdm etw an den ~ werfen** *or* **schmeißen** (*inf*) to chuck (*inf*) *or* sling (*inf*) sth at sb; **jdm Beschimpfungen/Beleidigungen an den ~ werfen** (*inf*) to hurl insults at sb *or* in sb's face; **jdm etw auf den ~ zusagen** to say sth straight out to sb; **den ~ hängenlassen** (*lit*) to hang one's head; (*fig*) to be downcast *or* despondent; **jdn vor den ~ stoßen** to offend *or* antagonize sb; **jdm den ~ zurechtsetzen** *or* **-rücken** to bring sb to his/her senses; **mit dem ~ durch die Wand wollen** (*inf*) to be determined to get *or* bent on getting one's own way regardless; **(jdm) zu ~(e) steigen** to go to sb's head; **ich war wie vor den ~ geschlagen** I was dumbfounded *or* thunderstruck; **über jds ~** (*acc*) **hinweg** over sb's head; **du hast wohl was am ~!** (*sl*) you must be off your head! (*inf*); **ein ~ Salat/Kohl** a head of lettuce/cabbage; **~ oder Zahl?** heads or tails?
(b) (*Einzelperson*) person ♦ **pro ~** per person *or* head *or* capita; **das Einkommen pro ~** the per capita income; **eine zehn ¨e starke Gruppe** a group of ten people.
(c) (*fig*) (*Verstand*) head; (*Denker*) thinker; (*leitende Persönlichkeit*) leader; (*Bandenführer*) brains *sing* ♦ **sich** (*dat*) **über etw** (*acc*) **den ~ zerbrechen** to rack one's brains over sth; **im ~ muß man's haben** (*inf*) you need brains, you have to have plenty up top (*inf*); **er ist nicht ganz richtig** *or* **klar im ~** (*inf*) he is not quite right in the head *or* up top (*inf*); **ein kluger/findiger ~** an

intelligent/ingenious person; **er ist ein fähiger ~** he has a good head on his shoulders, he's a very capable person; **die besten ~e** the best brains *or* minds.

(d) (*Sinn*) head, mind; (*Erinnerung*) memory ◆ **sich** (*dat*) **etw durch den ~ gehen lassen** to think about sth; **mir ist neulich in den ~ gekommen, daß ...** the other day it *or* the idea crossed my mind that ...; **nichts als Tanzen/ Fußball/Lesen** *etc* **im ~ haben** to think of nothing but dancing/football/ reading *etc*; **andere Dinge im ~ haben** to have other things on one's mind; **ich habe den ~ voll genug** (*inf*) I've got enough on my mind; **ich weiß kaum, wo mir der ~ steht** I scarcely know whether I'm coming or going; **einen kühlen ~ bewahren** *or* **behalten** to keep a cool head, to stay cool-headed, to keep one's cool (*inf*); **den ~ verlieren** to lose one's head, not to keep one's head; **den ~ nicht verlieren** to keep one's head, not to lose one's head; **sich** (*dat*) **etw aus dem ~ schlagen** to put sth out of one's mind; **jdm den ~ verdrehen** to turn sb's head; **der Gedanke will mir nicht aus dem ~** *or* **geht mir im ~ herum** I can't get the thought out of my head *or* mind; **es will mir nicht in den ~** I can't get my mind *or* head round it; **im ~** in one's head; **etw im ~ haben** to have sth in one's head; **etw im ~ rechnen** to work sth out in one's head *or* mentally; **ich habe die Melodie genau im ~** I know the tune exactly; **aus dem ~** from memory; **was man nicht im ~ hat, hat man in den Beinen** (*inf*) you'd/I'd forget your/my head if it wasn't screwed on (*inf*); **sie hat es sich** (*dat*) **in den ~ gesetzt, das zu tun** she has taken it into her head to do that, she has set her mind on doing that; **seinen ~ durchsetzen** to get one's own way; **seinen eigenen ~ haben** (*inf*) to have a mind of one's own; **es muß ja nicht immer alles nach deinem ~ gehen** you can't have things your own way all the time.

Kopf-: ~-an-~-Rennen *nt* neck-and-neck race; **~arbeit** *f* brain-work; **~arbeiter** *m* brain-worker; **~bahnhof** *m* terminus (station); **~ball** *m* (*Ftbl*) header; **~bedeckung** *f* headgear; **als ~bedeckung trug er ...** on his head he wore ...; **ohne ~bedeckung** without a hat; **~betrag** *m* per capita sum, sum per head; **~bild** *nt* (portrait of sb's) head.

Köpfchen *nt dim of* **Kopf** little head; (*fig hum*) brains ◆ **~, ~!** clever stuff!; **~ haben** to have brains, to be brainy (*inf*); **du bist aber ein kluges ~** (*iro*) clever *or* smart cookie, eh! (*inf*).

köpfeln (*Aus*) [1] *vi* (*einen Kopfsprung machen*) to dive (headfirst), to take a header.

[2] *vti siehe* **köpfen (c)**.

köpfen *vti* **(a)** *jdn* to behead, to decapitate; (*hum*) *Flasche Wein* to crack (open) ◆ **in Frankreich wird immer noch geköpft** they still behead *etc* people in France. **(b)** (*verschneiden*) *Bäume* to poll; *Jungtriebe* to cut off the heads of. **(c)** (*Ftbl*) to head ◆ **ins Tor ~** to head a goal, to head the ball in.

Kopf-: ~ende *nt* head; **~form** *f* shape of (the) head; **~füßer** *m* **-s, -** (*Zool*) cephalopod (*spec*); **~geld** *nt* head money; **~geldjäger** *m* bounty hunter; **~griff** *m* (*Rettungsschwimmen*) chinhold; (*Ringen*) headlock; **~grippe** *f* flu (and headache), (epidemic) encephalitis (*spec*); **~haar** *nt* hair on one's head; (*einzelnes*) hair from the head; **~haltung** *f* **eine gerade ~haltung haben** to hold one's head straight; **~haut** *f* scalp; **~hörer** *m* headphone.

-köpfig *adj suf* -headed ◆ **eine fünf~e Familie** a family of five.

Kopf-: ~jäger *m* head-hunter; **~jucken** *nt* itching of the scalp; **~keil** *m* (wedge-shaped) bolster; **~kissen** *nt* pillow; **~kissenbezug** *m* pillow case *or* slip; **~lage** *f* (*Med*) head presentation; **~länge** *f* **um eine ~länge** by a head; **k~lastig** *adj* (*lit, fig*) top-heavy; *Flugzeug* nose-heavy; **~lastigkeit** *f* top-heaviness; nose-heaviness; **~laus** *f* head louse; **~leiste** *f* (*Typ*) head rule; **k~los** *adj* (*fig*) in a panic, panicky, in a flap (*inf*); (*lit*) headless; **k~los werden** to lose one's head, to get into a flap (*inf*); **k~los handeln** to lose one's head; **~losigkeit** *f* (*fig*) panickiness; **~nicken** *nt* **-s,** *no pl* nod (of the head); **⚠~nuß** *f* (*inf*) clip *or* clout (round the earhole) (*inf*); **~prämie** *f* reward; **~putz** *m* headdress; **k~rechnen** *vi infin only* to do mental arithmetic; **~rechnen** *nt* mental arithmetic; **~salat** *m* lettuce; **k~scheu** *adj* timid, nervous, shy; **jdn k~scheu machen** to intimidate sb; **~schmerz** *m usu pl* headache; **~schmerzen haben** to have a headache; **sich** (*dat*) **über** *or* **um etw** (*acc*) *or* **wegen etw ~schmerzen machen** (*fig*) to worry about sth; **~schmerztablette** *f* aspirin, headache tablet; **~schmuck** *m* headdress; **⚠~schuß** *m* shot in the head; **~schütteln** *nt* **-s,** *no pl* shaking the head; **mit einem ~schütteln** with a shake of the *or* one's head; **sein ~schütteln zeigte mir, daß er ...** the way he shook his head told me that he ...; **k~schüttelnd** [1] *adj* shaking one's head; [2] *adv* with a shake of one's head, shaking one's head; **~schutz** *m* protection for the head; (*~schützer*) headguard; **~schützer** *m* **-s, -** headguard; **~seite** *f* (*von Münze*) heads, face side; (*von Zeitung*) front page; **~spiel** *nt* (*Ftbl*) heading; **~sprung** *m* header, dive; **einen ~sprung machen** to take a header, to dive (headfirst); **~stand** *m* headstand; **einen ~stand machen** to stand on one's head; **⚠k~stehen** *vi sep irreg aux sein* **(a)** (*lit*) to stand on one's head; **(b)** (*fig*) (*vor Ausgelassenheit*) to go wild (with excitement); (*vor Aufregung*) to be in a state of excitement; (*vor Empörung*) to be in a (state of) turmoil; (*durcheinander sein*) to be in a jumble, to be all topsy-turvy (*inf*); **~stein** *m* cobble-stone; **~steinpflaster** *nt* cobble-stones *pl*; **eine Gasse mit ~steinpflaster** a cobbled street; **~steuer** *f* poll tax; **~stimme** *f* (*Mus*) falsetto; (*Phon*) head voice; **~stoß** *m* (*Billiard*) massé; **~stück** *nt* (*Cook*) head end; **~stütze** *f* head-rest; (*Aut*) head restraint; **~tuch** *nt* (head)scarf; **k~über** *adv* (*lit, fig*) headfirst, headlong; **~verband** *m* (*Med*) head bandage; **~verletzung** *f* head injury; **~wäsche** *f* shampoo, hair-wash; **~weh** *nt siehe* **~schmerz**; **~wunde** *f* head wound; **~zahl** *f* number of persons; **~zeile** *f* (*Comput*) header; **~zerbrechen** *nt* **jdm ~zerbrechen machen** to be a worry to sb, to be a headache for sb (*inf*); **sich** (*dat*) **über etw** (*acc*) **~zerbrechen machen** to worry about sth.

Kopie [ko'piː, (*Aus*) 'koːpiə] *f* copy; (*fig*) carbon copy; (*Durchschlag auch*) carbon (copy); (*Ablichtung*) photocopy; (*Phot*) print; (*Film*) print, copy; (*von Statue*) copy, replica ◆ **das ist nicht das Original, sondern eine ~** it's not the original but a copy *or* imitation.

Kopier-: ~anstalt *f* (*Film*) printing laboratory, print lab (*inf*); **~apparat** *m siehe* **~gerät**; **~befehl** *m* (*Comput*) copy command.

kopieren* *vti* (*lit, fig*) to copy; (*nachahmen*) to imitate; (*ablichten*) to photocopy; (*durchpausen*) to trace; (*Phot, Film*) to print ◆ **oft kopiert, nie erreicht** often imitated but never equalled.

Kopierer *m* **-s, -** copier.

Kopier-: ~funktion *f* (*Comput*) copy function; **~gerät** *nt* photocopier; **k~geschützt** *adj* (*Comput, HiFi*) copy-protected; **~papier** *nt* photocopy paper; **~rad** *nt* (*Sew*) tracing wheel; **~rahmen** *m* printing frame; **~schutz** *m* (*Comput, HiFi*) copy protection; **mit ~schutz** copy-protected; **~sperre** *f* anti-copy device; **~stift** *m* indelible pencil; **~verfahren** *nt* photocopying process.

Kopilot(in *f*) *m* copilot.

Kopist(in *f*) *m* (*Nachahmer*) imitator; (*Art*) copyist.

Koppe *f* **-, -n** *siehe* **Kuppe**.

Koppel[1] *nt* **-s, -** *or* (*Aus*) *f* **-, -n** (*Mil*) belt.

Koppel[2] *f* **-, -n (a)** (*Weide*) paddock, enclosure ◆ **auf** *or* **in der ~** in the paddock *etc.* **(b)** (*Hunde~*) pack; (*Pferde~*) string. **(c)** (*Mus: Registerzug*) coupler.

Koppelgeschäft *nt* tie-in deal.

koppeln *vt* **(a)** (*zusammenbinden*) *Hunde* to tie *or* leash together; *Pferde* to tie *or* string together.

(b) (*verbinden*) to couple, to join (*etw an etw* (*acc*) sth to sth); *zwei Dinge* to couple *or* join together; *Raumschiffe auch* to link up; (*fig*) to link, to couple; (*als Bedingung*) to tie; *Ziele, Zwecke* to conjoin, to combine ◆ **eine Dienstreise mit einem Urlaub ~** to combine a business trip with a holiday; **einen Vertrag mit einer Klausel ~** to attach a clause to a contract.

(c) (*Elec*) to couple.

(d) (*Typ*) *Wort* to hyphenate.

Koppel-: ~rick *nt* **-s, -e** (*Pferderennen*) fence; **⚠~schloß** *nt* (*Mil*) belt buckle.

Kopp(e)lung *f, no pl* **(a)** (*Elec*) coupling. **(b)** (*Verbindung*) (*lit*) coupling, joining; (*fig, von Raumschiffen*) link-up. **(c)** (*Mus*) coupler.

Kopp(e)lungsmanöver *nt* (*Space*) docking manoeuvre ◆ **ein ~ durchführen** to link up.

Köpper *m* **-s, -** (*N Ger inf*) header ◆ **einen ~ machen** to take a header, to dive headfirst.

koppheister *adv* (*N Ger*) headfirst, headlong ◆ **~ schießen** to do a somersault.

Kopplung *f siehe* **Kopp(e)lung**.

Kopra *f* **-,** *no pl* copra.

Koproduktion *f* coproduction.

Koproduzent *m* coproducer.

Koprophagie [koprofa'giː] *f, no pl* (*Psych*) coprophagy.

Kopte *m* **-n, -n, Koptin** *f* Copt.

koptisch *adj* Coptic.

Kopula *f* **-, -s** *or* **-e** [lɛː] (*Gram*) copula.

Kopulation *f* (*Biol*) copulation, coupling; (*Hort*) splice grafting; (*old Jur: Trauung*) union.

kopulativ *adj* (*Gram*) copulative.

kopulieren* [1] *vt* (*Hort*) to splice-graft; (*old Jur: trauen*) to unite.

[2] *vi* (*koitieren*) to copulate.

kor *pret of* **küren**.

Koralle *f* **-, -n** coral.

Korallen-: ~bank *f* coral-reef; **~fischer** *m* coral fisherman; **~pilz** *m* goatsbeard; **~riff** *nt* coral-reef; **k~rot** *adj* coral(-red); **~tiere** *pl* coral.

Koran *m* **-s,** *no pl* Koran.

Koranschule *f* Koranic school.

Korb *m* **-(e)s, ¨e (a)** basket; (*Trag~ für Lasttiere auch*) pannier; (*Fisch~ auch*) creel; (*Bienen~*) hive; (*Förder~*) cage; (*Degen~, Säbel~*) basket hilt ◆ **ein ~ Äpfel** a basket of apples.

(b) (*~geflecht*) wicker ◆ **ein Sessel aus ~** a wicker(work) *or* basket(work) chair.

(c) (*inf: Abweisung*) refusal, rebuff ◆ **einen ~ bekommen, sich** (*dat*) **einen ~ holen** to get a refusal, to be turned down; **jdm einen ~ geben** to turn sb down.

Korb-: ~arbeit wickerwork *no pl*; **~ball** *m* basket-ball; **~blüt(l)er** *m* **-s, -** (*Bot*) composite (flower).

Körbchen *nt* **(a)** *dim of* **Korb** ◆ **ins ~!** (*baby-talk*) off to *or* time for bye-byes (*baby-talk*) or beddy-byes (*baby-talk*). **(b)** (*von Biene*) (pollen) basket; (*von Büstenhalter*) cup.

Korb-: ~flasche *f* demijohn; **~flechter(in** *f*) *m* **-s, -** *siehe* **~macher(in)**; **~flechterei** *f* basket-making; **~geflecht** *nt* basketwork, wickerwork; **~macher(in** *f*) *m* basket-maker; **~möbel** *pl* wicker(work) furniture; **~sessel** *m* wicker(work) chair; **~wagen** *m* bassinet; **~waren** *pl* wickerwork (articles); **~weide** *f* osier; **k~weise** *adv* by the basketful.

Kord *m* **-(e)s, -e** *siehe* **Cord**.

Kordel *f* **-, -n** cord.

Kordilleren *pl* (*Geog*) Cordilleras *pl*.

Kordon [kɔr'dõː, kɔr'doːn] *m* **-s, -s** *or* (*Aus*) **-e** [kɔr'doːnə] (*Mil, Bot*) cordon; (*Ordensband auch*) ribbon.

Kore *f* -, -n (*Archit*) caryatid.
Korea *nt* -s Korea.
Koreaner(in *f*) *m* -s, - Korean.
koreanisch *adj* Korean.
Koreanisch(e) *nt* Korean; *siehe auch* **Deutsch(e)**.
Koreastraße *f* **die** ~ the Korea Strait.
Koreferat *nt siehe* **Korreferat**.
Koreferent(in *f*) *m siehe* **Korreferent**.
kören *vt* to select for breeding purposes.
Korfiot(in *f*) *m* -en, -en Corfuan, Corfiote.
Korfu *nt* -s Corfu.
Körhengst *m* stud.
Koriander *m* -s, *no pl* coriander.
Korinth *nt* -s Corinth.
Korinthe *f* -, -n currant.
Korinthenkacker *m* (*sl*) fusspot (*inf*).
Korinther *m* -s, - Corinthian.
Korintherbrief *m* Epistle to the Corinthians, Corinthians *sing, no def art*.
korinthisch *adj* Corinthian.
Kork *m* -(e)s, -e (a) (*Bot*) cork. (b) *siehe* **Korken**.
Kork|eiche *f* cork oak *or* tree.
Korken *m* -s, - cork; (*aus Plastik*) stopper.
Korken-: ~zieher *m* -s, - corkscrew; **~zieherlocken** *pl* corkscrew curls *pl*.
korkig *adj* corky.
Korkmundstück *nt* cork filter.
Kormoran [kɔrmo'ra:n] *m* -s, -e cormorant.
Korn[1] *nt* -(e)s, ¨er (a) (*Samen~*) seed, grain; (*Pfeffer~*) corn; (*Salz~, Sand~, Tech, Phot, Typ*) grain; (*Hagel~*) stone; (*Staub~*) speck. (b) *no pl* (*Getreide*) grain, corn (*Brit*) ◆ **das ~ steht gut** the corn *etc* looks promising.
Korn[2] *m* -(e)s, - *or* -s (*Kornbranntwein*) corn schnapps.
Korn[3] *nt* -(e)s, -e (*am Gewehr*) front sight, bead ◆ **jdn/etw aufs ~ nehmen** (*lit*) to draw a bead on sb/sth; (*fig*) to hit out at sth; **jdn aufs ~ nehmen** (*fig*) to start keeping tabs on sb.
Korn-: ~ähre *f* ear of corn (*Brit*) *or* grain; **~blume** *f* cornflower; **k~blumenblau** *adj* cornflower blue; (*hum: volltrunken*) as drunk as a lord; **~branntwein** *m* (*form*) corn schnapps.
Körnchen *nt dim of* **Korn**[1] small grain, granule ◆ **ein ~ Wahrheit** a grain of truth.
Körndlbauer *m* (*Aus*) corn-growing (*Brit*) *or* grain-growing farmer.
körnen *vt* to granulate, to grain; (*aufrauhen*) to roughen.
Körner *m* -s, - centre punch.
Körner-: ~fresser *m* -s, - (*Zool*) grain-eating bird, granivore (*form*); (*inf*) health food freak (*inf*); **~futter** *nt* grain *or* corn (*Brit*) (for animal feeding).
Kornett[1] *nt* -s, -e *or* -s (*Mus*) cornet.
Kornett[2] *m* -(e)s, -e *or* -s (*old Mil*) cornet (*old*).
Kornfeld *nt* cornfield (*Brit*), grainfield.
körnig *adj* granular, grainy.
-körnig *adj suf* -grained.
kornisch *adj* Cornish.
Korn-: ~käfer *m* corn weevil; **~kammer** *f* (*lit, fig*) granary; **~rade** *f* (*Bot*) corn-cockle; **~speicher** *m* granary.
Körnung *f* (*Tech*) grain size; (*Phot*) granularity; (*Hunt*) decoy-place ◆ **Schmirgelpapier mit feiner ~** fine-grain sandpaper.
Korona *f* -, **Koronen** corona; (*inf*) crowd (*inf*), gang (*inf*).
Koronar- (*Med*) *in cpds* coronary.
Körper *m* -s, - (*alle Bedeutungen*) body; (*Schiffs~*) hull ◆ **~ und Geist** mind and body; **das braucht der ~** it's good for you; **am ganzen ~ beben** *or* **zittern/frieren** to tremble/to be cold all over.
Körper-: ~bau *m* physique, build; **~bautyp** *m* physical type; **~beherrschung** *f* physical control; **k~behindert** *adj* physically handicapped *or* disabled; **~behinderte(r)** *mf* physically handicapped *or* disabled person; **die ~behinderten** the physically handicapped, the disabled; **k~eigen** *adj* produced *or* occurring naturally in the body; **~ertüchtigung** *f* physical training, keep-fit exercises *pl*; **das dient der ~ertüchtigung** it helps keep you fit; **~fülle** *f* (*euph*) corpulence; **~geruch** *m* body odour, BO (*inf*); **~gewicht** *nt* weight; **~größe** *f* height; **~haltung** *f* posture, bearing; **~kontakt** *m* physical *or* bodily contact; **~kraft** *f* physical *or* bodily strength; **~kultur** *f* (a) (*DDR*) physical education *or* training; (b) (*~pflege*) personal hygiene; **~länge** *f* height; (*von Schlange etc*) (body) length.
körperlich *adj* physical; (*stofflich*) material, corporeal ◆ **~e Arbeit** manual work; **~e Züchtigung** corporal punishment; **sich ~ ertüchtigen** to keep oneself physically fit; **~e Vereinigung** (*geh*) physical union.
Körperlichkeit *f* corporeality.
Körper-: k~los *adj* bodiless, incorporeal; **~lotion** *f* body lotion; **~maße** *pl* measurements *pl*; **~öffnung** *f* (*Anat*) orifice of the body; **~pflege** *f* personal hygiene; **~puder** *m or nt* body powder; **~säfte** *pl* (*liter*) blood *sing*; (*~flüssigkeit*) body *or* bodily fluids *pl*.
Körperschaft *f* corporation, (corporate) body ◆ **gesetzgebende ~** legislative body; **~ des öffentlichen Rechts** public corporation *or* body.
Körperschaft(s)steuer *f* corporation tax.
Körper-: ~schwäche *f* physical weakness; **~sprache** *f* body language; **~spray** *m or nt* body spray; **~teil** *m* part of the body; **~temperatur** *f* body temperature; **~verletzung** *f* (*Jur*) bodily *or* physical injury; **fahrlässige ~verletzung** physical injury resulting from negligence; **schwere ~verletzung** grievous bodily harm; **~verletzung im Amt** *injury caused by a policeman/public official*; **~verletzung mit tödlichem Ausgang** manslaughter; **~wärme** *f* body heat.
Korporal *m* -s, -e *or* **Korporäle** corporal.
Korporation *f* (a) (*Studentenverbindung*) student society, fraternity (*US*). (b) (*Körperschaft*) corporation.
korporativ *adj Staat* corporate.
korporiert *adj pred* **~ sein** *to be a member of a students' society which fights duels*.
Korps [ko:ɐ] *nt* - [ko:ɐ(s)], - [ko:ɐs] (*Mil*) corps; (*Univ*) (duelling) corps.
Korps-: ~bruder *m* fellow member of a student (duelling) society; **~geist** *m* esprit de corps; **~student** *m* student belonging to a (duelling) society.
korpulent *adj* corpulent.
Korpulenz *f, no pl* corpulence.
Korpus[1] *m* -, -se (*Art*) body of Christ; (*hum inf: Körper*) body.
Korpus[2] *nt* -, **Korpora** (a) (*Ling*) corpus. (b) (*Mus*) resonance box.
Korpuskel *nt* -s, -n *or f* -, -n (*Phys*) particle, corpuscle.
Korreferat *nt* (a) (*Vortrag*) supplementary paper *or* report. (b) (*Prüfung*) second marking *or* assessment.
Korreferent(in *f*) *m* (a) (*Redner*) reader of a supplementary paper. (b) (*Prüfer*) second examiner.
korrekt *adj* correct; *Frage* civil.
korrekterweise *adv* to be correct, by rights.
Korrektheit *f* correctness.
Korrektiv *nt* corrective.
Korrektor *m*, **Korrektorin** *f* (*Typ*) proof-reader.
Korrektur *f* correction; (*Typ*) (*Vorgang*) proof-reading; (*Verbesserung*) proof correction; (*~fahne*) proof ◆ **~ lesen** to read *or* correct (the) proofs, to do (the) proof-reading (*bei etw* for sth), to proof-read (*bei etw* sth); **kann er ~ lesen?** can he proof-read?
Korrektur-: ~abzug *m* galley (proof); **~band** *nt* correction tape; **~bogen** *m* page proof; **~fahne** *f* galley (proof); **~flüssigkeit** *f* correction fluid; **~speicher** *m* correction memory; **~taste** *f* correction key; **~zeichen** *nt* proofreader's mark.
Korrelat *nt* correlate.
korrelieren* *vi* to correlate.
Korrepetitor *m* (*Mus*) repetiteur, coach.
Korrespondent(in *f*) *m* correspondent.
Korrespondenz *f* correspondence ◆ **mit jdm in ~ stehen** to be in correspondence with sb.
Korrespondenz-: ~büro *nt* news *or* press agency; **~schrift** *f* (*Comput*) letter quality.
korrespondieren* *vi* (a) (*in Briefwechsel stehen*) to correspond ◆ **~des Mitglied** corresponding member. (b) (*entsprechen*) to correspond (*mit* to, with). **~der Winkel** corresponding angle.
Korridor *m* -s, -e (*auch Luft~ etc*) corridor; (*Flur*) hall ◆ **der (Polnische) ~** (*Hist*) the Polish Corridor.
korrigierbar *adj* able to be corrected, corrigible (*form*) ◆ **ein nicht so leicht ~er Sprachfehler** a speech defect which is not so easy to put right *or* correct.
korrigieren* *vt* (*berichtigen*) to correct; *Aufsätze etc auch* to mark; *Meinung, Einstellung* to alter, to change ◆ **nach oben ~** to adjust upwards; *Gehaltsangebot etc auch* to top up; **nach unten ~** to adjust downwards; *Gehaltsforderung etc auch* to trim down.
korrodieren* *vti* (*vi: aux sein*) to corrode.
Korrosion *f* corrosion.
Korrosions-: k~beständig, k~fest *adj* corrosion-resistant; **k~frei** *adj* non-corrosive, non-corroding; **~schutz** *m* corrosion prevention.
korrosiv *adj* corrosive.
korrumpieren* *vt* to corrupt.
korrumpiert *adj* corrupt.
korrupt *adj* (*auch Comput*) corrupt.
Korruption *f, no pl* corruption.
Korsage [kɔr'za:ʒə] *f* -, -n corsage.
Korsar *m* -en, -en (*Hist*) corsair.
Korse *m* -n, -n Corsican.
Korselett [kɔrzə'lɛt] *nt* -(e)s, -e *or* -s corselet.
Korsett *nt* -s, -s *or* -e corset(s *pl*).
Korsettstange *f* stay.
Korsika *nt* -s Corsica.
Korsin *f* Corsican.
korsisch *adj* Corsican.
Korso *m* -s, -s (*Pferderennen*) horse-race; (*Umzug*) parade, procession; (*breite Straße*) avenue.
Kortex *m* -(es), **Kortizes** ['kɔrtitse:s] (*Anat*) cortex.
kortikal *adj* (*Anat*) cortical.
Kortison *nt* -s, -e (*Med*) cortisone.
Korund *m* -(e)s, -e (*Geol*) corundum.
Körung *f* selection for breeding purposes.
Korvette [kɔr'vɛtə] *f* (*Naut*) corvette; (*Sport*) jump to handstand.
Korvettenkapitän *m* lieutenant commander.
Koryphäe [kory'fɛ:ə] *f* -, -n genius; (*auf einem Gebiet*) eminent authority.
Kosak *m* -en, -en Cossack.
Kosakenmütze *f* cossack hat.
Koschenille [kɔʃə'nɪljə] *f* -, *no pl* cochineal.

koscher *adj* (*Rel, fig inf*) kosher ◆ **~ kochen/schlachten** to cook/slaughter according to kosher requirements.
K.-o.-Schlag [ka:'|o:-] *m* knockout blow ◆ **durch ~ siegen** to win by a knockout.
Koseform *f* affectionate *or* familiar form (*of proper name*).
kosen *vti* (*dated, geh*) **jdn/mit jdm ~** to fondle *or* caress sb; **~d** caressingly; **miteinander ~** to bill and coo.
Kose-: ~name *m* pet name; **~wort** *nt* term of endearment *or* affection.
K.-o.-Sieg [ka:'|o:-] *m* knock-out victory.
Kosinus *m* -, - *or* **-se** (*Math*) cosine.
Kosmetik *f* -, *no pl* beauty culture; (*Kosmetika, fig*) cosmetics *pl* ◆ **eine Reform, die sich nicht nur auf ~ beschränkt** a reform which is not merely cosmetic.
Kosmetiker(in *f*) *m* **-s, -** beautician, cosmetician.
Kosmetik-: ~institut *nt* beauty parlour; **~koffer** *m* vanity case; **~tuch** *nt* paper tissue.
Kosmetikum *nt* **-s, Kosmetika** cosmetic.
kosmetisch *adj* cosmetic ◆ **ein ~es Mittel** a cosmetic.
kosmisch *adj* cosmic ◆ **~ beeinflußt werden** to be influenced by the stars *or* the cosmos.
Kosmo-: ~biologie *f* space *or* cosmic biology; **~gonie** *f* cosmogony; **~loge** *m* cosmologist; **~logie** *f* cosmology; **~naut(in *f*)** *m* **-en, -en** cosmonaut; **~polit(in *f*)** *m* **-en, -en** cosmopolitan; **k~politisch** *adj* cosmopolitan.
Kosmos *m* -, *no pl* cosmos.
Kost *f* -, *no pl* **(a)** (*Nahrung, Essen*) food, fare ◆ **vegetarische/fleischlose ~** vegetarian/meatless diet; **geistige ~** (*fig*) intellectual fare; **leichte/schwere ~** (*fig*) easy/heavy going, heavy stuff (*inf*). **(b)** (*dated: Beköstigung*) board. **jdn in ~ nehmen** to take sb as a boarder; **(freie) ~ und Logis** *or* **Wohnung** (free) board and lodging.
kostbar *adj* (*wertvoll*) valuable, precious; (*luxuriös*) luxurious, sumptuous.
Kostbarkeit *f* **(a)** *siehe adj* value, preciousness; luxuriousness, sumptuousness. **(b)** (*Gegenstand*) treasure, precious object; (*Leckerbissen*) delicacy.
Kosten *pl* cost(s); (*Jur*) costs *pl*; (*Un~*) expenses *pl*; (*Auslagen auch*) outlay ◆ **die ~ tragen** to bear the cost(s); **auf ~ von** *or* **+gen** (*fig*) at the expense of; **auf ~ des Steuerzahlers** at the expense of the tax-payer, at the tax-payer's expense; **auf meine ~** (*lit, fig*) at my expense; **auf seine ~ kommen** to cover one's expenses; (*fig*) to get one's money's worth, to have a very good time; **~ spielen keine Rolle** money's no object.
kosten[1] *vti* **(a)** (*lit, fig*) to cost ◆ **was kostet das?** what *or* how much does it cost?, how much is it?; **was soll das ~?** what's it going to cost?; **das kostet/hat gekostet** (*inf*) it costs/it cost a bit *or* something; **koste es, was es wolle** whatever the cost; **das/die lasse ich mich etwas ~** I don't mind spending a bit of money on it/her; **jdn sein Leben/den Sieg ~** to cost sb his life/the victory; **was kostet die Welt?** (*inf*) the world's your/their *etc* oyster.
(b) (*in Anspruch nehmen*) *Zeit, Geduld etc* to take.
kosten[2] [1] *vt* (*probieren*) to taste, to try, to sample; (*fig*) to taste; *Freuden etc auch* to taste of (*liter*).
[2] *vi* to taste ◆ **willst du mal ~?** would you like a taste?; **von etw ~** to taste *etc* sth.
Kosten-: ~aufstellung *f* statement of costs; **~aufwand** *m* expense; **mit einem ~aufwand von 100.000 DM** at a cost of DM 100,000; **~bindung** *f* cost controls *pl*; **~dämpfung** *f* curbing cost expansion; **k~deckend** *adj* cost-effective; **~deckend arbeiten** to cover one's costs, to break even; **~deckung** *f* covering one's costs, breaking even; **~deckungsgrad** *m* level of cost-effectiveness; **~ersparnis** *f* cost saving; **~erstattung** *f* reimbursement of costs *or* expenses; **~explosion** *f* (*inf*) costs explosion; **~frage** *f* question of cost(s); **k~frei** *adj* cost-free, free of cost; **k~günstig** *adj* economical; **k~intensiv** *adj* (*Econ*) cost-intensive; **k~los** *adj, adv* free (of charge); **~miete** *f* rent which covers costs; **k~neutral** *adj* self-financing.
Kosten-Nutzen-Analyse *f* cost-benefit analysis.
Kosten-: k~pflichtig *adj* liable to pay costs, with costs; **eine Klage k~pflichtig abweisen** to dismiss a case with costs; **k~pflichtig verurteilt werden** to have costs awarded against one, to have to pay costs; **ein Kfz k~pflichtig abschleppen** to tow away a car at the owner's expense, to impound a car; **~planung** *f* costing; **~punkt** *m* cost question; **~punkt?** (*inf*) what'll it cost?, how much?; **~punkt: 100 DM** (*inf*) cost, DM 100; **~satz** *m* rate; ⚠**k~sparend** *adj* cost-saving; **etw k~sparend herstellen** to produce sth at low cost; **~stelle** *f* cost centre; **~voranschlag** *m* (costs) estimate; ⚠**~vorschuß** *m* advance.
Kost-: ~gänger *m* **-s, -** (*dated*) boarder; **~geld** *nt* board.
köstlich *adj* **(a)** *Wein, Speise* exquisite; *Luft* magnificent. **(b)** (*amüsant*) priceless. **~, wie er darauf reagiert hat** (*inf*) it was priceless the way he reacted; **du bist ja ~** (*inf*) you're priceless; **sich ~ amüsieren** to have a great time.
Köstlichkeit *f siehe adj* **(a)** *no pl* exquisiteness; magnificence. **(b)** *no pl* pricelessness. **(c)** (*Leckerbissen etc*) (culinary) delicacy.
Kost-: ~probe *f* (*von Wein, Käse*) taste; (*fig*) sample; **bei der ~probe** while tasting; **warst du auch bei der ~probe?** were you at the tasting too?; **k~spielig** *adj* costly, expensive.
Kostüm *nt* **-s, -e** **(a)** (*Theat: Tracht*) costume. **(b)** (*Schneider~*) costume (*dated*), suit. **(c)** (*Masken~*) fancy dress.
Kostüm-: ~ball *m* fancydress ball; **~bildner(in *f*)** *m* costume designer; **~fest** *nt siehe* **~ball**; **~film** *m* period film *or* picture.
kostümieren* *vr* to dress up.
Kostüm-: ~probe *f* (*Theat*) dress rehearsal; **~verleih** *m* (theatrical) costume agency.
Kostverächter *m*: **kein ~ sein** (*hum*) (*Feinschmecker sein*) to be fond of *or* to enjoy one's food; (*die Frauen lieben*) to be one for the ladies, to be a bit of a lad (*inf*).
Kot *m* **-(e)s,** *no pl* (*form*) excrement, faeces (*form*) *pl*; (*liter: Schmutz, Dreck*) mire, filth.
Kotangens *m* (*Math*) cotangent.
Kotau *m* **-s, -s** **(einen) ~ machen** (*pej*) to kowtow (*vor jdm* to sb).
Kote[1] *f* **-, -n** (*Surv*) spot height.
Kote[2] *f* **-, -n** (*Lappenzelt*) tent.
Kotelett ['kɔtlɛt, kɔt'lɛt] *nt* **-(e)s, -s** *or* (*rare*) **-e** chop, cutlet.
Kotelette [kotə'lɛtə] *f* (*usu pl*) (side)whisker, sideboard, sideburn (*US*).
koten *vi* (*form*) to defecate (*form*).
Köter *m* **-s, -** (*pej*) damn dog (*inf*).
Kotflügel *m* (*Aut*) wing.
kotig *adj* filthy.
K.-o.-Tropfen *pl* (*inf*) knock -out drops (*inf*).
Kotzbrocken *m* (*sl*) mean bastard (*Brit sl*), son of a bitch (*US vulg*).
Kotze *f* -, *no pl* (*vulg*) vomit, puke (*sl*).
kotzen *vi* (*vulg*) to throw up (*inf*), to puke (*sl*) ◆ **das ist zum K~** (*sl*) it makes you sick; **du bist zum K~** (*sl*) you make me sick, you make me want to throw up *or* puke (*sl*); **da kann man das (kalte) K~ kriegen** (*sl*) it makes you want to throw up *or* puke (*sl*).
kotzübel *adj* (*sl*) **mir ist ~** I feel like throwing up (*inf*).
KP [ka:'pe:] *f* **-, -s** *abbr of* **Kommunistische Partei.**
KPD [ka:pe:'de:] *f abbr of* **Kommunistische Partei Deutschlands.**
KPdSU [ka:pe:de:|ɛs'|u:] *f* - *abbr of* **Kommunistische Partei der Sowjetunion** Communist Party of the Soviet Union.
Krabbe *f* **-, -n** **(a)** (*Zool*) (*klein*) shrimp; (*größer*) prawn. **(b)** (*dated inf: Kind*) tot (*inf*), mite (*inf*) ◆ **eine süße kleine ~** a sweet little thing. **(c)** (*Archit*) crocket.
Krabbel-: ~alter *nt* crawling stage (*of a baby*); **~gruppe** *f* playgroup.
krabbeln [1] *vi aux sein* to crawl.
[2] *vt* (*kitzeln*) to tickle.
[3] *vti impers* (*kitzeln*) to tickle; (*jucken*) to itch; *siehe* **kribbeln.**
Krabbencocktail [-kɔkte:l] *m* prawn cocktail.
Krach *m* **-(e)s, ¨-e** **(a)** *no pl* (*Lärm*) noise, din, racket (*inf*); (*Schlag*) crash, bang ◆ **~ machen** to make a noise *etc*.
(b) (*inf: Zank, Streit*) row, quarrel, fight ◆ **mit jdm ~ haben** to have a row *etc* with sb, to row *or* quarrel *or* fight with sb; **mit jdm ~ kriegen** to get into trouble with sb, to have a row with sb; **~ schlagen** to make a fuss.
(c) (*Börsen~*) crash.
krach *interj* crash, bang.
krachen [1] *vi* **(a)** (*Lärm machen*) to crash, to bang; (*Holz*) to creak; (*Schuß*) to ring out; (*Donner*) to crash ◆ **~d fallen** *etc* to fall with a crash *or* bang; **..., daß es nur so krachte** (*lit*) with a bang *or* crash; (*fig*) with a vengeance; **sonst kracht's!** (*inf*) or there'll be trouble; **es hat gekracht** (*inf*) (*Zusammenstoß*) there's been a crash.
(b) *aux sein* (*inf*) (*aufplatzen*) to rip (open), to split; (*brechen*) to break; (*Eis*) to crack; (*Betrieb*) to crash.
(c) *aux sein* (*inf: aufprallen*) to crash.
[2] *vr* (*inf*) to have a row *or* fight *or* quarrel.
Kracher *m* **-s, -** banger (*Brit*), fire-cracker (*US*).
Kracherl *nt* **-s, -(n)** (*Aus inf*) pop (*inf*), fizzy pop (*inf*).
Krach-: k~ledern *adj* (*fig hum*) rustic; **~lederne** *f* **-n, -n** leather shorts *pl*, lederhosen *pl*; **~macher(in *f*)** *m* (*inf*) (*lit*) noisy person *or* character; (*fig*) trouble-maker; **hör auf, du ~macher!** must you make so much noise!
Krächzen *nt* **-s,** *no pl* croak(ing); (*von Vogel*) caw(ing).
krächzen *vi* to croak; (*Vogel*) to caw.
kracken ['krakn, 'krɛkn] *vt* (*Chem*) to crack.
Kräcker *m* **-s, -** (*Cook*) cracker.
Krad *nt* **-(e)s, ¨-er** (*Mil, dated*) motor-cycle.
Krad-: ~fahrer *m* (*dated*) motor-cyclist; **~melder** *m* (*Mil*) motor-cycle despatch rider.
Kraft *f* **-, ¨-e** **(a)** (*körperlich, sittlich*) strength *no pl*; (*geistig, schöpferisch*) powers *pl*; (*von Prosa, Stimme*) strength, power, force; (*von Muskeln, Ringkämpfer*) strength, power; (*Energie*) energy, energies *pl* ◆ **er weiß nicht wohin mit seiner ~** (*inf*) he's just bubbling over with energy; **er kann vor ~ nicht mehr laufen** (*hum*) he's so muscle-bound he can hardly move; **die ¨-e (mit jdm) messen** to try *or* pit one's strength (against sb); (*fig*) to pit oneself against sb; **wenn man alle ¨-e anspannt** *or* **zusammennimmt** if you summon up all your strength; **seine ¨-e sammeln** to build up *or* recover one's strength; **mit frischer ~** with renewed strength; **mit letzter ~** with one's last ounce of strength; **die ~ aufbringen, etw zu tun** to find the strength to do sth; **mit vereinten ¨-en werden wir ...** if we combine our efforts *or* join forces we will ...; **die ~ der Verzweiflung** the strength born of desperation; **das geht über meine ¨-e** it's more than I can take; **ich bin am Ende meiner ~** I can't take any more; **mit aller** *or* **voller ~** with all one's might *or* strength; **er will mit aller ~ durchsetzen, daß ...** he will do his utmost to ensure that ...; **aus eigener ~** by oneself; (*fig auch*) by one's own efforts, single-handedly; **nach (besten) ¨-en** to the best of one's ability; **er tat, was in seinen ¨-en stand** he did everything (with)in his power; **nicht/wieder bei ¨-en sein** not to be in very good shape/to have (got) one's strength back; **wieder zu ¨-en kommen** to regain one's strength.
(b) (*Phys: einer Reaktion etc*) force; (*der Sonne etc*) strength, power; (*no pl: Wirksamkeit, liter, Bibl: Macht*) power ◆ **die treibende ~** (*fig*) the driving force;

⚠: Informationen zur Rechtschreibreform im Anhang

das Gleichgewicht der ~̈e (*Pol*) the balance of power; **das Parallelogramm der ~̈e** (*Phys*) the parallelogram of forces; **die heilende ~ der Sonne** the healing power of the sun; **die tröstende ~ der Musik** the comforting power of music.
(c) (*usu pl: in Wirtschaft, Politik etc*) force.
(d) *no pl* (*Jur: Geltung*) force ◆ **in ~ sein/treten** to be in/come into force; **außer ~ sein/treten** to have ceased to be in force/to cease to be in force, to be no longer in force; **außer ~ setzen** to cancel, to annul.
(e) *no pl* (*Naut: Geschwindigkeit*) **halbe/volle ~ voraus!** half/full speed ahead.
(f) (*Arbeits~*) employee, worker; (*Haushalts~*) domestic help; (*Lehr~*) teacher ◆ **~̈e** staff, personnel *no pl*.

kraft *prep +gen* (*form*) by virtue of; (*mittels*) by use of ◆ **~ meines Amtes** by virtue of my office; **~ meiner Befugnisse** on the strength of *or* by virtue of my authority.

Kraft-: ~akt *m* strong-man act; (*fig*) show of strength; **~anstrengung** *f* exertion; **~arm** *m* (*Phys*) lever arm to which force is applied; **~aufwand** *m* effort; **unnützer ~aufwand** wasted effort, waste of energy; **~ausdruck** *m* swearword; **~ausdrücke** strong language; **~brühe** *f* beef tea; **~droschke** *f* (*form*) Hackney carriage (*form*), taxicab; **~einheit** *f* (*Phys*) unit of force.

Kräfteparallelogramm *nt* parallelogram of forces.

Kraftersparnis *f* saving of energy *or* effort.

Kräfte-: ~spiel *nt* power play; **~verfall** *m* loss of strength; **~verhältnis** *nt* (*Pol*) balance of power; (*von Mannschaften etc*) relative strength; **~verlagerung** *f* (*Pol*) power shift; **~verschleiß** *m* waste of energy.

Kraftfahrer(in *f*) *m* (*form*) motorist, driver; (*als Beruf*) driver.

Kraftfahr-: ~park *m* fleet of motor vehicles; **k~technisch** *adj attr* mechanical; **k~technische Ausbildung** training in motor mechanics; **~truppe** *f* (*Mil*) motorized unit.

Kraftfahrzeug *nt* motor vehicle.

Kraftfahrzeug-: ~brief *m* (vehicle) registration document, logbook (*Brit*); **~kennzeichen** *nt* (vehicle) registration; **~mechaniker** *m* motor mechanic; **~schein** *m* (vehicle) registration document; **~steuer** *f* motor vehicle tax, road tax (*Brit*); **~versicherung** *f* car insurance.

Kraft-: ~feld *nt* (*Phys*) force field; **~futter** *nt* concentrated feed(stuff).

kräftig [1] *adj* strong; *Mann, Geschmack, Muskel, Stimme auch* powerful; *Ausdrucksweise auch* powerful, forceful; *Haarwuchs, Pflanze auch* healthy; *Farbe auch* rich; *Schlag* hard, powerful, hefty (*inf*); *Händedruck* firm, powerful; *Fluch* violent; *Suppe, Essen* nourishing; (*groß*) *Portion* big, massive; *Preiserhöhung* big, massive; *Beifall* loud ◆ **~e Ausdrücke** strong language; **einen ~en Schluck nehmen** to take a good *or* big swig; **eine ~e Tracht Prügel** a good *or* sound *or* thorough beating.
[2] *adv* **(a)** *gebaut* strongly, powerfully; *zuschlagen, treten, pressen, drücken, blasen* hard; *klatschen* loudly; *lachen, mitsingen* heartily; *fluchen, niesen* violently ◆ **etw ~ schütteln/polieren/umrühren** to shake/polish/stir sth vigorously, to give sth a good shake/polish/stir; **jdn ~ verprügeln** to give sb a sound *or* good *or* thorough beating; **~ essen/trinken** to eat well/to drink a lot; **husten Sie mal ~** have a good cough; **er hat sich ~ dagegen gewehrt** he objected most strongly; (*körperlich*) he put up a strong resistance; **sich für etw ~ einsetzen** to support sth strongly *or* energetically.
(b) (*zur Verstärkung*) really ◆ **es hat ~ geregnet/geschneit** it really rained/snowed, it rained/snowed heavily; **die Preise sind ~ gestiegen** prices have gone up a lot, prices have really gone up; **jdn ~ ausschimpfen** to give sb a good bawling out (*inf*), to really give sb a bawling out (*inf*); **sich ~ täuschen** (*inf*) to be really *or* very much *or* greatly mistaken; **jdn ~ belügen** (*inf*) to tell sb a pack of lies; **sich ~ ausweinen** to have a good cry; **sich ~ ärgern** to get really *or* mighty (*inf*) annoyed.

kräftigen *vt* (*geh*) **jdn ~** to build up sb's strength; (*Luft, Bad etc*) to invigorate sb; (*Essen, Mittel etc*) to fortify sb.

Kräftigung *f* (*geh*) *siehe vt* strengthening; invigoration; fortification.

Kräftigungsmittel *nt* tonic.

Kraftlinien *pl* (*Phys*) lines of force *pl*.

kraftlos *adj* (*schwach*) feeble, weak; (*schlaff*) limp; (*machtlos*) powerless; (*Jur*) invalid ◆ **~ sank er zurück** he fell feebly back.

Kraftlos|erklärung *f* (*Jur*) invalidation, annulment.

Kraftlosigkeit *f siehe adj* feebleness, weakness; limpness; powerlessness; invalidity.

Kraft-: ~meier *m* **-s, -** (*inf*) muscle man (*inf*); (*fig*) strong-man; **~meierei** *f* strongarm tactics *pl*; **verbale ~meierei** tough talking; **~mensch** *m* strongman, muscle man (*inf*); **~messer** *m* **-s, -** dynamometer (*form*); (*auf Jahrmarkt*) test-your-strength machine; **~post** *f* post(al) bus service; **~probe** *f* test of strength; (*zwischen zwei Gruppen, Menschen*) trial of strength; **~protz** *m* (*inf*) muscle man (*inf*); **~rad** *nt* motor-cycle, motorbike; **~raum** *m* power training gym; **~sport** *m* sport(s *pl*) involving strength; **~sportler** *m* power athlete; **~spruch** *m* strong words *pl*; **~stoff** *m* fuel; **k~strotzend** *adj* exuding vitality, vigorous; *Pflanze* healthy-looking, vigorous; (*muskulös*) with bulging muscles; **ein k~strotzendes Baby** a big strong bouncing baby; **~training** *nt* power training; **~übertragung** *f* power transmission; **~vergeudung** *f siehe* **~verschwendung**; **~verkehr** *m* motor traffic; **~verschwendung** *f* waste of energy *or* effort; **k~voll** *adj* (*geh*) *Stimme* powerful; **~wagen** *m* motor vehicle; **~werk** *nt* power station; **~wort** *nt siehe* **~ausdruck**.

Kragdach *nt* overhanging roof.

Kragen *m* **-s, -** *or* (*S Ger, Sw auch*) **¨** collar ◆ **jdn am** *or* **beim ~ packen** to grab sb by the collar; (*fig inf*) to collar sb; **mir platzte der ~** (*inf*) I blew my top (*inf*); **jetzt platzt mir aber der ~!** this is the last straw!; **es geht ihm jetzt an den ~** (*inf*) he's in for it now (*inf*); *siehe* **Kopf**.

Kragen-: ~knopf *m* collar stud; **~nummer** *f siehe* **~weite**; **~spiegel** *m* (*Mil*) collar patch; **~weite** *f* (*lit*) collar size; **eine ~weite zu groß für jdn sein** (*fig inf*) to be too much for sb (to handle); **das ist nicht meine ~weite** (*fig inf*) that's not my cup of tea (*inf*).

Kragstein *m* (*Archit*) console.

Krähe *f* **-, -n** crow ◆ **eine ~ hackt der anderen kein Auge aus** (*Prov*) birds of a feather stick together (*Prov*).

krähen *vi* to crow; *siehe* **Hahn**.

Krähen-: ~fuß *m* (*Eisenkralle*) crowbar; **~füße** *pl* (*an den Augen*) crowsfeet *pl*; (*Schriftkrakel*) scrawl *sing*; **~nest** *nt* (*Naut*) crow's nest.

Krähwinkel *m* (*pej*) cultural backwater.

Krakau *nt* **-s** Cracow.

Krakauer *f* **-, -** *spicy smoked sausage with garlic.*

Krakauer(in *f*) *m* **-s, -** Cracovian.

Krake *m* **-n, -n** octopus; (*Myth*) Kraken.

Krakeel *m* **-s,** *no pl* (*inf*) row ◆ **~ machen** (*inf*) to kick up a row *or* racket (*inf*).

krakeelen* *vi* (*inf*) to make *or* kick up a row *or* racket (*inf*).

Krakeeler(in *f*) *m* **-s, -** (*inf*) rowdy (*inf*), rowdy type (*inf*).

Krakel *m* **-s, -** (*inf*) scrawl, scribble.

Krakelei *f* (*inf*) scrawl, scribble.

krakelig *adj* scrawly.

krakeln *vti* to scrawl, to scribble.

Kral *m* **-s, -e** kraal.

Kralle *f* **-, -n** claw; (*von Raubvogel auch*) talon; (*pej: Fingernagel*) claw, talon; (*sl: Hand*) paw (*inf*), mauler (*sl*); (*Park~*) wheel clamp ◆ **jdn/etw in seinen ~n haben** (*fig inf*) to have sb/sth in one's clutches; **(jdm) die ~n zeigen** (*fig*) to show (sb) one's claws; **jdn aus den ~n des Todes retten** to rescue sb from the jaws of death; **auf die ~** (*sl*) (cash) on the nail (*inf*).

krallen [1] *vr* **sich an jdn/etw ~** (*lit, fig*) to cling to sb/sth; (*Katze*) to dig its claws into sb/sth; **sich in etw** (*acc*) **~** to sink its claws into sth; (*mit Fingern*) to dig one's fingers into sth.
[2] *vt* **(a) die Finger in etw** (*acc*)**/um etw ~** to dig one's fingers into sth/to clutch sth; **er krallte vor Schmerz die Finger in die Decke** he clawed (at) the blanket in pain.
(b) (*sl*) to pinch (*inf*), to swipe (*inf*).
(c) (*Aut*) to clamp.
[3] *vi* to claw (*an +dat* at).

Kram *m* **-(e)s,** *no pl* (*inf*) (*Gerümpel*) junk; (*Zeug*) things *pl*, stuff (*inf*); (*Angelegenheit*) business ◆ **den ~ satt haben/hinschmeißen** to be fed up with/to chuck the whole thing *or* business (*inf*); **das paßt mir nicht in den ~** it's a confounded nuisance; **mach doch deinen ~ allein!** do it yourself!; **laß mich meinen ~ alleine machen** don't tell me what to do.

kramen [1] *vi* **(a)** to rummage about (*in +dat* in, *nach* for). **(b)** (*Sw inf*) to do a bit of shopping.
[2] *vt* **etw aus etw ~** to fish sth out of sth.

Krämer(in *f*) *m* **-s, -** small shopkeeper, grocer; (*Laden*) small general store, grocer's ◆ **ein Volk von ~n** a nation of shopkeepers.

Krämer-: ~geist *m*, **~seele** *f* small- *or* petty-minded person; **ein ~geist** *or* **eine ~seele sein** to be small- *or* petty-minded; **einen ~geist** *or* **eine ~seele haben** to have a small *or* petty mind.

Kramladen *m* (*pej inf*) tatty little shop (*inf*); (*Trödelladen*) junk shop.

Krampe *f* **-, -n** staple.

Krampen *m* **-s, -** staple; (*Aus: Spitzhacke*) pick(-axe).

Krampf *m* **-(e)s, ¨e (a)** (*Zustand*) cramp; (*Verkrampfung, Zuckung*) spasm; (*wiederholt*) convulsion(s *pl*); (*Anfall, Lach~*) fit ◆ **einen ~ haben/bekommen** to have/get (a) cramp. **(b)** *no pl* (*inf*) (*Getue*) palaver (*inf*); (*Unsinn*) nonsense, rubbish.

Krampf-: ~ader *f* varicose vein; **k~artig** *adj* convulsive.

krampfen [1] *vt Finger, Hand* to clench (*um etw* around sth) ◆ **die Finger in etw** (*acc*) **~** to dig one's fingers into sth.
[2] *vr* **sich um etw ~** to clench sth.
[3] *vi* **(a)** (*Krämpfe haben*) to have a convulsion/convulsions. **(b)** (*Sw inf: hart arbeiten*) to slave away (*inf*).

Krampf-: k~haft *adj Zuckung* convulsive; (*inf: angestrengt, verzweifelt*) frantic, desperate; *Lachen* forced *no adv*; **sich k~haft an etw** (*dat*) **festhalten** (*lit, fig inf*) to cling desperately to sth; **~husten** *m* (*Aus inf*) whooping cough; **k~lindernd** *adj* antispasmodic (*spec*); **k~lösend** *adj* antispasmodic (*spec*).

Krampus *m* **-** (*Aus*) *companion of St Nicholas.*

Kran *m* **-(e)s, ¨e** *or* **-e (a)** crane. **(b)** (*dial: Hahn*) tap, faucet (*US*).

Kranführer *m* crane driver *or* operator.

krängen *vi* (*Naut*) to heel (over).

Kranich *m* **-s, -e** (*Orn*) crane.

krank *adj, comp* **¨er**, *superl* **¨ste(r, s)** *or adv* **am ¨sten** ill *usu pred*, sick (*auch fig*), not well; (*leidend*) invalid; *Pflanze, Organ* diseased; *Zahn, Bein* bad; *Wirtschaft, Firma* ailing; (*Hunt*) *Wild* wounded ◆ **~ werden** to fall *or* be taken ill *or* sick; **schwer ~** seriously ill; **~ am Herzen/an der Seele** (*liter*) sick at heart (*liter*); **vor Aufregung/Angst ~** sick with excitement/fear; **vor Heimweh/Liebe ~** homesick/lovesick; **sich ~ melden** to let sb/one's boss *etc* know that one is sick *or* ill; (*telefonisch*) to phone in sick; (*esp Mil*) to report sick; **sie hat sich ~ gemeldet** she is off sick; **jdn ~ schreiben** to give sb a medical certificate; (*esp Mil*) to put sb on the sick-list; **er ist schon seit einem halben Jahr ~ geschrieben** he's been off sick for six months; **sich ~ stellen** to pretend to be ill *or* sick, to malinger; **das macht/du machst mich ~!** (*inf*) it gets/you get on my nerves! (*inf*), it drives/you drive me round the bend! (*inf*); **du bist**

wohl ~! (*inf iro*) there must be something wrong with you!; **der ~e Mann am Bosporus** the Sick Man of Europe.

kränkeln *vi* to be ailing (*auch Wirtschaft, Firma*), to be sickly, to be in bad *or* poor health ◆ **sie ~ leicht** they're often poorly.

kranken *vi* to suffer (*an +dat* from) ◆ **das krankt daran, daß** ... (*fig*) it suffers from the fact that ...

kränken [1] *vt* **jdn ~** to hurt sb('s feelings), to wound sb; **sie war sehr gekränkt** she was very hurt; **es kränkt mich, daß** ... it hurts *or* grieves me that ...; **jdn in seiner Ehre ~** to offend sb's pride; **~d** hurtful.
[2] *vr* **sich über etw** (*acc*) **~** (*dated, dial*) to feel upset about sth.

Kranken-: ~akte *f* medical file; **~anstalten** *pl* hospitals and/or clinics *pl*; **~auto** *nt siehe* **~wagen**; **~bericht** *m* medical report; **~besuch** *m* visit (to a sick person); (*von Arzt*) (sick) call; **~bett** *nt* sick-bed; **~geld** *nt* sickness benefit; (*von Firma*) sickpay; **~geschichte** *f* medical history; **~gymnastik** *f* physiotherapy; **~gymnastin** *f* physiotherapist.

Krankenhaus *nt* hospital ◆ **ins ~ gehen** (*als Patient*) to go into (the *US*) hospital; **im ~ liegen** to be in (the *US*) hospital; **jdn in einem ~ unterbringen** to put sb in a hospital; **an einem ~ sein** (*Arzt, Schwester etc*) to work in a hospital.

Krankenhaus- *in cpds* hospital; **~arzt** *m* hospital doctor; **~aufenthalt** *m* stay in hospital; **~kosten** *pl* hospital charges *pl or* costs *pl*; **~rechnung** *f* bill for hospital treatment; **k~reif** *adj* in need of hospital treatment; **jdn k~reif schlagen** to make a stretcher-case out of sb; **~seelsorger** *m* hospital chaplain.

Kranken-: ~kasse *f* (*Versicherung*) medical *or* health insurance; (*Gesellschaft*) medical *or* health insurance company; **ich bin in einer privaten ~kasse** I am in a private medical insurance scheme, I'm privately insured; **er ist in keiner ~kasse** he has no medical insurance; **~lager** *nt* (*Krankenbett*) sick-bed; (*Kranksein*) illness; **das Fieber warf ihn aufs ~lager** (*geh*) the fever confined him to his sick-bed; **~pflege** *f* nursing; **~pfleger** *m* orderly; (*mit Schwesternausbildung*) male nurse; **~pflegerin** *f* nurse; **~pflegeschülerin** *f* student nurse; **~saal** *m* ward; **~salbung** *f* (*Eccl*) anointing of the sick; **~schein** *m* medical insurance record card; **~schwester** *f* nurse; **~stand** *m* (*dial, Aus*) **im ~stand sein** to be sick *or* ill; **~stuhl** *m* invalid chair; (*Nachtstuhl*) commode; **~transport** *m* transportation of sick people; (*mittels Krankenwagen*) ambulance service; (*die Kranken selbst*) shipload/busload *etc* of sick people; **~versicherung** *f* medical *or* health insurance; **soziale/private ~versicherung** state *or* national/private health insurance; **~wagen** *m* ambulance; **~wärter** *m* orderly; **~zimmer** *nt* sick-room; (*im Krankenhaus*) hospital room.

Kranke(r) *mf decl as adj* sick person, invalid; (*Patient*) patient ◆ **die ~n** the sick.

krankfeiern *vi sep* (*inf*) to be off 'sick', to skive off work (*Brit inf*) ◆ **das K~ ist ein großes Problem** absenteeism is a great problem; **geh doch heute nicht ins Büro, feier doch krank** don't go in to the office today, say you're not feeling well; **ich glaube, ich muß morgen ~** I think I'll have to be off sick tomorrow.

krankhaft *adj* **(a)** *Stelle, Zelle* diseased; *Vergrößerung, Zustand* morbid; *Aussehen* sickly; *Augen* ill-looking ◆ **die Untersuchungen haben keinen ~en Befund ergeben** the examinations revealed no sign(s) of disease; **~er Befund der Leber** affected *or* diseased liver; **~e Veränderung** affection; **der ~e Zustand der britischen Wirtschaft** the ailing condition of the British economy; **das K~e an unserer Gesellschaft** the sickness affecting our society.
(b) (*seelisch*) pathological; *Mißtrauen, Eifersucht etc auch* chronic, morbid ◆ **sein Geiz/diese Vorstellung ist schon ~** his meanness/this idea is almost pathological *or* has reached almost pathological proportions.

Krankheit *f* (*lit, fig*) illness, sickness; (*eine bestimmte ~ wie Krebs, Masern etc auch*) disease; (*von Pflanzen*) disease ◆ **wegen ~** due to illness; **eine ~ durchmachen** to have *or* suffer from a disease/an illness; **(eine) ~ vorschützen, eine ~ vortäuschen** to pretend to be ill, to fake an illness; **sich** (*dat*) **eine ~ zuziehen** to catch *or* contract (*form*) an illness *or* a disease; **von einer ~ befallen werden** to catch *or* contract (*form*) an illness *or* a disease; (*Pflanze, Organ*) to become diseased; **nach langer/schwerer ~** after a long/serious illness; **während/seit meiner ~** during/since my illness; **das soll ein Auto sein? das ist eine ~!** (*fig inf*) call that a car? that's just an apology *or* a miserable excuse for one *or* that's just a joke!

-krankheit *f in cpds* disease.

Krankheits-: ~bild *nt* symptoms *pl*, syndrome (*spec*); **~erreger** *m* pathogene, disease-causing agent; **k~halber** *adv* due to illness; **~keim** *m* germ (of a/the disease).

kranklachen *vr* (*inf*) to kill oneself (laughing) (*inf*) ◆ **er hat sich bei dem Film krankgelacht** he just about killed himself (*inf*) *or* died laughing when he saw the film.

kränklich *adj* sickly, in poor *or* bad health.

Krank-: k~machen *vi sep* (*inf*) *siehe* **k~feiern**; **~meldung** *f* notification of illness *or* sickness.

Kränkung *f* **(a)** insult ◆ **etw als ~ empfinden** to take offence at sth, to be hurt by sth; **jdm eine ~ zufügen** to hurt sb. **(b)** (*Kränken*) offending, insulting ◆ **das war eine ~ seiner Gefühle** that hurt his feelings.

Kranz *m* **-es, ¨-e (a)** wreath; (*Sieger~, Dichter~, Braut~ auch*) garland; (*fig: von Geschichten, Anekdoten etc*) cycle ◆ **da kannst du dir gleich einen ~ schicken lassen** (*inf*) you'll be signing your own death warrant.
(b) (*kreisförmig Angeordnetes*) ring, circle; (*Haar~*) plaits *pl* round one's head; (*obs: von Mädchen*) bevy.
(c) (*Tech: Rad~*) rim; (*von Glocke auch*) lip.
(d) (*dial Cook*) ring.

Kranz|arterie *f* coronary artery.

Kränzchen *nt* small wreath/garland; (*fig: Kaffee~*) (coffee) circle.

kränzen *vt* (*liter*) to garland, to adorn (with garlands).

Kranz-: ~gefäß *nt* (*Anat*) coronary artery; **~geld** *nt* (*Jur*) *money paid by a man to a woman as a fine on having sexual intercourse with her under the pretence of an offer of marriage*; **~gesims** *nt* (*Archit*) cornice; **~jungfer** *f* (*dial*) bridesmaid; **~niederlegung** *f* wreath laying.

Krapfen *m* **-s, -, Kräppel** *m* **-s, -** (*dial Cook*) ≃ doughnut.

Krapp *m* **-(e)s,** *no pl* madder.

Krapp-: ~lack *m* madder paint; **~rot** *nt* madder red.

⚠ **kraß** *adj* (*auffallend*) *Widerspruch, Gegensatz* glaring, stark; *Farben* garish, glaring; *Dissonanz* harsh, jarring; *Unterschied* extreme; (*unerhört*) *Ungerechtigkeit, Lüge* blatant, gross; (*extrem*) *Fall, Haltung* extreme; *Materialist, Unkenntnis* crass; *Egoist* out-and-out, blatant; *Außenseiter* rank, complete; (*unverblümt*) *Schilderung, Worte, Stil* stark.

Krater *m* **-s, -** crater.

Krater-: ~landschaft *f* crater(ed) landscape; **~see** *m* (*Geol*) crater lake.

Krätten *m* **-s, -** (*S Ger, Sw*) (small) basket.

Kratz-: ~beere *f* (*dial*) *siehe* **Brombeere**; **~bürste** *f* wire brush; (*inf*) prickly character; **k~bürstig** *adj* (*inf*) prickly.

Krätzchen *nt* (*Mil sl*) forage cap.

Kratze *f* **-, -n** scraper; (*Tex*) carding machine.

Krätze[1] *f* **-,** *no pl* **(a)** (*Med*) scabies. **(b)** (*Tech*) scrapings *pl*, (metal) waste.

Krätze[2] *f* **-, -n** (*S Ger*) basket.

kratzen [1] *vti* **(a)** to scratch; (*ab~ auch*) to scrape (*von* off) ◆ **seinen Namen in die Wand ~** to scratch one's name on the wall; **der Pulli kratzt fürchterlich** the pullover scratches terribly *or* is terribly scratchy (*inf*); **der Rauch kratzt (mich) im Hals** the smoke irritates my throat; **es kratzt (mich) im Hals** my throat feels rough; **an etw** (*dat*) **~** (*fig*) to scratch away at sth.
(b) (*inf: stören*) to bother ◆ **das kratzt mich nicht** (*inf*), **das soll** *or* **kann mich nicht ~** (*inf*) I couldn't care less (about that), I don't give a damn (about that) (*inf*); **was kratzt mich das?** what do I care about that?; **das braucht dich doch nicht (zu) ~** it's nothing to do with you.
(c) (*Tex*) to card, to tease.
[2] *vr* to scratch oneself.

Kratzer *m* **-s, -** (*Schramme*) scratch.

Krätzer *m* **-s, -** (*inf*) rough *or* vinegary wine, plonk (*inf*) *no pl*; (*Aus*) sweet young Tirolean wine.

Kratzfuß *m* (*dated inf*) (low) bow (*with one foot drawn backwards*) ◆ **einen ~ machen** to bow low.

kratzig *adj* (*inf*) scratchy (*inf*).

krätzig *adj* scabious.

Kratz-: ~putz *m* sgraffito; **~wunde** *f* scratch.

krauchen *vi aux sein* (*dial*) to crawl.

kraueln, krauen *vt siehe* **kraulen[2]**.

Kraul *nt* **-(s),** *no pl* (*Schwimmen*) crawl ◆ **(im) ~ schwimmen** to do the crawl.

kraulen[1] (*Schwimmen*) *aux haben or sein* [1] *vi* to do *or* swim the crawl.
[2] *vt* **er hat** *or* **ist die Strecke/100 m gekrault** he did the stretch using the crawl/he did a 100m's crawl.

kraulen[2] *vt* to fondle ◆ **jdn am Kinn ~** to chuck sb under the chin; **jdn in den Haaren ~** to run one's fingers through sb's hair.

kraus *adj* crinkly; *Haar, Kopf* frizzy; *Stirn* wrinkled, furrowed; (*zerknittert*) crumpled, wrinkled; (*fig: verworren*) muddled, confused ◆ **die Stirn/Nase ~ ziehen** to wrinkle up *or* knit one's brow; (*mißbilligend*) to frown/to screw up one's nose.

Krause *f* **-, -n (a)** (*Hals~*) ruff; (*an Ärmeln etc*) ruffle, frill.
(b) (*inf*) (*Krausheit*) crinkliness; (*von Haar, Kopf*) frizziness; (*Frisur*) frizzy hair/hairstyle ◆ **im Regen bekomme ich eine ~** my hair goes frizzy in the rain.

Kräusel-: ~band *nt* decorative ribbon; **~krepp** *m* (*Tex*) crepe; (*Streifenkrepp*) seersucker.

kräuseln [1] *vt Haar* to make frizzy; (*mit Brennschere auch*) to crimp; (*mit Dauerwelle auch*) to frizz; (*Sew*) to gather (*in small folds*); (*Tex*) to crimp; *Stirn* to knit, to wrinkle; *Nase* to screw up; *Lippen* to pucker; *Wasseroberfläche* to ruffle.
[2] *vr* (*Haare*) to go frizzy; (*Stoff*) to go crinkly; (*Stirn, Nase*) to wrinkle up; (*Lippen*) to pucker; (*Wasser*) to ripple; (*Rauch*) to curl (up).

krausen *vtr Haar, Stirn, Nase,* (*Sew*) *siehe* **kräuseln**.

Kraus-: k~haarig *adj* frizzy-haired; **~kopf** *m* frizzy head; (*Frisur*) frizzy hair/hairstyle; (*Mensch*) curly-head.

Kraut *nt* **-(e)s, Kräuter (a)** (*Pflanze: esp Heil~, Würz~*) herb ◆ **dagegen ist kein ~ gewachsen** (*fig*) there is no remedy for that, there's nothing anyone can do about that.
(b) *no pl* (*grüne Teile von Pflanzen*) foliage, stems and leaves *pl*, herbage; (*von Gemüse*) tops *pl*; (*Kartoffel~*) potato foliage; (*Spargel~*) asparagus leaves *pl* ◆ **wie ~ und Rüben durcheinanderliegen** (*inf*) to lie (about) all over the place (*inf*); **ins ~ schießen** (*lit*) to run to seed; (*fig*) to get out of control, to run wild.
(c) *no pl* (*Rot~, Weiß~*) cabbage; (*Sauer~*) sauerkraut.
(d) (*pej: Tabak*) tobacco.

Kräuterbutter *f* herb butter.

Kräuter-: ~frau *f* herb woman; **~hexe** *f* (*pej*) herb woman; (*fig*) old hag (*pej*); **~käse** *m* herb cheese; **~likör** *m* herbal liqueur; **~mühle** *f* herb mill; **~sammler** *m* herbalist; **~tee** *m* herb(al) tea; **~weiblein** *nt* herb woman.

Kraut-: ~junker *m* (*pej*) country squire; **~kopf** *m* (*S Ger, Aus*) (head of) cabbage; **~salat** *m* ≃ coleslaw.

Krawall *m* **-s, -e** (*Aufruhr*) riot; (*inf*) (*Rauferei*) brawl; (*Lärm*) racket (*inf*), din (*inf*) ♦ **~ machen** (*inf*) to kick up a row; (*randalieren*) to go on the rampage; (*auch* **~ schlagen**: *sich beschweren*) to kick up a fuss.

Krawall-: ~bruder, ~macher *m* (*inf*) hooligan; (*Krakeeler*) rowdy.

Krawallo *m* **-s, -s** (*inf*) *siehe* **Krawallbruder**.

Krawatte *f* **-, -n** tie, necktie (*esp US*); (*kleiner Pelzkragen*) tippet; (*Ringkampf*) headlock.

Krawatten-: ~halter *m*, **~klemme** *f* tie clip; **~knoten** *m* tie knot; **~nadel** *f* tie-pin; **~zwang** *m* **da ist ~zwang** you have to wear a tie there; **der ~zwang ...** the fact that you have to wear a tie ...

kraxeln *vi aux sein* (*S Ger*) to clamber (up).

Kreation *f* (*Fashion etc*) creation.

kreativ *adj* creative.

Kreative(r) *mf decl as adj* (*inf*) creative person ♦ **er ist einer der ~n** he's one of the creators; **die ~n der Werbebranche** the creative people in advertising.

Kreativität [kreativi'tɛ:t] *f* creativity.

Kreatur *f* **(a)** (*lit, fig, pej*) creature; (*abhängiger Mensch*) minion, creature (*liter*). **(b)** *no pl* (*alle Lebewesen*) creation ♦ **die ~** all creation.

kreatürlich *adj* (*naturhaft*) natural; *Angst etc* animal *attr*.

Krebs *m* **-es, -e (a)** (*Taschen~, Einsiedler~*) crab; (*Fluß~*) crayfish, crawfish (*US*) ♦ **rot wie ein ~** red as a lobster. **(b)** (*Gattung*) crustacean; (*Hummer, Krabbe etc*) crayfish, crawfish (*US*). **(c)** (*Astron*) **der ~** Cancer, the Crab; (*Astrol*) Cancer. **(d)** (*Med*) cancer; (*Bot*) canker. **(e)** (*Typ inf*) return.

krebs-: ~artig *adj* (*Zool*) crablike; crayfish-like; crustaceous; (*Med*) cancerous; ⚠**~auslösend** *adj* carcinogenic.

krebsen *vi* **(a)** (*Krebse fangen*) to go crabbing, to catch crabs. **(b)** (*inf: sich abmühen*) to struggle; (*Umsatz, Industrie*) to languish ♦ **er hat es schwer zu ~** he really has to struggle, he finds it really hard going.

Krebs-: ⚠**k~erregend, k~erzeugend** *adj* carcinogenic; **k~erzeugend wirken** to cause cancer; **~forschung** *f* cancer research; **~früherkennung** *f* early detection of cancer; **~gang** *m* (*fig*) retrogression; **im ~gang gehen** to regress, to go backwards; **~geschwulst** *f* (*Med*) cancer, cancerous tumour *or* growth; **~geschwür** *nt* (*Med*) cancerous ulcer; (*fig*) cancer, cancerous growth; **~klinik** *f* cancer clinic; **k~krank** *adj* suffering from cancer; **k~krank sein** to have cancer; **~kranke(r)** *mf* cancer victim; (*Patient*) cancer patient; **k~rot** *adj* red as a lobster; **~schere** *f* claws *pl or* pincers *pl* of the crab/crayfish; **~tiere** *pl* crustaceans *pl*, crustacea *pl*; **~vorsorge, ~vorsorgeuntersuchung** *f* cancer check-up; **~zelle** *f* (*Med*) cancer cell.

Kredenz *f* (*dated, Aus*) sideboard.

kredenzen* *vt* (*liter*) **jdm etw ~** to proffer sb sth (*liter*).

Kredit[1] *m* **-(e)s, -e** credit; (*Darlehen auch*) loan; (*fig auch*) standing, (good) repute ♦ **auf ~** on credit; **einen ~ kündigen** to withdraw credit facilities *or* a credit; **er hat bei uns/der Bank ~** his credit is good with us/the bank; **in seiner Stammkneipe hat er ~** he gets credit at his local; **~ haben** (*fig*) to have standing *or* a good reputation.

Kredit[2] *nt* **-s, -s** (*Habenseite*) credit (side).

Kredit-: ~anstalt *f* credit institution, credit *or* loan bank; **~aufnahme** *f* borrowing; **sich zu einer ~aufnahme entschließen** to decide to obtain a loan; **~brief** *m* letter of credit; **k~fähig** *adj* credit-worthy; **~geber(in** *f*) *m* creditor; **~hai** *m* (*inf*) loan shark (*inf*).

kreditieren* *vt* **jdm einen Betrag ~, jdn für einen Betrag ~** to advance sb an amount, to credit sb with an amount.

Kredit-: ~institut *nt* bank; **~karte** *f* credit card; **~kartenorganisation** *f* credit card company; **~linie** *f* line of credit; **~nehmer(in** *f*) *m* borrower; **~politik** *f* lending policy; **k~politisch** *adj* on lending; **~rahmen** *m* credit range; **den ~rahmen ausschöpfen/sprengen** to use up/exceed the credit range; **k~würdig** *adj* credit-worthy.

Kredo *nt* **-s, -s** (*lit, fig*) creed, credo.

kregel *adj* (*dial*) lively.

Kreide *f* **-, -n** chalk; (*Geol: ~zeit*) Cretaceous (period) ♦ **eine ~** a piece of chalk; **bei jdm (tief) in der ~ sein** *or* **stehen** to be (deep) in debt to sb, to owe sb (a lot of) money.

Kreide-: k~bleich *adj* (as) white as chalk *or* a sheet; **~felsen** *m* chalk cliff; **~formation** *f* (*Geol*) Cretaceous (formation); **k~haltig** *adj* chalky, cretaceous (*spec*); **~stift** *m* chalk; **k~weiß** *adj siehe* **k~bleich**; **~zeichnung** *f* chalk drawing.

kreidig *adj* chalky.

kreieren* [kre'i:rən] *vt* (*Fashion, Theat etc, Eccl*) to create ♦ **jdn zum Kardinal ~** (*form*) to create *or* appoint sb (a) cardinal.

Kreis *m* **-es, -e (a)** circle ♦ **einen ~ beschreiben** *or* **schlagen** *or* **ziehen** to describe a circle; **einen ~ um jdn bilden** *or* **schließen** to form *or* make a circle around sb, to encircle sb; **im ~ (gehen/sitzen)** (to go round/sit) in a circle; **~e ziehen** (*lit*) to circle; **(weite) ~e ziehen** (*fig*) to have (wide) repercussions; **sich im ~ bewegen** *or* **drehen** (*lit*) to go *or* turn round in a circle; (*fig*) to go round in circles; **mir dreht sich alles im ~e** everything's going round and round, my head is reeling *or* spinning; **der ~ schließt sich** (*fig*) we *etc* come full circle, the wheel turns full circle; **störe meine ~e nicht!** (*fig*) leave me in peace!

(b) (*Elec: Strom~*) circuit.

(c) (*Bereich: von Interessen, Tätigkeit etc*) sphere; (*Ideen~*) body of ideas; (*Sagen~*) cycle ♦ **im ~ des Scheinwerferlichtes** in the arc *or* pool of light thrown by the headlamps.

(d) (*fig: von Menschen*) circle ♦ **der ~ seiner Leser** his readership, his readers *pl*; **weite ~e der Bevölkerung** wide sections of the population; **im ~e von Freunden/seiner Familie** among *or* with friends/his family, in the family circle; **eine Feier im engen** *or* **kleinen ~e** a celebration for a few close friends and relatives; **das kommt auch in den besten ~en vor** that happens even in the best society *or* the best of circles.

(e) (*Stadt~, Land~*) district; (*Gemeindewahl~*) ward; (*Landeswahl~*) constituency ♦ **~ Leipzig** Leipzig District, the District of Leipzig.

Kreis-: ~abschnitt *m* segment; **~ausschnitt** *m* sector; **~bahn** *f* (*Astron, Space*) orbit; **~bogen** *m* arc (of a circle).

kreischen *vi* (*old, hum: pret* **krisch**, *ptp* **gekrischen**) to screech; (*Vogel auch*) to squawk; (*Reifen, Bremsen auch*) to squeal; (*Mensch auch*) to shriek, to squeal.

Kreisel *m* **-s, -** (*Tech*) gyroscope; (*Spielzeug*) (spinning) top; (*inf: im Verkehr*) roundabout (*Brit*), traffic circle (*US*), rotary (*US*) ♦ **den ~ schlagen** to spin the top.

Kreisel-: ~bewegung *f* gyration; ⚠**~kompaß** *m* gyroscopic compass, gyrocompass.

kreiseln *vi* **(a)** *aux sein or haben* (*sich drehen*) to spin around, to gyrate. **(b)** (*mit Kreisel spielen*) to play with a top, to spin a top.

kreisen *vi aux sein or haben* to circle (*um* round, *über +dat* over); (*um eine Achse*) to revolve (*um* around); (*Satellit, Planet auch*) to orbit (*um etw* sth); (*Blut, Öl etc*) to circulate (*in +dat* through); (*fig: Gedanken, Wünsche, Gespräch*) to revolve (*um* around) ♦ **die Arme ~ lassen** to swing one's arms around (in a circle); **den Becher ~ lassen** to hand the cup round.

Kreis-: ~fläche *f* circle; (*~inhalt*) area of a/the circle; **k~förmig** *adj* circular; **sich k~förmig bewegen** to move in a circle; **k~förmig angelegt** arranged in a circle; **k~frei** *adj* **k~freie Stadt** *town which is an administrative district in its own right*; **~inhalt** *m* area of a/the circle; **~kolbenmotor** *m* rotary piston engine.

Kreislauf *m* (*Blut~, Öl~, von Geld*) circulation; (*der Natur, des Wassers*) cycle.

Kreislauf-: ~kollaps *m* circulatory collapse; **~mittel** *nt* cardiac stimulant; **~störungen** *pl* circulation *or* circulatory trouble *sing or* disorders *pl*.

Kreis-: ~linie *f* circle; **vom Mittelpunkt durch die ~linie** from the centre through the circumference (of a/the circle); **k~rund** *adj* (perfectly) circular; **~säge** *f* circular saw; (*inf: Hut*) boater.

kreißen *vi* (*old*) to be in labour ♦ **der Berg kreißt und gebiert eine Maus** (*prov*) the mountain laboured and brought forth a mouse.

Kreißsaal *m* delivery room.

Kreis-: ~stadt *f* chief town of a district, district town, ≃ county town (*Brit*); **~tag** *m* district assembly, ≃ county council (*Brit*); **~umfang** *m* circumference (of a/the circle); **~verkehr** *m* roundabout (*Brit*) *or* rotary (*US*) traffic; (*Kreisel*) roundabout (*Brit*), traffic circle (*US*), rotary (*US*); **im ~verkehr muß man ...** on a roundabout *etc* one must ...; **dort gibt es viel ~verkehr** there are a lot of roundabouts *etc* there; **~wehrersatzamt** *nt* district recruiting office.

Krematorium *nt* crematorium.

kremig *adj* creamy ♦ **etw ~ schlagen** to cream sth.

Kreml *m* **-s der ~** the Kremlin.

Kreml-: ~-Astrologe *m* (*Pol sl*) Kremlin watcher; **~chef** *m* Kremlin chief.

Krempe *f* **-, -n** (*Hut~*) brim ♦ **ein Hut mit breiter ~** a broad-brimmed hat.

Krempel[1] *m* **-s,** *no pl* (*inf*) (*Sachen*) stuff (*inf*), things *pl*; (*wertloses Zeug*) junk, rubbish ♦ **ich werfe den ganzen ~ hin** I'm chucking the whole lot *or* business in (*inf*); **dann kannst du deinen ~ allein machen** then you can (damn well *inf*) do it yourself.

Krempel[2] *f* **-, -n** carding machine.

Krempelarm *m* (*Fashion*) rolled sleeve.

krempeln *vt* **(a)** (*Tex*) to card. **(b)** *siehe* **hoch~, um~** *etc*.

Kren *m* **-s,** *no pl* (*Aus*) horse-radish.

Kreole *m* **-n, -n, Kreolin** *f* Creole.

kreolisch *adj* Creole.

krepieren* *vi aux sein* **(a)** (*platzen*) to explode, to go off. **(b)** (*sl: sterben*) to croak (it) (*sl*), to snuff it (*sl*), to kick the bucket (*inf*); (*inf: elend sterben*) to die a wretched death ♦ **das Tier ist ihm krepiert** (*inf*) the animal died on him (*inf*).

Krepp *m* **-s, -e** *or* **-s** crepe.

⚠ **Kreppapier** *nt getrennt* **Krepp-papier** crepe paper.

Kreppsohle *f* crepe sole.

Kresse *f* **-,** *no pl* cress.

Kreta *nt* **-s** Crete.

Kreter(in *f*) *m* **-s, -** Cretan.

Krethi und Plethi *pl no art* (*inf*) every Tom, Dick and Harry.

Kretin [kre'tɛ̃:] *m* **-s, -s** (*Med, pej*) cretin.

Kretinismus *m* (*Med*) cretinism.

kretisch *adj* Cretan.

Kreton [kre'to:n] *m* **-s, -e** (*Aus*), **Kretonne** [kre'tɔn] *m or f* **-, -s** (*Tex*) cretonne.

kreucht (*obs, poet*) *3 pers sing of* **kriechen** ♦ **alles was da ~ und fleucht** all living creatures, all things that do creep and fly (*poet*).

Kreuz[1] *nt* **-es, -e (a)** cross; (*als Anhänger etc*) crucifix ♦ **das ~ des Südens** (*Astron*) the Southern Cross; **jdn ans ~ schlagen** *or* **nageln** to nail sb to the cross; **ein ~ schlagen** *or* **machen** to make the sign of the cross; (*sich bekreuzigen auch*) to cross oneself; **zwei Gegenstände über ~ legen** to put two objects crosswise one on top of the other; **mit jdm über ~ sein** *or* **stehen** (*fig*) to be on bad terms with sb; **sein ~ auf sich nehmen** (*fig*) to take up one's cross; **es ist ein** *or* **ich habe mein ~ mit ihm/damit** he's/it's an awful problem;

ich mache drei ~e, wenn er geht (*inf*) it'll be such a relief when he has gone; **er machte ein ~ (als Unterschrift/am Rand)** he put a cross (for his signature/ in the margin); **zu ~e kriechen** (*fig*) to eat humble pie, to eat crow (*US*).
(b) (*Anat*) small of the back; (*von Tier*) back ◆ **ich habe Schmerzen im ~** I've got (a) backache; **ich hab's im ~** (*inf*) I have back trouble; **aufs ~ fallen** to fall on one's back; (*fig inf*) to be staggered (*inf*), to fall through the floor (*inf*); **jdn aufs ~ legen** to throw sb on his back; (*fig inf*) to take sb for a ride (*inf*); (*vulg*) *Mädchen* to lay sb (*sl*).
(c) (*Archit: Fenster~*) mullion and transom.
(d) (*Typ*) dagger, obelisk.
(e) (*Mus*) sharp.
(f) (*Autobahn~*) intersection.
(g) (*Cards*) (*Farbe*) clubs *pl*; (*Karte*) club ◆ **die ~-Dame** the Queen of Clubs.

Kreuz[2] *f*: **in die ~ und in die Quer** this way and that.

kreuz *adj*: **~ und quer** all over; **~ und quer durch die Gegend fahren** to drive/ travel all over the place.

Kreuz-: **~abnahme** *f* Descent from the Cross; **~band** *nt* **(a)** (*Anat*) crucial ligament; **(b)** (*Post: Streifband*) wrapper; **~bein** *nt* (*Anat*) sacrum; (*von Tieren*) rump-bone; **~blume** *f* (*Bot*) milkwort; (*Archit*) finial; **~blütler** *pl* cruciferous plants *pl*; **k~brav** *adj Kind* terribly good *or* well-behaved, as good as gold; *Benehmen, Karriere* faultless.

kreuzen [1] *vt* to cross (*auch Biol*) ◆ **die Degen** *or* **Klingen** *or* **Schwerter mit jdm ~** (*lit, fig*) to cross swords with sb; **die Arme ~** to fold *or* cross one's arms.
[2] *vr* to cross; (*Meinungen, Interessen*) to clash; (*Biol*) to interbreed ◆ **unsere Wege haben sich nie wieder gekreuzt** our paths have never crossed again.
[3] *vi aux haben or sein* (*Naut*) to cruise; (*Zickzack fahren*) to tack.

Kreuzer *m* **-s, - (a)** (*Naut*) cruiser. **(b)** (*Hist: Münze*) kreutzer.

Kreuzes-: **~tod** *m* (death by) crucifixion; **den ~tod erleiden** to die on the cross; **~zeichen** *nt* sign of the cross.

Kreuz-: **~fahrer** *m* (*Hist*) crusader; **~fahrt** *f* **(a)** (*Naut*) cruise; **eine ~fahrt machen** to go on a cruise; **(b)** (*Hist*) crusade; **~feuer** *nt* (*Mil, fig*) crossfire; **im ~feuer (der Kritik) stehen** (*fig*) to be under fire (from all sides); **ins ~feuer (der Kritik) geraten** (*fig*) to come under fire (from all sides); **k~fidel** *adj* (*inf*) happy as a sandboy (*inf*) *or* lark; **k~förmig** *adj* cross-shaped, cruciform (*form*); **etw k~förmig anordnen** to arrange sth crossways *or* crosswise; **~gang** *m* cloister; **~gelenk** *nt* (*Tech*) universal joint; **~gewölbe** *nt* (*Archit*) cross *or* groin vault.

kreuzigen *vt* to crucify.

Kreuzigung *f* crucifixion.

Kreuz-: **~knoten** *m* reef-knot; **k~lahm** *adj Pferd* broken-backed; (*inf*) *Mensch* exhausted; **~lähme -, -n** *f* (*Vet*) paralysis of the hindquarters; **~mast** *m* (*Naut*) mizzen mast; **~otter** *f* (*Zool*) adder, viper; **~rippengewölbe** *nt* (*Archit*) ribbed vault; **~ritter** *m* (*Hist*) crusader; (*vom deutschen Ritterorden*) knight of the Teutonic Order; **~schlitzschraube** *f* Phillips ® screw; **~schlitzschraubenzieher** *m* Phillips ® screwdriver, **~schlüssel** *m* wheel brace; **~schmerzen** *pl* backache *sing*, pains *pl* in the small of the back; **~schnabel** *m* (*Orn*) crossbill; **~spinne** *f* (*Zool*) garden *or* cross spider; **k~ständig** *adj* (*Bot*) decussate; **~stich** *m* (*Sew*) cross-stitch.

Kreuzung *f* **(a)** (*Straßen~*) crossroads *sing or pl* (*esp Brit*), intersection (*esp US*).
(b) (*das Kreuzen*) crossing; (*von Tieren auch*) cross-breeding, interbreeding.
(c) (*Rasse*) hybrid; (*Tiere auch*) cross, cross-breed.

kreuz|unglücklich *adj* absolutely miserable.

kreuzungsfrei *adj* without crossroads.

Kreuz-: **~verband** *m* (*Med*) crossed bandage; (*Build*) cross bond; **~verhör** *nt* cross-examination; **jdn ins ~verhör nehmen** to cross-examine sb; **~weg** *m* **(a)** (*Wegkreuzung, fig*) crossroads *sing*; **(b)** (*Rel: Christi Leidensweg*) way of the cross; (*Eccl: in Kirche auch*) stations of the cross *pl*; **den ~weg beten** to do the stations of the cross; **k~weise** *adv* crosswise, crossways; **du kannst mich k~weise!** (*sl*) (you can) get stuffed! (*sl*); **~worträtsel** *nt* crossword puzzle; **~zeichen** *nt* sign of the cross; **~zug** *m* (*lit, fig*) crusade.

Krevette [kre'vɛtə] *f* shrimp.

kribb(e)lig *adj* (*inf*) fidgety, edgy (*inf*); (*kribbelnd*) tingly (*inf*).

kribbeln [1] *vt* (*kitzeln*) to tickle; (*jucken*) to make itch; (*prickeln*) to make tingle.
[2] *vi* **(a)** (*jucken*) to itch, to tickle; (*prickeln*) to prickle, to tingle ◆ **auf der Haut ~** to cause a prickling sensation; (*angenehm*) to make the skin tingle; **es kribbelt mir im Fuß** (*lit*) I have pins and needles in my foot; **es kribbelt mir** *or* **mich (in den Fingern), etw zu tun** (*inf*) I'm itching/I get an itch to do sth.
(b) *aux sein* (*Insekten*) **~ (und krabbeln)** to scurry *or* swarm (around); **es kribbelt von Ameisen** the place is crawling *or* swarming *or* teaming with ants; **es kribbelt und krabbelt wie in einem Ameisenhaufen** it's like an ant-hill.

krickelig *adj* (*inf*) *siehe* **krakelig**.

Krickelkrakel *nt* **-s, -** *siehe* **Gekrakel**.

krickeln *vi* (*inf*) *siehe* **krakeln**.

Kricket *nt* **-s, -s** (*Sport*) cricket.

Krida *f* **-**, *no pl* faked bankruptcy.

kriechen *pret* **kroch**, *ptp* **gekrochen** *vi aux sein* to creep (*auch Pflanze, Tech*), to crawl (*auch Schlange*); (*langsam fahren*) to creep *or* crawl (along); (*fig: Zeit*) to creep by; (*fig: unterwürfig sein*) to grovel (*vor +dat* before), to crawl (*vor +dat* to) ◆ **aus dem Ei ~** to hatch (out); **ins Bett ~** (*inf*) to go to bed; (*sehr müde, erschöpft*) to crawl into bed; **unter die Bettdecke ~** to slip under the covers *or* blankets; *siehe* **Kreuz**[1], **Leim**.

Kriecher(in *f*) *m* **-s, -** (*inf*) groveller, bootlicker (*inf*), crawler (*inf*).

kriecherisch *adj* (*inf*) grovelling, servile, bootlicking *attr* (*inf*).

Kriech-: **~gang** *m* crawling gear; **~spur** *f* crawler lane; **~strom** *m* (*Elec*) leakage current; **~tier** *nt* (*Zool*) reptile.

Krieg *m* **-(e)s, -e** war; (*Art der Kriegsführung*) warfare ◆ **~ der Sterne** (*Pol*) Star Wars; **~ anfangen mit** to start a war with; **einer Partei** *etc* **den ~ ansagen** (*fig*) to declare war on a party *etc*; **~ führen (mit** *or* **gegen)** to wage war (on); **in ~ und Frieden** in war and in peace; **im ~(e)** in war; (*als Soldat*) away in the war, away fighting; **im ~ sein** *or* **stehen (mit)**, **~ haben mit** to be at war (with); **im ~e fallen, im ~ bleiben** (*inf*) to be killed in the war *or* in action; **in den ~ ziehen** to go to war; **in einem ständigen ~ leben** (*fig*) to be constantly feuding.

kriegen *vt* (*inf*) to get; *Zug, Bus, Schnupfen, Weglaufenden auch* to catch; *Schlaganfall, eine Spritze, Besuch auch* to have; *Junge, ein Kind* to have ◆ **sie kriegt ein Kind** she's going to have a baby; **graue Haare/eine Glatze ~** to get grey hairs, to go grey/bald; **sie** *or* **es ~** to get a hiding; **es mit jdm zu tun ~** to be in trouble with sb; **wenn ich dich kriege!** just you wait till I catch you!; **sie ~ sich** (*in Kitschroman*) boy gets girl; **dann kriege ich zuviel** then it gets too much for me; **was kriegt der Herr?** yes sir, what will you have?; **ich kriege ein Steak** I'll have a steak; **~ Sie schon?** are you being *or* have you been served *or* done (*inf*)?; **jdn dazu ~, etw zu tun** to get sb to do sth; **etw gemacht ~** to get sth done; **das kriege ich einfach nicht übersetzt** I just can't get it translated; **kann ich das bestätigt ~?** Can I have *or* get that confirmed?

Kriegen *nt* **-s**, *no pl* (game of) tag.

Krieger *m* **-s, -** warrior; (*Indianer~*) brave ◆ **alter ~** veteran (soldier), old campaigner *or* warhorse; **ein müder ~ sein** (*fig inf*) to have no go left in one.

Kriegerdenkmal *nt* war memorial.

kriegerisch *adj* warlike *no adv*; *Haltung auch* belligerent ◆ **eine ~e Auseinandersetzung** fighting *no pl*, military conflict.

Kriegerwitwe *f* war-widow.

Krieg-: ⚠**k~führend** *adj* belligerent, warring; **die ~führenden** the belligerents; **~führung** *f* warfare *no art*; (*eines Feldherrn*) conduct of the war.

Kriegs-: **~anleihe** *f* war loan; **~ausbruch** *m* outbreak of war; **es kam zum ~ausbruch** war broke out; **k~bedingt** *adj* resulting from *or* caused by (the) war; **~beginn** *m* start of the war; **~beil** *nt* tomahawk; **das ~beil begraben/ ausgraben** (*fig*) to bury the hatchet/to start a fight; **~bemalung** *f* (*lit, hum*) warpaint; **~berichterstatter** *m* war correspondent; **k~beschädigt** *adj* war-disabled; **~beschädigte(r)** *mf decl as adj* war-disabled (ex-serviceman/-woman); **~blinde(r)** *mf* war-blinded person; **die ~blinden** the war-blind; **~dienst** *m* (*old, form*) military service; **den ~dienst verweigern** to be a conscientious objector.

Kriegsdienst-: **~verweigerer** *m* **-s, -** conscientious objector; **~verweigerung** *f* refusal to fight in a war.

Kriegs-: **~einwirkung** *f* effects *pl or* aftermath *no pl* of war; **~ende** *nt* end of the war; **~entschädigungen** *pl* reparations *pl*; **~erklärung** *f* declaration of war; **~erlebnis** *nt* war-time experience; **~fall** *m* (eventuality of a) war; **dann träte der ~fall ein** then war would break out; **~film** *m* war film; **~flagge** *f* naval ensign; **~flotte** *f* navy, fleet; **~folge** *f* consequence of (a/the) war; **~freiwillige(r)** *mf* (wartime) volunteer; **~fuß** *m* (*inf*): **mit jdm auf ~fuß stehen** to be at loggerheads with sb; **~gebiet** *nt* war-zone; **~gefahr** *f* danger of war; **~gefahr zieht herauf** (*geh*) the war clouds are gathering; **~gefangene(r)** *mf* prisoner of war, P.O.W.; **~gefangenschaft** *f* captivity; **in ~gefangenschaft sein** to be a prisoner of war; **aus der ~gefangenschaft kommen** to return *or* be released from captivity; **~gegner** *m* **(a)** opponent of a/the war; (*Pazifist*) pacifist, opponent of war; **(b)** (*Gegner im Krieg*) war-time enemy; **~gerät** *nt* military equipment; **~gericht** *nt* (war-time) court-martial; **jdn vor ein ~gericht stellen** to court-martial sb; **~geschrei** *nt* war-cry; **~gewinnler(in** *f*) *m* **-s, -** (*pej*) war-profiteer; **~glück** *nt* (*liter*) fortunes of war *pl*; **dann verließ Hannibal sein ~glück** then the fortunes of war turned against *or* deserted Hannibal; **~gott** *m* god of war; **~göttin** *f* goddess of war; **~gräberfürsorge** *f* War Graves Commission; ⚠**~greuel** *pl* war atrocities *pl*; **~grund** *m* reason for war; **~hafen** *m* naval port *or* harbour; **~handwerk** *nt* (*old*) soldiering; **~held** *m* great warrior; (*in moderner Zeit*) military hero; **~herr** *m* (*Hist*): **oberster ~herr** commander-in-chief; **~hetze** *f* war-mongering; **~invalide(r)** *mf siehe* **~beschädigte(r)**; **~jahr** *nt* year of war; **die ~jahre** the war years; **im ~jahr 1945** (during the war) in 1945; **im dritten ~jahr** in the third year of the war; **~kamerad** *m* fellow soldier, war(-time) comrade; **~kasse** *f* war-chest; **~kind** *nt* war-baby; **~kosten** *pl* cost of the war *sing*; **~kunst** *f* art of war(fare); **~list** *f* (*old, liter*) ruse of war, stratagem; **~marine** *f* navy; **k~mäßig** *adj* for war; **~minister** *m* (*Hist, Pol pej*) minister of war; **~ministerium** *nt* (*Hist*) War Office (*Brit*), War Department (*US*); **k~müde** *adj* war-weary; **~opfer** *nt* war victim; **~pfad** *m* (*liter*): **auf dem ~pfad** on the war-path; **~rat** *m* council of war; **~rat halten** (*fig*) to have a pow-wow (*inf*); **~recht** *nt* conventions of war *pl*; (*Mil*) martial law; **~schäden** *pl* war damage; **~schauplatz** *m* theatre of war; **~schiff** *nt* warship, man-of-war; **~schuld** *f* war guilt; **~schulden** *pl* war debts *pl*; **~spiel** *nt* war game; **~spielzeug** *nt* war toy; **~stärke** *f* war establishment; **die Armee auf ~stärke bringen** to make the army ready for war; **~teilnehmer** *m* combatant; (*Staat*) combatant nation, belligerent; (*ehemaliger Soldat*) ex-serviceman; **~trauung** *f* war wedding; **~treiber** *m* **-s, -** (*pej*) war-monger; **k~tüchtig** *adj* (*old*) fit for active service; **k~untauglich** *adj* unfit for active service; **~verbrechen** *nt* war crime; **~verbrecher** *m* war criminal; **~verletzung** *f* war wound; **k~versehrt** *adj siehe* **k~beschädigt**; **k~verwendungsfähig** *adj* (*form*) fit for active service; **~wirren** *pl* (*geh*) chaos of war *sing*; **~wirtschaft** *f* war economy; **~zeit** *f* wartime; **in ~zeiten** in times of war; **sie erzählten von ihrer ~zeit** they told about their wartime experiences; **~zug** *m* (*old*) campaign, military expedition; **~zustand** *m* state of war; **im ~zustand** at war.

Kriek|ente *f* (green-winged) teal.

Krill *m* **-(s),** *no pl* (*Biol*) krill.

Krim *f* **- die ~** the Crimea.

Krimi *m* **-s, -s** (*inf*) (crime) thriller; (*mit Detektiv als Held*) detective novel; (*rätselhaft*) murder mystery, whodunnit (*inf*); (*moderner Film, Fernsehsendung*) crime series *sing*; crime film.

Kriminalbe|amte(r) *m* detective, CID officer (*Brit*).

Kriminale(r) *m decl as adj* (*sl*) plain-clothes man, detective, CID officer (*Brit*).

Kriminal-: ~film *m* crime thriller *or* film *or* movie (*esp US*); (*rätselhaft*) whodunnit (*inf*); **~gericht** *nt siehe* **Strafgericht**; **~groteske** *f* black comedy; **~hörspiel** *nt* radio thriller; (*rätselhaft*) murder mystery, whodunnit (*inf*).

kriminalisieren* *vt* to criminalize.

Kriminalist(in *f*) *m* criminologist.

Kriminalistik *f* criminology.

kriminalistisch *adj* criminological.

Kriminalität *f* crime; (*Ziffer*) crime rate.

Kriminal-: ~kommissar *m* detective superintendent; **~komödie** *f* comedy thriller; **~literatur** *f* crime literature; **~museum** *nt* crime museum; **~polizei** *f* criminal investigation department; **~polizist** *m* detective, CID officer (*Brit*); **~roman** *m siehe* **Krimi** (crime) thriller; detective novel; murder mystery, whodunnit (*inf*); **~stück** *nt* thriller; detective play; murder mystery, whodunnit (*inf*); **k~technisch** *adj* forensic.

kriminell *adj* (*lit, fig inf*) criminal ♦ **~ werden** to turn to crime, to become a criminal; (*junger Mensch auch*) to become delinquent.

Kriminelle(r) *mf decl as adj* criminal.

Kriminologe *m*, **Kriminologin** *f* criminologist.

Kriminologie *f* criminology.

kriminologisch *adj* criminological.

Krimkrieg *m* Crimean War.

Krimskrams *m* **-es,** *no pl* (*inf*) odds and ends *pl*, bits and pieces *pl*, rubbish.

Kringel *m* **-s, -** (*der Schrift*) squiggle; (*Cook: Zucker~ etc*) ring.

kringelig *adj* crinkly ♦ **sich ~ lachen** (*inf*) to laugh oneself silly (*inf*), to kill oneself (laughing) (*inf*).

kringeln *vr* to go frizzy, to curl ♦ **sich ~ vor Lachen** (*inf*) to kill oneself (laughing) (*inf*).

Krinoline *f* (*Hist*) crinoline.

Kripo *f* **-, -s** (*inf*) *abbr of* **Kriminalpolizei** ♦ **die ~** the cops (*inf*) *pl*, the CID (*Brit*).

Kripo- *in cpds* (*inf*) police.

Krippe *f* **-, -n (a)** (*Futter~*) (hay)rack, (hay)box ♦ **sich an die ~ drängen** (*fig*) to start jockeying for position; **an der ~ sitzen** (*fig*) to live a life of ease, to live in comfort. **(b)** (*Kinder~, Weihnachts~*) crib; (*Bibl auch*) manger. **(c)** (*Kinderhort*) crèche. **(d)** (*Astron*) manger.

Krippen-: ~spiel *nt* nativity play; **~tod** *m* cot death.

krisch (*old, hum*) *pret of* **kreischen**.

Krise *f* **-, -n** crisis ♦ **in eine ~ geraten** to enter a state of crisis; **er hatte eine schwere ~** he was going through a difficult crisis.

kriseln *vi impers* (*inf*) **es kriselt** there is a crisis looming, there is trouble brewing.

Krisen-: k~anfällig *adj* crisis-prone; **k~fest** *adj* stable, crisis-proof; **er hat sein Geld k~fest in Grundbesitz angelegt** he put his money in property to secure it against *or* to hedge against economic crises; **~gebiet** *nt* crisis area; **k~geschüttet** *adj* crisis-wracked; **~herd** *m* flash point, trouble spot; **~management** *nt* crisis management; **~manager** *m* crisis manager; **~sitzung** *f* emergency session; **~stab** *m* (special) action *or* crisis committee.

Krisis *f* **-, Krisen** (*liter*) *siehe* **Krise**.

krisselig *adj* (*dial*) curdled.

Kristall[1] *m* **-s, -e** crystal ♦ **~e bilden** to crystallize, to form crystals.

Kristall[2] *nt* **-s,** *no pl* (*~glas*) crystal (glass); (*~waren*) crystal-ware, crystal goods *pl*.

Kristallbildung *f* crystallization.

kristallen *adj* (made of) crystal; *Stimme* crystal-clear.

⚠ **Kristalleuchter** *m getrennt* **Kristall-leuchter** crystal chandelier.

Kristall-: ~gitter *nt* crystal lattice; **~glas** *nt* crystal glass.

kristallin, kristallinisch *adj* crystalline.

Kristallisation *f* crystallization.

Kristallisationspunkt *m* (*fig*) focal point.

kristallisieren* *vir* (*lit, fig*) to crystallize.

Kristall-: k~klar *adj* crystal-clear; **~leuchter, ~lüster** (*geh*) *m siehe* **Kristalleuchter**; **~nacht** *f* (*Hist*) Crystal night, *night of 9th/10th November 1938, during which the Nazis organized a pogrom throughout Germany, burning synagogues and breaking windows of Jewish shops.*

⚠ **Kristallüster** *m getrennt* **Kristall-lüster** *siehe* **Kristalleuchter**.

Kristall-: ~waren *pl* crystalware *sing*, crystal goods *pl*; **~zucker** *m* refined sugar (in) crystals.

Kriterium *nt* **(a)** criterion. **(b)** (*Radfahren*) circuit race.

Kritik *f* **-, -en (a)** *no pl* criticism (*an +dat* of) ♦ **an jdm/etw ~ üben** to criticize sb/sth; **Gesellschafts-/Literatur~** social/literary criticism; **unter aller ~ sein** (*inf*) to be beneath contempt.
(b) (*Rezensieren*) criticism; (*Rezension auch*) review, notice, crit (*inf*) ♦ **eine gute ~ haben** to get good reviews *etc*.
(c) *no pl* (*die Kritiker*) critics *pl*.
(d) *no pl* (*Urteilsfähigkeit*) discrimination ♦ **ohne jede ~** uncritically.
(e) (*Philos, kritische Analyse*) critique.

Kritikaster *m* **-s, -** (*dated pej*) caviller, fault-finder, criticaster (*rare*).

Kritiker(in *f*) *m* **-s, -** critic.

Kritik-: k~fähig *adj* able to criticize; **~fähigkeit** *f* critical faculty; **k~los** *adj* uncritical.

kritisch *adj* (*alle Bedeutungen*) critical ♦ **jdm/einer Sache ~ gegenüberstehen** to be critical of sb/sth, to regard *or* consider sb/sth critically; **dann wird es ~** it could be critical.

kritisieren* *vti* to criticize ♦ **er hat** *or* **findet an allem etw zu ~** he always has *or* finds something to criticize.

Kritizismus *m* (*Philos*) critical philosophy.

Krittelei *f* fault-finding *no pl*, cavilling *no pl*.

kritteln *vi* to find fault (*an +dat, über +acc* with), to cavil (*an +dat, über +acc* at).

Kritzelei *f* scribble; (*das Kritzeln*) scribbling; (*Männchenmalen etc*) doodle; doodling; (*an Wänden*) graffiti.

kritzeln *vti* to scribble, to scrawl; (*Männchen malen etc*) to doodle.

Kroate *m* **-n, -n, Kroatin** *f* Croat, Croatian.

Kroatien [kro'a:tsiən] *nt* **-s** Croatia.

kroatisch *adj* Croat, Croatian.

Kroatisch(e) *nt* Croatian; *siehe auch* **Deutsch(e)**.

Kroatzbeere *f* (*esp S Ger*) *siehe* **Brombeere**.

kroch *pret of* **kriechen**.

Krocket(spiel) ['krɔkət-, krɔ'kɛt-] *nt* **-s,** *no pl* croquet.

Krokant *m* **-s,** *no pl* (*Cook*) cracknel.

Krokette *f* (*Cook*) croquette.

Kroko *nt* **-s,** *no pl* crocodile leather.

Krokodil *nt* **-s, -e** crocodile.

Krokodilleder *nt* crocodile leather *or* skin.

Krokodilstränen *pl* crocodile tears *pl*.

Krokus *m* **-, -** *or* **-se** crocus.

Krönchen *nt dim of* **Krone**.

Krone *f* **-, -n (a)** crown; (*eines Grafen etc*) coronet ♦ **die ~** (*fig*) the Crown.
(b) (*Mauer~*) coping; (*Schaum~*) cap, crest; (*Zahn~*) crown, cap; (*an Uhr*) winder; (*Geweih~*) surroyal (antler); (*Baum~*) top; (*Ernte~*) harvest wreath *or* crown ♦ **die ~ der Schöpfung** the pride of creation, creation's crowning glory; **die ~ des Lebens** (*Bibl*) (a) crown of life; **die ~ des Ganzen war, daß ...** (*fig*) (but) what crowned *or* capped it all was that ...; **das setzt doch allem die ~ auf** (*inf*) that beats everything; **das setzt der Dummheit die ~ auf** (*inf*) that beats everything for stupidity; **einen in der ~ haben** (*inf*) to be tipsy, to have had a drop too much; **dabei fällt dir keine Perle** *or* **kein Stein** *or* **Zacken aus der ~** (*inf*) it won't hurt you.
(c) (*Währungseinheit*) (*Hist, in der CSSR*) crown; (*in Skandinavien*) krone; (*in Schweden*) krona.

krönen *vt* (*lit, fig*) to crown; *Bauwerk* to crown, to top, to cap ♦ **jdn zum König ~** to crown sb king; **von Erfolg gekrönt sein/werden** to be crowned with success; **gekrönte Häupter** crowned heads; **damit wurde eine glänzende Laufbahn gekrönt** this was the crowning achievement in *or* culmination of his career; **der ~de Abschluß** the culmination.

Kronen-: ~korken *m* crown cap; **~mutter** *f* (*Tech*) castle nut.

Kron-: ~erbe *m* heir to the Crown *or* Throne; **~gut** *nt* crown estate; **~kolonie** *f* crown colony; **~korken** *m* crown cap; **~land** *nt* crown land.

Krönlein *nt dim of* **Krone**.

Kron-: ~leuchter *m* chandelier; **~prätendent** *m* pretender (to the crown); **~prinz** *m* crown prince; (*in Großbritannien auch*) Prince of Wales; (*fig*) heir apparent; **~prinzessin** *f* crown princess; **~rat** *m* crown council.

Kronsbeere *f* (*N Ger*) *siehe* **Preiselbeere**.

Krönung *f* coronation; (*fig*) culmination; (*von Veranstaltung*) high point, culmination; (*Archit*) coping stone.

Kronzeuge *m* (*Jur*) person who gives *or* turns King's/Queen's evidence *or* (*US*) State's evidence; (*Hauptzeuge*) principal witness; (*fig*) main authority ♦ **~ sein, als ~ auftreten** to turn King's/Queen's/State's evidence; to appear as principal witness.

Kropf *m* **-(e)s, ⸚e (a)** (*von Vogel*) crop. **(b)** (*Med*) goitre ♦ **überflüssig wie ein ~** totally superfluous.

Kröpfchen *nt dim of* **Kropf (a)**.

kröpfen **1** *vt* (*füttern, nudeln*) to cram.
2 *vi* (*fressen: Raubvögel*) to gorge.

Kropftaube *f* pouter (pigeon).

Kroppzeug *nt* (*pej inf: Gesindel*) scum ♦ **dieses ganze ~** all this junk (*inf*).

⚠ **kroß** *adj* (*N Ger*) crisp; *Brötchen auch* crusty.

Krösus *m* **-, -se** Croesus ♦ **ich bin doch kein ~** (*inf*) I'm not made of money (*inf*).

Kröte *f* **-, -n (a)** (*Zool*) toad ♦ **eine freche (kleine) ~** (*inf*) a cheeky (little) minx (*inf*); **eine giftige ~** (*inf*) a spiteful creature. **(b) ~n** *pl* (*sl*) pennies (*inf*).

Krötentest *m* (*Med*) Hogben (pregnancy) test.

Krücke *f* **-, -n (a)** crutch; (*fig*) prop, stay ♦ **auf** *or* **an ~n** (*dat*) **gehen** to walk on crutches. **(b)** (*Schirm~*) crook. **(c)** (*zum Harken etc*) rake. **(d)** (*sl: Stock*) stick. **(e)** (*sl: Nichtskönner*) dead loss (*inf*), washout (*inf*).

Krückstock *m* walking-stick; *siehe* **Blinde(r)**.

krud(e) *adj* (*geh*) crude.

Krug *m* **-(e)s, ⸚e (a)** (*Milch~ etc*) jug, pitcher (*old*); (*Wein~ auch*) flagon; (*Bier~*) (beer-)mug, stein, tankard; (*Maß~*) litre mug; (*Kruke*) jar ♦ **der ~ geht**

⚠: for details of spelling reform, see supplement

so lange zum Brunnen, bis er bricht (*Prov*) one day you/they *etc* will come unstuck *or* to grief. **(b)** (*N Ger: Wirtshaus*) inn, pub (*Brit*).

Krügel *nt* **-s, -** (*Aus*) half-litre mug.

Kruke *f* **-, -n** stone jar; (*Wärm~*) bed-warmer, earthenware *or* stone hot-water bottle.

Krume *f* **-, -n** (*geh*) **(a)** (*Brot~*) crumb. **(b)** (*liter: Acker~*) (top)soil.

Krümel *m* **-s, - (a)** (*Brot~ etc*) crumb. **(b)** (*inf: Kind*) little one, tiny tot (*inf*).

krümelig *adj* crumbly.

krümeln *vti* to crumble; (*beim Essen*) to make crumbs.

krumm *adj* **(a)** crooked; (*verbogen auch*) bent; (*hakenförmig*) hooked; *Beine auch* bandy; *Rücken* hunched ♦ **~e Nase** hook(ed) nose; **~ gewachsen** crooked; **etw ~ biegen** to bend sth; **~ und schief** askew, skew-whiff (*inf*); **sich ~ und schief lachen** (*inf*) to fall about laughing (*inf*); **jdn ~ und lahm schlagen** to beat sb black and blue; **keinen Finger ~ machen** (*inf*) not to lift a finger; **eine ~e Hand machen** (*inf*) to hold one's hand out; **einen ~en Rücken machen** to stoop; (*fig*) to bow and scrape; **mach nicht solchen ~en Rücken!** straighten your shoulders, hold yourself straight; **steh/sitz nicht so ~ da!** stand/sit up straight, don't slouch; **~ gehen** to walk with a stoop.
(b) (*inf: unehrlich*) crooked (*inf*) ♦ **~er Hund** (*pej*) crooked swine; **ein ~es Ding drehen** (*sl*) to do something crooked; **er hat während seiner Zeit als Buchhalter viele ~e Dinger gedreht** (*sl*) while he was a book-keeper he got up to all sorts of crooked tricks *or* he was up to all sorts of fiddles (*inf*); **etw auf die ~e Tour versuchen** to try to fiddle (*inf*) *or* wangle (*inf*) sth; **er hat sie auf die ~e Tour herumgekriegt** he conned her (*inf*); **~e Wege gehen** to err from the straight and narrow.

krummbeinig *adj* bow-legged, bandy(-legged).

krümmen [1] *vt* to bend ♦ **die Katze krümmte den Buckel** the cat arched its back; **gekrümmte Oberfläche** curved surface.
[2] *vr* to bend; (*Fluß*) to wind; (*Straße*) to bend, to curve; (*Wurm*) to writhe ♦ **sich vor Lachen ~** to double up with laughter, to crease up (*inf*); **sich vor Schmerzen** (*dat*) **~** to double up *or* writhe with pain.

Krumm-: ~horn *nt* crumhorn, krummhorn; **k~lachen** *vr sep* (*inf*) to double up *or* fall about laughing *or* with laughter; ⚠**k~legen** *vr sep* (*inf*) to pinch and scrape (*inf*); **k~nasig** *adj* (*pej*) hook-nosed; ⚠**k~nehmen** *vt sep irreg* (*inf*) **(jdm) etw k~nehmen** to take offence at sth, to take sth amiss; **~säbel** *m* scimitar; **~schwert** *nt* scimitar; **~stab** *m* crook, crozier.

Krümmung *f* **(a)** (*das Krümmen*) bending. **(b)** (*Biegung*) (*von Weg, Fluß*) bend, turn; (*Math, Med, von Fläche*) curvature; (*Opt: von Linse*) curve, curvature, figure.

krump(e)lig *adj* (*dial*) creased, crumpled.

Kruppe *f* **-, -n** (*Zool*) croup, crupper.

Krüppel *m* **-s, -** cripple ♦ **ein seelischer/geistiger ~ sein** to be an emotional/intellectual cripple, to be emotionally/intellectually stunted; **zum ~ werden** to be crippled; **jdn zum ~ schlagen** to (beat and) cripple sb.

krüpp(e)lig *adj Mensch* crippled, deformed; *Wuchs* stunted; *siehe* **lachen**.

Krustazeen [krʊsta'tseːən] *pl* (*spec*) crustacea.

Kruste *f* **-, -n** crust; (*von Schweinebraten*) crackling; (*von Braten*) crisped outside.

krustig *adj* crusty; *Topf etc* encrusted.

Krux *f* **-,** *no pl siehe* **Crux**.

Kruzifix *nt* **-es, -e** crucifix ♦ **~!** (*inf*) Christ almighty!

Kruzitürken *interj* (*S Ger inf*) confound it, curse it.

Krypta ['krʏpta] *f* **-, Krypten** crypt.

Krypto-, krypto- [krʏpto-] *in cpds* crypto-.

Krypton ['krʏptɔn, krʏp'toːn] *nt* **-s,** *no pl* (*abbr* **Kr**) krypton.

KSZE [kaː|ɛstsɛt'|eː] *f* **-** *abbr of* **Konferenz über Sicherheit und Zusammenarbeit in Europa** CSCE.

Kuba *nt* **-s** Cuba.

Kubaner(in *f***)** *m* **-s, -** Cuban.

kubanisch *adj* Cuban.

Kübel *m* **-s, -** bucket, pail; (*für Jauche etc*) container; (*inf: im Gefängnis*) latrine *or* toilet bucket, crapper (*sl*); (*für Bäume*) tub ♦ **es regnet (wie) aus** *or* **in** *or* **mit ~n** it's bucketing down; **~ von Schmutz** *or* **Unrat** (*fig geh*) torrents of abuse.

kübeln *vi* (*inf: zechen*) to booze (*inf*).

Kuben *pl of* **Kubus**.

Kubik *nt* **-, -** (*Aut inf: Hubraum*) cc.

Kubik-: ~meter *m or nt* cubic metre; **~wurzel** *f* cube root; **~zahl** *f* cube number; **~zentimeter** *m or nt* cubic centimetre.

kubisch *adj* cubic(al); *Gleichung* cubic; *Lampen* cube-shaped.

Kubismus *m* (*Art*) cubism.

Kubist(in *f***)** *m* (*Art*) cubist.

kubistisch *adj* (*Art*) cubist(ic).

Kubus *m* **-, Kuben** *or* **-** cube.

Küche *f* **-, -n (a)** kitchen; (*klein*) kitchenette ♦ **es wurde alles aufgetischt, was ~ und Keller zu bieten hatten** he/they *etc* served up a meal fit for a king. **(b)** (*Kochkunst*) **gutbürgerliche ~** good home cooking. **(c)** (*Speisen*) meals *pl*, dishes *pl*, food ♦ **warme/kalte ~** hot/cold food.

Kuchen *m* **-s, -** cake; (*Torte auch*) gateau; (*mit Obst gedeckt*) (fruit) flan, gateau.

Küchen-: ~abfälle *pl* kitchen scraps *pl*; **~abzugshaube** *f* extractor hood; **~benutzung** *f* use of kitchen.

Kuchenblech *nt* baking sheet *or* tin.

Küchen-: ~bulle *m* (*Mil sl*) cookhouse wallah (*Mil sl*); **~chef** *m* chef; **~fee** *f* (*hum inf*) (lady) cook.

Kuchen-: ~form *f* cake tin; **~gabel** *f* pastry fork.

Küchen-: ~gerät *nt* kitchen utensil; (*kollektiv*) kitchen utensils *pl*; (*elektrisch*) kitchen appliance; **~geschirr** *nt* kitchenware *no pl*; **~handtuch** *nt* kitchen towel; **~herd** *m* (electric/gas) cooker; **~hilfe** *f* kitchen help; **~hobel** *m* slicer, cutter; **~junge** *m* (*dated*) apprentice cook *or* chef; **~kabinett** *nt* (*Pol*) inner circle; **~latein** *nt* dog Latin; **~maschine** *f* food processor; **~meister** *m siehe* **~chef**; **~messer** *nt* kitchen knife; **~personal** *nt* kitchen staff; **~schabe** *f* (*Zool*) cockroach; **~schrank** *m* (kitchen) cupboard.

Kuchenteig *m* cake mixture; (*Hefeteig*) dough.

Küchen-: ~tisch *m* kitchen table; **~tuch** *nt* kitchen towel; **~uhr** *f* kitchen clock; **~waage** *f* kitchen scales *pl*; **~wagen** *m* (*Mil*) mobile field-kitchen; **~zettel** *m* menu.

Küchlein *nt* **(a)** small cake. **(b)** (*Küken*) chick.

Kücken *nt* **-s, -** (*Aus*) *siehe* **Küken**.

kucken *vi* (*inf, N Ger*) *siehe* **gucken**.

Kuckuck *m* **-s, -e (a)** cuckoo. **(b)** (*inf: Siegel des Gerichtsvollziehers*) bailiff's seal (for distraint of goods). **(c)** (*euph inf: Teufel*) devil ♦ **zum ~ (noch mal)!** hell's bells! (*inf*); **hol's der ~!** botheration! (*inf*); **geh zum ~, scher dich zum ~** go to blazes (*inf*); **das weiß der ~** heaven (only) knows (*inf*).

kuckuck *interj* cuckoo.

Kuckucks-: ~ei *nt* cuckoo's egg; (*inf: außerehelich gezeugtes Kind*) illegitimate child; **man hat uns ein ~ei untergeschoben** (*inf*) we've been left holding the baby (*inf*); **~uhr** *f* cuckoo clock.

Kuddelmuddel *m or nt* **-s,** *no pl* (*inf*) muddle, mess, confusion; (*Aufsatz etc auch*) hotchpotch (*inf*).

Kufe *f* **-, -n (a)** (*von Schlitten, Schlittschuh etc*) runner; (*von Flugzeug*) skid. **(b)** (*Holzbottich*) tub.

Küfer *m* **-s, -** cellarman; (*S Ger: Böttcher*) cooper.

Kugel *f* **-, -n (a)** ball; (*geometrische Figur*) sphere; (*Erd~*) sphere, globe; (*Sport sl: Ball*) ball; (*Kegel~*) bowl; (*Gewehr~*) bullet; (*für Luftgewehr*) pellet; (*Kanonen~*) (cannon)ball; (*Sport: Stoß~*) shot; (*Murmel*) marble; (*Papier~*) ball; (*kleine*) pellet; (*Christbaum~*) glitter ball ♦ **sich** (*dat*) **eine ~ durch den Kopf jagen** *or* **schießen** to blow one's brains out; **eine ruhige ~ schieben** (*inf*) to have a cushy number *or* job (*inf*); (*aus Faulheit*) to swing the lead (*inf*); **rund wie eine ~** (*inf*) like a barrel; **die ~ rollt** the roulette wheels are spinning.
(b) (*Gelenk~*) head (of a bone).
(c) (*sl: Mark*) mark; ≃ quid (*Brit inf*), buck (*US inf*).

Kugel-: ~abschnitt *m* (*Math*) spherical segment; **~ausschnitt** *m* (*Math*) spherical sector; **~bauch** *m* pot belly, paunch; **~blitz** *m* (*Met*) ball-lightning; **~fang** *m* butt; **die Leibwächter sollen als ~fang dienen** the body-guards are meant to act as a bullet-screen; **k~fest** *adj siehe* **k~sicher**; **~fisch** *m* globefish, puffer; **~fläche** *f* (*Math*) spherical surface; **k~förmig** *adj* spherical; **~gelenk** *nt* (*Anat, Tech*) ball-and-socket joint; **~hagel** *m* hail of bullets.

kugelig *adj* **(a)** *siehe* **kugelförmig**. **(b)** (*inf*) **sich ~ lachen** to double up (laughing).

Kugel-: ~kopf *m* golf-ball; **~kopfschreibmaschine** *f* golf-ball typewriter.

Kugellager *nt* ball-bearing.

kugeln [1] *vi aux sein* (*rollen, fallen*) to roll.
[2] *vr* to roll (about) ♦ **sich (vor Lachen) ~** (*inf*) to double up (laughing); **ich könnte mich ~** (*inf*) it's killingly funny (*inf*).

Kugel-: ~regen *m siehe* **~hagel**; **k~rund** *adj* as round as a ball; (*inf*) *Mensch* tubby, barrel-shaped (*inf*); **~schreiber** *m* ballpoint (pen), biro ®; **~schreibermine** *f* refill (for a ballpoint pen); **k~sicher** *adj* bullet-proof; **~stoßen** *nt* **-s,** *no pl* shot-putting, putting the shot; **Sieger im ~stoßen** winner in the shot(-put); **~stoßer(in** *f***)** *m* **-s, -** shot-putter; **~ventil** *nt* (*Tech*) ball valve; **~wechsel** *m* exchange of shots.

Kuh *f* **-, ¨e** cow; (*pej sl: Mädchen, Frau*) cow (*sl*) ♦ **wie die ~ vorm neuen Tor dastehen** (*inf*) to be completely bewildered; **heilige ~** (*lit, fig*) sacred cow.

Kuh-: ~dorf *nt* (*pej inf*) one-horse town (*inf*); **~fladen** *m* cow-pat; **~fuß** *m* (*Tech*) crow-bar; **~glocke** *f* cowbell; **~handel** *m* (*pej inf*) horse-trading (*inf*) *no pl*; **ein ~handel** a bit of horse-trading; **k~handeln** *vi insep* (*inf*) to do horse-trading; **~haut** *f* cow-hide; **das geht auf keine ~haut** (*inf*) that is absolutely staggering *or* incredible; **~herde** *f* herd of cows; **~hirt(e)** *m* cowhand, cowherd; cowboy.

kühl *adj* (*lit, fig*) cool; (*abweisend*) cold ♦ **mir wird etwas ~** I'm getting rather chilly; **abends wurde es ~** in the evenings it got cool; **etw ~ lagern** to store sth in a cool place; **ein ~er Kopf** (*fig*) a cool-headed person; **einen ~en Kopf bewahren** to keep a cool head, to keep cool; **ein ~er Rechner** a cool, calculating person.

Kühl-: ~anlage *f* refrigeration plant, cold storage plant; **~becken** *nt* (*für Brennelemente*) cooling pond; **~box** *f* cold box.

Kuhle *f* **-, -n** (*N Ger*) hollow; (*Grube*) pit.

Kühle *f* **-,** *no pl* (*lit*) cool(ness); (*fig*) coolness; (*Abweisung*) coldness.

kühlen [1] *vt* to cool; (*auf Eis*) to chill; *siehe* **Mütchen**.
[2] *vi* to be cooling, to have a cooling effect ♦ **bei großer Hitze kühlt Tee am besten** in very hot weather tea cools you down best.

Kühler *m* **-s, -** (*Tech*) cooler; (*Aut*) radiator; (*inf: ~haube*) bonnet (*Brit*), hood (*US*); (*Sekt~*) ice bucket ♦ **ich hätte die alte Frau beinahe auf den ~ genommen** (*inf*) the old lady almost finished up on my bonnet; **jdm vor den ~ rennen** (*inf*) to run (out) right in front of sb *or* right under sb's front wheels.

Kühler-: ~figur *f* (*Aut*) radiator mascot; **~grill** *m* radiator grill; **~haube** *f* (*Aut*) *siehe* **Motorhaube**.

Kühl-: ~fach *nt siehe* **Gefrierfach**; **~haus** *nt* cold-storage depot; **~kette** *f* chain of cold storage units; **~lagerung** *f* cold storage; **~mittel** *nt* (*Tech*) coolant, cooling agent; **~ofen** *m* (*Tech*) annealing oven; **~raum** *m* cold store *or* storage room; **~rippe** *f* (*Aut*) cooling fin; **~schiff** *nt* refrigerator ship; **~schrank** *m* refrigerator, fridge (*Brit*), icebox (*US*); **~tasche** *f* cold bag; **~truhe** *f* (chest) freezer, deep freeze (*Brit*); (*in Lebensmittelgeschäft*) freezer (cabinet); **~turm** *m* (*Tech*) cooling tower.

Kühlung *f* (*das Kühlen*) cooling; (*Kühle*) coolness ◆ **zur ~ des Motors** to cool the engine; **sich** (*dat*) **~ verschaffen** to cool oneself (down); **er ging in den Schatten, um sich ~ zu verschaffen** he went into the shade to cool down *or* off; **auch bei ~ nur begrenzt haltbar** perishable even when kept in cold storage.

Kühl-: ~vitrine *f* refrigerated counter *or* cabinet; **~wagen** *m* **(a)** (*Rail*) refrigerator *or* refrigerated *or* cold storage wagon; **(b)** (*Lastwagen*) refrigerator *or* refrigerated *or* cold storage truck; **~wasser** *nt* coolant; (*Aut*) radiator water; **~wasserturm** *m* cooling tower; **~wirkung** *f* cooling effect.

Kuh-: ~magd *f* (*dated*) milkmaid, dairymaid; **~milch** *f* cow's milk; **~mist** *m* cow dung.

kühn *adj* (*lit, fig*) bold ◆ **eine ~ geschwungene Nase** an aquiline nose; **das übertrifft meine ~sten Erwartungen** it's beyond *or* it surpasses my wildest hopes or dreams.

Kühnheit *f* boldness.

Kuh-: ~pocken *pl* cowpox *sing*; **~scheiße** *f* (*sl*) cow-shit (*vulg*); **~stall** *m* cow-shed, byre; **~stallwärme** *f* (*fig*) cosy camaraderie; **k~warm** *adj Milch* warm *or* fresh from the cow; **~weide** *f* pasture.

kujonieren* *vt* (*old*) to bully, to harass.

k.u.k. ['ka:|ʊnt'ka:] *abbr of* **kaiserlich und königlich** imperial and royal.

Küken *nt* **-s, - (a)** (*Huhn*) chick; (*inf: junges Mädchen*) young goose (*inf*); (*inf: Nesthäkchen*) youngest child, baby of the family (*inf*); (*jüngste Person*) baby. **(b)** (*Tech*) plug.

Ku-Klux-Klan *m* **-s** Ku Klux Klan.

Kukuruz *m* **-(es),** *no pl* (*Aus*) maize, corn.

kulant *adj* obliging, accommodating; *Bedingungen* generous, fair.

Kulanz *f, no pl siehe adj* obligingness, accommodatingness; generousness, fairness.

Kulanzleistung *f* gesture of goodwill.

Kuli *m* **-s, -s (a)** (*Lastträger*) coolie; (*fig*) slave ◆ **wie ein ~ arbeiten** (*inf*) to work like a slave *or* black (*inf*). **(b)** (*inf: Kugelschreiber*) ballpoint, biro ®.

kulinarisch *adj* culinary; (*fig*) entertainment-orientated.

Kulisse *f* **-, -n** scenery *no pl*; (*Teilstück*) flat, piece of scenery; (*hinten*) backdrop; (*an den Seiten auch*) wing; (*fig: Hintergrund*) background, backdrop, back-cloth; (*St Ex*) unofficial market ◆ **die ~n für das Stück** the scenery for the play; **das ist alles nur ~** (*fig*) that is only a façade; **hinter den ~n** behind the scenes.

Kulissen-: ~maler *m* scene-painter; **~schieber(in** *f*) *m* **-s, -** scene-shifter.

Kuller-: ~augen *pl* (*inf*) big wide eyes *pl*; **~ball** *m* **(a)** (*baby-talk*) baby's little ball; **(b)** (*Sport inf*) easy ball; (*leicht zu haltender Schuß auch*) dolly (*inf*).

kullern *vti* (*vi: aux sein*) (*inf*) to roll.

Kulmination *f* culmination; (*fig auch*) apex ◆ **obere/untere ~** highest/lowest point.

Kulminationspunkt *m* (*Astron*) point of culmination; (*fig*) culmination, apex.

kulminieren* *vi* to culminate; (*fig auch*) to reach its peak.

Kult *m* **-(e)s, -e** cult; (*Verehrung*) worship ◆ **einen ~ mit jdm/etw treiben** to make a cult out of sb/sth, to idolize sb; **mit denen wird jetzt so ein ~ getrieben** they have become such cult figures.

Kult-: ~bild *nt* religious symbol; **~buch** *nt* cult book; **~figur** *f* cult figure; **~film** *m* cult film; **~gemeinschaft** *f* cult; **~handlung** *f* ritual(istic) act.

kultisch *adj* ritual(istic), cultic (*rare*) ◆ **er wird geradezu ~ verehrt** they almost make a god out of him.

kultivierbar *adj Land* cultiv(at)able ◆ **dieser Boden ist nur schwer ~** the soil is very hard to cultivate.

kultivieren* [kʊlti'vi:rən] *vt* (*lit, fig*) to cultivate.

kultiviert *adj* cultivated, cultured, refined; *Mensch, Geschmack, Unterhaltung auch* sophisticated ◆ **könnt ihr euch nicht etwas ~er unterhalten?** couldn't you make your language just a little more refined *etc*?; **in dieser Familie mußt du dich ein bißchen ~er benehmen als sonst** in this family you'll have to behave with a little more refinement *or* class (*inf*) than usual; **wenn Sie ~ reisen wollen** if you want to travel in style; **Kerzen beim Essen, das ist sehr ~** meals by candlelight, very civilized; **wenn man mal ~ essen will** if you want a civilized meal.

Kultivierung [kʊlti'vi:rʊŋ] *f* (*lit, fig*) cultivation.

Kult-: ~sprache *f* language of worship; **~stätte** *f* place of worship; **~symbol** *nt* ritual symbol.

Kultur *f* **(a)** (*no pl: Kunst und Wissenschaft*) culture ◆ **ein Volk von hoher ~** a highly cultured *or* civilized people; **er hat keine ~** he is uncultured.
(b) (*Lebensform*) civilization ◆ **dort leben verschiedene ~en harmonisch zusammen** different cultures live harmoniously together there.
(c) (*Bakterien~, Pilz~ etc*) culture.
(d) *no pl* (*von Mikroben etc*) culture; (*des Bodens auch*) cultivation.
(e) (*Bestand angebauter Pflanzen*) plantation.

Kultur-: ~abkommen *nt* cultural agreement; **~anthropologie** *f* cultural anthropology; **~arbeit** *f* cultural activities *pl*; **~attaché** *m* cultural attaché; **~austausch** *m* cultural exchange; **~autonomie** *f* independence in cultural (and educational) matters; **~banause** *m* (*inf*) philistine; **~beilage** *f* cultural *or* arts supplement *or* review; **~betrieb** *m* (*inf*) culture industry; **~beutel** *m* sponge *or* toilet bag (*Brit*), washbag; **~boden** *m* cultivated *or* arable land; **~denkmal** *nt* cultural monument.

kulturell *adj* cultural.

Kultur-: ~erbe *nt* cultural heritage; **~film** *m* documentary film; **~föderalismus** *m* (*Pol*) cultural and educational devolution; ⚠**~geographie** *f* human geography; **~geschichte** *f* history of civilization; **Sozial- und ~geschichte der Etrusker** social and cultural history of the Etruscans; **k~geschichtlich** *adj* historico-cultural, concerning the history of civilization; **~gut** *nt* cultural possessions *pl or* assets *pl*; **~haus** *nt* (*esp DDR*) arts centre; **k~historisch** *adj siehe* **k~geschichtlich**; **~hoheit** *f* independence in matters of education and culture; **~industrie** *f* culture industry; **~kampf** *m, no pl* cultural war; (*Hist*) Kulturkampf (*struggle between Church and State 1872-1887*); **~konsum** *m* (*inf*) consumption of culture, cultural consumption; **~kreis** *m* culture group *or* area; **~kritik** *f* critique of (our) civilization *or* culture; **~land** *nt* cultivated *or* arable land; **~landschaft** *f* land developed and cultivated by man; (*fig*) cultural landscape; **~leben** *nt* cultural life; **k~los** *adj* lacking culture; *Mensch auch* uncultured; **~losigkeit** *f* lack of culture; **~minister** *m siehe* **Kultusminister**; **~ministerium** *nt siehe* **Kultusministerium**; **~nation** *f* cultural nation; **~palast** *m* (*esp DDR*) palace of culture *or* the arts; (*pej*) cultured extravagance; **~pessimismus** *m* despair of civilization; **~pflanze** *f* cultivated plant; **~politik** *f* cultural and educational policy; **~politiker** *m* politician who concerns himself mainly with cultural and educational policies; **k~politisch** *adj* politico-cultural; **k~politische Fragen** matters with both a cultural and a political aspect; **~psychologie** *f* psychology of culture; **~revolution** *f* cultural revolution; **~schaffende(r)** *mf decl as adj* creative artist; **~schale** *f* Petri dish; **~schande** *f* crime against civilization, cultural outrage; (*fig inf*) insult to *or* offence against good taste; **~schock** *m* culture shock; **~soziologie** *f* cultural sociology, sociology of culture; **k~soziologisch** *adj* socio-cultural; **~sprache** *f* language of the civilized world; **~stätte** *f* place of cultural interest; **~steppe** *f* (*Geog*) cultivated steppe; **~stufe** *f* stage *or* level of civilization; **~teil** *m* (*von Zeitung*) arts section; **~träger** *m* vehicle of culture *or* civilization; **~volk** *nt* civilized people *sing or* nation; **~wandel** *m* cultural change; **~wissenschaft** *f* study of civilization; **~wissenschaften** cultural studies; **~zentrum** *nt* **(a)** (*Stadt*) centre of cultural life, cultural centre; **(b)** (*Anlage*) arts centre.

Kultus-: ~freiheit *f* religious freedom, freedom of worship; **~gemeinde** *f* religious community; **~minister** *m* minister of education and the arts; **~ministerium** *nt* ministry of education and the arts.

Kumme *f* **-, -n** (*N Ger*) bowl.

Kümmel *m* **-s, - (a)** *no pl* (*Gewürz*) caraway (seed). **(b)** (*inf: Schnaps*) kümmel.

Kümmelbranntwein *m* (*form*) kümmel.

kümmeln [1] *vt* to season with caraway (seeds).
[2] *vti* (*inf*) to tipple ◆ **einen ~** to have a little drink.

Kümmel-: ~öl *nt* caraway oil; **~türke** *m* (*pej sl: Türke*) Turk, wog (*pej inf*).

Kummer *m* **-s,** *no pl* (*Gram, Betrübtheit*) grief, sorrow; (*Unannehmlichkeit, Ärger*) trouble, problems *pl* ◆ **hast du ~?** is something wrong?, have you got problems?; **aus** *or* **vor ~ sterben** to die of sorrow *or* grief; **vor ~ vergehen** to be pining away with sorrow *or* grief; **vor ~ nahm er sich** (*dat*) **das Leben** in his grief *or* grief-stricken he took his life; **er fand vor ~ keinen Schlaf mehr** such was his grief *or* sorrow that he was unable to sleep; **jdm ~ machen** *or* **bereiten** to cause sb worry; **wenn das dein einziger ~ ist** if that's your only problem *or* worry; **wir sind (an) ~ gewöhnt** (*inf*) it happens all the time, nothing's ever perfect.

Kummerfalten *pl* wrinkles *pl* ◆ **das sind ~** that's the worry.

kümmerlich *adj* **(a)** (*karg, armselig*) wretched, miserable; *Reste, Ausbeute, Rente* miserable, meagre, paltry; *Lohn, Mahlzeit auch* measly (*inf*); *Aufsatz* scanty ◆ **sich ~ ernähren** to live on a meagre diet. **(b)** (*schwächlich*) puny.

Kümmerling *m* **(a)** (*Zool*) stunted person/plant/animal ◆ **die Pflanze war von Anfang an ein ~** the plant always was a sickly thing. **(b)** (*inf: Schwächling*) weakling, weed (*pej inf*).

kümmern[1] *vi* (*Hunt, Zool*) to become *or* grow stunted; (*fig*) to shrivel.

kümmern[2] [1] *vt* to concern ◆ **was kümmert mich die Firma?** why should I worry about the firm?, what do I care about the firm?; **was kümmert Sie das?** what business *or* concern is that of yours?; **was kümmert mich das?** what's that to me?
[2] *vr* **sich um jdn/etw ~** to look after sb/sth; **sich um einen Kranken/jds Kinder ~** to look after *or* take care of a sick person/sb's children; **sich um die Karten/das Essen ~** to look after *or* take care of *or* see to the tickets/the food; **sich darum ~, daß ...** to see to it that ...; **aber darum kümmert sich im Stadtrat ja keiner** but nobody on the council does anything about it; **kümmere dich nicht um Sachen, die dich nichts angehen** don't worry about things that don't concern you; **kümmere dich gefälligst um deine eigenen Angelegenheiten!** mind your own business!; **er kümmert sich nicht darum, was die Leute denken** he doesn't mind *or* isn't worried about *or* doesn't care (about) what people think; *siehe* **Dreck**.

Kümmernis *f* (*liter*) troubles *pl*, worries *pl*.

Kummer-: ~speck *m* (*inf*) *flab caused by overeating because of emotional problems*; **sie hat ganz schön ~speck angesetzt** she's been putting on weight, it's the worry making her eat too much; **k~voll** *adj* sorrowful, sad, woebegone *no adv*.

Kümmerwuchs *m* stunted growth.

Kummet *nt* **-s, -e** *siehe* **Kumt**.

Kümo *nt* **-s, -s** *abbr of* **Küstenmotorschiff** coaster.

Kumpan(in *f*) *m* **-s, -e** (*dated inf*) pal (*inf*), chum (*inf*), mate (*Brit inf*), buddy (*esp US inf*).
Kumpanei *f* (*pej*) chumminess.
Kumpel *m* **-s, -** *or* (*inf*) **-s** *or* (*Aus*) **-n** **(a)** (*Min: Bergmann*) pitman, miner. **(b)** (*inf: Arbeitskollege, Kamerad*) pal (*inf*), chum (*inf*), mate (*Brit inf*), buddy (*esp US inf*).
Kumt *nt* **-(e)s, -e** horse collar.
Kumulation *f* **(a)** (*von Ämtern*) plurality. **(b)** (*von Wahlstimmen*) accumulation.
kumulativ *adj* cumulative.
kumulieren* *vt* to accumulate ◆ **~de Bibliographie** cumulative bibliography.
Kumulierung *f* cumulative voting; (*von Wahlstimmen*) accumulation.
Kumulus *m* **-, Kumuli, Kumuluswolke** *f* cumulus (cloud).
kund *adj inv* (*obs*): **jdm etw ~ und zu wissen tun** to make sth known to sb.
kündbar *adj Vertrag* terminable; *Anleihe* redeemable ◆ **Beamte sind nicht ohne weiteres ~** civil servants cannot be given (their) notice *or* dismissed just like that; **die Mitgliedschaft ist sehr schwer ~** it is very difficult to terminate *or* cancel one's membership.
Kündbarkeit *f* (*von Vertrag*) terminability; (*von Anleihe*) redeemability ◆ **die ~ von Verträgen ist gesetzlich geregelt** the termination of contracts is controlled by law.
Kunde[1] *f* **-,** *no pl* (*geh*) news *sing*, tidings *pl* (*old*) ◆ **der Welt von etw ~ geben** to proclaim sth to the world; **von etw ~ geben** *or* **ablegen** to bear witness to sth.
Kunde[2] *m* **-n, -n** customer; (*pej inf*) customer (*inf*), character.
-kunde *f in cpds* science of.
künden [1] *vt* (*geh*) to announce, to herald.
[2] *vi* (*geh*) **von etw ~** to tell of sth, to bear witness to sth.
Kunden-: ~beratung *f* customer advisory service; **~dienst** *m* customer *or* after-sales service; (*Abteilung*) service department; **~fang** *m* (*pej*) touting *or* looking for customers; **auf ~fang sein** to be touting *or* looking for customers; **~karte** *f* (*von Firma, Organisation*) charge card; (*von Kaufhaus etc*) store card; (*von Bank*) bank card; **~kreis** *m* customers *pl*, clientèle; **~nummer** *f* customer number; **~sprache** *f* thieves' cant, argot; **~stock** *m* (*Aus*) *siehe* **~kreis**; **~werbung** *f* publicity aimed at attracting custom *or* customers.
Künder(in *f*) *m* **-s, -** (*rare*) messenger, harbinger (*obs, liter*).
kundgeben *sep irreg* [1] *vt* (*dated*) to make known, to announce; *Meinung, Gefühle* to express, to declare ◆ **etw ~** to announce sth (*jdm* to sb), to make sth known (*jdm* to sb).
[2] *vr* to be revealed.
Kundgebung *f* **(a)** (*Pol*) rally. **(b)** (*Bekanntgabe*) declaration, demonstration.
kundig *adj* (*geh*) well-informed, knowledgeable; (*sach~*) expert ◆ **einer Sache** (*gen*) **~ sein** to have a knowledge of sth.
-kundig *adj suf* with a good knowledge of.
kündigen [1] *vt Stellung* to hand in one's notice for; *Abonnement, Mitgliedschaft, Kredite* to cancel, to discontinue, to terminate; *Vertrag* to terminate; *Tarife* to discontinue; *Hypothek* (*Bank*) to foreclose (on); (*Hausbesitzer*) to terminate; (*strictly incorrect, Aus*) *Person* to sack (*inf*), to fire (*inf*), to dismiss ◆ **jdm die Wohnung ~, jdn aus einer Wohnung ~** (*Aus*) to give sb notice to quit his flat; **ich habe meine Wohnung gekündigt** I've given in notice that I'm leaving my flat, I've given in my notice for my flat; **die Stellung ~** to hand *or* give in one's notice; **jdm die Stellung ~** to give sb his/her notice; **jdm Kredite ~** to cancel *or* discontinue *or* terminate sb's credit; **Beträge über ... muß man ~** for sums in excess of ... notification must be given in advance; **jdm die Freundschaft ~** to break off a friendship with sb.
[2] *vi* (*Arbeitnehmer*) to hand *or* give in one's notice; (*Mieter*) to give in one's notice, to give notice ◆ **jdm ~** (*Arbeitgeber*) to give sb his notice, to dismiss sb; (*Arbeitnehmer*) to hand *or* give in one's notice to sb; (*Vermieter*) to give sb notice to quit; (*Mieter*) to give in one's notice to sb; **zum 1. April ~** to give *or* hand in one's notice for April 1st; (*Mieter*) to give notice for *or* give in one's notice for April 1st; (*bei Mitgliedschaft*) to cancel one's membership as of April 1st; **ihm ist zum 1. Februar gekündigt worden** he's been given his notice for *or* as from February 1st; (*bei Wohnung*) he's been given notice to quit for February 1st; **ich kann nur zum Ersten eines Monats ~** I have to give a clear month's notice; **bei jdm/einer Firma ~** to give *or* hand in one's notice to sb/a firm.
Kündigung *f* **(a)** (*Mitteilung*) (*von Vermieter*) notice to quit; (*von Mieter*) notice; (*von Stellung*) notice; (*von Vertrag*) termination; (*von Hypothek*) notice of foreclosure; (*von Anleihe*) notice of withdrawal; (*von Mitgliedschaft, Abonnement*) (letter of) cancellation.
(b) (*das Kündigen*) (*von Arbeitgeber*) dismissal; (*von Arbeitnehmer*) handing *or* giving in one's notice; (*von Vertrag*) termination; (*von Hypothek*) foreclosure; (*von Anleihe*) withdrawal; (*von Tarifen*) discontinuation; (*von Mitgliedschaft, Abonnement*) cancellation ◆ **wegen schlechten Betragens des Mieters entschloß sich der Vermieter zur ~** the landlord decided to give the tenant his notice (to quit) because of his bad behaviour; **ich drohte (dem Chef) mit der ~** I threatened to give *or* hand in my notice (to my boss), I threatened to quit; **ich erwäge eine ~ meiner Stelle** I'm considering handing *or* giving in my notice; **Vertrag mit vierteljährlicher ~** contract with three months' notice on either side; **vierteljährliche ~ haben** to have (to give) three months' notice.
Kündigungs-: ~frist *f* period of notice; **~geld** *nt* (*Fin*) deposits *pl* at notice; **~grund** *m* reason *or* grounds *pl* for giving notice; (*von Arbeitgeber auch*) grounds *pl* for dismissal; **~schutz** *m* protection against wrongful dismissal.
Kundin *f* customer.
kundmachen *vt sep* (*old, liter*) *siehe* **kundgeben 1.**
Kundmachung *f* (*Aus, Sw, S Ger*) *siehe* **Bekanntmachung.**
Kundschaft *f* **(a)** customers *pl* ◆ **~!** shop!, service!; **es ist ~ im Geschäft** there are customers in the shop.
(b) (*Erkundung*) reconnaissance ◆ **jdn auf ~ ausschicken** *or* **senden** (*Mil*) to send sb out to reconnoitre *or* on reconnaissance; **auf ~ (aus)gehen** (*Mil*) to go out on reconnaissance.
(c) *siehe* **Kunde**[1].
kundschaften *vi insep* (*Mil*) to reconnoitre.
Kundschafter *m* **-s, -** spy; (*Mil*) scout.
kundtun ['kʊnttuːn] *vt sep irreg* (*geh*) to make known, to proclaim.
kundwerden *vi sep irreg aux sein* (*liter*) to become known.
künftig [1] *adj* future ◆ **~en Jahres/Monats** next year/month; **das ~e Leben** the next life, the life to come; **meine ~e Frau/mein ~er Schwager** my future wife/brother-in-law, my wife-to-be/brother-in-law to be.
[2] *adv* in future.
Kungelei *f* (*inf*) fiddle (*inf*), fiddling *no pl* (*inf*).
kungeln *vti* (*inf*) to fiddle (*inf*) ◆ **mit denen hat er viel gekungelt** he did a lot of fiddles with them.
Kung-Fu *nt* **-,** *no pl* kung fu.
Kunst *f* **-, ⸚e** **(a)** art ◆ **die schönen ⸚e** fine art *sing*, the fine arts; *siehe* **bildend.**
(b) (*Können, Fertigkeit*) art, skill ◆ **seine ~ an jdm versuchen** to try *or* practise one's skills on sb; **mit seiner ~ am** *or* **zu Ende sein** to be at one's wits' end; **die ~ besteht darin, ...** the art *or* knack is in ...; **ärztliche ~** medical skill; *siehe* **Regel.**
(c) (*Kunststück*) trick ◆ **er wandte alle ⸚e der Rhetorik an** he used all the arts *or* tricks of rhetoric; **sie versuchte all ihre ⸚e an ihm** she used all her charms and wiles on him; **das ist keine ~!** it's like taking candy from a baby (*inf*); (*ein Kinderspiel*) it's a piece of cake (*inf*); **so einfach ist das, das ist die ganze ~** it's that easy, that's all there is to it.
(d) (*inf*) **das ist eine brotlose ~** there's no money in that; **was macht die ~?** (*inf*) how are things?, how's tricks? (*inf*).
Kunst- *in cpds* (*Art*) art; (*künstlich*) artificial; **~akademie** *f* college of art, art college; **~ausstellung** *f* art exhibition; **~banause** *m* (*pej*) philistine; **~darm** *m* artificial sausage skin; **~denkmal** *nt* work of art (*from an older culture*); **~druck** *m* art print; **~druckpapier** *nt* art paper; **~dünger** *m* chemical *or* artificial fertilizer.
Künstelei *f* affectation.
Kunst-: k~empfänglich *adj* artistic, appreciative of art; **~erzieher** *m* art teacher; **~erziehung** *f* (*Sch*) art; **~faser** *f* man-made *or* synthetic fibre; **~fehler** *m* professional error; (*weniger ernst*) slip; **wegen eines ärztlichen ~fehlers** because of medical malpractice; **k~fertig** *adj* (*geh*) skilful; **~fertigkeit** *f* skill, skilfulness; **~figur** *f* fictional character; **~flieger** *m* stunt *or* aerobatic pilot, stunt flyer; **~flug** *m* aerobatics *sing*, aerobatic *or* stunt flying; **ein ~flug** a piece of aerobatic *or* stunt flying; **~freund** *m* art lover, patron *or* lover of the arts; **~gegenstand** *m* objet d'art, art object; (*Gemälde*) work of art; **k~gemäß, k~gerecht** *adj* (*fachmännisch*) proficient, skilful; **~geschichte** *f* history of art, art history; **~gewerbe** *nt* arts and crafts *pl*; **ein Fachgeschäft für ~gewerbe** an arts and crafts shop, a craft shop; **~gewerbler(in** *f*) *m* **-s, -** artisan, craftsman/-woman; **k~gewerblich** *adj* **k~gewerbliche Gegenstände** craft objects; **k~gewerblicher Zweig** arts and crafts department; **~griff** *m* trick, dodge (*inf*); **~handel** *m* art trade; **~händler** *m* art dealer; **~handwerk** *nt* craft industry; **~harz** *nt* synthetic resin; **~herz** *nt* artificial heart; **k~historisch** [1] *adj* art-historical, relating to art history; **k~historisches Museum** art history museum; **k~historisches Interesse** interest in art history; [2] *adv* from the point of view of art history; **~hochschule** *f siehe* **~akademie**; **~honig** *m* artificial *or* synthetic honey; **~kenner** *m* art connoisseur; **~kritik** *f, no pl* art criticism; (*die Kritiker*) art critics *pl*; (*Rezension*) art review; **~kritiker** *m* art critic; **~leder** *nt* artificial *or* imitation leather.
Künstler(in *f*) *m* **-s, -** **(a)** artist; (*Unterhaltungs~*) artiste ◆ **bildender ~** visual artist. **(b)** (*Könner*) genius (*in +dat* at).
Künstler|eingang *m* stage door.
künstlerisch *adj* artistic.
Künstler-: ~kolonie *f* artists' colony, colony of artists; **~mähne** *f* (*inf*) mane of hair; **~name** *m* pseudonym; (*von Schriftsteller auch*) pen name, nom de plume; (*von Schauspieler auch*) stage name; **~pech** *nt* (*inf*) hard luck; **~tum** *nt* artistry, artistic genius; **~verband** *m* artists' association.
künstlich *adj* artificial; *Auge auch* glass; *Zähne, Wimpern, Fingernägel* false; *Faserstoffe* synthetic, man-made; *Diamanten* imitation, fake (*inf*) ◆ **~e Intelligenz** artificial intelligence; **jdn ~ ernähren** (*Med*) to feed sb artificially; **sich ~ aufregen** (*inf*) to get all worked up (*inf*) *or* excited about nothing; *siehe* **beatmen.**
Künstlichkeit *f* artificiality.
Kunst-: ~licht *nt* (*Phot*) artificial light; **~lied** *nt* composed *or* art song, kunstlied; **k~los** *adj* unsophisticated, simple; **~maler** *m* artist, painter; **~märchen** *nt* literary fairytale; **~pause** *f* (*als Spannungsmoment*) dramatic pause, pause for effect; (*iro: beim Stocken*) awkward pause, hesitation; **eine ~pause machen** to pause for effect; to pause awkwardly; **k~reich** *adj* (*geh*) *siehe* **k~voll**; **~reise** *f* art tour; **~reiter** *m* trick *or* circus rider; **~sammlung** *f* art collection; **~schätze** *pl* art treasures *pl*; **~schnee** *m* artificial snow;

~schneepiste *f* artificial snow piste; **~schwimmen** *nt* exhibition swimming; **~seide** *f* artificial silk; **~sinn** *m* artistic sense *or* taste, appreciation of *or* feeling for art; **k~sinnig** *adj* artistic, appreciative of art; **~sprache** *f* artificial *or* invented language; **~springen** *nt* diving.

Kunststoff *m* man-made *or* synthetic material *or* substance.

Kunststoff-: k~beschichtet *adj* synthetic-coated; **~karosserie** *f* fibre glass body.

Kunst-: k~stopfen *sep infin and ptp only* [1] *vt* to repair by invisible mending, to mend invisibly; [2] *vi* to do invisible mending; **~stück** *nt* trick; **~stück!** (*iro*) hardly surprising!, no wonder!; **das ist kein ~stück** (*fig*) there's nothing to it; (*keine große Leistung*) that's nothing to write home about; **~szene** *f* art scene; **~tischler** *m* cabinet-maker; **~turnen** *nt* gymnastics *sing*; **~verstand** *m* feeling for *or* appreciation of art, artistic taste *or* sense; **k~verständig** *adj* appreciative of art, having artistic sense *or* taste; **~verständnis** *nt siehe* **~verstand**; **k~voll** *adj* artistic, elaborate; **~werk** *nt* work of art; **~wissenschaft** *f* aesthetics *sing*, art; **~wort** *nt* artificial *or* made-up word.

kunterbunt *adj Sammlung, Gruppe etc* motley *attr*; (*vielfarbig auch*) multi- *or* many-coloured; *Programm* varied; *Leben* chequered ♦ **eine ~ zusammengewürfelte Gruppe** a motley assortment; **~ durcheinander** all jumbled up, higgledy-piggledy (*inf*); **hier geht es ~ zu** it's pretty chaotic here.

Kunz *m siehe* **Hinz**.

Kupfer *nt* **-s,** *no pl* (*abbr* **Cu**) **(a)** *no pl* (*Chem*) copper ♦ **etw in ~ stechen** to do a copper engraving, to engrave *or* etch sth on copper. **(b)** *no pl* (*Gegenstände aus ~, auch* **~geld**) copper. **(c)** *siehe* **Kupferstich**.

Kupfer- *in cpds* copper; **~blech** *nt* sheet copper; **~draht** *m* copper wire; **~druck** *m* copperplate engraving *or* etching; **~geld** *nt* coppers *pl*, copper coins *pl*; **k~haltig** *adj* containing copper, cupriferous (*form*).

kupf(e)rig *adj* coppery.

kupfern *adj* copper ♦ **~e Hochzeit** 7th wedding anniversary.

Kupfer-: k~rot *adj* copper-red, copper coloured; **~schmied** *m* coppersmith; **~stecher** *m* **-s, -** copper(plate) engraver; **mein lieber Freund und ~stecher** (*inf*) now then my dear old chap; **~stich** *m* **(a)** copperplate (engraving *or* etching); **(b)** (*Kunst*) copper(plate) engraving *or* etching; **~vitriol** *nt* blue vitriol; (*dated Chem*) copper sulphate.

kupieren* *vt Schwanz, Ohren* to crop, to dock; *Karten* to cut; (*form*) *Wein* to blend; (*Med*) *Krankheit* to check, to arrest.

Kupon [ku'põ:] *m* **-s, -s** coupon.

Kupon- [ku'põ-]: **~steuer** *f* (*Fin*) coupon tax; **~termin** *m* (*Fin*) coupon date.

Kuppe *f* **-, -n** (*Berg~*) (rounded) hilltop; (*von Straße*) hump; (*Finger~*) tip.

Kuppel *f* **-, -n** dome, cupola.

Kuppeldach *nt* domed *or* dome-shaped roof.

Kuppelei *f* (*Jur*) procuring, procuration.

Kuppelmutter *f* procuress, bawd.

kuppeln [1] *vt* **(a)** *siehe* **koppeln**. **(b)** (*Tech*) to couple.
[2] *vi* **(a)** (*Aut*) to operate *or* use the clutch. **(b)** (*inf: Paare zusammenführen*) to match-make.

Kuppelpelz *m*: **sich** (*dat*) **einen ~ verdienen** (*fig*) to arrange *or* make a match.

Kuppelung *f siehe* **Kupplung**.

Kuppler(in *f*) *m* **-s, -** matchmaker (*gen* for); (*Jur*) procurer/procuress.

Kupplung *f* **(a)** (*Tech*) coupling; (*Aut etc*) clutch ♦ **die ~ (durch)treten** to disengage the clutch; **die ~ kommen lassen** (*Aut*) to let the clutch up *or* in. **(b)** (*das Koppeln*) coupling.

Kupplungs- *in cpds* (*Aut*) clutch; **~belag** *m* clutch lining; **~pedal** *nt* clutch pedal; **~scheibe** *f* clutch plate; **~seil** *nt*, **~zug** *m* clutch cable.

Kur *f* **-, -en** (*in Badeort*) (health) cure; (*Haar~ etc*) treatment *no pl*; (*Schlankheits~, Diät~*) diet ♦ **er ist zur ~ in Baden-Baden** he's on a health cure *or* is taking a cure *or* the waters in Baden-Baden; **in** *or* **zur ~ fahren** to go to a health resort *or* spa; **eine ~ machen** to take *or* undergo a cure; (*Schlankheits~*) to diet; **ich mache zur Zeit eine ~ gegen meinen Ausschlag** I'm taking a course of treatment for my rash; **jdn zur ~ schicken** to send sb on a cure *or* to a health resort *or* spa.

Kür *f* **-, -en (a)** (*Sport*) free section ♦ **eine ~ laufen** to do the free skating; **eine ~ tanzen/turnen** to do the free section. **(b)** (*old: Wahl*) election.

Kurant(in *f*) *m* (*Sw*) *siehe* **Kurgast**.

⚠ **Küraß** *m* **-sses, -sse** cuirass.

Kürassier *m* **-s, -e** (*Mil Hist*) cuirassier.

Kurat *m* **-en, -en** curate.

Kuratel *f* **-, -en** (*obs*) (*Pflegschaft*) trusteeship; (*Vormundschaft*) guardianship ♦ **unter (jds)** (*dat*) **~ stehen** (*fig dated*) to be under sb's thumb; **jdn unter ~ stellen** (*old*) to keep a watch on sb.

kurativ *adj* (*Med*) curative.

Kurator *m* **(a)** (*Vormund*) guardian. **(b)** (*Verwalter einer Geldstiftung*) trustee. **(c)** (*Museum~*) curator. **(d)** (*Univ*) ≃ registrar.

Kuratorium *nt* **(a)** (*Vereinigung*) committee. **(b)** (*Amt*) curatorship.

Kur-: ~aufenthalt *m* stay at a health resort *or* spa; **~bad** *nt siehe* **Heilbad**.

Kurbel *f* **-, -n** crank; (*an Fenstern, Rolläden etc*) winder.

kurbeln *vti* to turn, to wind; (*inf: filmen*) to film, to shoot ♦ **wenn du daran kurbelst** ... if you turn *or* wind it ...; **die Markise vors Fenster ~** to wind up the awning in front of the window.

Kurbel-: ~stange *f siehe* **Pleuelstange**; **~welle** *f* crankshaft.

Kürbis *m* **-ses, -se** pumpkin; (*inf: Kopf*) nut (*inf*).

Kürbisflasche *f* gourd.

Kurde *m* **-n, -n, Kurdin** *f* Kurd.

Kurdistan *nt* **-s** Kurdistan.

kuren *vi* (*Sw, inf*) to take a cure; (*in Mineralbad*) to take the waters.

küren *pret* **kürte** *or* **kor** (*rare*), *ptp* **gekürt** *or* **gekoren** *vt* (*old, geh*) to choose, to elect (*zu* as).

Kurfürst *m* Elector, electoral prince.

Kurfürstentum *nt* electorate.

kurfürstlich *adj* electoral.

Kur-: ~gast *m* visitor to/patient at a health resort *or* spa; **~haus** *nt* assembly rooms *pl* (at a health resort *or* spa), spa rooms *pl*.

Kurie ['ku:riə] *f* **(a)** (*Eccl*) Curia. **(b)** (*Hist*) curia.

Kurier *m* **-s, -e** courier, messenger.

Kurierdienst *m* courier service.

kurieren* *vt* (*lit, fig*) to cure (*von* of) ♦ **von dieser Stadt/Idee/ihm bin ich kuriert** I've gone right off this town/idea/him.

kurios *adj* (*merkwürdig*) curious, strange, odd.

Kuriosa *pl of* **Kuriosum**.

Kuriosität *f* **(a)** (*Gegenstand*) curio(sity). **(b)** (*Eigenart*) peculiarity, oddity.

Kuriositätenkabinett *nt* collection of curios; (*fig*) collection of odd people.

Kuriosum *nt* **-s, Kuriosa** (*geh*) curious *or* strange *or* odd thing.

Kurkonzert *nt* concert (at a health resort *or* spa), spa concert.

Kürlauf *m* free skating.

Kur-: ~ort *m* health resort, spa; **~packung** *f* (*für Haare*) hair repair kit; **~park** *m* spa gardens *pl*; **~pfalz** *f* Palatinate, Palatine electorate; **k~pfälzisch** *adj* Palatine; **k~pfuschen** *vi insep* to play the quack; **~pfuscher** *m* (*pej inf*) quack (doctor); **~pfuscherei** *f* (*pej inf*) quackery; **~prinz** *m* heir of an Elector; **~promenade** *f* promenade (at a health resort *or* spa).

Kurre *f* **-, -n** (*Naut*) trawl (net).

kurrent *adj* (*Aus*) in gothic handwriting.

Kurrentschrift *f* **(a)** cursive writing *or* script. **(b)** (*Aus*) gothic handwriting.

Kurrikulum *nt* **-s, Kurrikula (a)** (*Lehrplan*) curriculum. **(b)** (*obs: Lebenslauf*) curriculum vitae.

Kurs *m* **-es, -e (a)** (*Naut, Aviat, fig*) course; (*Pol, Richtung auch*) line ♦ **harter/weicher ~** (*Pol*) hard/soft line; **den ~ ändern/beibehalten** (*lit, fig*) to change *or* alter/stick to *or* hold (one's) course; **den ~ halten** to hold (the) course; **~ nehmen auf** (*+acc*) to set course for, to head for; **auf (südwestlichen) ~ gehen/auf (südwestlichem) ~ sein** to set a/be on (a southwesterly) course; **~ haben auf** (*+acc*) to be heading for.
(b) (*Fin: Wechsel~*) rate of exchange, exchange rate; (*Börsen~, Aktien~*) price, (going) rate; (*Marktpreis*) market value *or* price, going rate ♦ **zum ~ von** at the rate of; **die ~e fallen/steigen** prices *or* rates are falling/rising; **hoch im ~ stehen** (*Aktien*)) to be high; (*fig*) to be popular (*bei* with).
(c) (*Lehrgang*) course (*in +dat, für* in) ♦ **einen ~ besuchen** *or* **mitmachen** to go to *or* attend a class.

Kurs-: ~änderung *f* (*lit, fig*) change of course; **~bericht** *m* (*Fin*) *siehe* **Börsenbericht**; **~bildung** *f* formation of rates; **~blatt** *nt siehe* **~zettel**; **~buch** *nt* (*Rail*) (railway) timetable, Bradshaw (*dated Brit*).

Kurschatten *m* **-s, -** (*hum inf*) romance from/at the spa.

Kürschner(in *f*) *m* **-s, -** furrier.

Kürschnerei *f* **(a)** (*Handwerk*) furrier's trade. **(b)** (*Werkstatt*) furrier's workshop.

Kurse *pl of* **Kursus**.

Kurs-: ~einbuße *f* decrease *or* fall in value; **das £ hat weitere ~einbußen hinnehmen müssen** the £ suffered further losses (on the exchange market); **~gewinn** *m* profit (on the stock exchange *or* (*bei Wechsel*) foreign exchange market); **der jüngste ~gewinn des Pfundes** the recent increase in the value of the pound; **einen ~gewinn haben** to make a profit.

kursieren* *vi aux haben or sein* to be in circulation, to circulate; (*fig*) to circulate, to go round.

kursiv *adj* italic ♦ **etw ~ drucken** to print sth in italics, to italicize sth; **Anmerkungen sind ~** notes are in italics.

Kursive [kʊr'zi:və] *f* **-, -n, Kursivschrift** *f* italics *pl* ♦ **in ~ gesetzt** printed in italics, italicized.

Kurs-: ~korrektur *f* (*lit, fig*) course correction *or* adjustment; (*St Ex*) corrective price *or* rate adjustment; **~leiter(in)** *m(f)* course tutor; **~makler** *m* (*St Ex*) market maker; **~notierung** *f* (market) quotation, quotation (of stock exchange prices).

kursorisch *adj*: **~e Lektüre** course reading.

Kurs-: ~pflege *f* price support; **~risiko** *nt* market risk; **~rückgang** *m* fall in prices; **~schwankung** *f* fluctuation in rates of exchange *or* exchange rates; (*St Ex*) fluctuation in market rates *or* prices; **~sicherung** *f* price support; **~sicherungsgeschäft** *nt* price support operation; **~sturz** *m* sharp fall in prices; **~system** *nt* (*Sch, Univ*) course system.

Kursus *m* **-, Kurse** (*geh: Lehrgang*) course.

Kurs-: ~verlust *m* (*Fin*) loss (on the stock exchange *or* foreign exchange market); **das Pfund mußte ~verluste hinnehmen** the pound suffered losses on the foreign exchange market; **~wagen** *m* (*Rail*) through coach; **~wechsel** *m* change of direction; **~wert** *m* (*Fin*) market value *or* price; **~zettel** *m* (*Fin*) stock exchange (price) list, list of quotations; **~zusatz** *m* excess supply and demand indicator.

Kurtaxe *f* **-, -n** visitors' tax (at health resort *or* spa).

Kurtisane *f* **-, -n** courtesan.

Kurtschatovium *nt, no pl* (*abbr* **Ku**) rutherfordium, kurchatovium.

Kür|übung *f* (*Sport*) free section.

⚠: for details of spelling reform, see supplement

Kurve ['kʊrvə, 'kʊrfə] *f* **-, -n** (*Math, inf: Körperrundung*) curve; (*Biegung, Straßen~*) bend; (*an Kreuzung*) corner; (*von Geschoß*) trajectory; (*statistisch, Fieber~ etc*) graph ◆ **die Straße macht eine ~** the road bends; **eine ~ fliegen** (*Aviat*) to bank, to do a banking turn; **die ~ kratzen** (*inf*) to scrape through (*inf*); (*schnell weggehen*) to make tracks (*inf*); **die ~ nicht kriegen** (*inf*) not to get round to it.

kurven ['kʊrvn, 'kʊrfn] *vi aux sein* (*inf*) (*Aviat*) to circle ◆ **durch Italien ~** to drive around Italy.

Kurven-: ~diagramm *nt* graph; **~lineal** *nt* curve template *or* templet, French curve; **k~reich** *adj Straße* bendy, winding; (*inf*) *Frau* curvaceous, shapely; **„k~reiche Strecke"** "(series of) bends"; **~technik** *f* (*Sport*) cornering technique.

Kurverwaltung *f* spa authorities *pl.*

kurvig ['kʊrvɪç] *adj* winding, twisting.

kurz [1] *adj, comp* **¨er**, *superl* **¨este(r, s)** short; *Zeit, Aufenthalt, Besuch, Bericht, Antwort etc auch* brief; *Blick, Folge* quick; *Gedächtnis auch* short-lived; (*klein und stämmig*) stocky, squat ◆ **etw ¨er machen** to make sth shorter, to shorten sth; **ich will es ~ machen** I'll make it brief, I'll be brief; **mach's ~!** make it brief *or* quick, be brief, keep it short; **~e Hosen** short trousers; (*Shorts*) shorts; **~e See** (*Naut*) choppy sea; **den ¨eren ziehen** (*fig inf*) to come off worst, to get the worst of it; **~ verliert, lang gewinnt** whoever draws the shortest (straw/match) loses; **in** *or* **mit ein paar ~en Worten** in a few brief words, briefly; **in ¨ester Frist** before very long; **Pippin der K~e** Pippin the Short.

[2] *adv, comp* **¨er**, *superl* **am ¨esten (a) ~ atmen** to breathe in *or* take short breaths; **X hat ~ abgespielt** (*Sport*) X's pass was short; **(zu) ~ schießen/werfen** *etc* to shoot/throw (too) short; **die Hundeleine ~ halten** to keep the dog on a short lead; **eine Sache ~ abtun** to dismiss sth out of hand; **zu ~ kommen** to come off badly, to get a raw deal (*inf*); **~ entschlossen** without a moment's *or* the slightest hesitation; **~ gesagt** in a nutshell, in a word; **sich ~ fassen** to be brief; **~ und bündig** concisely, tersely (*pej*); **~ und gut** in short, in a word; **~ und schmerzlos** (*inf*) short and sweet; **jdn/etw ~ und klein hauen** *or* **schlagen** to beat sb up/to smash sth to pieces.

(b) (*für eine ~e Zeit*) briefly ◆ **ich bleibe nur ~** I'll only stay for a short while; **darf ich mal ~ stören?** could I just interrupt for a moment *or* second?; **ich muß mal ~ weg** I'll just have to go for a moment *or* second; **darf ich mal ~ fragen ...?** could I just quickly ask ...?; **ich werde ~ mal gucken** I'll have a quick look.

(c) (*zeitlich, räumlich: nicht lang, nicht weit*) shortly, just ◆ **~ bevor/nachdem** shortly *or* just before/after; **~ vor Köln/Ostern** shortly *or* just before Cologne/Easter; **binnen ~em** (*form*) shortly, before long; **er hat den Wagen erst seit ~em** he's only had the car for a short *or* little while; **seit ~em gibt es Bier in der Kantine** recently there's been beer in the canteen; **über ~ oder lang** sooner or later; **(bis) vor ~em** (until) recently; **~ nacheinander** shortly after each other.

Kurz-: ~arbeit *f* short time; **k~arbeiten** *vi sep* to be on *or* to work short time; **~arbeiter** *m* short-time worker; **~arbeitergeld** *nt* short-time allowance; **k~ärm(e)lig** *adj* short-sleeved; **k~atmig** *adj* (*fig*) feeble, lame; (*Med*) short-winded; **~atmigkeit** *f* (*Med*) shortness of breath, dyspnoea (*spec*); (*fig*) time pressure; **~ausbildung** *f* short training course; **~auto** *nt* short-wheelbase car; **~brief** *m* memo letter.

Kürze *f* **-, -n (a)** *no pl* shortness; (*von Besuch, Bericht etc auch*) brevity, briefness; (*fig: Bündigkeit*) brevity, conciseness; (*fig: Barschheit*) abruptness, curtness, bluntness ◆ **in ~** shortly, soon; **in aller ~** very briefly; **der ~ halber** for the sake of brevity; **in der ~ liegt die Würze** (*Prov*) brevity is the soul of wit.
(b) (*Poet: Silbe*) short (syllable).

Kürzel *nt* **-s, -** (*stenographisches Zeichen*) shorthand symbol; (*Kurzwort*) contraction.

kürzen *vt Kleid, Rede etc* to shorten; *Buch auch* to abridge; (*Math*) *Bruch* to cancel (down); *Gehalt, Etat, Produktion* to cut (back).

Kurze(r)¹ *m decl as adj* (*inf*) **(a)** (*Schnaps*) schnapps, short. **(b)** (*Kurzschluß*) short(-circuit).

Kurze(r)² *m decl as adj* (*inf*) small child.

kurzerhand *adv* without further ado; *entlassen* on the spot ◆ **etw ~ ablehnen** to reject sth out of hand.

Kurz-: ~fassung *f* abridged version; **~film** *m* short (film); **~form** *f* shortened form (*von, zu* of, for); **k~fristig** [1] *adj* short-term; *Wettervorhersage* short-range; [2] *adv* (*auf kurze Sicht*) for the short term; (*für kurze Zeit*) for a short time; **etw k~fristig erledigen** to do sth without delay; **k~fristig seine Pläne ändern** to change one's plans at short notice; **k~fristig gesehen** looked at in the short term; ⚠**k~gefaßt** *adj* concise; **~geschichte** *f* short story; ⚠**k~geschnitten** *adj attr* cropped; **~haardackel** *m* short-haired dachshund; **k~haarig** *adj* short-haired; **k~halsig** *adj* short-necked; ⚠**k~halten** *vt sep irreg* **jdn k~halten** to keep sb short; **~hantel** *f* dumb-bell; **~läufer** *m* (*Fin*) short, short-dated bond; **k~lebig** *adj* short-lived, ephemeral.

kürzlich [1] *adv* recently, lately ◆ **erst** *or* **gerade ~** only *or* just recently, only a short time ago
[2] *adj* recent.

Kurz-: ~meldung *f* newsflash; **~nachrichten** *pl* the news headlines *pl*; (*in Zeitung auch*) the news in brief; **~parker** *m*: **„nur für ~parker"** "short-stay *or* short-term parking only"; **~parkzone** *f* short-stay parking zone; **~reise** *f* short trip; **~reisekoffer** *m* overnight bag; **k~schalten** *vr sep siehe* **k~schließen 2**; **k~schließen** *sep irreg* [1] *vt* to short-circuit; [2] *vr* (*in Verbindung treten*) to get in contact (*mit* with); ⚠**~schluß** *m* **(a)** short-circuit; **einen ~schluß haben/bekommen** to be short-circuited/to short-circuit; **(b)** (*fig: auch* **~schlußhandlung**) rash action; **das war ein ~schluß** *or* **eine ~schlußhandlung** something just went snap; ⚠**~schlußreaktion** *f* knee-jerk *or* rash reaction; **~schrift** *f* shorthand; **k~schriftlich** [1] *adj* shorthand; [2] *adv* in shorthand; **k~sichtig** *adj* (*lit, fig*) short-sighted; **~sichtigkeit** *f* (*lit, fig*) short-sightedness.

Kurzstrecken-: ~flugzeug *nt* short-haul *or* short-range aircraft; **~jet** *m* short-range jet; **~läufer** *m* (*Sport*) sprinter, short distance runner; **~rakete** *f* short-range missile; **~waffe** *f* short-range weapon.

kurz-: ⚠**~treten** *vi sep irreg* (*Mil*) to march with short steps; (*fig inf*) to go easy; **~um** *adv* in short, in a word.

Kürzung *f* shortening; (*eines Berichts, Buchs etc*) abridgement; (*von Gehältern, von Etat, der Produktion*) cut (*gen* in).

Kurz-: ~urlaub *m* short holiday; (*Mil*) short leave; **~wahlspeicher** *m* quick-dial number memory; **~waren** *pl* haberdashery (*Brit*), notions *pl* (*US*); **~weil** *f* **-,** *no pl* (*old*) pastime, diversion; **allerlei ~weil treiben** to amuse oneself; **zur ~weil** as a pastime; **k~weilig** *adj* entertaining; **~welle** *f* (*Rad*) short wave; **~wellensender** *m* short-wave transmitter; **~wort** *nt* abbreviation, abbreviated word.

Kurzzeit- *in cpds* short-term; **~effekt** *m* short-term effect; **~gedächtnis** *nt* short-term memory; **~speicher** *m* short-term memory.

kusch *interj* (*an Hund*) down.

kuschelig *adj* (*inf*) cosy, snug.

kuscheln *vr* **sich an jdn ~** to snuggle up *or* cuddle up to sb; **sich in etw** (*acc*) **~** to snuggle up *or* cuddle up in sth.

kuschen *vir* (*Hund etc*) to get down; (*fig*) to knuckle under.

Kusine *f* (female) cousin.

⚠ **Kuß** *m* **Kusses, Küsse** kiss ◆ **Gruß und ~ Dein X** (*hum inf*) love and kisses, yours X.

⚠ **Küßchen** *nt* little kiss, peck (*inf*) ◆ **gib ~** give us a kiss.

⚠ **küßdiehand, küß die Hand** *interj* (*Aus*) your servant (*old*); (*guten Tag auch*) how do you do?; (*auf Wiedersehen auch*) good day.

⚠ **kuß|echt** *adj Lippenstift* kiss-proof.

küssen [1] *vti* to kiss ◆ **jdm die Hand ~** to kiss sb's hand; **küß** *or* **küss die Hand** (*S Ger, Aus*) *siehe* **küßdiehand.**
[2] *vr* to kiss (each other).

⚠ **Kuß-: k~fest** *adj siehe* **k~echt**; **~hand** *f* **jdm eine ~hand zuwerfen** to blow sb a kiss; **mit ~hand!** with (the greatest) pleasure!, gladly!; **jdn/etw mit ~hand nehmen** (*inf*) to be only too glad to take sb/sth; **~mund** *m* puckered lips *pl.*

Küste *f* **-, -n** coast; (*Ufer*) shore ◆ **die zerklüftete ~ Schottlands** the jagged coastline *or* coast of Scotland.

Küsten- *in cpds* coastal; **~bewohner** *m* coast-dweller; **die ~bewohner Englands** people who live on the English coast; **~fischerei** *f* inshore fishing *or* fishery (*form*); **~gebiet** *nt* coastal area; **~gewässer** *pl*, **~meer** *nt* coastal waters *pl*; **~motorschiff** *nt* coaster; **~schiffahrt** *f* coastal shipping; **~strich** *m* stretch of coast; **~wacht** *f* coastguard.

Küster *m* **-s, -** verger, sexton.

Küsterei *f* verger's *or* sexton's house.

Kustode *m* **-n, -n, Kustos** *m* **-, Kustoden** (*in Museum*) curator.

Kutikula *f* **-, -s** (*spec*) cuticle, cuticula (*spec*).

Kutschbock *m* coach-box.

Kutsche *f* **-, -n** coach, carriage; (*inf: Auto*) jalopy (*inf*).

kutschen *vti* (*old*) *siehe* **kutschieren.**

Kutscher *m* **-s, -** coachman, driver.

Kutschermanieren *pl* (*pej*) manners like a navvy *pl.*

kutschieren* [1] *vi aux sein* to drive, to ride ◆ **durch die Gegend ~** (*inf*) to drive *or* ride around.
[2] *vt* to drive ◆ **jdn im Auto durch die Gegend ~** to drive sb around.

Kutschkasten *m* luggage compartment on a coach.

Kutte *f* **-, -n** habit.

Kuttel *f* **-, -n** *usu pl siehe* **Kaldaune.**

Kutter *m* **-s, -** (*Naut*) cutter.

Kuvert [ku'veːɐ, ku'vɛːɐ] *nt* **-s, -s** *or* [-'vɛrt] **-(e)s, -e (a)** (*Brief~*) envelope. **(b)** (*Gedeck*) cover.

kuvertieren* [kuvɛr'tiːrən] *vt* (*form*) to put into an envelope.

Kuvertüre [kuvɛr'tyːrə] *f* **-, -n** (*Cook*) (chocolate) coating.

Kuwait *nt* **-s** Kuwait.

Kuwaiter(in *f*) *m* **-s, -** Kuwaiti.

Kuwaiti *m* **-s, -s** Kuwaiti.

kuwaitisch *adj* Kuwaiti.

KV *abbr of* **Köchelverzeichnis.**

kW *abbr of* **Kilowatt.**

kWh *abbr of* **Kilowattstunde.**

Kybernetik *f* cybernetics *sing.*

Kybernetiker(in *f*) *m* **-s, -** cybernetician.

kybernetisch *adj* cybernetic.

Kykladen *pl* Cyclades *pl.*

kymrisch *adj* Cymric, Welsh.

Kyrie(eleison) ['kyːrie(e'laizɔn)] *nt* **-s, -s** Kyrie (eleison).

kyrillisch *adj* Cyrillic.

KZ [kaː'tsɛt] *nt* **-s, -s** *abbr of* **Konzentrationslager.**

KZler(in *f*) [kaː'tsɛtlɐ, -lərɪn] *m* **-s, -** (*inf*) concentration camp prisoner.

L

L, l [ɛl] *nt* **-, -** L, l.
l. *abbr of* **Liter.**
Lab *nt* **-(e)s, -e** rennin.
labb(e)rig *adj (dial) Bier, Suppe* watery; *Kaffee, Tee auch* weak; *Essen* mushy; *Stoff etc* floppy, limp; *Hose* flappy.
Label ['le:bl] *nt* **-s, -** label.
laben *(liter)* [1] *vt (Mensch)* to feast; *(Quelle)* to refresh.
[2] *vr* to feast (oneself) *(an +dat* on); *(an einer Quelle etc)* to refresh oneself *(mit, an +dat* with) ◆ **wir labten uns an dem Anblick** we drank in *or* feasted our eyes on the view.
labern *(inf)* [1] *vi* to prattle *or* jabber (on *or* away) *(inf)*.
[2] *vt* to talk ◆ **was laberst du denn da?** what are you prattling *etc* on about? *(inf)*.
labial *adj (Ling)* labial.
Labial(laut) *m* **-s, -e** labial.
labil *adj (physisch) Gesundheit* delicate; *Kreislauf* poor; *Patient* frail; *(psychisch) Mensch, Charakter* weak.
Labilität *f siehe adj* delicateness; poorness; frailness; weakness.
labiodental *adj (Ling)* labiodental.
Lab-: ~kraut *nt (Bot)* bedstraw; **~magen** *m (Zool)* abomasum *(spec)*, fourth stomach.
Labor *nt* **-s, -s** *or* **-e** laboratory, lab *(inf)*.
Laborant(in *f***)** *m* lab(oratory) technician.
Laboratorium *nt* laboratory.
Laborbefund *m* laboratory findings *pl*.
laborieren* *vi* to labour *(an +dat* at); *(leiden)* to be plagued *(an +dat* by).
Labor-: ~schiff *nt* laboratory ship; **~werte** *pl* laboratory results *pl*.
Labsal *nt* **-(e)s, -e,** *(Aus auch) f* **-, -e** *(old, liter)* refreshment.
Labskaus *nt* **-,** *no pl (N Ger) stew made of meat, fish and mashed potato.*
Labung *f (liter)* refreshment.
Labyrinth *nt* **-(e)s, -e** *(lit, Med)* labyrinth; *(fig auch)* maze.
labyrinthisch *adj* labyrinthine, maze-like.
Lach|anfall *m* laughing fit.
Lache[1] ['laxə, 'la:xə] *f* **-, -n** puddle; *(von Benzin, Blut etc auch)* pool.
Lache[2] *f* **-, -n** *(inf)* laugh.
lächeln *vi* to smile ◆ **verlegen/freundlich ~** to give an embarrassed/a friendly smile.
Lächeln *nt* **-s,** *no pl* smile.
lachen [1] *vi* to laugh *(über +acc* at) ◆ **jdn zum L~ bringen, jdn ~ machen** to make sb laugh; **zum L~ sein** *(lustig)* to be hilarious; *(lächerlich)* to be laughable; **mir ist nicht zum L~ (zumute)** I'm in no laughing mood; **daß ich nicht lache!** *(inf)* don't make me laugh! *(inf)*; **da kann ich doch nur ~** I can't help laughing (at that); **du hast gut ~!** it's all right for you to laugh! *(inf)*; **lach du nur!** you can laugh!; **gezwungen/verlegen ~** to give a forced/an embarrassed laugh; **wer zuletzt lacht, lacht am besten** *(Prov)* he who laughs last, laughs longest *(Prov)*; **die ~den Erben** *(hum)* the joyful heirs; **die Sonne** *or* **der Himmel lacht** the sun is shining brightly; **ihm lachte das Glück/der Erfolg** Fortune/success smiled on *or* favoured him; *siehe* **Dritte(r).**
[2] *vt* **da gibt es gar nichts zu ~** that's nothing to laugh about; *(es ist etwas Ernstes auch)* that's no laughing matter, that's not funny; **was gibt es denn da zu ~?** what's so funny about that?; **er hat bei seiner Frau nichts zu ~** *(inf)* he has a hard time of it with his wife; **wenn dieses Versehen herauskommt, hast du nichts zu ~** *(inf)* you won't have anything to laugh about *or* it won't be funny if that mistake comes to light; **das wäre doch gelacht** it would be ridiculous; **sich schief** *or* **scheckig ~, sich** *(dat)* **einen Ast** *or* **Bruch ~** *(inf)* to split one's sides (laughing) *(inf)*, to kill oneself *(inf)*, to laugh oneself silly *(inf)*; **sich** *(dat)* **eins ~** *(inf)* to have a little snigger.
Lachen *nt* **-s,** *no pl* laughter, laughing; *(Art des ~s)* laugh ◆ **vor ~ schreien** to shriek with laughter; **dir wird das ~ schon noch vergehen!** you'll soon be laughing on the other side of your face.
Lacher *m* **-s, - (a)** laugher ◆ **die ~ auf seiner Seite haben** to have the last laugh; *(einen Lacherfolg verbuchen)* to get a laugh. **(b)** *(inf: Lache)* laugh.
Lach|erfolg *m* **ein ~ sein, einen ~ haben** *or* **erzielen** to make everybody laugh.
lächerlich *adj* **(a)** ridiculous, absurd, ludicrous; *(komisch)* comical, funny ◆ **jdn/etw ~ machen** to make sb/sth look silly *or* stupid *(vor jdm* in front of sb); **jdn/sich ~ machen** to make a fool of sb/oneself *(vor jdm* in front of sb); **etw ins L~e ziehen** to make fun of sth. **(b)** *(geringfügig) Kleinigkeit, Anlaß* trivial, petty; *Preis* ridiculously *or* absurdly low.
lächerlicherweise *adv* ridiculously enough.
Lächerlichkeit *f* **(a)** *no pl* ridiculousness; *(von Argument etc auch)* absurdity ◆ **jdn der ~ preisgeben** to make a laughing stock of sb. **(b)** *(Geringfügigkeit)* triviality.
Lach-: ~gas *nt* laughing gas; **l~haft** *adj* ridiculous, ludicrous; *Ansichten, Argument auch* laughable; **~krampf** *m* paroxysm (of laughter); **einen ~krampf bekommen** to go (off) into fits of laughter; **~möwe** *f* black-headed gull; **~muskel** *m (Anat)* risorius; **das ist was für Ihre ~muskeln** this will really make you laugh.
Lachs [laks] *m* **-es, -e** salmon.
Lachsalve *f* burst *or* roar of laughter.
Lachs-: l~farben, l~farbig *adj* salmon pink, salmon(-coloured); **~forelle** *f* salmon *or* sea trout; **~schinken** *m smoked, rolled fillet of ham.*
Lachtaube *f* ringdove, Barbary dove.
Lack *m* **-(e)s, -e** *(Holz~, Nagel~)* varnish; *(Auto~)* paint; *(für Lackarbeiten)* lacquer; *siehe* **fertig.**
Lack-: ~affe *m (pej inf)* flash Harry *(inf)*; **~arbeit** *f* lacquerwork.
Lacke *f* **-, -n** *(Aus)* puddle.
Lackel *m* **-s, -** *(S Ger, Aus)* oaf.
lacken *vti (Tech)* to lacquer.
Lackfarbe *f* gloss paint.
Lackier|arbeiten *pl (von Möbeln etc)* varnishing; *(von Autos)* spraying.
lackieren* *vti Holz* to varnish; *Fingernägel auch* to paint; *Auto* to spray ◆ **am Ende war ich der Lackierte** *(inf)* I ended up looking a fool.
Lackierer(in *f***)** *m* **-s, -** varnisher; *(von Autos)* sprayer.
Lackiererei *f* **(a)** *(Auto~)* paint shop; *(Möbel~)* varnisher's. **(b)** *(Handwerk)* lacquerwork.
Lackierung *f* **(a)** *(das Lackieren) (von Autos)* spraying; *(von Möbeln)* varnishing. **(b)** *(der Lack) (von Auto)* paintwork; *(Holz~)* varnish; *(für Lackarbeiten)* lacquer.
Lackier-: ~werkstatt, ~werkstätte *f siehe* **Lackiererei (a).**
Lackleder *nt* patent leather.
lackmeiern *vt siehe* **gelackmeiert.**
Lackmus *nt or m* **-,** *no pl* litmus.
Lackmuspapier *nt* litmus paper.
Lack-: ~schaden *m* damage to the paintwork; **~schuh** *m* patent-leather shoe.
ladbar *adj (Comput)* loadable.
Lade *f* **-, -n** chest; *(inf: Schub~)* drawer.
Lade-: ~baum *m* derrick; **~brücke** *f* loading bridge; **~bucht** *f (Space)* loading bay; **~bühne** *f* loading ramp; **~fläche** *f* load area; **~gerät** *nt* battery charger; **~gewicht** *nt* load, capacity; **~gut** *nt (Ladung)* load; *(Fracht)* freight *no pl*; **~hemmung** *f* **das Gewehr hat ~hemmung** the gun is jammed; **er hatte plötzlich ~hemmung** *(inf)* he had a sudden mental block; **~höhe** *f* **Lkw mit einer ~höhe bis zu ... Meter** loads not exceeding ... metres (in height); **~klappe** *f* tailboard; **~kontrolle** *f (Aut)* (generator) charge indicator; **~luke** *f* cargo *or* loading hatch.
laden[1] *pret* **lud,** *ptp* **geladen** [1] *vt* **(a)** *(beladen)* to load ◆ **einen Sack Mehl auf den Rücken ~** to load *or* hump a sack of flour on one's back; **das Schiff hat Autos geladen** the ship has a cargo of cars; **der Lkw hat zuviel geladen** the lorry is overloaded; **Verantwortung/Schulden auf sich** *(acc)* **~** to saddle *or* load oneself with responsibility/debts; **eine schwere Schuld auf sich** *(acc)* **~** to place oneself under a heavy burden of guilt; **da habe ich ja etwas auf mich geladen** I've taken on more than I'd bargained for; **er hatte schon ganz schön geladen** *(inf)* he was already pretty tanked up *(inf)*.
(b) *Gewehr, Pistole* to load; *(Phys)* to charge ◆ **der Chef war mächtig geladen** *(inf)* the boss was absolutely hopping (mad) *(inf)*; **mit Spannung geladen** charged with tension.
(c) *(Comput)* to load.
[2] *vi* **(a)** *(auch Comput)* to load (up). **(b)** *(Phys)* to charge.
laden[2] *pret* **lud** *ptp* **geladen** *vt* **(a)** *(liter: einladen)* to invite ◆ **nur für geladene Gäste** by invitation only. **(b)** *(form: vor Gericht)* to summon.
Laden[1] *m* **-s, ¨** shop *(esp Brit)*, store *(US)*; *(inf: Betrieb)* outfit *(inf)* ◆ **der ~ läuft**

(*inf*) business is good; **es wird eine Zeit dauern, bis der ~ läuft** (*inf*) it will be some time before the business gets going *or* off the ground; **dann kann er den ~ zumachen** *or* **dichtmachen** (*inf*) he might as well shut up shop (and go home) (*inf*); **den ~ schmeißen** (*sl*) to run the show; (*zurechtkommen*) to manage; **den (ganzen) ~ hinschmeißen** (*inf*) to chuck the whole lot in (*inf*).

Laden² *m* **-s, ¨** *or* **-** shutter.

Laden-: ~besitzer *m* shopowner (*esp Brit*), shopkeeper (*esp Brit*), storekeeper (*US*); **~dieb** *m* shoplifter; **~diebstahl** *m* shoplifting; **~hüter** *m* non-seller; **~kasse** *f* cashdesk, till; **~kette** *f* chain of shops *or* stores; **~öffnungszeit** *f usu pl* shop (*esp Brit*) *or* store (*US*) opening hours *pl*; **~preis** *m* shop price; **~schild** *nt* shop (*esp Brit*) *or* store (*US*) sign.

⚠ **Ladenschluß** *m* **nach/vor ~** after/before the shops (*esp Brit*) *or* stores (*US*) shut; **kurz vor ~** (*lit, fig*) just before we/they shut up shop; **um fünf Uhr ist ~** the shops/stores shut at five o'clock.

⚠ **Ladenschluß-: ~gesetz** *nt law governing the hours of trading*; **~zeit** *f* (shop) closing time.

Laden-: ~straße *f* shopping street; **~tisch** *m* shop counter; **über den/unter dem ~tisch** over/under the counter; **~tochter** *f* (*Sw*) shop *or* sales assistant, salesgirl.

Lade-: ~platz *m* loading bay *or* area; **~rampe** *f* loading ramp; **~raum** *m* load room; (*Aviat, Naut*) hold; **~stock** *m* ramrod.

lädieren* *vt Kunstwerk, Briefmarke* to damage ♦ **lädiert sein** (*hum*)**/aussehen** (*hum*) to be/look the worse for wear.

Ladnerin *f* (*old: S Ger, Aus*) shop assistant.

Ladung *f* **(a)** load; (*von Schnee, Steinen, Unflätigkeiten etc*) whole load (*inf*); (*von Sprengstoff*) charge ♦ **eine geballte ~ Schnee/Dreck** (*inf*) a handful of snow/mud; **eine geballte ~ von Schimpfwörtern** a whole torrent of abuse. **(b)** (*Vorladung*) summons *sing*.

Lady ['le:di] *f* **-, -s** *or* **Ladies** lady; (*Adlige*) Lady.

Lafette *f* (*Mil*) (gun) carriage.

Laffe *m* **-n, -n** (*pej*) flash Harry (*inf*).

lag *pret of* **liegen**.

▼ **Lage** *f* **-, -n (a)** (*geographische ~*) situation, location ♦ **in günstiger ~** well-situated; **eine gute/ruhige ~ haben** to be in a good/quiet location.

(b) (*Art des Liegens*) position ♦ **eine bequeme ~ haben, sich in einer bequemen ~ befinden** to be lying comfortably, to be (lying) in a comfortable position.

▼ **(c)** (*Situation*) situation ♦ **dazu bin ich nicht in der ~** I'm not in a position to do that; **er wird wohl nie in die ~ kommen, das zu tun** he'll never be in a position to do it; **in der glücklichen/beneidenswerten ~ sein, etw zu tun** to be in the happy/enviable position of doing sth; **Herr der ~ sein/bleiben** to be/remain master of *or* in control of the situation; **die ~ der Dinge erfordert es, daß ...** the situation requires that ...; *siehe* **peilen**.

(d) (*Schicht*) layer.

(e) (*Mus*) (*Stimm~*) register; (*Ton~*) pitch; (*eines Instruments*) position ♦ **enge/weite ~** close/open harmony.

(f) (*Runde*) round ♦ **eine ~ schmeißen** (*sl*) to buy *or* get *or* stand a round.

Lage-: ~bericht *m* report; (*Mil*) situation report; **~besprechung** *f* discussion of the situation; **eine ~besprechung abhalten** to discuss the situation.

lagenweise *adv* in layers.

Lageplan *m* ground plan.

Lager *nt* **-s, - (a)** (*Unterkunft*) camp.

(b) (*liter: Schlafstätte*) bed ♦ **die Krankheit fesselte ihn wochenlang ans ~** the illness kept him abed for weeks; **sie wachten am ~ des Königs** they kept watch at the King's bedside.

(c) (*fig: Partei*) camp; (*von Staaten*) bloc ♦ **ins andere ~ überwechseln** to change camps *or* sides.

(d) *pl auch* **¨** (*Vorratsraum*) store(room); (*von Laden*) stockroom; (*~halle*) warehouse; (*Vorrat*) stock ♦ **am ~ sein** to be in stock; **etw auf ~ haben** to have sth in stock; (*fig*) *Witz etc* to have sth on tap (*inf*) *or* (at the) ready.

(e) (*Tech*) bearing.

(f) (*Geol*) bed.

Lager-: ~bestand *m* stock; **den ~bestand aufnehmen** to do the stocktaking; **~denken** *nt* (*Pol*) stereotype thinking, thinking in stereotypes; **l~fähig** *adj* non-perishable; **~feuer** *nt* campfire; **~gebühr** *f*, **~geld** *nt* storage charge; **~halle** *f* warehouse; **~haltung** *f* storekeeping; **~haltung rentiert sich bei uns nicht** it doesn't pay us to keep a large stock; **~haus** *nt* warehouse.

Lagerist(in *f*) *m* storeman/storewoman.

Lager-: ~koller *m* (*inf*) **er hat einen ~koller gekriegt** life in the camp turned his mind; **~leben** *nt* camp life; **~leiter** *m* camp commander; (*in Ferien ~ etc*) camp leader.

lagern [1] *vt* **(a)** (*aufbewahren*) to store ♦ **kühl ~!** keep *or* store in a cool place. **(b)** (*hinlegen*) *jdn* to lay down; *Bein etc* to rest ♦ **den Kopf/einen Kranken weich ~** to rest one's head/lay an invalid on something soft; **das Bein hoch ~** to put one's leg up; **die Kranken müssen bequem gelagert werden** the invalids must be bedded down *or* must lie comfortably; *siehe* **gelagert**.

[2] *vi* **(a)** (*Lebensmittel etc*) to be stored *or* kept.

(b) (*liegen*) to lie.

(c) (*von Truppen*) to camp, to be encamped.

[3] *vr* (*geh*) to settle oneself (down).

Lager-: ~raum *m* storeroom; (*in Geschäft*) stockroom; **~statt** *f* (*old liter*) bed, couch (*liter*); **~stätte** *f* **(a)** (*old liter*) *siehe* **~statt**; **(b)** (*Geol*) deposit; **~theorie** *f* (*Pol*) theory of political stereotypes.

Lagerung *f* storage; (*das Lagern auch*) storing.

Lagerverwalter *m* **(a)** stores supervisor. **(b)** *siehe* **Lagerleiter**.

Lageskizze *f* sketch-map.

Lagune *f* **-, -n** lagoon.

Lagunenstadt *f* town built on a lagoon; (*Venedig*) Venice.

lahm *adj* **(a)** (*gelähmt*) *Bein, Mensch* lame; (*inf: steif*) stiff ♦ **er ist auf dem linken Bein ~** he is lame in his *or* the left leg; **er hat ein ~es Bein** he is lame in one leg, he has a gammy leg (*inf*).

(b) (*inf: langsam, langweilig*) dreary, dull; *Ausrede, Entschuldigung* lame; *Geschäftsgang* slow, sluggish ♦ **eine ~e Ente sein** (*inf*) to have no zip (*inf*).

Lahm-: ~arsch *m* (*sl*) slowcoach (*Brit inf*), slowpoke (*US inf*); **l~arschig** *adj* (*sl*) bloody (*Brit inf*) *or* damn (*inf*) slow; **steh doch nicht so l~arschig herum!** get your finger out! (*sl*), get your arse in gear! (*vulg*).

lahmen *vi* to be lame (*auf +dat* in).

lähmen *vt* to paralyze; (*fig*) *Industrie auch* to cripple; *Verhandlungen, Verkehr* to hold up; *Freude, Fest etc* to spoil ♦ **er ist durch einen Unfall/an beiden Beinen gelähmt** he was paralyzed in an accident/is paralyzed in both legs; **vor Angst wie gelähmt sein** to be petrified, to be paralyzed with fear; **~des Entsetzen befiel die Zuschauer** the onlookers were paralyzed with horror.

Lahme(r) *mf decl as adj* (*old*) cripple.

lahmlegen *vt sep Verkehr, Produktion* to bring to a standstill *or* halt; *Industrie auch* to paralyze.

Lähmung *f* (*lit*) paralysis; (*fig*) immobilization.

Lähmungs|erscheinungen *pl* signs *pl* of paralysis.

Lahn *f* **-, -en** (*Aus*) avalanche.

Laib *m* **-(e)s, -e** (*esp S Ger*) loaf.

Laich *m* **-(e)s, -e** spawn.

laichen *vi* to spawn.

Laich-: ~platz *m* spawning ground; **~zeit** *f* spawning season.

Laie *m* **-n, -n** (*lit, fig*) layman, layperson ♦ **~n** the lay public; **die ~n** (*Eccl*) the laity; **da staunt der ~, der Fachmann wundert sich** (*hum inf*) that's a real turn-up for the book (*inf*).

Laien-: ~apostolat *nt* lay apostolate; **~bruder** *m* lay brother; **~bühne** *f* amateur dramatic society; (*Gebäude*) amateur theatre; **~darsteller** *m* amateur actor; **l~haft** *adj Arbeit* amateurish, unprofessional; *Urteil, Meinung* lay *attr only*; **~prediger, ~priester** *m* lay preacher; **~richter** *m* lay judge; **~schwester** *f* lay sister; **~spiel** *nt* amateur play; **~stand** *m* laity; **~theater** *nt* amateur theatre; (*Ensemble*) amateur theatre group; **~tum** *nt* laity; **er mußte sich zwischen Priestertum und ~tum entscheiden** he had to decide whether to become a priest or remain a layman.

laisieren* [lai'zi:rən] *vt* to unfrock.

Laisser-faire [lɛse'fɛ:r] *nt* **-**, *no pl* (*Econ, fig*) laisser- *or* laissez-faire.

Laizismus [lai'tsɪsmʊs] *m* laicism.

Lakai *m* **-en, -en** (*lit, fig*) lackey.

lakaienhaft *adj* servile.

Lake *f* **-, -n** brine.

Laken *nt* **-s, -** sheet.

lakonisch *adj* laconic.

Lakritz *m* **-es, -e** (*dial*), **Lakritze** *f* **-, -n** liquorice.

Laktose *f* **-,** *no pl* lactose.

lala *adv* (*inf*): **so ~** so-so (*inf*), not too bad (*inf*).

lallen *vti* to babble; (*Betrunkener*) to mumble.

Lama¹ *nt* **-s, -s** llama.

Lama² *m* **-(s), -s** (*Rel*) lama.

Lamaismus *m* Lamaism.

Lamakloster *nt* lamasery.

Lamäng *f*: **aus der (kalten) ~** (*sl*) just like that.

Lambda-Sonde *f* (*Aut*) Lambda probe.

Lamé *m* **-s, -s** (*Tex*) lamé.

Lamelle *f* **(a)** (*Biol*) lamella. **(b)** (*Tech*) commutator bar *or* segment; (*von Jalousien*) slat.

lamellenförmig *adj* lamellate, lamellar.

lamentieren* *vi* to moan, to complain.

Lamento *nt* **-s, -s** (*Mus*) lament ♦ **wegen etw ein ~ anstimmen** (*fig*) to bewail sth.

Lametta *nt* **-s,** *no pl* lametta; (*hum: Orden*) gongs *pl* (*inf*).

laminieren* *vt* (*Tex*) to draw; (*Typ*) to laminate.

Lamm *nt* **-(e)s, ¨er** lamb ♦ **das ~ Gottes** the Lamb of God.

Lammbraten *m* roast lamb.

Lämmerwölkchen *pl* fleecy *or* cotton-wool clouds *pl* (*inf*).

Lamm(e)sgeduld *f* patience of a saint.

Lamm-: ~fell *nt* lambskin; **~fleisch** *nt* lamb; **l~fromm** *adj Gesicht, Miene* innocent; **l~fromm sein** to be like a (little) lamb; **sie saßen l~fromm auf ihren Plätzen** they were sitting in their seats like little lambs *or* as good as gold.

Lammsgeduld *f siehe* **Lamm(e)sgeduld**.

Lammwolle *f* lambswool.

Lampe *f* **-, -n** light; (*Öl~, Steh~, Tisch~*) lamp; (*Glüh~*) bulb ♦ **die ~n auf der Straße** the street lights; **einen auf die ~ gießen** (*inf*) to wet one's whistle (*inf*); *siehe* **Meister**.

Lampen-: ~fieber *nt* stage fright; **~licht** *nt* artificial light; **~schirm** *m* lampshade.

Lampion [lam'piõ:, lam'piɔŋ] *m* **-s, -s** Chinese lantern.

LAN *nt* **-s, -s** (*Comput*) LAN.

lancieren* [lã'si:rən] *vt Produkt, Künstler* to launch; *Meldung, Nachricht* to put out ♦ **jdn/etw in etw** (*acc*) **~** to get sb/sth into sth; **sein Onkel hat ihn in diese**

➤ SPRACHE AKTIV: **Lage: c** → 39.2, 42.4, 43.4

hohe Stellung lanciert his uncle got him (into) that high position.

Land *nt* **-(e)s, ¨er (a)** (*Gelände, Festland*) land ◆ **ein Stück ~** a plot of land *or* ground; **~ bestellen/bebauen** to till the soil *or* land/to cultivate the land; **an ~ gehen** to go ashore; **jdn an ~ setzen** to put sb ashore; **an ~ schwimmen** to swim to the shore; **~ sehen** (*lit*) to see *or* sight land; **endlich können wir ~ sehen/sehe ich ~** (*fig*) at last we/I can see the light at the end of the tunnel; **kein ~ mehr sehen (können)** (*fig*) to be completely muddled *or* in a complete muddle; **etw/ein Boot/einen Fisch an ~ ziehen** to pull sth ashore/ to beach a boat/to land a fish; **einen Millionär/einen Auftrag an ~ ziehen** (*inf*) to land a millionaire/an order; **~ in Sicht!** land ahoy!; **~ unter!** land submerged!
(b) (*ländliches Gebiet*) country ◆ **aufs ~** (in)to the country; **auf dem ~(e)** in the country; **über ~ fahren** (*old*) to travel.
(c) (*Staat*) country, land (*esp liter*); (*Bundes~*) (*in BRD*) Land, state; (*in Österreich*) province ◆ **das ~ Hessen/Tirol** the state of Hesse/the province of Tyrol, Tyrol province; **außer ~es sein/gehen** to be out of/leave the country; **~ und Leute kennenlernen** to get to know the country and its inhabitants; **~e** *pl* (*poet*) lands *pl*; **in fernen ~en** (*liter*) in distant *or* far away lands; **durch die ~e ziehen** (*liter*) to roam abroad; **das ~ der unbegrenzten Möglichkeiten** the new world, the land of limitless opportunity; **das ~ der aufgehenden Sonne** the land of the rising sun; **aus aller Herren ¨er(n)** from all over the world, from the four corners of the earth; **der Frühling war ins ~ gezogen** (*liter*) spring had arrived; **seitdem waren viele Jahre ins ~ gegangen** *or* **gezogen** (*liter*) many years had passed since then.

Land-: l~ab *adv siehe* **l~auf**; **~adel** *m* landed gentry; **~ammann** *m* (*Sw*) *highest official in a Swiss canton*; **~arbeit** *f* agricultural work; **~arbeiter** *m* agricultural worker; **~aristokratie** *f* landed aristocracy; **~arzt** *m* country doctor.

Landauer *m* **-s, -** landau.

Land-: l~auf *adv*: **l~auf, l~ab** all over the country, the length and breadth of the country; **l~aus** *adv*: **l~aus, ~ein** all over the world; **~bau** *m siehe* **Ackerbau**; **~besitz** *m* landholding; **~besitz haben** to be a landowner, to own land; **~besitzer** *m* landowner; **~bevölkerung** *f* rural population; **~bewohner** *m* country dweller; **~bewohner sind ...** people who live in the country are ...; **~brot** *nt brown bread usually made from rye flour*; **~brücke** *f* land bridge; **~butter** *f* farm butter.

Lände *f* **-, -n** (*dial*) landing stage.

Lande-: ~anflug *m* approach; **~bahn** *f* runway; **~brücke** *f siehe* **Landungsbrücke**; **~erlaubnis** *f* landing permission, permission to land; **~fähre** *f* (*Space*) landing module.

Land-: ~eier *pl* farm eggs *pl*; **l~ein** *adv siehe* **l~aus**; **l~einwärts** *adv* inland.

Lande-: ~klappe *f* landing flap; **~kopf** *m* (*Mil*) beachhead; **~korridor** *m* (*Space*) re-entry corridor *or* window; **~manöver** *nt* landing manoeuvre.

landen [1] *vi aux sein* to land; (*inf: enden*) to land up; (*inf: Eindruck machen*) to get somewhere ◆ **weich ~** to make a soft landing; **alle anonymen Briefe ~ sofort im Papierkorb** all anonymous letters go straight into the wastepaper basket; **mit deinen Komplimenten kannst du bei mir nicht ~** your compliments won't get you anywhere *or* very far with me.
[2] *vt* (*lit, fig*) to land; *siehe* **Coup**.

länden *vt* (*dial*) *Leiche* to recover (*aus* from).

Land|enge *f* isthmus.

Lande-: ~piste *f* landing strip; **~platz** *m* (*für Flugzeuge*) place to land; (*ausgebaut*) landing strip; (*für Schiffe*) landing place.

Ländereien *pl* estates *pl*.

Länder-: ~finanzausgleich *m, no pl* balancing of federal budgets; **~kampf** *m* (*Sport*) international contest; (*~spiel*) international (match); **~kunde** *f* regional studies *pl*; **~name** *m* name of a/the country; **~spiel** *nt* international (match).

Landes-: ~bank *f* regional bank; **~beamte(r)** *m civil servant employed by a Land rather than the nation*; **~behörde** *f* regional authorities *pl*; **~bodenbrief** *m* land mortgage certificate; **~brauch** *m* national custom, custom of the country; **nach ~brauch ist es hier üblich ...** in this country it is customary ...; **~ebene** *f*: **auf ~ebene** at state level; **l~eigen** *adj* owned by the Land/province; **~farben** *pl* (*von Staat*) national colours *pl*; (*von Bundesland*) state colours *pl*/colours *pl* of the province; **~gericht** *nt siehe* **Landgericht**; **~grenze** *f* (*von Staat*) national boundary; (*von Bundesland*) state/ provincial boundary; **~hauptmann** *m* (*Aus*) *head of the government of a province*; **~hauptstadt** *f* capital of a Land/province, provincial capital; **~herr** *m* (*Hist*) sovereign, ruler; **~innere(s)** *nt* interior; **~kind** *nt* (*von Staat*) native of a/the country; (*von Bundesland*) native of a/the Land/ province; **~kirche** *f* national church; (*in Deutschland*) *established Protestant church in some Länder*; **~kunde** *f* regional studies *pl*; **l~kundig** *adj* **l~kundiger Reiseleiter** courier who knows the country; **l~kundlich** *adj Themen, Aspekte* regional; **~liste** *f* (*Parl*) *regional list of parliamentary candidates for election to Federal parliament*; **~mediengesetz** *nt law relating to the running and content of regional media*; **~meister** *m* (*Sport*) regional champion; **~mutter** *f* (*liter*) mother of the people (*liter*); **die britische ~mutter** the mother of the British nation (*liter*); **~rat** *m* (*BRD*) *highest official of an administrative district*; (*Sw*) *cantonal parliament*; **~recht** *nt* law of a Land/province; **~regierung** *f* government of a Land/provincial government; **~sprache** *f* national language; **der ~sprache unkundig sein** not to know the language.

Landesteg *m* landing stage.

Landes-: ~teil *m* region, area; **~tracht** *f* national dress *or* costume; **l~üblich** *adj* customary; **das ist dort l~üblich** that's the custom there; **~vater** *m* (*liter*) father of the people (*liter*); **~verrat** *m* treason; **~verteidigung** *f* national defence; **l~verwiesen** *adj* (*rare*) expelled, banished (*old*); (*exiliert*) exiled; **~zentralbank** *f* State Central Bank.

Lande-: ~übung *f* landing exercise; **~verbot** *nt* refusal of landing permission; **~verbot erhalten** to be refused landing permission *or* permission to land.

Land-: ~fahrer *m* (*form*) vagrant; **l~fein** *adj* (*dated*) spruced up; **~flucht** *f* migration from the land, emigration to the cities; **~frau** *f* countrywoman; **~friede(n)** *m* (*Hist*) King's/Queen's Peace; **~friedensbruch** *m* (*Jur*) breach of the peace; **~funk** *m* farming (radio) programme; **~gang** *m* shore leave; **~gemeinde** *f* country community; **~gericht** *nt* district court; **l~gestützt** *adj Raketen* land-based; **~gewinnung** *f* land reclamation; **~graf** *m* landgrave; **~gut** *nt* estate; **~haus** *nt* country house; **~heer** *nt* army; **~heim** *nt siehe* **Schullandheim**; **~jäger** *m* **(a)** (*Hist*) country policeman; **(b)** (*Wurst*) *pressed smoked sausage*; **~karte** *f* map; **~klima** *nt* continental climate; **~kreis** *m* administrative district; **~krieg** *m* land warfare; **Luft- und ~krieg** war in the air and on the ground; **See- und ~krieg** war at sea and on land; **~kriegsordnung** *f*: **Haager ~kriegsordnung** Hague Land Warfare Convention; **l~läufig** *adj* popular, common; **entgegen l~läufiger** *or* **der l~läufigen Meinung** contrary to popular opinion.

Ländle *nt* **-s,** *no pl* (*inf*) **das ~** Swabia.

Landleben *nt* country life.

Ländler *m* **-s, -** (*S Ger*) *country dance*.

Landleute *pl* country people *or* folk *pl*.

ländlich *adj* rural; *Tracht* country *attr*; *Tanz* country *attr*, folk *attr*; *Idylle* pastoral; *Stille, Frieden* of the countryside, rural.

Ländlichkeit *f* rural character *or* nature.

Land-: l~liebend *adj* country-loving *attr*; **~luft** *f* country air; **~macht** *f* land power; **~mann** *m, pl* **-männer** (*old, liter*) husbandman (*old, liter*); **~maschinen** *pl* agricultural machinery *sing or* machines *pl*; **~messer** *m siehe* **~vermesser**; **~nahme** *f* **-, -n** (*Hist*) acquisition of land; **~partie** *f* (*old*) country outing; **~pfarrer** *m* country parson; **~pfleger** *m* (*Bibl*) governor; **~plage** *f* plague; (*fig inf*) pest; **~pomeranze** *f* (*dated pej*) country cousin; **~praxis** *f* (*Med*) country practice; **~rat** *m head of the administration of a Landkreis*; **~ratte** *f* (*hum*) landlubber; **~reform** *f* land reform; **~regen** *m* steady rain; **~rücken** *m* ridge of land; **~sasse** *m* **-n, -n** (*Hist*) freeholder.

Landschaft *f* scenery *no pl*; (*Gemälde*) landscape; (*ländliche Gegend*) countryside ◆ **eine öde ~** a barren landscape *or* region; **die ~ um London** the countryside around London; **die ~en Italiens** the types of countryside in Italy; **wir sahen eine reizvolle ~** we saw some delightful scenery; **vor uns tat sich eine liebliche ~ auf** a lovely view appeared before us; **in der ~ herumstehen** (*inf*) to stand around; **da stand einsam ein Hochhaus in der ~ (herum)** (*inf*) there was one solitary skyscraper to be seen; **die politische ~** the political scene *or* landscape; **die kulinarische/kulturelle ~** the culinary/cultural scene.

landschaftlich *adj Schönheiten etc* scenic; *Besonderheiten* regional ◆ **das Dorf liegt ~ einmalig** (*inf*) the village is surrounded by the most fantastic scenery; **diese Gegend ist ~ ausgesprochen reizvoll** the scenery in this area is particularly delightful; **das ist ~ unterschiedlich** it differs from one part of the country to another *or* in various parts of the country; **„Klempner" heißt ~ auch „Spengler"** in some areas the word "Spengler" is used for "Klempner".

Landschafts-: ~bild *nt* view; (*Gemälde*) landscape (painting); (*Photographie*) landscape (photograph); **~form** *f* land form; **~gärtner** *m* landscape gardener; **~maler** *m* landscape painter; **~schutz** *m* protection of the countryside; **~schutzgebiet** *nt* nature reserve.

Land(schul)heim *nt siehe* **Schullandheim**.

Landser *m* **-s, -** (*dated inf*) private.

Landsitz *m* country seat.

Lands-: ~knecht *m* (*Hist*) lansquenet; **fluchen wie ein ~knecht** to swear like a trooper; **~mann** *m*, **~männin** *f*, *pl* **-leute** compatriot, fellow countryman/-woman; **~mannschaft** *f welfare and cultural association for Germans born in the eastern areas of the former Reich*.

Land-: ~stände *pl* (*Hist*) *body of representatives of various classes in medieval provincial politics*; **~straße** *f* country road; (*Straße zweiter Ordnung*) secondary *or* B (*Brit*) road; (*im Gegensatz zur Autobahn*) ordinary road; **~streicher(in** *f*) *m* **-s, -** (*pej*) tramp, hobo (*US*); **~streicherei** *f* vagrancy; **~streitkräfte** *pl* land forces *pl*; **~strich** *m* area; **ein flacher ~strich** a flat belt of land; **~sturm** *m conscripted militia in times of war*, ≃ Home Guard (*Brit*); **~tag** *m* Landtag (*state parliament*); **~tagswahlen** *pl* (West) German regional elections *pl*; **~truppen** *pl* land forces *pl*.

Landung *f* (*von Flugzeug, Truppen etc*) landing ◆ **zur ~ gezwungen werden** to be forced to land *or* forced down.

Landungs-: ~boot *nt* landing craft; **~brücke** *f* jetty, landing stage; **~steg** *m* landing stage; **~truppen** *pl* land assault forces *pl*.

Land-: ~urlaub *m* shore leave; **~(ver)messer** *m* land surveyor; **~vermessung** *f* land surveying; **~vogt** *m* (*Hist*) landvogt (*governor of a royal province*); **~volk** *nt* country people *pl or* folk *pl*.

landw. *abbr of* **landwirtschaftlich**.

Land-: l~wärts *adv* landwards; **~weg** *m* **auf dem ~weg** by land; **~wein** *m* vin ordinaire; **~wind** *m* offshore wind; **~wirt** *m* farmer.

Landwirtschaft *f* agriculture, farming; (*Betrieb*) farm; (*Landwirte*) farmers *pl* ◆ **~ betreiben** to farm; **~ haben** (*inf*) to have a farm.

landwirtschaftlich *adj* agricultural ◆ **~e Geräte** agricultural *or* farm implements.

Landwirtschafts- *in cpds* agricultural; **~berater** *m* agricultural adviser;

~brief *m (Fin)* agricultural bond; **~ministerium** *nt* ministry of agriculture; **~schule** *f* agricultural college.

Landzunge *f* spit (of land), promontory.

lang [1] *adj, comp* **-̈er,** *superl* **-̈ste(r, s)** **(a)** long; *Film, Roman, Aufenthalt, Rede auch* lengthy ◆ **das ist/war seit ~em geplant** that has been planned (for) a long time/was planned a long time ago; **vor ~er Zeit** a long time ago; **in nicht allzu ~er Zeit** before too *or* very long, in the not too distant future; **das hat die -̈ste Zeit gedauert!** that's gone on long enough!; **hier wird mir der Tag/die Zeit nicht ~** I won't get bored here; **etw -̈er machen** to make sth longer, to lengthen sth; **es ist eine ~e Strecke bis Bristol, jedenfalls -̈er, als ich gedacht hatte** it's a long way to Bristol, at least, further than I thought; **die Tage werden wieder -̈er** the days are drawing out *or* getting longer; **er machte ein ~es Gesicht** his face fell; **man sah überall nur ~e Gesichter** you saw nothing but long faces; **etw von ~er Hand vorbereiten** to prepare sth carefully; **des ~en und breiten** at great length; **einen ~en Hals machen** *(inf)* to crane one's neck.

(b) *(inf: groß gewachsen) Mensch* tall ◆ **eine ~e Latte, ein ~er Lulatsch, ein ~es Elend** *or* **Ende sein** to be a (real) beanpole *(inf)*; **er ist so ~ wie er dumm ist** he's as thick as two short planks *(inf)*.

[2] *adv, comp* **-̈er,** *superl* **am -̈sten** ◆ **der ~ erwartete Regen** the long-awaited rain; **der ~ ersehnte Tag/Urlaub** the longed-for day/holiday; **~ anhaltender Beifall** prolonged *or* long applause; **nur einen Augenblick ~** only for a moment *or* second; **zwei Stunden ~** for two hours; **mein ganzes Leben ~** all my life, my whole life; **~ und breit** at great length; *siehe* **entlang.**

lang-: ~ärm(e)lig *adj* long-sleeved; **~armig** *adj* long-armed; **~atmig** *adj* long-winded; **L~atmigkeit** *f* long-windedness; **~beinig** *adj* long-legged.

lange, lang *(S Ger, Aus) adv, comp* **-̈er,** *superl* **am längsten** **(a)** *(zeitlich)* a long time; *(in Fragen, Negativsätzen)* long ◆ **die Sitzung hat heute ~/nicht ~ gedauert** the meeting went on (for) a long time/didn't go on (for) long today; **wie ~ lernst du schon Deutsch/bist du schon hier?** how long have you been learning German (for)/been here (for)?; **es ist noch gar nicht ~ her, daß wir diese Frage diskutiert haben** we discussed this question not long ago, it's not long since we discussed this question; **er wird es nicht mehr ~ machen** *(inf)* he won't last long, he's not got long to go; **bis Weihnachten ist es ja noch ~ hin** it's still a long time till Christmas, we're a long way from Christmas; **je -̈er, je lieber** the more the better; *(zeitlich)* the longer the better.

(b) *(inf: längst)* **noch ~ nicht** not by any means, not by a long chalk *(inf)*; **~ nicht so ...** nowhere near as ..., not nearly as ...; **er verdient ~ nicht soviel** he doesn't earn nearly as much *or* anywhere near as much; **wenn er das schafft, kannst du das schon ~** if he can do it, you can do it easily.

Länge *f* **-, -n** **(a)** *(zeitlich, räumlich)* length; *(inf: von Mensch)* height ◆ **eine ~ von 10 Metern haben** to be 10 metres long *or* in length; **ein Seil von 10 Meter ~** a rope 10 metres long; **ein Vortrag/eine Fahrt von einer Stunde ~** an hour-long lecture/an hour's journey; **Bauarbeiten auf 5 km ~** road works for 5 kms; **etw der ~ nach falten** to fold sth lengthways *or* lengthwise; **der ~ nach hinfallen** to fall flat, to go sprawling; **in die ~ gehen** *(Kleidungsstücke)* to stretch; **in die ~ schießen** *or* **wachsen** to shoot up; **etw in die ~ ziehen** to protract sth, to drag sth out *(inf)*; **sich in die ~ ziehen** to go on and on; **der ~ nach hinfallen** to fall flat (on one's face); **einen Artikel in seiner vollen ~ abdrucken** to print an article in its entirety.

(b) *(Sport)* length ◆ **mit einer ~ gewinnen** to win by a length; **die anderen Wagen kamen mit einigen ~n Abstand** the other cars came in several lengths behind.

(c) *(in Buch, Film etc)* long-drawn-out passage/scene.

(d) *(Geog)* longitude ◆ **der Ort liegt auf** *or* **unter 20 Grad östlicher ~** the town has a longitude of 20 degrees east.

langen *(dial, inf)* [1] *vi* **(a)** *(sich erstrecken, greifen)* to reach *(nach* for, *in +acc* in, into) ◆ **bis an etw ~** to reach sth.

(b) *(fassen)* to touch *(an etw (acc)* sth).

(c) *(ausreichen)* to be enough; *(auskommen)* to get by, to manage ◆ **mir langt es** I've had/I have enough; **das Geld langt nicht** there isn't *or* we *etc* haven't enough money; **jetzt langt's mir aber!** I've had just about enough!; *siehe* **hinten.**

[2] *vt (reichen)* **jdm etw ~** to give *or* pass *or* hand sb sth; **jdm eine ~** to give sb a clip on the ear *(inf)*; **sich** *(dat)* **etw ~** to take sth.

Längen-: ~grad *m* **(a)** degree of longitude; **(b)** *(auch* **~kreis)** meridian; **~maß** *nt* measure of length, linear measure *(form)*.

länger *comp of* **lang, lange.**

längerfristig [1] *adj* longer-term.

[2] *adv* in the longer term; *planen* for the longer term.

Langerhanssche Inseln *pl (Med)* islets *pl* of Langerhans.

⚠**lang|ersehnt** *adj attr* longed-for.

Langeweile *f (gen)* - *or* **Langenweile,** *(dat)* - *or* **Langerweile,** *no pl* boredom ◆ **~ haben** to be bored.

Lang-: l~fädig *adj (Sw)* long-winded; **~finger** *m (hum)* pickpocket; **l~fing(e)rig** *adj* long-fingered; *(hum)* light-fingered; **~format** *nt* **Briefumschläge/Zigaretten im ~format** long envelopes/long(-length) cigarettes; **l~fristig** [1] *adj* long-term; [2] *adv* in the long term; *planen* for the long term; ⚠**l~gehegt** *adj attr Wunsch* long-cherished; **l~gehen** *vi sep irreg* **(a)** *(Weg etc)* **wo geht's hier ~?** where does this (road/path) go? **(b) sie weiß, wo es langgeht** she knows what's what; **hier bestimme ich, wo es langgeht** I decide what's what here; ⚠**l~gestreckt** *adj* long; *Dorf auch* strung-out; ⚠**l~gezogen** *adj* sustained; **l~glied(e)rig** *adj* long-limbed; **l~haarig** *adj* long-haired; **~haarige(r)** *mf decl as adj* long-haired man/woman *etc*; **so ein ~haariger** some long-haired type; **diese dreckigen ~haarigen** *(pej)* these long-haired layabouts; **~haarperücke** *f* long wig; **~hantel** *f* barbell; **~haus** *nt* nave; **~holz** *nt* uncut timber; **~holzwagen** *m* timber lorry *(Brit) or* truck; **l~jährig** [1] *adj Freundschaft, Bekannter, Gewohnheit* long-standing; *Erfahrung, Verhandlungen, Recherchen* many years of; *Mitarbeiter* of many years' standing; [2] *adv* for many years; **~lauf** *m (Ski)* cross-country skiing; **Sieger im ~lauf** winner of the cross-country (event); **~läufer** *m* **(a)** *(Ski)* cross-country skier; **(b)** *(Fin)* long(-dated security); **~laufski** *m* cross-country ski; **l~lebig** *adj* long-lasting; *Stoff, Waren etc auch* durable; *Gerücht* long-lived; *Melodie* enduring, long-lived; *Mensch, Tier* long-lived; **l~lebig sein** to last a long time *or* have a long life/be durable/long-lived/enduring/live to an old age *or* be long-lived; **~lebigkeit** *f siehe adj* long-lastingness; durability; long life; longevity; **l~legen** *vr sep* to have a lie-down; *(inf: hinfallen)* to fall flat on one's face; *(fig inf)* to be struck all of a heap *(inf)*.

länglich *adj* long, elongated.

Lang-: l~liegen *vi sep irreg (inf)* to be in bed; **l~mähnig** *adj* with a long mane, long-maned; *(inf) Mensch* long-haired; **~mut** *f* **-,** *no pl* patience, forbearance; **l~mütig** *adj* patient, forbearing; **~mütigkeit** *f* forbearance; **~ohr** *nt (hum)* rabbit, bunny *(inf)*; *(Häschen)* hare; **Meister ~ohr** Master Longears; **~pferd** *nt (Sport)* (long) horse.

längs [1] *adv* lengthways, lengthwise.

[2] *prep +gen* along ◆ **~ der Straße stehen Kastanien** chestnut trees line the road, there are chestnut trees along the road; **die Bäume ~ des Flusses** the trees along (the banks of) the river.

Längs|achse *f* longitudinal axis.

langsam [1] *adj* slow.

[2] *adv* **(a)** slowly ◆ **geh/fahr/sprich ~er!** slow down!, walk/drive/speak (a bit) more slowly *or* (a bit) slower! *(inf)*; **~, ~!, immer schön ~!** *(inf)* (take it) easy!, easy does it!; **~, aber sicher** slowly but surely.

(b) *(allmählich, endlich)* **es wird ~ Zeit, daß ...** it's about time *or* it's high time that ...; **~ müßtest du das aber wissen** it's about time *or* it's high time you knew that; **ich muß jetzt ~ gehen** I must be getting on my way, I'd better be thinking about going; **kannst du dich ~ mal entscheiden?** could you start making up your mind?; **~ (aber sicher) reicht es mir** I've just about had enough; **ist das ~ fertig?** is it ready yet?

Langsamkeit *f* slowness.

langsamtreten *vi sep irreg (inf)* to go easy *(inf)*; *(gesundheitlich auch)* to take things easy.

Lang-: ~schäfter *m* **-s, -** high boot; *(aus Gummi)* wader; **l~schäftig** *adj Stiefel* high; **~schiff** *nt* nave; **~schläfer** *m* late-riser; **~schrift** *f* longhand; **~seite** *f siehe* **Längsseite.**

Längs-: ~faden *m* warp; **~falte** *f* lengthways fold; ⚠**l~gestreift** *adj Stoff* with lengthways stripes; *Kleid, Vorhang etc auch* with vertical stripes; **~linie** *f* vertical line, line down.

Langspiel-: ~band *nt* long-playing tape; **~platte** *f* long-playing record.

Längs-: ~richtung *f* longitudinal direction; **in ~richtung zu etw verlaufen** to run longitudinally along sth; **l~schiffs** *adv* broadside on; **~schnitt** *m* longitudinal section; **~seite** *f* long side; *(Naut)* broadside; **l~seit(s)** *adv, prep +gen* alongside; **die beiden Boote lagen l~seit(s)** the boats were lying alongside one another; **~streifen** *pl* lengthways stripes *pl*; *(von Kleid, Vorhängen auch)* vertical stripes *pl*.

längst *adv* **(a)** *(seit langem, schon lange)* for a long time; *(vor langer Zeit)* a long time ago, long ago ◆ **er ist inzwischen ~ gestorben** he has been dead (for) a long time now; **als wir ankamen, war der Zug ~ weg** when we arrived the train had long since gone. **(b)** *siehe* **lange (b).**

Längstal ['lɛŋs-] *nt* longitudinal valley.

längstens *adv* **(a)** *(höchstens)* at the most. **(b)** *(spätestens)* at the latest.

längste(r, s) *superl of* **lang.**

langstielig *adj* long-stemmed.

Langstrecken-: ~flug *m* long-distance flight; **~flugzeug** *nt* long-range *or* long-haul aircraft; **~lauf** *m (Disziplin)* long-distance running; *(Wettkampf)* long-distance race; **~läufer(in** *f***)**, *(auch)* **Langstreckler(in** *f***)** *m* **-s, -** *(inf)* long-distance runner; **~rakete** *f* long-range missile; **~waffe** *f* long-range weapon.

Längswand *f* long wall.

Languste [laŋ'gʊstə] *f* **-, -n** crayfish, crawfish *(US)*.

langweilen *insep* [1] *vt* to bore.

[2] *vi* to be boring.

[3] *vr* to be/get bored ◆ **sich tödlich** *or* **zu Tode ~** to be/get bored to death *or* to tears; *siehe* **gelangweilt.**

Langweiler *m* **-s, -** bore; *(langsamer Mensch)* slowcoach *(Brit inf)*, slowpoke *(US inf)*.

langweilig *adj* **(a)** boring. **(b)** *(inf: langsam)* slow ◆ **er ist so ~ mit allem** he's so slow *or* such a slowcoach *(Brit inf) or* slowpoke *(US inf)* at everything.

Langweiligkeit *f siehe adj* **(a)** boringness. **(b)** slowness.

Lang-: ~welle *f* long wave; **l~wellig** *adj* long-wave; **l~wierig** *adj* long, lengthy; *Verhandlungen, Behandlung, Krankheit auch* prolonged; **l~wierig über etw** *(acc)* **beraten** to have lengthy *or* prolonged discussions about sth; **~wierigkeit** *f* lengthiness.

Langzeit- *in cpds* long-term; **~arbeitslose(r)** *mf decl as adj* long-term unemployed person; **~gedächtnis** *nt* long-term memory; **~programm** *nt* long-term programme; **~risiko** *nt* long-term risk; **~studie** *f* long-range study; **~wert** *m, no pl* long-term result; **~wirkung** *f* long-term effect.

⚠**langziehen** *vt sep irreg* to stretch; *siehe* **Ohr, Hammelbeine.**

Lanolin *nt* **-s,** *no pl* lanolin.
Lanthan *nt, no pl* (*abbr* **La**) lanthanum.
Lanze *f* **-, -n** lance; (*zum Werfen*) spear ◆ **für jdn eine ~ brechen** (*fig*) to take up the cudgels for sb, to go to bat for sb (*esp US*).
Lanzen-: ~spitze *f* tip of a lance/spear; **~stich** *m* lance/spear thrust; (*Wunde*) lance/spear wound; **er wurde von einem ~stich getroffen** he was hit by a lance/spear; **~stoß** *m* lance/spear thrust.
Lanzette *f* (*Med*) lancet.
Lanzett-: ~fisch *m,* **~fischchen** *nt* lancelet; **l~förmig** *adj* (*Bot*) lanceolate (*spec*).
Laos *nt* **-'** Laos.
Laote *m* **-n, -n, Laotin** *f* Laotian.
laotisch *adj* Laotian.
Laotse *m* **-s** Lao-Tse.
lapidar *adj* succinct.
Lapislazuli *m* **-, -** lapis lazuli.
Lappalie [-iə] *f* trifle, petty little matter.
Läppchen *nt* (small) cloth.
Lappe *m* **-n, -n, Lappin** *f* Lapp, Lapplander.
Lappen *m* **-s, -** (**a**) (*Stück Stoff*) cloth; (*Wasch~*) face cloth, flannel. (**b**) (*sl: Geldschein*) note, bill (*US*). (**c**) (*Hautstück*) fold of skin. (**d**) (*inf*) **jdm durch die ~ gehen** to slip through sb's fingers; **die Sendung ist mir durch die ~ gegangen** I missed the programme.
läppern *vr impers* (*inf*) **es läppert sich** it (all) mounts up.
lappig *adj* (*inf*) limp.
Lappin *f siehe* **Lappe.**
läppisch *adj* silly ◆ **wegen ~en zwei Mark macht er so ein Theater** (*inf*) he makes such a fuss about a mere two marks.
Lappland *nt* **-s** Lapland.
Lappländer(in *f*) *m* **-s, -** *siehe* **Lappe.**
lappländisch *adj* Lapp.
Lapsus *m* **-, -** mistake, slip; (*gesellschaftlich, diplomatisch*) faux pas ◆ **~ linguae** [-'lıŋguɛ] slip of the tongue; **mir ist ein ~ unterlaufen** *or* **passiert, ich habe einen ~ begangen** I've made a mistake/faux pas.
Laptop *m* **-s, -s** (*Comput*) laptop.
Lärche *f* **-, -n** larch.
large [larʒ] *adj* (*Sw*) generous.
Lärge *f* **-, -n** (*dial, pej*) Silesian.
Largo *nt* **-s, -s** *or* **Larghi** (*Mus*) largo.
larifari [1] *interj* nonsense, fiddlesticks, fiddle-de-dee.
[2] *adj inv* airy-fairy.
Larifari *nt* **-s,** *no pl* (*inf*) nonsense.
Lärm *m* **-(e)s,** *no pl* noise; (*Geräuschbelästigung auch*) din, row, racket; (*Aufsehen*) fuss ◆ **~ schlagen** (*lit*) to raise the alarm; (*fig*) to kick up a fuss, to raise a commotion; **„Viel ~ um nichts"** "Much Ado about Nothing"; **viel ~ um nichts machen** to make a lot of fuss *or* ado *or* a big to-do about nothing; **viel ~ um jdn/etw machen** to make a big fuss about sb/sth.
Lärm-: ~bekämpfung *f* noise abatement; **~belästigung** *f* noise pollution; **sie beschwerten sich wegen der unzumutbaren ~belästigung** they complained about the unacceptable noise level; **l~empfindlich** *adj* sensitive to noise.
lärmen *vi* to make a noise ◆ **~d** noisy.
Lärm-: l~geplagt *adj* plagued with noise; **l~geschädigt** *adj* suffering physical damage as a result of exposure to noise; ⚠**~meßgerät** *nt* noise meter.
larmoyant [larmoa'jant] *adj* (*geh*) lachrymose (*liter*).
Larmoyanz [larmoa'jants] *f* (*geh*) sentimentality.
Lärm-: ~quelle *f* source of noise/the noise; **~schäden, ~schädigungen** *pl* injuries caused by excessive noise; **~schutz** *m* noise prevention.
Lärmschutz-: ~maßnahmen *pl* noise prevention measures *pl*; **~wall** *m,* **~wand** *f* sound *or* noise barrier.
Lärvchen *nt* (**a**) *dim of* **Larve.** (**b**) (*dated inf: Gesicht*) baby-doll face.
Larve ['larfə] *f* **-, -n** (**a**) (*Tier~*) larva. (**b**) *siehe* **Maske.**
las *pret of* **lesen.**
Lasagne [la'zanjə] *pl* lasagne *sing.*
lasch *adj* (*inf*) (**a**) (*schlaff*) *Bewegungen* feeble; *Händedruck* limp. (**b**) *Erziehung, Polizei, Eltern* lax. (**c**) *Speisen* insipid, wishy-washy (*inf*).
Lasche *f* **-, -n** (*Schlaufe*) loop; (*Schuh~*) tongue; (*als Schmuck, Verschluß*) tab, flap; (*Tech*) splicing plate; (*von Kette*) sideplate; (*Rail*) fishplate.
Laschheit *f siehe adj* (**a**) feebleness; limpness. (**b**) laxity. (**c**) insipidity, wishy-washiness (*inf*).
Laser ['le:zɐ, 'la:zɐ] *m* **-s, -** laser.
Laser- *in cpds* laser; **~chirurgie** *f* laser surgery; **~drucker** *m* (*Typ*) laser (printer); **~-Kanone** *f* laser gun; **~strahl** *m* laser beam; **~technik** *f, no pl* laser technology; **~-Waffe** *f* laser weapon.
lasieren* *vt Bild, Holz* to varnish; *Glas* to glaze.
⚠**laß** *imper sing of* **lassen.**
Lassafieber *nt, no pl* Lassa fever.
lassen *pret* **ließ,** *ptp* **gelassen** [1] *vt* (**a**) (*unter~*) to stop; (*momentan aufhören*) to leave ◆ **laß das (sein)!** don't (do it)!; (*hör auf*) stop it!; **laß das Jammern** stop your moaning; **laß diese Bemerkungen!** that's enough of that kind of remark!; **~ wir das!** let's leave it *or* that!; **er kann das Rauchen/Trinken nicht ~** he can't stop smoking/drinking, he can't keep from smoking/drinking; **er kann es nicht ~!** he will keep on doing it!; **er hat es versucht, aber er kann es nicht ~** he's tried, but he can't help it *or* himself; **sich vor Freude nicht zu ~ wissen** *or* **~ können** to be delirious with joy; **dann ~ wir es eben** let's drop the whole idea; **ich will aber nicht! — dann ~ wir es eben** but I don't want to! — let's not bother then; **wenn du nicht willst, dann laß es doch** if you don't want to, then don't; **ich habe es dann doch gelassen** in the end I didn't; **tu, was du nicht ~ kannst!** if you must, you must!
(**b**) (*zurück~*) to leave ◆ **jdn allein ~** to leave sb alone; **er hat dort viel Geld gelassen** he left there with his pockets a lot lighter.
(**c**) (*über~*) **jdm etw ~** to let sb have sth; (*behalten ~*) to let sb keep sth; **das muß man ihr ~** (*zugestehen*) you've got to give *or* grant her that.
(**d**) (*hinein~, hinaus~*) to let (*in +acc* into, *aus* out of) ◆ **Wasser in die Badewanne (laufen) ~** to run water into the bath; **laß die Kinder nicht auf die Straße/auf das Sofa** don't let the children (go) onto the street/(get) on(to) the sofa.
(**e**) (*be~*) to leave ◆ **etw ~, wie es ist** to leave sth (just) as it is; **etw ungesagt/ungetan ~** (*geh*) to leave sth unsaid/undone.
(**f**) (*inf: los~*) to let go; (*in Ruhe ~*) to leave alone, to let be; (*gewähren ~*) to let.
[2] *modal aux vb ptp ~ Übersetzung hängt oft vom Vollverb ab, siehe auch dort* (**a**) (*veranlassen*) **etw tun ~** to have *or* get sth done; **sich** (*dat*) **etw schicken ~** to have *or* get sth sent to one; **ich muß mich mal untersuchen ~** I'll have to have a check-up; **sich** (*dat*) **einen Zahn ziehen ~** to have a tooth out; **jdm mitteilen/ausrichten ~, daß** ... to let sb know *or* have sb informed (*form*)/ leave a message for sb that ...; **er läßt Ihnen mitteilen, daß** ... he wants *or* wishes (*form*) you to know that ...; **jdn rufen** *or* **kommen ~** to send for sb; **mein Vater wollte mich studieren ~** my father wanted me to study; **eine Versammlung einberufen ~** to have a meeting called; **Goethe läßt Faust sagen:** ... Goethe has *or* makes Faust say: ...
(**b**) (*zu~*) **jdn etw wissen/sehen/hören ~** to let sb know/see/hear sth; **etw kochen ~** to boil sth; **sie hat mich nichts merken ~** she didn't show it/ anything; **einen Bart/sich** (*dat*) **die Haare wachsen ~** to grow a beard/one's hair, to let one's hair grow; **den Tee ziehen ~** to let the tea draw; **das Licht brennen ~** to leave the light on; **jdn warten ~** to keep sb waiting; **laß ihn nur kommen!** just let him show his face *or* come!
(**c**) (*erlauben*) to let, to allow ◆ **er hat sich überreden/nicht überreden ~** he let himself be *or* allowed himself to be persuaded/he was not to be persuaded; **ich lasse mich nicht belügen/zwingen** I won't be lied to/coerced.
(**d**) (*möglich sein*) **das Fenster läßt sich leicht öffnen** the window opens easily; **das Fenster läßt sich nicht öffnen** (*grundsätzlich nicht*) the window doesn't open; (*momentan nicht*) the window won't open; **das Wort läßt sich schwer/ nicht übersetzen** the word is hard to translate/can't be translated *or* is untranslatable; **das läßt sich machen** that's possible, that can be done; **es läßt sich essen/trinken** it's edible *or* eatable/drinkable; **hier läßt es sich bequem sitzen** it's comfortable sitting here; **das läßt sich nicht mehr feststellen** that can no longer be established; **das läßt sich nicht mehr ändern** nothing can be done about that now, it's too late to do anything about it now; **daraus läßt sich schließen** *or* **folgern, daß** ... one can conclude from this that ...
(**e**) (*als Imperativ*) **laß uns gehen!** let's go!; **laß uns alles vergessen!** let's forget everything!; **laß es dir gutgehen!** take care of yourself!; **laß dir das gesagt sein!** let me tell you this!; **lasset die Kindlein zu mir kommen** (*Bibl*) suffer the little children to come unto me (*Bibl*); **lasset uns beten** let us pray.
[3] *vi* (**a**) **laß mal, ich mache das schon** leave it, I'll do it; **laß mal, ich zahle das schon** no, that's all right, I'll pay; **ich lasse gern mit mir handeln** I'm quite willing to negotiate.
(**b**) (*ab~*) **von jdm/etw ~** to give sb/sth up.
lässig *adj* (*ungezwungen*) casual; (*nach~*) careless; (*sl: gekonnt*) cool (*sl*) ◆ **das hat er ganz ~ hingekriegt** (*sl*) pretty cool, the way he did that (*sl*).
Lässigkeit *f siehe adj* casualness; carelessness; coolness (*sl*).
⚠**läßlich** *adj* (*Eccl*) *Sünde* venial, pardonable.
Lasso *m or nt* **-s, -s** lasso.
⚠**laßt** *imper pl of* **lassen.**
Last *f* **-, -en** (**a**) load; (*Trag~ auch*) burden; (*lit, fig: Gewicht*) weight ◆ **Aufzug nur für ~en** goods lift *or* hoist; **des Lebens ~ und Mühe** (*liter*) the trials and tribulations of life.
(**b**) (*fig: Bürde*) burden ◆ **eine ~ für jdn sein, jdm zur ~ fallen/werden** to be/ become a burden on sb; **die ~ der Verantwortung/des Amtes** the burden of responsibility/the weight of office; **sich** (*dat*) **selbst eine ~ sein** to be a burden to oneself; **damit war uns eine schwere ~ vom Herzen** *or* **von der Seele genommen** that took a load off our minds; **jdm eine ~ abnehmen** to take a load off sb's shoulders; **jdm etw zur ~ legen** to accuse sb of sth.
(**c**) **~en** (*Kosten*) costs; (*des Steuerzahlers*) charges; **soziale ~en** welfare costs *or* charges; **die steuerlichen ~en für die kleinen Unternehmen** the tax burden for small concerns; **zu jds/eigenen ~en gehen** to be chargeable to sb/ payable oneself.
Last-: ~arm *m* (*Phys*) load arm; **~auto** *nt* van (*Brit*), panel truck (*US*).
lasten *vi* to weigh heavily (*auf +dat* on) ◆ **eine schwere Sorge hat auf ihr gelastet** a terrible worry weighed her down; **eine lähmende Schwüle lastete über der Stadt** (*geh*) an oppressive heat hung heavily over the town; **auf dem Haus lastet noch eine Hypothek** the house is still encumbered (with a mortgage) (*form*); **auf ihm lastet die ganze Verantwortung/Arbeit** all the responsibility rests on him/all the work falls on him.
Lasten-: ~aufzug *m* hoist, goods lift *or* elevator (*US*); **~ausgleich** *m system of financial compensation for losses suffered in the Second World War.*
lastend *adj* (*geh*) *Stille, Schwüle* oppressive.
Lasten-: l~frei *adj Grundstück* unencumbered; **~taxi** *nt van plus driver to rent.*

⚠: for details of spelling reform, see supplement

Laster[1] *m* **-s, -** (*inf*) lorry (*Brit*), truck.
Laster[2] *nt* **-s, -** vice; *siehe* **lang, Müßiggang.**
Lästerei *f* (*inf*) **(a)** *no pl* (*das Lästern*) running down (*über +acc* of), nasty comments *pl.* **(b)** (*Lästerwort*) nasty remark.
Lästerer *m* **-s, - (a) ein ~ sein** to have a vicious tongue (in one's head). **(b)** (*Gottes~*) blasphemer.
lasterhaft *adj* depraved.
Lasterhaftigkeit *f* depravity.
Lasterhöhle *f* den of vice *or* iniquity.
Lasterleben *nt* (*old, iro*) life of sin and depravity.
lästerlich *adj* malicious; (*gottes~*) blasphemous ◆ **~e Bemerkung** gibe (*über +acc* at).
Lästermaul *nt* (*inf*) *siehe* **Lästerer (a).**
lästern [1] *vi* **über jdn/etw ~** to make nasty remarks about sb/sth, to run sb/sth down; **wir haben gerade über dich gelästert** (*hum*) we were just talking about you, we were just taking your name in vain (*hum*).
[2] *vt* **(a)** to be nasty about. **(b)** *Gott* to blaspheme against, to curse.
Läster-: ~wort *nt, pl* **-worte (a)** gibe; **(b)** (*gegen Gott*) blasphemy; **~worte** blasphemous words; **~zunge** *f* vicious tongue.
Last|esel *m* pack mule.
Lastex ® *nt* **-,** *no pl* stretch fabric.
Lastex- ® *in cpds* stretch.
Last-: ~fahrzeug *nt* goods vehicle; **~fuhre** *f* **mit dem Mietwagen dürfen keine ~fuhren unternommen werden** the hired car is not to be used for the carriage of goods.
lästig *adj* tiresome; (*ärgerlich auch*) annoying, irksome, aggravating; *Husten, Kopfschuppen etc* troublesome ◆ **wie ~!** what a nuisance!; **jdm ~ sein** to bother sb; **der Regenschirm/dieser Verband ist mir ~** the umbrella is a nuisance/this bandage is bothering me; **jdm ~ fallen** to be a nuisance to sb; **jdm ~ werden** to become a nuisance (to sb); (*zum Ärgernis werden*) to get annoying (to sb).
Lästigkeit *f siehe adj* tiresomeness; irksomeness; troublesomeness.
Last-: ~kahn *m* barge; **~kraftwagen** *m* (*form*) heavy goods vehicle.
Last-Minute-: ~-Flug *m* late availability flight; **~-Reise** *f* late availability holiday.
Last-: ~schiff *nt* freighter, cargo ship; **~schrift** *f* debit; (*Eintrag*) debit entry; **~tier** *nt* beast of burden, pack animal; **~träger** *m* carrier, porter; **~wagen** *m* lorry (*Brit*), truck; **~wagenfahrer** *m* lorry (*Brit*) *or* truck driver; **~zug** *m* truck-trailer (*US*), juggernaut (*Brit inf*).
Lasur *f* (*auf Holz, Bild*) varnish; (*auf Glas, Email*) glaze.
Lasurstein *m siehe* **Lapislazuli.**
lasziv *adj* (*geh*) lascivious.
Laszivität *f* (*geh*) lasciviousness.
Lätare *no art* (*Eccl*) Laetare Sunday, 3rd Sunday before Easter.
Latein *nt* **-s** Latin ◆ **mit seinem ~ am Ende sein** to be stumped (*inf*).
Latein-: ~amerika *nt* Latin America; **~amerikaner(in** *f*) *m* Latin American; **l~amerikanisch** *adj* Latin-American.
Lateiner *m* **-s, -** Latin scholar; (*Sch*) Latin pupil.
lateinisch *adj* Latin.
Lateinschule *f* (*Hist*) grammar school.
latent *adj* latent; *Selbstmörder* potential ◆ **~ vorhanden sein** to be latent.
Latenz *f* latency.
Latenz-: ~periode *f* latency period; **~zeit** *f* latent period.
lateral *adj* (*Sci*) lateral.
Laterna magica *f* magic lantern.
Laterne *f* **-, -n** (*Leuchte, Archit*) lantern; (*Straßen~*) streetlight, streetlamp.
Laternen-: ~licht *nt* light of the streetlamp(s); **~pfahl** *m* lamp post.
Latex *m* **-, Latizes** latex.
Latifundium *nt usu pl* latifundium.
latinisieren* *vt* to latinize.
Latinist(in *f*) *m* Latinist, Latin scholar.
Latinum *nt* **-s,** *no pl* **kleines/großes ~** ≃ Latin O-/A-level (exam) (*Brit*).
Latium *nt* **-s** Latium.
Latrine *f* latrine.
Latsche *f* **-, -n** (*Bot*) *siehe* **Latschenkiefer.**
Latschen *m* **-s, -** (*inf*) (*Hausschuh*) slipper; (*pej: Schuh*) worn-out shoe.
latschen *vi aux sein* (*inf*) to wander; (*durch die Stadt etc*) to traipse; (*schlurfend*) to slouch along; *siehe* **Bremse**[1].
Latschenkiefer *f* mountain pine.
latschig *adj* (*inf*) *Gang* sloppy (*inf*).
Latte *f* **-, -n (a)** (*schmales Brett*) slat ◆ **nicht alle auf der ~ haben** (*sl*) to have a screw loose (*inf*). **(b)** (*Sport*) bar; (*Ftbl*) (cross)bar. **(c)** (*inf: Liste*) **eine (ganze) ~ von Wünschen/Vorstrafen** a whole string of things that he *etc* wants/of previous convictions; *siehe* **lang. (d)** (*sl*) **eine ~ haben** to have a hard-on (*sl*).
Latten-: ~holz *nt* lath wood; **~kreuz** *nt* corner of the goalpost; **~rost** *m* duckboards *pl*; (*in Bett*) slatted frame; ⚠**~schuß** *m* (*Ftbl*) shot against the bar; **nach dem ~schuß von Matthäus** after Matthäus hit the crossbar; **einen ~schuß haben** (*sl*) to be off one's rocker (*sl*); **~verschlag** *m* crate; (*abgeteilte Fläche*) enclosure; (*für Hühner etc*) run; **~zaun** *m* wooden fence, paling.
Lattich *m* **-s, -e** (*Bot*) lettuce.
Latüchte *f* **-, -n** (*hum*) *siehe* **Laterne.**
Latz *m* **-es, ¨-e** *or* (*Aus*) **-e** (*Lätzchen, bei Kleidung*) bib; (*Hosen~*) (front) flap ◆ **jdm eins vor den ~ knallen** (*sl*) *or* **ballern** (*sl*) to sock sb one (*sl*).
Lätzchen *nt* bib.
Latzhose *f* (pair of) dungarees *pl.*

lau *adj* **(a)** *Wind, Abend* mild. **(b)** (*~warm*) *Flüssigkeit* tepid, lukewarm; (*fig*) *Freundschaft, Begeisterung, Haltung* lukewarm, half-hearted.
Laub *nt* **-(e)s,** *no pl* leaves *pl*; (*an Bäumen etc auch*) foliage.
Laub-: ~baum *m* deciduous tree; **~blatt** *nt* (fallen) leaf; **~dach** *nt* leafy canopy (*liter*).
Laube *f* **-, -n (a)** (*Gartenhäuschen*) summerhouse. **(b)** (*Gang*) arbour, pergola; (*Arkade*) arcade; *siehe* **fertig.**
Lauben-: ~gang *m* arbour, pergola; **~kolonie** *f* area of allotments; **~pieper** *m* **-s, -** (*dial*) allotment gardener.
Laub-: ~fall *m* **vor dem ~fall** before the leaves fall; **~färbung** *f* colouring of the leaves; **~frosch** *m* (European) tree-frog; **~hölzer** *pl* deciduous trees *pl*; **~hüttenfest** *nt* Feast of Tabernacles, Sukkoth; **~krone** *f* tree-top; **~säge** *f* fretsaw; **~sägearbeit** *f* fretwork; ⚠**l~tragend** *adj* deciduous; **~wald** *m* deciduous wood/forest; **~werk** *nt* foliage (*auch Art*).
Lauch *m* **-(e)s, -e** allium (*form*); (*esp S Ger: Porree*) leek.
Lauchzwiebel *f* spring onion.
Laudatio [lau'da:tsio] *f* **-, Laudationes** encomium, eulogy.
Laue(ne) *f* **-, -(ne)n** (*esp Sw*) avalanche.
Lauer *f* **-,** *no pl*: **auf der ~ sein** *or* **liegen** to lie in wait; **sich auf die ~ legen** to settle down to lie in wait.
lauern *vi* (*lit, fig*) to lurk, to lie in wait (*auf +acc* for); (*inf*) to wait (*auf +acc* for) ◆ **ein ~der Blick** a furtive glance.
Lauf *m* **-(e)s, Läufe (a)** (*schneller Schritt*) run; (*Sport: Wett~*) race ◆ **sein ~ wurde immer schneller** he ran faster and faster; **im ~ innehalten** to stop running for a moment.
(b) (*Verlauf*) course ◆ **im ~e der Jahre** in the course of the years, over *or* through the years; **im ~e des Gesprächs** in the course of *or* during the conversation; **einer Entwicklung** (*dat*) **freien ~ lassen** to allow a development to take its (own) course; **sie ließ ihren Gefühlen freien ~** she gave way to her feelings; **den Dingen ihren ~ lassen** to let matters *or* things take their course; **das ist der ~ der Dinge** *or* **der Welt** that's the way of the world *or* the way things go; **die Dinge nahmen ihren ~** everything took its course.
(c) (*Gang, Arbeit*) running, operation; (*Comput*) run.
(d) (*Fluß~, Astron*) course ◆ **der obere/untere ~ der Donau** the upper/lower reaches of the Danube.
(e) (*Mus*) run.
(f) (*Gewehr~*) barrel ◆ **ein Tier vor den ~ bekommen** to get an animal in one's sights.
(g) (*Hunt: Bein*) leg.
Laufbahn *f* career ◆ **die ~ des Beamten einschlagen** to embark *or* enter on a career as a civil servant.
Laufband *nt* (*Förderband*) conveyor belt; (*in Flughafen etc*) travelator; (*Sportgerät*) treadmill.
Laufbursche *m* errand-boy, messenger boy.
laufen *pret* **lief,** *ptp* **gelaufen** [1] *vi aux sein* **(a)** (*rennen*) to run ◆ **lauf doch!** get a move on! (*inf*).
(b) (*inf*) (*gehen*) to go; (*seine Notdurft verrichten*) to run (to the toilet) (*inf*) ◆ **er läuft dauernd ins Kino/auf die Polizei** he's always off to the cinema/running to the police.
(c) (*zu Fuß gehen*) to walk ◆ **das Kind läuft schon** the child can already walk *or* is already walking; **das L~ lernen** to learn to walk; **er läuft sehr unsicher** he's very unsteady on his feet; **es sind noch/nur 10 Minuten zu ~** it's another/only 10 minutes' walk.
(d) (*fließen*) to run; (*schmelzen: Käse, Butter*) to melt ◆ **in Strömen ~** to stream *or* pour (in/out/down *etc*); **Wasser in einen Eimer/die Badewanne ~ lassen** to run water into a bucket/the bath; **das Bier muß ~** the beer must be kept flowing.
(e) (*undicht sein*) (*Gefäß, Wasserhahn*) to leak; (*Nase, Wunde*) to run ◆ **seine Nase läuft, ihm läuft die Nase** his nose is running, he's got a runny nose.
(f) (*in Betrieb sein*) to run, to go; (*Uhr*) to go; (*Elektrogerät*) (*eingeschaltet sein*) to be on; (*funktionieren*) to work ◆ **wir haben jetzt drei neue Maschinen ~** (*inf*) we've got three new machines going (*inf*); **er hat vier Mädchen ~** (*sl*) he's got four girls out on the game (*sl*) *or* hustling for him (*sl*).
(g) (*Comput*) to run ◆ **ein Programm ~ lassen** to run a program.
(h) (*fig: im Gange sein*) (*Prozeß, Verhandlung*) to go on, to be in progress; (*Bewerbung, Antrag*) to be under consideration; (*gezeigt werden*) (*Film*) to be on, to be showing; (*Stück*) to be on, to be playing ◆ **der Film lief schon, als wir ankamen** the film had already started when we arrived; **der Film läuft über drei Stunden** the film goes on for three hours; **etw läuft gut/schlecht** sth is going well/badly; **die Sache/das Geschäft läuft jetzt** it/the shop is going well now; **sehen, wie die Sache läuft** see how things go; **alles/die Dinge ~ lassen** to let everything/things slide; **die Sache ist gelaufen** (*sl*) it's in the bag (*inf*), it's all wrapped up (*inf*); **jdm zeigen, wie es läuft** (*inf*) to show sb the ropes (*inf*).
(i) (*gültig sein: Vertrag, Abkommen*) to run.
(j) (*bezeichnet werden*) **das Auto läuft unter meinem Namen** *or* **auf meinen Namen** the car is in my name; **das Konto läuft unter der Nummer ...** the number of the account is ...; **der Agent läuft unter dem Decknamen „Spinne"** the agent goes by the cover-name of "Spider"; **das läuft unter „Sonderausgaben"** that comes under "special expenses".
(k) (*sich bewegen*) to run ◆ **es lief mir eiskalt über den Rücken** a chill ran *or* went up my spine; **auf eine Mine ~** to hit a mine; **in den Hafen ~** to enter port; *siehe* **Geld, Stapel.**
(l) (*verlaufen: Fluß etc*) to run; (*Weg auch*) to go.
[2] *vt* **(a)** *aux haben or sein* (*Sport*) *Rekordzeit* to run; *Rekord* to set ◆ **Rennen ~** to

run (in races); **Ski/Schlittschuh/Rollschuh** *etc* ~ to ski/skate/rollerskate *etc*; *siehe* **Gefahr**.
(b) *aux sein (fahren: Auto etc) Geschwindigkeit, Strecke* to do.
(c) *aux sein (zu Fuß gehen)* to walk; *(schnell)* to run.
(d) **sich** *(dat)* **eine Blase ~** to give oneself a blister; **sich** *(dat)* **ein Loch in die Sohlen ~** to wear a hole in one's soles.
[3] *vr* **sich warm ~** to warm up; **sich heiß ~** to overheat; **sich müde ~** to tire oneself out; **in den Schuhen läuft es sich gut/schlecht** these shoes are good/bad for walking/running in; **zu zweit läuft es sich besser** it's better walking/running in twos.

laufend [1] *adj attr (ständig) Arbeiten, Ausgaben* regular; *Kredit* outstanding; *(regelmäßig) Wartung* routine; *Monat, Jahr, Konto (form)* current ♦ **10 DM das ~e Meter** DM 10 per metre; **~e Nummer** serial number; *(von Konto)* number; **auf dem ~en bleiben/sein** to keep (oneself)/be in the picture *or* up-to-date *or* informed; **jdn auf dem ~en halten** to keep sb posted *or* up-to-date *or* informed; **mit etw auf dem ~en sein** to be up-to-date on sth; *siehe* **Band**[1].
[2] *adv* continually, constantly.

laufenlassen *vt sep irreg (inf)* **jdn ~** to let sb go.

Läufer *m* **-s, - (a)** *(Sport)* runner; *(Hürden~)* hurdler; *(Ftbl)* halfback; *(dated: Laufbursche)* messenger-boy; *(Chess)* bishop ♦ **rechter/linker ~** *(Ftbl)* right/left half.
(b) *(Teppich)* rug; *(Treppen~, Tisch~)* runner.
(c) *(Tech) (Laufkatze)* crab; *(Laufgewicht)* sliding weight.
(d) *(Build)* stretcher.
(e) *(junges Schwein)* young pig.

Lauferei *f (inf)* running about *no pl*.

Läuferin *f siehe* **Läufer (a)**.

Läuferstange *f* stair-rod.

Lauf-: l~faul *adj* lazy; **er war während des Spiels l~faul** he didn't run around very much during the game; **~feuer** *nt*: **sich wie ein ~feuer verbreiten** to spread like wildfire; **~fläche** *f (von Reifen)* tread; **l~freudig** *adj* keen on running/walking; **~gewicht** *nt* sliding weight; **~gitter** *nt* playpen; **~graben** *m* approach trench.

läufig *adj* on heat.

Lauf-: ~junge *m* errand-boy; **~katze** *f (Tech)* crab; **~kran** *m* (overhead) travelling crane; **~kunde** *m* occasional customer; **~kundschaft** *f* occasional customers *pl*; **~masche** *f* ladder *(Brit)*, run; **~maschen aufnehmen** to mend ladders; **⚠~paß** *m*: **jdm den ~paß geben** *(inf)* to give sb his marching orders *(inf)*; *Freundin etc auch* to pack sb in *(inf)*; **~planke** *f (Naut)* gangplank; **~rad** *nt* traversing wheel; *(ohne Antrieb)* trailing wheel; *(in Turbine)* rotor; **~richtung** *f (Mech)* direction of travel; **~rolle** *f* roller; *(unter Möbeln)* castor; **~rost** *m* duckboards *pl*; **l~ruhig** *adj Motor* quiet; **~schritt** *m* trot; *(Mil)* double-quick, double-time; **im ~schritt** *(Mil)* at the double; **er näherte sich im ~schritt** he came trotting up; **~schuh** *m (inf)* walking shoe; **~stall** *m* **(a)** playpen; **(b)** *(für Tiere)* pen; **~steg** *m* catwalk; **~werk** *nt* running gear; *(Comput)* drive; **~zeit** *f* **(a)** *(von Wechsel, Vertrag)* term, period of validity; *(von Kredit)* period; **(b)** *(von Maschine) (Lebensdauer)* (operational) life; *(Betriebszeit)* running time; **(c)** *(Sport)* time; **(d)** *(Zool: Brunstzeit)* **während der ~zeit** while on heat; **~zettel** *m (an Akten, Maschinen)* docket.

Lauge *f* **-, -n** *(Chem)* lye, leach; *(Seifen~)* soapy water; *(Salz~)* salt solution.

Laugenbrezel *f* pretzel stick.

Lauheit, Lauigkeit *(rare) f* **(a)** *(von Wind, Abend)* mildness. **(b)** *(von Flüssigkeit)* tepidness, tepidity, lukewarmness; *(fig: von Freundschaft etc)* lukewarmness, half-heartedness.

Laune *f* **-, -n (a)** *(Stimmung)* mood ♦ **(je) nach (Lust und) ~** just as the mood *or* fancy takes one; **gute/schlechte ~ haben, (bei** *or* **in) guter/schlechter ~ sein** to be in a good/bad mood *or* temper; **jdn bei guter ~** *or* **bei ~** *(inf)* **halten** to keep sb happy *or* in a good mood; **was hat er für ~?** what sort of (a) mood is he in?; **seine ~ an jdm auslassen** to take one's temper out on sb.
(b) *(Grille, Einfall)* whim, caprice ♦ **die ~n des Glücks** the vagaries of fortune; **etw aus einer ~ heraus tun** to do sth on a whim.

launenhaft *adj* moody; *(unberechenbar)* capricious; *Wetter* changeable.

Launenhaftigkeit *f siehe adj* moodiness; capriciousness; changeability.

launig *adj (dated)* witty.

launisch *adj siehe* **launenhaft**.

Laureat(in *f***)** *m* **-en, -en** *(geh)* laureate.

Laus *f* **-, Läuse** louse; *(Blatt~)* greenfly; blackfly ♦ **jdm/sich eine ~ in den Pelz setzen** *(inf)* to land sb/oneself in it *(inf)*, to let sb/oneself in for it *(inf)*; **ihm ist (wohl) eine ~ über die Leber gelaufen** *or* **gekrochen** *(inf)* something's biting him *(inf)*.

Lausbub *m (dated)* rascal, scamp, scalliwag; *(jungenhaftes Mädchen)* tomboy.

Lausbubengesicht *nt (dated)* scampish *or* roguish face.

Lausbüberei *f (dated)* devilry, prank(s).

lausbübisch *adj (dated)* roguish, scampish, rascally; *Mädchen* tomboyish.

Lausch|angriff *m* bugging operation *(gegen* on).

lauschen *vi* **(a)** *(geh)* to listen *(dat, auf +acc* to). **(b)** *(heimlich zuhören)* to eavesdrop.

Läuschen ['lɔysçən] *nt dim of* **Laus**.

Lauscher *m* **-s, - (a)** eavesdropper ♦ **der ~ an der Wand hört seine eigene Schand** *(Prov)* people who listen at doors never hear any good of themselves. **(b)** *(Hunt: Ohr)* ear.

Lauscherin *f siehe* **Lauscher (a)**.

lauschig *adj Plätzchen* cosy, snug; *(im Freien)* secluded.

Lause-: ~bengel, ~junge *m (inf)* blighter *(Brit inf)*, little devil *(inf)*; *(wohlwollend)* scamp, rascal; **l~kalt** *adj (inf)* perishing *(inf)*, freezing (cold); **~kälte** *f (inf)* freezing *or* perishing *(inf)* cold.

lausen *vt* to delouse ♦ **jdn ~** *(inf: übervorteilen)* to fleece sb *(inf)*; **ich denk', mich laust der Affe!** *(sl)* well blow me down! *(inf)*, well I'll be blowed! *(inf)*.

Lauser *m* **-s, -** *(S Ger) siehe* **Lausbub**.

lausig *(inf)* [1] *adj* lousy *(sl)*, awful; *Kälte* freezing, perishing.
[2] *adv* awfully; *(vor Adjektiv auch)* damn(ed) *(sl)*, bloody *(Brit sl)*.

laut[1] *adj* **(a)** loud ♦ **~er sprechen** to speak louder *or* more loudly, to speak up; **~ auflachen** to burst out laughing, to laugh out loud; **etw ~(er) stellen** to turn sth up (loud).
(b) *(lärmend, voll Lärm)* noisy; *(auffällig, aufdringlich) Mensch* loudmouthed; *Farbe etc* loud ♦ **er wird niemals/wird immer gleich ~** he never/always gets obstreperous.
(c) *(hörbar)* out loud *pred, adv*, aloud *pred, adv* ♦ **etw ~ sagen** *(lit)* to say sth out loud; *(fig)* to shout sth from the rooftops, to tell sth to the whole world; **~ werden** *(bekannt)* to become known; **etw ~ werden lassen** to make sth known, to let sth be known.
(d) *(Hunt: windstill)* still.

laut[2] *prep +gen (geh) or dat* according to.

Laut *m* **-(e)s, -e** sound ♦ **heimatliche ~e** sounds of home; **wir hörten bayerische ~e** we heard Bavarian accents; **keinen ~ von sich** *(dat)* **geben** not to make a sound; **~ geben** *(Hund)* to give tongue.

lautbar *adj*: **~ werden** to become known.

Lautbildung *f* articulation.

Laute *f* **-, -n** lute.

lauten *vi* to be; *(Rede, Argumentation)* to go; *(Schriftstück)* to read, to go ♦ **dieser Erlaß lautet wörtlich: ...** the exact text of this decree is: ...; **auf den Namen ... ~** *(Paß)* to be in the name of ...; *(Scheck)* to be payable to *or* made out to ...; **die Anklage lautet auf Mord** the charge is (one of) murder.

läuten *vti* **(a)** to ring; *(Wecker)* to go (off) ♦ **es hat geläutet** the bell rang *or* went; **es läutet zur Stunde** *(Sch)* the bell is ringing *or* going for the next lesson; **jdn zu Grabe ~** *(liter)* to sound sb's funeral knell, to toll the bells for sb's funeral; **(nach) jdm ~** to ring for sb; *siehe* **Sturm**. **(b) er hat davon (etwas) ~ hören** *(inf)* he has heard something about it.

Lautenist(in *f***), Lautenspieler(in** *f***)** *m* lute-player, lutenist.

lauter [1] *adj* **(a)** *(liter: rein) Gold, Wein* pure.
(b) *(geh: aufrichtig) Mensch, Absichten* honourable; *Wahrheit* honest.
[2] *adv (nur)* nothing/nobody but ♦ **~ Unsinn/Angst/Freude** *etc* pure *or* sheer nonsense/fear/joy *etc*; **das sind ~ Lügen** that's nothing but lies, that's all a pack of lies; **vor ~ Rauch/Autos kann man nichts sehen** you can't see anything for all the smoke/cars.

Lauterkeit *f, no pl* **(a)** *(liter: Reinheit)* purity. **(b)** *(geh: Aufrichtigkeit)* honourableness.

läutern *vt (liter)* to purify; *(fig)* to reform.

Läuterung *f (liter)* purification; *(fig)* reformation.

Läut(e)werk *nt (Rail)* signal bell.

laut-: ~(ge)treu *adj* phonetic; **~hals** *adv* at the top of one's voice.

Laut-: ~lehre *f* phonetics *sing*; phonology; **l~lich** *adj* phonetic; **l~los** *adj* silent, soundless; noiseless; *(wortlos)* silent; *Stille* utter, complete; **~losigkeit** *f siehe adj* silence, soundlessness; noiselessness; silence; completeness; **l~malend** *adj* onomatopoeic; **~malerei** *f* onomatopoeia; *(Ausdruck auch)* onomatopoeic word; **~schrift** *f* phonetics *pl*; *(System auch)* phonetic alphabet *or* script.

Lautsprecher *m* (loud)speaker ♦ **über ~** over the loudspeaker(s).

Lautsprecher-: ~anlage *f* **öffentliche ~anlage** public address *or* PA system, tannoy ® *(Brit)*; **~box** *f* speaker; **~wagen** *m* loudspeaker car/van.

Laut-: ~stand *m (Ling)* stage of development of the sound system; **l~stark** *adj* loud; *(Rad, TV etc)* high-volume; *Partei, Protest* vociferous; **~stärke** *f siehe adj* loudness; volume; vociferousness; **das Radio auf volle ~stärke einstellen** to turn the radio right up *or* up as loud as it will go; **~stärkeregler** *m (Rad)* volume control; **l~treu** *adj siehe* **l~(ge)treu**.

Lautung *f (geh)* articulation.

Laut-: ~verschiebung *f* sound shift; **~wandel** *m* sound change.

Läutwerk *nt (Rail)* signal bell.

Lautzeichen *nt* phonetic symbol.

lauwarm *adj* slightly warm; *Flüssigkeit* lukewarm; *(fig)* lukewarm, half-hearted.

Lava ['la:va] *f* **-, Laven** ['la:vn] lava.

Lavabo *nt* **-(s), -s (a)** [la'va:bo] *(Rel)* lavabo. **(b)** ['la:vabo] *(Sw)* washbasin.

Lavendel [la'vɛndl] *m* **-s, -** lavender.

lavieren[1]* [la'vi:rən] *vi* **(a)** *(Naut)* to tack. **(b)** *(fig)* to manoeuvre.

lavieren[2]* [la'vi:rən] *vt (Art)* to wash ♦ **lavierte Zeichnung** wash drawing.

Lavoir [la'voa:ɐ] *nt* **-s, -s** *(old, Aus)* washbasin, washbowl.

Law and order [lɔ:ənd'ɔ:də] *no art* law and order.

Law-and-order- *in cpds* law-and-order; **~-Kurs** *m* law-and-order campaign; **~-Programm** *nt* law-and-order policy.

Lawine *f (lit, fig)* avalanche.

Lawinen-: l~artig *adj* like an avalanche; **l~artig anwachsen** to snowball; **~gefahr** *f* danger of avalanches; **~schutzwald** *m* barrier forest; **l~sicher** *adj Ort* secure from avalanches; **~verbauung** *f* avalanche barrier.

Lawrencium [lo-] *nt, no pl (abbr* **Lr)** lawrencium.

lax *adj* lax.

Laxheit *f* laxity, laxness.

Layout ['le:|aut] *nt* **-s, -s** layout.

Layouter(in *f***)** ['le:|autɐ, -ərın] *m* **-s, -** designer.

Lazarett *nt* **-(e)s, -e** *(Mil) (in Kaserne etc)* sick bay; *(selbständiges Krankenhaus)*

⚠: for details of spelling reform, see supplement

hospital.

Lazarett-: ~schiff *nt* hospital ship; **~zug** *m* hospital train.

Lazarus *m* **-, -se** (*Bibl*) Lazarus ♦ **armer ~!** poor beggar *or* devil.

LCD- [ɛltseː'deː] *in cpds* LCD; **~-Anzeige** *f* LCD display.

Leadsänger(in *f*) ['liːd-] *m* lead singer.

leasen ['liːzn] *vt* (*Comm*) to lease.

Leasing ['liːzɪŋ] *nt* **-s, -s** (*Comm*) leasing ♦ **etw im ~ bekommen** to lease sth.

Leasing- *in cpds* leasing; **~-Geber** *m* lessor; **~-Nehmer** *m* lessee.

Lebedame *f* courtesan.

Lebehoch *nt* **-(s), -(s)** ≃ three cheers ♦ **~ rufen** ≃ to give three cheers; **ein (dreifaches) ~ auf jdn ausbringen** ≃ to give sb three cheers.

Lebemann *m, pl* **-männer** roué, rake.

Leben *nt* **-s, - (a)** life ♦ **das ~** life; **das ~ des Menschen/der Tiere** *etc* the life of man/animals *etc*; **am ~ sein/bleiben** to be/stay alive; **das ~ als Briefträger** life as a postman, a postman's life; **das ~ Hemingways** Hemingway's life, the life of Hemingway; **das ~ vor/hinter sich** (*dat*) **haben** to have one's life ahead of *or* in front of *or* before/behind one; **solange ich am ~ bin** as long as I live; **sich des ~s freuen, das** *or* **sein ~ genießen** to enjoy life; **das** *or* **sein ~ verlieren** to lose one's life; **jdm das ~ retten** to save sb's life; **es geht um ~ und Tod, es ist eine Sache auf ~ und Tod** it's a matter of life and death; **wenn dir dein ~ lieb ist** if you value your life; **ein glückliches** *etc* **~ führen** to lead a happy *etc* life; **mit dem ~ davonkommen** to escape with one's life; **mit dem ~ spielen, sein ~ aufs Spiel setzen** to take one's life in one's hands, to dice with death; **mit dem ~ abschließen** to prepare for death; **einer Sache** (*dat*) **zu neuem ~ verhelfen** to breathe new life into sth, to revitalize sth; **etw ins ~ rufen** to bring sth into being; **jdn vom ~ zum Tode bringen** (*form*) *or* **befördern** (*inf*) to kill sb, to take sb's life, to take care of sb (*inf*); (*bei Hinrichtung auch*) to put sb to death; **seines ~s nicht mehr sicher sein** to fear for one's life; **ums ~ kommen** to die, to lose one's life; **sein ~ lassen (müssen)** to lose one's life; **jdn am ~ lassen** to spare sb's life; **um sein ~ laufen** *or* **rennen** to run for one's life *or* for dear life; **sich** (*dat*) **das ~ nehmen** to take one's (own) life; **jdn wieder ins ~ zurückrufen** to bring sb back to life; *Bewußtlosen* to revive sb, to bring sb round; **was ist das für ein ~?** what kind of (a) life is that?; **der Mann/die Frau meines ~s** my ideal man/woman; **etw für sein ~ gern tun** to love doing sth, to be mad about doing sth (*inf*); **etw für sein ~ gern essen/trinken** to be mad about sth (*inf*), to love sth; **jdn künstlich am ~ erhalten** to keep sb alive artificially; **ein ~ in Frieden/in Armut** *etc* a life of peace/poverty *etc*; **er hat es nie leicht gehabt im ~** he has never had an easy life; **ein ~ lang** one's whole life (long); **zum erstenmal** *or* **das erstemal im ~** for the first time in one's life; **ich habe noch nie im** *or* **in meinem ~ geraucht** I have never smoked (in) all my life *or* in my whole life; **nie im ~!** never!; **sich durchs ~ schlagen** to struggle through (life); **ins ~ treten** to go out into the world; **im ~ stehen** to have some standing in the world; (*nicht weltfremd sein*) to know what life is all about; **(draußen) im ~ ist das ganz anders** in real life it's very different; **ein Roman, den das ~ schrieb** a novel of real life; **ein Film nach dem ~** a film from real life; **das ~ geht weiter** life goes on; **unser ~ währet siebenzig Jahr ...** (*Bibl*) the days of our years are three score years and ten (*Bibl*); **so ist das ~ (eben)** that's life, such is life, that's the way the cookie crumbles (*inf*).
(b) (*Betriebsamkeit*) life ♦ **auf dem Markt herrscht reges ~** the market is a hive of activity; **in dieser Stadt ist wenigstens ~** at least there is some life in this town; **~ in etw** (*acc*) **bringen** (*inf*) to liven *or* brighten sth up; **voller ~ stecken** to be full of life; **es war überhaupt kein ~ in seinem Vortrag** there wasn't a spark of life in his lecture.

leben [1] *vi* (*alle Bedeutungen*) to live; (*am Leben sein*) to be alive; (*weiter~*) to live on ♦ **er lebt noch/nicht mehr** he is still/is no longer alive; **er hat nicht lange gelebt** he didn't live (for) long; **ich möchte nicht mehr ~** I don't want to go on living; **er wird nicht mehr lange zu ~ haben** he won't live much longer; **von etw ~** to live on sth; **es/lang lebe der König!** long live the King!; **so wahr ich lebe!** (*obs*) 'pon my life! (*obs*); **wie geht es dir? — man lebt (so)** (*inf*) how are you? — surviving; **lebst du noch?** (*hum inf*) are you still in the land of the living? (*hum*); **genug zu ~ haben** to have enough to live on; **~ und ~ lassen** to live and let live; **so was lebt, und Schiller mußte sterben!** (*hum inf*) some mothers do have 'em (*inf*), it's a sad case (*inf*); **zum L~ zu wenig, zum Sterben zuviel, davon kann man nicht ~ und nicht sterben** it's barely enough to keep body and soul together; **man lebt nur einmal!** you only live once; **einsam/christlich/gesund ~** to live *or* lead a lonely/Christian/healthy life; **allein/glücklich ~** to live alone/happily; **ganz für sich ~** to live a secluded life; **für etw ~, einer Sache** (*dat*) **~** (*geh*) to live for sth; **leb(e) wohl!** (*liter*) farewell! (*liter*); **hier lebt es sich gut** *or* **läßt es sich (gut) ~** it's a good life here; *siehe* **hoch, Ehe.**
[2] *vt* to live ♦ **jeder muß sein eigenes Leben ~** we've all got our own lives to live *or* lead.

lebend *adj* live *attr*, alive *pred*; *Wesen, Seele, Beispiel, Sprache* living ♦ **„Vorsicht, ~e Tiere"** "with care, live animals"; **ein noch ~er Zeuge** a witness who is still alive *or* living today; **ein Tier ~ fangen** to catch an animal alive; **~es Inventar** livestock; **die L~en** the living; **~es Bild** tableau.

Lebend-: ⚠l~gebärend *adj* viviparous, live-bearing; **~geburt** *f* live-birth; **~gewicht** *nt* live weight; (*von Rindern auch*) weight on the hoof.

lebendig *adj* **(a)** (*nicht tot*) live *attr*, alive *pred*; *Wesen* living ♦ **~e Junge** live young; **~e Junge gebären** to bear one's young live; **die L~en und die Toten** (*Bibl*) the Quick and the Dead (*Bibl*); **er ist dort ~ begraben** (*fig inf*) it's a living death for him there; **jdn bei ~em Leibe** *or* **jdn ~en Leibes** (*liter*) **verbrennen** to burn sb alive; **wieder ~ werden** to come back to life; **er nimmt's von den L~en** (*hum inf*) he'll have the shirt off your back (*inf*), it's daylight robbery what he charges (*inf*).
(b) (*fig: lebhaft*) lively *no adv*; *Darstellung, Szene, Bild, Erinnerung auch* vivid; *Glaube* deep, fervent.

Lebendigkeit *f, no pl* (*fig*) *siehe adj (b)* liveliness; vividness; depth, fervour.

Lebens-: ~abend *m* old age, autumn *or* twilight of one's life (*liter*); **~abschnitt** *m* phase in *or* of one's life; **~ader** *f* (*fig*) lifeline; **~alter** *nt* age; **ein hohes ~alter erreichen** to have a long life; (*Mensch auch*) to reach a ripe old age (*inf*); **~angst** *f* angst; **~anschauung** *f* philosophy of life; **~arbeitszeit** *f* working life; **~arbeitszeitverkürzung** *f* shortening of one's working life; **~art** *f, no pl* **(a)** *siehe* **~weise**; **(b)** (*Manieren*) manners *pl*; (*Stil*) style, savoir-vivre; **eine feine/kultivierte ~art haben** to have exquisite manners/style/to be cultivated; **~auffassung** *f* attitude to life; **~aufgabe** *f* life's work; **~baum** *m* (*Bot*) arbor vitae; (*fig, Art*) tree of life; **~bedingungen** *pl* living conditions *pl*; **l~bedrohend** *adj* life-threatening; **l~bejahend** *adj* positive; **eine l~bejahende Einstellung** a positive approach to life; **~bejahung** *f* positive attitude to life; **~berechtigung** *f* right to exist; (*von Menschen, Tieren auch*) right to live; **~bereich** *m* area of life; **~beschreibung** *f* biography; **~bild** *nt* (*fig*) picture of sb's life; **~dauer** *f* life(span); (*von Maschine*) life; **l~echt** *adj* true-to-life; **~elixier** *nt* elixir of life; **~ende** *nt* end of sb's/(one's) life, end; **~erfahrung** *f* experience of life; **l~erhaltend** *adj Geräte* life-support *attr*; **~erhaltungssystem** *nt* life-support system; **~erinnerungen** *pl* memoirs *pl*; **~erwartung** *f* life expectancy; **l~fähig** *adj* (*Med*) capable of life *or* of living, viable; (*fig*) capable of surviving, viable; **~fähigkeit** *f* (*Med*) ability to live, viability; (*fig*) ability to survive, viability; **~form** *f* (*Biol*) life-form; (*Psych, Philos*) form of life, type of man; (*Form menschlichen Zusammenlebens*) way of life; **~frage** *f* vital matter; **l~fremd** *adj* remote from *or* out of touch with life; **~freude** *f* joie de vivre, zest for life; **l~freudig** *adj* **l~freudig sein** to enjoy life; **l~froh** *adj* merry, full of the joys of life; **~führung** *f* life-style; **~gefahr** *f* (mortal) danger; **„~gefahr!"** "danger"; **es besteht ~gefahr** there is danger (to life); **er ist** *or* **schwebt in ~gefahr** his life is in danger, he is in danger of his life; (*Patient*) he is in a critical condition; **außer ~gefahr sein** to be out of danger; **etw unter ~gefahr** (*dat*) **tun** to risk one's life doing sth; **der Film wurde unter ~gefahr gedreht** the film was made at great personal risk to the crew; **l~gefährlich** *adj* highly dangerous; *Krankheit, Verletzung* critical; **~gefährte** *m*, **~gefährtin** *f* longtime companion, companion through life (*liter*); **~gefühl** *nt, no pl* feeling of being alive; **ein ganz neues ~gefühl haben** to feel (like) a different person; (*neuen Auftrieb haben*) to have a new lease of life; **~geister** *pl* (*hum inf*) **jds/seine ~geister auffrischen** *or* **wecken** to pep sb/oneself up (*inf*), to put some life into sb/oneself; **~gemeinschaft** *f* long-term relationship; (*Biol, Zool*) symbiosis; **⚠~genuß** *m* enjoyment of life; **~geschichte** *f* life-story, life-history; **~gewohnheit** *f* habit; **l~groß** *adj* lifesize; **~größe** *f* lifesize; **eine Figur in ~größe** a lifesize figure; **etw in ~größe malen** to paint sth lifesize; **da stand er in voller ~größe** (*hum*) there he was (as) large as life (and twice as ugly) (*inf*); **er erhob sich zu seiner vollen ~größe** (*hum*) he drew himself up to his full height; **~haltung** *f* **(a)** (*Unterhaltskosten*) cost of living; **(b)** (*~führung*) lifestyle.

Lebenshaltungs-: ~index *m* cost-of-living index; **~kosten** *pl* cost of living *sing*.

▼ **Lebens-: ~hilfe** *f* counselling; **er mißversteht Literatur als ~hilfe** he makes the mistake of thinking that literature can help him with the problems of life; **~hunger** *m* thirst for life; **l~hungrig** *adj* eager *or* thirsty for life; **~inhalt** *m* purpose in life, raison d'être; **etw zu seinem ~inhalt machen** to devote oneself to sth, to make sth one's mission in life; **das ist sein ganzer ~inhalt** his whole life revolves round it, it's the be-all and end-all of his existence; **~jahr** *nt* year of (one's) life; **in seinem fünften ~jahr** in the fifth year of his life; **nach Vollendung des 18. ~jahres** on attaining the age of 18; **~kamerad** *m siehe* **~gefährte**; **~kampf** *m* struggle for life *or* existence; **l~klug** *adj* streetwise; **~kraft** *f* vitality; **~kreis** *m* (*Lebensbereich*) sphere of life; **~künstler** *m* master *or* expert in the art of living; **er ist ein echter ~künstler** he really knows how to live *or* to enjoy life; **~lage** *f* situation; **in jeder ~lage** in any situation; **l~lang** *adj Freundschaft, Siechtum* lifelong; *Haft, Gefangenschaft* life *attr*, for life; **~lang** *nt* **-,** *no pl* life (sentence); **l~länglich** *adj Rente, Strafe* for life; *Gefangenschaft auch* life *attr*; **ein ~länglicher** (*inf*) a lifer (*sl*); **sie hat „l~länglich"** *or* **~länglich bekommen** (*inf*) she got life (*inf*); **l~länglich im Zuchthaus** *or* **hinter Gittern sitzen** (*inf*) to be inside for life *or* behind bars for life (*inf*); **~lauf** *m* life; (*bei Bewerbungen*) curriculum vitae, résumé (*US*); **~licht** *nt* **(a)** (*fig*) flame of life (*liter*); **jdm das ~licht ausblasen** *or* **auslöschen** (*liter*) to snuff out sb's life; **(b)** (*als Geburtstagskerze*) candle; **~linie** *f* lifeline; **~lüge** *f* sham existence; **mit einer ~lüge leben** to live a lie; **~lust** *f* zest for life, joie de vivre; **l~lustig** *adj* in love with life; **~mitte** *f* middle years *pl*; **die Krise in der ~mitte** the mid-life crisis.

Lebensmittel *pl* food *sing*, food(stuff)s *pl* (*form*); (*als Kaufware auch*) groceries *pl*.

Lebensmittel-: ~chemie *f* food chemistry; **l~gerecht** *adj* suitable for putting food in; **~geschäft** *nt* grocer's (shop); **~gesetz** *nt* food law; **~karte** *f* food ration-card; **~vergiftung** *f* food poisoning.

Lebens-: l~müde *adj* weary *or* tired of life; **ein ~müder** a potential suicide; **~müdigkeit** *f* weariness *or* tiredness of life; **~mut** *m* courage to face life; **l~nah** *adj* true-to-life; **~nerv** *m* (*fig*) **eine Industrie/eine Stadt an ihrem ~nerv treffen** to cripple an industry/a town; **der Tourismus ist der ~nerv Mallorcas** tourism is Majorca's lifeblood; **l~notwendig** *adj* essential, vitally necessary; *Organ, Sauerstoff etc* vital (for life), essential for life; **~notwendigkeit** *f* necessity of life, essential; **~ordnung** *f* way of life; (*Eccl*) canons and ordinances *pl* (*of the German Protestant Church*); **~pfad** *m*,

➤ SPRACHE AKTIV: **Lebenslauf** → 46.2

no pl (*liter*) path of (one's/sb's) life; **~philosophie** *f* philosophy of life; **~qualität** *f* quality of life; **~raum** *m* (*Pol*) lebensraum; (*Biol*) habitat; **~regel** *f* rule (of life); **~reise** *f, no pl* (*liter*) journey through life; **~retter** *m* rescuer; **du bist mein ~retter** you've saved my life; **~rettungsmedaille** *f* lifesaving medal; **~standard** *m* standard of living; **~stellung** *f* job for life; **~stil** *m* lifestyle, style of life; **l~tüchtig** *adj* able to cope with life; **⚠~überdruß** *m* weariness with life, world-weariness; **~umstände** *pl* circumstances *pl*; **damals waren die ~umstände schwierig** conditions made life difficult in those days; **~unterhalt** *m* **(a) seinen ~unterhalt verdienen** to earn one's living; **sie verdient den ~unterhalt für die Familie** she is the breadwinner of the family, she supports the family; **für jds ~unterhalt sorgen** to support sb; **etw zu seinem ~unterhalt tun** to do sth for a living *or* livelihood; **nur das Nötigste zum ~unterhalt haben** to have just enough to live on; **(b)** (*Unterhaltskosten*) cost of living; **l~untüchtig** *adj* unable to cope with life; **l~verlängernd** *adj Maßnahme* life-prolonging; **l~verneinend** *adj* negative; **eine l~verneinende Einstellung** a negative approach to life; **~versicherung** *f* life assurance *or* insurance; **eine ~versicherung abschließen** to take out a life assurance *or* insurance policy; **~wandel** *m* way of life; **einen einwandfreien/zweifelhaften** *etc* **~wandel führen** to lead an irreproachable/a dubious *etc* life; **~weg** *m* journey through life; **den gemeinsamen ~weg antreten** to begin one's life together; **alles Gute für den weiteren** *or* **ferneren ~weg** every good wish for the future; **~weise** *f* way of life; **~weisheit** *f* maxim; (*~erfahrung*) wisdom; **~wende** *f* (*geh*) turning-point in (one's/sb's) life; **~werk** *nt* life's work, lifework; **l~wert** *adj* worth living; **l~wichtig** *adj* essential, vital; *Organ, Bedürfnisse* vital; **l~wichtige Verbindungslinie** vital link, lifeline; **~wille** *m* will to live; **~zeichen** *nt* sign of life; **kein ~zeichen mehr von sich geben** to show no sign(s) of life; **~zeit** *f* life(time); **auf ~zeit** for life; **Beamter auf ~zeit** permanent civil servant; **Mitglied auf ~zeit** life member; **~ziel** *nt* goal *or* aim in life; **~zweck** *m* purpose in life.

Leber *f* **-, -n** liver ♦ **ich habe es mit der ~ zu tun** *or* **an der ~** (*inf*) I've got liver trouble; **frei** *or* **frisch von der ~ weg reden** (*inf*) to speak out *or* frankly; **sich** (*dat*) **etw von der ~ reden** (*inf*) to get sth off one's chest; *siehe* **Laus**.

Leber-: ~blümchen *nt* liverwort; **~entzündung** *f* hepatitis, inflammation of the liver; **~fleck** *m* mole; (*Hautfärbung*) liver spot; **~haken** *m* (*Sport*) hook to the liver; **~käs(e)** *m, no pl* ≃ meat loaf; **~knödel** *m* liver dumpling; **l~krank** *adj* suffering from a liver disorder; **~krebs** *m* cancer of the liver; **~leiden** *nt* liver disorder; **~pastete** *f* liver pâté; **~tran** *m* cod-liver oil; **~wert** *m* liver function reading; **~wurst** *f* liver sausage; *siehe* **beleidigt**.

Lebewesen *nt* living thing ♦ **kleinste ~** micro-organisms.

Lebewohl *nt* **-s,** *no pl* (*liter*) farewell (*liter*) ♦ **die Stunde des ~s** the hour of farewell; **jdm ~ sagen** to bid sb farewell *or* adieu.

lebhaft *adj* **(a)** (*voll Leben, rege*) lively *no adv*; *alter Mensch auch* sprightly; *Temperament auch* vivacious; *Gespräch, Streit auch* animated; (*Comm*) *Geschäfte auch* brisk; *Verkehr* brisk ♦ **es geht ~ zu** it is *or* things are lively; **das Geschäft geht ~** business is brisk *or* lively; **die Börse schloß ~** business was brisk *or* lively on the Stock Exchange at the close of the day.
(b) (*deutlich*) *Erinnerung, Vorstellungsvermögen* vivid; (*einfallsreich*) *Phantasie* lively ♦ **ich kann mir ~ vorstellen, daß** ... I can (very) well imagine that ...; **in ~er Erinnerung bleiben** to remain a vivid memory; **etw in ~er Erinnerung haben** to remember sth vividly.
(c) (*kräftig*) *Muster, Interesse, Beifall* lively; *Farben auch* bright ♦ **~ bedauern** to regret deeply, to be really sorry about.

Lebhaftigkeit *f siehe adj* **(a)** liveliness; sprightliness; vivaciousness; animation; briskness. **(b)** vividness; liveliness. **(c)** liveliness; brightness.

Leb-: ~kuchen *m* gingerbread; **l~los** *adj Körper, Augen* lifeless; *Straße auch* empty, deserted; **l~loser Gegenstand** inanimate object; **~losigkeit** *f siehe adj* lifelessness; emptiness; **~tag** *m* (*inf*) **mein/dein** *etc* **~tag** all my/your *etc* life, all my/your *etc* born days; **das habe ich mein ~tag noch nicht gesehen** *etc* I've never seen the like (of it) in all my life *or* in all my born days; **das werde ich mein ~tag nicht vergessen** I'll never forget that as long as I live; **~zeiten** *pl* **zu jds ~zeiten** (*Leben*) while sb is/was alive, in sb's lifetime; (*Zeit*) in sb's day; **schon zu ~zeiten eine Legende** a legend in his/her own lifetime.

lechzen *vi* (*Hund*) to pant, to have its tongue hanging out ♦ **nach etw ~** to thirst for *or* crave sth, to long for sth; **mit ~der Zunge** with one's tongue hanging out; *siehe* **Blut**.

Lecithin [lɛtsi'tiːn] *nt* **-s,** *no pl* lecithin.

leck *adj* leaky ♦ **~ sein** to leak; **~ schlagen** to hole.

Leck *nt* **-(e)s, -s** leak.

Leckage [le'kaːʒə] *f* **-, -n (a)** (*Gewichtsverlust*) leakage. **(b)** (*Leck*) leak.

Lecke *f* **-, -n** (*Hunt*) saltlick.

lecken¹ *vi* (*undicht sein*) to leak.

lecken² *vti* to lick ♦ **an jdm/etw ~** to lick sb/sth; **sich** (*dat*) **die Wunden ~** to lick one's wounds; *siehe* **Arsch, Finger, geleckt**.

lecker *adj Speisen* delicious, lovely, yummy (*inf*); (*inf*) *Mädchen* lovely, delectable.

Leckerbissen *m* **(a)** (*Speise*) delicacy, titbit. **(b)** (*fig*) gem.

Leckerei *f* **(a)** *siehe* **Leckerbissen (a)**. **(b)** (*Süßigkeit*) dainty.

Lecker-: ~maul, ~mäulchen *nt* (*inf*) sweet-toothed child/person *etc*; **ein ~maul sein** to have a sweet tooth.

leckschlagen *vti sep irreg siehe* **leck**.

Leckstein *m* licking stone.

LED [ɛl|eːdeː] *f* **-, -s** LED.

led. *abbr of* **ledig**.

⚠: for details of spelling reform, see supplement

Leder *nt* **-s, - (a)** leather; (*Fenster~ auch*) chamois, chammy; (*Wild~*) suede ♦ **in ~ gebunden** leather-bound; **zäh wie ~** as tough as old boots (*inf*); **vom ~ ziehen** (*inf*) to let rip (*inf*) *or* fly (*inf*).
(b) (*dated inf: Haut*) hide (*inf*) ♦ **jdm das ~ gerben** *or* **versohlen** to tan sb's hide; **jdm ans ~ wollen** to want to get one's hands on sb.
(c) (*inf: Fußball*) ball ♦ **am ~ bleiben** to stick with the ball.

Leder- *in cpds* leather; **l~artig** *adj Stoff* leather-like; **~band** *m* (*Buch*) leather-bound volume; **~fett** *nt* dubbin; **~garnitur** *f* leather-upholstered suite; **~haut** *f* (*Anat*) dermis (*spec*), derma (*spec*); (*um den Augapfel*) sclera (*spec*); **~hose** *f* lederhosen *pl*, leather/suede trousers *pl or* pants *pl*; (*von Tracht*) leather shorts *pl*; (*Bundhose*) leather breeches *pl*; **~jacke** *f* leather/suede jacket; **~mantel** *m* leather coat.

ledern [1] *adj* **(a)** (*aus Leder*) leather. **(b)** (*zäh*) *Fleisch, Haut* leathery; (*fig*) *Vortrag etc* dry (as dust).
[2] *vt* **(a)** (*gerben*) to tan. **(b)** (*putzen*) to leather.

Leder-: ~nacken *pl* leathernecks *pl*; **~rücken** *m* (*von Buch*) leather spine; **~schurz** *m* leather apron; **~waren** *pl* leather goods *pl*; **~zeug** *nt* leather gear; (*Mil*) leathers *pl*.

ledig *adj* **(a)** (*unverheiratet*) single; (*inf*) *Mutter* unmarried; *Kind* illegitimate. **(b)** (*geh: unabhängig*) free ♦ **(los und) ~ sein** to be footloose and fancy free; **aller Pflichten** (*gen*) **(los und) ~ sein** to be free of all commitments.

Ledige(r) *mf decl as adj* single person.

lediglich *adv* merely, simply.

Lee *f* **-,** *no pl* (*Naut*) lee ♦ **in ~ liegen** to be on the lee side; **nach ~ drehen** to turn to leeward.

leer *adj* empty; *Blätter, Seite auch* blank; *Gesichtsausdruck, Blick* blank, vacant ♦ **der ~e Raum** (*geh*) the cosmos; **eine ~e Stelle** an empty space; **vor einem ~en Haus** *or* **vor ~en Bänken spielen** (*Theat*) to play to an empty house; **ins L~e starren/treten** to stare/step into space; **ins L~e greifen** to clutch at thin air; **mit ~en Händen** (*fig*) empty-handed; **eine Zeile ~ lassen** to leave a line (blank *or* free); **~ laufen** (*Motor*) to idle; (*Maschine*) to run idle; (*Betrieb etc*) to be idle; **etw ~ machen** to empty sth; **den Teller ~ essen** to eat everything on the plate; **~ stehen** to stand empty; **einen Laden ~ kaufen** to buy a shop out.

Leere *f* **-,** *no pl* (*lit, fig*) emptiness ♦ **(eine) geistige ~** a mental vacuum; **(eine) gähnende ~** a yawning *or* gaping void.

leeren *vt* to empty; (*völlig auch*) to drain; *Briefkasten auch* to clear ♦ **jdm die Taschen ~** (*inf*) to clean sb out (*inf*).

Leer-: ~formel *f* empty phrase; **l~gefegt** *adj* (*fig*) **(wie) l~gefegt** *Straßen, Stadt etc* deserted; **~gewicht** *nt* unladen weight, tare; (*von Behälter*) empty weight of a container; **~gut** *nt* empties *pl*; **~lauf** *m* **(a)** (*Aut*) neutral; (*von Fahrrad*) freewheel; **im ~lauf fahren** to coast; **das Auto ist im ~lauf** the engine is in neutral; (*stehend mit laufendem Motor*) the engine is idling; **(b)** (*fig*) slack; **⚠l~laufen** *vi sep irreg aux sein* (*Faß etc*) to run dry; **l~laufen lassen** to empty, to drain; **~packung** *f* (empty) display package, dummy; **~position** *f* (*St Ex*) short position; **⚠l~stehend** *adj* empty; **~taste** *f* (*bei Schreibmaschine*) space-bar.

Leerung *f* emptying ♦ **die ~ der Mülltonnen erfolgt wöchentlich** the dustbins (*Brit*) *or* garbage cans (*US*) are emptied once a week; **nächste ~: 18 Uhr** (*an Briefkasten*) next collection (*Brit*) *or* pickup (*US*): 6 p.m.

Leerverkauf *m* (*St Ex*) short sale.

Lefze *f* **-, -n** *usu pl* chaps *pl*; (*von Pferd*) lip.

legal *adj* legal, lawful.

legalisieren* *vt* to legalize.

legalistisch *adj* legalistic.

Legalität *f* legality ♦ **(etwas) außerhalb der ~** (*euph*) (slightly) outside the law.

Legasthenie *f* dyslexia.

Legastheniker(in *f***)** *m* **-s, -** dyslexic.

legasthenisch *adj* dyslexic.

Legat¹ *nt* (*Jur*) legacy.

Legat² *m* **-en, -en** (*Eccl, Hist*) legate.

Legation *f* legation.

Legationsrat *m* counsellor to a legation.

Legato *nt* **-(s), -s** *or* **Legati** (*Mus*) legato.

Legebatterie *f* hen battery.

Leg(e)henne *f*, **Leg(e)huhn** *nt* layer, laying hen.

Legel *m* **-s, -** (*Naut*) cringle, grummet.

legen [1] *vt* **(a)** (*lagern*) to lay down; (*mit adv*) to lay; *Flasche etc* to lay on its side; (*zusammen~*) *Wäsche* to fold; (*dial*) *Kartoffeln etc* to plant, to put in; (*Sport*) to bring down.
(b) (*mit Raumangabe*) to put, to place ♦ **wir müssen uns ein paar Flaschen Wein in den Keller ~** we must lay down a few bottles of wine; **etw beiseite ~** to put sth aside *or* (*weglegen*) away; **etw in Essig** *etc* **~** to preserve sth in vinegar *etc*; **ein Tier an die Kette ~** to chain an animal (up); **jdn in Ketten/Fesseln ~** to put sb in chains, to chain sb; (*fig hum*) to (en)snare sb.
(c) (*mit Angabe des Zustandes*) **etw in Falten ~** to fold sth; **er legte die Stirn in Falten** he frowned, he creased his brow; **eine Stadt in Schutt und Asche ~** to reduce a town to rubble.
(d) (*verlegen*) *Fliesen, Leitungen, Schienen, Minen etc* to lay, to put down; *Bomben* to plant ♦ **Feuer** *or* **einen Brand ~** to start a fire; **sich** (*dat*) **die Haare ~ lassen** to have one's hair set; **sich** (*dat*) **Dauerwellen** *etc* **~ lassen** to have a perm *etc*, to have one's hair permed *etc*.
(e) *auch vi* (*Hühner*) to lay.
[2] *vr* **(a)** (*hin~*) to lie down (*auf +acc* on) ♦ **sich ins** *or* **zu** (*geh*) **Bett ~** to go to

bed, to retire (*form*); **sich in die Sonne ~** to lie in the sun; **leg dich!** (*zum Hund*) lie!; *siehe* **schlafen.**

(b) (*mit Ortsangabe*) (*nieder~*) (*Nebel, Rauch*) to settle (*auf +acc* on) ◆ **sich auf die Seite ~** to lie on one's side; (*Boot*) to heel over, to go over onto its side; **sich in die Kurve ~** to lean into the corner; **sich auf ein Spezialgebiet ~** to concentrate on *or* specialize in a particular field.

(c) (*Lärm*) to die down, to abate; (*Sturm, Wind auch, Kälte*) to let up; (*Rauch, Nebel*) to clear; (*Zorn, Begeisterung auch, Arroganz, Nervosität*) to wear off; (*Anfangsschwierigkeiten*) to sort themselves out ◆ **das Fieber legt sich bald** his *etc* temperature will come down/the fever will lessen soon.

legendär *adj* legendary; (*obskur*) apocryphal ◆ **er/das ist schon fast ~** he/it has already become almost legendary.

Legende *f* **-, -n** (*alle Bedeutungen*) legend ◆ **sich** (*dat*) **eine ~ zulegen** to assume a false identity.

legenden|umwoben *adj* fabled, surrounded by legends.

leger [le'ʒeːɐ, le'ʒɛːɐ] *adj* casual, informal.

Legezeit *f* laying season *or* time.

Legföhre *f siehe* **Latschenkiefer.**

Leggings, Leggins *pl* leggings *pl.*

Leghenne *f siehe* **Leg(e)henne.**

legieren* *vt* (a) *Metall* to alloy. (b) (*Cook*) *Suppe etc* to thicken.

Legierung *f* alloy; (*Verfahren*) alloying.

Legion *f* legion ◆ **die Zahl der Toten war ~** (*geh*) the number of the dead was legion (*liter*).

Legionär *m* legionary, legionnaire.

Legionärskrankheit *f* Legionnaire's disease.

legislativ *adj* legislative.

Legislative *f* legislature, legislative assembly *or* body.

Legislatur *f* (a) (*rare: Gesetzgebung*) legislation; (*obs: gesetzgebende Gewalt*) legislature. (b) (*inf*) *siehe* **Legislaturperiode.**

Legislaturperiode *f* parliamentary/congressional term.

legitim *adj* legitimate.

Legitimation *f* identification; (*Berechtigung*) authorization; (*eines Kindes*) legitimation.

legitimieren* [1] *vt Beziehung, Kind* to legitimize; (*berechtigen*) to entitle; (*berechtigt erscheinen lassen*) to justify, to warrant; (*Erlaubnis geben*) to authorize.

[2] *vr* to show (proof of) authorization; (*sich ausweisen*) to identify oneself, to show proof of one's identity.

Legitimität *f, no pl* legitimacy.

Legostein ® *m* Lego ® brick.

Leguan *m* **-s, -e** iguana.

Lehen *nt* **-s, -** (*Hist*) fief, feoff, feu (*Scot*) ◆ **jdm ein Gut zu ~ geben** to enfeoff sb.

Lehens- *in cpds siehe* **Lehns-.**

Lehm *m* **-(e)s, -e** loam; (*Ton*) clay.

Lehm-: ~bau *m*, **~bauweise** *f* clay building; **~boden** *m* clay soil; **l~farben, l~farbig** *adj* clay-coloured; **~hütte** *f* mud hut.

lehmig *adj* loamy; (*tonartig*) claylike, clayey.

Lehm-: ~packung *f* mudpack; **~ziegel** *m* clay brick.

Lehn *nt* **-s, -** *siehe* **Lehen.**

Lehnbildung *f* (*Ling*) loan formation.

Lehne *f* **-, -n** (a) (*Arm~*) arm(-rest); (*Rücken~*) back(-rest). (b) (*old, S Ger: Berghang*) slope.

lehnen [1] *vt* to lean (*an +acc* against).

[2] *vi* to be leaning (*an +dat* against).

[3] *vr* to lean (*an +acc* against, *auf +acc* on) ◆ **„nicht aus dem Fenster ~!"** (*Rail*) "do not lean out of the window".

Lehnsdienst *m* (*Hist*) vassalage.

Lehnsessel *m siehe* **Lehnstuhl.**

Lehns-: ~herr *m* (*Hist*) feudal lord; **~mann** *m*, *pl* **-männer** *or* **-leute** (*Hist*) vassal; **~pflicht** *f* (*Hist*) feudal duty.

Lehnstuhl *m* easy-chair.

Lehnswesen *nt* (*Hist*) feudal system, feudalism.

Lehn-: ~übersetzung *f* (*Ling*) loan-translation; **~wort** *nt* (*Ling*) loan-word, borrowing.

Lehramt *nt* **das ~** the teaching profession; **ein/sein ~ ausüben** to hold a teaching post; **Prüfung für das höhere ~** examination for secondary school teachers; **sein ~ ernst nehmen** (*Univ*) to take one's teaching responsibilities seriously.

Lehramts-: ~anwärter, ~kandidat *m* prospective teacher; **~studium** *nt* teacher training.

Lehr-: ~anstalt *f* (*form*) educational establishment; **höhere ~anstalt** establishment of secondary education; **~auftrag** *m* (*als Sonderlehrer*) special teaching post; **einen ~auftrag für etw haben** (*Univ*) to give lectures on sth; **l~bar** *adj* teachable; **~barkeit** *f* teachability; **~beauftragte(r)** *mf* (*Univ*) **~beauftragter für etw sein** to give lectures on sth; **~befähigung** *f* teaching qualification; **~behalt** *m* (*Aus*) *siehe* **~mittel**; **~berechtigung** *f* **jdm die ~berechtigung erteilen** to register sb as a teacher; **ihm wurde die ~berechtigung entzogen** he was struck off the register of teachers; **für Latein hat er keine ~berechtigung** he isn't qualified to teach Latin; **~beruf** *m* (a) (*als Lehrer*) teaching profession; **den ~beruf ergreifen** to go into teaching; (b) (*Beruf mit ~zeit*) trade requiring an apprenticeship, skilled trade; **~betrieb** *m* (*Univ*) teaching; **~brief** *m* (a) (*Zeugnis*) apprenticeship certificate; (b) (*Lektion*) correspondence lesson; **~bub, ~bursche** *m* (*dial*) *siehe* **Lehrling**; **~buch** *nt* textbook; **l~buchgerecht** *adj* (a) **die l~buchgerechte Bearbeitung eines Textes** the editing of a text for a school edition; (b) (*gutausgeführt*) text-book *attr*, perfect; **~dichtung** *f* didactic poetry.

Lehre *f* **-, -n** (a) (*das Lehren*) teaching.

(b) (*von Christus, Buddha, Marx etc*) teachings *pl*; (*christlich, buddhistisch, marxistisch etc*) (*Lehrmeinung*) doctrine; (*das Lehren*) teaching; (*von Galilei, Kant, Freud etc*) theory; (*von Schall, Leben etc*) science ◆ **die christliche ~** Christian doctrine/teaching.

(c) (*negative Erfahrung*) lesson; (*Ratschlag*) (piece of) advice; (*einer Fabel*) moral ◆ **seine ~(n) aus etw ziehen** to learn a lesson from sth; (*aus einer Fabel etc*) to draw a moral from sth; **laß dir das eine ~ sein, laß es dir zur ~ dienen!** let that be a lesson to you!

(d) (*dated*) (*Berufs~*) apprenticeship; (*in nichthandwerklichem Beruf*) training ◆ **bei jdm die ~ (durch)machen** *or* **in die ~ gehen** to serve one's apprenticeship with *or* under sb; **du kannst bei ihm noch in die ~ gehen** (*fig*) he could teach you a thing or two.

(e) (*Tech*) gauge; (*Muster*) template.

lehren *vti* to teach; (*Univ auch*) to lecture (*ein Fach* in a subject) ◆ **die Wissenschaft lehrt, daß ...** science tells us that ...; **jdn** *or* **jdm** (*inf*) **lesen** *etc* **~** to teach sb to read *etc*; **die Zukunft wird es ~** time (alone) will tell; **ich werde dich ~, so frech zu antworten!** I'll teach you to answer back! (*inf*).

Lehrer(in *f*) *m* **-s, -** teacher; (*Privat~, Nachhilfe~ auch*) tutor; (*Flug~, Fahr~ etc*) instructor/instructress ◆ **er ist ~** he's a (school)teacher; **~ für Philosophie/Naturwissenschaften** teacher of philosophy/science; (*in der Schule*) philosophy/science teacher.

Lehrer|ausbildung *f* teacher training.

Lehrerin *f siehe* **Lehrer.**

Lehrer-: ~kollegium *nt* (teaching)staff; **in diesem ~kollegium** amongst the teaching staff of this school; **~mangel** *m* teacher shortage; **~schaft** *f* (*form*) (teaching) staff; **~schwemme** *f* surplus of teachers; **~seminar** *nt* (*für Referendare, inf: Pädagogische Hochschule*) teacher training college; (*Kurs*) in-service course for teachers; **~zimmer** *nt* staff (*esp Brit*) *or* teachers' room.

Lehr-: ~fach *nt* subject; **~film** *m* educational film; **~freiheit** *f* freedom to teach what one sees fit; **~gang** *m* course (*für* in); **~gebäude** *nt* (*fig*) system of theories; (*Eccl*) doctrinal system; **~gegenstand** *m* subject; **~geld** *nt* (*Hist*) (apprenticeship) premium; **(teures) ~geld für etw zahlen müssen** (*fig*) to pay dearly for sth; **laß dir dein ~geld zurückgeben!** (*hum inf*) go to the bottom of the class! (*hum inf*); **~gerüst** *nt* centring; **l~haft** *adj* didactic; **~herr** *m* master (of an apprentice); **~jahr** *nt* year as an apprentice; **~jahre sind keine Herrenjahre** (*Prov*) life's not easy at the bottom; **~junge** *m siehe* **Lehrling**; **~kanzel** *f* (*Aus*) *siehe* **~stuhl**; **~körper** *m* (*form*) teaching staff; (*Univ auch*) academic staff; **~kraft** *f* (*form*) teacher.

Lehrling *m* (*dated*) apprentice; (*in nichthandwerklichem Beruf*) trainee.

Lehr-: ~mädchen *nt* (*dated*) *siehe* **Lehrling**; **~meinung** *f* opinion; (*von einer bestimmten Gruppe vertreten*) school of thought; (*Eccl*) doctrine; **~meister** *m* master; **seinen ~meister finden** to meet one's master; **du bist mir ein schöner ~meister** you're a fine example; **~methode** *f* teaching method; **~mittel** *nt* teaching aid; *pl auch* teaching materials; **~plan** *m* (teaching) curriculum; (*für ein Schuljahr*) syllabus; **~probe** *f* demonstration lesson, crit (*inf*); **~programm** *nt* teaching programme; **l~reich** *adj* (*informativ*) instructive; *Erfahrung* educational; **~satz** *m* (*Math, Philos*) theorem; (*Eccl*) dogma; **~schwimmbecken** *nt* beginners' *or* teaching pool; **~stelle** *f* position for *or* (*aus Sicht des Lehrlings*) as an apprentice/a trainee; **wir haben zwei ~stellen zu vergeben** we have vacancies for two apprentices; **~stoff** *m* subject; (*eines Jahres*) syllabus; **das ist ~stoff der dritten Klasse** that's on the syllabus for the third year; **~stuhl** *m* (*Univ*) chair (*für* of); **jdn auf einen ~stuhl berufen** to offer sb a chair; **~tochter** *f* (*Sw*) *siehe* **Lehrling**; **~verhältnis** *nt* contractual relationship (*between apprentice and master/trainee and employer*); **in einem ~verhältnis stehen** (*form*) to be apprenticed (*bei* to); **~vertrag** *m* indentures *pl*; contract as a trainee; **~werk** *nt* (*form*) textbook; (*Buchreihe*) series of textbooks; **~werkstatt** *nt* training workshop; **~zeit** *f* apprenticeship.

Leib *m* **-(e)s, -er** (a) (*Körper*) body ◆ **der ~ des Herrn** (*Eccl*) the Body of Christ; **Gefahr für ~ und Leben** (*geh*) danger to life and limb; **~ und Leben wagen** (*geh*) to risk life and limb; **mit ~ und Seele** heart and soul; *wünschen* with all one's heart; **mit ~ und Seele singen/dabei sein** to sing one's heart out/put one's heart and soul *or* one's whole heart into it; **etw am eigenen ~(e) erfahren** *or* **(ver)spüren** to experience sth for oneself; **kein Hemd mehr am ~ haben** to be completely destitute; **keinen trockenen Faden am ~ haben** (*inf*) to be soaked to the skin (*inf*); **der hat vielleicht einen Ton am ~!** (*inf*) talk about rude!; **am ganzen ~(e) zittern/frieren/schwitzen** to shake/freeze/sweat all over; **sich** (*dat*) **alles an den ~ hängen** (*inf*) to spend everything on clothes; **die Rolle ist ihr wie auf den ~ geschrieben** the part is tailor-made for her; **der Beruf ist ihr wie auf den ~ geschnitten** that job is tailor-made for her *or* suits her to a T (*inf*); **kein Herz im ~e haben** to have no heart at all, to be completely heartless; **sich** (*dat*) **jdn/etw vom ~e halten** to keep *or* hold sb/sth at bay; **halt ihn mir vom ~** keep him away from me; **jdm vom ~ bleiben** to keep away from sb; **geh mir vom ~!** get away (from) me!; (*laß mich in Ruhe*) get off my back! (*inf*); **bleib mir damit vom ~e!** (*inf*) stop pestering me with it (*inf*); *siehe* **rücken.**

(b) (*old, dial: Bauch*) stomach; (*Mutter~*) womb ◆ **ich habe noch nichts im ~e** I haven't eaten yet.

Leib-: ~arzt *m* personal physician; **~binde** *f* truss; (*nach Geburt*) abdominal binder.

Leibchen *nt* **(a)** (*old*) bodice. **(b)** (*Unterhemd*) vest (*Brit*), undershirt (*US*); (*Hemdchen*) top.

Leib-: l~eigen *adj siehe* **Leibeigenschaft** unfree, in bondage; serf *attr*; villein *attr*; **l~eigen sein** not to be a free man/woman; to be a serf/villein; **~eigene(r)** *mf decl as adj* bond(s)man/bond(s)woman; serf; villein; **er behandelt seine Frau wie eine ~eigene** he treats his wife as though she were one of his possessions; **~eigenschaft** *f* bondage; (*im Mittelalter*) serfdom; (*von Höhergestellten, mit Eigentum*) villeinage.

leiben *vi*: **wie er leibt und lebt** to the life, to a T (*inf*).

Leibes-: ~erziehung *f* physical education; **~frucht** *f* (*geh*) unborn child, fruit of (one's/sb's) womb (*poet*); **~kraft** *f*: **aus ~kräften schreien** *etc* to shout *etc* with all one's might (and main); **~übung** *f* (physical) exercise; **~übungen** (*Schulfach*) physical education *no pl*; **~visitation** *f* body check; (*Mil*) physical inspection, medical.

Leib-: ~garde *f* (*Mil*) bodyguard; **die ~garde der englischen Königin** the Queen's Guards *pl*; **~gardist** *m* soldier of a bodyguard; (*Brit*) lifeguard; **~gericht** *nt* favourite meal.

leibhaft (*rare*), **leibhaftig** [1] *adj* personified, incarnate ◆ **die ~e Güte** *etc* goodness *etc* personified *or* incarnate; **(wie) der ~e Teufel** *or* **der L~e** (as) the devil himself.
[2] *adv* in person, in the flesh.

Leibkoch *m* personal chef.

leiblich *adj* **(a)** (*körperlich*) physical, bodily ◆ **die ~en Genüsse** the pleasures of the flesh; **die ~e Hülle** (*geh*) the mortal remains *pl*. **(b)** *Mutter, Vater* natural; *Kind* by birth; *Bruder, Schwester* full; *Verwandte* blood; (*emph: eigen*) (very) own.

Leib-: ~pacht *f* (*old*) life tenancy, lease for life; **~rente** *f* life annuity; **~riemen** *m* (*old*) belt; **~schmerzen** *pl* (*old, dial*) stomach pains *pl*; **~speise** *f* favourite food; **~wache** *f* bodyguard; **~wächter** *m* bodyguard; **~wäsche** *f* underwear, underclothes *pl*; **~weh** *nt* (*old*) stomach-ache.

Leich *m* **-(e)s, -e** (*Liter*) lay.

Leiche *f* **-, -n (a)** body, corpse; (*menschlich auch*) stiff (*sl*); (*inf: Bier~, Schnaps~*) drunken body (*inf*) ◆ **die Insassen konnten nur noch als ~n geborgen werden** the passengers were dead when the rescuers arrived; **eine lebende** *or* **wandelnde ~** (*inf*) a corpse; **wie eine lebende** *or* **wandelnde ~ aussehen** to look like death (warmed up *inf*); **er geht über ~n** (*inf*) he'd stick at nothing, he'd sell his own grandmother (*inf*); **nur über meine ~!** (*inf*) over my dead body!
(b) (*S Ger*) (*Beerdigung*) funeral; (*Leichenschmaus*) funeral meal ◆ **die ~ begießen** (*inf*) to drink the dead man's health.
(c) (*Typ*) omission.

Leichen-: ~begängnis (*form*), **~begräbnis** *nt* funeral; **~beschauer** *m* **-s, -** doctor conducting a post-mortem; **~bittermiene** *f* (*inf*) mournful *or* doleful expression; **⚠l~blaß** *adj* deathly pale, as pale as death; **~fledderei** *f* robbing of dead people; **das ist die reinste ~fledderei** (*fig*) what vultures!; **~fledderer** *m* **-s, -** person who robs dead people; (*fig*) vulture; **~frau** *f* layer-out; **~halle** *f*, **~haus** *nt* mortuary; **~hemd** *nt* shroud; **~konservierung** *f* preservation of corpses; **~öffnung** *f* autopsy; **~rede** *f* funeral oration (*liter*) *or* address; **~schändung** *f* desecration of corpses; (*sexuell*) necrophilia; **~schau** *f* post-mortem (examination); **~schauhaus** *nt* morgue; **~schmaus** *m* funeral meal; **~starre** *f* rigor mortis *no art*; **~tuch** *nt* shroud; **~verbrennung** *f* cremation; **~wagen** *m* hearse; **~zug** *m* funeral procession.

Leichnam *m* **-s, -e** (*form*) body.

leicht [1] *adj* **(a)** (*von geringem Gewicht, nicht schwerfällig, Mil*) light; (*aus ~em Material*) *Koffer, Kleidung* lightweight ◆ **einen ~en Gang haben** to have an easy walk; **mit ~er Hand** lightly; (*fig*) effortlessly; **eine ~e Hand mit jdm/für etw haben** to have a way with sb/sth; **~en Fußes** (*liter*) with a spring in one's step; **~ zu tragen** light; **gewogen und zu ~ befunden** (*fig*) tried and found wanting; **jdn um einiges ~er machen** to relieve sb of some of his money; **das Haus/Auto ist ~ gebaut** the house is built of light materials/the car is lightly built; **ein zu ~ gebautes Haus/Auto** a flimsily built house/car; **~ bekleidet sein** to be scantily clad *or* dressed; **~ gekleidet sein** to be (dressed) in light clothes; *siehe* **Feder**.
(b) (*schwach, geringfügig, nicht wichtig*) slight; *Regen, Wind, Frost, Schläge, Schlaf, Berührung, Atmen* light; (*Jur*) *Diebstahl, Vergehen etc* minor, petty ◆ **~ gewürzt/gesalzen** lightly seasoned/salted; **zu ~ gewürzt/gesalzen** not seasoned/salted enough; **~ waschen** to wash gently.
(c) (*von geringem Gehalt*) *Essen, Musik, Lektüre etc* light.
(d) (*ohne Schwierigkeiten, einfach*) easy ◆ **~er Absatz** (*Comm*) quick turnover (*von* in); **mit dem werden wir (ein) ~es Spiel haben** he'll be a pushover (*inf*) *or* walkover (*inf*), he'll be no problem; **keinen ~en Stand haben** not to have an easy time (of it) (*bei, mit* with); **sie hat es immer ~ gehabt (im Leben)** she's always had it easy *or* had an easy time of it; **man hat's nicht ~, aber ~ hat's einen** (*inf*) it's a hard life; **das ist** *or* **geht ganz ~** it's quite easy *or* simple; **das ist ihr ein ~es** (*geh*) that will present no problem to *or* for her; **nichts ~er als das!** nothing (could be) easier *or* simpler; **die Aufgabe ist ~ zu lösen** *or* **läßt sich ~ lösen** the exercise is easy to do; **~ zu beantworten/verstehen** easily answered/understood, easy to answer/understand; **er ist ~ herumzukriegen/zu überzeugen** he's easy to win round/convince, he's easily won round/convinced; **~ begreifen** to understand quickly *or* readily; **mach es dir nicht zu ~** (*bequem*) don't make things too easy for yourself; (*sei gewissenhaft auch*) don't take the easy way out; (*vereinfache es nicht*) don't over-simplify things; **das ist ~er gesagt als getan** that's easier said than done; **du hast ~ reden/lachen** it's all very well *or* it's all right for you to talk/laugh.
(e) (*moralisch locker*) *Lebenswandel* loose ◆ **~es Mädchen** tart (*inf*).
(f) (*unbeschwert*) *Herz, Gefühl* light ◆ **etw ~en Herzens** *or* **Sinnes tun** to do sth with a light heart; **sich ~ und beschwingt fühlen** to be walking on air, to be up in the clouds; **mir ist so ~ ums Herz** my heart is so light; **mir ist jetzt viel ~er** I feel a lot easier now; **nimm das nicht zu ~** don't take it too lightly.
[2] *adv* (*schnell, unversehens*) easily ◆ **er wird ~ böse/ist ~ beleidigt** *etc* he is quick to get angry/take offence *etc*, he gets angry/takes offence *etc* easily; **~ zerbrechlich** very fragile; **man kann einen Fehler ~ übersehen** it's easy to miss a mistake, mistakes are easily missed; **das ist ~ möglich** that's quite possible; **das kann ich mir ~ vorstellen** *or* **denken** I can easily *or* well imagine (it); **~ entzündlich sein** (*Gas, Brennstoff*) to be highly inflammable; (*Haut*) to become easily inflamed; **man hat ~ etwas gesagt, was man nachher bereut** it's easy to say something (without thinking) that you regret later; **das passiert mir so ~ nicht wieder** I won't let that happen again in a hurry (*inf*); **das passiert mir so ~ nicht wieder, daß ich dir Geld borge** I won't lend you money again in a hurry (*inf*).

Leicht-: ~athlet *m* (track and field) athlete; **~athletik** *f* (track and field) athletics; **l~athletisch** [1] *adj* athletic *attr*; [2] *adv* as regards (track and field) athletics; **~baustoff** *m* lightweight building material; **~bau(weise** *f*) *m* lightweight construction; **in ~bauweise** using lightweight materials; **~benzin** *nt* benzine; **⚠l~beschwingt** *adj attr Musik* light; **l~beschwingte Melodien** melodies for easy listening; **~beton** *m* lightweight concrete; **⚠l~bewaffnet** *adj attr* lightly armed; **⚠l~entzündlich** *adj attr Brennstoff etc* highly inflammable; **l~entzündliche Haut** skin which easily becomes inflamed.

Leichter *m* **-s, -** (*Naut*) lighter.

leichtern *vt* (*Naut*) to lighten (*form*).

Leicht-: ⚠l~fallen *vi sep irreg aux sein* to be easy (*jdm* for sb); **Sprachen sind mir schon immer l~gefallen** I've always found languages easy; **l~fertig** *adj* thoughtless; (*moralisch*) easygoing; **l~fertig handeln** to act without thinking; **etw l~fertig aufs Spiel setzen** to risk sth without giving it a thought; **~fertigkeit** *f siehe adj* thoughtlessness; easygoing nature; **l~flüssig** *adj attr* (easily) fusible; **~fuß** *m* (*old*): **(Bruder) ~fuß** adventurer; **l~füßig** *adj* (*liter*) light-footed; **l~gängig** *adj Getriebe* smooth; *Motor auch* smooth-running; **⚠l~geschürzt** *adj attr* (*hum*) scantily clad *or* dressed; **~gewicht** *nt* (*Sport, fig*) lightweight; **Weltmeister im ~gewicht** world lightweight champion; **~gewichtler** *m* **-s, -** (*Sport*) lightweight; **~gewichtsklasse** *f* lightweight class; **l~gläubig** *adj* credulous; (*leicht zu täuschen*) gullible; **~gläubigkeit** *f siehe adj* credulity; gullibility.

Leichtheit *f siehe adj* **(a)** lightness. **(b)** slightness; lightness. **(c)** lightness. **(d)** easiness.

leichtherzig *adj* light-hearted.

leichthin *adv* lightly.

Leichtigkeit *f* ease ◆ **mit ~** easily, with no trouble (at all).

Leicht-: ~industrie *f* light industry; **~kraftrad** *nt* moped; **l~lebig** *adj* happy-go-lucky, easygoing; **~lebigkeit** *f* happy-go-lucky *or* easygoing nature; **~lohngruppe** *f group of (usually female) workers paid less than workers in comparable jobs*; **⚠l~machen** *vt sep* **jdm etw l~machen** to make sth easy for sb; **sich** (*dat*) **etw l~machen, sich** (*dat*) **es mit etw l~machen** (*es sich bequem machen*) to make things easy for oneself with sth; (*nicht gewissenhaft sein*) to take it easy with sth; (*vereinfachen*) to over-simplify sth; **er machte es sich** (*dat*) **leicht und vermied eine Entscheidung** he took the easy way out and avoided making a decision; **~matrose** *m* ordinary seaman; **~metall** *nt* light metal; **⚠l~nehmen** *vt sep irreg* **etw l~nehmen** (*nicht ernsthaft behandeln*) to take sth lightly; (*sich keine Sorgen machen*) not to worry about sth; **~öl** *nt* light oil.

Leichtsinn *m* (*unvorsichtige Haltung*) foolishness; (*Unbesorgtheit, Sorglosigkeit*) thoughtlessness ◆ **sträflicher ~** criminal negligence; **unverzeihlicher ~** unforgivable stupidity; **das ist (ein) ~** that's foolish *or* silly; **so ein ~!** how silly/thoughtless (can you get)!

leichtsinnig *adj* foolish; (*unüberlegt*) thoughtless ◆ **~ mit etw umgehen** to be careless with sth.

Leichtsinnigkeit *f siehe adj* foolishness; thoughtlessness.

Leichtsinnsfehler *m* careless mistake, slip.

Leicht-: ⚠l~verdaulich *adj attr* easily digestible; **⚠l~verderblich** *adj attr* perishable; **⚠l~verletzt** *adj attr* slightly injured; (*in Gefecht etc auch*) slightly wounded; **~verletzte(r)** *mf decl as adj* slightly injured/wounded person; **⚠l~verständlich** *adj attr* readily *or* easily understandable; **⚠l~verwundet** *adj attr* slightly wounded; **~verwundete(r)** *mf decl as adj* slightly wounded soldier *etc*; **die ~verwundeten** the walking wounded; **~wasserreaktor** *m* light water reactor.

▼ **leid** *adj pred* **(a) etw tut jdm ~** sb is sorry about *or* for sth; **es tut jdm ~, daß ...** sb is sorry that ...; **tut mir ~!** (I'm) sorry!; **es tut mir ~, daß ich so spät gekommen bin** I'm sorry for coming so late *or* (that) I came so late; **es tut mir nur ~, daß ...** I'm only sorry that ..., my only regret is that ..., I only regret that ...; **es tut uns ~, Ihnen mitteilen zu müssen ...** we regret to have to inform you ...; **es tut einem ~, zu sehen, wie ...** it makes you feel sorry when you see how ...; **er/sie tut mir ~** I'm sorry for him/her, I pity him/her; **er/sie kann einem ~ tun** you can't help feeling sorry *or* you can't (help) but feel sorry for him/her; **du kannst einem ~ tun** you really are to be pitied; **es kann einem ~ tun, wenn ...** you can't help feeling sorry when ...; **es tut mir um ihn/darum ~** I'm sorry about him/that; **das wird dir noch ~ tun** you'll regret it, you'll be sorry.
(b) (*überdrüssig*) **jdn/etw ~ sein** to be tired of sb/sth; **das lange Warten bin**

⚠: for details of spelling reform, see supplement

➤ SPRACHE AKTIV: **leid: a** → 39.3, 45.1, 45.3, 48.1

ich ~ geworden I'm tired of all this waiting.

Leid *nt* **-(e)s,** *no pl* **(a)** (*Kummer, Sorge*) sorrow, grief *no indef art*; (*Unglück*) misfortune; (*Böses, Schaden*) harm ◆ **jdm in seinem tiefen ~ beistehen** to stand by sb in his/her (hour of) affliction *or* sorrow; **um jdn ~ tragen** (*geh*) to mourn sb; **ihm ist großes ~ widerfahren** he has suffered great misfortune; **viel ~ erfahren/ertragen (müssen)** to suffer/have to suffer a great deal; **es soll dir kein ~ geschehen** *or* **zugefügt werden** you will come to no harm, no harm will come to you; **jdm ein ~ antun** (*liter*) to harm sb; (*moralisch*) to wrong sb, to do sb wrong; **jdm sein ~ klagen** to tell sb one's troubles, to cry on sb's shoulder; *siehe* **antun.**
(b) (*Sw: Begräbnis*) funeral.
(c) (*Sw: Trauerkleidung*) mourning ◆ **(um jdn) ~ tragen, im ~ sein** to wear mourning (for sb), to be in mourning.

Leideform *f* (*Gram*) passive (voice).

leiden *pret* **litt,** *ptp* **gelitten** [1] *vt* **(a)** (*ertragen müssen*) *Schaden, Hunger, Schmerz, Unrecht etc* to suffer ◆ **viel zu ~ haben** to have a great deal to bear *or* endure.
(b) (*geh: zulassen, dulden*) to allow, to permit, to suffer (*old*) ◆ **er ist bei allen wohl gelitten** everybody holds him in high regard *or* great esteem.
(c) ich kann *or* **mag ihn/es** *etc* **(gut) ~** I like him/it *etc* (very much); **ich kann** *or* **mag ihn/es** *etc* **nicht (gut) ~** I don't like him/it *etc* very much, I'm not very fond of him/it *etc.*
[2] *vi* to suffer (*an +dat, unter +dat* from) ◆ **die Farbe hat durch die grelle Sonne sehr gelitten** the harsh sun hasn't done the paint any good; *siehe* **leidend.**

Leiden *nt* **-s, - (a)** suffering; (*Kummer auch*) tribulation ◆ **das sind (nun mal) die Freuden und ~ des Lebens!** ah, the ups and downs *or* the trials and tribulations of life!; **du siehst aus wie das ~ Christi** (*inf*) you look like death warmed up (*inf*).
(b) (*Krankheit*) illness; (*Beschwerden*) complaint ◆ **das ist ja eben das ~!** (*inf*) that's just the trouble.
(c) (*hum inf: Mensch*) **ein langes ~** a beanpole (*inf*).

-leiden *nt in cpds* complaint, condition.

leidend *adj* (*kränklich*) ailing; (*inf*) *Miene* long-suffering ◆ **~ aussehen** to look ill; **sich ~ fühlen** (*form*) to feel ill.

Leidende(r) *mf decl as adj* sufferer ◆ **die ~n** the afflicted *pl.*

Leidenschaft *f* passion ◆ **seine ~ für etw entdecken** to develop a passion for sth; **etw mit ~ tun** to do sth with passionate enthusiasm; **ich koche mit großer ~** cooking is a great passion of mine, **er ist Lehrer aus ~** he teaches for the love of it.

leidenschaftlich *adj* passionate; *Liebhaber auch* ardent; *Rede auch* impassioned ◆ **etw ~ gern tun** to be mad about (*inf*) *or* passionately fond of doing sth.

Leidenschaftlichkeit *f* passion; (*im Beruf*) dedication; (*bei Hobby*) burning enthusiasm.

leidenschaftslos *adj* dispassionate.

Leidens-: ~druck *m, no pl* mental trauma; **~gefährte** *m,* **~gefährtin** *f,* **~genosse** *m,* **~genossin** *f* fellow-sufferer; **~geschichte** *f* tale of woe; **die ~geschichte (Christi)** (*Bibl*) Christ's Passion; **~miene** *f* (*hum inf*) (long-)suffering expression; **~weg** *m* life of suffering; **Christi ~weg** Christ's suffering; **seinen ~weg gehen** to bear one's cross.

▼ **leider** *adv* unfortunately ◆ **~ Gottes ja!, ja ~!** (yes,) more's the pity (*inf*), I'm afraid so, yes, unfortunately; **~ (Gottes) nein/nicht!** unfortunately not, I'm afraid not, no, worse luck (*inf*); **ich kann ~ (Gottes) nicht kommen** unfortunately *or* I'm afraid I can't come.

leidgeprüft *adj* sorely afflicted.

leidig *adj attr* tiresome ◆ **wenn bloß das ~e Geld nicht wäre** if only we didn't have to worry about money.

leidlich [1] *adj* reasonable, fair.
[2] *adv* reasonably ◆ **wie geht's? — danke, ~!** how are you? — not too bad *or* all right, thanks; **sie ist noch so ~ davongekommen** she didn't come out of it too badly.

Leidtragende(r) *mf decl as adj* **(a)** (*Hinterbliebener eines Verstorbenen*) bereaved ◆ **ein ~r** a bereaved person. **(b)** (*Benachteiligter*) **der/die ~** the sufferer, the one to suffer.

Leidwesen *nt*: **zu jds ~** (much) to sb's disappointment *or* chagrin.

Leier *f* **-, -n (a)** (*Mus*) lyre; (*Dreh~*) hurdy-gurdy ◆ **es ist immer dieselbe** *or* **die alte** *or* **die gleiche ~** (*inf*) it's always the same old story. **(b)** (*Astron*) Lyra.

Leierkasten *m* barrel-organ, hurdy-gurdy.

Leierkastenmann *m, pl* **-männer** organ-grinder.

leiern [1] *vt Drehorgel* to grind, to play; (*inf: kurbeln*) to wind; (*inf*) *Gedicht, Gebete* to drone (out).
[2] *vi* (*Drehorgel spielen*) to grind *or* play a barrel-organ; (*inf: drehen*) to crank (*an etw* (*dat*) sth); (*inf: beim Beten, Gedichteaufsagen*) to drone.

Leierschwanz *m* lyrebird.

Leih-: ~arbeit *f, no pl* casual labour; **~arbeiter** *m* casual worker; **~auto** *nt* hire(d) car; **~bibliothek, ~bücherei** *f* lending library.

Leihe *f* **-, -n** (*das Verleihen*) lending; (*das Vermieten*) hiring; (*das Verpfänden*) pawning; (*inf: Leihhaus*) pawnshop ◆ **etw in ~** *or* **in die ~** (*inf*) **geben** to pawn *or* pop (*inf*) sth; **etw in ~ nehmen** to take sth in pawn.

leihen *pret* **lieh,** *ptp* **geliehen** *vt Geld* to lend; *Sachen auch* to loan; (*von jdm ent~*) to borrow; (*mieten, aus~*) to hire ◆ **ich habe es (mir) geliehen** I've borrowed/hired it, I've got it on loan/hire; **jdm seinen Beistand/sein Ohr/seine Aufmerksamkeit ~** (*geh*) to lend sb one's support/one's ear/one's attention.

Leih-: ~flasche *f* returnable bottle; **~gabe** *f* loan; **dieses Bild ist eine ~gabe der Tate Gallery** this picture is on loan from the Tate Gallery; **~gebühr** *f* hire *or* rental charge; (*für Buch*) lending charge; **~haus** *nt* pawnshop; **~mutter** *f* surrogate mother; **~mutterschaft** *f* surrogate motherhood, surrogacy; **~schein** *m* (*in der Bibliothek*) borrowing slip; (*im ~haus*) pawn ticket; **~schwangerschaft** *f* surrogate pregnancy; **~stimme** *f* (*Pol*) tactical vote; **~verkehr** *m* **ein Buch über den auswärtigen ~verkehr bestellen** to order a book on inter-library loan; **im ~verkehr erhältlich** available on loan; **~wagen** *m* hire(d) car; **l~weise** *adv* on loan.

Leim *m* **-(e)s, -e** glue; (*zum Vogelfangen*) (bird)lime ◆ **jdn auf den ~ führen** *or* **locken** (*inf*) to take sb in; **jdm auf den ~ gehen** *or* **kriechen** (*inf*) to be taken in by sb; **aus dem ~ gehen** (*inf*) (*Sache*) to fall apart *or* to pieces; (*Mensch*) to lose one's figure.

leimen *vt* (*zusammenkleben*) to glue (together); (*mit Leim bestreichen*) to spread with glue; (*zum Vogelfangen*) to lime; (*inf*) *Ehe* to patch up (*inf*) ◆ **jdn ~** (*inf*) to take sb for a ride (*inf*); **der Geleimte** the mug (*inf*).

Leimfarbe *f* distemper.

leimig *adj* sticky, gluey.

Leimrute *f* lime twig.

Leimung *f, no pl* sizing.

Lein *m* **-(e)s, -e** flax.

Leine *f* **-, -n** cord; (*Tau, Zelt~*) rope; (*Schnur*) string; (*Angel~, Wäsche~, Naut*) line; (*Hunde~*) lead, leash ◆ **Hunde bitte an der ~ führen!** dogs should *or* must be kept on a leash; **den Hund an die ~ nehmen** to put the dog on the lead; **jdn an der ~ halten** *or* **haben** (*inf*) to keep sb on a tight rein; **jdn an die ~ legen** to hook sb (*inf*), to drag sb to the altar (*inf*); **jdn an die lange ~ legen** to give sb his/her head; **~ ziehen** (*sl*) to clear out (*sl*), to push off (*inf*).

leinen *adj* linen; canvas; cloth.

Leinen *nt* **-s, -** linen; (*grob, segeltuchartig*) canvas; (*als Bucheinband*) cloth.

Leinen- *in cpds* linen; canvas; cloth; **~band** *m* cloth(-bound) volume; **ein Buch als ~band haben** to have the cloth-bound edition of a book; **~schlafsack** *m* sheet sleeping bag; **~tasche** *f* canvas bag; **~tuch** *nt* linen (cloth); (*grob, segeltuchartig*) canvas; **~zeug** *nt* linen.

Leineweber *m* linen weaver.

Leineweberei *f* (*Fabrik*) linen mill; (*Herstellung*) linen weaving.

Lein-: ~kraut *nt* toadflax; **~öl** *nt* linseed oil; **~pfad** *m* towpath; **~samen** *m* linseed; **~tuch** *nt* (*S Ger, Aus, Sw*) sheet.

Leinwand *f* **-,** *no pl* canvas; (*Film, für Dias*) screen ◆ **wenn der Film über die ~ läuft** when the film is being shown *or* screened; **Dias auf die ~ werfen** to show *or* project slides.

leise *adj* **(a)** quiet; *Stimme, Schritt, Klopfen auch* soft; *Radio auch* low; (*aus der Ferne*) faint ◆ **auf ~n Sohlen** treading softly; **das Radio (etwas) ~r stellen** to turn the radio down (slightly); **... sagte er mit ~r Stimme** ... he said in a low voice *or* quietly; **sprich doch ~r!** keep your voice down a bit.
(b) (*gering, schwach*) slight, faint; *Schlaf, Regen, Berührung* light; *Wind, Wellenschlag* light, gentle ◆ **nicht die ~ste Ahnung haben** not to have the slightest *or* faintest *or* foggiest (*inf*) (idea); **ich habe nicht die ~ste Veranlassung, ...** there isn't the slightest *or* faintest reason why I ...
(c) (*sanft, zart*) soft, gentle; *Musik* soft.

Leisetreter *m* **-s, -** (*pej, inf*) pussyfoot(er) (*pej, inf*); (*Duckmäuser*) creep (*pej inf*).

Leiste *f* **-, -n (a)** (*Holz~ etc*) strip (of wood/metal *etc*); (*Zier~*) trim; (*Umrandung*) border; (*zur Bilderaufhängung, zur Führung von Arbeitsstücken etc*) rail; (*Scheuer~*) skirting (board), baseboard (*US*). **(b)** (*Anat*) groin.

leisten *vt* **(a)** (*erringen, erreichen*) to achieve; *Arbeit, Überstunden* to do; (*Maschine, Motor*) to manage ◆ **etwas/viel/nichts ~** (*Mensch*) (*arbeiten*) to do something/a lot/nothing; (*schaffen auch*) to get something/a lot/nothing done; (*vollbringen*) to achieve something/a great deal/nothing; (*Maschine*) to be quite good/very good/no good at all; (*Auto, Motor etc*) to be quite powerful/very powerful/have no power; **Großartiges/Erstaunliches/Überragendes** *etc* **~** to do *or* achieve something really great/amazing/excellent; **gute/ganze Arbeit ~** to do a good/thorough job; **in meiner Position muß ich schon etwas ~** in my position I have to do my work and do it well; **er leistet genau soviel wie ich** he's just as efficient as I am; **was eine Mutter alles ~ muß** the things that a mother has to cope with; **er hat immer das Gefühl, nichts zu ~** he always has the feeling that he isn't doing a good job; **seine Arbeit ~** to do one's work well; **ich muß genauso meine Arbeit ~ wie jeder andere auch** I've got my job to do like everybody else.
(b) *in festen Verbindungen mit n siehe auch dort* **(jdm) Beistand/Hilfe ~** to lend (sb) one's support/give sb some help; **jdm gute Dienste ~** (*Gegenstand*) to serve sb well; (*Mensch*) to be useful to sb; **Folge ~** to comply (*dat* with); **Zahlungen ~** to make payments; **jdm eine Garantie/Gewähr ~** to give sb a guarantee (*für/auf etw* (*acc*) for/on sth, *dafür, daß* ... that ...).
(c) sich (*dat*) **etw ~** to allow oneself sth; (*sich gönnen*) to treat oneself to sth; (*kaufen*) to buy sth; **sich** (*dat*) **etw ~ können** to be able to afford sth; **sich** (*dat*) **eine Frechheit/Frechheiten ~** to be cheeky *or* impudent; **er leistete sich die Frechheit, ungebeten zu erscheinen** he had the cheek *or* effrontery to turn up uninvited; **da hast du dir ja was (Schönes** *or* **Nettes) geleistet** (*iro*) you've really done it now; **er hat sich tolle Sachen/Streiche geleistet** he got up to the craziest things/pranks.

Leisten *m* **-s, -** (*Schuh~*) last ◆ **alle/alles über einen ~ schlagen** (*fig*) to measure everyone/everything by the same yardstick; *siehe* **Schuster.**

Leisten-: ~bruch *m* (*Med*) hernia, rupture; **~gegend** *f* inguinal region (*form*), groin.

Leistung *f* **(a)** (*Geleistetes*) performance; (*großartige, gute, Sociol*) achieve-

➤ SPRACHE AKTIV: **leider** → 36.3, 39.2, 39.3, 45.3, 47.2, 47.4, 48.3, 52.4, 52.5

ment; (*Ergebnis*) result(s); (*geleistete Arbeit*) work *no pl* ◆ **eine große ~ vollbringen** to achieve a great success; **das ist eine ~!** that's quite *or* really something (*inf*) *or* quite an achievement *or* quite a feat; **das ist keine besondere ~** that's nothing special; **nach ~ bezahlt werden** to be paid on results; **nicht das Geschlecht, nur die ~ zählt** your sex isn't important, it's how you do the job that counts; **das liegt weit unter der üblichen ~** that is well below the usual standard; **die ~en sind besser geworden** the levels of performance have improved; (*in Fabrik, Schule auch*) the standard of work has improved; **seine schulischen/sportlichen ~en haben nachgelassen** his school work/athletic ability has deteriorated; **er ist auf seine sportlichen ~en stolz** he's proud of his athletic achievement(s); **eine ~ der Technik** a feat of engineering; **schwache ~!** poor show! (*dated inf*), that's not very good.
(b) (*~sfähigkeit*) capacity; (*eines Motors, einer Energiequelle*) power; (*einer Fabrik, Firma*) potential output.
(c) (*Jur*) (*Übernahme einer Verpflichtung*) obligation; (*Zahlung*) payment ◆ **die ~en des Reiseveranstalters** what the travel company offers; **~ eines Ersatzes** obligation to provide a replacement.
(d) (*Aufwendungen*) (*einer Versicherung, Krankenkasse, sozial*) benefit; (*Dienst~*) service; (*Zahlungs~*) payment.

Leistungs-: ~abfall *m* (*in bezug auf Qualität*) drop in performance; (*in bezug auf Quantität*) drop in productivity; **~ausfall** *m* loss of productivity; **~bilanz** *f* (*einer Firma*) current balance including investments; (*eines Landes*) balance of payments including invisible trade; **~druck** *m* pressure (to do well); **~fach** *nt* (*Sch*) special subject; **l~fähig** *adj* (*konkurrenzfähig*) competitive; (*produktiv*) efficient, productive; *Motor* powerful; *Maschine* productive; (*Fin*) able to pay, solvent; *Mensch* able, capable; *Arbeiter* efficient; *Organe, Verdauungssystem etc* functioning properly; **~fähigkeit** *f siehe adj* competitiveness; efficiency, productivity; power(fulness); capacity; ability to pay, solvency; ability, capability; efficiency; capacity; **das übersteigt meine ~fähigkeit** that's more than I can manage; **l~feindlich** *adj* **hohe Steuern sind l~feindlich** high taxes inhibit productivity; **l~fördernd** *adj* conducive to efficiency; (*in Schule, Universität etc*) conducive to learning; **~gesellschaft** *f* meritocracy, achievement-orientated society (*pej*); **~grenze** *f* upper limit; **~klage** *f* (*Jur*) suit for fulfilment of obligations; **~klasse** *f* (*Sport*) class; **~kontrolle** *f* (*Sch, Univ*) assessment; (*in der Fabrik*) productivity check; **zur ~kontrolle** (in order) to assess progress/check productivity; **~kraft** *f* power; **eine hohe ~kraft haben** to be very powerful; **~kurs** *m* (*Sch*) set; **~kurve** *f* productivity curve; **~lohn** *m* piece rates *pl*; **~merkmal** *nt* performance feature; **~messer** *m* (*Phys*) power output meter; (*Elec*) wattmeter; **~messung** *f* assessment of achievement; (*in Fabrik*) measuring *or* assessment of productivity; (*Phys, Elec*) measurement of power; **~motivation** *f* achievement motivation; **l~orientiert** *adj* achievement-orientated; **~prämie** *f* productivity bonus; **~prinzip** *nt* achievement principle; **~prüfung** *f* (*Sch*) achievement test; (*Tech*) performance test; **~schau** *f* exhibition, show; **~sport** *m* competitive sport; **l~stark** *adj* (*konkurrenzfähig*) highly competitive; (*produktiv*) highly efficient *or* productive; *Motor* very powerful; *Maschine* highly productive; **~steigerung** *f siehe* **Leistung (a, b)** increase in performance/achievement *etc*; **~stufe** *f* (*Sch*) special subject class; **~test** *m siehe* **~prüfung**; **~vermögen** *nt* capabilities *pl*; **~wettkampf** *m* competition; **~wille** *m* motivation; **~zulage** *f*, **~zuschlag** *m* productivity bonus; **~zwang** *m* pressure to do well.

Leit-: ~artikel *m* leader; **l~artikeln*** *vti insep* (*inf*) to lead; **~artikler(in** *f***)** *m* **-s, -** leader-writer; **~bild** *nt* model; **~bündel** *nt* (*Bot*) vascular bundle.

leiten *vt* **(a)** (*in bestimmte Richtung lenken*) to lead; (*begleiten, führen auch*) to conduct; (*fig*) *Leser, Schüler etc* to guide; *Verkehr* to route; *Gas, Wasser* to conduct; (*um~*) to divert ◆ **etw an die zuständige Stelle ~** to pass sth on to the proper authority; **sich von jdm/etw ~ lassen** (*lit, fig*) to (let oneself) be guided by sb/sth; *von Vorstellung, Idee, Emotion, Gesichtspunkt* to be governed by sth; **das Öl wird (durch Rohre) zum Hafen geleitet** the oil is piped to the port.
(b) (*verantwortlich sein für*) to be in charge of; (*administrativ auch*) to run; *Expedition, Partei, Regierung, Bewegung etc auch* to lead, to head; *Betrieb auch* to manage; *Orchester, Theatergruppe etc* to direct, to run; *Sitzung, Diskussion, Gespräch, Verhandlungen* to lead; (*als Vorsitzender*) to chair; *Geschick(e)* to determine, to guide.
(c) (*Phys*) *Wärme, Strom, Licht* to conduct ◆ **(etw) gut/schlecht ~** to be a good/bad conductor (of sth).

leitend *adj* leading; *Gedanke, Idee* central, dominant; *Stellung, Position* managerial; *Ingenieur, Beamter* in charge; (*Phys*) conductive ◆ **nicht ~** (*Phys*) non-conductive; **~e(r) Angestellte(r)** executive; **ein ~er Beamter** a senior official; **die ~e Hand** (*fig*) the guiding hand.

Leiter[1] *f* **-, -n** (*lit, fig*) ladder; (*Steh~*) steps *pl*, stepladder; (*Sport*) wall-bars *pl* ◆ **an der ~ turnen** to work on the wall-bars.

Leiter[2] *m* **-s, -** **(a)** leader; (*von Hotel, Restaurant, Geschäft*) manager; (*Abteilungs~ in Firma*) head; (*von Schule*) head (*esp Brit*), principal (*esp US*); (*von Orchester, Chor, Theatergruppe etc*) director; (*von Kirchenchor*) choirmaster ◆ **kaufmännischer/künstlerischer ~** sales/artistic director.
(b) (*Phys*) conductor.

Leiterbahn *f* (*Comput*) strip conductor.

Leiterin *f siehe* **Leiter**[2] **(a)**.

Leiter-: ~platte *f* (*Comput*) circuit board; **~sprosse** *f* rung; **eine ~sprosse des Erfolgs höher kommen** to climb one rung higher up the ladder of success; **~wagen** *m* hand-cart.

Leit-: ~faden *m* (*fig*) main connecting thread *or* theme; (*Fachbuch*) introduction; (*Gebrauchsanleitung*) manual; **l~fähig** *adj* (*Phys*) conductive; **~fähigkeit** *f* (*Phys*) conductivity; **~feuer** *nt* beacon; **~fossil** *nt* index fossil; **~gedanke** *m* central idea; **er machte diesen Spruch zum ~gedanken seines Lebens** he made this saying his motto in life; **~gerade** *f* (*Math*) directrix; **~gewebe** *nt* (*Biol*) vascular tissue; **~hammel** *m* bellwether; (*fig inf*) leader, bellwether (*liter*); **~hund** *m* (*Hunt*) leader of the pack; **~idee** *f siehe* **~gedanke**; **~linie** *f* (*im Verkehr*) broken (white) line; (*fig*) broad outline; (*Bestimmung*) guideline; (*Math*) directrix; **~motiv** *nt* (*Mus, Liter, fig*) leitmotif; **~pfosten** *m* reflector post; **~planke** *f* crash-barrier; **~preis** *m* guide price; **~satz** *m* basic principle; **~schiene** *f* guide rail; **~spindel** *f* (*Tech*) lead screw; **~spruch** *m* motto; **~stelle** *f* regional headquarters *pl*; **~stern** *m* (*lit*) lodestar; (*fig auch*) guiding star; **~strahl** *m* (*Aviat, Mil, Space*) control beam; (*Math*) radius vector; **~tier** *nt* leader (*of a herd etc*); **~ton** *m* (*Mus*) leading note; **~trieb** *m* leader.

Leitung *f* **(a)** *no pl siehe vt (a)* leading; conducting; guiding; routing; conducting; diversion, diverting.
(b) *no pl* (*von Menschen, Organisationen etc*) *siehe vt (b)* running; leadership; management; direction; leadership; chairmanship; (*einer Schule*) headship (*esp Brit*), principalship (*esp US*) ◆ **die ~ einer Sache** (*gen*) **haben** to be in charge of sth/to run/lead/manage/direct/lead/chair sth; (*Sch*) to be the head *or* principal of sth; **unter der ~ von jdm** (*Mus*) conducted by sb; **die ~ des Gesprächs hat Horst Bauer** Horst Bauer is leading the discussion.
(c) (*die Leitenden*) leaders *pl*; (*eines Betriebes etc*) management *sing or pl*; (*einer Schule*) head teachers *pl*.
(d) (*für Gas, Wasser, Elektrizität etc bis zum Haus*) main; (*für Gas, Wasser im Haus*) pipe; (*für Elektrizität im Haus*) wire; (*dicker*) cable; (*Überlandleitung für Elektrizität*) line; (*Telefon~*) (*Draht*) wire; (*dicker*) cable; (*Verbindung*) line ◆ **die ~ ist ganz fürchterlich gestört** (*Telec*) it's a terrible line, there's a lot of interference on the line; **gehen Sie aus der ~!** (*inf*) get off the line; **da ist jemand in der ~** (*inf*) there's somebody else on the line; **eine lange ~ haben** (*hum, inf*) to be slow on the uptake, to be slow to catch on; **bei dir steht wohl jemand** *or* **du stehst wohl auf der ~** (*hum, inf*) you're slow on the uptake, you're slow to catch on.

Leitungs-: ~anästhesie *f* (*Med*) nerve-block *or* conduction anaesthesia; **~draht** *m* wire; **~mast** *m* (*Elec*) (electricity) pylon; **~netz** *nt* (*Elec*) (electricity) grid; (*für Wasser, Gas*) mains system; (*Telec*) (telephone) network; **~rohr** *nt* main; (*im Haus*) (supply) pipe; **~wasser** *nt* tapwater, mains water; **~widerstand** *m* (*Elec*) resistance.

Leit-: ~vermögen *nt* (*Phys*) conductivity; **~währung** *f* reserve currency; **~werk** *nt* (*Aviat*) tail unit, empennage (*spec*); **~wert** *m* conductance; **~wort** *nt* motto.

Leitzins *m* base rate.

Leitzins-: ~erhöhung *f* increase in the base rate; **~satz** *m* bank rate.

Leitz-Ordner ® *m* lever-arch file.

Lektion *f* lesson ◆ **jdm eine ~ erteilen** (*fig*) to teach sb a lesson.

Lektor *m*, **Lektorin** *f* (*Univ*) foreign language assistant, lector; (*Verlags~*) editor.

Lektorat *nt* (*im Verlag*) editorial office; (*Gutachten*) editorial report.

Lektüre *f* **-, -n** (*no pl: das Lesen*) reading; (*Lesestoff*) reading matter ◆ **das wird zur ~ empfohlen** that is recommended reading; **das ist eine gute/interessante** *etc* **~** it makes good/interesting *etc* reading, it's a good/an interesting *etc* read; **das ist eine schlechte ~** it doesn't make good reading, it's not a good read; **das ist keine (passende) ~ für dich/Kinder** that's not suitable reading for you/children, that's not suitable for you/children to read; **ich muß noch (etwas) leichte ~ besorgen** I've still got to get something light to read.

Lemma *nt* **-s, -ta** lemma.

Lemming *m* lemming.

Lende *f* **-, -n** (*Anat, Cook*) loin.

Lenden-: ~braten *m* loin roast; **~gegend** *f* lumbar region; **l~lahm** *adj* (*dated*) *Pferd* broken-backed; **er ist l~lahm** his back is crippling him; **~schurz** *m* loincloth; **~stück** *nt* piece of loin; **~wirbel** *m* lumbar vertebra.

Leninismus *m* Leninism.

Leninist(in *f***)** *m* Leninist.

leninistisch *adj* Leninist.

Lenk-: ~achse *f* pivoted axle; **l~bar** *adj* (*Tech*) steerable; *Kind* tractable; *Rakete* guided; **leicht/schwer l~bar sein** to be easy/difficult to steer, to have light/heavy steering; **das Kind ist leicht/schwer l~bar** the child can be easily guided/won't be guided; **~computer** *m* guide computer.

lenken *vt* **(a)** (*führen, leiten*) to direct, to guide; (*fig: beeinflussen*) *Sprache, Presse etc* to influence; *Kind* to guide ◆ **gelenkte Wirtschaft** planned economy.
(b) *auch vi* (*steuern*) *Auto, Flugzeug, Schiff etc* to steer; *Pferde* to drive ◆ **sich leicht ~ lassen** to be easy to steer/drive.
(c) (*fig*) *Schritte, Gedanken, seine Aufmerksamkeit, Blick* to direct (*auf +acc* to); *jds Aufmerksamkeit auch, Blicke* (*auf sich*) to draw (*auf +acc* to); *Verdacht* to throw; (*auf sich*) to draw (*auf +acc* onto); *Gespräch* to lead, to steer; *Schicksal* to guide ◆ **seine Schritte heimwärts ~** (*liter, hum inf*) to wend one's way homewards, to turn one's steps to home (*both liter, hum*).

Lenker *m* **-s, -** **(a)** (*Fahrrad~ etc*) handlebars *pl*. **(b)** (*Tech*) guide; (*Lenkung*) steering gear. **(c)** (*Mensch*) driver; (*fig*) guide.

Lenk-: ~getriebe *nt* steering gear; **~rad** *nt* (steering) wheel; **jdm ins ~rad greifen** to grab the (steering) wheel from sb.

Lenkrad-: ~schaltung *f* (*Aut*) column(-mounted) (gear) change *or* shift (*US*); ⚠**~schloß** *nt* (*Aut*) steering(-wheel) lock.

Lẹnkstange *f (von Fahrrad etc)* handlebars *pl*.

Lẹnkung *f* (a) *siehe vt (das Lenken)* direction, directing, guidance, guiding; influencing; *(das Steuern)* steering; driving; *(fig)* direction, directing; drawing; throwing; drawing; leading, steering. (b) *(Tech: Lenkeinrichtung)* steering.

Lẹnk-: ~verhalten *nt (von Auto)* steering *no indef art*; **~waffe** *f* guided missile.

Lẹntivirus *nt or m* lentivirus.

Lẹnz *m* **-es, -e** *(liter) (Frühling)* spring(time), springtide *(liter)* ◆ **der ~ des Lebens** the springtime of one's life *(liter)*; **sie zählt 20 ~e** she has seen 20 summers *(liter, hum)*; **einen ~ schieben** *or* **haben, sich** *(dat)* **einen (faulen** *or* **schönen) ~ machen** *(all inf)* to laze about, to swing the lead *(inf)*.

lẹnzen *(Naut)* [1] *vt (leerpumpen)* to pump out.
[2] *vi (vor dem Wind segeln)* to scud.

Lẹnz-: ~pumpe *f (Naut)* bilge-pump; **~tag** *m (liter)* spring day.

Leopard *m* **-en, -en** leopard.

Lẹpra *f* **-,** *no pl* leprosy.

Leprom *nt* **-s, -e** leprous lesion.

lepros, leprös *adj* leprous.

Lepröse(r) *mf decl as adj* leper.

Leprosorium *nt* leprosarium.

leptosom *adj (form)* asthenic *(form)*, leptosome *(form)*.

Lẹrche *f* **-, -n** lark.

Lẹrn-: l~bar *adj* learnable; **~begier(de)** *f* eagerness to learn; **l~begierig** *adj* eager to learn; **l~behindert** *adj* educationally handicapped; **~behinderte(r)** *mf* educationally handicapped child/boy/girl; **~diskette** *f* tutorial disk *or* diskette; **~eifer** *m siehe* **~begier(de)**; **l~eifrig** *adj siehe* **l~begierig**.

lẹrnen [1] *vt* (a) to learn ◆ **lesen/schwimmen** *etc* **~** to learn to read/swim *etc*; **Stenographie/Schreibmaschine ~** to learn shorthand/typing *or* to type; **~, etw zu tun** to learn to do sth; *(sich Fähigkeit, Können aneignen auch)* to learn how to do sth; **etw von/bei jdm ~** to learn sth from sb; **jdn lieben/schätzen ~** to come *or* learn to love/appreciate sb; **er lernt's nie/wird's nie ~** he never learns/he'll never learn; *siehe* **Hänschen**.
(b) *Beruf* to learn; *Bäcker, Schlosser etc* to train as, to learn the trade of ◆ **das will gelernt sein** it's a question of practice; **gelernt ist gelernt** *(Prov)* once you've learnt something ...; **lerne was, so kannst/bist du was** *(prov)* it never hurt anyone to learn anything; *siehe* **gelernt**.
[2] *vi* (a) *(Kenntnisse erwerben)* to learn; *(arbeiten)* to study; *(Schulaufgaben machen)* to do (one's) homework ◆ **die Mutter lernte drei Stunden mit ihm** his mother spent three hours helping him with his homework; **lerne fleißig in der Schule** work hard at school; **von ihm kannst du noch ~!** he could teach you a thing or two; **man lernt nicht für die Schule, sondern fürs Leben** *(Prov)* learning is not just for school but for life.
(b) *(sich in der Ausbildung befinden)* to go to school; *(in Universität)* to study; *(in Beruf)* to train ◆ **er lernt bei der Firma Braun** he's training at Braun's, Braun's are training him.
[3] *vr* **der Text/die Rolle lernt sich leicht/schwer/schnell** the text/part is easy/hard to learn/doesn't take long to learn.

Lẹrner *m* learner.

Lẹrn-: ~hilfe *f* educational aid; **~kurve** *f (Psych)* learning curve; **~maschine** *f* teaching machine; **~mittel** *pl* schoolbooks and equipment *pl*; **~mittelfreiheit** *f* free provision of schoolbooks and equipment; **~programm** *nt (Comput: für Software)* tutorial program; (didaktisches Programm) learning program; **⚠~prozeß** *m* learning process; **~psychologie** *f* psychology of learning; **~schwester** *f* student nurse; **~ziel** *nt* learning goal.

Les-: ~art *f (lit, fig)* version; **l~bar** *adj* legible; *Buch* readable.

Lẹsbe *f* **-, -n** *(sl)* lesbian.

Lesbierin ['lɛsbiərɪn] *f* lesbian.

lẹsbisch *adj* lesbian.

Lese *f* **-, -n** *(Ernte)* harvest; *(Weinart)* vintage; *(Beeren~)* picking.

Lese-: ~abend *m* evening of readings; **~brille** *f* reading glasses *pl*; **~buch** *nt* reader; **~ecke** *f* reading *or* readers' corner; **~gerät** *nt (Comput)* reading device, reader; **~geschwindigkeit** *f (auch Comput)* reading speed; **~karte** *f* reader's ticket; **~kopf** *m (Comput)* read head; **~kreis** *m* reading circle; **~lampe** *f* reading lamp; **~liste** *f* reading list; **~mappe** *f (Zeitschrift)* magazine in a folder.

lesen¹ *pret* **las**, *ptp* **gelesen** [1] *vti* (a) to read *(auch Comput)*; *(Eccl) Messe* to say ◆ **hier/in der Zeitung steht** *or* **ist zu ~, daß** ... it says here/in the paper that ...; **die Schrift ist kaum zu ~** the writing is scarcely legible; *siehe* **Leviten**.
(b) *(deuten) Gedanken* to read ◆ **jdm (sein Schicksal) aus der Hand ~** to read sb's palm; **in den Sternen ~** to read *or* see in the stars; **aus ihren Zeilen habe ich einen Vorwurf/eine gewisse Unsicherheit gelesen** I could tell from what she had written that she was reproaching me/felt a certain amount of uncertainty; **etw in jds Augen/Miene** *(dat)* **~** to see sth in sb's eyes/from sb's manner; **es war in ihrem Gesicht zu ~** it was written all over her face, you could see it in her face.
[2] *vi (Univ)* to lecture *(über +acc* on).
[3] *vr (Buch, Bericht etc)* to read ◆ **bei diesem Licht liest es sich nicht gut** this light isn't good for reading (in); **sich in den Schlaf ~** to read oneself to sleep.

lesen² *pret* **las**, *ptp* **gelesen** *vt* (a) *(sammeln) Trauben, Beeren* to pick; *(nach der Ernte) Ähren* to glean. (b) *(ver~) Erbsen, Linsen etc* to sort; *Salat* to clean.

lesenswert *adj* worth reading.

Lese-: ~probe *f* (a) *(Theat)* reading; (b) *(Ausschnitt aus Buch)* extract, excerpt; **~pult** *nt* lectern.

Leser(in *f*) *m* **-s, -** reader ◆ **seine Romane haben viele ~ gefunden** his novels have gained a large readership.

Leseratte *f (inf)* bookworm *(inf)*.

Leserbrief *m* (reader's) letter ◆ **einen ~ an eine Zeitung schreiben** to write a letter to a newspaper; „**~e**" "letters to the editor", "readers' letters".

Leserei *f (inf)* reading ◆ **kannst du jetzt nicht endlich mit der ~ aufhören?** can't you take your nose out of your books? *(inf)*.

Lesering ® *m* book club.

Leser-: ~kreis *m* readership; **l~lich** *adj* legible; **~lichkeit** *f* legibility; **~schaft** *f* readership; **~wunsch** *m* wish(es) of the readers; **auf vielfachen ~wunsch** at the request of many readers; **~zuschrift** *f siehe* **~brief**.

Lese-: ~saal *m* reading room; **~speicher** *m (Comput)* read-only memory, ROM; **~stoff** *m* reading material; **ich brauche noch ~stoff** I need something to read; **~stück** *nt* reading passage; **~wut** *f* craze for reading; **von (der) ~wut gepackt sein** to have caught the reading bug *(inf)*; **~zeichen** *nt* bookmark(er); **~zimmer** *nt* reading room; **~zirkel** *m* magazine subscription club.

Lesung *f (Dichter~, Parl)* reading; *(Eccl auch)* lesson.

Lethargie *f (Med, fig)* lethargy.

lethargisch *adj (Med, fig)* lethargic.

Lethe *f* **-** *(Myth)* Lethe; *(poet: Vergessenheit)* waters *pl* of oblivion.

Lẹtte *m* **-n, -n, Lẹttin** *f* Lett, Latvian.

Lẹtten *m* **-s, -** (potter's) clay.

Lẹtter *f* **-, -n** character.

lẹttisch *adj* Lettish, Latvian.

Lẹttisch(e) *nt* Latvian; *siehe auch* **Deutsch(e)**.

Lẹttland *nt* Latvia.

Lẹttner *m* **-s, -** *(Archit)* choir screen.

Lẹtzt *f*: **zu guter ~** finally, in the end.

lẹtztemal *adv* **das ~** (the) last time; **zum letztenmal** (for) the last time.

letzt|ẹndlich *adv* at (long) last.

lẹtztens *adv* recently ◆ **erst ~, ~ erst** just *or* only recently.

lẹtzte(r, s) *adj* (a) *(örtlich, zeitlich)* last; *(endgültig, aller~ auch)* final; *(restlich)* last (remaining) ◆ **~(r) werden** to be last; **als ~(r) (an)kommen/(weg)gehen/fertig sein** to arrive/leave/finish last, to be the last to arrive/leave/finish; **als ~(r) gehen** to be the last to go; *(in Reihenfolge auch)* to go last; *(in Prozession etc)* to bring up the rear; **auf dem ~n Platz** *or* **an ~r Stelle liegen** to be (lying) last; *(in Tabelle, Liga auch)* to be (lying) bottom; **den ~n beißen die Hunde** *(Prov)* (the) devil take the hindmost *(prov)*; **er wäre der ~, dem ich** ... he would be the last person I'd ...; **das ist das ~, was ich tun würde** that's the last thing I'd do; **das ~ Wort haben** *or* **behalten** to have the last word; **mein ~s Geld** the last of my money; **die ~n zwei Tage/Jahre** *etc* the last two days/years *etc*; *(vor heute/diesem Jahr auch)* the past two days/years *etc*; **in ~r Zeit** recently; **jdm die ~ Ehre erweisen, jdm das ~ Geleit geben** to pay one's last respects to sb; **die ~n Dinge** death and the life to come; **die Lehre der ~n Dinge** eschatology; **das ~ und höchste Ziel meines Lebens/des Werkes** the ultimate aim of my life/of the work; **der L~ Wille** last will and testament.
(b) **zum dritten und zum ~n** *(bei Auktion)* for the (third and) last time of asking; **bis aufs ~** completely, totally; **bis ins ~** (right) down to the last detail; **etw bis ins ~ kennen** to know sth like the back of one's hand; **bis zum ~n** to the utmost; **am** *or* **zum ~n** last; **fürs ~** lastly.
(c) *(neueste) Mode, Nachricht, Neuigkeit etc* latest.
(d) *(schlechtester)* most terrible ◆ **das ist der ~ Schund/Dreck** that's absolute trash; **er ist der ~ Mensch** *(inf)* he's a terrible person; **jdn wie den ~n Dreck/Sklaven** *etc* **behandeln** to treat sb like dirt *or* as though he/she *etc* were the scum of the earth/to treat sb like a slave *etc*.

Lẹtzte(r) *mf decl as adj* last; *(dem Rang nach)* lowest ◆ **der ~ seines Stammes** the last of his line; **der ~ des Monats** the last (day) of the month; **der/die ~ in der Klasse sein** to be bottom of the class; **die ~n werden die Ersten sein** *(Bibl)* the last shall be first *(Bibl)*.

lẹtztere(r, s) *adj* the latter; *siehe* **welch**.

Lẹtzte(s) *nt decl as adj* last thing ◆ **es geht ums ~** everything is at stake; **sein ~s (her)geben** to give one's all, to do one's utmost; **bis zum ~n gehen** to do all that one possibly can; **das ist ja das ~!** *(inf)* that really is the limit.

Lẹtzt-: l~genannt *adj* the last-named; **l~hin** *adv siehe* **letztens**; **l~instanzlich** *adj Urteil* in the court of last instance; *(fig)* in the last instance; **l~jährig** *adj attr* last year's *no art*; **l~lich** *adv* in the end; **das ist l~lich egal** it comes down to the same thing in the end; **l~malig** *adj attr* last; **l~mals** *adv* for the last time; **l~möglich** *adj attr* last possible; **~nummernspeicher** *m* last number redial; **l~willig** *adj (form)* **l~willige Verfügung** last will and testament; **l~willig verfügen, daß** ... to state in one's last will and testament that ...

Leu *m* **-en, -en** *(obs, poet)* lion.

Leucht-: ~anzeige *f* illuminated display; **~boje** *f* light-buoy; **~diode** *f* light-emitting diode; **~diodenanzeige** *f* LED display.

Leuchte *f* **-, -n** *(Leuchtkörper)* light; *(old: Laterne)* lamp, lantern; *(inf: Mensch)* genius ◆ **auf einem Gebiet/in einem Fach eine ~ sein** to shine in a particular field/subject.

leuchten *vi* (a) to shine; *(Flammen, Feuer, Lava, Zifferblatt)* to glow; *(auf~)* to flash.
(b) *(Mensch)* **mit einer Lampe in/auf etw** *(acc) etc* **~** to shine a lamp into/onto *etc* sth; **mußt du mir direkt in die Augen ~?** do you have to shine that

thing straight into my eyes?; **kannst du (mir) nicht mal ~?** can you point *or* shine the lamp/torch *etc* (for me)?; **leuchte mal hierher!** shine some light over here.

leuchtend *adj* (*lit, fig*) shining; *Farbe* bright, radiant ◆ **etw in den ~sten Farben schildern/preisen** to paint sth/speak of sth in glowing colours.

Leuchter *m* **-s, -** (*Kerzen~*) candlestick; (*Arm~*) candelabra; (*Kron~*) chandelier; (*Wand~*) sconce.

Leucht-: ~farbe *f* fluorescent colour/paint/dye/ink; **~feuer** *nt* navigational light; **~gas** *nt* town gas; ⚠**~geschoß** *nt* flare; **~käfer** *m* glow-worm; **~kraft** *f* brightness; (*von Birne etc auch*) luminous power (*form*); (*von Stern auch*) luminosity (*form*); **~kugel** *f* flare; **~patrone** *f* flare; **~pistole** *f* flare pistol; **~pult** *nt* light box; **~rakete** *f* signal rocket; **~reklame** *f* neon sign; **~röhre** *f* fluorescent tube; **~schirm** *m* fluorescent screen; **~schrift** *f* neon writing; **eine ~schrift** a neon sign.

Leuchtspur *f* trail of light.

Leuchtspur-: ⚠**~geschoß** *nt* (*Mil*) tracer bullet; **~munition** *f* (*Mil*) tracer bullets *pl*.

Leucht-: ~stift *m* highlighter; **~tonne** *f siehe* **~boje**; **~turm** *m* lighthouse; **~zeiger** *m* luminous hand; **~zifferblatt** *nt* luminous face *or* dial.

➤ **leugnen** [1] *vt* to deny ◆ **~, etw getan zu haben** to deny having done sth; **es ist nicht zu ~, daß ...** it cannot be denied that ...; **der Angeklagte leugnete die Tat** the defendant denied the offence; (*vor Gericht*) the defendant pleaded not guilty.
[2] *vi* to deny everything.

Leugnung *f* denial.

Leukämie *f* leukaemia.

Leukämiekranke(r) *mf decl as adj* leukaemia sufferer.

leukämisch *adj* leukaemic.

Leukoplast ® *nt* **-(e)s, -e** sticking plaster, elastoplast ® (*Brit*), bandaid ®.

Leukozyten *pl* leucocytes *pl* (*spec*), white corpuscles *pl*.

Leukozytenzählung *f* blood count (*of the white corpuscles*).

Leumund *m* **-(e)s,** *no pl* reputation, name.

Leumundszeugnis *nt* character reference.

Leutchen *pl* (*inf*) people *pl*, folk *pl* (*inf*) ◆ **kommt, ~!** come on everyone *or* folks (*inf*).

Leute *pl* **(a)** people *pl*; (*inf: Eltern auch*) folk(s) *pl* (*inf*) ◆ **arme/reiche/alte/junge ~** poor/rich/old/young people *or* folk(s) (*inf*); **alle ~** everybody; **kleine ~** (*fig*) ordinary people *or* folk (*inf*); **die kleinen ~** (*hum, inf: Kinder*) the little ones; **die ~ waren von dem Stück begeistert** people were enthusiastic about the play; **was sollen denn die ~ davon denken?** what will people think?; **aber liebe ~!** (*inf*) come on now! (*inf*); **~, ~!** (*inf*) dear me, (dear) oh dear; **kommt, ~!** come on folks; **aber die Sache ist doch in aller ~ Mund!** but everybody's talking about it!; **es ist nicht wie bei armen ~n** (*hum inf*) we're not on the breadline yet (*hum inf*); **ich kenne meine ~!** (*inf*) I know them/him *etc*; **etw unter die ~ bringen** (*inf*) *Gerücht, Geschichte* to spread sth around, to put sth about; *Geld* to spend sth; **unter die ~ kommen** (*inf*) (*Mensch*) to meet people; (*Gerüchte etc*) to go around, to go *or* do the rounds (*inf*); **das sind wohl nicht die richtigen ~** they're not the right kind of people.
(b) (*Mannschaft, Arbeiter etc*) **der Offizier ließ seine ~ antreten** the officer ordered his men to fall in; **dafür brauchen wir mehr ~** we need more people/staff *etc* for that.

Leuteschinder *m* **-s, -** slavedriver.

Leutnant *m* **-s, -s** *or* **-e** (second) lieutenant; (*bei der Luftwaffe*) pilot officer (*Brit*), second lieutenant (*US*) ◆ **~ zur See** sub-lieutenant (*Brit*), lieutenant junior grade (*US*); **jawohl, Herr ~!** yes, sir; (*Naut*) aye aye, sir.

leutselig *adj* (*umgänglich*) affable; (*pej: freundlich-herablassend*) genial.

Leutseligkeit *f siehe adj* affability; geniality.

Levante [le'vantə] *f* **-,** *no pl* Levant.

levantinisch *adj* Levantine.

Leviathan, Leviatan [le'via:tan, levia'ta:n] *m* **-s** (*Myth*) leviathan.

Levit [le'vi:t] *m* **-en, -en** (*Bibl*) Levite; (*Eccl*) deacon.

Leviten [le'vi:tən] *pl*: **jdm die ~ lesen** (*inf*) to haul sb over the coals (*inf*), to read sb the riot act (*inf*).

Levkoje [lɛf'ko:jə] *f* **-, -n** (*Bot*) stock.

Lex *f* **-, Leges** (parliamentary) bill ◆ **~ Smythe/Braun** *etc* Smythe's/Braun's *etc* bill.

Lexem *nt* **-s, -e** (*Ling*) lexeme.

lexikalisch *adj* lexical.

⚠**Lexikographie** *f* lexicography.

⚠**Lexikograph(in** *f*) *m* lexicographer.

⚠**lexikographisch** *adj* lexicographic(al).

Lexikologe *m*, **Lexikologin** *f* lexicologist.

Lexikologie *f* lexicology.

lexikologisch *adj* lexicological.

Lexikon *nt* **-s, Lexika** encyclopedia; (*Wörterbuch*) dictionary, lexicon.

lfd. *abbr of* **laufend.**

Liaison [liɛ'zõ:] *f* **-, -s** liaison.

Liane *f* **-, -n** liana.

Libanese *m* **-n, -n, Libanesin** *f* Lebanese.

libanesisch *adj* Lebanese.

Libanon *m* **-(s) der ~** (*Land*) the Lebanon; (*Gebirge*) the Lebanon Mountains *pl*.

Libanonzeder *f* cedar of Lebanon.

Libelle *f* (*Zool*) dragonfly; (*in Wasserwaage*) spirit level.

liberal *adj* liberal.

Liberale(r) *mf decl as adj* (*Pol*) Liberal.

liberalisieren* *vt* to liberalize.

Liberalisierung *f* liberalization.

Liberalismus *m* liberalism.

liberalistisch *adj* liberalist.

Liberalität *f* liberalness, liberality.

Libero *m* **-s, -s** (*Ftbl*) sweeper.

Libertin [libɛr'tɛ̃] *m* **-s, -s** (*old, geh*) libertine (*old*).

libidinös *adj* (*Psych*) libidinous, libidinal.

Libido *f* **-,** *no pl* (*Psych*) libido.

Librettist(in *f*) *m* librettist.

Libretto *nt* **-s, -s** *or* **Libretti** libretto.

Libyen *nt* **-s** Libya.

Libyer(in *f*) *m* **-s, -** Libyan.

libysch *adj* Libyan.

Licht *nt* **-(e)s, -er** *or* (*rare*) **-e (a)** *no pl* light ◆ **~ machen** (*anschalten*) to turn *or* switch *or* put on a light; (*anzünden*) to light a candle/lantern *etc*; **das ~ ist an** *or* **brennt** the light is on *or* is burning/the candle is burning; **das ~ des Tages/der Sonne** the light of day/the sun; **ich möchte es noch bei ~ fertigbekommen** I'd like to get it finished in daylight *or* while it's still light; **~ ins Zimmer lassen** to let (the/some) light into the room; **in der ganzen Stadt fiel das ~ aus** all the lights in the town went out; **etw gegen das ~ halten** to hold sth up to the light; **gegen das ~ fotografieren** to take a photograph into the light; **bei ~e besehen** *or* **betrachtet** (*lit*) in the daylight; (*fig*) in the cold light of day; **das ist nicht das richtige ~** that's not the right sort of light; **das Bild hängt hier nicht im richtigen ~** the light is wrong for the picture here; **du nimmst mir das ganze ~ weg** you're in the *or* my light; **jdm im Licht stehen** (*lit*) to stand in sb's light; **(jdm) aus dem ~ gehen** to move *or* get out of the *or* sb's light; **~ und Schatten** light and shade (*auch Art*); **wo ~ ist, ist auch Schatten** (*Prov*) there's no joy without sorrow (*prov*); **das ~ der Welt erblicken** (*geh*) to (first) see the light of day; **das ~ scheuen** (*lit*) to shun the light (of day); **Geschäfte, die das ~ scheuen** shady deals; *siehe* **Scheffel.**
(b) (*fig*) light; (*Könner*) genius ◆ **das ~ der Wahrheit/Erkenntnis** *etc* the light of truth/knowledge *etc*; **~ in eine (dunkle) Sache bringen** to cast *or* shed some light on a matter; **im ~(e) unserer Erfahrungen** in the light of our experiences; **etw ans ~ bringen/zerren** to bring/drag sth out into the open; **ans ~ kommen** to come *or* get out, to come to light; **jdn hinters ~ führen** to pull the wool over sb's eyes, to lead sb up the garden path; **mir geht ein ~ auf(, warum ...)** now it's dawned on me (why ...), now I see (why ...); **etw in milderem ~ sehen** to see sth in a more favourable light; **ein schiefes/schlechtes** *or* **kein gutes ~ auf jdn/etw werfen** to show sb/sth in the wrong/a bad light; **in ein schiefes** *or* **falsches ~ geraten** to be seen in the wrong light; **etw ins rechte/falsche ~ rücken** *or* **setzen** *or* **stellen** to show sth in a favourable/an unfavourable light; (*richtigstellen/falsch darstellen*) to show sth in its true light/put a wrong complexion on sth.
(c) (*Lichtquelle*) light; (*Kerze*) candle ◆ **~er führen** (*Naut*) to display *or* show lights; **jdm ein ~ aufstecken** *or* **aufsetzen** (*fig inf*) to put sb wise (*inf*).
(d) (*Hunt*) eye (*of deer etc*).

licht *adj* **(a)** (*hell*) light; (*liter*) *Morgen* bright ◆ **am ~en Tag** in broad daylight; **es wird schon ~** (*geh*) it is getting light, (the) day is dawning (*liter*); **einen ~en Augenblick** *or* **Moment haben** to have a lucid moment; (*fig inf*) to have a brainwave (*inf*); **auch ich habe ~e Augenblicke** even I have my lucid moments.
(b) *Wald* sparse; *Haar auch* thin ◆ **eine ~e Stelle im Wald** a sparsely-wooded spot in the forest.
(c) (*Tech*) **~e Höhe/Weite** headroom/(internal) width; **~er Durchmesser** internal diameter.

Licht-: ~anlage *f* lights *pl*; **er hat sich** (*dat*) **eine ganze ~anlage gebastelt** he put together a whole lighting system; **~behandlung** *f* (*Med*) phototherapy; **l~beständig** *adj* lightproof; *Farben, Stoff* non-fade; **~bild** *nt* (*Dia*) transparency, slide; (*form: Foto*) photograph; **~bildervortrag** *m* illustrated talk *or* lecture; **~blick** *m* (*fig*) ray of hope; **~bogen** *m* arc; **l~brechend** *adj* (*Opt*) refractive; **~brechung** *f* refraction; **~brücke** *f* lighting rig; **~bündel** *nt* pencil (of rays); **~druck** *m* (*Typ*) collotype; (*Phys*) light pressure; **l~durchlässig** *adj* pervious to light, light-transmissive (*form*); (*durchsichtig*) transparent; (*durchscheinend*) translucent.

Lichte *f* **-,** *no pl* (internal) width.

Licht-: l~echt *adj* non-fade; **~echtheit** *f* non-fade properties *pl*; **~effekt** *m* lighting effect; **~einfall** *m* incidence of light; **~einwirkung** *f* action of light; **l~elektrisch** *adj* photoelectric; **l~empfindlich** *adj* sensitive to light; (*Tech auch*) photosensitive; **~empfindlichkeit** *f* sensitivity to light; photosensitivity; (*Phot*) film speed.

lichten[1] [1] *vt Wald* to thin (out).
[2] *vr* (*Reihen, Wald, Dickicht, Haare*) to thin (out); (*Nebel*) to clear, to lift; (*Wolken, Dunkel*) to lift; (*Bestände*) to go down, to dwindle; (*fig: Angelegenheit*) to be cleared up.

lichten[2] *vt Anker* to weigh.

Lichter-: ~baum *m* Christmas tree; **~fest** *nt* **(a)** (*liter: Weihnachten*) Yule (*old*), Christmas; **(b)** (*jüdisches Fest*) Festival of Lights, Hanuk(k)ah; **~glanz** *m* blaze of lights; **in festlichem ~glanz erstrahlen** to be a blaze of festive lights; **l~loh** *adv* **l~loh brennen** (*lit*) to be ablaze; (*fig: Herz*) to be aflame; **~meer** *nt* (*liter*) sea of light; **das ~meer von New York** the sea of light that is New York.

Licht-: ~filter *nt or m* (light) filter; **~geschwindigkeit** *f* speed of light;

⚠: for details of spelling reform, see supplement

➤ SPRACHE AKTIV: leugnen: 1 → 42.1

~gestalt *f (fig)* shining light; **~griffel** *m (Comput)* light pen; **~hof** *m* **(a)** *(Archit)* air well; **(b)** *(Phot)* halation *(spec)*; **(c)** *(des Mondes)* halo; **~hupe** *f (Aut)* flash (of the headlights); **jdn durch ~hupe warnen** to warn sb by flashing one's lights; **~jahr** *nt* light year; **~kegel** *m (Phys)* cone of light; *(von Scheinwerfer)* beam (of light); **er stand im ~kegel** he stood in the spotlight/the beam of the headlights; **~kreis** *m* circle *or* pool of light; **~leitung** *f* lighting wire; **l~los** *adj* dark; **ein l~loser Raum** a room which doesn't get any light; **~mangel** *m* lack of light; **~maschine** *f (für Gleichstrom)* dynamo; *(für Drehstrom)* alternator; **~mast** *m* lamppost; ⚠**~meß** *no art* **Mariä ~meß** Candlemas; ⚠**~meßverfahren** *nt (Mil)* flash ranging; **~nelke** *f* catchfly, lychnis *(form)*; **~orgel** *f* clavilux, colour organ; **~pause** *f* photocopy; *(bei Blaupausverfahren)* blueprint; **~punkt** *m* point of light; **~quant** *nt* photon; **~quelle** *f* source of light; **~reklame** *f* neon sign; **~satz** *m (Typ)* film-setting, photocomposition; **in ~satz hergestellt** film-set; **~schacht** *m* air shaft; **~schalter** *m* light switch; **~schein** *m* gleam of light; **l~scheu** *adj* averse to light; *(fig) Gesindel* shady; **~schimmer** *m* gleam of light; **~schranke** *f* photoelectric barrier.

Lichtschutz-: ~faktor *m* protection factor; **~filter** *m* light filter.

Licht-: ~setzmaschine *f (Typ)* photosetting machine; **~signal** *nt* light signal; **~spielhaus, ~spieltheater** *nt (dated)* cinema, picture palace *(old)*; **l~stark** *adj (Opt)* intense; *(Phot)* fast; **~stärke** *f (Opt)* luminous intensity; *(Phot)* speed; **~stift** *m (Comput)* light pen; **~stock** *m siehe* **Wachsstock**; **~strahl** *m* beam *or* ray of light; *(fig)* ray of sunshine; **~strom** *m (Opt)* luminous *or* light flux; **l~undurchlässig** *adj* opaque.

Lichtung *f* clearing, glade.

Licht-: ~verhältnisse *pl* lighting conditions *pl*; **~wechsel** *m* change of light; *(Astron)* light variation; **~weg** *m* light path; **l~wendig** *adj (Bot)* phototropic.

Lid *nt* **-(e)s, -er** eyelid.

Lid-: ~rand, ~schatten *m* eye-shadow; **~schlag** *m* blink; **~strich** *m* eye-liner.

lieb *adj* **(a)** *(liebenswürdig, hilfsbereit)* kind; *(nett, reizend)* nice; *(niedlich) Kerl(chen), Ding* sweet, lovely, cute *(inf)*; *(artig) Kind, Schulklasse* good ◆ **(es sendet Dir) (viele) ~e Grüße Deine Silvia** love Silvia; **~e Grüße an Deine Eltern** give my best wishes to your parents; **sich ~ um jdn kümmern** to be very kind to sb; **er hat mir wirklich ~ geholfen** it was really sweet the way he helped me; **würdest du (bitte) so ~ sein und das Fenster aufmachen** *or*, **das Fenster aufzumachen?, sei bitte so ~ und mache das Fenster auf** would you do me a favour *or* (would you) be a love *(Brit inf) or* an angel *(inf)* and open the window; **willst du wohl (endlich) ~ sein?!** are you going to be good *or* to behave now?; **bei jdm ~ Kind sein** *(pej)* to be sb's (little) darling *or* pet; **beim Lehrer ~ Kind sein** *(pej)* to be teacher's pet; **sich bei jdm ~ Kind machen** *(pej)* to suck up to sb, to worm one's way into sb's good books.
(b) *Gast, Besuch (angenehm)* pleasant; *(willkommen)* welcome ◆ **bei uns bist du jederzeit ein ~er Gast** you're always welcome, we're always pleased to see you.
(c) *(angenehm)* **etw ist jdm ~** sb likes sth; **es wäre mir ~, wenn ...** I'd be glad if ..., I'd like it if ...; **es ist mir ~, daß ...** I'm glad that ...; **es wäre ihm ~er** he would prefer it; *siehe auch* **lieber 2, liebste(r, s) 2.**
(d) *(geliebt, geschätzt)* dear, beloved *(iro, form)*; *(in Briefanrede)* dear; *(bei Anrede von Publikum etc) not translated* ◆ **~e Monika, das geht doch nicht** (my) dear Monika, that's just not on; **~e Brüder und Schwestern** *(Rel)* dearly beloved; **der ~e Gott** the Good Lord; **~er Gott** *(Anrede)* dear God *or* Lord; **unsere L~e Frau** *(Eccl)* Our Lady; **L~e Anna, ~er Klaus! ...** Dear Anna and Klaus, ...; **(mein) L~es** (my) love *or* pet, honey *(esp US)*; **jdn ~ behalten** to stay fond of sb; **er ist mir ~ und wert** *or* **teuer** he's very dear to me; **den ~en langen Tag** *(inf)* the whole livelong day; **das ~e Geld!** the money, the money!; **(ach) du ~er Himmel/~er Gott/~e Güte/~e Zeit/~es Lieschen** *or* **Lottchen/~es bißchen** *(inf)* good heavens *or* Lord!, goodness me!; *siehe* **Not.**
(e) ~ste(r, s) favourite; **sie ist mir die ~ste von allen** she is my favourite.

lieb|äugeln *vi insep* **mit etw ~** to have one's eye on sth; **mit einem neuen Auto ~** to be toying with the idea of getting a new car; **mit dem Gedanken ~, etw zu tun** to be toying *or* flirting with the idea of doing sth.

Liebchen *nt (old)* sweetheart.

Liebe *f* **-, -n (a)** love *(zu jdm, für jdn* for *or* of sb, *zu etw* of sth) ◆ **die große ~** the love of one's life, the real thing *(inf)*; **Heirat aus ~** love-match; **aus ~ zu jdm/einer Sache** for the love of sb/sth; **ein Kind der ~** *(liter)* a love child; **etw mit viel ~ tun** to do sth with loving care; **in ~** with love; **in ~ Dein Theobald** with all my love, Theobald; **~ macht blind** *(Prov)* love is blind *(Prov)*.
(b) *(Sex)* sex ◆ **eine Nacht der ~** a night of love; **von der ~ leben** *(Prostituierte etc)* to live off sex *or* off one's favours *(euph)*; **ein Meister der ~** an expert at love-making *or* in love; **sie/er ist gut in der ~** *(inf)* she/he is good at making love.
(c) *(inf: Gefälligkeit)* favour ◆ **tu mir doch bitte die ~ und ...** would you do me a favour and ...
(d) *(Geliebte(r))* love ◆ **sie ist eine alte ~ von mir** she is an old flame of mine.

Liebe-: l≈bedürftig *adj* **l≈bedürftig sein, ein l≈bedürftiges Wesen haben** *or* **sein** to need a lot of love *or* affection; **~dienerei** *f (pej)* subservience, fawning *(gegenüber* to); **l≈dienern** *vi insep (pej)* to fawn *(jdm* to sb); **l≈leer** *adj Leben, Dasein* loveless.

Liebelei *f (inf)* flirtation; affair.

lieben *vti* to love; *(als Liebesakt)* to make love *(jdn* to sb) ◆ **etw nicht ~** not to like sth; **ich liebe es nicht, wenn man mich unterbricht** I do not like being interrupted; **das liebe ich (gerade)!** *(iro)* marvellous, isn't it? *(iro)*; **etw ~d gern tun** to love to do sth; **sich** *or* **einander ~** to love one another *or* each other; *(euph)* to make love.

Liebende(r) *mf decl as adj* lover.

⚠ **liebenlernen** *vt sep* to come to love.

liebenswert *adj* lovable, endearing.

liebenswürdig *adj* kind; *(liebenswert)* charming ◆ **würden Sie so ~ sein und die Tür schließen?** would you be so kind as to shut the door?

liebenswürdigerweise *adv* kindly.

Liebenswürdigkeit *f* **(a)** *(Höflichkeit)* politeness; *(Freundlichkeit)* kindness ◆ **würden Sie die ~ haben, das zu tun** *or* **und das tun?** *(form)* would you be kind *or* good enough to do that?, would you have the goodness to do that? **(b)** *(iro: giftige Bemerkung)* charming remark *(iro)*.

Liebe(r) *mf decl as adj* dear ◆ **meine ~n** my dears.

▼ **lieber** **1** *adj comp of* **lieb.**
▼ **2** *adv comp of* **gern (a)** *(vorzugsweise)* rather, sooner ◆ **das tue ich ~** *(im Augenblick)* I would *or* I'd rather *or* sooner do that; *(grundsätzlich auch)* I prefer doing that; **das würde ich ~ tun** I would *or* I'd rather *or* sooner do that, I would prefer to do that; **ich trinke ~ Wein als Bier** I prefer wine to beer; **(das möchte ich) ~ nicht!** I would *or* I'd sooner *or* rather not, I would *or* I'd prefer not to; **er sieht es ~, wenn du das nicht tust** he would *or* he'd prefer you not to do that, he would *or* he'd prefer it if you didn't do that, he would *or* he'd sooner *or* rather you didn't do that; *(grundsätzlich)* he prefers you not to do that, he prefers it if you don't do that.
▼ **(b)** *(besser, vernünftigerweise)* better ◆ **bleibe ~ im Bett** you had *or* you'd better stay in bed, I would *or* I'd stay in bed if I were you; **ich hätte ~ lernen/nachgeben** *etc* **sollen** I would have done better *or* I'd have done better to have studied/given in *etc*; **sollen wir gehen? — ~ nicht!** should we go? — better not; **nichts ~ als das** there's nothing I'd rather do/have.

Liebes- *in cpds* love; **~abenteuer** *nt* amorous adventure; **~affäre** *f* (love-) affair; **~akt** *m* love *or* sex act; **~apfel** *m (obs)* tomato; **~bande** *pl (liter)* bonds of love *pl*, **~beziehung** *f* romantic attachment; (sexual) relationship; **~bote** *m* messenger of love; **~brief** *m* love letter; **~dienerin** *f (inf)* lady of the night *(euph)*; **~dienst** *m* labour of love; *(fig: Gefallen)* favour; **jdm einen ~dienst erweisen** to do sb a service of love/a favour; **~entzug** *m, no pl* withdrawal of affection; **~erklärung** *f* declaration of love; **jdm eine ~erklärung machen** to declare one's love to sb; **~film** *m* love film; **~gedicht** *nt* love poem; **~geschichte** *f* **(a)** *(Liter)* love story; **(b)** *(inf: Liebschaft)* love-affair; **~gott** *m* god of love; **~göttin** *f* goddess of love; **~handel, ~händel** *m (obs)* love-affair; **~heirat** *f* love-match; **~kummer** *m* lovesickness; **~kummer haben** to be lovesick; **vor ~kummer konnte sie nicht mehr essen** she was so lovesick that she couldn't eat; **~leben** *nt* love-life; **~lied** *nt* love song; **~müh(e)** *f*: **das ist vergebliche** *or* **verlorene ~müh(e)** that is futile; **~nest** *nt (inf)* love-nest; **~paar** *nt* lovers *pl*; **~roman** *m* romantic novel; **~spiel** *nt* loveplay; **~szene** *f* love scene; **l~toll** *adj* love-stricken, lovelorn; **~töter** *pl (hum)* long johns *pl*, passion-killers *pl (hum)*; **~trank** *m (liter)* love potion; **l~trunken** *adj (geh)* in an ecstasy of love; **~verhältnis** *nt* (sexual) relationship, liaison.

liebevoll *adj* loving.

lieb-: ⚠~gewinnen* *vt sep irreg* to get *or* grow fond of; **⚠~geworden** *adj attr* well-loved; *Brauch, Angewohnheit* favourite; **ein mir ~gewordenes Land** a country of which I've grown very fond; **⚠~haben** *vt sep irreg* to love; *(weniger stark)* to be (very) fond of.

Liebhaber(in *f***)** *m* **-s, - (a)** lover. **(b)** *(Interessent, Freund)* enthusiast; *(Sammler)* collector ◆ **ein ~ von etw** a lover of sth; **das ist nur etwas für ~** it's an acquired taste; **das ist ein Wein/Auto für ~** that is a wine/car for connoisseurs.

Liebhaberei *f (fig: Steckenpferd, Hobby)* hobby ◆ **etw aus ~ tun** to do sth as a hobby.

Liebhaber-: ~preis *m* collector's price; **~stück** *nt* collector's item; **~wert** *m* collector's value.

liebkosen* *vt insep (liter)* to caress, to fondle.

Liebkosung *f (liter)* caress.

lieblich *adj* charming, lovely, delightful; *Duft, Geschmack, Wein* sweet.

Lieblichkeit *f* loveliness, delightfulness; sweetness ◆ **ihre ~, Prinzessin Sylvia** *(im Fasching)* Her Sweetness Princess Sylvia *(title of carnival princess)*.

Liebling *m* darling; *(bevorzugter Mensch)* favourite.

▼ **Lieblings-** *in cpds* favourite.

Lieb-: l~los *adj Ehemann, Eltern* unloving; *Bemerkung, Behandlung* unkind; *Benehmen* inconsiderate; **l~los gekocht/zubereitet** *etc* cooked/prepared *etc* any old how *(inf)*; **~losigkeit** *f* **(a)** *(no pl: liebloses Wesen) siehe adj* unlovingness; unkindness; inconsiderateness; **(b)** *(Äußerung)* unkind remark; *(Tat)* unkind act; **~losigkeiten** *(Benehmen)* unkind behaviour *sing*; **~reiz** *m (liter)* charm; **l~reizend** *adj (liter)* charming; **~schaft** *f* affair.

liebsten *adv*: **am ~**; *siehe* **liebste(r, s) 2.**

liebste(r, s) **1** *adj superl of* **lieb.**
2 *adv superl of* **gern**: **am ~n** best; **am ~n hätte/würde ich ...** what I'd like most would be (to have) .../would be to ..., most of all *or* best of all I'd like (to have) .../I'd like to ...; **am ~n lese ich Kriminalromane/esse ich scharfe Speisen/gehe ich ins Kino** most *or* best of all I like detective novels/spicy food/going to the cinema; **am ~n hätte ich ihm eine geklebt!** *(inf)* I could have stuck one on him *(sl)*; **das würde ich am ~n tun** that's what I'd like to do best, that's what I'd prefer to do.

Liebste(r) *mf decl as adj* sweetheart.

Liebstöckel *m or nt* **-s, -** *(Bot)* lovage.

Liechtenstein ['lıçtnʃtain] *nt* **-s** Liechtenstein.

Liechtensteiner(in *f***)** *m* **-s, -** Liechtensteiner.

➤ SPRACHE AKTIV: **lieber: 2** → 31, 34.1, 34.2, 34.4, 35.5, 36.3 **2b** → 33.3 **Lieblings-** → 34.1, 34.3

liechtensteinisch *adj* Liechtenstein, of/from Liechtenstein.

Lied *nt* **-(e)s, -er** song; (*Kirchen~*) hymn; (*Weihnachts~*) carol ◆ **das Ende vom ~** (*fig inf*) the upshot *or* outcome (of all this); **das ist dann immer das Ende vom ~** it always ends like that; **es ist immer dasselbe** *or* **das alte** *or* **gleiche ~** (*inf*) it's always the same old story (*inf*); **davon kann ich ein ~ singen** *or* **weiß ich ein ~ zu singen** I could tell you a thing or two about that (*inf*).

Lieder-: ~abend *m* evening of songs; (*von Sänger*) song recital; **~buch** *nt siehe* **Lied** songbook; hymnbook; book of carols; **~dichter** *m* lyrical poet; (*des Mittelalters*) minstrel; **~handschrift** *f* collection of ballads.

Liederjan *m* **-(e)s, -e** (*dated inf*) wastrel.

liederlich *adj* (*schlampig*) slovenly *attr, pred*; (*nachlässig auch*) sloppy; (*unmoralisch*) *Leben, Mann* dissolute, dissipated; *Frau, Mädchen* loose ◆ **ein ~es Frauenzimmer** (*pej*) a slut; **Bruder L~** (*old*) wastrel.

Liederlichkeit *f siehe adj* slovenliness; sloppiness; dissoluteness; looseness.

Lieder-: ~macher(in *f*) *m* singer-songwriter; **~zyklus** *m* song cycle.

lief *pret of* **laufen**.

Lieferant *m* supplier; (*Auslieferer*) deliveryman.

Lieferanten|eingang *m* tradesmen's entrance; (*von Warenhaus etc*) goods entrance.

Liefer-: ~auto *nt siehe* **~wagen**; **l~bar** *adj* (*vorrätig*) available; (*zustellbar*) deliverable (*rare*); **die Ware ist sofort l~bar** the article can be supplied/delivered at once; **diese Sachen sind auch kurzfristig l~bar** these goods can be supplied/delivered at short notice; **~bedingungen** *pl* conditions *or* terms of supply/delivery; **~firma** *f* supplier; (*Zusteller*) delivery firm; **~frist** *f* delivery period; **die ~frist einhalten** to meet the delivery date; **~monat** *m* (*Comm*) contract month, delivery month.

liefern *vti* **(a)** to supply; (*zustellen*) to deliver (*in +acc* to) ◆ **jdm etw ~** to supply sb with sth/deliver sth to sb; **wir ~ nicht ins Ausland/nach Frankreich** we don't supply the foreign market/(to) France; **eine Firma, die wegen Streiks nicht mehr ~ kann** a firm which, because of a strike, cannot deliver any more.
(b) (*zur Verfügung stellen*) to supply; *Beweise, Gesprächsstoff, Informationen, Sensationen auch* to provide, to furnish; *Ertrag* to yield; (*inf: stellen*) to provide ◆ **jdm eine Schlacht/ein Wortgefecht ~** to do battle/verbal battle with sb; **sie lieferten sich eine regelrechte Schlacht** they had a real battle; (*Sport*) they put up a real fight; **ein spannendes Spiel ~** (*Sport*) to put on an exciting game; **jdm eine gute/schlechte Partie ~** to give/not to give sb a good game; *siehe* **geliefert**.

Liefer-: ~schein *m* delivery note; **~termin** *m* delivery date.

Lieferung *f* **(a)** (*Versand, Versandgut*) delivery; (*Versorgung*) supply ◆ **bei ~ zu bezahlen** payable on delivery; **Zahlung bis 14 Tage nach ~** account payable within 14 days of delivery. **(b)** (*von Buch*) instalment.

Lieferungsbedingungen *pl siehe* **Lieferbedingungen**.

Liefer-: ~vertrag *m* contract of sale, sale contract; **ein ~vertrag über 5.000 Lastwagen** a contract to supply/deliver 5,000 lorries; **~wagen** *m* van, panel truck (*US*); (*offen*) pick-up; **~zeit** *f* delivery period, lead time (*Comm*); **~zettel** *m* delivery order.

Liege *f* **-, -n** couch; (*Camping~*) camp bed; (*für Garten*) lounger.

Liege-: ~deck *nt* (*Naut*) sundeck; **~geld** *nt* (*Naut*) demurrage; **~karte** *f* (*Rail*) couchette ticket; **~kur** *f* rest-cure.

liegen *pret* **lag**, *ptp* **gelegen** *aux haben or* (*S Ger*) *sein vi* **(a)** (*flach~, ausgebreitet sein*) to lie; (*Flasche etc*) to lie on its side; (*inf: krank sein*) to be laid up (*inf*) ◆ **das lange L~** lying a long time; (*von Mensch*) lying in bed for a long time; **hart/weich ~** to lie on hard/soft ground, to lie on a hard/soft surface, to lie on a hard/soft bed *etc*; **in diesem Bett liegt es sich** *or* **liegt man hart/weich** this bed is hard/soft; **unbequem ~** to lie uncomfortably *or* in an uncomfortable position; **auf den Knien ~** to be kneeling *or* on one's knees; **im Bett/Krankenhaus ~** to be in bed/hospital; **auf dem Boden ~** to lie on the floor; (*zum Schlafen*) to sleep on the floor; **zu Bett ~** (*form*) to have retired (*form*); (*krank sein*) to have taken to one's bed (*form*); **der Kranke muß unbedingt ~** the patient really must lie down; **der Kopf muß hoch/tief ~** the head must be higher/lower than the rest of the body; **flach ~** (*lit*) to lie flat; (*inf: krank sein*) to be laid up; **verstreut ~** to be *or* lie scattered; **der Vogel/das Flugzeug liegt ganz ruhig in der Luft** the bird/plane is flying quite smoothly; **in der Kurve ~** (*Auto*) to hold the corner; (*Rennfahrer*) to corner; **der Wagen liegt gut auf der Straße** the car holds the road well; **auf dem Boden haben sie teure Teppiche ~** they have expensive carpets on the floor; **etw ~ lassen** to leave sth (there); **einen Ort links/rechts ~ lassen** to pass by a place.
(b) (*sich befinden, sein*) to be ◆ **das Schiff liegt am Kai** the ship is (tied up) alongside the quay; **ich habe noch einen guten Wein im Keller ~** I have a good wine in the cellar; **ein Lächeln lag auf ihrem Gesicht** there was a smile on her face; **die Preise ~ zwischen 60 und 80 Mark** the prices are between 60 and 80 marks; **der zweite Läufer liegt weit hinter dem ersten** the second runner is *or* is lying a long way behind the first; **die Betonung liegt auf der zweiten Silbe** the stress is *or* lies on the second syllable; **seine Fähigkeiten ~ auf einem anderen Gebiet** his abilities lie in a different direction; **in jds Absicht** (*dat*) **~** to be sb's intention; **es liegt in seiner Gewalt, das zu tun** it is *or* lies within his power to do that.
(c) (*einen bestimmten Rang haben*) to be ◆ **an erster Stelle der Hitparade ~** to be number one (in the hit parade), to top the charts; **auf den hintersten Plätzen/in Führung/an der Spitze ~** to be at the bottom/in the lead/right out in front.
(d) (*lasten*) **auf dieser Familie scheint ein Fluch zu ~** there seems to be a curse on this family; **die Verantwortung/Schuld dafür liegt bei ihm** the responsibility/blame for that lies *or* rests with him; **die Schuld liegt schwer auf mir** my guilt weighs heavily on me; **damit liegt die ganze Arbeit auf mir** that means all the work falls on me; **das liegt ganz bei dir** that is completely up to you; **die Entscheidung liegt beim Volk/bei Ihnen** the decision rests with the people/you.
(e) (*eine bestimmte Lage haben*) to be; (*Haus, Stadt etc auch*) to be situated *or* located, to lie ◆ **nach Süden/der Straße ~** to face south/the road; **das Haus liegt ganz ruhig** the house is in a very quiet position *or* location; **das liegt doch auf dem Weg/ganz in der Nähe** it's on the way/quite nearby.
(f) (*sich verhalten*) to be ◆ **so, wie die Dinge jetzt ~** as things are *or* stand at the moment; **damit liegst du (gold)richtig** (*inf*) you're (dead (*inf*) *or* absolutely) right there; **bei mir ~ Sie richtig (damit)** (*inf*) you've come to the right person (for that).
(g) (*begraben sein*) to lie.
(h) (*Schnee*) to lie; (*Hitze, Nebel auch*) to hang ◆ **die Stadt lag in dichtem Nebel** the town was enveloped in thick fog, thick fog hung *or* lay over the town; **der Schnee liegt 50 cm hoch** the snow is 50 cm deep; **der Schnee bleibt nicht ~** the snow isn't lying.
(i) (*wichtig sein*) **es liegt mir viel/wenig/nichts daran** that matters a lot/doesn't matter much/at all to me, that is important/isn't very/at all important to me; **es liegt mir viel an ihm/an meinem Beruf** he/my job is very important *or* matters a lot to me; **mir liegt an einer schnellen Fertigstellung des Hauses/an guten Beziehungen** I am concerned that the house should be finished quickly/that there should be good relations; **was liegt (dir) schon daran?** what does it matter (to you)?
(j) (*begründet sein*) **an jdm/etw ~** to be because of sb/sth; **woran liegt es?** why is that?, what is the reason (for that)?; **das liegt daran, daß ...** that is because..., the reason for that is that...; **an mir soll es nicht ~!** I'll go along with that; **an mir soll es nicht ~, daß** *or* **wenn die Sache schiefgeht** it won't be my fault if things go wrong.
(k) (*geeignet sein, passen*) **jdm liegt etw nicht** sth doesn't suit sb; (*jds Art, Lebensart, Beruf*) sth doesn't appeal to sb; (*Mathematik etc*) sb has no aptitude for sth; **Krankenschwester liegt mir nicht** (*inf*) nursing isn't my cup of tea (*inf*) *or* doesn't appeal to me; **diese Rolle liegt ihr** she suits *or* fits the part, the part suits her.
(l) (*angeordnet sein*) (*Falten*) to lie; (*Haare*) to stay in place ◆ **der Stoff liegt quer/90 cm breit** the material is on the cross/is 90 cm wide.

⚠ **liegenbleiben** *vi sep irreg aux sein* **(a)** (*nicht aufstehen*) to remain lying (down) ◆ **(im Bett) ~** to stay in bed; **er blieb bewußtlos auf dem Boden liegen** he lay unconscious on the floor; **bleib liegen!** don't get up!, stay down!
(b) (*vergessen werden*) to be *or* get left behind ◆ **mein Schirm muß irgendwo liegengeblieben sein** I must have left my umbrella somewhere.
(c) (*nicht verkauft werden*) not to sell, to be left unsold ◆ **wenn uns diese Sachen ~** if we are left with these things (on our hands).
(d) (*Auto*) to conk out (*inf*).
(e) (*nicht ausgeführt werden*) to get *or* be left (undone), not to get done.

liegend *adj* (*Art*) reclining ◆ **~ aufbewahren** to store flat; *Flasche etc* to store on its side; **~e Güter** immovable property *sing* (*form*), real estate.

Liegende *f* **-n, -n** (*Art*) reclining figure.

⚠ **liegenlassen** *vt sep irreg, ptp* **-** *or* (*rare*) **liegengelassen** (*nicht erledigen*) to leave; (*vergessen*) to leave (behind); (*herum~*) to leave lying about *or* around ◆ **sie hat alles liegengelassen, um dem Kind zu helfen** she dropped everything to (go and) help the child; *siehe* **links, stehenlassen**.

Liegenschaft(en *pl*) *f* real estate *sing*, property *sing*.

Liege-: ~platz *m* place to lie; (*auf Schiff, in Zug etc*) berth; (*Ankerplatz*) moorings *pl*; (*von großem Schiff*) berth; **~sitz** *m* reclining seat; (*auf Boot*) couchette; **~statt** *f* (*old, dial*) bed; **~stuhl** *m* (*mit Holzgestell*) deck chair; (*mit Metallgestell*) lounger; **~stütz** *m* (*Sport*) press-up; **~stütze machen** to do press-ups; **in den ~stütz!** press-ups!; **~wagen** *m* (*Rail*) couchette coach *or* car (*esp US*); **~wagen buchen** to book a couchette; **~wiese** *f* lawn (*for sunbathing*); **~zeit** *f* **(a)** (*Naut*) lay days *pl* (*form*); **(b)** rest period.

lieh *pret of* **leihen**.

Liek *nt* **-(e)s, -en** (*Naut*) boltrope.

lies *imper sing of* **lesen**.

Lieschen [liːsçən] *nt* Liz(zie) ◆ **~ Müller** (*inf*) the average woman in the street; *siehe* **fleißig, lieb**.

ließ *pret of* **lassen**.

Lift *m* **-(e)s, -e** *or* **-s** (*Personen~*) lift (*Brit*), elevator (*esp US*); (*Güter~*) lift (*Brit*), hoist; (*Ski~*) ski lift.

Liftboy [ˈlɪftbɔy] *m* **-s, -s** liftboy (*Brit*), elevator boy (*US*).

liften *vt* to lift ◆ **sich** (*dat*) **das Gesicht ~ lassen** to have a facelift.

Lift-off [lɪftˈɒf] *m* **-(s), -s** lift-off.

Liga *f* **-, Ligen** league.

Ligatur *f* ligature; (*Mus: Verbindung zweier Noten*) tie.

Light pen [ˈlaɪtpɛn] *m* **- -s, - -s** light pen.

Lignin *nt* **-s, -e** lignin(e).

Liguster *m* **-s, -** privet.

liieren* **1** *vt* to bring *or* get together; *Firmen etc* to get to work together ◆ **liiert sein** to have joined forces; (*Firmen etc*) to be working together; (*Pol*) to be allied; (*ein Verhältnis haben*) to have a relationship.
2 *vr* to join forces; (*Firmen etc*) to work together; (*Pol*) to enter into an alliance; (*ein Verhältnis eingehen*) to get together, to form a liaison.

Likör *m* **-s, -e** liqueur.

lila *adj inv* purple.

Lila *nt* **-s,** (*inf*) **-s** purple.

⚠: for details of spelling reform, see supplement

Lilie [-iə] *f* lily ◆ **keusch wie eine ~** as pure as the driven snow.
Liliput- *in cpds* miniature.
Liliputaner(in *f*) *m* **-s, -** dwarf, midget; (*Bewohner von Liliput*) Liliputian.
Limbo *m* **-s, -s** limbo.
Limburger (Käse) *m* **-s, -** Limburger, Limburg cheese.
Limerick *m* **-(s), -s** limerick.
Limes *m* **-, -** (a) *no pl* (*Hist*) limes. (b) (*Math*) limit.
Limit *nt* **-s, -s** *or* **-e** limit; (*Fin*) ceiling ◆ **jdm ein ~ setzen** to set sb a limit.
limitieren* *vt* (*form*) to limit; (*Fin*) to put a ceiling on.
Limo *f* **-, -s** (*inf*) lemonade.
Limonade *f* lemonade; (*in weiterem Sinn*) soft drink.
Limone *f* **-, -n** lime.
Limousine [limu'zi:nə] *f* saloon (*Brit*), sedan (*US*).
lind *adj* (a) (*liter*) balmy; *Regen* gentle. (b) (*Sw*) **~ (gewürzt)** lightly spiced.
Lindan *nt* **-** lindane.
Linde *f* **-, -n** linden *or* lime (tree); (~*nholz*) limewood.
Lindenblütentee *m* lime blossom tea.
lindern *vt* to ease, to relieve, to alleviate; *Hustenreiz, Sonnenbrand etc auch* to soothe.
Linderung *f siehe vt* easing, relief, alleviation; soothing.
Linderungsmittel *nt* pain reliever, analgesic.
Lind-: l~grün *adj* lime green; **~wurm** *m* (*Myth*) lindworm (*type of wingless dragon*).
Lineal *nt* **-s, -e** ruler ◆ **einen Strich mit dem ~ ziehen** to rule a line, to draw a line with a ruler; **er geht, als ob er ein ~ verschluckt hätte** (*inf*) he walks with his back as stiff as a ramrod *or* as straight as a die.
linear *adj* linear.
Lineatur *f siehe* **Liniatur.**
Liner ['laɪnɐ] *m* **-s, -** (*Naut*) liner.
lingual *adj* (*form*) lingual.
Linguist(in *f*) *m* linguist.
Linguistik *f* linguistics *sing.*
linguistisch *adj* linguistic.
Liniatur *f* ruling, lines *pl.*
▼ **Linie** [-iə] *f* (a) (*auch Sport, Pol, Naut, Abstammung, Straßenmarkierung*) line; (*Umriß auch*) outline ◆ **ein Schreibblock mit ~n** a ruled *or* lined notepad; **die ~n (in) seiner Hand** the lines of *or* on his hand; **in einer ~ stehen** to be in a line; **sich in einer ~ aufstellen** to line up; **die Buchstaben halten nicht ~** (*Typ*) the letters are not in line; **auf der gleichen ~** along the same lines; **einer Sache** (*dat*) **fehlt die klare ~** there's no clear line to sth; **eine klare ~ für sein Leben finden, seinem Leben eine klare ~ geben** to give one's life a clear sense of direction; **eine ~ ziehen zwischen ...** (+*dat*) (*fig*) to draw a distinction between ...; **auf der ganzen ~** (*fig*) all along the line; **auf ~ bleiben** (*fig*) to toe the line; **sie hat ein Gesicht mit klaren/verschwommenen ~n** she has clear-cut/ill-defined features; **auf die (schlanke) ~ achten** to watch one's figure; **die männliche/weibliche ~ eines Geschlechts** the male/female line of a family; **in erster/zweiter ~ kommen** (*fig*) to come first/second, to take first/second place; **in erster ~ muß die Arbeitslosigkeit bekämpft werden** the fight against unemployment must come first *or* take priority; *siehe* **erste(r, s).**
(b) (*Mil*) (*Stellung*) line; (*Formation*) rank ◆ **in ~ antreten!** fall in!; **in ~ zu drei Gliedern** in ranks three deep; **die feindliche/vorderste ~** the enemy lines *pl*/front line.
(c) (*Verkehrsverbindung, -strecke*) route; (*Bus~, Eisenbahn~ auch*) line ◆ **fahren Sie mit der ~ 2** take a *or* the (number) 2; **auf einer ~ verkehren** to work a route; **die ~ Köln-Bonn** the Cologne-Bonn line.
Linien- [-iən]: **~blatt** *nt* ruled sheet (*placed under writing-paper*), line guide; **~bus** *m* public service bus, regular bus; **~dampfer** *m* regular service steamer; **~dienst** *m* regular service; (*Aviat*) scheduled service; **~flug** *m* scheduled flight; **~flugzeug** *nt* scheduled (service) plane; **~führung** *f* lines *pl*; **~maschine** *f* scheduled flight; **mit einer ~maschine** on a scheduled flight; **~netz** *nt* network of routes; **das ~netz der U-Bahn/der Straßenbahnen** the underground (system)/the tram system; **~papier** *nt* lined *or* ruled paper; **~richter** *m* (*Sport*) linesman; (*Tennis*) line judge; **~schiff** *nt* regular service ship; **l~treu** *adj* loyal to the party line; **l~treu sein** to follow *or* toe the party line; **~verkehr** *m* regular traffic; (*Aviat*) scheduled traffic; **im ~verkehr fliegen/fahren** to fly on scheduled services/operate on regular services.
linieren*, liniieren* *vt* to rule, to draw *or* rule lines on ◆ **liniert** lined, feint (*spec*).
Linierung, Liniierung *f* ruling.
link *adj* (*inf*) *Typ* underhanded, double-crossing; *Masche, Tour* dirty, low-down (*US inf*) ◆ **komm mir nicht so ~** stop messing me around (*inf*); **ein ganz ~er Hund** (*pej*) a nasty piece of work (*pej inf*); **ein ganz ~es Ding drehen** to get up to a bit of no good (*inf*).
Linke *f* **-n, -n** (a) (*Hand*) left hand; (*Seite*) left(-hand) side; (*Boxen*) left ◆ **zur ~n (des Königs) saß ...** to the left (of the king) *or* on the (king's) left sat ... (b) (*Pol*) Left.
linken *vt* (*inf: hereinlegen*) to con (*inf*).
Linke(r) *mf decl as adj* (*Pol*) left-winger, leftist (*pej*), lefty (*pej inf*).
linke(r, s) *adj attr* (a) left; *Rand, Spur etc auch* left-hand ◆ **die ~ Seite** the left(-hand) side; (*von Stoff*) the wrong side, the reverse (side); **auf der ~n Seite** on the left-hand side, on the left; **~r Hand, zur ~n Hand** to *or* on the *or* one's left; **~ Masche** (*Stricken*) purl (stitch); **eine ~ Masche stricken** to purl one; **zwei ~ Hände haben** (*inf*) to have two left hands (*inf*); **das mache ich mit der ~n Hand** (*inf*) I can do that with my eyes shut (*inf*); **er ist heute mit dem ~n Bein** *or* **Fuß zuerst aufgestanden** (*inf*) he got out of bed on the wrong side this morning (*inf*).
(b) (*Pol*) left-wing, leftist (*pej*), lefty (*pej inf*); *Flügel* left.
linkerseits *adv* to the left, on the left-hand side.
linkisch *adj* clumsy, awkward.
links [1] *adv* (a) on the left; *schauen, abbiegen* (to the) left ◆ **nach ~** (to the) left; **von ~** from the left; **~ von etw** (to *or* on the) left of sth; **~ von jdm** to *or* on sb's left; **sich ~ halten** to keep to the left; **weiter ~** further to the left; **sich ~ einordnen** to move into *or* take the left-hand lane; **jdn ~ liegenlassen** (*fig inf*) to ignore sb; **weder ~ noch rechts schauen** (*lit*) to look neither left nor right; (*fig*) not to let oneself be distracted; **~ von der Mitte** (*Pol*) (to the) left of centre; **~ stehen** *or* **sein** (*Pol*) to be left-wing *or* on the left *or* a left-winger; **Augen ~!** (*Mil*) eyes left!; **~ um!** (*Mil*) left about turn; **~ schwenkt, marsch!** (*Mil*) left wheel!
(b) (*verkehrt*) *bügeln* on the reverse *or* wrong side; *tragen* reverse *or* wrong side out; *liegen* reverse *or* wrong side up ◆ **~ stricken** to purl; **eine (Masche) ~, drei (Maschen) rechts** purl one, knit three; **der Pullover ist nur ~ gestrickt** the pullover is knitted all in purl.
[2] *prep +gen* on *or* to the left of.
Links-: ~abbieger *m* motorist/cyclist/car *etc* turning left; **~abbiegerspur** *f* left-hand turn-off lane; **~abweichler** *m* (*Pol inf*) left-wing dissenter; **~außen** *m* **-, -** (*Ftbl*) outside left; (*Pol*) extreme left-winger; **l~bündig** *adj* (*Typ*) ranged *or* flush left; **~drall** *m* (*lit*) (*im Gewehrlauf*) anticlockwise rifling; (*von Geschoß, Billardball*) swerve to the left; (*von Auto, Pferd*) pull to the left; (*fig*) leaning to the left; **einen ~drall haben** to swerve/pull/lean to the left; (*fig*) leaning to the left; **l~drehend** *adj* (*Chem*) laevorotatory (*spec*); **~extremist** *m* left-wing extremist; **~gang** *m* (*Tech*) left-handed thread; **l~gängig** *adj* (*Tech*) left-handed; **l~gerichtet** *adj* (*Pol*) left-wing orientated *no adv*; **~gewinde** *nt* left-handed thread; **~haken** *m* left hook; **~händer(in *f*)** *m* **-s, -** left-hander, left-handed person/player *etc*; **~händer sein** to be left-handed; **l~händig** *adj, adv* left-handed; **~händigkeit** *f* left-handedness; **l~her** *adv* (*old*) from the left; **l~heran** *adv* over to the left; **l~herum** *adv* (round) to the left; *sich drehen etc* anti-clockwise; **l~hin** *adv* (*old*) (to the) left; **~intellektuelle(r)** *mf* left-wing intellectual; **~kurve** *f* (*von Straße*) left-hand bend; (*von Bahn auch*) left-hand curve; **l~lastig** *adj* (*lit*) *Boot* listing to the left; *Auto* down at the left; (*fig*) leftist (*pej*), leaning to the left; **l~läufig** *adj Gewinde* left-handed; *Schrift* right-to-left; **~partei** *f* left-wing party; **l~radikal** *adj* (*Pol*) radically left-wing; **die ~radikalen** the left-wing radicals; **~radikalismus** *m* (*Pol*) left-wing radicalism; **l~rheinisch** *adj* to *or* on the left of the Rhine; **~ruck, ~rutsch, ~schwenk** *m* (*Pol*) shift to the left; **l~rum** *adv* (*inf*) *siehe* **l~herum**; **l~seitig** *adj* on the left(-hand) side; **l~seitig gelähmt** paralyzed in the left side; **l~um** *adv* (*Mil*) to the left; **l~um machen** (*inf*) to do a left turn; **l~um kehrt!** to the left about turn!; **~verkehr** *m, no pl* driving on the left *no def art*; **in Großbritannien ist ~verkehr** they drive on the left in Britain; **im ~verkehr muß man ...** when driving on the left one must ...
Linnen *nt* **-s, -** (*liter*) *siehe* **Leinen.**
linnen *adj* (*liter*) *siehe* **leinen.**
Linoleum [li'no:leʊm] *nt* **-s,** *no pl* linoleum, lino.
Linol-: ~säure *f* linoleic acid; **~schnitt** *m* (*Art*) linocut.
Linon [li:'nõ] *m* **-(s), -s** cotton/linen lawn.
Linse *f* **-, -n** (a) (*Bot, Cook*) lentil. (b) (*Opt*) lens.
linsen *vi* (*inf*) to peep, to peek (*inf*); (*Sch*) to copy (*bei* off, from).
Linsen-: ~gericht *nt* lentil dish; (*Bibl, fig*) mess of potage; **~suppe** *f* lentil soup.
Lippe *f* **-, -n** lip; (*Bot auch*) labium ◆ **eine (große** *or* **dicke) ~ riskieren** (*sl*) to be brazen; **das bringe ich nicht über die ~n** I can't bring myself to say it; **es wird** *or* **soll kein Wort über meine ~n kommen** not a word shall cross *or* pass my lips; **er brachte kein Wort über die ~n** he couldn't say *or* utter a word; **das Wort erstarb ihm auf den ~n** (*liter*) the word froze on his lips; *siehe* **hängen.**
Lippen-: ~bekenntnis *nt* lip-service; **ein ~bekenntnis ablegen** to pay lip-service (to one's ideals *etc*); **~blütler** *m* **-s, -** (*Bot*) labiate; **~laut** *m* (*Ling*) labial; **~pflegestift** *m* lip salve stick, lipcare stick; **~stift** *m* lipstick.
liquid *adj siehe* **liquide.**
Liquida *f* **-, Liquidä** *or* **Liquiden** (*Ling*) liquid.
Liquidation *f* (*form*) (a) (*Auflösung*) liquidation ◆ **in ~ treten** to go into liquidation; **sie haben die ~ beschlossen** they decided to go into liquidation. (b) (*Rechnung*) account.
liquid(e) *adj* (*Econ*) *Geld, Mittel* liquid; *Firma, Geschäftsmann* solvent ◆ **ich bin nicht ~** (*inf*) I'm out of funds (*inf*), I'm short of the ready (*inf*).
liquidieren* *vt* (a) *Geschäft* to put into liquidation, to wind up; *Betrag* to charge ◆ **einen Kontrakt in bar ~** to settle a contract in cash. (b) *Firma* to liquidate; *jdn* to eliminate.
Liquidierung *f* (*von Firma*) liquidation; (*von Person*) elimination.
Liquidität *f* (*Econ*) liquidity.
lismen *vti* (*Sw*) to knit.
lispeln *vti* to lisp; (*flüstern*) to whisper.
Lissabon *nt* **-s** Lisbon.
Lissaboner *adj attr* Lisbon.
Lissaboner(in *f*) *m* native of Lisbon; (*Einwohner*) inhabitant of Lisbon.
List *f* **-, -en** (*Täuschung*) cunning, artfulness; (*trickreicher Plan*) trick, ruse ◆ **mit ~ und Tücke** (*inf*) with a lot of coaxing; **zu einer ~ greifen, (eine) ~ anwenden** to use a bit of cunning, to resort to a ruse.

➤ SPRACHE AKTIV: **Linie: a** → 53.5

Liste *f* **-, -n** (*Aufstellung*) list; (*Wähler~*) register; (*von Parteien*) (party) list (*of candidates under the proportional representation system*) ◆ **sich in eine ~ eintragen** *or* **(ein)schreiben** to put oneself *or* one's name (down) on a list.
Listen-: ~führer *m* list keeper; **~platz** *m* (*Pol*) place on the party list (*of candidates under the proportional representation system*); **~preis** *m* list price; **~wahl** *f electoral system in which a vote is cast for a party rather than a specific candidate.*
listig *adj* cunning, crafty, wily *no adv.*
listigerweise *adv* cunningly, craftily.
Litanei *f* (*Eccl, fig*) litany ◆ **eine ~ von Klagen/Beschwerden** *etc* a long list *or* catalogue of complaints; **immer dieselbe ~ beten** to go on about the same old things all the time (*inf*).
Litauen *nt* **-s** Lithuania.
Litauer(in *f*) *m* **-s, -** Lithuanian.
litauisch *adj* Lithuanian.
Liter *m or nt* **-s, -** litre.
literarhistorisch *adj* literary historical *attr*; *Buch, Artikel auch* relating to literary history ◆ **~ interessant** of interest to literary history.
literarisch *adj* literary.
Literat *m* **-en, -en** man of letters; (*Schriftsteller*) literary figure ◆ **die ~en** literati (*form*).
Literatur *f* literature.
Literatur-: ~angabe *f* bibliographical reference; (*Zusammenfassung*) bibliography; **~denkmal** *nt* literary monument; **~gattung** *f* literary genre; **~geschichte** *f* history of literature; **l~geschichtlich** *adj siehe* **literarhistorisch**; **~hinweis** *m* literary reference (*auf +acc* to); **~kritik** *f* literary criticism; (*Kritikerschaft*) literary critics *pl*; **~kritiker** *m* literary critic; **~papst** *m* literary pundit; **~preis** *m* prize *or* award for literature, literary prize *or* award; **~verzeichnis** *nt* bibliography; **~wissenschaft** *f* literary studies *pl*; **vergleichende ~wissenschaft** comparative literature; **~wissenschaftler** *m* literary *or* literature specialist.
Liter-: ~flasche *f* litre bottle; **~leistung** *f* power output per litre; **~maß** *nt* litre measure; **l~weise** *adv* (*lit*) by the litre; (*fig*) by the gallon.
⚠ **Litfaßsäule** *f* advertising column.
Lithium *nt, no pl* (*abbr* **Li**) lithium.
⚠ **Litho-: ~graph** *m* lithographer; **~graphie** *f* **(a)** (*Verfahren*) lithography; **(b)** (*Druck*) lithograph; **l~graphieren*** *vt* to lithograph; **l~graphisch** *adj* lithographic(al).
litt *ptp of* **leiden.**
Liturgie *f* liturgy.
liturgisch *adj* liturgical.
Litze *f* **-, -n** braid; (*Elec*) flex.
live [laif] *adj pred, adv* (*Rad, TV*) live.
Live-Sendung [laif-] *f* live programme *or* broadcast.
Livree [li'vre:] *f* **-, -n** [-e:ən] livery.
livriert [li'vri:ɐt] *adj* liveried.
Lizenz *f* licence (*Brit*), license (*US*) ◆ **eine ~ dafür haben, etw zu tun** to have a licence to do sth, to be licensed to do sth; **etw in ~ herstellen** to manufacture sth under licence.
Lizenz-: ~abgabe *f* licence fee; (*im Verlagswesen*) royalty; **~abkommen** *nt* licensing agreement; **~ausgabe** *f* licensed edition; **~geber** *m* licenser; (*Behörde*) licensing authority; **~gebühr** *f* licence fee; (*im Verlagswesen*) royalty.
lizenzieren* *vt* (*form*) to license.
Lizenz-: ~inhaber *m* licensee, licence holder; **er ist ~inhaber** he has a licence, he is licensed; **~nehmer** *m* licensee; **~presse** *f* (*Pol*) licensed press; **~spieler** *m* (*Ftbl*) professional player; **~träger** *m* licensee.
Lkw, LKW ['ɛlka:ve:, ɛlka:'ve:] *m* **-(s), -(s)** *abbr of* **Lastkraftwagen.**
Lob *nt* **-(e)s,** *no pl* praise ◆ **~ verdienen** to deserve praise *or* to be praised; **(viel) ~ für etw bekommen** to come in for (a lot of) praise for sth, to be (highly) praised for sth; **ein ~ der Köchin** (my/our) compliments to the chef!; **Gott sei ~ und Dank** praise be to God, God be praised; **zum ~e Gottes** in praise of the Lord; **über jedes ~ erhaben sein** to be beyond praise; **sein eigenes ~ singen** (*inf*) to sing one's own praises, to blow one's own trumpet (*inf*); **jdm ~ spenden** *or* **zollen** to praise sb.
Lobby ['lɔbi] *f* **-, -s** *or* **Lobbies** lobby.
Lobbyismus [lɔbi'ɪsmʊs] *m* lobbyism.
Lobbyist(in *f*) [lɔbi'ɪst(ɪn)] *m* lobbyist.
loben *vt* to praise ◆ **sein neues Werk wurde allgemein sehr gelobt** his new work was universally acclaimed; **jdn/etw ~d erwähnen** to commend sb/sth; **das lob ich mir** that's what I like (to see/hear *etc*); **seinen Fleiß lob ich mir** his diligence is most laudable; **da lob ich mir doch ein gutes Glas Wein** I always say you can't beat a good glass of wine; *siehe* **Abend, Klee.**
lobenswert *adj* praiseworthy, laudable.
lobesam *adj* (*obs*) virtuous.
Lobeshymne *f* (*fig*) hymn of praise, panegyric.
Lob-: ~gesang *m* song *or* hymn of praise; **einen ~gesang auf jdn/etw anstimmen** (*fig*) to sing sb's praises/the praises of sth; **~hudelei** *f* (*pej*) gushing; **l~hudeln** *vi insep* **jdm l~hudeln** (*pej*) to gush over sb (*inf*).
löblich *adj* (*dated, iro*) commendable, laudable.
Lob-: ~lied *nt* song *or* hymn of praise; **ein ~lied auf jdn/etw anstimmen** *or* **singen** (*fig*) to sing sb's praises; **~preis** *m* (*liter*) praise *no art*; **l~preisen** *vt insep ptp* **l~(ge)priesen** (*liter*) *Gott* to praise, to glorify; **~rede** *f* eulogy, panegyric; **eine ~rede auf jdn halten** (*lit*) to make a speech in sb's honour; (*fig*) to eulogize *or* extol sb; **sich in ~reden über jdn/etw ergehen** to eulogize *or* extol sb/sth; **~redner** *m* (*lit*) speaker; (*fig*) eulogist; **l~singen** *vi insep irreg ptp* **l~gesungen** *+dat Gott* to praise; (*fig*) to sing the praises of; **~spruch** *m* eulogy (*über +acc* of), encomium (*form*); (*Gedicht*) panegyric.
Loch *nt* **-(e)s, ⸚er** (*Öffnung, Lücke*) hole; (*in Zahn auch*) cavity; (*in Reifen auch*) puncture; (*Luft~*) gap; (*Billard*) pocket; (*fig inf: elende Wohnung*) dump (*inf*), hole (*inf*); (*inf: Gefängnis*) jug (*sl*), clink (*sl*), can (*esp US sl*); (*vulg: Vagina*) cunt (*vulg*), hole (*sl*) ◆ **sich** (*dat*) **ein ~ in den Kopf/ins Knie** *etc* **schlagen** to gash one's head/knee *etc*, to cut one's head/knee *etc* open; **jdm ein ~** *or* **⸚er in den Bauch fragen** (*inf*) to pester the living daylights out of sb (with all one's questions) (*inf*); **sie redet einem ein ~** *or* **⸚er in den Bauch** (*inf*) she could talk the hind legs off a donkey (*inf*); **ein ~** *or* **⸚er in die Luft gucken** *or* **starren** *or* **in die Wand stieren** (*inf*) to gaze into space *or* thin air; **ein großes ~ in jds (Geld)beutel** (*acc*) *or* **Tasche** (*acc*) **reißen** (*inf*) to make a big hole in sb's pocket.
Loch|eisen *nt* punch.
lochen *vt* to punch holes/a hole in; to perforate; *Fahrkarte* to punch, to clip ◆ **gelochter Schreibblock** tear-off file pad.
Locher *m* **-s, - (a)** punch. **(b)** (*Mensch*) punch-card operator.
löcherig *adj* full of holes, holey ◆ **ganz ~ sein** to be full of holes.
löchern *vt* (*inf*) to pester (to death) with questions (*inf*) ◆ **er löchert mich seit Wochen, wann ...** he's been pestering me for weeks wanting to know when ...
Loch-: ~kamera *f* pinhole camera; **~karte** *f* punch card; **~kartenmaschine** *f* punch card machine; **~säge** *f* keyhole saw; **~stickerei** *f* broderie anglaise; **~streifen** *m* (punched) paper tape.
Lochung *f* punching; perforation.
Loch-: ~zange *f* punch; **~ziegel** *m* airbrick.
Locke[1] *f* **-, -n** (*Haar*) curl ◆ **~n haben** to have curly hair.
Locke[2] *f* **-, -n** (*Pfeife*) (bird) call.
locken[1] *vtr Haar* to curl ◆ **gelocktes Haar** curly hair.
locken[2] *vt* **(a)** *Tier* to lure ◆ **die Henne lockte ihre Küken** the hen called to its chicks.
(b) *jdn* to tempt; (*mit Ortsangabe*) to lure ◆ **es lockt mich in den Süden** I can feel the call of the south; **jdn in einen Hinterhalt ~** to lead *or* lure sb into a trap; **das Angebot lockt mich sehr** I'm very tempted by the offer; *siehe* **Falle, Tasche.**
löcken *vi*: **wider den Stachel ~** (*geh*) to kick against the pricks.
lockend *adj* tempting, enticing, alluring.
Locken-: ~kopf *m* curly hairstyle; (*Mensch*) curlyhead; **~pracht** *f* (magnificent) head of curls; **~schere** *f* curling tongs *pl or* irons *pl* (*old*); **~stab** *m* (electric) curling tongs *pl*; **~wickel, ~wickler** *m* **-s, -** (hair-) curler; **das Haar auf ~wickel drehen** to put one's hair in curlers.
locker *adj* (*lit, fig*) loose; *Schnee, Erdreich auch* loose-packed; *Kuchen, Schaum* light; (*nicht gespannt*) slack; *Haltung, Sitzweise* relaxed; (*sl*) cool (*sl*) ◆ **~ werden** (*lit, fig*) to get loose; (*Muskeln, Mensch*) to loosen up; (*Seil*) to get *or* go slack; (*Verhältnis*) to get more relaxed; (*Kuchen*) to be light; **etw ~ machen** to loosen sth/make sth light/slacken sth; **jdn ~ machen** to relax sb; **etw ~ lassen** to slacken sth off; *Bremse* to let sth off; **~ sitzen** (*Ziegel, Schraube etc*) to be loose; (*Mensch*) to relax, to sit in a relaxed position; **eine ~e Hand haben** (*fig*) (*schnell züchtigen*) to be quick to hit out; (*beim Schreiben*) to have a flowing hand; **bei ihr sitzt die Hand ziemlich ~** she's quick to lash out (*inf*); **bei ihm sitzt der Revolver/das Messer ~** he's trigger-happy/he'd pull a knife at the slightest excuse; **ein ~er Vogel** (*inf*) *or* **Zeisig** (*dated inf*) a bit of a lad (*inf*) *or* rake (*dated*), a gay dog (*dated*); **das mache ich ganz ~** (*sl*) I can do it just like that (*inf*).
Lockerheit *f, no pl* looseness; (*von Kuchen etc*) lightness; (*von Seil etc*) slackness.
locker-: ~lassen *vi sep irreg* (*inf*) **nicht ~lassen** not to give *or* let up; **~machen** *vt sep* (*inf*) *Geld* to shell out (*inf*), to part with; **bei jdm 100 Mark ~machen** to get sb to shell out (*inf*) *or* part with 100 marks.
lockern [1] *vt* **(a)** (*locker machen*) to loosen; *Griff auch* to relax; *Seil,* (*lit, fig*) *Zügel* to slacken.
(b) (*entspannen*) *Arme, Beine, Muskeln* to loosen up; (*fig*) *Vorschriften, Atmosphäre* to relax.
[2] *vr* to work itself loose; (*Sport*) to loosen up; (*zum Warmwerden*) to limber up; (*Verkrampfung, Spannung*) to ease off; (*Atmosphäre, Beziehungen, Mensch*) to get more relaxed.
Lockerung *f siehe vt* **(a)** loosening; relaxation; slackening. **(b)** loosening up; relaxation; (*von Beziehungen*) easing, relaxation.
Lockerungs-: ~mittel *nt* raising agent; **~übung** *f* loosening-up exercise; (*zum Warmwerden*) limbering-up exercise.
lockig *adj Haar* curly; *Mensch* curlyheaded.
Lock-: ~mittel *nt* lure; **~pfeife** *f* (bird) call; (*für Hund*) whistle; **~ruf** *m* call; **~spitzel** *m* agent provocateur; **~stoff-Falle** *f* pheromone-baited insect trap.
Lockung *f* lure; (*Versuchung*) temptation.
Lockvogel *m* decoy (bird); (*fig*) lure, decoy.
Lockvogel|angebot *nt* inducement.
Loddel *m* **-s, -** (*inf*) ponce (*inf*), pimp.
Lode *f* **-, -n** sapling.
Loden *m* **-s, -** loden (cloth).
Lodenmantel *m* loden (coat).
lodern *vi* (*lit, fig*) to blaze; (*empor~*) to blaze up ◆ **in seinen Augen loderte Haß/Gier** his eyes blazed with hatred/greed.
Löffel *m* **-s, - (a)** (*als Besteck*) spoon; (*als Maßangabe*) spoonful; (*von Bagger*)

bucket ◆ **den ~ abgeben** (*inf*) *or* **wegschmeißen** (*sl*) *or* **aus der Hand legen** (*inf*) to kick the bucket (*inf*); *siehe* **balbieren.**
(b) (*Hunt*) ear; (*inf: von Mensch auch*) lug (*Brit sl*) ◆ **jdm ein paar hinter die ~ hauen** (*inf*), **jdm eins hinter die ~ geben** to give sb a clout round the ear(s); **sich** (*dat*) **etw hinter die ~ schreiben** (*inf*) to get sth into one's head (*inf*); **sperr doch deine ~ auf** (*inf*) pin back your lugholes (*Brit sl*), listen properly.
Löffelbagger *m* excavator, mechanical shovel.
löffeln *vt* to spoon; (*mit der Kelle*) to ladle.
Löffel-: ~stiel *m* spoon-handle; **l~weise** *adv* by the spoonful.
Löffler *m* **-s, -** (*Zool*) spoonbill.
Loft *nt* **-s, -s** (*Build*) luxury attic flat (*Brit*) *or* apartment (*esp US*).
log *abbr of* **Logarithmus.**
log *pret of* **lügen.**
Log *nt* **-s, -e** (*Naut*) log.
Logarithmentafel *f* log table.
logarithmieren* [1] *vt* to find the log(arithm) of.
[2] *vi* to find log(arithm)s/the log(arithm).
logarithmisch *adj* logarithmic.
Logarithmus *m* logarithm.
Logbuch *nt* log(book).
Loge ['lo:ʒə] *f* **-, -n (a)** (*Theat*) box. **(b)** (*Freimaurer~*) lodge. **(c)** (*Pförtner~*) lodge.
Logen- ['lo:ʒən-]: **~bruder** *m* lodge brother; **~meister** *m* master of a/the lodge; **~platz** *m* (*Theat*) seat in a box.
Logger *m* **-s, -** (*Naut*) lugger.
Loggia ['lɔdʒa] *f* **-, Loggien** [-iən] (*Bogenhalle*) loggia; (*Balkon auch*) balcony.
Logglas *nt* log glass.
Logierbesuch [lo'ʒi:ɐ-] *m* (*dated*) house-guest(s *pl*).
logieren* [lo'ʒi:rən] (*dated*) [1] *vi* to stay; (*als Zimmerherr*) to lodge.
[2] *vt* **jdn ~** to put sb up.
Logiergast [lo'ʒi:ɐ-] *m* (*dated*) (*Besuch*) house-guest; (*Untermieter*) lodger.
Logik *f* logic ◆ **in der ~** in logic; **du hast vielleicht eine ~!** your logic is a bit quaint; **dieser Aussage fehlt die ~** this statement is illogical *or* is lacking in logic.
Logiker(in *f***)** *m* **-s, -** logician.
Logis [lo'ʒi:] *nt* **-, -** (*dated*) lodgings *pl*, rooms *pl*; (*Naut*) forecastle, crew's quarters *pl* ◆ **Kost und ~** board and lodging; **bei jdm in** *or* **zu ~ wohnen** to lodge with sb.
logisch *adj* logical; (*inf: selbstverständlich*) natural ◆ **gehst du auch hin? — ~** are you going too? — of course.
logischerweise *adv* logically.
Logistik *f* **(a)** (*Math*) logic. **(b)** (*Mil*) logistics *sing*.
logistisch *adj* logistic.
Logleine *f* (*Naut*) logline.
logo *interj* (*sl*) you bet (*inf*).
Logo *nt* **-(s), -s** (*Firmen~*) logo.
Logopäde *m* **-n, -n, Logopädin** *f* speech therapist.
Logopädie *f* speech therapy.
Logotype *f* **-, -n** logotype.
Lohe¹ *f* **-, -n** (*liter*) raging flames *pl*.
Lohe² *f* **-, -n** (*Gerbrinde*) tan.
lohen¹ *vi* (*liter*) to blaze.
lohen² *vt* *Felle* to tan.
Loh-: ~gerber *m* tanner; **~gerbung** *f* tanning.
Lohn *m* **-(e)s, ¨-e (a)** (*Arbeitsentgelt*) wage(s), pay *no pl, no indef art* ◆ **wieviel ~ bekommst du?** how much do you get (paid)?, what are your wages?; **bei jdm in ~ und Brot stehen** (*old*) to be in sb's employ (*old*); **jdn um ~ und Brot bringen** (*old*) to deprive sb of a living *or* livelihood.
(b) (*fig: Belohnung/Vergeltung*) reward; (*Strafe*) punishment ◆ **als** *or* **zum ~ für** ... as a reward/punishment for ...; **sein verdienter ~** one's just reward; **das ist nun der ~ für meine Mühe!** (*iro*), **das ist ein schlechter ~ für all die Mühe** that's what I get *or* that's all the thanks I get for my trouble.
Lohn-: ~abbau *m* reduction of earnings; **l~abhängig** *adj* on a payroll; **~abhängige(r)** *mf* worker; **~abkommen** *nt* wages *or* pay agreement; **~abrechnung** *f* wages slip; *siehe* **Abrechnung**; **~abzug** *m* deduction from one's wages; **~arbeit** *f* labour; **~ausfall** *m* loss of earnings; **~ausgleich** *m* wage adjustment; **bei vollem ~ausgleich** with full pay; **~auszahlung** *f* payment of wages; **~buchhalter** *m* wages clerk; **~buchhaltung** *f* wages accounting; wages office; **~büro** *nt* wages office; **~empfänger** *m* wage-earner.
lohnen [1] *vir* to be worthwhile, to be worth it ◆ **es lohnt (sich), etw zu tun** it is worth *or* worthwhile doing sth; **die Mühe lohnt sich** it is worth the effort, the effort is worthwhile; **der Film lohnt sich wirklich** the film is really worth seeing; **Fleiß lohnt sich immer** hard work always pays (off) *or* is always worthwhile; **das lohnt sich nicht für mich** it's not worth my while.
[2] *vt* **(a)** to be worth ◆ **das Ergebnis lohnt die Mühe** the result makes all the effort worthwhile *or* amply repays all the effort.
(b) jdm etw ~ to reward sb for sth; **er hat mir meine Hilfe mit Undank gelohnt** he repaid my help with ingratitude.
löhnen [1] *vi* (*inf: viel bezahlen*) to pay up, to cough up (*inf*), to shell out (*inf*).
[2] *vt* **(a)** (*inf: bezahlen*) to shell out (*inf*). **(b)** (*old: mit Lohn versehen*) to pay.
lohnend *adj* rewarding; (*nutzbringend*) worthwhile; (*einträglich*) profitable; (*sehens-/hörenswert*) worth seeing/hearing.
lohnenswert *adj* worthwhile ◆ **es ist ~, etw zu tun** it is worth(while) doing sth.
Lohn-: ≈erhöhung *f* wage *or* pay rise, rise; **≈forderung** *f* wage demand *or* claim; **≈fortzahlung** *f* continued payment of wages; **≈gefälle** *nt* pay differential; **≈gruppe** *f* wage group; **≈herr** *m* (*old*) employer; **l≈intensiv** *adj* wage-intensive; **≈kosten** *pl* wage costs *pl*; **≈kürzung** *f* wage cut; **≈liste** *f* payroll; **~nebenkosten** *pl* additional wage costs *pl*; **≈poker** *nt* (*fig*) wages haggling; **≈politik** *f* pay policy; **~-Preis-Spirale** *f* (*Econ*) wage-price spiral; **≈runde** *f* pay round; **≈senkung** *f* cut in wages *or* pay; **≈skala** *f* pay *or* wages scale; **≈steuer** *f* income tax (*paid on earned income*).
Lohnsteuer-: ~jahresausgleich *m* annual adjustment of income tax; **beim letzten ~jahresausgleich habe ich 100 DM zurückbekommen** at the end of the last tax year I got back DM 100; **≈karte** *f* (income) tax card.
Lohn-: ~stopp *m* wages *or* pay freeze; **~streifen** *m* pay slip; **~stückkosten** *pl* (*Comm*) unit wage costs *pl*; **~tarif** *m* wage rate; **~tüte** *f* pay packet.
Löhnung *f* **(a)** (*Auszahlung*) payment; (*auch* **~stag** *m*) pay day. **(b)** (*Lohn*) pay.
Lohn-: ~verhandlung *f* pay *or* wage negotiations *pl*; **~verzicht** *m* **Lohnverzicht üben** to take a cut in wages; **wir mußten einen Lohnverzicht hinnehmen** we had to accept a cut in wages; **~zahlung** *f* payment of wages; **~zettel** *m* pay slip.
Loipe *f* **-, -n** cross-country ski run.
Lok *f* **-, -s** *abbr of* **Lokomotive** engine.
lokal *adj* **(a)** (*örtlich*) local ◆ **~es Rechnernetz** (*Comput*) local area network. **(b)** (*Gram*) of place.
Lokal *nt* **-s, -e (a)** (*Gaststätte*) pub (*esp Brit*), bar; (*auf dem Land auch*) inn (*Brit*); (*Restaurant*) restaurant. **(b)** (*Versammlungsraum*) meeting place.
Lokal- *in cpds* local; **~anästhesie** *f* (*Med*) local anaesthesia; **~augenschein** *m* (*Aus Jur*) *siehe* **~termin**; **~derby** *nt* local derby.
Lokale(s) *nt decl as adj* local news.
Lokalfernsehen *nt* local television.
Lokalisation *f siehe vt* **(a)** location. **(b)** localization; limiting.
lokalisieren* *vt* **(a)** (*Ort feststellen*) to locate. **(b)** (*Med*) to localize; (*auf einen Ort*) to limit (*auf +acc* to).
Lokalisierung *f siehe* **Lokalisation.**
Lokalität *f* **(a)** (*örtliche Beschaffenheit*) locality; (*Raum*) facilities *pl* ◆ **sich mit den ~en auskennen** to know the district; **die ~en verlassen** to leave the premises.
(b) (*hum inf: Lokal*) pub (*esp Brit*), bar.
(c) (*hum inf: WC*) cloakroom (*euph*), washroom, bathroom (*US*).
Lokal-: ~kolorit *nt* local colour; **~nachrichten** *pl* local news *sing*; **~patriotismus** *m* local patriotism; **~reporter** *m* local reporter; **~satz** *m* (*Gram*) (adverbial) clause of place; **~teil** *m* local section; **~termin** *m* (*Jur*) visit to the scene of the crime; **~verbot** *nt* ban; **~verbot haben** to be barred *or* banned from a pub/bar; **~zeitung** *f* local newspaper.
Lokativ *m* (*Gram*) locative (case).
Lokführer *m abbr of* **Lokomotivführer.**
Lokogeschäft *nt* (*St Ex*) spot deal.
Lokomotive *f* locomotive, (railway) engine.
Lokomotiv-: ~führer *m* engine driver, engineer (*US*); **~schuppen** *m* engine-shed.
Lokopreis *m* (*St Ex*) spot price.
Lokus *m* **-** *or* **-ses, -** *or* **-se** (*inf*) toilet, bathroom (*esp US*).
Lombard *m or nt* **-(e)s, -e** (*Fin*) loan on security.
Lombardgeschäft *nt* loan on security.
lombardieren *vt* (*Fin*) to accept as collateral.
Lombard-: ~kasse *f* guaranty authority; **~kredit** *m* collateral loan; **~satz** *m* rate for loans on security.
London *nt* London.
Londoner *adj attr* London.
Londoner(in *f***)** *m* **-s, -** Londoner.
Longdrink ['lɔŋdrɪŋk] *m* long drink.
Longe ['lõ:ʒə] *f* **-, -n** (*für Pferde*) lunge; (*für Akrobaten*) harness.
longieren* [lõ'ʒi:rən] *vt* *Pferd* to lunge.
Look [lʊk] *m* **-s, -s** (*Mode*) look.
Looping ['lu:pɪŋ] *m or nt* **-s, -s** (*Aviat*) looping the loop ◆ **einen ~ machen** to loop the loop.
⚠ **Lorbaß** *m* **-sses, -sse** (*dial inf*) sly devil (*inf*), sharp one (*inf*).
Lorbeer *m* **-s, -en (a)** (*lit: Gewächs*) laurel; (*als Gewürz*) bayleaf; (*~kranz*) laurel wreath.
(b) ~en *pl* (*fig: Erfolg*) laurels *pl* ◆ **sich auf seinen ~en ausruhen** (*inf*) to rest on one's laurels; **seine ersten ~en ernten** to win one's first laurels; **damit kannst du keine ~en ernten** that's no great achievement.
Lorbeer-: ~baum *m* laurel (tree); **~blatt** *nt* bayleaf; **~kranz** *m* laurel wreath.
Lordose *f* **-, -n** (*Med*) lordosis (*spec*).
Lore *f* **-, -n (a)** (*Rail*) truck, wagon; (*Kipp~*) tipper, dumper. **(b)** (*Kohlenmaß: 200 Zentner*) 10,000 kilos (of coal).
Lorgnette [lɔrn'jetə] *f* lorgnette.
Lorgnon [lɔrn'jõ:] *nt* **-s, -s** lorgnon.
Los *nt* **-es, -e (a)** (*für Entscheidung*) lot; (*in der Lotterie, auf Jahrmarkt etc*) ticket ◆ **das Große ~ gewinnen** *or* **ziehen** (*lit, fig*) to hit the jackpot; **etw durch das ~ entscheiden** *or* **bestimmen** *or* **ermitteln** to decide sth by drawing *or* casting lots; **jdn durch das ~ bestimmen** to pick sb by drawing lots; **etw durch das ~ gewinnen** to win sth in a lottery *or* (*bei Tombola*) raffle *or* (*auf Jahrmarkt*) tombola; **das ~ hat mich getroffen** it fell to my lot.
(b) *no pl* (*Schicksal*) lot ◆ **er hat ein hartes** *or* **schweres ~** his is a hard *or* not

an easy lot; **das gleiche ~ erfahren** to share the same lot; **jds ~ teilen** to share sb's lot.

los [1] *adj pred* **(a)** (*nicht befestigt*) loose ◆ **der Hund ist von der Leine ~** the dog is off the lead.

(b) (*frei*) **jdn/etw ~ sein** (*inf*) to be rid *or* shot (*inf*) of sb, to have got *or* gotten (*US*) rid of sb; **ich bin mein ganzes Geld ~** (*inf*) I'm cleaned out (*inf*).

(c) (*inf*) **etwas ist ~/es ist nichts ~** (*geschieht*) there's something/nothing going on *or* happening; (*nicht in/in Ordnung*) there's something/nothing wrong *or* the matter, something's/nothing's up; **mit jdm/etw ist etwas/nichts ~** there's something/nothing wrong *or* the matter with sb/sth; **mit jdm/etw ist nichts (mehr) ~** (*inf*) sb/sth isn't up to much (any more), sb/sth is a dead loss (now) (*inf*); **etwas ~ machen** (*sl*) to make sth happen; **was ist denn hier/da ~?** what's going on *or* what's up here/there (then)?; **was ist ~?** what's up?, what's wrong?, what's the matter?; **was ist da abends ~?** what is there going on there in the evenings?; **wo ist denn hier was ~?** where's the action here (*inf*)?; **als mein Vater das hörte, da war was ~!** when my father got to hear of it, you should have heard him.

[2] *adv* **(a)** (*Aufforderung*) **~!** come on!; (*geh/lauf schon*) go on!, get going!; **nun aber ~!** let's get going; (*zu andern*) get going *or* moving (*inf*); **nichts wie ~!** let's get going; **(na) ~, mach schon!** (come on,) get on with it; **~, schreib/fahr** *etc* **doch endlich** come on, start writing/driving *etc*; **auf die Plätze** *or* **Achtung, fertig, ~** on your marks, get set, go!, ready, steady, go!

(b) (*weg*) **sie wollen ~ vom Reich/Kapitalismus** they want to break away from the Reich/from capitalism; **wir wollen früh ~** we want to leave *or* to be off early.

los- *pref +vb* (*anfangen zu*) to start *+prp*; (*bei Verben der Bewegung auch*) *infin+* off; (*befreien von, loslösen*) *infin+* off.

-los *adj suf* -less.

lösbar *adj* soluble.

los-: ~bellen *vi sep* (*Hund*) to start barking; (*Mensch*) to start yelling; **~binden** *vt sep irreg* to untie (*von* from); **~brechen** *sep irreg* [1] *vt* to break off; [2] *vi aux sein* (*Gelächter etc*) to break out; (*Sturm, Gewitter*) to break.

Lösch-: ~arbeit *f usu pl* fire-fighting operations *pl*; **l~bar** *adj* **(a)** *Feuer, Flammen* extinguishable; *Kalk* slakable; *Durst* quenchable; *Schrift, Tonband* erasable; **die Hypothek/Schuld/Eintragung/das Konto ist l~bar** the mortgage/debt can be paid off/the entry can be deleted/the account can be closed; **(b)** (*Naut*) unloadable; **~blatt** *nt* sheet *or* piece of blotting paper; **~eimer** *m* fire-bucket.

löschen [1] *vt* **(a)** *Feuer, Brand, Flammen, Kerze* to put out, to extinguish; *Licht auch* to switch out *or* off, to turn out *or* off; *Kalk, Durst* to slake; *Durst* to quench; *Schrift (an Tafel), Tonband* to wipe *or* rub off, to erase; *Hypothek, Schuld* to pay off; *Eintragung, Zeile* to delete; *Konto* to close; *Firma, Name* to strike off; (*aufsaugen*) *Tinte* to blot; (*Comput*) *Speicher, Bildschirm* to clear; *Daten, Information* to erase, to delete.

(b) (*Naut*) *Ladung* to unload.

[2] *vi* **(a)** (*Feuerwehr etc*) to put out a/the fire.

(b) (*aufsaugen*) to blot.

(c) (*Naut*) to unload.

Löscher *m* **-s, -** (fire) extinguisher; (*Tinten~*) blotter.

Lösch-: ~fahrzeug *nt* fire engine; **~kalk** *m* slaked lime; **~mannschaft** *f* team of firemen/fire-fighters; **~mittel** *nt* (fire-)extinguishing agent; **~papier** *nt* (piece of) blotting paper; **~schaum** *m* extinguishant foam; **~taste** *f* (*Comput*) delete key.

Löschung *f* **(a)** (*von Schuld, Hypothek*) paying off; (*von Eintragung*) deletion; (*von Konto*) closing; (*von Firma, Namen*) striking off; (*Comput: von Daten*) erasing, deletion.

(b) (*Naut*) (*von Ladung*) unloading.

Lösch-: ~wasser *nt, no pl* water for firefighting; **~zug** *m* set of fire-fighting appliances.

losdonnern *vi sep* (*lit, fig*) to start to thunder.

lose *adj* (*lit, fig*) loose; (*nicht gespannt*) *Seil* slack; (*schelmisch*) *Streich* mischievous ◆ **etw ~ verkaufen** to sell sth loose; *siehe* **Maul, Zunge**.

Loseblatt|ausgabe *f* loose-leaf edition.

Lösegeld *nt* ransom (money).

los|eisen *sep* (*inf*) [1] *vt* to get *or* prise away (*bei* from) ◆ **jdn von einer Verpflichtung ~** to get sb out of an obligation.

[2] *vr* to get away (*bei* from); (*von Verpflichtung etc*) to get out (*von* of).

losen *vi* to draw lots (*um* for) ◆ **wir ~, wer** ... we'll draw lots to decide who ...

lösen [1] *vt* **(a)** (*losmachen, abtrennen, entfernen*) to remove (*von* from); *Boot* to cast off (*von* from); (*ab~*) *Fleisch, Briefmarken, Tapete etc auch* to get off (*von etw* sth); (*heraus~ auch*) to get out (*aus* of); (*aufbinden*) *Knoten, Fesseln, Gürtel, Haare* to undo; *Arme* to unfold; *Hände* to unclasp; *Handbremse* to take *or* let off; *Husten, Krampf* to ease; *Muskeln* to loosen up; (*lit, fig: lokkern*) to loosen ◆ **sie löste ihre Hand aus der seinen** she slipped her hand out of his; *siehe* **gelöst**.

(b) (*klären, Lösung finden für*) to solve; *Konflikt, Schwierigkeiten* to resolve.

(c) (*annullieren*) *Vertrag* to cancel; *Verlobung* to break off; *Verbindung, Verhältnis* to sever; *Ehe* to dissolve.

(d) (*zergehen lassen*) to dissolve.

(e) (*kaufen*) *Karte* to buy, to get.

[2] *vr* **(a)** (*sich losmachen*) to detach oneself (*von* from); (*sich ab~ auch*) to come off (*von etw* sth); (*Knoten, Haare*) to come undone; (*Schuß*) to go off; (*Husten, Krampf, Spannung*) to ease; (*Schleim, Schmutz*) to loosen; (*Atmosphäre*) to relax; (*Muskeln*) to loosen up; (*lit, fig: sich lockern*) to (be)come loose ◆ **sich von jdm ~** to break away from sb; **sich von etw ~** *von Verpflichtungen* to free oneself of sth; *von Vorstellung, Vorurteilen, Gedanken* to rid oneself of sth; *von Partnern, Vaterland, Vergangenheit* to break with sth *or* away from sth; **das Boot hat sich von der Verankerung gelöst** the boat has broken (away from) its moorings; **eine Gestalt löste sich aus der Dunkelheit** (*liter*) a figure detached itself *or* emerged from the darkness.

(b) (*sich aufklären*) to be solved ◆ **sich von selbst ~** (*Mordfall*) to solve itself; (*Problem auch*) to clear itself up, to resolve itself.

(c) (*zergehen*) to dissolve (*in +dat* in) ◆ **ihre Anspannung/ihr Schmerz löste sich in Tränen** her tension/pain found relief in tears.

los-: ~fahren *vi sep irreg aux sein* **(a)** (*abfahren*) to set off; (*Fahrzeug*) to move off; (*Auto*) to drive off; **(b)** (*inf: schimpfen, anfallen*) **auf jdn ~fahren** to lay into sb (*inf*), to attack sb; **~gehen** *vi sep irreg aux sein* **(a)** (*weggehen*) to set off; (*Schuß, Bombe etc*) to go off; **(mit dem Messer) auf jdn ~gehen** to go for sb (with a knife); **(b)** (*inf: anfangen*) to start; (*Geschrei der Menge*) to go up; **gleich geht's ~** it's just about to start; (*bei Streit*) any minute now; **jetzt geht's ~!** here we go!; (*Vorstellung*) it's starting!; (*Rennen*) they're off!; (*Reise, Bewegung*) we're/you're off!; **jetzt geht's wieder ~ (mit ihren Klagen)** here we go again (with all her moans); **geht's bald ~?** will it start soon?; (*Reise etc*) are we off soon?; **bei drei geht's ~** you/they *etc* start on the count of three; **jetzt geht's aber ~!** (*sl*) you're kidding! (*inf*); (*bei Frechheit*) do you mind!; **(c)** (*inf: abgehen*) to come off; **~haben** *vt sep irreg* (*inf*) **etwas/nichts ~haben** to be pretty clever (*inf*)/pretty stupid (*inf*); **~heulen** *vi sep* to burst out crying; **~kaufen** *vt sep* to buy out; *Entführten* to ransom; **~knüpfen** *vt sep* to untie, to undo; **~kommen** *vi sep irreg aux sein* (*Mensch*) to get away (*von* from); (*sich befreien*) to free oneself, to get free (*von* from); **das Boot kam von der Sandbank ~/nicht ~** the boat came off/wouldn't come off the sandbank; **von Schulden ~kommen** to get out of debt; **~kriegen** *vt sep* (*inf*) (*ablösen*) to get off; (*~werden*) *Mensch* to get rid *or* shot (*inf*) of; **~lachen** *vi sep* to burst out laughing; **laut ~lachen** to laugh out loud; **~lassen** *vt sep irreg* **(a)** (*nicht mehr festhalten*) to let go of; (*fig: nicht fesseln*) *Mensch* to let go; **der Gedanke/die Frage** *etc* **läßt mich nicht mehr ~** the thought/problem haunts me *or* won't go out of my mind; **das Buch läßt mich nicht mehr ~** I can't put the book down; **(b)** (*inf*) (*abfeuern*) *Feuerwerk, Bombe* to let off; (*fig*) *Rede, Witze, Geschichte* to come out with; *Beschwerden, Schimpfkanonade* to launch into; *Schrift* to launch; *Brief* to send off; **(c) jdn (auf jdn) ~lassen** (*fig inf*) to let sb loose (on sb); **die Hunde auf jdn ~lassen** to put *or* set the dogs on(to) sb; **und so was läßt man nun auf die Menschheit ~!** (*hum inf*) what a thing to unleash on an unsuspecting world; **wehe, wenn sie ~gelassen ...** (*hum inf*) once let them off the leash ...; **~laufen** *vi sep irreg aux sein* (*zu laufen anfangen*) to start to run; (*weggehen*) to run out; **~legen** *vi sep* (*inf*) to get going *or* started; (*mit Schimpfen*) to let fly (*inf*) *or* rip (*inf*); **er legte gleich mit seinen Ideen ~** he started on about his ideas; **nun leg mal ~ und erzähle ...** now come on and tell me/us ...

löslich *adj* soluble ◆ **leicht/schwer ~** readily/not readily soluble.

los-: ~lösen *sep* [1] *vt* to remove (*von* from); (*ablösen auch*) to take off (*von etw* sth); (*herauslösen auch*) to take out (*aus* of); (*lockern*) to loosen; [2] *vr* to detach oneself (*von* from); (*sich ablösen auch*) to come off (*von etw* sth); (*lockern*) to become loose; **sich von jdm ~lösen** to break away from sb; **~machen** *sep* [1] *vt* **(a)** to free; (*~binden*) to untie; *Handbremse* to let *or* take off; **jdn von einer Kette ~machen** to unchain sb; **(b) einen** *or* **was ~machen** (*sl*) to have some action (*inf*); [2] *vi* **(a)** (*Naut*) to cast off; **(b)** (*inf: sich beeilen*) to step on it (*inf*), to get a move on (*inf*); [3] *vr* to get away (*von* from); **der Hund hat sich ~gemacht** the dog has got loose; **~müssen** *vi sep irreg* (*inf*) to have to go.

Losnummer *f* ticket number.

los-: ~platzen *vi sep aux sein* (*inf*) (*lachen*) to burst out laughing; (*spontan, vorzeitig äußern*) to start yapping (*inf*); **mit etw ~platzen** to burst out with sth; **platz nicht immer gleich ~** think before you speak; **~prusten** *vi sep* (*inf*) to explode (with laughter); **~quatschen** *vi sep* (*inf*) to prattle away (*inf*); **~rasen** *vi sep aux sein* (*inf*) to race *or* tear off; **~reißen** *sep irreg* [1] *vt* to tear *or* rip off (*von etw* sth)/down (*von* from)/out (*aus* of)/up; **jdn ~reißen** to tear sb away; [2] *vr* **sich (von etw) ~reißen** (*Hund etc*) to break free *or* loose (from sth); (*fig*) to tear oneself away (from sth); **~rennen** *vi sep irreg aux sein* (*inf*) to run off; (*anfangen zu laufen*) to start to run.

Löß *m* **-es** *or* **-sses, -e** *or* **-sse** (*Geol*) loess.

lossagen *vr sep* **sich von etw ~** to renounce sth; **sich von jdm/seiner Vergangenheit ~** to dissociate oneself from *or* break with sb/the *or* one's past.

Lossagung *f siehe vr* renunciation (*von* of); dissociation (*von* from).

Lößboden *m* loess soil.

los-: ~schicken *vt sep* to send off; **~schießen** *vi sep irreg* **(a)** (*zu schießen anfangen*) to open fire; **schieß ~!** (*fig inf*) fire away! (*inf*); **(b)** *aux sein* (*schnell starten*) to shoot *or* race off; **auf jdn ~schießen** to race towards sb; **~schlagen** *sep irreg* [1] *vi* to hit out; (*Mil*) to (launch one's) attack; **auf jdn/aufeinander ~schlagen** to go for sb/one another *or* each other; [2] *vt* **(a)** (*abschlagen*) to knock off; **(b)** (*inf: verkaufen*) to get rid of; **~schnallen** *vt sep* to unbuckle; **~schrauben** *vt sep* to unscrew; (*lockern auch*) to loosen; **~springen** *vi sep irreg aux sein* to jump; **auf jdn/etw ~springen** to leap for sb/sth; **~steuern** *vi sep aux sein* **auf jdn/etw ~ steuern** to head *or* make for sb/sth; **~stürzen** *vi sep aux sein* to rush off; **auf jdn/etw ~stürzen** to pounce on sb/sth.

Lost *m* **-(e)s,** *no pl* (*Chem*) mustard gas.

los-: ~tigern *vi sep aux sein* (*inf*) to toddle off (*inf*); **~trennen** *vt sep siehe* **abtrennen**; **~treten** *vt sep irreg* to kick off.

Lostrommel *f* drum (*containing lottery tickets*).

Losung[1] *f* **(a)** (*Devise, Parole*) motto. **(b)** (*Kennwort*) password.

Losung[2] *f (Hunt)* droppings *pl*.
Lösung *f* **(a)** solution (*gen* to); (*das Lösen*) solution (*gen* of); (*eines Konfliktes, von Schwierigkeiten*) resolving ◆ **zur ~ dieser Schwierigkeiten** to resolve these problems. **(b)** (*Annullierung*) (*eines Vertrages*) cancellation; (*von Beziehungen, einer Verlobung*) breaking off; (*einer Verbindung, eines Verhältnisses*) severing, severance; (*einer Ehe*) dissolving. **(c)** (*Chem*) solution.
Lösungsmittel *nt* solvent.
Losungswort *nt* password.
Losverkäufer *m* ticket seller (*for lottery, raffle etc*).
loswerden *vt sep irreg aux sein* to get rid of; *Gedanken* to get away from, to get out of one's mind; *Angst etc auch* to rid oneself of; *Hemmungen auch, Geld* (*beim Spiel etc*), *Hab und Gut* to lose; *Geld* (*ausgeben*) to spend ◆ **er wird seine Erkältung einfach nicht los** he can't shake off *or* get rid of his cold.
losziehen *vi sep irreg aux sein* **(a)** (*aufbrechen*) to set out *or* off (*in +acc, nach* for). **(b) gegen jdn/etw ~** (*inf*) to lay into sb/sth (*inf*).
Lot[1] *nt* **-(e)s, -e (a)** (*Senkblei*) plumbline; (*Naut auch*) sounding line ◆ **im ~ sein** to be in plumb.
(b) (*old*) *old unit of weight varying between 16 and 50 gram.*
(c) (*Lötmetall*) solder.
(d) (*Math*) perpendicular ◆ **das ~ fällen** to drop a perpendicular; **seine Finanzen wieder ins ~ bringen** to put one's finances back on an even keel; **die Sache ist wieder im ~** things have been straightened out; **die Sache wieder ins (rechte) ~ bringen** to put things right, to put the record straight (*inf*).
Lot[2] *m* **-s** (*Bibl*) Lot.
Löt|apparat *m* soldering appliance.
lötbar *adj* solderable.
loten *vt* to plumb.
löten *vti* to solder.
Lothringen *nt* **-s** Lorraine.
Lothringer(in *f*) *m* **-s,** - Lorrainer ◆ **~ Kreuz** Cross of Lorraine.
lothringisch *adj* of Lorraine, Lorrainese.
Lotion [lo'tsio:n] *f* **-, -en** lotion.
Löt-: ~kolben *m* soldering iron; **~lampe** *f* blowlamp.
Lotleine *f* plumbline.
Lötmetall *nt* solder.
Lotophage [loto'fa:gə] *m* **-n, -n** (*Myth*) lotus-eater.
Lotos *m* **-,** - lotus.
Lotos-: ~blume *f* lotus (flower); **~sitz** *m* lotus position.
lotrecht *adj* (*Math*) perpendicular.
Lotrechte *f* (*Math*) perpendicular.
Lötrohr *nt* blowpipe.
Lotse *m* **-n, -n** (*Naut*) pilot; (*Flug~*) air-traffic *or* flight controller; (*Aut*) navigator; (*fig*) guide.
lotsen *vt* to guide; *Schiff auch* to pilot ◆ **jdn irgendwohin ~** (*inf*) to drag sb somewhere (*inf*); *siehe* **Geld.**
Lotsen-: ~boot *nt* pilot boat; **~dienst** *m* pilot service; (*Aut*) driver-guide service; **~geld** *nt* pilotage; **~zwang** *m* compulsory pilotage.
Löt-: ~stein *m* sal ammoniac block; **~stelle** *f* soldered point.
Lotte *f* - *abbr of* **Charlotte.**
Lotterbett *nt* (*old, hum*) old bed.
Lotterie *f* lottery; (*Tombola*) raffle.
Lotterie-: ~gewinn *m* lottery/raffle prize *or* (*Geld*) winnings *pl*; **~los** *nt* lottery/raffle ticket; **~spiel** *nt* (*lit*) lottery; (*fig*) gamble.
lott(e)rig *adj* (*inf*) slovenly *no adv*; *Mensch, Arbeit auch* sloppy (*inf*) ◆ **~ herumlaufen** to go around looking a mess (*inf*).
Lotterleben *nt* (*inf*) dissolute life.
lottern *vi* (*inf*) **(a)** to lead a dissolute life. **(b)** (*S Ger, Sw: lose sein*) to wobble.
Lotterwirtschaft *f* (*inf*) muddle, slovenly mess.
Lotto *nt* **-s, -s (a)** national lottery ◆ **(im) ~ spielen** to do the national lottery; **du hast wohl im ~ gewonnen** you must have won the pools (*Brit*). **(b)** (*Gesellschaftsspiel*) lotto.
Lotto-: ~geschäft *nt*, **~laden** *m* (*inf*) Lotto agency; **~gewinn** *m* Lotto win; (*Geld*) Lotto winnings *pl*; **~schein** *m* Lotto coupon; **~- und Totoannahmestelle** *f* Lotto and football pools agency; **~zahlen** *pl* winning Lotto numbers *pl*.
lottrig *adj* (*inf*) *siehe* **lott(e)rig.**
Lötung *f* (*das Löten*) soldering; (*Lötstelle*) soldered joint.
Lotus *m* **-,** - (*Bot*) **(a)** (*Hornklee*) birdsfoot trefoil. **(b)** *siehe* **Lotos.**
Lötzinn *m* solder.
Louisdor [lui'do:ɐ] *m* **-s, -e** *or* (*bei Zahlenangaben*) - (*Hist*) louis (d'or).
Low-Budget-: ['loʊbʌdʒət-] **~Produktion** *f* low-budget production; **~Sendung** *f* low-budget programme.
Löwe *m* **-n, -n** lion ◆ **der ~** (*Astron*) Leo, the Lion; (*Astrol*) Leo; **im Zeichen des ~n geboren sein** to be/have been born under (the sign of) Leo; **~ sein** to be (a) Leo; **sich in die Höhle des ~n begeben** (*inf*) to beard the lion in his den (*prov*).
Löwen-: ~anteil *m* (*inf*) lion's share; **~bändiger** *m* lion-tamer; **~grube** *f* (*Bibl*) lions' den; **~herz** *nt*: **Richard ~herz** *m* Richard (the) Lionheart; **~jagd** *f* lion hunt; **~mähne** *f* (*lit*) lion's mane; (*fig*) flowing mane; **~maul** *nt*, **~mäulchen** *nt* snapdragon, antirrhinum; **~mut** *m* (*liter*) leonine courage (*liter*); **mit ~mut** as brave as a lion; **~zahn** *m* dandelion.
Löwin *f* lioness.
loyal [loa'ja:l] *adj* loyal (*jdm gegenüber* to sb) ◆ **einen Vertrag ~ auslegen** to interpret a contract faithfully.
Loyalität [loajali:'tɛ:t] *f* loyalty (*jdm gegenüber* to sb).
LP [ɛl'pe:] *f* **-, -s** LP.
LPG [ɛlpe:'ge:] *f* **-, -s** (*DDR*) *abbr of* **Landwirtschaftliche Produktionsgenossenschaft.**
LSD [ɛl|ɛs'de:] *nt* **-(s)** LSD.
lt. *abbr of* **laut**[2].
Luch *f* **-, ¨-e** *or nt* **-(e)s, -e** (*dial*) marsh.
Luchs [lʊks] *m* **-es, -e** lynx ◆ **Augen wie ein ~ haben** (*inf*) to have eyes like a hawk, to be eagle-eyed.
Luchs|augen *pl* (*inf*) eagle eyes *pl*.
luchsen ['lʊksn] *vi* (*inf*) to peep.
Lücke *f* **-, -n** (*lit, fig*) gap; (*zwischen Wörtern auch, auf Formularen etc*) space; (*Ungereimtheit, Unvollständigkeit etc*) hole; (*Gesetzes~*) loophole; (*in Versorgung*) break ◆ **~n (im Wissen) haben** to have gaps in one's knowledge; **sein Tod hinterließ eine schmerzliche ~** (*geh*) his death has left a void in our lives.
Lücken-: ~büßer *m* (*inf*) stopgap; **~büßer spielen** to be used as a stopgap; **l~haft** *adj* full of gaps; *Bericht, Sammlung, Beweis etc auch* incomplete; *Kenntnisse auch* sketchy; *Versorgung* deficient; *Gesetz, Alibi* full of holes; **sein Wissen ist sehr l~haft** there are great gaps in his knowledge; **~haftigkeit** *f siehe adj* incompleteness; sketchiness; deficiency; **wegen der ~haftigkeit des Berichts/des Gesetzes** because of all the gaps in the report/loop-holes in the law; **l~los** *adj* complete; *Kenntnisse, (Mil) Abwehr* perfect; *Versorgung, Überlieferung* unbroken; **~losigkeit** *f siehe adj* completeness; perfection; unbrokenness; **~test** *m* (*Sch*) completion test.
Lucullus *m* - *siehe* **Lukull.**
lud *pret of* **laden**[1] *and* **laden**[2].
Lude *m* **-n, -n** (*sl*) ponce (*inf*), pimp.
Luder *nt* **-s, - (a)** (*Hunt: Aas*) bait. **(b)** (*inf*) minx ◆ **armes/dummes ~** poor/stupid creature; **so ein ordinäres ~!** what a common little hussy!
Luderjan *m* **-(e)s, -e** (*inf*) *siehe* **Liederjan.**
Ludwig *m* - Ludwig; (*frz. Königsname*) Louis.
Lues ['lu:ɛs] *f* **-,** *no pl* (*Med*) syphilis, lues (*spec*).
luetisch ['lue:tɪʃ] *adj* (*Med*) syphilitic, luetic (*spec*).
Luft *f* **-,** (*liter*) **¨-e (a)** air *no pl* ◆ **die ¨-e** *pl* (*liter*) the skies, the air *sing*; **frische ~ hereinlassen** to let some fresh air in; **im Zimmer ist schlechte ~** the room is stuffy, the air *or* it is stuffy in the room; **bei schlechter ~ kann ich nicht schlafen** I can't sleep when it's stuffy; **dicke ~** (*inf*) a bad atmosphere; **~ an etw** (*acc*) **kommen lassen** to let the air get to sth; **an** *or* **in die/der (frischen) ~** in the fresh air; **an die (frische) ~ gehen/kommen, (frische) ~ schnappen** (*inf*) *or* **schöpfen** (*geh*) to get out in the fresh air, to get some fresh air; **die ~ ist rein** (*inf*) the coast is clear; **die ~ reinigen** (*lit, fig*) to clear the air; **jetzt ist das Flugzeug in der ~** the plane is now airborne *or* in the air; **aus der ~** from the air; **die ~ aus etw lassen** to let the air out of sth; **jdn an die (frische) ~ setzen** (*inf*) to show sb the door; (*Sch*) to send sb out; (*entlassen*) to give sb the push (*inf*); **in die ~ fliegen** (*inf*) to explode, to go up; **etw in die ~ jagen** (*inf*) *or* **sprengen** to blow sth up; **gleich** *or* **leicht** *or* **schnell in die ~ gehen** (*fig*) to be quick to blow one's top (*inf*), to be very explosive; **es liegt ein Gewitter/etwas in der ~** there's a storm brewing/something in the air; **in die ~ starren** *or* **gucken** to stare into space *or* thin air; **jdn/etw in der ~ zerreißen** (*inf*) to tear sb/sth to pieces; **das kann sich doch nicht in ~ aufgelöst haben** it can't have vanished into thin air; **in der ~ hängen** (*Sache*) to be (very much) up in the air; (*Mensch*) to be in (a state of) limbo, to be dangling; **die Behauptung ist aus der ~ gegriffen** this statement is (a) pure invention; **vor Freude in die ~ springen** to jump for *or* with joy; **von ~ und Liebe/von ~ leben** to live on love/air; **jdn wie ~ behandeln** to treat sb as though he/she just didn't exist; **er ist ~ für mich** I'm not speaking to him.
(b) (*Atem*) breath ◆ **der Kragen schnürt mir die ~ ab** this collar is choking me, I can't breathe in this collar; **nach ~ schnappen** to gasp for breath *or* air; **die ~ anhalten** (*lit*) to hold one's breath; **nun halt mal die ~ an!** (*inf*) (*rede nicht*) hold your tongue!, put a sock in it! (*inf*); (*übertreibe nicht*) come off it! (*inf*), come on! (*inf*); **keine ~ mehr kriegen** not to be able to breathe; **tief ~ holen** (*lit, fig*) to take a deep breath; **... da mußte ich erst mal tief ~ holen** (*fig: war perplex*) it really made me gasp; **mir blieb vor Schreck/Schmerz die ~ weg** I was breathless with shock/pain; **wieder ~ bekommen** *or* **kriegen/haben** (*nach Sport etc*) to get/have got one's breath back; (*nach Schnupfen etc*) to be able to breathe again; (*fig*) to get/have a chance to catch one's breath.
(c) (*Wind*) breeze ◆ **linde/laue ¨-e** (*liter*) gentle/warm breezes; **sich** (*dat*) **~ machen** (*fächeln*) to fan oneself; **sich** (*dat*) **~ machen** (*fig*), **seinem Herzen ~ machen** to get everything off one's chest; **seinem Ärger/Zorn** *etc* **~ machen** to give vent to one's annoyance/anger *etc*.
(d) (*fig: Spielraum, Platz*) space, room ◆ **zwischen Wand und Regal etwas ~ lassen** to leave a space between the wall and the bookcase.
Luft-: ~abwehr *f* (*Mil*) anti-aircraft defence; **~abwehrrakete** *f* anti-aircraft missile; **~alarm** *m* air-raid alarm; **~angriff** *m* air-raid (*auf +acc* on); **einen ~angriff auf eine Stadt fliegen** to bomb a town, to carry out an air-raid on a town; **~aufklärung** *f* aerial reconnaissance; **~aufnahme** *f* aerial photo(graph); **~ballon** *m* balloon; **~belastung** *f, no pl* atmospheric pollution; **~betankung** *f* (*Aviat*) in-flight refuelling; **~bewegung** *f* movement of the air; **~bild** *nt* aerial picture; **~bläschen** [-blɛ:sçən] *nt* (*Anat*) air-sac; **~blase** *f* air bubble, bubble of air; **~-Boden-Flugkörper** *m* air-to-surface ballistic missile; **~bremse** *f* air-brake; **~brücke** *f* airlift; **über eine ~brücke** by airlift.
Lüftchen *nt* breeze.
Luft-: l~dicht *adj* airtight *no adv*; **die Ware ist l~dicht verpackt** the article is in airtight packaging; **ein l~dicht verschlossener Behälter** an airtight con-

tainer, a container with an airtight seal; **~druck** *m* air pressure; **~druckwelle** *f* (*Met*) pressure wave; (*Knallwelle*) blast; **l~durchlässig** *adj* pervious to air; **~durchlässigkeit** *f* perviousness to air.

lüften [1] *vt* **(a)** to air; (*ständig, systematisch*) to ventilate. **(b)** (*hochheben*) *Hut, Schleier* to raise, to lift.
[2] *vi* (*Luft hereinlassen*) to let some air in; (*Betten, Kleider etc*) to air.

Lüfter *m* fan.

Luftfahrt *f* aeronautics *sing*; (*mit Flugzeugen*) aviation *no art*.

Luftfahrt-: **~gesellschaft** *f* airline (company); **~ingenieur** *m* aviation engineer; **~karte** *f* aviation chart; **~medizin** *f* aeromedicine; **~schau** *f* air show.

Luft-: **~fahrzeug** *nt* aircraft; **~feuchtigkeit** *f* (atmospheric) humidity; **~filter** *nt or m* air filter; **~flotte** *f* air fleet; **~fracht** *f* air freight; **~geist** *m* (*Myth*) spirit of the air; **l~gekühlt** *adj* air-cooled; **l~gestützt** *adj Flugkörper* air-launched; **l~getrocknet** *adj* air-dried; **~gewehr** *nt* air-rifle, airgun; **~hauch** *m* (*geh*) gentle breeze; **~herrschaft** *f* air supremacy; **~hoheit** *f* air sovereignty; **~hülle** *f* mantle of air; **l~hungrig** *adj* longing for fresh air; **ein l~hungriger Mensch** a fresh-air fanatic.

luftig *adj Zimmer* airy; *Plätzchen* breezy; *Kleidung* light ◆ **in ~er Höhe** (*liter*) at a dizzy height.

Luftikus *m* **-(ses), -se** (*inf*) happy-go-lucky sort of fellow.

Luft-: **~kampf** *m* air *or* aerial battle; **~kissen** *nt* air cushion; (*von ~kissenboot*) cushion of air; **~kissenboot, ~kissenfahrzeug** *nt* hovercraft; **~klappe** *f* ventilation flap; **~korridor** *m* air corridor; **~kreuz** *nt*, **~kreuzung** *f* centre of air routes; **~krieg** *m* aerial warfare; **~- und Seekrieg** warfare at sea and in the air; **~kühlung** *f* air-cooling; **~kurort** *m* (climatic) health resort; **~landetruppe** *f* airborne troops *pl*; **l~leer** *adj* (**völlig**) **l~leer sein** to be a vacuum; **l~leerer Raum** vacuum; **~linie** *f* **200 km** *etc* **~linie** 200 km *etc* as the crow flies; **~loch** *nt* airhole; (*Aviat*) air pocket; **~mangel** *m* lack of air; **~masche** *f* (*Sew*) chain-stitch; **~massen** *pl* air masses *pl*; **~matratze** *f* airbed, lilo ®; **~pirat** *m* (aircraft) hijacker, skyjacker (*esp US*).

Luftpost *f* airmail ◆ **mit ~** by airmail.

Luftpost-: **~leichtbrief** *m* aerogramme, airletter (*Brit*); **~papier** *nt* airmail paper.

Luft-: **~pumpe** *f* air *or* pneumatic pump; (*für Fahrrad*) (bicycle) pump; **~raum** *m* airspace; **~recht** *nt* air traffic law; **~reifen** *m* pneumatic tyre; **~reinhaltung** *f* prevention of air pollution; **~reiniger** *m* air purifier; **~rettungsdienst** *m* air rescue service; **~röhre** *f* (*Anat*) windpipe, trachea; **~röhrenschnitt** *m* tracheotomy; **~sack** *m* (*Aut*) air bag; (*Orn*) air sac; **~schacht** *m* ventilation shaft; **~schaukel** *f* swingboat; **~schicht** *f* (*Met*) layer of air; **~schiff** *nt* airship; **~schiffahrt** *f* aeronautics *sing*; **~schlacht** *f* air battle; **die ~schlacht um England** the Battle of Britain; **~schlange** *f* (paper) streamer; **~schlitz** *m* (*Aut*) ventilation slit; ⚠**~schloß** *nt* (*fig*) castle in the air, pipe dream; **~schlösser bauen** to build castles in the air; **~schneise** *f* air lane; **~schraube** *f* propeller, airscrew.

Luftschutz *m* anti-aircraft defence.

Luftschutz-: **~bunker, ~keller, ~raum** *m* air-raid shelter; **~übung** *f* air-raid drill.

Luft-: **~sieg** *m* air victory; **~sperre** *f* (*Mil*) aerial barrage; **~spiegelung** *f* mirage; **~sprung** *m* jump in the air; **vor Freude einen ~sprung** *or* **~sprünge machen** to jump for *or* with joy; **~straße** *f* air route; **~streitkräfte** *pl* air force *sing*; **~strom** *m* stream of air; **~strömung** *f* current of air; **~stützpunkt** *m* airbase; **~tanken** *nt* in-flight refuelling; **~taxi** *nt* air taxi; **~temperatur** *f* air temperature; **~torpedo** *m* aerial torpedo; **l~trocken** *adj* air-dry; **~überwachung** *f* air surveillance; **~überwachungsflugkörper** *m* airborne warning and control system; **~- und Raumfahrtindustrie** *f* aerospace industry; **~- und Raumfahrttechnik** *f* aerospace technology.

Lüftung *f* airing; (*ständig, systematisch*) ventilation.

Lüftungs-: **~klappe** *f* ventilation flap; **~schacht** *m siehe* **Luftschacht**.

Luft-: **~unterstützung** *f* (*Mil*) air support; **~veränderung** *f* change of air; **~verflüssigung** *f* liquefaction of air; **~verkehr** *m* air traffic; **~verkehrsgesellschaft** *f* airline; **~verkehrslinie** *f* air route; **~verpestung** *f* (*pej*), **~verschmutzung** *f* air pollution; **~versorgung** *f* air supplies *pl*; **~verteidigung** *f* air defence; **~waffe** *f* (*Mil*) air force; **die (deutsche) ~waffe** the Luftwaffe; **~waffenstützpunkt** *m* air-force base; **~weg** *m* (*Flugweg*) air route; (*Atemweg*) respiratory tract; **etw auf dem ~weg befördern** to transport by air; **~widerstand** *m* air resistance; **~widerstandsbeiwert** *m* drag coefficient; **~zufuhr** *f* air supply; **~zug** *m* wind, (mild) breeze; (*in Gebäude*) draught.

Lug *m*: **~ und Trug** lies *pl* (and deception).

Lüge *f* **-, -n** lie, fib, falsehood ◆ **jdn einer ~ beschuldigen** to accuse sb of lying; **das ist alles ~** that's all lies; **jdn/etw ~n strafen** to give the lie to sb/sth, to belie sth; **~n haben kurze Beine** (*prov*) truth will out (*prov*).

lugen *vi* (*dial*) to peep, to peek.

lügen *pret* **log**, *ptp* **gelogen** [1] *vi* to lie, to fib ◆ **ich müßte ~, wenn ...** I would be lying if ...; **wie gedruckt ~** (*inf*) to lie like mad (*inf*); **wer einmal lügt, dem glaubt man nicht, und wenn er auch die Wahrheit spricht** (*Prov*) remember the boy who cried 'wolf' (*prov*).
[2] *vt* **das ist gelogen!, das lügst du doch!** (*inf*) that's a lie!, you're lying!; *siehe* **Blaue**[2].

Lügen-: **~bericht** *m* fabrication; **~bold** *m* **-(e)s, -e** (*dated inf*) (inveterate) liar; **~detektor** *m* lie detector; **~gebäude** *or* **~gespinst** (*geh*), **~gewebe** (*liter*) *nt* tissue *or* web of lies; **~geschichte** *f* pack of lies; **l~haft** *adj Erzählung* made-up, mendacious (*form*); *Bericht auch* false; **seine l~haften Geschichten** his tall stories; **~haftigkeit** *f siehe adj* mendacity (*form*), mendaciousness (*form*); falseness; **~kampagne** *f* campaign of lies; **~märchen** *nt* tall story, cock-and-bull story; **~maul** *nt* (*pej inf*) liar; **~propaganda** *f* propagandist lies *pl*, mendacious propaganda.

Lügerei *f* lying *no pl*, fibbing *no pl*.

Lügner(in *f*) *m* **-s, -** liar.

lügnerisch *adj Mensch* lying *attr*, untruthful, mendacious.

Lukas *m* **-** Luke.

Lukas|evangelium *nt* Gospel according to St. Luke, St. Luke's Gospel.

Luke *f* **-, -n** hatch; (*Dach~*) skylight.

lukrativ *adj* lucrative.

Lukull *m* **-**, **Lukullus** *m* **-** (*lit*) Lucullus; (*fig*) (*gen* **Lukulls**) epicure, gourmet, gastronome.

lukullisch *adj* epicurean.

Lulatsch *m* **-(es), -e** (*hum inf*) **langer ~** beanpole (*inf*).

Lulle *f* **-, -n** (*sl*) fag (*Brit inf*), cig (*inf*), gasper (*Brit sl*).

lullen *vt* (*dated*) **ein Kind in den Schlaf ~** to lull a child to sleep.

Lumbago *f* **-,** *no pl* lumbago.

lumbecken *vt* (*Typ*) to adhesive-bind.

Lumberjack ['lʌmbədʒæk] *m* **-s, -s** (*dated*) lumber jacket.

Lumme *f* **-, -n** guillemot.

Lümmel *m* **-s, -** (*pej*) **(a)** lout, oaf ◆ **du ~, du** you rascal *or* rogue you. **(b)** (*hum: Penis*) willie (*inf*).

Lümmelei *f* (*inf*) sprawling about; (*Flegelei*) rudeness *no pl*.

lümmelhaft *adj* (*pej*) ill-mannered.

lümmeln *vr* (*inf*) to sprawl; (*sich hin~*) to flop down.

Lump *m* **-en, -en** (*pej*) rogue, blackguard (*dated*).

lumpen [1] *vt* (*inf*) **sich nicht ~ lassen** to splash out (*inf*).
[2] *vi* (*old, dial*) to go/be out on the tiles (*inf*).

Lumpen *m* **-s, -** **(a)** rag. **(b)** (*S Ger: Lappen*) cloth.

Lumpen-: **~gesindel** *nt* (*pej*) rabble *pl* (*pej*), riffraff *pl* (*pej*); **~händler** *m* rag-and-bone man; **~pack** *nt* (*pej inf*) *siehe* **~gesindel**; **~proletariat** *nt* (*Sociol*) lumpenproletariat; **~sammler** *m* **(a)** *siehe* **~händler**; **(b)** (*hum*) last bus/tram/train, drunks' special (*hum*).

Lumperei *f* (*inf*) mean *or* dirty trick.

lumpig *adj* **(a)** *Kleidung* ragged, tattered ◆ **~ herumlaufen** to go around in rags. **(b)** *Gesinnung, Tat* shabby, mean. **(c)** *attr* (*inf: geringfügig*) paltry, measly (*inf*) ◆ **~e 10 Mark** 10 paltry *or* measly (*inf*) marks.

Lunatismus *m* (*Psych*) sleepwalking, somnambulism (*form*).

Lunch [lanʃ, lantʃ] *m* **-(es)** *or* **-s, -e(s)** *or* **-s** lunch, luncheon (*form*).

lunchen ['lanʃn, 'lantʃn] *vi* (*geh*) to lunch (*form*).

Lüneburger Heide *f* Lüneburg Heath.

Lunge *f* **-, -n** lungs *pl*; (*~nflügel*) lung ◆ **(auf) ~ rauchen** to inhale; **sich** (*dat*) **die ~ aus dem Hals** *or* **Leib schreien** (*inf*) to yell till one is blue in the face (*inf*); **sich** (*dat*) **die ~ aus dem Leib husten** (*inf*) to cough one's lungs out (*inf*); **die (grünen) ~n einer Großstadt** the lungs of a city; *siehe* **eisern**.

Lungen-: **~bläschen** *nt* pulmonary alveolus (*spec*); **~braten** *m* (*Aus*) *siehe* **Lendenbraten**; **~embolie** *f* pulmonary embolism (*spec*); **~emphysem** *nt* pulmonary emphysema; **~entzündung** *f* pneumonia; **~fisch** *m* lungfish; **~flügel** *m* lung; **~haschee** *nt* (*Cook*) *hash made with calf's lights*; **~heilstätte** *f* TB *or* tuberculosis sanatorium; **l~krank** *adj* tubercular; **l~krank sein** to have a lung disease; **~kranke(r)** *mf decl as adj* TB case; **~krankheit** *f* lung *or* pulmonary (*form*) disease; **~krebs** *m* lung cancer; **~sanatorium** *nt* tuberculosis sanatorium; **~tuberkulose** *f* tuberculosis (of the lung), TB; **~tumor** *m* lung tumour; **~zug** *m* deep drag (*inf*); **einen ~zug machen** to inhale deeply, to take a deep drag (*inf*).

lungern *vi* (*inf*) to loaf or hang about (*inf*).

Lunte *f* **-, -n** **(a)** (*Hist*) fuse ◆ **~ riechen** (*Verdacht schöpfen*) to smell a rat (*inf*); (*Gefahr wittern*) to smell (*inf*) *or* sense danger. **(b)** (*Hunt: Fuchsschwanz*) brush.

Lupe *f* **-, -n** magnifying glass ◆ **so etwas/solche Leute kannst du mit der ~ suchen** things/people like that are few and far between; **jdn/etw unter die ~ nehmen** (*inf*) (*beobachten*) to keep a close eye on sb/sth; (*prüfen*) to examine sb/sth closely.

lupenrein *adj* (*lit*) *Edelstein* flawless; *Diamant auch* of the first water; (*fig*) *Vergangenheit etc auch* unimpeachable, unblemished; *Gentleman, Intellektueller* through and through *pred* ◆ **das Geschäft war nicht ganz ~** the deal wouldn't stand close scrutiny *or* wasn't quite all above-board; **ein ~er KP-Mann** a communist with an unblemished party record.

lupfen, lüpfen *vt* (*S Ger, Aus, Sw*) to lift, to raise.

Lupine *f* lupin.

Lurch *m* **-(e)s, -e** amphibian.

Lure *f* **-, -n** lur.

Lurex ® *nt* **-,** *no pl* lurex ®.

Lusche *f* **-, -n** (*Cards*) low card; (*fig*) cipher.

Lust *f* **-, ⸚e** **(a)** *no pl* (*Freude*) pleasure, joy ◆ **er hat die ~ daran verloren, die ~ daran ist ihm vergangen** he has lost all interest in it; **da kann einem die (ganze)** *or* **alle ~ vergehen, da vergeht einem die ganze ~** it puts you off; **jdm die ~ an etw** (*dat*) **nehmen** to take all the fun out of sth for sb; **ich habe immer mit ~ und Liebe gekocht** I've always enjoyed cooking; **sie ging mit/ohne ~ (und Liebe) an die Arbeit** she set to work enthusiastically/without enthusiasm.
(b) *no pl* (*Neigung*) inclination ◆ **zu etw ~ (und Liebe) haben** to feel like sth; **ich habe keine ~, das zu tun** I don't really want to do that; (*bin nicht dazu aufgelegt*) I don't feel like doing that; **ich habe keine ~ zu arbeiten** I'm not in

the mood to work *or* for working, I don't feel like work *or* working; **ich habe ~, das zu tun** I'd like to do that; (*bin dazu aufgelegt*) I feel like doing that; **ich habe jetzt keine ~** I'm not in the mood just now; **ich hätte ~ dazu** I'd like to; **das mache ich erst, wenn ich ~ dazu habe** I'll do that when I feel like it *or* when I'm in the mood; **hast du ~?** how about it?; **auf etw** (*acc*) **~ haben** to feel like *or* to fancy sth; **mach, wie du ~ hast** (*inf*) do as you like; **er kann bleiben, solange er ~ hat** he can stay as long as he likes; **~ kriegen, etw zu tun** to feel like doing sth; **ich habe nicht übel ~, ... zu ...** I've a good *or* half a mind to ...; **ganz** *or* **je nach ~ und Laune** (*inf*) just depending on how I/you *etc* feel *or* on my/your *etc* mood.
(c) (*sinnliche Begierde*) desire; (*sexuell auch*) lust (*usu pej*) ◆ **~ haben** to feel desire; **er/sie hat ~** (*inf*) he's/she's feeling like a bit (*inf*); **seinen ¨en leben** *or* **frönen** to indulge one's desires/lusts (*pej*).

Lustbarkeit *f* (*dated*) festivity, junketing (*old*).

lustbetont *adj* pleasure-orientated, governed by the pleasure principle; *Beziehung, Mensch* sensual ◆ **~ unterrichten** to teach in such a way that learning is fun.

Luster *m* **-s, -** (*Aus*) *siehe* **Lüster (a)**.

Lüster *m* **-s, - (a)** (*Leuchter*) chandelier. **(b)** (*Stoff, Glanzüberzug*) lustre.

Lüsterklemme *f* (*Elec*) connector.

lüstern *adj* lecherous, lascivious ◆ **nach etw ~ sein** to lust after *or* for sth.

Lüsternheit *f* lecherousness, lasciviousness.

Lust-: ~film *m* (*dated*) comedy film; **~garten** *m* (*old*) pleasance; **~gefühl** *nt* feeling of pleasure; (*sexuell auch*) desire; **~gewinn** *m* pleasure; **~greis** *m* (*hum*) dirty old man (*inf*), old lecher.

lustig *adj* (*munter*) merry, jolly; *Mensch auch* jovial; (*humorvoll*) funny, amusing; (*emsig*) happy, merry, cheerful ◆ **es wurde ~** things got quite merry; **seid ~!** liven up and have a bit of fun; **L~e Person** (*Theat*) clown, fool, buffoon; **Die L~e Witwe** the Merry Widow; **Bruder L~** (*old*) jolly *or* merry fellow (*dated*); **das ist ja ~!, das finde ich aber ~!** (*iro*) (that's) very *or* most amusing (*iro*); **das kann ja ~ werden!** (*iro*) that's going to be fun (*iro*); **das kannst du tun, so lange du ~ bist** (*inf*) you can do that as long as you like *or* please; **sich über jdn/etw ~ machen** to make fun of sb/sth.

Lustigkeit *f siehe adj* merriness, jolliness (*dated*); joviality; funniness.

Lustknabe *m* (*old, hum*) catamite.

Lüstling *m* debauchee, lecher ◆ **ein alter ~** an old lecher, a debauched old man.

Lust-: l~los *adj* unenthusiastic; (*Fin*) *Börse* slack, dull; **~molch** *m* (*hum inf*) sex maniac (*inf*); (*bewundernd*) sexy beast (*inf*), sexpot (*inf*); **~mord** *m* sex murder; **~mörder** *m* sex killer *or* murderer; **~objekt** *nt* sex object; **~prinzip** *nt* (*Psych*) pleasure principle; ⚠**~schloß** *nt* summer residence; **~spiel** *nt* comedy; **~spieldichter** *m* comedy-writer, writer of comedies; **~verlust** *m, no pl* loss of sexual drive; **l~voll** [1] *adj* full of relish; [2] *adv* with relish; **l~wandeln** *vi insep aux sein or haben* (*liter*) to (take a) stroll, to promenade (*old*).

Lutetium *nt, no pl* (*abbr* **Lu**) lutetium.

luth. *abbr of* **lutherisch.**

Lutheraner(in *f*) *m* **-s, -** Lutheran.

Lutherbibel *f* Lutheran translation (*of the Bible*).

Lutherisch, Luthersch, lutherisch *adj* Lutheran.

lutschen *vti* to suck (*an etw* (*dat*) sth).

Lutscher *m* **-s, -** lollipop.

Lutschtablette *f* (*Med*) lozenge.

lütt *adj* (*N Ger*) wee (*esp Scot*).

Lüttich *nt* **-s** Liège.

Luv [lu:f] *f* **-,** *no pl* (*Naut*) windward *or* weather side ◆ **nach/in ~** to windward.

luven ['lu:vn, 'lu:fn] *vi* (*Naut*) to luff (up).

Luvseite *f* windward side.

Lux *nt* **-, -** (*Phys*) lux.

Luxation *f* (*Med*) dislocation.

Luxemburg *nt* **-s** Luxembourg.

Luxemburger(in *f*) *m* **-s, -** Luxembourger.

luxemburgisch *adj* Luxembourgian.

luxuriös *adj* luxurious ◆ **ein ~es Leben** a life of luxury.

Luxus *m* **-,** *no pl* luxury; (*pej: Verschwendung, Überfluß*) extravagance ◆ **im ~ leben** to live in (the lap of) luxury; **den ~ lieben** to love luxury; **mit etw ~ treiben** to be extravagant with sth, to lash out on sth (*inf*); **ich leiste mir den ~ und ...** I'll treat myself to the luxury of ...

Luxus- *in cpds* luxury; **~ausführung** *f* de luxe model; **~ausgabe** *f* de luxe edition; **~dampfer** *m* luxury cruise ship; **~frau** *f* (*inf*) piece of class (*inf*), classy woman; **~körper** *m* (*hum*) beautiful body; **~limousine** *f* limousine; **~restaurant** *nt* first-class restaurant; **~schlitten** *m* (*inf*) classy car (*inf*) *or* job (*sl*); **~weibchen** *nt* (*pej*) classy piece (*inf*); **~zug** *m* pullman (train).

Luzern *nt* **-s** Lucerne.

Luzerne *f* **-, -n** (*Bot*) lucerne.

luzid *adj* (*liter*) lucid; (*durchsichtig*) translucent.

Luzifer ['lu:tsifɛr] *m* **-s** Lucifer.

luziferisch [lutsi'fe:rɪʃ] *adj* diabolical, satanic.

Lymph-: ~drainage *f* lymphatic drainage; **~drüse** *f* lymph(atic) gland.

Lymphe ['lʏmfə] *f* **-, -n** lymph.

Lymphknoten *m* lymph node, lymph(atic) gland.

Lymphknoten-: ~entzündung *f* inflammation of the lymph node; **~schwellung** *f* swelling of the lymph node.

Lymphozyt *m* **-en, -en** lymphocyte.

lynchen ['lʏnçn, 'lɪnçn] *vt* (*lit*) to lynch; (*fig*) to kill.

Lynch- ['lʏnç-]**: ~justiz** *f* lynch-law; **~mord** *m* lynching.

Lyoner *f* **-, -** (*Wurst*) pork/veal sausage.

Lyra *f* **-, Lyren** (*Mus*) lyre ◆ **die ~** (*Astron*) Lyra, the Lyre.

Lyrik *f* **-,** *no pl* lyric poetry *or* verse.

Lyriker(in *f*) *m* **-s, -** lyric poet, lyricist.

lyrisch *adj* (*lit, fig*) lyrical; *Dichtung, Dichter* lyric.

Lyzeum [ly'tse:ʊm] *nt* **-s, Lyzeen** [ly'tse:ən] **(a)** (*Gymnasium*) girls' grammar school (*Brit*), girls' high school. **(b)** (*Sw: Oberstufe*) upper school.

M

M, m [ɛm] *nt* **-, -** M, m.
m *abbr of* **Meter.**
MA. *abbr of* **Mittelalter.**
Mäander *m* **-s, -** *(Geog, Art)* meander.
mäandrisch *adj* meandering ◆ **sich ~ schlängeln** to meander; **~ verziert** *(Art)* decorated with meanders.
Maar *nt* **-(e)s, -e** *(Geol)* maar *(spec)*, volcanic lake.
Maas *f* **-** Meuse, Maas.
Maastricht-Vertrag *m* Maastricht Treaty.
Maat *m* **-(e)s, -e** *or* **-en** *(Naut)* (ship's) mate.
Mach *nt* **-(s), -** *(Phys)* Mach.
Machandel *m* **-s, -, Machandelbaum** *m (N Ger)* juniper (tree).
Mach|art *f* make; *(Muster)* design; *(lit, fig: Stil)* style.
machbar *adj* feasible, possible.
Mache *f* **-, -n** *(inf)* **(a)** *(Technik)* structure.
(b) *(Vortäuschung)* sham ◆ **reine** *or* **pure ~ sein** to be (a) sham.
(c) etw in der ~ haben *(inf)* to be working on sth, to have sth on the stocks; **in der ~ sein** *(inf)* to be in the making; **der Film war noch in der ~** *(inf)* the film was still being made; **jdn in der ~ haben/in die ~ nehmen** *(sl)* to be having/to have a go at sb *(inf)*; *(verprügeln auch)* to be working *or* doing/to work *or* do sb over *(inf)*.
machen [1] *vt* **(a)** *(tun)* to do ◆ **was macht dein Bruder (beruflich)?** what does your brother do for a living?; **was habe ich nur falsch gemacht?** what have I done wrong?; **gut, wird gemacht** right, shall do *(inf) or* I'll get that done; **das läßt sich ~/nicht ~, das ist zu/nicht zu ~** that can/can't be done; **ich mache dir das schon** I'll do that for you; **(da ist) nichts zu ~** *(geht nicht)* (there's) nothing to be done; *(kommt nicht in Frage)* nothing doing; **wie man's macht, ist's verkehrt** whatever you do is wrong; **ich mache das schon** *(bringe das in Ordnung)* I'll see to that; *(erledige das)* I'll do that; **was machst du da?** what are you doing (there)?; **was machst du denn hier?** what (on earth) are you doing here?; **was macht denn das Fahrrad hier im Hausflur?** what's this bicycle doing here in the hall?; **er macht, was er will** he does what he wants; **ich muß noch so viel ~** I still have so much to do; **ich kann da auch nichts ~** I can't do anything about it either; **was hast du denn nun wieder gemacht?** what have you done now?; **ich mache es wohl am besten so, daß ich etwas früher komme** I'd do *or* be best to come a bit earlier; **es ist schon gut gemacht, wie ...** it's good the way ...; **so etwas macht man nicht** that sort of thing just isn't done; **wie ~ Sie das nur?** how do you do it?; **damit/mit ihr kann man etwas ~** you could do something with it/her; *siehe* **gemacht.**
(b) *(herstellen, anfertigen, zu Erfolg verhelfen)* to make ◆ **sich/jdm etw ~ lassen** to have sth made for oneself/sb; **Bilder** *or* **Fotos ~** to take photos; **mach mir mal einen (guten) Preis!** make me an offer, give me a price; **er ist für den Beruf wie gemacht** he's made for the job; **Bier wird aus Gerste gemacht** beer is made from barley; **aus Holz gemacht** made of wood.
(c) was macht die Arbeit? how's the work going?; **was macht dein Bruder?** how is your brother doing?, how are things with your brother?
(d) *(verursachen) Schwierigkeiten, Arbeit* to make *(jdm* for sb); *Mühe, Schmerzen, Aufregung* to cause *(jdm* for sb) ◆ **jdm Angst/Mut/Sorgen/Freude ~** to make sb afraid/brave/worried/happy; **jdm Hoffnung/Mut/Kopfschmerzen ~** to give sb hope/courage/a headache; **das macht Appetit/Hunger** that gives you an appetite/makes you hungry; *siehe* **schaffen[2].**
(e) *(hervorbringen) Laut, Geräusch* to make; *miau, aua, brumm, mäh* to go; *Grimassen, böse Miene* to pull ◆ **wie macht das Kindchen/feine Hündchen?** say please/sit up and beg.
(f) *(bilden, formen, darstellen) Kreuzzeichen, Kreis* to make; *(zeichnen) Kreis, Kurve auch* to draw ◆ **die Straße macht einen Knick** the road bends.
(g) *(bewirken)* to do; (+*infin*) to make ◆ **das macht die Kälte** it's the cold that does that; **jdn lachen/weinen/etw vergessen ~** to make sb laugh/cry/forget sth; **~, daß etw geschieht** to make sth happen; **mach, daß er gesund wird!** make him get better; **das ~ die vielen Zigaretten, daß du hustest** it's all those cigarettes you smoke that make you cough; **(viel) von sich reden ~** to be much talked about; **mach, daß du hier verschwindest!** (you just) get out of here!
(h) *(veranstalten) Fest, Party* to have, to give; *Seminar, Kurs* to do, to give; *Gruppenreise* to do.
(i) *(besuchen, teilnehmen an) Kurs, Seminar, (inf) Sehenswürdigkeiten, London* to do.
(j) *(zubereiten) Kaffee, Glühwein, Salat, Pfannkuchen* to make; *Frühstück, Abendessen auch* to get ◆ **jdm einen Drink ~** to get sb a drink; *(Cocktail)* to make *or* mix sb a drink; **das Essen ~** to get the meal.
(k) *(mit unpersönlichem Objekt)* **mach's kurz!** make it *or* be brief; **mach's gut!** all the best; **er wird's nicht mehr lange ~** *(inf)* he won't last long; **es mit jdm ~** *(inf: Verkehr haben)* to make *or* do it with sb *(inf)*; **es jdm ~** *(sl: befriedigen)* to bring sb off *(sl)*; **mit mir kann man's ja ~!** *(inf)* the things I put up with! *(inf)*; **das läßt er nicht mit sich ~** he won't stand for that.
(l) *(ausmachen, schaden)* to matter ◆ **macht nichts!** (it) doesn't matter; **macht das was?** does that matter?; **das macht durchaus etwas** it does indeed matter; **das macht mir doch nichts!** that doesn't matter to me; **der Regen/die Kälte** *etc* **macht mir nichts** I don't mind the rain/cold *etc*; **die Kälte macht dem Motor nichts** the cold doesn't hurt the engine; **es macht mir nichts, durch den Regen zu gehen** I don't mind walking in the rain.
(m) *(gewinnen, erzielen) Punkte, Freispiel, Preis* to get, to win; *Doktor, Diplom etc (studieren für)* to do; *(abschließen)* to get, to do; *(verdienen) Gewinne, Defizit* to make.
(n) *in Verbindung mit adj siehe auch dort* to make ◆ **jdn nervös/unglücklich ~** to make sb nervous/unhappy; **etw größer/kleiner ~** to make sth bigger/smaller; **etw sauber/schmutzig ~** to get sth clean/dirty; **etw leer/kürzer ~** to empty/shorten sth; **einen Stuhl frei ~** to vacate a chair; **jdn alt/jung ~** *(aussehen lassen)* to make sb look old/young; **jdn wieder sehend ~** to make sb see again; **mach's dir doch bequem/gemütlich** make yourself comfortable/at home; **mach es ihm nicht noch schwerer** don't make it harder for him; **er macht es sich** *(dat)* **nicht leicht** he doesn't make it easy for himself.
(o) *(in Verbindung mit prep)* **etw aus jdm/etw ~** *(darstellen, interpretieren als)* to make sth of sb/sth; *(verwandeln in)* to make sth (out) of sb/out of sth, to turn *or* make sb/sth into sth; **was soll ich aus dieser Sache ~?** *(verstehen, interpretieren)* what am I meant to make of this?; **eine große Sache aus etw ~** to make a big thing of sth; **aus dem Haus könnte man schon etwas ~** you could really make something of that house; **jdn/etw zu etw ~** *(verwandeln in)* to turn sb/sth into sth; *(Rolle, Image, Status geben)* to make sb/sth sth; **jdm etw zur Hölle/Qual** *etc* **~** to make sth hell/a misery *etc* for sb; **jdn zum Wortführer/Sklaven/zu seiner Frau ~** to make sb spokesman/a slave/one's wife.
(p) *(Funktionsverb) siehe auch n* **auf jdn/etw Jagd ~** to hunt sb/sth; **Schicht/Nachtdienst ~** to work shifts/do night duty; **jdm die Rechnung ~** to make up sb's bill; **einen Spaziergang/Kopfsprung/Handstand ~** to go for a walk/to take a header/to do a handstand; **Pause/Halt ~** to have a break/call a halt; **ein Fragezeichen/einen Strich ~** to put a question mark/dash; **das Geschirr ~** to do the dishes; **eine Prüfung ~** to do *or* take an exam; **ein Spiel ~** to play a game.
(q) *(ordnen, reparieren, säubern)* to do ◆ **die Küche muß mal wieder gemacht werden** *(gereinigt, gestrichen)* the kitchen needs doing again; **das Auto/den Kühlschrank ~ lassen** to have the car/refrigerator seen to *or* done; **er macht mir die Haare/Zähne** *(inf)* he does my hair/teeth; **das Bett ~** to make the bed; **mach den Fleck aus den Hosen** get that stain out of your trousers.
(r) *(inf: ergeben)* to make; *(Math)* to be ◆ **drei und fünf macht** *or* **~ acht** three and five make(s) *or* is *or* are eight; **fünf mal vier macht** *or* **~ zwanzig** five fours are twenty, five times four is twenty; **das macht (zusammen) 23** altogether that's 23; **was** *or* **wieviel macht sechs geteilt durch zwei?** what is six divided by two?; **100 cm ~ einen Meter** 100 cm make a metre; **was macht die Rechnung?** how much is the bill?, what does the bill come to?
(s) *(kosten)* to be ◆ **was** *or* **wieviel macht das (alles zusammen)?** how much is that altogether?, what does that come to *or* make altogether?
(t) *(inf: eine bestimmte Rolle übernehmen) Dolmetscher, Schiedsrichter etc* to be; *(Theat)* to play ◆ **den Ghostwriter für jdn ~** to act as sb's ghost writer, to ghost for sb.
(u) *(inf: Notdurft verrichten)* to do ◆ **groß/klein ~** to do a big/little job *(babytalk)*; **einen Haufen** *or* **sein Geschäft ~** to do one's business *(euph)*; *siehe* **Aa, Pipi** *etc.*
(v) *(inf: legen)* to put ◆ **er machte sich** *(dat)* **Zucker in den Kaffee** he put some sugar in his coffee, he sugared his coffee.
[2] *vi* **(a)** *(inf: sich beeilen)* to get a move on *(inf)* ◆ **mach schon/mach (mal 'n bißchen) schnell/schneller!** get a move on! *(inf)*, hurry up; **ich mach ja schon!**

⚠: for details of spelling reform, see supplement

I am hurrying; **sie machten, daß sie nach Hause kamen** they hurried home.
(b) (*inf*) **in etw** (*dat*) **~** (*beruflich*) to be in sth; (*pej: sich interessiert zeigen an*) to be into sth (*sl*); **er macht in Politik/Malerei** he's in politics/doing some painting; **auf etw** (*acc*) **~** to play sth; **jetzt macht sie auf große Dame** she's playing the lady now; **sie macht auf verständnisvoll/gebildet** *etc* she's doing her understanding/cultured *etc* bit (*inf*); **jetzt macht sie auf beleidigt** now she's playing the injured innocent; **er macht auf Schau** he's out for effect.
(c) laß ihn nur ~ (*hindre ihn nicht*) just let him do it; (*verlaß dich auf ihn*) just leave it to him; **laß mich mal ~** let me do it; (*ich bringe das in Ordnung*) let me see to that; **gut, mache ich** right, will do (*inf*) *or* I'll do that.
(d) (*inf: Notdurft verrichten*) to go to the toilet; (*Hund etc*) to do its business (*euph*) ◆ **(sich** *dat*) **in die Hosen ~** (*lit, fig*) to wet oneself; **ins Bett ~** to wet the bed.
(e) (*dial: fahren, reisen*) to go ◆ **nach Amerika ~** to go to America.
(f) das macht müde/gesund/schlank that makes you tired/healthy/slim; **das Kleid macht alt/schlank** that dress makes you look old/slim.
3 *vr* **(a)** (*sich entwickeln*) to come on *or* along ◆ **wie macht sich der Garten?** how is the garden coming on *or* along?
(b) (*passen*) to look ◆ **der Schal macht sich sehr hübsch zu dem Kleid** the scarf looks very pretty with that dress.
(c) sich an etw (*acc*) **~** to get down to sth/doing sth; **sich auf den Weg ~** to get going; **sich über das Essen ~** (*inf*) to get stuck in (*inf*).
(d) sich verständlich/wichtig ~ to make oneself understood/important; **sich bei jdm beliebt/verhaßt ~** to make oneself popular with/hated by sb.
(e) sich (*dat*) **viel aus jdm/etw ~** to like sb/sth; **sich** (*dat*) **wenig aus jdm/etw ~** not to be very keen on sb/sth; **sich** (*dat*) **nichts aus etw ~** (*sich nicht ärgern*) not to let sth bother one; (*keinen Wert legen auf*) not to be very keen on sth; **mach dir nichts daraus** don't let it bother you; **sich** (*dat*) **einen schönen Abend/ein paar gemütliche Stunden ~** to have a nice evening/a few pleasant hours; **sich** (*dat*) **ein Vergnügen aus etw ~** to take delight in sth; **sich** (*dat*) **Umstände/Mühe ~** to go to a lot of bother/trouble; **sich** (*dat*) **Sorgen/Hoffnungen ~** to worry/get hopeful; **sich** (*dat*) **jdn zum Freund/Feind ~** to make sb one's friend/enemy; **sich** (*dat*) **etw zur Aufgabe/zum Grundsatz/Motto ~** to make sth one's job/a principle/a motto.
(f) sich zum Fürsprecher *etc* **~** to make oneself spokesman *etc*.

Machenschaften *pl* wheelings and dealings *pl*, machinations *pl*.
Macher *m* **-s, -** (*inf*) doer, man of action.
-macher(in *f*) *m in cpds* -maker.
Macherlohn *m* labour charge; (*bei Kleidung*) making-up charge.
Machete *f* **-, -n** machete.
machiavellistisch [makiavɛl-] *adj* Machiavellian.
Machismo [ma'tʃɪsmo] *m* **-s,** *no pl* machismo.
Macho ['matʃo] *m* **-s, -s** macho (*inf*).
Macht *f* **-, ¨-e (a)** *no pl* (*Einfluß, Kraft*) power; (*Stärke auch*) might ◆ **die ~ der Gewohnheit/Verhältnisse/des Schicksals** the force of habit/circumstance(s)/destiny; **alles, was in unserer ~ steht, alles in unserer ~ Stehende** everything (with)in our power; **es stand nicht in seiner ~, zu ...** it was not *or* did not lie within his power to ...; **mit aller ~** with might and main, with all one's might; **~ geht vor Recht** (*Prov*) might is right (*Prov*).
(b) *no pl* (*Herrschaft, Befehlsgewalt*) power ◆ **die ~ ergreifen/erringen** to seize/gain power; **an die ~ gelangen** (*form*) *or* **kommen** to come to power; **an der ~ sein/bleiben** to be/remain in power; **seine ~ behaupten** to maintain control, to continue to hold sway; **die ~ übernehmen** to assume power, to take over.
(c) (*dated: Heeres~*) forces *pl*.
(d) (*außerirdische Kraft, Groß~*) power ◆ **die ¨-e der Finsternis** (*old, liter*) the Powers of Darkness (*old, liter*).
Macht-: ~anspruch *m* claim to power; **~ausübung** *f* exercise of power; **jdn an der ~ausübung hindern** to prevent sb from exercising his power; **~befugnis** *f* power, authority *no pl*; **~bereich** *m* sphere of influence *or* control; **~block** *m* power bloc.
Mächtegruppierung *f* grouping of the powers.
Macht-: ~entfaltung *f* display of power; **zur Zeit der größten ~entfaltung** at the height *or* peak of its power; **~ergreifung** *f* seizure of power; **~fülle** *f* power *no indef art*; **~gier** *f* lust for power; **~haber** *m* **-s, -** ruler; (*pej*) dictator; **die ~haber in Ruritanien** the rulers of *or* powers-that-be in Ruritania; **~hunger** *m* (*liter*) craving *or* hunger for power; **m~hungrig** *adj* (*liter*) power-hungry; **m~hungrig sein** to crave power.
mächtig 1 *adj* **(a)** (*einflußreich*) powerful ◆ **die M~en (dieser Erde)** the powerful (of this world).
(b) (*sehr groß*) mighty; *Baum, Felsen auch, Körper* massive; *Stimme, Wirkung, Schlag, Schultern auch* powerful; *Essen* heavy; (*inf: enorm*) *Hunger, Durst, Glück* terrific (*inf*), tremendous ◆ **~e Angst** *or* **einen ~en Bammel haben** (*inf*) to be scared stiff.
(c) (*liter*) **seiner selbst** (*gen*) *or* **seiner Sinne** (*gen*) **nicht ~ sein** not to be in control of oneself; **einer Sprache** (*gen*) **~ sein** to have a good command of a language.
2 *adv* (*inf: sehr*) terrifically (*inf*), tremendously; *schneien, brüllen, sich beeilen* like mad (*inf*) ◆ **sich ~ anstrengen** to make a terrific (*inf*) *or* tremendous effort; **da hast du dich ~ getäuscht** you've made a big mistake there.
Mächtigkeit *f* (*Größe*) mightiness; (*von Baum, Felsen auch, von Körper*) massiveness; (*von Stimme, Wirkung, Schlag, Schultern auch*) powerfulness; (*von Essen*) heaviness; (*Geol, Min*) thickness.
Macht-: ~kampf *m* power struggle, struggle for power; **m~los** *adj* powerless; (*hilflos*) helpless; **gegen diese Argumente war ich m~los** I was powerless against these arguments; **~losigkeit** *f, no pl* powerlessness; helplessness; ⚠**~mißbrauch** *m* abuse *or* misuse of power; **~mittel** *nt* instrument of power; **~monopol** *nt* monopoly of power; **~politik** *f* power politics *pl*; **~position** *f* position of power; **~probe** *f* trial of strength; **~stellung** *f* position of power; (*einflußreiche Stellung auch*) powerful position; **~streben** *nt* striving for power; **~struktur** *f* power structure; **~techniker** *m* power-monger; **~übernahme** *f* takeover (*durch* by); **~verhältnisse** *pl* balance of power *sing*; **~verschiebung** *f* shift of power; **m~voll** *adj* powerful; **~vollkommenheit** *f* absolute power; **~wechsel** *m* changeover of power; **~wort** *nt* word (*gen* from); **ein ~wort sprechen** to exercise one's authority.
Machwerk *nt* (*pej*) sorry effort ◆ **das ist ein ~ des Teufels** that is the work of the devil.
Mach-Zahl *f* (*Phys*) Mach number.
Macke *f* **-, -n** (*inf*) **(a)** (*Tick, Knall*) quirk ◆ **eine ~ haben** (*sl*) to be cracked (*inf*), to have a screw loose (*inf*). **(b)** (*Fehler, Schadstelle*) fault; (*bei Maschinen auch*) defect; (*bei Kartoffeln etc*) bad patch.
Macker *m* **-s, -** (*inf*) fellow (*inf*), bloke (*Brit inf*), guy (*inf*) ◆ **spiel hier nicht den ~** don't come the tough guy here (*inf*).
MAD [ɛm|aː'deː] *m* - *abbr of* **Militärischer Abschirmdienst** ≃ MI5 (*Brit*), CIA (*US*).
Madagaskar *nt* **-s** Madagascar; (*Pol: heutzutage*) Malagasy Republic.
Madagasse *m* **-n, -n, Madagassin** *f* Madagascan; Malagasy.
madagassisch *adj* Madagascan; Malagasy.
Madam *f* **-, -s** *or* **-en (a)** (*hum dated*) lady ◆ **meine ~** my old woman *or* lady (*inf*). **(b)** (*in Bordell*) madam.
Mädchen *nt* girl; (*Tochter auch*) daughter; (*dated: Freundin*) girl(friend); (*Dienst~*) maid ◆ **ein unberührtes ~** a virgin; **ein ~ für alles** (*inf*) a dogsbody; (*im Haushalt auch*) a maid-of-all-work; *siehe* **spät, leicht.**
Mädchen-: ~buch *nt* book for girls; **m~haft** *adj* girlish; **sich m~haft kleiden** to dress like a girl; **m~haft aussehen** to look like a (young) girl; **~handel** *m* white slave trade; **~händler** *m* white slaver, white slave trader; **~klasse** *f* girls' class *or* form; **~kleidung** *f* girls' clothing *or* clothes *pl*; **~name** *m* **(a)** (*Vorname*) girl's name; **~namen** girls' names; **(b)** (*von verheirateter Frau*) maiden name; **~pensionat** *nt* girls' boarding school; **diese Kaserne ist kein ~pensionat!** (*hum*) these barracks aren't a finishing school; **~schule** *f* girls' school; **~zimmer** *nt* (*dated*) maid's room; (*für Tochter*) girl's room.
Made *f* **-, -n** maggot ◆ **wie die ~ im Speck leben** (*inf*) to live *or* be in clover, to live in (the lap of) luxury.
Madeira(wein) [ma'deːra-] *m* **-s, -s** Madeira.
Mädel *nt* **-s, -(s)** (*dial*), **Mad(e)l** *nt* **-s, -n** (*Aus*) lass (*dial*), girl; *siehe auch* **Mädchen.**
Madenwurm *m* threadworm.
Mäderl *nt* **-s, -n** (*Aus*) little lass (*dial*) *or* girl.
madig *adj* maggoty; *Obst auch* worm-eaten ◆ **jdn/etw ~ machen** (*inf*) to run sb/sth down; **jdm etw ~ machen** (*inf*) to put sb off sth.
Madjar [ma'djaːɐ] *m* **-en, -en** Magyar.
Madl *nt* **-s, -n** (*Aus*), **Mädle** *nt* **-s, -** (*S Ger*) *siehe* **Mädel.**
Madonna *f* **-, Madonnen** Madonna.
Madonnen-: ~bild *nt* (picture of the) Madonna; **m~haft** *adj* madonna-like.
Madrid *nt* **-s** Madrid.
Madrider *adj attr* Madrid.
Madrider(in *f*) *m* native of Madrid; (*Einwohner*) inhabitant of Madrid.
Madrigal *nt* **-s, -e** madrigal.
Maestro [ma'ɛstro] *m* **-s, -s** *or* **Maestri** maestro.
Ma(f)fia *f* **-,** *no pl* Mafia.
⚠**Ma(f)fia-Boß** *m* Mafia boss.
Mafioso *m* **-, Mafiosi** mafioso.
Magazin *nt* **-s, -e (a)** (*Lager*) storeroom; (*esp für Sprengstoff, Waffen, old: Speicher auch*) magazine; (*Bibliotheks~*) stockroom. **(b)** (*am Gewehr*) magazine. **(c)** (*Zeitschrift*) magazine, journal; (*TV, Rad*) magazine programme.
Magaziner *m* **-s, -** (*Sw*), **Magazineur** [-'nøːɐ] *m* (*Aus*) storeman.
Magazinsendung *f* (*Rad, TV*) magazine programme.
Magd *f* **-, ¨-e (a)** (*old*) (*Dienst~*) maid; (*Landarbeiterin*) farm lass *or* girl; (*Kuh~*) milkmaid. **(b)** (*liter: Mädchen, Jungfrau*) maid(en) (*old, liter*) ◆ **Maria, die reine ~/die ~ des Herrn** Mary, the holy virgin/the handmaid of the Lord.
Mägd(e)lein *nt* (*obs, poet*) maid(en) (*old, liter*).
Magen *m* **-s, ¨** *or* **-** stomach, tummy (*inf*) ◆ **mit leerem ~, auf nüchternen ~** on an empty stomach; **(die) Liebe geht durch den ~** (*Prov*) the way to a man's heart is through his stomach (*prov*); **etw liegt jdm (schwer** *or* **wie Blei** *or* **bleiern) im ~** (*inf*) sth lies heavily on sb's stomach; (*fig*) sth preys on sb's mind; **jdm auf den ~ schlagen** (*inf*) to upset sb's stomach, to give sb an upset stomach; (*fig*) to upset sb; **sich** (*dat*) **den ~ verderben** *or* **verkorksen** (*inf*) to get an upset stomach, to upset one's stomach; *siehe* **umdrehen, knurren.**
Magen-: ~beschwerden *pl* stomach *or* tummy (*inf*) trouble *sing*; **~bitter** *m* bitters *pl*; **~blutung** *f* stomach bleeding *or* haemorrhaging; ⚠**~-Darm-Katarrh** *m* gastroenteritis; **~-Darm-Trakt** *m* gastro-intestinal tract; **~drücken** *nt* **-s, -** stomach-ache; **~gegend** *f* stomach region; **~geschwür** *nt* stomach ulcer; **~grube** *f* pit of the stomach; **ein Schlag in die ~grube** a blow in the solar plexus; **~knurren** *nt* **-s,** *no pl* tummy (*inf*) *or* stomach rumbles *pl*; **~krampf** *m* stomach cramp; **m~krank** *adj* with stomach trouble; **m~krank sein** to have stomach trouble; **jdn m~krank machen** to give sb stomach trouble; **~krebs** *m* stomach cancer, cancer of the

stomach; **~leiden** *nt* stomach disorder *or* complaint; **m~leidend** *adj siehe* **m~krank**; **~mittel** *nt* stomachic (*spec*); **jdm ein ~mittel verschreiben** to give sb something for his stomach; **~saft** *m* gastric juice; **~säure** *f* gastric acid; **~schleimhaut** *f* stomach lining; **~schleimhautentzündung** *f* gastritis; **~schmerzen** *pl* stomach-ache *sing*, tummy-ache *sing* (*inf*); (*Krämpfe auch*) stomach pains *pl*; **~spiegelung** *f* gastroscopy (*spec*); **~spülung** *f* irrigation of the stomach.

Magenta *nt* -, *no pl* magenta.

Magen-: ~verstimmung *f* upset stomach, stomach upset; **~weh** *nt* (*S Ger*) *siehe* **~schmerzen**.

mager *adj* **(a)** (*fettarm*) *Fleisch* lean; *Kost* low-fat, low in fat ◆ **~ essen** to be on a low-fat diet.
(b) (*dünn*) thin, skinny (*inf*); (*abgemagert*) emaciated; (*Typ*) *Druck* roman.
(c) (*unfruchtbar*) *Boden, Felder* poor, infertile.
(d) (*dürftig*) meagre; *Ernte, Ertrag auch* lean; (*Tech*) *Mischung* weak; *Ergebnis* poor ◆ **die sieben ~en Jahre** the seven lean years.

Magerkeit *f, no pl siehe adj* **(a)** leanness; low fat level (*gen* in). **(b)** thinness, skinniness (*inf*); emaciation. **(c)** poorness.

Mager-: ~milch *f* skimmed milk; **~quark** *m* low-fat curd cheese; **~sucht** *f* (*Med*) anorexia.

Magie *f, no pl* magic.

Magier ['maːgiɐ] *m* **-s, -** magician ◆ **die drei ~** the three Magi.

Maginot-Linie, Maginotlinie [maʒi'no-] *f* Maginot Line.

magisch *adj* magic(al); *Quadrat,* (*Tech*) *Auge,* (*Econ*) *Dreieck,* (*Phys*) *Zahlen* magic ◆ **nach ~en Vorstellungen** according to various concepts of magic; **mit ~er Gewalt** with magical force; (*fig*) as if by magic; **von jdm/etw ~ angezogen werden** to be attracted to sb/sth as if by magic.

Magister *m* **-s, - ~ (Artium)** (*Univ*) M.A., Master of Arts; **~ (pharmaciae)** (*abbr* **Mag. pharm.**) (*Aus*) M. Sc. *or* Master of Science in pharmacology.

Magistrat *m* **-(e)s, -e** municipal authorities *pl*.

Magma *nt* **-s, Magmen** (*Geol*) magma.

magna cum laude ['magna'kʊm'laudə] *adv* (*Univ*) magna cum laude.

Magnat *m* **-en, -en** magnate (*auch Hist*).

Magnesia *f* **-**, *no pl* (*Chem*) magnesia; (*Sport*) chalk.

Magnesium *nt* **-s**, *no pl* (*abbr* **Mg**) magnesium.

Magnet *m* **-s** *or* **-en, -e(n)** (*lit, fig*) magnet.

Magnet- *in cpds* magnetic; **~aufzeichnung** *f* magnetic recording; **~bahn** *f* magnetic railway; **~band** *nt* magnetic tape; **~berg** *m* (*liter*) *mountain believed to draw ships to their doom by its magnetic properties;* **~bildverfahren** *nt* video recording; **~eisenstein** *m* lodestone, magnetite; **~feld** *nt* magnetic field.

magnetisch *adj* (*lit, fig*) magnetic ◆ **eine ~e Anziehungskraft auf jdn ausüben** (*fig*) to have a magnetic attraction for sb.

magnetisieren* *vt Metall* to magnetize; *jdn* to use animal magnetism on.

Magnetismus *m, no pl* magnetism; (*Mesmerismus*) animal magnetism; (*heutzutage*) *form of healing where the illness is supposedly drawn out by the magnetic power of the healer.*

Magnet-: ~karte *f* magnetic card; (*Bank etc auch*) cashpoint card; **~kartenleser** *m* magnetic card reader; **~kern** *m* (magnet) core; ⚠**~kompaß** *m* magnetic compass; **~nadel** *f* magnetic needle.

Magneto-: ⚠**~phon** ® *nt* **-(e)s, -e** steel tape recorder, magnetophone ®; ⚠**~phonband** ® *nt* steel recording tape; **~sphäre** *f* magnetosphere.

Magnet-: ~platte *f* (*Comput*) magnetic disk; **~pol** *m* magnetic pole; **~schalter** *m* (*Aut*) solenoid switch; **~schwebebahn** *f* magnetic levitation railway; **~spule** *f* coil; **~streifen** *m* magnetic strip; **~streifenkarte** *f* magnetic stripe card; **~tonband** *nt* magnetic tape; **~tongerät** *nt* magnetic (sound) recorder; **~tonverfahren** *nt* magnetic (sound) recording; **~zündung** *f* (*Aut*) magneto ignition.

Magnifikat *nt* **-(s)**, *no pl* magnificat.

Magnifizenz *f* (*Univ*) **(Euer** *or* **Eure)/Seine ~** Your/His Magnificence (*title given to German university rectors*).

Magnolie [mag'noːliə] *f* magnolia.

Magnumflasche *f* magnum (bottle).

Magyar [ma'djaːɐ] *m* **-en, -en** (*Aus, liter*) Magyar.

magyarisch [ma'djaːrɪʃ] *adj* (*Aus, liter*) Magyar.

mäh *interj* baa.

Mahagoni *nt* **-s**, *no pl* mahogany.

Maharadscha *m* **-s, -s** maharaja(h).

Maharani *f* **-, -s** maharani.

Mähbinder *m* reaper-binder, reaping-and-binding machine.

Mahd[1] *f* **-, -en** (*dial*) reaping; (*das Abgemähte*) cut grass.

Mahd[2] *nt* **-(e)s, ¨-er** (*Sw, Aus*) mountain pasture.

Mähder *m* **-s, -** (*dial*) *siehe* **Mäher**.

Mähdrescher *m* combine (harvester).

mähen[1] [1] *vt Gras* to cut; (*für Heu*), *Getreide auch* to reap; *Rasen* to mow.
[2] *vi* to reap; (*Rasen ~*) to mow.

mähen[2] *vi* (*Schaf*) to bleat.

Mäher *m* **-s, -** mower; (*von Getreide*) reaper.

Mahl *nt* **-(e)s, -e** *or* **¨-er** (*liter*) meal, repast (*form*); (*Gast~*) banquet ◆ **beim ~e sitzen** (*liter*) to be at table.

mahlen *pret* **mahlte**, *ptp* **gemahlen** [1] *vt* to grind.
[2] *vi* to grind; (*Räder*) to spin.

Mahl-: ~gang *m* (*Tech*) pair of millstones; **~gut** *nt* material to be ground; (*Getreide*) grain (to be ground), grist.

mählich *adj* (*poet*) *siehe* **allmählich**.

⚠: for details of spelling reform, see supplement

Mahl-: ~statt, ~stätte *f* (*Hist*) *meeting place of the Teutons;* **~stein** *m* millstone; (*prähistorisch*) quern; **~strom** *m siehe* **Malstrom**; **~zahn** *m* grinder.

Mahlzeit *f* meal ◆ **~!** (*inf*) *greeting used around mealtimes;* (*guten Appetit*) enjoy your meal; **(prost) ~!** (*iro inf*) that's just great (*inf*) *or* swell (*esp US inf*).

Mähmaschine *f* mower; (*Rasen~ auch*) mowing machine; (*Getreide~*) reaper.

Mahn-: ~bescheid, ~brief *m* reminder.

Mähne *f* **-, -n** (*lit, fig*) mane ◆ **du hast wieder eine ~!** (*inf*) you're looking rather wild and woolly again (*inf*).

mahnen [1] *vt* **(a)** (*erinnern*) to remind (*wegen, an +acc* of); (*warnend, mißbilligend*) to admonish (*wegen, an +acc* on account of); *Schuldner* to send a reminder to ◆ **jdn schriftlich/brieflich ~** to remind sb in writing/by letter; **gemahnt werden** (*Schuldner*) to receive a reminder; **eine ~de Stimme** (*liter*) an admonishing *or* admonitory voice.
(b) (*auffordern*) **jdn zur Eile/Geduld/Ruhe** *etc* **~** to urge *or* (*warnend, mißbilligend*) admonish sb to hurry/be patient/be quiet *etc*; **jdn zur Mäßigkeit ~** to urge sb to be moderate, to urge moderation on sb.
[2] *vi* **(a)** (*wegen Schulden etc*) to send a reminder.
(b) zur Eile/Geduld ~ to urge haste/patience; **der Lehrer mahnte zur Ruhe** the teacher called for quiet; **die Uhr mahnte zur Eile** the clock indicated that haste was called for.

Mahn-: ~mal *nt* (*liter*) memorial; **~ruf** *m* (*liter*) exhortation; **~schreiben** *nt* reminder.

Mahnung *f* **(a)** (*Ermahnung*) exhortation; (*warnend, mißbilligend*) admonition. **(b)** (*geh: warnende Erinnerung*) reminder ◆ **zur ~ an** (*+acc*) in memory of. **(c)** (*Mahnbrief*) reminder.

Mahn-: ~verfahren *nt* collection proceedings *pl*; **~wache** *f* (*Pol*) picket; **eine demonstrative ~wache** a protest picket; **jdn als institutionelle ~wache einstellen** to appoint sb as an official watchdog.

Mähre *f* **-, -n** (*old, pej*) nag, jade.

Mähren *nt* **-s** Moravia.

mährisch *adj* Moravian.

Mai *m* **-(e)s** *or* **-** *or* (*poet*) **-en, -e** May ◆ **der Erste ~** May Day; **des Lebens ~** (*poet*) the springtime of one's life (*poet*); **wie einst im ~** (as if) in the first bloom *or* flush of youth, as if young again; *siehe auch* **März**.

Mai- *in cpds* May; (*Pol*) May Day; **~andacht** *f* May devotions *pl*; **~baum** *m* maypole; **~bowle** *f* white wine punch (*flavoured with woodruff*).

Maid *f* **-, -en** (*old, liter*) maid(en) (*old, liter*); (*hum*) wench (*old, hum*).

Mai-: ~feier *f* May Day celebrations *pl*; **~feiertag** *m* (*form*) May Day *no art*; **~glöckchen** *nt* lily of the valley; **~käfer** *m* cockchafer; **~königin** *f* Queen of (the) May; **~kundgebung** *f* May Day rally.

Mailand *nt* **-s** Milan.

Mailänder *adj attr* Milan ◆ **die ~ Scala** La Scala.

Mailänder(in *f*) *m* **-s, -** Milanese.

mailändisch *adj* Milanese.

Mailbox [meːl'bɔks] *f* **-, -en** (*Comput*) mailbox.

Mailing ['meɪlɪŋ] *nt* **-s, -s** mailing, mailshot ◆ **etw per Mailing erhalten** to receive sth in a mailing; **ein Mailing an alle Kunden durchführen** to send a mailshot to all customers.

Main *m* **-s** Main.

Mainlinie *f line formed by the River Main roughly dividing North and South Germany.*

Mais *m* **-es**, *no pl* maize, (Indian) corn (*esp US*).

Mais-: ~brei *m* thick maize porridge; **~brot** *nt* corn bread.

Maischbottich *m* mash tub; (*für Wein*) fermenting vat.

Maische *f* **-, -n** (*Bier~*) mash; (*Wein~*) must; (*Schnaps~*) wort.

maischen *vt* to mash; *Trauben* to ferment.

Mais-: ~flocken *pl* cornflakes *pl*; **m~gelb** *adj* corn-coloured; **~kolben** *m* corn cob; (*Gericht*) corn on the cob; **~korn** *nt* grain of maize *or* corn (*esp US*); (*als Sammelbegriff*) maize *or* corn (*esp US*) grain; **~mehl** *nt* maize *or* corn (*esp US*) meal.

Maisonette [mezo'nɛt], **Maisonette-Wohnung** *f* maisonette.

Maisstärke *f* cornflour, cornstarch (*US*).

Maître de plaisir [mɛtrə(d)plɛ'ziːr] *m* **- - -, -s - -** (*old, hum*) Master of Ceremonies.

Maître d'hôtel [mɛtrədo'tɛl] *m* **- -, -s -** maître d'hôtel.

Majestät *f* **(a)** (*Titel*) Majesty ◆ **Seine/Ihre/Eure** *or* **Euer ~** His/Her/Your Majesty; **die (kaiserlichen** *etc*) **~en** ... their (Imperial *etc*) Majesties ... **(b)** (*liter*) majesty, grandeur.

majestätisch *adj* majestic.

Majestäts-: ~beleidigung *f* lèse-majesté; **~verbrechen** *nt* (*Jur*) crime against the crown.

Majolika *f* **-, -s** *or* **Majoliken** majolica.

Majonäse *f* **-, -n** *siehe* **Mayonnaise**.

Major *m* **-s, -e** (*Mil*) major; (*in Luftwaffe*) squadron leader (*Brit*), major (*US*).

Majoran *m* **-s, -e** marjoram.

Majorat *nt* (*old*) **(a)** (*Jur*) primogeniture. **(b)** (*Erbgut*) *estate to which the eldest son is entitled.*

Majorette *f* majorette.

majorisieren* *vt* to outvote.

Majorität *f* majority ◆ **die ~ haben** to have a majority.

Majoritäts-: ⚠**~beschluß** *m* majority decision; **~prinzip** *nt siehe* **Mehrheitsgrundsatz**.

Majorsrang *m* (*Mil*) rank of major ◆ **im ~ sein** to hold the rank of major.

Majorz *m* **-es**, *no pl* (*Sw*) first-past-the-post system; (*Mehrheit*) majority.

Majuskel *f* **-, -n** (*geh*) majuscule (*spec*), capital (letter).
MAK *abbr of* **Maximale Arbeitsplatzkonzentration** *maximum permitted exposure level of pollution at the place of work* ◆ **~-Liste** *list of products or materials which are harmful to health.*
makaber *adj* macabre; *Witz, Geschichte* sick.
Makedonien [-iən] *nt* **-s** Macedonia.
Makedonier(in *f***)** [-iɐ, -iərɪn] *m* **-s, -** Macedonian.
makedonisch *adj* Macedonian.
Makel *m* **-s, - (a)** (*Schandfleck*) stigma ◆ **ohne ~** without a stain on one's reputation; (*Rel*) unblemished; **ein ~ auf seiner blütenreinen Weste** a blot on his escutcheon; **mit einem ~ behaftet sein** (*liter*) to be stigmatized.
(b) (*Fehler*) blemish; (*bei Waren*) flaw, defect ◆ **ohne ~** without blemish, flawless.
Mäkelei *f* carping *no pl*, fault-finding *no pl* (*an +dat, über +acc* about, over).
mäk(e)lig *adj* (*inf*) finicky (*inf*).
makellos *adj Reinheit, Frische* spotless; *Charakter, Lebenswandel, Gesinnung* unimpeachable; *Figur, Haut, Frisur* perfect, flawless; *Kleidung, Haare* immaculate; *Alibi* watertight.
Makellosigkeit *f* (*Reinheit*) spotlessness; (*moralisch*) unimpeachability; (*von Haut*) flawlessness; (*von Kleidung*) immaculateness.
makeln **1** *vi* to act as a broker.
2 *vt* to be a broker for.
mäkeln *vi* (*inf*) (*nörgeln*) to carp, to cavil (*an +dat* at); (*zu wählerisch sein*) to be finicky (*inf*) (*an +dat* about, over).
Make-up [meːk'|ap] *nt* **-s, -s** make-up; (*flüssig*) foundation, liquid make-up ◆ **sie braucht zwei Stunden fürs ~** she needs two hours for her *or* to put on her make-up.
Makkabäer *pl* Maccabees *pl.*
Makkaroni *pl* macaroni *sing.*
Makler(in *f***)** *m* **-s, -** broker; (*Grundstücks~*) estate agent; (*fig*) middleman ◆ **der ehrliche ~** (*fig*) the honest broker.
Mäkler *m* **-s, - (a)** *siehe* **Makler. (b)** (*inf*) (*nörglerisch*) fault-finder, carper; (*wählerisch*) fusspot (*inf*).
Maklergebühr *f* broker's commission, brokerage.
Mako *m or f or nt* **-(s), -s** (*Tex*) Egyptian cotton.
Makrele *f* **-, -n** mackerel.
Makro *nt* **-s, -s** (*Comput*) macro.
Makro- *in cpds* macro-; **~befehl** *m* (*Comput*) macro command; **m~biotisch** *adj* macrobiotic; **~klima** *nt* macro-climate; **~kosmos** *m* macrocosm.
Makrone *f* **-, -n** macaroon.
Makro-: ~ökonomie *f* macro-economics *sing*; **~phage** *f* **-, -n** (*Med: Freßzelle*) macrophage; **m~zephal** *adj* megacephalic.
Makulatur *f* (*Typ*) wastepaper; (*fig pej*) rubbish ◆ **~ reden** (*inf*) to talk rubbish (*inf*) *or* trash (*inf*).
Makulaturbogen *m* (*Typ*) waste *or* spoiled sheet.
makulieren* *vt* to pulp.
Mal[1] *nt* **-(e)s, -e** *or* (*poet*) **¨er (a)** (*Fleck*) mark; (*fig liter: Kennzeichen auch*) brand, sign. **(b)** (*liter: Ehren~*) memorial, monument. **(c)** (*Sport*) (*Schlagball*) base; (*Rugby*) posts *pl*; (*~feld*) touch.
Mal[2] *nt* **-(e)s, -e** time ◆ **das eine ~** once; **erinnerst du dich an das eine ~ in Düsseldorf?** do you remember that time in Düsseldorf?; **nur das eine ~** just (the) once; **(nur) dieses eine ~** (just) this once; **das eine oder andere ~** now and then *or* again, from time to time; **ein/kein einziges ~** once/not once; **wenn du bloß ein einziges ~ auf mich hören würdest** if you would only listen to me for once; **manch liebes ~, manches liebe ~** (*dated*) many a time; **ein für alle ~e** once and for all; **ein über das** *or* **ums andere ~, ein ~ über das** *or* **ums andere ~** time after time; **voriges** *or* **das vorige ~** the time before; **das soundsovielte** *or* **x-te ~** (*inf*) the umpteenth (*inf*) *or* nth time; **ein erstes ~** (*liter*) for the first time ever; **ein letztes ~** (*liter*) one last time; **als ich letztes** *or* **das letzte ~ in London war** (the) last time I was in London; **beim ersten ~(e)** the first time; **beim zweiten/letzten** *etc* **~** the second/last *etc* time; **zum ersten/letzten** *etc* **~** for the first/last *etc* time; **zu verschiedenen ~en** at various times; **zu wiederholten ~en** repeatedly, time and again; **von ~ zu ~** each *or* every time; **er wird von ~ zu ~ besser/dümmer** he gets better and better/more and more stupid, he gets better/more stupid each *or* every time; **für dieses ~** for the time being, for now; **mit einem ~e** all at once, all of a sudden, suddenly.
mal[1] *adv* (*Math*) times; (*bei Maßangaben*) by ◆ **zwei ~ zwei** (*Math*) two times two, two twos, twice two.
mal[2] *adv* (*inf*) *siehe* **einmal.**
-mal *adv suf* times.
Malachit *m* **-s, -e** malachite.
Malaga(wein) *m* **-s, -s** malaga.
Malaie [ma'laiə] *m* **-n, -n, Malaiin** [ma'laiɪn] *f* Malay.
malaiisch [ma'laiɪʃ] *adj* Malayan, Malay *attr* ◆ **M~er Bund** (*Hist*) Federation of Malaya.
Malaiisch(e) [ma'laiiʃ(ə)] *nt* Malay; *siehe auch* **Deutsch(e).**
Malaise [ma'lɛːzə] *f* **-, -n** *or* (*Sw*) *nt* **-s, -** (*geh*) malaise.
Malaria *f* **-,** *no pl* malaria.
Malawi *nt* **-s** Malawi.
Malawier(in *f***)** [-iɐ, -iərɪn] *m* **-s, -** Malawian.
malawisch *adj* Malawian, Malawi *attr.*
Malaysia [ma'laizia] *nt* **-s** Malaysia.
Malaysier(in *f***)** [ma'laiziɐ, -iərɪn] *m* **-s, -** Malaysian.
malaysisch [ma'laizɪʃ] *adj* Malaysian.
Malbuch *nt* colouring book.
Malediven [male'diːvn] *pl* Maldives *pl*, Maldive Islands *pl.*
malen **1** *vti* to paint; (*inf: zeichnen*) to draw; (*inf: langsam schreiben*) to write with painstaking care ◆ **sich ~ lassen** to have one's portrait painted; **etw rosig/schwarz** *etc* **~** (*fig*) to paint a rosy/black *etc* picture of sth; **er hat während des Vortrags (Männchen) gemalt** he was doodling during the talk; **er malt** (*als Beruf*) he's a painter *or* an artist; *siehe* **Teufel.**
2 *vr* **(a)** to paint *or* do a self-portrait, to paint a picture of oneself.
(b) (*fig liter*) to show itself, to be reflected.
Maler *m* **-s, -** painter; (*Kunst~ auch*) artist.
Malerei *f* (*no pl: Malkunst*) art; (*Bild*) painting; (*Zeichnung*) drawing.
Malerfarbe *f* paint.
Malerin *f* (woman) painter, artist.
malerisch *adj* **(a)** (*bildnerisch*) in painting; *Talent, Können* as a painter ◆ **das ~e Schaffen Leonardos** Leonardo's painting; **seine ~en Mittel** his technique as a painter.
(b) (*pittoresk*) picturesque; *Altstadt, Fachwerkhaus auch* quaint; *Landschaft auch* scenic ◆ **~ auf das Sofa drapiert** draped artistically *or* decoratively over the sofa.
Maler-: ~leinwand *f* artist's canvas; **~meister** *m* (master) painter; **~schule** *f* school of painting.
Malheur [ma'løːɐ] *nt* **-s, -s** *or* **-e** mishap ◆ **ihm ist ein kleines ~ passiert** (*inf*) he's had a little accident (*auch euph*) *or* a mishap; **das ist doch kein ~!** it's not serious.
Mali *nt* **-s** Mali.
Malier(in *f***)** [-iɐ, -iərɪn] *m* **-s, -** Malian.
maligne *adj* (*Med*) malignant.
maliziös *adj* (*liter*) malicious.
Malkasten *m* paintbox.
mall *adj* (*Naut*) variable; (*N Ger inf*) barmy (*inf*), batty (*inf*).
Mallorca [ma'lɔrka, ma'jɔrka] *nt* **-s** Majorca, Mallorca.
mallorquinisch [malɔr'kiːnɪʃ] *adj* Majorcan.
malnehmen *vti sep irreg* to multiply (*mit* by).
Maloche *f* **-,** *no pl* (*sl*) graft (*sl*) ◆ **auf ~ sein** to be grafting (*sl*); **du mußt zur ~** you've got to go to work.
malochen* *vi* (*sl*) to graft (*sl*), to sweat away (*inf*).
Malocher(in *f***)** *m* **-s, -** (*sl*) grafter (*inf*).
Malstift *m* crayon.
Malstrom *m* Maelstrom; (*fig liter*) maelstrom.
Malta *nt* **-s** Malta.
Maltechnik *f* painting technique.
Malteser *m* **-s, -** Maltese.
Malteser-: ~kreuz *nt* Maltese cross (*auch Tech*); **~orden** *m* (Order of the) Knights *pl* of Malta *or* of St John; **~ritter** *m* Knight of Malta, (Knight) Hospitaller.
maltesisch *adj* Maltese.
Maltose *f* **-,** *no pl* maltose.
malträtieren* *vt* to ill-treat, to maltreat.
Malus *m* **-ses, -** *or* **-se** (*Insur*) supplementary (high-risk) premium; (*Univ*) minus point ◆ **sein ~ ist ihr Bonus** his loss is her gain.
Malve ['malvə] *f* **-, -n** (*Bot*) mallow; (*Stockrose*) hollyhock.
malvenfarbig, malvenfarben *adj* mauve.
Malvinen [mal'viːnən] *pl* Malvinas *pl.*
Malz *nt* **-es,** *no pl* malt; *siehe* **Hopfen.**
Malz-: ~bier *nt* malt beer, ≃ stout; **~bonbon** *nt or m* malt lozenge.
Malzeichen *nt* multiplication sign.
mälzen *vti* to malt.
Mälzer *m* **-s, -** maltster.
Mälzerei *f* malthouse, malting.
Malz-: ~extrakt *m* malt extract; **~kaffee** *m coffee substitute made from barley malt*; **~zucker** *m* maltose, malt sugar.
Mama[1] *f* **-, -s** (*inf*) mummy, mommy (*US*).
Mama[2] *f* **-, -s** (*dated*) mama (*dated*).
Mama-: ~kind *nt* (*pej*) mummy's boy/girl; **~söhnchen** *nt* (*pej*) mummy's darling.
Mameluck *m* **-en, -en** (*Hist*) mameluke.
Mami *f* **-, -s** (*inf*) *siehe* **Mama**[1]**.**
Mammographie *f* **-,** *no pl* mammography.
Mammon *m* **-s,** *no pl* Mammon ◆ **der schnöde ~** Mammon, filthy lucre; **dem ~ dienen** to serve Mammon.
Mammonsdiener *m* (*pej*) servant of Mammon.
Mammut *nt* **-s, -s** *or* **-e** mammoth.
Mammut- *in cpds* (*lit, fig*) mammoth; (*lange dauernd*) marathon; **~baum** *m* sequoia, giant redwood; ⚠**~prozeß** *m* marathon trial.
mampfen *vti* (*inf*) to munch, to chomp (*inf*) ◆ **ich brauche was zu ~** I want something to eat.
Mamsell *f* **-, -en** *or* **-s** (*dated hum*) lady; (*old: Wirtschafterin*) housekeeper.
man[1] *indef pron dat* **einem,** *acc* **einen (a)** you, one; (*ich*) one; (*wir*) we ◆ **~ kann nie wissen** you *or* one can never tell, there's no knowing; **das tut ~ nicht** that's not done; **~ wird doch wohl noch fragen dürfen** there's no law against asking.
(b) (*jemand*) somebody, someone ◆ **~ hat mir gesagt ...** I was told ..., somebody told me ...; **~ hat mir erklärt, daß ...** it was explained *or* somebody explained to me that ...; **~ hat festgestellt, daß ...** it has been established that ...

(c) *(die Leute)* they *pl*, people *pl* ◆ **früher glaubte ~** they *or* people used to believe; **~ will die alten Häuser niederreißen** they want to pull down the old houses; **diese Farbe trägt ~ nicht mehr** this colour isn't worn any more; **~ hat öfters versucht, ...** many attempts have been made ...
(d) **~ wende sich an ...** apply to ...; *siehe* **nehmen.**

man² *adv (N Ger inf)* just ◆ **denn ~ los!** let's go then!; **~ sachte!** (just) take it easy!; **jetzt ~ schnell!** we'd/you'd *etc* better hurry.

Management ['mænɪdʒmənt] *nt* **-s, -s** management.

Management-Buyout [-baɪaut] *nt* **-s, -s** management buyout.

managen ['mɛnɪdʒn] *vt (inf)* to manage; *(hinkriegen auch)* to fix ◆ **ich manage das schon!** I'll manage *or* fix it somehow!

Manager(in *f*) ['mɛnɪdʒɐ, -ərɪn] *m* **-s, -** manager.

Managerkrankheit *f (inf)* executivitis *(hum)*, stress disease.

manch *indef pron* **(a)** *inv (in Zusammensetzung mit ein, eine(r, s), substantiviertem Adjektiv und (liter) Substantiv)* many a ◆ **~ eine(r), ~ ein Mensch** many a person, (a good) many people, quite a few people; **~ einem kann man nie Vernunft beibringen** you can never teach sense to some people; **~ anderer** many another; **~ Schönes** *(geh)* many a beautiful thing; **~ Erlebnis/schöne Geschichte/Kind** *(all liter)* many an experience/a lovely story/a child.
(b) *(adjektivisch)* **~e(r, s)** a good many *+pl*, a fair number of *+pl*, quite a few *+pl*, many a *+sing*; *(pl: einige)* some *+pl*; **~er, der ...** many a person who ..., many *pl* who ..., a good many people *pl* who ..., some (people) *pl* who ...; **~e hundert Mark** some *or* several hundreds of marks; **~es Schöne** a number of *or* quite a few *or* a good many beautiful things.
(c) *(substantivisch)* **~e(r)** a good many (people/men/women *etc*) *pl*, many a person/man/woman *etc*; *(pl: einige)* some (people/men/women *etc*); **~es** *(vieles)* a good many things, a number of things, quite a few things *all pl*; *(einiges)* some things *pl*; **so** *or* **gar** *(old)* **~es** a good many things *pl*, quite a few things *pl*; **in ~em hat er recht** he's right about a lot of/some things.

manchen|orts *adv siehe* **mancherorts.**

mancherlei *adj inv (adjektivisch mit pl n)* various, a number of; *(substantivisch)* various things *pl*, a number of things.

mancher|orts, mancher|orten *adv* in a number of places, in many a place.

Manchester [man'ʃɛstɐ] *m* **-s,** *no pl (Tex)* broad-ribbed cord(uroy).

manchmal *adv* sometimes.

Mandant(in *f*) *m (Jur)* client.

Mandarin *m* **-s, -e** *(Hist)* mandarin.

Mandarine *f* mandarin (orange), tangerine.

Mandat *nt* **(a)** *(Auftrag, Vollmacht)* mandate *(auch Pol)*, authorization *(gen* from); *(von Anwalt)* brief; *(Parl: Abgeordnetensitz)* seat ◆ **sein ~ niederlegen** *(Parl)* to resign one's seat; **imperatives ~** *(Pol)* fixed mandate. **(b)** *siehe* **Mandatsgebiet.**

Mandatar *m* **(a)** *(rare: Beauftragter)* mandatary *(form)*, agent. **(b)** *(Aus)* member of parliament, representative.

Mandatarstaat *m* mandatary.

Mandats-: ~gebiet *nt* mandated territory, mandate; **~macht** *f* mandatory power; **~träger** *m* mandate holder; **~verlust** *m* loss of a seat.

Mandel *f* **-, -n (a)** almond. **(b)** *(Anat)* tonsil. **(c)** *(obs Measure)* fifteen.

Mandel-: ~augen *pl (poet)* almond eyes *pl*; **m~äugig** *adj (poet)* almond-eyed; **~baum** *m* almond tree; **~entzündung** *f* tonsillitis; **m~förmig** *adj* almond-shaped; **~kern** *m* almond (kernel); **~kleie** *f* almond meal; **~öl** *nt* almond oil.

Manderl *(Aus)*, **Mandl** *(S Ger) nt* **-s, -n** *(inf)* **(a)** *(Männchen)* little man. **(b)** *(Vogelscheuche)* scarecrow.

Mandoline *f* mandolin.

Mandragora *f* **-, Mandragoren** *(Bot)* mandrake.

Mandrill *m* **-s, -e** *(Zool)* mandrill.

Mandschu *nt* **-(s),** *no pl (Ling)* Manchu.

Mandschurei *f* **- die ~** Manchuria.

mandschurisch *adj* Manchurian.

Manege [ma'ne:ʒə] *f* **-, -n** ring, arena.

mang *prep +dat or acc (N Ger inf)* among(st).

Mangan [maŋ'ga:n] *nt* **-s,** *no pl (abbr* **Mn)** manganese.

Manganat [maŋga'na:t] *nt (Chem)* manganate.

Mangan- [maŋ'ga:n-]: **~eisen** *nt* ferro-manganese; **~erz** *nt* manganese ore; **~stahl** *m* manganese steel.

Mangel¹ *f* **-, -n** mangle; *(Heiß~)* rotary iron ◆ **durch die ~ drehen** to put through the mangle; *(fig inf)* to put through it *(inf)*; *Prüfling etc auch* to put through the mill; **jdn in die ~ nehmen/in der ~ haben** *(fig inf)* to give sb a going-over *(inf)*; *(ausfragen auch)* to give sb a grilling *(inf)*.

Mangel² *m* **-s, ¨ (a)** *(Fehler)* fault; *(bei Maschine auch)* defect; *(Unzulänglichkeit auch)* shortcoming; *(Charakter~)* flaw.
(b) *no pl (das Fehlen)* lack *(an +dat* of); *(Knappheit auch)* shortage *(an +dat* of); *(Med auch)* deficiency *(an +dat* of) ◆ **aus ~** *or* **wegen ~s an** (*+dat)* for lack of, due to a lack of; **wegen ~s an Beweisen** for lack of evidence; **~ an Vitamin C** lack of vitamin C, vitamin C deficiency; **es besteht** *or* **herrscht ~ an etw** *(dat)* there is a lack/shortage of sth; **~ an etw** *(dat)* **haben** *or* **leiden** *(liter)* to be short of sth, to lack sth, to have a lack of sth.
(c) *no pl (Entbehrung)* privation, need, want ◆ **~ leiden** *(liter)* to go short, to suffer hardship *or* privation; **keinen ~ leiden** to want for nothing.

-mangel *m in cpds* shortage of ...; *(Med)* ... deficiency.

Mängelbericht *m* list of faults.

Mangel-: ~beruf *m* undersubscribed *or* understaffed profession; **~erscheinung** *f (Med)* deficiency symptom; **eine ~erscheinung sein** *(fig)* to be in short supply *(bei* with).

mangelfrei, mängelfrei *adj* free of faults *or* defects.

mangelhaft *adj (unzulänglich, schlecht)* poor; *Beleuchtung, Ausrüstung auch* inadequate; *Informationen, Interesse* insufficient; *(fehlerhaft) Sprachkenntnisse, Ware* faulty; *(Schulnote auch)* unsatisfactory.

Mangelhaftigkeit *f siehe adj* poorness; inadequacy; insufficiency; faultiness.

Mängelhaftung *f (Jur)* liability for faults *or* defects.

Mangelkrankheit *f* deficiency disease.

mangeln¹ [1] *vt Wäsche* to (put through the) mangle; *(heiß ~)* to iron, to press.
[2] *vi* to use the mangle/rotary iron.

mangeln² [1] *vi impers* **es mangelt an etw** *(dat)* there is a lack of sth; *(unzureichend vorhanden auch)* there is a shortage of sth; **er ließ es an nichts ~** he made sure that he/they *etc* lacked nothing *or* that nothing was lacking; **es mangelt jdm an etw** *(dat)* sb lacks sth; **es mangelt ihm an Selbstvertrauen/Erfahrung** he is lacking in *or* he lacks self-confidence/experience; **~des Selbstvertrauen/Verständnis** *etc* a lack of self-confidence/understanding *etc*; **wegen ~der Aufmerksamkeit** through not paying attention; **das Kino wurde wegen ~der Sicherheit geschlossen** the cinema was closed because of inadequate safety precautions.
[2] *vi* **etw mangelt jdm/einer Sache** sb/sth lacks sth; *(Verständnis, Selbstvertrauen, Erfahrung auch)* sb is lacking in sth.

Mängelrüge *f (Admin)* point of criticism.

mangels *prep +gen (form)* for lack of.

Mangel-: ~ware *f* scarce commodity, commodity in short supply; **~ware sein** *(fig)* to be a rare thing; *(Ärzte, gute Lehrer etc)* not to grow on trees; **~wäsche** *f* ironing *(to be done in a rotary iron)*.

Mango ['maŋgo] *f* **-, -nen** [maŋ'go:nən] *or* **-s** *(auch* **~pflaume)** mango.

Mangobaum *m* mango tree.

Mangold ['maŋgɔlt] *m* **-(e)s, -e** mangel(-wurzel).

Mangrove [maŋ'gro:və] *f* **-, -n** mangrove.

Mangrovensumpf *m* mangrove swamp.

Manie *f (Med, fig)* mania; *(fig auch)* obsession.

Manier *f* **-, -en (a)** *no pl (Art und Weise)* manner; *(eines Künstlers etc)* style ◆ **in überzeugender ~** in a most convincing manner. **(b) ~en** *pl (Umgangsformen)* manners; **~en lernen** to learn (some) manners, to learn (how) to behave; **was sind das für ~en** *(inf)* that's no way to behave. **(c)** *(Angewohnheit)* affectation.

manieriert *adj* affected; *Benehmen auch* mannered.

Manieriertheit *f siehe adj* affectation; manneredness.

Manierismus *m (Liter, Art)* mannerism.

manierlich [1] *adj Kind* well-mannered, well-behaved; *Benehmen* good; *Aussehen, Frisur, Kleidung* respectable.
[2] *adv essen* politely; *sich benehmen* properly; *sich kleiden* respectably.

Manifest *nt* **-(e)s, -e (a)** manifesto. **(b)** *(Naut)* manifest.

manifest *adj (liter)* manifest.

Manifestant(in *f*) *m (Sw)* demonstrator.

Manifestation *f* manifestation; *(offenkundiger Beweis)* demonstration; *(Sw: Kundgebung)* demonstration.

manifestieren* *(geh)* [1] *vt* to demonstrate, to manifest.
[2] *vi (Sw)* to demonstrate.
[3] *vr* to manifest oneself.

Maniküre *f* **-, -n (a)** *(Handpflege)* manicure. **(b)** *(Handpflegerin)* manicurist.

maniküren* *vt* to manicure.

Manila *nt* **-s** Manil(l)a.

Manila-: ~hanf *m* Manil(l)a (hemp); **~zigarre** *f* Manil(l)a (cigar).

Maniok *m* **-s, -s** *(Bot)* cassava.

Maniokwurzel *f* cassava root.

Manipulant *m* manipulator; *(Aus: Amtshelfer)* assistant.

Manipulation *f* manipulation; *(Trick)* manoeuvre.

Manipulator *m (Tech)* manipulator; *(fig)* conjurer, magician.

manipulierbar *adj* manipulable ◆ **leicht/schwer ~** easily manipulated/difficult to manipulate.

Manipulierbarkeit *f* manipulability.

manipulieren* *vt* to manipulate.

Manipulierung *f* manipulation.

manisch *adj* manic ◆ **~-depressiv, ~-melancholisch** manic-depressive; **~-melancholische Krankheit** manic depression.

Manitu *m* **-s** Manitou.

Manko *nt* **-s, -s (a)** *(Comm: Fehlbetrag)* deficit ◆ **~ haben** *(inf) or* **machen** *(inf)* to be short *(inf)*; **~ machen** *(inf: bei Verkauf)* to make a loss. **(b)** *(fig: Nachteil)* shortcoming.

Mann *m* **-(e)s, ¨er (a)** man ◆ **ein Überschuß an ¨ern** a surplus of males *or* men; **der böse** *or* **schwarze ~** the bogeyman; **ein feiner ~** a (perfect) gentleman; **ein ~ aus dem Volk(e)** a man of the people; **der erste ~** *or* **der ~ an der Spitze sein** *(fig sl)* to be in charge; **der ~ im Mond(e)** the man in the moon; **ein ~ der Feder/Wissenschaft** a man of letters/science; **ein ~ des Todes** a dead man, a man marked for death; **ein ~ von Wort** a man of his word; **wo ¨er noch ¨er sind** where men are men; **er ist unser ~** he's the man for us, he's our man; **er ist nicht der ~ dafür** *or* **danach** he's not the man for that; *(nicht seine Art)* he's not the sort; **drei ~ hoch** *(inf)* three of them together; **wie ein ~** as a *or* one man; **auf den ~ dressiert sein** to be trained to go for people; **etw an den ~ bringen** *(inf)* to get rid of sth; **seinen ~ stehen** to hold one's own; *(auf eigenen Füßen stehen)* to stand on one's own two feet; **einen**

kleinen ~ im Ohr haben (*hum sl*) to be crazy (*inf*); **und ein ~, ein Wort, er hat's auch gemacht** and, as good as his word, he did it; **~ an ~** close together, next to one another; **~ für ~** (*einzeln hintereinander*) one after the other; (*allesamt*) every single one; **~ gegen ~** man against man; **pro ~** per head; **ein Gespräch unter ¨ern** *or* **von ~ zu ~** a man-to-man talk; *siehe* **Mannen, Not, tot** *etc.*

(b) (*Ehe~*) husband ◆ **jdn an den ~ bringen** (*inf*) to marry sb off (*inf*), to find sb a husband; **~ und Frau werden** to become man and wife.

(c) *pl* **Leute** (*Besatzungsmitglied*) hand, man ◆ **20 ~** 20 hands *or* men; **mit ~ und Maus untergehen** to go down with all hands; (*Passagierschiff*) to go down with no survivors.

(d) *pl* **Leute** (*Teilnehmer, Sport, Cards*) player, man ◆ **auf den ~ spielen** to play the ball at one's opponent; (*beim Zuspielen*) to pass accurately; **den dritten ~ spielen** (*Cards*) to play *or* take the third hand.

(e) (*inf: als Interjektion*) (my) God (*inf*); (*auffordernd, bewundernd, erstaunt auch*) hey, (hey) man (*sl*) ◆ **~, das kannst du doch nicht machen!** hey, you can't do that!; **mach schnell, ~!** hurry up, man!; **~, oh ~!** oh boy! (*inf*); **(mein) lieber ~!** my God! (*inf*); (*erstaunt, bewundernd auch*) wow! (*inf*).

mannbar *adj* **(a)** *Junge* sexually mature; (*mutig*) brave. **(b)** *Mädchen* marriageable.

Männchen *nt dim of* **Mann (a)** little man; (*Zwerg*) man(n)ikin ◆ **~ malen** to draw (little) matchstick men, ≃ to doodle. **(b)** (*Biol*) male; (*Vogel~ auch*) cock. **(c) ~ machen** (*Tier*) to sit up on its hind legs; (*Hund*) to (sit up and) beg; (*pej inf*) (*Mensch*) to grovel; (*hum: Soldat*) to jump smartly to attention.

Männe *m* **-,** *no pl* **(a)** (*dial*) *dim of* **Hermann. (b)** (*inf: Ehemann*) hubby (*inf*).

Mannen *pl* (*Hist: Gefolgsleute*) men *pl.*

Mannequin [manə'kɛ̃:, 'manəkɛ̃] *nt* **-s, -s** (fashion) model.

Männer *pl of* **Mann.**

Männer- *in cpds* men's; (*eines Mannes*) man's; **~bekanntschaft** *f usu pl* man friend, boyfriend; **von ~bekanntschaften leben** to earn one's living from prostitution; **~beruf** *m* male profession; **~bund** *m* male organization; **~chor** *m* male-voice choir; **~domäne** *f* male domain; **technische Berufe sind noch immer ~domäne** the technical professions remain a male preserve; **~fang** *m* **auf ~fang ausgehen/sein** to go/be looking for a man/men; (*zwecks Heirat*) to go/be husband-hunting; **~freund** *m* (*Mann*) man's man; (*Frau*) friend of the male sex; **~freundschaft** *f* friendship between men; **er hat immer ~freundschaften vorgezogen** he has always preferred friendship(s) with other men; **~gesangverein** *m* male choral society; **~gesellschaft** *f* (*Sociol*) male-dominated society; (*Gesellschaft von Männern*) all-male company; ⚠**~haß** *m* hatred of men; **~haus** *nt* men's house; **~herrschaft** *f* male domination; **~magazin** *nt* magazine for men; **m~mordend** *adj* man-eating; **~sache** *f* (*Angelegenheit*) man's business; (*Arbeit*) job for a man, man's job; **~sachen** men's affairs; **Fußball war früher ~sache** football used to be a male preserve; **~stimme** *f* man's voice; (*Mus*) male voice; **~treu** *f* **-, -** (*Bot*) speedwell; ⚠**~überschuß** *m* surplus of men; **~welt** *f* (*dated*) men *pl.*

Mannes-: ~alter *nt* manhood *no art*; **im besten ~alter sein** to be in one's prime *or* in the prime of (one's) life; **~jahre** *pl* years of manhood *pl*; **in die ~jahre kommen** to reach manhood; **~kraft** *f* (*dated, hum*) virility.

Mannesmannrohr ® *nt* seamless metal tube, Mannesmann tube.

Mannes-: ~stolz *m* masculine pride; **~würde** *f* (*old*) accoutrements of manhood *pl*; (*hum*) dignity as a man.

mannhaft *adj* manly *no adv*; (*tapfer*) manful, valiant; (*entschlossen*) resolute; *Widerstand* stout.

Mannhaftigkeit *f, no pl siehe adj* manliness; manfulness, valour; resolution; stoutness.

mannigfach *adj attr* manifold, multifarious.

mannigfaltig *adj* diverse, varied.

Männlein *nt dim of* **Mann** little man; (*Zwerg*) man(n)ikin ◆ **~ und Weiblein** (*hum inf*) boys and girls.

männlich *adj* **(a)** male; *Reim, Wort* masculine. **(b)** (*fig: mannhaft*) *Stärke, Mut, Entschluß, Wesen* manly; *Auftreten, Stimme auch* masculine; *Frau* masculine, mannish.

Männlichkeit *f* (*fig*) manliness; (*von Auftreten, Stimme auch*) masculinity; (*von Frau*) masculinity, mannishness.

Männlichkeitswahn *m* machismo.

Mannloch *nt* (*Tech*) manhole.

Mannsbild *nt* (*dated pej*) fellow, male.

Mannschaft *f* (*Sport, fig*) team; (*Naut, Aviat*) crew ◆ **~(en)** (*Mil*) men *pl.*

Mannschafts- *in cpds* (*Sport*) team; **~aufstellung** *f* team line-up; (*das Aufstellen*) selection of the team; **~dienstgrad** *m* (*Mil*) other rank *usu pl*; **~führer** *m* (*Sport*) (team) captain; **~geist** *m* team spirit; **~kampf** *m* (*Sport*) team event; **~kost** *f* (*Sport*) team fare; (*Mil*) troops' rations *pl*; (*Naut, Aviat*) crew's rations *pl*; **~raum** *m* (*Sport*) team quarters *pl*; (*Mil*) men's quarters *pl*; (*Naut*) crew's quarters *pl*; (*Umkleideraum*) changing rooms *pl*; **~sieger** *m* (*Sport*) winning team; **~spiel** *nt,* **~sport** *m* team sport; **~verpflegung** *f siehe* **~kost**; **~wagen** *m* police van; (*Mil*) troop carrier; **~wertung** *f* (*Sport*) team score.

Manns-: m~hoch *adj* as high as a man; **der Schnee liegt m~hoch** the snow is six feet deep; **~leute** *pl* (*dated inf*) men *pl*; **~person** *f* (*dated pej*) *siehe* **~bild**; **m~toll** *adj* man-mad (*inf*); **~tollheit** *f* nymphomania; **~volk** *nt* (*dated inf*) men *pl.*

Mannweib *nt* (*pej*) masculine *or* mannish woman.

Manometer *nt* (*Tech*) pressure gauge ◆ **~!** (*inf*) wow! (*inf*), boy oh boy! (*inf*).

Manöver [ma'nø:vɐ] *nt* **-s, -** (*lit, fig*) manoeuvre ◆ **ins ~ gehen** *or* **ziehen** to go on manoeuvres; **nach größeren ~n ...** (*Mot, fig etc*) after a lot of manoeuvring ...

Manöver-: ~gelände *nt* exercise area; (*ständig*) ranges *pl*; **~kritik** *f* (*fig*) inquest, post-mortem; **~schaden** *m* damage resulting from military manoeuvres.

manövrieren* [manø'vri:rən] *vti* (*lit, fig*) to manoeuvre.

Manövrier- [manø'vri:ɐ]: **m~fähig** *adj* manoeuvrable; **~fähigkeit** *f* manoeuvrability; **m~unfähig** *adj* disabled.

Mansarde *f* **-, -n** garret; (*Boden*) attic.

Mansarden- *in cpds* attic.

Mansch *m* **-es,** *no pl* (*inf*) (*Brei*) mush; (*Schlamm*) mud.

manschen *vi* (*inf*) to mess around (*inf*).

Manschette *f* **(a)** (*Ärmelaufschlag*) cuff.

(b) (*Umhüllung*) frill.

(c) (*Tech: Dichtung*) sleeve.

(d) (*Sport: Würgegriff*) stranglehold ◆ **~n haben** (*inf*) to be scared stupid (*inf*); **vor seinem Vater/der Prüfung hat er mächtige ~n** (*inf*) his father/the thought of the exam scares him stupid; **~n kriegen** (*inf*) to get cold feet.

Manschettenknopf *m* cufflink.

Mantel *m* **-s, ¨ (a)** coat; (*loser ~*) cloak; *siehe* **Wind.**

(b) (*Tech*) (*Glocken~*) cope; (*Rohr~*) jacket; (*Geschoß~*) jacket, casing; (*Kabel~*) casing; (*Reifen~*) outer tyre, casing.

(c) (*Math*) curved surface.

(d) (*Fin*) share certificate.

(e) (*Comm: Firmen~*) form.

(f) (*Zool*) mantle, pallium.

(g) (*fig*) cloak, mantle ◆ **etw mit dem ~ der christlichen Nächstenliebe zudecken** to forgive and forget sth.

Mäntelchen *nt dim of* **Mantel** ◆ **einer Sache** (*dat*) **ein ~ umhängen** to cover sth up; *siehe* **Wind.**

Mantel- *in cpds* (*Tex*) coat; ⚠**~geschoß** *nt* jacketed bullet; **~gesetz** *nt siehe* **Rahmengesetz**; **~pavian** *m* sacred *or* hamadryas baboon; **~stoff** *m* coating, coat fabric; **~tarifvertrag** *m* (*Ind*) general agreement on conditions of employment; **~tiere** *pl* tunicates *pl* (*spec*); **~- und Degen-Film** *m* swashbuckling film.

Mantsch *m* **-es,** *no pl* (*inf*) *siehe* **Mansch.**

mantschen *vi* (*inf*) *siehe* **manschen.**

Manual *nt* **-s, -e (a)** (*Mus*) manual. **(b)** (*old Comm*) daily ledger.

manuell *adj Arbeit* manual ◆ **etw ~ bedienen** to operate sth manually *or* by hand.

Manufaktur *f* (*old, Sociol*) **(a)** *no pl* manufacture. **(b)** (*Fabrik*) factory, manufactory (*old*).

Manufakturwaren *pl* manufactured goods *pl*; (*Textilien*) textiles *pl.*

Manuskript *nt* **-(e)s, -e** manuscript; (*Rad, Film, TV*) script.

Maoismus *m* Maoism.

Maoist(in *f*) *m* Maoist.

maoistisch *adj* Maoist.

Maori *m* **-(s), -(s)** Maori.

Mappe *f* **-, -n** (*Aktenhefter*) folder, file; (*Aktentasche*) briefcase; (*Schul~*) (school) bag; (*Feder~, Bleistift~*) pencil case.

Mär *f* **-, -en** (*old*) *siehe* **Mär(e).**

Marabu *m* **-s, -s** (*Orn*) marabou.

Marabut *m* **-(s), -(s)** (*Rel*) marabout.

Maracuja *f* **-, -s** passion fruit.

Marathon[1] *m* **-s, -s** marathon.

Marathon[2] *nt* **-s, -s** (*fig*) marathon.

Marathon- *in cpds* marathon; **~lauf** *m* marathon; **~läufer** *m* marathon runner.

Märchen *nt* **-s, -** fairytale, fairy story; (*inf*) tall story.

Märchen- *in cpds* fairytale; **~buch** *nt* book of fairytales; **~erzähler** *m* teller of fairytales; (*fig*) storyteller; **~film** *m* film of a fairytale; **m~haft** *adj* fairytale *attr*, fabulous; (*fig*) fabulous, fantastic; **~land** *nt* fairyland; **~prinz** *m* Prince Charming; (*fig auch*) fairytale prince; **~stunde** *f* story time.

Marder *m* **-s, -** marten.

Marder-: ~fell *nt,* **~pelz** *m* marten (fur).

Mär(e) *f* **-(e), -en** (*old*) (*Nachricht*) tidings *pl*, news; (*Märchen*) (fairy)tale; (*hum inf*) fairy story.

Margarete *f* **-** Margaret.

Margarine [(*Aus*) -'ri:n] *f* margarine.

Marge ['marʒə] *f* **-, -n** (*Comm*) margin.

Margerite *f* **-, -n** daisy, marguerite.

marginal *adj* marginal.

Marginalie [-iə] *f usu pl* marginalia *pl.*

Maria *f* **-** Mary ◆ **die Mutter ~** the Virgin Mary, Our (Blessed) Lady.

Mariä: ~ Empfängnis *f* the Immaculate Conception; **~ Geburt** *f* (the) Nativity of Mary; **~ Himmelfahrt** *f* Assumption.

Mariatheresientaler, Maria-Theresien-Taler [-te're:ziən-] *m* Maria Theresa thaler, Levant dollar.

Marie *f* **-** Mary; (*sl: Geld*) dough (*sl*), bread (*sl*).

Marien- [-i:ən]: **~altar** *m* Lady altar; **~bild** *nt* picture of the Virgin Mary; **~dichtung** *f* hymns and poems *pl* in praise of the Virgin Mary; **~fest** *nt* Lady Day; **~käfer** *m* ladybird; **~kult** *m* Mariolatry (*form*), cult of the Virgin Mary; **~leben** *nt* (*Art, Liter*) Life of the Virgin Mary; **~verehrung** *f* adoration *or* veneration of the Virgin Mary.

Marihuana [mari'hua:na] *nt* **-s,** *no pl* marijuana.

⚠: Informationen zur Rechtschreibreform im Anhang

Marille *f* **-, -n** (*Aus*) apricot.
Marinade *f* (*Cook*) marinade; (*Soße*) mayonnaise-based sauce. **~n** *pl* (*Fischkonserven*) canned *or* tinned (*Brit*) fish.
Marine *f* navy.
Marine- *in cpds* naval; **m~blau** *adj* navy blue; **~flieger** *m* naval pilot; **~flugzeug** *nt* naval aircraft *or* plane; **~infanterie** *f* marines *pl*; **~infanterist** *m* marine; **~maler** *m* marine *or* seascape painter; **~minister** *m* minister of naval affairs; **~ministerium** *nt* ministry of naval affairs.
Mariner *m* **-s, -** (*inf*) sailor.
Marine-: ~soldat *m* marine; **~truppen** *pl* marines *pl*; **~wesen** *nt* navy; **ein Begriff aus dem ~wesen** a nautical term.
marinieren* *vt Fisch, Fleisch* to marinate, to marinade ◆ **marinierter Hering** pickled herring.
Marionette *f* marionette, puppet; (*fig*) puppet.
Marionetten- *in cpds* puppet; **~spieler** *m* puppeteer; **~theater** *nt* puppet theatre.
maritim *adj* maritime.
Mark[1] *nt* **-(e)s,** *no pl* (*Knochen~*) marrow; (*Bot: Gewebe~*) medulla, pith ◆ **Brühe mit ~** (*Cook*) consommé with beef marrow; **bis ins ~** (*fig*) to the core; **jdn bis ins ~ treffen** (*fig*) to cut sb to the quick; **es geht mir durch ~ und Bein** (*inf*) *or* **durch ~ und Pfennig** (*hum inf*) it goes right through me; **kein ~ in den Knochen haben** (*fig*) to have no guts *or* backbone; **jdm das ~ aus den Knochen saugen** (*liter*) to bleed sb dry.
Mark[2] *f* **-, -en (a)** (*Grenzland*) borderland, march (*rare*) ◆ **die ~ Brandenburg, die ~** (*inf*) the Mark Brandenburg, the Brandenburg Marches; **die ~en** (*Hist*) the Marches.
(b) (*Rugby*) touch.
Mark[3] *f* **-,** *or* (*hum*) **¨er** mark ◆ **Deutsche ~** German mark, deutschmark; **~ der DDR** (East German) mark; **vier ~ zwanzig** four marks twenty (pfennigs); **mit jeder ~ rechnen, die** *or* **jede ~ umdrehen** to think twice before spending anything; **mit jeder ~ rechnen müssen** to have to count every penny.
markant *adj* (*ausgeprägt*) clear-cut; *Schriftzüge* clearly defined; (*hervorstechend*) *Kinn etc* prominent; (*auffallend*) *Erscheinung, Persönlichkeit* striking.
Mark Aurel *m* **- -** Marcus Aurelius.
markdurchdringend *adj* (*geh*) bloodcurdling.
Marke *f* **-, -n (a)** (*bei Lebens- und Genußmitteln*) brand; (*bei Industriegütern*) make ◆ **du bist (vielleicht) eine ~!** (*inf*) you're a right *or* fine one (*inf*); **eine komische ~** (*fig inf*) a queer *or* rum customer *or* character.
(b) (*Brief~*) stamp ◆ **zehn ~n à** *or* **zu fünfzig** ten fifty-pfennig stamps.
(c) (*Essen~*) voucher; (*Rabatt~*) (trading) stamp; (*Lebensmittel~*) coupon; (*old: Renten~*) stamp ◆ **~n kleben** (*inf*) to buy one's stamps.
(d) (*Erkennungs~*) disc, tag; (*Garderoben~*) cloakroom counter *or* (*Zettel*) ticket *or* check (*US*); (*Polizei~*) badge; (*Spiel~*) chip; (*Pfand~ etc*) token; *siehe* **Hundemarke.**
(e) (*Rekord~*) record; (*Wasserstands~*) watermark.
märken *vt* (*Aus*) *Wäsche* to mark.
Marken-: ~album *nt* (*inf*) stamp album; **~artikel** *m* proprietary article; **~butter** *f* non-blended butter, best quality butter; **~erzeugnis, ~fabrikat** *nt* proprietary article; **m~frei** *adj* **(a)** (*ohne Marken*) unrationed, not on coupons; **(b)** (*ohne Warenzeichen*) non-branded; **~hersteller** *m* manufacturer of proprietary goods; **~name** *m* brand *or* proprietary name; **~piraterie** *f* brand name piracy; **~schutz** *m* protection of trademarks; **~ware** *f siehe* **~artikel.**
Marker *m* **-s, -(s) (a)** (*Med*) marker. **(b)** (*Markierstift*) highlighter.
mark|erschütternd *adj siehe* **markdurchdringend.**
Marketender(in *f*) *m* **-s, -** (*Hist*) sutler.
Marketenderware *f* (*Mil*) goods *pl or* (*einzelner Artikel*) article sold at army stores.
Marketing *nt* **-s,** *no pl* marketing.
Mark- (*Hist*): **~graf** *m* margrave; **~gräfin** *f* margravine; **m~gräflich** *adj* margravial; **~grafschaft** *f* margravate.
markieren* [1] *vt* (*lit, fig, Sport*) to mark; (*inf: vortäuschen*) to play ◆ **den starken Mann ~** to come the strong man; **den Dummen** *or* **Dusseligen ~** (*inf*) to act daft (*inf*).
[2] *vi* (*inf: so tun, als ob*) to put it on (*inf*) ◆ **markier doch nicht!** stop putting it on.
Markierstift *m* highlighter.
Markierung *f* marking; (*Zeichen*) mark.
Markierungs-: ~linie *f* (marking) line; **~punkt** *m* marker; **~zeichen** *nt* (*Comput*) marker.
markig *adj* (*kraftvoll, kernig*) vigorous, pithy; (*iro: pathetisch*) grandiloquent, bombastic.
Markigkeit *f* vigour, pithiness; (*iro*) grandiloquence, bombast.
märkisch *adj* of/from the Mark Brandenburg.
Markise *f* **-, -n** awning, (sun)blind.
Markknochen *m* (*Cook*) marrowbone.
Markscheide *f* (*Min*) boundary line.
Markscheide-: ~kunde, ~kunst *f* mine surveying.
Markscheider *m* **-s, -** mine surveyor.
Mark-: ~schein *m* mark note *or* bill (*US*); **10-~-Schein** *or* **Zehnmarkschein** ten-mark note *or* bill (*US*); **~stein** *m* (*lit, fig*) milestone; (*an Feldern etc*) boundary stone; **~stück** *nt* (one-) mark piece; **m~stückgroß** *adj* the size of a one-mark piece.
Markt *m* **-(e)s, ¨e (a)** market; (*Jahr~*) fair ◆ **zum** *or* **auf den ~ gehen** to go to (the) market/to the fair; **~ abhalten** to hold *or* have a market; **dienstags/jede Woche einmal ist ~** *or* **wird ~ abgehalten** there is a market every Tuesday/week.
(b) (*Comm*) market; (*Warenverkehr*) trade ◆ **auf dem** *or* **am ~** on the market; **auf den ~ bringen** to put on the market; **etw in großen Mengen auf den ~ werfen** to flood the market with sth; **auf den ~ gebracht werden** to come on the market.
(c) (*~platz*) marketplace, market square ◆ **am ~** in the marketplace; **am ~ wohnen** to live on the marketplace.
(d) (*geh:* **~flecken**) small market town.
Markt- *in cpds* market; **~absprache** *f* marketing agreement; **~analyse** *f* market analysis; **~anteil** *m* market share, share of the market; **m~beherrschend** *adj* **m~beherrschend sein, eine m~beherrschende Stellung einnehmen** to control *or* dominate the market; **~bericht** *m* (*Fin*) stock market report; **~bude** *f* market stall; **m~fähig** *adj* marketable; **~fahrer** *m* (*Aus*) (travelling) marketman; **~flecken** *m* small market town; **~forscher(in** *f*) *m* market researcher; **~forschung** *f* market research; **~frau** *f* market woman, (woman) stallholder; **~führer** *m* market leader; **m~gängig** *adj* marketable; *Preis* current; **m~gerecht** *adj* in line with *or* geared to market requirements; **~halle** *f* covered market; **~helfer** *m* market hand; **~lage** *f* state of the market; **~lücke** *f* gap in the market; **in eine ~lücke stoßen** to fill a gap in the market; **~macht** *f, no pl* market power; **~nische** *f* (market) niche; **~ordnung** *f* market regulations *pl*; **~ort** *m* (small) market town; **~platz** *m* marketplace, market square; **am/auf dem ~platz** on/in the marketplace; **~preis** *m* market price; **~psychologie** *f* marketing psychology; **~recht** *nt* (*Hist*) market rights *pl*; **m~reif** *adj Produkt* ready for the market; **~reife** *f* **ein Produkt zur ~reife entwickeln** to develop a product into a marketable commodity; **~schreier** *m* barker, market crier; **m~schreierisch** *adj* loud and vociferous; (*fig*) blatant; **~stand** *m* market stall *or* stand; **~studie** *f* market survey; **~weib** *nt* (*pej*) market woman; (*fig*) fish-wife; **~wert** *m* market value; **~wirtschaft** *f* market economy; *siehe* **frei**; **m~wirtschaftlich** *adj attr* free enterprise; **m~wirtschaftliche Prinzipien** market principles.
Markus *m* **-** Mark.
Markus|evangelium *nt* St Mark's Gospel, Gospel according to St Mark.
Marmarameer *nt* Sea of Marmara.
Marmel *f* **-, -n** marble.
Marmelade *f* jam; (*Orangen~*) marmalade.
Marmeladen-: ~brot *nt* jam sandwich; (*Scheibe*) slice of bread and jam; **~glas** *nt* jam-jar.
marmeln *vi* to play marbles.
Marmor *m* **-s, -e** marble.
Marmor- *in cpds* marble; **~bild** *nt* (*liter*) marble statue; **~bruch** *m* marble quarry.
marmorieren* *vt* to marble ◆ **mit marmoriertem Schnitt** with marbled edges, marbled.
Marmorkuchen *m* marble cake.
marmorn *adj* marble.
marode *adj* (*inf*) washed-out (*inf*); *Wirtschaft etc* ailing.
Marodeur [-'dø:ɐ] *m* marauder.
marodieren* *vi* to maraud.
Marokkaner(in *f*) *m* **-s, -** Moroccan.
marokkanisch *adj* Moroccan.
Marokko *nt* **-s** Morocco.
Marone[1] *f* **-, -n, Maroni** *f* **-, -** (sweet *or* Spanish) chestnut.
Marone[2] *f* **-, -n, Maronenpilz** *m* chestnut boletus, boletus badius (*spec*).
Maronibrater *m* **-s, -** (*Aus*) chestnut man (*inf*), chestnut vendor.
Maronit *m* **-en, -en** Maronite.
Marotte *f* **-, -n** quirk ◆ **das ist ihre ~** that's one of her little quirks.
Marquis [mar'ki:] *m* **-, -** marquis, marquess.
Marquise [mar'ki:zə] *f* **-, -n** marquise, marchioness.
Mars[1] *m* **-,** *no pl* (*Myth, Astron*) Mars.
Mars[2] *m* **-, -e** (*Naut*) top.
Marsbewohner *m* Martian.
marsch *interj* **(a)** (*Mil*) march ◆ **vorwärts ~!** forward march!; **(im Laufschritt,) ~! ~!** (at the double,) quick march! **(b)** (*inf*) off with you ◆ **~ ins Bett!** off to bed with you at the double *or* chop, chop (*inf*)!; **raus hier, ~! ~!** get out of here at the double *or* chop, chop (*inf*)!
Marsch[1] *m* **-(e)s, ¨e (a)** (*das Marschieren*) march; (*Wanderung*) hike ◆ **einen ~ machen** to go on a march/hike; **sich in ~ setzen** to move off. **(b)** (*~musik*) march. **jdm den ~ blasen** (*inf*) to give sb a rocket (*inf*).
Marsch[2] *f* **-, -en** marsh, fen.
Marschall *m* **-s, Marschälle** (field) marshal.
Marschallstab *m* (field) marshal's baton ◆ **den ~ im Tornister haben** (*fig*) to be a potential leader of men.
Marsch-: ~befehl *m* (*Mil*) (*für Truppen*) marching orders *pl*; (*für einzelnen*) travel orders *pl*; **m~bereit** *adj* ready to move; **~boden** *m* marshy soil.
Marschendorf *nt* fenland village.
Marsch-: m~fertig *adj siehe* **m~bereit**; **~flugkörper** *m* cruise missile; **~gepäck** *nt* pack.
marschieren* *vi aux sein* to march; (*fig*) to march off, to take oneself off ◆ **getrennt ~, vereint schlagen** to unite for the attack.
Marsch-: ~kolonne *f* column; ⚠**~kompaß** *m* compass; **~land** *nt* marsh(land), fen; **m~mäßig** *adj Ausrüstung etc* marching *attr*; (*für Wanderung*) hiking *attr*; **m~mäßig angezogen** dressed for marching/hiking; **~musik** *f* military marches *pl*; **~order** *f* (*Mil*) marching orders *pl*; (*fig*) go-

⚠: for details of spelling reform, see supplement

ahead; **~ordnung** *f* marching order; **~pause** *f* halt; **~richtung, ~route** *f* (*lit*) route of march; (*fig*) line of approach; **~tempo** *nt* marching time; (*Mus*) march time *or* tempo; **~verpflegung** *f* rations *pl*; (*Mil*) field rations *pl*; **~ziel** *nt* destination.

Marseille [mar'zɛ:j, mar'sɛ:j] *nt* **-s** Marseilles.

Marsfeld *nt* (*in Rom*) Campus Martius; (*in Paris*) Champs de Mars.

Marshallplan ['marʃal-] *m* (*Pol*) Marshall Plan.

Marsmensch *m* Martian.

Marssegel *nt* (*Naut*) topsail.

Marstall *m* **-(e)s, Marställe** (*Hist*) royal stables *pl*.

Marter *f* **-, -n** (*liter*) torment ◆ **das kann zur ~ werden** it can be a painful ordeal.

Marter-: ~gerät, ~instrument *nt* instrument of torture.

Marterl *nt* **-s, -n** (*S Ger, Aus*) *wayside shrine with a crucifix.*

martern (*liter*) 1 *vt* to torture, to torment ◆ **jdn zu Tode ~** to torture sb to death.
2 *vr* to torment *or* torture oneself.

Marter-: ~pfahl *m* stake; **~tod** *m* (*liter*) *siehe* **Märtyrertod**.

Marterung *f* (*liter*) torment.

martialisch [mar'tsia:lɪʃ] *adj* (*geh*) martial, warlike.

Martin-Horn ® *nt siehe* **Martinshorn**.

Martini *nt* **-**, *no pl* (*Eccl*) Martinmas.

Martins-: ~fest *nt*, **~tag** *m siehe* **Martini**.

Martinshorn ® *nt* (*von Polizei und Feuerwehr*) siren ◆ **mit ~** with its siren blaring *or* going.

Märtyrer, Martyrer (*Eccl*) *m* **-s, -** (*Eccl, fig*) martyr ◆ **jdn zum ~ machen** to make a martyr of sb; **sich als ~ aufspielen** (*pej*) to make a martyr of oneself.

Märty(re)rin, Marty(re)rin (*Eccl*) *f* martyr.

Märtyrer-: ~krone *f* martyr's crown; **~tod** *m* martyr's death; **den ~tod sterben** to die a martyr's death; **~tum** *nt* martyrdom.

Martyrium *nt* **(a)** (*Opfertod*) martyrdom; (*fig*) ordeal. **(b)** (*Grabkirche*) martyry.

Marxismus *m* Marxism.

Marxismus-Leninismus *m* Marxism-Leninism.

Marxist(in *f*) *m* Marxist.

marxistisch *adj* Marxist.

Marxsch *adj attr* Marxian ◆ **die ~e Dialektik** Marx's *or* Marxian dialectic.

März *m* **-(es)** *or* **-en** (*liter*), **-e** March ◆ **im ~** in March; **im Monat ~** in the month of March; **heute ist der zweite ~** today is the second of March *or* is March the second *or* March second (*US*); (*geschrieben*) today is 2nd March *or* March 2nd; **am ersten ~ fahren wir nach ...** on the first of March we are going to ...; **in diesem ~** this March; **im Laufe des ~** during March; **der ~ war sehr warm** March was very warm; **Anfang/Ende/Mitte ~** at the beginning/end/in the middle of March; **den 4. ~ 1973** March 4th, 1973, 4th March 1973.

Märzbecher, Märzenbecher *m* (*Bot*) snowflake; (*inf: Narzisse*) narcissus.

Märzen *nt* **-(s), -, März(en)bier** *nt strong light beer.*

Marzipan *nt* [martsi'pa:n, (*Aus*) 'martsipa:n] **-s, -e** marzipan.

März-: ~revolution *f* (*Hist*) *Revolution of March 1848*; **~veilchen** *nt* sweet violet.

Masche *f* **-, -n (a)** (*Strick~, Häkel~*) stitch; (*von Netz*) hole; (*von Kettenhemd*) link; (*Lauf~*) ladder (*Brit*), run ◆ **die ~n eines Netzes** the mesh *sing* of a net; **dir läuft eine ~ am Bein/Strumpf (runter)** you've got a ladder *or* run (in your stocking); **(jdm) durch die ~n schlüpfen** to slip through sb's/the net; (*fig auch*) to slip through sb's fingers; **durch die ~n des Gesetzes schlüpfen** to slip through a loophole in the law.
(b) (*S Ger, Aus: Schleife*) bow.
(c) (*inf*) (*Trick*) trick, dodge (*inf*); (*Eigenart*) fad, craze ◆ **die ~ raushaben** to know how to do it; **er versucht es immer noch auf die alte ~** he's still trying the same old trick; **das ist *die* ~!** that's the thing!; **das ist seine neueste ~** *or* **die neueste ~ von ihm** that's his latest (fad *or* craze).

Maschen-: ~draht *m* wire netting; **~drahtzaun** *m* wire-netting fence; **m~fest** *adj Strümpfe* non-run; **~netz** *nt* mesh, net; **~werk** *nt* (*fig*) **sich im ~werk von etw verfangen** to become enmeshed in sth.

Maschin- (*Aus*) *in cpds siehe* **Maschine(n)-**.

Maschine *f* machine; (*Motor*) engine; (*Flugzeug*) plane; (*Schreib~*) typewriter; (*inf: Motorrad*) bike ◆ **eine bloße ~ sein** (*fig*) to be no more than a machine; **zur ~ werden** (*fig*) to become a machine; **etw auf** *or* **mit der ~ schreiben** to type sth; **ich habe den Brief meiner Sekretärin in die ~ diktiert** my secretary typed the letter as I dictated it; *siehe* **maschine(n)schreiben**.

maschinell 1 *adj Herstellung, Bearbeitung* mechanical, machine *attr*.
2 *adv* mechanically, by machine; *Übersetzung* machine *attr*.

Maschinen-: ~antrieb *m* machine drive; **mit ~antrieb** machine-driven, mechanically driven; **~arbeit** *f* machine work; **~bau** *m* mechanical engineering; **~bauer** *m* mechanical engineer; **~bauingenieur** *m* mechanical engineer; **~defekt** *m* mechanical fault; **~diktat** *nt typing directly from dictation*; **~element** *nt* machine component; **~fabrik** *f* engineering works *sing or pl*; **~garn** *nt* machine thread; **m~geschrieben** *adj* typewritten, typed; **~geschütz** *nt* machine-gun; **m~gestrickt** *adj* machine-knitted; **~gewehr** *nt* machine-gun; **mit ~gewehr(en) beschießen** to machine-gun; **~gewehr-Schütze** *m* machine-gunner; **~haus** *nt* machine room; **~industrie** *f* engineering industry; **~kraft** *f* mechanical power; **m~lesbar** *adj* machine-readable; **~lesbarkeit** *f* machine-readability; **m~mäßig** *adj* in terms of machinery; **m~mäßige Ausstattung** machinery; **~meister** *m* (*Aufseher*) machine minder; (*Theat*) stage technician; (*Typ*) pressman; **~öl** *nt* lubricating oil; **~park** *m* plant; **~pistole** *f* submachine gun; **~raum** *m* plant room; (*Naut*) engine-room; **~revision** *f* (*Typ*) press proof; **~saal** *m* machine room; (*Typ*) pressroom; (*in Setzerei*) caseroom; **~satz** *m* **(a)** machine unit; **(b)** (*Typ*) machine setting *or* composition; **~schaden** *m* mechanical fault; (*Aviat etc*) engine fault; **~schlosser** *m* machine fitter.

Maschine(n)-: ⚠**m~schreiben** *vi sep irreg* (*Kleinschreibung nur bei infin und ptp*) to type; **sie schreibt Maschine** she types; **~schreiben** *nt* typing, typewriting; **~schreiber** *m* typist.

Maschinen-: ~schrift *f* typescript, typing; (*Schriftart*) typeface; **in ~schrift** typed, typewritten; **m~schriftlich** *adj* typewritten *no adv*; **~setzer** *m* machine compositor *or* typesetter; **~sprache** *f* machine language; **~stürmer** *m* **-s, -** machine wrecker; (*Hist*) Luddite; **~stürmerei** *f* Luddism; **~teil** *nt* machine part; **~-(und-)Traktoren-Station** *f* (*DDR*) agricultural machinery centre; **~wärter** *m* machine minder; **~zeitalter** *nt* machine age.

Maschinerie *f* **(a)** (*dated: Mechanismus*) piece of machinery. **(b)** (*Bühnen~*) stage machinery. **(c)** (*fig: Getriebe*) machinery.

Maschinist(in *f*) *m* (*Schiffs~*) engineer; (*Eisenbahn~*) engine-driver, engineer (*US*).

Maser[1] *f* **-, -n** vein ◆ **Holz mit feinen ~n** wood with a fine grain.

Maser[2] ['me:zɐ, 'ma:zɐ] *m* **-s, -** (*Phys*) maser.

Maserholz *nt* grained wood.

maserig *adj* grained.

masern 1 *vt* to grain.
2 *vi* to become grained.

Masern *pl* measles *sing* ◆ **die ~ haben** to have (the) measles.

Maserung *f* grain.

Maske *f* **-, -n (a)** (*lit, fig, Sport, Med*) mask ◆ **sein Gesicht wurde** *or* **erstarrte zur ~** his face froze (into a mask); **die ~ abnehmen** *or* **ablegen** to take off one's mask, to unmask; (*fig*) to drop all pretence, to let fall one's mask; **die ~ fallen lassen** *or* **abwerfen** (*fig*) to throw off one's mask; **jdm die ~ herunterreißen** *or* **vom Gesicht reißen** (*fig*) to unmask sb; **ohne ~** (*fig*) undisguised; **unter der ~ von etw** (*fig*) under the guise of sth; **das ist alles nur ~** that's all just pretence.
(b) (*Theat: Aufmachung*) make-up ◆ **~ machen** to make up.
(c) (*maskierte Person*) mask, domino (*old*); (*fig*) phony (*inf*).
(d) (*Typ, Comput*) mask.
(e) (*Tech*) frame.

Masken-: ~ball *m* masked ball; **~bildner** *m* make-up artist; **m~haft** *adj* mask-like, like a mask; **~kleid, ~kostüm** *nt* fancy-dress costume; **~spiele** *pl* (*Liter*) masques *pl*; **~verleih** *m* fancy-dress hire, theatrical costumier; **~zug** *m* carnival procession.

Maskerade *f* (*Verkleidung*) costume; (*old*) masquerade.

maskieren* 1 *vt* **(a)** (*verkleiden*) to dress up; (*unkenntlich machen*) to disguise. **(b)** (*verbergen*) to mask, to disguise.
2 *vr* to dress up; (*sich unkenntlich machen*) to disguise oneself ◆ **sich als jd/etw ~** (*fig*) to masquerade as sb/sth.

maskiert *adj* masked.

Maskierung *f* **(a)** (*das Verkleiden*) dressing up; (*Sich-Unkenntlichmachen*) disguising oneself. **(b)** (*Verkleidung*) fancy-dress costume; (*von Spion etc*) disguise. **(c)** (*Verhüllung*) masking.

Maskottchen *nt* (lucky) mascot.

maskulin *adj* **(a)** (*Gram, Poet*) masculine. **(b)** [masku'li:n] (*betont männlich*) masculine.

Maskulinum *nt* **-s, Maskulina** masculine noun.

Maso *m* **-s**, *no pl* (*sl*) *abbr of* **Masochismus**.

Masochismus *m* **-**, *no pl* masochism.

Masochist(in *f*) *m* masochist.

masochistisch *adj* masochist.

maß *pret of* **messen**.

Maß[1] *nt* **-es, -e (a)** (*~einheit*) measure (*für* of); (*Zollstock*) rule; (*Bandmaß*) tape measure ◆ **~e und Gewichte** weights and measures; **das ~ aller Dinge** (*fig*) the measure of all things; **das richtige** *or* **rechte ~ halten** (*fig*) to strike the right balance; **mit zweierlei** *or* **verschiedenem ~ messen** (*fig*) to operate a double standard; **das ~ ist voll** (*fig*) that's enough (of that), enough's enough; **und, um das ~ vollzumachen ...** (*fig*) and to cap it all ...; **in reichem ~(e)** abundantly; **in reichem ~(e) vorhanden sein** to be abundant; (*Energie, Zeit etc*) to be plentiful; **er hat sich in reichem ~e erkenntlich gezeigt** he gave abundant proof of his gratitude; **das (übliche) ~ überschreiten, über das übliche ~ hinausgehen** to overstep the mark; **die edlen ~e dieser Plastik** (*geh*) the noble proportions of this statue.
(b) (*Meßgröße*) measurement; (*von Zimmer, Möbelstück auch*) dimension ◆ **ihre ~e sind: ...** her measurements *or* vital statistics are ...; **sich** (*dat*) **etw nach ~ anfertigen lassen** to have sth made to measure *or* order (*US*); **~ nehmen** to measure up; **bei jdm ~ nehmen** to measure sb, to take sb's measurements; **Schuhe/Hemden nach ~** shoes/shirts made to measure *or* order (*US*), custom (*US*) shoes/shirts.
(c) (*Ausmaß*) extent, degree ◆ **ein solches/gewisses ~ an** *or* **von ...** such a degree/a certain degree of ...; **in hohem ~(e)** to a high degree; **in solchem ~(e)** *or* **in einem ~(e), daß ...** to such an extent that ...; **in nicht geringem ~(e)** in no small measure; **in großem ~e** to a great extent; **in vollem ~e** fully; **in demselben** *or* **gleichem ~e wie die Produktion steigt, steigt auch der Verbrauch** when production increases, consumption increases accordingly; **die Bäcker verlangen eine Lohnerhöhung in demselben** *or* **in gleichem**

~e wie die Fleischer the bakers are demanding a pay rise comparable to *or* with that of the butchers; **in besonderem ~e** especially; **in gewissem/höherem** *or* **stärkerem/beschränktem ~** to a certain/greater/limited degree *or* extent; **in höchstem ~e** extremely; **über alle ~en** (*liter*) beyond (all) measure.
(d) (*Mäßigung*) moderation ◆ **in** *or* **mit ~en** in moderation; **weder ~ noch Ziel kennen** to know no bounds; **ohne ~ und Ziel** immoderately.

Maß² *f* **-, -** (*S Ger, Aus*) litre (tankard) of beer ◆ **zwei ~ Bier** two litres of beer.

Massage [ma'sa:ʒə] *f* **-, -n** massage ◆ **~n nehmen** to have massage treatment.

Massage-: ~institut *nt siehe* **~salon; ~praxis** *f* physiotherapy centre; **~salon** *m* (*euph*) massage parlour; **~stab** *m* vibrator.

Massaker *nt* **-s, -** massacre.

massakrieren* *vt* (*dated, inf*) to massacre.

Maß-: ~analyse *f* (*Chem*) volumetric analysis; **~angabe** *f* measurement; (*bei Hohlmaßen*) volume *no pl*; **Gläser in Restaurants müssen eine ~angabe haben** glasses in restaurants must show how much they hold; **~anzug** *m* made-to-measure *or* bespoke *or* made-to-order (*US*) *or* custom (*US*) suit; **~arbeit** *f* (*inf*) **das war ~arbeit** that was a neat bit of work.

Masse *f* **-, -n (a)** (*Stoff*) mass; (*Cook*) mixture ◆ **die ~ für den Guß der Glocke** the molten metal for casting the bell; **die wogenden ~n ihres Körpers** the heaving bulk of her body.
(b) (*große Menge*) heaps *pl* (*inf*), stacks *pl* (*inf*); (*von Besuchern etc*) host ◆ **die (breite) ~ der Bevölkerung** *etc* the bulk of the population *etc*; **eine ganze ~** (*inf*) a lot *or* a great deal; **sie kamen in wahren ~n** they came in droves *or* in their thousands; **die ~ muß es bringen** (*Comm*) the profit only comes with quantity.
(c) (*Menschenmenge*) crowd.
(d) (*Bevölkerungs~*) masses *pl* (*auch pej*) ◆ **die namenlose** *or* **graue** *or* **breite ~** the masses *pl*; **der Geschmack der ~** the taste of the masses.
(e) (*Konkurs~*) assets *pl*; (*Erb~*) estate.
(f) (*Phys*) mass.

Massegläubiger *m* (*Jur*) preferential creditor.

Maß-: ~einheit *f* unit of measurement; **~einteilung** *f* (measuring) scale.

Massekabel *nt* ground cable.

Massel *m* **-s,** *no pl* (*sl*) **~ haben** to be dead lucky (*inf*).

Massen- *in cpds* mass; **~absatz** *m* bulk selling; **das ist kein Artikel für den ~absatz** that isn't intended for the mass market; **~andrang** *m* crush; **~angebot** *nt* glut; **sie waren im ~angebot auf dem Markt** there was a glut of them on the market; **~anziehung** *f* (*Phys*) gravitation; **~arbeitslosigkeit** *f* mass unemployment; **~artikel** *m* mass-produced article; **~aufgebot** *nt* large body; **in einem ~aufgebot erscheinen** to turn up in force; **~auflauf** *m, no pl* crowds *pl* of people; **es gab einen ~auflauf am Unfallort** huge crowds of people gathered at the scene of the accident; **~bedarf** *m* requirements *pl* of the masses; (*Comm*) requirements *pl* of the mass market; **~bedarfsgüter** *pl* basic consumer goods *pl*; **~beeinflussung** *f* mass propaganda; **~beförderungsmittel** *nt* means of mass transportation *sing*; **~entlassung** *f* mass redundancy; **~fabrikation, ~fertigung** *f* mass production; **~gesellschaft** *f* faceless society; **~grab** *nt* mass grave; **~güter** *pl* bulk goods *pl*; **m~haft** *adj* on a huge *or* massive scale; **m~haft Fanbriefe/Sekt** *etc* (*inf*) masses of fan letters/champagne *etc* (*inf*); **~herstellung** *f siehe* **~produktion; ~karambolage** *f* multiple (car) crash, pile-up (*inf*); **~kommunikationsmittel** *nt* mass medium *usu pl*; **~medien** *pl* mass media *pl*; **~mord** *m* mass murder; **~mörder** *m* mass murderer; **~partei** *f* party of the masses; **~presse** *f* popular press; **~produktion** *f* mass production; **~psychologie** *f* crowd psychology; **~psychose** *f* mass hysteria; **~quartier** *nt* camp; **~speicher** *m* (*Comput*) disk capacity, mass storage (device); **~sterben** *nt* mass of deaths; **~szene** *f* crowd scene; **~terror** *m* mass terror; **~tierhaltung** *f* intensive livestock farming; **~verkehrsmittel** *nt* means of mass transportation *sing*.

Massenvernichtung *f* mass extermination.

Massenvernichtungs-: ~lager *nt* extermination camp; **~mittel** *pl* means of mass extermination *pl*; **~waffe** *f* weapon of mass destruction.

Massen-: ~versammlung *f* mass meeting; **~wahn** *m* mass hysteria; **~ware** *f* mass-produced article; **m~weise** *adj siehe* **m~haft; ~wirkung** *f* mass effect.

Masseur [ma'sø:ɐ] *m* masseur.

Masseurin [-'sø:rɪn] *f* (*Berufsbezeichnung*) masseuse.

Masseuse [-'sø:zə] *f* (*in Eros-Center etc*) masseuse.

Maßgabe *f* (*form*) stipulation ◆ **mit der ~, daß ...** with the proviso that ..., on (the) condition that ...; **nach ~** (*+gen*) according to.

maßgebend, maßgeblich *adj* (*entscheidend, ausschlaggebend*) *Einfluß, Bedingungen* decisive; *Meinung, Ansicht* definitive; *Text* definitive, authoritative; *Fachmann* authoritative; (*wichtig*) *Persönlichkeit* leading; *Beteiligung* substantial; (*zuständig*) competent ◆ **~e Kreise** influential circles; **von ~er Seite** from the corridors of power; **das/seine Meinung ist hier nicht ~** that/his opinion doesn't weigh *or* signify here; **das war für mich nicht ~** that didn't weigh with me.

maßgeschneidert *adj Anzug* made-to-measure, made-to-order (*US*), custom *attr* (*US*).

Maßhalte-: ~appell *m*, **~parole** *f* appeal for moderation.

⚠ **maßhalten** *vi sep irreg* to be moderate, to practise moderation.

massieren¹* [1] *vt* to massage.
[2] *vi* to give (a) massage.

⚠: for details of spelling reform, see supplement

massieren²* [1] *vt* to mass.
[2] *vr* to amass; (*Truppen*) to mass.

massig [1] *adj* massive, huge.
[2] *adv* (*inf: sehr viel*) **~ Arbeit/Geld** *etc* masses *or* stacks of work/money *etc* (*inf*).

mäßig *adj* **(a)** moderate; *Preise auch* reasonable ◆ **in etw** (*dat*) **~ sein** to be moderate in sth; **etw ~ tun** to do sth in moderation; **~ essen** to eat with moderation; **~ rauchen** to be a moderate smoker, to smoke in moderation; **~, aber regelmäßig** in moderation but regularly.
(b) (*unterdurchschnittlich*) *Leistung, Schulnote etc* mediocre, indifferent; *Begabung, Beifall* moderate; *Gesundheit* middling, indifferent.

-mäßig *adj, adv suf* -wise.

mäßigen [1] *vt* (*mildern*) *Anforderungen* to moderate; *Sprache auch* to tone down; *Zorn, Ungeduld* to curb, to check ◆ **sein Tempo ~** to slacken one's pace, to slow down; *siehe* **gemäßigt.**
[2] *vr* (*im Essen, Trinken, Temperament*) to restrain *or* control oneself; (*Sturm*) to abate, to die down ◆ **~ Sie sich!** control yourself!; **sich in seinem Temperament ~** to control *or* restrain oneself; **~ Sie sich in Ihren Worten!** tone down your language!

Massigkeit *f* massiveness, hugeness.

Mäßigkeit *f* **(a)** (*beim Essen, Trinken*) moderation, restraint; (*von Forderungen, Preisen etc*) moderateness ◆ **~ üben** to exercise *or* show moderation *or* restraint. **(b)** (*Mittelmäßigkeit*) mediocrity; (*von Begabung, Beifall*) moderateness.

Mäßigung *f* restraint; (*beim Essen etc auch*) moderation.

massiv *adj* **(a)** (*pur, nicht hohl, stabil*) solid. **(b)** (*heftig*) *Beleidigung* gross; *Drohung, Kritik* heavy; *Anschuldigung* severe ◆ **~ werden** (*inf*) to turn nasty.

Massiv *nt* **-s, -e** (*Geol*) massif.

Massivität *f* massiveness.

Maß-: ~kleidung *f* made-to-measure *or* made-to-order (*US*) *or* custom (*US*) clothing; **~krug** *m* litre beer mug; (*Steinkrug*) stein; **~lieb** *nt* **-(e)s, -e, ~liebchen** *nt* daisy, marguerite.

maßlos [1] *adj* extreme; (*übermäßig*) *Forderungen auch* excessive; (*grenzenlos*) *Trauer, Freude, Ehrgeiz auch* boundless; *Mensch* (*in Forderungen etc auch, in Essen etc*) immoderate ◆ **er war ~ in seiner Wut/Freude** *etc* his rage/joy *etc* knew no bounds; **er raucht/trinkt ~** he smokes/drinks to excess.
[2] *adv* (*äußerst*) extremely; *übertreiben* grossly, hugely ◆ **es ist alles ~ traurig** (*inf*) it's all very *or* terribly (*inf*) sad.

Maßlosigkeit *f siehe adj* extremeness; excessiveness; boundlessness; lack of moderation.

Maßnahme *f* **-, -n** measure ◆ **~n treffen, um etw zu tun** to take steps *or* measures to do sth; **~n gegen jdn/etw treffen** *or* **ergreifen** to take measures against sb/sth; **vor ~n zurückschrecken** to shrink from taking action; **sich zu ~n gezwungen sehen** to be forced to take action.

Maßregel *f* rule.

maßregeln *vt insep* (*zurechtweisen*) to reprimand, to rebuke, to reprove; (*bestrafen*) to discipline; (*Sport*) to penalize.

Maßreg(e)lung *f* **(a)** *no pl siehe vt* reprimanding, rebuking, reproval; disciplining; penalizing. **(b)** (*Rüge*) reprimand, rebuke; (*von Beamten*) disciplinary action; (*Sport*) penalty.

Maßschneider *m* bespoke *or* custom (*US*) tailor.

Maßstab *m* **(a)** (*Lineal*) ruler; (*Zollstock*) rule.
(b) (*Karten~*) scale ◆ **die Karte hat einen kleinen/großen ~** it's a small-/large-scale map, the map is on a small/large scale; **beim/im ~ 1:1000** on a scale of 1:1000; **im ~ 1:25000 gezeichnet** drawn to a scale of 1:25000; **etw in verkleinertem ~ darstellen** to scale sth down.
(c) (*fig: Richtlinie, Kriterium*) standard ◆ **einen hohen/strengen ~ anlegen** to apply a high/strict standard (*an +acc* to); **für jdn als** *or* **zum ~ dienen, für jdn einen ~ abgeben** to serve as a model for sb; **sich** (*dat*) **jdn/etw zum ~ nehmen** to take sb/sth as a yardstick, to take sth as a benchmark; **das ist für mich kein ~** I don't take that as my yardstick *or* benchmark.

maßstäblich *adj* scale *attr*, to scale.

maßstab(s)-: ~gerecht, ~getreu *adj* (true) to scale; **eine ~gerechte Karte** an accurate scale map.

Maß-: ~system *nt* system of measures; **m~voll** *adj* moderate; **~vorlage** *f* (*Ftbl*) spot-on (*inf*) *or* accurate pass; **~werk** *nt* (*Archit*) tracery.

Mast¹ *m* **-(e)s, -en** *or* **-e** (*Naut, Rad, TV*) mast; (*Stange*) pole; (*Elec*) pylon.

Mast² *f* **-, -en** (*das Mästen*) fattening; (*Futter*) feed; (*Schweine~*) mast.

Mast-: ~baum *m* mast; **~darm** *m* rectum.

mästen [1] *vt* to fatten.
[2] *vr* (*inf*) to gorge *or* stuff (*inf*) oneself.

Mästerei *f* (*Schweine~*) pig fattening unit.

Mast- *in cpds* (*zu mästen*) feeder; (*gemästet*) fattened; **~futter** *nt* (fattening) feed; (*für Schweine*) mast.

Mastino *m* **-s, Mastini** mastiff.

Mast-: ~korb *m* (*Naut*) top; **~kur** *f* (*hum inf*) fattening diet; **~schwein** *nt* (*zu mästen*) porker; (*gemästet*) fattened pig; **er sieht wie ein ~schwein aus** he looks like a little (fat) piggy.

Mästung, Mastung *f* fattening.

Masturbation *f* masturbation.

masturbieren* *vti* to masturbate.

Masurka *f* **-, -s** *siehe* **Mazurka.**

Matador *m* **-s, -e** (*Stierkämpfer*) matador; (*fig*) kingpin.

Match [metʃ] *nt or m* **-(e)s, -e(s)** match.

Match-: ~ball *m* (*Tennis*) match point; **~beutel, ~sack** *m* duffel bag.

Mate ['ma:tə] *m* **-,** *no pl* maté, Paraguay tea.

Mater *f* -, -n (*Typ*) *siehe* **Matrize.**
Material *nt* -s, -ien [-iən] material; (*Bau~, Utensilien, Gerät*) materials *pl*; (*Beweis~, Belastungs~*) evidence ◆ **rollendes ~** (*Rail*) rolling stock.
Material-: ~ausgabe *f* (**a**) (*Raum*) stores *pl*; (**b**) (*Vorgang*) issue of stores and equipment; **~bedarf** *m* material requirements *pl*; **~fehler** *m* material defect, defect in the material.
Materialisation *f* materialization.
materialisieren* *vtr* to materialize.
Materialismus *m* materialism.
Materialist(in *f*) *m* materialist.
materialistisch *adj* materialist(ic); (*pej*) materialistic.
Material-: ~kosten *pl* cost of materials *sing*; **~prüfung** *f* testing of materials; **~sammlung** *f* collection of material; **ich habe jetzt die ~sammlung abgeschlossen** I have now finished collecting *or* gathering the material; **~schaden** *m* material defect, defect in the material; **~schlacht** *f* (*Mil*) matériel battle.
Materie [-iə] *f* (**a**) *no pl* (*Phys, Philos*) matter *no art*. (**b**) (*Stoff, Thema*) subject-matter *no indef art* ◆ **die ~ beherrschen** to know one's stuff.
materiell *adj* (**a**) (*Philos*) material, physical; *Recht* substantive. (**b**) (*wirtschaftlich*) financial; *Vorteile auch* material; (*gewinnsüchtig*) materialistic ◆ **~ eingestellt sein** to be materialistic; **nur ~e Interessen haben** to be only interested in material things.
matern *vt* (*Typ*) to make a plate for.
Matetee ['ma:tə-] *m siehe* **Mate.**
Math. *abbr of* **Mathematik.**
Mathe *f* -, *no pl* (*Sch sl*) maths *sing* (*Brit inf*), math (*US inf*).
Mathematik *f* mathematics *sing no art*.
Mathematiker(in *f*) *m* -s, - mathematician.
mathematisch *adj* mathematical.
Matinee *f* -, -n [-e:ən] matinée.
Matjeshering, Matjes *m* -, - (*inf*) young herring.
Matratze *f* -, -n mattress ◆ **~ horchen** (*sl*) to have a kip (*inf*).
Matratzenlager *nt* **für die Kinder ein ~ herrichten** to put down a mattress for the children.
Mätresse *f* mistress.
matriarchalisch *adj* matriarchal.
Matriarchat *nt* matriarchy, matriarchate.
Matrikel *f* -, -n (*old, Aus*) register; (*Univ: Aufnahmeverzeichnis*) matriculation register ◆ **Student mit kleiner/großer ~** occasional/full-time student.
Matrikelnummer *f* (*Univ*) registration *or* matriculation number.
Matrix *f* -, **Matrizen** *or* **Matrizes** [ma'tri:tse:s] (*Math, Med, Biol*) matrix.
Matrixdrucker *m* dot-matrix (printer).
Matrize *f* -, -n (*Typ*) matrix, mould; (*für Schreibmaschine*) stencil ◆ **etw auf ~ schreiben** to stencil sth.
Matrone *f* -, -n matron.
matronenhaft *adj* matronly.
Matrose *m* -n, -n sailor; (*als Rang*) rating (*Brit*), ordinary seaman.
Matrosen- *in cpds* sailor; **~anzug** *m* sailor suit; **~mütze** *f* sailor's cap; **~uniform** *f* sailor's uniform.
matsch *adj pred* (*dial*) (**a**) *Obst* rotten, bad. (**b**) (*Cards*) beaten ◆ **~ werden** to be beaten. (**c**) **sich ~ fühlen** to feel whacked (*inf*).
Matsch *m* -(e)s, *no pl* (*inf: breiige Masse*) mush; (*Schlamm*) mud, sludge; (*Schnee~*) slush.
Matsch|auge *nt* (*sl*) black eye, shiner (*inf*).
matschen *vi* (*inf*) to splash (about *or* around).
matschig *adj* (*inf: breiig*) gooey (*inf*), mushy; (*schlammig*) muddy, sludgy; *Schnee* slushy.
Matschwetter *nt* (*inf*) muddy/slushy weather *or* conditions *pl*.
matt *adj* (**a**) (*schwach*) *Kranker* weak; *Stimme, Lächeln auch* faint; *Glieder* weary ◆ **sich ~ fühlen** to have no energy.
(**b**) (*glanzlos*) *Augen, Metall, Farbe* dull; (*nicht glänzend*) *Farbe, Papier* mat(t); (*trübe*) *Licht* dim, subdued; *Glühbirne* opal, pearl; *Spiegel* cloudy, dull.
(**c**) (*undurchsichtig*) *Glas* frosted, opaque.
(**d**) (*fig*) *Ausdruck, Witz, Rede, Schluß* lame, feeble; *Echo* faint; (*St Ex: flau*) slack.
(**e**) (*Chess*) (check)mate ◆ **jdn ~ setzen** to checkmate sb (*auch fig*), to mate sb.
Matt *nt* -s, -s (*Chess*) (check)mate.
mattblau *adj* pale blue.
Matte[1] *f* -, -n mat ◆ **auf der ~ stehen** (*inf: bereit sein*) to be there and ready for action; **du mußt um sechs bei mir auf der ~ stehen** you must be at my place at six; **jdn auf die ~ legen** to floor sb; (*fig inf*) to make mincemeat of sb (*inf*).
Matte[2] *f* -, -n (*liter, Sw, Aus*) alpine meadow.
Matterhorn *nt* -s **das Matterhorn** the Matterhorn.
Matt-: ~glanz *m* mat(t) finish; **~glas** *nt* frosted *or* ground glass; **~gold** *nt* dull gold; (*Farbe*) pale gold.
Matthäi [ma'tɛ:i] *gen of* **Matthäus** ◆ **bei ihm ist ~ am letzten** he's had it (*inf*).
Matthäus [ma'tɛ:ʊs] *m* **Matthäi** Matthew.
Matthäus|evangelium *nt* St Matthew's Gospel, Gospel according to St Matthew.
Mattheit *f siehe adj* (**a**) weakness; faintness; weariness; lack of energy. (**b**) dullness; mat(t) finish; dimness; opal *or* pearl finish; cloudiness. (**c**) opacity. (**d**) lameness, feebleness; faintness; slackness.
mattieren* *vt* to give a mat(t) finish to ◆ **mattiert sein** to have a mat(t) finish; **mattierte Gläser** frosted glasses.
Mattigkeit *f* weariness; (*von Kranken*) weakness.
Matt-: ~lack *m* dull *or* mat(t) lacquer *or* varnish; **~papier** *nt* mat(t) *or* unglazed paper.
Mattscheibe *f* (**a**) (*Phot*) focus(s)ing screen; (*inf: Fernseher*) telly (*Brit inf*), (goggle-) box (*Brit inf*), tube (*US inf*).
(**b**) (*inf*) **eine ~ haben/kriegen** (*dumm sein*) to be soft/go soft in the head (*inf*); (*nicht klar denken können*) to have/get a mental block; **als ich das gesagt habe, muß ich wohl eine ~ gehabt haben** I can't have been really with it when I said that (*inf*).
Matur, Maturum *nt* -s, *no pl* (*old*) **Matura** *f* -, *no pl* (*Aus, Sw*) *siehe* **Abitur.**
Maturand(in *f*) *m* -en, -en (*old, Sw*), **Maturant(in** *f*) *m* (*Aus*) *siehe* **Abiturient(in).**
maturieren* *vi* (*Aus: Abitur machen*) to take one's school-leaving exam, to graduate (from high school) (*US*).
Maturität *f* (*Sw: Hochschulreife*) matriculation exam(ination).
Maturitäts- *in cpds siehe* **Reife-.**
Matz *m* -es, ¨e (*dated inf*) laddie (*inf*).
Mätzchen *nt* (*inf*) (**a**) antic ◆ **~ machen** to play *or* fool around (*inf*); **mach keine ~, schmeiß die Kanone weg!** don't try anything funny, just drop the gun! (**b**) *dim of* **Matz.**
Matze *f* -, -n, **Matzen** *m* -s, - (*Cook*) matzo.
mau *adj pred* (*inf*) poor, bad ◆ **mir ist ~** I feel poorly (*inf*); **die Geschäfte gehen ~** business is slack.
Mauer *f* -, -n (**a**) wall ◆ **etw mit einer ~ umgeben** to wall sth in; **in den ~n der Stadt** (*fig*) in the city. (**b**) (*fig: des Schweigens etc*) wall ◆ **die ~n einreißen** to tear down the barriers.
Mauer-: ~assel *f* woodlouse; **~blümchen** *nt* (*fig inf*) (*beim Tanzen*) wallflower; (*schüchternes Mädchen*) shy young thing; **~brecher** *m* -s, - (*Mil*) battering ram; **~haken** *m* (*Bergsteigen*) piton, peg; **~krone** *f* wall coping.
mauern [1] *vi* (**a**) to build, to lay bricks. (**b**) (*Cards*) to hold back; (*Ftbl sl*) to stonewall (*sl*), to play defensively; (*fig*) to stall, to stonewall (*esp Parl*).
[2] *vt* to build; (*mit Zement verfugen*) to build with mortar ◆ **der Beckenrand muß gemauert werden** the edge of the pool must be bedded in mortar.
Mauer-: ~schwalbe *f*, **~segler** *m* swift; **~speis** *m* -es, *no pl*, **~speise** *f* (*esp S Ger*) *siehe* **Mörtel**; **~stein** *m* building stone; **~verband** *m* bond; **~vorsprung** *m* projection on a/the wall; **~werk** *nt* (**a**) (*Steinmauer*) stonework, masonry; (*Ziegelmauer*) brickwork; **ein mittelalterliches ~werk** a medieval stone structure; (**b**) (*die Mauern*) walls *pl*; **~ziegel** *m* (building) brick.
Mauke *f* -, *no pl* (*Vet*) malanders *pl*.
Mauken *pl* (*dial inf*) hooves *pl* (*hum*).
Maul *nt* -(e)s, **Mäuler** mouth; (*von Löwen etc*) jaws *pl*; (*sl: von Menschen*) gob (*sl*) ◆ **ein böses** *or* **ungewaschenes** *or* **gottloses ~** (*inf*) an evil *or* a wicked *or* malicious tongue; **ein loses** *or* **lockeres ~ haben** (*sl*) (*frech sein*) to be an impudent so-and-so (*inf*); (*indiskret sein*) to be a blabbermouth (*inf*), to have a loose tongue; **jdm übers ~ fahren** (*sl*) to choke sb off (*inf*); **das ~ zu weit aufreißen** *or* **zu voll nehmen** (*sl*) to be too cocksure (*inf*); **ein großes ~ haben** (*sl*) to have a big mouth, to be a big-mouth (*inf*); **(hungrige) Mäuler stopfen** (*inf*) to feed *or* fill (hungry) mouths; **darüber werden sich die Leute das ~ zerreißen** (*inf*) that will start people's tongues wagging; **dem Volk** *or* **den Leuten aufs ~ schauen** (*inf*) to listen to what people really say; (*Meinung ermitteln*) to sound out public opinion, to listen to the man in the street; **halt's ~!** (*sl*), **~ halten!** (*sl*) shut your face *or* trap *or* gob (*all sl*); **jdm das ~ stopfen** (*sl*) to shut sb up; **sich** (*dat*) **das ~ verbrennen** (*inf*) to talk one's way *or* oneself into trouble.
Maul-: ~affen *pl* (*dated inf*): **~affen feilhalten** to stand gawping *or* gaping; **~beerbaum** *m* mulberry (tree); **~beere** *f* mulberry.
maulen *vi* (*inf*) to moan.
Maul-: ~esel *m* mule, hinny; **m~faul** *adj* (*inf*) uncommunicative; **~held** *m* (*pej*) loud-mouth (*inf*), show-off; **~hurerei** *f* (*geh*) foul-mouthedness.
-mäulig *adj suf* -mouthed.
Maulkorb *m* (*lit, fig*) muzzle ◆ **einem Hund/jdm einen ~ umhängen** to put a muzzle on a dog, to muzzle a dog/sb.
Maulkorb- (*fig inf*): ⚠**~erlaß** *m* decree muzzling freedom of speech; **~gesetz** *nt* law muzzling freedom of speech.
Maul-: ~schelle *f* (*dated inf*) slap in the face; **~sperre** *f*: **er kriegte die ~sperre** (*inf*) his mouth dropped open; **~taschen** *pl* (*Cook*) pasta squares *pl*; **~tier** *nt* mule; **~- und Klauenseuche** *f* (*Vet*) foot-and-mouth disease.
Maulwurf *m* -(e)s, **Maulwürfe** (*auch fig*) mole.
Maulwurfs-: ~haufen, ~hügel *m* mole-hill.
maunzen *vi* (*S Ger*) (*winseln*) to whine; (*Katze*) to mewl.
Maure *m* -n, -n (*Hist*) Moor.
Maurer(in *f*) *m* -s, - bricklayer, brickie (*inf*) ◆ **~ lernen** to learn bricklaying *or* to be a bricklayer; **pünktlich wie die ~** (*hum*) super-punctual; **pünktlich wie die ~ ließ er seinen Kugelschreiber fallen** bang on the dot he put down his pen.
Mau(r)er|arbeit *f* bricklaying (work) *no pl*.
Maurer-: ~geselle *m* journeyman bricklayer; **~hammer** *m* bricklayer's hammer; **~handwerk** *nt* bricklaying.
Mau(r)erkelle *f* (bricklayer's) trowel.
Maurer-: ~kolonne *f* bricklaying gang; **~meister** *m* master builder; **~polier** *m* foreman bricklayer.
Mauretanien [-iən] *nt* -s Mauritania, Mauretania.
Mauretanier(in *f*) [-iɐ, -iərɪn] *m* -s, - Mauritanian.
mauretanisch *adj* Mauritanian.
Maurin *f* (*Hist*) Moor.
maurisch *adj* Moorish.

Mauritier(in *f*) [mau'ri:tsiɐ, -iərɪn] *m* **-s, -** Mauritian.
Mauritius [mau'ri:tsiʊs] *nt* - Mauritius.
Maus *f* **-, Mäuse** **(a)** mouse ♦ **weiße ~** (*fig inf*) traffic cop (*inf*); **weiße Mäuse sehen** (*fig inf*) to see pink elephants (*inf*). **(b)** (*fig dated: Frau*) **kleine ~** little mouse; **eine graue ~** (*inf*) a mouse (*inf*). **(c)** (*Comput*) mouse. **(d) Mäuse** *pl* (*sl: Geld*) bread (*sl*), dough (*sl*).
Mauschelei *f* (*inf*) (*Korruption*) fiddle (*inf*) ♦ **das war bestimmt ~** it was definitely a fiddle.
mauscheln 1 *vi* (*jiddisch sprechen*) to talk Yiddish.
2 *vti* (*manipulieren*) to fiddle (*inf*).
Mauscheln *nt* **-s** (*Cards*) cheat.
Mäuschen ['mɔysçən] *nt* **(a)** little mouse ♦ **da möchte ich mal ~ sein** *or* **spielen** (*inf*) I'd like to be a fly on the wall. **(b)** (*fig*) sweetheart (*inf*), love (*Brit inf*), honey (*esp US*). **(c)** *siehe* **Musikantenknochen.**
mäuschenstill ['mɔysçən-] *adj* dead quiet; *Mensch auch* (as) quiet as a mouse; (*reglos*) stock-still.
Mäusebussard *m* (common) buzzard.
Mausefalle, Mäusefalle (*rare*) *f* mouse-trap; (*fig*) police roadblock ♦ **in eine ~ kommen** *or* **geraten** to get caught in a police roadblock.
Mäusegift *nt* mouse poison.
Mauseloch, Mäuseloch (*rare*) nt mouse-hole ♦ **sich in ein ~ verkriechen** (*fig*) to crawl into a hole in the ground.
Mäusemelken *nt*: **das/es ist zum ~** (*dated inf*) it's enough to drive you up the wall (*inf*).
mausen 1 *vi* to catch mice ♦ **diese Katze maust gut** the cat is a good mouser.
2 *vt* (*dated inf*) to pinch (*inf*), to nick (*Brit inf*).
Mauser *f* **-,** *no pl* (*Orn*) moult ♦ **in der ~ sein** to be moulting.
Mausergewehr *nt* Mauser (rifle).
Mäuserich *m* (*hum*) Mr Mouse (*hum*).
mausern *vr* **(a)** (*Orn*) to moult. **(b)** (*inf*) to blossom out (*inf*).
Mauser(pistole) *f* **-, -n** Mauser.
mausetot *adj* (*inf*) stone-dead, as dead as a doornail.
mausgrau *adj* **(a)** (*~farben*) mouse-grey. **(b)** (*unauffällig*) mousy.
mausig *adj*: **sich ~ machen** (*inf*) to get uppish *or* bolshie *or* stroppy (*all inf*).
Mausklick *m* **-s, -s** (*Comput*) mouse click ♦ **etw per Mausklick steuern/ aktivieren** to control/activate sth by clicking the mouse.
Mausloch *nt siehe* **Mauseloch.**
Mausmatte *f* (*Comput*) mouse pad.
Mausoleum [-'le:ʊm] *nt* **-s, Mausoleen** [-'le:ən] mausoleum.
Maussteuerung *f* (*Comput*) mouse control.
Maut *f* **-, -en** (*S Ger, Aus*) toll.
Maut-: **~gebühr** *f* toll(-charge); **~schranke** *f* toll barrier (*Brit*), turnpike (*US*); **~stelle** *f* tollgate; **~straße** *f* toll-road, turnpike (*US*).
max. *abbr of* **maximal.**
maxi *adj pred* maxi ♦ **~ tragen** to wear a maxi.
Maxi- *in cpds* maxi-.
maximal 1 *adj* maximum.
2 *adv* (*höchstens*) at most ♦ **bis zu ~ $ 100** up to a maximum of $100.
Maximal- *in cpds* maximum.
Maxime *f* **-, -n** (*Liter, Philos*) maxim.
maximieren* *vt* (*Econ*) to maximize.
Maximierung *f* (*Econ*) maximization.
Maximum *nt* **-s, Maxima** maximum (*an +dat* of).
Maxi-Single [-sɪŋgl] *f* twelve-inch single.
Maya ['ma:ja] *m* **-(s), -(s)** Maya.
Mayonnaise [majɔ'nɛ:zə] *f* **-, -n** mayonnaise.
Mazedonien [-iən] *nt* **-s** *siehe* **Makedonien.**
Mäzen *m* **-s, -e** patron.
Mäzenatentum *nt* **(a)** (*Kunstförderung*) patronage (of the arts). **(b)** (*Wesen eines Mäzens*) spirit of patronage.
Mazurka *f* **-, -s** mazurka.
MB [ɛm'be:] *abbr of* **Megabyte** MB.
MByte, Mbyte *abbr of* **Megabyte** mbyte.
MdB, M.d.B. [ɛm'de:'be:] *m* **-s, -s** *abbr of* **Mitglied des Bundestages** Member of the "Bundestag".
MdL, M.d.L. [ɛm'de:'|ɛl] *m* **-s, -s** *abbr of* **Mitglied des Landtages** Member of the "Landtag".
m.E. *abbr of* **meines Erachtens** in my opinion.
mech. *abbr of* **mechanisch.**
Mechanik *f* **(a)** *no pl* (*Phys*) mechanics *sing.* **(b)** (*rare*) *siehe* **Mechanismus.**
Mechaniker(in *f*) *m* **-s, -** mechanic.
mechanisch *adj* (*alle Bedeutungen*) mechanical ♦ **~er Webstuhl** power loom.
mechanisieren* *vt* to mechanize.
Mechanisierung *f* mechanization.
⚠ **Mechanisierungsprozeß** *m* process of mechanization.
Mechanismus *m* mechanism; (*Methode, Arbeitsablauf*) machinery.
mechanistisch *adj* (*Philos, Psych*) mechanistic.
meck *interj* (*Ziege*) **~, ~!** meh, meh!
Meckerei *f* (*inf*) moaning, grumbling, grousing.
Meckerer *m* **-s, -** (*inf*) moaner, grumbler, grouser.
Mecker-: **~fritze** (*inf*) *m* belly-acher (*inf*), wailing Willie (*inf*); **~liese** *f* (*inf*) moaning Minny (*inf*).
meckern *vi* (*Ziege*) to bleat; (*inf: Mensch*) to moan, to bleat (*inf*), to grouse.
Meckerziege *f* (*sl*) sourpuss (*inf*), ratbag (*inf*).

Mecklenburg-Vorpommern *nt* Mecklenburg-West Pomerania.
med. *abbr of* **medizinisch.**
Medaille [me'daljə] *f* **-, -n** (*Gedenkmünze*) medallion; (*bei Wettbewerben*) medal.
Medaillen- [me'daljən-]: **~gewinner** *m* medallist, medal winner; **~spiegel** *m* medals table.
Medaillon [medal'jõ:] *nt* **-s, -s** **(a)** (*Bildchen*) medallion; (*Schmuckkapsel*) locket. **(b)** (*Cook*) médaillon.
medial *adj* (*Gram*) middle; (*Med*) medial, median; (*Psych*) mediumistic.
Mediävistik [medie'vɪstɪk] *f* medieval studies *sing or pl.*
Mediävist(in *f*) [medie'vɪst(ɪn)] *m* medievalist.
Medien ['me:diən] *pl* media *pl.*
Medien-: **~berater** *m* press adviser; **~forschung** *f* media research; **m~gerecht** *adj* suited to the media; **~gesetz** *nt* media law; **~gigant** *m* media giant; **~konzern** *m* media concern; **~landschaft** *f, no pl* media landscape; **~politik** *f* (mass) media policy; **~referent** *m* press officer; **~rummel** *m* media excitement; **~verbund** *m* **etw im ~verbund lernen** to learn sth using the multi-media system; **m~wirksam** *adj* effective in media terms ♦ **eine medienwirksame Kampagne** an effective campaign in media terms; **etw medienwirksam präsentieren** to present sth effectively in media terms.
Medikament *nt* medicine.
Medikamenten-: ⚠**~mißbrauch** *m* drug abuse; **~sucht** *f, no pl* drug dependency.
medikamentös *adj* medicinal.
Medikus *m* **-, Medizi** *or* **-se** (*hum*) quack (*hum inf*), doc (*inf*); (*esp Student*) medic (*inf*).
mediokcr *adj* (*geh*) mediocre.
Meditation *f* meditation.
meditativ *adj* (*liter*) meditative ♦ **in ~er Versunkenheit** lost in meditation.
mediterran *adj* Mediterranean.
meditieren* *vi* to meditate.
Medium *nt* medium; (*Gram*) middle (voice).
Medizin *f* **-, -en** **(a)** *no pl* (*Heilkunde*) medicine. **(b)** (*inf: Heilmittel*) medicine ♦ **das ist ~ für ihn** that's his medicine; (*fig: Lektion, Denkzettel*) that'll teach him a lesson.
Medizinal-: **~assistent** *m* houseman (*Brit*), intern (*US*); **~rat** *m* medical officer of health; **~statistik** *f* medical statistics *pl.*
Medizinball *m* (*Sport*) medicine ball.
Mediziner(in *f*) *m* **-s, -** **(a)** doctor. **(b)** (*Univ*) medic (*inf*).
medizinisch *adj* **(a)** (*ärztlich*) medical ♦ **M~e Fakultät** school *or* faculty of medicine; **M~e Klinik** clinic for internal medicine; **~-technische Assistentin, ~-technischer Assistent** medical technician. **(b)** (*heilend*) *Kräuter, Bäder* medicinal; *Shampoo* medicated.
Medizin-: **~mann** *m, pl* **-männer** medicine man, witchdoctor; (*hum: Arzt*) quack (*inf*), medico (*US inf*); **~schränkchen** *nt* medicine cabinet *or* cupboard; **~student** *m* medical student; **~studium** *nt* study of medicine.
Meduse *f* **-, -n** **(a)** (*Myth*) Medusa. **(b)** (*Zool*) medusa (*spec*), jellyfish.
Medusenhaupt *nt* **(a)** (*Liter*) head of Medusa. **(b)** (*Med*) caput medusae (*spec*).
Meer *nt* **-(e)s, -e** **(a)** sea; (*Welt~*) ocean ♦ **am ~(e)** by the sea; **diesseits/ jenseits des ~es** at home/across the sea; **übers ~ fahren** to travel (across) the seas; **ans ~ fahren** to go to the sea(side); **über dem ~** above sea-level. **(b)** (*liter: riesige Menge*) sea.
Meer-: **~busen** *m* gulf, bay; **Bottnischer ~busen** Gulf of Bothnia; **~enge** *f* straits *pl*, strait.
Meeres-: **~algen** *pl* seaweed, marine algae *pl* (*spec*); **~arm** *m* arm of the sea, inlet; **~biologe** *m* marine biologist; **~boden** *m siehe* **~grund**; **~fauna** *f* marine fauna; **~fisch** *m* saltwater fish; **~flora** *f* marine flora; **~forschung** *f* oceanography; **~freiheit** *f* (*Jur*) freedom of the seas; **~grund** *m* seabed, sea bottom, bottom of the sea; **~höhe** *f siehe* **~spiegel**; **~klima** *nt* maritime climate; **~kunde** *f* oceanography; **m~kundlich** *adj* oceanographic(al); **~leuchten** *nt* marine phosphorescence; **~oberfläche** *f* surface of the sea; **~schildkröte** *f* turtle; **~spiegel** *m* sea-level; **über/unter dem ~spiegel** above/below sea-level; **~stille** *f* calm (at sea); **~strand** *m* (*liter*) seashore, strand (*poet*); **~straße** *f* waterway; **~strömung** *f* ocean current; **~tiefe** *f* depth (of the sea *or* ocean); **~tier** *nt* marine creature; **~ufer** *nt* seashore, coast.
Meer-: **~gott** *m* (*Myth*) sea-god; **~göttin** *f* sea-goddess; **m~grün** *adj* sea-green; **~jungfer, ~jungfrau** *f* mermaid; **~katze** *f* long-tailed monkey, guenon; **~rettich** *m* horseradish; **~salz** *nt* sea salt; **~schaum** *m* (*Miner*) meerschaum; **~schaumpfeife** *f* meerschaum (pipe); **~schweinchen** *nt* guineapig, cavy (*spec*); **m~umschlungen** *adj* (*poet*) seagirt (*poet*), seabound; **~ungeheuer** *nt* sea-monster; **m~wärts** *adv* seawards.
Meerwasser *nt* sea water.
Meerwasser-: **~aufbereitung** *f* treatment of sea water; **~entsalzung** *f* desalination of sea water; **~entsalzungsanlage** *f* desalination plant.
Meeting ['mi:tɪŋ] *nt* **-s, -s** (*esp DDR Pol, Sport*) meeting.
Mega- *in cpds* mega-; **~bit** *nt* megabit; **~bit-Chip** *m* megabit chip; **~byte** [-'baɪt] *nt* megabyte; **~hertz** *nt* megahertz.
Megalith *m* **-en, -en** (*Archeol*) megalith.
Megalith-: **~grab** *nt* (*Archeol*) dolmen, megalithic tomb; **~kultur** *f* (*Hist*) megalithic culture.
Megalo-: **m~man** *adj* (*geh*) megalomanic; **~manie** *f* (*geh*) megalomania; **~polis** [mega'lo:polɪs] *f* **-, -polen** [megalo'po:lən] megalopolis.

⚠: for details of spelling reform, see supplement

⚠**Megaphon** [mega'fo:n] *nt* megaphone.
Megäre *f* **-, -n** **(a)** *(Myth)* Megaera. **(b)** *(fig liter)* shrew, termagant *(liter)*.
Megastar *m (inf)* megastar.
Mega-: ~tonne *f* megaton; **~tonnenbombe** *f* megaton bomb; **~watt** *nt indecl* megawatt.
Mehl *nt* **-(e)s, -e** flour; *(gröber)* meal; *(Knochen~)* bonemeal; *(Pulver, Zement~)* powder.
Mehl-: m~artig *adj* floury, mealy; **~beere** *f* berry of the whitebeam; **~brei** *m* pap, flummery.
mehlig *adj Äpfel, Kartoffeln* mealy.
Mehl-: ~kleister *m* flour paste; **~kloß** *m* dumpling; **~papp** *m (inf)* mush *(inf)*; **~sack** *m* flour bag; **wie ein ~sack** *(inf)* like a sack of potatoes; **~schwitze** *f (Cook)* roux; **~speise** *f* **(a)** *(Gericht)* flummery; **(b)** *(Aus) (Nachspeise)* sweet, dessert; *(Kuchen)* pastry; **~suppe** *f* gruel; **~tau** *m (Bot)* mildew.
mehr [1] *indef pron inv comp of* **viel, sehr** more ◆ **was wollen Sie ~?** what more do you want?; **zu ~ hat es nicht gelangt** *or* **gereicht** that was all I/you *etc* could manage; **~ will er nicht bezahlen** he doesn't want to pay (any) more; **ist das alles, ~ kostet das nicht?** is that all it costs?; **je ~ er hat, je ~ er will** *(Prov)* the more he has, the more he wants; **sich für ~ halten** *(inf)* to think one is something more; **mit ~ oder weniger Erfolg** with a greater or lesser degree of success.
[2] *adv* **(a)** *(in höherem Maße)* more ◆ **immer ~** more and more; **~ oder weniger** *or* **minder** *(geh)* more or less; **~ lang als breit** more long than wide, longer than it is/they are wide; **~ ein juristisches Problem** more (of) a legal problem; **war er frech/sind Sie beleidigt/hat es Ihnen geschmeckt? — ~ als das** was he cheeky/are you insulted/did you like it? — "cheeky/insulted/like" is not the word for it; **würden Sie das gerne tun? — ja, nichts ~ als das** would you like to? — there's nothing I'd rather do.
(b) *(+neg: sonst, länger)* **ich habe kein Geld ~** I have no more money, I haven't any more money; **du bist doch kein Kind ~!** you're not a child any longer *or* any more!, you're no longer a child!; **es hat sich keiner ~ beworben** nobody else has applied; **es besteht keine Hoffnung ~** there's no hope left; **kein Wort ~!** not another word!; **es war niemand ~ da** there was no-one left, everyone had gone; **daran erinnert sich niemand ~** nobody can remember that any more; **wenn niemand ~ einsteigt, ...** if nobody else gets in ...; **das benutzt man nicht ~** that's not used any more *or* any longer, it's no longer used; **er lebt nicht ~** he is dead; **das darf nicht ~ vorkommen** that must not *or* never happen again; **nicht ~** not any longer, not any more, no more, no longer; **nicht ~ lange** not much longer; **wenn unser Opa nicht ~ ist** *(euph)* when Grandpa is no longer with us; **nichts ~** nothing more; **ich kann nichts ~ sagen** I can say nothing more, I can't say anything more; **nie ~** never again, nevermore *(liter)*; **ich will dich nie ~ wiedersehen** I never want to see you again, I don't ever want to see you again.
Mehr *nt* **-,** *no pl* **(a)** *(esp Sw: Mehrheit)* majority. **(b)** *(Zuwachs)* increase ◆ **mit einem ~ an Mühe** with more effort; **auf das ~ oder Weniger an Erfahrung kommt es nicht an** it's not a question of having more or less experience.
Mehr-: ~arbeit *f* overtime, extra time *or* work; **~aufwand** *m* additional expenditure; **~ausgabe** *f* extra *or* additional expense(s *pl*); **m~bändig** *adj* in several volumes, multi-volume; **~bedarf** *m* greater need *(an +dat* of, for); *(Comm)* increased demand, increase in *or* extra demand *(an +dat* for); **~belastung** *f* excess load; *(fig)* extra *or* additional burden; **~benutzer-** *in cpds (Comput) siehe* **~platz-**; **~bereichsöl** *nt (Aut)* multigrade oil; **~betrag** *m* **(a)** *(zusätzliche Zahlung)* extra *or* additional amount; **(b)** *(Überschuß)* surplus; **m~deutig** *adj* ambiguous, equivocal; **~deutigkeit** *f* ambiguity, equivocalness; **m~dimensional** *adj* multi-dimensional; **~einnahme** *f* additional revenue.
mehren [1] *vt (liter) (vergrößern)* to augment, to increase; *(fördern)* to further.
[2] *vr (geh: sich vermehren)* to multiply ◆ **seid fruchtbar und mehret Euch!** *(Bibl)* be fruitful and multiply!
Mehrer *m* **-s, -** *(liter)* augmenter *(form)*.
mehrere *indef pron* several; *(verschiedene auch)* various.
mehreres *indef pron* several *or* various things *pl*.
mehrerlei *indef pron inv* **(a)** *(substantivisch)* several things *pl*. **(b)** *(adjektivisch)* several kinds of.
Mehr-: ~erlös *m siehe* **~einnahme**; **~ertrag** *m* additional yield, increase in yield.
mehrf. *abbr of* **mehrfach**.
mehrfach [1] *adj* multiple; *(zahlreich)* numerous; *(wiederholt)* repeated ◆ **ein ~er Millionär** a multimillionaire; **der ~e Meister im 100-m-Lauf** the man who has several times been the 100 metres champion; **die Unterlagen in ~er Ausfertigung einsenden** to send in several copies of the documents.
[2] *adv (öfter)* many *or* several times; *(wiederholt)* repeatedly.
Mehrfache(s) *nt decl as adj* **das ~** *or* **ein ~s des Kostenvoranschlags** several times the estimated cost; **verdient er wirklich mehr? — ja, ja, das ~** *or* **ein ~s** does he earn more? — oh yes, several times as much.
Mehrfach-: ~fahrschein *m* multi-journey ticket; **~-Kino-Komplex** *m* multi-screen cinema; **~stecker** *m (Elec)* multiple adaptor; **~täter** *m* multiple offender.
Mehr-: ~fahrtenkarte *f siehe* **Mehrfachfahrschein**; **~familienhaus** *nt* multiple dwelling *(form)*, house for several families; **~farbendruck** *m* **(a)** *no pl (Verfahren)* colour *or* polychromatic *(form)* printing; **(b)** *(Druck)* colour *or* polychromatic *(form)* print; **m~farbig** *adj* multicoloured, polychromatic *(form)*; **~gepäck** *nt* excess baggage; **~gewicht** *nt* additional *or* excess weight; *(Übergewicht)* excess weight.
Mehrheit *f* **(a)** *no pl (größerer Teil)* majority *(with sing or pl vb)* ◆ **weitaus in der ~** in the vast majority.
(b) *(Stimmenmehrheit)* majority ◆ **die absolute/einfache** *or* **relative ~** an absolute/a simple *or* relative majority; **die ~ haben** *or* **besitzen/gewinnen** *or* **erringen** to have/win *or* gain a majority; **die ~ der Stimmen auf sich vereinigen** to secure a majority of votes; **die ~ verlieren** to lose one's majority; **mit zwei Stimmen ~** with a majority of two.
mehrheitlich *adj* **wir sind ~ der Ansicht, daß ...** the majority of us think(s) that ...; **der Stadtrat hat ~ beschlossen ...** the town council has reached a majority decision ...
Mehrheits-: ~beschaffer *m (Pol)* junior coalition partner *(securing majority)*; ⚠**~beschluß** *m*, **~entscheidung** *f* majority decision; **m~fähig** *adj* capable of winning a majority; **~führer** *m* leader of the majority faction; **~grundsatz** *m* principle of majority rule; **~parteien** *pl* majority parties *pl*; **~prinzip** *nt* principle of majority rule; **~wahl** *f* first-past-the-post election; **~wahlrecht** *nt* first-past-the-post system, majority vote system.
Mehr-: m~jährig *adj attr* of several years; **m~jährige Klinikerfahrung** several years of clinical experience; **~kampf** *m (Sport)* multi-discipline event; **~kämpfer** *m (Sport)* all-round athlete, all rounder; **~kosten** *pl* additional costs *pl*; *(in Hotel etc)* additional expenses *pl*; **~ladegewehr** *nt*, **~lader** *m* **-s, -** repeater, repeater rifle; **m~malig** *adj attr* repeated; **m~mals** *adv* several times, repeatedly; **~parteiensystem** *nt* multi-party system; **~phasenstrom** *m (Elec)* multiphase *or* polyphase current.
Mehrplatz- *in cpds (Comput)* multi-user; **m~fähig** *adj (Comput)* capable of supporting multi-user operation; **~rechner** *m (Comput)* multi-user system.
Mehr-: m~silbig *adj* polysyllabic, multisyllabic; **m~sprachig** *adj* multilingual, polyglot; **m~sprachig aufwachsen** to grow up multilingual *or* speaking several languages; **~sprachigkeit** *f* multilingualism; **m~stimmig** *adj (Mus)* for several voices; **m~stimmiges Lied** part-song; **m~stimmig singen** to sing in harmony; **~stimmigkeit** *f (Mus)* polyphony; **m~stöckig** *adj* multistorey; **m~stöckig bauen** to build *or* erect multistorey buildings; **~stufenrakete** *f* multistage rocket; **m~stufig** *adj* multistage; **m~stündig** *adj attr* lasting several hours; **mit m~stündiger Verspätung eintreffen** to arrive several hours late; **m~tägig** *adj attr Konferenz* lasting several days; **nach m~tägiger Abwesenheit** after an absence of several days, after several days' absence; **m~teilig** *adj* in several parts.
Mehrung *f (liter)* increase.
Mehrverbrauch *m* additional consumption.
Mehrweg- *in cpds* reusable; **~flasche** *f* returnable bottle; **~system** *nt* (bottle *or* packaging) return system; **~verpackung** *f* reusable packaging.
Mehr-: ~wert *m (Econ)* added value; **m~wertig** *adj (Chem)* polyvalent, multivalent; **~wertsteuer** *f* value added tax, VAT; **m~wöchig** *adj attr* lasting several weeks; *Abwesenheit* of several weeks.
Mehrw. St. *abbr of* **Mehrwertsteuer**.
Mehr-: ~zahl *f, no pl* **(a)** *(Gram)* plural; **(b)** *(Mehrheit)* majority; **m~zeilig** *adj* of several lines; **m~zellig** *adj* multicellular.
Mehrzweck- *in cpds* multipurpose.
meiden *pret* **mied**, *ptp* **gemieden** *vt* to avoid.
Meierei *f* **(a)** *(dial: Molkerei)* dairy (farm). **(b)** *(old: Pachtgut)* leasehold farm.
Meile *f* **-, -n** mile; *(old: 4,8 km)* league ◆ **das riecht man drei ~n gegen den Wind** *(inf)* you can smell *or* tell that a mile off *(inf)*.
Meilen-: m~lang [1] *adj* mile-long; [2] *adv* for miles; **~stein** *m (lit, fig)* milestone; **~stiefel** *pl siehe* **Siebenmeilenstiefel**; **m~weit** [1] *adj* of many miles; **m~weite Sandstrände** miles and miles of sandy beaches; [2] *adv* for miles; **m~weit auseinander/entfernt** *(lit, fig)* miles apart/away; **~zahl** *f* mileage; **~zähler** *m* mileometer, clock *(inf)*.
Meiler *m* **-s, -** *(Kohlen~)* charcoal kiln *or* pile; *(dated: Atom~)* (atomic) pile.
mein [1] *poss pron* **(a)** *(adjektivisch)* my ◆ **~ verdammtes Auto** this damn *(inf)* car of mine; **ich trinke so ~e fünf Flaschen Bier pro Tag** I drink my five bottles of beer a day.
(b) *(old: substantivisch)* mine ◆ **~ und dein verwechseln** *(euph)* to take what doesn't belong to one.
[2] *pers pron gen of* **ich** *(old, poet)* of me.
Mein|eid *m* perjury *no indef art* ◆ **einen ~ leisten** *or* **ablegen** to perjure oneself, to commit perjury.
mein|eidig *adj* perjured ◆ **~ werden** to commit perjury, to perjure oneself.
Mein|eidige(r) *mf decl as adj* perjurer.
▼ **meinen** [1] *vi (denken, glauben)* to think ◆ **ich würde/man möchte ~** I/one would think; **ich meine, ...** I think ..., I reckon ... *(inf)*; **~ Sie?** (do) you think so?, do you reckon? *(inf)*; **wie ~ Sie?** I beg your pardon?; **ich meine nur so** *(inf)* it was just a thought; **wie Sie ~!** as you wish; *(drohend auch)* have it your own way; **wenn du meinst!** if you like, I don't mind; **man sollte ~** one would have thought.
[2] *vt* **(a)** *(der Ansicht sein)* to think ◆ **was ~ Sie dazu?** what do you think *or* say?; **~ Sie das im Ernst?** are you serious about that?; **das will ich ~!** I quite agree!; **das sollte man ~!** one would think so.
▼ **(b)** *(sagen wollen)* to mean; *(inf: sagen)* to say ◆ **was ~ Sie damit?, wie ~ Sie das?** what *or* how do you mean?; *(drohend)* (just) what do you mean by that?
(c) *(geh: bedeuten)* to mean.
(d) *(bezeichnen wollen)* to mean ◆ **damit bin ich gemeint** that's meant for me, they mean/he means *etc* me.
(e) *(beabsichtigen)* to mean, to intend ◆ **so war es nicht gemeint** it wasn't meant like that; **sie meint es gut** she means well; **sie meint es nicht böse** she

means no harm, she doesn't mean any harm; **die Sonne hat es aber heute wieder gut gemeint!** the sun's done its best for us again today.
meiner *pers pron gen of* **ich** of me.
meine(r, s) *poss pron (substantivisch)* mine ◆ **der/die/das ~** *(geh)* mine; **ich tu das M~** *(geh)* I'll do my bit; **das M~** *(geh: Besitz)* what is mine; **die M~n** *(geh: Familie)* my people, my family.
meinerseits *adv* as far as I'm concerned, for my part ◆ **ich ~** I personally *or* myself, I for my part; **Vorschläge/Einwände ~** suggestions/objections from me; **ganz ~!** the pleasure's (all) mine; *(iro)* so do/are you.
meines-: ~gleichen *pron inv (meiner Art)* people such as I *or* me, people like me *or* myself; *(gleichrangig)* my own kind, my equals; **Leute** *or* **Menschen ~gleichen** *(meiner Art)* people like me *or* myself; *(gleichrangig)* people of my own kind, my equals; **~teils** *adv* for my part.
meinet-: ~halben *(dated)*, **~wegen** *adv* **(a)** *(wegen mir)* because of me, on account of me, on my account; *(mir zuliebe auch)* for my sake; *(um mich)* about me; *(für mich)* on my behalf; **(b)** *(von mir aus)* as far as I'm concerned; **~wegen!** if you like; **wenn Ihr das tun wollt, ~wegen, aber ...** if you want to do that, fair enough *(inf)*, but ...; **~willen** *adv*: **um ~willen** for my sake, on my account.
meinige *poss pron* **der/die/das ~** *(form, old)* mine; **die M~n** *(geh)* my family, my people.
meins *poss pron* mine.
▼ **Meinung** *f* opinion; *(Anschauung auch)* view; *(Urteil)* judgement, estimation ◆ **eine vorgefaßte ~** a preconceived idea; **nach meiner ~, meiner ~ nach** in my opinion *or* view; **ich bin der ~, daß ...** I'm of the opinion that ..., I take the view that ...; **seine ~ ändern** to change one's opinion *or* mind; **einer ~ sein** to share the same opinion, to think the same; **was ist Ihre ~ dazu?** what's your opinion *or* view (about *or* on that)?; **von seiner ~ eingenommen sein** to be opinionated; **das ist auch meine ~!** that's just what I think; **jdm (kräftig** *or* **vernünftig) die ~ sagen** *(inf)* to give sb a piece of one's mind *(inf)*.
Meinungs-: ~äußerung *f* (expression of) opinion; **~austausch** *m* exchange of views *(über +acc* on, about); **m~bildend** *adj* opinion-forming; **m~bildend wirken** to shape public opinion; **~bildung** *f* formation of opinion; **der Prozeß der ~bildung ist noch nicht abgeschlossen** we have not yet formed an opinion; **~forscher** *m* (opinion) pollster; **~forschung** *f* (public) opinion polling *or* research; **~forschungsinstitut** *nt* opinion research institute; **~freiheit** *f* freedom of speech; **~führer** *m* spokesperson; **die Rolle als ~führer verlieren** *(Pol)* to no longer set the (political) agenda; **~klima** *nt* climate of public opinion; **m~los** *adj* without opinions, viewless; **m~los sein** to have no opinions; **~mache** *f (pej inf)* propaganda; **~macher** *m (inf)* opinion-maker, opinion-leader; **~manipulation** *f* manipulation of (public) opinion; **~monopol** *nt* monopoly of opinion; **~umfrage** *f* (public) opinion poll; **~umschwung** *m* swing of opinion; **~verschiedenheit** *f* difference of opinion, disagreement.
Meise *f* **-, -n** titmouse ◆ **eine ~ haben** *(sl)* to be crackers *(inf)*.
Meisenring *m* bird-feeding ring.
Meißel *m* **-s, -** chisel.
meißeln *vti* to chisel.
Meiß(e)ner *adj* **~ Porzellan** Dresden *or* Meissen china.
meist *adv siehe* **meistens**.
Meist-: m~begünstigt *adj (Econ)* most-favoured; **~begünstigung** *f (Econ)* most-favoured-nation treatment; **~begünstigungsklausel** *f (Econ Pol)* most-favoured-nation clause; **m~bietend** *adj* highest bidding; **~bietender** highest bidder; **m~bietend versteigern** to sell *or* auction (off) to the highest bidder.
meisten: am ~ *adv* **(a)** *superl of* **viel** the most. **(b)** *superl of* **sehr** most of all ◆ **am ~ bekannt** best known.
meistens *adv* mostly, more often than not; *(zum größten Teil)* for the most part.
meistenteils *adv siehe* **meistens**.
Meister *m* **-s, - (a)** *(Handwerks~)* master (craftsman); *(in Laden)* boss *(inf)*; *(in Fabrik)* foreman, boss *(inf)*; *(sl: als Anrede)* guv *(Brit sl)*, chief *(Brit sl)*, mac *(US sl)*; *(Sport)* champion; *(Mannschaft)* champions *pl* ◆ **seinen ~ machen** to take one's master craftsman's diploma.
(b) *(Lehr~, Künstler)* master *(auch fig)* ◆ **alter ~** *(Art)* old master; **~ vom Stuhl** *(fig)* Master of the Lodge; **er hat seinen ~ gefunden** *(fig)* he's met his match; **~ einer Sache** *(gen) or* **in etw** *(dat)* past master at sth; **es ist noch kein ~ vom Himmel gefallen** *(Prov)* no-one is born a master.
(c) *(old liter)* master ◆ **~ Zwirn** Snip, the tailor; **~ Knieriem** *or* **Pfriem/Lampe** Master Cobbler/Hare; **~ Urian** Old Nick.
meiste(r, s) *indef pron superl of* **viel (a)** *(adjektivisch)* **die ~n Leute** most people; **die ~n Leute, die ...** most people who ..., most of the people who ...; **du hast die ~ Zeit** you have (the) most time. **(b)** *(substantivisch)* **die ~n** most people; **die ~n (von ihnen)** most (of them), the majority (of them); **das ~** most of it; **du hast das ~** you have (the) most.
Meister- *in cpds* master; **~brief** *m* master craftsman's diploma *or* certificate; **~gesang** *m (Liter)* poetry of the meistersingers; **m~haft** [1] *adj* masterly; [2] *adv* in a masterly manner; **er versteht es m~haft, zu lügen** he is brilliant at lying; **~hand** *f*: **von ~hand** by a master hand.
Meisterin *f (Handwerks~)* master craftswoman; *(Frau von Handwerksmeister)* master craftsman's wife; *(in Fabrik)* forewoman; *(Sport)* champion ◆ **Frau ~!** madam!
Meister-: ~klasse *f* master class; **~leistung** *f* masterly performance; *(iro)* brilliant achievement.
meisterlich *adj siehe* **meisterhaft**.
meistern *vt* to master; *Schwierigkeiten* to overcome ◆ **sein Leben ~** to come to grips with one's life.
Meisterprüfung *f* examination for master craftsman's diploma *or* certificate.
Meisterschaft *f* **(a)** *(Sport)* championship; *(Veranstaltung)* championships *pl*. **(b)** *no pl (Können)* mastery ◆ **es zu wahrer ~ bringen** *(als Künstler etc)* to become really proficient *or* expert, to achieve real mastery *or* proficiency; *(als Dieb etc)* to get it down to a fine art.
Meisterschaftsspiel *nt (Sport)* league match.
Meister-: ~schule *f* school for master craftspeople; **~schüler** *m (Art, Mus)* pupil *in a master class*; ⚠**~schuß** *m* brilliant shot; **~schütze** *m* marksman, crack shot; **~singer** *m (Hist)* meistersinger, mastersinger; **~stück** *nt (von Handwerker) work done to qualify as master craftsman*; *(fig)* masterpiece; *(geniale Tat)* master stroke; **~titel** *m (im Handwerk)* title of master craftsman; *(Sport)* championship title.
Meisterung *f, no pl* mastery.
Meisterwerk *nt* masterpiece.
Meist-: ~gebot *nt* highest bid, best offer; **m~gebräuchlich** *adj attr* commonest; **m~gefragt** *adj attr* most popular, most in demand; *Wohngegend auch* most sought-after; **m~gekauft** *adj attr* best-selling; **m~gelesen** *adj attr* most widely read; **m~genannt** *adj attr* most frequently mentioned.
Mekka *nt* **-s** *(Geog, fig)* Mecca.
Melancholie [melaŋko'li:] *f* melancholy.
Melancholiker(in *f***)** [melaŋ'ko:likɐ, -ərɪn] *m* **-s, -** melancholic.
melancholisch [melaŋ'ko:lɪʃ] *adj* melancholy.
Melanesien [-iən] *nt* **-s** Melanesia.
Melanesier(in *f***)** [-iɐ, -iərɪn] *m* **-s, -** Melanesian.
melanesisch *adj* Melanesian.
Melange [me'lã:ʒə] *f* **-, -n (a)** *(rare: Mischung)* blend. **(b)** *(Aus: Milchkaffee)* white coffee *(Brit)*, coffee with milk.
Melanin *nt* **-s, -e** *(Chem)* melanin.
Melanom *nt* **-s, -e** *(Med)* melanoma.
Melasse *f* **-, -n** molasses.
Melde-: ~amt, ~büro *(inf) nt* registration office; **~behörde** *f* registration authorities *pl*; **~fahrer** *m (Mil)* dispatch rider; **~frist** *f* registration period.
▼ **melden** [1] *vt* **(a)** *(anzeigen) Unfall, Verlust, ansteckende Erkrankungen* to report; *(berichten)* to report; *(registrieren)* to register; *(denunzieren)* to report ◆ **eine Geburt/Änderungen (der Behörde** *dat***) ~** to notify the authorities of a birth/changes; **wie soeben gemeldet wird** *(Rad, TV)* according to reports just coming in; **das wird gemeldet!** *(Sch)* I'll tell on you *(Sch inf)*; **(bei jdm) nichts zu ~ haben** *(inf)* to have no say; **er hat hier nichts zu ~** *(inf)* he has no say in this; **melde gehorsamst** *(old Mil)* beg to report.
(b) *(ankündigen)* to announce ◆ **ich ging zur Sekretärin und ließ mich beim Direktor ~** I went to the secretary and asked her to tell the director that I was there; **wen darf ich ~?** who(m) shall I say (is here)?, who(m) shall I announce?
[2] *vi (Cards)* to meld.
[3] *vr* **(a)** to report *(zu* for) ◆ **sich freiwillig ~** *(Mil)* to volunteer; **sich zu** *or* **für etw ~** *(esp Mil)* to sign up for *or* volunteer for sth; *(für Arbeitsplatz)* to apply for sth; *(für Lehrgang)* to enrol *or* sign on for sth; **sich krank/zum Dienst ~** to report sick/for work; **sich auf eine Anzeige ~** to answer an advertisement; **sich polizeilich** *or* **bei der Polizei ~** to register with the police.
(b) *(fig: sich ankündigen)* to announce one's presence; *(Alter)* to make itself *or* its presence felt; *(Sport, zur Prüfung)* to enter (one's name) *(zu* for); *(Winter, Dunkelheit)* to draw *or* set in; *(durch Handaufheben)* to put one's hand up, to hold up one's hand; *(Rad, TV)* to come on the air.
▼ **(c)** *(esp Telec: antworten)* to answer ◆ **bitte ~!** *(Telec)* come in, please; **es meldet sich niemand** there's no answer.
(d) *(von sich hören lassen)* to get in touch *(bei* with) ◆ **melde dich wieder** keep in touch; **seitdem hat er sich nicht mehr gemeldet** he hasn't been heard of since; **wenn du was brauchst, melde dich** if you need anything give a shout *(inf) or* let me know.
Melde-: ~pflicht *f* **(a)** *(beim Ordnungsamt)* compulsory registration, obligation to register *(when moving house)*; **polizeiliche ~pflicht** obligation to register with the police; **(b) ~pflicht des Arztes** the doctor's obligation to notify the authorities *(of people with certain contagious diseases)*; **m~pflichtig** *adj* **(a)** obliged to register; **(b)** *Krankheit* notifiable.
Melder *m* **-s, -** *siehe* **Meldefahrer**.
Melde-: ~schein *m* registration form; ⚠**~schluß** *m* closing date; **~stelle** *f* place of registration; **~zettel** *m (Aus)* certificate of registration.
Meldung *f* **(a)** *(Mitteilung)* announcement.
(b) *(Press, Rad, TV)* report *(über +acc* on, about) ◆ **~en in Kürze** news headlines *pl*; **~en vom Sport** sports news *sing*.
(c) *(dienstlich)* report ◆ **(eine) ~ machen** to make a report.
(d) *(bei der Polizei)* report.
(e) *(Sport, Examens~)* entry ◆ **seine ~ zurückziehen** to withdraw.
(f) *(Comput)* (on-screen) message.
meliert *adj Haar* greying, streaked with grey; *Wolle* flecked ◆ **sein Haar war grau ~** his hair was streaked with grey.
Melisse *f* **-, -n** balm.
Melissengeist ® *m* medicinal spirit.
Melk- *in cpds* milking.
melken *pret* **melkte** *or (old)* **molk**, *ptp* **gemolken** *or (rare)* **gemelkt** *vti* **(a)**

➤ SPRACHE AKTIV: **Meinung** → 29.2, 33.1, 33.2, 33.3, 34.5, 38.1, 39.1, 40.1, 40.4, 41, 53.3, 53.5 **melden: 3c** → 27.5, 27.7

to milk ◆ **frisch gemolkene Milch** milk fresh from the cow. **(b)** (*fig inf*) to milk (*inf*), to fleece (*inf*).

Melker *m* **-s, -** milker.

Melkerei *f* (*Milchwirtschaft*) dairy (farm).

Melkerin *f* milkmaid.

Melodie *f* melody; (*Weise auch*) tune ◆ **nach der ~ von ...** to the tune of ...

Melodien- [-'di:ən-]: **~folge** *f*, **~reigen** *m* (*Rad*) medley of tunes.

Melodik *f* **(a)** (*Theorie*) melodics *sing*. **(b)** (*musikalische Eigenart*) musical idiom.

melodiös *adj* (*geh*) melodious.

melodisch *adj* melodic, tuneful.

Melodram(a) *nt* **-s, Melodramen** (*liter*) melodrama (*auch fig*).

melodramatisch *adj* melodramatic (*auch fig*).

Melone *f* **-, -n (a)** melon. **(b)** (*Hut*) bowler (*Brit*), derby (*US*).

Membran(e) *f* **-, Membrane** *or* **Membranen (a)** (*Anat*) membrane. **(b)** (*Phys, Tech*) diaphragm.

Memento *nt* **-s, -s** (*liter*) admonition, warning.

Memme *f* **-, -n** (*inf*) cissy (*sl*), yellow-belly (*sl*).

memmenhaft *adj* (*inf*) lily-livered (*inf*), yellow-bellied (*sl*).

Memo *nt* **-s, -s** memo.

Memoire [me'moa:r(ə)] *nt* **-s, -s** (*Pol*) *siehe* **Memorandum**.

Memoiren [me'moa:rən] *pl* memoirs *pl*.

Memorandum *nt* **-s, Memoranden** *or* **Memoranda** (*Pol*) memorandum.

memorieren* *vt* (*old*) **(a)** to memorize, to commit to memory. **(b)** (*aufsagen*) to recite (from memory).

Menage [me'na:ʒə] *f* **-, -n (a)** (*Gewürzständer*) cruet (set). **(b)** (*Aus: Verpflegung*) rations *pl*.

Menagerie [menaʒə'ri:] *f* menagerie.

Menarche *f* **-,** *no pl* (*Med*) menarche (*spec*), first menstruation.

Mendelevium [mɛnde'le:viʊm] *nt, no pl* (*abbr* **Md**) mendelevium.

mendeln *vi* (*Biol*) to mendelize (*spec*), to conform to Mendel's laws.

Mendelsche Regeln *pl* (*Biol*) Mendel's laws *pl*.

Menetekel *nt* **-s, -** (*liter*) warning sign, portent ◆ **das ~ an der Wand** the writing on the wall.

Menge *f* **-, -n (a)** (*Quantum*) amount, quantity ◆ **in ~n zu** in quantities of.
(b) (*inf*) (*große Anzahl*) lot, load (*inf*); (*Haufen auch*) pile (*inf*), heap (*inf*) ◆ **eine ~** a lot, lots (*inf*); **eine ~ Zeit/Häuser** a lot *or* lots (*inf*) of time/houses; **jede ~** masses *pl* (*inf*), loads *pl* (*inf*); **jede ~ Zeit/Geld** masses (*inf*) *or* loads (*inf*) of time/money; **wir haben jede ~ getrunken** we drank an enormous amount *or* a hell of a lot (*inf*); **es gab Wein jede ~** there was masses *or* loads of wine (*inf*); **eine ganze ~** quite a lot; **sie bildet sich eine ~ auf ihre Schönheit ein** she's incredibly conceited about her looks; **Bücher in ~n** any amount of books; *siehe* **rauh**.
(c) (*Menschen~*) crowd; (*geh: Masse*) mass; (*das Volk*) people; (*pej: Pöbel*) mob.
(d) (*Math*) set.

mengen [1] *vt* (*geh*) to mix (*unter +acc* with).
[2] *vr* to mingle (*unter +acc* with); (*fig: sich einmischen*) to meddle, to interfere (*in +acc* with, in).

Mengen-: **~angabe** *f* quantity, indication of quantity; **~begriff** *m* uncountable noun; (*Math*) concept of the set; **~lehre** *f* (*Math*) set theory; **m~mäßig** *adj* as far as quantity is concerned, quantitative; **~preis** *m* bulk price; **~rabatt** *m* bulk *or* quantity discount; **~verhältnis** *nt* relative proportions *pl* (*zwischen* of), quantitative ratio (*form*) (*zwischen* between).

Menhir *m* **-s, -e** (*Archeol*) standing stone, menhir.

Meningitis [menɪŋ'gi:tɪs] *f* **-, Meningitiden** (*Med*) meningitis.

Meniskus *m* **-, Menisken** (*Anat, Phys*) meniscus; (*Phot auch*) meniscal lens.

⚠**Meniskusriß** *m* torn meniscus.

Menjoubärtchen ['mɛnʒu-] *nt* pencil moustache.

Menkenke *f* **-, -s** *or* **-n** (*dial*) fuss.

Mennige *f* **-,** *no pl* minium, red lead.

Menopause *f* (*Med*) menopause.

Mensa *f* **-, Mensen** (*Univ*) canteen, refectory (*Brit*), commons (*US*).

Mensa|essen *nt* (*Univ*) (*Mahlzeit*) college meal, commons (*US*); (*Kost*) college food, commons (*US*).

Mensch[1] *m* **-en, -en (a)** (*Person*) person, man/woman ◆ **ein anderer ~ werden** to become a different man/woman *or* person; **ein neuer ~ werden** to become a new person *or* man/woman; **von ~ zu ~** man-to-man/woman-to-woman; **es war kein ~ da** there was nobody *or* not a soul there; **als ~** as a person; **des ~en Wille ist sein Himmelreich** (*Prov*) do what you want if it makes you happy (*inf*); **das konnte kein ~ ahnen!** no-one (on earth) could have foreseen that!; **viel unter (die) ~en kommen** to meet a lot of people, to get around (a lot); **man muß die ~en nehmen, wie sie sind** you have to take people as they are *or* come.
(b) (*als Gattung*) **der ~** man; **die ~en** man *sing*, human beings *pl*, people *pl*; **die Ruritanier sind gutmütige ~en** the Ruritanians are a good-natured race *or* are good-natured people; **ein Tier, das keine ~en mag** an animal that doesn't like people *or* humans; **~ bleiben** (*inf*) to stay human; **ich bin auch nur ein ~!** I'm only human; **wer so etwas macht, ist kein ~ mehr** somebody who does something like that is not human; **wie die ersten/letzten ~en** (*inf*) like animals; **~ und Tier** man and beast; **alle ~en müssen sterben** we are all mortal; **alle ~en haben tierische Gelüste** all human beings have animal cravings.
(c) (*die Menschheit*) **die ~en** mankind, man; **des ~en Sohn** (*Bibl*) the Son of Man; **Jesus ist gekommen, um die ~en zu retten** Jesus came to save mankind; **alle ~en** everyone; **so sind die ~en** that's human nature.
(d) (*inf: als Interjektion*) hey; (*erstaunt auch*) wow, blimey (*Brit sl*) ◆ **~, hat die Beine!** hey *or* wow! has she got a pair of legs! (*inf*); **~, das habe ich ganz vergessen** damn (*inf*), I completely forgot; **~, da habe ich mich aber getäuscht** boy, was I wrong! (*inf*); **~, habe ich mich beeilt/geärgert!** boy, did I rush/was I angry! (*inf*); **~ Meier!** golly! (*inf*), gosh! (*inf*).

Mensch[2] *nt* **-(e)s, -er** (*sl*) cow (*sl*); (*liederlich*) slut.

Mensch ärgere dich nicht *nt* **- - - -,** *no pl* (*Spiel*) ludo (*Brit*), aggravation (*US*).

menscheln *vi impers* **(a) es menschelt** there's no escaping (from) one's humanity. **(b)** (*in Märchen*) **es menschelt** I smell *or* sense a human.

Menschen- *in cpds* human; **~affe** *m* ape, anthropoid (ape); **m~ähnlich** *adj* man-like, like a human being/human beings; **~alter** *nt* **(a)** (*30 Jahre*) generation; **(b)** (*Lebensdauer*) lifetime; **~ansammlung** *f* gathering (of people); **~art** *f* **(a) nach ~art** like human beings/a human being; **(b)** (*menschliche Schwäche*) human nature; **~auflauf** *m* crowd (of people); **~feind** *m* misanthropist; **m~feindlich** *adj Mensch* misanthropic; *Landschaft etc* hostile to man, inhospitable; **~fleisch** *nt* human flesh; **~fresser(in** *f*) *m* **-s, - (a)** (*inf: Kannibale*) cannibal; (*Raubtier*) man-eater; **ich bin doch kein ~fresser!** I won't eat you!; **(b)** (*Myth*) ogre; **~fresserei** *f* (*inf*) cannibalism; **~freund** *m* philanthropist; **m~freundlich** *adj Mensch* philanthropic, benevolent; *Gegend* hospitable; **diese Affenart ist nicht sehr m~freundlich** this species of ape does not like humans; **~freundlichkeit** *f* philanthropy, benevolence; **aus reiner ~freundlichkeit** from the sheer goodness of one's heart; **~führung** *f* leadership; **~gedenken** *nt* **der kälteste Winter seit ~gedenken** the coldest winter in living memory; **hier hat sich seit ~gedenken nichts geändert** nothing has changed here from time immemorial; **~gestalt** *f* human form; **ein Teufel** *or* **Satan** *or* **Scheusal in ~gestalt** a devil in disguise; **~gewühl** *nt* milling crowd; **~hai** *m* man-eating shark, man-eater; **~hand** *f* human hand; **von ~hand geschaffen** fashioned by the hand of man; **das liegt nicht in ~hand** that is beyond man's control; **~handel** *m* slave trade; (*Jur*) trafficking (in human beings); **~händler** *m* slave trader; (*Jur*) trafficker (in human beings); ⚠**~haß** *m* misanthropy, hatred of people; **~hasser** *m* **-s, -** *siehe* **~feind**; **~jagd** *f* manhunts *pl*, man-hunting; **eine ~jagd** a manhunt; **~jäger** *m* manhunter; **~kenner** *m* judge of character, connoisseur of human nature; **~kenntnis** *f, no pl* knowledge of human nature; **~kenntnis haben** to know human nature; **~kette** *f* human chain; **~kind** *nt* creature, soul; **~kunde** *f* anthropology; **~leben** *nt* human life; **ein ~leben lang** a whole lifetime; **~leben beklagen** to report fatalities; **~leben waren nicht zu beklagen** there was no loss of life, no fatalities were reported; **Verluste an ~leben** loss of human life; **das Unglück hat zwei ~leben gefordert** the accident claimed two lives; **m~leer** *adj* deserted; **~liebe** *f* **(a)** (*Bibl*) human love; **(b)** (*Nächsten~*) love of mankind, philanthropy; **aus reiner ~liebe** from the sheer goodness of one's heart; **tätige ~liebe** concrete humanitarianism, active philanthropy; **~masse** *f* crowd *or* mass (of people); **~material** *nt* (*Mil sl*) manpower; **~menge** *f* crowd (of people); **m~möglich** *adj* humanly possible; **das m~mögliche tun** to do all that is humanly possible; **~opfer** *nt* **(a)** human sacrifice; **(b)** (*~leben*) **es waren ~opfer zu beklagen** there were (some) fatalities; **~raub** *m* (*Jur*) kidnapping; **~räuber** *m* (*Jur*) kidnapper.

Menschenrecht *nt* human right ◆ **die Allgemeine Erklärung** *or* **Deklaration der ~e** the Universal Declaration of Human Rights.

Menschenrechts-: **~kommission** *f* Commission on Human Rights; **~konvention** *f* Human Rights Convention; **~verletzung** *f* violation of human rights.

Menschen-: **~scheu** *f* fear of people; **krankhafte ~scheu** anthropophobia (*spec*); **m~scheu** *adj* afraid of people; **~schinder** *m* slavedriver; **~schlag** *m* (*inf*) kind of people, breed (*inf*); **~seele** *f* human soul; **keine ~seele** (*fig*) not a (living) soul.

Menschenskind *interj* good heavens, heavens above.

Menschen-: **~sohn** *m* (*Bibl*) Son of Man; **m~unmöglich** *adj* absolutely impossible; **das ~unmögliche versuchen/vollbringen** to attempt/achieve the impossible; **m~unwürdig** *adj* beneath human dignity; *Behandlung* inhumane; *Behausung* unfit for human habitation; ⚠**m~verachtend** *adj* inhuman, contemptuous of human life; **~verächter** *m* despiser of mankind; **~verachtung** *f* contempt for mankind; **~verstand** *m* human understanding *no art*; **gesunder ~verstand** common sense; **~werk** *nt* (*old, liter*) work of man; **alles ~werk ist vergänglich** all works of men are transient; **~würde** *f* human dignity *no art*; **m~würdig** *adj Behandlung* humane; *Unterkunft* fit for human habitation; **m~würdig leben** to live in conditions fit for human beings; **m~würdige Entlohnung** decent living wage.

Menschewik *m* **-en, -en** *or* **-i** (*Hist*) Menshevik.

Menschewismus *m* (*Hist*) Menshevism.

Menschheit *f* **die ~** mankind, humanity; **zum Wohle der ~** for the benefit of mankind *or* the human race; **Verdienste um die/im Namen der ~** services to/in the name of humanity.

Menschheits-: **~entwicklung** *f* development of mankind; **~geschichte** *f* history of the human race *or* of mankind.

menschlich *adj* **(a)** human ◆ **das ~e Leben** human life; **der ~e Körper/Geist** the human body/mind; **die ~e Gesellschaft/Gemeinschaft** the society of man/the human community; **jede ~e Hilfe kam zu spät für sie** she was beyond human help; **sie ist mir ~ sympathisch** I like her as a person.
(b) (*inf: zivilisiert*) human ◆ **(einigermaßen) ~ aussehen** (*inf*) to look more or

less human; **sich wieder ~ fühlen** to feel more human (again).
(c) (*human*) *Behandlung etc* humane ◆ **eine ~e Seite haben** to have a human side to one.
Menschlichkeit *f, no pl* humanity *no art* ◆ **aus reiner ~** on purely humanitarian grounds.
Menschwerdung *f* **(a)** (*Bibl*) incarnation. **(b)** (*Biol*) anthropogenesis.
Mensen *pl of* **Mensa**.
Menstruation [mɛnstrua'tsio:n] *f* menstruation.
menstruieren* *vi* to menstruate.
Mensur *f* (*Univ*) (students') fencing bout ◆ **eine ~ schlagen** *or* **fechten** to fight a duel.
mental *adj Einstellung, Reaktion* mental ◆ **mentales Training** mental training, mind training; **körperlich und mental** physically and mentally.
Mentalität *f* mentality.
Menthol *nt* **-s, -e** menthol.
Mentor *m* **(a)** (*dated, geh*) mentor. **(b)** (*Sch*) ≃ tutor.
Menü, Menu *nt* **-s, -s (a)** (*Tages~*) set meal *or* menu, table d'hôte (*form*) ◆ **~ essen** to have one of the set meals, to have the set menu; **~ des Tages** (set) meal of the day. **(b)** (*Comput*) menu.
Menuett *nt* **-s, -e** (*Tanz, Kunstmusik*) minuet.
Menü-, Menu- (*Comput*) *in cpds* menu; **~anzeige** *f* menu display; **~führung** *f* menu-driven operation; **m~gesteuert** *adj* menu-driven; **~leiste** *f* menu strip; **~steuerung** *f siehe* **~führung**; **~zeile** *f* menu line.
mephistophelisch *adj* (*liter*) Mephistophelian.
Mergel *m* **-s, -** (*Geol*) marl.
Mergelboden *m* (*Geol*) marly *or* marlaceous (*spec*) soil.
merg(e)lig *adj* marly, marlaceous (*spec*).
Meridian *m* **-s, -e** (*Astron, Geog*) meridian.
Meridiankreis *m* (*Astron*) meridian circle.
Merino *m* **-s, -s, Merinoschaf** *nt* merino (sheep).
Merinowolle *f* merino wool.
Meriten *pl* (*geh*) merits *pl* ◆ **sich** (*dat*) **~ um etw erwerben** to receive plaudits for sth; **auf seinen alten ~ ruhen** to rest on one's laurels *or* on one's past merits.
merkantil *adj* (*Hist, geh*) mercantile.
Merkantilismus *m* (*Hist*) mercantilism.
merkantilistisch *adj* (*Hist*) mercantilist(ic).
Merk-: m~bar *adj* **(a)** (*wahrnehmbar*) noticeable; **(b)** (*zu behalten*) retainable; **leicht/schwer m~bar** easy/difficult to remember *or* retain; **~blatt** *nt* leaflet; (*mit Anweisungen auch*) instructions *pl*; **~buch** *nt siehe* **Notizbuch**.
merken **1** *vt* **(a)** (*wahrnehmen, entdecken*) to notice; (*spüren*) to feel; (*erkennen*) to realize ◆ **ich merke nichts!** I can't feel anything!; **davon habe ich nichts gemerkt** I didn't notice anything; **jdn etw ~ lassen** to make sb feel sth; **seine Gefühle ~ lassen** to let one's feelings show; **hat er dich etwas ~ lassen?** did you notice anything in the way he behaved?; **woran hast du das gemerkt?** how could you tell that?; **wie soll ich das ~?** how am I supposed to tell (that)?; **du merkst auch alles!** (*iro*) nothing escapes you, does it?, you *are* observant(, aren't you)?; **das merkt jeder/keiner!** everyone/no-one will notice!; **das ist kaum zu ~, davon merkt man kaum etwas** it's hardly noticeable; **das ist zu ~** you can tell; **ich merke keinen Unterschied** I can't tell the difference; (*weil es keinen gibt*) I can't see a difference.
(b) (*im Gedächtnis behalten*) to remember, to retain ◆ **das kann man leicht ~** that's easy to remember; **merke: ...** NB *or* note: ...
2 *vr* **(a)** (*im Gedächtnis behalten*) **sich** (*dat*) **jdn/etw ~** to remember sb/sth; **das werde ich mir ~!, ich werd's mir ~!** (*inf*) I'll remember that, I won't forget that; **das hat er sich gemerkt** he's taken that/it to heart; **merk dir das!** mark my words!
(b) (*im Auge behalten*) to remember, to make a note of ◆ **sich** (*dat*) **eine Autonummer ~** to make a (mental) note of a licence number; **~ Sie sich** (*dat*) **den Mann!** keep an eye on that man; **diesen Schriftsteller wird man sich** (*dat*) **~ müssen** this author is someone to take note of.
Merk-: ~fähigkeit *f* memory; **~heft** *nt* notebook.
merklich *adj* noticeable, marked, distinct ◆ **kein ~er Unterschied** no noticeable difference.
Merkmal *nt* **-s, -e** characteristic, feature; (*Biol, Zool*) distinctive mark *or* marking ◆ **„besondere ~e: ..."** "distinguishing marks: ...".
Merk- (*Sch*): **~satz** *m* mnemonic (sentence); **~spruch** *m* mnemonic (*form*), memory aid.
Merkur *m* **-s,** *no pl* (*Myth, Astron*) Mercury; (*obs: Quecksilber*) quicksilver, mercury.
Merk-: ~vers *m* (*Sch*) jingle, mnemonic (rhyme) (*form*); **m~würdig** *adj* strange, odd, curious; **er hat sich ganz m~würdig verändert** he has undergone a curious change; **m~würdigerweise** *adv* strangely *or* oddly *or* curiously enough.
Mesalliance [meza'liã:s] *f* **-, -n** (*liter*) misalliance, mésalliance (*liter*).
meschugge *adj* (*sl*) nuts (*sl*), barmy (*Brit sl*), meshuga (*US sl*).
Meskalin *nt* **-s,** *no pl* mescalin(e).
Mesmerismus *m, no pl* mesmerism.
Mesner *m* **-s, -** (*dial*) *siehe* **Küster**.
Mesolithikum *nt* **-s,** *no pl* (*Geol*) Mesolithic period.
mesolithisch *adj* (*Geol*) Mesolithic.
Meson *nt* **-s, -en** [-'o:nən] (*Phys*) meson, mesotron.
Mesopotamien [-iən] *nt* **-s** Mesopotamia.
Mesopotamier(in *f*) [-iɐ, -iərın] *m* **-s, -** Mesopotamian.
mesopotamisch *adj* Mesopotamian.
Mesozephale(r) *mf decl as adj* mesocephalic.
Mesozoikum [-'tso:ikʊm] *nt* (*Geol*) Mesozoic.
⚠**Meß-: ~band** *nt siehe* **Bandmaß**; **m~bar** *adj* measurable; **~becher** *m* (*Cook*) measuring jug; **~buch** *nt* (*Eccl*) missal, Mass book; **~daten** *pl* readings *pl*; **~diener** *m* (*Eccl*) server, acolyte (*form*).
Messe[1] *f* **-, -n** (*Eccl, Mus*) mass ◆ **in die** *or* **zur ~ gehen** to go to mass; **die ~ lesen** *or* **halten** to say mass; **für jdn eine ~ lesen lassen** to have a mass said for sb; **die hohe ~** High Mass.
Messe[2] *f* **-, -n** (trade) fair ◆ **auf der ~** at the fair.
Messe[3] *f* **-, -n** (*Naut, Mil*) mess.
Messe- *in cpds* fair; **~angebot** *nt* exhibits *pl* (at a/the fair), fair exhibits *pl*; **~gast** *m* visitor to a/the fair, fair visitor; **~gelände** *nt* exhibition centre; **~halle** *f* fair pavilion.
messen *pret* **maß**, *ptp* **gemessen** **1** *vti* to measure; (*Tech: anzeigen auch*) to gauge; *Verlauf* to time; (*abschätzen*) *Entfernung etc* to judge, to gauge ◆ **jds Blutdruck/Temperatur ~** (*Arzt etc*) to take sb's blood pressure/temperature; (*Instrument*) to measure sb's blood pressure/temperature; **während ich lief, maß er die Zeit** I ran and he timed me *or* took the time; **seine Kräfte/Fähigkeiten mit jdm ~** to match one's strength/skills against sb's, to try *or* measure one's strength/skills with sb; **seine Kräfte/Fähigkeiten an etw** (*dat*) **~** to test one's strength/skills on sth; **etw an etw** (*dat*) **~** (*ausprobieren*) to try sth out on sth; (*vergleichen*) to compare sth with sth; **jdn mit den Blicken ~** (*geh*) to look sb up and down.
2 *vr* **(a)** (*mit* against) (*geh: im Wettkampf*) to compete; (*in geistigem Wettstreit, es jdm gleichtun wollen*) to pit oneself.
(b) sich mit jdm/etw nicht ~ können to be no match for sb/sth.
Messeneuheit *f* trade fair first.
Messer *nt* **-s, -** knife; (*Tech auch*) cutter, blade; (*Rasier~*) (cut-throat) razor ◆ **jdm ein ~ in den Leib stoßen, jdm ein ~ in den Bauch jagen** (*inf*) to stick a knife into sb; **unter dem ~ sein** (*Med inf*) to be under the knife; **jdm das ~ an die Kehle setzen** (*lit, fig*) to hold a knife to sb's throat; **die ~ wetzen** (*fig*) to get ready *or* prepare for the kill; **damit würden wir ihn ans ~ liefern** (*fig*) that would be putting his head on the block; **jdn der Mafia ans ~ liefern** to shop sb (*Brit sl*) *or* inform on sb to the Mafia; **ins (offene) ~ laufen** to walk straight into the trap; **ein Kampf/sich bekämpfen bis aufs ~** (*fig*) a fight/to fight to the finish; **auf des ~s Schneide stehen** (*fig*) to be *or* hang (very much) in the balance, to be on a razor-edge *or* razor's edge; **es steht auf des ~s Schneide, ob ...** it's touch and go *or* it's very much in the balance whether ...; **es wird eine Nacht der langen ~ geben** (*fig*) heads will roll; *siehe* **locker**.
Messer- *in cpds* knife; **~griff** *m*, **~heft** *nt* knife handle; **~held** *m* (*inf*) knifer (*inf*); **~rücken** *m* back of a/the knife; **m~scharf** *adj* (*lit, fig*) razor-sharp; **m~scharf schließen** (*iro*) to conclude with incredible logic (*iro*); **~schmied** *m* cutler; **~schneide** *f* knife edge; **~spitze** *f* knife point; **eine ~spitze (voll)** (*Cook*) a pinch; **~stecher(in** *f*) *m* **-s, -** knifer (*inf*); **~stecherei** *f* knife fight; **zur** *or* **in eine ~stecherei ausarten** to end up in a knife fight; **~stich** *m* knife thrust; (*Wunde*) stab wound; **~werfer** *m* knife-thrower.
Messe-: ~stadt *f* (town with an) exhibition centre; **~stand** *m* stand (at the/a fair).
⚠**Meß-: ~fühler** *m* probe, detector; (*Met*) gauge; **~gerät** *nt* **(a)** (*für Öl, Druck etc*) measuring instrument, gauge; **(b)** (*Eccl*) Mass requisites *pl*; **~gewand** *nt* chasuble; **~glas** *nt* graduated measure.
messianisch *adj* (*Rel, Philos*) Messianic.
Messias *m* **-, -se** (*Rel, fig*) Messiah.
Messing *nt* **-s,** *no pl* brass ◆ **mit ~ beschlagen** brass-bound.
Messing- *in cpds* brass; **~blech** *nt* sheet brass; **~schild** *nt* brass plate.
⚠**Meß-: ~instrument** *nt* gauge; **~opfer** *nt* (*Eccl*) Sacrifice of the Mass; **~ordnung** *f* (*Eccl*) ordinary (of the Mass); **~platte** *f* (*Surv*) surveyor's staff *or* rod; **~stab** *m* **(a)** (*Surv*) surveyor's staff; **(b)** (*Aut: Ölmeßstab etc*) dipstick; **~technik** *f* measurement technology, metrology; **~tisch** *m* (*Surv*) surveyor's table; **~tischblatt** *nt* ordnance survey map.
Messung *f* **(a)** (*das Messen*) measuring; (*das Ablesen*) reading; (*von Blutdruck*) taking; (*Tech: das Anzeigen*) gauging. **(b)** (*Meßergebnis*) measurement; (*Ableseergebnis*) reading.
⚠**Meß-: ~wein** *m* (*Eccl*) Communion wine; **~wert** *m* measurement; (*Ableseergebnis*) reading; **~zahl** *f* measurement; **~zylinder** *m* measuring cylinder, graduated measure.
Mestize *m* **-n, -n** mestizo.
Mestizin *f* mestiza.
Met *m* **-(e)s,** *no pl* mead.
Metall *nt* **-s, -e (a)** metal. **(b)** (*geh: der Stimme*) metallic ring *or* timbre.
Metall- *in cpds* metal-; **~arbeiter** *m* metalworker; **m~artig** *adj* metallic; **~bearbeitung** *f* metal processing, metalworking.
metallen *adj* metal; (*geh*) *Klang, Stimme* metallic.
Metaller(in *f*) *m* **-s, -** (*inf*) metalworker.
Metall-: ~ermüdung *f* metal fatigue; **~geld** *nt* specie, metallic currency; **m~haltig** *adj* metalliferous, metalline.
metallic *adj* metallic.
Metallic- *in cpds* metallic.
metallisch *adj* metal; (*metallartig*), (*fig*) *Stimme, Klang* metallic ◆ **~ glänzen** to gleam like metal; **~ schmecken** to have a metallic taste.
Metall-: ~kunde *f* metallurgy; **~säge** *f* hacksaw.
Metallurg(e) *m* **-(e)n, -(e)n, Metallurgin** *f* metallurgist.
Metallurgie *f* metallurgy.
metallurgisch *adj* metallurgic(al).
Metall-: ⚠**m~verarbeitend** *adj* **die m~verarbeitende Industrie** the metal-

processing industry; ~**verarbeitung** *f* metal processing; ~**waren** *pl* hardware *sing* (*Brit*), metalware *sing* (*US*).
Metamorphose [-'fo:zə] *f* -, -n metamorphosis.
Metapher [me'tafɐ] *f* -, -n (*Liter, Poet*) metaphor.
Metaphorik [-'fo:rɪk] *f* (*Liter, Poet*) imagery.
metaphorisch *adj* (*Liter, Poet*) metaphoric(al).
Metaphysik *f* metaphysics *sing*.
metaphysisch *adj* metaphysical.
Metapsychologie *f* metapsychology.
Metasprache *f* metalanguage.
Metastase [meta'sta:zə] *f* -, -n (*Med*) metastasis.
Metathese, Metathesis *f* -, **Metathesen** (*Ling*) metathesis.
Meteor *m or nt* -s, -e meteor.
Meteor|eisen *nt* meteoric iron.
Meteorit *m* -en, -en meteorite.
Meteorologe *m*, **Meteorologin** *f* meteorologist; (*im Wetterdienst*) weather forecaster, weatherman/-woman (*inf*).
Meteorologie *f* meteorology.
meteorologisch *adj* meteorological.
Meteorstein *m siehe* **Meteorit**.
Meter *m or nt* -s, - (a) metre (*Brit*), meter (*US*) ◆ **in einer Entfernung von 40 ~(n)** at a distance of 40 metres; **in 500 ~ Höhe** at a height of 500 metres; **nach ~n** by the metre. (b) (*Meterstab*) metric measure. (c) (*inf*) *siehe* **Metermaß**.
Meter-: **m~dick** *adj* metres thick; **m~hoch** *adj Wellen etc* enormous; **m~lang** *adj* metres long; **m~lange Lochstreifen** yards and yards of punch tape; ~**maß** *nt* (a) (*Bandmaß*) tape measure, measuring tape; (b) (*Stab*) (metre) rule; ~**ware** *f* (*Tex*) piece goods; **m~weise** *adv* by the metre; **m~weit** *adj* (*breit*) metres wide; (*lang*) metres long; **er schoß m~weit vorbei** his shot was yards *or* miles (*inf*) off target.
Methadon *nt* -s, *no pl* methadone.
Methan *nt* -s, *no pl*, **Methangas** *nt* methane.
Methanol *nt* -s, *no pl siehe* **Methylalkohol**.
▼ **Methode** *f* -, -n (a) method ◆ **etw mit ~ machen** to do sth methodically *or* systematically; **das hat ~** (*inf*) there's (a) method behind it; **er hat (so) seine ~n** (*inf*) he's got his methods.
(b) **~n** *pl* (*Sitten*) behaviour ◆ **was sind denn das für ~n?** what sort of way is that to behave?
Methodenlehre *f siehe* **Methodologie**.
Methodik *f* methodology.
Methodiker(in *f*) *m* -s, - methodologist.
methodisch *adj* methodical.
Methodist(in *f*) *m* Methodist.
methodistisch *adj* Methodist.
Methodologie *f* methodology.
methodologisch *adj* methodological.
Methusalem *m* -s Methuselah ◆ **alt wie ~** old as Methuselah.
Methyl|alkohol *m* methyl *or* wood alcohol.
Metier [me'tie:] *nt* -s, -s (*hum*) job, profession ◆ **sich auf sein ~ verstehen** to be good at one's job.
Metonymie *f* (*Liter*) metonymy.
metonymisch *adj* (*Liter*) metonymical.
Metrik *f* (*Poet, Mus*) metrics *sing*.
metrisch *adj* (*Sci*) metric; (*Poet, Mus auch*) metrical.
Metro *f* -, -s metro.
Metronom *nt* -s, -e (*Mus*) metronome.
Metropole *f* -, -n (a) (*größte Stadt*) metropolis. (b) (*Zentrum*) capital, centre. (c) (*Pol: Mutterland*) home country.
Metropolit *m* -en, -en metropolitan.
Metrum *nt* -s, **Metren** metre (*Brit*), meter (*US*).
Mett *nt* -(e)s, *no pl* (*Cook dial*) (lean) minced pork/beef.
Mettage [mɛ'ta:ʒə] *f* -, -n (*Typ*) make-up; (*Arbeitsort*) make-up room.
Mette *f* -, -n (*Eccl*) matins *sing*; (*Abend~*) vespers *sing*.
Metteur(in *f*) [-'tø:ɐ, -'tø:rɪn] *m* (*Typ*) make-up man/woman.
Mettwurst *f* (smoked) pork/beef sausage.
Metze *f* -, -n (*obs: Hure*) strumpet (*old*).
Metzelei *f* butchery, slaughter.
metzeln *vt* to slaughter, to butcher; (*S Ger: schlachten*) to slaughter.
Metzelsuppe *f* (*S Ger*) meat broth.
Metzger(in *f*) *m* -s, - butcher.
Metzger- *siehe* **Fleischer-**.
Metzgerei *f* butcher's (shop).
Meuchel-: ~**mord** *m* (treacherous) murder; ~**mörder** *m* (treacherous) assassin.
meucheln *vt* (*old*) to assassinate.
meuchlerisch *adj* (*old*) murderous; *Mörder* treacherous.
meuchlings *adv* treacherously.
Meute *f* -, -n pack (of hounds); (*fig pej*) mob ◆ **die ~ loslassen** *or* **loskoppeln** to release the hounds.
Meuterei *f* mutiny; (*fig auch*) rebellion.
meutern *vi* to mutiny; (*inf auch*) to rebel; (*dial inf: meckern*) to moan, to grouch (*inf*) ◆ **die ~den Soldaten** the mutinous soldiers.
Mexikaner(in *f*) *m* -s, - Mexican.
mexikanisch *adj* Mexican.
Mexiko *nt* -s Mexico ◆ **~ City, ~-Stadt** Mexico City.
MEZ *abbr of* **mitteleuropäische Zeit**.
Mezzosopran *m* mezzo-soprano.
MG [ɛm'ge:] *nt* -(s), -(s) *abbr of* **Maschinengewehr**.
MHz *abbr of* **Megahertz**.
miau *interj* miaow.
miauen* *vi* to miaow.
mich [1] *pers pron acc of* **ich** me.
[2] *reflexive pron* myself ◆ **ich fühle ~ wohl** I feel fine.
Michael ['mɪçae:l, 'mɪçaɛl] *m* -s Michael.
Michaeli(s) [mɪça'e:li, mɪça'e:lɪs] *nt* -, - Michaelmas.
Michel *m* -s Mike, Mick ◆ **der deutsche ~** (*fig*) the plain honest German.
Michigansee ['mɪʃɪgən-] *m* Lake Michigan.
mick(e)rig *adj* (*inf*) pathetic; *Betrag auch* paltry; *altes Männchen* puny.
Mickymaus ['mɪki-] *f* Mickey Mouse.
midi *adj pred* (*Fashion*) midi.
Midi- *in cpds* midi; **~-Anlage** *f*, **~-System** *nt* midi (system).
mied *pret of* **meiden**.
Mieder *nt* -s, - (a) (*Leibchen*) bodice. (b) (*Korsage*) girdle.
Mieder-: ~**höschen** *nt* pantie-girdle; ~**waren** *pl* corsetry *sing*.
Mief *m* -s, *no pl* (*inf*) fug; (*muffig*) stale air; (*Gestank*) stink, pong (*Brit inf*) ◆ **der ~ der Provinz/des Kleinbürgertums** (*fig*) the oppressive claustrophobic atmosphere of the provinces/petty bourgeoisie.
miefen *vi* (*inf*) to stink, to pong (*Brit inf*); (*furzen*) to make a smell ◆ **hier mieft es** there's a pong in here; (*muffig*) the air in here is so stale; **was mieft denn hier so?** what's this awful pong?
Miene *f* -, -n (*Gesichtsausdruck*) expression, face, mien (*liter*) ◆ **eine finstere ~ machen** to look grim; **gute ~ zum bösen Spiel machen** to grin and bear it; **~ machen, etw zu tun** to make a move to do sth; **seine ~ verfinsterte** *or* **verdüsterte sich** his face darkened; **sich** (*dat*) **etw mit eisiger ~ anhören** to listen to sth in stony silence; *siehe* **verziehen**[1].
Mienenspiel *nt* facial expressions *pl* ◆ **ein lebhaftes ~ haben** to express a lot with one's face.
mies *adj* (*inf*) rotten (*inf*), lousy (*inf*); *Lokal auch* crummy (*inf*); *Laune auch* foul ◆ **jdn/etw ~ machen** to run sb/sth down; **mir ist ~** I feel lousy *or* rotten (*inf*); **in den M~en sein** (*inf*) to be in the red.
Miesepeter *m* -s, - (*inf*) misery-guts (*inf*).
miesepet(e)rig *adj* (*inf*) miserable, grouchy (*inf*).
Miesmacher *m* (*inf*) kill-joy.
Miesmacherei *f* (*inf*) belly-aching (*sl*).
Miesmuschel *f* mussel.
Miet-: ~**ausfall** *m* loss of rent; ~**auto** *nt* hire(d) car; ~**beihilfe** *f* rent allowance *or* subsidy/rebate.
Miete[1] *f* -, -n (*für Wohnung*) rent; (*für Gegenstände*) rental; (*für Dienstleistungen*) charge ◆ **rückständige ~** (rent) arrears; **zur ~ wohnen** to live in rented accommodation; **das ist die halbe ~** (*inf*) that's half the battle.
Miete[2] *f* -, -n (*Kartoffel~*) clamp (*Brit*), pit; (*Schober*) stack.
mieten *vt* to rent; *Boot, Auto auch* to hire.
Mieter(in *f*) *m* -s, - tenant; (*Untermieter*) lodger.
Miet|erhöhung *f* rent increase.
Mieterschaft *f* tenants *pl*.
Mieter-: ~**schutz** *m* rent control; ~**schutzgesetz** *nt* Rent Act.
Miet-: ~**ertrag** *m* rent(al) (income); **m~frei** *adj* rent-free; ~**garantie** *f* proof of ability to pay rent; ~**partei** *f* tenant (and family); ~**recht** *nt* rent law; ~**rückstände** *pl* rent arrears *pl*.
Miets-: ~**haus** *nt* block of (rented) flats (*Brit*), apartment house (*US*); ~**kaserne** *f* (*pej*) tenement house.
Miet-: ~**spiegel** *m* rent level; ~**verhältnis** *nt* tenancy; ~**vertrag** *m* lease; (*von Auto*) rental agreement; ~**wagen** *m* hire car, hired car; ~**wert** *m* letting *or* rental value; ~**wohnung** *f* rented flat (*Brit*) *or* apartment (*US*); ~**wucher** *m* exorbitant rent; **~wucher ist strafbar** charging exorbitant rent(s) is a punishable offence; ~**zahlung** *f* payment of the rent; ~**zins** *m* (*form, S Ger, Aus*) rent.
Mieze *f* -, -n (*inf*) (a) (*Katze*) pussy (*inf*). (b) (*Mädchen*) chick (*inf*), bird (*Brit inf*); (*als Anrede*) baby (*inf*), honey (*inf*).
Mieze-: ~**kätzchen** *nt* (*baby-talk*) (little) pussy(-cat); ~**katze** *f* (*baby-talk*) pussy(-cat).
MiG [mɪg] *f* -s, -s (*Mil*) MiG.
Migräne *f* -, *no pl* migraine.
Migräne|anfall *m* attack of migraine.
Mikado[1] *nt* -s, -s (*Spiel*) pick-a-stick.
Mikado[2] *m* -s, -s (*old: Kaiser von Japan*) mikado.
Mikro *nt* -s, -s (*inf*) *abbr of* **Mikrofon** mike (*inf*).
Mikro- *in cpds* micro-.
Mikrobe *f* -, -n microbe.
Mikrochip ['mi:krotʃɪp] *m* microchip.
Mikrocomputer *m* microcomputer, micro.
Mikro|elektronik *f* microelectronics *sing*.
Mikrofiche ['mi:krofi:ʃ] *m or nt* -s, -s microfiche.
Mikrofon *nt* -s, -e microphone.
Mikrokosmos *m* microcosm.
Mikrometer *nt* micron; (*Gerät*) micrometer.
Mikron *nt* -s, - micron.
Mikro|organismus *m* microorganism.
⚠ **Mikrophon** *nt* -s, -e microphone.
Mikro-: ~**prozessor** *m* microprocessor; ~**sekunde** *f* microsecond;

➤ SPRACHE AKTIV: Methode: a → 39.2

⚠: Informationen zur Rechtschreibreform im Anhang

~sender *m* microtransmitter.
Mikroskop *nt* **-s, -e** microscope.
Mikroskopie *f* microscopy.
mikroskopieren* [1] *vt* (*rare*) to examine under *or* with the microscope. [2] *vi* to work with a/the microscope.
mikroskopisch *adj* microscopic ♦ **etw ~ untersuchen** to examine sth under the microscope; **~ klein** (*fig*) microscopically small.
Mikrowelle *f* microwave.
Mikrowellenherd *m* microwave (oven).
Mikrozensus *m* sample census.
Mikrozephale(r) *mf decl as adj* microcephalic.
Milan *m* **-s, -e** (*Orn*) kite.
Milbe *f* **-, -n** mite.
Milch *f* **-,** *no pl* (*alle Bedeutungen*) milk; (*Fischsamen*) milt, soft roe ♦ **dicke ~** curd(s); **~ geben** (*Kuh*) to yield milk; **das Land, wo ~ und Honig fließt** the land of *or* flowing with milk and honey; **aussehen wie ~ und Blut** to have a peaches-and-cream complexion.
Milch- *in cpds* milk; **m~artig** *adj* milky; **~bar** *f* milk bar; **~bart** *m* (*inf*) downy *or* fluffy beard, bum-fluff (*inf*); (*fig pej: Jüngling*) milksop; **~brei** *m* ≃ milk pudding; **~brötchen** *nt roll made with milk and sugar*; **~drüse** *f* mammary gland; **~eiweiß** *nt* lactoprotein; **~fett** *nt* milk fat; **~flasche** *f* milk bottle; **~frau** *f* (*inf*) dairywoman; ⚠**~gebiß** *nt* milk teeth *pl*; **~geschäft** *nt* dairy; **~gesicht** *nt* (*inf*) baby face; **~glas** *nt* frosted glass; **~handel** *m* dairy business; **~händler** *m* dairyman.
milchig *adj* milky.
Milch-: ~kaffee *m* milky coffee; **~kanne** *f* milk can; (*größer*) (milk) churn; **~kuh** *f* milk *or* milch (*spec*) cow; (*fig inf*) milch cow, ever-open purse; **~laden** *m siehe* **~geschäft**; **~mädchen** *nt* (*~verkäuferin*) dairy girl; (*~kassiererin*) milk girl; **~mädchenrechnung** *f* (*inf*) naïve fallacy; **~mann** *m, pl* **-männer** milkman; **~mixgetränk** *nt* milk shake.
Milchner *m* **-s, -** milter.
Milch-: ~produkt *nt* milk product; **~pulver** *nt* dried *or* powdered milk; **~pumpe** *f* breast pump; **~quote** *f* (*in der EG*) milk quota; **~reis** *m* round-grain rice; (*als Gericht*) rice pudding; **~saft** *m* (*Bot*) latex; **~säure** *f* lactic acid; **~schorf** *m* cradle cap; **~see** *m* (*in der EG*) milk lake; **~speise** *f* milky *or* milk-based food; **~straße** *f* Milky Way; **~straßensystem** *nt* Milky Way system *or* galaxy; **~suppe** *f* **(a)** ≃ warm blancmange; **(b)** (*dated inf: Nebel*) pea-souper (*inf*); **~tüte** *f* milk carton; **~wirtschaft** *f* dairy farming; **~zahn** *m* milk tooth; **~zucker** *m* lactose.
mild(e) *adj* **(a)** (*sanft, lind*) *Wetter, Abend* mild; *Luft auch* gentle. **(b)** (*nachsichtig, barmherzig*) *Behandlung, Beurteilung, Richter* lenient; *Worte* mild ♦ **jdn ~ stimmen** to put sb in a mild mood; **~ ausfallen** to be lenient; **eine ~e Gabe** alms *pl*; **~ gesagt/ausgedrückt** to put it mildly. **(c)** *Käse, Zigaretten* mild; *Seife auch* gentle; *Speisen* light.
Milde *f* **-,** *no pl siehe adj* **(a)** mildness; gentleness. **(b)** leniency ♦ **~ walten lassen** to be lenient.
mildern [1] *vt* (*geh*) *Schmerz* to ease, to soothe, to alleviate; *Furcht* to calm; *Strafe, Urteil* to moderate, to mitigate; *Gegensätze* to reduce, to make less crass *or* severe; *Ausdrucksweise, Zorn* to moderate ♦ **~de Umstände** (*Jur*) mitigating *or* extenuating circumstances. [2] *vr* (*Wetter*) to become milder; (*Gegensätze*) to become less crass; (*Zorn*) to abate; (*Schmerz*) to ease.
Milderung *f, no pl* (*von Schmerz*) easing, soothing, alleviation; (*von Ausdruck, des Klimas*) moderation; (*von Strafe*) moderation, mitigation ♦ **spüren Sie schon eine ~?** can you feel any easing (of the pain)?
Milderungsgrund *m* mitigating cause *or* circumstance.
Mild-: m~herzig *adj* (*old*) *siehe* **barmherzig**; **m~tätig** *adj* (*geh*) charitable; **er war sein ganzes Leben lang m~tätig** he performed charitable deeds throughout his life; **~tätigkeit** *f* (*geh*) charity.
Milieu [mi'liø:] *nt* **-s, -s** (*Umwelt*) environment, milieu; (*Lokalkolorit*) atmosphere; (*Verbrecher~*) underworld; (*von Prostitution*) world of prostitutes.
Milieu-: m~geschädigt, m~gestört *adj* maladjusted (*due to adverse social factors*); **~schaden** *m* effects *pl* of adverse social factors; **~schilderung** *f* background description; **~studien** *pl* **~studien treiben** (*usu hum*) to study the locals (*hum*); **~theorie** *f* (*Sociol*) environmentalism *no art*; **~wechsel** *m* change of environment; (*Abwechslung*) change of scene.
militant *adj* militant.
Militanz *f, no pl* militancy.
Militär[1] *nt* **-s,** *no pl* military, armed forces *pl* ♦ **beim ~ sein** (*inf*) to be in the forces; **zum ~ einberufen werden** to be called up; **zum ~ müssen** (*inf*) to have to join up; **zum ~ gehen** to join up; **(gegen jdn) ~ einsetzen** to use the military (against sb); **wir sind doch hier nicht beim ~!** we're not in the army, you know!; **da geht es zu wie beim ~** the place is run like an army camp.
Militär[2] *m* **-s, -s** (army) officer.
Militär- *in cpds* military; **~arzt** *m* army doctor; medical officer; **~dienst** *m* military service; **(seinen) ~dienst ableisten** to do national service; **~geistliche(r)** *m* (army) chaplain; **~gericht** *nt* military court, court martial; **Internationales ~gericht** International Military Tribunal; **vor ein ~gericht gestellt werden** to be tried by a court martial; **wenn Sie das machen, werden Sie vor ein ~gericht gestellt** if you do that you'll be court-martialled; **~hilfe** *f* military aid.
Militaria *pl* things military *pl.*
militärisch *adj* military ♦ **~ grüßen** to give the military salute; **jdm ~e** *or* **die ~en Ehren erweisen** to give sb military honours; **mit allen ~en Ehren** with full military honours; **einen Konflikt ~** *or* **mit ~en Mitteln lösen** to resolve a conflict with the use of troops; **es geht dort streng ~ zu** it's very regimented there; **~ abgehackt sprechen** to speak in a clipped military fashion; **sich ~ geben** to behave in a military fashion.
militarisieren* *vt* to militarize.
Militarismus *m, no pl* militarism.
Militarist(in *f*) *m* militarist.
militaristisch *adj* militaristic.
Militär-: ~seelsorge *f* spiritual welfare of the armed forces; **~wesen** *nt* military affairs *pl*; **~wissenschaft** *f* military science.
Military ['mɪlɪtərɪ] *f* **-, -s** (*Sport*) three-day event.
Militärzeit *f* army days *pl*, days *pl* as a soldier.
Miliz *f* **-, -en** militia; (*in Osteuropa: Polizei*) police.
Milizionär(in *f*) *m* militiaman/-woman; (*in Osteuropa: Polizist*) policeman/-woman.
Milizsoldat *m* (*old*) militiaman.
Mill. *abbr of* **Million(en).**
mille: pro ~ *siehe* **Promille.**
Mille *f* **-, -** (*sl*) grand (*sl*) ♦ **5 ~** 5 grand (*sl*).
Millennium *nt* (*geh*) millennium.
Milliardär(in *f*) *m* multi-millionaire, billionaire.
Milliarde *f* **-, -n** thousand millions (*Brit*), billion (*US*) ♦ **zwei ~n Mark** two thousand million marks (*Brit*), two billion marks (*US*); **~n (von) Menschen** thousands of millions of people, billions of people.
Milliardenbetrag *m* (amount of) thousands of millions (*Brit*), billions (*US*).
Milliardstel *nt* **-s, -** thousand millionth (*Brit*) *or* billionth (*US*) part.
milliardstel *adj* thousand millionth (*Brit*), billionth (*US*) ♦ **ein ~ Meter** a *or* one thousand millionth of a metre (*Brit*), a *or* one billionth of a meter (*US*), a *or* one bicron (*US*).
milliardste(r, s) *adj* thousand millionth (*Brit*), billionth (*US*).
Milli- *in cpds* milli-; **~bar** *nt* **-s, -** millibar; **~gramm** *nt* milligramme; **~meter** *m or nt* millimetre; **~meterpapier** *nt* graph paper.
Million *f* million ♦ **eine ~ Londoner ist** *or* **sind unterwegs** a million Londoners are on their way; **zwei ~en** two millions; **zwei ~en Einwohner** two million inhabitants.
Millionär(in *f*) *m* millionaire(ss) ♦ **vom Tellerwäscher zum ~** from rags to riches; **es zum ~ bringen** to make a million.
Millionen-: ~auflage *f* million copies *pl*; millions of copies; **~auftrag** *m* contract worth millions; **~erbe** *m,* **~erbin** *f* inheritor of millions; **m~fach** [1] *adj* millionfold; [2] *adv* a million times; **~geschäft** *nt* multi-million-pound industry; **ein ~geschäft abschließen** to conclude a (business) deal worth millions; **~gewinn** *m* **(a)** (*Ertrag*) profit of millions; **manche Firmen haben ~gewinne gemacht** some firms have made profits running into millions; **(b)** (*Lotterie~*) prize of a million; **~heer** *nt* army of millions; **m~mal** *adv* a million times; **~schaden** *m* damage *no pl* amounting to *or* running into millions; **m~schwer** *adj* (*inf*) worth a few million; **~stadt** *f* town with over a million inhabitants.
Millionstel *nt* **-s, -** millionth part.
millionstel *adj* millionth.
millionste(r, s) *adj* millionth.
Millirem *nt* **-s, -** millirem.
Milz *f* **-, -en** spleen.
Milzbrand *m* (*Med, Vet*) anthrax.
Mime *m* **-n, -n** (*old, liter*) mime (*old*), Thespian.
mimen (*old*) [1] *vt* to mime ♦ **er mimt den Unschuldigen/den Kranken** (*inf*) he's acting the innocent/he's playing at being sick. [2] *vi* to play-act.
Mimesis *f* **-, Mimesen** (*Liter, Philos*) mimesis.
mimetisch *adj* (*Liter, Philos*) mimetic.
Mimik *f, no pl* facial expression ♦ **etw durch ~ ausdrücken** to express sth facially.
Mimiker(in *f*) *m* **-s, -** mime(r).
Mimikry ['mɪmikri] *f* **-,** *no pl* (*Zool, fig*) mimicry.
mimisch *adj* mimic.
Mimose *f* **-, -n** mimosa ♦ **empfindlich wie eine ~ sein** to be oversensitive.
mimosenhaft *adj* (*fig*) oversensitive.
Min., min. *abbr of* **Minute(n).**
min. *abbr of* **minimal.**
Minarett *nt* **-s, -e** *or* **-s** minaret.
minder *adv* less ♦ **mehr oder ~** more or less; **nicht mehr und nicht ~** neither more nor less, no more and no less; **nicht ~ wichtig als** no less important than; **und das nicht ~** and no less so.
Minder-: m~begabt *adj* less gifted; **~begabte** *pl decl as adj* less gifted people/ones *pl*; **m~begütert** *adj* less well-off; **~begüterte** *pl decl as adj* people *pl* in the lower income brackets; **~belastete(r)** *m decl as adj* (*Jur*) less incriminated person; **m~bemittelt** *adj* (*dated*) less well-off; **geistig m~bemittelt** (*iro*) mentally less gifted; **~bemittelte** *pl decl as adj* (*dated*) people *pl* with a limited income; (*iro*) not very bright people *pl*; **~einnahme** *f* decrease in receipts.
mindere(r, s) *adj attr* lesser; *Güte, Qualität* inferior.
Mindergewicht *nt* short weight.
Minderheit *f* minority.
Minderheiten- (*Pol*): **~frage** *f* minorities problem; **~schutz** *m* protection of minorities.
Minderheits- (*Pol*): **~rechte** *pl* rights of minorities *pl*; **~regierung** *f*

minority government.
Minder-: m~jährig *adj* who is (still) a minor; **~jährige(r)** *mf decl as adj* minor; **~jährigkeit** *f* minority.
mindern [1] *vt (herabsetzen) Würde, Verdienste* to diminish; *(verringern) Wert, Qualität* to reduce, to diminish, to erode; *Rechte* to erode; *Freude, Vergnügen* to detract from, to lessen.
[2] *vr siehe vt* to diminish; to be reduced, to diminish; to be eroded; to lessen.
Minderung *f siehe vb* diminishing *no indef art*; reduction (*gen* in); erosion; lessening.
Minderwert *m (Jur)* decrease in value.
minderwertig *adj* inferior; *Waren, Material auch* poor- *or* low-quality; *Arbeit auch* poor(-quality); *Qualität auch* low; *Charakter* low, base.
Minderwertigkeit *f siehe adj* inferiority; poor *or* low quality; poorness; lowness, baseness ◆ **die ~ der Qualität** the low quality.
Minderwertigkeits-: ~gefühl *nt* feeling of inferiority; **~gefühle haben** to feel inferior; **~komplex** *m* inferiority complex.
Minderzahl *f* minority ◆ **in der ~ sein** to be in the minority.
Mindest- *in cpds* minimum; **~abstand** *m* minimum distance; **~alter** *nt* minimum age; **~betrag** *m* minimum amount; **Waren für einen ~betrag von DM 20** goods to a minimum value of DM 20.
mindestens *adv* at least.
mindeste(r, s) *superl of* **wenig** [1] *adj attr* least, slightest; *Ahnung auch* faintest, foggiest *(inf)* ◆ **nicht die ~ Angst** not the slightest *or* least trace of fear; **er hat nicht das ~ bißchen Arbeit geleistet** he didn't do a single stroke (of work); **das ~** the (very) least; **ich verstehe nicht das ~ von (der) Kunst** I don't know the slightest thing about art; **das wäre das ~ gewesen** that's the least he/she *etc* could have done.
[2] *adv* **zum ~n** at least, at the very least; **(nicht) im ~n** (not) in the least; **das bezweifle ich nicht im ~n** I don't doubt that at all *or* in the slightest.
Mindest-: ~einkommen *nt* minimum income; **~forderung** *f* minimum demand; **~gebot** *nt (bei Auktionen)* reserve *or* knockdown price; **~geschwindigkeit** *f* minimum speed; **~größe** *f* minimum size; *(von Menschen)* minimum height; **~haltbarkeitsdatum** *nt* best-before date; **~lohn** *m* minimum wage; **~maß** *nt* minimum, minimum amount (*an +dat* of); **sich auf das ~maß beschränken** to limit oneself to the (absolute) minimum; **~preis** *m* minimum price; **~reserve** *f (Fin)* minimum reserves *pl*; **~reservesatz** *m (Fin)* minimum reserve ratio; **~strafe** *f* minimum penalty; **~umtausch** *m* minimum obligatory exchange; **~urlaub** *m* minimum holiday entitlement; **~wert** *m* minimum value; **im ~wert von** to a minimum value of; **~zinssatz** *m* minimum lending rate, MLR.
Mine *f* **-, -n (a)** *(Min)* mine ◆ **in den ~n arbeiten** to work down *or* in the mines.
(b) *(Mil)* mine ◆ **auf eine ~ laufen** to strike *or* hit a mine.
(c) *(Bleistift~)* lead; *(Kugelschreiber~, Filzstift~)* reservoir; *(Farb~)* cartridge; *(austauschbar)* refill ◆ **die ~ ist leer/läuft aus** the biro/felt-tip has run out/is leaking; **eine neue ~** a refill/new lead.
Minen-: ~feld *nt (Mil)* minefield; **~leger** *m* **-s, -** *(Mil, Naut)* mine-layer; **~räumboot** *nt* minesweeper; **~sperre** *f (Mil)* mine barrage; **~suchboot** *nt*, **~sucher** *m (inf)* minesweeper; **~werfer** *m (old Mil) siehe* **Mörser.**
Mineral *nt* **-s, -e** *or* **-ien** [-iən] mineral.
Mineral-: ~bad *nt* mineral bath; *(Ort)* spa; *(Schwimmbad) swimming-pool fed from a mineral spring*; **~brunnen** *m* mineral spring; **~dünger** *m* inorganic fertilizer.
Mineraliensammlung [-liən-] *f* collection of minerals.
mineralisch *adj* mineral.
Mineraloge *m*, **Mineralogin** *f* mineralogist.
Mineralogie *f* mineralogy.
mineralogisch *adj* mineralogical.
Mineral-: ~öl *nt* (mineral) oil; **~ölgesellschaft** *f* oil company; **~ölsteuer** *f* tax on oil; **~quelle** *f* mineral spring; **~salz** *nt* mineral salt; **~wasser** *nt* mineral water.
mini *adj inv (Fashion)* mini ◆ **~ tragen/gehen** to wear a mini(-skirt/-dress *etc*).
Mini- *in cpds* mini-.
Miniatur *f (Art)* miniature; *(fig Liter)* thumb-nail sketch.
Miniatur- *in cpds* miniature; **~ausgabe** *f* miniature version; *(Buch)* miniature edition; **~bild** *nt* miniature; **~bildnis** *nt* miniature portrait; **~format** *nt* miniature format; **eine Bibel in ~format** a miniature Bible; **~gemälde** *nt* miniature; **~maler** *m* miniaturist; **~malerei** *f* miniature painting; **~staat** *m* tiny state *or* country.
Mini-: ~bar *f (im Hotel etc)* mini-bar; **~bikini** *m* scanty bikini; **~bus** *m* minibus; **~car** *m* minicab; **~computer** *m* minicomputer; **~golf** *nt* crazy golf; **~-Kassette** *f* mini-cassette.
minimal [1] *adj Unterschied, Arbeitsaufwand* minimal; *Verlust, Verbesserung, Steigerung* marginal; *Gewinn* very small; *Preise, Benzinverbrauch, Gehalt* very low ◆ **mit ~er Anstrengung** with a minimum of effort.
[2] *adv (wenigstens)* at least; *(geringfügig)* minimally, marginally.
Minimal- *in cpds* minimum; **~betrag** *m* minimum amount; **~forderung** *f* minimum demand; **~konsensus** *m* basic area of agreement; **~programm** *nt* basic programme.
minimieren* *vt* to minimize.
Minimierung *f* minimization.
Minimum *nt* **-s, Minima** minimum (*an +dat* of) ◆ **barometrisches ~** *(Met)* barometric low.
Mini-: ~pille *f* mini-pill; **~rock** *m* mini-skirt; **~spion** *m* miniaturized bugging device.
Minister(in *f*) *m* **-s, -** *(Pol)* minister *(Brit)* (*für* of), secretary (*für* for).
Minister|amt *nt* ministerial office.
Ministerial-: ~beamte(r) *m* ministry official; **~direktor** *m* head of a government department, permanent secretary *(Brit)*; **~dirigent, ~rat** *m* assistant head of government department, assistant secretary *(Brit)*.
ministeriell *adj attr* ministerial.
Ministerium *nt* ministry *(Brit)*, department.
Minister-: ~konferenz *f* conference of ministers, ministerial conference; **~präsident** *m* prime minister; *(eines Bundeslandes)* leader of a Federal German state; **~rat** *m* council of ministers; *(von EG)* Council of Ministers; **~sessel** *m* ministerial post.
Ministrant *m (Eccl)* server.
ministrieren* *vi (Eccl)* to serve, to act as server.
Minna *f* **-,** *no pl (dated: Hausangestellte)* maid; *(fig inf)* skivvy *(inf)* ◆ **jdn zur ~ machen** *(inf)* to give sb a piece of one's mind, to tear a strip off sb *(inf)*; *siehe* **grün.**
Minne *f* **-,** *no pl (Liter, Hist)* courtly love.
Minne-: ~dienst *m* homage rendered by a knight to his lady; **~gesang** *m siehe* **~sang**; **~lied** *nt* minnelied; **~sang** *m* minnesong; **~sänger, ~singer** *m* minnesinger.
minoisch *adj* Minoan.
Minorität *f siehe* **Minderheit.**
Minuend *m* **-en, -en** *(Math)* minuend.
minus [1] *prep +gen* minus, less; *(Math)* minus.
[2] *adv* minus; *(Elec)* negative ◆ **~ 10 Grad, 10 Grad ~** minus 10 degrees, 10 degrees below (zero); **~ machen** *(inf)* to make a loss.
Minus *nt* **-, - (a)** *(Fehlbetrag)* deficit; *(auf Konto)* overdraft; *(fig: Nachteil)* bad point; *(in Beruf etc)* disadvantage. **(b)** (*~zeichen*) minus (sign).
Minus-: ~pol *m* negative pole; **~punkt** *m* minus *or* penalty point; *(fig)* minus point; **ein ~punkt für jdn sein** to count against sb, to be a point against sb; **~temperatur** *f* temperature below freezing *or* zero; **~zeichen** *nt* minus sign.
Minute *f* **-, -n** minute; *(fig: Augenblick auch)* moment ◆ **es ist 10 Uhr und 21 ~n** *(form)* it is 21 minutes past 10 o'clock; **auf die ~ (genau/pünktlich)** (right) on the dot; **in letzter ~** at the last moment *or* minute; **~ auf** *or* **um ~ verging** *or* **verstrich** *or* **verrann** *(liter)* the minutes ticked by *or* went by; **auf die ~ kommt es nicht an** a few minutes one way or another don't matter; **es vergeht keine ~, ohne daß** ... not a moment goes by without ...
Minuten-: m~lang [1] *adj attr* several minutes of; [2] *adv* for several minutes; **~schnelle** *f*: **in ~schnelle** in minutes, in a matter of minutes; **~zeiger** *m* minute-hand.
minutiös [minu'tsiø:s], **minuziös** *adj (geh) Nachbildung, Mensch* meticulous; *Schilderung auch, Fragen* detailed.
Minze *f* **-, -n** *(Bot)* mint.
Mio. *abbr of* **Million(en)** m.
mir *pers pron dat of* **ich** to me; *(nach Präpositionen)* me ◆ **ein Freund von ~** a friend of mine; **von ~ aus!** *(inf)* I don't mind, fair enough; **~ nichts, dir nichts** *(inf)* *(unhöflich)* without so much as a by-your-leave; **es war ~ nichts, dir nichts weg** the next thing I knew it had gone; **wie du ~, so ich dir** *(prov)* tit for tat *(inf)*; *(als Drohung)* I'll get my own back (on you); **und das ~!** why me (of all people)?; **daß ihr ~ nicht an die Bücher geht!** *(inf)* don't you touch those books!; **du bist ~ vielleicht einer!** *(inf)* you're a right one, you are! *(inf)*; *siehe auch* **ihm.**
Mirabelle *f* mirabelle, small yellow plum.
Mirakel *nt* **-s, -** *(old liter)* miracle.
Misanthrop *m* **-en, -en** *(geh)* misanthropist.
Misanthropie *f (geh)* misanthropy.
Misch-: ~arbeitsplatz *m (Comput)* mixed work station; **m~bar** *adj* mixable, miscible *(form)*; **m~bar sein** to mix; **~batterie** *f* mixer tap; **~brot** *nt bread made from more than one kind of flour*; **~ehe** *f* mixed marriage.
mischen [1] *vt* to mix; *Tabak-, Tee-, Kaffeesorten auch* to blend; *Karten* to shuffle; *(Comput) Dateien* to merge; *siehe* **gemischt.**
[2] *vr (sich vermengen)* to mix ◆ **sich unter jdn/etw ~** to mix *or* mingle with sb/mix with sth; **sich in etw** *(acc)* **~** to meddle *or* interfere with sth; **sich in das Gespräch ~** to butt *or* cut into the conversation.
[3] *vi (Cards)* to shuffle ◆ **wer mischt?** whose shuffle is it?
Mischer *m* **-s, -** *(inf)* **(a)** *siehe* **Mischpult. (b)** *siehe* **Mischtrommel.**
Misch-: ~farbe *f* mixed *or* blended colour; *(Phys)* secondary colour; **~finanzierung** *f* mixed financing; **~form** *f* mixture; *(von zwei Elementen auch)* hybrid (form); **~futter** *nt (Agr) siehe* **Kraftfutter**; **~gas** *nt mixture of coal gas and water gas*; **~gewebe** *nt* mixed fibres *pl*; **~kalkulation** *f* mixed calculation; **~konzern** *m* conglomerate; **~kultur** *f* **(a)** *(Agr)* mixed cultivation; **~kulturen anbauen** to grow different crops side by side *or* in the same field; **(b)** *(Sociol)* mixed culture.
Mischling *m* **(a)** *(Mensch)* half-caste, half-breed. **(b)** *(Zool)* half-breed.
Mischlingskind *nt* half-caste child.
Misch-: ~masch *m* **-(e)s, -e** *(inf)* hotchpotch, mishmash (*aus* of); *(Essen auch)* concoction; **sie redet einen fürchterlichen ~masch** she speaks a horrible jumble *or* hotchpotch of different languages; **~maschine** *f* cement-mixer; **~poke, ~poche** *f* **-,** *no pl (sl)* clan *(inf)*, mob *(inf)*; **~pult** *nt (Rad, TV)* mixing desk *or* panel; *(von Band)* sound mixer; **~rasse** *f* **(a)** *(Tiere)* crossbreed; **(b)** *(Menschen)* mixed race; **~trommel** *f* (drum in) cement-mixer.
Mischung *f* **(a)** *(das Mischen)* mixing; *(von Tee-, Kaffee-, Tabaksorten auch)*

blending. **(b)** (*lit, fig: Gemischtes*) mixture; (*von Tee etc auch*) blend; (*von Süßigkeiten etc auch*) assortment; (*fig auch*) combination (*aus* of). **(c)** (*Chem*) *siehe* **Gemisch.**

Mischungsverhältnis *nt* ratio/proportions (of a mixture).

Misch-: ~volk *nt* mixed race; **~wald** *m* mixed (deciduous and coniferous) woodland; **~wort** *nt* hybrid word.

miserabel *adj* (*inf*) lousy (*inf*); *Gesundheit* miserable, wretched; *Gefühl* ghastly; *Benehmen* dreadful; *Leistungen auch* pathetic; (*gemein*) *Kerl etc* nasty.

Misere *f* **-, -n** (*von Leuten, Wirtschaft etc*) plight; (*von Hunger, Krieg etc*) misery, miseries *pl* ◆ **in einer ~ stecken** to be in a terrible *or* dreadful state; (*Mensch*) to be in a mess, to have run into trouble; **jdn aus einer ~ herausholen** to get sb out of trouble *or* a mess; **das war eine einzige ~** that was a real disaster; **es ist eine ~, wie/daß ...** it is dreadful how/that ...; **es ist die ~ des Alltags, daß ...** it is one of life's hardships that ...

Miserere *nt* **-(s),** *no pl* **(a)** (*Eccl*) miserere. **(b)** (*Med*) faecal vomiting.

Misogyn *m* **-s** *or* **-en, -en** (*liter*) misogynist.

Mispel *f* **-, -n** medlar (tree).

⚠ **Miß, Miss** *f* **-, Misses** Miss.

⚠ **miß** *imper sing of* **messen.**

⚠ **miß|achten*** *vt insep* **(a)** (*ignorieren*) *Warnung, Ratschlag* to ignore, to disregard; *Gesetz, Verbot* to flout. **(b)** (*geringschätzen*) *jdn* to despise; *Hilfe, Angebot* to disdain.

⚠ **Miß|achtung** *f* **(a)** *siehe vt (a)* disregard; flouting. **(b)** (*Geringschätzung*) disrespect (*gen* for); disdain (*gen* of, for).

⚠ **mißbehagen*** *infin auch* **mißzubehagen** *vi insep +dat* **das mißbehagte ihm** that was not to his liking; **es mißbehagt mir, schon wieder umziehen zu müssen** it ill suits me to have to move again.

⚠ **Mißbehagen** *nt* (*geh*) (*Unbehagen*) uneasiness; (*Mißfallen*) discontent(ment) ◆ **jdm ~ bereiten** to cause sb uneasiness/discontent(ment).

⚠ **mißbilden** *ptp* ⚠**mißgebildet** *vt insep* to deform.

⚠ **Mißbildung** *f* deformity, malformation.

⚠ **mißbilligen*** *vt insep* to disapprove of, to object to.

⚠ **mißbilligend** *adj* disapproving.

⚠ **Mißbilligung** *f* disapproval.

⚠ **Mißbrauch** *m* abuse; (*falsche Anwendung*) misuse; (*von Notbremse, Feuerlöscher etc*) improper use; (*geh: einer Person*) sexual assault (*gen* on) ◆ **~ zur Unzucht** (*Jur*) *sexual offence committed by person in position of authority over victim*; **vor ~ wird gewarnt** use only as directed; (*an Notbremse etc*) do not misuse; **unter ~ seines Amtes** in abuse of his office.

⚠ **mißbrauchen*** *vt insep* to abuse; *Güte auch* to impose upon; (*geh: vergewaltigen*) to assault ◆ **den Namen Gottes ~** (*liter*) to take the Lord's name in vain; **jdn für** *or* **zu etw ~** to use sb for sth *or* to do sth; **jdn zu allem möglichen ~** to impose on sb.

⚠ **mißbräuchlich** *adj* (*form*) *Benutzung* improper; *Anwendung auch* incorrect.

⚠ **mißdeuten*** *vt insep* to misinterpret.

⚠ **Mißdeutung** *f* misinterpretation.

missen *vt* (*geh*) to go *or* do without; *Erfahrung* to miss ◆ **das möchte ich nicht ~** I wouldn't do without it/miss it (for the world); **ich möchte meine Kinder nicht ~** I could not do without my children.

⚠ **Miß|erfolg** *m* failure; (*Theat, Buch etc auch*) flop.

⚠ **Miß|ernte** *f* crop failure.

Missetat *f* (*old, liter*) misdeed, misdemeanour.

Missetäter(in *f*) *m* (*old, liter*) culprit; (*Verbrecher auch*) wrongdoer.

⚠ **mißfallen*** *vi insep irreg +dat* to displease ◆ **es mißfällt mir, wie er ...** I dislike the way he ...

⚠ **Mißfallen** *nt* **-s,** *no pl* displeasure (*über +acc* at), disapproval (*über +acc* of) ◆ **jds ~ erregen** to incur sb's displeasure.

⚠ **Mißfallens-: ~äußerung** *f* expression of disapproval *or* displeasure; **~bekundung, ~kundgebung** *f* expression *or* demonstration of disapproval *or* displeasure.

⚠ **mißfällig** *adj* (*rare*) *Bemerkung* disparaging, deprecatory.

⚠ **Mißgeburt** *f* deformed person/animal; (*fig inf*) failure ◆ **das Kind ist eine ~** the child was born deformed.

⚠ **mißgelaunt** *adj* (*geh*) bad-tempered, ill-humoured.

⚠ **Mißgeschick** *nt* mishap; (*Pech, Unglück*) misfortune ◆ **ein kleines ~** a slight mishap; **vom ~ verfolgt werden** (*geh*) to be dogged by misfortune.

⚠ **Mißgestalt** *f* (*liter*) misshapen figure.

⚠ **mißgestalt** (*liter*), ⚠**mißgestaltet** (*geh*) *adj* misshapen.

⚠ **mißgestimmt** *adj* (*geh*) ill-humoured ◆ **~ sein** to be in an ill humour.

⚠ **mißglücken*** *vi insep aux sein* to fail, to be unsuccessful ◆ **der Versuch ist (ihm) mißglückt** the/his attempt was a failure *or* failed; **er wollte mich überraschen, aber es ist ihm mißglückt** he wanted to surprise me but he failed.

⚠ **mißgönnen*** *vt insep* **jdm etw ~** to (be)grudge sb sth; **sie mißgönnt es ihm, daß er erfolgreich ist** she (be)grudges him his success, she resents his success.

⚠ **Mißgriff** *m* mistake.

⚠ **Mißgunst** *f* resentment, enviousness (*gegenüber* of).

⚠ **mißgünstig** *adj* resentful (*auf +acc* towards).

⚠ **mißhandeln*** *vt insep* to ill-treat, to maltreat.

⚠ **Mißhandlung** *f* ill-treatment, maltreatment; (*Kindes~*) cruelty (to children).

⚠ **Mißhelligkeit** *f* (*geh*) disagreement, difference.

Missingsch *nt* **-,** *no pl mixture of High and Low German.*

Mission *f* (*Eccl, Pol, fig*) mission; (*diplomatische Vertretung*) legation, mission (*US*); (*Gruppe*) delegation ◆ **~ treiben** to do missionary work; **in der ~ tätig sein** to be a missionary.

Missionar(in *f*), **Missionär(in** *f*) (*Aus*) *m* missionary.

missionarisch *adj* missionary.

Missionarsstellung *f* (*fig*) missionary position.

missionieren* [1] *vi* to do missionary work, to proselytize; (*fig*) to preach, to proselytize.
[2] *vt Land, Mensch* to (work to) convert, to proselytize; (*fig*) to convert, to proselytize.

Missionierung *f* conversion, proselytization.

Missions-: ~chef *m* head of a legation/leader of a delegation; **~gesellschaft** *f* missionary society; **~schule** *f* mission school; **~schwester** *f* nun working at a mission.

⚠ **Mißklang** *m* discord (*auch Mus*), dissonance; (*Mißton*) discordant note ◆ **ein ~** (*fig*) a note of discord, a discordant note.

⚠ **Mißkredit** *m, no pl* discredit ◆ **jdn/etw in ~ bringen** to bring sb/sth into discredit, to discredit sb/sth; **in ~ geraten** *or* **kommen** to be discredited.

⚠ **mißlang** *pret of* **mißlingen.**

⚠ **mißlaunig** *adj* bad-tempered, ill-humoured.

⚠ **mißlich** *adj* (*geh*) awkward, difficult; *Umstand auch, Verzögerung* unfortunate, regrettable ◆ **das ist ja eine ~e Sache** that is a bit awkward/unfortunate; **es steht ~ um dieses Vorhaben** the outlook for this plan is not good.

⚠ **Mißlichkeit** *f siehe adj* awkwardness, difficulty; unfortunate nature.

⚠ **mißliebig** *adj* unpopular ◆ **sich (bei jdm) ~ machen** to make oneself unpopular (with sb); **~e Ausländer** foreigners who have fallen out of favour.

⚠ **mißlingen** *pret* ⚠**mißlang,** *ptp* ⚠**mißlungen** *vi aux sein* to fail, to be unsuccessful ◆ **der Versuch ist ihr mißlungen** her attempt failed *or* was unsuccessful; **das ist ihr mißlungen** she failed; **ihm mißlingt alles** everything he does goes wrong; **ein mißlungener Versuch** an unsuccessful attempt.

⚠ **Mißlingen** *nt* **-s,** *no pl* failure.

⚠ **mißlungen** *ptp of* **mißlingen.**

⚠ **Mißmanagement** *nt* mismanagement.

⚠ **Mißmut** *m* sullenness, moroseness; (*Unzufriedenheit*) displeasure, discontent ◆ **seinen ~ über etw** (*acc*) **zeigen/äußern** to show/express one's displeasure *or* discontent at sth.

⚠ **mißmutig** *adj* sullen, morose; (*unzufrieden*) discontented; *Äußerung, Aussehen* disgruntled ◆ **mach nicht so ein ~es Gesicht** don't look so morose.

⚠ **mißraten*** [1] *vi insep irreg aux sein* to go wrong; (*Kind*) to become wayward ◆ **der Kuchen ist mir ~** my cake went wrong *or* was a failure.
[2] *adj Kind* wayward ◆ **der ~e Kuchen** the cake which went wrong.

⚠ **Mißstand** *m* disgrace *no pl*, outrage; (*allgemeiner Zustand*) bad *or* deplorable state of affairs *no pl*; (*Ungerechtigkeit*) abuse; (*Mangel*) defect ◆ **einen ~/~̈e beseitigen** to remedy something which is wrong/things which are wrong; **~̈e in der Regierung/im Management anprangern** to inveigh against misgovernment/mismanagement.

⚠ **Mißstimmung** *f* **(a)** (*Uneinigkeit*) friction, discord ◆ **eine ~** a note of discord, a discordant note. **(b)** (*Mißmut*) ill feeling *no indef art.*

⚠ **Mißton** *m* (*Mus, fig*) discordant note; (*fig auch*) note of discord ◆ **~̈e** (*Klang*) discordant sound; (*fig*) discord.

⚠ **mißtönend,** ⚠**mißtönig** (*rare*) *adj* discordant; *Stimme, Instrument* unpleasant(-sounding).

⚠ **mißtrauen*** *vi insep +dat* to mistrust, to be suspicious *or* wary of.

⚠ **Mißtrauen** *nt* **-s,** *no pl* mistrust, distrust (*gegenüber* of); (*esp einer Sache, Handlung gegenüber*) suspiciousness (*gegenüber* of) ◆ **~ gegen jdn/etw haben** *or* **hegen** (*liter*), **jdm/etw ~ entgegenbringen** to mistrust sb/sth, to be suspicious of sb/sth.

⚠ **Mißtrauens-** (*Parl*): **~antrag** *m* motion of no confidence; **~votum** *nt* vote of no confidence.

⚠ **mißtrauisch** *adj* mistrustful, distrustful; (*argwöhnisch*) suspicious.

⚠ **Mißvergnügen** *nt* (*geh*) displeasure, disgruntlement.

⚠ **mißvergnügt** *adj* (*geh*) disgruntled, displeased.

⚠ **Mißverhältnis** *nt* discrepancy, disparity; (*in Proportionen*) imbalance ◆ **seine Leistung steht im ~ zu seiner Bezahlung** there is a discrepancy *or* disparity between the work he does and his salary.

⚠ **mißverständlich** *adj* unclear ◆ **~e Ausdrücke** expressions which could be misunderstood *or* misleading.

⚠ **Mißverständnis** *nt* **(a)** misunderstanding; (*falsche Vorstellung*) misconception. **(b)** *usu pl* (*Meinungsverschiedenheit*) misunderstanding, disagreement.

⚠ **mißverstehen*** *infin auch* **mißzuverstehen** *vt insep irreg* to misunderstand ◆ **Sie dürfen mich nicht ~** please do not misunderstand me; **in nicht mißzuverstehender Weise** unequivocally.

⚠ **Mißwahl, Misswahl** *f* beauty contest.

⚠ **Mißweisung** *f* (*form*) (*von Kompaß*) magnetic declination *or* variation; (*von Radar*) indication error.

⚠ **Mißwirtschaft** *f* maladministration, mismanagement.

⚠ **Mißwuchs** *m* malformed growth, malformation.

Mist *m* **-es,** *no pl* **(a)** (*Tierkot*) droppings *pl*; (*Pferde~, Kuh~ etc*) dung; (*Dünger*) manure; (*~haufen*) manure *or* muck heap ◆ **~ streuen** *or* **fahren** to spread manure *or* muck (*inf*); **das ist nicht auf seinem ~ gewachsen** (*inf*) he didn't think that up himself.
(b) (*inf*) (*Unsinn*) rubbish, nonsense; (*Schund*) rubbish, trash ◆ **~!** blow!, blast! (*inf*); **so ein ~!** (*inf*) what a darned *or* blasted nuisance (*inf*); **er hat einen ~ geredet** he talked a load of rubbish; **da hat er ~ gemacht** *or* **gebaut** (*sl*) he really messed that up (*inf*); **allerlei ~ machen** to do all sorts of stupid things; **mach keinen ~!** (*sl*) don't be a fool!

Mistbeet *nt* (*Hort*) hotbed.

Mistel *f* **-, -n** mistletoe *no pl.*
Mistelzweig *m* sprig of mistletoe ◆ **ein Kuß unterm ~** a kiss under the mistletoe.
misten[1] [1] *vt* **(a)** *Stall* to muck out; *Acker* to manure. **(b)** *(inf) siehe* **ausmisten.**
[2] *vi (im Stall)* to do the mucking out; *(düngen)* to do the manuring.
misten[2] *vi impers (Naut)* **es mistet** it is misting over.
Mist-: ~gabel *f* pitchfork *(used for shifting manure)*; **~grube** *f siehe* **Jauche(n)grube; ~haufen** *m* manure heap; **~käfer** *m* dung beetle; **~kerl** *m (inf)* dirty swine *(inf)*; **~stück, ~vieh** *nt (sl) (Mann)* bastard *(sl)*; *(Frau auch)* bitch *(sl)*; **~wagen** *m* dung cart; **~wetter** *nt (inf)* lousy weather.
Miszellen *pl (liter)* short articles *or* items ◆ **das fällt unter ~** that comes under miscellaneous.
mit [1] *prep +dat* **(a)** with; *(versehen mit auch)* and ◆ **Tee ~ Zitrone** lemon tea, tea with lemon; **~ dem Hut in der Hand** (with) his hat in his hand; **ein Topf ~ Suppe** a pot of soup; **ein Kleid ~ Jacke** a dress and jacket; **wie wär's ~ einem Bier?** *(inf)* how about a beer?
(b) *(~ Hilfe von)* with ◆ **~ einer Zange** with *or* using a pair of pliers; **~ der Bahn/dem Bus/dem Auto** by train/bus/car; **ich fahre ~ meinem eigenen Auto zur Arbeit** I drive to work in my own car; **~ der Post** by post; **~ Gewalt** by force; **~ Bleistift/Tinte/dem Kugelschreiber schreiben** to write in pencil/ink/ballpoint; **~ dem nächsten Flugzeug/Bus kommen** to come on the next plane/bus; **~ etwas Liebe/Verständnis** with a little love/understanding; **~ einem Wort** in a word.
(c) *(zeitlich)* **~ dem Glockenschlage sechs** at *or* on the stroke of six, at six on the dot; **~ achtzehn Jahren** at (the age of) eighteen; **~ einem Mal** all at once, suddenly, all of a sudden; **~ heutigem Tage** *(form)* as from today; **~ beginnendem Sommer** at the start of summer; **~ der Zeit** in time.
(d) *(bei Maß-, Mengenangaben)* **~ 1 sec Vorsprung gewinnen** to win by 1 sec; **etw ~ 50.000 DM versichern** to insure sth for DM 50,000; **~ 80 km/h** at 80 km/h; **~ 4:2 gewinnen** to win 4-2.
(e) *(einschließlich)* with, including ◆ **~ mir waren es 5** there were 5 with *or* including *or* counting me.
(f) *(Begleitumstand, Art und Weise, Eigenschaft)* with ◆ **er ~ seinem Herzfehler kann das nicht** he can't do that with his heart condition; **du ~ deinen dummen Ideen** *(inf)* you and your stupid ideas; **~ Muße** at (one's) leisure; **ein junger Dichter, Rosenholz ~ Namen** *(old)* a young poet, Rosenholz by name *or* called Rosenholz; **~ einem Schlage** in a flash; **~ lauter Stimme** in a loud voice; **~ Verlust** at a loss.
(g) *(betreffend)* **was ist ~ ihr los?** what's the matter *or* what's up with her?; **wie geht** *or* **steht es ~ deiner Arbeit?** how is your work going?, how are you getting on with your work?; **~ meiner Reise wird's nichts** my trip is off.
[2] *adv* **er wollte ~** *(inf)* he wanted to come too; **er war ~ dabei** he went *or* came too; **er ist ~ der Beste der Gruppe/Mannschaft** he is one of *or* among the best in the group/the team; **das gehört ~ dazu** that's part and parcel of it; **etw ~ in Betracht ziehen** to consider sth as well.
Mit|angeklagte(r) *mf* co-defendant.
Mit|arbeit *f* cooperation, collaboration; *(Hilfe auch)* assistance; *(Teilnahme)* participation *(auch Sch)* ◆ **~ bei/an etw** work on sth; **er ist an einer ~ bei diesem Projekt interessiert** he is interested in working on this project; **unter ~ von** in collaboration with.
mit|arbeiten *vi sep (mithelfen)* to cooperate *(bei* on); *(bei Projekt etc)* to collaborate ◆ **an** *or* **bei etw ~** to work on sth; **er hat beim Bau des Hauses mitgearbeitet** he helped build the house; **beim Unterricht ~** to take an active part in lessons; **seine Frau arbeitet mit** *(inf)* his wife works too.
Mit|arbeiter(in *f)* *m (Betriebsangehöriger)* employee; *(Kollege)* colleague; *(an Projekt etc)* collaborator ◆ **die ~ an diesem Projekt/bei dieser Firma** those who work on this project/for this firm; **freier ~** freelance.
Mit|arbeiterstab *m* staff.
Mitbegründer *m* co-founder.
mitbekommen* *vt sep irreg* **(a) etw ~** to get *or* be given sth to take with one; *Rat, Ausbildung* to get *or* be given sth; *(als Mitgift)* to be given sth as a dowry. **(b)** *(inf) (verstehen)* to get *(inf)*; *(bemerken)* to realize ◆ **hast du das noch nicht ~?** *(erfahren)* you mean you didn't know that?
mitbenutzen*, mitbenützen* *(S Ger) vt sep* to share (the use of).
Mitbenutzung *f* joint use.
Mitbesitz *m* co-ownership, joint ownership/property ◆ **~ an etw** *(dat)* **haben** to have a share in the ownership of sth.
Mitbesitzer(in *f)* *m* joint owner, co-owner.
mitbestimmen* *sep* [1] *vi* to have a say *(bei* in); to participate *(bei* in) ◆ **~d sein** *or* **wirken** to have an influence *(bei, für* on).
[2] *vt* to have an influence on.
Mitbestimmung *f* co-determination, participation *(bei* in) ◆ **~ der Arbeiter** *or* **am Arbeitsplatz** worker participation.
Mitbestimmungs-: ~gesetz *nt* worker participation law; **~recht** *nt* right of participation *(in decision making etc)*.
Mitbewerber *m* (fellow) competitor; *(für Stelle)* (fellow) applicant.
Mitbewohner *m* (fellow) occupant ◆ **die ~ in unserem Haus** the other occupants of the house.
mitbringen *vt sep irreg* **(a)** *(beim Kommen bringen)* to bring; *Freund, Begleiter* to bring along; *(beim Zurückkommen)* to bring back ◆ **jdm etw ~** to bring sth for sb *or* sb sth; **jdm etw von der Stadt/vom Bäcker ~** to bring (sb) sth back from town/fetch (sb) sth from the baker's; **was sollen wir der Gastgeberin ~?** what should we take to our hostess?; **die richtige Einstellung ~** to have the right attitude; **bringt gute Laune mit** come ready to enjoy yourselves; **Sie haben schönes Wetter mitgebracht!** lovely weather you've brought with you!
(b) *Mitgift, Kinder* to bring with one ◆ **etw in die Ehe ~** to have sth when one gets married; **sie hat ein ansehnliches Vermögen in die Ehe mitgebracht** she brought a considerable fortune with her when she got married; **meine Frau hat den Hund in die Ehe mitgebracht** my wife had the dog before our marriage; **sie hat zwei Kinder aus der ersten Ehe mitgebracht** she has two children from her first marriage.
(c) *(fig) Befähigung, Voraussetzung etc* to have, to possess.
Mitbringsel *nt (Geschenk)* small present; *(Andenken)* souvenir.
Mitbürger *m* fellow citizen ◆ **meine Stuttgarter ~** my fellow citizens from Stuttgart; *(in Anrede)* fellow citizens of Stuttgart; **die älteren ~** senior citizens.
mitdenken *vi sep irreg (Gedankengänge/Beweisführung mitvollziehen)* to follow sb's train of thought/line of argument ◆ **zum Glück hat er mitgedacht** luckily he did not let me/us *etc* forget; **du denkst ja mit!** good thinking; **denk mal mit** help me/us *etc* think.
mitdürfen *vi sep irreg* **wir durften nicht mit** we weren't allowed to go along.
Mit|eigentum *nt siehe* **Mitbesitz.**
Mit|eigentümer(in *f)* *m siehe* **Mitbesitzer(in).**
mit|einander *adv* with each other, with one another; *(gemeinsam)* together ◆ **alle ~!** all together; **wir haben lange ~ geredet** we had a long talk; **sie reden nicht mehr ~** they are not talking (to each other *or* one another) any more; **guten Tag ~** *(esp S Ger)* hello everybody *or* all.
Mit|einander *nt* **-s,** *no pl* cooperation ◆ **ein ~ ist besser als ein Gegeneinander** it is better to work with each other than against each other.
mit|empfinden* *sep irreg* [1] *vt* to feel too, to share.
[2] *vi* **mit jdm ~** to feel for sb, to sympathize with sb.
Mit|empfinden *nt* sympathy.
Mit|erbe *m,* **Mit|erbin** *f* joint heir ◆ **außer ihm sind es noch 4 ~n** there are 4 other heirs apart from him.
mit|erleben *vt sep Krieg* to live through; *(im Fernsehen)* to watch.
mit|essen *sep irreg* [1] *vt Schale etc* to eat as well; *Mahlzeit* to share.
[2] *vi* **(bei jdm) ~** to eat *or* have a meal with sb; **willst du nicht ~?** why don't you have something to eat too?
Mit|esser *m* **-s, -** blackhead.
mitfahren *vi sep irreg aux sein* to go (with sb) ◆ **sie fährt mit** she is going too/with me/us *etc*; **(mit jdm) ~** to go with sb; *(auf Reise auch)* to travel with sb; *(mitgenommen werden)* to get a lift with sb, to be given a lift by sb; **jdn ~ lassen** to allow sb to go; *(jdn mitnehmen)* to give sb a lift; **kann ich (mit Ihnen) ~?** can you give me a lift?; **er fährt jeden Morgen mit mir im Auto mit** I give him a lift in my car every morning; **wieviel Leute können bei dir ~?** how many people can you take (with you)?; **ich fahre nicht gern mit ihr im Auto mit** I don't like going in her car.
Mitfahrer *m* fellow-passenger; *(vom Fahrer aus gesehen)* passenger.
Mitfahrerzentrale *f* agency for arranging lifts.
Mitfahrgelegenheit *f* lift ◆ **~en nach Rom** lifts offered to Rome.
mitfühlen *vi sep siehe* **mitempfinden.**
mitfühlend *adj* sympathetic, compassionate.
mitführen *vt sep Papiere, Ware etc* to carry (with one); *(Fluß)* to carry along.
mitgeben *vt sep irreg* **jdn jdm ~** to send sb along with sb; **jdm etw ~** to give sb sth to take with them; *Rat, Erziehung* to give sb sth; **das gebe ich dir noch mit** take that (with you) too.
Mitgefangene(r) *mf* fellow prisoner.
Mitgefühl *nt* sympathy.
mitgehen *vi sep irreg aux sein* **(a)** to go too *or* along ◆ **mit jdm ~** to go with sb; *(begleiten auch)* to accompany sb; **gehen Sie mit?** are you going (too)?; **ich gehe bis zur Ecke mit** I'll go to the corner with you/him *etc*; **mit der Zeit ~** to move with the times.
(b) *(fig: Publikum etc)* to respond (favourably) *(mit* to) ◆ **man merkt, wie die Zuhörer richtig (mit ihm) ~** you can see that the audience is really with him.
(c) *(inf)* **etw ~ lassen** to lift *or* pinch sth *(inf)*.
Mitgift *f* **-, -en** dowry.
Mitgiftjäger *m (inf)* dowry-hunter.
Mitglied *nt* member *(gen, bei, in +dat* of) ◆ **~ eines Komitees sein** to sit on *or* be a member of a committee.
Mitglieder-: ~liste *f* list of members; **~versammlung** *f* general meeting.
Mitglieds-: ~ausweis *m* membership card; **~beitrag** *m* membership subscription *or* fee *or* dues *pl.*
Mitgliedschaft *f* membership.
Mitgliedsstaat *m* member state *or* country.
mithaben *vt sep irreg* **etw ~** to have sth (with one); **jdn ~** to have brought sb with one; **hast du alles mit?** have you got everything?
➤ **mithalten** *vi sep irreg (sich beteiligen)* to join in *(mit* with); *(bei Leistung, Tempo etc nachkommen)* *(mit* with) to keep up, to keep pace; *(bei Versteigerung)* to stay in the bidding ◆ **in der Kneipe hat er immer feste mitgehalten** in the pub he would always drink as much as the rest; **bei einer Diskussion ~ können** to be able to hold one's own in a discussion; **er kann so erstklassig Englisch, da kann keiner ~** he speaks such excellent English, no-one can touch him *(inf)*; **ich halte mit** *(mitmachen)* count me in (on that).
mithelfen *vi sep irreg* to help ◆ **beim Bau des Hauses ~** to help build the house; **hilf doch ein bißchen mit** give us *or* lend us a hand.
Mitherausgeber *m* co-editor, joint editor; *(Verlag)* co-publisher.
Mithilfe *f* assistance, aid ◆ **unter ~ der Kollegen** with the aid *or* assistance of

colleagues.
mithin *adv (dated)* therefore, consequently.
mithören *sep* [1] *vt* to listen to (too); *Gespräch* to overhear; *(heimlich)* to listen in on; *Vorlesung* to attend, to go to ◆ **ich habe alles mitgehört** I heard everything.
[2] *vi (zusammen mit jdm)* to listen (too); *(Radio hören, Gespräch belauschen)* to listen in *(bei* on); *(zufällig)* to overhear ◆ **Feind hört mit** *(Mil prov)* careless talk costs lives; *(fig hum)* someone may be listening.
[3] *vi impers* **es hört jd mit** sb is listening.
Mit|inhaber *m (von Haus etc)* joint owner, co-owner; *(von Firma auch)* joint proprietor.
mitkämpfen *vi sep* to fight ◆ **mit jdm ~** to fight alongside sb.
Mitkämpfer *m (im Krieg)* comrade-in-arms; *(Sport)* team-mate; partner.
mitklingen *vi sep irreg (Ton, Saite)* to sound, to resonate ◆ **bei dem ersten Lied klangen eigenartige Töne mit** there were some odd notes in the first song; **in ihrer Äußerung klang ein leichter Vorwurf mit** there was a slight note of reproach in her remark; **Assoziationen, die bei diesem Wort ~** associations contained in this word.
mitkommen *vi sep irreg aux sein* **(a)** to come along *(mit* with); *(Sendung, Brief etc)* to come, to arrive ◆ **kommst du auch mit?** are you coming too?; **ich kann nicht ~** I can't come; **komm doch mit!** (do) come with us/me *etc*!, why don't you come too?; **kommst du mit ins Kino?** are you coming to the cinema (with me/us)?; **bis zum Bahnhof ~** to come as far as the station; **ich bin gerade noch mit dem Zug mitgekommen** I just caught the train.
(b) *(inf) (mithalten)* to keep up; *(verstehen)* to follow ◆ **da komme ich nicht mit** that's beyond me; **sie kommt in der Schule/in Französisch gut mit** she is getting on well at school/with French.
mitkönnen *vi sep irreg (inf)* **(a)** to be able to come/go *(mit* with). **(b)** *(usu neg)* *(inf: verstehen)* to be able to follow ◆ **da kann ich nicht mehr mit** I can't follow that.
mitkriegen *vt sep (inf) siehe* **mitbekommen.**
mitlaufen *vi sep irreg aux sein* to run *(mit* with); *(Rad, Zeiger etc)* to turn ◆ **er läuft beim 100-m-Lauf mit** he's running in the 100 metres.
Mitläufer *m (Pol, pej)* fellow traveller.
Mitlaut *m* consonant.
Mitleid *nt, no pl* pity, compassion *(mit* for); *(Mitgefühl)* sympathy *(mit* with, for).
Mitleidenschaft *f*: **jdn/etw in ~ ziehen** to affect sb/sth (detrimentally).
mitleidig *adj* pitying; *(mitfühlend)* sympathetic; *Mensch auch* compassionate ◆ **~ lächeln** to smile pityingly.
Mitleid(s)-: m~los *adj* pitiless, heartless; **~losigkeit** *f* pitilessness, heartlessness; **m~voll** *adj* sympathetic, compassionate.
mitlernen *vti sep* to learn too; *(durch jdn lernen)* to learn *(mit* from).
mitlesen *vti sep irreg* to read too; *Text* to follow ◆ **etw (mit jdm) ~** to read sth at the same time as sb.
mitmachen *vti sep* **(a)** *(teilnehmen) Spiel, Singen etc* to join in; *Reise, Expedition, Ausflug* to go on; *Kurs* to do; *Mode* to follow ◆ **etw** *or* **bei etw ~** to join in sth; **er hat schon viele Partys mitgemacht** he has been to lots of parties; **er macht alles mit** he always joins in (all the fun); **jede Mode ~** to follow every fashion; **bei der Mode** *or* **da mache ich nicht mit** that's not my scene *(inf)*; **meine Augen/meine Beine machen nicht mehr mit** my eyes/legs are giving up; **wenn das Wetter mitmacht** if the weather cooperates.
(b) *(inf: einverstanden sein)* **da kann ich nicht ~** I can't go along with that; **da macht mein Chef nicht mit** my boss won't go along with that; **das mache ich nicht mehr mit** I've had quite enough (of that); **ich mache das nicht mehr lange mit** I won't take that much longer.
(c) *(erleben)* to live through; *(erleiden)* to go through ◆ **sie hat viel mitgemacht** she has been through a lot in her time.
Mitmensch *m* fellow man *or* creature, neighbour ◆ **wir müssen in jedem den ~en sehen** we must see people as neighbours.
mitmenschlich *adj Kontakte, Probleme etc* human; *Verhalten* considerate.
mitmischen *vi sep (sl) (sich beteiligen)* to be involved *(in +dat, bei* in); *(sich einmischen)* to interfere *(in +dat, bei* in sth).
mitmüssen *vi sep irreg* to have to go/come too.
Mitnahme *f -, no pl* **die ~ von etw empfehlen** to recommend sb to take sth with them.
Mitnahmemarkt *m* cash and carry.
mitnehmen *vt sep irreg* **(a)** to take (with one); *(ausleihen)* to borrow; *(kaufen)* to take ◆ **jdn (im Auto) ~** to give sb a lift; **der Bus konnte nicht alle ~** the bus couldn't take everyone; **sie nimmt alles mit, was sich bietet** she makes the most of everything life has to offer; **(das ist) zum M~** please take one; **einmal Pommes frites zum M~** a bag of chips to take away *(Brit)*, French fries to go *(US)*.
(b) *(erschöpfen) jdn* to exhaust, to weaken; *(beschädigen)* to be bad for ◆ **mitgenommen aussehen** to look the worse for wear.
(c) *(stehlen)* to walk off with.
(d) *(inf) Sehenswürdigkeit, Veranstaltung* to take in.
mitnichten *adv (old)* not at all, by no means, in no way.
Mitra *f -,* **Mitren** *(Eccl)* mitre.
Mitrauchen *nt* passive smoking.
Mitraucher *m* passive smoker.
mitrechnen *vt sep* to count; *Betrag* to count in.
mitreden *sep* [1] *vi (Meinung äußern)* to join in *(bei etw* sth); *(mitbestimmen)* to have a say *(bei* in) ◆ **da kann er nicht ~** he wouldn't know anything about that; **da kann ich ~** I should know; **da kann ich aus Erfahrung ~** I know from my own experience; **sie will überall ~** *(inf)* she always has to have her say.
[2] *vt* **da möchte ich auch ein Wörtchen ~** I'd like to have some say (in this) too; **Sie haben hier nichts mitzureden** this is none of your concern.
mitreisen *vi sep aux sein* to go/travel too *(mit* with).
Mitreisende(r) *mf* fellow passenger/traveller.
mitreißen *vt sep irreg (Fluß, Lawine)* to sweep *or* carry away; *(Fahrzeug)* to carry along ◆ **der Schauspieler/seine Rede hat alle mitgerissen** everyone was carried away by the actor's performance/his speech.
mitreißend *adj Rhythmus, Enthusiasmus* infectious; *Reden, Marschmusik* rousing; *Film, Fußballspiel* thrilling, exciting.
mitsamt *prep +dat* together with.
mitschicken *vt sep (in Brief etc)* to enclose.
mitschleifen *vt sep* to drag along.
mitschleppen *vt sep* **jdn/etw ~** to drag *or* cart *(inf)* sb/sth with one *or* along.
mitschneiden *vt sep irreg* to record.
Mitschnitt *m* recording.
mitschreiben *sep irreg* [1] *vt* **etw ~** to write *or* take sth down; *(Sekretärin)* to take sth down.
[2] *vi* to take notes ◆ **nicht so schnell, ich kann nicht mehr ~** not so fast, I can't keep up.
Mitschrift *f* record; *(von Vorlesung etc)* notes *pl* ◆ **zur ~** for the record; **nicht zur ~ bestimmt** *or* **gedacht** off the record.
Mitschuld *f* share of the blame *or* responsibility *(an +dat* for); *(an einem Verbrechen)* complicity *(an +dat* in) ◆ **ihn trifft eine ~** a share of the blame falls on *or* must be taken by him; *(an Verbrechen)* he is implicated *(an +dat* in).
mitschuldig *adj (an Verbrechen)* implicated *(an +dat* in); *(an Unfall)* partly responsible *or* to blame *(an +dat* for) ◆ **sich ~ machen** to incur (some) blame *(an +dat* for); *(an Verbrechen)* to become implicated *(an +dat* in).
Mitschuldige(r) *mf* accomplice; *(Helfershelfer)* accessory.
Mitschüler *m* school-friend; *(in derselben Klasse)* class-mate.
mitschwingen *vi sep irreg (lit)* to resonate too ◆ **was bei** *or* **in diesem Wort mitschwingt** the overtones *or* associations contained in *or* conjured up by this word; **in seiner Stimme schwang ein Ton von Enttäuschung mit** there was a note of disappointment in his voice.
mitsingen *sep irreg* [1] *vt* to join in (singing).
[2] *vi* to join in the singing, to sing along ◆ **in einer Oper/einem Chor** *etc* **~** to sing in an opera/choir *etc.*
mitspielen *vi sep* **(a)** to play too; *(in Mannschaft etc)* to play *(bei* in) ◆ **in einem Film/bei einem Theaterstück ~** to be in a film/play; **bei einem Orchester ~** to play in an orchestra; **wer spielt mit?** who wants to play?; *(in Mannschaft)* who's playing?; *(Theat etc)* who's in it?
(b) *(fig inf: mitmachen)* to play along *(inf)*.
(c) *(Gründe, Motive)* to play a part *or* role *(bei* in), to be involved *(bei* in).
(d) *(Schaden zufügen)* **er hat ihr übel/schlimm/arg/hart mitgespielt** he has treated her badly; **das Leben hat ihr übel** *etc* **mitgespielt** she has had a hard life, life has been hard to her.
Mitspieler *m (Sport)* player; *(Theat)* member of the cast ◆ **seine ~** his team-mates; the other members of the cast.
Mitsprache *f* a say.
Mitspracherecht *nt* right to a say in a matter ◆ **jdm ein ~ einräumen** *or* **gewähren** to allow *or* grant sb a say *(bei* in); **bei dieser Entscheidung möchte ich ein ~** I want to have a say in this matter.
mitsprechen *sep irreg* [1] *vt Gebet* to join in (saying) ◆ **etw (mit jdm) ~** to say sth with *or* at the same time as sb.
[2] *vi* to join in ◆ **bei etw ~** to join in sth; *(mitbestimmen)* to have a say in sth; **sie will überall ~** she always wants to have her say.
Mitstreiter *m (geh)* comrade-in-arms.
⚠ **mittag** *adv* **gestern/heute/morgen ~** at midday yesterday/today/tomorrow, yesterday/today/tomorrow lunchtime; **Dienstag ~** midday Tuesday, Tuesday (at) midday, Tuesday lunchtime.
Mittag[1] *m* **-(e)s, -e (a)** midday ◆ **gegen ~** around *or* about midday *or* noon; **über ~** at midday, at lunchtime(s); **jeden ~** every day at midday, every lunchtime; **jeden ~ gegen halb eins** every day at half past twelve; **des ~s** *(geh)* around noon *or* midday; **eines ~s** *(geh)* one day around noon *or* midday; **zu ~ essen** to have lunch *or* dinner *or* one's midday meal; **etwas Warmes zu ~ essen** to have a cooked lunch.
(b) *(old, liter: Süden)* south.
(c) *(inf: Pause)* lunch-hour, lunch-break ◆ **~ machen/haben** to take/have one's lunch-hour *or* lunch-break; **sie macht gerade ~** she's (off) at lunch.
Mittag[2] *nt* **-s,** *no pl (inf)* lunch.
Mittag|essen *nt* lunch, midday meal ◆ **er kam zum ~** he came to lunch; **sie saßen beim ~** they were having lunch *or* their midday meal.
mittägig *adj attr* midday.
mittäglich [1] *adj attr* midday, lunchtime; *Schläfchen* afternoon.
[2] *adv* at lunchtimes.
mittags *adv* at lunchtime ◆ **die Deutschen essen ~ warm** the Germans have a hot meal at midday; **~ (um) 12 Uhr, (um) 12 Uhr ~** at 12 noon, at 12 o'clock midday; **sonnabends ~** Saturday lunchtime.
Mittags-. ~ausgabe *f* midday *or* lunchtime edition; **~brot** *nt (dial)* lunch; **~glut** *(liter)*, **~hitze** *f* midday *or* noonday heat, heat of midday; **~mahl** *nt (liter)*, **~mahlzeit** *f* midday meal; **~pause** *f* lunch-hour, lunch-break; **~pause machen/haben** to take/have one's lunch-hour *or* lunch-break; *(Geschäft etc)* to close at lunchtime; **~ruhe** *f* period of quiet (after lunch); *(in Geschäft)* midday-closing; **~ruhe halten** to have a period of quiet after lunch; to close for lunch; **~schlaf** *m* afternoon nap; **~sonne** *f* midday

sun; **~stunde** *f* midday, noon; **um die** *or* **zur** (*geh*) **~stunde** around midday *or* noon; **~tisch** *m* **(a)** dinner-table; **den ~tisch decken** to lay the table for lunch; **am ~tisch sitzen** to be sitting (at the table) having lunch; **(b)** (*im Restaurant*) businessman's lunch; **~zeit** *f* lunchtime; **während** *or* **in der ~zeit** at lunchtime; **um die ~zeit** around midday *or* lunch-time; **zur ~zeit** (*geh*) at midday.

Mittäter(in *f*) *m* accomplice.

Mittäterschaft *f* complicity ◆ **die ~ leugnen** *or* **abstreiten** to deny complicity.

Mittdreißiger(in *f*) *m* man/woman in his/her mid-thirties.

Mitte *f* **-, -n (a)** (*Mittelpunkt, mittlerer Teil*) middle; (*fig auch, von Kreis, Kugel etc*) centre; (*der Stadt, Sport*) centre ◆ **das Reich der ~** (*liter*) the Middle Kingdom; **ein Buch bis zur ~ lesen** to read half of a book; **~ August** in the middle of August; **~ des Jahres/des Monats** halfway through the year/month; **er ist ~ Vierzig** *or* **der Vierziger** he's in his mid-forties; **die goldene ~** the golden mean; **die rechte ~** a happy medium; **in der ~** in the middle; (*zwischen zwei Menschen*) in between (them/us *etc*); (*zwischen Ortschaften*) halfway, midway; **sie nahmen sie in die ~** they took her between them; *siehe* **ab.**
(b) (*Pol*) centre ◆ **die linke/rechte ~** centre-left/-right; **in der ~ stehen** to be moderate; **in der ~ zwischen** midway between.
(c) (*Gruppe, Gesellschaft*) **einer aus unserer ~** one of us *or* our number; **ich möchte gern in eurer ~ sein** I would like to be with you; **in unserer ~** with us, in our midst, among(st) us; **wir haben ihn in unserer ~ willkommen geheißen** we welcomed him into our midst; **er wurde aus unserer ~ gerissen** he was taken from our midst *or* from amongst us.

mitteilbar *adj* communicable.

▼ **mitteilen** *sep* [1] *vt* **jdm etw ~** to tell sb sth; (*benachrichtigen*) to inform sb of *or* about sth, to communicate sth to sb (*form*); (*bekanntgeben*) to announce sth to sb; (*Comm, Admin*) to inform *or* notify sb of sth; **wir erlauben uns, Ihnen mitzuteilen, daß** ... we beg to inform you that ...; **teile ihm die Nachricht schonend mit** break the news to him gently.
[2] *vr* **(a)** to communicate (*jdm* with sb) ◆ **er kann sich gut/schlecht ~** he finds it easy/difficult to communicate.
(b) (*geh: Stimmung*) to communicate itself (*jdm* to sb).

mitteilsam *adj* communicative; (*pej*) talkative, garrulous.

Mitteilung *f* (*Bekanntgabe*) announcement; (*Erklärung*) statement; (*Benachrichtigung*) notification; (*Comm, Admin*) communication; (*an Mitarbeiter etc*) memo; (*von Korrespondenten, Reporter etc*) report ◆ **jdm (eine) ~ (von etw) machen** (*form*) to inform sb (of sth), to report (sth) to sb; (*bekanntgeben*) to announce sth to sb; (*Erklärung abgeben*) to make a statement (about sth) to sb; (*benachrichtigen*) to inform *or* notify sb (of sth); **eine ~ bekommen, daß** ... to hear that ...

Mitteilungsbedürfnis *nt* need to talk to other people.

mittel *adj siehe* **mittlere(r, s).**

Mittel[1] *nt* **-s, - (a)** (*Math: Durchschnitt*) average ◆ **im ~** on average; **arithmetisches/geometrisches ~** arithmetical/geometrical mean.
(b) (*~ zum Zweck, Transport~ etc*) means *sing*; (*Maßnahme, Methode*) way, method; (*Werbe~, Propaganda~, zur Verkehrskontrolle*) device; (*Lehr~*) aid ◆ **~ und Wege finden** to find ways and means; **~ zum Zweck** a means to an end; **kein ~ unversucht lassen** to try everything; **~ gegen die Inflation** ways of beating inflation; **als letztes** *or* **äußerstes ~** as a last resort; **zu anderen ~n greifen, andere ~ anwenden** to use *or* employ other means *or* methods; **ihm ist jedes ~ recht** he will do anything (to achieve his ends); **ihm war jedes ~ recht, dazu war ihm jedes ~ recht** he did not care how he did it *or* what means he used to achieve his ends; **er ist in der Wahl seiner ~ nicht zimperlich** he is not fussy about what methods he chooses; **etw mit allen ~n verhindern/bekämpfen** to do one's utmost *or* everything one can to prevent/oppose sth; **etw mit allen ~n versuchen** to try one's utmost to do sth; **sie hat mit allen ~n gekämpft, um** ... she fought tooth and nail to ...
(c) *pl* (*Geld~*) funds *pl*, resources *pl*; (*Privat~*) means *pl*, resources *pl*.
(d) *meist nicht übersetzt* (*Medikament, kosmetisch*) preparation; (*Med auch*) drug; (*Medizin*) medicine; (*Putz~*) cleaning agent; (*Flecken~*) spot *or* stain remover; (*Wasch~*) detergent; (*Haarwasch~*) shampoo ◆ **welches ~ nimmst du?** what do you use *or* (*Med: einnehmen*) take?; **ein ~ zum Einreiben** something *or* a lotion/an ointment/a cream to be rubbed in; **das ist ein ~ gegen (meinen) Durchfall/(meine) Schuppen** that is for (my) diarrhoea/dandruff; **~ zum Putzen** cleaning things *pl or* stuff; **sich** (*dat*) **ein ~ (gegen Kopfschmerzen/Husten** *etc*) **verschreiben lassen** to get the doctor to prescribe something (for headaches/a cough *etc*); **welches ~ hat der Arzt dir verschrieben?** what did the doctor give you?; **es gibt kein ~ gegen Schnupfen** there is no cure for the common cold; **das beste ~ für** *or* **gegen etw** the best cure *or* remedy for sth.
(e) (*Phys, Chem*) *siehe* **Medium.**

Mittel[2] *f* **-,** *no pl* (*Typ*) 14 point (type), English (type).

Mittel-: ~achse *f* (*von Fläche, Körper*) central axis; (*von Auto*) central axle; **m~aktiv** *adj* (*Atommüll etc*) intermediate-level; **~alter** *nt* Middle Ages *pl*; **da herrschen Zustände wie im ~alter!** (*inf*) it is positively medieval there; **m~alterlich** *adj* medieval; **~amerika** *nt* Central America (and the Caribbean); **m~amerikanisch** *adj* Central American; **m~bar** *adj* indirect (*auch Jur*); *Schaden* consequential; **~bau** *m* **(a)** (*Gebäude*) central block; **(b)** (*Univ*) non-professorial teaching staff; **m~deutsch** *adj* (*Geog, Ling*) Central German; (*dated Pol*) East German; **~deutsch(e)** *nt* Central German dialects *pl*; **~deutschland** *nt Germany east of the Harz Mountains excluding Pomerania etc*; (*dated Pol: Land*) East Germany; **~ding** *nt* (*Mischung*) cross; **ein/kein ~ding** (*weder das eine noch das andere*) something/nothing in between; **~europa** *nt* Central Europe; **~europäer** *m* Central European; **ich, als normaler ~europäer** (*inf*) any average person like myself; **m~europäisch** *adj* Central European; **m~europäische Zeit** Central European Time; **m~fein** *adj Erbsen etc* medium-sized; *Kaffee, Mehl etc* medium-ground; **~feld** *nt* (*Sport*) midfield; (*die Spieler auch*) midfield players *pl*; **~finger** *m* middle finger; **m~fristig** *adj Finanzplanung, Kredite* medium-term; *Voraussage* medium-range; **~gebirge** *nt* low mountain range; **~gewicht** *nt* middleweight; **Meister im ~gewicht** middleweight champion; **m~groß** *adj* medium-sized; **m~hochdeutsch** *adj* Middle High German; **~hochdeutsch(e)** *nt* Middle High German; **~klasse** *f* **(a)** (*Comm*) middle of the market; **ein Wagen der ~klasse** a mid-range car; **(b)** (*Sociol*) middle classes *pl*; **~klassewagen** *m* mid-range *or* middle of the range car; **m~ländisch** *adj* Mediterranean; **das ~ländische Meer** (*form*) the Mediterranean Sea; **~läufer** *m* (*Sport*) centre-half; **~linie** *f* centre line; **m~los** *adj* without means; (*arm*) impoverished; **~losigkeit** *f* lack of means; (*Armut*) impoverishment; **~maß** *nt* mediocrity *no art*; **das (gesunde) ~maß** the happy medium; **seine Leistungen bewegen sich im ~maß** *or* **gehen nicht über das ~maß hinaus** his performance is no more than mediocre; **m~mäßig** [1] *adj* mediocre; *Schriftsteller, Spieler etc auch* indifferent; **als Redner gibt er eine recht m~mäßige Figur ab** he's a pretty mediocre *or* indifferent speaker; [2] *adv* indifferently; **wie gefällt es dir hier? — so m~mäßig** how do you like it here? — so-so; **~mäßigkeit** *f* mediocrity.

Mittelmeer *nt* Mediterranean (Sea), Med (*inf*).

Mittelmeer- *in cpds* Mediterranean; **~raum** *m* Mediterranean (region), Med (*inf*).

Mittel|ohr-: ~entzündung, ~(ver)eiterung *f* inflammation of the middle ear, otitis (media) (*spec*).

Mittel-: m~prächtig *adj* (*hum inf*) reasonable, not bad *pred*, so-so *pred* (*inf*); (*ziemlich schlecht*) pretty awful (*inf*); **~punkt** *m* (*Math, räumlich*) centre; (*fig: visuell*) focal point; **er muß immer ~punkt sein** *or* **stehen** he always has to be the centre of attention; **er steht im ~punkt des Interesses** he is the centre of attention; **~punktschule** *f school at the centre of a rural catchment area.*

mittels (*geh*), **mittelst** (*old*) *prep +gen or dat* by means of.

Mittel-: ~scheitel *m* centre parting (*Brit*) *or* part (*US*); **~schicht** *f* (*Sociol*) middle class; **~schiff** *nt* (*Archit*) nave; **~schule** *f* **(a)** (*inf: Realschule*) ≃ secondary modern school (*Brit*), junior high (*US*); **(b)** (*Sw, Aus, inf: Oberschule*) secondary school, high school (*US*); **m~schwer** *adj Text* of medium difficulty *pred*; *Verletzungen* moderately severe.

Mittels-: ~mann *m*, *pl* **-männer** *or* **-leute, ~person** (*form*) *f* intermediary.

mittelst *prep* (*old*) *siehe* **mittels.**

Mittel-: ~stand *m* middle classes *pl*; **m~ständig** *adj* (*Bot*) perigynous (*spec*); **m~ständisch** *adj* **(a)** middle-class; **(b)** *Betrieb* medium-sized; **(c)** (*Pol*) centrist; **~ständler** *m* **-s, - (a)** middle-class person; **(b)** (*Comm*) medium-sized company; **(c)** (*Pol*) centrist; **~steinzeit** *f* Mesolithic period; **~stellung** *f* medium setting; (*fig*) intermediate position; **~stimme** *f* (*Mus*) middle part.

Mittelstrecke *f* (*Sport*) middle-distance event; (*Aviat*) medium haul; (*von Rakete etc*) medium range.

Mittelstrecken-: ~flugzeug *nt* medium-haul aircraft; **~lauf** *m* middle-distance race; (*Disziplin*) middle-distance running; **~läufer(in** *f*) *m* middle-distance runner; **~rakete** *f* intermediate-range *or* medium-range missile; **~waffe** *f* intermediate-range weapon.

Mittel-: ~streifen *m* central reservation (*Brit*), median (strip) (*US*); **~stück** *nt* middle *or* centre part; (*von Braten etc*) middle; **~stufe** *f* (*Sch*) middle school (*Brit*), junior high (*US*); **~stürmer** *m* (*Sport*) centre-forward; **~teil** *m or nt* middle section; **~weg** *m* middle course; **der goldene ~weg** the happy medium, the golden mean; **einen ~weg einschlagen** to steer a middle course; **einen ~weg suchen** to try to find a happy medium; **~welle** *f* (*Rad*) medium wave(band); **auf ~welle senden** to broadcast on the medium waveband *or* on (the) medium wave; **~wert** *m* mean; **~wort** *nt* (*Gram*) participle; **~wort der Gegenwart/Vergangenheit** present/past participle.

mitten *adv* **~ an/in/auf/bei etw** (right) in the middle of sth; **~ aus etw** (right) from the middle of sth; (*aus Gedränge etc auch*) from the midst of sth; **~ durch etw** (right) through the middle of sth; **~ darin/darein** (right) in the middle of it; **~ darunter** (*räumlich*) right under it/them; (*dabei*) right amongst *or* in the middle of it/them; **~ (hin)durch** right through the middle; **~ im Urwald** in the middle *or* depths of the jungle; **~ in der Luft/im Atlantik** in mid-air/mid-Atlantic; **~ ins Gesicht** right in the face; **es ist noch ~ in der Nacht** it's still the middle of the night; **~ im Leben** in the middle of life; **~ in** *or* **bei der Arbeit** when I *etc* am/was *etc* in the middle of working; **~ beim Frühstück/Essen sein** to be in the middle of (one's) breakfast/of eating; **~ unter uns** (right) in our midst; **der Stock brach ~ entzwei** the stick broke clean in two.

mitten-: ~drin *adv* (right) in the middle of it; **~drin in der Stadt/der Arbeit** (right) in the middle of the town/one's work; **~drin, etw zu tun** (right) in the middle of doing sth; **~drunter** *adv* (*räumlich*) right at the bottom; (*dabei*) (right) amongst it/them; **er ist immer ~drunter** (*fig*) he's always in the middle of things; **~durch** *adv* (right) through the middle; **~mang** (*dial inf*) [1] *prep +dat or* (*sl*) *acc* among; [2] *adv* (right) in the middle of it/them.

Mitternacht *f* midnight *no art.*

mitternächtig, mitternächtlich *adj attr* midnight ◆ **zu ~er Stunde** (*geh*) at the midnight hour.

Mitternachts-: ~sonne *f* midnight sun; **~stunde** *f* witching hour; **~vase** *f* (*hum*) chamberpot.

Mittfünfziger(in *f*) *m* man/woman in his/her mid-fifties.
Mittler *m* **-s, -** mediator; (*liter: Ideen, Sprache etc*) medium.
Mittler|amt *nt* mediatory position.
mittlere(r, s) *adj attr* **(a)** (*dazwischenliegend*) middle ◆ **der/die/das ~** the middle one; **der M~ Osten** the Middle East; **der ~ Weg** (*fig*) the middle course.
(b) (*den Mittelwert bildend*) medium; (*mittelschwer*) *Kursus, Aufgabe* intermediate; (*durchschnittlich*) average; (*Math*) mean ◆ **von ~m Wert** of medium value; **~r Beamter** *person in the section of the civil service for which the entry requirement is the Abitur,* ≃ civil servant of the administrative class (*Brit*); **~n Alters** middle-aged; *siehe* **Reife.**
Mittler-: ~rolle *f* role of mediator, mediatory role; **m~weile** *adv* in the meantime; **ich habe mich m~weile daran gewöhnt** I've got used to it in the meantime.
mit-: ~tragen *sep irreg* [1] *vt* to help (to) carry; [2] *vi* to help to carry it/them/everything; **~trinken** *sep irreg* [1] *vt* to drink with us/them *etc*; **er wollte nichts ~trinken** he didn't want to join us/them *etc* in a drink; [2] *vi* to have a drink with us/them *etc.*
Mitt-: m~schiffs *adv* (*Naut*) (a)midships; **~sechziger(in** *f*) *m* man/woman in his/her mid-sixties; **~siebziger(in** *f*) *m* man/woman in his/her mid-seventies; **~sommer** *m* midsummer; **~sommernacht** *f* Midsummer's Night.
mittun *vi sep irreg* (*inf*) to join in.
Mitt-: ~vierziger(in *f*) *m* man/woman in his/her mid-forties; **m~wegs** *adv* (*old*) midway; **~woch** *m* **-s, -e** Wednesday; *siehe auch* **Dienstag; m~wochs** *adv* on Wednesdays; *siehe auch* **dienstags.**
mit|unter *adv* from time to time, now and then *or* again, (every) once in a while.
mit|unterschreiben* *vti sep irreg* to sign too.
mitver|antwortlich *adj* jointly responsible *pred.*
Mitver|antwortlichkeit *f* joint responsibility.
Mitver|antwortung *f* share of the responsibility ◆ **~ haben** to have *or* bear a share of the responsibility; **die** *or* **jede ~ ablehnen** to abnegate (all) responsibility.
mitverdienen* *vi sep* to (go out to) work as well.
Mitverfasser *m* co-author.
Mitverschulden *nt* **ihm wurde ein ~ nachgewiesen** he was shown to have been partially *or* partly to blame; **ihn trifft ein ~ an diesem Vorfall** he was partially *or* partly to blame for this incident.
Mitverschwor(e)ne(r) *mf decl as adj* fellow thinker/idealist *etc*, crony (*hum inf*); (*pej, bei Verbrechen*) conspirator.
Mitverschwörer *m* conspirator.
mitversichern* *vt sep* to include in the insurance.
Mitwelt *f* **die ~** the people *or* those about one; **es dauerte lange, bis die ~ seine Leistungen würdigte** it was a long time before his contemporaries learnt to appreciate his achievements.
mitwirken *vi sep* to play a part (*an +dat, bei* in); (*Fakten, Faktoren etc auch*) to contribute (*an +dat, bei* to); (*beteiligt sein*) to be involved (*an +dat, bei* in); (*Schriftsteller, Regisseur etc*) to collaborate (*an +dat, bei* on); (*mitspielen*) (*Schauspieler, Diskussionsteilnehmer*) to take part (*an +dat, bei* in); (*in Film*) to appear (*an +dat, bei* in); (*Tänzer, Orchester, Chor*) to perform (*an +dat, bei* in) ◆ **ohne das M~ des Ministers wäre das unmöglich gewesen** it would have been impossible without the minister's involvement.
Mitwirkende(r) *mf decl as adj* participant (*an +dat, bei* in); (*Mitspieler*) performer (*an +dat, bei* in); (*Schauspieler*) actor (*an +dat, bei* in) ◆ **die ~n** (*Theat*) the cast *pl.*
Mitwirkung *f* (*Beteiligung, Mitarbeit*) involvement (*an +dat, bei* in); (*Zusammenarbeit*) cooperation (*an +dat, bei* in); (*an Buch, Film*) collaboration (*an +dat, bei* on); (*Teilnahme*) (*an Diskussion, Projekt*) participation (*an +dat, bei* in); (*von Schauspieler*) appearance (*an +dat, bei* in); (*von Tänzer, Orchester, Chor*) performance (*an +dat, bei* in) ◆ **unter ~ von** with the assistance *or* aid *or* help of.
Mitwisser(in *f*) *m* **-s, -** (*Jur*) accessory (*gen* to) ◆ **~ sein** to know about it; **~ einer Sache** (*gen*) **sein** to know about sth; **jdn zum ~ machen** to tell sb (all) about it; (*Jur*) to make sb an accessory; **er wollte nicht so viele ~ haben** he didn't want so many people to know about it.
Mitwisserschaft *f* **er wurde wegen ~ angeklagt** he was charged with being an accessory (to the crime); **an seiner ~ kann kein Zweifel bestehen** there can be no doubt that he was an accessory (to it) (*Jur*) *or* that he knew about it.
mitwollen *vi sep* to want to go/come along.
mitzählen *vti sep siehe* **mitrechnen.**
mitziehen *vi sep irreg aux sein* (*fig inf*) to go along with it.
Mixbecher *m* (cocktail) shaker.
mixen *vt Getränke,* (*Rad, TV*) to mix.
Mixer *m* **-s, -** **(a)** (*Bar~*) cocktail waiter. **(b)** (*Küchen~*) blender; (*Rührmaschine*) mixer. **(c)** (*Film, Rad, TV*) mixer.
Mixgetränk *nt* mixed drink; (*alkoholisch*) cocktail; (*Milch~*) milkshake.
Mixtur *f* (*Pharm, Mus, fig*) mixture.
ml *abbr of* **Milliliter** millilitre.
mm *abbr of* **Millimeter.**
Mnemo- [mnemo-]: **~technik** *f* mnemonics *sing*; **m~technisch** *adj* mnemonic.
Mob *m* **-s,** *no pl* (*pej*) mob.
Mobbing *nt no pl* harassment in the workplace.
Möbel *nt* **-s, -** (*~stück*) piece of furniture. **~** *pl* furniture *sing* ◆ **~ rücken** to shift the furniture.
Möbel- *in cpds* furniture; **~lager** *nt* furniture showroom; **~packer** *m* furniture packer, removal man; **~schreiner** *m* cabinetmaker; **~spedition** *f* removal firm; **~stoff** *m* furnishing fabric; **~stück** *nt* piece of furniture; **~tischler** *m* cabinetmaker; **~wagen** *m* removal van (*Brit*) *or* truck, pantechnicon.
mobil *adj* **(a)** mobile; (*Comm, Jur*) *Vermögen, Kapital* movable ◆ **~es Vermögen** movables *pl*; **~ machen** (*Mil*) to mobilize. **(b)** (*inf: flink, munter*) lively. **jdn ~ machen** to liven sb up.
Mobile ['moːbilə] *nt* **-s, -s** mobile.
Mobilfunk *m* cellular radio.
Mobilfunknetz *nt* cellular network.
Mobiliar *nt* **-s,** *no pl* furnishings *pl.*
Mobilien [-iən] *pl* (*old*) furnishings *pl*; (*Jur*) chattels *pl*, movables *pl.*
mobilisieren* *vt* (*Mil, fig*) to mobilize; (*Comm*) *Kapital* to make liquid ◆ **die Straße** *or* **den Mob ~** to rouse the mob.
Mobilität *f* mobility (*auch Sociol*); (*geistige ~*) agility.
Mobil-: ~machung *f* (*Mil*) mobilization; **die ~machung ausrufen/beschließen** to mobilize/decide to mobilize; **~telefon** *nt* portable phone.
möbl. *abbr of* **möbliert** furnished.
möblieren* *vt* to furnish ◆ **neu ~** to refurnish; **ein möbliertes Zimmer** a furnished room; **ein möblierter Herr** (*hum inf*) a lodger; **möbliert wohnen** to live in furnished accommodation.
Mocca *m* **-s, -s** *siehe* **Mokka.**
mochte *pret of* **mögen.**
Möchtegern- *in cpds* (*iro*) would-be.
mod. *abbr of* **modern.**
modal *adj* (*Gram*) modal.
Modalität *f* **(a)** *usu pl* (*von Plan, Vertrag etc*) arrangement; (*von Verfahren, Arbeit*) procedure. **(b)** (*Philos*) modality.
Modal- (*Gram*): **~satz** *m* (adverbial) clause of manner; **~verb** *nt* modal verb.
Modder *m* **-s,** *no pl* (*N Ger*) mud.
modd(e)rig *adj* (*N Ger*) muddy.
Mode *f* **-, -n** fashion; (*Sitte*) custom ◆ **~n** (*Kleider*) fashions, fashionwear *sing*, apparel *sing* (*esp US*); **~ sein** to be fashionable *or* the fashion *or* in vogue; (*Sitte*) to be the custom; **das ist jetzt ~** that's the latest fashion; **Radfahren/Alaska wird jetzt große ~** cycling/Alaska is becoming very fashionable nowadays; **in ~/aus der ~ kommen** to come into/go out of fashion; **die ~** *or* **alle ~n mitmachen, mit** *or* **nach der ~ gehen, sich nach der ~ richten** to keep up with the latest fashions; **sich nach der ~ kleiden** to dress in the height of fashion; **wir wollen keine neuen ~n einführen** (*inf*) we don't want any new-fangled ideas.
Mode-: ~artikel *m* **(a)** fashion accessory; **(b)** (*in Zeitung*) fashion article; **~arzt** *m* fashionable doctor; **~ausdruck** *m* in-phrase, trendy expression (*inf*); (*Wort*) in-word, vogue *or* trendy (*inf*) word; ⚠**m~bewußt** *adj* fashion-conscious; **~farbe** *f* fashionable colour, in-colour (*inf*); **m~gerecht** *adj* fashionable; **~geschäft** *nt* fashion shop; **~haus** *nt* fashion house; **~heft, ~journal** *nt* fashion magazine; **~krankheit** *f* fashionable complaint.
Model[1] ['mɔdl] *nt* **-s, -s** (*Fashion*) model.
Model[2] *nt* **-s, -** (*Cook*) wooden mould.
Modell *nt* **-s, -e** **(a)** model; (*naturgetreue Nachbildung auch*) mock-up. **(b)** (*Art, Foto~*) model ◆ **zu etw ~ stehen** to be the model for sth; **jdm ~ stehen/sitzen** to sit for sb.
Modell-: ~eisenbahn *f* model railway; (*als Spielzeug*) train set; **~flugzeug** *nt* model aeroplane *or* airplane (*US*).
modellieren* *vti* to model.
Modelliermasse *f* modelling clay.
Modell-: ~kleid *nt* model (dress); **~versuch** *m* (*esp Sch*) experiment; **~zeichnung** *f* drawing of a model; (*Art*) drawing from a model.
modeln *vt* to model.
Modem *nt* **-s, -e** modem.
Moden-: ~schau *f* fashion show; **~zeitung** *f* fashion magazine.
Mode-: ~puppe *f*, **~püppchen** *nt* model type (*inf*).
Moder *m* **-s,** *no pl* mustiness; (*geh: Verwesung*) decay; (*Schimmel*) mildew ◆ **es riecht nach ~** it smells musty; **in ~ übergehen** to decay; (*Grabsteine etc*) to become mildewed.
Moderation *f* (*Rad, TV*) presentation ◆ **die ~ heute abend hat:** ... tonight's presenter is ...
Moderator *m*, **Moderatorin** *f* presenter.
Modergeruch *m* musty odour.
moderieren* *vti* (*Rad, TV*) to present ◆ **das M~** the presentation.
mod(e)rig *adj Geruch* musty.
modern[1] *vi aux sein or haben* to rot.
modern[2] *adj* modern *no adv*; (*zeitgemäß*) *Maschine, Vorrichtung auch* up-to-date *no adv*; (*modisch*) fashionable; *Politik, Ansichten, Eltern, Lehrer* progressive ◆ **~ sein** (*Kleidung, Möbel*) to be fashionable; **~ werden** to come into fashion, to become fashionable; **ein ~ eingerichtetes Zimmer** a modern room; **der ~e Mensch** modern man.
Moderne *f* **-,** *no pl* (*geh*) modern age ◆ **das Zeitalter der ~** the modern age.
modernisieren* [1] *vt Gebäude* to modernize; *Gesetz, Arbeitsmethoden, Betrieb auch* to bring up to date; *Kleidung* to revamp, to make more fashionable. [2] *vi* to get up to date.

Modernismus *m* modernism.
modernistisch *adj* modernistic.
Modernität *f* (*geh*) modernity.
Mode-: ~sache *f* **das ist reine ~sache** it's just the fashion; **~salon** *m siehe* **~haus**; **~schau** *f siehe* **Modenschau**; **~schmuck** *m* costume jewellery; **~schöpfer(in** *f*) *m* fashion designer, couturier/couturière; **~schrei** *m* **der letzte ~schrei** the latest fashion; **~schriftsteller** *m* popular writer; **~tanz** *m* popular dance; **~torheit** *f* fashion fad; **~wort** *nt* in-word, vogue *or* trendy (*inf*) word, buzzword; **~zeichner** *m* fashion illustrator; **~zeitschrift** *f siehe* **Modenzeitung.**
Modi *pl of* **Modus.**
Modifikation *f* modification.
modifizieren* *vt* to modify.
Modifizierung *f* modification.
modisch *adj* stylish, fashionable, modish.
Modistin *f* milliner.
Modul[1] *m* **-s, -n** (*Archit*) module; (*Math*) modulus.
Modul[2] *nt* **-s, -e** (*Comput*) module.
modular *adj* (*Comput*) modular.
Modulation *f* modulation.
modulieren* *vt* to modulate.
Modus *m* **-, Modi (a)** way ◆ **~ vivendi** (*geh*) modus vivendi. **(b)** (*Gram*) mood. **(c)** (*Comput*) mode.
Mofa *nt* **-s, -s** small moped, motor-assisted bicycle (*form*).
Mogelei *f* cheating *no pl*.
mogeln *vi* to cheat ◆ **beim Kartenspiel/bei der Prüfung ~** to cheat at cards/in an exam; **nicht ~!** no cheating!
Mogel-: ~packung *f* misleading packaging; **den Wählern eine ~packung verkaufen** (*fig*) to sell the electorate false promises; **~zettel** *m* (*Sch*) crib.
▼ **mögen** *pret* **mochte,** *ptp* **gemocht** [1] *vt* to like ◆ **~ Sie ihn/Operettenmusik?** do you like him/operetta?; **ich mag ihn/Operettenmusik nicht** I don't like *or* care for him/operetta; **sie mag das (gern)** she (really) likes that; **sie mag kein Sauerkraut** she doesn't like sauerkraut; **was möchten Sie, bitte?** what would you like?; (*Verkäufer*) what can I do for you?; **~ Sie eine Praline/etwas Wein?** (*form*) would you like *or* care for a chocolate/some wine?; **nein danke, ich möchte lieber Tee** no thank you, I would prefer tea *or* rather have tea.
[2] *vi* **(a)** (*wollen*) (*eine Praline/etwas Wein etc* ~) to like one/some; (*etw tun* ~) to like to ◆ **ich mag nicht mehr** I've had enough; (*bin am Ende*) I can't take any more; **kommen Sie mit? — ich möchte gern, aber** ... are you coming too? — I'd like to, but ...
(b) (*gehen/fahren wollen*) to want to go ◆ **ich möchte (gern) nach Hause** I want to go home; **ich möchte lieber in die Stadt** I would prefer to go *or* I would rather go into town.
▼ [3] *ptp* **~** *modal aux vb* **(a)** (*im Konjunktiv: Wunsch*) to like to *+infin* ◆ **möchten Sie etwas essen?** would you like *or* care for something to eat?; **wir möchten (gern) etwas trinken** we would like something to drink; **ich möchte gern Herrn Schmidt sprechen** I would like to speak to Mr Schmidt; **hier möchte ich nicht wohnen** (*würde nicht gern*) I wouldn't like to live here; (*will nicht*) I don't want to live here; **ich möchte dazu nichts sagen** I don't want to say anything about that, no comment; **ich hätte gern/lieber dabeisein ~** I would like *or* have liked/prefer *or* have preferred to have been there; **das möchte ich auch wissen** I'd like to know that too; **möge er/mögest du Erfolg haben** (*old*) may he/you be successful.
(b) (*im Konjunktiv: einschränkend*) **man möchte meinen, daß** ... you would think that ...; **ich möchte fast sagen** ... I would almost say ...
(c) (*geh: Einräumung*) **es mag wohl sein, daß er recht hat, aber** ... he may well be right, but ...; **wie dem auch sein mag** however that may be; **was sie auch sagen mag** whatever she says; **oder wie er auch heißen mag** or whatever he is *or* might be *or* may be called; **es mag für dieses Mal hingehen** it's all right this time; **mag kommen was da will** come what may; **mag es schneien, soviel es will** it can snow *or* let it snow as much as it likes; **von mir aus mag er warten** as far as I'm concerned he can wait; **man mag es tun, wie man will, aber** ... you can do it how you like, but ...
(d) (*Vermutung*) **es mochten etwa fünf Stunden vergangen sein** about five hours must *or* would have passed; **sie mag/mochte etwa zwanzig sein** she must *or* would be/have been about twenty; **wie alt mag sie sein?** how old might *or* would she be?, how old is she, I wonder?; **wo mag sie das gehört haben?** where could *or* might she have heard that?; **was mag das wohl heißen?** what might that mean?
(e) (*wollen*) to want ◆ **sie mag nicht bleiben** she doesn't want to stay.
(f) (*Aufforderung, indirekte Rede*) **(sagen Sie ihm,) er möchte zu mir kommen** would you tell him to come and see me; **Sie möchten zu Hause anrufen** you should call home; **du möchtest dich brieflich melden** you should write.
Mogler(in *f*) *m* **-s, -** cheat.
▼ **möglich** [1] *adj* **(a)** possible; (*ausführbar auch*) feasible ◆ **alles ~e** everything you *or* one can think of; **alles M~e tun** to do everything possible *or* everything one can; **aus allen ~en Richtungen** from all directions; **er hat allen ~en Blödsinn gemacht** he did all sorts of stupid things; **so viel/bald wie ~** as much/soon as possible; **das ist schon** *or* **wohl** *or* **durchaus ~** that's quite possible; **wenn es irgend ~ ist** if (it's) at all possible; **können Sie es ~ machen, daß Sie schon morgen kommen** *or* **schon morgen zu kommen?** could you manage to come tomorrow?; **es war mir nicht ~ mitzukommen** I couldn't manage to come, it wasn't possible for me to come; **das ist doch nicht ~!** that's impossible; **nicht ~!** never!, impossible!; **das wäre woanders nicht ~** that couldn't happen anywhere else; **ist denn so was ~?** would you credit it? (*inf*); **er tat sein ~stes** he did his utmost *or* all he could.
(b) (*attr: eventuell*) *Kunden, Interessenten, Nachfolger* potential, possible ◆ **alle ~en Fälle** every eventuality; **alles M~e bedenken** to consider everything.
[2] *adv siehe* **möglichst.**
möglicherweise *adv* possibly ◆ **~ kommt er morgen** he may *or* might (possibly) come tomorrow; **ich habe meinen Regenschirm ~ im Bus vergessen** I may *or* might (possibly) have left my umbrella on the bus; **da liegt ~ ein Mißverständnis vor** it's possible that there is a misunderstanding, there is possibly a misunderstanding.
▼ **Möglichkeit** *f* **(a)** possibility; (*no pl: Ausführbarkeit auch*) feasibility ◆ **es besteht die ~, daß** ... there is a possibility that ..., it is possible that ...; **es besteht die ~ zu kündigen** it would (always) be possible to hand in your notice; **alle ~en in Betracht ziehen** to take all the possibilities into account; **nach ~** if possible; **ist denn das die ~?, ist es die ~!** (*inf*) it's impossible!, I don't believe it!
▼ **(b)** (*Aussicht*) chance; (*Gelegenheit auch*) opportunity ◆ **die ~ haben, etw zu tun** to have the *or* a chance/the *or* an opportunity to do sth *or* of doing sth; **er hatte keine andere ~** he had no other choice *or* alternative.
möglichst *adv* **~ genau/schnell/oft** as accurately/quickly/often as possible; **in ~ kurzer Zeit** as quickly as possible.
Mogul *m* **-s, -n** *or* **-e** (*Hist, fig*) mogul.
Mohair, Mohär [mo'hɛːɐ] *m* **-s, -e** (*Tex*) mohair.
Mohammedaner(in *f*) [mohame'daːnɐ, -ərɪn] *m* **-s, -** Mohammedan.
mohammedanisch [mohame'daːnɪʃ] *adj* Mohammedan.
Mohikaner [mohi'kaːnɐ] *m* **-s, -** Mohican ◆ **der letzte ~, der Letzte der ~** (*lit*) the last of the Mohicans; (*fig*) the very last one.
Mohn *m* **-(e)s, -e (a)** poppy. **(b)** (*~samen*) poppy seed.
Mohn- *in cpds* poppy; (*Cook*) (poppy)seed; **~blume** *f* poppy; **~kuchen** *m* poppy-seed cake.
Mohr *m* **-en, -en** (*old*) (blacka)moor (*old*) ◆ **Othello, der ~ von Venedig** Othello, the Moor of Venice; **schwarz** *or* **braungebrannt wie ein ~** (*dated inf*) as brown as a berry; **der ~ hat seine Schuldigkeit getan, der ~ kann gehen** (*prov*) as soon as you've served your purpose they've no further interest in you.
Möhre *f* **-, -n** carrot.
Mohrenkopf *m small chocolate-covered cream cake.*
Mohrrübe *f* carrot.
⚠ **Moiré** [moa're:] *m or nt* **-s, -s** (*Tex*) moiré.
mokant *adj* (*geh*) sardonic, mocking.
Mokassin *m* **-s, -s** moccasin.
Mokick *nt* **-s, -s** moped with a kick-starter.
mokieren* *vr* to sneer (*über +acc* at).
Mokka *m* **-s, -s** mocha.
Mokka-: ~löffel *m* coffee spoon; **~tasse** *f*, ⚠ **~täßchen** *nt* coffee cup.
Molar(zahn) *m* **-s, -en** molar (tooth).
Molch *m* **-(e)s, -e** salamander.
Moldau *f* **- (a)** (*Fluß*) Vltava. **(b)** (*Republik*) Moldavia.
Mole *f* **-, -n** (*Naut*) mole.
Molekül *nt* **-s, -e, Molekel** (*old*) *nt* **-s, -** *or f* **-, -n** molecule.
molekular *adj* molecular.
Molekular-: ~biologe *m* molecular biologist; **~biologie** *f* molecular biology.
molk *pret of* **melken.**
Molke *f* **-,** *no pl* **Molken** (*dial*) *m* **-s,** *no pl* whey.
Molkerei *f* dairy.
Molkerei-: ~butter *f* blended butter; **~genossenschaft** *f* dairy cooperative; **~produkt** *nt* dairy product.
Moll *nt* **-, -** (*Mus*) minor (key) ◆ **in ~ übergehen** to go into the minor; **a-~** A minor; **a-~-Tonleiter** scale of A minor; **Violinkonzert Nummer 4 a-~** violin concerto Number 4 in A minor; **alles in ~ sehen** to see only the gloomy side of things.
Molle *f* **-, -n** beer ◆ **eine ~ mit Korn** a beer and a (glass of) schnapps.
mollert *adj* (*Aus inf*) plump.
mollig *adj* (*inf*) **(a)** cosy; (*warm, behaglich auch*) snug. **(b)** (*rundlich*) plump.
Moll-: ~tonart *f* minor key; **~tonleiter** *f* minor scale.
Molluske *f* **-, -n** (*spec*) mollusc.
Moloch *m* **-s, -e** Moloch.
Molotowcocktail ['moːlotɔfkɔkteːl] *m* Molotov cocktail.
Molukken *pl* (*Geog*) Moluccas *pl*, Spice Islands *pl*.
Molybdän *nt* **-s,** *no pl* (*abbr* **Mo**) molybdenum.
Moment[1] *m* **-(e)s, -e** moment ◆ **jeden ~** any time *or* minute *or* moment; **einen ~, bitte** one minute *or* moment please; **kleinen ~!** just a second *or* tick (*inf*)!; **~ mal!** just a minute!; **im ~** at the moment; **im letzten/richtigen** *etc* **~** at the last/right *etc* moment; **im ersten ~** for a moment.
Moment[2] *nt* **-(e)s, -e (a)** (*Bestandteil*) element. **(b)** (*Umstand*) fact; (*Faktor*) factor. **(c)** (*Phys*) moment; (*Kraftwirkung*) momentum.
momentan [1] *adj* **(a)** (*vorübergehend*) momentary. **(b)** (*augenblicklich*) present *attr*.
[2] *adv* **(a)** (*vorübergehend*) for a moment, momentarily. **(b)** (*augenblicklich*) at the moment, at present.
Moment|aufnahme *f* (*Phot*) photo(graph).
Monaco ['moːnako, mo'nako] *nt* **-s** Monaco.
Monade *f* (*Philos*) monad.
Monadenlehre, Monadologie *f* (*Philos*) monadology.

➤ SPRACHE AKTIV: **mögen: 1** → 34.2, 34.3, 34.4 **3a** → 35.3, 35.4, 35.5, 36.3 **möglich: 1a** → 36.1, 39.2, 42.3, 43.3, 46.6

Monarch(in *f*) *m* **-en, -en** monarch.
Monarchie *f* monarchy.
monarchisch *adj* monarchic(al).
Monarchist(in *f*) *m* monarchist.
monarchistisch *adj* monarchistic.
Monat *m* **-(e)s, -e** month ♦ **der ~ Mai** the month of May; **sie ist im sechsten ~ (schwanger)** she's over five months pregnant *or* gone (*inf*), she's in the sixth month; **was verdient er im ~?** how much does he earn a month?; **am 12. dieses** *or* **des laufenden ~s** on the 12th (of this month); **auf ~e hinaus** months ahead; **jdn zu drei ~en (Haft) verurteilen** to sentence sb to three months' imprisonment, to send sb down for three months (*inf*); **von ~ zu ~** month by month.
monatelang [1] *adj attr Verhandlungen, Kämpfe* which go/went *etc* on for months ♦ **seine ~e Abwesenheit** his months of absence; **nach ~em Warten** after waiting for months *or* months of waiting; **mit ~er Verspätung** months late.
[2] *adv* for months.
-monatig *adj suf* -month ♦ **ein drei~er Urlaub** a three-month holiday.
monatlich *adj* monthly ♦ **~ stattfinden** to take place every month.
-monatlich *adj suf* **zwei-/drei~** every two/three months; **all~** every month.
Monats-: ~anfang *m* beginning of the month; **~binde** *f* sanitary towel; **~blutung** *f* menstrual period; **~einkommen** *nt* monthly income; **~ende** *nt* end of the month; **~erste(r)** *m decl as adj* first (day) of the month; **~frist** *f* **innerhalb** *or* **binnen ~frist** within a month; **~gehalt** *nt* monthly salary; **ein ~gehalt** one month's salary; **~hälfte** *f* half of the month; **~karte** *f* monthly season ticket; **~lohn** *m* monthly wage; **~lohn bekommen** to be paid monthly; **~mitte** *f* middle of the month; **~name** *m* name of the/a month; **~rate** *f* monthly instalment; **~schrift** *f* monthly (journal *or* periodical); **~wechsel** *m* monthly allowance.
monat(s)weise [1] *adv* every month, monthly.
[2] *adj* monthly.
Mönch *m* **-(e)s, -e** monk; (*Bettel~ auch*) friar ♦ **wie ein ~ leben** to live like a monk.
mönchisch *adj* monastic ♦ **ein ~es Leben führen** (*fig*) to live like a monk.
Mönchs-: ~kapuze *f* cowl; **~kloster** *nt* monastery; (*von Bettelmönchen*) friary; **~kutte** *f* monk's/friar's habit; **~leben** *nt* monastic life; **~orden** *m* monastic order.
Mönch(s)tum *nt* monasticism.
Mönchs-: ~wesen *nt* monasticism; **~zelle** *f* monastic cell.
Mond *m* **-(e)s, -e (a)** moon ♦ **den ~ anbellen** (*fig*) to bay at the moon; **auf** *or* **hinter dem ~ leben** (*inf*) to be *or* live behind the times; **du lebst wohl auf dem ~!** (*inf*) where have you been?; **drei Meilen hinter dem ~** (*inf*) in the Stone Age (*hum*); **in den ~ gucken** (*inf*) to go empty-handed; **deine Uhr geht nach dem ~** (*inf*) your watch/clock is way out (*inf*).
(b) (*old: Monat*) moon (*old*), month.
mondän *adj* chic.
Mond-: ~aufgang *m* moonrise; **~auto** *nt* moon buggy *or* rover; **~bahn** *f* moon's orbit, orbit of the moon; (*Space*) lunar orbit; **m~beschienen** *adj* (*geh*) bathed in moonlight, moonlit.
Mondenschein, Mondesglanz *m* (*poet*) moonlight.
Mond-: ~finsternis *f* eclipse of the moon, lunar eclipse; **~gebirge** *nt* mountains of the moon *pl*; **~gesicht** *nt* moonface; (*gemalt*) *simple representation of a face*; **~gestein** *nt* moon rocks *pl*; **~göttin** *f* moon goddess; **m~hell** *adj* moonlit; **m~hell erleuchtet** lit by the moon, moonlit; **~jahr** *nt* lunar year; **~kalb** *nt* (*dated inf: Dummkopf*) mooncalf; **~krater** *m* lunar crater; **~(lande)fähre** *f* (*Space*) lunar module; **~landschaft** *f* lunar landscape; **~landung** *f* lunar *or* moon landing; **~licht** *nt* moonlight; **m~los** *adj* (*geh*) moonless; **~nacht** *f* (*geh*) moonlit night; **~oberfläche** *f* surface of the moon; **~phasen** *pl* phases of the moon *pl*; **~schein** *m* moonlight; **der kann mir mal im ~schein begegnen!** (*inf*) he can get stuffed (*sl*); **~sichel** *f* (*liter*) crescent moon; **~sonde** *f* (*Space*) lunar probe; **~stein** *m* moonstone; **m~süchtig** *adj* **m~süchtig sein** to sleepwalk; **~süchtigkeit** *f* sleepwalking, somnambulism (*form*); **~umlaufbahn** *f* (*Space*) lunar orbit; **~untergang** *f* moonset.
Monegasse *m* **-n, -n, Monegassin** *f* Monegasque.
monegassisch *adj* Monegasque.
monetär *adj* monetary.
Monetarismus *m* (*Econ*) monetarism.
Monetarist(in *f*) *m* (*Econ*) monetarist.
Moneten *pl* (*sl*) bread *sing* (*sl*), dough *sing* (*sl*) ♦ **~ machen** to make some bread (*sl*) *or* dough (*sl*).
Mongole *m* **-n, -n, Mongolin** *f* Mongolian, Mongol.
Mongolei *f* **die ~** Mongolia; **die Innere/Äußere ~** Inner/Outer Mongolia.
Mongolen-: ~falte *f* epicanthus; **~fleck** *m* Mongolian spot.
mongolid *adj* Mongoloid.
Mongolide(r) *mf decl as adj* Mongoloid.
Mongolin *f siehe* **Mongole.**
mongolisch *adj* Mongolian.
Mongolismus *m* (*Med*) mongolism.
mongoloid *adj* (*Med*) mongoloid.
Mongoloide(r) *mf decl as adj* (*Med*) mongol.
monieren* [1] *vt* to complain about ♦ **sie hat moniert, daß ...** she complained that ...
[2] *vi* to complain.
Monismus *m* (*Philos*) monism.

Monitor *m* (*TV, Phys*) monitor.
Mono-, mono- *in cpds* mono-.
Mono-: m~chrom [mono'kroːm] *adj* monochrome; **m~color** *adj* (*Aus*) **eine m~colore Regierung** a single-party government; **m~gam** *adj* monogamous; **~gamie** *f* monogamy; **~gramm** *nt* monogram; ⚠**~graphie** *f* monograph; **m~kausal** [1] *adj* monocausal; [2] *adv* **ein Problem m~kausal sehen** to attribute a problem to a single cause.
Monokel *nt* **-s, -** monocle.
Monokultur *f* (*Agr*) monoculture.
Monolith *m* **-en, -e(n)** monolith.
monolithisch *adj* (*auch fig*) monolithic.
Monolog *m* **-(e)s, -e** (*Liter, fig*) monologue; (*Selbstgespräch*) soliloquy ♦ **einen ~ sprechen** to hold a monologue/give a soliloquy; **einen ~ halten** (*fig*) to hold a monologue, to talk on and on.
monologisch *adj* monologic(al).
monologisieren* *vi siehe n* to hold a monologue; to soliloquize.
monoman *adj* (*liter*) monomaniacal.
Monomane *m* **-n, -n, Monomanin** *f* (*liter*) monomaniac.
Monomanie *f* (*liter*) monomania; (*fig*) obsession.
Monophthong [mono'ftɔŋ] *m* **-s, -e** (*Ling*) monophthong.
Monopol *nt* **-s, -e** monopoly (*auf +acc, für* on).
Monopol- *in cpds* monopoly; **~bildung** *f* monopolization *no pl*.
monopolisieren* *vt* (*lit, fig*) to monopolize.
Monopolisierung *f* monopolization.
Monopolist(in *f*) *m* monopolist.
Monopol-: ~kapital *nt* (*Kapital*) monopoly capital; (*Kapitalisten*) monopoly capitalism; **~kapitalismus** *m* monopoly capitalism; **~kapitalist** *m* monopolist; **m~kapitalistisch** *adj* monopolistic; **~stellung** *f* monopoly.
Monopoly ® *nt* **-**, *no pl* Monopoly ®.
Monotheismus [monote'ɪsmʊs] *m* monotheism.
monoton *adj* monotonous.
Monotonie *f* monotony.
Monoxid (*spec*), **Monoxyd** *nt* monoxide.
Monster *nt* **-s, -** (*inf*) *siehe* **Monstrum.**
Monster- *in cpds* (*usu pej*) mammoth, monster; **~film** *m* mammoth (film) production.
Monstranz *f* (*Eccl*) monstrance.
Monstren *pl of* **Monstrum.**
monströs *adj* monstrous; (*riesig groß*) monster.
Monstrosität *f* monstrosity; (*riesige Größe*) monstrous size; (*Ungeheuer*) monster.
Monstrum *nt* **-s, Monstren** *or* (*geh*) **Monstra** (*Ungeheuer*) monster; (*fig: Mißbildung*) monstrosity; (*inf: schweres Möbel*) hulking great piece of furniture (*inf*).
Monsun *m* **-s, -e** monsoon.
Monsunregen *m* monsoon rain.
Montag *m* Monday; *siehe* **Dienstag, blau.**
Montage [mɔn'taːʒə] *f* **-, -n (a)** (*Tech*) (*Aufstellung*) installation; (*von Gerüst*) erection; (*Zusammenbau*) assembly; (*Typ*) stripping ♦ **auf ~** (*dat*) **sein** to be away on a job. **(b)** (*Art, Liter*) montage; (*Film*) editing.
Montage-: ~band *nt* assembly line; **~halle** *f* assembly shop; **~werk** *nt* assembly plant.
montags *adv* on Mondays; *siehe* **dienstags.**
Montags|auto *nt* (*hum*) problem car.
Montan-: ~industrie *f* coal and steel industry; **~union** *f* European Coal and Steel Community.
Monte Carlo [-'karlo] *nt* Monte Carlo.
Monteur(in *f*) [mɔn'tøːɐ, -'tøːrɪn] *m* (*Tech*) fitter; (*Aut*) mechanic; (*Heizungs~, Fernmelde~, Elektro~*) engineer; (*Elec*) electrician.
Monteur|anzug [-'tøːɐ-] *m* boiler suit.
montieren* *vt* **(a)** (*Tech*) to install; (*zusammenbauen*) to assemble; (*befestigen*) *Kotflügel, Autoantenne* to fit (*auf or an +acc* to); *Dachantenne* to put up; (*aufstellen*) *Gerüst* to erect.
(b) (*Art, Film, Liter*) *Einzelteile* to create a montage from ♦ **aus etw montiert sein** to be a montage of sth.
Montur *f* (*inf*) (*hum: Arbeitskleidung*) gear (*inf*), rig-out (*inf*); (*Aus: Uniform*) uniform.
Monument *nt* monument.
monumental *adj* monumental.
Monumental- *in cpds* monumental.
Moonboots ['muːnbuːts] *pl* moon boots *pl*.
Moor *nt* **-(e)s, -e** bog; (*Hoch~*) moor.
Moor-: ~bad *nt* mud-bath; **~boden** *m* marshy soil; **~huhn** *nt* grouse.
moorig *adj* boggy.
Moor-: ~kolonie *f* fen community; **~kultur** *f* cultivation of peat bogs; **~land** *nt* marshland; (*Hoch~*) moorland; **~packung** *f* mudpack; **~siedlung** *f siehe* **~kolonie.**
Moos[1] *nt* **-es, -e** moss ♦ **von ~ überzogen** overgrown with moss, moss-grown; **~ ansetzen** to become covered with moss, to become moss-grown; (*fig*) to become hoary with age.
Moos[2] *nt* **-es,** *no pl* (*sl*) bread (*sl*), dough (*sl*).
moos-: ~bedeckt *adj* moss-covered; **~grün** *adj* moss-green.
moosig *adj* mossy.
Moos-: ~rose *f*, **~röschen** *nt* moss rose.
⚠**Mop** *m* **-s, -s** mop.

➤ SPRACHE AKTIV: **Möglichkeit: a** → 39.2, 42.3, 43.3 **b** → 46.1

Möp *m* **-s, -s** *or f* **-, -s: ein fieser** *or* **eine fiese ~** *(dial sl)* a nasty piece of work *(inf)*.
Moped *nt* **-s, -s** moped.
Mopedfahrer *m* moped rider.
Moppel *m* **-s, -** *(inf)* tubby *(inf)*.
moppen *vt* to mop.
Mops *m* **-es, ¨-e (a)** *(Hund)* pug (dog). **(b)** *(Dickwanst)* roly-poly *(inf)*, dumpling *(inf)*. **(c) ¨-e** *pl (sl: Geld)* bread *sing (sl)*, dough *sing (sl)*. **(d) ¨-e** *pl (sl: Busen)* tits *pl (sl)*.
mopsen *vt (dated inf)* to nick *(Brit inf)*, to pinch *(inf)*.
Mops-: m~fidel *adj (dated inf)* chirpy *(inf)*; **~gesicht** *nt (inf)* pug-face, puggy face *(inf)*.
mopsig *adj (inf)* **(a)** *Gesicht* puggy *(inf)*. **(b)** *(frech)* **sich ~ machen, ~ werden** to get cheeky *(esp Brit)* or fresh *(esp US)*.
Moral *f* **-,** *no pl* **(a)** *(Sittlichkeit)* morals *pl*; *(gesellschaftliche Norm auch)* morality ◆ **eine hohe/keine ~ haben** to have high moral standards/no morals; **private ~** personal morals; **die ~ sinkt/steigt** moral standards are declining/rising; **die bürgerliche/sozialistische ~** bourgeois/socialist morality; **gegen die (geltende) ~ verstoßen** to violate the (accepted) moral code; **eine doppelte ~** double standards *pl*, a double standard; **~ predigen** to moralize *(jdm* to sb).
(b) *(Lehre, Nutzanwendung)* moral ◆ **und die ~ von der Geschicht'** and the moral of this story.
(c) *(Ethik)* ethics *pl*, moral code ◆ **nach christlicher ~** according to Christian ethics *or* the Christian (moral) code.
(d) *(Disziplin: von Volk, Soldaten)* morale ◆ **die ~ sinkt** morale is falling *or* getting lower.
Moral- *in cpds* moral; **~apostel** *m (pej)* upholder of moral standards.
Moralin *nt* **-s,** *no pl (hum)* priggishness.
moralinsauer *adj (hum)* priggish.
moralisch *adj* moral ◆ **ein ~ hochstehender Mensch** a person of high moral standing; **das war eine ~e Ohrfeige für die Regierung** that was one in the eye for the government *(inf)*; **einen/seinen M~en haben** *(inf)* to have (a fit of) the blues *(inf)*, to be down in the dumps *(inf)*.
moralisieren* *vi* to moralize.
Moralismus *m (geh)* morality ◆ **einem unbestechlichen ~ leben** to live a life of incorruptible morality.
Moralist(in *f***)** *m* moralist.
moralistisch *adj* moralistic.
Moralität *f* morality; *(Theat)* morality play.
Moral-: ~kodex *m* moral code; **~philosophie** *f* moral philosophy; **~prediger** *m* moralizer; **~predigt** *f* homily, sermon; **~predigten halten** to moralize; **jdm eine ~predigt halten** to give sb a homily *or* sermon; **~theologie** *f* moral theology.
Moräne *f* **-, -n** *(Geol)* moraine.
Morast *m* **-(e)s, -e** *or* **Moräste** *(lit, fig)* mire, quagmire; *(Sumpf auch)* morass.
morastig *adj* marshy; *(schlammig)* muddy.
Moratorium *nt* moratorium.
morbid *adj (Med)* morbid; *(fig geh)* degenerate.
Morbidität *f* morbidity, morbidness; *(fig geh)* degeneracy.
Morbus-Down-Syndrom [-'daʊn-] *nt* Down's syndrome.
Morchel *f* **-, -n** *(Bot)* morel.
Mord *m* **-(e)s, -e** murder, homicide *(US)* *(an +dat* of); *(an Politiker etc)* assassination *(an +dat* of) ◆ **wegen ~es** for murder *or* homicide *(US)*; **„~ an altem Mann"** "old man slain *or* murdered"; **politischer ~** political killing; **auf ~ sinnen** *(old liter)* to devise murderous schemes; **das ist ja ~!** *(inf)* it's (sheer) murder! *(inf)*; **dann gibt es ~ und Totschlag** *(inf)* all hell will be let loose *(inf)*, there'll be hell to pay *(inf)*; **von ~ und Totschlag handeln** to be full of violence.
Mord-: ~anklage *f* murder charge, charge of homicide *(US)*; **~anklage erheben** to lay a murder charge *or* a charge of homicide *(US)*; **unter ~anklage stehen** to be on a murder charge *or* charge of homicide *(US)*; **~anschlag** *m* assassination *(auf +acc* of); *(erfolglos)* assassination attempt *(auf +acc* on), attempted assassination *(auf +acc* of); **einen ~anschlag verüben** to carry out an assassination attempt; **einen ~anschlag auf jdn verüben** to assassinate/try to assassinate sb; **~brenner** *m (old liter)* arsonist, incendiary; **~bube** *m (obs)* murderer; **~drohung** *f* threat on one's life, murder threat.
morden *vti (liter)* to murder, to kill, to slay *(liter)* ◆ **das sinnlose M~** senseless killing.
Mörder *m* **-s, -** murderer *(auch Jur)*, killer; *(Attentäter)* assassin.
Mörder-: ~bande *f* gang *or* bunch of murderers *or* killers; **~grube** *f*: **aus seinem Herzen keine ~grube machen** to speak frankly; **~hand** *f (old, liter)*: **durch ~hand fallen/sterben** to die *or* perish *(old)* at the hands of a murderer.
Mörderin *f* murderer, murderess, killer; *(Attentäterin)* assassin.
mörderisch [1] *adj (fig) (schrecklich)* dreadful, terrible, murderous; *Tempo auch* breakneck *attr*; *Preise* iniquitous; *Konkurrenzkampf* cutthroat.
[2] *adv (inf: entsetzlich)* dreadfully, terribly, murderously ◆ **~ fluchen** to curse like blazes *(inf)*; **~ schreien** to scream blue murder *(inf)*.
Mord-: ~fall *m* murder *or* homicide *(US)* (case); **der ~fall Dr. Praun** the Dr Praun murder *or* homicide *(US)* (case); **~gier** *f (geh)* desire to kill; **m~gierig** *adj (geh)* bloodthirsty; **~instrument** *nt* murder weapon.
mordio *interj (old) siehe* **zetermordio, Zeter.**
Mord-: ~kommission *f* murder squad, homicide squad *or* division *(US)*; **~lust** *f* desire to kill; ⚠**~prozeß** *m* murder trial.
Mords- *in cpds (inf)* incredible, terrible, awful; *(toll, prima)* hell of a *(inf)*; **~ding** *nt (inf)* whopper *(inf)*; **~dusel** *m (inf)* tremendous stroke of luck; **einen ~dusel haben** to be dead lucky *(inf)*; **~gaudi** *f (S Ger inf)* whale of a time *(inf)*; **~geld** *nt (inf)* fantastic amount of money; **~glück** *nt (inf) siehe* **~dusel**; **~kerl** *m (inf)* **(a)** *(verwegener Mensch)* hell of a guy *(inf)*; **(b)** *(starker Mann)* enormous fellow *or* guy *(inf)*; **~krach** *m (inf)* hell of a *(inf)* or fearful *or* terrible din; **~lärm** *m (inf)* hell of a *(inf)* or fearful *or* terrible noise; **m~mäßig** *(inf)* [1] *adj* incredible; [2] *adv (+vb)* incredibly, terribly, awfully; *(+adj, ptp auch)* helluva *(sl)*, bloody *(Brit sl)*; **~wut** *f (inf)* terrible temper *or* rage; **eine ~wut im Bauch haben** to be in a hell of a *(inf)* or terrible temper *or* rage.
Mord-: ~tat *f (liter)* murderous deed; **~verdacht** *m* suspicion of murder; **unter ~verdacht** *(dat)* **stehen** to be suspected of murder; **~waffe** *f* murder weapon.
Mores ['mo:re:s] *pl*: **jdn ~ lehren** *(dated inf)* to teach sb some manners.
Morgen *m* **-s, - (a)** *(Tagesanfang)* morning ◆ **am ~, des ~s** *(geh)* in the morning; **gegen ~** towards (the) morning; **bis in den ~ (hinein)** into the wee small hours *or* the early hours; **am nächsten** *or* **den nächsten ~** the next morning; **eines ~s** one morning; **den ganzen ~ (über)** the whole morning; **es wird ~** day is breaking; **der ~ dämmert** *or* **bricht an, der ~ graut** *or* **zieht herauf** *(all liter)* dawn is breaking; **guten ~!** good morning; **~!** *(inf)* morning, hello, hi *(inf)*; **(jdm) guten ~ sagen** to say good morning (to sb); *(morgens kurz besuchen)* to say hello to sb; **schön** *or* **frisch wie der junge ~** *(liter)* fresh as a daisy.
(b) *no pl (old, liter: Osten)* East.
(c) *(liter: Zukunft)* dawn ◆ **der ~ einer neuen Zeit bricht an** a new age is dawning.
(d) *(Measure)* ≃ acre ◆ **drei ~ Land** three acres of land.
morgen *adv* **(a)** tomorrow ◆ **~ früh/mittag/abend** tomorrow morning/lunchtime/evening; **~ in acht Tagen** tomorrow week, a week (from) tomorrow; **~ um diese(lbe) Zeit** this time tomorrow; **bis ~/~ früh!** see you tomorrow/in the morning; **Kartoffeln gibt es erst wieder ~** we/they *etc* won't have any potatoes till tomorrow; **hast du ~ Zeit?** are you free tomorrow?; **~, ~, nur nicht heute, sagen alle faulen Leute** *(Prov)* tomorrow never comes *(Prov)*; **~ ist auch (noch) ein Tag!** *(Prov)* there's always tomorrow; **die Technik von ~** the technology of tomorrow.
(b) gestern ~ yesterday morning.
Morgen- *in cpds* morning; **~ausgabe** *f* morning edition; **~dämmerung** *f siehe* **~grauen.**
morgendlich *adj* morning *attr*; *(früh~)* early morning *attr* ◆ **die ~e Stille** the quiet of the early morning; **~ frisch aussehen** to look as fresh as a daisy.
Morgen-: ~dunst *m* early morning mist; **~frühe** *f* early morning; **sie brachen in aller ~frühe auf** they left at break of dawn; **~gabe** *f (Hist) gift given to a bride by her husband after the wedding night*; **~grauen** *nt* **-s, -** dawn, daybreak; **im** *or* **beim ~grauen** in the first light of dawn; **~gymnastik** *f* morning exercises *pl*; **~gymnastik machen** to do one's morning exercises; **~land** *nt (old, liter)* Orient, East; **die Weisen aus dem ~land** the Three Wise Men from the East; **~länder(in** *f***)** *m* **-s, -** *(old, iro)* Oriental; **m~ländisch** *adj (old, iro)* Oriental, Eastern; **~licht** *nt* early morning light; **~luft** *f* early morning air; **~luft wittern** *(fig inf)* to see one's chance; **~mantel** *m* dressing-gown; *(für Damen auch)* housecoat; **~muffel** *m (inf)* **er ist ein schrecklicher ~muffel** he's terribly grumpy in the mornings *(inf)*; **~nebel** *m* early morning mist; **~post** *f* morning post *(Brit)* or mail; **~rock** *m* housecoat; **~rot** *nt* **-s,** *no pl*, **~röte** *f* **-, -n** sunrise; *(fig)* dawn(ing); **~rot deutet auf schlechtes Wetter hin** red sky in the morning, shepherd's warning *(prov)*.
morgens *adv* in the morning ◆ **(um) drei Uhr ~, (um) drei Uhr** at three o'clock in the morning, at three a.m.; **~ und abends** morning and evening; *(fig: dauernd)* morning, noon and night; **von ~ bis mittags/abends** in the morning/from morning to night; **nur ~** mornings only; **Freitag ~** on Friday morning.
Morgen-: ~sonne *f* morning sun; **~sonne haben** to get *or* catch the morning sun; **~stern** *m* morning star; *(Schlagwaffe auch)* flail; **~stunde** *f* morning hour; **zu früher ~stunde** early in the morning; **bis in die frühen ~stunden** into the early hours *or* wee small hours; **~stund(e) hat Gold im Mund(e)** *(Prov)* the early bird catches the worm *(Prov)*; **~zug** *m* early (morning) train.
morgig *adj attr* tomorrow's ◆ **die ~e Veranstaltung/Zeitung** tomorrow's event/paper; **der ~e Tag** tomorrow; **sein ~er Besuch** his visit tomorrow.
moribund *adj (Med, fig)* moribund.
Moritat ['mo:rita:t] *f* **-, -en (a)** *(Vortrag)* street ballad. **(b)** *(Geschehen)* murderous deed.
Mormone *m* **-n, -n, Mormonin** *f* Mormon.
mormonisch *adj* Mormon.
Morphem [mɔr'fe:m] *nt* **-s, -e** morpheme.
Morpheus ['mɔrfɔys] *m* **-'** Morpheus ◆ **in ~' Armen ruhen** *(liter)* to be in the arms of Morpheus *(liter)*.
Morphin [mɔr'fi:n] *nt* **-s,** *no pl (Chem) siehe* **Morphium.**
Morphinismus *m* morphine addiction.
Morphinist(in *f***)** *m* morphine addict.
Morphium ['mɔrfiʊm] *nt* **-s,** *no pl* morphine, morphia.
morphiumsüchtig *adj* addicted to morphine.
Morphologie [mɔrfolo'gi:] *f* morphology.
morphologisch [mɔrfo'lo:gɪʃ] *adj* morphological.
morsch *adj (lit, fig)* rotten; *Knochen* brittle; *Gebäude* ramshackle.
Morse-: ~alphabet *nt* Morse (code); **im ~alphabet** in Morse (code);

~apparat *m* Morse telegraph.
morsen [1] *vi* to send a message in Morse (code). [2] *vt* to send in Morse (code).
Mörser *m* **-s, -** mortar (*auch Mil*) ◆ **etw im ~ zerstoßen** to crush sth with a pestle and mortar.
Morsezeichen *nt* Morse signal.
Mortadella *f* **-,** *no pl* mortadella, baloney (*US*).
Mortalität *f, no pl* mortality rate.
Mörtel *m* **-s, -** (*zum Mauern*) mortar; (*Putz*) stucco.
Mosaik *nt* **-s, -e(n)** (*lit, fig*) mosaic.
Mosaik- *in cpds* mosaic; **m~artig** *adj* like a mosaic, tessellated *no adv*; **~fußboden** *m* mosaic *or* tessellated floor; **~stein** *m* tessera.
mosaisch *adj* Mosaic.
Mosambik [mosam'bɪk, -'bi:k] *nt* **-s** Mozambique.
Moschee *f* **-, -n** [-'e:ən] mosque.
Moschus *m* **-,** *no pl* musk.
Moschus|ochse *m* musk-ox.
Möse *f* **-, -n** (*vulg*) cunt (*vulg*).
Mosel[1] *f* **-** (*Geog*) Moselle.
Mosel[2] *m* **-s, -, Moselwein** *m* Moselle (wine).
mosern *vi* (*dial inf*) to gripe (*inf*), to belly-ache (*inf*) ◆ **er hat immer was zu ~** he always has something to gripe *or* belly-ache about (*inf*).
Moses[1] *m* **-** *or* (*liter*) **Mosis** Moses ◆ **bin ich ~?** (*hum inf*) don't ask me; *siehe* **Buch**.
Moses[2] *m* **-, -** (*Naut inf*) ship's boy.
Moskau *nt* **-s** Moscow.
Moskauer *adj attr* Moscow *attr*.
Moskauer(in *f***)** *m* **-s, -** Muscovite.
Moskito *m* **-s, -s** mosquito.
Moskitonetz *nt* mosquito net.
Moskowiter *adj attr* Muscovite.
Moskowiter(in *f***)** *m* **-s, -** Muscovite.
Moslem *m* **-s, -s** Moslem.
moslemisch *adj attr* Moslem.
Most *m* **-(e)s,** *no pl* **(a)** (unfermented) fruit juice; (*für Wein*) must. **(b)** (*S Ger, Sw: Obstwein*) fruit wine; (*Birnen~*) perry; (*Apfel~*) cider.
Most|apfel *m* cider apple.
Mostgewicht *nt* specific gravity of the must.
Mostrich *m* **-s,** *no pl* (*dial*) mustard.
Motel *nt* **-s, -s** motel.
Motette *f* (*Mus*) motet.
Motion *f* **(a)** (*Sw: Antrag*) motion. **(b)** (*Gram: Abwandlung*) inflexion (for gender).
Motiv *nt* **-s, -e (a)** (*Psych, Jur, fig*) motive ◆ **das ~ einer Tat** the motive for a deed; **aus welchem ~ heraus?** for what motive/reason?, what are your/his *etc* motives?; **ohne erkennbares ~** without any apparent motive. **(b)** (*Art, Liter*) subject; (*Leit~, Topos, Mus*) motif.
Motivation [-va'tsio:n] *f* motivation.
Motiv-: **~forschung** *f* motivation research; **m~gleich** *adj* with the same theme *or* motif; **m~gleich sein** to have the same motif.
motivieren* [moti'vi:rən] *vt* **(a)** (*begründen*) **etw (jdm gegenüber) ~** to give (sb) reasons for sth; (*rechtfertigend*) to justify sth (to sb); *Verhalten, Sinneswandel, Abwesenheit* to account for sth (to sb). **(b)** (*anregen*) to motivate.
Motivierung *f* motivation; (*erklärende Rechtfertigung*) explanation.
Moto-Cross *nt* **-, -e** motocross.
Motor ['mo:tɔr, mo'to:ɐ] *m* **-s, -en** [mo'to:rən] motor; (*von Fahrzeug*) engine; (*fig*) driving force (*gen* in).
Motor-: **~antrieb** *m* motor drive; **mit ~antrieb** motor-driven; **~block** *m* engine block; **~boot** *nt* motorboat.
Motor(en)-: **~geräusch** *nt* sound of the/an engine/engines; **~lärm** *m* noise *or* roar of (the) engines; **~öl** *nt* engine oil.
Motorhaube *f* bonnet (*Brit*), hood (*US*); (*Aviat*) engine cowling.
-motorig *adj suf* -engined.
Motorik *f* (*Physiol*) motor activity; (*Lehre*) study of motor activity.
Motoriker(in *f***)** *m* **-s, -** (*Pysch*) motor type.
motorisch *adj* (*Physiol*) motor *attr*.
motorisieren* *vt* to motorize; *Landwirtschaft* to mechanize; (*mit Motor ausstatten*) to fit with an engine ◆ **sich ~** to get motorized, to buy a car/motorcycle *etc*.
Motorisierung *f, no pl siehe vt* motorization; mechanization; fitting with an engine.
Motor-: **~jacht** *f* motor yacht; **~kühlung** *f* engine cooling system; **~leistung** *f* engine performance.
Motorrad ['mo:tɔrra:t, mo'to:ɐra:t] *nt* motorbike, motorcycle ◆ **fahren Sie (ein) ~?** do you ride a motorbike?
Motorrad-: **~fahrer** *m* motorcyclist; **~rennen** *nt* motorcycle race; (*Sportart*) motorcycle racing; **~rennfahrer** *m* motorcycle racer; **~sport** *m* motorcycle racing.
Motor-: **~raum** *m* engine compartment; **~roller** *m* (motor) scooter; **~säge** *f* power saw; **~schaden** *m* engine trouble *no pl*; **~schiff** *nt* motor vessel *or* ship; **~schlitten** *m* motorized sleigh; **~sport** *m* motor sport.
Motte *f* **-, -n (a)** moth ◆ **von ~n zerfressen** moth-eaten; **angezogen wie die ~n vom Licht** attracted like moths to a flame; **du kriegst die ~n!** (*sl*) blow me! (*inf*). **(b)** (*dated inf: Mädchen*) **eine kesse/flotte ~** a cheeky/bright young thing (*inf*).
Motten-: **m~fest** *adj* mothproof; **~kiste** *f* (*fig*) **etw aus der ~kiste hervorholen** to dig sth out; **aus der ~kiste des 19. Jahrhunderts stammen** (*inf*) to be a relic of the 19th century; **~kugel** *f* mothball; **~pulver** *nt* moth powder; **m~zerfressen** *adj* moth-eaten.
Motto *nt* **-s, -s (a)** (*Wahlspruch*) motto ◆ **unter dem ~ ... stehen** to have ... as a *or* one's motto. **(b)** (*in Buch*) epigraph. **(c)** (*Kennwort*) password.
motzen *vi* (*sl*) to beef (*inf*), to grouse (*inf*) ◆ **was hast du jetzt zu ~?** what are you beefing *or* grousing about now? (*inf*).
mouillieren* [mu'ji:rən] *vt* (*Ling*) to palatalize.
Mountainbike *nt* **-s, -s** mountain bike.
moussieren* [mʊ'si:rən] *vi* to effervesce.
Möwe *f* **-, -n** seagull, gull.
Mozambique [mozam'bɪk, -'bi:k] *nt* **-s** *siehe* **Mosambik**.
Mozart-: **~kugel** *f* chocolate truffle with liqueur; **~schleife** *f* Mozart cravat.
MP (a) [ɛm'pe:] *abbr of* **Militärpolizei** Military Police. **(b)** [ɛm'pi:] *abbr of* **Maschinenpistole**.
Mrd. *abbr of* **Milliarde**.
MS [ɛm'|ɛs] *abbr of* **Multiple Sklerose** MS.
MS-: **~-krank** *adj* suffering from MS; **~-kranke(r)** *mf decl as adj* MS sufferer, person with MS.
Ms., Mskr. *abbr of* **Manuskript** ms.
MTA [ɛmte:'|a:] *mf abbr of* **medizinisch-technische Assistentin, medizinisch-technischer Assistent**.
mtl. *abbr of* **monatlich**.
Mücke *f* **-, -n (a)** (*Insekt*) mosquito, midge, gnat ◆ **aus einer ~ einen Elefanten machen** (*inf*) to make a mountain out of a molehill. **(b)** (*sl: Geld*) **(ein paar) ~n** (some) dough (*sl*).
Muckefuck *m* **-s,** *no pl* (*inf*) coffee substitute, ersatz coffee.
mucken [1] *vi* (*inf*) to mutter ◆ **ohne zu ~** without a murmur. [2] *vr* to make a sound.
Mucken *pl* (*inf*) moods *pl* ◆ **(seine) ~ haben** to be moody; (*Sache*) to be temperamental; (*zu diesem Zeitpunkt*) (*Mensch*) to be in one of one's moods; (*Sache*) to play up; **jdm die ~ austreiben** to sort sb out (*inf*).
Mückenstich *m* mosquito *or* gnat bite.
Mucker *m* **-s, - (a)** (*dated*) creep (*inf*). **(b)** (*sl: Musiker*) (session) musician.
muck(i)sch *adj* (*dial*) peeved.
Mucks *m* **-es, -e** (*inf*) sound ◆ **einen/keinen ~ sagen** to make/not to make a sound; (*widersprechend*) to say/not to say a word; **ohne einen ~** (*widerspruchslos*) without a murmur.
mucksen *vr* (*inf*) **sich nicht ~** not to budge (*inf*), not to move (a muscle); (*sich nicht äußern*) not to make a sound; (*Mensch*) not to say a dickybird (*inf*), not to make a sound.
mucksmäuschenstill [-'mɔysçən-] *adj* (*inf*) (as) quiet as a mouse.
Mud, Mudd *m* **-s,** *no pl* (*Naut*) mud.
müde *adj* **(a)** tired; (*erschöpft auch*) weary; *Haupt* weary ◆ **sich ~ laufen** to tire oneself out running about. **(b)** (*überdrüssig*) tired, weary ◆ **einer Sache** (*gen*) **~ werden** to tire *or* weary of sth, to grow tired *or* weary of sth; **einer Sache** (*gen*) **~ sein** to be tired *or* weary of sth; **des Wartens ~ sein** to be tired of waiting; **ich bin es ~, das zu tun** I'm tired *or* weary of doing that; **sie wird nicht ~, das zu tun** she never tires *or* wearies of doing that; **~ abwinken** to make a weary gesture (with one's hand); **keine ~ Mark** (*inf*) not a single penny.
-müde *adj suf* tired *or* weary of ...
Müdigkeit *f* (*Schlafbedürfnis*) tiredness; (*Schläfrigkeit*) sleepiness; (*Erschöpfung auch*) weariness, fatigue ◆ **die ~ überwinden** to overcome one's tiredness; **sich** (*dat*) **die ~ vertreiben, gegen die ~ ankämpfen** to fight one's tiredness; **vor ~** (*dat*) **umfallen** to drop from exhaustion; **nur keine ~ vorschützen!** (*inf*) don't (you) tell me you're tired.
Mudschaheddin, Mudschahidin *m* **-(s), -** Mujaheddin.
Müesli ['my:ɛsli] *nt* **-s, -s** (*Sw*) muesli.
Muezzin [mu'ɛtsi:n] *m* **-s, -s** muezzin.
Muff[1] *m* **-s,** *no pl* (*N Ger*) **(a)** (*Schimmel, Moder*) mildew. **(b)** (*Modergeruch*) musty smell, mustiness; (*fig: Rückständigkeit*) fustiness.
Muff[2] *m* **-(e)s, -e** muff.
Muffe *f* **-, -n (a)** (*Tech*) sleeve. **(b)** (*sl*) **~ kriegen/haben** to be scared stiff (*inf*), to get/have the shits (*sl*); **ihm geht die ~ (eins zu hunderttausend)** he's scared stiff (*inf*).
Muffel *m* **-s, - (a)** (*Hunt: Maul*) muzzle. **(b)** (*inf: Murrkopf*) grouch, grouser.
-muffel *m in cpds* (*inf*) stick-in-the-mud where ... is/are concerned (*inf*).
muff(e)lig *adj* (*inf*) grumpy.
muffeln [1] *vi* (*inf*) (*mürrisch sein*) to be grumpy. [2] *vti* (*mürrisch reden*) to mutter.
müffeln (*dial*) *vi* (*inf*) to smell musty ◆ **es müffelt** there's a musty smell.
Muffensausen *nt* (*sl*): **~ kriegen/haben** to get/be scared stiff (*inf*).
muffig *adj* **(a)** *Geruch* musty. **(b)** *Gesicht* grumpy.
müffig *adj* (*dial*) musty.
mufflig *adj* (*inf*) grumpy.
Mufti *m* **-s, -s** mufti.
Mugel *m* **-s, -n, Mugl** *m* **-s, -(n)** (*Aus inf*) hillock, hummock.
muh *interj* moo.
Mühe *f* **-, -n** trouble; (*Anstrengung auch*) effort; (*Arbeitsaufwand auch*) bother ◆ **ohne ~** without any trouble *or* bother; **nur mit ~** only just; **mit Müh und Not** (*inf*) with great difficulty; **er kann mit Müh und Not seinen Namen schrei-**

ben (*inf*) he can just about write his name; **nur mit Müh und Not kriegt sie mal einen Blumenstrauß von ihm** (*inf*) she's lucky to get a bunch of flowers from him; **alle/viel ~ haben** to have a tremendous amount of/a great deal of trouble *or* bother (*etw zu tun* doing sth); **wenig/keine ~ haben** not to have much trouble *or* bother (*etw zu tun* doing sth); **mit jdm/etw seine ~ haben** to have a great deal of trouble *or* bother with sb/sth; **es ist der** (*gen*) *or* **die ~ wert, es lohnt die ~** it's worth the trouble *or* bother (*etw zu tun* of doing sth); **die kleine ~ hat sich gelohnt** it was worth the little bit of trouble; **sich** (*dat*) **etwas/mehr/keine ~ geben** to take some/more/no trouble; **er hat sich** (*dat*) **große ~ gegeben** he has taken great pains *or* a lot of trouble; **gib dir keine ~!** (*sei still*) save your breath; (*hör auf*) don't bother, save yourself the trouble; **sich** (*dat*) **die ~ machen/nicht machen, etw zu tun** to take the trouble to do sth, to go to the trouble *or* bother of doing sth/not to bother to do sth; **machen Sie sich** (*dat*) **keine ~!** (please) don't go to any trouble *or* bother; **sie hatte sich die ~ umsonst gemacht** her efforts were wasted; **jdm ~ machen** to give sb some trouble *or* bother; **wenn es Ihnen keine ~ macht** if it isn't any *or* too much trouble *or* bother; **viel ~ auf etw** (*acc*) **verwenden** to take a lot of trouble *or* bother with sth; **es hat viel ~ gekostet** it took a great deal of trouble; **verlorene ~** a waste of effort.

mühelos *adj* effortless; *Sieg, Aufstieg auch* easy.

Mühelosigkeit *f siehe adj* effortlessness; ease.

muhen *vi* to moo, to low.

mühen *vr* to strive (*um* for) ♦ **sosehr er sich auch mühte** ... strive as he might ...

mühevoll *adj* laborious, arduous; *Leben* arduous.

Muhkuh *f* (*baby-talk*) moo-cow (*baby-talk*).

Mühlbach *m* mill-stream.

Mühle *f* -, **-n** **(a)** mill; (*Kaffee~*) grinder. **(b)** (*fig*) (*Routine*) treadmill; (*Bürokratie*) wheels of bureaucracy *pl*. **(c)** (*~spiel*) nine men's morris. **(d)** (*inf*) (*Flugzeug*) crate (*inf*); (*Auto auch*) banger (*inf*), jalopy (*inf*); (*Fahrrad*) bone-shaker (*inf*).

Mühl(en)- *in cpds* mill; **~graben** *m* mill race; **~rad** *nt* millwheel; **~stein** *m* millstone.

Mühlespiel *nt* **das ~** nine men's morris.

Muhme *f* -, **-n** (*obs*) aunt.

Mühsal ['my:za:l] *f* -, **-e** (*geh*) tribulation; (*Strapaze*) toil ♦ **die ~e des Lebens** the trials and tribulations of life.

mühsam ['my:za:m] 1 *adj Aufstieg, Weg, Leben* arduous; *Aufgabe, Amt auch* laborious.

2 *adv* with difficulty ♦ **nur ~ vorwärtskommen** to make painfully slow progress; **~ verdientes Geld** hard-earned money.

mühselig ['my:ze:lɪç] *adj* arduous, toilsome (*liter*) ♦ **Ihr M~en und Beladenen** (*Bibl*) ye that labour and are heavy laden; **sich ~ ernähren** *or* **durchschlagen** to toil for one's living.

Mukoviszidose *f* - *no pl* (*Med*) mucoviscidosis (*spec*), cystic fibrosis.

Mulatte *m* **-n, -n, Mulattin** *f* mulatto.

Mulde *f* -, **-n** **(a)** (*Geländesenkung*) hollow. **(b)** (*Trog*) trough. **(c)** (*für Bauschutt*) skip.

Muli *nt or m* **-s, -(s)** **(a)** (*Maultier*) mule. **(b)** (*Ind inf: Gabelstapler*) fork-lift (*inf*).

Mull *m* **-(e)s, -e** **(a)** (*Torf~*) garden peat. **(b)** (*Gewebe*) muslin; (*Med*) gauze.

Müll *m* **-(e)s,** *no pl* (*Haushalts~*) rubbish, garbage (*esp US*), trash (*US*), refuse (*form*); (*Gerümpel*) rubbish, junk, garbage (*esp US*); (*Industrie~*) waste; (*inf: Unsinn*) rubbish (*inf*), trash (*inf*) ♦ **etw in den ~ werfen** to throw sth out; **„~ abladen verboten"** "dumping prohibited", "no tipping" (*Brit*).

Müll-: ~abfuhr *f* (*~abholung*) refuse *or* garbage (*US*) *or* trash (*US*) collection; (*Stadtreinigung*) refuse *etc* collection department; **~abladeplatz** *m* rubbish dump *or* tip (*Brit*), dump.

Mullah *m* **-s, -s** Mullah.

Müllberg *m* rubbish heap.

Mullbinde *f* gauze bandage.

Müll-: ~container *m* rubbish *or* garbage (*US*) skip, dumpster (*US*); **~deponie** *f* waste disposal site (*form*), sanitary (land)fill (*US form*); **~eimer** *m* rubbish bin (*Brit*), garbage can (*US*).

Müller *m* **-s,** - miller.

Müllerin *f* (*obs*) miller's wife ♦ **~ Art** (*Cook*) meunière; **Forelle (nach) ~ Art** trout meunière.

Müll-: ~fahrer *m siehe* **~mann**; **~grube** *f* rubbish (*Brit*) *or* refuse pit; **~haufen** *m* rubbish *or* garbage (*US*) *or* trash (*US*) heap; **~kasten** *m* (*dial*) *siehe* **~tonne**; **~kippe** *f* rubbish *or* garbage (*US*) dump; **~kutscher** (*N Ger*), **~mann** *m, pl* **-männer** *or* **Mülleute** (*inf*) dustman (*Brit*), trash collector (*US*); **~schaufel, ~schippe** *f* dustpan; **~schlucker** *m* **-s,** - refuse chute; **~sortierung** *f, no pl* sifting of waste; **~tonne** *f* dustbin (*Brit*), ashcan (*US*), trashcan (*US*); **~tüte** *f* bin liner.

Müllverbrennungs-: ~anlage *f* incinerating plant; **~ofen** *m* incinerator.

Müll-: ~verfüllung *f, no pl* waste relocation; **~verwertung** *f* refuse utilization; **~verwertungswerk** *nt* waste reprocessing plant; **~wagen** *m* dustcart (*Brit*), garbage truck (*US*).

Mullwindel *f* gauze nappy (*Brit*) *or* diaper (*US*).

mulmig *adj* **(a)** (*morsch*) *Holz etc* rotten. **(b)** (*inf: bedenklich*) uncomfortable ♦ **es wird ~** things are getting (a bit) uncomfortable; **ich hatte ein ~es Gefühl im Magen, mir war ~ zumute** (*lit*) I felt queasy; (*fig*) I had butterflies (in my tummy) (*inf*).

Multi *m* **-s, -s** (*inf*) multinational (organization).

Multi- *in cpds* multi-; **m~funktional** *adj* multi-function(al); **~funktionstastatur** *f* (*Comput*) multi-functional keyboard; **m~kulturell** *adj* multicultural; **multikulturelle Gesellschaft** multicultural society; **m~lateral** *adj* multilateral; **~media** *pl* multimedia *pl*; **m~medial** *adj* multimedia *attr*; **~millionär** *m* multimillionaire; **m~national** *adj* multinational.

multipel *adj* multiple ♦ **multiple Sklerose** multiple sclerosis.

Multiplikand *m* **-en, -en** (*Math*) multiplicand.

Multiplikation *f* multiplication.

Multiplikationszeichen *nt* multiplication sign.

Multiplikator *m* (*Math, fig*) multiplier.

multiplizierbar *adj* multipliable.

multiplizieren* 1 *vt* (*lit, fig*) to multiply (*mit* by).

2 *vr* (*fig*) to multiply.

Multitalent *nt* all-rounder.

Mumie ['mu:miə] *f* mummy ♦ **wie eine wandelnde ~** (*inf*) like death warmed up (*inf*).

mumienhaft [-iən-] *adj* like a mummy.

mumifizieren* *vt* to mummify.

Mumm *m* **-s,** *no pl* (*inf*) **(a)** (*Kraft*) strength. **(b)** (*Mut*) spunk (*dated inf*), guts *pl* (*inf*).

Mummelgreis *m* (*inf*) old dodderer (*inf*).

Mümmelmann *m, pl* **-männer** (*hum*) hare.

mummeln 1 *vti* **(a)** (*undeutlich reden*) to mumble. **(b)** (*behaglich kauen*) to chew slowly, to munch.

2 *vtr* (*einhüllen*) **jdn/sich in etw** (*acc*) **~** to wrap *or* muffle sb/oneself up in sth; **sich ins Bett ~** to huddle up in bed.

mümmeln *vi* to nibble.

Mummenschanz *m* **-es,** *no pl* masquerade.

Mumpitz *m* **-es,** *no pl* (*inf*) balderdash (*dated inf*).

Mumps *m or* (*inf*) *f* **-,** *no pl* (the) mumps *sing*.

München *nt* **-s** Munich.

Münch(e)ner *adj attr* Munich ♦ **das ~ Abkommen** (*Hist*) the Munich Agreement.

Münch(e)ner(in *f*) *m* **-s,** - native of Munich; (*Einwohner*) inhabitant of Munich.

Münchhausen *m* **-s, -(s)** (*fig*) yarn-spinner.

Münchhaus(en)iade *f* cock-and-bull story, tall story.

Mund *m* **-(e)s, ¨er** *or* (*rare*) **-e** *or* **¨e** mouth; (*inf: Mundwerk*) tongue ♦ **ein Glas an den ~ setzen** to raise a glass to one's mouth *or* lips; **~ und Nase aufsperren** to gape (with astonishment *or* amazement); **etw in den ~ nehmen** to put sth in one's mouth; **dieses Wort nehme ich nicht in den ~** I never use that word; **den ~ aufmachen** *or* **auftun** (*lit, fig*) to open one's mouth; (*fig: seine Meinung sagen*) to speak up; **einen großen ~ haben** (*fig*) (*aufschneiden*) to talk big (*inf*); (*frech sein*) to be cheeky (*esp Brit*) *or* fresh (*esp US*); **jdm den ~ verbieten** to order sb to be quiet; **halt den ~!** shut up! (*inf*), hold your tongue!; **er kann den ~ einfach nicht halten** (*inf*) he can't keep his big mouth shut (*inf*); **jdm über den ~ fahren** to cut sb short; **jdm den ~ stopfen** (*inf*) to shut sb up (*inf*); **Sie haben mir das in den ~ gelegt** you're putting words into my mouth; **in aller ~e sein** to be on everyone's lips; **wie aus einem ~e** with one voice; **von ~ zu ~ gehen** to be passed on from person to person; **und das** *or* **so etwas aus deinem/seinem** *etc* **~(e)!** and (that) coming from you/him *etc* too!; **an jds ~(e)** (*dat*) **hängen** (*fig*) to hang on sb's every word; **Sie nehmen mir das Wort aus dem ~(e)** you've taken the (very) words out of my mouth; **jdm nach dem ~(e) reden** (*inf*) to say what sb wants to hear; **sie ist nicht auf den ~ gefallen** (*inf*) she's never at a loss for words; **den ~ (zu/reichlich) voll nehmen** (*inf*) to talk (too/pretty) big (*inf*); **den ~ aufreißen** (*sl*) to talk big (*inf*).

Mund|art *f* dialect ♦ **~ sprechen** to speak dialect.

Mund|art-: ~dichter *m* dialect poet; **~dichtung** *f* dialect poetry/literature.

Mund|art(en)forschung *f* dialect research.

mund|artlich *adj* dialect(al) ♦ **das Wort wird ~ gebraucht** it's a dialect word, the word is used in dialect.

Mund|art-: ~sprecher *m* dialect speaker; **~wörterbuch** *nt* dialect dictionary.

Mund-: ~atmung *f* oral breathing; **~dusche** *f* water jet.

Mündel *nt or* (*Jur*) *m* **-s,** - ward.

mündelsicher *adj* ≃ gilt-edged *no adv*.

munden *vi* (*liter*) **jdm trefflich/köstlich ~** to taste excellent/delicious to sb; **sich** (*dat*) **etw ~ lassen** to savour sth; **es mundete ihm nicht, es wollte ihm nicht ~** he found it unpalatable.

münden *vi aux sein or haben* (*Bach, Fluß*) to flow (*in +acc* into); (*Straße, Gang*) to lead (*in +acc, auf +acc* into); (*fig: Fragen, Probleme*) to lead (*in +acc or dat* to) ♦ **die B 3 mündet bei Celle in die B 1** the B3 joins the B1 at Celle.

Mund-: m~faul *adj* (*inf*) too lazy to say much; **sei doch nicht so m~faul!** make an effort and say something!; **~fäule** *f* (*Med*) stomatitis; **~flora** *f* (*Med*) (bacterial) flora of the oral cavity *or* mouth; **m~gerecht** *adj* bite-sized; **etw m~gerecht schneiden** to cut sth into bite-sized pieces; **jdm etw m~gerecht machen** (*fig*) to make sth attractive *or* palatable to sb; **~geruch** *m* bad breath, halitosis; **etwas gegen ~geruch tun** to do something about one's (bad) breath; **~harmonika** *f* mouth organ, harmonica; **~höhle** *f* oral cavity.

mundig *adj* (*geh*) appetizing, savoury; *Wein* full-bodied.

mündig *adj* of age; (*fig*) mature, responsible ♦ **~ werden** to come of age, to reach *or* attain one's majority; **jdn (für) ~ erklären** to declare sb of age; **der**

~e Bürger the politically mature citizen.
Mündigkeit *f* majority; (*fig*) maturity, responsibility.
Mündigkeits|erklärung *f siehe* **Volljährigkeitserklärung.**
Mündig-: ⚠m~sprechen *vt sep irreg* to declare of age; **~sprechung** *f* declaration of (one's/sb's) majority.
mündlich *adj* verbal; *Prüfung, Leistung* oral ◆ **~e Verhandlung** (*Jur*) hearing; **einen Fall ~ verhandeln** (*Jur*) to hear a case; **etw durch ~e Überlieferung weitergeben** to pass sth on by word of mouth; **das M~e** (*inf: Sch, Univ*) (*in Fremdsprache*) the oral; (*bei Dissertation etc*) the viva (voce); **alles andere** *or* **weitere ~!** I'll tell you the rest when I see you.
Mund-: ~orgel *f* cheng; **~pflege** *f* oral hygiene *no art*; **~propaganda** *f* verbal propaganda; **~raub** *m* (*Jur*) theft of comestibles for personal consumption; **~schenk** *m* (*Hist*) cupbearer; (*fig*) wine-waiter; **~schleimhaut** *f* mucous membrane of the oral cavity *or* mouth; **~schutz** *m* mask (over one's mouth); **~spalte** *f* oral fissure.
M-und-S-Reifen ['ɛmʊnt'ɛs-] *m* winter tyre.
Mund-: ~stellung *f* position of the mouth, embouchure; **~stück** *nt* (*von Pfeife, Blasinstrument*) mouthpiece; (*von Zigarette*) tip; **ohne/mit ~stück** untipped/tipped; **m~tot** *adj* (*inf*) **jdn m~tot machen** to silence sb; **~tuch** *nt* serviette, napkin.
Mündung *f* (*von Fluß, Rohr etc*) mouth; (*Trichter~*) estuary; (*von Straße*) end; (*Gewehr~, Kanonen~*) muzzle ◆ **die ~ des Missouri in den Mississippi** the confluence of the Missouri and the Mississippi, the point where the Missouri flows into the Mississippi; **die ~ der Straße auf die B 11** the point where the road joins the B11.
Mündungsfeuer *nt* flash from the muzzle.
Mund-: ~verkehr *m* oral intercourse; **~voll** *m* **ein/ein paar ~voll** a mouthful/a few mouthfuls; **~vorrat** *m* provisions *pl*; **~wasser** *nt* mouthwash; **~werk** *nt* (*inf*) **ein gutes** *or* **flinkes ~werk haben** to be a fast talker (*inf*); **ein böses ~werk haben** to have a vicious tongue (in one's head); **ein freches/loses** *or* **lockeres/großes ~werk haben** to be cheeky (*esp Brit*) *or* fresh (*esp US*)/have a big mouth (*inf*)/talk big (*inf*); **der mit seinem großen ~werk!** him with all his big talk (*inf*); **ihr ~werk steht nie still** her tongue never stops wagging (*inf*); **~winkel** *m* corner of one's mouth; **~-zu-~-Beatmung** *f* mouth-to-mouth resuscitation.
Munition *f* ammunition; (*Mil: als Sammelbegriff*) munitions *pl* ◆ **~ fassen** (*Mil*) to be supplied with ammunition/munitions; **keine ~ mehr haben** (*lit, fig*) to have run out of ammunition; **seine ~ verschießen** (*lit*) to use up one's ammunition; (*fig*) to shoot one's bolt.
munitionieren* *vt* to provide with ammunition.
Munitions-: ~depot *nt* munitions *or* ammunition dump *or* store; **~fabrik** *f* munitions *or* ordnance factory; **~lager** *nt siehe* **~depot**; **~zug** *m* (*Rail*) ammunition train.
munkeln *vti* **man munkelt** *or* **es wird gemunkelt, daß ...** it's rumoured *or* there's a rumour that ...; **ich habe ~ hören, daß ...** I've heard it rumoured that ...; **man munkelt allerlei, allerlei wird gemunkelt** you hear all kinds of rumours; **im Dunkeln ist gut ~** darkness is the friend of thieves/lovers.
Mun-Sekte *f* Moonies *pl*.
Münster *nt* **-s, -** minster, cathedral.
munter *adj* **(a)** (*lebhaft*) lively *no adv*; *Farben* bright, gay; (*fröhlich*) cheerful, merry ◆ **~ werden** to liven up; **~ und vergnügt** bright and cheery; **~ drauflos reden/gehen** to prattle away merrily/to go at it with a will.
(b) (*wach*) awake; (*aufgestanden*) up and about ◆ **jdn ~/wieder ~ machen** to wake sb up/to wake sb up (again).
Munterkeit *f* (*Lebhaftigkeit*) liveliness; (*von Farben*) brightness; (*Fröhlichkeit*) cheerfulness, merriness.
Muntermacher *m* (*Med inf*) stimulant, pick-me-up (*inf*).
Münz-: ~anstalt *f* mint; **~automat** *m* slot machine.
Münze *f* **-, -n (a)** (*Geldstück*) coin; (*Münzsystem*) coinage ◆ **jdm etw mit** *or* **in gleicher ~ heimzahlen** (*fig*) to pay sb back in his own coin for sth; *siehe* **bar.**
(b) (*Münzanstalt*) mint.
Münz|einwurf *m* (coin) slot.
münzen *vt* to mint, to coin ◆ **das war auf ihn gemünzt** (*fig*) that was aimed at *or* meant for him.
Münz(en)sammlung *f* coin *or* numismatic (*form*) collection.
Münz-: ~fälscher *m* (*Jur*) counterfeiter (*of coins*); **~fälschung** *f* (*Jur*) counterfeiting of coins; **~fernsprecher** *m* (*form*) pay phone; (*Telefonzelle auch*) callbox (*Brit*); **~fund** *m* find of coins; **~gaszähler** *m* slot gas meter; **~geld** *nt* coin; **~gewicht** *nt* coin weight; **~hoheit** *f* prerogative of coinage; **~kunde** *f* numismatics *sing*; **~sammlung** *f siehe* **Münz(en)sammlung**; **~schacht** *f* coin slot; **~spielautomat** *m*, **~spielgerät** *nt* (*form*) coin-operated gaming machine (*form*), slot machine; **~system** *nt* coinage; **~tank** *m* coin-operated petrol (*Brit*) *or* gas(oline) (*US*) pump; **~telefon** *nt siehe* **~fernsprecher**; **~wechsler** *m* change machine; **~wesen** *nt* coinage.
Mur *f* **-, -en** (*Aus*) mud.
Muräne *f* **-, -n** moray.
mürb(e) *adj* **(a)** crumbly; *Gestein etc auch* friable; (*zerbröckelnd*) crumbling; *Holz, Stoff auch* rotten.
(b) *Fleisch* tender; (*abgehangen*) well-hung ◆ **~ klopfen** to tenderize, to hammer.
(c) *Obst* soft ◆ **etw ~ werden lassen** to let sth ripen.
(d) (*fig: zermürbt*) **jdn ~ machen** to wear sb down; **~ werden/sein** to be worn down; **jdn ~ kriegen** to break sb.
Mürbeteig *m* short(-crust) pastry.
Mure *f* **-, -n** (*Geol*) mudflow.

⚠: for details of spelling reform, see supplement

Murkel *m* **-s, -** (*dial inf*) squirt (*inf*), shrimp (*inf*).
murk(e)lig *adj* (*dial inf*) tiny, wee (*esp Scot*).
Murks *m* **-es,** *no pl* (*inf*) **~ machen** to bungle things (*inf*), to botch things up (*inf*); **das ist ~!** that's a botch-up (*inf*); **so ein ~!** what a botch-up! (*inf*).
murksen *vi* (*inf*) to fiddle around; (*vermurksen*) to bungle things (*inf*), to botch things up (*inf*).
Murkserei *f* (*inf*) botching things up (*inf*) ◆ **eine ~** a botch-up (*inf*).
Murmel *f* **-, -n** marble.
murmeln [1] *vti* to murmur; (*undeutlich*) to mumble; (*brummeln*) to mutter ◆ **etw vor sich** (*acc*) **hin ~** to mutter sth to oneself.
[2] *vi* (*mit Murmeln spielen*) to play marbles.
Murmeltier *nt* marmot; *siehe* **schlafen.**
murren *vi* to grumble (*über +acc* about) ◆ **etw ohne M~** *or* **ohne zu ~ ertragen** to put up with sth without grumbling.
mürrisch *adj* (*abweisend*) sullen, morose, surly; (*schlechtgelaunt*) grumpy.
Mus *nt or m* **-es, -e** mush; (*Apfel~, Kartoffel~*) puree; (*Pflaumen~*) jam ◆ **~ aus Kartoffeln machen** to cream *or* mash potatoes; **sie wurden fast zu ~ zerdrückt** *or* **zerquetscht** (*inf*) they were (nearly) squeezed to death; **jdn zu ~ schlagen** (*inf*) to make mincemeat of sb (*inf*).
Muschel *f* **-, -n (a)** mussel (*auch Cook*), bivalve; (*Schale*) shell. **(b)** (*Ohr~*) external ear, pinna. **(c)** (*Telec*) (*Sprech~*) mouthpiece; (*Hör~*) ear-piece.
Muschel-: ~bank *f* mussel bed; **~kalk** *m* Muschelkalk (*spec*).
Muschi *f* **-, -s** (*sl*) pussy (*sl*).
Muschkote *m* **-n, -n** (*Mil sl*) private.
Muse *f* **-, -n** (*Myth*) Muse ◆ **die heitere** *or* **leichte ~** (*fig*) light entertainment; **von der ~ geküßt werden** (*fig*) to be inspired.
museal *adj* (*geh*) museum *attr* ◆ **das Haus sieht zu ~ aus** the house looks too much like a museum.
Musel-: ~man(in *f*) *m* **-en, -en, ~mann** *m*, *pl* **-männer** (*dated*), **~männin** *f* (*dated*) *siehe* **Moslem.**
Musen-: ~almanach *m* (*old*) *poetry periodical published in the 17th and 18th centuries*; **~tempel** *m* (*old, liter*) theatre.
Museum [mu'ze:ʊm] *nt* **-s, Museen** [mu'ze:ən] museum.
Museums-: ~diener *m* (*dated*) museum attendant; **~führer** *m* museum guide; **m~reif** *adj* (*hum*) antique; **m~reif sein** to be almost a museum piece; **~stück** *nt* museum piece.
Musical ['mju:zikl] *nt* **-s, -s** musical.
Musicbox ['mju:zik-] *f* **-, -en** *siehe* **Musikbox.**
Musik *f* **-, -en (a)** music ◆ **die ~ lieben** to love music; **etw in ~ setzen** (*geh*) to set *or* put sth to music; **~ machen** to play some music; **das ist ~ in meinen Ohren** (*fig*) that's music to my ears. **(b)** (*~kapelle*) band. **hier ist die ~!** (*fig inf*) this is where it's at (*sl*).
Musik|akademie *f* musical academy, academy of music.
Musikalien [-iən] *pl* music *sing*.
Musikalienhandlung [-iən-] *f* music shop (*Brit*) *or* store.
musikalisch *adj* musical ◆ **jdn ~ ausbilden** to give sb a musical training *or* a training in music.
Musikalität *f, no pl* musicalness, musicality.
Musikant(in *f*) *m* musician, minstrel (*old*).
Musikantenknochen *m* funny bone (*Brit*), crazy bone (*US*).
Musik-: ~automat *m* musical box (*Brit*), music box (*US*); (*~box*) jukebox; **m~begeistert** *adj* fond of music, music-loving *attr*; **~begleitung** *f* musical accompaniment; **unter ~begleitung** accompanied by music, to the accompaniment of music; **~berieselung** *f* (*inf*) constant background music; **~betrieb** *m* music industry; **~box** *f* jukebox; **~drama** *nt* music drama.
Musiker(in *f*) *m* **-s, -** musician.
Musik-: ~erziehung *f* (*form*) musical education; **~freund** *m* music-lover; **~geschichte** *f* history of music; **~hochschule** *f* college of music; **~instrument** *nt* musical instrument; **~kapelle** *f* band; **~kassette** *f* music cassette; **~konserve** *f* (*inf*) canned music *no pl*; **~korps** *nt* music corps *sing*; **~kritik** *f* music criticism; (*Rezension auch*) music crit; (*Kritikerschaft*) music critics *pl*; **~kritiker** *m* music critic; **~lehrer** *m* music teacher; **~lexikon** *nt* encyclopaedia/dictionary of music; **~liebhaber** *m* music-lover; **~programm** *nt* music station; (*Sendung*) music programme; **~saal** *m* music room; **~sendung** *f* music programme; **~stück** *nt* piece of music; **~stunde** *f* music lesson; **~theater** *nt* music theatre; **~truhe** *f* radiogram, radio-phonograph (*US*); **~unterricht** *m* music lessons *pl*; (*Sch*) music.
Musikus *m* **-, Musizi** (*hum*) musician.
Musik-: ~werk *nt* (*geh*) musical composition *or* work; **~wissenschaft** *f* musicology; **~wissenschaftler** *m* musicologist; **~zimmer** *nt* music room.
musisch *adj Fächer, Gymnasium* (fine) arts *attr*; *Begabung* for the arts; *Erziehung* in the (fine) arts; *Veranlagung, Mensch* artistic.
Musizi *pl of* **Musikus.**
musizieren* *vi* to play a musical instrument ◆ **sie saßen auf dem Marktplatz und musizierten** they sat in the market place playing their instruments; **sonntags abends wird bei uns immer musiziert** we always have a musical evening on Sundays.
Muskat *m* **-(e)s, -e** *siehe* **Muskatnuß.**
Muskatblüte *f* mace.
Muskateller(wein) *m* **-s, -** muscatel.
⚠ **Muskatnuß** *f* nutmeg.
Muskel *m* **-s, -n** muscle ◆ **(viele) ~n haben** to be muscular; **seine ~n spielen lassen** (*lit, fig*) to flex one's muscles.

Muskel-: ~dystrophie *f* muscular dystrophy; **~faser** *f* muscle fibre; ⚠**~faserriß** *m* torn muscle fibre; **~kater** *m* aching muscles *pl*; **~kater haben** to be stiff; **er hatte (einen) ~kater in den Beinen** his legs were stiff; **~kraft** *f* physical strength; **~krampf** *m* muscle cramp *no indef art*; **~mann** *m*, **~paket** *nt*, **~protz** *m* (*inf*) muscleman (*inf*); ⚠**~riß** *m* torn muscle; **sich** (*dat*) **einen ~riß zuziehen** to tear a muscle; **~schmerzen** *pl* muscle pains *pl*; **~schwund** *m* muscular atrophy *or* wasting; **~spiel** *nt* muscle play; **~starre** *f* muscular rigidity; **~zerrung** *f* pulled muscle.

Muskete *f* **-, -n** musket.

Musketier *m* **-s, -e** musketeer.

Muskulatur *f* muscular system, musculature (*spec*).

muskulös *adj* muscular ◆ **~ gebaut sein** to have a muscular build.

Müsli *nt* **-(s), -s** muesli.

Muslim *m* **-s, -s** *siehe* **Moslem.**

⚠ **Muß** *nt* **-,** *no pl* **es ist ein/kein ~** it's/it's not a must.

⚠ **Muß-Bestimmung,** ⚠**Mußbestimmung** *f* fixed regulation.

Muße *f* **-,** *no pl* leisure ◆ **(die) ~ für etw finden** to find the time and leisure for sth; **dafür fehlt mir die ~** I don't have the time or leisure; **sich** (*dat*) **~ gönnen** to allow oneself some (time for) leisure; **etw mit ~ tun** to do sth in a leisurely way.

⚠ **Muß|ehe** *f* (*inf*) shotgun wedding (*inf*).

▼ **müssen** [1] *modal aux vb pret* **mußte,** *ptp* **~ (a)** (*Zwang*) to have to; (*Notwendigkeit auch*) to need to; **ich muß** (*Zwang*) I have to, I must *only pres tense*, I've got to (*esp Brit*); (*Notwendigkeit auch*) I need to; **ich muß nicht** (*Zwang*) I don't have to, I haven't got to (*esp Brit*); (*Notwendigkeit auch*) I don't need to, I needn't; **muß er?** must he?, does he have to?, has he got to? (*esp Brit*); **mußtest du?** did you have to?; **das hat er tun/nicht tun ~** he had to/didn't have to do it; **er hatte es tun ~** he had had to do it; **es mußte ins Haus gebracht werden** it had to be brought inside; **das muß irgendwann mal gemacht werden** it will have to be done some time; **er sagte, er müsse bald gehen** he said he would have to go soon; **ich hätte es sonst allein tun ~** otherwise I would have had to do it alone; **dafür ~/müßten Sie einen Polizisten fragen** you'll/you'd have *or* need to ask a policeman about that; **ich muß jeden Tag um sechs Uhr aufstehen** I have to get up at six every day; **ich muß jetzt gehen** *or* **weg** (*inf*) I must be going *or* be off now, I must go now, I'll have to go now; **man mußte lachen/weinen** *etc* you couldn't help laughing/crying *etc*, you had to laugh/cry *etc*; **wir ~ Ihnen leider mitteilen, daß ...** we regret to (have to) inform you ...; **muß das (denn) sein?** is that (really) necessary?; must you/he?, do you/does he have to?; **das muß sein** it's necessary; I do/he does have to; **das mußte (ja so) kommen** that had to happen, that was bound to happen; **das muß man sich** (*dat*) **mal vorstellen!** (just) imagine that!, think of that!; **jetzt muß ich dir mal was sagen** now let me tell you something; **was habe ich da hören ~?** what's this I hear?

(b) (*sollen*) **das müßte ich/müßtest du eigentlich wissen** I/you ought to *or* should know that; **ich hätte es gestern tun ~** I ought to *or* should have done it yesterday; **das mußt du nicht tun!** you oughtn't to *or* shouldn't do that; **„Zuspätkommende ~ sich beim Pförtner melden"** "latecomers should report *or* are required to report (*form*) to the porter".

▼**(c)** (*Vermutung, Wahrscheinlichkeit*) **es muß geregnet haben** it must have rained; **es muß wahr sein** it must be true, it has *or* it's got to be true; **es muß nicht wahr sein** it needn't be true; **er muß es gewesen sein** it must have been him, it has *or* it's got to have been him; **es müßten zehntausend Zuschauer im Stadion gewesen sein** there must have been ten thousand spectators in the stadium; **er müßte schon da sein** he should be there by now; **so muß es gewesen sein** that's how it must have been; **was ~ bloß die Leute (von uns) denken!** what must people think (of us); **was muß bloß in ihm vorgehen?** what goes on in his mind?

(d) (*Wunsch*) **(viel) Geld müßte man haben!** if only I were rich!; **man müßte noch mal von vorn anfangen können!** if only one could begin again!; **man müßte noch mal zwanzig sein!** oh, to be twenty again!

[2] *vi pret* **mußte,** *ptp* **gemußt (a)** to have to go ◆ **ich muß jetzt zur Schule** I must *or* I've got to (*esp Brit*) *or* I have to go to school now; **wann müßt ihr zur Schule?** when do you have to go to school?; **der Brief muß heute noch zur Post** the letter must be *or* has to be mailed today.

(b) (*inf*) **ich muß mal** I need to go to the loo (*Brit inf*) *or* bathroom (*esp US*).

(c) (*gezwungen sein*) to have to ◆ **hast du gewollt? — nein, gemußt** did you want to? — no, I had to; **kein Mensch muß ~** there's no such thing as 'must'.

Mußestunde *f* hour of leisure ◆ **seine ~n** one's leisure hours.

⚠ **Mußheirat** *f* (*inf*) *siehe* **Mußehe.**

müßig *adj* (*untätig*) idle; *Leben, Tage, Stunden* of leisure; (*überflüssig, unnütz*) futile, pointless, otiose (*form*).

Müßig-: ~gang *m* (*liter*) *siehe adj* idleness; **dem ~gang leben, sich dem ~gang hingeben** to lead a life of idleness *or* an idle life; **~gang ist aller Laster Anfang** (*Prov*) the devil finds work for idle hands (*Prov*); **~gänger(in** *f*) *m* **-s, -** idler.

Müßigkeit *f siehe adj* futility, pointlessness, otiosity (*form*).

⚠ **mußte** *pret of* **müssen.**

⚠ **Muß-Vorschrift** *f siehe* **Muß-Bestimmung.**

Mustang *m* **-s, -s** mustang.

Muster *nt* **-s, - (a)** (*Vorlage, Dessin*) pattern; (*für Brief, Bewerbung etc*) specimen ◆ **nach einem ~ stricken** *etc* to knit *etc* from a pattern.

(b) (*Probestück*) sample; (*Buch, Korrekturfahne etc*) specimen ◆ **~ ohne Wert** sample of no commercial value.

(c) (*fig: Vorbild*) model (*an +dat* of); (*Verhaltens~*) pattern ◆ **als ~ dienen** to serve as a model; **er ist ein ~ von einem Schüler/Ehemann/Staatsbürger** he is a model student/husband/citizen; **ein ~ an Tugend** a paragon of virtue.

Muster- *in cpds* model; **~beispiel** *nt* classic *or* prime example; **~betrieb** *m* model factory/farm *etc*; **~buch** *nt* pattern book; **~dorf** *nt* model village; **~ehe** *f* perfect marriage; **~exemplar** *nt* fine specimen; **ein ~exemplar von einer Frau/einem Idioten** a model wife/a perfect idiot; **~gatte** *m* model husband; **m~gültig** *adj* exemplary; **~gültigkeit** *f* exemplariness; **~gut** *nt* model farm; **m~haft** *adj* exemplary; **er hat sich m~haft verhalten** his conduct was exemplary; **~knabe** *m* (*iro*) paragon; **~koffer** *m* sample case; **~kollektion** *f* collection of samples; (*Fashion*) collection of models; **~ländle** *nt* (*inf*) **das ~ländle** Baden-Württemberg; **~messe** *f* trade fair.

mustern *vt* **(a)** (*betrachten*) to scrutinize, to look over, to survey ◆ **jdn kühl/skeptisch ~** to survey *or* eye sb coolly/sceptically; **jdn von oben bis unten ~** *or* **von Kopf bis Fuß ~** to look sb up and down, to scrutinize sb from head to toe.

(b) (*Mil: inspizieren*) to inspect, to review.

(c) (*Mil: für Wehrdienst*) **jdn ~** to give sb his/her medical.

(d) *Stoff siehe* **gemustert.**

Muster-: ~packung *f* sample pack; (*Attrappe*) display pack; ⚠**~prozeß** *m* test case; **~schüler** *m* model pupil; (*fig*) star pupil; **~schutz** *m* protection of patterns and designs; **~sendung** *f* selection of samples; **~stadt** *f* model town; **~stück** *nt* (*usu iro*) *siehe* **~exemplar.**

Musterung *f* **(a)** pattern. **(b)** (*Mil*) (*von Truppen*) inspection, review; (*von Rekruten*) medical examination for military service. **(c)** (*durch Blicke*) scrutiny.

Musterungs-: ⚠**~ausschuß** *m* recruiting *or* draft (*US*) board; **~bescheid** *m* notification of the recruiting *or* draft (*US*) board's decision; **~kommission** *f siehe* **~ausschuß.**

Mut *m* **-(e)s,** *no pl* **(a)** courage, pluck (*inf*); (*Zuversicht*) heart ◆ **~ fassen** to pluck up courage; **~/keinen ~ haben** to have (a lot of/some)/not to have any courage; **mit frischem ~** with new heart; **nur ~!** don't lose heart!, cheer up!, keep your pecker up! (*Brit inf*); **jdm den ~ nehmen** to discourage sb, to make sb lose heart; **den ~ verlieren** to lose heart; **~/wieder ~ bekommen** to gain confidence/to take heart; **jdm ~ zusprechen** *or* **machen** to encourage sb; **das gab ihr wieder neuen ~** that gave her new heart; **ihm sank der ~** his heart sank; **mit dem ~ der Verzweiflung** with the courage born of desperation *or* despair; **der ~ zum Leben** the will to live; **der ~ zur Lücke** (*hum*) the courage to admit when one doesn't know something.

(b) (*old: Laune, Stimmung*) spirits *pl* ◆ **frohen/guten ~es sein** to be of good cheer (*old*), to be in good spirits; **mit frohem ~** with good cheer (*old*).

Mutation *f* **(a)** mutation. **(b)** (*Med*) breaking of the voice ◆ **er hat die ~ gerade hinter sich** his voice has just broken.

Mutbeweis *m* proof of his *etc* courage.

Mütchen *nt* **sein ~ an jdm kühlen** (*inf*) to take it out on sb (*inf*).

muten *vi* (*Min*) to divine.

Muter(in *f*) *m* (*Min*) diviner.

mutieren* *vi* **(a)** (*sich erblich ändern*) to mutate. **(b)** (*Med, Aus*) **er hat schon mutiert** his voice has already broken.

mutig *adj* (*tapfer*) courageous, brave, plucky (*inf*) ◆ **dem M~en gehört die Welt** (*Prov*) fortune favours the brave (*Prov*).

Mut-: m~los *adj* (*niedergeschlagen*) discouraged *no adv*, disheartened *no adv*; (*bedrückt*) despondent, dejected; **jdn m~los machen** to discourage sb, to make sb lose heart; **~losigkeit** *f siehe adj* discouragement, disheartenment; despondency, dejection.

mutmaßen *vti insep* to conjecture ◆ **es wurde viel über seine Abwesenheit gemutmaßt** there was a lot of conjecture as to the reason for his absence.

mutmaßlich [1] *adj attr Vater* presumed; *Täter, Terrorist* suspected.

[2] *adv* **alle Fahrgäste sind ~ ums Leben gekommen** it is presumed that all the passengers were killed; **~ soll er der Vater sein** he is presumed to be the father.

Mutmaßung *f* conjecture ◆ **wir müssen uns auf ~en stützen** we can only conjecture.

Mutprobe *f* test of courage.

Muttchen *nt* (*inf*) **(a)** (*Mutter*) mummy (*inf*), mommy (*US inf*). **(b)** (*biedere Hausfrau*) little housewife. **(c)** (*alte Frau*) grandma.

Mutter[1] *f* **-, ¨** mother ◆ **sie ist jetzt ~** she's a mother now; **~ werden** to have a baby; **sie ist ~ von drei Kindern** she's a mother of three; **als Frau und ~** as a wife and a mother; **~ Natur/Erde** (*liter*) Mother Nature/Earth; **die ~ der Kompanie** (*Mil hum*) the sergeant-major; **wie bei ~n** (*dial*) just like (at) home; (*Essen*) just like mother makes/used to make.

Mutter[2] *f* **-, -n** (*Tech*) nut.

Mütterberatungsstelle *f* child welfare clinic.

Mutter-: ~bindung *f* (*Psych*) mother fixation; **~boden** *m* topsoil; **~brust** *f* mother's breast; (*Ernährung*) mother's milk; **an der ~brust** at one's mother's breast; **da war ich ja noch an der ~brust!** I was just a babe-in-arms then.

Mütterchen *nt* **(a)** *siehe* **Muttchen (a). (b)** *siehe* **Muttchen (c). (c) ~ Rußland** Mother Russia.

Mutter-: ~erde *f* topsoil; (*liter: Heimaterde*) native soil; **~fahrzeug** *nt* (*Space*) parent ship; **~figur** *f* mother figure; **~freuden** *pl* the joys of motherhood *pl*.

Müttergenesungs-: ~heim *nt rest centre for mothers, especially of large families*; **~werk** *nt organization providing rest for mothers.*

Mutter-: ~gesellschaft *f* (*Comm*) parent company; **~gewinde** *nt* (*Tech*) female thread; **~glück** *nt* **das ~glück** the joy of motherhood; **~gottes** *f* **-,** *no pl* Mother of God; (*Abbild*) Madonna; **~gottesbild(nis)** *nt* (image of

➤ SPRACHE AKTIV: **müssen: 1a** → 37.1, 37.2, 37.3, 39.3, 42.1, 42.4, 45.1, 48.1, 48.3 **1c** → 27.7, 42.2

the) Madonna; **~haus** *nt* (*Rel*) training centre; (*von Kloster*) mother house; **~herz** *nt* maternal heart; **~instinkt** *m* maternal instinct; **~kirche** *f* mother church; **~komplex** *m* mother complex; **~korn** *nt* (*Bot*) ergot; **~kuchen** *m* (*Anat*) placenta; **~kult** *m* mother cult; **~land** *nt* mother country; **~leib** *m* womb.

Mütterlein *nt siehe* **Mütterchen (a, b).**

mütterlich *adj* **(a)** maternal; *Seite, Linie auch* distaff ◆ **die ~en Pflichten** one's duties as a mother; **auf ~er Seite** on his/her *etc* mother's side, on the distaff side. **(b)** (*liebevoll besorgt*) motherly *no adv* ◆ **jdn ~ umsorgen** to mother sb.

mütterlicherseits *adv* on his/her *etc* mother's side, on the distaff side ◆ **sein Großvater ~** his maternal grandfather.

Mütterlichkeit *f* motherliness.

Mutter-: ~liebe *f* motherly love; **m~los** *adj* motherless; **~mal** *nt* birthmark, mole; **~milch** *f* mother's milk; **etw mit der ~milch einsaugen** (*fig*) to learn sth from the cradle; **~mord** *m* matricide; **~mund** *m* (*Anat*) cervix, neck of the uterus *or* womb.

Mutternschlüssel *m* (*Tech*) spanner.

Mutter-: ⚠~paß *m document held by expectant mothers in which the details of the pregnancy are entered*; **~pferd** *nt* dam; **~pflanze** *f* parent (plant); **~platine** *f* (*Comput*) *siehe* **Hauptplatine**; **~recht** *nt* (*Sociol*) matriarchy; **m~rechtlich** *adj* (*Sociol*) matriarch(al); **~schaf** *nt* ewe.

Mutterschaft *f* motherhood; (*nach Entbindung*) maternity.

Mutterschafts-: ~geld *nt* maternity grant; **~hilfe** *f* maternity benefit; **~urlaub** *m* maternity leave.

Mutter-: ~schiff *nt* (*Space*) parent ship; **~schutz** *m* legal protection of expectant and nursing mothers; **~schutzgesetz** *nt* law for the protection of expectant and nursing mothers; **~schwein** *nt* sow; **m~seelenallein** *adj, adv* all alone, all on one's own; **~söhnchen** *nt* (*pej*) mummy's boy; **~sprache** *f* native language, mother tongue; **Gälisch ist seine ~sprache** Gaelic is his native language, he's a native speaker of Gaelic; **~sprachler(in *f*)** *m* native speaker; **~stelle** *f*: **bei jdm ~stelle vertreten** to be like a mother to sb; (*Jur*) to stand in loco parentis to sb.

Müttersterblichkeit *f* mortality in childbirth.

Mutter-: ~stute *f* dam; **~tag** *m* Mother's Day; **~tier** *nt* mother (animal); (*Zuchttier*) brood animal; **~witz** *m* (*Schläue*) mother wit; (*Humor*) natural wit.

Mutti *f* **-, -s** (*inf*) mummy, mum, mommy (*US*).

Mutwille *m* **-ns,** *no pl* **(a)** (*geh: Übermut*) mischief ◆ **aus bloßem** *or* **reinem ~n** out of pure mischief. **(b)** (*böse Absicht*) malice ◆ **etw mit** *or* **aus ~n tun** to do sth out of malice.

mutwillig [1] *adj* **(a)** (*geh: übermütig*) *Streiche, Dummheiten* mischievous. **(b)** (*böswillig*) malicious; *Beschädigung, Zerstörung auch* wilful.
[2] *adv* (*absichtlich*) *zerstören etc* wilfully.

Mutwilligkeit *f siehe* **Mutwille.**

Mütze *f* **-, -n** cap ◆ **die ~ ziehen** to doff one's cap; (*fig*) to take one's hat off (*vor jdm* to sb); **was auf die ~ kriegen** (*inf*) to get a ticking-off (*inf*); (*verprügelt etc werden*) to get thumped (*inf*); **eine ~ voll Schlaf** (*inf*) a good kip (*inf*).

Mützenschirm *m* peak.

MW *abbr of* **Megawatt.**

MwSt., MWSt. *abbr of* **Mehrwertsteuer** VAT.

Mykenä, Mykene *nt* **-s** Mycenae.

mykenisch *adj* Mycenean.

Myriade *f* (*lit, fig*) myriad.

⚠**Myrrhe** ['mʏrə] *f* **-, -n** myrrh.

⚠**Myrrhen|öl** *nt* oil of myrrh.

Myrte *f* **-, -n** myrtle.

Myrtenkranz *m* myrtle wreath.

Mysterien- [-iən-] (*Hist*): **~kult** *m* mystery cult; **~spiel** *nt* (*Theat*) mystery play.

mysteriös *adj* mysterious.

Mysterium *nt* (*alle Bedeutungen*) mystery.

Mystifikation *f* mystification.

mystifizieren* *vt* to mysticize.

Mystifizierung *f* mystification.

Mystik *f* mysticism *no art.*

Mystiker(in *f*) *m* **-s, -** mystic.

mystisch *adj* mystic(al); (*fig: geheimnisvoll*) mysterious.

Mystizismus *m* mysticism.

Mythen-: ~bildung *f* **zur ~bildung beitragen** to help to create a myth; **m~haft** *adj* mythical.

mythisch *adj* mythical.

Mythologie *f* mythology.

mythologisch *adj* mythologic(al).

Mythos, Mythus *m* **-, Mythen** (*lit, fig*) myth ◆ **er war zeitlebens von einem ~ umgeben** he was a legend in his time.

⚠: for details of spelling reform, see supplement

N, n [ɛn] *nt* **-, -** N, n ◆ **n-te** nth.
N *abbr of* **Norden.**
'n [n] *(inf) abbr of* **ein, einen.**
na¹ *interj (inf)* **(a)** *(Frage, Anrede)* well; *(Aufforderung)* then ◆ **~, kommst du mit?** well, are you coming?, are you coming then?
(b) *(zögernde Zustimmung, Resignation)* well ◆ **~ ja** well; **~ ja, aber nur noch zehn Minuten** well yes *or* I suppose so, but only another ten minutes; **~ gut, ~ schön** all right, OK *(inf)*.
(c) *(Bestätigung, Erleichterung)* well ◆ **~ also!, ~ eben!** (well,) there you are (then)!; **~ und ob!** *(auf jeden Fall)* you bet! *(inf)*, not half! *(inf)*; *(und wie auch)* and how! *(inf)*.
(d) *(Beschwichtigung)* come (on) (now).
(e) *(Ermahnung)* now; *(Zurückweisung)* well ◆ **~ (~)!** now, now!, now then!; **~ warte!** just you wait!; **~ so was** *or* **so etwas!** well, I never!; **~ und?** so what?; **~ ich danke!** no thank you!
(f) *(Zweifel)* well ◆ **~, wenn das mal klappt!** well, if it comes off.
na² *adv (S Ger, Aus inf) siehe* **nein.**
Nabe *f* **-, -n** hub.
Nabel *m* **-s, -** *(Anat)* navel, umbilicus *(spec)*; *(Bot)* hilum ◆ **der ~ der Welt** *(fig)* the hub of the universe, the centre of the world.
Nabel-: ~binde *f* umbilical bandage; **~bruch** *m* umbilical hernia; **~schau** *f* **~schau betreiben** to be bound up in oneself; **~schnur** *f*, **~strang** *m (Anat)* umbilical cord.
Nabob *m* **-s, -s** nabob.
nach [1] *prep +dat* **(a)** *(örtlich)* to ◆ **ich nahm den Zug ~ Mailand** *(bis)* I took the train to Milan; *(in Richtung)* I took the Milan train *or* the train for Milan; **das Schiff/der Zug fährt ~ Kiel** the boat is bound for Kiel, the boat/train is going to Kiel; **er ist schon ~ London abgefahren** he has already left for London; **~ Osten/Westen** eastward(s)/westward(s), to the east/west; **von Osten ~ Westen** from (the) east to (the) west; **~ links/rechts** (to the) left/right; **von links ~ rechts** from (the) left to (the) right; **~ jeder Richtung** *or* **allen Richtungen** *(lit)* in all directions; *(fig)* on all sides; **~ hinten/vorn** to the back/front; *(in Wagen/Zug etc auch)* to the rear/front; **~ ... zu** towards ...; **~ Norden zu** *or* **hin** to(wards) the north.
(b) *in Verbindung mit vb siehe auch dort* **~ jdm/etw suchen** to look for sb/sth; **sich ~ etw sehnen** to long for sth; **~ etw schmecken/riechen** to taste/smell of sth.
(c) *(zeitlich)* after ◆ **fünf (Minuten) ~ drei** five (minutes) past *or* after *(US)* three; **~ Christi Geburt** *or* **unserer Zeitrechnung** *(esp DDR)* AD, anno Domini *(form)*; **sie kam ~ zehn Minuten** she came ten minutes later *or* after ten minutes; **~ zehn Minuten war sie wieder da** she was back in ten minutes *or* ten minutes later; **~ zehn Minuten wurde ich schon unruhig** after ten minutes I was getting worried; **was wird man ~ zehn Jahren über ihn sagen?** what will people be saying about him in ten years (time)?; **~ Empfang** *or* **Erhalt** *or* **Eingang** on receipt; **drei Tage ~ Empfang** three days after receipt; **~ allem, was geschehen ist** after all that has happened.
(d) *(Reihenfolge)* after ◆ **eine(r, s) ~ dem/der anderen** one after another *or* the other; **die dritte Straße ~ dem Rathaus** the third road after *or* past the town hall; **ich komme ~ Ihnen!** I'm *or* I come after you; **(bitte) ~ Ihnen!** after you!; **der Leutnant kommt ~ dem Major** *(inf)* a lieutenant comes after a major; **~ „mit" steht der Dativ** "mit" is followed by *or* takes the dative.
(e) *(laut, entsprechend)* according to; *(im Einklang mit)* in accordance with ◆ **~ dem Gesetz, dem Gesetz ~** according to the law; **~ römischem Gesetz** according to *or* under Roman law; **~ Artikel 142c** under article 142c; **manche Arbeiter werden ~ Zeit, andere ~ Leistung bezahlt** some workers are paid by the hour, others according to productivity; **etw ~ Gewicht kaufen** to buy sth by weight; **~ Verfassern/Gedichtanfängen** in order of *or* according to authors/first lines; **die Uhr ~ dem Radio stellen** to put a clock right by the radio; **seinem Wesen** *or* **seiner Natur ~ ist er sehr sanft** he's very gentle by nature; **seiner Veranlagung ~ hätte er Musiker werden sollen** with his temperament he should have been a musician; **ihrer Sprache ~ (zu urteilen)** from her language, judging by her language; **~ dem, was er gesagt hat** from *or* according to what he's said; **~ allem, was ich gehört habe** from what I've heard; **~ allem, was ich weiß** as far as I know; **Knödel ~ schwäbischer Art** Swabian dumplings.
(f) *(angelehnt an)* after ◆ **~ dem Russischen** after the Russian; **~ einem Gedicht von Schiller** after a poem by Schiller.
(g) er wurde ~ seinem Großvater genannt he was called after *or* for *(US)* his grandfather.
[2] *adv* **(a)** *(räumlich)* **mir ~!** *(old liter)* follow me!
(b) *(zeitlich)* **~ und ~** little by little, gradually; **~ wie vor** still; **wir treffen uns ~ wie vor im „Goldenen Handschuh"** we still meet in the "Golden Glove" as always.
nach|äffen *vt sep (pej)* Moden, Ideen to ape; *jdn* to take off, to mimic; *(imitieren)* to copy.
Nach|äfferei *f (pej) siehe vt* aping; mimicry; copying.
nach|ahmen *vt sep* to imitate; *(karikieren)* to take off, to mimic; *(nacheifern auch)* to emulate; *(kopieren)* to copy.
nach|ahmenswert *adj* exemplary.
Nach|ahmer(in *f*) *m* **-s, -** imitator; *(eines großen Vorbilds)* emulator; *(pej: Art, Liter)* copyist.
Nach|ahmer-: ~medikament, ~präparat *nt* generic drug.
Nach|ahmung *f siehe vt* **(a)** *(das Imitieren)* imitation; taking off, mimicking; emulation; copying ◆ **etw zur ~ anraten** *or* **empfehlen** to recommend sth as an example. **(b)** *(die Imitation)* imitation; take-off, impression; emulation; copy.
Nach|ahmungs-: ~täter *m* copy-cat criminal; **~trieb** *m* imitative instinct.
nach|arbeiten *sep* [1] *vt* **(a)** *(aufholen)* to make up. **(b)** *(überarbeiten)* to work over; *(Art etc)* to touch up. **(c)** *(nachbilden)* to copy, to reproduce.
[2] *vi* **wir müssen morgen ~** we'll have to make up the work tomorrow.
Nachbar ['naxbaːɐ] *m* **-n** *or* **-s, -n** neighbour; *(in ~wohnung, ~haus auch)* next-door neighbour ◆ **Herr X war beim Konzert mein ~** Mr X sat next to me at the concert; **ich war eben bei ~s** *(inf)* I've just been round to the neighbours; **~s Garten** the next-door garden; **die lieben ~n** *(iro)* the neighbours.
Nachbar-: ~dorf *nt* neighbouring village; **~haus** *nt* house next door, neighbouring house; **in unserem ~haus, bei uns im ~haus** in the house next door (to us).
Nachbarin *f* neighbour.
Nachbarland *nt* neighbouring country.
nachbarlich *adj (freundlich)* neighbourly *no adv*; *(benachbart)* neighbouring *no adv*.
Nachbarschaft *f (Gegend)* neighbourhood; *(Nachbarn)* neighbours *pl*; *(Nähe)* vicinity ◆ **gute ~ halten** *or* **pflegen** to keep on good terms with the neighbours.
Nachbarschaftshilfe *f* neighbourly help ◆ **man ist ja wohl zu ein bißchen ~ verpflichtet** you have to help your neighbours a bit.
Nachbars-: ~familie *f* next-door family, family next door; **~frau** *f* lady next door; **~kind** *nt* child next door; **~leute** *pl* neighbours *pl*; *(von nebenan auch)* people next door *pl*.
Nachbarstadt *f* neighbouring town.
Nachbeben *nt* aftershock.
nachbehandeln* *vt sep (Med)* **jdn/etw ~** to give sb after-care, to give sb/sth follow-up treatment.
Nachbehandlung *f (Med)* follow-up treatment *no indef art*.
nachbereiten* *vt sep (Sch)* to assess *or* evaluate afterwards.
nachbessern *sep* [1] *vt* to retouch; *Gesetz, Beschluß* to amend.
[2] *vi* to make improvements.
Nachbesserungsklausel *f* clause improving the terms of a/the contract.
nachbestellen* *vt sep* to order some more; *(Comm)* to reorder, to put in a repeat order for; *(nachträglich)* to put in *or* make a late order for ◆ **ich habe gerade noch Sekt/noch zwei Flaschen Sekt nachbestellt** I've just ordered some more champagne/another two bottles of champagne.
Nachbestellung *f (gen* for) repeat order; *(nachträgliche Bestellung)* late order.
nachbeten *vt sep (inf)* to repeat parrot-fashion, to parrot.
Nachbeter *m (inf)* echoer, parrot *(inf)*.
nachbezahlen* *sep* [1] *vt* to pay; *(später)* to pay later ◆ **Steuern ~** to pay back-tax.
[2] *vi* to pay the rest.
Nachbild *nt (Opt)* after-image.
nachbilden *vt sep* to copy; *(exakt)* to reproduce ◆ **einer Sache** *(dat)*

nachgebildet sein to be modelled on sth, to be a copy/reproduction of sth.
Nachbildung *f* copy; (*exakt*) reproduction.
nachblättern *vi sep* to have a quick look ◆ **in etw** (*dat*) ~ to flick through sth again.
nachbleiben *vi sep irreg aux sein* (*dial*) to stay behind.
nachblicken *vi sep siehe* **nachsehen 1 (a).**
Nachblutung *f* (*Med*) secondary haemorrhage; (*nach Operation*) post-operative haemorrhage; (*nach Geburt*) post-partum haemorrhage.
nachbohren *sep* [1] *vt Öffnung* to drill out.
[2] *vi* (*lit*) to drill out some more; (*fig inf*) to probe.
Nachbrenner *m* (*Aviat*) after-burner.
nachbringen *vt sep irreg* (*hinterherbringen*) to bring afterwards; (*zusätzlich servieren*) to bring some more ◆ **er brachte mir den Schirm nach** he came after me with my umbrella.
nachchristlich *adj* **in den ersten ~en Jahrhunderten** in the first centuries AD.
nachdatieren* *vt sep* to postdate.
nachdem *conj* **(a)** (*zeitlich*) after. **(b)** (*modal*) *siehe* **je¹ 3 (b). (c)** (*S Ger: kausal*) since.
nachdenken *vi sep irreg* to think (*über +acc* about) ◆ **darüber darf man gar nicht ~** it doesn't bear thinking about; **laut ~** to think aloud, to think out loud; **denk doch mal nach!** think about it!; **denk mal gut** *or* **scharf nach!** think carefully!
Nachdenken *nt* thought, reflection ◆ **nach langem ~** after (giving the matter) considerable thought; **gib mir ein bißchen Zeit zum ~** give me a bit of time to think (about it).
nachdenklich *adj Mensch, Miene* thoughtful, pensive; *Geschichte, Worte* thought-provoking ◆ **jdn ~ stimmen** *or* **machen** to set sb thinking; **~ gestimmt sein** to be in a thoughtful mood.
Nachdenklichkeit *f, no pl* thoughtfulness, pensiveness.
nachdichten *vt sep* (*Liter*) to give a free rendering of.
Nachdichtung *f* (*Liter*) free rendering.
nachdrängen *vi sep aux sein* to push from behind ◆ **jdm ~** to throng after sb (*liter*).
Nachdruck *m* **(a)** *no pl* (*Betonung*) stress, emphasis; (*Tatkraft*) vigour, energy ◆ **besonderen ~ darauf legen, daß ...** to put special emphasis on the fact that ..., to stress *or* emphasize particularly that ...; **etw mit ~ betreiben/sagen** to pursue sth with vigour/to say sth emphatically.
(b) (*das Nachdrucken*) reprinting; (*das Nachgedruckte*) reprint ◆ **„~ verboten"** "no part of this publication may be reproduced without the prior permission of the publishers".
nachdrucken *vt sep* to reprint.
nachdrücklich *adj* emphatic; *Warnung auch* firm ◆ **~ auf etw** (*dat*) **bestehen** to insist firmly (up)on sth; **jdm ~ raten** *or* **jdm den ~en Rat geben, etw zu tun** to advise sb strongly *or* to urge sb to do sth; **jdn ~ warnen** to give sb a firm warning.
Nachdrücklichkeit *f* insistence.
nachdrucksvoll *adj* emphatic.
nachdunkeln *vi sep aux sein* to get *or* grow darker; (*Bild*) to darken.
Nachdurst *m* (*nach Alkoholgenuß*) dehydration ◆ **~ haben** to be dehydrated.
nach|eifern *vi sep* **jdm/einer Sache ~** to emulate sb/sth.
nach|eifernswert *adj* worth emulating, worthy of emulation.
nach|eilen *vi sep aux sein* **jdm/einer Sache ~** to run *or* hurry after sb/sth.
nach|einander *adv* (*räumlich*) one after another *or* the other; (*zeitlich auch*) in succession ◆ **zweimal ~** twice running *or* in a row; **kurz/unmittelbar ~** shortly/immediately after each other.
nach|empfinden* *vt sep irreg* **(a)** *Stimmung* to feel; *Gedicht, Lied* to relate to ◆ **niemand kann Werthers Schmerz ~** no-one can really feel Werther's grief; **ich kann (Ihnen) Ihre Entrüstung ~** I can understand how horrified you must be/have been; **das kann ich ihr ~** I can understand her feelings *or* how she feels/felt. **(b)** (*nachgestalten*) to adapt (*dat* from).
Nachen *m* **-s, -** (*liter*) barque (*poet*).
Nach|erbe *m* remainderman (*spec*).
Nach|ernte *f* second harvest; (*Ähren ~*) gleaning; (*Ertrag*) gleanings *pl* ◆ **~ halten** to glean the remains of the harvest.
nach|erzählen* *vt sep* to retell ◆ **dem Türkischen nacherzählt** (*geh*) adapted from the Turkish.
Nach|erzählung *f* retelling; (*Sch*) (story) reproduction.
nach|exerzieren* *vi sep* (*Mil*) to do extra drill.
Nachf. *abbr of* **Nachfolger.**
Nachfahr *m* **-s, -en** (*liter*) descendant.
nachfahren *vi sep irreg aux sein* to follow (on) ◆ **jdm ~** to follow sb.
⚠ **Nachfaßaktion** *f* (*in der Werbung*) follow-up campaign.
nachfassen *sep* [1] *vi* **(a)** (*nachgreifen*) to get a firmer grip; (*noch einmal zufassen*) to regain one's grip. **(b)** (*inf: nachforschen*) to probe a bit deeper. **(c)** (*inf: Essen ~*) to have a second helping.
[2] *vt* (*inf: nachholen*) to have a second helping of ◆ **Essen ~** to have a second helping.
Nachfeier *f* continuation of the party; (*später*) celebration *held some time after the event.*
nachfeiern *vi sep* (*weiterfeiern*) to carry on celebrating; (*auch vt: später feiern*) to celebrate later.
nachfeilen *vt sep* to file off.
nachfinanzieren* *vt sep* to find additional finance for.
Nachfolge *f, no pl* **(a)** succession ◆ **jds/die ~ antreten** to succeed sb/succeed.
(b) (*Nacheiferung*) emulation ◆ **in der ~ seines Lehrmeisters** in emulation of his master; **die ~ Christi** the imitation of Christ.
nachfolgen *vi sep aux sein* **(a)** (*hinterherkommen*) to follow (on) ◆ **jdm ~** to follow sb; **jdm im Amt ~** to succeed sb in office; **sie ist ihrem Gatten nachgefolgt** (*euph*) she has gone to join her husband (*euph*). **(b)** *+dat* (*Anhänger sein*) to follow.
nachfolgend *adj* following ◆ **wie im ~en ausgeführt** as detailed below; **~es, das N~e** the following; **können/konnten Sie aus den ~en Beispielen etwas entnehmen?** can/could you gather anything from the following/subsequent examples?
Nachfolge- *in cpds* follow-up; **~modell** *nt* (*von Produkt, Auto*) successor, follow-up model (*gen* to); **~organisation** *f* successor organization.
Nachfolger(in *f*) *m* **-s, -** (*im Amt etc*) successor ◆ **Friedrich Reißnagel ~** successors to Friedrich Reißnagel.
Nachfolgestaat *m* succession state.
nachfordern *vt sep* to put in another demand for.
Nachforderung *f* subsequent demand.
nachforschen *vi sep* to try to find out; (*polizeilich etc*) to carry out an investigation (*dat* into); (*amtlich etc*) to make enquiries (*dat* into).
Nachforschung *f* enquiry; (*polizeilich etc*) investigation ◆ **~en anstellen** to make enquiries.
Nachfrage *f* **(a)** (*Comm*) demand (*nach, in +dat* for) ◆ **danach besteht eine rege/keine ~** there is a great/no demand for it. **(b)** (*Erkundigung*) enquiry ◆ **danke der ~** (*form*) thank you for your concern; (*inf*) nice of you to ask.
➤ **nachfragen** *vi sep* to ask, to enquire.
Nachfrage-: ~schub *m* surge in demand; **~überhang** *m* surplus demand.
Nachfrist *f* extension ◆ **jdm eine ~ setzen** to extend sb's deadline, to give *or* grant sb an extension.
nachfühlen *vt sep siehe* **nachempfinden.**
nachfüllen *vt sep leeres Glas etc* to refill; *halbleeres Glas, Batterie etc* to top up ◆ **darf ich (Ihr Glas) ~?** can I fill/top you up?, would you like a refill?
Nachfüllpack *m*, **Nachfüllpackung** *f* refill pack ◆ **etwas im Nachfüllpack kaufen** to buy the refill pack of sth.
nachgären *vi sep irreg aux haben or sein* to be lagered.
Nachgärung *f* lagering.
nachgeben *sep irreg* [1] *vi* **(a)** to give way (*dat* to); (*federn*) to give; (*fig*) (*Mensch*) to give in *or* way (*dat* to); (*aufgeben*) to give up *or* in.
(b) (*Comm: Preise, Kurse*) to drop, to fall.
[2] *vt* (*noch mehr geben*) **darf ich Ihnen noch etwas Gemüse ~?** may I give you a few more vegetables?; **er ließ sich** (*dat*) **Fleisch ~** he had another helping of meat.
nachgeboren *adj* **(a)** (*mit großem Altersunterschied*) late(r)-born ◆ **die N~en** (*geh*) future generations. **(b)** (*nach Tod des Vaters geboren*) posthumous.
Nachgebühr *f* excess (postage).
Nachgeburt *f* (*Gewebe*) afterbirth; (*Vorgang*) expulsion of the afterbirth.
Nachgefühl *nt* feeling.
nachgehen *vi sep irreg aux sein* **(a)** *+dat* (*hinterhergehen*) to follow; *jdm auch* to go after.
(b) (*Uhr*) to be slow ◆ **deine Uhr geht fünf Minuten nach** your clock is five minutes slow.
(c) *+dat* (*ausüben*) *Beruf* to practise; *Studium, Vergnügungen, Interesse etc* to pursue; *Geschäften* to go about ◆ **welcher Tätigkeit gehen Sie nach?** what is your occupation?
(d) *+dat* (*erforschen*) to investigate, to look into.
(e) *+dat* (*zu denken geben*) to haunt.
nachgelassen *adj Werke, Briefe, Papiere* posthumously published ◆ **seine ~en, bis heute nicht veröffentlichten Fragmente** the fragments he left which remain unpublished to this day.
nachgemacht *adj Gold, Leder etc* imitation; *Geld* counterfeit.
nachge|ordnet *adj* (*form*) *Behörde, Dienststelle* subordinate.
nachgerade *adv* (*geradezu*) practically, virtually; (*nach wie vor*) still.
nachgeraten* *vi sep irreg aux sein* **jdm ~** to take after sb; **sie ist ganz ihrer Mutter ~** she's just like her mother.
Nachgeschmack *m* (*lit, fig*) aftertaste ◆ **einen üblen ~ hinterlassen** (*fig*) to leave a bad *or* nasty taste in one's *or* the mouth.
nachgestellt *adj* (*Gram*) postpositive.
nachgewiesenermaßen *adv siehe* **erwiesenermaßen.**
nachgiebig *adj* **(a)** *Material* pliable; *Boden, Wand etc* yielding ◆ **~ sein** to be pliable/to give. **(b)** (*fig*) *Mensch, Haltung* soft; (*entgegenkommend*) accommodating, compliant ◆ **sie behandelt die Kinder zu ~** she's too soft with the children; **jdn ~ machen** to soften sb up.
Nachgiebigkeit *f siehe adj* **(a)** pliability; softness. **(b)** softness; compliance.
nachgießen *vti sep irreg Wasser, Milch* to add ◆ **er trinkt so schnell, daß man ständig ~ muß** he drinks so fast that you keep having to top up his glass; **darf ich Ihnen (noch etwas Wein) ~?** would you like some more (wine)?
nachglühen *vi sep* to go on glowing.
nachgreifen *vi sep irreg siehe* **nachfassen 1.**
nachgrübeln *vi sep* to think (*über +acc* about); (*sich Gedanken machen*) to ponder (*über +acc* on), to muse (*über +acc* about).
nachgucken *vti sep siehe* **nachsehen.**
nachhaken *vi sep* (*inf*) to dig deeper ◆ **bei jdm ~** to pump sb (*inf*).
Nachhall *m* reverberation; (*fig*) (*Anklang*) response (*auf +acc* to); (*Nachklang*) echo ◆ **künstlicher ~** echo effect, artificial echo; **das Echo hatte einen langen ~** the echo went on reverberating a long while.

⚠: for details of spelling reform, see supplement

➤ SPRACHE AKTIV: **nachfragen** → 46.1, 48.1

nachhallen *vi sep* to reverberate.

nachhaltig *adj* lasting *no adv*; *Widerstand* sustained *no adv* ◆ **ihre Gesundheit hat sich ~ gebessert** there has been a lasting improvement in her health.

nachhängen *vi sep irreg +dat* to give oneself up to, to abandon oneself to ◆ **seinen Erinnerungen ~** to lose oneself in one's memories.

Nachhauseweg *m* way home.

nachhelfen *vi sep irreg* to help ◆ **jdm ~** to help sb, to give sb a hand; **sie hat ihrer Schönheit etwas nachgeholfen** she has improved a little on Mother Nature *or* given nature a helping hand; **er hat dem Glück ein bißchen nachgeholfen** he engineered himself a little luck; **meine Güte, bist du braun! — na, ich hab' auch ein bißchen nachgeholfen** good heavens, you're brown! — well, I did help it *or* things along a bit.

nachher *adv* **(a)** (*danach*) afterwards; (*später auch*) later ◆ **bis ~** see you later! **(b)** (*inf: möglicherweise*) **~ stimmt das gar nicht** that might not be true at all, (it) could be that's not true at all.

Nachhilfe *f* help, assistance; (*Sch*) private coaching *or* tuition *or* tutoring (*US*).

Nachhilfe-: ~lehrer *m* private tutor, crammer (*inf*); **~stunde** *f* private lesson; **~unterricht** *m* private coaching *or* tuition *or* tutoring (*US*).

⚠ **nachhinein** *adv*: **im ~** afterwards; (*rückblickend*) in retrospect; *siehe* **klug**.

nachhinken *vi sep aux sein* (*fig inf*) to lag behind ◆ **hinter jdm/etw ~** to lag behind sb/sth.

Nachholbedarf *m* **einen ~ an etw** (*dat*) **haben** to have a lot to catch up on in the way of sth, to have a lot of sth to catch up on.

nachholen *vt sep* **(a)** (*nachkommen lassen*) to get sb to join one; (*von Übersee auch*) to fetch *or* get sb over. **(b)** (*aufholen*) *Versäumtes* to make up.

Nachhut ['na:xhu:t] *f* **-, -en** (*Mil*) rearguard ◆ **bei der ~** in the rearguard.

Nach|impfung *f* (*Zweitimpfung*) reinoculation; (*Wiederholungsimpfung*) booster.

nach|industriell *adj* (*Sociol*) post-industrial.

nachjagen *vi sep aux sein +dat* to chase (after); *Vergnügungen, dem Glück auch* to pursue.

nachkauen *vt sep* (*inf*) to regurgitate.

Nachkauf *m* further purchase ◆ **10 Jahre ~ garantiert** availability guaranteed for 10 years.

nachkaufen *vt sep* to buy later ◆ **kann man diese Knöpfe auch ~?** is it possible to buy replacements for these buttons?

Nachkaufgarantie *f* availability guarantee.

Nachklang *m* **der ~ der Mandolinen** the sound of the mandolines dying away; **ein ferner ~ von Mallarmé** a distant echo of Mallarmé.

nachklassisch *adj* post-classical.

nachklingen *vi sep irreg aux sein* (*Ton, Echo*) to go on sounding; (*Worte, Erinnerung*) to linger on, to linger ◆ **die Melodie klang noch lange in mir nach** the tune stayed in my head for some time.

Nachkomme *m* **-n, -n** descendant ◆ **ohne ~n** without issue (*form*).

▼ **nachkommen** *vi sep irreg aux sein* **(a)** (*später kommen*) to follow *or* come (on) later ◆ **jdm ~** to follow sb; **wir kommen gleich nach** we'll follow *or* come in just a couple of minutes; **Sie können Ihre Familie/Ihr Gepäck ~ lassen** you can let your family join you later/have your luggage sent on (after).
(b) (*mitkommen, Schritt halten*) to keep up ◆ **ich komme nicht nach!** I can't keep up (with you/them *etc*).
▼ **(c)** *+dat* (*erfüllen*) *seiner Pflicht* to fulfil, to carry out; *einer Anordnung, Forderung, einem Wunsch* to comply with.

Nachkommenschaft *f* descendants *pl*, issue (*form*) ◆ **seine zahlreiche ~** his numerous progeny *pl or* descendants.

Nachkömmling *m* **(a)** (*Nachzügler*) late arrival, latecomer; (*Kind*) afterthought (*hum*). **(b)** (*old: Nachkomme*) descendant.

nachkontrollieren* *vt sep* to check (over).

Nachkriegs- *in cpds* post-war; **n~deutsch** *adj* postwar German; **~deutschland** *nt* postwar Germany.

Nachkühlstrang *m* (*bei Kraftwerk*) cooling phase.

Nachkur ['na:xku:ɐ] *f* follow-up cure.

nachladen *vti sep irreg* to reload.

⚠ **Nachlaß** *m* **-lasses, -lasse** *or* **-lässe (a)** (*Preis~*) discount, reduction (*auf +acc* on). **(b)** (*Erbschaft*) estate ◆ **den ~ eröffnen** to read the will; **literarischer ~** unpublished works *pl*; **Gedichte aus dem ~** unpublished poems.

nachlassen *sep irreg* [1] *vt* **(a)** *Preis, Summe* to reduce ◆ **10% vom Preis ~** to give a 10% discount *or* reduction.
(b) (*locker lassen*) *Zügel, Seil* to slacken; *Schraube* to loosen.
(c) (*old: hinterlassen*) to bequeath; *siehe* **nachgelassen**.
[2] *vi* to decrease, to diminish; (*Interesse auch*) to flag, to wane; (*Sehvermögen, Gehör auch*) to deteriorate; (*Regen, Sturm, Nasenbluten*) to ease off *or* up; (*Leistung, Geschäfte*) to fall *or* drop off; (*Preise*) to fall, to drop ◆ **nicht ~!** keep it up!; **er hat in letzter Zeit sehr nachgelassen** he hasn't been nearly as good recently; **er hat in** *or* **mit seinem Eifer sehr nachgelassen** he's lost a lot of his enthusiasm; **das hat nachgelassen** it's got better; **sobald die Kälte nachläßt** as soon as it gets a bit warmer.

Nachlassenschaft *f siehe* **Hinterlassenschaft**.

⚠ **Nachlaß-: ~gericht** *nt* probate court; **~gläubiger** *m* (*Jur*) creditor of the estate.

nachlässig *adj* careless, negligent; *Arbeit auch* slipshod; (*unachtsam*) thoughtless ◆ **~ gekleidet** carelessly dressed.

nachlässigerweise *adv* thoughtlessly.

Nachlässigkeit *f siehe adj* carelessness; thoughtlessness.

⚠ **Nachlaß-: ~pfleger, ~verwalter** *m* executor; **~verwaltung** *f* administration of the estate.

nachlaufen *vi sep irreg aux sein +dat* **jdm/einer Sache ~** to run after sb/sth; (*fig auch*) to chase sb/sth; **den Mädchen ~** to chase girls.

nachleben *vi sep* **jdm ~** to model one's life on sb's; **einem Ideal ~** to live according to an ideal.

nachlegen *sep* [1] *vt* **noch Kohlen/Holz ~** to put some more coal/wood on (the fire).
[2] *vi* to make up the fire.

Nachlese *f* second harvest; (*Ähren~*) gleaning; (*Ertrag*) gleanings *pl*; (*Liter*) further selection.

nachlesen *sep irreg* [1] *vt* **(a)** *Ähren* to glean ◆ **Beeren/Kartoffeln ~** to gather late berries/potatoes.
(b) (*in einem Buch*) to read; (*nachschlagen*) to look up; (*nachprüfen*) to check up ◆ **man kann das in der Bibel ~** it says so in the Bible.
[2] *vi* **(a)** to have a second harvest; (*Ähren ~*) to glean.
(b) (*nachschlagen*) to look it up; (*nachprüfen*) to check up.

nachliefern *sep* [1] *vt* (*später liefern*) to deliver at a later date; (*zuzüglich liefern*) to make a further delivery of; (*inf: später abgeben*) *Unterlagen* to hand in later ◆ **könnten Sie mir noch einen Zentner ~?** could you deliver another hundredweight?
[2] *vi* to make further deliveries.

Nachlieferung *f* delivery ◆ **wir warten auf die ~** we're waiting for the rest to be delivered.

nachlösen *sep* [1] *vi* to pay on the train/when one gets off; (*zur Weiterfahrt*) to pay the extra.
[2] *vt Fahrkarte* to buy on the train/when one gets off; (*zur Weiterfahrt*) to buy another.

Nachlöseschalter *m* excess fares (counter).

nachm. *abbr of* **nachmittags** p.m.

nachmachen *vt sep* **(a)** (*nachahmen*) to copy; (*nachäffen*) to take off, to mimic ◆ **sie macht mir alles nach** she copies everything I do; **das mach' mir mal einer nach!, das macht mir so schnell keiner nach!, das soll erst mal einer ~!** I'd like to see anyone else do that!
(b) (*fälschen*) *Unterschrift* to forge; *Geld auch* to counterfeit; (*imitieren*) to copy; *siehe* **nachgemacht**.
(c) (*inf: nachholen*) to make up.

nachmalen *vt sep* to copy; (*übermalen*) to touch up.

nachmalig *adj* (*old*) **der ~e Präsident** the future president; **der ~e Präsident X** President X, as he was to become.

nachmals *adv* (*old*) later, subsequently.

nachmessen *sep irreg* [1] *vt* to measure again; *Temperatur* to take again; (*prüfend messen*) to check.
[2] *vi* to check.

Nachmieter *m* next tenant ◆ **unser ~** the tenant after us; **wir müssen einen ~ finden** we have to find someone to take over the flat *etc*.

Nachmittag *m* afternoon ◆ **am ~** in the afternoon; **am heutigen ~** this afternoon; **am ~ des 14. Oktober** on the afternoon of October 14th; **im Laufe** *or* **während des ~s** during *or* in the course of the afternoon; (*heute*) sometime this afternoon; **vom ~ an** from about two o'clock; **bis zum ~** till the afternoon; **des ~s** (*geh*) in the afternoon.

⚠ **nachmittag** *adv* **gestern/morgen/Dienstag/heute ~** yesterday/tomorrow/Tuesday/this afternoon.

nachmittägig *adj attr* afternoon.

nachmittäglich *adj no pred* afternoon *attr* ◆ **die ~ stattfindenden Kurse** the afternoon courses.

nachmittags *adv* in the afternoon; (*jeden Nachmittag*) in the afternoon(s) ◆ **von ~ an** from about two o'clock; **Dienstag** *or* **dienstags ~** every Tuesday afternoon, on Tuesday afternoons; **er ißt immer erst ~** he never eats till (the) afternoon.

Nachmittags-: ~schlaf *m* **~schlaf halten** to have a sleep after lunch; **~schläfchen** *nt* (*inf*) **sein ~schläfchen halten** to have one's afternoon nap *or* post-prandial snooze (*hum*); **~sendung** *f* (*TV*) afternoon programme *or* show (*esp US*); **~stunde** *f* hour of the afternoon; **~vorstellung** *f* matinée (performance).

Nachmusterung *f* (*Mil*) medical re-examination.

Nachnahme *f* **-, -n** cash *or* collect (*US*) on delivery, COD; (*inf: ~sendung*) COD parcel ◆ **etw als** *or* **per ~ schicken** to send sth COD.

Nachnahme-: ~gebühr *f* COD charge; **~sendung** *f* COD parcel.

Nachname *m* surname, family *or* last name ◆ **wie heißt du mit ~n?** what is your surname?

nachnehmen *vti sep irreg* to take (some) more.

nachplappern *vt sep* to repeat parrot-fashion ◆ **jdm alles ~** to repeat everything sb says parrot-fashion.

Nachporto *nt* excess (postage).

nachprägen *vt sep* (*nachträglich prägen*) to mint *or* strike some more; (*fälschen*) to forge ◆ **es wurden 200 Stück nachgeprägt** a further 200 copies were struck.

nachprüfbar *adj* verifiable ◆ **die Ergebnisse sind jederzeit ~** the results can be verified *or* checked at any time.

Nachprüfbarkeit *f* verifiability.

nachprüfen *sep* [1] *vt* **(a)** *Aussagen, Tatsachen* to verify, to check. **(b)** *Kandidaten* (*nochmals prüfen*) to re-examine; (*später prüfen*) to examine at a later date.
[2] *vi* to check.

Nachprüfung *f* **(a)** (*von Aussagen, Tatsachen*) check (*gen* on) ◆ **bei der ~ der**

Meldungen when the reports were checked. **(b)** (*nochmalige Prüfung*) re-examination; (*Termin*) re-sit; (*spätere Prüfung*) later examination.
nachrasen *vi sep aux sein +dat* to race *or* chase after.
nachrechnen *vti sep* to check ◆ **rechne noch einmal nach!** you'd better do your sums again, you'd better check your arithmetic.
Nachrede *f* **(a)** (*Verunglimpfung*) **üble ~** (*Jur*) defamation of character; **jdn in üble ~ bringen** to damage sb's reputation, to bring sb into ill repute; **üble ~ über jdn verbreiten** *or* **führen** to cast aspersions on sb's character; **in üble ~ geraten** *or* **kommen** to get a bad reputation. **(b)** (*Epilog*) epilogue.
nachreden *vt sep* **(a)** (*wiederholen*) to repeat ◆ **er redet dir alles nach** he repeats everything you say. **(b) jdm (etwas) Übles/Schlechtes ~** to speak ill/badly of sb.
Nachredner *m* later *or* subsequent speaker ◆ **mein ~** the speaker after me.
nachreichen *vt sep* to hand in later.
Nachreife *f* afterripening.
nachreifen *vi sep aux sein* to afterripen.
nachreisen *vi sep aux sein* **jdm ~** to follow sb.
nachreiten *vi sep irreg aux sein +dat* to ride after.
nachrennen *vi sep irreg aux sein* (*inf*) *siehe* **nachlaufen.**
Nachricht *f* **-, -en (a)** (*Mitteilung, Botschaft*) message; (*Meldung*) (piece of) news ◆ **eine ~** a message; some news, a piece of news; **die ~en** the news *sing* (*auch Rad, TV*); **~en hören** to listen to the news; **„Sie hören ~en"** "this *or* here is the news"; **das sind aber schlechte ~en** that's bad news; **wer teilt ihm diese unangenehme ~ mit?** who's going to break this unpleasant (piece of) news to him?; **die letzte ~ von ihm kam aus Indien** the last news of him was from India; **~ erhalten, daß** ... to receive (the) news that ...; **wir geben Ihnen ~** we'll let you know.
(b) (*Bestätigung*) confirmation ◆ **wir sind bezüglich unserer Bestellung immer noch ohne ~** we are still awaiting confirmation of our order.
Nachrichten-: ~agentur *f* news agency; **n~arm** *adj* **in n~armen Monaten** in the silly season; **~büro** *nt* news agency; **~dienst** *m* **(a)** (*Rad, TV*) news service; **(b)** (*Pol, Mil*) intelligence (service); **n~dienstlich** *adj Erkenntnisse etc* intelligence *attr*, *Vorschriften etc* intelligence service *attr*; **n~dienstlich erfaßt sein** to be on the files of the intelligence service; **~magazin** *nt* news magazine; **~redaktion** *f* news department *or* room; **wie wir von der ~redaktion erfahren,** ... as we hear from the news desk, ...; **~satellit** *m* (tele)communications satellite; news satellite; **~sperre** *f* news blackout *or* embargo; **~sprecher** *m* newsreader, newscaster; **~technik** *f* telecommunications *sing*; **~übermittlung** *f* communication; **~verbindung** *f* line of communication (*zu* with, to); **~wesen** *nt* communications *pl*.
nachrichtlich *adv* (*form*) **~ an** *+acc* copy to.
nachrücken *vi sep aux sein* to move up; (*auf Stelle, Posten*) to succeed (*auf +acc* to); (*Mil*) to advance ◆ **dem Feind/nach Hanoi ~** to advance on the enemy/on Hanoi.
Nachrücker(in *f*) *m* **-s, -** successor, replacement.
Nachrückerphase *f* period of succession, transition period.
Nachruf *m* obituary.
nachrufen *vti sep irreg +dat* to shout after.
Nachruhm *m* fame after death.
nachrühmen *vt sep* **jdm etw ~** to praise sb for sth.
nachrüsten *sep* [1] *vi* (*Mil*) to deploy new arms; (*modernisieren*) to modernize.
[2] *vt Kraftwerk etc* to modernize; *Auto etc* to refit.
Nachrüstsatz *m* (*Aut*) additional component; (*von Spiel*) supplement.
Nachrüstung *f* **(a)** (*Mil*) deployment of new arms; (*Modernisierung*) arms modernization. **(b)** (*Tech: von Kraftwerk etc*) modernization; (*von Auto etc*) refit.
Nachrüstungs-: ~abkommen *nt* (*Mil*) agreement to deploy new arms; ⚠**~beschluß** *m* (*Mil*) decision to deploy new arms.
nachsagen *vt sep* **(a)** (*wiederholen*) to repeat ◆ **jdm alles ~** to repeat everything sb says; **das ist kein Grund für dich, es nachzusagen** that's no reason for you to say it too.
(b) jdm etw ~ to accuse sb of sth; **jdm Schlechtes ~** to speak ill of sb; **man kann ihr nichts ~** you can't say anything against her; **ihm wird nachgesagt, daß** ... it's said that he ...; **das kannst du mir nicht ~** you can't accuse me of that; **das lasse ich mir nicht ~!** I'm not having that said of me!
Nachsaison *f* off-season.
nachsalzen *sep* [1] *vt* to add more salt to.
[2] *vi* to add more salt.
Nachsatz *m* **(a)** (*Nachschrift*) postscript; (*Nachtrag*) afterthought ◆ **in einem ~ sagte er, daß** ... he added, as an afterthought, that ... **(b)** (*Gram*) clause in sentence final position.
nachschaffen *vt sep irreg* to reproduce.
nachschauen *vti sep siehe* **nachsehen 1, 2 (a).**
nachschenken *vti sep* **jdm etw ~** to top sb up with sth; **darf ich Ihnen noch (etwas) ~?** may I top you up *or* top up your glass *or* give you a refill?; **darf ich (dir) noch etwas Wein ~?** can I give you a little *or* a drop more wine?; **hat der Ober schon nachgeschenkt?** has the waiter already topped up *or* refilled the glasses?
nachschicken *vt sep* to send on, to forward ◆ **bitte ~!** please forward.
nachschieben *vt sep irreg Erklärung, Begründung etc* to provide afterwards ◆ **einer Sache** (*dat*) **etw ~** to follow sth up with sth; **nachgeschobene Gründe** rationalizations.
nachschießen *sep irreg* [1] *vi* **(a)** (*Ftbl*) to shoot again. **(b)** (*Geld ~*) to add something to it.
[2] *vt Geld* to add (to it).
Nachschlag *m* **(a)** (*Mus*) nachschlag (*spec*), *turn ending a trill* ◆ **freier ~** *any grace note following the main note.* **(b)** (*inf*) second helping.
nachschlagen *sep irreg* [1] *vt Stelle, Zitat* to look up.
[2] *vi* **(a)** *aux sein* (*ähneln*) **jdm ~** to take after sb. **(b)** (*Ftbl*) (*sich revanchieren*) to retaliate; (*von hinten foulen*) to foul (one's opponent) from behind. **(c)** (*in Lexikon*) to look.
Nachschlagewerk *nt* reference book *or* work.
nachschleichen *vi sep irreg aux sein +dat* to creep after.
nachschleifen[1] *vt sep* (*hinterherschleifen*) to drag along.
nachschleifen[2] *vt sep irreg* **eine Linse/ein Messer ~** to grind a lens a little more/to sharpen up a knife.
nachschleppen *vt sep* **jdm etw ~** to lug sth after sb.
nachschleudern *vt sep* (*fig*) **jdm etw ~** to fling *or* hurl sth after sb.
Nachschlüssel *m* duplicate key; (*Dietrich*) skeleton key.
nachschmeißen *vt sep irreg* (*inf*) **jdm etw ~** to fling sth after sb; **das ist ja nachgeschmissen!** it's a real bargain.
nachschnüffeln *vi sep* (*inf*) to poke *or* sniff around (*inf*) ◆ **jdm ~** to spy on sb.
nachschreiben *vt sep irreg* (*nachträglich schreiben*) to write later; (*abschreiben*) to write out.
Nachschrift *f* (*Protokoll*) transcript; (*Zugefügtes*) (*abbr* **NS**) postscript, PS ◆ **er hat eine ~ der Vorlesung angefertigt** he wrote up the lecture afterwards.
Nachschub ['na:xʃu:p] *m* (*Mil*) supplies *pl* (*an +dat* of); (*Material*) reinforcements *pl*.
Nachschub- (*Mil*): **~basis** *f* supply base; **~linie** *f* supply line; **~weg** *m* supply route.
⚠**Nachschuß** *m* **(a)** (*Comm*) additional payment; (*St Ex*) marginal call. **(b)** (*Ftbl*) second shot.
nachschütten *vt sep Kies, Sand* to tip in (some) more; *Kohlen* to put on (some) more; (*inf: nachgießen*) to pour (some) more.
nachschwatzen, nachschwätzen (*S Ger, Aus*) *vt sep* (*inf*) *siehe* **nachplappern.**
nachschwingen *vi sep irreg siehe* **nachklingen.**
nachsehen *sep irreg* [1] *vi* **(a) jdm/einer Sache ~** to follow sb/sth with one's eyes, to watch sb/sth; (*hinterherschauen*) to gaze after sb/sth.
(b) (*gucken*) to have a look (and see), to look and see; (*nachschlagen*) to (have a) look.
[2] *vt* **(a)** to (have a) look at; (*prüfen*) to check; *Schulaufgaben etc* to mark; (*nachschlagen*) to look up.
(b) (*verzeihen*) **jdm etw ~** to forgive sb (for) sth.
Nachsehen *nt*: **das ~ haben** to be left standing; (*keine Chance haben*) not to get a look-in (*inf*), not to get anywhere; (*nichts bekommen*) to be left empty-handed.
Nachsende-: ~anschrift *f* forwarding address; **~antrag** *m application to have one's mail forwarded.*
nachsenden *vt sep irreg* to forward ◆ **bitte ~!** please forward.
nachsetzen *sep* [1] *vi* **jdm ~** to pursue sb.
[2] *vt* **(a)** *Fuß* to drag. **(b)** *siehe* **nachstellen 1 (a).**
Nachsicht *f* **-,** *no pl* (*Milde*) leniency, clemency; (*Geduld*) forbearance ◆ **er wurde ohne ~ bestraft** he was punished without mercy; **er kennt keine ~** he knows no mercy; **~ üben** *or* **haben** to be lenient/forbearing; **jdn mit ~ behandeln** to show leniency *or* clemency to sb, to be forbearing with sb; **jdn um ~ bitten** to ask sb to be lenient/forbearing.
nachsichtig, nachsichtsvoll *adj* (*milde*) lenient; (*geduldig*) forbearing (*gegen, mit* with).
Nachsichtigkeit *f siehe* **Nachsicht.**
Nachsilbe *f* suffix.
nachsingen *vt sep irreg* to sing.
nachsinnen *vi sep irreg* to ponder (*über +acc* over, about).
nachsitzen *vi sep irreg* (*Sch*) **~ (müssen)** to be kept in, to have detention; **jdn ~ lassen** to keep sb in, to give sb detention.
Nachsommer *m* Indian summer.
Nachsorge *f* (*Med*) after-care.
Nachsorgeklinik *f* after-care clinic.
nachspähen *vi sep* **jdm ~** to watch sb closely.
Nachspann *m* **-s, -e** credits *pl*.
Nachspeise *f* dessert, sweet (*Brit*) ◆ **als ~** for dessert.
Nachspiel *nt* (*Theat*) epilogue; (*Mus*) closing section, postlude (*form*); (*fig*) sequel ◆ **das geht nicht ohne ~ ab** that's bound to have repercussions; **das wird noch ein unangenehmes ~ haben** that will have unpleasant consequences; **ein gerichtliches ~ haben** to have legal repercussions.
nachspielen *sep* [1] *vt* to play.
[2] *vi* (*Sport*) to play extra time (*Brit*) *or* overtime (*US*); (*wegen Verletzungen*) to play injury time ◆ **der Schiedsrichter ließ ~** the referee allowed extra time (*Brit*) *or* overtime (*US*)/injury time.
nachspionieren* *vi sep* (*inf*) **jdm ~** to spy on sb.
nachsprechen *sep irreg* [1] *vt* to repeat ◆ **jdm etw ~** to repeat sth after sb.
[2] *vi* **wir mußten ihm ~** we had to repeat what he said.
nachspülen *vti sep* to rinse ◆ **ein Bier zum N~** (*inf*) a beer to wash it down.
nachspüren *vi sep +dat* to track *or* hunt down; *einem Tier* to track; *einer Fährte* to follow; *einem Verbrechen, Fehler* to go *or* look into.
nächst *prep +dat* (*geh*) (*örtlich*) next to, beside; (*außer*) apart *or* aside from.
nächstbeste *adj attr* **der/die/das ~** ... the first ... I/you *etc* see; **der ~ Zug/Job** the first train/job that comes along.

⚠: for details of spelling reform, see supplement

➤ SPRACHE AKTIV: **Nachricht: a** → 27.6, 51.3, 51.4

nachstehen *vi sep irreg* **jdm ~** to take second place to sb; **keinem ~** to be second to none (*in +dat* in); **jdm in nichts** (*dat*) **~** to be sb's equal in every way; **jdm an Intelligenz** (*dat*) **nicht ~** to be every bit as intelligent as sb.

nachstehend *adj attr Bemerkung, Ausführungen* following; (*Gram*) postpositive (*form*) ◆ **im ~en** below, in the following; **im ~en der Kläger genannt** here(in)after referred to as the plaintiff; **~es müssen Sie beachten** you must take note of the following; **das ~e Adjektiv** the adjective which follows the noun.

nachsteigen *vi sep irreg aux sein* **jdm ~** (*lit*) to climb up after sb; (*fig inf*) to run after *or* chase sb.

nachstellen *sep* [1] *vt* (a) (*Gram*) **im Französischen wird das Adjektiv (dem Substantiv) nachgestellt** in French the adjective is put after the noun.
(b) (*Tech*) (*neu einstellen*) to adjust; (*zurückstellen*) to put back.
(c) **einen Vorfall/den Unfallhergang ~** to reconstruct an incident/the accident.
[2] *vi* **jdm ~** to follow sb; (*aufdringlich umwerben*) to pester sb; **einem Tier ~** to hunt an animal.

Nachstellung *f* (a) (*Gram*) postposition (*form*). (b) (*Tech*) adjustment; (*Zurückstellung*) putting back. (c) *usu pl* (*old*) (*Verfolgung*) - pursuit *no pl*; (*Aufdringlichkeit*) pestering *no pl*; (*Versuchung*) temptation, snare.

Nächstenliebe *f* brotherly love; (*Barmherzigkeit*) compassion ◆ **~ üben** to love one's neighbour as oneself; *siehe* **Mantel**.

nächstens *adv* (a) (*das nächste Mal*) (the) next time; (*bald einmal*) some time soon, before long. (b) (*am Ende*) next.

nächste(r, s) *adj superl of* **nah(e)** (a) (*nächstgelegen*) nearest ◆ **der ~ Nachbar/das ~ Telefon** the nearest neighbour/telephone; **ist dies der ~ Weg zum Bahnhof?** is this the shortest *or* quickest way to the station?; **in ~r Nähe/Entfernung** in the immediate vicinity/not far away; **aus ~r Entfernung/Nähe** from close by; *sehen, betrachten* at close quarters; *schießen* at close range.
(b) (*unmittelbar folgend*) next ◆ **im ~n Haus** next door.
(c) (*zeitlich*) next ◆ **~s Mal** next time; **bis zum ~n Mal!** till the next time!, see you (some time)!; **Dienstag ~r Woche** Tuesday next week; **Ende ~en Monats** at the end of next month; **am ~en Morgen/Tag(e)** (the) next morning/day; **~r Tage, in den ~n Tagen** in the next few days; **bei ~er** *or* **bei der ~n Gelegenheit** at the earliest opportunity; **in ~r Zukunft** in the near future; **in den ~n Jahren** in the next few years; **in ~r Zeit** some time soon.
(d) *Angehörige, Freunde etc* closest ◆ **die ~n Verwandten** the immediate family; **der ~ Angehörige** the next of kin.
(e) (*in Adverbialkonstruktionen*) **am ~n** closest; (*räumlich auch*) nearest; **fürs ~** for the time being.

Nächste(r) *mf decl as adj* (a) next one ◆ **der n~e, bitte** next please, first please (*US, Scot*). (b) (*Mitmensch*) neighbour (*fig*) ◆ **jeder ist sich selbst der ~** (*Prov*) it's every man for himself; **du sollst deinen ~n lieben wie dich selbst** (*Bibl*) (thou shalt) love thy neighbour as thyself.

Nächste(s) *nt decl as adj* **das ~** the next thing; (*das erste*) the first thing; **als ~s** next/first; **das ~ wäre, ...** the next/first thing *or* step would be ...

nächst-: ~folgend *adj attr* next; **~gelegen** *adj attr* nearest; **~höher** *adj attr* one higher; **die ~höhere Klasse** one class higher; **~jährig** *adj attr* next year's; **~liegend** *adj attr* (*lit*) nearest; (*fig*) most obvious; **das N~liegende** the most obvious thing (to do); **~möglich** *adj attr* next possible.

nachstreben *vi sep* **jdm/einer Sache ~** to emulate sb/to strive after sth.

nachstürzen *vi sep aux sein* (*Geröll*) to cave in ◆ **jdm ~** (*fig*) to dash *or* rush after sb.

nachsuchen *vi sep* (a) to look ◆ **such mal nach, ob ...** (have a) look and see if ... (b) (*form: beantragen*) **um etw ~** to request sth (*bei jdm* of sb), to apply for sth (*bei jdm* to sb).

Nachsuchung *f* (*form*) (*um* for) application, request.

Nacht *f* -, ⸚e (*lit, fig*) night ◆ **es wird/ist/war ~** it's getting/it is/was dark; **als die ~ hereinbrach** at nightfall, as night fell; **in der** *or* **bei ~** at night; **in der ~ vom 12. zum 13. April** during the night of April 12th to 13th; **in der ~ auf Dienstag** during Monday night; **diese ~** tonight; **des ~s** (*geh*) at night; **spät in der ~** late in the *or* at night; **in tiefster ~** at dead of night; **bis tief in die ~** *or* **bis in die späte ~ arbeiten** to work late *or* far into the night; **vor der ~** (*S Ger*) before evening; **über ~** (*lit, fig*) overnight; **über ~ bleiben** to stay the night; **zu(r) ~ essen** (*S Ger, Aus*) to have supper; **sich** (*dat*) **die ~ um die Ohren schlagen** (*inf*) to make a night of it; **die ~ zum Tage machen** to stay up all night (working *etc*); **eines ~s** one night; **letzte** *or* **vergangene ~** last night; **ganze ⸚e** for nights (on end); **gute ~!** good night!; **na, dann gute ~!** (*inf*) what a prospect!, what an outlook!; **bei ~ und Nebel** (*inf*) at dead of night; **es wurde mir ~ vor den Augen** everything went black; **die ~ des Wahnsinns/der Barbarei/des Krieges** (*liter*) the darkness of insanity/barbarism/war (*liter*); **es wurde ~ über Deutschland** (*liter*) the sun went down on Germany (*liter*).

⚠ **nacht** *adv* **heute ~** tonight; (*letzte~*) last night; **Dienstag ~** (on) Tuesday night; **12 Uhr ~** (*Aus*) midnight.

nachtanken *sep* [1] *vi* to get some more (petrol *or* gas *US*).
[2] *vt* **fünf Liter ~** to put in another five litres.

Nacht- *in cpds* night; **~arbeit** *f* night-work; **~asyl** *nt* night shelter; **~ausgabe** *f* late final (edition); **~blindheit** *f* night blindness; **~dienst** *m* (*von Person*) night duty; (*von Apotheke*) all-night service; **~dienst haben** (*Person*) to be on night duty; (*Apotheke*) to be open all night.

➤ **Nachteil** *m* -(e)s, -e disadvantage; (*Schaden auch*) detriment ◆ **~e von** *or* **durch etw haben** to lose by sth; **jdm ~e bringen** to bring sb disadvantages, to be disadvantageous to sb; **im ~ sein, sich im ~ befinden** to be at a disadvantage (*jdm gegenüber* with sb); **daraus entstanden** *or* **erwuchsen ihm ~e** this brought its disadvantages for him; **der ~, allein zu leben** the disadvantage of living alone; **er hat sich zu seinem ~ verändert** he has changed for the worse; **das soll nicht Ihr ~ sein** you won't lose by it; **zu jds ~** to sb's disadvantage/detriment.

nachteilig *adj* (*ungünstig*) disadvantageous; (*schädlich*) detrimental ◆ **es ist nichts N~es über ihn bekannt** nothing unfavourable is known about him; **er hat sich sehr ~ über mich geäußert** he spoke very unfavourably about me; **jdn ~ behandeln** to treat sb unfavourably.

nächtelang *adv* night after night, for nights (on end).

nachten *vi impers* (*Sw, poet*) **es nachtet** it's growing dark, darkness *or* night is falling.

Nacht-: ~essen *nt* (*S Ger, Aus*) supper; **~eule** *f* (*fig inf*) night owl; **~falter** *m* moth; **~flug** *m* night flight; **~flugverbot** *nt* ban on night flights; **~frost** *m* night frost; **~gebet** *nt* evening prayer; **sein/das ~gebet sprechen** to say one's bedtime prayers; **~geschirr** *nt* (*old, hum*) chamber pot; **~gespenst** *nt* ghost (*that walks at night*); **~gewand** *nt* (*geh*) nightrobe; **~hemd** *nt* (*Damennachthemd*) nightie, nightdress; (*Herrennachthemd*) nightshirt; **~himmel** *m* night sky, sky at night.

Nachtigall *f* -, -en nightingale ◆ **~, ick hör' dir trapsen** (*hum dial*) I see it all now, now I see what you're/he's *etc* after.

nächtigen *vi* (*geh*) to spend the night.

Nachtisch *m* dessert, sweet (*Brit*); (*zu Hause auch*) pudding.

Nacht-: ~kästchen *nt* (*S Ger, Aus*) *siehe* **~tisch**; **~klub** *m* night club; **~lager** *nt* (*Unterkunft*) place for the night; (*Mil auch*) bivouac; **sein ~lager aufschlagen** to settle *or* bed down for the night; (*Mil*) to bivouac; **~leben** *nt* night life.

nächtlich *adj attr* (*jede Nacht*) nightly; (*in der Nacht*) night ◆ **die ~e Stadt** the town at night; **zu ~er Stunde** at a late hour; **~e Ruhestörung** (*Jur*) *breach of the peace during the night*.

Nacht-: ~lokal *nt* night club *or* spot; **~luft** *f* night air; **~mahl** *nt* (*Aus*) supper; **n~mahlen** *vi insep* (*Aus*) to have supper; **~mahr** *m* -(e)s, -e (*old, liter*) nightmare; **~mensch** *m* night person; **~mütze** *f* nightcap (*lit*).

nachtönen *vi sep* to resound.

Nacht-: ~portier *m* night porter; **~programm** *nt* late-night programme; **~quartier** *nt* **ein ~quartier** somewhere for the night, a place to sleep; **sein ~quartier aufschlagen** to bed down (for the night).

Nachtrag *m* -(e)s, **Nachträge** postscript; (*zu einem Buch*) supplement.

nachtragen *vt sep irreg* (a) (*hinterhertragen*) **jdm etw ~** (*lit*) to go after sb with sth, to take sth after sb; (*fig*) to hold sth against sb, to bear sb a grudge for sth. (b) (*hinzufügen*) to add; *Summe* to enter up.

nachtragend *adj* unforgiving.

nachträglich *adj* (*zusätzlich*) additional; (*später*) later; (*verspätet*) belated; (*nach dem Tod*) posthumous.

Nachtrags- *in cpds* supplementary; **~haushalt** *m* (*Pol*) supplementary budget.

nachtrauern *vi sep +dat* to mourn.

Nachtruhe *f* night's rest *or* sleep; (*in Anstalten*) lights-out.

nachts *adv* at night ◆ **dienstags ~** (on) Tuesday nights.

Nacht-: ~schalter *m* night desk; **~schatten** *m, no pl* (*Bot*) nightshade; **~schattengewächs** *nt* (*Bot*) solanum (*spec*); (*fig inf*) night bird; **~schicht** *f* night shift; **~schicht haben** to be on night shift *or* nights; **n~schlafend** *adj*: **bei** *or* **zu n~schlafender Zeit** *or* **Stunde** in the middle of the night; **~schwärmer** *m* (*Zool*) moth; (*fig hum*) night owl; **~schwester** *f* night nurse; **~sichtgerät** *nt* night vision aid; **~speicherofen** *m* storage heater; **~strom** *m* off-peak electricity; **~stuhl** *m* (*old*) commode.

nachts|über *adv* by night.

Nacht-: ~tarif *m* (*Verkehrsmittel*) night fares *pl*; (*Strom etc*) off-peak rate; **~tier** *nt* nocturnal animal; **~tisch** *m* bedside table; **~tischlampe, ~tischleuchte** *f* bedside lamp; **~topf** *m* chamber pot.

nachtun *vt sep irreg* **es jdm ~** to copy *or* emulate sb.

Nacht-: ~-und-Nebel-Aktion *f* cloak-and-dagger operation; **~vogel** *m* nocturnal *or* night bird; **~vorstellung** *f* late-night performance; **~wache** *f* night-watch; (*im Krankenhaus*) night duty; **bei einem Kranken ~wache halten** to sit with a patient through the night; **~wache haben** to be on night duty *or* on nights; **~wächter** *m* (*Hist*) (night) watch; (*in Betrieben etc*) night watchman; (*inf*) dope (*inf*); **n~wandeln** *vi insep aux sein or haben* to sleepwalk, to walk in one's sleep; **~wanderung** *f* night ramble *or* walk; **~wandler(in** *f*) *m* -s, - sleepwalker; **n~wandlerisch** *adj* **mit n~wandlerischer Sicherheit** with instinctive assurance; **~zeit** *f* night-time; **~zeug** *nt* night things *pl*; **~zug** *m* night train; **~zuschlag** *m* night supplement.

Nach|untersuchung *f* (*weitere Untersuchung*) further examination; (*spätere Untersuchung*) check-up.

Nachverbrennung *f* (*Tech*) after-burning *no pl*.

nachverlangen* *vt sep* **20 DM ~** to demand an additional DM 20.

nachversichern* *vt sep* **Sie müssen neuerworbene Wertgegenstände ~** you must revise your insurance to cover newly-acquired valuables.

nachvollziehbar *adj* comprehensible.

nachvollziehen* *vt sep irreg* to understand, to comprehend.

nachwachsen *vi sep irreg aux sein* to grow again ◆ **die neue Generation, die jetzt nachwächst** the young generation who are now taking their place in society.

nachwachsend *adj* (*Rohstoff*) renewable; (*Generation*) up-and-coming, younger.

➤ SPRACHE AKTIV: **Nachteil** → 53.3, 53.4

Nachwahl *f (Pol)* ≃ by-election.

Nachwehen *pl* after-pains *pl*; *(fig)* painful aftermath *sing.*

nachweinen *vi sep +dat* to mourn ♦ **dieser Sache weine ich keine Träne nach** *or* **nicht nach** I won't shed any tears over that.

Nachweis *m* **-es, -e** *(Beweis)* proof *(gen, für, über +acc* of); *(Zeugnis)* certificate; *(Zahlungs~)* proof of payment *(über +acc* of) ♦ **als** *or* **zum ~** as proof; **den ~ für etw erbringen** *or* **führen** *or* **liefern** to furnish proof of sth; **der ~ seiner Bedürftigkeit ist ihm geglückt** he succeeded in proving his need.

-nachweis *m in cpds (Vermittlungsstelle)* agency; *(Aufstellung)* directory, list.

nachweisbar *adj (beweisbar)* provable; *Fehler, Irrtum* demonstrable; *(Tech)* detectable ♦ **dem Angeklagten ist keinerlei Schuld ~** it cannot be proved that the accused is in any way guilty.

nachweisen *vt sep irreg (beweisen, aufzeigen)* to prove; *Staatsangehörigkeit, Identität auch* to establish proof of; *(Tech)* to detect ♦ **die Polizei konnte ihm nichts ~** the police could not prove anything against him; **dem Angeklagten konnte seine Schuld nicht nachgewiesen werden** the accused's guilt could not be proved.

nachweislich *adj* provable; *Fehler, Irrtum* demonstrable ♦ **er war ~ in London** it can be proved that he was in London.

Nachwelt *f* **die ~** posterity.

nachwerfen *vt sep irreg* **jdm etw ~** *(lit)* to throw sth after *or* at sb; **das ist nachgeworfen** *(inf)* that's dirt cheap *(inf)* or a gift.

nachwiegen *sep irreg* [1] *vt* to weigh again.
[2] *vi* to check the weight.

nachwinken *vi sep* **jdm ~** to wave (goodbye) to sb.

Nachwinter *m* late winter.

nachwirken *vi sep* to continue to have an effect.

Nachwirkung *f* after-effect; *(fig)* consequence.

Nachwort *nt* epilogue.

Nachwuchs *m* **(a)** *(fig: junge Kräfte)* young people *pl* (in the profession/sport *etc*) ♦ **es mangelt an ~** there's a lack of young blood; **der wissenschaftliche ~** the new generation of academics, the up-and-coming academics.
(b) *(hum: Nachkommen)* offspring *pl.*

Nachwuchs-: ~autor *m* up-and-coming young author; **~kraft** *f* junior member of the staff; **~parlamentarier** *m* junior parliamentarian; **~schauspieler(in** *f*) *m* talented young actor/actress; **~sorgen** *pl* recruitment problems *pl*; **~spieler** *m (Sport)* junior.

nachzahlen *vti sep* to pay extra; *(später zahlen)* to pay later ♦ **20 Pfennig ~** to pay 20 pfennigs extra.

nachzählen *vti sep* to check.

Nachzahlung *f (nachträglich)* back-payment; *(zusätzlich)* additional payment.

nachzeichnen *vt sep siehe* **nachziehen 1 (b).**

Nachzeitigkeit *f (Gram)* posteriority.

nachziehen *sep irreg* [1] *vt* **(a)** *(hinterherziehen)* **etw ~** to pull *or* drag sth behind one; **das rechte Bein ~** to drag one's right leg.
(b) *Linie, Umriß* to go over; *Lippen* to paint over *or* in; *Augenbrauen* to pencil over *or* in.
(c) *Schraube, Seil* to tighten (up).
[2] *vi* **(a)** *aux sein +dat (folgen)* to follow.
(b) *(Schach etc)* to make the next move; *(inf: gleichtun)* to follow suit.

nachzotteln *vi sep aux sein (inf)* to lag behind.

Nachzug *m* **(a)** *(Rail)* relief train. **(b)** *(von Familie, Ehepartner)* joining one's family *(in country of immigration)* ♦ **der ~ wurde nur Kindern unter 10 gestattet** only children under 10 were allowed to join their families.

Nachzügler(in *f*) ['na:xtsy:klɐ, -ərın] *m* **-s, -** latecomer, late arrival *(auch fig).*

Nackedei *m* **-(e)s, -e** *or* **-s** *(hum inf)* naked body *or* person; *(Kind)* little bare monkey *(hum inf).*

Nacken *m* **-s, -** (nape of the) neck ♦ **den ~ beugen** *(fig)* to submit; **jdm den ~ steifen** to encourage sb, to back sb up; **jdn im ~ haben** *(inf)* to have sb after one *or* on one's tail; **jdm im ~ sitzen** *(inf)* to breathe down sb's neck; **ihm sitzt die Furcht/der Geiz im ~** he's frightened out of his wits *(inf)*/he's a miserly so-and-so *(inf)*; **den ~ steif halten** *(inf)* to stand one's ground, to stand fast; **er hat einen starren/störrischen/unbeugsamen ~** he's an obstinate/hard-headed/unbending character.

nackend *adj (inf) Mensch* naked.

Nacken-: ~haar *nt* hair at the nape of the neck; **~hebel** *m (Sport)* nelson; **~rolle** *f* bolster; **~schlag** *m* rabbit-punch; *(fig)* hard knock; **~schutz** *m* neck guard; **~starre** *f* stiffness of the neck; **~starre kriegen** to get a stiff neck; **~stütze** *f (Aut)* headrest, head restraint.

nackig, nackert *(Aus) adj (inf)* bare; *Mensch auch* starkers *pred (inf).*

nackt *adj* **(a)** *Mensch* naked, nude *(esp Art)*; *Arm, Kinn, Haut etc* bare; *neugeborenes Tier* naked ♦ **~ herumlaufen** to run around naked *or* in the nude; **~ baden/schlafen** to bathe/sleep in the nude; **er stand ganz ~ da** he was standing there stark naked *or* absolutely starkers *(inf).*
(b) *(unbewachsen, unbedeckt) Erde, Wand* bare; *Schwert* naked.
(c) *(fig) (unverblümt)* naked; *Wahrheit auch* plain; *Wirklichkeit* stark; *Tatsachen, Zahlen* bare ♦ **mit ~en Worten** without mincing one's words; **die ~e Armut** naked *or* sheer poverty; **das ~e Leben retten** to escape with one's bare life.

Nackt-: ~baden *nt* nude bathing, swimming in the nude; **~badestrand** *m* nudist beach.

Nackte(r) *mf decl as adj* nude.

Nackt-: ~heit *f* nakedness; *(von Mensch auch)* nudity; *(Kahlheit)* bareness; *(von Landschaft auch)* starkness; **~kultur** *f* nudism, naturism; **~modell** *nt* nude model; **~schnecke** *f* slug; **~tänzerin** *f* nude dancer.

Nadel *f* **-, -n (a)** needle; *(Grammophon~, Gravier~, Radier~ auch)* stylus; *(Steck~, Comput: von Drucker)* pin; *(Häkel~)* hook; *(inf: Spritze)* needle ♦ **mit ~ und Faden umgehen können** to be able to wield a needle and thread; **er sitzt wie auf ~n** *(inf)* he's like a cat on hot bricks *(inf)*; **an der ~ hängen** *(sl)* to be hooked on heroin; **von der ~ kommen** *(sl)* to kick the habit.
(b) *(Haar~, Hut~, Krawatten~)* pin; *(Brosche)* brooch.
(c) *(Blatt~, Eis~, Kristall~)* needle.

Nadel-: ~abweichung *f* magnetic deviation *or* declination; **~arbeit** *f* needlework *no pl*; **eine ~arbeit** a piece of needlework; **~baum** *m* conifer; **~brief** *m* packet of needles; **~büchse** *f* pin tin; **~drucker** *m* dot-matrix printer; **~einfädler** *m* **-s, -** needle-threader; **~filz** *m* needle felting; **n~förmig** *adj* needlelike, needle-shaped; **~hölzer** *pl* conifers *pl*; **~kissen** *nt* pin-cushion; **~kopf** *m* pin-head.

nadeln *vi (Baum)* to shed (its needles).

Nadel-: ~öhr *nt* eye of a needle; *siehe* **Kamel**; **~spitze** *f* point *or* tip (of a needle); *(Handarbeit)* needle-point (lace); **~stärke** *f* size of needle; **~stich** *m* prick; *(beim Nähen, Med)* stitch; **jdm ~stiche versetzen** *(fig)* to needle sb; **eine Politik der ~stiche** a policy of pinpricks; **~streifen** *pl* pinstripes *pl*; **~streifenanzug** *m* pinstripe(d) suit; **~wald** *m* coniferous forest.

Nadir *m* **-s,** *no pl* nadir.

-Nadler *m suf* **-s, -** *(Comput inf)* **24-~** 24-pin printer.

Nagel *m* **-s, ¨** nail *(auch Anat)*; *(Zwecke)* tack; *(aus Holz)* peg; *(an Schuhen)* hobnail, stud; *(Med)* pin ♦ **sich** *(dat)* **etw unter den ~ reißen** *or* **ritzen** *(inf)* to pinch sth *(inf)*; **etw an den ~ hängen** *(fig)* to chuck sth in *(inf)*; **den ~ auf den Kopf treffen** *(fig)* to hit the nail on the head; **¨~ mit Köpfen machen** *(inf)* to do the job *or* thing properly; *siehe* **Sarg, brennen.**

Nagel-: ~bett *nt (Anat)* bed of the nail; **~bohrer** *m* gimlet; **~brett** *nt (von Fakir)* bed of nails; **~bürste** *f* nailbrush; **~feile** *f* nailfile; **n~fest** *adj siehe* **niet- und n~fest**; **~haut** *f* cuticle; **~hautentferner** *m* **-s, -** cuticle-remover.

Nägelkauen *nt* **-s,** *no pl* nail-biting.

Nagel-: ~knipser *m* **-s, -** nail clippers *pl*; **~kopf** *m* head (of a/the nail); **~lack** *m* nail varnish *or* polish; **~lackentferner** *m* nail varnish remover.

nageln *vt* to nail *(an +acc, auf +acc* (on)to); *Teppich auch* to tack; *(Med)* to pin; *(mit Nägeln versehen)* to hobnail *or* stud.

Nagel-: n~neu *adj (inf)* brand new; **~pflege** *f* nail care; **~pflege machen** to give oneself a manicure; **~probe** *f (fig)* acid test; **~reiniger** *m* **-s, -** nail-cleaner; **~schere** *f* (pair of) nail-scissors *pl*; **~schuh** *m* hobnailed boot; *(Bergstiefel)* climbing boot; **~zange** *f* nail clippers *pl*; *(Tech)* (pair of) pincers *pl.*

nagen [1] *vi (lit, fig)* to gnaw *(an +dat* at); *(knabbern)* to nibble *(an +dat* at); *(Rost, Wasser)* to eat *(an +dat* into) ♦ **an einem Knochen ~** to gnaw (on *or* at) a bone.
[2] *vt* to gnaw ♦ **wir haben nichts zu ~ noch zu beißen** *(old)* we've eaten our last crust.

nagend *adj Hunger* gnawing; *Zweifel, Gewissen* nagging.

Nager *m* **-s, -**, **Nagetier** *nt* rodent.

nah *adj, adv siehe* **nah(e) 1, 2.**

Näh|arbeit *f* sewing *no pl* ♦ **eine ~** a piece of sewing.

Nah|aufnahme *f (Phot)* close-up.

nah(e) [1] *adj, comp* **näher**, *superl* **nächste(r, s) (a)** *(örtlich)* near *pred*, close *pred*, nearby ♦ **der N~e Osten** the Middle East; **von ~em** from close to, at close quarters; **jdm ~ sein** to be near (to) sb; **Gott ist uns ~** *(liter)* God is nigh *(liter)*; **Rettung/Hilfe ist nah** help is at hand.
(b) *(zeitlich)* near *pred*, approaching, nigh *(liter) pred* ♦ **die ~e Zukunft** the near future.
(c) *(eng) Freund, Beziehung etc* close.
[2] *adv, comp* **näher**, *superl* **am nächsten (a)** *(örtlich)* near, close ♦ **~e an** near *or* close to; **~e bei** close to *or* by, near; **~ beieinander** close together; **~ liegend** nearby; **~ vor** right in front of; **von ~ und fern** from near and far; **jdm zu ~ treten** *(fig)* to offend sb; **jdm/einer Sache zu ~ kommen** to get too close to sb/sth; *siehe* **daran.**
(b) *(zeitlich)* **mein Prüfungstermin rückt allmählich ~** my examination is getting close; **Weihnachten steht ~ bevor** Christmas is just (a)round the corner *or* is almost upon us; **~ bevorstehend** approaching; **sie ist ~ an (die) Achtzig** she's almost *or* nearing eighty.
(c) *(eng)* closely ♦ **mit jdm ~ verwandt sein** to be a near relative of sb's, to be closely related to sb.
[3] *prep +dat* near (to), close to ♦ **der Ohnmacht/dem Wahnsinn** *etc* **~e sein** to be on the verge of fainting/madness.

Nähe *f* **-,** *no pl* **(a)** *(örtlich) (Nahesein)* nearness, closeness, proximity; *(Umgebung, Nachbarschaft)* vicinity, neighbourhood ♦ **in meiner ~/der ~ des Gebäudes** near me/the building, in the vicinity of the building; **aus der ~** from close to, at close quarters. **(b)** *(zeitlich)* closeness.

nahebei *adv* nearby, close to *or* by.

⚠ **nahebringen** *vt sep irreg +dat (fig)* **jdm etw ~** to bring sth home to sb, to impress sth on sb; **jdn jdm ~** to bring sb close to sb.

⚠ **nahegehen** *vi sep irreg aux sein +dat (fig)* to upset.

Nah|einstellung *f (Film)* close-up (shot).

⚠ **nahekommen** *vi sep irreg aux sein +dat (fig)* **jdm ~** *(vertraut werden)* to get on close terms with sb, to get close to sb; **jdm/einer Sache ~** *(fast gleichen)* to come close *or* near to sb/sth; **sich** *or* **einander ~** to become close; **das kommt der Wahrheit schon eher nahe** that is getting nearer the truth.

⚠**nahelegen** *vt sep (fig)* **jdm etw ~** to suggest sth to sb; **jdm ~, etw zu tun** to advise sb to do sth; **er legte es mir nahe, von mir aus zu kündigen** he put it to me that I should resign.

⚠**naheliegen** *vi sep irreg (fig: Idee, Frage, Lösung)* to suggest itself ◆ **die Vermutung/die Annahme/der Verdacht liegt nahe, daß ...** it seems reasonable to suppose/assume/suspect that ...; **der Gedanke lag nahe, ihn zum Teilhaber zu machen** the idea of making him a partner seemed to suggest itself.

⚠**naheliegend** *adj Gedanke, Lösung* which suggests itself; *Verdacht, Vermutung* natural ◆ **das N~e wäre ...** the obvious thing to do would be ...; **aus ~en Gründen** for obvious reasons.

nahen *vir aux sein (liter)* to approach *(jdm/einer Sache* sb/sth), to draw near *or* nigh *(liter) (jdm/einer Sache* to sb/sth).

nähen [1] *vt* to sew; *(mit Stichen befestigen auch)* to stitch; *Kleid* to make; *Wunde, Verletzten* to stitch (up), to suture *(spec)* ◆ **mit der Maschine/mit der** *or* **von Hand genäht** machine-/hand-sewn, sewn by machine/hand; **sich** *(dat)* **die Finger wund ~** to sew one's fingers to the bone; *siehe* **doppelt**.
[2] *vi* to sew.
[3] *vr* **dieser Stoff näht sich sehr gut/schlecht** this material is very easy/difficult to sew.

näher *comp of* **nah(e)** [1] *adj* **(a)** *(örtlich)* closer, nearer ◆ **jdm/einer Sache ~** closer to *or* nearer (to) sb/sth; **dieser Weg ist ~** this road is shorter *or* quicker; **die ~e Umgebung** the immediate vicinity.
(b) *(zeitlich)* closer, sooner *pred*.
(c) *(genauer) Auskünfte, Einzelheiten* further *attr*, more detailed *or* precise.
(d) *(enger) Verwandter, Bekannter, Beziehungen* closer ◆ **die ~e Verwandtschaft** the immediate family.
[2] *adv* **(a)** *(örtlich, zeitlich)* closer, nearer ◆ **~ kommen** *or* **rücken** to come *or* draw nearer, to approach; **bitte treten Sie ~** just step up!; *(Beamter, Arzt)* please come over here.
(b) *(genauer)* more closely; *besprechen, erklären, ausführen* in more detail ◆ **ich habe mir das Bild ~ angesehen** I had a closer look at the picture; **sich mit etw ~ befassen** *or* **beschäftigen** to go into sth; **jdn/etw ~ kennenlernen** to get to know sb/sth better; **ich kenne ihn nicht ~** I don't know him well; **der Sache** *(dat)* **~ kommen** to be nearer the mark.

⚠**näherbringen** *vt sep irreg +dat* **jdm etw ~** to give sb an understanding of sth.

Näherei *f* **(a)** *(no pl: das Nähen)* sewing; *(Näharbeit)* piece of sewing. **(b)** *(Betrieb)* sewing works *sing or pl*; *(für Kleider)* garment factory.

Nähere(s) *nt decl as adj* details *pl*; *(über Stellenangebot etc)* further details *pl* ◆ **ich kann mich des N~n nicht entsinnen** *(geh)* I can't remember the (precise) details.

Nah|erholungsgebiet *nt* recreational area *(close to a town)*.

Näherin *f* seamstress.

⚠**näherkommen** *vi sep irreg aux sein (fig)* **jdm ~** to get closer to sb; **sie sind sich** *or* **einander nähergekommen** they've become closer.

⚠**näherliegen** *vi sep irreg (fig)* to be more obvious; *(Verdacht auch)* to be more natural ◆ **ich denke, daß diese Entscheidung näherliegt** I think this is the more obvious decision; **das N~de** the more obvious course.

nähern [1] *vr* **sich (jdm/einer Sache) ~** to approach (sb/sth), to get closer *or* draw nearer (to sb/sth); **der Abend näherte sich seinem Ende** the evening was drawing to a close.
[2] *vt* to bring *or* draw closer.

⚠**näherstehen** *vi sep irreg +dat (fig)* to be closer to.

⚠**nähertreten** *vi sep irreg aux sein +dat (fig)* to get closer to ◆ **ich werde Ihrem Vorschlag ~** *(form)* I shall give full consideration to your proposal.

Näherung *f (Math)* approximation.

Näherungswert *m (Math)* approximate value.

⚠**nahestehen** *vi sep irreg +dat (fig)* to be close to; *(Pol)* to sympathize with ◆ **sich ~** *(Menschen, Ideen)* to be close; **wir stehen uns (geistig) sehr nahe** our views are very close; **dem Präsidenten ~de Quellen** sources close to the president; **eine den Konservativen ~de Zeitung** a paper with Conservative sympathies *or* leanings.

nahezu *adv* nearly, almost, virtually ◆ **das ist ja ~ Wucher** that's little short of profiteering.

Nähfaden *m*, **Nähgarn** *nt* (sewing) cotton *or* thread.

Nahkampf *m (Mil)* close combat, hand-to-hand fighting ◆ **beim ~ sein** *(fig sl)* to be in a clinch *(inf)*.

Nahkampf-: ~mittel, ~waffen *pl* close- *or* short-range weapons *pl*.

Näh-: ~kästchen *nt*, **~kasten** *m* work-box, sewing box; **aus dem ~kästchen plaudern** *(inf)* to give away private details; **~korb** *m* work-basket, sewing basket.

nahm *pret of* **nehmen**.

Näh-: ~maschine *f* sewing machine; **~nadel** *f* needle.

Nah|ost *m* **in/aus ~** in/from the Middle East.

nah|östlich *adj attr* Middle East(ern).

Nähr-: ~boden *m (lit)* fertile soil; *(für Bakterien)* culture medium; *(fig)* breeding-ground; **ein guter ~boden** *(lit)* fertile *or* good soil *or* land; **diese Ideen fanden keinen guten ~boden** these ideas didn't take root; **~brühe** *f siehe* **~lösung**; **~creme** *f* skin food.

nähren *(geh)* [1] *vt* to feed; *(fig) (steigern)* to increase, to feed; *Hoffnungen* to build up; *(haben)* to nurse; *Hoffnungen* to nurture, to nurse ◆ **er sieht gut genährt aus** he looks well-fed; **das Handwerk nährt seinen Mann** there's a good living to be made as a craftsman; **er nährt den süßen Traum, berühmt zu werden** he has fond hopes of becoming famous.
[2] *vr* to feed oneself; *(Tiere)* to feed ◆ **sich von** *or* **mit etw ~** to live on sth; *siehe* **bleiben**.
[3] *vi* to be nourishing.

nahrhaft *adj Kost* nourishing, nutritious; *Boden* fertile, rich ◆ **ein ~es Essen** a square meal.

Nähr-: ~kraft *f* nutritional value; **~lösung** *f* nutrient solution; **~mittel** *pl* cereal products *pl*; **~stoff** *m usu pl* nutrient, nutriment.

Nahrung *f, no pl* food ◆ **flüssige/feste ~** liquids/solids *pl*; **geistige ~** intellectual stimulation; **sie verweigerten jegliche ~** they refused all nourishment; **einer Sache** *(dat)* **(neue) ~ geben** to help to nourish *or* feed sth; **dadurch fand** *or* **erhielt die ganze Sache neue ~** that just added fuel to the fire; **dem Feuer ~ geben** *(liter)* to build up the fire.

Nahrungs-: ~aufnahme *f* eating, ingestion (of food) *(form)*; **die ~aufnahme verweigern** to refuse food *or* sustenance; **~kette** *f (Biol)* food chain; **~mangel** *m* food shortage.

Nahrungsmittel *nt* food(stuff).

Nahrungsmittel-: ~chemie *f* food chemistry; **~chemiker** *m* food chemist; **~vergiftung** *f* food poisoning.

Nahrungs-: ~suche *f* search for food; ⚠**~- und Genußmittelindustrie** *f* food and allied industries *pl*; **~verweigerung** *f* refusal of food, refusal to eat; **durch ~verweigerung** by refusing food *or* to eat.

Nährwert *m* nutritional value ◆ **hat das einen praktischen ~?** *(inf)* does that have any practical value?; **das hat doch keinen (praktischen) ~** *(inf)* it's pretty pointless.

Nähseide *f* sewing-silk, silk thread.

Naht *f* -, **¨e** seam; *(Tech auch)* join; *(Med)* stitches *pl*, suture *(spec)*; *(Anat)* suture ◆ **aus allen ¨en platzen** to be bursting at the seams.

Nähtisch(chen *nt***)** *m* sewing-table.

nahtlos *adj (lit) Teil, Anzug* seamless; *(fig) Übergang* smooth, imperceptible ◆ **Vorlesung und Diskussion gingen ~ ineinander über** there was a smooth transition from the lecture to the discussion.

Nahtstelle *f* **(a)** *(lit) siehe* **Naht**. **(b)** *(fig)* link.

Nahverkehr *m* local traffic ◆ **der öffentliche ~** local public transport; **im ~** on local runs *or* journeys.

Nahverkehrs-: ~mittel *pl* means of local transport *pl*; **~zug** *m* local train.

nahverwandt *adj attr* closely-related ◆ **N~e** close relatives.

Nähzeug *nt* sewing kit, sewing things *pl*.

Nahziel *nt* immediate aim *or* objective.

naiv *adj* naive; *(ungekünstelt auch)* ingenuous ◆ **die N~e** *(Theat)* the Ingénue.

Naivität [naivi'tɛ:t] *f* naivety.

Naivling *m (inf)* simpleton ◆ **wie kann man bloß so ein ~ sein!** how can anyone be so naive!

Najade *f* naiad.

Name *m* **-ns, -n, Namen** *m* **-s, -** *(Benennung)* name; *(fig: Ruf)* name, reputation ◆ **ein angenommener ~** an assumed name; *(von Autoren etc)* a pen name, a nom de plume, a pseudonym; **der volle ~** his/her/their full name; **mit ~n, des ~ns** *(geh)* by the name of, called; **dem ~n nach** by name; **ich kenne das Stück nur dem ~n nach** I've heard of the play but that's all; **dem ~n nach müßte sie Jugoslawin sein** judging by her name she must be Yugoslavian; **auf jds ~n** *(acc)* in sb's name; **unter dem ~n** under the name of; **er war unter dem ~n Schmidt bekannt** he was known under *or* by the name of Schmidt, he was known as Schmidt; **er nannte seinen ~n** he gave his name; **Ihr ~, bitte?** your *or* the name, please?; **wie war doch gleich Ihr (werter) ~?** what was the name?; **dazu gebe ich meinen ~n nicht her** I won't lend my name to that; **der ~ tut nichts zur Sache** his/my *etc* name's irrelevant; **einen ~n haben** *(fig)* to have a name; **sich** *(dat)* **einen ~n machen** to make a name for oneself; **die Dinge** *or* **das Kind** *(inf)* **beim (rechten) ~n nennen** to call a spade a spade, to face facts; **im ~n** *(+gen)* on *or* in *(US)* behalf of; **im ~n des Volkes** in the name of the people; **im ~n des Gesetzes** in the name of the law; **in Gottes ~n!** *(inf)* for heaven's sake *(inf)*.

Namen-: ~gebung *f siehe* **Namen(s)gebung**; **~gedächtnis** *nt* memory for names; **~kunde** *f* science of names, onomastics *(spec) sing*; **~liste** *f siehe* **Namen(s)liste**.

namenlos [1] *adj* **(a)** nameless *(auch fig)*, unnamed; *Helfer* anonymous ◆ **er will ~ bleiben** he wishes to remain anonymous; **die Millionen der N~en** the nameless millions. **(b)** *(geh: unsäglich)* nameless, unspeakable, unutterable.
[2] *adv (geh: äußerst)* unspeakably, unutterably.

namens [1] *adv (mit Namen)* by the name of, called, named.
[2] *prep +gen (form: im Auftrag)* in the name of.

Namen(s)- *in cpds* name; **~änderung** *f* change of name; **~gebung** *f* naming; **eine unglückliche ~gebung für eine Ware** an unfortunate choice of name for a product; **~liste** *f* list of names, name list; **~nennung** *f* naming names; **auf ~nennung wollen wir doch verzichten** we don't need to name names; **~papier** *nt (Fin)* registered security; **~register** *nt* list of names, name list; **~schild** *nt* nameplate; **~schuldverschreibung** *f (Fin)* registered bond; **~tag** *m* name day, Saint's day; **~verzeichnis** *nt* list of names, name list; **~vetter** *m* namesake; **~zeichen** *nt* initials *pl*; **~zug** *m* signature; *(Monogramm)* monogram.

namentlich [1] *adj* by name ◆ **wir bitten, von einer ~en Aufführung der Spender abzusehen** we would request you to refrain from naming the donors; **~e Abstimmung** roll call vote; **~er Aufruf** roll call.
[2] *adv* (e)specially, in particular, particularly.

Namen-: ~verzeichnis *nt siehe* **Namen(s)verzeichnis**; **~wechsel** *m* change of name.

namhaft *adj* **(a)** *(bekannt)* famous, well-known ◆ **~ machen** *(form)* to identify. **(b)** (*beträchtlich*) considerable, substantial.

Namibia *nt* **-s** Namibia.

namibisch *adj* Namibian.

nämlich [1] *adv* **(a)** namely, to wit (*Jur, hum*); (*geschrieben*) viz. **(b)** (*denn*) **es ging nicht schneller, wir haben ~ einen Umweg machen müssen** we couldn't be any quicker, we had to make a detour you see.
[2] *adj* **der/die/das ~e** (*old*) the same.

nannte *pret of* **nennen.**

Nano-: ~gramm *nt* nanogram; **~meter** *m or nt* nanometer; **~sekunde** *f* nanosecond.

nanu *interj* well I never ◆ **~, wer ist das denn?** hello (hello), who's this?

Napalm *nt* **-s,** *no pl* napalm.

Napalmbombe *f* napalm bomb.

Napf *m* **-(e)s, ¨-e** bowl.

Napfkuchen *m* ≃ ring-shaped poundcake.

Naphtha ['nafta] *nt* **-s** *or f* **-,** *no pl* naphtha.

Naphthalin [nafta'li:n] *nt* **-s,** *no pl* naphthalene.

napoleonisch *adj* Napoleonic.

Nappa(leder) *nt* **-(s), -s** napa leather.

Narbe *f* **-, -n (a)** (*lit, fig*) scar; (*Pocken~*) pock(mark) ◆ **eine ~ hinterlassen** to leave a scar; **die ~ bleibt, auch wenn die Wunde heilt** (*Prov*) deep down, I/you *etc* still bear the scars. **(b)** (*Bot*) stigma. **(c)** (*Gras~*) turf. **(d)** (*Leder~*) grain.

Narben *m* **-s, -** grain.

Narben-: ~bildung *f* scarring; **~gesicht** *nt* scarred face; (*als Name*) scarface.

narbig *adj* scarred.

Narkose *f* **-, -n** an(a)esthesia ◆ **jdm eine ~ geben** to put sb under an(a)esthetic; **in der ~ liegen** to be under an(a)esthetic; **ohne ~** without an(a)esthetic; **aus der ~ aufwachen** to come out of the an(a)esthetic.

Narkose-: ~apparat *m* an(a)esthetic apparatus *no indef art*; **~arzt** *m* an(a)esthetist; **~maske** *f* an(a)esthetic mask; **~zwischenfall** *m* complication during an(a)esthesia.

Narkotikum *nt* **-s, Narkotika** (*Med*) narcotic.

narkotisch *adj* narcotic; *Düfte* overpowering ◆ **der süße Geruch wirkte ~ auf uns** the sweet smell had a druglike effect on us.

narkotisieren* *vt* (*lit, fig*) to drug.

Narr *m* **-en, -en** fool; (*Hof~ auch*) jester ◆ **den ~en spielen** to act *or* play the fool; **die ~en werden nicht alle** (*Prov*) there's one born every minute (*inf*); **jdn zum ~en haben** *or* **halten** to make a fool of sb; **ein verliebter ~** somebody blinded by love; **er ist ein verliebter ~** he is love's dupe *or* fool; **dieser verliebte ~** this love-lorn fool; *siehe* **fressen.**

narrativ *adj* narrative.

narren *vt* (*geh*) **jdn ~** (*zum besten haben*) to make a fool of *or* fool sb; (*täuschen*) to dupe *or* fool sb.

Narren-: ~freiheit *f* freedom to do whatever one wants; **sie hat bei ihm ~freiheit** he gives her (a) free rein; **n~haft** *adj* foolish; **~hände** *pl*: **~hände beschmieren Tisch und Wände** (*Prov*) only fools go round defacing things; **~haus** *nt* madhouse; **du gehörst ins ~haus** you need locking up *or* putting away; **~kappe** *f* fool's *or* jester's cap; **n~sicher** *adj* foolproof; **~streich** *m* (*old*) prank; (*dumme Tat*) act of stupidity; **~zepter** *nt* jester's *or* fool's sceptre, bauble; **das ~zepter führen** to carry the fool's sceptre.

Narretei *f* (*geh*) folly.

Narrheit *f* **(a)** *no pl* folly, stupidity. **(b)** (*Streich*) prank; (*dumme Tat*) act of stupidity, stupid thing to do.

Närrin *f* fool.

närrisch *adj* foolish, silly; (*verrückt*) mad; (*inf: sehr*) madly ◆ **die ~en Tage** *Fasching and the period leading up to it*; **das ~e Treiben** *Fasching celebrations*; **sich wie ~ gebärden** to act like a madman, to act crazy; **ganz ~ auf jdn/etw sein** (*inf*) to be crazy about *or* mad (keen) on sb/sth (*inf*).

⚠ **Narziß** *m* **-sses, -sse** (*liter*) Narcissus.

Narzisse *f* **-, -n** narcissus.

⚠ **Narzißmus** *m* narcissism.

⚠ **Narzißt** *m* **-en, -en** (*Psych*) narcissist.

⚠ **narzißtisch** *adj* narcissistic.

Nasa, NASA ['na:za] *f* **-** NASA.

Nasal *m* **-s, -e** nasal.

nasal *adj* nasal ◆ **~er Ton** nasal twang.

Nasallaut *m* nasal (sound).

naschen [1] *vi* to eat sweet things; (*heimlich kosten*) to pinch a bit (*inf*) ◆ **darf ich mal ~?** can I try a bit?; **an etw** (*dat*) **~** to pinch a bit of sth; (*anknabbern*) to (have a) nibble at sth; **er hat von allem nur genascht** he only had a taste of everything; **die Kinder haben den ganzen Tag nur genascht** the children have been nibbling all day.
[2] *vt* to nibble ◆ **sie nascht gern Süßigkeiten** she has a sweet tooth; **hast du was zum N~?** have you got something for my sweet tooth?

Näschen ['nɛ:sçən] *nt dim of* **Nase.**

Nascher(in *f*) *m* **-s, -** nibbler; (*der Süßes mag*) sweet-eater.

Nascherei *f* **(a)** *no pl* nibbling; (*von Süßigkeiten*) sweet-eating. **(b) ~en** *pl* (*Süßigkeiten*) sweets and biscuits *pl* (*Brit*), candy and cookies *pl* (*US*).

Nasch-: n~haft *adj* fond of sweet things; **die Kinder sind so n~haft** the children are always nibbling at things; **sei nicht so n~haft** you and your sweet tooth; **~haftigkeit** *f* fondness for sweet things; **~katze** *f* (*inf*) guzzler; **ich bin halt so eine alte ~katze** I've got such a sweet tooth; **~sucht** *f* craving for sweet things; **~werk** *nt, no pl* (*old*) dainties *pl*, sweetmeats *pl* (*old*).

Nase *f* **-, -n (a)** (*Organ, Sinn, fig*) nose ◆ **durch die ~ reden** to talk through one's nose; **mir blutet die ~, meine ~ blutet** I've got a nosebleed, my nose is bleeding; **jdm/sich die ~ putzen** to wipe sb's/one's nose; **sich** (*dat*) **die ~ putzen** (*sich schnäuzen*) to blow one's nose; **pro ~** (*hum*) per head; **es liegt vor deiner ~** (*inf*) it's right in front of *or* right under your nose (*inf*); **wir haben die Weinberge genau vor der ~** (*inf*) the vine slopes are right on our doorstep; **(immer) der ~ nachgehen** (*inf*) to follow one's nose; **eine gute ~ für etw haben** (*inf*) to have a good nose for sth; **die richtige ~ für etw haben** (*inf*) to have a nose for sth; **faß dich an deine eigene ~!** (*inf*) you can (*iro*) *or* can't talk!; **jdm etw/die Würmer aus der ~ ziehen** (*inf*) to drag sth/it all out of sb; **jdm etw unter die ~ reiben** (*inf*) to rub sb's nose *or* face in sth (*inf*); **jdm auf der ~ herumtanzen** (*inf*) to play sb up (*inf*); **seine ~ gefällt mir nicht** (*inf*) I don't like his face; **es muß nicht immer nach deiner ~ gehen** (*inf*) you can't always have things your way; **ihm wurde ein Neuer vor die ~ gesetzt** (*inf*) they put a new man over him; **ich sah es ihm an der ~ an** (*inf*) I could see it on *or* written all over his face (*inf*); **auf der ~ liegen** (*inf*) (*krank sein*) to be laid up; (*hingefallen sein*) to be flat on one's face (*inf*); **steck deine ~ ins Buch!** (*inf*) get on with your book; **auf die ~ fallen** (*lit, fig*) *or* **fliegen** (*inf*) to fall flat on one's face; **jdm etw vor der ~ wegschnappen** (*inf*) just to beat sb to sth; **die Katze hat dem Hund das Futter vor der ~ weggeschnappt** the cat took the dog's food away right from under its nose; **der Zug fuhr ihm vor der ~ weg** (*inf*) he missed the train by inches *or* seconds; **jdm die Tür vor der ~ zuschlagen** (*inf*) to slam the door in sb's face; **jdm eine (lange) ~ drehen** *or* **machen** (*inf*) to cock a snook at sb, to thumb one's nose at sb; **jdm etw unter die ~ halten** to shove sth right under sb's nose (*inf*); **jdn mit der ~ draufstoßen** (*inf*) to point it out to sb; (*überdeutlich werden*) to make it more than obvious to sb; **jdm eins auf die ~ geben** (*lit*) to punch sb on the nose; (*fig*) to tell sb what's what, to put sb in his place; **die ~ voll haben** (*inf*) to be fed up (*inf*), to have had enough; **die ~ von jdm/etw voll haben** (*inf*) to be sick (to death) of sb/sth (*inf*), to be fed up to the back teeth with sb/sth (*inf*); **jdn an der ~ herumführen** (*als Täuschung*) to lead sb by the nose; (*als Scherz*) to pull sb's leg; **jdm etw auf die ~ binden** (*inf*) to tell sb all about sth; **jdm auf die ~ binden, daß ...** (*inf*) to tell sb that ...; **das werde ich ihm gerade auf die ~ binden** (*iro*) you think I'd tell him that!; **er steckt seine ~ in alles (hinein)** (*inf*) he pokes his nose into everything; **er sieht nicht weiter als seine ~** (*inf*) he can't see further than the end of his nose; **die ~ vorn haben** (*inf*) to be ahead by a nose; (*in Forschung etc auch*) to be one step ahead; *siehe* **Mund, Wind, hoch.**
(b) (*Mech*) handle, horn.
(c) (*Farbtropfen*) run.
(d) (*Halbinsel*) promontory, headland, naze; (*Fels~*) overhang.

nas(e)lang *adv*: **alle ~** all the time, again and again.

näseln *vi* to talk *or* speak through one's nose.

näselnd *adj* nasal.

Nasen-: ~atmung *f* breathing through the nose; **~bär** *m* coati; **~bein** *nt* nose bone, nasal bone; **~bluten** *nt* a nosebleed/nosebleeds; **ich habe ~bluten** my nose is bleeding, I have a nosebleed; **~flügel** *m* side of the nose; **seine ~flügel fingen an zu zittern** his nose *or* nostrils began to twitch; **~höhle** *f* nasal cavity; **~länge** *f* (*fig*) **mit einer** *or* **um eine ~länge gewinnen** to win by a nose; **jdm eine ~länge voraus sein** to be a hair's breadth ahead of sb; **~loch** *nt* nostril; **verliebte ~löcher machen** (*hum*) to make eyes; **~ring** *m* (nose) ring; **~rücken** *m* bridge *or* ridge of the nose; **~scheidewand** *f* nasal septum (*spec*); **~schleim** *m* nasal mucus; **~schleimhaut** *f* mucous membrane (of the nose); **~schmuck** *m* nose ornament(s); **~spitze** *f* tip of the/sb's nose; **ich seh es dir an der ~spitze an** I can tell by your face, I can see it written all over your face; **~spray** *m or nt* nasal *or* nose spray; **~stüber** *m* **-s, -** bump on the nose; **jdm einen ~stüber versetzen** (*lit*) to bop sb on the nose; (*fig*) to tick *or* tell sb off; **~tropfen** *pl* nose drops *pl*; **~wurzel** *f* bridge (of the nose).

Nase-: ~rümpfen *nt* wrinkling (up) *or* screwing up one's nose; **auf etw** (*acc*) **mit ~rümpfen reagieren** to turn one's nose up at sth; **n~rümpfend** *adj* **er sagte n~rümpfend** screwing up *or* wrinkling (up) his nose, he said; **die n~rümpfenden Eltern** the disapproving parents; **n~weis** *adj* cheeky, saucy; (*vorlaut*) forward, precocious; (*neugierig*) nos(e)y (*inf*), inquisitive; **~weis** *m* **-es, -e** (*Vorlauter*) cheeky (*esp Brit*) *or* precocious brat *or* monkey (*inf*); (*Neugieriger*) nos(e)y parker (*inf*); (*Überschlauer*) know-all, clever dick (*Brit inf*), wiseguy (*inf*).

nasführen *vt insep* **jdn ~** (*als Täuschung*) to lead sb by the nose; (*als Scherz*) to pull sb's leg (*inf*); **ich war der/die Genasführte** I was the dupe.

Nashorn *nt* rhinoceros, rhino.

-nasig *adj suf* -nosed.

⚠ **Naß** *nt* **Nasses,** *no pl* (*liter, hum*) water; (*Getränk*) liquid ◆ **hinein ins kühle ~** (*hum*) into the foaming brine; **gierig trank er das erfrischende ~** (*liter*) eagerly he drank of the refreshing waters (*liter*).

⚠ **naß** *adj, comp* **nasser** *or* **nässer,** *superl* **nasseste(r, s)** *or* **nässeste(r, s)** *or* (*adv*) **am nassesten** *or* **nässesten** wet ◆ **etw ~ machen** to make sth wet; (*für bestimmten Zweck*) to wet sth; *Bügelwäsche* to dampen sth; **sich ~ machen** (*inf*) to wet oneself; **das Bett ~ machen** to wet the bed; **nun mach dich bloß nicht ~!** (*sl*) keep your shirt (*inf*) *or* hair (*Brit inf*) on!, don't get your knickers in a twist! (*Brit sl*); **durch und durch ~** wet through; **mit nassen Augen** with moist eyes, moist-eyed; **wie ein nasser Sack** (*sl*) like a wet rag (*inf*); **ein nasses Grab** (*fig*) a watery grave; **der nasse Tod** (*fig*) a watery death.

Nassauer *m* **-s, -** (*inf*) sponger (*inf*), scrounger.

nassauern *vi* (*inf*) to sponge (*inf*), to scrounge (*bei jdm* on *or* off sb).

Nässe *f* -, *no pl* wetness, damp(ness), moisture ◆ **in der ~ stehen** to stand in the wet; „**vor ~ schützen**" "keep dry"; **vor ~ triefen** to be dripping *or* wringing wet.
nässen [1] *vi* (*Wunde*) to weep, to discharge.
[2] *vt* (*liter: feucht machen*) to dampen, to wet, to moisten; *Bett* to wet.
⚠**Naß-**: **n~forsch** *adj* (*inf*) brash; **n~kalt** *adj* cold *or* chilly and damp, raw; **~rasur** *f* **die ~rasur** wet shaving; **eine ~rasur** a wet shave; **~wäsche** *f* wet washing; **~zelle** *f* wet cell.
Nastuch ['na:stu:x] *nt* (*S Ger, Aus, Sw*) handkerchief.
Natal *nt* **-s** Natal.
Nation *f* nation ◆ **die Vereinten ~en** the United Nations.
national *adj* national; (*patriotisch*) nationalist(ic) ◆ **die Inflation muß ~ eingedämmt werden** inflation must be checked nationally *or* at the national level.
National- *in cpds* national; ⚠**n~bewußt** *adj* nationally conscious; ⚠**~bewußtsein** *nt* national consciousness; **~bibliothek** *f* national library; **~charakter** *m* national character; **~china** *nt* Nationalist China; **n~chinesisch** *adj* Chinese Nationalist; **~einkommen** *nt* national income; **~elf** *f* international (football) team; **die italienische ~elf** the Italian (international) team, the Italian eleven; **er hat dreimal in der ~elf gespielt** he's played for his country three times, he's been capped three times; **~epos** *nt* national epic; **~farben** *pl* national colours *pl*; **~feiertag** *m* national holiday; **~flagge** *f* national flag; **~garde** *f* National Guard; **~gefühl** *nt* national feeling *or* sentiment; **~gericht** *nt* national dish; **~getränk** *nt* national drink; **~held** *m* national hero; **~hymne** *f* national anthem.
nationalisieren* [natsionali'zi:rən] *vt* **(a)** (*einbürgern*) to naturalize. **(b)** (*verstaatlichen*) to nationalize.
Nationalisierung *f* **(a)** naturalization. **(b)** nationalization.
Nationalismus [natsiona'lɪsmʊs] *m* nationalism.
Nationalist(in *f*) [natsiona'lɪst(ɪn)] *m* nationalist.
nationalistisch [natsiona'lɪstɪʃ] *adj* nationalist(ic).
Nationalität [natsionali'tɛ:t] *f* nationality.
Nationalitäten-: **~frage** *f* problem of different nationalities (within one state); **~staat** *m* multinational state.
Nationalitätskennzeichen *nt* nationality sticker *or* (*aus Metall*) plate.
National- [natsio'na:l-]: **~mannschaft** *f* international team; **er spielt in der schottischen ~mannschaft** he plays for Scotland *or* in the Scotland team; **~ökonomie** *f* economics *sing*; **~park** *m* national park; **~preis** *m* (*DDR*) *annual award for achievement in science, arts and technology*; national prize *or* award; **~preisträger** *m* (*DDR*) national prize *or* award holder; **~rat** *m* **(a)** (*Sw*) National Council; (*Aus*) National Assembly; **(b)** (*Sw*) member of the National Council, ≃ MP; (*Aus*) deputy of *or* to the National Assembly, ≃ MP; **~sozialismus** *m* National Socialism; **~sozialist** *m* National Socialist; **~spieler** *m* international (footballer *etc*); **~staat** *m* nation-state; **n~staatlich** *adj* of a nation-state/nation-states; *Ordnung* as a nation-state; **~stolz** *m* national pride; **~straße** *f* national highway; **~theater** *nt* national theatre; **~tracht** *f* national dress *or* costume; **~versammlung** *f* National Assembly.
NATO, Nato *f* -: **die ~** NATO.
Nato-: ⚠**~-Doppelbeschluß** *m* NATO twin-track policy; **~-Stützpunkt** *m* NATO base.
Natrium *nt no pl* (*abbr* **Na**) sodium.
Natron *nt* **-s**, *no pl sodium compound, esp bicarbonate of soda* ◆ **kohlensaures ~** sodium carbonate; **doppeltkohlensaures ~** bicarbonate of soda, sodium bicarbonate, bicarb (*inf*).
Natronlauge *f* caustic soda, sodium hydroxide.
Natter *f* **-, -n** adder, viper; (*fig*) snake, serpent ◆ **eine ~ am Busen nähren** (*liter*) to nurture a viper at one's breast *or* bosom.
Natternbrut *f*, **Natterngezücht** *nt* (*fig*) viper's brood.
Natur *f* **(a)** *no pl* (*Kosmos, Schöpfungsordnung*) nature ◆ **sie ist ein Meisterwerk der ~** she is one of Nature's masterpieces; **die drei Reiche der ~** the three kingdoms of nature, the three natural kingdoms; **~ und Kultur** nature and civilization; **wider die ~ sein** to be unnatural *or* against nature.
(b) *no pl* (*freies Land*) countryside ◆ **die freie ~, Gottes freie ~** (*liter*) the open country(side); **in der freien ~** in the open countryside.
(c) *no pl* (*~zustand*) nature ◆ **ist ihr Haar gefärbt? — nein das ist alles ~** is her hair dyed? — no, it's natural; **sie sind von ~ so gewachsen** they grew that way naturally; **ich bin von ~ aus schüchtern** I am shy by nature; **sein Haar ist von ~ aus blond** his hair is naturally blond; **zurück zur ~!** back to nature; **nach der ~ zeichnen/malen** to draw/paint from nature.
(d) (*Beschaffenheit, Wesensart*) nature; (*Mensch*) type ◆ **es liegt in der ~ der Sache** *or* **der Dinge** it is in the nature of things; **das geht gegen meine ~** it goes against the grain; **das entspricht nicht meiner ~, das ist meiner ~ zuwider** it's not in my nature; **eine Frage allgemeiner ~** a question of a general nature; **zurückhaltender ~ sein** to be of a retiring nature; **das ist ihm zur zweiten ~ geworden** it's become second nature to him; **eine eiserne ~ haben** to have a cast-iron constitution; **sie ist eine gutmütige ~** she's a good-natured type *or* soul.
natur *adj inv* (*Cook*) **Schnitzel/Fisch ~** *cutlet/fish not cooked in breadcrumbs*; **Zitrone ~** freshly-squeezed lemon juice.
Naturalien [-iən] *pl* **(a)** natural produce ◆ **in ~ bezahlen** to pay in kind; **Handel mit ~** barter(ing) with goods. **(b)** (*Naturgeschichte*) natural history specimens *pl*.
naturalisieren* *vt* **(a)** (*Jur*) to naturalize. **(b)** (*Biol, Zool*) **naturalisiert werden, sich ~** to be naturalized, to naturalize.
Naturalisierung *f* naturalization.
Naturalismus *m* naturalism.
Naturalist(in *f*) *m* naturalist.
naturalistisch *adj* naturalistic; *Maler etc* naturalist(ic).
Naturallohn *m* payment in kind.
Natur-: **~apostel** *m* (*hum*) health fiend (*inf*); **~beobachtung** *f* observation of nature; **~beschreibung** *f* description of nature; **~bursche** *m* nature-boy (*inf*); **~denkmal** *nt* natural monument.
nature [na'ty:ɐ] (*Sw*), **naturell** (*geh*) *adj inv* (*Cook*) *siehe* **natur**.
Naturell *nt* **-s, -e** temperament, disposition.
Natur-: **~ereignis** *nt* (impressive) natural phenomenon, phenomenon of nature; **~erscheinung** *f* natural phenomenon; **~erzeugnis** *nt siehe* **~produkt**; **~farbe** *f* **(a)** natural colour; **(b)** (*auch* **~farbstoff**) natural dye; **n~farben** *adj* natural-coloured; **~faser** *f* natural fibre; **~forscher** *m* natural scientist; **~forschung** *f* natural science; **~freund** *m* nature-lover; **~gas** *nt* natural gas; **~gefühl** *nt* feeling for nature; **n~gegeben** *adj* (*lit*) natural; (*fig auch*) normal; **n~gemäß** *adj* natural; **n~gemäß ist es im Mittelmeerraum wärmer als in Skandinavien** in the nature of things it is warmer in the Mediterranean than in Scandinavia; **~geschichte** *f* natural history; **n~geschichtlich** *adj* natural history; **~gesetz** *nt* law of nature; **n~getreu** *adj* lifelike, true to life; (*in Lebensgröße*) life-size, full-scale; **etw n~getreu wiedergeben** to reproduce sth true to life; **n~haft** *adj* (*geh*) natural; **~heilkunde** *f* nature healing; **~heilverfahren** *nt* natural cure *or* remedy; **~katastrophe** *f* natural disaster; **~kind** *nt* child of nature; **~kostladen** *m* health food shop; **~kraft** *f* natural energy *or* force; **~kunde** *f* natural history; **n~kundlich** *adj Forschung, Zeitschrift* natural history; **~landschaft** *f* natural *or* virgin landscape; **~lehre** *f* (*Sch*) (physical) science; **~lehrpfad** *m* nature trail.
natürlich [1] *adj* (*alle Bedeutungen*) natural ◆ **in seiner ~en Größe** life-size; **eines ~en Todes sterben** to die from *or* of natural causes, to die a natural death; **es ist doch (nur zu) ~, daß** ... it's (only) natural that ...; **~e Person** (*Jur*) natural person; **~e Zahl** natural number; **die ~ste Sache (von) der Welt** the most natural thing in the world; **es geht nicht mit ~en Dingen zu** *or* **nicht ~ zu** there's something odd *or* fishy (*inf*) going on, I smell a rat (*inf*); **~e Grenze** natural frontier *or* boundary; **~e Auslese** (*Biol*) natural selection.
[2] *adv* **(a)** naturally ◆ **die Krankheit verlief ganz ~** the illness took its natural course.
(b) (*selbstverständlich*) naturally, of course ◆ **~!** naturally!, of course!, certainly!, sure! (*esp US*), surely!
natürlicherweise *adv* naturally, of course.
Natürlichkeit *f* naturalness.
Natur-: **~mensch** *m* child of nature; **~notwendigkeit** *f* physical inevitability; **~park** *m siehe* **~(schutz)park**; **~philosophie** *f* philosophy of nature; **~produkt** *nt* natural product; **~produkte** natural produce *sing*; **~recht** *nt* natural right; **n~rein** *adj* natural, pure, unadulterated; **~schätze** *pl* natural resources *pl*; **~schauspiel** *nt* natural spectacle, spectacle of nature; **~schutz** *m* conservation, nature conservancy; **unter ~schutz stehen** to be listed, to be legally protected; **~schutzgebiet** *nt* nature reserve; **~(schutz)park** *m* ≃ national park; **~seide** *f* natural silk; **~stein** *m* natural stone; **~talent** *nt* natural prodigy; **sie ist ein ~talent** she is a natural; **~theater** *nt* open-air theatre; **~treue** *f* trueness to life, faithfulness, fidelity; **~trieb** *m* (natural) instinct; **n~verbunden** *adj* nature-loving, attached to nature; **~verehrung** *f* nature worship; **~volk** *nt* primitive people.
naturw. *abbr of* **naturwissenschaftlich**.
Natur-: **n~widrig** *adj* unnatural, against nature; (*nicht normal*) abnormal; **~wissenschaft** *f* natural sciences *pl*; (*Zweig*) natural science; **~wissenschaftler** *m* (natural) scientist; **n~wissenschaftlich** *adj* scientific; **~wunder** *nt* miracle of nature, natural wonder; **~zustand** *m* natural state.
'nauf *adv* (*dial*) *siehe* **hinauf**.
'naus *adv* (*dial*) *siehe* **hinaus**.
Nautik *f*, *no pl* nautical science, navigation.
nautisch *adj* navigational; *Instrumente auch, Ausbildung, Ausdruck* nautical ◆ **~e Meile** nautical *or* sea mile.
Navigation [naviga'tsio:n] *f* navigation.
Navigations-: **~fehler** *m* navigational error; **~offizier** *m* navigation officer; **~raum** *m* charthouse, chartroom.
Navigator [navi'ga:tɔr] *m* (*Aviat*) navigator, navigation officer.
navigieren* [navi'gi:rən] *vti* to navigate.
Nazarener *m* **-s, -** Nazarene.
Nazi *m* **-s, -s** Nazi.
Nazismus *m* **(a)** (*pej: Nationalsozialismus*) Nazi(i)sm. **(b)** (*Ausdruck*) Nazi term *or* expression.
nazistisch *adj* (*pej*) Nazi.
Nazizeit *f* Nazi period.
NB [ɛn'be:] *abbr of* **nota bene** NB.
n.Br. *abbr of* **nördlicher Breite**.
NC [ɛn'tse:] *m* **-(s), -(s)** (*Univ*) *abbr of* **Numerus clausus**.
NC-Fach *nt* (*Univ*) subject with restricted entry.
n.Chr. *abbr of* **nach Christus** AD.
NDR [ɛnde:'|ɛr] *m* **-s** *abbr of* **Norddeutscher Rundfunk**.
ne *adv* (*inf*) no, nope (*inf*), nay (*old, dial*).
'ne (*inf*) *abbr of* **eine**.

⚠: Informationen zur Rechtschreibreform im Anhang

Neandertaler *m* **-s, -** Neanderthal man.

Neapel *nt* **-s** Naples.

Neapolitaner(in *f***)** *m* **-s, -** Neapolitan; (*Aus: Waffel*) waffle.

nebbich *interj* (*sl*) (*schade*) shame; (*nun, wenn schon*) so what.

Nebel *m* **-s, -** mist; (*dichter*) fog; (*mit Abgasen*) smog; (*Mil: künstlich*) smoke; (*Astron*) nebula; (*fig*) mist, haze ♦ **über der ganzen Sache lag ein ~** (*fig*) the whole affair was shrouded in mystery; **bei ~** in mist/fog; *siehe* **Nacht**.

Nebel-: ~auflösung *f* **nach ~auflösung** after the fog has lifted; **~bank** *f* fog bank; **~bildung** *f* fog; **stellenweise ~bildung** foggy patches; **~fleck** *m* **(a)** (*Astron*) nebula; **(b)** (*Zool*) leucoma (*spec*), clouding (of the eye); **~granate** *f* smoke grenade *or* canister.

nebelhaft *adj* (*fig*) nebulous ♦ **es liegt in ~er Ferne** it's in the dim distance.

Nebelhorn *nt* (*Naut*) foghorn.

neb(e)lig *adj* misty; (*bei dichterem Nebel*) foggy.

Nebel-: ~kammer *f* (*Phys*) cloud chamber; **~krähe** *f* hooded crow; **~meer** *nt* sea of mist; **~monat** *m* (*liter*) November.

nebeln *vi impers* **es nebelt** it's misty/foggy.

Nebel-: ~scheinwerfer *m* (*Aut*) fog lamp; **~schleier** *m* (*geh*) veil of mist; ⚠**~(schluß)leuchte** *f* (*Aut*) rear fog-light; **~schwaden** *m usu pl* waft of mist.

Nebelung *m* **-s, -e** (*obs*) November.

Nebel-: ~wand *f* wall *or* bank of fog; (*Mil*) smokescreen; **~werfer** *m* (*Mil*) multiple rocket launcher; **~wetter** *nt* misty/foggy weather.

neben *prep* **(a)** (*örtlich: +dat/acc*) beside, next to ♦ **er fuhr ~ dem Zug her** he kept level with the train; **er ging ~ ihr** he walked beside her; **ich stelle ihn ~ die größten Denker des 17. Jahrhunderts** I rank him among *or* with the greatest thinkers of the 17th century.
(b) (*außer: +dat*) apart from, besides, aside from (*esp US*) ♦ **du sollst keine anderen Götter haben ~ mir** (*Bibl*) thou shalt have no other gods before me (*Bibl*); **~ anderen Dingen** along with *or* as well as *or* amongst other things.
(c) (*verglichen mit: +dat*) compared with *or* to.

Neben-: ~abrede *f* (*Jur*) supplementary agreement, sub-agreement; **~absicht** *f* **eine ~absicht haben** *or* **verfolgen** to have a secondary aim *or* objective; **~altar** *m* side altar; **~amt** *nt* **(a)** (*Nebenberuf*) secondary *or* additional office; **(b)** (*Telec*) branch *or* local exchange; **n~amtlich** *adj Tätigkeit* secondary, additional; **das macht er nur n~amtlich** he does that just as a secondary occupation.

neben|an *adv* next door ♦ **die Tür ~** the next door.

Neben-: ⚠**~anschluß** *m* (*Telec*) extension; **~arbeit** *f* **(a)** (*Zusatzarbeit*) extra work *no indef art, no pl*, extra job; **(b)** (*Zweitberuf*) second *or* extra job, sideline, side job; **~arm** *m* branch; **~ausgabe** *f* incidental expense; **~ausgaben** incidentals, incidental expenses; **~ausgang** *m* side exit; **~bedeutung** *f* secondary meaning *or* connotation.

nebenbei *adv* **(a)** (*gleichzeitig*) at the same time ♦ **etw ~ machen** to do sth on the side.
(b) (*außerdem*) additionally, in addition ♦ **die ~ entstandenen Kosten** the additional expenses.
(c) (*beiläufig*) incidentally ♦ **~ bemerkt** *or* **gesagt** by the way, incidentally, by the by(e); **das mache ich so ~** (*inf*) that's just a sideline; (*kein Problem*) I'll do that with no bother (*inf*).

Neben-: ~beruf *m* second *or* extra job, sideline, side job; **er ist im ~beruf Nachtwächter** he has a second job as a night watchman, he moonlights as a night watchman (*inf*); **n~beruflich** [1] *adj* extra, supplementary; **n~berufliche Arbeit/Tätigkeit** extra work/job, sideline, side job; [2] *adv* as a second job, as a sideline (*inf*), as a side job (*inf*); **er verdient n~beruflich mehr als hauptberuflich** he earns more from his second job *or* from his moonlighting (*inf*) than he does from his main job; **~beschäftigung, ~betätigung** *f* **(a)** (*Zweitberuf*) second *or* extra job, sideline, side job; **(b)** (*Ablenkung*) **beim Fernsehen brauche ich immer eine kleine ~beschäftigung** I always need something else to do while I'm watching television; **~betrieb** *m* **(a)** branch industry; **(b)** (*Filiale*) (*Büro*) branch (office); (*Werk*) subsidiary factory; **~buhler(in** *f***)** *m* rival; **~buhlerschaft** *f, no pl* rivalry; **~darsteller(in** *f***)** *m* supporting actor/actress; **die ~darsteller** the supporting cast *sing*; **~dinge** *pl* secondary matters *pl*.

neben|einander *adv* **(a)** (*räumlich*) side by side; (*bei Rennen*) neck and neck ♦ **sie gingen ~ durchs Ziel** they were neck and neck at the finish; **drei ~, zu dritt ~** three abreast. **(b)** (*zeitlich*) simultaneously, at the same time.

Neben|einander *nt* **-s,** *no pl* juxtaposition.

neben|einanderher *adv* side by side ♦ **sie leben nur noch ~** (*Ehepaar etc*) they're just two people living in the same house.

⚠**neben|einander-: ~legen** *vt sep* to lay side by side *or* next to each other; **~reihen** *vt sep* to place *or* put side by side *or* next to each other; **~schalten** *vt sep* (*Elec*) to put in parallel; **~setzen** *vt sep* to place *or* put side by side *or* next to each other; **~sitzen** *vi sep irreg* (*S Ger: aux sein*) to sit side by side *or* next to each other; **~stellen** *vt sep* to place *or* put side by side *or* next to each other; (*fig: vergleichen*) to compare.

Neben-: ~eingang *m* side entrance; **~einkünfte, ~einnahmen** *pl* additional *or* supplementary income, extra money; **~erscheinung** *f* concomitant; (*von Krankheit*) secondary symptom; **~erwerb** *m* second occupation; **~fach** *nt* (*Sch, Univ*) subsidiary (subject), minor (*US*); **~flügel** *m* side wing; ⚠**~fluß** *m* tributary; **~form** *f* (*Biol*) variety; (*Ling*) variant; **~frage** *f* side issue; **~frau** *f* concubine; **~gebäude** *nt* **(a)** (*Zusatzgebäude*) annex(e), outbuilding; **(b)** (*Nachbargebäude*) neighbouring *or* adjacent building; **~gedanke** *m* ulterior motive; **~g(e)leis** *nt* (*Rail*) siding, sidetrack (*US*); **~geräusch** *nt* (*Rad, Telec*) interference, noise; (*bei Plattenspieler*) noise; **~geschäft** *nt* sideline; **~gestein** *nt* (*Min*) country rock; **~gewerbe** *nt siehe* **~erwerb**; **~handlung** *f* (*Liter*) subplot; **~haus** *nt* house next door, neighbouring house.

nebenher *adv* **(a)** (*zusätzlich*) in addition, on the side. **(b)** (*gleichzeitig*) at the same time, simultaneously.

nebenher- *pref* alongside, beside it/him *etc*.

nebenhin *adv* (*beiläufig*) in passing, by the way, casually.

Neben-: ~höhle *f* (*Physiol*) sinus (of the nose); **~höhlenentzündung** *f* (*Med*) sinusitis; **~klage** *f* (*Jur*) incidental action; **~kläger** *m* (*Jur*) joint plaintiff; **~kosten** *pl* additional costs *pl*; **~kriegsschauplatz** *m* secondary theatre of war; **~linie** *f* **(a)** (*Familie*) collateral line; **(b)** (*Rail*) branch line; **~mann** *m, pl* **~männer Ihr ~mann** the person next to you, your neighbour; **~niere** *f* suprarenal gland *or* capsule, adrenal body.

neben|ordnen *vt sep infin and ptp only* (*Gram*) to coordinate.

Neben-: ~ordnung *f* (*Gram*) coordination; **~person** *f* minor character; **~platz** *m* next seat; **auf meinem ~platz** in the seat next to me; **~produkt** *nt* by-product; **~raum** *m* (*benachbart*) adjoining *or* next room; (*weniger wichtig*) side room; **~rolle** *f* supporting rôle; (*fig*) minor rôle; **das spielt für mich nur eine ~rolle** that's only of minor concern to me; **~sache** *f* minor matter, trifle, triviality; **das ist ~sache** that's irrelevant *or* not the point; **n~sächlich** *adj* minor, peripheral; **etw als n~sächlich abtun** to dismiss sth as irrelevant *or* beside the point; **~sächliches** *nt* minor matters *pl*, trifles *pl*, trivia(lities) *pl*; **es ist doch völlig n~sächlich, wann er kommt** it doesn't matter a bit *or* it's quite irrelevant when he comes; **~sächlichkeit** *f* triviality; **~saison** *f* low season; **~satz** *m* (*Gram*) subordinate clause.

nebenschalten *vt sep* (*Elec*) to wire *or* connect in parallel.

Neben-: ⚠**~schluß** *m* (*Tech*) parallel connection, side (of a parallel circuit); **~sonne** *f* mock sun, sundog, parhelion (*spec*); **n~stehend** *adj* **n~stehende Erklärungen/Verbesserung** explanations/correction in the margin; **n~stehende Abbildung** illustration opposite; **im ~stehenden wird erklärt ...** the marginal note explains ...; **~stelle** *f* (*Telec*) extension; (*Comm*) branch; (*Post*) sub-post office; **~strafe** *f* additional penalty; **~straße** *f* (*in der Stadt*) side street; (*Landstraße*) minor road, by-road; **~strecke** *f* (*Rail*) branch *or* local line; **~thema** *nt* (*Mus*) minor theme; **~tisch** *m* adjacent table; **am ~tisch** at the next table; **sie saßen an einem ~tisch** they were sitting at a table near us; **~ton** *m* (*Ling*) secondary stress; **~ursache** *f* secondary cause; **~verdienst** *m* secondary *or* side (*inf*) income; **~weg** *m* byway; **auf ~wegen** (*lit, fig*) by a roundabout route; **~winkel** *m* (*Math*) adjacent angle; **~wirkung** *f* side effect; **~wohnung** *f* **(a)** next(-door) flat, flat next door; **in einer ~wohnung** in one of the flats next door; **(b)** (*Zweitwohnung*) second flat; **~zimmer** *nt* next *or* adjoining room; **in einem ~zimmer** in an adjoining room; **~zweck** *m* secondary aim.

neblig *adj siehe* **neb(e)lig**.

nebst *prep +dat* together with ♦ **viele Grüße, Onkel Otto ~ Familie** greetings from Uncle Otto and family.

nebulos, nebulös *adj* nebulous ♦ **er redete so ~es Zeug** he was so vague *or* woolly (*inf*).

⚠**Necessaire** [nesɛ'sɛːɐ] *nt* **-s, -s** (*Kulturbeutel*) vanity bag *or* case; (*zur Nagelpflege*) manicure case; (*Nähzeug*) sewing bag.

necken [1] *vt* to tease ♦ **jdn mit jdm/etw ~** to tease sb about sb/sth.
[2] *vr* **sich** *or* **einander ~, sich mit jdm ~** to tease each other, to have a tease (*inf*); **was sich neckt, das liebt sich** (*Prov*) teasing is a sign of affection.

Neckerei *f* teasing *no pl*.

neckisch *adj* (*scherzhaft*) merry, teasing; *Einfall, Melodie* amusing; *Unterhaltung* bantering; (*inf: kokett, keß*) *Kleid, Frisur* coquettish, saucy; *Spielchen* mischievous, naughty ♦ **~!** (*inf*) kinky! (*inf*).

nee *adv* (*inf*) no, nope (*inf*) ♦ **~, so was!** no, really!

Neer *f* **-, -en** (*N Ger*) eddy.

Neffe *m* **-n, -n** nephew.

Negation *f* negation.

Negativ *nt* (*Phot*) negative.

negativ *adj* negative ♦ **jdm auf eine Frage ~ antworten** to answer sb's question in the negative; **sich ~ zu etw stellen** to adopt a negative attitude towards sth; **sich ~ zu etw äußern** to speak negatively about sth; **ich beurteile seine Arbeit sehr ~** I have a very negative view of his work; **die Untersuchung verlief ~** the examination proved negative; **etw ~ (auf)laden** to put a negative charge on sth.

Negativ-: ~bild *nt* negative; **~druck** *m* reversing out; **~film** *m* negative (film).

Negativität *f* negativity, negativeness.

Negativkopie *f* (*Typ*) negative copy.

Neger *m* **-s, - (a)** negro ♦ **angeben wie zehn nackte ~** (*inf*) to shoot one's big mouth off (*inf*). **(b)** (*TV sl*) (*Gedächtnishilfe*) idiot card; (*Verdunklungstafel*) gobo.

neger *adj pred* (*Aus inf*) broke (*inf*).

Negerin *f* negress, negro woman.

Neger-: ~krause *f* (*dated*) frizzy hair; ⚠**~kuß** *m* chocolate marshmallow.

Negerlein *nt dim of* **Neger** little negro.

Neger-: ~musik *f* negro music; **~sklave** *m* negro slave.

negieren* *vt* (*verneinen*) *Satz* to negate; (*bestreiten*) *Tatsache, Behauptung* to deny.

⚠**Negligé, Négligé** [negli'ʒeː] (*Sw*) *nt* **-s, -s** negligee, négligé.

negrid *adj Rasse* negrid.

negroid *adj* negroid.

nehmen *pret* **nahm**, *ptp* **genommen** *vti* **(a)** (*ergreifen*) to take ♦ **etw in die**

Hand ~ (*lit*) to pick sth up; (*fig*) to take sth in hand; **etw an sich** (*acc*) **~** (*aufbewahren*) to take care *or* charge of sth, to look after sth; (*sich aneignen*) to take sth (for oneself).

(b) (*wegnehmen*) to take; *Schmerz* to take away, to relieve; (*versperren*) *Blick, Sicht* to block ◆ **jdm etw ~** to take sth (away) from sb; **jdm die Hoffnung/den Glauben/seine Illusionen/die Freude ~** to take away sb's hope/faith/illusions/joy, to rob *or* deprive sb of his hope/faith/illusions/joy; **um ihm die Angst zu ~** to stop him being afraid; **ihm sind seine Illusionen genommen worden** he was robbed *or* deprived of his illusions, his illusions were shattered; **er ließ es sich** (*dat*) **nicht ~, mich persönlich hinauszubegleiten** he insisted on showing me out himself; **diesen Erfolg lasse ich mir nicht ~** I won't be robbed of this success; **woher ~ und nicht stehlen?** (*inf*) where on earth am I going to find any/one *etc*?; **sie ~ sich** (*dat*) **nichts** (*inf*) there's nothing to choose between them, one's as good as the other.

(c) (*benutzen*) *Auto, Zug etc* to take; *Bürste, Zutaten, Farbe* to use ◆ **man nehme ...** (*Cook*) take ...; **sich** (*dat*) **etw ~** *Zimmer, Wohnung* to take sth; (*sich bedienen auch*) to help oneself to sth; **sich** (*dat*) **einen Anwalt/eine Hilfe ~** to get a lawyer/some help; **~ Sie sich doch bitte!** please help yourself.

(d) (*annehmen*) *Geschenk* to take; (*berechnen*) to charge ◆ **was ~ Sie dafür?** how much will you take for it?; **jdn zu sich ~** to take sb in; **Gott hat ihn zu sich genommen** (*euph*) he has been called home to his maker; **etw ~, wie es kommt** to take sth as it comes; **jdn ~, wie er ist** to take sb as he is; **etw auf sich** (*acc*) **~** to take sth upon oneself; **er ist immer der N~de** he does all the taking, with him it's just take take take (*inf*); **die N~den und die Gebenden** the takers and the givers.

(e) (*einnehmen*) to take; *Essen auch* to have ◆ **sie nimmt Rauschgift/die Pille** she's on *or* she takes drugs/the pill; **etw zu sich ~** to take sth, to partake of sth (*liter*); **der Patient hat nichts zu sich ~ können** the patient has been unable to take nourishment.

(f) (*auffassen*) to take; (*behandeln*) to handle, to treat ◆ **wenn Sie das so ~ wollen** if you care *or* choose to take it that way; **etw für ein** *or* **als Zeichen ~** to take sth as a sign *or* an omen; **wie man's nimmt** (*inf*) depending on your point of view; **wissen, wie man jdn ~ muß** *or* **soll** to know how to take sb.

(g) (*auswählen*) to take; *Essen, Menü auch* to have ◆ **sich** (*dat*) **einen Mann/eine Frau ~** to take a husband/wife.

(h) *Hürde, Festung, Stadt, Frau* to take; *Schwierigkeiten* to overcome ◆ **das Auto nahm den Berg im dritten Gang** the car took the hill in third gear.

(i) *in festen Verbindungen mit n siehe dort.*

Nehmer *m* **-s, -** **(a)** recipient. **(b)** (*Käufer*) taker.

Nehrung *f* spit (of land).

Neid *m* **-(e)s,** *no pl* envy, jealousy ◆ **aus ~** out of envy *or* jealousy; **der ~ der Besitzlosen** (*inf*) sour grapes (*inf*); **grün (und gelb) vor ~** (*inf*) green with envy; **das muß ihm der ~ lassen** (*inf*) you have to say that much for him, give the devil his due; **jds** (*acc*) *or* **bei jdm ~ erregen** to make sb jealous *or* envious, to arouse sb's jealousy; **vor ~ platzen** (*inf*) *or* **vergehen** to die of envy.

neiden *vt* **jdm etw ~** to envy sb (for) sth.

Neider *m* **-s, -** envious *or* jealous person ◆ **reiche Leute haben viele ~** rich people are much envied.

Neid-: n~erfüllt *adj* filled with *or* full of envy *or* jealousy, envious, jealous; **~hammel** *m* (*inf*) jealous *or* envious person; **der alte/du alter ~hammel!** he's/you're just jealous.

neidisch, neidig (*S Ger, Aus*) *adj* jealous, envious ◆ **auf jdn/etw ~ sein** to be jealous of sb/sth; **etw ~** *or* **mit ~en Blicken betrachten** to look enviously at sth, to cast covetous glances at sth.

neidlos *adj* ungrudging, without envy.

Neige *f* **-, -n** **(a)** (*Überrest*) remains *pl* ◆ **das Glas bis zur ~ leeren** (*liter*) to drain the cup to the dregs; **den Kelch bis zur ~ leeren** *or* **trinken** (*fig liter*) to drain the bitter cup (*liter*); **etw bis zur ~ auskosten** (*genießen*) to savour sth to the full; **etw bis zur bitteren ~ auskosten** *or* **kennenlernen** to suffer sth to the full.

(b) *no pl* (*geh: Ende*) **zur ~ gehen** to draw to an end *or* a close; **die Sonne geht zur ~** the sun is sinking; **die Vorräte gehen zur ~** the provisions are fast becoming exhausted.

▼ **neigen** [1] *vt* (*beugen*) *Kopf, Körper* to bend; (*zum Gruß*) to bow; (*kippen*) *Behälter, Glas* to tip, to tilt, to incline ◆ **die Bäume ~ ihre Zweige bis zur Erde** (*geh*) the trees bow their branches to the ground; **geneigte Ebene** sloping surface, slope, incline.

[2] *vr* (*Ebene*) to slope, to incline; (*Mensch*) to bend; (*liter: sich verneigen*) to bow; (*unter Last: Bäume etc*) to bow; (*Gebäude etc*) to lean; (*kippen*) to tip (up), to tilt (up); (*Schiff*) to list; (*liter: Tag, Leben*) to draw to a close *or* an end ◆ **sich nach vorne/hinten ~** (*Mensch*) to lean *or* bend forward/backwards; (*Auto*) to tilt forward/backwards; (*Schiff, Wippe*) to dip/tilt up; **ein leicht zur Seite geneigtes Gebäude** a building which is leaning *or* tilting over slightly; **mit seitwärts geneigtem Kopf** with his/her head held on *or* to one side; **die Waagschale neigt sich zu seinen Gunsten** (*geh*) the scales are tipping in his favour, the tide is turning in his favour.

▼ [3] *vi* **zu etw ~** to tend to sth, to have a tendency to sth; (*für etw anfällig sein*) to be susceptible *or* prone to sth; **er neigt zum Alkohol** he has a taste *or* predilection for alcohol, he has a tendency to drink; **er neigt zum Sozialismus** he tends *or* leans towards socialism, he has socialist leanings; **zu der Ansicht** *or* **Annahme ~, daß ...** to tend *or* lean towards the view that ..., to be inclined to take the view that ...; **ich neige eher zur klassischen Musik** I tend rather towards classical music; *siehe* **geneigt.**

Neigung *f* **(a)** (*das Neigen*) inclination; (*Gefälle auch*) incline, slope, gradient (*esp Rail*); (*Schräglage auch*) tilt; (*von Schiff*) list; (*von Magnetnadel*) dip; (*Astron*) inclination.

(b) (*Tendenz*) tendency; (*Med auch*) proneness; (*Hingezogensein, Veranlagung*) leaning *usu pl*; (*Hang, Lust*) inclination ◆ **er hat eine ~ zum Geiz/zum Trinken/zur Kritik** he has a tendency to be mean/to drink/to criticize, he inclines *or* tends to be mean/to drink/to criticize; **künstlerische/politische ~en** artistic/political leanings; **etw aus ~ tun** to do sth by inclination; **keine/geringe ~ verspüren, etw zu tun** to have *or* feel no/little inclination to do sth.

(c) (*Zuneigung*) affection, fondness ◆ **zu jdm eine ~ fassen** to take a liking to sb; **jds ~ erwidern** to return sb's affection.

Neigungs-: ~ehe *f* love match; **~messer** *m* **-s, -** inclinometer; **~winkel** *m* angle of inclination.

nein *adv* no; (*Überraschung*) no ◆ **kommt er? — ~!** is he coming? — no, (he isn't); **ich sage nicht ~** I wouldn't say no; **~ und abermals ~** for the last time - no!; **~, ~ und nochmals ~** I won't say it again - no, spelt NO!; **Hunderte, ~ Tausende** hundreds, no *or* nay (*liter*) thousands; **~, so was!** well I never!, you don't say!; **~ doch!** no!; **o ~!, aber ~!** certainly not!, of course not!; **~, daß du dich auch mal wieder sehen läßt!** fancy seeing you again; **~ wie nett, mich mal zu besuchen!** well, how nice of you to visit me.

Nein *nt* **-s,** *no pl* no ◆ **bei seinem ~ bleiben** to stick to one's refusal, to remain adamant; **mit Ja oder ~ stimmen** to vote yes *or* aye (*Pol*) or no *or* nay (*US Pol*).

Nein-: ~sager(in *f***)** *m* **-s, -** **er ist ein ewiger ~sager** he always says no; **~stimme** *f* (*Pol*) no(-vote), nay (*US*).

Nekro-: ~log *m* **-(e)s, -e** (*liter*) obituary (notice), necrology (*form*); **~philie** *f* necrophilia; **~pole** *f* **-, -n** necropolis.

Nektar *m* **-s,** *no pl* (*Myth, Bot, Frucht~*) nectar.

Nektarine *f* nectarine.

Nelke *f* **-, -n** **(a)** pink; (*gefüllt*) carnation. **(b)** (*Gewürz*) clove.

Nelson *m* **-(s), -(s)** (*Sport*) nelson.

'nem *abbr of* **einem.**

Nemesis *f* **-,** *no pl* nemesis.

'nen *abbr of* **einen.**

nennbar *adj* specifiable; *Gefühl, Phänomen, Gedanke etc* nam(e)able ◆ **nicht ~** unspecifiable; unnam(e)able.

Nennbetrag *m* (*Comm*) *siehe* **Nennwert.**

nennen *pret* **nannte,** *ptp* **genannt** [1] *vt* **(a)** (*bezeichnen*) to call; (*einen bestimmten Namen geben auch*) to name ◆ **jdn nach jdm ~** to name sb after *or* for (*US*) sb; **Friedrich II., genannt „der Große"** Frederick II, known as "Frederick the Great"; **das nenne ich Mut!** that's what I call courage!; **das nennst du schön?** you call that beautiful?; *siehe* **eigen.**

(b) (*angeben, aufzählen*) to name ◆ **die genannten Namen** the names mentioned; **können Sie mir einen guten Anwalt ~?** could you give me the name of a good lawyer?; *siehe* **Name.**

(c) (*erwähnen*) to mention ◆ **das (weiter oben) Genannte** the above; **das genannte Schloß** the above-mentioned castle, the castle referred to.

[2] *vr* to call oneself; (*heißen*) to be called, to call oneself ◆ **er nennt sich nur so** that's just what he calls himself; **und so was nennt sich Liebe/modern** (*inf*) and they call that love/modern; **und so was nennt sich modern/Dichter** (*inf*) and he calls himself modern/a poet.

nennenswert *adj* considerable, not inconsiderable ◆ **nicht ~** negligible, not worth mentioning; **keine ~en Schwierigkeiten** no great difficulties, no difficulties worth mentioning; **nichts N~es** nothing worth mentioning, nothing of any consequence.

Nenner *m* **-s, -** (*Math*) denominator ◆ **etw auf einen (gemeinsamen) ~ bringen** (*lit, fig*) to reduce sth to a common denominator.

Nenn-: ~fall *m* nominative; **~form** *f* infinitive; **~onkel** *m* **er ist kein richtiger Onkel, sondern nur ein ~onkel** he's not a proper uncle, I just call him uncle; **~tante** *f siehe* **~onkel.**

Nennung *f* (*das Nennen*) naming; (*Sport*) entry.

Nenn-: ~wert *m* (*Fin*) nominal *or* face *or* par value; **zum ~wert** at par; **über/unter dem ~wert** above/below par; **n~wertlos** *adj Aktie* nonpar; **~wort** *nt siehe* **Substantiv.**

neo-, Neo-, *in cpds* neo-.

Neodym *nt, no pl* (*abbr* **Nd**) neodymium.

Neologismus *m* neologism.

Neon *nt no pl* (*abbr* **Ne**) neon.

Neo-: ~nazi *m* neo-nazi; **~nazismus** *m* neo-nazism; **n~nazistisch** *adj* neo-nazi.

Neon-: ~licht *nt* neon light; **~reklame** *f* neon sign; **~röhre** *f* neon tube *or* strip.

Neoprenanzug *m* wet suit.

Nepal *nt* **-s** Nepal.

Nepalese *m* **-, -n, Nepalesin** *f* Nepalese.

nepalesisch *adj* Nepalese.

Nepotismus *m* nepotism.

Nepp *m* **-s,** *no pl* (*inf*) **so ein ~!, das ist ja ~!** that's daylight *or* highway robbery! (*inf*), it's a rip-off (*sl*).

neppen *vt* (*inf*) to fleece (*inf*), to rip off (*sl*) ◆ **da bist du aber geneppt worden!** they must have seen you coming (*inf*).

Nepplokal *nt* (*inf*) clipjoint (*inf*).

Neptun *m* **-s** Neptune.

Neptunium *nt, no pl* (*abbr* **Np**) neptunium.

'ner *abbr of* **einer.**

Nerv [nɛrf] *m* **-s** *or* **-en, -en** nerve; (*Bot auch*) vein; (*obs: Sehne*) sinew ◆ **leicht**

➤ SPRACHE AKTIV: **neigen: 3 → 53.1**

die ~en verlieren to scare easily, to get nervous easily; er hat trotz allem die ~en behalten *or* nicht verloren in spite of everything he kept calm *or* didn't lose his cool (*sl*); (*Selbstbeherrschung verlieren*) in spite of everything he didn't lose control; die ~en sind mit ihm durchgegangen he lost control *or* his cool (*sl*), he snapped (*inf*); gute/schlechte *or* schwache ~en haben to have strong *or* good/bad *or* weak nerves; der hat (vielleicht) ~en! (*inf*) he's got a cheek (*inf*) *or* nerve! (*inf*); er hat ~en wie Drahtseile *or* Bindfäden *or* Stricke he has nerves of steel; es geht *or* fällt mir auf die ~en (*inf*) it gets on my nerves; jdm den (letzten) ~ töten *or* rauben (*inf*) to break *or* shatter sb's nerve; den ~ haben, etw zu tun to have the nerve to do sth; jdn am ~ treffen to touch a raw nerve; das kostet ~en it's a strain on the nerves; das kostete ihn ~en it was a strain on his nerves.

nerven ['nɛrfn] (*inf*) [1] *vt* jdn ~ to get on sb's nerves ◆ genervt sein (*nervös sein*) to be worked up; (*gereizt sein*) to be irritated.
[2] *vi* das nervt it gets on your nerves.

Nerven- ['nɛrfn-]: **~anspannung** *f* nervous tension; **~arzt** *m* neurologist; **n~aufreibend** *adj* nerve-racking; **~bahn** *f* nerve; **~belastung** *f* strain on the nerves; **n~beruhigend** *adj* sedative; **~beruhigungsmittel** *nt* sedative, tranquillizer; **~bündel** *nt* fascicle; (*fig inf*) bag *or* bundle of nerves (*inf*); **~chirurgie** *f* neurosurgery; **~entzündung** *f* neuritis; **~faser** *f* nerve fibre; **~gas** *nt* (*Mil*) nerve gas; **~gift** *nt* neurotoxin; **~heilanstalt** *f* psychiatric *or* mental hospital; **~heilkunde** *f* neurology; **~kitzel** *m* (*fig*) thrill; etw als einen äußersten ~kitzel empfinden to get a big thrill *or* kick (*inf*) out of sth, to find sth really thrilling; **~klinik** *f* psychiatric clinic; **~kostüm** *nt* (*hum*) ein starkes/schwaches ~kostüm haben to have strong/weak nerves; **~kraft** *f* strong nerves *pl*; es erforderte einige ~kraft it took strong nerves; meine ~kraft ist erschöpft my nerves can't take any more; **n~krank** *adj* (*geistig*) mentally ill *or* disturbed; (*körperlich*) suffering from a nervous disease; **~krankheit** *f* (*geistig*) mental illness *or* disorder; (*körperlich*) nervous disease *or* disorder; **~krieg** *m* (*fig*) war of nerves; **~lähmung** *f* neuroparalysis; **~leiden** *nt* nervous complaint *or* condition; **~mittel** *nt* sedative, tranquillizer; **~nahrung** *f* (*fig*) das ist ~nahrung it's good for my *etc* nerves; **~probe** *f* trial; **~sache** *f* (*inf*) question of nerves; reine ~sache! it's all a question of nerves; **~säge** *f* (*inf*) pain (in the neck) (*inf*); **n~schädigend** *adj* damaging to the nerves; **~schmerz** *m* neuralgia *no pl*; **~schock** *m* nervous shock; **n~schwach** *adj* with weak nerves, neurasthenic; **~schwäche** *f* weak nerves *pl*, neurasthenia; **n~stärkend** *adj* nerve-strengthening, tonic; **~strang** *m* nerve fibre; **~system** *nt* nervous system; **~zelle** *f* nerve cell; **~zentrum** *nt* (*Physiol, fig*) nerve centre; **~zusammenbruch** *m* nervous breakdown, crack-up (*inf*).

nervig ['nɛrvɪç] *adj* (a) *Faust, Hand, Gestalt* sinewy, wiry. (b) (*inf*) *Musik, Lärm* irritating ◆ Mensch, wie ~! God, how irritating!; der ist vielleicht ~ he gets on your nerves.

nervlich ['nɛrflɪç] *adj* der ~e Zustand des Patienten the state of the patient's nerves; er ist ~ erschöpft his nerves are at breaking point; ~ bedingt nervous.

nervös [nɛr'vøːs] *adj* nervous; (*aufgeregt auch*) jumpy (*inf*), jittery (*inf*), on edge ◆ die Krankheit ist rein ~ bedingt the illness is purely nervous in origin; jdn ~ machen to make sb nervous; (*ärgern*) to get on sb's nerves.

Nervosität [nɛrvozi'tɛːt] *f* nervousness; (*Stimmung*) tension.

nervtötend ['nɛrf-] *adj* (*inf*) *Geräusch, Gerede* nerve-racking; *Arbeit* soul-destroying.

Nerz *m* -es, -e mink.

Nerzmantel *m* mink coat.

Nessel[1] *f* -, -n (*Bot*) nettle ◆ ~n (*Quaddeln*) nettle rash; sich in die ~n setzen (*inf*) to put oneself in a spot (*inf*).

Nessel[2] *m* -s, - (*auch* ~tuch, ~stoff) (untreated) cotton.

Nessel-: **~ausschlag** *m*, **~fieber** *nt* nettle rash; **~schlafsack** *m* sheet sleeping bag; **~tier** *nt* cnidarian (*spec*).

Nest *nt* -(e)s, -er (a) (*Brutstätte*) nest.
(b) (*fig: Schlupfwinkel*) hideout, lair ◆ ein ~ von Dieben a den of thieves; das ~ leer finden to find the bird/birds has/have flown.
(c) (*fig: Heim*) nest, home ◆ sein eigenes ~ beschmutzen to foul one's own nest; sich ins warme ~ setzen (*inf*) to marry (into) money/to move straight into a good job; da hat er sich ins warme ~ gesetzt (*inf*) he's got it made (*inf*).
(d) (*fig inf: Bett*) bed ◆ raus aus dem ~! rise and shine! (*inf*), show a leg! (*inf*).
(e) (*pej inf: Ort*) (*schäbig*) dump (*inf*), hole (*inf*), one-horse town (*inf*); (*klein*) little place.

Nest-: **~bau** *m* nest-building; **~beschmutzer** *m* (*pej*) runner-down (*inf*) *or* denigrator of one's family/country; **~beschmutzung** *f* (*pej*) running-down (*inf*) *or* denigration of one's family/country.

nesteln [1] *vi* an etw (*dat*) ~ to fumble *or* fiddle (around) with sth.
[2] *vt* (*rare*) to fasten.

Nest-: **~flüchter** *m* -s, - *bird that leaves the nest early*; (*fig*) *person who leaves the family home at an early age*; **~häkchen** *nt* baby of the family; **~hocker** *m* -s, - *bird that stays a long time in its nest*; (*fig*) *person who stays with his parents for a long time*.

Nestor *m* Nestor; (*fig*) doyen.

Nestorin *f* (*fig*) doyenne.

Nest-: **n~warm** *adj* warm from the nest; **~wärme** *f* (*fig*) happy home life.

nett *adj* nice; (*hübsch auch*) pretty, cute ◆ ein ganz ~es Sümmchen a nice little sum; eine ~e Stange Geld kosten (*inf*) to cost a pretty penny (*inf*) *or* tidy sum (*inf*); das kann ja ~ werden! (*iro*) that'll be nice *or* great (*inf*) (I don't think!); sei so ~ und räum' auf! would you mind clearing up?, would you like to clear up?; Oma war so ~ und hat schon abgewaschen Grandma very nicely *or* kindly did the washing-up; ~, daß Sie gekommen sind! nice *or* good of you to come; das war (nicht) ~ von ihm that was(n't very) nice of him; was N~eres ist dir wohl nicht eingefallen? (*iro*) you do say/do some nice things.

netterweise *adv* kindly.

Nettigkeit *f* (a) *no pl* (*nette Art*) kindness, goodness. (b) (*nette Worte*) ~en nice *or* kind words *or* things.

netto *adv* (*Comm*) net ◆ ich verdiene ~ £ 200 *or* £ 200 ~ im Monat I earn £200 net a month, I net £200 a month.

Netto- *in cpds* net; **~ertrag** *m* net profit; **~kurs** *m* net rate.

Netz *nt* -es, -e (a) net; (*Spinnen~*) web; (*Haar~*) (hair)net; (*Einkaufs~*) string bag, net bag; (*Gepäck~*) (luggage) rack; (*fig: von Lügen, Heuchelei*) tissue, web; (*Maschenwerk*) netting ◆ Fische mit dem ~ fangen to catch fish with nets, to net fish; ans ~ gehen (*Sport*) to go up to the net; ins ~ gehen (*Ftbl*) to go into the (back of the) net; (*Tennis*) to hit the net; ins ~ schlagen to play into the net; ~! (*Tennis*) let!; in jds ~ geraten (*fig*) to fall into sb's clutches; sich im eigenen ~ verstricken to be caught in one's own trap, to be hoist with one's own petard (*prov*); jdm ins ~ gehen (*fig*) to fall into sb's trap; jdm durchs ~ gehen (*fig*) to give sb the slip.
(b) (*System*) network; (*Strom~*) mains *sing or pl*; (*Überland~*) (national) grid; (*Comput*) network ◆ das soziale ~ the social security net; ans ~ gehen to be connected to the grid; Strom geht ins ~ the grid is supplied with electricity; das Werk mußte vom ~ genommen werden the power station had to be shut down.
(c) (*Math*) net; (*Kartengitter*) grid.
(d) (*Anat*) omentum (*spec*), caul (of the stomach).

Netz-: ⚠**~anschluß** *m* (*Elec*) mains connection; **n~artig** *adj* netlike, reticular (*form*); **~auge** *nt* compound eye; **~ball** *m* (*Tennis etc*) netball.

netzen *vti* to moisten, to wet.

Netz-: **~flügler** *m* -s, - neuropter (*spec*), ≃ lacewing; die ~flügler the Neuroptera (*spec*); **~frequenz** *f* mains frequency; **~gardine** *f* net curtain; **~garn** *nt* netting yarn; **~gerät** *nt* mains receiver; **~gewebe** *nt* gauze; **~gewölbe** *nt* (*Archit*) fan vault.

Netzhaut *f* retina.

Netzhaut-: **~ablösung** *f* detachment of the retina; **~entzündung** *f* retinitis.

Netz-: **~hemd** *nt* string vest (*Brit*) *or* undershirt (*US*); **~karte** *f* (*Rail*) unlimited travel ticket, runabout ticket (*Brit*); **~magen** *m* (*Zool*) second stomach; **~plan** *m* critical path (diagram); **~plantechnik** *f* critical path method; **~spannung** *f* mains voltage; **~spiel** *nt* net game; **~strümpfe** *pl* fish-net stockings *pl*; **~teil** *nt* mains adaptor.

Netzwerk *nt* necklace; (*Elec, Comput, fig*) network; (*aus Draht*) netting.

Netzwerk- (*Comput*): **~karte** *f* network card; **~server** *m* network server; **~treiber** *m* network driver.

neu *adj* new; *Seite, Kräfte, Hoffnung, Truppen auch* fresh; (*kürzlich entstanden auch*) recent; *Wäsche, Socken* clean; *Wein* young ◆ das N~e Testament the New Testament; die N~e Welt the New World; jdm zum ~en Jahr Glück wünschen to wish sb (a) happy new year; ein ~er Anfang a fresh *or* new start; ~eren Datums of (more) recent date; ~e Hoffnung schöpfen to take new *or* fresh hope; eine ~e Mode/ein ~er Tanz a new fashion/dance; die ~(e)ste Mode/der ~(e)ste Tanz the latest fashion/dance; die ~esten Nachrichten the latest news; die ~eren Sprachen modern languages; ein ganz ~er Wagen a brand-new car; das ist mir ~! that's new(s) to me; mir ist die Sache ~ this is all new to me; schlechte Laune ist mir ~ an ihm it's something new for me to see him in a bad mood; sich wie ein ~er Mensch fühlen to feel like a new person; eine ~e Bearbeitung a revised edition; (*von Oper etc*) a new version; Geschichte der ~eren Zeit recent *or* modern history; in ~erer Zeit in modern times; erst in ~erer Zeit only recently; viele alte Leute finden sich in der ~en Zeit nicht mehr zurecht a lot of old people can't get on in the modern world; seit ~(e)stem recently; seit ~(e)stem gibt es ... since recently there has been ...; aufs ~e (*geh*) afresh, anew; auf ein ~es! (*als Toast*) (here's) to the New Year!; (*Aufmunterung*) let's try again; der/die N~e the newcomer, the new man/boy/woman/girl; the new president/pope *etc*; the new guy (*inf*); die N~en the newcomers, the new people; N~e Welle new wave; was ist das N~e an dem Buch? what's new about the book?; das N~(e)ste in der Mode/auf dem Gebiet der Weltraumforschung the latest in fashion/in the field of space research; weißt du schon das N~(e)ste? have you heard the latest (news)?; was gibt's N~es? (*inf*) what's the latest?, what's new?; das N~(e)ste vom Tage the latest news, up-to-the-minute news; das N~(e)ste vom N~en the very latest (things); von ~em (*von vorn*) from the beginning, afresh, from scratch; (*wieder*) again; ~ beginnen to make a fresh start *or* start again from scratch; die Rollen ~ besetzen to re-cast the rôles; die Akten ~ ordnen to re-order the files; das Buch ist ~ erschienen the book is a recent publication *or* has recently *or* just come out *or* appeared; er ist ~ hinzugekommen he's joined (him/them) recently; ein Zimmer ~ einrichten to refurnish a room; sich/jdn ~ einkleiden to buy oneself/sb a new set of clothes.

Neu-: **~anfertigung** *f* (*das ~anfertigen*) making (up), production (from scratch); (*Produkt*) newly-made article; die ~anfertigung eines Anzugs dauert vier Wochen it takes four weeks to make up a suit; **~ankömmling** *m* newcomer; **~anschaffung** *f* new purchase *or* acquisition; eine ~anschaffung würde sich rentieren it would be worth buying a new machine/part *etc*; **n~apostolisch** *adj* New Apostolic.

neu|artig *adj* new ◆ ein ~es Wörterbuch a new type of dictionary; es ist ganz ~ it is of a completely new type, it is a completely new departure.

Neu|artigkeit *f* novelty.

Neu-: ~auflage *f* reprint; (*mit Verbesserungen*) new edition; **~ausgabe** *f* new edition.

Neubau *m* new house/building.

Neubau-: ~gebiet *nt* development area; **~siedlung** *f* new housing estate; **~viertel** *nt* new district; **~wohnung** *f* newly-built flat.

Neu-: ⚠n≈bearbeitet *adj attr* new; **≈bearbeitung** *f* revised edition; (*von Oper etc*) new version; (*das ~bearbeiten*) revision; reworking; **≈beginn** *m* new beginning(s); **≈belebung** *f* revival; **≈besetzung** *f* replacement; (*Theat*) recasting; **in der ~besetzung** in the recast version; **eine ~besetzung dieses Postens wurde nötig** it was necessary to find a replacement for this position; **≈bildung** *f* (*neues Gebilde*) new entity; (*Ling*) neologism; (*Med*) renewal, repair; **eine staatliche ~bildung** a newly-formed state; **bei der ~bildung von Begriffen** in the formation of new concepts; **≈bürger** *m* new citizen; **~-Delhi** *nt* **-s** New Delhi; **n≈deutsch** *adj* (*usu pej*) new German, neo-German; **≈druck** *m* reprint; **≈einrichtung** *f* refurnishing; (*Möbel*) new furniture *or* furnishings *pl*; **≈einstellung** *f* new appointment; **≈einstudierung** *f siehe* **~inszenierung**.

Neuenburg *nt* (*Kanton*) Neuchâtel.

Neu-: ~england *nt* New England; **n≈englisch** *adj* modern English; **⚠n≈entdeckt** *adj attr* newly *or* recently discovered; **≈entdeckung** *f* rediscovery; (*Mensch*) new discovery; (*Ort*) newly discovered place; **⚠n≈entwickelt** *adj attr* newly developed; **≈entwicklung** *f* new development.

neuerdings *adv* recently; (*rare: von neuem*) again.

Neuerer *m* **-s, -** innovator.

neuerlich [1] *adv* lately, recently, of late; (*rare: nochmals*) again. [2] *adj* recent; (*wiederholt*) further.

Neu-: ⚠n~eröffnet *adj attr* newly-opened; (*wiedereröffnet*) reopened; **~eröffnung** *f* (*Wiedereröffnung*) reopening; **die ~eröffnung der Fluglinie** the opening of the new airline; **es gab zwanzig Geschäftsschließungen und nur zwei ~eröffnungen** twenty shops were closed and only two new ones opened; **~erscheinung** *f* (*Buch*) new *or* recent publication; (*Schallplatte, CD*) new release; (*Neuheit*) new *or* recent phenomenon.

Neuerung *f* innovation; (*Reform*) reform.

neuerungssüchtig *adj* over-anxious to carry out reforms, reform-mad (*inf*).

Neu|erwerbung *f* new acquisition ◆ **die ~ von Büchern** the acquisition of new books.

neu(e)stens *adv* lately, recently.

Neu-: ≈fassung *f* new *or* revised version; **~fundland** *nt* Newfoundland; **~fundländer** *m* **-s, -** (*Hund*) Newfoundland (dog); **⚠n≈gebacken** *adj attr* fresh- *or* newly-baked; (*fig*) newly-fledged, brand-new; **⚠n≈geboren** *adj* newborn; **sich wie n~geboren fühlen** to feel (like) a new man/woman; **≈geborene(s)** *nt decl as adj* newborn child; **≈geburt** *f* (*~geborenes*) newborn child/animal; (*~erscheinung*) new phenomenon; (*Wiedergeburt*) rebirth; **die ~geburten** the newborn; **⚠n≈geschaffen** *adj attr* newly created; **⚠n≈gestalten*** *vt sep* to rearrange, to reorder; *Platz, Stadion* to redesign, to give a new layout; **≈gestaltung** *f siehe vt* rearrangement, reordering; redesigning, new layout; **die ~gestaltung eines alten Themas** the reworking of an old theme; **⚠n≈gewählt** *adj attr* newly elected.

Neugier(de) *f* **-**, *no pl* curiosity, inquisitiveness; (*pej auch*) nosiness (*inf*) ◆ **aus ~** out of curiosity; **seine ~ befriedigen** to satisfy one's curiosity.

neugierig *adj* inquisitive, curious (*auf +acc* about); (*pej*) prying, nos(e)y (*inf*); (*gespannt*) longing *or* curious to know ◆ **ein N~er** an inquisitive person; (*pej auch*) a nos(e)y parker (*inf*); **jdn ~ machen** to excite *or* arouse sb's curiosity; **ich bin ~, ob** I wonder if; **da bin ich aber ~!** this should be interesting, I can hardly wait (*inf*); **sei nicht so ~!** don't be so inquisitive *or* nos(e)y (*inf*) *or* such a nos(e)y parker (*inf*)!

Neu-: ≈gliederung *f* reorganization, restructuring; **≈gotik** *f* Gothic revival, neo-Gothic style; **n≈gotisch** *adj* neo-Gothic; **n≈griechisch** *adj* Modern Greek; **≈griechisch(e)** *nt* Modern Greek; *siehe auch* **Deutsch(e)**; **≈gründung** *f* (*Wiederbegründung*) re-establishment, refoundation; **die ~gründung von Universitäten** the founding of new universities; **der Verein ist eine ~gründung** the club was only recently founded; **≈gruppierung** *f* regroupment, rearrangement; **~guinea** *nt* New Guinea.

Neuheit *f* **(a)** *no pl* novelty ◆ **es wird bald den Reiz der ~ verlieren** the novelty will soon wear off. **(b)** innovation, new thing/idea ◆ **dieses Gerät ist eine ~ auf dem Markt** this apparatus has only recently come on(to) the market.

neuhochdeutsch *adj* New High German ◆ **das N~e** New High German.

Neuigkeit *f* (piece of) news ◆ **die ~en** the news *sing*; **die ~ des Tages** the big news of the day.

Neu|inszenierung *f* new production.

Neujahr *nt* New Year ◆ **jdm zu(m) ~ gratulieren** to wish sb a Happy New Year; **~ begehen** *or* **feiern** to celebrate the New Year; **Pros(i)t ~!** (here's) to the New Year!

Neujahrs-: ~abend *m* New Year's Eve, Hogmanay (*Scot*); **~empfang** *m* New Year reception; **~fest** *nt* New Year's Day; (*Feier*) New Year celebrations *pl*; **~glückwunsch** *m* New Year greeting; **~karte** *f* New Year card; **~tag** *m* New Year's day.

Neu-: ~kaledonien *nt* **-s** New Caledonia; **~kaledonier(in *f*)** *m* **-s, -** New Caledonian; **≈land** *nt, no pl* virgin land *or* territory, uncultivated land; (*fig*) new territory *or* ground; **er betrat wissenschaftliches ~land** he broke new ground in science; **n≈lateinisch** *adj* neo-Latin, new Latin.

neulich [1] *adv* recently, the other day ◆ **~ abend(s)** the other evening. [2] *adj* (*strictly incorrect*) recent.

Neuling *m* newcomer, new man/woman/boy/girl; (*pej auch*) beginner, greenhorn (*inf*).

neumodisch *adj* (*pej*) new-fangled (*pej*), fashionable ◆ **~ unterrichten** to teach in a new-fangled way/to teach new-fangled stuff.

Neumond *m* new moon ◆ **bei ~** at new moon; **heute ist ~** there's a new moon today.

Neun *f* **-, -en** nine ◆ **die ~ ist eine heilige Zahl** nine is a sacred number; **er hat die ~ ausgespielt** he played the nine; **ach du grüne ~e!** (*inf*) well I'm blowed! (*inf*); *siehe auch* **Vier**.

neun *num* nine. (*beim Kegeln*) **alle ~(e)!** strike!; **er warf alle ~(e)** he got a strike; *siehe auch* **vier**.

Neun|auge *nt* lamprey.

Neun-: ~eck *nt* nonagon; **n~eckig** *adj* nonagonal.

Neunerprobe *f* (*Math*) casting out nines.

Neun-: n~hundert *num* nine hundred; *siehe auch* **vierhundert**; **n≈mal** *adv* nine times; *siehe auch* **viermal**; **n≈malklug** *adj* (*iro*) smart-aleck *attr*, **du bist ein ganz ~malkluger!** you're a real smart-aleck; **n≈schwänzig** *adj*: **die n~schwänzige Katze** the cat-o'-nine-tails; **n~tausend** *num* nine thousand; *siehe auch* **viertausend**.

Neuntel *nt* **-s, -** ninth; *siehe auch* **Viertel**[1].

neuntens *adv* ninth(ly), in the ninth place.

neunte(r, s) *adj* ninth; *siehe auch* **vierte(r, s)**.

neunzehn *num* nineteen; *siehe auch* **vierzehn**.

neunzehnte(r, s) *adj* nineteenth; *siehe auch* **vierte(r, s)**.

neunzig *num* ninety ◆ **auf ~ sein** (*inf*) to be in a blind fury *or* a filthy temper (*inf*); *siehe auch* **vierzig**.

Neunziger(in *f*) *m* **-s, -** (*Mensch*) ninety-year-old, nonagenarian; *siehe auch* **Vierziger(in)**.

neunzigste(r, s) *adj* ninetieth; *siehe* **vierte(r, s)**.

Neu-: ~ordnung *f* reorganization, reordering; (*Reform*) reform; **~orientierung** *f* reorientation; **~philologe** *m* modern linguist; **~philologie** *f* modern languages *sing or pl*; **~prägung** *f* (*Münze*) new minting; (*Begriff*) new coinage.

Neuralgie *f* neuralgia.

neuralgisch *adj* neuralgic ◆ **ein ~er Punkt** a trouble area; **diese Kreuzung/Zypern ist ein ~er Punkt** this crossroads/Cyprus is a trouble area *or* trouble spot.

Neuraltherapie *f* neural therapy.

Neurasthenie *f* neurasthenia.

Neurastheniker(in *f*) *m* **-s, -** neurasthenic.

neurasthenisch *adj* neurasthenic.

Neu-: ~reg(e)lung *f* adjustment, revision; **eine ~regelung des Verkehrs** a new traffic management scheme; **n~reich** *adj* nouveau riche; **~reiche(r)** *mf* nouveau riche; **die ~reichen** the nouveaux riches.

Neuritis *f* **-, Neuritiden** neuritis.

Neuro- *in cpds* neuro; **~chirurgie** *f* neurosurgery; **~loge** *m* neurologist; **~logie** *f* neurology; **~login** *f* neurologist; **n~logisch** *adj* neurological.

Neuron *nt* **-s, -e(n)** [-'roːnə(n)] neuron.

Neuro-: ~pathie *f* neuropathy; **~pathologie** *f* neuropathology.

Neurose *f* **-, -n** neurosis.

Neurotiker(in *f*) *m* **-s, -** neurotic.

neurotisch *adj* neurotic.

Neu-: ≈satz *m* (*Typ*) new setting; **≈schnee** *m* fresh snow; **über Nacht gab es ~schnee** there was fresh snow *or* a fresh snowfall overnight; **≈schöpfung** *f* new creation; (*Ausdruck*) invention; **~seeland** *nt* New Zealand; **n~seeländisch** *adj* New Zealand; **≈silber** *nt* nickel silver; **≈sprachler(in *f*)** *m* **-s, -** modern linguist; **n≈sprachlich** *adj* modern language; **n~sprachlicher Zweig** (*Sch*) modern language side; **n~sprachliches Gymnasium** ≃ grammar school (*Brit*), high school (*esp US, Scot*) *stressing modern languages*; **≈stadt** *f* new town.

neustens *adv siehe* **neu(e)stens**.

Neutöner(in *f*) *m* **-s, -** (*Mus*) exponent of the New Music.

neutral *adj* neutral; (*rare: Gram*) neuter ◆ **die N~en** (*Pol*) the neutrals.

Neutralisation *f* neutralization ◆ **die ~ eines Rennens** (*Sport*) the suspension of a race.

neutralisieren* *vt* to neutralize ◆ **das Rennen wurde neutralisiert** (*Sport*) the race was suspended.

Neutralisierung *f* neutralization.

Neutralismus *m* (*Pol*) neutralism.

Neutralität *f* neutrality.

Neutralitäts-: ~abkommen *nt* treaty of neutrality; **~politik** *f* policy of neutrality; **~zeichen** *nt* sign of neutrality.

Neutrino *nt* **-s** neutrino.

Neutron *nt* **-s, -en** [nɔy'troːnən] neutron.

Neutronen- *in cpds* neutron; **~bombe** *f* neutron bomb; **~strahlen** *pl* neutron rays *pl*; **~strahlung** *f* neutron radiation.

Neutrum *nt* **-s, Neutra** *or* **Neutren** (*Gram, fig*) neuter ◆ **ein ~** (*Gram*) a neuter noun; **sie wirkt auf mich wie ein ~** I don't think of her as a woman.

Neu-: ~veranlagung *f* (*Fin*) reassessment; **⚠n~vermählt** *adj* newly married *or* wed; **die ~vermählten** the newly-weds; **~verschuldung** *f* new borrowings *pl*; **~wagen** *m* new car; **~wahl** *f* (*Pol*) new election, re-election; **die ~wahl des Präsidenten** the election of a new president; **n~weltlich** *adj* (*geh*) new world; **~wert** *m* value when new; **n~wertig** *adj* as new; **~wertversicherung** *f* new-for-old insurance, replacement value insurance; **~zeit** *f* modern age *or* era, modern times *pl*; **Literatur/**

Gesellschaft der ~zeit modern literature/society; **n~zeitlich** *adj* modern; **~züchtung** *f* new breed; (*Pflanze*) new variety; **die ~züchtung von Tieren/Pflanzen** the breeding/cultivation of new types of animal/plant; **~zugang** *m* new entry; **~zulassung** *f* (*Aut*) ≃ registration of a new vehicle; **die meisten gestohlenen Autos waren ~zulassungen** most of the stolen cars were *or* had new registrations.

New Age [njuːˈeɪdʒ] *nt* -, *no pl* new age.

Newcomer [njuːˈkamɐ] *m* **-(s), -** newcomer.

New Wave [njuːˈweːv] *f* -, *no pl* new wave.

New York [ˈnjuːˈjɔːk] *nt* **-s** New York.

New Yorker *adj attr* New York.

New Yorker(in *f*) *m* New Yorker.

Nibelungentreue *f* unshakeable loyalty.

nicht *adv* **(a)** (*Verneinung*) not ◆ **er raucht ~** (*augenblicklich*) he is not *or* isn't smoking; (*gewöhnlich*) he does not *or* doesn't smoke; **alle lachten, nur er ~** everybody laughed except him, everybody laughed, only he didn't; **kommst du? — nein, ich komme ~** are you coming? — no, I'm not (coming); **ich weiß auch ~, warum** I really don't know why; **ich kann das ~ — ich auch ~** I can't do it — neither *or* nor can I; **~ mehr** *or* **länger** not any longer; **~ mehr als** no *or* not more than; **~ mehr und ~ weniger als** no more and no less than; **~ heute und ~ morgen** neither today nor tomorrow; **~ ihn meinte ich, sondern sie** I didn't mean him, I meant her, it's not him I meant but her; **er ~!** not him, not he (*form*); **~ (ein)mal** not even.

(b) (*Bitte, Gebot, Verbot*) **~ berühren!** do not touch; (*gesprochen*) don't touch; **ärgere dich ~!** don't be angry, do not be angry (*often liter*); **~ rauchen!** no smoking; **~!** don't!, no!; **tu's ~!** don't do it!; **~ doch!** stop it!, don't!; **bitte ~!** please don't; **nur das ~!** anything but that!; **nun wein mal ~ gleich!** now don't start crying.

(c) (*rhetorisch*) **er kommt/sie kommen** *etc*, **~ (wahr)?** he's coming/they're coming *etc*, isn't he/aren't they? *or* is he not/are they not?; **er kommt ~, ~ wahr?** he isn't coming, is he?; **ich darf kommen, ~ (wahr)?** I can come, can't I *or* can I?; **das ist schön, ~ (wahr)?** it's nice, isn't it?; **jetzt wollen wir Schluß machen, ~?** let's leave it now, right *or* OK?

(d) (*doppelte Verneinung*) **~ uninteressant/unschön** *etc* not uninteresting/unattractive *etc*.

(e) (*Verwunderung, Resignation etc*) **was die Kinder ~ alles wissen!** the things children know about!; **was ich ~ alles durchmachen muß!** the things I have to go through!

Nicht-, nicht- *pref* non-.

Nicht-: ~achtung *f* (+*gen* for) disregard, lack of regard; **jdn mit ~achtung strafen** to send sb to Coventry; **~achtung des Gerichts** contempt of court; **n~amtlich** *adj* unofficial; **~anerkennung** *f* non-recognition; **~angriffspakt** *m* non-aggression pact; **~arier** *m* non-Aryan; **~beachtung, ~befolgung** *f* non-observance; **~benutzung** *f* (*form*) non-utilization (*form*); **bei ~benutzung der Maschine** when the machine is not in use *or* being used; **n~berufstätig** *adj attr* non-employed; **~bezahlung** *f* non-payment; **n~christlich** *adj* non-Christian.

Nichte *f* **-, -n** niece.

Nicht-: n~ehelich *adj* (*Jur*) *Kinder, Abstammung* illegitimate; *Mutter* unmarried; *Vater* natural; **n~eheliche Beziehungen zu jdm unterhalten** to cohabit with sb; **Kinder aus n~ehelichen Beziehungen** children born outside wedlock (*form*); **~einhaltung** *f* non-compliance (+*gen* with), non-observance (+*gen* of); **~einmischung** *f* (*Pol*) non-intervention, non-interference; **~erfüllung** *f* (*Jur*) non-fulfilment (*gen* of), default; **~erscheinen** *nt* non-appearance, failure to appear; **~fachmann** *m* non-specialist, non-expert; **n~flüchtig** *adj* (*Chem, Comput*) non-volatile; **~gebrauch** *m siehe* **~benutzung**; **~gefallen** *nt*: **bei ~gefallen (zurück)** if not satisfied (return); **n~geschäftsfähig** *adj attr siehe* **geschäftsunfähig**.

nichtig *adj* **(a)** (*Jur: ungültig*) invalid, void ◆ **etw für ~ erklären** to declare sth invalid; *Ehe auch* to annul sth; **dadurch** *or* **hierdurch ist der Vertrag ~ geworden** the treaty has thereby become invalid; *siehe* **null**.

(b) (*unbedeutend*) trifling, trivial; *Versuch* vain; *Drohung* empty, vain ◆ **die ~en Dinge dieser Welt** (*liter*) the vain things *or* the vanities (*liter*) of this life.

Nichtigkeit *f* **(a)** (*Jur: Ungültigkeit*) voidness, invalidity, nullity. **(b)** (*Bedeutungslosigkeit*) triviality, vainness, emptiness. **(c)** *usu pl* (*Kleinigkeit*) trifle, triviality, trivia *pl*.

Nichtigkeits-: ~erklärung *f* (*Jur*) annulment; **~klage** *f* (*Jur*) nullity suit.

Nicht-: ~kombattant *m* (*form*) non-combatant; **⚠n~leitend** *adj* (*Elec*) non-conducting; **~leiter** *m* **-s, -** (*Elec*) non-conductor; **~metall** *nt* non-metal; **n~metallisch** *adj* nonmetallic; **~mitglied** *nt* non-member; **n~öffentlich** *adj attr* not open to the public, private; **n~öffentliche Sitzung/Konferenz** meeting/conference in camera (*Jur*) *or* behind closed doors; **⚠n~organisiert** *adj attr Arbeiter* non-organized, non-union(ized); **~raucher** *m* (*auch Rail*) non-smoker; **ich bin ~raucher** I don't smoke, I'm a non-smoker; **„~raucher"** "no smoking" (*Brit*), "non-smoking car" (*US*); **~raucherabteil** *nt* no-smoking compartment; **~raucherzone** *f* non-smoking area; **⚠n~rostend** *adj attr* rustproof, non-rust; *Stahl* stainless.

Nichts *nt* **(a)** -, *no pl* (*Philos*) nothingness; (*Leere*) emptiness, void; (*Kleinigkeit*) trifle, triviality, trivia *pl* ◆ **etw aus dem ~ erschaffen/aufbauen** to create sth out of nothing(ness) *or* the void/to build sth up from nothing; **dieser Schriftsteller ist aus dem ~ aufgetaucht** this author sprang up from nowhere; **vor dem ~ stehen** to be left with nothing; **alle seine Hoffnungen endeten im ~** (*liter*) all his hopes came to nothing *or* nought.

(b) -es, -e (*Mensch*) nobody, nonentity, (mere) cipher.

nichts *indef pron inv* nothing; (*fragend, bedingend auch*) not ... anything ◆ **ich weiß ~** I know nothing, I don't know anything; **~ als** nothing but; **~ (anderes) als** nothing/not ... anything but *or* except; **~ von Bedeutung** nothing of (any) importance; **~ Besseres/Neues** *etc* nothing better/new *etc*; **~ da!** (*inf*) (*weg da*) no you don't!; (*ausgeschlossen*) nothing doing (*inf*), no chance (*inf*); **~ zu danken!** don't mention it, not at all; **für** *or* **um ~** for nothing; **das ist ~ für mich** that's not (for) me, that's not my thing (*inf*) *or* not my cup of tea (*Brit inf*); **für ~ und wieder ~** (*inf*) for nothing at all, for damn all (*sl*); **~ zu machen** nothing doing (*inf*), you've had that (*inf*), nix (*sl*); **(es war) ~ mehr zu machen** there was nothing more that could be done; **~ mehr** nothing more, not ... anything more; **ich weiß ~ Näheres** *or* **Genaues** I don't know any details; **das war wohl ~** (*sl*) that's not much good, you can't win them all (*inf*); **~ wie raus/rein/hin** *etc* (*inf*) let's get out/in/over there *etc* (on the double); **aus ~ wird ~** (*Prov*) you can't make something out of nothing; **ich mag** *or* **will ~ mehr davon hören** I don't want to hear any more about it; **er ist zu ~ nutze** *or* **zu gebrauchen** he's useless *or* hopeless.

⚠nichts|ahnend *adj* unsuspecting.

Nicht-: ~schwimmer *m* non-swimmer; **sie ist ~schwimmer** she's a non-swimmer; **~schwimmerbecken** *nt* pool for non-swimmers.

nichts-: ~destotrotz *adv* notwithstanding (*form*), nonetheless; **~destoweniger** *adv* nevertheless, nonetheless.

Nichtsein, Nicht-Sein *nt* non-existence, non-being.

⚠Nichtseßhafte(r) *mf decl as adj* (*form*) person of no fixed abode (*form*).

Nichts-: ~könner *m* washout (*inf*), incompetent person; **er ist ein ~könner** he's (worse than) useless; **~nutz** *m* **-es, -e** good-for-nothing, useless bungler; **n~nutzig** *adj* useless, hopeless; (*unartig*) good-for-nothing; **⚠n~sagend** *adj Buch, Rede, Worte* empty, meaningless; *Vergnügen* trivial, trite, frivolous; *Mensch* insignificant; *Gesichtsausdruck* blank, vacant, expressionless; *Erklärung, Redensart* meaningless; **~tuer(in *f*)** *m* **-s, -** idler, loafer; **~tun** *nt* idleness, inactivity; (*Muße*) leisure; **das süße ~tun** dolce far niente, idle bliss; **viel Zeit mit ~tun verbringen** to spend a lot of time doing nothing; **n~würdig** *adj* base, despicable; *Mensch auch* worthless; **(du) ~würdiger!** (*old, liter*) vile *or* base wretch! (*old, liter*).

Nicht-: ~tänzer *m* non-dancer; **ich bin ~tänzer** I don't dance; **~trinker** *m* non-drinker; **er ist ~trinker** he doesn't drink; **~übereinstimmung** *f* discrepancy (+*gen* in, of, between); (*Meinungsunterschied*) differences *pl*, disagreement; **~veranlagungsbescheid** *m* (*Fin*) non-assessment declaration; **~veranlagungsbescheinigung** *f* (*Fin*) non-assessment note; **~verbreitung** *f* (*von Kernwaffen*) non-proliferation; **~vorhandensein** *nt* absence; **~wählbarkeit** *f* ineligibility (for office); **~wissen** *nt* ignorance; **sich mit ~wissen entschuldigen** to plead ignorance; **~zahlung** *f* (*form*) non-payment; **im Falle der ~zahlung, bei ~zahlung** in default of payment; **n~zielend** *adj siehe* **intransitiv**; **~zustandekommen** *nt* (*form*) non-completion; **~zutreffende(s)** *nt decl as adj* **(etwas) ~zutreffendes** something incorrect; **~zutreffendes (bitte) streichen!** (please) delete as applicable.

Nickel *nt*, *no pl* (*abbr* **Ni**) nickel.

Nickelbrille *f* metal-rimmed glasses *pl*.

nicken *vi* **(a)** (*lit, fig*) to nod ◆ **mit dem Kopf ~** to nod one's head; **ein leichtes N~** a slight nod. **(b)** (*inf: schlummern*) to snooze, to doze, to nod.

Nickerchen *nt* (*inf*) nap, snooze, forty winks (*inf*) ◆ **ein ~ machen** to take *or* have forty winks *or* a nap *or* a snooze.

Nicki *m* **-s, -s** velour pullover.

nid *prep* +*dat* (*old*) beneath, under, 'neath (*poet*).

nie *adv* never ◆ **~ im Leben** never ever; **machst du das? — ~ im Leben!** will you do it? — not on your life; **~ und nimmer** never ever; **~ wieder** *or* **mehr** never again; **ein ~ wiedergutzumachender Fehler** a mistake that can never be put right; **fast ~** hardly ever.

nieder [1] *adj attr* **(a)** (*esp S Ger: niedrig*) low ◆ **die ~e Jagd** small game hunting.

(b) (*weniger bedeutend*) lower; *Beamte auch* minor; (*geringer*) *Geburt, Herkunft* lowly; *Volk* common; *Klasse, Stand* lower; (*Comput*) *Programmiersprache* lower(-level) ◆ **der ~e Adel** the gentry, the lower *or* lesser aristocracy; **Hohe und N~e** (*liter*)/**hoch und ~** (*liter*) (both) the high and the low.

(c) *Triebe, Instinkt* low, base; *Arbeit* menial.

(d) (*primitiv*) *Kulturstufe* low, primitive; *Entwicklungsstufe* low, early.

[2] *adv* down ◆ **die Waffen ~!** lay down your arms; **auf und ~** up and down; **das Auf und N~** (*lit*) the bobbing up and down; (*fig*) the ups and (the) downs *pl*; **~ mit dem Kaiser!** down with the Kaiser!

Nieder-, nieder- *pref* (*Geog*) lower.

niederbeugen *sep* [1] *vt* (*lit, fig*) to bow down. [2] *vr* to bend down.

niederbrennen *vti sep* (*irreg*) (*vi: aux sein*) to burn down.

niederbringen *vt sep irreg Bohrung* to sink.

niederbrüllen *vt sep Redner* to shout down.

niederbügeln *vt sep* (*inf*) *Person, Einwand, Argument* to demolish ◆ **jdn rhetorisch ~** to demolish sb with rhetoric.

niederdeutsch *adj* **(a)** (*Geog*) North German. **(b)** (*Ling*) Low German.

Niederdeutsch(e) *nt* Low German; *siehe auch* **Deutsch(e)**.

niederdonnern *vi sep aux sein* (*Lawine*) to thunder down.

Niederdruck *m* (*Tech*) low pressure.

niederdrücken *vt sep* **(a)** (*lit*) to press down; *Taste, Hebel auch* to press, to push, to depress (*form*). **(b)** (*bedrücken*) **jdn ~** to depress sb, to get sb down (*inf*); **~d** depressing; *siehe* **niedergedrückt**.

niederfahren *vi sep irreg aux sein* (*liter*) to descend.

niederfallen *vi sep irreg aux sein* (*liter*) to fall *or* drop down.

⚠: for details of spelling reform, see supplement

Niederfrequenz *f* low frequency; (*Akustik*) audio frequency.
Niedergang *m* **(a)** (*liter: der Sonne*) setting, going down (*poet*); (*fig: Verfall*) decline, fall. **(b)** (*Naut*) companionway.
niedergedrückt *adj* depressed, dejected.
niedergehen *vi sep irreg aux sein* to descend; (*Aviat*) to descend, to come down; (*Fallschirmspringer*) to drop; (*Vorhang*) to fall, to drop; (*Regen*) to fall; (*Gewitter*) to break (*auch fig*); (*Boxer*) to go down.
niedergeschlagen 1 *ptp of* **niederschlagen**.
2 *adj* dejected, despondent.
Niedergeschlagenheit *f* dejection, despondency.
niederhalten *vt sep irreg* to hold *or* keep down; *Volk* to oppress; (*Mil*) to pin *or* hold down.
niederhauen *vt sep irreg Baum* to cut *or* chop down, to fell; *Gegner* to floor, to knock down, to fell.
niederholen *vt sep Segel, Flagge* to haul down, to lower; *Ballon* to bring down.
Niederholz *nt, no pl* underwood, underbrush.
niederkämpfen *vt sep Feuer* to fight down *or* back; *Feind* to overcome; *Tränen* to fight back.
niederkauern *vir* (*vi: aux sein*) to crouch *or* cower down.
niederknallen *vt sep* to shoot down.
niederknien *vi sep aux sein* to kneel down.
niederknüppeln *vt sep* to club down.
niederkommen *vi sep irreg aux sein* (*old*) to be delivered (*old*) (*mit* of).
Niederkunft *f* -, ¨-e (*old*) delivery.
Niederlage *f* **(a)** (*Mil, Sport, fig*) defeat; (*Mißerfolg*) failure, defeat ◆ **eine ~ einstecken müssen** *or* **erleiden** to suffer a defeat; **jdm eine ~ zufügen** *or* **beibringen** to defeat sb, to inflict a defeat on sb. **(b)** (*Lager*) warehouse, store, depot. **(c)** (*Filiale*) branch (office).
Niederlande *pl*: **die ~** the Netherlands *sing or pl*, the Low Countries *pl*.
Niederländer(in *f*) *m* **-s, -** Dutchman/Dutchwoman *etc* ◆ **die ~** the Dutch.
niederländisch *adj* Dutch, Netherlands.
Niederländisch(e) *nt* Dutch; *siehe auch* **Deutsch(e)**.
niederlassen *vr sep irreg* **(a)** to sit down; (*sich niederlegen*) to lie down; (*Vögel*) to land, to alight.
(b) (*Wohnsitz nehmen*) to settle (down).
(c) (*Praxis, Geschäft eröffnen*) to set up in business, to establish oneself, to set up shop (*inf*) ◆ **sich als Arzt/Rechtsanwalt ~** to set up (a practice) as a doctor/lawyer; **die niedergelassenen Ärzte** general practitioners, GPs; **die niedergelassenen Rechtsanwälte** lawyers in private practice.
Niederlassung *f* **(a)** *no pl* (*das Niederlassen*) settling, settlement; (*eines Arztes etc*) establishment, setting-up. **(b)** (*Siedlung*) settlement. **(c)** (*Comm*) registered office; (*Zweigstelle*) branch.
Niederlassungsbewilligung *f* (*Sw*) residence permit.
niederlegen *sep* 1 *vt* **(a)** *Gegenstand, Menschen* to lay *or* put *or* set down; *Last auch* to cast off; (*liter, Bibl*) *Kranz, Blumen* to lay; *Waffen* to lay down.
(b) (*aufgeben*) *Dienst, Amt, Mandat* to resign (from), to give up; *Krone, Regierung, Führung* to renounce, to give up ◆ **die Arbeit ~** (*aufhören*) to stop work(ing); (*streiken*) to down tools.
(c) (*schriftlich festlegen*) to write *or* set down.
(d) (*rare: einreißen*) *Mauer, Gebäude* to pull down; *Baum* to fell, to cut down.
2 *vr* to lie down ◆ **da legst' di' nieder!** (*S Ger inf*) well I'm blowed! (*inf*), by the 'eck! (*N Engl dial*).
Niederlegung *f* **(a)** (*von Kranz*) laying.
(b) (*von Amt, Dienst, Mandat*) resignation (from); (*von Kommando*) resignation (of); (*der Krone*) abdication ◆ **~ der Arbeit** industrial action.
(c) (*schriftlich*) setting-out ◆ **eine schriftliche ~ meiner Gedanken** setting out *or* putting down my thoughts in writing.
niedermachen, niedermetzeln *vt sep* to massacre, to butcher.
niedermähen *vt sep* (*lit, fig*) to mow down.
Nieder|österreich *nt* Lower Austria.
niederprasseln *vi sep aux sein* (*Regen, Hagel etc*) to beat down, to hammer down; (*fig: Beschimpfungen, Vorwürfe*) to rain *or* hail down.
niederreißen *vt sep irreg jdn* to pull *or* drag down; *Gebäude* to pull *or* knock down; (*fig*) *Schranken* to tear down.
Niederrhein *m* Lower Rhine.
niederrheinisch *adj* Lower Rhine.
niederringen *vt sep irreg* to fight down; (*im Ringkampf auch*) to floor.
Niedersachsen *nt* Lower Saxony.
niedersausen *vi sep aux sein* to rain *or* hail down.
niederschießen *sep irreg* 1 *vt* to shoot down.
2 *vi aux sein* (*Vogel etc*) to shoot *or* plummet down.
Niederschlag *m* **(a)** (*Met*) precipitation (*form*); (*Chem*) precipitate; (*Bodensatz*) sediment, dregs *pl* ◆ **radioaktiver ~** (radioactive) fallout; **für morgen sind heftige ¨-e gemeldet** tomorrow there will be heavy rain/hail/snow; **in diesem Gedicht haben seine eigenen Erfahrungen ihren ~ gefunden** his own experiences are reflected *or* find expression in this poem.
(b) (*Mus*) downbeat.
(c) (*Boxen*) knockdown blow; (*über 10 Sekunden*) knockout, KO ◆ **~ bis 10** knockout, KO; **Sieg durch ~** win by a knockout.
niederschlagen *sep irreg* 1 *vt* **(a)** *jdn* to knock down, to fell; (*Regen, Hagel*) *Getreide* to beat down, to flatten; *Kragen, Hutkrempe* to turn down; *Aufstand, Revolte* to quell, to put down, to suppress; *Augen, Blick* to lower, to cast down (*liter*); *siehe auch* **niedergeschlagen**.
(b) (*erlassen*) *Steuerschuld* to waive ◆ **ein Verfahren ~** (*Jur*) to dismiss a case.
(c) (*Chem*) to precipitate.
2 *vr* (*Flüssigkeit*) to condense; (*Bodensatz*) to settle; (*Chem*) to precipitate; (*Met*) to fall ◆ **die Untersuchung schlug sich in einer Reform nieder** the investigation resulted in a reform; **sich in etw** (*dat*) **~** (*Erfahrungen etc*) to find expression in sth.
Niederschlags-: n~arm *adj* with low precipitation (*form*); low-rainfall *attr*, with little snow; **die Südinsel ist n~ärmer** the south island has a lower rainfall/less snow *or* a lower level of precipitation (*form*); **n~frei** *adj* dry, without precipitation (*form*); **~menge** *f* rainfall/snowfall, precipitation (*form*); **n~reich** *adj* with a lot of precipitation (*form*), high rainfall *attr*, with a lot of snow.
Niederschlagung *f* (*von Strafverfahren*) dismissal; (*eines Aufstands*) suppression.
niederschmettern *vt sep* to smash *or* batter down; (*fig*) to shatter.
niederschmetternd *adj Nachricht, Ergebnis* shattering.
niederschreiben *vt sep irreg* to write down.
niederschreien *vt sep irreg* to shout down.
Niederschrift *f* (*das Niederschreiben*) writing down; (*Niedergeschriebenes*) notes *pl*; (*Schulaufsatz*) composition, essay; (*Protokoll*) (*einer Sitzung*) minutes *pl*; (*Jur*) record; (*von Bandaufzeichnung*) transcript ◆ **er brauchte viel Zeit für die ~ seiner Gedanken** he needed a lot of time to write down his thoughts; **die erste ~ eines Gedichts/Romans** the first draft of a poem/novel.
niedersetzen *sep* 1 *vt Kind, Glas* to put *or* set down; *Last auch* to cast off (*liter, Bibl*).
2 *vr* to sit down; (*Vogel*) to perch, to settle, to alight.
niedersinken *vi sep irreg aux sein* (*geh*) to sink down.
Niederspannung *f* (*Elec*) low voltage *or* tension.
niederstechen *vt sep irreg* to stab *or* knife (down).
niedersteigen *vti sep irreg aux sein* (*liter*) to descend.
niederstimmen *vt sep* to vote down.
niederstoßen *sep irreg* 1 *vt* to knock down.
2 *vi aux sein* (*Raubvogel*) to shoot *or* plummet down.
niederstrecken *sep* (*geh*) 1 *vt* to lay low.
2 *vr* to lie down, to stretch out.
niederstürzen *vi sep aux sein* to crash down.
niedertourig [-tu:rɪç] *adj Motor, Maschine* low-revving ◆ **~ fahren** to drive with low revs.
Niedertracht *f, no pl* despicableness, vileness; (*als Rache*) malice, spite ◆ **so viel ~ hätte ich ihm nicht zugetraut** I would not have suspected him of such a despicable *or* vile act; **die ~, mit der er bei seinen Betrügereien vorgegangen ist** the despicable way he went about his deceptions.
niederträchtig *adj* despicable, vile; (*rachsüchtig*) malicious, spiteful ◆ **jdn ~ verraten** to betray sb in a despicable way.
Niederträchtigkeit *f* **(a)** *no pl siehe* **Niedertracht**. **(b)** (*Tat*) despicable/malicious behaviour *no pl* ◆ **das ist eine ~** that's despicable.
niedertrampeln *vt sep* to trample underfoot.
niedertreten *vt sep irreg* to tread *or* trample down; *Erde* to tread *or* stamp down; *Teppich* to wear (down).
Niederung *f* (*Senke*) depression; (*Mündungsgebiet*) flats *pl*; (*sumpfig*) marsh ◆ **die ~en des Lebens** the dark *or* seamy side of life; **in solche ~en begebe ich mich nicht** (*fig*) I will not sink to such depths.
niederwalzen *vt sep* to flatten.
niederwärts *adv* (*obs*) down, downward(s).
niederwerfen *sep irreg* 1 *vt* to throw *or* hurl *or* cast (*liter*) down; *Aufstand* to suppress, to put down; *Gegner* (*lit*) to throw down, to floor; (*fig*) to defeat, to overcome ◆ **er wurde von einer Krankheit niedergeworfen** he was laid low by *or* with an illness.
2 *vr* to throw oneself down, to prostrate oneself.
Niederwerfung *f* (*von Aufstand*) suppression.
Niederwild *nt* small game.
niederzwingen *vt sep irreg* (*lit*) to force down; (*fig*) to defeat, to vanquish ◆ **er zwang seinen Gegner auf die Knie nieder** (*lit, fig*) he brought his enemy to his knees.
niedlich *adj* sweet, cute, pretty little *attr* ◆ **das Kätzchen lag so ~ auf meinem Bett** the kitten looked so sweet lying on my bed.
Niednagel *m* agnail.
niedrig *adj* **(a)** (*tief*) low ◆ **~ fliegen** to fly low.
(b) (*gering*) low; *Stand, Herkunft, Geburt auch* lowly, humble ◆ **~ste Preise** lowest *or* rock-bottom prices; **ich schätze seine Chancen sehr ~ ein** I don't think much of his chances, I think his chances are very slim *or* small; **von jdm ~ denken, jdn ~ einschätzen** to have a low *or* poor opinion of sb.
(c) (*gemein*) low *no adv*, base.
Niedrigkeit *f* **(a)** lowness ◆ **die ~ der Häuser** the low-built style of the houses. **(b)** (*von Gedanken, Beweggründen*) lowness, baseness.
Niedriglohnland *nt* low-wage country.
Niedrig-: ⚠**n~stehend** *adj Volk, Kultur* undeveloped, primitive; **~strahlung** *f* low-level radiation; **~wasser** *nt* (*Naut*) low tide, low water.
niemals *adv* never.
niemand *indef pron* nobody, no-one ◆ **es war ~ zu Hause** there was nobody *or* no-one at home, there wasn't anybody *or* anyone at home; **~ anders** *or* **anderer** (*S Ger*) **kam** nobody else came; **~ anders** *or* **anderer** (*S Ger*) **war da** there wasn't anybody else there, nobody else was there; **ich habe ~ anders** *or* **anderen** (*S Ger*) **gesehen** I didn't see anybody else; **herein kam ~ anders** *or* **anderer** (*S Ger*) **als der Kanzler selbst** in came the Chancellor himself, no

less, in came none other than the Chancellor himself; **~ Fremdes** no strangers, not ... any strangers; **er hat es ~(em) gesagt** he hasn't told anyone, he has told no-one; **sag das ~(em)!** don't tell anybody.
Niemand *m* **-s,** *no pl* **er ist ein ~** he's a nobody.
Niemandsland *nt* no man's land.
Niere *f* **-, -n** kidney ◆ **künstliche ~** kidney machine, artificial kidney; **es geht mir an die ~n** (*inf*) it gets me down.
Nieren- *in cpds* (*Anat*) renal; **~becken** *nt* pelvis of the kidney; **~beckenentzündung** *f* pyelitis (*spec*); **~entzündung** *f* nephritis (*spec*); **n~förmig** *adj* kidney-shaped; **~kolik** *f* renal colic; **n~krank** *adj* suffering from a kidney disease; **~krankheit** *f,* **~leiden** *nt* kidney disease; **~schale** *f* kidney dish; **~schützer** *m* kidney belt; **~stein** *m* kidney stone, renal calculus (*spec*); **~steinzertrümmerer** *m* **-s, -** lithotripter (*spec*); **~tasche** *f* bum bag; **~tisch** *m* kidney-shaped table; **~wärmer** *m* **-s, -** kidney warmer.
nieseln *vi impers* to drizzle.
Nieselpriem *m* **-s, -e** (*inf*) misery-guts (*inf*), moaner.
Nieselregen *m* drizzle.
niesen *vi* to sneeze.
Niespulver *nt* sneezing powder.
Nieß-: ~brauch *m* (*Jur*) usufruct; **~braucher, ~nutzer** *m* **-s, -** (*Jur*) usufructuary.
Nieswurz *f* **-,** *no pl* (*Bot*) hellebore.
Niet *m* **-(e)s, -e** (*spec*), **Niete** *f* **-, -n** rivet; (*auf Kleidung*) stud.
Niete *f* **-, -n** (*Los*) blank; (*inf: Mensch*) dead loss (*inf*), wash-out (*inf*) ◆ **eine ~ ziehen** (*lit*) to draw a blank; **mit ihm haben wir eine ~ gezogen** he is a dead loss.
nieten *vt* to rivet.
Nietenhose *f* (pair of) studded jeans *pl*.
niet- und nagelfest *adj* (*inf*) nailed *or* screwed down.
Niger[1] *m* **-s** (*Fluß*) Niger.
Niger[2] *nt* **-s** (*Staat*) Niger.
Nigeria *nt* **-s** Nigeria.
Nigerianer(in *f*) *m* **-s, -** Nigerian.
Nigger *m* **-s, -** (*pej*) nigger (*pej*), coon (*pej*).
Nigrer(in *f*) *m* **-s, -** person from Niger.
Nihilismus [nihi'lɪsmʊs] *m* nihilism.
Nihilist(in *f*) [nihi'lɪst(ɪn)] *m* nihilist.
nihilistisch [nihi'lɪstɪʃ] *adj* nihilistic.
Nikolaus *m* **(a)** (*Name*) Nicholas. **(b) -, -e** *or* (*hum inf*) **Nikoläuse** St Nicholas; (*~tag*) St Nicholas' Day.
Nikotin *nt* **-s,** *no pl* nicotine.
Nikotin-: n~arm *adj* low-nicotine; **n~frei** *adj* nicotine-free; **~gehalt** *m* nicotine content; **n~haltig** *adj* containing nicotine; **Zigarren sind n~haltiger als Zigaretten** cigars contain more nicotine than cigarettes; **~vergiftung** *f* nicotine poisoning.
Nil *m* **-s** Nile.
Nil-: ~delta *nt* Nile Delta; **~pferd** *nt* hippopotamus, hippo.
Nimbus *m* **-, -se** (*Heiligenschein*) halo, aureole; (*fig*) aura ◆ **sich mit dem ~ der Anständigkeit umgeben** to surround oneself with an aura of respectability; **im ~ der Heiligkeit stehen** to be thought of as a saint.
nimm *imper sing of* **nehmen.**
nimmer *adv* **(a)** (*liter: niemals*) never. **(b)** (*S Ger, Aus*) = **nicht mehr.**
Nimmerleinstag *m siehe* **Sankt-Nimmerleins-Tag.**
nimmermehr *adv* (*liter*) nevermore (*liter*), never again ◆ **nie und ~** never ever.
nimmermüde *adj attr* tireless, untiring.
Nimmersatt *m* **-(e)s, -e** glutton ◆ **ein ~ sein** to be insatiable.
nimmersatt *adj* gluttonous, insatiable.
Nimmerwiedersehen *nt* (*inf*) **auf ~!** I don't *or* I never want to see you again; **ich habe meinen Koffer da stehen lassen — na dann, auf ~** I left my case there — well, you've seen the last of that; **auf ~ verschwinden** to disappear never to be seen again; **ich habe es ihm geborgt, hoffentlich nicht auf ~** I lent it to him, not permanently I hope *or* I hope not for ever.
Nimrod *m* **-s, -e** Nimrod.
Niob(ium) *nt, no pl* (*abbr* **Nb**) niobium.
Nippel *m* **-s, -** (*Tech*) nipple.
nippen *vti* to nip (*an +dat* at) ◆ **vom Wein ~** to sip (at) the wine.
Nippes, Nippsachen *pl* ornaments *pl*, knick-knacks *pl*, bric-à-brac *sing*.
Nippflut, Nippzeit *f* neap tide.
Nippon *nt* **-s** Japan.
nirgendhin *adv siehe* **nirgendwohin.**
nirgends *adv* nowhere, not ... anywhere ◆ **ihm gefällt es ~** he doesn't like it anywhere; **überall und ~** here, there and everywhere; **er ist überall und ~ zu Hause** he has no real home; **er fühlt sich ~ so wohl wie** ... there's nowhere *or* there isn't anywhere he feels so happy as ...
nirgend(s)her *adv* from nowhere, not ... from anywhere.
nirgend(s)hin *adv siehe* **nirgendwohin.**
nirgendwo *adv siehe* **nirgends.**
nirgendwohin *adv* nowhere, not ... anywhere ◆ **wohin gehst du? — ~** where are you going? — nowhere; **wenn man ~ gehen kann, um zu übernachten** if you've got nowhere *or* if you haven't got anywhere to spend the night.
Nirosta ® *m* **-,** *no pl* stainless steel.
Nirwana, Nirvana *nt* **-(s)** nirvana.

Nische *f* **-, -n** niche, alcove; (*Koch~ etc*) recess.
Nisse *f* **-, -n** nit.
Nissenhütte *f* Nissen hut.
nisten [1] *vi* to nest; (*fig*) to take possession (*in +dat* of) ◆ **dieses Vorurteil nistete in seinem Hirn** this prejudice lodged in his mind.
[2] *vr* **Haß nistete sich in ihr Herz** (*liter*) hatred gripped *or* filled her heart.
Nist-: ~kasten *m* nest(ing) box; **~platz** *m* nesting place; **~zeit** *f* nesting time, (the) nesting season.
Nitrat *nt* nitrate.
nitrieren* *vt* to nitrate.
Nitrit *nt* **-s, -e** nitrite.
Nitro- ['nitro] *in cpds* nitro; **~benzol** *nt* nitrobenzene; **~glyzerin** *nt* nitroglycerine; **~lack** *m* nitrocellulose paint; **~verdünnung** *f* cellulose thinner; **~vergiftung** *f* nitrate poisoning.
Niveau [ni'voː] *nt* **-s, -s** (*lit, fig*) level ◆ **auf gleichem ~ liegen** to be on the same level; **intelligenzmäßig steht er auf dem ~ eines Dreijährigen** he has the mental age of a three-year-old; **diese Schule hat ein hohes ~** this school has high standards; **seine Arbeit hat ein sehr schlechtes ~** the level *or* standard of his work is very poor; **unter ~** below par; **unter meinem ~** beneath me; **~/kein/wenig ~ haben** to be of a high/low/fairly low standard; (*Mensch*) to be cultured/not at all/not very cultured; **ein Hotel mit ~** a hotel with class.
Niveau- [ni'voː]: **~linie** *f* contour line; **n~los** *adj* mediocre; **~unterschied** *m* (*lit, fig*) difference of level; **n~voll** *adj* high-class.
nivellieren* [nivɛ'liːrən] [1] *vt* (*lit, fig*) to level off *or* out.
[2] *vi* (*Surv*) to level.
Nivellierung [nivɛ'liːrʊŋ] *f* (*Surv*) levelling; (*Ausgleichung*) levelling out.
nix *indef pron* (*inf*) *siehe* **nichts.**
Nix *m* **-es, -e** water-sprite; (*mit Fischschwanz*) merman.
Nixe *f* **-, -n** water-sprite, water-nymph, nix(ie); (*mit Fischschwanz*) mermaid; (*hum: Bade~*) bathing belle.
Nizza *nt* **-s** Nice.
NN *abbr of* **Normalnull.**
NNO *abbr of* **Nordnordost** NNE.
NNW *abbr of* **Nordnordwest** NNW.
NO *abbr of* **Nordosten.**
nobel *adj* (*edelmütig*) noble; (*inf*) (*großzügig*) generous, lavish; (*kostspielig*) extravagant; (*elegant*) posh (*inf*) ◆ **~ geht die Welt zugrunde** (*iro*) there's nothing like bowing out in style; **sich ~ zeigen** (*inf*) to be generous; **er zeigte sich sehr ~ und verzieh ihm** he nobly forgave him; **ein nobler Kunde** (*iro inf*) a pleasant customer, a nice type of person.
Nobelherberge *f* (*inf*) posh *or* classy hotel (*inf*).
Nobelium *nt, no pl* (*abbr* **No**) nobelium.
Nobelpreis *m* Nobel prize.
Nobelpreisträger *m* Nobel prize winner.
Noblesse [no'blɛsə] *f* **-,** *no pl* (*geh*) noblesse ◆ **dafür hat er zu viel ~** he's much too high-minded for that.
noch [1] *adv* **(a)** (*weiterhin, bis jetzt, wie zuvor*) still ◆ **~ nicht** still not, not yet; **bist du fertig? — ~ nicht** are you ready? — not yet; **er ist ~ nicht da** he still isn't here, he isn't here yet; **immer ~, — immer** still; **sie ist immer ~ nicht fertig** she still isn't ready (yet), she isn't ready yet; **er dachte ~ lange an sie** it was a long time before he stopped thinking of her; **du bist ~ zu klein** you're still too young; **er schläft ~** he's still asleep, he is sleeping yet (*liter*); **~ nie** never; **das habe ich ~ nie gehört** I've never known that (before); **ich gehe kaum ~ aus** I hardly go out any more; **ich möchte gerne ~ bleiben** I'd like to stay on longer.
(b) (*irgendwann*) some time, one day ◆ **er wird sich (schon) ~ daran gewöhnen** he'll get used to it (some time *or* one day); **das kann ~ passieren** that just might happen, that might still happen; **er wird ~ kommen** he'll come (yet).
(c) (*eben, nicht später als*) **das muß ~ vor Dienstag fertig sein** it has to be ready by Tuesday; **ich habe ihn ~ vor zwei Tagen gesehen** I saw him only two days ago; **er ist ~ am selben Tag gestorben** he died the very same day; **ich tue das ~ heute** *or* **heute ~** I'll do it today *or* this very day; **~ im 18. Jahrhundert** as late as the 18th century; **gerade ~** (only) just; **~ gestern war er frisch und munter** (only) yesterday he was still bright and cheerful; **~ keine drei Tage** not three days.
(d) (*einschränkend*) (only) just ◆ **(gerade) ~ gut genug** (only) just good enough.
(e) (*außerdem, zusätzlich*) **wer war ~ da?** who else was there?; **(gibt es) ~ etwas?** (is there) anything else?; **ich will ~ etwas sagen** there's something else *or* another thing I want to say; **~ etwas Fleisch** some more meat, a bit more meat; **~ einer** another (one); **~ ein Bier** another beer; **~ zwei Bier** two more beers, another two beers; **~ einmal** *or* **mal** (once) again, once more; **und es regnete auch ~** *or* **~ dazu** and on top of that it was raining; **dumm und ~ dazu frech** stupid and cheeky with it (*inf*); **ich gebe Ihnen ~ zwei dazu** I'll give you two extra; **~ ein Wort!** (not) another word!
(f) (*bei Vergleichen*) even, still, yet ◆ **~ größer** even *or* still *or* yet bigger; **er will ~ mehr haben** he wants even *or* still more; **das ist ~ besser** that's even better, that's better still *or* still better; **das ist ~ viel wichtiger als** ... that is far more important yet *or* still than ...; **seien sie auch ~ so klein** however small they may *or* might be; **und wenn du auch ~ so bittest** ... however much you ask ...
(g) (*inf*) **wir fanden Fehler ~ und ~er** (*hum inf*) we found tons (*inf*) *or* loads (*inf*) of mistakes; **Geld ~ und ~er** (*hum inf*) heaps and heaps of money (*inf*);

er kann ~ und ~̈er erzählen he can go on telling stories for ever; **ich kann Ihnen Beispiele ~ und ~̈er geben** I can give you any number of examples; **sie hat ~ und ~̈er versucht,** ... she tried again and again to ...
[2] *conj* (*weder ... ~ ...*) nor ◆ **nicht X, ~ Y, ~ Z** not X nor Y nor Z.
Nochgeschäft *nt* (*Fin*) option to double.
nochmalig *adj attr* renewed ◆ **eine ~e Überprüfung** another check.
nochmals *adv* again.
Nockenwelle *f* camshaft.
Nocturne [nɔk'tʏrn] *nt* **-s, -s** *or f* **-, -s, Nokturne** *f* **-, -n** (*Mus*) *siehe* **Notturno.**
No-future- [no'fju:tʃɐ] *in cpds* no-future; **~-Generation** *f* no-future generation.
NOK [ɛn|o:'ka] *nt* **-s** *abbr of* **Nationales Olympisches Komitee.**
nölen *vi* (*N Ger inf*) to moan.
nolens volens ['no:lɛns 'vo:lɛns] *adv* (*geh*) like it or not *or* no, willy-nilly.
Nolimetangere ['no:lime'taŋgərə] *nt* **-, -** (*Bot*) touch-me-not.
Nomade *m* **-n, -n** (*lit, fig*) nomad.
Nomaden- *in cpds* nomadic; **n~haft** *adj* (*lit, fig*) nomadic; **~tum** *nt* nomadism.
Nomadin *f* (*lit, fig*) nomad.
nomadisch *adj* nomadic.
nomadisieren* *vi* to lead a nomadic existence ◆ **~de Stämme** nomadic tribes.
Nomen *nt* **-s, Nomina** (*Gram*) noun ◆ **n~ est omen** (*geh*) true to your/his *etc* name.
Nomenklatur *f* nomenclature.
Nomina *pl of* **Nomen.**
nominal *adj* nominal.
Nominal- *in cpds* (*Gram, Fin*) nominal; **~stil** *m* nominal style; **~wert** *m* (*Fin*) nominal *or* face *or* par value; **~zins** *m* (*Fin*) nominal interest rate.
Nomination *f* (*Eccl*) nomination.
Nominativ *m* nominative.
nominell *adj* nominal.
nominieren* *vt* to nominate.
Nonchalance [nõʃa'lã:s] *f* **-,** *no pl* (*geh*) nonchalance.
nonchalant [nõʃa'lã:] *adj* (*geh*) nonchalant.
Nonius *m* **-, Nonien** [-iən] *or* **-se** vernier (scale).
Nonkonformist(in *f*) *m* nonconformist.
nonkonformistisch *adj* nonconformist.
Nonne *f* **-, -n (a)** nun. **(b)** (*Schmetterling*) nun moth. **(c)** (*Dachziegel*) concave tile.
Nonnen-: n~haft *adj* nunnish; **sie lebte n~haft** she lived like a nun; **sie tut so n~haft** she pretends to be so chaste; **~kloster** *nt* convent, nunnery (*old, hum*).
Nonplus|ultra *nt* **-s,** *no pl* (*geh*) ultimate, non plus ultra.
Nonsens *m* **-(es),** *no pl* nonsense.
⚠**nonstop** [nɔn'ʃtɔp, nɔn'stɔp] *adv* non-stop.
⚠**Nonstop-** *in cpds* non-stop; **~betrieb** *m*: **im ~betrieb** non-stop; **~flug** *m* non-stop flight; **~kino** *nt* cinema with a continuous programme.
nonverbal *adj* non-verbal.
Noppe *f* **-, -n** (*Gummi~*) nipple, knob; (*von Tischtennisschläger auch*) pimple; (*Knoten*) burl; (*Schlinge*) loop ◆ **Garn mit ~n** bouclé; **ein Teppich mit ~n** a loop pile carpet.
noppen *vt* (*entfernen*) *Rohgewebe* to burl; *siehe* **genoppt.**
Nord *m* **-(e)s,** (*rare*) **-e (a)** (*Naut, Met, liter*) north ◆ **aus** *or* **von/nach ~** from the/to the north. **(b)** (*liter: Wind*) north wind.
Nord- *in cpds* (*in Ländernamen*) (*politisch*) North; (*geographisch auch*) the North of ..., Northern; **~afrika** *nt* North Africa; **~amerika** *nt* North America; **~atlantik** *m* North Atlantic; **~atlantikpakt** *m* North Atlantic Treaty; **n~atlantisch** *adj* North Atlantic; **n~atlantisches Verteidigungsbündnis** NATO Alliance; **n~deutsch** *adj* North German; *Dialekt, Spezialität, Mentalität auch* Northern German; **die n~deutsche Tiefebene** the North German lowlands *pl*; **die ~deutschen** the North Germans; **~deutschland** *nt* North(ern) Germany, the North of Germany.
Norden *m* **-s,** *no pl* north; (*von Land*) North ◆ **aus dem ~, von ~ (her)** from the north; **gegen** *or* **gen** (*liter*) *or* **nach ~** north(wards), to the north; **der Balkon liegt nach ~** the balcony faces north(wards); **nach ~ hin** to the north; **im ~ der Stadt/des Landes** in the north of the town/country; **im hohen ~** in the far north; **weiter** *or* **höher im ~** further north; **im ~ Frankreichs** in the north of France, in northern France.
norden *vt Karte* to orient(ate).
Nord-: ~england *nt* the North of England; **n~friesisch** *adj* North Fri(e)sian; **~halbkugel** *f* northern hemisphere; **n~irisch** *adj* Northern Irish; **~irland** *nt* Northern Ireland, Ulster.
nordisch *adj Wälder* northern; *Völker, Sprache* nordic ◆ **~e Kombination** (*Ski*) nordic combined.
Nordist(in *f*) *m* expert on/student of nordic languages.
Nordistik *f* nordic studies *sing.*
Nord-: ~kap *nt* North Cape; **~korea** *nt* North Korea; **~küste** *f* north(ern) coast; **~länder(in** *f*) *m* **-s, -** northern; (*Skandinavier*) Scandinavian.
nördlich [1] *adj* northern; *Kurs, Wind, Richtung* northerly ◆ **der ~e Polarkreis** the Arctic Circle; **der ~e Wendekreis** the Tropic of Cancer; **52 Grad ~er Breite** 52 degrees north.
[2] *adv* (to the) north ◆ **~ von Köln (gelegen)** north of Cologne; **es liegt ~er** *or* **weiter ~** it is further (to the) north.
[3] *prep +gen* (to the) north of.
Nordlicht *nt* northern lights *pl*, aurora borealis; (*fig hum: Mensch*) Northerner.
Nordnord-: ~ost *m* **(a)** (*Naut, Met, liter*) north-north-east, nor'-nor'-east (*Naut*); **(b)** (*liter: Wind*) nor'-nor'-easterly; **~osten** *m* north-north-east, nor'-nor'-east (*Naut*); **n~östlich** *adj* north-north-east(erly), nor'-nor'-east(erly) (*Naut*); **~west** *m* **(a)** (*Naut, Met, liter*) north-north-west, nor'-nor'-west (*Naut*); **(b)** (*liter: Wind*) nor'-nor'-westerly; **~westen** *m* north-north-west, nor'-nor'-west (*Naut*); **n~westlich** *adj* north-north-west(erly), nor'-nor'-west(erly) (*Naut*).
Nord|ost *m* **(a)** (*Met, Naut, liter*) north-east, nor'-east (*Naut*) ◆ **aus ~** from the north-east. **(b)** (*liter: Wind*) north-east(erly) wind, north-easter, nor'-easter (*Naut*).
Nord|ost- *in cpds* north-east; (*bei Namen*) North-East.
Nord|osten *m* north-east; (*von Land*) North East ◆ **aus** *or* **von ~** from the north-east; **nach ~** to the north-east, north-east(wards).
nord|östlich [1] *adj Gegend* north-eastern; *Wind* north-east(erly).
[2] *adv* (to the) north-east.
[3] *prep +gen* (to the) north-east of.
Nord-Ostsee-Kanal *m* Kiel Canal.
Nordpol *m* North Pole.
Nordpolar-: ~gebiet *nt* Arctic (Zone); **~meer** *nt* Arctic Ocean.
Nordrhein-Westfalen *nt* North Rhine-Westphalia.
nordrhein-westfälisch *adj* North Rhine-Westphalian.
Nordsee *f* North Sea.
Nord-: ~seite *f* north(ern) side; (*von Berg*) north(ern) face; **~staaten** *pl* (*Hist*) northern states *pl*, Union; **~stern** *m* North Star, Polar Star; **~-Süd-Gefälle** *nt* north-south divide; **~wand** *f* (*von Berg*) north face.
nordwärts *adv* north(wards) ◆ **der Wind dreht ~** the wind is moving round to the north.
Nordwest *m* **(a)** (*Met, Naut, liter*) north-west ◆ **aus ~** from the north-west. **(b)** (*liter: Wind*) north-west(erly) wind, north-wester, nor'-wester (*Naut*).
Nordwest- *in cpds* north-west; (*bei Namen*) North-West.
Nordwesten *m* north-west; (*von Land*) North-West ◆ **aus** *or* **von ~** from the north-west; **nach ~** to the north-west, north-west(wards).
nordwestlich [1] *adj Gegend* north-western; *Wind* north-west(erly).
[2] *adv* (to the) north-west ◆ **~ von** (to the) north-west of.
[3] *prep +gen* (to the) north-west of.
Nordwind *m* north wind.
Nörgelei *f* moaning, grumbling; (*Krittelei*) carping.
nörg(e)lig *adj* grumbly (*inf*), moaning; (*krittelig*) carping.
nörgeln *vi* to moan, to grumble; (*kritteln*) to carp, to niggle (*an +dat* about) ◆ **er hat immer an allem zu ~** he always finds something to moan about.
Nörgler(in *f*) *m* **-s, -** grumbler, moaner; (*Krittler*) carper, niggler.
Norm *f* **-, -en (a)** norm; (*Größenvorschrift*) standard (specification) ◆ **als ~ gelten, die ~ sein** to be (considered) normal, to be the usual thing. **(b)** (*Leistungssoll*) quota, norm ◆ **die ~ erreichen** to achieve one's quota, to meet one's target. **(c)** (*Typ*) signature (*at foot of page*).
normal *adj* normal; *Format, Maß, Gewicht* standard ◆ **benimm dich doch mal ~!** act like a normal human being, can't you?; **bist du noch ~?** (*inf*) have you gone mad?
Normal- *in cpds* **(a)** (*üblich*) normal; **(b)** (*genormt*) standard; **~benzin** *nt* regular (petrol (*Brit*) *or* gas *US*).
Normale *f* **-(n), -n** (*Math*) normal.
normalerweise *adv* normally, usually.
Normal-: ~fall *m* normal case; **im ~fall** normally, usually; **~film** *m* standard film; **~gewicht** *nt* normal weight; (*genormt*) standard weight.
normalisieren* [1] *vt* to normalize.
[2] *vr* to return *or* get back to normal.
Normalisierung *f* normalization.
Normalität *f* normality, normalcy.
Normal-: ~maß *nt* standard (measure); **~null** *nt* **-s,** *no pl* (*abbr* **NN**) ≃ sea level; **~spur** *f* (*Rail*) standard gauge; **~uhr** *f* (*old*) (synchronized) clock; **~verbraucher** *m* average consumer; **(geistiger) ~verbraucher** (*inf*) middlebrow; **Otto ~verbraucher** (*inf*) Joe Bloggs (*Brit inf*), the man on the Clapham Omnibus (*Brit hum inf*), John Doe (*US*); **~zeit** *f* standard time; **~zustand** *m* normal state; (*normale Verhältnisse*) normal conditions *pl*; (*Chem, Phys*) natural state.
Normandie *f* **-** Normandy.
Normanne *m* **-n, -n, Normannin** *f* Norman.
normannisch *adj* Norman.
normativ *adj* normative.
Normativbestimmungen *pl* (*Jur*) basic stipulations *pl.*
Normblatt *nt* standard specifications sheet.
normen *vt* to standardize.
Normenkontrollklage *f* (*Jur*) *legal proceedings brought to ask for judicial review.*
normieren* *vt siehe* **normen.**
Normierung *f* standardization.
Norm-: ~schrift *f* standard print/handwriting; **~teil** *nt* (*Tech*) standard part.
Normung *f* (*Tech*) standardization.
normwidrig *adj* deviant; (*Tech*) non-standard.
Norwegen *nt* **-s** Norway.
Norweger(in *f*) *m* **-s, -** Norwegian.

Norwegerpullover *m* Norwegian pullover.
norwegisch *adj* Norwegian.
Norwegisch(e) *nt* Norwegian; *siehe auch* **Deutsch(e)**.
Nostalgie *f* nostalgia.
nostalgisch *adj* nostalgic.
Not *f* **-, ¨-e** **(a)** *no pl* (*Mangel, Elend*) need(iness), want, poverty ◆ **hier herrscht große ~** there is great poverty here; **eine Zeit der ~** a time of need, a lean time; **aus ~** out of poverty; **~ leiden** to suffer deprivation; **jds ~** (*acc*) **lindern** to improve sb's lot; **in ~ leben** to live in poverty; **wenn ~ am Mann ist** if you/they *etc* are short (*inf*); (*im Notfall*) in an emergency; **~ macht erfinderisch** (*Prov*) necessity is the mother of invention (*Prov*); **in der ~ frißt der Teufel Fliegen** *or* **schmeckt jedes Brot** (*Prov*) beggars can't be choosers (*prov*); **~ kennt kein Gebot** (*Prov*) necessity knows no law (*Prov*); *siehe* **Geldnot, Zeitnot**.
(b) (*Bedrängnis*) distress *no pl*, affliction; (*Problem*) problem ◆ **die ¨-e des Alltags** the problems of everyday living; **in seiner ~** in his hour of need; **in unserer ~ blieb uns nichts anderes übrig** in this emergency we had no choice; **jdm seine ~ klagen** to tell sb one's troubles, to cry on sb's shoulder (*inf*); **in ~ sein** to be in distress; **in ~ geraten** to get into serious difficulties; **Freunde in der ~ (gehen tausend auf ein Lot)** (*Prov*) a friend in need (is a friend indeed) (*Prov*); **der/als Retter in der ~** sb's knight/like a knight in shining armour; **Hilfe in höchster ~** help in the nick of time; **in Ängsten und ¨-en schweben** to be in fear and trembling; **jdm in der ~ beistehen** to help sb in *or* through times of trouble *or* in his need.
(c) *no pl* (*Sorge, Mühe*) difficulty, trouble ◆ **er hat seine liebe ~ mit ihr/damit** he really has problems with her/it, he really has his work cut out with her/it (*inf*); **die Eltern hatten ~, ihre fünf Kinder zu ernähren** the parents had difficulty in feeding their five children; **es hat** *or* **damit hat's keine ~** (*old*) there's no rush; *siehe* **knapp, Mühe**.
(d) (*Zwang, Notwendigkeit*) necessity ◆ **der ~ gehorchend** bowing to necessity; **etw nicht ohne ~ tun** not to do sth without having to; **zur ~** if necessary, if need(s) be; (*gerade noch*) at a pinch, just about; **aus der ~ eine Tugend machen** to make a virtue (out) of necessity.
⚠ **not** *adj* (*geh*) **~ tun** *or* **sein** to be necessary; **ihm tat Hilfe ~** he needed help; **uns allen täte ein bißchen mehr Bescheidenheit ~** we could all benefit from a little more modesty.
Notabeln *pl* (*geh*) notabilities *pl*.
nota bene *adv* (*geh*) please note, let it be noted.
Not|anker *m* sheet anchor.
Notar *m* notary public.
Notariat *nt* notary's office.
notariell *adj* notarial ◆ **~ beglaubigt** legally certified.
Notarin *f siehe* **Notar**.
Not-: ~arzt *m* emergency doctor; **~arztwagen** *m* emergency doctor's car; **den ~arztwagen rufen** to call the emergency doctor.
Notation *f* (*Comput, Mus*) notation.
Not-: ~aufnahme *f* casualty (unit); **~aufnahmelager** *nt* reception centre, transit camp; **~ausgang** *m* emergency exit; **~behelf** *m* stopgap (measure), makeshift; **~beleuchtung** *f* emergency lighting; **~bremse** *f* emergency brake, communication cord (*Brit*); **die ~bremse ziehen** to pull the emergency brake; (*Ftbl sl: foulen*) to hack sb down, to commit a blatant foul; **~bremsung** *f* emergency stop; **~brücke** *f* temporary bridge; **~dienst** *m* **~dienst haben** (*Apotheke*) to be open 24 hours; (*Arzt*) to be on call.
Notdurft *f* **-,** *no pl* **(a)** (*euph geh*) call of nature (*euph*) ◆ **seine ~ verrichten** to relieve oneself, to answer the *or* a call of nature (*euph*). **(b)** (*old*) need. **des Lebens ~** the bare necessities of life; **des Leibes ~** enough to keep body and soul together.
notdürftig *adj* (*kaum ausreichend*) meagre, poor; (*behelfsmäßig*) makeshift *no adv*, rough and ready *no adv*; *Kleidung* scanty ◆ **wir konnten uns mit den Einheimischen ~ verständigen** we could just about communicate with the natives; **damit Sie sich wenigstens ~ verständigen können** so that you can at least communicate to some extent; **nachdem wir den Reifen ~ geflickt hatten** when we had patched up the tyre in a makeshift *or* rough-and-ready way.
Note *f* **-, -n** **(a)** (*Mus*) note ◆ **ganze ~** semibreve (*Brit*), whole note (*US*); **halbe ~** minim (*Brit*), half note (*US*); **~n** *pl* music; **~n lesen** to read music; **nach ~n spielen/singen** to play/sing from music; **nach ~n** (*fig inf*) thoroughly.
(b) (*Sch*) mark.
(c) (*Pol*) note.
(d) (*Bank~*) (bank)note.
(e) *no pl* (*Eigenart*) (*in bezug auf Gespräch, Brief etc*) note; (*in bezug auf Beziehungen, Atmosphäre*) tone, character; (*in bezug auf Einrichtung, Kleidung*) touch ◆ **das ist meine persönliche ~** that's my trademark; **einer Sache** (*dat*) **eine persönliche ~ verleihen** to give sth a personal touch; **ein Parfüm mit einer herben ~** a perfume with something tangy about it *or* with a tangy quality.
Notebook ['no:tbuk] *m or nt* **-s, -s** (*Comput*) notebook (computer).
Notebookcomputer *m* notebook computer.
Noten-: ~austausch *m* (*Pol*) exchange of notes; **~bank** *f* issuing bank, bank of issue; **~blatt** *nt* sheet of music; **~deckung** *f* (*Fin*) (bank)note cover; **~heft** *nt* (*mit Noten*) book of music; (*ohne Noten*) manuscript book; **~linie** *f* lines *pl* (of a stave); **Papier mit ~linien** manuscript paper; **~papier** *nt* manuscript paper; **~presse** *f* money press; **~pult** *nt* music stand; **~schlüssel** *m* clef; **~schrift** *f* musical notation; **~ständer** *m* music stand; **~umlauf** *m* (*Fin*) circulation (of banknotes); **~wechsel** *m* (*Pol*) exchange of notes.
Notfall *m* emergency ◆ **für den ~ nehme ich einen Schirm mit** I'll take an umbrella (just) in case; **im ~** if necessary, if need(s) be; **bei einem ~** in case of emergency.
notfalls *adv* if necessary, if need(s) be.
Notflagge *f* distress flag.
notgedrungen 1 *adj* essential, imperative.
2 *adv* of necessity, perforce ◆ **ich muß mich ~ dazu bereit erklären** I'm forced to agree, I've no choice but to agree, I must perforce agree.
Not-: ~geld *nt* emergency money; **~gemeinschaft** *f* emergency organization; **im Luftschutzbunker waren wir alle eine ~gemeinschaft** in the air raid shelter we were all brothers in misfortune; **~groschen** *m* nest egg; **sich** (*dat*) **eine Summe als ~groschen zurücklegen** to put some money away for a rainy day; **~hafen** *m* harbour of refuge; **wegen der Epidemie mußte das Schiff einen ~hafen anlaufen** because of the epidemic the ship had to make an emergency stop; **~helfer** *m* (*Rel*) auxiliary saint; **~hilfe** *f* assistance in an emergency.
notieren* 1 *vti* **(a)** (*Notizen machen*) to note down, to make a note of; (*schnell*) to jot down ◆ **ich notiere (mir) den Namen** I'll make a note of the name; **Fräulein, bitte ~ Sie!** please take a note/a letter/a memo, Miss X; **was möchten Sie bestellen? ich notiere** what would you like to order? I'll make a note of it *or* I'll take it down.
(b) (*vormerken*) (*Comm*) *Auftrag* to note, to book ◆ **zu welchem Termin waren Sie notiert?** what time was your appointment?; **jdn ~** to put sb's name *or* sb down.
(c) (*St Ex: festlegen*) to quote (*mit* at).
2 *vi* (*St Ex: wert sein*) to be quoted (*auf +acc* at).
Notierung *f* **(a)** (*Comm*) note. **(b)** (*St Ex*) quotation. **(c)** (*Mus*) notation.
➤ **nötig** 1 *adj* necessary ◆ **das für die Reise ~e Geld** the necessary money for the journey, the money needed *or* necessary for the journey; **ist das unbedingt ~?** is that really *or* absolutely necessary?; **es ist nicht ~, zu sagen, wie ...** it's not necessary *or* there's no need to say how ...; **es ist nicht ~, daß er kommt** it's not necessary *or* there's no need for him to come, he doesn't need to come; **das war wirklich nicht ~** that really wasn't necessary, there was no need for that; (*nach spitzer Bemerkung auch*) that was uncalled for; **die ~en Unkosten** the unavoidable costs; **wenn ~** if necessary, if need(s) be; **etw ~ haben** to need sth; **etw bitter ~ haben** to need sth badly; **er hat das natürlich nicht ~** (*iro*) but, of course, he's different; **ich habe es nicht ~, mich von dir anschreien zu lassen** I don't need *or* have to let you shout at me; **die haben's gerade ~** (*inf*) that's the last thing they need; **du hast es gerade ~, so zu reden** (*inf*) you can *or* can't talk (*inf*), you're a fine one to talk (*inf*); **das habe ich nicht ~!** I can do without that, I don't need that; **etw ~ machen** to necessitate sth, to make sth necessary; **das N~e** the necessary; **das Nötigste** the (bare) necessities *or* essentials; **alles zum Bergsteigen unbedingt N~e** everything necessary *or* needed for mountaineering.
2 *adv* (*dringend*) **etw ~ brauchen** to need something urgently; **ich muß mal ~** (*inf*) I'm dying to go (*inf*).
nötigen *vt* (*geh: zwingen*) to force, to compel; (*Jur*) to coerce; (*auffordern*) to urge, to press ◆ **jdn ins Zimmer ~** to force sb to go into a room; **sich ~ lassen** to need prompting *or* urging; **lassen Sie sich nicht (erst) ~!** don't wait to be asked; *siehe* **genötigt**.
nötigenfalls *adv* (*form*) *siehe* **notfalls**.
Nötigung *f* (*Zwang*) compulsion; (*Jur*) coercion ◆ **~ zum Diebstahl** coercion to commit theft.
Notiz *f* **-, -en** **(a)** (*Vermerk*) note; (*Zeitungs~*) item ◆ **sich** (*dat*) **~en machen** to make *or* take notes; **sich** (*dat*) **eine ~ von etw machen** to make a note of sth. **(b) ~ nehmen von** to pay attention to, to take notice of; **keine ~ nehmen von** to ignore; **nimm keine ~!** take no notice, don't take any notice.
Notiz-: ~block *m* notepad, jotter; **~buch** *nt* notebook; **~zettel** *m* piece of paper; **er hinterließ mir einen ~zettel mit seiner Adresse** he left me a note of his address on a piece of paper.
Not-: ~jahr *nt* year of need, difficult year; **~kühlsystem** *nt* emergency cooling system.
Notlage *f* crisis; (*Elend*) plight ◆ **in ~n** in an emergency; **die wirtschaftliche ~ Großbritanniens** Great Britain's economic plight; **jds ~** (*acc*) **ausnützen** to exploit sb's situation; **in eine ~ geraten** to get into serious difficulties; **sich in einer ~ befinden** to find oneself in serious difficulties.
notlanden *pret* **notlandete** *ptp* **notgelandet,** *infin auch* **notzulanden** *vi aux sein* to make a forced landing *or* an emergency landing.
Notlandung *f* forced *or* emergency landing.
⚠ **notleidend** *adj* needy; (*Comm*) *Wechsel, Wertpapier* dishonoured ◆ **die N~en** the needy.
Not-: ~leine *f* emergency cord; **~lösung** *f* compromise *or* less-than-ideal solution; (*provisorisch*) temporary solution; **~lüge** *f* white lie; **~maßnahme** *f* emergency measure; **~nagel** *m* (*fig inf*) last resort; **~opfer** *nt* emergency levy.
notorisch *adj* notorious.
Not-: ~ruf *m* (*Telec*) (*Gespräch*) emergency call; (*Nummer*) emergency number; **~rufsäule** *f* emergency telephone; **~rutsche** *f* (*Aviat*) escape chute.
notschlachten *pret* **notschlachtete,** *ptp* **notgeschlachtet,** *infin auch* **notzuschlachten** *vt* to destroy, to put down.
Not-: ~schlachtung *f* putting down; **~schrei** *m* (*liter*) cry of distress, cry for help; **~signal** *nt* distress signal; **~situation** *f* emergency; **~sitz** *m* fold-

away seat, tip-up seat.
Notstand *m* crisis; (*Pol*) state of emergency; (*Jur*) emergency ◆ **innerer ~** domestic *or* internal state of emergency; **äußerer ~** threat of invasion *or* attack; **ziviler ~** disaster; **übergesetzlicher ~** *emergency situation in which a law no longer holds*; **den ~ ausrufen** to declare a state of emergency; **einen ~ beheben** to end *or* put an end to a crisis.
Notstands-: ~gebiet *nt* (*wirtschaftlich*) depressed *or* deprived area; (*bei Katastrophen*) disaster area; **~gesetze** *pl*, **~verfassung** *f* (*Pol*) emergency laws *pl*.
Not-: ~stromaggregat *nt* emergency power generator; **~taufe** *f* emergency baptism; **n~taufen** *pret* **n~taufte,** *ptp* **n~getauft,** *infin auch* **n~zutaufen** *vt* **jdn n~taufen** to administer an emergency baptism to sb.
Notturno *nt* **-s, -s** *or* **Notturni** nocturne.
Not-: ~unterkunft *f* emergency accommodation; **~verband** *m* emergency *or* first-aid dressing; **~verordnung** *f* emergency decree.
notwassern *pret* **notwasserte,** *ptp* **notgewassert,** *infin auch* **notzuwassern** *vi* to ditch (*Aviat sl*), to make a crash-landing in the sea.
Notwehr *f, no pl* self-defence ◆ **aus/in ~** in self-defence.
notwendig *adj* necessary; (*unvermeidlich auch*) inevitable ◆ **~ brauchen** to need urgently; **es folgt ~** it necessarily follows; **es mußte ~ zum Zusammenstoß kommen** the collision was inevitable; **es ist ~, daß sie selbst kommt** it is necessary that she come(s) herself; **das N~e** the necessary, what is necessary; **ich habe alles N~e erledigt** I've done everything (that's) necessary; **das N~ste** the (bare) necessities *or* essentials; **sich auf das N~ste beschränken** to stick to essentials.
notwendigerweise *adv* of necessity, necessarily, inevitably.
Notwendigkeit *f* **(a)** *no pl* necessity ◆ **mit ~** of necessity; **die ~, etw zu tun** the necessity of doing sth. **(b)** (*notwendige Sache*) necessity, essential.
Notzeichen *nt* distress signal.
Notzucht *f* (*Jur*) rape ◆ **~ begehen** *or* **verüben** to commit rape (*an +dat* on).
notzüchtigen, *pret* **notzüchtigte,** *ptp* **genotzüchtigt,** *infin auch* **notzuzüchtigen** *vt* (*Jur*) to rape, to ravish, to violate.
Notzuchtverbrechen *nt* crime of rape.
Nougat, Nugat ['nu:gat] *m or nt* **-s, -s** nougat.
Nova *pl of* **Novum.**
Novelle [no'vɛlə] *f* **(a)** novella. **(b)** (*Pol*) amendment.
novellieren* [novɛ'li:rən] *vt* (*Pol*) to amend.
Novellierung [novɛ'li:rʊŋ] *f* (*Pol*) amendment.
Novellist(in *f*) [novɛ'lɪst(ɪn)] *m* novella writer.
novellistisch [novɛ'lɪstɪʃ] *adj* novella-like ◆ **den Stoff ~ behandeln** to use the material for *or* in a novella.
November [no'vɛmbɐ] *m* **-s, -** November; *siehe* **März.**
novemberlich [no'vɛmbɐlɪç] *adj* November-like.
Novene [no've:nə] *f* **-, -n** novena.
Novität [novi'tɛ:t] *f* (*geh*) innovation, novelty; (*Buch*) new publication; (*Theat*) new play.
Novize [no'vi:tsə] *m* **-n, -n,** *f* **-, -n** novice.
Noviziat [novi'tsia:t] *nt* novitiate.
Novizin *f* novice.
Novum ['no:vʊm] *nt* **-s, Nova** ['no:va] novelty.
NPD [ɛnpe:'de:] *f* - *abbr of* **Nationaldemokratische Partei Deutschlands.**
Nr. *abbr of* **Numero, Nummer** No.
NS *abbr of* **Nachschrift** PS; **nationalsozialistisch.**
NT *abbr of* **Neues Testament** NT.
Nu *m*: **im ~** in no time, in a flash *or* trice.
nu *adv* (*dial inf*) *siehe* **nun.**
Nuance ['nyã:sə] *f* **-, -n** (*kleiner Unterschied*) nuance; (*Kleinigkeit*) shade ◆ **um eine ~ zu laut** a shade too loud.
nuancenreich *adj* full of nuances.
nuancieren* [nyã'si:rən] *vt* to nuance.
'nüber *adv* (*dial*) *siehe* **hinüber.**
nüchtern *adj* **(a)** (*ohne Essen*) **der Patient muß ~ sein** the patient must have an empty stomach; **eine Medizin ~ einnehmen** to take a medicine on an empty stomach; **mit ~em/auf ~en Magen** with/on an empty stomach; **das war ein Schreck auf ~en Magen** (*hum*) my heart skipped a beat.
(b) (*nicht betrunken*) sober ◆ **wieder ~ werden** to sober up.
(c) (*sachlich, vernünftig*) down-to-earth *no adv*, rational; *Mensch auch* no-nonsense *attr*; *Zahlen, Tatsachen* bare, plain.
(d) (*schmucklos*) sober; *Essen* (*fade*) dull, insipid; (*nicht gewürzt*) plain.
Nüchternheit *f* **(a) überzeugen Sie sich von der ~ des Patienten** make sure that the patient's stomach is empty.
(b) (*Unbetrunkenheit*) soberness, sobriety.
(c) (*Sachlichkeit, Vernünftigkeit*) rationality.
(d) (*Schmucklosigkeit*) soberness; (*von Essen*) (*Fadheit*) dul(l)ness, insipidness, insipidity; (*Ungewürztheit*) plainness.
Nuckel *m* **-s, -** (*inf*) (*auf Fläschchen*) teat (*Brit*), nipple (*US*); (*Schnuller*) dummy (*Brit*), pacifier (*US*).
nuckeln *vi* (*inf*) (*Mensch*) to suck (*an +dat* at); (*Tier*) to suckle (*an +dat* from) ◆ **am Daumen ~** to suck one's thumb.
Nuckelpinne *f* (*inf*) old banger (*Brit inf*) *or* crate (*inf*).
Nucki *m* **-s, -** (*Sw*) dummy (*Brit*), pacifier (*US*).
Nudel *f* **-, -n** *usu pl* **(a)** (*als Beilage*) pasta *no pl*; (*als Suppeneinlage, chinesische*) noodle; (*Faden~*) vermicelli *pl*. **(b)** (*inf: Mensch*) (*dick*) dumpling (*inf*); (*komisch*) character.
Nudel-: ~brett *nt* pastryboard; **n~dick** *adj* (*inf*) podgy (*inf*); **~holz** *nt* rolling pin.
nudeln *vt Gans* to force-feed; (*inf*) *Kind* to stuff (*inf*), to overfeed ◆ **ich bin genudelt** (*inf*) I'm full to bursting (*inf*).
Nudel-: ~suppe *f* noodle soup; **~teig** *m* pasta/noodle dough.
Nudismus *m* nudism.
Nudist(in *f*) *m* nudist.
Nudität *f usu pl* (*geh*) nude (picture).
Nugat *m or nt siehe* **Nougat.**
nuklear *adj attr* nuclear.
Nuklear- *in cpds* nuclear; **~macht** *f* nuclear power; **~medizin** *f* nuclear medicine; **~park** *m* nuclear arsenal; **~test** *m* nuclear test.
Nukle|insäure *f* nucleic acid.
Nukleon *nt* **-s, Nukleonen** nucleon.
Nukleus ['nu:kleʊs] *m* **-, Nuklei** ['nu:klei] nucleus.
Nuklid *nt* **-s, -e** nuclide.
Null[1] *f* **-, -en (a)** (*Zahl*) nought, naught (*US*), zero; (*Gefrierpunkt*) zero ◆ **die ~** the figure nought, zero; **das Thermometer steht auf ~** the thermometer is at *or* on zero; **gleich ~ sein** to be absolutely nil *or* zero; **in ~ Komma nichts** (*inf*) in less than no time; **~ Komma ~** (*sl*) damn-all (*sl*), sweet Fanny Adams (*Brit sl*); **jdn auf ~ bringen** (*inf*) to fix sb for good (*inf*); **seine Stimmung sank auf** *or* **unter ~** (*inf*) he sank into the depths of gloom; **im Jahre ~** in the year nought; **die Stunde ~** the new starting point.
(b) (*inf: Mensch*) dead loss (*inf*).
Null[2] *m or nt* **-(s), -s** (*Cards*) nullo.
null *num* zero; (*inf: kein*) zero (*sl*); (*Telec*) O [əʊ] (*Brit*), zero (*US*); (*Sport*) nil, nothing; (*Tennis*) love ◆ **~ Komma eins** (nought) point one; **es ist ~ Uhr zehn** it's ten past twelve *or* midnight; **zwei Minuten ~ Sekunden** (*bei Zeitansagen*) two minutes precisely; (*bei Rennen*) two minutes dead *or* flat; **~ Grad** zero degrees; **~ Fehler** no *or* zero (*sl*) mistakes; **es steht ~ zu ~** there's no score; **das Spiel wurde ~ zu ~ beendet** the game was a goalless draw; **~ zu eins** one-nil, one-nothing; **~ und nichtig** (*Jur*) null and void; **für ~ und nichtig erklären** (*Jur*) to declare null and void, to annul.
null|achtfünfzehn, null|achtfuffzehn (*inf*) **1** *adj inv* run-of-the-mill (*inf*).
2 *adv* in a run-of-the-mill way.
Null|achtfünfzehn-, Null|achtfuffzehn- *in cpds* (*inf*) run-of-the-mill.
Null-Bock- (*sl*) *in cpds* apathetic; **~-Generation** *f* "couldn't care less" generation.
Nulldiät *f* starvation diet.
⚠ **Nulleiter** *m getrennt*: **Null-leiter** (*Elec*) earth (wire) (*Brit*), ground (wire) (*US*).
⚠ **Nullinie** *f getrennt*: **Null-linie** zero, nought, naught (*US*).
Null-: ~menge *f* (*Math*) empty set; **~meridian** *m* Greenwich *or* prime Meridian.
Null-Null *nt or m* **-,** *no pl* (*inf*) loo (*Brit inf*), restroom (*US*).
Nullnummer *f* (*von Zeitung etc*) pilot.
⚠ **Nullösung** *f getrennt*: **Null-lösung** (*Pol*) zero option.
Null ouvert [u've:ɐ] *m or* (*rare*) *nt* **- -, - -s** (*Cards*) null ouvert.
Nullpunkt *m* zero ◆ **absoluter ~** absolute zero; **die Stimmung sank unter den ~** the atmosphere froze; **seine Karriere hatte den ~ erreicht** his career had reached rock-bottom; **auf dem ~ angekommen sein** (*fig*) to have sunk to *or* reached rock-bottom.
Nullrunde *f* **in diesem Jahr gab es eine ~ für Beamte** there has been no pay increase this year for civil servants; **die Arbeitgeber bestehen auf einer ~** the employers are insisting that there should be no pay increase this time.
Null-: ~spiel *nt* (*Cards*) nullo; **~stellung** *f* zero position; **in der ~stellung sein** to be on zero; **~tarif** *m* (*für Verkehrsmittel*) free travel; (*freier Eintritt*) free admission; **zum ~tarif** (*hum*) free of charge; **~wachstum** *nt* (*Pol*) zero growth.
Nulpe *f* **-, -n** (*sl*) clot (*inf*), dope (*sl*), jerk (*sl*).
Numerale *nt* **-s, Numeralia** *or* **Numeralien** [-liən] (*Gram*) numeral.
Numeri *pl of* **Numerus.**
⚠ **numerieren*** *vt* to number.
⚠ **Numerierung** *f* numbering.
⚠ **numerisch** *adj* numeric(al).
Numero *nt* **-s, -s** (*old, hum*) **~ eins/zwei** number one/two.
Numerus *m* **-, Numeri** (*Gram*) number ◆ **~ clausus** (*Univ*) restricted entry.
Numismatik *f* numismatics *sing*.
➤ **Nummer** *f* **-, -n** (*Math, von Zeitschrift, Varieté~*) number; (*Größe*) size; (*inf: Mensch*) character; (*sl: Koitus*) screw (*sl*); (*mit Prostituierter*) trick (*sl*) ◆ **unser Haus hat die ~ 25** our house is number 25; **Bahnhofstraße ~ 15** number 15 Bahnhofstraße; **nur eine ~ unter vielen sein** (*fig*) to be a cog (in the machine); **er hat eine ruhige ~** (*inf*) he's onto a cushy number (*inf*); **auf ~ Sicher gehen** (*inf*) to play (it) safe; **auf** *or* **in ~ Sicher sein** (*sl*) to be in the jug (*sl*) *or* can (*US sl*); **Gesprächsthema ~ eins** the number one talking point; **sie ist die ~ eins in Hollywood** she's number one *or* the number one star in Hollywood; **eine ~ abziehen** (*sl*) to put on an act; **eine ~ machen** *or* **schieben** (*sl*) to have it off *or* away (*sl*).
Nummern-: ~konto *nt* (*Fin*) numbered account; **~scheibe** *f* (*Telec*) dial; **~schild** *nt* (*Aut*) number plate, registration plate (*Brit*), license plate (*US*); **~speicher** *m* (*Telec*) memory.
nun **1** *adv* **(a)** (*jetzt*) now ◆ **von ~ an** from now on, as from *or* of now, from here on in (*US*); **~ und nimmer(mehr)** (*liter*) nevermore (*liter*); **~, da er da ist, können wir anfangen** now that he's here we can get started; **~ erst, erst ~** only now; **~ ist aber genug!** now that's enough; **~ endlich** (now) at last; **was ~?** what now?; **was ~ (schon wieder)?** what (is it) now?

➤ SPRACHE AKTIV: **Nummer** → 27.1, 27.3, 27.4, 27.7

(b) (*danach*) then ◆ **~ erst ging er** only then did he go.
(c) **ich bin ~ eben dumm** I'm just stupid, that's all; **er will ~ mal nicht** he simply doesn't want to; **wir hatten uns ~ eben entschlossen, zu gehen ...** after all, we had decided to go ...; **dann muß ich das ~ wohl tun!** then I'll just have to do it; **~, wenn's unbedingt sein muß** well, if I/you *etc* really must; **~, du hast ja recht, wenn du das sagst, aber ...** well *or* OK (*inf*) *or* fair enough (*inf*), what you say is true but ...; **das ist ~ (ein)mal so** that's just the way things are; **~ ja** *or* **gut, aber ...** all right *or* OK (*inf*), but ...; **~ ja** well yes; **~ gut** (well) all right, (well) OK (*inf*); **~, meinetwegen** well, as far as I'm concerned; **er mag ~ wollen oder nicht** (*liter*) whether he wants to or not *or* no; **~ gerade erst** *or* **erst recht!** just for that (I'll do it)!; **~ taten wir's gerade erst nicht** *or* **erst recht nicht** just because they/he/she *etc* said/did that, we didn't do it.
(d) (*Folge*) now ◆ **das hast du ~ davon!** (it) serves you right.
(e) (*Aufforderung*) come on, go on ◆ **~ denn** (*geh*) well then; **~, wird's bald?** (*inf*) come on then, hurry up then.
(f) (*bei Fragen*) well ◆ **~?** well?
(g) (*beschwichtigend*) come on ◆ **~, ~!** (*warnend*) come on now, come, come, now, now; (*tröstend*) there, there.
[2] *conj* (*obs*) since (that *obs*), now that.

nunmehr *adv* (*geh*) (*jetzt*) now, at this point; (*von jetzt an*) henceforth (*form*), from now on, as from *or* of now ◆ **die ~ herrschende Partei** the currently ruling party.

nunmehrig *adj attr* (*form*) present, current.

'nunter *adv* (*dial*) *abbr of* **hinunter**.

Nuntius ['nʊntsiʊs] *m* **-, Nuntien** ['nʊntsiən] nuncio.

nur *adv* **(a)** (*einschränkend*) only, just ◆ **er ist ein sehr schneller Arbeiter, ~ müßte er etwas gründlicher sein** he is a very fast worker but *or* only he should be rather more thorough; **ich habe ~ ein Stück Brot gegessen** I've only eaten a piece of bread, I've eaten only *or* just a piece of bread; **alle, ~ ich nicht** everyone except *or* but me; **~ ich weiß** I'm the only one who knows, only I know; **~ schade, daß ...** it's just a pity that ...; **~ daß** it's just that, only; **~ noch zwei Minuten** only *or* just two minutes left *or* to go; **der Kranke ißt fast ~ noch Obst** the sick man eats virtually nothing but fruit these days; **nicht ~ ..., sondern auch** not only *or* just ... but also; **alles, ~ das nicht!** anything but that!; **warum möchtest du das denn wissen? — ach, ~ so!** why do you want to know? — oh I just do *or* oh just because *or* oh no special reason; **ich hab' das ~ so gesagt** I was just talking; **warum hast du das gemacht? — ~ so** why did you do that? — I just did; **~ kann man nie wissen, ob ...** only *or* but you never can *or* can never tell if ...
(b) (*verstärkend*) just ◆ **wie schnell er ~ redet** doesn't he speak fast!; **daß es ~ so krachte** making a terrible din; **er fuhr, so schnell er ~ (fahren) konnte** he drove just as fast as he possibly could, he drove for all he was worth.
(c) (*mit Fragepronomen*) -ever, on earth (*inf*) ◆ **was/wer/wie** *etc* **~?** but what/who/how *etc*?; **was hat er ~?** whatever *or* what on earth is the matter with him?; **wie kannst du ~ (so etwas sagen)?** how could you (say such a thing)?; **sie bekommt alles, was sie ~ will** she gets whatever she wants.
(d) (*Wunsch, Bedingung*) **wenn er ~ (erst) käme** if only he would come, if he would only come; **wüßte ich ~, wie** if only I knew how, if I only knew how; **es wird klappen, wenn er ~ nicht die Nerven verliert** it will be all right as long as *or* so long as (*inf*) *or* provided (that) he doesn't lose his nerve.
(e) (*mit Negationen*) just, ... whatever you do ◆ **laß das ~ niemand wissen!** just don't let anyone find out, (but) don't let anyone find out whatever you do; **sagen Sie das ~ nicht Ihrer Frau!** just don't tell your wife (whatever you do).
(f) (*Aufforderung*) just ◆ **geh ~!** just go, go on; **~ zu!** go on; **sieh ~** just look; **~ her damit!** (*inf*) let's have it; **sagen Sie es ~, Sie brauchen es ~ zu sagen** just say (the word), you only have to say (the word); **er soll ~ lachen!** let him laugh.
(g) **~ mehr** (*dial, esp Aus*) only ... left; **ich habe ~ mehr eine Mark** I've only one mark left.

Nurhausfrau *f* full-time housewife.

Nürnberg *nt* **-s** Nuremberg ◆ **jdm etw mit dem ~er Trichter beibringen** (*inf*) to drum sth into sb.

nuscheln *vti* (*inf*) to mutter, to mumble.

⚠**Nuß** *f* **-, Nüsse (a)** nut ◆ **eine harte ~ zu knacken haben** (*fig*) to have a tough nut to crack. **(b)** (*inf: Mensch*) drip (*sl*), jerk (*sl*) ◆ **eine taube ~** a dead loss (*inf*), a wash-out (*inf*); **eine doofe ~** a stupid twit (*Brit inf*) *or* clown (*inf*). **(c)** (*inf: Kopf~*) punch (in the head).

⚠**Nuß-: ~baum** *m* (*Baum*) walnut tree; (*Holz*) walnut; **n~braun** *adj* nut-brown, hazel; **~knacker** *m* nutcracker, (pair of) nutcrackers *pl*; **~kohle** *f* nut coal; **~schale** *f* nutshell; (*fig: Boot*) cockleshell, frail little boat.

Nüster *f* **-, -n** nostril.

Nut *f* **-, -en** (*spec*), **Nute** *f* **-, -n** groove, flute, chase; (*zur Einfügung*) rabbet, slot; (*Keil~*) keyway, key seat ◆ **~ und Feder** tongue and groove; **~ und Zapfen** mortise and tenon.

nuten *vt siehe* **Nut** to groove, to flute; to rabbet, to slot; to cut a keyway in, to key seat.

Nutria *f* **-, -s** (*Tier, Pelz*) coypu, nutria (*rare*).

Nutte *f* **-, -n** (*inf*) tart (*inf*), pro (*Brit sl*), hooker (*esp US sl*).

Nut- und Federbrett *nt* tongue and groove board.

nutz *adj* (*S Ger, Aus*) *siehe* **nütze**.

Nutz *m*: **zu ~ und Frommen** *+gen* (*old liter*) for the greater good of (*form*).

Nutzanwendung *f* practical application; (*einer Geschichte*) moral.

nutzbar *adj* us(e)able, utilizable; *Bodenschätze* exploitable; *Boden* fertile, productive ◆ **~ machen** to make us(e)able *or* utilizable; *Sonnenenergie* to utilize, to harness, to turn to good use; *Sümpfe* to reclaim; *Bodenschätze* to exploit.

Nutzbarkeit *f siehe adj* us(e)ability, utilizability; exploitability; fertility, productivity.

Nutzbarmachung *f* utilization; (*von Sümpfen*) reclamation; (*von Bodenschätzen*) exploitation.

Nutzbau *m* **-(e)s, -ten** functional building.

nutzbringend *adj* profitable ◆ **etw ~ anwenden** to use sth profitably *or* to good effect, to put sth to good use, to turn sth to good account.

nütze, nutz (*S Ger, Aus*) *adj pred* **zu etw/nichts ~ sein** to be useful for sth/to be no use for anything.

Nutzeffekt *m* effectiveness, efficiency.

Nutzen *m* **-s, - (a)** use; (*Nützlichkeit*) usefulness ◆ **es hat keinen ~, das zu tun** there's no use *or* point (in) doing that; **zum ~ der Öffentlichkeit** for the benefit of the public; **jdm von ~ sein** to be useful *or* of use to sb; (*einer anderen Person auch*) to be of service to sb.
(b) (*Vorteil*) advantage, benefit; (*Gewinn*) profit ◆ **jdm ~ bringen** (*Vorteil*) to be of advantage to sb; (*Gewinn*) to bring sb profit, to prove profitable to sb; **sich** (*dat*) **großen ~ von etw versprechen** to expect to benefit *or* profit greatly from sth; **von etw ~ haben** to gain *or* profit by sth; **aus etw ~ ziehen** to reap the benefits of sth.

nutzen, nützen [1] *vi* to be of use, to be useful (*jdm zu etw* to sb for sth) ◆ **die Ermahnungen haben genützt/nichts genützt** the warnings had the desired effect/didn't do any good; **es nützt nichts** it's no use *or* good, it's useless; **alle Anstrengungen haben nichts genützt** all our efforts were useless *or* in vain; **da nützt alles nichts** there's nothing to be done; **das nützt (mir/dir) nichts** that won't help (me/you); **das nützt niemandem** that's of no use to anybody; **es nützt wenig** it isn't much use *or* good; **wozu soll das alles ~?** what's the use *or* point of that?
[2] *vt* to make use of, to use; *Gelegenheit* to take advantage of ◆ **nütze den Tag!** gather ye rosebuds while ye may (*liter*).

Nutzer(in *f*) *m* user.

nutzergerecht *adj* user-friendly.

Nutz-: ~fahrzeug *nt* farm vehicle; military vehicle *etc*; (*Comm*) commercial vehicle, goods vehicle; (*Straßenbahn etc*) public vehicle; **~fläche** *f* utilizable *or* us(e)able floor space; (*Agr*) (agriculturally) productive land; **~garten** *m* vegetable *or* kitchen garden; **~gegenstand** *m* article of purely practical value; **~holz** *nt* (utilizable) timber; **~last** *f* payload; **~leistung** *f* efficiency, effective capacity *or* output; (*Aut*) performance.

nützlich *adj* useful; *Hinweis, Wissen, Kenntnisse, Buch auch* helpful ◆ **~ für die Gesundheit** beneficial for the health; **er könnte dir eines Tages sehr ~ werden** he might be very useful to you one day; **sich ~ machen** to make oneself useful; **kann ich Ihnen ~ sein?** may I be of service to you?

Nützlichkeit *f* usefulness, utility (*form*); (*Vorteil*) advantage; (*Dienlichkeit*) usefulness, helpfulness.

Nützlichkeits-: ~denken *nt* utilitarian thinking; **~prinzip** *nt* utility principle.

Nützling *m* beneficial insect.

nutzlos *adj* **(a)** useless; (*unergiebig, vergeblich*) futile, vain *attr*, in vain *pred* ◆ **es ist völlig ~, das zu tun** it's absolutely useless *or* pointless *or* futile doing that; **er hat seine Zeit ~ mit Spielen zugebracht** he frittered away *or* wasted his time playing.
(b) (*unnötig*) needless ◆ **sein Leben ~ aufs Spiel setzen** to risk one's life needlessly *or* unnecessarily.

Nutzlosigkeit *f* uselessness; (*Uneinträglichkeit, Vergeblichkeit*) futility, vainness.

Nutznießer(in *f*) *m* **-s, -** beneficiary; (*Jur*) usufructuary.

Nutznießung *f* (*Jur*) usufruct.

Nutz-: ~pflanze *f* useful plant; **~tier** *nt* working animal.

Nutzung *f* (*Gebrauch*) use; (*das Ausnutzen*) exploitation; (*Jur: Ertrag*) benefit; (*Einkommen*) revenue (*+gen* from), return(s) (*+gen* on) ◆ **ich habe ihm meinen Garten zur ~ überlassen** I gave him the use of my garden; **die ~en aus etw ziehen** (*Jur*) to enjoy the benefit of sth.

Nutzungs-: ~dauer *f* (useful) life; **~recht** *nt* (*Jur*) usufruct; **~vertrag** *m* *contract granting use*; (*im Verlagswesen*) rights contract.

n.u.Z. *abbr of* **nach unserer Zeitrechnung** by our calendar.

NW *abbr of* **Nordwesten** NW.

Nylon ® ['nailɔn] *nt* **-(s),** *no pl* nylon.

Nylons ['nailɔns] *pl* nylons *pl*, nylon stockings *pl*.

Nylonstrumpf ['nailɔn-] *m* nylon (stocking).

Nymphchen ['nʏmf-] *nt* nymphet.

Nymphe ['nʏmfə] *f* **-, -n** (*Myth*) nymph; (*fig*) sylph; (*Zool*) nymph(a) ◆ **die ~n** (*Anat*) the nymphae *pl*.

Nymphomanie [nʏmfo-] *f* nymphomania.

Nymphomanin [nʏmfo-] *f* nymphomaniac.

nymphomanisch [nʏmfo-] *adj* nymphomaniac.

O, o [oː] *nt* **-, -** O, o.

O *abbr of* **Osten.**

o *interj* oh ◆ **~ Sünder!** (*liter*) O sinner.

Oase *f* **-, -n** oasis; (*fig*) haven, oasis.

ob [1] *conj* **(a)** (*indirekte Frage*) if, whether ◆ **wir gehen spazieren, ~ es regnet oder nicht** we're going for a walk whether it rains or not; **Sie müssen kommen, ~ Sie (nun) wollen oder nicht** like it or not, you have to come; **~ reich, ~ arm** whether rich or poor; **~ er (wohl) morgen kommt?** I wonder if he'll come tomorrow?; **~ wir jetzt Pause machen?** shall we have a break now?; **~ ich nicht lieber gehe?** maybe I'd better go, hadn't I better go?; **~ ich keine Angst gehabt hätte, fragte er** hadn't I been afraid, he asked; **er hat gefragt, ~ du's geklaut hast — ~ ich was?** (*inf*) he asked if you pinched it — if I what?; **kommst du mit? — was? — ~ du mitkommen willst?** are you coming? — what? — are you coming?; **~ Sie mir wohl mal helfen können?** could you possibly help me?, I wonder if you could help me?
(b) (*verstärkend*) **und ~** (*inf*) you bet (*inf*), of course; **und ~ ich das gesehen habe!** you bet (*inf*) *or* of course I saw it!
(c) (*vergleichend*) **als ~** as if; **(so) tun als ~** (*inf*) to pretend; **tu nicht so als ~!** stop pretending!
(d) ~ ... auch, ~ ... gleich (*liter*) even though.
[2] *prep + gen* **(a)** (*old, liter*) on account of.
(b) (*in Ortsnamen*) (up)on.

OB [oːˈbeː] *m* **-s, -s** *abbr of* **Oberbürgermeister.**

o.B. *abbr of* **ohne Befund.**

Obacht *f* **-,** *no pl* (*esp S Ger*) **~!** watch out!, look out!, careful!; **~ geben auf** (*+acc*) (*aufmerken*) to pay attention to; (*bewachen*) to keep an eye on; **du mußt ~ geben, daß du keine Fehler machst** you must be careful not to make any mistakes; **gib** *or* **hab doch ~!** (*inf*) be careful!, watch it! (*inf*).

ÖBB *abbr of* **Österreichische Bundesbahnen.**

Obdach *nt, no pl* (*geh*) shelter ◆ **jdm (ein) ~ gewähren** *or* **geben** to give *or* offer sb shelter; **kein ~ haben** to be homeless; (*vorübergehend*) to have no shelter.

Obdach-: o~los *adj* homeless; **o ~los werden** to be made homeless; **die Flüchtlinge zogen o~los umher** the refugees wandered about with no home to go to; **~lose(r)** *mf decl as adj* homeless person; **die ~losen** the homeless.

Obdachlosen-: ~asyl, ~heim *nt* hostel/shelter for the homeless; **~siedlung** *f* settlement for the homeless.

Obdachlosigkeit *f* homelessness.

Obduktion *f* post-mortem (examination), autopsy.

obduzieren* *vt* to carry out *or* do a post-mortem *or* autopsy on.

O-Beine *pl* (*inf*) bow *or* bandy legs *pl*.

o-beinig *adj* bow- *or* bandy-legged.

Obelisk *m* **-en, -en** obelisk.

oben *adv* **(a)** (*am oberen Ende*) at the top; (*an der Oberfläche*) on the surface; (*im Hause*) upstairs; (*in der Höhe*) up ◆ **(hier) ~!** (*auf Kisten etc*) this way *or* this side up!; **so ist das Leben, mal bist du ~, mal bist du unten** that's life, sometimes you're up, sometimes you're down; **~ und unten (von etw) verwechseln** to get sth upside down; **wo ist ~ (bei dem Bild)?** which is the top (of the picture)?, which is the right way up (for the picture)?; **die Leute, die ~ wohnen** the people on the floor above us/you *etc or* (who live) upstairs; **wir möchten lieber ~ wohnen** we'd rather live high(er) up; **möchten Sie lieber ~ schlafen?** (*im oberen Bett*) would you like the top bunk *or* to sleep on top?; **wir wohnen rechts ~** *or* **~ rechts** we live on the top floor to the right; **~ rechts** *or* **rechts ~ (in der Ecke)** in the top right-hand corner; **die Abbildung ~ links** *or* **links ~ auf der Schautafel** the illustration on the top left *or* in the top left-hand corner of the diagram; **der ist ~ nicht ganz richtig** (*inf*) he's not quite right up top (*inf*); **Kleid/Kellnerin mit ~ ohne** (*inf*) topless dress/waitress; **~ ohne gehen** *or* **tragen** (*inf*) to be topless; **ganz ~** right at the top; **ganz ~ auf dem Stapel/in der Rangordnung** right at the top of the pile/of the hierarchy; **hier/dort ~** up here/there; **die ganze Sache steht mir bis hier ~** (*inf*) I'm sick to death of *or* fed up to the back teeth with the whole thing (*inf*); **bis ~ (hin)** to the top; **hoch ~** high (up) above; **beim Festessen saß er weiter ~ an der Tafel** at the banquet he sat nearer the top of the table; **~ auf dem Berg/der Leiter/dem Dach** on top of the mountain/ladder/roof; **~ am Himmel** up in the sky; **~ im Himmel** up in heaven, in heaven above (*liter*); **~ in Schottland** up in Scotland; **~ im Norden** up (in the) north; **~ herum** round the top; (*von Frau*) up top; (*von Jacke*) round the chest; **nach ~** up, upwards; (*im Hause*) upstairs; **der Fahrstuhl fährt nach ~** the lift is going up; **wir sind mit dem Fahrstuhl nach ~ gefahren** we went up in the lift; **die Bergsteiger sind auf dem Weg nach ~** the climbers are on their way up; **der Weg nach ~** (*fig*) the road to the top; **endlich hat sie den Weg nach ~ geschafft** (*fig*) she finally got to the top *or* made it (to the top); **nach ~ zu** *or* **hin** towards the top; **von ~ (her)** down; (*im Hause*) down(stairs); **ich komme gerade von ~** (*am Berg*) I've just come from the top; (*im Hause*) I've just been upstairs; **von ~ (aus) hat man eine schöne Aussicht** there's a nice view from the top; **von ~ bis unten** from top to bottom; (*von Mensch*) from top to toe; **jdn von ~ bis unten mustern** to look sb up and down; **jdn von ~ herab behandeln** to be condescending to sb, to treat sb condescendingly; **jdn von ~ herab ansehen** to look down on sb; **weiter ~** further up; **das Gehöft liegt weiter ~ (am Berg/im Tal)** the farm is further *or* higher up (the mountain/valley).
(b) (*inf: die Vorgesetzten*) **die da ~** the powers that be (*inf*), the top brass (*inf*); **das wird ~ entschieden** that's decided higher up; **er will sich nur ~ beliebt machen** he's just sucking up to the management (*inf*); **etw nach ~ (weiter)melden/weitergeben** to report sth/to pass sth on to a superior; **der Befehl kommt von ~** it's orders from above.
(c) (*vorher*) above ◆ **siehe ~** see above; **wie ~ erwähnt** as mentioned above; **der ~ schon erwähnte Herr** the above-mentioned *or* aforementioned gentleman; **der weiter ~ erwähnte Fall** the case referred to before *or* above.

oben-: ~an *adv* at the top *or* on (the) top; **sein Name steht ~an (auf der Liste)** his name is (at the) top (of the list); **an der Tafel saß er ~an** he sat at the top of the table; **er will immer ~an sein** (*fig*) he always wants to be on top; **~auf** *adv* on (the) top; (*an der Oberfläche*) on the top *or* surface; **gestern war er krank, aber heute ist er wieder ~auf** (*inf*) he wasn't well yesterday, but he's back on form today; **sie ist immer ~auf** (*inf*) she is always bright and cheery (*inf*); **~drauf** *adv* (*inf*) on top; **~drein** *adv* (*inf*) on top of everything (*inf*); ⚠**~erwähnt** *adj attr* above-mentioned; **~hin** *adv* superficially; **etw nur so ~hin sagen** to say sth lightly *or* casually *or* in an offhand way; **~-ohne** *adj attr* topless; **O~-ohne-Bedienung** *f* topless waitress service.

Ober *m* **-s, -** **(a)** (*Kellner*) waiter ◆ **Herr ~!** waiter! **(b)** (*Cards*) ≃ Queen.

Ober- *in cpds* (*Geog*) Upper; (*im Rang*) senior, chief; (*fig*) first class; **~arm** *m* upper arm; **~arzt** *m* senior physician; **~aufseher** *m* (head) supervisor, superintendent; (*im Gefängnis*) head warden *or* guard; **~aufsicht** *f* supervision, superintendence; **die ~aufsicht haben** to be in *or* have overall control (*über +acc* of); **~bau** *m* **(a)** (*von Brücke*) superstructure; **(b)** (*Rail*) permanent way; **~befehl** *m* (*Mil*) supreme command; **den ~befehl haben** to be commander-in-chief *or* supreme commander, to be in supreme command (*über +acc* of); **~befehlshaber** *m* (*Mil*) commander-in-chief, supreme commander; **~begriff** *m* generic term; **~bekleidung** *f* outer clothing, top clothes; **~bett** *nt* quilt; **~bürgermeister** *m* mayor; (*von englischer Großstadt*) Lord Mayor; (*Scot*) provost; **~deck** *nt* upper *or* top deck; **o~deutsch** *adj* (*Ling*) Upper German.

obere(r, s) *adj attr Ende, Stockwerke, (Schul)klassen* upper, top; *Flußlauf* upper ◆ **die O~n** (*inf*) the top brass (*inf*), the bosses; (*Eccl*) the superiors; **die ~en Zehntausend** (*inf*) high society; *siehe* **oberste(r, s).**

Ober-: o~faul *adj* (*inf*) very peculiar *or* odd *or* funny (*inf*); **~feld** *m* (*sl*) sarge (*sl*); **~feldwebel** *m* **(a)** (*Heer*) staff sergeant (*Brit*), first sergeant (*US*); **(b)** (*Luftwaffe*) flight sergeant (*Brit*), master sergeant (*US*).

Oberfläche *f* surface; (*Tech, Math*) surface area ◆ **an die ~ kommen** (*lit*) to come to the surface, to surface; (*fig*) to emerge; **an der ~ schwimmen** to float; **an der ~ bleiben** (*lit*) to remain on the surface; **die Unterhaltung plätscherte an der ~ dahin** the conversation never got beyond small talk.

oberflächlich *adj* **(a)** (*an der Oberfläche*) superficial ◆ **~e Verletzung** surface wound; **er ist nur ~ verletzt** he's only got superficial injuries.
(b) (*flüchtig*) superficial; *Kenntnisse auch* shallow ◆ **bei ~er Betrachtung** at a quick glance; **seine Kenntnisse sind nur ~** his knowledge doesn't go very deep *or* far *or* doesn't go beyond the surface; **~ arbeiten** to work superficially; **eine Arbeit ~ machen** to do a job superficially, to skip through a piece of work; **etw ~ lesen** to skim through sth; **er ist sehr ~ in seiner Arbeit** his work is very superficial; **jdn (nur) ~ kennen** to know sb (only) slightly, to have a nodding acquaintance with sb; **etw (nur) ~ kennen** to have (only) a shallow *or* superficial knowledge of sth; **nach ~er Schätzung** at a

rough estimate *or* guess.
(c) *(seicht) Mensch, Unterhaltung* superficial, shallow.

Oberflächlichkeit *f* superficiality.

Ober-: ~förster *m* head forester; **~franken** *nt* **-s** Upper Franconia; **o~gärig** *adj Bier* top fermented; **~gefreite(r)** *m* **(a)** *(Heer)* lance-corporal *(Brit)*, private first class *(US)*; **(b)** *(Luftwaffe)* senior aircraftsman *(Brit)*, airman first class *(US)*; **(c)** *(Marine)* seaman first class *(Brit)*, seaman *(US)*; ⚠**~geschoß** *nt* upper *or* top floor; **im zweiten ~geschoß** on the second *(Brit) or (US)* third floor; **~grenze** *f* upper limit; **o~halb** [1] *prep +gen* above;
[2] *adv* above; **o~halb von Basel** above Basel; **weiter o~halb** further *or* higher up; **~hand** *f (fig)* upper hand; **die ~hand gewinnen** *or* **bekommen** to get *or* gain the upper hand *(über +acc* over); to get the better (of sb/sth); **die ~hand haben** to have the upper hand; **~haupt** *nt (Repräsentant)* head; *(Anführer)* leader; **~haus** *nt (Pol)* upper house; *(in GB)* House of Lords; **~hemd** *nt* shirt; **~herr** *m (old)* sovereign; **~herrschaft** *f* sovereignty, supremacy *(über +acc* over); **unter der ~herrschaft Englands** under English rule; **~hirte** *m* spiritual head *or* leader; **~hoheit** *f* supremacy, sovereignty, overlordship; **die ~hoheit über jdn gewinnen** to gain *or* win supremacy over sb.

Oberin *f* **(a)** *(im Krankenhaus)* matron. **(b)** *(Eccl)* Mother Superior.

Ober-: ~ingenieur *m* chief engineer; **~inspektor** *m* senior inspector; **o~irdisch** *adj* above ground; **~kellner** *m* head waiter; **~kiefer** *m* upper jaw; **~kirchenrat** *m* **(a)** church assembly; **(b)** member of the church assembly; **~klasse** *f* **(a)** *(Sch)* **~klassen** *pl* top classes *or* forms; **(b)** *(Sociol)* upper class; **~kleid** *nt (liter)* outer garment(s); **~kleidung** *f* outer clothing; **~kommandierende(r)** *m decl as adj* Commander-in-Chief, Supreme Commander; **~kommando** *nt (~befehl)* Supreme Command; *(Befehlsstab)* headquarters *pl*; **~körper** *m* trunk, upper part of the body; **mit bloßem** *or* **freiem** *or* **nacktem ~körper** stripped to the waist; **den ~körper frei machen** to strip to the waist; **~land** *nt (Geog)* uplands; **das Berner ~land** the Bernese Oberland; **~landesgericht** *nt provincial high court and court of appeal*; **~länge** *f* upstroke; *(Typ)* ascender; **o~lastig** *adj (Naut)* top-heavy; **~lauf** *m* upper reaches *pl*; **am ~lauf des Rheins** in the upper reaches of the Rhine; **~leder** *nt* (leather) uppers *pl*; **~lehrer** *m (old)* senior primary school teacher; **~leitung** *f* **(a)** *(Führung)* direction; **die ~leitung eines Projekts haben** to be in overall charge of a project; **(b)** *(Elec)* overhead cable; **~leutnant** *m* **(a)** *(Heer)* lieutenant *(Brit)*, first lieutenant *(US)*; **(b)** *(Luftwaffe)* flying officer *(Brit)*, first lieutenant *(US)*; **(c)** *(Marine)* **~leutnant zur See** lieutenant; **~licht** *nt (hochgelegenes Fenster)* small, high window; *(Lüftungsklappe, über einer Tür)* fanlight, transom (window); **~lid** *nt* upper lid; **~liga** *f (Sport)* top *or* first league; **~lippe** *f* upper lip; **~maat** *m (Naut)* ≃ leading seaman; **~material** *nt (von Schuh)* upper; **~meister** *m* **(a)** *head of craft guild*; **(b)** *(bei Polizei)* ≃ sergeant.

Oberösterreich *nt* Upper Austria.

Ober-: ~postdirektion *f (Behörde)* regional post office (administration); *(Bezirk)* postal area *or* district; **~postdirektion Köln** Cologne postal district; **~priester** *m* high priest; **~prima** *f top form of German grammar school*; ≃ upper sixth *(Brit)*, ≃ senior grade *(US)*; **~primaner** *m* ≃ sixth former *(Brit)*, ≃ senior *(US)*; **o~rheinisch** *adj* upper Rhine; **die ~rheinische Tiefebene** the upper Rhine valley; **im O~rheinischen** along *or* around the upper Rhine; **~richter** *m (Sw)* ≃ high court judge.

Obers *nt* **-,** *no pl (Aus)* cream.

Ober-: ~schenkel *m* thigh; **~schenkelbruch** *m* broken thighbone *or* femur, fracture of the thighbone *or* femur; **~schenkelhals** *m* head of the thighbone *or* femur; **~schenkelknochen** *m* thighbone, femur; **~schicht** *f* top layer; *(Sociol)* upper strata (of society) *pl*; **o~schlächtig** *adj Mühle* overshot; **~schule** *f (old: Gymnasium)* grammar school *(Brit)*, high school *(US)*; *(DDR: weiterführende Schule)* secondary school; **~schüler** *m (old: Gymnasiast)* grammar school pupil *(Brit)*, high school student *(US)*; *(DDR: an weiterführenden Schulen)* secondary school pupil; **~schulrat** *m* school inspector, HMI *(Brit inf)*; **~schurke** *m (inf)* chief villain, baddy *(inf)*; **~schwester** *f* senior nursing officer; **~seite** *f* top (side); **~sekunda** *f seventh year of German secondary school*; **~sekundaner** *m pupil in seventh year of German secondary school*.

Oberst *m* **-en, -e(n) (a)** *(Heer)* colonel. **(b)** *(Luftwaffe)* group captain *(Brit)*, colonel *(US)*.

Ober-: ~staatsanwalt *m* public prosecutor, procurator fiscal *(Scot)*, district attorney *(US)*; **~stadt** *f* upper town, upper part of a town; **~stadtdirektor** *m* town clerk; **~steiger** *m* head foreman (in a mine).

oberste(r, s) *adj* **(a)** *(ganz oben) Stockwerk, Schicht* topmost, uppermost, very top ♦ **das O~e zuunterst kehren** to turn everything *or* things upside down.
(b) *Gebot, Gesetz, Prinzip* supreme; *Dienstgrad* highest, most senior, top ♦ **die ~n Kreise der Gesellschaft** the upper circles *or* echelons of society; **O~es Gericht, O~er Gerichtshof** supreme court; *(in GB)* High Court (of Justice); *(in USA)* Supreme Court.

Oberstimme *f* soprano; *(Knaben~)* treble; *(Diskant)* descant.

Oberstleutnant *m* **(a)** *(Heer)* lieutenant colonel. **(b)** *(Luftwaffe)* wing commander *(Brit)*, lieutenant colonel *(US)*.

Ober-: ~stübchen *nt (inf)*: **er ist nicht ganz richtig im ~stübchen** he's not quite right up top *(inf)*; **~studiendirektor** *m* headmaster *(Brit)*, principal *(US)*; **~studienrat** *m* senior teacher; **~stufe** *f* upper school; *(Univ)* advanced level; **~teil** *nt or m* upper part, top; **~tertia** *f fifth year of German secondary school*; **~tertianer** *m pupil in fifth year of German secondary school*; **~töne** *pl (Mus, fig)* overtone(s); **~trottel** *m (inf)* prize *or* first-class idiot; **~volta** *nt* **-s** Upper Volta; **~wasser** *nt* **(a)** *(von Wehr)* backwater; **(b)** *(fig inf)* **sobald sein älterer Bruder dabei ist, hat er (wieder) ~wasser** as soon as his elder brother is there he opens up *or* out (again); **seitdem wir unser Geschäft renoviert haben, bekommen wir ~wasser** since we did up the shop we've been going great guns *(inf)*; **~weite** *f* bust measurement; **sie hat ~weite 94** she has a 38-inch bust; **die hat eine ganz schöne ~weite!** she's very well endowed.

obgleich *conj* although, (even) though.

Obhut *f* **-,** *no pl (geh) (Aufsicht)* care; *(Verwahrung)* keeping, care ♦ **jdn/etw jds ~** *(dat)* **anvertrauen** to place *or* put sb/sth in sb's care; **jdn in ~ nehmen** to take care of sb, to look after sb; **jdn bei jdm in ~ geben** to put *or* place sb in sb's care.

obige(r, s) *adj attr* above ♦ **vergleiche ~ Abbildung** compare the illustration above *or* the above illustration; **der O~** *(form)* the above *(form)*.

Objekt *nt* **-(e)s, -e** *(auch Gram)* object; *(Comm: Grundstück etc)* property; *(Phot)* subject ♦ **das ~ der Untersuchung** the object under examination.

objektiv *adj* objective ♦ **~ über etw** *(acc)* **urteilen** to make an objective judgement about sth, to judge sth objectively; **etw ~ betrachten** to view sth objectively.

Objektiv *nt* (object) lens, objective.

objektivieren* [ɔpjɛkti'viːrən] [1] *vi* to objectify.
[2] *vt Problem* to treat objectively, to objectivize.

Objektivität *f* objectivity ♦ **sich um größte ~ bemühen** to try to be as objective as possible.

Objekt-: ~satz *m (Gram)* object clause; **~schutz** *m* protection of property; **~träger** *m* slide.

Oblate *f* **-, -n** wafer; *(Eccl)* host.

obliegen *sep or (esp S Ger, Aus)** *insep irreg aux haben or sein (+dat)* [1] *vi (old) einer Aufgabe, seinen Studien* to apply oneself to *(form)*.
[2] *vi impers (form)* **es obliegt ihm** it's incumbent upon him *(form)*; **ihm oblag die Betreuung der Flüchtlinge** he was responsible for looking after the refugees.

Obliegenheit *f (form)* duty, obligation, incumbency *(form)*.

obligat *adj* obligatory ♦ **der ~e Dudelsackpfeifer** the obligatory bagpiper; **mit ~em Cembalo** *(Mus)* with (a) cembalo obligato.

Obligation *f (auch Fin)* obligation ♦ **die Firma übernimmt keine ~** the firm is under *or* accepts no obligation.

obligatorisch *adj* obligatory; *Fächer, Vorlesung* compulsory; *Qualifikationen* necessary, requisite.

Obligo *nt* **-s, -s** *(Fin)* guarantee ♦ **ohne ~** without recourse.

Obmann *m, pl* **-männer** *or* **-leute, Obmännin** *f* representative.

Oboe [o'boːə] *f* **-, -n** oboe.

Oboist(in *f*) [obo'ɪst(ɪn)] *m* oboist, oboe player.

Obolus *m* **-, -se** contribution.

Obrigkeit *f* **(a)** *(als Begriff)* authority. **(b)** *(Behörden)* **die ~** the authorities *pl*; **die geistliche/weltliche ~** the spiritual/secular authorities.

obrigkeitlich *adj* authoritarian.

Obrigkeitsstaat *m* authoritarian state.

Obrist *m* colonel.

obschon *conj (liter)* although, albeit *(nur in verbloser Konstruktion)*.

Observanz [ɔpzɛr'vants] *f* observance ♦ **ein Orden (von) der strengen ~** a strict *or* closed order.

Observatorium [ɔpzɛrva'toːriʊm] *nt* observatory.

observieren* [ɔpzɛr'viːrən] *vt (form)* to observe ♦ **er ist schon einige Monate observiert worden** he has been under surveillance for several months.

obsiegen *vi sep or insep* *(obs, Jur)* to prevail *(dat* over).

obskur *adj* **(a)** *(unbekannt)* obscure. **(b)** *(verdächtig) Gestalten, Kneipe, Gassen* suspect, dubious ♦ **diese ~en Gestalten der Unterwelt** these twilight figures of the underworld.

Obskurantismus *m* obscurantism.

obsolet *adj (liter)* obsolete.

Obst *nt* **-(e)s,** *no pl* fruit; *siehe* **danken**.

Obst-: ~bau *m* fruit-growing; **~baum** *m* fruit-tree; **~garten** *m* orchard.

obstinat *adj (geh)* obstinate.

Obst-: ~jahr *nt* **ein gutes ~jahr** a good year for fruit; **~kuchen** *m* fruit flan/tart.

Obstler *m* **-s, -** *(dial)* fruit schnapps.

Obstmesser *nt* fruit-knife.

Obstruktion *f* **(a)** *(Med)* obstruction, blockage.
(b) *(Pol)* obstruction, filibuster ♦ **das Regierungsprogramm scheiterte an der ~ der Opposition** the Government's programme failed because of the Opposition's obstructive *or* filibustering tactics *or* obstructionism; **~ betreiben** to obstruct, to block, to filibuster.

Obst-: ~saft *m* fruit juice; **~tag** *m* **legen Sie jede Woche einen ~tag ein** eat only fruit one day a week; **meine Frau hat heute ihren ~tag** my wife's on her fruit diet today; **~torte** *f* fruit flan/tart; **~wasser** *nt* fruit schnapps; **~wein** *m* fruit wine.

obszön *adj* obscene.

Obszönität *f* obscenity.

Obus *m* **-ses, -se** *(inf)* trolley *(inf)*, trolley bus.

obwalten* *vi sep or insep (form: herrschen)* to prevail.

obwohl *conj* although, (even) though.

obzwar *conj (rare) siehe* **obwohl**.

Ochs(e) ['ɔks(ə)] *m* **-n, -n (a)** ox, bullock ♦ **~ am Spieß** roast ox; **er stand da wie der ~ vorm Scheunentor** *or* **am Berg** *(inf)* he stood there like a cow at a

⚠: for details of spelling reform, see supplement

five-barred gate (*inf*). **(b)** (*inf: Dummkopf*) twit (*Brit inf*), ass (*inf*), dope (*inf*).

ochsen ['ɔksn] (*Sch sl*) [1] *vt* to swot up (*inf*), to mug up (*inf*).
[2] *vi* to swot (up) (*inf*), to mug (up) (*inf*), to cram (*inf*).

Ochsen- ['ɔksn-]: **~frosch** *m* bullfrog; **~gespann** *nt* yoke of oxen; **~schwanzsuppe** *f* oxtail soup; **~tour** *f* (*inf*) **(a)** (*Schinderei*) slog (*inf*), sweat (*inf*); **(b) er brauchte sich nicht über die ~tour heraufzudienen** he did not have to work his way up the hard way; **~ziemer** *m* bull's pizzle, bullwhip.

ochsig ['ɔksɪç] *adv* (*S Ger inf*) really hard ◆ **~ viel** an awful lot.

Öchsle ['œksla] *nt* **-s, -** *measure of alcohol content of drink according to its specific gravity.*

Ocker *m or nt* **-s, -** ochre.

ockerbraun, ockergelb *adj* ochre.

OCR-Schrift [o:tse:'|ɛr-] OCR font.

od. *abbr of* **oder.**

Ode *f* **-, -n** ode.

öd(e) *adj* **(a)** (*verlassen*) *Stadt, Strand* deserted, empty, abandoned; (*unbewohnt*) desolate, empty, bleak; (*unbebaut*) waste, barren ◆ **öd und leer** dreary and desolate. **(b)** (*fig: fade*) dull, dreary, tedious; *Dasein, Stunden auch* barren.

Öde *f* **-, -n** (*liter*) **(a)** (*einsame Gegend*) desert, wasteland. **(b)** (*Langeweile*) barrenness, dreariness, monotony.

Odem *m* **-s,** *no pl* (*poet, Bibl*) breath.

Ödem *nt* **-s, -e** oedema, edema.

oder *conj* **(a)** or ◆ **~ aber** or else; **~ auch** or even *or* maybe *or* perhaps; **eins ~ das andere** one or the other, it's either or; **entweder ... ~** either ... or.
(b) (*in Fragen*) **so war's doch, ~ (etwa) nicht?** that was what happened, wasn't it?, wasn't that how it happened?, it happened like that, didn't it?; **du kommst doch, ~?** you're coming, aren't you?; **der Mörder hat sein Opfer nie vorher gesehen, ~ doch?** the murderer had never seen his victim before, or had he?; **~ soll ich lieber mitkommen?** maybe I should come along?; **lassen wir es so, ~?** let's leave it at that, right *or* OK?

Oder *f* **-** Oder.

Oder-Neiße-(Friedens)grenze (*DDR*), **Oder-Neiße-Linie** *f* Oder-Neisse-Line.

ödipal *adj* oedipal.

Ödipuskomplex *m* Oedipus complex.

Odium *nt* **-s,** *no pl* (*liter*) odium.

Ödland *nt* wasteland.

Odyssee *f* **-, -n** [-e:ən] (*Liter*) Odyssey; (*fig*) odyssey.

OECD-Land [o:|e:tse:'de:-] *nt* OECD member country.

Oeuvre ['ø:vʀ, 'ø:vrə] *nt* **-, -s** (*Liter*) work, works *pl.*

OEZ *abbr of* **Osteuropäische Zeit.**

Öfchen *nt dim of* **Ofen.**

Ofen *m* **-s, ¨** **(a)** (*Heiz~*) heater; (*Elektro~, Gas~ auch*) fire; (*Öl~, Petroleum~ auch*) stove; (*Kohle~*) stove; (*Heizungs~*) boiler ◆ **hinter dem ~ hocken** to be a stay-at-home; **jetzt ist der ~ aus** (*sl*) that's it (*inf*), that does it (*inf*).
(b) (*Herd*) oven, stove; (*Kohle~*) stove, range; (*Back~*) oven.
(c) (*Tech*) furnace, oven; (*Brenn~*) kiln; (*Trocken~*) drying oven *or* kiln; (*Hoch~*) blast furnace; (*Schmelz~*) smelting furnace.

Ofen-: ~bank *f* fireside (bench), hearth; **auf der ~bank** by the hearth *or* fire *or* fireside; **~blech** *nt tray for catching falling coals*; **~ecke** *f* inglenook; **o~fertig** *adj Gericht* oven ready; **o~frisch** *adj Brot* oven fresh; **~heizung** *f* stove heating; **Zimmer mit ~heizung** room with stove (heater); **~klappe** *f* **(a)** *siehe* **~tür; (b)** (*Lüftungsklappe*) damper; **~loch** *nt* stove door; **~rohr** *nt* stovepipe; (*old inf: Zylinder*) stovepipe (hat); **~röhre** *f* (slow) oven; **~schirm** *m* firescreen; **~setzer** *m* stove fitter; **~tür** *f* stove door.

Off *nt* **-** (*TV, Theat*) offstage ◆ **aus dem ~** offstage; **eine Stimme aus dem ~** a voice off; **aus dem ~ kommen** to come onstage, to come from offstage.

offen *adj* **(a)** open; *Bein* ulcerated; *Flamme, Licht* naked; *Feuer* open; *Haare* loose ◆ **ein ~er Brief** an open letter; **er geht mit ~em Hemd** he wears an open neck; **die Haare ~ tragen** to wear one's hair loose; **der Laden hat bis 7 Uhr ~** the shop is *or* stays open until 7 o'clock; **das Turnier ist für alle ~** the tournament is open to everybody; **die Teilnahme ist für alle ~** anyone can take part; **~er Wein** wine by the carafe/glass; **Wein ~ verkaufen** to sell wine on draught; **auf ~er Strecke** (*Straße*) on the open road; (*Rail*) between stations; **wir hielten auf ~er Strecke** we stopped in the middle of nowhere; **auf ~er Straße** in the middle of the street; (*Landstraße*) on the open road; **auf ~er See** on the open sea; **Beifall auf ~er Szene** spontaneous applause, an outburst of applause; **bei ~er Szene** *or* **Bühne verwandelt sich das Bild** the scene changed without a curtain; **~e Flanke** (*Mil*) open *or* exposed flank; **~e Stadt** (*Mil*) open *or* undefended town; **endlich lag das Ziel ~ vor ihnen (da)** at last their goal lay before them; **mit ~em Munde dastehen** (*fig*) to stand gaping; **mit ~em Munde atmen** to breathe with one's mouth open; **~e Türen einrennen** (*fig*) to kick at an open door; **Tag der ~en Tür** open day; **ein ~es Haus haben** *or* **führen** to keep open house; **überall ~e Türen finden** (*fig*) to find a warm welcome everywhere; **Haus der ~en Tür** open house; **Politik der ~en Tür** open-door policy; **jdn mit ~en Armen empfangen** to greet *or* welcome sb with open arms; **mit ~en Augen** *or* **Sinnen durchs Leben gehen** to go through life with one's eyes open; **eine ~e Hand haben** (*fig*) to be open-handed; **allem Neuen gegenüber ~ sein** to be open *or* receptive to (all) new ideas; **~e Handelsgesellschaft** general partnership; *siehe* **Buch, Karte.**
(b) (*frei*) *Stelle* vacant ◆ **~e Stellen** vacancies; (*Press auch*) "situations vacant".
(c) (*unerledigt, unentschieden*) *Frage, Ausgang, Partie* open; *Rechnung* outstanding.
(d) (*aufrichtig, freimütig*) *Mensch, Bekenntnis, Aussprache* open ◆ **er hat einen ~en Blick** he's got an open *or* honest face; **er hat keinen ~en Blick** he's got a shifty look in his eyes; **~ gestanden** *or* **gesagt** to tell you the truth, quite honestly, to be frank; **etw ~ eingestehen** *or* **zugeben** to confess *or* admit (to) sth openly *or* frankly; **seine Meinung ~ sagen** to speak one's mind, to say what one thinks; **~ mit jdm reden** to speak openly to sb, to be frank with sb; **ein ~es Wort mit jdm reden** to have a frank talk with sb.

offenbar [1] *adj* obvious ◆ **sein Zögern machte ~, daß ...** it showed *or* was obvious from the way he hesitated that ...; **~ werden** to become obvious *or* clear, to emerge.
[2] *adv* (*vermutlich*) apparently ◆ **er hat ~ den Zug verpaßt** he must have missed the train; **da haben Sie sich ~ geirrt** you seem to have made a mistake.

offenbaren* *insep ptp auch* (*old*) **geoffenbart** [1] *vt* to reveal.
[2] *vr* **(a)** (*erweisen*) to show *or* reveal itself/oneself ◆ **sich als etw ~** to show oneself to be sth. **(b)** (*kundtun*) **sich jdm ~** to reveal oneself to sb; (*Liebe erklären*) to reveal one's feelings to sb.

Offenbarung *f* revelation.

Offenbarungs|eid *m* (*Jur*) oath of disclosure *or* manifestation ◆ **den ~ leisten** (*lit*) to swear an oath of disclosure *or* manifestation; **mit diesem Programm hat die Partei ihren ~ geleistet** with this programme the party has revealed its political bankruptcy.

⚠ **offen-: ~bleiben** *vi sep irreg aux sein* to remain open; **alle ~gebliebenen Probleme** all unsolved *or* remaining problems; **~halten** *vt sep irreg* to keep open; **die Ohren ~halten** to keep one's ear to the ground *or* open; **jdm eine Stelle** *or* **eine Stelle für jdn ~halten** to keep a job open for sb.

Offenheit *f* openness, frankness, candour ◆ **schonungslose ~** brutal frankness.

offen-: ~herzig *adj* **(a)** open, frank, candid; *Mensch auch* open-hearted, outspoken; **(b)** (*hum inf*) *Kleid* revealing; **sie ist ja heute wieder sehr ~herzig** she's being very revealing again today (*hum inf*); **O~herzigkeit** *f* openness, frankness, candour; **~kundig** *adj* obvious, clear; *Beweise* clear; *Lüge, Interesse* obvious, manifest; **es ist ~kundig, daß ~ ...** it is obvious *or* clear *or* evident that ...; ⚠**~lassen** *vt sep irreg* to leave open; **O~marktpolitik** *f* (*Fin*) free market policy; **~sichtlich** *adj* obvious; *Irrtum, Lüge auch* blatant; *Unterschied auch* clear; **es war ~sichtlich, daß er uns mied** it was plain *or* evident *or* obvious he was avoiding us, he was obviously avoiding us; **er hat sich da ganz ~sichtlich vertan** he's obviously *or* clearly *or* evidently made a mistake there.

offensiv *adj* offensive.

Offensive *f* offensive ◆ **in die ~ gehen** to take the offensive.

Offensiv-: ~krieg *m* offensive war; **~rakete** *f* offensive missile; **~waffe** *f* offensive weapon.

⚠ **offenstehen** *vi sep irreg* (*S Ger auch: aux sein*) **(a)** (*Tür, Fenster*) to be open; (*Knopf*) to be undone.
(b) (*Comm: Rechnung, Betrag*) to be *or* remain unpaid *or* unsettled, to be outstanding.
(c) jdm ~ (*fig: zugänglich sein*) to be open to sb; **die (ganze) Welt steht ihm offen** he has the (whole) world at his feet, the world's his oyster; **es steht ihr offen, sich uns anzuschließen** she's free to join us; **die Teilnahme an der Veranstaltung steht auch Nichtmitgliedern offen** the function is also open to non-members.

öffentlich *adj* **(a)** (*allgemein zugänglich, sichtbar*) *attr* public; *pred* open to the public, public; *adv* in public, publicly ◆ **etw ~ bekanntmachen** to make sth public, to publicize sth; **~ versteigern** to sell by public auction, to auction publicly; **eine Persönlichkeit des ~en Lebens** a person in public life *or* in the public eye; **im ~en Leben stehen** to be in public life; **jdn ~ anschuldigen/hinrichten** to accuse/execute sb publicly; **ein ~es Haus** (*euph*) a house of ill repute (*euph*).
(b) *attr* (*die Allgemeinheit betreffend*) *Wohl, Interesse* public ◆ **die ~e Meinung/Moral** public opinion/morality; **die ~e Ordnung** law and order; **~es Recht** (*Jur*) public law; **Anstalt des ~en Rechts** public institution.
(c) (*staatlich*) public ◆ **~e Schule** state school, public school (*US*); **die ~e Hand** (central/local) government; **Ausgaben der ~en Hand** public spending; **etw in die ~e Hand überführen** to take sth into public ownership, to take sth under public control.

Öffentlichkeit *f* **(a) der Verteidiger bestand auf der ~ der Verhandlung** the defence counsel insisted that the trial take place in public; **~ der Rechtsprechung** administration of justice in open court; **~ der Prüfungen war eine Hauptforderung der Studenten** one of the students' main demands was that exams should be open to the public; **die ~ einer Versammlung herstellen** to make a meeting public.
(b) (*Allgemeinheit*) the (general) public ◆ **die ~ scheuen** to shun publicity; **in** *or* **vor aller ~** in public; **unter Ausschluß der ~** in secret *or* private; (*Jur*) in camera; **als er das erstemal vor die ~ trat** when he made his first public appearance; **mit etw an** *or* **vor die ~ treten, etw vor die ~ bringen** to bring sth to the public eye *or* before the public; **etw der ~ übergeben** (*form*) (*eröffnen*) to declare sth officially open; (*veröffentlichen*) to publish sth.

Öffentlichkeits-: ~arbeit *f* public relations work; **ö~scheu** *adj* publicity-shy; **ö~wirksam** *adj* **ö~wirksam sein** to be effective (as) publicity, to be good publicity.

öffentlich-rechtlich *adj attr* (under) public law.

offerieren* *vt* (*Comm, form*) to offer.

Offerte *f* **-, -n** (*Comm*) offer.

Offizialdelikt *nt* (*Jur*) *offence for which proceedings are brought directly by the* *public prosecutor's department.*

offiziell *adj Meinung, Erklärung, Besuch* official; *Einladung, Besuch auch* formal ♦ **etw ~ bekanntgeben** to announce sth officially; **wie von ~er Seite verlautet** according to official sources; **auf dem Empfang ging es schrecklich ~ zu** the reception was terribly formal.

Offizier *m* **-s, -e** officer ♦ **~ werden** to become an officer, to get *or* be given *or* gain a commission; (*als Beruf*) to become *or* be an army officer; **erster/zweiter ~** first/second officer.

Offiziers-: ~anwärter *m* officer cadet; **~kasino** *nt* officers' mess; **~korps** *nt* officer corps, the officers *pl*; **~messe** *f* officers' mess; **~patent** *nt* (*old*) commission.

offiziös *adj* semiofficial.

Off-Kino *nt* arts *or* repertory (*US*) cinema.

Off-line-Betrieb [ɔf'lain-] *m* (*Comput*) off-line mode.

öffnen [1] *vt* to open ♦ **jdm den Blick für etw ~** to open sb's eyes to sth, to make sb aware *or* conscious of sth; **eine Leiche ~** to open (up) a corpse; **das Museum wird um 10 geöffnet** the museum is open *or* opens at 10; **„hier ~"** "open this end *or* here"; **eine Datei ~** (*Comput*) to open a file.
[2] *vi* to open ♦ **es hat geklingelt, könnten Sie mal ~?** that was the doorbell, would you answer it *or* would you get it?; **der Nachtportier öffnete mir** the night porter opened the door for me.
[3] *vr* (*Tür, Blume, Augen*) to open; (*weiter werden*) to open out ♦ **die Erde öffnete sich** the ground opened (up); **nach Norden hin öffnete sich die Schlucht** the gully widens *or* opens out further north; **das Tal öffnet sich nach Süden** the valley opens *or* is open to the south; **die Landschaft öffnet sich** the landscape opens out.

Öffner *m* **-s, -** opener.

Öffnung *f* **(a)** *no pl* (*das Öffnen*) opening ♦ **~ der Leiche** post-mortem, autopsy; **eine Politik der ~** a policy of openness. **(b)** (*offene Stelle*) opening.

Öffnungs-: ~kurs *m* (*Pol*) process of opening up; **~politik** *f* policy of openness; **~zeiten** *pl* hours of business *pl*.

Offsetdruck ['ɔfsɛt-] *m* offset (printing).

oft *adv, comp* **¨er**, (*rare*) *superl* **am ¨esten** (*häufig*) often, frequently; (*in kurzen Abständen*) frequently ♦ **der Bus fährt nicht ~, die Bahn verkehrt ¨er** the bus doesn't go very often, the train goes more often; **schon so ~, ~ genug** often enough; **wie ~ fährt der Bus?** how often *or* frequently does the bus go?; **wie ~ warst du schon in Deutschland?** how often *or* how many times have you been to Germany?; **wie ~ wir das schon gehört haben!** how often we've heard that!, how many times have we heard that before!; **des ¨eren** quite often *or* frequently; **je ¨er ...** the more often ...

öfter(s) *adv* on occasion, (every) once in a while; (*wiederholt*) from time to time, (every) now and then ♦ **~ mal was Neues** (*inf*) variety is the spice of life (*prov*).

oftmals *adv* (*geh*) often, oft (*poet*), oftimes (*poet*).

oh *interj siehe* **o**.

Oheim, Ohm *m* **-s, -e** (*old*) uncle.

OHG *abbr of* **Offene Handelsgesellschaft**.

Ohm *nt* **-(s), -** ohm ♦ **~sches Gesetz** Ohm's Law.

ohne [1] *prep +acc* **(a)** without ♦ **~ (die) Vororte hat die Stadt 100.000 Einwohner** the city has 100,000 inhabitants excluding *or* not including *or* not counting the suburbs; **~ mich!** count me out!; **er ist nicht ~** (*inf*) he's not bad (*inf*), he's got what it takes (*inf*); **die Sache ist (gar) nicht (so) ~** (*inf*) (*interessant*) it's not bad; (*schwierig*) it's not that easy (*inf*); **~ ihn wären wir immer noch dort** without him *or* but for him *or* if it weren't for him we'd still be there; **~ etw sein** to be without *or* minus (*inf*) sth; **~ Auto** without a *or* one's car; **er ist ~ jede Begabung (für Musik)** he lacks *or* is without any (musical) talent; **~ einen** *or* **jeden Pfennig Geld** penniless, without a penny *or* dime (*US*), without two halfpennies to rub together; **ich rauche immer ~** (*inf*) I always smoke untipped cigarettes.
(b) ich hätte das ~ weiteres getan I'd have done it without a second thought *or* without thinking twice about it; **so etwas kann man ~ weiteres sagen** it's quite all right to say that; **so etwas kann man in feiner Gesellschaft nicht ~ weiteres sagen** you can't say that sort of thing in polite society; **ich würde ~ weiteres sagen, daß ...** I would not hesitate to say that ...; **er hat den Brief ~ weiteres unterschrieben** he signed the letter just like that *or* straight away; **das Darlehen ist ~ weiteres bewilligt worden** the loan was granted without any bother *or* problem *or* straight away; **ihm können Sie ~ weiteres vertrauen** you can trust him implicitly; **das läßt sich ~ weiteres arrangieren** that can easily be arranged; **hast du das Geld gekriegt? — ja, ~ weiteres** did you get the money? — yes, no bother (*inf*); **dem Kerl kann man nicht ~ weiteres glauben** you can't just believe anything *or* whatever that guy says; **das kann man nicht ~ weiteres voraussetzen** you can't just assume that automatically; **diesem Vorschlag kann ich nicht ~ weiteres zustimmen** I can't accept the suggestion without some qualification; **du kannst doch nicht so ~ weiteres aus der Schule weglaufen** you can't just run away from school like that.
[2] *conj* **~ zu zögern** without hesitating; **~ daß ich ihn darum gebeten hätte, kam er mich besuchen** he came to see me without my *or* me inviting him; **wer redet, ~ gefragt zu sein** ... anybody who talks without being asked ...

ohne-: ~dem (*old*), **~dies** *adv siehe* **~hin**; **≈einander** *adv* without one another, without each other; **~gleichen** *adj inv* unparalleled; **ein Erfolg ~gleichen** an unparalleled success; **diese Frechheit ist ~gleichen!** I've never known such a cheek *or* nerve!; **seine Frechheit ist ~gleichen** I've never known anybody have such a nerve; **er singt ~gleichen** as a singer he is without compare *or* he's in a class by himself; **~hin** *adv* anyway; **wir sind ~hin zu viel Leute** there are too many of us already *or* as it is; **es ist ~hin schon spät** it's already late, it's late enough already, it's late enough as it is; **das hat ~hin keinen Zweck** there is no point in (doing) that anyway.

Ohnmacht *f* **-, -en (a)** (*Med*) faint, swoon (*old*) ♦ **in ~ fallen** to faint, to swoon (*old*); **aus der ~ erwachen** to come round *or* to, to recover consciousness. **(b)** (*geh: Machtlosigkeit*) powerlessness, helplessness, impotence.

ohnmächtig *adj* **(a)** (*bewußtlos*) unconscious ♦ **~ werden** to faint, to pass out; **Hilfe, sie ist ~!** help, she's fainted!; **~ sank sie in seine Arme** she fainted *or* collapsed unconscious into his arms.
(b) (*geh: machtlos*) powerless, impotent, helpless ♦ **~e Wut, ~er Zorn** impotent *or* helpless rage; **einer Sache** (*dat*) **~ gegenüberstehen** to stand *or* be helpless in the face of sth; **~ zusehen** to look on helplessly.

Ohnmachts|anfall *m* (*lit, fig*) fainting fit ♦ **als ich das hörte, habe ich fast einen ~ bekommen** (*inf*) when I heard that I nearly fainted *or* nearly passed out.

oho *interj* oho, hello; *siehe* **klein**.

Ohr *nt* **-(e)s, -en** ear ♦ **seine ~en sind nicht mehr so gut** his hearing isn't too good any more; **auf einem ~(e) taub sein** to be deaf in one ear; **auf dem ~ bin ich taub** (*fig*) nothing doing (*inf*), I won't hear of it; **bei jdm ein aufmerksames/geneigtes/offenes ~ finden** to find sb a ready/willing/sympathetic listener; **jdm ein geneigtes ~ leihen** *or* **schenken** to lend sb one's ear *or* a willing ear; **lange ~en machen** (*inf*) to prick up one's ears; **ein musikalisches ~ haben** to have a musical ear *or* an ear for music; **ein scharfes** *or* **feines ~ haben** to have a good ear; **die ~en hängenlassen** (*inf*) to look down in the mouth (*inf*) *or* downhearted *or* down in the dumps (*inf*); **die ~en anlegen** to put its ears back; **mach** *or* **sperr die ~en auf!** (*inf*) wash *or* clean out your ears (*inf*); **mir klingen die ~en** my ears are burning; **jdm die ~en volljammern** (*inf*) to keep (going) on *or* moaning at sb; **die Wände haben ~en** walls have ears; **ganz ~ sein** (*hum*) to be all ears; **sich aufs ~ legen** *or* **hauen** (*inf*) to turn in (*inf*), to hit the hay (*inf*), to kip down (*inf*); **sich** (*dat*) **die Mütze schief aufs ~ setzen** to wear one's cap at a jaunty angle *or* tipped over one ear; **sitzt er auf seinen ~en?** (*inf*) is he deaf or something?; **jdn bei den ~en nehmen, jdm die ~en langziehen** (*inf*) to tweak sb's ear(s); **für deutsche/englische ~en klingt das komisch** that sounds odd to German/English ears; **diese Nachricht war nicht für fremde ~en bestimmt** this piece of news was not meant for other ears; **jdm eins hinter die ~en geben** (*inf*) to give sb a clip round the ear; **jdm etw um die ~en hauen** (*inf*) *or* **schlagen** (*inf*) to hit sb over the head with sth; **schreib es dir hinter die ~en** (*inf*) will you (finally) get that into your (thick) head (*inf*), has that sunk in? (*inf*); **noch naß** *or* **feucht** *or* **nicht trocken hinter den ~en sein** to be still wet behind the ears; **jdm etw ins ~ sagen** to whisper sth in sb's ear; **die Melodie geht (leicht) ins ~** the tune is very catchy; **du hast wohl Dreck/Watte in den ~en!** (*inf*) are you deaf or something?, is there something wrong with your ears?; **ich habe seine Worte noch deutlich im ~** I can still hear his words clearly, his words are still ringing in my ears; **jdm in den ~en liegen** to badger sb, to keep on at sb (*inf*); **mit halbem ~(e) hin-** *or* **zuhören** to half listen *or* listen with half an ear; **jdn übers ~ hauen** to take sb for a ride (*inf*), to pull a fast one on sb (*inf*); **bis über die** *or* **beide ~en verliebt sein** to be head over heels in love; **viel um die ~en haben** (*inf*) to have a lot on (one's plate) (*inf*), to be rushed off one's feet (*inf*); **es ist mir zu ~en gekommen** it has come to my ears (*form*); **zum einen ~ hinein und zum anderen wieder hinaus gehen** (*inf*) to go in one ear and out the other (*inf*); **dein Wort in Gottes ~** God willing.

Öhr *nt* **-(e)s, -e** eye.

Ohren-: ~arzt *m* ear specialist; *siehe* **Hals-Nasen-Ohren-**; **~beichte** *f* (auricular) confession; **o~betäubend** *adj* (*fig*) earsplitting, deafening; **~entzündung** *f* ear infection; **~klappe** *f* earflap; **~kriecher** *m siehe* **Ohrwurm**; **~sausen** *nt* (*Med*) buzzing in one's ears; **~schmalz** *nt* earwax; **~schmaus** *m* **das Konzert war ein richtiger ~schmaus** the concert was a real delight to hear *or* a feast *or* treat for the ears; **moderne Musik ist oft kein ~schmaus** modern music is often far from easy on the ears; **~schmerzen** *pl* earache; **~schützer** *pl* earmuffs *pl*; **~sessel** *m* wing chair; **~stöpsel** *m* ear plug; **~zeuge** *m* earwitness.

Ohrfeige *f* **-, -n** slap (on *or* round the face); (*als Strafe*) box on *or* clip round the ears ♦ **jdm eine ~ geben** *or* **verabreichen** to slap sb's face; **eine ~ bekommen** to get a slap round the face; **wenn du nicht gleich ruhig bist, bekommst du eine ~** if you don't shut up I'll box your ears.

ohrfeigen *vt insep* **jdn ~** to slap *or* hit sb, to box sb's ears; **ich könnte mich selbst ~, daß ich das gemacht habe** I could hit *or* kick myself for doing it.

Ohrfeigengesicht *nt* (*inf*) fish face (*inf*) ♦ **er hat so ein richtiges ~** he's got the sort of face you'd like to put your fist into.

Ohr-: ~gehänge *nt* (*form*) drop earrings; (*hum*) dangly earrings; **~hänger** *m* earring; **~läppchen** *nt* (ear)lobe; **~muschel** *f* (outer) ear, auricle (*form*).

Ohropax ® *nt* **-, -** ear plugs *pl*.

Ohr-: ~ring *m* earring; **~stecker** *m* stud earring; **~wurm** *m* earwig; **der Schlager ist ein richtiger ~wurm** (*inf*) that's a really catchy record (*inf*).

oje, ojemine, ojerum (*old*) *interj* oh dear.

Okapi *nt* **-s, -s** okapi.

okay [o'ke:] *interj* okay, OK.

Okay [o'ke:] *nt* **-s, -s** okay, OK.

okkult *adj* occult ♦ **das O~e** the occult.

Okkultismus *m* occultism.

Okkupant *m* occupier ♦ **die ~en** the occupying forces *or* powers.

Okkupation *f* occupation.

okkupieren* *vt* to occupy.

Öko- *in cpds* eco-, ecological; (*Umwelt betreffend auch*) environmental;

~**bauer** *m (inf)* ecologically-minded farmer; ~**kriminelle(r)** *mf* environmental vandal; ~**krise** *f* ecological crisis; ~**laden** *m* wholefood shop.
Ökologe *m*, **Ökologin** *f* ecologist.
Ökologie *f* ecology.
Ökologiebewegung *f* ecology movement.
ökologisch *adj* ecological, environmental.
Ökonom *m* **(a)** economist. **(b)** *(obs)* bailiff.
Ökonomie *f* **(a)** *(Wirtschaftlichkeit)* economy ◆ **durch kluge ~ hat er das Unternehmen wieder auf die Beine gestellt** by clever economies he put the concern back on its feet again.
(b) *(Wirtschaft)* economy.
(c) *(Wirtschaftswissenschaft)* economics *sing* ◆ **politische ~ studieren** to study political economy.
ökonomisch *adj* **(a)** economic. **(b)** *(sparsam)* economic(al).
Öko-: ~**papier** *nt* recycled paper; ~**-Partei** *f* ecology party; ~**pazifismus** *m* environmental pacifism; ~**-Politiker(in** *f*) *m* ecologist politician; ~**sphäre** *f* ecosphere; ~**system** *nt* ecosystem.
Oktaeder [ɔkta'|e:dɐ] *nt* **-s, -** octohedron.
Oktanzahl *f* octane number *or* rating ◆ **Benzin mit einer hohen ~** high octane petrol.
Oktav *nt* **-s, -e** octavo.
Oktavband *m* octavo volume.
Oktave [ɔk'ta:və] *f* **-, -n** octave.
Oktett *nt* **-s, -e** octet.
Oktober *m* **-s, -** October; *siehe* **März**.
Oktoberfest *nt Munich beer festival.*
Oktoberrevolution *f* October Revolution.
oktroyieren* [ɔktroa'ji:rən] *vt (geh)* to force, to impose *(jdm etw* sth on sb).
Okular *nt* **-s, -e** eyepiece, ocular.
okulieren* *vt Obstbäume, Rosen* to graft, to bud.
Okumene *f* **-,** *no pl* ecumenical movement.
ökumenisch *adj* ecumenical ◆ ~**es Konzil** Ecumenical Council.
Okzident *m* **-s,** *no pl (liter)* occident.
Öl *nt* **-(e)s, -e** oil ◆ **auf ~ stoßen** to strike oil; **~ fördern** to extract oil; **ätherische ~e** *(Chem)* essential oils; **in ~ malen** to paint in oils; **~ auf die Wogen gießen** *(prov)* to pour oil on troubled waters; **~ ins Feuer gießen** *(prov)* to add fuel to the fire *(prov)*.
Öl-: ~**abscheider** *m* oil separator; ~**baum** *m* olive tree; ~**berg** *m* **(a)** Mount of Olives; **(b)** *(Art) sculpture or painting showing Christ with 12 sleeping Apostles on the Mount of Olives*; ~**bild** *nt* oil painting, oil; ~**bohrung** *f* oil drilling, drilling for oil.
Oldie ['ouldi] *m* **-s, -s** *(inf: Schlager)* (golden) oldie *(inf)*.
Öl-: ~**druck** *m* **(a)** *(Bild)* oleograph; **(b)** *(Tech)* oil pressure; ~**druckbremse** *f* hydraulic brake.
Oldtimer ['ouldtaɪmə] *m* **-s, - (a)** *(Auto)* veteran car; *(Rail)* historic train; *(Aviat)* veteran plane, old bus *or* crate *(pej inf)*. **(b)** *(Sport)* veteran, old timer. **(c)** *(Pferd)* old *or* retired racehorse.
Ole|ander *m* **-s, -** oleander.
ölen *vt* to oil ◆ **wie geölt** *(inf)* like clockwork *(inf)*; **wie ein geölter Blitz** *(inf)* like (a streak of) greased lightning *(inf)*.
Öl-: ~**exportland** *nt* oil-exporting country; ~**farbe** *f* oil-based paint; *(Art)* oil (paint *or* colour); **mit ~farben malen** to paint in oils *or* oil colours; ~**feld** *nt* oil field; ~**film** *m* film of oil; ~**förderland** *nt* oil-producing country; ~**gemälde** *nt* oil painting; ~**gesellschaft** *f* oil company; ~**götze** *m (inf)* **wie ein ~götze** like a stuffed *or* tailor's dummy *(inf)*; ~**heizung** *f* oil-fired central heating.
ölig *adj* oily; *(fig auch)* greasy.
Oligarchie *f* oligarchy.
Öl|industrie *f* oil industry.
oliv *adj pred* olive(-green) ◆ **ein Kleid in O~** an olive-green dress.
Olive [o'li:və] *f* **-, -n** olive.
Oliven-: ~**baum** *m* olive tree; **o~farben, o~farbig** *adj attr* olive green; ~**hain** *m* olive grove; ~**öl** *nt* olive oil.
olivgrün *adj* olive-green.
Öl-: ~**kanal** *m* oil duct; ~**kanne** *f*, ~**kännchen** *nt* oil can; ~**konzern** *m* oil company; ~**krise** *f* oil crisis; ~**kuchen** *m* oil cake; ~**kühlung** *f* oil cooling; **mit ~kühlung** oil-cooled.
oll *adj (N Ger inf)* old ◆ **das sind ~e Kamellen** *(inf)* that's nothing new, that's old hat *(inf)*; **je ~er, je doller** *(prov inf)* there's no fox like an old fox *(prov inf)*.
Öllache *f* oil slick.
Olle(r) *mf decl as adj (N Ger)* **der ~** the old man; **mein ~r** *(inf)* my *or* the old man *(inf)*; **meine ~** *(inf)* my old woman *(inf)*, the old lady *(inf)*.
Öl-: ~**lieferant** *m* oil producer; ~**malerei** *f* oil painting; ⚠~**meßstab** *m* *(Aut)* dip stick; ~**mühle** *f* oil mill; ~**multi** *m (inf)* oil conglomerate; ~**ofen** *m* oil stove *or* heater; ~**papier** *nt* oil paper; ~**pest** *f* oil pollution; ~**plattform** *f* oil-rig; ~**quelle** *f* oil well; **ö~reich** *adj* oil-rich; ~**sardine** *f* sardine; **6 Leute im Wagen, da sitzt ihr ja wie die ~sardinen** *(inf)* with 6 people in the car, you must be crammed in like sardines *(inf)*; ~**schalter** *m (Elec)* oil switch; ~**scheich** *m (pej)* oil sheik; ~**schicht** *f* layer of oil; ~**schiefer** *m* oil shale; ~**stand** *m* oil level; ~**standsanzeiger** *m* oil pressure gauge; ~**teppich** *m* oil slick.
Ölung *f* oiling ◆ **die Letzte ~** *(Eccl)* extreme unction, the last rites.
Öl-: ~**verbrauch** *m* oil consumption; ~**verknappung** *f* oil shortage; ~**vorkommen** *nt* oil deposit; ~**wanne** *f (Aut)* sump *(Brit)*, oil pan *(US)*; ~**wechsel** *m* oil change; **ich muß mit dem Wagen zum ~wechsel** I must take my car in for an oil change; **den ~wechsel machen** to change the oil, to do an oil change.
Olymp *m* **-s (a)** *(Berg)* Mount Olympus ◆ **die Götter des ~** the gods of *or* on Mount Olympus. **(b)** *(Theat)* **der ~** the gods.
Olympia *nt* **-(s),** *no pl (liter) siehe* **Olympiade**.
Olympiade *f* **(a)** *(Olympische Spiele)* Olympic Games *pl*, Olympics *pl*. **(b)** *(liter: Zeitraum)* Olympiad.
Olympia-: ~**medaille** *f* Olympic medal; ~**sieger** *m* Olympic champion *or* gold-medallist; ~**stadion** *nt* Olympic stadium.
Olympier [o'lʏmpiɐ] *m* **-s, -** *(liter)* Olympian *(liter)*.
Olympionike *m* **-n, -n** *(liter)* Olympic athlete.
olympisch *adj* **(a)** *(den Olymp betreffend)* Olympian *(auch fig)* ◆ **die ~en Götter, die O~en** *(liter)* the gods of *or* on Mount Olympus, the Olympian deities *(liter)*. **(b)** *(die Olympiade betreffend)* Olympic ◆ **die O~en Spiele** the Olympic Games.
Öl-: ~**zeug** *nt* oilskins *pl*; ~**zweig** *m (lit, fig)* olive-branch.
Oma *f* **-, -s** *(inf)* granny *(inf)*, grandma *(inf)* ◆ **die alte ~ da drüben** the old dear *(inf) or* old granny *(inf)* over there.
Oman *nt* **-s** Oman.
Omaner(in *f*) *m* **-s, -** Omani.
omanisch *adj* Omani.
Ombudsmann *m, pl* **-männer** ombudsman.
Omelett [ɔm(ə)'lɛt] *nt* **-(e)s, -e** *or* **-s, Omelette** *f* **-, -n** omelette.
Omen *nt* **-s, -** *or* **Omina** omen.
ominös *adj (geh)* ominous, sinister.
Omnibus *m* bus; *(im Überlandverkehr)* bus, coach *(Brit)*.
Omnibus-: ~**linie** *f* bus route; ~**verkehr** *m (Stadtverkehr)* bus service; *(Überlandverkehr)* bus *or* coach *(Brit)* service.
omnipotent *adj (liter)* omnipotent.
Omnipotenz *f, no pl (liter)* omnipotence.
Onanie *f* masturbation, onanism.
onanieren* *vi* to masturbate.
Onanist *m* masturbator.
Ondit [õ'di:] *nt* **-, -s** *(geh)* **einem ~ zufolge** as the rumour has it, as is being noised abroad *(liter)*.
ondulieren* *vt* to crimp.
Onkel *m* **-s, - (a)** uncle.
(b) *(Kindersprache: erwachsener Mann)* uncle ◆ **sag dem ~ guten Tag!** say hallo to the nice man!; **sieh mal den komischen ~ da!** look at the funny (old) man *or* guy *(inf)* over there!; **der ~ Doktor** the nice doctor.
(c) *(inf)* **der große** *or* **dicke ~** your/his *etc* big toe; **über den ~ gehen** to walk pigeon-toed.
Onkel-: ~**ehe** *f cohabitation of widow with a man so that she keeps pension rights etc*; **o~haft** *adj* avuncular.
Onkologe *m*, **Onkologin** *f* oncologist.
Onkologie *f (Med)* oncology.
online ['ɔnlaın] *adj pred (Comput)* on line ◆ **~ arbeiten** to work on line.
Online- [ɔn'lain-] *(Comput)*: ~**-Betrieb** *m* on-line mode; ~**-Datenbank** *f* on-line database; ~**-Dienst** *m* on-line service; ~**-Service** *m siehe* **Online-Dienst**.
ONO *abbr of* **Ostnordost** ENE.
Onomasiologie *f* onomastics *sing*.
onomatopoetisch [onomatopo'e:tɪʃ] *adj (form)* onomatopoetic.
ontisch *adj* ontic.
Ontogenese *f* **-,** *no pl* ontogenesis, ontogeny.
ontogenetisch *adj* ontogenetic, ontogenic.
Ontologie *f* ontology.
ontologisch *adj* ontological ◆ **der ~e Gottesbeweis** the ontological proof *or* argument.
Onyx *m* **-(es), -e** onyx.
OP [o:'pe:] *m* **-s, -s** *abbr of* **Operationssaal**.
o.P. *abbr of* **ordentlicher Professor**.
Opa *m* **-s, -s** *(inf)* grandpa *(inf)*, grandad *(inf)*; *(fig)* old grandpa *or* grandad ◆ **na ~, nun mach mal schneller!** come on grandpa, hurry up!
opak *adj* opaque.
Opal *m* **-s, -e** opal.
Op-art *f* **-,** *no pl* op art.
Opazität *f* opacity.
OPEC ['o:pɛk] *f* **- die ~** OPEC; ~**-Länder** OPEC countries *pl*.
Oper *f* **-, -n** opera; *(Ensemble)* Opera; *(Opernhaus)* Opera, Opera House ◆ **in die ~ gehen** to go to the opera; **an die** *or* **zur ~ gehen** to take up opera-singing, to become an opera singer.
Operateur [-'tø:ɐ] *m* **(a)** *(Med)* surgeon. **(b)** *(old: im Kino)* projectionist.
Operation *f* operation.
Operations-: ~**narbe** *f* operation scar; ~**saal** *m* operating theatre *(Brit) or* room *(US)*; ~**schwester** *f* theatre sister *(Brit)*, operating room nurse *(US)*.
operativ *adj* **(a)** *(Med)* operative, surgical ◆ **das ist nur durch einen ~en Eingriff zu beseitigen** that can only be removed by (means of) surgery; **eine Geschwulst ~ entfernen** to remove a growth surgically *or* by surgery.
(b) *(Mil) Pläne, Planung, Stab* operational, strategic ◆ **~ denken** to think strategically.
Operator *m*, **Operatorin** *f* (computer) operator.
Operette *f* operetta.
Operettenkaiser *m (hum)* stage emperor.
operieren* [1] *vt Patienten, Krebs, Magen* to operate on ◆ **jdn am Magen ~** to

operate *or* perform an operation on sb's stomach; **der Blinddarm muß sofort operiert werden** that appendix must be operated on at once *or* needs immediate surgery.
[2] *vi* **(a)** *(Med)* to operate ◆ **die Ärzte haben drei Stunden an ihm operiert** the doctors operated on him for three hours; **sich ~ lassen** to have an operation.
(b) *(Mil)* to operate.
(c) *(fig: arbeiten)* to operate ◆ **Arbeiter, die mit großen Maschinen ~** workers who operate large machines; **wir müssen in den Verhandlungen sehr vorsichtig ~** we must go *or* tread very carefully in the negotiations.
Opern-: ~arie *f* (operatic) aria; **~ball** *m* opera ball; **~glas** *nt* opera glasses *pl*; **~haus** *nt* opera house; **~sänger** *m* opera singer; **~text** *m* libretto.
Opfer *nt* **-s, - (a)** *(~gabe)* sacrifice *(auch fig)* ◆ **zum** *or* **als ~** as a sacrifice; **die Gottheit verlangte zehn Jungfrauen zum** *or* **als ~** the god demanded the sacrifice of ten virgins; **sie brachten ein ~ aus Wein und Wasser dar** they made an offering of water and wine; **jdm etw zum ~ bringen** *or* **als ~ darbringen** to offer sth as a sacrifice to sb, to make a sacrificial offering of sth to sb; **für ihre Kinder scheut sie keine ~** she sacrifices everything for her children, for her children she considers no sacrifice too great; **wir müssen alle ~ bringen** we must all make sacrifices.
(b) *(geschädigte Person)* victim ◆ **jdm/einer Sache zum ~ fallen** to be (the) victim of sb/sth; **sie fiel seinem Charme zum ~** she fell victim to his charm; **ein ~ einer Sache** *(gen)* **werden** to be a victim of sth, to fall victim to sth; **täglich werden 28 Kinder ~ des Straßenverkehrs** every day 28 children are the victims of road accidents; **das Erdbeben forderte viele ~** the earthquake took a heavy toll *or* claimed many victims.
Opfer-: o~bereit *adj* ready *or* willing to make sacrifices; **~bereitschaft** *f* readiness *or* willingness to make sacrifices; **o~freudig** *adj* willing to make sacrifices; **~gabe** *f* *(liter)* (sacrificial) offering; *(Eccl)* offering; **~gang** *m* *(liter)* sacrifice of one's honour/life; **~lamm** *nt* sacrificial lamb; **der Bräutigam schritt wie ein ~lamm zum Altar** the groom walked to the altar like a lamb to the slaughter; **~mut** *m* self-sacrifice.
opfern [1] *vt* **(a)** *(als Opfer darbringen)* to sacrifice, to immolate *(form)*; *Tiere auch* to make a sacrifice of; *Feldfrüchte etc* to offer (up) ◆ **sein Leben ~** to give up *or* sacrifice one's life.
(b) *(fig: aufgeben)* to give up, to sacrifice.
[2] *vi* to make a sacrifice, to sacrifice ◆ **einem Gotte ~** *(liter)* to pay homage to *(liter)* *or* worship a god.
[3] *vr* **(a)** *(sein Leben hingeben)* to sacrifice oneself *or* one's life.
(b) *(inf: sich bereit erklären)* to be a martyr *(inf)* ◆ **wer opfert sich, die Reste aufzuessen?** who's going to be a martyr and eat up the remains?, who's going to volunteer to eat up the remains?
Opfer-: ~pfennig *m* small contribution; **~stätte** *f* sacrificial altar; **~stock** *m* offertory box; **~tier** *nt* sacrificial animal; **~tod** *m* self-sacrifice, death; **er rettete durch seinen ~tod den anderen das Leben** by sacrificing his own life, he saved the lives of the others; **Christus starb den ~tod (für unsere Sünden)** Christ gave up his life (for our sins).
Opferung *f* *(das Opfern)* sacrifice; *(Eccl)* offertory.
Opfer-: ~wille *m* spirit of sacrifice; **o~willig** *adj* self-sacrificing, willing to make sacrifices.
Opiat *nt* opiate.
Opium *nt* **-s,** *no pl* opium.
Opium-: ~höhle *f* opium den; **~raucher** *m* opium smoker.
Opponent(in *f*) *m* opponent.
opponieren* *vi* to oppose *(gegen jdn/etw* sb/sth), to offer opposition *(gegen* to) ◆ **ihr müßt auch immer ~** do you always have to oppose *or* be against everything?
opportun *adj* *(geh)* opportune.
Opportunismus *m* opportunism.
Opportunist(in *f*) *m* opportunist.
opportunistisch *adj* opportunistic, opportunist ◆ **~ handeln** to act in an opportunist fashion; **da hat er sehr ~ gehandelt** that was very opportunist(ic) of him; **~e Infektion** *(Med)* secondary infection.
Opportunität *f* *(geh)* opportuneness, appropriateness.
Opposition *f* opposition ◆ **etw aus (lauter) ~ tun** to do sth out of *or* from (sheer) contrariness; **diese Gruppe macht ständig ~ (gegen den Klassenlehrer)** *(inf)* this group is always making trouble (for the teacher).
oppositionell *adj* *Gruppen, Kräfte* opposition.
OP-Schwester [oːˈpeː-] *f abbr of* **Operationsschwester.**
Optativ *m* optative.
optieren* *vi* *(Pol form)* **~ für** to opt for.
Optik *f* **(a)** *(Phys)* optics.
(b) *(Linsensystem)* lens system ◆ **du hast wohl einen Knick in der ~!** *(sl)* can't you see straight? *(inf)*, are you blind?; **das ist eine Frage der ~** *(fig)* it depends on your point of view; **in** *or* **aus seiner ~** in his eyes.
(c) *(Mode, Aussehen)* look; *(Schein)* appearances *pl* ◆ **das ist nur hier wegen der ~** it's just here because it looks good *or* for visual *or* optical effect; **die Partei muß sehen, daß sie die ~ ihrer Politik ein bißchen verbessert** the party must try to present their policies in a better light; **etw in die rechte ~ bringen** to put sth into the right perspective.
Optiker(in *f*) *m* **-s, -** optician.
optimal *adj* optimal, optimum *attr.*
optimieren* *vt* to optimize.
Optimismus *m* optimism.
Optimist(in *f*) *m* optimist.
optimistisch *adj* optimistic.
Optimum *nt* **-s, Optima** optimum.
Option [ɔpˈtsioːn] *f* **(a)** *(Wahl)* option *(für* in favour of). **(b)** *(Anrecht)* option *(auf +acc* on).
Options-: ~anleihe *f* optional bond; **~ausübung** *f* exercise (of option); **~empfänger** *m* grantee (of an option); **~fixierer** *m* option issuer; **~frist** *f* option period; **~preis** *m* option price; **~recht** *nt* option right; **~schein** *m* warrant.
optisch *adj* visual; *Gesetze, Instrumente* optical ◆ **~er Eindruck** visual *or* optical effect; **~e Täuschung** optical illusion.
opulent *adj* *Kostüme, Geldsumme* lavish; *Mahl auch* sumptuous.
Opus *nt* **-,** *(rare) pl* **Opera** work; *(Mus, hum)* opus; *(Gesamtwerk)* (complete) works *pl*, opus.
Orakel *nt* **-s,** - oracle ◆ **das ~ befragen** to consult the oracle; **er spricht in ~n** *(fig)* he speaks like an oracle, he has an oracular way of putting things.
orakelhaft *adj* *(liter)* oracular, delphic *(liter)*.
orakeln* *vi* **(a)** *(rätseln)* **wir haben lange orakelt, was der Satz bedeuten sollte** we spent a long time trying to figure out what the sentence meant *or* trying to decipher the sentence. **(b)** *(über die Zukunft)* to prognosticate *(hum)*.
oral *adj* oral.
Oral|erotik *f* oral eroticism.
Orange[1] [oˈrãːʒə] *f* **-, -n** *(Frucht)* orange.
Orange[2] [oˈrãːʒə] *nt* **-,** - *or (inf)* **-s** orange.
orange [oˈrãːʒə] *adj inv* orange ◆ **ein ~** *or* **~ner** *(inf)* **Rock** an orange skirt.
Orangeade [orãˈʒaːdə] *f* orangeade.
Orangeat [orãˈʒaːt] *nt* candied (orange) peel.
orange(n)- [oˈrãːʒə(n)-]: **~farben, ~farbig** *adj* orange(-coloured).
Orangenmarmelade [oˈrãːʒən-] *f* orange marmalade.
Orangerie [orãʒəˈriː] *f* orangery.
Orang-Utan *m* **-s, -s** orang-utan, orang-outang.
Oranien [-iən] *nt* **-s** Orange ◆ **Wilhelm von ~** William of Orange.
Oranjefreistaat [oˈranjə-] *m* Orange Free State.
Oratorium *nt* **(a)** *(Mus)* oratorio. **(b)** *(Betraum)* oratory.
Orbit *m* **-s, -s** orbit.
Orchester [ɔrˈkɛstɐ, *(old)* ɔrˈçɛstɐ] *nt* **-s, - (a)** orchestra. **(b)** *(~raum)* orchestra (pit).
Orchestergraben *m* orchestra pit.
orchestral [ɔrkɛsˈtraːl, *(old)* ɔrçɛsˈtraːl] *adj* orchestral.
orchestrieren* [ɔrkɛsˈtriːrən, *(old)* ɔrçɛsˈtriːrən] *vt* to orchestrate.
Orchestrierung *f* orchestration.
Orchidee *f* **-, -n** [-ˈdeːən] orchid.
Orden *m* **-s, - (a)** *(Gemeinschaft)* (holy) order ◆ **in einen ~ (ein)treten, einem ~ beitreten** to become a monk/nun.
(b) *(Ehrenzeichen)* decoration; *(Mil auch)* medal ◆ **~ tragen** to wear one's decorations; **jdm einen ~ (für etw) verleihen** to decorate sb (for sth); **einen ~ bekommen** to be decorated, to receive a decoration.
ordengeschmückt *adj* decorated, covered in decorations *or* *(Mil auch)* medals.
Ordens-: ~band *nt* ribbon; *(Mil)* medal ribbon; **~bruder** *m* **(a)** *(Eccl)* monk; **meine ~brüder** my brother monks; **(b)** *(von Ritterorden etc)* brother member (of an order); **~burg** *f medieval castle built by a religious order*; **~frau** *f* *(old)* nun; **~geistliche(r)** *m* priest in a religious order; **~kleid** *nt* *(liter)* habit; **~meister** *m* master of an order; **~regel** *f* rule (of the order); **~schwester** *f* nursing sister *or* nun; **~tracht** *f* habit.
ordentlich *adj* **(a)** *Mensch, Zimmer* tidy, neat, orderly ◆ **in ihrem Haushalt geht es sehr ~ zu** she runs a very orderly household; **kannst du die Wörter nicht ~ untereinander schreiben?** can't you write the words neatly *or* tidily under one another?; **bei ihr sieht es immer ~ aus** her house always looks neat and tidy; **~ arbeiten** to be a thorough and precise worker.
(b) *(ordnungsgemäß)* **~es Gericht** court of law, law court; **~es Mitglied** full member; **~er Professor** (full) professor.
(c) *(anständig)* respectable ◆ **sich ~ benehmen** to behave properly.
(d) *(inf: tüchtig)* **~ essen/trinken** to eat/drink (really) well *or* heartily; **ihr habt sicher Hunger, greift ~ zu** you're sure to be hungry, tuck in; **ein ~es Frühstück** a proper *or* good breakfast; **wir haben ~ gearbeitet** we really got down to it; **eine ~e Tracht Prügel** a real beating, a proper hiding.
(e) *(inf: richtig)* real, proper.
(f) *(annehmbar, ganz gut)* *Preis, Leistung* reasonable.
Order *f* **-, -s** *or* **-n (a)** *(Comm: Auftrag)* order ◆ **an ~ lautend** made out to order.
(b) *(dated: Anweisung)* order ◆ **jdm ~ erteilen** to order *or* direct *or* instruct sb; **sich an eine ~ halten** to keep to one's orders; **ich habe meine ~, und daran halte ich mich** orders are orders, I have my orders and I'm sticking to them.
ordern *vt* *(Comm)* to order.
Ordinalia *pl* ordinals *pl.*
Ordinalzahl *f* ordinal number.
ordinär *adj* **(a)** *(gemein, unfein)* vulgar, common. **(b)** *(alltäglich)* ordinary ◆ **was, Sie wollen so viel für eine ganz ~e Kiste?** what, you're wanting that much for a perfectly ordinary box *or* for that old box? **(c)** *(old Comm: regulär)* *Preis* regular, normal.
Ordinariat *nt* **(a)** *(Univ)* chair. **(b) Bischöfliches ~** bishop's palace; *(Amt)* bishopric.
Ordinarius *m* **-, Ordinarien** [-iən] **(a)** *(Univ)* professor *(für* of). **(b)** *(Eccl)* bishop, ordinary. **(c)** *(old Sch)* form *or* class teacher.
Ordinate *f* **-, -n** ordinate.

⚠: for details of spelling reform, see supplement

Ordinaten|achse *f* axis of ordinates.

Ordination *f* **(a)** (*Eccl*) ordination, ordaining. **(b)** (*old Med*) (*Verordnung*) prescription; (*Sprechstunde*) surgery. **(c)** (*Aus*) (doctor's) surgery (*Brit*) *or* office (*US*).

ordinieren* [1] *vt* **(a)** (*Eccl*) to ordain ◆ **sich ~ lassen** to be ordained. **(b)** (*old Med*) to prescribe.
[2] *vi* (*old Med*) to hold *or* have surgery (hours).

ordnen [1] *vt* **(a)** *Gedanken, Einfälle, Material* to order, to organize; *Demonstrationszug, Verkehrswesen* to organize; *Akten, Finanzen, Hinterlassenschaft, Privatleben* to put in order, to straighten out; *siehe* **geordnet**.
(b) (*sortieren*) to order, to arrange.
[2] *vr* to get into order ◆ **allmählich ordnete sich das Bild** (*fig*) the picture gradually became clear, things gradually fell into place; **die Menge ordnete sich zu einem Festzug** the crowd formed itself into a procession.

Ordner *m* **-s, -** **(a)** steward; (*bei Demonstration auch*) marshal. **(b)** (*Akten~*) file.

➤ **Ordnung** *f* **(a)** (*das Ordnen*) ordering ◆ **bei der ~ der Papiere** when putting the papers in order.
(b) (*geordneter Zustand*) order ◆ **~ halten** to keep things tidy; **du mußt mal ein bißchen ~ in deinen Sachen halten** you must keep your affairs a bit more in order, you must order your affairs a bit more; **in dem Aufsatz sehe ich keine ~** I can see no order *or* coherence in the essay; **~ schaffen, für ~ sorgen** to sort things out, to put things in order, to tidy things up; **seid ruhig, sonst schaff ich gleich mal ~** (*inf*) be quiet or I'll come and sort you out (*inf*); **Sie müssen mehr für ~ in Ihrer Klasse sorgen** you'll have to keep more discipline in your class, you'll have to keep your class in better order; **auf ~ halten** *or* **sehen** to be tidy; **etw in ~ halten** to keep sth in order; *Garten, Haus etc auch* to keep sth tidy; **etw in ~ bringen** (*reparieren*) to fix sth; (*herrichten*) to put sth in order; (*bereinigen*) to clear sth up, to sort sth out; **ich finde es (ganz) in ~, daß ...** I think *or* find it quite right that ...; **ich finde es nicht in ~, daß ...** I don't think it's right that ...; **(das ist) in ~!** (*inf*) (that's) OK (*inf*) *or* all right!; **geht in ~** (*inf*) sure (*inf*), that's all right *or* fine *or* OK (*inf*); **Ihre Bestellung geht in ~** we'll see to your order, we'll put your order through; **der ist in ~** (*inf*) he's OK (*inf*) *or* all right (*inf*); **da ist etwas nicht in ~** there's something wrong there; **mit ihm/der Maschine ist etwas nicht in ~** there's something wrong *or* the matter with him/the machine; **die Maschine ist (wieder) in ~** the machine's fixed *or* in order *or* all right (again); **es ist alles in bester** *or* **schönster ~** everything's fine, things couldn't be better; **jdn zur ~ rufen** to call sb to order; **ein Kind zur ~ anhalten** *or* **erziehen** to teach a child tidy habits; **~ muß sein!** we must have order!; **~ ist das halbe Leben** (*Prov*) tidiness *or* a tidy mind is half the battle; **hier** *or* **bei uns herrscht ~** we like to have a little order around here; **hier herrscht ja eine schöne ~** (*iro*) this is a nice mess; *siehe* **Ruhe**.
(c) (*Gesetzmäßigkeit*) routine ◆ **alles muß (bei ihm) seine ~ haben** (*räumlich*) he has to have everything in its right *or* proper place; (*zeitlich*) he does everything according to a fixed schedule; **das Kind braucht seine ~** the child needs a routine.
(d) (*Vorschrift*) rules *pl* ◆ **sich an eine ~ halten** to stick *or* keep to the rules; **ich frage nur der ~ halber** it's only a routine *or* formal question, I'm only asking as a matter of form; **der ~ gemäß** according to the rules *or* the rule book.
(e) (*Rang, Biol*) order ◆ **Straße erster ~** first-class road; **das war ein Fauxpas erster ~** (*inf*) that was a faux pas of the first order *or* first water (*inf*); **ein Stern fünfter ~** a star of the fifth magnitude.

Ordnungs-: **~amt** *nt* ≃ town clerk's office; **~fanatiker** *m* fanatic for order; **nicht alle Deutschen sind ~fanatiker** not all Germans have a mania *or* passion for order; **o~gemäß** *adj* according to *or* in accordance with the rules, proper; **ich werde mich selber um die o~gemäße Abfertigung ihrer Bestellung kümmern** I will see to it myself that your order is properly *or* correctly dealt with; **der Prozeß ist o~gemäß abgelaufen** the trial took its proper course; **o~halber** *adv* as a matter of form, for the sake of form; **~hüter** *m* (*hum*) custodian of the law (*hum*); **~liebe** *f* love of order; **o~liebend** *adj* tidy, tidy-minded; **~ruf** *m* call to order; **in der Debatte mußte der Präsident mehrere ~rufe erteilen** during the debate the chairman had to call the meeting to order several times; **einen ~ruf bekommen** to be called to order; **~sinn** *m* idea *or* conception of tidiness *or* order; **~strafe** *f* fine; **jdn mit einer ~strafe belegen** to fine sb; **o~widrig** *adj* irregular; *Parken, Verhalten* (*im Straßenverkehr*) illegal; **o~widrig handeln** to go against *or* infringe rules *or* regulations; **~widrigkeit** *f* infringement (*of law or rule*); **~zahl** *f* **(a)** (*Math*) ordinal number; **(b)** (*Phys*) atomic number.

⚠ **Ordonnanz** *f* orderly.

⚠ **Ordonnanz|offizier** *m* aide-de-camp, ADC.

Organ *nt* **-s, -e** **(a)** (*Med, Biol*) organ ◆ **kein ~ für etw haben** (*inf*) not to have any feel for sth.
(b) (*inf: Stimme*) voice.
(c) (*fig: Zeitschrift*) organ, mouthpiece.
(d) (*Behörde*) organ, instrument; (*Beauftragter*) agent; (*der Polizei*) branch, division ◆ **die ausführenden ~e** the executors; **wir sind nur ausführendes ~** we are only following orders; **beratendes ~** advisory body.

Organbank *f* organ bank.

Organigramm *nt* **-s, -e** organization chart.

Organisation *f* organization.

Organisations-: **~plan** *m* organization chart; **~programmierer** *m* (*Comput*) application programmer; **~talent** *nt* talent *or* flair for organization; **er ist ein ~talent** he has a talent *or* flair for organizing.

Organisator *m*, **Organisatorin** *f* organizer.

organisatorisch *adj* organizational ◆ **eine ~e Höchstleistung** a masterpiece of organization; **er ist ein ~es Talent** he has a gift for organizing *or* organization; **das hat ~ gar nicht geklappt** organizationally, it was a failure.

organisch *adj Chemie, Verbindung, Salze* organic; *Erkrankung, Leiden* physical ◆ **ein ~es Ganzes** an organic whole; **sich ~ einfügen** to merge, to blend (*in +acc* with, into).

organisieren* [1] *vti* **(a)** to organize ◆ **er kann ausgezeichnet ~** he's excellent at organizing. **(b)** (*sl: stehlen*) to lift (*sl*), to get hold of.
[2] *vr* to organize.

organisiert *adj* organized.

Organismus *m* organism.

Organist(in *f*) *m* (*Mus*) organist.

Organ-: **~klage** *f action brought against the Bundestag or Bundesrat by a Land or political party*; **~spende** *f* organ donation; **~spender** *m* donor (*of an organ*); **~spenderausweis** *m* donor card; **~verpflanzung** *f* transplant(ation) (*of organs*).

Organza *m* **-s,** *no pl* organza.

Orgasmus *m* orgasm.

orgastisch *adj* orgasmic.

Orgel *f* **-, -n** (*Mus*) organ.

orgeln *vi* **(a)** (*inf: Orgel spielen*) to play the organ. **(b)** (*Hunt: Hirsch*) to bell.

Orgelpfeife *f* organ pipe ◆ **die Kinder standen da wie die ~n** (*hum*) the children were standing in order of height *or* were standing like a row of Russian dolls.

orgiastisch *adj* orgiastic.

Orgie [-iə] *f* orgy ◆ **~n feiern** (*lit*) to have orgies/an orgy; (*fig*) to go wild; (*Phantasie etc*) to run riot.

Orient ['o:riɛnt, o'riɛnt] *m* **-s,** *no pl* **(a)** (*liter*) Orient ◆ **das Denken des ~s** Eastern thought; **der Vordere ~** the Near East; **vom ~ zum Okzident** from east to west. **(b)** (*inf*) ≃ Middle East.

Orientale [oriɛn'ta:lə] *m* **-n, -n, Orientalin** *f* person from the Middle East.

orientalisch [oriɛn'ta:lɪʃ] *adj* Middle Eastern.

Orientalist(in *f*) [oriɛnta'lɪst(ɪn)] *m* ≃ specialist in Middle Eastern and oriental studies.

Orientalistik [oriɛnta'lɪstɪk] *f* ≃ Middle Eastern studies ◆ **~ studieren** ≃ to do Middle Eastern studies.

orientieren* [oriɛn'ti:rən] [1] *vti* **(a)** (*unterrichten*) to put sb in the picture (*über +acc* about) ◆ **unser Katalog orientiert (Sie) über unsere Sonderangebote** our catalogue gives (you) information on *or* about our special offers; **darüber ist er gut/falsch/ nicht orientiert** he is well/wrongly/ not informed on *or* about that.
(b) (*ausrichten*) (*lit, fig*) to orient, to orientate (*nach, auf +acc* to, towards) ◆ **ein positivistisch orientierter Denker** a positivistically orientated thinker; **links orientiert sein** to tend to the left; **links orientierte Gruppen** left-wing groups.
(c) (*hinweisen*) (*auf +acc* to) to orient, to orientate.
[2] *vr* **(a)** (*sich unterrichten*) to inform oneself (*über +acc* about *or* on).
(b) (*sich zurechtfinden*) to orientate oneself (*an +dat, nach* by), to find *or* get one's bearings ◆ **in einer fremden Stadt kann ich mich gar nicht ~** I just can't find my way around in a strange city; **von da an kann ich mich alleine ~** I can find my own way from there.
(c) (*sich einstellen*) to adapt *or* orientate (oneself) (*an +dat, auf +acc* to).

Orientierung [oriɛn'ti:rʊŋ] *f* **(a)** (*Unterrichtung*) information ◆ **zu Ihrer ~** for your information. **(b)** (*das Zurechtfinden*) orientation ◆ **hier fällt einem die ~ schwer** it's difficult to find *or* get one's bearings here; **die ~ verlieren** to lose one's bearings. **(c)** (*das Ausrichten*) orientation.

Orientierungs-: **~punkt** *m* point of reference; **~sinn** *m* sense of direction; **~stufe** *f* (*Sch*) *period during which pupils are selected to attend different schools*.

Orig. *abbr of* **Original**.

Original *nt* **-s, -e** **(a)** original. **(b)** (*Mensch*) character.

original *adj* original ◆ **~ Meißener Porzellan** real *or* genuine Meissen porcelain; **~ aus USA** guaranteed from USA.

Original-: **~ausgabe** *f* first edition; **~einzug** *m* (*bei Kopierer*) automatic sheet feed; **~fassung** *f* original (version); **in der englischen ~fassung** in the original English version; **o~getreu** *adj* true to the original; **etw o~getreu nachmalen** to paint a very faithful copy of sth; **die Kopie sieht sehr o~getreu aus** the copy looks very like the original.

Originalität *f, no pl* **(a)** (*Echtheit*) authenticity, genuineness. **(b)** (*Urtümlichkeit*) originality.

Original-: **~ton** *m* original soundtrack; (*fig*) **im ~ton Thatcher** in Thatcher's own words; **~übertragung** *f* live broadcast; **~verpackung** *f* original packaging; **in ~verpackung** (*ungeöffnet*) unopened.

originär *adj Idee* original.

originell *adj* (*selbständig*) *Idee, Argumentation, Interpretation* original; (*neu*) novel; (*geistreich*) witty ◆ **das hat er sich** (*dat*) **sehr ~ ausgedacht** that's a very original idea of his; **er ist ein ~er Kopf** he's got an original mind; **das finde ich ~ (von ihm)** that's pretty original/witty.

Orkan *m* **-(e)s, -e** **(a)** hurricane ◆ **der Sturm schwoll zum ~ an** the storm increased to hurricane force. **(b)** (*fig*) storm ◆ **ein ~ des Beifalls brach los** thunderous applause broke out.

Orkan-: **o~artig** *adj Wind* gale-force; *Beifall* thunderous; **~stärke** *f* hurricane force.

Ornament *nt* decoration, ornament ◆ **der Fries ist reines ~** the frieze is purely ornamental *or* decorative; **eine Vase mit figürlichen ~en** a vase decorated with figures.

ornamental *adj* ornamental.

ornamentieren* *vt* to embellish, to ornament.

Ornat *m* **-(e)s, -e** regalia *pl*; (*Eccl*) vestments *pl*; (*Jur*) official robes *pl* ◆ **in vollem ~** (*inf*) dressed up to the nines (*inf*).

Ornithologe *m*, **Ornithologin** *f* ornithologist.

Orpheus *m* - Orpheus.

orphisch *adj* Orphic.

Ort[1] *m* **-(e)s, -e (a)** (*Platz, Stelle*) place ◆ **~ des Treffens** meeting place, venue; **hier bin ich wohl nicht am rechten ~** I've obviously not come to the right place; **ein ~ der Stille/des Friedens** a place of quiet/of peace; **ein ~ der Einkehr** a place for thinking quietly; **~ der Handlung** (*Theat*) scene of the action; **an den ~ der Tat** *or* **des Verbrechens zurückkehren** to return to the scene of the crime; **hier ist nicht der ~, darüber zu sprechen** this is not the (time or) place to talk about that; **am angegebenen ~** in the place quoted, loc cit *abbr*; **ohne ~ und Jahr** without indication of place and date of publication; **an ~ und Stelle** on the spot, there and then; **an ~ und Stelle ankommen** to arrive (at one's destination); **das ist höheren ~s entschieden worden** (*hum, form*) the decision came from higher places *or* from above; **höheren ~s ist das bemerkt worden** (*hum, form*) it's been noticed in high places.
(b) (*~schaft*) place ◆ **in einem kleinen ~ in Cornwall** in a little spot in Cornwall; **jeder größere ~ hat ein Postamt** a place of any size has a post office; **~e über 100.000 Einwohner** places with more than *or* with over 100,000 inhabitants; **er ist im ganzen ~ bekannt** everyone knows him, the whole village/town *etc* knows him; **wir sind mit dem halben ~ verwandt** we're related to half the people in the place; **am ~** in the place; **das beste Hotel am ~** the best hotel in town; **wir haben keinen Arzt am ~** we have no resident doctor; **am ~ wohnen** to live in the same village/town; **mitten im ~** in the centre (of the place/town); **der nächste ~** the next village/town *etc*; **von ~ zu ~** from place to place.

Ort[2] *m* **-(e)s, ¨er (a)** position; (*Geometrie*) locus. **(b)** (*Min*) coal face, (working) face ◆ **vor ~** at the (coal) face; (*fig*) on the spot; **Wartungsarbeiten vor ~ durchführen** to carry out on-the-spot *or* on-site servicing.

Örtchen *nt* **das (stille) ~** (*inf*) the smallest room (*inf*).

orten *vt U-Boot, Flugzeug* to locate, to fix the position of, to get a fix on; *Heringsschwarm* to locate.

orthodox *adj* (*lit, fig*) orthodox.

Orthodoxie *f* orthodoxy.

⚠ **Orthographie** *f* orthography.

⚠ **orthographisch** *adj* orthographic(al) ◆ **er schreibt nicht immer ~ richtig** his spelling is not always correct.

Orthopäde *m* **-n, -n**, **Orthopädin** *f* orthopaedist, orthopaedic specialist.

orthopädisch *adj* orthopaedic.

örtlich *adj* local ◆ **das ist ~ verschieden** it varies from place to place; **der Konflikt war ~ begrenzt** it was limited to a local encounter; **jdn/etw ~ betäuben** to give sb/sth a local anaesthetic; **er war nur ~ betäubt** he was only under *or* had only had a local anaesthetic.

Örtlichkeit *f* locality ◆ **sich mit der ~/den ~en vertraut machen** to get to know the place; **er ist mit den ~en gut vertraut** he knows his way about; **die ~en** (*euph*) the cloakroom (*euph*).

Orts-: ~angabe *f* place of publication; (*bei Anschriften*) (name of the) town; **ohne ~angabe** no place of publication indicated; **o~ansässig** *adj* local; **eine schon lange o~ansässige Familie** a long established local family; **sind Sie schon lange o~ansässig?** have you been living here *or* locally for a long time?; **die ~ansässigen** the local residents; **~bestimmung** *f* **Fehler bei der ~bestimmung** navigational error; **die ~bestimmung mit dem Kompaß** getting one's bearings with a compass; **die ~bestimmung einer Partei vornehmen** to locate a party's political position.

Ortschaft *f* **-, -en** village; town ◆ **geschlossene ~** built-up *or* restricted area.

Orts-: o~fest *adj* fixed; **o~fremd** *adj* non-local; **ich bin hier o~fremd** I'm a stranger here; **ein ~fremder** a stranger; **~gespräch** *nt* (*Telec*) local call; **~gruppe** *f* local branch *or* group; **~kenntnis** *f* local knowledge; **(gute) ~kenntnisse haben** to know one's way around (well); **~klasse** *f classification of area according to cost of living for estimating salary weighting allowances*; **~krankenkasse** *f* **Allgemeine ~krankenkasse** *compulsory medical insurance scheme for workers, old people etc*; **o~kundig** *adj* **nehmen Sie sich einen o~kundigen Führer** get a guide who knows his way around; **ich bin nicht sehr o~kundig** I don't know my way around very well; **ein ~kundiger** somebody who knows his way around *or* who knows the place; **~mitte** *f* centre; **~name** *m* place name; **~netz** *nt* (*Telec*) local (telephone) exchange area; (*Elec*) local grid; **~netzkennzahl** *f* (*Telec*) dialling code; **~schild** *nt* place name sign; **~sinn** *m* sense of direction; **~tarif** *m* (*bei Briefen*) local postal charge; (*Telec*) charge for local phone-call; **o~üblich** *adj* local; **o~übliche Mieten** standard local rents; **das ist hier o~üblich** it is usual *or* customary here, it is (a) local custom here; **~verband** *m* local committee; **~verkehr** *m* local traffic; **selbst im ~verkehr hat der Brief noch drei Tage gebraucht** even a local letter took three days; **Gebühren im ~verkehr** (*Telec*) charges for local (phone) calls; (*von Briefen*) local postage rates; **~zeit** *f* local time; **~zulage** *f*, **~zuschlag** *m* (local) weighting allowance.

Ortung *f* locating ◆ **bei (der) ~ eines feindlichen U-Boots ...** when locating an *or* fixing the position of *or* getting a fix on an enemy submarine ...

O-Saft *m* (*inf*) orange juice.

Öse *f* **-, -n** loop; (*an Kleidung*) eye; *siehe* **Haken**.

⚠: for details of spelling reform, see supplement

Ösenzange *f* eyelet punch.

Oslo *nt* **-s** Oslo.

Osloer(in *f*) [ˈɔsloːɐ, -ərɪn] *m* person from Oslo.

Osmane *m* **-n, -n** Ottoman.

osmanisch *adj* Ottoman.

Osmium *nt, no pl* (*abbr* **Os**) osmium.

Osmose *f* **-**, *no pl* osmosis.

OSO *abbr of* **Ostsüdost**.

Ossi *m* **-s, -s** (*inf*) Easterner, East German.

Ost *m* **-(e)s**, *no pl* (*liter*) **(a)** East ◆ **aus ~ und West** from East and West; **von ~ nach West** from East to West; **der Wind kommt aus ~** the wind is coming from the East; **wo ~ und West zusammentreffen** where East and West meet, where East meets West; **10 Mark ~** (*inf*) 10 East German marks.
(b) (*liter: ~wind*) East *or* easterly wind.

Ost- *in cpds* (*bei Ländern, Erdteilen*) (*als politische Einheit*) East; (*geographisch auch*) Eastern, the East of ...; (*bei Städten, Inseln*) East; **~afrika** *nt* East Africa; **~asien** *nt* Eastern Asia; **~-Berlin** *nt* East Berlin; **~berliner** [1] *m* East Berliner; [2] *adj attr* East Berlin; **~besuch** *m* (*inf*) visit from East Germany; **~block** *m* Eastern bloc; **~blockland** *nt*, **~blockstaat** *m* country belonging to the Eastern bloc, Eastern bloc country, Iron Curtain country; **o~deutsch** *adj* East German; **~deutschland** *nt* (*Pol*) East Germany; (*Geog*) Eastern Germany.

Osten *m* **-s**, *no pl* **(a)** east; (*von Land*) East ◆ **der Ferne ~** the Far East; **der Nahe ~** the Middle East, the Near East; **der Mittlere ~** *area stretching from Iran and Iraq to India*, Middle East; **im Nahen und Mittleren ~** in the Middle East; **aus dem ~, von ~ her** from the east; **gegen** *or* **gen** (*liter*) *or* **nach ~** east(wards), to the east; **nach ~ (hin)** to the east; **im ~ der Stadt/des Landes** in the east of the town/country; **weiter in ~** further east; **im ~ Frankreichs** in the east of France, in eastern France.
(b) (*Pol*) **der ~** (*Ostdeutschland*) East Germany; (*Ostblock*) the East; East Berlin.

ostentativ *adj* pointed ◆ **der Botschafter drehte sich ~ um und verließ den Raum** the ambassador pointedly turned round and left the room.

Osteoporose *f* - *no pl* (*Med*) osteoporosis.

Oster-: ~ei *nt* Easter egg; **~feiertag** *m* Easter holiday; **am 2. ~feiertag** on Easter Monday; **über die ~feiertage fahren wir weg** we're going away over the Easter weekend; **~fest** *nt* Easter; **das jüdische ~fest** the Jewish Feast of the Passover; **~feuer** *nt bonfire lit on Easter Saturday*; **~glocke** *f* daffodil; **~hase** *m* Easter bunny; **~insel** *f* Easter Island; **~lamm** *nt* paschal lamb.

österlich *adj* Easter.

Oster-: ~marsch *m* Easter peace march; **~montag** *m* Easter Monday; **~morgen** *m* Easter morning.

Ostern *nt* **-, -** Easter ◆ **frohe** *or* **fröhliche ~!** Happy Easter!; **ein verregnetes ~, verregnete ~** a rainy Easter; **an ~** on Easter day; **zu ~** at Easter; **(zu** *or* **über) ~ fahren wir weg** we're going away at *or* over Easter; **wenn ~ und Pfingsten auf einen Tag fällt** (*hum*) if pigs could fly (*hum*).

Österreich *nt* **-s** Austria ◆ **~-Ungarn** (*Hist*) Austria-Hungary.

Österreicher(in *f*) *m* **-s, -** Austrian ◆ **er ist ~** he's (an) Austrian.

österreichisch *adj* Austrian ◆ **~-ungarisch** (*Hist*) Austro-Hungarian; **das Ö~e** (*Ling*) Austrian.

Oster-: ~sonntag *m* Easter Sunday; **~spiel** *nt* Easter (passion) play.

Osterweiterung *f* (*von Nato, EU*) eastward expansion.

Osterwoche *f* Easter week.

Ost-: ~europa *nt* East(ern) Europe; **o~europäisch** *adj* East European; **~friese** *m*, **~friesin** *f* East Frisian; **o~friesisch** *adj* East Frisian; **~friesische Inseln** *pl* East Frisian Islands; **~friesland** *nt* **-s** East Frisia; **~geld** *nt* (*inf*) East German money; **o~germanisch** *adj* (*Ling*) East Germanic; **~goten** *pl* (*Hist*) Ostrogoths *pl*.

ostinat *adj* (*Mus*) **~er Baß** ground bass, bass ostinato.

Ostinato *nt or m* **-s, -s** *or* **Ostinati** ostinato.

Ost-: o~indisch *adj* East Indian; **~indische Kompanie** East India Company; **~jude** *m* East European Jew; **~kirche** *f* Orthodox *or* Eastern Church; **~kolonisation** *f* (*Hist*) *German medieval colonization of Eastern Europe*; **~küste** *f* East coast.

Ostler(in *f*) *m* **-s, -** (*inf*) East German.

östlich [1] *adj Richtung, Winde* easterly; *Gebiete* eastern ◆ **30° ~er Länge** 30° (longitude) east.
[2] *adv* **~ von Hamburg/des Rheins** (to the) east of Hamburg/of the Rhine.
[3] *prep +gen* (to the) east of.

Ost-: ~mark *f* **(a)** (*Hist*) Austria; **(b)** (*inf*) East German Mark; **~nordost(en)** *m* east-north-east; **~politik** *f* Ostpolitik, *West German foreign policy regarding the Eastern block especially East Germany and East Berlin*; **~preuße** *m* East Prussian; **~preußen** *nt* East Prussia; **o~preußisch** *adj* East Prussian.

Östrogen *nt* **-s, -e** oestrogen (*Brit*), estrogen (*US*).

Ost-: ~rom *nt* (*Hist*) Eastern (Roman) Empire, Byzantine Empire; **o~römisch** *adj* Byzantine.

Ostsee *f*: **die ~** the Baltic (Sea).

Ostsee- *in cpds* Baltic.

Ost-: ~staaten *pl* (*in USA*) the Eastern *or* East coast states; **~südost(en)** *m* east-south-east; **~verträge** *pl* (*Pol*) *political, social and economic agreements made between East and West Germany in 1970*; **o~wärts** *adv* eastwards; **~-West-Achse** *f* East-West link; **~-West-Verhandlungen** *pl* East-West negotiations; **~wind** *m* east *or* easterly wind.

OSZE [oːǀɛstsɛtˈǀeː] *f abbr of* **Organisation für Sicherheit und Zusammenarbeit in Europa** OSCE.

oszillieren* *vi* to oscillate.
⚠ **Oszillograph** *m* oscillograph.
O-Ton *m abbr of* **Originalton.**
Otter[1] *m* **-s, -** otter.
Otter[2] *f* **-, -n** viper, adder.
Otterngezücht *nt (Bibl)* brood of vipers.
Ottomane *f* **-, -n** ottoman.
Ottomotor *m* internal combustion engine, otto engine.
ÖTV [øːteːˈfau] *abbr of* **Gewerkschaft Öffentliche Dienste, Transport und Verkehr** ≃ TGWU *(Brit).*
out [aut] *adj pred Mode* out.
outen [ˈautn] *(inf)* [1] *vt (als Homosexuellen)* to out *(inf); (als Trinker, Spitzel etc)* to reveal, to expose ◆ **er wurde von der Presse als Geheimdienstler geoutet** he was exposed *or* unmasked by the press as a secret service agent.
[2] *vr* to come out *(inf)* ◆ **du solltest dich endlich ~** you really should come out at last *(inf);* **er outete sich als Schwuler** he came out *(inf).*
Outing [ˈautɪŋ] *nt* **-s** *(inf)* outing *(inf)* ◆ **er hat Angst vor dem ~** *(geoutet zu werden)* he's afraid of being outed *(inf); (sich zu outen)* he's afraid of coming out *(inf);* **sie hat ihr ~ unbeschadet überstanden** she survived her outing unscathed *(inf).*
Ouvertüre [uvɛrˈtyːrə] *f* **-, -n** overture.
oval [oˈvaːl] *adj* oval.
Oval [oˈvaːl] *nt* **-s, -e** oval.
Ovation [ovaˈtsioːn] *f* ovation ◆ **jdm eine ~** *or* **~en darbringen** to give sb an ovation *or* a standing ovation.
Overall [ˈouvərɔːl] *m* **-s, -s** overalls *pl.*
Overhead- [ˈoːvɐhɛd-]: **~folie** *f* transparency; **~projektor** *m* overhead projector.
Overkill [ˈoːvɐkɪl] *m* **-(s)** overkill.
ÖVP [øːfauˈpeː] *f* **-** *abbr of* **Österreichische Volkspartei.**
Ovulation [ovulaˈtsioːn] *f* ovulation.
Ovulationshemmer *m* **-s, -** ovulation inhibitor.
Oxid, Oxyd *nt* **-(e)s, -e** oxide.
Oxidation, Oxydation *f* oxidation.
oxidieren*, oxydieren* *vti (vi: aux sein or haben)* to oxidize.
Ozean *m* **-s, -e** ocean ◆ **ein ~ von Tränen** an ocean of tears.
Ozeandampfer *m* ocean steamer.
Ozeanien [-iən] *nt* **-s** Oceania.
ozeanisch *adj Flora* oceanic; *Sprachen* Oceanic.
⚠ **Ozeanographie** *f* oceanography.
Ozeanriese *m (inf)* ocean liner.
Ozelot *m* **-s, -e** ocelot.
Ozon *nt or (inf) m* **-s,** *no pl* ozone.
Ozon- *in cpds* ozone; **~hülle** *f* ozone layer; **~loch** *nt* hole in the ozone layer; **~schicht** *f* ozone layer; **~schild** *m* ozone shield; **~wert** *m* ozone level.

P

P, p [peː] *nt* **-, -** P, p.

Paar *nt* **-s, -e** pair; (*Mann und Frau auch*) couple ◆ **ein ~ Schuhe** a pair of shoes; **zwei ~ Socken** two pairs of socks; **ein ~ Ochsen** a yoke of oxen; **ein ~ Würstchen** a couple of *or* two sausages; **ein ~ bilden** to make *or* form a pair; **ein ~ mit jdm bilden** to pair off with sb; **ein ~ werden** (*liter*) to become man and wife (*form*), to be made one (*liter*); **ein ungleiches ~** an odd pair; (*Menschen auch*) an odd *or* unlikely couple.

paar *adj inv* **ein ~** a few; (*zwei oder drei auch*) a couple of; **ein ~ Male** a few times, a couple of times, once or twice; **schreiben Sie mir ein ~ Zeilen** drop me a line; **die ~ Pfennige, die es kostet ...** the few pence that it costs ...; **der Bus fährt alle ~ Minuten** there's a bus every few minutes; **wenn er alle ~ Minuten mit einer Frage kommt ...** if he comes along with a question every other minute ...; **du kriegst ein ~!** (*inf*) I'll land you one! (*inf*).

paaren [1] *vt Tiere* to mate, to pair; (*Sport*) to match ◆ **in seinen Bemerkungen sind Witz und Geist gepaart** his remarks show a combination of wit and intellect, in his remarks wit is coupled with intellect.
[2] *vr* (*Tiere*) to mate, to copulate; (*fig*) to be coupled *or* combined.

Paarhufer *pl* (*Zool*) cloven-hoofed animals *pl*, even-toed ungulates *pl* (*spec*).

paarig *adj* in pairs ◆ **~e Blätter** paired leaves.

Paar-: ~lauf *m*, **~laufen** *nt* pair-skating, pairs *pl*; **p~laufen** *vi sep irreg aux sein infin, ptp only* to pair-skate.

paarmal *adv* **ein ~** a few times; (*zwei oder dreimal auch*) a couple of times.

Paarreim *m* (*Poet*) rhyming couplet.

Paarung *f* **(a)** (*Sport, fig liter*) combination; (*Sport: Gegnerschaft*) draw, match. **(b)** (*Kopulation*) mating, copulation; (*Kreuzung*) crossing, mating.

Paarungszeit *f* mating season.

Paar-: p~weise *adv* in pairs, in twos; **~zeher** *m siehe* **~hufer**.

Pacht *f* **-, -en** lease; (*Entgelt*) rent ◆ **etw in ~ geben** to lease sth (out), to let out sth on lease; **etw in ~ nehmen** to take sth on lease, to lease sth; **etw in** *or* **zur ~ haben** to have sth on lease *or* (on) leasehold.

Pachtbrief *m* lease.

pachten *vt* to take a lease on, to lease ◆ **du hast das Sofa doch nicht für dich gepachtet** (*inf*) don't hog the sofa (*inf*), you haven't got a monopoly on the sofa (*inf*); **er tat so, als hätte er die Weisheit für sich (allein) gepachtet** (*inf*) he behaved as though he was the only clever person around.

Pächter(in *f*) *m* **-s, -** tenant, leaseholder, lessee (*form*) ◆ **er ist ~ auf einem Bauernhof** *or* **eines Bauernhofs** he's a tenant farmer.

Pacht-: ~ertrag *m* net rent; **~geld** *nt* rent; **~grundstück** *nt* leasehold property; **~gut** *nt*, **~hof** *m* smallholding.

Pachtung *f* leasing.

Pacht-: ~vertrag *m* lease; **p~weise** *adv* leasehold, on lease; **~zins** *m* rent.

Pack[1] *m* **-(e)s, -e** *or* **⸚e** (*von Zeitungen, Büchern, Wäsche*) stack, pile; (*zusammengeschnürt*) bundle, pack ◆ **zwei ~(e) Spielkarten** two packs of (playing) cards.

Pack[2] *nt* **-s,** *no pl* (*pej*) rabble *pl* (*pej*), riffraff *pl* (*pej*) ◆ **~ schlägt sich, ~ verträgt sich** (*Prov*) rabble like that are at each other's throats one minute and friends again the next.

Päckchen *nt* package, (small) parcel; (*Post*) small packet; (*Packung*) packet, pack ◆ **ein ~ Zigaretten** a packet *or* pack (*esp US*) of cigarettes; **ein ~ Spielkarten** a pack of (playing) cards; **ein ~ aufgeben** to post *or* mail a small parcel; **jeder hat sein ~ zu tragen** (*fig inf*) we all have our cross to bear.

Pack|eis *nt* pack ice.

packeln *vi* (*Aus inf*) *siehe* **paktieren (b)**.

packen [1] *vti* **(a)** *Koffer* to pack; *Paket* to make up; (*verstauen*) to stow *or* pack (away) ◆ **Sachen in ein Paket ~** to make things up into a parcel; **etw ins Paket ~** to put *or* pack sth into the parcel; **etw in Holzwolle/Watte ~** to pack sth (up) in wood shavings/to pack *or* wrap sth (up) in cotton wool; **jdn ins Bett ~** (*inf*) to tuck sb up (in bed); *siehe* **Watte**.
(b) (*fassen*) to grab (hold of), to seize, to grasp; (*Gefühle*) to grip, to seize ◆ **jdn am** *or* **beim Kragen ~** (*inf*) to grab *or* seize sb by the collar; **von der Leidenschaft gepackt** in the grip of passion; **jdn bei der Ehre ~** to appeal to sb's sense of honour; **den hat es aber ganz schön gepackt** (*inf*) he's got it bad(ly) (*inf*).
(c) (*fig: mitreißen*) to grip, to thrill, to enthrall ◆ **das Theaterstück hat mich gepackt** I was really gripped by the play.
(d) (*sl: schaffen*) to manage ◆ **hast du die Prüfung gepackt?** did you (manage to) get through the exam?
(e) (*inf: gehen*) **~ wir's!** let's go.
(f) (*inf: kapieren*) **er packt es nie** he'll never get it (*inf*).
[2] *vr* (*inf*) to clear off ◆ **packt euch (fort)!** clear off! (*inf*), beat it! (*inf*); **pack dich nach Hause!** clear off home! (*inf*).

Packen *m* **-s, -** heap, pile, stack; (*zusammengeschnürt*) package, bundle ◆ **ein ~ Arbeit** (*inf*) a pile of work.

Packer(in *f*) *m* **-s, -** packer; (*Hunt*) boarhound.

Packerei *f* **(a)** packing department. **(b)** *no pl* (*inf*) packing.

Pack-: ~esel *m* pack-ass, pack-mule; (*fig*) packhorse; **~leinen** *nt*, **~leinwand** *f* burlap, gunny, bagging; **~material** *nt* packing material; **~papier** *nt* wrapping *or* brown paper; **~pferd** *nt* packhorse; **~raum** *m siehe* **Packerei (a)**; **~sattel** *m* pack-saddle; **~tasche** *f* saddle-bag; **~tier** *nt* pack animal, beast of burden.

Packung *f* **(a)** (*Schachtel*) packet, pack; (*von Pralinen*) box ◆ **eine ~ Zigaretten** a packet *or* pack (*esp US*) of cigarettes. **(b)** (*Med*) compress, pack; (*Kosmetik*) beauty pack. **(c)** (*Tech*) gasket; (*Straßenbau*) pitching *no pl*, ballast *no pl*. **(d)** (*inf: Niederlage*) thrashing, hammering (*inf*).

Packungsbeilage *f* (*bei Medikamenten*) enclosed instructions *pl* for use.

Pack-: ~wagen *m* luggage van (*Brit*), baggage car (*US*); **~zettel** *m* packing slip, docket.

Pädagoge *m*, **Pädagogin** *f* educationalist, pedagogue (*form*).

Pädagogik *f* education, educational theory, pedagogy (*rare*).

pädagogisch *adj* educational, pedagogical (*form*) ◆ **P~e Hochschule** college of education, teacher-training college (*for primary teachers*); **eine ~e Ausbildung** a training in education, a pedagogical training; **seine ~en Fähigkeiten** his ability to teach, his teaching ability; **das ist nicht sehr ~** that's not a very educationally sound thing to do; **~ falsch** wrong from an educational point of view.

pädagogisieren* [1] *vt* (*pädagogisch ausrichten*) to bring into line with educational *or* pedagogical theory.
[2] *vi* (*inf*) (*über Pädagogik reden*) to talk education.

Paddel *nt* **-s, -** paddle.

Paddel-: ~boot *nt* canoe; **~bootfahrer** *m* canoeist.

paddeln *vi aux sein or haben* to paddle; (*als Sport*) to canoe; (*schwimmen*) to dog-paddle.

Paddler(in *f*) *m* **-s, -** canoeist.

Päderast *m* **-en, -en** pederast.

Päderastie *f* pederasty.

Pädiatrie *f* p(a)ediatrics *sing*.

pädiatrisch *adj* p(a)ediatric.

Pädophile(r) *mf decl as adj* paedophile (*Brit*), pedophile (*US*).

Pädophilie *f* paedophilia (*Brit*), pedophilia (*US*).

paff *interj* bang.

paffen [1] *vi* (*inf*) **(a)** (*heftig rauchen*) to puff away. **(b)** (*nicht inhalieren*) to puff ◆ **du paffst ja bloß!** you're just puffing at it!
[2] *vt* to puff (away) at.

Page [ˈpaːʒə] *m* **-n, -n** (*Hist*) page; (*Hotel~*) page (boy), bellboy, bellhop (*US*).

Pagen-: frisur *f*, **~kopf** *m* page-boy (hair style *or* cut).

paginieren* *vt* to paginate.

Pagode *f* **-, -n** pagoda.

pah *interj* bah, pooh, poof.

Paillette [paiˈjɛtə] *f* sequin.

Pak *f* **-, -s** *abbr of* **Panzerabwehrkanone** anti-tank gun.

Paket *nt* **-s, -e** (*Bündel*) pile, stack; (*zusammengeschnürt*) bundle, package; (*Packung*) packet; (*Post*) parcel; (*fig: von Angeboten, Gesetzesvorschlägen*) package; (*Aktien~*) dossier; (*Comput*) package.

Paket-: ~adresse *f* stick-on address label; **~annahme** *f* parcels office; **~ausgabe** *f* parcels office; **~boot** *nt* packet (boat), mailboat; **~karte** *f* dispatch form; **~post** *f* parcel post; **~schalter** *m* parcels counter.

Pakistan *nt* **-s** Pakistan.

Pakistaner(in *f*) *m* **-s, -, Pakistani** *m* **-(s), -(s)** Pakistani.

pakistanisch *adj* Pakistani.

Pakt *m* **-(e)s, -e** pact, agreement ◆ **einen ~ (ab)schließen (mit)** to make a pact *or* agreement *or* deal (*inf*) (with); **einem ~ beitreten** to enter into an agreement.

⚠: for details of spelling reform, see supplement

paktieren* *vi* **(a)** (*old: Bündnis schließen*) to make a pact *or* an agreement. **(b)** (*pej*) to make a deal (*inf*).
Paladin *m* **-s, -e** (*Hist*) paladin; (*pej*) (*Gefolgsmann*) henchman, hireling; (*Land*) satellite.
Palais [pa'lɛː] *nt* **-, -** palace.
paläo- *pref* palaeo-.
Palast *m* **-(e)s, Paläste** (*lit, fig*) palace.
palast|artig *adj* palatial.
Palästina *nt* **-s** Palestine.
Palästinenser(in *f*) **-s, -** Palestinian.
Palästinensertuch *nt* keffiyeh, kaffiyeh.
palästinensisch, palästinisch *adj* Palestinian.
Palast-: ~revolution *f* (*lit, fig*) palace revolution; **~wache** *f* palace guard.
palatal *adj* palatal.
Palatallaut *m* palatal (sound).
Palatschinke *f* **-, -n** (*Aus*) stuffed pancake.
Palaver [pa'laːvɐ] *nt* **-s, -** (*lit, fig inf*) palaver.
palavern* [pa'laːvɐn] *vi* (*lit, fig inf*) to palaver.
Paletot ['palәto] *m* **-s, -s** (*obs*) greatcoat, overcoat.
Palette *f* **(a)** (*Malerei*) palette; (*fig*) range. **(b)** (*Stapelplatte*) pallet.
paletti *adv* (*sl*) OK (*inf*).
Palisade *f* palisade.
Palisaden-: ~wand *f*, **~zaun** *m* palisade, stockade.
Palisander(holz *nt*) *m* **-s, -** jacaranda.
Palladium *nt, no pl* (*abbr* **Pd**) palladium.
Palliativ(um) *nt* (*Med*) palliative.
Palme *f* **-, -n** palm ♦ **die ~ des Sieges erringen** (*liter*) to bear off *or* carry off the palm (*liter*); **jdn auf die ~ bringen** (*inf*) to make sb see red (*inf*), to make sb's blood boil (*inf*).
Palmfett *nt* (*Palmbutter*) palm butter; (*Palmöl*) palm oil.
Palmin ® *nt* **-s,** *no pl* cooking fat (*made from coconut oil*).
Palm-: ~kätzchen *nt* pussy willow, catkin; **~lilie** *f* yucca; **~öl** *nt* palm oil; **~sonntag** *m* Palm Sunday; **~wedel** *m siehe* **~zweig**; **~wein** *m* palm wine; **~zweig** *m* palm leaf.
Pampa *f* **-, -s** pampas *pl*.
Pampasgras *nt* pampas grass.
Pampe *f* **-,** *no pl* paste; (*pej*) slop (*inf*), mush (*inf*).
Pampelmuse *f* **-, -n** grapefruit.
Pamphlet *nt* **-(e)s, -e** lampoon.
pampig *adj* (*inf*) **(a)** (*breiig*) gooey (*inf*); *Kartoffeln* soggy. **(b)** (*frech*) stroppy (*inf*).
Pan *m* **-s** (*Myth*) Pan.
pan- *pref* pan- ♦ **~amerikanisch** pan-American; **~arabisch** pan-Arab; **P~slawismus** pan-Slavism.
Panama *nt* **-s, -s** **(a)** Panama. **(b)** (*auch* **~hut**) Panama (hat).
Panamakanal *m* Panama Canal.
panaschieren* [1] *vi* (*Pol*) to split one's ticket.
[2] *vt* **panaschierte Blätter** variegated leaves.
panchromatisch [pankro'maːtɪʃ] *adj* panchromatic.
Panda *m* **-s, -s** panda.
Pandämonium *nt* (*Myth, fig*) pandemonium.
Pandekten *pl* (*Jur*) Pandects *pl*, Digest.
Pandemie *f* (*Med*) pandemic.
Paneel *nt* **-s, -e** (*form*) (*einzeln*) panel; (*Täfelung*) panelling, wainscoting.
paneelieren* *vt* (*form*) to panel.
Panflöte *f* panpipes *pl*, Pan's pipes *pl*.
päng *interj* bang.
Panier *nt* **-s, -e** (*obs*) banner, standard ♦ **Freiheit sei euer ~!** (*liter*) let freedom be your watchword *or* motto! (*liter*); **unter dem ~ der Freiheit kämpfen** (*liter*) to fight under the banner of freedom; **sich** (*dat*) **etw aufs ~ schreiben** (*fig*) to take *or* adopt sth as one's motto.
panieren* *vt* to bread, to coat with breadcrumbs.
Paniermehl *nt* breadcrumbs *pl*.
Panik *f* **-, -en** panic ♦ **(eine) ~ brach aus** *or* **breitete sich aus** panic broke out *or* spread, there was panic; **in ~ ausbrechen** to panic, to get into a panic; **von ~ ergriffen** panic-stricken; **nur keine ~!** don't panic!; **die ~, die ihn zu überwältigen drohte** the feeling of panic that threatened to overwhelm him.
Panik-: ~kauf *m* (*Comm*) panic buying; **~mache** *f* (*inf*) panicmongering; **~stimmung** *f* state of panic; **~verkauf** *m* (*Comm*) panic selling.
panisch *adj no pred* panic-stricken ♦ **~e Angst** panic-stricken fear, terror; **sie hat ~e Angst vor Schlangen** she's terrified of snakes, snakes scare her out of her wits; **er hatte eine ~e Angst zu ertrinken** he was terrified of drowning; **~er Schrecken** panic; **sich ~ fürchten (vor)** to be terrified *or* petrified (by); **sie rannten ~ durcheinander** they ran about in panic.
Pankreas *nt* **-, Pankreaten** (*Anat*) pancreas.
Panne *f* **-, -n** **(a)** (*Störung*) hitch (*inf*), breakdown, trouble *no indef art*; (*Reifen~*) puncture, flat (tyre), blow-out (*inf*) ♦ **ich hatte eine ~ mit dem Fahrrad, mein Fahrrad hatte eine ~** I had some trouble with my bike/I had a puncture *etc*; **ich hatte eine ~ mit dem Auto, mein Auto hatte eine ~** my car broke down/I had a puncture *etc*; **mit der neuen Maschine passieren dauernd ~n** things keep going wrong with the new machine, the new machine keeps breaking down.
(b) (*fig inf*) slip, boob (*Brit inf*), goof (*US inf*) ♦ **mit jdm/etw eine ~ erleben** to have (a bit of) trouble with sb/sth; **uns ist eine ~ passiert** we've made a slip *etc or* we've slipped up *or* boobed (*Brit inf*) *or* goofed (*US inf*); **da ist eine ~ passiert mit dem Brief** something has gone wrong with the letter.
Pannen-: ~dienst *m*, **~hilfe** *f* breakdown service; **~koffer** *m* emergency toolkit; **~kurs** *m* car maintenance course.
Pan|optikum *nt* **-s, Pan|optiken** (*von Kuriositäten*) collection of curios; (*von Wachsfiguren*) waxworks *pl*.
Panorama *nt* **-s, Panoramen** panorama.
Panorama-: ~aufnahme *f* panorama, panoramic view; **~bus** *m* coach with panoramic windows, panorama coach; **~gemälde** *nt* panoramic painting; **~spiegel** *m* (*Aut*) panoramic mirror.
panschen [1] *vt* to adulterate; (*verdünnen*) to water down, to dilute.
[2] *vi* (*inf*) to splash (about).
Panscher *m* **-s, -** (*inf*) **(a)** (*pej*) adulterator. **(b) du bist vielleicht ein ~!** you're a messy thing!
Panscherei *f siehe vb* **(a)** adulteration; watering down, dilution. **(b)** splashing (about) ♦ **was für eine ~ du gemacht hast!** what a flood *or* mess you've made!
Pansen *m* **-s, -** (*Zool*) rumen; (*N Ger inf*) belly (*inf*).
Pantalons [pãta'lõːs] *pl* (*Hist*) pantaloons *pl*.
Pantheismus *m* pantheism.
Pantheist *m* pantheist.
pantheistisch *adj* pantheistic.
⚠ **Panther** *m* **-s, -** panther.
Pantine *f* (*N Ger*) clog; *siehe* **kippen**.
Pantoffel *m* **-s, -n** slipper ♦ **unterm ~ stehen** (*inf*) to be henpecked; **unter den ~ kommen** *or* **geraten** (*inf*) to become a henpecked husband.
Pantoffelblume *f* slipper flower, calceolaria.
Pantöffelchen *nt* slipper.
Pantoffel-: ~held *m* (*inf*) henpecked husband; **~kino** *nt* (*inf*) telly (*Brit inf*), (goggle-)box (*Brit inf*), tube (*US inf*); **~tierchen** *nt* (*Biol*) slipper animalcule, paramecium (*spec*).
Pantolette *f* slip-on (shoe).
Pantomime[1] *f* **-, -n** mime.
Pantomime[2] *m* **-n, -n** mime.
pantomimisch *adj Darstellung* in mime ♦ **sich ~ verständlich machen** to communicate with gestures *or* in sign language.
pantschen *vti siehe* **panschen**.
Panzer *m* **-s, -** **(a)** (*Mil*) tank ♦ **die deutschen ~** the German tanks *pl or* armour *sing*.
(b) (*Hist: Rüstung*) armour *no indef art*, suit of armour.
(c) (*Panzerung*) armour plating, armour plate.
(d) (*von Schildkröte, Insekt*) shell; (*dicke Haut*) armour.
(e) (*fig*) shield ♦ **sich mit einem ~ (gegen etw) umgeben** to harden oneself (against sth); **sich mit einem ~ aus etw umgeben** to put up *or* erect a defensive barrier of sth; **ein ~ der Gleichgültigkeit** a wall of indifference.
Panzer-: ~abwehr *f* anti-tank defence; (*Truppe*) anti-tank unit; **~abwehrkanone** *f* anti-tank gun; **~besatzung** *f* tank crew; **p~brechend** *adj* armour-piercing; **~division** *f* armoured division; **~falle** *f* tank trap; **~faust** *f* bazooka; **~glas** *nt* bulletproof glass; **~graben** *m* anti-tank ditch; **~granate** *f* armour-piercing shell; **~grenadier** *m* armoured infantryman; **~hemd** *nt* coat of mail; **~kampfwagen** *m* armoured vehicle; **~kette** *f* tank-track; **~kreuzer** *m* (*Naut*) (armoured) cruiser.
panzern [1] *vt* to armour-plate ♦ **gepanzerte Fahrzeuge** armoured vehicles.
[2] *vr* (*lit*) to put on one's armour; (*fig*) to arm oneself.
Panzer-: ~platte *f* armour plating *no pl*, armour plate; **~schrank** *m* safe; **~spähwagen** *m* armoured scout car; **~sperre** *f* anti-tank obstacle, tank trap; **~truppe** *f* tanks *pl*, tank division; **~turm** *m* tank turret.
Panzerung *f* armour plating; (*fig*) shield.
Panzer-: ~wagen *m* armoured car; **~weste** *f* bulletproof vest.
Papa[1] *m* **-s, -s** (*inf*) daddy (*inf*), pa (*US inf*), pop(s) (*US inf*).
Papa[2] *m* **-s, -s** papa.
Papagallo *m* **-s, Papagalli** (*pej*) (Latin) wolf *or* romeo.
Papagei *m* **-s, -en** parrot ♦ **er plappert alles wie ein ~ nach** he repeats everything parrot fashion, he parrots everything he/she *etc* says.
Papageienkrankheit *f* (*Med*) parrot fever, psittacosis.
Paparazzo *m* **-s, Paparazzi** (*inf*) paparazzo.
Papaya *f* **-, -s** papaya.
Paper ['peɪpә] *nt* **-s, -** paper.
Paperback ['peɪpәbæk] *nt* paperback.
Papeterie [papɛtә'riː] *f* (*Sw*) stationer's.
Papi *m* **-s, -s** (*inf*) daddy (*inf*).
Papier *nt* **-s, -e** **(a)** *no pl* (*Material*) paper ♦ **ein Blatt ~** a sheet *or* piece of paper; **das existiert nur auf dem ~** it only exists on paper; **das steht nur auf dem ~** that's only on paper, that's only in theory; **seine Gedanken zu ~ bringen** to set *or* put one's thoughts down on paper *or* in writing, to commit one's thoughts to paper; **~ ist geduldig** (*Prov*) you can say what you like on paper, you can write what you like.
(b) (*politisches Dokument, Schriftstück*) paper.
(c) ~e *pl* (identity) papers *pl*; (*Urkunden*) documents *pl* ♦ **er hatte keine ~e bei sich** he had no *or* he was carrying no means of identification on him; **seine ~e bekommen** (*entlassen werden*) to get one's cards.
(d) (*Fin, Wert~*) security.
Papier-: ~deutsch *nt* officialese, gobbledygook (*inf*); **~einzug** *m* paper feed.
papier(e)n *adj* **(a)** (*lit form*) paper. **(b)** (*fig*) *Stil, Sprache* prosy, bookish.

Papier-: ~fabrik *f* paper mill; **~fetzen** *m* scrap *or* (little) bit of paper; **~format** *nt* paper size; **~geld** *nt* paper money; **~korb** *m* (waste)paper basket *or* bin; **~kram** *m* (*inf*) bumf (*inf*); **~krieg** *m* (*inf*) **vor lauter ~krieg kommen wir nicht zur Forschung** there's so much paperwork we can't get on with our research; **erst nach einem langen ~krieg** after going through a lot of red tape; **einen ~krieg (mit jdm) führen** to go through a lot of red tape (with sb); ⚠**~maché** [papiema'ʃeː] *nt* **-s, -s** *siehe* **Pappmaché**; **~manschette** *f* paper frill; (*am Ärmel*) false cuff; **~mühle** *f* paper mill; **~schere** *f* paper scissors *pl*; **~schlange** *f* streamer; **~schnitzel** *m or nt* scrap of paper; (*Konfetti*) confetti; **~serviette** *f* paper serviette *or* napkin; **~taschentuch** *nt* paper hanky *or* handkerchief, tissue; **~tiger** *m* (*fig*) paper tiger; ⚠**p~verarbeitend** *adj attr* paper-processing; **~verschwendung** *f* waste of paper; **~vorschub** *m* paper feed; **~währung** *f* paper currency; **~waren** *pl* stationery *no pl*; **~warengeschäft** *nt*, **~warenhandlung** *f* stationer's (shop); **~zuführung** *f* (*Comput*) sheetfeed.

Papist(in *f*) *m* (*pej*) papist (*pej*).

papistisch *adj* (*Hist*) papal; (*pej*) popish.

Papp *m* **-s,** *no pl* (*S Ger*) *siehe* **Pappe (b)**.

papp *adj* (*inf*) **ich kann nicht mehr ~ sagen** I'm full to bursting (*inf*), I'm about to go pop (*inf*).

Papp-: ~band *m* (*Einband*) pasteboard; (*Buch*) hardback; **~becher** *m* paper cup; **~deckel** *m* (thin) cardboard; **einen ~deckel unterlegen** to put a piece of cardboard underneath.

Pappe *f* **-, -n (a)** (*Pappdeckel*) cardboard; (*Dach~*) roofing felt ♦ **dieser linke Haken war nicht von ~** (*inf*) that left hook really had some weight *or* force behind it, that was no mean left hook; **X ist ein guter Sprinter, aber Y ist auch nicht von ~** (*inf*) X is good but Y is no mean sprinter either.
(b) (*S Ger inf*) (*Leim*) glue; (*Brei*) paste; (*pej*) slop (*pej inf*), mush (*pej inf*) ♦ **ich kann diese ~ von Porridge nicht essen** I can't eat this porridge muck (*pej inf*).

Papp|einband *m* pasteboard.

Pappel *f* **-, -n** poplar.

Pappel|allee *f* avenue of poplars.

päppeln *vt* (*inf*) to nourish.

pappen (*inf*) [1] *vt* to stick, to glue (*an or auf +acc* on).
[2] *vi* (*inf*) (*klebrig sein*) to be sticky; (*Schnee*) to pack ♦ **der Leim pappt gut** the glue sticks *or* holds well; **das Hemd pappt an mir** my shirt is sticking to me.

Pappen-: ~deckel *m* (*S Ger*) *siehe* **Pappdeckel**; **~heimer** *pl*: **ich kenne meine ~heimer** (*inf*) I know you lot/that lot (inside out) (*inf*); **~stiel** *m* (*fig inf*): **das ist doch ein ~stiel** (*billig*) that's chicken feed (*inf*); (*leicht*) that's child's play (*inf*); **das ist keinen ~stiel wert** that's not worth a thing *or* a penny *or* a straw; **das hab ich für einen ~stiel gekauft** I bought it for a song *or* for next to nothing.

papperlapapp *interj* (*inf*) rubbish, (stuff and) nonsense.

pappig *adj* (*inf*) sticky.

Papp-: ~kamerad *m* (*Mil sl*) silhouette target; **~karton** *m* (*Schachtel*) cardboard box; (*Material*) cardboard; ⚠**~maché** ['papmaʃeː] *nt* **-s, -s** papier-mâché; **~nase** *f* false nose; **~schachtel** *f* cardboard box; **~schnee** *m* wet *or* sticky snow; **~teller** *m* paper plate.

Paprika *m* **-s, -(s)** (*no pl*: *Gewürz*) paprika; (*~schote*) pepper.

Paprikaschote *f* pepper; (*rote ~ auch*) pimento (*US*) ♦ **gefüllte ~n** stuffed peppers.

Paps *m* **-,** *no pl* (*inf*) dad (*inf*), daddy (*inf*), pops (*US inf*).

Papst *m* **-(e)s, ¨-e** pope; (*fig*) high priest.

päpstlich *adj* papal; (*fig pej*) pontifical ♦ **~er als der Papst sein** to be more Catholic than the Pope, to be more royal than the king.

Papst-: ~tum *nt, no pl* papacy; **~wahl** *f* papal elections *pl*; **~würde** *f* papal office.

Papua *m* **-(s), -(s)** Papuan.

Papua-Neuguinea [-gi'neːa] *nt* Papua New Guinea.

papuanisch *adj* Papuan.

Papyrus *m* **-, Papyri** papyrus.

Papyrusrolle *f* papyrus (scroll).

Parabel *f* **-, -n (a)** (*Liter*) parable. **(b)** (*Math*) parabola, parabolic curve.

parabolisch *adj* **(a)** (*Liter*) parabolic ♦ **eine ~e Erzählung** a parable. **(b)** (*Math*) parabolic.

Parabol-: ~antenne *f* satellite dish, parabolic receiving dish; **~spiegel** *m* parabolic reflector *or* mirror.

Parade *f* **(a)** (*Mil*) parade, review ♦ **die ~ abnehmen** to take the salute.
(b) (*Sport: Fechten, Boxen*) parry; (*Ballspiele*) save; (*Reiten*) check ♦ **jdm in die ~ fahren** (*fig*) to cut sb off short.

Parade-: ~anzug *m* (*Mil*) dress uniform; (*inf: gute Kleidung*) best bib and tucker (*inf*), Sunday best (*inf*); **~beispiel** *nt* prime example; **~bett** *nt* fourposter (bed).

Paradeiser *m* **-s, -** (*Aus*) tomato.

Parade-: ~kissen *nt* scatter cushion; **~marsch** *m* **(a)** parade step; (*Stechschritt*) goose-step; **im ~marsch marschieren** to march in parade step/to goose-step; **(b)** (*Marschmusik*) (military) march; **~pferd** *nt* show horse; (*fig*) showpiece; **~platz** *m* parade ground; **~schritt** *m siehe* **~marsch (a)**; **~stück** *nt* (*fig*) showpiece; (*Gegenstand auch*) pièce de résistance; **~uniform** *f* dress uniform.

paradieren* *vi* to parade ♦ **mit etw ~** (*fig*) to show off *or* flaunt sth.

Paradies *nt* **-es, -e (a)** (*lit, fig*) paradise ♦ **die Vertreibung aus dem ~** the expulsion from Paradise; **hier ist es so schön wie im ~** it's like paradise here, this is paradise; **da haben sie wie im ~ gelebt** they were living in paradise; **ein ~ für Kinder** a children's paradise, a paradise for children; **das ~ auf Erden** heaven on earth.
(b) (*Archit*) galilee.

paradiesisch *adj* (*fig*) heavenly, paradisiac(al) (*liter*) ♦ **hier ist es ~ schön** it's (like) paradise here, this is paradise; **sich ~ wohl fühlen** to be blissfully happy, to be in paradise; **~ leere Strände** blissfully empty beaches.

Paradiesvogel *m* bird of paradise.

Paradigma *nt* **-s, Paradigmen** paradigm.

paradigmatisch *adj* paradigmatic.

paradox *adj* paradoxical.

Paradox *nt* **-es, -e, Paradoxon** *nt* **-s, Paradoxa** paradox.

paradoxerweise *adv* paradoxically.

Paradoxie *f* paradox, paradoxicalness.

Paraffin *nt* **-s, -e** (*Chem*) (*~öl*) (liquid) paraffin; (*~wachs*) paraffin wax.

⚠**Paragraph** *m* (*Jur*) section; (*Abschnitt*) paragraph.

⚠**Paragraphen-: ~reiter** *m* (*inf*) pedant, stickler for the rules; **p~weise** *adv* in paragraphs; **~werk** *nt* rules and regulations *pl*; **~zeichen** *nt* paragraph (marker).

Parallaxe *f* **-, -n** (*Math*) parallax.

parallel *adj* parallel ♦ **~ laufen** to run parallel; **der Weg (ver)läuft ~ zum Fluß** the path runs *or* is parallel to the river; **die Entwicklung dort verläuft ~ zu der in der BRD** the development there is parallel to *or* parallels that of (West) Germany; **~ schalten** (*Elec*) to connect in parallel.

Paralleldrucker *m* (*Comput*) parallel printer.

Parallele *f* **-, -n** (*lit*) parallel (line); (*fig*) parallel ♦ **eine ~ zu etw ziehen** (*lit*) to draw a line parallel to sth; (*fig*) to draw a parallel to sth.

Parallel-: ~erscheinung *f* parallel; **~fall** *m* parallel (case).

Parallelismus *m* parallelism.

Parallelität *f* parallelism.

Parallel-: ~klasse *f* parallel class; **~kreis** *m* parallel (of latitude).

Parallelogramm *nt* **-s, -e** parallelogram.

Parallel-: ~schaltung *f* parallel connection; **~schwung** *m* (*Ski*) parallel turn.

Paralyse *f* **-, -n** (*Med, fig*) paralysis.

paralysieren* *vt* (*Med, fig*) to paralyse.

Paralytiker(in *f*) *m* **-s, -** (*Med*) paralytic.

paralytisch *adj* paralytic.

Parameter *m* **-s, -** parameter.

Paramedizin *f* alternative medicine.

paramilitärisch *adj* paramilitary.

Paranoia [para'nɔya] *f* **-,** *no pl* paranoia.

paranoid [parano'iːt] *adj* paranoid.

Paranoiker(in *f*) [para'noːikɐ, -ərɪn] *m* **-s, -** paranoiac.

paranoisch [para'noːɪʃ] *adj* paranoiac.

⚠**Paranuß** *f* (*Bot*) Brazil nut.

Paraphe *f* **-, -n** (*form*) (*Namenszug*) signature; (*Namenszeichen*) initials *pl*; (*Stempel*) signature stamp.

paraphieren* *vt* (*Pol*) to initial.

Paraphrase *f* paraphrase; (*Mus*) variation.

paraphrasieren* *vt* to paraphrase; (*Mus*) to write variations on.

Parapsychologie *f* parapsychology.

Parasit *m* **-en, -en** (*Biol, fig*) parasite.

parasitär, parasitisch *adj* (*Biol, fig*) parasitic(al) ♦ **~ leben** to live parasitically.

Parasol *m or nt* **-s, -s** *or* **-e** (*old*) parasol, sunshade.

parat *adj Antwort, Beispiel etc* ready, prepared; *Werkzeug etc* handy, ready ♦ **halte dich ~** be ready; **er hatte immer eine Ausrede ~** he always had an excuse ready *or* on tap (*inf*), he was always ready with an excuse; **seine stets ~e Ausrede** his ever-ready excuse.

parataktisch *adj* (*Ling*) coordinated; (*ohne Konjunktion*) paratactic(al).

Parataxe *f* **-, -n** (*Ling*) coordination; (*ohne Konjunktion*) parataxis.

Pärchen *nt* (courting) couple ♦ **ihr seid mir so ein ~!** (*iro*) you're a fine pair!

pärchenweise *adv* in pairs.

Parcours [par'kuːɐ] *m* **-, -** show-jumping course; (*Sportart*) show-jumping ♦ **einen ~ reiten** to jump a course; **sie reitet nicht gern ~** she doesn't like show-jumping.

pardauz *interj* (*old*) whoops.

Pardon [par'dõː] *m or nt* **-s,** *no pl* **(a)** pardon ♦ **jdn um ~ bitten** to ask sb's pardon; **jdm kein(en) ~ geben** (*old*) to show sb no mercy, to give sb no quarter.
(b) (*inf*) **kein ~ kennen** to be ruthless; **wenn er sich** (*dat*) **was in den Kopf gesetzt hat, gibt's kein ~** *or* **kennt er kein ~** once he's set on something he's merciless *or* ruthless; **das Zeug räumst du auf, da gibt's kein ~** you'll clear that stuff up and that's that! (*inf*).

pardon [par'dõː] *interj* (*Verzeihung*) sorry; (*nicht verstanden*) sorry, beg pardon, pardon me (*US*) ♦ **o ~!** sorry!, I'm so sorry!; (*empört*) excuse me!

Parenthese *f* **-, -n** parenthesis ♦ **in ~** in parenthesis *or* parentheses; **etw in ~ setzen** to put sth in parentheses.

parenthetisch *adj* parenthetic(al).

par excellence [parɛksɛ'lãːs] *adv* par excellence.

Parforce- [par'fɔrs]: **~jagd** *f* hunt, course; (*Jagdart*) coursing; **wir machen eine ~jagd** we're going hunting *or* going on a hunt; **~ritt** *m* forced ride.

Parfum [par'fœ̃ː] *nt* **-s, -s, Parfüm** *nt* **-s, -e** *or* **-s** perfume, scent.

Parfümerie *f* perfumery.

Parfümfläschchen *nt* scent *or* perfume bottle.

parfümieren* [1] *vt* to scent, to perfume.

⚠: for details of spelling reform, see supplement

[2] *vr* to put perfume *or* scent on ◆ **du parfümierst dich zu stark** you put too much scent *or* perfume on.
Parfümzerstäuber *m* scent spray, perfume *or* scent atomizer.
pari *adv (Fin)* par ◆ **al ~** at par (value), at nominal value; **über ~** above par, at a premium; **unter ~** below par, at a discount; **die Chancen stehen ~ (~)** the odds are even *or* fifty-fifty.
Paria *m* **-s, -s** *(lit, fig)* pariah.
parieren* [1] *vt* **(a)** *(Fechten, fig)* to parry; *(Ftbl)* to deflect. **(b)** *(Reiten)* to rein in.
[2] *vi* to obey, to do what one is told ◆ **aufs Wort ~** to jump to it.
Parikurs *m (Fin)* par of exchange.
Paris *nt* **-** Paris.
Pariser[1] *m* **-s, - (a)** Parisian. **(b)** *(inf: Kondom)* French letter *(inf)*.
Pariser[2] *adj attr* Parisian, Paris.
Pariserin *f* Parisienne.
Parität *f (Gleichstellung)* parity, equality; *(von Währung)* parity, par of exchange; *(Comput)* parity.
paritätisch *adj* equal ◆ **~e Mitbestimmung** equal representation.
Park *m* **-s, -s (a)** park; *(von Schloß)* grounds *pl.* **(b)** *(rare) siehe* **Fuhrpark.**
Parka *m* **-(s), -s** *or f* **-, -s** parka.
Park-and-ride System ['pa:kənd'raɪd-] *nt* park and ride system.
Park-: ~anlage *f* park; **p~artig** *adj* park-like; **~bahn** *f (Space)* parking orbit; **~bank** *f* park bench; **~bucht** *f* parking bay; **~deck** *nt* parking level.
parken *vti (auch Comput)* to park ◆ **ein ~des Auto** a parked car; **„P~ verboten!"** "No Parking"; **sein Auto parkte ...** his car was parked ...
Parkett *nt* **-s, -e (a)** *(Fußboden)* parquet (flooring) ◆ **ein Zimmer mit ~ auslegen** to lay parquet (flooring) in a room; **sich auf jedem ~ bewegen können** *(fig)* to be able to move in any society; **auf dem internationalen ~** in international circles.
(b) *(Tanzfläche)* (dance) floor ◆ **eine tolle Nummer aufs ~ legen** *(inf)* to put on a great show; *siehe* **Sohle.**
(c) *(Theat)* stalls *pl*, parquet *(US)* ◆ **das ~ klatschte Beifall** there was applause from the stalls; **wir sitzen ~** *(inf)* we sit in the stalls.
Parkett(fuß)boden *m* parquet floor.
parkettieren* *vt* to lay with parquet, to lay *or* put down parquet in, to parquet.
Parkett-: ~platz, ~sitz *m (Theat)* seat in the stalls *or* parquet *(US)*.
Park-: ~gebühr *f* parking fee; **~haus** *nt* multi-storey car park.
parkieren* *vti (Sw) siehe* **parken.**
Parkingmeter *m (Sw)* parking meter.
Parkinsonsche Krankheit *f*, **Parkinsonismus** *m* Parkinson's disease.
Park-: ~kralle *f* wheel clamp; **~landschaft** *f* parkland; **~licht** *nt* parking light; **~lücke** *f* parking space; **~möglichkeit** *f* parking facility; **~platz** *m* car park, parking lot *(esp US)*; *(für Einzelwagen)* (parking) space, place to park; **bewachter/unbewachter ~platz** car park with/without an attendant; **~platznot** *f* dearth of parking spaces; **~raum** *m* parking space; **~raumnot** *f* shortage of parking space; **~scheibe** *f* parking disk; **~schein** *m* carpark ticket; **~studium** *nt (Univ)* interim course of study *(while waiting for a place)*; **~sünder(in** *f***)** *m* parking offender; **~uhr** *f* parking meter; **~verbot** *nt* parking ban; **hier ist ~verbot** there's no parking *or* you're not allowed to park here; **~verbotsschild** *nt* no-parking sign; **~wächter** *m (Aut)* car-park attendant; *(von Anlagen)* park keeper *or* attendant; **~zeit** *f* parking time.
Parlament *nt* parliament ◆ **das ~ auflösen** to dissolve parliament; **jdn ins ~ wählen** to elect sb to parliament.
Parlamentär *m* peace envoy, negotiator.
Parlamentärflagge *f* flag of truce.
Parlamentarier(in *f***)** [-iɐ, -iərɪn] *m* **-s, -** parliamentarian.
parlamentarisch *adj* parliamentary ◆ **~ regieren** to govern by a parliament; **~er Staatssekretär im Verteidigungsministerium** *non-Cabinet minister with special responsibility for defence*; **der P~e Rat** the Parliamentary Council; **~e Demokratie** parliamentary democracy.
Parlamentarismus *m* parliamentarianism.
Parlaments-: ⚠~ausschuß *m* parliamentary committee; **⚠~beschluß** *m* vote *or* decision of parliament; **~ferien** *pl* recess; **in die ~ferien gehen** to go into recess; **~gebäude** *nt* parliamentary building(s); *(in London)* Houses of Parliament *pl*; *(in Washington)* Capitol; **~mitglied** *nt* member of parliament; *(in GB)* Member of Parliament, MP; *(in USA)* Congressman; **~sitzung** *f* sitting (of parliament); **~wahl** *f usu pl* parliamentary election(s).
parlieren* *vi* to talk away ◆ **er ist so schüchtern, ich hätte nie geglaubt, daß er so ~ könnte** he's so shy I'd never have believed that he could talk so fluently.
Parmaschinken *m* Parma ham.
Parmesan(käse) *m* **-s,** *no pl* Parmesan (cheese).
⚠ **Parnaß** *m* **-sses** *(liter)* (Mount) Parnassus.
Parodie *f* parody, take-off *(auf +acc* on, *zu* of) ◆ **er ist nur noch eine ~ seiner selbst** he is now only a parody of his former self; **eine ~ von jdm geben** to do a parody *or* take-off of sb, to take sb off.
parodieren* *vt* **(a)** *(Parodie schreiben auf)* to parody. **(b)** *(karikieren)* to take off, to parody.
Parodist *m* parodist; *(von Persönlichkeiten)* impersonator.
parodistisch *adj* parodistic *(liter)* ◆ **~e Sendung** parody, take-off; **er hat ~e Fähigkeiten** he's good at taking people off, he's a good impersonator; **~e Literatur** literary parodies.
Parodontose *f* **-, -n** periodontosis *(spec)*, shrinking gums.
Parole *f* **-, -n (a)** *(Mil)* password. **(b)** *(fig: Wahlspruch)* motto, watchword; *(Pol)* slogan.
Paroli *nt*: **jdm ~ bieten** *(geh)* to defy sb.
Parsing *nt* **-s** *(Comput)* parsing.
Part *m* **-s, -e (a)** *(Anteil)* share. **(b)** *(Theat, Mus)* part.
Partei *f* **(a)** *(Pol)* party ◆ **bei** *or* **in der ~** in the party; **die ~ wechseln** to change parties; **als Bundespräsident steht er über den ~en** as Federal President he takes no part in party politics.
(b) *(Jur)* party ◆ **die streitenden ~en** the disputing parties; **die vertragsschließenden ~en** the contracting parties; **meine ~** my client.
(c) *(fig)* **~ sein** to be bias(s)ed; **jds ~** *(acc) or* **für jdn ~ ergreifen** *or* **nehmen** to take sb's side *or* part, to side with sb; **gegen jdn ~ ergreifen** *or* **nehmen** to side *or* to take sides against sb; **es mit keiner ~ halten, es mit keiner von beiden ~en halten** to be on neither side, to be neutral; **es mit beiden ~en halten** to run with the hare and hunt with the hounds *(prov)*; **ein Richter sollte über den ~en stehen** a judge should be impartial.
(d) *(im Mietshaus)* tenant, party *(form)*.
Partei-: ~abzeichen *nt* party badge; **~anhänger** *m* party supporter; **~apparat** *m* party machinery *or* apparatus; **⚠~ausschlußverfahren** *nt* expulsion proceedings *pl*; **~bonze** *m (pej)* party bigwig *or* boss; **~buch** *nt* party membership book; **das richtige ~buch haben** to belong to the right party; **~chef** *m* party leader *or* boss; **~chinesisch** *nt (pej)* party jargon.
Parteienfinanzierung *f* party financing.
Partei-: ~frau *f (Pol)* female politician; **~freund** *m* fellow party member; **~führer** *m* party leader; **~führung** *f* leadership of a party; *(Vorstand)* party leaders *pl or* executive; **~gänger** *m* **-s, -** party supporter *or* follower; **~genosse** *m* party member; **p~intern** *adj* internal party; **etw p~intern lösen** to solve sth within the party.
parteiisch *adj* bias(s)ed, partial.
⚠ **Parteikongreß** *m* convention, party congress.
parteilich *adj* **(a)** *(rare: parteiisch)* bias(s)ed. **(b)** *(eine Partei betreffend)* party ◆ **Maßnahmen, die nicht ~ gebunden sind** measures which are independent of party politics. **(c)** *(DDR: linientreu)* in accordance with party thought.
Parteilichkeit *f* bias, partiality.
Parteilinie *f* party line ◆ **auf die ~ einschwenken** to toe the party line.
parteilos *adj Abgeordneter, Kandidat* independent, non-party ◆ **der Journalist war ~** the journalist wasn't attached to *or* aligned with any party.
Parteilose(r) *mf decl as adj* independent.
Parteilosigkeit *f* independence ◆ **~ ist oft ein Vorteil** it's often an advantage not to belong to any party.
Partei-: ~mitglied *nt* party member; **~nahme** *f* **-, -n** partisanship; **~organ** *nt* party organ; **~politik** *f* party politics *pl*; **p~politisch** *adj* party political; **~präsidium** *nt* party executive committee; **~programm** *nt* (party) manifesto *or* programme; **~spende** *f* party donation; **~spendenaffäre** *f* party donations scandal; **~tag** *m* party conference *or* convention.
Parteiungen *pl (old)* factions *pl.*
Partei-: ~versammlung *f* party meeting; **~volk** *nt* grass roots *pl* of the party; **~vorsitzende(r)** *mf* party leader; **~vorstand** *m* party executive; **~wesen** *nt* party system; **~zugehörigkeit** *f* party membership; **was hat er für eine ~zugehörigkeit?** what party does he belong to?
parterre [par'tɛr] *adv* on the ground *(Brit) or* first *(US)* floor.
Parterre [par'tɛr] *nt* **-s, -s (a)** *(von Gebäude)* ground floor *(Brit)*, first floor *(US)* ◆ **im ~ wohnen** to live on the ground floor. **(b)** *(old Theat)* rear stalls, pit *(Brit)*, parterre *(US)*.
Parterrewohnung *f* ground-floor flat *(Brit)*, first-floor apartment *(US)*.
⚠ **partial-** [par'tsia:l] *in cpds* partial.
Partie *f* **(a)** *(Teil, Ausschnitt)* part; *(eines Buchs auch)* section.
(b) *(Theat)* part, role; *(Mus)* part.
(c) *(Sport)* game; *(Fechten)* round ◆ **eine ~ Schach spielen** to play *or* have a game of chess; **die ~ verloren geben** *(lit, fig)* to give the game up as lost.
(d) *(old: Land~)* outing, trip ◆ **eine ~ machen** to go on *or* for an outing *or* a trip.
(e) *(Comm)* lot, batch.
(f) *(inf)* catch ◆ **eine gute ~ (für jdn) sein** to be a good catch (for sb); **eine gute ~ (mit jdm) machen** to marry (into) money.
(g) mit von der ~ sein to join in, to be in on it; **da bin ich mit von der ~** count me in, I'm with you.
(h) *(Aus: Arbeitergruppe)* gang.
⚠ **partiell** [par'tsiɛl] *adj* partial ◆ **diese Lösung ist ~ richtig** this solution is partly *or* partially right.
partienweise [par'ti:ən-] *adv (Comm)* in lots.
Partikel *f* **-, -n** *(Gram, Phys)* particle.
Partikelschleuder *f (Phys)* particle accelerator.
Partikularismus *m* particularism.
Partikularist(in *f***)** *m* particularist.
partikularistisch *adj* particularistic.
Partisan(in *f***)** *m* **-s** *or* **-en, -en** partisan.
Partisanen-: ~kampf *m* guerrilla warfare; *(Kampfhandlung)* guerrilla battle; **~krieg** *m* partisan war; *(Art des Krieges)* guerrilla warfare.
Partita *f* **-, Partiten** *(Mus)* partita.
partitiv *adj (Gram)* partitive.
Partitur *f (Mus)* score.
Partizip *nt* **-s, -ien** [-iən] *(Gram)* participle ◆ **~ Präsens/Perfekt** present/past participle.

Partizipation *f* participation (*an +dat* in).
Partizipationsgeschäft *nt* (*Comm*) transaction conducted by several parties.
Partizipial-: ~konstruktion *f* participial construction; **~satz** *m* participial clause.
partizipieren* *vi* to participate (*an +dat* in).
Partner(in *f*) *m* **-s, -** partner; (*Film*) co-star ◆ **als jds ~ spielen** (*in Film*) to play opposite sb; (*Sport*) to be partnered by sb, to be sb's partner; *siehe* **Gesprächspartner.**
Partnerschaft *f* partnership; (*Städte~*) twinning.
partnerschaftlich *adj* **~es Verhältnis** (relationship based on) partnership; **in unserer Ehe haben wir ein ~es Verhältnis** our marriage is a partnership; **~e Zusammenarbeit** working together as partners; **in gutem ~em Einvernehmen** in a spirit of partnership; **das haben wir ~ gelöst** we solved it together *or* jointly.
Partner-: ~staat *m* partner (country); **~stadt** *f* twin town; **~tausch** *m* **(a)** (*Tanz, Tennis*) change of partners; **(b)** (*sexuell*) partner-swopping; **~wahl** *f* choice of partner; **jetzt ist ~wahl** (*beim Tanz*) take *or* choose your partners, please!; **~wechsel** *m siehe* **~tausch (a).**
partout [par'tu:] *adv* (*dated*) **er will ~ ins Kino gehen** he insists on going to the cinema; **sie will ~ nicht nach Hause gehen** she just doesn't want to go home.
Party ['pa:ɐti] *f* **-, -s** *or* **Parties** party ◆ **eine ~ geben** *or* **veranstalten** to give *or* have a party; **bei** *or* **auf einer ~** at a party; **auf eine** *or* **zu einer ~ gehen** to go to a party.
Party-: ~löwe *m* (*iro*) socialite; **~service** *m* party catering service.
Parvenü [parve'ny:, -və'ny:] *m* **-s, -s** (*dated*) parvenu, upstart.
Parze *f* **-, -n** (*Myth*) Parca ◆ **die ~n** the Fates.
Parzelle *f* plot, lot, parcel of land.
parzellieren* *vt* to parcel out.
Pasch *m* **-(e)s, -e** *or* **¨e** (*beim Würfelspiel*) doublets *pl*; *siehe* **Viererpasch.**
Pascha *m* **-s, -s** pasha ◆ **wie ein ~** like Lord Muck (*inf*).
Paspel *f* **-, -n** piping *no pl.*
paspelieren*, paspeln *vt* to pipe.
⚠ **Paß** *m* **Passes, Pässe (a)** passport. **(b)** (*im Gebirge etc*) pass. **(c)** (*Ballspiele*) pass. **(d)** (*Reitsport*) *siehe* **Paßgang.**
passabel *adj* passable, reasonable; *Aussehen auch* presentable ◆ **mir geht's ganz ~** I'm OK (*inf*), I'm all right.
Passage [pa'sa:ʒə] *f* **-, -n** (*alle Bedeutungen*) passage; (*Ladenstraße*) arcade.
Passagier [pasa'ʒi:ɐ] *m* passenger ◆ **ein blinder ~** a stowaway.
Passagier-: ~dampfer *m* passenger steamer; **~flugzeug** *nt* passenger aircraft, air-liner; **~liste** *f* passenger list.
Passah ['pasa] **-s,** *no pl,* **Passahfest** *nt* (Feast of the) Passover.
⚠ **Paß|amt** *nt* passport office.
Passant(in *f*) *m* passer-by.
Passat(wind) *m* **-s, -e, Passatströmung** *f* trade wind.
⚠ **Paßbild** *nt* passport photo(graph).
⚠ **passé** [pa'se:] *adj pred* passé ◆ **diese Mode ist längst ~** this fashion went out long ago; **die Sache ist längst ~** that's all ancient history (*inf*), that's all in the past.
Passe *f* **-, -n** yoke.
passen[1] [1] *vi* **(a)** (*die richtige Größe, Form haben*) to fit ◆ **die Schuhe ~ (mir) gut** the shoes fit (me) well *or* are a good fit (for me); **dieser Schlüssel paßt nicht (ins Schloß)** this key doesn't *or* won't fit (the lock); **der Deckel paßt nicht** the lid doesn't *or* won't fit (on); **wie angegossen ~** to fit like a glove.
(b) (*harmonieren*) **zu etw ~** to go with sth; **zu etw im Ton ~** to match sth; **zu jdm ~** (*Mensch*) to be suited to sb, to suit sb; **zueinander ~** to go together; (*Menschen auch*) to be suited (to each other), to suit each other, to be well matched; **sie paßt gut zu ihm** she suits him well, she's well suited to him, she's just right for him; **das paßt zu ihm, so etwas zu sagen** that's just like him to say that; **es paßt nicht zu dir, Bier zu trinken** it doesn't look right for you to drink beer, you don't look right drinking beer; **diese Einstellung paßt gut zu ihm** that attitude is typical of him *or* is just like him; **so ein formeller Ausdruck paßt nicht in diesen Satz** such a formal expression is out of place *or* is all wrong in this sentence; **das Rot paßt da nicht** the red is all wrong there; **das Bild paßt besser in das andere Zimmer** the picture would look *or* go better in the other room; **er paßt nicht in diese Welt/in dieses Team** he doesn't fit *or* is out of place in this world/in this team.
(c) (*genehm sein*) to suit, to be suitable *or* convenient ◆ **er paßt mir einfach nicht** I just don't like him; **Sonntag paßt uns nicht** Sunday is no good for us; **das paßt mir gar nicht** (*kommt ungelegen*) that isn't at all convenient, that doesn't suit me at all; (*gefällt mir nicht*) I don't like that at all, I don't think much of that; **das paßt mir gar nicht, daß du schon gehst** I don't want you to go now; **wenn's dem Chef paßt ...** if it suits the boss ..., if the boss gets the idea into his head ...; **du kannst doch nicht einfach kommen, wann es dir paßt** you can't just come when it suits you *or* when you like; **das könnte dir so ~!** (*inf*) you'd like *or* love that, wouldn't you?; **ihre Raucherei paßt mir schon lange nicht** this smoking of hers has been annoying me for a long time.
[2] *vr* (*inf*) to be proper ◆ **ein solches Benehmen paßt sich nicht hier** you can't behave like that here.
[3] *vt* to fix.
passen[2] *vi* (*Cards*) to pass ◆ **(ich) passe!** (I) pass!; **bei dieser Frage muß ich ~** (*fig*) I'll have to pass on this question.
passen[3] *vti* (*Ftbl*) to pass.
passend *adj* **(a)** (*in Größe, Form*) **gut/schlecht ~** well-/ill-fitting; **er trägt kaum mal einen ~en Anzug** he hardly ever wears a suit that fits; **ein ~er Schlüssel (zu diesem Schloß)** a key that fits *or* to fit (this lock).
(b) (*in Farbe, Stil*) matching ◆ **etwas dazu P~es** something that goes with it *or* to go with it *or* to match; **ich muß jetzt dazu ~e Schuhe kaufen** now I must buy some matching shoes *or* some shoes to go with it *or* that go with it; **eine im Ton genau dazu ~e Tasche** a bag which matches it exactly.
(c) (*genehm*) *Zeit, Termin* convenient, suitable ◆ **er kam zu jeder ~en und unpassenden Zeit** he came at any time, no matter how inconvenient.
(d) (*angemessen*) *Bemerkung, Benehmen, Kleidung* suitable, appropriate, fitting; *Wort* right, proper ◆ **sie trägt zu jeder Gelegenheit einen ~en Hut** she always wears a hat to suit *or* match the occasion; **er findet immer das ~e Wort** he always knows the right thing to say.
(e) *Geld* exact ◆ **haben Sie es ~?** have you got it exactly?, have you got the right money?
Passepartout [paspar'tu:] *m or nt* **-s, -s** (*alle Bedeutungen*) passe-partout.
⚠ **Paß-: ~form** *f* fit; **eine gute ~form haben** to be a good fit; **~foto** *nt* passport photo(graph); **~gang** *m* amble; **im ~gang gehen** to amble; **~gänger** *m* **-s, -** ambler; **~höhe** *f* top of the pass.
passierbar *adj* passable; *Fluß, Kanal* negotiable.
passieren* [1] *vt* **(a)** *auch vi* to pass ◆ **der Zug passierte die Brücke/zwei Stationen** the train crossed *or* went *or* passed over the bridge/went through *or* passed (through) two stations; **die Grenze ~** to cross (over) *or* pass (over *or* through) the border; **die Zensur ~** to get through the censor, to be passed by the censor; **jdn ungehindert ~ lassen** to let sb pass.
(b) (*Cook*) to strain.
[2] *vi aux sein* (*sich ereignen*) to happen (*mit* to) ◆ **ihm ist etwas Schreckliches passiert** something terrible has happened to him; **ihm ist beim Bergsteigen etwas passiert** he had an accident while mountaineering; **ist ihm etwas passiert?** has anything happened to him?; **beim Sturz ist ihm erstaunlicherweise nichts passiert** miraculously he wasn't hurt *or* injured in the fall; **was ist denn passiert?** what's the matter?; **es wird dir schon nichts ~** nobody's going to hurt you, nothing is going to happen to you; **es ist ein Unfall passiert** there has been an accident; **das kann auch nur mir ~!** that could only happen to me!, just my luck!; **daß mir das ja nicht mehr** *or* **nicht noch mal passiert!** see that it doesn't happen again!; **jetzt ist es passiert! ich hatte dich gewarnt** now it's happened! I warned you; **jetzt ist es passiert! jetzt kriegen wir Ärger** that's done it *or* torn it (*inf*), now we'll be in trouble; **so was ist mir noch nie passiert!** that's never happened to me before!; (*empört*) I've never known anything like it!
Passier-: ~schein *m* pass, permit; **~schlag** *m* (*Tennis*) passing shot; **~sieb** *nt* strainer; **~stelle** *f* crossing point.
Passion *f* passion; (*religiös*) Passion ◆ **er ist Jäger aus ~** he has a passion for hunting.
passioniert *adj* enthusiastic, passionate.
Passions-: ~blume *f* passion flower; **~spiel** *nt* Passion play; **~woche** *f* Holy Week, Passion Week; **~zeit** *f* (*Karwoche*) Holy *or* Passion Week; (*Fastenzeit*) Lent.
passiv *adj* passive ◆ **sich ~ verhalten** to be passive; **~e Bestechung** corruption *no pl*, corrupt practices *pl*; **~es Mitglied** non-active member; **~es Rauchen** passive smoking; **~er Widerstand** passive resistance; **~er Wortschatz** passive vocabulary; **~e Handelsbilanz** (*Comm*) adverse trade balance; *siehe* **Wahlrecht.**
Passiv *nt* **-s, -e** (*Gram*) passive (voice) ◆ **das Verb steht im ~** the verb is in the passive (voice).
Passiva [pa'si:va], **Passiven** [pa'si:vn] *pl* (*Comm*) liabilities *pl.*
Passiv-: ~bildung *f* (*Gram*) formation of the passive; **~fähigkeit** *f* (*Gram*) ability to form the passive; **~geschäft** *nt* (*Fin*) deposit business.
Passivität [pasivi'tɛ:t] *f* passiveness, passivity; (*Chem*) passivity.
Passiv-: ~posten *m* (*Comm*) debit entry; **~rauchen** *nt* passive smoking; **~saldo** *m* (*Comm*) debit account; **~seite** *f* (*Comm*) debit side.
Passivum *nt* (*Gram*) *siehe* **Passiv.**
⚠ **Paß-: ~kontrolle** *f* passport control; **~kontrolle!** (your) passports please!; **durch die ~kontrolle gehen** to go through passport control; **~photo** *nt siehe* **~foto; ~stelle** *f* passport office; **~straße** *f* (mountain) pass.
Passung *f* (*Tech*) fit.
Passus *m* **-, -** passage.
⚠ **Paßwort** *nt* (*Comput*) password.
⚠ **Paßzwang** *m* requirement to carry a passport ◆ **es besteht kein ~** you don't have to carry a passport.
Paste *f* **-, -n, Pasta** *f* **-, Pasten** paste.
Pastell *nt* **-s, -e** pastel ◆ **in ~ arbeiten** to work in pastels; **ein schönes ~** a beautiful pastel (drawing).
Pastell-: ~farbe *f* pastel (crayon); (*Farbton*) pastel (shade *or* colour); **p~farben** *adj* pastel(-coloured); **etw p~farben streichen** to paint sth in pastel colours *or* in pastels; **~maler** *m* pastellist; **~malerei** *f* drawing in pastels, pastel drawing; **~stift** *m* pastel (crayon); **~ton** *m* pastel shade *or* tone.
Pastetchen *nt* vol-au-vent.
Pastete *f* **-, -n (a)** (*Schüssel~*) pie; (*Pastetchen*) vol-au-vent; (*ungefüllt*) vol-au-vent case. **(b)** (*Leber~ etc*) pâté.
Pasteurisation [pastøriza'tsio:n] *f siehe* **Pasteurisierung.**
pasteurisieren* [pastøri'zi:rən] *vt* to pasteurize.
Pasteurisierung [pastøri'zi:rʊŋ] *f* pasteurization.
Pastille *f* **-, -n** pastille.

Pastor *m siehe* **Pfarrer(in)**.
pastoral *adj* pastoral.
Pastorale *nt* **-s, -s** *or f* **-, -n** (*Mus*) pastorale; (*Art*) pastoral ◆ **Beethovens ~** Beethoven's Pastoral Symphony.
Pastorin *f siehe* **Pfarrer(in)**.
Pate *m* **-n, -n (a)** (*Taufzeuge*) godfather, godparent; (*Firmzeuge*) sponsor ◆ **bei einem Kind ~ stehen** to be a child's godparent/sponsor; **bei etw ~ gestanden haben** (*fig*) to be the force behind sth.
(b) (*obs: Täufling*) godchild.
Patene *f* **-, -n** (*Eccl*) paten.
Paten-: ~kind *nt* godchild; godson; goddaughter; **~onkel** *m* godfather; **~schaft** *f* godparenthood; sponsorship; **er übernimmt die ~schaft für das Kind** he's going to be the child's godfather; **er nahm seine ~schaft nicht ernst** he didn't take his responsibilities as godfather *or* godparent very seriously; **~sohn** *m* godson; **~stadt** *f* twin(ned) town.
patent *adj* ingenious, clever; *Lösung auch* neat; (*praktisch*) *Mensch, Messer auch* handy (*inf*); *Werkzeug auch* nifty (*inf*) ◆ **ein ~er Kerl** a great guy/girl (*inf*); **sie ist eine ~e Frau** she's a tremendous woman.
Patent *nt* **-(e)s, -e (a)** (*Erfindung, Urkunde*) patent; (*inf: Mechanismus*) apparatus ◆ **der Reißverschluß, so ein blödes ~** this zip, the stupid thing; **etw als** *or* **zum ~ anmelden, ein ~ auf** *or* **für etw anmelden** to apply for a patent on *or* for sth; **ein ~ auf eine Erfindung haben** to have a patent on an invention; **„zum ~ angemeldet"** patent pending. **(b)** (*Ernennungsurkunde*) commission. **(c)** (*Sw*) permit, licence.
Patent-: ~amt *nt* Patent Office; **~anmeldung** *f* application for a patent.
Patentante *f* godmother.
Patent-: ~anwalt *m* patent agent *or* attorney; **p~fähig** *adj* patentable; **~geber** *m* patentor; **~gebühr** *f* (*bei Anmeldung*) (patent) filing fee; (*jährlich*) patent annuity; **~gesetz** *nt* Patents Act.
patentierbar *adj* patentable.
patentieren* *vt* to patent ◆ **sich** (*dat*) **etw ~ lassen** to take out a patent on sth, to have sth patented.
Patent-: ~inhaber *m* patentee, patent-holder; **~lösung** *f* (*fig*) easy answer, patent remedy; **bei der Kindererziehung gibt es keine ~lösung** there's no instant recipe for success in bringing up children.
Patentochter *f* goddaughter.
Patent-: ~recht *nt* patent law; **~register** *nt* Patent Rolls *pl*; **~rezept** *nt* (*fig*) *siehe* **~lösung**; **~schrift** *f* patent specification; **~schutz** *m* patent right, protection by (letters) patent; **~urkunde** *f* letters patent *pl*; **⚠~verschluß** *m* swing stopper.
Pater *m* **-s, -** *or* **Patres** (*Eccl*) Father.
Paternoster[1] *nt* **-s, -** (*Gebet*) Lord's Prayer, paternoster.
Paternoster[2] *m* **-s, -** (*Aufzug*) paternoster.
pathetisch *adj* emotional; *Beschreibung auch* dramatic; *Rede, Stil auch* emotive; *Gehabe auch* histrionic ◆ **das war zu ~ gespielt** it was overacted.
Pathologe *m*, **Pathologin** *f* pathologist.
Pathologie *f* pathology.
pathologisch *adj* pathological.
Pathos *nt* **-,** *no pl* emotiveness, emotionalism ◆ **ein Gedicht mit ~ vortragen** to read a poem with feeling; **die Rede enthielt zuviel falsches ~** the speech contained too much false emotionalism; **mit viel ~ in der Stimme** in a voice charged with emotion; **mit viel ~ versuchte sie, ihn zu überzeugen** she made a highly emotional attempt to persuade him.
Patience [pa'siã:s] *f* **-, -n** patience *no pl* ◆ **~n legen** to play patience; **eine ~ legen** to play (a game of) patience.
Patient(in *f*) [pa'tsiɛnt(ɪn)] *m* **-en, -en** patient ◆ **ich bin ~ von** *or* **bei Dr. X** I'm Dr X's patient, I'm being treated by Dr X.
Patin *f* godmother, godparent; (*Firm~*) sponsor.
Patina *f* **-,** *no pl* (*lit, fig*) patina ◆ **~ ansetzen** (*lit*) to patinate, to become coated with a patina; (*fig*) to take on a hallowed air of tradition.
patinieren* *vt* to patinate, to coat with a patina.
Patres *pl of* **Pater**.
Patriarch *m* **-en, -en** (*lit, fig*) patriarch.
patriarchalisch *adj* (*lit, fig*) patriarchal ◆ **er regiert ~** he rules patriarchally.
Patriarchat *nt* patriarchy.
Patriot(in *f*) *m* **-en, -en** patriot.
patriotisch *adj* patriotic ◆ **~ gesinnt** patriotically-minded, patriotic.
Patriotismus *m* patriotism.
Patrize *f* **-, -n** punch.
Patriziat *nt* patriciate.
Patrizier(in *f*) [-iɐ, -iərɪn] *m* patrician.
Patriziergeschlecht *nt* patrician family.
patrizisch *adj* patrician.
Patron *m* **-s, -e (a)** (*Eccl*) patron saint. **(b)** (*old: Schirmherr*) patron. **(c)** (*inf*) **frecher ~** cheeky beggar (*inf*).
Patronage [patro'na:ʒə] *f* **-, -n** patronage.
Patronat *nt* patronage (*über +acc* of) ◆ **unter jds ~** (*dat*) **stehen** to be under sb's patronage.
Patrone *f* **-, -n** (*Film, Mil, von Füller*) cartridge; (*Tex*) point paper design.
Patronen-: ~gurt *m* ammunition belt; **~gürtel** *m* cartridge belt, bandolier; **~hülse** *f* cartridge case; **~rahmen** *m* (cartridge) clip; **~tasche** *f* ammunition pouch.
Patronin *f* **(a)** (*Eccl*) patron saint. **(b)** (*old: Schirmherrin*) patron, patroness.
Patronym *nt* **-s, -e**, **Patronymikon** *nt* **-s**, **Patronymika** patronymic.
Patrouille [pa'trʊljə] *f* **-, -n** patrol ◆ **~ gehen** to patrol.
Patrouillen- [pa'trʊljən-]: **~boot** *nt* patrol boat; **~gang** *m* patrol.
patrouillieren* [patrʊl'ji:rən] *vi* to patrol.
patsch *interj* splash, splat; (*bei Ohrfeige*) smack ◆ **wenn du so frech bist, macht's gleich ~!** if you go on being so cheeky you'll get a good smack.
Patsch *m* **-es, -e** (*inf*) smack, slap.
Patsche *f* **-, -n** (*inf*) **(a)** (*Hand*) paw (*inf*), mitt (*inf*).
(b) (*Matsch*) mud; (*Schneematsch*) slush; (*fig*) jam (*inf*), fix (*inf*), (tight) spot (*inf*) ◆ **in der ~ sitzen** *or* **stecken** to be in a jam *etc*; **jdm aus der ~ helfen, jdn aus der ~ ziehen** to get sb out of a jam *etc*; **jdn in der ~ (sitzen) lassen** to leave sb in the lurch.
(c) (*Feuer~*) beater; (*Fliegen~*) swat.
patschen *vi* **(a)** to splash ◆ **das Baby patschte mit der Hand in die Suppe** the baby went splat *or* splash with his hand in the soup; **er ist durch die Pfützen gepatscht** he splashed *or* went splashing through the puddles.
(b) (*inf*) **das Baby patschte auf den Tisch/an die Möbel** the baby smacked *or* slapped the table/the furniture (with its hands); **die Kinder ~ mit den Händen** the children clap their hands (together); **der Hund patschte über den Flur** the dog padded across the hall; **er patschte der Sekretärin auf den Hintern** he gave his secretary a pat on the bottom, he patted his secretary on the bottom.
Patsch-: ~hand *f* (*inf*), **~händchen** *nt* (*inf*) paw (*inf*), mitt (*inf*); (*von Kindern*) (little) hand; **⚠p~naß** *adj* (*inf*) soaking *or* dripping wet; **p~naß ist es draußen!** it's soaking wet outside.
patt *adj pred, adv* (*Chess, fig*) in stalemate ◆ **das Spiel endete ~** the game ended in (a) stalemate; **jetzt sind wir beide ~** now we've both reached a stalemate.
Patt *nt* **-s, -s** (*lit, fig*) stalemate ◆ **ein ~ erreichen** to reach *or* come to (a) stalemate.
Pattsituation *f* (*lit, fig*) stalemate ◆ **aus einer ~ herauskommen** to get out of a stalemate, to break the deadlock.
patzen *vi* (*inf*) to slip up, to boob (*Brit inf*), to goof (*US inf*) ◆ **der Pianist/Schauspieler hat gepatzt** the pianist/actor fluffed a passage/his lines *or* boobed *etc*.
Patzen *m* **-s, -** (*Aus*) blotch, splodge; (*Tinte auch*) blot.
Patzer *m* **-s, -** (*inf: Fehler*) slip, boob (*Brit inf*), goof (*US inf*) ◆ **mir ist ein ~ unterlaufen** I made a slip *or* boob.
patzig *adj* (*inf*) snotty (*inf*), insolent.
Paukant *m* (*Univ sl*) duellist.
Paukboden *m* (*Univ sl*) duelling floor.
Pauke *f* **-, -n (a)** (*Mus*) kettledrum, timpani *pl* ◆ **jdn mit ~n und Trompeten empfangen** to roll out the red carpet for sb, to give sb the red-carpet treatment; **mit ~n und Trompeten durchfallen** (*inf*) to fail miserably *or* dismally; **auf die ~ hauen** (*inf*) (*angeben*) to blow one's own trumpet, to brag; (*feiern*) to paint the town red.
(b) (*dated Sch: Schule*) swot-shop (*dated sl*).
pauken [1] *vi* **(a)** (*inf: Pauke spielen*) to drum. **(b)** (*von Korpsstudenten*) to fence. **(c)** (*inf: lernen*) to swot (*inf*), to cram (*inf*) ◆ **meine Mutter hat immer mit mir gepaukt** my mother always helped me with my swotting.
[2] *vt* to swot up (*inf*) ◆ **mit jdm Geschichtszahlen ~** to help sb swot up their dates.
Pauken-: ~schlag *m* drum beat; **wie ein ~schlag** (*fig*) like a thunderbolt; **die Sinfonie mit dem ~schlag** the Surprise Symphony; **~schläger** *m* drummer; **⚠~schlegel** *m* drumstick; **~spieler** *m* drummer.
Pauker *m* **-s, - (a)** (*inf: Paukenspieler*) drummer. **(b)** (*Sch inf: Lehrer*) teacher ◆ **da geht unser ~** there's sir (*inf*).
Paukerei *f* **(a)** (*inf: das Paukespielen*) drumming. **(b)** (*Sch inf*) swotting (*inf*) ◆ **ich hab diese ~ satt** I'm fed up with school.
Paukist(in *f*) *m* timpanist.
Paulusbrief *m* Paul's Epistle.
Pausbacken *pl* chubby cheeks *pl*.
pausbäckig *adj* chubby-cheeked.
pauschal *adj* **(a)** (*vorläufig geschätzt*) estimated; (*einheitlich*) flat-rate *attr only*; (*inklusiv*) inclusive ◆ **ich schätze die Baukosten ~ auf etwa eine Million DM** I'd estimate the overall building costs to be DM1 million; **die Werkstatt berechnet ~ pro Inspektion 60 DM** the garage has a flat rate of DM60 per service; **die Einkommensteuer kann ~ festgesetzt werden** income tax can be set at a flat rate; **die Gebühren werden ~ bezahlt** the charges are paid in a lump sum; **Strom berechnen wir Ihnen ~** we'll charge you a flat rate for electricity; **die Reisekosten verstehen sich ~** the travelling costs are inclusive; **alle bekommen ~ £6 pro Woche mehr** there will be an across-the-board increase of £6 a week, they'll get £6 a week more across the board.
(b) (*fig*) **so ~ kann man das nicht sagen** that's much too sweeping a statement; **ein Volk ~ verurteilen** to condemn a people wholesale *or* lock, stock and barrel; **diese Probleme hat er ganz ~ in einem kurzen Kapitel behandelt** he treated these problems all lumped together in a single short chapter.
Pauschale *f* **-, -n** (*Einheitspreis*) flat rate; (*vorläufig geschätzter Betrag*) estimated amount.
Pauschalgebühr *f* (*Einheitsgebühr*) flat rate (charge); (*vorläufig geschätzter Betrag*) estimated charge.
pauschalieren* *vt* to estimate at a flat rate *or* in a lump sum.
Pauschal-: ~preis *m* (*Einheitspreis*) flat rate; (*vorläufig geschätzter Betrag*) estimated price; (*Inklusivpreis*) inclusive *or* all-in price; **~reise** *f* package holiday/tour; **~steuer** *f* (*vorläufige Steuer*) estimated tax; (*einheitliche Steuer*) tax at a flat rate; **~summe** *f* lump sum; **~tarif** *m* flat rate; **~urteil** *nt* sweeping statement; **er neigt sehr zu ~urteilen** he tends to make sweeping

statements; **~versicherung** *f* comprehensive insurance *no pl.*

Pauschbetrag *m* flat rate.

Pause *f* **-, -n (a)** (*Unterbrechung*) break; (*Rast*) rest; (*das Innehalten*) pause; (*Theat*) interval, intermission; (*Sch*) break, recess (*US*); (*Pol*) recess ◆ **(eine) ~ machen, eine ~ einlegen** (*sich entspannen*) to take *or* have *or* make a break; (*rasten*) to rest, to have *or* take a rest; (*innehalten*) to pause, to make a pause; **nach einer langen ~ sagte er ...** after a long silence he said ...; **immer wieder entstanden ~n in der Unterhaltung** the conversation was full of gaps *or* silences; **ohne ~ arbeiten** to work non-stop *or* without stopping *or* continuously; **die große ~** break, recess (*US*); (*in einer Grundschule*) playtime.
(b) (*Mus*) rest ◆ **die ~n einhalten** to make the rests; **eine halbe/ganze ~** a minim (*Brit*) *or* half-note (*US*)/semi-breve (*Brit*) *or* whole-note (*US*) rest.
(c) (*Durchzeichnung*) tracing; (*Photokopie*) (photo)copy.

pausen *vt* to trace.

Pausen-: ~brot *nt* something to eat at break; **~füller** *m* stopgap; **~halle** *f* break *or* recess (*US*) hall; **~hof** *m* playground, schoolyard; **p~los** *adj no pred* non-stop, continuous, incessant; **er arbeitet p~los** he works non-stop; **~pfiff** *m* (*Sport*) time-out whistle; (*zur Halbzeit*) half-time whistle; **~stand** *m* half-time score; score at the interval; **~zeichen** *nt* (*Mus*) rest; (*Rad*) call sign.

pausieren* *vi* to (take *or* have a) break ◆ **der Torwart mußte wegen einer Verletzung ~** the goalkeeper had to rest up because of injury.

Pauspapier *nt* tracing paper; (*Kohlepapier*) carbon paper.

Pavian ['pa:via:n] *m* **-s, -e** baboon.

Pavillon ['pavıl'jõ:] *m* **-s, -s** pavilion.

Pay-TV ['peıte:fau] *nt* pay TV.

Pazifik *m* **-s** Pacific.

pazifisch *adj* Pacific ◆ **der P~e Ozean** the Pacific (Ocean).

Pazifismus *m* pacifism.

Pazifist(in *f*) *m* pacifist.

pazifistisch *adj* pacifist.

PC [pe:'tse:] *m* **-s, -s** *abbr of* **Personalcomputer** PC.

PDS [pe:de:'|ɛs] *f* - *abbr of* **Partei des Demokratischen Sozialismus.**

Pech *nt* **-(e)s, -e (a)** (*Stoff*) pitch ◆ **schwarz wie ~** (as) black as pitch; **ihr Haar ist schwarz wie ~** her hair is jet black; **die beiden halten zusammen wie ~ und Schwefel** (*inf*) the two are as thick as thieves *or* are inseparable.
(b) *no pl* (*inf: Mißgeschick*) bad *or* hard *or* tough (*inf*) luck ◆ **bei etw ~ haben** to be unlucky in *or* with sth, to have bad *or* tough (*inf*) *or* lousy (*inf*) luck in *or* with sth; **~ gehabt!** tough! (*inf*); **sie ist vom ~ verfolgt** bad luck follows her around; **das ist sein ~!** that's his hard *or* bad *or* tough (*inf*) luck!; **so ein ~!** just my/our *etc* luck!

Pech-: ~blende *f* (*Min*) pitchblende; **~draht** *m* waxed thread; **~fackel** *f* (pitch) torch, link; **~kohle** *f* bituminous coal; **p~(raben)schwarz** *adj* (*inf*) pitch-black; *Haar* jet-black; **~strähne** *f* (*inf*) run *or* streak of bad luck, unlucky patch; **eine ~strähne haben** to have a run *or* streak of bad luck, to go through an unlucky patch; **~vogel** *m* (*inf*) unlucky person, walking disaster area (*hum inf*); (*Frau auch*) Calamity Jane.

Pedal *nt* **-s, -e** pedal ◆ **(fest) in die ~e treten** to pedal (hard).

Pedant *m* pedant.

Pedanterie *f* pedantry.

pedantisch *adj* pedantic.

Peddigrohr *nt* cane.

Pedell *m* **-s, -e** (*old*) (*Sch*) caretaker, janitor; (*Univ*) porter.

Pediküre *f* **-, -n (a)** *no pl* (*Fußpflege*) pedicure. **(b)** (*Fußpflegerin*) chiropodist.

pediküren* *vt* to give a pedicure to.

Peeling ['pi:lıŋ] *nt* **-s, -s** (*Hautpflege*) peeling, exfoliation.

Peep-Show ['pi:pʃo:] *f* peep show.

Pegasus *m* - Pegasus.

Pegel *m* **-s, -** (*in Flüssen, Kanälen, Meer*) water depth gauge; (*Elec*) level recorder.

Pegelstand *m* water level.

Peil-: ~anlage *f* direction finding equipment, direction-finder; (*Naut*) sounding equipment; **~antenne** *f* directional antenna.

peilen *vt Wassertiefe* to sound, to plumb; *U-Boot, Sender, Standort* to get a fix on, to get *or* take the bearings of; *Richtung* to plot; (*entdecken*) to detect ◆ **die Lage ~** (*inf*) to see how the land lies, to see which way the wind's blowing; **über den Daumen ~** (*inf*) to guess roughly; **über den Daumen gepeilt** (*inf*) roughly speaking, at a rough estimate.

Peiler *m* **-s, -** detector.

Peil-: ~funk *m* radio direction finder; **~gerät** *nt* direction finder; **~lot** *nt* plumb-line; **~sender** *m* tracking device; **~station** *f* direction finding station.

Peilung *f* (*von Wassertiefe*) sounding, plumbing; (*von U-Boot, Sender*) locating; (*von Richtung*) plotting ◆ **was für eine ~ haben wir für das U-Boot?** what's our bearing on the submarine?

Pein *f* **-,** *no pl* agony, suffering ◆ **seine Leben war nur eine einzige ~** his life was one long torment; **jdm das Leben zur ~ machen** to make sb's life a misery.

peinigen *vt* to torture; (*fig*) to torment ◆ **jdn bis aufs Blut ~** to torture sb till he bleeds; (*fig*) to torment sb mercilessly; **von Schmerzen/Zweifeln gepeinigt** tormented by pain/doubt, racked with pain/doubt.

Peiniger(in *f*) *m* **-s, -** (*liter*) torturer; (*fig*) tormentor.

Peinigung *f* (*liter*) torture; (*fig*) torment.

peinlich *adj* **(a)** (*unangenehm*) (painfully) embarrassing; *Lage, Fragen auch* awkward; *Überraschung* nasty ◆ **ich habe das ~e Gefühl, daß ...** I have a terrible feeling that ...; **es war ihm ~(, daß ...)** he was *or* felt embarrassed (because ...); **es ist mir sehr ~, aber ich muß es Ihnen einmal sagen** I don't know how to put it, but you really ought to know; **es ist mir sehr ~, aber die Arbeit ist immer noch nicht fertig** I'm really sorry but the work still isn't finished; **das ist mir ja so ~** I feel awful about it; **~ berührt sein** (*hum*) to be profoundly shocked (*iro*); **~ wirken** to be embarrassing, to cause embarrassment; **es war so schlecht, daß es schon ~ war** (*inf*) it was so bad it was really painful (*inf*).
(b) (*gewissenhaft*) painstaking, meticulous; *Sparsamkeit* careful ◆ **in seinem Zimmer/auf seinem Schreibtisch herrschte ~e** *or* **~ste Ordnung** his room/his desk was meticulously *or* scrupulously tidy; **jdn einem ~en Verhör unterziehen** to question sb very closely; **~ sauber** scrupulously *or* meticulously clean; **der Koffer wurde ~ genau untersucht** the case was gone through very thoroughly *or* was given a very thorough going-over (*inf*); **er vermied es ~st, davon zu sprechen** he was at pains not to talk about it; **etw ~st geheimhalten** to keep sth strictly secret *or* top secret.

Peinlichkeit *f* **(a)** (*Unangenehmheit*) awkwardness, embarrassment ◆ **die ~ der Situation/seines Benehmens** the awkwardness of the situation, the embarrassing *or* awkward situation/his embarrassing behaviour; **diese ~en auf der Bühne** these embarrassing *or* painful (*inf*) scenes on stage.
(b) (*Gewissenhaftigkeit*) thoroughness, meticulousness, painstakingness.

peinsam *adj* (*hum*) painful, embarrassing.

peinvoll *adj* (*old*) painful.

Peitsche *f* **-, -n** whip ◆ **er gab seinem Pferd die ~** he whipped his horse on; *siehe* **Zuckerbrot.**

peitschen *vti* to whip; (*fig*) to lash.

Peitschen-: ~hieb *m* stroke, lash; **~knall** *m* crack of a whip; **~leuchte** *f* street lamp; **~schlag** *m* lash of a whip; **~schnur** *f* (whip)lash, thong; **~stiel** *m* whip handle, whipstock.

pejorativ *adj* pejorative.

Pekinese *m* **-n, -n** pekinese, peke (*inf*).

Peking *nt* **-s** Peking.

Pektin *nt* **-s, -e** pectin.

pekuniär *adj* (*dated*) pecuniary, financial.

Pelerine *f* (*old*) pelerine (*old*), cape.

Pelikan *m* **-s, -e** pelican.

Pelle *f* **-, -n** (*inf*) skin ◆ **der Chef sitzt mir auf der ~** (*inf*) I've got the boss on my back (*inf*); **er geht mir nicht von der ~** (*inf*) he won't stop pestering me; *siehe* **rücken.**

pellen (*inf*) [1] *vt Kartoffeln, Wurst* to skin, to peel; *siehe* **Ei.**
[2] *vr* (*Mensch, Körperhaut*) to peel ◆ **meine Haut pellt sich** my skin's peeling, I'm peeling.

Pellkartoffeln *pl* potatoes *pl* boiled in their jackets.

Peloponnes *m* **-(es)** *or f* - Peloponnese.

Pelz *m* **-es, -e** fur; (*nicht gegerbt auch*) pelt, hide, skin; (*Kleidung*) fur; (*fig: Haarwuchs*) fur *no pl* ◆ **jdm eins auf den ~ brennen** (*inf*) to singe sb's hide; **sich** (*dat*) **die Sonnen auf den ~ brennen lassen** (*inf*) to toast oneself (*inf*); *siehe* **rücken.**

Pelz-: ~besatz *m* fur trimming; **p~besetzt** *adj* trimmed with fur, fur-trimmed; **~futter** *nt* fur lining; **p~gefüttert** *adj* fur-lined, lined with fur; **~händler** *m* furrier; (*Fellhändler*) fur trader; **~handschuh** *m* fur glove.

pelzig *adj* furry; *Zunge* furred(-over), furry.

Pelz-: ~imitation *f* imitation fur; **~jäger** *m* skin-hunter; (*Fallensteller*) (fur-) trapper; **~kragen** *m* fur collar; **~mantel** *m* fur coat; **~mütze** *f* fur hat; **~stiefel** *m* fur *or* furry (*inf*) boot; (*p~gefüttert*) fur-lined boot; **~stoff** *m* fur fabric; **~tier** *nt* animal with a valuable fur, animal prized for its fur; **~tiere jagen** to hunt animals for their fur; (*mit Fallen*) to go trapping; **~tierfarm** *f* fur farm; **~tierjäger** *m siehe* **~jäger**; **~tierzucht** *f* fur-farming; **p~verbrämt** *adj* (*liter*) *siehe* **p~besetzt**; **~waren** *pl* furs; **~werk** *nt* fur.

Pen-Club *m* PEN Club.

Pendant [pã'dã:] *nt* **-s, -s** counterpart, opposite number.

Pendel *nt* **-s, -** pendulum ◆ **keiner kann das ~ der Zeit aufhalten** time and tide wait for no man (*prov*); **das ~ schlug nach der entgegengesetzten Seite aus** (*fig*) the pendulum swung in the other direction.

Pendel-: ~ausschlag *m* swing of a/the pendulum; **~flugdienst** *m* shuttle service.

pendeln *vi* **(a)** (*schwingen*) to swing (to and fro), to oscillate (*form*) ◆ **er ließ die Beine ~** he let his legs dangle, he dangled his legs. **(b)** *aux sein* (*hin- und herfahren*) (*Zug, Fähre etc*) to run *or* operate a shuttle-service, to shuttle; (*Mensch*) to commute; (*fig*) to vacillate, to fluctuate.

Pendel-: ~schlag *m* swing of the pendulum; **er spielte zum ~schlag des Metronoms** he played in time to the metronome; **der ~schlag der Zeit** the march of time; **~schwingung** *f* swing of the pendulum; (*Phys auch*) oscillation (of a pendulum); **~tür** *f* swing door; **~uhr** *f* pendulum clock; **~verkehr** *m* shuttle service; (*Berufsverkehr*) commuter traffic.

Pendler(in *f*) *m* **-s, -** commuter.

Penes *pl of* **Penis.**

penetrant *adj* **(a)** *Gestank, Geschmack* penetrating, pungent; *Gestank, Parfüm auch* overpowering ◆ **das schmeckt ~ nach Knoblauch** you can't taste anything for garlic, it has a very strong taste of garlic.
(b) (*fig: aufdringlich*) pushing, insistent ◆ **der Typ war mir zu ~** he was too pushing *or* pushy (*inf*) for my liking; **seine Selbstsicherheit ist schon ~** his self-confidence is overpowering; **ein ~er Kerl** a pest, a nuisance.

Penetranz *f, no pl* (*von Geruch, Geschmack*) pungency; (*fig: Aufdringlichkeit*) insistence, aggressiveness ◆ **er ist von einer unausstehlichen ~** he's unbearably

overpowering.
Penetration *f* penetration.
penetrieren* *vt* to penetrate.
peng *interj* bang.
penibel *adj* **(a)** pernickety (*inf*), precise, exact. **(b)** (*dial: peinlich*) *Lage, Angelegenheit* painful, embarrassing.
Penicillin [penitsɪˈliːn] *nt* **-s, -e** *siehe* **Penizillin.**
Penis *m* **-, -se** *or* **Penes** penis.
Penizillin *nt* **-s, -e** penicillin.
Pennäler(in *f***)** *m* **-s, -** (*dated*) high-school boy/girl, grammar-school boy/girl (*Brit*).
Pennbruder *m* (*inf*) tramp, bum (*inf*), hobo (*US*).
Penne *f* **-, -n (a)** (*Sch sl*) school. **(b)** (*inf: Herberge*) doss house (*inf*), flophouse (*inf*).
pennen *vi* (*inf*) to kip (*inf*) ◆ **ich habe gerade ein bißchen gepennt** I've just been having a kip (*inf*) *or* sleep, I've just been kipping (*inf*); **der Meier pennt schon wieder im Unterricht** Meier's having a little sleep again during the lesson; **du bist daran, penn nicht!** it's your turn, wake up!
Penner(in *f***)** *m* **-s, -** (*inf*) **(a)** tramp, bum (*inf*), hobo (*US*). **(b)** (*verschlafener Mensch*) sleepyhead (*inf*).
Pensa, Pensen *pl of* **Pensum.**
Pension [pãˈzioːn, pãˈsioːn, pɛnˈzioːn] *f* **-, -en (a)** (*Fremdenheim*) guest-house, pension.
(b) *no pl* (*Verpflegung, Kostgeld*) board ◆ **halbe/volle ~** half/full board; **die ~ pro Tag macht 30 DM** half/full board is DM 30 a day.
(c) (*Ruhegehalt*) pension, superannuation.
(d) *no pl* (*Ruhestand*) retirement ◆ **in ~ gehen** to retire, to go into retirement; **in ~ sein** to be retired, to be in retirement.
Pensionär(in *f***)** [pãzioˈnɛːɐ, -ɛːərɪn, pãsioˈnɛːɐ, -ɛːərɪn, penzioˈnɛːɐ, -ɛːərɪn] *m* **(a)** (*Pension beziehend*) pensioner; (*im Ruhestand befindlich*) retired person. **(b)** (*Pensionsgast*) paying guest; (*ständiger Pensionsgast*) boarder.
Pensionat [pãzioˈnaːt, pãsioˈnaːt, penzioˈnaːt] *nt* (*dated*) boarding school.
pensionieren* [pãzioˈniːrən, pãsioˈniːrən, pensioˈniːrən] *vt* to pension off, to retire ◆ **sich ~ lassen** to retire.
pensioniert *adj* retired, in retirement.
Pensionierung *f* (*Zustand*) retirement; (*Vorgang*) pensioning-off ◆ **die Firma entschloß sich zur ~ der älteren Mitarbeiter** the firm decided to pension off the older workers.
Pensionist [pãzioˈnɪst, pãsioˈnɪst, pɛnsioˈnɪst] *m* (*S Ger, Aus*) *siehe* **Pensionär(in) (a).**
Pensions-: ~alter *nt* retiring *or* retirement age; **~anspruch** *m* right to a pension; **p~berechtigt** *adj* entitled to a pension; **~fonds** *m* pension fund; **~gast** *m* paying guest; **~kasse** *f siehe* **~fonds**; **~preis** *m* price for full board; **~preis DM 21** full board DM21; **p~reif** *adj* (*inf*) ready for retirement; **~rückstellungen** *pl* pension reserve(s).
Pensum *nt* **-s, Pensa** *or* **Pensen** workload; (*Sch*) curriculum ◆ **tägliches ~** daily quota; **er hat sein ~ nicht geschafft** he didn't achieve his target; **ein hohes** *or* **großes ~ an Arbeit** a heavy workload.
Pentagon *nt* **-s, -e** pentagon.
Pentagramm *nt* pentagram.
Pentameter *m* (*Poet*) pentameter.
Pentateuch *m* **-s** Pentateuch.
Penthouse [ˈpenthaus] *nt* **-, -s, Penthouse-Wohnung** *f* penthouse (flat).
Pentium *m* **-(s), -s** (*Comput: Chip*) Pentium chip; (*Computer*) Pentium PC.
Pentium-Prozessor *m* Pentium processor.
Pep *m* **-(s),** *no pl* (*inf*) pep (*inf*), life ◆ **etw mit ~ machen** to put a bit of pep (*inf*) *or* life *or* zip (*inf*) into doing sth; **das Kleid hat ~** that dress has style *or* flair.
Peperoni *pl* chillies *pl*.
Pepita *m or nt* **-s, -s** shepherd('s) check *or* plaid.
peppig *adj* (*inf*) lively, upbeat.
Pepsin *nt* **-s, -e** pepsin.
Peptid *nt* **-(e)s, -e** peptide.
per *prep* **(a)** (*mittels, durch*) by ◆ **~ Adresse** (*Comm*) care of, c/o; **mit jdm ~ du sein** (*inf*) to be on Christian-name terms *or* first-name terms with sb; **~ procura** (*Comm*) per procura, pp *abbr*, for; **~ pedes** (*hum*) on shanks's pony (*hum*), on foot; **~ se** per se; **~ definitionem** by definition.
(b) (*Comm: gegen*) against ◆ **~ cassa, ~ Kasse** (*old*) against cash.
(c) (*Comm: bis, am*) by.
(d) (*Comm: pro*) per.
perennierend *adj* perennial.
perfekt *adj* **(a)** (*vollkommen*) perfect ◆ **~ Englisch sprechen** to speak perfect English, to speak English perfectly.
(b) *pred* (*abgemacht*) settled ◆ **etw ~ machen** to settle *or* conclude sth; **die Sache ~ machen** to clinch the deal, to settle the matter; **der Vertrag ist ~** the contract is signed, sealed and delivered (*inf*), the contract is all settled; **damit war die Niederlage ~** total defeat was then inevitable.
Perfekt *nt* **-s, -e, Perfektum** *nt* **-s, Perfekta** perfect (tense).
Perfektion *f* perfection ◆ **das war Artistik in höchster ~** that was the epitome of artistry, that was perfect artistry.
perfektionieren* [pɛrfɛktsioˈniːrən] *vt* to perfect.
Perfektionismus [pɛrfɛktsioˈnismʊs] *m* perfectionism.
Perfektionist(in *f***)** [pɛrfɛktsioˈnɪst(ɪn)] *m* perfectionist.
perfektionistisch [pɛrfɛktsioˈnɪstɪʃ] *adj* perfectionist.
perfektiv *adj* perfective.
perfid(e) *adj* (*liter*) perfidious.
Perfidie *f* (*liter*) perfidy.
Perforation *f* perforation.
perforieren* *vt* to perforate.
Performance [pəːˈfɔːməns] *f* **-, -s** [-mənsɪz] (*Theat*) performance.
Performanz *f no pl* (*Ling*) performance.
Pergament *nt* **(a)** (*präparierte Tierhaut*) parchment; (*Kalbs~ auch*) vellum ◆ **dieses Buch ist in ~ gebunden** this book is vellum-bound *or* bound in vellum. **(b)** (*Handschrift*) parchment. **(c)** (*~papier*) greaseproof paper.
Pergamentband *m* vellum(-bound) book.
pergamenten *adj* (*liter*) parchment; (*aus Kalbshaut*) vellum.
Pergament-: ~papier *nt* greaseproof paper; **~rolle** *f* (parchment) scroll; **~rücken** *m* vellum spine.
Pergola *f* **-, Pergolen** arbour, bower.
Periode *f* **-, -n** period (*auch Physiol*); (*von Wetter auch*) spell; (*Math*) repetend; (*Elec*) cycle ◆ **0,33 ~** 0.33 recurring; **ihre ~ ist ausgeblieben** she didn't get *or* have her period; **~n pro Sekunde** cycles per second.
Periodensystem *nt* periodic system; (*Tafel*) periodic table.
Periodikum *nt* **-s, Periodika** *usu pl* periodical.
periodisch *adj* periodic(al); (*regelmäßig*) regular; (*Phys*) periodic ◆ **~er Dezimalbruch** recurring fraction.
periodisieren* *vt* to divide up into periods.
Periodizität *f* periodicity; (*Math: von Bruch*) recurrence.
Peripetie *f* peripeteia.
peripher *adj* (*liter*) peripheral.
Peripherie *f* periphery; (*von Kreis*) circumference; (*von Stadt*) outskirts *pl* ◆ **an der ~ Bonns** in *or* on the outskirts of Bonn.
Peripheriegerät *nt* peripheral.
Periskop *nt* **-s, -e** periscope.
periskopisch *adj* periscopic.
Peristaltik *f* peristalsis.
Perle *f* **-, -n (a)** (*Muschel~*) pearl ◆ **~n vor die Säue werfen** (*prov*) to cast pearls before swine (*prov*); *siehe* **Krone. (b)** (*aus Glas, Holz etc*) bead; (*Luftbläschen*) bubble; (*von Wasser, Schweiß*) bead, drop, droplet. **(c)** (*fig*) pearl, gem; (*dated inf: Hausmädchen*) maid.
perlen *vi* (*sprudeln*) to sparkle, to bubble, to effervesce; (*fallen, rollen*) to trickle, to roll ◆ **~des Lachen** (*liter*) rippling *or* bubbling laughter; **der Tau perlt auf den Blättern** drops *or* beads of dew glisten on the leaves; **der Schweiß perlte ihm von/auf der Stirn** beads of sweat were running down/stood out on his forehead; **Wasser perlt auf einer Fettschicht** water forms into droplets on a greasy surface.
Perlen-: ~auster *f* pearl oyster; **p~besetzt** *adj* set with pearls; **p~bestickt** *adj* embroidered *or* decorated with pearls; **~fischer** *m* pearl fisher, pearler; **~fischerei** *f* pearl fishing; **~kette** *f*, **~kollier** *nt* string of pearls, pearl necklace, pearls *pl*; **~schnur** *f* string of beads, beads *pl*; **~stickerei** *f* beadwork; **~taucher** *m* pearl diver.
Perl-: ~fang *m* (*Knitting*) knit one, purl one; **~garn** *nt* mercerized yarn; **p~grau** *adj* pearl grey; **~huhn** *nt* guinea fowl; **~muschel** *f* pearl oyster; **~mutt** *nt* **-s,** *no pl*, **~mutter** *f* **-,** *no pl or nt* **-s,** *no pl* mother-of-pearl; **~mutterknopf, ~muttknopf** *m* (mother-of-)pearl button; **p~muttern** *adj* mother-of-pearl; (*fig*) pearly.
Perlon ® *nt* **-s,** *no pl* ≃ nylon.
Perlonstrümpfe *pl* nylons *pl*, nylon stockings *pl*.
Perl-: ~schrift *f* (*Typ*) pearl; **~wein** *m* sparkling wine; **~zwiebel** *f* cocktail *or* pearl onion.
permanent *adj* permanent.
Permanenz *f* permanence ◆ **in ~** continually, constantly.
permeabel *adj* (*Bot, Phys, Tech*) permeable.
permissiv *adj* permissive.
Permissivität *f, no pl* permissiveness.
perniziös *adj* malignant.
Perpendikel *m or nt* **-s, -** (*von Uhr*) pendulum.
perpetuieren *vt* to perpetuate.
Perpetuum mobile *nt* **- -, - -(s)** perpetual motion machine.
perplex *adj* dumbfounded, thunderstruck.
Perron [peˈrõː] *m* **-s, -s** (*old, Sw, Aus*) platform.
Persenning *f* **-, -e(n)** tarpaulin, tarp (*US inf*).
Perser(in *f***)** *m* **-s, - (a)** (*Mensch*) Persian. **(b)** (*inf*) *siehe* **Perserteppich.**
Perserteppich *m* Persian carpet; (*Brücke*) Persian rug.
Pershing [ˈpəːʃɪŋ] *f* **-, -s** (*inf*), **Pershing-Rakete** *f* Pershing missile.
Persianer *m* **-s, - (a)** (*Pelz*) Persian lamb. **(b)** (*auch* **~mantel**) Persian lamb (coat).
Persien [-iən] *nt* **-s** Persia.
Persiflage [pɛrziˈflaːʒə] *f* **-, -n** pastiche, satire (*gen, auf +acc* on, of).
persiflieren* *vt* to satirize, to write a pastiche of.
Persilschein *m* (*hum inf*) clean bill of health (*inf*); denazification certificate ◆ **jdm einen ~ ausstellen** to absolve sb of all responsibility.
persisch *adj* Persian ◆ **P~er Golf** Persian Gulf.
Person *f* **-, -en (a)** (*Einzel~*) person, individual ◆ **jede ~ bezahlt** ... each person *or* everybody pays ...; **~en** people, persons (*form*); **eine aus 6 ~en bestehende Familie** a family of 6; **pro ~** per person; **die eigene ~** oneself; **was seine eigene ~ betrifft** as for himself; **ich für meine ~** ... I myself ..., as for myself I ..., I for my part ...; **in (eigener) ~ erscheinen** to appear in person *or* personally; **er ist Finanz- und Außenminister in einer ~** he's the Chancellor of the Exchequer and Foreign Secretary rolled into one; **jdn zur ~ vernehmen** (*Jur*) to question sb concerning his identity; **von ~ bekannt** (*Jur*) of

known identity; **natürliche/juristische ~** (*Jur*) natural/juristic *or* artificial person; **die drei göttlichen ~en** the Holy Trinity, God in three persons; **eine hochgestellte ~** a high-ranking personage *or* person.
(b) (*Mensch*) person; (*pej: Frau*) female ◆ **sie ist die Geduld in ~** she's patience personified; **Tiere treten in Fabeln als ~en auf** animals figure in fables as human beings *or* as people; **die ~ des Königs ist unantastbar** (the person of) the king is inviolable; **es geht um die ~ des Kanzlers, nicht um das Amt** it concerns the chancellor as a person, not the office; **lassen wir seine ~ aus dem Spiel** let's leave personalities out of it; **wir müssen die ~ von der Sache trennen** we must keep the personal and the factual aspects separate.
(c) (*Liter, Theat*) character ◆ **die ~en der Handlung** the characters (in the action); (*Theat auch*) the dramatis personae; **eine stumme ~** a non-speaking part.
(d) (*Gram*) person.

Personal *nt* **-s,** *no pl* personnel, staff; (*Dienerschaft auch*) servants *pl*; (*Liter: Romanfiguren*) characters *pl* ◆ **fliegendes ~** aircrew; **ständiges ~** permanent staff; **ausreichend/ungenügend mit ~ versehen sein** to be adequately staffed/understaffed.

Personal-: ~abbau *m* reductions *pl* in staff *or* personnel, personnel *or* staff cuts *pl*; **~abteilung** *f* personnel (department); **~akte** *f* personal file; **~angaben** *pl* particulars *pl*; **~ausweis** *m* identity card; **~bestand** *m* number of staff *or* employees *or* personnel; **~büro** *nt siehe* **~abteilung; ~chef** *m* personnel manager, head of the personnel department; **~computer** *m* personal computer; **~decke** *f* personnel cover; **eine dünne ~decke** a very tight personnel situation; **~direktor** *m* personnel director; **~einsparung** *f* personnel reduction *or* cut-down; **~gesellschaft** *f* unlimited company.

Personalien [-iən] *pl* particulars *pl*.

personalisieren* *vti* to personalize ◆ **er personalisiert immer alles** he always personalizes everything *or* reduces everything to a personal level.

Personalisierung *f* personalization.

Personalität *f* personality.

Personal-: ~kartei *f* personnel index; **~kosten** *pl* personnel costs *pl*; **~leiter** *m siehe* **~chef; ~politik** *f* staff *or* personnel policy; **~pronomen** *nt* personal pronoun; **~rabatt** *m* staff discount; **~rat** *m* (*Ausschuß*) *staff council for civil servants*; (*einzelner*) *representative on a staff council for civil servants*; **~union** *f* personal union; **er ist Kanzler und Parteivorsitzender in ~union** he is at the same time Prime Minister and party chairman; **~vertretungsgesetz** *nt* employees' representation law.

Persona non grata *f, no pl* persona non grata.

Persönchen *nt* (*inf*) little lady (*inf*).

personell *adj* staff *attr*, personnel *attr* ◆ **die Verzögerungen unserer Produktion sind ~ bedingt** the delays in production are caused by staff *or* personnel problems; **unsere Schwierigkeiten sind rein ~** our difficulties are simply to do with staffing *or* personnel.

Personen-: ~aufzug *m* (passenger) lift (*Brit*), elevator (*US*); **~auto** *nt siehe* **~kraftwagen; ~beförderung** *f* carriage *or* conveyance of passengers; **die Bahn hat ein finanzielles Defizit bei der ~beförderung** the railways' passenger(-carrying) services show a deficit; **~beschreibung** *f* (personal) description; **p~bezogen** *adj Daten, Informationen* personal; **~gedächtnis** *nt* memory for faces; **~gesellschaft** *f* partnership; **~kraftwagen** *m* (*form*) (private) car, motorcar (*form*), automobile (*US*); **~kreis** *m* group of people; **~kult** *m* personality cult; **mit Che Guevara wird viel ~kult getrieben** a great personality cult has been built up around Che Guevara; **~rufanlage** *f* pager, bleeper; **~schaden** *m* injury to persons; **~schaden ist bei dem Unfall nicht entstanden** no-one was injured *or* received any injuries in the accident; **~schutz** *m* personal security; **~stand** *m* marital status; **~standsregister** *nt* register of births, marriages and deaths; **~verkehr** *m* passenger services *pl*; **~versicherung** *f* personal injury insurance; **~verzeichnis** *nt* register (of persons); (*Liter*) list of characters; **~waage** *f* scales *pl*, pair of scales; **~wagen** *m* (*Aut*) (private) car, automobile (*US*); **~zahl** *f* number of persons (*form*) *or* people; **~zug** *m* (*Gegensatz: Schnellzug*) slow *or* stopping train; (*Gegensatz: Güterzug*) passenger train.

Personifikation *f* personification.

personifizieren* *vt* to personify ◆ **er läuft herum wie das personifizierte schlechte Gewissen** he's going around with guilt written all over his face.

Personifizierung *f* personification.

persönlich [1] *adj* personal; *Atmosphäre, Umgangsformen* friendly ◆ **~e Auslagen** out-of-pocket *or* personal expenses; **~e Meinung** personal *or* one's own opinion; **~ werden** to get personal; **~es Fürwort** personal pronoun.
[2] *adv* personally; (*auf Briefen*) private (and confidential) ◆ **der Chef ~** the boss himself *or* in person *or* personally; **etw ~ meinen/nehmen** *or* **auffassen** to mean/take sth personally; **er interessiert sich ~ für seine Leute** he takes a personal interest in his people; **Sie müssen ~ erscheinen** you are required to appear in person *or* personally; **~ haften** (*Comm*) to be personally liable.

Persönlichkeit *f* **(a)** *no pl* (*Charakter*) personality ◆ **er besitzt wenig ~** he hasn't got much personality. **(b)** (*bedeutender Mensch*) personality. **er ist eine ~** he's quite a personality; **~en des öffentlichen Lebens** public figures.

Persönlichkeits-: ~entfaltung *f* personality development, development of the personality; **~merkmal** *nt* personality trait; **~profil** *nt* psychological profile; **~test** *m* personality test; **~veränderung** *f* personality change; **~wahl** *f electoral system in which a vote is cast for a candidate rather than a party*; **diese Wahl war eine reine ~wahl** (*inf*) this election boiled down to a question of the candidates' personalities.

Perspektiv *nt* small telescope, perspective (*obs*).

Perspektive [-'ti:və] *f* (*Art, Opt*) perspective; (*Blickpunkt*) angle; (*Gesichtspunkt*) point of view, angle; (*fig: Zukunftsausblick*) prospects *pl* ◆ **aus dieser ~ wirkt das Haus viel größer** the house looks much bigger from this angle; **das eröffnet ganz neue ~n für uns** that opens new horizons for us.

perspektivisch [-'ti:vɪʃ] *adj* perspective *attr*, in perspective ◆ **die Zeichnung ist nicht ~** the drawing is not in perspective; **~e Verkürzung** foreshortening.

perspektivlos *adj* without prospects.

Perspektivlosigkeit *f* lack of prospects.

Peru *nt* **-s** Peru.

Peruaner(in *f***)** *m* **-s, -** Peruvian.

peruanisch *adj* Peruvian.

Perücke *f* **-, -n** wig.

pervers [pɛr'vɛrs] *adj* perverted, warped (*inf*) ◆ **ein ~er Mensch** a pervert.

Perversion [pɛrvɛr'zio:n] *f* perversion.

Perversität [pɛrvɛrzi'tɛ:t] *f* perversion.

pervertieren* [pɛrvɛr'ti:rən] [1] *vt* to pervert, to warp.
[2] *vi aux sein* to become *or* get perverted.

Pervertiertheit *f* pervertedness, perversion.

pesen *vi aux sein* (*inf*) to belt (*inf*), to charge (*inf*).

Pessar *nt* **-s, -e** pessary; (*zur Empfängnisverhütung*) cap, diaphragm.

Pessimismus *m* pessimism ◆ **immer dieser ~!** you're/he's *etc* always so pessimistic!, this eternal pessimism!

Pessimist(in *f***)** *m* pessimist.

pessimistisch *adj* pessimistic ◆ **etw ~ beurteilen** to take a pessimistic view of sth, to view sth pessimistically.

Pest *f* **-,** *no pl* (*Hist, Med*) plague, pestilence, pest ◆ **sich wie die ~ ausbreiten** to spread like the plague *or* like wildfire; **jdn/etw wie die ~ hassen** (*inf*) to loathe (and detest) sb/sth, to hate sb's guts (*inf*); **jdn wie die ~ meiden** (*inf*) to avoid sb like the plague; **wie die ~ stinken** (*inf*) to stink to high heaven (*inf*); **jdm die ~ an den Hals wünschen** (*inf*) to wish sb would drop dead (*inf*).

Pest-: p~artig *adj* (*Med*) pestilential; (*fig*) *Gestank* fetid, miasmic (*liter*); **sich p~artig verbreiten** to spread like the plague; **~beule** *f* plague spot; **~geruch, ~gestank** *m* (foul) stench, stink; **~hauch** *m* (*poet*) miasma (*liter*), fetor (*liter*).

Pestilenz *f* (*old*) pestilence.

Pestizid *nt* **-(e)s, -e** pesticide.

Pest-: p~krank *adj* sick of the plague (*old*), plague-stricken; **~kranke(r)** *mf* person with *or* who has the plague; **die ~kranken** those who had (been stricken by) the plague.

PET [pe:|e:'te:] *abbr nt of* **Polyethylenterephthalat** PET, polyethylene terephthalate.

Petersilie [-iə] *f* parsley ◆ **du siehst aus, als wäre dir die ~ verhagelt** (*inf*) you look as though you've lost a pound and found a sixpence (*inf*).

Peterskirche *f* St Peter's.

Peterwagen *m* (*inf*) police *or* patrol car, panda car (*Brit*).

PET-Flasche *f* PET bottle.

Petition *f* petition.

Petitionsrecht *nt* right to petition.

Petrischale *f* Petri dish.

Petro-: ~chemie *f* petrochemistry; **p~chemisch** *adj* petrochemical; **~dollar** *m* petrodollar.

Petroleum [pe'tro:leum] *nt* **-s,** *no pl* paraffin (oil), kerosene (*esp US*).

Petroleum-: ~kocher *m* paraffin stove, primus (stove); **~lampe** *f*, **~licht** *nt* paraffin *or* oil *or* kerosene (*esp US*) lamp.

Petrus *m* **-** (*Bibl*) Peter.

Petschaft *nt* **-s, -e** (*old*) seal.

Petticoat ['pɛtiko:t] *m* **-s, -s** stiff(ened) petticoat.

Petting *nt* **-s, -s** petting.

petto *adv*: **etw in ~ haben** (*inf*) to have sth up one's sleeve (*inf*).

Petunie [-iə] *f* petunia.

Petz *m* **-es, -e** (*liter*) **Meister ~** (Master) Bruin.

Petze *f* **-, -n** (*Sch sl*) sneak (*Sch sl*), telltale (tit) (*Sch sl*).

petzen (*inf*) [1] *vt* **der petzt alles** he always tells; **er hat gepetzt, daß ...** he (went and) told that ...; **er hat's dem Lehrer gepetzt** he told sir (*Sch sl*).
[2] *vi* to tell (tales).

Petzer *m* **-s, -** (*inf*) *siehe* **Petze**.

Petzliese *f siehe* **Petze**.

peu à peu [pøa'pø] *adv* (*inf*) gradually, little by little.

Pf *abbr of* **Pfennig**.

Pfad *m* **-(e)s, -e** path, track; (*Comput*) path ◆ **den ~ der Tugend wandeln** (*liter*) to follow the path of virtue; **neue ~e in der Medizin** new directions in medicine.

Pfader -s, - (*Sw*), **Pfadfinder** *m* (boy) scout ◆ **er ist bei den ~n** he's in the (Boy) Scouts.

Pfadfinderbewegung *f* (Boy) Scout movement, (Boy) Scouts *pl*.

Pfadfinderin *f* girl guide (*Brit*), girl scout (*US*).

Pfaffe *m* **-n, -n** (*pej*) cleric (*pej*), parson.

pfäffisch *adj* (*pej*) sanctimonious (*pej*).

Pfahl *m* **-s, ⸚e** post; (*Zaun~ auch*) stake; (*Stütze auch*) support; (*Palisade*) palisade, pale, stake; (*Brücken~*) pile, pier; (*Marter~*) stake ◆ **jdm ein ~ im Fleisch sein** (*liter*) to be a thorn in sb's flesh.

Pfahl-: ~bau *m* **-s, -ten (a)** *no pl* (*Bauweise*) building on stilts; **im ~bau** on stilts; **(b)** (*Haus*) pile dwelling, house built on stilts; **~brücke** *f* pile bridge; **~dorf** *nt* pile village.

pfählen *vt* **(a)** *(Hort)* to stake. **(b)** *(hinrichten)* to impale.

Pfahl-: ~werk *nt (Stützwand)* pilework; *(Palisade)* palisade, paling; **~wurzel** *f* taproot.

Pfalz *f* **-, -en (a)** *no pl (Rhein~)* Rhineland *or* Lower Palatinate, Rheinpfalz. **(b)** *no pl (Ober~)* Upper Palatinate. **(c)** *(Hist) (Burg)* palace; *(Gebiet eines Pfalzgrafen)* palatinate.

Pfälzer(in *f*) *m* **-s, - (a)** person from the Rhineland/Upper Palatinate ◆ **er ist (ein) ~** he comes from the (Rhineland/Upper) Palatinate. **(b)** *(Wein)* *wine from the Rhineland Palatinate.*

Pfalz-: ~graf *m (Hist)* count palatine; **p~gräflich** *adj* of a/the count palatine.

pfälzisch *adj* Palatine, of the (Rhineland) Palatinate.

Pfand *nt* **-(e)s, ¨er** security, pledge; *(beim Pfänderspiel)* forfeit; *(Flaschen~)* deposit; *(fig)* pledge ◆ **etw als ~ geben, etw zum ~ setzen** *(liter)* to pledge sth, to give sth as (a) security; *(fig)* to pledge sth; *(beim Pfänderspiel)* to pay sth as a forfeit; **ich gebe mein Wort als ~** I pledge my word; **etw gegen ~ leihen** to lend sth against a security *or* pledge; **auf der Flasche ist ~** there's something (back) on the bottle *(inf)*, there's a deposit on the bottle; **auf der Flasche ist 20 Pf ~** there's 20Pf (back) on the bottle *(inf)*; **ein ~ einlösen** to redeem a pledge; **etw als ~ behalten** to keep sth as (a) security, to hold sth in pledge.

pfändbar *adj (Jur)* distrainable *(form)*, attachable *(form)* ◆ **der Fernseher ist nicht ~** the bailiffs can't take the television.

Pfandbrief *m (von Bank, Regierung)* bond, debenture.

pfänden *vt (Jur)* to impound, to seize, to distrain upon *(form)* ◆ **man hat ihm die Möbel gepfändet** the bailiffs *or* they took away his furniture; **jdn ~** to impound *or* seize some of sb's possessions; **jdn ~ lassen** to get the bailiffs onto sb.

Pfänderspiel *nt* (game of) forfeits.

Pfand-: ~flasche *f* returnable bottle; **~haus** *nt* pawnshop, pawnbroker's; **~leihe** *f* **(a)** *(das Leihen)* pawnbroking; **(b)** *(~haus)* pawnshop, pawnbroker's; **~leiher** *m* **-s, -** pawnbroker; **~recht** *nt* right of distraint *(an +dat* upon) *(form)*, lien *(an +dat* on) *(form)*; **wenn du deine Miete nicht bezahlst, hat der Vermieter ein ~recht an deinen Möbeln** if you don't pay your rent the landlord is entitled to seize *or* impound your furniture; **~schein** *m* pawn ticket.

Pfändung *f* seizure, distraint *(form)*, attachment *(form)* ◆ **der Gerichtsvollzieher kam zur ~** the bailiff came to seize *or* impound their possessions.

Pfändungs-: ~befehl *m*, **~verfügung** *f* distress warrant.

Pfanne *f* **-, -n** *(Cook)* pan; *(Anat)* socket; *(Dach~)* pantile; *(Zünd~)* pan ◆ **ein paar Eier in die ~ schlagen** *or* **hauen** *(inf)* to bung a couple of eggs in the pan *(inf)*, to fry up a couple of eggs; **jdn in die ~ hauen** *(sl)* to do the dirty on sb *(inf)*; *(vernichtend schlagen)* to wipe the floor with sb *(inf)*, to give sb a thrashing *(inf)* or hammering *(Brit sl)*; *(ausschimpfen)* to bawl sb out *(inf)*, to give sb a bawling-out *(inf)*.

Pfannengericht *nt (Cook)* fry-up.

Pfann(en)kuchen *m* pancake ◆ **Berliner ~** (jam) doughnut; **wie ein ~ aufgehen** *(inf)* to turn into *or* to get to be a real dumpling *(inf)* *or* roly-poly *(inf)*.

Pfarr|amt *nt* priest's office.

Pfarrbezirk *m*, **Pfarre** *f* **-, -n** *(old)* parish.

Pfarrei *f (Gemeinde)* parish; *(Amtsräume)* priest's office.

Pfarrer(in *f*) *m* **-s, -** *(katholisch, evangelisch)* parish priest; *(anglikanisch auch)* vicar; *(von Freikirchen)* minister; *(Gefängnis~, Militär~ etc)* chaplain, padre ◆ **guten Morgen, Herr ~!** good morning, *(katholisch)* Father *or (evangelisch, anglikanisch)* Vicar *or (von Freikirchen)* Mr ... *or (Gefängnis etc)* Padre; **als nächster wird Herr ~ Schmidt sprechen** the Reverend Michael Schmidt is going to speak next.

Pfarr-: ~gemeinde *f siehe* **Pfarrei**; **~haus** *nt (anglikanisch)* vicarage; *(methodistisch, Scot)* manse; *(katholisch)* presbytery; **~helfer** *m* curate; **~kind** *nt* parishioner; **~kirche** *f* parish church; **~stelle** *f* parish, (church) living, benefice.

Pfau *m* **-(e)s** *or* **-en, -en** peacock ◆ **er stolziert daher wie ein ~** he struts around like a peacock; **aufgedonnert wie ein ~** *(inf)* dressed *or* done up to the nines *(inf)*.

Pfauen-: ~auge *nt (Tag~)* peacock butterfly; *(Nacht~)* peacock moth; **~feder** *f* peacock feather; **~henne** *f* peahen.

Pfeffer *m* **-s, -** pepper ◆ **~ und Salz** *(lit)* salt and pepper; *(Stoffmuster)* pepper-and-salt; **das brennt wie ~** that's red-hot; *(Schmerz)* that really stings; **er kann hingehen** *or* **bleiben, wo der ~ wächst!** *(inf)* he can go to hell *(sl)*, he can take a running jump *(inf)*; **sie hat ~ im Hintern** *(inf)* *or* **Arsch** *(vulg)* she's got lots of get-up-and-go *(inf)*.

pfeff(e)rig *adj* peppery.

Pfeffer-: ~korn *nt* peppercorn; **~kuchen** *m* gingerbread; **~kuchenhäuschen** *nt* gingerbread house.

Pfefferminz(bonbon) *nt* **-es, -(e)** peppermint.

Pfefferminze *f* **-,** *no pl* peppermint.

Pfefferminz-: ~geschmack *m* peppermint flavour; **~likör** *m* crème de menthe; **~plätzchen** *nt* peppermint; **~tee** *m* peppermint tea.

Pfeffermühle *f* pepper-mill.

pfeffern *vt* **(a)** *(Cook)* to season with pepper, to pepper; *siehe* **gepfeffert**. **(b)** *(inf) (heftig werfen)* to fling, to hurl; *(hinauswerfen)* to chuck out *(inf)*, to sling out *(inf)* ◆ **jdm eine ~, jdm eine gepfefferte Ohrfeige geben** to give sb a clout *(inf)*, to clout sb one *(inf)*.

Pfeffer-: ⚠~nuß *f* gingerbread biscuit; **~steak** *nt* pepper steak; **~strauch** *m* pepper (plant); **~-und-Salz-Muster** *nt* pepper-and-salt (pattern).

Pfeifchen *nt dim of* **Pfeife (b)**.

Pfeife *f* **-, -n (a)** whistle; *(Quer~)* fife *(esp Mil)*, piccolo; *(Bootsmanns~, Orgel~)* pipe ◆ **nach jds ~ tanzen** to dance to sb's tune. **(b)** *(zum Rauchen)* pipe ◆ **eine ~ rauchen** to smoke *or* have a pipe; **~ rauchen** to smoke a pipe. **(c)** *(inf: Versager)* wash-out *(inf)*.

pfeifen *pret* **pfiff**, *ptp* **gepfiffen** *vti* to whistle *(dat* for); *(auf einer Trillerpfeife)* to blow one's whistle; *(Mus: auf einer Pfeife spielen)* to pipe; *(inf) Spiel* to ref *(inf)* ◆ **mit P~ und Trommeln zogen sie durch die Stadt** they made their way through the town amid piping and drumming *or* with pipes piping and drums beating; **auf dem letzten Loch ~** *(inf) (erschöpft sein)* to be on one's last legs *(inf)*; *(finanziell)* to be on one's beam ends *(inf)*; **ich pfeife darauf!** *(inf)* I couldn't care less, I don't give a damn *(inf)*; **ich pfeife auf seine Meinung** *(inf)* I couldn't care less about what he thinks; **das ~ ja schon die Spatzen von den Dächern** that's common knowledge, it's all over town; **~der Atem** wheezing; **sein Atem ging ~d** his breath was coming in wheezes *or* wheezily; *siehe* **Wald**.

Pfeifen-: ~deckel *m* pipe lid; **~kopf** *m* bowl (of a pipe); **~reiniger** *m* pipe-cleaner; **~ständer** *m* pipe stand *or* rack; **~stiel** *m* pipe stem; **~stopfer** *m* tamper; **~tabak** *m* pipe tobacco; **~werk** *nt* pipes *pl*, pipework.

Pfeifer *m* **-s, -** piper, fifer *(esp Mil)*.

Pfeiferei *f (inf)* whistling.

Pfeif-: ~kessel *m* whistling kettle; **~konzert** *nt* barrage *or* hail of catcalls *or* whistles; **~ton** *m* whistle, whistling sound *or* tone.

Pfeil *m* **-s, -e** arrow; *(bei Armbrust auch)* bolt; *(Wurf~)* dart ◆ **~ und Bogen** bow and arrow; **die ~e seines Spotts** *(liter)* the barbs of his mockery; **alle seine ~e verschossen haben** *(fig)* to have run out of arguments, to have shot one's bolt; **Amors ~** Cupid's arrow *or* dart; **er schoß wie ein ~ davon** he was off like a shot.

Pfeiler *m* **-s, -** *(lit, fig)* pillar; *(Brücken ~ auch)* pier; *(von Hängebrücke)* pylon; *(Stütz~)* buttress.

Pfeil-: p~förmig *adj* arrow-shaped, V-shaped; **p~förmig angeordnet** arranged in the shape of an arrow *or* in a V; **p~gerade** *adj* as straight as a die; **eine p~gerade Linie** a dead-straight line; **sie kam p~gerade auf uns zu** she made a beeline for us, she headed straight for us; **der Vogel flog p~gerade von einem Baum zum nächsten** the bird flew straight as an arrow from one tree to the next; **~gift** *nt* arrow poison; **~köcher** *m* quiver; **p~schnell** *adj* as quick as lightning, as swift as an arrow *(liter)*; **er startete p~schnell** he was off like a shot; **⚠~schuß** *m* arrowshot; **durch einen ~schuß getötet** killed by an arrow; **~schütze** *m* bowman, archer; **~spitze** *f* arrowhead, tip of an arrow; **~taste** *f (Comput)* arrow key; **~wurfspiel** *nt* darts *pl*; **~wurz** *f* arrowroot *no pl*.

Pfennig *m* **-s, -e** *or (nach Zahlenangabe)* **-** pfennig *(one hundredth of a mark)* ◆ **30 ~** 30 pfennigs; **er hat keinen ~ Geld** he hasn't got a penny to his name *or* two pennies to rub together *or* a dime *(US)*; **es ist keinen ~ wert** *(fig)* it's not worth a thing *or* a red cent *(US)*; **dem/dafür gebe ich keinen ~** *(lit)* I won't give him/it a penny; **für seine Chancen/Gesundheit** *etc* **gebe ich keinen ~** I don't give much for his chances *(inf)*, I wouldn't put much money on his chances *(inf)*; **nicht für fünf ~** *(inf)* not the slightest (bit of); **er hat nicht für fünf ~ Anstand/Verstand** *(inf)* he hasn't an ounce of respectability/intelligence; **das interessiert mich nicht für fünf ~** *(inf)* that doesn't interest me in the slightest; **auf den ~ sehen** *(fig)* to watch *or* count every penny; **mit dem** *or* **jedem ~ rechnen müssen** *(fig)* to have to watch *or* count every penny; **jeden ~ (dreimal) umdrehen** *(fig inf)* to think twice about every penny one spends; **wer den ~ nicht ehrt, ist des Talers nicht wert** *(Prov)* take care of the pennies, and the pounds will look after themselves *(Prov)*; *siehe* **Heller**.

Pfennig-: ~absatz *m* stiletto heel; **~betrag** *m* (amount in) pence *or* pennies; **es war nur ein ~betrag** it was only a matter of pence *or* pennies; **~fuchser** *m* **-s, -** *(inf)* skinflint *(inf)*, miser *(inf)*; **p~groß** *adj* **ein p~großes Geschwür** a boil the size of a sixpence; **~stück** *nt* pfennig (piece); **p~weise** *adv* penny by penny, one penny at a time; *siehe* **Groschen**.

Pferch *m* **-es, -e** fold, pen.

pferchen *vt* to cram, to pack.

Pferd *nt* **-(e)s, -e** *(Tier, Turngerät)* horse; *(Reit~ auch)* mount; *(beim Schachspiel)* knight, horse *(US inf)* ◆ **zu ~e** on horseback; **aufs falsche/richtige ~ setzen** *(lit, fig)* to back the wrong/right horse; **die ~e gehen ihm leicht durch** *(fig)* he flies off the handle easily *(inf)*; **immer langsam** *or* **sachte mit den jungen ~en** *(inf)* hold your horses *(inf)*; **wie ein ~ arbeiten** *(inf)* to work like a Trojan; **das hält ja kein ~ aus** *(inf)* it's more than flesh and blood can stand; **keine zehn ~e brächten mich dahin** *(inf)* wild horses wouldn't drag me there; **mit ihm kann man ~e stehlen** *(inf)*, **er ist ein Kerl zum ~e stehlen** *(inf)* he's a great sport *(inf)*; **er ist unser bestes ~ im Stall** he's our best man; **ich glaub, mich tritt ein ~** *(sl)* blow me down *(inf)*, struth *(sl)*.

Pferde-: ~apfel *m* piece of horse-dung; **~äpfel** horse-droppings *pl or* dung *no pl*; **~bahn** *f* horse-drawn tram, horsecar *(US)*; **p~bespannt** *adj* horse-drawn; **~bremse** *f* horsefly; **~decke** *f* horse blanket; **~dieb** *m* horse thief; **~droschke** *f* hackney-cab; **~fleisch** *nt* horsemeat *or* -flesh; **~fliege** *f siehe* **~bremse**; **~fuhrwerk** *nt* horse and cart; **~fuß** *m (fig: des Teufels)* cloven hoof; **die Sache hat aber einen ~fuß** there's just one snag; **⚠~gebiß** *nt* horsey mouth *or* teeth; **~gesicht** *nt* horsey face, face like a horse; **~haar** *nt* horsehair; **~händler** *m* horse dealer; **~huf** *m* horse's hoof; **~knecht** *m* groom; **~koppel** *f* paddock; **~länge** *f* length; **~rennbahn** *f* race course *or* track; **~rennen** *nt (Sportart)* (horse-)racing; *(einzelnes Rennen)* (horse-)race; **~schlachter** *m* knacker; **~schlachterei** *f* knacker's; **~schlitten** *m* horse-drawn sleigh; **~schwanz** *m* horse's tail; (*Frisur*) pony-tail; **~sport** *m* equestrian sport; **~stall** *m* stable; **~stärke** *f* horse power *no pl*, hp *abbr*; **~wagen** *m* (*für Personen*) horse and carriage, trap, horse-buggy (*US*); (*für Lasten*) horse and cart; **~zucht** *f* horse breeding; (*Gestüt*) stud-farm; **~züchter** *m* horse breeder.

pfiff *pret of* **pfeifen**.

Pfiff *m* **-s, -e (a)** whistle; (*Theat auch*) catcall.
(b) (*Reiz*) flair, style ◆ **der Soße fehlt noch der letzte ~** the sauce still needs that extra something; **einem Kleid den richtigen ~ geben** to add flair to a dress, to give a dress real style.
(c) (*inf: Trick*) **jetzt hast du den ~ heraus** you've got the knack *or* hang of it now (*inf*); **das ist ein Ding mit 'nem ~** there's a special knack to it.

Pfifferling *m* chanterelle ◆ **er kümmert sich keinen ~ um seine Kinder** (*inf*) he doesn't give *or* care a fig *or* give a damn about his children (*inf*); **keinen ~ wert** (*inf*) not worth a thing.

pfiffig *adj* smart, sharp, cute.

Pfiffigkeit *f* sharpness, cuteness.

Pfiffikus *m* **- *or* -ses, -se** (*dated*) crafty thing (*inf*).

Pfingsten *nt* **-, -** Whitsun, Pentecost (*Eccl*) ◆ **zu *or* an ~** at Whitsun.

Pfingst-: ~ferien *pl* Whit(sun) holiday(s); **~fest** *nt siehe* **Pfingsten**.

pfingstlich *adj no pred* Whit(sun) *attr* ◆ **die Wiesen sehen schon ~ aus** the fields have taken on a spring-time look.

Pfingst-: ~montag *m* Whit Monday; **~ochse** *m* **herausgeputzt wie ein ~ochse** (*inf*) dressed *or* done up to the nines (*inf*); **~rose** *f* peony; **~sonntag** *m* Whit Sunday, Pentecost (*Eccl*); **~woche** *f* Whit week; **~zeit** *f* Whitsun(tide).

Pfirsich *m* **-s, -e** peach.

Pfirsich-: ~baum *m* peach tree; **~blüte** *f* peach blossom; **p~farben** *adj* peach(-coloured); **~haut** *f* (*lit*) peach skin; (*fig*) peaches-and-cream complexion.

Pflanze *f* **-, -n (a)** (*Gewächs*) plant. **(b)** (*inf: Mensch*) **er/sie ist eine komische *or* seltsame ~** he/she is an odd bird (*inf*); **eine Berliner ~** (*dated*) a typical Berlin lass.

pflanzen 1 *vt* to plant ◆ **einem Kind etw ins Herz ~** (*liter*) to implant sth in the heart of a child (*liter*).
2 *vr* (*inf*) to plant (*inf*) *or* plonk (*inf*) oneself.

Pflanzen-: ~butter *f* vegetable butter; **~farbstoff** *m* vegetable dye; **~faser** *f* plant fibre; **~fett** *nt* vegetable fat; ⚠**p~fressend** *adj attr* herbivorous; **~fresser** *m* herbivore; **~kost** *f* vegetable foodstuffs *pl*; **~kunde, ~lehre** *f* botany; **~margarine** *f* vegetable margarine; **~öl** *nt* vegetable oil; **~reich** *nt* vegetable kingdom; **~schädling** *m* pest; garden pest; **~schutz** *m* protection of plants; (*gegen Ungeziefer*) pest control; **~schutzmittel** *nt* pesticide; **~welt** *f* plant world; **die ~welt des Mittelmeers** the plant life *or* the flora of the Mediterranean.

Pflanzer(in *f*) *m* **-s, -** planter.

Pflanzkartoffel *f* seed potato.

pflanzlich *adj attr* vegetable.

Pflänzling *m* seedling.

Pflanz-: ~schale *f* planting dish; **~trog** *m* plant trough.

Pflanzung *f* (*das Pflanzen*) planting; (*Plantage*) plantation.

Pflaster *nt* **-s, - (a)** (*Heft~*) (sticking-)plaster; (*fig: Entschädigung*) sop (*auf +acc* to) ◆ **das ~ erneuern** to put on a fresh *or* new (piece of) (sticking-)plaster.
(b) (*Straßen~*) (road) surface; (*Kopfstein~*) cobbles *pl* ◆ **~ treten** (*inf*) to trudge the streets, to trudge *or* traipse around; **ein gefährliches *or* heißes ~** (*inf*) a dangerous place; **ein teures ~** (*inf*) a pricey place (*inf*).

Pflasterer *m* **-s, -** road worker.

Pflaster-: ~maler *m* pavement artist; **p~müde** *adj* (*inf*) dead on one's feet (*inf*).

pflastern *vt* **(a)** *Straße, Hof* to surface; (*mit Kopfsteinpflaster*) to cobble; (*mit Steinplatten*) to pave ◆ **eine Straße neu ~** to resurface a road; *siehe* **Vorsatz**.
(b) (*inf: ohrfeigen*) **jdm eine ~** to sock sb (one) (*inf*); **du kriegst gleich eine gepflastert** I'll sock you one in a minute (*inf*).

Pflasterstein *m* (*Kopfstein*) cobble(stone); (*Steinplatte*) paving stone, flagstone; (*inf: Pfefferkuchen*) ≃ gingerbread.

Pflasterung *f* surfacing; (*mit Kopfsteinpflaster*) cobbling; (*mit Steinplatten*) paving; (*Pflaster*) surface; (*Kopfsteinpflaster*) cobbles *pl*; (*Steinplatten*) paving *no pl*.

Pflaume *f* **-, -n (a)** plum ◆ **getrocknete ~** prune. **(b)** (*inf: Mensch*) dope (*inf*), twit (*Brit inf*). **(c)** (*vulg*) cunt (*vulg*).

Pflaumen-: ~baum *m* plum(tree); **~kern** *m* plum stone; **~kompott** *nt* stewed plums *pl*; **~kuchen** *m* plum tart; **~mus** *nt* plum jam; **p~weich** *adj* (*inf*) soft; (*pej*) *Haltung* spineless.

Pflege *f* **-,** *no pl* care; (*von Kranken auch*) nursing; (*von Garten auch*) attention; (*von Beziehungen, Künsten*) fostering, cultivation; (*von Maschinen, Gebäuden*) maintenance, upkeep ◆ **jdn/etw in ~ nehmen** to look after sb/sth; **jdn/etw in ~ geben** to have sb/sth looked after; **sie gaben den Hund bei den Nachbarn in ~** they gave their dog to the neighbours to look after; **ein Kind in ~ nehmen** (*dauernd*) to foster a child; **ein Kind in ~ geben** to have a child fostered; (*von Behörden*) to foster a child out (*zu jdm* with sb); **die ~ von jdm/etw übernehmen** to look after sb/sth; **der Garten/Kranke braucht viel ~** the garden/sick man needs a lot of care and attention; **das Kind/der Hund hat bei uns gute ~** the child/dog is well looked after *or* cared for by us; **jdm gute ~ angedeihen lassen** to take good care of sb, to look after sb well.

Pflege-: p~bedürftig *adj* in need of care (and attention); **wenn alte Leute p~bedürftig werden** when old people start to need looking after; **~eltern** *pl* foster parents *pl*; **~fall** *m* case for nursing *or* care; **sie ist ein ~fall** she needs constant care; **~geld** *nt* (*für ~kinder*) boarding-out allowance; (*für Kranke*) attendance allowance; **~heim** *nt* nursing home; **~kind** *nt* foster child; **~kosten** *pl* nursing fees *pl*; **~kostenversicherung** *f* private nursing insurance; **p~leicht** *adj* easy-care; (*fig auch*) easy to handle; **~mittel** *nt* (*Kosmetikum*) cosmetic care product; (*Aut*) cleaning product; **~mutter** *f* foster mother.

pflegen 1 *vt* to look after, to care for; *Kranke auch* to nurse; *Garten, Blumen, Rasen auch* to tend; *Haar, Bart auch* to groom; *Beziehungen, Kunst, Freundschaft* to foster, to cultivate; *Maschinen, Gebäude, Denkmäler* to maintain, to keep up ◆ **etw regelmäßig ~** to attend to sth regularly, to pay regular attention to sth; *siehe* **gepflegt, Umgang**.
2 *vi* (*gewöhnlich tun*) to be in the habit (*zu* of), to be accustomed (*zu* to) ◆ **sie pflegte zu sagen** she used to say, she was in the habit of saying; **zum Mittagessen pflegt er Bier zu trinken** he's in the habit of drinking beer with his lunch, he usually drinks beer with his lunch; **wie es so zu gehen pflegt** as usually happens; **wie man zu sagen pflegt** as they say.
3 *vr* **(a)** to care about one's appearance.
(b) (*sich schonen*) to take it *or* things easy (*inf*).

Pflegepersonal *nt* nursing staff.

Pfleger *m* **-s, -** (*im Krankenhaus*) orderly; (*voll qualifiziert*) (male) nurse; (*Vormund*) guardian; (*Nachlaß~*) trustee.

Pflegerin *f* nurse.

pflegerisch *adj* nursing.

Pflege-: ~satz *m* hospital and nursing charges *pl*; **~serie** *f* (*Kosmetika*) line of cosmetic products; **~sohn** *m* foster son; **~station** *f* nursing ward; **~tochter** *f* foster daughter; **~vater** *m* foster father; **~versicherung** *f siehe* **~kostenversicherung**.

pfleglich *adj* careful ◆ **etw ~ behandeln** to treat sth carefully *or* with care.

Pflegling *m* foster child; (*Mündel*) ward.

Pflegschaft *f* (*Vormundschaft*) guardianship, tutelage (*form*); (*Vermögens~*) trusteeship.

Pflicht *f* **-, -en (a)** (*Verpflichtung*) duty ◆ **ich habe die traurige ~ ...** it is my sad duty ...; **als Abteilungsleiter hat er die ~, ...** it's his duty *or* responsibility as head of department ...; **Rechte und ~en** rights and responsibilities; **seine ~ erfüllen** to do one's duty; **der ~ gehorchen** (*geh*) to obey the call of duty; **jdn in die ~ nehmen** to remind sb of his duty; **eheliche ~en** conjugal *or* marital duties; **die bürgerlichen ~en** one's civic duties *or* responsibilities; **die ~ ruft** duty calls; **ich habe es mir zur ~ gemacht** I've taken it upon myself, I've made it my duty; **ich tue nur meine ~** I'm only doing my duty; **etw nur aus ~ tun** to do sth merely because one has to; **das/Schulbesuch ist ~** you have to do that/to go to school, it's/going to school is compulsory; **es ist seine (verdammte *inf*) ~ und Schuldigkeit(, das zu tun)** he damn well *or* jolly well ought to (do it) (*inf*).
(b) (*Sport*) compulsory section *or* exercises *pl* ◆ **bei der ~** in the compulsory section *or* exercises.

Pflicht-: ~besuch *m* duty visit; ⚠**p~bewußt** *adj* conscientious, conscious of one's duties; **er ist sehr p~bewußt** he takes his duties very seriously, he has a great sense of duty; ⚠**~bewußtsein** *nt* sense of duty; **~eifer** *m* zeal; **p~eifrig** *adj* zealous.

Pflichtenheft *nt* (*Anforderungsprofil, für Geräte*) specification; (*für Arbeitsstelle*) job description.

Pflichtenkreis *m* duties *pl*.

Pflicht-: ~erfüllung *f* fulfilment of one's duty; **~exemplar** *nt* deposit copy; **~fach** *nt* compulsory subject; **Deutsch ist ~fach** German is compulsory *or* is a compulsory subject; **~gefühl** *nt siehe* **~bewußtsein**; **p~gemäß** *adj* dutiful; **ich teile Ihnen p~gemäß mit** it is my duty to inform you; **p~getreu** *adj* dutiful; **~jahr** *nt a year's compulsory community service for girls during Nazi period*; **~kür** *f* compulsory exercise; **~lauf** *m* (*Eiskunstlauf*) compulsory figures *pl*; **~lektüre** *f* compulsory reading; (*Sch auch*) set book(s); **p~schuldig** *adj* dutiful; **~teil** *m or nt* statutory portion (*of a deceased person's estate that must be left, eg to a child*); **p~treu** *adj* dutiful; **~treue** *f* devotion to duty; **~übung** *f* compulsory exercise; **p~vergessen** *adj* irresponsible; **~vergessenheit** *f* neglect of duty, irresponsibility; **~verletzung** *f* breach of duty; **~versäumnis** *f* neglect *or* dereliction of duty *no pl*; **er machte sich häufiger ~versäumnisse schuldig** he was frequently guilty of neglecting his duties; **p~versichert** *adj* compulsorily insured; **~versicherte(r)** *mf* compulsorily insured person; **~versicherung** *f* compulsory insurance; **~verteidiger** *m counsel for the defence appointed by the court and paid from the legal aid fund*; **~vorlesung** *f* compulsory lecture; **p~widrig** *adj* contrary to duty; **er hat sich p~widrig verhalten** he behaved in a manner contrary to (his) duty.

Pflock *m* **-(e)s, ¨-e** peg; (*für Tiere*) stake ◆ **einen ~ *or* ein paar ¨-e zurückstecken** (*fig*) to back-pedal a bit.

pflücken *vt* to pick, to pluck; (*sammeln*) to pick.

Pflücker(in *f*) *m* **-s, -** picker.

Pflug *m* **-es, ¨-e** plough (*Brit*), plow (*US*) ◆ **unter dem ~** under the plough.

Pflugbogen *m* (*Ski*) snowplough (*Brit*) *or* snowplow (*US*) turn.

pflügen *vti* (*lit, fig*) to plough (*Brit*), to plow (*US*); (*lit auch*) to till (*liter*) ◆ **das Schiff pflügte die Wellen** (*liter*) the ship ploughed (through) the waves.

Pflüger *m* **-s, -** ploughman (*Brit*), plowman (*US*).

Pflug-: ~schar *f* **-, -en** ploughshare (*Brit*), plowshare (*US*); **~sterz** *m* plough-handle (*Brit*), plow-handle (*US*).

Pfortader *f* portal vein.

Pforte *f* **-, -n** (*Tor*) gate; (*Geog*) gap ◆ **das Theater hat seine ~n für immer geschlossen** the theatre has closed its doors for good; **Nepal, die ~ zum**

Himalaya Nepal, the gateway to the Himalayas; **die ~n des Himmels** (*liter*) the gates *or* portals (*liter*) of Heaven.

Pförtner *m* **-s, -** (*Anat*) pylorus.

Pförtner(in *f*) *m* **-s, -** porter; (*von Fabrik*) gateman; (*von Wohnhaus, Behörde*) doorman; (*von Schloß*) gatekeeper.

Pförtnerloge [-lo:ʒə] *f* porter's office; (*in Fabrik*) gatehouse; (*in Wohnhaus, Büro*) doorman's office.

Pfosten *m* **-s, -** post; (*senkrechter Balken*) upright; (*Fenster~*) jamb; (*Tür~*) jamb, doorpost; (*Stütze*) support, prop; (*Ftbl*) (goal)post, upright.

⚠ **Pfostenschuß** *m* (*Ftbl*) **das war nur ein ~** it hit the (goal)post *or* upright.

Pfötchen *nt dim of* **Pfote** little paw ◆ **(gib) ~!** shake hands!

Pfote *f* **-, -n (a)** paw. **(b)** (*inf: Hand*) mitt (*inf*), paw (*inf*) ◆ **sich** (*dat*) **die ~n verbrennen** (*inf*) to burn one's fingers; **seine ~n überall drin haben** (*fig inf*) to have a finger in every pie (*inf*). **(c)** (*inf: schlechte Handschrift*) scribble, scrawl.

Pfriem *m* **-(e)s, -e** awl.

Pfropf *m* **-(e)s, -e** *or* **¨-e, Pfropfen** *m* **-s, -** (*Stöpsel*) stopper; (*Kork, Sekt~*) cork; (*Watte~ etc*) plug; (*von Faß, Korbflasche*) bung; (*Med: Blut~*) (blood) clot; (*verstopfend*) blockage ◆ **er hat einen ~ im Ohr** his ears are bunged up (*inf*) *or* blocked up.

pfropfen *vt* **(a)** *Pflanzen* to graft. **(b)** (*verschließen*) *Flasche* to bung. **(c)** (*inf: hineinzwängen*) to cram ◆ **er pfropfte den Korken in die Flasche** he shoved the cork in the bottle (*inf*); **gepfropft voll** jam-packed (*inf*), crammed full.

Pfröpfling *m* graft, scion.

Pfropf-: ~messer *nt* grafting knife; **~reis** *nt* graft, scion.

Pfründe *f* **-, -n** (*Kirchenamt*) (church) living, benefice; (*Einkünfte auch*) prebend; (*fig*) sinecure.

Pfuhl *m* **-s, -e** (*liter*) mudhole; (*fig*) (quag)mire, slough (*liter*).

Pfühl *m or nt* **-(e)s, -e** (*poet, dial*) (*Kissen*) pillow; (*weiches Bett*) downy *or* feather bed.

pfui *interj* (*Ekel*) ugh, yuck; (*Mißbilligung*) tut tut; (*zu Hunden*) oy, hey; (*Buhruf*) boo ◆ **faß das nicht an, das ist ~** (*inf*) don't touch it, it's dirty *or* nasty; **~ Teufel** *or* **Deibel** *or* **Spinne** (*all inf*) ugh, yuck; **~ schäme dich** shame on you!; **da kann ich nur ~ sagen** it's simply disgraceful.

Pfuiruf *m* boo.

Pfund *nt* **-(e)s, -e** *or* (*nach Zahlenangabe*) **- (a)** (*Gewicht*) (*in Deutschland*) 500 grams, half a kilo(gram); (*in UK*) pound ◆ **drei ~ Äpfel** three pounds of apples; **er bewegte seine ~e mit Mühe** he moved his great bulk with effort. **(b)** (*Währungseinheit*) pound ◆ **in ~** in pounds; **zwanzig ~ Sterling** twenty pounds sterling; **das ~ sinkt** sterling/the pound is falling; **mit seinem ~e wuchern** (*liter*) to make the most of one's opportunities *or* chances.

Pfund- *in cpds* pound; **~betrag** *m* amount in pounds, sterling sum.

-pfünder *m* **-s, -** *in cpds* -pounder; (*Brot*) -pound loaf.

pfundig *adj* (*dated inf*) great *no adv*, fantastic, swell *no adv* (*US*) ◆ **das hast du ~ gemacht** you've made a great job of that.

-pfündig *adj suf* -pound.

Pfunds- *in cpds* (*inf*) great (*inf*), swell (*US inf*), super (*inf*); **~kerl** *m* (*inf*) great guy (*inf*).

pfundweise *adv* by the pound.

Pfusch *m* **-(e)s,** *no pl* (*inf*) *siehe* **Pfuscherei.**

Pfusch|arbeit *f* (*inf*) slapdash work ◆ **sie haben richtige ~ geleistet** they did a really sloppy job (*inf*).

pfuschen *vi* **(a)** to bungle; (*einen Fehler machen*) to slip up, to come unstuck (*inf*) ◆ **jdm ins Handwerk ~** to poke one's nose into *or* meddle in sb's affairs. **(b)** (*Sch*) to cheat.

Pfuscher(in *f*) *m* **-s, -** (*inf*) bungler, botcher (*inf*).

Pfuscherei *f* (*das Pfuschen*) bungling *no pl*; (*gepfuschte Arbeit*) botch-up (*inf*), botched-up job.

Pfütze *f* **-, -n** puddle.

PH [pe:'ha:] *f* **-, -s** *abbr of* **Pädagogische Hochschule.**

Phalanx *f* **-, Phalangen** (*Hist*) phalanx; (*fig*) battery.

Phallen, Phalli *pl of* **Phallus.**

phallisch *adj* phallic.

Phallus *m* **-, -se** *or* **Phalli** *or* **Phallen** phallus.

Phallus-: ~kult *m* phallus worship; **~symbol** *nt* phallic symbol.

Phänomen *nt* **-s, -e** phenomenon ◆ **dieser Mensch ist ein ~** this person is phenomenal *or* is an absolute phenomenon.

phänomenal *adj* phenomenal.

Phänomenologie *f* phenomenology.

Phänotyp *m* **-s, -en, Phänotypus** *m* phenotype.

⚠ **Phantasie** *f* **(a)** *no pl* (*Einbildung*) imagination ◆ **er hat ~** he's got imagination; **eine schmutzige ~ haben** to have a dirty mind; **in seiner ~** in his mind *or* imagination; **er spielt ohne ~** he plays unimaginatively *or* without any imagination. **(b)** *usu pl* (*Trugbild*) fantasy.

⚠ **Phantasie-: p~arm** *adj* unimaginative, lacking in imagination; **p~begabt** *adj* imaginative; **~bild** *nt* fantasy (picture); **~gebilde** *nt* **(a)** (*phantastische Form*) fantastic form; **(b)** (*Einbildung*) figment of the *or* one's imagination; **p~los** *adj* unimaginative, lacking in imagination; **~losigkeit** *f* lack of imagination, unimaginativeness; **p~reich** *adj siehe* **p~voll.**

⚠ **phantasieren*** [1] *vi* to fantasize (*von* about); (*von Schlimmem*) to have visions (*von* of); (*Med*) to be delirious; (*Mus*) to improvise ◆ **er phantasiert von einem großen Haus auf dem Lande** he has fantasies about a big house in the country.

[2] *vt Geschichte* to dream up; (*Mus*) to improvise ◆ **was phantasierst du denn da?** (*inf*) what are you (going) on about? (*inf*); **er hat das alles phantasiert** that's all just (in) his imagination; **er phantasiert, daß die Welt untergeht** he has visions of the world coming to an end; **sie phantasiert, daß sie auswandern will** she fantasizes about emigrating.

⚠ **Phantasie-: p~voll** *adj* highly imaginative; **~vorstellung** *f* figment of the imagination.

⚠ **Phantast** *m* **-en, -en** dreamer, visionary.

⚠ **Phantasterei** *f* fantasy.

⚠ **phantastisch** *adj* fantastic; (*unglaublich auch*) incredible.

Phantom *nt* **-s, -e (a)** (*Trugbild*) phantom ◆ **einem ~ nachjagen** (*fig*) to tilt at windmills. **(b)** (*Modell*) (*für Unterricht*) anatomical model, manikin; (*beim Fechten*) dummy.

Phantom-: ~bild *nt* identikit (picture); **~schmerz** *m* phantom limb pain.

Pharao *m* **-s, Pharaonen** Pharaoh.

Pharaonen- *in cpds* of the Pharaohs.

Pharisäer *m* **-s, -** (*Hist*) pharisee; (*fig auch*) hypocrite.

pharisäerhaft, pharisäisch *adj* pharisaic(al); (*fig auch*) holier-than-thou, self-righteous.

Pharisäertum *nt* (*fig*) self-righteousness.

pharm. *abbr of* **pharmazeutisch.**

Pharma-: ~hersteller *m* drug manufacturer; **~industrie** *f* pharmaceuticals industry.

Pharmakologe *m*, **Pharmakologin** *f* pharmacologist.

Pharmakologie *f* pharmacology.

pharmakologisch *adj* pharmacological.

Pharma-: ~markt *m* pharmaceuticals market; **~produkt** *nt* pharmaceutical product; **~produzent** *m* pharmaceuticals producer; **~referent** *m* medical representative; **~rückstände** *pl* pharmaceutical effluents *pl*; **~unternehmen** *nt* pharmaceuticals company.

Pharmazeut(in *f*) *m* **-en, -en** pharmacist, druggist (*US*).

Pharmazeutik *f siehe* **Pharmazie.**

pharmazeutisch *adj* pharmaceutical ◆ **~-technische Assistentin, ~-technischer Assistent** pharmaceutical assistant.

Pharmazie *f* pharmacy, pharmaceutics *sing*.

Phase *f* **-, -n** phase.

Phasen-: p~gleich *adj* in phase; **~gleichheit** *f* phase coincidence; **~spannung** *f* voltage to neutral, phase voltage; **~verschiebung** *f* phase difference *or* displacement.

-phasig *adj suf* -phase.

Phenol *nt* **-s,** *no pl* phenol.

Phenolgas *nt* phenol gas.

Pheromon *nt* **-s, -e** pheromone.

Philanthrop *m* **-en, -en** philanthropist.

Philanthropie *f* philanthropy.

philanthropisch *adj* philanthropic(al).

Philatelie *f* philately.

Philatelist(in *f*) *m* philatelist.

philatelistisch *adj* philatelic.

Philharmonie *f* (*Orchester*) philharmonia, philharmonic (orchestra); (*Konzertsaal*) philharmonic hall.

Philharmoniker *m* **-s, -** (*Musiker*) member of a philharmonic orchestra ◆ **die ~** the philharmonic (orchestra).

philharmonisch *adj* philharmonic.

Philippika *f* **-, Philippiken** (*Hist*) Philippic; (*fig*) philippic.

Philippine *m* **-n, -n, Philippinin** *f* Filipino.

Philippinen *pl* Philippines *pl*, Philippine Islands *pl*.

philippinisch *adj* Filipino.

Philister *m* **-s, -** (*lit*) Philistine; (*fig*) philistine.

philisterhaft *adj* (*fig*) philistine ◆ **sich ~ verhalten** to behave like a philistine.

Philologe *m*, **Philologin** *f* philologist.

Philologie *f* philology.

philologisch *adj* philological.

Philosoph(in *f*) *m* **-en, -en** philosopher.

Philosophie *f* philosophy.

philosophieren* *vi* to philosophize (*über +acc* about).

philosophisch *adj* philosophical.

Phimose *f* **-, -n** phimosis.

Phiole *f* **-, -n** phial, vial.

Phlegma *nt* **-s,** *no pl* apathy, torpor, torpidity.

Phlegmatiker(in *f*) *m* **-s, -** apathetic person.

phlegmatisch *adj* apathetic.

Phlox [flɔks] *m* **-es, -e** *or f* **-, -e** phlox.

Phobie [fo'bi:] *f* phobia (*vor +dat* about).

⚠ **Phon** [fo:n] *nt* **-s, -s** phon.

Phonem *nt* **-s, -e** phoneme.

Phonetik *f* phonetics *sing*.

Phonetiker(in *f*) *m* **-s, -** phonetician.

phonetisch *adj* phonetic ◆ **~e Schrift** phonetic transcription *or* script; **etw ~ schreiben** to write *or* transcribe sth phonetically *or* in phonetics.

Phönix *m* **-(es), -e** phoenix ◆ **wie ein ~ aus der Asche steigen** to rise like a phoenix from the ashes.

Phönizier(in *f*) [-iɐ, -iərɪn] *m* **-s, -** Phoenician.

phönizisch *adj* Phoenician.

Phono-: ~branche *f* hi-fi industry; **~graph** *m* phonograph.

Phonologie *f* phonology.

phonologisch *adj* phonological.
Phonotypistin *f* audio-typist.
⚠**Phon-**: **p~stark** *adj Lautsprecher* powerful; *Lärm* loud; **~stärke** *f* decibel; **~zahl** *f* decibel level.
Phosgen [fɔs'ge:n] *nt* **-s**, *no pl* phosgene.
Phosphat [fɔs'fa:t] *nt* phosphate.
phosphat- [fɔs'fa:t-]: **~frei** *adj* phosphate-free; **~haltig** *adj* containing phosphates.
Phosphor ['fɔsfɔr] *m* **-s**, *no pl* (*abbr* **P**) phosphorus.
Phosphoreszenz *f* phosphorescence.
phosphoreszieren* *vi* to phosphoresce.
phosphorhaltig *adj* phosphorous.
phosphorig *adj* **~e Säure** phosphorous acid.
Phosphor-: **~säure** *f* phosphoric acid; **~vergiftung** *f* phosphorus poisoning.
phot. *abbr of* **photographisch.**
Photo[1] *nt* **-s, -s** *siehe* **Foto**[1].
Photo[2] *m* **-s, -s** (*inf*) *siehe* **Foto**[2].
Photo- *in cpds* photo; *siehe auch* **Foto-**; **~chemie** *f* photochemistry; **p~elektrisch** *adj* photoelectric.
Photograph *m siehe* **Fotograf.**
Photographie *f siehe* **Fotografie.**
photographieren* *vti siehe* **fotografieren.**
Photographin *f siehe* **Fotografin.**
Photon *nt* **-s, -en** photon.
Photo-: **~synthese** *f* photosynthesis; **p~trop** *adj* phototropic; **p~voltaisch** [-vɔl'ta:ɪʃ] *adj* photovoltaic; **~zelle** *f* photoelectric cell.
Phrase *f* **-, -n** phrase; (*pej*) empty *or* hollow phrase ◆ **abgedroschene ~** cliché, hackneyed phrase; **das sind alles nur ~n** that's just (so many) words, that's just talk; **leere** *or* **hohle ~n** empty *or* hollow words *or* phrases; **~n dreschen** (*inf*) to churn out one cliché after another.
Phrasen-: **~drescher** *m* (*pej*) windbag; **~drescherei** *f* (*pej*) phrase-mongering; (*Geschwafel*) hot air, **p~haft** *adj* empty, hollow; **er drückt sich p~haft aus** he speaks in empty phrases; **p~reich** *adj* cliché-ridden.
Phraseologie *f* phraseology; (*Buch*) dictionary of idioms.
phraseologisch *adj* phraseological ◆ **~es Wörterbuch** dictionary of idioms.
phrasieren* *vt* to phrase.
Phrasierung *f* phrasing.
pH-Wert [pe:'ha:-] *m* pH-value.
Physik *f* **-**, *no pl* physics *sing.*
physikalisch *adj* physical ◆ **~e Experimente durchführen** to carry out physics experiments *or* experiments in physics; **das ist ~ nicht erklärbar** that can't be explained by physics; **~e Therapie** physiotherapy, physical therapy.
Physiker(in *f*) *m* **-s, -** physicist; (*Student auch*) physics student.
Physiksaal *m* physics lab *or* laboratory.
Physikum *nt* **-s**, *no pl* (*Univ*) *preliminary examination in medicine.*
Physiognomie [fyziogno'mi:] *f* (*liter*) physiognomy.
physiognomisch [fyzio'gno:mɪʃ] *adj* physiognomical.
Physiologe *m*, **Physiologin** *f* physiologist.
Physiologie *f* physiology.
physiologisch *adj* physiological.
Physiotherapeut *m* physiotherapist.
Physiotherapie *f* physiotherapy, physical therapy.
physisch *adj* physical.
Pi *nt* **-(s), -s** pi ◆ **etw ~ mal Daumen** (*inf*) *or* **Schnauze** (*sl*) **machen** to do sth off the top of one's head.
Pianino *nt* **-s, -s** pianino, cottage *or* piccolo piano.
Pianist(in *f*) *m* pianist.
Piano *nt* **-s, -s** (*geh: Klavier*) piano.
Pianoforte *nt* **-s, -s** pianoforte.
picheln *vi* (*inf*) to booze (*inf*), to knock it back (*inf*).
Picke *f* **-, -n** pick(axe).
Pickel *m* **-s, -** **(a)** spot, pimple. **(b)** (*Spitzhacke*) pick(axe); (*Eis~*) ice axe.
Pickelhaube *f* spiked (leather) helmet.
pick(e)lig *adj* spotty, pimply.
picken *vti* to peck (*nach* at).
Picknick *nt* **-s, -s** *or* **-e** picnic ◆ **zum ~ fahren** to go for a picnic; **~ machen** to have a picnic.
picknicken *vi* to (have a) picnic.
Piefke *m* **-s, -s** **(a)** (*Aus inf: Deutscher*) Kraut (*inf*), Jerry (*inf*). **(b) ein kleiner ~** a (little) pipsqueak.
pieken, pieksen *vti* (*inf*) to prick ◆ **es hat nur ein bißchen gepiekt** it was just a bit of a prick, I/he *etc* just felt a bit of a prick.
piekfein, pikfein *adj* (*inf*) posh (*inf*), swish (*inf*).
pieksauber *adj* (*inf*) spotless, clean as a whistle *or* a new penny.
pieksen *vti siehe* **pieken.**
piep *interj* tweet(-tweet), chirp(-chirp), cheep(-cheep) ◆ **er traute sich nicht mal ~ zu sagen** *or* **machen** (*inf*) he wouldn't have dared (to) say boo to a goose (*inf*).
Piep *m* **-s, -e** (*inf*) **er sagt keinen ~** he doesn't say a (single) word; **keinen ~ mehr machen** to have had it (*inf*); **du hast ja einen ~!** you're off your head (*inf*).
piepe, piep|egal *adj pred* (*inf*) all one (*inf*) ◆ **das ist mir ~!** (*inf*) I couldn't care less (*inf*), it's all one to me (*inf*).

piepen, piepsen *vi* (*Vogel*) to cheep, to chirrup; (*Kinderstimme*) to pipe, to squeak; (*Maus*) to squeak; (*Funkgerät etc*) to bleep ◆ **bei dir piept's wohl!** (*inf*) are you off your head?; **es war zum P~!** (*inf*) it was a scream (*inf*); **mit ~der Stimme** in a piping voice.
Piepen *pl* (*dated sl*) lolly (*inf*), dough (*sl*).
Piepmatz *m* (*baby-talk: Vogel*) dickybird (*baby-talk*).
piepsen *vi siehe* **piepen.**
Piepser *m* **-s, -** (*inf*) **(a)** *siehe* **Piep. (b)** (*Telec*) bleeper.
piepsig *adj* (*inf*) squeaky.
Piepsstimme *f* (*inf*) squeaky voice.
Piepvogel *m* (*baby-talk*) dickybird (*baby-talk*).
Pier *m* **-s, -s** *or* **-e** *or f* **-, -s** jetty, pier.
piesacken *vt* (*inf*) (*quälen*) to torment; (*belästigen*) to pester ◆ **er piesackt mich schon den ganzen Tag, daß ich ihn mitnehme** he's been pestering me all day to take him with me.
Piesepampel *m* **-s, -** (*inf*) square (*inf*).
Pietà [pie'ta] *f* **-, -s** pietà.
Pietät [pie'tɛ:t] *f* (*Ehrfurcht vor den Toten*) reverence *no pl*; (*Achtung*) respect (*gegenüber jdm/etw, vor etw* (*dat*) for sb/sth); (*Frömmelei*) piety ◆ **das verstößt gegen jede ~** that goes against every feeling of respect *or* sense of reverence.
pietätlos [pie'tɛ:t-] *adj* irreverent, lacking in respect, impious.
Pietätlosigkeit [pie'tɛ:t-] *f* irreverence, impiety; (*Tat*) impious act ◆ **das ist eine ~ sondergleichen!** that shows a complete lack of reverence!
pietätvoll [pie'tɛ:t-] *adj* pious, reverent.
Pietismus [pie'tɪsmʊs] *m* Pietism; (*pej*) pietism, piety, piousness.
Pietist(in *f*) [pie'tɪst(ɪn)] *m* Pietist; (*pej auch*) holy Joe (*inf*).
pietistisch [pie'tɪstɪʃ] *adj* pietistic; (*pej auch*) pious.
piff paff *interj* bang bang, pow pow (*inf*).
Pigment *nt* pigment.
Pigmentation *f* pigmentation.
Pigmentfleck *m* pigmentation mark.
pigmentieren* (*form*) **[1]** *vi* to become pigmented, to pigment. **[2]** *vt* to pigment.
Pik[1] *m* (*inf*) **einen ~ auf jdn haben** to have something *or* a grudge against sb.
Pik[2] *nt* **-s, -** (*Cards*) (*no pl: Farbe*) spades *pl*; (*~karte*) spade ◆ **~-As** ace of spades; **dastehen wie ~-Sieben** (*inf*) to look completely bewildered *or* at a loss.
pikant *adj* piquant; *Witz, Geschichte auch* racy.
Pikanterie *f* **(a)** *siehe adj* piquancy; raciness. **(b)** (*Bemerkung*) piquant *or* racy remark.
Pike *f* **-, -n** pike ◆ **von der ~ auf dienen** (*fig*) to rise from the ranks, to work one's way up; **etw von der ~ auf lernen** (*fig*) to learn sth starting from the bottom.
Pikee *m or nt* **-s, -s** piqué.
pikieren* *vt Blumen* to prick out, to transplant; *Bäume* to transplant.
pikiert *adj* (*inf*) put out, peeved, piqued ◆ **sie machte ein ~es Gesicht** she looked put out *or* peeved; **~ reagieren** to get put out *or* peeved.
Pikkolo *m* **-s, -s** **(a)** (*Kellnerlehrling*) apprentice *or* trainee waiter. **(b)** (*fig: kleine Ausgabe*) mini-version, baby; (*auch* **~flasche**) *quarter bottle of champagne.* **(c)** (*Mus: auch* **~flöte**) piccolo.
pikobello *adj* (*inf*) immaculate, impeccable ◆ **ein Zimmer ~ aufräumen** to make a room look immaculate.
Piktogramm *nt* **-s, -e** pictogram.
Pilger(in *f*) *m* **-s, -** pilgrim.
Pilgerfahrt *f* pilgrimage ◆ **auf ~ gehen** to go on a pilgrimage.
pilgern *vi aux sein* to make a pilgrimage; (*inf: gehen*) to make *or* wend one's way.
Pilgerschaft *f* pilgrimage.
Pilger-: **~stab** *m* pilgrim's staff; **~zug** *m* procession of pilgrims.
Pille *f* **-, -n** pill, tablet; (*Antibaby~*) pill ◆ **die ~ danach** the morning-after pill; **eine ~ (ein)nehmen** *or* **schlucken** to take a pill; **sie nimmt die ~** she's on the pill, she takes the pill; **das war eine bittere ~ für ihn** (*fig*) that was a bitter pill for him (to swallow); **jdm eine bittere ~ versüßen** *or* **verzuckern** (*fig*) to sugar *or* sweeten the pill for sb.
Pillen-: **~dreher** *m* **(a)** (*Zool*) scarab; **(b)** (*inf: Apotheker*) chemist, druggist (*US*); **~knick** *m birth-rate slump caused by the pill.*
Pilot(in *f*) *m* **-en, -en** pilot.
Pilot-: **~anlage** *f* pilot plant; **~ballon** *m* pilot balloon; **~film** *m* pilot film; **~projekt** *nt* pilot scheme; **~studie** *f* pilot study.
Pils **-, -**, **Pils(e)ner** *nt* **-s, -** pils, pilsner.
Pilz *m* **-es, -e** **(a)** fungus; (*giftig*) toadstool; (*eßbar*) mushroom; (*Mikro~*) mould; (*Atom~*) mushroom cloud ◆ **in die ~e gehen** (*inf*) to go mushrooming *or* mushroom-picking; **wie ~e aus der Erde** *or* **aus dem Boden schießen** *or* **sprießen** to spring up like mushrooms, to mushroom.
(b) (*Haut~*) ringworm; (*Fuß~ auch*) athlete's foot.
pilzförmig *adj* mushroom-shaped ◆ **der Rauch stieg ~ auf** the smoke climbed up in a mushroom-shaped cloud.
Pilz-: **~kopf** *m* (*inf*) Beatle; (*Frisur*) Beatle haircut; **~krankheit** *f* fungal disease; **~kunde** *f* mycology; **p~tötend** *adj* fungicidal; **~vergiftung** *f* fungus poisoning.
Pimmel *m* **-s, -** (*inf: Penis*) willie (*inf*).
pimp(e)lig *adj* (*inf*) (*wehleidig*) soppy (*inf*); (*verweichlicht auch*) namby-pamby (*inf*), cissyish.
Pimperlinge *pl* (*dated inf*) **die paar ~** the odd penny.
pimpern (*sl*) **[1]** *vt* to have it off with (*sl*).

⚠: for details of spelling reform, see supplement

[2] vi to have it off (sl).
Pimpf m -(e)s, -e (a) (inf) squirt (pej). (b) (Hist) member of Hitlerian organization for 10 — 14-year-olds.
pimplig adj siehe **pimp(e)lig.**
Pin m -s, -s (Comput: von Stecker) pin.
pingelig adj (inf) finicky (inf), fussy, nit-picking (inf).
Pingpong nt -s, -s (inf) ping-pong.
Pinguin ['pɪŋgui:n] m -s, -e penguin.
Pinie ['pi:niə] f pine (tree).
pink adj pred pink.
Pinkel m -s, - (inf) **ein feiner** or **vornehmer ~** a swell, Lord Muck (inf).
pinkeln vi (inf) to pee (inf), to piddle (inf) ♦ **ich muß mal ~** I need a pee (inf).
Pinkelpause f (inf) break ♦ **der Bus hielt zu einer ~** the bus made a toilet stop or a convenience stop.
Pinke(pinke) f -, no pl (dated sl) dough (sl), lolly (inf) ♦ **heute gibt's ~** payday today!
pinkfarben adj pink.
Pinne f -, -n (a) (inf: Stift) pin. (b) (für Kompaßnadel) pivot. (c) (Ruder ~) tiller.
Pinnwand f notice board (Brit), bulletin board (US).
Pinscher m -s, - pinscher; (inf: Mensch) self-important little pipsqueak (inf).
Pinsel m -s, - (a) brush; (Hunt) tuft of hair. (b) (inf) **ein eingebildeter ~** a self-opinionated twit (inf), a jumped-up so-and-so (inf). (c) (sl: Penis) willie (inf).
Pinselei f (pej) daubing (pej); (Gemälde auch) daub (pej).
Pinselführung f brushwork.
pinseln vti (inf: streichen) to paint (auch Med); (pej: malen) to daub; (inf: schreiben) to pen.
Pinselstrich m stroke (of a brush), brushstroke.
Pinte f -, -n (a) (inf: Lokal) boozer (Brit inf). (b) (Measure) pint.
Pin-up-girl [pɪn'apgœrl] nt -s, -s pin-up (girl).
Pinzette f (pair of) tweezers pl.
Pionier m -s, -e (a) (Mil) sapper, engineer. (b) (fig) pioneer. (c) (DDR) member of a political organization similar to the Boy Scouts.
Pionier-: **~arbeit** f pioneering work; **~geist** m pioneering spirit.
Pipapo nt -s, no pl (inf) **das ganze ~** the whole caboodle (inf); **eine Party mit allem ~** a party with all the works.
Pipeline ['paiplain] f -, -s pipeline.
Pipette f pipette.
Pipi nt or m -s, -s (baby-talk) wee(-wee) (baby-talk) ♦ **~ machen** to do or have a wee(-wee).
Pipi-: **~fax** nt or m -, no pl (inf) nonsense; **~mädchen** nt (pej) bimbo (inf).
Piranha [pi'ranja] m -(s), -s piranha.
Pirat m -en, -en pirate; (Luft~) hijacker.
Piraten-: **~akt** m act of piracy; **~schiff** nt pirate ship; **~sender** m pirate radio station.
Piraterie f (lit, fig) piracy.
Pirol m -s, -e oriole.
Pirouette [pi'ruɛtə] f pirouette.
Pirsch f -, no pl stalk ♦ **auf (die) ~ gehen** to go stalking.
pirschen vi to stalk, to go stalking.
Pirschgang m stalk ♦ **auf ~ gehen** to go stalking.
pispern vi (dial) to whisper.
⚠ **Piß** m **Pisses**, no pl (vulg) piss (vulg), slash (Brit sl).
Pisse f -, no pl (vulg) piss (vulg).
pissen vi (vulg) to (have a) piss (vulg); (regnen) to piss down (vulg).
Pissoir [pɪ'soa:ɐ] nt -s, -s or -e (dated) urinal.
⚠ **Pißpott** m (sl) potty (inf).
Pistazie [pɪs'ta:tsiə] f pistachio.
Piste f -, -n (Ski) piste, (ski-)run; (Rennbahn) track, circuit; (Aviat) runway, tarmac; (behelfsmäßig) landing-strip, air-strip; (im Zirkus) barrier.
Pisten-: **~raupe** f piste caterpillar or basher (inf); **~sau** f (Ski sl), **~schreck** m (Ski inf) hooligan on the piste.
Pistole f -, -n (a) pistol ♦ **jdn mit vorgehaltener ~ zwingen** to force sb at gun-point; **jdn auf ~n fordern** to challenge sb to a duel (with pistols); **jdm die ~ auf die Brust setzen** (fig) to hold a pistol to sb's head; **wie aus der ~ geschossen** (fig) like a shot.
(b) (Hist: Goldmünze) pistole.
Pistolen-: **~griff** m pistol butt; **~kugel** f (pistol) bullet; ⚠**~schuß** m pistol shot; **~tasche** f holster.
Pit-Bull-Terrier m pit bull-terrier.
⚠ **pitsch(e)naß**, ⚠ **pitsch(e)patsch(e)naß** (inf) adj soaking (wet); Kleidung, Mensch auch dripping (wet).
pitsch, patsch interj pitter-patter.
pittoresk adj picturesque.
Pixel nt -s, -s (Comput) pixel.
Pizza f -, -s pizza.
Pizzeria f -, -s pizzeria.
Pkw ['pe:ka:ve:] m -s, -s siehe **Personenkraftwagen.**
pl., Pl. abbr of **Plural** pl.
Placebo [pla'tse:bo] nt -s, -s placebo.
⚠ **placieren*** [pla'tsi:rən] vt, ⚠ **Placierung** f siehe **plazieren, Plazierung.**
placken vr (inf) to slave (away) (inf).
Placken m -s, - (dial) patch.
Plackerei f (inf) grind (inf).
pladdern (N Ger) [1] vi aux sein (Regen) to pelt (down).
[2] vi impers to pelt down.

plädieren* vi (Jur, fig) to plead (für, auf +acc for).
Plädoyer [plɛdoa'je:] nt -s, -s (Jur) address to the jury, summation (US), summing up; (fig) plea.
Plafond [pla'fõ:] m -s, -s (lit, fig) ceiling.
Plage f -, -n (a) plague. (b) (fig: Mühe) nuisance ♦ **sie hat ihre ~ mit ihm** he's a trial for her; **man hat schon seine ~ mit dir** you do make life difficult, you are a nuisance; **zu einer ~ werden** to become a nuisance.
Plagegeist m nuisance, pest.
plagen [1] vt to plague, to torment; (mit Bitten und Fragen auch) to pester, to harass ♦ **dich plagt doch etwas, heraus mit der Sprache** something's worrying or bothering you, out with it; **ein geplagter Mann** a harassed man.
[2] vr (a) (leiden) to be troubled or bothered (mit by) ♦ **schon die ganze Woche plage ich mich mit meinem Heuschnupfen** I've been bothered or troubled all week by my hay fever, my hay fever's been bothering or troubling me all week.
(b) (arbeiten) to slave or slog away (inf); (sich Mühe geben) to go to or take a lot of trouble or great pains (mit over or with).
Plagiat nt plagiarism ♦ **da hat er ein ~ begangen** that's a plagiarism, he plagiarized that.
Plagiator m plagiarist.
plagiieren* vti to plagiarize.
Plaid [ple:t] nt or m -s, -s tartan travelling rug.
Plakafarbe ® f poster paint.
Plakat nt -(e)s, -e (an Litfaßsäulen etc) poster, bill; (aus Pappe) placard.
Plakat-: **~ankleber** m -s, - billposter, billsticker; **~farbe** f poster paint.
plakatieren* vt to placard; (fig) to broadcast.
plakativ adj Wirkung striking, bold; Sprache pithy.
Plakat-: **~maler** m poster painter or artist; **~säule** f advertisement pillar; **~schrift** f block lettering; **~träger** m sandwich-man; **~werbung** f poster advertising.
Plakette f (Abzeichen) badge; (Münze) commemorative coin; (an Wänden) plaque.
plan adj flat, level; Ebene, Fläche plane attr.
Plan[1] m -(e)s, ¨e (a) plan ♦ **die ¨e zur Renovierung der Stadt** the plans for the renovation of the city; **den ~ fassen, etw zu tun** to form the intention of doing sth, to plan to do sth; **wir haben den ~, ...** we're planning to ...; **¨e machen** or **schmieden** to make plans, to plan; **nach ~ verlaufen** to run or go according to plan.
(b) (Stadt~) (street-)map, town plan; (Grundriß, Bau~) plan, blueprint; (Zeittafel) schedule, timetable.
Plan[2] m -(e)s, ¨e (obs: ebene Fläche) plain ♦ **auf dem ~ erscheinen, auf den ~ treten** (fig) to arrive or come on the scene; **jdn auf den ~ rufen** (fig) to bring sb into the arena.
Plane f -, -n tarpaulin, tarp (US inf); (von LKW) hood; (Schutzdach) canopy, awning.
Plänemacher m planner ♦ **er ist ein großer ~** he's a great one for making plans.
➤ **planen** vti to plan; Attentat, Verbrechen auch to plot.
Planer(in f) m -s, - planner.
Plan|erfüllung f realization of a/the plan ♦ **uns trennen nur noch 5% von der ~** we're only 5% short of our planned target.
planerisch adj planning ♦ **~e Ausarbeitung** working out of the plans; **~ vorgehen** to proceed methodically; **ein Projekt ~ betreuen** to be in charge of the planning of a project; **~ hat das Team versagt** the team's planning was a failure.
Planet m -en, -en planet.
planetarisch adj planetary.
Planetarium nt planetarium.
Planeten-: **~bahn** f planetary orbit; **~system** nt planetary system.
Planetoid m -en, -en planetoid, asteroid.
Plan-: **~feststellungsverfahren** nt (Build) planning permission hearings pl; **p~gemäß** adj siehe **p~mäßig.**
planieren* vt Boden to level (off); Werkstück to planish.
Planierraupe f bulldozer.
Planke f -, -n plank, board; (Leit~) crash barrier ♦ **~n** (Umzäunung) fencing, boarding (gen round).
Plänkelei f (old Mil) skirmish; (fig auch) squabble.
plänkeln vi (old Mil) to skirmish, to engage in skirmishes; (fig) to squabble, to have a squabble.
Plankton nt -s, no pl plankton.
planlos adj unmethodical, unsystematic; (ziellos) random.
Planlosigkeit f lack of planning.
planmäßig adj (wie geplant) as planned, according to plan; (pünktlich) on schedule, as scheduled; (methodisch) methodical ♦ **~e Ankunft/Abfahrt** scheduled time of arrival/departure; **wir sind ~ um 7 angekommen** we arrived on schedule or as scheduled or on time at 7; **~ kommt der Zug um 7 Uhr an** the train is scheduled to arrive or is due in at 7 o'clock.
Planmäßigkeit f (Methodik) methodicalness, method; (Pünktlichkeit) punctuality; (Regelmäßigkeit) regularity.
Planquadrat nt grid square.
Planschbecken nt paddling pool.
planschen vi to splash around.
Planscherei f splashing around.
Plan-: **~soll** nt output target; **~stelle** f post.
Plantage [plan'ta:ʒə] f -, -n plantation.

➤ SPRACHE AKTIV: **planen** → 35.2, 52.5

Planung *f* planning ◆ **diese Straße ist noch in ~** this road is still being planned; **schon in der ~** in *or* at the planning stage.

Planungs-: ~abteilung *f* planning department; **~kommission** *f* planning commission.

Plan-: ~wagen *m* covered wagon; **~wirtschaft** *f* planned economy.

Plapperei *f* (*inf*) chatter(ing), prattling.

Plappermaul *nt* (*inf*) (*Mund*) big mouth (*inf*); (*Kind*) chatterbox (*inf*); (*Schwätzer*) tittle-tattler (*inf*), blabber (*inf*).

plappern [1] *vi* to prattle, to chatter; (*Geheimnis verraten*) to talk, to blab (*inf*). [2] *vt* **was plapperst du denn da für Blödsinn?** don't talk rubbish.

Plappertasche *f* (*inf*) tittle-tattler (*inf*).

Plaque [plak] *f* **-, -s** plaque.

plärren *vti* (*inf: weinen*) to howl, to bawl; (*Radio*) to blare (out); (*schreien*) to yell, to shriek; (*unschön singen*) to screech.

Pläsier *nt* **-s, -e** (*dated*) pleasure, delight ◆ **nun laß ihm doch sein ~** let him have his bit of fun.

Pläsierchen *nt*: **jedem Tierchen sein ~** (*hum*) each to his own.

Plasma *nt* **-s, Plasmen** plasma.

Plastik[1] *nt* **-s, -s** (*Kunststoff*) plastic.

Plastik[2] *f* **(a)** (*Bildhauerkunst*) sculpture, plastic art (*form*). **(b)** (*Skulptur*) sculpture. **(c)** (*Med*) plastic surgery. **(d)** (*fig: Anschaulichkeit*) vividness.

Plastik-: ~beutel *m* plastic bag, carrier bag; **~bombe** *f* plastic bomb; **~folie** *f* plastic film; **~geld** *nt* (*inf*) plastic money; **mit ~geld bezahlen** to pay with plastic (*inf*); **~material** *nt* plastic; **~sprengstoff** *m* plastic explosive; **sie benutzten ~sprengstoff** they used plastic explosives; **~tüte** *f* plastic bag.

Plastilin *nt* **-s, -e** plasticine ®.

plastisch *adj* **(a)** (*knetbar*) malleable, plastic, workable.
(b) (*dreidimensional*) three-dimensional, 3-D; (*fig: anschaulich*) vivid ◆ **~es Vorstellungsvermögen** ability to imagine things in three dimensions; **~ hervortreten** to stand out; **~e Sprache** vivid *or* graphic language; **sich** (*dat*) **einen Gegenstand ~ vorstellen** to form a concrete mental image of an object; **das kann ich mir ~ vorstellen** I can just imagine *or* picture it.
(c) (*Art*) plastic ◆ **die ~e Kunst** plastic art; **~e Arbeiten** sculptures, plastic works.
(d) (*Med*) plastic.

Plastizität *f, no pl* **(a)** (*Formbarkeit*) malleability, plasticity, workability. **(b)** (*fig: Anschaulichkeit*) vividness, graphicness.

Platane *f* **-, -n** plane tree.

Plateau [pla'to:] *nt* **-s, -s (a)** plateau; (*Tafelland auch*) tableland. **(b)** (*von Schuh*) platform.

Plateausohle [pla'to:-] *f* platform sole.

Platin *nt* **-s,** *no pl* (*abbr* **Pt**) platinum.

platinblond *adj* platinum blonde.

Platine *f* **-, -n** (*Comput*) circuit board.

⚠ **Platitüde** *f* **-, -n** platitude.

Plato(n) *m* **-** Plato.

Platoniker *m* **-s, -** Platonist.

platonisch *adj* Platonic, Platonist; (*nicht sexuell*) platonic; (*geh: unverbindlich*) non-committal.

platsch *interj* splash, splosh.

platschen *vi* (*inf*) to splash; (*regnen*) to pelt, to pour.

plätschern *vi* (*Bach*) to babble, to splash; (*Brunnen*) to splash; (*Regen*) to patter; (*planschen*) to splash (about *or* around) ◆ **eine ~de Unterhaltung** light conversation.

⚠ **platschnaß** *adj* (*inf*) soaking (wet); *Kleidung, Mensch auch* dripping (wet), drenched.

platt *adj* **(a)** (*flach*) flat ◆ **etw ~ drücken** to press sth flat, to flatten sth; **einen P~en** (*inf*) *or* **einen ~en Reifen haben** to have a flat (*inf*) *or* a flat tyre; **das ~e Land** the flat country; (*nicht Stadt*) the country.
(b) (*fig: geistlos*) *Bemerkung, Witz* flat, boring, dull; *Mensch* dull, uninspired.
(c) (*inf: verblüfft*) **~ sein** to be flabbergasted (*inf*); **da bist du ~, nicht?** that's surprised you.

Platt *nt* **-(s),** *no pl* (*inf*) Low German, Plattdeutsch.

Plättbrett *nt* (*dial*) ironing-board; (*sl*) skinny Lizzy (*inf*).

Plättchen *nt* little tile; (*Computers*) microchip.

plattdeutsch *adj* Low German.

Plattdeutsch(e) *nt* Low German, Plattdeutsch; *siehe auch* **Deutsch(e)**.

Platte *f* **-, -n (a)** (*Holz~*) piece of wood, wood *no pl*, board; (*zur Wandverkleidung*) panel; (*Tischtennis~*) ping-pong table; (*Glas~/Metall~/Plastik~*) piece *or* sheet of glass/metal/plastic; (*Beton~, Stein~*) slab; (*zum Pflastern*) paving stone, flagstone; (*Kachel, Fliese*) tile; (*Grab~*) gravestone, slab; (*Herd~*) hotplate; (*Tisch~*) (table-)top; (*ausziehbare*) leaf; (*Felsen~*) shelf, ledge; (*Geog: ebenes Land*) flat or low land; (*Druckstock*) plate; (*Phot*) plate; (*Gebiß*) (dental) plate; (*Gedenktafel*) plaque; (*Comput*) disk ◆ **ein Ereignis auf die ~ bannen** to capture an event on film; **die ~ putzen** (*inf*) to hop it (*inf*).
(b) (*Fleisch-, Gemüseteller*) serving-dish, plate; (*Torten~*) cake plate; (*mit Fuß*) cake-stand ◆ **eine ~ Aufschnitt** a plate of selected cold meats; **kalte ~** cold dish.
(c) (*Schall~*) record, disc ◆ **etw auf ~ sprechen/aufnehmen** to make a record of sth, to record sth; **eine ~ mit Marschmusik** a record of march music.
(d) (*fig inf*) **die ~ kenne ich schon** I've heard all that before, I know that line; **er legte die alte ~ auf** he started on his old theme; **leg doch mal eine neue ~ auf!** change the record, can't you!; **die ~ hat einen Sprung** the record's stuck.
(e) (*inf: Glatze*) bald head; (*kahle Stelle*) bald spot *or* patch.

Plätte *f* **-, -n** (*N Ger inf*), **Plätt|eisen** *nt* (*dial, Hist*) iron, smoothing iron (*Hist*).

plätten *vt* (*dial*) to iron, to press; *siehe* **geplättet**.

Platten-: ~bau *m* **-s, -ten** (*inf: Haus*) *building made from prefabricated slabs*; **~kondensator** *m* plate condenser; **~label** [-'leɪbl] *nt* record label; **~laufwerk** *nt* (*Comput*) disk drive; **~leger** *m* **-s, -** paver; **~sammlung** *f* record collection; **~see** *m* **der ~see** Lake Balaton; **~spieler** *m* record-player; **~teller** *m* turntable; **~wechsler** *m* **-s, -** autochanger, record changer; **~weg** *m* paved path.

Plätterei *f* (*dial*) **(a)** (*Betrieb*) *business which does ironing*. **(b)** (*inf: das Plätten*) ironing.

Plätterin *f* ironer, presser.

Platt-: ~fisch *m* flatfish; **~form** *f* **-, -en** platform; (*fig: Grundlage*) basis; **~fuß** *m* flat foot; (*inf: Reifenpanne*) flat (*inf*); **p~füßig** *adj, adv* flat-footed; **~heit** *f* **(a)** *no pl* (*Flachheit*) flatness; (*Geistlosigkeit auch*) dullness; **(b)** *usu pl* (*Redensart etc*) commonplace, platitude, cliché.

plattieren* *vt Metall* to plate.

Platt-: p~machen *vt sep* (*sl: dem Erdboden gleichmachen*) to level; (*pleite gehen lassen*) *Firma* to bankrupt; (*heruntermachen*) to take out (*inf*); (*mundtot machen*) to silence; (*töten*) to do in (*inf*); **p~nasig** *adj* flat-nosed; **~stich** *m* satin stitch; **~stickerei** *f* satin stitch embroidery.

Plättwäsche *f* (*dial*) ironing.

Platz *m* **-es, ¨-e (a)** (*freier Raum*) room, space ◆ **~ für jdn/etw schaffen** to make room for sb/sth; **~ für etw finden** to find room *or* space for sth; **es wird ~ finden** there'll be room *or* space for it; **~ greifen** to spread, to gain ground; **~ einnehmen** *or* **brauchen** to take up *or* occupy room *or* space; **~ für etw (frei) lassen** to leave room *or* space for sth; **das Buch hat keinen ~ mehr im Regal** there's no more room *or* space on the bookshelf for that book; **mehr als 10 Leute haben hier nicht ~** there's not room *or* space for more than 10 people here; **jdm den (ganzen) ~ wegnehmen** to take up all the room; **jdm ~ machen** to make room for sb; (*vorbeigehen lassen*) to make way for sb (*auch fig*); **~ machen** to get out of the way (*inf*); **mach mal ein bißchen ~** make a bit of room; **~ für jdn/etw bieten** to hold sb/sth, to have room for sb/sth; **~ da!** (*inf*) (get) out of the way there! (*inf*), gangway! (*inf*).
(b) (*Sitzplatz*) seat ◆ **~ nehmen** to take a seat; **bitte ~ nehmen zum Mittagessen** please take your seats for lunch; **behalten Sie doch bitte ~!** (*form*) please remain seated (*form*); **ist hier noch ein ~ frei?** is there a free seat here?; **dieser ~ ist belegt** *or* **besetzt** this seat's taken, this is somebody's seat; **sich von seinem ~ erheben** (*geh*) to rise (*form*); **der Saal hat 2.000 ¨-e** the hall seats 2,000 *or* has seating for 2,000 *or* has 2,000 seats; **mit jdm den ~ tauschen** *or* **wechseln** to change places with sb; **erster/zweiter ~** front/rear stalls; **~!** (*zum Hund*) sit!
(c) (*Stelle, Standort, Rang, Sport*) place ◆ **das Buch steht nicht an seinem ~** the book isn't in (its) place; **etw (wieder) an seinen ~ stellen** to put sth (back) in (its) place; **fehl** *or* **nicht am ~e sein** to be out of place; **auf die ¨-e, fertig, los!** (*beim Sport*) on your marks, get set, go!, ready, steady, go!; **er wich nicht vom ~(e)** he wouldn't yield (an inch); **seinen ~ behaupten** to stand one's ground, to hold one's own; **alles hat seinen festen ~** everything has its proper place; **das Buch hat einen festen ~ auf der Bestsellerliste** the book is firmly established on the bestseller list; **die Literatur hat einen festen ~ in ihrem Leben** literature is very much a part of her life; **ihr ~ ist an der Seite ihres Mannes** her (proper) place is at her husband's side; **den ersten ~ einnehmen** (*fig*) to take first place, to come first; **auf ~ zwei** in second place; **jdn auf ~ drei/den zweiten ~ verweisen** to beat sb into third/second place; **jdn auf die ¨-e verweisen** (*fig*) to beat sb; **auf ~ wetten** to make a place bet; **ein ~ an der Sonne** (*lit, fig*) a place in the sun.
(d) (*Arbeits~, Studien~ etc*) place ◆ **im Kindergarten sind noch ein paar ¨-e frei** there are still a few vacancies *or* places left in the kindergarten; **wir haben noch einen freien ~ im Büro** we've still got one vacancy in the office.
(e) (*umbaute Fläche*) square ◆ **auf dem ~** in *or* on the square; **ein freier ~ vor der Kirche** an open space in front of the church.
(f) (*Sport~*) playing field; (*Ftbl, Hockey*) pitch, field; (*Handball~, Tennis~*) court; (*Golf~*) (golf) course, (golf) links *pl* ◆ **einen Spieler vom ~ stellen** *or* **verweisen** to send a player off; **auf gegnerischem/eigenem ~** away/at home.
(g) (*Ort*) town, place; (*Handels~*) centre ◆ **das erste Hotel** *or* **Haus am ~** the best hotel in town *or* in the place.
(h) (*Lager~*) (store *or* storage) yard.
(i) (*Bau~*) site.

Platz-: ~angst *f* (*Psych*) agoraphobia; (*inf: Beklemmung*) claustrophobia; **~angst bekommen** to get claustrophobic *or* claustrophobia; **~anweiser(in** *f*) *m* **-s, -** usher(ette).

Plätzchen *nt* **(a)** *dim of* **Platz** spot, little place. **(b)** (*Gebäck*) biscuit (*Brit*), cookie (*US*).

platzen *vi aux sein* **(a)** (*aufreißen*) to burst; (*Naht, Hose, Augenbraue, Haut*) to split; (*explodieren: Granate, Bombe*) to explode; (*einen Riß bekommen*) to crack ◆ **mir ist unterwegs ein Reifen geplatzt** I had a blow-out on the way, a tyre burst on the way; **ihm ist eine Ader geplatzt** he burst a blood-vessel; **wenn du so weiterißt, platzt du!** if you go on eating like that you'll burst; **wir sind vor Lachen fast geplatzt** we split our sides laughing, we laughed till our sides ached *or* split; **ins Zimmer ~** (*inf*) to burst into the room; **jdm ins Haus ~** (*inf*) to descend on sb; **(vor Wut/Neid/Ungeduld) ~** (*inf*) to be bursting (with rage/envy/impatience); *siehe* **Kragen, Naht.**
(b) (*inf: scheitern*) (*Plan, Geschäft*) to fall through; (*Freundschaft*) to break up; (*Theorie*) to fall down, to collapse; (*Spionagering, Verschwörung*) to collapse; (*Wechsel*) to bounce (*inf*) ◆ **die Verlobung ist geplatzt** the engagement is (all)

off; **etw ~ lassen** *Plan* to make sth fall through; *Freundschaft, Verlobung* to break sth up; *Theorie* to explode sth; *Spionagering* to break sth up, to smash sth; *Wechsel* to make sth bounce (*inf*).

Platz-: ~halter *m* place-marker; (*fig*) custodian; (*Comput*) free variable parameter, free definable parameter; **~herren** *pl* (*Sport inf*) home team; **~hirsch** *m* (*lit, fig*) dominant male; **~karte** *f* (*Rail*) seat reservation (ticket); **ich bestelle mir eine ~karte** I'll reserve (myself) a seat, I'll get a seat reservation; **~konzert** *nt* open-air concert; **~mangel** *m* shortage *or* lack of space *or* room; **wir leiden sehr unter ~mangel** we're terribly short of space *or* room, we've a space problem; **~miete** *f* (*Theat*) season ticket; (*Sport*) ground rent; **~patrone** *f* blank (cartridge); ⚠**p~raubend** *adj* space-consuming; **~regen** *m* cloudburst; **das ist nur ein ~regen** it's only a (passing) shower; **~reservierung** *f* seat reservation; ⚠**p~sparend** *adj* space-saving *attr*; **etw p~sparend stapeln** to stack sth away compactly *or* with a minimum use of space; **das ist p~sparender** that saves more space; **~verweis** *m* sending-off; **es gab drei ~verweise** three players were sent off; **~wahl** *f* toss-up; **die ~wahl haben/verlieren** to win/lose the toss; **die ~wahl vornehmen** to toss up; **~wart** *m* (*Sport*) groundsman; **~wechsel** *m* change of place; (*Sport*) change of position; **~wette** *f* place bet; **~wunde** *f* cut, laceration.

Plauderei *f* chat, conversation; (*Press*) feature; (*TV, Rad*) chat show.

Plauderer *m* **-s, -, Plauderin** *f* conversationalist.

plauderhaft *adj Ton* conversational, chatty.

plaudern *vi* to chat, to talk (*über +acc, von* about); (*verraten*) to talk ♦ **mit ihm läßt sich gut ~** he's easy to talk to; *siehe* **Schule**.

Plauder-: ~stündchen *nt* chat; **ein angenehmes ~stündchen zubringen** to have a pleasant chat *or* a cosy little chat; **~tasche** *f* (*inf*) chatterbox (*inf*); **~ton** *m* conversational *or* chatty tone.

Plausch *m* **-(e)s, -e** (*inf*) chat ♦ **das war ein ~** (*Sw: Freude, Amüsement*) that was a good laugh.

plauschen *vi* (*inf*) to chat, to have a chat *or* a natter (*Brit inf*).

plausibel *adj* plausible ♦ **jdm etw ~ machen** to make sth clear to sb, to explain sth to sb.

Plausibilität *f* plausibility.

Plausibilitätskontrolle *f* (*von Daten, Statistik*) plausibility check.

plauz *interj* (*old*) crash, bang.

Plauz *m* **-es, -e** (*inf*) (*Geräusch*) bang, crash; (*Fall*) fall.

Plauze *f* **-, -n** (*dial inf*) chest ♦ **es auf der ~ haben** (*inf*) to have a chesty cough, to be chesty (*inf*).

Playback ['pleɪbæk] *nt* **-s, -s** (*Band*) (*bei der Schallplatte*) backing track; (*TV*) recording; (*~verfahren*) (*bei der Schallplatte*) double-tracking *no pl*; (*TV*) miming *no pl* ♦ **ein ~ von einem Lied machen** to double-track a song; (*TV*) to prerecord a song, to make a recording of a song; **etw im ~ machen** to double-track sth; (*TV*) to mime to (a recording of) sth.

Play-: ~boy ['ple:bɔɪ] *m* **-s, -s** playboy; **~girl** ['ple:gœɐl] *nt* **-s, -s** playgirl.

Plazenta *f* **-, -s** *or* **Plazenten** placenta.

Plazet *nt* **-s, -s** approval, OK (*inf*) ♦ **sein ~ zu etw geben** to approve *or* OK sth, to give sth one's approval *or* OK.

Plazeur(in *f*) [pla'tsøːɐ, -'øːrɪn] *m* (*Fin*) securities investor.

⚠**plazieren*** [1] *vt* **(a)** (*Platz anweisen*) to put; *Soldaten, Wächter* to put, to place, to position; (*Tennis*) to seed ♦ **der Kellner plazierte uns in die** *or* **der Nähe der Band** the waiter directed *or* showed us to a place *or* put us near the band.
(b) (*zielen*) *Ball* to place, to position; *Schlag, Faust* to land ♦ **gut plazierte Aufschläge** well-placed *or* well-positioned services; **ein (gut) plazierter Schlag** a well-placed *or* well-aimed blow; **plaziert schießen** to position one's shots well; **er hat plaziert in die rechte Torecke geschossen** he tucked the ball away neatly in the right corner of the goal.
(c) (*anlegen*) *Geld* to put, to place.
[2] *vr* **(a)** (*inf: sich setzen, stellen etc*) to plant oneself (*inf*).
(b) (*Sport*) to be placed, to get a place; (*Tennis*) to be seeded ♦ **der Läufer konnte sich gut/nicht ~** the runner was well-placed/wasn't even placed.

⚠**Plazierung** *f* (*bei Rennen*) order; (*Tennis*) seeding; (*Platz*) place ♦ **welche ~ hatte er?** where did he come in?, what position did he come in?

Plebejer(in *f*) *m* **-s, -** (*lit, fig*) plebeian, pleb (*inf*).

plebejisch *adj* (*lit*) plebeian *no adv*; (*fig auch*) plebby (*inf*), common ♦ **sich ~ benehmen** to behave like a pleb (*inf*).

Plebiszit *nt* **-(e)s, -e** plebiscite.

Plebs[1] *f* **-,** *no pl* (*Hist*) plebs *pl*.

Plebs[2] *m* **-es,** *no pl* (*pej*) plebs *pl*.

pleite *adj pred, adv* (*inf*) *Mensch* broke (*inf*); *Firma auch* bust (*inf*) ♦ **~ gehen** to go bust.

Pleite *f* **-, -n** (*inf*) bankruptcy, collapse; (*fig*) flop (*inf*), washout (*inf*) ♦ **~ machen** to go bankrupt *or* bust (*inf*); **damit/mit ihm haben wir eine ~ erlebt** it/he was a disaster.

Pleitegeier *m* (*inf*) **(a)** (*drohende Pleite*) vulture ♦ **über der Firma schwebt der ~** the vultures are *or* the threat of bankruptcy is hovering over the firm. **(b)** (*Bankrotteur*) bankrupt.

Plektron, Plektrum *nt* **-s, Plektren** *or* **Plektra** plectrum.

Plempe *f* **-, -n** (*dial*) dishwater (*inf*).

plempern *vi* (*inf*) **(a)** (*trödeln*) to dawdle. **(b)** (*verschütten*) to splash.

plemplem *adj pred* (*sl*) nuts (*sl*), round the bend (*Brit inf*) ♦ **jdn ~ machen** to drive sb round the bend (*inf*) *or* up the wall (*inf*).

Plena *pl of* **Plenum**.

Plenar-: ~saal *m* chamber; **~sitzung, ~versammlung** *f* plenary session.

Plenum *nt* **-s, Plena** plenum.

Pleonasmus *m* pleonasm.

pleonastisch *adj* pleonastic.

Pleuelstange *f* connecting rod.

Plexiglas ® *nt* acrylic glass.

plieren, plinkern *vi* (*N Ger*) to screw up one's eyes.

Plissee *nt* **-s, -s** pleats *pl*, pleating *no pl*.

Plissee-: ~falte *f* pleat; **~rock** *m* pleated skirt.

plissieren* *vt* to pleat.

PLO [peː|ɛl'|oː] *f* **-** PLO.

PLO-Führung *f* PLO leadership.

Plombe *f* **-, -n (a)** (*Siegel*) lead seal. **(b)** (*Zahn~*) filling.

plombieren* *vt* **(a)** (*versiegeln*) to seal, to put a seal on. **(b)** *Zahn* to fill ♦ **er hat mir zwei Zähne plombiert** he did two fillings.

Plombierung *f* **(a)** (*das Versiegeln*) sealing; (*Vorrichtung*) seal. **(b)** (*beim Zahn*) filling.

Plörre *f* **-, -n** (*dial*) dishwater.

Plot *m or nt* **-s, -s** (*Liter*) plot.

Plotter *m* **-s, -** (*Comput*) plotter.

plötzlich [1] *adj* sudden.
[2] *adv* suddenly, all of a sudden ♦ **aber etwas ~!** (*inf*) make it snappy! (*inf*), look sharp! (*inf*); **das kommt alles so ~** (*inf*) it all happens so suddenly.

Plötzlichkeit *f* suddenness.

Pluderhose *f* harem pants *pl*, Turkish trousers *pl*.

Plumeau [ply'moː] *nt* **-s, -s** eiderdown, quilt.

plump *adj Figur, Hände, Form* ungainly *no adv*; *Bewegung, Gang auch* awkward; *Ausdruck* clumsy; *Bemerkung* crass; *Mittel, Schmeichelei, Lüge, Betrug* obvious, crude ♦ **der Film ist sehr ~ (gemacht)** the film is very crudely made; **etw ~ ausdrücken** to express sth clumsily; **sich ~ verhalten** to behave crassly; **~e Annäherungsversuche** very obvious advances.

Plumpheit *f siehe adj* ungainliness; awkwardness; clumsiness; crassness; obviousness, crudeness.

plumps *interj* bang; (*lauter*) crash ♦ **~, da lag er** crash, he'd fallen over.

Plumps *m* **-es, -e** (*inf*) (*Fall*) fall, tumble; (*Geräusch*) bump, thud ♦ **einen ~ machen** (*baby-talk*) to fall; **mit einem ~ ins Wasser fallen** to fall into the water with a splash.

plumpsen *vi aux sein* (*inf*) to tumble, to fall ♦ **ich habe es ~ gehört** I heard a bang; **ich ließ mich einfach aufs Bett ~** I just flopped (down) onto the bed; **er plumpste ins Wasser** he went splash into the water, he fell into the water with a splash.

Plumpsklo(sett) *nt* (*inf*) earth closet.

⚠**plump-vertraulich** [1] *adj* hail-fellow-well-met.
[2] *adv* in a hail-fellow-well-met sort of way.

Plunder *m* **-s,** *no pl* junk, rubbish.

Plünd(e)rer *m* **-s, -** looter, plunderer.

Plundergebäck *nt* flaky pastry.

plündern *vti* to loot, to plunder, to pillage; (*ausrauben*) to raid; *Obstbaum* to strip ♦ **jemand hat unsere** *or* **auf unserer Obstplantage geplündert** somebody's raided our orchard.

Plünderung *f* looting, pillage, plunder.

Plural *m* **-s, -e** plural ♦ **im ~ stehen** to be (in the) plural; **den ~ zu etw bilden** to form the plural of sth.

Pluraletantum *nt* **-s, -s** *or* **Pluraliatantum** plural noun.

pluralisch *adj* plural.

Pluralismus *m* pluralism.

pluralistisch *adj* pluralistic.

Pluralität *f* plurality; (*Mehrheit*) majority, plurality (*US*).

plus [1] *prep +gen* plus.
[2] *adv* plus ♦ **bei ~ 5 Grad** *or* **5 Grad ~** at 5 degrees (above freezing *or* zero); **~ minus 10** plus or minus 10; **das Ergebnis war ~ minus null** nothing was gained, nothing was lost; **mit ~ minus null abschließen** to break even.
[3] *conj* **Karl ~ Ehefrau** (*inf*) Karl plus wife.

Plus *nt* **-, - (a)** (*~zeichen*) plus (sign) ♦ **ein ~ machen** to put a plus (sign).
(b) (*Phys inf: ~pol*) positive (pole).
(c) (*Comm*) (*Zuwachs*) increase; (*Gewinn*) profit; (*Überschuß*) surplus.
(d) (*fig: Vorteil*) advantage ♦ **das ist ein ~ für dich** that's a point in your favour; **das können Sie als ~ für sich buchen** that's one up to *or* for you (*inf*), you've scored a point there (*inf*).

Plüsch *m* **-(e)s, -e** plush ♦ **Stofftiere aus ~** soft toys made of fur fabric.

Plüsch- *in cpds* plush; **~bär** *m* furry teddy bear.

plüschig *adj* plush.

Plüschtier *nt* ≃ soft toy.

Plus-: ~pol *m* (*Elec*) positive pole; **~punkt** *m* (*Sport*) point; (*Sch*) extra mark; (*fig*) advantage; **einen ~punkt machen** to win a point; **deine Erfahrung ist ein ~punkt für dich** your experience counts in your favour *or* is a point in your favour; **~quamperfekt** *nt* pluperfect, past perfect.

plustern [1] *vt Federn* to fluff up.
[2] *vr* to fluff oneself up.

Pluszeichen *nt* plus sign.

Plutokrat(in *f*) *m* **-en, -en** plutocrat.

Plutokratie *f* plutocracy.

Plutonium *nt, no pl* (*abbr* **Pn**) plutonium.

Plutonium-: ~gewinnung *f* plutonium extraction; **~wirtschaft** *f* plutonium industry.

PLZ [peː|ɛl'tsɛt] *f abbr of* **Postleitzahl**.

Pneu [pnøː] *m* **-s, -s** (*esp Sw*) tyre.

pneumatisch [pnɔy'maːtɪʃ] *adj* pneumatic ◆ **~e Kammer** pressure chamber.
Po *m* **-s, -s** (*inf*) *siehe* **Popo.**
Pöbel *m* **-s,** *no pl* rabble, mob.
Pöbelei *f* vulgarity, bad language *no pl.*
Pöbel-: p~haft *adj* uncouth, vulgar; **~herrschaft** *f* mob rule.
pöbeln *vi* to swear, to use bad language.
pochen *vi* to knock; (*leise auch*) to tap; (*heftig*) to thump, to bang; (*Herz*) to pound, to thump; (*Blut*) to throb, to pound ◆ **auf etw** (*acc*) **~** (*fig*) to insist on sth; **auf sein (gutes) Recht ~** to insist on *or* stand up for one's rights.
pochieren* [pɔ'ʃiːrən] *vt Ei* to poach.
Pocke *f* **-, -n** pock ◆ **~n** *pl* smallpox.
Pocken-: ~narbe *f* pockmark; **p~narbig** *adj* pockmarked; **~(schutz)impfung** *f* smallpox vaccination.
Pocket- *in cpds* pocket.
Podest *nt or m* **-(e)s, -e** (*Sockel*) pedestal (*auch fig*); (*Podium*) platform; (*Treppenabsatz*) landing.
Podex *m* **-es, -e** (*hum inf*) posterior (*hum inf*), behind (*inf*).
Podium *nt* (*lit, fig*) platform; (*des Dirigenten*) podium; (*bei Diskussion*) panel.
Podiums-: ~diskussion *f*, **~gespräch** *nt* panel discussion, brains trust.
Poem *nt* **-s, -e** (*usu pej*) poem, doggerel (*pej*) *no indef art.*
Poesie [poe'ziː] *f* (*lit, fig*) poetry.
Poesie|album *nt* autograph book.
Poet(in *f*) *m* **-en, -en** (*old: Dichter*) poet, bard (*liter*); (*pej*) poetaster, versifier.
Poetaster [poe'tastɐ] *m* **-s, -** (*old pej*) poetaster.
Poetik *f* poetics *sing.*
poetisch *adj* poetic ◆ **eine ~e Ader haben** to have a poetic streak.
pofen *vi* (*sl*) to kip (*inf*).
Pogrom *nt or m* **-s, -e** pogrom.
Pogromstimmung *f* bloodthirsty mood.
Pointe ['poɛ̃ːtə] *f* **-, -n** (*eines Witzes*) punch-line; (*einer Geschichte*) point ◆ **die ~ einer Geschichte begreifen** to get the (main) point of a story.
pointieren* [poɛ̃'tiːrən] *vt* to emphasize, to stress.
pointiert [poɛ̃'tiːɐt] *adj* trenchant, pithy.
Pokal *m* **-s, -e** (*zum Trinken*) goblet; (*Sport*) cup ◆ **das Endspiel um den ~** the cup final.
Pokal-: ~sieger *m* cup-winners *pl*; **~spiel** *nt* cup-tie.
Pökel *m* **-s, -** brine, pickle.
Pökel-: ~fleisch *nt* salt meat; **~hering** *m* salt *or* pickled herring.
pökeln *vt Fleisch, Fisch* to salt, to pickle.
Poker *nt* **-s,** *no pl* poker.
Pokergesicht *nt*, **Pokermiene** *f* poker face ◆ **ein Pokergesicht machen, eine Pokermiene aufsetzen** to put on a poker-faced *or* deadpan expression.
pokern *vi* to play poker ◆ **um etw ~** (*fig*) to haggle for sth.
pol. *abbr. of* **politisch, polizeilich.**
Pol *m* **-s, -e** pole ◆ **der ruhende ~** (*fig*) the calming influence.
polar *adj* polar ◆ **~e Kälte** arctic coldness; **~ entgegengesetzt** diametrically opposed, poles apart *pred.*
Polar- *in cpds* polar; **~fuchs** *m* arctic fox.
polarisieren* [1] *vt* to polarize.
[2] *vr* to polarize, to become polarized.
Polarisierung *f* polarization.
Polarität *f* polarity.
Polar-: ~kreis *m* polar circle; **nördlicher/südlicher ~kreis** Arctic/Antarctic circle; **~licht** *nt* polar lights *pl*; **~stern** *m* Pole Star, North Star, Polaris; **~zone** *f* Frigid Zone, polar region.
Polder *m* **-s, -** polder.
Polderdeich *m* polder dyke.
Pole *m* **-n, -n** Pole ◆ **er ist ~** he's Polish, he's a Pole.
Polemik *f* polemics *sing*; (*Streitschrift*) polemic ◆ **die ~ dieses Artikels** the polemic nature of this article; **seine ~ ist kaum mehr erträglich** his polemics are becoming unbearable.
Polemiker(in *f*) *m* **-s, -** controversialist, polemicist.
polemisch *adj* polemic(al).
polemisieren* *vi* to polemicize ◆ **~ gegen** to inveigh against.
polen *vt* to polarize.
Polen *nt* **-s** Poland ◆ **noch ist ~ nicht verloren** (*prov*) the day is *or* all is not yet lost.
Polente *f* **-,** *no pl* (*inf*) cops *pl* (*inf*), fuzz *pl* (*inf*).
Police [po'liːsə] *f* **-, -n** (insurance) policy.
Polier *m* **-s, -e** site foreman.
polieren* *vt* to polish; *Schuhe auch* to shine; (*fig*) to polish *or* brush up ◆ **jdm die Fresse** *or* **Schnauze** *or* **Visage ~** (*sl*) to smash sb's face in (*sl*).
Polier-: ~mittel *nt* polish; **~scheibe** *f* polishing wheel *or* disc; **~tuch** *nt* polishing cloth; **~wachs** *nt* wax polish.
Poliklinik *f* (*Krankenhaus*) clinic (*for outpatients only*); (*Abteilung*) outpatients' department, outpatients *sing.*
Polin *f* Pole, Polish woman.
Polio *f* **-,** *no pl* polio, poliomyelitis.
Polit-: ~barometer *nt* (*fig*) political barometer; **~bühne** *f* political stage; **~büro** *nt* Politburo.
Politesse *f* (woman) traffic warden.
Politik *f* **(a)** *no pl* politics *sing*; (*politischer Standpunkt*) politics *pl* ◆ **welche ~ vertritt er?** what are his politics?; **in die ~ gehen** to go into politics; **über ~ sprechen** to talk (about) politics.
(b) (*bestimmte ~*) policy ◆ **eine ~ der starken Hand treiben** to take a tough line; **eine ~ verfolgen** *or* **betreiben** to pursue a policy; **ihre gesamte ~** all their policies.
Politika *pl of* **Politikum.**
Politiker(in *f*) *m* **-s, -** politician ◆ **führender ~** leading politician, statesman.
Politikum *nt* **-s, Politika** political issue.
Politikverdrossenheit *f* disenchantment with politics ◆ **die wachsende ~ der Bevölkerung** the people's growing disenchantment with politics.
Politikwissenschaft *f siehe* **Politologie.**
politisch *adj* political; (*klug*) politic, judicious ◆ **jdn ~ schulen** to educate sb politically; **er ist ein P~er** he's a political prisoner.
politisieren* [1] *vi* to talk politics, to politicize.
[2] *vt* to politicize; *jdn* to make politically aware.
Politisierung *f* politicization.
Polit|ökonomie *f* political economy.
Politologe *m*, **Politologin** *f* political scientist.
Politologie *f* political science, politics *sing.*
Politur *f* (*Poliermittel*) polish; (*Glanz*) shine, polish; (*das Polieren*) polishing.
Polizei *f* police *pl*; (*Gebäude*) police station ◆ **auf die** *or* **zur ~ gehen** to go to the police; **er ist bei der ~** he's in the police (force); *siehe* **dumm.**
Polizei- *in cpds* police; **~aktion** *f* police operation; **~apparat** *m* police force; **~aufgebot** *nt* police presence; **~aufsicht** *f* police supervision; **unter ~aufsicht stehen** to have to report regularly to the police; **~beamte(r)** *m* police official; (*Polizist*) police officer; **~behörde** *f* police authorities *pl*; **sich bei der ~behörde anmelden** to register with the police; **~chef** *m* chief constable, chief of police (*US*); **~dienststelle** *f* (*form*) police station; **~direktion** *f* police headquarters *pl*; **~funk** *m* police radio; **~griff** *m* wrist-hold, police hold; **er wurde im ~griff abgeführt** they put a wrist-hold on him and led him away, he was frogmarched away; **~haft** *f* detention; **~hund** *m* police dog; **~kette** *f* police cordon; **~knüppel** *m* truncheon; **~kommissar** *m* (police) inspector.
polizeilich *adj no pred* police *attr* ◆ **diese Regelung ist ~ angeordnet** this is a police regulation, this regulation is by order of the police; **~es Führungszeugnis** *certificate issued by the police, stating that the holder has no criminal record*; **er wird ~ überwacht** he's being watched by the police; **sich ~ melden** to register with the police; **~ verboten** against the law; **„Parken ~ verboten"** "police notice — no parking".
Polizei-: ~präsident *m* chief constable, chief of police (*US*); **~präsidium** *nt* police headquarters *pl*; **~revier** *nt* **(a)** (*~wache*) police station; **ins** *or* **aufs ~revier gehen** to go (down) to the (police) station; **(b)** (*Bezirk*) (police) district, precinct (*US*), patch (*inf*); **~schutz** *m* police protection; **~sirene** *f* (police) siren, hee-haw (*inf*); **~spitzel** *m* (police) informer, nark (*Brit sl*); **~staat** *m* police state; **~streife** *f* police patrol; **~stunde** *f* closing time; **~verordnung** *f* police regulation; **~wache** *f siehe* **~revier (a)**; **~wesen** *nt* police force; **p~widrig** *adj* illegal; **sich p~widrig verhalten** to break the law.
Polizist *m* policeman.
Polizistin *f* policewoman.
Polka *f* **-, -s** polka.
Polkappe *f* polar icecap.
Pollen *m* **-s, -** pollen.
Pollenflug *m* pollen count.
Poller *m* **-s, -** capstan, bollard.
Pollution *f* (*Med*) (seminal) emission.
polnisch *adj* Polish ◆ **~e Wirtschaft** (*inf*) shambles *sing.*
Polnisch(e) *nt* Polish; *siehe auch* **Deutsch(e).**
Polo *nt* **-s, -s** polo.
Polohemd *nt* sports shirt; (*für Frau*) casual blouse.
Polonaise [polo'nɛːzə], **Polonäse** *f* **-, -n** polonaise.
Polonium *nt, no pl* (*abbr* **Po**) polonium.
Polster *nt or* (*Aus*) *m* **-s, - (a)** cushion; (*Polsterung*) upholstery *no pl*; (*bei Kleidung*) pad, padding *no pl* ◆ **das ~ vom Sessel muß erneuert werden** the chair needs re-upholstering; **seine Jacke als ~ für seinen Kopf benutzen** to use one's jacket as a pillow.
(b) (*fig*) (*Fett~*) flab *no pl* (*inf*), layer of fat; (*Bauch*) spare tyre; (*Geldreserve*) reserves *pl* ◆ **sie hat ein ganz schönes ~ am Hintern** she's pretty well-upholstered *or* well-padded behind.
Pölsterchen *nt* (*inf*) **(a)** (*Rücklage*) nest-egg. **(b)** (*Fettpolster*) (layer of) fat; (*an Hüften*) spare tyre ◆ **sie hat einige ~** she's well-upholstered *or* well-padded.
Polsterer *m* **-s, -** upholsterer.
Polster-: ~garnitur *f* three-piece suite; **~möbel** *pl* upholstered furniture.
polstern *vt* to upholster; *Kleidung, Tür* to pad ◆ **etw neu ~** to re-upholster sth; **sie ist gut gepolstert** she's well-upholstered *or* well-padded; **sie ist finanziell gut gepolstert** she's not short of the odd penny.
Polster-: ~sessel *m* armchair, easy chair; **~sitz** *m* upholstered *or* padded seat; **~stoff** *m* upholstery *or* upholstering fabric; **~stuhl** *m* upholstered *or* padded chair; **~tür** *f* padded door.
Polsterung *f* (*Polster*) upholstery; (*das Polstern*) upholstering.
Polter|abend *m party on the eve of a wedding, at which old crockery is smashed to bring good luck*, ≃ shower (*US*).
Polterer *m* **-s, -** noisy person; (*beim Sprechen*) ranter, blusterer.
Poltergeist *m* poltergeist.
poltern *vi* **(a)** to crash about; (*~d umfallen*) to go crash ◆ **die Kinder ~ oben** the children are crashing about *or* banging about upstairs *or* are making a din *or* racket (*inf*) upstairs; **was hat da eben so gepoltert?** what was that crash *or* bang?; **es fiel ~d zu Boden** it crashed to the floor, it fell with a

crash to the floor; **es polterte fürchterlich, als er** ... there was a terrific crash *or* bang when he ...; **es poltert (an der Tür/vor dem Haus)** there's a real racket (*inf*) *or* din going on (at the door/in front of the house); **an die Tür ~** to thump *or* bang on the door.
(b) *aux sein* (*sich laut bewegen*) to crash, to bang ◆ **über das Pflaster ~** to clatter over the cobbles.
(c) (*inf: schimpfen*) to rant (and rave), to carry on (*inf*).
(d) (*inf: Polterabend feiern*) *to celebrate on the eve of a wedding.*
Poly-: ~amid *nt* **-(e)s, -e** polyamide; **p~chloriert** [-klo'ri:ɐt] *adj* polychlorinated; **~ester** *m* **-s, -** polyester; **p~gam** *adj* polygamous; **~gamie** *f* polygamy; **p~glott** *adj* polyglot *no adv.*
Polynesien [-iən] *nt* **-s** Polynesia.
Polynesier(in *f*) [-iɐ, -iərɪn] *m* **-s, -** Polynesian.
polynesisch *adj* Polynesian.
Polyp *m* **-en, -en (a)** (*Zool*) polyp. **(b)** (*Med*) **~en** adenoids. **(c)** (*hum inf*) (*Polizist*) cop (*inf*).
Poly-: ~technikum *nt* polytechnic, poly (*inf*); **p~technisch** *adj* polytechnic.
Pomade *f* hair-cream; (*Hist, für krause Haare*) pomade.
pomadig *adj* (*inf*) **(a)** *Haare* smarmed down (*inf*), Brylcreemed ®. **(b)** (*schleimig*) smarmy (*inf*). **(c)** (*langsam*) sluggish.
Pomeranze *f* **-, -n** Seville *or* bitter orange.
Pommer(in *f*) *m* **-n, -n** Pomeranian.
Pommern *nt* **-s** Pomerania.
Pommes frites [pɔm'frits] *pl* chips *pl* (*Brit*), French fries *pl* (*US*), French fried potatoes *pl* (*form*).
Pomp *m* **-(e)s,** *no pl* pomp.
pompös *adj* grandiose.
Poncho *m* **-s, -s** poncho.
Pond *nt* **-s, -** (*Phys*) weight of 1 gramme mass under standard gravity.
Pontifex *m* **-, Pontifizes** Pontifex.
Pontifikal|amt *nt* Pontifical Mass.
Pontifikat *nt or m* **-(e)s, -e** pontificate.
Pontius ['pɔntsiʊs] *m*: **von ~ zu Pilatus** from pillar to post.
Ponton [põ'tõ:, pɔn'tõ:, 'pɔntõ] *m* **-s, -s** pontoon.
Pontonbrücke *f* pontoon bridge.
Pony[1] ['pɔni] *nt* **-s, -s** pony.
Pony[2] ['pɔni] *m* **-s, -s** (*Frisur*) fringe, bangs *pl* (*US*).
Ponyfrisur *f* hairstyle with a fringe *or* with bangs (*US*) ◆ **sie hat eine ~** she has a fringe/bangs.
Pool [pu:l] *m* **-s, -s** pool; (*Fin*) pool ◆ **~ der Arbeitslosen** pool of unemployed.
Pool(billard) ['pu:l(bɪljart)] *nt* pool, pocket billiards *no pl.*
Pop *m* **-s,** *no pl* (*Mus*) pop; (*Art*) pop-art; (*Mode*) pop fashion.
Popanz *m* **-es, -e (a)** (*Schreckgespenst*) bogey, bugbear ◆ **etw als ~ hinstellen** to make a bogey *or* bugbear of sth. **(b)** (*willenloser Mensch*) puppet.
Popcorn [-kɔ:n] *nt* **-s,** *no pl* popcorn.
Pope *m* **-n, -n** priest; (*pej*) cleric.
Popel *m* **-s, -** (*inf*) (*Nasen~*) bogey (*baby-talk*), (piece of) snot (*sl*); (*Mensch*) pleb (*inf*), prole (*inf*).
pop(e)lig *adj* (*inf*) **(a)** (*knauserig*) stingy (*inf*) ◆ **~e zwei Mark** a lousy two marks (*inf*). **(b)** (*dürftig*) crummy (*inf*) ◆ **ihre Wohnung war recht ~ eingerichtet** her flat had really crummy furniture. **(c)** (*spießig*) small-minded, narrow-minded.
Popelin *m* **-s, -e, Popeline** *f* **-, -** poplin.
popeln *vi* (*inf*) **(in der Nase) ~** to pick one's nose.
Pop-: ~gruppe *f* pop group; **~musik** *f* pop music.
Popo *m* **-s, -s** (*inf*) bottom, behind (*inf*), botty (*baby-talk*).
Poposcheitel *m* (*inf*) middle *or* centre parting.
Popper *m* **-s, -** preppie.
popperhaft *adj* preppie.
poppig *adj* (*inf*) (*Art, Mus*) pop *no adv; Kleidung* trendy.
Pop-: ~sänger *m* pop singer; **~star** *m* pop star; **~szene** *f* pop scene.
populär *adj* popular (*bei* with).
popularisieren* *vt* to popularize.
Popularität *f* popularity.
populärwissenschaftlich *adj* popular science ◆ **seine Bücher sind mehr ~** his books are rather more popular science; **etw ~ darstellen** to present sth in a popular scientific way.
Population *f* (*Biol, Sociol*) population.
Populismus *m* (*Pol*) populism.
Populist(in *f*) *m* populist.
populistisch *adj* populist.
Pore *f* **-, -n** pore.
porig *adj Gestein* porous ◆ **die Haut ist ~** the skin has pores.
-porig *adj suf* with ... pores.
Porno *m* **-s, -s** (*inf*) porn (*inf*).
Porno- *in cpds* (*inf*) porn (*inf*); **~film** *m* porn *or* blue film.
⚠**Pornographie** *f* pornography.
⚠**pornographisch** *adj* pornographic.
porös *adj* (*durchlässig*) porous; (*brüchig: Gummi, Leder*) perished ◆ **~ werden** to perish.
Porosität *f* porosity.
Porree ['pɔre] *m* **-s, -s** leek.
Port[1] *m* **-(e)s, -e (a)** (*poet*) haven (*poet*). **(b)** (*~wein*) port.
Port[2] *m* **-s, -s** (*Comput*) port.
portabel *adj* portable.
Portabilität *f* portability.
Portable ['pɔrtəbl] *nt* **-s, -s** portable TV *or* television (set).
Portal *nt* **-s, -e** portal.
Portefeuille [pɔrt(ə)'fø:j] *nt* **-s, -s** (*Pol, obs*) portfolio; (*obs: Brieftasche*) wallet.
⚠**Portemonnaie** [pɔrtmɔ'ne:, pɔrtmɔ'nɛ:] *nt* **-s, -s** purse.
Porti *pl of* **Porto.**
Portier [pɔr'tie:] *m* **-s, -s** porter; *siehe* **Pförtner(in).**
portieren* *vt* (*Sw, Pol*) to put up.
Portierloge [pɔr'tie:lo:ʒə] *f* porter's lodge; *siehe* **Pförtnerloge.**
Portion *f* **(a)** (*beim Essen*) portion, helping ◆ **eine halbe ~** a half portion; (*fig inf*) a half-pint (*inf*); **eine zweite ~** a second helping; **eine ~ Kaffee** a pot of coffee; **eine ~ Butter** a portion of butter.
(b) (*fig inf: Anteil*) amount ◆ **er besitzt eine ganze ~ Frechheit** he's got a fair amount of cheek (*inf*); **sie brachte eine gute ~ Geduld auf** she showed a fair amount of patience (*inf*).
portionenweise, portionsweise *adv* in helpings *or* portions.
Porto *nt* **-s, -s** *or* **Porti** postage *no pl* (*für* on, for); (*für Kisten etc*) carriage ◆ **~ zahlt Empfänger** postage paid; **das ~ für den Brief macht eine Mark** the postage on *or* for the letter is one mark.
Porto-: ~auslagen *pl* postal *or* postage expenses *pl*; **p~frei** *adj* post free, postage paid; **~kasse** *f* ≃ petty cash (*for postal expenses*); **p~pflichtig** *adj* liable *or* subject to postage.
Porträt, Portrait [pɔr'trɛ:] *nt* **-s, -s** (*lit, fig*) portrait.
Porträt|aufnahme *f* portrait photo(graph).
porträtieren*, portraitieren* *vt* (*fig*) to portray ◆ **jdn ~** to paint a portrait of sb, to paint sb's portrait.
Porträtist(in *f*), **Portraitist(in** *f*) *m* portrait painter, portraitist.
Porträt-, Portrait-: ~maler *m* portrait painter, portraitist; **~malerei** *f* portraiture; ⚠**~photographie** *f* portrait photo(graph); **~studie** *f* sketch for a portrait.
Portugal *nt* **-s** Portugal.
Portugiese *m*, **-n, -n, Portugiesin** *f* Portuguese.
portugiesisch *adj* Portuguese.
Portugiesisch(e) *nt* Portuguese; *siehe auch* **Deutsch(e).**
Portwein *m* port.
Porzellan *nt* **-s, -e** (*Material*) china, porcelain; (*Geschirr*) china ◆ **unnötig ~ zerbrechen** *or* **zerschlagen** (*fig*) to cause a lot of unnecessary bother *or* trouble.
Porzellan- *in cpds* china, porcelain; **~erde** *f* china clay, kaolin; **~geschirr** *nt* china, crockery; **~laden** *m* china shop; *siehe* **Elefant**; **~manufaktur** *f* porcelain *or* china factory; (*Herstellung*) porcelain *or* china production.
Posaune *f* **-, -n** trombone; (*fig*) trumpet ◆ **die ~n des Jüngsten Gerichts** the last trump.
posaunen* (*inf*) **1** *vi* (*Posaune spielen*) to play the trombone.
2 *vti* (*fig: laut sprechen*) to bellow, to bawl, to yell ◆ **etw in alle Welt** *or* **in die Gegend ~** to shout sth from the rooftops *or* hilltops, to tell *or* proclaim sth to the whole world.
Posaunen-: ~bläser *m* trombonist, trombone player; **~chor** *m* trombone band (*usually connected with a church*); **~engel** *m* (*lit*) cherub with a trumpet; (*fig*) (little) chubby-cheeks (*inf*).
Posaunist(in *f*) *m siehe* **Posaunenbläser.**
Pose *f* **-, -n** pose.
posieren* *vi* to pose ◆ **er posiert in der Rolle des Wohltäters** he's playing the benefactor.
Position *f* position; (*Comm: Posten einer Liste*) item ◆ **in gesicherter ~ sein** to have a secure position.
positionieren* *vt* (*Comput*) to position.
Positionierung *f* positioning.
Positions-: ~lampe *f*, **~licht** *nt* navigation light; **~papier** *nt* (*Pol*) policy document.
positiv *adj* positive ◆ **eine ~e Antwort** an answer in the affirmative, an affirmative (answer); **etw ~ wissen** to know sth for certain *or* for a fact, to be positive; **ich weiß nichts P~es** I don't know anything definite; **~ zu etw stehen** to be in favour of sth; **sich ~ zu einer Sache äußern** to respond *or* react positively to sth.
Positiv[1] *m* (*Gram*) positive.
Positiv[2] *nt* **(a)** (*Phot*) positive. **(b)** (*Orgel*) harmonium.
Positivismus *m* positivism.
positivistisch *adj* positivist.
Positur *f* posture; (*stehend auch*) stance ◆ **sich in ~ setzen/stellen** to take up *or* adopt a posture; **sie setzte sich vor ihrem Chef in ~** she sat neatly posed for her boss; **sich in ~ werfen** to strike a pose.
Posse *f* **-, -n** farce.
Possen *m* **-s, -** (*dated*) prank, tomfoolery *no pl* ◆ **~ reißen** to lark *or* fool *or* clown around; **jdm einen ~ spielen** to play a prank on sb; **mit jdm ~ treiben** (*old*) to play pranks on sb; **er tat es mir zum ~** he did it just to annoy me.
Possen-: p~haft *adj* farcical; **~reißer** *m* **-s, -** clown, buffoon; **~spiel** *nt* (*liter*) pranks *pl.*
possessiv *adj* possessive.
Possessiv(pronomen) *nt* **-s, -e, Possessivum** *nt* possessive pronoun.
possierlich *adj* comical, funny.
Post *f* **-, -en (a)** post, mail; (*~amt, ~wesen*) post office ◆ **war die ~ schon da?** has the post *or* mail come yet?; **ist ~ für mich da?** is there any post *or* mail for me?, are there any letters for me?; **er las seine ~** he read his mail; **etw**

mit der ~ schicken to send sth by post *or* mail; **etw auf die ~ geben** to post *or* mail sth; **auf die** *or* **zur ~ gehen** to go to the post office; **mit gleicher ~** by the same post; **mit getrennter ~** under separate cover; **mit der ersten ~ kommen** to come with *or* in the first post, to come first post; **etw durch die ~ beziehen** to order sth by post.
(b) (*~kutsche*) mail coach; (*~bus*) mail bus.

Post|abholer *m* **-s, -** *someone who collects his mail from a PO box.*

postalisch *adj* postal.

Postament *nt* pedestal, base.

Post-: ~amt *nt* post office; **~anschrift** *f* postal address; **~anweisung** *f* *remittance paid in at a Post Office and delivered by post,* ≃ postal (*Brit*) *or* money order; **~auto** *nt* post-office van; (*Lieferwagen*) mail van (*Brit*) *or* truck (*US*); (*Bus*) mail bus; **~beamte(r)** *m,* **~beamtin** *f* post office official; **~bedienstete(r)** *mf* (*form*) post office worker; **~bezirk** *m* postal district *or* area *or* zone (*US*); **~boot** *nt* mail boat, packet (boat); **~bote** *m* postman, mailman (*US*); **~bus** *m* mail bus.

Pöstchen *nt dim of* **Posten** little position *or* job.

Postdienst *m* postal service, the mails *pl* (*US*).

Posten *m* **-s, - (a)** (*Anstellung*) post, position, job.
(b) (*Mil: Wachmann*) guard; (*am Eingang auch*) sentry; (*Stelle*) post ♦ **~ stehen** to stand guard; (*am Eingang auch*) to stand sentry; **~ beziehen** to take up one's post; **~ aufstellen** to post guards, to mount a guard.
(c) **auf dem ~ sein** (*aufpassen*) to be awake; (*gesund sein*) to be fit; **nicht ganz auf dem ~ sein** to be (a bit) under the weather, to be off-colour; *siehe* **verloren, ausharren.**
(d) (*Streik~*) picket ♦ **~ aufstellen** to set up pickets *or* a picket-line.
(e) (*Comm: Warenmenge*) quantity, lot.
(f) (*Comm: im Etat*) item, entry.

Posten-: ~dienst *m* guard duty; **~dienst haben** to be on guard duty; **~kette** *f* cordon.

Poster ['pɔstɐ] *nt* **-s, -(s)** poster.

Postf. *abbr of* **Postfach.**

Post-: ~fach *nt* post-office *or* PO box; **~fachnummer** *f* (PO *or* post-office) box number; **p~fertig** *adj* ready for posting *or* for the post; **~flugzeug** *nt* mail plane; **p~frisch** *adj* mint; **~gebühr** *f* postal (and telephone) charge *or* rate; **~geheimnis** *nt* secrecy of the post.

Postgiro- [-ʒiːro]: **~amt** *nt* National Giro office (*Brit*); **~konto** *nt* National *or* Post Office Giro account (*Brit*).

Post-: ~halterei *f* coaching house *or* inn; **~horn** *nt* post-horn.

posthum *adj* posthumous.

postieren* [1] *vt* to post, to station, to position.
[2] *vr* to station *or* position oneself.

Postillion [pɔstɪl'joːn, 'pɔstɪljoːn] *m* **-s, -e** mail coach driver.

⚠**Postillon d'amour** [pɔstijõda'muːr] *m* **- -, -s -** go-between.

Postkarte *f* postcard, postal card (*US*), postal (*US inf*).

Postkarten-: ~format *nt,* **~größe** *f* postcard size; **in ~größe** postcard sized.

Post-: ~kasten *m* pillar box (*Brit*), postbox, mailbox (*US*); **~kutsche** *f* mail coach, stagecoach; **p~lagernd** [1] *adj* to be called for; [2] *adv* poste restante (*Brit*), general delivery (*US*); **~leitzahl** *f* post(al) code, Zip code (*US*).

Postler(in *f***)** *m* **-s, -** (*inf*) post office official/worker.

Post-: ~meister *m* postmaster; **~minister** *m* postmaster general; **p~modern** *adj* postmodern; **~moderne** *f* postmodern era; **p~nuklear** *adj* post-nuclear; **~paket** *nt* parcel (*sent by post*); **~sache** *f* matter sent postage paid *no pl*; **~sack** *m* mailbag; **~schalter** *m* post office counter; **~scheck** *m* (Post Office *or* National) Giro cheque (*Brit*); **~scheckamt** *nt siehe* **~giroamt; ~scheckkonto** *nt siehe* **~girokonto; ~skript** *nt* **-(e)s, -e, ~skriptum** *nt* **-s, -e** *or* **~skripta** postscript, PS; **~sparbuch** *nt* Post Office savings book; **~sparkasse** *f* Post Office savings bank; **~stelle** *f* sub post office; **~stempel** *m* postmark; **Datum des ~stempels** date as postmark; **~überweisung** *f* Girobank transfer.

Postulat *nt* (*Annahme*) postulate; (*Eccl: Probezeit*) postulancy.

postulieren* *vt* to postulate.

postum *adj siehe* **posthum.**

Post-: ~vermerk *m* postmark; **~wagen** *m* (*Rail*) mail car *or* van (*Brit*); **p~wendend** *adv* by return (of post), by return mail; **~wertzeichen** *nt* (*form*) postage stamp (*form*); **~wesen** *nt* Post Office; **~wurfsendung** *f* direct-mail advertising; **~zug** *m* mail train; **~zustellung** *f* postal *or* mail delivery; **~zustellungsurkunde** *f* registered post certificate.

Pot *nt* **-s,** *no pl* (*sl: Haschisch*) pot (*sl*).

⚠**Potemkinsch** *adj* sham ♦ **~e Dörfer** façade, sham.

potent *adj* potent; (*fig*) *Phantasie* powerful; *Mensch* high-powered.

Potentat *m* **-en, -en** potentate.

⚠**Potential** [poten'tsiaːl] *nt* **-s, -e** potential.

⚠**potentiell** [poten'tsiɛl] *adj* potential ♦ **er ist ~ mein Gegner** he's a potential opponent, he's potentially my opponent.

Potenz *f* **(a)** (*Med*) potency; (*fig*) ability ♦ **schöpferische ~** creative power.
(b) (*Math*) power ♦ **zweite/dritte ~** square/cube; **eine Zahl in die sechste ~ erheben** to raise a number to the power of six *or* to the sixth power; **die zweite/dritte ~ zu zwei ist vier/acht** the square/cube of two is four/eight, two to the power of two/three is four/eight; **die sechste ~ zu zwei** two to the sixth (power); **in höchster ~** (*fig*) to the highest degree.

potenzieren* *vt* (*Math*) to raise to the power of; (*fig: steigern*) to multiply, to increase ♦ **2 potenziert mit 4** 2 to the power of 4, 2 to the fourth.

Potpourri ['pɔtpuri] *nt* **-s, -s** (*Mus*) potpourri, medley (*aus +dat* of); (*fig*) potpourri, assortment.

Pott *m* **-(e)s, ¨-e** (*inf*) pot; (*Schiff*) ship, tub (*hum inf*) ♦ **mit etw zu ~e kommen** to see sth through; (*anfangen*) to get down to sth.

Pott-: ~asche *f* potash; **~fisch** *m* sperm whale; ⚠**p~häßlich** *adj* (*inf*) ugly as sin, plug-ugly (*inf*); **~wal** *m* sperm whale.

potz Blitz, potztausend *interj* (*old*) upon my soul (*old*).

Poularde [pu-] *f* poulard(e).

poussieren [pu'siːrən] [1] *vi* (*dated inf: flirten*) to flirt.
[2] *vt* (*old: schmeicheln*) **jdn ~** to curry favour with sb.

power ['poːvɐ] *adj* (*inf*) poor; *Essen, Geschenke* meagre ♦ **der Ring sieht ~ aus** the ring looks cheap.

Power ['pauɐ] *f* **-,** *no pl* (*inf*) power.

Powerfrau ['pauɐ-] *f* (*sl*) high-powered career woman.

powern ['pauɐn] *vi* (*sl*) to get things moving.

PR [peː'|ɛr] *abbr of* **Public Relations** PR.

prä-, prae- *pref* pre-.

Prä|ambel *f* preamble (*gen* to).

Pracht *f* **-,** *no pl* splendour, magnificence; (*fig: Herrlichkeit*) splendour ♦ **in seiner vollen** *or* **ganzen ~** in all its splendour *or* magnificence; **große ~ entfalten** to put on a show *or* display of great splendour; **es ist eine wahre ~** it's (really) marvellous *or* fantastic; **er kann singen, daß es eine ~ ist** he can sing marvellously *or* fantastically.

Pracht-: ~ausgabe *f* de luxe edition; **~bau** *m* splendid *or* magnificent building; **~entfaltung** *f* display of splendour, magnificent display; **zur vollen ~entfaltung kommen** to display its/their full splendour; **~exemplar** *nt* splendid *or* prime specimen, beauty (*inf*); (*von Buch: ~ausgabe*) de luxe copy; (*fig: Mensch*) fine specimen; **mein ~exemplar von Sohn** (*iro*) my brilliant son (*iro*).

prächtig *adj* (*prunkvoll*) splendid, magnificent; (*großartig*) splendid, marvellous.

Pracht-: ~kerl *m* (*inf*) great guy (*inf*), good bloke (*Brit inf*); (*~exemplar*) beauty (*inf*); **~straße** *f* boulevard, magnificent avenue; **~stück** *nt siehe* **~exemplar; p~voll** *adj siehe* **prächtig; ~weib** *nt* (*inf*) fine specimen of a woman *or* of womanhood.

Prädestination *f* predestination.

prädestinieren* *vt* to predestine, to predetermine ♦ **sein diplomatisches Geschick prädestinierte ihn zum Politiker** with his diplomatic skill he was predestined to be a politician; **er ist für diese Aufgabe wie prädestiniert** he seems to have been made for the job.

Prädikat *nt* (*Gram*) predicate; (*Bewertung*) rating; (*Sch: Zensur*) grade; (*Rangbezeichnung*) title ♦ **Wein mit ~** special quality wine.

prädikativ *adj* predicative.

Prädikativ(um) *nt* predicative noun/adjective/pronoun.

Prädikats-: ~nomen *nt* predicative noun/pronoun; **~wein** *m* top quality wine.

prädisponieren* *vt* to predispose (*für* to).

Prä|emptivschlag *m* (*Mil*) pre-emptive strike.

Präfekt *m* **-en, -en** prefect.

Präferenz *f* (*geh*) preference.

Präfix *nt* **-es, -e** prefix.

Prag *nt* **-s** Prague ♦ **~er Frühling** (*Pol*) Spring of Prague.

Präge *f* **-, -n, Präge|anstalt** *f* mint.

prägen *vt* **(a)** to stamp; *Münzen* to mint, to strike; *Leder, Papier, Metall* to emboss; (*erfinden*) *Begriffe, Wörter* to coin ♦ **seine Worte prägten sich ihr ins Herz** (*liter*) his words engraved themselves in her heart (*liter*).
(b) (*fig: formen*) *Charakter* to shape, to mould; (*Erlebnis, Kummer, Erfahrungen*) *jdn* to leave its/their mark on ♦ **ein vom Leid geprägtes Gesicht** a face marked by suffering; **das moderne Drama ist durch Brecht geprägt worden** Brecht had a forming *or* formative influence on modern drama.
(c) (*kennzeichnen*) *Stadtbild, Landschaft etc* to characterize.

prägend *adj Erlebnis* formative.

PR-Agentur [peː'|ɛr-] *f* PR agency.

Präge-: ~ort *m* mint; **~stempel** *m* die, stamp; **~stock** *m* punch.

Pragmatiker(in *f***)** *m* **-s, -** pragmatist.

pragmatisch *adj* pragmatic.

Pragmatismus *m* pragmatism.

prägnant *adj* succinct, concise, terse.

Prägnanz *f* succinctness, conciseness, terseness.

Prägung *f* **(a)** *siehe vt (a, b)* stamping; minting, striking; embossing; coining; shaping, moulding. **(b)** (*auf Münzen*) strike; (*auf Leder, Metall, Papier*) embossing. **(c)** (*Eigenart*) character; (*von Charakter*) mould.

prähistorisch *adj* prehistoric.

prahlen *vi* (*mit* about) to boast, to brag, to swank (*inf*).

Prahler(in *f***)** *m* **-s, -** boaster, bragger, braggart.

Prahlerei *f* (*Großsprecherei*) boasting *no pl*, bragging *no pl*; (*das Zurschaustellen*) showing-off, swank (*inf*) ♦ **~en** boasts, showing-off, swanking (*inf*).

prahlerisch *adj* (*großsprecherisch*) boastful, bragging *attr*; (*großtuerisch*) swanky (*inf*).

Prahlhans *m* **-es, -hänse** (*inf*) show-off.

Prahm *m* **-(e)s, -e** *or* **¨-e** barge, lighter.

präjudizieren* *vt insep* (*Jur*) to prejudge.

Praktik *f* (*Methode*) procedure, method; (*usu pl: Kniff*) practice, trick ♦ **undurchsichtige ~en** shady *or* dark practices.

Praktika *pl of* **Praktikum.**

praktikabel *adj* practicable, practical.

Praktikant(in *f*) *m student doing a period of practical training*, trainee.
Praktiker(in *f*) *m* **-s, -** practical man/woman; (*auf wissenschaftlichem Gebiet auch*) practician; (*inf: praktischer Arzt*) GP ♦ **was halten Sie als ~ von der Pädagogik?** what do you, as a practising teacher, think of educational theory?
Praktikum *nt* **-s, Praktika** practical, (period of) practical training.
praktisch [1] *adj* practical; (*nützlich auch*) handy ♦ **sie hat einen ~en Verstand** she's practically minded; **~er Arzt** general practitioner; **~es Jahr** practical year; **~e Ausbildung** practical *or* in-job training; **~es Beispiel** concrete example.
[2] *adv* (*in der Praxis*) in practice; (*geschickt*) practically; (*so gut wie*) practically, virtually.
praktizieren* [1] *vi* to practise ♦ **ein ~der Katholik** a practising Catholic.
[2] *vt* (**a**) (*pej: ausführen*) to put into practice, to practise. (**b**) (*inf: geschickt an eine Stelle bringen*) to conjure.
Prälat *m* **-en, -en** prelate.
Präliminarien [-iən] *pl* preliminary talks *or* discussions *pl*.
Praline *f*, **Praliné, Pralinee** (*Aus*) *nt* **-s, -s** chocolate, chocolate candy (*US*).
prall *adj Sack, Beutel, Brieftasche* bulging; *Segel* billowing, full; *Tomaten* firm; *Euter* swollen, full; *Luftballon* hard; *Wange* full, chubby; *Brüste* full, well-rounded; *Hintern* well-rounded; *Arme, Schenkel* big strong *attr*; *Sonne* blazing ♦ **~gefüllt** filled to bursting; **das Segel war ~ vom Wind gefüllt** the sail billowed out in the wind; **ihre Brüste wölbten sich ~ unter dem Pullover** her breasts curved firmly under her sweater; **die Hose spannte sich ~ über ihrem Hintern** her trousers stretched tightly over her bottom; **die Sonne brannte ~ auf den Strand** the sun blazed *or* beat down onto the beach.
Prall *m* **-(e)s, -e** collision (*gegen* with).
prallen *vi aux sein* **gegen etw ~** to collide with sth, to crash into sth; (*Ball*) to bounce against *or* off sth; **er prallte mit dem Kopf gegen die Windschutzscheibe** he hit *or* crashed his head on *or* against the windscreen; **die Sonne prallte gegen** *or* **auf die Fenster** the sun beat *or* blazed down on the windows.
Prallheit *f* (*von Ballon*) hardness; (*von Brüsten, Hintern*) fullness, well-roundedness; (*von Euter*) fullness, swollenness ♦ **die ~ der Segel** the fullness of the sails, the billowing sails.
prallvoll *adj* full to bursting; *Brieftasche* bulging.
Präludium *nt* prelude; (*sexuell*) foreplay.
Prämie [-iə] *f* premium; (*Belohnung*) bonus; (*Preis*) prize.
Prämien- [-iən]: **p~begünstigt** *adj* concession- *or* premium-carrying, with benefit of premiums; **~geschäft** *nt* (*Handel*) option dealing; (*Abschluß*) option; **p~los** *nt* winning premium bond; **p~sparen** *vi sep infin, ptp only to save on a system benefiting from government premiums in addition to interest.*
prämieren*, prämiieren* *vt* (*auszeichnen*) to give an award; (*belohnen*) to give a bonus ♦ **etw mit dem ersten Preis/mit 1000 Mark ~** to award sth first prize/a prize of 1000 marks *or* a 1000 mark prize.
Prämierung, Prämiierung *f* (**a**) (*das Prämieren*) **für diesen Film kommt eine ~ nicht in Frage** we can't possibly give this film an award. (**b**) (*Veranstaltung*) presentation ♦ **die ~ der Preisträger** the presentation to the prizewinners.
Prämisse *f* **-, -n** premise.
pränatal *adj attr* prenatal; *Vorsorge* antenatal.
prangen *vi* (*liter*) to be resplendent ♦ **an der Tür prangte ein Schild/sein Name in großen Lettern** a notice hung resplendent on the door/his name was emblazoned in big letters on the door.
Pranger *m* **-s, -** stocks *pl*, pillory ♦ **jdn/etw an den ~ stellen** (*fig*) to pillory sb/sth; **am ~ stehen** (*lit*) to be in the stocks *or* pillory; (*fig*) to be being pilloried.
Pranke *f* **-, -n** (*Tier~*) paw; (*inf: Hand*) paw (*inf*), mauler (*inf*).
Prankenhieb *m* swipe *or* blow from a paw ♦ **ein ~ des Löwen streckte die Antilope nieder** one blow *or* swipe from the lion's paw laid the antelope low.
PR-Anzeige [pe:'|ɛr-] *f* promotional advert.
Präparat *nt* preparation; (*für Mikroskop*) slide preparation.
Präparator *m*, **Präparatorin** *f* lab technician.
präparieren* [1] *vt* (**a**) (*konservieren*) to preserve. (**b**) (*Med: zerlegen*) to dissect. (**c**) (*geh: vorbereiten*) to prepare.
[2] *vr* (*dated*) to prepare (oneself), to do one's preparation (*für, auf +acc* for).
Präposition *f* preposition.
präpositional *adj* prepositional.
Prärie *f* prairie.
Präriewolf *m* prairie wolf, coyote.
Präsens *nt* **-, Präsenzien** [-iən] present (tense).
präsent *adj* (*anwesend*) present; (*geistig rege*) alert ♦ **etw ~ haben** to have sth at hand; **sein Name ist mir nicht ~** his name escapes me.
Präsent *nt* **-s, -e** present, gift.
präsentabel *adj* presentable.
Präsentation *f* presentation.
präsentieren* [1] *vt* to present ♦ **jdm etw ~** to present sb with sth; **präsentiert das Gewehr!** present arms!
[2] *vr* (*sich zeigen*) to present oneself; (*sich vorstellen auch*) to introduce oneself.
[3] *vi* (*Mil*) to present arms.
Präsentierteller *m* (*old*) salver ♦ **auf dem ~ sitzen** (*fig*) to be on show.
Präsenz *f* **-,** *no pl* (*geh*) presence ♦ **die ständig abnehmende ~ im Büro** the constantly decreasing numbers in the office.
Präsenz-: **~bibliothek** *f* reference library; **~liste** *f* (attendance) register.
Praseodym *nt, no pl* (*abbr* **Pr**) praseodymium.
Präser *m* **-s, -** (*inf*) *abbr of* **Präservativ**.
Präservativ [prɛzɛrva'ti:f] *nt* contraceptive, condom, sheath.
Präsident(in *f*) *m* president ♦ **Herr/Frau ~** Mister/Madam President.
Präsidentenwahl *f* presidential election.
Präsidentschaft *f* presidency.
Präsidentschaftskandidat *m* presidential candidate.
präsidieren* *vi* to preside ♦ **einem Ausschuß ~** to preside over *or* be president of a committee.
Präsidium *nt* (*Vorsitz*) presidency; (*Führungsgruppe*) committee; (*Polizei~*) (police) headquarters *pl* ♦ **ins ~ gewählt werden** to be elected to the committee; **das ~ übernehmen** to take the chair.
prasseln *vi* (**a**) *aux sein* to clatter; (*Regen, Hagel*) to drum; (*fig: Vorwürfe, Fragen*) to rain *or* hail down. (**b**) (*Feuer*) to crackle.
prassen *vi* (*schlemmen*) to feast; (*in Luxus leben*) to live the high life.
Prasser *m* **-s, -** glutton; (*Verschwender*) spendthrift.
Prasserei *f* (*Schlemmerei*) feasting; (*Luxusleben*) high life.
Prätendent *m* pretender.
prätentiös [prɛtɛn'tsiø:s] *adj* pretentious.
Präteritum *nt* **-s, Präterita** preterite.
Pratze *f* **-, -n** (*S Ger inf*) paw; (*fig: Hand*) paw (*inf*), mauler (*sl*).
präventiv [prɛvɛn'ti:f] *adj* prevent(at)ive.
Präventiv-: **~behandlung** *f* (*Med*) preventive treatment; **~krieg** *m* preventive *or* pre-emptive war; **~maßnahme** *f* preventive measure; **~medizin** *f* preventive medicine; **~schlag** *m* (*Mil*) pre-emptive strike.
Praxis *f* **-, Praxen** (**a**) (*no pl*) practice; (*Erfahrung*) experience; (*Brauch*) practice, custom ♦ **in der ~** in practice; **die ~ sieht anders aus** the facts are different; **eine Idee in die ~ umsetzen** to put an idea into practice; **ein Mann der ~** a man with practical experience; **ein Beispiel aus der ~** an example from real life; **das lernt man erst durch die ~** you only learn that by doing it, that's only learnt through practical experience; **seine langjährige ~** his long years of experience.
(**b**) (*eines Arztes, Rechtsanwalts*) practice.
(**c**) (*Behandlungsräume, Sprechstunde*) surgery (*Brit*), doctor's office (*US*); (*Anwaltsbüro*) office.
praxis-: **~fern, ~fremd** *adj* impractical; **~nah** *adj* practical; **~orientiert** *adj* practical.
Präzedenzfall *m* precedent ♦ **einen ~ schaffen** to set *or* create *or* establish a precedent.
präzis(e) *adj* precise.
präzisieren* *vt* to state more precisely; (*zusammenfassen*) to summarize.
Präzision *f* precision.
Präzisions- *in cpds* precision; **~arbeit** *f* precision work; **~arbeit leisten** to work with precision; **~schütze** *m* marksman.
predigen [1] *vt* (**a**) to preach ♦ **solche Leute ~ immer Moral** people like that are always preaching (about) *or* sermonizing about morality.
(**b**) (*fig*) **jdm etw ~** to lecture sb on sth; **sie predigt ihm andauernd, daß er sich die Zähne putzen soll** she keeps lecturing him on the importance of cleaning his teeth.
[2] *vi* to give a sermon, to preach; (*fig: mahnen*) to preach, to sermonize ♦ **tauben Ohren ~** to preach to deaf ears.
Prediger(in *f*) *m* **-s, -** preacher/woman preacher.
Predigt *f* **-, -en** (*lit, fig*) sermon ♦ **jdm eine lange ~ über etw** (*acc*) **halten** (*fig*) to give sb a long sermon on *or* about sth.
Predigttext *m* text for a sermon.
Preis *m* **-es, -e** (**a**) price (*für* of); (*Fahrgeld*) fare (*für* for); (*Gebühr, Honorar*) fee (*für* of) ♦ **der ~ für die Hose beträgt 70 Mark** the price of the trousers is 70 marks; **(weit) unter(m) ~** cut-price; **etw unter ~ verkaufen/verschleudern** to sell/flog (*Brit inf*) sth off cheap; **zum halben ~** half-price; **um jeden ~** (*fig*) at all costs; **ich gehe um keinen ~ hier weg** (*fig*) I'm not leaving here at any price; **auch um den ~ seines eignen Glücks** even at the expense of his own happiness.
(**b**) (*bei Wettbewerben*) prize; (*Auszeichnung*) award ♦ **in diesem Rennen ist kein ~ ausgesetzt** there's no prize in *or* for this race; **den ersten ~ gewinnen** to win (the) first prize; **jdm einen ~ zusprechen** *or* **zuerkennen** *or* **verleihen** to award *or* give sb a prize/to give sb an award.
(**c**) (*Belohnung*) reward ♦ **einen ~ auf jds Kopf aussetzen** to put a price on sb's head.
(**d**) *no pl* (*liter: Lob*) praise (*auf +acc* of) ♦ **ein Gedicht zum ~ von ...** a poem in praise of ...
Preis-: **~abbau** *m* price reduction; **~absprache** *f* price-fixing *no pl*; **~änderung** *f* price change; **~angabe** *f* price quotation; **alle Kleider sind mit ~angabe** all dresses are priced, the prices of all dresses are given; **~anstieg** *m* rise in prices; **~aufgabe** *f* prize competition; **~aufschlag** *m* supplementary charge, supplement; **~auftrieb** *m* price increase; **~ausschreiben** *nt* competition; **~bewegung** *f* movement of prices; ⚠**p~bewußt** *adj* price-conscious; **~bildung** *f* price fixing; **~bindung** *f* price fixing; **~bindung der zweiten Hand** retail price maintenance; **~brecher** *m* (*Produkt*) (all-time) bargain, snip (*inf*); (*Firma*) undercutter; **diese Firma wirkt als ~brecher auf dem Markt** this firm undercuts the market; **~disziplin** *f* price restraint; **~einbruch** *m* price collapse.
Preiselbeere *f* cranberry.
preis|empfindlich *adj* price-sensitive.
preisen *pret* **pries**, *ptp* **gepriesen** *vt* (*geh*) to extol, to praise, to laud (*liter*)

◆ **Gott sei gepriesen** praise be to God; **sich glücklich ~** to consider *or* count *or* think oneself lucky.

Preis-: **~entwicklung** *f* price trend; **~erhöhung** *f* price increase; **~ermäßigung** *f* price reduction; **~explosion** *f* price explosion; **~frage** *f* **(a)** question of price; **(b)** (*beim ~ausschreiben*) prize question (*in a competition*); (*inf: schwierige Frage*) sixty-four-thousand dollar question (*inf*), big question; **~gabe** *f* (*geh*) (*Aufgabe*) surrender, relinquishment, abandoning; (*von Geheimnis*) betrayal, divulgence; **sie wurden zur ~gabe ihrer Position gezwungen** they were forced to surrender *or* abandon *or* relinquish their position.

preisgeben *vt sep irreg* (*geh*) **(a)** (*ausliefern*) to expose, to leave to the mercy of ◆ **jdm/einer Sache preisgegeben sein** to be exposed to *or* at the mercy of sb/sth. **(b)** (*aufgeben*) to abandon, to relinquish; *Gebiete auch* to surrender. **(c)** (*verraten*) to betray; *Geheimnis auch* to divulge.

Preis-: **~gefälle** *nt* price gap; **~gefüge** *nt* price structure; **p~gekrönt** *adj* award-winning; **p~gekrönt werden** to be given an award; **~gericht** *nt* jury, team of judges; **~gestaltung** *f* pricing; **eine ganz andere ~gestaltung** a totally different price structure; **~grenze** *f* price limit; **p~günstig** *adj* inexpensive; **etw p~günstig bekommen** to get sth at a low *or* good price; **~index** *m* price index; **~klasse** *f* price range; **die gehobene ~klasse** the upper price range; **~kontrolle** *f* price control; **~krieg** *m* price war; **~lage** *f* price range; **in jeder ~lage** at all prices, at prices to suit every pocket; **in der mittleren ~lage** in the medium-priced range; **~lawine** *f* (*inf*) snowballing prices *pl*; **~-Leistungsverhältnis** *nt* cost effectiveness.

preislich *adj no pred* price *attr*, in price ◆ **dieses Angebot ist ~ sehr günstig** this offer is a bargain; **die Waren sind nur ~ verschieden** the goods only differ in price.

Preis-: **~liste** *f* price list; ⚠**~nachlaß** *m* price reduction; **10% ~nachlaß bei Barbezahlung** 10% off cash sales; **~niveau** *nt* price level; **~politik** *f* pricing policy; **~rätsel** *nt* prize competition; **~richter** *m* judge (*in a competition*), jury-member; **~schießen** *nt* shooting competition *or* contest, shoot; **~schild** *nt* price-tag; **~schlager** *m* (all-time) bargain; **~schwankung** *f* price fluctuation; **~senkung** *f* price cut; **~spanne** *f* price margin; **p~stabil** *adj* stable in price; **~stabilität** *f* stability of prices; **~steigerung** *f* price increase; **~steigerungsrate** *f* rate of price increases; **~stopp** *m* price freeze; **~sturz** *m* sudden fall *or* drop in prices; **~träger(in** *f*) *m* prizewinner; (*Kultur~*) award-winner; *siehe* **Nobelpreis**; **~treiber** *m person who forces prices up*; **~treiberei** *f* forcing up of prices; (*Wucher*) profiteering; **das ist nur ein Vorwand für die ~treiberei der Industrie** that's only an excuse for industry to force up prices; **~überwachung** *f siehe* **~kontrolle**; **~verfall** *m* drop-off in prices; **~vergleich** *m* price comparison; **einen ~vergleich machen** to shop around; **~verleihung** *f* presentation (of prizes/awards); **p~wert** *adj* good value *pred*; **ein (sehr) p~wertes Angebot** a (real) bargain; **ein p~wertes Kleid** a dress which is good value (for money); **hier kann man p~wert einkaufen** you get good value (for money) here.

prekär *adj* (*peinlich*) awkward, embarrassing; (*schwierig*) precarious.

Prell-: **~ball** *m game similar to volleyball in which the ball is bounced over the net*; **~bock** *m* (*Rail*) buffers *pl*, buffer-stop; **der ~bock sein** (*fig*) to be the scapegoat *or* fallguy (*esp US inf*).

prellen [1] *vt* **(a)** to bruise; (*anschlagen*) to hit. **(b)** (*fig inf: betrügen*) to swindle, to cheat ◆ **jdm um etw ~** to swindle *or* cheat sb out of sth; **die Zeche ~** to avoid paying the bill. **(c)** (*Sport*) to bounce.
[2] *vr* to bruise oneself ◆ **ich habe mich am Arm geprellt** I've bruised my arm.

Prellerei *f* swindle, fraud.

⚠**Prellschuß** *m* ricochet, ricocheting bullet.

Prellung *f* bruise, contusion.

Premier [prəˈmieː, pre-] *m* **-s, -s** premier.

Premiere [prəˈmieːrə, pre-, -ˈmiɛːrə] *f* **-, -n** premiere.

Premieren-: **~besucher** *pl*, **~publikum** *nt* premiere audience *no pl*; **~kino** *nt* first-run cinema.

Premierminister [prəˈmieː-, pre-] *m* prime minister.

Presbyterianer(in *f*) *m* Presbyterian.

presbyterianisch *adj* Presbyterian.

preschen *vi aux sein* (*inf*) to tear, to dash.

Presse *f* **-, -n (a)** (*mechanische ~*) press; (*Sch sl: Privatschule*) crammer (*sl*) ◆ **in die ~ gehen** to go to press; **frisch** *or* **eben aus der ~** hot from the press. **(b)** (*Zeitungen*) press ◆ **eine gute ~ haben** to have *or* get a good press.

Presse-: **~agentur** *f* press *or* news agency; **~amt** *nt* press office; **~attaché** *m* press attaché; **~ausweis** *m* press card; **~bericht** *m* press report; **~büro** *nt siehe* **~agentur**; **~dienst** *m* news service; **~empfang** *m* press reception; **~erklärung** *f* statement to the press, press release; **~fotograf** *m* press photographer; **~freiheit** *f* freedom of the press; **~gesetz** *nt* press law; **~jargon** *m* journalese; **~kampagne** *f* press campaign; **~karte** *f* press *or* review ticket; **~kommentar** *m* press commentary; **~konferenz** *f* press conference; **~meldung** *f* press report; **~mitteilung** *f* press release *or* announcement.

pressen [1] *vt* **(a)** to press; *Obst auch* to squeeze; *hohe Töne* to squeeze out; (*fig: zwingen*) to force (*in +acc* into); (*fig dated: unterdrücken*) to oppress. **(b)** (*Naut*) **Segel ~** to make too much sail.
[2] *vi* (*Sänger*) to squeeze the/one's notes out.

Presse-: **~notiz** *f* paragraph in the press; **~organ** *nt* organ; **~recht** *nt* press laws *pl*; **~referent** *m* press officer; **~sprecher** *m* press officer; **~stelle** *f* press office; **~stimme** *f* press commentary; (*kulturell*) press review; **~tribüne** *f* press box; (*Parl*) press gallery; **~vertreter** *m* representative of the press; **~wesen** *nt* press; **~zar** *m* (*inf*) press baron.

⚠**Preßglas** *nt* pressed glass.

pressieren* (*S Ger, Aus, Sw*) [1] *vi* to be in a hurry.
[2] *vi impers* **es pressiert** it's urgent; **(bei) ihm pressiert es immer** he's always in a hurry.

Pression *f* pressure.

⚠**Preßkohle** *f siehe* **Brikett**.

⚠**Preßluft** *f* compressed air.

⚠**Preßluft-**: **~bohrer** *m* pneumatic drill; **~hammer** *m* pneumatic *or* air hammer.

Prestige [prɛsˈtiːʒə] *nt* **-s**, *no pl* prestige ◆ **~ verlieren** to lose (one's) prestige.

Prestige-: **~frage** *f* question *or* matter of prestige; **~gewinn** *m* gain in prestige; **~sache** *f siehe* **~frage**; **~verlust** *m* loss of prestige.

Pretiosen [preˈtsioːzn] *pl* (*geh*) valuables *pl*.

Preuße *m* **-n, -n**, **Preußin** *f* Prussian ◆ **so schnell schießen die ~n nicht** (*inf*) things don't happen that fast.

Preußen *nt* **-s** Prussia.

preußisch *adj* Prussian.

preußischblau *adj* Prussian blue.

preziös *adj* (*geh*) precious.

PR-Fachmann [peːˈ|ɛr-] *m* PR specialist.

Pricke *f* **-, -n** (*Naut*) shallows marker.

prickeln *vi* (*kribbeln*) to tingle; (*kitzeln*) to tickle; (*Bläschen bilden*) to sparkle, to bubble ◆ **die Limonade prickelt in der Nase** the lemonade's tickling my nose; **ein angenehmes P~ auf der Haut** a pleasant tingling of the skin; **ich spürte ein P~ in meinem Bein** I had pins and needles in my leg.

prickelnd *adj siehe vi* tingling; tickling; sparkling, bubbling; (*fig: würzig*) piquant; (*fig: erregend*) *Gefühl* tingling ◆ **der ~e Reiz der Neuheit** the thrill of novelty; **etwas P~es für den Gaumen** something to titillate the tastebuds (*hum*), something tasty for the palate.

Priel *m* **-(e)s, -e** narrow channel (*in North Sea mud flats*), tideway.

Priem *m* **-(e)s, -e** quid of tobacco.

priemen *vi* to chew tobacco.

pries *pret of* **preisen**.

Priester *m* **-s, -** priest.

Priester|amt *nt* priesthood.

Priesterin *f* priestess.

priesterlich *adj* priestly *no adv*; *Kleidung auch* clerical.

Priester-: **~rock** *m* cassock; **~schaft** *f* priesthood; **~seminar** *nt* seminary; **~tum** *nt* priesthood; **~weihe** *f* ordination (to the priesthood); **die ~weihe empfangen** to be ordained (to the priesthood *or* as a priest).

prima *adj inv* **(a)** (*inf*) fantastic (*inf*), great *no adv* (*inf*) ◆ **das hast du ~ gemacht** you did that fantastically (well) *or* beautifully *or* just great. **(b)** (*Comm*) first-class, top-quality.

Prima *f* **-, Primen** (*Sch*) *eighth and ninth year of German secondary school*; (*Aus*) *first year of secondary school*.

Prima-: **~ballerina** *f* prima ballerina; **~donna** *f* **-, -donnen** prima donna.

Primaner(in *f*) *m* **-s, -** (*Sch*) ≃ sixth-former; (*Aus*) first-former.

primär *adj* primary.

Primär-: **~energie** *f* primary energy; **~literatur** *f* primary literature *or* sources *pl*.

Primar- (*Sw*): **~lehrer** *m* primary school teacher; **~schule** *f* primary *or* junior school.

Primas *m* **-, -se** *or* **Primaten** (*Eccl*) primate; (*in Zigeunerkapelle*) first violin.

Primat[1] *m or nt* **-(e)s, -e** priority, primacy (*vor +dat* over); (*des Papstes*) primacy; (*Erstgeburtsrecht*) primogeniture.

Primat[2] *m* **-en, -en** (*Zool*) primate.

Primaten *pl of* **Primas, Primat[2]**.

Primel *f* **-, -n** (*Wald~*) (wild) primrose; (*Schlüsselblume*) cowslip; (*farbige Garten~*) primula; (*mit verzweigtem Stiel*) polyanthus ◆ **wie eine ~ eingehen** (*fig*) to fade *or* wither away.

Primen *pl of* **Prima**.

Primi *pl of* **Primus**.

primitiv *adj* primitive; *Maschine auch* crude.

Primitive(r) *mf decl as adj* primitive person; (*Art*) primitive.

Primitivität *f siehe adj* primitiveness; crudeness.

Primitivling *m* (*pej inf*) peasant (*pej inf*), primitive (*pej inf*).

Primus *m* **-, -se** *or* **Primi** top of the class *or* form, top *or* star pupil.

Primzahl *f* prime (number).

Printmedium *nt usu pl* printed medium ◆ **die Werbung in Fernsehen und Printmedien** advertising on television and in printed media.

Prinz *m* **-en, -en** prince ◆ **wie ein ~ leben** (*inf*) to live like a lord *or* a king; **unser kleiner ~** (*inf*) our son and heir (*inf*).

Prinzessin *f* princess ◆ **eine ~ auf der Erbse** (*fig*) a hot-house plant.

Prinzgemahl *m* prince consort.

Prinzip *nt* **-s, -ien** [-iən] *or* (*rare*) **-e** principle ◆ **aus ~** on principle; **das hat er aus ~ getan** he did it on principle *or* as a matter of principle; **im ~** in principle; **das funktioniert nach einem einfachen ~** it works on a simple principle; **nach einem ~ handeln** to act according to a principle; **er ist ein Mann von** *or* **mit ~ien** he is a man of principle.

Prinzipal *m* **-s, -e** (*old*) (*Geschäftsinhaber*) proprietor; (*Lehrherr*) master.

prinzipiell *adj* (*im Prinzip*) in principle; (*aus Prinzip*) on principle ◆ **~ bin ich einverstanden** I agree in principle; **das tue ich ~ nicht** I won't do that on principle.

Prinzipien- [-iən-]: **p~fest** *adj* firm-principled; **er ist ein p~fester Mann** he's a man of very firm principles; **~frage** *f* matter *or* question of principle;

p~los *adj* unprincipled; **~losigkeit** *f* lack of principle(s); **~reiter** *m* (*pej*) stickler for one's principles; **~reiterei** *f* (*pej*) going-on about principles (*pej*); **~streit** *m* dispute about principles.
Prinzregent *m* prince regent.
Prior *m* prior.
Priorin *f* prioress.
Priorität *f* priority **~en** *pl* (*Comm*) preference shares *pl*, preferred stock (*US*) ◆ **~ vor etw** (*dat*) **haben** to have *or* take priority *or* precedence over sth; **~en setzen** to establish one's priorities; **die richtigen ~en setzen** to get one's priorities right.
Prioritätenliste *f* list of priorities.
Prise *f* -, **-n** **(a)** (*kleine Menge*) pinch ◆ **eine ~ Humor** a touch of humour. **(b)** (*Naut*) prize.
Prisma *nt* **-s, Prismen** prism.
prismatisch *adj* prismatic.
Prismen *pl of* **Prisma.**
Prismenglas *nt* prismatic telescope.
Pritsche *f* **-, -n** **(a)** (*Narren~*) fool's wand. **(b)** (*von LKW*) platform. **(c)** (*Liegestatt*) plank bed.
Pritschenwagen *m* platform truck.
privat [pri'va:t] *adj* private; *Telefonnummer auch* home *attr* ◆ **~ ist der Chef sehr freundlich** the boss is very friendly out(side) of work; **~ ist er ganz anders** he's quite different socially; **jdn ~ sprechen** to speak to sb in private *or* privately; **jdn ~ unterbringen** to put sb up privately; **ich sagte es ihm ganz ~** I told him quite confidentially *or* in absolute confidence; **etw an P~ verkaufen** (*Comm*) to sell sth to the public *or* to private individuals; **~ versichert sein** to be privately insured; **~ behandelt werden** to have private treatment; **~ liegen** to be in a private ward.
Privat- *in cpds* private; **~adresse** *f* private *or* home address; **~angelegenheit** *f* private matter; **das ist meine ~angelegenheit** that's my own business, that's a private matter; **~besitz** *m* private property; **viele Gemälde sind in ~besitz** many paintings are privately owned *or* in private ownership; **~detektiv** *m* private detective *or* investigator *or* eye (*inf*); **~dozent** *m* outside lecturer; **~eigentum** *nt* private property; **~fernsehen** *nt* commercial television; **~funk** *m* commercial broadcasting; **~gelehrte(r)** *m* scholar; **~gespräch** *nt* private conversation *or* talk; (*am Telefon*) private call.
Privatier [priva'tie:] *m* **-s, -s** (*dated*) man of independent *or* private means.
Privat-: ~initiative *f* private initiative; **~interesse** *nt* private interest.
privatisieren* [privati'zi:rən] [1] *vt* to privatize.
[2] *vi* to live on a private income *or* on independent means.
Privatisierung *f* privatization.
Privat-: ~klage *f* private action *or* suit; **~kläger** *m* private litigant; **~klinik** *f* private clinic *or* hospital, nursing-home; **~leben** *nt* private life; **~lehrer** *m* private tutor; **~mann** *m, pl* **~leute** private person *or* individual; **~mittel** *pl* private means *pl*; **~patient** *m* private patient; **~person** *f* private individual *or* person; **~quartier** *nt* private quarters *pl*; **~recht** *nt* private *or* civil law; **p~rechtlich** *adj Klage, Verfahren* private *or* civil law *attr*; **p~rechtlich ist die Frage ganz eindeutig** the matter is quite clear in private *or* civil law; **~sache** *f* private matter; **das ist meine ~sache** that's my own business, that's a private matter; **~schule** *f* private school; (*Eliteschule auch*) public school (*Brit*); **~sekretär** *m* private secretary; **~sektor** *m* private sector; **~unternehmen** *nt* private enterprise; **~unterricht** *m* private tuition; **~vergnügen** *nt* (*inf*) private pleasure; **~vermögen** *nt* private fortune; **~versicherung** *f* private insurance; **~weg** *m* private way; **~wirtschaft** *f* private industry; **~wohnung** *f* private flat (*Brit*) *or* apartment (*US*)/house.
Privileg [privi'le:k] *nt* **-(e)s, -ien** [-iən] *or* **-e** privilege.
privilegieren* [privile'gi:rən] *vt* to favour, to privilege ◆ **die privilegierten Schichten** the privileged classes.
pro *prep* per ◆ **~ Jahr** per annum (*form*), a *or* per year; **~ Person** per person; **~ Kopf** per person, per capita (*form*); **~ Stück** each, apiece.
Pro *nt* **(das) ~ und (das) Kontra** the pros and cons *pl*.
Proband *m* **-en, -en** guinea-pig, experimentee.
probat *adj no adv* (*dated*) tried, proved, tested.
Probe *f* **-, -n** **(a)** (*Prüfung*) test ◆ **eine ~ auf etw** (*acc*) **machen** to test sth, to do a test on sth; **die ~ (auf eine Rechnung) machen** to check a calculation; **wenn du die ~ gemacht hättest** if you'd checked it *or* given it a check; **ein Beamter auf ~** a probationary civil servant; **er ist auf ~ angestellt** he's employed for a probationary period; **jdn/etw auf ~ nehmen** to take sb/sth on trial; **jdn/etw auf die ~ stellen** to put sb/sth to the test, to try sb/sth; **meine Geduld wurde auf eine harte ~ gestellt** my patience was sorely tried; **jdn/etw einer ~ unterziehen** to subject sb/sth to a test; **zur ~** for a trial, to try out.
(b) (*Theat*) rehearsal ◆ **~n abhalten** to rehearse, to hold rehearsals.
(c) (*Teststück, Beispiel*) sample ◆ **er gab eine ~ seines Könnens** he showed what he could do.
Probe-: ~abzug *m* proof; **~alarm** *m* practice alarm; **heute ist ~alarm** the alarms will be tested today; **~angebot** *nt* trial offer; **~arbeit** *f* test *or* specimen piece, trial work *no pl*; **~belastung** *f* stress test; **~bohrung** *f* test drill, probe; **~druck** *m* trial print; **~exemplar** *nt* specimen (copy); ⚠**p~fahren** *sep irreg infin, ptp only* [1] *vt* to test-drive; [2] *vi aux sein* to go for a test drive *or* run; **~fahrt** *f* test drive *or* run/trial sail; **eine ~fahrt machen** to go for a test drive *etc*; **~flug** *m* test flight; **p~halber** *adv* for a test; **~jahr** *nt* probationary year; **~lauf** *m* test *or* trial run; (*Sport*) practice run; **~lehrer** *m* (*Aus*) probationary teacher.
proben *vti* to rehearse.
Proben-: ~arbeit *f* rehearsals *pl*; **~entnahme** *f* sampling.
Probe-: ~nummer *f* trial copy; **~seite** *f* specimen *or* sample page; **~sendung** *f* sample pack; **~stück** *nt* sample, specimen; **p~weise** *adv* on a trial basis; **ich habe mir p~weise einen anderen Kaffee gekauft** I've bought another kind of coffee to try (out); **~zeit** *f* probationary *or* trial period.
probieren* [1] *vt* (*versuchen*) to try, to have a go *or* try at; (*kosten*) *Speisen, Getränke* to try, to taste, to sample; (*prüfen*) to try (out), to test ◆ **~ Sie es noch mal!** try (it) again!, have another go *or* try!; **laß es mich mal ~!** let me try!, let me have a try *or* a go!
[2] *vi* **(a)** (*versuchen*) to try, to have a try *or* go ◆ **Kinder lernen durch P~** children learn by trial and error; **P~ geht über Studieren** (*Prov*) the proof of the pudding is in the eating (*Prov*).
(b) (*kosten*) to have a taste, to try ◆ **probier mal** try some, have a taste.
Probierer(in *f*) *m* **-s, -** taster.
Probierglas *nt* **(a)** taster, tasting glass. **(b)** *siehe* **Reagenzglas.**
▼ **Problem** *nt* **-s, -e** problem ◆ **vor einem ~ stehen** to be faced *or* confronted with a problem; **das wird zum ~** it's becoming (something of) a problem.
Problematik *f* (*Schwierigkeit*) problem, difficulty (*gen* with); (*Fragwürdigkeit*) questionability, problematic nature ◆ **die ~ der modernen Soziologie** the problems of modern sociology.
problematisch *adj* problematic; (*fragwürdig*) questionable.
Problem-: ⚠**~bewußtsein** *nt* appreciation of the difficulties *or* problem; **~kind** *nt* problem child; **~kreis** *m* problem area; **p~los** *adj* trouble-free, problem-free; **p~los ablaufen** to go smoothly *or* without any problems; **p~orientiert** *adj* (*auch Comput*) problem-orientated; **~stellung** *f* way of looking at a problem; **dieses Buch ist von der ~stellung her interessant** this book looks at *or* approaches the problem in an interesting way; **~stück** *nt* problem play.
Procedere [pro:'tse:dərə] *nt* **-, -** (*geh*) proceedings *pl*.
Produkt *nt* **-(e)s, -e** (*lit, fig*) product ◆ **landwirtschaftliche ~e** agricultural produce *no pl or* products; **das ~ aus 2 mal 2** the product of 2 × 2; **ein ~ seiner Phantasie** a figment of his imagination.
Produkten-: ~handel *m* produce business *or* trade; **~markt** *m* produce market.
Produkthaftung *f* product liability.
Produktion *f* production.
Produktions- *in cpds* production; **~anlagen** *pl* production plant; **~ausfall** *m* loss of production; **~beschränkung** *f* limitation of production; **~genossenschaft** *f* (*DDR*) collective, cooperative; **landwirtschaftliche ~genossenschaft** collective farm; **~kosten** *pl* production costs *pl*; **~kraft** *f* production capacity; **~leistung** *f* (potential) output, production capacity; **~leiter** *m* production manager; **p~mäßig** [1] *adj* production *attr*; [2] *adv* in terms of production; **~menge** *f* output; **~mittel** *pl* means of production *pl*; **p~reif** *adj* ready to go into production; **~rückgang** *m* drop in production; **~stand** *m* production level; **~stätte** *f* production centre; **~zweig** *m* line of production.
produktiv *adj* productive.
Produktivität *f* productivity.
Produktivkräfte *pl* (*Sociol*) productive forces *pl*, forces of production *pl*.
Produkt-: ~manager(in) *m(f)* product manager; **~palette** *f* product spectrum; **~piraterie** *f* product piracy.
Produzent(in *f*) *m* producer.
produzieren* [1] *vt* **(a)** *auch vi* to produce. **(b)** (*inf: hervorbringen*) *Lärm* to make; *Entschuldigung* to come up with (*inf*); *Romane* to churn out (*inf*) ◆ **wer hat denn das produziert?** who's responsible for that?
[2] *vr* (*pej*) to show off.
Prof. *abbr of* **Professor.**
Pro Familia *f family planning organization.*
profan *adj* (*weltlich*) secular, profane; (*gewöhnlich*) mundane.
Profanbau *m* secular building.
profanieren* *vt* (*form*) to profane.
Profession *f* (*old form*) profession ◆ **eine ~ ausüben** to ply a trade (*old*), to follow a profession (*form*).
Professional [pro'fɛʃənəl] *m* **-s, -s** professional.
Professionalität *f* professionalism.
professionell *adj* professional ◆ **eine P~e** (*inf*) a pro (*inf*), a tart (*inf*).
Professor *m* **(a)** (*Hochschul~*) professor. **(b)** (*Aus, S Ger: Gymnasial~*) master/mistress ◆ **Herr ~!** Sir!; **Frau ~!** Miss!
professoral *adj* (*geh*) professorial.
Professorenschaft *f* professors *pl*.
Professorin *f* (lady) professor.
Professur *f* chair (*für* in, of).
Profi *m* **-s, -s** (*inf*) pro (*inf*).
Profil *nt* **-s, -e** **(a)** (*von Gesicht*) profile; (*Archit*) elevation; (*fig: Ansehen*) image ◆ **im ~** in profile; **~ haben** *or* **besitzen** (*fig*) to have a (distinctive *or* personal) image; **die Partei hat in den letzten Jahren mehr ~ bekommen** over the last few years the party has sharpened its image; **dadurch hat er an ~ gewonnen/verloren** that improved/damaged his image; **psychisches ~** state of mind.
(b) (*von Reifen, Schuhsohle*) tread.
(c) (*Querschnitt*) cross-section; (*Längsschnitt*) vertical section; (*Geog*) (vertical) section; (*Aviat*) wing section; (*fig: Skizze*) profile ◆ **im ~** in section.
Profilager *nt* (*Sport inf*) **ins ~ (über)wechseln** to turn *or* go professional.

profilieren* [1] *vt* (*mit Profil versehen*) *Schuhsohlen, Reifen* to put a tread on; (*fig: scharf umreißen*) to define.
[2] *vr* (*sich ein Image geben*) to create a distinctive personal image for oneself; (*Besonderes leisten*) to distinguish oneself ◆ **er will sich akademisch/politisch** *etc* **~** he wants to make a mark for himself academically/in politics *etc*, he wants to make his mark academically/in politics *etc*.
profiliert *adj Schuhe, Reifen* with a tread, treaded; (*fig: scharf umrissen*) clear-cut *no adv*; (*fig: hervorstechend*) distinctive ◆ **ein ~er Politiker/Wissenschaftler** a politician/scientist who has made his mark.
Profilierung *f* (*das Sich-Profilieren*) making one's mark *no art*.
profillos *adj Politiker, Firma* lacking any distinct (personal) image; *Sohle, Reifen* treadless.
Profil-: ~neurose *f* (*hum*) neurosis about one's image, image neurosis; **~sohle** *f* sole with a tread, treaded sole; **~stahl** *m* sectional steel.
Profit *m* **-(e)s, -e** profit ◆ **~ aus etw schlagen** *or* **ziehen** (*lit*) to make a profit from *or* out of sth; (*fig*) to reap the benefits *or* to profit from sth; **den/keinen ~ von etw haben** to profit/not to profit from sth; **ohne/mit ~ arbeiten** to work unprofitably/profitably.
profitabel *adj* profitable.
Profit-: ⚠p~bringend *adj* profitable; **~denken** *nt* profit orientation; **~gier** *f* greed for profit, profit lust; **p~gierig** *adj* greedy for profit, profit-greedy.
profitieren* *vti* to profit; (*fig auch*) to gain ◆ **viel/etwas ~** (*lit*) to make a large profit/to make something of a profit; (*fig*) to profit greatly/somewhat; **davon hat er wenig profitiert** (*lit*) he didn't make much of a profit from it; (*fig*) he didn't profit much *or* didn't gain a great deal from it; **dabei kann ich nur ~** I only stand to gain from it, I can't lose; **und was profitierst du dabei** *or* **davon?** what do you stand to gain from *or* by it?
Profit-: ⩳jäger, ⩳macher *m* (*inf*) profiteer; **~macherei** *f* (*inf*) profiteering; **⩳maximierung** *f* maximization of profit(s *pl*); **⩳streben** *nt* profit seeking.
pro forma *adv* as a matter of form, for appearance's sake.
Pro-forma-Rechnung *f* pro forma invoice.
profund *adj* (*geh*) profound, deep ◆ **er ist ein ~er Kenner** *+gen* he has a profound *or* deep knowledge of ...
Prognose *f* **-, -n** prediction, prognosis; (*Wetter~*) forecast ◆ **eine ~ stellen/wagen** to give *or* make/venture a prediction *or* prognosis.
prognostisch *adj* prognostic.
prognostizieren* *vt* to predict, to prognosticate (*form*).
Programm *nt* **-s, -e** programme, program (*US, Comput*); (*Tagesordnung*) agenda; (*Theat: Vorstellungsablauf auch*) bill; (*TV: Sender*) channel; (*Sendefolge*) programmes *pl*; (*gedrucktes Radio~, TV-~*) programme guide; (*Verlags~*) list; (*beim Pferderennen*) card; (*Kollektion*) range ◆ **nach ~** as planned; **auf dem ~ stehen** to be on the programme/agenda; **ein ~ für den Urlaub machen** to work out a programme for one's holidays; **für heute habe ich schon ein ~** I've already got something planned for today; **unser ~ für den heutigen Abend** our programmes for this evening.
Programm|anbieter *m* (*TV*) programme maker.
programmatisch *adj* programmatic.
Programm-: ~folge *f* order of programmes *or* (*Theat*) acts; **~füller** *m* (*inf*) (programme) filler; **p~gemäß** *adj* according to plan *or* programme; **~gestaltung** *f* programme planning; **~heft** *nt* programme; **~hinweis** *m* (*Rad, TV*) programme announcement; **wir bringen noch einige ~hinweise für morgen** and now a look at some of tomorrow's programmes.
programmierbar *adj* programmable.
programmieren* *vt* **(a)** (*auch vi*) to programme, to program (*US, Comput*); (*fig auch*) to condition ◆ **auf etw** (*acc*) **programmiert sein** (*fig*) to be geared *or* conditioned to sth; **programmiertes Lernen** programmed learning. **(b)** (*entwerfen*) to draw up a programme for; (*planen*) to schedule, to plan.
Programmierer(in *f*) *m* **-s, -** programmer.
Programmierfehler *m* programming error.
Programmiersprache *f* programming language.
Programmierung *f* programming; (*fig auch*) conditioning.
Programm-: ~kino *nt* arts *or* repertory (*US*) cinema; **~punkt** *m* item on the agenda; (*TV*) programme; (*bei Show*) act.
⚠**Programmusik** *f getrennt:* **Programm-musik** programme music.
Programm-: ~speicher *m* (*von Compact Disc etc*) programmable memory; **~übersicht** *f* run-down of the programmes; **~vorschau** *f* preview (*für* of); (*Film*) trailer; **~zeitschrift** *f* programme guide; **~zettel** *m* programme.
⚠**Progreß** *m* **-sses, -sse** progress.
Progression *f* progression.
progressiv *adj* progressive.
Progymnasium *nt* secondary school (*for pupils up to 16*).
Prohibition *f* Prohibition.
Projekt *nt* **-(e)s, -e** project.
Projektgruppe *f* project team.
projektieren* *vt* (*entwerfen*) to plan, to project, to lay plans for; (*planen*) to project.
Projektil *nt* **-s, -e** (*form*) projectile.
Projektion *f* projection.
Projektions-: ~apparat *m siehe* **Projektor**; **~ebene** *f* plane of projection; **~fläche** *f* projection surface; **~lampe** *f* projection lamp; **~schirm** *m* projection screen.
Projektleiter *m* project leader.
Projektor *m* projector.

projizieren* *vt* to project.
Proklamation *f* proclamation.
proklamieren* *vt* to proclaim.
Pro-Kopf- *in cpds* per capita; **~-Einkommen** *nt* per capita income.
Prokrustesbett *nt* Procrustean bed.
Prokura *f* **-, Prokuren** (*form*) procuration (*form*), general commercial power of attorney ◆ **jdm ~ erteilen** to grant sb general commercial power of attorney.
Prokurist(in *f*) *m* holder of a general power of attorney, ≃ company secretary (*Brit*).
Prolet *m* **-en, -en** (*pej*) prole (*pej*), pleb (*pej*).
Proletariat *nt* proletariat.
Proletarier [-iɐ] *m* **-s, -** proletarian ◆ **~ aller Länder, vereinigt euch!** workers of the world, unite!
proletarisch *adj* proletarian.
proletarisieren* *vt* to proletarianize.
proletenhaft *adj* (*pej*) plebeian (*pej*), plebby (*pej inf*).
Prolo *m* **-s, -s** (*sl*) prole (*esp Brit pej inf*) pleb (*pej inf*).
Prolog *m* **-(e)s, -e** prologue.
Prolongation *f* (*St Ex*) carryover.
Prolongations- (*St Ex*): **~geschäft** *nt* carryover; **~satz** *m* carryover rate.
prolongieren* [prolɔŋ'giːrən] *vt* to prolong, to extend.
Promenade *f* (*old: Spaziergang*) promenade, constitutional (*old, hum*); (*Spazierweg*) promenade.
Promenaden-: ~deck *nt* promenade deck; **~konzert** *nt* promenade concert; **~mischung** *f* (*hum*) mongrel, cross-breed.
promenieren* *vi aux sein* (*geh*) to promenade.
prometheisch [prome'teːɪʃ] *adj* (*liter*) Promethean (*liter*).
Prometheus *m* **-** Prometheus.
Promethium *nt, no pl* (*abbr* **Pm**) promethium.
Promi *m* **-s, -s** (*Pol sl*) star politician.
Promille *nt* **-(s), -** thousandth (part); (*inf: Alkoholspiegel*) alcohol level ◆ **er hat zuviel ~ (im Blut)** he has too much alcohol in his blood, his alcohol level is too high; **0,8 ~** 80 millilitres alcohol level.
Promille-: ~grenze *f* legal (alcohol) limit; **~messer** *m* Breathalyzer ®.
prominent *adj* prominent.
Prominente(r) *mf decl as adj* prominent figure, VIP.
Prominenten- *in cpds* posh; **~herberge** *f* (*inf*) posh hotel (*inf*); **~suite** *f* VIP suite.
Prominenz *f* VIP's *pl*, prominent figures *pl*.
promisk *adj* promiscuous.
Promiskuität [promɪskui'tɛːt] *f* promiscuity.
Promotion[1] *f* (*Univ*) doctorate, PhD ◆ **während seiner ~** while he was doing his doctorate *or* PhD; **nach seiner ~** after he got his PhD; **jds ~ befürworten** to recommend sb for a doctorate.
Promotion[2] [prə'moʊʃən] *f* (*Comm*) promotion.
Promotor *m*, **Promotorin** *f* promoter.
promovieren* [promo'viːrən] [1] *vi* to do a doctorate *or* a doctor's degree *or* a PhD (*über +acc* in); (*Doktorwürde erhalten*) to receive a doctorate *etc*.
[2] *vt* to confer a doctorate *or* the degree of doctor on.
prompt [1] *adj* prompt.
[2] *adv* promptly; (*natürlich*) naturally, of course.
Promptheit *f* promptness, promptitude (*form*).
Pronomen *nt* **-s, -** *or* **Pronomina** pronoun.
pronominal *adj* pronominal.
Pronominal-: ~adjektiv *nt* pronominal adjective; **~adverb** *nt* pronominal adverb.
prononciert [pronõ'siːɐt] *adj* (*geh*) (*deutlich*) distinct, clear; (*nachdrücklich*) definite.
Propädeutik *f* preparatory course.
propädeutisch *adj* preparatory.
Propaganda *f* **-,** *no pl* propaganda; (*dated: Werbung*) publicity ◆ **~ für etw machen** *or* **treiben** to make propaganda for sth; **~ mit etw machen** to make propaganda out of sth; **das ist (doch) alles nur ~** that's just (so much) propaganda.
Propaganda-: ~apparat *m* propaganda machine; **~feldzug** *m* propaganda campaign; (*Werbefeldzug*) publicity campaign; **~rummel** *m* (*inf*) deluge *or* torrent *or* flood of propaganda; **p~wirksam** *adj* effective *or* good propaganda *pred*; **etw p~wirksam ausnützen** to make effective propaganda out of sth.
Propagandist(in *f*) *m* **(a)** propagandist. **(b)** (*Comm*) demonstrator.
propagandistisch *adj* propagandist(ic) ◆ **etw ~ ausnutzen** to use sth as propaganda.
propagieren* *vt* to propagate.
Propan *nt* **-s,** *no pl* propane.
Propangas *nt* propane gas.
Propeller *m* **-s, -** (*Luftschraube*) propeller, prop (*inf*), airscrew; (*Schiffsschraube*) propeller, screw.
Propeller-: ~antrieb *m* propeller-drive; **ein Flugzeug mit ~antrieb** a propeller-driven plane; **~flugzeug** *nt*, **~maschine** *f* propeller-driven plane; **~turbine** *f* turboprop.
proper *adj* (*inf*) trim, neat, (clean and) tidy.
Prophet *m* **-en, -en** prophet ◆ **der ~ gilt nichts in seinem Vaterland** (*Prov*) a prophet is without honour in his own country (*Prov*); *siehe* **Berg**.
Prophetie [profe'tiː] *f* prophecy.

Prophetin *f* prophetess.
prophetisch *adj* prophetic.
prophezeien* *vt* to prophesy; (*vorhersagen auch*) to predict, to foretell ◆ **Kassandra hat den Trojanern ihren Untergang prophezeit** Cassandra prophesied that the Trojans would meet their downfall; **das kann ich dir ~!** I can promise you that!
Prophezeiung *f* prophecy.
Prophylaktikum *nt* **-s, Prophylaktika** (*Med*) prophylactic; (*Präservativ*) contraceptive.
prophylaktisch *adj* prophylactic (*form*), preventive.
Prophylaxe *f* **-, -n** prophylaxis.
Proportion *f* proportion.
proportional [proportsio'na:l] *adj* proportional, proportionate ◆ **die Steuern steigen ~ (zu** *or* **mit) dem Einkommen** taxes increase in proportion to *or* proportionally to income; **umgekehrt ~** (*Math*) in inverse proportion.
Proportional-: ~druck *m* proportional printing; **~schrift** *f* proportional spacing; **~zone** *f* (*Fin*) flat rate tax bracket.
proportioniert [proportsio'ni:ɐt] *adj* proportioned.
Proporz *m* **-es, -e** proportional representation *no art.*
Proppen *m* **-s, -** (*N Ger*) **(a)** *siehe* **Pfropfen. (b)** (*inf: Mensch*) dumpling (*inf*).
proppe(n)voll *adj* (*inf*) jam-packed (*inf*).
Propst *m* **-(e)s, ¨e** provost.
Prorektor *m* (*old Sch*) deputy rector; (*Univ*) deputy vice-chancellor.
Prosa *f* **-,** *no pl* prose; (*fig*) prosaicness.
Prosadichtung *f* prose writing.
Prosaiker [pro'za:ikɐ] *m* **-s, - (a)** (*old*) *siehe* **Prosaist(in). (b)** (*fig: nüchterner Mensch*) prosaic person.
prosaisch [pro'za:ɪʃ] *adj* **(a)** (*nüchtern*) prosaic. **(b)** (*Liter*) prose *attr*, prosaic (*form*) ◆ **ein Thema ~ bearbeiten** to treat a subject in prose.
Prosaist(in *f***)** [proza'ɪst(ɪn)] *m*, **Prosaschriftsteller(in** *f***)** *m* prosewriter.
Proselyt *m* **-en, -en** (*liter*) proselyte ◆ **~en machen** to proselytize.
Proseminar *nt an introductory seminar course for students in their first and second year.*
prosit *interj* your health ◆ **~ Neujahr!** (here's to) the New Year!
Prosit *nt* **-s, -s** toast ◆ **ein ~ der Köchin!** here's to the cook!; **auf jdn ein ~ ausbringen** to toast sb, to drink to sb, to drink sb's health; **sie rief mir ein ~ zu** she called out 'cheers' to me.
Prosodie *f* prosody.
prosodisch *adj* prosodic.
Prospekt [pro'spɛkt] *m* **-(e)s, -e (a)** (*Reklameschrift*) brochure, pamphlet (*gen* about); (*Werbezettel*) leaflet; (*Verzeichnis*) catalogue. **(b)** (*Ansicht*) view, prospect (*old*). **(c)** (*Theat*) back-drop, back-cloth.
prospektieren* [prospɛk'ti:rən] *vt* to prospect (in).
prospektiv [prospɛk'ti:f] *adj* prospective.
Prospektmaterial [pro'spɛkt-] *nt* brochures *pl*, pamphlets *pl*, literature.
prosperieren* [prospe'ri:rən] *vi* (*geh*) to prosper.
Prosperität [prosperi'tɛ:t] *f* (*geh*) prosperity.
prost *interj* cheers, cheerio; (*hum: beim Niesen*) bless you ◆ **na denn ~!** cheers then!, bottoms up! (*hum*); *siehe* **Mahlzeit.**
Prostata *f* **-,** *no pl* prostate gland; (*inf: Prostataleiden*) prostate.
prosten *vi* to say cheers.
prösterchen *interj* (*hum*) cheers, bottoms up (*hum*).
prostituieren* [prostitu'i:rən] **1** *vr* (*lit, fig*) to prostitute oneself. **2** *vt* (*old*) to prostitute.
Prostituierte [prostitu'i:ɐtə] *f* **-n, -n** prostitute.
Prostitution [prostitu'tsio:n] *f* prostitution.
Proszenium *nt* proscenium.
Protactinium *nt, no pl* (*abbr* **Pa**) protactinium.
Protagonist(in *f***)** *m* (*lit, fig*) protagonist.
⚠ **Protegé** [prote'ʒe:] *m* **-s, -s** protégé.
protegieren* [prote'ʒi:rən] *vt Schriftsteller, Projekt* to sponsor; *Land, Regime* to support ◆ **er wird vom Chef protegiert** he's the boss's protégé.
Protein *nt* **-s, -e** protein.
Protektion *f* (*Schutz*) protection; (*Begünstigung*) patronage ◆ **unter jds ~** (*dat*) **stehen** (*Schutz*) to be under sb's protection; (*Begünstigung*) to be under sb's patronage.
Protektionismus [protɛktsio'nɪsmʊs] *m* **(a)** (*Econ*) protectionism. **(b)** (*Günstlingswirtschaft*) nepotism.
protektionistisch *adj* protectionist.
Protektor *m*, **Protektorin** *f* (*old: Beschützer*) protector; (*Schirmherr*) patron.
Protektorat *nt* (*Schirmherrschaft*) patronage; (*Schutzgebiet*) protectorate.
Protest *m* **-(e)s, -e (a)** protest ◆ **(scharfen) ~ gegen jdn/etw erheben** to make a (strong) protest against sb/sth; **etw aus ~ tun** to do sth in protest *or* as a protest; **unter ~** protesting; (*gezwungen*) under protest.
(b) (*Fin*) **~ mangels Annahme/Zahlung** protest for non-acceptance/non-payment; **einen Wechsel zu ~ gehen lassen** to protest a bill.
Protest|aktion *f* protest.
Protestant(in *f***)** *m* Protestant.
protestantisch *adj* Protestant.
Protestantismus *m* Protestantism.
Protest-: ~bewegung *f* protest movement; **~demonstration** *f* (protest) demonstration, demo (*inf*).
protestieren* **1** *vi* to protest (*gegen* against, about).
2 *vt* (*Fin*) to protest.
Protestkundgebung *f* (protest) rally.
Protestler(in *f***)** *m* **-s, -** (*inf*) protester.
Protest-: ~marsch *m* protest march; **~note** *f* (*Pol*) letter of protest; **~sänger** *m* protest singer; **~schreiben** *nt* letter of protest; **~song** *m* protest song; **~stimme** *f* protest vote; **~streik** *m* protest strike; **~sturm** *m* storm of protest; **~versammlung** *f* protest meeting; **~wähler** *m* protest voter; **~welle** *f* wave of protest.
Prothese *f* **-, -n (a)** artificial limb/joint, prosthesis (*Med, form*); (*Gebiß*) set of dentures. **(b)** (*Ling*) prothesis.
Prothesenträger(in *f***)** *m* **(a)** person with an artificial limb ◆ **er ist ~** he has an artificial limb. **(b)** (*Gebiß*) denture-wearer.
Prothetik *f* (*Med*) prosthetics *sing.*
prothetisch *adj* prosthetic.
Protokoll *nt* **-s, -e (a)** (*Niederschrift*) record; (*Bericht*) report; (*von Sitzung*) minutes *pl*; (*bei Polizei*) statement; (*bei Gericht*) transcript ◆ **das ~ aufnehmen** to take sth down; (*bei Sitzung*) to take (down) the minutes; (*bei Polizei*) to take (down) sb's statement; (*bei Gericht*) to keep a record of the proceedings, to make a transcript of the proceedings; **(das) ~ führen** (*bei Sitzung*) to take *or* keep the minutes; (*bei Gericht*) to keep a record of *or* make a transcript of the proceedings; (*beim Unterricht*) to write a report; **etw zu ~ geben** to have sth put on record; (*bei Polizei*) to say sth in one's statement; **etw zu ~ nehmen** to take sth down, to record sth; **wenn man auf Dienstreise ist, muß man über alle Ausgaben ~ führen** on a business trip one must keep a record *or* (check)list of all expenses.
(b) (*diplomatisch*) protocol.
(c) (*Strafzettel*) ticket.
(d) (*Comput*) protocol.
Protokollant(in *f***)** *m* secretary; (*Jur*) clerk (of the court).
protokollarisch *adj* **(a)** (*protokolliert*) on record; (*in Sitzung*) minuted ◆ **folgende Maßnahmen wurden ~ festgelegt** the following measures were agreed on. **(b)** (*zeremoniell*) **~e Vorschriften** rules of protocol; **~ ist das so geregelt, daß ...** protocol requires that ...; **diese Vorschriften sind rein ~** these are merely rules of protocol.
Protokoll-: ~chef *m* head of protocol; **~führer** *m siehe* **Protokollant(in).**
protokollieren* **1** *vi* (*bei Sitzung*) to take the minutes (down); (*bei Polizei*) to take a/the statement down; (*in der Schule*) to write notes.
2 *vt* to take down; *Sitzung* to minute; *Bemerkung auch* to put *or* enter in the minutes; *Stunde* to write up.
Proton *nt* **-s, Protonen** proton.
Proto- *in cpds* proto-; **~plasma** *nt* protoplasm; **~typ** *m* (*Erstanfertigung*) prototype; (*Inbegriff auch*) archetype.
Protz *m* **-es** *or* **-en, -e(n)** (*inf*) swank (*inf*).
protzen *vi* (*inf*) to show off ◆ **mit etw ~** to show sth off.
Protzerei *f* (*inf*) showing off, swanking (*inf*).
protzig *adj* (*inf*) swanky (*inf*), showy (*inf*).
Provenienz [prove'niɛnts] *f* (*geh*) provenance.
Provenzale [provɛn'tsa:lə, provɛn'sa:lə, provã'sa:lə] *m* **-n, -n, Provenzalin** *f* Provençal.
provenzalisch [provɛn'tsa:lɪʃ, provɛn'sa:lɪʃ] *adj* Provençal.
Proviant [pro'viant] *m* **-s,** (*rare*) **-e** provisions *pl*, supplies *pl* (*esp Mil*); (*Reise~*) food for the journey ◆ **sich mit ~ versehen** to lay in provisions/to buy food for the journey.
Proviantlager *nt* supply camp.
Provinz [pro'vɪnts] *f* **-, -en** province; (*im Gegensatz zur Stadt*) provinces *pl* (*auch pej*), country ◆ **das ist finsterste** *or* **hinterste ~** (*pej*) it's so provincial, it's a cultural backwater.
Provinz- *in cpds* provincial; **~bewohner** *m* provincial.
provinziell [provɪn'tsiɛl] *adj* provincial (*auch pej*).
Provinzler(in *f***)** [pro'vɪntslɐ, -ərɪn] *m* **-s, -** (*pej*) provincial.
provinzlerisch [pro'vɪntslərɪʃ] *adj* (*pej*) provincial.
Provision [provi'zio:n] *f* commission; (*bei Bank*) bank charges *pl* ◆ **auf ~** on commission.
Provisionsbasis *f* commission basis ◆ **auf ~ arbeiten** to work on a commission basis.
Provisor [pro'vi:zɔr] *m* (*old*) *manager of a chemist's shop.*
provisorisch [provi'zo:rɪʃ] *adj* provisional, temporary ◆ **~e Regierung** caretaker *or* provisional government; **das ist alles noch sehr ~ in unserem Haus** things are still very makeshift in our house; **Straßen mit ~em Belag** roads with a temporary surface; **wir wollen es ~ so lassen** let's leave it like that for the time being; **ich habe den Stuhl ~ repariert** I've fixed the chair up for the time being.
Provisorium [provi'zo:riʊm] *nt* stop-gap, temporary *or* provisional arrangement.
provokant [provo'kant] *adj* provocative, provoking.
Provokateur(in *f***)** [provoka'tø:ɐ, -'tø:rɪn] *m* troublemaker; (*Pol auch*) agitator, agent provocateur.
Provokation [provoka'tsio:n] *f* provocation.
provokativ, provokatorisch [provoka-] *adj* provocative, provoking.
provozieren* [provo'tsi:rən] *vti* to provoke.
Prozedur *f* **(a)** (*Vorgang*) procedure ◆ **ein Auto zu bauen ist eine lange ~** making a car is a lengthy procedure *or* business.
(b) (*pej*) carry-on (*inf*), palaver (*inf*) ◆ **die ganze ~, bis man endlich zur Universität zugelassen wird** all the rigmarole (*inf*) before you are finally admitted to university; **die ~ beim Zahnarzt** the ordeal at the dentist's.
Prozent *nt* **-(e)s, -e** *or* (*nach Zahlenangaben*) **-** per cent *no pl* ◆ **~e** percentage; **fünf ~** five per cent; **wieviel ~?** what percentage?; **zu zehn ~** at ten per cent;

zu hohen ~en at a high percentage; **etw in ~en ausdrücken** to express sth as a percentage *or* in per cent; **dieser Whisky hat 35 ~ (Alkoholgehalt)** this whisky contains 35 per cent alcohol; **~e (in einem Geschäft) bekommen** to get a discount (in a shop).
Prozentbasis *f* percentage *or* (*von Vertreter auch*) commission basis ◆ **auf ~ arbeiten** to work on a commission basis.
-prozentig *adj suf* per cent ◆ **hoch~** high percentage.
Prozent-: ~punkt *m* point; **~rechnung** *f* percentage calculation; **~satz** *m* percentage; (*Zins*) rate of interest, interest rate.
prozentual *adj* percentage *attr* ◆ **~er Anteil** percentage; **etw ~ ausdrücken/ rechnen** to express/calculate sth as a percentage *or* in percentages; **sich an einem Geschäft ~ beteiligen** to have a percentage (share) in a business; **~ gut abschneiden** to get a good percentage; **die Beteiligung war ~ sehr hoch** that's a very high percentage.
prozentuell *adj* (*esp Aus*) *siehe* **prozentual.**
Prozentzeichen *nt* percent sign.
Prozeß *m* **-sses, -sse (a)** (*Straf~*) trial; (*Rechtsfall*) (court) case ◆ **einen ~ gewinnen/verlieren** to win/lose a case; **gegen jdn einen ~ anstrengen** to take *or* institute legal proceedings against sb, to bring an action against sb; **er führt zur Zeit gegen fünf Firmen einen ~** at the moment he's taking five companies to court *or* is involved in legal action against five companies; **es ist sehr teuer, einen ~ zu führen** going to court *or* taking legal action is very expensive; **es zum ~ kommen lassen** to go to court; **es kann zum ~ kommen** it might come to a court case; **mit jdm im ~ liegen** to be involved in a court case *or* in a law-suit *or* in litigation (*form*) with sb; **jdm den ~ machen** (*inf*) to take sb to court; **mit jdm/etw kurzen ~ machen** (*fig inf*) to make short work of sb/sth (*inf*).
(b) (*Vorgang*) process.
Prozeß-: ~akten *pl* case files *pl*; **p~fähig** *adj* able *or* entitled to take legal action; **~fähigkeit** *f* ability *or* entitlement to take legal action; **p~führend** *adj* **p~führende Partei** litigant; **~führung** *f* handling of a case; **~hansel** *m* (*inf*) someone who is always going to law.
prozessieren* *vi* to go to court ◆ **er prozessiert mit fünf Firmen** he's got cases going on against five firms; **sie haben jahrelang gegen mich prozessiert** they've been bringing an action against me for years, they've had a case going on against me for years.
Prozession *f* procession.
Prozeß-: ~kosten *pl* legal costs *pl*; **er mußte die ~kosten tragen** he had to pay costs; **~lawine** *f* spate of trials.
Prozessor *m* (*Comput*) processor.
Prozeß-: ~ordnung *f* code *or* rules of procedure, legal procedure; **~recht** *nt* procedural law; **~sprache** *f* (*Comput*) processing language; **p~süchtig** *adj* litigious; **p~unfähig** *adj* not entitled to take legal action; **~unfähigkeit** *f* inability to take legal action; **~verschleppung** *f* protraction of a case; **~vollmacht** *f, no pl* power of attorney (*for a lawsuit*); (*Formular*) letter of attorney; **~wärme** *f* heat of reaction.
prüde *adj* prudish.
Prüderie *f* prudishness, prudery.
prüfen [1] *vt* **(a)** (*auch vi*) (*Sch, Univ*) *jdn* to examine; *Kenntnisse auch* to test ◆ **jdn in etw** (*dat*) **~** to examine sb in sth; **wer hat bei dir geprüft?** who examined you?; **morgen wird in Englisch geprüft** the English exams are tomorrow; **schriftlich geprüft werden** to have a written examination; **ein staatlich geprüfter Dolmetscher** a qualified interpreter.
(b) (*überprüfen*) to check (*auf +acc* for); (*untersuchen*) to examine, to check; (*durch Ausprobieren*) to test; (*auf die Probe stellen*) to test; *Alibi* to check (out), to check up on; *Geschäftsbücher* to audit, to check, to examine; *Lebensmittel, Wein* to inspect, to test ◆ **es wird geprüft, ob alle anwesend sind** they check *or* there's a check to see if everyone is present; **den Wein auf sein Aroma ~** to sniff *or* test the bouquet of the wine; **Metall auf den Anteil an Fremdstoffen ~** to check the level of impurities in metal; **jdn auf seine Ehrlichkeit ~** to test *or* try sb's honesty; **wir werden die Beschwerde/Sache ~** we'll look into *or* investigate the complaint/matter; **sie wollte ihn nur ~** she only wanted to test him; **drum prüfe, wer sich ewig bindet** (*prov*) marry in haste, repent at leisure (*Prov*).
(c) (*erwägen*) to consider ◆ **etw nochmals ~** to reconsider *or* review sth.
(d) (*mustern*) to scrutinize ◆ **ein ~der Blick** a searching look.
(e) (*heimsuchen*) to try, to afflict ◆ **ein schwer geprüfter Vater** a sorely tried *or* much afflicted father.
[2] *vr* (*geh*) to search one's heart ◆ **du mußt dich selber ~, ob ...** you must decide for yourself *or* you must enquire of yourself (*liter*) whether ...
Prüfer(in *f*) *m* **-s, -** examiner; (*Wirtschafts~*) inspector.
Prüf-: ~gerät *nt* testing apparatus *or* equipment; **~lampe** *f* control light tester.
Prüfling *m* examinee, (examination) candidate.
Prüf-: ~röhrchen *nt* test tube; **~stand** *m* test bed; (*Space*) test stand; **auf dem ~stand sein** to be being tested; **~standlauf** *m* test run; **~stein** *m* (*fig*) touchstone (*für* of *or* for), measure (*für* of).
Prüfung *f* **(a)** (*Sch, Univ*) exam, examination ◆ **eine ~ machen** to take *or* do an exam.
(b) (*Überprüfung*) check, checking *no indef art*; (*Untersuchung*) examination, checking *no indef art*; (*durch Ausprobieren*) test, testing *no indef art*; (*von Geschäftsbüchern*) audit, examination, checking *no indef art*; (*von Lebensmitteln, Wein*) inspection, testing *no indef art* ◆ **eine gründliche ~ einer Maschine vornehmen** to check *or* examine *or* test a machine thoroughly, to give a machine a thorough check *or* examination *or* test; **nach der ~ wird das Auto ...** after being checked *or* tested the car is ...; **bei nochmaliger ~ der Rechnung** on re-checking the account; **er führt (Wirtschafts)~en bei Firmen durch** he audits firms' books; **nach/bei ~ Ihrer Beschwerde/dieser Sache ...** after/on looking into *or* investigating your complaint/the matter.
(c) (*Erwägung*) consideration ◆ **die ~ seiner Entscheidung** the reconsideration of one's decision.
(d) (*Heimsuchung*) test, trial.
Prüfungs-: ~anforderung *f* examination requirement; **~angst** *f* exam nerves *pl*; **~arbeit** *f* dissertation; **~aufgabe** *f* exam(ination) question; ⚠**~ausschuß** *m* board of examiners, examining board; (*bei Sachen*) board of inspectors; **~frage** *f* examination question; **~gebühr** *f* examination fee; **~kandidat** *m siehe* **Prüfling**; **~kommission** *f siehe* **~ausschuß**; **~ordnung** *f* exam(ination) regulations *pl*; **~termin** *m* (*Sch, Univ*) date of examination *or* test; (*Jur*) meeting of creditors; **~unterlagen** *pl* exam(ination) papers *pl*; **~zeugnis** *nt* exam(ination) certificate.
Prüfverfahren *nt* test procedure.
Prügel *m* **-s, - (a)** (*Stock*) club, cudgel. **(b)** *pl* (*inf: Schläge*) beating, thrashing ◆ **~ bekommen** *or* **beziehen** (*lit, fig*) to get a beating *or* thrashing; *siehe* **Tracht.**
Prügelei *f* (*inf*) fight, punch-up (*Brit inf*).
Prügelknabe *m* (*fig*) whipping boy.
prügeln [1] *vti* to beat ◆ **unser Lehrer prügelt grundsätzlich nicht** our teacher doesn't use corporal punishment on principle.
[2] *vr* to fight ◆ **sich mit jdm ~** to fight sb; **Eheleute, die sich ~** married people who come to blows; **sich um etw** (*acc*) **~** to fight over *or* for sth.
Prügel-: ~strafe *f* corporal punishment; **~szene** *f* fight; (*Theat*) fight scene.
Prunk *m* **-s,** *no pl* (*Pracht*) splendour, magnificence, resplendence; (*von Saal, Rokoko auch*) sumptuousness; (*von Stadt, Gebäude auch*) grandeur; (*von höfischer Zeremonie auch*) pomp and circumstance, pageantry ◆ **Ludwig XIV liebte ~** Louis XIV had a passion for grandeur; **der ~ im Saal** the splendour *or* magnificence *or* resplendence of the hall; **die Schlösser sind voller ~** the castles are sumptuously appointed; **großen ~ entfalten** to put on a show of great splendour.
Prunk- *in cpds* magnificent, resplendent; **~bett** *nt* four-poster bed; magnificent bed.
prunken *vi* to be resplendent ◆ **mit etw ~** to flaunt sth, to make a great show of sth.
Prunk-: ~gemach *nt* state apartment; **p~los** *adj* unostentatious, modest; **~saal** *m* sumptuous *or* palatial room; **~stück** *nt* showpiece; **~sucht** *f* great love of splendour, passion for the grand scale; **p~süchtig** *adj* **p~süchtig sein** to have a craving for splendour; **p~voll** *adj* splendid, magnificent.
prusten *vi* (*inf*) to snort ◆ **vor Lachen ~** to snort with laughter; **sie prustete laut vor Lachen** she gave a loud snort (of laughter).
PS [pe:'|ɛs] *nt* **~** *abbr of* **Pferdestärke** hp.
P.S., PS [pe:'|ɛs] *nt* **-, -** *abbr of* **Postskript(um)** PS.
Psalm *m* **-s, -en** psalm.
Psalmist *m* psalmist.
Psalter *m* **-s, - (a)** (*Eccl*) psalter. **(b)** (*Mus*) psaltery.
pseudo- *in cpds* pseudo.
Pseudokrupp *m* (*Med*) pseudo-croup.
Pseudonym *nt* **-s, -e** pseudonym; (*eines Schriftstellers auch*) nom de plume, pen-name.
psst *interj* pst; (*ruhig*) sh, hush.
Psychagoge *m*, **Psychagogin** *f* educational psychotherapist.
Psyche *f* **-, -n** psyche; (*Myth*) Psyche.
psychedelisch *adj* psychedelic.
Psychiater(in *f*) *m* **-s, -** psychiatrist.
Psychiatrie *f* psychiatry.
psychiatrisch *adj* psychiatric ◆ **~ betrachtet** from a psychiatric point of view, (considered) psychiatrically.
psychisch *adj Belastung, Auswirkungen, Defekt* emotional, psychological; *Phänomen, Erscheinung* psychic; *Vorgänge* psychological ◆ **~e Erkrankung** mental illness; **eine ~ bedingte Krankheit** a psychologically determined illness; **~ gestört** emotionally *or* psychologically disturbed; **jdn ~ beanspruchen** to make emotional *or* psychological demands on sb; **er ist ~ völlig am Ende** his nerves can't take any more; **~ unter großem Druck stehen, unter großem ~en Druck stehen** to be under a great deal of emotional *or* psychological pressure, to have a great deal of emotional *or* psychological pressure on one.
Psycho- *in cpds* psycho-; **~analyse** *f* psychoanalysis; **~analytiker** *m* psychoanalyst; **p~analytisch** *adj* psychoanalytic(al); **jdn p~analytisch behandeln** to psychoanalyze sb; **~diagnostik** *f* psychodiagnostics *sing*; **~drama** ['psy:ço-] *nt* psychodrama; **p~gen** *adj* psychogenic; **~gramm** *nt* **-s, -e** profile (*auch fig*), psychograph; **~kinese** *f* psychokinesis; **~loge** *m*, **~login** *f* psychologist; **~logie** *f* psychology; **p~logisch** *adj* psychological; **p~logische Kampf-** *or* **Kriegsführung** psychological warfare; **p~logisieren*** *vt* to psychologize; **~neurose** *f* psychoneurosis; **~path(in *f*)** *m* **-en, -en** psychopath; **~pathie** *f* psychopathy; **p~pathisch** *adj* psychopathic; **p~pathisch reagieren** to react psychopathically; **~pharmakon** *nt* **-s, -pharmaka** *usu pl* psychiatric drug.
Psychose *f* **-, -n** psychosis.
Psycho-: ~somatik *f* psychosomatics *sing*; **p~somatisch** *adj* psychosomatic; **~terror** ['psy:ço-] *m* psychological terror; **~therapeut** *m* psychotherapist; **p~therapeutisch** *adj* psychotherapeutic; **~therapie** *f* psycho-

⚠: for details of spelling reform, see supplement

therapy.
Psychotiker(in *f*) *m* **-s, -** psychotic.
psychotisch *adj* psychotic.
PTA [pe:te:'|a:] *abbr of* **pharmazeutisch-technische Assistentin, pharmazeutisch-technischer Assistent.**
Ptolemäer [ptole'mɛ:ɐ] *m* **-s, -** Ptolemy.
ptolemäisch [ptole'mɛ:ɪʃ] *adj* Ptolemaic.
Ptolemäus [ptole'mɛ:ʊs] *m* **-** Ptolemy.
pubertär *adj* of puberty, adolescent ◆ **ein Junge im ~en Alter** a boy at the age of puberty *or* in puberty; **~ bedingte Störungen** disorders caused by puberty, adolescent disorders.
Pubertät *f* puberty ◆ **er steckt mitten in der ~** he's going through his adolescence.
Pubertäts-: ~alter *nt* age of puberty; **im ~alter** at the age of puberty; **~erscheinung** *f* symptom of puberty *or* adolescence; **~störungen** *pl* adolescent disturbances *pl*, growing-up problems *pl* (*inf*); **~zeit** *f* puberty (period).
pubertieren* *vi* to reach puberty ◆ **~d** pubescent.
Public-Domain-Programm [pʌblɪkdo'meɪn-] *nt* (*Comput*) public domain program.
Publicity [pʌ'blɪsɪtɪ] *f* **-**, *no pl* publicity.
publicity-: ~scheu *adj* **er ist ~scheu** he shuns publicity; **~trächtig** *adj* which generates (a lot of) publicity.
Public Relations [pʌblɪkrɪ'leɪʃənz] *pl* public relations *pl.*
publik *adj pred* public ◆ **~ werden** to become public knowledge; **die Sache ist längst ~** that's long been common knowledge.
Publikation *f* publication.
Publikum *nt* **-s**, *no pl* public; (*Zuschauer, Zuhörer*) audience; (*Sport*) crowd ◆ **er muß ja immer ein ~ haben** (*fig*) he always has to have an audience; **das ~ in dem Lokal ist sehr gemischt** you get a very mixed group of people using this pub, the customers in this pub are very mixed; **in diesem Lokal verkehrt ein sehr schlechtes ~** this pub attracts a very bad type of customer *or* a very bad clientele; **sein ~ finden** to find a public.
Publikums-: ~erfolg *m* success with the public, popular success; **~geschmack** *m* public *or* popular taste; **~interesse** *nt* interest of the public; **~liebling** *m* darling of the public; **~magnet** *m* crowd-puller; **~renner** *m* **-s, -** (*inf*) hit with the public (*inf*); **~verkehr** *m* **~verkehr im Rathaus ist von 8 bis 12 Uhr** the town hall is open to the public from 8 till 12 o'clock; **„heute kein ~verkehr"** "closed today for public business"; **wir haben heute viel ~verkehr** we've a lot of people coming in today; **p~wirksam** *adj* **p~wirksam sein** to have public appeal; **ein Stück p~wirksam inszenieren** to produce a play in a popular way *or* with a view to public appeal; **sehr p~wirksame Tricks** tricks with great public appeal *or* appeal to the public.
publizieren* *vti* to publish ◆ **er hat in verschiedenen Fachzeitschriften publiziert** he's had things *or* work published *or* he has been published in various journals.
Publizist(in *f*) *m* publicist; (*Journalist*) journalist.
Publizistik *f* journalism.
publizistisch *adj* journalistic ◆ **sich ~ betätigen** to write for newspapers.
Publizität *f* publicity.
publizitätspflichtig *adj* declarable.
Puck *m* **-s, -s** puck.
puckern *vi* (*inf*) to throb ◆ **es puckert im Zahn** my tooth's throbbing.
Pudding *m* **-s, -s** *thick custard-based dessert often flavoured with vanilla, chocolate etc*, ≃ blancmange ◆ **kaltgerührter ~** instant whip.
Puddingpulver *nt* custard powder.
Pudel *m* **-s, - (a)** (*Hund*) poodle ◆ **das ist des ~s Kern** (*fig*) that's what it's really all about; *siehe* **begossen. (b)** (*inf: Fehlwurf beim Kegeln*) miss.
Pudel-: ~mütze *f* bobble cap *or* hat, pom-pom hat (*inf*); **p~nackt** *adj* (*inf*) stark-naked, starkers *pred* (*inf*); ⚠**p~naß** *adj* dripping *or* soaking wet, drenched; **p~wohl** *adj* (*inf*) **sich p~wohl fühlen** to feel completely contented; **nach der Sauna fühle ich mich p~wohl** after the sauna I feel like a million dollars (*inf*) *or* on top of the world (*inf*).
Puder *m or* (*inf*) *nt* **-s, -** powder.
Puderdose *f* powder tin; (*für Gesichtspuder*) (powder) compact.
puderig *adj* powdery.
pudern [1] *vt* to powder ◆ **sich** (*dat*) **das Gesicht ~** to powder one's face.
[2] *vr* (*Puder auftragen*) to powder oneself; (*Puder benutzen*) to use powder ◆ **ich muß mich noch ~** I still have to powder my nose *or* face; **sich stark ~** to use a lot of powder.
Puder-: ~quaste *f* powder puff; **~zucker** *m* icing sugar.
pueril [pue'ri:l] *adj* (*geh*) puerile; (*knabenhaft*) boyish.
Puertoricaner(in *f*) [puɛrtori'ka:nɐ, -ərɪn] *m* **-s, -** Puerto Rican.
puertoricanisch [puɛrtori'ka:nɪʃ] *adj* Puerto Rican.
Puerto Rico [pu'ɛrto'ri:ko] *nt* **- -s** Puerto Rico.
puff *interj* bang.
Puff[1] *m* **-(e)s, ⸚e (a)** (*Stoß*) thump, blow; (*in die Seite*) prod, dig; (*vertraulich*) nudge ◆ **einen ~** *or* **einige ⸚e aushalten können** (*fig*) to be thick-skinned. **(b)** (*Geräusch*) bang.
Puff[2] *m* **-(e)s, -e (a)** (*Wäsche~*) linen basket. **(b)** (*Bausch*) puff. **(c)** (*Sitz~*) pouf(fe).
Puff[3] *m or nt* **-s, -s** (*inf*) brothel, whorehouse (*sl*), cathouse (*esp US inf*).
Puff|ärmel *m* puff(ed) sleeve.
puffen [1] *vt* **(a)** (*schlagen*) to thump, to hit; (*in die Seite*) to prod, to dig; (*vertraulich stoßen*) to nudge. **(b)** *Rauch* to puff. **(c)** *Ärmel* to puff.
[2] *vi* (*inf: puff machen*) to go bang; (*leise*) to go phut (*inf*); (*Rauch, Abgase*) to puff.
Puffer *m* **-s, - (a)** (*Rail, Comput*) buffer. **(b)** (*Cook*) *siehe* **Kartoffelpuffer.**
Puffer-: ~speicher *m* (*Comput*) buffer memory; **~staat** *m* buffer state; **~zone** *f* buffer zone.
Puff-: ~gegend *f* (*inf*) red-light district; **~mais** *m* popcorn; **~mutter** *f* (*inf*) madam(e), bawd; **~reis** *m* puffed rice; **~straße** *f* (*inf*) brothel street.
puh *interj* (*Abscheu*) ugh; (*Erleichterung*) phew.
pulen [1] *vi* (*inf*) to pick ◆ **in der Nase ~** to pick one's nose; **an einem Loch ~** to pick (at) a hole.
[2] *vt* (*N Ger*) *Krabben* to shell; *Erbsen auch* to pod.
Pulk *m* **-s, -s** *or* (*rare*) **-e (a)** (*Mil*) group. **(b)** (*Menge*) (*von Menschen*) throng; (*von Dingen*) pile.
Pull-down-Menü *nt* (*Comput*) pull-down menu.
Pulle *f* **-, -n** (*inf*) bottle ◆ **eine ~ Schnaps** a bottle of schnapps; **volle ~ fahren** (*sl*) to drive flat out (*inf*) *or* full pelt (*inf*).
pullen *vi* (*Naut*) to row.
pulle(r)n *vi* (*inf*) to pee (*inf*).
Pulli *m* **-s, -s** (*inf*), **Pullover** [pʊ'lo:vɐ] *m* **-s, -** jumper (*Brit*), pullover, sweater, jersey.
Pullunder *m* **-s, -** tank top, slipover.
Puls *m* **-es, -e** (*lit, fig*) pulse ◆ **sein ~ geht** *or* **schlägt regelmäßig** his pulse is regular; **jdm den ~ fühlen** to feel *or* take sb's pulse; **sein Ohr am ~ der Zeit haben** to have one's finger on the pulse of the time(s).
Puls|ader *f* artery ◆ **sich** (*dat*) **die ~(n) aufschneiden** to slash one's wrists.
pulsen *vi* (*liter*) to pulse, to pulsate, to throb.
pulsieren* *vi* (*lit, fig*) to pulsate, to throb ◆ **~der Gleichstrom** intermittent direct current.
Puls-: ~schlag *m* pulse-beat; (*fig*) pulse; (*das Pulsieren*) throbbing, pulsing, pulsation; **an der Börse fühlt man den ~schlag der Wirtschaft** at the stock exchange you have your finger on the pulse of the economy; **in Schwabing spürte sie den ~schlag der Großstadt** in Schwabing she felt the throbbing *or* puls(at)ing of the city; **den ~schlag der Zeit spüren** to feel life pulsing around one; **in der Einsamkeit der Berge, fern vom ~schlag der Zeit** in the loneliness of the mountains, far from the throb of civilization; **~wärmer** *m* **-s, -** wristlet; **~zahl** *f* pulse count.
Pult *nt* **-(e)s, -e** desk.
Pulver ['pʊlfɐ, -lvɐ] *nt* **-s, -** powder; (*Schieß~*) gunpowder, powder; (*sl: Geld*) dough (*sl*) ◆ **er hat das ~ nicht erfunden** (*fig*) he'll never set the Thames on fire (*prov*); **sein ~ verschossen haben** (*fig*) to have shot one's bolt.
Pulver-: ~dampf *m* gunsmoke, gunpowder smoke; **~fabrik** *f* gunpowder factory; ⚠**~faß** *nt* barrel of gunpowder, powder barrel *or* keg; (*fig*) powder keg, volcano; **(wie) auf einem ~faß sitzen** (*fig*) to be sitting on (top of) a volcano; **Nordirland gleicht einem ~faß** Northern Ireland is like a powder keg; **p~fein** *adj* finely ground.
pulv(e)rig ['pʊlf(ə)rɪç, -lv(ə)rɪç] *adj* powdery *no adv* ◆ **den Kaffee ~ mahlen** to grind the coffee to a powder.
Pulverisator [pʊlveri'za:tɔr] *m* pulverizer.
pulverisieren* [pʊlveri'zi:rən] *vt* to pulverize, to powder.
Pulver-: ~kaffee *m* (*inf*) instant coffee; **~kammer** *f* (*Hist*), **~magazin** *nt* magazine; **~mühle** *f siehe* **~fabrik.**
pulvern ['pʊlfɐn] [1] *vt* to pulverize, to powder ◆ **zu Silvester werden Millionenbeträge in die Luft gepulvert** on New Year's Eve vast sums of money go up in smoke.
[2] *vi* (*inf*) to shoot.
Pulver-: ~schnee *m* powder snow; **~turm** *m* (*Hist*) magazine.
Puma *m* **-s, -s** puma.
Pummel *m* **-s, -** (*inf*), **Pummelchen** *nt* (*inf*) dumpling (*inf*), pudding (*inf*), roly-poly (*inf*).
pumm(e)lig *adj* (*inf*) chubby, plump.
Pump *m* **-(e)s**, *no pl* (*inf*) credit, tick (*inf*) ◆ **etw auf ~ kaufen** to buy sth on credit *or* on tick; **auf ~ leben** to live on credit *or* tick.
Pumpe *f* **-, -n (a)** pump. **(b)** (*inf: Herz*) ticker (*inf*).
pumpen *vti* **(a)** to pump. **(b)** (*inf: entleihen*) to borrow; (*verleihen*) to lend, to loan ◆ **(sich** *dat*) **Geld bei jdm ~** to borrow money from *or* off (*inf*) sb.
Pumpenschwengel *m* pump handle.
pumpern *vi* (*S Ger, Aus inf*) to thump, to hammer ◆ **sein Herz pumperte vor Aufregung** his heart was thumping (away) *or* hammering away with excitement.
Pumpernickel *m* **-s, -** pumpernickel.
Pumphose *f* baggy breeches *pl*, knickerbockers *pl*; (*Unterhose*) knickerbockers *pl.*
Pumps [pœmps] *m* **-, -** pump.
Pump-: ~speicherkraftwerk, ~speicherwerk *nt* pumped storage works *sing or pl*; **~station** *f* pumping station.
puncto *prep +gen*: **in ~ X** where X *or* in so far as X is concerned.
Punier(in *f*) ['pu:niɐ, -iərɪn] *m* **-s, -** Phoenician.
punisch *adj* Punic.
Punk [paŋk] *m* **-s**, *no pl* punk.
Punker(in *f*) ['paŋkɐ, -ərɪn] *m* **-s, -** punk.
Punkt *m* **-(e)s, -e (a)** (*Tupfen*) spot, dot ◆ **grüne ~e in den Augen** green flecks in one's eyes; **das Schiff war nur noch ein kleiner ~ in der Ferne** the ship was only a small speck *or* dot *or* spot in the distance.
(b) (*Satzzeichen*) full stop, period (*esp US*); (*Typ*) point; (*auf dem i, Mus, Aus-*

lassungszeichen, von ~linie, Comput) dot ◆ **einen ~ setzen** *or* **machen** to put a full stop; **der Satz endet mit drei ~en** the sentence ends with a row of dots *or* with suspension points; **nun mach aber mal einen ~!** *(inf)* come off it! *(inf)*; **einen ~ hinter eine Angelegenheit setzen** to make an end to a matter; **ohne ~ und Komma reden** *(inf)* to talk nineteen to the dozen *(inf)*, to rattle on and on *(inf)*; **und sagte, ~, ~, ~** and said dot, dot, dot.
(c) *(Stelle)* point ◆ **zwischen den ~en A und B** between (the) points A and B; **~ 12 Uhr** at 12 o'clock on the dot; **wir sind auf** *or* **an dem ~ angelangt, wo ...** we have reached the stage *or* point where ...; **ein dunkler ~** *(fig)* a dark chapter; **bis zu einem gewissen ~** up to a certain point; *siehe* **tot**.
(d) *(Bewertungseinheit)* point, mark; *(bei Prüfung)* mark ◆ **nach ~en siegen/führen** to win/lead on points.
(e) *(bei Diskussion, von Vertrag etc)* point ◆ **in diesem ~** on this point; **etw ~ für ~ widerlegen** to disprove sth point by point; **etw in allen ~en widerlegen** to refute sth in every respect; **der strittige ~** the disputed point, the area of dispute; **sein Aufsatz ist in vielen ~en anfechtbar** many points in his essay are disputable; **etw auf den ~ bringen** to get to the heart of sth; **damit brachte er das Problem auf den ~** he put his finger on it *or* on the problem.
Punktball *m* punchball, punchbag.
Pünktchen *nt* little dot *or* spot ◆ **drei ~** three dots; **da fehlt aber auch nicht das ~ auf dem i!** *(fig)* it's got every i dotted and every t crossed.
Punkt-: ~feuer *nt (Mil)* precision fire; **p~gleich** *adj (Sport)* level; **die beiden Mannschaften liegen p~gleich** the two teams are lying level (on points) *or* are level pegging; **der Boxkampf ging p~gleich aus** the fight ended in *or* was a draw; **~gleichheit** *f (Sport)* level score; **bei ~gleichheit** if the scores are level; **wegen ~gleichheit** because the score was level.
punktieren* *vt* **(a)** *(Med)* to aspirate. **(b)** *(mit Punkten versehen)* to dot; *Fläche auch* to stipple ◆ **einen Umriß ~** to dot in an outline; **punktierte Linie** dotted line.
Punktion *f (Med)* aspiration.
Punktlandung *f* precision landing.
pünktlich [1] *adj* **(a)** punctual. **(b)** *(genau)* exact, precise, meticulous.
[2] *adv* on time ◆ **er kam ~ um 3 Uhr** he came punctually at 3 o'clock *or* at 3 o'clock sharp; **der Zug kommt immer sehr ~** the train is always dead on time *or* very punctual; **~ dasein** to be there on time; **es wird ~ erledigt** it will be promptly dealt with; *(rechtzeitig)* it will be dealt with on time.
Pünktlichkeit *f* punctuality ◆ **~ ist die Höflichkeit der Könige** *(Prov)* punctuality is the politeness of princes.
Punkt-: ~linie *f* dotted line; **~matrix** *f (Comput)* dot matrix; **~niederlage** *f* defeat on points, points defeat.
punkto *prep +gen* **~ X** where X *or* as far as X is concerned; **~ meiner Anfrage** concerning *or* reference *(Comm) or* re *(Comm)* my enquiry.
Punkt-: ~richter *m* judge; **~schrift** *f* Braille; **p~schweißen** *vti sep infin, ptp only (Tech)* to spot-weld; **~sieg** *m* win on points, points win; **~sieger** *m* winner on points; **~spiel** *nt* league game, game decided on points.
punktuell *adj* selective, dealing with certain points ◆ **wir haben uns nur ~ mit diesem Thema befaßt** we only dealt with certain *or* selected points of this topic; **einige ~e Ergänzungen anbringen** to expand a few points; **~e Verkehrskontrollen** spot checks on traffic; **die Kontrollen erfolgten nur ~** they only did spot checks.
Punktum *interj* and that's flat, and that's that ◆ **Schluß, aus, ~!** and that's/that was the end of that!
Punkt-: ~wertung *f* points system; **in der ~wertung liegt er vorne** he's leading on points; **~zahl** *f* score.
Punsch *m* **-es, -e** (hot) punch.
Punschglas *nt* punch cup.
Punze *f* **-, -n (a)** *(Tech)* punch. **(b)** *(Aus: Gütezeichen)* hallmark.
punzen *vt* **(a)** *(Tech)* to punch. **(b)** *(Aus) Gold* to hallmark.
Pup *m* **-(e)s, -e** *siehe* **Pups**.
pupen *vi siehe* **pupsen**.
Pupille *f* **-, -n** pupil.
Pupillen-: ~erweiterung *f* dilation of the pupil; **~verengung** *f* contraction of the pupil, miosis *(spec)*.
Püppchen *nt* **(a)** *(kleine Puppe)* little doll *or* dolly *(inf)*. **(b)** *(hübsches Mädchen)* little sweetie; *(Teenager)* dolly bird *(inf)* ◆ **ein süßes kleines ~** a sweet little thing.
Puppe *f* **-, -n (a)** *(Kinderspielzeug)* doll, dolly *(inf)*; *(Marionette)* puppet, marionette; *(Schaufenster~, Mil: Übungs~)* dummy; *(inf: Mädchen)* doll *(inf)*, bird *(esp Brit inf)*; *(als Anrede)* baby *(inf)*, doll *(esp US inf)* ◆ **die ~n tanzen lassen** *(inf)* to paint the town red *(inf)*, to live it up *(inf)*; **bis in die ~n schlafen** *(inf)* to sleep to all hours.
(b) *(Zool)* pupa.
Puppen- *in cpds* doll's; **~doktor** *m* dolls' doctor; **~gesicht** *nt* baby-doll face; **p~haft** *adj* doll-like; **~haus** *nt* doll's house, dollhouse *(US)*; **~spiel** *nt* puppet show; **~spieler** *m* puppeteer; **~stube** *f* doll's house, dollhouse *(US)*; **~theater** *nt* puppet theatre; **~wagen** *m* doll's pram.
puppern *vi (inf) (zittern)* to tremble, to shake, to quake; *(klopfen)* to thump, to thud.
puppig *adj (inf)* **(a)** *(niedlich)* cute. **(b)** *(einfach)* easy.
Pups *m* **-es, -e, Pupser** *m* **-s, -** *(inf: Furz)* rude noise/smell.
pupsen *vi (inf)* to make a rude noise/smell.
Pupser *m siehe* **Pups**.
pur *adj (rein)* pure; *(unverdünnt)* neat, straight; *(bloß, völlig)* sheer, pure ◆ **~er Unsinn** absolute nonsense; **~er Wahnsinn** sheer *or* pure *or* absolute madness; **~er Zufall** sheer *or* mere coincidence; **Whisky ~** straight *or* neat whisky.
Püree *nt* **-s, -s** puree; *(Kartoffel~)* mashed *or* creamed potatoes *pl*.
Purgatorium *nt* purgatory.
pürieren* *vt* to puree.
purifizieren* *vt (liter)* to purify.
Purismus *m* purism.
Purist(in *f***)** *m* purist.
puristisch *adj* puristic.
Puritaner(in *f***)** *m* **-s, -** Puritan.
puritanisch *adj (Hist)* Puritan; *(pej)* puritanical.
Puritanismus *m* Puritanism.
Purpur *m* **-s,** *no pl* crimson ◆ **den ~ tragen** *(fig)* to wear the purple.
Purpur-: p~farben, p~farbig *adj* crimson; **der Morgenhimmel strahlte p~farben** the morning sky shone a deep crimson; **~mantel** *m* crimson *or* purple robe.
purpurn *adj (liter)* crimson.
purpurrot *adj* crimson (red).
Purzelbaum *m* somersault ◆ **einen ~ machen** *or* **schlagen** *or* **schießen** to turn *or* do a somersault.
purzeln *vi aux sein* to tumble ◆ **über etw** *(acc)* **~** to trip *or* fall over sth.
Puschen *m* **-s, -** *(N Ger)* slipper.
puschen, pushen ['pʊʃən] *vt* to push.
pusselig *adj (inf) Mensch* pernickety *(inf)*, finicky *(inf)*, fussy; *Arbeit, Aufgabe* fiddly *(inf)*.
pusseln *vi (inf)* **(a)** to fuss ◆ **sie pusselt den ganzen Tag im Haus** she fusses about the house all day. **(b)** *(herumbasteln)* to fiddle about.
⚠ **Pußta** *f* **-, Pußten** puszta *(plain in Hungary)*.
Puste *f* **-,** *no pl (inf)* puff *(inf)*, breath ◆ **außer ~ sein** to be puffed out *(inf)*, to be out of puff *(inf)*; **(ja) ~(kuchen)!** *(inf)* no chance! *(inf)*; *siehe* **ausgehen**.
Pusteblume *f (inf)* dandelion.
Pustekuchen *interj (inf)* fiddlesticks *(inf)*.
Pustel *f* **-, -n** *(Pickel)* spot, pimple; *(Med)* pustule.
pusten *(inf)* [1] *vi (blasen)* to puff, to blow; *(keuchen)* to puff (and pant).
[2] *vt* **(a)** *(blasen)* to puff, to blow. **(b)** *(inf)* **dem werd' ich was ~!** I'll tell him where he can get off! *(inf)*.
Pusterohr *nt (inf)* pea-shooter.
putativ *adj (geh)* putative.
Pute *f* **-, -n** turkey (hen) ◆ **dumme ~** *(inf)* silly goose *(inf)*; **eingebildete ~** *(inf)* conceited *or* stuck-up little madam *(inf)*.
Putenschnitzel *nt (Cook)* turkey breast in breadcrumbs.
Puter *m* **-s, -** turkey (cock).
puterrot *adj* scarlet, bright red ◆ **~ werden** to go as red as a beetroot *(inf)*, to go scarlet *or* bright red.
Putsch *m* **-(e)s, -e** coup (d'état), revolt, putsch.
putschen *vi* to rebel, to revolt ◆ **in Südamerika wird permanent geputscht** they're always having coups *or* revolts in South America; **sich an die Macht ~** to take power by a military coup.
Putschist(in *f***)** *m* rebel.
Putschversuch *m* attempted coup (d'état).
Pütt *m* **-s, -s** *(dial)* pit, mine.
Putte *f* **-, -n** *(Art)* cherub.
putten *vt* to putt.
put(t) put(t) *interj* chick, chick, chick.
Putz *m* **-es,** *no pl* **(a)** *(dated: Kleidung)* finery; *(Besatz)* frills and furbelows *pl* ◆ **in vollem ~ erscheinen** to arrive all dressed up in one's Sunday best.
(b) *(Build)* plaster; *(Rauh~)* roughcast ◆ **eine Mauer mit ~ verkleiden** *or* **bewerfen** to plaster *or* roughcast a wall; **unter ~** under the plaster.
(c) auf den ~ hauen *(inf) (angeben)* to show off; *(ausgelassen feiern)* to have a rave-up *(inf)*; *(meckern)* to kick up a fuss *(inf)*.
Putzdienst *m* cleaning duty ◆ **~ haben** to be on cleaning duty.
putzen [1] *vt* **(a)** to clean; *(scheuern auch)* to scrub; *(polieren auch)* to polish; *(wischen auch)* to wipe; *Gemüse* to clean; *Pferd* to brush down, to groom; *Docht* to trim ◆ **die Schuhe ~** to clean *or* polish one's shoes; **Fenster ~** to clean the windows; **sich** *(dat)* **die Nase ~** to wipe one's nose; *(sich schneuzen)* to blow one's nose; **sich** *(dat)* **die Zähne ~** to clean *or* brush one's teeth; **einem Baby den Hintern/die Nase ~** to wipe a baby's bottom/nose.
(b) *(dated: schmücken)* to decorate.
(c) *Mauer* to roughcast, to plaster.
[2] *vr* **(a)** *(sich säubern)* to wash *or* clean oneself.
(b) *(dated: sich schmücken)* to dress *or* do oneself up.
Putzerei *f* **(a)** *no pl (inf)* cleaning ◆ **hör doch endlich mal auf mit der ~!** will you stop all this damn cleaning! *(inf)*. **(b)** *(Aus: Reinigung)* dry cleaner's.
Putzfrau *f* cleaner, cleaning lady, char(woman) *(Brit)*.
putzig *adj (inf) (komisch)* funny, comical, amusing; *(niedlich)* cute; *(merkwürdig)* funny, strange, odd.
Putz-: ~kolonne *f* team of cleaners; **~lappen** *m* cloth; *(Staubtuch)* duster; **~leder** *nt* chamois *or* chammy (leather), wash-leather; **~macherin** *f (dated)* milliner; **~mann** *m* cleaning man; **~mittel** *nt (zum Scheuern)* cleanser, cleansing agent; *(zum Polieren)* polish; **~mittel** *pl* cleaning things *pl*; **p~munter** *adj (inf)* full of beans *(inf)*; **~schere** *f* wick trimmer; **~stelle** *f* cleaning job; **~sucht** *f (dated)* obsession with dressing up; **p~süchtig** *adj (dated)* excessively fond of dressing up; **~tag** *m* cleaning day; **~teufel** *m (inf: Frau)* maniac for housework; **sie ist ein richtiger ~teufel** she's excessively house-proud; **vom ~teufel besessen sein, den ~teufel haben** to have a mania for keeping things clean, to have the cleaning bug *(inf)*; **~tuch** *nt*

(*Staubtuch*) duster; (*Wischlappen*) cloth; **~wolle** *f* wire *or* steel wool; **~wut** *f* obsession with cleaning; **~zeug** *nt* cleaning things *pl.*
puzzeln [pʌzəln] *vi* to do a jigsaw (puzzle).
Puzzle ['pazl, 'pasl] *nt* **-s, -s** jigsaw (puzzle).
Puzzle- ['pazl-, 'pasl-]: **~spiel** *nt* jigsaw (puzzle); **~teil** *nt* **die ~teile wollen nicht passen** the pieces of the puzzle won't fit together.
PVC [pe:fau'tse:] *nt* **-(s)** PVC.
PX-Laden [pe:'ɪks-] *m* (*US Mil*) PX store.
Pygmäe [pʏ'gmɛ:ə] *m* **-n, -n** Pygmy.
pygmäenhaft *adj* pygmy-like, pygmy *attr.*
Pyjama [py'dʒa:ma, py'ʒa:ma, pi'dʒa:ma, pi'ʒa:ma] *m* **-s, -s** pair of pyjamas (*Brit*) *or* pajamas (*US*) *sing*, pyjamas *pl* (*Brit*), pajamas *pl* (*US*) ◆ **wo ist mein ~?** where are my pyjamas?; **im ~** in his pyjamas.
Pyjamahose *f* pyjama (*Brit*) *or* pajama (*US*) trousers *pl.*
Pykniker(in *f*) *m* **-s, -** stocky person.
pyknisch *adj* stockily built.
Pylon *m* **-en, -en, Pylone** *f* **-, -n** (*Archit, von Brücken*) pylon; (*Absperrmarkierung*) traffic cone.
Pyramide *f* **-, -n** pyramid.
pyramidenförmig *adj* pyramid-shaped *no adv*, pyramidal (*form*) ◆ **~ konstruiert** built in the shape of a pyramid.
Pyrenäen [pyre'nɛ:ən] *pl* **die ~** the Pyrenees *pl.*
Pyrenäenhalb|insel *f* Iberian Peninsula.
Pyro-: **~lyse** *f* **-, -n** pyrolysis; **~mane** *m* **-n, -n**, **~manin** *f* pyromaniac; **~manie** *f* pyromania; **~technik** *f* pyrotechnics *sing*; **~techniker** *m* pyrotechnist; **p~technisch** *adj* pyrotechnic.
Pyrrhussieg ['pʏrʊs-] *m* Pyrrhic victory.
pythagoreisch [pytago're:ɪʃ] *adj* Pythagorean ◆ **~er Lehrsatz** Pythagoras's theorem, law of Pythagoras.
Python(schlange *f*) ['py:tɔn-] *m* **-s, -s** python.

Q, q [kuː] *nt* **-, -** Q, q.
qkm *abbr of* **Quadratkilometer.**
qm *abbr of* **Quadratmeter.**
Qu-, qu- [kv-].
qua *adv (geh)* qua.
quabbelig *adj Frosch, Qualle* slimy; *Pudding* wobbly.
quabbeln *vi* to wobble.
Quackelei *f (inf)* nattering *(inf)*, chattering, blethering *(inf)*.
Quacksalber *m* **-s, -** *(pej)* quack (doctor).
Quacksalberei *f* quackery, quack medicine.
quacksalbern *vi insep* to quack *(rare)* ◆ **sowas nenne ich ~** I'd call that quack medicine *or* quackery.
Quaddel *f* **-, -n** hives *pl*, rash; *(durch Insekten)* bite; *(von Sonne)* heat spot.
Quader *m* **-s, -** *or f* **-, -n** *(Math)* cuboid, rectangular solid; *(Archit: auch* **~stein***)* ashlar, square stone block.
Quadrant *m* quadrant.
Quadrat[1] *nt (Fläche, Potenz)* square ◆ **eine Zahl ins ~ erheben** to square a number; **vier zum ~** four squared; **drei Meter im ~** three metres square.
Quadrat[2] *nt* **-(e)s, -e(n)** *(Typ)* quad, quadrat.
Quadrat- *in cpds* square; **~arsch** *m (inf)* great big bum *(Brit inf) or* backside *(inf)*.
quadratisch *adj Form* square; *(Math) Gleichung* quadratic.
Quadrat-: ~latschen *pl (inf) (Schuhe)* clodhoppers *(inf)*, beetle-crushers *(inf)*; *(Füße)* plates of meat *(Brit sl)*; **~meter** *m or nt* square metre; **~schädel** *m (inf: Kopf)* big head, great bonce *(Brit inf)*.
Quadratur *f* quadrature ◆ **die ~ des Kreises** *or* **Zirkels** the squaring of the circle; **das käme der ~ des Kreises** *or* **Zirkels gleich** that's like trying to square the circle.
Quadrat-: ~wurzel *f* square root; **~zahl** *f* square number.
quadrieren* *vt Zahl* to square.
Quadriga *f* **-, Quadrigen** four-horsed chariot.
Quadrille [kvaˈdrɪljə, ka-] *f* **-, -n** quadrille.
⚠ **Quadrophonie** *f* quadrophonic sound, quadrophony ◆ **in ~** in quadrophonic, in quad *(inf)*.
⚠ **quadrophonisch** *adj* quadrophonic.
Quai [kɛː, keː] *m or nt* **-s, -s** *siehe* **Kai.**
quak *interj (von Frosch)* croak; *(von Ente)* quack.
quaken *vi (Frosch)* to croak; *(Ente)* to quack; *(inf: Mensch)* to squawk *(inf)*, to screech *(inf)*.
quäken *vti (inf)* to screech, to squawk.
Quäker(in *f***)** *m* **-s, -** Quaker.
Qual *f* **-, -en** *(Schmerz) (körperlich)* pain, agony; *(seelisch)* agony, anguish ◆ **tapfer ertrug er alle ~en** he bore all his suffering *or* pain bravely; **jds ~(en) lindern** *or* **mildern** *(liter)* to lessen sb's suffering; **unter großen ~en sterben** to die in agony *or* great pain; **sein Leben war eine einzige ~** his life was a living death; **es ist eine ~, das mit ansehen zu müssen** it is agonizing to watch; **die letzten Monate waren für mich eine ~** the last few months have been sheer agony for me; **jeder Schritt/das Bücken wurde ihm zur ~** every step/bending down was agony for him; **er machte ihr den Aufenthalt/das Leben/die Tage zur ~** he made her stay/her life/her days a misery; **es bereitete ihm ~en, sie so leiden zu sehen** it tormented him to see her suffering so; **die ~en des Gewissens** *(geh)***/des Zweifels** agonies of conscience/of doubt *or* indecision; **die ~en, die sie um ihn** *or* **seinetwegen ausgestanden hat** the suffering she has gone through because of him.
quälen [1] *vt* to torment; *Tiere auch* to tease; *(inf) Motor* to punish; *(mit Bitten etc)* to pester, to plague ◆ **jdn zu Tode ~** to torture sb to death; **~de Ungewißheit/Zweifel** agonizing uncertainty/doubts, agonies of uncertainty/doubt; **~der Schmerz** agonizing *or* excruciating pain; *siehe* **gequält.**
[2] *vr* **(a)** *(seelisch)* to torture *or* torment oneself; *(leiden)* to suffer, to be in agony.
(b) *(sich abmühen)* to struggle ◆ **sie quälte sich in die enge Hose** she struggled into *or* squeezed herself into her tight slacks; **er mußte sich ~, damit er das schaffte** it took him a lot of effort *or* it was a struggle for him to do it; **sich durch ein Buch ~** to struggle *or* plough *or* wade through a book; **ich quäle mich jeden Morgen aus dem Bett** it's a struggle for me to get out of bed every morning; **er quälte sich aus dem Sessel** he heaved himself out of the chair; **das Auto quälte sich über den Berg** the car laboured *or* struggled over the hill.
Quälerei *f* **(a)** *(Grausamkeit)* atrocity, torture; *(seelische, nervliche Belastung)* agony, torment ◆ **diese Tierversuche sind in meinen Augen ~** in my view these experiments on animals are cruel; **das ist doch eine ~ für das Tier** that is cruel to the animal; **die letzten Monate waren eine einzige ~** the last few months were sheer agony *or* were one long agony.
(b) *(mühsame Arbeit)* struggle ◆ **das war vielleicht eine ~!** that was really a struggle *or* hard going.
quälerisch *adj attr* tormenting, agonizing.
Quälgeist *m (inf)* pest *(inf)*.
Qualifikation *f* qualification ◆ **für diese Arbeit fehlt ihm die nötige ~** he lacks the necessary qualifications for this work; **er hat die ~ zu diesem Amt** he has the qualifications *or* is qualified for this office; **mit diesem Sieg gelang der Mannschaft die ~** the team qualified with this win; **zur ~ fehlten ihr nur wenige Zentimeter/Sekunden** she only needed a few more centimetres/seconds to qualify.
Qualifikations-: ~runde *f* qualifying round; **~spiel** *nt* qualifying match *or* game.
qualifizieren* [1] *vt* **(a)** *(befähigen)* to qualify *(für, zu* for).
(b) *(geh: differenzieren)* to qualify.
(c) *(geh: einstufen)* to designate, to label, to qualify ◆ **man hat den Artikel als minderwertig qualifiziert** the article has been designated *or* labelled poor quality.
[2] *vr* **(a)** *(allgemein, Sport)* to qualify ◆ **er hat sich zum Facharbeiter qualifiziert** he qualified as a specialist.
(b) *(sich erweisen)* to show *or* reveal oneself *(als* to be).
qualifiziert *adj* **(a)** *Arbeiter, Nachwuchs* qualified; *Arbeit* expert, professional.
(b) *(Pol) Mehrheit* requisite.
Qualität *f* quality ◆ **dieses Leder ist in der ~ besser als das andere** this leather is better quality than that; **von der ~ her** as far as quality is concerned, for quality; **die Ware ist von ausgezeichneter ~** the product is (of) top quality.
qualitativ *adj* qualitative.
Qualitäts- *in cpds* quality; **~arbeit** *f* quality work; **unsere Firma hat sich durch (ihre) ~arbeit einen Namen gemacht** our firm made its name by the quality of its work *or* has got itself a reputation for quality; **~erzeugnis** *nt* quality product; **~kontrolle** *f* quality check *or* control; **~ware** *f* quality goods *pl*; **~wein** *m wine of certified origin and quality.*
Qualle *f* **-, -n** jellyfish.
Qualm *m* **-(e)s,** *no pl* (thick *or* dense) smoke; *(Tabaks~)* fug.
qualmen [1] *vi* **(a)** to give off smoke, to smoke ◆ **es qualmt aus dem Schornstein/hinten aus dem Auto** clouds of smoke are coming *or* billowing from the chimney/from the back of the car.
(b) *(inf: Mensch)* to smoke ◆ **sie qualmt einem die ganze Bude voll** she fills the whole place with smoke.
[2] *vt (inf) Zigarette, Pfeife* to puff away at *(inf)*.
Qualmerei *f (inf)* smoking; *(von Ofen)* smoke.
qualmig *adj* smoke-filled, smoky.
qualvoll *adj* painful; *Schmerzen* agonizing, excruciating; *Vorstellung, Gedanke* agonizing; *Anblick* harrowing.
Quant *nt* **-s, -en** quantum.
quanteln *vt* to quantize.
Quanten *pl* **(a)** *pl of* **Quant, Quantum. (b)** *(sl: Füße)* feet, plates of meat *(Brit sl)*.
Quanten-: ~mechanik *f* quantum mechanics *sing*; **~physik** *f* quantum physics *sing*; **~sprung** *m* quantum leap; **~theorie** *f* quantum theory.
Quantität *f* quantity.
quantitativ *adj* quantitative.
Quantum *nt* **-s, Quanten** *(Menge, Anzahl)* quantum, quantity; *(Anteil)* quota, quantum *(an +dat* of).
Quappe *f* **-, -n (a)** *(Kaul~)* tadpole. **(b)** *(Aal~)* burbot.
Quarantäne *f* **-, -n** quarantine ◆ **in ~ liegen** *or* **sein** to be in quarantine; **unter ~ stellen** *Personen* to put in quarantine; *Gebiet, Stadt auch* to put under quarantine, to quarantine off; **über das Gebiet wurde sofort ~ verhängt** the area was immediately placed in *or* under quarantine *or* was quarantined

off.

Quarantänestation *f* quarantine *or* isolation ward.

Quark¹ *m* **-s,** *no pl* **(a)** quark.
(b) (*inf: Unsinn*) rubbish; (*unbedeutende Sache*) (little) trifle ◆ **so ein ~!** stuff and nonsense!; **~ reden** to talk rubbish; **das geht ihn einen ~ an!** it's none of his business!

Quark² *nt* **-s, -s** (*Phys*) quark.

Quark-: ~kuchen *m siehe* **Käsekuchen; ~speise** *f pudding made with curd cheese, sugar, milk, fruit etc;* **~tasche** *f*, **~teilchen** *nt curd cheese turnover.*

Quart¹ *f* **-, -en (a)** (*Mus: auch* **~e**) fourth ◆ **ein Sprung über eine ~ nach oben/unten** a jump up/down a fourth. **(b)** (*Fechten*) quarte.

Quart² *nt* **-s, -e (a)** (*old: Maß*) ≃ quart. **(b)** (*Typ*) *no pl siehe* **Quartformat.**

Quarta *f* **-, Quarten** (*Sch*) *third year of German secondary school.*

Quartal *nt* **-s, -e** quarter (year) ◆ **Kündigung zum ~** quarterly notice date; **es muß jedes ~ bezahlt werden** it has to be paid quarterly *or* every quarter.

Quartal(s)-: ⚠~abschluß *m* end of the quarter; **~säufer** *m* periodic heavy drinker; **sein Vater ist ein ~säufer** every so often his father goes on a binge (*inf*); **q~weise** *adj* quarterly.

Quartaner(in *f*) *m* **-s, -** (*Sch*) *pupil in third year of German secondary school.*

Quartär *nt* **-s,** *no pl* quaternary.

Quartband *m* quarto volume.

Quarte *f* **-, -n** *siehe* **Quart¹ (a).**

Quarten *pl of* **Quart¹, Quarta, Quarte.**

Quartett *nt* **-(e)s, -e (a)** (*Mus*) quartet. **(b)** (*Cards*) (*Spiel*) ≃ happy families; (*Karten*) set of four cards.

Quartformat *nt* quarto (format).

Quartier *nt* **-s, -e (a)** (*Unterkunft*) accommodation ◆ **wir sollten uns ein ~ suchen** we should look for accommodation *or* a place to stay; **die Jugendlichen sind in verschiedenen ~en untergebracht/auf mehrere ~e verteilt worden** the youngsters have been accommodated *or* given accommodation *or* put up in various different places; **wir hatten unser ~ in einem alten Bauernhof** we stayed in an old farmhouse.
(b) (*Mil*) quarters *pl*, billet ◆ **bei jdm in ~ liegen** to be quartered *or* billeted with *or* on sb; **~ machen** to arrange quarters *or* billets.
(c) (*Stadtviertel*) district, quarter.

Quartier-: ~macher *m* (*Mil*) billeting officer; **~meister** *m* (*old Mil*) quartermaster.

Quarz *m* **-es, -e** quartz.

Quarz-: ~glas *nt* quartz glass; **q~haltig** *adj* quartziferous (*form*), which contains quartz; **~lampe** *f* quartz lamp; **~uhr** *f* quartz clock/watch.

Quasar *m* **-s, -e** quasar.

quasi [1] *adv* virtually.
[2] *pref* quasi ◆ **~-wissenschaftlich** quasi-scientific.

Quasselei *f* (*inf*) gabbling (*inf*), gabbing (*inf*), blethering (*inf*).

quasseln *vti* to gabble (*inf*), to blether (*inf*) ◆ **was quasselst du denn da für ein dummes Zeug?** what are you blethering about now? (*inf*).

Quassel: ~bude *f* (*pej inf: Parlament etc*) talking shop (*inf*); **~strippe** *f* (*inf*) chatterbox (*inf*); (*beleidigend*) windbag (*inf*), blabbermouth (*inf*).

Quast *m* **-(e)s, -e** (*dial*) wide paint brush.

Quaste *f* **-, -n** (*Troddel*) tassle; (*von Pinsel*) brush, bristles *pl*; (*Schwanz~*) tuft; *siehe* **Puderquaste.**

Quästur *f* (*Univ*) bursary.

Quatember *m* **-s, -** (*Eccl*) Ember day.

quatsch *interj* squelch.

Quatsch *m* **-es,** *no pl* **(a)** (*inf: Unsinn*) rubbish ◆ **das ist der größte ~, den ich je gehört habe** that is the biggest load of rubbish I have ever heard; **ach ~!** rubbish!; **so ein ~!** what (a load of) rubbish; **~ mit Soße!** stuff and nonsense!
(b) (*inf: Dummheiten*) nonsense ◆ **hört doch endlich mit dem ~ auf!** stop being so stupid *or* silly!; **was soll denn der ~!** what's all this nonsense in aid of then!; **laß den ~** cut it out! (*inf*); **~ machen** to mess about *or* around (*inf*); **mach damit keinen ~** don't mess about *or* around with it (*inf*), don't do anything stupid with it; **mach keinen ~, sonst knallt's** don't try anything silly *or* funny or I'll shoot; **mach keinen ~!, du kannst doch jetzt nicht krank werden** don't be silly, you can't get ill now!

quatschen¹ (*inf*) [1] *vti* (*dummes Zeug reden*) to gab (away) (*inf*), to blather (*inf*), to gabble (*inf*) ◆ **sie quatscht mal wieder einen Blödsinn** she's talking a load of nonsense *or* rubbish again.
[2] *vi* **(a)** (*plaudern*) to blather (*inf*), to chatter, to natter (*Brit inf*) ◆ **er hat stundenlang gequatscht** he blathered *or* gabbled on for hours; **ich hab' mit ihm am Telefon gequatscht** I had a good natter with him on the phone.
(b) (*etw ausplaudern*) to squeal (*inf*), to talk.

quatschen² *vi* (*Schlamm*) to squelch.

Quatscherei *f* (*inf*) blathering (*inf*), yacking (*inf*); (*in der Schule*) chattering.

Quatsch-: ~kopf *m* (*pej inf*) (*Schwätzer*) windbag (*inf*); (*Dummkopf*) fool, twit (*Brit inf*); **⚠q~naß** *adj* (*inf*) soaking *or* dripping wet.

Quecke *f* **-, -n** couch grass.

Quecksilber *nt* **(a)** (*abbr* **Hg**) mercury, quicksilver ◆ **~ im Leib haben** (*fig*) to have ants in one's pants (*inf*). **(b)** (*dated: Mensch*) fidget.

Quecksilber- *in cpds* mercury; **~dampflampe** *f* mercury-vapour lamp; **q~haltig** *adj* mercurial.

quecksilb(e)rig *adj* (*fig*) fidgety, restless.

Quell *m* **-(e)s, -e** (*poet*) spring, source.

Quelle *f* **-, -n (a)** spring; (*von Fluß auch*) source; (*Erdöl~, Gas~*) well ◆ **heiße ~n** hot springs; **eine ~ erschließen** to develop *or* exploit a source.
(b) (*fig*) (*Ursprung*) source; (*für Waren*) source (of supply), supplier ◆ **die ~ allen Übels** the root of all evil; **eine ~ der Freude** a source of pleasure; **~n der Weisheit** fountain of knowledge; **aus zuverlässiger/sicherer ~** from a reliable/trustworthy source; **an der ~ sitzen** (*fig*) to be well-placed; to be able to get inside information; **kannst du mir einige Bücher besorgen, du sitzt doch an der ~?** can you get me some books, after all you can get them from source.

quellen [1] *vi pret* **quoll,** *ptp* **gequollen** *aux sein* **(a)** (*herausfließen*) to pour, to stream, to well ◆ **der Bauch quillt ihm aus der Hose** his stomach hangs out *or* bulges out over his trousers; **die Augen quollen ihm aus dem Kopf** his eyes were popping out of his head.
(b) (*Holz, Reis, Erbsen*) to swell ◆ **lassen Sie die Bohnen über Nacht ~** leave the beans to soak overnight.
[2] *vt pret* **quellte,** *ptp* **gequellt** (*rare*) *Erbsen* to soak.

Quellen-: ~angabe *f* reference; **achten Sie bei der ~angabe darauf, daß ...** make sure when doing *or* giving the references that ...; **~forschung** *f* source research; **~kritik** *f* verification of sources; **~sammlung** *f* (collection of) source material; (*~werk*) source book; **~steuer** *f* (*Econ*) tax at source; **~studium** *nt* study of sources; **ich bin immer noch mit dem ~studium beschäftigt** I am still studying the sources.

Quell-: ⚠~fluß *m* source (river); **~gebiet** *nt* headwaters *pl*; **~programm** *nt* (*Comput*) source program; **~sprache** *f* source language; **~wasser** *nt* spring water.

Quengelei *f* (*inf*) whining.

queng(e)lig *adj* whining ◆ **die Kinder wurden ~** the children started to whine; **er ist sonst nicht so ~** he doesn't usually whine so much.

quengeln *vi* (*inf*) to whine.

Quengler *m* **-s, -** (*inf*) whiner.

⚠**Quentchen** *nt* (*old*) tiny bit, spot ◆ **ein ~ Salz** a speck *or* dash of salt; **ein ~ Glück** a modicum of luck; **ein ~ Mut** a scrap of courage; **kein ~** not a jot, not an iota.

quer *adv* (*schräg*) crossways, crosswise, diagonally; (*rechtwinklig*) at right angles ◆ **sollen wir den Teppich lieber ~ legen?** why don't we lay the carpet crosswise *or* crossways *or* diagonally?; **er legte sich ~ aufs Bett** he lay down across the bed; **die Spur verläuft ~ zum Hang** the path runs across the slope; **die Straße/Linie verläuft ~** the road/the line runs at right angles; **der Wagen stand ~ zur Fahrbahn** the car was at right angles to the road; **der Lastzug lag ~ über der Straße** the truck was lying (diagonally/at right angles) across the road; **wenn Sie sich ~ stellen, habe ich mit meinem Wagen auch noch Platz** if you park diagonally/at right angles I'll have room to park my car too; **~ durch etw gehen/laufen** *etc* to cross sth, to go through sth; **~ über etw** (*acc*) **gehen/laufen** to cross sth, to go across sth; **der Hund ist ~ über die Wäsche gelaufen** the dog ran straight *or* right over *or* across the washing; **die Kamera ~ nehmen** to hold the camera lengthways *or* crossways; **den Stoff ~ nehmen** to use the cross-grain of the material; *siehe* **kreuz.**

Quer-: q~ab *adv* (*Naut*) abeam; **~balken** *m* crossbeam; (*von Türrahmen*) transom, lintel; (*Sport*) crossbar; (*Her*) bar; (*Mus*) *line joining quavers etc;* **q~beet** *adv* (*inf*) (*wahllos*) at random; (*durcheinander*) all over the place (*inf*); (*~feldein*) across country; **~denker** *m* open-minded thinker; **q~durch** *adv* straight through.

Quere *f* **-,** *no pl* **der ~ nach** widthways, breadthways; **jdm in die ~ kommen** to cross sb's path; **es muß ihm etwas in die ~ gekommen sein, sonst hätte er sich nicht verspätet** something must have cropped up otherwise he would not be late; **der Lastwagen kam mir in die ~** the lorry got in my way.

Querele *f* **-, -n** *usu pl* (*geh*) dispute, quarrel.

queren *vti* to cross.

querfeldein *adv* across country.

Querfeldein-: ~lauf *m* cross-country (run); (*Wettbewerb*) cross-country (race); **~rennen** *nt* cross-country; (*Auto~*) autocross; (*Motorrad~*) motocross; (*Fahrrad~*) cyclecross; (*Pferde~*) point-to-point.

Quer-: ~flöte *f* (transverse) flute; **~format** *nt* oblong format; **wenn du das Photo im ~format machst** if you take the photo lengthways; **⚠q~gehen** *vi sep irreg aux sein* (*inf*) to go wrong; **heute geht mir alles q~** I can't do a thing right today; **⚠q~gestreift** *adj attr* horizontally striped, cross-striped; **~holz** *nt siehe* **~balken; ~kopf** *m* (*inf*) awkward so-and-so (*inf*) *or* customer (*inf*); **q~köpfig** *adj* awkward, perverse; **~lage** *f* (*Med*) transverse presentation, crossbirth; **~latte** *f* crossbar; **⚠q~legen** *vr sep* (*fig inf*) to be awkward; **⚠~paß** *m* cross; **~pfeife** *f* fife; **~ruder** *nt* aileron; **⚠q~schießen** *vi sep irreg* (*inf*) to be awkward, to spoil things; **~schiff** *nt* transept; **~schläger** *m* ricochet (shot).

Querschnitt *m* (*lit, fig*) cross-section.

Querschnitt(s)-: q~gelähmt *adj* paraplegic; **seit dem Autounfall ist er q~gelähmt** since the car accident he has been paralyzed from the waist down; **~gelähmte(r)** *mf* paraplegic; **~lähmung** *f* paraplegia; **~zeichnung** *f* sectional drawing.

Quer-: ⚠q~schreiben *vt sep irreg* (*Fin*) *Wechsel* to accept, to underwrite; **⚠~schuß** *m* (*fig*) objection; **⚠q~stellen** *vr sep* (*fig inf*) to be awkward; **~straße** *f* **das ist eine ~straße zur Hauptstraße** it runs at right angles to the high street; **in dieser ~straße muß das Geschäft sein** the shop must be down this turning; **bei** *or* **an der zweiten ~straße fahren Sie links ab** turn (off to the) left at the second junction, go left at the second turning; **die ~straßen zur Königstraße sehen alle gleich aus** the streets (going) off Königstraße all look the same; **~streifen** *m* horizontal stripe; **~strich** *m* (horizontal) stroke *or* line; (*Typ inf: Gedankenstrich*) dash; (*Bruchstrich*) line; **einen ~strich durch etw machen** to put a line through sth; (*streichen auch*) to cross sth out;

er macht beim T nie die ~striche he always forgets to cross his T's; **≈summe** *f (Math)* sum of digits of a number; **die ~summe bilden** to add the digits in a number; **≈treiber** *m (inf)* troublemaker, awkward customer *(inf)*; **~treiberei** *f (inf)* awkwardness, troublemaking.
Querulant(in *f***)** *m* grouser *(inf)*, grumbler.
querulieren* *vi* to grouse *(inf)*, to grumble.
Quer-: ~verbindung *f* connection, link; *(von Eisenbahn)* connecting line; *(von Straße)* link road; **hier läßt sich doch eine ~verbindung zur deutschen Geschichte herstellen** you can surely make a connection here with German history, you can surely link this up with German history; **~verweis** *m* cross-reference.
quetschen [1] *vt (drücken)* to squash, to crush; *(aus einer Tube)* to squeeze; *Kartoffeln* to mash; *(Med: usu pass)* to crush ◆ **etw in etw** *(acc)* ~ to squeeze *or* squash sth into sth; **jdn halbtot ~** to crush sb (nearly) to death; **jdm/sich den Finger ~** to squash sb's/one's finger; **du hast mir den Finger in der Tür gequetscht** you caught my finger in the door.
[2] *vr (sich klemmen)* to be caught *or* squashed *or* crushed; *(sich zwängen)* to squeeze (oneself) ◆ **du kannst dich noch ins Auto ~** you can still squeeze into the car.
Quetsch-: ~falte *f (Fashion)* box pleat; **~kommode** *f (hum inf)* squeeze box *(inf)*.
Quetschung, Quetschwunde *f (Med)* bruise, contusion *(form)* ◆ **der Fahrer kam mit ~en davon** the driver escaped with bruises *or* bruising; **~ innerer Organe** internal bruising.
Queue [kø:] *nt or m* **-s, -s** *(Billard)* cue.
quicklebendig *adj (inf) Kind* lively, active; *ältere Person auch* spry.
quiek *interj* squeak.
quiek(s)en *vi* to squeal, to squeak.
quietschen *vi (Tür, Schloß)* to squeak; *(Reifen, Mensch)* to squeal ◆ **das Kind quietschte vergnügt** *or* **vor Vergnügen** *(inf)* the child squealed with delight; **das** *or* **es war zum Q~!** *(inf)* it was a (real) scream! *(inf)*.
quietschfidel, quietschvergnügt *adj (inf)* happy as a sandboy.
quill *imper sing of* **quellen.**
Quinta *f* **-, Quinten** *(Sch) second year of German secondary school.*
Quintaner(in *f***)** *m* **-s, -** *(Sch) pupil in second year of German secondary school.*
Quint *f* **-, -en (a)** *(Mus: auch* **Quinte***)* fifth. **(b)** *(Fechten)* quinte.
Quinten *pl of* **Quinta, Quinte.**
Quint|essenz *f* quintessence.
Quintett *nt* **-(e)s, -e** quintet.
Quintole *f* **-, -n** quintuplet.
Quirl *m* **-s, -e (a)** *(Cook)* whisk, beater. **(b)** *(Bot)* whorl, verticil. **(c)** *(dated inf: Mensch)* live wire *(inf)*.
quirlen *vt* to whisk, to beat.
quirlig *adj* lively, effervescent.
Quisling *m (Pol pej)* quisling.
quitt *adj* **~ sein (mit jdm)** to be quits *or* even (with sb); **jdn/etw ~ sein** *(dial)* to be rid of sb/sth.
Quitte *f* **-, -n** quince.
quitte(n)gelb *adj* (sickly) yellow.
quittieren* [1] *vt* **(a)** *(bestätigen) Betrag, Rechnung, Empfang* to give a receipt for ◆ **lassen Sie sich** *(dat)* **die Rechnung ~** get a receipt for the bill. **(b)** *(beantworten)* to meet, to answer, to counter. **(c)** *(verlassen) Dienst* to quit, to resign.
[2] *vi* **(a)** *(bestätigen)* to sign. **(b)** *(old: zurücktreten)* to quit, to resign.
Quittung *f* **(a)** receipt ◆ **gegen ~** on production of a receipt; **eine ~ über 500 Mark** a receipt for 500 marks; **eine ~ ausstellen (über** *or* **für etw)** to make out *or* give a receipt (for sth).
(b) *(fig)* **das ist die ~ für Ihre Unverschämtheit** that is what you get for being so insolent, that's what comes of being so insolent; **das ist die ~ dafür, daß ...** that's the price you have to pay for ...; **jetzt haben Sie die ~!** now you have paid the penalty!; **du wirst die ~ für deine Faulheit bekommen** you'll pay the penalty for being lazy.
Quittungsblock *m* receipt book.
Quivive [ki'vi:f] *nt, no pl* **auf dem ~** on the qui vive, on the alert.
Quiz [kvɪs] *nt* **-, -** quiz.
Quizmaster ['kvɪsma:stɐ] *m* **-s, -** quizmaster.
quoll *pret of* **quellen.**
Quorum *nt* **-s,** *no pl* quorum.
Quote *f* **-, -n (a)** *(Statistik) (Anteilsziffer)* proportion; *(Rate)* rate. **(b)** *(Econ, Quantum)* quota.
Quotelung *f* apportionment.
Quotenregelung *f* quota system.
Quotient [kvo'tsiɛnt] *m* quotient.
quotieren* *vt (Comm) Preis, Kurs* to quote.
Quotierung *f (Comm)* quotation.
QWERTY-Tastatur ['kverti-] *f* QWERTY keyboard.
QWERTZ-Tastatur ['kverts-] *f* QWERTZ keyboard.

R, r [ɛr] *nt* -, - R, r ◆ **das R rollen** to roll one's r's.
Rabatt *m* **-(e)s, -e** discount ◆ **mit 10% ~** at *or* with (a) 10% discount.
Rabatte *f* (*Beet*) border.
Rabattmarke *f* (*Comm*) (trading) stamp.
Rabatz *m* **-es,** *no pl* (*inf*) row, din, shindy (*sl*).
Rabauke *m* **-n, -n** (*inf*) hooligan, lout (*inf*), rowdy (*inf*).
Rabaukentum *nt* hooliganism, rowdyism.
Rabbi *m* **-(s), -s,** *or* **Rabbinen, Rabbiner** *m* **-s,** - rabbi.
rabbinisch *adj* rabbinical.
Rabe *m* **-n, -n** raven ◆ **wie ein ~ stehlen** (*inf*) to thieve like a magpie.
Raben-: ~aas *nt* (*dated inf*) bad lot (*inf*); **~eltern** *pl* (*inf*) bad parents *pl*; **~mutter** *f* (*inf*) bad mother; **r~schwarz** *adj Nacht* pitch-black, black as pitch; *Augen, Seele auch* coal-black, black as coal; *Haare* jet-black, raven (-black); **~vater** *m* (*inf*) bad father.
rabiat *adj Kerl* violent, rough; *Autofahrer* breakneck, wild; *Geschäftsleute* ruthless; *Umgangston* aggressive; *Methoden, Konkurrenz* ruthless, cut-throat ◆ **~ werden** (*wütend*) to go wild; (*aggressiv*) to get violent *or* physical (*inf*).
Rabulist(in *f*) *m* sophist, quibbler.
Rabulisterei, Rabulistik *f* sophistry, quibbling.
rabulistisch *adj* sophistic, quibbling.
Rache *f* **-,** *no pl* revenge, vengeance ◆ **die ~ des kleinen Mannes** (*inf*) sweet revenge; **Tag der ~** (*liter*) day of reckoning; **das ist die ~ für deine Untat** this is the retribution for your misdeed; **auf ~ sinnen** to contemplate *or* plot revenge; **~ schwören** to swear vengeance; **(an jdm) ~ nehmen** *or* **üben** to take revenge *or* have one's revenge (on *or* upon sb); **etw aus ~ tun** to do sth in revenge; **~ ist Blutwurst** (*inf*) you'll/he'll *etc* be sorry (*inf*); **~ ist süß** (*prov*) revenge is sweet (*prov*).
Rache-: ~akt *m* act of revenge *or* vengeance; **~durst** *m* thirst *or* longing for revenge *or* vengeance; **r~durstig** *adj* thirsting *or* longing for revenge *or* vengeance; **~engel** *m* avenging angel; **~gefühl** *nt* feeling of bitter resentment; **~gefühle haben** to harbour bitter resentment; **~göttin** *f* avenging goddess, goddess of vengeance; **wie eine ~göttin** like a Fury.
Rachen *m* **-s,** - throat, pharynx (*spec*); (*von großen Tieren*) jaws *pl*; (*fig*) jaws *pl*, abyss, maw ◆ **jdm etw in den ~ werfen** *or* **schmeißen** (*inf*) to shove sth down sb's throat (*inf*); **jdm den ~ stopfen** (*inf*) to give sb what he/she wants.
rächen [1] *vt jdn, Untat* to avenge (*etw an jdm* sth on sb) ◆ **er schwor, diese Schmach zu ~** he swore to seek vengeance for *or* to avenge this dishonour; **dieses Unrecht werde ich noch an ihm ~** I intend to avenge myself on him for this injustice.
[2] *vr* (*Mensch*) to get one's revenge, to take revenge *or* vengeance (*an jdm für etw* on sb for sth); (*Schuld, Sünde, Untat*) to be avenged ◆ **deine Faulheit/Unehrlichkeit wird sich ~** you'll pay for being so lazy/dishonest.
Rachen-: ~blütler *m* **-s,** - (*Bot*) figwort; **~höhle** *f* pharynx, pharyngeal cavity; **~katarrh** *m* pharyngitis; **~mandel** *f* pharyngeal tonsil; **~putzer** *m* (*hum inf*) gutrot (*inf*).
Racheplan *m* plan of revenge ◆ **Rachepläne schmieden** to plot revenge.
Rächer(in *f*) *m* **-s,** - avenger.
Racheschwur *m* oath of revenge *or* vengeance.
Rach-: ~gier *f siehe* **~sucht**; **r~gierig** *adj siehe* **r~süchtig**.
Rachitis *f* **-,** *no pl* rickets, rachitis (*spec*).
rachitisch *adj* rickety, rachitic (*spec*); *Symptom* of rickets.
Rach-: ~sucht *f* vindictiveness; **r~süchtig** *adj* vindictive.
Racker *m* **-s,** - (*inf: Kind*) rascal, scamp, monkey (*all inf*).
Rackerei *f siehe* **Plackerei**.
rackern *vir* (*inf*) to slave (away) (*inf*).
Racket ['rɛkət, ra'kɛt] *nt* **-s, -s** (*Aus*) *siehe* **Rakett**.
Raclette [ra'klɛt] *nt or f* **-s, -s** raclette.
Rad¹ *nt* **-(e)s, ⸚er (a)** wheel; (*Rolle*) castor; (*Zahn~*) gearwheel; (*Sport*) cartwheel ◆ **ein ~ schlagen** (*Sport*) to do *or* turn a cartwheel; **der Pfau schlägt ein ~** the peacock is fanning out its tail *or* spreading its tail *or* opening its fan; **jdn aufs ~ flechten** (*Hist*) to break sb on the wheel; **alle ⸚er greifen ineinander, ein ~ greift ins andere** (*fig*) it all knits together, all the parts knit together; **nur ein ~** *or* **Rädchen im Getriebe sein** (*fig*) to be only a cog in the works; **das ~ der Geschichte** the wheels of history; **das ~ der Geschichte** *or* **Zeit läßt sich nicht zurückdrehen** you can't turn *or* put the clock back; **unter die ⸚er kommen** *or* **geraten** (*inf*) to get *or* fall into bad ways; **das fünfte ~ am Wagen sein** (*inf*) to be in the way; **ein ~ abhaben** (*inf*) to have a screw loose (*inf*).
(b) (*Fahr~*) bicycle, bike (*inf*), cycle ◆ **mit dem ~ fahren/kommen** to go/come by bicycle; *siehe* **radfahren**.
Rad² *nt* **-(s),** - (*Maßeinheit*) rad.
Rad|achse *f* axle(tree).
Radar *m or nt* **-s,** *no pl* radar.
Radar- *in cpds* radar; **~abwehrnetz** *nt* (*Mil*) radar defence network; **~anlage** *f* radar (equipment) *no indef art*; **~falle** *f* speed trap; **~gerät** *nt* radar unit; **r~gesteuert** *adj* radar-controlled; **~kontrolle** *f* radar speed check; **~schirm** *m* radar screen, radarscope.
Radau *m* **-s,** *no pl* (*inf*) row, din, racket (*inf*) ◆ **~ machen** to kick up a row; (*Unruhe stiften*) to cause *or* make trouble.
Radaubruder *m* (*inf*) rowdy (*inf*), hooligan, yobbo (*Brit inf*).
Rad|aufhängung *f* (*Aut*) (wheel) suspension.
Radaumacher *m* (*inf*) *siehe* **Radaubruder**.
Radball *m, no pl* bicycle polo.
Rädchen *nt dim of* **Rad** small wheel; (*für Schnittmuster*) tracing wheel; (*Cook*) pastry wheel; *siehe* **Rad**.
Raddampfer *m* paddle-steamer.
Rade *f* **-, -n** corncockle.
radebrechen *vti insep* to speak broken English/German *etc* ◆ **er radebrechte auf Italienisch, er wolle ...** he said in broken Italian that he wanted ...
radeln¹ *vi aux sein* (*inf*) to cycle.
radeln², rädeln *vt Schnittmuster* to trace; (*Cook*) to cut out.
Rädelsführer *m* ringleader.
-räd(e)rig *adj suf* -wheeled.
rädern *vt* (*Hist*) to break on the wheel; *siehe* **gerädert**.
Räderwerk *nt* (*Mech*) mechanism, works *pl*; (*fig*) machinery, cogs *pl*.
⚠ **radfahren** *vi sep irreg aux sein* (*Kleinschreibung nur bei infin und ptp*) **(a)** to cycle ◆ **ich fahre Rad** I ride a bicycle; **kannst du ~?** can you ride a bike?; **R~ verboten** no cycling. **(b)** (*pej inf: kriechen*) to crawl (*inf*), to suck up (*inf*).
Radfahrer *m* **(a)** cyclist. **(b)** (*pej inf*) crawler (*inf*).
Radfahr-: ~sport *m siehe* **Radsport**; **~weg** *m siehe* **Radweg**.
Radgabel *f* fork.
Radi *m* **-s,** - (*S Ger, Aus*) radish ◆ **einen ~ kriegen** (*inf*) to get a rocket (*inf*), to catch it (*inf*).
radial *adj* radial.
Radialgeschwindigkeit *f* (*Astron*) radial velocity.
Radiator *m* radiator.
Radicchio [ra'dɪkjo] *m* **-s, -dicchi** [-'diki] radicchio.
radieren* *vti* **(a)** to rub out, to erase ◆ **auf dieser Seite hat er dreimal radiert** he's rubbed three things out on this page, there are three erasures on this page. **(b)** (*Art*) to etch.
Radierer *m* **-s, - (a)** (*inf*) *siehe* **Radiergummi**. **(b)** (*Art*) etcher.
Radier-: ~gummi *m* rubber (*Brit*), eraser (*esp US, form*); **~kunst** *f* (*Art*) etching; **~messer** *nt* (steel) eraser, erasing knife; **~nadel** *f* (*Art*) etching needle.
Radierung *f* (*Art*) etching.
Radieschen [ra'di:sçən] *nt* radish ◆ **sich (*dat*) die ~ von unten an-** *or* **besehen** (*hum sl*) to be pushing up the daisies (*hum*).
radikal *adj* radical; *Vereinfachung, Methode auch* drastic; *Vertilgung, Entfernen* total; *Verneinung* categorical; *Ablehnung* flat, categorical ◆ **mit diesen Mißbräuchen muß ~ Schluß gemacht werden** a definitive stop must be put to these abuses; **etw ~ verneinen/ablehnen** to deny sth categorically/to refuse sth flatly; **~ vorgehen** to be drastic; **~ gegen etw vorgehen** to take radical steps against sth.
Radikal *nt* **-s, -e** (*Math*) root; (*Chem*) radical.
⚠ **Radikalen|erlaß** *m ban on the employment of radical teachers and civil servants.*
Radikale(r) *mf decl as adj* radical.
radikalisieren* *vt* to radicalize.
Radikalisierung *f* radicalization.
Radikalismus *m* (*Pol*) radicalism.
Radikalkur *f* (*inf*) drastic remedy, kill-or-cure remedy.
Radio *nt or* (*Sw, S Ger auch*) *m* **-s, -s** radio, wireless (*esp Brit*) ◆ **~ hören** to listen to the radio; **im ~** on the radio.

⚠: Informationen zur Rechtschreibreform im Anhang

Radio- *in cpds* radio; **r~aktiv** *adj* radioactive; **r~aktiv machen** to activate, to make radioactive; **r~aktiver Niederschlag** (radioactive) fall-out; **~aktivität** *f* radioactivity; **≈amateur** *m* radio ham (*inf*) *or* amateur; **≈apparat** *m siehe* **~gerät**; **≈astronomie** *f* radio astronomy; **≈biologie** *f* radiobiology; **≈chemie** *f* radiochemistry; **≈durchsage** *f* radio announcement; **≈empfänger** *m* radio (set); (*von Funkamateur*) radio receiver; **≈gehäuse** *nt* radio cabinet; (*von Kofferradio*) casing; **≈gerät** *nt* radio (set); **≈geschäft** *nt* electrical shop; **~gramm** *nt* (*Med*) X-ray (photograph), radiograph (*esp US*); ⚠**~graphie** *f* radiography; **~isotop** *nt* radioisotope; **~karbonmethode** *f* radiocarbon (dating) technique *or* method; ⚠**≈kompaß** *m* (*Aviat, Naut*) radio compass, automatic direction finder; **~loge** *m*, **~login** *f* (*Med*) radiologist; **~logie** *f* (*Med*) radiology; **r~logisch** *adj* radiological; **~lyse** *f* radiolysis; **≈mechaniker** *m* radio technician *or* engineer; **~metrie** *f* radiometry; **~nuklid** *m* (*Phys*) radionuclide; **≈quelle** *f* (*Astron*) radio source; **≈recorder** *m* radio recorder; **≈röhre** *f* radio valve (*esp Brit*) *or* tube (*esp US*); **≈sender** *m* (*Rundfunkanstalt*) radio station; (*Sendeeinrichtung*) radio transmitter; **≈sendung** *f* radio programme; **~skopie** *f* radioscopy; **≈sonde** *f* (radio-equipped) weather balloon, radiosonde; **≈station** *f* radio *or* broadcasting station; **≈strahlung** *f* radio signal; **≈technik** *f* radio technology; **≈techniker** *m siehe* **~mechaniker**; **~telegrafie** *f* radiotelegraphy; **~teleskop** *nt* radio telescope; **≈therapeut** *m* radiotherapist; **≈therapie** *f* radiotherapy; **≈übertragung** *f* (radio) broadcast *or* transmission; **≈wecker** *m* radio alarm (clock).

Radium *nt, no pl* (*abbr* **Ra**) radium.

Radium-: ~behandlung, ~bestrahlung *f* (*Med*) *siehe* **~therapie**; **r~haltig** *adj* containing radium; **r~haltig sein** to contain radium; **~strahlen** *pl* (*Phys, Med*) radium rays *pl*; **~therapie** *f* radium therapy *or* treatment.

Radius *m* **-, Radien** [-iən] radius.

Rad-: ~kappe *f* hub cap; **~kasten** *m* wheel casing; (*Naut*) paddle-box; **~kranz** *m* rim (of a/the wheel); **~lager** *nt* wheel bearing.

Radler(in *f***)** *m* **-s, -** (*inf*) cyclist.

Radlerhose *f* cycling shorts *pl*.

Radlermaß *f* (*S Ger inf*) shandy.

Rad-: ~macher *m siehe* **Stellmacher**; **~mantel** *m* (*Bereifung*) bicycle tyre; **~nabe** *f* (wheel) hub.

Radon *nt* **-s,** *no pl* (*abbr* **Rn**) radon.

Rad-: ~rennbahn *f* cycle (racing) track; **~rennen** *nt* (*Sportart*) cycle racing; (*einzelnes Rennen*) cycle race; **~rennfahrer** *m* racing cyclist; **~rennsport** *m* cycle racing; **~schaufel** *f* blade (of a wheel); ⚠**r~schlagen** *vi sep irreg* (*Kleinschreibung nur bei infin und ptp*) to do *or* turn cartwheels; **ich schlage ~** I do cartwheels; **~schuh** *m* brake; **~sport** *m* cycling; **~sportler** *m* cyclist; **~stand** *m* (*Aut, Rail*) wheelbase; **~sturz** *m* (*Aut*) camber; **~tour** *f* bike ride; (*länger*) cycling *or* cycle tour; **~wechsel** *m* wheel change; **(einen) ~wechsel machen** to change a wheel, to do a wheel change; **~weg** *m* cycleway.

RAF [ɛr|aː'|ɛf] *f abbr of* **Rote-Armee-Fraktion.**

Raffel *f* **-, -n** (*dial*) **(a)** (*Reibeisen*) grater. **(b)** (*Tex*) hackle, flax comb.

raffeln *vti* (*dial*) **(a)** to grate. **(b)** (*Tex*) to comb, to hackle.

raffen *vt* **(a)** (*anhäufen*) to pile, to heap ◆ **er will immer nur Geld ~** he's always after money; **sein ganzes Leben hat er nur Geld gerafft** he spent his whole life making money; **etw an sich** (*acc*) **~** to grab *or* snatch sth. **(b)** *Stoff, Gardine* to gather; *langes Kleid, Rock* to gather up. **(c)** (*sl: verstehen*) to suss (*inf*).

Raff-: ~gier *f* greed, avarice; **r~gierig** *adj* greedy, grasping.

Raffinade *f* (*Zucker*) refined sugar.

Raffination *f* (*von Öl, Zucker*) refining.

Raffinement [rafinə'mãː] *nt* **-s, -s** (*geh*) *siehe* **Raffinesse (b).**

Raffinerie *f* refinery.

Raffinesse *f* **(a)** (*Feinheit*) refinement, finesse *no pl* ◆ **ein Auto mit allen ~n** a car with all the refinements. **(b)** (*Schlauheit, Durchtriebenheit*) cunning *no pl*, craftiness *no pl*, wiliness *no pl* ◆ **mit allen ~n** with all one's cunning.

raffinieren* *vt Zucker, Öl* to refine.

raffiniert *adj* **(a)** *Zucker, Öl* refined.
(b) (*inf*) *Kleid, Frisur, Apparat, Kleidung* fancy (*inf*), stylish; *Apparat* fancy (*inf*) ◆ **sie kleidet sich sehr ~** she certainly knows how to dress.
(c) (*schlau*) clever, cunning; (*durchtrieben auch*) crafty ◆ **sie ist eine ~e Frau** she knows all the tricks in the book; **ein ~es Luder** *or* **Weib** (*pej*) a cunning bitch (*inf*).

Raffiniertheit *f siehe adj* (*b, c*) fanciness (*inf*), stylishness; fanciness (*inf*); cleverness, cunning; craftiness.

Raffke *m* **-s, -s** (*inf*) money-grubber (*inf*).

RAF- [ɛr|aː'|ɛf-]: **~-Kader** *m* unit of the Red Army Faction; **~-Mitglied** *nt* member of the Red Army Faction.

Rafting *nt* **-** *no pl* rafting.

Rage ['raːʒə] *f* **-,** *no pl* **(a)** (*Wut*) rage, fury ◆ **jdn in ~ bringen** to infuriate sb; **in ~ kommen** *or* **geraten** to get *or* become furious, to fly into a rage *or* fury. **(b)** (*inf: Aufregung, Eile*) hurry, rush.

ragen *vi* to rise, to tower, to loom; (*heraus~*) to jut.

Ragionenbuch [ra'dʒoːnən-] *nt* (*Sw*) business register.

Raglan- *in cpds* raglan; **~ärmel** *m* raglan sleeve; **~schnitt** *m* raglan style.

Ragout [ra'guː] *nt* **-s, -s** ragout.

Ragtime ['ræg-] *m* **-(s),** *no pl* ragtime.

Rah(e) *f* **-(e), -(e)n** (*Naut*) yard.

Rahm *m* **-(e)s,** *no pl* (*dial*) cream; *siehe* **abschöpfen.**

Rähmchen *nt dim of* **Rahmen** (*Dia~*) mount.

rahmen *vt* to frame; *Dias* to mount.

Rahmen *m* **-s, - (a)** frame; (*vom Schuh*) welt.
(b) (*fig*) (*Bereich, Liter: ~handlung*) framework; (*Atmosphäre*) setting; (*Größe*) scale ◆ **im ~** within the framework (*gen* of); **seine Verdienste wurden im ~ einer kleinen Feier gewürdigt** his services were honoured in a small ceremony; **im ~ des Möglichen** within the bounds of possibility; **im ~ bleiben** not to go too far; **aus dem ~ fallen** to go too far; **mußt du denn immer aus dem ~ fallen!** do you always have to show yourself up?; **ein Geschenk/Getränk, das aus dem ~ des Üblichen fällt** a present/drink with a difference; **dieses Buch fällt aus dem ~ unserer normalen Produktion** this book is outside our usual line (of business); **in den ~ von etw passen, sich in den ~ von etw einfügen** to fit (in) *or* blend in with sth, to go with sth; **den ~ von etw sprengen, über den ~ von etw hinausgehen** to go beyond the scope of sth; **das würde den ~ sprengen** it would be beyond my/our *etc* scope; **einer Feier einen würdigen/den richtigen ~ geben** to provide the appropriate setting for a celebration; **in größerem/kleinerem ~** on a large/small scale; **die Feier fand nur in engem** *or* **in engstem ~ statt** the celebration was just a small-scale affair.

Rahmen-: ~antenne *f* frame aerial (*esp Brit*) *or* antenna; **~bedingung** *f* basic condition; **~erzählung** *f* (*Liter*) framework story; **~gesetz** *nt general outline of a law providing guidelines for specific elaboration*; **~handlung** *f* (*Liter*) background story, story which forms the framework; **~plan** *m* framework, outline plan; **~programm** *nt* **(a)** framework; (*von Veranstaltung etc*) supporting acts *pl*; **(b)** *siehe* **~plan**; **~richtlinien** *pl* guidelines *pl*; **~tarifvertrag** *m siehe* **Manteltarifvertrag**; **~vertrag** *m* (*Ind*) general agreement.

rahmig *adj* (*dial*) creamy.

Rahmkäse *m* cream cheese.

Rahsegel *nt* (*Naut*) square sail.

Rain *m* **-(e)s, -e** (*liter*) margin, marge (*poet*).

räkeln *vr siehe* **rekeln.**

Rakeltiefdruck *m* photogravure, rotogravure.

Rakete *f* **-, -n** rocket (*auch Space*); (*Mil auch*) missile ◆ **ferngelenkte** *or* **ferngesteuerte ~** guided missile.

⚠**Raketen-** *in cpds* rocket; (*Mil auch*) missile; **~abschuß** *m* (rocket) launch(ing); **~(abschuß)basis** *f* (*Mil*) missile *or* rocket base; (*Space*) launch(ing) site.

Raketen|abwehr *f* antimissile defence.

Raketen|abwehr-: ~rakete *f* antimissile missile; **~schirm** *m* nuclear defence umbrella; **~stellung** *f* antimissile position; **~system** *nt* missile-defence system; **~waffe** *f* antimissile weapon.

Raketen-: ~antrieb *m* rocket propulsion; **mit ~antrieb** rocket-propelled; **~apparat** *m* rocket(-line) apparatus; **~basis** *f siehe* **~(abschuß)basis**; **r~bestückt** *adj* missile-carrying *or* -equipped; **~flugzeug** *nt* rocket-propelled aircraft; ⚠**~geschoß** *nt* missile; **~satz** *m* set of rockets/missiles; **~silo** *m* rocket silo; **~start** *m* (rocket) launch(ing); (*Start mittels Raketen*) rocket-assisted take-off; **~stufe** *f* stage (of a rocket/missile); **~stützpunkt** *m* missile base; **~versuchsgelände** *nt* rocket range; (*Space*) launch(ing) site; **~werfer** *m* rocket launcher; **~zeitalter** *nt* space age.

Rakett *nt* **-s, -s** *or* **-e** (*old Sport*) racket, racquet.

Rallye ['rali, 'rɛli] *f* **-, -s** rally ◆ **eine ~ fahren** to drive in a rally; **~ fahren** to go rallying.

Rallyefahrer *m* rally-driver.

RAM [ram] *nt* **-s, -s** (*Comput*) RAM.

Rambazamba *nt* **-s,** *no pl* (*inf*) **~ machen** to kick up a fuss.

Rambo *m* **-s, -s** Rambo, tough guy.

Ramm-: ~bock *m siehe* **Ramme**; **r~dösig** *adj* (*inf*) giddy, dizzy.

Ramme *f* **-, -n** ram(mer); (*für Pfähle*) pile-driver.

Rammelei *f* **(a)** (*inf: Gedränge*) crush, scrum (*inf*). **(b)** (*sl*) banging away (*sl*).

rammeln 1 *vt siehe* **gerammelt.**
2 *vir* (*dial: herumtoben*) to charge about *or* around.
3 *vi* (*Hunt*) to mate; (*sl*) to have it off *or* away (*sl*).

rammen *vt* to ram.

Rammler *m* **-s, -** buck.

Rampe *f* **-, -n (a)** ramp. **(b)** (*Theat*) apron, forestage.

Rampenlicht *nt* (*Theat*) footlights *pl* ◆ **sie möchte im ~ stehen** (*Theat*) she'd like to go on the stage; (*fig*) she wants to be in the limelight; **im ~ der Öffentlichkeit stehen** (*fig*) to be in the limelight.

ramponieren* *vt* (*inf*) to ruin; *Möbel* to bash about (*inf*) ◆ **er sah ziemlich ramponiert aus** he looked the worse for wear (*inf*).

Ramsch *m* **-(e)s,** *no pl* **(a)** (*inf*) junk, rubbish, trash. **(b)** (*Skat*) **(einen) ~ spielen** to play (a) ramsch.

ramschen 1 *vi* **(a)** (*inf*) to buy cheap junk. **(b)** (*beim Skat*) to play (a) ramsch.
2 *vt* (*Comm*) to buy up.

Ramsch-: ~händler *m* (*pej*) junk dealer; **~laden** *m* (*pej*) junk shop; **~verkauf** *m* oddments sale; **~ware** *f* (*pej*) trashy goods *pl*, rubbish.

RAM-Speicher *m* (*Comput*) RAM memory.

ran *interj* (*inf*) come on, go it (*inf*) ◆ **~ an den Feind!** let's go get 'em! (*inf*); **~ an die Bouletten** (*sl*) get stuck in (*inf*); *siehe* **heran.**

Ranch [rɛntʃ, raːntʃ] *f* **-, -(e)s** ranch.

Rancher ['rɛntʃɐ, 'raːntʃɐ] *m* **-s, -(s)** rancher.

Rand[1] *m* **-es, ¨er (a)** edge; (*von Weg, Straße, Schwimmbecken etc auch*) side; (*von Brunnen, Tasse*) top, rim, brim; (*von Abgrund*) brink ◆ **voll bis zum ~** full to the brim, brimful; **am ~e** *erwähnen, zur Sprache kommen* by the way, in passing;

⚠: for details of spelling reform, see supplement

interessieren marginally; *beteiligt sein* marginally, on the fringe; *miterleben* on the sidelines; **etw am ~e bemerken** *or* **vermerken** to mention sth in passing *or* in parentheses; **am ~e des Waldes** at the edge of the forest; **am ~e der Stadt** on the outskirts of the town; **am ~e der Verzweiflung/des Wahnsinns** on the verge of despair/madness; **am ~e des Grabes/Todes** at death's door; **am ~e des Untergangs** *or* **Ruins** on the brink *or* verge of ruin; **am ~e eines Krieges** on the brink of war; **die Schweizer haben den Krieg nur am ~e miterlebt** the Swiss were only marginally involved in the war *or* only experienced the war from the sidelines; **er hat die Russische Revolution noch am ~e miterlebt** he was around at the beginning/end of the Russian Revolution; **eine kleine Szene am ~e des Krieges** a small incident on the fringe of the war; **am ~e der Gesellschaft/der politischen Landschaft** on the fringes of society/the political scene.

(b) (*Umrandung*) border; (*Teller~*) edge, side; (*Brillen~*) rim; (*von Hut*) brim; (*Seiten~, Buch~, Heft~*) margin ◆ **wenn er so über die ~̈er seiner Brille schielt** when he peers over the top of his glasses like that; **mit schwarzem ~** black-edged, with a black border; **etw an den ~ schreiben** to write sth in the margin.

(c) (*Schmutz~*) ring; (*um Augen auch*) circle; (*in der Badewanne auch*) tidemark ◆ **rote ~̈er um die Augen haben** to have red rims around one's eyes.

(d) (*fig*) **das versteht sich am ~e** that goes without saying; **sie waren außer ~ und Band** there was no holding them, they were going wild; **allein komme ich damit nicht zu ~e** I can't manage (it) by myself; **halt den ~!** (*sl*) shut your face (*sl*).

Rand[2] *m* **-s, -(s)** (*Währung*) rand.

Randale *f* rioting ◆ **~ machen** to riot.

randalieren* *vi* to rampage (about) ◆ **~de Jugendliche** (young) hooligans; **~de Studenten** rioting students; **die Jugendlichen zogen ~d durch die Straßen** the youths rampaged *or* went on the rampage *or* ran wild through the streets; **die Gefangenen fingen an zu ~** the prisoners started to get violent.

Randalierer *m* **-s, -** hooligan, trouble-maker.

Rand-: ~ausgleich *m* (*Comput*) justification; **~auslöser** *m* margin release; **~bemerkung** *f* note in the margin, marginal note; (*fig*) (passing) comment; **etw in einer ~bemerkung erwähnen** (*fig*) to mention sth in passing.

Rande *f* **-, -n** (*Sw*) beetroot.

Rand|einstellung *f* margin setting.

rändeln *vt Münze* to mill.

-ränd(e)rig *adj suf* -edged.

rändern *vt* to edge, to border.

Rand-: ~erscheinung *f* matter of peripheral importance; (*Nebenwirkung*) side effect; **das Problem des ... ist nur eine ~erscheinung** the problem of ... is only of peripheral importance; **~figur** *f* minor figure; **~gebiet** *nt* (*Geog*) edge, fringe; (*Pol*) border territory; (*fig*) subsidiary; **r~genäht** *adj Schuhe* welted; **~glosse** *f* marginal note; **~gruppe** *f* fringe group.

-randig *adj suf* -edged.

Rand-: r~los *adj Brille* rimless; *Hut* brimless; **~persönlichkeit** *f* (*Sociol*) marginal man; **~staat** *m* border state; **die ~staaten des Mittelmeers** the countries around *or* bordering on the Mediterranean; **die ~staaten der Nordsee** the North Sea countries; **r~ständig** *adj Personen* marginal; *Bevölkerungsgruppen* minority; **~ständige(r)** *mf decl as adj* marginal person; **~stein** *m siehe* **Bordstein**; **~steller** *m* **-s, -** margin stop; **r~voll** *adj Glas* full to the brim; *Flugzeug etc* packed; (*inf: betrunken*) smashed (*inf*); **~zone** *f* peripheral zone *or* area; **in der ~zone** on the periphery; **diese Staaten sind vorerst noch ~zonen der Weltpolitik** these states are still on the periphery *or* perimeter of world politics.

Ranft *m* **-(e)s, ~̈e** (*dial*) crust, heel (*US, Scot, dial*).

rang *pret of* **ringen**.

Rang *m* **-(e)s, ~̈e (a)** (*Mil*) rank; (*in Firma*) position; (*gesellschaftliche Stellung auch*) position, station (*dated*) ◆ **im ~(e) eines Hauptmanns stehen** to have the rank of captain; **im ~ höher/tiefer stehen** to have a higher/lower rank/position, to rank higher/lower; **einen hohen ~ bekleiden** to hold a high office; (*Mil*) to have a high rank; **ein Mann von ~ und Würden** a man of considerable *or* high standing, a man of status; **ein Mann ohne ~ und Namen** a man without any standing or reputation; **jdm den ~ streitig machen** (*fig*) to challenge sb's position; **jdm den ~ ablaufen** (*fig*) to outstrip sb.

(b) (*Qualität*) quality, class ◆ **ein Künstler/Wissenschaftler von ~** an artist/scientist of standing, a top artist/scientist; **von hohem ~** high-class; **ein Essen ersten ~es** a first-class *or* first-rate meal; **minderen ~es** low-class, second-rate.

(c) (*Theat*) circle ◆ **erster/zweiter ~** dress/upper circle, first/second circle; **wir sitzen (erster/zweiter) ~ Mitte** (*inf*) we're sitting in the middle of the (dress/upper) circle; **vor leeren/überfüllten ~̈en spielen** to play to an empty/a packed house.

(d) ~̈e *pl* (*Sport*) stands *pl*.

(e) (*Gewinnklasse*) prize category.

Rang-: ~abzeichen *nt* (*Mil*) badge of rank, insignia; **~älteste(r)** *m* (*Mil*) senior officer.

Range *f* **-, -n** urchin.

rangehen *vi sep irreg aux sein* (*inf*) to get stuck in (*inf*) ◆ **geh ran!** go on!; **der geht aber ran wie Blücher!** he's a fast worker (*inf*); *siehe* **herangehen**.

Rangelei *f* (*inf*) *siehe* **Gerangel**.

rangeln (*inf*) [1] *vi* to scrap; (*um Sonderangebote auch*) to tussle (*um* for); (*um Posten*) to wrangle (*um* for).

[2] *vr* to sprawl about.

Rang-: ~folge *f* order of rank (*esp Mil*) *or* standing; **nach der ~folge, der ~folge nach** in order of rank (*esp Mil*) *or* standing; **r~hoch** *adj* senior; (*Mil auch*) high-ranking; **~höchste(r)** *mf decl as adj* senior person/member *etc*; (*Mil*) highest-ranking officer.

Rangierbahnhof [rã'ʒiːɐ-] *m* marshalling yard.

rangieren* [rã'ʒiːrən] [1] *vt* **(a)** (*Rail*) to shunt, to switch (*US*).

(b) (*inf: abschieben*) to shove (*inf*), to shunt (*inf*).

[2] *vi* (*Rang einnehmen*) to rank ◆ **er rangiert gleich hinter** *or* **unter dem Abteilungsleiter** he comes directly beneath the head of department; **seine Familie rangiert nur am Rande in seinem Leben** his family take second place; **die Mathilde rangiert bei mir unter „ferner liefen"** (*inf*) as far as I'm concerned Mathilde is an "also-ran"; **der Intelligenz nach rangiert er ganz vorne** he's quite high up the list as far as intelligence goes; **an erster/letzter Stelle ~** to come first/last, to take first/last place.

Rangierer [rã'ʒiːrɐ] *m* **-s, -** (*Rail*) shunter.

Rangier- [rã'ʒiːɐ-]: **~gleis** *nt* siding, sidetrack (*US*); **~lok(omotive), ~maschine** *f* shunter, switcher (*US*).

Rang-: ~liste *f* **(a)** (*Mil*) active list; **(b)** (*Sport*) (results) table; **er steht auf der ~liste der weltbesten Boxer** he ranks among the world's top boxers; **~loge** *f* (*Theat*) box (in the circle); **r~mäßig** *adj* according to rank; **r~mäßig stehe ich unter ihm** I'm lower than him in rank; **~ordnung** *f* hierarchy; (*Mil*) (order of) ranks; **~stufe** *f* rank; **auf der gleichen ~stufe stehen** to be of *or* to have the same rank; **~unterschied** *m* social distinction; (*Mil*) difference of rank; **wir machen hier keine ~unterschiede** we're not status-conscious here.

ranhalten *vr sep irreg* (*inf*) **(a)** (*sich beeilen, sich umtun*) to get a move on (*inf*). **(b)** (*schnell zugreifen*) to dig in (*inf*), to get stuck in (*inf*).

ranhauen *vi sep irreg* (*sl*) to get stuck in (*inf*).

rank *adj* (*liter*) **~ und schlank** slender and supple; *Mädchen auch* slim and sylphlike.

Ranke *f* **-, -n** tendril; (*von Brom-, Himbeeren*) branch; (*von Erdbeeren*) stalk; (*von Weinrebe*) shoot.

Ränke *pl* (*liter*) intrigue, cabal (*liter*) ◆ **~ schmieden** to hatch a plot, to intrigue, to cabal (*liter*).

ranken [1] *vr* **sich um etw ~** to entwine itself around sth; (*fig: Geschichten etc*) to have grown up around sth.

[2] *vi aux haben or sein* **an etw** (*dat*) **~** to entwine itself around sth.

Ranken-: ~gewächs *nt* climbing plant, climber; (*Efeu etc*) creeper; **~werk** *nt* (*Art*) arabesques *pl*; (*fig*) embellishment.

Ränke-: ~schmied *m* (*liter*) intriguer; **~spiel** *nt* (*liter*) intrigue, cabal (*liter*); **r~süchtig, r~voll** *adj* (*liter*) scheming, caballing (*liter*).

rankig *adj* (*Bot*) climbing.

Ranking ['raŋkɪŋ] *nt* **-, -s** (*inf: Rangordnung*) ranking.

ranklotzen *vi sep* (*sl*) to get stuck in (*inf*).

rankommen *vi sep irreg aux sein* (*inf*) **an etw** (*acc*) **~** to get at sth; **an die Helga ist nicht ranzukommen** you won't get anywhere with Helga (*inf*); **an unseren Chef ist schwer ran zukommen** our boss isn't very easy to get at (*inf*); **niemanden an sich ~ lassen** to be standoffish (*inf*), to keep oneself to oneself; *siehe* **herankommen**.

Rankünе *f, no pl* (*geh, old*) grudge, rancour.

ranlassen *vt sep irreg* (*inf*) **jdn ~** to let sb have a go; **sie läßt jeden ran** (*sl*) she's anybody's (*inf*), she's an easy lay (*sl*); **sie läßt keinen mehr (an sich** *acc***) ran** (*sl*) she won't let anybody near her.

ranmachen *vr sep* (*inf*) *siehe* **heranmachen**.

rann *pret of* **rinnen**.

rannte *pret of* **rennen**.

ranschmeißen *vr sep irreg* (*inf*) **sich an jdn ~** to fling oneself at sb (*inf*).

Ranschmeißer *m* **-s, -** (*sl*) fast worker (*inf*), goer (*sl*).

Ranunkel *f* (*Bot*) ranunculus.

Ranzel *nt or m* **-s, -** (*old, dial*) knapsack, pack ◆ **sein** *or* **den ~ schnüren** (*liter*) to pack up one's belongings.

Ranzen *m* **-s, - (a)** (*Schul~*) satchel. **(b)** (*inf: Bauch*) belly (*inf*), gut (*sl*) ◆ **sich** (*dat*) **den ~ voll schlagen** to stuff oneself (*inf*) *or* one's face (*sl*). **(c)** (*inf: Buckel*) hunchback, hump(back) ◆ **jdm (ordentlich) den ~ vollhauen** to give sb a (good) thrashing.

ranzig *adj* rancid.

Rap [rap] *m* **-(s), -s** (*Mus*) rap.

rapid(e) *adj* rapid.

Rapier *nt* **-s, -e** rapier.

Rappe *m* **-n, -n** black horse; *siehe* **Schuster**.

Rappel *m* **-s, -** (*inf*) **(a)** (*Fimmel*) craze; (*Klaps*) crazy mood ◆ **seinen ~ kriegen** to get one of one's crazes/crazy moods; **du hast wohl einen ~!** you must be crazy!

(b) (*Wutanfall*) **einen ~ haben/kriegen** to be in a foul *or* filthy mood *or* temper/to throw a fit; **dabei kann man ja einen ~ kriegen** it's enough to drive you mad *or* up the wall (*inf*).

rapp(e)lig *adj* (*inf*) **(a)** (*verrückt*) crazy, cracked (*inf*) ◆ **bei dem Lärm kann man ja ~ werden** the noise is enough to drive you crazy *or* round the twist (*inf*).

(b) (*nervös, unruhig*) jumpy (*inf*).

rappeln *vi* (*inf*) (*lärmen*) to rattle; (*Aus: verrückt sein*) to be crazy ◆ **es rappelt an der Tür** somebody is shaking *or* rattling the door; **bei dir rappelt's wohl!** (*inf*) are you crazy?; **bei dem rappelt's manchmal** he just flips sometimes (*sl*).

Rappen *m* **-s, -** (*Sw*) centime.

rappen ['rapn] *vi* (*Mus*) to rap.

Rapper(in *f***)** ['rapɐ, rɪn-] *m* **-s, -** (*Mus*) rapper.

Rapport *m* -(e)s, -e **(a)** (*old*) report ◆ **sich zum ~ melden** to report; **er ist beim Kommandeur zum ~** he's making a report to the commander. **(b)** (*Psych*) rapport.

Raps *m* -es, -e (*Bot*) rape.

Raps|öl *nt* rape(seed) oil.

Raptus *m* -, -se (*Med*) fit, raptus (*spec*).

Rapunzel *f* -, -n **(a)** (*Bot*) corn salad, lamb's lettuce. **(b)** (*Märchen*) Rapunzel.

Rapunzelsalat *m* corn salad.

rar *adj* rare ◆ **sich ~ machen** (*inf*) to keep *or* stay away; (*sich zurückziehen*) to make oneself scarce.

Rarität *f* rarity.

Raritäten-: ~händler *m* dealer in rare objects; **~kabinett** *nt* collection of rare objects *or* curios.

rasant *adj* **(a)** *Schuß-, Flugbahn* level, flat.
(b) (*inf*) *Tempo, Spurt* terrific, lightning *attr* (*inf*); *Auto, Fahrer* fast; *Aufstieg, Karriere* meteoric; *Entwicklung, Zerfall* rapid ◆ **das ist vielleicht ein ~es Auto** this car really can shift (*inf*); **sie fuhr ~ die Straße hinunter** she tore *or* raced down the street; **sie haben das Presto in ~em Tempo gespielt** they really raced *or* rattled (*inf*) through the presto.
(c) (*inf: imponierend*) *Frau* vivacious; *Leistung* terrific.

Rasanz *f, no pl* **(a)** (*Mil*) levelness, flatness.
(b) (*inf: Geschwindigkeit*) speed ◆ **er jagte mit unheimlicher ~ davon** he tore off at a terrific speed *or* lick (*inf*); **er nahm die Kurve mit gekonnter ~** he took the bend fast and well *or* with daredevil skill; **etw mit ~ tun** to do sth in great style.

rasch [1] *adj* **(a)** (*schnell*) quick, rapid, swift; *Tempo* great.
(b) (*übereilt*) rash, (over-)hasty.
[2] *adv* **(a)** quickly, rapidly, swiftly ◆ **nicht so ~!** not so fast *or* quick; **~ machen** to hurry (up), to get a move on (*inf*); **ich habe so ~ wie möglich gemacht** I was as quick *or* fast as I could be; **ein bißchen ~, bitte!** make it quick, be quick.
(b) mit etw ~ bei der Hand sein to be rash *or* (over-)hasty about sth, to be too quick off the mark with sth (*inf*).

rascheln *vi* to rustle ◆ **es raschelt (im Stroh/Laub)** there's something rustling (in the straw/leaves); **mit etw ~** to rustle sth.

Raschheit *f* **(a)** quickness, rapidity, swiftness. **(b)** (*Übereiltheit*) rashness, (over-)hastiness.

rasen *vi* **(a)** (*wüten, toben*) to rave; (*Sturm*) to rage ◆ **er raste vor Schmerz/Wut** he was going wild with pain/he was mad with rage; **er raste vor Eifersucht** he was half-crazed with jealousy; **die Zuschauer rasten vor Begeisterung** the spectators were/went wild with excitement.
(b) *aux sein* (*sich schnell bewegen*) to race, to tear; (*Puls*) to race ◆ **der Rennwagen raste in die Menge/gegen einen Baum** the racing car crashed *or* smashed into the crowd/a tree; **das Auto raste in den Fluß** the car crashed into the river; **ras doch nicht so!** (*inf*) don't go so fast!; **die Zeit rast** time flies.
(c) *aux sein* (*inf: herumhetzen*) to race *or* run around.

Rasen *m* -s, - lawn, grass *no indef art, no pl*; (*von Sportplatz*) turf, grass; (*Sportplatz*) field, pitch; (*Tennis*) court ◆ **einen ~ anlegen** to lay a lawn; **„bitte den ~ nicht betreten"** "please keep off the grass"; **jetzt deckt ihn der kühle** *or* **grüne ~ zu** (*liter*) now he lies beneath the green sward (*liter*); **unter dem grünen ~ ruhen** (*liter*) to be at rest in God's green acre (*liter*).

Rasen-: ~bank *f* grassy bank; **r~bedeckt, r~bewachsen** *adj* grassy, grass-covered, covered with grass.

rasend [1] *adj* **(a)** (*enorm*) terrific; *Eile auch* tearing; *Hunger, Durst auch* raging; *Beifall auch* wild, rapturous; *Eifersucht* burning; *Schmerz auch* excruciating ◆ **~e Kopfschmerzen** a splitting headache.
(b) (*wütend*) furious, livid, raging ◆ **jdn ~ machen** to make sb furious *or* livid *or* wild (*inf*); **er macht mich noch ~** he'll drive me crazy; **ich könnte ~ werden** I could scream; **es ist zum R~werden** it's absolutely infuriating *or* maddening.
[2] *adv* (*inf*) terrifically, enormously; *weh tun, sich beeilen, applaudieren* like mad (*inf*) *or* crazy (*inf*); *lieben, verliebt, eifersüchtig sein* madly (*inf*) ◆ **~ viel Geld** heaps *or* pots of money (*inf*); **~ gern!** I'd simply love to!

Rasende(r) *mf decl as adj* madman/madwoman, maniac.

Rasen-: ~fläche *f* lawn; **~mäher** *m*, **~mähmaschine** *f* lawn-mower; **~platz** *m* (*Ftbl etc*) field, pitch; (*Tennis*) grass court; **~spiel** *nt* (*Sport*) *game played on grass*, outdoor game; **~sport** *m sport played on grass*, outdoor sport; **~sprenger** *m* -s, - (lawn) sprinkler; **~stück** *nt* patch of grass; **~walze** *f* (lawn) roller.

Raser(in *f*) *m* -s, - (*inf*) speed maniac (*inf*) *or* merchant (*inf*).

Raserei *f* **(a)** (*Wut*) fury, rage, frenzy. **(b)** (*inf: schnelles Fahren, Gehen*) mad rush.

Rasier- *in cpds* shaving; **~apparat** *m* razor; (*elektrisch auch*) shaver; **~creme** *f* shaving cream.

rasieren* [1] *vt* **(a)** to shave ◆ **sich ~ lassen** to have a shave; **sie rasiert sich** (*dat*) **die Beine** she shaves her legs. **(b)** (*inf: streifen*) to scrape.
[2] *vr* to (have a) shave ◆ **sich naß/trocken ~** to have a wet shave/to use an electric shaver.

Rasier-: ~klinge *f* razor blade; **~messer** *nt* (open) razor, cut-throat razor; **~pinsel** *m* shaving brush; **~schale** *f* shaving mug; **~schaum** *m* shaving foam; **~seife** *f* shaving soap; **~wasser** *nt* aftershave/pre-shave (lotion); **~zeug** *nt* shaving things *pl or* tackle (*inf*) *or* equipment.

Räson [rɛ'zõ:] *f* -, *no pl* **er will keine ~ annehmen** he refuses to *or* won't listen to reason; **jdn zur ~ bringen** to make sb listen to reason, to make sb see sense.

räsonieren* *vi* (*old*) to grumble.

Raspel *f* -, -n **(a)** (*Holzfeile*) rasp. **(b)** (*Cook*) grater.

raspeln *vt* to grate; *Holz* to rasp; *siehe* **Süßholz.**

raß, räß *adj* (*S Ger, Sw*) *Most, Speise* sharp; *Witz* earthy; *Pferd* fiery; *Kellnerin* buxom; (*Sw*) *Mensch* wild.

Rasse *f* -, -n (*Menschen~*) race; (*Tier~*) breed; (*fig*) spirit, hot-bloodedness ◆ **das Mädchen hat ~** she's a hot-blooded girl; **das Pferd/der Hund hat ~** that horse/dog has spirit.

Rasse-: ~hund *m* pedigree *or* thoroughbred dog; **~katze** *f* pedigree cat.

Rassel *f* -, -n rattle.

Rasselbande *f* (*dated inf*) mischievous bunch (*inf*).

rasseln *vi* **(a)** to rattle ◆ **mit** *or* **an etw** (*dat*) **~** to rattle sth. **(b)** *aux sein* (*inf*) **durch eine Prüfung ~** to flunk an exam (*inf*).

Rassen- *in cpds* racial; ⚠**~bewußtsein** *nt* racial consciousness; **~diskriminierung** *f* racial discrimination; **~doktrin** *f* racial doctrine; **~forschung** *f* ethnogeny (*form*), racial research; **~frage** *f* race *or* racial problem; ⚠**~haß** *m* race *or* racial hatred; **~hygiene** *f* (*NS*) eugenics *sing*; **r~hygienisch** *adj* (*NS*) eugenical; **~kampf** *m* racial struggle; **~konflikt** *m* racial conflict; **~krawall** *m* race *or* racial riot; **~kreuzung** *f* (*von Tieren*) cross-breeding; (*Tier*) crossbreed, crossbred; **~kunde** *f* ethnogeny (*form*), study of race; **~merkmal** *nt* racial characteristic; **~mischung** *f* mixture of races; (*bei Tieren*) cross-breeding; (*Tier*) crossbreed, crossbred; **~problem** *nt siehe* **~frage**; **~schande** *f Nazi term for sexual relations with a non-Aryan*; **~schranke** *f* racial barrier, barrier of race; (*Farbige betreffend*) colour bar; **~theorie** *f* racial theory, theory of race; **~trennung** *f* racial segregation; **~unruhen** *pl* racial disturbances *pl*; **~vorurteil** *nt* racial prejudice; **~vorurteile haben** to be racially biased.

Rasse-: ~pferd *nt* thoroughbred (horse); **r~rein** *adj siehe* **reinrassig**; **~reinheit** *f* racial purity; **~vieh** *nt* thoroughbred *or* pure-bred animal(s).

rassig *adj Pferd, Auto* sleek; *Frau* vivacious and hot-blooded; *Erscheinung, Gesichtszüge* sharp, striking; *Wein* spirited, lively; *Zigeuner, Spanier* fiery, hot-blooded.

rassisch *adj* racial ◆ **jdn ~ verfolgen** to persecute sb because of his/her race.

Rassismus *m* racialism, racism.

Rassist(in *f*) *m* racist.

rassistisch *adj* racialist, racist.

Rast *f* -, *no pl* rest, repose (*liter*) ◆ **~ machen** to stop (to eat); (*Mil*) to make a halt; **die schöne Aussicht lädt zur ~** (*liter*) the beautiful view invites repose (*liter*); **er gönnt sich keine ~** he won't rest, he allows himself no respite; **ohne ~ und Ruh** (*liter*) without pause for rest, without respite.

Rastalocken *pl* dreadlocks *pl*.

Raste *f* -, -n notch.

rasten *vi* to rest; (*Mil*) to make a halt ◆ **er hat nicht gerastet und geruht, bis ...** (*liter*) he did not rest until ...; **wer rastet, der rostet** (*Prov*) you have to keep active; you have to keep in practice.

Raster *nt* -s, - (*Archit*) grid; (*Typ*) halftone *or* raster screen; (*Phot: Gitter*) screen; (*TV*) raster; (*fig*) framework ◆ **es paßt nicht in das ~, es fällt durch das ~** it doesn't fit into the scheme of things; **ein grobes ~** (*fig*) a rough criterion.

Raster-: ~ätzung *f* halftone (engraving); **~bild** *nt* (*Typ*) halftone picture; (*TV*) frame; **~druck** *m* (*Typ*) halftone printing; **~fahndung** *f* computer search.

rastern *vt* (*Typ*) to print in halftone; (*TV*) to scan.

Rasterpunkt *m* (*Typ*) (halftone) dot; (*TV*) picture element; (*Typ*) halftone screening.

Rasterung *f* (*TV*) scanning.

Rast-: ~haus *nt* (travellers') inn; (*an Autobahn: auch* **~hof**) service area (*including motel*); **r~los** *adj* (*unruhig*) restless; (*unermüdlich*) tireless, untiring; **r~los tätig sein** to work tirelessly *or* ceaselessly; **~losigkeit** *f* restlessness; **~platz** *m* resting place, place to rest; (*an Autostraßen*) picnic area; **~stätte** *f* service area, services *pl*.

Rasur *f* **(a)** (*Bart~*) shave; (*das Rasieren*) shaving. **(b)** (*radierte Stelle*) erasure.

▼ **Rat** *m* -(e)s **(a)** *pl* **Ratschläge** (*Empfehlung*) advice *no pl*, counsel *no pl* (*liter*) ◆ **ein ~** a piece of advice; **jdm einen ~ geben** to give sb a piece of advice; **jdm den ~ geben, etw zu tun** to advise sb to do sth; **jdn um ~ fragen, sich** (*dat*) **bei jdm ~ holen** to ask sb's advice *or* sb for advice; **gegen jds ~ handeln** to go against *or* act against *or* ignore sb's advice; **auf jds ~** (*acc*) **(hin)** on *or* following sb's advice; **jdm mit ~ und Tat beistehen** *or* **zur Seite stehen** to support sb *or* back sb up in (both) word and deed; **da ist guter ~ teuer** it's hard to know what to do.
(b) *no pl* (*Beratung*) **mit jdm zu ~e gehen** (*liter*) to seek sb's advice, to consult sb; **ich muß erst mit mir zu ~e gehen** I'll have to consider it first; **jdn/etw zu ~e ziehen** to consult sb/sth; **einen Anwalt/Arzt zu ~e ziehen** to take legal/medical advice, to consult a lawyer/doctor; **einen Kollegen zu ~e ziehen** to get a second opinion, to consult a colleague; **mit jdm ~ halten** (*liter*) *or* **pflegen** (*liter*) to take counsel with sb (*liter*).
(c) *no pl* (*Abhilfe*) **~ (für etw) wissen** to know what to do (about sth); **~ schaffen** (*liter*) to show what is to be done; **sie wußte sich** (*dat*) **keinen ~ mehr** she was at her wits' end; **sich** (*dat*) **keinen ~ mit etw wissen** not to know what to do about sth.
(d) *pl* ¨e (*Körperschaft*) council; (*Sowjet*) soviet ◆ **der ~ der Gemeinde/Stadt** ≃ the district council; **der Große ~** (*Sw*) the cantonal parliament; **der Hohe ~** (*Bibl*) the Sanhedrin; **den ~ einberufen** to call a council meeting; **im ~ sitzen** to be on the council.
(e) *pl* ¨e (*Person*) senior official; *siehe* **wissenschaftlich, geheim.**

⚠: for details of spelling reform, see supplement

➤ SPRACHE AKTIV: **Rat: a** → 28.1, 29.1, 29.2, 38.3

Rate *f* **-, -n** instalment *(Brit)*, installment *(US)* ◆ **auf ~n kaufen** to buy in instalments *or* on hire purchase *(Brit) or* on the installment plan *(US)*; **in ~n zahlen** to pay in instalments.

▼ **raten** *pret* **riet**, *ptp* **geraten** *vti* **(a)** *(Ratschläge geben)* to advise ◆ **jdm gut/richtig/schlecht ~** to give sb good/correct/bad advice; **jdm zu etw ~** to recommend sth to sb, to advise sb to do/take/buy *etc* sth; **jdm ~, etw nicht zu tun** to advise sb not to do sth, to advise sb against doing sth; **zu dieser langen Reise kann ich dir nicht ~** I must advise you against making this long journey; **das würde ich dir nicht ~** I wouldn't advise *or* recommend it; **das möchte ich dir nicht ~** *or* **geraten haben** I wouldn't advise *or* recommend it, I wouldn't if I were you; **das möchte ich dir auch geraten haben!** you better had *(inf)*, see that you do/are *(inf)*; **was** *or* **wozu ~ Sie mir?** what do you advise *or* recommend?; **laß dir ~!** take some advice, be advised; **ich weiß mir nicht zu ~** *(old)* I'm at a loss; **wem nicht zu ~ ist, dem ist auch nicht zu helfen** *(prov)* a bit of advice never hurt anybody; **ich halte es für geraten** I think it would be advisable.
(b) *(erraten, herausfinden)* to guess; *Kreuzworträtsel etc* to solve, to do ◆ **hin und her ~** to make all sorts of guesses; **rate mal!** (have a) guess; **dreimal darfst du ~** I'll give you three guesses *(auch iro)*; **das rätst du nie!** you'll never guess!; **(gut) geraten!** good guess!; **falsch geraten!** wrong!; **das kann ich nur ~** I can only make a guess, I can only guess at it; **das hab' ich nur so geraten** I was only guessing, it was only a guess.

Raten-: **~kauf** *m (Kaufart)* hire purchase *(Brit)*, HP *(Brit inf)*, the installment plan *(US)*; **durch viele ~käufe** by buying a lot of items on hire purchase *etc*; **r~sparen** *vi sep infin only siehe* **prämiensparen**; **~sparvertrag** *m (Fin)* premium-aided saving; **r~weise** *adv* in instalments; **~zahlung** *f (Zahlung einer Rate)* payment of an instalment; *(Zahlung in Raten)* payment by instalments.

Rater *m* **-s, -** *(inf)* guesser; *(von Rätsel)* solver of riddles.

Räteregierung *f* soviet government.

Raterei *f* **(a)** *(das Schätzen)* guessing ◆ **laß mal die ~** must we have these guessing games? **(b)** *(Rätselraten)* puzzle-solving.

Räterepublik *f* soviet republic *(esp in Bavaria 1919)*.

Ratespiel *nt* guessing game; *(TV)* quiz; *(Beruferaten etc auch)* panel game.

Rat-: **~geber** *m* adviser, counsellor *(form)*; **~haus** *nt* town hall; *(einer Großstadt)* city hall; **~haussaal** *m* council chamber; **Konzert im ~haussaal** concert in the town hall.

Ratifikation *f* ratification.

ratifizieren* *vt* to ratify.

Ratifizierung *f* ratification.

Rätin *f siehe* **Rat (e)**.

Ratio ['ra:tsio] *f* **-**, *no pl* reason ◆ **es ist ein Gebot der ~, zu ...** reason demands that ..., it's only rational to ...

Ration [ra'tsio:n] *f* ration ◆ **jeder bekommt eine bestimmte ~** everyone gets fixed rations; **eiserne ~** iron rations *pl*.

rational [ratsio'na:l] *adj* rational.

rationalisieren* [ratsionali'zi:rən] *vti* to rationalize.

Rationalisierung [ratsionali'zi:rʊŋ] *f* rationalization.

Rationalisierungs-: **~fachmann** *m* efficiency expert, time and motion (study) expert *or* man; **~maßnahme** *f* rationalization *or* efficiency measure; **~schutz** *m* job protection measures *pl*.

Rationalismus [ratsiona'lɪsmʊs] *m* rationalism.

Rationalist [ratsiona'lɪst] *m* rationalist.

rationalistisch [ratsiona'lɪstɪʃ] *adj* rationalist(ic).

Rationalität [ratsionali'tɛ:t] *f* rationality; *(Leistungsfähigkeit)* efficiency.

rationell [ratsio'nɛl] *adj* efficient.

rationenweise [ratsio:nən-] *adv* in rations.

rationieren* [ratsio'ni:rən] *vt* to ration.

Rationierung [ratsio'ni:rʊŋ] *f* rationing.

Rationierungssystem *nt* rationing system.

rationsweise [ratsi'o:ns-] *adv siehe* **rationenweise**.

ratlos *adj* helpless ◆ **ich bin völlig ~(, was ich tun soll)** I'm at a complete loss (as to what to do), I just don't know what to do; **~e Eltern** parents who are at a loss to know what to do with their children; **sie machte ein ~es Gesicht** she looked helpless *or* at a loss; **einer Sache** *(dat)* **~ gegenüberstehen** to be at a loss when faced with sth; **sie sahen sich ~ an** they looked at each other helplessly.

Ratlosigkeit *f* helplessness ◆ **in meiner ~** ... not knowing what to do ..., being at a loss ...

Rätoromane *m* Rhaetian.

rätoromanisch *adj* Rhaetian; *Sprache* Rhaeto-Romanic.

Rätoromanisch(e) *nt* Rhaeto-Romanic; *siehe auch* **Deutsch(e)**.

ratsam *adj* advisable ◆ **ich halte es für ~, das zu tun** I think it (would be) advisable to do that.

⚠ **Ratsbeschluß** *m* decision of the local council.

ratsch *interj* rip.

Ratsche, Rätsche *f* **-, -n** *(S Ger, Aus)* rattle.

ratschen, rätschen *vi (S Ger, Sw)* **(a)** *(mit der Ratsche)* to rattle. **(b)** *(inf: schwatzen)* to blather *(inf)*.

▼ **Ratschlag** *m* piece *or* bit of advice ◆ **ein guter ~** a good piece of advice, good advice; **Ratschläge** advice; **drei Ratschläge** three pieces of advice; **deine klugen Ratschläge kannst du dir sparen** keep your advice for yourself; **jdm einen ~ geben** *or* **erteilen** to give sb a piece of advice *or* some advice.

ratschlagen *vi insep* to deliberate, to consult (together).

⚠ **Ratschluß** *m (liter)* decision ◆ **Gottes ~** the will of God; **Gottes unerforschlichem ~ hat es gefallen** ... it has pleased the Lord in his mysterious wisdom ...

Ratsdiener *m (old)* (town hall) porter.

Rätsel *nt* **-s, - (a)** riddle; *(Kreuzwort~)* crossword (puzzle); *(Silben~, Bilder~ etc)* puzzle ◆ **jdm ein ~ aufgeben** to give *or* ask sb a riddle; **das plötzliche Verschwinden des Zeugen gab der Polizei ~ auf** the sudden disappearance of the witness baffled the police.
(b) *(fig: Geheimnis)* riddle, mystery, enigma *(um* of) ◆ **die Polizei konnte das ~ lösen** the police have solved the riddle *or* mystery; **vor einem ~ stehen** to be faced with a riddle *or* mystery, to be baffled; **es ist mir ein ~, wie ...** it's a mystery to me how ..., it baffles *or* beats *(inf)* me how ...; **er ist mir ein ~** he's a mystery *or* an enigma to me; **in ~n sprechen** to talk in riddles; **das ist des ~s Lösung!** that's the answer.

Rätsel-: **~ecke** *f* puzzle corner; **~frage** *f (Quizfrage)* question; **r~haft** *adj* mysterious; *Gesichtsausdruck, Lächeln auch* enigmatic; **auf r~hafte Weise** mysteriously; **es ist mir r~haft** it's a mystery to me, it baffles me; **~haftigkeit** *f* mysteriousness; **~heft** *nt* puzzle book; **~löser** *m* **-s, -** puzzle-solver.

rätseln *vi* to puzzle (over sth), to rack one's brains.

Rätsel-: **~raten** *nt* guessing game; **~raten ist nicht meine starke Seite** guessing isn't/guessing games aren't my forte; **r~voll** *adj (geh)* mysterious; **~zeitung** *f siehe* **~heft**.

Rats-: **~herr** *m* councillor *(esp Brit)*, councilman *(US)*; **~keller** *m* rathskeller *(US) (cellar bar/restaurant under the town hall)*; **~sitzung** *f* council meeting; **~stube** *f bar/restaurant near the town hall*.

⚠ **ratsuchend** *adj* seeking advice ◆ **sich ~ an jdn wenden** to turn to sb for advice; **R~e** people/those wanting *or* seeking advice.

Ratsversammlung *f* **(a)** *siehe* **Ratssitzung**. **(b)** *(Rat)* council.

Rattan *nt* **-s**, *no pl* rattan.

Ratte *f* **-, -n** rat ◆ **eine widerliche ~** *(sl)* a dirty rat *(sl)*; **die ~n verlassen das sinkende Schiff** *(prov)* the rats are leaving the sinking ship; *siehe* **schlafen**.

Ratten-: **~bekämpfung** *f* rat control; **~fänger** *m* rat-catcher; *(Hund)* ratter; *(fig)* rabble-rouser; **der ~fänger von Hameln** the Pied Piper of Hamelin; **~gift** *nt* rat poison; **~schwanz** *m* **(a)** *(lit)* rat's tail; **(b)** *usu pl (inf: Zopf)* bunch; **(c)** *(fig inf: Serie, Folge)* string.

rattern *vi (als Bewegungsverb: aux sein)* to rattle, to clatter; *(Maschinengewehr)* to chatter.

ratzekahl *adv (inf)* completely, totally ◆ **alles ~ aufessen** *(Vorräte)* to eat the cupboard bare *(inf)*; *(Portion)* to polish off the lot *(inf)*.

ratzen *vi (dial inf)* to kip *(inf)* ◆ **ich hab' vielleicht geratzt** I had a really good kip *(inf)*.

Raub *m* **-(e)s**, *no pl* **(a)** *(das Rauben)* robbery ◆ **auf ~ ausgehen** *(Tiere)* to go out hunting *or* on the prowl; *(Räuber)* to go out pillaging.
(b) *(Entführung)* abduction ◆ **der ~ der Sabinerinnen** the rape of the Sabine women.
(c) *(Beute)* booty, loot, spoils *pl* ◆ **ein ~ der Flammen werden** *(liter)* to fall victim to the flames.

Raub-: **~bau** *m, no pl* overexploitation (of natural resources); *(am Wald)* overfelling; *(an Äckern)* overcropping; *(an Weideland)* overgrazing; **~bau an etw** *(dat)* **treiben** to overexploit *etc* sth; **am Fischbestand eines Flusses ~bau treiben** to overfish a river; **mit seiner Gesundheit ~bau treiben** to ruin one's health; **~druck** *m* pirate(d) copy; *(das Drucken)* pirating.

rauben [1] *vt* **(a)** *(wegnehmen)* to steal ◆ **jdm etw ~** to rob sb of sth.
(b) *(entführen)* to abduct, to carry off.
(c) *(fig)* **jdm etw ~** to rob sb of sth; **das hat uns viel Zeit geraubt** it cost us a lot of time; **jdm einen Kuß ~** to steal a kiss from sb; **jdm die Unschuld ~** *(obs, iro)* to take sb's virginity; **du raubst mir noch die letzten Nerven!** you'll drive me mad *or* crazy *(inf)*.
[2] *vi* to rob, to plunder, to pillage.

Räuber *m* **-s, -** robber, brigand *(old)*; *(bei Banküberfall etc auch)* raider; *(Wegelagerer)* highwayman ◆ **Ali Baba und die vierzig ~** Ali Baba and the forty thieves; **unter die ~ fallen** *or* **geraten** to fall among thieves; **der Fuchs ist ein ~** the fox is a beast of prey *or* a predator; **~ und Gendarm** cops and robbers.

Räuberbande *f* robber band, band of robbers; *(pej)* bunch of thieves.

Räuberei *f (inf)* robbery.

Räuber-: **~geschichte** *f* **(a)** story about robbers; **(b)** *(fig)* cock-and-bull story *(inf)*; **~gesindel** *nt (pej)* thieving riffraff; **~hauptmann** *m* robber-chief; **~höhle** *f* **(a)** *(lit)* robbers' cave; **(b)** *(fig inf) (Spelunke)* low dive *(inf)*; *(Durcheinander)* pigsty.

räuberisch *adj* rapacious, predatory ◆ **~er Diebstahl** *(Jur) theft in which force or the threat of violence is used to remain in possession of the stolen goods*; **~e Erpressung** *(Jur)* armed robbery, *robbery using the threat of violence*; **in ~er Absicht** with intent to rob.

räubern *vi (inf)* to thieve ◆ **in der Speisekammer ~** to raid the larder.

Räuber-: **~pistole** *f siehe* **~geschichte (b)**; **~zivil** *nt (hum inf)* scruffy old clothes *pl (inf)*.

Raub-: **~fisch** *m* predatory fish, predator; **~gier** *f (liter)* rapacity; **r~gierig** *adj (liter)* rapacious; **~katze** *f* (predatory) big cat; **~kopie** *f* pirate(d) copy; **~krieg** *m* war of conquest; **der ~krieg gegen unser Land** the rape of our country; **~mord** *m* robbery with murder; **~mörder** *m* robber and murderer; **~pressung** *f* pirate(d) copy; **~ritter** *m* robber baron.

Raubtier *nt* predator, beast of prey.

Raubtier-: **~haus** *nt* lion house; **~käfig** *m* lion's/tiger's *etc* cage.

Raub-: **~überfall** *m* robbery; *(auf Bank etc auch)* raid; **einen ~überfall auf jdn**

begehen to hold sb up; „~überfall auf Taxifahrer" "taxi-driver attacked and robbed"; ~vogel *m* bird of prey, predator; ~wild *nt* (*Hunt*) predatory game; ~zeug *nt* (*Hunt*) vermin *pl*; ~zug *m* series *sing* of robberies; (*pej: Angriffskrieg*) rape (*nach, gegen* of); (*von Tieren*) hunting excursion; auf ~zug gehen (*Einbrecher*) to commit a series of robberies; (*Tier*) to go hunting *or* on the prowl.

Rauch *m* **-(e)s,** *no pl* smoke; (*giftig auch*) fumes *pl* ♦ in ~ und Flammen aufgehen to go up in smoke *or* flames; in ~ aufgehen (*lit, fig*), sich in ~ auflösen (*fig*) to go up in smoke; Würste in den ~ hängen to hang sausages up to smoke; kein ~ ohne Feuer (*Prov*) there's no smoke without fire (*prov*).

Rauch-: ~abzug *m* smoke outlet; r~arm *adj* smokeless; r~bar *adj* smok(e)able; hast du was ~bares? have you got anything to smoke?; ~bildung *f siehe* ~entwicklung; ~bombe *f* smoke bomb.

rauchen [1] *vi* (*Rauch abgeben*) to smoke, to give off smoke ♦ sie sah, daß es in unserer Küche rauchte she saw smoke in/coming from our kitchen; mir raucht der Kopf my head's spinning.
[2] *vti* to smoke ♦ möchten Sie ~? do you want to smoke?; (*Zigarette anbietend*) would you like a smoke *or* a cigarette?; nach dem Essen rauche ich gern I like a *or* to smoke after a meal; eine ~ to have a smoke; hast du was zu ~? have you got a smoke?; „R~ verboten" "no smoking"; sich (*dat*) das R~ an-/abgewöhnen to take up/give up smoking; viel *or* stark ~ to be a heavy smoker, to smoke a lot; ~ Sie? do you smoke?

Rauchentwicklung *f* production *or* formation of smoke ♦ mit großer/geringer ~ with high/low smoke levels.

Raucher *m* **-s, -** (a) smoker. (b) (*Rail: ~abteil*) smoker, smoking compartment.

Räucher|aal *m* smoked eel.

Raucher-: ~abteil *nt* smoking compartment, smoker; ~bein *nt* hardening of the arteries (in the leg) (*caused by smoking*).

Räucher-: ⚠~faß *nt* (*Eccl*) censer; ~gefäß *nt* incense burner; ~hering *m* kipper, smoked herring.

Raucherhusten *m* smoker's cough.

Raucherin *f* smoker.

Räucher-: ~kammer *f* smoking chamber, smokehouse; ~kerze *f* incense cone; ~lachs *m* smoked salmon.

räuchern [1] *vt* to smoke.
[2] *vi* (*inf: mit Weihrauch*) to burn incense.

Räucher-: ~schinken *m* smoked ham; ~speck *m* ≃ smoked bacon; ~stäbchen *nt* joss stick; ~waren *pl* smoked foods *pl*.

Rauch-: ~fahne *f* smoke trail, trail of smoke; ~fang *m* (a) (~*abzug*) chimney hood; (b) (*Aus*) chimney; ~fangkehrer *m* (*Aus*) (chimney) sweep; r~farben, r~farbig *adj* smoke-coloured; ⚠~faß *nt* (*Eccl*) censer; ~fleisch *nt* smoked meat; r~frei *adj* smokeless; ~gase *pl* fumes *pl*; ~gasentschwefelung *f* flue gas desulphurization; ~gasentschwefelungsanlage *f* flue gas desulphurization plant; r~geschwängert *adj* smoke-filled, heavy with smoke; r~geschwärzt *adj* blackened by smoke, smoke-blackened; ~glas *nt* smoked glass; ~glocke *f* pall of smoke.

rauchig *adj* smoky.

Rauch-: r~los *adj* smokeless; ~pilz *m* mushroom cloud; ~quarz *m* smoky quartz, cairngorm; ~salon *m* smoking *or* smoke room; ~säule *f* column *or* pillar of smoke; ~schleier *m* veil of smoke; ~schwaden *pl* drifts of smoke *pl*; ~schwalbe *f* swallow; ~service *nt* smoker's set; ~signal *nt* smoke signal; ~tabak *m* (*form*) tobacco; ~tisch(chen *nt*) *m* smoker's table; ~topas *m siehe* ~quarz; ~utensilien *pl* smoker's requisites *pl*; ~verbot *nt* smoking ban, ban on smoking; hier herrscht ~verbot smoking is not allowed here, there's no smoking here; ~vergiftung *f* fume poisoning; eine ~vergiftung erleiden to be overcome by fumes; ~verzehrer *m* **-s, -** smoke dispeller, *small, often ornamental device for neutralizing tobacco smoke*; ~vorhang *m*, ~wand *f* smokescreen; ~waren[1] *pl* tobacco (products *pl*); ~waren[2] *pl* (*Pelze*) furs *pl*; ~warenhändler *m* furrier; ~wolke *f* cloud of smoke; ~zeichen *nt* smoke signal; ~zimmer *nt* smoking *or* smoke room.

Räude *f* **-, -n** (*Vet*) mange.

räudig *adj* mangy ♦ du ~er Hund! (*old inf*) you dirty dog!

rauf *adv* (*inf*) ~! (get) up!; *siehe* herauf, hinauf.

Raufbold *m* **-(e)s, -e** (*dated*) ruffian, roughneck.

Raufe *f* **-, -n** hay rack.

raufen [1] *vt Unkraut* to pull up; *Flachs* to pull ♦ sich (*dat*) die Haare ~ to tear (at) one's hair.
[2] *vir* to scrap, to fight.

Rauferei *f* scrap, rough-house (*inf*) ♦ nur eine harmlose ~ just a harmless little scrap.

Rauf-: ~handel *m* (*old, form*) affray (*form*); ~lust *f* pugnacity; r~lustig *adj* ready for a fight *or* scrap, pugnacious.

⚠**rauh** *adj* (a) rough ♦ eine ~e Schale haben (*fig*) to be a rough diamond.
(b) *Hals, Kehle* sore; *Stimme* husky; (*heiser*) hoarse; (*unfreundlich*) rough.
(c) (*nicht mild, streng*) *Wetter* rough, raw; *Wind, Luft* raw; *See* rough; *Klima, Winter* harsh, raw; (*unwirtlich*) *Gebiet* bleak, stark; *Stadt* tough ♦ im ~en Norden in the rugged north; (die) ~e Wirklichkeit harsh reality, the hard facts *pl*; hier herrschen ja ~e Methoden their/his *etc* methods are brutal.
(d) (*barsch, grob*) *Benehmen, Wesen* rough; (*hart*) *Mann* tough, rugged; *Sitten auch* rough-and-ready; *Ton, Worte, Behandlung auch* harsh ♦ ~, aber herzlich bluff; *Begrüßung, Ton* rough but jovial; er ist ~, aber herzlich he's a rough diamond; in unserer Familie geht es ~, aber herzlich zu we're a pretty hale and hearty lot in our family.

(e) (*inf*) in ~en Mengen by the ton (*inf*), galore (*inf*); Zucker in ~en Mengen sugar by the ton, sugar galore.

⚠**Rauh-:** ~bein *nt* (*inf*) rough diamond; r~beinig *adj* (*inf*) rough-and-ready.

⚠**Rauheit** *f, no pl siehe adj* (a) roughness. (b) soreness; huskiness; hoarseness; roughness. (c) roughness, rawness; rawness; roughness; harshness; bleakness; toughness. (d) roughness; toughness; rough-and-readiness; harshness.

⚠**rauhen** *vt siehe* aufrauhen.

⚠**Rauh-:** ~fasertapete *f* woodchip paper; ~futter *nt* roughage; ~haardackel *m* wire-haired dachshund; r~haarig *adj* coarse-haired; *Hund auch* wire-haired; *Fell, Wolle* coarse; ~putz *m* roughcast; ~reif *m* hoarfrost, white frost; (*gefrorener Nebel*) rime.

Raum *m* **-(e)s, Räume** (a) *no pl* (*Platz*) room, space; (*Weite*) expanse ♦ ~ schaffen to make some space *or* room; auf engstem ~ leben to live in a very confined space; einer Sache (*dat*) ~ geben (*geh*) to yield to sth; eine Frage in den ~ stellen to pose a question; eine Frage im ~ stehen lassen to leave a question unresolved *or* hanging.
(b) (*Spielraum*) room, scope.
(c) (*Zimmer*) room.
(d) (*Gebiet, Bereich*) area; (*fig*) sphere ♦ der ~ Frankfurt the Frankfurt area; im geistigen ~ in the intellectual sphere; ~ gewinnen (*Mil, fig*) to gain ground.
(e) *no pl* (*Phys, Space*) space *no art* ♦ der offene *or* leere ~ the void; *siehe* luftleer.

Raum-: ~anzug *m* spacesuit; ~aufteilung *f* floor plan; ~ausstatter(in *f*) *m* **-s, -** interior decorator; ~bild *nt* stereoscopic *or* 3-D picture; ~bildverfahren *nt* stereoscopy.

Räumboot *nt* minesweeper.

Raum|einheit *f* unit of volume.

räumen [1] *vt* (a) (*verlassen*) *Gebäude, Gebiet* to clear, to evacuate; (*Mil: Truppen*) to move out of, to withdraw from; *Wohnung* to vacate, to move out of; *Hotelzimmer* to vacate, to check out of; *Sitzplatz* to vacate, to give up ♦ wir müssen die Wohnung bis Mittwoch ~ we have to be out of the flat by Wednesday; *siehe* Feld.
(b) (*leeren*) *Gebäude, Straße, Warenlager* to clear (*von* of) ♦ „wir ~" "clearance sale"; wegen Einsturzgefahr mußte das Gebäude geräumt werden the building had to be evacuated *or* cleared because of the danger of it collapsing.
(c) (*woanders hinbringen*) to shift, to move; (*entfernen*) *Schnee, Schutt auch* to clear (away); *Minen* to clear; (*auf See*) to sweep, to clear ♦ räum deine Sachen in den Schrank put your things away in the cupboard; er hat seine Sachen aus dem Schrank geräumt he cleared his things out of the cupboard; *siehe* Weg.
[2] *vi* (*auf~*) to clear up; (*um~*) to rearrange things ♦ in etw (*dat*) ~ to rummage around in sth.

Raum-: ~entweser *m* **-s, -** (*form*) pest exterminator; ~ersparnis *f* space-saving; aus Gründen der ~ersparnis to save space, for reasons of space; ~fähre *f* space shuttle; ~fahrer *m* spaceman, astronaut; (*sowjetisch*) cosmonaut.

Raumfahrt *f* space travel *no art or* flight *no art* ♦ die Ausgaben für die ~ erhöhen to increase the space budget; mit der Entwicklung der ~ with the development of space technology; das Zeitalter der ~ the space age.

Raumfahrt- *in cpds* space; ~behörde *f* space authority; ~ingenieur *m* astronautical engineer; ~medizin *f* space medicine; ~programm *nt* space programme; ~station *f* space station; ~technik *f* space technology; ~zeitalter *nt* space age; ~zentrum *nt* space centre.

Raumfahrzeug *nt* spacecraft.

Räumfahrzeug *nt* bulldozer; (*für Schnee*) snow-clearer.

Raum-: ~flug *m* space flight; (*Forschungsflug auch*) space mission; ~forschung *f* space research; ~gestaltung *f* interior design; ~gewinn *m* extra space gained; der ~gewinn war nicht sehr groß we didn't gain much space; ~gitter *nt* (*Min*) (crystal *or* space) lattice; ~gleiter *m* orbiter; r~greifend *adj* far-reaching, extensive; eine r~greifende Skulptur a sculpture of great presence; ~inhalt *m* volume, (cubic) capacity; ~kapsel *f* space capsule; ~klang *m* stereoscopic sound; ~labor *nt* space lab; ~lehre *f* geometry.

räumlich *adj* (a) (*den Raum betreffend*) spatial ♦ ~e Verhältnisse physical conditions; ~e Nähe physical closeness, spatial proximity; wir wohnen ~ sehr beengt we live in very cramped conditions; rein ~ ist das unmöglich (just) from the point of view of space it's impossible.
(b) (*dreidimensional*) three-dimensional ♦ ~es Anschauungsvermögen capacity to think in three dimensions; ~ sehen to see in three dimensions *or* three-dimensionally; ich kann mir das nicht ~ vorstellen I can't really picture it.

Räumlichkeit *f* (a) *no pl* three-dimensionality. (b) ~en *pl* premises *pl* ♦ dazu fehlen uns die ~en our premises aren't big enough.

Raum-: ~mangel *m* lack of space *or* room; ~maß *nt* unit of volume; ~meter *m or nt* cubic metre (*of stacked wood*); ~mission *f* space mission; ~not *f* shortage of space; ~ordnung *f* environmental planning; ~ordnungsplan *m* development plan; ~pflegerin *f* cleaner, cleaning lady.

Räumpflug *m* snowplough, snowplow (*US*).

Raum-: ~planung *f* (*das Planen*) development planning; (*Plan*) development plan; ~schiff *nt* spaceship; ~schiffahrt *f siehe* ~fahrt; ~sonde *f* space probe; ⚠r~sparend *adj siehe* platzsparend; ~station *f* space station; ~transporter *m* space shuttle.

Räumtrupp *m* clearance gang *or* workers *pl*.

⚠: for details of spelling reform, see supplement

Räumung *f* clearing; (*von Wohnung, Gebäude*) vacation; (*wegen Gefahr etc*) evacuation; (*unter Zwang*) eviction; (*von Lager, Vorräten, Geschäft*) clearance ◆ **„wegen ~ alle Preise radikal herabgesetzt!"** "all prices reduced to clear".
Räumungs-: ~arbeiten *pl* clearance operations *pl*; **~befehl** *m* eviction order; **~frist** *f* (period of) notice; **~klage** *f* action for eviction; **~verkauf** *m* clearance sale.
Raumverschwendung *f* waste of space.
raunen *vti* (*liter*) to whisper ◆ **es ging ein R~ durch die Menge** a murmur went through the crowd.
raunzen *vi* (*inf: S Ger, Aus*) to grouse (*inf*), to grouch (*inf*).
Raunzer *m* **-s, -** (*inf: S Ger, Aus*) grouse(r) (*inf*), grouch(er) (*inf*).
Raupe *f* **-, -n** **(a)** caterpillar. **(b)** (*Planier~*) caterpillar; (*Kette*) caterpillar track *or* tread.
Raupen-: ~fahrzeug *nt* caterpillar (vehicle); **~kette** *f* caterpillar track; **~schlepper** *m* caterpillar (tractor).
raus *adv* (*inf*) **~!** (get) out!; *siehe* **heraus, hinaus.**
Rausch *m* **-(e)s, Räusche** **(a)** (*Trunkenheit*) intoxication, inebriation; (*Drogen~*) state of euphoria, high (*sl*) ◆ **sich** (*dat*) **einen ~ antrinken** to get drunk; **einen ~ haben** to be drunk; **etw im ~ tun/sagen** to do/say sth under the influence *or* while one is drunk; **seinen ~ ausschlafen** to sleep it off.
(b) (*liter: Ekstase*) ecstasy, transport (*liter*), rapture; (*Blut~, Mord~ etc*) frenzy ◆ **im ~ der Leidenschaft** inflamed with passion; **im ~ der Gefühle** in an ecstasy of emotion; **der ~ der Geschwindigkeit** the thrill of speed.
rausch|arm *adj* (*Rad*) low-noise.
Rauschebart *m* (*inf*) big bushy beard; (*Mann*) man with a big bushy beard, beardy (*hum inf*).
rauschen *vi* **(a)** (*Wasser, Meer, Wasserfall*) to roar; (*sanft*) to murmur; (*Brandung*) to boom, to roar; (*Baum, Wald*) to rustle; (*Wind*) to murmur; (*Seide*) to rustle, to swish; (*Korn*) to swish; (*Regen*) to pour *or* swoosh down; (*Radio, Lautsprecher etc*) to hiss; (*Muschel*) to sing; (*Applaus*) to resound ◆ **im ~den Walde** in the gently murmuring forest; **mit ~den Flügeln** with a swish or swoosh of its wings; **~de Feste** glittering parties; **eine ~e Ballnacht** a glittering ball.
(b) *aux sein* (*sich bewegen*) (*Bach*) to rush; (*Bumerang, Geschoß*) to whoosh.
(c) *aux sein* (*inf: Mensch*) to sweep ◆ **sie rauschte in das/aus dem Zimmer** she swept into/out of the room.
Rauscher *m* **-s, -** (*dial*) sweet cider (*half fermented*).
Rausch-: r~frei *adj* low-noise; **~freiheit** *f, no pl* low-noise performance.
Rauschgift *nt* drug, narcotic; (*Drogen*) drugs *pl*, narcotics *pl* ◆ **~ nehmen** to take drugs; (*regelmäßig auch*) to be on drugs.
Rauschgift-: ~dezernat *nt* narcotics *or* drug squad; **~handel** *m* drug trafficking; **~händler** *m* drug trafficker; **~sucht** *f* drug addiction; **r~süchtig** *adj* drug-addicted; **er ist r~süchtig** he's addicted to drugs, he's a drug addict; **~süchtige(r)** *mf* drug addict.
Rausch-: ~gold *nt* gold foil; **~goldengel** *m* ≃ Christmas tree fairy; **r~haft** *adj* (*fig*) ecstatic; **~mittel** *nt* (*form*) intoxicant (*form*).
raus|ekeln *vt sep* (*inf*) to freeze out (*inf*).
rausfeuern *vt sep* (*inf*) to chuck *or* sling out (*inf*).
rausfliegen *vi sep irreg aux sein* (*inf*) to be chucked *or* slung out (*inf*); (*entlassen werden auch*) to be given the boot (*inf*) *or* the push (*inf*).
rauskriegen *vt sep* (*inf*) to get out; (*herausfinden*) to find out; (*lösen können*) to be able to do.
rauspauken *vt sep* (*inf*) **jdn ~** to get sb out of trouble *or* off the hook (*inf*); **mein Anwalt hat mich rausgepaukt** my lawyer got me off.
räuspern *vr* to clear one's throat.
rausreißen *vt sep irreg* (*inf*) **jdn ~** to save sb, to save sb's bacon (*inf*), to get sb out of trouble; **der Mittelstürmer/das hat noch alles rausgerissen** the centre-forward/that saved the day.
rausschmeißen *vt sep irreg* (*inf*) to chuck *or* sling *or* kick out (*all inf*); (*entlassen auch*) to give the boot (*inf*); (*wegwerfen*) to chuck out *or* away (*inf*); *Geld* to chuck away (*inf*), to chuck down the drain (*inf*) ◆ **das ist rausgeschmissenes Geld** that's money down the drain (*inf*).
Rausschmeißer(in *f*) *m* **-s, -** (*inf*) bouncer; (*letzter Tanz*) last number *or* dance.
⚠ **Rausschmiß** *m* **-sses, -sse** (*inf*) booting out (*inf*) ◆ **man drohte uns mit dem ~** they threatened us with the boot (*inf*) *or* push (*inf*).
Raute *f* **-, -n** **(a)** (*Bot*) rue. **(b)** (*Math*) rhombus; (*Her*) lozenge.
rautenförmig *adj* rhomboid, diamond-shaped, lozenge-shaped.
Ravioli [ravi'o:li] *pl* ravioli *sing.*
Rayon [rɛ'jõ:] *m* **-s, -s** (*Aus*) department; (*old*) region.
Razzia ['ratsia] *f* **-, Razzien** ['ratsiən] raid, swoop (*inf*) ◆ **die Polizei machte in ein paar Lokalen ~** the police swooped on (*inf*) *or* raided *or* made a raid on three or four bars.
Re *nt* **-s, -s** (*Cards*) redouble ◆ **~ ansagen** to redouble.
Reader ['ri:dɐ] *m* **-s, -** (*Lehrbuch*) reader.
Reagens *nt* **-, Reagenzien** [-iən], **Reagenz** *nt* **-es, -ien** [-iən] (*Chem*) reagent.
Reagenz-: ~glas, ~röhrchen *nt* (*Chem*) test-tube.
reagieren* *vi* to react (*auf +acc* to) ◆ **auf etw** (*acc*) **verärgert ~** to react angrily to sth; **miteinander ~** (*Chem*) to react (together).
Reaktion *f* **(a)** reaction (*auf +acc* to). **(b)** (*Pol pej*) reaction ◆ **ein Vertreter der ~** a representative of reactionary thinking.
reaktionär [reaktsio'nɛ:ɐ] *adj* (*Pol pej*) reactionary.
Reaktionär(in *f*) [reaktsio'nɛ:ɐ, -ərɪn] *m* (*pej*) reactionary.
Reaktions-: ~fähigkeit *f* reactions *pl*; (*Chem*) reactivity; **Alkohol vermindert die ~fähigkeit** alcohol slows down the *or* one's reactions; **r~freudig** *adj* highly reactive; **~geschwindigkeit** *f* speed of reaction; **r~schnell** *adj* with fast reactions; **er bremste r~schnell** he reacted quickly and braked; **r~schnell sein** to have fast reactions; **r~träge** *adj* of low reactivity; **~verlauf** *m* (*Chem*) course of the reaction; **~wärme** *f* (*Chem*) heat of reaction; **~zeit** *f* reaction time.
reaktiv *adj* (*geh*) reactive ◆ **er verhält sich nur ~** he doesn't act — he only reacts.
reaktivieren* [reakti'vi:rən] *vt* (*Sci*) to reactivate; (*Agr, Biol, fig*) to revive; *Kenntnisse, Können* to brush up, to polish up; *Glieder* to rehabilitate; (*Mil*) to call up again.
Reaktivierung *f siehe vt* reactivation; revival; brushing *or* polishing up; rehabilitation; new call-up.
Reaktor *m* reactor.
Reaktor-: ~block *m* reactor block; **~kern** *m* reactor core; **~sicherheit** *f* reactor safety; **~unglück** *nt* nuclear disaster.
real *adj* real; (*wirklichkeitsbezogen*) realistic.
Real-: ~büro *nt* (*Aus*) estate agency; **~einkommen** *nt* real income; **~enzyklopädie** *f* specialist dictionary/encyclopaedia; **~gymnasium** *nt* ≃ grammar school (*Brit*), high school (*esp US*) (*stressing modern languages, maths and science*).
Realien [re'a:liən] *pl* realities *pl*, real facts *pl*; (*old Sch*) science and modern languages *pl.*
Real-: ~index *m* (*dated*) subject index; **~injurie** [-iə] *f* (*Jur*) ≃ assault.
Realisation *f* (*Verwirklichung, Fin*) realization; (*TV, Rad, Theat*) production.
realisierbar *adj* **(a)** practicable, feasible, realizable. **(b)** (*Fin*) realizable.
Realisierbarkeit *f* practicability, feasibility, realizability.
realisieren* *vt* **(a)** *Pläne, Ideen, Programm* to carry out; (*TV, Rad, Theat*) to produce. **(b)** (*Fin*) to realize; *Verkauf* to make, to conclude. **(c)** (*verstehen*) to realize.
Realisierung *f siehe* **Realisation.**
Realismus *m* realism.
Realist(in *f*) *m* realist.
realistisch *adj* realistic.
Realität *f* **(a)** reality ◆ **die ~ anerkennen** to face facts; **~en** *pl* (*Gegebenheiten*) realities *pl*, facts *pl.* **(b) ~en** *pl* (*Aus: Grundstücke*) real estate.
Realitäten-: ~händler, ~vermittler *m* (*Aus*) (real) estate agent, realtor (*US*).
Realitäts-: r~feindlich *adj* (*pej*) **r~feindlich sein** to refuse to accept the realities of the situation; **r~fern** *adj* unrealistic; **~ferne** *f* lack of contact with reality; **r~fremd** *adj* out of touch with reality; **r~nah** *adj* realistic; **~nähe** *f* realism; **~sinn** *m* sense of realism; **er hat einen gesunden ~sinn** he has a firm hold on reality.
realiter [re'a:litɐ] *adv* (*geh*) in reality, in (point of) fact.
Reality-Fernsehen, Reality-TV [ri'ælɪti-] *nt* real-life TV, reality TV (*esp US*).
Real-: ~kanzlei *f* (*Aus*) *siehe* **~büro**; **~kapital** *nt* physical assets *pl*, non-monetary capital; **~katalog** *m* subject catalogue; **~konkurrenz** *f* (*Jur*) **in ~konkurrenz mit** in conjunction with; **~kredit** *m* (*Fin*) collateral loan; **~lexikon** *nt* specialist dictionary/encyclopaedia; **~lohn** *m* real wages *pl.*
Realo *m* **-s, -s** (*Pol sl*) political realist (*of the Green Party*).
Real-: ~politik *f* political realism, Realpolitik; **~politiker** *m* political realist; **r~politisch** *adj* politically realistic, pragmatic; **~schule** *f* ≃ secondary school, secondary modern school (*Brit*); (*Aus*) ≃ grammar school (*Brit*), high school (*US*); **~schüler** *m* ≃ secondary modern pupil (*Brit*), student at secondary school (*US*); (*Aus*) ≃ grammar school pupil (*Brit*), high school student (*US*); **~wert** *m* (*Fin*) real value.
Re|animation *f* (*Med*) resuscitation.
re|animieren* *vt* (*Med*) to resuscitate.
Rebe *f* **-, -n** (*Ranke*) shoot; (*Weinstock*) vine.
Rebell(in *f*) *m* **-en, -en** rebel.
rebellieren* *vi* to rebel, to revolt.
Rebellion *f* rebellion, revolt.
rebellisch *adj* rebellious.
Rebensaft *m* (*liter*) wine, juice of the vine (*liter*), grape (*liter*).
Rebhuhn *nt* (common) partridge.
Reb-: ~laus *f* phylloxera (*spec*), vine pest; **~ling** *m* young vine; **~schnur** *f* (*Aus*) rope; **~sorte** *f* type of vine; **~stock** *m* vine.
Rebus *m or nt* **-, -se** rebus, picture puzzle.
Rechaud [re'ʃo:] *m or nt* **-s, -s** spirit burner; tea/coffee *etc* warmer; (*für Fondue*) spirit burner.
Rechen *m* **-s, -** (*S Ger*) (*Harke*) rake; (*Gitter an Bächen, Flüssen*) grill.
rechen *vt* (*S Ger*) to rake.
Rechen-: ~anlage *f* computer; **~art** *f* type of calculation; **die vier ~arten** the four arithmetical operations; **~aufgabe** *f* sum, (arithmetical) problem; **~automat** *m* (automatic) adding machine, comptometer; **~brett** *nt* abacus; **~buch** *nt* arithmetic book; **~exempel** *nt* sum; **das ist doch ein ganz einfaches ~exempel** it's a matter of simple arithmetic; **~fehler** *m* miscalculation, (arithmetical) error *or* mistake; **~funktion** *f* (*Comput*) computational function; **~geschwindigkeit** *f* (*Comput*) processing speed; **~heft** *nt* arithmetic book; **~künstler** *m* mathematical genius *or* wizard (*inf*); **~lehrer** *m* arithmetic teacher; **~maschine** *f* adding machine; **~operation** *f* calculation.
Rechenschaft *f* account ◆ **jdm über etw** (*acc*) **~ geben** *or* **ablegen** to account to sb for sth, to give *or* render account to sb for sth (*liter*); **sich** (*dat*) **über etw**

(*acc*) ~ **ablegen** to account to oneself for sth; **jdm ~ schuldig sein** *or* **schulden** to be accountable to sb, to have to account to sb; **dafür bist du mir ~ schuldig** you owe me an explanation for that; **jdn (für etw) zur ~ ziehen** to call sb to account (for *or* over sth); **(von jdm) ~ verlangen** *or* **fordern** to demand an explanation *or* account (from sb).

Rechenschafts-: ~bericht *m* report; **~legung** *f* report; **jdm gegenüber zur ~legung verpflichtet sein** to be accountable to sb.

Rechen-: ~schieber, ~stab *m* slide-rule; **~stunde** *f* arithmetic lesson; **~tabelle** *f* ready-reckoner; **~tafel** *f* arithmetic slate; (*an der Wand*) (squared) blackboard; **~werk** *nt* (*Comput*) arithmetic unit; **~zeit** *f* (*Comput*) computer time; **~zentrum** *nt* computer centre.

Recherche [re'ʃɛrʃə, rə-] *f* -, -n investigation, enquiry ◆ **~n anstellen** to make investigations *or* enquiries (*über etw (acc)* about *or* into sth).

Recherchenjournalismus [re'ʃɛrʃən-, rə-] *m* investigative journalism.

recherchieren* [reʃɛr'ʃi:rən, rə-] *vti* to investigate.

rechnen [1] *vt* **(a)** (*addieren etc*) to work out, to calculate; *Aufgabe* to work out ◆ **wir ~ gerade Additionsbeispiele** we're doing addition sums at the moment; **rund gerechnet** in round figures; **was für einen Unsinn hast du da gerechnet!** how did you get that absurd result?, how did you work that out?

(b) (*einstufen*) to count ◆ **jdn/etw zu etw ~, jdn/etw unter etw** (*acc*) **~** to count sb among sth, to class sb/sth as sth; **er wird zu den größten Physikern** *or* **unter die größten Physiker gerechnet** he is rated as *or* is reckoned to be one of the greatest physicists, he is counted among the greatest physicists.

(c) (*veranschlagen*) to estimate, to reckon ◆ **wir hatten nur drei Tage gerechnet** we were only reckoning on three days; **für vier Personen rechnet man ca. zwei Pfund Fleisch** for four people you should reckon on about two pounds of meat; **das ist zu hoch/niedrig gerechnet** that's too high/low (an estimate).

(d) (*einberechnen*) to include, to count, to take into account ◆ **alles in allem gerechnet** all in all, taking everything into account; **den Ärger/die Unkosten mit dazu gerechnet** what with all the trouble/expense too *or* on top of that.

[2] *vi* **(a)** (*addieren etc*) to do *or* make a calculation/calculations; (*esp Sch*) to do sums ◆ **falsch/richtig ~** to go wrong *or* make a mistake (in one's calculations)/to calculate correctly; **(da hast du) falsch gerechnet!** you got that wrong; **gut/schlecht ~ können** to be good/bad at sums (*esp Sch*) *or* arithmetic *or* with figures; **~ lernen** to learn arithmetic.

(b) (*eingestuft werden*) to count ◆ **er rechnet noch als Kind** he still counts as a child.

(c) (*sich verlassen*) **auf jdn/etw ~** to reckon *or* count on sb/sth.

(d) mit jdm/etw ~ (*erwarten, einkalkulieren*) to reckon on *or* with sb/sth; (*berücksichtigen*) to reckon with sb/sth; **du mußt damit ~, daß es regnet** you must reckon on *or* with it raining; **mit ihm/dieser Partei wird man ~ müssen** he/this party will have to be reckoned with; **damit hatte ich nicht gerechnet** I wasn't expecting that, I hadn't reckoned on *or* with that; **mit so etwas muß man ~** you have to reckon on *or* with that sort of thing happening; **er rechnet mit einem Sieg** he reckons he'll win; **mit allem/dem Schlimmsten ~** to be prepared for anything/the worst; **wir hatten nicht mehr mit ihm/seinem Kommen gerechnet** we hadn't reckoned on him coming any more; **damit ~ müssen, daß** ... to have to be prepared for the fact that ..., to have to expect that ...; **ich rechne morgen fest mit dir** I'll be expecting you tomorrow.

(e) (*inf: haushalten*) to be thrifty, to economize ◆ **seine Frau kann gut ~** his wife knows how to economize, his wife is thrifty.

[3] *vr* to pay off, to turn out to be profitable ◆ **etw rechnet sich schlecht/nicht** sth is barely/not economical.

Rechnen *nt* **-s,** *no pl* arithmetic; (*esp Sch*) sums *pl.*

Rechner *m* **-s, - (a)** arithmetician ◆ **ein guter ~ sein** to be good at arithmetic *or* figures. **(b)** (*Elektronen~*) computer; (*Taschen~*) calculator.

Rechnerei *f* (*inf*) calculation ◆ **das ist eine furchtbare ~** it's incredibly difficult to work out; **die ganze ~ überlasse ich ihm** I leave all the calculations *or* figurework to him.

rechner-: ~gesteuert *adj* computer-controlled; **~gestützt** *adj* computer-aided.

rechnerisch *adj* arithmetical ◆ **ein ~es Beispiel** an example with some figures; **ich bin rein ~ überzeugt, aber** ... I'm convinced as far as the figures go but ...

Rechnerverbund *m* computer network ◆ **um den ~ zu erleichtern** to make networking easier; **sie arbeiten im ~** they use networking *or* a computer network.

▼ **Rechnung** *f* **(a)** (*Berechnung*) calculation; (*als Aufgabe*) sum ◆ **die ~ geht nicht auf** (*lit*) the sum doesn't work out; (*fig*) it won't work (out); *siehe* **Strich**.

▼ **(b)** (*schriftliche Kostenforderung*) bill (*Brit*), check (*US*); (*von Firma auch*) invoice; (*für Kundenkonto*) statement of account ◆ **das geht auf meine ~** I'm paying, this one's on me; **auf ~ kaufen/bestellen** to buy/order on account; **laut ~** as per invoice; **laut ~ vom 5. Juli** as per our invoice of July 5th; **auf** *or* **für eigene ~** on one's own account; **(jdm) etw in ~ stellen** to charge (sb) for sth; **einer Sache** (*dat*) **~ tragen, etw in ~ ziehen** to take sth into account, to bear sth in mind; **auf seine ~ kommen** to have one's money's worth; **wenn du das glaubst, dann hast du die ~ ohne den Wirt gemacht** (*inf*) if you think that, you've got another think coming; **aber er hatte die ~ ohne den Wirt gemacht** (*inf*) but there was one thing he hadn't reckoned with.

Rechnungs-: ⚠**~abschluß** *m* making-up of (the) accounts; **den ~abschluß machen** to do the books; **~amt** *nt* audit office; **~art** *f siehe* **Rechenart**; **~betrag** *m* (total) amount of a bill *or* check (*US*)/invoice/account; **~buch** *nt* account(s) book *or* ledger; **~einheit** *f* unit of account; **~führer** *m* chief accountant; **~führung** *f siehe* **Buchführung**; **~hof** *m* ≃ Auditor-General's office (*Brit*), audit division (*US*); **~jahr** *nt* financial *or* fiscal year; **~legung** *f* tendering of account; **~prüfer** *m* auditor; **~prüfung** *f* audit; **~wesen** *nt* (*Führung*) accountancy, bookkeeping; (*Prüfung*) auditing.

▼ **Recht** *nt* **-(e)s, -e (a)** (*Rechtsordnung, sittliche Norm*) law; (*Gerechtigkeit auch*) justice ◆ **~ sprechen** to administer *or* dispense justice; **nach geltendem/englischem ~** in law/in *or* under *or* according to English law; **~ muß ~ bleiben** (*Naturrecht*) fair's fair; (*Gesetz*) the law's the law; **für das ~ kämpfen** to fight for justice; **das Schwurgericht hat für ~ erkannt ...** the court has reached the following verdict *or* has decided ...; **von ~s wegen** legally, as of right; (*inf: eigentlich*) by rights (*inf*).

(b) ~e *pl* (*form: Rechtswissenschaft*) jurisprudence ◆ **Doktor der** *or* **beider ~e** Doctor of Laws.

▼ **(c)** (*Anspruch, Berechtigung*) right (*auf +acc* to) ◆ **sein ~ fordern** to demand one's rights; **seine ~e geltend machen** to insist on one's rights; **ich nehme mir das ~, das zu tun** I shall make so bold as to do that; **sein ~ bekommen** *or* **erhalten** *or* **kriegen** (*inf*) to get one's rights, to get what is one's by right; **zu seinem ~ kommen** (*lit*) to gain one's rights; (*fig*) to come into one's own; **auch das Vergnügen muß zu seinem ~ kommen** there has to be a place for pleasure too; **der Körper verlangt sein ~ (auf Schlaf)** the body demands its due *or* its rightful sleep; **gleiches ~ für alle!** equal rights for all!; **gleiche ~e, gleiche Pflichten** equal rights, equal duties; **das ~ des Stärkeren** the law of the jungle; **mit** *or* **zu ~** rightly, with justification; **und (das) mit ~** and rightly so; **Sie stellen diese Frage ganz zu ~** you are quite right to ask this question; **im ~ sein** to be in the right; **das ist mein gutes ~** it's my right; **es ist unser gutes ~, zu erfahren** ... we have every right to know ...; **woher nimmt er das ~, das zu sagen?** what gives him the right to say that?; **mit welchem ~?** by what right?; *siehe* **vorbehalten**.

▼ **recht** [1] *adj* **(a)** (*richtig*) right ◆ **mir ist es ~, es soll mir ~ sein** it's all right *or* OK (*inf*) by me; **ganz ~!** quite right; **ist schon ~!** (*inf*) that's all right, that's OK (*inf*); **alles, was ~ ist** (*empört*) there is a limit, fair's fair; (*anerkennend*) you can't deny it; **ich will zum Bahnhof, bin ich hier ~?** (*esp S Ger*) I want to get to the station, am I going the right way?; **bin ich hier ~ bei Schmidts?** (*esp S Ger*) is this the Smiths' place (all right *inf*)?; **hier geht es nicht mit ~en Dingen zu** there's something odd *or* not right here; **ich habe keine ~e Lust** I don't particularly feel like it; **ein ~er Narr** (*old*) a real *or* right fool; **nichts R~es** no good; **aus dem Jungen kann nichts R~es werden** that boy will come to no good; **aus ihm ist nichts R~es geworden** (*beruflich etc*) he never really made it; **er hat nichts R~es gelernt** he didn't learn any real trade; **nach dem R~en sehen** to see that everything's OK (*inf*); **Tag, ich wollte nur mal nach dem R~en sehen** hello, I just thought I'd come and see how you're doing *or* how things are; **es ist nicht mehr als ~ und billig** it's only right and proper; **was dem einen ~ ist, ist dem andern billig** (*Prov*) what's sauce for the goose is sauce for the gander (*Prov*).

▼ **(b) ~ haben** to be right; **er hat ~ bekommen** he was right; **~ behalten** to be right; **er will immer ~ behalten** he always has to be right; **ich hatte ~, und ich habe ~ behalten** I was right and I'm still right; **jdm ~ geben** to agree with sb, to admit that sb is right; **~ daran tun, zu** ... to be *or* do right to ...

[2] *adv* **(a)** (*richtig*) properly; (*wirklich*) really ◆ **verstehen Sie mich ~** don't get me wrong (*inf*), don't misunderstand me; **ich verstehe ihn nicht so ~, wie kann er nur ...?** I just don't understand him, how can he ...?; **wenn ich Sie ~ verstehe** if I understand you rightly *or* aright (*form*); **sehe/höre ich ~?** am I seeing/hearing things?; **ich werde daraus nicht ~ klug** I don't really *or* rightly know what to make of it; **das geschieht ihm ~** it serves him right; **nun** *or* **jetzt mache ich es erst ~ (nicht)** now I'm definitely (not) going to do it; **du kommst gerade ~, um ...** you're just in time to ...; **das ist** *or* **kommt mir gerade ~** (*inf*) that suits me fine; **du kommst mir gerade ~** (*iro*) you're all I needed; **gehe ich ~ in der Annahme, daß ...?** am I right *or* correct in assuming that ...?; **es hat mir nicht mehr ~ gefallen** I didn't really like it any more; **hat es dir gefallen? — nicht so ~** did you like it? — not really; **ich weiß nicht ~** I don't really *or* rightly know; **man kann ihm nichts ~ machen** you can't do anything right for him; **man kann es nicht allen ~ machen** you can't please all of the people all of the time; **ich mache es Ihnen (auch) ~** (*inf*) I'll make it worth your while; **sie versuchte, es ihm immer ~ zu machen** she always tried to do everything right for him.

(b) (*ziemlich, ganz*) quite, fairly, pretty (*inf*) ◆ **~ viel** quite a lot.

(c) (*sehr*) very, right (*dial*) ◆ **~ herzlichen Dank!** thank you very much indeed.

Rechte *f* **-n, -n (a)** (*Hand*) right hand; (*Boxen*) right. **(b)** (*Pol*) right, Right.

Recht-: ~eck *nt* rectangle; **r~eckig** *adj* rectangular.

Rechtehandregel *f* (*Phys*) right-hand rule.

rechten *vi* (*geh*) to argue, to dispute.

Rechtens *gen of* **Recht** (*form*) **es ist ~/nicht ~, daß er das gemacht hat** he was/was not within his rights to do that; **die Sache war nicht ~** the matter was not right *or* (*Jur*) legal.

rechte(r, s) *adj attr* **(a)** right, right-hand ◆ **~r Hand** on *or* to the right; **auf der ~n Seite** on the right-hand side, on the right; **jds ~ Hand sein** to be sb's right-hand man. **(b) ein ~r Winkel** a right angle. **(c)** (*konservativ*) right-wing, rightist ◆ **der ~ Flügel** the right wing. **(d)** (*beim Stricken*) plain ◆ **eine ~ Masche stricken** to knit one.

rechterseits *adv* on the right-hand side.

rechtfertigen *insep* [1] *vt* to justify; (*berechtigt erscheinen lassen auch*) to warrant ◆ **das ist durch nichts zu ~** that can in no way be justified, that is

➤ SPRACHE AKTIV: **Rechnung: b** → 47.5 **Recht: c** → 53.6 **recht: 1a** → 36.2 **1b** → 38.1, 40.3

completely unjustifiable.
[2] *vr* to justify oneself.

Rẹchtfertigung *f siehe vt* justification; warranting ◆ **zu meiner ~** in my defence, in justification of what I did/said *etc.*

Rẹchtfertigungs-: ~grund *m (Jur)* justification; **~schrift** *f* apologia; **~versuch** *m* attempt at self-justification.

Recht-: r~gläubig *adj* orthodox; **~gläubigkeit** *f* orthodoxy; **~haber** *m* **-s, -** *(pej)* know-all *(inf)*, self-opinionated person; **~haberei** *f (pej)* know-all attitude *(inf)*, self-opinionatedness; **r~haberisch** *adj* know-all *attr (inf)*, self-opinionated; **er ist so r~haberisch** he's such a know-all *(inf)*, he's so self-opinionated; **r~haberisch bestand er darauf** he insisted on it in his self-opinionated way.

rẹchtlich *adj* **(a)** *(gesetzlich)* legal ◆ **~ verpflichtet** bound by law, legally obliged; **~ zulässig** permissible in law, legal; **~ nicht zulässig** not permissible in law, illegal; **~ unmöglich** impossible for legal reasons; **jdn ~ belangen** to take sb to court, to take legal action against sb.
(b) *(old: redlich)* honest, upright, upstanding *(old)* ◆ **~ denken/handeln** to think/act in an honest *etc* way.

Rẹcht-: r~los *adj* **(a)** without rights; **(b)** *Zustand* lawless; **~lose(r)** *mf decl as adj* person with no rights; *(Vogelfreier)* outlaw; **~losigkeit** *f* **(a)** *(von Mensch)* lack of rights; **in völliger ~losigkeit leben** to have no rights whatever; **(b)** *(in Land)* lawlessness; **r~mäßig** *adj (legitim)* lawful, legitimate; *Erben, Thronfolger, Besitzer auch* rightful; *(dem Gesetz entsprechend)* legal, in accordance with the law; **für r~mäßig erklären** to legitimize; to declare legal; **jdm etw r~mäßig zuerkennen** to recognize sb's legal right *or* entitlement to sth; **~mäßigkeit** *f (Legitimität)* legitimacy; *(Legalität)* legality.

rẹchts [1] *adv* **(a)** on the right ◆ **nach ~** (to the) right; **von ~** from the right; **~ von etw** (on *or* to the) right of sth; **~ von jdm** to *or* on sb's right; *(Pol)* to the right of sb; **weiter ~** further to the right; **sich ~ einordnen** to move into *or* take the right-hand lane; **~ vor links** right before left *(rule of the priority system for driving)*; **sich ~ halten** to keep (to the) right; **Augen ~!** *(Mil)* eyes right!; **~ schwenkt, marsch!** *(Mil)* right wheel!; **~ stehen** *or* **sein** *(Pol)* to be right-wing *or* on the right *or* a right-winger; **ich weiß nicht mehr, wo ~ und links ist** *(inf)* I don't know whether I'm coming or going *(inf)*.
(b) ~ stricken to knit (plain); **ein ganz ~ gestrickter Pullover** a pullover knitted in garter stitch; **zwei ~, zwei links** *(beim Stricken)* knit two, purl two, two plain, two purl.
[2] *prep +gen* **~ des Rheins** to *or* on the right of the Rhine.

Rechts- *in cpds (Jur)* legal; **~abbieger** *m* **-s, -** motorist/cyclist/car *etc* turning right; **die Spur für ~abbieger** the right-hand turn-off lane; **~abbiegerspur** *f* right-hand turn-off lane; **~abweichler** *m* **-s, -** *(Pol inf)* right-wing dissenter; **~angelegenheit** *f* legal matter; **~anspruch** *m* legal right *or* entitlement; **einen ~anspruch auf etw** *(acc)* **haben** to be legally entitled to sth, to have a legal right *etc* to sth; **aus etw einen ~anspruch ableiten** to use sth to create a legal precedent; **~anwalt** *m* lawyer, attorney *(US)*; *(als Berater auch)* solicitor *(Brit)*; *(vor Gericht auch)* barrister *(Brit)*; *(vor Gericht auch)* advocate *(Scot)*; **sein ~anwalt behauptete vor Gericht, ...** his counsel maintained in court ...; **sich** *(dat)* **einen ~anwalt nehmen** to get a lawyer *or* an attorney *(US) etc*; **~auffassung** *f* **(a)** conception of legality; **(b)** *(Auslegung)* interpretation of the law; **~auskunft** *f* legal advice; **~ausleger** *m (Boxen)* southpaw; *(Pol hum)* extreme right-winger (of a party); **~außen** *m* **-, -** *(Ftbl)* outside-right; *(Pol inf)* extreme right-winger; **~beistand** *m* legal advice; *(Mensch)* legal adviser; **~belehrung** *f siehe* **~mittelbelehrung**; **~berater** *m* legal adviser; **~beratung(sstelle)** *f* ≃ citizens' advice bureau *(Brit)*; **~beugung** *f* perversion of the course of justice; **~brecher(in** *f***)** *m* **-s, -** law-breaker, criminal; **~bruch** *m* breach *or* infringement of the law; **r~bündig** *adj (Typ)* ranged *or* flush right; **der Brief ist r~bündig geschrieben** the letter has justified margins.

rẹchtschaffen [1] *adj* **(a)** *(ehrlich, redlich)* honest, upright. **(b)** *(inf: stark, groß)* **~en Durst/Hunger haben** to be really thirsty/hungry, to be parched *(inf)*/to be starving *(inf)*.
[2] *adv* really, tremendously ◆ **sich ~ bemühen** to try really *etc* hard.

Rẹchtschaffenheit *f* honesty, uprightness.

rẹchtschreiben *vi infin only* to spell.

Rẹchtschreiben *nt* spelling.

Rẹchtschreib-: ~fehler *m* spelling mistake; **~hilfe** *f (Comput)* spelling aid; **~kontrolle, ~prüfung** *f (Comput)* spelling check, spell check; *(Programm)* spelling checker, spell checker; **~reform** *f* spelling reform.

Rẹchtschreibung *f* spelling.

Rẹchts-: ~drall *m (im Gewehrlauf)* clockwise rifling; *(von Geschoß, Billardball)* swerve to the right; *(von Auto, Pferd)* pull to the right; *(Pol inf)* leaning to the right; **einen ~drall haben** to swerve/pull/lean to the right; **r~drehend** *adj (Chem)* dextrorotatory *(spec)*; **~drehung** *f* turn to the right.

rẹchtseitig *adj siehe* **rechtsseitig**.

Rẹchts|empfinden *nt* sense of justice.

Rẹchtser(in *f***)** *m* **-s, -** *(dial) siehe* **Rechtshänder(in)**.

Rẹchts-: r~extrem *adj* right-wing extremist *attr*; **~extremismus** *m* right-wing extremism; **~extremist** *m* right-wing extremist; **r~fähig** *adj (Jur)* legally responsible, having legal capacity *(form)*; **~fähigkeit** *f (Jur)* legal responsibility *or* capacity *(form)*; **~fall** *m* court case; *(in der ~geschichte auch)* legal case; **~frage** *f* legal question *or* issue; **r~frei** *adj* **r~freier Raum** unlegislated area; **~frieden** *m (Jur)* peace under the law; **~gang**[1] *m (Jur)* legal procedure; **im ersten ~gang** at the first courtcase; **~gang**[2] *m (Tech)* right-handed thread; **r~gängig** *adj (Tech)* right-handed; **~gefühl** *nt siehe* **~empfinden**; **~gelehrsamkeit** *f (old) siehe* **~wissenschaft**; **~gelehrte(r)** *mf* jurist, legal scholar; **r~gerichtet** *adj (Pol)* right-wing; **~geschäft** *nt* legal transaction; **einseitiges/mehrseitiges ~geschäft** unilateral/multilateral legal transaction; **~geschichte** *f* legal history; *(Geschichte der ~wissenschaft auch)* history of law; **~gewinde** *nt* right-handed thread; **~grund** *m* legal justification; **~grundlage** *f* legal basis; **~grundsatz** *m* legal maxim; **r~gültig** *adj* legally valid, legal; *Vertrag auch* legally binding; **~gültigkeit** *f* legal validity, legality; **~gut** *nt* something enjoying legal protection, legally protected right; **~gutachten** *nt* legal report; **~haken** *m (Boxen)* right hook; **~handel** *m (liter)* lawsuit; **~händer(in** *f***)** *m* **-s, -** right-handed person, right-hander *(esp Sport)*; **~händer sein** to be right-handed; **r~händig** *adj* right-handed; **~händigkeit** *f* right-handedness; **~handlung** *f* legal act; **r~hängig** *adj (Jur)* sub judice *pred*; **~hängigkeit** *f* state of being sub judice; **r~her** *adv* from the right; **r~heran** *adv* over to the right; **r~herum** *adv* (round) to the right; *sich drehen etc auch* clockwise; **~hilfe** *f* (mutual) assistance in law enforcement; **~hilfeabkommen** *nt* law enforcement treaty; **r~hin** *adv* (to the) right; **~klarheit** *f* clear legal principles *pl*; **~kraft** *f, no pl* force of law; *(Gültigkeit: von Vertrag etc)* legal validity; **~kraft erlangen** to become law, to come into force; **die ~kraft eines Urteils** the finality *or* legal force of a verdict; **r~kräftig** *adj* having the force of law; *Urteil* final; *Vertrag* legally valid; **r~kräftig sein/werden** *(Verordnung)* to have the force of law/to become law; *(Urteil)* to be/become final; *(Gesetz)* to be in/come into force; **r~kundig** *adj* familiar with *or* versed in the law; **~kurve** *f (von Straße)* right-hand bend; *(von Bahn auch)* right-hand curve; **~lage** *f* legal position; **r~lastig** *adj* listing to the right; *Auto auch* down at the right; *(fig)* leaning to the right; **r~lastig sein** to list to/be down at/lean to the right; **r~läufig** *adj Gewinde* right-handed; *Schrift* left-to-right; **~lehre** *f siehe* **~wissenschaft**; **~lehrer** *m (form)* professor of jurisprudence *(form)*; ⚠**~mißbrauch** *m* abuse of the law; **~mittel** *nt* means of legal redress; **~mittel einlegen** to lodge an appeal; **~mittelbelehrung** *f* statement of rights of redress *or* appeal; **~nachfolge** *f* legal succession; **~nachfolger** *m* legal successor; **~norm** *f* legal norm; **~ordnung** *f* **eine ~ordnung** a system of laws; **die ~ordnung** the law; **~partei** *f* right-wing party; **~pflege** *f* administration of justice; **~pfleger** *m official with certain judicial powers*; **~philosophie** *f* philosophy of law.

Rẹchtsprechung *f* **(a)** *(Rechtspflege)* administration of justice; *(Gerichtsbarkeit)* jurisdiction. **(b)** *(richterliche Tätigkeit)* administering *or* dispensation of justice. **(c)** *(bisherige Urteile)* precedents *pl*.

Rẹchts-: r~radikal *adj* radical right-wing; **die ~radikalen** the right-wing radicals; **~radikalismus** *m* right-wing radicalism; **~referendar** *m* articled clerk; **~referendar sein** to be under articles; **r~rheinisch** *adj* to *or* on the right of the Rhine; **~ruck, ~rutsch** *m (Pol)* swing to the right; **r~rum** *adv (inf)* to the right; **~sache** *f* legal matter; *(Fall)* case; **~schutz** *m* legal protection; **~schutzversicherung** *f* legal costs insurance; **r~seitig** *adj* on the right(-hand) side; **r~seitig gelähmt** paralysed in the right side; **~sprache** *f* legal terminology *or* language; **~spruch** *m* verdict; **~staat** *m* state under the rule of law; **r~staatlich** *adj* of a state under the rule of law; **r~staatliche Ordnung** law and order; **seine r~staatliche Gesinnung** his predisposition for law and order; **~staatlichkeit** *f* rule of law; *(einer Maßnahme)* legality; ⚠**r~stehend** *adj attr* right-hand, on the right; *(Pol)* right-wing, on the right; **~stellung** *f* legal position; **~steuerung** *f* right-hand drive; **~streit** *m* lawsuit; **~titel** *m* legal title.

rẹchtsuchend *adj attr* seeking justice.

rechts|ụm *adv (Mil)* to the right ◆ **~ (kehrt)!** *(Mil)* right about turn!

Rẹchts-: ~unsicherheit *f* uncertainty (about one's legal position); **r~verbindlich** *adj* legally binding; *Auskunft* legally valid; **~verbindlichkeit** *f siehe adj* legal bindingness; legal validity; **~verdreher** *m* **-s, -** *(pej)* shyster *(inf)*, Philadelphia lawyer *(US)*; *(hum inf)* legal eagle *(inf)*; **~vergleichung** *f* comparative law; **~verhältnis** *nt* facts of the case *pl*; **~verkehr** *m* driving on the right *no def art*; **in Deutschland ist ~verkehr** in Germany they drive on the right; **im ~verkehr muß man ...** when driving on the right one must ...; **~verletzung** *f* infringement *or* breach of the law; **~verordnung** *f* ≃ statutory order; **~vertreter** *m* legal representative; **~weg** *m* legal action; **den ~weg beschreiten** *or* **einschlagen** to have recourse to *or* take legal action, to go to law; **unter Ausschluß des ~weges** without possibility of recourse to legal action; **der ~weg ist ausgeschlossen** ≃ the judges' decision is final; **r~widrig** *adj* illegal; **~widrigkeit** *f* illegality; **~wissenschaft** *f* jurisprudence.

Rẹcht-: r~wink(e)lig *adj* right-angled; **r~zeitig** [1] *adj (früh genug)* timely; *(pünktlich)* punctual; **um r~zeitige Anmeldung wird gebeten** you are requested to apply in good time; [2] *adv (früh genug)* in (good) time; *(pünktlich)* on time; **gerade noch r~zeitig ankommen** to arrive *or* be just in time; **~zeitigkeit** *f siehe adj* timeliness; punctuality.

Recital [riː'saitl] *nt* **-s, -s** *(Mus)* recital.

Rẹck *nt* **-(e)s, -e** *(Sport)* horizontal bar.

Rẹcke *m* **-n, -n** *(obs)* warrior.

rẹcken [1] *vt* **(a)** *(aus-, emporstrecken)* to stretch ◆ **den Kopf/Hals ~** to crane one's neck; **die Glieder ~** to stretch (oneself), to have a stretch. **(b)** *(dial: glattziehen)* **etw ~** to pull the creases out of sth.
[2] *vr* to stretch (oneself) ◆ **sich ~ und strecken** to have a good stretch.

Rẹck-: ~stange *f* horizontal bar; **~turnen** *nt* bar exercises *pl*.

Recorder [re'kɔrdɐ] *m* **-s, -** (cassette) recorder.

recycelbar [riː'saikəlbaːr] *adj* recyclable.

recyceln* [riː'saikəln] *vt* to recycle.

Recycling [riː'saikliŋ] *nt* **-s,** *no pl* recycling.

Recycling-: ~hof *m* recycling plant; **~papier** *nt* recycled paper; **~werk** *nt* recycling plant.

Red. *abbr of* **Redakteur** ed; **Redaktion.**

Redakteur(in *f*) [-'tøːɐ, -'tøːrɪn] *m* editor.

Redaktion *f* **(a)** (*das Redigieren*) editing ◆ **die ~ dieses Buches hatte XY** this book was edited by XY. **(b)** (*Personal*) editorial staff. **(c)** (*~sbüro*) editorial office(s) ◆ **der Reporter rief seine ~ an** the reporter phoned his office *or* paper.

redaktionell [redaktsio'nɛl] *adj* editorial ◆ **die ~e Leitung im Ressort Wirtschaft hat Herr Müller** Herr Müller is the editor responsible for business and finance; **etw ~ überarbeiten** to edit sth.

Redaktions-: ~geheimnis *nt* press secret; **~konferenz** *f* editorial conference; **⚠~schluß** *m* time of going to press; (*Einsendeschluß*) copy deadline; **diese Nachricht ist vor/nach ~schluß eingegangen** this news item arrived before/after the paper went to press *or* bed (*sl*); **„nach ~schluß eingegangen"** "stop-press (news)".

Redaktor *m* (*Sw*) editor.

Redaktrice [-'triːsə] *f* -, **-n** (*Aus*) editor.

Rede *f* -, **-n (a)** speech; (*Ansprache*) address ◆ **die Kunst der ~** (*form*) the art of rhetoric; **eine ~ halten** *or* **schwingen** (*sl*) to make *or* give a speech; **die ~ des Bundeskanzlers** the Chancellor's speech, the speech given by the Chancellor; **der langen ~ kurzer Sinn** (*prov*) the long and the short of it.
(b) (*Äußerungen, Worte*) words *pl*, language *no pl* ◆ **seine frechen ~n** his cheek; **große ~n führen** *or* **schwingen** (*sl*) to talk big (*inf*); **das ist meine ~!** that's what I've always said; **das ist nicht der ~ wert** it's not worth mentioning; **(es ist) nicht der ~ wert!** don't mention it, it was nothing.
(c) (*das Reden, Gespräch*) conversation, talk ◆ **jdm in die ~ fallen** to interrupt sb; **die ~ fiel** *or* **kam auf** (*+acc*) the conversation *or* talk turned to; **die in ~ stehende Person** (*form*) the person in question *or* under discussion; **es war von einer Gehaltserhöhung die ~** there was talk *or* mention of a salary increase; **von Ihnen war eben die ~** we were just talking about you; **aber davon war doch nie die ~** but no-one was ever talking about that; **wovon ist die ~?** what are you/we *etc* talking about?; **von einer Gehaltserhöhung kann keine ~ sein** there can be no question of a salary increase; **von Großzügigkeit kann keine ~ sein, das war nur ...** there's no question of it being generosity, it was just ...; **davon kann keine ~ sein** it's out of the question.
(d) (*Ling, Liter*) speech ◆ **direkte/indirekte ~** direct/indirect speech *or* discourse (*US*); **gebundene/ungebundene ~** verse/prose; **in freier ~** without (consulting) notes.
(e) (*Gerücht, Nachrede*) rumour ◆ **kümmere dich doch nicht um die ~n der Leute!** don't worry (about) what people say; **es geht die ~, daß** there's a rumour that, rumour has it that.
(f) (*Rechenschaft*) **(jdm) ~ (und Antwort) stehen** to justify oneself to sb; **(jdm) für etw ~ und Antwort stehen** to account (to sb) for sth; **jdn zur ~ stellen** to take sb to task.

Rede-: ~duell *nt* verbal exchange *or* duel; **~figur** *f* (*Liter*) figure of speech; **⚠~fluß** *m* volubility; **er stockte plötzlich in seinem ~fluß** his flow of words suddenly stopped; **ich will Ihren ~fluß nicht unterbrechen, aber ...** I don't wish to interrupt your flow but ...; **~freiheit** *f* freedom of speech; **~gabe** *f* eloquence; **r~gewandt** *adj* eloquent; **~kunst** *f* **die ~kunst** rhetoric.

reden [1] *vi* **(a)** (*sprechen*) to talk, to speak ◆ **R~ während des Unterrichts** talking in class; **mit sich selbst/jdm ~** to talk *or* speak to oneself/sb; **wie redst du denn mit deiner Mutter!** that's no way to talk *or* speak to your mother; **so lasse ich nicht mit mir ~!** I won't be spoken to like that!; **sie hat geredet und geredet** she talked and talked; **mit jdm über jdn/etw ~** to talk *or* speak to *or* with sb about sb/sth; **~ wir nicht mehr davon** *or* **darüber** let's not talk *or* speak about it any more, let's drop it (*inf*); **~ Sie doch nicht!** (*inf*) come off it! (*inf*); **(viel) von sich ~ machen** to become (very much) a talking point; **das Buch/er macht viel von sich ~** everyone is talking about the book/him; **viel R~s von einer Sache machen** to make a great to-do about sth; **du hast gut** *or* **leicht ~!** it's all very well for you (to talk); **ich habe mit Ihnen zu ~!** I would like to speak *or* talk to you, I would like a word with you; **ich rede gegen eine Wand** *or* **Mauer** it's like talking to a brick wall (*inf*); **darüber läßt** *or* **ließe sich ~** that's a possibility; (*über Preis, Bedingungen*) I think we could discuss that; **darüber läßt** *or* **ließe sich eher ~** that's more like it, now you're talking; **er läßt mit sich ~** he could be persuaded; (*in bezug auf Preis*) he's open to offers; (*gesprächsbereit*) he's open to discussion; **sie läßt nicht mit sich ~** she is adamant; (*bei eigenen Forderungen auch*) she won't take no for an answer; **R~ ist Silber, Schweigen ist Gold** (*Prov*) (speech is silver but) silence is golden (*Prov*); **das ist ja mein R~ (seit 33)** (*inf*) I've been saying that for (donkey's *inf*) years; *siehe* **Wasserfall.**
(b) (*klatschen*) to talk (*über +acc* about) ◆ **schlecht von jdm ~** to talk *or* speak ill of sb; **in so einem Dorf wird natürlich viel geredet** in a village like that naturally people talk a lot.
(c) (*eine Rede halten*) to speak ◆ **er redet nicht gerne öffentlich** he doesn't like public speaking; **er kann nicht/gut ~** he is no/a good talker *or* (*als Redner*) speaker.
(d) (*euph: gestehen, aussagen*) to talk ◆ **jdn zum R~ bringen** to get sb to talk, to make sb talk; **er will nicht ~** he won't talk.
[2] *vt* **(a)** to talk; *Worte* to say ◆ **einige Worte ~** to say a few words; **kein Wort ~** not to say *or* speak a word; **sich** (*dat*) **etw von der Seele** *or* **vom Herzen ~** to get sth off one's chest; **jdm/einer Sache das Wort ~** to speak (out) in favour of sb/sth.
(b) (*klatschen*) to say ◆ **es kann dir doch nicht egal sein, was über dich geredet wird** it must matter to you what people say about you; **Schlechtes von jdm** *or* **über jdn ~** to say bad things about sb; **damit die Leute wieder was zu ~ haben** so that people have something to talk about again.
[3] *vr* **sich heiser ~** to talk oneself hoarse; **sich in Zorn** *or* **Wut ~** to talk oneself into a fury.

Redens|art *f* (*Phrase*) hackneyed expression, cliché; (*Redewendung*) expression, idiom; (*Sprichwort*) saying; (*leere Versprechung*) empty promise ◆ **das ist nur so eine ~** it's just a way of speaking; **bloße ~en** empty talk.

Redenschreiber(in *f*) *m* speechwriter.

Rederei *f* **(a)** (*Geschwätz*) chattering *no pl*, talking *no pl* ◆ **du mit deiner ~, du bist doch zu feige dazu** you're all talk, you're too scared to do it. **(b)** (*Klatsch*) gossip *no pl*, talk *no pl* ◆ **zu ~en Anlaß geben** to make people talk, to give rise to gossip.

Rede-: ~schwall *m* torrent *or* flood of words; **~strom** *m* flow of words; **~verbot** *nt* ban on speaking; **jdm ~verbot erteilen** to ban sb from speaking; **(allgemeines) ~verbot!** no talking!; **~weise** *f* style *or* manner (of speaking); **~wendung** *f* idiom, idiomatic expression.

redigieren* *vt* to edit.

Rediskontgeschäft *nt* rediscount.

Rediskontierung *f* rediscounting.

redlich *adj* honest ◆ **~ denken** to be honest; **~ handeln** to be honest, to act honestly; **er meint es ~** he is being honest; **sich** (*dat*) **etw ~ verdient haben** to have really *or* genuinely earned sth; *Geld, Gut* to have acquired sth by honest means; **~ (mit jdm) teilen** to share (things) equally (with sb); **sich ~ durchs Leben schlagen** to make an honest living.

Redlichkeit *f* honesty.

Redner(in *f*) *m* **-s, -** speaker; (*Rhetoriker*) orator ◆ **ich bin kein (großer) ~ aber** ... unaccustomed as I am to public speaking ...

Redner-: ~bühne *f* platform, rostrum; **~gabe** *f* gift of oratory.

rednerisch *adj* rhetorical, oratorical ◆ **~e Begabung** talent for public speaking; **~ begabt sein** to be a gifted speaker.

Rednerpult *nt* lectern.

redselig *adj* talkative.

Redseligkeit *f* talkativeness.

Reduktion *f* **(a)** (*Einschränkung*) diminution; (*von Preisen, Ausgaben, Verbrauch*) reduction (*gen* in). **(b)** (*Zurückführung*) reduction (*auf +acc* to). **(c)** (*Chem*) reduction.

Reduktions-: ~mittel *nt* (*Chem*) reducing agent; **~ofen** *m* (*Metal*) reducing furnace.

redundant *adj* redundant ◆ **er drückt sich ~ aus** a lot of what he says is redundant.

Redundanz *f* redundancy, redundance *no pl.*

Reduplikation *f* reduplication.

reduplizieren* *vt* to reduplicate.

reduzierbar, reduzibel *adj* reducible (*auf +acc* to).

reduzieren* [1] *vt* **(a)** (*einschränken*) to reduce. **(b)** (*zurückführen*) to reduce (*auf +acc* to). **(c)** (*Chem*) to reduce.
[2] *vr* to decrease, to diminish.

Reduzierung *f siehe* **Reduktion.**

Reede *f* -, **-n** (*Naut*) roads *pl*, roadstead ◆ **auf der ~ liegen** to be (lying) in the roads.

Reeder *m* **-s, -** ship owner.

Reederei *f* shipping company.

Reedereiflagge *f* house flag.

reell *adj* **(a)** (*ehrlich*) honest, straight, on the level (*inf*); (*Comm*) *Geschäft, Firma* solid, sound; *Preis* realistic, fair; *Bedienung* good ◆ **das ist etwas R~es!** it's the real thing. **(b)** (*wirklich, echt*) real. **(c)** (*Math*) *Zahlen* real.

Reep *nt* **-(e)s, -e** (*N Ger*) rope.

Reet *nt* **-s,** *no pl* (*N Ger*) reed.

Reet-: ~dach *nt* thatched roof; **r~gedeckt** *adj* thatched.

REFA-Fachmann, REFA-Mann ['reːfa-] (*inf*) *m* time and motion expert *or* man (*inf*), work-study man (*inf*).

Refektorium *nt* (*Eccl*) refectory.

Referat *nt* **(a)** (*Univ*) seminar paper; (*Sch*) project ◆ **ein ~ vortragen** *or* **halten** to give *or* read *or* present a seminar paper/to present a project. **(b)** (*Admin: Ressort*) department.

Referendar(in *f*) *m* trainee (in civil service); (*Studien~*) student teacher; (*Gerichts~*) articled clerk.

Referendarzeit *f* traineeship; (*Studien~*) teacher training; (*Gerichts~*) time under articles.

Referendum *nt* **-s, Referenden** *or* **Referenda** referendum.

Referent(in *f*) *m* (*Sachbearbeiter*) consultant, expert; (*Redner, Berichterstatter*) speaker; (*Univ: Gutachter*) examiner.

▼ **Referenz** *f* reference ◆ **jdn als ~ angeben** to give sb as a referee.

referieren* *vi* to (give a) report, to give a review (*über +acc* on).

Reff *nt* **-(e)s, -e** (*Naut*) reef.

reffen *vt* (*Naut*) to reef.

Refinanzierung *f* financing of financing, rediscounting.

Reflektant(in *f*) *m* (*dated*) (*Kauflustiger*) prospective purchaser; (*Stellungsbewerber*) applicant.

reflektieren* [1] *vt* to reflect.
[2] *vi* **(a)** (*nachdenken*) to reflect, to ponder (*über +acc* (up)on). **(b)** (*streben nach*) **auf etw** (*acc*) **~** to be interested in sth. **(c)** (*Phys*) to reflect ◆ **entblendete Rückspiegel ~ nicht** tinted rear-view mirrors eliminate dazzle.

Reflektor *m* reflector.

reflektorisch [1] *adj* **(a)** (*motorisch*) reflex. **(b)** (*geistig*) reflective.
[2] *adv* by reflex action.

➤ SPRACHE AKTIV: Referenz → 46.5

Reflex *m* **-es, -e (a)** *(Phys)* reflection. **(b)** *(Physiol)* reflex. **(c)** *(Sociol)* reflection.
Reflexbewegung *f* reflex action.
Reflexion *f* **(a)** *(Phys)* reflection. **(b)** *(Überlegung)* reflection ◆ **über etw** *(acc)* **~en anstellen** to reflect on sth.
Reflexionswinkel *m (Phys)* angle of reflection.
reflexiv *adj (Gram)* reflexive.
Reflexiv *nt* **-s, -e, Reflexivum** *nt* reflexive (pronoun/verb).
Reflexivpronomen *nt* reflexive pronoun.
Reflexzonenmassage *f* reflexology.
Reform *f* **-, -en** reform.
Reformation *f* Reformation.
Reformationsfest *nt* Reformation Day *(Oct 31st)*.
Reformator *m* Reformer.
reformatorisch *adj* reforming.
Reform-: r~bedürftig *adj* in need of reform; **~bestrebungen** *pl* striving for *or* after reform; **~bewegung** *f* reform movement; **~eifer** *m* reforming zeal.
Reformer(in *f***)** *m* **-s, -** reformer.
reformerisch *adj* reforming.
Reform-: r~freudig *adj* avid for reform; **~gesetz** *nt* reform bill *or* law; **~haus** *nt* health food shop.
reformieren* *vt* to reform.
reformiert *adj (Eccl)* Reformed.
Reformierte(r) *mf decl as adj* member of the Reformed Church.
Reformismus *m (Pol)* reformism.
Reformist(in *f***)** *m (Pol)* reformist.
reformistisch *adj (Pol)* reformist.
Reform-: ~kurs *m* policy of reform; **einen ~kurs steuern** to follow a policy of reform; **auf ~kurs gehen** to embark on a policy of reform; **~plan** *m* plan for reform.
Refrain [rəˈfrɛ̃ː, re-] *m* **-s, -s** *(Mus)* chorus, refrain.
refraktär *adj (Med, liter)* refractory.
Refraktion *f (Phys)* refraction.
Refraktor *m (Phys, Opt)* refractor.
Refugium *nt (geh)* refuge.
Regal[1] *nt* **-s, -e (a)** *(Bord)* shelves *pl*; *(Typ)* stand. **(b)** *(Mus) (tragbare Orgel)* regal; *(Orgelteil)* vox humana.
Regal[2] *nt* **-s, -ien** [-iən] *(Jur)* regale *(spec)*.
Regatta *f* **-, Regatten** regatta.
Regattastrecke *f* regatta course.
Reg. Bez. *abbr of* **Regierungsbezirk.**
rege *adj* **(a)** *(betriebsam)* active, busy; *Verkehr* busy; *Handel* flourishing; *Briefwechsel* lively ◆ **ein ~s Treiben** a busy to-and-fro, a hustle and bustle; **auf dem Marktplatz herrschte ein ~s Treiben** the market place was bustling with activity *or* life; **Tendenz ~** *(St Ex)* brisk activity; **~ werden** to become active.
(b) *(lebhaft)* lively; *Unterhaltung auch* animated; *Phantasie auch* vivid; *Interesse auch* avid ◆ **ein ~r Geist** a lively soul; *(Verstand)* an active mind; **körperlich und geistig ~ sein** to be mentally and physically active, to be active in mind and body; **noch sehr ~ sein** to be very active still; **in ihm wurde die Hoffnung ~** *(liter)* his hopes rose; **in ihm wurde der Gedanke ~** *(liter)* the thought stirred within him; **~ Beteiligung** lively participation; *(zahlreich)* good attendance *or* turnout.
(c) *(zahlreich)* numerous; *(häufig)* frequent ◆ **~r Besuch** high attendance; **das Museum wurde nach der Eröffnung ~ besucht** when it opened the museum was very well visited.
Regel *f* **-, -n (a)** *(Vorschrift, Norm)* rule; *(Verordnung)* regulation ◆ **die ~n der ärztlichen Kunst** the rules of the medical profession; **nach allen ~n der Kunst** *(fig)* thoroughly; **sie überredete ihn nach allen ~n der Kunst,** ... she used every trick in the book to persuade him ...
(b) *(Gewohnheit)* habit, rule ◆ **sich** *(dat)* **etw zur ~ machen** to make a habit *or* rule of sth; **in der ~** as a rule; **zur ~ werden** to become a habit.
(c) *(Monatsblutung)* period; *(Menstruation)* menstruation *no art* ◆ **die ~ haben/bekommen** to have/get one's period, to menstruate; **sie hat mit zehn ihre ~ bekommen** her periods started when she was ten.
Regel-: ~arbeitszeit *f* core working hours *pl*; **r~bar** *adj (steuerbar)* adjustable; *(klärbar)* easily arranged; **~detri** *f* **-,** *no pl (Math)* rule of three; **~fall** *m* rule; **im ~fall** as a rule; **r~los** *adj (ungeregelt)* irregular; *(unordentlich)* disorderly, haphazard; *Leben* disorderly; **in r~loser Folge** at irregular intervals; **ein r~loses Durcheinander** a disorderly confusion; **~losigkeit** *f siehe adj* irregularity; disorderliness, haphazardness; disorderliness; **r~mäßig** *adj* regular; *Lebensweise auch* well-ordered, orderly; **r~mäßig spazierengehen** to take regular walks; **r~mäßige Beschwerden** regularly recurring complaints; **er kommt r~mäßig zu spät** he's always late; **~mäßigkeit** *f* regularity; **er kommt mit sturer ~mäßigkeit zu spät** he is persistently late.
regeln [1] *vt* **(a)** *(regulieren) Verkehr* to control; *Temperatur etc auch* to regulate; *siehe* **geregelt.**
(b) *(erledigen)* to see to; *(endgültig)* to settle; *Problem etc* to sort out; *(in Ordnung bringen) Unstimmigkeiten* to settle, to resolve; *Finanzen* to put in order ◆ **das läßt sich ~** that can be arranged; **das werde ich schon ~** I'll see to it.
(c) *(festsetzen, einrichten)* to settle ◆ **wir haben die Sache so geregelt** ... we have arranged things like this ...; **gesetzlich geregelt sein** to be laid down by law.
[2] *vr* to sort itself out, to resolve itself.
Regel-: r~recht [1] *adj* real, proper; *Betrug, Erpressung, Beleidigung etc* downright; **er wollte einen r~rechten Prozeß** he wanted a full-blown trial; **das Spiel artete in eine r~rechte Schlägerei aus** the match degenerated into a regular brawl; [2] *adv* really; *unverschämt, beleidigend* downright; **~studienzeit** *f period of time within which a student must complete his studies*; **~technik** *f* control engineering; **~techniker** *m* control engineer.
Regelung *f* **(a)** *(Regulierung)* regulation, control(ling).
(b) *(Erledigung)* settling, settlement; *(von Unstimmigkeiten)* resolution ◆ **ich habe die ~ meiner finanziellen Angelegenheiten meinem Bruder übertragen** I have entrusted my brother with the management of my financial affairs; **ich werde für die ~ dieser Angelegenheit sorgen** I shall see to this matter.
(c) *(Abmachung)* arrangement; *(Bestimmung)* ruling ◆ **wir haben eine ~ gefunden** we have come to an arrangement.
Regelungstechnik *f* control engineering.
Regel-: r~widrig *adj* against the rules; *(gegen Verordnungen verstoßend)* against the regulations; **r~widriges Verhalten im Verkehr** breaking the traffic regulations; **r~widrige Transaktion** irregular transaction; **ein r~widriger Einwurf/Elfmeter** a foul throw-in/an improperly taken penalty; **~widrigkeit** *f* irregularity; *(Verstoß auch)* breach of the rules; *(Verstoß gegen Verordnungen auch)* breach of regulations.
regen [1] *vt (bewegen)* to move ◆ **keinen Finger (mehr) ~** *(fig)* not to lift a finger (any more).
[2] *vr (Mensch, Glied, Baum etc)* to move, to stir; *(Gefühl, Gewissen, Zweifel, Wind etc)* to stir ◆ **unter den Zuhörern regte sich Widerspruch** there were mutterings of disapproval from the audience; **kein Lüftchen regt sich** *(poet)* not a breeze stirs the air; **reg dich!** look lively!; **sich nicht/kaum ~ können** not/hardly to be able to move; *(fig)* not to have enough/to have just enough to keep body and soul together; **sich ~ bringt Segen** *(Prov)* hard work brings its own reward.
Regen *m* **-s, -** rain; *(fig: von Schimpfwörtern, Blumen etc)* shower ◆ **in den ~ kommen** to be caught in the rain; **es gibt bald ~** it's going to rain soon; **so ein ~!** what *or* some rain!; **in/bei strömendem ~** in the pouring rain; **ein warmer ~** *(fig)* a windfall; **jdn im ~ stehenlassen** *(fig)* to leave sb out in the cold; **vom ~ in die Traufe kommen** *(prov)* to fall out of the frying-pan into the fire *(prov)*.
Regen-: r~arm *adj* dry, rainless; **~bö** *f* rainy squall.
Regenbogen *m* rainbow.
Regenbogen-: ~farben *pl* colours *pl* of the rainbow; **in allen ~farben schillern** to shine like shot silk, to iridesce *(liter)*; **r~farbig, r~farben** *adj* rainbow-coloured; **~haut** *f (Anat)* iris; **~hautentzündung** *f* iritis *(spec)*, inflammation of the iris; **~presse** *f* trashy *or* pulp magazines *pl*; **~trikot** *nt (Sport)* multi-coloured jersey.
Regen-: ~dach *nt* canopy; *(hum: ~schirm)* brolly *(Brit inf)*, bumbershoot *(US inf)*; **r~dicht** *adj* rainproof.
Regeneration *f* regeneration; *(fig auch)* revitalization.
regenerationsfähig *adj* capable of regeneration; *(fig auch)* capable of regenerating itself *or* of revitalization.
regenerativ *adj* regenerative.
Regenerator *m (Tech)* regenerator.
regenerieren* [1] *vr (Biol)* to regenerate; *(fig)* to revitalize *or* regenerate oneself/itself; *(nach Anstrengung, Schock etc)* to recover.
[2] *vt (Biol)* to regenerate; *(fig auch)* to revitalize.
Regenerierung *f siehe* **Regeneration.**
Regen-: ~fall *m usu pl* (fall of) rain; **ein ~fall** rain, a shower; **tropische ~fälle** tropical rains; **⚠~faß** *nt* water-butt, rain barrel; **~flut** *f usu pl* torrential rain *usu sing*, torrent of rain; **r~frei** *adj* rainless; **⚠~guß** *m* downpour; **~haut** ® *f* plastic mac *(Brit inf) or* raincoat; **~hut** *m* waterproof hat, rainhat; **~kleidung** *f* rainwear; **~mantel** *m* raincoat, mac *(Brit inf)*, mac(k)intosh *(esp Brit)*; **~pfeifer** *m* plover; **r~reich** *adj* rainy, wet; **~rinne** *f siehe* **Dachrinne**; **~schatten** *m (Geog)* rain shadow; **~schauer** *m* shower (of rain); **~schirm** *m* umbrella; *siehe* **gespannt**; **r~schwer** *adj* **r~schwere Wolken** black *or* rain clouds, clouds heavy with rain.
Regent(in *f***)** *m* sovereign, reigning monarch; *(Stellvertreter)* regent.
Regen-: ~tag *m* rainy day; **~tonne** *f* water-butt, rain barrel; **~tropfen** *m* raindrop.
Regentschaft *f* reign; *(Stellvertretung)* regency ◆ **die ~ antreten** to ascend the throne; *(als Stellvertreter)* to become regent; **die ~ übernehmen** to take over as regent.
Regen-: ~wald *m (Geog)* rain forest; **~wasser** *nt* rainwater; **~wetter** *nt* rainy weather, rain; **er macht ein Gesicht wie drei** *or* **sieben Tage ~wetter** *(inf)* he's got a face as long as a month of Sundays *(inf)*; **~wolke** *f* rain cloud; **~wurm** *m* earthworm; **~zeit** *f* rainy season, rains *pl*.
Reggae [ˈrɛgeː] *m* **-(s),** *no pl* reggae.
Regie [reˈʒiː] *f* **(a)** *(künstlerische Leitung)* direction; *(Theat, Rad, TV auch)* production *(Brit)* ◆ **die ~ bei etw haben** *or* **führen** to direct/produce sth; *(fig)* to be in charge of sth; **die ~ bei diesem Film/dieser Sendung führte** *or* **hatte Heinz Krüger** this film/programme was directed/produced by Heinz Krüger; **unter der ~ von** directed/produced by; **„~: A.G. Meier"** "Producer/Director A.G. Meier".
(b) *(Leitung, Verwaltung)* management ◆ **etw in eigener ~ führen** to control sth directly *or* personally; **etw in eigene ~ nehmen** to take *or* assume direct *or* personal control of sth; **etw in eigener ~ tun** to do sth oneself.
Regie- [reˈʒiː-]: **~anweisung** *f* (stage) direction; **~assistent** *m* assistant producer/director; **~betrieb** *m (Admin)* state-owned factory; **~fehler** *m (fig)* slip-up; **~film** *m* **sein erster ~film** the first film he directed; **~pult** *nt (Rad)* control desk *or* console.

regieren* 1 *vi (herrschen)* to rule; *(Monarch auch, fig)* to reign ◆ **der R~de Bürgermeister von Berlin** the Mayor of West Berlin.
2 *vt (beherrschen, lenken) Staat* to rule (over), to govern; *(Monarch auch)* to reign over; *Markt, Fahrzeug* to control; *(Gram)* to govern.

Regierung *f* **(a)** *(Kabinett)* government ◆ **die ~ Wilson** the Wilson government.
(b) *(Herrschaft)* government; *(Zeitabschnitt)* period of government; *(nichtdemokratisch)* rule; *(von Monarch)* reign; *(Führung)* leadership ◆ **an die ~ kommen** to come to power; *(durch Wahl auch)* to come into *or* take office; **jdn an die ~ bringen** to put sb into power; *(durch Wahl auch)* to put sb into office; **die ~ antreten** to take power; *(nach Wahl auch)* to take office.

Regierungs-: **r~amtlich** *adj* governmental; **~anhänger** *m* government supporter; **~antritt** *m* coming to power; *(nach Wahl auch)* taking of office; **bei ~antritt** when the government took power/office; **~bank** *f* government bench; **~beamte(r)** *m* government official; **~bezirk** *m primary administrative division of a "Land",* ≃ region *(Brit),* ≃ county *(US)*; **~bildung** *f* formation of a government; **~chef** *m* head of a/the government; **der belgische ~chef** the head of the Belgian government; **~direktor** *m* senior government official; **~erklärung** *f* inaugural speech; *(in GB)* King's/Queen's Speech; **~fähigkeit** *f* ability to govern; **r~feindlich** *adj* anti-government *no adv*; **sich r~feindlich verhalten/äußern** to act/speak against the government; **~form** *f* form *or* type of government; **r~freundlich** *adj* pro-government *no adv*; **~geschäfte** *pl* government business *sing*; **~hauptstadt** *f* administrative capital; **~kreise** *pl* government circles *pl*; **~krise** *f* government(al) crisis; **~partei** *f* ruling *or* governing party, party in power; **~präsident** *m chief administrator of a ~bezirk,* ≃ chairman of the regional council *(Brit),* ≃ county manager *(US)*; **~präsidium** *nt highest authority in a ~bezirk,* ≃ regional council *(Brit) or* board *(US)*; **~rat** *m* senior civil servant; *(Sw: Organ)* legislature; **~sitz** *m* seat of government; **~sprecher** *m* government spokesman; **~system** *nt* system of government, governmental system; **r~treu** *adj* loyal to the government; **~umbildung** *f* cabinet reshuffle; **~vorlage** *f* government bill; **~wechsel** *m* change of government; **~zeit** *f* rule; *(von Monarch auch)* reign; *(von gewählter Regierung, Präsident)* period *or* term of office.

Regime [re'ʒiːm] *nt* **-s, -s** *(pej)* regime.

Regime-: **~anhänger** *m* supporter of the regime; **~gegner** *m* opponent of the regime; **~kritiker** *m* critic of the regime, dissident.

Regiment *nt* **-(e)s, -e** *or (Einheit)* **-er (a)** *(old: Herrschaft)* rule ◆ **das ~ führen** *(inf)* to be the boss *(inf)*, to give the orders; **ein strenges** *or* **straffes ~ führen** *(inf)* to be strict; *(Vorgesetzter etc auch)* to run a tight ship *(inf)*; **der Winter führt ein strenges ~** the winter is harsh and stern. **(b)** *(Mil)* regiment.

Regiments- *in cpds* regimental; **~kommandeur** *m* regimental commander.

Region *f* region; *siehe* **schweben.**

regional *adj* regional ◆ **~ verschieden** *or* **unterschiedlich sein** to vary from one region to another.

Regionalismus *m* regionalism.

Regional-: **~liga** *f* regional league *(lower leagues of professional clubs)*; **~programm** *nt (TV, Rad)* regional station *or (TV auch)* channel; *(Sendung)* regional programme; **~schnellbahn** *f (Rail)* high-speed regional railway.

Regisseur(in *f)* [reʒɪ'søːɐ, -'søːrɪn] *m* director; *(Theat, Rad, TV auch)* producer *(Brit)*.

Register *nt* **-s, - (a)** *(amtliche Liste)* register ◆ **ein ~ (über etw** *acc***) führen** to keep a register (of sth); **etw ins ~ (eines Amtes** *etc***) eintragen** to register sth (with an office *etc*).
(b) *(Stichwortverzeichnis)* index.
(c) *(Mus)* register; *(von Orgel auch)* stop ◆ **alle ~ spielen lassen** *or* **ziehen** *(fig)* to pull out all the stops; **andere ~ ziehen** *(fig)* to get tough.
(d) *(fig inf)* **ein langes/altes ~** a tall/an old type *(inf)*.

Register-: **~tonne** *f (Naut)* register ton; **~zug** *m (Mus: bei Orgel)* stop.

Registrator *m (old)* registrar.

Registratur *f* **(a)** *(das Registrieren)* registration. **(b)** *(Büro)* records office. **(c)** *(Aktenschrank)* filing cabinet. **(d)** *(Mus: bei Orgel)* stops *pl*.

Registrierballon *m (Met)* sounding balloon.

registrieren* *vti* **(a)** *(eintragen, verzeichnen)* to register; *(zusammenzählen)* to calculate ◆ **sie ist registriert** she is a registered prostitute. **(b)** *(inf: zur Kenntnis nehmen)* to note. **sie hat überhaupt nicht registriert, daß ich nicht da war** the fact that I wasn't there didn't register with her at all.

Registrier-: **~kasse** *f* cash register; **~stelle** *f* registration office.

Registrierung *f* registration.

Reglement [reglə'mãː] *nt* **-s, -s** *(old)* rules *pl*, conventions *pl*.

reglementarisch 1 *adj* regulation.
2 *adv* according to (the) regulations ◆ **etw ~ festlegen** to make a regulation about sth.

reglementieren* *vt* to regulate; *jdn* to regiment.

Reglementierung *f siehe vt* regulation; regimentation.

reglement- [reglə'mãː-]: **~mäßig** *adj (old)* according to regulation(s); **~widrig** *adj (old)* contrary to regulations.

Regler *m* **-s, -** regulator, control; *(Elektromotor, Fernsteuerung)* control(ler); *(von Benzinmotor)* governor.

Reglette *f (Typ)* lead.

reglos *adj* motionless.

regnen *vti impers* to rain ◆ **es regnet in Strömen** it's pouring (with rain); **es regnet Glückwünsche/Proteste** congratulations/protests are pouring in; **es regnete Vorwürfe** reproaches hailed down.

regnerisch *adj* rainy.

⚠ **Regreß** *m* **-sses, -sse (a)** *(Philos)* regress. **(b)** *(Jur)* recourse, redress ◆ **einen ~ auf jdn** *or* **an jdm nehmen** to have recourse against sb.

⚠ **Regreß|anspruch** *m (Jur)* claim for compensation.

Regression *f* regression, retrogression.

regressiv *adj (Biol)* regressive, retrogressive; *(fig)* retrograde, retrogressive ◆ **die Ausweitung verlief ~** the expansion dropped off.

⚠ **Regreß-:** **~pflicht** *f* liability for compensation; **r~pflichtig** *adj* liable for compensation.

regsam *adj* active, alert, lively.

regulär *adj (üblich)* normal; *(vorschriftsmäßig)* proper, regular; *Arbeitszeit* normal, basic, regular ◆ **~e Truppen** regular troops, regulars; **~e Bankgeschäfte** normal banking transactions; **etw ~ kaufen/verkaufen** *(zum normalen Preis)* to buy/sell sth at the normal price; *(auf normale Weise)* to buy/sell sth in the normal way.

Regulation *f (Biol)* regulation.

Regulations-: **~störung** *f (Biol)* malfunction of a regulatory system; **~system** *nt (Biol)* regulatory system.

regulativ *adj* regulatory, regulative ◆ **in etw** *(acc)* **~ eingreifen** to regulate sth.

Regulativ *nt* counterbalance *(Med)* ◆ **als ~ wirken** to have a regulating effect.

Regulator *m* wall clock.

regulierbar *adj* regul(at)able, adjustable.

regulieren* 1 *vt* **(a)** to regulate; *(nachstellen auch)* to adjust.
(b) *Rechnung, Forderung* to settle.
2 *vr* to become more regular ◆ **sich von selbst ~** to be self-regulating.

Regulierhebel *m (Tech)* regulating lever.

Regulierung *f* regulation; *(Nachstellung auch)* adjustment.

Regung *f (Bewegung)* movement; *(des Gefühls, des Gewissens, von Mitleid)* stirring ◆ **ohne jede ~** without a flicker (of emotion); **einer ~ des Herzens folgen** *(liter)* to follow the dictates of one's heart *(liter)*; **zu keiner ~ fähig sein** *(fig)* to be paralyzed; **eine menschliche ~ verspüren** *(hum)* to have to answer a call of nature *(hum)*.

regungslos *adj* motionless.

Regungslosigkeit *f* motionlessness.

Reh *nt* **-s, -e** deer; *(im Gegensatz zu Hirsch etc)* roedeer ◆ **scheu wie ein ~** (as) timid as a fawn.

Reha- *in cpds abbr of* **Rehabilitations-**.

Rehabilitand *m* **-en, -en** person undergoing rehabilitation.

Rehabilitation *f* rehabilitation; *(von Ruf, Ehre)* vindication.

Rehabilitations-: **~klinik** *f* rehabilitation clinic; **~zentrum** *nt* rehabilitation centre.

rehabilitieren* 1 *vt* to rehabilitate; *Ruf, Ehre* to vindicate.
2 *vr* to rehabilitate *(form) or* vindicate oneself.

Rehabilitierung *f siehe* **Rehabilitation.**

Reh-: **~bock** *m* roebuck; **~braten** *m* roast venison; **r~braun** *adj* russet; *Augen* hazel; **~geiß** *f* doe *(of the roedeer)*; **~kalb, ~kitz** *nt* fawn *or* kid (of the roedeer); **~keule** *f (Cook)* haunch of venison; **~leder** *nt* deerskin; **r~ledern** *adj* deerskin.

Rehling *m (Bot dial)* chanterelle.

Reh-: **~posten** *m (Hunt: grober Schrot)* buckshot; **~rücken** *m (Cook)* saddle of venison; **~wild** *nt (Hunt)* roedeer.

Reibach *m* **-s,** *no pl (inf)* killing *(inf)* ◆ **einen ~ machen** *(inf)* to make a killing *(inf)*.

Reibe *f* **-, -n** *(Cook)* grater.

Reib|eisen *nt* rasp; *(Cook)* grater; *(fig: zänkisches Weib)* shrew ◆ **rauh wie ein ~** *(inf)* like sandpaper.

Reibe-: **~kuchen** *m (Cook dial)* ≃ potato fritter; **~laut** *m (Ling)* fricative.

reiben *pret* **rieb,** *ptp* **gerieben** 1 *vti* **(a)** to rub ◆ **etw blank ~** to rub sth till it shines; **etw** *or* **an etw** *(dat)* **~** to rub sth; **sich** *(dat)* **die Augen (vor Müdigkeit) ~** to rub one's eyes (because one is tired); **sie rieb dem Kranken die Salbe in die Haut** she rubbed the ointment into the patient's skin; **jdm den Rücken ~** to rub sb's back; **sich** *(dat)* **die Hände ~** to rub one's hands.
(b) *(zerkleinern)* to grate.
2 *vr* to rub oneself *(an +dat* on, against); *(sich verletzen)* to scrape oneself *(an +dat* on) ◆ **ich würde mich ständig an ihm ~** there would always be friction between him and me; **sich an etw** *(dat)* **wund ~** to scrape oneself raw on sth; **ich habe mich beim Radfahren wund gerieben** I got chafed cycling.

Reiberei *f usu pl (inf)* friction *no pl* ◆ **(kleinere) ~en** (short) periods of friction; **ihre ständigen ~en** the constant friction between them.

Reibfläche *f (für Streichholz)* striking surface; *(von Reibe)* scraping surface.

Reibung *f* **(a)** *(das Reiben)* rubbing; *(Phys)* friction. **(b)** *(fig)* friction *no pl* ◆ **es kommt zu ~en** friction occurs.

Reibungs-: **~elektrizität** *f* frictional electricity; **~fläche** *f (fig)* source of friction; **(viele) ~flächen bieten** to be a potential cause of friction; **r~los** *adj* frictionless; *(fig inf)* trouble-free; **r~los verlaufen** to go off smoothly *or* without a hitch; **~verlust** *m* friction(al) loss; **~wärme** *f (Phys)* frictional heat; **~widerstand** *m (Phys)* frictional resistance.

Reich *nt* **-(e)s, -e (a)** *(Herrschaft(sgebiet), Imperium)* empire; *(König~)* realm, kingdom ◆ **das ~ der aufgehenden Sonne** *(liter)* the land of the rising sun; **das Deutsche ~** the German Reich; *(bis 1919 auch)* the German Empire; **das Dritte ~** the Third Reich; **das himmlische ~** *(liter)* the Kingdom of Heaven, the Heavenly Kingdom; **das ~ Gottes** the Kingdom of God.
(b) *(Bereich, Gebiet)* realm ◆ **das ~ der Tiere/Pflanzen** the animal/vegetable

kingdom; **das ~ der Natur** the world *or* realm of nature; **das ist mein ~** *(fig)* that is my domain; **da bin ich in meinem ~** that's where I'm in my element.

reich *adj* **(a)** *(vermögend, wohlhabend)* rich, wealthy; *Erbschaft* substantial; *Partie, Heirat* good ◆ **~ heiraten** *(inf)* to marry (into) money.
(b) *(kostbar)* costly *no adv*, rich; *Schmuck* costly *no adv*, expensive ◆ **~ geschmückt** richly decorated; *Mensch* richly adorned; **ein ~ ausgestattetes Haus** a richly *or* lavishly furnished house; **eine ~ ausgestattete Bibliothek** a well stocked library; **~ mit Vorräten ausgestattet** well *or* amply stocked up with supplies.
(c) *(ergiebig, üppig)* rich, copious; *Ernte auch* bountiful, abundant; *Mahl* sumptuous, lavish ◆ **jdn ~ belohnen** to reward sb well, to give sb a rich reward; **damit bin ich ~ belohnt** *(fig)* I am richly *or* amply rewarded; **jdn ~ beschenken** to shower sb with presents; **eine mit Kindern ~ beschenkte Familie** a family blessed with many children; **~ an etw** *(dat)* **sein** to be rich in sth; **~ an Fischen/Wild/Steinen** abounding with *or* full of fish/game/stones; **er ist ~ an Erfahrungen/guten Einfällen** he has had a wealth of experiences/he is full of good ideas.
(d) *(groß, vielfältig)* large, copious; *Auswahl* wide, large; *Erfahrungen, Kenntnisse* wide; *Blattwerk, Vegetation* rich, luxuriant ◆ **eine ~e Fülle** a rich abundance; **in ~em Maße vorhanden sein** to abound, to be found in large quantities; **~ illustriert** richly *or* copiously illustrated.

⚠**reichbegütert** *adj* wealthy, affluent.

▼ **reichen** 1 *vi* **(a)** *(sich erstrecken)* to stretch, to extend *(bis zu* to), to reach *(bis zu etw* sth); *(Stimme)* to carry *(bis zu* to), to reach *(bis zu jdm/etw* sb/sth); *(Kleidungsstück)* to reach *(bis zu etw* sth) ◆ **sein Swimmingpool reicht bis an mein Grundstück** his swimming pool comes right up to my land; **der Garten reicht bis ans Ufer** the garden stretches *or* extends *or* goes right down to the riverbank; **das Wasser reicht mir bis zum Hals** the water comes up to my neck; **jdm bis zur Schulter ~** to come up to sb's shoulder; **er reicht mit dem Kopf bis zur Decke** his head reaches *or* touches the ceiling; **so weit der Himmel reichte** in the whole sky; **so weit ~ meine Beziehungen/Fähigkeiten nicht** my connections are not that extensive/my skills are not that wide-ranging; **... aber sein Arm reichte nicht so weit** ... but his arm wouldn't reach that far; **so weit das Auge reicht** as far as the eye can see.
▼ **(b)** *(langen)* to be enough, to suffice *(form)*; *(zeitlich auch)* to last ◆ **der Saal reicht nicht für so viele Leute** the room isn't big enough *or* won't suffice *(form)* for so many people; **der Zucker reicht nicht** there won't be enough sugar; **reicht mein Geld noch bis zum Monatsende?** will my money last until the end of the month?; **reicht das Licht zum Lesen?** is there enough light to read by?; **dazu reicht meine Geduld/~ meine Fähigkeiten nicht** I haven't got enough patience/I'm not skilled enough for that; **das muß für vier Leute ~** that will have to be enough *or* suffice *(form) or* do *(inf)* for four people; **das sollte eigentlich ~** that should be enough, that should do *(inf)*; **mir reicht's** *(inf)* *(habe die Nase voll)* I've had enough *(inf)*; *(habe genug gehabt)* that's enough for me; **als das dann noch passierte, reichte es ihm** when that happened it was just too much for him; **jetzt reicht's (mir aber)!** that's the last straw!; *(Schluß)* that's enough!; **das reicht ja, um den Geduldigsten aus der Fassung zu bringen!** it's enough to try the patience of a saint!; **es reichte ja schon, daß er frech war** it was bad enough that he was cheeky, his being cheeky was bad enough.
(c) *(inf)* **mit dem Essen/der Zeit** *etc* **~** to have enough food/time *etc.*
2 *vt* *(entgegenhalten)* to hand; *(geben auch)* to give; *(herüber~, hinüber~ auch)* to pass (over); *(anbieten)* to serve; *(Eccl) Abendmahl* to give, to administer ◆ **jdm etw ~** to hand/give/pass sb sth, to hand/give/pass sth to sb; **sie reichte mir die Wange zum Kuß** she proffered her cheek for a kiss; **jdm die Hand ~** to hold out one's hand (to sb); **sich die Hände ~** to join hands; *(zur Begrüßung)* to shake hands; **es wurden Erfrischungen gereicht** refreshments were served; *siehe* **Hand**.

Reiche(r) *mf decl as adj* rich *or* wealthy man/woman *etc* ◆ **die ~n** the rich *or* wealthy.

Reich-: ⚠**r~geschmückt** *adj attr* richly adorned; *Gegenstand auch* richly decorated; **r~haltig** *adj* extensive; *Auswahl auch* wide, large; *Essen* rich; *Informationen* comprehensive; *Programm* varied; **~haltigkeit** *f siehe adj* extensiveness; wideness; richness; comprehensiveness; variety; **die ~haltigkeit der Auswahl** the range of choice.

reichlich 1 *adj* **(a)** *(sehr viel, groß)* ample, large, substantial; *Vorrat auch* plentiful; *Portion, Trinkgeld auch* generous; *Geschenke* numerous.
(b) *(mehr als genügend) Zeit, Geld, Platz* ample, plenty of; *Belohnung* ample.
(c) *(inf: mindestens)* good ◆ **eine ~e Stunde** a good hour.
2 *adv* **(a)** *(sehr viel) belohnen, sich eindecken* amply; *verdienen* richly ◆ **jdn ~ beschenken** to give sb lots of *or* numerous presents; **~ Trinkgeld geben** to tip generously.
(b) *(mehr als genügend)* **~ Zeit/Geld haben** to have plenty of *or* ample time/money; **~ vorhanden sein** to abound, to exist in plenty; **mehr als ~ belohnt/bezahlt** more than amply rewarded/paid more than enough; **der Mantel ist ~ ausgefallen** the coat is on the big side; **das war ~ gewogen/abgemessen** that was very generously weighed out/measured out; **das ist ~ gerechnet** that's a generous estimate.
(c) *(inf: mindestens)* **~ 1.000 Mark** a good 1,000 marks.
(d) *(inf: ziemlich)* pretty.

Reichs-: **~abt** *m (Hist) abbot of an abbey under imperial protection*; **~acht** *f (Hist)* outlawry in the Emperor's name; **~adler** *m (Her, Hist)* imperial eagle; **~apfel** *m (Her, Hist)* imperial orb; **~bahn** *f* state railway; *(DDR)* East German State Railways; **~gebiet** *nt* prewar Germany; **im ~gebiet** inside Germany's prewar boundaries; **~gericht** *nt (Hist)* German supreme court *(until 1945)*; **~grenze** *f* border of the empire; prewar German border; **~gründung** *f* foundation of the Reich *or* Prussian Empire; **~hauptstadt** *f (1933-45)* capital of the Reich; *(vor 1933)* imperial capital; **~insignien** *pl (Hist)* imperial regalia *pl*; **~kanzler** *m (bis 1918)* Imperial Chancellor; *(1918-34)* German Chancellor; **~kleinodien** *pl (Hist)* imperial regalia *pl*; **~konkordat** *nt* Reich Concordat; **~mark** *f* reichsmark, (old) German mark; **~präsident** *m* German president *(until 1934)*; **~regierung** *f* German government *(until 1945)*; **~stadt** *f (Hist)* free city (of the Holy Roman Empire); **freie ~stadt** free city; **~stände** *pl (Hist)* estates of the Empire *pl*; **~tag** *m* Parliament; *(in Deutschland 1871-1945)* Reichstag; *(in Deutschland vor 1871, in Japan)* Imperial Diet; **~tagsbrand** *m* burning of the Reichstag; **r~unmittelbar** *adj (Hist)* self-governing under the Kaiser; **~vogt** *m (Hist)* protector; **~wehr** *f* German army *(1921-35)*.

Reichtum *m* **(a)** wealth *no pl*, richness *no pl*; *(Besitz)* riches *pl* ◆ **zu ~ kommen** to become rich, to make one's fortune; **~̈er erwerben** to gain riches; **die ~̈er der Erde/des Meeres** the riches of the earth/sea; **der innere** *or* **seelische ~** richness of spirit; **damit kann man keine ~̈er gewinnen** you won't get rich that way.
(b) *(fig: Fülle, Reichhaltigkeit)* wealth, abundance *(an +dat* of) ◆ **der ~ an Fischen** the abundance of fish.

⚠**reichverziert** *adj attr* richly ornamented.

Reichweite *f (von Geschoß, Sender)* range; *(greifbare Nähe)* reach; *(fig: Einflußbereich)* scope ◆ **in ~** within range/the reach *(gen* of); **jd ist in ~** sb is nearby *or* around; **außer ~** out of range/reach *(gen* of); **innerhalb der ~** *+gen* within range/the scope of; **außerhalb der ~** *+gen* outside the range of/beyond the scope of.

Reif[1] *m* **-(e)s,** *no pl siehe* **Rauhreif**.

Reif[2] *m* **-(e)s, -e** *(old, liter)* *(Stirn~, Diadem)* circlet; *(Arm~)* bangle; *(Fingerring)* ring; *(im Rock)* hoop.

reif *adj* **(a)** *(voll entwickelt) Früchte, Getreide* ripe; *Mensch, Ei* mature ◆ **der Pickel/das Geschwür ist ~** *(inf)* the spot/abscess has come to a head.
(b) *(erfahren, älter)* mature ◆ **in ~(er)em Alter, in den ~eren Jahren** in one's mature(r) years; **die ~ere Jugend** those of mellower years; **im ~eren Alter von ...** at the ripe old age of ...
(c) *(vorbereitet)* ready, ripe; *(durchdacht) Urteil, Arbeit, Gedanken* mature ◆ **~ zur Veröffentlichung** ready *or* ripe for publication; **die Zeit ist ~/noch nicht ~** the time is ripe/not yet ripe; **eine ~e Leistung** *(inf)* a brilliant achievement.
(d) **für etw ~ sein** *(inf)* to be ready for sth; **~ sein** *(sl)* to be in for it *(inf) or* for the high jump *(inf)*.

Reife *f* **-,** *no pl* **(a)** *(das Reifen)* ripening.
(b) *(das Reifsein)* ripeness; *(Geschlechts~, von Ei)* maturity ◆ **zur ~ kommen** to ripen; *(geh: Mädchen)* to come to *or* reach maturity; **zur ~ bringen** to ripen.
(c) *(fig: von Menschen, Gedanken etc)* maturity ◆ **ihm fehlt die (sittliche) ~** he lacks maturity, he's too immature.
(d) **mittlere ~** *(Sch) first public examination in secondary school*, ≃ O-Levels *pl* *(Brit)*; **Zeugnis der ~** *(form) siehe* **Reifezeugnis**.

Reifegrad *m* degree of ripeness.

reifen[1] *vi impers* **es reift** there has been/will be a frost.

reifen[2] 1 *vt Obst* to ripen; *jdn* to mature ◆ **das hat ihn zum Manne gereift** *(liter)* that made a man out of him; *siehe* **gereift**.
2 *vi aux sein* **(a)** *(Obst)* to ripen; *(Mensch, Ei)* to mature ◆ **er reifte zum Manne** he became a man.
(b) *(fig: Plan, Entscheidung)* to mature ◆ **zur Wirklichkeit ~** to come to fruition, to become reality; **zur Gewißheit ~** to harden into certainty.

Reifen *m* **-s, -** tyre *(Brit)*, tire *(US)*; *(Spiel~, von Faß, von Rock)* hoop; *(Arm~)* bangle ◆ **(den) ~ treiben/spielen** to bowl a hoop.

Reifen-: **~defekt** *m siehe* **~panne**; **~druck** *m* tyre pressure; **~panne** *f* puncture, flat; *(geplatzt auch)* blowout; **~profil** *nt* tyre tread; **~schaden** *m* **(a)** faulty tyre; **(b)** *siehe* **~panne**; **~wechsel** *m* tyre-change.

Reife-: **~prüfung** *f (Sch) siehe* **Abitur**; **~zeit** *f* ripening time; *(von Ei)* period of incubation; *(Pubertät)* puberty *no def art*; **~zeugnis** *nt (Sch) "Abitur" certificate*, ≃ A-Level certificate *(Brit)*, high-school graduation certificate *(US)*.

reiflich *adj* thorough, careful ◆ **nach ~er Überlegung** after careful consideration, upon mature reflection *(liter)*; **sich** *(dat)* **etw ~ überlegen** to consider sth carefully.

Reifrock *m (Hist)* farthingale, hoop skirt.

Reifung *f* ripening; *(von Ei)* maturing, maturation.

⚠**Reifungsprozeß** *m* process of ripening; *(von Ei)* maturation process.

Reigen *m* **-s, -** round dance, roundel(ay) *(old)*; *(fig geh)* round ◆ **den ~ eröffnen** *or* **anführen** *(fig geh)* to lead off; **den ~ beschließen** *(fig geh)* to bring up the rear; **ein bunter ~ von Melodien** a varied selection of melodies.

Reihe *f* **-, -n** **(a)** *(geregelte Anordnung)* row, line; *(Sitz~, beim Stricken)* row; *(fig: von Beispielen, Reden)* series *sing* ◆ **in ~n antreten** to line up; *(Mil)* to fall in; **in ~n zu (je) drei antreten/marschieren** to line up/march in rows of three *or* in threes; **sich in einer ~ aufstellen** to line up, to form a row *or* line; **sich in die/eine ~ stellen** to join the row *or* line/to line up; *(Mil)* to fall in; **in einer ~ stehen** to stand in a row *or* line; **in Reih und Glied antreten** to line up in formation; **sie standen in Reih und Glied vor dem Lehrer** they stood lined up in front of their teacher; **aus der ~ tanzen** *(fig inf)* to be different; *(gegen Konventionen verstoßen)* to step out of line; **die ~ herumgehen** *(Gegenstand)* to be passed around, to go the rounds; **die ~n schließen** *(Mil)* to close ranks; **die ~n lichten sich** *(fig)* the ranks are thinning; **in den eigenen ~n** within our/their *etc* own ranks; **die ~ eröffnen** *(fig)* to start off; **in einer ~ mit jdm stehen** *(fig)* to be on a par with sb; **sich in eine ~ mit jdm stellen** *(fig)* to put

oneself on a par *or* on an equal footing with sb.
(b) (*Reihenfolge*) **er ist an der ~** it's his turn, he's next; (*beim Spiel etc auch*) it's his go; **die ~ ist an jdm** it's sb's turn; **er kommt an die ~** he's next, it's his turn *or* him (*inf*) next; **warte, bis du an die ~ kommst** wait till it's your turn/go; **er kommt immer außer der ~** he always comes just when he pleases; **der ~ nach, nach der ~** in order, in turn; **sie sollen der ~ nach hereinkommen** they are to come in one by one *or* one at a time; **erzähl mal der ~ nach, wie alles war** tell us how it was in the order it all happened; **außer der ~** out of order; (*bei Spielen auch*) out of turn; (*zusätzlich, nicht wie gewöhnlich*) out of the usual way of things; **wenn ich das Auto mal außer der ~ brauche** if I should happen to need the car at a time when I don't normally have it; **es kommt ganz selten vor, daß ich mal außer der ~ da bin** it's very rare for me to be there out of my routine.
(c) (*Serie, Math, Mus*) series *sing*; (*Biol: Ordnung*) order.
(d) (*unbestimmte Anzahl*) number ◆ **in die ~ der Mitgliedsstaaten eintreten** to join the ranks of the member states; **in der ~ der Stars** amongst the ranks of the stars; **eine ganze ~ (von)** a whole lot (of); **eine ganze ~ von Beispielen** a whole string of examples.
(e) (*inf: Ordnung*) **aus der ~ kommen** (*in Unordnung geraten*) to get out of order; (*verwirrt werden*) to lose one's equilibrium; (*gesundheitlich*) to fall ill; **wieder in die ~ kommen** to get one's equilibrium back; (*gesundheitlich*) to get back on form; **nicht in der ~ sein** not to be well *or* one hundred per cent (*inf*); **in die ~ bringen** to put in order, to put straight; **etw auf die ~ kriegen** (*inf*) to handle sth, to get sth together.

reihen [1] *vt* **(a) Perlen auf eine Schnur ~** to string beads (on a thread); **sie reihte die Pilzstücke auf einen Faden** she strung the pieces of mushroom up (on a thread).
(b) (*Sew*) to tack.
[2] *vr* **etw reiht sich an etw** (*acc*) sth follows (after) sth; **eine Enttäuschung reihte sich an die andere** let-down followed let-down.

Reihen *m* **-s, -** (*S Ger*) instep.

Reihen-: ~dorf *nt village built along a road*, ribbon development (*spec*); **~fabrikation, ~fertigung** *f* serial production.

Reihenfolge *f* order; (*notwendige Aufeinanderfolge*) sequence ◆ **der ~ nach** in sequence; **in zwangloser ~** in no particular *or* special order; **alphabetische/zeitliche ~** alphabetical/chronological order.

Reihen-: ~haus *nt* terraced house (*Brit*), town house (*US*); **~(haus)siedlung** *f* estate of terraced houses; **~schaltung** *f* (*Elec*) series connection; **in ~schaltung** in series; **~untersuchung** *f* mass screening; **r~weise** *adv* **(a)** (*in Reihen*) in rows; **(b)** (*fig: in großer Anzahl*) by the dozen; **sie sind r~weise ohnmächtig geworden** they fainted by the dozen, dozens of them fainted; **~zahl** *f* (*Math*) member of a series.

Reiher *m* **-s, -** heron ◆ **kotzen wie ein ~** (*sl*) to spew *or* puke one's guts up (*sl*).

Reiher-: ~feder *f* heron's feather; (*als Hutschmuck*) aigrette; **~horst** *m* heron's nest.

reihern *vi* (*sl*) to puke (up) (*sl*), to spew up (*sl*).

Reiherschnabel *m* (*Bot*) common stork's-bill.

Reihgarn *nt* tacking thread.

-reihig *adj suf* -rowed ◆ **zwei~e Jacke** double-breasted jacket.

reih|um *adv* round ◆ **es geht ~** everybody takes their turn; **etw ~ gehen lassen** to pass sth round.

Reim *m* **-(e)s, -e** rhyme ◆ **ein ~ auf „Hut"** a rhyme for "hat"; **~e bilden** *or* **machen** *or* **drechseln** (*hum*) *or* **schmieden** (*hum*) to make *or* write rhymes, to versify (*hum*); **etw in ~e bringen** to make sth rhyme; **sich** (*dat*) **einen ~ auf etw** (*acc*) **machen** (*inf*) to make sense of sth; **ich mache mir so meinen ~ darauf** (*inf*) I can put two and two together (*inf*), I think I can see what's going on; **ich kann mir keinen ~ darauf machen** (*inf*) I can't make head (n)or tail of it, I can see no rhyme (n)or reason in it.

Reim|art *f* type of rhyme.

reimen [1] *vt* to rhyme (*auf +acc, mit* with) ◆ **ich kann das Wort nicht ~** I can't find a rhyme for this word *or* anything to rhyme with this word.
[2] *vi* to make up rhymes, to rhyme (*liter*), to versify (*hum*).
[3] *vr* to rhyme (*auf +acc, mit* with) ◆ **das reimt sich nicht** (*fig*) it doesn't hang together *or* make sense.

Reimer *m* **-s, -** (*pej*) rhymester, versifier.

Reimerei *f* **(a)** (*das Reimen*) versifying. **(b)** (*Gedicht*) doggerel *no pl* ◆ **eine ~** a piece of doggerel.

Reim-: ~lexikon *nt* rhyming dictionary; **r~los** *adj* unrhymed, nonrhyming; **~paar** *nt* rhyming couplet.

Re|import *m* (*Fin, Comm*) reimportation.

Reim-: ~schema *nt* rhyming pattern, rhyme scheme; **~schmied** *m* (*hum*) rhymester, versifier; **~wort** *nt, pl* **-wörter** rhyme; **ein ~wort zu etw finden** to find a rhyme for sth *or* a word to rhyme with sth.

rein[1] *adv* (*inf*) = **herein, hinein.**

rein[2] [1] *adj* **(a)** pure; (*absolut, völlig auch*) sheer; *Wahrheit* plain, straight, unvarnished; *Gewinn* clear ◆ **das ist die ~ste Freude/der ~ste Hohn** *etc* it's pure *or* sheer joy/mockery *etc*; **er ist der ~ste Künstler/Akrobat** he's a real artist/acrobat; **das Kind ist der ~ste Vater** (*dial*) the child is just like his father; **er ist die ~ste Bestie** he's an absolute *or* downright brute; **mit ihren Kindern hat sie nicht immer die ~ste Freude** she doesn't find her children exactly an unmixed blessing; **die ~e Arbeit kostet ...** the work alone costs ...; **er ist ein Demokrat ~sten Wassers** *or* **von ~stem Wasser** he is the archetypal *or* a pure democrat; **jdm ~en Wein einschenken** (*fig*) to give it to sb straight (from the shoulder); **eine ~e Jungenklasse** an all boys' class; **eine ~e Industriestadt** a purely industrial town.
(b) (*sauber*) clean; *Haut, Teint* clear, pure ◆ **etw ~ machen** to clean sth; **~ Schiff!** (*Naut*) ≃ swab the decks!; **~ klingen** to make a pure sound; **~ singen** to have a pure voice; **~en Tisch machen** (*fig*) to get things straight, to sort things out; **ich habe ~e Hände** (*fig*) my hands are clean; **die Hände ~ behalten** (*fig*) to keep one's nose clean (*inf*); *siehe* **Weste.**
(c) (*klar, übersichtlich*) **etw ins ~e schreiben** to write out a fair copy of sth, to write sth out neatly; **etw ins ~e bringen** to clear sth up; **die Sache ist ins ~e gekommen** things are cleared up, things have cleared themselves up; **mit sich selbst ins ~e kommen** to get things straight with oneself, to straighten *or* sort things out with oneself; **mit etw ins ~e kommen** to get straight about sth; **mit jdm/sich selbst im ~en sein** to have got things straightened *or* sorted out with sb/oneself; **mit etw im ~en sein** to have got sth straightened *or* sorted out; **mit seinem Gewissen im ~en sein** to have a clear conscience; **er ist mit sich selbst nicht im ~en** he is at odds with himself.
(d) (*unschuldig*) pure; *Gewissen* clear ◆ **er ist ~ von Schuld** (*old*) he is free of guilt; **dem R~en ist alles ~** (*prov*) to the pure all things are pure.
[2] *adv* **(a)** (*ausschließlich*) purely ◆ **~ hypothetisch gesprochen** speaking purely hypothetically.
(b) (*inf: ganz, völlig*) absolutely ◆ **~ alles/unmöglich** absolutely everything/impossible; **~ gar nichts** absolutely nothing, sweet Fanny Adams (*sl*).

Rein(e) *f* **-, -en** (*S Ger, Aus: Cook*) ≃ casserole.

Reineclaude [rɛnə'klo:də] *f* **-, -n** *siehe* **Reneklode.**

Rein|einnahme *f siehe* **Reinertrag.**

Reineke Fuchs *m* (*Liter*) Reynard the Fox.

Rein(e)machefrau *f* cleaner, cleaning lady.

reinemachen *vi sep* to do the cleaning, to clean.

Reinemachen *nt* **-s,** *no pl* (*inf*) cleaning.

Rein-: r~erbig *adj* (*Biol*) homozygous (*spec*); **~erlös, ~ertrag** *m* net profit(s) *or* proceeds *pl*.

Reinette [re'nɛtə] *f siehe* **Renette.**

rein(e)weg *adv* (*inf*) completely, absolutely ◆ **das ist ~ eine Frechheit/erlogen** it's a downright cheek/lie; **das ist ~ zum Verrücktwerden** it's enough to drive you absolutely mad.

Reinfall *m* (*inf*) disaster (*inf*); (*Pleite auch*) flop (*inf*) ◆ **mit der Waschmaschine/dem Kollegen haben wir einen ~ erlebt** the washing machine/this colleague was a real disaster.

reinfallen *vi sep irreg aux sein* (*inf*) *siehe* **hereinfallen, hineinfallen.**

Re|infektion *f* reinfection.

Reingeschmeckte(r) *mf decl as adj* (*S Ger*) outsider.

Rein-: ~gewicht *nt* net(t) weight; **~gewinn** *m* net(t) profit; **~haltung** *f* keeping clean; (*von Wasser auch, von Rasse*) keeping pure; **die ~haltung des Spielplatzes** keeping the playground clean.

Reinheit *f* purity; (*Sauberkeit*) cleanness; (*von Haut*) clearness.

Reinheits-: ~gebot *nt* beer/wine/milk/food purity regulations *pl*; **~grad** *m* (*Chem*) (degree of) purity.

reinigen [1] *vt* **(a)** (*saubermachen, putzen*) to clean; (*chemisch auch*) to dry-clean ◆ **etw chemisch ~** to dry-clean sth; **sich** (*dat*) **die Hände ~** to clean one's hands.
(b) (*säubern*) to purify; *Metall* to refine; *Blut auch* to cleanse ◆ **ein ~des Gewitter** (*fig inf*) a row which clears/cleared the air.
(c) (*zensieren*) *Text* to clean up, to bowdlerize; *Sprache* to purify ◆ **eine Sprache/einen Text von etw ~** to purify *or* purge a language/text of sth.
[2] *vr* to clean itself; (*Mensch*) to cleanse oneself ◆ **normalerweise kann ein Fluß sich von selbst ~** normally a river can cleanse itself *or* keep itself clean; **sich von einer Schuld/einem Verdacht ~** (*liter*) to cleanse oneself of a sin (*liter*)/to clear oneself of suspicion.

Reiniger *m* **-s, -** cleaner.

Reinigung *f* **(a)** (*das Saubermachen*) cleaning. **(b)** (*chemische ~*) (*Vorgang*) dry cleaning; (*Anstalt*) (dry) cleaner's. **(c)** (*das Säubern*) purification; (*von Metall*) refining; (*von Blut auch*) cleansing. **(d)** (*von Text*) cleaning up, bowdlerization; (*von Sprache*) purification. **(e)** (*Rel*) purification.

Reinigungs-: ~creme *f* cleansing cream; **~milch** *f* cleansing milk; **~mittel** *nt* cleansing agent.

Re|inkarnation *f* reincarnation.

reinkriechen *vi sep irreg aux sein* (*fig sl*) **jdm hinten ~** to suck up to sb (*inf*).

reinkriegen *vt sep* (*inf*) to get in.

Reinkultur *f* (*Biol*) cultivation of pure cultures ◆ **Kitsch/Faschismus** *etc* **in ~** (*inf*) pure unadulterated rubbish/fascism.

reinlegen *vt sep* (*inf*) *siehe* **hereinlegen, hineinlegen.**

⚠**reinleinen** *adj* pure linen.

reinlich *adj* **(a)** (*sauberkeitsliebend*) cleanly. **(b)** (*ordentlich*) neat, tidy. **(c)** (*gründlich, klar*) clear.

Reinlichkeit *f siehe adj* **(a)** cleanliness. **(b)** neatness, tidiness. **(c)** clearness.

Rein-: ≈luftgebiet *nt* pollution-free zone; **≈machefrau** *f siehe* **Rein(e)machefrau; r≈rassig** *adj* of pure race, pure-blooded; *Tier* purebred, thoroughbred; **≈rassigkeit** *f* racial purity; (*von Tier*) pure breeding; **r≈reiten** *vt sep irreg* **jdn (ganz schön) r~reiten** (*inf*) to get sb into a (right) mess (*inf*); **~schiff** *nt* (*Naut*): **~schiff machen** ≃ to swab the decks; **≈schrift** *f* writing out a fair copy *no art*; (*Geschriebenes*) fair copy; **etw/Notizen in ~schrift schreiben** to write out a fair copy of sth/to write up notes; **r≈schriftlich** *adj* **r~schriftliches Exemplar** fair copy; ⚠**r≈seiden** *adj* pure silk; **r≈tun** *vr* (*inf*) **sich** (*dat*) **etw r~tun** to imagine sth; **das muß man sich mal r~tun** just imagine that; **≈vermögen** *nt* net assets *pl*; **r≈waschen** *sep irreg* [1] *vt* (*von* of) to clear; (*von Sünden*) to cleanse; [2] *vr* (*fig*) to clear oneself; (*von Sünden*) to cleanse oneself; **r≈weg** *adv siehe* **rein(e)weg; r≈wollen** *adj* pure

⚠: for details of spelling reform, see supplement

wool; **r~würgen** *vt (inf) Essen etc* to force down; **jdm einen r~würgen** to do the dirty on sb *(inf)*; **r~ziehen** *vr (inf)* **sich** *(dat)* **etw r~ziehen** *Drogen* to take sth; *Musik* to listen to sth; *Film* to watch sth; *Getränk* to knock sth back; *Essen* to guzzle sth down; *(vorstellen)* to imagine sth; *(akzeptieren)* to take sth in; **~zucht** *f (von Tieren)* inbreeding; *(von Bakterien)* cultivation of pure cultures.

Reis[1] *nt* **-es, -er** *(old, liter) (Zweig)* twig, sprig; *(Pfropf~)* scion.

Reis[2] *m* **-es, -e** rice ◆ **Huhn auf ~** chicken with rice.

Reis-: ~auflauf *m* rice pudding; **~bau** *m* rice-growing *no art,* cultivation of rice; **~besen** *m siehe* **Reisigbesen**; **~branntwein** *m siehe* **~schnaps**; **~brei** *m* ≈ creamed rice; **~bündel** *nt siehe* **Reisigbündel**.

Reise *f* **-, -n** journey, trip; *(Schiffs~)* voyage; *(Space)* voyage, journey; *(Geschäfts~)* trip ◆ **seine ~n durch Europa** his travels through Europe; **eine ~ mit der Eisenbahn/dem Auto** a train/car journey, a journey by rail/car; **eine ~ zu Schiff** a sea voyage; *(Kreuzfahrt)* a cruise; **er plant eine ~ durch Afrika** he's planning to travel through Africa; **eine ~ machen** to go on a journey; **wir konnten die geplante ~ nicht machen** we couldn't go away as planned; **er hat in seinem Leben viele interessante ~n gemacht** he has travelled to a lot of interesting places in his lifetime; **wann machst du die nächste ~?** when are you off (on your travels) again?, when's the next trip?; **ich muß mal wieder eine ~ machen** I must go away again; **die ~ nach Afrika habe ich allein gemacht** I travelled to Africa by myself; **auf ~n sein** to be away (travelling); **er ist viel auf ~n** he does a lot of travelling; **jeden Sommer gehen wir auf ~n** we go away every summer; **er geht viel auf ~n** he travels a lot; **jdn auf die ~ schicken** to see sb off on his/her journey; **wohin geht die ~?** where are you off to?; **die letzte ~ antreten** *(euph liter)* to enter upon one's last journey *(liter)*; **glückliche** *or* **gute ~!** bon voyage!, have a good journey!; **wenn einer eine ~ tut, so kann er was erzählen** *(prov)* strange things happen when you're abroad.

Reise-: ~andenken *nt* souvenir; **~antritt** *m* start of a/the journey; **vor/bei ~antritt** before/at the start of a/the journey; **~apotheke** *f* first aid kit; **~bedarf** *m* travel requisites *pl*; **~begleiter** *m* travelling companion; *(~leiter)* courier; *(für Kinder)* chaperon; **~bekanntschaft** *f* acquaintance made while travelling; **~bericht** *m* report *or* account of one's journey; *(Buch)* travel story; *(Film)* travel film, travelogue; *(in Tagebuch)* holiday diary; **~beschränkungen** *pl* travel restrictions *pl*; **~beschreibung** *f* description of a journey/one's travels *etc*; traveller's tale, travel book *or* story/film; *(Film)* travelogue; **~büro** *nt* travel agency; **~bürokaufmann** *m* travel agent; **~car** *m (Sw)* coach *(Brit)*, bus; **~eindrücke** *pl* travel impressions *pl*; **~erleichterungen** *pl* easing of travel restrictions; **~fachkraft** *f* travel agent; **r~fertig** *adj* ready (to go *or* leave); **r~fertige Gäste warten bitte in der Hotelhalle** would guests who are ready to leave please wait in the hotel foyer; **~fieber** *nt (fig)* travel nerves *pl*; **~flughöhe** *f* cruising altitude; **~führer** *m (Buch)* guidebook; *(Person) siehe* **~leiter**; **~gefährte** *m* travelling companion; **~geld** *nt* fare; **~genehmigung** *f* travel permit; **~gepäck** *nt* luggage, baggage *(esp US, Aviat)*; **~gepäckversicherung** *f* baggage insurance; **~geschwindigkeit** *f* cruising speed; **~gesellschaft** *f* (tourist) party; *(im Bus auch)* coach party; *(inf: Veranstalter)* tour operator; **eine japanische ~gesellschaft** a party of Japanese tourists; **~koffer** *m* suitcase.

Reisekosten *pl* travelling expenses *pl*.

Reisekosten-: ~abrechnung *f* claim for travelling expenses; **~vergütung** *f* payment *or* reimbursement of travelling expenses; **die Firma übernimmt volle ~vergütung** the firm will pay all (your) travelling expenses; **100 Mark ~vergütung** 100 marks (in respect of) travelling expenses.

Reise-: ~krankheit *f* travel sickness; **~land** *nt* holiday destination; **~leiter** *m* courier; **~leitung** *f (das Leiten)* organization of a/the tourist party; *(~leiter)* courier(s); **möchten Sie die ~leitung für eine Englandtour übernehmen?** would you like to take a party for a tour of England?; **wegen schlechter ~leitung** because of the poor way in which the party was run; **~lektüre** *f* reading-matter (for a journey); **etw als ~lektüre mitnehmen** to take sth to read on the journey; **~lust** *f* travel urge, wanderlust; **mich packt die ~lust** I've got itchy feet *(inf) or* the travel bug *(inf)*; **r~lustig** *adj* fond of *or* keen on travel(ling), travel-mad *(inf)*; **~mitbringsel** *nt* souvenir.

reisen *vi aux sein* to travel ◆ **in den Urlaub ~** to go away on holiday; **in etw** *(dat)* **~** *(Comm)* to travel in sth; **viel gereist sein** to have travelled a lot, to be well-travelled.

Reisende(r) *mf decl as adj* traveller; *(Fahrgast)* passenger; *(Comm)* (commercial) traveller, travelling salesman.

Reise-: ⚠~necessaire *nt (für Nagelpflege)* travelling manicure set; *(Nähzeug)* travelling sewing kit; **~onkel** *m (hum inf)* globetrotter *(hum)*; **⚠~paß** *m* passport; **~pläne** *pl* plans *pl* (for a/the journey); **meine Mutter schmiedet dauernd irgendwelche ~pläne** my mother is always planning some journey *or* trip or other; **~prospekt** *m* travel brochure; **~proviant** *m* food for the journey, provisions *pl (usu hum)*.

Reiserei *f* (endless) travelling around.

Reise-: ~route *f* route, itinerary; **~ruf** *m* personal message; **~scheck** *m* traveller's cheque *(Brit)*, traveler's check *(US)*; **~schilderung** *f* description of a journey/one's travels; *(Buch)* travel story; **~schreibmaschine** *f* portable typewriter; **~spesen** *pl* travelling expenses *pl*; **~stipendium** *nt* travelling scholarship; **~tablette** *f* travel sickness pill; **~tante** *f (hum inf)* globetrotter *(hum)*; **~tasche** *f* holdall, travelling bag; **~veranstalter** *m* tour operator; **~verkehr** *m* holiday traffic; **~versicherung** *f* travel insurance; **~vorbereitungen** *pl* travel preparations *pl*, preparations for a/the journey; **~wecker** *m* travelling alarm clock; **~welle** *f* **die ~welle setzt ein** the holiday season is underway; **die ~welle nach Süden** the wave of holidaymakers heading south, the surge of holidaymakers to the south; **~wetter** *nt* travelling weather; **~wetterbericht** *m* holiday weather forecast; **~zeit** *f* time for travelling; **die beste ~zeit für Ägypten** the best time to go to Egypt; **~ziel** *nt* destination.

Reis-: ~feld *nt* paddy-field; **~holz** *nt (old) siehe* **Reisig**.

Reisig *nt* **-s,** *no pl* brushwood, twigs *pl*.

Reisig-: ~besen *m* besom; **~bündel** *nt* bundle of twigs, faggot.

Reis-: ~korn *nt* grain of rice; **~mehl** *nt* ground rice; **~papier** *nt (Art, Cook)* rice paper.

Reiß|aus *m*: **~ nehmen** *(inf)* to clear off *(inf)*, to make oneself scarce *(inf)*, to take to one's heels.

Reiß-: ~blei *nt* graphite; **~brett** *nt* drawing-board; **~brettstift** *m siehe* **~zwecke**.

Reis-: ~schleim *m* rice water; **~schnaps** *m* rice spirit.

reißen *pret* **riß**, *ptp* **gerissen** 1 *vt* **(a)** *(zer~)* to tear, to rip ◆ **ein Loch ins Kleid ~** to tear *or* rip a hole in one's dress.

(b) *(ab~, ent~, herunter~, weg~)* to tear, to pull, to rip *(etw von etw* sth off sth); *(mit~, zerren)* to pull, to drag ◆ **jdn zu Boden ~** to pull *or* drag sb to the ground; **jdn/etw in die Tiefe ~** to pull *or* drag sb/sth down into the depths; **der Fluß hat die Brücke mit sich gerissen** the river swept the bridge away; **jdn aus der Gefahr ~** to snatch sb from danger; **aus diesem Leben gerissen** snatched from this life; **jdn aus seinen Gedanken ~** to interrupt sb's thoughts; *(aufmuntern)* to make sb snap out of it; **jdn aus dem Schlaf/seinen Träumen ~** to wake sb from his sleep/dreams; **in etw** *(dat)* **Lücken ~** to make gaps in sth; **jdn ins Verderben ~** to ruin sb; **hin und her gerissen werden/sein** *(fig)* to be torn.

(c) etw an sich *(acc)* **~** to seize sth; *Macht auch* to usurp sth; *Unterhaltung* to monopolize sth; *siehe* **Nagel**.

(d) *(Sport) (Gewichtheben)* to snatch; *(Hochsprung, Pferderennen)* to knock off *or* down.

(e) *(töten)* to take, to kill.

(f) *(inf: machen) Witze* to crack *(inf)*; *Possen* to play.

(g) *(Aus sl)* **jdm eine ~** to clout sb (one) *(inf)*; **einen Stern ~** to fall; **damit kannst du nichts ~** that's not going to impress anybody.

(h) *(Wunde beibringen)* **sich** *(dat)* **eine Wunde an etw** *(dat)* **~** to cut oneself on sth; **sich** *(dat)* **etw blutig ~** to tear sth open.

2 *vi* **(a)** *aux sein (zer~)* to tear, to rip; *(Muskel)* to tear; *(Seil)* to tear, to break, to snap; *(Risse bekommen)* to crack ◆ **mir ist die Kette/der Faden gerissen** my chain/thread has broken *or* snapped; **da riß mir die Geduld** *or* **der Geduldsfaden** then my patience gave out *or* snapped; **es reißt mir in allen Gliedern** *(inf)* I'm aching all over; **wenn alle Stricke** *or* **Stränge ~** *(fig inf)* if the worst comes to the worst, if all else fails.

(b) *(zerren)* *(an +dat* at) to pull, to tug; *(wütend)* to tear.

(c) *(Sport) (Gewichtheben)* to snatch; *(Hochsprung, Pferderennen)* to knock the bar off *or* down.

3 *vr* **(a)** *(sich verletzen)* to cut oneself *(an +dat* on).

(b) *(sich los~)* to tear oneself/itself.

(c) *(inf)* **sich um jdn/etw ~** to scramble to get sb/sth.

Reißen *nt* **-s,** *no pl* **(a)** *(Gewichtheben: Disziplin)* snatch. **(b)** *(inf: Glieder~)* ache.

reißend *adj Fluß* torrential, raging; *Tier* rapacious; *Schmerzen* searing; *Verkauf, Absatz* massive ◆ **~en Absatz finden** to sell like hot cakes *(inf)*.

Reißer *m* **-s, -** *(Theat, Film, Buch: inf)* thriller; *(inf: Ware)* hot item *(inf) or* line *(inf)*, big seller.

reißerisch *adj* sensational.

Reiß-: ~feder *f (Art)* (drawing) pen; **r~fest** *adj* tearproof; **~festigkeit** *f* (tensile) strength; **~kohle** *f (Art)* charcoal; **~leine** *f* ripcord; **~nagel** *m siehe* **~zwecke**; **~schiene** *f* T-square; **~stift** *m siehe* **~zwecke**; **~verschluß** *m* zip(-fastener) *(Brit)*, zipper; **den ~verschluß an etw** *(dat)* **auf-/zumachen** to zip sth up/to unzip sth; **~verschlußprinzip** *nt* principle of alternation; **~wolf** *m* shredder, shredding machine; **~wolle** *f* shoddy; **~zahn** *m* fang, carnassial (tooth) *(spec)*; **~zeug** *nt* drawing instruments *pl*; **~zirkel** *m* drawing compass(es); **~zwecke** *f* drawing pin *(Brit)*, thumb tack *(US)*.

Reis-: ~tag *m* day of eating only rice *(as part of a diet)*; **~wein** *m* rice wine.

Reit-: ~anzug *m* riding-habit; **~bahn** *f* arena.

reiten *pret* **ritt**, *ptp* **geritten** 1 *vi aux sein* **(a)** to ride ◆ **auf etw** *(dat)* **~** to ride (on) sth; **im Schritt/Trab/Galopp ~** to ride at a walk/trot/gallop; **geritten kommen** to ride up, to come riding up; **das Schiff reitet vor Anker** *(Naut)* the ship is riding at anchor; **auf diesem Messer kann man ~!** *(inf)* you couldn't cut butter with this knife!

(b) *(sl: koitieren)* to ride *(sl)*.

2 *vt* to ride ◆ **Schritt/Trab/Galopp ~** to ride at a walk/trot/gallop; **ein schnelles Tempo ~** to ride at a fast pace; **sich** *(dat)* **Schwielen ~** to get saddle-sore; **jdn zu Boden** *or* **über den Haufen** *(inf)* **~** to trample sb down; **Prinzipien ~** *(inf)* to insist on one's principles.

reitend *adj* mounted ◆ **~e Artillerie** horse artillery.

Reiter *m* **-s, - (a)** rider, horseman; *(Mil)* cavalryman ◆ **ein Trupp preußischer ~** a troop of Prussian horse. **(b)** *(an Waage)* rider; *(Kartei~)* index-tab. **(c)** *(Mil: Absperrblock)* barrier ◆ **spanische ~** *pl* barbed-wire barricade.

Reiter-: ~angriff *m* cavalry charge; **~aufzug** *m* cavalcade.

Reiterei *f* **(a)** *(Mil)* cavalry. **(b)** *(inf: das Reiten)* riding.

Reiterin *f* rider, horsewoman.

Reiterregiment *nt* cavalry regiment.

Reitersmann *m, pl* **-männer** *(liter)* horseman.

Reiterstandbild *nt* equestrian statue.

⚠: Informationen zur Rechtschreibreform im Anhang

Reit-: ~gerte *f* riding crop; **~hose** *f* riding-breeches *pl*; (*Hunt, Sport*) jodhpurs *pl*; **~jacke** *f* riding jacket; **~kleid** *nt* riding-habit; **~knecht** *m* (*old*) groom; **~kunst** *f* horsemanship, riding skill; **~peitsche** *f* riding whip; **~pferd** *nt* saddle-horse, mount; **~sattel** *m* (riding) saddle; **~schule** *f* riding school; **~sitz** *m* riding position; (*rittlings*) straddling position; **im ~sitz sitzen** to sit astride (*auf etw (dat)* sth); **~sport** *m* (horse-)riding, equestrian sport (*form*); **~stall** *m* riding-stable; **~stiefel** *m* riding-boot; **~stunde** *f* riding lesson; **~tier** *nt* mount, animal used for riding; **~turnier** *nt* horse show; (*Geländereiten*) point-to-point; **~- und Fahrturnier** *nt* horse show; **~unterricht** *m* riding lessons *pl*; **~weg** *m* bridle-path; **~zeug** *nt* riding equipment *or* things *pl*.

Reiz *m* **-es, -e (a)** (*Physiol*) stimulus ◆ **einen ~ auf etw** (*acc*) **ausüben** to act as a stimulus on sth.
(b) (*Verlockung*) attraction, appeal; (*des Unbekannten, Fremdartigen, der Großstadt auch*) lure; (*Zauber*) charm ◆ **der ~ der Neuheit/des Verbotenen** the lure *or* appeal of novelty/forbidden fruits; **(auf jdn) einen ~ ausüben** to have *or* hold great attraction(s) (for sb); **das erhöht den ~** it adds to the thrill *or* pleasure; **einen/keinen ~ für jdn haben** to appeal/not to appeal to sb; **seinen** *or* **den ~ verlieren** to lose all one's/its charm; **an ~ verlieren** to be losing one's/its charm *or* attraction *or* appeal, to begin to pall; **seine ~e spielen lassen** to display one's charms; **weibliche ~e** feminine charms; **seine ~e zeigen** (*euph, iro*) to reveal one's charms.

Reiz-: ~auslöser *m* stimulant; (*von krankhaftem Zustand*) irritant; **r~bar** *adj* (*empfindlich*) sensitive, touchy (*inf*); (*erregbar*) irritable; (*Med*) irritable, sensitive; **leicht r~bar sein** to be very sensitive/irritable; (*ständig erregbar auch*) to be quick-tempered *or* hot-tempered; **r~bare Schwäche** (*Med*) irritability; (*fig*) sensitive spot *or* point; **~barkeit** *f siehe adj* sensitiveness, sensitivity, touchiness (*inf*); irritability; irritability, sensitivity; **~behandlung** *f* (*Med*) stimulation therapy; **r~empfänglich** *adj* responsive; (*Physiol*) receptive to stimuli; **~empfänglichkeit** *f* responsiveness; (*Physiol*) receptiveness to stimuli.

reizen [1] *vt* **(a)** (*Physiol*) to irritate; (*stimulieren*) to stimulate.
(b) (*verlocken*) to appeal to ◆ **jds/den Gaumen ~** to make sb's/one's mouth water; **jds Verlangen ~** to waken *or* rouse sb's desire; **es würde mich ja sehr ~, ...** I'd love to ...; **es reizt mich, nach Skye zu fahren** I've got an itch to go to Skye; **es hat mich ja immer sehr gereizt, ...** I've always had an itch to ...; **Ihr Angebot reizt mich sehr** I find your offer very tempting; **sie versteht es, Männer zu ~** she knows how to appeal to men.
(c) (*ärgern*) to annoy; *Tier auch* to tease; (*herausfordern*) to provoke ◆ **ein gereiztes Nashorn** a rhinoceros when provoked; **jds Zorn ~** to arouse sb's anger; **die Kinder reizten sie bis zur Weißglut** the children really made her see red; *siehe* **gereizt**.
(d) (*Skat*) to bid.
[2] *vi* **(a)** (*Med*) to irritate; (*stimulieren*) to stimulate ◆ **auf der Haut** *etc* **~** to irritate the skin *etc*; **der Rauch reizt zum Husten** the smoke makes you cough; **zum Widerspruch ~** to invite contradiction.
(b) (*Skat*) to bid ◆ **hoch ~** (*lit, fig*) to make a high bid.

reizend *adj* charming ◆ **es ist ~ (von dir)** it is charming *or* lovely (of you); **das ist ja ~** (*iro*) (that's) charming.

Reiz-: ~gas *nt* irritant gas; **~husten** *m* chesty cough; (*nervös*) nervous cough.

Reizker *m* **-s, -** (*Bot*) saffron milk-cap.

Reiz-: ~klima *nt* bracing climate; (*fig*) charged atmosphere; **r~los** *adj* dull, uninspiring; **das ist ja r~los** that's no fun; **~losigkeit** *f* dullness, uninspiring nature; **~mittel** *nt* (*Med*) stimulant; **~schwelle** *f* (*Physiol*) stimulus *or* absolute threshold; (*Comm*) sales resistance; **~stoff** *m* irritant; **~thema** *nt* controversial issue; **~therapie** *f* (*Med*) stimulation therapy; **~überflutung** *f* overstimulation.

Reizung *f* **(a)** (*Med*) stimulation; (*krankhaft*) irritation. **(b)** (*Herausforderung*) provocation.

Reiz-: r~voll *adj* charming, delightful; *Aufgabe, Beruf* attractive; **die Aussicht ist nicht gerade r~voll** the prospect is not particularly enticing *or* appealing; **es wäre r~voll, mal dahin zu fahren/das ganz anders zu machen** it would be lovely to go there some time/it would be interesting to do it quite differently; **~wäsche** *f* (*inf*) sexy underwear; **~wort** *nt* emotive word.

Rekapitulation *f* recapitulation.

rekapitulieren* *vt* to recapitulate.

Rekelei *f* (*inf*) lolling about (*inf*).

rekeln *vr* (*inf*) (*sich herumlümmeln*) to loll about (*inf*); (*sich strecken*) to stretch ◆ **sich noch ein paar Minuten im Bett ~** to stretch out in bed for a few more minutes; **er rekelte sich im behaglichen Sessel vor dem Feuer** he snuggled down in the comfy chair in front of the fire; **die Katze rekelte sich behaglich in der Sonne** the cat lay lazily sunning itself.

Reklamation *f* query; (*Beschwerde*) complaint ◆ **„spätere ~en können nicht anerkannt werden"** "we regret that money cannot be refunded after purchase".

Reklame *f* **-, -n (a)** (*Werbewesen, Werbung*) advertising ◆ **~ für jdn/etw machen** to advertise sb/sth; (*fig*) to do a bit of advertising for sb/sth; **mit jdm/etw ~ machen** (*pej*) to show sb off/to show off about sth; **das ist keine gute ~ für die Firma** it's not a very good advertisement for the company.
(b) (*Einzelwerbung*) advertisement, advert (*Brit inf*), ad (*inf*); (*TV, Rad auch*) commercial.

Reklame-: ~artikel *m* free gift, sales gimmick (*often pej*); (*Probe*) (free) sample; **~broschüre** *f* (advertising) brochure, handout; **~broschüren** advertising literature; **~feldzug** *m* advertising campaign; **~film** *m* advertising film, commercial; **~plakat** *nt* (advertising) poster, advertisement; **~rummel** *m* (*pej*) (advertising) ballyhoo (*inf*); **~schild** *nt* advertising sign; **~sendung** *f* commercial break, commercials *pl*; **eine verkappte ~sendung** a disguised commercial; **~spot** *m* (advertising) spot, commercial; **~tafel** *f* hoarding; **~trick** *m* sales trick; **~trommel** *f*: **die ~trommel für jdn/etw rühren** (*inf*) to beat the (big) drum for sb/sth; **~zettel** *m* (advertising) leaflet, handout.

reklamieren* [1] *vi* (*Einspruch erheben*) to complain, to make a complaint ◆ **bei jdm wegen etw ~** to complain to sb about sth; **die Rechnung kann nicht stimmen, da würde ich ~** the bill can't be right, I would query it.
[2] *vt* **(a)** (*bemängeln*) to complain about (*etw bei jdm* sth to sb); (*in Frage stellen*) *Rechnung, Rechnungsposten* to query (*etw bei jdm* sth with sb).
(b) (*in Anspruch nehmen*) **jdn/etw für sich ~** to lay claim to sb/sth, to claim sb/sth as one's own.

rekommandieren* [1] *vt* (*Aus*) *Brief, Sendung* to register ◆ **einen Brief rekommandiert aufgeben** to register a letter, to send a letter by registered mail.
[2] *vr* (*obs, Aus*) **sich jdm ~** to present one's compliments to sb.

Rekompens, (*Aus Admin*) **Rekompenz** *f* compensation.

rekonstruieren* *vt* to reconstruct.

Rekonstruktion *f* reconstruction.

Rekonvaleszent(in *f*) [rekɔnvalɛs'tsɛnt(ɪn)] *m* convalescent.

Rekonvaleszenz [rekɔnvalɛs'tsɛnts] *f* convalescence.

Rekord *m* **-s, -e** record ◆ **das Zeitalter der ~e** the age of superlatives; (*des Fortschritts*) the age of achievement.

Rekord- *in cpds* record; **~brecher(in** *f*) *m* record breaker; **~halter, ~inhaber** *m* record-holder; **~lauf** *m* record(-breaking) run.

Rekordler *m* **-s, -** (*inf*) record-holder.

Rekord-: ~marke *f* (*Sport, fig*) record; **die bisherige ~marke im Weitsprung war ...** till now the long-jump record stood at *or* was ...; **auf der ~marke (von)** at the record *or* (*fig*) record level (of); **~versuch** *m* attempt on the/a record; **~zeit** *f* record time.

Rekrut *m* **-en, -en** (*Mil*) recruit.

Rekruten-: ~ausbildung *f* (*Mil*) basic training; **~aushebung** *f* (*old Mil*) levy (*old*).

rekrutieren* [1] *vt* (*Mil, fig*) to recruit.
[2] *vr* (*fig*) **sich ~ aus** to be recruited *or* drawn from.

Rekrutierung *f* recruitment, recruiting.

Rekrutierungsstelle *f* (*Mil*) recruiting centre.

Rekta *pl of* **Rektum**.

rektal *adj* (*Med*) rectal ◆ **~ einführen** to insert through the rectum; **Temperatur ~ messen** to take the temperature rectally.

Rektifikation *f* **(a)** (*old*) correction; (*Berichtigung auch*) rectification. **(b)** (*Chem, Math*) rectification.

rektifizieren* *vt* **(a)** (*old*) to correct; (*berichtigen auch*) to rectify. **(b)** (*Chem, Math*) to rectify.

Rektion *f* (*Gram*) government ◆ **die ~ eines Verbs** the case governed by a verb.

Rektor *m*, **Rektorin** *f* (*Sch*) headteacher, principal (*esp US*); (*Univ*) vice-chancellor, rector (*US*); (*von Fachhochschule*) principal.

Rektorat *nt* (*Sch*) (*Amt, Amtszeit*) headship, principalship (*esp US*); (*Zimmer*) headmaster's/-mistress's study, principal's room (*esp US*); (*Univ*) vice-chancellorship, rectorship (*US*); vice-chancellor's *or* rector's (*US*) office; (*in Fachhochschule*) principalship; principal's office.

Rektoratsrede *f* (*Univ*) (vice-chancellor's *or* rector's *US*) inaugural address.

Rektorin *f siehe* **Rektor**.

Rektum *nt* **-s, Rekta** (*form*) rectum.

rekurrieren* *vi* **(a)** (*old Jur*) to appeal. **(b)** (*liter: auf etw zurückkommen*) to return (*auf +acc* to).

Rekurs *m* **-es, -e** (*old Jur*) appeal.

Rel. *abbr of* **Religion**.

Relais [rə'lɛː] *nt* **-** [rə'lɛː(s)], **-** [rə'lɛːs] (*Elec*) relay.

Relaisstation *f* (*Elec*) relay station.

Relation *f* relation ◆ **in einer/keiner ~ zu etw stehen** to bear some/no relation to sth.

relational *adj* (*Comput*) relational.

relativ [1] *adj* relative ◆ **~e Mehrheit** (*Parl*) simple majority; **alles ist ~** everything is relative.
[2] *adv* relatively.

Relativ *nt* relative pronoun.

Relativ|adverb *nt* relative adverb.

relativieren* [relati'viːrən] (*geh*) [1] *vt Begriff, Behauptung etc* to qualify.
[2] *vi* to see things *or* to think in relative terms.

Relativismus [-'vɪsmʊs] *m* relativism.

relativistisch [-'vɪstɪʃ] *adj* relativistic.

Relativität [relativi'tɛːt] *f* relativity.

Relativitätstheorie *f* theory of relativity, relativity theory *no art*.

Relativ-: ~pronomen *nt* relative pronoun; **~satz** *m* relative clause.

Relativum [-'tiːvʊm] *nt* (*form*) relative pronoun.

relaxt [riː'lɛkst] *adj* (*sl*) relaxed, laid-back (*sl*).

Relegation *f* (*form*) expulsion.

relegieren* *vt* (*form*) to expel.

relevant [rele'vant] *adj* relevant.

Relevanz [rele'vants] *f* relevance.

Relief [reli'ɛf] *nt* **-s, -s** *or* **-e** relief.

Relief-: ~druck *m* relief printing; **~karte** *f* relief map.
Religion *f* religion; (*Schulfach*) religious instruction *or* education, RI (*inf*), RE (*inf*) ◆ **~sehr gut, Kopfrechnen schwach** (*inf*) virtuous but stupid.
Religions-: ~bekenntnis *nt* denomination; **~buch** *nt* religion *or* religious textbook; **~ersatz** *m* substitute for religion; **~freiheit** *f* religious freedom, freedom of worship; **~friede(n)** *m* religious peace; **~führer** *m* religious leader; **~gemeinschaft** *f* religious community; **~geschichte** *f* history of religion; **~krieg** *m* religious war, war of religion; **~lehre** *f* religious education *or* instruction; **~lehrer** *m* teacher of religious education, RI *or* RE teacher (*inf*); **r~los** *adj* not religious; (*bekenntnislos*) non-denominational; **~stifter** *m* founder of a religion; **~streit** *m* religious controversy; **~stunde** *f* religious education *or* instruction lesson, RI *or* RE lesson (*inf*); **~unterricht** *m* **(a)** *siehe* **~lehre**; **(b)** *siehe* **~stunde**; **~wissenschaft** *f* religious studies *pl*; **vergleichende ~wissenschaft** comparative religion; **~zugehörigkeit** *f* religious affiliation, religion.
religiös *adj* religious ◆ **~ erzogen werden** to have *or* receive a religious upbringing.
Religiosität *f* religiousness ◆ **ein Mensch von tiefer ~** a deeply religious person.
Relikt *nt* **-(e)s, -e** relic.
Reling *f* **-, -s** *or* **-e** (*Naut*) (deck) rail.
Reliquiar *nt* reliquary.
Reliquie [-iə] *f* relic.
Reliquienschrein [-iən-] *m* reliquary.
Relocate-Funktion [ri:lo'ke:t-] *f* relocate function.
Rem, rem *nt* **-, -** (*Einheit*) rem.
Remake ['ri:meɪk] *nt* **-s, -s** remake.
Remanenz *f* (*Phys*) remanence, residual magnetism.
Rembours [rã'bu:ɐ] *m* **-, -** (*Fin*) reimbursement, payment.
Remboursgeschäft [rã'bu:ɐ-] *nt* (*Fin*) documentary credit trading/transaction.
Remigrant(in *f*) *m* returning/returned emigrant.
remilitarisieren* *vti* to remilitarize.
Reminiszenz *f* (*geh*) (*Erinnerung*) memory (*an +acc* of); (*Ähnlichkeit*) similarity, resemblance (*an +acc* to) ◆ **ich habe aus seinem Vortrag ~en an Spengler herausgehört** I found his lecture in some ways reminiscent of Spengler.
remis [rə'mi:] *adj inv* drawn ◆ **~ spielen** to draw; **die Partie ist ~** the game has ended in a draw *or* has been drawn; **die Vereine trennten sich ~** the clubs held each other to a draw.
Remis [rə'mi:] *nt* **-** [rə'mi:(s)], **-** [rə'mi:s] *or* **-en** [rə'mi:zn] **(a)** (*Schach, Sport*) draw ◆ **gegen jdn ein ~ erzielen** to hold sb to a draw. **(b)** (*fig*) stalemate, deadlock ◆ **mit einem ~** in stalemate *or* deadlock.
Remise *f* **-, -n** (*old*) shed, outbuilding.
Remission *f* (*Med, old: Erlaß*) remission; (*Comm*) remittance.
Remittende *f* **-, -n** (*Comm*) return.
Remittent(in *f*) *m* (*Fin*) payee.
remittieren* [1] *vt* (*Comm*) *Waren* to return; *Geld* to remit.
[2] *vi* (*Med: nachlassen*) to remit (*form*).
Remmidemmi *nt* **-s,** *no pl* (*sl*) (*Krach*) row, rumpus (*inf*); (*Trubel*) rave-up (*sl*) ◆ **~ machen** to make a row *etc*/to have a rave-up (*sl*).
Remoulade [remu'la:də], **Remouladensoße** *f* (*Cook*) remoulade.
Rempelei *f* (*inf*) barging (*inf*), jostling, pushing and shoving; (*im Sport*) pushing.
rempeln *vti* (*inf*) to barge (*jdn* into sb) (*inf*), to jostle, to elbow; (*im Sport*) to barge (*jdn* into sb); (*foulen*) to push.
REM-Phase *f* REM sleep.
Rem(p)ter *m* **-s, -** (*in Klöstern*) refectory; (*in Burgen*) banquet(ing) hall.
Remuneration *f* (*Aus*) (*Gratifikation*) bonus; (*Vergütung*) remuneration.
Ren *nt* **-s, -e** reindeer.
Renaissance [rənɛ'sã:s] *f* **-, -en** **(a)** (*Hist*) renaissance. **(b)** (*fig*) revival, rebirth; (*von Kunstformen auch*) renaissance.
Renaissance- [rənɛ'sã:s-] *in cpds* renaissance; **~mensch** *m* renaissance man *no art*.
Rendezvous [rãde'vu:, 'rã:devu] *nt* **-** [-'vu:(s)], **-** [-'vu:s] rendezvous (*liter, hum*), date (*inf*); (*Space*) rendezvous.
Rendezvousmanöver *nt* (*Space*) rendezvous manoeuvre.
Rendite *f* **-, -n** (*Fin*) yield, return on capital.
Renegat *m* **-en, -en** (*Eccl, Pol*) renegade.
Reneklode *f* **-, -n** greengage.
Renette *f* rennet.
renitent *adj* awkward, refractory.
Renitenz *f* awkwardness, refractoriness.
Renke *f* **-, -n** whitefish.
Renn- *in cpds* race; **~bahn** *f* (race)track; **~boot** *nt* powerboat.
rennen *pret* **rannte,** *ptp* **gerannt** [1] *vi aux sein* **(a)** (*schnell laufen*) to run; (*Sport*) (*Mensch, Tier*) to run, to race; (*Auto etc*) to race ◆ **um die Wette ~** to have a race; **ins Verderben** *or* **Unglück ~** to rush headlong into disaster; **(aufs Klo) ~** (*inf*) to run (to the loo *Brit inf* *or* bathroom *US*).
(b) (*inf: hingehen*) to run (off) ◆ **sie rennt wegen jeder Kleinigkeit zum Chef** she goes running (off) to the boss at the slightest little thing; **er rennt zu jedem Fußballspiel** he goes to every football match; **sie rennt jeden Tag in die Kirche** she goes running off to church every day.
(c) (*stoßen*) **an** *or* **gegen jdn/etw ~** to run *or* bump *or* bang into sb/sth; **er rannte mit dem Kopf gegen ...** he bumped *or* banged his head against ...; **mit dem Kopf durch/gegen die Wand ~** (*fig*) to bang one's head against a brick wall.
[2] *vt* **(a)** *aux haben or sein* (*Sport*) to run.
(b) jdn zu Boden *or* **über den Haufen ~** to knock sb down *or* over; **sich** (*dat*) **(an etw) ein Loch in den Kopf ~** to crack one's head (against sth).
(c) (*stoßen*) *Messer etc* to run.
Rennen *nt* **-s, -** running; (*Sport*) (*Vorgang*) racing; (*Veranstaltung*) race ◆ **totes ~** dead heat; **gehst du zum ~?** (*bei Pferde~, Hunde~ etc*) are you going to the races?, are you going racing?; (*bei Auto~ etc*) are you going to the racing?; **gut im ~ liegen** (*lit, fig*) to be well placed; **das ~ ist gelaufen** (*lit*) the race is over; (*fig*) it's all over; **das ~ machen** (*lit, fig*) to win (the race); **aus dem ~ ausscheiden** (*lit, fig*) to drop out; **das ~ aufgeben** (*lit*) to drop out (of the race); (*fig auch*) to throw in the towel.
Renner *m* **-s, -** (*inf: Verkaufsschlager*) winner, worldbeater; (*Pferd auch*) flier.
Rennerei *f* (*inf*) (*lit, fig: das Herumrennen*) running around; (*Hetze*) mad chase (*inf*) ◆ **die ~, bis ich endlich meinen Paß kriegte** all that running around until I finally got my passport; **nach meinem Umzug hatte ich tagelange ~en** after moving I was running around for days; **diese ~ zum Klo** this running to the loo (*Brit inf*) *or* bathroom (*US*).
Renn-: ~fahrer *m* (*Radfahrer*) racing cyclist; (*Motorradfahrer*) racing motorcyclist; (*Autofahrer*) racing driver; **~jacht** *f* racing yacht; **~leiter** *m* race organizer; **~leitung** *f* organization of a race meeting; (*die ~leiter*) race organizers *pl*; **~lenkstange** *f* drop handlebars *pl*; **~maschine** *f* racer; **~pferd** *nt* racehorse; **aus einem Ackergaul kann man kein ~pferd machen** (*prov*) you can't make a silk purse out of a sow's ear (*Prov*); **~piste** *f* (race)track; **~platz** *m* racecourse; **~rad** *nt* racing bicycle *or* bike (*inf*); **~rodeln** *nt* bob(sleigh) racing; **~schlitten** *m* bob(sleigh), bobsled; **~schuhe** *pl* (*Sport*) spikes *pl*; **~sport** *m* racing; **~stall** *m* (*Tiere, Zucht*) stable; **~strecke** *f* (*~bahn*) (race)track; (*zu laufende Strecke*) course, distance; **eine ~strecke von 100 km** a 100 km course, a distance of 100km; **~tag** *m* day of the race; **das Rennen erstreckt sich über drei ~tage** the race is a three-day event; **~veranstaltung** *f* races *pl*, race meeting; **~wagen** *m* racing car; **~wette** *f* bet (on a race); **Ergebnisse der ~wetten** betting results.
Renommee *nt* **-s, -s** reputation, name.
Renommierclub *m* posh club.
renommieren* *vi* to show off, to swank (*inf*); (*aufschneiden auch*) to brag.
Renommier-: ~figur *f* famous name; **~schule** *f* (*inf*) posh *or* classy school (*inf*); **~stück** *nt* pride and joy, showpiece.
renommiert *adj* renowned, famed, famous (*wegen* for).
renovieren* [reno'vi:rən] *vt* to renovate; (*tapezieren etc*) to redecorate, to do up (*inf*).
Renovierung [reno'vi:rʊŋ] *f* renovation.
rentabel *adj* profitable; *Firma auch* viable ◆ **es ist nicht ~, das reparieren zu lassen** it is not worth(while) having it repaired; **~ wirtschaften** (*gut einteilen*) to spend one's money sensibly; (*mit Gewinn arbeiten*) to make *or* show a profit; **~ kalkulieren** (*gut einteilen*) to budget sensibly; (*Gewinn einplanen*) to think in terms of profit(s), to go for profit(s); **das ist eine rentable Sache** *or* **Angelegenheit** it will pay (off).
Rentabilität *f* profitability; (*von Firma auch*) viability.
Rentabilitäts-: ~gesichtspunkte *pl* profitability point of view; **~grenze** *f* limit of profitability; **~prüfung** *f* investigation into profitability; **~rechnung** *f* profitability calculation; **~schwelle** *f* break-even point.
Rent|amt *nt* (*old, Admin*) bursary.
Rente *f* **-, -n** (*Alters~, Invaliden~*) pension; (*aus Versicherung, Lebens~*) annuity; (*aus Vermögen*) income, (*St Ex: ~npapier*) fixed-interest security ◆ **auf ~ gehen** (*inf*)/**sein** (*inf*) to start drawing one's pension/to be on a pension; **jdn auf ~ setzen** (*inf*) to pension sb off (*inf*).
Renten-: ~alter *nt* retirement age; **~anhebung** *f* pension increase; **~anpassung** *f* tying of pensions to the national average wage; **~anpassungsgesetz** *nt* law tying pensions to the national average wage; **~anspruch** *m* right to a pension; **~basis** *f* annuity basis; **~bemessungsgrundlage** *f* basis of calculation of a/the pension/pensions; **~berechnung** *f* calculation of a/the pension/pensions; **r~berechtigt** *adj* entitled to a pension; *Alter* pensionable; **~bescheid** *m* notice of the amount of one's pension; **~besteuerung** *f* taxation of pensions; **~empfänger** *m* pensioner; **~erhöhung** *f* pension increase; **~finanzierung** *f* financing of pensions; **~fonds** *m* fixed-income fund; **~mark** *f* (*Hist*) rentenmark; **~markt** *m* market in fixed-interest securities; **~optionshandel** *m* bond option dealing; **~papier** *nt* fixed-interest security; **r~pflichtig** *adj* responsible for paying a pension; **~politik** *f* pension policy; **~reform** *f* reform of pensions; **~versicherung** *f* pension scheme; **~versicherungsbeitrag** *m* pension scheme contribution; **~werte** *pl* fixed-interest securities *pl*; **~zahltag** *m* pension day.
Rentier[1] *nt siehe* **Ren.**
Rentier[2] [ren'tie:] *m* **-s, -s** (*old*) man of private means, gentleman of leisure; (*mit staatlicher Rente*) pensioner.
rentieren* *vir* to be worthwhile; (*Geschäft, Unternehmen etc auch, Maschine*) to pay ◆ **es hat sich doch rentiert, daß ich noch ein bißchen dageblieben bin** it was worth(while) staying on a bit; **das rentiert (sich) nicht** it's not worth it; **ein Auto rentiert sich für mich nicht** it's not worth my having a car.
rentierlich *adj* profitable, viable.
Rentner(in *f*) *m* **-s, -** pensioner; (*Alters~ auch*) senior citizen, old age pensioner (*Brit*).
re|okkupieren* *vt* (*Mil*) to reoccupy.
Re|organisation, Re|organisierung *f* reorganization.

⚠: Informationen zur Rechtschreibreform im Anhang

re|organisieren* *vt* to reorganize.

Rep *m* **-s, -s(e)** *usu pl abbr of* **Republikaner** (*inf*) Republican, *member of the right-wing German Republikaner party.*

reparabel *adj* repairable.

Reparation *f* reparations *pl* ◆ **~en leisten** *or* **zahlen** to pay *or* make reparations.

Reparations-: ⚠**~ausschuß** *m* reparations committee; **~zahlungen** *pl* reparations *pl*.

Reparatur *f* repair ◆ **~en am Auto** car repairs; **~en am Haus vornehmen** to do some repairs on *or* to the house; **in ~** being repaired; **er übernimmt ~en von Schuhen** he does shoe repairs, he mends shoes; **etw in ~ geben** to have sth repaired *or* mended; *Auto* to have sth repaired.

Reparatur-: **r~anfällig** *adj* prone to break down; **r~bedürftig** *adj* in need of repair; **~kosten** *pl* repair costs *pl*; **~werkstatt** *f* workshop; (*Auto~*) garage.

reparieren* *vt* to repair, to mend; *Auto* to repair.

Repartierung *f* (*Fin*) scaling down, allotment.

repatriieren* *vt* **(a)** (*wieder einbürgern*) to renaturalize. **(b)** (*heimschicken*) to repatriate.

Repatriierung *f siehe vt* renaturalization; repatriation.

Repertoire [repɛr'toaːɐ] *nt* **-s, -s** repertory, repertoire (*auch fig*).

Repertoire- [repɛr'toaːɐ-]: **~stück** *nt* repertory *or* stock play; **~theater** *nt* repertory theatre, rep (*inf*).

Repetent *m* (*form, Aus*) *pupil who has to repeat a year.*

repetieren* [1] *vt* **(a)** (*old*) *Stoff, Vokabeln* to revise. **(b)** (*wiederholen*) to repeat; (*form, Aus*) *Klasse* to repeat, to take again; *Jahr* to repeat, to stay down for.
[2] *vi* **(a)** (*old*) to do revision, to revise. **(b)** (*form, Aus*) to stay down, to repeat a class.

Repetiergewehr *nt* (*old*) repeating rifle.

Repetition *f* **(a)** (*old: von Stoff etc*) revision. **(b)** (*Wiederholung*) repetition ◆ **im Falle einer ~ muß der Schüler ...** (*form, Aus*) if it is necessary to repeat a class *or* to stay down for a year the pupil must ...

Repetitor *m* (*Univ*) coach, crammer (*inf*).

Repetitorium *nt* (*Buch*) revision book; (*Unterricht*) revision *or* cramming (*inf*) course.

Replik *f* **-, -en (a)** (*Jur*) replication; (*fig geh*) riposte, reply. **(b)** (*Art*) replica.

replizieren* *vti* **(a)** (*Jur*) to reply; (*fig geh auch*) to ripost. **(b)** (*Art*) to make a replica of.

Report *m* **-(e)s, -e (a)** report; (*Enthüllungsbericht auch*) exposé ◆ **Schulmädchen-/Fensterputzer~** Confessions of a Schoolgirl/Window-Cleaner. **(b)** (*St Ex*) contango.

Reportage [repɔr'taːʒə] *f* **-, -n** report.

Reporter(in *f*) *m* **-s, -** reporter ◆ **Sport-/Wirtschafts~** sports/economics correspondent.

Reportgeschäft *nt* (*Fin*) contango.

Reposition *f* (*Med*) resetting.

repräsentabel *adj* impressive, prestigious; *Frau* (highly) presentable.

Repräsentant(in *f*) *m* representative.

Repräsentantenhaus *nt* (*US Pol*) House of Representatives.

Repräsentanz *f* **(a)** (*Pol*) representation. **(b)** (*Geschäftsvertretung*) branch.

Repräsentation *f* **(a)** (*Stellvertretung*) representation.
(b) der ~ dienen to create a good image, to have good prestige value, to make the right impression; **die Diplomatenfrau fand die Pflichten der ~ sehr anstrengend** the diplomat's wife found her life of official and social functions very tiring; **die einzige Funktion des Monarchen ist heute die ~** the sole function of the monarch today is that of an official figurehead.

repräsentativ *adj* **(a)** (*stellvertretend, typisch*) representative (*für* of).
(b) *Haus, Auto, Ausstattung* prestigious; *Erscheinung auch* presentable, personable ◆ **zu ~en Zwecken** for purposes of prestige.
(c) die ~en Pflichten eines Botschafters the social duties of an ambassador; **seine Stellung schließt ~e Pflichten ein** his job includes being a public/social representative of his company; **der ~e Aufwand des Königshauses/der Firma** the expenditure for maintaining the royal household's/company's image; **ein großes Konferenzzimmer für ~e Zwecke** a large conference room to provide a suitable setting for functions.

Repräsentativ|umfrage *f* representative survey.

repräsentieren* [1] *vt* to represent.
[2] *vi* to perform official duties ◆ **eine Diplomatenfrau muß ~ können** a diplomat's wife must be able to perform social duties.

Repressalie [-iə] *f* reprisal ◆ **~n anwenden** *or* **ergreifen** to take reprisals.

Repression *f* repression.

repressionsfrei *adj* free of repression.

repressiv *adj* repressive.

Reprise *f* **-, -n (a)** (*Mus*) recapitulation; (*TV, Rad*) repeat; (*Film, Theat*) rerun; (*nach längerer Zeit*) revival. **(b)** (*Mil*) recapture.

Reprivatisierung [reprivati'ziːrʊŋ] *f* denationalization.

Repro *f* **-, -s** (*Typ sl*) *abbr of* **Reproduktion.**

Reproduktion *f* reproduction; (*Typ auch*) repro (*sl*).

Reproduktions-: **~faktor** *m* (*Econ*) production factor; ⚠**~prozeß** *m* reproductive process; **~technik** *f* reproduction technology.

reproduktiv *adj* reproductive ◆ **er arbeitet rein ~** he merely reproduces what others have done.

reproduzierbar *adj* reproducible.

Reproduzierbarkeit *f* reproducibility.

reproduzieren* *vt* to reproduce.

Repro- *in cpds* repro; **~film** *m* repro film; **~fotografie** *f* repro photography; ⚠**~graphie** *f* (*Typ*) reprography.

Reptil *nt* **-s, -ien** [-iən] reptile.

Reptilienfonds [-iən-] *m* slush fund.

Republik *f* **-, -en** republic.

Republikaner(in *f*) *m* **-s, -** republican.

republikanisch *adj* republican.

Republik-: **~flucht** *f* (*DDR*) illegal crossing of the border; **r~flüchtig** *adj* (*DDR*) illegally emigrated; **r~flüchtig werden** to cross the border illegally; **~flüchtling** *m* (*DDR*) illegal emigrant.

Repunze *f* **-, -n** hallmark, plate-mark.

Reputation *f* (*old*) (good) reputation.

reputierlich *adj* (*old*) reputable, of good *or* high renown (*old, liter*).

Requiem ['reːkviɛm] *nt* **-s, -s** *or* (*Aus*) **Requien** ['reːkviən] requiem.

requirieren* *vt* (*Mil*) to requisition, to commandeer.

Requisit *nt* **-s, -en** equipment *no pl*, requisite (*form*) ◆ **ein unerläßliches ~** an indispensable piece of equipment; **~en** (*Theat*) props, properties (*form*).

Requisiteur(in *f*) [-'tøːɐ, -'tøːrɪn] *m* (*Theat*) props *or* property manager.

Requisition *f* requisition(ing), commandeering.

Requisitionsschein *m* (*Mil*) requisition order.

resch *adj* (*Aus*) (*knusprig*) *Brötchen etc* crisp, crunchy, crispy; (*fig: lebhaft*) *Frau* dynamic.

Reseda -, Reseden, Resede *f* **-, -n** (*Gattung*) reseda; (*Garten~*) mignonette.

reservat [rezɛr'vaːt] *adj* (*Aus*) classified.

Reservat [resɛr'vaːt] *nt* **(a)** (*old: Sonderrecht*) right, discretionary power ◆ **sich** (*dat*) **das ~ vorbehalten, etw zu machen** to reserve the right to do sth. **(b)** (*Wildpark*) reserve. **(c)** (*für Volksstämme*) reservation.

Reservation [resɛrva'tsioːn] *f* **(a)** (*old: Sonderrecht*) *siehe* **Reservat (a). (b)** (*für Volksstämme*) reservation.

Reservatrecht [rezɛr'vaːt-] *nt* discretionary power.

Reserve [re'zɛrvə] *f* **-, -n (a)** (*Vorrat*) reserve(s) (*an +dat* of); (*Geld*) savings *pl*; (*Mil, Sport*) reserves *pl* ◆ **(noch) etw in ~ haben** to have sth (still) in reserve; **in ~ liegen** (*Mil*) to stay back in reserve.
(b) (*Zurückhaltung*) reserve; (*Bedenken*) reservation ◆ **jdn aus der ~ locken** to break down sb's reserve, to bring sb out of his shell (*inf*); **aus der ~ heraustreten** to lose one's reserve, to come out of one's shell (*inf*).

Reserve-: **~bank** *f* (*Sport*) substitutes *or* reserves bench; **er saß nur auf der ~bank** he only sat on the bench; **~fonds** *m* reserve fund; **~kanister** *m* spare can; **~mann** *m, pl* **-männer** *or* **-leute** (*Sport*) reserve; **~offizier** *m* reserve officer; **~rad** *nt* spare (wheel); **~reifen** *m* spare (tyre); **~spieler** *m* (*Sport*) reserve; (*Kricket*) 12th man; **~tank** *m* reserve tank; **~truppen** *pl* reserves *pl*; **~übung** *f* (army) reserve training *no pl*.

reservieren* [rezɛr'viːrən] *vt* to reserve.

reserviert *adj Platz, Mensch* reserved.

Reserviertheit *f* reserve, reservedness.

▼ **Reservierung** *f* reservation.

Reservist [rezɛr'vɪst] *m* reservist.

Reservoir [rezɛr'voaːɐ] *nt* **-s, -e** reservoir; (*fig auch*) pool.

Reset-Taste [riː'sɛt-] *f* (*Comput*) reset key.

resident *adj* (*Comput*) resident.

Resident *m* envoy, resident (*rare*).

Residenz *f* **(a)** (*Wohnung*) residence, residency. **(b)** (*Hauptstadt*) royal seat *or* capital.

Residenzstadt *f* royal seat *or* capital.

residieren* *vi* to reside.

residual *adj* (*geh*) residual.

Residuum *nt* **-s, Residuen** [re'ziːduən] (*geh*) residue, residuum (*form*).

Resignation *f* (*geh*) resignation ◆ **(über etw** *acc*) **in ~ verfallen, sich der ~ überlassen** to become resigned (to sth).

resignieren* *vi* to give up ◆ **resigniert** resigned; **... sagte er ~d** *or* **resigniert ...** he said with resignation *or* in a resigned way.

resistent *adj* (*auch Med*) resistant (*gegen* to).

Resistenz *f* (*auch Med*) resistance (*gegen* to).

resistieren* *vi* (*Med*) to resist.

resolut *adj* determined.

Resolution *f* (*Pol*) (*Beschluß*) resolution; (*Bittschrift*) petition.

Resonanz *f* **(a)** (*Mus, Phys*) resonance. **(b)** (*fig*) response (*auf +acc* to) ◆ **keine/wenig/große ~ finden** to meet with *or* get no/little/a good response.

Resonanz-: **~boden** *m* sounding-board; **~kasten** *m* soundbox.

Resopal ® *nt* **-s,** *no pl* Formica ®.

resorbieren* *vt* to absorb.

Resorption *f* absorption.

resozialisieren* *vt* to rehabilitate.

Resozialisierung *f* rehabilitation.

resp. *abbr of* **respektive.**

▼ **Respekt** *m* **-s,** *no pl* (*Achtung*) respect; (*Angst*) fear ◆ **jdm ~ einflößen** (*Achtung*) to command *or* inspire respect from sb; (*Angst*) to put the fear of God into sb; **vor jdm den ~ verlieren** to lose one's respect for sb; **bei allem ~ (vor jdm/etw)** with all due respect (to sb/for sth); **vor jdm/etw ~ haben** (*Achtung*) to respect sb/sth, to have respect for sb/sth; (*Angst*) to be afraid of sb/sth; **sich** (*dat*) **~ verschaffen** to make oneself respected; **allen ~!** well done!

respektabel *adj* respectable.

respekt-: ⚠**~einflößend** *adj* authoritative; **ein wenig ~einflößender Mensch** a person who commands *or* inspires little respect; **~heischend** *adj*

demanding respect.
respektieren* *vt* to respect; *Wechsel* to honour.
respektive [rɛspɛk'tiːvə] *adv* (*geh, Comm*) **(a)** (*jeweils*) and ... respectively ◆ **Fritz und Franz verdienen 40 ~ 50 Mark pro Tag** Fritz and Franz earn 40 and 50 marks per day respectively.
(b) (*anders ausgedrückt*) or rather; (*genauer gesagt*) (or) more precisely.
(c) (*oder*) or.
Respekt-: **r~los** *adj* disrespectful, irreverent; **eine r~lose Person** an irreverent person; **~losigkeit** *f* **(a)** (*no pl: Verhalten*) disrespect(fulness), lack of respect, irreverence; **(b)** (*Bemerkung*) disrespectful remark *or* comment.
Respektsperson *f* person to be respected; (*Beamter etc*) person in authority.
Respekt-: **~tage** *pl* (*Comm*) days of grace; **r~voll** *adj* respectful; **r~widrig** *adj* disrespectful, irreverent.
Respiration *f* (*form*) respiration.
Respirations|apparat, Respirator *m* respirator.
respirieren* *vi* (*form*) to respire.
Ressentiment [rɛsãti'mãː, rə-] *nt* **-s, -s** resentment *no pl*, feeling of resentment (*gegen* against).
Ressort [rɛ'soːɐ] *nt* **-s, -s** department ◆ **in das ~ von jdm/etw fallen** to be sb's/sth's department.
Ressort-: **r~mäßig** *adj* departmental, on a departmental basis; **ich weiß nicht, wo der Antrag r~mäßig hingehört** I don't know which department the application comes under; **~minister** *m* department minister; **der ~minister für die Polizei** the minister responsible for the police.
Ressource [rɛ'sʊrsə] *f* **-, -n** (*auch Comput*) resource; **erneuerbare ~** renewable resources.
Rest *m* **-(e)s, -e** **(a)** rest ◆ **die ~e einer Kirche/Stadt/Kultur** the remains *or* remnants of a church/city/civilization; **90% sind schon fertig, den ~ mache ich** 90% is done, I'll do the rest *or* remainder; **am Anfang hatte ich 25 Schüler, die 3 hier sind noch der ~ (davon)** at the beginning I had 25 pupils, these 3 are what's left *or* all that is left; **der letzte ~** the last bit; **der letzte ~ vom Schützenfest** (*hum*) the last little bit; **bis auf einen ~** except for a little bit *or* a small amount; **dieser kleine ~** this little bit that's left (over); **der kümmerliche ~** (*von meinem Geld*) all that's left, the miserable remains; (*vom Essen*) the sad remnants; **der ~ ist für Sie** (*beim Bezahlen*) keep the change; **jdm/einer Sache den ~ geben** (*inf*) to finish sb/sth off; **sich** (*dat*) **den ~ holen** (*inf*) to make oneself really ill.
(b) **~e** *pl* (*Essens~*) left-overs *pl*.
(c) (*Stoff~*) remnant.
(d) (*Math*) remainder ◆ **2 ~ 3** 2 and 3 over, 2 remainder 3.
Rest- *in cpds* remaining; **~abschnitt** *m* remaining part.
Restant *m* (*Comm*) **(a)** (*Schuldner*) defaulter. **(b)** (*Ladenhüter*) slow *or* slow-moving line.
Rest|auflage *f* remainder(ed) stock, remainders *pl*.
Restaurant [rɛsto'rãː] *nt* **-s, -s** restaurant.
Restaurateur(in *f*) [rɛstora'tøːɐ, -'tøːrɪn] *m* (*old*) restaurateur.
Restauration[1] *f* restoration ◆ **die ~** (*Hist*) the Restoration.
Restauration[2] [rɛstora'tsioːn] *f* (*old, Aus*) inn, tavern (*old*); (*im Bahnhof*) refreshment rooms *pl*.
Restaurations-: **~betrieb** *m* catering business; **~zeit** *f* period of ultra-conservatism; **die ~zeit** (*Hist*) the Restoration.
Restaurator *m*, **Restauratorin** *f* restorer.
restaurieren* [1] *vt* to restore.
[2] *vr* (*old*) to partake of some refreshment (*old, form*).
Restaurierung *f* restoration.
Rest-: **~bestand** *m* remaining stock; **wir haben noch einen kleinen ~bestand an Bikinis** we still have a few bikinis left; **~betrag** *m* balance.
Reste-: **~essen** *nt* left-overs *pl*; **~verkauf** *m* remnants sale.
restituieren* *vt* (*form*) to make restitution of (*form*).
Restitution *f* (*form*) restitution (*form*).
Restitutions-: **~edikt** *nt* Edict of Restitution; **~klage** *f* action for a retrial.
Restlaufzeit *f* (*Fin*) remaining term.
restlich *adj* remaining, rest of the ... **die ~en** the rest.
restlos [1] *adj* complete, total.
[2] *adv* completely, totally; *begeistert* wildly.
Rest-: **~menge** *f* residue; **~posten** *m* (*Comm*) remaining stock; **ein ~posten** remaining stock; **ein großer ~posten Bücher/Zucker** a lot of books/sugar left in stock; **„~posten"** "reduced to clear".
Restriktion *f* (*form*) restriction.
Restriktionsmaßnahme *f* restriction, restrictive measure.
restriktiv *adj* (*geh*) restrictive.
Rest-: **~risiko** *nt* residual risk; **~summe** *f* balance, amount remaining; **~wert** *m* residual; **~zahlung** *f* final payment, payment of the balance.
Resultante *f* **-, -n** (*Math*) resultant.
Resultat *nt* result; (*von Prüfung auch*) results *pl* ◆ **zu einem ~ kommen** to come to *or* arrive at a conclusion.
resultatlos *adj* fruitless, without result ◆ **das Spiel verlief ~** the game was undecided *or* ended in a draw.
resultieren* *vi* (*geh*) to result (*in +dat* in) ◆ **aus etw ~** to be the result of sth, to result from sth; **aus dem Gesagten resultiert, daß** ... from what was said one must conclude that ...; **die daraus ~den** ... the resulting ...
Resultierende *f* **-n, -n** (*Math*) resultant.
Resümee, Resumé (*Aus, Sw*) [rezy'meː] *nt* **-s, -s** (*geh*) summary, résumé; (*am Ende einer Rede auch*) recapitulation.
resümieren* *vti* (*geh*) to summarize, to sum up; (*am Ende einer Rede auch*) to recapitulate.
Retardation *f* retardation.
retardieren* *vt* to retard ◆ **ein ~des Moment** a delaying factor *or* element.
retirieren* *vi aux sein* (*old Mil, hum*) to beat a retreat.
Retorte *f* **-, -n** (*Chem*) retort ◆ **aus der ~** (*inf*) synthetic; **Baby aus der ~** test-tube baby.
Retortenbaby *nt* test-tube baby.
retour [re'tuːɐ] *adv* (*Aus, dial*) back.
Retourbillett [re'tuːɐbɪl'jɛt] *nt* (*Sw*) return (ticket), round-trip ticket (*US*).
Retoure [re'tuːrə] *f* **-, -n** *usu pl* (*Aus*) return.
Retour- [re'tuːɐ-]: **~gang** *m* (*Aus*) reverse (gear); **~karte** *f* (*Aus*) return (ticket), round-trip ticket (*US*); **~kutsche** *f* (*inf*) (*Worte*) retort; (*Handlung*) retribution.
retournieren* [retʊr'niːrən] *vt* (*old, Aus*) to return.
Retourspiel [re'tuːɐ-] *nt* (*Aus*) return (match).
retrospektiv (*liter*) [1] *adj* retrospective.
[2] *adv* in retrospect.
Retrospektive *f* (*liter*) retrospective.
Retrovirus *nt* retrovirus.
retten [1] *vt* to save; (*aus Gefahr auch, befreien*) to rescue; (*Comput*) *Datei* to recover ◆ **jdm das Leben ~** to save sb's life; **jdn vor jdm/etw ~** to save sb from sb/sth; **ein ~der Gedanke** a bright idea that saved the situation *or* his/our *etc* bacon (*inf*); **der Patient/die alte Kirche** *etc* **ist noch/nicht mehr zu ~** the patient/the old church can still be saved *or* is not yet past saving/is past saving; **er hat wieder geheiratet? er ist nicht mehr zu ~** he got married again? he's beyond redemption *or* past saving *or* helping; **bist du noch zu ~?** (*inf*) are you out of your mind, have you gone completely round the bend? (*inf*).
[2] *vr* to escape ◆ **sich auf/unter etw** (*acc*)/**aus etw ~** to escape onto/under/from sth; **sich vor jdm/etw ~** to escape (from) sb/sth; **sich durch die Flucht ~** to escape; **sich vor etw nicht mehr ~ können** *or* **zu ~ wissen** (*fig*) to be swamped with sth; **rette sich, wer kann!** (it's) every man for himself!
Retter(in *f*) *m* **-s, -** rescuer, saviour (*liter*), deliverer (*liter*); (*Rel*) Saviour ◆ **ach mein ~!** oh my hero!; *siehe* **Not**.
Rettich *m* **-s, -e** radish.
Rettung *f* rescue, deliverance (*liter*); (*von Waren*) recovery; (*Rel*) salvation, deliverance ◆ **die ~ und Erhaltung historischer Denkmäler** the saving and preservation of historical monuments; **Gesellschaft zur ~ Schiffbrüchiger** Lifeboat Service; **die ~ kam in letzter Minute** the situation was saved in the last minute; (*für Schiffbrüchige etc*) help came in the nick of time; **auf ~ hoffen** to hope to be saved, to hope for deliverance (*liter*); **an seine (eigene) ~ denken** to worry about one's own safety; **Trinker, für die jegliche ~ ...** alcoholics for whom any salvation ...; **für den Patienten/unsere Wirtschaft gibt es keine ~ mehr** the patient/our economy is beyond saving, our economy is beyond salvation; **das war meine ~** that saved me, that was my salvation; **das war meine ~, daß ...** I was saved by the fact that ...; **das war meine letzte ~** that was my last hope; (*hat mich gerettet*) that was my salvation, that saved me.
Rettungs-: **~aktion** *f* rescue operation; **~anker** *m* sheet anchor; (*fig*) anchor; **~arzt** *m siehe* **Notarzt**; **~boje** *f* lifebelt; (*Hosenboje*) breeches buoy; **~boot** *nt* lifeboat; **~dienst** *m* rescue service; **~floß** *nt* life-raft; **~flugwacht** *f* air rescue service; **~flugzeug** *nt* rescue aircraft; **~gerät** *nt* rescue equipment *no pl or* apparatus *no pl*; **~gürtel** *m* lifebelt; **~hubschrauber** *m* rescue helicopter; **~insel** *f* inflatable life-raft; **~kommando** *nt* rescue squad; **~leine** *f* lifeline; **~leiter** *f* rescue ladder; **r~los** [1] *adj* beyond saving; *Lage* hopeless, irredeemable; *Verlust* irrecoverable; [2] *adv verloren* hopelessly, irretrievably; **~mannschaft** *f* rescue team *or* party; **~medaille** *f* lifesaving medal; **~ring** *m* lifebuoy, lifebelt; (*hum: Bauch*) spare tyre (*hum*); **~schwimmen** *nt* lifesaving; **~schwimmer** *m* lifesaver; (*am Strand*) lifeguard; **~station, ~stelle** *f* rescue centre; (*für Erste Hilfe*) first-aid post; (*mit ~booten*) lifeboat *or* coastguard station; **~trupp** *m siehe* **~kommando**; **~versuch** *m* rescue attempt *or* bid; (*von Arzt etc*) attempt to save sb; **~wagen** *m* ambulance; **~wesen** *nt* rescue services *pl*.
Retusche *f* **-, -n** (*Phot*) retouching.
Retuscheur(in *f*) [retʊ'ʃøːɐ, -'ʃøːrɪn] *m* retoucher.
retuschieren* *vt* (*Phot*) to retouch, to touch up (*inf, auch fig*).
Reue *f* **-,** *no pl* remorse (*über +acc* at, about), repentance (*auch Rel*) (*über +acc* of), rue (*old, liter*) (*über +acc* at, of); (*Bedauern*) regret (*über +acc* at, about).
reuelos *adj* unrepentant.
reuen *vt* (*liter*) **etw reut jdn** sb regrets *or* rues (*liter, old*) sth; **es reut mich, daß ich das getan habe** I regret *or* rue (*liter, old*) having done that.
reuevoll *adj siehe* **reumütig**.
reuig *adj* (*liter*) *siehe* **reumütig**.
reumütig *adj* (*voller Reue*) remorseful, repentant; *Sünder, Missetäter* contrite, penitent; (*betreten, zerknirscht*) rueful ◆ **~ gestand er** ... full of remorse he confessed ...; **du wirst bald ~ zu mir zurückkommen, sagte der Ehemann** you'll soon come back feeling sorry, said the husband.
Reuse *f* **-, -n** fish trap.
re|üssieren* *vi* (*old*) to succeed, to be successful (*bei, mit* with).
Revanche [re'vãːʃ(ə)] *f* **-, -n** **(a)** (*Sport*) revenge; (*~partie*) return match ◆ **du mußt ihm ~ geben!** you'll have to let him have his revenge, you'll have to give him a return match. **(b)** *no pl* (*Pol*) revenge, vengeance.
Revanche- [re'vãːʃə-]: **~krieg** *m* war of revenge; **r~lüstern** *adj* revanchist; **~partie** *f* (*Sport*) return match; **~politik** *f* (*pej*) revanchist policy/politics

pl; **~spiel** *nt* (*Sport*) return match.

revanchieren* [revã'ʃi:rən] *vr* **(a)** (*sich rächen*) to get one's revenge, to get one's own back (*bei jdm für etw* on sb for sth).
(b) (*sich erkenntlich zeigen*) to reciprocate ◆ **ich werde mich bei Gelegenheit mal ~** I'll return the compliment some time; (*für Hilfe*) I'll do the same for you one day, I'll return the favour one day; **das Problem bei Geschenken/Einladungen ist, daß man meint, sich ~ zu müssen** the problem with getting presents/invitations is that one always feels one has to give something (back) in return/to invite somebody back (in return); **sich bei jdm für eine Einladung/seine Gastfreundschaft ~** to return sb's invitation/hospitality.

Revanchismus [revã'ʃɪsmʊs] *m* revanchism.

Revanchist(in *f*) [revã'ʃɪst(ɪn)] *m* revanchist.

revanchistisch [revã'ʃɪstɪʃ] *adj* revanchist.

Reverenz [reve'rɛnts] *f* (*old*) (*Hochachtung*) reverence; (*Verbeugung*) obeisance, reverence (*old*) ◆ **jdm seine ~ erweisen** to show one's reverence *or* respect for sb; **seine ~en machen** to make one's obeisances (*old*), to bow.

Revers[1] [re've:ɐ, re'vɛ:ɐ, rə'-] *nt or m* -, - (*an Kleidung*) lapel, revere, revers (*esp US*).

Revers[2] [re'vɛrs] *m* **-es, -e** *or* [re'vɛ:ɐ, rə'vɛ:ɐ] *m* -, - (*old: Rückseite*) reverse.

Revers[3] [re'vɛrs] *m* **-es, -e** (*Erklärung*) declaration.

reversibel [revɛr'zi:bl] *adj* reversible.

Reversion [revɛr'zio:n] *f* (*Biol, Psych*) reversion.

revidieren* [revi'di:rən] *vt* to revise; *Korrekturen* to check; (*Comm*) to audit, to check.

Revier [re'vi:ɐ] *nt* **-s, -e** **(a)** (*Polizei~*) (*Dienststelle*) (police) station, station house (*US*); (*Dienstbereich*) beat, district, precinct (*US*), patch (*inf*); (*von Prostituierter*) beat, patch (*inf*).
(b) (*Zool: Gebiet*) territory ◆ **die Küche ist mein ~** the kitchen is my territory *or* preserve.
(c) (*Hunt: Jagd~*) hunting ground, shoot.
(d) (*old: Gebiet, Gegend*) district, area.
(e) (*Mil: Kranken~*) sick-bay ◆ **auf dem** *or* **im ~ liegen** to be in the sick-bay.
(f) (*Min: Kohlen~*) (coal)mine ◆ **im ~ an der Ruhr** in the mines of the Ruhr; **das ~** the Ruhr; the Saar.

Revier-: ~förster *m* forester, forest ranger (*US*); **~försterei** *f* forester's lodge; **r~krank** *adj* (*Mil*) hospitalized, in the sick-bay; **~wache** *f* duty room; **~wachtmeister** *m* station sergeant.

Revirement [revirə'mã:, revɪr'mã:] *nt* **-s, -s** (*Pol*) reshuffle.

Revision [revi'zio:n] *f* **(a)** (*von Meinung, Politik etc*) revision.
(b) (*Comm: Prüfung*) audit.
(c) (*Typ: letzte Überprüfung*) final (proof-)read ◆ **~ lesen** to do the final (proof-)read.
(d) (*Jur: Urteilsanfechtung*) appeal (*an +acc* to).

Revisionismus [revizio'nɪsmʊs] *m* (*Pol*) revisionism.

Revisionist(in *f*) [revizio'nɪst(ɪn)] *m* (*Pol*) revisionist.

revisionistisch [revizio'nɪstɪʃ] *adj* (*Pol*) revisionist.

Revisions-: ~bogen *m* page-proof; **~frist** *f* time for appeal; **~gericht** *nt* court of appeal, appeal court; **~verhandlung** *f* appeal hearing.

Revisor [re'vi:zɔr] *m* (*Comm*) auditor; (*Typ*) proof-reader.

Revolte [re'vɔltə] *f* **-, -n** revolt.

revoltieren* [revɔl'ti:rən] *vi* to revolt, to rebel; (*fig: Magen*) to rebel.

Revolution [revolu'tsio:n] *f* (*lit, fig*) revolution ◆ **eine ~ der Moral** a moral revolution, a revolution in morals.

revolutionär [revolutsio'nɛ:ɐ] *adj* (*lit, fig*) revolutionary.

Revolutionär(in *f*) [revolutsio'nɛ:ɐ, -'nɛ:ərɪn] *m* revolutionary.

revolutionieren* [revolutsio'ni:rən] *vt* to revolutionize.

Revolutions- *in cpds* revolutionary.

Revoluzzer(in *f*) [revo'lʊtsɐ, -ərɪn] *m* **-s, -** (*pej*) would-be revolutionary.

Revolver [re'vɔlvɐ] *m* **-s, -** revolver, gun.

Revolver-: ~blatt *nt* (*pej*) scandal sheet; **~griff** *m* butt (of a/the revolver); **~held** *m* (*pej*) gunslinger; **~lauf** *m* barrel (of a/the revolver); **~mündung** *f* mouth (of a/the revolver); **plötzlich starrte er in eine ~mündung** he suddenly found himself staring down the barrel of a revolver; **~presse** *f* (*pej*) gutter press.

Revue [rə'vy:] *f* **-, -n** [-y:ən] **(a)** (*Theat*) revue.
(b) (*rare: Zeitschrift*) review.
(c) (*old, Mil*) review ◆ **etw ~ passieren lassen** (*fig*) to let sth parade before one, to pass sth in review.

Revuetänzerin [rə'vy:-] *f* chorus-girl.

Reykjavik ['raikjavi:k] *nt* **-s** Reykjavik.

Rezensent(in *f*) *m* reviewer.

rezensieren* *vt* to review.

Rezension *f* review, write-up (*inf*).

Rezensions|exemplar *nt* review copy.

rezent *adj* **(a)** (*Biol*) living; (*Ethnologie*) *Kulturen* surviving. **(b)** (*dial: säuerlich, pikant*) tart, sour.

Rezept *nt* **-(e)s, -e** **(a)** (*Med*) prescription; (*fig*) cure, remedy (*für, gegen* for) ◆ **auf ~** on prescription. **(b)** (*Cook, fig*) recipe.

Rezept-: ~block *m* prescription pad; **r~frei** [1] *adj* available without prescription; [2] *adv* over the counter, without a prescription.

Rezeption *f* **(a)** (*liter: Übernahme*) adoption. **(b)** (*von Hotel: Empfang*) reception.

rezeptiv *adj* receptive ◆ **der Kritiker als ~er Mensch** the critic as one who assimilates *or* receives ideas.

Rezept-: ~pflicht *f* prescription requirement; **der ~pflicht unterliegen** to be available only on prescription; **dafür besteht jetzt keine ~pflicht mehr** you don't need a prescription for it now; **r~pflichtig** *adj* available only on prescription, ethical (*spec*); **etw r~pflichtig machen** to put sth on prescription.

Rezeptur *f* (*form*) dispensing.

⚠ **Rezeß** *m* **-sses, -sse** (*Jur*) written settlement *or* agreement.

Rezession *f* (*Econ*) recession.

rezessiv *adj* (*Biol*) recessive.

reziprok *adj* (*Math, Gram*) reciprocal ◆ **sich ~ zueinander verhalten** to be in a reciprocal relationship.

Rezitation *f* recitation.

Rezitations|abend *m* poetry evening.

Rezitativ *nt* (*Mus*) recitative.

Rezitator *m*, **Rezitatorin** *f* reciter.

rezitieren* *vti* to recite.

R-Gespräch ['ɛr-] *nt* transfer *or* reverse charge call (*Brit*), collect call ◆ **ein ~ führen** to make a transfer charge call *etc*, to transfer *or* reverse the charges (*Brit*), to call collect (*US*).

Rh [ɛr'ha:] *abbr of* **Rhesusfaktor positiv.**

rh [ɛr'ha:] *abbr of* **Rhesusfaktor negativ.**

Rhabarber *m* **-s**, *no pl* (*auch Gemurmel*) rhubarb.

Rhapsodie *f* (*Mus, Liter*) rhapsody.

rhapsodisch *adj* (*Mus, Liter*) rhapsodic(al).

Rhein *m* **-s** Rhine.

Rhein-: r~ab(wärts) *adv* down the Rhine; **~armee** *f* British Army of the Rhine; **r~auf(wärts)** *adv* up the Rhine; **~bund** *m* (*Hist*) Confederation of the Rhine; **~fall** *m* Rhine Falls *pl*, Falls of the Rhine *pl*.

rheinisch *adj attr* Rhenish, Rhineland.

Rhein-: ~länder *m* **-s, -** **(a)** Rhinelander; **(b)** (*Tanz*) ≃ schottische; **~länderin** *f siehe* **~länder (a)**; **r~ländisch** *adj* Rhenish, Rhineland; **~land-Pfalz** *nt* Rhineland-Palatinate; **~wein** *m* Rhine wine, Rhenish (wine); (*weißer auch*) hock.

Rhenium *nt*, *no pl* (*abbr* **Re**) rhenium.

Rhesus-: ~affe *m* rhesus monkey; **~faktor** *m* (*Med*) rhesus *or* Rh factor; **~(faktor) positiv/negativ** rhesus positive/negative.

Rhetorik *f* rhetoric.

Rhetoriker(in *f*) *m* **-s, -** rhetorician (*form*), master of rhetoric; (*Redner*) orator.

rhetorisch *adj* rhetorical ◆ **~e Frage** rhetorical question.

Rheuma *nt* **-s**, *no pl* rheumatism.

Rheumamittel *nt* (*inf*) cure for rheumatism *or* the rheumatics (*inf*).

Rheumatiker(in *f*) *m* **-s, -** rheumatic, rheumatism sufferer.

rheumatisch *adj* rheumatic.

Rheumatismus *m* rheumatism.

Rheumatologe *m*, **Rheumatologin** *f* rheumatologist.

Rhinozeros *nt* **-(ses), -se** rhinoceros, rhino (*inf*); (*inf: Dummkopf*) fool, twit (*Brit inf*), sap (*inf*).

Rhizom *nt* **-s, -e** (*Bot*) rhizome.

Rhodesien [-iən] *nt* **-s** Rhodesia.

Rhodesier(in *f*) [-iɐ, -iərɪn] *m* **-s, -** Rhodesian.

rhodesisch *adj* Rhodesian.

Rhodium *nt*, *no pl* (*abbr* **Rh**) rhodium.

Rhododendron [rodo'dɛndrɔn] *m or nt* **-s, Rhododendren** rhododendron.

Rhodos ['ro:dɔs, 'rɔdɔs] *nt* **-** Rhodes.

Rhomben *pl of* **Rhombus.**

rhombisch *adj* rhomboid(al).

Rhomboid *nt* **-(e)s, -e** rhomboid.

Rhombus *m* **-, Rhomben** rhombus, rhomb.

Rhythmik *f* rhythmics *sing*; (*inf: Rhythmus*) rhythm.

Rhythmiker(in *f*) *m* **-s, -** rhythmist.

rhythmisch *adj* rhythmic(al) ◆ **~e Prosa** rhythmic prose; **~e Gymnastik** rhythmics *sing*, music and movement.

rhythmisieren* *vt* to make rhythmic, to put rhythm into ◆ **rhythmisiert** rhythmic.

Rhythmus *m* (*Mus, Poet, fig*) rhythm.

RIAS *abbr of* **Rundfunk im amerikanischen Sektor** broadcasting station in the American sector (of Berlin).

Ribis(e)l *f* **-, -n** (*Aus*) *siehe* **Johannisbeere.**

Ribonukle|insäure *f* (*abbr* **RNS**) ribonucleic acid.

Richt-: ~antenne *f* directional aerial (*esp Brit*) *or* antenna; **~baum** *m tree used in the topping-out ceremony*; **~beil** *nt* executioner's axe; **~blei** *nt* plumbline, plummet.

richten [1] *vt* **(a)** (*lenken*) to direct (*auf +acc* towards), to point (*auf +acc* at, towards); *Gewehr auch* to train (*auf +acc* on); *Scheinwerfer auch* to turn (*auf +acc* on); *Augen, Blicke, Aufmerksamkeit* to direct, to turn (*auf +acc* towards), to focus (*auf +acc* on); *Pläne, Wünsche, Tun* to direct (*auf +acc* towards) ◆ **den Kurs nach Norden/Osten** *etc* **~** to set *or* steer a northerly/easterly *etc* course; **die Augen gen Himmel ~** (*liter*) to raise *or* lift one's eyes heavenwards (*liter*) *or* to heaven (*liter*); **richt euch!** (*Mil*) right dress!; (*Sch*) get in a straight line!; **einen Verdacht gegen jdn ~** to suspect sb.
(b) (*aus~*) **etw nach jdm/etw ~** to suit *or* fit sth to sb/sth; *Lebensstil, Verhalten* to orientate sth to sb/sth.
(c) (*adressieren*) *Briefe, Anfragen* to address, to send (*an +acc* to); *Bitten, Forderungen, Gesuch* to address, to make (*an +acc* to); *Kritik, Vorwurf* to level, to

⚠: for details of spelling reform, see supplement

direct, to aim (*gegen* at, against).
(d) (*S Ger*) (*zurechtmachen*) to prepare, to get ready; (*in Ordnung bringen*) to do, to fix; (*reparieren*) to fix; *Essen auch* to get, to fix; *Haare* to do; *Tisch* to lay (*Brit*), to set; *Betten* to make, to do ◆ **jdm ein Bad ~** (*form, S Ger*) to draw (*form*) *or* run a bath for sb.
(e) (*einstellen*) to set; (*S Ger: geradebiegen*) to straighten (out), to bend straight.
(f) (*Aus pej*) **sich's** (*dat*) **~** to get oneself off (*inf*).
(g) (*old: hinrichten*) to execute, to put to death ◆ **sich selbst ~** (*liter*) to find death by one's own hand (*liter*); **sich von selbst ~** (*fig*) to condemn oneself; *siehe* **zugrunde.**
[2] *vr* **(a)** (*sich hinwenden*) to focus, to be focussed (*auf +acc* on), to be directed (*auf +acc* towards); (*Gedanken, Augen auch*) to turn, to be turned (*auf +acc* towards).
(b) (*sich wenden*) to consult (*an jdn* sb); (*Maßnahme, Vorwurf etc*) to be directed *or* aimed (*gegen* at).
(c) (*sich anpassen*) to follow (*nach jdm/etw* sb/sth) ◆ **sich nach den Vorschriften ~** to go by the rules; **sich nach jds Wünschen ~** to comply with *or* go along with sb's wishes; **mir ist es egal, ob wir früher oder später gehen, ich richte mich nach dir** I don't mind if we go earlier or later, I'll fit in with you *or* I'll do what you do; **wir ~ uns ganz nach unseren Kunden** we are guided entirely by our customers' wishes; **warum sollte die Frau sich immer nach dem Mann ~?** why should the woman always do what the man wants?; **sich nach den Sternen/der Wettervorhersage/dem, was er behauptet, ~** to go by the stars/the weather forecast/what he maintains; **und richte dich (gefälligst) danach!** (*inf*) (kindly) do as you're told.
(d) (*abhängen von*) to depend (*nach* on).
(e) (*S Ger: sich zurechtmachen*) to get ready ◆ **für die Party brauchst du dich nicht extra zu ~** you don't have to get specially done up for the party (*inf*).
[3] *vi* (*liter: urteilen*) to judge (*über jdn* sb), to pass judgement (*über +acc* on) ◆ **milde/streng ~** to be mild/harsh in one's judgement; **richtet nicht, auf daß ihr nicht gerichtet werdet!** (*Bibl*) judge not, that ye be not judged (*Bibl*).

Richter(in *f*) *m* **-s, -** judge ◆ **jdn/etw vor den ~ bringen** to take sb/sth to court; **der gesetzliche ~** the right to a fair trial; **die ~** the Bench, the judiciary, the judges *pl*; **das Buch der ~** (*Bibl*) (the Book of) Judges; **sich zum ~ aufwerfen** *or* **machen** (*fig*) to set (oneself) up in judgement; **der höchste ~** (*liter: Gott*) the Supreme Judge; **vor dem höchsten ~ stehen** (*liter: vor Gott*) to stand before the Judgement Seat *or* the Throne of Judgement.

Richter-: ~amt *nt* judicial office; **das ~amt ausüben** to sit on the Bench; **~gesetz** *nt law defining the functions and powers of judges.*

Richterin *f siehe* **Richter.**

Richter-: r~lich *adj attr* judicial; **~schaft** *f* judiciary, Bench; **~-Skala** *f* (*Geol*) Richter scale; **~spruch** *m* **(a)** (*Jur*) ≈ judgement; **(b)** (*Sport*) judges' decision; (*Pferderennen*) stewards' decision; **~stuhl** *m* Bench; **der ~stuhl (Gottes)** the Judgement Seat, the Throne of Judgement.

Richt-: ~fest *nt* topping-out ceremony; **~feuer** *nt* (*Naut*) leading lights *pl*; (*Aviat*) approach lights *pl.*

Richtfunk *m* directional radio.

Richtfunk-: ~bake *f* (*Naut*) directional radio beacon; **~verbindung** *f* micro-wave link.

Richtgeschwindigkeit *f* recommended speed.

➤ **richtig** [1] *adj* **(a)** right *no comp*; (*zutreffend auch*) correct ◆ **eine ~e Erkenntnis/Voraussetzung** *etc* a correct realization/presupposition *etc*; **der ~e Mann am ~en Ort** the right man for the job; **ich halte es für ~/das ~ste,** ... I think it would be right/best ...; **nicht ganz ~ (im Kopf) sein** (*inf*) to be not quite right (in the head) (*inf*); **bin ich hier ~ bei Müller?** (*inf*) is this right for the Müllers?; **der Junge ist ~** (*inf*) that boy's all right (*inf*) *or* OK (*inf*).
(b) (*wirklich, echt*) real, proper ◆ **der ~e Vater/die ~e Mutter** the real father/mother; **ein ~er Drache/Idiot** *etc* a real *or* proper *or* right (*inf*) dragon/idiot *etc.*
[2] *adv* **(a)** (*korrekt*) correctly, right; *passen, funktionieren, liegen etc auch* properly ◆ **die Uhr geht ~** the clock is right *or* correct; **habe ich ~ gehört?** (*iro*) do my ears deceive me?, am I hearing things?; (*Gerücht betreffend*) is it right what I've heard?; **wenn man es ~ nimmt** (*inf*) really, actually, properly speaking; **du kommst gerade ~!** you're just in time; (*iro*) you're just what I need.
(b) (*inf: ganz und gar*) really, proper (*dial*), real (*esp US inf*); *sich schämen, verlegen, schlagen auch* thoroughly.
(c) (*wahrhaftig*) right, correct ◆ **du bist doch Konrads Schwester — ~!** you're Konrad's sister — (that's) right; **das ist doch Paul! — ach ja, ~** that's Paul — oh yes, so it is; **wir dachten, es würde gleich regnen und ~, kaum** ... we thought it would soon start raining and, sure enough, scarcely ...

Richtige(r) *mf decl as adj* right person/man/woman *etc*; (*zum Heiraten auch*) Mr/Miss Right ◆ **du bist mir der ~!** (*iro*) you're a fine *or* right one (*inf*), some mothers do have them! (*inf*); **sechs ~ im Lotto** six right in the lottery.

Richtige(s) *nt decl as adj* right thing ◆ **das ist das ~** that's right; **das ist genau das ~** that's just right *or* the thing *or* the job (*inf*); **das ist auch nicht das ~** that's not right either; **ich habe nichts ~s gegessen/gelernt** I haven't had a proper meal/I didn't really learn anything; **ich habe noch nicht das ~/endlich was ~s gefunden** I haven't found anything right *or* suitable/at last I've found something suitable.

richtiggehend [1] *adj attr Uhr, Waage* accurate; (*inf: regelrecht*) real, regular (*inf*), proper.
[2] *adv* (*inf*) **~ intelligent** really intelligent; **das ist ja ~ Betrug** that's downright deceit.

Richtigkeit *f* correctness, accuracy; (*von Verhalten, Vorgehen, einer Entscheidung*) rightness, correctness ◆ **an der ~ von etw zweifeln, bei etw an der ~ zweifeln** (*inf*) to doubt whether sth is correct *or* right; **die ~ einer Abschrift bescheinigen** to certify a copy as being accurate; **das hat schon seine ~** it's right enough; **es wird schon seine ~ haben** it's bound to be right *or* OK (*inf*).

Richtig-: ⚠r~liegen *vi sep irreg* (*inf*) to fit in; **bei jdm r~liegen** to get on well with sb; *siehe* **liegen (f); ⚠r~stellen** *vt sep* to correct; **ich muß Ihre Behauptung r~stellen** I must put you right there; **~stellung** *f* correction.

Richt-: ~kanonier *m* (*Mil*) gun-layer; **~kranz** *m*, **~krone** *f* (*Build*) *wreath used in the topping-out ceremony*; **~linie** *f* guideline; **~maß** *nt siehe* **Eichmaß; ⚠~mikrophon** *nt* directional microphone *or* mike (*inf*); **~platz** *m* place of execution; **~preis** *m* recommended price; **unverbindlicher ~preis** recommended price; **~scheit** *nt* (*Build*) (spirit) level; **~schnur** *f* **(a)** (*Build*) guide line; (*senkrecht*) plumb-line; **(b)** (*fig: Grundsatz*) guiding principle; **~spruch** *m* (*old*) judgement; **~stätte** *f* (*old*) place of execution; **~strahlantenne** *f*, **~strahler** *m* beam *or* directional antenna.

Richtung *f* **(a)** direction ◆ **in ~ Hamburg/Süden** towards Hamburg/the south, in the direction of Hamburg/in a southerly direction; (*auf Autobahn*) towards Hamburg/on the southbound carriageway (*Brit*) *or* lane; **in nördliche ~** northwards, towards the north, in a northerly direction; **die Autobahn/der Zug ~ Hamburg** the Hamburg autobahn/train; **nach allen ~en/in alle ~en** in all directions; **die ~ ändern** *or* **wechseln** to change direction(s); **die ~ anzeigen** to indicate the direction, to point the way; (*mit Fahrzeug*) to indicate which way one is going to turn; **eine ~ nehmen** *or* **einschlagen** to head *or* drive/walk *etc* in a direction; **eine neue ~ bekommen** to change course, to take a new turn *or* direction; **einem Gespräch eine bestimmte ~ geben** to turn a conversation in a particular direction; **er will sich nach keiner ~ hin festlegen** he won't commit himself in any way at all; **in jeder ~** each way, in each direction; (*fig: in jeder Hinsicht*) in every respect; **irgend etwas in der** *or* **dieser ~** something along those/these lines.
(b) (*Tendenz*) trend; (*in der Kunst, einer Partei auch*) line; (*die Vertreter einer ~*) movement; (*Denk~, Lehrmeinung*) school of thought ◆ **die herrschende ~** the prevailing trend; **Picasso begann eine völlig neue ~ in der Malerei** Picasso started a completely new direction in painting; **die beiden ~en in der katholischen Kirche** the two lines of thought in the Catholic church; **sie gehören den verschiedensten politischen ~en an** they have the most varied political sympathies; **die ganze ~ paßt uns nicht!** that's not the sort of thing we want.

richtunggebend *adj* pointing the way; (*in der Mode*) trendsetting ◆ **für jdn/etw ~ sein** to set the pattern for sb/sth.

Richtungs-: ~änderung *f* change of *or* in direction; **~kampf** *m* (*Pol*) factional dispute; **r~los** *adj* lacking a sense of direction; **~losigkeit** *f* lack of a sense of direction; **~streit** *m* (*Pol*) factional dispute; **~wechsel** *m* (*lit, fig*) change of direction.

richtungweisend *adj* pointing the way ◆ **~ sein** to point the way (ahead).

Richt-: ~waage *f siehe* **Wasserwaage; ~wert** *m* guideline; **~zahl** *f* approximate figure.

Ricke *f* **-, -n** doe.

rieb *pret of* **reiben.**

riechen *pret* **roch**, *ptp* **gerochen** [1] *vti* to smell ◆ **gut/schlecht ~** to smell good/bad; **nach etw ~** to smell of sth; **an jdm/etw ~** to smell sb/sth, to sniff (at) sb/sth; **ich rieche Gas** I (can) smell gas; **ich rieche das Gewürz gern** I like the smell of this spice; **aus dem Mund ~** to have bad breath; **riech mal** have a sniff *or* smell; **das riecht nach Betrug/Verrat** (*fig inf*) that smacks of deceit/treachery; **Lunte** *or* **den Braten ~** (*fig sl*) to smell a rat (*inf*); **ich kann das nicht ~** (*inf*) I can't stand the smell of it; (*fig: nicht leiden*) I can't stand it; **jdn nicht ~ können** (*inf*) not to be able to stand sb, to hate sb's guts (*inf*); **das konnte ich doch nicht ~!** (*inf*) how was I (supposed) to know?, I'm not psychic (*inf*).
[2] *vi* (*Geruchssinn haben*) to have a sense of smell, to be able to smell ◆ **nicht mehr ~ können** to have lost one's sense of smell.
[3] *vi impers* to smell ◆ **es riecht angebrannt** there's a smell of burning, there's a burning smell; **es riecht nach Gas** there's a smell of gas.

Riecher *m* **-s, -** (*inf*) **einen guten** *or* **den richtigen ~ (für etw) haben** (*inf*) to have a nose (for sth) (*inf*); **da habe ich doch den richtigen ~ gehabt!** I knew it all along!

Riech-: ~fläschchen *nt* (bottle of) smelling salts *pl*; **~kolben** *m* (*sl*) hooter (*sl*), conk (*sl*), s(c)hnozzle (*sl*); **~nerv** *m* olfactory nerve; **~organ** *nt* organ of smell, olfactory organ; **~salz** *nt* smelling salts *pl*; **~stoff** *m* aromatic substance.

Ried *nt* **-s, -e (a)** (*Schilf*) reeds *pl.* **(b)** (*S Ger: Moor*) marsh.

Riedgras *nt* sedge.

rief *pret of* **rufen.**

Riefe *f* **-, -n** groove, channel; (*in Säulen*) flute.

riefeln, riefen *vt* to groove, to channel; *Säule* to flute.

Riege *f* **-, -n** (*Sport*) team, squad.

Riegel *m* **-s, - (a)** (*Verschluß*) bolt ◆ **den ~ an etw** (*dat*) **vorlegen** to bolt sth; **vergiß nicht, den ~ vorzulegen!** don't forget to bolt the door *etc*; **den ~ an etw** (*dat*) **zurückschieben** to unbolt sth; **einer Sache** (*dat*) **einen ~ vorschieben** (*fig*) to put a stop to sth, to clamp down on sth; **ein ~ gegen aggressive Politik** a restraint on *or* against aggressive policies; *siehe* **Schloß.**
(b) (*Schokolade*) bar; (*Seife auch*) cake.
(c) (*Sew*) (*Lasche*) tab; (*von Jackett*) strap; (*für Haken*) eye; (*am Knopfloch*) bar tack.

Riegel-: ~bau *m* (*Sw*) half-timbering; (*Gebäude*) half-timbered building; **~stellung** *f* (*Mil*) switch line *or* position; **~werk** *nt* (*dial*) half-timbering.

➤ SPRACHE AKTIV: **richtig: 1a** → 38.1, 40.2, 41, 53.6

Riegen-: ~führer *m* team *or* squad leader *or* captain; **r~weise** *adv* in teams *or* squads.
Riemchenschuh *m* strap shoe.
Riemen[1] *m* **-s, -** (*Treib~, Gürtel*) belt; (*an Schuhen, Kleidung, Koffer~, Gepäck~*) strap; (*Schnürsenkel*) leather shoelace; (*Peitschen~*) thong; (*vulg: Penis*) prick (*vulg*), cock (*vulg*) ◆ **jdn mit einem ~ verdreschen** to strap sb, to give sb the strap *or* belt; **den ~ enger schnallen** (*fig*) to tighten one's belt; **sich am ~ reißen** (*fig inf*) to get a grip on oneself.
Riemen[2] *m* **-s, -** (*Sport*) oar ◆ **die ~ einlegen** to ship oars; **sich in die ~ legen** (*lit, fig*) to put one's back into it.
Riemen-: ~antrieb *m* belt-drive; **~werk** *nt* strapping.
Ries *nt* **-es, -e** (*Measure*) German ream, ≃ 2 reams.
Riese[1]: **das macht nach Adam ~ DM 3,50** (*hum inf*) the way I learned it at school that makes DM 3.50.
Riese[2] *m* **-n, -n** (*lit, fig*) giant; (*sl: Tausendmarkschein*) 1000 mark note, big one (*esp US sl*) ◆ **ein böser ~** an ogre; **ein ~ von Mensch** *or* **von einem Menschen** a giant of a man/woman.
Rieselfelder *pl* sewage farm.
rieseln *vi aux sein* (*Wasser, Sand*) to trickle; (*Regen*) to drizzle; (*Schnee*) to float *or* flutter down ◆ **der Kalk rieselt von der Wand** lime is crumbling off the wall; **Schuppen ~ ihm vom Kopf** dandruff is flaking off his head; **ein angenehmes Lustgefühl rieselte durch seinen Körper** a pleasurable sensation ran *or* thrilled through his body; **ein Schauder rieselte mir über den Rücken/durch alle Glieder** a shiver went down my spine/through me.
Riesen- *pref* gigantic, enormous, colossal; (*Zool, Bot etc auch*) giant; **~ameise** *f* carpenter ant; **~arbeit** *f* (*Pensum*) gigantic *etc* job; (*Anstrengung*) gigantic *etc* effort; **~chance** *f* tremendous chance; **~erfolg** *m* gigantic *etc* success; (*Theat, Film*) smash hit; **~fräulein** *nt* giantess; **~gebirge** *nt* (*Geog*) Sudeten Mountains *pl*; **~gestalt** *f* **(a)** (*Größe*) gigantic *etc* frame; **(b)** (*Riese*) giant; **r~groß, r~haft** *adj siehe* **riesig**; **~hai** *m* basking shark; **~hunger** *m* (*inf*) enormous appetite; **ich habe einen ~hunger** (*inf*) I could eat a horse (*inf*); **~kraft** *f* gigantic *etc* strength; **mit ~kräften** with a colossal *or* an enormous effort; **~rad** *nt* big *or* Ferris wheel; **~salamander** *m* giant salamander; **~schildkröte** *f* giant tortoise; **~schlange** *f* boa; **~schritt** *m* giant step *or* stride; **sich mit ~schritten nähern** (*fig*) to be drawing on apace; **~slalom** *m* giant slalom; **~trara** *nt* (*inf*) ballyhoo, great fuss *or* to-do (*inf*); **~werk** *nt* colossal work; (*Gesamtwerk*) colossal works *pl*; **~wuchs** *m* giantism; (*Med auch*) gigantism.
riesig [1] *adj* gigantic, colossal, enormous.
[2] *adv* (*inf: sehr*) enormously, tremendously, immensely.
Riesin *f* giantess.
Riesling *m* Riesling.
riet *pret of* **raten.**
Riff[1] *nt* **-(e)s, -e** (*Felsklippe*) reef.
Riff[2] *m* **-(e)s, -s** (*Mus*) riff.
Riffel *f* **-, -n** (*Tex*) (flax) hackle, flax comb.
riffeln *vt* **(a)** *Flachs* to comb. **(b)** (*Tech*) *siehe* **riefeln.**
Rigg *nt* **-s,** *no pl* (*Naut*) rigging.
Riggung *f* (*Naut*) rigging.
rigide *adj* (*geh*) rigid.
Rigidität *f* (*Med, Psych*) rigidity.
Rigole *f* **-, -n** (*Agr*) (drainage) trench.
Rigorismus *m* (*geh*) rigour.
rigoristisch *adj* (*geh*) rigorous.
rigoros *adj* rigorous ◆ **ich bleibe dabei, da bin ich ganz ~** I'm sticking to that, I'm adamant.
Rigorosität *f* rigorousness.
Rigorosum *nt* **-s, Rigorosa** *or* (*Aus*) **Rigorosen** (*Univ*) (doctoral *or* PhD) viva.
Rikscha *f* **-, -s** rickshaw.
Rille *f* **-, -n** groove; (*in Säule*) flute.
Rillen-: r~förmig *adj* groove-like; **~profil** *nt* tread.
rillig *adj* (*rare*) fluted.
Rimesse *f* (*Fin*) remittance.
rin- *pref* (*dial*) *siehe* **herein-, hinein-.**
Rind *nt* **-(e)s, -er (a)** (*Tier*) cow ◆ **~er** cattle *pl*; **10 ~er** 10 head of cattle. **(b)** (*inf: Rindfleisch*) beef ◆ **vom ~** beef *attr*; **Hackfleisch vom ~** minced (*Brit*) *or* ground (*US*) beef, mince.
Rinde *f* **-, -n** (*Baum~*) bark; (*Brot~*) crust; (*Käse~*) rind; (*Anat*) cortex.
rindenlos *adj Baum* barkless; *Käse* rindless.
Rinder-: ~bouillon *f* beef stock *or* bouillon (*form*); **~braten** *m* (*roh*) joint of beef; (*gebraten*) roast beef *no indef art*; **~bremse** *f* horsefly; **~brühe** *f* beef broth; **~brust** *f* brisket (of beef); **~filet** *nt* fillet of beef; **~herde** *f* herd of cattle; **~hirt** *m* cowherd; (*in Nordamerika*) cowboy; (*in Südamerika*) gaucho; (*in Australien*) drover.
rindern *vi* (*Kuh*) to be on *or* in heat.
Rinder-: ~pest *f* (*Vet*) rinderpest; **~seuche** *f* epidemic cattle disease; (*BSE*) mad cow disease; **~talg** *m* beef dripping; **~wahn(sinn)** *m* mad cow disease; **~zucht** *f* cattle farming *or* raising; **~zunge** *f* ox tongue.
Rind-: ~fleisch *nt* beef; **~fleischbrühe** *f* beef broth.
Rinds- *in cpds* (*Aus, S Ger*) *siehe* **Rinder-**; **~leder** *nt* leather; **r~ledern** *adj attr* leather; **~stück** *nt* (*Cook*) joint of beef.
Rindvieh *nt* **(a)** *no pl* cattle ◆ **10 Stück ~** 10 head of cattle. **(b)** *pl* **Rindviecher** (*sl*) ass (*inf*).
Ring *m* **-(e)s, -e (a)** ring; (*Ketten~*) link; (*Wurf~*) quoit; (*Einweck~*) seal, rubber; (*Rettungs~*) lifebuoy, lifebelt ◆ **die ~e tauschen** *or* **wechseln** to exchange rings.
(b) (*Kreis*) (*Jahres~, Rauch~*) ring; (*auf dem Wasser, von Menschen auch*) circle; (*~ straße*) ring road.
(c) (*Sport*) (*Box~*) ring; (*von Schießscheibe*) ring, circle ◆ **~e** (*Turnen*) rings; **acht ~e schießen** to score an eight; **~ frei!** seconds out *or* away!; (*fig*) clear the decks!
(d) (*Astron, Met, Chem*) ring.
(e) (*Vereinigung*) circle, group; (*von Großhändlern, Erzeugern*) group; (*Bande*) ring.
(f) (*liter: Kreislauf*) circle, cycle ◆ **der ~ schließt sich** the circle is completed *or* closed, the wheel comes *or* turns full circle.
Ring-: r~artig *adj* ring-like; **~bahn** *f* circle line; **~buch** *nt* ring binder; **~bucheinlage** *f* loose-leaf pad.
Ringel *m* **-s, -** ring; (*Locke*) ringlet.
Ringelblume *f* marigold.
Ringelchen *nt* (*inf*) little ring.
Ringel-: ~gans *f* marsh goose; **~gedicht** *nt siehe* **Rondeau.**
ring(e)lig *adj* ringleted.
Ringellocke *f* ringlet ◆ **~n tragen** to wear one's hair in ringlets, to have ringlets.
ringeln [1] *vt* (*Pflanze*) to (en)twine; *Schwanz etc auch* to curl; *siehe* **geringelt.**
[2] *vr* to go curly, to curl; (*Rauch*) to curl up(wards) ◆ **die Schlange ringelte sich durch das Unterholz** the snake wriggled through the undergrowth; **der Schwanz des Schweins ringelt sich** the pig has a curly tail; **die Schlange ringelte sich um den Baum** the snake coiled *or* curled itself around the tree.
Ringel-: ~natter *f* grass snake; **~pie(t)z** *m* **-es, -e** (*hum inf*) hop (*inf*); **~pie(t)z mit Anfassen** hop (*inf*); **~reigen, ~reihen** *m* ring-a-ring-o' roses; **einen ~reigen tanzen** to play ring-a-ring-o' roses; **~schwanz** *m*, **~schwänzchen** *nt* (*inf*) curly tail; **~spiel** *nt* (*Aus*) merry-go-round, roundabout (*Brit*); **~taube** *f* woodpigeon, ringdove; **~wurm** *m* ringed worm, annelid (*spec*).
ringen *pret* **rang,** *ptp* **gerungen** [1] *vt* **die Hände ~** to wring one's hands; **er rang ihr das Messer aus der Hand** he wrenched *or* wrested the knife from her hand; **ein Schluchzen rang sich aus ihrer Brust** (*liter*) a sob was wrung from her breast (*liter*).
[2] *vi* **(a)** (*lit, fig: kämpfen*) to wrestle ◆ **mit sich/dem Tode ~** to wrestle with oneself/death; **mit den Tränen ~** to struggle *or* fight to keep back one's tears.
(b) (*streben*) **nach** *or* **um etw ~** to struggle for sth; **er rang um Fassung** he struggled to maintain his composure; **ums Überleben ~** (*liter*) to struggle to survive.
Ringen *nt* **-s,** *no pl* (*Sport*) wrestling; (*fig*) struggle.
Ringer(in *f*) *m* **-s, -** wrestler.
Ringergriff *m* wrestling hold.
ringerisch *adj* wrestling *attr.*
Ring-: ~fahndung *f* dragnet; **~finger** *m* ring finger; **r~förmig** *adj* ring-like; **der Wallgraben umschließt die Stadt r~förmig** the rampart rings *or* encircles the town; **r~förmige Verbindungen** (*Chem*) cyclic *or* ring compounds; **~kampf** *m* fight; (*Sport*) wrestling match; **~kämpfer** *m* wrestler; **~lein** *nt* ring; **~leitung** *f* (*Elec etc*) ring main; **~lotte** *f* **-, -n** (*Aus*) *siehe* **Reneklode**; **~mauer** *f* circular wall; **die ~mauer rund um die Burg** the wall encircling *or* surrounding the castle; **~muskel** *m* sphincter; **~ordner** *m* ring binder; **~panzer** *m* articulated *or* jointed armour; **~richter** *m* (*Sport*) referee.
rings *adv* (all) around ◆ **die Stadt ist ~ von Bergen umgeben** the town is completely surrounded *or* encircled by mountains, there are mountains all around the town; **ich bin ~ um die Kirche gegangen** I went all the way round (the outside of) the church; **wir mußten uns alle ~ im Kreis aufstellen** we all had to get into *or* make a circle.
Ring-: ~scheibe *f* (*Sport*) target (*marked with concentric rings*); **~sendung** *f* (*Rad, TV*) link up (transmission).
ringsherum *adv* all (the way) around.
Ringstraße *f* ring road.
rings-: ~um *adv* (all) around; **~um konnte ich nichts sehen** I could see nothing around me; **~umher** *adv* around.
Ring-: ~tausch *m* exchange of rings; (*von Wohnungen*) *three-way house exchange*; **~tennis** *nt* (*Sport*) quoits *sing*, deck tennis; **~vorlesung** *f series of lectures by different speakers*; **~wall** *m siehe* **~mauer.**
Rinne *f* **-, -n** (*Rille*) groove; (*Furche, Abfluß~, Fahr~*) channel; (*Dach~, inf: Rinnstein*) gutter; (*Geog*) gap.
rinnen *pret* **rann,** *ptp* **geronnen** *vi aux sein* (*fließen*) to run ◆ **das Blut rann ihm in Strömen aus der Wunde** blood streamed from his wound; **die Zeit rinnt (dahin)** (*liter*) time is slipping away (*liter*); **das Geld rinnt ihm durch die Finger** (*fig*) money slips through his fingers.
Rinn-: ~sal *nt* **-(e)s, -e** rivulet; **~stein** *m* (*Gosse*) gutter; (*old: Ausguß*) drain; **jdn aus dem ~stein holen** *or* **auflesen** (*fig*) to pick sb out of the gutter; **im ~stein enden** to come to a sorry end.
Rippchen *nt* (*Cook*) *slightly cured pork rib.*
Rippe *f* **-, -n (a)** (*Anat, Cook*) rib ◆ **bei ihm kann man die ~n zählen** (*inf*) you could play a tune on his ribs (*inf*); **er hat nichts auf den ~n** (*inf*) he's just skin and bones; ... **damit du was auf die ~n kriegst** (*inf*) ... to put a bit of flesh on you; **ich kann es mir nicht aus den ~n schneiden** (*inf*), **ich kann es doch nicht durch die ~n schwitzen** (*inf*) I can't just produce it from nowhere.
(b) (*Blatt~, Gewölbe~, Boots~*) rib.

(c) (*von Heizkörper, Kühlaggregat*) fin.
(d) (*von Apfelsine*) segment; (*von Schokolade*) row (of squares).

rippen *vt* to rib.

Rippen-: ~bogen *m* (*Anat*) costal arch; **~bruch** *m* broken *or* fractured rib; **~fell** *nt* pleura; **~fellentzündung** *f* pleurisy; **~gewölbe** *nt* (*Archit*) ribbed vaulting; **~quallen** *pl* ctenophorans *pl* (*spec*); **~speer** *m or nt* (*Cook*) spare rib; **Kaßler** *or* **Kasseler ~speer** *slightly cured pork spare rib*; **~stoß** *m* nudge, dig in the ribs; (*schmerzhaft*) thump (*inf*) *or* dig in the ribs; **ein freundschaftlicher ~stoß** (*fig*) a quiet *or* friendly word; **~strickpulli** *m* ribbed sweater; **~stück** *nt* (*Cook*) *joint of meat including ribs*.

Rippli *pl* (*Sw*) ribs *pl*.

Rippspeer *m siehe* **Rippenspeer**.

rips *interj* **~, raps!** rip!

Rips *m* **-es, -e** (*Tex*) rep.

Risiko *nt* **-s, -s** *or* **Risiken** *or* (*Aus*) **Risken** risk ◆ **auf eigenes ~** at one's own risk; **bitte, Sie können das machen, aber auf eigenes ~** do it by all means, but on your own head be it; **ohne ~** without risk; **etw ohne ~ tun** to do sth without taking a risk; **es ist nicht ohne ~, das zu tun** there is a risk involved in doing that, doing that is not without risk; **die Sache ist ohne ~** there's no risk involved; **als gutes ~ gelten** to be a good (credit) risk.

Risiko-: ~bereitschaft *f* **sie hat eine hohe ~bereitschaft** she is prepared to take high risks; **~faktor** *m* risk factor; **~freude** *f siehe* **~bereitschaft**; **r~freudig** *adj* venturesome, prepared to take risks; **~gruppe** *f* (high-)risk group; **~kapital** *nt* (*Fin*) risk *or* venture capital; **~lebensversicherung** *f* (renewable) term life insurance; **~versicherung** *f* term insurance.

riskant *adj* risky, chancy (*inf*) ◆ **das ist mir zu ~** that's too risky *or* chancy for me.

riskieren* *vt* (a) (*aufs Spiel setzen*) to risk ◆ **etwas/nichts ~** to take risks *or* chances/no risks *or* chances; **seine Stellung/sein Geld ~** to risk losing one's job/money, to put one's job/money at risk; **sein Geld bei etw ~** to risk one's money on sth.
(b) (*wagen*) to venture ◆ **traust du dich, hier runterzuspringen? — ja, ich riskier's!** do you think you dare jump down? — yes, I'll risk *or* chance it!; **in Gegenwart seiner Frau riskiert er kein Wort** when his wife is present he dare not say a word.

Rispe *f* **-, -n** (*Bot*) panicle.

rispenförmig, rispig *adj* (*Bot*) panicled, paniculate.

⚠ **riß** *pret of* **reißen**.

⚠ **Riß** *m* **Risses, Risse** (a) (*in Stoff, Papier etc*) tear, rip; (*in Erde, Gestein*) crevice, fissure; (*Sprung in Wand, Behälter etc*) crack; (*Haut~*) chap; (*fig: Kluft*) rift, split ◆ **die Freundschaft hat einen (tiefen) ~ bekommen** a rift has developed in their friendship; **durch das Volk geht ein tiefer ~** there is a deep split in the people, the people are deeply divided.
(b) (*Archit: Zeichnung*) sketch, sketch plan.
(c) (*Hunt: Raubwildbeute*) kill.

rissig *adj Boden, Wand, Leder* cracked; *Haut, Hände* chapped.

⚠ **Rißwunde** *f* laceration, lacerated wound.

Rist *m* **-(e)s, -e** (a) (*am Fuß*) instep; (*an der Hand*) back (of the hand). (b) (*beim Pferd*) withers *pl*.

rite *adv* (*Univ*) *lowest pass grade in doctoral examinations*.

Riten *pl of* **Ritus**.

ritsch *interj* **~, ratsch!** rip!

ritt *pret of* **reiten**.

Ritt *m* **-(e)s, -e** ride ◆ **einen ~ machen** to go for a ride; **in scharfem ~ jagte er über die Felder** riding furiously he chased across the fields.

Rittberger *m* **-s, -** (*Eiskunstlauf*) Rittberger.

Ritter *m* **-s, -** (a) (*im Mittelalter, im alten Rom*) knight; (*Kavalier*) cavalier ◆ **fahrender ~** knight errant; **jdn zum ~ schlagen** to knight sb, to dub sb knight; **der ~ von der traurigen Gestalt** the Knight of the Sorrowful Countenance; **ein ~ ohne Furcht und Tadel** (*lit*) a doughty knight; (*fig*) a knight in shining armour.
(b) (*Adelstitel*) ≃ Sir ◆ **X ~ von Y** ≃ Sir X of Y.
(c) (*Ordensträger*) knight.
(d) (*Schmetterling*) swallowtail.
(e) (*Cook*) **arme ~** *pl sweet French toast soaked in milk*.

Ritter-: ~burg *f* knight's castle; **~gut** *nt* ≃ manor; **~gutsbesitzer** *m* ≃ lord of the manor; **r~haft** *adj siehe* **r~lich**; **~kreuz** *nt* (*Mil*) Knight's Cross; **~kreuz mit Eichenlaub** ≃ Knight's Cross with bar; **~kreuzträger** *m* holder of the Knight's Cross; **r~lich** *adj* (*lit*) knightly; (*fig*) chivalrous; **~lichkeit** *f* chivalry, chivalrousness; **~orden** *m* order of knights; **der Deutsche ~orden** the Teutonic Order; **~roman** *m* (*Liter*) romance of chivalry; **~rüstung** *f* knight's armour; **~schaft** *f* (a) (*die Ritter*) knights *pl*, knighthood; (b) (*Ritterehre*) knighthood; **~schlag** *m* (*Hist*) dubbing; **den ~schlag empfangen** to be knighted, to be dubbed knight; **(jdm) den ~schlag erteilen** to confer a knighthood (on sb).

Rittersmann *m*, *pl* **-leute** (*poet*) knight.

Ritter-: ~sporn *m* (*Bot*) larkspur, delphinium; **~stand** *m* knighthood; **in den ~stand erhoben werden** to be raised to the knighthood, to be knighted; **~tum** *nt* knighthood; **~-und-Räuber-Roman** *m* (*Liter*) *late eighteenth century sentimental novel about knights and robbers*, romance of chivalry; **~wesen** *nt* knighthood; **~zeit** *f* Age of Chivalry.

rittlings *adv* astride (*auf etw (dat)* sth).

Rittmeister *m* (*old Mil*) cavalry captain, captain (of horse).

Ritual *nt* **-s, -e** *or* **-ien** [-iən] (*lit, fig*) ritual.

Rituale *nt* **-,** *no pl* (*Eccl*) ritual ◆ **~ Romanum** missal.

Ritualhandlung *f* ritual act.

Ritualien [-iən] *pl* (*Eccl*) ritual objects *pl*.

Ritualmord *m* ritual murder.

rituell *adj* ritual.

Ritus *m* **-, Riten** rite; (*fig*) ritual.

Ritz *m* **-es, -e** (a) (*Kratzer*) scratch. (b) (*Spalte*) chink, crack.

Ritze *f* **-, -n** (*Riß, Po~*) crack; (*Fuge*) join, gap ◆ **auf der ~ schlafen** (*hum inf*) to sleep in the middle.

Ritzel *nt* **-s, -** (*Tech*) pinion.

ritzen [1] *vt* to scratch; (*einritzen*) *Initialen, Namen etc auch* to carve ◆ **die Sache ist geritzt** (*inf*) it's all fixed up.
[2] *vr* to scratch oneself.

Ritzer *m* **-s, -** (*inf*) scratch.

Rivale [ri'va:lə] *m* **-n, -n, Rivalin** [ri'va:lɪn] *f* rival.

rivalisieren* [rivali'zi:rən] *vi* **mit jdm ~** to compete with sb; **34 ~de Parteien** 34 rival parties.

Rivalität [rivali'tɛ:t] *f* rivalry.

Riviera [ri'vie:ra] *f* **-** Riviera.

Rizinus *m* **-, -** *or* **-se** (a) (*Bot*) castor-oil plant. (b) (*auch* **~öl**) castor oil.

RNS [ɛr|ɛn'|ɛs] *abbr of* **Ribonukleinsäure** RNA.

Roadie [ro:dɪ] *m* **-s, -s** roadie.

Roadster ['ro:tstɐ] *m* **-s, -** open two-seater sports car, roadster (*US*).

Roastbeef ['ro:stbi:f] *nt* **-s, -s** (*roh*) beef; (*gebraten*) roast beef.

Robbe *f* **-, -n** seal.

robben *vi aux sein* (*Mil*) to crawl.

Robben-: ~fang *m* sealing, seal hunting; **~fänger** *m* sealer, seal hunter; **~jagd** *f siehe* **~fang**.

Robe *f* **-, -n** (a) (*Abendkleid*) evening gown ◆ **in großer ~** in evening dress. (b) (*Amtstracht*) (official) robe *or* robes *pl*.

Robinie [-iə] *f* robinia.

Robinsonade *f* Robinsonade; (*Sport*) flying save (*towards attacker*).

roboten *vi* (*sl*) to slave (*inf*).

Roboter ['rɔbɔtɐ, ro'bɔtɐ] *m* **-s, -** (a) robot. (b) (*sl: Schwerstarbeiter*) slave (*inf*). (c) (*Sport*) ball-feeder.

Robotertechnik, Robotik *f* robotics *sing or pl*.

robust *adj Mensch, Gesundheit* robust; *Material* tough.

Robustheit *f siehe adj* robustness; toughness.

roch *pret of* **riechen**.

Rochade [rɔ'xa:də, rɔ'ʃa:də] *f* (*Chess*) castling; (*Ftbl*) switch-over, change of position ◆ **die kleine** *or* **kurze/große** *or* **lange ~** castling king's side/queen's side.

Röcheln *nt* **-s,** *no pl* groan; (*Todes~*) death rattle ◆ **das ~ der Verletzten** the groans *or* groaning of the wounded.

röcheln *vi* to groan; (*Sterbender*) to give the death rattle.

Rochen *m* **-s, -** ray.

rochieren* [rɔ'xi:rən, rɔ'ʃi:rən] *vi* to castle; (*Ftbl*) to change *or* switch positions.

Rock[1] *m* **-(e)s, ⸚e** (a) (*Damen~*) skirt; (*Schotten~*) kilt; (*Sw: Kleid*) dress. (b) (*geh: Herren~*) jacket ◆ **den bunten ~ anziehen** (*old*) to take the King's shilling (*old*); **der grüne ~ (des Försters)** (*old*) the green coat of a forester; **der schwarze ~ (des Geistlichen)** (*old*) the black gown *or* cassock of a priest.

Rock[2] *m* **-s,** *no pl* (*Mus*) rock.

Rock-: ~aufschlag *m* lapel; **~band** *f* rock band; **~barde** *m* rock poet.

Röckchen *nt dim of* **Rock**.

rocken *vi* (*Mus*) to rock.

Rocken *m* **-s, -** (*Tex*) distaff.

Rocker *m* **-s, -** rocker.

Rock-: ~falte *f* (*von Damenrock*) inverted pleat; (*von Jackett*) vent; **~festival** *nt* rock festival; **~futter** *nt* skirt lining.

rockig *adj Musik* rock-like.

Rock-: ~musik *f* rock music; **~röhre** *f* (*sl*) rock singer; **~saum** *m* hem of a/the skirt; **~schoß** *m* coat-tail; **an jds ~schößen hängen, sich jdm an die ~schöße hängen** (*inf*) to cling to sb's coat-tails (*inf*); **~schuppen** *m* (*sl*) rock venue, rock club; **~star** *m* rock star; **~zipfel** *m*: **der Mutter am ~zipfel** *or* **an Mutters ~zipfel hängen** (*inf*) to cling to (one's) mother's apron-strings (*inf*).

Rodehacke *f* mattock.

Rodel *m* **-s, -,** (*S Ger, Aus*) *f* **-, -n** sledge, toboggan, sleigh.

Rodelbahn *f* toboggan-run.

rodeln *vi aux sein or haben* to toboggan (*auch Sport*), to sledge.

Rodel-: ~schlitten *m* toboggan, sledge; **~sport** *m* tobogganning.

roden *vt Wald, Land* to clear; *Kartoffeln* to lift.

Rodeo *m or nt* **-s, -s** rodeo.

Rodler(in *f*) *m* **-s, -** tobogganer; (*Sport auch*) tobogganist.

Rodung *f* (*das Roden, Siedlung*) clearing.

Rogen *m* **-s, -** roe.

Rog(e)ner *m* **-s, -** spawner.

Rogenstein *m* (*Geol*) oolite, oolitic limestone.

Roggen *m* **-s,** *no pl* rye.

roh *adj* (a) (*ungebraten, ungekocht*) raw; *Milch* ordinary.
(b) (*unbearbeitet*) *Bretter etc* rough; *Stein auch* undressed, unhewn; *Diamant auch* uncut; *Eisen, Metall* crude; *Felle* untreated ◆ **etw aus dem ~en arbeiten** (*Art*) to work sth from the rough; **die Statue/das Bild/das Manuskript ist im ~en fertig** the rough shape of the statue/the rough sketch of the picture/the rough draft of the manuscript is finished; *siehe* **Ei**.
(c) (*unkultiviert, brutal*) rough ◆ **~e Gewalt** brute force; **wo ~e Kräfte sinnlos**

walten ... (*prov*) brute force does it.

Roh-: ~bau *m* **(a)** (*Bauabschnitt*) shell (of a/the house); **das Haus ist im ~bau fertig(gestellt)** the house is structurally complete; **die ~bauten** the shells of the unfinished houses; **(b)** *siehe* **Klinkerbau; ~baumwolle** *f* raw cotton; **~benzin** *nt* naphtha; **~bilanz** *f* trial balance sheet; **~bogen** *m* unbound sheet; **~diamant** *m* rough *or* uncut *or* unpolished diamond; **~einnahme** *f siehe* **~ertrag; ~eisen** *nt* pig iron.

⚠ **Roheit** *f* **(a)** *no pl* (*Eigenschaft*) roughness; (*Brutalität auch*) brutality. **(b)** (*Tat*) brutality. **(c)** (*ungekochter Zustand*) rawness.

Roh-: ~entwurf *m* rough draft; **~ertrag** *m* gross proceeds *pl*.

roherweise *adv* roughly.

Roh-: ~faser *f* raw fibre; **~gewicht** *nt* gross weight; **~gummi** *m or nt* raw rubber; **~kost** *f* raw fruit and vegetables *pl*; **~köstler(in** *f*) *m* **-s, -** *person who prefers fruit and vegetables uncooked*; **~leder** *nt* rawhide, untanned leather; **~ling** *m* **(a)** (*Grobian*) brute, ruffian; **(b)** (*Tech*) blank; **~material** *nt* raw material; **~öl** *nt* crude oil; **~produkt** *nt* raw material; **~produktenhändler** *m siehe* **Schrotthändler.**

Rohr *nt* **-(e)s, -e (a)** (*Schilf~*) reed; (*Röhricht, Schilf*) reeds *pl*; (*Zucker~*) cane; (*für Stühle etc*) cane, wicker *no pl* ◆ **aus ~ geflochtene Stühle** wicker(work) *or* basketwork *or* cane chairs; **wie ein schwankendes ~ im Wind** (*liter*) like a reed in the wind (*liter*); **spanisches ~** (*old*) cane.
(b) (*Tech, Mech*) pipe; (*Geschütz~*) (gun) barrel; (*Blas~*) blowpipe ◆ **aus allen ~en feuern** to fire with all its guns.
(c) (*dial, Aus: Backröhre*) oven.

Rohr-: ~ammer *f* (*Orn*) reed bunting; **~blatt** *nt* (*Mus*) reed; **~bruch** *m* burst pipe.

Röhrchen *nt* tube; (*Chem*) test tube; (*inf: zur Alkoholkontrolle*) breathalyzer ◆ **ins ~ blasen** (*inf*) to be breathalyzed, to have *or* take a breathalyzer test.

Rohrdommel *f* **-, -n** (*Orn*) bittern.

Röhre *f* **-, -n (a)** (*Ofen~*) warming oven; (*Back~*) oven; (*Drainage~*) drainage pipe ◆ **in die ~ gucken** (*inf*) to be left out.
(b) (*Neon~*) (neon) tube *or* strip; (*Elektronen~*) valve (*Brit*), tube (*US*); (*fig: Fernseher*) telly (*Brit inf*), box (*Brit inf*), tube (*US inf*) ◆ **in die ~ gucken** *or* **glotzen** (*inf*) to watch telly (*Brit inf*) *or* the tube (*US inf*), to sit in front of the box (*Brit inf*).
(c) (*Höhlung, Hohlkörper*) tube; (*in Knochen*) cavity.
(d) (*Hunt: Gang im Tierbau*) gallery.

röhren *vi* (*Hunt*) to bell; (*Motorrad, Mensch*) to roar.

Röhren-: ~blütler *pl* (*Bot*) tubiflorae *pl* (*spec*); **r~förmig** *adj* tubular; *Hosenbein* drainpipe *attr*; **~hose** *f* (*inf*) drainpipe trousers *pl*; **~knochen** *m* long bone; **~pilz** *m siehe* **Röhrling.**

Rohr-: ~flöte *f* (*Mus*) reed pipe; (*Orgel~*) rohrflöte, rohr flute; (*Pan~*) pan pipes *pl*; **~geflecht** *nt* wickerwork, basketwork.

Röhricht *nt* **-s, -e** (*old*) reeds *pl*, reed bed.

Rohr-: ~kolben *m* (*Bot*) reed mace, cat's tail; **~krepierer** *m* **-s, -** (*Mil sl*) barrel burst; **zum ~krepierer werden, ein ~krepierer sein** (*fig*) to backfire; **~leger** *m* **-s, -** pipe fitter; **~leitung** *f* pipe, conduit; **~leitungssystem** *nt* network *or* system of pipes.

Röhrling *m* (*Bot*) boletus.

Rohr-: ~matte *f* rush *or* reed mat; **~möbel** *pl* cane furniture *sing*; **~muffe** *f* (*Tech*) socket; **~netz** *nt* network of pipes; **~palme** *f* calamus; **~post** *f* pneumatic dispatch system; **~sänger** *m* (*Orn*) warbler; **~spatz** *m*: **schimpfen wie ein ~spatz** (*inf*) to make a fuss; (*Schimpfwörter gebrauchen*) to curse and swear; **~stock** *m* cane; **~stuhl** *m* basketwork *or* wickerwork chair; **~zange** *f* pipe wrench; **~zucker** *m* cane sugar.

Roh-: ~seide *f* wild silk; **r~seiden** *adj* wild silk.

Rohstoff *m* raw material; (*St Ex*) commodity.

Rohstoff-: ~börse *f* commodities market; **~fonds** *m* commodity fund; **~mangel** *m* shortage of raw materials; **~markt** *m siehe* **~börse; ~preis** *m* commodity price; **~quelle** *f* source of raw materials; **~reserven** *pl* reserves of raw materials *pl*.

Roh-: ~tabak *m* tobacco; (*ungetrocknet*) uncured tobacco; (*ungeschnitten*) leaf tobacco; **~übersetzung** *f* rough translation; **~zucker** *m* crude *or* unrefined sugar; **~zustand** *m* natural *or* unprocessed state *or* condition; **das Denkmal/Manuskript ist noch im ~zustand** the memorial/manuscript is still in a fairly rough state.

rojen *vti* (*Naut*) to row.

Rokoko *nt* **-(s),** *no pl* Rococo period; (*Stil*) Rococo, rococo.

⚠ **Rolladen** *m* **-s, Rolläden** *or* **-** *getrennt* **Roll-laden** (*an Fenster, Tür etc*) shutters *pl*; (*von Schreibtisch*) roll top.

Roll-: ~bahn *f* (*Aviat*) taxiway; (*Start-, Landebahn*) runway; **~braten** *m* (*Cook*) roast; **~brett** *nt siehe* **Skateboard.**

Röllchen *nt* little roll; (*von Garn*) reel.

Rolle *f* **-, -n (a)** (*Zusammengerolltes*) roll; (*Garn~, Zwirn~*) reel, bobbin (*spec*); (*Papier~*) reel; (*Urkunde*) scroll ◆ **eine ~ Garn/Zwirn** a reel of thread; **eine ~ Bindfaden** a ball of string; **eine ~ Film** a roll of film; (*im Kino*) a reel of film.
(b) (*walzenförmig*) roller; (*an Möbeln, Kisten*) caster, castor; (*an Flaschenzug*) pulley; (*Gardinen~*) runner.
(c) (*dial: Wäschemangel*) roller iron.
(d) (*Sport*) forward roll; (*Aviat*) roll ◆ **eine ~ machen** to do a forward roll/roll; **die ~ rückwärts** the backward roll.
(e) (*Theat, Film, fig*) role, part; (*Sociol*) role ◆ **es war ein Spiel mit vertauschten ~n** (*fig*) it was a situation where the roles were reversed; **ein Stück mit verteilten ~n lesen** to read a play with the parts cast *or* (*in Schule*) given out; **der literarische Kreis liest jeden Dienstag ein Stück mit verteilten ~n** the literary circle has a play-reading every Tuesday; **eine Ehe mit streng verteilten ~n** a marriage with strict allocation of roles; **jds ~ bei etw** (*fig*) sb's role *or* part in sth; **in der ~ von jdm/etw auftreten** to appear in the role of sb/sth; **er gefällt sich** (*dat*) **in der ~ des** ... (*fig*) he likes to think of *or* see himself in the role of the ...; **sich in die ~ eines anderen versetzen** (*fig*) to put oneself in sb else's place; **bei** *or* **in etw** (*dat*) **eine ~ spielen** to play a part in sth; (*Mensch auch*) to play a role in sth; **als Verteidiger hat er eine klägliche ~ gespielt** as a defence counsel he was not up to much *or* he left much to be desired; **etw spielt eine große ~ (bei jdm)** sth is very important (to sb); **es spielt keine ~, (ob)** ... it doesn't matter (whether) ..., it doesn't make any difference (whether) ..., whether ... doesn't come into it; **das spielt hier keine ~** that does not concern us now, that is irrelevant; **bei ihm spielt Geld keine ~** with him money is no object; **aus der ~ fallen** (*fig*) to say the wrong thing; to do the wrong thing; **du bist aber gestern wirklich aus der ~ gefallen!** you really behaved badly yesterday!; **seine ~ ausgespielt haben** (*fig*) to have played one's part.

rollen 1 *vi* **(a)** *aux sein* to roll; (*Flugzeug*) to taxi ◆ **der Stein kommt ins R~** (*fig*) the ball has started rolling; **etw/den Stein ins R~ bringen** (*fig*) to set *or* start sth/the ball rolling; **es werden einige Köpfe ~** heads will roll.
(b) mit den Augen ~ to roll one's eyes.
2 *vt* to roll; *Teig* to roll out; *Teppich, Papier* to roll up; (*dial: mangeln*) *Wäsche, Bettücher* to mangle.
3 *vr* to curl up; (*Schlange auch*) to curl itself up.

Rollen-: ~besetzung *f* (*Theat, Film*) casting; **~bild** *nt* (*Sociol*) role model; **~erwartung** *f* (*Sociol*) role expectation; **~fach** *nt* (*Theat*) character *or* type part; **der jugendliche Liebhaber ist sein ~fach** he's a character actor specializing in the young lover; **r~förmig** *adj* cylindrical; **~gedicht** *nt* (*Liter*) dramatic monologue; **r~gelagert** *adj* mounted on roller bearings; **~konflikt** *m* role conflict; **~lager** *nt* roller bearings *pl*; **~-Offset-Verfahren** *nt* rotary offset process; **~prüfstand** *m* (*Tech*) rolling road dynamometer; **r~spezifisch** *adj* role-specific; **~spiel** *nt* (*Sociol*) role play; **~tausch** *m* exchange of roles; (*Sociol auch*) role reversal; **~verhalten** *nt* (*Sociol*) behavioural role; **~verständnis** *nt* understanding of one's role; **~verteilung** *f* (*Sociol*) role allocation; **~zug** *m siehe* **Flaschenzug.**

Roller *m* **-s, - (a)** scooter. **(b)** (*Naut: Welle*) roller. **(c)** (*Aus: Rollo*) (roller) blind. **(d)** (*Orn*) **Harzer ~** canary, roller. **(e)** (*Walze*) roller.

Rollerblades ['ro:lǝbleɪdz] ® *pl* rollerblades *pl*.

Rollerfahren *nt* riding a scooter.

rollern *vi aux sein* to ride one's scooter.

Roll-: ~feld *nt* runway; **~film** *m* roll film; **~fuhrdienst** *m* road-rail haulage; **~geld** *nt* carriage, freight charge; **~gerste** *f* (*Agr*) pot-barley, hulled barley; **~gut** *nt* (*Rail*) freight; **~hockey** *nt* roller-skate hockey.

Rolli *m* **-s, -s** (*Fashion inf*) roll neck.

rollig *adj* (*inf*) *Katze* on heat.

Roll-: ~kommando *nt* raiding party; **~kragen** *m* roll *or* polo neck; **~kragenpullover** *m* polo-neck sweater; **~kunstlauf** *m* roller-skating; **~kur** *f* (*Med*) *treatment for stomach disorders where the patient takes medicine, lies for 5 minutes on his back, 5 minutes on his side, then on his front etc*; **~mops** *m* rollmops.

Rollo *nt* **-s, -s** (roller) blind.

Roll-: ~schinken *m* smoked ham; **~schnellauf** *m* speed (roller-)skating; **~schrank** *m* roll-fronted cupboard.

Rollschuh *m* roller-skate ◆ **~ laufen** to roller-skate.

Rollschuh-: ~bahn *f* roller-skating rink; **~laufen** *nt* roller-skating; **~läufer** *m* roller-skater; **~sport** *m* roller-skating.

Roll-: ~sitz *m* (*im Rennboot*) sliding seat; **~splitt** *m* loose chippings *pl*; **~sport** *m siehe* **~schuhsport; ~steg** *m* travolator, moving pavement (*Brit*), mobile walkway (*US*); (*Naut*) gangplank, gangway.

Rollstuhl *m* wheelchair.

Rollstuhl-: ~fahrer *m* wheelchair user; **r~gerecht** *adj* suitable for wheelchairs.

Roll-: ~tabak *m* tobacco plug; **~treppe** *f* escalator; **~werk** *nt* (*Archit*) cartouche, scrollwork.

ROM [rɔm] *nt* **-s, -s** (*Comput*) ROM.

Rom *nt* **-s** Rome ◆ **~ ist auch nicht an einem Tag erbaut worden** (*prov*) Rome wasn't built in a day (*Prov*); **viele Wege führen nach ~** (*Prov*) all roads lead to Rome (*Prov*); **das sind Zustände wie im alten ~** (*inf*) (*unmoralisch*) it's disgraceful; (*primitiv*) it's medieval (*inf*).

Roma *pl* (*Zigeuner*) Romany.

Roman *m* **-s, -e** novel; (*höfisch, ritterlich etc auch*) romance ◆ **ich könnte einen ~ schreiben!** (*inf*) I could write a book about it!; **(jdm) einen ganzen ~ erzählen** (*inf*) to give sb a long rigmarole (*inf*); **erzähl keine ~e!** (*inf*) don't tell stories! (*inf*).

roman|artig *adj* novelistic.

Roman|autor *m*, **Romancier** [romã'sie:] *m* **-s, -s** novelist.

Romane *m* **-n, -n** person speaking a Romance language.

Romanentum *nt* Latin nature.

Roman-: r~haft *adj* like a novel; **~heft** *nt* cheap pulp novel, penny dreadful (*dated*); **~held** *m* hero of a/the novel.

Romanik *f* (*Archit, Art*) Romanesque period; (*Stil*) Romanesque (style).

Romanin *f siehe* **Romane.**

romanisch *adj Volk, Sprache* Romance; (*Art*) Romanesque.

Romanist(in *f*) *m* (*Univ*) teacher/student/scholar of Romance languages and literature.

Romanistik *f* (*Univ*) Romance languages and literature.

romanistisch *adj* Romance.

⚠: for details of spelling reform, see supplement

Roman-: ~leser *m* novel reader; **~literatur** *f* fiction, novels *pl*; **~schreiber** *m (inf)* novelist; *(pej)* scribbler; **~schriftsteller** *m* novelist.
Romantik *f* **(a)** *(Liter, Art, Mus)* Romanticism; *(Epoche)* Age of Romanticism, Romantic period. **(b)** *(fig)* romance, romanticism; *(Gefühl, Einstellung)* romanticism ♦ **keinen Sinn für ~ haben** to have no sense of romance.
Romantiker(in *f)* *m* **-s, -** *(Liter, Art, Mus)* Romantic; *(fig)* romantic.
romantisch *adj* romantic; *(Liter etc)* Romantic.
romantisieren* *vt* to romanticize.
romantsch, romaun(t)sch *adj siehe* **rätoromanisch.**
Romanze *f* **-, -n** *(Liter, Mus, fig)* romance.
Römer[1] *m* **-s, -** *(Weinglas)* *wineglass in various sizes with clear glass bowl and green or brown coiled stem.*
Römer[2] *m* **-s der ~** *town hall of Frankfurt am Main.*
Römer(in *f)* *m* **-s, -** Roman ♦ **die alten ~** the (ancient) Romans.
Römer-: ~brief *m* Letter *or* Epistle of Paul to the Romans, Romans *sing, no art*; **~reich** *nt* Roman Empire; **~straße** *f* Roman road; **~topf** ® *m (Cook)* ≃ (chicken) brick; **~tum** *nt* Roman culture *etc*; **die Haupttugenden des ~tums** the main virtues of Rome; **das ~tum hat zahlreiche griechische Elemente absorbiert** Rome absorbed many elements from Greece.
Romfahrer *m* pilgrim to Rome.
römisch *adj* Roman ♦ **~ 12** 12 in Roman numerals.
römisch-katholisch *adj* Roman Catholic.
⚠**Rommé** [rɔ'meː, 'rɔme] *nt* **-s,** *no pl* rummy.
Rondeau *nt* **-s, -s (a)** [rõ'doː] *(Liter, Mus)* rondeau, rondel. **(b)** [rɔn'doː] *(Aus: Rondell)* circular flowerbed.
Rondell *nt* **-s, -e (a)** *(Archit)* round tower. **(b)** circular flowerbed.
Rondo *nt* **-s, -s** *(Mus)* rondo.
röntgen *vt* to X-ray; *Körperteil auch* to take an X-ray of.
Röntgen *nt* **-s,** *no pl* X-raying ♦ **er ist zur Zeit beim ~** he's being X-rayed at the moment.
Röntgen-: ~apparat *m* X-ray equipment *no indef art, no pl*; **~aufnahme** *f* X-ray (plate); **~augen** *pl (hum)* X-ray eyes *pl (hum)*; **~behandlung, ~bestrahlung** *f* radiotherapy, X-ray treatment *or* therapy; **~diagnostik** *f* X-ray diagnosis; **~film** *m* X-ray film.
röntgenisieren* *vt (Aus) siehe* **röntgen.**
Röntgenlaser [-'leːzɐ] *m* X-ray laser.
Röntgenogramm *nt* **-s, -e** X-ray (plate), radiograph *(esp US)*.
⚠**Röntgenographie** *f* radiography.
Röntgenologe *m*, **Röntgenologin** *f* radiologist, roentgenologist *(form)*.
Röntgenologie *f* radiology, roentgenology *(form)*.
Röntgenoskopie *f* radioscopy.
Röntgen-: ⚠**~paß** *m* X-ray registration card; **~reihenuntersuchung** *f* X-ray screening; **~röhre** *f* X-ray tube; **~strahlen** *pl* X-rays *pl*; **jdn mit ~strahlen behandeln** to treat sb with X-rays, to give sb X-ray treatment; **~therapie** *f siehe* **~behandlung**; **~untersuchung** *f* X-ray examination.
rören *vi siehe* **rö(h)ren.**
rosa *adj inv* pink ♦ **ein ~** *or* **~nes** *(inf)* **Kleid** a pink dress; **die Welt durch eine ~(rote) Brille sehen** to see the world through rose-coloured *or* rose-tinted glasses; **in ~(rotem) Licht** in a rosy light; **er malt die Zukunft ~rot** he paints a rosy picture of the future.
Rosa *nt* **-s, -s** pink.
rosa-: ~farben, ~farbig, ~rot *siehe* **rosa.**
rösch *adj (S Ger: knusprig)* *Brot* crusty; *Fleisch* crisp; *Mädchen* bonnie *(esp N Engl, Scot)*.
Röschen ['røːsçən] *nt* (little) rose; *(von Rosenkohl)* Brussel(s) sprout.
Rose *f* **-, -n (a)** *(Blume)* rose; *(Kompaßblatt auch)* compass card; *(Archit)* rose window ♦ **er ist nicht auf ~n gebettet** *(fig)* life isn't a bed of roses for him; **keine ~ ohne Dornen** *(prov)* no rose without a thorn *(prov)*. **(b)** *(Med)* erysipelas *(spec)*, rose. **(c)** *(Hunt: am Hirschgeweih)* burr.
rosé *adj inv* pink ♦ **Schuhe in ~** pink shoes.
Rosé *m* **-s, -s** rosé (wine).
Rosen-: r≈artig *adj* rose-like, rosaceous *(spec)*; **≈blatt** *nt* rose petal; **≈duft** *m* scent *or* perfume of roses; **r≈farben, r≈farbig** *adj* rose-coloured, pink, rosy; **≈garten** *m* rose garden; **≈gewächse** *pl* rosaceae *pl (spec)*; **≈holz** *nt* rosewood; **≈käfer** *m* rose chafer, rose beetle; **≈knospe** *f* rosebud; **≈kohl** *m* Brussel(s) sprouts *pl*; **≈kranz** *m (Eccl)* rosary; **den ~kranz beten** to say a rosary; **≈kreu(t)zer** *pl (Rel)* Rosicrucians *pl*; **≈kriege** *pl (Hist)* the Wars of the Roses *pl*; **~montag** *m Monday preceding Ash Wednesday*; **~montagszug** *m Carnival parade which takes place on the Monday preceding Ash Wednesday*; **≈öl** *nt* attar of roses; **≈quarz** *m* rose quartz; **r≈rot** *adj Wangen, Lippen* rosy (red); **Schneeweißchen und ~rot** *(Liter)* Snow White and Rose Red; **≈stock** *m* rose (tree); **≈strauch** *m* rosebush; **≈zucht** *f* rose-growing; **≈züchter** *m* rose-grower.
Rosette *f* rosette.
Roséwein *m* rosé wine.
rosig *adj (lit, fig)* rosy ♦ **etw in ~em Licht sehen** *(inf)* to see sth in a rosy light; **etw in ~en Farben schildern** *(inf)* to paint a glowing *or* rosy picture of sth, to show sth in a rosy light.
Rosine *f* raisin ♦ **(große) ~n im Kopf haben** *(inf)* to have big ideas; **sich** *(dat)* **die (besten** *or* **größten) ~n (aus dem Kuchen) herauspicken** *(inf)* to take the pick of the bunch.
Rosinenbomber *m (hum)* *plane which flew food etc into Berlin during the 1948 airlift.*
Röslein *nt* (little) rose.
Rosmarin *m* **-s,** *no pl* rosemary.

⚠**Roß** *nt* **Rosses, Rosse** *or (S Ger, Aus, Sw)* **Rösser** *(liter)* steed; *(S Ger, Aus, Sw)* horse; *(inf: Dummkopf)* dolt *(inf)* ♦ **~ und Reiter nennen** *(fig geh)* to name names; **der Ritter hoch zu ~** *(liter)* the knight astride his steed *(liter)*; *siehe* **hoch.**
Roß-: ~apfel *m (hum inf)* horse droppings *pl*; **~breiten** *pl (Naut)* horse latitudes *pl*.
Rössel, ⚠**Rößl** *nt* **-s, -** *(Chess)* knight; *(S Ger: Pferd)* horse.
Rosselenker *m (poet)* reinsman *(liter)*.
Rösselsprung *m* **(a)** *(Chess)* knight's move. **(b)** *(Rätselart)* *type of crossword puzzle in which certain individual letters make up a phrase or saying.*
⚠**Roß-: ~haar** *nt* horsehair; **~haarmatratze** *f* horsehair mattress; **~käfer** *m siehe* **Mistkäfer**; **~kastanie** *f* horse chestnut; **~kastanienextrakt** *m extract of horse chestnut used as a medicament for varicose veins*; **~kur** *f (hum)* drastic cure, kill-or-cure remedy; **eine ~kur (durch)machen** to follow a drastic cure.
⚠**Rößli(spiel), Rössliritti** *nt* **-s, -** *(Sw)* merry-go-round, roundabout *(Brit)*.
Roß-: ~schlächter *m* horse butcher; **~schlächterei** *f* horse butchery; **~täuscher** *m (old, fig)* horse-trader; **~täuscherei** *f (fig)* horse-trading *no pl*.
Rost[1] *m* **-(e)s,** *no pl (auch Bot)* rust ♦ **~ ansetzen** to start to rust.
Rost[2] *m* **-(e)s, -e** *(Ofen~)* grill; *(Gitter~)* grating, grille; *(dial: Bett~)* base, frame ♦ **auf dem ~ braten** *(Cook)* to barbecue, to grill on charcoal.
Rost-: ~ansatz *m* signs of rust *pl*; **r~beständig** *adj* rust-resistant; **~bildung** *f* rust formation; **~braten** *m (Cook)* ≃ roast; **~bratwurst** *f* barbecue sausage; **r~braun** *adj* russet; *Haar* auburn.
Röstbrot [*S Ger:* 'røːst, *N Ger:* 'rœst-] *nt siehe* **Toast.**
Röste [*S Ger:* 'røːstə, *N Ger:* 'rœstə] *f* **-, -n** *(Metal)* roasting.
rosten *vi aux sein or haben* to rust, to get rusty *(auch fig)* ♦ **alte Liebe rostet nicht** *(Prov)* old love never dies; *siehe* **rasten.**
rösten [*S Ger:* 'røːstən, *N Ger:* 'rœstən] *vt* **(a)** *Kaffee* to roast; *Brot* to toast ♦ **sich in der Sonne ~ lassen** to lie in the sun and bake. **(b)** *Erz* to roast, to calcine.
Rösterei [*S Ger:* røːst'-, *N Ger:* rœst'-] *f* roast(ing) house ♦ **frisch aus der ~** fresh from the roast, freshly roasted.
Rost-: r~farben, r~farbig *adj siehe* **r~braun**; **~fleck** *m* spot *or* patch of rust, rust spot *or* patch; **r~frei** *adj (Stahl)* stainless.
röstfrisch [*S Ger:* 'røːst-, *N Ger:* 'rœst-] *adj Kaffee* freshly roasted.
Rösti [*S Ger:* 'røːsti, *N Ger:* 'rœsti] *pl fried grated potatoes.*
rostig *adj (lit, fig)* rusty.
Röstkartoffeln [*S Ger:* 'røːst-, *N Ger:* 'rœst-] *pl siehe* **Bratkartoffeln.**
Rost-: ~krankheiten *pl (Bot)* rust diseases *pl*; **~laube** *f (hum)* rust-heap *(hum)*; **r~rot** *adj* rust-coloured, russet.
Rostschutz *m* anti-rust protection.
Rostschutz-: ~farbe *f* anti-rust paint; **~mittel** *nt* rust-proofer.
Rost|umwandler *m (Aut)* rust converter.
Röstzwiebeln [*S Ger:* 'røːst-, *N Ger:* 'rœst-] *pl* fried onions *pl*.
rot *adj comp* **¨er** *or (esp fig)* **-er,** *superl* **¨este(r, s)** *or (esp fig)* **-este(r, s),** *adv* **am ¨esten** *or (esp fig)* **am -esten** red *(auch Pol)* ♦ **~e Bete** *or* **Rüben** beetroot; **~e Karte** *(Ftbl)* red card; **das R~e Kreuz** the Red Cross; **der R~e Halbmond** the Red Crescent; **der R~e Löwe** the Red Lion; **der R~e Platz** Red Square; **das R~e Meer** the Red Sea; **die R~e Armee** the Red Army; **die R~en** *(pej)* the reds; **in den ~en Zahlen stecken** to be in the red; **Gewalt zieht sich wie ein ~er Faden durch die Geschichte** violence runs like a thread through history; **~ werden** to blush, to go red *(inf)*; **bis über beide Ohren ~ werden** to blush furiously, to turn crimson; **~ wie ein Krebs** red as a lobster; **~e Ohren bekommen** *(hum)*, **einen ~en Kopf bekommen** *or* **kriegen** *(inf)* to blush, to go red *(inf)*; **~ (angehaucht) sein** *(Pol inf)* to have left-wing leanings; **sich** *(dat)* **etw ~ (im Kalender) anstreichen** *(inf)* to make sth a red-letter day; **den Tag werde ich mir ~ im Kalender anstreichen** that will be a red-letter day; *siehe* **Grütze, rotsehen, Tuch, Hahn.**
Rot *nt* **-s, -s** *or* **-** red; *(Wangen~)* rouge ♦ **bei** *or* **auf ~** at red; **bei ~ anhalten!** stop (when the lights are) at red, stop when the lights are (at) red; **die Ampel stand auf ~** the lights were (at) red; **bei ~ über die Ampel fahren** to jump *or* shoot *(inf)* the lights.
Röt *nt* **-(e)s,** *no pl (Geol)* upper layer of bunter sandstone.
Rotarier [ro'taːriɐ] *m* **-s, -** rotarian.
Rot|armist *m* soldier in *or* of the Red Army ♦ **die ~en zogen durch die Stadt** the Red Army moved through the town.
Rotation *f (Phys, Pol)* rotation; *(Math auch)* curl.
Rotations-: ~achse *f (Math, Phys)* axis of rotation; **r~bedingt** *adj* subject to a rota system; **~druck** *m (Typ)* rotary (press) printing; **~fläche** *f (Math, Phys)* surface of revolution; **~maschine, ~presse** *f (Typ)* rotary press; **~prinzip** *nt (Pol)* rota system.
Rot-: ~auge *nt (Zool)* roach; **r~bäckig, r~backig** *adj* rosy-cheeked; **~barsch** *m* rosefish; **~bart** *m* red-beard; **Kaiser ~bart** Emperor Frederick Barbarossa; **r~bärtig** *adj* red-bearded; **r~blond** *adj Haar* sandy; *Mann* sandy-haired; *Frau, Tönung, (Frauen) haar* strawberry blonde; **r~braun** *adj* reddish brown; **~buche** *f* (common) beech; **~dorn** *m* hawthorn.
Röte *f* **-,** *no pl* redness, red; *(Erröten)* blush ♦ **die ~ des Abendhimmels** the red glow of the evening sky; **die ~ stieg ihr ins Gesicht** her face reddened.
Rote-Armee-Fraktion *f* Red Army Faction.
Rote Khmer *pl* Khmer Rouge *pl*.
Rötel *m* **-s, -** red chalk.
Röteln *pl* German measles *sing*.
röten [1] *vt* to redden, to make red; *Himmel* to turn red ♦ **die frische Luft rötete ihre Wangen** the fresh air gave her rosy cheeks *or* made her cheeks (go) red; **ein gerötetes Gesicht** a flushed face.

[2] *vr* to turn *or* become red, to flush.

Rot-: ≈filter *nt or m (Phot)* red filter; **≈front** *f (Pol)* red front; **≈fuchs** *m* red fox; *(Pferd)* sorrel *or* bay (horse); *(fig inf)* carrot-top *(inf)*; **≈gardist** *m* Red Guard; **⚠r≈gerändert** *adj* red-rimmed; **r≈-grün** *adj* red-green; **die r~-grüne Koalition** the Red-Green coalition; **r≈gesichtig** *adj* florid, red-faced; **⚠r≈glühend** *adj Metall* red-hot; **der r~glühende Abendhimmel** the red glow of the evening sky; **≈glut** *f (Metal)* red heat; **~grünblindheit** *f* red-green colour-blindness; **⚠≈guß** *m (Metal)* red brass; **r≈haarig** *adj* red-haired; **≈haut** *f (dated hum)* redskin; **≈hirsch** *m* red deer.

rotieren* *vi (auch Pol)* to rotate ◆ **anfangen zu ~** *(sl)* to get into a flap *(inf)*; **am R~ sein** *(sl)* to be rushing around like a mad thing *(inf)*.

Rot-: ~kabis *m (Sw)* red cabbage; **~käppchen** *nt (Liter)* Little Red Riding-hood; **~kehlchen** *nt* robin; **~kohl** *m* red cabbage; **~kopf** *m (inf)* redhead; **~kraut** *nt (S Ger, Aus)* red cabbage.

Rotkreuz-: ~lotterie *f* Red Cross lottery; **~sammlung** *f* Red Cross appeal *or* collection; **~schwester** *f* Red Cross nurse.

Rotlauf *m* **-s,** *no pl (Vet)* swine erysipelas *(spec)*.

rötlich *adj* reddish.

Rotlicht *nt* red light.

Rotlicht-: ~-Milieu *nt* demi-monde; **~revier, ~viertel** *nt* red-light district.

Rotor *m* rotor.

Rotorflügel *m (Aviat)* rotor blade.

Rot-: ~schwanz *m,* **~schwänzchen** *nt* redstart; **r~sehen** *vi sep irreg (inf)* to see red *(inf)*; **~sehen** *nt* **-s,** *no pl (Med)* erythropsia *(spec)*; **~stift** *m* red pencil; **den ~stift ansetzen** *(fig)* to cut sth back drastically; **dem ~stift zum Opfer fallen** *(fig)* to be scrapped *or* rejected *or* cancelled; **~tanne** *f* Norway spruce.

Rotte *f* **-, -n** gang; *(bei Jugendorganisation)* troop; *(Mil)* rank; *(Mil Aviat, Mil Naut)* pair *(of planes/ships operating together)*; *(von Hunden etc)* pack; *(Hunt: von Sauen)* herd, sounder *(spec)*.

Rotten-: ~führer *m (von Arbeitern)* foreman; *(bei Jugendorganisation)* troop-leader; **r~weise** *adv* in groups; **die Hunde fielen r~weise über das Reh her** packs of dogs attacked the deer.

Rottweiler *m* **-s, -** Rottweiler.

Rotunde *f* **-, -n** *(Archit)* rotunda.

Rötung *f* reddening.

Rot-: ⚠r~verheult *adj* **r~verheulte Augen** eyes red from crying; **r~wangig** *adj* rosy-cheeked; **~wein** *m* red wine; **r~welsch** *adj* argot, thieves' cant; **~welsch(e)** *nt decl as adj* argot, thieves' cant; **~wild** *nt* red deer; **~wurst** *f* ≃ black pudding.

Rotz *m* **-es,** *no pl* **(a)** *(sl)* snot *(inf)* ◆ **jdm ~ auf die Backe schmieren** *(sl)* to suck up to sb *(inf)*; **~ und Wasser heulen** *(inf)* to blubber; **Baron** *or* **Graf ~** *(inf)* Lord Muck *(inf)*; **der ganze ~** *(sl)* the whole bloody *(Brit)* *or* goddam *(US)* show *(sl)*.
(b) *(Vet)* glanders *sing,* farcy ◆ **den ~ haben** to have glanders.
(c) *(Bot)* soft rot.

Rotzbengel, Rotzbub *(S Ger, Aus) m (inf)* snotty-nosed brat *(inf)*.

rotzen *vi (sl)* to blow one's nose.

Rotz-: ~fahne *f (sl)* snot-rag *(sl)*; **r~frech** *adj (inf)* cocky *(inf)*.

rotzig *adj* **(a)** *(sl: lit, fig)* snotty *(sl)*. **(b)** *(Vet)* glanderous.

Rotz-: ~junge *m (inf)* snotty-nosed kid *(inf)*; **~lappen** *m (sl)* snot-rag *(sl)*; **~löffel** *(Aus),* **~lümmel** *(sl) m* cheeky brat *(inf)*; **~nase** *f* **(a)** *(sl)* snotty nose *(inf)*; **(b)** *(inf: Kind)* snotty-nosed brat *(inf)*; **r~näsig** *adj (sl)* **(a)** snotty-nosed *(inf)*; **(b)** *(frech)* snotty *(sl)*; **~nigel** *m (Aus inf)* snotty-nosed brat *(inf)*.

Rotzunge *f (Zool)* witch flounder.

Rouge [ruːʒ] *nt* **-s, -s** rouge, blusher.

Roulade [ru'laːdə] *f (Cook)* ≃ beef olive.

Rouleau [ru'loː] *nt* **-s, -s** *siehe* **Rollo.**

Roulett(e) [ru'lɛt(ə)] *nt* **-s, -** *or* **-s** roulette.

roulieren* [ru'liːrən] *vt (Sew)* to roll.

Route ['ruːtə] *f* **-, -n** route ◆ **wir sind die ~ über Bremen gefahren** we took the Bremen route.

Routine [ru'tiːnə] *f* **(a)** *(Erfahrung)* experience; *(Gewohnheit, Trott)* routine ◆ **das ist bei mir zur ~ geworden** that has become routine for me. **(b)** *(Comput)* routine.

Routine-: ~angelegenheit *f* routine matter; **r~mäßig** [1] *adj* routine; [2] *adv* **ich gehe r~mäßig zum Zahnarzt** I make a routine visit to the dentist's; **das wird r~mäßig überprüft** it's checked as a matter of routine; **ich werde das r~mäßig abwickeln** I'll deal with it in the usual way; **~sache** *f* routine matter; **~untersuchung** *f* routine examination.

routiniert [ruti'niːɐt] *adj* experienced.

Rowdy ['raudi] *m* **-s, -s** *or* **Rowdies** hooligan; *(zerstörerisch)* vandal; *(lärmend)* rowdy (type); *(Verkehrs~)* roadhog *(inf)*.

Rowdytum ['rauditu:m] *nt, no pl* hooliganism; vandalism ◆ **das ~ im Verkehr bekämpfen** to combat roadhogs.

Royalismus [roaja'lɪsmʊs] *m* royalism.

Royalist(in *f*) [roaja'lɪst(ɪn)] *m* royalist.

royalistisch [roaja'lɪstɪʃ] *adj* royalist.

Rubbel-: ~lotterie *f* scratch card lottery; **~massage** *f* body scrub.

rubbeln *vti* to rub.

Rübchen *nt dim of* **Rübe** small turnip ◆ **Teltower ~** *(Cook) glazed turnip with bacon.*

Rübe *f* **-, -n (a)** turnip ◆ **gelbe ~** *(S Ger, Sw: Mohr~)* carrot; **rote ~** beetroot; **weiße ~** white turnip; **jdn über die ~n jagen** *(sl)* to send sb packing *(inf)*; *siehe* **Kraut.**
(b) *(sl: Kopf)* nut *(inf)* ◆ **eins auf die ~ bekommen** *or* **kriegen** to get a bash on the nut *(inf)*; **jdm eins über die ~ ziehen** to give sb a bash *or* crack on the nut *(inf)*; **die ~ (für etw) hinhalten** to take the rap (for sth) *(inf)*; **jdm die ~ abhacken** *(fig)* to have sb's guts for garters *(sl)*; **~ ab!** off with his/her head!

Rubel *m* **-s, -** rouble ◆ **der ~ rollt** *(inf)* the money's rolling in *(inf)*.

Rüben-: r~artig *adj* turnip-like; **~saft** *m,* **~kraut** *nt* sugar beet syrup; **~zucker** *m* beet sugar.

rüber- *in cpds (inf) siehe auch* **herüber-, hinüber-; ~bringen** *vt sep irreg (inf) Botschaft, Feeling* to get across, to communicate; **~kommen** *vi sep* **(a)** *siehe* **herüberkommen; (b)** *(inf)* **sie kam gut ~** she came across well; **es kam viel/nichts ~ bei dem Meeting** a lot/not much came out of the meeting; **~ziehen** *sep irreg* [1] *vti siehe* **herüberziehen;**
[2] *vt (inf: schlagen)* **jdm eine ~ziehen** to give sb one *(inf)*, to stick one on sb *(sl)*.

Rübezahl *m* **-s** *spirit of the Sudeten Mountains.*

Rubidium *nt, no pl (abbr* **Rb)** rubidium.

Rubikon *m* **-s** Rubicon ◆ **den ~ überschreiten** *(fig geh)* to cross the Rubicon.

Rubin *m* **-s, -e** ruby.

rubinrot *adj* ruby-red, ruby.

Rüb-: ~kohl *m siehe* **Kohlrabi; ~öl** *nt* rapeseed oil, rape oil.

Rubrik *f* **(a)** *(Kategorie)* category ◆ **das gehört in die ~ „Militaria"** this belongs under the category *or* heading "military". **(b)** *(Zeitungs~)* section, column.

rubrizieren* *vt* to categorize, to put under a heading/headings.

Rubrizierung *f* categorization.

Rübsame(n) *m* **-(n)s,** *no pl (Bot)* rape.

Ruch *m* **-(e)s, ⸚e** *(geh)* **jdn/etw in den ~ bringen** to bring sb/sth into disrepute; **ein ~ von Korruption** the smell *or* whiff of corruption.

Ruch-: r~bar *adj* **r~bar werden** *(geh)* to become known; **r~los** *adj (old, liter)* dastardly *(liter)*; **~losigkeit** *f (old, liter)* dastardliness *(liter)*.

ruck *interj siehe* **hau ruck, ruck, zuck.**

Ruck *m* **-(e)s, -e** jerk, tug; *(von Fahrzeug)* jolt, jerk; *(Pol)* swing, shift ◆ **auf einen** *or* **mit einem ~** in one go, with one heave; **er stand mit einem ~ auf** he sprang to his feet, he stood up suddenly; **sich** *(dat)* **einen ~ geben** *(inf)* to make an effort, to give oneself a kick up the backside *(hum inf)*; **etw in einem ~ erledigen** to do sth at one fell swoop.

Rück-: ~ansicht *f* back *or* rear view; **~antwort** *f* reply, answer; **um ~antwort wird gebeten** please reply; **Telegramm mit ~antwort** reply-paid telegram.

ruck|artig [1] *adj* jerky ◆ **das Auto machte einige ~e Bewegungen** the car jerked a few times.
[2] *adv* jerkily ◆ **er stand ~ auf** he shot to his feet.

Rück-: ~äußerung *f* reply, answer; **~berufung** *f* recall; **~besinnung** *f* recollection; **die ~besinnung auf die Werte der Vergangenheit** thinking back to past values, the recollection of past values; **r~bezüglich** *adj (Gram)* reflexive; **~bildung** *f (Ling)* back-formation; *(Biol)* degeneration; **~blende** *f* flashback; **~blick** *m* look back *(auf +acc* at); **im ~blick auf etw** *(acc)* looking back on sth; **einen ~blick auf etw** *(acc)* **werfen** to look back on *or* at sth; **r~blickend** *adj* retrospective; **r~blickend läßt sich sagen, daß ...** in retrospect *or* retrospectively *or* looking back we can say that ...; **ein auf das vergangene Jahr r~blickender Bericht** a report that looks back at *or* over the last year; **r~datieren*** *vt sep infin, ptp only* to backdate; **~deckungsversicherung** *f (Econ) firm's private pension plan for employees*; **r~drehend** *adj (Met) Wind* backing.

rucken *vi (Fahrzeug)* to jerk, to jolt; *(Taube)* to coo.

Rücken *m* **-s, -** *(Anat, Stuhl~, Hand~, Sew)* back; *(Nasen~)* ridge; *(Fuß~)* instep; *(Messer~)* blunt edge, back; *(Hügel~, Berg~)* crest; *(Buch~)* spine ◆ **auf dem/den ~** on one's back; **ich bin ja auf den ~ gefallen!** *(fig)* you could have knocked me down with a feather *(inf)*; **den Feind im ~ haben** to have the enemy in one's rear; **die Sonne im ~ haben** to have the sun behind one *or* in one's back; **den Wind im ~ haben** to have a tail *or* following wind; **er hat doch die Firma des Vaters im ~** but he's got his father's firm behind him; **ich habe nicht gern jemanden im ~** I don't like having somebody sitting/standing right behind my back; **jdm die Hände auf den ~ binden** to tie sb's hands behind his back; **mit dem ~ zur Tür/Wand** with one's back to the door/wall; **mit dem ~ zur Wand stehen** *(fig) (aus Feigheit)* to cover oneself; *(aus Unterlegenheit)* to have one's back to the wall; **der verlängerte ~** *(hum inf)* one's posterior *(hum inf)*; **~ an ~** back to back; **ein schöner ~ kann auch entzücken** *(hum inf)* you've got a lovely back; **hinter jds ~** *(dat) (fig)* behind sb's back; **jdm/einer Sache den ~ kehren** *(lit, fig) or* **zuwenden** *(lit) or* **wenden** *(fig) or* **zudrehen** *(lit)* to turn one's back on sb/sth; **den ~ wenden** to turn one's back; **jdm in den ~ fallen** *(fig)* to stab sb in the back; *(Mil)* to attack sb from the rear; **sich** *(dat)* **den ~ freihalten** *(inf) or* **decken** to cover oneself; **jdm den ~ decken** *(fig inf)* to back sb up *(inf)*; **schon viele Jahre/viel Erfahrung auf dem ~ haben** *(inf)* to be getting on in years/to have a lot of experience under one's belt *(inf)*; **auf seinen ~ geht viel** *(inf)* he can take it; **jdm den ~ stärken** *or* **steifen** *(fig inf)* to give sb encouragement; *siehe* **breit.**

rücken [1] *vi aux sein* to move; *(Platz machen)* to move up *or (zur Seite auch)* over; *(weiter~: Zeiger)* to move on *(auf +acc* to) ◆ **näher ~** to move *or* come closer; *(Zeit)* to come *or* get closer; **ins Feld** *(old)* **/ins Manöver/an die Front ~** to take the field/to go off on manoeuvres/to go up to the front; **mit etw ~** to move sth; **sie rückten ungeduldig mit den Stühlen** they shuffled their chairs about impatiently; **an etw** *(dat)* **~** *an Uhrzeiger* to move sth; *an Krawatte* to pull sth (straight); *(schieben)* to push at sth; *(ziehen)* to pull at sth; **an jds Seite** *(acc)* **~** to move up close beside sb; **an jds Stelle** *(acc)* **~** to

take sb's place; **nicht von der Stelle ~** not to budge an inch (*inf*); **in weite Ferne ~** to recede into the distance; **jdm auf den Leib** *or* **Pelz** (*inf*) *or* **Balg** (*inf*) *or* **die Pelle** (*sl*) ~ (*zu nahe kommen*) to crowd sb; (*sich jdn vorknöpfen*) to get on at sb; (*hum: besuchen*) to move in on sb; **einer Sache** (*dat*) **zu Leibe ~** to have a go at sth, to tackle sth; *siehe* **Bude**.
[2] *vt* to move; *siehe* **Licht**.

Rücken-: ~deckung *f* (*fig*) backing; **jdm ~deckung geben** to back sb; **~flosse** *f* dorsal fin; **~flug** *m* (*Aviat*) inverted flight; **~kraulen** *nt* (*Sport*) back crawl, backstroke; **r~kraulen** *vi sep infin only* to do *or* swim back crawl *or* backstroke; **~lage** *f* supine position; **er mußte 3 Monate in ~lage verbringen** he had to spend 3 months lying (flat) on his back *or* in a supine position (*form*); **er schläft in ~lage** he sleeps on his back; **~lehne** *f* back, back-rest; **~mark** *nt* spinal cord; **~mark(s)entzündung** *f* myelitis; **~muskel** *m* back muscle; **~muskulatur** *f* back muscles *pl*, muscles of the/one's back *pl*; **~schmerz(en** *pl*) *m* backache; **ich habe ~schmerzen** I've got backache, my back aches; **~schwimmen** *nt* backstroke, swimming on one's back; **r~schwimmen** *vi sep infin only* to swim on one's back, to do the *or* swim backstroke; **~stärkung** *f* (*fig*) moral support; **~stück** *nt* (*Cook*) (*vom Rind*) chine; (*vom Reh, Hammel*) saddle; **ein schönes ~stück** a nice piece of back; **~trage** *f* carrying-frame.

Rück|entwicklung *f* (*allgemein*) fall-off (*gen* in); (*Biol*) degeneration.

Rücken-: ~wind *m* tail *or* following wind; **~wirbel** *m siehe* **Brustwirbel**.

Rück-: ~erinnerung *f* memory (*an +acc* of); **r~erstatten*** *vt sep infin, ptp only* to refund; *Ausgaben* to reimburse; **~erstattung** *f* refund; reimbursement; **~fahrkarte** *f*, **~fahrschein** *m* return ticket, round-trip ticket (*US*); **~fahrscheinwerfer** *m* (*Aut*) reversing light; **~fahrt** *f* return journey; **~fall** *m* (*Med, fig*) relapse; (*Jur*) subsequent offence, repetition of an/the offence; **ein ~fall in alte Gewohnheiten** a relapse into one's old habits; **Diebstahl im ~fall** a repeated case of theft; **r~fällig** *adj* (*Med, fig*) relapsed; (*Jur*) recidivistic (*form*); **ein r~fälliger Dieb** a thief who repeats his offence; **r~fällig werden** (*Med*) to have a relapse; (*fig*) to relapse; (*Jur*) to lapse back into crime; **~fällige(r)** *mf decl as adj* (*Med, fig*) person who relapses/has relapsed; (*Jur*) subsequent offender, recidivist (*form*); **~falltäter** *m* recidivist (*form*), recidivistic offender (*form*); **~flug** *m* return flight; **⚠~fluß** *m* reflux, flowing back; (*von Investitionen, Kapital*) return; **~forderung** *f* **~forderung des Geldes/des Buches** demand for the return of the money/the book; **~fracht** *f* return load; **~frage** *f* question; **nach ~frage bei der Zentrale ...** after querying *or* checking this with the exchange ...; **bei jdm ~frage halten** to query it/sth with sb; **r~fragen** *vi sep infin, ptp only* to inquire, to check; **ich habe im Fundbüro r~gefragt** I inquired *or* checked at the lost-property office; **ich muß beim Chef r~fragen** I'll have to check with the boss *or* query it with the boss; **~front** *f* back, rear façade; **~führgebühr** *f* (*bei Leihwagen*) drop-off charge; **~führung** *f* (**a**) (*Deduktion*) tracing back; **die ~führung der Probleme auf** (*+acc*) tracing the problems back to; (**b**) (*von Menschen*) repatriation, return; (**c**) (*Fin: von Kredit*) repayment; **~gabe** *f* return; **~gaberecht** *nt* right of return; **~gang** *m* fall, drop (*gen* in); **einen ~gang** *or* **~gänge zu verzeichnen haben** to report a drop *or* fall; **r~gängig** *adj* (**a**) (*Comm: zurückgehend*) declining, falling, dropping; (**b**) **r~gängig machen** (*widerrufen*) to undo; *Bestellung, Geschäft, Vertrag, Termin* to cancel; *Verlobung, Hochzeit* to call off; *chemischen Prozeß* to reverse; **~gängigmachung** *f* (*form*) cancellation; (*Chem*) reversal; **~gebäude** *nt* rear building; **r~gebildet** *adj* (*Biol*) degenerate; **~gewinnung** *f* recovery; (*von Land, Gebiet*) reclaiming, reclamation; (*aus verbrauchten Stoffen*) recycling; **~gliederung** *f* (*Pol*) reintegration.

Rückgrat *nt* **-(e)s, -e** spine, backbone ◆ **er ist ein Mensch ohne ~** (*fig*) he's a spineless creature, he's got no backbone; **das ~ der Wirtschaft** the backbone *or* mainstay of the economy; **jdm das ~ stärken** (*inf*) to give sb encouragement *or* a boost; **jdm das ~ brechen** to break *or* ruin sb.

Rückgratverkrümmung *f* curvature of the spine.

Rück-: ~griff *m* (**a**) **durch einen ~griff auf jdn/etw** by reverting to sb/sth; **wenn ein ~griff auf vorhandene Reserven nicht möglich ist** if it is not possible to fall back on available resources; **erlauben Sie mir einen ~griff auf bereits Gesagtes** allow me to revert to something that has already been said; (**b**) (*Jur*) *siehe* **Regreß**; **~halt** *m* (**a**) (*Unterstützung*) support, backing; **an jdm einen ~halt haben** to find a support in sb; (**b**) (*Einschränkung*) **ohne ~halt** without reservation; **~haltebecken** *nt* storage pond; **r~haltlos** *adj* complete; *Unterstützung auch* unqualified; *Vertrauen auch* implicit; **sich r~haltlos zu etw bekennen** to proclaim one's total allegiance to sth; **~hand** *f* (*Sport*) backhand; **~hand spielen** to play backhand; **er kann erstklassig ~hand spielen** he has a first-rate backhand; **den Ball (mit der) ~hand schlagen** to hit the ball (on one's) backhand; **~handschlag** *m* (*Sport*) backhand (stroke).

ruckizucki *adv* (*inf*) *siehe* **ruck, zuck**.

Rückkampf *m* (*Sport*) return match.

Rückkauf *m* repurchase.

Rückkaufs-: ~recht *nt* right of repurchase; **~wert** *m* repurchase value.

Rückkehr *f* **-,** *no pl* return ◆ **bei seiner ~** on his return; **jdn zur ~ (nach X/zu jdm) bewegen** to persuade sb to return (to X/to sb).

Rückkehr-: ~förderungsgesetz, ~hilfegesetz *nt law encouraging the return of immigrants to their native country*; **r~willig** *adj* willing to return.

Rück-: r~koppeln *vti sep infin, ptp only* (*alle Bedeutungen*) to feed back; **~kopp(e)lung** *f* feedback; **~kreuzung** *f* back-cross; (*Vorgang*) back crossing; **~kunft** *f* **-,** *no pl* (*liter*) return; **~lage** *f* (*Fin: Reserve*) reserve, reserves *pl*; (*Ersparnisse auch*) savings *pl*; **~lauf** *m*, *no pl* (*Tech*) reverse running; (*von Maschinenteil*) return travel; (*Gegenströmung*) countercurrent; (*TV*) flyback; (*Naut*) slip; (*beim Tonband*) fast rewind; (*von Schußwaffe*) recoil; (*von Pfandflaschen, Fragebögen*) returns *pl*; **ein guter ~lauf** a good number of returns; **r~läufig** *adj* declining, falling, dropping; *Tendenz* downward; **eine r~läufige Entwicklung** a decline, a falling off; **r~läufiges Wörterbuch** reverse index; **~licht** *nt* tail *or* rear light; (*bei Fahrrad auch*) back light; **r~lings** *adv* (*r~wärts*) backwards; (*von hinten*) from behind; (*auf dem Rücken*) on one's back; **~marsch** *m* (*Mil*) march back; (*~zug*) retreat.

Rückmelde-: ~frist *f* (*Univ*) re-registration period; **~gebühren** *pl* (*Univ*) re-registration fee.

Rück-: ~meldung *f* (**a**) (*Univ*) re-registration; (**b**) (*Comput*) echo; **~nahme** *f* **-, -n** taking back; **die ~nahme des Gerätes ist unmöglich** it is impossible for us to take this set back; **ich bestehe auf der ~nahme des Gerätes** I must insist that you take this set back; **~nahmepreis** *m* repurchase price; **⚠~paß** *m* (*Sport*) return pass; **~porto** *nt* return postage; **~prall** *m* rebound; (*von Kugel, Stein etc*) ricochet; **~prämie** *f* (*Fin*) put premium; **~prämiengeschäft** *nt* (*Fin*) put.

Rückreise *f* return journey.

Rückreise-: ~verkehr *m* homebound traffic; **~visum** *nt* return visa.

Rück-: ~ruf *m* (**a**) (*am Telefon*) **Herr X hat angerufen und bittet um ~ruf** Mr X called and asked you to call (him) back; (**b**) (*Jur*) rescission of permission to manufacture under licence; **~rufaktion** *f* call-back campaign.

Rucksack *m* rucksack.

Rucksacktourist(in *f*) *m* backpacker.

Rück-: ~schalttaste *f siehe* **~(stell)taste**; **~schau** *f* reflection (*auf +acc* on); (*in Medien*) review (*auf +acc* of); **~schau halten** to reminisce, to reflect; **auf etw** (*acc*) **~schau halten** to look back on sth; **in ~schau auf das vergangene Jahr ...** looking back on the past year ...; **~schein** *m* ≃ recorded delivery slip; **~schlag** *m* (**a**) (*von Ball*) rebound; (*von Gewehr*) recoil; (*fig*) set-back; (*bei Patient*) relapse; (**b**) (*Biol*) atavism; **~schläger** *m* (*Sport*) receiver; **~schlagventil** *nt* check valve; **⚠~schluß** *m* conclusion; **den ~schluß gestatten, daß ...** to admit of the conclusion that ...; **den ~schluß ziehen, daß ...** to draw the conclusion *or* to conclude that ...; **~schlüsse ziehen** (*euph*) to draw one's own conclusions (*aus* from); **~schritt** *m* (*fig*) retrograde step, step backwards; **ein gesellschaftlicher ~schritt** a retrograde social step, a social step backwards; **r~schrittlich** *adj* reactionary; *Entwicklung* retrograde.

Rückseite *f* back; (*von Blatt Papier, Geldschein auch*) reverse; (*von Buchseite, Münze*) reverse, verso; (*von Zeitung*) back page; (*von Mond auch*) far side; (*von Gebäude auch*) rear ◆ **siehe ~** see over(leaf).

rückseitig *adj* on the back *or* reverse ◆ **die ~en Bemerkungen** the remarks overleaf; **der Garten liegt ~** the garden is at the back; **das Papier soll auch ~ beschrieben werden** you should write on both sides of the paper.

rucksen *vi* (*Taube*) to coo.

Rücksendung *f* return.

Rücksicht *f* **-, -en** (*Schonung, Nachsicht*) consideration ◆ **~en** *pl* (*Gründe, Interessen*) considerations *pl*; **aus** *or* **mit ~ auf jdn/etw** out of consideration for sb/sth; **ohne ~ auf jdn/etw** with no consideration for sb/sth; **ohne ~ auf Verluste** (*inf*) regardless; **auf jdn/etw ~ nehmen** to consider sb/sth, to show consideration for sb/sth; **er kennt keine ~** he's ruthless; **da kenne ich keine ~!** I can be ruthless.

rücksichtlich *prep +gen* (*old*) in view of.

Rücksichtnahme *f* **-,** *no pl* consideration.

Rücksichts-: r~los *adj* (**a**) inconsiderate, thoughtless; (*im Verkehr*) reckless; **er verfolgt r~los seine Interessen** he follows his own interests without consideration for others; (**b**) (*unbarmherzig*) ruthless; **~losigkeit** *f* (**a**) inconsiderateness *no pl*, thoughtlessness *no pl*; **das ist doch eine ~losigkeit!** how inconsiderate *or* thoughtless; (**b**) ruthlessness; **r~voll** *adj* considerate, thoughtful (*gegenüber, gegen* towards).

Rück-: ~sitz *m* (*von Fahrrad, Motorrad*) pillion; (*von Auto*) back seat; **~spiegel** *m* (*Aut*) rear(-view) *or* driving mirror; (*außen*) outside mirror; **~spiel** *nt* (*Sport*) return match; **~sprache** *f* consultation; **laut ~sprache mit Herrn Müller ...** I have consulted Herr Müller and he informs me that ...; **~sprache mit jdm nehmen** *or* **halten** to confer with *or* consult (with) sb; **r~spulen** *vt sep infin, ptp only Tonband, Film* to rewind.

Rückspul-: ~automatik *f* (*von Kamera, Video etc*) automatic rewind; **~knopf** *m* (*von Kamera*) rewind knob; **~taste** *f* (*von Tonbandgerät*) rewind key.

Rückstand *m* (**a**) (*Überrest*) remains *pl*; (*bei Verbrennung, Bodensatz*) residue.
(**b**) (*Verzug*) delay; (*bei Aufträgen*) backlog ◆ **im ~ sein/in ~ geraten** to be/fall behind; (*bei Zahlungen auch*) to be/get in arrears *pl*; **seinen ~ aufholen** to make up for one's delay/to catch up on a backlog; (*bei Zahlungen*) to catch up on one's payments; (*in Leistungen*) to catch up.
(**c**) (*Außenstände*) arrears *pl* ◆ **wie hoch ist mein ~?** how much are my arrears?; **~̈e eintreiben/bezahlen** to collect/pay arrears.
(**d**) (*Sport*) amount by which one is behind ◆ **mit 0:2 im ~ sein** to be 2 goals/points *etc* down; **ihr ~ gegenüber dem Tabellenführer beträgt 4 Punkte** they are 4 points behind the leader.

rückständig *adj* (**a**) (*überfällig*) *Betrag* overdue; *Mensch* in arrears ◆ **~er Betrag** amount overdue. (**b**) (*zurückgeblieben*) *Land, Mensch* backward; *Methoden, Ansichten auch* antiquated ◆ **~ denken** to have antiquated ideas.

Rückständigkeit *f*, *no pl* backwardness.

rückstand(s)frei *adj* without residue; *Verbrennung auch* clean ◆ **ein Diamant verbrennt ~** a diamond burns without leaving any residue; **dieses Öl verbrennt nahezu ~** this oil burns cleanly.

Rück-: ~stau *m* (*von Wasser*) backwater; (*von Autos*) tailback; **~(stell)taste** *f* (*an Schreibmaschine, Computer*) backspace key; **~stellung** *f* (*Fin*) reserve; **~stoß** *m* repulsion; (*bei Gewehr*) recoil; (*von Rakete*) thrust; **~stoßantrieb** *m* (*Aviat*) reaction propulsion; **r~stoßfrei** *adj Geschütze* recoilless; **~strahler** *m* **-s, -** reflector; **~strom** *m* (*Elec*) reverse current; (*von Menschen, Fahrzeugen*) return; **der ~strom der Urlauber aus Italien** the stream of holiday makers returning from Italy; **~tabulator** *m* (*an Schreibmaschine*) tab left (key); **~taste** *f siehe* **~(stell)taste**; **~transport** *m* return transport; (*bei Schreibmaschine*) return.

Rücktritt *m* **(a)** (*Amtsniederlegung*) resignation; (*von König*) abdication ♦ **seinen ~ einreichen** *or* **erklären** to hand in *or* tender (*form*) one's resignation. **(b)** (*Jur*) (*von Vertrag*) withdrawal (*von* from), rescission (*form*) (*von* of) ♦ **~ vom Versuch** abandonment of intent. **(c)** (*inf*) *siehe* **Rücktrittbremse**.

Rücktrittbremse *f* backpedal *or* coaster brake.

Rücktritts-: ~drohung *f* threat to resign/abdicate; **~frist** *f* period for withdrawal; **~gesuch** *nt* resignation; **das ~gesuch einreichen** to tender one's resignation (*form*); **~klausel** *f* withdrawal clause; **~recht** *nt* right of withdrawal; **~vorbehalt** *m* option of withdrawal.

Rück-: r~übersetzen* *vt sep infin, ptp only* to translate back into the original language; **~übersetzung** *f* retranslation into the original language; **r~vergüten*** *vt sep infin, ptp only* to refund (*jdm etw* sb sth); **~vergütung** *f* refund; **~versicherer** *m* reinsurer; (*fig*) hedger; **r~versichern*** *sep* [1] *vti* to reinsure; [2] *vr* to check (up *or* back); **~versicherung** *f* reinsurance; **~versicherungsvertrag** *m* (*Hist*) Reinsurance Treaty; **~verweis** *m* reference back; **r~verweisen*** *vti sep irreg infin, ptp only* to refer back; **~wand** *f* (*von Zimmer, Gebäude etc*) back wall; (*von Möbelstück etc*) back; **~wanderer** *m* returning emigrant, remigrant; **~wanderung** *f* remigration; **r~wärtig** *adj* back; *Tür, Eingang, Ausgang auch,* (*Mil*) rear; **r~wärtige Verbindungen** (*Mil*) lines of communication.

rückwärts *adv* **(a)** (*zurück, rücklings*) backwards ♦ **Rolle/Salto ~** backward roll/back somersault; **~ einparken** to back *or* reverse into a parking space. **(b)** (*Aus: hinten*) behind, at the back ♦ **von ~** from behind.

Rückwärts-: ~drehung *f* reverse turn; **~fahren** *nt* reversing; **~gang** *m* reverse gear; **den ~gang einlegen** to change into reverse, to put the car *etc* into reverse; **im ~gang fahren** to reverse; ⚠**r~gewandt** *adj* (*fig*) backward-looking, retrogressive.

Rückweg *m* way back ♦ **auf dem ~ vorbeikommen** to call in on one's way back; **den ~ antreten, sich auf den ~ begeben** to set off back; **sich auf den ~ machen** to head back; **jdm den ~ abschneiden** to cut off sb's line of retreat.

ruckweise *adv* jerkily ♦ **sich ~ bewegen** to jerk, to move jerkily.

Rück-: ~wendung *f* return (*zu, auf +acc* to); **r~wirkend** *adj* (*Jur*) retrospective; *Lohn-, Gehaltserhöhung* backdated; **es wird r~wirkend vom 1. Mai bezahlt** it will be backdated to the 1st May; **das Gesetz tritt r~wirkend vom 1. Januar in Kraft** the law is made retrospective to the 1st January; **~wirkung** *f* repercussion; **eine Zahlung/Gesetzesänderung mit ~wirkung vom ...** a payment backdated to/an amendment made retrospective to ...; **r~zahlbar** *adj* repayable; **~zahlung** *f* repayment; **~zieher** *m* **-s, -** (*inf*) **einen ~zieher machen** to back out (*inf*); **r~zielend** *adj* (*Gram rare*) reflexive.

ruck, zuck [1] *interj* (*beim Ziehen*) heave; (*beim Schieben*) push.
[2] *adv* in a flash; (*Imperativ*) jump to it ♦ **das geht ~, ~** it won't take a second; **wenn er nicht gehorcht, fliegt er raus, das geht ~, ~** if he doesn't obey he'll be out, just like that.

Ruckzuck *nt* **-s,** *no pl* (*inf*) **etw mit ~ machen** to do sth at the double (*inf*).

Rückzug *m* (*Mil*) retreat ♦ **auf dem ~** in the retreat; **den ~ antreten** (*lit, fig*) to retreat, to beat a retreat; *siehe* **blasen**.

Rückzugs-: ~gebiet *nt* retreat; **~gefecht** *nt* (*Mil, fig*) rearguard action.

Rüde *m* **-n, -n** (*Männchen*) dog, male; (*Hetzhund*) hound.

rüde, rüd (*Aus*) *adj* impolite; *Antwort* curt, brusque ♦ **das war sehr ~ von dir** that was a very rude thing to do.

Rudel *nt* **-s, -** (*von Hunden, Wölfen*) pack; (*von Wildschweinen, Hirschen*) herd; (*fig dated*) swarm, horde ♦ **in ~n auftreten** to go round in packs/herds/swarms *or* hordes.

rudelweise *adv* in packs/herds/swarms *or* hordes.

Ruder *nt* **-s, -** (*von ~boot, Galeere etc*) oar; (*Naut, Aviat: Steuer~*) rudder; (*fig: Führung*) helm ♦ **das ~ fest in der Hand haben** (*fig*) to be in control of the situation; **die ~ auslegen/einziehen** to put out/ship oars; **am ~ sein** (*lit, fig*)/ **ans ~ kommen** (*fig*) to be at/to take over (at) the helm; **sich in die ~ legen** (*lit, fig*), **sich für etw in die ~ legen** (*fig*) to put one's back into it/sth; **das ~ herumwerfen** (*fig*) to change course *or* tack; **aus dem ~ laufen** (*fig*) to get out of hand.

Ruder-: ~bank *f* rowing seat; (*in Galeere*) rowing bench; **~blatt** *nt* (oar) blade; **~boot** *nt* rowing boat, rowboat (*esp US*); **~dolle** *f* rowlock.

Ruderer *m* **-s,** - oarsman, rower.

Rudergänger *m* **-s, -** (*Naut*) helmsman.

Ruderhaus *nt* (*Naut*) wheelhouse, pilot house.

-rud(e)rig *adj suf* -oared.

Ruderin *f* oarswoman, rower.

rudern [1] *vi* **(a)** *aux haben or sein* to row. **(b)** (*Schwimmvögel*) to paddle ♦ **mit den Armen ~** (*fig*) to flail *or* wave one's arms about.
[2] *vt* to row.

Ruder-: ~pinne *f* tiller; **~regatta** *f* rowing regatta; **~schlag** *m* stroke; **~sport** *m* rowing *no def art*; **~stange** *f* tiller.

Rudiment *nt* rudiment.

rudimentär *adj* rudimentary; (*Biol*) *Organ auch* vestigial ♦ **~ ausgebildet** rudimentary.

Rudrer(in *f*) *m* **-s, -** *siehe* **Ruderer, Ruderin**.

Ruf *m* **-(e)s, -e (a)** (*Aus~, Vogel~, fig: Auf~*) call; (*lauter*) shout; (*Schrei, gellend*) cry ♦ **ein ~ ertönte** a cry rang out; **in den ~ „...“ ausbrechen** to burst into cries *or* shouts of "..."; **der ~ des Muezzins** the call of the muezzin; **der ~ der Wildnis** the call of the wild; **dem ~ des Herzens/Gewissens folgen** (*fig*) to obey the voice of one's heart/conscience; **der ~ nach Freiheit/Gerechtigkeit** (*fig*) the call for freedom/justice; **der ~ nach dem Henker** (*fig*) the call to bring back hanging/the chair *etc*; **der ~ zu den Waffen** the call to arms; **der ~ zur Ordnung** (*fig*) the call to order.
(b) (*Ansehen, Leumund*) reputation ♦ **einen guten ~ haben** *or* **genießen, sich eines guten ~es erfreuen** (*geh*) to have *or* enjoy a good reputation; **dem ~ nach** by reputation; **eine Firma von ~** a firm with a good reputation *or* of high repute, a firm with a good name; **sich** (*dat*) **einen ~ als etw erwerben** to build up a reputation *or* make a name for oneself as sth; **ein Mann von schlechtem ~** a man with a bad reputation *or* of low repute, a man with a bad name; **von üblem** *or* **zweifelhaftem ~** with a bad reputation; **von üblem** *or* **zweifelhaftem ~ sein** to have a bad reputation; **jdn/etw in schlechten ~ bringen** to give sb/sth a bad name; **jdn bei jdm in schlechten ~ bringen** to bring sb into disrepute with sb; **sie/das ist besser als ihr/sein ~** she/it is better than she/it is made out to be, she/it is not as black as she/it is painted; **ist der ~ erst ruiniert, lebt man völlig ungeniert** (*prov*) you live freely if you haven't a reputation to lose.
(c) (*Univ: Berufung*) offer of a chair *or* professorship ♦ **er hat einen ~ nach Mainz erhalten** he has been offered a chair *or* professorship at Mainz.
(d) (*Fernruf*) telephone number ♦ **„~: 2785“** "Tel: 2785".

Rufe, Rüfe *f* **-, -n** (*Sw*) **(a)** (*Steinlawine*) rockfall; (*Erdrutsch*) landslide. **(b)** (*auf Wunde*) scab.

rufen *pret* **rief**, *ptp* **gerufen** [1] *vi* to call; (*Mensch: laut ~*) to shout; (*Gong, Glocke, Horn etc*) to sound (*zu* for) ♦ **um Hilfe ~** to call *or* cry for help; **die Pflicht ruft** duty calls; **die Arbeit ruft** my/your *etc* work is waiting; **nach jdm/etw ~** to call for sb/sth; **nach dem Henker ~** (*fig*) to call for the return of hanging/the chair *etc*.
[2] *vi impers* **es ruft eine Stimme** a voice is calling; **es hat gerufen** somebody called.
[3] *vt* **(a)** to call; (*aus~*) to cry; (*Mensch: laut ~*) to shout ♦ **jdm/sich etw in Erinnerung** *or* **ins Gedächtnis ~** to bring back (memories of) sth to sb/to recall sth; **jdn zur Ordnung ~** to call sb to order; **jdn zur Sache ~** to bring sb back to the point; **jdn zu den Waffen ~** to call sb to arms; **bravo/da capo ~** to shout hooray/encore; **sich heiser ~** to shout oneself hoarse.
(b) (*kommen lassen*) to send for; *Arzt, Polizei auch, Taxi* to call ♦ **jdn zu sich ~** to send for sb; **Gott hat sie zu sich gerufen** God has called her to Him; **Sie haben mich ~ lassen?** you called, sir/madam?; **~ Sie ihn bitte!** please send him to me; **jdn zu Hilfe ~** to call on sb to help; **du kommst wie gerufen** you're just the man/woman I wanted; **das kommt mir wie gerufen** that's just what I needed; (*kommt mir gelegen*) that suits me fine (*inf*).

Rufen *nt* **-s,** *no pl* calling *no indef art*; (*von Mensch: laut*) shouting *no indef art* ♦ **haben Sie das ~ nicht gehört?** didn't you hear him/her *etc* calling/shouting?

Rufer *m* **-s, - der ~ im Streit** (*liter*) the leader in battle; **der ~ in der Wüste** the voice (crying) in the wilderness.

Ruferei *f* (*inf*) *siehe* **Rufen**.

Rüffel *m* **-s, -** (*inf*) telling- *or* ticking-off (*inf*).

rüffeln *vt* (*inf*) to tell *or* tick off (*inf*).

Ruf-: ~mord *m* character assassination; **~mordkampagne** *f* smear campaign; **~name** *m* forename (by which one is generally known); **~nummer** *f* telephone number; **~nummernspeicher** *m* (*von Telefon*) memory; **~reservierung** *f* (*von Telefax*) polling; **~säule** *f* (*für Taxi*) telephone; (*Mot: Not~*) emergency telephone; **~weite** *f*: **in ~weite** within earshot, within calling distance; **außer ~weite** out of earshot; **~zeichen** *nt* **(a)** (*Telec*) call sign; (*von Telefon*) ringing tone; **(b)** (*Aus*) exclamation mark.

Rugby ['rakbi] *nt* **-,** *no pl* rugby, rugger (*inf*).

Rugbyspiel *nt* (*Veranstaltung*) rugby match ♦ **das ~** (*Sportart*) rugby.

Rüge *f* **-, -n** (*Verweis*) reprimand, rebuke; (*Kritik*) criticism *no indef art*; (*scharfe Kritik*) censure *no indef art* ♦ **jdm eine ~ erteilen** to reprimand *or* rebuke/criticize/censure sb (*für, wegen* for).

rügen *vt* (*form*) *jdn* to reprimand (*wegen, für* for); *etw* to reprehend ♦ **ich muß dein Verhalten ~** I must reprimand you for your behaviour.

rügenswert *adj* reprehensible.

Ruhe *f* **-,** *no pl* **(a)** (*Schweigen, Stille*) quiet, silence ♦ **~!** quiet!, silence!; **~, bitte!** quiet, please; **gebt ~!** be quiet!; **ihr sollt ~ geben!** once and for all — (will you) be quiet!; **jdn zur ~ ermahnen** to tell sb to be quiet; **sich** (*dat*) **~ verschaffen** to get quiet *or* silence; **es herrscht ~** all is silent, silence reigns (*liter*); (*fig: Disziplin, Frieden*) all is quiet; **~ halten** (*lit, fig*) to keep quiet *or* silent; **die ~ der Natur** the stillness of nature; **himmlische ~** heavenly peace; **~ und Frieden** peace and quiet; **in ~ und Abgeschiedenheit** in peaceful seclusion; **die ~ vor dem Sturm** (*fig*) the calm before the storm.
(b) (*Ungestörtheit, Frieden*) peace, quiet; (*~stätte*) resting place ♦ **~ ausstrahlen** to radiate a sense of calm; **in ~ und Frieden leben** to live a quiet life; **~ und Ordnung** law and order; **~ ist die erste Bürgerpflicht** (*prov*) the main thing is to keep calm/quiet; **die ~ wiederherstellen** to restore order; **ich brauche meine ~** I need a bit of peace; **laß mich in ~!** leave me in peace, stop bothering me; **ich will meine ~ haben!, mei Ruh will i ham!** (*S Ger*) leave *or* let me alone *or* be; **dann hat die liebe Seele Ruh** (*prov*) then perhaps we'll get a bit of peace; **vor jdm ~ haben wollen** to want a rest from sb; (*endgültig*) to want to get *or* be rid of sb; **jdm keine ~ lassen** *or* **gönnen** (*Mensch*) not to give sb any peace; **keine ~ geben** to keep on and on; **das läßt ihm keine ~** he

⚠: for details of spelling reform, see supplement

can't stop thinking about it; **zur ~ kommen** to get some peace; (*solide werden*) to settle down; **jdn zur ~ kommen lassen** to give sb a chance to rest; **keine ~ finden (können)** to know no peace, not to be able to find any peace of mind; **jdn zur letzten ~ betten** (*liter*) to lay sb to rest (*liter*); **die letzte ~ finden** (*liter*) to be laid to rest (*liter*).
(c) (*Erholung*) rest, repose (*liter*); (*~ stand*) retirement; (*Stillstand*) rest ♦ **der Patient braucht viel ~** the patient needs a great deal of rest; **das Pendel befindet sich in ~** the pendulum is stationary; **jdm keine ~ gönnen** not to give sb a minute's rest; **sich zur ~ begeben** (*form*), **zur ~ gehen** to retire (to bed) (*form*); **angenehme ~!** sleep well!; **sich zur ~ setzen** to retire.
(d) (*Gelassenheit*) calm(ness); (*Disziplin*) quiet, order ♦ **die ~ weghaben** (*inf*) to be unflappable (*inf*); **~ bewahren** to keep calm; **die ~ selbst sein** to be calmness itself; **jdn aus der ~ bringen** to throw sb (*inf*); **sich nicht aus der ~ bringen lassen, nicht aus der ~ zu bringen sein** not to (let oneself) get worked up; **er trank noch in aller ~ seinen Kaffee** he drank his coffee as if he had all the time in the world; **überlege es dir in aller ~** think about it calmly; **sich** (*dat*) **etw in ~ ansehen** to look at sth in one's own time; **immer mit der ~** (*inf*) don't panic.

Ruhe-: ~bank *f* bench, seat; **~bedürfnis** *nt* need for quiet/peace/rest; **r~bedürftig** *adj* in need of quiet/peace/rest; **~bett** *nt* bed; **~gehalt** *nt* (*form*) superannuation; **~geld** *nt* (*form*), ⚠**~genuß** *m* (*Aus*) pension; **~kissen** *nt* bolster; *siehe* **Gewissen**; **~lage** *f* (*von Mensch*) reclining position; (*Med: bei Bruch*) immobile position; (*Tech*) (*von Maschine*) resting position; (*von Zeiger*) neutral position; (*Unbeweglichkeit*) immobility; **sich in ~lage befinden** (*Mensch, Maschine*) to be at rest; (*Wein*) to be kept still; (*unbeweglich sein*) to be immobile; **r~liebend** *adj* fond of peace and quiet; **r~los** *adj* restless; **eine r~lose Zeit** a time of unrest; **~losigkeit** *f* restlessness; **~masse** *f* (*Phys*) rest mass.

ruhen [1] *vi* **(a)** (*aus~*) to rest ♦ **nach dem Essen soll man ruhn oder tausend Schritte tun** (*Prov*) after a meal one should either rest or take some exercise; **ich möchte etwas ~** I want to take a short rest, I want to rest a little; **nicht (eher) ~** *or* **nicht ~ und rasten, bis ...** (*fig*) not to rest until ...; **ich wünsche wohl zu ~!** (*form*) I wish you a good night (*form*); **(ich) wünsche, wohl geruht zu haben!** (*form*) I trust that you slept well (*form*).
(b) (*geh: liegen*) to rest (*an or auf +dat* on); (*Gebäude auch*) to be supported (*auf +dat* by); (*Fluch*) to lie (*auf +dat* on) ♦ **möge Gottes Segen auf dir ~** may God's blessing be with you; **auf ihm ruht ein Verdacht** suspicion hangs over him (*liter*).
(c) (*stillstehen*) to stop; (*Maschinen*) to stand idle; (*Arbeit auch, Verkehr*) to cease; (*Waffen*) to be laid down; (*unterbrochen sein: Verfahren, Verhandlung, Vertrag*) to be suspended ♦ **laß die Arbeit jetzt ~** (*geh*) leave your work now.
(d) (*tot und begraben sein*) to lie, to be buried ♦ **„hier ruht (in Gott) ..."** "here lies ..."; **„ruhe in Frieden!"** "Rest in Peace"; **„ruhe sanft!"** "rest eternal".
[2] *vr impers* **hier ruht es sich gut** this is good to rest on.

ruhend *adj* resting; *Kapital* dormant; *Maschinen* idle; *Verkehr* stationary ♦ **~e Venus** Venus reclining.

⚠**ruhenlassen** *vt sep irreg Vergangenheit, Angelegenheit* to let rest; *Verhandlungen, Prozeß* to adjourn; *Teig* to allow to rest.

Ruhe-: ~pause *f* break; (*wenig Betrieb, Arbeit*) slack *or* quiet period; **eine ~pause einlegen** to take *or* have a break; **~platz** *m* resting place; **~posten** *m* sinecure; **~punkt** *m* place of rest; **~raum** *m* rest room; **~sitz** *m* (*Haus*) retirement home; **er hat seinen ~sitz in Ehlscheid aufgeschlagen** he has retired to Ehlscheid; **~stand** *m* retirement; **im ~stand sein/leben** to be retired; **er ist Bankdirektor im ~stand** he is a retired bank director; **in den ~stand treten** *or* **gehen** to retire, to go into retirement; **jdn in den ~stand versetzen** to retire sb; **~ständler(in *f*)** *m* **-s, -** retired person; **~standsbeamte(r)** *m* retired civil servant; **~statt, ~stätte** *f* resting-place; **letzte ~stätte** last *or* final resting-place; **~stellung** *f* (*von Körper*) resting position; (*von beweglichem Gegenstand*) resting point; (*von Maschinen*) off position; **der Arm muß in ~stellung bleiben** the arm must not be moved; **r~störend** *adj* **r~störender Lärm** (*Jur*) disturbance of the peace; **~störer** *m* disturber of the peace; **~störung** *f* (*Jur*) disturbance of the peace; **~tag** *m* rest-day, day off; (*von Geschäft etc*) closing day; **einen ~tag einlegen** to have a day's rest, to take a day off; **„Mittwoch ~tag"** "closed (on) Wednesdays"; **~zeit** *f* rest period; (*Saison*) off-season.

ruhig [1] *adj* **(a)** (*still*) quiet; *Wetter, Meer* calm ♦ **seid ~!** be quiet!; **ihr sollt ~ sein!** (will you) be quiet!; **sitz doch ~!** sit still!
(b) (*geruhsam*) quiet; *Urlaub, Feiertage, Leben auch* peaceful; *Farbe* restful; (*ohne Störung*) *Überfahrt, Verlauf* smooth; (*Tech auch*) smooth ♦ **gegen 6 Uhr wird es ~er** it quietens down around 6 o'clock; **das Flugzeug liegt ~ in der Luft** the plane is flying smoothly; **alles geht seinen ~en Gang** everything is going smoothly.
(c) (*gelassen*) calm; *Gewissen* easy ♦ **nur ~ (Blut)!** keep calm, take it easy (*inf*); **bei ~er Überlegung** on (mature) consideration; **du wirst auch noch ~er!** you'll calm down one day; **du kannst/Sie können ganz ~ sein** I can assure you.
(d) (*sicher*) *Hand, Blick* steady.
(e) (*teilnahmslos*) calm ♦ **etw ~ mitansehen** to stand by and watch sth; **~ dabeistehen** just to stand by.
[2] *adv* **du kannst ~ hierbleiben** feel free to stay here, you're welcome to stay here if you want; **ihr könnt ~ gehen, ich passe schon auf** you just go and I'll look after things; **man kann ~ behaupten/sagen/annehmen, daß ...** (*mit Recht*) one may well assert/say/assume that ..., one need have no hesitation in *or* about asserting/saying/assuming that ...; **die können ~ etwas mehr zahlen** (*leicht*) they could easily pay a little more; **wir können ~ darüber sprechen** we can talk about it if you want; **du könntest ~ mal etwas für mich tun!** it's about time you did something for me!

Ruhm *m* **-es,** *no pl* glory; (*Berühmtheit*) fame; (*Lob*) praise ♦ **des ~es voll sein** to be full of praise (*über +acc* for); **mit etw keinen ~ ernten** (*inf*) not to win any medals with *or* for sth; **sich in seinem ~ sonnen** to rest on one's laurels; *siehe* **bekleckern**.

ruhmbedeckt *adj* covered with glory.

rühmen [1] *vt* (*preisen, empfehlen*) to praise, to sing the praises of; *Tugenden, Schönheit auch* to extol ♦ **jdn ~d erwähnen** to give sb an honourable mention; **etw ~d hervorheben** to single sth out for *or* give sth special praise.
[2] *vr* **sich einer Sache** (*gen*) **~** (*prahlen*) to boast about sth; (*stolz sein*) to pride oneself on sth; **sich einer Sache** (*gen*) **~ können** to be able to boast of sth; **die Stadt rühmt sich eines eigenen Schwimmbads** (*iro*) the town boasts its own swimming pool; **ohne mich zu ~** without wishing to boast.

rühmenswert *adj* praiseworthy, laudable.

Ruhmes-: ~blatt *nt* (*fig*) glorious chapter; **~halle** *f* hall of fame; **~tag** *m* glorious day; **~tat** *f* glorious deed.

rühmlich *adj* praiseworthy, laudable; *Ausnahme* notable ♦ **kein ~es Ende finden** *or* **nehmen** to meet a bad end; **sich ~ hervortun** to distinguish oneself.

Ruhm-: r~los *adj* inglorious; **r~reich** *adj* (*liter*) glorious; **~sucht** *f* thirst for glory; **r~süchtig** *adj* thirsting for glory; **r~voll** *adj* glorious.

Ruhr[1] *f* - (*Geog*) Ruhr.

Ruhr[2] *f* **-,** *no pl* (*Krankheit*) dysentery.

Rühr|ei *nt* scrambled egg; (*als Gericht*) scrambled eggs *pl*.

rühren [1] *vi* **(a)** (*um~*) to stir.
(b) **an etw** (*acc*) **~** (*anfassen*) to touch sth; (*fig: erwähnen*) to touch on sth; **daran wollen wir nicht ~** let's not go into it; (*in bezug auf Vergangenes*) let sleeping dogs lie; **rühret nicht daran!** (*liter*) let us not dwell on that.
(c) **von etw ~** to stem from sth; **das rührt daher, daß ...** that is because ...; **daher rührt sein Mißtrauen!** so that is the reason for his distrust!
[2] *vt* **(a)** (*um~*) *Teig, Farbe* to stir; (*schlagen*) *Eier* to beat.
(b) (*bewegen*) to move ♦ **er rührte kein Glied** he didn't stir at all; **er rührte keinen Finger** *or* **keine Hand, um mir zu helfen** (*inf*) he didn't lift a finger to help me (*inf*).
(c) (*Gemüt bewegen*) to move; *Herz* to stir ♦ **das kann mich nicht ~!** that leaves me cold; (*stört mich nicht*) that doesn't bother me; **jdn zu Tränen ~** to move sb to tears; **sie war äußerst gerührt** she was extremely moved *or* touched.
(d) (*Mus*) *Trommel* to strike, to beat.
(e) **ihn hat der Schlag gerührt** (*inf*) he was thunderstruck; **ich glaubte, mich rührt der Schlag** (*inf*) you could have knocked me down with a feather (*inf*); *siehe* **Donner**.
[3] *vr* **(a)** (*sich bewegen*) (*Blatt, Mensch*) to stir; (*Körperteil*) to move; (*sich von der Stelle bewegen*) to move; (*aktiv sein*) to buck up (*inf*); (*sich beeilen*) to bestir oneself, to get a move on (*inf*) ♦ **rührt Euch!** (*Mil*) at ease!; **~ lassen** (*Mil*) to give the order to stand at ease; **kein Lüftchen rührte sich** the air was still, there was not the slightest breeze; **er rührt sich nicht mehr** (*inf*) he won't get up again; **hier kann man sich nicht ~** you can't move in here; **nichts hat sich gerührt** nothing happened.
(b) (*Gewissen, Mitleid, Reue*) to stir, to be awakened; (*inf: sich melden*) to say something ♦ **sie hat sich schon 2 Jahre nicht gerührt** (*inf*) I haven't heard from her for 2 years.

Rühren *nt* **-s,** *no pl* stirring ♦ **ein menschliches ~ (verspüren)** (to feel) a stirring of human pity; (*hum*) (to have to answer) a *or* the call of nature (*hum*).

rührend *adj* touching ♦ **das ist ~ von Ihnen** that is sweet of you.

Ruhrgebiet *nt* Ruhr (area).

rührig *adj* active.

ruhrkrank *adj* suffering from dysentery.

Rühr-: ~löffel *m* mixing spoon; **~maschine** *f* mixer; (*in Bäckerei*) mixing machine; **~michnichtan** *nt* **-, -** (*Bot*) touch-me-not.

Ruhrpott *m* (*inf*) Ruhr (Basin *or* Valley).

Rühr-: r~selig *adj* (*pej*) touching, tear-jerking (*pej inf*); **~seligkeit** *f, no pl* sentimentality; **~stück** *nt* (*Theat*) melodrama; **~teig** *m* sponge mixture.

Rührung *f, no pl* emotion ♦ **vor ~ nicht sprechen können** to be choked with emotion.

Ruin *m* **-s,** *no pl* ruin ♦ **vor dem ~ stehen** to be on the brink *or* verge of ruin; **seinem/dem ~ entgegengehen** to be on the way to ruin; **das ist mein ~!** that will be my ruin *or* the ruin of me; **du bist noch mein ~!** (*hum inf*) you'll be the ruin of me.

Ruine *f* **-, -n** (*lit, fig*) ruin.

Ruinen-: ~feld *nt* sea of debris; **r~haft** *adj* ruined; **~stadt** *f* ruined city.

ruinieren* *vt* to ruin ♦ **sich ~** to ruin oneself.

ruinös *adj* ruinous.

Rülps *m* **-es, -e** (*dial*) *siehe* **Rülpser**.

rülpsen *vi* to belch ♦ **das R~** belching.

Rülpser *m* **-s, -** (*inf*) belch.

Rülpswasser *nt* (*sl*) gassy stuff (*inf*).

rum *adv* (*inf*) *siehe* **herum**.

Rum [(*S Ger, Aus auch*) ru:m] *m* **-s, -s** rum.

Rumäne *m* **-n, -n, Rumänin** *f* Romanian.

Rumänien [-iən] *nt* **-s** Romania.

rumänisch *adj* Romanian.

Rumänisch(e) *nt* Romanian; *siehe auch* **Deutsch(e)**.

Rumba *f* **-, -s** *or* (*inf*) *m* **-s, -s** rumba ♦ **~ tanzen** to (dance the) rumba.

⚠: Informationen zur Rechtschreibreform im Anhang

Rumbakugel, Rumbarassel *f* maraca.

rumflachsen *vi sep* (*inf*) to have a laugh, to joke around.

rumkommen *vi sep irreg* (*inf*) **(a)** *siehe* **herumkommen. (b) dabei kommt nichts rum** nothing will come out of it.

rumkriegen *vt sep* (*inf*) **jdn ~** to talk sb round.

Rummel *m* **-s,** *no pl* **(a)** (*inf*) (*Betrieb*) (hustle and) bustle; (*Getöse*) racket (*inf*); (*Aufheben*) fuss (*inf*) ◆ **der ganze ~** the whole business *or* carry-on (*inf*); **den ~ kennen** to know all about it; **großen ~ um jdn/etw machen** to make a great fuss *or* to-do about sb/sth (*inf*).
(b) (*~platz*) fair ◆ **auf den ~ gehen** to go to the fair.

Rummelplatz *m* (*inf*) fairground.

Rummy ['rœmi] *nt* **-s, -s** (*Aus*) rummy.

rumoren* [1] *vi* to make a noise; (*Mensch*) to rumble about; (*Bauch*) to rumble; (*Gewissen*) to play up; (*Gedanke*) to float about ◆ **etw rumort in den Köpfen** sth is going through people's minds.
[2] *vi impers* **es rumort in meinem Magen** *or* **Bauch** *or* **mir im Leib** my stomach's rumbling; **es rumort im Volk** (*fig*) there is growing unrest among the people.

rump(e)lig *adj* (*inf*) *siehe* **holp(e)rig.**

Rumpelkammer *f* (*inf*) junk room (*inf*).

rumpeln *vi* **(a)** (*Geräusch machen*) to rumble ◆ **er fiel ~d die Treppe hinunter** he fell down the stairs with a clatter. **(b)** *aux sein* (*sich polternd bewegen*) to rumble; (*Mensch*) to clatter.

Rumpelstilzchen *nt* **-s** Rumpelstiltskin.

Rumpf *m* **-(e)s, ¨-e** trunk; (*Sport*) body; (*von geschlachtetem Tier*) carcass; (*Statue*) torso; (*von Schiff*) hull; (*von Flugzeug*) fuselage ◆ **~ beugt/streckt!** (*Sport*) bend/stretch.

Rumpfbeuge *f* forward bend.

rümpfen *vt* **die Nase ~** to turn up one's nose (*über +acc* at).

Rumpfparlament *nt* (*Hist*) Rump (Parliament).

Rumpsteak ['rumpste:k] *nt* rump steak.

rums *interj* bang.

Rum-: ~topf *m* rumpot (*soft fruit in rum*); **~verschnitt** *m* blended rum.

Run [ran] *m* **-s, -s** run (*auf +acc* on).

rund [1] *adj* round; *Figur, Arme* plump; *Ton, Klang* full; *Wein* mellow ◆ **du wirst mit jedem Jahr ~er** you're getting bigger *or* plumper every year; **~e 50 Jahre/2000 Mark** a good 50 years/2,000 marks; **ein ~es Dutzend Leute** a dozen or more people; **das Kind machte ~e Augen** the child's eyes grew round; **Konferenz am ~en Tisch** round-table talks *pl*; **die Sache wird ~** it all works out.
[2] *adv* **(a)** (*herum*) (a)round ◆ **~ um** right (a)round; **~ um die Uhr** right (a)round the clock.
(b) (*ungefähr*) (round) about, roughly ◆ **~ gerechnet 200** call it 200.
(c) (*fig: glattweg*) *abschlagen, ablehnen* flatly.
(d) (*Aut*) **der Motor läuft ~** the engine runs smoothly.

Rund-: ~bank *f* circular bench; **~bau** *m* rotunda; **~blick** *m* panorama; **~bogen** *m* (*Archit*) round arch; **~brief** *m* circular.

Runde *f* **-, -n (a)** (*Gesellschaft*) company ◆ **sich zu einer gemütlichen ~ treffen** to meet informally.
(b) (*Rundgang*) walk, turn; (*von Wachmann*) rounds *pl*; (*von Briefträger etc*) round ◆ **die/seine ~ machen** to do the/one's rounds; (*Gastgeberin*) to circulate; (*herumgegeben werden*) to be passed round; **das Gerücht machte die ~** the rumour did the rounds *or* went around; **eine ~ durch die Lokale machen** to go on a pub crawl; **eine ~ machen** to go for a walk; (*mit Fahrzeug*) to go for a ride; **eine ~ um etw machen** to go for a walk *or* take a turn round sth; (*mit Fahrzeug*) to ride round sth; **zwei ~n um etw machen** to do two circuits of sth.
(c) (*Sport*) (*bei Rennen*) lap; (*von Turnier, Wettkampf*) round; (*Gesprächs~, Verhandlungs~*) round ◆ **seine ~n drehen** *or* **ziehen** to do one's laps; **über die ~n kommen** (*Sport, fig*) to pull through; **etw über die ~n bringen** (*fig*) to manage sth, to get through sth; **eine ~ schlafen** (*inf*) to have a kip (*inf*).
(d) (*von Getränken*) round ◆ **(für jdn) eine ~ spendieren** *or* **ausgeben** *or* **schmeißen** (*sl*) to buy *or* stand (sb) a round.
(e) (*liter: Umkreis*) surroundings *pl* ◆ **in die/der ~** round about.

runden [1] *vt Lippen* to round.
[2] *vr* (*lit: rund werden*) (*Bauch*) to become round; (*Gesicht auch*) to become full; (*Lippen*) to grow round; (*fig: konkrete Formen annehmen*) to take shape ◆ **sich zu etw ~** (*fig*) to develop into sth.

Rund-: △**~erlaß** *m* circular (directive); **r~erneuern*** *vt sep infin, ptp only* to remould; **r~erneuerte Reifen** remoulds; **~erneuerung** *f* remoulding; **~fahrt** *f* tour; **eine ~fahrt machen/an einer ~fahrt teilnehmen** to go on a tour; **~flug** *m* (*Besichtigungsflug*) sightseeing flight; (*Reiseroute*) round trip; **~frage** *f* survey (*an +acc, unter +dat* of).

Rundfunk *m* broadcasting; (*besonders Hörfunk*) radio, wireless (*esp Brit dated*); (*Organisation*) broadcasting company *or* corporation ◆ **der ~ überträgt etw** sth is broadcast; **im/über ~** on the radio; **~ hören** to listen to the radio; **beim ~ arbeiten** *or* **(tätig) sein** to work *or* be in broadcasting.

Rundfunk- *in cpds* radio; **~ansager** *m* (radio) announcer; **~anstalt** *f* broadcasting corporation; **~durchsage** *f* special announcement (on the radio); **~empfang** *m* radio reception; **~empfänger** *m* radio receiver; **~gebühr** *f* radio licence fee; **~gerät** *nt* radio set; **~gesellschaft** *f* broadcasting company; **~hörer** *m* (radio) listener; **~programm** *nt* (*Kanal, inf: Sendung*) radio programme; (*Sendefolge*) radio programmes; (*gedrucktes ~programm*) radio programme guide; **~satellit** *m* TV satellite; **~sender** *m* **(a)** (*Sendeanlage*) radio transmitter; **(b)** (*Sendeanstalt*) radio station; **~sendung** *f* radio programme; **~sprecher** *m* radio announcer; **~station** *f* radio station; **~technik** *f* radiotechnology; **~techniker** *m* radio engineer; **~teilnehmer** *m* owner of a radio set; **~übertragung** *f* radio broadcast; **~zeitschrift** *f* radio programme guide.

Rundgang *m* (*Spaziergang*) walk; (*zur Besichtigung*) tour (*durch* of); (*von Wachmann*) rounds *pl*; (*von Briefträger etc*) round ◆ **einen ~ machen** to go for a walk; to go on a tour; **seinen ~ machen** to do one's rounds/round.

rundgehen *vi sep irreg* (*inf*) **(a) jetzt geht's rund** this is where the fun starts (*inf*); **wenn er das erfährt, geht's rund** there'll be all hell let loose when he finds out (*inf*); **es geht rund, wenn sie zu Besuch kommen** there's never a dull moment when they come to visit; **es geht rund im Büro** there's a lot on at the office.
(b) (*herumgehen*) to do the rounds ◆ **die Neuigkeit ist schon rundgegangen** the news has already got round.

Rund-: ~gesang *m* (*Mus*) chorus song (*in which a different person sings each verse*); (*Kanon*) round; **~halspullover** *m* crewneck sweater; **~heit** *f* roundness; **r~heraus** *adv* flatly, bluntly, straight out; **r~heraus gesagt** frankly; **r~herum** *adv* all round; (*fig inf: völlig*) totally; **~kopfschraube** *f* round-headed *or* button-head (*US*) screw; **~kurs** *m* circuit; **r~lich** *adj* plump; **~lichkeit** *f* plumpness; **~ling** *m circular village grouped round a green,* nuclear village; **~reise** *f* tour (*durch* of); **~rücken** *m* (*Med*) round shoulders *pl*; **~ruf** *m* **per ~ruf** with a series of phonecalls; **~schädel** *m* shorthead; **~schau** *f* (*Rad, TV*) magazine programme; **~schnitt** *m* round haircut; **~schreiben** *nt* circular; **~sicht** *f* panorama; **~stricknadel** *f* circular needle; **~stück** *nt* (*N Ger*) roll.

rundum *adv* all around; (*fig*) completely, totally.

Rundum-: ~schlag *m* (*lit, fig*) sweeping blow; **~sicht** *f* panoramic view.

Rundung *f* curve.

Rund-: ~wanderweg *m* circular route; **r~weg** *adv siehe* **r~heraus; ~zange** *f* round-nosed pliers *pl*.

Rune *f* **-, -n** rune.

Runen- *in cpds* runic; **~reihe** *f* runic alphabet; **~schrift** *f* runic writing; **~stein** *m* rune-stone; **~zeichen** *nt* runic character.

Runge *f* **-, -n** stake.

Runkelrübe *f*, **Runkel** *f* **-, -n** (*Aus*) mangel-wurzel.

Runologe *m*, **Runologin** *f* runologist.

runter *adv* (*inf*) *siehe* **herunter, hinunter** ◆ **~!** down!

runter- *pref* (*inf*) down; **~hauen** *vt sep* (*inf*) **(a)** (*ohrfeigen*) **jdm eine** *or* **ein paar ~hauen** to give sb a clip round the ear; **(b)** (*schreiben*) **einen Text ~hauen** to bang out a text (*inf*); **~holen** *vt sep* to get down; **jdm/sich einen ~holen** (*sl*) to jerk sb/(oneself) off (*sl*); **~kommen** *vi sep irreg aux sein* (*sl: von Drogen*) to come off drugs/heroin *etc*; **~lassen** *vt sep irreg siehe* **herunterlassen; die Hosen ~lassen** (*sl*) to come clean (*inf*); △**~sein** *vi sep irreg aux sein* (*Zusammenschreibung nur bei infin und ptp*) (*inf*) (*erschöpft sein*) to be run down; (*sl: vom Rauschgift etc*) to be off drugs/heroin *etc*; **gesundheitlich ~sein** to be under the weather (*inf*), to feel off (*inf*); **mit den Nerven ~sein** to be at the end of one's tether (*inf*).

Runzel *f* **-, -n** wrinkle; (*auf Stirn auch*) line ◆ **~n bekommen** (*Mensch*) to get wrinkles; (*Haut*) to get *or* become wrinkled.

runz(e)lig *adj* wrinkled; *Stirn auch* lined.

runzeln [1] *vt Stirn* to wrinkle, to crease; *Brauen* to knit.
[2] *vr* to become wrinkled.

runzlig *adj siehe* **runz(e)lig.**

Rüpel *m* **-s, -** lout, yob(bo) (*Brit sl*).

Rüpelei *f* (*rüpelhafte Art*) loutishness; (*rüpelhafte Handlung/Bemerkung*) loutish act/remark *etc.*

rüpelhaft *adj* loutish.

rupfen *vt Gänse, Hühner, Enten* to pluck; *Gras, Unkraut* to pull up ◆ **jdn ~** (*fig inf*) to fleece sb (*inf*), to take sb to the cleaners (*inf*); **wie ein gerupftes Huhn aussehen** to look like a shorn sheep; *siehe* **Hühnchen.**

Rupfen *m* **-s, -** (*Tex*) gunny; (*für Wandbehänge*) hessian.

Rupie ['ru:piə] *f* rupee.

ruppig *adj* (*grob*) rough; *Benehmen, Antwort* gruff; *Äußeres* scruffy (*inf*); *Autofahren* wild ◆ **~ spielen** to play rough.

Ruprecht *m* Rupert; *siehe* **Knecht.**

Rüsche *f* **-, -n** ruche, frill.

Rush-hour ['rʌʃ-auə] *f* **-,** *no pl* rush hour.

Ruß *m* **-es,** *no pl* soot; (*von Kerze*) smoke; (*von Petroleumlampe*) lampblack.

rußbedeckt *adj* covered in *or* with soot.

Russe *m* **-n, -n** Russian, Russian man/boy.

Rüssel *m* **-s, -** snout (*auch sl: Nase*); (*Elefanten~*) trunk; (*von Insekt*) proboscis.

rüsselförmig *adj* snoutlike; trunklike; proboscidean (*spec*).

rußen [1] *vi* (*Öllampe, Kerze*) to smoke; (*Ofen*) to produce soot ◆ **es rußt** there's a lot of soot; **eine stark ~de Lampe** a very smoky lamp.
[2] *vt* (*Sw, S Ger*) **den Ofen/den Kamin ~** to clean the soot out of the stove/to sweep the chimney.

Russen-: r~freundlich *adj* pro-Russian; **ein r~freundlicher Mensch** a Russophile; **~kittel** *m* smock; **~stiefel** *m* Cossack boot.

Ruß-: r~farben, r~farbig *adj* soot-black; **~fleck** *m* sooty mark; **~flocke** *f* soot particle; **r~geschwärzt** *adj* soot-blackened.

rußig *adj* sooty.

Russin *f* Russian, Russian woman/girl.

russisch *adj* Russian ◆ **~es Roulett** Russian roulette; **~e Eier** (*Cook*) egg(s) mayonnaise; **~er Salat** (*Cook*) Russian salad; **R~es Brot** (*Cook*) alphabet biscuits.

Russisch(e) *nt* Russian; *siehe auch* **Deutsch(e).**

⚠ **Rußland** *nt* **-s** Russia.

rüsten [1] *vi* (*Mil*) to arm ◆ **zum Krieg/Kampf ~** to arm for war/battle; **gut/ schlecht gerüstet sein** to be well/badly armed; **um die Wette ~** to be involved in an arms race.
[2] *vr* to prepare (*zu* for); (*lit, fig: sich wappnen*) to arm oneself (*gegen* for) ◆ **sich zur Abreise/zum Fest ~** to get ready to leave/to prepare for the festival.
[3] *vt* **(a)** (*old: vorbereiten*) to prepare; *Nachtlager auch* to make ready.
(b) (*Build*) *Haus* to scaffold.

Rüster *f* **-, -n** elm.

rüstern *adj attr* elm.

Rüster(n)holz *nt* elm(wood).

rüstig *adj* sprightly.

Rüstigkeit *f* sprightliness.

rustikal *adj* rustic ◆ **sich ~ einrichten** to furnish one's home in a rustic *or* farmhouse style.

Rüstkammer *f* (*Mil, fig*) armoury.

Rüstung *f* **(a)** (*das Rüsten*) armament; (*Waffen*) arms *pl*, weapons *pl*. **(b)** (*Ritter~*) armour.

Rüstungs- *in cpds* arms; **~begrenzung** *f* arms limitation; **~begrenzungsverhandlungen** *pl* arms limitation talks *pl*; **~beschränkung** *f siehe* **~begrenzung**; **~betrieb** *m*, **~fabrik** *f* armaments *or* ordnance factory; **~gegner** *m* supporter of disarmament; **~industrie** *f* armaments industry; **~kontrolle** *f* arms control; **~kontrollverhandlungen** *pl* arms control talks *pl*; **~produktion** *f* arms production; **~wettlauf** *m* arms race.

Rüstzeug *nt, no pl* **(a)** (*old*) *siehe* **Handwerkszeug. (b)** (*fig*) qualifications *pl*.

Rute *f* **-, -n (a)** (*Gerte*) switch; (*esp Stock zum Züchtigen*) cane, rod; (*Birken~*) birch (rod); (*von Gertenbündel*) birch ◆ **jdn mit einer ~ schlagen** to cane/birch sb, to beat sb with a cane/birch; **mit eiserner ~ regieren** (*fig*) to rule with a rod of iron.
(b) (*Wünschel~*) (divining *or* dowsing) rod; (*Angel~*) (fishing) rod ◆ **mit der ~ gehen** to go divining.
(c) (*Hunt: Schwanz*) tail.
(d) (*Tierpenis*) penis; (*sl: von Mann*) cock (*vulg*), prick (*vulg*).
(e) (*Aus: Schneebesen*) whisk.
(f) (*old: Measure*) rod.

Ruten-: ~bündel *nt* (*Hist*) fasces *pl*; **~gänger(in** *f***)** *m* **-s, -** diviner, dowser; **~gehen** *nt* dowsing; **~hieb** *m* stroke (of the birch).

Ruthenium *nt, no pl* (*abbr* **Ru**) ruthenium.

Rütlischwur *m* (*Hist*) *oath taken on the Rütli Mountain by the founders of Switzerland.*

rutsch *interj* whee, whoomph.

Rutsch *m* **-es, -e** slip, slide, fall; (*Erd~*) landslide; (*von Steinen*) rockfall; (*fig Pol*) shift, swing; (*inf: Ausflug*) trip, outing ◆ **guten ~!** (*inf*) have a good new year!; **in einem ~** in one go.

Rutschbahn *f*, **Rutsche** *f* **-, -n** (*Mech*) chute; (*Kinder~*) slide.

rutschen *vi aux sein* **(a)** (*gleiten*) to slide; (*aus~, entgleiten*) to slip; (*Aut*) to skid; (*fig: Preise, Kurse*) to slip; (*Regime, Hierarchie*) to crumble ◆ **auf dem Stuhl hin und her ~** to fidget *or* shift around on one's chair.
(b) (*inf: rücken*) to move *or* shove (*inf*) up ◆ **zur Seite ~** to move *or* shove (*inf*) up *or* over; **ein Stück(chen) ~** to move *or* shove (*inf*) up a bit.
(c) (*herunter~*) to slip down; (*Essen, Tablette*) to go down; *siehe* **Herz.**
(d) (*auf Rutschbahn*) to slide ◆ **darf ich mal ~?** can I have a go on the slide?
(e) (*~d kriechen*) to crawl ◆ **auf den Knien gerutscht kommen** (*fig inf*) to go down on one's bended knees; **auf den Knien ~** (*lit*) to move along on one's knees.

Rutscher *m* **-s, -** (*Aus*) (*Abstecher*) small detour; (*kleine Strecke*) stone's throw.

Rutsch-: r~fest *adj* non-slip; **~gefahr** *f* danger of skidding; **„~gefahr"** "slippery road".

rutschig *adj* slippery, slippy (*inf*).

Rutsch-: ~partie *f* (*hum inf*) (*das Ausrutschen*) slip; (*von Auto*) skid; (*auf ~bahn*) slide; **eine ~partie machen** (*ausrutschen*) to slip; (*mit Auto*) to skid; (*auf ~bahn*) to slide; **das war eine schöne ~partie** (*auf vereister Straße*) we were sliding all over the place; **r~sicher** *adj* non-slip.

Rüttelei *f* shaking; (*von Fahrzeug, Zug*) jolting; (*von Fenstern, Türen*) rattling ◆ **die Fahrt war eine einzige ~** we were jolted about the whole way.

rütteln [1] *vt* to shake (about); *Getreide etc* to riddle, to sieve ◆ **jdn am Arm/an der Schulter ~** to shake sb's arm/shoulder, to shake sb by the arm/ shoulder.
[2] *vi* to shake; (*Fahrzeug*) to jolt; (*Fenster, Tür: im Wind*) to rattle ◆ **an etw** (*dat*) **~** *an Tür, Fenster etc* to rattle (at) sth; (*fig*) *an Grundsätzen, Glauben* to shake sth; **daran ist nicht** *or* **daran gibt es nichts zu ~** (*inf*) there's no doubt about that.

Rüttelsieb *nt* sieve, riddle.

S

S, s [ɛs] *nt* **-, -** S, s.
S *abbr of* **Süden** S.
S. *abbr of* **Seite** p.
s. *abbr of* **siehe** see.
SA [ɛs'|aː] *f* **-,** *no pl (NS) abbr of* **Sturmabteilung.**
s.a. *abbr of* **siehe auch.**
Saal *m* **-(e)s, Säle** hall; (*für Sitzungen etc*) room; (*Lese~*) reading room; (*Tanz~, Ball~*) ballroom; (*für Hochzeiten, Empfänge*) function suite; (*Theater~*) auditorium.
Saal-: ~ordner *m* usher; **~schlacht** *f (inf)* brawl, punch-up (*inf*); **~tochter** *f (Sw)* waitress.
Saar *f* - Saar.
Saar-: ~gebiet, ~land *nt* Saarland; **~länder(in** *f*) *m* **-s, -** Saarlander; **s~ländisch** *adj* (of the) Saarland.
Saat *f* **-, -en (a)** (*das Säen*) sowing.
(b) (*Samen, ~gut*) seed(s) (*auch fig*) ◆ **wenn die ~ aufgeht** (*lit*) when the seed begins to grow; (*fig*) when the seeds bear fruit; **die ~ für etw legen** (*fig*) to sow the seed(s) of sth; **wie die ~, so die Ernte** (*prov*)/**ohne ~ keine Ernte** (*prov*) as you sow, so shall you reap (*Prov*).
(c) (*junges Getreide*) young crop(s), seedlings *pl*.
Saatenstand *m* state of the crop(s).
Saat-: ~feld *nt* cornfield (*Brit*), grainfield; **~gut** *nt, no pl* seed(s); **~kartoffel** *f* seed potato; **~korn** *nt* seed corn; **~krähe** *f* rook; **~zeit** *f* seedtime, sowing time.
Saba *nt* **-s** (*Hist*) Sheba ◆ **die Königin von ~** the Queen of Sheba.
Sabbat *m* **-s, -e** Sabbath.
Sabbat-: ~jahr *nt (Rel)* sabbatical year; **~schänder** *m* **-s, -** desecrator of the Sabbath.
Sabbel *m* **-s,** *no pl (dial) siehe* **Sabber.**
sabbeln *vti (dial) siehe* **sabbern.**
Sabber *m* **-s,** *no pl (dial)* slobber, saliva, slaver.
Sabberei *f (inf) (dial)* slobbering; (*fig: Geschwätz*) drivel (*inf*).
Sabberlätzchen *nt (dial)* bib.
sabbern (*inf*) [1] *vi* to slobber, to slaver ◆ **vor sich hin ~** (*fig*) to mutter away to oneself. [2] *vt* to blather (*inf*) ◆ **dummes Zeug ~** to talk drivel (*inf*).
Säbel *m* **-s, -** sabre; (*Krumm~*) scimitar ◆ **jdn auf ~ fordern** to challenge sb to a (sabre) duel; **mit dem ~ rasseln** (*fig*) to rattle the sabre.
Säbel-: ~beine *pl (inf)* bow *or* bandy legs *pl*; **s~beinig** *adj (inf)* bow-legged, bandy-legged; **~fechten** *nt* sabre fencing; **~gerassel** *nt siehe* **~rasseln;** **~hieb** *m* stroke of one's sabre.
säbeln (*inf*) [1] *vt* to saw away at.
[2] *vi* to saw away (*an +dat* at).
Säbel-: ~rasseln *nt* **-s,** *no pl* sabre-rattling; **s~rasselnd** *adj* sabre-rattling; ⚠**~raßler(in** *f*) *m* **-s, -** sabre-rattler.
Sabinerinnen *pl* **der Raub der ~** the rape of the Sabines *or* the Sabine women.
Sabotage [zabo'taːʒə] *f* **-, -n** sabotage ◆ **~ treiben** to perform acts of sabotage.
Sabotage|akt *m* act of sabotage.
Saboteur(in *f*) [-'tøːɐ, -'tøːrɪn] *m* saboteur.
sabotieren* *vt* to sabotage.
Sa(c)charin *nt* **-s,** *no pl* saccharin.
Sach-: ~anlagevermögen *nt (Econ)* tangible fixed assets *pl*; **~bearbeiter** *m* specialist; (*Beamter*) official in charge (*für* of); **der ~bearbeiter für Anträge ist nicht da** the person who deals with applications isn't here; **~bereich** *m* (specialist) area; **~beschädigung** *f* damage to property; **s~bezogen** *adj Wissen, Fragen, Angaben* relevant, pertinent; **~buch** *nt* non-fiction book; **s~dienlich** *adj* useful; **es ist nicht s~dienlich, wenn ...** it won't help the matter if ...
▼ **Sache** *f* **-, -n (a)** thing; (*Gegenstand auch*) object; (*Jur: Eigentum*) article of property. **~n** *pl (inf: Zeug)* things *pl*; (*Jur*) property ◆ **der Mensch wird zur ~** man is reduced to *or* becomes an object; **das liegt in der Natur der ~** that's in the nature of things; **~n gibt's(, die gibt's gar nicht)!** (*inf*) would you credit it! (*inf*).
▼ **(b)** (*Angelegenheit*) matter; (*Rechtsstreit, ~fall*) case; (*Aufgabe*) job ◆ **eine ~ der Polizei/der Behörden** a matter for the police/authorities; **es ist ~ der Polizei/der Behörden, das zu tun** it's up to the police/authorities *or* it's for the police/authorities to do that; **das mit dem Präsidenten war eine unangenehme ~** that was an unpleasant business with the president; **das ist eine ganz tolle/unangenehme ~** it's really fantastic/unpleasant; **die ~ macht sich** (*inf*) things are coming along; **ich habe mir die ~ anders vorgestellt** I had imagined things differently; **das ist eine andere ~** that's a different matter, that's a different kettle of fish (*inf*); **das ist meine/seine ~** that's my/his affair *or* business; **in ~n** *or* **in der ~ A gegen B** (*Jur*) in the case (of) A versus B; **das ist nicht jedermanns ~** it's not everyone's cup of tea (*inf*); **er versteht seine ~** he knows what he's doing *or* what he's about (*inf*); **er macht seine ~ gut** he's doing very well; (*beruflich*) he's doing a good job; **diese Frage können wir nicht hier mitbesprechen, das ist eine ~ für sich** we can't discuss this question now, it's a separate issue all to itself; **und was hat deine Frau gesagt?/was meinen Sie zu diesen Streiks? — das ist eine ~ für sich** and what did your wife say?/what do you think about these strikes? — that's another story; **das ist so eine ~** (*inf*) it's a bit tricky, it's a bit of a problem; **das ist 'ne ~** (*inf: prima*) great (*inf*); **der ~ zuliebe** for the love of it; **die ~ mit der Bank ist also geplatzt** so the bank job fell through; **er ist für illegale ~n nicht zu haben** you won't get him to do anything illegal; **solche ~n liegen mir nicht** I don't like things like that.
(c) (*Vorfall*) business, affair. **~n** *pl (Vorkommnisse)* things *pl* ◆ **die ~ mit dem verschwundenen Schlüssel** the business *or* affair with the disappearing key; **machst du bei der ~ mit?** are you with us?; **bei der ~ mache ich nicht mit** I'll have nothing to do with it; **was hat die Polizei zu der ~ gesagt?** what did the police say about it *or* about all this business?; **das ist (eine) beschlossene ~** it's (all) settled; **die ~ hat geklappt/ist schiefgegangen** everything *or* it worked/went wrong; **mach keine ~n!** (*inf*) don't be silly *or* daft! (*inf*); **was machst du bloß für ~n!** (*inf*) the things you do!; **was sind denn das für ~n?** what's all this?
(d) (*Frage, Problem*) matter, question; (*Thema*) subject; (*Ideal, Anliegen*) cause ◆ **eine ~ der Erziehung/des Geschmacks** a matter *or* question of education/taste; **mehr kann ich zu der ~ nicht sagen** that's all I can say on the subject; **um die ~ herumreden** to talk (all) round the subject; **zur ~!** let's get on with it; (*Parl, Jur etc*) come to the point!; **das tut nichts zur ~** that doesn't matter; **sich (***dat***) seiner ~ sicher** *or* **gewiß sein** to be sure of one's ground; **bei der ~ sein** to be with it (*inf*), to be on the ball (*inf*); **sie war nicht bei der ~** her mind was elsewhere; **bei der ~ bleiben** to keep one's mind on the job; (*bei Diskussion*) to keep to the point.
(e) (*Sachlage*) things *pl, no art* ◆ **so steht die ~ also** so that's the way things are; **die ~ ist die, daß ...** the thing is that ...; **jdm sagen, was ~ ist** (*inf*) to tell sb what's what; **neben der ~ liegen** to be beside the point.
(f) (*Tempo*) **mit 60/100 ~n** (*inf*) at 60/100.
-sache *f in cpds* a matter of ...
Sach|einlage *f (Econ)* contribution in kind.
Sachenrecht *nt (Jur)* law of property.
Sachertorte *f a rich chocolate cake,* sachertorte.
Sach-: ~frage *f* factual question; **~- und Personalfragen** questions relating to work and to personnel matters; **s~fremd** *adj* irrelevant; **~gebiet** *nt* subject area; **s~gemäß, s~gerecht** *adj* proper; **bei s~gemäßer Anwendung** if used properly; **etw s~gemäß machen** to do sth properly; **~katalog** *m* subject index; **~kenner** *m* expert (*in +dat* on); **~kenner auf einem** *or* **für ein Gebiet sein** to be an expert in a field; **~kenntnis** *f* (*in bezug auf Wissensgebiet*) knowledge of the/his subject; (*in bezug auf ~lage*) knowledge of the facts; **~kunde** *f, no pl* **(a)** *siehe* **~kenntnis; (b)** (*Schulfach*) general knowledge; **s~kundig** *adj* (well-)informed *no adv*; **sich s~kundig machen** to inform oneself; **s~kundig antworten** to give an informed answer; **~kundige(r)** *mf decl as adj siehe* **~kenner**; **~lage** *f* situation, state of affairs; **~leistung** *f* payment in kind; (*bei Krankenkasse etc*) benefit in kind.
sachlich *adj* **(a)** (*faktisch*) *Irrtum, Angaben* factual; *Unterschied auch* material; *Grund, Einwand* practical; (*sachbezogen*) *Frage, Wissen* relevant ◆ **rein ~ hast du recht** from a purely factual point of view you are right.
(b) (*objektiv*) *Kritik, Bemerkung* objective; (*nüchtern, unemotional*) matter-of-fact ◆ **bleiben Sie mal ~** don't get carried away; (*nicht persönlich werden*) don't get personal, stay objective.
(c) (*schmucklos*) functional, businesslike.

➤ SPRACHE AKTIV: **Sache: b** → 33.2

sächlich *adj* (*Gram*) neuter.
Sachlichkeit *f* **(a)** *siehe adj (b)* objectivity; matter-of-factness ◆ **mit ~ kommt man weiter** you get on better if you stay objective. **(b)** (*Schmucklosigkeit*) functionality ◆ **die Neue ~** (*Art, Archit*) the new functionalism.
Sach-: ~mängel *pl* material defects *pl*; **~mängelhaftung** *f* liability for material defects; **~mittel** *pl* (*form*) materials *pl*; (*Zubehör*) equipment *no pl*; **~register** *nt* subject index; **~schaden** *m* damage (to property); **bei dem Unfall hatte ich nur ~schaden** only my car was damaged in the accident.
Sachse ['zaksə] *m* **-n, -n, Sächsin** ['zɛksın] *f* Saxon.
sächseln ['zɛksln] *vi* (*inf*) to speak with a Saxon accent *or* in the Saxon dialect.
Sachsen ['zaksn] *nt* **-s** Saxony.
Sachsen-Anhalt *nt* **-s** Saxony-Anhalt.
sächsisch ['zɛksıʃ] *adj* Saxon ◆ **~er Genitiv** Saxon genitive.
Sächsisch(e) ['zɛksıʃ(ə)] *nt* Saxon (dialect); *siehe auch* **Deutsch(e)**.
Sachspende *f* gift ◆ **wir bitten um Geld- und ~n** we are asking for donations of money, food and clothes.
sacht(e) *adj* (*leise*) soft; (*sanft*) gentle; (*vorsichtig*) cautious, careful; (*allmählich*) gentle, gradual ◆ **mit ~n Schritten** softly; **~, ~!** (*inf*) take it easy!
Sach-: ~verhalt *m* **-(e)s, -e** facts *pl* (of the case); **~verstand** *m* expertise; ⚠**~verständigenausschuß** *m* committee of experts; **~verständigengutachten** *nt* specialist report; **~verständige(r)** *mf decl as adj* expert, specialist; (*Jur*) expert witness; **~verzeichnis** *nt siehe* **~register**; **~walter(in *f*)** *m* **-s, -** (*geh*) (*Verwalter*) agent; (*Treuhänder*) trustee; (*fig: Fürsprecher*) champion; **~wert** *m* real *or* intrinsic value; **~werte** *pl* material assets *pl*; **~wörterbuch** *nt* specialist dictionary; **~wörterbuch der Kunst/Botanik** dictionary of art/botany, art/botanical dictionary; **~zwang** *m* practical constraint; **~zwängen unterliegen** *or* **unter ~zwängen** (*dat*) **stehen** to be constrained by circumstances.
Sack *m* **-(e)s, ¨-e** **(a)** sack; (*aus Papier, Plastik*) bag ◆ **drei ~ Kartoffeln/Kohlen** three sacks of potatoes/sacks *or* bags of coal; **in ~ und Asche** in sackcloth and ashes; **mit ~ und Pack** (*inf*) with bag and baggage; **den ~ schlägt man, und den Esel meint man** (*Prov*) to kick the dog and mean the master (*prov*); **ihr habt wohl (zu Hause) ¨-e vor der Tür** (*sl*) were you born in a field?; **ich habe in den ~ gehauen** (*sl*) I chucked it (in) (*sl*), I packed it in (*inf*); **jdn in den ~ stecken** (*fig inf*) to put sb in the shade.
(b) (*Anat, Zool*) sac.
(c) (*S Ger, Aus: Hosentasche*) (trouser (*Brit*) or pants *US*) pocket ◆ **Geld im ~ haben** to have money in one's pocket.
(d) (*vulg: Hoden*) balls *pl* (*sl*).
(e) (*sl: Kerl, Bursche*) sod (*Brit sl*), bastard (*sl*), cunt (*vulg*) ◆ **fauler ~** lazy bugger (*Brit sl*) *or* bastard (*sl*).
Sackbahnhof *m* terminus.
Säckel *m* **-s, -** (*S Ger*) (*Beutel*) bag; (*Hosentasche*) pocket; (*Geld~*) moneybag ◆ **tief in den ~ greifen müssen** to have to dig deep (into one's pockets); **sich** (*dat*) **den ~ füllen** to line one's (own) pockets; *siehe* **Staats~**.
sacken[1], **säckeln** (*dial*) *vt* to put into sacks, to sack.
sacken[2] *vi aux sein* (*lit, fig*) to sink; (*Flugzeug*) to lose height; (*durchhängen*) to sag ◆ **in die Knie ~** to sag at the knees.
sackerlot, sackerment *interj* (*old*) *siehe* **sapperlot**.
säckeweise *adj* by the sack/bag.
Sack-: s~förmig *adj* like a sack, sack-like; **~gasse** *f* dead end, blind alley, cul-de-sac (*esp Brit*); (*fig*) dead end; **in eine ~gasse geraten** (*fig*) to finish up a blind alley; (*Verhandlungen*) to reach an impasse; **in einer ~gasse stecken** (*fig*) to be (stuck) up a blind alley; (*mit Bemühungen etc*) to have come to a dead end; **~hüpfen** *nt* **-s,** *no pl* sack-race; **~karre** *f* barrow, hand-cart; **~kleid** *nt* sack dress; **~leinen** *nt*, **~leinwand** *f* sacking, burlap (*US*); **~pfeife** *f siehe* **Dudelsack**; **~träger** *m* carrier; **~tuch** *nt* **(a)** *siehe* **~leinen**; **(b)** (*S Ger, Aus, Sw: Taschentuch*) handkerchief.
Sadismus *m* **(a)** *no pl* sadism. **(b)** (*Handlung*) sadistic act.
Sadist(in *f*) *m* sadist.
sadistisch *adj* sadistic.
Sadomasochismus *m* sado-masochism.
säen *vti* to sow; (*fig*) to sow (the seeds of) ◆ **dünn** *or* **spärlich** *or* **nicht dick gesät** (*fig*) thin on the ground, few and far between.
Safari *f* **-, -s** safari ◆ **eine ~ machen** to go on safari.
Safari-: ~anzug *m* safari suit; **~park** *m* safari park.
Safe [ze:f] *m or nt* **-s, -s** safe.
Saffian *m* **-s,** *no pl*, **Saffianleder** *nt* morocco (leather).
Safran *m* **-s, -e** (*Krokus, Gewürz*) saffron.
safrangelb *adj* saffron (yellow).
Saft *m* **-(e)s, ¨-e** (*Obst~*) (fruit) juice; (*Pflanzen~*) sap; (*Braten~, Fleisch~*) juice; (*Flüssigkeit*) liquid; (*Husten~ etc*) syrup; (*Magen~*) juices *pl*; (*old: Körper~*) humour (*old*); (*inf: Strom, Benzin*) juice (*inf*) ◆ **roter ~** lifeblood; **Blut ist ein ganz besonderer ~** blood is a very special stuff; **der ~ der Reben** the juice of the grape; **im ~ stehen** (*liter*) to be full of sap; **die ¨-e der Natur** (*liter*) the vital forces of nature; **von ~ und Kraft** (*fig*) dynamic, vital, vibrant; **ohne ~ und Kraft** (*fig*) wishy-washy (*inf*), effete; *siehe* **schmoren**.
Saftbraten *m* (*Cook*) roast.
Säftchen *nt dim of* **Saft** (*Frucht~*) juice; (*pej: Arznei*) mixture, medicine.
saftig *adj* **(a)** (*voll Saft*) *Obst, Fleisch* juicy; *Wiese, Grün* lush. **(b)** (*inf: kräftig*) *Witz* juicy (*inf*); *Rechnung, Ohrfeige* hefty (*inf*); *Brief, Antwort, Ausdrucksweise* potent ◆ **da habe ich ihm einen ~en Brief geschrieben** so I wrote him a pretty potent letter *or* one hell of a letter (*inf*).
Saftigkeit *f* (*von Obst, Witz*) juiciness; (*von Wiese etc*) lushness.
Saft-: ~kur *f* fruit-juice diet; **~laden** *m* (*pej inf*) dump (*pej inf*); **s~los** *adj* not juicy, juiceless; **~presse** *f* fruit-press; **~sack** *m* (*sl*) stupid bastard (*sl*) *or* bugger (*Brit sl*); **~tag** *m* juice day; **einen ~tag haben/einlegen** to have a day on juices only.
saft- und kraftlos *adj* wishy-washy (*inf*), effete.
Saga *f* **-, -s** saga.
sagbar *adj* sayable.
Sage *f* **-, -n** legend; (*altnordische*) saga ◆ **es geht die ~, daß ...** legend has it that ...; (*Gerücht*) rumour has it that ...
Säge *f* **-, -n** **(a)** (*Werkzeug*) saw. **(b)** (*Aus: ~werk*) sawmill.
Säge-: ~blatt *nt* saw blade; **~bock** *m* sawhorse; **~fisch** *m* sawfish; **~maschine** *f* mechanical saw; **~mehl** *nt* sawdust; **~messer** *nt* serrated knife; **~mühle** *f* sawmill.
sagen *vt* **(a)** (*äußern*) to say ◆ **jdm etw ~** to say sth to sb; (*mitteilen, ausrichten*) to tell sb sth; **sich** (*dat*) **etw ~** to say sth to oneself; **das hättest du dir selbst ~ können** *or* **müssen!** you might have known *or* realised that!; **im Vertrauen gesagt** in confidence; **unter uns gesagt** between you and me (and the gatepost *hum inf*); **genauer/deutlicher gesagt** to put it more precisely/clearly; **könnten Sie mir ~ ...?** could you tell me ...?; **ich sag's ihm** I'll tell him; **sag mir, was du liest, und ich sage dir, wer du bist** (*prov*) tell me what you read and I'll tell you what kind of person you are; **jdm etw ~ lassen** to ask somebody to tell sb sth; **ich habe mir ~ lassen, ...** I've been told ...; **was ich mir von ihm nicht alles ~ lassen muß!** the things I have to take from him!; **das kann ich Ihnen nicht ~** I couldn't say, I don't know; **das kann ich noch nicht ~** (that) I can't say yet; **so was sagt man doch nicht!** you mustn't say things like that; (*bei Schimpfen, Fluchen*) (watch *or* mind your) language!; **sag nicht so etwas** *or* **so was!** (*inf*) don't say things like that!, don't talk like that!; **wie kannst du so etwas ~?** how can you say such things?; **das sage ich nicht!** I'm not saying *or* telling; **was ich noch ~ wollte, ...** (*inf*) there's something else I wanted to say ...; **oh, was ich noch ~ wollte, vergiß nicht ...** (*inf*) by the way, don't forget ...; **dann will ich nichts gesagt haben** in that case forget I said anything; **wie ich schon sagte** as I said before; **ich sage, wie es ist** I'm just telling you the way it is; **es ist nicht zu ~** it doesn't bear thinking about!; (*entrüstet*) there just aren't any words to describe it!; **um nicht zu ~** not to say, to call the shots (*inf*); **sag an, ...** (*old, liter*) pray tell (*old*).
(b) (*befehlen*) **jdm ~, er solle etw tun** to tell sb to do sth; **hat er im Betrieb etwas zu ~?** does he have a say in the firm?; **du hast hier (gar) nichts zu ~** that isn't for you to say; **das S~ haben** to have the say, to call the shots (*inf*); **hier habe ich das S~** what I say goes!; **laß dir von mir ~** *or* **gesagt sein, .../laß dir das gesagt sein** let me tell you, take it from me; **er läßt sich** (*dat*) **nichts ~** he won't be told, you can't tell him anything; **das laß ich mir von dem nicht ~** I won't take that from him; **sie ließen es sich** (*dat*) **nicht zweimal ~** they didn't need to be told a second time *or* to be told twice.
(c) (*Meinung äußern*) to say ◆ **was ~ Sie dazu?** what do you think about it?; **was soll man dazu ~?** what can you say?; **haben Sie dazu etwas zu ~?** do you have anything to say (about *or* on that)?; **das möchte** *or* **will ich nicht ~** I wouldn't say that; **das würde ich (wieder) nicht ~** I wouldn't say that; **ich sag's ja immer ...** I always say ..., I've always said ...; **ich möchte fast ~, ...** I'd almost say ..., one could almost say ...; **wenn ich so ~ darf** if I may say so; **sag, was du willst, ...** (*inf*) say what you like ...; **da soll noch einer ~, ...** never let it be said ...
(d) (*bedeuten, meinen*) to mean ◆ **was will er damit ~?** what does he mean (by that)?; **willst du vielleicht ~, daß ...** are you trying to tell me *or* to say that ...?, do you mean to tell me *or* to say that ...?; **ich will damit nicht ~, daß ...** I don't mean to imply *or* to say that ...; **damit ist nichts gesagt** that doesn't mean anything; **damit ist alles gesagt** that says everything, that says it all; **sein Gesicht sagte alles** it was written all over his face; **damit ist nicht gesagt, daß ...** that doesn't mean (to say) that ...; **das hat nichts zu ~** that doesn't mean anything; **sagt dir der Name etwas?** does the name mean anything to you?
(e) (*Redewendungen*) **~ Sie mal/sag mal, ...** tell me, ..., say, ...; **du, Veronika, sag mal, wollen wir ...** hey, Veronika, listen, shall we ...; **sag mal, Peter, kannst du mir fünf Mark leihen?** (say,) Peter, can you lend me five marks?; **sag mal, willst du nicht endlich Schluß machen?** come on *or* hey, isn't it time to stop?; **nun ~ Sie/sag mal selber, ist das nicht unpraktisch?** you must admit that's impractical; **wem ~ Sie das!** you don't need to tell *me* that!; **sag bloß!** you don't say, get away (*Brit inf*); **was Sie nicht ~!** you don't say!; **ich sage gar nichts mehr!** I'm not saying another word; (*verblüfft*) good heavens!, did you ever! (*inf*); **das kann man wohl ~** you can say that again!; **ich muß schon ~** I must say; **das muß man ~** you have to *or* you must admit that; **wie man so sagt** as they say, as the saying goes; **das ist nicht gesagt** that's by no means certain; **das ist schnell gesagt** I can tell you in two words; (*leicht gesagt*) that's easily said; **leichter gesagt als getan** easier said than done; **gesagt, getan** no sooner said than done; **wie (schon) gesagt** as I/you *etc* said; **ich bin, ~ wir, in einer Stunde da** I'll be there in, let's say, an hour; **sage und schreibe 100 Mark** 100 marks, would you believe it; *siehe* **offen, Dank, Meinung**.
sägen 1 *vti* to saw.
2 *vi* (*inf*) to snore, to saw wood (*US inf*).
Sagen-: ~dichtung *f* sagas *pl*; **s~haft** *adj* **(a)** (*nach Art einer Sage*) legendary; **(b)** (*enorm*) fabulous; **(c)** (*inf: hervorragend*) fantastic (*inf*), terrific (*inf*); **~kreis** *m* group of sagas; **s~umwoben** *adj* legendary; **~welt** *f* mythology, legend.
Sägerei *f* **(a)** *siehe* **Sägewerk**. **(b)** *no pl* (*inf*) sawing.
Säge-: ~späne *pl* wood shavings *pl*; **~werk** *nt* sawmill; **~zahn** *m* saw

tooth.
Sago *m or nt* **-s,** *no pl* sago.
Sagopalme *f* sago palm.
sah *pret of* **sehen.**
Sahara [za'ha:ra, 'za:hara] *f* - Sahara (Desert).
Sahel *m* **-(s)** Sahel.
Sahne *f* **-,** *no pl* cream.
Sahne-: **~baiser** *nt* cream meringue; **~bonbon** *m or nt* toffee; **~eis** *nt* icecream; **~käse** *m* cream cheese; **~torte** *f* cream gateau.
sahnig *adj* creamy ♦ **etw ~ schlagen** to whip *or* beat sth until creamy.
Saibling *m* char(r).
Saison [zɛ'zõ:, zɛ'zɔŋ] *f* **-, -s** *or* (*Aus*) **-en** season ♦ **außerhalb der ~, in der stillen** *or* **toten ~** in the off-season.
saisonal [zɛzo'na:l] *adj* seasonal.
Saison- [zɛ'zõ:] *in cpds* seasonal; **~arbeit** *f* seasonal work; **~arbeiter** *m* seasonal worker; **s~bedingt** *adj* seasonal; **~beginn** *m* start of the season; **s~bereinigt** *adj* seasonally adjusted; **~beschäftigung** *f* seasonal job; **~betrieb** *m* (*Hochsaison*) high season; (*~geschäft*) seasonal business; **~eröffnung** *f* opening of the season; **~geschäft** *nt* seasonal business; **~gewerbe** *nt* seasonal trade; **~industrie** *f* seasonal industry; ⚠**~schluß** *m* end of the season; **~schwankung** *f* seasonal fluctuation; **~stellung** *f* seasonal job; **in ~stellung gehen** to take a seasonal job; **~wanderung** *f* (*Econ*) seasonal movement of labour; **~zuschlag** *m* in-season supplement.
Saite *f* **-, -n** **(a)** (*Mus, Sport*) string. **(b)** (*fig liter*) **eine ~ in jdm berühren** *or* **anschlagen, eine ~ in jdm zum Klingen bringen** to strike a chord in sb; **eine empfindliche ~ berühren** to touch a tender *or* sore spot; **andere ~n aufziehen** (*inf*) to get tough.
Saiten-: **~instrument** *nt* string(ed) instrument; **~klang** *m* (*liter*) sound of strings; **~spiel** *nt, no pl* playing of a stringed instrument.
-saitig *adj suf* -stringed.
Sakko *m or nt* **-s, -s** sports jacket (*Brit*), sport coat (*US*); (*aus Samt etc*) jacket.
sakra *interj* (*S Ger, Aus*) good God, my God.
sakral *adj* sacred, sacral.
Sakralkunst *f* religious art, sacral art.
Sakrament *nt* sacrament ♦ **das ~ der Taufe** the sacrament of baptism; **~ (noch mal)!** (*sl*) Jesus Christ! (*sl*).
sakramental *adj* sacramental.
Sakrament(s)häuschen *nt* tabernacle.
Sakrileg *nt* **-s, -e, Sakrilegium** *nt* (*geh*) sacrilege.
sakrisch *adv* (*dial inf*) damned (*inf*); *schreien* like hell (*inf*).
Sakristei *f* sacristy.
sakrosankt *adj* sacrosanct.
säkular *adj* **(a)** (*weltlich*) secular. **(b)** (*zeitüberdauernd*) timeless.
Säkularisation *f* secularization.
säkularisieren* *vt* to secularize.
Säkulum *nt* **-s, Säkula** (*geh*) century.
Salamander *m* **-s, -** salamander.
Salami *f* **-, -s** salami.
Salamitaktik *f* (*inf*) policy of small steps.
Salär *nt* **-s, -e** (*old, Sw*) salary.
Salat *m* **-(e)s, -e** **(a)** (*Pflanze, Kopf~*) lettuce. **(b)** (*Gericht*) salad ♦ **da haben wir den ~!** (*inf*) now we're in a fine mess *or* a pretty pickle (*inf*).
Salat-: **~besteck** *nt* salad servers *pl*; **~gurke** *f* cucumber; **~kartoffel** *f* potato *used for potato salad*; **~kopf** *m* (head of) lettuce; **~öl** *nt* salad oil; **~pflanze** *f* **(a)** (*Setzling*) lettuce (plant); **(b)** (*Sorte*) salad; **~platte** *f* salad; **~schleuder** *f* salad drainer; **~schüssel** *f* salad bowl; **~soße** *f* salad dressing.
Salbaderei *f* (*pej geh*) sanctimonious prating.
salbadern* *vi* to prate.
Salbe *f* **-, -n** ointment.
Salbei *m* **-s,** *no pl* or *f* **-,** *no pl* sage.
salben *vt* (*liter*) to anoint ♦ **jdn zum König ~** to anoint sb king.
Salb|öl *nt* consecrated oil.
Salbung *f* anointing, unction.
salbungsvoll *adj* (*pej*) unctuous (*pej*).
Salchow *m* (*Eiskunstlauf*) salchow.
saldieren* *vt* (*Comm*) to balance; (*Aus*) to confirm payment.
Saldo *m* **-s, -s** *or* **Saldi** *or* **Salden** (*Fin*) balance ♦ **per ~** (*lit, fig*) on balance; **per ~ bezahlen/remittieren** to pay off the balance in full; **in ~ bleiben/sein** to stay/be in debt.
Saldo|übertrag, Saldovortrag *m* (*Fin*) balance brought forward *or* carried forward.
Säle *pl of* **Saal.**
Saline *f* salt-works *sing or pl.*
salisch *adj* (*Hist*) Salian, Salic.
Salizylsäure *f* salicylic acid.
Salm *m* **-(e)s, -e** **(a)** (*Lachs*) salmon. **(b)** (*inf: Gerede*) rigmarole (*inf*).
Salmiak *m or nt* **-s,** *no pl* sal ammoniac, ammonium chloride.
Salmiak-: **~geist** *m* (liquid) ammonia; **~pastille** *f bitter-tasting lozenge*, liquorice imp ®.
Salmonellen *pl* salmonellae *pl.*
Salmonellenvergiftung *f* salmonella (poisoning).
Salmonellose *f* **-, -n** salmonellosis.
Salomo(n) *m* **-s** *or* (*geh*) **Salomonis** Solomon.
salomonisch *adj* of Solomon; *Urteil* worthy of a Solomon ♦ **ein wahrhaft ~es Urteil!** a real Solomon!
Salon [za'lõ:, za'lɔŋ] *m* **-s, -s** **(a)** (*Gesellschaftszimmer*) drawing room; (*Naut*) saloon. **(b)** (*Friseur~, Mode~, Kosmetik~ etc*) salon. **(c)** (*Hist: literarischer etc Zirkel*) salon. **(d)** (*auf Messe*) stand, exhibition stand. **(e)** (*Kunst~*) exhibition room.
Salon- [za'lõ:-]: **~anarchist** *m* (*pej*) drawing-room revolutionary; **s~fähig** *adj* (*iro*) socially acceptable; *Leute, Aussehen* presentable; **ein nicht s~fähiger Witz** an objectionable joke; (*unanständig auch*) a rude *or* naughty joke; **nicht s~fähige Ausdrucksweise** uncouth language, not the sort of language to be used in polite society; **~löwe** *m* socialite, society man, social lion; **~musik** *f* palm court music; **~wagen** *m* (*Rail*) Pullman (carriage), special coach.
salopp *adj* **(a)** (*nachlässig*) sloppy, slovenly; *Manieren* slovenly; *Ausdruck, Sprache* slangy. **(b)** (*ungezwungen*) casual.
Salpeter *m* **-s,** *no pl* saltpetre, nitre.
salpet(e)rig *adj* nitrous.
Salpetersäure *f* nitric acid.
Salto *m* **-s, -s** *or* **Salti** somersault; (*Turmspringen auch*) turn ♦ **ein anderthalbfacher ~** a one-and-a-half somersault *or* turn; **einen ~ mortale machen** (*Zirkus*) to perform a death-defying leap; (*Aviat*) to loop the loop; **ein logischer/gedanklicher ~ mortale** a logical/an intellectual leap.
Salut *m* **-(e)s, -e** (*Mil*) salute ♦ **~ schießen** to fire a salute; **21 Schuß ~** 21-gun salute.
salutieren* *vti* (*Mil*) to salute.
⚠**Salutschuß** *m* **man gab** *or* **feuerte fünf Salutschüsse ab** a five-gun salute was fired.
Salve ['zalvə] *f* **-, -n** salvo, volley; (*Ehren~*) salute; (*fig*) (*Lach~*) burst of laughter; (*von Applaus*) volley, burst ♦ **eine ~ auf jdn abschießen** (*lit, fig*) to fire a salvo *or* volley at sb.
salvieren *vt* (*geh*) to exculpate.
Salz *nt* **-es, -e** salt ♦ **in ~ legen** to salt down *or* away; **das ~ der Erde** (*liter*) the salt of the earth; **das ist das ~ in der Suppe** (*fig*) that's what gives it that extra something; **wie eine Suppe ohne ~** (*fig*) like ham without eggs (*hum*); **er gönnt einem nicht das ~ in der Suppe** he even begrudges you the air you breathe.
Salz-: **s~arm** *adj* (*Cook*) low-salt, with a low salt content; **s~arm essen/leben** to eat low-salt food/to live on a low-salt diet; **~bergwerk** *nt* salt mine; **~brezel** *f* pretzel.
salzen *vt pret* **salzte,** *ptp* **gesalzen** to salt; *siehe* **gesalzen.**
Salz-: ⚠**~faß,** ⚠**~fäßchen** *nt* salt cellar; **~fleisch** *nt* (*Cook*) salt meat; **s~frei** *adj* salt-free; *Diät auch* no-salt *attr*; **~gebäck** *nt* savoury biscuits *pl*; **~gurke** *f* pickled gherkin; **s~haltig** *adj* salty, saline; **~hering** *m* salted herring.
salzig *adj* salty, salt.
Salzigkeit *f* saltiness.
Salz-: **~kartoffeln** *pl* boiled potatoes *pl*; **~korn** *nt* grain of salt; **~lake** *f* brine; **s~los** *adj* salt-free; **s~los essen** not to eat salt; **~lösung** *f* saline solution; **~mandel** *f* salted almond; **~säule** *f*: **zur ~säule erstarren** (*Bibl*) to turn into a pillar of salt; (*fig*) to stand as though rooted to the spot; **~säure** *f* hydrochloric acid; **~see** *m* salt lake; **~sieder** *m* **-s, -** (*Hist*) saltmaker; **~siederei** *f* (*Hist*) saltworks *sing or pl*; **~sole** *f* brine; **~stange** *f* pretzel stick; **~stock** *m* salt mine; **~streuer** *m* **-s, -** salt shaker, salt cellar; **~wasser** *nt* salt water; **~wüste** *f* salt desert, salt flat.
SA-Mann *m, pl* **SA-Leute** [ɛs'|a:-] storm-trooper, SA-man.
Sämann *m, pl* **Sämänner** (*old liter*) sower.
Samariter *m* **-s, -** **(a)** (*Bibl, fig*) Samaritan ♦ **der Barmherzige ~** the good Samaritan. **(b)** (*Angehöriger des Arbeiter-Samariterbunds*) first-aid volunteer, ≃ St John's Ambulance man (*Brit*).
Samariterdienst *m* act of mercy ♦ **jdm einen ~ erweisen** to be a good Samaritan to sb.
Samarium *nt, no pl* (*abbr* **Sm**) samarium.
Samba *m* **-s, -s** *or f* **-, -s** samba.
Sambesi *m* **-(s)** Zambesi.
Sambia *nt* **-s** Zambia.
Sambier(in *f*) [-iɐ, -iərɪn] *m* **-s, -** Zambian.
sambisch *adj* Zambian.
Same *m* **-ns, -n** (*liter*) *siehe* **Samen.**
Samen *m* **-s, -** **(a)** (*Bot, fig*) seed; (*fig auch*) seeds *pl.* **(b)** (*Menschen~, Tier~*) sperm. **(c)** (*liter, Bibl: Nachkommen*) seed (*liter, Bibl*).
Samen-: **~anlage** *f* (*Bot*) ovule; **~bank** *f* sperm bank; **~blase** *f* seminal vesicle; ⚠**~erguß** *m* ejaculation, emission of semen, seminal discharge *or* emission; **~faden** *m* spermatozoon; **~flüssigkeit** *f* semen, seminal fluid; **~händler** *m* seedsman, seed merchant; **~handlung** *f* seed shop; **~kapsel** *f* seed capsule; **~korn** *nt* seed; **~leiter** *m* vas deferens; **~spender** *m* sperm donor; **~strang** *m* spermatic cord; ⚠**s~tragend** *adj* seed-bearing; **~zelle** *f* sperm cell; **~zwiebel** *f* seed onion.
Sämereien *pl* seeds *pl.*
sämig *adj* thick, creamy.
Sämischleder *nt* chamois (leather).
Sämling *m* seedling.
Sammel-: **~album** *nt* (collector's) album; ⚠**~anschluß** *m* (*Telec*) private (branch) exchange; (*von Privathäusern*) party line; **~band** *m* anthology; **~becken** *nt* collecting tank; (*Geol*) catchment area; (*fig*) melting pot (*von* for); **~begriff** *m* (*Gram*) collective name *or* term; **~bestellung** *f* joint *or* collective order; **~bezeichnung** *f siehe* **~begriff**; **~büchse** *f* collecting tin

or box; **~depot** *nt* (*Fin*) collective securities deposit; **~fahrschein** *m*, **~karte** *f* (*für mehrere Fahrten*) multi-journey ticket; (*für mehrere Personen*) group ticket; **~mappe** *f* file.

sammeln [1] *vt* to collect; *Holz, Ähren, Fakten, Material, Erfahrungen auch* to gather; *Blumen, Pilze etc* to pick, to gather; *Truppen, Anhänger* to gather, to assemble ◆ **neue Kräfte ~** to build up one's energy again; **seine Gedanken ~** to collect one's thoughts.
[2] *vr* **(a)** (*zusammenkommen*) to gather, to collect; (*sich anhäufen: Wasser, Geld etc*) to collect, to accumulate; (*Lichtstrahlen*) to converge, to meet.
(b) (*sich konzentrieren*) to collect *or* compose oneself *or* one's thoughts; *siehe* **gesammelt.**
[3] *vi* to collect (*für* for).

Sammel-: ~name *m siehe* **~begriff**; **~nummer** *f* (*Telec*) private exchange number, switchboard number; ⚠**~paß** *m* group passport; **~platz** *m* **(a)** (*Treffpunkt*) assembly point; **(b)** (*Lagerplatz*) collecting point; (*Deponie*) dump; **~punkt** *m* **(a)** (*Treffpunkt*) assembly point; **(b)** (*Opt*) focus; **~sendung** *f* joint consignment; **Güter als ~sendung schicken** to send goods part-load; **~stecker** *m* (*Elec*) plugboard; **~stelle** *f siehe* **~platz.**

Sammelsurium *nt* conglomeration.

Sammel-: ~tasse *f* ornamental cup, saucer and plate; **~transport** *m* (*von Gütern*) general shipment; (*von Personen*) group transport; **~visum** *nt* collective visa; **~wut** *f* collecting mania.

Sammet *m* **-s, -e** (*obs, Sw*) velvet.

Sammler(in *f*) *m* **-s, -** collector; (*von Beeren*) picker; (*von Holz*) gatherer.

Sammlerfleiß *m* collector's enthusiasm ◆ **diese Kollektion ist mit großem ~ zusammengetragen** it has taken a lot of hard work to put this collection together.

Sammlung *f* **(a)** collection. **(b)** (*fig: Konzentration*) composure ◆ **ihm fehlt die innere ~** he lacks composure; **zur ~ (meiner Gedanken)** to collect myself *or* my thoughts.

Sammlungsbewegung *f* coalition movement.

Samos(wein) *m* **-, -** Samian wine, wine from Samos.

Samowar *m* **-s, -e** samovar.

Samstag *m* **-(e)s, -e** Saturday; *siehe* **Dienstag.**

samstägig *adj* Saturday.

samstags *adv* on Saturdays.

samt [1] *prep +dat* along *or* together with ◆ **sie kam ~ Katze** (*hum*) she came complete with cat.
[2] *adv* **~ und sonders** the whole lot (of them/us/you), the whole bunch (*inf*); **die Teilnehmer wurden ~ und sonders verhaftet** all the participants were arrested, the whole lot of them.

Samt *m* **-(e)s, -e** velvet ◆ **in ~ und Seide** (*liter*) in silks and satins; **zart wie ~ und Seide** (*liter*) as soft as silk.

Samt- *in cpds* velvet; **s~artig** *adj* velvety, like velvet; **~band** *nt* velvet ribbon; **~blume** *f* (*Bot*) marigold.

samten *adj* (*liter*) velvet.

Samthandschuh *m* velvet glove ◆ **jdn mit ~en anfassen** (*inf*) to handle sb with kid gloves (*inf*).

samtig *adj* velvety.

sämtlich *adj* (*alle*) all; (*vollständig*) complete ◆ **~e Unterlagen waren verschwunden, die Unterlagen waren ~ verschwunden** all the *or* every one of the documents had disappeared, the documents had all disappeared; **Schillers ~e Werke** the complete works of Schiller; **~e Anwesenden** all those present; **sie mußten ~en Besitz zurücklassen** they had to leave all their possessions behind.

Samt-: ~pfötchen *nt* (*inf*) velvet paw; **~pfötchen machen** (*Katze*) to draw in/have drawn in its claws; (*fig*) to go all soft; **s~weich** *adj* (as) soft as velvet, velvet-soft, velvety.

Sanatorium *nt* sanatorium.

Sand *m* **-(e)s, -e** sand; (*Scheuer~*) scouring powder ◆ **mit ~ bestreuen** to sand; **das/die gibt's wie ~ am Meer** (*inf*) there are heaps of them (*inf*); **auf ~ laufen** *or* **geraten** to run aground; **auf ~ bauen** (*fig*) to build upon sandy ground; **jdm ~ in die Augen streuen** (*fig*) to throw dust in sb's eyes; **~ ins Getriebe streuen** to throw a spanner in the works; **im ~e verlaufen** (*inf*) to peter out, to come to naught *or* nothing; **den Kopf in den ~ stecken** to stick *or* bury *or* hide one's head in the sand; **etw in den ~ setzen** (*inf*) *Projekt, Prüfung* to blow sth (*inf*); *Geld* to squander sth.

Sandale *f* **-, -n** sandal.

Sandalette *f* high-heeled sandal.

Sand- *in cpds* sand; **~bank** *f* sandbank, sandbar; **~boden** *m* sandy soil; **~dorn** *m* (*Bot*) sea buckthorn.

Sandelholz *nt* sandalwood.

sandeln *vi* (*S Ger, Aus, Sw*) to play in the sand.

Sandel|öl *nt* sandalwood oil.

Sand-: s~farben, s~farbig *adj* sand-coloured; **~grube** *f* sandpit (*esp Brit*), sandbox (*US*); (*Golf*) bunker, sand trap; **~haufen** *m* pile *or* heap of sand; (*~kasten*) sandpit (*esp Brit*), sandbox (*US*); **~hose** *f* sand column *or* spout, dust devil.

sandig *adj* sandy.

Sandinist(in *f*) *m* Sandinista.

Sand-: ~kasten *m* sandpit (*esp Brit*), sandbox (*US*); (*Mil*) sand table; **~kastenspiele** *pl* (*Mil*) sand-table exercises *pl*; (*fig*) tactical manoeuvrings *pl*; **~korn** *nt* grain of sand; **~kuchen** *m* (*Cook*) sand-cake (*a Madeira-type cake*); (*von Kindern*) mud pie; **~mann** *m*, **~männchen** *nt* (*in Geschichten*) sandman; **~meer** *nt* (*geh*) sea of sand; **~papier** *nt* sandpaper; **~platz** *m* (*Tennis*) clay court; **~sack** *m* sandbag; (*Boxen*) punchbag.

Sandstein *m* sandstone ◆ **ein Haus aus rotem ~** a red sandstone house, a brownstone (house) (*US*).

Sandstein- *in cpds* sandstone; **~fels(en)** *m* sandstone cliff.

Sand-: ~strahl *m* jet of sand; **etw mit ~strahl abblasen** *or* **reinigen** to sandblast sth; **s~strahlen** *vti insep* to sandblast; **~strahlgebläse** *nt* sandblasting equipment *no indef art, no pl*; **~strand** *m* sandy beach; **~sturm** *m* sandstorm.

sandte *pret of* **senden**[1].

Sand-: ~uhr *f* hour-glass; (*Eieruhr*) egg-timer; **~weg** *m* dirt road, track.

Sandwich ['zɛntvɪtʃ] *nt or m* **-(s), -(e)s** sandwich.

Sandwich-: ~bauweise *f* sandwich construction; **~mann** *m, pl* **-männer** (*hum*) sandwichman; **~wecken** *m* (*Aus*) *long thin white loaf*, French loaf.

Sandwüste *f* sandy waste; (*Geog*) (sandy) desert.

sanft *adj* gentle; *Berührung, Stimme, Farbe, Licht, Wind, Regen auch* soft; *Unterlage, Haut* soft; *Schlaf, Tod* peaceful ◆ **sich ~ anfühlen** to feel soft; **mit ~er Gewalt** gently but firmly; **mit ~er Hand** with a gentle hand; **von ~er Hand** by a woman's fair hand; **sie lächelte ~** she smiled softly; **sie schaute das Kind mit ~en Augen an** she looked tenderly at the child; **~ schlafen** to be sleeping peacefully; **er ist ~ entschlafen** he passed away peacefully, he fell gently asleep (*auch iro*); **~ wie ein Lamm** (as) gentle as a lamb; *siehe* **ruhen.**

Sänfte *f* **-, -n** litter; (*esp im 17., 18. Jh. Europas*) sedan-chair; (*in Indien*) palanquin; (*auf Elefant*) howdah.

Sänftenträger *m* litter-bearer; sedan bearer; palanquin bearer.

Sanftheit *f siehe adj* gentleness; softness.

sänftigen *vt* (*obs*) *siehe* **besänftigen.**

Sanftmut *f, no pl* (*liter*) gentleness.

sanftmütig *adj* (*liter*) gentle; (*Bibl*) meek.

sang *pret of* **singen.**

Sang *m* **-(e)s, ⸚e** (*old liter*) (*Gesang*) song; (*das Singen*) singing ◆ **mit ~ und Klang** (*lit*) with drums drumming and pipes piping; (*fig iro*) *durchfallen* disastrously, catastrophically; *entlassen werden* with a lot of hullabaloo; **ohne ~ und Klang** (*inf*) without any ado, quietly; **ohne ~ und Klang verschwinden** to just simply disappear.

Sänger *m* **-s, - (a)** singer; (*esp Jazz~, Pop~ auch*) vocalist. **(b)** (*old liter: Dichter*) bard (*old*), poet ◆ **da(rüber) schweigt des ~s Höflichkeit** modesty forbids me to say. **(c)** (*Singvogel*) songbird, songster.

Sänger-: ~bund *m* choral union; **~fest** *nt* choral festival.

Sängerin *f* singer; (*esp Jazz~, Pop~*) vocalist.

Sanges-: ~bruder *m* (*inf*) chorister; **~freude, ~lust** *f* (*dated*) love of song *or* singing; **s~freudig, s~lustig** *adj* (*dated*) fond of singing, song-loving.

Sanguiniker(in *f*) [zaŋ'gui:nikɐ, -ərɪn] *m* **-s, -** (*Psych*) sanguine person.

sanguinisch [zaŋ'gui:nɪʃ] *adj* (*Psych*) sanguine.

sang- und klanglos *adv* (*inf*) without any ado, quietly ◆ **sie ist ~ verschwunden** she just simply disappeared.

Sani *m* **-s, -s** (*Mil inf*) medical orderly.

sanieren* [1] *vt* **(a)** (*gesunde Lebensverhältnisse schaffen*) to renovate; *Stadtteil* to redevelop.
(b) (*Econ*) *Unternehmen, Wirtschaft* to put (back) on it's feet, to put on an even keel, to rehabilitate.
[2] *vr* **(a)** (*inf: Mensch*) to line one's own pocket (*inf*) ◆ **bei dem Geschäft hat er sich saniert** he made a killing on the deal (*inf*).
(b) (*Unternehmen, Wirtschaft, Industrie*) to put itself on an even keel, to put itself (back) in good shape.

Sanierung *f* **(a)** *siehe vt (a)* renovation; redevelopment.
(b) (*Econ*) rehabilitation ◆ **Maßnahmen zur ~ des Dollars** measures to put the dollar back on an even keel *or* on its feet again.
(c) (*inf: Bereicherung*) self-enrichment ◆ **er ist nur auf die eigene ~ bedacht** he is only interested in lining his own pocket (*inf*).

Sanierungs-: ~gebiet *nt* redevelopment area; **~gewinn** *m profit from property speculation in a redevelopment area*; **~maßnahme** *f* (*für Gebiete etc*) redevelopment measure; (*Econ*) rehabilitation measure; **~plan** *m* redevelopment plan *or* scheme; (*Econ*) rehabilitation plan.

sanitär *adj no pred* sanitary ◆ **~e Anlagen** sanitation (facilities), sanitary facilities; **ein Haus ~ ausstatten** to install sanitation in a house.

Sanität *f* (*Aus, Sw*) **(a)** medical service; (*Krankenpflege*) nursing. **(b)** (*inf: Krankenwagen*) ambulance.

Sanitäter *m* **-s, -** first-aid attendant; (*Mil*) (medical) orderly; (*in Krankenwagen*) ambulance man.

Sanitäts-: ~auto *nt* ambulance; **~dienst** *m* (*Mil*) medical duty; (*Heeresabteilung*) medical corps; **~flugzeug** *nt* ambulance plane, air ambulance; **~gefreite(r)** *m* (medical) orderly; **~kasten** *m* first-aid box *or* kit; **~kompanie** *f* medical company; **~offizier** *m* (*Mil*) Medical Officer, MO; **~truppe** *f* medical corps; **~wagen** *m* ambulance; **~wesen** *nt* (*Mil*) medical service.

sank *pret of* **sinken.**

Sanka ['zaŋka] *m* **-s, -s** (*Mil inf*) ambulance.

Sankt *adj inv* saint ◆ **~ Nikolaus** Santa (Claus), Father Christmas; (*Rel*) St *or* Saint Nicholas.

Sankt Gallen *nt* (*Kanton, Stadt*) St Gall.

Sanktion *f* sanction.

sanktionieren* *vt* to sanction.

Sanktionierung *f* sanctioning.

Sankt-Lorenz-Strom *m* St Lawrence river.

Sankt-Nimmerleins-Tag *m* (*hum*) never-never day ◆ **ja ja, am ~** yes yes, and pigs might fly (*hum*).

sann *pret of* **sinnen.**

San(n)yas(s)in *mf* **-(s), -(s)** sannyasin.

Sansibar *nt* **-s** Zanzibar.

Sanskrit *nt* **-s,** *no pl* Sanskrit.

Saphir *m* **-s, -e** sapphire.

sapperlot, sapperment *interj* (*old*) stap me (*old*), upon my soul (*old*).

sapphisch ['zapfɪʃ, 'zafɪʃ] *adj* Sapphic.

Sarabande *f* **-, -n** (*Mus*) saraband.

Sarazene *m* **-n, -n, Sarazenin** *f* Saracen.

sarazenisch *adj* Saracen.

Sarde *m* **-n, -n, Sardin** *f* Sardinian.

Sardelle *f* anchovy.

Sardellen-: ~butter *f* anchovy butter; **~paste** *f* anchovy paste.

Sardin *f siehe* **Sarde.**

Sardine *f* sardine.

Sardinenbüchse *f* sardine-tin ♦ **wie in einer ~** (*fig inf*) like sardines (*inf*).

Sardinien [-iən] *nt* **-s** Sardinia.

Sardinier(in *f***)** [-iɐ, -iərɪn] *m* **-s, -** Sardinian.

sardinisch, sardisch *adj* Sardinian.

sardonisch *adj* (*liter*) sardonic.

Sarg *m* **-(e)s, ⸚e** coffin, casket (*US*) ♦ **ein Nagel zu jds ~ sein** (*hum inf*) to be a nail in sb's coffin; **du kannst dir schon deinen ~ machen lassen** (*hum inf*) you'd better start arranging your funeral.

Sarg-: ~deckel *m* coffin lid, casket lid (*US*); **~nagel** *m* coffin nail; (*fig inf auch: Zigarette*) cancer-stick (*hum inf*); **~tischler** *m* coffin-maker, casket-maker (*US*); **~träger** *m* pall-bearer.

Sari *m* **-(s), -s** sari.

Sarin *nt* **-s** *no pl* (*Chem*) sarin.

Sarkasmus *m* sarcasm.

sarkastisch *adj* sarcastic.

Sarkom *nt* **-s, -e** (*Med*) sarcoma.

Sarkophag *m* **-(e)s, -e** sarcophagus.

Sarong *m* **-(s), -s** sarong.

saß *pret of* **sitzen.**

Satan *m* **-s, -e** (*Bibl, fig*) Satan ♦ **dieses Weib ist ein ~** this woman is a (she-) devil.

satanisch *adj* satanic.

Satanismus *m* Satanism.

Satans-: ~braten *m* (*hum inf*) young devil; **~kult** *m* satan-cult; **~pilz** *m* Satan's mushroom, boletus satanas (*spec*).

Satellit *m* **-en, -en** (*alle Bedeutungen*) satellite.

Satelliten- *in cpds* satellite; **~abwehrwaffe** *f* anti-satellite weapon; **~bahn** *f* satellite orbit; **~bild** *nt* (*TV*) satellite picture; **~fernsehen** *nt* satellite television; **~foto** *nt* satellite picture; **~schüssel** *f* (*TV inf*) satellite dish; **~staat** *m* satellite state; **~stadt** *f* satellite town; **~station** *f* space station; **~übertragung** *f* (*Rad, TV*) satellite transmission.

Satin [za'tɛ̃:] *m* **-s, -s** satin; (*Baumwoll~*) sateen.

satinieren* *vt Papier* to glaze; (*Typ*) to satin-coat.

Satinpapier [za'tɛ̃:-] *nt* glazed paper.

Satire *f* **-, -n** satire (*auf +acc* on).

Satiriker(in *f***)** *m* **-s, -** satirist.

satirisch *adj* satirical.

Satisfaktion *f* (*old*) satisfaction ♦ **ich verlange** *or* **fordere ~!** I demand satisfaction.

satisfaktionsfähig *adj* (*old*) capable of giving satisfaction.

Satrap *m* **-en, -en** (*Hist*) satrap.

satt *adj* **(a)** (*gesättigt*) *Mensch* replete (*hum, form*), full (up) (*inf*); *Magen, Gefühl* full; (*sl: betrunken*) smashed (*sl*), bloated (*sl*) ♦ **~ sein** to have had enough (to eat), to be full (up) (*inf*); **~ werden** to have enough to eat; **von so was kann man doch nicht ~ werden** it's not enough to satisfy you *or* fill you up; **das macht ~** it's filling; **sich (an etw** *dat***) ~ essen** to eat one's fill (of sth); (*überdrüssig werden auch*) to have had one's fill (of sth); **sie haben nicht ~ zu essen** (*inf*) they don't have enough to eat; **wie soll sie ihre Kinder ~ kriegen?** (*inf*) how is she supposed to feed her children?; **er ist kaum ~ zu kriegen** (*inf: lit, fig*) he's insatiable; **er konnte sich an ihr nicht ~ sehen/hören** he could not see/hear enough of her; **~ sank er in den Sessel zurück** having eaten his fill he sank back into his chair; **wie ein ~er Säugling** (*inf*) with a look of contentment, like a contented cow (*inf*).
(b) jdn/etw ~ haben *or* **sein** to be fed up with sb/sth (*inf*); **jdn/etw ~ bekommen** *or* **kriegen** (*inf*) to get fed up with sb/sth (*inf*).
(c) (*blasiert, übersättigt*) well-fed; (*selbstgefällig*) smug.
(d) (*kräftig, voll*) *Farben, Klang* rich, full; (*inf*) *Applaus* resounding; (*inf*) *Mehrheit* comfortable; **~e 100 Mark/10 Prozent** (*inf*) a cool 100 marks/10 per cent (*inf*).

Sattel *m* **-s, ⸚ (a)** saddle ♦ **ohne/mit ~ reiten** to ride bareback *or* without a saddle/with a saddle; **sich in den ~ schwingen** to swing (oneself) into the saddle; (*auf Fahrrad*) to jump onto one's bicycle; **sich im ~ halten** (*lit, fig*) to stay in the saddle; **jdn aus dem ~ heben** (*herunterhelfen*) to help sb (to) dismount; (*lit, fig: zu Fall bringen*) to unseat sb; **jdn in den ~ heben** (*lit*) to lift sb into the saddle; (*fig*) to help sb to power; **er ist in allen ⸚n gerecht** *or* **sicher** (*fig*) he can turn his hand to anything; **fest im ~ sitzen** (*fig*) to be firmly in the saddle.
(b) (*Berg~*) saddle; (*Geigen~*) nut; (*Nasen~*) bridge.

Sattel-: ~dach *nt* saddle roof; **~decke** *f* saddlecloth; **s~fest** *adj* **s~fest sein** (*Reiter*) to have a good seat; **in etw** (*dat*) **s~fest sein** (*fig*) to have a firm grasp of sth; **~gurt** *m* girth; **~knopf** *m* pommel.

satteln *vt Pferd* to saddle (up) ♦ **für etw gesattelt sein** (*fig*) to be ready for sth.

Sattel-: ~nase *f* saddlenose; **~pferd** *nt* saddle horse; **~platz** *m* paddock; **~schlepper** *m* articulated lorry (*Brit*), artic (*Brit inf*), semitrailer (*US*), semi (*US inf*); **~tasche** *f* saddlebag; (*Gepäcktasche am Fahrrad, aus Stroh*) pannier; **~zeug** *nt* saddlery; **~zug** *m siehe* **~schlepper.**

Sattheit *f* **(a)** (*Gefühl*) feeling of repletion *or* of being full. **(b)** (*von Farben*) richness, fullness.

sättigen 1 *vt* **(a)** *Hunger, Neugier* to satisfy, to satiate; *jdn* to make replete; (*ernähren*) to feed, to provide with food ♦ **ich bin gesättigt** I am *or* feel replete. **(b)** (*Comm, Chem*) to saturate.
2 *vi* to be filling.
3 *vr* **sich an etw** (*dat*) *or* **mit etw ~** to eat one's fill of sth.

sättigend *adj Essen* filling.

Sättigung *f* **(a)** (*geh*) (*Sattsein*) repletion ♦ **die ~ der Hungrigen** the feeding of the hungry; **das Essen dient nicht nur der ~** eating does not only serve to satisfy hunger. **(b)** (*Chem, Comm, von Farbe*) saturation.

Sättigungs-: ~grad *m* degree of saturation; **~punkt** *m* saturation point.

Sattler(in *f***)** *m* **-s, -** saddler; (*Polsterer*) upholsterer.

Sattlerei *f siehe* **Sattler** saddlery; upholstery; (*Werkstatt*) saddler's; upholsterer's.

Sattler-: ~geselle *m* journeyman saddler/upholsterer; **~meister** *m* master saddler/upholsterer.

sattsam *adv* amply; *bekannt* sufficiently.

saturieren* 1 *vt* (*liter*) to satisfy, to content.
2 *vr* (*geh*) to do well for oneself.

saturiert *adj* (*geh*) *Markt* saturated; *Klasse* prosperous ♦ **~ leben** to prosper, to live prosperously.

Saturn *m* **-s** (*Myth, Astron*) Saturn ♦ **die Ringe des ~s** the rings of Saturn.

Saturnalien [-iən] *pl* (*Hist*) Saturnalia *pl.*

Satyr *m* **-s** *or* **-n, -n** *or* **-e** satyr.

Satz *m* **-es, ⸚e (a)** sentence; (*Teilsatz*) clause; (*Jur: Gesetzabschnitt*) clause ♦ **ich kann nur ein paar ⸚e Italienisch** I only know a few phrases of Italian; **mitten im ~** in mid-sentence; **abhängiger/selbständiger ~** subordinate/principal clause; **eingeschobener ~** appositional phrase.
(b) (*Lehr~, Philos*) proposition; (*Math*) theorem ♦ **der ~ des Pythagoras** Pythagoras' theorem.
(c) (*Typ*) (*das Setzen*) setting; (*das Gesetzte*) type *no pl* ♦ **etw in ~ geben** to send sth for setting; **in ~ gehen** to go for setting; **das Buch ist im ~** the book is being set.
(d) (*Mus*) movement.
(e) (*Boden~*) dregs *pl*; (*Kaffee~*) grounds *pl*; (*Tee~ auch*) leaves *pl.*
(f) (*Zusammengehöriges*) set; (*Hunt: Wurf*) litter.
(g) (*Sport*) set; (*Tischtennis*) game.
(h) (*Tarif~*) charge; (*Spesen~*) allowance.
(i) (*Sprung*) leap, jump ♦ **einen ~ machen** *or* **tun** to leap, to jump; **mit einem ~** in one leap *or* bound.

Satz-: ~aussage *f* (*Gram*) predicate; **~ball** *m* (*Sport*) set point; (*Tischtennis*) game point; **~bau** *m* sentence construction; **~befehl** *m* (*Typ*) typographical command; **~ergänzung** *f* (*Gram*) object; **~fehler** *m* (*Typ*) printer's error; **~gefüge** *nt* (*Gram*) complex sentence; **~gegenstand** *m* (*Gram*) subject; **~glied** *nt* part of a/the sentence; **~herstellung** *f* (*Typ*) typesetting.

-sätzig *adj suf* (*Mus*) in ... movements.

Satz-: ~lehre *f* (*Gram*) syntax; **~melodie** *f* (*Phon*) intonation; **~reihe** *f* compound sentence; **~spiegel** *m* (*Typ*) type area, area of type; **~teil** *m* part or constituent of a/the sentence.

Satzung *f* constitution, statutes *pl*; (*Vereins~*) rules *pl.*

satzungsgemäß *adj* according to the statutes/rules.

Satz-: ~verbindung *f* clause construction; **~verlust** *m* (*Tennis*) loss of a set; **s~weise** *adj* **(a)** (*Ling*) sentence by sentence; **eine Sprache lernt man besser s~weise** you are better to learn a language in phrases; **(b)** (*Tech*) in sets; **~zeichen** *nt* punctuation mark; **~zusammenhang** *m* context of the sentence.

Sau *f* **-, Säue** *or* (*Hunt*) **-en (a)** sow; (*inf: Schwein*) pig; (*Hunt*) wild boar ♦ **die ~ rauslassen** *or* **losmachen** (*fig sl*) to let it all hang out (*sl*); (*sich äußern*) to speak out; **wie eine gestochene ~ bluten** (*sl*) to bleed like a (stuck) pig (*inf*); **wie eine gesengte ~** (*sl*) like a maniac (*inf*).
(b) (*pej inf: Schmutzfink*) dirty swine (*inf*); (*Frau auch*) bitch (*sl*) ♦ **du alte ~!** (*vulg*) you dirty bastard (*sl*), you son-of-a-bitch (*esp US sl*); (*Frau auch*) you dirty bitch (*sl*).
(c) (*fig sl*) **da war keine ~ zu sehen** there wasn't a bloody (*Brit sl*) *or* goddamn (*sl*) soul to be seen; **jdn zur ~ machen** to bawl sb out (*inf*); **unter aller ~** bloody (*Brit sl*) *or* goddamn (*sl*) awful *or* lousy.

Sau-: ~arbeit *f* (*sl*) bloody (*Brit sl*) *or* damn (*inf*) awful job; (*schlampige Arbeit*) lousy piece of work (*inf*); **~bande** *f* (*inf*) gang of hoodlums (*inf*).

sauber 1 *adj* **(a)** (*rein, reinlich*) clean ♦ **~ sein** (*Hund etc*) to be house-trained; (*Kind*) to be (potty-)trained; **etw ~ putzen** to clean sth; **~ singen/spielen** to sing/play on key.
(b) (*ordentlich*) neat, tidy; (*Aus, S Ger: hübsch*) *Mädel* pretty; (*exakt*) accurate.
(c) (*anständig*) honest, upstanding ♦ **~ bleiben** to keep one's hands clean; **bleib ~!** (*sl*) keep your nose clean (*inf*).
(d) (*inf: großartig*) fantastic, great ♦ **~! ~!** that's the stuff! (*inf*); **du bist mir ja ein ~er Freund!** (*iro*) a fine friend *you* are! (*iro*); **eine ~e Gesellschaft!** (*iro*) a

bunch of crooks; **das ist ja ~!** (*iro*) that's great (*iro*).
2 *adv* (*Aus, S Ger: verstärkend*) really and truly.

⚠ **sauberhalten** *vt sep irreg* to keep clean.

Sauberkeit *f* **(a)** (*Hygiene, Ordentlichkeit*) cleanliness; (*Reinheit*) (*von Wasser, Luft etc*) cleanness; (*von Tönen*) accuracy. **(b)** (*Anständigkeit*) honesty, upstandingness.

Sauberkeitsfimmel *m* (*pej*) mania for cleanliness, thing about cleanliness (*inf*).

säuberlich *adj* neat and tidy ◆ **fein ~** neatly and tidily.

⚠ **saubermachen** *vt sep* to clean.

Saubermann *m* (*inf*) cleanliness freak (*inf*), Mr Clean (*inf*) ◆ **die Saubermänner** (*fig: moralisch*) the squeaky-clean brigade (*inf*).

säubern *vt* **(a)** to clean ◆ **er säuberte seinen Anzug von den Blutflecken** he cleaned the bloodstains off his jacket; **das Wasser (von Verschmutzung) ~** to cleanse the water.
(b) (*fig euph*) *Partei, Buch* to purge (*von* of); *Saal,* (*Mil*) *Gegend* to clear (*von* of).

Säuberung *f siehe vt* **(a)** cleaning; cleansing. **(b)** purging; clearing; expurgation; (*Pol: Aktion*) purge.

Säuberungs|aktion *f* cleaning-up operation; (*Pol*) purge.

Sau-: **s~blöd, s~blöde** *adj* (*sl*) bloody (*Brit sl*) *or* damn (*inf*) stupid; **sich s~blöd anstellen** to behave like a bloody (*Brit sl*) *or* damn (*inf*) idiot; **~bohne** *f* broad bean.

Sauce ['zo:sə] *f* **-, -n** *siehe* **Soße**.

Sauciere [zo'sie:rə, -'sie:rə] *f* **-, -n** sauce boat.

Saudi *m* **-(s), -(s)** Saudi.

Saudi-: **~araber** *m* Saudi; **~-Arabien** *nt* Saudi Arabia; **s~arabisch** *adj* Saudi *attr,* Saudi-Arabian.

saudumm *adj* (*inf*) damn stupid (*inf*) ◆ **sich ~ benehmen** to behave like a stupid idiot (*inf*).

sauen *vi* **(a)** to litter. **(b)** (*inf: Dreck machen*) to make a mess. **(c)** *aux sein* (*S Ger inf: rennen*) to run.

sauer *adj* **(a)** (*nicht süß*) sour; *Wein, Bonbons* acid(ic), sharp; *Obst auch* sharp, tart ◆ **saure Drops** acid drops; *siehe* **aufstoßen**.
(b) (*verdorben*) off *pred*; *Milch auch* sour; *Geruch* sour, sickly ◆ **es roch so ~** there was a sickly smell; **~ werden** (*Milch, Sahne*) to go sour *or* off, to turn (sour).
(c) (*mit Säure zubereitet*) *Gurke, Hering* pickled; *Sahne* soured ◆ **~ einlegen** to pickle.
(d) (*sumpfig*) *Wiese, Boden* acidic.
(e) (*Chem*) acid(ic) ◆ **~ reagieren** to react acidically; **saurer Regen** acid rain.
(f) (*inf: schlecht gelaunt*) (*auf* +*acc* with) mad (*inf*), cross ◆ **eine ~e Miene machen** to look sour *or* annoyed; **~ reagieren** to get annoyed.
(g) (*unerfreulich, unter Schwierigkeiten*) **das habe ich mir ~ erworben** I got that the hard way; **~ erworbenes Geld** hard-earned money; **jdm das Leben ~ machen** to make sb's life a misery, to make life miserable for sb; **gib ihm Saures!** (*sl*) let him have it! (*inf*).

Sauer-: **~ampfer** *m* sorrel; **~braten** *m* braised beef (marinaded in vinegar), sauerbraten (*US*); **~brunnen** *m* **(a)** (*Heilquelle*) acidic spring; **(b)** (*Wasser*) acidic mineral water.

Sauerei *f* (*sl*) **(a)** (*Unflätigkeit*) **~en erzählen** to tell filthy stories; **eine einzige ~** a load of filth. **(b) das ist eine ~!, so eine ~!** it's a bloody (*Brit sl*) *or* downright disgrace *or* scandal. **(c)** (*Dreck*) mess ◆ **(eine) ~ machen** to make a mess.

Sauer-: **~kirsche** *f* sour cherry; **~klee** *m* wood sorrel, oxalis; **~kohl** *m* (*dial*), **~kraut** *nt* sauerkraut, pickled cabbage.

säuerlich *adj* (*lit, fig*) sour; *Wein auch* sharp; *Obst auch* sharp, tart.

Säuerlichkeit *f siehe adj* sourness; sharpness; tartness.

Säuerling *m* **(a)** *siehe* **Sauerbrunnen**. **(b)** (*Bot*) *siehe* **Sauerampfer**.

Sauermilch *f* sour milk.

säuern 1 *vt Brot, Teig* to leaven.
2 *vi* to go *or* turn sour, to sour.

Sauerstoff *m, no pl* (*abbr* **O**) oxygen.

Sauerstoff- *in cpds* oxygen; **~apparat** *m* breathing apparatus; **s~arm** *adj* low in oxygen; (*zu wenig*) oxygen-deficient; **~entzug** *m* (*Med*) oxygen deficiency; (*Chem*) deoxygenation; **~flasche** *f* oxygen cylinder *or* (*kleiner*) bottle; **~gerät** *nt* breathing apparatus; (*Med*) (*für künstliche Beatmung*) respirator; (*für Erste Hilfe*) resuscitator; **s~haltig** *adj* containing oxygen; **~mangel** *m* lack of oxygen; (*akut*) oxygen deficiency; **~maske** *f* oxygen mask; **~patrone** *f* oxygen cartridge; **~zelt** *nt* oxygen tent; **~zufuhr** *f* oxygen supply; **mittels ~zufuhr** by supplying oxygen.

Sauer-: **s~süß** *adj siehe* **süßsauer**; **~teig** *m* sour dough; **~topf** *m* (*old, hum*) sourpuss (*inf*); **s~töpfisch** *adj* (*old, hum*) sour; *Mensch auch* sour-faced.

Säuerung *f* leavening.

Sauf-: **~aus** *m* **-, -**, **~bold** *m* **-(e)s, -e** (*old pej*) sot (*old*), drunkard; **~bruder** *m* (*pej inf*) (*Kumpan*) drinking companion; (*Säufer*) soak (*inf*), boozer (*inf*).

saufen *pret* **soff**, *ptp* **gesoffen** *vti* **(a)** (*Tiere*) to drink. **(b)** (*sl: Mensch*) to booze (*inf*), to drink ◆ **das S~** boozing; **sich dumm/zu Tode ~** to drink oneself silly/to death; **wie ein Loch** *or* **Bürstenbinder** (*dated*) **~** to drink like a fish.

Säufer(in *f*) *m* **-s, -** (*inf*) boozer (*inf*), drunkard.

Sauferei *f* (*inf*) **(a)** (*Trinkgelage*) booze-up (*inf*). **(b)** *no pl* (*Trunksucht*) boozing (*inf*).

Säufer-: **~leber** *f* (*inf*) gin-drinker's liver (*inf*); **~nase** *f* boozer's nose; **~wahn(sinn)** *m* the DT's *pl* (*inf*).

Sauf-: **~gelage** *nt* (*pej inf*) drinking bout, booze-up (*inf*); **~kumpan, ~kumpel** *m* (*pej inf*) drinking pal.

Saufraß *m* (*sl*) muck (*inf*).

Säug|amme *f* (*old*) wet nurse.

Saugbagger *m* suction dredger.

saugen *pret* **sog** *or* **saugte**, *ptp* **gesogen** *or* **gesaugt** *vti* to suck; (*Pflanze, Schwamm*) to draw up, to absorb; (*inf: mit Staubsauger*) to vacuum ◆ **an etw** (*dat*) **~** to suck sth; *an Pfeife* to draw on sth; *siehe* **Finger**.

säugen *vt* to suckle.

Sauger *m* **-s, -** **(a)** (*auf Flasche*) teat (*Brit*), nipple (*US*); (*Schnuller*) dummy (*Brit*), pacifier (*US*). **(b)** (*inf: Staub~*) vacuum (cleaner).

Säuger *m* **-s, -**, **Säugetier** *nt* mammal.

Saug-: **s~fähig** *adj* absorbent; **~fähigkeit** *f* absorbency; **~flasche** *f* (*form*) feeding bottle; **~glocke** *f* (*Med*) vacuum extractor, ventouse (*spec*); **~glockengeburt** *f* (*Med*) suction *or* ventouse (*spec*) delivery.

Säugling *m* baby, infant (*form*).

Säuglings- *in cpds* baby, infant (*form*); **~alter** *nt* babyhood; **das Kind ist noch im ~alter** the child is still a baby; **~fürsorge** *f* infant welfare; **~heim** *nt* home for babies; **~pflege** *f* babycare; **~schwester** *f* infant nurse; **~sterblichkeit** *f* infant mortality.

Saug-: **~massage** *f* suction *or* vacuum massage; **~napf** *m* sucker; **~organ** *nt* suctorial organ (*form*); **~pumpe** *f* suction pump; (*für Brust*) breast pump; **~reflex** *m* sucking reflex; **~rohr, ~röhrchen** *nt* pipette; **~rüssel** *m* (*Zool*) proboscis; **~würmer** *pl* trematodes *pl* (*spec*).

Sau-: **~hatz** *f* (*Hunt*) wild boar hunt; **~haufen** *m* (*sl*) bunch of layabouts (*inf*); **~hirt** *m* (*old*) swineherd (*old*); **~hund** *m* (*dated sl*) bastard (*sl*).

säuisch *adj* (*sl*) *Benehmen, Witze* filthy, swinish (*sl*).

Sau-: **~jagd** *f siehe* **~hatz**; **s~kalt** *adj* (*sl*) bloody (*Brit sl*) *or* damn (*inf*) cold; **~kälte** *f* (*sl*) bloody (*Brit sl*) *or* damn (*inf*) freezing weather; **~kerl** *m* (*sl*) bastard (*sl*); **~klaue** *f* (*sl*) scrawl (*inf*).

Säule *f* **-, -n** column; (*Rauch~, Wasser~ auch, inf: Pfeiler, fig: Stütze*) pillar ◆ **die ~n des Herkules** the Pillars of Hercules.

Säulen-: ⚠**~abschluß** *m* capital; **~bau** *m* building with columns; **s~förmig** *adj* like a column/columns, columnar (*form*); **~fuß** *m* base; **~gang** *m* colonnade; (*um einen Hof*) peristyle; **~halle** *f* columned hall; **~heilige(r)** *mf* stylite; **~ordnung** *f* order (of columns); **die dorische ~ordnung** the Doric Order; **~portal** *nt* colonnaded doorway; **~reihe** *f* row of columns; **~schaft** *m* shaft of a column; **~tempel** *m* colonnaded temple.

Saulus *m* **-** (*Bibl*) Saul ◆ **vom ~ zum Paulus werden** (*fig liter*) to have seen the light.

Saum *m* **-(e)s, Säume** (*Stoffumschlag*) hem; (*Naht*) seam; (*fig: Wald~*) edge ◆ **ein schmaler ~ am Horizont** a thin band of cloud on the horizon.

saumäßig (*sl*) 1 *adj* lousy (*inf*); (*zur Verstärkung*) hell of a (*inf*).
2 *adv* lousily (*inf*); (*zur Verstärkung*) like hell (*inf*) ◆ **das hat er ~ gemacht** he made a real mess of it.

säumen[1] *vt* (*Sew*) to hem; (*fig geh*) to line.

säumen[2] *vi* (*liter*) to tarry (*liter*).

säumig *adj* (*geh*) *Schuldner* defaulting; *Zahlung* outstanding, overdue; *Schüler* dilatory ◆ **~ sein/bleiben/werden** to be/remain/get behind.

Säumnis *f* (*obs*) delay.

Saum-: **~pfad** *m* mule track; **s~selig** *adj* (*old liter*) dilatory; **~seligkeit** *f* (*old liter*) dilatoriness; **~stich** *m* hemstitch; **~tier** *nt* pack animal.

Sauna *f* **-, -s** *or* **Saunen** sauna.

saunieren *vi* to have a sauna.

Saupreuße *m* (*S Ger sl*) Prussian swine.

Säure *f* **-, -n** **(a)** (*Chem, Magen~*) acid. **(b)** *siehe* **sauer (a)** sourness; acidity, sharpness; sharpness, tartness ◆ **dieser Wein hat zuviel ~** this wine is too sharp.

Säure-: **s~arm** *adj* low in acid; **~bad** *nt* acid bath; **s~beständig, s~fest** *adj* acid-resistant; **s~frei** *adj* acid-free; **~gehalt** *m* acid content.

⚠ **Sauregurkenzeit** *f* bad time *or* period; (*in den Medien*) silly season.

Säure-: **s~haltig** *adj* acidic; **s~löslich** *adj* acid-soluble.

Saure(s) *nt decl as adj siehe* **sauer (g)**.

Säure-: **~vergiftung** *f* acid poisoning; **~zünder** *m* acid fuse.

Saurier [-iɐ] *m* **-s, -** dinosaur, saurian (*spec*).

Saus *m*: **in ~ und Braus leben** to live like a lord.

Sause *f* **-, -n** (*inf*) pub crawl ◆ **eine ~ machen** to go on a pub crawl.

säuseln 1 *vi* (*Wind*) to murmur, to sigh; (*Blätter*) to rustle; (*Mensch*) to purr ◆ **mit ~der Stimme** in a purring voice.
2 *vt* to murmur, to purr.

sausen *vi* **(a)** (*Ohren, Kopf*) to buzz; (*Wind*) to whistle; (*Sturm*) to roar ◆ **ihr sauste das Blut in den Ohren** (*geh*) the blood pounded in her ears; **mir ~ die Ohren, es saust mir in den Ohren** my ears are buzzing.
(b) *aux sein* (*Geschoß, Peitsche*) to whistle.
(c) *aux sein* (*inf: Mensch*) to tear (*inf*), to charge (*inf*); (*Fahrzeug*) to roar ◆ **saus mal schnell zum Bäcker** nip round (*Brit*) *or* run round to the baker's; **in den Graben ~** to fly into the ditch; **durch eine Prüfung ~** to fail *or* flunk (*inf*) an exam.
(d) einen ~ lassen (*sl*) to let off (*sl*) (a fart *vulg*).

⚠ **sausenlassen** *vt sep irreg* (*inf*) **jdn/etw ~** to drop sb/sth; **das Kino heute abend laß ich sausen** I'll not bother going to the cinema tonight.

Sauser *m* **-s, -** (*S Ger*) fermented apple/grape juice.

Sausewind *m* **(a)** (*dated inf*) (*lebhaft*) live wire (*inf*); (*unstet*) restless person. **(b)** (*baby-talk: Wind*) wind.

Sau-: **~stall** *m* (*sl*) (*unordentlich*) pigsty (*inf*); (*chaotisch*) mess; **~wetter** *nt* (*sl*)

bloody (*Brit sl*) *or* damn (*inf*) awful weather; **s~wohl** *adj pred* (*sl*) bloody (*Brit sl*) *or* really good; **mir ist** *or* **ich fühle mich s~wohl** I feel bloody (*Brit sl*) *or* really good; **~wut** *f* (*sl*) flaming rage (*inf*); **eine ~wut (im Bauch) haben** to be flaming mad; **eine ~wut auf jdn/etw haben** to be flaming mad at sb/sth.
Savanne [za'vanə] *f* -, -n savanna(h).
saven [se:vn] *vti* (*Comput inf*) to save.
Savoyen [za'vɔyən] *nt* -s Savoy.
Saxophon *nt* -(e)s, -e saxophone, sax (*inf*).
Saxophonist(in *f*) *m* saxophone player, saxophonist.
SB- [ɛs'be:-] *in cpds* self-service.
S-Bahn ['ɛs-] *f abbr of* **Schnellbahn, Stadtbahn.**
S-Bahnhof ['ɛs-] *m* suburban line station.
S-Bahn-Netz ['ɛs-] *nt* suburban rail network.
SBB *abbr of* **Schweizerische Bundesbahn.**
s. Br. *abbr of* **südlicher Breite.**
scannen ['skɛnən] *vt* to scan.
Scanner ['skɛnɐ] *m* (*Med, Comput*) scanner.
Scanner-Kasse ['skɛnɐ-] *f* electronic scanning cash register.
sch *interj* shh; (*zum Fortscheuchen*) shoo.
Schabau *m* -s, *no pl* (*dial*) spirits *pl*.
Schabe *f* -, -n cockroach.
Schabefleisch *nt* (*Cook dial*) minced steak (*Brit*), ground beef (*US*) (*often eaten raw*).
Schab(e)messer *nt* scraping knife, scraper.
schaben *vt* to scrape; *Fleisch* to chop finely; *Leder, Fell* to shave.
Schaber *m* -s, - scraper.
Schabernack *m* -(e)s, -e (a) prank, practical joke ◆ **jdm einen ~ spielen/mit jdm einen ~ treiben** to play a prank on sb; **allerlei ~ treiben** to get up to all sorts of pranks; **ich bin zu jedem ~ bereit** I'm always ready for a laugh. (b) (*Kind*) monkey (*inf*).
schäbig *adj* (a) (*abgetragen*) shabby. (b) (*niederträchtig*) mean, shabby; (*geizig*) mean, stingy; *Bezahlung* poor, shabby.
Schäbigkeit *f siehe adj* (a) shabbiness. (b) meanness, shabbiness; stinginess; poorness; (*Verhalten*) mean *or* shabby behaviour *no pl*.
Schablone *f* -, -n (a) stencil; (*Muster*) template.
(b) (*fig pej*) (*bei Arbeit, Arbeitsweise*) routine, pattern; (*beim Reden*) cliché ◆ **in ~n denken** to think in a stereotyped way; **in ~n reden** to speak in clichés; **etw geht nach ~** sth follows the same routine; **der Präsident lächelte, aber das war reine ~** the President smiled but it was just a matter of convention; **das ist alles nur ~** that's all just for show.
schablonenhaft 1 *adj* (*pej*) *Denken, Vorstellungen, Argumente* stereotyped; *Ausdrucksweise* clichéd.
2 *adv* in stereotypes/clichés.
Schabmesser *nt siehe* **Schab(e)messer.**
Schabracke *f* -, -n (a) (*Satteldecke*) saddlecloth. (b) (*altes Pferd*) nag; (*sl: alte Frau*) hag. (c) (*Querbehang*) pelmet.
Schabsel *pl* shavings *pl*.
Schach *nt* -s, *no pl* chess; (*Stellung im Spiel*) check ◆ **kannst du ~ (spielen)?** can you play chess?; **~ (dem König)!** check; **~ und matt** checkmate; **im ~ stehen** *or* **sein** to be in check; **jdm ~ bieten** (*lit*) to put sb in check, to check sb; (*fig*) to thwart sb; **jdn in ~ halten** (*fig*) to stall sb; (*mit Pistole etc*) to cover sb, to keep sb covered.
Schach-: ~aufgabe *f* chess problem; **~brett** *nt* chessboard; **s~brettartig** *adj* chequered; **Platten s~brettartig anlegen** to lay tiles in a chequered pattern *or* like a chessboard; **die Straßen sind s~brettartig angeordnet** the roads are laid out like a grid; **~brettmuster** *nt* chequered pattern.
Schacher *m* -s, *no pl* (*pej*) (*das Feilschen*) haggling (*um* over); (*Wucher*) sharp practice; (*fig Pol auch*) horse-trading (*um* about) ◆ **~ treiben** to indulge in haggling *etc*.
Schächer *m* -s, - (*Bibl*) thief.
Schacherei *f* (*pej*) *siehe* **Schacher.**
Schacherer *m* -s, - (*pej*) haggler; (*Wucherer*) sharper; (*Pol*) horse-trader.
schachern *vi* (*pej*) **um etw ~** to haggle over sth.
Schach-: ~feld *nt* square (on a chessboard); **~figur** *f* chess piece, chessman; (*fig*) pawn; **s~matt** *adj* (*lit*) (check)mated; (*fig: erschöpft*) exhausted, shattered (*inf*); **s~matt!** (check)- mate; **jdn s~matt setzen** (*lit*) to (check)mate sb; (*fig*) to snooker sb (*inf*); **~partie** *f* game of chess; **~spiel** *nt* (*Spiel*) game of chess; (*Spielart*) chess *no art*; (*Brett und Figuren*) chess set; **~spieler** *m* chess player.
Schacht *m* -(e)s, ⸚e shaft; (*Brunnen~*) well; (*Straßen~*) manhole; (*Kanalisations~*) drain.
Schachtel *f* -, -n (a) box; (*Zigaretten~*) packet ◆ **eine ~ Streichhölzer/Pralinen** a box of matches/chocolates. (b) (*sl: Frau*) bag (*sl*).
Schachtel-: ~halm *m* (*Bot*) horsetail; **~satz** *m* complicated *or* multi-clause sentence.
schächten *vt* to slaughter according to religious rites ◆ **das rituelle Schächten von Tieren** the ritual slaughter of animals.
Schach-: ~turnier *nt* chess tournament; **~zug** *m* (*fig*) move.
Schade *m* (*old*): **es soll dein ~ nicht sein** it will not be to your disadvantage.
schade *adj pred* **(das ist aber) ~!** what a pity *or* shame; **es ist (zu) ~, daß ...** it's a (real) pity *or* shame that ...; **es ist ~ um jdn/etw** it's a pity *or* shame about sb/sth; **um sie ist es nicht ~** she's no great loss; **für etw zu ~ sein** to be too good for sth; **sich** (*dat*) **für etw zu ~ sein** to consider oneself too good for sth; **sich** (*dat*) **für nichts zu ~ sein** to consider nothing (to be) beneath one.
Schädel *m* -s, - skull ◆ **ein kahler ~** a bald head; **jdm den ~ einschlagen** to beat sb's skull *or* head in; **jdm den ~ spalten/zertrümmern** to split *or* cleave/crush sb's skull; **sich** (*dat*) **den ~ einrennen** (*inf*) to crack one's skull; **mir brummt der ~** (*inf*) my head is going round and round; (*vor Kopfschmerzen*) my head is throbbing; **einen dicken ~ haben** (*fig inf*) to be stubborn.
Schädel-: ~basisbruch *m* fracture at the base of the skull; **~bruch** *m* fractured skull; **~decke** *f* top of the skull; **~lage** *f* vertex presentation; **~naht** *f* suture.
schaden *vi* +*dat* to damage, to harm; *einem Menschen* to harm, to hurt; *jds Ruf* to damage ◆ **sich** (*dat*) **selbst ~** to harm *or* hurt oneself, to do oneself harm; **das/Rauchen schadet Ihrer Gesundheit/Ihnen** that/smoking is bad for your health/you; **das schadet nichts** it does no harm; (*macht nichts*) that doesn't matter; **es kann nichts ~, wenn ...** it would do no harm if ...; **das kann nicht(s) ~** that won't do any harm, it wouldn't hurt; **das schadet dir gar nichts** it serves you right; **was schadet es, wenn ...?** what harm can it do if ...?
Schaden *m* -s, ⸚ (a) (*Beschädigung, Zerstörung*) damage *no pl, no indef art* (*durch* caused by); (*Personen~*) injury; (*Verlust*) loss; (*Unheil, Leid*) harm ◆ **einen ~ verursachen** to cause damage; **ich habe einen ~ am Auto** my car has been damaged; **zu jds ~ gereichen** (*geh*) to be to sb's detriment; **es soll sein ~ nicht sein** it will not be to his disadvantage; **es ist nicht zu deinem ~** it won't do you any harm; **den ~ von etw haben** to suffer for sth; **zu ~ kommen** to suffer; (*physisch*) to be hurt *or* injured; **nicht zu ~ kommen** not to come to any harm; **an etw** (*dat*) **~ nehmen** to damage *or* harm sth; **jdm/einer Sache ~ zufügen** to harm sb/to harm *or* damage sth; **geringe/einige ⸚ aufweisen** to have suffered little/some damage; **aus** *or* **durch ~ wird man klug** (*Prov*) you learn by *or* from your mistakes; **wer den ~ hat, braucht für den Spott nicht zu sorgen** (*Prov*) don't mock the afflicted.
(b) (*Defekt*) fault; (*körperlicher Mangel*) defect ◆ **⸚ an der Lunge** lung damage; **⸚ aufweisen** to be defective; (*Organ*) to be damaged; **ein ~ an der Leber** a damaged liver.
Schaden-: ~ersatz *m siehe* **Schadensersatz**; **~feststellung** *f* assessment of damage; **~freiheitsrabatt** *m* no claims bonus; **~freude** *f* malicious joy, gloating; **... sagte er mit ~freude ...** he gloated; **s~froh** *adj* gloating.
Schadensbegrenzung *f* damage limitation.
Schadens|ersatz *m* compensation, damages *pl* ◆ **jdn auf ~ verklagen** to claim compensation from sb; **~ leisten** to pay compensation.
Schadens|ersatz-: ~anspruch *m* claim for compensation; **~klage** *f* action for damages; **s~pflichtig** *adj* liable for compensation.
Schadens-: ~fall *m* **im ~fall** (*Insur*) in the event of a claim; **~regulierung** *f* settlement of damages.
schadhaft *adj no adv* faulty, defective; (*beschädigt*) damaged; (*abgenutzt*) *Kleidung* worn; *Zähne* decayed; *Gebäude* dilapidated.
Schadhaftigkeit *f siehe adj* faultiness, defectiveness; damaged/worn/decayed/dilapidated state.
schädigen *vt* to damage; *jdn* to hurt, to harm; *Firma auch* to hurt ◆ **man muß die Firma ~, wo man nur kann** (*iro*) you've got to get what you can out of the firm.
Schädigung *f siehe vt* (*gen* done to) damage; hurt, harm.
schädlich *adj* harmful; *Wirkung, Einflüsse* detrimental, damaging ◆ **~ für etw sein** to be damaging to sth; **~es Tier** pest.
Schädlichkeit *f* harmfulness.
Schädling *m* pest.
Schädlings-: ~bekämpfung *f* pest control *no art*; **~bekämpfungsmittel** *nt* pesticide.
schadlos *adj* **sich an jdm/etw ~ halten** to take advantage of sb/sth; **wir halten uns dafür am Bier ~** (*hum*) ... but we'll make up for it on the beer.
Schadstoff *m* harmful substance.
Schadstoff-: s~arm *adj* **s~arm sein** to contain a low level of harmful substances; **~belastung** *f* (*von Umwelt*) pollution; **~gehalt** *m* level of harmful substances (*gen* in); (*der Luft*) pollution content (*gen* of); **~konzentration** *f* concentration of harmful substances.
Schaf *nt* -(e)s, -e sheep; (*inf: Dummkopf*) twit (*Brit inf*), dope (*inf*) ◆ **das schwarze ~ sein** to be the black sheep (*in* +*dat, gen* of); **~e zählen** (*fig*) to count sheep; *siehe* **Bock**[1] **(a).**
Schafbock *m* ram.
Schäfchen *nt* lamb, little sheep; (*inf: Dummerchen*) silly billy (*inf*) ◆ **~ *pl*** (*Gemeinde, Anvertraute*) flock *sing*; **sein ~ ins trockene bringen** (*prov*) to see oneself all right (*inf*); **sein ~ im trockenen haben** to have feathered one's own nest.
Schäfchenwolken *pl* cotton-wool clouds *pl*, fleecy clouds *pl*.
Schäfer *m* -s, - shepherd.
Schäferdichtung *f* (*Liter*) pastoral poetry.
Schäferei *f* (a) (*Schafhaltung*) sheep-rearing *or* -farming. (b) (*Betrieb*) sheep farm.
Schäferhund *m* alsatian (dog) (*Brit*), German shepherd (dog) (*US*).
Schäferin *f* shepherdess.
Schäfer-: ~roman *m* (*Liter*) pastoral novel; **~stündchen** *nt* (*euph hum*) bit of hanky-panky (*hum inf*).
Schaffell *nt* sheepskin.
Schaffen *nt* -s, *no pl* **die Freude am ~** the joy of creation; **sein musikalisches/künstlerisches ~** his musical/artistic works *pl or* creations *pl*; **der Künstler bei seinem ~** the artist at work; **auf dem Höhepunkt seines ~s** at the peak of his creative powers *or* prowess.
schaffen[1] *pret* **schuf,** *ptp* **geschaffen** *vt* (a) to create ◆ **die ~de Natur** the creative power of nature; **der ~de Mensch** the creative human being; **dafür**

⚠: for details of spelling reform, see supplement

➤ SPRACHE AKTIV: schade → 45.3

ist er wie geschaffen he's just made for it; wie ihn Gott geschaffen hatte as God made him.
(b) *pret auch* schaffte (*herstellen*) to make; *Bedingungen, Möglichkeiten, System, Methode* to create ◆ Raum *or* Platz ~ to make room; Ruhe ~ to establish order; Linderung ~ to bring relief (*für* to).

schaffen[2] 1 *vt* (a) (*bewältigen, zustande bringen*) *Aufgabe, Hürde, Portion etc* to manage; *Prüfung* to pass ◆ ~ wir das zeitlich? are we going to make it?; schaffst du's noch? (*inf*) can you manage?; wir haben's geschafft we've managed it; (*Arbeit erledigt*) we've done it; (*gut angekommen*) we've made it; so, das hätten wir *or* das wäre geschafft! there, that's done; das ist nicht zu ~ that can't be done; das hast du wieder mal geschafft you've done it again; wir haben nicht viel geschafft *or* geschafft gekriegt (*inf*) we haven't managed to do much *or* haven't got much done; er schafft es noch, daß ich ihn rauswerfe/er rausgeworfen wird he'll end up with me throwing him out/(by) being thrown out.
(b) (*inf: überwältigen*) jdn to see off (*inf*) ◆ das hat mich geschafft it took it out of me; (*nervlich*) it got on top of me; geschafft sein to be shattered (*inf*); die schafft keiner (*sl*) she can't get enough (from anyone).
(c) (*bringen*) etw in etw (*acc*) ~ to put sth in sth; wie sollen wir das in den Keller/auf den Berg ~? how will we manage to get that into the cellar/up the mountain?; etw aus etw ~ to get sth out of sth; einen Koffer zum Bahnhof ~ to take a case to the station; alte Zeitungen auf den Boden ~ to put old newspapers in the attic; etw aus der Welt ~ to settle sth (for good); sich (*dat*) jdn/etw vom Hals(e) *or* Leib(e) ~ to get sb/sth off one's back; *siehe* beiseite.
(d) (*verursachen*) Ärger, Unruhe, Verdruß to cause, to create.
2 *vi* (a) (*tun*) to do ◆ ich habe damit nichts zu ~ that has nothing to do with me; was haben Sie dort zu ~? what do you think you're doing (there)?; sich (*dat*) an etw (*dat*) zu ~ machen to fiddle about with sth; sich mit etw zu ~ machen to busy oneself with sth.
(b) (*zusetzen*) jdm (sehr *or* schwer) zu ~ machen to cause sb (a lot of) trouble; (*bekümmern*) to worry sb (a lot); das macht ihr heute noch zu ~ she still worries about it today.
(c) (*S Ger: arbeiten*) to work.

Schaffens-: ~drang *m* energy; (*von Künstler*) creative urge; ~freude *f* (creative) zest *or* enthusiasm; s~freudig *adj* (creatively) enthusiastic; *Künstler* creative; ~kraft *f* creativity.

Schaffer *m* -s, - (*inf*) hard worker.

Schaffhausen *nt* (*Kanton, Stadt*) Schaffhausen.

Schaffleisch *nt* mutton.

Schaffner(in *f*) *m* -s, - (a) (*im Bus*) conductor; (*Rail*) ticket collector; (*im Zug*) guard (*Brit*), conductor (*US*), ticket inspector; (*im Schlafwagen*) attendant. (b) (*old*) (*Verwalter*) major-domo; (*Wirtschafterin*) housekeeper.

schaffnerlos *adj* without a conductor *etc* ◆ ~e Busse one-man buses.

Schaffung *f* creation.

Schaf- *siehe auch* Schafs-; ~garbe *f* yarrow; ~herde *f* flock of sheep; ~hirt *m* shepherd; ~hürde *f* sheep pen, (sheep)fold.

Schäflein *nt* (*lit, fig*) lamb; (*pl fig*) flock *sing or pl*.

Schafott *nt* -(e)s, -e scaffold.

Schaf-: ~pelz *m siehe* Schafspelz; ~scherer(in *f*) *m* -s, - sheepshearer; ~schur *f* sheepshearing.

Schafs-: ~käse *m* sheep's milk cheese; ~kopf *m* (a) sheep's head; (*pej: Dummkopf*) blockhead, dolt, numskull; (b) (*Cards*) *German card game, a simplified version of skat*; ~milch *f* sheep's milk; ~pelz *m* sheepskin; *siehe* Wolf.

Schafstall *m* sheepfold.

Schaft *m* -(e)s, ¨e shaft (*auch Archit*); (*von Gewehr*) stock; (*von Stiefel*) leg; (*von Schraube, Schlüssel*) shank; (*Bot*) stalk.

Schaftstiefel *pl* high boots *pl*; (*Mil*) jackboots *pl*.

Schaf-: ~weide *f* sheep pasture; ~wolle *f* sheep's wool; ~zucht *f* sheep breeding *no art*.

Schah *m* -s, -s Shah.

Schakal *m* -s, -e jackal.

Schäker *m* -s, - (*inf*) flirt; (*Witzbold*) joker.

Schäkerei *f* (*inf*) flirting; (*Witzelei*) fooling around.

Schäkerin *f* (*inf*) flirt, coquette; (*Witzbold*) joker.

schäkern *vi* to flirt; (*necken*) to play about.

Schal *m* -s, -s *or* -e scarf; (*Umschlagtuch*) shawl.

schal *adj Getränk* flat; *Wasser, Geschmack* stale; (*fig: geistlos*) *Witz* stale, weak; *Leben* empty; *Gerede* vapid, empty.

Schälchen *nt dim of* Schale[1] (small) bowl.

Schale[1] *f* -, -n bowl; (*flach, zum Servieren etc*) dish; (*von Waage*) pan; (*Sekt~*) champagne glass; (*esp S Ger, Aus: Tasse*) cup.

Schale[2] *f* -, -n (*von Obst, Gemüse*) skin; (*abgeschält*) peel *no pl*; (*Rinde*) (*von Käse*) rind; (*von Nüssen, Eiern, Muscheln*) shell; (*von Getreide*) husk, hull; (*Hunt*) hoof; (*fig: äußeres Auftreten*) appearance ◆ sich in ~ werfen *or* schmeißen (*inf*) to get dressed up; (*Frau auch*) to get dolled up (*inf*); in seiner rauhen ~ steckt ein guter Kern beneath that rough exterior (there) beats a heart of gold (*prov*); *siehe* rauh.

schälen 1 *vti* to peel; *Tomate, Mandel* to skin; *Erbsen, Eier, Nüsse* to shell; *Getreide* to husk.
2 *vr* to peel; (*Schlange*) to slough its skin ◆ sich aus den Kleidern ~ to peel off (one's clothes); ich schäle mich auf der Nase my nose is peeling.

Schal(en)|obst *nt* nuts *pl*.

Schalen-: ~sessel *m* shell chair; ~sitz *m* bucket seat; ~wild *nt siehe* Schalwild.

Schalheit *f* flatness; (*von Wasser, Geschmack*) staleness; (*fig: Geistlosigkeit, von Witz*) staleness, weakness.

Schalholz *nt* shuttering wood.

Schalk *m* -(e)s, -e *or* ¨e joker ◆ ihm sitzt der ~ im Nacken he's in a devilish mood; ihr schaut der ~ aus den Augen she (always) has a roguish *or* mischievous look on her face.

schalkhaft *adj* roguish, mischievous.

Schalkhaftigkeit *f* roguishness, mischievousness.

Schalkragen *m* shawl collar; (*mit losen Enden*) scarf collar.

Schall *m* -s, -e *or* ¨e sound ◆ Ruhm vergeht wie ~ und Rauch (*geh*) fame is but a transient shadow; Name ist ~ und Rauch what's in a name?; das ist alles ~ und Rauch it's all hollow words.

Schall-: ~becher *m* (*Mus*) bell; ~boden *m* sound(ing)-board; s~dämmen *vt* to soundproof; s~dämmend *adj* sound-deadening; ~dämmung *f* sound absorption; (*Abdichtung gegen Schall*) soundproofing; s~dämpfend *adj Wirkung* sound-muffling *or* -deadening; *Material* soundproofing; ~dämpfer *m* sound absorber; (*von Auto*) silencer (*Brit*), muffler (*US*); (*von Gewehr etc*) silencer; (*Mus*) mute; ~dämpfung *f* sound absorption; (*Abdichtung gegen Schall*) soundproofing; (*von Auto etc*) silencing; s~dicht *adj* soundproof; s~dicht abgeschlossen sein to be fully soundproofed.

⚠ **Schalleiter** *m getrennt:* Schall-leiter conductor of sound.

schallen *pret* schallte *or* (*old*) scholl, *ptp* geschallt *or* (*old*) geschollen *vi* to sound; (*Stimme, Glocke, Beifall*) to ring (out); (*widerhallen*) to resound, to echo ◆ das Schlagen der Turmuhr schallte zu uns herüber we could hear the church clock ring out.

schallend *adj Beifall, Ohrfeige* resounding; *Gelächter* ringing ◆ ~ lachen to roar with laughter.

Schall-: ~geschwindigkeit *f* speed of sound; ~grenze, ~mauer *f* sound barrier; ~leiter *m siehe* Schalleiter; ~messung *f* sound ranging.

Schallplatte *f* record.

Schallplatten-: ~album *nt* record case; ~archiv *nt* (gramophone) record archive; ~aufnahme *f* (gramophone) recording.

Schall-: ~schirm *m siehe* ~wand; s~schluckend *adj* sound-absorbent; *Material* soundproofing; ~schutzfenster *nt* soundproof window; s~sicher *adj* soundproof; s~tot *adj Raum* completely soundproof, anechoic (*spec*); ~trichter *m* horn; (*von Trompeten etc*) bell; ~wand *f* baffle (*of loudspeaker etc*); ~welle *f* soundwave; ~wort *nt* onomatopoeic word.

Schalmei *f* shawm.

Schal|obst *nt siehe* Schal(en)obst.

Schalotte *f* -, -n shallot.

schalt *pret of* schelten.

Schalt-: ~anlage *f* switchgear; ~bild *nt* circuit diagram, wiring diagram; ~brett *nt* switchboard, control panel.

schalten 1 *vt* (a) to switch, to turn; (*in Gang bringen*) to switch *or* turn on; *Leitung* to connect ◆ etw auf „2" ~ to turn *or* switch sth to "2"; etw auf die höchste Stufe ~ to turn sth on full, to turn sth full on *or* up; in Reihe/parallel ~ (*Elec*) to connect in series/in parallel; das Gerät läßt sich schwer ~ *or* schaltet sich schwer this device has a difficult switch (to operate); das Auto läßt sich spielend ~ *or* schaltet sich leicht it's easy to change gear in this car.
(b) *Werbespot, Zeitungsanzeige* to place.
2 *vi* (a) (*Gerät*) to switch (*auf* +*acc* to); (*Aut*) to change gear ◆ in den 2. Gang ~ to change *or* shift (*US*) (up/down) into 2nd gear.
(b) (*fig: verfahren, handeln*) ~ und walten to bustle around; frei ~ (und walten) können to have a free hand (to do as one pleases); jdn frei ~ und walten lassen to give sb a free hand, to let sb manage things as he sees fit.
(c) (*inf: begreifen*) to latch on (*inf*), to get it (*inf*), to get the message (*inf*); (*reagieren*) to react.

Schalter *m* -s, - (a) (*Elec etc*) switch. (b) (*in Post, Bank, Amt*) counter; (*mit Fenster auch*) window; (*im Bahnhof*) ticket window.

Schalter-: ~beamte(r) *m* counter clerk; (*im Bahnhof*) ticket clerk; ~dienst *m* counter duty; ~halle *f*, ~raum *m* (*in Post*) hall; (*in Bank*) (banking) hall; (*im Bahnhof*) booking *or* ticket hall; ~stunden *pl* hours of business *pl*, business hours *pl*.

Schalt-: s~faul *adj* (*inf*) reluctant to change gear; ~getriebe *nt* manual transmission, stick shift (*US*); ~hebel *m* switch lever; (*Aut*) gear lever, gear-shift (lever); an dem ~hebel der Macht sitzen to hold the reins of power.

Schaltier *nt* crustacean.

Schalt-: ~jahr *nt* leap year; alle ~jahre (*inf*) once in a blue moon; ~kasten *m* switchbox; ~knüppel *m* (*Aut*) gear lever; (*Aviat*) joystick; ~kreis *m* (*Tech*) (switching) circuit; ~pause *f* (*TV, Rad*) pause (*before going over to another region or station*); ~plan *m siehe* ~bild; ~pult *nt* control desk; ~satz *m* (*Ling*) parenthetic clause; ~schritt *m* (*von Schreibmaschine*) horizontal spacing; ~skizze *f siehe* ~bild; ~stelle *f* (*fig*) coordinating point; ~tafel *f siehe* ~brett; ~tag *m* leap day

Schaltung *f* switching; (*Elec*) wiring; (*Aut*) gear change, gearshift.

Schaltzentrale *f* (*lit*) control centre; (*fig*) nerve centre.

Schalung *f* formwork, shuttering.

Schaluppe *f* -, -n sloop.

Schalwild *nt* hoofed game.

Scham *f* -, *no pl* (a) shame ◆ er wurde rot vor ~ he went red with shame; die ~ stieg ihm ins Gesicht (*old*) a blush of shame mounted to his cheeks; ich hätte vor ~ (in den Boden) versinken können I wanted the floor to swallow me up *or* to open up under me; er versteckte sich vor ~ he hid himself in

shame; **aus falscher ~** from a false sense of shame; **nur keine falsche ~!** (*inf*) no need to feel *or* be embarrassed!, no need for embarrassment!; **sie hat kein bißchen ~ (im Leibe)** she doesn't have an ounce of shame (in her); **ohne ~** unashamedly.
(b) (*geh: Genitalien*) private parts *pl*; (*von Frau*) pudenda *pl*.

Schamane *m* **-n, -n** shaman.

Scham-: ~bein *nt* pubic bone; **~berg** *m* (*geh*) *siehe* **~hügel**; **~bogen** *m* pubic arch.

schämen *vr* to be ashamed ♦ **du solltest dich ~!, du sollst dich was ~** (*inf*) you ought to be ashamed of yourself!; **sich einer Sache** (*gen*) *or* **für** *or* **wegen etw ~** to be ashamed of sth; **sich jds/einer Sache** *or* **wegen jdm/etw** (*inf*) **~** to be ashamed of sb/sth; **sich für jdn ~** to be ashamed for sb; **sich vor jdm ~** to be *or* feel ashamed in front of sb; **ich schäme mich so vor ihm** he makes me feel so ashamed; **schäme dich!** shame on you!

Scham-: ~fuge *f* pubic symphysis (*spec*); **~gefühl** *nt* sense of shame; **ganz ohne ~gefühl sein** to have no (sense of) shame; **~gegend** *f* pubic region; **~grenze** *f* **keine ~grenze haben** to have no sense of shame; **da liegt meine ~grenze** that's going too far for me; **~haar** *nt* pubic hair; **s~haft** *adj* modest; (*verschämt*) bashful, coy; **die heutige Jugend ist nicht sehr s~haft** today's young people have very little modesty; **~haftigkeit** *f* modesty; **~hügel** *m* mount of Venus, mons veneris (*form*); **~lippen** *pl* labia *pl*, lips *pl* of the vulva; **s~los** *adj* shameless; (*unanständig auch*) indecent; (*unverschämt auch*) brazen; *Frechheit, Lüge* brazen, barefaced; **sich s~los zeigen** to flaunt oneself brazenly *or* shamelessly; **sich s~los kleiden** to dress indecently; **s~lose Reden führen** to make indecent remarks; **~losigkeit** *f siehe adj* shamelessness; indecency; brazenness.

Schamott *m* **-s,** *no pl* **(a)** (*inf*) junk (*inf*), trash (*inf*), rubbish. **(b)** (*Aus, S Ger*) *siehe* **Schamotte**.

Schamotte *f* **-,** *no pl* fireclay.

Schamotte-: ~stein *m* firestone; **~ziegel** *m* firebrick.

schamottieren* *vt* to line with firebricks.

Schampus *m* **-s,** *no pl* (*dated inf*) champers *sing* (*dated inf*).

Scham-: s~rot *adj* red (with shame); **s~rot werden** *or* **anlaufen** to turn red *or* to blush *or* flush with shame; **~röte** *f* flush *or* blush of shame; **die ~röte stieg ihr ins Gesicht** her face flushed with shame; **~teile** *pl* private parts *pl*, genitals *pl*.

schandbar *adj* shameful, disgraceful.

Schande *f* **-,** *no pl* disgrace; (*Unehre auch*) shame, ignominy ♦ **er ist eine ~ für seine Familie** he is a disgrace to his family; **das ist eine (wahre) ~!** this is a(n absolute) disgrace!; **~!** (*euph inf*) sugar! (*euph inf*), hell! (*inf*); **es ist doch keine ~, Gefühle zu zeigen** *or* **wenn man Gefühle zeigt** there is no shame *or* disgrace in showing one's feelings; **~ über jdn bringen** to bring disgrace *or* shame upon sb, to disgrace sb; **~ über dich!** (*dated*) shame on you!; **er hat das arme Mädchen in ~ gebracht** he brought shame *or* dishonour upon the poor girl, he dishonoured the poor girl; **jdm/einer Sache ~ machen** to be a disgrace to sb/sth; **mach mir keine ~** don't show me up (*inf*), don't be a disgrace to me; **zu meiner (großen) ~ muß ich gestehen, ...** to my great *or* eternal shame I have to admit that ...; *siehe* **Schimpf**.

schänden *vt Leichnam, Grab, Denkmal* to violate, to defile; *Heiligtum auch* to desecrate; *Sabbat, Sonntag etc* to violate, to desecrate; *Frauen, Kinder* to violate; *Ansehen, Namen* to dishonour, to discredit, to sully.

Schand-: ~fleck *m* blot (*in +dat* on); (*Gebäude etc auch*) eyesore; **er war der ~fleck der Familie** he was the disgrace of his family; **~geld** *nt* ridiculous *or* extortionate price.

schändlich *adj* disgraceful, shameful ♦ **jdn ~ im Stich lassen/betrügen** shamefully to leave sb in the lurch/to deceive sb shamefully.

Schändlichkeit *f* disgracefulness, shamefulness.

Schand-: ~mal *nt* brand, stigma; **~maul** *nt* (*pej*) malicious *or* evil tongue; **er ist ein ~maul** he has a malicious *or* an evil tongue; **~pfahl** *m* pillory; **~tat** *f* scandalous *or* disgraceful deed; (*hum*) prank, escapade; **zu jeder ~tat bereit sein** (*inf*) to be always ready for mischief *or* a lark (*inf*).

Schändung *f siehe vt* violation, defilement; desecration; violation; dishonouring, discrediting, sullying.

schanghaien* *vt* (*Naut*) to shanghai.

Schani *m* **-s, -** (*Aus inf*) **(a)** (*Freund*) mate (*inf*), buddy (*US inf*). **(b)** (*Diener*) servant.

Schank *f* **-, -en** (*Aus*) bar.

Schank-: ~betrieb *m* bar service; **nach 24**[00] **kein ~betrieb mehr** the bar closes at 12 midnight; **~bier** *nt* draught beer.

Schanker *m* **-s, -** chancre.

Schank-: ~erlaubnis *f* licence (*of publican*) (*Brit*), excise license (*US*); **~fräulein** *nt* (*Aus*) barmaid; **~konzession** *f siehe* **~erlaubnis**; **~stube** *f* (public) bar (*Brit*), saloon (*US*); **~tisch** *m* bar; **~wirt** *m* (*old*) taverner (*old*), publican (*Brit*), saloon keeper (*US*), barkeeper (*US*); **~wirtschaft** *f* (*old, Aus*) tavern (*old*), public house (*Brit*), saloon (*US*).

Schanz-: ~arbeit *f* trench digging, trenchwork; **~arbeiten** entrenchments, trenchwork; **~bau** *m siehe* **Schanzenbau**.

Schanze *f* **-, -n** (*Mil*) fieldwork, entrenchment; (*Naut*) quarterdeck; (*Sport*) (ski-)jump ♦ **sein Leben in die ~ schlagen** (*geh*) to risk one's life, to put one's life at risk *or* in jeopardy.

schanzen *vi* (*Mil*) to dig (trenches).

Schanzen-: ~bau *m* construction of fieldwork *or* entrenchments; **~rekord** *m* (*Sport*) ski-jump record.

Schanzwerk *nt* entrenchment.

Schar[1] *f* **-, -en** crowd, throng (*liter*); (*von Vögeln*) flock; (*von Insekten, Heuschrecken etc*) swarm; (*Reiter~, Soldaten~ etc*) band, company; (*von Jägern*) party; (*Pfadfinder*) company, troop; (*von Engeln*) host, band, throng (*liter*) ♦ **~en von Hausfrauen stürzten sich auf die Sonderangebote** hordes *or* crowds of housewives descended on the special offers; **die Schlachtenbummler verließen das Stadion in (hellen) ~en** the away supporters left the stadium in droves *or* swarmed away from the stadium; **die Menschen kamen in (hellen) ~en nach Lourdes** people flocked to Lourdes.

Schar[2] *f* **-, -en** (*Pflug~*) (plough)share (*Brit*), (plow)share (*US*).

Scharade *f* charade ♦ **~ spielen** to play charades.

Scharbockskraut *nt* (lesser) celandine.

Schäre *f* **-, -n** skerry.

scharen **[1]** *vt* **Menschen/Anhänger um sich ~** to gather people/to rally supporters around one.
[2] *vr* **sich um jdn ~** to gather around sb; (*Anhänger auch*) to rally around sb.

scharenweise *adv* (*in bezug auf Menschen*) in droves ♦ **die Heuschrecken/Vögel fielen ~ über die Saat her** swarms of locusts/whole flocks of birds descended on the seedcrop; **~ drängten sich die Leute vor dem Schaufenster** people crowded *or* thronged in front of the shop window.

scharf *adj, comp* **¨-er,** *superl* **¨-ste(r, s)** *or adv* **am ¨-sten** **(a)** *Kante, Kurve* sharp; *Messer, Klinge auch* keen *attr* (*liter*); (*durchdringend*) *Wind* keen, biting, cutting; *Kälte* biting; *Luft* raw, keen; *Frost* sharp, keen; *Ton* piercing, shrill ♦ **das „s" wird oft ~ ausgesprochen** "s" is often voiceless *or* pronounced as an "s" and not a "z"; **das ~e s** (*inf, Aus*) the "scharfes s" (*German symbol ß*); **ein Messer ~ machen** to sharpen a knife.
(b) (*stark gewürzt*) hot; (*mit Salz, Pfeffer*) highly seasoned; *Geruch, Geschmack* pungent, acrid; *Käse* strong, sharp; *Alkohol* (*stark*) strong; (*brennend*) fiery; (*ätzend*) *Waschmittel, Lösung* caustic ♦ **~ nach etw riechen** to smell strongly of sth; **~ würzen** to season highly, to make hot (*inf*); **Fleisch ~ anbraten** to sear meat; **~e Sachen** (*inf*) hard stuff (*inf*).
(c) (*hart, streng*) *Mittel, Maßnahmen* tough, severe, drastic; (*inf*) *Prüfung, Untersuchung* strict, tough; *Lehrer, Polizist* tough; *Bewachung* close, tight; *Hund* fierce ♦ **jdn ~ bewachen** to guard sb closely.
(d) (*schonungslos, stark*) *Worte, Kritik* sharp, biting, harsh; *Widerstand, Konkurrenz* fierce, tough; *Gegner, Protest* strong, fierce; *Auseinandersetzung* bitter, fierce ♦ **eine ~e Zunge haben** to have a sharp tongue, to be sharp-tongued; **jdn/etw in ~er Form kritisieren** to criticize sb/sth in strong terms; **etw in ¨~ster Form** *or* **aufs ¨~ste verurteilen** to condemn sth in the strongest possible terms; **das ist ja das ¨~ste!** (*sl*) this is too much! (*inf*); **das ¨~ste war, mich zu belügen** (*sl*) worst of all, I was lied to.
(e) (*deutlich, klar, genau*) sharp; *Unterschied auch* marked; *Brille, Linse* sharply focusing; *Augen auch* keen; *Töne* clear, precise; *Verstand, Intelligenz, Gehör auch* keen, acute; *Beobachter* keen ♦ **etw ~ einstellen** *Bild, Diaprojektor etc* to bring sth into focus; *Sender* to tune sth in (properly); **~ eingestellt** in (sharp) focus; (properly) tuned in; **~ sehen/hören** to have sharp eyes/ears; **~ aufpassen/zuhören** to pay close attention/to listen closely; **jdn ~ ansehen** to give sb a scrutinizing look; (*mißbilligend*) to look sharply at sb; **etw ~ umreißen** (*fig*) to outline sth precisely *or* clearly; **~ nachdenken** to have a good *or* long think, to think long and hard; **~ kalkulieren** to calculate exactly; **ein ~es Auge für etw haben** (*fig*) to have a keen *or* sharp eye for sth; **mit ~em Blick** (*fig*) with penetrating insight.
(f) (*heftig, schnell*) *Ritt, Trab* hard ♦ **~ reiten** to ride hard; **ein ~es Tempo fahren** (*inf*) to drive hell for leather (*inf*), to drive at quite a lick (*inf*); **einen ~en Stil fahren** (*inf*) to drive hard; **~ bremsen** to brake sharply *or* hard.
(g) (*echt*) *Munition etc, Schuß* live ♦ **etw ~ machen** to arm sth; **~e Schüsse abgeben** to shoot *or* fire live bullets; **das Gewehr war ~ geladen** the rifle was loaded with live ammunition; **~ schießen** (*lit*) (*mit ~er Munition*) to shoot with live ammunition; (*auf den Mann*) to aim to hit; (*fig*) to let fly; **in der Diskussion wurde ziemlich ~ geschossen** (*inf*) the discussion became rather heated, sparks flew in the discussion.
(h) (*sl*) (*geil*) randy (*Brit inf*), horny (*inf*); (*aufreizend*) *Frau, Kleidung, Bilder* sexy (*inf*); *Film* sexy (*inf*), blue *attr*; (*aufregend*) *Auto, Film* cool (*inf*), great (*inf*) ♦ **~ werden** to get turned on (*inf*), to get randy (*Brit inf*) *or* horny (*inf*); **jdn ~ machen** to turn sb on (*inf*); **auf jdn/etw ~ sein** (*inf*) to be keen on *or* hot for (*sl*) sb/sth, to fancy sb/sth (*inf*); **der Kleine/Alte ist ~ wie Nachbars Lumpi** *or* **tausend Russen** *or* **sieben Sensen** he's a randy little/old beggar (*sl*); *siehe* **~machen**.

Scharfblick *m* (*fig*) perspicacity, keen insight, penetration.

Schärfe *f* **-, -n** *siehe adj (a-e)* **(a)** sharpness; keenness; shrillness.
(b) hotness; pungency; causticity.
(c) toughness, severity; closeness, tightness ♦ **mit ~ vorgehen** to take tough *or* severe *or* drastic measures.
(d) sharpness, harshness; ferocity, toughness; bitterness ♦ **ich möchte in aller ~ sagen, daß ...** I'm going to be quite harsh (about this) and say that ...
(e) sharpness; sharp focus; keenness; clarity; (*an Kamera, Fernsehen*) focus; (*an Radio*) tuning ♦ **dem Bild fehlt die ~** the picture lacks sharpness (of focus) *or* definition.

Scharf|einstellung *f* focusing.

schärfen *vt* (*lit, fig*) to sharpen.

Schärfen|einstellung *f* focusing control.

Scharf-: s~kantig *adj* with sharp edges, sharp-edged; **s~machen** *vt sep* (*inf*) to stir up, to get up in arms; **~macher** *m* (*inf*) rabble-rouser, agitator; **~macherei** *f* (*inf*) rabble-rousing, agitation; **~richter** *m* executioner; **~schütze** *m* marksman; **s~sichtig** *adj* keen- *or* sharp-sighted; (*fig*) perspicacious, clear-sighted; **~sinn** *m* astuteness, acumen, keen percep-

tion; **s~sinnig** *adj Bemerkung* astute, penetrating; *Detektiv etc* astute, sharp-witted; **wie er s~sinnig bemerkte** as he so astutely remarked.
Schärfung *f (lit, fig)* sharpening.
Scharia *f - no pl (islamische Rechtsordnung)* sharia.
Scharlach *m* **-s,** *no pl* **(a)** scarlet. **(b)** *(~fieber)* scarlet fever.
Scharlach-: s~farben *adj* scarlet; **~fieber** *nt* scarlet fever; **s~rot** *adj* scarlet (red).
Scharlatan *m* **-s, -e** charlatan; *(Arzt auch)* quack.
Scharlatanerie *f* charlatanism.
Scharmützel *nt* **-s, -** *(old)* skirmish, brush with the enemy.
Scharnier -s, -e, Scharniergelenk *nt* hinge.
Schärpe *f* **-, -n** sash.
scharren *vti* to scrape; *(Pferd, Hund)* to paw; *(Huhn)* to scratch; *(verscharren)* to bury (hurriedly) ◆ **mit dem Huf ~** to paw the ground.
Scharte *f* **-, -n** nick; *(in Bergkamm)* wind-gap; *(Schieß~)* embrasure; *(in Kampfwagen)* gunport ◆ **eine ~ auswetzen** *(fig)* to make amends, to patch things up.
Scharteke *f* **-, -n** *(pej)* (old) hag; *(Buch)* tattered old volume.
schartig *adj* jagged, notched.
scharwenzeln* *vi aux sein or haben (inf)* to dance attendance (*um* (up)on).
Schaschlik *nt* **-s, -s** (shish-)kebab.
schassen *vt (inf)* to chuck out *(inf)*, to boot out *(inf)*.
Schatten *m* **-s, -** *(lit, fig)* shadow; *(schattige Stelle)* shade; *(Geist)* shade ◆ **im ~ sitzen** to sit in the shade; **40 Grad im ~** 40 degrees in the shade; **~ geben** *or* **spenden** to give *or* provide shade; **einen ~ auf etw** *(acc)* **werfen** *(lit)* to cast a shadow on sth; *(fig)* to cast a shadow *or* cloud (up)on sth; **aus dem ~ ans Licht treten** *(lit, fig)* to come out of the shadows; **große Ereignisse werfen ihre ~ voraus** great events are often foreshadowed; **in jds ~** *(dat)* **stehen** *(fig)* to stand *or* be in sb's shadow; **im ~ bleiben** *(fig)* to remain in the background *or* shadows; **jdn/etw in den ~ stellen** *(fig)* to put sb/sth in the shade, to overshadow *or* eclipse sb/sth; **man kann nicht über seinen eigenen ~ springen** *(fig)* the leopard cannot change his spots *(prov)*; **sich vor seinem eigenen ~ fürchten** *(fig)* to be afraid of one's own shadow; **nur noch ein ~ (seiner selbst) sein** to be (only) a shadow of one's former self; **die ~ des Todes/der Nacht** *(liter)* the shades of death/night *(liter)*; **Reich der ~** *(liter)* realm of shades *(liter)*; **es fiel nicht der leiseste ~ des Verdachts auf ihn** not a shadow of suspicion fell on him; **nicht der ~ eines Beweises** not the slightest proof; **~ unter den Augen** shadows under the eyes; **du hast ja einen ~** *(sl)* you must be nuts *(sl)*; *siehe* **Licht.**
Schatten-: ~bild *nt* silhouette; *(in ~spiel)* shadow picture, shadow(graph); **~boxen** *nt* shadow-boxing; **~dasein** *nt* shadowy existence; **~druck** *m (Comput)* shadow printing; **s~haft** *adj* shadowy, shadow-like; *(fig: vage)* shadowy, fuzzy, vague; **~kabinett** *nt (Pol)* shadow cabinet; **s~los** *adj* shadowless; **~morelle** *f* morello cherry; **s~reich** *adj* shady; **~reich** *nt (liter)* realm of shadows *(liter) or* shades *(liter)*; ⚠**~riß** *m* silhouette; **~seite** *f* shady side; *(von Planeten)* dark side; *(fig: Nachteil)* drawback, disadvantage; **die ~seite(n) des Lebens** the dark side of life, life's dark side; *(in Milieu, Slums etc)* the seamy side of life; ⚠**s~spendend** *adj attr* shady; **~spiel** *nt* shadow play *or* show; *(Art)* contrast, shadow play; **~wirtschaft** *f* black economy.
schattieren* *vt* to shade.
Schattierung *f (lit, fig)* shade; *(das Schattieren)* shading ◆ **aller politischen ~en** of every political shade.
schattig *adj* shady.
Schatulle *f* **-, -n** casket; *(Geld~)* coffer; *(pej inf)* bag *(inf)*.
Schatz *m* **-es, ⸚e (a)** *(lit, fig)* treasure. **⸚e** *pl (Boden~)* natural resources *pl*; *(Reichtum)* riches *pl*, wealth *sing* ◆ **nach ⸚en graben** to dig for (buried) treasure; **du bist ein ~!** *(inf)* you're a (real) treasure *or* gem!; **für alle ⸚e der Welt** *(fig)* for all the money in the world, for all the tea in China.
(b) *(Liebling)* sweetheart; *(als Anrede)* love, darling.
Schatz-: ~amt *nt* Treasury; **~anweisung** *f* treasury bond.
schätzbar *adj* assessable ◆ **gut/schlecht/schwer ~** easy/hard/difficult to assess *or* estimate.
Schätzchen *nt* darling.
➤ **schätzen** [1] *vt* **(a)** *(veranschlagen)* to estimate, to assess (*auf +acc* at); *Wertgegenstand, Gemälde etc* to value, to appraise; *(annehmen)* to reckon, to think ◆ **die Besucherzahl wurde auf 500.000 geschätzt** the number of visitors was estimated at *or* to be 500,000; **wie alt ~ Sie mich denn?** how old do you reckon I am *or* would you say I am, then?; **was schätzt du, wie lange/wie viele/wie alt ...?** how long/how many/how old ... do you reckon *or* would you say ...?; **was/wieviel schätzt du denn?** what/how much do you reckon it is *or* would you say it was?; **ich hätte sie älter geschätzt** I'd have said she was older, I'd have thought her older; *siehe* **hoch.**
➤ **(b)** *(würdigen)* to regard highly, to value ◆ **jdn ~** to think highly of sb, to hold sb in high regard *or* esteem; **mein geschätzter Kollege** *(form)* my esteemed colleague *(form)*; **etw zu ~ wissen** to appreciate sth; **das schätzt er (überhaupt) nicht** he doesn't care for *or* appreciate that (at all); **sich glücklich ~** to consider *or* deem *(form)* oneself lucky.
[2] *vi (veranschlagen, raten)* to guess ◆ **schätz mal** have a guess.
⚠**schätzenlernen** *vt sep* to come to appreciate *or* value.
schätzenswert *adj* estimable.
Schätzer *m* **-s, -** valuer; *(Insur)* assessor.
Schatz-: ~fund *m* find *(of treasure)*, treasure-trove *(Jur)*; **~gräber** *m* **-s, -** treasure-hunter; **~kammer** *f* treasure chamber *or* vault; **~kanzler** *m (Pol)* minister of finance, Chancellor of the Exchequer *(Brit)*, secretary to the Treasury *(US)*; **~kästchen, ~kästlein** *nt* casket, (small) treasure chest; *(fig: als Buchtitel etc)* treasury; **~meister** *m* treasurer; **~obligation** *f (Fin)* treasury bond.
Schätzpreis *m* valuation price.
Schatzschein *m (Fin)* treasury note.
Schätzung *f* estimate; *(das Schätzen)* estimation; *(von Wertgegenstand)* valuation, appraisal ◆ **nach meiner ~** ... I reckon that ...; *(ungefähr)* approximately, roughly.
schätzungsweise *adv (so vermutet man)* it is estimated *or* thought; *(ungefähr)* approximately, roughly; *(so schätze ich)* I think, I reckon ◆ **die Inflationsrate wird sich ~ verdoppeln** it is thought *or* estimated (that) the rate of inflation will double; **es werden ~ 3.000 Zuschauer kommen** an estimated 3,000 spectators will come; **das wird ~ länger dauern** I think *or* reckon (that) that'll take longer; **wann wirst du ~ kommen?** when do you think *or* reckon you'll come?
Schatzwechsel *m (Fin)* treasury bill.
Schätzwert *m* estimated value.
Schau *f* **-, -en (a)** *(Vorführung)* show; *(Ausstellung auch)* display, exhibition ◆ **etw zur ~ stellen** *(ausstellen)* to put sth on show, to display *or* exhibit *or* show sth; *(fig)* to make a show of sth, to parade sth; *(protzen mit)* to show off sth; **sich zur ~ stellen** to make a spectacle *or* exhibition of oneself; **etw zur ~ tragen** to display sth.
(b) *(inf)* **eine ~ abziehen** to put on a display *or* show; *(Theater machen)* to make a big show *(inf)*; **das war eine ~!** that was really great *or* fantastic *(inf)*; **das ist nur ~** it's only show; **er macht nur (eine) ~** he's (only) putting it on; **jdm die ~ stehlen** *or* **klauen** to steal the show from sb.
Schau-: ~bild *nt* diagram; *(Kurve)* graph; **~bude** *f* (show) booth; **~bühne** *f (old)* theatre; *(fig)* stage, scene.
Schauder *m* **-s, -** shudder; *(vor Angst, Kälte auch)* shiver ◆ **ein ~ lief mir über den Rücken** a shiver/shudder ran down my spine.
schauder-: ~bar *adj (hum)* terrible, dreadful, awful; ⚠**~erregend** *adj* terrifying, fearsome, horrifying; *Vorstellung, Vision, Geschichte auch* horrific; **~haft** *adj (lit)* horrible, ghastly, terrible; *(fig inf)* terrible, dreadful, awful.
schaudern *vi (vor Grauen, Abscheu)* to shudder; *(vor Kälte, Angst auch)* to shiver; *(vor Ehrfurcht)* to tremble, to quiver ◆ **mich schauderte bei dem Anblick/Gedanken** I shuddered/shivered/trembled *or* quivered at the sight/thought (of it); **ihr schaudert vor ihm** he makes her shudder/shiver.
schauen [1] *vi (esp dial)* to look ◆ **verärgert/traurig** *etc* **~** to look angry/sad *etc*; **auf etw** *(acc)* **~** to look at sth; **um sich ~** to look around (one); **die Sonne schaut durch die Wolken** the sun is peeping *or* shining through the clouds *or* from behind the clouds; **jdm (fest) in die Augen ~** to look sb (straight) in the eye; **jdm (verliebt) in die Augen ~** to gaze (adoringly) into sb's eyes; **ihm schaut der Ärger/Zorn/Schrecken aus den Augen** annoyance/anger/fright is written all over his face; **nach jdm/etw ~** *(suchen)* to look for sb/sth; *(sich kümmern um)* to look after sb/sth; **da schaust du aber!** there, see!, there you are!; **schau, schau!** *(inf)*, **da schau her!** *(S Ger)* well, well!, what do you know! *(inf)*, how about that! *(inf)*; **schau, daß du ...** see *or* mind (that) you ...
[2] *vt (geh)* to see, to behold *(old, liter)*; *(erkennen)* to see ◆ **Gott ~** to see God.
Schauer *m* **-s, - (a)** *(Regen~)* shower. **(b)** *(Schauder)* shudder.
Schauergeschichte *f* horror story; *(Liter)* gothic tale *or* story; *(inf: Lügengeschichte)* horror story.
Schauerleute *pl of* **Schauermann.**
schauerlich *adj* **(a)** horrific, horrible; *Anblick, Schrei, Erzählung auch* spine-chilling, bloodcurdling; *(gruselig)* eerie, creepy *(inf)*. **(b)** *(inf: fürchterlich)* terrible, dreadful, awful.
Schauerlichkeit *f siehe adj (a)* horribleness; eeriness, creepiness *(inf)*.
Schauer-: ~mann *m, pl* **-leute** docker, longshoreman *(US)*; **~märchen** *nt (inf)* horror story.
schauern [1] *vi* to shudder.
[2] *vt impers* **mich schauert** I shudder; **mich schauert bei dem bloßen Gedanken** the very thought (of it) makes me shudder.
Schauerroman *m (lit, fig inf)* horror story; *(Liter auch)* Gothic novel.
Schaufel *f* **-, -n** shovel; *(kleiner: für Mehl, Zucker)* scoop; *(Kehricht~)* dustpan; *(von Bagger)* scoop; *(von Schaufelrad)* paddle; *(von Wasserrad, Turbine)* vane; *(Geweih~)* palm; *(Hunt: von Auerhahn)* fan ◆ **zwei ~n (voll) Sand/Kies** two shovel(ful)s of sand/gravel.
schaufelförmig *adj* shaped like a shovel, shovel-shaped.
schaufeln *vti* to shovel; *Grab, Grube* to dig; *siehe* **Grab.**
Schaufel-: ~rad *nt (von Dampfer)* paddlewheel; *(von Turbine)* vane wheel, impeller; **~raddampfer** *m* paddle-steamer; **s~weise** *adv* in shovelfuls.
Schaufenster *nt* display window; *(von Geschäft auch)* shop window.
Schaufenster-: ~auslage *f* window display; **~bummel** *m* window-shopping expedition; **einen ~bummel machen** to go window-shopping; **~dekorateur** *m* window-dresser; **~gestaltung** *f* window-dressing; **~krankheit** *f* intermittent claudication; **~puppe** *f* display dummy.
Schau-: ~fliegen *nt* stunt flying; *(Veranstaltung)* air display; **~flug** *m* stunt flight; **~geschäft** *nt* show business; **~kampf** *m* exhibition bout *or* fight; **~kasten** *m* showcase.
Schaukel *f* **-, -n** swing.
schauk(e)lig *adj Brücke* swaying *attr*; *Überfahrt* rough; *Auto, Fahrt* bouncy ◆ **ein ~es Boot** a boat which rocks.
schaukeln [1] *vi* **(a)** *(mit Schaukel)* to swing; *(im Schaukelstuhl)* to rock ◆ **auf** *or* **mit dem Stuhl ~** to swing *or* rock back and forth in one's chair, to tip one's chair back and forth.
(b) *(sich hin und her bewegen)* to swing *or* sway (to and fro *or* back and

forth); (*sich auf und ab bewegen*) to rock up and down; (*Fahrzeug*) to bounce (up and down); (*Schiff*) to rock, to pitch and toss.
(c) *aux sein* (*sich ~d bewegen*) (*Schiff*) to pitch and toss; (*gemütlich fahren*) to jog along.
[2] *vt* to rock ◆ **jdn durch die Gegend ~** (*inf*) to take sb for a spin round the place (*inf*); **wir werden das Kind** *or* **das** *or* **die Sache schon ~** (*inf*) we'll manage it.
[3] *vi impers* **bei der Überfahrt/im Auto hat es geschaukelt** the boat pitched and tossed on the way over/it was a bouncy ride.

Schaukel-: ~pferd *nt* rocking horse; **~politik** *f* seesaw(ing) politics *pl*/policy; **~stuhl** *m* rocking chair.

Schau-: ~laufen *nt* exhibition skating; (*Veranstaltung*) skating display; **s~lustig** *adj* curious; **~lustige** *pl decl as adj* (curious) onlookers *pl*, rubbernecks *pl* (*US inf*).

Schaum *m* **-s, Schäume** foam, froth; (*Seifen~, Shampoo~*) lather; (*von Waschmittel*) lather, suds *pl*; (*Cook: auf Speisen, Getränken*) froth; (*auf Marmelade, Flüssen, Sümpfen*) scum; (*von Bier*) head, froth ◆ **~ vor dem Mund haben** (*lit, fig*) to froth *or* foam at the mouth; **etw zu ~ schlagen** (*Cook*) to beat *or* whip sth until frothy; **~ schlagen** (*fig inf*) to be all hot air.

Schaum-: ~bad *nt* bubble *or* foam bath; **~blase** *f* bubble.

schäumen [1] *vi* to foam, to froth; (*Seife, Shampoo, Waschmittel*) to lather (up); (*Limonade, Wein*) to bubble; (*inf: wütend sein*) to foam at the mouth ◆ **das Waschmittel schäumt stark/schwach** it's a high-/low-lather detergent; **vor Wut ~** to be foaming with rage.
[2] *vt* **Kunststoff ~** to produce foam synthetics.

Schaum-: ~festiger *m* mousse; **~feuerlöscher** *m* foam fire extinguisher; **~gummi** *nt or m* foam rubber.

schaumig *adj siehe* **Schaum** foamy, frothy; lathery; lathery, sudsy; frothy; scummy; frothy.

Schaum-: ~kelle *f* skimmer; **~krone** *f* whitecap, white crest *or* horse; **~löffel** *m* skimmer; **~löscher** *m*, **~löschgerät** *nt* foam extinguisher.

Schäummittel *nt* foaming agent.

Schaum-: ~schläger *m* (*fig inf*) hot-air merchant (*inf*); **~schlägerei** *f* (*fig inf*) hot air (*inf*); **~stoff** *m* foam material; **~wein** *m* sparkling wine.

Schau-: ~platz *m* scene; **vom ~platz berichten** to give an on-the-spot report; **am ~platz sein** to be on *or* at the scene *or* on the spot; **auf dem ~platz erscheinen** to appear on the scene; **vom ~platz (der Politik) abtreten** to leave the (political) scene *or* arena; ⚠**~prozeß** *m* show trial.

schaurig *adj* gruesome; *Schrei* spine-chilling, bloodcurdling; (*inf: sehr schlecht*) dreadful, abysmal (*inf*), awful.

Schaurigkeit *f siehe adj* gruesomeness; spine-chillingness; dreadfulness.

schaurig-schön *adj* gruesomely beautiful; (*unheimlich*) eerily beautiful.

Schauspiel *nt* (a) (*Theat*) drama, play. (b) (*fig*) spectacle. **wir wollen doch den Leuten kein ~ bieten** let's not make a spectacle of ourselves.

Schauspieler *m* actor, player; (*fig*) (play-)actor.

Schauspielerei *f* acting; (*fig: Verstellung*) play-acting.

Schauspielerin *f* (*lit*) actress; (*fig*) (play-)actress.

schauspielerisch [1] *adj* acting.
[2] *adv* as regards acting, as far as (the) acting is/was concerned.

schauspielern *vi insep* to act; (*fig*) to (play-)act.

Schauspiel-: ~haus *nt* playhouse, theatre; **~kunst** *f* dramatic art, drama; (*in bezug auf Schauspieler*) acting; **~schule** *f* drama school; **~schüler** *m* drama student; **~unterricht** *m* acting *or* drama lessons *pl or* classes *pl*.

Schau-: ~steller(in *f***)** *m* **-s, -** showman; **~stück** *nt* showpiece; **~tafel** *f* (*zur Information*) (notice)board; (*~bild*) diagram; **~tanz** *m* exhibition dance; **~turnen** *nt* gymnastic display.

Scheck *m* **-s, -s** *or* (*rare*) **-e** cheque (*Brit*), check (*US*) ◆ **mit (einem)** *or* **per ~ bezahlen** to pay by cheque; **ein ~ auf** *or* **über DM 200** a cheque for DM 200.

Scheck-: ~betrug *m* cheque/check fraud; **~betrüger** *m* cheque/check fraud; **~buch** *nt* chequebook (*Brit*), checkbook (*US*).

Schecke *m* **-n, -n** *or f* **-, -n** (*Pferd*) dappled horse/pony; (*Rind*) spotted ox/bull/cow.

Scheck-: ~fälschung *f* cheque/check forgery; **~heft** *nt siehe* **~buch**.

scheckig *adj* spotted; *Pferd* dappled; (*inf: kunterbunt*) gaudy; (*verfärbt*) blotchy, patchy.

Scheck-: ~karte *f* cheque card (*Brit*), check card (*US*), banker's card; **~verkehr** *m* cheque/check transactions *pl*.

scheel *adj* (a) (*old: schielend*) cross-eyed. (b) (*mißgünstig*) envious, jealous; (*abschätzig*) disparaging ◆ **ein ~er Blick** a dirty look; **jdn ~ ansehen** to give sb a dirty look; (*abschätzig*) to look askance at sb.

Scheffel *m* **-s, -** (*Gefäß, Hohlmaß*) ≃ bushel (*contains anything from 30 to 300 litres*); (*Flächenmaß*) *area between 12 and 42 ares* ◆ **sein Licht unter den ~ stellen** (*inf*) to hide one's light under a bushel.

scheffeln [1] *vt Gold, Orden* to pile up, to accumulate; *Geld* to rake in (*inf*).
[2] *vi* **er scheffelt seit Jahren** he's been raking it in for years (*inf*).

scheffelweise *adv* in large quantities, by the sackful ◆ **~ Geld verdienen** to be raking it in (*inf*).

scheibchenweise *adv* (*fig*) bit by bit, little by little, a bit *or* little at a time.

Scheibe *f* **-, -n** (a) disc; (*Schieß~*) target; (*Eishockey*) puck; (*Wähl~*) dial; (*Tech*) (*Unterleg~, Dichtungs~*) washer; (*Kupplungs~, Brems~*) disc; (*Töpfer~*) wheel; (*inf: Schallplatte*) disc (*inf*).
(b) (*abgeschnittene ~*) slice; (*Längs~: von Orange etc*) segment ◆ **etw in ~n schneiden** to slice sth (up), to cut sth (up) into slices; **von ihm könntest du dir eine ~ abschneiden** (*fig inf*) you could take a leaf out of his book (*inf*).
(c) (*Glas~*) (window)pane; (*Fenster, von Auto*) window; (*inf: Windschutz~*) windscreen (*Brit*), windshield (*US*); (*Spiegel~*) glass.
(d) (*euph inf*) **~!** sugar! (*euph inf*).

Scheiben-: ~bremse *f* disc brake; **~honig** *m* comb honey; **~honig!** (*euph inf*) sugar! (*euph inf*); **~kleister** *interj* (*euph inf*) sugar! (*euph inf*); **~kupplung** *f* disc *or* plate clutch; **~schießen** *nt* target shooting; **~waschanlage** *f* windscreen (*Brit*) *or* windshield (*US*) washers *pl*; **s~weise** *adv* in slices; **~wischer** *m* windscreen (*Brit*) *or* windshield (*US*) wiper; **~wischerblatt** *nt* windscreen (*Brit*) *or* windshield (*US*) wiper blade.

Scheich *m* **-s, -e** sheik(h); (*inf*) bloke (*Brit inf*), guy (*inf*).

Scheichtum *nt* sheik(h)dom.

Scheide *f* **-, -n** (a) sheath; (*von Schwert auch*) scabbard; (*Vagina*) vagina ◆ **das Schwert aus der ~ ziehen** to unsheathe *or* draw one's sword; **das Schwert in die ~ stecken** to put up *or* sheathe one's sword. (b) (*obs, fig: Grenze*) border.

Scheide-: ~anstalt *f* separating works *sing or pl*; **~linie** *f* (*lit*) border(line); (*fig*) dividing line; **~mittel** *nt* (*Chem*) separating agent.

scheiden *pret* **schied**, *ptp* **geschieden** [1] *vt* (a) (*geh: trennen*) to separate; (*voneinander ~ auch*) to divide; (*Chem*) to separate (out); *siehe* **Geist, Spreu**.
(b) (*auflösen*) *Ehe* to dissolve; *Eheleute* to divorce ◆ **eine geschiedene Frau** a divorced woman, a divorcee; **sich ~ lassen** to get divorced, to get a divorce; **er will sich von ihr ~ lassen** he wants to divorce her *or* to get a divorce (from her); **er läßt sich nicht von ihr ~** he won't give her a divorce; **von dem Moment an waren wir (zwei) geschiedene Leute** (*inf*) after that it was the parting of the ways for us (*inf*).
[2] *vi aux sein* (*liter*) (*sich trennen*) to part; (*weggehen*) to depart ◆ **aus dem Dienst/Amt ~** to retire from service/one's office; **aus dem Leben ~** to depart this life; **S~ tut weh** (*prov*) parting is such sweet sorrow (*Prov*).
[3] *vr* (*Wege*) to divide, to part, to separate; (*Meinungen*) to diverge, to part company.

Scheiden-: ~abstrich *m* vaginal smear; **~krampf** *m* vaginal cramp, vaginismus (*form*); **~vorfall** *m* prolapse of the vagina.

Scheide-: ~wasser *nt* (*Chem*) nitric acid, aqua fortis; **~weg** *m* (*fig*) crossroads *sing*; **am ~weg stehen** to be at a crossroads.

Scheidung *f* (a) (*das Scheiden*) separation. (b) (*Ehe~*) divorce ◆ **die ~ dieser Ehe** the dissolution of this marriage; **in ~ leben** *or* **liegen** to be in the middle of divorce proceedings, to be getting a divorce; **die ~ einreichen** to file a petition for divorce.

Scheidungs-: ~grund *m* grounds *pl* for divorce; (*hum: Mensch*) reason for his/her *etc* divorce; **~klage** *f* petition for divorce; ⚠**~prozeß** *m* divorce proceedings *pl*; **~recht** *nt* divorce law(s *pl*); **~urkunde** *f* divorce certificate; **~urteil** *nt* decree of divorce; **~waise** *f* (*inf*) child of divorced parents.

Schein[1] *m* **-s,** *no pl* (a) (*Licht*) light; (*matt*) glow; (*von Gold, Schwert etc*) gleam, glint ◆ **einen (hellen) ~ auf etw** (*acc*) **werfen** to shine (brightly) on sth, to cast a (bright) light on sth.
(b) (*An~*) appearances *pl*; (*Vortäuschung*) pretence, sham ◆ **~ und Sein** appearance and reality; **das ist mehr ~ als Sein** it's all (on the) surface; **der ~ trügt** *or* **täuscht** appearances are deceptive; **dem ~ nach** on the face of it, to all appearances; **den ~ wahren** to keep up appearances; **etw nur zum ~ tun** only to pretend to do sth, to make only a pretence *or* a show of doing sth.

Schein[2] *m* **-s, -e** (*Geld~*) note, bill (*US*); (*Bescheinigung*) certificate; (*Univ*) (end of semester) certificate; (*Fahr~*) ticket ◆ **~e machen** (*Univ*) to get certificates.

Schein-: ~angriff *m* feint (attack); **~asylant(in)** *m(f)* bogus asylum-seeker; **s~bar** *adj* apparent, seeming *attr*; (*vorgegeben*) feigned, ostensible; **er hörte s~bar interessiert zu** he listened with apparent *or* seeming/feigned interest; **~blüte** *f* illusory flowering; (*Econ*) illusory boom; **~dasein** *nt* phantom existence; **~ehe** *f* fictitious *or* sham marriage.

▼ **scheinen** *pret* **schien**, *ptp* **geschienen** *vi* (a) (*leuchten*) to shine.
▼ (b) *auch vi impers* (*den Anschein geben*) to seem, to appear ◆ **es scheint, daß .../als (ob) ...** it seems *or* appears that .../as if ...; **mir scheint, (daß) ...** it seems *or* appears to me that ...; **wie es scheint** as it seems *or* would appear, apparently; **es scheint nur so** it only seems *or* appears to be like that; **er kommt scheint's nicht mehr** (*dial inf*) it would seem that he won't come now, seemingly he's not coming now; **du hast scheint's vergessen, daß ...** (*dial inf*) you seem to have forgotten that ...

Schein-: ~firma *f* dummy *or* fictitious firm; **~friede** *m* phoney peace, peace in name only, semblance *no pl* of peace; **~gefecht** *nt* mock *or* sham fight; **~grund** *m* spurious reason; (*Vorwand*) pretext; **s~heilig** *adj* hypocritical; (*Arglosigkeit vortäuschend*) innocent; **s~heilig tun** to be hypocritical; (*Arglosigkeit vortäuschen*) to act innocent, to play *or* act the innocent; **~heilige(r)** *mf siehe adj* hypocrite; sham; **~heiligkeit** *f siehe adj* hypocrisy; feigned innocence; **~schwangerschaft** *f* false pregnancy; **~tod** *m* apparent death, suspended animation; **s~tot** *adj* in a state of apparent death *or* of suspended animation; **~werfer** *m* (*zum Beleuchten*) floodlight; (*im Theater*) spotlight; (*Such~*) searchlight; (*Aut*) (head)light, headlamp; **~werferlicht** *nt siehe* **~werfer** floodlight(ing); spotlight; searchlight (beam); light *or* beam of the headlights *or* headlamps; (*fig*) limelight; **im ~werferlicht (der Öffentlichkeit) stehen** (*fig*) to be in the glare of publicity; **ein Problem in das ~werferlicht rücken** to spotlight *or* highlight a problem; **~widerstand** *m* sham resistance; (*Elec*) impedance, apparent resistance.

Scheiß *m* **-,** *no pl* (*sl*) shit (*vulg*), crap (*vulg*) ◆ **ein ~** a load of shit (*vulg*) *or* crap (*vulg*); **~ machen** (*herumalbern*) to bugger (*sl*) *or* mess (*inf*) about; (*Fehler machen*) to make a balls-up (*vulg*); **mach keinen ~!** don't do anything so bloody (*Brit sl*) *or* damn (*inf*) silly; **red' doch keinen ~!** don't talk crap! (*vulg*), cut (out) the crap! (*vulg*).

⚠: for details of spelling reform, see supplement

➤ SPRACHE AKTIV: **scheinen: b** → 33.2, 38.2, 39.2, 41, 53.4, 53.5

Scheiß- *in cpds (sl)* bloody *(Brit sl)*, bleeding *(Brit sl)*, damn(ed) *(inf)*, fucking *(vulg)*.

Scheißdreck *m (vulg: Kot)* shit *(vulg)*, crap *(vulg)*; *(sl) (blödes Gerede, schlechtes Buch, schlechte Ware etc)* load of shit *(vulg)*; *(unangenehme Sache, Arbeit)* effing thing *(sl)*, bloody thing *(Brit sl)*; *(Angelegenheiten)* effing business *(sl)*, bloody business *(Brit sl)* ♦ **~!** shit! *(vulg)*; **wegen jedem ~** about every effing *(sl) or* bloody *(Brit sl)* little thing; **das geht dich einen ~ an** it's none of your effing *(sl) or* bloody *(Brit sl)* business, it's got bugger-all to do with you *(sl)*; **einen ~ werd' ich tun!** like (bloody *Brit sl*) hell I will!; **sich einen ~ um jdn/etw kümmern** not to give a shit *(vulg) or* a bloody damn *(Brit sl)* about sb/sth.

Scheiße *f -, no pl (vulg: Kot)* shit *(vulg)*, crap *(vulg)*; *(sl) (unangenehme Lage)* shit *(vulg)*; *(Unsinn)* shit *(vulg)*, crap *(vulg)* ♦ **~ sein** to be bloody awful *(Brit sl) or* goddamn *(sl)* awful; *(ärgerlich)* to be a bloody *(Brit sl) or* goddamn *(sl)* nuisance; **das ist doch alles ~** it's all a bloody mess *(Brit sl)*, it's all shit *(vulg)*; *(Unsinn)* it's all a load of shit *(vulg)*; **in der ~ sitzen** to be in the shit *(vulg)*, to be up shit creek *(vulg)*; *siehe auch* **Scheiß**.

scheiß|egal *adj (sl)* **das ist mir doch ~!** I don't give a shit *(vulg) or* a bloody damn *(Brit sl)*.

scheißen *pret* **schiß**, *ptp* **geschissen** *vi (vulg)* to shit *(vulg)*, to crap *(vulg)* ♦ **sich** *(dat)* **vor Angst in die Hosen ~** to have *or* get the shits *(vulg)*, to shit oneself *(vulg)*; **auf etw** *(acc)* **~** *(fig)* not to give a shit about sth *(vulg)*; **scheiß der Hund drauf** to hell with that! *(sl)*, bugger that! *(sl)*.

Scheißer *m -s, - (sl: Arschloch)* bugger *(sl)*; *(inf: Kosename)* chubby cheeks *sing (hum inf)*.

Scheißerei *(sl)*, **Scheißeritis** *(hum inf) f* **die ~** the runs *(inf)*, the shits *(vulg)*.

Scheiß-: s~freundlich *adj (sl)* as nice as pie *(iro inf)*; **~haus** *nt (vulg)* shithouse *(vulg)*; **~kerl** *m (sl)* bastard *(sl)*, sod *(sl)*, son-of-a-bitch *(US sl)*, mother(fucker) *(US vulg)*; **s~vornehm** *adj (sl)* bloody posh *(Brit sl)*.

Scheit *m -(e)s, -e or (Aus, Sw)* **-er** log, piece of wood.

Scheitel *m -s, - (a) (Haar~)* parting *(Brit)*, part *(US)*; *(liter: Haupthaar)* locks *pl* ♦ **vom ~ bis zur Sohle** from top to toe. **(b)** *(höchster Punkt)* vertex.

scheiteln *vt* to part.

Scheitel-: ~punkt *m* vertex; **~wert** *m* peak (value); **~winkel** *m* vertical angle.

scheiten *vt (Sw) Holz* to chop.

Scheiterhaufen *m* (funeral) pyre; *(Hist: zur Hinrichtung)* stake ♦ **die Hexe wurde auf dem ~'verbrannt** the witch was burned at the stake.

scheitern *vi aux sein* **(a)** *(an +dat* because of) *(Mensch, Unternehmen)* to fail; *(Verhandlungen, Ehe)* to break down; *(Plan, Vorhaben auch)* to fall through; *(Regierung)* to founder *(an +dat* on); *(Mannschaft)* to be defeated *(an +dat* by); *siehe* **Existenz. (b)** *(Schiff)* to be wrecked.

Scheitern *nt -s, no pl siehe vi* **(a)** failure; breakdown; falling through; foundering; defeat ♦ **das war zum ~ verurteilt** *or* **verdammt** that was doomed to failure; **etw zum ~ bringen** to make sth fail/break down/fall through. **(b)** wrecking.

Scheitholz *nt* firewood.

Schelf *m or nt* **-s, -e** *(Geog)* (continental) shelf.

Schelfmeer *nt* shelf sea.

Schellack *m -(e)s, -e* shellac.

Schelle *f -, -n* **(a)** bell; *(dial: Klingel)* (door)bell. **(b)** *(Tech)* clamp. **(c)** *(Hand~)* handcuff. **(d)** *(dial) siehe* **Ohrfeige. (e)** *(Cards)* **~n** *pl* ≃ diamonds *sing or pl (shaped like bells on traditional German cards)*.

schellen *vi* to ring *(nach jdm* for sb) ♦ **es hat geschellt** the bell has gone; **bei jdm** *or* **an jds Tür** *(dat)* **~** to ring at sb's door.

Schellen-: ~baum *m (Mus)* Turkish crescent, pavillon chinois; **~bube** *m* ≃ jack *or* knave of diamonds; **~geläut(e)** *nt* jingling (of bells); **mit ~geläute fuhr der Pferdeschlitten vorbei** the sleigh passed by with its bells jingling; **~kappe** *f* cap and bells, fool's cap; **~könig** *m* ≃ king of diamonds; **~ober** *m* ≃ queen of diamonds *(a man on traditional German cards)*; **~unter** *m* ≃ jack *or* knave of diamonds.

Schellfisch *m* haddock.

Schelm *m -(e)s, -e (dated: Spaßvogel)* rogue, wag *(dated)*; *(obs: Gauner)* knave *(obs)*; *(Liter)* picaro ♦ **den ~ im Nacken haben** to be up to mischief; **ein ~, der Böses denkt** honi soit qui mal y pense *(prov)*, evil to him who evil thinks *(prov)*.

Schelmen-: ~gesicht *nt* mischievous face; **~roman** *m* picaresque novel; **~streich** *m (dated)* roguish prank; **~stück** *nt (dated)* knavery *(old)*; *(obs: Missetat)* villainous deed *(old)*.

schelmisch *adj* mischievous.

Schelte *f -, -n* scolding; *(Kritik)* attack ♦ **er hat ~ bekommen** he got a scolding.

schelten *pret* **schalt**, *ptp* **gescholten** [1] *vt* to scold, to chide ♦ **jdn einen Dummkopf ~** to call sb a blockhead.
[2] *vi (schimpfen)* to curse ♦ **über** *or* **auf jdn/etw ~** to curse sb/sth, to rail at sb/sth *(old)*; **mit jdm ~** to scold sb.

Scheltwort *nt* word of abuse ♦ **~e** words of abuse, invective *sing*.

Schema *nt -s,* **Schemen** *or* **-ta** scheme; *(Darstellung)* diagram; *(Ordnung, Vorlage auch)* plan; *(Muster)* pattern; *(Philos, Psych)* schema ♦ **nach ~ F** in the same (old) way; **etw nach einem ~ machen** to do sth according to a pattern.

schematisch *adj* schematic; *(mechanisch)* mechanical.

schematisieren* *vti* to schematize.

Schematismus *m* schematism.

Schemel *m -s, -* stool.

Schemen *m -s, -* silhouette; *(Gespenst)* spectre.

schemenhaft [1] *adj* shadowy.
[2] *adv* **etw ~ sehen/zeichnen** to see the outlines of sth/to sketch sth in; **die Bäume hoben sich ~ gegen den Himmel ab** the trees were silhouetted against the sky.

⚠ **Schenke** *f -, -n* tavern, inn.

Schenkel *m -s, - (a) (Anat) (Ober~)* thigh ♦ **sich** *(dat)* **auf die ~ schlagen** to slap one's thighs; **dem Pferd die ~ geben** to press a horse on; *siehe* **Unterschenkel. (b)** *(von Zirkel)* leg; *(von Zange, Schere)* shank; *(Math: von Winkel)* side.

Schenkel-: ~bruch *m* fracture of the thigh(bone) *or* femur; **~hals** *m* neck of the femur; **~halsbruch** *m* fracture of the neck of the femur.

schenken [1] *vt* **(a)** *(Geschenk geben)* **jdm etw ~** to give sb sth *or* give sth to sb (as a present *or* gift); **sich** *(dat)* **(gegenseitig) etw ~** to give each other sth (as a present *or* gift); **etw geschenkt bekommen/sich** *(dat)* **etw ~ lassen** to get sth as a present *or* gift; **etw zum Geburtstag/zu Weihnachten geschenkt bekommen** to get sth for one's birthday/for Christmas; **zu Weihnachten hat er nichts geschenkt bekommen** he didn't get anything *or* any presents for Christmas; **so was kaufe ich nicht, das lasse ich mir immer ~** I don't buy anything like that, I always like to get these things as presents; **ich möchte nichts geschenkt haben!** *(lit)* I don't want any presents!; *(fig: bevorzugt werden)* I don't want any special treatment!; **ich nehme nichts geschenkt!** I'm not accepting any presents!; **das ist geschenkt!** *(inf) (ist ein Geschenk)* it's a present; *(nicht der Rede wert)* that's no great shakes *(inf)*; *(sl: nichts wert)* forget it! *(inf)*; **das ist (fast) geschenkt!** *(inf: billig)* that's dirt cheap *(inf) or* a give-away *(inf)*; **das möchte ich nicht mal geschenkt haben!** I wouldn't want it if it was given to me; **einem geschenkten Gaul sieht man nicht ins Maul** *(Prov)* don't look a gift horse in the mouth *(Prov)*.
(b) *(erlassen)* **jdm etw ~** to let sb off sth; **ihm ist nie etwas geschenkt worden** *(fig)* he never had it easy.
(c) *in Verbindung mit n siehe auch dort* **jdm die Freiheit/das Leben ~** *(begnadigen)* to set sb free/to spare sb's life; **einem Kind das Leben ~** *(geh)* to give birth to a child; **jdm seine Liebe/seine Aufmerksamkeit** *etc* **~** to give sb one's love/one's attention *etc*; **jdm/einer Sache (keinen) Glauben ~** to give (no) credence to sb/sth; **jdm Vertrauen ~** to put one's trust in sb.
[2] *vi* to give presents.
[3] *vr* **(a) sich** *(dat)* **etw ~** to skip sth *(inf)*; **deine Komplimente kannst du dir ~!** you can keep your compliments *(inf)*; **sich** *(dat)* **die Mühe ~** to save oneself the trouble; **er hat sich** *(dat)* **nichts geschenkt** he spared no pains; **die beiden haben sich nichts geschenkt** neither was giving anything away.
(b) sich jdm ~ *(liter: Frau)* to give oneself to sb.

Schenkung *f (Jur)* gift.

Schenkungs-: ~steuer *f* gift tax; **~urkunde** *f* deed of gift.

scheppern *vi (dial)* to clatter ♦ **es hat gescheppert** there was a clatter; *(loser Gegenstand)* there was a rattle; *(Autounfall)* there was a bang; *(Ohrfeige)* he/she got a clip round the ear.

Scher *m -(e)s, -e (S Ger, Aus, Sw)* mole.

Scherbe *f -, -n* fragment, (broken) piece; *(Glas~, Porzellan~, Keramik~)* broken piece of glass/china/pottery; *(Archeol)* shard, potsherd ♦ **etw in ~n schlagen** to shatter sth; **in ~n gehen** to break, to shatter; *(fig)* to fall *or* go to pieces; **~n machen** to break something; *(fig)* to put one's foot in it; **die ~n zusammenkehren** to sweep up the (broken) pieces; *(fig)* to pick up the pieces; **es hat ~n gegeben** *(fig)* there was lots of trouble; *(bei Streit)* sparks flew; **die ~n unseres Glücks** the shattered remains of our happiness; **~n bringen Glück** *(Prov)* broken crockery brings you luck.

Scherben *m -s, - (S Ger, Aus) siehe* **Scherbe**.

Scherben-: ~gericht *nt* ostracism; **über jdn ein ~gericht abhalten** *(geh)* to ostracize sb; **~haufen** *m* pile of smashed crockery; **er stand vor dem ~haufen seiner Ehe** he was faced with the ruins of his marriage.

Schere *f -, -n* **(a)** *(Werkzeug) (klein)* scissors *pl*; *(groß)* shears *pl*; *(Draht~)* wire-cutters *pl*; *(fig: Kluft)* divide ♦ **eine ~** a pair of scissors/shears/wire-cutters. **(b)** *(Zool)* pincer; *(von Hummer, Krebs etc auch)* claw. **(c)** *(Turnen, Ringen)* scissors *sing*.

scheren[1] *pret* **schor**, *ptp* **geschoren** *vt* to clip; *Schaf, (Tech)* to shear; *Haare* to crop; *Bart (rasieren)* to shave; *(stutzen)* to trim ♦ **er war/seine Haare waren kurz geschoren** his hair was cropped short; *siehe* **kahlscheren, Kamm**.

scheren[2] *vtr* **(a) sich nicht um jdn/etw ~** not to care *or* bother about sb/sth; **was schert mich das?** what do I care (about that)?, what's that to me?; **er scherte sich nicht im geringsten darum** he couldn't have cared less about it; *siehe* **Teufel**.
(b) *(inf)* **scher dich (weg)!** scram! *(inf)*, beat it! *(inf)*; **scher dich heim!** go home!; **scher dich ins Bett!** get to bed!; **es ist Zeit, daß du dich nach Hause scherst** it's time you were off home.

Scheren-: ~fernrohr *nt* binocular periscope; **~gitter** *nt* concertina barrier; **~schlag** *m* scissors kick; **~schleifer** *m* scissor(s) grinder, knife grinder; **~schnitt** *m* silhouette.

Schererei *f usu pl (inf)* trouble *no pl*.

Scherflein *nt (Bibl)* mite ♦ **sein ~ (zu etw) beitragen** *or* **dazu geben** *or* **beisteuern** *(Geld)* to contribute one's mite (towards sth); *(fig)* to do one's bit (for sth) *(inf)*.

Scherge *m -n, -n* **(a)** *(geh: Büttel)* thug. **(b)** *(obs) siehe* **Häscher**.

Schergendienst *m* dirty work.

Scher-: ~kopf *m* shaving head; **~maus** *f (Aus, S Ger)* vole; *(Sw)* mole; **~messer** *nt* shearing knife; **~wind** *m (Met)* wind shear; **~wolle** *f* fleece.

Scherz[1] *m -es, -e* joke, jest; *(Unfug)* tomfoolery *no pl* ♦ **aus** *or* **zum/im ~** as a joke/in jest; **einen ~ machen** to make a joke; *(Streich)* to play a joke; **mach keine ~e!** *(inf)* you're joking!, you must be kidding! *(inf)*; **mit so etwas macht**

man keine ~e you don't joke *or* make jokes about things like that; **seine ~e über jdn/etw machen** to make *or* crack jokes about sb/sth; **seine ~e (mit jdm) treiben** to play jokes; **... und solche ~e** (*inf*) ... and what have you (*inf*); **(ganz) ohne ~!** (*inf*) no kidding! (*inf*).

Scherz² *m* **-es, -e, Scherzel** *nt* **-s, -** (*Aus*) hunk of bread; (*Endstück*) heel.

Scherz|artikel *m usu pl* joke (article).

scherzen *vi* (*old, geh*) to joke, to jest; (*albern*) to banter; (*nicht ernst nehmen*) to trifle (*mit* with) ◆ **mir scheint, du scherzt** you can't be serious; **ich scherze nicht** (*old, geh*) I'm not joking; **Sie belieben wohl zu ~!** (*old, geh*) surely you are in jest (*old, liter*); **mit jdm/etw ist nicht zu ~** one can't trifle with sb/sth.

Scherz-: ~frage *f* riddle; **~gedicht** *nt* humorous poem; **s~haft** *adj* jocular, jovial; *Angelegenheit* joking; (*spaßig*) *Einfall* playful; **etw s~haft sagen/meinen/aufnehmen** to say sth jokingly *or* as a joke *or* in jest/to mean sth as a joke/to take sth as a joke; **~keks** *m* (*inf*) joker (*inf*).

Scherzo ['skɛrtso] *nt* **-s, -s** *or* **Scherzi** scherzo.

Scherzwort *nt* witticism, jocular *or* joking remark.

schesen *vi aux sein* (*dial*) to rush.

scheu *adj* (*schüchtern*) shy; (*ängstlich*) *Reh, Tier auch* timid; (*zaghaft*) *Versuche, Worte* cautious ◆ **jdn ~ machen** to make sb shy; (*ängstigen*) to frighten *or* scare sb; **mach doch die Pferde** *or* **Gäule nicht ~** (*fig inf*) keep your hair on (*inf*); **~ werden** (*Pferd*) to be frightened.

Scheu *f* **-,** *no pl* fear (*vor +dat* of); (*Schüchternheit*) shyness; (*von Reh, Tier*) shyness, timidity; (*Hemmung*) inhibition; (*Ehrfurcht*) awe ◆ **seine ~ verlieren** to lose one's inhibitions; **ohne jede ~** without any inhibition; *sprechen* quite freely.

scheuchen *vt* to shoo (away); (*verscheuchen*) to frighten *or* scare away *or* off.

scheuen [1] *vt Kosten, Arbeit* to shy away from; *Menschen, Licht* to shun ◆ **weder Mühe noch Kosten ~** to spare neither trouble nor expense; **keine Mühe ~** to go to endless trouble.
[2] *vr* **sich vor etw** (*dat*) **~** (*Angst haben*) to be afraid of sth; (*zurückschrecken*) to shy away from sth; **sich (davor) ~, etw zu tun** (*Angst haben*) to be afraid of doing sth; (*zurückschrecken*) to shrink back from doing sth; **und ich scheue mich nicht, das zu sagen** and I'm not afraid of saying it.
[3] *vi* (*Pferd etc*) to shy (*vor +dat* at).

Scheuer *f* **-, -n** barn.

Scheuer-: ~besen *m* scrubbing broom; **~bürste** *f* scrubbing brush; **~frau** *f* char (*Brit*), cleaning woman; **~lappen** *m* floorcloth; **~leiste** *f* skirting board (*Brit*), baseboard (*US*).

scheuern [1] *vti* **(a)** (*putzen*) to scour; (*mit Bürste*) to scrub.
(b) (*reiben*) to chafe ◆ **der Rucksack scheuert mich am Rücken** the rucksack is chafing my back; **der Kragen scheuert am Hals** the collar chafes at the neck.
(c) jdm eine ~ (*inf*) to clout sb one (*inf*).
[2] *vr* **sich (an etw** *dat***) ~** to rub (against sth); **sich** (*acc*) **(wund) ~** to chafe oneself.

Scheuer-: ~sand *m* scouring powder; **~tuch** *nt* floorcloth.

Scheuklappe *f* blinker ◆ **~n haben** *or* **tragen** (*lit, fig*) to be blinkered, to wear blinkers; **mit ~n herumlaufen** *or* **durchs Leben laufen** to be wearing blinkers.

Scheune *f* **-, -n** barn.

Scheunen-: ~drescher *m*: **wie ein ~drescher fressen** (*inf*) to eat like a horse (*inf*); **~tor** *nt* barn door; *siehe* **Ochse**.

Scheusal *nt* **-s, -e** *or* (*inf*) **Scheusäler** monster.

scheußlich *adj* dreadful; (*abstoßend häßlich*) hideous ◆ **es hat ~ weh getan** (*inf*) it hurt dreadfully (*inf*), it was horribly *or* terribly painful.

Scheußlichkeit *f siehe adj* dreadfulness; hideousness.

Schi *m* **-s, -er** *or* **-** *siehe* **Ski**.

Schicht *f* **-, -en (a)** (*Lage*) layer; (*dünne~*) film; (*Geol, Sci auch*) stratum; (*Farb~*) coat; (*der Gesellschaft*) level, stratum ◆ **breite ~en der Bevölkerung** large sections of the population; **aus allen ~en (der Bevölkerung)** from all walks of life.
(b) (*Arbeitsabschnitt, -gruppe etc*) shift ◆ **er hat jetzt ~, er ist auf ~** (*inf*) he's on shift; **zur ~ gehen** to go on shift; **er muß ~ arbeiten** he has to work shifts.

Schicht-: ~arbeit *f* shift-work; **~arbeiter** *m* shift-worker.

schichten [1] *vt* to layer; *Holz, Heu, Bücher etc* to stack.
[2] *vr* (*Geol*) to form layers; (*Gestein*) to stratify.

schichtenspezifisch *adj* (*Sociol*) specific to a particular social stratum.

Schicht-: ~lohn *m* shift(-work) rates *pl*; **~stoff** *m* laminate; **~stoffplatte** *f* laminated sheet.

Schichtung *f* layering; (*von Holz, Heu, Büchern etc*) stacking; (*Sociol, Geol, Met*) stratification.

Schicht-: ~unterricht *m* teaching in shifts; **~wechsel** *m* change of shifts; **um 6 Uhr ist ~wechsel bei uns** we change shifts at six o'clock; **s~weise** *adv* in layers; (*Farbe, Lack*) in coats.

schick *adj* elegant, smart; *Frauenmode* chic; *Haus, Wohnung auch, Möbel* stylish; *Auto* smart; (*inf: prima*) great (*inf*).

Schick *m* **-s,** *no pl* style; (*von Frauenmode, Frau auch*) chic.

schicken [1] *vti* to send ◆ **(jdm) etw ~** to send sth (to sb), to send (sb) sth; **jdn einkaufen/Bier holen ~** to send sb to do the shopping/to fetch *or* for some beer; **(jdn) nach jdm/etw ~** to send (sb) for sb/sth.
[2] *vr, vr impers* (*sich ziemen*) to be fitting *or* proper ◆ **das schickt sich nicht für ein Mädchen** it does not befit *or* become a girl.
[3] *vr* (*old: sich abfinden*) **sich in etw** (*acc*) **~** to resign *or* reconcile oneself to sth; **schließlich schickte er sich drein** eventually he became reconciled to this.

Schickeria *f* **-,** *no pl* (*iro*) in-people *pl*.

Schicki, Schickimicki *m* **-(s), -s** (*sl*) trendy.

schicklich *adj Kleidung etc* proper, fitting; *Verhalten* seemly, becoming ◆ **es ist nicht ~ zu pfeifen** it is unseemly *or* unbecoming to whistle.

Schicksal *nt* **-s, -e** fate, destiny; (*Pech*) fate ◆ **das ~ wollte es, (daß)** ... as fate would have it, ...; **~ spielen** to play at fate; **die ~e der Flüchtlinge** the fate of the refugees; **manche schweren ~e** many a difficult fate; **das sind (schwere) ~e** those are tragic cases; **er hat ein schweres ~ gehabt** *or* **durchgemacht** fate has been unkind to him; **(das ist) ~** (*inf*) that's life; **jdn seinem ~ überlassen** to leave *or* abandon sb to his fate; **sein ~ herausfordern** to tempt fate *or* providence; **dem ~ haben wir es zu verdanken, daß** ... we have to thank our good fortune that ...; **das ~ hat es gut mit uns gemeint** fortune has smiled on us.

schicksalhaft *adj* fateful.

Schicksals-: ~frage *f* fateful question; **~gefährte** *m* companion in misfortune; **~gemeinschaft** *f* **wir waren eine ~gemeinschaft** we shared a common destiny; **~glaube** *m* fatalism; **~göttin** *f* goddess of destiny; **die ~göttinnen** the Fates; (*Nornen*) the Norns; **~schlag** *m* great misfortune, stroke of fate; **~tragödie** *f* tragedy of fate *or* destiny; **~wende** *f* change in fortune.

Schickse *f* **-, -n** (*pej inf*) floozy (*pej inf*).

Schickung *f* (*liter*) act of providence.

Schiebe-: ~bühne *f* traverser; (*Theat*) sliding stage; **~dach** *nt* sunroof; **~fenster** *nt* sliding window.

schieben *pret* **schob**, *ptp* **geschoben** [1] *vt* **(a)** to push, to shove; *Fahrrad, Rollstuhl etc auch* to wheel ◆ **etw von sich** (*dat*) **~** (*fig*) to put sth aside; *Schuld, Verantwortung* to reject sth; **etw vor sich** (*dat*) **her ~** (*fig*) to put off sth; **etw von einem Tag auf den andern ~** to put sth off from one day to the next; **etw auf jdn/etw ~** to blame sb/sth for sth, to put the blame onto sb/sth; **die Schuld/Verantwortung auf jdn ~** to put the blame on sb/the responsibility at sb's door.
(b) (*stecken*) to put; *Hände auch* to slip ◆ **jdm/sich etw in den Mund ~** to put sth into sb's/one's mouth.
(c) (*inf: handeln mit*) to traffic in; *Drogen* to push (*inf*).
(d) (*inf*) **Wache/Dienst ~** to do guard duty/duty; *siehe* **Kohldampf** *etc*.
(e) (*Rail*) to shunt.
[2] *vi* **(a)** to push, to shove.
(b) (*inf*) **mit etw/Drogen ~** to traffic in sth/push (*inf*) drugs.
(c) (*inf: begünstigen*) to wangle (*inf*) ◆ **da wurde viel geschoben** there was a lot of wangling (*inf*) going on.
[3] *vr* **(a)** (*mit Anstrengung*) to push, to shove ◆ **sich an die Spitze ~** to push one's way to the front.
(b) (*sich bewegen*) to move.

Schieber *m* **-s, - (a)** slide; (*am Ofen etc*) damper; (*inf: Bettpfanne*) bedpan; (*Eßbesteck für Kinder*) pusher. **(b)** (*inf: Tanz*) shuffle. **(c)** (*Schwarzhändler*) black marketeer; (*Waffen~*) gun-runner; (*Drogen~*) pusher (*inf*).

Schieberei *f* (*inf*) **(a)** (*Drängelei*) pushing, shoving. **(b)** (*Begünstigung*) wangling (*inf*).

Schieber-: ~geschäft *nt* shady deal; (*Schwarzhandel*) *siehe* **Schieber (c)** black marketeering; trafficking; pushing (*inf*); **~mütze** *f* flat cap.

Schiebe-: ~sitz *m* sliding seat; **~tür** *f* sliding door; **~wand** *f* sliding partition (wall).

Schieblehre *f* calliper rule.

Schiebung *f* (*Begünstigung*) string-pulling; (*Sport*) rigging; (*Schiebergeschäfte*) shady deals *pl* ◆ **der ~ bezichtigt werden** to be accused of rigging; **das war doch ~** that was rigged *or* a fix; **die Zuschauer riefen „~!"** the spectators shouted "fix!"

schiech [ʃiːç] *adj* (*Aus*) **(a)** (*häßlich*) ugly. **(b)** (*bang*) **jdm wird ~** sb gets scared.

schied *pret of* **scheiden**.

schiedlich *adv*: **~ und friedlich** amicably.

Schieds-: ~gericht *nt*, **~gerichtshof** *m* court of arbitration; **s~gerichtlich** [1] *adj* arbitral; [2] *adv* by arbitration; **~mann** *m, pl* **-leute** arbitrator, arbiter; **~richter** *m* arbitrator, arbiter, umpire; (*Fußball, Eishockey, Boxen*) referee; (*Hockey, Tennis, Federball, Kricket, Mil*) umpire; (*Preisrichter*) judge; **~richterentscheidung** *f* (*Sport*) referee's/umpire's decision; **s~richterlich** *adj siehe* **~richter** arbitrational, arbitral, umpiring; refereeing; judging; **das muß s~richterlich entschieden werden** the arbitrator/arbiter *etc* decides; **s~richtern** *vi insep* (*inf*) *siehe* **~richter** to arbitrate, to umpire; to referee; to judge; **~spruch** *m* (arbitral) award; **~stelle** *f* arbitration service; **~verfahren** *nt* arbitration proceedings *pl*.

schief *adj* crooked, not straight *pred*; (*nach einer Seite geneigt*) lopsided, tilted; *Winkel* oblique; *Blick, Lächeln* wry; *Absätze* worn(-down); (*fig: unzutreffend*) inappropriate; *Deutung* wide of the mark, inappropriate; *Bild* distorted ◆ **~ laufen** to walk lopsidedly; **das Bild hängt ~** the picture is crooked *or* isn't straight; **~e Ebene** (*Phys*) inclined plane; **auf die ~e Bahn geraten** *or* **kommen** (*fig*) to leave the straight and narrow; **du siehst die Sache ganz ~!** (*fig*) you're looking at it all wrong!; **jdn ~ ansehen** (*fig*) to look askance at sb; **einen ~en Mund** *or* **ein ~es Gesicht ziehen** (*fig inf*) to pull a (wry) face; **der S~e Turm von Pisa** the Leaning Tower of Pisa; *siehe* **Licht**.

Schiefe *f* **-,** *no pl* crookedness; (*Neigung*) lopsidedness, tilt; (*von Ebene*) inclination; (*von Winkel*) obliqueness.

Schiefer *m* **-s, -** (*Gesteinsart*) slate; (*esp Aus: Holzsplitter*) splinter.

Schiefer-: ~bruch *m* slate quarry; **~dach** *nt* slate roof; **s~grau** *adj* slate-grey; **~kasten** *m* pencil box; **~platte** *f* slate; **~stift** *m* slate pencil; **~tafel** *f* slate.

schief-: ⚠~gehen *vi sep irreg aux sein* to go wrong; **es wird schon ~gehen!** (*hum*) it'll be OK (*inf*); **⚠~gewickelt** *adj pred* (*inf*) on the wrong track; **da**

⚠: for details of spelling reform, see supplement

➤ SPRACHE AKTIV: **schicken: 1 → 48.1, 48.3**

bist du ~gewickelt you've got a surprise coming to you there (*inf*).
Schiefheit *f siehe adj* crookedness; lopsidedness, tilt; obliqueness; wryness; inappropriateness; distortion.
schief-: **~lachen** *vr sep* (*inf*) to kill oneself (laughing) (*inf*); **~lage** *f* (*fig*) difficulties *pl*; ⚠**~laufen** *sep irreg* [1] *vt siehe* **~treten**; [2] *vi aux sein* (*inf*) to go wrong; ⚠**~liegen** *vi sep irreg* (*inf*) to be wrong; **mit einer Meinung ~liegen** to be on the wrong track; ⚠**~treten** *vt sep irreg Absätze* to wear down; **die Schuhe ~treten** to wear down the heels of one's shoes; **~wink(e)lig** *adj* oblique-angled.
schiel|äugig *adj* cross-eyed, squint-eyed, boss-eyed.
schielen *vi* to squint, to be cross-eyed *or* boss-eyed ◆ **auf** *or* **mit einem Auge ~** to have a squint in one eye; **auf etw** (*acc*) **~** (*inf*) to steal a glance at sth; **nach jdm/etw ~** (*inf*) to look at sb/sth out of the corner of one's eye; (*begehrlich*) to eye sb/sth up; (*heimlich*) to sneak a look at sb/sth.
schien *pret of* **scheinen**.
Schienbein *nt* shin; (*~knochen*) shinbone ◆ **jdm gegen** *or* **vor das ~ treten** to kick sb on the shin(s).
Schienbein-: **~schoner, ~schutz, ~schützer** *m* shin-pad, shin-guard.
Schiene *f* -, -n (a) rail; (*Med*) splint; (*von Lineal*) edge, guide; (*von Winkelmesser*) blade ◆ **auf oberster ~ backen** (*im Backofen*) to bake at the top of the oven; **~n** (*Rail*) track *sing*, rails *pl*; **aus den ~n springen** to leave *or* jump the rails.
(b) (*fig*) **auf der Tennis-~** on the tennis circuit; **auf der politischen ~** along political lines; **ein Problem auf der politischen/pragmatischen ~ lösen** to solve a problem by political means/pragmatically; **auf der emotionalen ~** on an emotional level.
schienen *vt Arm, Bein* to put in a splint/splints, to splint.
Schienen-: **~bahn** *f* (a) track transport; (b) *siehe* **~fahrzeug**; **~bremse** *f* slipper brake; **~bus** *m* rail bus; **~fahrzeug** *nt* track vehicle; **s~gleich** *adj* **s~gleicher Straßenübergang** level crossing (*Brit*), grade crossing (*US*); **~netz** *nt* (*Rail*) rail network; **~räumer** *m* -s, - track clearer; **~strang** *m* (section of) track; **~weg** *m* railway (*Brit*) *or* railroad (*US*) line; **etw auf dem ~weg versenden** to send sth by rail.
schier[1] *adj* pure; (*fig*) sheer.
schier[2] *adv* (*beinahe*) nearly, almost.
Schierling *m* hemlock.
Schierlingsbecher *m* (cup of) hemlock.
Schieß-: **~befehl** *m* order to fire *or* shoot; **~bude** *f* shooting gallery; **~budenfigur** *f* target figure *or* doll; (*fig inf*) clown; **du siehst ja aus wie eine ~budenfigur** you look like something out of a pantomime; **~eisen** *nt* (*sl*) shooting iron (*sl*).
schießen *pret* **schoß**, *ptp* **geschossen** [1] *vt* to shoot; *Kugel, Rakete* to fire; (*Ftbl etc*) to kick; *Tor auch* to score; (*mit Stock, Schläger*) to hit ◆ **jdn in den Kopf ~** to shoot sb in the head; **etw an der Schießbude ~** to win sth at the shooting gallery; **ein paar Bilder ~** (*Phot inf*) to take a few shots; **sie hat ihn zum Krüppel geschossen** she shot and crippled him.
[2] *vi* (a) to shoot ◆ **auf jdn/etw ~** to shoot at sb/sth; **nach etw ~** to shoot at sth; **aufs Tor/ins Netz ~** to shoot *or* kick at goal/into the net; **das ist zum S~** (*inf*) that's a scream (*inf*).
(b) *aux sein* (*in die Höhe ~*) to shoot up; (*Samenstand entwickeln*) to run to seed ◆ **die Pflanzen/Kinder sind in die Höhe geschossen** the plants/children have shot up; **aus dem Boden ~** (*lit, fig*) to spring *or* sprout up; *siehe* **Kraut**.
(c) *aux sein* (*inf: sich schnell bewegen*) to shoot ◆ **er ist** *or* **kam um die Ecke geschossen** he shot round the corner; **jdm durch den Kopf ~** (*fig*) to flash through sb's mind.
(d) *aux sein* (*Flüssigkeit*) to shoot; (*spritzen*) to spurt ◆ **das Blut schoß ihm ins Gesicht** blood rushed *or* shot to his face; **die Tränen schossen ihr in die Augen** tears flooded her eyes.
(e) *aux sein* (*S Ger, Aus: verbleichen*) to fade.
[3] *vr* to have a shoot-out.
Schießerei *f* gun battle, shoot-out; (*das Schießen*) shooting.
Schieß-: **~gewehr** *nt* (*hum*) gun; **~hund** *m*: **wie ein ~hund aufpassen** (*inf*) to keep a close watch, to watch like a hawk; **~kunst** *f* marksmanship *no pl*; **~platz** *m* (shooting *or* firing) range; **~prügel** *m* (*sl*) iron (*sl*); **~pulver** *nt* gunpowder; **~scharte** *f* embrasure; **~scheibe** *f* target; **~sport** *m* shooting; **~stand** *m* shooting range; (*~bude*) shooting gallery; **~übung** *f* shooting *or* target practice *no pl*.
Schiet *m* -s, *no pl* (*N Ger inf*) *siehe* **Scheiße**.
Schiff *nt* -(e)s, -e (a) ship ◆ **das ~ der Wüste** (*geh*) the ship of the desert; **das ~ des Staates** (*geh*) the ship of state; *siehe* **klar**. (b) (*Archit*) (*Mittel~*) nave; (*Seiten~*) aisle; (*Quer~*) transept. (c) (*in Kohleherd*) boiler. (d) (*Typ: Setz~*) galley.
⚠**Schiffahrt** *f getrennt*: **Schiff-fahrt** shipping; (*~skunde*) navigation.
Schiffahrts-: **~gesellschaft** *f* shipping company; **~kunde** *f* navigation; **~linie** *f* (a) (*Schiffsweg*) shipping route; (b) (*Unternehmen*) shipping line; **~recht** *nt* maritime law; **~straße** *f*, **~weg** *m* (*Kanal*) waterway; (*~linie*) shipping route *or* lane.
Schiff-: **s~bar** *adj* navigable; **~barkeit** *f* navigability; **~barmachung** *f* (*von Fluß*) canalization; **~bau** *m* shipbuilding; **~bauer** *m* shipwright; **~bruch** *m* shipwreck; **~bruch erleiden** (*lit*) to be shipwrecked; (*fig*) to fail; (*Unternehmen*) to founder; **s~brüchig** *adj* shipwrecked; **s~brüchig werden** to be shipwrecked; **~brüchige(r)** *mf decl as adj* shipwrecked person.
Schiffchen *nt* (a) (*zum Spielen*) little boat. (b) (*Mil, Fashion*) forage cap. (c) (*Tex, Sew*) shuttle. (d) (*Bot*) keel, carina (*spec*). (e) (*für Weihrauch*) boat.
schiffen [1] *vi* (a) *aux sein* (*old*) (*Schiff fahren*) to ship (*old*), to go by ship; (*Schiff steuern*) to steer. (b) (*sl: urinieren*) to piss (*sl*).
[2] *vi impers* (*sl: regnen*) to piss down (*sl*).
Schiffer(in *f*) *m* -s, - boatman, sailor; (*von Lastkahn*) bargee; (*Kapitän*) skipper.
Schiffer-: **~klavier** *nt* accordion; **~knoten** *m* sailor's knot; **~mütze** *f* yachting cap; **~scheiße** *f* (*vulg*) **frech/geil/dumm wie ~scheiße** cheeky as hell (*inf*)/randy (*Brit*) *or* horny as hell (*sl*)/thick as pigshit (*vulg*).
Schiffs- *in cpds* ship's; **~arzt** *m* ship's doctor; **~bauch** *m* bilge; **~besatzung** *f* ship's company.
Schiffschaukel *f* swing boat.
Schiffs-: **~eigner** *m* (*form*) shipowner; **~junge** *m* ship's boy; **~kapitän** *m* ship's captain; **~karte** *f* chart; **~koch** *m* ship's cook; **~körper** *m* (*form*) hull; **~ladung** *f* shipload; **~makler** *m* ship-broker; **~mannschaft** *f* ship's crew; **~modell** *nt* model ship; **~papiere** *pl* ship's papers *pl*; **~raum** *m* hold; **~register** *nt* register of shipping; **~rumpf** *m* hull; **~schnabel** *m* bow; **~schraube** *f* ship's propeller; **~tagebuch** *nt* ship's log; **~tau** *nt* (ship's) rope; **~taufe** *f* christening *or* naming of a/the ship; **~verbindung** *f* connecting boat service; **~verkehr** *m* shipping; **~werft** *f* shipyard; **~zwieback** *m* ship's biscuit.
Schiit *m* -en, -en Shiite.
schiitisch *adj* Shiite.
Schikane *f* -, -n (a) harassment; (*von Mitschülern*) bullying *no pl* ◆ **diese neuerlichen ~n an der Grenze** this recent harassment at the border; **das hat er aus reiner ~ gemacht** he did it out of sheer bloody-mindedness; **die Schüler brauchen sich nicht alle ~n gefallenzulassen** the pupils don't have to put up with being messed around (*inf*).
(b) **mit allen ~n** (*inf*) with all the trimmings.
(c) (*Sport*) chicane.
schikanieren* *vt* to harass; *Ehepartner, Freundin etc* to mess around; *Mitschüler* to bully ◆ **ich lasse mich nicht weiter von diesem Weibsstück ~** I won't let this female mess me around any more (*inf*); **er hat mich einmal so schikaniert, daß** ... he once gave me such a rough time that ...
schikanös *adj Mensch* bloody-minded; *Maßnahme etc* harassing; *Mitschüler, Ehemann, Vorgesetzter* bullying ◆ **jdn ~ behandeln** to mess sb around, to give sb a rough time.
Schild[1] *m* -(e)s, -e shield; (*Wappen~*) escutcheon; (*von ~kröte*) shell, carapace (*spec*) ◆ **etwas/nichts Gutes im ~e führen** (*fig*) to be up to something/to be up to no good.
Schild[2] *nt* -(e)s, -er (*Aushang, Waren~, Verkehrs~*) sign; (*Wegweiser*) signpost; (*Namens~, Tür~*) nameplate; (*Kennzeichen*) number plate (*Brit*), license plate (*US*); (*Preis~*) ticket; (*Etikett, an Käfig, Gepäck etc*) label; (*Plakette*) badge; (*Plakat*) placard; (*von Plakatträger*) board; (*an Monument, Haus, Grab*) plaque; (*von Mütze*) peak ◆ **im Fenster stand ein ~** there was a sign *or* notice in the window.
Schildbürger(in *f*) *m* (*Liter*) ≃ Gothamite; (*hum*) fool.
Schildbürgerstreich *m* foolish act ◆ **das war ein ~** that was a stupid thing to do, that was a bit Irish (*hum inf*).
Schildchen *nt siehe* **Schild**[2] small sign; small plate *etc*.
Schilddrüse *f* thyroid gland ◆ **an der ~ leiden** to have a thyroid complaint.
Schilddrüsenhormon *nt* thyroid hormone.
Schilderer *m* -s, - portrayer.
Schilder-: **~haus, ~häuschen** *nt* sentry-box; **~maler** *m* sign-writer.
schildern *vt Ereignisse, Erlebnisse, Vorgänge* to describe; (*skizzieren*) to outline; *Menschen, Landschaften* to portray ◆ **es ist kaum zu ~** it's almost impossible to describe; **es ist kaum zu ~, wie frech er war** he was indescribably cheeky; **~ Sie den Verlauf des Unfalls** give an account of how the accident happened.
Schilderung *f* (*Beschreibung*) description; (*Bericht, von Zeuge*) account; (*literarische ~*) portrayal.
Schilderwald *m* (*hum*) forest *or* jungle of traffic signs.
Schild-: **~knappe** *m* (*Hist*) squire, shield-bearer; **~kröte** *f* (*Land~*) tortoise; (*Wasser~*) turtle; **~krötensuppe** *f* turtle soup; **~laus** *f* scale insect; **~patt** *nt* -s, *no pl* tortoiseshell; **~wache** *f* (*old*) sentry; **~wache stehen** to stand sentry.
Schilf *nt* -(e)s, -e reed; (*mit ~ bewachsene Fläche*) reeds *pl*.
Schilf-: **~dach** *nt* thatched roof; **~gras** *nt*, **~rohr** *nt siehe* **Schilf**.
Schiller *m* -s, *no pl* (a) (*Schimmer, Glanz*) shimmer. (b) (*Wein*) rosé (wine).
Schiller-: **~kragen** *m* Byron collar; **~locke** *f* (a) (*Gebäck*) cream horn; (b) (*Räucherfisch*) strip of smoked rock-salmon.
schillern *vi* to shimmer.
schillernd *adj Farben, Stoffe* shimmering; (*in Regenbogenfarben*) iridescent; (*fig*) *Charakter* enigmatic ◆ **~e Seide** shot silk.
Schillerwein *m* rosé (wine).
Schilling *m* -s, - *or* (*bei Geldstücken*) **-e** shilling; (*Aus*) schilling.
schilpen *vi* to twitter, to chirp.
schilt *imper sing of* **schelten**.
Schimäre *f* -, -n chimera.
schimärisch *adj* chimerical.
Schimmel[1] *m* -s, - (*Pferd*) white horse, grey ◆ **ein weißer ~** (*hum*) a pleonasm.
Schimmel[2] *m* -s *no pl* (*auf Nahrungsmitteln*) mould; (*auf Leder, Papier etc*) mildew.
schimm(e)lig *adj siehe* **Schimmel**[2] mouldy; mildewy ◆ **~ riechen** to smell mouldy; **~ werden** to go mouldy; to become covered with mildew.
schimmeln *vi aux sein or haben* (*Nahrungsmittel*) to go mouldy; (*Leder, Papier etc*) to go mildewy.

⚠: Informationen zur Rechtschreibreform im Anhang

Schimmel-: ~pilz *m* mould; **~reiter** *m* (*Myth*) ghost rider.
Schimmer *m* **-s,** *no pl* glimmer, gleam; (*von Licht auf Wasser, Perlen, Seide*) shimmer; (*von Metall*) gleam; (*im Haar*) sheen ◆ **beim ~ der Lampe/Kerzen** by *or* in the soft glow of the lamp/glimmer of the candles; **keinen (blassen) ~ von etw haben** (*inf*) not to have the slightest idea *or* the faintest (*inf*) about sth.
schimmern *vi* to glimmer, to gleam; (*Licht auf Wasser auch, Perlen, Seide*) to shimmer; (*Metall*) to gleam ◆ **der Stoff/ihr Haar schimmert rötlich** the material/her hair has a tinge of red.
schimmlig *adj siehe* **schimm(e)lig.**
Schimpanse *m* **-n, -n** chimpanzee, chimp (*inf*).
Schimpf *m* **-(e)s,** *no pl* (*liter*) insult, affront ◆ **mit ~ und Schande** in disgrace.
schimpfen [1] *vi* to get angry; (*sich beklagen*) to moan, to grumble, to bitch (*inf*); (*fluchen*) to swear, to curse; (*Vögel, Affen etc*) to bitch (*inf*) ◆ **mit jdm ~** to scold sb, to tell sb off; **heute hat der Lehrer (fürchterlich) geschimpft, weil ich ...** the teacher told me off today because I ... (*inf*); **auf** *or* **über jdn/etw ~** to bitch (*inf*) about sb/sth, to curse (about *or* at) sb/sth; **vor sich hin ~** to grumble.
[2] *vt* (*aus~*) to tell off, to scold ◆ **jdn einen Idioten ~** to call sb an idiot.
[3] *vr* **sich etw ~** (*inf*) to call oneself sth.
Schimpferei *f* cursing and swearing; (*Geschimpfe*) scolding; (*Beschimpfung*) row, set-to (*inf*), slanging match (*inf*); (*das Murren*) moaning, grumbling, bitching (*inf*); (*von Vögeln, Affen etc*) bitching (*inf*).
Schimpfkanonade *f* barrage of abuse.
schimpflich *adj* (*geh*) (*beleidigend*) insulting; (*schmachvoll*) humiliating ◆ **jdn ~ verjagen** to drive sb away in disgrace.
Schimpf-: ~name *m* nickname; **Tricky Dicky war sein ~name** they dubbed him Tricky Dicky; **~wort** *nt* swearword; **mit ~wörtern um sich werfen** to curse and swear.
Schinakel *nt* **-s, -(n)** (*Aus inf*) (*Ruderboot*) rowing boat; (*klappriges Fahrzeug*) rattletrap (*inf*).
Schind|anger *m* (*old*) knacker's yard.
Schindel *f* **-, -n** shingle.
Schindeldach *nt* shingle roof.
schinden *pret* **schindete** *or* (*rare*) **schund,** *ptp* **geschunden** [1] *vt* **(a)** (*quälen*) *Gefangene, Tiere* to maltreat; (*ausbeuten*) to overwork, to drive hard; *Maschine, Motor, Auto* to flog ◆ **der geschundene Leib Christi** the broken body of Christ.
(b) (*inf: herausschlagen*) *Zeilen* to pad (out); *Arbeitsstunden* to pile up ◆ **Zeit ~** to play for time; **(bei jdm) Eindruck ~** to make a good impression (on sb), to impress (sb); **Mitleid ~** to get some sympathy.
[2] *vr* (*hart arbeiten*) to struggle; (*sich quälen*) to strain ◆ **sich mit etw ~** to slave away at sth.
Schinder *m* **-s, - (a)** (*old: Abdecker*) knacker. **(b)** (*fig: Quäler*) slavedriver.
Schinderei *f* **(a)** (*old: Abdeckerei*) knacker's yard. **(b)** (*Plakkerei*) struggle; (*Arbeit*) slavery *no indef art.*
Schindluder *nt* (*inf*) **mit jdm ~ treiben** to make sb suffer; **mit etw ~ treiben** to misuse sth; **mit seiner Gesundheit/seinen Kräften ~ treiben** to abuse one's health/strength.
Schindmähre *f* (*old*) nag.
Schinken *m* **-s, - (a)** ham; (*gekocht und geräuchert auch*) gammon. **(b)** (*pej inf*) hackneyed and clichéed play/book/film; (*großes Buch*) tome; (*großes Bild*) great daub (*pej inf*).
Schinken-: ~brötchen *nt* ham roll; **~röllchen** *nt* roll of ham; **~speck** *m* bacon; **~wurst** *f* ham sausage.
Schinn *m* **-s,** *no pl*, **Schinnen** *pl* (*N Ger*) dandruff *no pl.*
Schintoismus *m* (*Rel*) shintoism.
Schippe *f* **-, -n (a)** (*esp N Ger: Schaufel*) shovel, spade ◆ **jdn auf die ~ nehmen** (*fig inf*) to pull sb's leg (*inf*); **dem Tod von der ~ springen** (*inf*) to be snatched from the jaws of death. **(b)** (*Cards*) spades.
schippen *vt* to shovel ◆ **Schnee ~** to clear the snow.
schippern *vi aux sein* (*inf*) to sail.
Schiri *m* **-s, -s** (*Ftbl inf*) ref (*inf*).
Schirm *m* **-(e)s, -e (a)** (*Regen~*) umbrella; (*Sonnen~*) sunshade, parasol; (*von Pilz*) cap.
(b) (*Mützen~*) peak ◆ **eine Mütze mit ~** a peaked cap.
(c) (*Röntgen~, Wand~, Ofen~*) screen; (*Lampen~*) shade.
(d) (*liter: Schutz*) **unter seinem Schutz und ~** under his protection; **jdm** *or* **jds ~ und Schild sein** to be sb's protector.
Schirm-: ~akazie *f* umbrella thorn; **~bild** *nt* X-ray (picture); **~bildaufnahme** *f* (*form*) X-ray; **~bildstelle** *f* X-ray unit.
schirmen *vt* (*geh*) to shield, to protect (*vor +dat* from, *gegen* against).
Schirm-: ~futteral *nt* umbrella cover *or* case; **~herr(in** *f*) *m* patron; (*Frau auch*) patroness; **~herrschaft** *f* patronage; **unter der ~herrschaft von** under the patronage of; (*von Organisation*) under the auspices of; **die ~herrschaft übernehmen** to become patron; **~hülle** *f* umbrella cover; **~mütze** *f* peaked cap; **~pilz** *m* parasol mushroom; **~ständer** *m* umbrella stand.
Schirokko *m* **-s, -s** sirocco.
Schisma [ˈʃɪsma, ˈsçɪ-] *nt* **-s, Schismen** *or* (*geh*) **-ta** (*Eccl, Pol*) schism.
Schismatiker(in *f*) [ʃɪsˈmaːtikɐ, -ərɪn, sçɪ-] *m* **-s, -** (*liter*) schismatic.
schismatisch [ʃɪsˈmaːtɪʃ, sçɪ-] *adj* (*geh*) schismatic.
⚠ **schiß** *pret of* **scheißen.**
⚠ **Schiß** *m* **-sses,** *no pl* (*sl*) shit (*vulg*), crap (*vulg*) ◆ **(fürchterlichen) ~ haben** to be shit scared (*vor +dat* of) (*vulg*); **~ kriegen** to get the shits (*vulg*).
schizophren *adj* **(a)** (*Med*) schizophrenic. **(b)** (*pej: widersinnig*) contradictory, topsy-turvy.
Schizophrenie *f* **(a)** (*Med*) schizophrenia. **(b)** (*pej: Widersinn*) contradictoriness ◆ **das ist die reinste ~** that's a flat contradiction.
Schlabberei *f* (*inf*) slurping, slobbering.
schlabberig *adj* (*inf*) slithery, slimy; *Maul* slobbery; *Brei, Suppe* watery.
Schlabbermaul *nt* (*inf: von Hund*) slobbery mouth.
schlabbern (*inf*) [1] *vi* to slobber, to slurp ◆ **er schlabberte beim Essen** he slobbered *or* slurped his food.
[2] *vt* to slurp.
Schlacht *f* **-, -en** battle ◆ **die ~ bei** *or* **um X** the battle of X; **in die ~ gehen** *or* **ziehen** to go into battle; **jdm eine ~ liefern** to fight sb, to battle with sb; **die Kelten lieferten den Römern eine ~, die ...** the Celts gave the Romans a battle that ...
Schlachtbank *f*: **jdn (wie ein Lamm) zur ~ führen** to lead sb (like a lamb) to the slaughter.
schlachten [1] *vt Schwein, Kuh* to slaughter, to butcher; *Huhn, Kaninchen, Opfertier etc* to slaughter, to kill; (*hum*) *Sparschwein* to break into.
[2] *vi* to do one's slaughtering ◆ **unser Fleischer schlachtet selbst** our butcher does his own slaughtering; **heute wird geschlachtet** we're/they're *etc* slaughtering today.
Schlachten-: ~bummler *m* (*inf: Sport*) visiting *or* away supporter *or* fan; **~maler** *m* painter of battle scenes.
Schlachter(in *f*) *m* **-s, -** (*esp N Ger*) butcher.
Schlächter(in *f*) *m* **-s, -** (*dial, fig*) butcher.
Schlachterei *f* (*esp N Ger*) butcher's (shop).
Schlächterei *f* **(a)** (*dial*) butcher's (shop). **(b)** (*fig: Blutbad*) slaughter, butchery *no pl*, massacre.
Schlachterladen, Schlächterladen *m* (*dial*) *siehe* **Schlachterei.**
Schlacht-: ~feld *nt* battle-field; **auf dem ~feld bleiben** (*lit*) to fall in battle; (*fig*) (*nach Schlägerei etc*) to be left lying; (*esp Pol*) to be finished; **das ~feld räumen** (*aufräumen*) to clear the (battle-)field; (*verlassen*) to leave the (battle-)field; (*fig*) to drop out of contention; **das Zimmer sieht aus wie ein ~feld** the room looks like a battle-field *or* looks as if a bomb has hit it (*inf*); **~fest** *nt a country feast to eat up meat from freshly slaughtered pigs*; **~gesang** *m* battle song; **~getümmel** *nt* thick of the battle, fray; **~gewicht** *nt* dressed weight; **~gewühl** *nt siehe* **~getümmel; ~haus** *nt*, **~hof** *m* slaughter-house, abattoir; **~kreuzer** *m* battle cruiser; **~linie** *f* battle line; **~messer** *nt* butcher's knife; **~opfer** *nt* sacrifice; (*Mensch*) human sacrifice; **~ordnung** *f* battle formation; **~plan** *m* battle plan; (*für Feldzug*) campaign plan; (*fig auch*) plan of action; **~platte** *f* (*Cook*) *ham, German sausage, made with meat from freshly slaughtered pigs and served with sauerkraut*; **s~reif** *adj* (*lit, fig*) ready for the slaughter; ⚠**~roß** *nt* (*liter*) warhorse, charger; (*fig inf*) heavyweight; **~ruf** *m* battle cry; **~schiff** *nt* battleship; **~tag** *m* slaughtering day.
Schlachtung *f siehe vt* slaughter(ing), butchering; killing.
Schlachtvieh *nt, no pl* animals *pl* for slaughter; (*Rinder auch*) beef cattle *pl.*
Schlacke *f* **-, -n** (*Verbrennungsrückstand*) clinker *no pl*; (*Aschenteile auch*) cinders *pl*; (*Metal*) slag *no pl*; (*Geol*) scoria *pl* (*spec*), slag *no pl*; (*Physiol*) waste products *pl.*
Schlacken-: ~bahn *f* (*Sport*) cinder track; **s~frei, s~los** *adj* (*ohne Verbrennungsrückstand*) non-clinker *attr*, clinker-free; (*ohne Stoffwechselrückstand*) free of waste products; **Anthrazit brennt s~frei** anthracite burns without clinkering.
schlackern *vi* (*inf*) to tremble, to shake; (*vor Angst auch*) to quake; (*Kleidung*) to hang loosely, to be baggy ◆ **mit den Knien ~** to tremble at the knees; **mit den Ohren ~** (*fig*) to be (left) speechless.
Schlaf *m* **-(e)s,** *no pl* sleep; (*Schläfrigkeit auch*) sleepiness ◆ **einen leichten/festen/tiefen ~ haben** to be a light/sound/deep sleeper; **keinen ~ finden** to be unable to sleep; **um seinen ~ kommen/gebracht werden** to lose sleep; (*überhaupt nicht schlafen*) not to get any sleep; **jdn um seinen ~ bringen** to keep sb awake; **halb im ~e** half asleep; **im ~ reden** to talk in one's sleep; **ein Kind in den ~ singen** to sing a child to sleep; **sich** (*dat*) **den ~ aus den Augen reiben** to rub the sleep out of one's eyes; **in tiefstem ~ liegen** to be sound *or* fast asleep; **aus dem ~ erwachen** (*geh*) to awake, to waken (from sleep); **den ewigen** *or* **letzten ~ schlafen** (*euph*) to sleep one's last sleep; **den Seinen gibt's der Herr im ~** the devil looks after his own; **es fällt mir nicht im ~(e) ein, das zu tun** I wouldn't dream of doing that; **das macht** *or* **tut** *or* **kann er im ~** (*fig inf*) he can do that in his sleep.
Schlaf-: ~anzug *m* pyjamas *pl* (*Brit*), pajamas *pl* (*US*); **s~bedürftig** *adj* **(besonders) s~bedürftig sein** to need a lot of sleep; **Kinder sind s~bedürftiger als Erwachsene** children need more sleep than adults.
Schläfchen *nt* nap, snooze ◆ **ein ~ machen** to have a nap *or* snooze.
Schlafcouch *f* studio couch, sofa bed.
Schläfe *f* **-, -n** temple ◆ **graue ~n** greying temples.
schlafen *pret* **schlief,** *ptp* **geschlafen** [1] *vi* to sleep; (*nicht wach sein auch*) to be asleep; (*euph: tot sein*) to be asleep (*euph*); (*geh: Stadt, Land auch*) to be quiet, to slumber (*liter*); (*inf: nicht aufpassen*) (*bei bestimmter Gelegenheit*) to be asleep; (*immer*) not to pay attention ◆ **er schläft immer noch** he's still asleep, he's still sleeping; **tief** *or* **fest ~** (*zu diesem Zeitpunkt*) to be fast *or* sound asleep; (*immer*) to be a deep *or* sound sleeper; **~ gehen** to go to bed; **sich ~ legen** to lie down to sleep; **jdn ~ legen** to put sb to bed; **schläfst du schon?** are you asleep?; **jetzt wird (aber) geschlafen!** go to sleep this minute; **lange ~** to sleep for a long time; (*spät aufstehen*) to sleep late, to have a long lie (in); **schlaf gut** *or* (*geh*) **wohl** sleep well; **hast du gut geschlafen?** did you sleep well?, did you have a good sleep?; **mittags** *or* **über Mittag ~** to have an

afternoon nap; ~ wie ein Murmeltier *or* Bär *or* Sack *or* Stein *or* eine Ratte (*all inf*) to sleep like a log; bei jdm ~ to stay overnight with sb; er kann nachts nicht mehr ~ (*fig*) he can't sleep nights; das läßt ihn nicht ~ (*fig*) it preys on his mind, it gives him no peace; darüber muß ich erst mal ~ (*fig: überdenken*) I'll have to sleep on it; mit jdm ~ (*euph*) to sleep with sb; sie schläft mit jedem she sleeps around; schlaf nicht! wake up!

[2] *vr impers* auf dieser Matratze schläft es sich schlecht this mattress is terrible to sleep on.

Schläfenbein *nt* temporal bone.

schlafend [1] *adj* sleeping ◆ im ~en Zustand asleep.
[2] *adv* asleep ◆ sich ~ stellen to pretend to be asleep.

Schlafengehen *nt* going to bed ◆ vor dem ~ before going to bed.

Schlafenszeit *f* bedtime.

Schlaf|entzug *m* sleep deprivation.

Schläfer(in *f*) *m* -s, - sleeper; (*fig*) dozy person (*inf*).

schlaff *adj* limp; (*locker*) *Seil, Segel* loose, slack; *Moral* lax, loose; *Disziplin* lax; *Haut* flabby, loose; *Muskeln* flabby, floppy; (*erschöpft*) worn-out, shattered (*inf*), exhausted; (*energielos*) listless, floppy.

Schlaffheit *f siehe adj* limpness; looseness, slackness; flabbiness, floppiness; exhaustion; listlessness.

Schlaf-: ~gelegenheit *f* place to sleep; wir haben ~gelegenheit für mehrere Leute we can put up several people; **~gemach** *nt* (*liter*) bedchamber (*liter*).

Schlafittchen *nt*: jdn am *or* beim ~ nehmen *or* kriegen (*inf*) to take sb by the scruff of the neck; (*zurechtweisen*) to give sb a dressing down (*inf*).

Schlaf-: ~kammer *f* (*dial*) bedroom; **~krankheit** *f* sleeping sickness; **~lied** *nt* lullaby; **s~los** *adj* (*lit, fig*) sleepless; s~los liegen to lie awake; **~losigkeit** *f* sleeplessness, insomnia (*Med*); sie verbrachte die folgenden Nächte in ~losigkeit she spent the following nights unable to sleep; **~mittel** *nt* sleeping drug *or* pill; (*fig iro*) soporific; diese Zeitung ist das reinste ~mittel this newspaper just sends you to sleep; **~mittelvergiftung** *f* (poisoning from an) overdose of sleeping pills, ≃ barbiturate poisoning; **~mütze** *f* (a) nightcap; (b) (*inf*) dope (*inf*); diese ~mützen im Parlament that dozy lot in Parliament (*inf*); **s~mützig** *adj* (*inf*) dozy (*inf*), dopey (*inf*); **~pille** *f* (*inf*) sleeping pill; **~raum** *m* dormitory, dorm (*inf*).

schläfrig *adj* sleepy; *Mensch auch* drowsy; (*fig auch: träge*) lethargic.

Schläfrigkeit *f siehe adj* sleepiness; drowsiness; lethargy.

Schlaf-: ~rock *m* dressing-gown; Äpfel im ~rock baked apples in puff pastry; Würstchen im ~rock ≃ sausage roll; **~saal** *m* dormitory; **~sack** *m* sleeping-bag; **~sacktourist** *m* backpacker; **~sessel** *m* reclining seat; **~sofa** *nt* sofabed, bed-settee (*Brit*); **~stadt** *f* dormitory town; **~stelle** *f* place to sleep; **~störung** *f* sleeplessness, insomnia; **~stube** *f* (*dial*) bedroom; **~sucht** *f* hypersomnia; **~tablette** *f* sleeping pill; **~trunk** *m* (*old*) sleeping draught (*old*); (*hum inf: Alkohol*) nightcap; **s~trunken** [1] *adj* (*geh*) drowsy, half asleep; [2] *adv* drowsily, half-asleep.

Schlafwagen *m* sleeping-car, sleeper.

Schlafwagen-: ~karte *f* sleeper ticket; **~platz** *m* berth; **~schaffner** *m* sleeping-car attendant.

Schlaf-: s~wandeln *vi insep aux sein or haben* to sleepwalk, to walk in one's sleep, to somnambulate (*form*); **~wandler(in *f*)** *m* -s, - sleepwalker, somnambulist (*form*); **s~wandlerisch** *adj* (*geh*) sleepwalking *attr*, somnambulatory (*form*); mit s~wandlerischer Sicherheit *wählen, Fragen beantworten* intuitively, instinctively; das Kind lief mit s~wandlerischer Sicherheit durch den dichten Verkehr the child ran through the heavy traffic with instinctive assurance; **~zimmer** *nt* bedroom; **~zimmerblick** *m* (*hum inf*) come-to-bed eyes *pl* (*inf*); **~zimmergeschichte** *f* (*inf*) sexual adventure, bedroom antic (*inf*).

Schlag *m* -(e)s, ⸚e (a) (*lit, fig*) blow; (*Faust~ auch*) punch; (*mit der Handfläche*) smack, slap; (*leichter*) pat; (*Handkanten~, Judo etc*) chop (*inf*); (*Ohrfeige*) cuff, clout; (*mit dem Fuß, Huf*) kick; (*Ftbl sl: Schuß*) shot; (*mit Rohrstock etc*) stroke; (*Peitschen~*) stroke, lash; (*einmaliges Klopfen*) knock; (*dumpf*) thump, thud; (*leichtes Pochen*) tap; (*Glocken~*) chime; (*Standuhr~*) stroke; (*von Metronom*) tick, beat; (*Gehirn~, ~anfall, Kolben~, Ruder~, Schwimmen, Tennis*) stroke; (*Herz~, Puls~, Trommel~, Wellen~*) beat; (*Blitz~*) bolt, stroke; (*Donner~*) clap; (*Strom~*) shock ◆ man hörte die ⸚e des Hammers/der Trommeln you could hear the clanging of the hammer/beating of the drums; ⸚e kriegen to get a hiding *or* thrashing *or* beating; zum entscheidenden ~ ausholen (*fig*) to strike the decisive blow; ~ auf ~ (*fig*) in quick succession, one after the other; ~ *or* s~ (*Aus*) acht Uhr (*inf*) at eight on the dot (*inf*), on the stroke of eight; ein ~ ins Gesicht (*lit, fig*) a slap in the face; ein ~ ins Kontor (*inf*) a nasty shock *or* surprise; ein ~ ins Wasser (*inf*) a washout (*inf*), a let-down (*inf*); ein ~ aus heiterem Himmel a bolt from the blue; mit einem *or* auf einen ~ (*inf*) all at once; (*auf einmal, zugleich auch*) in one go; mit einem ~ berühmt werden to become famous overnight; die haben keinen ~ getan (*inf*) they haven't done a stroke (of work); einen ~ weghaben (*sl*) (*blöd sein*) to have a screw loose (*inf*); (*betrunken sein*) to be tiddly (*inf*); ihn hat der ~ getroffen (*Med*) he had a stroke; ich dachte, mich rührt *or* trifft der ~ (*inf*) I was flabbergasted (*inf*) *or* thunderstruck; ich glaube, mich trifft der ~ I don't believe it; wie vom ~ gerührt *or* getroffen sein to be flabbergasted (*inf*) *or* thunderstruck (*inf*), to be knocked all of a heap (*inf*).
(b) (*inf: Wesensart*) type (of person *etc*) ◆ vom ~ der Südländer sein to be a Southern type; vom gleichen ~ sein to be cast in the same mould; (*pej*) to be tarred with the same brush; vom alten ~ of the old school.
(c) (*Vogel~*) song.
(d) (*dated: Wagen~*) door.
(e) (*Tauben~*) cote.
(f) (*Aus: ~sahne*) cream.
(g) (*inf: Portion*) helping.
(h) (*sl*) er hat ~ bei Frauen he has a way with the ladies.

Schlag-: ~abtausch *m* (*Boxen*) exchange of blows; (*fig*) (verbal) exchange; offener ~abtausch public exchange (of views); **~ader** *f* artery; **~anfall** *m* stroke; **s~artig** [1] *adj* sudden, abrupt; [2] *adv* suddenly; **~ball** *m* rounders *sing*; (*Ball*) rounders ball; **s~bar** *adj* beatable; diese Mannschaft ist durchaus s~bar this team is by no means invincible *or* unbeatable; **~baum** *m* barrier; **~bohrer** *m*, **~bohrmaschine** *f* hammer drill; **~bolzen** *m* firing pin.

Schläge *pl of* Schlag.

Schlägel *m* -s, - (*Min*) (miner's) hammer ◆ ~ und Eisen crossed hammers, *miner's symbol*.

schlagen *pret* **schlug**, *ptp* **geschlagen** [1] *vti* (a) to hit; (*hauen*) to beat; (*einmal zu~, treffen auch*) to strike; (*mit der flachen Hand*) to slap, to smack; (*leichter*) to pat; (*mit der Faust*) to punch; (*mit Schläger*) to hit; (*treten*) to kick; (*mit Hammer, Pickel etc*) *Nagel, Loch* to knock ◆ jdn bewußtlos ~ to knock sb out *or* unconscious; (*mit vielen Schlägen*) to beat sb unconscious; etw in Stücke *or* kurz und klein ~ to smash sth up *or* to pieces; nach jdm/etw ~ to hit out *or* lash out at sb; um sich ~ to lash out; mit dem Hammer auf den Nagel ~ to hit the nail with the hammer; mit der Faust an die Tür/auf den Tisch ~ to beat *or* thump on the door/table with one's fist; gegen die Tür ~ to hammer on the door; jdm *or* (*rare*) jdn auf die Schulter ~ to slap sb on the back; (*leichter*) to pat sb on the back; jdm *or* (*rare*) jdn auf den Kopf ~ to hit sb on the head; jdm ein Buch auf den Kopf ~ to hit sb on the head with a book; jdm etw aus der Hand ~ to knock sth out of sb's hand; jdm *or* (*rare*) jdn ins Gesicht ~ to hit/slap/punch sb in the face; ihm schlug das Gewissen his conscience pricked him; einer Sache (*dat*) ins Gesicht ~ (*fig*) to be a slap in the face for sth; *siehe* grün, Boden, Wahrheit *etc*.
(b) *Teig, Eier* to beat; (*mit Schneebesen*) to whisk; *Sahne* to whip ◆ ein Ei in die Pfanne/die Suppe ~ to crack an egg into the pan/beat an egg into the soup.
(c) (*läuten*) to chime; *Stunde* to strike ◆ die Uhr hat 12 geschlagen the clock has struck 12; eine geschlagene Stunde a full hour; wissen, was es *or* die Uhr *or* Glocke geschlagen hat (*fig inf*) to know what's what (*inf*); *siehe* dreizehn.
(d) (*heftig flattern*) mit den Flügeln ~, die Flügel ~ (*liter*) to beat *or* flap its wings.
(e) (*Chess*) to take, to capture.
[2] *vt* (a) (*besiegen, übertreffen*) *Gegner, Rekord* to beat ◆ jdn in etw (*dat*) ~ to beat sb at sth; unsere Mannschaft schlug den Gegner (mit) 2:1 our team beat their opponents (by) 2-1; na ja, ehe ich mich ~ lasse! (*hum inf*) yes, I don't mind if I do, I suppose you could twist my arm (*hum inf*); sich geschlagen geben to admit that one is beaten, to admit defeat.
(b) (*liter: treffen*) das Schicksal schlug sie hart fate dealt her a hard blow; ein vom Schicksal geschlagener Mann a man dogged by fate.
(c) (*Bibl: bestrafen*) to strike (down), to smite (*Bibl*) ◆ mit Blindheit (*lit, fig*)/Dummheit geschlagen sein to be blind/dumb.
(d) (*fällen*) to fell.
(e) (*fechten*) *Mensuren* to fight.
(f) (*liter: krallen, beißen*) seine Fänge/Zähne in etw (*acc*) ~ to sink one's talons/teeth into sth.
(g) (*Hunt: töten*) to kill.
(h) (*spielen*) *Trommel* to beat; (*liter*) *Harfe, Laute* to pluck, to play ◆ das S~ der Trommeln the beat(ing) of the drums.
(i) (*prägen*) *Münzen* to mint, to coin; *Medaillen auch* to strike.
(j) (*hinzufügen*) to add (*auf +acc, zu* to); *Gebiet* to annexe.
(k) *in Verbindung mit n siehe auch dort. Kreis, Bogen* to describe; *Purzelbaum, Rad* to do; *Alarm, Funken* to raise; *Krach* to make ◆ Profit aus etw ~ to make a profit from sth; (*fig*) to profit from sth; eine Schlacht ~ to fight a battle.
(l) den Kragen nach oben ~ to turn up one's collar; die Hände vors Gesicht ~ to cover one's face with one's hands.
(m) (*wickeln*) to wrap.
[3] *vi* (a) (*Herz, Puls*) to beat; (*heftig*) to pound, to throb ◆ sein Puls schlug unregelmäßig his pulse was irregular.
(b) *aux sein* (*auftreffen*) mit dem Kopf auf/gegen etw (*acc*) ~ to hit one's head on/against sth.
(c) *aux sein* (*gelangen*) ein leises Wimmern schlug an sein Ohr he could hear a faint whimpering.
(d) (*Regen*) to beat; (*Wellen auch*) to pound.
(e) *aux sein or haben* (*Flammen*) to shoot out (*aus* of); (*Rauch*) to pour out (*aus* of).
(f) (*Blitz*) to strike (*in etw* (*acc*) sth).
(g) (*singen: Nachtigall, Fink*) to sing.
(h) *aux sein* (*inf: ähneln*) er schlägt sehr nach seinem Vater he takes after his father a lot; *siehe* Art.
(i) (*betreffen*) in jds Fach/Gebiet (*acc*) ~ to be in sb's field/line.
(j) *aux sein* (*esp Med: in Mitleidenschaft ziehen*) auf die Augen/Nieren *etc* ~ to affect the eyes/kidneys; jdm auf die Augen *etc* ~ to affect sb's eyes *etc*.
[4] *vr* (a) (*sich prügeln*) to fight; (*sich duellieren*) to duel (*auf +dat* with) ◆ als Schuljunge habe ich mich oft geschlagen I often had fights when I was a schoolboy; sich mit jdm ~ to fight (with) sb, to have a fight with sb; (*duellieren*) to duel with sb; sich um etw ~ (*lit, fig*) to fight over sth; er schlägt sich nicht um die Arbeit he's not too keen on work.
(b) (*sich selbst ~*) to hit *or* beat oneself.
(c) (*sich bewähren*) to do, to fare ◆ sich tapfer *or* gut ~ to make a good showing.

(d) *(sich begeben)* **sich nach rechts/links/Norden ~** to strike out to the left/right/for the North; **sich auf jds Seite** *(acc)* **~** to side with sb; *(die Fronten wechseln)* to go over to sb; **sich zu einer Partei ~** to throw in one's lot with a party; *siehe* **Leben, Busch.**
(e) *(Mech)* **sich auf etw** *(acc)* **~** to affect sth.
schlagend *adj (treffend) Bemerkung, Vergleich* apt, appropriate; *(überzeugend) Beweis* striking, convincing ◆ **etw ~ beweisen/widerlegen** to prove/refute sth convincingly; *siehe* **Verbindung, Wetter**[2]**.**
Schlager *m* **-s, - (a)** *(Mus)* pop-song; *(erfolgreich)* hit-song, hit. **(b)** *(inf) (Erfolg)* hit; *(Waren)* bargain; *(Verkaufs~, Buch)* bestseller.
Schläger *m* **-s, - (a)** *(Tennis~, Federball~)* racquet *(Brit)*, racket *(US)*; *(Hockey~, Eishockey~)* stick; *(Golf~)* club; *(Kricket~, Baseball~)* bat; *(Tischtennis)* bat, paddle; *(Polo~)* mallet.
(b) *(Spieler) (Kricket)* batsman; *(Baseball)* batter.
(c) *(Raufbold)* thug, ruffian.
(d) *(Waffe) straight-bladed sabre used by students in duelling bouts.*
Schlägerbande *f* gang of thugs.
Schlägerei *f* fight, brawl.
Schlägerin *f siehe* **Schläger (b, c).**
Schlagermusik *f* pop music.
Schlägermütze *f* cap.
Schlager-: ~parade *f* hit-parade; **~sänger** *m* pop singer; **~sendung** *f* pop music programme; **~text** *m* (pop music) lyrics *pl*; **~texter** *m* writer of pop music lyrics, lyricist.
Schlägertyp *m (inf)* thug.
Schlag-: s~fertig *adj* quick-witted; **~fertigkeit** *f* quick-wittedness; **~instrument** *nt* percussion instrument; **~kraft** *f (lit, fig)* power; *(Boxen)* punch(ing power); *(Mil)* strike power; **s~kräftig** *adj Boxer, Armee, Argumente* powerful; *Beweise* clear-cut; **~licht** *nt (Art, Phot)* highlight; **s~lichtartig** *adj* **etw s~lichtartig beleuchten** to give a sudden insight into sth; **s~lichtartig deutlich werden** to become clear at a stroke; **~loch** *nt* pothole; **~mann** *m, pl* **-männer** *(Rudern)* stroke; *(Kricket)* batsman; *(Baseball)* batter; **~obers** *nt* **-, -** *(Aus)*, **~rahm** *m (S Ger) siehe* **~sahne**; **~ring** *m* **(a)** knuckleduster; **(b)** *(Mus)* plectrum; **~sahne** *f* (whipping) cream; *(geschlagen)* whipped cream; **~schatten** *m (Art, Phot)* shadow *(of person or object)*; **~seite** *f (Naut)* list; **~seite haben** *(Naut)* to be listing, to have a list; *(hum inf)* to be half-seas over *(inf)*; **~stock** *m (form)* truncheon, baton, nightstick *(US)*; **~stöcke einsetzen** to charge with batons; **~stockeinsatz** *m (form)* baton charge; **~werk** *nt* striking mechanism *(of a clock)*; **~wetter** *nt (Min)* firedamp; **~wort** *nt* **(a)** *pl* **~wörter** *(Stichwort)* headword; **(b)** *pl* **~worte** *(Parole)* catchword, slogan; **~wortkatalog** *m* subject catalogue; **~zeile** *f* headline; **~zeilen machen** *(inf)* to hit the headlines; **s~zeilen** *vt* to headline; **~zeug** *nt* drums *pl*; *(in Orchester)* percussion *no pl*; **~zeuger(in** *f***)** *m* **-s, -** drummer; *(inf: im Orchester)* percussionist; **~zeugspieler** *m* percussionist.
schlaksig *(esp N Ger inf)* **1** *adj* gangling, gawky.
2 *adv* in a gangling way, gawkily.
Schlamassel *m or nt* **-s, -** *(inf) (Durcheinander)* mix-up; *(mißliche Lage)* mess ◆ **der** *or* **das (ganze) ~** *(Zeug)* the whole lot *or* whole caboodle *(inf)*; **da haben wir den ~** now we're in a right mess *(inf)*.
Schlamm *m* **-(e)s, -e** *or* **¨-e** mud; *(Schlick auch)* sludge.
Schlammbad *nt* mudbath.
schlämmen *vt* **(a)** *(reinigen) Hafenbecken* to dredge; *Kreide* to wash. **(b)** *(weißen) Wand* to whitewash.
schlammig *adj* muddy; *(schlickig auch)* sludgy.
Schlämmkreide *f* whiting.
Schlammschlacht *f (inf)* mudbath.
Schlampe *f* **-, -n** *(pej inf)* slut *(inf)*.
schlampen *vi (inf)* to be sloppy (in one's work) ◆ **bei einer Arbeit ~** to do a piece of work sloppily; **die Behörden haben wieder einmal geschlampt** (once again) the authorities have done a sloppy job.
Schlamper(in *f***)** *m* **-s, -** *(S Ger inf)* sloppy person; *(unordentlich)* untidy person.
Schlamperei *f (inf)* sloppiness; *(schlechte Arbeit)* sloppy work; *(Unordentlichkeit)* untidiness ◆ **das ist eine ~!** that's a disgrace.
schlampig, schlampert *(Aus, S Ger) adj (inf)* sloppy, careless; *Arbeit auch* slipshod; *(unordentlich)* untidy; *(liederlich)* slovenly.
schlang *pret of* **schlingen**[1] *and* **schlingen**[2]**.**
Schlange *f* **-, -n (a)** snake, serpent *(liter)*; *(fig: Frau)* Jezebel ◆ **die ~** *(Astron)* Serpens, the Serpent; **eine falsche ~** a snake in the grass; **sich winden wie eine ~** *(fig)* to go through all sorts of contortions.
(b) *(Menschen~, Auto~)* queue *(Brit)*, line *(US)* ◆ **~ stehen** to queue (up) *(Brit)*, to stand in line *(US)*.
(c) *(Tech)* coil.
schlängelig *adj Weg* winding.
Schlängellinie *f* wavy line.
schlängeln *vr (Weg)* to wind (its way), to snake; *(Fluß auch)* to meander; *(Schlange)* to wriggle ◆ **sich um etw ~** to wind around sth; **sich durch etw ~** *(fig)* to worm one's way *or* wriggle through sth; **eine geschlängelte Linie** a wavy line.
Schlangen-: s~artig *adj* snakelike; **~beschwörer** *m* **-s, -** snake-charmer; ⚠**~biß** *m* snakebite; **~brut** *f (old liter)* brood of vipers *(liter)*; **~fraß** *m (pej inf)* muck *no indef art*; **~gezücht** *nt* brood of vipers; **~gift** *nt* snake venom *or* poison; **s~haft** *adj* snake-like; **~haut** *f* snake's skin; *(Leder)* snakeskin; **~leder** *nt* snakeskin; **~linie** *f* **(in) ~linien fahren** to swerve about; **~mensch** *m* contortionist.

Schlangestehen *nt* queuing *(Brit)*, standing in line *(US)*.
schlank *adj* slim; *Hals, Bäume auch* slender ◆ **~ werden** to slim; **ihr Kleid macht sie ~** her dress makes her look slim; **Joghurt macht ~** yoghourt is slimming *or* is good for the figure; **sich ~ machen** *(fig)* to breathe in; *siehe* **Linie.**
Schlankheit *f siehe adj* slimness; slenderness.
Schlankheitskur *f* diet; *(Med)* course of slimming treatment ◆ **eine ~ machen/anfangen** to be/go on a diet.
schlankweg *adv (inf) ablehnen, sagen* point-blank, flatly.
schlapp *adj (inf) (erschöpft, kraftlos)* worn-out, shattered *(inf)*; *(energielos)* listless, floppy; *(nach Krankheit etc)* run-down; *(feige) Haltung, Gesinnung, Mensch* lily-livered *(inf)*, yellow *(inf)* ◆ **sich ~ lachen** *(inf)* to laugh oneself silly.
Schlappe *f* **-, -n** *(inf)* set-back; *(esp Sport)* defeat ◆ **eine ~ erleiden** *or* **einstecken (müssen)** to suffer a set-back/defeat; **jdm eine ~ beibringen** *or* **erteilen** to defeat sb.
schlappen **1** *vi aux sein or haben (inf) (lose sitzen)* to be baggy; *(Schuhe)* to flap.
2 *vt (Tier)* to lap.
Schlappen *m* **-s, -** *(inf)* slipper.
Schlappheit *f (Erschöpfung)* exhaustion, fatigue; *(Energielosigkeit)* listlessness, floppiness; *(Feigheit)* cowardice, yellowness *(inf)*.
Schlapp-: ~hut *m* floppy hat; **s~machen** *vi sep (inf)* to wilt; *(zusammenbrechen, ohnmächtig werden)* to collapse; **die meisten Manager machen mit 40 s~** most managers are finished by the time they're 40; **Leute, die bei jeder Gelegenheit s~machen, können wir nicht gebrauchen** we can't use people who can't take it *or* who can't stand the pace *(inf)*; **~ohr** *nt (hum: Kaninchen)* bunny (rabbit) *(inf)*; **~ohren** *pl* floppy ears *pl*; **~schwanz** *m (pej inf)* wimp *(inf)*.
Schlaraffenland *nt* Cockaigne, land of milk and honey.
schlau *adj* clever, smart; *Mensch, Idee auch* shrewd; *(gerissen)* cunning, crafty, wily; *Sprüche* clever ◆ **er ist ein ~er Kopf** he has a good head on his shoulders; **ein ~er Bursche** a crafty *or* cunning devil *(inf)*; **sie tut immer so ~** she always thinks she's so clever *or* smart; **ein ~es Buch** *(inf)* a clever book; **etw ~ anfangen** *or* **anstellen** to manage sth cleverly; **ich werde nicht ~ aus ihm/dieser Sache** I can't make him/it out; *siehe* **Fuchs.**
Schlaube *f* **-, -n** *(dial)* skin.
Schlauberger *m* **-s, -** *(inf)* clever-dick *(inf)*, smart-alec *(inf)*.
Schlaubergerei *f, no pl (iro inf)* know-all attitude.
Schlauch *m* **-(e)s, Schläuche (a)** hose; *(Garten~ auch)* hosepipe; *(Fahrrad~, Auto~)* (inner) tube; *(Wein~ etc)* skin ◆ **das Zimmer ist ein richtiger ~** the room is really narrow; **auf dem ~ stehen** *(inf)* to be at a loose end. **(b)** *(inf: Strapaze)* slog *(inf)*, grind. **(c)** *(sl: Übersetzungshilfe)* crib *(inf)*.
Schlauch-: s~artig *adj* tube-like, tubular; **~boot** *nt* rubber dinghy.
schlauchen **1** *vt* **(a)** *(inf) (Reise, Arbeit etc)* **jdn** to wear out; *(Chef, Feldwebel etc)* to drive hard. **(b)** *(sl) Zigaretten, Geld* to scrounge *(inf)*.
2 *vi* **(a)** *(inf: Kraft kosten)* to wear you/one *etc* out, to take it out of you/one *etc (inf)*. **(b)** *(sl: schmarotzen)* to scrounge *(inf)*.
schlauchlos *adj Reifen* tubeless.
Schläue *f* **-,** *no pl* cunning, craftiness, slyness.
schlauerweise *adv* cleverly, shrewdly; *(gerissen)* craftily, cunningly, slyly ◆ **wenn du das wußtest, hättest du mich ~ benachrichtigen können** if you'd had any sense, you would have informed me.
Schlaufe *f* **-, -n** *(an Kleidungsstück, Schuh etc)* loop; *(Aufhänger)* hanger.
Schlauheit, Schlauigkeit *(rare) f siehe* **schlau** cleverness, smartness; shrewdness; cunning, craftiness, guile; easiness, cushiness *(inf)*; *(Bemerkung)* clever remark.
Schlaukopf *m*, **Schlaule** *nt* **-s, -** *(S Ger inf)*, **Schlaumeier** *m siehe* **Schlauberger.**
Schlawiner *m* **-s, -** *(hum inf)* villain, rogue.
schlecht **1** *adj* **(a)** bad; *Zustand, Aussprache, Geschmack, Zensur, Leistung auch* poor; *Qualität auch* poor, inferior; *Luft auch* stale; *Zeiten auch* hard ◆ **das S~e in der Welt/im Menschen** the evil in the world/in man; **das ist ein ~er Scherz** that is a dirty trick; **er ist in Latein ~er als ich** he is worse at Latin than I am; **sich zum S~en wenden** to take a turn for the worse; **nur S~es von jdm** *or* **über jdn sagen** not to have a good word to say for sb.
(b) *pred (ungenießbar)* off ◆ **die Milch/das Fleisch ist ~** the milk/meat has gone off *or* is off; **~ werden** to go off.
(c) *(gesundheitlich etc) Zustand* poor; *Nieren, Herz* bad; *Durchblutung* bad, poor ◆ **jdm ist (es) ~** sb feels sick *or* ill; **es ist zum S~werden** *(fig inf)* it makes *or* is enough to make you sick *(inf)*; **in ~er Verfassung sein** to be in a bad way; **~ aussehen** *(Mensch)* to look bad *or* sick *or* ill; *(Lage)* to look bad; **mit jdm/etw sieht es ~ aus** sb/sth looks in a bad way; **damit sieht es ~ aus** things look bad; *siehe* **schlechtgehen.**
2 *adv* **(a)** badly ◆ **sich ~ vertragen** *(Menschen)* to get along badly; *(Dinge, Farben etc)* not to go well together; **die beiden können sich ~ leiden** the two of them don't get along (with each other); **an jdm ~ handeln** to do sb wrong, to wrong sb; **~ über jdn sprechen/von jdm denken** to speak/think ill of sb.
(b) *(mit Schwierigkeiten) hören, sehen* badly; *lernen, begreifen* with difficulty ◆ **er kann ~ nein sagen** he finds it hard to say no, he can't say no; **da kann man ~ nein sagen** you can hardly say no *or* it's hard to say no to that; **heute geht es ~** today is not very convenient; **das läßt sich ~ machen, das geht ~** that's not really possible *or* on *(inf)*; **er ist ~ zu verstehen** he is hard to understand; **sie kann sich ~ anpassen** she finds it difficult *or* hard to adjust; **das kann ich ~ sagen** it's hard to say, I can't really say; **sie kann es sich ~ leisten, zu ...** she can ill afford to ...; **ich kann sie ~ sehen** I can't see her very

⚠: for details of spelling reform, see supplement

well.
(c) *in festen Redewendungen* **auf jdn/etw ~ zu sprechen sein** not to have a good word to say for sb/sth; **~ gerechnet** at the very least; **~ und recht, mehr ~ als recht** (*hum*) after a fashion.
(d) (*inf*) **er hat nicht ~ gestaunt** he wasn't half surprised (*inf*).

⚠**schlecht-: ~beraten** *adj attr* ill-advised; **~bezahlt** *adj attr* low-paid, badly paid.

schlechterdings *adv* (*völlig*) absolutely; (*nahezu*) virtually.

schlecht-: ⚠**~gehen** *vi impers sep irreg aux sein* **es geht jdm ~** sb is in a bad way; (*finanziell*) sb is doing badly; **wenn er das erfährt, geht's dir ~** if he hears about that you'll be for it (*inf*); ⚠**~gelaunt** *adj attr* bad-tempered; **~hin** *adv* (*vollkommen*) quite, absolutely; (*als solches, in seiner Gesamtheit*) as such, per se; **er gilt als** *or* **ist der romantische Komponist ~hin** he is the epitome of the Romantic composer; **Studenten/die deutsche Sprache ~hin** students/the German language as such *or* per se.

Schlechtigkeit *f* (a) *no pl* badness; (*qualitativ auch*) inferiority. (b) (*schlechte Tat*) misdeed.

Schlecht-: ⚠**s~machen** *vt sep* to denigrate, to run down; **s~weg** *adv siehe* **s~hin**; **~wetter** *nt* bad weather; **~wettergeld** *nt* bad-weather money *or* pay; **~wetterperiode** *f* spell of bad weather.

schlecken (*Aus, S Ger*) [1] *vti siehe* **lecken**[2].
[2] *vi* (*Süßigkeiten essen*) to eat sweets (*Brit*) *or* candies (*US*) ◆ **Lust auf was zum S~ haben** to feel like eating something sweet.

Schleckerei *f* (*Aus, S Ger*) (a) *no pl* (*das Lecken*) licking. (b) *no pl* (*das Naschen*) eating sweet things ◆ **die ~ der Kinder** the children eating sweet things. (c) (*Leckerbissen*) delicacy; (*Süßigkeit*) sweet (*Brit*), sweetie (*Brit inf*), candy (*US*).

Schleckermaul *nt* (*hum inf*) **sie ist ein richtiges ~** she really has a sweet tooth.

⚠**Schlegel** *m* **-s, -** (a) stick; (*Trommel~ auch*) drumstick. (b) (*Min*) miner's hammer. (c) (*S Ger, Aus: Cook*) leg; (*von Geflügel auch*) drumstick.

Schlehdorn *m* blackthorn, sloe.

Schlehe *f* **-, -n** sloe.

Schlei *m* **-(e)s, -e** *siehe* **Schleie**.

schleichen *pret* **schlich**, *ptp* **geschlichen** [1] *vi aux sein* to creep; (*heimlich auch*) to sneak, to steal; (*Fahrzeug*) to crawl; (*fig: Zeit*) to crawl (by) ◆ **um das Haus ~** to prowl around the house.
[2] *vr* (a) to creep, to sneak, to steal; (*fig: Mißtrauen*) to enter ◆ **sich in jds Vertrauen** (*acc*) **~** to worm one's way into sb's confidence; **sich in jds Herz** (*acc*) **~** (*Zweifel etc*) to enter sb's heart.
(b) (*Aus: weggehen*) to go away ◆ **schleich dich** get lost (*inf*).

schleichend *adj attr* creeping; *Krankheit, Gift* insidious; *Fieber* lingering.

Schleicher *m* **-s, -** hypocrite.

Schleicherei *f* hypocrisy, insincerity.

Schleich-: ~handel *m* illicit trading (*mit* in); **der ~handel mit Waffen/Alkohol** gun-running/bootlegging; **~händler** *m siehe* **~handel** illicit trader; gun-runner/bootlegger; **~pfad, ~weg** *m* secret *or* hidden path; **auf ~wegen** (*fig*) on the quiet, surreptitiously; **~werbung** *f* a plug; **~werbung vermeiden** to avoid making plugs.

Schleie *f* **-, -n** (*Zool*) tench.

Schleier *m* **-s, -** (*lit, fig*) veil; (*von Wolken, Nebel auch*) haze ◆ **das Photo hat einen ~** the photo is foggy *or* fogged; **die Berggipfel waren in ~ von Nebel gehüllt** the mountain tops were veiled in mist; **einen ~ vor den Augen haben/wie durch einen ~ sehen** to have a mist in front of one's eyes; **den ~ (des Geheimnisses) lüften** to lift the veil of secrecy; **einen ~ über etw** (*acc*) **ziehen** *or* **breiten** (*fig*) to draw a veil over sth; **der ~ des Vergessens** the veil of oblivion; **den ~ nehmen** (*liter*) to take the veil.

Schleier-: ~eule *f* barn owl; **s~haft** *adj* (*inf*) baffling, mysterious; **es ist mir völlig s~haft** it's a complete mystery to me; **~kraut** *nt* (*Bot*) gypsophila; **~schwanz** *m* goldfish; **~tanz** *m* veil-dance.

Schleifbank *f* grinding machine.

Schleife *f* **-, -n** (a) loop (*auch Aviat, Comput, beim Schlittschuhlaufen*); (*Fluß~*) bow, horse-shoe bend; (*Straßen~*) twisty bend. (b) (*von Band*) bow; (*Schuh~*) bow(-knot); (*Fliege*) bow tie; (*Kranz~*) ribbon.

schleifen[1] [1] *vt* (a) (*lit, fig*) to drag; (*ziehen auch*) to haul; (*Mus*) *Töne, Noten* to slur ◆ **jdn vor Gericht ~** (*fig*) to drag *or* haul sb into court; **jdn ins Konzert ~** (*hum inf*) to drag sb along to a concert.
(b) (*niederreißen*) to raze (to the ground).
[2] *vi* (a) *aux sein or haben* to trail, to drag.
(b) (*reiben*) to rub ◆ **die Kupplung ~ lassen** (*Aut*) to slip the clutch; **die Zügel ~ lassen** (*lit, fig*) to slacken the reins.

schleifen[2] *pret* **schliff**, *ptp* **geschliffen** *vt* (a) *Rasiermesser, Messer, Schere* to sharpen, to whet; *Beil, Sense auch* to grind; *Werkstück, Linse* to grind; *Parkett* to sand; *Edelstein, Glas* to cut; *siehe* **geschliffen**. (b) (*inf: drillen*) **jdn ~** to drill sb hard.

Schleifer *m* **-s, -** (a) grinder; (*Edelstein~*) cutter. (b) (*Mus*) slurred note. (c) (*Mil sl*) slave-driver.

Schleiferei *f* (a) *no pl siehe* **schleifen**[2] (a) whetting; grinding; sanding; cutting. (b) (*Werkstatt*) grinding shop. (c) (*Mil sl: Drill*) square-bashing (*inf*).

Schleiferin *f siehe* **Schleifer (a)**.

Schleif-: ~lack *m* (coloured) lacquer *or* varnish; **~lackmöbel** *pl* lacquered furniture *sing*; **~maschine** *f* grinding machine; **~papier** *nt* abrasive paper; **~rad** *nt*, **~scheibe** *f* grinding wheel; **~stein** *m* grinding stone, grindstone; **er sitzt da wie ein Affe auf dem ~stein** (*sl*) he looks a proper idiot *or* a proper Charlie (*inf*) sitting there.

Schleifung *f* razing.

Schleim *m* **-(e)s, -e** (a) slime; (*Med*) mucus; (*in Atemorganen auch*) phlegm; (*Bot*) mucilage. (b) (*Cook*) gruel.

Schleim-: ~absonderung *f* mucous secretion; **~beutel** *m* (*Physiol*) bursa (*spec*); **~drüse** *f* mucous gland; (*von Schnecken etc*) slime gland.

schleimen *vi* to leave a coating *or* film; (*fig inf: schmeicheln*) to fawn, to crawl (*inf*).

Schleimer(in *f*) *m* **-s, -** (*inf*) crawler (*inf*).

Schleimhaut *f* mucous membrane.

schleimig *adj* (a) slimy; (*Med*) mucous; (*Bot*) mucilaginous. (b) (*pej: unterwürfig*) slimy (*inf*).

Schleimigkeit *f* (*pej*) sliminess (*inf*).

Schleim-: s~lösend *adj* expectorant; **~pilz** *m* slime mould *or* fungus; **~scheißer** *m* (*sl*) bootlicker (*inf*), arse-licker (*vulg*); **~suppe** *f* gruel.

schlemmen [1] *vi* (*üppig essen*) to feast, to have a feast; (*üppig leben*) to live it up.
[2] *vt* to feast on.

Schlemmer(in *f*) *m* **-s, -** gourmet, bon vivant.

Schlemmerei *f* feasting; (*Mahl*) feast.

schlemmerhaft, schlemmerisch *adj* gourmandizing, gluttonous (*pej*).

Schlemmermahl *nt* feast, banquet.

schlendern *vi aux sein* to stroll, to amble.

Schlendrian *m* **-(e)s,** *no pl* (*inf*) casualness, inefficiency; (*Trott*) rut.

Schlenker *m* **-s, -** swerve ◆ **einen ~ machen** to swerve.

schlenk(e)rig *adj* swinging, flapping ◆ **er geht ~** he flaps along.

schlenkern [1] *vti* to swing, to dangle ◆ **mit den Beinen ~, die Beine ~** to swing *or* dangle one's legs.
[2] *vi* (*Auto*) to swerve, to sway.

schlenzen *vi* (*Sport*) to scoop.

Schlepp *m* (*Naut, fig*): **jdn/etw in ~ nehmen** to take sb/sth in tow; **in** *or* **im ~ haben** to have in tow.

Schleppdampfer *m* tug(boat).

Schleppe *f* **-, -n** (a) (*von Kleid*) train. (b) (*Hunt*) drag.

schleppen [1] *vt* (*tragen*) *Lasten* to lug, to schlepp (*US sl*); (*zerren*) to drag, to haul, to schlepp (*US sl*); *Auto, Schiff* to tow; (*fig*) to drag; (*inf*) *Kleidung* to wear continually ◆ **jdn vor den Richter ~** to haul sb (up) before the judge.
[2] *vi* (*inf: nachschleifen*) to drag, to trail.
[3] *vr* to drag *or* haul oneself; (*Verhandlungen etc*) to drag on.

schleppend *adj Gang* dragging, shuffling; *Bedienung, Abfertigung* sluggish, slow; *Absatz, Nachfrage* slack, sluggish; *Gesang* dragging, slow ◆ **wehmütig ~e Klänge** melancholy languorous sounds; **die Unterhaltung kam nur ~ in Gang** conversation was very slow to start *or* started sluggishly; **nach ein paar Stunden wurde die Unterhaltung immer ~er** after a few hours the conversation began to drag more and more.

Schleppenträger *m* trainbearer.

Schlepper *m* **-s, -** (a) (*Aut*) tractor. (b) (*Naut*) tug. (c) (*sl: Zuhälter, für Lokal*) tout.

Schlepperei *f* (*inf*) lugging around *or* about.

Schlepp-: ~kahn *m* lighter, (canal) barge; **~lift** *m* ski tow; **~lohn** *m* (*Naut*) towage; **~netz** *nt* trawl (net); **~netzfahndung** *f* dragnet; **~schiff** *nt* tug(boat); **~tau** *nt* (*Naut*) tow rope; (*Aviat*) dragrope, trail rope; **ein Schiff/jdn ins ~tau nehmen** to take a ship/sb in tow.

Schlesien [-iən] *nt* **-s** Silesia.

Schlesier(in *f*) [-iɐ, -iərɪn] *m* **-s, -** Silesian.

schlesisch *adj* Silesian.

Schleswig-Holstein *nt* **-s** Schleswig-Holstein.

Schleuder *f* **-, -n** (a) (*Waffe*) sling; (*Wurfmaschine*) catapult, onager; (*Zwille*) catapult, slingshot (*US*). (b) (*Zentrifuge*) centrifuge; (*für Honig*) extractor; (*Wäsche~*) spin-drier.

Schleuder-: ~ball *m* (*Sport*) (a) *heavy leather ball with a strap attached, swung round the head and then thrown*; (b) *no pl a game using such a ball*; **~gefahr** *f* (*Mot*) risk of skidding; **„Achtung ~gefahr"** "slippery road ahead"; **~honig** *m* extracted honey; **~maschine** *f* (*Wurfmaschine*) catapult, onager; (*für Milch etc*) centrifuge; (*für Honig*) extractor.

schleudern [1] *vt* (a) (*werfen*) to hurl, to sling, to fling ◆ **jdm etw ins Gesicht** *or* **an den Kopf ~** to hurl *or* fling sth in sb's face.
(b) (*Tech*) to centrifuge, to spin; *Honig* to extract; *Wäsche* to spin-dry ◆ **die Maschine schleudert nicht mehr** the machine isn't spinning *or* extracting.
[2] *vi aux sein or haben* (*Aut*) to skid ◆ **ins S~ kommen** *or* **geraten** to go into a skid; (*fig inf*) to run into trouble.

Schleuder-: ~preis *m* giveaway price, throwaway price; **immer noch die alten ~preise** we're still practically giving it/them away; **~sitz** *m* (*Aviat*) ejection *or* ejector seat; (*fig*) hot seat; **~spur** *f* skidmark; **~start** *m* (*Aviat*) catapult start; **~ware** *f* cut-price goods *pl*, cheap goods *pl*.

schleunig *adj attr usu superl* prompt, speedy; *Schritte* quick, rapid ◆ **nur ~stes Eingreifen kann jetzt helfen** only immediate measures can help now.

schleunigst *adv* at once, straight away, immediately ◆ **verschwinde, aber ~!** beat it, on the double!; **ein Bier, aber ~!** a beer, and make it snappy!

Schleuse *f* **-, -n** (*für Schiffe*) lock; (*zur Regulierung des Wasserlaufs*) sluice, floodgate; (*für Abwasser*) sluice ◆ **der Himmel öffnete seine ~n** (*liter*) the floodgates of heaven opened, the rain sluiced down.

schleusen *vt Schiffe* to pass through a lock, to lock; *Wasser* to channel; (*langsam*) *Menschen* to filter; *Antrag* to channel; (*fig: heimlich*) to smuggle ◆ **er wurde in den Saal geschleust** he was smuggled into the hall.

Schleusen-: ~geld *nt* lock dues *pl*, lockage; **~kammer** *f* (lock) basin; **~meister** *m* lockmaster; **~tor** *nt* (*für Schiffe*) lock gate; (*zur Regulierung des*

Wasserlaufs) sluice gate, floodgate; **~wärter** *m* lock keeper.

Schleusung *f* lockage, locking ◆ **bei der ~ größerer Schiffe** when putting bigger ships through the locks.

Schlich *m* **-(e)s, -e** *usu pl* ruse, trick, wile *usu pl* ◆ **alle ~e kennen** to know all the tricks; **jdm auf** *or* **hinter die ~e kommen** to catch on to sb, to get on to sb, to get wise to sb.

schlich *pret of* **schleichen.**

schlicht *adj* simple ◆ **die ~e Wahrheit/Tatsache** the plain *or* simple truth/fact; **~ und einfach** plain and simple; **das ist ~ und einfach nicht wahr** that's just simply not true; **der ~e Menschenverstand** basic common sense; **das geht über den ~en Menschenverstand** this is beyond the normal human mind *or* beyond human comprehension; **er sagte ~ und ergreifend nein** he said quite simply no; **diese Gedichte sind ~ und ergreifend** (*iro*) these poems are not exactly brilliant; **unser Abschied war ~ und ergreifend** our parting was short and sweet.

schlichten *vti* **(a)** *Streit* (*vermitteln*) to mediate, to arbitrate (*esp Ind*); (*beilegen*) to settle ◆ **zwischen zwei Ländern ~** to mediate between two countries; **er wollte ~d in den Streit eingreifen** he wanted to intervene in the quarrel (to settle it).
(b) (*glätten*) *Werkzeug, Leder, Gewebe* to dress; *Holz* to smooth (off).

Schlichter(in *f*) *m* **-s, -** mediator; (*Ind*) arbitrator.

Schlichtfeile *f* smooth-cut file.

Schlichtheit *f* simplicity.

Schlichthobel *m* smoothing plane.

Schlichtung *f siehe vti (a)* mediation, arbitration; settlement.

Schlichtungs-: ⚠**~ausschuß** *m* arbitration *or* conciliation commission; **~stelle** *f* arbitration *or* conciliation board; **~verhandlungen** *pl* arbitration (negotiations); **~versuch** *m* attempt at mediation *or* arbitration.

Schlick *m* **-(e)s, -e** silt, ooze, mud; (*Öl~*) slick.

schlickig *adj* muddy, slimy.

schliddern *vi aux haben or sein* (*N Ger*) *siehe* **schlittern.**

schlief *pret of* **schlafen.**

Schliere *f* **-, -n** streak, schlieren *pl* (*Tech*).

schließbar *adj* (*rare*) closable; (*zu~*) lockable.

Schließe *f* **-, -n** fastening, fastener.

schließen *pret* **schloß,** *ptp* **geschlossen** [1] *vt* **(a)** (*zumachen*) to close, to shut; (*verriegeln*) to bolt; (*Betrieb einstellen*) to close *or* shut down; *Stromkreis* to close ◆ **eine Lücke ~** (*lit*) to close a gap; (*fig auch*) to fill a gap; **die Reihen ~** (*Mil*) to close ranks.
(b) (*beenden*) *Versammlung* to close, to conclude, to wind up; *Brief* to conclude, to close.
(c) (*eingehen*) *Vertrag, Bündnis* to conclude; *Frieden auch* to make; *Bündnis auch* to enter into; *Freundschaft* to form ◆ **wo wurde Ihre Ehe geschlossen?** where did your marriage take place?; **wer hat Ihre Ehe geschlossen?** who married you?
(d) (*geh: umfassen*) **etw in sich** (*dat*) **~** (*lit, fig*) to contain sth, to include sth; (*indirekt*) to imply sth; **jdn in die Arme ~** to embrace sb; **laß dich in die Arme ~** let me embrace you; **jdn/etw in sein Herz ~** to take sb/sth to one's heart.
(e) (*befestigen*) **etw an etw** (*acc*) **~** to fasten sth to sth; **daran schloß er eine Bemerkung** he added a remark (to this).
[2] *vr* to close, to shut; (*Wunde*) to close; (*fig geh: Wunde*) to heal ◆ **daran schließt sich eine Diskussion** this is followed by a discussion; **sich um etw ~** to close around sth.
[3] *vi* **(a)** to close, to shut; (*Betrieb einstellen*) to close *or* shut down; (*Schlüssel*) to fit ◆ **die Tür schließt nicht** the door doesn't *or* won't close *or* shut; **„geschlossen"** "closed".
(b) (*enden*) to close, to conclude; (*St Ex*) to close ◆ **leider muß ich jetzt ~** (*in Brief*) I'm afraid I must conclude *or* close now; **die Börse schloß munter** the market closed on a lively note.
(c) (*schlußfolgern*) to infer ◆ **aus etw auf etw** (*acc*) **~** to infer sth from sth; **auf etw** (*acc*) **~ lassen** to indicate sth, to suggest sth; **von sich auf andere ~** to judge others by one's own standards; *siehe* **geschlossen.**

Schließer(in *f*) *m* **-s, -** (*inf*) jailer, warder.

Schließ-: **~fach** *nt* left-luggage locker; (*Post~*) post-office box, PO box; (*Bank~*) safe-deposit box; **~korb** *m* hamper.

schließlich *adv* (*endlich*) in the end, finally, eventually; (*immerhin*) after all ◆ **er kam ~ doch** he came after all; **~ und endlich** at long last; **~ und endlich bist du doch kein Kind mehr** after all you're not a child any more.

Schließmuskel *m* (*Anat*) sphincter.

Schließung *f* **(a)** (*das Schließen*) closing, shutting; (*Betriebseinstellung*) closure.
(b) (*Beendigung*) (*einer Versammlung*) closing, breaking-up; (*von Debatte etc*) conclusion, closing; (*Geschäftsschluß*) closing(-time); (*Parl*) closure.
(c) (*Vereinbarung*) (*von Frieden, Vertrag, Ehe*) conclusion; (*von Bündnis auch*) forming.

Schliff *m* **-(e)s, -e** (*von Glas, von Edelstein*) (*Prozeß*) cutting; (*Ergebnis*) cut; (*fig: Umgangsformen*) refinement, polish ◆ **jdm ~ beibringen** *or* **geben** to give sb some polish *or* refinement; **einer Sache/jdm den letzten ~ geben** (*fig*) to put the finishing touch(es) to sth/to perfect sb.

schliff *pret of* **schleifen**[2].

schlimm *adj* **(a)** (*moralisch*) bad, wicked; (*unartig auch*) naughty ◆ **es gibt S~ere als ihn** there are worse than him; **ein ~er Bösewicht** (*old*) an out-and-out villain; **Sie sind ja ein ganz S~er!** you *are* naughty *or* wicked.
(b) (*inf: krank, entzündet*) bad.
(c) (*übel*) bad; *Krankheit auch* nasty; *Wunde auch* nasty, ugly; *Nachricht auch* awful, terrible ◆ **sich ~ verletzen** to hurt oneself badly; **~, ~!** terrible, terrible!; **das war ~** that was awful *or* terrible; **mit der neuen Frisur siehst du ~ aus** you look awful with that new hairdo; **~ genug, daß ...** it is/was bad enough that ...; **das finde ich nicht ~** I don't find that so bad; **eine ~e Geschichte** (*inf*) a nasty state of affairs; **eine ~e Zeit** bad times *pl*; **das ist halb so/nicht so ~!** that's not so bad!, it doesn't matter!; **er ist ~ dran** (*inf*) he's in a bad way; **es steht ~ (um ihn)** things aren't looking too good (for him); **zu Anfang war es ~ für ihn** in the beginning he had a hard time of it; **ist es ~** *or* **etwas S~es?** is it bad?; **wenn es ganz ~ kommt** if things get really bad; **wenn es nichts S~eres ist!** if that's all it is!; **es gibt S~eres** it *or* things could be worse; **es hätte ~er kommen können** it *or* things could have been worse; **~er kann es nicht mehr werden** things can hardly get any worse; **um so** *or* **desto ~er** all the worse; **im ~sten Fall** if the worst comes to the worst; **das S~ste** the worst; **was aber das S~ste ist, ...** but the worst of it is that ...; **das S~ste liegt hinter uns** the worst (of it) is behind us.

schlimmstenfalls *adv* at (the) worst ◆ **~ wird er nur sein Geld verlieren** at worst, he will only lose his money; **~ kann ich dir £ 100 leihen** if the worst comes to the worst I can lend you £100.

Schlinge *f* **-, -n** loop; (*an Galgen*) noose; (*Med: Armbinde*) sling; (*Falle*) snare ◆ **~n legen** to set snares; **den Kopf** *or* **sich aus der ~ ziehen** (*fig*) to get out of a tight spot; **(bei jdm) die ~ zuziehen** (*fig*) to tighten the noose (on sb).

Schlingel *m* **-s, -** rascal.

schlingen[1] *pret* **schlang,** *ptp* **geschlungen** (*geh*) [1] *vt* (*binden*) *Knoten* to tie; (*umbinden*) *Schal* to wrap; (*flechten auch*) to plait ◆ **die Arme um jdn ~** to wrap one's arms around sb, to hug sb.
[2] *vr* **sich um etw ~** to coil (itself) around sth; (*Pflanze auch*) to twine (itself) around sth.

schlingen[2] *pret* **schlang,** *ptp* **geschlungen** *vi* to gobble, to gulp, to bolt one's food.

Schlingerbewegung *f* rolling (motion).

schlingern *vi* (*Schiff*) to roll; (*fig*) to lurch from side to side.

Schlinggewächs *nt*, **Schlingpflanze** *f* creeper.

Schlips *m* **-es, -e** tie, necktie (*US*) ◆ **mit ~ und Kragen** (*inf*) wearing a collar and tie; **jdm auf den ~ treten** (*inf*) to tread on sb's toes; **sich auf den ~ getreten fühlen** (*inf*) to feel offended, to be put out (*inf*).

Schlitten *m* **-s, -** **(a)** sledge, sled; (*Pferde~*) sleigh; (*Rodel~*) toboggan ◆ **~ fahren** to go tobogganing; **mit jdm ~ fahren** (*inf*) to have sb on the carpet (*inf*), to give sb a bawling out (*inf*).
(b) (*Tech*) (*Schreibmaschinen~*) carriage; (*zum Stapellauf*) cradle.
(c) (*sl: Auto*) car, motor (*inf*).

Schlitten-: **~bahn** *f siehe* **Rodelbahn**; **~fahren** *nt* sledging; (*Rodeln*) tobogganing; (*mit Pferde~ etc*) sleighing; **~fahrt** *f* sledge ride; (*mit Rodel*) toboggan ride; (*mit Pferde~ etc*) sleigh ride; **~partie** *f* sleigh ride.

Schlitterbahn *f* slide.

schlittern *vi* **(a)** *aux sein or haben* (*absichtlich*) to slide. **(b)** *aux sein* (*ausrutschen*) to slide, to slip; (*Wagen*) to skid; (*fig*) to slide, to stumble ◆ **in den Konkurs/Krieg ~** to slide into bankruptcy/war.

Schlittschuh *m* (ice-)skate ◆ **~ laufen** *or* **fahren** (*inf*) to (ice-) skate.

Schlittschuh-: **~laufen** *nt* (ice-)skating; **~läufer** *m* (ice-) skater; **~schritt** *m* skating step.

Schlitz *m* **-es, -e** slit; (*Einwurf~*) slot; (*Hosen~*) fly, flies *pl*; (*Kleider~*) slit; (*Jackett~*) vent.

Schlitz-: **~auge** *nt* slit *or* slant eye; (*pej: Chinese*) Chink (*pej*); **s~äugig** *adj* slit- *or* slant-eyed; **er grinste s~äugig** he grinned a slant- *or* slit-eyed grin.

schlitzen *vt* to slit.

Schlitz-: **~ohr** *nt* (*fig*) sly fox; **s~ohrig** *adj* (*fig*) shifty, crafty; ⚠**~verschluß** *m* (*Phot*) focal-plane shutter.

schlohweiß *adj Haare* snow-white.

⚠**schloß** *pret of* **schließen.**

⚠**Schloß** *nt* **-sses, ¨sser** **(a)** castle; (*Palast*) palace; (*großes Herrschaftshaus*) mansion, stately home; (*in Frankreich*) château ◆ **Schlösser und Burgen** castles and stately homes; **Schlösser im Mond** (*fig*) castles in the air, castles in Spain.
(b) (*Tür~, Gewehr~ etc*) lock; (*Vorhänge~*) padlock; (*an Handtasche etc*) fastener, clasp ◆ **ins ~ fallen** to lock (itself); **die Tür ins ~ werfen** to slam the door shut; **hinter ~ und Riegel sitzen/bringen** to be/put behind bars.

⚠**Schloß-:** **s~artig** *adj* palatial; **~berg** *m* castle *etc* hill; **~besitzer** *m* owner of a castle *etc.*

⚠**Schlößchen** *nt dim of* **Schloß** small castle *etc.*

Schlosser(in *f*) *m* **-s, -** fitter, metalworker; (*für Schlösser*) locksmith.

Schlosserei *f* **(a)** (*~handwerk*) metalworking. **(b)** (*~werkstatt*) metalworking shop.

Schlosser-: **~handwerk** *nt* metalworking; **~meister** *m* master fitter; **~werkstatt** *f* metalworking shop.

⚠**Schloß-:** **~garten** *m* castle *etc* gardens *pl*; **~herr** *m* owner of a castle *etc*; (*Adliger*) lord of the castle; **~hof** *m* courtyard; **~hund** *m* (*obs: Kettenhund*) watchdog; **heulen wie ein ~hund** (*inf*) to howl one's head off (*inf*); **~kapelle** *f* castle *etc* chapel; **~park** *m* castle *etc* grounds *pl*, estate; **~platz** *m* castle *etc* square; **~vogt** *m* (*Hist*) castellan; **~wache** *f* castle *etc* guard.

Schlot *m* **-(e)s, -e** *or* (*rare*) **¨e** **(a)** (*Schornstein*) chimney (stack), smokestack; (*Naut, Rail auch*) funnel; (*von Vulkan*) chimney ◆ **rauchen** *or* **qualmen wie ein ~** (*inf*) to smoke like a chimney (*inf*). **(b)** (*inf: Flegel*) slob (*inf*), peasant (*inf*).

schlott(e)rig *adj* (*inf*) **(a)** (*zitternd*) shivering *attr*; (*vor Angst, Erschöpfung*) trembling *attr.* **(b)** *Kleider* baggy.

schlottern *vi* **(a)** (*zittern*) to shiver; (*vor Angst, Erschöpfung*) to tremble ◆ **an**

allen Gliedern ~ to shake all over; **er schlotterte mit den Knien** he was shaking at the knees, his knees were knocking. **(b)** *(Kleider)* to hang loose, to be baggy.

Schlucht *f* **-, -en** gorge, ravine.

schluchzen *vti (lit, fig)* to sob.

Schluchzer *m* **-s, -** sob.

Schluck *m* **-(e)s, -e** *or (rare)* **¨e** drink; *(ein bißchen)* drop; *(das Schlucken)* swallow; *(großer)* gulp; *(kleiner)* sip ♦ **der erste ~ war mir ungewohnt** the first mouthful tasted strange; **er stürzte das Bier in einem ~ herunter** he downed the beer in one gulp *or* in one go; **etw ~ für ~ austrinken** to drink every drop; **einen (kräftigen) ~ nehmen** to take a (long) drink *or* swig *(inf)*.

Schluck|auf *m* **-s,** *no pl* hiccups *pl* ♦ **einen/den ~ haben** to have (the) hiccups.

Schluckbeschwerden *pl* difficulties *pl* in swallowing.

Schlückchen *nt dim of* **Schluck** drop; *(von Alkohol auch)* nip.

schlückchenweise *adv* in short sips ♦ **~ trinken** to sip.

schlucken [1] *vt* **(a)** to swallow; *(hastig)* to gulp down; *(sl) Alkohol* to booze *(inf)*.
(b) *(inf: absorbieren, kosten)* to swallow up; *Benzin, Öl* to guzzle.
(c) *(inf: hinnehmen) Beleidigung* to swallow, to take.
(d) *(inf: glauben)* to swallow *(inf)*.
[2] *vi* to swallow; *(hastig)* to gulp; *(sl)* to booze *(inf)* ♦ **da mußte ich erst mal trocken** *or* **dreimal ~** *(inf)* I had to take a deep breath *or* to count to ten.

Schlucken *m* **-s,** *no pl siehe* **Schluckauf.**

Schlucker *m* **-s, -** *(inf)*: **armer ~** poor devil.

Schluck-: ~impfung *f* oral vaccination; **~specht** *m (inf)* boozer *(inf)*; **s~weise** *adv* in sips.

Schluder|arbeit *f (inf)* botched-up *or* sloppy job *(inf)*.

Schluderei *f (inf)* sloppiness, bungling ♦ **das ist eine ~!** how sloppy can you get!

schlud(e)rig *adj (inf) Arbeit* sloppy, slipshod *no adv* ♦ **~ arbeiten** to work sloppily *or* in a slipshod way.

Schlud(e)rigkeit *f (inf)* sloppiness.

schludern *(inf)* [1] *vt* to skimp ♦ **das ist geschludert!** this is a sloppy piece of work!
[2] *vi* to do sloppy work, to work sloppily.

schludrig *adj (inf) siehe* **schlud(e)rig.**

schlug *pret of* **schlagen.**

Schlummer *m* **-s,** *no pl (liter)* (light) slumber *(liter)*.

Schlummerlied *nt (geh)* cradlesong, lullaby.

schlummern *vi (geh)* to slumber *(liter)*; *(fig auch)* to lie dormant.

Schlummer-: ~rolle *f* bolster; **~taste** *f (an Radiowecker)* snooze button.

Schlund *m* **-(e)s, ¨e** *(Anat)* pharynx, gullet; *(fig liter)* maw *(liter)*.

schlunzen *vi (dial) siehe* **schludern.**

Schlupf *m* **-(e)s,** *no pl (Elec, Naut)* slip; *(Tech)* slip, slippage.

schlüpfen *vi aux sein* to slip; *(Küken)* to hatch (out).

Schlüpfer *m* **-s, -** panties *pl*, knickers *pl*.

Schlupfloch *nt* hole, gap; *(Versteck)* hideout, lair; *(fig)* loophole.

schlüpfrig *adj* **(a)** slippery. **(b)** *(fig) Bemerkung* lewd, risqué.

Schlüpfrigkeit *f siehe adj* slipperiness; lewdness.

Schlupf-: ~wespe *f* ichneumon (fly) *(form)*; **~winkel** *m* hiding place; *(fig)* quiet corner.

schlurfen *vi aux sein* to shuffle.

schlürfen [1] *vt* to slurp; *(mit Genuß)* to savour ♦ **er schlürfte die letzten Tropfen** he slurped up the last drops.
[2] *vi* to slurp.

⚠ **Schluß** *m* **-sses, ¨sse (a)** *no pl (Ende)* end; *(eines Romans, Gedichts, Theaterstücks auch)* ending, conclusion; *(hinterer Teil)* back, end, rear ♦ **~!** that'll do!, stop!; **~ für heute!** that's it *or* all for today, that'll do for today; **~ damit!** stop it!, that'll do!; **... und damit ~!** ... and that's that!, ... and that's the end of it!; **nun ist aber ~!, ~ jetzt!** that's enough now!; **dann ist ~** that'll be it; **~ folgt** to be concluded; **am/zum ~ des Jahres** at the end of the year; **zum ~ sangen wir ...** at the end we sang ...; **zum ~ hat sie's dann doch erlaubt** finally *or* in the end she allowed it after all; **bis zum ~ bleiben** to stay to the end; **zum ~ kommen** to conclude; **zum ~ möchte ich noch darauf hinweisen, daß ...** to conclude *or* in conclusion I would like to point out that ...; **~ machen** *(inf) (aufhören)* to finish, to call it a day *(inf)*; *(zumachen)* to close, to shut; *(Selbstmord begehen)* to put an end to oneself, to end it all; *(Freundschaft beenden)* to break *or* call it off; **ich muß ~ machen** *(in Brief)* I'll have to finish off now; *(am Telefon)* I'll have to go now; **mit etw ~ machen** to stop *or* end sth, to finish with sth *(inf)*; **mit der Arbeit ~ machen** to stop *or* leave off work.
(b) *no pl (das Schließen)* closing.
(c) *(Folgerung)* conclusion ♦ **aus etw den ~ ziehen, daß ...** to draw the conclusion *or* to conclude from sth that ...; **ich ziehe meine Schlüsse daraus!** I can draw my own conclusions!
(d) *(Tech)* **die Tür hat einen guten/schlechten ~** the door is a good/bad fit.
(e) *(Mus)* cadence.
(f) *(St Ex)* minimum amount allowed for dealing.

⚠ **Schluß-: ~abrechnung** *f* final statement *or* account; **~akkord** *m* final chord; **~akt** *m (lit, fig)* final act; **~akte** *f (Pol)* final agreement; **~ansprache** *f* closing address *or* speech; **~bemerkung** *f* final observation, concluding remark; **~bestimmung** *f* final clause; **~bilanz** *f (lit)* final balance (sheet); *(fig)* final position.

Schlüssel *m* **-s, -** *(lit, fig)* key; *(Chiffren~ auch)* cipher; *(Sch: Lösungsheft)* key; *(Tech)* spanner, wrench; *(Verteilungs~)* ratio (of distribution); *(Mus)* clef.

Schlüssel-: ~anhänger *m* keyring pendant; **~bein** *nt* collarbone, clavicle *(form)*; **~blume** *f* cowslip; **~brett** *nt* keyboard; **~bund** *m or nt* key ring; bunch of keys; **~dienst** *m* key cutting service; **~erlebnis** *nt (Psych)* crucial experience; **s~fertig** *adj Neubau* ready for moving into, ready for occupancy; **~figur** *f* key figure; **~gewalt** *f (Jur) a wife's power to represent her husband in matters concerning the household*; *(Eccl)* power of the keys; **~industrie** *f* key industry; **~kind** *nt (inf)* latchkey child *(inf)*; **~loch** *nt* keyhole; **~position** *f* key position; **~ring** *m* key ring; **~roman** *m* roman à clef; **~stellung** *f* key position; **~tasche** *f* key wallet; **~wort** *nt* keyword; *(für Schloß)* combination, code.

⚠ **Schluß-: s~endlich** *adv (geh)* to conclude, in conclusion *or* closing; ▼ **~ergebnis** *nt* final result; **s~folgern** *vi insep* to conclude, to infer; **~folgerung** *f* conclusion, inference; **~formel** *f (in Brief)* complimentary close; *(bei Vertrag)* final clause.

schlüssig *adj* conclusive ♦ **sich** *(dat)* **(über etw** *acc*) **~ sein** to have made up one's mind (about sth).

Schlüssigkeit *f* conclusiveness.

⚠ **Schluß-: ~kapitel** *nt* concluding *or* final chapter; **~kommuniqué** *nt* final communiqué; **~kurs** *m (St Ex)* closing prices *pl*; **~läufer** *m* last runner; *(in Staffel)* anchor(man); **~licht** *nt* rear light, tail light; *(inf: bei Rennen etc)* tailender, back marker; **~licht der Tabelle/in der Klasse sein** to be bottom of the table/class; **das ~licht bilden** *(fig) (beim Laufen etc)* to bring up the rear; *(in einer Tabelle)* to be bottom of the league; **~mann** *m, pl* **-männer** *(Sport sl)* goalie *(inf)*, keeper *(inf)*; **~notierung** *f (St Ex)* closing quotation; **~pfiff** *m* final whistle; **~phase** *f* final stages *pl*; **~punkt** *m*: **einen ~punkt unter etw** *(acc)* **setzen** to round off sth; *(bei etwas Unangenehmem)* to write sth off; **~rechnung** *f* **(a)** *(Comm)* final account *or* settlement; **(b)** *(Math: Dreisatz)* computation using the rule of three; **~runde** *f (Boxen etc, fig)* final round; *(in Rennsport, Leichtathletik)* final lap; *(bei Ausscheidungskämpfen)* final heat; *(Endausscheidung)* final(s); **~rundenteilnehmer** *m* finalist; **~satz** *m* closing *or* concluding sentence; *(Logik)* conclusion; *(Mus)* last *or* final movement; **~schein** *m (Comm)* contract note; **~sprung** *m* standing jump; *(beim Turnen)* finishing jump; **~stand** *m* final result; *(von Spiel auch)* final score; **~stein** *m (Archit, fig)* keystone; **~strich** *m (fig)* final stroke; **einen ~strich unter etw** *(acc)* **ziehen** to consider sth finished; **~tag** *m (St Ex)* settlement day; **~verkauf** *m* (end-of-season) sale; **~wort** *nt* closing words *or* remarks *pl*; *(~rede)* closing *or* concluding speech; *(Nachwort)* postscript.

Schmach *f* **-,** *no pl (geh)* disgrace, ignominy, shame *no indef art*; *(Demütigung auch)* humiliation ♦ **etw als ~ empfinden** to see sth as a disgrace; to feel humiliated by sth.

schmachten *vi (geh)* **(a)** *(leiden)* to languish ♦ **vor Durst ~** to be parched; **vor Hunger ~** to starve. **(b)** *(sich sehnen)* **nach jdm/etw ~** to pine *or* yearn for sb/sth.

schmachtend *adj* yearning, soulful; *Liebhaber* languishing.

Schmachtfetzen *m (dated hum)* tear-jerker *(inf)*.

schmächtig *adj* slight, frail, weedy *(pej)*.

Schmächtigkeit *f* slightness, frailty, weediness *(pej)*.

Schmacht-: ~lappen *m (dated hum)* Romeo *(inf)*; **~locke** *f (dated hum)* kiss-curl.

schmachvoll *adj (geh) Niederlage* ignominious; *(demütigend auch) Frieden* humiliating.

Schmackes *pl (dial inf)* **(a)** *(Schläge)* **~ kriegen** to get a smacking. **(b)** *(Schwung)* **er knallte das Buch mit ~ auf den Tisch** he slammed *or* banged *(inf)* the book down on the table; **das muß man mit ~ machen!** *(richtig zuschlagen)* give it a good clout *(inf)* *or* bang *(inf)*.

schmackhaft *adj (wohlschmeckend)* palatable, tasty; *(appetitanregend)* appetizing ♦ **jdm etw ~ machen** *(fig)* to make sth palatable to sb.

Schmackhaftigkeit *f* palatability.

Schmäh *m* **-s, -(s)** *(Aus inf) (Trick)* con *(inf)*, dodge *(inf)* ♦ **einen ~ führen** *(Witze machen)* to clown around; **jdn am ~ halten** to make a fool out of sb.

Schmähbrief *m* defamatory *or* abusive letter.

schmähen *vti (geh)* to abuse, to revile *(liter)*, to vituperate against *(liter)*.

schmählich *adj (geh)* ignominious, shameful; *(demütigend)* humiliating.

Schmäh-: ~rede *f (geh)* invective, diatribe; **~reden (gegen jdn) führen** to launch diatribes (against sb); **~schrift** *f* defamatory piece of writing; *(Satire)* lampoon.

Schmähung *f (geh)* abuse, vituperation *(liter)* ♦ **(gegen jdn) ~en und Verwünschungen ausstoßen** to hurl abuse (at sb).

Schmähwort *nt, pl* **-e** *(liter)* abusive word, term of abuse ♦ **~e** abuse *sing*, invective *sing*.

schmal *adj, comp* **-er** *or* **¨er**, *superl* **-ste(r, s)** *or* **¨ste(r, s)**, *adv superl* **am -sten** *or* **¨sten (a)** narrow; *Hüfte, Taille auch, Mensch* slim, slender; *Band, Buch* slim; *Gelenke, Lippen* thin ♦ **er ist sehr ~ geworden** he has got very thin. **(b)** *(fig: karg)* meagre, slender ♦ **~e Kost** slender fare.

schmalbrüstig *adj* narrow-chested; *(fig)* limited.

schmälern *vt* to diminish, to reduce, to lessen; *(heruntermachen)* to detract from, to belittle, to diminish.

Schmälerung *f siehe vt* diminishing, reduction, lessening; detraction, belittlement ♦ **eine ~ seines Ruhms** a detraction from *or* diminishing of his fame.

Schmal-: ~film *m* cine-film; **~filmkamera** *f* cine-camera; **~hans** *m (inf)*: **bei ihnen/uns ist ~hans Küchenmeister** their/our cupboard is nearly always bare; **s~lippig** *adj* thin-lipped; **s~schult(e)rig** *adj* narrow-shouldered; **~seite** *f* narrow side; **~spur** *f (Rail)* narrow gauge; **~spur-** *in cpds (pej)* small-time; **~spurbahn** *f* narrow-gauge railway; **s~spurig** *adj (Rail) Strecke* narrow-gauge.

Schmalz¹ *nt* **-es, -e (a)** fat; *(Schweine~)* lard; *(Braten~)* dripping. **(b)** *siehe* **Ohren~**.

Schmalz² *m* **-es,** *no pl (pej inf)* schmaltz *(inf)*.

schmalzen *vti* to drool; *Lied* to croon.

schmalzig *adj (pej inf)* schmaltzy *(inf)*, slushy *(inf)*.

Schmalzler *m* **-s, -** *(S Ger)* snuff.

Schmankerl *nt* **-s, -n** *(S Ger, Aus) siehe* **Leckerbissen**.

Schmant *m* **-(e)s,** *no pl (dial)* **(a)** *(Sahne)* cream. **(b)** *(Matsch)* muck.

schmarotzen* *vi* to sponge, to scrounge, to freeload *(esp US)* *(bei* on, off); *(Biol)* to be parasitic *(bei* on).

Schmarotzer(in *f***)** *m* **-s, -** *(Biol)* parasite; *(fig auch)* sponger, scrounger, freeloader *(esp US)*.

schmarotzerhaft, schmarotzerisch *adj (Biol, fig)* parasitic.

Schmarotzertum *nt, no pl (Biol, fig)* parasitism.

Schmarre *f* **-, -n** *(dial)* cut, gash; *(Narbe)* scar.

Schmarr(e)n *m* **-s, - (a)** *(S Ger, Aus) (Cook) pancake cut up into small pieces.* **(b)** *(inf: Quatsch)* rubbish, tripe *(inf)* ◆ **das geht dich einen ~ an!** that's none of your business!

Schmatz *m* **-es, -e** *(inf: Kuß)* smacker.

schmatzen *vi* to eat noisily ◆ **er aß ~d seine Suppe** he slurped his soup; **schmatz nicht so!** don't make so much noise when you eat!; **mit den Lippen ~** to smack one's lips; **Oma küßte das Kind ~d** grandma gave the child a real smacker of a kiss.

schmauchen [1] *vt* to puff away at.
[2] *vi* to puff away.

Schmaus *m* **-es, Schmäuse** *(dated)* feast.

schmausen *(geh)* [1] *vi* to feast.
[2] *vt* to feast on.

schmecken [1] *vi* **(a)** *(Geschmack haben)* to taste *(nach* of); *(gut ~)* to be good, to taste good *or* lovely; *(probieren auch)* to have a taste ◆ **ihm schmeckt es** *(gut finden)* he likes it; *(Appetit haben)* he likes his food; **ihm schmeckt es nicht** *(keinen Appetit)* he's lost his appetite, he's off his food; **das schmeckt ihm nicht** *(lit, fig)* he doesn't like it; **die Arbeit schmeckt ihm nicht** this work doesn't agree with him, he has no taste for this work; **wie schmeckt die Ehe?** how does marriage agree with you?; **nach etw ~** *(fig)* to smack of sth; **das schmeckt nach nichts** it's tasteless; **das schmeckt nach mehr!** *(inf)* it tastes more-ish *(hum inf)*; **schmeckt es (Ihnen)?** do you like it?, is it good?; are you enjoying your food *or* meal? *(esp form)*; **das hat ge schmeckt** that was good; **und das schmeckt!** and it tastes so good, and it's so good; **das schmeckt nicht (gut)** it doesn't taste good *or* nice; **es schmeckt mir ausgezeichnet** it is *or* tastes really excellent; **Hauptsache, es schmeckt** *(inf)* the main thing is it tastes nice; **es sich ~ lassen** to tuck in.
(b) *(S Ger, Aus, Sw: riechen)* to smell.
[2] *vt* **(a)** to taste; *(probieren auch)* to have a taste of ◆ **etw zu ~ bekommen** *(fig inf)* to have a taste of sth.
(b) *(S Ger, Aus, Sw: riechen)* to smell; *(fig: ahnen)* to sense.

Schmeichelei *f* flattery; *(Komplimente auch)* flattering remark *or* compliment ◆ **so eine ~!** such flattery!

schmeichelhaft *adj* flattering; *Bemerkung auch* complimentary.

schmeicheln *vi* **(a)** to flatter *(jdm* sb); *(um etw zu erreichen auch)* to butter up *(inf)* *(jdm* sb) ◆ **es schmeichelt mir, daß ...** it flatters me that ..., I find it flattering that ...; **... sagte sie ~d** ... she wheedled; **sich** *(dat)* **~ ...** *(geh)* to flatter oneself (that) ... **(b)** *(verschönen)* to flatter ◆ **das Bild ist aber geschmeichelt!** the picture is very flattering.

Schmeichelwort *nt, pl* **-e** *(geh)* flattery, honeyed word.

Schmeichler(in *f***)** *m* **-s, -** flatterer; *(Kriecher)* sycophant, fawner.

schmeichlerisch *adj* flattering; *(lobhudelnd auch)* unctuous, fawning, sycophantic.

schmeißen *pret* **schmiß**, *ptp* **geschmissen** *(inf)* [1] *vt* **(a)** *(werfen)* to sling *(inf)*, to chuck *(inf)*, to fling; *Tür* to slam ◆ **sich auf etw** *(acc)* **~** to throw oneself into sth; **die Frauen schmissen sich auf die Sonderangebote** the women made a rush at the special offers; **sich jdm an den Hals ~** *(fig)* to throw oneself at sb; **er schmiß sich mutig zwischen die beiden** he courageously flung *or* threw *or* hurled himself between the two.
(b) *(spendieren)* **eine Runde** *or* **Lage ~** to stand a round; **eine Party ~** *(sl)* to throw a party.
(c) *(managen)* **den Laden ~** to run the (whole) show; **die Sache ~** to handle it.
[2] *vi (werfen)* to throw, to chuck *(inf)* ◆ **mit Steinen ~** to throw *or* chuck *(inf)* stones; **mit etw um sich ~** to throw sth about, to chuck sth around *(inf)*; **mit Fremdwörtern um sich ~** to bandy loanwords *or* foreign words about.

Schmeißfliege *f* bluebottle.

Schmelz *m* **-(e)s, -e** *(Glasur)* glaze; *(Zahn~)* enamel; *(geh) (einer Farbe)* lustre, glow; *(Wohllaut)* melodiousness, mellifluousness.

Schmelz-: s~bar *adj* fusible, meltable; **Eisen ist leicht s~bar** iron is easily melted *or* melts easily; **~barkeit** *f* fusibility.

Schmelze *f* **-, -n (a)** *(Metal)* melt. **(b)** *(Schmelzen)* melting; *(Metal: von Erz)* smelting. **(c)** *(Schmelzhütte)* smelting plant *or* works *sing or pl.*

schmelzen *pret* **schmolz**, *ptp* **geschmolzen** [1] *vi aux sein (lit, fig: erweichen)* to melt; *(Reakturkern)* to melt down; *(fig: schwinden auch)* to melt away ◆ **es ist ihr gelungen, sein hartes Herz zum S~ zu bringen** she succeeded in melting his heart of stone.
[2] *vt Metall, Fett* to melt; *Erz* to smelt.

schmelzend *adj (geh) Gesang, Ton, Stimme* mellifluous.

Schmelzerei *f siehe* **Schmelzhütte**.

Schmelz-: ~farbe *f (Tech)* vitrifiable pigment *or* colour; **~glas** *nt* enamel; **~hütte** *f* smelting plant *or* works *sing or pl*; **~käse** *m* cheese spread; **~ofen** *m* melting furnace; *(für Erze)* smelting furnace; **~punkt** *m* melting point; **~tiegel** *m (lit, fig)* melting pot; **~wärme** *f (Metal)* heat of fusion; **~wasser** *nt* melted snow and ice; *(Geog, Phys)* meltwater.

Schmer *m or nt* **-s,** *no pl (old, dial)* pork fat.

Schmer-: ~bauch *m (inf)* paunch, potbelly; **s~bäuchig** *adj (inf)* paunchy, potbellied.

Schmerle *f* **-, -n** loach.

Schmerz *m* **-es, -en** pain *pl rare*; *(Kummer auch)* grief *no pl* ◆ **ihre ~en** her pain; **dumpfer ~** ache; **stechender ~** stabbing pain; **sie schrie vor ~en** she cried out in pain; **~en haben** to be in pain; **~en in der Nierengegend/in den Ohren/im Hals haben** to have a pain in the kidneys/to have ear-ache/to have a sore throat; **wo haben Sie ~en?** where does it hurt?, where's the pain?; **wenn den Patient wieder ~en bekommt ...** if the patient starts feeling pain again ...; **jdm ~en bereiten** to cause sb pain; *(seelisch auch)* to pain sb; **mit ~en** *(fig)* regretfully; **jdn/etw mit ~en erwarten** to wait impatiently for sb/sth; **unter ~en** painfully; *(fig)* regretfully; **jdn mit ~(en) erfüllen** *(fig)* to grieve *or* hurt sb.

Schmerz-: s~betäubend *adj* pain-killing; **s~empfindlich** *adj Mensch* sensitive to pain; *Wunde, Körperteil* tender; **~empfindlichkeit** *f siehe adj* sensitivity to pain; tenderness.

-schmerzen *pl in cpds* pain in the ...; *(Bauch~, Ohren~, Kopf~)* -ache; *(Hals~, Gelenk~)* sore ...

schmerzen *(geh)* [1] *vt* to hurt, to pain; *(körperlich)* to hurt.
[2] *vi* to hurt; *(Wunde etc)* to be sore; *(Kopf, Bauch auch)* to ache ◆ **mir schmerzt der Kopf** my head aches; **es schmerzt** *(lit, fig)* it hurts; **eine ~de Stelle** a painful spot *or* area.

Schmerzens-: ~geld *nt (Jur)* damages *pl*; **~laut** *m (geh)* cry of pain; **~schrei** *m* scream of pain.

Schmerz-: s~erfüllt *adj (geh)* racked with pain; *(seelisch)* grief-stricken; **s~frei** *adj* free of pain; *Operation* painless; **~grenze** *f* pain barrier; **s~haft** *adj (lit, fig)* painful; **~kranke(r)** *mf person suffering from chronic pain*; **s~lich** *adj (geh)* painful; *Lächeln* sad; **es ist mir sehr s~lich, Ihnen mitteilen zu müssen, daß ...** it is my painful duty to inform you that ...; **s~lindernd** *adj* pain-relieving, analgesic; **~linderung** *f* relief *or* alleviation of pain; **s~los** *adj (lit, fig)* painless; **s~loser** less painful; *siehe* **kurz**; **~losigkeit** *f (lit, fig)* painlessness; **~mittel** *nt* pain-killing drug, pain-killer; **~schwelle** *f* pain threshold; **s~stillend** *adj* pain-killing, pain-relieving, analgesic *(Med)*; **s~stillendes Mittel** pain-killing drug, pain-killer, analgesic *(Med)*; **~tablette** *f* pain-killer, ≃ aspirin *(inf)*; **s~unempfindlich** *adj* insensitive to pain; *Körperteil auch* numb; **s~verzerrt** *adj* pain-racked, agonized; **s~voll** *adj (fig)* painful.

Schmetterball *m* smash.

Schmetterling *m (Zool, inf: Schwimmart)* butterfly ◆ **kannst du ~ schwimmen?** can you do the butterfly?

Schmetterlings-: ~blütler *m* **-s, - die ~blütler** the papilionaceae *(spec)*; **ein ~blütler** a member of the papilionaceae family *(spec)*; **~netz** *nt* butterfly net; **~stil** *m* butterfly stroke.

schmettern [1] *vt* **(a)** *(schleudern)* to smash; *Tür* to slam; *(Sport) Ball* to smash ◆ **etw in Stücke ~** to smash sth to pieces.
(b) *Lied* to bellow out; *(Vogel)* to sing, to warble.
[2] *vi* **(a)** *(Sport)* to smash, to hit a smash.
(b) *(Trompete etc)* to blare (out); *(Sänger)* to bellow; *(Vogel)* to sing, to warble.

Schmied *m* **-(e)s, -e** (black)smith; *siehe* **Glück**.

schmiedbar *adj* malleable.

Schmiede *f* **-, -n** smithy, forge.

Schmiede-: ~arbeit *f (das Schmieden)* forging; *(Gegenstand)* piece of wrought-iron work; **~eisen** *nt* wrought iron; **s~eisern** *adj* wrought-iron; **~hammer** *m* blacksmith's hammer; **~kunst** *f* skill in wrought-iron work.

schmieden *vt* to forge *(zu* into); *(fig: zusammenfügen auch)* to mould; *(ersinnen) Plan* to hatch, to concoct; *(hum) Verse* to concoct ◆ **geschmiedet sein** *(Gartentür etc)* to be made of wrought-iron; **jdn in Ketten ~** *(liter)* to bind sb in chains.

Schmiedin *f siehe* **Schmied**.

schmiegen [1] *vr* **sich an jdn ~** to cuddle *or* snuggle up to sb; **sich an/in etw** *(acc)* **~** to nestle *or* snuggle into sth; **die Weinberge/Häuser ~ sich an die sanften Hänge** the vineyards/houses nestle into the gentle slopes; **sich um etw ~** to hang gracefully on sth; *(Haare)* to fall gracefully round sth.
[2] *vt* **etw an/in etw** *(acc)* **~** to nestle sth into sth; **etw um etw ~** to wrap sth around sth; **die an den Felsen geschmiegte Kapelle** the chapel nestled *or* nestling in the cliffs.

schmiegsam *adj* supple; *Stoff* soft; *(fig: anpassungsfähig)* adaptable, flexible.

Schmiere *f* **-, -n (a)** *(inf)* grease; *(Salbe)* ointment; *(feuchter Schmutz auch)* mud; *(pej: Schminke)* paint; *(Aufstrich)* spread.
(b) *(pej) (Wanderbühne)* (troop of) barnstormers; *(schlechtes Theater)* flea-pit.
(c) *(sl)* **~ stehen** to be the look-out, to keep cave *(dated Brit Sch sl)*.

schmieren [1] *vt* **(a)** *(streichen)* to smear; *Butter, Aufstrich* to spread; *Brot* to butter; *Salbe, Make-up* to rub in *(in +acc* -to); *(einfetten, ölen)* to grease; *(Tech) Achsen, Gelenke etc* to grease, to lubricate ◆ **es geht** *or* **läuft wie geschmiert** it's going like clockwork; **jdm eine ~** *(inf)* to clout sb one *(inf)*.
(b) *(pej: schreiben)* to scrawl.

(c) (*inf: bestechen*) **jdn ~** to grease sb's palm (*inf*).
[2] *vi* (a) (*pej*) (*schreiben*) to scrawl; (*malen*) to daub.
(b) (*Stift, Radiergummi, Scheibenwischer*) to smear.
(c) (*inf: bestechen*) to give a bribe/bribes.

Schmieren-: ~komödiant *m* (*pej*) ham (actor); **~komödie** *f* (*pej*) slapstick farce, pantomime; (*fig*) pantomime, farce; **~schauspieler** *m* barnstormer; (*pej*) ham (actor); **~theater** *nt* (*pej*) (troop of) barnstormers; (*schlechtes Theater*) flea-pit.

Schmierer(in *f*) *m* **-s, -** (*pej inf*) scrawler, scribbler; (*von Parolen*) slogan dauber; (*in Toiletten, an Gebäuden*) graffiti writer; (*Maler*) dauber; (*Autor, Journalist*) hack, scribbler.

Schmiererei *f* (*pej inf*) (*Geschriebenes*) scrawl, scribble; (*Parolen etc*) graffiti *pl*; (*Malerei*) daubing; (*Schriftstellerei*) scribbling; (*das Schmieren von Parolen etc*) scrawling, scribbling; (*von Stift, Scheibenwischer etc*) smearing.

Schmierestehen *nt* (*sl*) keeping look-out.

Schmier-: ~fett *nt* (lubricating) grease; **~fink** *m* (*pej*) (a) (*Autor, Journalist*) hack, scribbler; (*Skandaljournalist*) muckraker (*inf*); (b) (*Schüler*) messy writer, scrawler; **~geld** *nt* (*inf*) bribe, bribe-money; **~heft** *nt* jotter, rough-book.

schmierig *adj* greasy; *Restaurant auch* grimy; (*fig*) (*unanständig*) dirty, filthy; (*schleimig*) greasy, smarmy (*inf*).

Schmier-: ~käse *m* (*dated*) cheese spread; **~mittel** *nt* lubricant; **~öl** *nt* lubricating oil; **~papier** *nt* rough *or* jotting paper; **~seife** *f* soft soap.

Schmierung *f* lubrication.

Schmierzettel *m* piece of rough *or* jotting paper.

schmilz *imper sing of* **schmelzen.**

Schminke *f* **-, -n** make-up.

schminken [1] *vt* to make up ◆ **sich** (*dat*) **die Lippen/Augen ~** to put on lipstick/eye make-up.
[2] *vr* to make oneself up, to put on make-up ◆ **sich selten/zu stark ~** to wear make-up rarely/to wear too much make-up.

Schmink-: ~koffer *m* vanity case; **~täschchen** *nt* make-up bag; **~tisch** *m* dressing table.

Schmirgel *m* **-s,** *no pl* emery.

schmirgeln [1] *vt* to sand, to rub down.
[2] *vi* to sand.

Schmirgel-: ~papier *nt* sandpaper; **~scheibe** *f* sanding disc.

⚠**Schmiß** *m* **-sses, -sse** (a) (*Fechtwunde*) gash, wound; (*Narbe*) duelling scar. (b) (*dated: Schwung*) dash, élan ◆ **~ haben** (*Musik etc*) to go with a swing; (*Mensch*) to have go (*inf*).

⚠**schmiß** *pret of* **schmeißen.**

schmissig *adj* (*dated*) dashing; *Musik auch* spirited.

Schmock *m* **-(e)s, -e** *or* **-s** (*pej*) hack (*inf*).

Schmok *m* **-s,** *no pl* (*N Ger*) smoke.

schmöken *vti* (*N Ger*) to smoke.

Schmöker *m* **-s, -** book (*usu of light literature*); (*dick*) tome.

schmökern (*inf*) [1] *vi* to bury oneself in a book; (*in Büchern blättern*) to browse.
[2] *vt* to bury oneself in.

Schmoll|ecke *f siehe* **Schmollwinkel.**

schmollen *vi* to pout; (*gekränkt sein*) to sulk ◆ **mit jdm ~** to be annoyed with sb.

Schmoll-: ~mund *m* pout; **einen ~mund machen** to pout; **~winkel** *m* (*inf*) **im ~winkel sitzen** to have the sulks (*inf*); **sich in den ~winkel zurückziehen** to go off into a corner to sulk.

schmolz *pret of* **schmelzen.**

Schmonzes *m* **-, -** (*dated*) balderdash (*dated*), tripe (*inf*).

Schmor-: ~brand *m* smouldering fire; **~braten** *m* pot-roast.

schmoren [1] *vt* to braise; *Braten auch* to pot-roast.
[2] *vi* (a) (*Cook*) to braise; (*inf: schwitzen*) to roast, to swelter ◆ **jdn (im eigenen Saft** *or* **Fett) ~ lassen** to leave sb to stew (in his/her own juice). (b) (*unbearbeitet liegen*) to lie there.

Schmorfleisch *nt* (*Cook*) braising steak; (*Braten*) pot roast.

Schmu *m* **-s,** *no pl* (*inf*) cheating; (*esp mit Geld auch*) fiddling (*inf*) ◆ **das ist ~!** that's a cheat *or* a fiddle! (*inf*); **~ machen** to cheat; to fiddle (*inf*); **bei der Abrechnung/Prüfung ~ machen** to fiddle the expenses/cheat in the exam.

schmuck *adj* (*dated*) *Haus etc* neat, tidy; *Schiff* neat, trim; *Bursche, Mädel* smart, spruce; *Paar* smart.

Schmuck *m* **-(e)s,** (*rare*) **-e** (a) (*~stücke*) jewellery (*Brit*) *no pl*, jewelry *no pl*.
(b) (*Verzierung*) decoration; (*fig*) embellishment ◆ **der ~ am Christbaum** the decorations on the Christmas tree; **im ~ der Blumen/Fahnen** (*liter*) decked with flowers/flags; **Natürlichkeit ist der schönste ~ eines Mädchens** naturalness is the greatest adornment a girl can have.

schmücken [1] *vt* to decorate, to adorn; *Rede* to embellish ◆ **die mit Blumenkränzen geschmückten Tänzerinnen** the dancers adorned with garlands of flowers; **mit Juwelen geschmückt** bejewelled; **~des Beiwerk/Beiwort** embellishment.
[2] *vr* (*zum Fest etc*) (*Mensch*) to adorn oneself; (*Stadt*) to be decorated ◆ **sich mit Blumenkränzen ~** to garland oneself with flowers; *siehe* **fremd.**

Schmuck-: ~gegenstand *m* ornament; (*Ring etc*) piece of jewellery; **~kassette** *f*, **~kästchen** *nt*, **~kasten** *m* jewellery box; **ihr Haus war ein ~kästchen** her house was a picture; **s~los** *adj* plain; *Fassade* unadorned; *Einrichtung, Stil auch* simple; (*fig*) *Stil, Prosa etc* simple, unadorned; **~losigkeit** *f siehe adj* plainness; unadornedness; simplicity; simplicity, unadornedness; **~sachen** *pl* jewellery (*Brit*) *sing*, jewelry *sing*; **~stein** *m* (*Edelstein*) precious stone, gem; (*Halbedelstein*) semi-precious stone; **~stück** *nt* (*Ring etc*) piece of jewellery; (*~gegenstand*) ornament; (*fig: Prachtstück*) gem; (*fig inf*) (*Frau*) better half (*inf*); (*Freundin, als Anrede*) sweetheart (*inf*); **~waren** *pl* jewellery (*Brit*) *sing*, jewelry *sing*.

Schmuddel *m* **-s,** *no pl* (*N Ger inf*) (*Schmutz*) mess; (*auf Straße*) dirt, mud.

Schmuddelei *f* (*inf*) mess *no pl*.

schmudd(e)lig *adj* messy; (*schmutzig auch*) dirty; (*schmierig, unsauber*) filthy; (*schlampig*) *Bedienung* sloppy; *Frau, Schüler* sloppy, slovenly.

Schmuddel-: ~kind *nt* (*fig*) (street) urchin; **~look** [-luk] *m* (*iro*) urchin look (*iro*).

Schmuggel *m* **-s,** *no pl* smuggling ◆ **~ treiben** to smuggle; **der ~ von Heroin** heroin smuggling.

Schmuggelei *f* smuggling *no pl* ◆ **seine kleinen ~en** his small-scale smuggling.

schmuggeln *vti* (*lit, fig*) to smuggle ◆ **mit etw ~** to smuggle sth.

Schmuggeln *nt* **-s,** *no pl* smuggling.

Schmuggelware *f* smuggled goods *pl*, contraband *no pl*.

Schmuggler(in *f*) *m* **-s, -** smuggler ◆ **~ von Rauschgift/Waffen** drug-smuggler/arms smuggler, gun-runner.

Schmuggler-: ~bande *f* smuggling ring, ring of smugglers; **~pfad** *m* smugglers' path.

schmunzeln *vi* to smile.

Schmunzeln *nt* **-s,** *no pl* smile.

Schmus *m* **-es,** *no pl* (*inf*) (*Unsinn*) nonsense; (*Schmeicheleien*) soft-soap (*inf*) ◆ **~ erzählen** to talk nonsense.

Schmusekurs *m* (*inf*) friendly overtures *pl* ◆ **mit jdm auf ~ gehen** to cosy up to sb; **der ~ zwischen SPD und Unternehmern** the friendly noises between the SPD and the employers; **sich auf ~ begeben** to try to ingratiate oneself.

schmusen *vi* (*inf*) (*zärtlich sein*) to cuddle; (*mit Freund, Freundin auch*) to canoodle (*inf*) ◆ **mit jdm ~** to cuddle sb; to canoodle with sb (*inf*).

Schmusepuppe *f* cuddly toy.

Schmuser(in *f*) *m* **-s, -** (*zärtlicher Mensch*) affectionate person ◆ **er ist ein kleiner ~** he likes a cuddle.

schmusig *adj* (*inf*) smoochy (*inf*).

Schmutz *m* **-es,** *no pl* (a) dirt; (*Schlamm auch*) mud ◆ **die Handwerker haben viel ~ gemacht** the workmen have made a lot of mess; **sie leben in ~** they live in real squalor; **der Stoff nimmt leicht ~ an** the material dirties easily.
(b) (*fig*) filth, dirt, smut ◆ **~ und Schund** obscene *or* offensive material; **jdn/etw in den ~ ziehen** *or* **zerren** to drag sb/sth through the mud; *siehe* **bewerfen.**

Schmutzblatt *nt* (*Typ*) half-title (page).

schmutzen *vi* to get dirty.

Schmutz-: ~fänger *m* dust trap; **~fink** *m* (*inf*) (*unsauberer Mensch*) dirty slob (*inf*); (*Kind*) mucky pup (*inf*); (*fig*) (*Mann*) dirty old man; (*Journalist*) muckraker (*inf*); **~fleck** *m* dirty mark; **~fracht** *f* dirty cargo.

schmutzig *adj* (*unsauber, unanständig*) dirty, filthy; *Geschäft* dirty, sordid; *Witze, Geschichten auch* smutty ◆ **sich ~ machen** to get oneself dirty; **Geld ist doch nicht ~** money is money no matter where it comes from; **~e Wäsche (vor anderen Leuten) waschen** to wash one's dirty linen in public; **~e Reden führen** to use bad *or* foul language.

Schmutzigkeit *f siehe adj* dirtiness, filthiness; dirtiness, sordidness; smuttiness; (*Witz, Bemerkung*) dirty *etc* joke/remark.

Schmutz-: ~kampagne *f* smear campaign; **~literatur** *f* dirty *or* smutty literature; **~titel** *m* (*Typ*) half-title; **~wäsche** *f* dirty washing; **~wasser** *nt* dirty water.

Schnabel *m* **-s, ¨** (a) (*Vogel~*) beak, bill.
(b) (*von Kanne*) spout; (*von Krug*) lip; (*von Schiff*) prow.
(c) (*Mus: Mundstück*) mouthpiece.
(d) (*inf: Mund*) mouth ◆ **halt den ~!** shut your mouth (*inf*) *or* trap (*sl*); **den ~ aufreißen** (*vor Erstaunen*) to gape; (*reden*) to open one's big mouth (*inf*); **mach doch den ~ auf** say something; **reden, wie einem der ~ gewachsen ist** to say exactly what comes into one's head; (*unaffektiert*) to talk naturally.

Schnäbelei *f* (*lit, fig*) billing and cooing.

Schnabelhieb *m* peck.

schnäbeln *vi* (*lit, fig*) to bill and coo.

Schnabel-: ~schuh *m* pointed shoe (with turned-up toe); **~tasse** *f* feeding cup; **~tier** *nt* duckbilled platypus.

schnabulieren* *vi* (*inf: essen*) to nibble.

Schnack *m* **-(e)s, -s** (*N Ger inf*) (*Unterhaltung*) chat; (*Ausspruch*) silly *or* amusing phrase ◆ **das ist ein dummer ~** that's a silly phrase.

schnackeln *vi* (*S Ger*) (*Mensch*) to shake ◆ **mit den Fingern ~** to snap *or* click one's fingers; **jdm ~ die Knie** sb's knees are trembling *or* shaking; **es hat (bei jdm) geschnackelt** it's clicked.

schnacken *vi* (*N Ger*) to chat.

Schnackerl *m or nt* **-s,** *no pl* (*Aus*) hiccup ◆ **den ~ haben** to have (the) hiccups.

Schnake *f* **-, -n** (a) (*inf: Stechmücke*) gnat, midge. (b) (*Weberknecht*) daddy-longlegs.

Schnalle *f* **-, -n** (a) (*Schuh~, Gürtel~*) buckle. (b) (*an Handtasche, Buch*) clasp. (c) (*Aus, S Ger: Tür~*) handle. (d) (*sl: Flittchen*) tarty type (*inf*).

schnallen *vt* (a) to strap; *Gürtel* to buckle, to fasten; *siehe* **Gürtel.** (b) (*inf: begreifen*) **etw ~** to catch on to sth; **hast du das noch immer nicht geschnallt?** have you still not caught on?

Schnallenschuh *m* buckled shoe.

schnalzen *vi* **mit der Peitsche ~** to crack one's whip, to give a crack of one's whip; **mit der Zunge ~** to click one's tongue.

⚠: Informationen zur Rechtschreibreform im Anhang

Schnalzer *m* **-s, -** (*inf*) (*mit Zunge*) click; (*von Peitsche*) crack.
Schnalzlaut *m* (*Ling*) click.
schnapp *interj* snap; *siehe* **schnipp**.
Schnäppchen *nt* bargain ◆ **ein ~ machen** to get a bargain.
schnappen [1] *vi* **(a) nach jdm/etw ~** to snap *or* take a snap at sb/sth; (*greifen*) to snatch *or* grab at sb/sth; *siehe* **Luft**.
(b) *aux sein* (*sich bewegen*) to spring up ◆ **die Tür schnappt ins Schloß** the door snaps *or* clicks shut.
[2] *vt* (*inf*) **(a)** (*ergreifen*) to snatch, to grab ◆ **jdn am Arm ~** to grab sb's arm *or* sb by the arm; **schnapp dir einen Zettel** grab a piece of paper (*inf*).
(b) (*fangen*) to catch, to nab (*inf*).
Schnapper *m* **-s, -** (*inf*) (*von Hund etc*) snap.
Schnäpper *m* **-s, -** (*Med*) lancet.
Schnapp-: ~feder *f* spring catch; **~hahn** *m* (*Hist*) highwayman; **~messer** *nt* clasp-knife; ⚠**~schloß** *nt* (*an Tür*) springlock; (*an Schmuck*) spring clasp; ⚠**~schuß** *m* (*Foto*) snap(shot); ⚠**~verschluß** *m* snap lock.
Schnaps *m* **-es, ¨e** (*klarer ~*) schnapps; (*inf: Branntwein*) spirits *pl*; (*inf: Alkohol*) drink, booze (*inf*), liquor (*esp US inf*) ◆ **ich möchte lieber einen ~ trinken** I'd rather have a short (*inf*).
Schnaps-: ~brenner *m* distiller; **~brennerei** *f* **(a)** (*Gebäude*) distillery; **(b)** *no pl* (*das Brennen*) distilling of spirits *or* liquor; **~bruder** *m* (*inf*) boozer (*inf*).
Schnäpschen ['ʃnɛpsçən] *nt* (*inf*) little drink, wee dram (*esp Scot*).
schnapseln (*Aus*), **schnapsen** *vi* (*inf*) to booze (*inf*).
Schnaps-: ~fahne *f* (*inf*) boozy breath (*inf*); **~flasche** *f* bottle of booze (*inf*) *or* spirits *or* liquor; **~glas** *nt* small glass for spirits; **~idee** *f* (*inf*) crazy *or* crackpot idea; **~laden** *m* off-licence (*Brit*), liquor store (*US*); **~leiche** *f* (*inf*) drunk; **~nase** *f* (*inf*) boozer's nose (*inf*); **~zahl** *f* (*inf*) *multi-digit number with all digits identical*.
schnarchen *vi* to snore.
Schnarcher(in *f*) *m* **-s, -** snorer.
Schnarre *f* **-, -n** rattle.
schnarren *vi* (*Wecker, Radio, Saite etc*) to buzz; (*Maschine, Spinnrad etc*) to clatter; (*Uhrwerk*) to creak; (*Vogel*) to croak ◆ **mit ~der Stimme** in a rasping *or* grating voice.
Schnatter-: ~gans, ~liese *f*, **~maul** *nt* (*all inf*) chatterbox.
schnattern *vi* (*Gans*) to gabble; (*Ente*) to quack; (*Affen*) to chatter, to gibber; (*inf: schwatzen*) to natter (*inf*) ◆ **sie schnattert vor Kälte** her teeth are chattering with (the) cold.
schnauben *pret* **schnaubte** *or* (*old*) **schnob**, *ptp* **geschnaubt** *or* (*old*) **geschnoben** [1] *vi* **(a)** (*Tier*) to snort. **(b) vor Wut/Entrüstung ~** to snort with rage/indignation.
[2] *vt* **(a) Unverschämtheit, schnaubte er** disgraceful, he snorted. **(b)** (*liter: Pferd etc*) to breathe.
[3] *vr* **sich** (*dat*) **die Nase ~, sich ~** to blow one's nose.
schnaufen *vi* **(a)** (*schwer atmen*) to wheeze; (*keuchen*) to puff, to pant; (*fig*) (*Lokomotive*) to puff; (*inf: Auto*) to struggle. **(b)** (*esp S Ger: atmen*) to breathe. **(c)** *aux sein* (*sich keuchend bewegen: Auto*) to struggle ◆ **ich bin in den fünften Stock geschnauft** (*inf*) I went/came puffing and panting up to the fifth floor.
Schnaufer *m* **-s, -** (*inf*) breath ◆ **ein ~ frische Luft** a breath of fresh air; **den letzten ~ tun** to breathe one's last, to kick the bucket (*inf*), to snuff it (*inf*).
Schnauferl *nt* **-s, -** *or* (*Aus*) **-n** (*hum: Oldtimer*) veteran car.
Schnaufpause *f* (*Aus, S Ger*) short breather (*inf*).
Schnauzbart *m* walrus moustache.
Schnäuzchen *nt dim of* **Schnauze** nose.
Schnauze *f* **-, -n (a)** (*von Tier*) muzzle ◆ **eine feuchte ~ haben** to have a wet nose; **mit einer Maus in der ~** with a mouse in its mouth.
(b) (*Ausguß an Kaffeekanne etc*) spout; (*an Krug etc*) lip.
(c) (*inf*) (*von Fahrzeugen*) front; (*von Flugzeug, Schiff*) nose.
(d) (*sl: Mund*) gob (*sl*), trap (*sl*) ◆ **~!** shut your gob (*sl*) *or* trap (*sl*); **auf die ~ fallen** to fall flat on one's face; (*fig*) to come a cropper (*inf*); **jdm die ~ einschlagen** *or* **polieren** *or* **lackieren** to smash sb's face in (*sl*); **die ~ (gestrichen) voll haben** to be fed up to the back teeth (*inf*); **eine große ~ haben** to have a big mouth, to be a big-mouth (*inf*); **die ~ halten** to hold one's tongue; **etw frei nach ~ machen** to do sth any old how (*inf*).
schnauzen *vi* (*inf*) to shout; (*jdn anfahren*) to snap, to bark.
Schnauzer *m* **-s, - (a)** (*Hundeart*) schnauzer. **(b)** (*inf*) *siehe* **Schnauzbart**.
Schneck *m* **-s, -en** (*Aus, S Ger*) *siehe* **Schnecke (a, b)**.
Schnecke *f* **-, -n (a)** (*Zool, fig*) snail; (*Nackt~*) slug; (*Cook auch*) escargot ◆ **wie eine ~ kriechen** to crawl at a snail's pace; **jdn zur ~ machen** (*inf*) to give sb a real bawling-out (*inf*).
(b) (*Anat*) cochlea (*spec*).
(c) (*Archit, an Säule*) volute; (*Treppe*) spiral staircase.
(d) (*Tech*) (*Schraube*) worm, endless screw; (*Förder~*) worm *or* screw conveyor.
(e) *usu pl* (*Frisur*) earphone.
(f) (*Cook: Gebäck*) ≃ Chelsea bun.
Schnecken-: s~förmig *adj* spiral; (*Archit*) *ornament* scroll-shaped; **~gehäuse, ~haus** *nt* snail-shell; **sich in sein ~haus zurückziehen** (*fig inf*) to retreat into one's shell; **~post** *f* (*hum inf*) **du bist wohl mit der ~post gefahren?** you must have crawled your way here; **~tempo** *nt* (*inf*) **im ~tempo** at a snail's pace; **dein ~tempo kenn' ich schon** I know how slowly you do things.
Schnee *m* **-s,** *no pl* **(a)** (*auch TV*) snow ◆ **vom ~ eingeschlossen sein** to be snowbound; **im Jahre ~** (*Aus*) ages ago; **das ist ~ von gestern** that's old hat.
(b) (*Ei~*) whisked egg-white ◆ **Eiweiß zu ~ schlagen** to whisk the egg-white(s) till stiff.
(c) (*sl: Heroin, Kokain*) snow (*sl*).
Schnee-: ~anzug *m* snow suit; **s~arm** *adj* **s~arme Gebiete** areas with little snowfall.
Schneeball *m* snowball; (*Bot*) snowball, guelder rose.
Schneeball-: ~effekt *m* snowball effect; **~prinzip** *nt* snowball effect; **~schlacht** *f* snowball fight; **eine ~schlacht machen** to have a snowball fight; **~system** *nt* accumulative process; (*Comm*) pyramid selling; **das vermehrt sich nach dem ~-system** it snowballs.
Schnee-: s~bedeckt *adj* snow-covered; *Berg auch* snow-capped; **~besen** *m* (*Cook*) whisk; **s~blind** *adj* snow-blind; **~blindheit** *f* snow blindness; **~brille** *f* snow-goggles *pl*; **~decke** *f* blanket *or* (*Met*) covering of snow; ⚠**~-Eule** *f* snowy owl; **~fall** *m* snowfall, fall of snow; **dichter ~fall behindert die Sicht** heavy falling snow is impairing visibility; **~flocke** *f* snowflake; **~fräse** *f* snow blower; **s~frei** *adj* free of snow; **~gans** *f* snow goose; **~gestöber** *nt* (*leicht*) snow flurry; (*stark*) snowstorm; **~glätte** *f* hard-packed snow *no pl*; **~glöckchen** *nt* snowdrop; **~grenze** *f* snow-line; **~hase** *m* blue hare; **~hemd** *nt* (*Mil*) *white anorak for camouflage in snow*; **~hütte** *f* hut made of snow; **~kanone** *f* snow cannon; **~kette** *f* (*Aut*) snow chain; **~könig** *m*: **sich freuen wie ein ~könig** to be as pleased as Punch; **~kristall** *m* snow crystal; **~landschaft** *f* snowy landscape; **~mann** *m*, *pl* **-männer** snowman; **~matsch** *m* slush; **~mobil** *nt* snowmobile; **~pflug** *m* (*Tech, Ski*) snowplough (*Brit*), snowplow (*US*); **~raupe** *f* snow cat; **~regen** *m* sleet; **~schaufel, ~schippe** *f* snow-shovel, snowpusher (*US*); **~schläger** *m* whisk; **~schmelze** *f* thaw; **~schuh** *m* snow-shoe; (*dated: Ski*) ski; **~sturm** *m* snowstorm; (*stärker*) blizzard; **~treiben** *nt* driving snow; **~verhältnisse** *pl* snow conditions *pl*; **~verwehung** *f* snowdrift; ⚠**~wächte** *f* snow cornice; **~wasser** *nt* water from melting snow, snowmelt (*US*); **~wehe** *f* snowdrift; **s~weiß** *adj* snow-white, as white as snow; *Haare* snowy-white; *Hände* lily-white; *Gewissen* clear.
Schnee-: ~weißchen, ~wittchen *nt* Snow White.
Schneid *m* **-(e)s,** *no pl*, (*Aus*) *f* **-,** *no pl* (*inf*) guts *pl* (*inf*), nerve, courage ◆ **~/keinen ~ haben** to have/not to have guts (*inf*); **den ~ verlieren** to lose one's nerve.
Schneidbrenner *m* (*Tech*) oxyacetylene cutter, cutting torch.
Schneide *f* **-, -n** (sharp *or* cutting) edge; (*von Messer, Schwert*) blade; *siehe* **Messer**.
schneiden *pret* **schnitt**, *ptp* **geschnitten** [1] *vi* to cut; (*Med*) to operate; (*bei Geburt*) to do an episiotomy ◆ **jdm ins Gesicht/in die Hand** *etc* **~** to cut sb on the face/on the hand; **der Wind/die Kälte schneidet** the wind is biting/it is bitingly cold; **jdm ins Herz** *or* **in die Seele ~** to cut sb to the quick.
[2] *vt* **(a)** *Papier etc, Haare,* (*fig: meiden*) to cut; *Getreide auch* to mow; (*klein~*) *Schnittlauch, Gemüse etc* to chop; (*Sport*) *Ball* to slice, to cut; (*schnitzen*) *Namen, Figuren* to carve; (*Math auch*) to intersect with; (*Weg*) to cross ◆ **eine Kurve ~** to cut a corner; **sein schön/scharf geschnittenes Gesicht** his clean-cut/sharp features *or* face; **Gesichter** *or* **Grimassen ~** to make *or* pull faces; **die Luft ist zum S~** (*fig inf*) the air is very bad; **die Atmosphäre ist zum S~** (*fig inf*) you could cut the atmosphere with a knife; **jdn ~** (*beim Überholen*) to cut in on sb; (*ignorieren*) to cut sb dead; **weit/eng geschnitten sein** (*Sew*) to be cut wide/narrow.
(b) *Film, Tonband* to edit.
(c) (*inf: operieren*) to operate on; *Furunkel* to lance ◆ **jdn ~** to cut sb open (*inf*); (*bei Geburt*) to give sb an episiotomy; **geschnitten werden** (*bei Geburt*) to have an episiotomy.
[3] *vr* **(a)** (*Mensch*) to cut oneself ◆ **sich in den Finger** *etc* **~** to cut one's finger *etc*; *siehe* **Fleisch**.
(b) (*inf: sich täuschen*) **da hat er sich aber geschnitten!** he's made a big mistake, he's very mistaken.
(c) (*Linien, Straßen etc*) to intersect.
schneidend *adj* biting; *Hohn, Bemerkung auch* cutting; *Wind, Kälte auch* piercing, bitter; *Schmerz* sharp, searing; *Stimme, Ton* piercing.
Schneider *m* **-s, - (a)** (*Beruf*) tailor; (*Damen~*) dressmaker; *siehe* **frieren**.
(b) (*Cards*) **einen ~ machen** to score half (the full) points; **im ~ sein** to have less than half points; **aus dem ~ sein** to have slightly more than half points; (*fig*) to be out of the woods.
(c) (*Gerät*) cutter; (*inf: für Brot etc*) slicer.
(d) (*Schnake*) daddy-longlegs.
Schneideraum *m* (*Film~*) cutting room, editing suite.
Schneiderei *f* **(a)** *no pl* (*Handwerk*) tailoring; (*für Damen*) dressmaking. **(b)** (*Werkstatt*) tailor's/dressmaker's.
Schneider-: ~geselle *m* journeyman tailor/dressmaker; **~handwerk** *nt* tailoring *no art*; dressmaking *no art*.
Schneiderin *f siehe* **Schneider (a)**.
Schneider-: ~kostüm *nt* tailored suit; **~kreide** *f* tailor's chalk; **~lehrling** *m* tailor's/dressmaker's apprentice; **~meister** *m* master tailor/dressmaker.
schneidern [1] *vi* (*beruflich*) to be a tailor/dressmaker; (*als Hobby*) to do dressmaking.
[2] *vt* to make, to sew; *Herrenanzug* to tailor, to make.
Schneider-: ~puppe *f* tailor's/dressmaker's dummy; **~sitz** *m* **im ~sitz sitzen** to sit cross-legged; **~werkstatt** *f* tailor's/dressmaker's workshop.
Schneide-: ~tisch *m* (*Film*) editing *or* cutting table; **~werkzeug** *nt* cutting tool; **~zahn** *m* incisor.
schneidig *adj* dashing, sharp; *Musik* rousing; *Tempo* fast.

⚠: for details of spelling reform, see supplement

Schneidigkeit *f* (*von Mensch*) dashing character; (*von Musik*) rousing character *or* tempo; (*von Tempo*) speed.

schneien [1] *vi impers* to snow.
[2] *vt impers* **es schneit dicke Flocken** big flakes (of snow) are falling; **es schneite Konfetti** confetti rained down.
[3] *vi aux sein* (*fig*) to rain down ◆ **jdm ins Haus ~** (*inf*) (*Besuch*) to drop in on sb; (*Rechnung, Brief*) to arrive through one's letterbox *or* in the post.

Schneise *f* **-, -n** break; (*Wald~*) aisle, lane; (*Feuer~*) firebreak; (*Flug~*) path.

schnell *adj* quick; *Bedienung, Fahrt, Tempo, Läufer auch* fast; *Auto, Zug, Verkehr, Fahrer, Strecke* fast; *Schritte, Puls, Verbesserung auch* fast, rapid; *Abreise, Bote, Hilfe* speedy; *Antwort auch* speedy, prompt; *Genesung, Besserung* quick, rapid, speedy ◆ **~ gehen/fahren** to walk/drive quickly *or* fast; **etw in ~em Tempo singen** to sing sth quickly *or* fast; **er kam in ~em Lauf dahergerannt** he came running up quickly; **sie wird ~ böse/ist ~ verärgert** she loses her temper quickly, she is quick to get angry; **er ist sehr ~ mit seinem Urteil/seiner Kritik** he's very quick to judge/to criticize; **nicht so ~!** not so fast!; **kannst du das vorher noch ~ machen?** (*inf*) can you do that quickly first?; **ich muß mir nur noch ~ die Haare kämmen** I must just give my hair a quick comb; **sein Puls ging ~** his pulse was very fast; **das geht ~** (*grundsätzlich*) it doesn't take long; **das mache ich gleich, das geht ~** I'll do that now, it won't take long; **das ging ~** that was quick; **es ist mit dem Patienten ~ gegangen** it was all over quickly; **mit dicker Wolle geht es ~, einen Pullover zu stricken** knitting a pullover with thick wool is very quick; **an der Grenze ist es ~ gegangen** things went very quickly at the border; **das ging alles viel zu ~** it all happened much too quickly *or* fast; **das werden wir ~ erledigt haben** we'll soon have that finished; **~ machen!** hurry (up)!; **das werde ich so ~ nicht vergessen/wieder tun** *etc* I won't forget that/do that *etc* again in a hurry; **das werden wir ~ sehen** (*bald*) we'll soon see about that; **diese dünnen Gläser gehen ~ kaputt** these thin glasses break easily; **~es Geld/eine ~e Mark (machen)** (*inf*) (to make) a fast buck (*inf*); *siehe* **Schnelle**.

⚠ **Schnelläufer** *m getrennt*: **Schnell-läufer** (*Sport*) sprinter; (*Astron*) high-velocity star; (*Tech*) high-speed machine.

Schnell-: **~bahn** *f* high-speed railway; **~bauweise** *f* high-speed building methods *pl*; **~boot** *nt* speedboat; **~dienst** *m* express service; **~drucker** *m* high-speed printer.

Schnelle *f* **-, -n** **(a)** *no pl* (*Schnelligkeit*) quickness, speed. **(b)** (*Strom~*) rapids *pl*. **(c) etw auf die ~ machen** to do sth quickly *or* in a rush; **das läßt sich nicht auf die ~ machen** we can't rush that, that will take time; **Sex/ein Bier auf die ~** (*inf*) a quickie (*inf*).

⚠ **schnellebig** *adj getrennt*: **schnell-lebig** *Zeit* fast-moving.

schnellen *vi aux sein* (*lit, fig*) to shoot ◆ **in die Höhe ~** to shoot up; **ein Gummiband ~ lassen** to flick a rubber band.

Schnellfeuer *nt* (*Mil*) rapid fire.

Schnellfeuer-: **~geschütz** *nt* automatic rifle; **~gewehr** *nt* automatic pistol; **~waffe** *f* rapid-fire weapon.

Schnell-: **s~füßig** *adj* (*geh*) fleet-footed (*liter*), fleet of foot (*liter*); **~gaststätte** *f* fast-food restaurant, cafeteria, fast-food store (*US*); **~gericht** *nt* **(a)** (*Jur*) summary court; **(b)** (*Cook*) convenience food; **~hefter** *m* spring folder.

Schnelligkeit *f* (*von Auto, Verkehr, Abreise*) speed; (*von Bewegung, Tempo auch*) quickness; (*von Schritten, Besserung, Verbesserung auch, von Puls*) rapidity; (*von Bote, Hilfe*) speediness; (*von Antwort*) speediness, promptness.

Schnell-: ⚠**~imbiß** *m* **(a)** (*Essen*) (quick) snack; **(b)** (*Raum*) snack-bar; **~kochplatte** *f* high-speed ring; **~kochtopf** *m* (*Dampfkochtopf*) pressure cooker; (*Wasserkochtopf*) ≃ electric kettle; **~kraft** *f* (*von Feder, Sprungbrett*) springiness, resilience; (*von Sportler, Fischen*) ability to jump; **~kurs** *m* crash course; **~läufer** *m siehe* **Schnelläufer**; **s~lebig** *adj siehe* **schnellebig**; **~paket** *nt* express parcel; **~presse** *f* high-speed printing machine *or* press; **~reinigung** *f* express cleaning service; **~rücklauf** *m* fast rewind; **~schrift** *f* (*Comput*) draft quality.

schnellstens *adv* as quickly as possible.

Schnell-: **~straße** *f* expressway; **~suchlauf** *m* rapid search; **~verfahren** *nt* (*Jur*) summary trial; (*Mil*) summary court-martial; **im ~verfahren abgeurteilt werden** to be sentenced by a summary trial/court-martial; **~verkehr** *m* fast traffic; (*im Transportwesen*) express service; **etw im ~verkehr schicken** to send sth express delivery; **~vorlauf** *m* fast forward; **~zug** *m* fast train; **~zugzuschlag** *m* supplementary charge for travel on a fast train; (*inf: Karte*) supplementary ticket.

Schnepfe *f* **-, -n** snipe; (*pej inf*) silly cow (*sl*).

schnetzeln *vt* (*S Ger, Sw*) *Frucht, Gemüse* to slice; *Fleisch* to shred.

⚠ **schneuzen** [1] *vr* to blow one's nose.
[2] *vt* **einem Kind/sich die Nase ~** to blow a child's/one's nose.

Schnickschnack *m* **-s,** *no pl* (*inf*) (*Unsinn*) twaddle (*inf*) *no indef art*, poppycock (*inf*) *no indef art*; (*Kinkerlitzchen*) paraphernalia (*inf*) *no indef art* ◆ **ach ~!** (*dated*) balderdash! (*dated inf*), fiddlesticks! (*dated inf*).

schniefen *vi* (*dial*) (*bei Schnupfen*) to sniff(le); (*beim Weinen*) to sniffle, to snivel.

schniegeln (*inf*) [1] *vt Kleidung, Kinder, Auto* to spruce up.
[2] *vr* to get spruced up, to spruce oneself up; *siehe* **geschniegelt**.

schnieke *adj* (*N Ger sl: schick*) swish (*inf*).

schnipp *interj* snip ◆ **~, schnapp** snip, snip.

Schnippchen *nt* (*inf*) **jdm ein ~ schlagen** to play a trick on sb, to trick sb; **dem Tod ein ~ schlagen** to cheat death.

Schnippel *m or nt* **-s, -** (*inf*) *siehe* **Schnipsel**.

schnippeln *vti* (*inf*) to snip (*an +dat* at); (*mit Messer*) to hack (*an +dat* at) ◆ **an ihr haben die Ärzte schon was geschnippelt!** she has already been hacked about a bit by the doctors (*inf*).

schnippen [1] *vi* **mit den Fingern ~** to snap one's fingers.
[2] *vt* **etw von etw ~** to flick sth off *or* from sth.

schnippisch *adj* saucy, pert.

Schnipsel *m or nt* **-s, -** (*inf*) scrap; (*Papier~*) scrap *or* bit of paper.

schnipseln *vti* (*inf*) *siehe* **schnippeln**.

schnipsen *vti* (*inf*) *siehe* **schnippen**.

schnitt *pret of* **schneiden**.

Schnitt *m* **-(e)s, -e** **(a)** cut; (*Kerbe auch*) notch, nick; (*Med auch*) incision; (*von Heu, Getreide*) crop ◆ **Blumen für den ~** flowers (suitable) for cutting.
(b) (*Haar~*) (hair)cut ◆ **einen kurzen ~ bitte** cut it short please.
(c) (*Sew*) cut; (*~muster*) pattern.
(d) (*Form*) (*von Edelstein*) cut; (*von Gesicht, Augen*) shape; (*von Profil*) line.
(e) (*Film*) editing *no pl* ◆ **der Film ist jetzt beim ~** the film is now being edited *or* cut; **~: L. Schwarz** editor — L. Schwarz.
(f) (*Math*) (*~punkt*) (point of) intersection; (*~fläche*) section; (*inf: Durch~*) average ◆ **im ~** on average; *siehe* **golden**.
(g) (*Längs~, Quer~*) section ◆ **im ~ gezeichnet** drawn in section.
(h) (*inf: Gewinn*) profit.
(i) (*Typ*) (*das Beschneiden*) cut; (*Buchrand*) (trimmed) edge ◆ **dann kommt das gebundene Buch zum ~** then the bound book is cut *or* trimmed.
(j) (*Hort: von Bäumen etc*) cutting *no indef art*.

Schnitt-: **~blumen** *pl* cut flowers *pl*; (*im Garten*) flowers (suitable) for cutting; **~bohnen** *pl* French *or* green beans *pl*.

Schnitte *f* **-, -n** slice; (*belegt*) open sandwich; (*zusammengeklappt*) sandwich ◆ **womit soll ich dir die ~ belegen?** what shall I put on your (slice of) bread?

Schnitt|ebene *f* (*Math*) sectional plane.

Schnitter(in *f*) *m* **-s, -** reaper.

Schnitt-: **s~fest** *adj Tomaten* firm; **~fläche** *f* section.

schnittig *adj* smart; *Mann, Auto, Formen auch* stylish; *Tempo auch* snappy (*inf*) ◆ **er ist ganz schön ~ gefahren** he nipped *or* zipped along (*inf*).

Schnitt-: **~lauch** *m, no pl* chives *pl*; **~lauchlocken** *pl* (*hum inf*) straight hair; **~linie** *f* (*Math*) line of intersection; (*Sew*) cutting line; **~menge** *f* (*Math*) intersection; **~muster** *nt* (*Sew*) (paper) pattern; **~musterbogen** *m* (*Sew*) pattern chart; **~punkt** *m* (*von Straßen*) intersection; (*Math auch*) point of intersection; **~stelle** *f* cut; (*Comput*) interface; **~winkel** *m* angle of intersection; **~wunde** *f* cut; (*tief*) gash.

Schnitz *m* **-es, -e** (*S Ger, Aus*) piece; (*von Orange auch*) segment; (*von Apfel auch*) slice.

Schnitz|arbeit *f siehe* **Schnitzerei**.

Schnitzel[1] *nt or m* **-s, -** (*Papier~*) bit *or* scrap of paper; (*Holz~*) shaving; (*Fetzen, Karotten~, Kartoffel~*) shred, sliver ◆ **~** *pl* (*Abfälle*) scraps *pl*.

Schnitzel[2] *nt* **-s, -** (*Cook*) veal/pork cutlet, schnitzel.

Schnitzeljagd *f* paper-chase.

schnitzeln *vt Gemüse* to shred; *Holz* to chop (up) (into sticks).

schnitzen *vti* to carve ◆ **wir haben in der Schule S~ gelernt** we learnt wood carving at school; *siehe* **Holz**.

Schnitzer *m* **-s, -** **(a)** wood carver. **(b)** (*inf*) (*in Benehmen*) blunder, boob (*Brit inf*), goof (*US inf*); (*Fehler*) howler (*inf*).

Schnitzerei *f* (wood-)carving.

Schnitzerin *f siehe* **Schnitzer (a)**.

Schnitz-: **~kunst** *f* (art of) wood carving; **~messer** *nt* wood-carving knife; **~werk** *nt* (wood) carving.

schnob (*old*) *pret of* **schnauben**.

schnodd(e)rig *adj* (*inf*) rude and offhand, brash.

Schnodd(e)rigkeit *f* (*inf*) brashness.

schnöd(e) *adj* (*niederträchtig*) despicable, contemptible, base; *Geiz, Verrat* base; *Gewinn* vile; *Behandlung, Ton, Antwort* contemptuous, disdainful ◆ **~r Mammon/~s Geld** filthy lucre; **jdn ~ verlassen** to leave sb in a most despicable fashion.

Schnödigkeit *f* **(a)** (*Gemeinheit*) despicableness, contemptibleness, baseness; (*Geringschätzung*) contempt *no pl*, disdain *no pl*. **(b)** (*gemeine Handlung, Bemerkung*) despicable *or* contemptible thing (to do/say).

Schnorchel *m* **-s, -** (*von U-Boot, Taucher*) snorkel; (*~maske*) snorkel mask.

Schnörkel *m* **-s, -** flourish; (*an Möbeln, Säulen*) scroll; (*fig: Unterschrift*) squiggle (*hum*), signature.

schnörkelig *adj* ornate; *Schrift auch* full of flourishes; *Rede auch* flowery.

schnörkellos *adj* without frills.

schnorren *vti* (*inf*), to cadge (*inf*) to scrounge (*inf*) (*bei* from).

Schnorrer(in *f*) *m* **-s, -** (*inf*) cadger (*inf*), scrounger (*inf*).

Schnösel *m* **-s, -** (*inf*) snotty(-nosed) little upstart (*inf*).

schnöselig *adj* (*inf*) *Benehmen, Jugendlicher* snotty (*inf*), snotty-nosed (*inf*).

Schnuckelchen *nt* (*inf*) sweetheart, pet, baby (*esp US*).

schnuckelig *adj* (*inf*) (*gemütlich*) snug, cosy; *Wärme* cosy; (*niedlich*) cute.

Schnüffelei *f* (*inf*) **(a)** (*von Hund, Mensch*) snuffling *no pl*, sniffing *no pl*; (*von Mensch auch*) sniffling *no pl*. **(b)** (*fig: das Spionieren*) snooping *no pl* (*inf*).

schnüffeln *vi* **(a)** (*schnuppern, riechen*) to sniff; (*Hund auch*) to snuffle ◆ **an etw** (*dat*) **~** to sniff (at) sth. **(b)** (*bei Erkältung etc*) to sniffle, to snuffle. **(c)** (*fig inf: spionieren*) to snoop around (*inf*), to nose around *or* about (*inf*). **(d)** (*von Drogen*) to sniff.

Schnüffler(in *f*) *m* **-s, -** (*inf*) (*fig*) snooper (*inf*), Nosey Parker (*inf*); (*Detektiv*) sleuth (*inf*), private eye (*inf*); (*von Drogen*) glue-sniffer.

Schnuller *m* **-s, -** (*inf*) dummy (*Brit*), pacifier (*US*); (*auf Flasche*) teat (*Brit*), nipple (*US*).

Schnulze f -, -n (inf) schmaltzy film/book/song (inf) ◆ **das sind alles ~n** it's all schmaltz (inf).

schnulzig adj (inf) slushy, soppy, schmaltzy (all inf).

schnupfen vti Kokain to snort, to sniff ◆ **Tabak ~** to take snuff; **willst du auch ~?** would you like some snuff too?

Schnupfen m -s, - cold, headcold ◆ **(einen) ~ bekommen, sich (dat) einen ~ holen** (inf) to catch (a) cold; **(einen) ~ haben** to have a cold.

Schnupfer(in f) m -s, - snuff-taker.

Schnupf-: ~tabak m snuff; **~tabak(s)dose** f snuffbox; **~tuch** nt (S Ger) handkerchief, hanky (inf).

schnuppe adj pred (inf) **jdm ~ sein** to be all the same to sb; **das Wohl seiner Angestellten ist ihm völlig ~** he couldn't care less (inf) about the welfare of his employees.

schnuppern [1] vi (Hund, Mensch) to sniff; (Hund auch) to snuffle ◆ **an etw** (dat) **~** to sniff (at) sth.
[2] vt to sniff.

Schnur f -, ⸚e (Bindfaden) string; (Kordel, an Vorhang) cord; (Litze) braid no indef art, no pl, piping no indef art, no pl; (Zelt~) guy (rope); (Angel~) (fishing) line; (Kabel) flex, lead.

Schnür-: ~band nt lace; **~boden** m (Theat) flies pl.

Schnürchen nt dim of **Schnur** bit of string ◆ **es läuft** or **geht** or **klappt alles wie am ~** everything's going like clockwork; **etw wie am ~ hersagen** to say or recite sth off pat.

schnüren [1] vt Paket, Strohbündel to tie up; Schuhe auch, Mieder to lace (up); Körper to lace in ◆ **Schuhe zum S~** lace-up shoes, lace-ups.
[2] vi (a) (inf: eng sein) to be too tight. (b) aux sein (Hunt) to run in a straight line.
[3] vr (Frauen) to lace oneself up or in.

Schnur-: s~gerade adj (dead) straight; **s~gerade auf jdn/etw zugehen** to make a bee-line for sb/sth (inf), to go straight up to sb/sth; **~keramik** f (Archeol) string ceramics sing.

Schnürleibchen nt siehe **Schnürmieder**.

schnurlos adj Telefon cordless.

Schnürl- (Aus): **~regen** m pouring or streaming rain; **~samt** m corduroy.

Schnürmieder nt lace-up corset.

Schnurrbart m moustache (Brit), mustache (US).

schnurrbärtig adj with a moustache, mustachioed.

Schnurre f -, -n (a) (Erzählung) funny story. (b) (Posse) farce.

schnurren vi (Katze) to purr; (Spinnrad etc) to hum, to whirr.

Schnurrhaare pl whiskers pl.

Schnürriemen m siehe **Schnürsenkel**.

schnurrig adj amusing, droll; alter Mann quaint, funny.

Schnür-: ~schuh m lace-up or laced shoe; **~senkel** m shoelace; (für Stiefel) bootlace; **~stiefel** m lace-up or laced boot.

schnurstracks adv straight, directly ◆ **du gehst jetzt ~ nach Hause!** you are to go straight home (now), you are to go home directly; **~ auf jdn/etw zugehen** to make a bee-line for sb/sth (inf), to go straight up to sb/sth.

schnurz adj (inf) **das ist ihm ~** he couldn't care less (about it) (inf), he couldn't give a darn (about it) (inf).

Schnute f -, -n (inf) (Mund) mouth; (Schmollmund) pout; (pej: Mundwerk) big mouth (inf) ◆ **eine ~ ziehen** or **machen** to pout, to pull a face.

schob pret of **schieben**.

Schober m -s, - (S Ger, Aus) (a) (Scheune) barn. (b) (Heuhaufen) haystack or -rick.

Schock[1] nt -(e)s, -e (obs) three score (old).

Schock[2] m -(e)s, -s or (rare) -e (Schreck, elektrisch) shock ◆ **unter ~ stehen** to be in (a state of) shock.

schockant adj (dated) shocking.

Schock-: ~behandlung f shock therapy; (elektrisch auch) electro-convulsive therapy; **~einwirkung** f state of shock; **unter ~einwirkung stehen** to be in (a state of) shock.

schocken vt (inf) to shock ◆ **jdn elektrisch ~** (Med) to give sb an electric shock, to administer an electric shock to sb (form).

Schocker m -s, - (inf) shock film/novel, film/novel aimed to shock.

Schockfarbe f electric colour.

schockieren* vti to shock; (stärker) to scandalize ◆ **sich leicht ~ lassen** to be easily shocked; **~d** shocking; **schockiert sein** to be shocked (über +acc at).

Schock-: ~therapie f shock therapy; (elektrisch auch) electro-convulsive therapy; **s~weise** adv (obs) by the three score (old).

schofel, schof(e)lig adj (inf) Behandlung, Ausrede mean, rotten no adv (inf); Spende, Geschenk, Mahlzeit miserable.

Schöffe m -n, -n ≃ juror.

Schöffen-: ~amt nt ≃ jury service; **~bank** f ≃ jury bench; **~gericht** nt court (with jury); **einen Fall vor einem ~gericht verhandeln** ≃ to try a case by jury.

Schöffin f ≃ juror.

schoflig adj (inf) siehe **schofel**.

Schokolade f chocolate.

Schokoladen- in cpds chocolate; **s~braun** adj chocolate-coloured; ⚠**~guß** m chocolate icing; **~raspel** f chocolate flake; **~riegel** m chocolate bar; **~seite** f (fig) attractive side; **sich von seiner ~seite zeigen** to show oneself at one's best.

Schokoriegel m chocolate bar.

Scholastik f scholasticism.

Scholastiker(in f) m -s, - scholastic.

scholastisch adj scholastic.

scholl (old) pret of **schallen**.

Scholle[1] f -, -n (Fisch) plaice.

Scholle[2] f -, -n (Eis~) (ice) floe; (Erd~) clod (of earth) ◆ **mit der ~ verbunden sein** (fig) to be a son of the soil.

Scholli m: **mein lieber ~!** (inf) (drohend) now look here!; (erstaunt) my goodness me!, my oh my!

schon adv (a) (bereits) already; (in Fragen: überhaupt ~) ever ◆ **er ist ~ da** he's there already, he's already there; **ist er ~ da?** is he there yet?; **warst du ~ dort?** have you been there yet?; (je) have you ever been there?; **danke, ich habe ~** (inf) no thank you, I have some (already); **ich habe den Film ~ gesehen** I've already seen that film, I've seen that film before; **ich werde ~ bedient** I'm (already) being served; **mußt du ~ gehen?** must you go already or so soon?; **ich bin ~ drei Jahre alt** I'm *three* (years old); **er wollte ~ die Hoffnung aufgeben, als ...** he was just about to give up hope when ...
(b) (mit Zeitangaben) **ich warte nun ~ seit drei Wochen** I've already been waiting (for) three weeks; **~ vor drei Wochen** three weeks ago; **~ am frühen Morgen** early in the morning; **~ damals** even then; **~ damals, als ...** even when ...; **~ früher wußte man ...** even in years gone by they knew ...; **~ vor 100 Jahren/im 13. Jahrhundert** as far back as 100 years ago/as early or as far back as the 13th century; **das haben wir ~ gestern** or **gestern ~ gemacht** we did that yesterday; **~ am nächsten Tag** the very next day; **es ist ~ 11 Uhr** it's 11 o'clock already; **der Briefträger kommt ~ um 6 Uhr** the postman comes as early as 6 o'clock; **kommt er ~ heute?** will he come today (already)?
(c) **~ (ein)mal** before; (in Fragen: je) ever; **ich habe das ~ mal gehört** I've heard that before; **warst du ~ (ein)mal dort?** have you ever been there?; **ich habe Sie ~ (ein)mal gesehen** I've met or seen you before somewhere; **ich habe dir ~ *(ein)mal* gesagt, daß ...** I've already told you once that ...; **das habe ich dir doch ~ *hundertmal* gesagt** I've told you that a hundred times (before); **ich habe das Buch ~ zweimal gelesen** I've read that book twice already; **das habe ich ~ oft gehört** I've heard that often; **das ist ~ längst vorbei/vergessen** that's long past/forgotten; **das ist ~ längst erledigt** that was done a long time ago or was done ages ago; **ich bin ~ lange fertig** I've been ready for ages; **wie lange wartest du ~?** how long have you been waiting?; **wartest du ~ lange?** have you been waiting (for) long?; **wie ~ so oft** as so often (before); **wie ~ erwähnt** as has (already) been mentioned; **~ immer** always; **ich habe ~ immer dunkle Haare** I've always had dark hair; **~ wieder zurück** back already; **da ist sie ~ wieder** (zum x-ten Male) there she is again, she's back again; (~ zurück) she's back already; **was, ~ wieder?** what — *again*?; **was denn nun ~ wieder?** what is it *now*?, *now* what is it?
(d) (allein, bloß) just; (ohnehin) anyway ◆ **allein ~ das Gefühl ...** just the very feeling ...; **~ die Tatsache, daß ...** just the fact that ..., the very fact that ...; **wenn ich das ~ sehe/höre/lese!** if I even see/hear/read that!; **~ deswegen** if only because of that; **~ weil** if only because.
(e) (bestimmt) all right ◆ **du wirst ~ sehen** you'll see (all right); **das wirst du ~ noch lernen** you'll learn that one day; **sie wird es ~ machen** (don't worry,) she'll do it (all right); (schaffen) she'll manage it all right.
(f) (ungeduldig) **hör ~ auf damit!** will you stop that!; **so antworte ~!** come on, answer; **geh ~** go on; **nun sag ~!** come on, tell me/us etc; **mach ~!** get a move on! (inf), get on with it!; **wenn doch ~ ...!** if only ...; **ich komme ja ~!** I'm just coming!, I'm on my way! (inf).
(g) (tatsächlich, allerdings) really ◆ **das ist ~ eine Frechheit!** what a cheek!, that's a real cheek!; **das ist ~ etwas, (wenn ...)** it's really something (if ...); **da gehört ~ Mut/Geschick etc dazu** that takes real courage/skill etc; **da müßten wir ~ großes Glück haben** we'd be very lucky; **du müßtest ~ etwas mehr arbeiten** you really ought to work a bit harder; **das ist ~ möglich** that's quite possible, that's not impossible; **das mußt du ~ machen!** you really ought to do that.
(h) (bedingt) siehe **wenn, wennschon**.
(i) (einschränkend) **~** or **ja ~, aber ...** (inf) yes (well), but ...; **da haben Sie ~ recht, aber ...** yes, you're right (there), but ...
(j) (in rhetorischen Fragen) **was macht das ~, wenn ...** what(ever) does it matter if ...; (was hilft das ~) what(ever) use is it if ...; **wer fragt ~ danach, ob ...** who wants to know if ...; **aber wer fragt ~ danach** (resignierend) but, no-one wants to know; **500 km, was ist das ~ bei den heutigen Flugverbindungen?** 500 km is nothing with today's air travel; **10 Mark, was ist das ~, was sind heute ~ 10 Mark?** 10 marks goes nowhere these days, what's 10 marks these days?; **die paar Tropfen, was ist das ~, das ist doch kein Regen** a few drops, what are you talking about, that's not rain; **3 Seiten schreiben, was ist das ~?** write 3 pages? that's nothing.
(k) (inf: Füllwort) **und wenn ~!, na wenn ~!** so what? (inf); **~ gut!** all right, okay (inf); **ich verstehe ~** I understand; **ich weiß ~** I know; **danke, es geht ~** thank you, I/we etc will manage; **so kannst du das ~ gar nicht machen!** that's even more impossible, you *certainly* can't do that; **für Krimis gebe ich kein Geld aus, und für Pornoheftchen ~ gar nicht** I won't spend money on thrillers and certainly not on pornography.

schön [1] adj (a) (hübsch anzusehen) beautiful, lovely; Mann handsome ◆ **das S~e** beauty; **~es Fräulein** (old, hum) my pretty one or maid (old); **na, ~es Kind** (inf) well then, beautiful (inf).
(b) (nett, angenehm) good; Erlebnis, Stimme, Musik, Wetter auch lovely; Gelegenheit great, splendid ◆ **die ~en Künste** the fine arts; **die ~e Literatur** belles-lettres; **das ist ein ~er Tod** that's a good way to die; **eines ~en Tages** one fine day; **(wieder) in ~ster Ordnung** (nach Krach etc) back to normal (again); **in ~ster Eintracht/Harmonie** in perfect harmony; **das S~e beim Skilaufen ist ...** the nice thing about skiing is ...; **das S~ste daran ist ...** the beauty of it is ...,

⚠: for details of spelling reform, see supplement

the nicest *or* best thing about it is ...; **~e Ferien/~en Urlaub!** have a good *or* nice holiday; **~es Wochenende** have a good *or* nice weekend; **~en guten Tag** a very good morning/evening *etc* to you; **war es ~ im Urlaub/bei Tante Veronika?** did you have a nice *or* good holiday/did you have a nice *or* good time at Aunty Veronika's?; ~, daß du gekommen bist (how) nice of you to come; **~er, heißer Kaffee** nice hot coffee; **ein ~er frischer Wind** a nice fresh wind.

(c) (*iro*) *Unordnung* fine, nice, lovely; *Überraschung, Wetter* lovely; *Unsinn, Frechheit* absolute ◆ **da hast du etwas S~es angerichtet** you've made a fine *or* nice *or* lovely mess/muddle; **du bist mir ein ~er Freund/Vater/Held** *etc* a fine friend/father/hero *etc* you are, you're some friend/father/hero *etc*; **du machst** *or* **das sind mir ja ~e Sachen** *or* **Geschichten** here's *or* this is a pretty state of things, here's a pretty kettle of fish (*inf*); **von dir hört man ~e Sachen** *or* **Geschichten** I've been hearing some nice *or* fine things about you; **das wäre ja noch ~er** (*inf*) that's (just) too much!; **es wird immer ~er** (*inf*) things are going from bad to worse; *siehe* **Bescherung.**

(d) (*inf: gut*) nice ◆ **das war nicht ~ von dir** (*inf*) that wasn't very nice of you; **zu ~, um wahr zu sein** (*inf*) too good to be true; ~, ~, **(also) ~, sehr ~, na ~** fine, okay, all right; **~ und gut, aber** ... (that's) all well and good but ..., that's all very well but ...

(e) (*beträchtlich, groß*) *Erfolg* great; *Strecke, Stück Arbeit, Alter* good ◆ **ein ~es Stück weiterkommen** to make good progress; **eine ganz ~e Leistung/Arbeit/Menge** quite an achievement/quite a lot of work/quite a lot; **das hat eine ~e Stange Geld gekostet** (*inf*) that cost a pretty penny.

[2] *adv* **(a)** (*bei Verben*) (*gut*) well; *sich waschen, verarbeiten lassen* easily; *scheinen* brightly; *schreiben* beautifully; (*richtig, genau*) *ansehen, durchlesen etc* carefully ◆ **sich ~ anziehen** to get dressed up; **es ~ haben** to be well off; (*im Urlaub etc*) to have a good time (of it); **etw am ~sten machen** to do sth best; *siehe* **danke, bitte.**

(b) (*angenehm*) **~ weich/warm/stark** *etc* nice and soft/warm/strong *etc.*

(c) (*bei Wünschen*) **schlaf ~** sleep well; **amüsiere dich ~** have a nice *or* good time; **erhole dich ~** have a good rest; *siehe* **grüßen.**

(d) (*inf: brav, lieb*) nicely ◆ **iß mal ~ deinen Teller leer** eat it all up nicely (now), be a good girl/boy and eat it all up; **sag ~ „Guten Tag"** say "hallo" nicely; **sei ~ still/ordentlich** *etc* (*als Aufforderung*) be nice and quiet/tidy *etc*; **sei ~ brav** be a good boy/girl; **fahr ~ langsam** drive nice and slowly; *siehe* **bleibenlassen.**

(e) (*inf: sehr, ziemlich*) (*vor Verb, Partizip*) really; (*vor Adjektiv auch*) pretty ◆ **sich** (*dat*) **~ weh tun** to hurt oneself a lot; **sich ~ täuschen** to make a big mistake; **sich ~ ärgern** to be very angry; **jdn ~ erschrecken** to give sb quite a *or* a real fright; **ganz ~ teuer/kalt** pretty expensive/cold; **~ weit weg** a long *or* good way off, quite a distance away; **ganz ~ lange** quite a while; **~ viel Geld kosten** to cost a pretty penny.

Schonbezug *m* (*für Matratzen*) mattress cover; (*für Möbel*) loose cover; (*für Autositz*) seat cover.

Schöndruck *m* (*Typ*) first printing.

Schöne *f* **-n, -n** (*liter, hum: Mädchen*) beauty, belle (*liter, hum*) ◆ **nun, ihr beiden ~n** (*inf*) now, my beauties (*inf*).

schonen [1] *vt Gesundheit, Herz, Körperteil, Buch, Kleider* to look after, to take care of; *eigene Nerven* to go easy on; *jds Nerven, Gefühle, Kraft* to spare; *Gegner, Kind* to be easy on; (*nicht stark beanspruchen*) *Teppich, Schuhsohlen* to save; (*Mensch*) *Bremsen, Auto* to go easy on; *Füße,* (*iro*) *Gehirn* to save; (*schützen*) to protect ◆ **ein Waschmittel, das die Hände/Wäsche schont** a detergent that is kind to your hands/washing; **ein Licht, das die Augen schont** lighting that is easy on *or* kind to the eyes; **sie trägt eine Schürze, um ihre Kleider zu ~** she wears an apron to save her clothes; **er muß den Arm noch ~** he still has to be careful with *or* look after his arm; **um seine Nerven/die Nerven seiner Mutter zu ~** for the sake of his/his mother's nerves; **ein Beruf, der die Nerven nicht gerade schont** a job that isn't exactly easy on the nerves; **du brauchst mich nicht zu ~, sag ruhig die Wahrheit** you don't need to spare me *or* my feelings — just tell me the truth.

[2] *vr* to look after *or* take care of oneself; (*Patient auch*) to take things easy.

schönen *vt* **(a)** *Farbe* to brighten. **(b)** *Wein* to clarify. **(c)** *Statistik, Zahlen* to dress up.

schonend *adj* gentle; (*rücksichtsvoll*) considerate; *Waschmittel auch, Politur* mild ◆ **jdm etw ~ beibringen** to break sth to sb gently; **jdn ~ behandeln** to be *or* go easy on sb; *Kranken* to treat gently; **etw ~ behandeln** to treat sth with care, to look after sth.

Schoner[1] *m* **-s, -** (*Naut*) schooner.

Schoner[2] *m* **-s, -** cover; (*für Rückenlehnen*) antimacassar, chairback; (*Ärmel~*) sleeve-protector.

Schön-: s~färben *sep* [1] *vt* (*fig*) to gloss over; [2] *vi* to gloss things over; **~färber** *m* (*fig*) someone who tends to gloss things over; **~färberei** *f* (*fig*) glossing things over.

Schon-: ~frist *f* period of grace; **eine ~frist von 12 Tagen** 12 days' grace; **~gang** *m* (*bei Waschmaschine*) gentle action wash.

Schöngeist *m* aesthete.

schöngeistig *adj* aesthetic ◆ **~e Literatur** belletristic literature.

Schönheit *f* beauty.

Schönheits-: ~chirurgie *f* cosmetic surgery; **~fehler** *m* blemish; (*von Gegenstand*) flaw; **~fleck** *m* beauty spot; **~ideal** *nt* ideal of beauty; **~königin** *f* beauty queen; **~konkurrenz** *f* beauty contest; **~korrektur** *f* correction of an imperfection/imperfections; (*fig*) cosmetic alteration; **~operation** *f* cosmetic operation; **~pflästerchen** *nt* (artificial) beauty spot; **~pflege** *f* beauty care; **~salon** *m* beauty parlour *or* salon; **~sinn** *m* sense of beauty; **~wettbewerb** *m* beauty contest.

Schonkost *f* light diet; (*Spezialdiät*) special diet.

Schönling *m* (*pej*) pansy (*inf*), pretty boy (*inf*).

Schön-: s~machen *sep* [1] *vt Kind* to dress up; *Wohnung, Straßen* to decorate; [2] *vr* to get dressed up, to dress (oneself) up; (*sich schminken*) to make (oneself) up; [3] *vi* (*Hund*) to sit up (and beg); **s~reden** *vi sep* to use flattery; **das ~reden** smooth talking, flattery; **~redner** *m* flatterer, smooth-talker.

Schönschreibdrucker *m* letter-quality printer.

Schönschreiben *nt* (*Sch*) writing.

Schönschreibheft *nt* writing book; (*mit vorgedruckten Buchstaben*) copy-book.

Schönschrift *f* **in ~** in one's best (copy-book) (hand)writing.

schönstens *adv* most beautifully; *bitten, fragen* respectfully ◆ **jdn ~ grüßen** to give sb one's kindest regards.

Schön-: ~tuerei *f* flattery, blandishments *pl*, soft-soap (*inf*); **s~tun** *vi sep irreg* **jdm s~tun** (*schmeicheln*) to flatter *or* soft-soap (*inf*) sb; (*sich lieb Kind machen*) to pay court to sb, to play *or* suck (*inf*) up to sb.

Schonung *f* **(a)** (*Waldbestand*) (protected) forest plantation area.

(b) (*das Schonen*) (*von Gefühlen, Kraft*) sparing; (*von Teppich, Schuhsohlen, Kleider*) saving; (*das Schützen*) protection ◆ **der Patient/Arm braucht noch ein paar Wochen ~** the patient/arm still needs looking after for a few weeks; **zur ~ meiner Gefühle/der Gefühle anderer** to spare my feelings/the feelings of others; **auf ~ seiner Gesundheit/Nerven Wert legen** to value one's health/to attach importance to the state of one's nerves; **zur ~ Ihrer Augen/Waschmaschine** to look after your eyes/washing machine; **zur ~ des Getriebes** to give your gears a longer life.

(c) (*Nachsicht, Milde*) mercy.

Schonungs-: s~bedürftig *adj* in need of care; (*in bezug auf Gefühle, Nerven*) in need of careful handling; **s~los** *adj* ruthless, merciless; *Wahrheit* blunt; *Kritik* savage; **~losigkeit** *f* ruthlessness, mercilessness; (*von Kritik*) savageness; **mit einer solchen ~losigkeit** so ruthlessly, so mercilessly; so savagely; **s~voll** *adj* gentle.

Schonwald *m* protected woodland.

Schönwetter *nt* (*lit*) fine weather ◆ **~ machen** (*fig inf*) to smooth things over; **bei jdm um ~ bitten** (*fig inf*) to be as nice as pie to sb (*inf*).

Schönwetter-: ~front *f* warm front; **~periode** *f* period of fine weather; **~wolke** *f* (*inf*) cloud that means good weather.

Schonzeit *f* close season; (*fig*) honeymoon period.

Schopf *m* **-(e)s, ¨e** (shock of) hair; (*von Vogel*) tuft, crest ◆ **jdn beim ~ packen** to grab sb by the hair; **eine Gelegenheit beim ~ ergreifen** *or* **packen** *or* **fassen** to seize *or* grasp an opportunity with both hands.

schöpfen *vt* **(a)** *auch vi* (*aus* from) *Wasser* to scoop; *Suppe* to ladle; *Papier* to dip ◆ **Wasser aus einem Boot ~** to bale out a boat.

(b) *Atem* to draw, to take; *Mut, Kraft* to summon up; *Vertrauen, Hoffnung* to find ◆ **Vertrauen/Hoffnung/Mut** *etc* **aus etw ~** to draw confidence/hope/courage *etc* from sth.

(c) *auch vi* (*old: schaffen*) *Kunstwerk* to create; *neuen Ausdruck, Wörter auch* to coin, to invent.

Schöpfer *m* **-s, - (a)** creator; (*Gott*) Creator ◆ **seinem ~ danken** to thank one's Maker *or* Creator. **(b)** (*inf: Schöpflöffel*) ladle. **(c)** (*Papier~*) paper maker.

Schöpfer-: ~geist *m* creative spirit; (*Rel*) Holy Spirit; **~hand** *f* (*Rel*) Hand of the Creator.

Schöpferin *f siehe* **Schöpfer (a, c).**

schöpferisch *adj* creative ◆ **~er Augenblick** moment of inspiration, creative moment; **~e Pause** (*hum*) pause for inspiration; **~ tätig sein** to be creative.

Schöpferkraft *f* creative power, creativity.

Schöpf-: ~kelle *f*, **~löffel** *m* ladle.

Schöpfung *f* creation; (*Wort, Ausdruck*) coinage, invention ◆ **die ~** (*Rel*) the Creation; (*die Welt*) Creation; *siehe* **Herr, Krone.**

Schöpfungs-: ~bericht *m*, **~geschichte** *f* story of the Creation; **~tag** *m* (*Rel*) day of the Creation.

schöppeln *vti* (*dial*) **(einen) ~** to have a drink.

Schoppen *m* **-s, - (a)** (*old: Flüssigkeitsmaß*) half-litre (measure); (*S Ger: Glas Wein*) glass of wine; (*S Ger: Glas Bier*) ≃ half-pint of beer, glass of beer.

(b) (*dial: Beisammensein*) **zum ~ gehen** to go for a drink; **sich beim ~ treffen** to meet for *or* over a drink.

(c) (*S Ger, Sw: Babyfläschchen*) bottle.

schoppenweise *adv* (*dial*) by the glass(ful).

Schöps *m* **-es, -e** (*Aus*) *siehe* **Hammel.**

Schöpserne(s) *nt decl as adj* (*Aus*) lamb; mutton.

schor *pret of* **scheren**[1].

Schorf *m* **-(e)s, -e (a)** crust, scaly skin; (*Wund~*) scab. **(b)** (*Pflanzenkrankheit*) scab.

schorfig *adj* **(a)** *Wunde* that has formed a scab; *Haut* scaly. **(b)** *Pflanzen* scabby.

Schorle *f* **-, -n** *or nt* **-s, -s** spritzer.

Schornstein *m* chimney; (*von Schiff, Lokomotive*) funnel, (smoke)stack; (*von Fabrik auch*) stack ◆ **etw in den ~ schreiben** (*inf*) to write sth off (as a dead loss *inf*); **damit der ~ raucht** (*inf*) to keep body and soul together.

Schornstein-: ~brand *m* chimney fire; **~feger(in** *f***), ~kehrer(in** *f***)** *m* **-s, -** chimney-sweep.

Schose *f* **-, -n** (*dated inf*) *siehe* **Chose.**

⚠ **schoß** *pret of* **schießen.**

⚠ **Schoß**[1] *m* **-sses, -sse** (*Bot*) shoot.

Schoß[2] **-es, ¨e** *m* **(a)** lap ◆ **die Hände in den ~ legen** (*lit*) to put one's hands

in one's lap; (*fig*) to sit back (and take it easy); **das ist ihm nicht in den ~ gefallen** (*fig*) it wasn't handed (to) him on a plate, it didn't just fall into his lap; *siehe* **Abraham**.
(b) (*liter*) (*Mutterleib*) womb; (*Scheide*) vagina ◆ **im ~e der Familie/Kirche** in the bosom of one's family/of the church; **im ~ der Erde** in the bowels of the earth.
(c) (*an Kleidungsstück*) tail.

Schoß[3] *f* **-, -en** *or* **¨-e** (*Aus*) skirt.
Schößchen *nt dim of* **Schoß**[2] **(c)**.
Schößchenjacke *f* peplum jacket.
Schoß-: ~hund *m* lap-dog; **~kind** *nt* spoilt child; **Mamas ~kind** mummy's little boy/girl; **ein ~kind des Glücks** (*geh*) a child of Fortune.
⚠**Schößling** *m* (*Bot*) shoot.
Schot *f* **-, -en, Schote** *f* **-, -n** (*Naut*) sheet.
Schote *f* **-, -n (a)** (*Bot*) pod ◆ **~n** (*inf: Erbsen*) peas (in the pod). **(b)** (*inf*) yarn, tall story.
Schott *nt* **-(e)s, -e(n)** (*Naut*) bulkhead ◆ **die ~en dichtmachen** (*inf*) to close up shop.
Schotte *m* **-n, -n** Scot, Scotsman ◆ **er ist ~** he's a Scot, he's Scottish; **die ~n** the Scots, the Scottish.
Schotten-: ~karo, ~muster *nt* tartan; **Rock mit** *or* **im ~muster** tartan skirt; **~preis** *m* (*hum*) rock-bottom price; **~rock** *m* tartan skirt; kilt.
Schotter *m* **-s, -** gravel; (*im Straßenbau*) (road-)metal; (*Rail*) ballast; (*inf: Geld*) dough (*inf*).
Schotterdecke *f* gravel surface.
schottern *vt siehe n* to gravel (over); to metal; to ballast.
Schotterstraße *f* gravel road.
Schottin *f* Scot, Scotswoman ◆ **sie ist ~** she's a Scot, she's Scottish; **die ~nen** Scottish women, Scotswomen.
schottisch *adj* Scottish, Scots.
Schottland *nt* **-s** Scotland.
schraffieren* *vt* to hatch.
Schraffierung, Schraffur *f* hatching.
schräg [1] *adj* **(a)** (*schief, geneigt*) sloping; *Schrift auch* slanting; *Augen* slanted, slanting; *Kante* bevelled.
(b) (*nicht gerade, nicht parallel*) oblique; *Linie auch* diagonal.
(c) (*inf: verdächtig*) suspicious, fishy (*inf*) ◆ **ein ~er Vogel** a queer fish (*inf*).
(d) *Musik, Vorstellungen, Leute* weird.
[2] *adv* **(a)** (*geneigt*) at an angle; *halten* on the slant, slanting; (*krumm auch*) skew, off the straight, skew-whiff (*inf*) ◆ **den Hut ~ aufsetzen** to put one's hat on at an angle; **~ stehende Augen** slanting *or* slanted eyes.
(b) (*nicht gerade, nicht parallel*) obliquely; *überqueren, gestreift* diagonally; (*Sew*) on the bias; *schneiden* on the cross *or* bias ◆ **~ gegenüber/hinter** diagonally opposite/behind; **~ rechts/links** diagonally to the right/left; **~ rechts/links abbiegen** (*Auto, Fähre*) to bear *or* fork right/left; **die Straße biegt ~ ab** the road forks off; **~ gedruckt** in italics; **den Kopf ~ halten** to hold one's head at an angle *or* cocked to one side; **~ parken** to park at an angle; **die Sonne schien ~ ins Fenster** the sun slanted in through the window; **jdn ~ ansehen** *or* **angucken** (*lit*) to look at sb out of the corner of one's eye; (*fig*) to look askance at sb; **~ zum Hang queren/fahren** to traverse; **~ zum Fadenlauf** on the bias.
Schrägband *nt siehe* **Schrägstreifen (b)**.
Schräge *f* **-, -n (a)** (*schräge Fläche*) slope, sloping surface; (*schräge Kante*) bevel(led edge). **(b)** (*Schrägheit*) slant, angle; (*von Dach auch*) pitch, slope; (*im Zimmer*) sloping ceiling ◆ **eine ~ haben** to be on the slant, to slope, to slant; (*Zimmer*) to have a sloping ceiling.
schrägen *vt* to chamfer; *Kanten* to bevel.
Schrägheck *nt* (*am Auto*) coupé back; (*Auto*) coupé.
Schrägheit *f* slant, angle; (*von Wand auch*) slope; (*von Dach auch*) pitch, slope; (*von Schrift, Augen*) slant.
Schräg-: ~kante *f* bevelled edge; **~lage** *f* angle, slant; (*von Flugzeug*) bank(ing); (*im Mutterleib*) oblique position; **etw in ~lage bringen/aufbewahren** to put/keep sth at an angle *or* on the slant; **das Baby ist in ~lage** the baby is in an oblique position; **s~laufend** *adj* diagonal, oblique; **~linie** *f* diagonal line, oblique (line); **~schrift** *f* (*Handschrift*) slanting hand(writing) *or* writing; (*Typ*) italics *pl*; **~streifen** *m* **(a)** (*Muster*) diagonal stripe; **(b)** (*Sew*) bias binding; **~strich** *m* oblique.
schrak (*old*) *pret of* **schrecken**.
Schramme *f* **-, -n** scratch.
Schrammelmusik *f popular Viennese music for violins, guitar and accordion.*
Schrammeln *pl* (*Aus*) *quartet playing Schrammelmusik.*
schrammen [1] *vt* to scratch ◆ **sich** (*dat*) **den Arm/sich ~** to scratch one's arm/oneself.
[2] *vi* **über den Boden ~** to scrape across the floor; **haarscharf am Bankrott ~** to come within an inch of bankruptcy.
Schrank *m* **-(e)s, ¨-e** cupboard, closet (*US*); (*Kleider~*) wardrobe; (*für Bücher*) bookcase; (*im Wohnzimmer, Vitrinen~, Medizin~ auch*) cabinet; (*Platten~*) record cabinet; (*Umkleide~, Mil: Spind*) locker; (*inf: Mann*) giant; *siehe* **Tasse**.
Schrankbett *nt* fold-away bed.
Schränkchen *nt dim of* **Schrank** small cupboard; (*Arznei~, im Badezimmer*) cabinet; (*neben dem Bett*) bedside cupboard *or* cabinet.
Schranke *f* **-, -n (a)** barrier; (*Barrikade*) barricade; (*Rail: Gatter*) gate; (*fig*) (*Grenze*) limit; (*Hindernis*) barrier ◆ **vor den ~n des Gerichts** before the court; **keine ~n kennen** to know no bounds; (*Mensch*) not to know when to stop; **er kennt keine ~n mehr** there's no restraining him; **sich in ~n halten** to keep *or* to remain within reasonable limits; **meine Begeisterung hält sich in ~n** I'm not exactly overwhelmed by it; **etw in ~n halten** to keep sth within reasonable limits *or* bounds; **einer Sache** (*dat*) **(enge) ~n setzen** to put a limit on sth; **seiner Geduld sind keine ~n gesetzt** his patience knows no bounds.
(b) ~n *pl* (*Hist*) lists *pl* ◆ **jdn in die ~n fordern** (*fig*) to challenge sb; **jdn in seine ~n (ver)weisen** (*fig*) to put sb in his place.
Schranken *m* **-s, -** (*Aus*) (level-crossing) barrier.
Schranken-: s~los *adj* (*fig*) *Weiten* boundless, unbounded, unlimited; *Verhalten, Forderungen, Ansprüche* unrestrained, unbridled; **~losigkeit** *f siehe adj* boundlessness; unrestraint (*gen* in), unrestrainedness; **~wärter** *m* gatekeeper (*at level crossing*).
Schrank-: ~fach *nt* shelf; **im obersten ~fach** on the top shelf; **s~fertig** *adj Wäsche* washed and ironed; **~koffer** *m* wardrobe trunk; **~spiegel** *m* wardrobe mirror; **~wand** *f* wall unit.
Schränkzange *f* saw set pliers.
Schrapnell *nt* **-s, -e** *or* **-s** shrapnel.
Schrapper *m* **-s, -** scraper.
Schrat, Schratt *m* **-(e)s, -e** forest demon.
Schraubdeckel *m* screw(-on) lid.
Schraube *f* **-, -n (a)** screw; (*ohne Spitze*) bolt ◆ **bei ihr ist eine ~ locker** (*inf*) she's got a screw loose (*inf*). **(b)** (*Naut, Aviat*) propeller, prop (*inf*). **(c)** (*Sport*) twist. **(d) alte ~** (*pej inf*) old bag (*inf*).
schrauben *vti* to screw ◆ **etw höher/niedriger ~** to screw sth up/down; **etw fester ~** to screw sth tighter; **etw in die Höhe ~** (*fig*) *Preise, Rekorde* to push sth up; *Ansprüche, Erwartungen* to raise; **etw niedriger ~** (*fig*) to lower sth; **das Flugzeug schraubte sich in die Höhe** the plane spiralled upwards; *siehe* **geschraubt**.
Schrauben-: ~bolzen *m* bolt; **~dampfer** *m* propeller-driven steamer; **~dreher** *m siehe* **~zieher**; **~gewinde** *nt* screw thread; **~kopf** *m* screw head; **~mutter** *f* nut; **~schlüssel** *m* spanner; **~windung** *f* screw thread; (*Umdrehung*) turn; **~zieher** *m* **-s, -** screwdriver.
Schraub-: ~fassung *f* screw fixture (*on light bulb*); **~stock** *m* vice; **etw wie ein ~stock umklammern** (*fig*) to clasp sth in a vice-like grip; ⚠**~verschluß** *m* screw top *or* cap.
Schrebergarten *m* allotment (*Brit*), garden plot.
Schreck *m* **-s,** (*rare*) **-e** fright, scare ◆ **vor ~** in fright; *zittern* with fright; **zu meinem großen ~(en)** to my great horror *or* dismay; **einen ~(en) bekommen** to get a fright *or* scare; **jdm einen ~(en) einjagen** to give sb a fright *or* scare; **der ~ fuhr mir in die Glieder** *or* **Knochen** my knees turned to jelly (*inf*); **mir sitzt** *or* **steckt der ~ noch in allen Gliedern** *or* **Knochen** my knees are still like jelly (*inf*); **auf den ~ (hin)** to get over the fright; **sich vom ersten ~ erholen** to recover from the initial shock; **mit dem ~(en) davonkommen** to get off *or* escape with no more than a fright; **ach du ~** (*inf*) (oh) crumbs! (*inf*), blast! (*inf*); **o ~ laß nach** (*hum inf*) for goodness sake! (*inf*), for heaven's sake! (*inf*).
Schreckbild *nt* terrible *or* awful vision, nightmare.
schrecken *pret* **schreckte**, *ptp* **geschreckt** [1] *vt* **(a)** (*ängstigen*) to frighten, to scare; (*stärker*) to terrify ◆ **jdn aus dem Schlaf/aus seinen Träumen ~** to startle sb out of his sleep/dreams.
(b) (*Cook*) to dip quickly in cold water.
[2] *pret auch* (*old*) **schrak**, *ptp auch* (*old*) **geschrocken** *vi* **(a)** *aux sein* **aus dem Schlaf/aus den Gedanken ~** to be startled out of one's sleep/be startled.
(b) (*Hunt*) to start up.
Schrecken *m* **-s, - (a)** (*plötzliches Erschrecken*) *siehe* **Schreck**.
(b) (*Furcht, Entsetzen*) terror, horror ◆ **einer Sache** (*dat*) **den ~ nehmen** to make a thing less frightening *or* terrifying; **er war der ~ der ganzen Lehrerschaft** he was the terror of all the teachers; **das Gleichgewicht des ~s** the balance of terror; *siehe* **Ende**.
⚠**schrecken|erregend** *adj* terrifying, horrifying.
Schreckens-: ⚠**s~blaß, s~bleich** *adj* as white as a sheet *or* ghost; **~botschaft** *f* terrible *or* alarming piece of news; **~herrschaft** *f* (reign of) terror; **~kammer** *f* chamber of horrors; **~nachricht** *f* terrible news *no pl or* piece of news; **~tat** *f* atrocity; **~vision** *f* terrifying *or* terrible vision, nightmare.
Schreck-: ~gespenst *nt* nightmare; **das ~gespenst des Krieges/der Inflation** the bogey of war/inflation; **s~haft** *adj* easily startled; *Mensch auch* jumpy (*inf*); **~haftigkeit** *f* nervousness; jumpiness (*inf*).
schrecklich *adj* terrible, dreadful; (*inf: sehr, groß auch*) awful, frightful; *Freude* great ◆ **er war ~ in seinem Zorn** (*geh*) his wrath was terrible (to behold) (*liter*); **sich ~ freuen** (*inf*) to be terribly *or* awfully *or* frightfully pleased; **~ gerne!** (*inf*) I'd absolutely love to; **~ schimpfen** to swear dreadfully *or* terribly.
Schrecknis *nt* (*old*) horror(s *pl*), terror(s *pl*).
Schreck-: ~schraube *f* (*pej inf*) (old) battle-axe (*inf*); (*in bezug auf Äußeres*) dolled-up old bag (*sl*); ⚠**~schuß** *m* (*lit*) warning shot; **einen ~schuß abgeben** (*lit, fig*) to give *or* fire a warning shot; ⚠**~schußpistole** *f* blank gun; **~sekunde** *f* moment of shock.
Schrei *m* **-(e)s, -e** cry, shout; (*brüllender*) yell; (*gellender*) scream; (*kreischender*) shriek; (*von Vogel, von Wild*) cry, call; (*von Esel*) bray; (*von Eule etc*) screech; (*von Hahn*) crow ◆ **einen ~ ausstoßen** to give a cry *or* shout/yell/scream *or* shriek; **einen ~ unterdrücken** to suppress a cry; **ein spitzer ~** a sharp cry; **der ~ nach Freiheit/Rache** the call for freedom/revenge; **ein ~ der Entrüstung** an (indignant) outcry; **der letzte ~** (*inf*) the latest thing, all the rage (*inf*); **nach dem letzten ~ gekleidet** (*inf*) dressed in the latest style *or* in the height of fashion.

Schreib-: ~art *f* style; **~bedarf** *m* writing materials *pl*, stationery; **alles, was Sie für Ihren ~bedarf brauchen** everything you need in the way of writing materials *or* stationery; **~block** *m* (writing) pad.

Schreibe *f* (*inf*) writing.

schreiben *pret* **schrieb**, *ptp* **geschrieben** 1 *vt* **(a)** to write; (*ausstellen*) *Scheck auch, Rechnung* to make out, to write out; (*mit Schreibmaschine*) to type (out); *Klassenarbeit, Übersetzung, Examen* to do; (*berichten: Zeitung etc*) to say; (*nieder~*) to write (down) ◆ **sie schreibt einen guten Stil** she has *or* writes a good style; **jdm** *or* **an jdn einen Brief ~** to write a letter to sb, to write sb a letter; **jdm ein paar Zeilen ~** to write *or* drop sb a few lines, to write a few lines to sb; **etw auf Diskette ~** to write sth to disk; **sich** (*dat*) **etw von der Seele** *or* **dem Herzen ~** to get sth off one's chest; **wo steht das geschrieben?** where does it say that?; **es steht geschrieben** (*Rel*) it is written; **es steht Ihnen auf der Stirn** *or* **im Gesicht geschrieben** it's written all over your face; *siehe* **Handschrift, Stern[1], krank, gesund.**
(b) (*orthographisch*) to spell ◆ **ein Wort falsch ~** to misspell a word, to spell a word wrong(ly); **etw groß/klein ~** to write *or* spell sth with a capital/small letter.
(c) (*Datum*) **wir ~ heute den 10. Mai** today is the 10th May; **den Wievielten ~ wir heute?** what is the date today?; **man schrieb das Jahr 1939** the year was 1939, it was (in) 1939.
(d) (*verbuchen*) **jdm etw auf sein (Bank)konto/die Rechnung ~** to credit sth to sb's (bank) account/to put sth on sb's bill.
2 *vi* to write; (*Schriftsteller sein auch*) to be a writer; (*tippen*) to type; (*berichten*) to say ◆ **jdm ~** to write to sb, to write sb (*US*); **ich schrieb ihm, daß ...** I wrote and told him that ...; **er schreibt orthographisch richtig** his spelling is correct; **an einem Roman** *etc* **~** to be working on *or* writing a novel *etc*; **über etw** (*acc*) **~** (*abhandeln*) to write about sth; (*Univ auch*) to work on sth; **ich kann nicht mit der Maschine ~** I can't type; **wieviel Silben schreibt sie pro Minute?** what is her (typing) speed?, how many words a minute can *or* does she do?; **mit Bleistift ~** to write in pencil, to write with a pencil; **hast du was zum S~?** have you something *or* anything to write with?
3 *vr impers* to write ◆ **mit diesem Kuli schreibt es sich gut/schlecht** this biro writes well/doesn't write properly; **auf diesem Papier schreibt es sich gut/schlecht** this paper is easy *or* good/difficult to write on.
4 *vr* **(a)** (*korrespondieren*) to write (to one another *or* to each other), to correspond ◆ **ich schreibe mich schon lange mit ihm** (*inf*) I've been writing to him for a long time.
(b) (*geschrieben werden*) to be spelt ◆ **wie schreibt er sich?** how does he spell his name?, how is his name spelt?; **wie schreibt sich das?** how is that spelt?, how do you spell that?
(c) (*dated: heißen*) to call oneself ◆ **seit wann schreibst du dich wieder mit deinem Mädchennamen?** how long have you been calling yourself by your maiden name again?

Schreiben *nt* **-s, - (a)** *no pl* writing. **(b)** (*Mitteilung*) communication (*form*); (*Brief auch*) letter.

Schreiber *m* **-s, - (a)** (*Verfasser*) writer, author; (*Brief~*) (letter-)writer; (*Hist*) scribe; (*Angestellter, Gerichts~*) clerk; (*Sw: Schriftführer*) secretary; (*pej: Schriftsteller*) scribbler.
(b) (*inf: Schreibgerät*) writing implement ◆ **einen/keinen ~ haben** to have something/nothing to write with.
(c) (*Tech*) (*Fahrten~*) tachograph; (*an Meßgerät*) recording instrument, recorder; (*Fern~*) teleprinter, telex.

Schreiberei *f* (*inf*) (*das Schreiben, Geschriebenes*) writing *no indef art*; (*Schriftverkehr*) paperwork *no indef art, no pl*; (*pej: von Schriftsteller*) scribbling.

Schreiberin *f siehe* **Schreiber (a).**

Schreiberling *m* (*pej*) (*Schriftsteller*) scribbler; (*kleiner Angestellter*) pen-pusher.

Schreib-: s~faul *adj* lazy (about letter-writing); **ich bin s~faul** I'm no great letter-writer, I'm a poor correspondent; **~faulheit** *f* laziness (about letter-writing); **~feder** *f* (pen) nib; (*Federhalter*) ink pen; (*Gänse~*) quill (pen); **~fehler** *m* (spelling) mistake; (*aus Flüchtigkeit*) slip of the pen; (*Tippfehler*) (typing) mistake *or* error; **~gerät** *nt* writing implement; (*Tech*) recording instrument, recorder; **s~geschützt** *adj* (*Comput*) write-protected; **~heft** *nt* exercise book; (*Schönschreibheft*) copy-book; **~kraft** *f* typist; **~krampf** *m* writer's cramp; **einen ~krampf (in der Hand) bekommen** to get writer's cramp; **~-/Lesekopf** *m* (*Comput*) read-write head; **~maschine** *f* typewriter; **auf** *or* **mit der ~maschine schreiben** to type; **mit der ~maschine geschrieben** typewritten, typed; **~maschinenpapier** *nt* typing paper; **~material** *nt* writing materials *pl*, stationery *no pl*; **~papier** *nt* (typing) paper; (*Briefpapier*) writing paper, letter paper, notepaper; **~pult** *nt* (writing) desk; **~schrift** *f* cursive (hand)writing, script; (*Typ*) script; **~schutz** *m* (*Comput*) write protection; **s~schützen** *vt* (*Comput*) to write-protect; **~stelle** *f* (*Comput*) cursor position; **~stellenmarke** *f* (*Comput: Cursor*) cursor; **~stift** *m* (*auch Comput*) pen; **~stube** *f* (*Hist*) writing room; (*Büro*) (typists') office, typing room; (*Mil*) orderly room; **~tafel** *f* (*Hist*) tablet; (*für Schüler*) slate; (*Wandtafel*) blackboard; **~tisch** *m* desk; **~tischtäter** *m* mastermind *or* brains *sing* behind the scenes (of a/the crime); **~übung** *f* writing exercise.

Schreibung *f* spelling ◆ **falsche ~ eines Namens** misspelling of a name.

Schreib-: s~unkundig *adj* unable to write; **~unterlage** *f* pad; (*auf ~tisch*) desk pad; **ein Buch als ~unterlage benutzen** to use a book to rest (one's paper) on; **~waren** *pl* stationery *sing*, writing materials *pl*; **~warenhändler** *m* stationer; **~warenhandlung** *f* stationer's (shop), stationery shop; **~weise** *f* (*Stil*) style; (*Rechtschreibung*) spelling; **~werk** *nt* typing mechanism; **~werkaufzug** *m* carriage return; **~zeug** *nt* writing things *pl*; **~zimmer** *nt* (*Büro*) (typists') office, typing room; (*von Schriftsteller*) study.

schreien *pret* **schrie**, *ptp* **geschrie(e)n** 1 *vi* to shout, to cry out; (*gellend*) to scream; (*vor Angst, vor Schmerzen*) to cry out/to scream; (*kreischend*) to shriek; (*brüllen*) to yell; (*inf: laut reden*) to shout; (*inf: schlecht und laut singen*) to screech; (*heulen, weinen: Kind*) to howl; (*jammern*) to moan; (*Esel*) to bray; (*Vogel, Wild*) to call; (*Eule, Käuzchen etc*) to screech; (*Hahn*) to crow ◆ **vor Lachen ~** to roar *or* hoot with laughter; (*schrill*) to scream with laughter; **es war zum S~** (*inf*) it was a scream (*inf*) *or* a hoot (*inf*); **nach jdm ~** to shout for sb; **nach etw ~** (*fig*) to cry out for sth; *siehe* **Hilfe.**
2 *vt Befehle etc* to shout (out) ◆ **jdm etw ins Gesicht ~** to shout sth in sb's face.
3 *vr* **sich heiser ~** to shout oneself hoarse; (*Baby*) to cry itself hoarse; **sich** (*dat*) **die Kehle heiser** *or* **aus dem Hals ~** (*inf*) to shout oneself hoarse, to shout one's head off (*inf*).

schreiend *adj Farben* loud, garish, gaudy; *Unrecht* glaring, flagrant.

Schreier(in *f*) *m* **-s, -** (*inf*) (*Baby*) bawler (*inf*); (*Unruhestifter*) rowdy, noisy troublemaker; (*fig: Nörgler*) moaner, grouser (*inf*).

Schreierei *f* (*inf*) bawling (*inf*) *no pl*, yelling *no pl*.

Schrei-: ~hals *m* (*inf*) (*Baby*) bawler (*inf*); (*Unruhestifter*) rowdy, noisy troublemaker; **~krampf** *m* screaming fit.

Schrein *m* **-(e)s, -e** (*geh*) shrine; (*Reliquien~ auch*) reliquary; (*old: Sarg*) coffin.

Schreiner(in *f*) *m* **-s, -** (*esp S Ger*) carpenter.

schreinern (*esp S Ger*) 1 *vi* to do carpentry ◆ **mein Mann kann gut ~** my husband is good at carpentry *or* woodwork *or* is a good carpenter.
2 *vt* to make.

schreiten *pret* **schritt**, *ptp* **geschritten** *vi aux sein* (*geh*) (*schnell gehen*) to stride; (*liter: Zeit*) to march on; (*feierlich gehen*) to walk; (*vorwärts*) to proceed; (*stolzieren*) to strut, to stalk ◆ **im Zimmer auf und ab ~** to stride *or* pace up and down the room; **zu etw ~** (*fig*) to get down to sth, to proceed with sth; **es wird Zeit, daß wir zur Tat ~** it's time we got down to work *or* action; **zum Äußersten ~** to take extreme measures; **zur Abstimmung/Wahl ~** to proceed *or* go to a vote.

schrie *pret of* **schreien.**

schrieb *pret of* **schreiben.**

Schrieb *m* **-s, -e** (*inf*) missive (*hum*).

Schrift *f* **-, -en (a)** writing; (*Hand~ auch*) handwriting; (*~system*) script; (*Typ*) type, typeface, font ◆ **gotische** *or* **deutsche ~ schreiben** to write in the Roman/Cyrillic alphabet *or* in (the) Cyrillic script; **er hat eine schlechte ~** he has bad handwriting, he writes *or* has a poor hand.
(b) (*~stück*) document; (*Bericht*) report; (*Eingabe*) petition.
(c) (*Broschüre*) leaflet; (*Buch*) work; (*kürzere Abhandlung*) paper ◆ **seine früheren ~en** his early writings *or* works; **Schopenhauers sämtliche ~en** the complete works of Schopenhauer; **die (Heilige) ~** the (Holy) Scriptures *pl*.

Schrift-: ~art *f* (*Hand~*) script; (*Typ*) type, typeface; **~auslegung** *f* (*Bibl*) interpretation (of the Bible); **~bild** *nt* script; **~deutsch** *nt* (*nicht Umgangssprache*) written German; (*nicht Dialekt*) standard German; **~deutung** *f* graphology.

Schriften-: ~nachweis *m*, **~verzeichnis** *nt* bibliography.

Schrift-: ~form *f* (*Jur*) **dieser Vertrag erfordert die ~form** this contract must be drawn up in writing; **~führer** *m* secretary; (*Protokollführer auch*) clerk; **~gelehrte(r)** *m* (*Bibl*) scribe; **~gießer** *m* typefounder; **~grad** *m* type size; ⚠**~guß** *m* typefounding; **~höhe** *f* x-height (*spec*), height of the type; **~kunst** *f* calligraphy; **~leiter** *m* editor; **~leitung** *f* (*Redaktionsstab*) editorial staff *pl*; (*Redaktionsleitung*) editorship; **~lesung** *f* (*Eccl*) lesson.

schriftlich 1 *adj* written ◆ **in ~er Form/auf ~em Wege** in writing; **die ~e Prüfung, das S~e** (*inf*) the written exam; **ich habe nichts S~es darüber** I haven't got anything in writing.
2 *adv* in writing ◆ **ich bin ~ eingeladen worden** I have had a written invitation; **ich muß mich bei ihm ~ für das Geschenk bedanken** I must write and thank him for the present; **etw ~ festhalten/niederlegen/machen** (*inf*) to put sth down in writing; **das kann ich Ihnen ~ geben** (*fig inf*) I can tell you that for free (*inf*).

Schrift-: ~linie *f* (*Typ*) type line; **~probe** *f* (*Hand~*) specimen of one's handwriting; (*Typ*) specimen (proof); **~rolle** *f* scroll; **~sachverständige(r)** *mf* handwriting expert; **~satz** *m* **(a)** (*Jur*) legal document; **(b)** (*Typ*) form(e); **~setzer** *m* typesetter, compositor, comp (*Typ sl*); **~sprache** *f* (*nicht Umgangssprache*) written language; (*nicht Dialekt*) standard language; **die französische ~sprache** written/(good) standard French; **s~sprachlich** *adj Ausdruck, Konstruktion* used in the written language; **s~sprachlich würde man ... sagen** in the written language one would say ...

Schriftsteller *m* **-s, -** author, writer.

Schriftstellerei *f* writing.

Schriftstellerin *f* author(ess), writer.

schriftstellerisch *adj* literary ◆ **~ tätig sein** to write; **er ist ~ begabt** he has literary talent *or* talent as a writer.

schriftstellern* *vi insep* (*inf*) to try one's hand at writing *or* as an author ◆ **der ~de General Patschke** General Patschke, who also writes in his free time.

Schriftstellername *m* pen name, nom de plume.

Schrift-: ~stück *nt* paper; (*Jur*) document; **~tum** *nt*, *no pl* literature; **~verkehr** *m* correspondence; **im ~verkehr stehen** to be in correspondence; **~wechsel** *m siehe* **~verkehr**; **~zeichen** *nt* character; **~zug** *m usu pl* stroke; (*Duktus*) hand.

➤ SPRACHE AKTIV: **schreiben: 1a** → 48.1, 48.2

schrill *adj Ton, Stimme* shrill; *(fig) Mißton, Mißklang* jarring; *Fest, Musik* brash; *Farbe* garish ♦ **sie lachte ~ auf** she gave a shriek *or* screech of laughter; **~ angezogen sein** to be loudly dressed.

schrillen *vi* to shrill; *(Stimme auch)* to sound shrilly.

Schrippe *f* **-, -n** *(dial)* (bread) roll.

schritt *pret of* **schreiten.**

Schritt *m* **-(e)s, -e (a)** *(lit, fig)* step; *(weit ausholend)* stride; *(hörbar)* footstep ♦ **mit schnellen/langsamen ~en** quickly/slowly, with quick/slow steps; **mit schleppenden ~en** dragging one's feet, with dragging feet; **sie näherte sich ihm mit trippelnden ~en** she tripped towards him; **einen ~ zurücktreten/zur Seite gehen** to step back/aside *or* to one side; **~ vor ~ setzen** to put one foot in front of the other; **ein paar ~e spazierengehen** to go for *or* take a short walk *or* stroll; **einen ~ machen** *or* **tun** to take a step; **kleine** *or* **kurze/große** *or* **lange ~e machen** to take small steps/long strides; **ich habe seit Wochen keinen/kaum einen ~ aus dem Haus getan** I haven't/have hardly set foot outside the house for weeks; **die ersten ~e machen** *or* **tun** to take one's first steps; *(fig)* to take the first step; **den ersten ~ tun** *(fig)* to make the first move; *(etw beginnen)* to take the first step; **den ~ tun** *(fig)* to take the plunge; **~e gegen jdn/etw unternehmen** to take steps against sb/sth; **im gleichen ~ und Tritt** *(lit, fig)* in step; **auf ~ und Tritt** *(lit, fig)* wherever *or* everywhere one goes; **~ um** *or* **für ~** step by step; *(fig auch)* little by little, gradually; **Politik der kleinen ~e** step-by-step *or* gradualistic policy.

(b) *(Gang)* walk, gait; *(Tempo)* pace ♦ **~ halten** *(lit, fig)* to keep pace, to keep up; **mit der Zeit ~ halten** to keep abreast of the times; **einen schnellen/unwahrscheinlichen ~ am Leib** *(inf) or* **an sich** *(dat)* **haben** to walk quickly/incredibly quickly; **gemessenen/leichten/langsamen ~es** *(geh)* with measured/light/slow step(s) *or* tread; **seinen ~** *or* **seine ~e beschleunigen/verlangsamen** *(geh)* to increase/slow one's pace, to speed up/slow down; **den ~ anhalten** to stop.

(c) *(~geschwindigkeit)* walking pace ♦ **(im) ~ fahren** to go at a crawl, to drive at walking speed; **„~fahren"** "dead slow"; **im ~ reiten/gehen** to walk.

(d) *(Maßangabe)* ≃ yard ♦ **mit zehn ~** *or* **~en Abstand** at a distance of ten paces; **sich** *(dat)* **jdn drei ~(e) vom Leib halten** *(inf)* to keep sb at arm's length.

(e) *(Hosen~)* crotch; *(~weite)* crotch measurement.

Schrittempo *nt getrennt* **Schritt-tempo** walking speed ♦ **im ~ fahren** to crawl along; **„~"** "dead slow".

Schrittlänge *f* length of one's stride.

Schrittmacher *m (Sport, Med)* pacemaker; *(fig auch)* pacesetter ♦ **die Universitäten waren ~ der Revolution** the universities were in the van(guard) of *or* led the way in the revolution.

Schrittmacher-: ~dienste *pl (fig)* **jdm ~dienste leisten** to smooth the path *or* way for sb; **~maschine** *f (Sport)* pacemaker.

Schritt-: ~tempo *nt siehe* **Schrittempo**; **s~weise** [1] *adv* gradually, little by little; [2] *adj* gradual; **~weite** *f (Sew: von Hose)* (waist-to-)crotch measurement; *(von Kleid, Rock)* hemline; **~zähler** *m* pedometer.

schroff *adj (rauh, barsch)* curt, brusque; *(kraß, abrupt) Übergang, Bruch* abrupt; *(steil, jäh) Fels, Klippe* precipitous, steep ♦ **das ~e Nebeneinander von Arm und Reich** the stark juxtaposition of rich and poor; **~e Gegensätze** stark *or* sharp contrasts.

Schroffheit *f siehe adj* curtness, brusqueness; abruptness; precipitousness, steepness; *(schroffes Wort)* curt remark.

schröpfen *vt (Blut absaugen)* to bleed, to cup *(old)* ♦ **jdn ~** *(fig)* to fleece sb *(inf)*, to rip sb off *(sl)*.

Schröpfkopf *m (Med)* cupping glass.

Schrot *m or nt* **-(e)s, -e (a)** whole-corn/-rye *etc* meal; *(Weizen)* wholemeal *(Brit)*, wholewheat *(US)* ♦ **ein Schotte von echtem ~ und Korn** a true Scot; **er ist ein Bauer von echtem ~ und Korn** he is a farmer through and through; **vom alten ~ und Korn** *(fig)* of the old school.

(b) *(Hunt)* shot ♦ **einem Hasen eine Ladung ~ aufbrennen** *(inf)* to pepper a hare with shot.

Schrot-: ~brot *nt* whole-corn/-rye *etc* bread; wholemeal *(Brit) or* wholewheat *(US)* bread; **~büchse** *f (Hunt)* shotgun; **~effekt** *m (Elec)* shot effect.

schroten *vt Getreide* to grind coarsely; *Alteisen* to break up.

Schrot-: ~flinte *f* shotgun; **~korn** *nt* **(a)** grain; **(b)** *(Hunt)* pellet; **~kugel** *f* pellet; **~ladung** *f* round of shot; **~mehl** *nt* whole-corn/-rye *etc* flour; *(Weizen)* wholemeal *(Brit) or* wholewheat *(US)* flour; **~meißel** *m* blacksmith's chisel; **~säge** *f* crosscut saw; ⚠**~schuß** *m* round of shot *or* pellets.

Schrott *m* **-(e)s,** *no pl* scrap metal; *(aus Eisen auch)* old iron; *siehe* **fahren.**

Schrott-: ~halde *f* scrap heap; **~handel** *m* scrap trade; **~händler** *m* scrap dealer *or* merchant; **~haufen** *m (lit)* scrap heap; *(fig: Auto)* pile *or* heap of scrap; **~platz** *m* scrap yard; **s~reif** *adj* ready for the scrap heap, only fit for scrap; *siehe* **fahren**; **~wert** *m* scrap value.

schrubben [1] *vti* to scrub ♦ **das Deck ~** to swab *or* scrub the deck/decks. [2] *vr* to scrub oneself.

Schrubber *m* **-s, -** (long-handled) scrubbing brush.

Schrulle *f* **-, -n (a)** quirk ♦ **was hast du dir denn da für eine ~ in den Kopf gesetzt?** *(inf)* what strange idea have you got into your head now? **(b)** *(pej: alte Frau)* old crone.

schrullenhaft, schrullig *adj* odd, cranky.

Schrullenhaftigkeit, Schrulligkeit *f* crankiness.

Schrumpel *f* **-, -n** *(dial)* wrinkle.

schrump(e)lig *adj (inf)* wrinkled.

schrumpeln *vi aux sein (inf)* to go wrinkled.

schrumpfen *vi aux sein* **(a)** *(lit)* to shrink; *(Leber, Niere)* to atrophy; *(Muskeln)* to waste, to atrophy; *(Metall, Gestein etc)* to contract; *(runzlig werden)* to get wrinkled.

(b) *(fig)* to shrink; *(Kapital auch, Exporte, Mitgliederschaft, Interesse)* to dwindle; *(Währung)* to depreciate; *(Industriezweig)* to decline.

Schrumpf-: ~kopf *m* shrunken head; **~leber** *f* cirrhosis of the liver; **~niere** *f* cirrhosis of the kidney.

Schrumpfung *f* shrinking; *(Raumverlust)* shrinkage; *(von Fundamenten, Metall)* contraction; *(Med)* atrophy(ing); *(von Kapital, Arbeitskräften, Exporten)* dwindling, diminution; *(von Währung)* depreciation; *(von Industriezweig etc)* decline.

schrumplig *adj siehe* **schrump(e)lig.**

Schrund *m* **-(e)s, ¨-e** *(Berg~)* crevasse.

Schrunde *f* **-, -n** *(in der Haut)* crack; *(durch Kälte)* chap; *(Fels~, Gletscherspalte)* crevasse.

schrundig *adj* cracked; *(durch Kälte)* chapped.

schruppen *vt* **(a)** *(Tech) (mit Feile)* to rough-file; *(mit Hobel)* to rough-plane; *(mit Maschine)* to rough-machine. **(b)** *siehe* **schrubben.**

Schrupp-: ~feile *f* rough file; **~hobel** *m* jack plane.

Schub *m* **-(e)s, ¨-e (a)** *(Stoß)* push, shove. **(b)** *(Phys) (Vortriebskraft)* thrust; *(Scherung)* shear. **(c)** *(Med)* phase. **(d)** *(Anzahl)* batch. **(e)** *(Kegel~)* throw ♦ **alle neune auf einen ~** a strike; **auf zwei ¨-e** in two throws. **(f)** *(inf: ~fach)* drawer.

schubbern *vti (N Ger)* to scratch.

Schuber *m* **-s, -** slipcase.

Schub-: ~fach *nt* drawer; **~haft** *f (Jur) siehe* **Abschiebehaft**; **~karre** *f*, **~karren** *m* wheelbarrow; **~kasten** *m* drawer; **~kraft** *f (Phys)* thrust; *(Scherung)* shearing stress.

Schublade *f* **-, -n** drawer.

Schubladengesetz *nt (Pol pej) law kept in reserve to deal with a special situation.*

Schubladkasten *m (Aus)* chest of drawers.

Schublehre *f* vernier calliper.

Schubs *m* **-es, -e** *(inf)* shove *(inf)*, push; *(Aufmerksamkeit erregend)* nudge ♦ **jdm einen ~ geben** to give sb a shove *(inf) or* push/nudge; *(fig)* to give sb a prod.

Schubschiff *nt* tug (boat) *(which pushes).*

schubsen *vti (inf)* to shove *(inf)*, to push; *(Aufmerksamkeit erregend)* to nudge.

schubweise *adv* in batches; *(Med)* in phases.

schüchtern *adj* shy; *(scheu auch)* bashful ♦ **einen ~en Versuch unternehmen** *(iro)* to make a half-hearted attempt.

Schüchternheit *f* shyness; *(Scheu auch)* bashfulness.

schuckeln *vi (inf, dial) siehe* **wackeln.**

schuf *pret of* **schaffen**[1]**.**

Schufa *f abbr of* **Schutzgemeinschaft für allgemeine Kreditsicherung** ≃ credit investigation company.

Schuft *m* **-(e)s, -e** heel *(inf)*, cad, blackguard *(old)*.

schuften *vi (inf)* to graft (away) *(sl)*, to slave away ♦ **wie ein Pferd ~** *(inf)* to work like a horse *or* a Trojan.

Schufterei *f (inf)* graft *(sl)*, hard work.

schuftig *adj* mean, shabby.

Schuftigkeit *f* meanness, shabbiness ♦ **das war eine ~ von ihm** that was a mean thing he did, that was mean of him.

Schuh *m* **-(e)s, -e (a)** shoe ♦ **jdm etw in die ~e schieben** *(inf)* to lay the blame for sth at sb's door, to put the blame for sth on sb; **wissen, wo jdn der ~ drückt** to know what is bothering *or* troubling sb; **wo drückt der ~?** what's the trouble?, what's bothering you? **(b)** *(Brems~ etc)* shoe.

Schuh- *in cpds* shoe; **~absatz** *m* heel (of a/one's shoe); **~anzieher** *m* shoehorn; **~band** *nt* shoelace.

Schühchen *nt dim of* **Schuh.**

Schuh-: ~creme *f* shoe polish *or* cream; **~größe** *f* shoe size; **~haus** *nt* shoe shop; **~löffel** *m* shoehorn; **~macher** *m* shoemaker; *(Flickschuster)* cobbler; **~nummer** *f (inf)* shoe size; **jds ~nummer sein** *(fig)* to be sb's cup of tea *(inf)*; **ein paar/mindestens zwei ~nummern zu groß für jdn** *(fig)* out of sb's league; **~plattler** *m* **-s, -** *Bavarian folk dance*; **~putzer** *m* bootblack, shoeshine boy *(US)*; **jdn wie einen ~putzer behandeln** to treat sb like dirt; **ich bin doch nicht dein ~putzer!** I'm not your slave!; **~putzmittel** *nt* shoe polish; **~riemen** *m* strap (of a/one's shoe); *(Schnürsenkel)* shoelace; **~sohle** *f* sole (of a/one's shoe); **~sohlen sparen** to save shoe-leather; **~spanner** *m* shoetree; **~waren** *pl* footwear *sing*; **~werk** *nt, no pl* footwear; **~wichse** *f (inf)* shoe polish; **~zeug** *nt, no pl* footwear.

Schuko-®: ~steckdose *f* safety socket; **~stecker** *m* safety plug.

Schul-: ~abgänger(in *f***)** *m* **-s, -** school-leaver; **~alter** *nt* school age; **im ~alter** of school age; **ins ~alter kommen** to reach school age; **~amt** *nt* education authority; **~anfang** *m* beginning of term; *(~eintritt)* first day at school; **morgen ist ~anfang** school starts tomorrow; **~anfänger** *m* child just starting school; **~arbeit** *f* **(a)** *usu pl* homework *no pl*, prep *no pl (Brit inf)*; **(b)** *(Aus)* test; **~arzt** *m* school doctor; **~aufgaben** *pl* homework *sing*; **~aufsatz** *m* class essay; **~aufsicht** *f* supervision of schools; **die ~aufsicht obliegt dem Kultusministerium** the Department of Education is responsible for schools; **~aufsichtsbehörde** *f* education authority; **~ausflug** *m* school outing *or* trip; **~ausgabe** *f* school edition; **~bank** *f* school desk; **die ~bank drücken** *(inf)* to go to school; **~beginn** *m (~jahrsbeginn)* beginning of the school year; *(nach Ferien)* beginning of term; **(der) ~beginn ist um neun** school starts at nine; **~behörde** *f* education authority;

⚠: for details of spelling reform, see supplement

~beispiel *nt (fig)* classic example (*für* of); **~besuch** *m* school attendance; **~bildung** *f* (school) education; **~bub** *m (S Ger, Aus)* schoolboy; **~buch** *nt* schoolbook, textbook; **~buchverlag** *m* educational publishing company; **~bus** *m* school bus.

⚠**schuld** *adj pred* **~ sein** *or* **haben** to be to blame (*an +dat* for); **er war** *or* **hatte ~ an dem Streit** the argument was his fault, he was to blame for the argument; **das Wetter/ich war ~ daran, daß wir zu spät kamen** the weather/I was to blame for us being late, it was my fault that we were late; **bin ich denn ~, wenn ...?** is it my fault if ...?; **du hast** *or* **bist selbst ~** that's your own fault, that's nobody's fault but your own; **jdm/einer Sache ~ geben** to blame sb/sth; **er gab ihr ~, daß es nicht klappte** he blamed her for it not working *or* for the fact that it didn't work.

▼ **Schuld** *f* **-, -en (a)** *no pl (Ursache, Verantwortlichkeit)* **die ~ an etw** *(dat)* **haben** *or* **tragen** *(geh)* to be to blame for sth; **die ~ auf sich** *(acc)* **nehmen** to take the blame; **jdm die ~ geben** *or* **zuschreiben** *or* **zuschieben** to blame sb; **die ~ auf jdn abwälzen** *or* **schieben** to put the blame on sb; **die ~ bei anderen suchen** to try to blame somebody else; **die ~ liegt bei mir** I am to blame (for that); **das ist meine/deine ~** that is my/your fault, I am/you are to blame (for that); **das ist meine eigene ~** it's my own fault, I've nobody but *or* only myself to blame; **durch meine/deine ~** because of me/you.
(b) *no pl (~haftigkeit, ~gefühl)* guilt; *(Unrecht)* wrong; *(Rel: Sünde)* sin; *(im Vaterunser)* trespasses *pl* ◆ **die Strafe sollte in einem angemessenen Verhältnis zur ~ stehen** the punishment should be appropriate to the degree of culpability; **sich frei von ~ fühlen** to consider oneself completely blameless; **ich bin mir keiner ~ bewußt** I'm not aware of having done anything wrong; **ich bin mir meiner ~ bewußt** I know that I have done wrong; **ihm konnte seine ~ nicht nachgewiesen werden** his guilt could not be proved; **ihm konnte keine ~ nachgewiesen werden** it couldn't be proved that he had done anything wrong; **~ auf sich** *(acc)* **laden** to burden oneself with a deep sense of guilt; **seine ~ sühnen** to atone for one's sins; **für seine ~ büßen** to pay for one's sin/sins; **~ und Sühne** crime and punishment.
(c) *(Zahlungsverpflichtung)* debt ◆ **ich stehe tief in seiner ~** *(lit)* I'm deeply in debt to him; *(fig)* I'm deeply indebted to him; **~en machen** to run up debts; **~en haben** to be in debt; **DM 10.000 ~en haben** to have debts totalling *or* of DM10,000, to be in debt to the tune of DM10,000; **in ~en geraten** to get into debt; **mehr ~en als Haare auf dem Kopf haben** *(inf)* to be up to one's ears in debt *(inf)*; **das Haus ist frei von ~en** the house is unmortgaged.

Schuld-: ~anerkenntnis *nt* admission of one's guilt; *(~schein)* promissory note, IOU; **~bekenntnis** *nt* confession; **s~beladen** *adj* burdened with guilt; **~beweis** *m* proof *or* evidence of one's guilt; ⚠**s~bewußt** *adj Mensch* feeling guilty; *Gesicht, Miene* guilty; ⚠**~bewußtsein** *nt* feelings of guilt *pl*; **~buch** *nt (Econ)* Debt Register; **~buchforderung** *f (Econ)* Debt Register Claims.

schulden *vt* to owe ◆ **das schulde ich ihm** I owe him that, I owe it to him; **jdm Dank ~** to owe sb a debt of gratitude.

Schulden-: ~dienst *m (Econ)* debt servicing; **s~frei** *adj* free of debt(s); *Besitz* unmortgaged; **~last** *f* debts *pl*; **~macher** *m (inf)* habitual debtor; **er ist ein notorischer/ewiger ~macher** he is notorious for/is forever running up debts; **~masse** *f (Jur)* aggregate liabilities *pl*; **~tilgung** *f* discharge of one's debt(s).

Schuld-: ~fähigkeit *f (Jur)* **verminderte ~fähigkeit** diminished responsibility; **~forderung** *f* claim; **~frage** *f* question of guilt; **s~frei** *adj* blameless; **~gefängnis** *nt (Hist)* debtors' prison; **~gefühl** *nt* sense *no pl or* feeling of guilt; **~haft** *f (Hist)* imprisonment for debt; **s~haft** *adj (Jur)* culpable.

Schul-: ~diener *m (old)* school janitor *or* caretaker; **~dienst** *m* (school-) teaching *no art*; **in den ~dienst treten** *or* **gehen** to go into teaching; **im ~dienst (tätig) sein** to be a teacher, to be in the teaching profession.

schuldig *adj* **(a)** *(schuldhaft, straffällig, schuldbeladen)* guilty; *(verantwortlich)* to blame *pred (an +dat* for); *(Rel)* sinful ◆ **einer Sache** *(gen)* **~ sein** to be guilty of sth; **jdn einer Tat** *(gen)* **(für) ~ erklären** *or* **befinden** *(Jur)* to find sb guilty of *or* to convict sb of an offence; **sich einer Sache** *(gen)* **~ machen** to be guilty of sth; **jdn ~ sprechen** to find *or* pronounce sb guilty, to convict sb; **sich ~ bekennen** to admit one's guilt; *(Jur)* to plead guilty; **~ geschieden sein** to be the guilty party in a/the divorce; **an jdm ~ werden** *(geh)* to wrong sb.
(b) *(geh: gebührend)* due ◆ **jdm die ~e Achtung/den ~en Respekt zollen** to give sb the attention/respect due to him/her.
(c) *(verpflichtet)* **jdm etw** *(acc)* **~ sein** *(lit, fig)* to owe sb sth; **ich muß Ihnen 2 Mark ~ bleiben** I'll have to owe you 2 marks; **was bin ich Ihnen ~?** how much *or* what do I owe you?; **jdm Dank ~ sein** to owe sb a debt of gratitude; **sie blieb mir die Antwort ~/nicht ~** she didn't answer me *or* didn't have an answer/she hit back at me; **er blieb ihr nichts ~** *(fig)* he gave (her) as good as he got.

Schuldige(r) *mf decl as adj* guilty person; *(zivilrechtlich)* guilty party.

Schuldiger *m* **-s, -** *(Bibl)* trespasser ◆ **wie auch wir vergeben unseren ~n** as we forgive those who trespass against us.

Schuldigkeit *f, no pl* duty ◆ **seine ~ tun** to do one's duty.

Schuldigsprechung *f* conviction.

Schul-: ~direktor *m* headmaster *(esp Brit)*, principal; **~direktorin** *f* headmistress *(esp Brit)*, principal.

Schuld-: ~komplex *m* guilt complex; **s~los** *adj (an Verbrechen)* innocent *(an +dat* of); *(an Fehler, Unglück etc)* blameless, free from blame; **er war vollständig s~los an dem Unglück** he was in no way to blame for the accident; **s~los geschieden sein** to be the innocent party in a/the divorce.

Schuldner(in *f***)** *m* **-s, -** debtor.

Schuldnerstaat *m* debtor nation.

Schuld-: ~prinzip *nt (Jur)* principle of the guilty party; **~recht** *nt (Jur)* law of contract; **~schein** *m* IOU, promissory note; **~scheindarlehen** *f* loan against borrower's note; **~spruch** *m* verdict of guilty; **~turm** *m (Hist)* debtors' prison; **~unfähigkeit** *f (Jur)* incapacity; **~verhältnis** *nt (Jur)* relationship of debenture; **~verschreibung** *f (Fin)* debenture bond; **~zuweisung** *f* accusation, assignment of guilt.

Schule *f* **-, -n (a)** *(Lehranstalt, Lehrmeinung, künstlerische Richtung)* school ◆ **in die** *or* **zur ~ kommen/gehen** to start school/go to school; **er hat nie eine ~ besucht** he has never been to school; **auf** *or* **in der ~** at school; **die ~ wechseln** to change schools; **von der ~ abgehen** to leave school; **sie ist an der ~** she is a (school)teacher; **die ~ ist aus** school is over, the schools are out; **er ist bei Brecht in die ~ gegangen** *(fig)* he was greatly influenced by Brecht; **darin hat er bei seinen Eltern eine gute ~ gehabt** his parents have given him a good schooling in that; **durch eine harte ~ gegangen sein** *(fig)* to have learned in a hard school; **~ machen** to become the accepted thing; **aus der ~ plaudern** to tell tales out of school *(inf)*; **ein Kavalier der alten ~** a gentleman of the old school.
(b) *(Reiten)* school of riding; *siehe* **hoch.**

schulen *vt* to train; *Auge, Gedächtnis, Pferd auch* to school; *(Pol)* to give political instruction to.

Schul-: ~englisch *nt* schoolboy/schoolgirl English; **zwei Jahre ~englisch** two years' English at school; **mein ~englisch** the English I learnt at school; **s~entlassen** *adj* **kaum s~entlassen, begann er ...** hardly had he left school when he began ...; **die s~entlassene Jugend** the young people who have recently left school; **~entlassene** *pl* school-leavers *pl*; **~entlassung** *f* **der Tag der ~entlassung** the day one leaves school; **nach seiner/der ~entlassung** after leaving school; **~entlassungsfeier** *f* school-leavers' day; **~entlassungszeugnis** *nt* school-leaving certificate.

Schüler(in *f***)** *m* **-s, -** schoolboy/schoolgirl; *(einer bestimmten Schule)* pupil; *(einer Oberschule auch)* student; *(Jünger)* follower, disciple ◆ **als ~ habe ich ...** when I was at school I ...; **alle ~ und ~innen dieser Stadt** all the schoolchildren of this town; **ein ehemaliger ~ (der Schule)** an old boy *or* pupil (of the school).

Schüler-: ~austausch *m* school *or* student exchange; **~ausweis** *m* (school) student card; **s~haft** *adj* schoolboyish/schoolgirlish; *(pej)* childish, puerile; **~heim** *nt* (school) boarding house.

Schülerin *f siehe* **Schüler(in).**

Schüler-: ~karte *f* school season-ticket; **~lotse** *m pupil acting as road-crossing warden*; **~mitverwaltung** *f* school *or* student council; **~parlament** *nt* inter-school student council; **~schaft** *f* pupils *pl*; **~sprache** *f* school slang; **~vertretung** *f* pupil *or* student representation; **~zeitung** *f* school magazine.

Schul-: ~erziehung *f* schooling; **~fach** *nt* school subject; **~feier** *f* school function; **~ferien** *pl* school holidays *pl (Brit) or* vacation; **~fernsehen** *nt* schools' *or* educational television; **~fest** *nt* school function; **~film** *m* educational film; **s~frei** *adj* **ein s~freier Nachmittag** an afternoon when one doesn't have to go to school; **nächsten Samstag ist s~frei** there's no school next Saturday; **die Kinder haben morgen s~frei** the children don't have to go to school tomorrow; **~freund** *m* schoolfriend; **~funk** *m* schools' radio; **~gebäude** *nt* school building; **~gebrauch** *m*: **zum** *or* **für den ~gebrauch** for use in schools; **~gegenstand** *m (Aus)* school subject; **~gelände** *nt* school grounds *pl*; **~geld** *nt* school fees *pl*; **~gelehrsamkeit** *f (old, pej)* booklearning; **~gesetz** *nt* education act; **~grammatik** *f* (school) grammar book *or* grammar *(inf)*; **~haus** *nt* schoolhouse; **~heft** *nt* exercise book; **~hof** *m* school playground *(Brit)*, schoolyard.

schulisch *adj Leistungen, Probleme, Verbesserung* at school; *(rein akademisch)* scholastic; *Angelegenheiten* school *attr* ◆ **seine ~en Leistungen/Probleme** his progress/problems at school; **er hat ~ große Fortschritte gemacht** he has improved greatly at school; **~e Angelegenheiten** school matters; **aus ~er Sicht** from the school angle.

Schul-: ~jahr *nt* school year; *(Klasse)* year; **ihre ~jahre** her schooldays; **~jugend** *f* schoolchildren *pl*; **~junge** *m* schoolboy; **~kamerad** *m* schoolmate, schoolfriend; **~kenntnisse** *pl* knowledge *sing* acquired at school; **~kind** *nt* schoolchild; **~klasse** *f* (school) class; **~landheim** *nt country house used by school classes for short visits*; **~lehrer** *m* schoolteacher; **~leiter** *m* headmaster *(esp Brit)*, principal; **~leiterin** *f* headmistress *(esp Brit)*, principal; **~lektüre** *f* book/books read in schools; **~lektüre sein** to be read in schools; **~mädchen** *nt* schoolgirl; **~mappe** *f* schoolbag; **s~mäßig** *adj Unterricht, Kurs, Lehrbuch* didactic; **s~mäßig gekleidet** dressed for school; **es war alles s~mäßig reglementiert** everything was regimented just like in school; **~medizin** *f* orthodox medicine; **~mediziner** *m* orthodox medical practitioner; **~meinung** *f* received opinion; **~meister** *m (old, hum, pej)* schoolmaster; **s~meisterlich** *adj (pej)* schoolmasterish; **sich s~meisterlich aufspielen** to play the schoolmaster; **s~meistern** *insep* **1** *vt* to lecture (at *or* to); **2** *vi* to lecture; **~ordnung** *f* school rules *pl*; **~pflicht** *f* compulsory school attendance *no art*; **allgemeine ~pflicht** compulsory school attendance for all children; **es besteht ~pflicht** school attendance is compulsory; **s~pflichtig** *adj Kind* required to attend school; **~politik** *f* education policy; **~psychologe** *m* educational psychologist; **~ranzen** *m* (school) satchel; **~rat** *m* schools inspector; **~reform** *f* educational reform; **~reife** *f* school readiness *(spec)*; **die ~reife haben** to be ready to go to school; **~reifetest** *m* school readiness test; **~schiff** *nt* training ship; ⚠**~schluß** *m* end of school; *(vor den Ferien)* end of term; **~schluß ist um 13[10]** school finishes at 13.10; **kurz nach ~schluß** just after school finishes/finished; **~schwänzen** *nt* truancy; **~schwänzer** *m* **-s, -** truant;

➤ SPRACHE AKTIV: **Schuld: a** → 45.2

⚠: Informationen zur Rechtschreibreform im Anhang

~**speisung** *f* free school meals *pl*; ~**sport** *m* school sport; ~**sprecher(in** *f*) *m* head boy/girl (*Brit*); ~**sprengel** *m* (*Aus*) (school) catchment area; ⚠~**streß** *m* stress at school; **im ~streß sein** to be under stress at school; ~**stunde** *f* (school) period *or* lesson; ~**system** *nt* school system; ~**tag** *m* schoolday; **der erste ~tag** the/one's first day at school; ~**tasche** *f* schoolbag.

Schulter *f* -, -**n** shoulder ◆ **mit gebeugten/hängenden ~n gehen** to be round-shouldered, to have round/sloping shoulders; (*fig: niedergeschlagen*) to look careworn/down in the mouth *or* downcast; **breite ~n haben** (*lit*) to be broad-shouldered, to have broad shoulders; (*fig*) to have a broad back; **er ließ die ~n hängen** he was slouching; (*niedergeschlagen*) he hung his head; **sich** (*dat*) **eine Jacke über die ~n hängen** to put a jacket round one's shoulders; **sich** (*dat*) **den Fotoapparat über die ~ hängen** to sling one's camera over one's shoulder; **jdm die Hand auf die ~ legen** to put one's hand on sb's shoulder; **jdm auf die ~ klopfen** *or* **schlagen** to give sb a slap on the back, to clap sb on the back; (*lobend*) to pat sb on the back; **sich** (*dat*) **selbst auf die ~ klopfen** (*fig*) to blow one's own trumpet; **jdm** *or* **jdn um die ~ fassen** to put one's arm round sb's shoulders; **~ an ~** (*dichtgedrängt*) shoulder to shoulder; (*gemeinsam, solidarisch*) side by side; **die** *or* **mit den ~n zucken** to shrug one's shoulders; **jdn auf die ~ legen** *or* **werfen** to get sb in a shoulder-press; **die Verantwortung ruht auf seinen ~n** the responsibility rests on his shoulders *or* lies at his door; **etw auf die leichte ~ nehmen** to take sth lightly; *siehe* **kalt**.

Schulter-: ~**blatt** *nt* shoulder blade; **s~frei** *adj Kleid* off-the-shoulder; (*ohne Träger*) strapless; (*mit Nackenträger*) halterneck; **sie war/kam s~frei** her shoulders were bare, she was wearing a dress which left her shoulders bare; ~**gelenk** *nt* shoulder joint; ~**höhe** *f* shoulder height; **in ~höhe** at shoulder level *or* height.

-schult(e)rig *adj suf* -shouldered.

Schulter-: ~**klappe** *f* (*Mil*) epaulette; **s~lang** *adj* shoulder-length.

schultern *vt* to shoulder ◆ **das Gewehr ~** to shoulder arms.

Schulter-: ~**polster** *nt* shoulder pad; ~**riemen** *m* shoulder strap; ⚠~**schluß** *m, no pl* shoulder-to-shoulder stance, solidarity; (*Solidarisierung*) closing of ranks; ~**sieg** *m* (*Sport*) fall; ~**stand** *m* (*Sport*) shoulder stand; ~**stück** *nt* (a) (*Mil*) epaulette; (b) (*Cook*) piece of shoulder; ~**wurf** *m* (*Sport*) shoulder-throw.

Schultheiß *m* -**en**, -**en** (*Hist*) mayor.

Schulträger *m* (*form*) **der ~ (dieser Schule) ist der Staat** the school is supported *or* maintained by the State.

-schultrig *adj suf siehe* **-schult(e)rig**.

Schul-: ~**tüte** *f large conical bag of sweets given to children on their first day at school*; ~**typ** *m* type of school.

Schulung *f* (*Ausbildung, Übung*) training; (*von Auge, Gedächtnis, Pferd auch*) schooling; (*Pol*) political instruction.

Schulungs-: ~**diskette** *f* tutorial diskette; ~**kurs** *m* training course; ~**lager** *nt* training camp.

Schul-: ~**uniform** *f* school uniform; ~**unterricht** *m* school lessons *pl*; ~**versager** *m* failure at school; ~**wanderung** *f* school hike; ~**weg** *m* way to/from school; (*Entfernung*) distance to/from school; (*Route*) route to/from school; **ich habe einen ~weg von 20 Minuten** it takes me 20 minutes to get to/from school; ~**weisheit** *f* (*pej*) booklearning; ~**wesen** *nt* school system; ~**wissen** *nt* knowledge acquired at school; ~**wörterbuch** *nt* school dictionary.

Schulze *m* -**n**, -**n** (*Hist*) *siehe* **Schultheiß**.

Schul-: ~**zeit** *f* (~*jahre*) schooldays *pl*; **nach 13jähriger ~zeit** after 13 years at school; **seit der ~zeit** since we/they were at school, since our/their schooldays; ~**zeitung** *f* school magazine; ~**zentrum** *nt* school complex; ~**zeugnis** *nt* school report; ~**zwang** *m siehe* ~**pflicht**; ~**zwecke** *pl*: **für ~zwecke, zu ~zwecken** for school; (*als geeignetes Lehrmittel*) for use in schools.

schummeln *vi* (*inf*) to cheat ◆ **in Latein/beim Kartenspiel ~** to cheat in Latin/at cards.

Schummelzettel *m* (*Sch sl*) crib.

schumm(e)rig *adj Beleuchtung* dim; *Raum* dimly-lit ◆ **bei ~em Licht** in the half-light; **es war schon ~** it was already getting dark.

schummern [1] *vi impers* (*N Ger*) **es schummert** dusk is falling.
[2] *vt* (*Geog*) to shade (in).

Schummerstunde *f* (*N Ger*) twilight hour.

Schummerung *f* (*Geog*) shading.

schummrig *adj siehe* **schumm(e)rig**.

schund (*rare*) *pret of* **schinden**.

Schund *m* -**(e)s**, *no pl* (*pej*) trash, rubbish ◆ **was für ~/einen ~ hast du denn da?** what's that trash/trashy book you're reading?; *siehe* **Schmutz**.

Schund-: ~**literatur** *f* trash, trashy *or* pulp literature; ~**roman** *m* trashy *or* pulp novel.

Schunkellied *nt* German drinking song.

schunkeln *vi* to link arms and sway from side to side.

Schupfen *m* -**s**, - (*esp S Ger*) *siehe* **Schuppen**.

Schupfer *m* -**s**, - (*Aus*) *siehe* **Schubs**.

Schupo[1] *f* -, *no pl abbr of* **Schutzpolizei**.

Schupo[2] *m* -**s**, -**s** (*dated inf*) *abbr of* **Schutzpolizist** cop (*inf*), copper (*Brit inf*).

Schuppe *f* -, -**n** (a) (*Bot, Zool*) scale; (*von Ritterrüstung, Tierpanzer*) plate ◆ **es fiel mir wie ~n von den Augen** the scales fell from my eyes. (b) (*Kopf~*) **~n** *pl* dandruff *sing*.

Schuppen *m* -**s**, - (a) shed; (*Flugzeug~*) hangar. (b) (*inf*) (*Haus, Wohnung etc*) joint (*sl*), hole (*pej inf*), hovel (*pej*); (*übles Lokal*) dive (*inf*).

schuppen [1] *vt Fische* to scale.
[2] *vr* to flake.

Schuppen-: **s~artig** *adj* scale-like; **die Ziegel sind s~artig angeordnet** the tiles are arranged so that they overlap; ~**bildung** *f, no pl* dandruff; ~**flechte** *f* (*Med*) psoriasis (*spec*); **s~förmig** *adj siehe* **s~artig**; ~**panzer** *m* scale armour; ~**tier** *nt* scaly ant-eater.

schuppig *adj* scaly; (*abblätternd auch*) flaking ◆ **die Haut löst sich ~ ab** his *etc* skin is flaking (off).

Schup(p)s *m* -**es**, -**e** *siehe* **Schubs**.

schup(p)sen *vti siehe* **schubsen**.

Schur *f* -, -**en** (*das Scheren*) shearing; (*geschorene Wolle*) clip.

Schür|eisen *nt siehe* **Schürhaken**.

schüren *vt* (a) *Feuer, Glut* to rake, to poke. (b) (*fig*) to stir up; *Zorn, Eifersucht, Leidenschaft, Haß* to fan the flames of.

schürfen [1] *vi* (*Min*) to prospect (*nach* for) ◆ **tief ~** (*fig*) to dig deep.
[2] *vt Bodenschätze* to mine.
[3] *vtr* to graze oneself ◆ **sich** (*dat*) **die Haut ~, sich ~** to graze oneself *or* one's skin; **sich am Knie ~** to graze one's knee.

Schürf-: ~**grube** *f*, ~**loch** *nt* (*Min*) test pit; ~**recht** *nt* mining rights *pl*; ~**wunde** *f* graze, abrasion.

Schürhaken *m* poker.

schurigeln *vt* (*inf*) (*hart anfahren*) to lay into (*inf*); (*schikanieren*) to bully.

Schurke *m* -**n**, -**n** (*dated*) villain, scoundrel, rogue.

Schurkenstreich *m*, **Schurkentat**, **Schurkerei** *f* (*old*) (piece of) villainy.

schurkisch *adj* (*dated*) base, despicable.

schurren *vi* (*dial*) (*Schlitten*) to grate ◆ **mit den Füßen ~** to shuffle one's feet; (*beim Gehen*) to drag one's feet.

Schurwolle *f* virgin wool ◆ **„reine ~"** "pure new wool".

Schurz *m* -**es**, -**e** loincloth; (*von Schmied, Arbeiter etc, dial*) apron.

Schürze *f* -, -**n** apron; (*Frauen~, Kinder~ mit Latz auch*) pinafore, pinny (*inf*) ◆ **sich** (*dat*) **eine ~ umbinden** to put an apron on; **er ist hinter jeder ~ her** (*dated inf*), **er läuft jeder ~ nach** (*dated inf*) he runs after anything in a skirt (*inf*).

schürzen *vt* (a) (*dated*) *Rock* to gather (up). (b) (*geh: schlingen*) *Knoten* to tie; *Faden* to knot, to tie a knot in. (c) (*geh: aufwerfen*) **die Lippen/den Mund ~** (*zum Pfeifen*) to purse one's lips; (*verführerisch*) to pout; **ihr geschürzter Mund** her pursed lips/her pout.

Schürzen-: ~**band** *nt siehe* ~**zipfel**; ~**jäger** *m* (*inf*) philanderer, one for the girls (*inf*); ~**zipfel** *m* apron-string; **er hängt der Mutter noch am ~zipfel** he's still tied to his mother's apron strings.

⚠**Schuß** *m* -**sses**, ⚠**-̈sse** (a) shot; (~ *Munition*) round ◆ **sechs ~** *or* **Schüsse** six shots/rounds; **zum ~ kommen** to have a chance to shoot; **ein ~ ins Schwarze** (*lit, fig*) a bull's-eye; **weit vom ~ sein** (*fig inf*) to be miles from where the action is (*inf*); **er ist keinen ~ Pulver wert** (*fig*) he is not worth tuppence (*inf*); **das war ein (schöner) ~ vor den Bug** (*fig*) that was a warning not to be ignored; **ein ~ in den Ofen** (*sl*) a complete waste of time.
(b) (*Min: Sprengung*) blast, charge.
(c) (*Ftbl*) kick; (*zum Tor auch*) shot ◆ **zum ~ kommen** to get the ball; (*zum Tor*) to get a chance to shoot.
(d) (*Ski*) schuss ◆ **im ~ fahren** to schuss.
(e) (*Spritzer*) (*von Wein, Essig etc*) dash; (*von Whisky*) shot; (*von Humor, Leichtsinn etc auch*) touch.
(f) (*Tex: Querfäden*) weft, woof.
(g) (*sl: mit Rauschgift*) shot ◆ **einen ~ setzen** *or* **drücken** to shoot up (*sl*); **sich** (*dat*) **den goldenen ~ setzen** to OD (*sl*).
(h) (*inf*) **in ~ sein/kommen** to be in/get into (good) shape; (*Mensch, Sportler auch*) to be on form/get into good form; (*Schüler, Klasse*) to be/get up to the mark; (*Party*) to be going well/get going; **etw in ~ bringen/halten** to knock sth into shape/keep sth in good shape; *Schulklasse* to bring/keep sth up to the mark; *Party* to get/keep sth going.

⚠**Schuß-**: ~**bereich** *m* (firing) range; **im ~bereich** within range; **s~bereit** *adj* ready to fire; *Gewehr auch* cocked.

Schussel *m* -**s**, - (*inf*) *or f* -, -**n** (*inf*) dolt (*inf*); (*zerstreut*) scatterbrain (*inf*); (*ungeschickt*) clumsy clot (*inf*).

Schüssel *f* -, -**n** bowl; (*Servier~ auch*) dish; (*Wasch~*) basin ◆ **vor leeren ~n sitzen** (*nach dem Essen*) to sit staring at the dirty dishes; (*in Notzeit*) to go hungry.

schusselig *adj* (*inf*) daft; (*zerstreut*) scatterbrained (*inf*), muddle-headed (*inf*); (*ungeschickt*) clumsy, all thumbs *pred*.

Schusseligkeit *f* (*inf*) daftness; (*Zerstreutheit*) muddleheadedness (*inf*); (*Ungeschick*) clumsiness.

schusseln *vi* (*inf*) (*zerstreut sein*) to be scatterbrained (*inf*) *or* muddle-headed (*inf*); (*ungeschickt vorgehen*) to be clumsy; (*sich ungeschickt bewegen*) to bumble (*inf*).

Schusser *m* -**s**, - (*dial*) marble.

⚠**Schuß-**: ~**faden** *m* (*Tex*) weft thread; ~**fahrt** *f* (*Ski*) schuss; (*das ~fahren*) schussing; ~**feld** *nt* field of fire; (*Übungsplatz*) firing range; **s~fest** *adj* bulletproof; **s~frei** *adj* clear for firing; ~**geschwindigkeit** *f* velocity (*of bullet etc*); ~**kanal** *m* (*Med*) path of a/the bullet through the body.

⚠**schußlig** *adj* (*inf*) *siehe* **schusselig**.

⚠**Schußligkeit** *f* (*inf*) *siehe* **Schusseligkeit**.

⚠**Schuß-**: ~**linie** *f* line of fire; (*fig auch*) firing line; ~**richtung** *f* direction of fire; **s~sicher** *adj* bulletproof; ~**verletzung** *f* bullet wound; ~**waffe** *f* firearm; ~**waffengebrauch** *m* (*form*) use of firearms; ~**wechsel** *m* exchange of shots *or* fire; **~weite** *f* range (of fire); **in/außer ~weite** within/out of range; **~winkel** *m* angle of fire; **~wunde** *f* bullet wound; **~zahl** *f* (*Tex*) number of weft threads.

Schuster *m* **-s, -** shoemaker; (*Flick~*) cobbler ◆ **auf ~s Rappen** (*hum*) by Shanks's pony; **~, bleib bei deinem Leisten!** (*Prov*) cobbler, stick to your last (*Prov*).

Schuster-: ~ahle *f* shoemaker's awl; **~draht** *m* waxed thread.

Schusterei *f* **(a)** (*Werkstatt*) shoemaker's; (*von Flickschuster*) cobbler's. **(b)** (*pej inf: Pfuscherei*) botching (*inf*).

Schuster-: ~handwerk *nt* shoemaking; cobbling; **~junge** *m* **(a)** (*old: ~lehrling*) shoemaker's/cobbler's apprentice; **(b)** (*Typ*) widow.

schustern *vi* **(a)** to cobble *or* repair *or* mend shoes. **(b)** (*pej inf*) to do a botch job (*inf*).

Schuster-: ~pech *nt* shoemaker's *or* cobbler's wax; **~pfriem(en)** *m siehe* **~ahle**; **~werkstatt** *f* shoemaker's/cobbler's workshop.

Schute *f* **-, -n (a)** (*Naut*) lighter. **(b)** (*Damenhut*) poke (bonnet).

Schutt *m* **-(e)s,** *no pl* (*Trümmer, Bau~*) rubble; (*Geol*) debris, detritus (*spec*) ◆ **„~ abladen verboten"** "no tipping"; **eine Stadt in ~ und Asche legen** to reduce a town to rubble; **in ~ und Asche liegen** to be in ruins.

Schutt|abladeplatz *m* tip, dump.

Schütt-: ~beton *m* cast concrete; **~boden** *m* strawloft; (*für Getreide*) granary.

Schütte *f* **-, -n (a)** (*Bund*) stock. **(b)** (*Behälter*) *wall-mounted drawer-like canister for sugar, flour etc.*

Schüttel-: ~becher *m* (cocktail) shaker; **~frost** *m* (*Med*) shivering fit, fit of the shivers (*inf*); **~lähmung** *f* (*Med*) Parkinson's disease.

schütteln [1] *vt* to shake; (*rütteln*) to shake about, to jolt (about) ◆ **den** *or* **mit dem Kopf ~** to shake one's head; **von Angst geschüttelt werden** to be gripped with fear; **von Fieber geschüttelt werden** to be racked with fever; *siehe* **Hand, Staub.**

[2] *vr* to shake oneself; (*vor Kälte*) to shiver (*vor* with); (*vor Ekel*) to shudder (*vor* with, in) ◆ **sich vor Lachen ~** to shake with laughter.

Schüttel-: ~reim *m* goat rhyme, *rhyme in which the consonants of the rhyming syllables are transposed in the next line*; **~rutsche** *f* (*Tech*) vibrating chute; **~sieb** *nt* riddle.

schütten [1] *vt* to tip; *Flüssigkeiten* to pour; (*ver~*) to spill.

[2] *vi impers* (*inf*) **es schüttet** it's pouring (with rain), it's pouring (down), it's bucketing (down) (*inf*).

schütter *adj Haar* thin.

Schüttgut *nt* bulk goods *pl*.

Schutt-: ~halde *f* (*~haufen*) rubble tip; (*Geol*) scree slope; **~haufen** *m* pile *or* heap of rubble; **etw in einen ~haufen verwandeln** to reduce sth to a pile of rubble; **~kegel** *m* (*Geol*) cone of scree *or* debris; **~mulde** *f* skip; **~platz** *m* tip.

Schütt-: ~stein *m* (*S Ger, Sw*) sink; **~stroh** *nt* bedding straw.

Schutz *m* **-es,** *no pl* protection (*vor +dat, gegen* against, from); (*Zuflucht auch*) shelter, refuge (*vor +dat, gegen* from); (*der Natur, Umwelt etc*) conservation; (*esp Mil: Deckung*) cover ◆ **jdn um ~ bitten** to ask sb for protection; **bei jdm ~ suchen** to look to sb for protection; to seek shelter *or* refuge with sb; **unter einem Baum ~ suchen** to shelter under a tree, to take *or* seek refuge under a tree; **im ~(e) der Nacht** *or* **Dunkelheit/des Artilleriefeuers** under cover of night *or* darkness/artillery fire; **zum ~ von Leib und Leben** for the protection of life and limb: **jdn/etw als ~ mitnehmen** to take sb/sth with one for protection; **zum ~ der Augen** to protect the eyes; **jdn in ~ nehmen** (*fig*) to take sb's part, to stand up for sb; **zu ~ und Trutz zusammenstehen** (*old, liter*) to stand together.

Schutz-: ~anstrich *m* protective coat; **~anzug** *m* protective clothing *no indef art, no pl*; **~ärmel** *m* sleeve-protector; **~aufsicht** *f* (*Jur*) supervision by a social worker; **s~bedürftig** *adj* in need of protection; **~befohlene(r)** *mf decl as adj siehe* **Schützling**; **~behauptung** *f* lie to cover oneself; **~blech** *nt* mudguard; **~brief** *m* **(a)** (letter of) safe-conduct; **(b)** *siehe* **Auslandsschutzbrief**; **~brille** *f* protective goggles *pl*; **~bündnis** *nt* defensive alliance; **~dach** *nt* porch; (*an Haltestelle*) shelter; **~deck** *nt* shelter deck.

Schütze *m* **-n, -n (a)** marksman; (*Schießsportler*) rifleman; (*Hunt*) hunter; (*Bogen~*) archer; (*Hist*) bowman, archer; (*Ftbl: Tor~*) scorer ◆ **er ist der beste ~** he is the best shot.

(b) (*Mil: Dienstgrad*) private; (*Maschinengewehr~*) gunner.

(c) (*Astrol*) Sagittarius *no art*; (*Astron auch*) Archer ◆ **sie ist ~** she's Sagittarius *or* a Sagittarian.

(d) (*Weberschiffchen*) shuttle.

Schützen *m* **-s, -** (*Tex*) shuttle.

schützen [1] *vt* to protect (*vor +dat, gegen* from, against); (*Zuflucht bieten auch*) to shelter (*vor +dat, gegen* from); (*absichern: Versicherung etc auch*) to safeguard; (*esp Mil: Deckung geben*) to cover ◆ **urheberrechtlich/gesetzlich/patentrechtlich geschützt** protected by copyright/registered/patented; **ein geschützter Platz** a sheltered spot *or* place; **vor Hitze/Sonnenlicht ~!** keep away from heat/sunlight; **vor Nässe ~!** keep dry; **Gott schütze dich!** (*old*) (may) the Lord protect *or* keep you.

[2] *vi* to give *or* offer protection (*vor +dat, gegen* against, from); (*Zuflucht bieten auch*) to give *or* offer shelter (*vor +dat, gegen* from); (*esp Mil: Deckung geben*) to give cover.

[3] *vr* to protect oneself (*vor +dat, gegen* from, against); (*sich absichern auch*) to safeguard oneself (*vor +dat, gegen* against) ◆ **er weiß sich zu ~** he knows how to look after himself.

Schützen-: ~anger *m siehe* **~wiese**; **~bruder** *m member of a rifle club.*

schützend *adj* protective ◆ **ein ~es Dach** (*gegen Wetter*) a shelter; **ein ~es Dach über sich** (*dat*) **haben** to be under cover; **der ~e Hafen** (*lit*) the protection of the harbour; (*fig*) a/the safe haven; **seine ~e Hand über jdn halten** *or* **breiten** to take sb under one's wing.

Schützenfest *nt fair featuring shooting matches.*

Schutz|engel *m* guardian angel.

Schützen-: ~gesellschaft, ~gilde *f siehe* **~verein**; **~graben** *m* trench; **~haus** *nt* clubhouse (*of a rifle club*); **~hilfe** *f* (*fig*) support; **jdm ~hilfe geben** to back sb up, to support sb; **~kette** *f* (*Mil*) firing line; **~könig** *m champion rifleman at a Schützenfest*; **~linie** *f* (*Mil*) firing line; **~loch** *nt* (*Mil*) foxhole; **~panzer(wagen)** *m* armoured personnel carrier; **~platz** *m siehe* **~wiese**; **~verein** *m* rifle *or* shooting club; **~wiese** *f fairground at which a rifle club holds its competitions*; **~zug** *m* procession of riflemen.

Schutz-: ~farbe, ~färbung *f* (*Biol*) protective *or* adaptive colouring; **~frist** *f* term of copyright; **~gebiet** *nt* (*Pol*) protectorate; **~gebühr** *f* (token) fee; **~gebühren** *pl* (*euph sl*) protection money *sing*; **~geist** *m* (*Myth*) protecting *or* tutelary (*liter*) spirit; **~geländer** *nt* guard-rail; **~geld** *nt* protection money; **~gitter** *nt* (*um Denkmal etc*) protective barrier; (*vor Maschine, Fenster, Tür*) protective grille; (*um Leute zu schützen*) safety barrier/grille; (*vor Kamin*) (fire)guard; (*Elec*) screen grid; **~gott** *m* tutelary god (*liter*); **~göttin** *f* (*Myth*) tutelary goddess (*liter*); **~hafen** *m* port of refuge; (*Winterhafen*) winter harbour; **~haft** *f* (*Jur*) protective custody; (*Pol*) preventive detention; **~handschuh** *m* protective glove; **~haube** *f* protective hood; (*für Schreibmaschine*) cover; **~haut** *f* protective covering; **~heilige(r)** *mf* patron saint; **~helm** *m* safety helmet; (*von Bauarbeiter auch*) hard hat (*inf*); **~herr** *m* patron; **~herrschaft** *f* (*Pol*) protection, protectorate; (*Patronat*) patronage; **~hülle** *f* protective cover; (*Buchumschlag*) dust cover *or* jacket; **~hütte** *f* shelter, refuge; **s~impfen** *pret* **s~impfte,** *ptp* **s~geimpft,** *infin auch* **s~zuimpfen** *vt* to vaccinate, to inoculate; **~impfung** *f* vaccination, inoculation; **~kappe** *f* (protective) cap; **~karton** *m* cardboard box; (*für Buch*) slipcase; **~klausel** *f* protective *or* let-out clause; **~kleidung** *f* protective clothing; **~kontakt** *m* (*Elec*) safety contact; **~kontakt(steck)dose** *f* (*Elec*) *siehe* **Schukosteckdose**; **~kontaktstecker** *m* (*Elec*) *siehe* **Schukostecker**; **~leiste** *f* protective strip; (*~planke*) guard-rail.

Schützling *m* protégé; (*esp Kind*) charge.

schutzlos *adj* (*wehrlos*) defenceless; (*gegen Kälte etc*) without protection, unprotected ◆ **jdm/einer Sache ~ ausgeliefert** *or* **preisgegeben sein** to be at the mercy of sb/sth, to be defenceless/without protection against sb/sth.

Schutzlosigkeit *f* defencelessness; unprotectedness.

Schutz-: ~macht *f* (*Pol*) protecting power, protector; **~mann** *m, pl* **-leute** (*dated*) policeman, constable (*Brit*); **~mantel** *m* (*Tech*) protective casing; (*gegen Strahlen*) radiation shield; (*der Haut*) protective layer; **~marke** *f* trademark; **~maske** *f* (protective) mask; **~maßnahme** *f* precaution, precautionary measure; (*vorbeugend*) preventive measure; **~mauer** *f* protecting wall; (*von Festung*) defensive wall; **~mechanismus** *m* (*esp Psych*) protective mechanism; **~mittel** *nt* means of protection *sing*; (*Substanz*) protective substance; (*Med auch*) prophylactic (*gegen* for); **~netz** *nt* (*im Zirkus*) safety net; (*an Damenfahrrad*) skirt guard; (*gegen Stechmücken etc*) mosquito net; **~patron** *m* saint; **~polizei** *f* (*form*) police force, constabulary (*Brit form*); **~polizist** *m* (*form*) police officer, (police) constable (*Brit*), policeman; **~raum** *m* shelter; **~schicht** *f* protective layer; (*Überzug*) protective coating; **~schild** *m* shield; (*an Geschützen*) gun shield; **~schirm** *m* (*Tech*) protective screen; **~staffel** *f* (*Hist*) SS; ⚠**s~suchend** *adj* seeking protection; (*nach Obdach*) seeking refuge *or* shelter; **~truppe** *f* (*Hist*) colonial army *or* force; **~umschlag** *m* dust cover *or* jacket; **~-und-Trutz-Bündnis** *nt* (*old*) defensive and offensive alliance; **~verband** *m* **(a)** protective association; **der ~verband der ...** (*in Namen*) the Association for the Protection of ...; **(b)** (*Med*) protective bandage *or* dressing; **~vorrichtung** *f* safety device; **~wald** *m* barrier woodland; **~wall** *m* protective wall (*gegen* to keep out), barrier; **~weg** *m* (*Aus*) pedestrian crossing; **s~würdig** *adj* worthy of protection; *Gebäude, Sitten* worth preserving, worthy of preservation; **~zoll** *m* protective duty *or* tariff.

Schwa *nt* **-s,** *no pl* (*Ling*) schwa.

schwabbelig *adj* (*inf*) *Körperteil* flabby; *Gelee* wobbly.

schwabbeln *vi* (*inf*) to wobble (about).

Schwabbelscheibe *f* (*Tech*) buffing wheel.

Schwabe *m* **-n, -n** Swabian.

schwäbeln *vi* (*inf*) to speak Swabian *or* the Swabian dialect; (*mit Akzent*) to speak with a Swabian accent.

Schwaben *nt* **-s** Swabia.

Schwabenstreich *m* piece of folly.

Schwäbin *f* Swabian (woman/girl).

schwäbisch *adj* Swabian ◆ **die S~e Alb** the Swabian mountains *pl*; **das S~e Meer** (*hum*) Lake Constance.

schwach *adj, comp* **¨er,** *superl* **¨ste(r, s)** *or adv* **am ¨sten** weak (*auch Gram*); *Mensch, Greis, Begründung, Versuch, Aufführung, Alibi, Widerstand auch* feeble; *Konstitution auch* frail; *Gesundheit, Beteiligung, Gedächtnis* poor; *Ton, Anzeichen, Hoffnung, Bewegung* faint, slight; *Gehör* poor, dull; *Stimme auch* feeble; faint; *Licht* poor, dim; *Wind* light; (*Comm*) *Nachfrage, Geschäft* slack, poor ◆ **~e Augen** weak *or* poor (eye)sight; **das ist ein ~es Bild** (*inf*) *or* **eine ~e Leistung** (*inf*) that's a poor show (*inf*); **ein ~es Lob** faint praise; **jds ~e Seite/Stelle** sb's weak point/spot; **ein ~er Trost** cold *or* small comfort; **in einem ~en Augenblick, in einer ~en Stunde** in a moment of weakness, in a weak moment; **jdn ~ machen** (*inf*) to soften sb up, to talk sb round; **mach mich nicht ~!** (*inf*) don't say that! (*inf*); **in etw** (*dat*) **~ sein** to be weak in sth; **auf ~en Beinen** *or*

Füßen stehen (*fig*) to be on shaky ground; (*Theorie*) to be shaky; **alles, was in meinen ~en Kräften steht** everything within my power; **jdn an seiner ~en** *or* **~̈sten Stelle treffen** to strike at *or* hit sb's weak spot; **mir wird ~** (*lit*) I feel faint; (*fig inf*) it makes me sick (*inf*); **nur nicht ~ werden!** don't weaken!; **~̈er werden** to grow weaker, to weaken; (*Augen*) to fail, to grow worse; (*Stimme*) to grow fainter; (*Licht*) to (grow) dim; (*Ton*) to fade; (*Nachfrage*) to fall off, to slacken; **~ besiedelt** *or* **bevölkert** sparsely populated; **~ besucht** poorly attended; **~ gesalzen/gesüßt** slightly salted/sweetened; **die S~en** the weak; **der S~̈ere** the weaker (person); (*gegenüber Gegner*) the underdog.

schwach-: ~aktiv *adj* (*Atommüll etc*) low-level; ⚠**~besiedelt,** ⚠**~bevölkert** *adj attr* sparsely populated; ⚠**~betont** *adj attr* weakly stressed; ⚠**~bewegt** *adj attr Meer* gently rolling; **schon bei ~bewegtem Meer werde ich seekrank** as soon as there's the slightest swell I get sea-sick; **~brüstig** *adj* (*hum*) feeble.

▼ **Schwäche** *f* **-, -n (a)** *no pl siehe adj* weakness; feebleness; frailty; poorness; faintness, slightness; dullness; dimness; lightness; slackness ◆ **eine ~ überkam sie** a feeling of weakness came over her; **sie brach vor ~ zusammen** she was so weak she collapsed.
(b) (*Nachteil, Fehler*) weakness.
▼ **(c)** (*Vorliebe*) weakness (*für* for).
(d) (*Charaktermangel*) weakness, failing ◆ **menschliche ~n** human failings *or* frailties; **jeder Mensch hat seine ~n** we all have our little weaknesses *or* failings.

Schwäche-: ~anfall *m* sudden feeling of weakness; **~gefühl** *nt* feeling of weakness.

schwächen [1] *vt* (*lit, fig*) to weaken.
[2] *vr* to weaken oneself.
[3] *vi* **etw schwächt** sth has a weakening effect.

Schwäche-: ~punkt *m* low point; **einen ~punkt erreichen** to reach a low point *or* low ebb (in the day); **~zustand** *m* condition of weakness *or* debility (*spec*), weak condition.

Schwachheit *f* **(a)** *no pl* (*fig*) weakness, frailty ◆ **~, dein Name ist Weib** (*prov*) frailty, thy name is woman! (*prov*). **(b)** *no pl* (*rare: Kraftlosigkeit*) *siehe* **Schwäche (a)**. **(c)** (*inf*) **bilde dir nur keine ~en ein!** don't fool *or* kid yourself! (*inf*).

Schwach-: ~kopf *m* (*inf*) dimwit (*inf*), idiot, thickie (*inf*); **s~köpfig** *adj* (*inf*) daft, idiotic.

schwächlich *adj* weakly; (*zart auch*) puny.

Schwächlichkeit *f siehe adj* weakness; puniness.

Schwächling *m* (*lit, fig*) weakling.

Schwachmatikus *m* **-, -se** *or* **Schwachmatiker** *m* (*hum inf*) weakling.

Schwach-: ~punkt *m* weak point; ⚠**s~radioaktiv** *adj* with low-level radioactivity; **s~sichtig** *adj* (*Med*) poor- or weak-sighted; **~sichtigkeit** *f* (*Med*) dimness of vision, amblyopia (*spec*); **~sinn** *m* (*Med*) mental deficiency, feeble-mindedness (*dated*); (*fig inf*) (*unsinnige Tat*) idiocy *no indef art*; (*Quatsch*) rubbish (*inf*); **leichter/mittelschwerer/schwerer ~sinn** mild/severe to moderate/profound mental deficiency, moronism/imbecility/idiocy; **s~sinnig** *adj* (*Med*) mentally deficient, feeble-minded (*dated*); (*fig inf*) daft, idiotic; **~sinnige(r)** *mf decl as adj* mental defective, feeble-minded person (*dated*); (*fig inf*) idiot, moron (*inf*), imbecile (*inf*); **~stelle** *f* weak point.

Schwachstrom *m* (*Elec*) low-voltage *or* weak current.

Schwachstrom-: ~leitung *f* low-voltage (current) line; **~technik** *f* (*dated*) communications engineering *or* technology.

Schwächung *f* weakening.

Schwade *f* **-, -n, Schwaden**[1] *m* **-s, -** swath(e), windrow (*spec*).

Schwaden[2] *m* **-s, -** *usu pl* cloud.

Schwadron *f* **-, -en** (*Mil Hist*) squadron.

Schwadroneur [ʃvadroˈnøːɐ] *m* blusterer.

schwadronieren* *vi* to bluster.

Schwafelei *f* (*pej inf*) drivel *no pl* (*inf*), twaddle *no pl* (*inf*); (*das Schwafeln*) drivelling *or* blethering on (*inf*).

schwafeln (*pej inf*) [1] *vi* to drivel (on), to blether (on), to talk drivel (*all inf*); (*in einer Prüfung*) to waffle (*inf*).
[2] *vt* **dummes Zeug ~** to talk drivel (*inf*); **was schwafelst du da?** what are you drivelling *or* blethering on about? (*inf*).

Schwafler(in *f*) *m* **-s, -** (*pej inf*) wind-bag, gas-bag, blether (*all inf*).

Schwager *m* **-s, ~̈ (a)** brother-in-law. **(b)** (*obs: Postillion*) coachman.

Schwägerin *f* sister-in-law.

Schwägerschaft *f* (*Jur*) relationship by marriage, affinity (*spec*).

Schwaige *f* **-, -n** (*S Ger, Aus*) *siehe* **Sennhütte**.

Schwaiger *m* **-s, -** (*S Ger, Aus*) *siehe* **Senner**.

Schwälbchen *nt dim of* **Schwalbe**.

Schwalbe *f* **-, -n** swallow ◆ **eine ~ macht noch keinen Sommer** (*Prov*) one swallow doesn't make a summer (*Prov*).

Schwalben-: ~nest *nt* **(a)** swallow's nest; **(b)** (*Mil*) (bandsman's) epaulette; **(c)** (*Naut*) sponson; **(d)** (*Cook*) bird's nest soup; **~nestersuppe** *f* bird's nest soup; **~schwanz** *m* **(a)** (*Zool*) swallowtail (butterfly); **(b)** (*inf*) (*Frack*) swallow-tailed coat, swallow-tails *pl*, cutaway; (*Frackschoß*) (swallow-)tails *pl*; **(c)** (*Tech*) dovetail; **mit einem ~schwanz verbinden** to dovetail; **~wurz** *f* **-, -e** (*Bot*) swallowwort.

Schwall *m* **-(e)s, -e** flood, torrent; (*von Worten auch*) effusion.

schwamm *pret of* **schwimmen**.

Schwamm *m* **-(e)s, ~̈e (a)** sponge ◆ **etw mit dem ~ abwischen** to sponge sth (down), to wipe sth with a sponge; **~ drüber!** (*inf*) (let's) forget it! **(b)** (*dial: Pilz*) fungus; (*eßbar*) mushroom; (*giftig*) toadstool. **(c)** (*Haus~*) dry rot ◆ **den ~ haben** to have dry rot. **(d)** (*Feuer~*) touchwood, tinder, punk *all no pl*.

Schwämmchen *nt* **(a)** *dim of* **Schwamm**. **(b)** (*Med*) thrush.

Schwammerl *nt* **-s, -(n)** (*S Ger, Aus inf*) *siehe* **Schwamm (b)**.

schwammig *adj* **(a)** (*lit*) spongy. **(b)** (*fig*) *Gesicht, Hände* puffy, bloated; (*vage*) *Begriff* woolly.

Schwan *m* **-(e)s, ~̈e** swan ◆ **mein lieber ~!** (*inf*) (*überrascht*) my goodness!; (*drohend*) my lad/girl.

schwand *pret of* **schwinden**.

schwanen *vi impers* **ihm schwante etwas** he had forebodings, he sensed something might happen; **mir schwant nichts Gutes** I don't like it, I've a feeling something nasty is going to happen.

Schwanen-: ~gesang *m* (*fig*) swansong; **~hals** *m* swan's neck; (*fig*) swan-like neck; (*Tech*) goose-neck, swan-neck; **~jungfrau** *f* (*Myth*) swan maiden; **~see** *m* Swan Lake; **~teich** *m* swan pond; **s~weiß** *adj* (*geh*) lily-white.

schwang *pret of* **schwingen**.

Schwang *m*: **im ~(e) sein** to be in vogue, to be "in" (*inf*); (*in der Entwicklung*) to be afoot; **in ~ kommen** to come into vogue.

schwanger *adj* pregnant ◆ **~ sein** *or* **gehen** to be pregnant; **mit etw ~ gehen** (*fig*) to be big with sth; **mit großen Ideen ~ gehen** (*fig*) to be full of great ideas.

Schwangere *f decl as adj* pregnant woman.

schwängern *vt* to make pregnant, to impregnate (*form*) ◆ **mit etw geschwängert sein** (*fig*) to be impregnated with sth; **die Luft war mit Rauch/Weihrauch geschwängert** the air was thick with smoke/heavy *or* impregnated with incense.

Schwangerschaft *f* pregnancy.

Schwangerschafts-: ~abbruch *m* termination of pregnancy, abortion; **~gymnastik** *f* antenatal exercises *pl*; **~nachweis** *m* pregnancy test; **~narbe** *f*, **~streifen** *m* stretch mark; **~test** *m* pregnancy test; **~unterbrechung** *f siehe* **~abbruch**; **~verhütung** *f* contraception.

Schwängerung *f* **die ~ einer Frau** making a woman pregnant.

schwank *adj* (*poet*): **~en Schrittes** with faltering steps, shakily, falteringly.

Schwank *m* **-(e)s, ~̈e** (*Liter*) merry *or* comical tale; (*Theat*) farce ◆ **ein ~ aus der Jugendzeit** (*hum*) a tale of one's youthful exploits.

schwanken *vi* **(a)** (*wanken, sich wiegen*) to sway; (*Schiff*) (*auf und ab*) to pitch; (*seitwärts*) to roll; (*beben*) to shake, to rock ◆ **der Boden schwankte unter meinen Füßen** (*lit, fig*) the ground rocked beneath my feet.
(b) *aux sein* (*gehen*) to stagger, to totter.
(c) (*Preise, Temperatur, Stimmung etc*) to fluctuate, to vary; (*Gesundheit, Gebrauch*) to vary; (*Phys, Math*) to fluctuate; (*Kompaßnadel etc*) to swing, to oscillate.
(d) (*hin und her gerissen werden*) to vacillate; (*wechseln*) to alternate ◆ **sie schwankte zwischen Stolz und Mitleid** she alternated between pride and pity.
(e) (*zögern*) to hesitate; (*sich nicht schlüssig sein*) to waver, to vacillate ◆ **~, ob** to hesitate as to whether, to be undecided (as to) whether.
(f) ins S~ kommen *or* **geraten** (*Baum, Gebäude etc*) to start to sway; (*Erde*) to start to shake *or* rock; (*Preise, Kurs, Temperatur etc*) to start to fluctuate *or* vary; (*Autorität, Überzeugung etc*) to begin to waver; (*Institution*) to begin to totter.

schwankend *adj* **(a)** *siehe vi (a)* swaying; pitching; rolling; shaking, rocking ◆ **auf ~en Füßen/~em Boden stehen** (*fig*) to be shaky/to be on shaky ground.
(b) *Mensch* staggering; *Gang* rolling; *Schritt* unsteady.
(c) *siehe vi (c)* fluctuating *esp attr*, varying; oscillating; *Kurs, Gesundheit auch* unstable.
(d) (*unschlüssig*) uncertain, wavering *attr*, (*zögernd*) hesitant; (*unbeständig*) vacillating, unsteady ◆ **jdn ~ machen** to make sb waver; **~ werden** to waver; **sie ist sehr ~ in ihren Entschlüssen** she vacillates a lot.

Schwankung *f* **(a)** (*hin und her*) swaying *no pl*; (*auf und ab*) shaking *no pl*, rocking *no pl* ◆ **um die ~en des Turms zu messen** to measure the extent to which the tower sways.
(b) (*von Preisen, Temperatur, Stimmung etc*) fluctuation, variation (*gen* in); (*von Kompaßnadel etc*) oscillation ◆ **seelische ~en** fluctuations in one's mental state, mental ups and downs (*inf*).

Schwankungsbereich *m* range.

Schwanz *m* **-es, ~̈e (a)** (*lit, fig*) tail; (*inf: von Zug*) (tail-)end ◆ **den ~ zwischen die Beine klemmen und abhauen** (*lit, fig sl*) to put one's tail between one's legs and run; **den ~ hängen lassen** (*lit*) to let its tail droop; (*fig inf*) to be down in the dumps (*inf*); **das Pferd** *or* **den Gaul beim** *or* **am ~ aufzäumen** to do things back to front; **kein ~** (*inf*) not a (blessed) soul (*inf*); *siehe* **treten**.
(b) (*sl: Penis*) prick (*vulg*), cock (*vulg*).

Schwänzchen *nt dim of* **Schwanz**.

Schwänzelei *f siehe vi* **(a)** tail-wagging. **(b)** crawling (*inf*). **(c)** sashaying (*esp US inf*).

schwänzeln *vi* **(a)** (*Hund: mit dem Schwanz wedeln*) to wag its tail. **(b)** (*fig pej: Mensch*) to crawl (*inf*). **(c)** *aux sein* (*geziert gehen*) to sashay (*esp US inf*).

schwänzen (*inf*) [1] *vt Stunde, Vorlesung* to skip (*inf*), to cut (*inf*); *Schule* to play truant *or* hooky (*esp US inf*) from, to skive off (*Brit sl*).
[2] *vi* to play truant, to play hooky (*esp US inf*), to skive (*Brit sl*).

Schwanz-: ~ende *nt* end *or* tip of the tail; (*fig*) tail-end; (*von Flugzeug*) tail; **~feder** *f* tail feather; **~flosse** *f* tail *or* caudal fin; (*Aviat*) tail fin; **s~lastig** *adj* (*Aviat*) tail-heavy; **s~los** *adj* tail-less (*auch Aviat*); **~lurch** *m* (*Zool*) caudate (*spec*), urodele (*spec*); **~meise** *f* (*Orn*) long-tailed tit; **~spitze** *f* tip of the/its tail; **~stachel** *m* (*Zool*) sting (in the tail); **~wirbel** *m* (*Anat*) caudal vertebra.

schwapp *interj* slosh, splash; (*schwups*) slap, smack.

Schwapp *m* **-(e)s, -e** slosh, splash.

schwappen *vi* **(a)** to slosh around. **(b)** *aux sein* (*über~*) to splash, to slosh ◆ **die Modewelle schwappt nach Europa** the fashion spills over into Europe.

schwaps *interj siehe* **schwapp**.

Schwaps *m* **-(e)s, -e** *siehe* **Schwapp**.

schwären *vi* (*liter*) to fester ◆ **eine ~de Wunde** (*lit, fig*) a festering sore.

Schwarm *m* **-(e)s, ¨e (a)** swarm; (*Flugzeugformation*) flight.
(b) (*inf*) (*Angebeteter*) idol; (*Schauspieler, Popsänger auch*) heart-throb (*inf*); (*Vorliebe*) passion, big thing (*inf*) ◆ **der neue Englischlehrer ist ihr ~** she's got a crush on the new English teacher (*inf*).

schwärmen *vi* **(a)** *aux sein* to swarm.
(b) (*begeistert reden*) to enthuse (*von* about), to go into raptures (*von* about) ◆ **für jdn/etw ~** (*außerordentlich angetan sein*) to be mad *or* wild *or* crazy about sb/sth (*inf*); (*verliebt sein, verehren auch*) to worship sb/sth, to be smitten with sb/sth (*liter, hum*); **ins S~ kommen** *or* **geraten** to go *or* fall into raptures; **ich schwärme nicht gerade für ihn** (*iro*) I'm not exactly crazy about him (*inf*).

Schwärmer *m* **-s, - (a)** (*Begeisterter*) enthusiast, zealot; (*Phantast*) dreamer, visionary; (*sentimentaler ~*) sentimentalist. **(b)** (*Zool*) hawkmoth, sphinx moth. **(c)** (*Feuerwerkskörper*) jumping jack.

Schwärmerei *f* (*Begeisterung*) enthusiasm; (*in Worten ausgedrückt*) effusion *no pl*; (*Leidenschaft*) passion; (*Verzückung*) rapture ◆ **sich in ~en über jdn/etw ergehen** to go into raptures over sb/sth; **sich in ~en verlieren** to get *or* become carried away.

Schwärmerin *f siehe* **Schwärmer (a)**.

schwärmerisch *adj* (*begeistert*) enthusiastic; *Worte, Übertreibung* effusive; (*verliebt*) infatuated, gooey (*inf*); (*verzückt*) enraptured; *Illusion, Glaube, Gemüt* fanciful ◆ **die Romantiker hatten alle etwas S~es** the Romantics were all filled with a great emotional passion.

Schwarm-: ~geist *m* (*Phantast*) visionary; (*Eiferer*) zealot; **s~weise** *adv* in swarms.

Schwärmzeit *f* swarming time.

Schwarte *f* **-, -n (a)** (*Speck~*) rind; (*Hunt: Haut*) skin, hide; (*Abfallholz*) slab ◆ **arbeiten, daß** *or* **bis die ~ kracht** (*inf*) *or* **knackt** (*inf*) to work oneself into the ground (*inf*). **(b)** (*inf*) (*Buch*) old book, tome (*hum*); (*Gemälde*) daub(ing) (*pej*); (*Sch sl*) crib (*inf*).

Schwartenmagen *m* (*Cook*) brawn.

schwartig *adj* (*rare*) rindy.

schwarz *adj, comp* **¨er**, *superl* **¨este(r, s)** *or adv* **am ¨esten (a)** (*lit, fig*) black; (*schmutzig auch*) dirty; (*stark sonnengebräunt*) deeply tanned, brown ◆ **~e Blattern** *or* **Pocken** smallpox; **~e Diamanten** black diamonds; **der S~e Erdteil** the Dark Continent; **der S~e Freitag** Black Friday; **~es Gold** (*fig*) black gold; **~er Humor** black humour; **~er Kaffee/Tee** black coffee/tea; **die S~e Kunst** (*Buchdruckerkunst*) (the art of) printing; (*Magie*) the Black Art; **~e Liste** blacklist; **jdn auf die ~e Liste setzen** to blacklist sb, to put sb on the blacklist; **~es Loch** black hole; **~e Magie** Black Magic; **der ~e Mann** (*Schornsteinfeger*) the (chimney-)sweep; (*Kinderschreck*) the bogeyman; (*dated: die ~e Rasse*) the Black Man, the Negro; **das S~e Meer** the Black Sea; **eine ~e Messe** a Black Mass; **S~er Peter** (*Cards*) *children's card-game;* **jdm den S~en Peter zuschieben** *or* **zuspielen** (*fig*) (*die Verantwortung abschieben*) to pass the buck to sb (*inf*), to leave sb holding the baby; (*etw Unangenehmes abschieben*) to give sb the worst of the deal; **das ~e Schaf (in der Familie)** the black sheep (of the family); **eine ~e Seele** a black *or* evil soul; **~er Star** (*Med*) amaurosis (*spec*); **ein ~er Tag** a black day; **der ~e Tod** the Black Death; **die S~e Witwe** the Black Widow (spider); **etw ~ auf weiß haben** to have sth in black and white; **~ von Menschen** crowded *or* black with people; **~ wie die Nacht/wie Ebenholz** jet-black; **in den ~en Zahlen** in the black; **sich ~ ärgern** to get extremely annoyed, to get hopping mad (*inf*); **er wurde ~ vor Ärger** his face went black; **mir wurde ~ vor den Augen** everything went black, I blacked out; **er kam ~ wie ein Neger aus dem Urlaub zurück** he came back from his holidays as brown as a berry; **~ werden** (*Cards*) to lose every trick, to be whitewashed (*inf*); **da kannst du warten/schreien, bis du ~ wirst** (*inf*) you can wait till the cows come home (*inf*)/shout until you're blue in the face (*inf*).
(b) (*inf: ungesetzlich*) illicit ◆ **der ~e Markt** the black market; **~e Geschäfte machen** to do shady deals; **sich** (*dat*) **etw ~ besorgen** to get sth illicitly/on the black market; **~ über die Grenze gehen** to cross the border illegally; **etw ~ verdienen** to earn sth on the side (*inf*).
(c) (*inf: katholisch*) Catholic, Papist (*pej*) ◆ **dort wählen alle ~** they all vote conservative there.

Schwarz *nt* **-,** *no pl inv* black ◆ **in ~ gehen** to wear black.

Schwarz-: ~afrika *nt* Black Africa; **~arbeit** *f* illicit work, work on the side (*inf*); (*nach Feierabend*) moonlighting (*inf*); **s~arbeiten** *vi sep* to do illicit work, to work on the side (*inf*); to moonlight (*inf*); **~arbeiter** *m* person doing illicit work *or* work on the side (*inf*); moonlighter (*inf*); **s~äugig** *adj* dark-eyed; *Schönheit auch* sloe-eyed (*liter*); **~beere** *f* (*S Ger, Aus*) *siehe* **Heidelbeere**; **s~blau** *adj* bluish black, inky blue; *Tinte* blue-black; **~blech** *nt* black plate; **s~braun** *adj* dark brown; **~brenner** *m* illicit distiller, moonshine distiller (*inf*); **~brennerei** *f* illicit still, moonshine still (*inf*); **~brot** *nt* (*braun*) brown rye bread; (*schwarz, wie Pumpernickel*) black bread, pumpernickel; **~bunte** *f* **-n, -n** Friesian; **~dorn** *m* (*Bot*) blackthorn; **~drossel** *f* blackbird.

Schwarze *f* **-n, -n** (*Negerin*) black woman; (*Schwarzhaarige*) brunette.

Schwärze *f* **-, -n (a)** (*no pl: Dunkelheit*) blackness. **(b)** (*Farbe*) black dye; (*Drucker~*) printer's ink.

schwärzen *vtr* to blacken.

Schwarze(r) *m decl as adj* (*Neger*) black; (*Schwarzhaariger*) dark man/boy; (*pej sl: Katholik*) Catholic, Papist (*pej*); (*Aus: schwarzer Mokka*) black (mocha) coffee ◆ **die ~n** (*pej sl*) the Conservatives.

Schwarz|erde *f* (*Geol*) black earth.

Schwarze(s) *nt decl as adj* black ◆ **das kleine ~** (*inf*) one's *or* a little black dress; **ins ~ treffen** (*lit, fig*) to score a bull's-eye; **jdm nicht das ~ unter den Nägeln gönnen** (*dated*) to begrudge sb the very air he/she breathes.

Schwarz-: s~fahren *vi sep irreg aux sein* (*ohne zu zahlen*) to travel without paying, to dodge paying the fare (*inf*); (*ohne Führerschein*) to drive without a licence; **~fahrer** *m* fare dodger (*inf*); driver without a licence; **~fahrt** *f* ride without paying; drive without a licence; **sie wurde bei einer ~fahrt geschnappt** she was caught travelling without a ticket *or* taking a free ride (*inf*)/driving without a licence; **~fäule** *f* (*Bot*) black rot; **~film** *m* (*Typ*) film; **~filter** *m* (*Phot*) black filter; **~geld** *nt* illegal earnings *pl*; **⚠s~gestreift** *adj attr* with black stripes; **s~grau** *adj* grey-black, greyish-black; **s~haarig** *adj* black-haired; **eine ~haarige** a brunette; **~handel** *m, no pl* black market; (*Tätigkeit*) black-marketeering; **im ~handel** on the black market; **~händler** *m* black marketeer; **~hemden** *pl* (*Hist*) Blackshirts *pl*; **s~hören** *vi sep* (*Rad*) to use a radio without having a licence; **~hörer** *m* (*Rad*) radio-owner without a licence; **~kittel** *m* (*inf*) wild boar; (*pej: Geistlicher*) priest.

schwärzlich *adj* blackish; *Haut* dusky.

Schwarz-: s~malen *sep* [1] *vi* to be pessimistic; [2] *vt* to be pessimistic about; **~maler** *m* pessimist; **~malerei** *f* pessimism; **~markt** *m* black market; **~markthändler** *m* black marketeer; **~marktpreis** *m* black-market price; **~meerflotte** *f* Black Sea fleet; **~pappel** *f* black poplar; **~pulver** *nt* black (gun)powder; **~rock** *m* (*pej*) priest; **~-Rot-Gold** *nt*: **die Fahne/Farben ~-Rot-Gold** the black-red-and-gold flag/colours (*of Germany*); **s~rotgolden** *adj Fahne* black-red-and-gold; **s~schlachten** *sep* [1] *vi* to slaughter pigs *etc* illegally *or* illicitly; [2] *vt* to slaughter illegally *or* illicitly; **s~sehen** *sep irreg* [1] *vt* to be pessimistic about; [2] *vi* **(a)** to be pessimistic; **für jdn/etw s~-sehen** to be pessimistic about sb/sth; **(b)** (*TV*) to watch TV without a licence; **~seher** *m* **(a)** pessimist; **(b)** (*TV*) licence-dodger (*inf*); **~seherei** *f* pessimism; **s~seherisch** *adj* pessimistic, gloomy; **~sender** *m* pirate (radio) station; **~specht** *m* black woodpecker; **~storch** *m* black stork.

Schwärzung *f* blackening.

Schwarz-: ~wald *m* Black Forest; **~wälder** *adj attr* Black Forest; **~wälder(in** *f*) *m* **-s, -** inhabitant of/person from the Black Forest; **~wälder Kirsch** *m*, **~wälder Kirschwasser** *nt* kirsch; **~wälder Kirschtorte** *f* Black Forest gateau.

schwarzweiß *adj* black-and-white *attr*, black and white.

Schwarzweiß-: ~aufnahme *f* black-and-white (shot); **~empfänger** *m* black-and-white *or* monochrome set; **~fernsehen** *nt* black-and-white *or* monochrome television; **~fernseher** *m* black-and-white *or* monochrome television (set); **~film** *m* black-and-white film; **~foto** *nt* black-and-white (photo); **~gerät** *nt* black-and-white *or* monochrome set; **⚠s~malen** *vti sep* (*fig*) to depict in black and white (terms); **das kann man doch nicht so s~malen** it's not as black and white as that; **~malerei** *f* (*fig*) black-and-white portrayal; **die ~malerei älterer Geschichtsbücher** the way older history books make everything seem black and white *or* reduce everything to black and white (terms); **s~rot** *adj* black-white-and-red (*the colours of the German imperial flag*); **~rot** *nt*: **die Farben/Fahne ~rot** the black-white-and-red colours/flag; **zeichnung** *f* black-and-white (drawing).

Schwarz-: ~wild *nt* wild boars *pl*; **~wurzel** *f* viper's grass; (*Cook*) salsify.

Schwatz *m* **-es, -e** (*inf*) chat, chinwag (*inf*) ◆ **auf einen ~ kommen** to come (round) for a chat.

Schwatzbase, (*S Ger*) **Schwätzbase** *f* (*inf*) gossip.

Schwätzchen *nt dim of* **Schwatz**.

schwatzen *vti* (*N Ger*) to talk; (*pej*) (*unaufhörlich*) to chatter; (*über belanglose, oberflächliche Dinge, kindisch*) to prattle; (*Unsinn reden*) to blether (*inf*); (*klatschen*) to gossip ◆ **über Politik ~** to prate on about politics (*pej*); **dummes Zeug ~** to talk a lot of rubbish (*inf*) *or* drivel (*inf*).

schwätzen *vti* (*S Ger, Aus*) *siehe* **schwatzen**.

Schwätzer *m* **-s, -** (*pej*) chatterer; (*Kind, Schüler*) chatterbox; (*Schwafler*) wind-bag, gas-bag, bletherer (*all inf*); (*Klatschmaul*) gossip.

Schwätzerei *f* (*pej*) (*Gerede, im Unterricht*) talk, chatter; (*über Belanglosigkeiten, kindisch*) prattle; (*Unsinn*) drivel (*inf*); (*Klatsch*) gossip.

Schwätzerin *f* (*pej*) chatterer, chatterbox; (*Schwaflerin*) bletherer (*inf*), wind-bag (*inf*); (*Klatschbase*) gossip.

schwätzerisch *adj* windy (*inf*), gassy (*inf*).

schwatzhaft *adj* (*geschwätzig*) talkative, garrulous; (*klatschsüchtig*) gossipy.

Schwatzhaftigkeit *f siehe adj* talkativeness, garrulousness; gossipy nature.

Schwebe *f* **-,** *no pl* **sich in der ~ halten** (*Ballon*) to hover, to float in the air; (*Waage*) to balance; (*fig*) to hang in the balance; **in der ~ sein/bleiben** (*fig*) to be/remain in the balance, to be/remain undecided; (*Jur, Comm*) to be/ remain pending.

Schwebe-: ~bahn *f* suspension railway; (*Seilbahn*) cable railway; **~balken, ~baum** *m* (*Sport*) beam.

schweben *vi* **(a)** to hang; (*in der Luft, in Flüssigkeit auch*) to float; (*an Seil etc auch*) to be suspended, to dangle; (*sich unbeweglich in der Luft halten: Geier etc*) to hover; (*nachklingen, zurückbleiben: Klänge, Parfüm*) to linger (on) ◆ **und der Geist Gottes schwebte über den Wassern** (*Bibl*) and the Spirit of the Lord moved over the waters (*Bibl*); **ihr war, als ob sie schwebte** she felt she was walking *or* floating on air; **etw schwebt jdm vor Augen** (*fig*) sb envisages sth, sb has sth in mind; (*Bild*) sb sees sth in his mind's eye; **in großer Gefahr ~** to be in great danger; **in höheren Regionen** *or* **Sphären** *or* **über den Wolken ~** to have one's head in the clouds.

(b) *aux sein* (*durch die Luft gleiten*) to float, to sail; (*hoch~*) to soar; (*nieder~*) to float down; (*an Seil etc*) to swing; (*mit Fahrstuhl*) to soar, to zoom; (*sich leichtfüßig bewegen*) to glide, to float.

(c) (*schwanken*) to hover, to waver; (*Angelegenheit*) to hang *or* be in the balance, to be undecided; (*Jur*) to be pending.

schwebend *adj* (*Tech, Chem*) suspended; (*fig*) *Fragen etc* unresolved, undecided; *Verfahren,* (*Comm*) *Geschäft* pending; (*Comm*) *Schulden* floating; (*Poet*) *Betonung* hovering.

Schwebe-: ~zug *m* hovertrain; **~zustand** *m* (*fig*) state of suspense; (*zwischen zwei Stadien*) in-between state.

Schweb-: ~fliege *f* hover-fly; **~staub** *m* floating dust; **~stoff** *m* suspended matter; (*in Luft*) airborne particles *pl.*

Schwede *m* **-n, -n** Swede ◆ **alter ~** (*inf*) (my) old fruit (*Brit inf*) *or* chap.

Schweden *nt* **-s** Sweden.

Schweden-: ~platte *f* (*Cook*) smorgasbord; **~punsch** *m* arrack punch, Swedish punch; **~stahl** *m* Swedish steel.

Schwedin *f* Swede, Swedish girl/woman.

schwedisch *adj* Swedish ◆ **hinter ~en Gardinen** (*inf*) behind bars; **hinter ~e Gardinen kommen** (*inf*) to be put behind bars.

Schwedisch(e) *nt* Swedish; *siehe auch* **Deutsch(e).**

Schwefel *m* **-s,** *no pl* (*abbr* **S**) sulphur, brimstone (*old, Bibl*).

Schwefel- *in cpds* sulphur; **s~artig** *adj* sulphur(e)ous; **~blume, ~blüte** *f* flowers of sulphur; **~dioxid** *nt* sulphur dioxide; **s~gelb** *adj* sulphurous yellow; **s~haltig** *adj* containing sulphur, sulphur(e)ous; **~hölzchen** *nt* (*old*) match, lucifer (*old*).

schwefelig *adj siehe* **schweflig.**

Schwefel-: ~kies *m* iron pyrites *sing or pl*; **~kohlenstoff** *m* carbon disulphide.

schwefeln *vt* to sulphurize.

Schwefelsäure *f* sulphuric acid.

Schwefelung *f* sulphurization.

Schwefel-: ~verbindung *f* sulphur compound; **~wasserstoff** *m* hydrogen sulphide, sulphuretted hydrogen.

schweflig *adj* sulphurous ◆ **es roch ~** there was a smell of sulphur.

Schweif *m* **-(e)s, -e** (*auch Astron*) tail.

schweifen [1] *vi aux sein* (*lit geh, fig*) to roam, to wander, to rove ◆ **warum in die Ferne ~ ...?** why roam so far afield ...?; **seine Gedanken in die Vergangenheit ~ lassen** to let one's thoughts roam *or* wander over the past.

[2] *vt Bretter, Blechgefäß* to curve.

Schweif-: ~haar *nt* tail hair(s); **~säge** *f* fretsaw; **~stern** *m* comet.

Schweifung *f* curving; (*geschweifte Form*) curve.

schweifwedeln *vi insep* (*Hund*) to wag its tail; (*fig old: liebedienern*) to fawn.

Schweige-: ~geld *nt* hush-money; **~marsch** *m* silent march (of protest); **~minute** *f* one minute('s) silence.

schweigen *pret* **schwieg,** *ptp* **geschwiegen** *vi* to be silent; (*still sein auch*) to keep quiet; (*sich nicht äußern auch*) to remain silent, to say nothing; (*aufhören: Musik, Geräusch, Wind*) to cease, to stop ◆ **~ Sie!** be silent *or* quiet!; **kannst du ~?** can you keep a secret?; **seit gestern ~ die Waffen** yesterday the guns fell silent; **plötzlich schwieg er** suddenly he fell *or* went silent; **er kann ~ wie ein Grab** he knows how to keep quiet; **auf etw** (*acc*)**/zu etw ~** to make no reply to sth; **ganz zu ~ von ..., von ... ganz zu ~** to say nothing of ...

Schweigen *nt* **-s,** *no pl* silence ◆ **jdn zum ~ bringen** to silence sb (*auch euph*); **(es herrscht) ~ im Walde** (there is) dead silence; *siehe* **reden.**

schweigend *adj* silent ◆ **die ~e Mehrheit** the silent majority; **~ über etw** (*acc*) **hinweggehen** to pass over sth in silence; **~ zuhören** to listen in silence *or* silently.

Schweigepflicht *f* pledge of secrecy; (*von Anwalt*) requirement of confidentiality ◆ **die ärztliche ~** medical confidentiality *or* secrecy; **die priesterliche ~** a priest's duty to remain silent; **unter ~ stehen** to be bound to observe confidentiality.

Schweiger *m* **-s, -** man of few words ◆ **der große ~** the strong silent type; (*als Beiname*) the silent.

schweigsam *adj* silent, quiet; (*als Charaktereigenschaft*) taciturn, reticent; (*verschwiegen*) discreet.

Schweigsamkeit *f siehe adj* silence, quietness; taciturnity, reticence; discretion, discreetness.

Schwein *nt* **-s, -e (a)** pig, hog (*US*); (*Fleisch*) pork ◆ **~e** *pl* pigs *pl*, hogs *pl* (*US*), swine *pl*; **sich wie die ~e benehmen** (*inf*) to behave like pigs (*inf*); **bluten wie ein ~** (*sl*) to bleed like a stuck pig; **mit jdm (zusammen) ~e gehütet haben** (*hum*) to be on familiar terms (with sb).

(b) (*inf: Mensch*) pig (*inf*), swine; (*gemein, Schweinehund*) swine (*inf*), bastard (*sl*) ◆ **ein armes/faules ~** a poor/lazy sod *or* bastard (*all sl*); **kein ~** nobody, not one single person.

(c) *no pl* (*inf: Glück*) **~ haben** to be lucky; **~ gehabt!** that's a bit of luck.

Schweinchen *nt dim of* **Schwein** little pig; (*baby-talk*) piggy(-wiggy) (*baby-talk*); (*fig inf: kleiner Schmutzfink*) mucky pup (*inf*).

Schweine-: ~bande *f* (*fig inf*) pack; **~bauch** *m* (*Cook*) belly of pork; **~braten** *m* joint of pork; (*gekocht*) roast pork; **~bucht** *f* (*Geog*) **die ~bucht** the Bay of Pigs; **~fett** *nt* pig fat; **~filet** *nt* fillet of pork; **~fleisch** *nt* pork; **~fraß** *m* (*fig sl*) muck (*inf*); **~futter** *nt* pig feed; (*flüssig*) pig swill; **~geld** *nt* (*sl*) **ein ~geld** a packet (*inf*); **~haltung** *f* pig-keeping; **~hirt(e)** *m* (*esp liter*) swineherd (*esp old, liter*); **~hund** *m* (*sl*) bastard (*sl*), swine (*inf*); **den inneren ~hund überwinden** (*inf*) to conquer one's weaker self; **~kerl** *m* (*sl*) swine (*inf*), bastard (*sl*); **~koben, ~kofen** *m* pigsty; **~kotelett** *nt* pork chop; **~mast** *f* pig-fattening; (*Futter*) pig food; **~mästerei** *f* piggery; **~mett** *nt* (*N Ger Cook*) minced (*Brit*) *or* ground (*US*) pork; **~pack** *nt* (*pej sl*) vermin; **~pest** *f* (*Vet*) swine fever.

Schweinerei *f* (*inf*) **(a)** *no pl* mess ◆ **es ist eine ~, wenn ...** it's disgusting if ...; **so eine ~!** how disgusting!; **Fische zu schuppen, ist eine ~** scaling fish is a messy business.

(b) (*Skandal*) scandal; (*Gemeinheit*) dirty *or* mean trick (*inf*) ◆ **ich finde es eine ~, wie er sie behandelt** I think it's disgusting the way he treats her; **(so eine) ~!** what a dirty trick! (*inf*).

(c) (*Zote*) smutty *or* dirty joke; (*unzüchtige Handlung*) indecent act ◆ **~en machen** to do dirty *or* filthy things; **das Buch besteht nur aus ~en** the book is just a lot of dirt *or* filth.

(d) (*iro: Leckerbissen*) delicacy.

Schweine-: ~rippchen *nt* (*Cook*) cured pork chop; **~rotlauf** *m* (*Vet*) swine erysipelas (*spec*).

schweinern *adj* pork ◆ **S~es** pork.

Schweine-: ~rüssel *m* pig's snout; **~schmalz** *nt* dripping; (*als Kochfett*) lard; **~schnitzel** *nt* pork cutlet, escalope of pork; **~stall** *m* (*lit, fig*) pigsty, pig pen (*esp US*); (*korruptes System*) corrupt shambles *sing*; **~zucht** *f* pig-breeding; (*Hof*) pig farm; **~züchter** *m* pig-breeder.

Schwein|igel *m* (*inf*) dirty pig (*inf*) *or* so-and-so (*inf*).

Schwein|igelei *f* (*inf*) (*Witz*) dirty *or* smutty joke; (*Bemerkung*) dirty *or* smutty remark; (*das Schweinigeln*) dirty *or* smutty jokes *pl*/remarks *pl.*

schwein|igeln *vi insep* (*inf*) (*Witze erzählen*) to tell dirty jokes; (*Bemerkungen machen*) to make dirty *or* smutty remarks; (*Schmutz machen*) to make a mess.

schweinisch *adj* (*inf*) *Benehmen* piggish (*inf*), swinish (*inf*); *Witz* dirty ◆ **benimm dich nicht so ~!** stop behaving like a pig!

Schweinkram *m* (*inf*) dirt, filth.

Schweins-: ~augen, ~äuglein *pl* (*inf*) piggy eyes *pl* (*inf*); **~blase** *f* pig's bladder; **~borste** *f* pig's bristle; **~füße** *pl* (*Cook dial*) (pig's) trotters *pl*; **~galopp** *m*: **im ~galopp davonlaufen** (*hum inf*) to go galumphing off (*inf*); **~haxe** *f* (*S Ger Cook*) knuckle of pork; **~kopf** *m* (*Cook*) pig's head; **~leder** *nt* pigskin; **s~ledern** *adj* pigskin; **~ohr** *nt* **(a)** pig's ear; (*Gebäck*) (kidney-shaped) pastry; **(b)** (*Bot*) (*Kalla*) calla (lily); (*Pilz*) cantharellus clavatus (*spec*); **~stelze** *f* (*Aus*) *siehe* **~füße.**

Schweiß *m* **-es,** *no pl* sweat; (*von Mensch auch*) perspiration; (*Hunt*) blood ◆ **in ~ geraten** *or* **kommen** to break into a sweat, to start sweating/perspiring; **der ~ brach ihm aus allen Poren** he was absolutely dripping with sweat; **der ~ brach ihm aus** he broke out in a sweat; **naß von ~** soaked with perspiration *or* sweat; **kalter ~** cold sweat; **das hat viel ~ gekostet** it was a sweat (*inf*); **im ~e seines Angesichts** (*Bibl, liter*) in the sweat of his brow (*Bibl, liter*); **die Früchte seines ~es** (*liter*) the fruits of his toil *or* labour(s).

Schweiß-: ~absonderung *f* perspiration; **~apparat** *m* welding equipment *no indef art, no pl*; **~ausbruch** *m* sweating *no indef art, no pl*; **~band** *nt* sweatband; **s~bar** *adj* (*Tech*) weldable; **s~bedeckt** *adj* covered in sweat; **~bläschen** *pl* (*Med*) prickly heat *sing*, miliaria *sing* (*spec*); **~brenner** *m* (*Tech*) welding torch; **~brille** *f* (*Tech*) welding goggles *pl*; **~draht** *m* (*Tech*) welding rod *or* wire; **~drüse** *f* (*Anat*) sweat *or* perspiratory (*form*) gland.

schweißen [1] *vt* (*Tech*) to weld.

[2] *vi* **(a)** (*Tech*) to weld. **(b)** (*Hunt*) to bleed.

Schweißer(in *f***)** *m* **-s, -** (*Tech*) welder.

Schweiß-: ~fährte *f* (*Hunt*) trail of blood, blood track; **~flamme** *f* welding flame; **~fleck** *m* sweat stain, perspiration mark; **~fuß** *m* sweaty foot; **s~gebadet** *adj* bathed in sweat; *Mensch auch* bathed in perspiration; **~geruch** *m* smell of sweat *or* perspiration; **~hund** *m* (*Hunt*) bloodhound.

schweißig *adj* sweaty; (*Hunt*) *Tier* bleeding; *Fährte* bloody.

Schweiß-: ~naht *f* (*Tech*) weld, welded joint; **s~naß** *adj* sweaty; **~perle** *f* bead of perspiration *or* sweat; **~roboter** *m* welding robot; **~stahl** *m* welding steel; **~stelle** *f* weld; **~technik** *f* welding (engineering); **s~treibend** *adj* causing perspiration, sudorific (*spec*); **s~treibendes Mittel** sudorific (*spec*); **s~triefend** *adj* dripping with perspiration *or* sweat; **~tropfen** *m* drop of sweat *or* perspiration; **~tuch** *nt* **(a)** (*obs: Taschentuch*) handkerchief; **(b) das ~tuch der Veronika** the sudarium, Veronica's veil; **s~überströmt** *adj* streaming *or* running with sweat.

Schweißung *f* welding; (*Naht, Stelle*) weld.

Schweiz *f* **-** **die ~** Switzerland.

Schweizer [1] *m* **-s, - (a)** Swiss. **(b)** (*Melker*) dairyman. **(c)** (*Eccl: Pförtner*) beadle. **(d)** (*päpstlicher Leibgardist*) Swiss Guard.

[2] *adj attr* Swiss ◆ **~ Käse** Swiss cheese.

Schweizer-: ~degen *m* (*Typ*) compositor-printer; **~deutsch** *nt* Swiss German; **s~deutsch** *adj* Swiss-German; **~franken** *m* Swiss franc.

Schweizergarde *f* Swiss Guard.

Schweizerin *f* Swiss (woman/girl).

schweizerisch *adj* Swiss.

Schwelbrand *m* smouldering fire.

schwelen [1] *vi* (*lit, fig*) to smoulder.

[2] *vt Rasen* to burn off (slowly); *Koks* to carbonize at a low temperature.

schwelgen *vi* to indulge oneself (*in +dat* in) ◆ **von S~ und Prassen hat er nichts gehalten** he had no time for self-indulgence and feasting; **wir schwelgten in Kaviar und Sekt** we feasted on caviar and champagne; **in Farben/Worten ~** to revel in colour/in the sound of words; **im Überfluß ~** to live in the lap of luxury; **in Gefühlen** *etc* **~** to revel in one's emotions; **in Erinnerungen ~** to indulge in reminiscences.

Schwelgerei *f* high living *no pl*, indulgence *no pl*; (*Schlemmerei*) feasting *no pl*.

schwelgerisch *adj* (*üppig*) *Mahl, Farbe* sumptuous; *Akkorde auch* voluptuous; (*genießerisch*) self-indulgent.

Schwel-: **~kohle** *f* high-bituminous brown coal; **~koks** *m* low-temperature coke.

Schwelle *f* -, -n (a) (*Tür~, fig, Psych*) threshold; (*Stein etc*) sill; (*auf Straße*) ramp ◆ **einen/keinen Fuß über die ~ setzen** to set foot/not to set foot in sb's house; **er darf mir nicht mehr über die ~ kommen, er darf meine ~ nie wieder betreten** he shall *or* may not darken my door again (*liter*), he may not cross my threshold again (*liter*); **an der ~ einer neuen Zeit** on the threshold of a new era; **an der ~ des Grabes** *or* **Todes** at death's door.
(b) (*Rail*) sleeper (*Brit*), tie (*US*).
(c) (*Geog*) rise.

schwellen [1] *vi pret* **schwoll**, *ptp* **geschwollen** *aux sein* to swell; (*lit: Körperteile auch*) to swell up ◆ **der Wind schwoll zum Sturm** the wind grew into a storm; **ihm schwoll der Kamm** (*inf*) (*vor Eitelkeit, Übermut*) he got swollen-headed (*esp Brit*) *or* swell-headed (*esp US*) *or* above himself; (*vor Wut*) he saw red; *siehe* **geschwollen**.
[2] *vt* (*geh*) *Segel* to swell *or* belly (out); (*fig*) *Brust* to swell.

Schwellen|angst *f* (*Psych*) fear of entering a place; (*fig*) fear of embarking on something new.

schwellend *adj* (*geh*) swelling; *Lippen* full.

Schwellen-: **~land** *nt* fast-developing nation; **~macht** *f* rising power; **~wert** *m* (*Phys, Psych*) threshold value.

Schweller *m* -s, - (*Mus*) swell.

Schwellkörper *m* (*Anat*) erectile tissue.

Schwellung *f* swelling; (*von Penis*) tumescence (*spec*).

Schwelung *f* (*Tech*) low-temperature carbonization.

Schwemmboden *m siehe* **Schwemmland**.

Schwemme *f* -, -n (a) (*für Tiere*) watering place. (b) (*Überfluß*) glut (*an +dat* of). (c) (*Kneipe*) bar, public bar (*Brit*). (d) (*Aus: im Warenhaus*) bargain basement.

-schwemme *f in cpds* glut of.

schwemmen *vt* (*treiben*) *Sand etc* to wash; *Vieh* to water; (*wässern*) *Felle* to soak; (*Aus: spülen*) *Wäsche* to rinse.

Schwemm-: **~land** *nt* alluvial land; **~sand** *m* alluvial sand.

Schwengel *m* -s, - (*Glocken~*) clapper; (*Pumpen~*) handle; (*sl: Penis*) dong (*US sl*), tool (*sl*).

Schwenk *m* -(e)s, -s (*Drehung*) wheel; (*Film*) pan, panning shot; (*fig*) about-turn ◆ **einen ~ machen** (*Kolonne*) to swing *or* wheel around.

Schwenk-: **~arm** *m* swivel arm; **s~bar** *adj* swivelling; *Lampe auch* swivel *attr*; *Geschütz* traversable; **~bereich** *m* jib range.

schwenken [1] *vt* (a) (*schwingen*) to wave; (*herumfuchteln mit auch*) to brandish.
(b) *Lampe etc* to swivel; *Kran* to swing, to slew; *Geschütz auch* to traverse, to swing; *Kamera* to pan.
(c) (*Cook*) *Kartoffeln, Nudeln* to toss.
(d) *Tanzpartnerin* to swing round, to spin (round).
[2] *vi aux sein* to swing; (*Kolonne von Soldaten, Autos etc*) to wheel; (*Geschütz auch*) to traverse; (*Kamera*) to pan; (*fig*) to swing over, to switch ◆ **links schwenkt!** (*Mil*) left wheel!

Schwenker *m* -s, - balloon glass.

Schwenk-: **~flügel** *m* (*Tech*) swing-wing; **~kartoffeln** *pl* sauté potatoes *pl*; **~kran** *m* swing crane; **~sockel** *m* (*Comput*) swivel base.

Schwenkung *f* swing; (*Mil*) wheel; (*von Kran auch*) slewing; (*von Geschütz*) traverse; (*von Kamera*) pan(ning) ◆ **eine ~ vollziehen** (*Mil*) to wheel; (*fig*) to swing around.

▼ **schwer** [1] *adj* (a) (*lit, fig*) heavy; (*massiv*) *Gold* solid ◆ **ein 10 kg ~er Sack** a sack weighing 10 kgs *or* 10 kgs in weight; **~ beladen/bewaffnet sein** to be heavily laden/armed; **~ auf jdm/etw liegen/lasten** to lie/weigh heavily on sb/sth; **die Beine wurden mir ~** my legs grew heavy; **er ist fünf Millionen ~** (*inf*) he is worth five million.
(b) (*stark*) *Fahrzeug, Maschine* powerful; *Artillerie, Kavallerie, Wein, Parfüm* heavy; *Zigarre* strong; (*nährstoffreich*) *Boden* rich ◆ **~es Wasser** (*Phys*) heavy water; *siehe* **Geschütz**.
(c) (*heftig*) *Sturm, See, Angriff, Artilleriefeuer* heavy; *Winter* hard, severe.
(d) (*ernst*) *Sorge, Bedenken, Unrecht, Unfall, Verlust, Krankheit* serious, grave; *Fehler, Enttäuschung, Beleidigung auch* big; *Zeit, Leben, Schicksal* hard; *Leiden, Belastungsprobe, Strafe, Buße* severe; *Musik* heavy ◆ **~ erkältet sein** to have a heavy cold; **~e Verluste** heavy losses; **~ geprüft sein** to be sorely tried; **S~es erlebt** *or* **durchgemacht haben** to have been through (some) hard times, to have had a hard time (of it); **~ verletzt/krank sein** to be seriously wounded/ill; **~ stürzen/verunglücken** to have a heavy fall/serious accident; **~ bestraft werden** to be punished severely; **das war ein ~er Schlag für ihn** it was a hard blow for him; *siehe* **Stunde**.
(e) (*hart, anstrengend*) *Amt, Aufgabe, Dienst, Arbeit, Tag* hard; *Geburt, Tod* difficult ◆ **es ~ haben** to have a hard time (of it); **~ schuften müssen** to have to work hard; **er lernt ~** he's a slow learner; **~ hören** to be hard of hearing.
▼ (f) (*schwierig*) *Frage, Entscheidung, Übung* hard, difficult, tough ◆ **~ zu sehen/sagen** hard *or* difficult to see/say; **sich ~ entschließen können** to find it hard *or* difficult to decide.
(g) (*inf: enorm*) **~es Geld machen** to make a packet (*inf*).
[2] *adv* (*inf: sehr*) really; *gekränkt, verletzt* deeply ◆ **da mußte ich ~ aufpassen** I really had to watch out; **~ reich** stinking rich (*inf*); **~ betrunken** rolling drunk (*inf*); **~ verdienen** to earn a packet (*inf*); **sich ~ blamieren** to make a proper fool of oneself; **ich werde mich ~ hüten** there's no way (I will) (*inf*); **~ im Irrtum sein** to be badly *or* seriously mistaken; **er ist ~ in Ordnung** he's OK (*inf*), he's a good bloke (*Brit inf*) *or* guy (*inf*).

Schwer-: **~arbeit** *f* heavy labour; **~arbeiter** *m* labourer; **~athlet** *m* weight-lifter; boxer; wrestler; **~athletik** *f weight-lifting sports, boxing, wrestling etc*; **~behinderte(r)** *mf* seriously handicapped person; ⚠**s~beladen** *adj attr* heavily-laden; **~benzin** *nt* heavy benzene, naphtha; ⚠**s~bepackt** *adj attr* heavily-loaded *or* -laden; ⚠**s~beschädigt** *adj attr* (seriously) disabled; **~beschädigte(r)** *mf* disabled person; ⚠**s~bewaffnet** *adj attr* heavily armed; **s~blütig** *adj* serious, ponderous; **ein s~blütiger Mensch** a ponderous (sort of) person.

Schwere *f* -, *no pl siehe adj* (a) heaviness. (b) power; heaviness; strength; richness. (c) heaviness; hardness, severity. (d) seriousness, gravity; hardness; severity ◆ **die ganze ~ des Gesetzes** the full severity of the law. (e) hardness; difficulty. (f) (*Phys: Schwerkraft*) gravitation.

Schwere-: **~feld** *nt* field of gravity, gravitational field; **s~los** *adj* weightless; **~losigkeit** *f* weightlessness.

Schwerenöter *m* -s, - (*dated*) philanderer.

⚠**schwer|erziehbar** *adj attr* maladjusted.

⚠**schwerfallen** *vi sep irreg aux sein* to be difficult *or* hard (*jdm* for sb) ◆ **das dürfte dir doch nicht ~** you shouldn't find that too difficult *or* hard.

schwerfällig *adj* (*unbeholfen*) *Gang, Bewegungen* clumsy, heavy, awkward; (*langsam*) *Verstand* slow, dull, ponderous; *Stil, Übersetzung* awkward, ponderous, cumbersome ◆ **~ gehen/sprechen** to walk/speak clumsily *or* awkwardly.

Schwerfälligkeit *f siehe adj* clumsiness, heaviness, awkwardness; slowness, dullness, ponderousness; cumbersomeness.

Schwer-: **s~geprüft** *adj attr* sorely afflicted; **~gewicht** *nt* (a) (*Sport, fig*) heavyweight; (b) (*Nachdruck*) stress, emphasis; **das ~gewicht verlagern** to shift the emphasis; **das ~gewicht auf etw** (*acc*) **legen** to put the stress *or* emphasis on sth; **s~gewichtig** *adj* heavyweight; **~gewichtler(in** *f***)** *m* -s, - (*Sport*) heavyweight; **s~hörig** *adj* hard of hearing; **~hörigkeit** *f* hardness of hearing; **~industrie** *f* heavy industry; **~industrielle(r)** *mf* industrialist (*in heavy industry*); **~kraft** *f* gravity; ⚠**s~krank** *adj attr* seriously *or* critically *or* dangerously ill; **~kranke(r)** *mf* seriously *or* critically *or* dangerously ill patient; ⚠**s~kriegsbeschädigt** *adj attr* seriously disabled (*in war*); **~kriegsbeschädigte(r)** *mf* seriously disabled ex-serviceman/woman *or* war veteran (*US*).

schwerlich *adv* hardly, scarcely.

Schwer-: ⚠**s~löslich** *adj attr* not easily dissoluble; ⚠**s~machen** *vt sep* (a) **jdm das Herz s~machen** to make sb's heart sad *or* heavy; **jdm das Leben s~machen** to make life difficult *or* hard for sb; (b) **es jdm/sich s~machen** to make it *or* things difficult *or* hard for sb/oneself; **~metall** *nt* heavy metal.

Schwermut *f* -, *no pl* melancholy.

schwermütig *adj* melancholy.

⚠**schwernehmen** *vt sep irreg* **etw ~** to take sth hard.

Schwer|öl *nt* heavy oil.

Schwerpunkt *m* (*Phys*) centre of gravity; (*fig*) (*Zentrum*) centre, main focus; (*Hauptgewicht*) main emphasis *or* stress ◆ **er hat Französisch mit ~ Linguistik studiert** he studied French with the main emphasis *or* main stress on linguistics; **den ~ einer Sache** (*gen*) **bilden** to occupy the central position in sth; **den ~ auf etw** (*acc*) **legen** to put the main emphasis *or* stress on sth.

-schwerpunkt *m in cpds* main emphasis in *or* of.

Schwerpunkt-: **~bildung** *f* concentration; **~industrie** *f* main industry; **s~mäßig** *adj* **eine s~mäßige Betrachtung** a look at the main points; **s~mäßig konzentrieren wir uns auf ...** principally we concentrate on ...; **~programm** *nt* programme *or* plan of main points of emphasis; **~streik** *m* pinpoint strike; **~verlagerung** *f* shift of emphasis.

Schwer-: **s~reich** *adj attr* (*inf*) stinking rich (*inf*); **~spat** *m* heavy spar, barite, barytes *sing*.

Schwerst-: **~arbeiter** *m* heavy labourer; **~beschädigte(r)** *mf* totally disabled person.

Schwert *nt* -(e)s, -er (a) sword ◆ **das ~ ziehen** *or* **zücken** to draw one's sword; **sich mit dem ~ gürten** (*liter*) to gird (on) one's sword. (b) (*von Segelboot*) centreboard.

Schwert|adel *m* (*Hist, fig*) military nobility.

Schwerter-: **~geklirr** *nt* (*liter*) ring(ing) *or* clash(ing) of swords; **~tanz** *m* sword dance.

Schwert-: **~fisch** *m* swordfish; **s~förmig** *adj* sword-shaped; *Blatt auch* gladiate (*spec*); **~griff** *m* (sword) hilt; **~hieb** *m* sword stroke, stroke *or* blow of the sword; **~klinge** *f* sword blade; **~knauf** *m* (sword) pommel; **~leite** *f* -, -n (*Hist*) accolade; **~lilie** *f* (*Bot*) iris; **~schlucker** *m* -s, - sword-swallower; **~streich** *m siehe* **~hieb**; **~tanz** *m siehe* **Schwertertanz**; **~träger** *m* (*Zool*) swordtail.

⚠**schwertun** *vr sep irreg* (*inf*) **sich** (*dat*) **mit** *or* **bei etw ~** to make heavy weather of sth (*inf*).

Schwertwal *m* killer whale.

Schwer-: **~verbrecher** *m* criminal, felon (*esp Jur*); ⚠**s~verdaulich** *adj attr Speisen* indigestible; (*fig auch*) difficult; ⚠**s~verdient** *adj attr Geld* hard-earned; **~verkehr** *m* heavy goods traffic; **~verkehrsabgabe** *f* heavy goods vehicle supplement; ⚠**s~verletzt** *adj attr* seriously injured; **~verletzte(r)** *mf* serious casualty; (*bei Unfall etc auch*) seriously injured person; ⚠**s~verständlich** *adj attr* difficult *or* hard to understand, incomprehensible; ⚠**s~verträglich** *adj attr Speisen* indigestible; *Medikament*

➤ SPRACHE AKTIV: **schwer: 1f** → 33.3, 53.3, 53.6

not easily assimilable *or* assimilated; ⚠**s~verwundet** *adj attr* seriously wounded; **~verwundete(r)** *mf* major casualty; **~wasserreaktor** *m* heavy water reactor; **s~wiegend** *adj* (*fig*) serious.

Schwester *f* **-, -n** sister; (*Kranken~*) nurse; (*Stations~*) sister; (*Ordens~*) nun, sister; (*Gemeinde~*) district nurse; (*inf: ~firma*) sister *or* associate(d) company.

Schwesterchen *nt* little sister, baby sister.

Schwester-: ~firma *f* sister *or* associate(d) company; **~herz** *nt* (*inf*) (dear) sister, sis (*inf*).

Schwesterlein *nt siehe* **Schwesterchen.**

schwesterlich *adj* sisterly.

Schwesterliebe *f* sisterly love.

Schwestern-: ~heim *nt* nurses' home; **~helferin** *f* nursing auxiliary (*Brit*) *or* assistant (*US*); **~liebe** *f* sisterly love; **~orden** *m* sisterhood; **~paar** *nt* two sisters *pl*; **~schaft** *f* nursing staff; (*von Orden*) sisterhood; **~schule** *f* nurses' training college; **~tracht** *f* nurse's uniform; **~wohnheim** *nt* nurses' home.

Schwester-: ~partei *f* sister party; **~schiff** *nt* sister ship.

Schwibbogen *m* (*Archit*) flying buttress.

schwieg *pret of* **schweigen.**

Schwieger-: ~eltern *pl* parents-in-law *pl*; **~leute** *pl* (*inf*) in-laws *pl* (*inf*); **~mama** (*inf*), **~mutter** *f* mother-in-law; **~papa** *m* (*inf*) *siehe* **~vater; ~sohn** *m* son-in-law; **~tochter** *f* daughter-in-law; **~vater** *m* father-in-law.

Schwiele *f* **-, -n** callus; (*Vernarbung*) welt.

schwielig *adj Hände* callused.

schwiem(e)lig *adj* (*dial inf*) dizzy.

schwierig *adj* difficult; (*schwer zu lernen etc auch*) hard ♦ **er ist ein ~er Fall** he is a problem.

Schwierigkeit *f* difficulty ♦ **in ~en geraten** *or* **kommen** to get into difficulties *or* trouble; **jdm ~en machen** to make difficulties *or* trouble for sb; **es macht mir überhaupt keine ~en** it won't be at all difficult for me; **warum mußt du bloß immer ~en machen!** why must you always be difficult *or* make difficulties!; **jdn in ~en** (*acc*) **bringen** to create difficulties for sb; **mach keine ~en!** (*inf*) don't be difficult, don't make any trouble; **ohne ~en** without any difficulty; **ohne große ~(en)** without any great difficulty; **~en haben, etw zu tun** to have difficulties doing sth.

Schwierigkeitsgrad *m* degree of difficulty.

schwill *imper sing of* **schwellen.**

Schwimm-: ~bad *nt* swimming pool; (*Hallenbad*) swimming baths *pl*; **~bagger** *m* dredger; **~bahn** *f* lane; **~bassin, ~becken** *nt* (swimming) pool; **~bewegungen** *pl* swimming action *sing*; (*~züge*) swimming strokes *pl*; **~blase** *f* (*Zool*) air bladder; **~dock** *nt* floating dock.

schwimmen *pret* **schwamm,** *ptp* **geschwommen** *aux sein* [1] *vi* (**a**) *auch aux haben* to swim ♦ **~ gehen** to go swimming *or* for a swim; **er ist über den Fluß geschwommen** he swam (across) the river.

(**b**) (*auf dem Wasser treiben*) to float ♦ **seine Schiffe ~ auf allen Meeren** his ships are afloat on every ocean.

(**c**) (*inf: überschwemmt sein, triefen*) (*Boden*) to be swim ming (*inf*), to be awash ♦ **in Fett** (*dat*) **~** to be swimming in fat; **in seinem Blut ~** to be soaked in blood; **in Tränen ~** to be bathed in tears; **in** *or* **im Geld ~** to be rolling in it *or* in money (*inf*).

(**d**) (*fig: unsicher sein*) to be at sea, to flounder.

(**e**) **es schwimmt mir vor den Augen** I feel giddy *or* dizzy, everything's going round.

[2] *vt auch aux haben* (*Sport*) to swim.

Schwimmen *nt* **-s,** *no pl* swimming ♦ **zum ~ gehen** to go swimming; **ins ~ geraten** *or* **kommen** (*fig*) to begin to flounder.

schwimmend *adj* floating ♦ **~es Fett** deep fat; **im ~en Fett aufbraten** to deep-fry.

Schwimmer *m* **-s, -** (**a**) swimmer. (**b**) (*Tech, Angeln*) float.

Schwimmerbecken *nt* swimmer's pool.

Schwimmerin *f* swimmer.

Schwimm-: s~fähig *adj Material* buoyant; *Fahrzeug, Flugzeug* amphibious; *Boot, Floß* floatable; **s~fähig sein** to be able to float; (*Material*) to float, to be buoyant; **~fest** *nt* swimming gala; **~flosse** *f* fin; (*von Taucher auch, von Wal, Robbe*) flipper; **~flügel** *m* water wing; **~fuß** *m* web-foot, webbed foot; **~gürtel** *m* swimming *or* cork belt; **~halle** *f* swimming bath(s *pl*), (indoor) swimming pool; **~haut** *f* (*Orn*) web; **~hilfe** *f* swimming aid; **~käfer** *m* diving beetle; **~kissen** *nt* water wing; **~kran** *m* floating crane; **~lage** *f* swimming position; **~lehrer** *m* swimming instructor; **~sport** *m* swimming *no art*; **~stadion** *nt* swimming stadium, international swimming pool; **~stil** *m* stroke; (*Technik*) (swimming) style; **~stoß** *m* stroke; **~übungen** *pl* swimming exercises *pl*; **~unterricht** *m* swimming lessons *pl*; **~verein** *m* swimming club; **~versuch** *m* (*fig*) **die ersten ~versuche** the/one's first tentative steps; **~vogel** *m* waterbird, waterfowl; **~weste** *f* life jacket.

Schwindel *m* **-s,** *no pl* (**a**) (*Gleichgewichtsstörung*) dizziness; (*esp nach Drehen auch*) giddiness.

(**b**) (*Lüge*) lie; (*Betrug*) swindle, fraud; (*Vertrauensmißbrauch*) con (*inf*) ♦ **die Berichte über das perfekte Haarwuchsmittel sind reiner ~** the reports about this perfect hair-restorer are a complete swindle *or* fraud *or* con (*inf*); **mit den Subventionen wird viel ~ getrieben** a lot of swindling *or* cheating goes on with the subsidies; **das ist alles ~, was er da sagt** what he says is all a pack of lies *or* a big con (*inf*); **glaub doch nicht an diesen ~!** don't be taken in!; **den ~ kenne ich!** (*inf*), **auf den ~ falle ich nicht herein!** (*inf*) that's an old trick.

(**c**) (*inf: Kram*) **der ganze ~** the whole caboodle (*inf*) *or* shoot (*inf*); **ich will von dem ganzen ~ nichts mehr wissen!** I don't want to hear another thing about the whole damn business (*inf*).

Schwindel|anfall *m* dizzy turn, attack of dizziness.

Schwindelei *f* (*inf*) (*leichte Lüge*) fib (*inf*); (*leichter Betrug*) swindle ♦ **seine ständige ~** his constant fibbing (*inf*).

Schwindel-: ⚠**s~erregend** *adj* (**a**) causing dizziness, vertiginous (*form*); **in s~erregender Höhe** at a dizzy height; (**b**) *Preise* astronomical; **~firma** *f* bogus firm *or* company; **s~frei** *adj* **Wendy ist nicht s~frei** Wendy can't stand heights, Wendy suffers from vertigo; **sie ist völlig s~frei** she has a good head for heights, she doesn't suffer from vertigo at all; **~gefühl** *nt* feeling of dizziness; (*esp nach Drehen auch*) feeling of giddiness.

schwind(e)lig *adj* dizzy; (*esp nach Drehen*) giddy ♦ **mir ist** *or* **ich bin ~** I feel dizzy/giddy; **mir wird leicht ~** I get dizzy/giddy easily.

schwindeln [1] *vi* (**a**) **mir** *or* **mich** (*rare*) **schwindelt** I feel dizzy *or* (*esp vom Drehen*) giddy; **mir schwindelte der Kopf, mein Kopf schwindelte** my head was reeling; **der Gedanke macht mich ~** (*fig*) my head reels *or* I feel dizzy at the thought; **in ~der Höhe** at a dizzy height; **ein ~der Abgrund** a yawning abyss *or* chasm.

(**b**) (*inf: lügen*) to fib (*inf*), to tell fibs (*inf*).

[2] *vt* (*inf*) **das hat sie geschwindelt** she was lying; **das ist alles geschwindelt** it's all lies.

[3] *vr* **sich durch die Kontrollen/in den Saal ~** to con *or* wangle one's way through the checkpoint/into the hall (*inf*); **sich durchs Leben/durch die Schule ~** to con one's way through life/school.

Schwindel-: ~preis *m* astronomical *or* exorbitant price; **~unternehmen** *nt siehe* **~firma.**

schwinden *pret* **schwand,** *ptp* **geschwunden** *vi aux sein* (**a**) (*abnehmen*) to dwindle; (*Schönheit*) to fade, to wane; (*allmählich ver~*) (*Hoffnung auch, Erinnerung, Angst, Zeit*) to fade away; (*Kräfte*) to fade, to fail ♦ **im S~ begriffen sein** to be dwindling; (*Schönheit*) to be on the wane; **ihm schwand der Mut, sein Mut schwand** his courage failed him; **ihm schwanden die Sinne** (*liter*) he grew faint; **aus den Augen ~** to fade from view; **aus der Erinnerung ~** to fade from (one's) memory.

(**b**) (*verblassen: Farben*) to fade; (*leiser werden: Ton auch*) to fade *or* die away; (*sich auflösen: Dunkelheit*) to fade away, to retreat (*liter*).

(**c**) (*Tech: Holz, Metall, Ton*) to shrink, to contract.

Schwindler(in *f*) *m* **-s, -** swindler; (*Hochstapler*) con-man, con merchant (*inf*); (*Lügner*) liar, fibber (*inf*), fraud.

schwindlerisch *adj* fraudulent.

schwindlig *adj siehe* **schwind(e)lig.**

Schwindsucht *f* (*dated*) consumption ♦ **die (galoppierende) ~ haben** (*dated*) to have galloping consumption; (*fig hum*) to suffer from a sort of wasting disease.

schwindsüchtig *adj* (*dated*) consumptive; (*fig hum*) shrinking, ailing.

Schwindsüchtige(r) *mf* (*dated*) consumptive.

Schwingboden *m* sprung floor.

Schwinge *f* **-, -n** (*liter: Flügel*) wing, pinion (*poet*) ♦ **auf den ~n der Poesie/Begeisterung** on wings of poetry/passion.

schwingen *pret* **schwang,** *ptp* **geschwungen** [1] *vt* to swing; (*drohend*) *Schwert, Stock etc* to brandish; *Hut, Zauberstab, Fahne* to wave ♦ **die Gläser** *or* **den Becher ~** (*hum*) to quaff a glass (*old, hum*); **Rahm ~** (*Sw*) to whip cream; *siehe* **geschwungen, Klappe, Rede, Tanzbein.**

[2] *vr* **sich auf etw** (*acc*) **~** to leap *or* jump onto sth, to swing oneself onto sth; **sich über etw** (*acc*) **~** to vault across *or* over sth, to swing oneself over sth; **sich in etw** (*acc*) **~** to vault into sth, to swing oneself into sth; **sich in die Luft** *or* **Höhe ~** (*geh*) to soar (up) into the air; **sich auf den Thron ~** (*fig*) to usurp the throne; **die Brücke schwingt sich elegant über das Tal** the bridge sweeps elegantly over the valley.

[3] *vi* (**a**) to swing.

(**b**) (*vibrieren: Brücke, Saite*) to vibrate; (*Wellen*) to oscillate.

(**c**) (*geh*) (*nachklingen*) to linger ♦ **in ihren Worten schwang leichte Kritik** her words had a tone of mild criticism.

Schwingen *nt* **-s,** *no pl* (*Sw Sport*) (*kind of*) wrestling.

Schwinger *m* **-s, -** (*Boxen*) swing; (*Sw*) wrestler.

Schwing-: ~flügel *m* casement window; **~hebel** *m* (*Aut*) rocker arm; **~schleifer** *m* (orbital) sander; **~tür** *f* swing door.

Schwingung *f* (*Phys*) vibration; (*von Wellen*) oscillation; (*fig*) vibration ♦ **in ~ kommen** to begin to swing *or* (*Saite*) to vibrate *or* (*Wellen*) to oscillate; **etw in ~(en) versetzen** to set sth swinging; to start sth vibrating; to start sth oscillating.

Schwingungs-: ~dämpfer *m* (*Tech*) vibration damper; **~dauer** *f* (*Phys*) time of vibration; period (of oscillation); **~kreis** *m* (*Rad*) resonant circuit; **~weite** *f* (*Phys*) amplitude; **~zahl** *f* (*Phys*) frequency of oscillation.

schwipp *interj* **~, schwapp** splish-splash.

Schwipp-: ~schwager *m* (*inf*) sister-in-law's husband; sister-in-law's/brother-in-law's brother; **~schwägerin** *f* (*inf*) brother-in-law's wife; brother-in-law's/sister-in-law's sister.

Schwips *m* **-es, -e** (*inf*) **einen (kleinen) ~ haben** to be tiddly (*Brit inf*) *or* (slightly) tipsy.

schwirren *vi aux sein* to whizz; (*Bienen, Fliegen etc*) to buzz ♦ **unzählige Gerüchte ~ durch die Presse** the press is buzzing with countless rumours; **die Gedanken/Zahlen schwirrten mir durch den Kopf** thoughts/figures were whirling around in *or* buzzing through my head; **mir schwirrt der Kopf** my

⚠: for details of spelling reform, see supplement

head is buzzing.

Schwitzbad *nt* Turkish bath; (*Dampfbad*) steam bath.

Schwitze *f* -, -n (*Cook*) roux.

schwitzen [1] *vi* (*lit, fig*) to sweat; (*Mensch auch*) to perspire; (*Fenster*) to steam up ◆ **Gott sei Dank, daß du kommst, wir haben vielleicht geschwitzt!** (*inf*) thank God you've come, we were really in a sweat (*inf*).
[2] *vt* (a) *Harz* to sweat; *siehe* **Rippe**.
(b) (*Cook*) *Mehl* to brown in fat.
[3] *vr* **sich halb tot ~** (*inf*) to get drenched in sweat; **sich naß ~** to get drenched in sweat; **wir schleppen diese Kisten und ~ uns halb tot** we've been sweating away with these crates (*inf*).

Schwitzen *nt* -s, *no pl* sweating; (*von Mensch auch*) perspiration.

schwitzig *adj siehe* **verschwitzt**.

Schwitz-: ~kasten *m* (*Ringen*) headlock; **jdn in den ~kasten nehmen** to get sb in a headlock, to put a headlock on sb; **~kur** *f* sweating cure; **~packung** *f* hot pack; **~wasser** *nt* condensation.

Schwof *m* -(e)s, -e (*inf*) hop (*inf*), shindig (*dated inf*), dance.

schwofen *vi* (*inf*) to dance ◆ **~ gehen** to go to a hop (*inf*) *or* shindig (*dated inf*) *or* dance.

schwoll *pret of* **schwellen**.

schwören *pret* **schwor**, *ptp* **geschworen** *vti* to swear ◆ **ich schwöre es(, so wahr mir Gott helfe)** I swear it (so help me God); **auf die Bibel/die Verfassung** *etc* **~** to swear on the Bible/the Constitution *etc*; **er schwor bei Gott/seiner Ehre, nichts davon gewußt zu haben** he swore by God/by *or* on his honour that he knew nothing about it; **ich kann darauf ~, daß ...** I could swear to it that ...; **ich hätte ~ mögen** *or* **geschworen, daß ...** I could have sworn that ...; **jdm/sich etw ~** to swear sth to sb/oneself; **ich spreche nie mehr mit ihm, das habe ich mir geschworen** I have sworn never to speak to him again; **er macht das nie wieder, das hat er ihr geschworen** he has sworn to her that he'll never do it again; **aber das hast du mir geschworen!** but you swore ...!; **sie schworen sich** (*dat*) **ewige Liebe** they swore (each other) eternal love; **auf jdn/etw ~** (*fig*) to swear by sb/sth.

Schwuchtel *f* -, -n (*sl*) queen (*sl*).

schwul *adj* (*inf*) gay, queer (*pej inf*).

schwül *adj* (*lit, fig*) *Tag, Schönheit, Stimmung* sultry; *Wetter, Tag etc auch* close, muggy; (*dumpf-sinnlich*) *Träume, Phantasien* sensuous; *Beleuchtung* murky.

Schwüle *f* -, *no pl siehe adj* sultriness; closeness, mugginess; sensuousness ◆ **in dieser ~** in this sultry weather.

Schwulen- (*inf*): **~bar** *f*, **~lokal** *nt* gay bar; **~strich** *m* (*sl*) gay *or* queer (*pej*) beat (*inf*).

Schwule(r) *mf decl as adj* (*inf*) gay, queer (*pej inf*), fag (*US pej sl*).

Schwulität *f* (*inf*) trouble *no indef art*, difficulty ◆ **in ~en geraten** *or* **kommen** to get into a fix (*inf*); **jdn in ~en bringen** to get sb into trouble *or* hot water (*inf*).

Schwulst *m* -(e)s, *no pl* (*pej*) (*in der Sprache*) bombast, fustian, pompousness; (*in der Kunst*) bombast, ornateness, floridness.

schwulstig *adj* (a) *siehe* **geschwollen**. (b) (*esp Aus*) *siehe* **schwülstig**.

schwülstig *adj* (*pej*) *Stil, Redeweise* bombastic, fustian, pompous.

schwumm(e)rig *adj* (*inf*) (*nervös*) uneasy, apprehensive; (*dial: schwindelig*) dizzy, giddy; (*unwohl*) funny (*inf*) ◆ **mir wird ~** I feel uneasy/dizzy/funny (*inf*).

Schwund *m* -(e)s, *no pl* (a) (*Abnahme, Rückgang*) decrease (*gen* in), decline (*gen* in), dwindling (*gen* of). (b) (*von Material*) shrinkage; (*Tech: Abfall*) waste ◆ **~ machen** (*inf*) to produce scrap. (c) (*Rad*) fading. (d) (*Med*) atrophy. (e) (*Ling: von Vokal etc*) loss.

Schwund-: ~ausgleich *m* (*Rad*) automatic frequency control, anti-fade device; **~stufe** *f* (*Ling*) zero grade.

Schwung *m* -(e)s, ¨-e (a) swing; (*ausholende Handbewegung*) flourish; (*Sprung*) leap ◆ **jdm/etw einen ~ geben** to give sb/sth a push; **etw in ~ setzen** to set sth in motion.
(b) *no pl* (*fig: Elan*) verve, zest; (*von Mensch auch*) go (*inf*); (*lit: Antrieb*) momentum ◆ **in ~ kommen** (*lit: Schlitten etc*) to gather *or* gain momentum; (*fig auch*) to get going; **jdn/etw in ~ bringen** (*lit, fig*) to get sb/sth going; **die Sache** *or* **den Laden in ~ bringen** (*inf*) to get things going; **~ in die Sache** *or* **den Laden bringen** (*inf*) to put a bit of life into things, to liven things up; **jdm/etw ~ geben** (*lit*) to give sb/sth momentum; (*fig auch*) to get sb/sth going; **in ~ sein** (*lit: Schlitten etc*) to be going full speed *or* full pelt (*inf*); (*fig*) to be in full swing; **etw mit ~ tun** to do sth with zest; **voller/ohne ~** full of/lacking life *or* verve *or* zest.
(c) (*Linienführung*) sweep.
(d) *no pl* (*inf: Menge*) (*Sachen*) stack, pile (*inf*); (*Leute*) bunch.

Schwung-: ~feder *f* (*Orn*) wing feather; **s~haft** *adj Handel* flourishing, roaring; **sich s~haft entwickeln** to grow hand over fist; **~kraft** *f* centrifugal force; **s~los** *adj* lacking in verve *or* zest, lacking life; *Mensch auch* lacking go (*inf*); **~rad** *nt* flywheel.

schwungvoll *adj* (a) *Linie, Bewegung, Handschrift* sweeping. (b) (*mitreißend*) *Rede, Aufführung* lively ◆ **es hätte etwas ~er gespielt werden müssen** it should have been played with somewhat more zest *or* verve.

schwupp *interj* in a flash, as quick as a flash ◆ **~! da ist er hingefallen** bang! down he fell; **und ~ hatte der Zauberer ...** and hey presto, the conjurer had ...

Schwupp *m* -s, -e (*inf: Stoß*) push ◆ **in einem ~** in one fell swoop.

schwuppdiwupp, schwups *interj siehe* **schwupp**.

Schwups *m* -es, ¨-e (*inf*) *siehe* **Schwupp**.

Schwur *m* -(e)s, ¨-e (*Eid*) oath; (*Gelübde*) vow.

Schwur-: ~finger *pl thumb, first finger and second finger, raised in swearing an oath*; **~gericht** *nt court with a jury*; **vor das ~gericht kommen** to be tried by jury; **~gerichtsverfahren** *nt* trial by jury *no def art*.

Schwyz *nt* (*Kanton*) Schwyz.

Schwyzerdütsch, Schwyzertütsch ['ʃvi:tsɐty:tʃ] *nt* -(s), *no pl* (*Sw*) Swiss German.

Science-fiction ['saiənsfikʃən] *f* -, -s science fiction, sci-fi (*inf*).

Scientologe [saiəntɔ'lo:gə] *m*, **Scientologin** *f* Scientologist.

scientologisch *adj* Scientologist.

Scientology [saiən'tɔlədʒi] *f* - *no pl* Scientology.

Scientology-Kirche *f* Church of Scientology.

Scirocco [ʃi'rɔko] *m* -s, -s *siehe* **Schirokko**.

Scotchterrier ['skɔtʃtɛriɐ] *m* Scotch terrier, Scottie.

Scriptgirl ['skriptgø:ɐl, -gœrl] *nt* (*Film*) script girl.

scröllen *vti* (*Comput*) to scroll.

Scrotum *nt* -s, **Scrota** (*Med*) scrotum.

Scylla ['stsyla] *f* -, *no pl* (*Myth*) *siehe* **Szylla**.

SDR [ɛsde:'|ɛr] *m* - *abbr of* **Süddeutscher Rundfunk**.

SDS [ɛsde:'|ɛs] *m* - *abbr of* **Sozialistischer Deutscher Studentenbund**.

Seal [si:l] *m or nt* -s, -s sealskin.

Sealskin ['si:lskin] *m or nt* -s, -s (a) sealskin. (b) imitation sealskin.

Séance [se'ã:sə] *f* -, -n séance.

⚠ **Seborrhöe** [zebɔ'rø] *f* -, *no pl* dandruff, seborrh(o)ea (*spec*).

sec *abbr of* **Sekunde**.

sechs [zɛks] *num* six; *siehe auch* **vier**.

Sechs- [zɛks-] *in cpds* six; *siehe auch* **vier-**; **~achteltakt** *m* (*Mus*) six-eight time **~eck** *nt* hexagon; **s~eckig** *adj* hexagonal.

Sechser ['zɛksɐ] *m* -s, - (a) (*obs*) six-kreutzer/-groschen *etc* piece; (*dial inf*) five-pfennig piece ◆ **nicht für einen ~ Verstand haben** not to have a scrap *or* a ha'p'orth (*Brit*) of sense; **einen ~ im Lotto haben** to get a six in the German national lottery (*i.e. the top prize*). (b) six; *siehe auch* **Vierer**.

sechserlei ['zɛksɐ'lai] *adj inv* six kinds of; *siehe auch* **viererlei**.

Sechserpack *m* -s, -s six-pack.

Sechs- [zɛks-]: **s~fach** [1] *adj* sixfold; [2] *adv* sixfold, six times; *siehe auch* **vierfach**; **~füßer** *m* -s, - (*Zool*) hexapod; **s~hundert** *num* six hundred; **~kampf** *m gymnastic competition with six events*; **s~mal** *adv* six times; **s~spurig** *adj* six-lane; **~tagerennen** *nt* six-day (bicycle) race; **s~tägig** *adj* six-day; **s~tausend** *num* six thousand; **ein ~tausender** *a mountain six thousand metres in height*.

Sechstel ['zɛkstl] *nt* -s, - sixth; *siehe auch* **Viertel**[1].

sechstens ['zɛkstns] *adv* sixth(ly), in the sixth place.

sechste(r, s) ['zɛkstə] *adj* sixth ◆ **einen ~n Sinn für etw haben, den ~n Sinn haben** to have a sixth sense (for sth); *siehe auch* **vierte(r, s)**.

Sechsundsechzig ['zɛks|ʊnt'zɛçtsɪç] *nt* -, *no pl* (*Cards*) sixty-six.

Sechszylinder ['zɛks-] *m* six-cylinder car/engine.

sechzehn ['zɛçtse:n] *num* sixteen; *siehe auch* **vierzehn**.

Sechzehntel(note *f*) *nt* -s, - (*Mus*) semiquaver (*Brit*), sixteenth note (*US*).

sechzig ['zɛçtsɪç] *num* sixty; *siehe auch* **vierzig**.

Sechziger(in *f*) *m* -s, - sixty-year-old, sexagenarian.

Secondhandladen [sɛkənd'hɛnd-] *m* secondhand shop.

SED [ɛs|e:'de:] *f* - *abbr of* **Sozialistische Einheitspartei Deutschlands**.

Sedativ(um) *nt* (*Pharm*) sedative.

Sedezformat *nt* (*Typ*) sextodecimo.

Sediment *nt* (*Geol*) sediment.

sedimentär *adj* (*Geol*) sedimentary.

Sedimentgestein *nt* (*Geol*) sedimentary rock.

See[1] *f* -, -n [ze:ən] sea ◆ **rauhe** *or* **schwere ~** rough *or* heavy seas; **an der ~** by the sea, at the seaside; **an die ~ fahren** to go to the sea(side); **auf hoher ~** on the high seas; **auf ~** at sea; **in ~ gehen** *or* **stechen** to put to sea; **zur ~ fahren** to be a merchant seaman; **zur ~ gehen** to go to sea.

See[2] *m* -s, -n [ze:ən] lake; (*in Schottland*) loch; (*Teich*) pond.

See-: ~aal *m* (a) (*Zool*) conger (eel); (b) (*Comm*) dogfish; **~adler** *m* sea eagle; **~alpen** *pl* (*Geog*) Maritime Alps *pl*; **~amt** *nt* (*Admin*) maritime court; **~anemone** *f* sea anemone; **~bad** *nt* (a) (*Kurort*) seaside resort; (b) (*Bad im Meer*) bathe *or* swim in the sea; **~bär** *m* (a) (*hum inf*) seadog (*inf*); (b) (*Zool*) fur seal; **~beben** *nt* seaquake; **s~beschädigt** *adj* (*form*) *Schiff* damaged at sea; **~boden** *m* bottom *or* bed of a/the sea/lake; **der ~boden des Loch Ness** the bottom *or* bed of Loch Ness; ⚠**~-Elefant** *m* sea-elephant; **s~erfahren** *adj Volk* experienced at navigation *or* seafaring; **s~fahrend** *adj attr Volk* seafaring; **~fahrer** *m* seafarer; **Sindbad der ~fahrer** Sinbad the Sailor.

Seefahrt *f* (a) (*Fahrt*) (sea) voyage; (*Vergnügungs~*) cruise. (b) (*Schiffahrt*) seafaring *no art* ◆ **ungeeignet für die ~ in ...** unsuited for navigation *or* sailing in ...; **die ~ lernen** to learn to sail; **die Regeln der ~** the rules of the sea.

Seefahrts-: ~amt *nt* (*esp DDR*) shipping board; **~buch** *nt* (seaman's) registration book; **~schule** *f* merchant navy training college.

See-: s~fest *adj* (a) *Mensch* not subject to seasickness; **s~fest sein** to be a good sailor; (b) *siehe* **s~tüchtig**; (c) *Ladung* fit for sea transport; **~fisch** *m* salt-water fish; **~fischerei** *f* sea fishing; **~fracht** *f* sea freight; **~frachtbrief** *m* (*Comm*) bill of lading; **~funk(dienst)** *m* shipping radio service; **~gang** *m* swell; **starker** *or* **hoher ~gang** heavy *or* rough seas *or* swell; **~gefahr** *f* (*Comm*) sea-risk; **~gefecht** *nt* sea *or* naval battle; **~geltung** *f* (*Hist*) naval prestige; **~gemälde** *nt* seascape; **s~gestützt** *adj* (*Mil*) sea-based; *Flugkörper auch* sea-launched; **~gras** *nt* (*Bot*) eelgrass, sea grass *or* hay; **~grasmatratze** *f* sea grass mattress; **s~grün** *adj* sea-green; **~hafen** *m* seaport; **~handel** *m* maritime trade; **~hase** *m* lumpsucker; **~herrschaft** *f* naval *or* maritime supremacy; **~höhe** *f* sea level; **~hund** *m* seal; **~hundsfell** *nt* sealskin; **~igel** *m* sea urchin; **~jungfer** *f* (*Zool*) dragonfly; **~jungfrau** *f* (*Myth*) mermaid; **~kadett** *m* (*Mil*) naval cadet; **~kanal** *m* (maritime) canal; **~karte** *f* sea *or* nautical chart; **~katze** *f* catfish; **s~klar** *adj* ready to sail; **~klima** *nt* maritime climate; **s~krank** *adj* seasick; **Paul wird leicht s~krank** Paul is a bad sailor; **~krankheit** *f* seasickness; **~krieg(führung** *f*) *m* naval war(fare); **~kriegsrecht** *nt* laws of naval warfare *pl*; **~kuh** *f* (*Zool*) seacrow, manatee; **~lachs** *m* (*Cook*) pollack.

Seel|amt *nt* (*Sw Eccl*) *siehe* **Seelenamt.**

Seeland *nt* **-s** (*Geog*) **(a)** (*dänisch*) Zealand, Seeland. **(b)** (*niederländisch*) Zeeland.

Seelchen *nt* (*inf*) dear soul.

Seele *f* **-, -n (a)** (*Rel, fig*) soul; (*Herzstück, Mittelpunkt*) life and soul ◆ **seine ~ aushauchen** (*euph liter*) to breathe one's last (*liter*); **in tiefster** *or* **innerster ~** (*geh*) in one's heart of hearts; **mit ganzer ~** with all one's soul; **von ganzer ~** with all one's heart (and soul); **aus tiefster** *or* **innerster ~** with all one's heart and with all one's soul; *danken* from the bottom of one's heart; **jdm aus der ~** *or* **aus tiefster ~ sprechen** to express exactly what sb feels; **das liegt mir auf der ~** it weighs heavily on my mind; **sich** (*dat*) **etw von der ~ reden** to get sth off one's chest; **sich** (*dat*) **die ~ aus dem Leib reden** (*inf*) to talk until one is blue in the face (*inf*); **das tut mir in der ~ weh** I am deeply distressed; **zwei ~n und ein Gedanke** (*prov*) two minds with but a single thought; **zwei ~n wohnen in meiner Brust** (*liter*) I am torn; **dann/nun hat die liebe** *or* **arme ~ Ruh** that'll put him/us *etc* out of his/our misery; **meiner Seel!** (*old*) upon my soul! (*old*).

(b) (*Mensch*) soul ◆ **eine ~ von Mensch** *or* **von einem Menschen** an absolute dear.

(c) (*von Feuerwaffen*) bore.

(d) (*von Tau*) core.

Seelen-: ~achse *f* axis (of the bore); **~adel** *m* (*liter*) nobility of mind; **~amt** *nt* (*Eccl*) requiem; **~arzt** (*hum*), **~doktor** (*hum inf*) *m* head-shrinker (*hum inf*), shrink (*inf*), trick-cyclist (*hum sl*); **~drama** *nt* psychological drama; **~forscher** *m* psychologist; **~freund(in** *f*) *m* (*geh*) soul mate; **~friede(n)** *m* (*geh*) peace of mind; **~größe** *f* (*geh*) greatness of mind, magnanimity; **s~gut** *adj* kind-hearted; **~güte** *f* (*geh*) kind-heartedness; **~heil** *nt* spiritual salvation, salvation of one's soul; (*fig*) spiritual welfare; **~hirt(e)** *m* (*geh, iro*) pastor; **~kunde** *f* (*dated*) psychology; **~leben** *nt* inner life; **er versteht ihr ~leben überhaupt nicht** he does not understand her emotions *or* feelings at all; **~lehre** *f* (*dated*) psychology; **s~los** *adj* soulless; **~massage** *f* (*hum inf*) gentle persuasion; **~messe** *f* (*Eccl*) requiem mass; **~not, ~pein, ~qual** *f* (*geh*) (mental) anguish; **~regung** *f* sign of emotion, emotional reaction *or* response; **~ruhe** *f* calmness, coolness; **in aller ~ruhe** calmly; (*kaltblütig*) as cool as you please; **s~ruhig** *adv* calmly; (*kaltblütig*) as cool as you please, as cool as a cucumber (*inf*); **~tröster** *m* (*hum*) (*Schnaps*) pick-me-up (*inf*); (*Mensch*) com forter; **~verkäufer** *m* (*Hist*) seller of souls; (*fig pej*) (*Heuerbaas*) press-gang officer; (*Schiff*) death trap; **s~verwandt** *adj* congenial (*liter*); **sie waren s~verwandt** they were kindred spirits; **~verwandtschaft** *f* affinity, congeniality of spirit (*liter*); **s~voll** *adj* soulful; **~wanderung** *f* (*Rel*) transmigration of souls, metempsychosis; **~wärmer** *m* **-s, -** (*hum: Schnaps*) pick-me-up (*inf*); **~zustand** *m* psychological *or* mental state.

See-: ~leute *pl of* **~mann**; **~lilie** *f* sea lily.

seelisch *adj* (*Rel*) spiritual; (*geistig*) mental, psychological; *Erschütterung, Belastung* emotional; *Grausamkeit* mental ◆ **~ bedingt sein** to be psychologically conditioned, to have psychological causes; **~e Kraft zu etw haben** to have the strength of mind for sth; **~e Abgründe** the blackest depths of the human soul.

See-: ~lotse *m* pilot; **~löwe** *m* sea lion.

Seelsorge *f, no pl* spiritual welfare ◆ **in der ~ arbeiten** to do spiritual welfare work with a church.

Seelsorger(in *f*) *m* **-s, -** pastor.

seelsorgerisch, seelsorg(er)lich *adj* pastoral.

See-: ~luft *f* sea air; **~macht** *f* naval *or* sea *or* maritime power.

Seemann *m, pl* **-leute** sailor, seaman, mariner (*esp liter*).

seemännisch [1] *adj Ausbildung, Sprache etc* nautical; *Tradition auch* seafaring ◆ **das ist typisch ~** that is typical of sailors.

[2] *adv* nautically ◆ **~ heißen sie ...** in nautical *or* sailors' language they are called ...

Seemanns-: ~amt *nt* shipping board; **~ausdruck** *m* nautical *or* sailors' term; **~brauch** *m* seafaring custom; **~gang** *m* sailor's walk; **~garn** *nt, no pl* (*inf*) sailor's yarn; **~garn spinnen** to spin a yarn; **~heim** *nt* sailors' home; **~lied** *nt* sea shanty; **~los** *nt* a sailor's lot; **~mission** *f* mission to seamen, seamen's mission; **~sprache** *f* nautical *or* sailors' slang; **~tod** *m* sailor's death; **den ~tod sterben** to die a sailor's death.

See-: s~mäßig *adj Verpackung* seaworthy; **~meile** *f* nautical *or* sea mile; **~mine** *f* (sea) mine; **~nelke** *f* sea anemone.

Seengebiet ['ze:ən-] *nt* lakeland district.

Seenot *f, no pl* distress ◆ **in ~ geraten** to get into distress.

Seenot-: ~kreuzer *m* (motor) lifeboat; **~(rettungs)dienst** *m* sea rescue service; **~zeichen** *nt* nautical distress signal.

Seenplatte ['ze:ən-] *f lowland plain full of lakes.*

See-: ≈nymphe *f* mermaid; **≈otter** *m* sea otter; **≈pferd(chen)** *nt* seahorse; **≈räuber** *m* pirate; (*in Mittelamerika im 17., 18. Jh. auch*) buccaneer; **~räuberei** *f* piracy; **≈räuberschiff** *nt* pirate (ship); buccaneer; **≈recht** *nt* maritime law; **≈reise** *f* (sea) voyage; (*Kreuzfahrt*) cruise; **≈rose** *f* waterlily; **≈sack** *m* seabag, sailor's kitbag; **≈salz** *nt* sea *or* bay salt; **≈sand** *m* sea sand; **≈schaden** *m* damage at sea, average (*spec*); **≈schiff** *nt* seagoing *or* ocean-going ship *or* vessel; **≈schiffahrt** *f* maritime *or* ocean shipping; **≈schildkröte** *f* sea turtle; **≈schlacht** *f* naval *or* sea battle; **≈schlange** *f* sea snake; (*Myth*) sea serpent; **≈schwalbe** *f* tern; **≈sieg** *m* naval victory; **≈sperre** *f* naval blockade; **≈stadt** *f* seaside town; **≈stern** *m* (*Zool*) starfish; **≈straßenordnung** *f* rules of the road (at sea) *pl*, international regulations for preventing collisions at sea *pl* (*form*); **≈streitkräfte** *pl* naval forces *pl*, navy; **≈stück** *nt* (*Art*) seascape; **≈tang** *m* seaweed; **≈taucher** *m* (*Orn*) grebe; **≈teufel** *m* (*Zool*) monkfish; **≈transport** *m* shipment *or* transport by sea, sea transport; **s≈tüchtig** *adj* seaworthy; **≈tüchtigkeit** *f* seaworthiness; **≈ufer** *nt* lakeside; (*von großem See auch*) (lake) shore; **≈ungeheuer** *nt* sea monster; **s≈untüchtig** *adj* unseaworthy; **≈verkehr** *m* maritime traffic; **≈versicherung** *f* marine insurance; **≈vogel** *m* sea bird; **≈volk** *nt* (*Nation*) seafaring nation *or* people; (*inf: ~leute*) seafaring people *pl*; **≈walze** *f* (*Zool*) sea-cucumber; **s≈wärts** *adv* (*in Richtung Meer*) seaward(s), toward(s) the sea; (*in Richtung (Binnen)see*) toward(s) the lake; **≈wasser** *nt* (*Meerwasser*) sea water; (*Wasser eines Sees*) lake water; **≈weg** *m* sea route; **auf dem ≈weg reisen** to go *or* travel by sea; **≈wesen** *nt* maritime affairs *pl, no art*; **≈wetterdienst** *m* meteorological service, Met Office (*Brit inf*); **≈wind** *m* sea breeze, onshore wind; **≈wolf** *m* (*Zool*) wolf-fish; **≈zeichen** *nt* navigational aid; **≈zunge** *f* sole.

Segel *nt* **-s, -** sail ◆ **mit vollen ~n** under full sail *or* canvas; (*fig*) with gusto; **unter ~ gehen** (*Naut*) to set sail; **die ~ streichen** (*Naut*) to strike sail; (*fig*) to give in.

Segel-: ≈boot *nt* sailing boat (*Brit*), sailboat (*US*); **≈fahrt** *f* sail; **s≈fliegen** *vi infin only* to glide; **s≈fliegen gehen** to go gliding; **≈fliegen** *nt* gliding; **≈flieger** *m* glider pilot; **~fliegerei** *f* gliding; **≈flug** *m* (*no pl: ~fliegerei*) gliding; (*Flug im ~flugzeug*) glider flight; **≈flugplatz** *m* gliding field; **≈flugzeug** *nt* glider; (*leichter gebaut auch*) sailplane; **≈jacht** *f* (sailing) yacht, sailboat (*US*); **≈karte** *f* chart; **s≈klar** *adj pred* ready to sail; **≈klasse** *f* (*Sport*) (yacht) class; **≈klub** *m* sailing club; **≈macher** *m* sailmaker.

segeln *vti* **(a)** *aux haben or sein* (*lit, fig*) to sail ◆ **eine Strecke ~** to sail a course; **eine Regatta ~** to sail in a regatta; **als junger Mensch hat er viel gesegelt** in his younger days he did a lot of sailing *or* he sailed a lot; **~ gehen** to go for a sail.

(b) *aux sein* (*inf*) **durch eine Prüfung ~** to flop in an exam (*inf*), to fail (in) an exam.

Segeln *nt* **-s,** *no pl* sailing.

Segel-: ~ohren *pl* (*hum*) flappy ears *pl* (*inf*); **~partie** *f* sail, sailing trip; **~regatta** *f* sailing *or* yachting regatta; **~schiff** *nt* sailing ship *or* vessel; **~schulschiff** *nt* training sailing ship; **~sport** *m* sailing *no art*; **~törn** *m* cruise (on a yacht etc); **~tuch** *nt* canvas.

Segen *m* **-s, - (a)** (*lit, fig*) blessing; (*Eccl: Gnadengebet auch*) benediction ◆ **es ist ein ~, daß ...** it is a blessing that ...; **über jdn/etw den ~ sprechen** to give sb/sth one's blessing; (*Eccl auch*) to pronounce one's blessing upon sb/sth; **jdm den ~ erteilen** *or* **spenden** to give sb one's blessing *or* benediction; **meinen ~ hat er, er hat meinen ~** he has my blessing.

(b) (*Heil, Erfolg*) blessing, boon, godsend ◆ **das bringt keinen ~** no good will come of it; **ein wahrer ~** a real blessing *or* boon; **zum ~ der Menschheit werden** to be for *or* redound to (*liter*) the benefit of mankind.

(c) (*liter: Ertrag, Lohn*) fruits *pl.*

(d) (*inf*) **der ganze ~** the whole lot *or* shoot (*inf*).

Segen-: ⚠s~bringend *adj* beneficent; **~erteilung** *f* (*Eccl*) benediction, blessing; **⚠s~spendend** *adj* beneficent.

Segens-: s~reich *adj* beneficial; *Tätigkeit* beneficent; **~wunsch** *m* (*liter*) blessing; **herzliche ~wünsche** congratulations and best wishes.

Segler *m* **-s, - (a)** (*Segelsportler*) yachtsman, sailor. **(b)** (*Schiff*) sailing vessel. **(c)** (*Orn*) swift.

Seglerin *f* yachtswoman.

Seglermütze *f* sailor's cap.

Segment *nt* segment.

segmental *adj* segmental.

segmentär *adj* segmentary.

segmentieren* *vt* to segment.

Segmentierung *f* segmentation.

segnen *vt* (*Rel*) to bless ◆ **~d die Hände erheben** to raise one's hands in blessing; *siehe* **gesegnet.**

Segnung *f* (*Rel*) blessing, benediction.

Segregation *f* (*Sociol*) segregation.

sehbehindert *adj* partially sighted.

sehen *pret* **sah,** *ptp* **gesehen** [1] *vt* **(a)** to see; (*an~ auch*) to look at; *Fernsehsendung auch* to watch ◆ **gut/schlecht zu ~ sein** to be easily seen/difficult to see; **sieht man das?** does it show?; **das kann man ~** you can see that, you can tell that (just by looking); **siehst du irgendwo mein Buch?** can you see my book anywhere?; **von ihm war nichts mehr zu ~** he was no longer to be seen; **da gibt es nichts zu ~** there is nothing to see *or* to be seen; **darf ich das mal ~?** can I have a look at that?, can I see that?; **das muß man gesehen haben** it has to be seen to be believed; (*läßt sich nicht beschreiben*) you have to see it for yourself; **ich kann den Mantel/den Menschen nicht mehr ~** I can't stand the sight of that coat/him any more; **jdn kommen/weggehen ~** to see sb coming/leaving; **jdn/etw zu ~ bekommen** to get to see sb/sth; **Sie ~ jetzt eine Direktübertragung ...** we now bring you a live broadcast ...; **Sie sahen eine Direktübertragung ...** that was *or* you have been watching a live broadcast ...; **den möchte ich ~, der ...** I'd like to meet the man who ...; **da sieht man es mal wieder!** that's typical!, it all goes to show (*inf*); **hat man so was schon gesehen!** (*inf*) did you ever see anything like it!; **ich sehe was, was du nicht siehst** (*Spiel*) I spy with my little eye.

(b) (*treffen*) to see ◆ **sich** *or* **einander** (*acc*) ~ to see each other; **also, wir ~ uns morgen** right, I'll see you tomorrow; **ich freue mich, Sie zu ~!** nice to see you.

(c) (*erkennen, feststellen, glauben*) to see ◆ **sich/jdn als etw ~** to see oneself/sb as sth; **etw in jdm ~** to see sth in sb; **das müssen wir erst mal ~** that remains to be seen; **das sehe ich noch nicht** (*inf*) I still don't see that happening; **(ob er tatsächlich kommt,) das wird man noch ~** we'll see (if he actually does come); **das wollen wir (doch) erst mal ~!** we'll see about that!; **das wollen wir (doch) erst mal ~, ob ...** we'll see if ...

(d) (*betrachten, beurteilen*) to see; (*deuten, interpretieren auch*) to look at ◆ **wie siehst du das?** how do you see it?; **das darf man nicht so ~** you shouldn't look at it like that, that's not the way to look at it; **du siehst das/ihn nicht richtig** you've got it/him wrong; **das sehe ich anders, so sehe ich das nicht** that's not how I see it; **rein menschlich/dienstlich gesehen** looking at it personally/officially, from a purely personal/official point of view; **so gesehen** looked at *or* regarded in this way; **du hast wohl keine Lust, oder wie sehe ich das?** (*inf*) you don't feel like it, do you *or* right?

(e) sich ~ lassen to put in an appearance, to appear; **er hat sich schon lange nicht mehr zu Hause ~ lassen** he hasn't shown up at home (*inf*) *or* put in an appearance at home for a long time; **er läßt sich kaum noch bei uns ~** he hardly comes to see us any more; **lassen Sie sich doch mal wieder ~!** do come again; **er kann sich in der Nachbarschaft nicht mehr ~ lassen** he can't show his face in the neighbourhood any more; **kann ich mich in diesem Anzug ~ lassen?** do I look all right in this suit?; **das neue Rathaus kann sich ~ lassen** the new town hall is certainly something to be proud of.

[2] *vr* **sich betrogen/getäuscht/enttäuscht ~** to see oneself cheated/deceived/to feel disappointed; **sich genötigt** *or* **veranlaßt ~, zu ...** to see *or* find it necessary to ...; **sich gezwungen ~, zu ...** to see *or* find oneself obliged to ...; **sich in der Lage ~, zu ...** (*form*) to see *or* find oneself in a position to ... (*form*).

[3] *vi* **(a)** to see ◆ **siehe oben/unten** see above/below; **siehe!** (*esp Bibl*)/**sehet!** (*old, liter, Bibl*) lo! (*Bibl*), behold! (*Bibl*); **sieh(e) da!** (*liter*) behold! (*liter*); **siehst du (wohl)!, siehste!** (*inf*) you see!; **sieh doch!** look (here)!; **~ Sie mal!** look!; **er sieht gut/schlecht** he can/cannot see very well; **scharf/weit ~ (können)** to be able to see clearly/a long way; **~den Auges** (*geh*) with open eyes, with one's eyes open; **willst du mal ~?** do you want to see *or* look?, do you want to have a look?; **laß mal ~** let me see *or* look *or* have a look, give us a look (*inf*); **jdm über die Schulter ~** to look over sb's shoulder; **na siehst du** (there you are,) you see?; **wie ich sehe ...** I (can) see (that) ...; **Sie sind beschäftigt, wie ich sehe** I can see you're busy; **ich sehe schon, du willst nicht** I can see you don't want to; **wir werden schon ~** we'll see; **da kann man mal ~, da kannste mal ~** (*inf*) that just shows (you) (*inf*) *or* goes to show (*inf*); **wir wollen ~** we'll have to see; **mal ~, ob ...** (*inf*) let's see if ...; **mal ~!** (*inf*) we'll see; **jeder muß ~, wo er bleibt** (it's) every man for himself; **sieh, daß du ...** make sure *or* see (that) you ...

(b) (*herausragen*) **aus etw ~** to be sticking *or* peeping *or* peeking (*inf*) out of sth; **das Boot sah kaum aus dem Wasser** the boat hardly showed above the water.

(c) (*zeigen, weisen*) to look ◆ **das Fenster sieht auf den Garten** the window looks onto the garden.

(d) nach jdm ~ (*jdn betreuen*) to look after sb; (*jdn besuchen*) to go/come to see sb; **nach etw ~** to look after sth; **ich muß nur mal eben nach den Kartoffeln ~** I've just got to (have a) look at the potatoes; **nach der Post ~** to see if there are any letters.

(e) auf etw (*acc*) **~** to pay attention to sth, to care about sth; **darauf ~, daß** ... to make sure (that) ...

Sehen *nt* **-s,** *no pl* seeing; (*Sehkraft*) sight, vision ◆ **als Photograph muß man richtiges, bewußtes ~ lernen** as a photographer one has to learn to see correctly and consciously; **ich kenne ihn nur vom ~** I only know him by sight.

sehenswürdig, sehenswert *adj* worth seeing ◆ **ein ~es Schloß** a castle (which is) worth seeing.

Sehenswürdigkeit *f* sight ◆ **die Kneipe ist wirklich eine ~!** that pub is really (a sight) worth seeing!; **die ~en (einer Stadt) besichtigen** to go sightseeing (in a city), to see the sights (of a city).

Seher ['zeːɐ] *m* **-s, -** (*liter*) seer; (*Hunt*) eye.

Seher-: ~blick *m* (*geh*) prophetic eye; **den ~blick haben** to have a prophetic eye; **~gabe** *f* (*geh*) gift of prophecy, prophetic gift.

Seherin ['zeːərɪn] *f* seer.

seherisch ['zeːərɪʃ] *adj attr* prophetic.

Seh-: ~fehler *m* visual *or* sight defect; **~feld** *nt siehe* **Gesichtsfeld**; **~kraft** *f* (eye)sight; **~kreis** *m siehe* **Gesichtskreis**; **~loch** *nt* (*Opt*) pupil.

Sehne *f* **-, -n (a)** (*Anat*) tendon, sinew. **(b)** (*Bogen~*) string. **(c)** (*Math*) chord.

sehnen *vr* **sich nach jdm/etw ~** to long *or* yearn (*liter*) for sb/sth; (*schmachtend*) to pine for sb/sth; **mit ~dem Verlangen** (*geh*) with longing *or* yearning.

Sehnen *nt* **-s,** *no pl siehe* **Sehnsucht**.

Sehnen-: ~reflex *m* tendon reflex; **~scheidenentzündung** *f* tendovaginitis (*spec*), inflammation of a tendon and its sheath; **~zerrung** *f* pulled tendon.

Sehnerv *m* optic nerve.

sehnig *adj Gestalt, Mensch* sinewy, wiry; *Fleisch* stringy.

sehnlich *adj* ardent; *Erwartung* eager ◆ **sein ~ster Wunsch** his fondest *or* most ardent (*liter*) wish; **sich** (*dat*) **etw ~st wünschen** to long for sth with all one's heart; **wir alle hatten sie ~(st) erwartet** we had all been (most) eagerly awaiting her.

Sehnsucht *f* **-, ¨e** longing, yearning (*nach* for); (*schmachtend*) pining ◆ **~ haben** to have a longing *or* yearning.

sehnsüchtig *adj* longing, yearning; *Verlangen, Wunsch etc* ardent; *Erwartung, Ungeduld* eager; *Brief* full of longing *or* yearning ◆ **der dritte Satz hat etwas seltsam S~es** the third movement has a strangely yearning quality.

sehnsuchtsvoll *adj* longing, yearning; *Blick, Augen, Brief, Schilderung, Musik* wistful.

Seh|organ *nt* visual organ.

sehr *adv, comp* **(noch) mehr,** *superl* **am meisten (a)** (*mit adj, adv*) very ◆ **~ verbunden!** (*dated form*) much obliged; **er ist ~ dafür/dagegen** he is very much in favour of it, he is all for it/he is very much against it; **hat er ~ viel getrunken?** did he drink very much?; **er hat ~ viel getrunken** he drank a lot; **~ zu meiner Überraschung** very much to my surprise; **es geht ihm ~ viel besser** he is very much better; **wir haben ~ viel Zeit/Geld** we have plenty of time/money *or* a lot of time/money *or* lots of time/money; **wir haben nicht ~ viel Zeit/Geld** we don't have very much time/money.

(b) (*mit vb*) very much, a lot ◆ **so ~** so much; **jdn so ~ schlagen/zusammenschlagen, daß ...** to hit sb so hard that/to beat sb up so much *or* so badly that ...; **sich über etw** (*acc*) **so ~ ärgern/freuen, daß ...** to be so (very) annoyed/pleased about sth that ...; **~ verwurzelt sein** to be very deeply rooted; **wie ~** how much; **wie ~ er sich auch ...** however much he ...; **sich ~ vorsehen** to be very careful *or* very much on the lookout; **sich** (*dat*) **etw ~ überlegen** to consider sth very carefully; **sich ~ anstrengen** to try very hard; **es lohnt sich ~** it's very *or* well worthwhile; **~ weinen** to cry a lot *or* a great deal; **hat sie ~ geweint?** did she cry very much *or* a lot?; **es regnet ~** it's raining hard *or* heavily; **regnet es ~?** is it raining very much *or* a lot?; **freust du dich? — ja, ~!** are you pleased? — yes, very; **freust du dich darauf? — ja, ~** are you looking forward to it? — yes, very much; **tut es weh? — ja, ~/nein, nicht ~** does it hurt? — yes, a lot/no, not very much *or* not a lot; **~ sogar!** yes, very much so (in fact); **zu ~** too much; **man sollte sich nicht zu ~ ärgern** one shouldn't get too annoyed.

sehren *vt* (*old, dial*) *siehe* **verletzen**.

Seh-: ~rohr *nt* periscope; **~schärfe** *f* keenness of sight, visual acuity; **~schlitz** *m* slit; (*von Panzer etc*) observation slit; **~schwäche** *f* poor eyesight; **~störung** *f* visual defect; **wenn ~störungen auftreten** when the vision becomes disturbed; **~test** *m* eye test; **~vermögen** *nt* powers of vision *pl*; **~weite** *f siehe* **Sichtweite**.

sei *imper sing, 1. and 3. pers sing subjunc of* **sein**.

seibern *vi* (*dial*) *siehe* **sabbern**.

Seich *m* **-(e)s,** *no pl*, **Seiche** *f* **-,** *no pl* **(a)** (*dial sl*) piss (*vulg*). **(b)** (*inf: Geschwätz*) *siehe* **Geseich(e)**.

seichen *vi* **(a)** (*dial sl*) to piss (*vulg*). **(b)** (*inf*) *siehe* **schwafeln**.

seicht *adj* (*lit, fig*) shallow ◆ **die ~e Stelle** the shallows *pl*.

Seichtheit *f* (*lit, fig*) shallowness.

Seichtigkeit *f* (*fig*) shallowness *no pl.* **er sagte nur ~en** everything he said was so shallow.

seid *2. pers pl present, imper pl of* **sein**.

Seide *f* **-, -n** silk.

Seidel *nt* **-s, - (a)** (*Gefäß*) stein, (beer) mug. **(b)** (*S Ger: altes Maß*) half-litre, ≃ pint.

Seidelbast *m* (*Bot*) daphne.

seiden *adj attr* (*aus Seide*) silk, silken (*liter*).

Seiden- *in cpds* silk; **s~artig** *adj* silky, silk-like; **~atlas** *m* silk satin; **~band** *nt* silk ribbon; **~faden** *m*, **~garn** *nt* silk thread; **~gewebe** *nt* silk fabric; **~glanz** *m* silky *or* silken sheen; **~papier** *nt* tissue paper; (*Phot*) satin-finished paper; **~raupe** *f* silkworm; **~raupenzucht** *f* silkworm breeding; **~schwanz** *m* (*Orn*) waxwing; **~spinner** *m* **(a)** (*Zool*) silk(worm) moth; **(b)** (*als Beruf*) silk spinner; **~spinnerei** *f* **(a)** silk spinning; **(b)** (*Betrieb*) silk mill; **~stoff** *m* silk cloth *or* fabric; **~straße** *f* (*Hist*) silk road; **~strumpf** *m* silk stocking; **s~weich** *adj* soft as silk, silky soft.

seidig *adj* (*wie Seide*) silky, silken.

Seiende(s) *nt decl as adj* (*Philos*) being *no art*.

Seife *f*, **-, -n (a)** soap. **(b)** (*Geol*) alluvial deposit.

seifen *vt* **(a)** (*ein~, ab~*) to soap. **(b)** (*Min*) to wash.

Seifen-: ~blase *f* soap-bubble; (*fig*) bubble; **~blasen machen** to blow (soap-) bubbles; **~flocken** *pl* soapflakes *pl*; **~kistenrennen** *nt* soap-box derby; **~lauge** *f* (soap)suds *pl*; **~napf** *m* shaving mug; **~oper** *f* (*inf*) soap (opera); **~pulver** *nt* soap powder; **~schale** *f* soap dish; **~schaum** *m* lather; **~spender** *m* soap dispenser; **~wasser** *nt* soapy water.

seifig *adj* soapy; (*fig*) soppy.

Seigerschacht *m* (*Min*) perpendicular shaft.

Seihe *f* **-, -n** *siehe* **Seiher**.

seihen *vt* (*sieben*) to sieve; (*S Ger, Aus: Flüssigkeit abgießen von*) to strain.

Seiher *m* **-s, -** (*esp S Ger, Aus*) strainer, colander.

Seihtuch *nt* (muslin) cloth.

Seil *nt* **-(e)s, -e** rope; (*Kabel*) cable; (*Hoch~*) tightrope, high-wire ◆ **auf dem ~ tanzen** (*fig*) to be walking a tightrope.

Seil-: ~bahn *f* cable railway; (*Bergseilbahn auch*) funicular; **~brücke** *f* rope bridge.

Seiler *m* **-s, -** ropemaker.

Seilerbahn *f* ropewalk.
Seilerei *f* **(a)** (*Seilerhandwerk*) ropemaking. **(b)** (*Seilerwerkstatt*) ropewalk, ropery (*rare*).
Seilerwaren *pl* rope goods *pl*.
Seil-: ~fähre *f* cable ferry; **s~hüpfen** *vi sep aux sein* to skip; **~schaft** *f* (*Bergsteigen*) rope, roped party; **~schwebebahn** *f* cable railway; (*Bergseilbahn auch*) funicular; **s~springen** *vi sep irreg aux sein* to skip; **~tanz** *m* tightrope *or* high-wire act; **s~tanzen** *vi sep* to walk the tightrope *or* high-wire; **~tänzer** *m* tightrope walker, high-wire performer; **~winde** *f* winch; **~ziehen** *nt siehe* **Tauziehen.**
Seim *m* **-(e)s, -e** viscous *or* glutinous substance.
seimig *adj* viscous, glutinous.
Sein *nt* **-s,** *no pl* being *no art*; (*Philos*) (*Existenz, Da~ auch*) existence *no art*; (*Wesen, So~*) essence, suchness ◆ **~ und Schein** appearance and reality; **~ oder Nichtsein** to be or not to be.
sein[1] *pret* **war,** *ptp* **gewesen** *aux sein* [1] *vi* **(a)** to be ◆ **wir waren** we were; **wir sind gewesen** we have been, we've been; **sei (mir)/seien Sie (mir) nicht böse, aber ...** don't be angry (with me) but ...; **sei/seid so nett und ...** be so kind as to ...; **du bist wohl verrückt!** (*inf*) you must be crazy; **ist das heiß/kalt!** that's really hot/cold!, is that hot/cold!; **das wäre gut** that would *or* that'd (*inf*) be a good thing; **es wäre schön gewesen** it would *or* it'd (*inf*) have been nice; **die Arbeit will sofort erledigt ~** (*geh*) this work must be done immediately; **er ist Lehrer/Inder/ein Verwandter/der Chef** he is a teacher/(an) Indian/a relative/the boss; **was sind Sie (beruflich)?** what do you do?; **er ist immer noch nichts** he still hasn't become anything; **Liverpool ist Fußballmeister/eine große Stadt** Liverpool are football champions/is a large town; **in der Küche sind noch viele** there's (*inf*) *or* there are still plenty in the kitchen; **drei und vier ist** *or* **sind sieben** three and four is *or* are seven; **x sei 4** let x be *or* equal 4; **wenn ich Sie/er wäre** if I were *or* was you/him *or* he (*form*); **er war es nicht** it wasn't him; **niemand will es gewesen ~** nobody admits that it was him/her *or* them (*inf*); **das kann schon ~** that may well be; **und das wäre?** and what would *or* might that be?; **das wär's!** that's all, that's it; **wie war das noch?** what was that again?; **wie war das noch mit dem Witz?** how did that joke go now?; **bist du's/ist er's?** is that you/him?; **wer ist da?** who's there?; **ist da jemand?** is (there) anybody there?; **er ist aus Genf/aus guter Familie** he is *or* comes from Geneva/a good family; **morgen bin ich im Büro/in Rom** I'll *or* I will *or* I shall be in the office/in Rome tomorrow; **waren Sie mal in Rom?** have you ever been to Rome?; **wir waren baden/essen** we went swimming/out for a meal; **wo warst du so lange?** where have you been all this time?, what kept you?; **er war vier Jahre hier, bevor er ...** he had been here for four years before he ...; **es sind über zwanzig Jahre her, daß ...** it is more than twenty years since ...
(b) (*mit infin +zu*) **du bist nicht zu sehen** you cannot be seen; **das war ja vorauszusehen** that was to be expected; **das war nicht vorauszusehen** we couldn't have known that; **der Brief ist persönlich abzugeben** the letter is to be delivered by hand; **wie ist das zu verstehen?** how is that to be understood?; **er ist nicht zu ersetzen** he cannot be replaced; **ein eigener Garten ist nicht zu unterschätzen** a garden of one's own is not to be underestimated; **mit ihr ist ja nicht zu sprechen** you can't talk to her.
(c) was ist? what's the matter?, what is it?; **ist was?** what is it?; (*paßt dir was nicht*) is something the matter?; **was ist mit dir/ihm?** what *or* how about you/him?; (*was hast du/hat er?*) what's wrong *or* the matter *or* up (*inf*) with you/him?; **das kann nicht ~** that can't be (true); **wie wäre es mit ...?** how about ...?, what about ...?; **sei es, daß ..., sei es, daß ...** whether ... or ...; **nun, wie ist es?** well, how *or* what about it?; **wie wäre es, wenn wir ihn besuchen würden?** what about *or* how about going to see him?, why don't we go to see him?; **das brauchte nicht zu ~** it need not *or* never have happened *or* have been (*dial, liter*).
(d) (*dasein, existieren*) to be ◆ **wenn du nicht gewesen wärest ...** if it hadn't been for you ...; **er ist nicht mehr** (*euph*) he is no more (*euph liter*); **alles, was (bis jetzt/damals) war** all that has/had been (*liter*).
(e) (*in unpersönlicher Konstruktion*) **mir ist schlecht** *or* **übel** I feel ill; **mir ist kalt** I'm cold; **was ist Ihnen?** what's the matter with you?; **mir ist, als wäre ich zehn Jahre jünger** I feel ten years younger; **mir ist, als hätte ich ihn früher schon einmal gesehen** I have a feeling I've seen him before.
[2] *v aux* to have ◆ **er ist/war jahrelang krank gewesen** he has/had been *or* he's/he'd been ill for years; **sie ist gestern nicht zu Hause gewesen** she was not *or* wasn't at home yesterday; **er ist verschwunden** he has *or* he's disappeared; **er ist gestern verschwunden** he disappeared yesterday; **er ist eben/gestern fünf Kilometer gelaufen** he has just run five kilometres/he ran five kilometres yesterday; **er ist geschlagen worden** he has been beaten.
sein[2] [1] *poss pron* **(a)** (*adjektivisch*) (*bei Männern*) his; (*bei Dingen, Abstrakta*) its; (*bei Mädchen*) her; (*bei Tieren*) its, his/her; (*bei Ländern, Städten*) its, her; (*bei Schiffen*) her, its; (*auf „man" bezüglich*) one's (*Brit*), his (*US*), your ◆ **wenn man ~ Leben betrachtet** when one looks at one's *or* his (*US*) life, when you look at your life; **jeder hat ~e Probleme** everybody has his *or* their (*inf*) problems; **~e komische Frau** that peculiar wife of his, his peculiar wife; **mein und ~ Freund** my friend and his; **~e zwanzig Zigaretten** his/her/one's twenty cigarettes; **er wiegt gut ~e zwei Zentner** (*inf*) he weighs a good two hundred pounds; **er ist gut ~e zwei Meter** (*inf*) he's a good two metres.
(b) (*old: substantivisch*) his.
[2] *pers pron gen of* **er, es**[1] (*old, poet*) **ich werde ewig ~ gedenken** I shall remember him forever.
seiner *pers pron gen of* **er, es**[1] (*geh*) **gedenke ~** remember him; **er war ~ nicht mächtig** he was not in command of himself.
seine(r, s) *poss pron* (*substantivisch*) his ◆ **der/die/das ~** (*geh*) his; **das S~ tun** (*geh*) to do one's (*Brit*) *or* his (*US*) bit; **er hat das S~ getan** (*geh*) he did his bit; **jedem das S~** each to his own; **sie ist die S~ geworden** (*geh*) she has become his (*liter*); **die S~n** (*geh*) his family, his people; (*auf „man" bezüglich*) one's (*Brit*) *or* his (*US*) family *or* people; **das S~** (*geh: Besitz*) what is his; (*auf „man" bezüglich*) what is one's own (*Brit*) *or* his (*US*).
seiner-: ~seits *adv* (*von ihm*) on his part; (*er selbst*) for his part; **~zeit** *adv* at that time; (*rare: künftig*) one day; **~zeitig** *adj attr* (*Aus*) then *attr*.
seines *poss pron siehe* **seine(r, s).**
seinesgleichen *pron inv* (*gleichgestellt*) his equals *pl*; (*auf „man" bezüglich*) one's (*Brit*) *or* his (*US*) equals; (*gleichartig*) his kind *pl*; of one's own kind; (*pej*) the likes of him *pl* ◆ **jdn wie ~ behandeln** to treat sb as an equal *or* on equal terms; **das hat nicht** *or* **sucht ~** it is unparalleled; (*Kunstwerk auch*) it has no equal.
seinet-: ~halben (*dated*), **~wegen** *adv* **(a)** (*wegen ihm*) because of him, on account of him, on his account; (*ihm zuliebe auch*) for his sake; (*um ihn*) about him; (*für ihn*) on his behalf; **(b)** (*von ihm aus*) as far as he is concerned; **~willen** *adv*: **um ~willen** for his sake, for him.
seinige *poss pron* **der/die/das ~** (*form, old*) *siehe* **seine(r, s).**
⚠ **seinlassen** *vt sep irreg* **etw ~** (*aufhören*) to stop sth/doing sth; (*nicht tun*) to drop sth, to leave sth; **jdn/etw ~** to leave sb/sth alone, to let sb/sth be; **laß es sein!** stop that!; **du hättest es ~ sollen** you should have left well alone; **sie kann es einfach nicht ~** she just can't stop herself.
seins *poss pron* his.
Seinslehre *f* (*Philos*) ontology.
seismisch *adj* seismic.
Seismogramm *nt* seismogram.
⚠ **Seismograph** *m* seismograph.
Seismologe *m*, **Seismologin** *f* seismologist.
Seismologie *f* seismology.
seit [1] *prep +dat* (*Zeitpunkt*) since; (*Zeitdauer*) for, in (*esp US*) ◆ **~ wann?** since when?; **~ Jahren** for years; **ich habe ihn ~ Jahren nicht gesehen** I haven't seen him for *or* in (*esp US*) years; **ich bin ~ zwei Jahren hier** I have been here for two years; **schon ~ zwei Jahren nicht mehr** not for two years, not since two years ago; **wir warten schon ~ zwei Stunden** we have been *or* we've been waiting (for) two hours; **~ etwa einer Woche** since about a week ago, for about a week.
[2] *conj* since.
seitdem [1] *adv* since then ◆ **~ ist die Strecke nicht mehr in Betrieb** the line has been closed down since then.
[2] *conj* since.
Seite *f* **-, -n** **(a)** (*auch Abstammungslinie, Charakterzug*) side ◆ **die hintere/vordere ~** the back/front; **zu** *or* **auf beiden ~n des Fensters/des Hauses/der Straße** on both sides of the window/house/street; **mit der ~ nach vorn** sideways on; **~ an ~** side by side; **an jds ~** (*dat*)**gehen** to walk at *or* by sb's side *or* beside sb; **halt dich an meiner ~!** stay by my side; **er ging** *or* **wich uns nicht von der ~** he never left our side; **ich kann mich nicht an Ihrer ~ zeigen** I can't be seen with you; **jdn von der ~ ansehen** to give sb a sidelong glance; **auf die** *or* **zur ~ gehen** *or* **treten** to step aside; **an der ~ (einer Reihe) sitzen** to sit at the end (of a row); **zur ~ sprechen/sehen** to speak/look to one side; **zur ~** (*Theat*) aside; **die ~n wechseln** (*Sport*) to change ends *or* over; (*fig*) to change sides; **jdn auf seine ~ bringen** *or* **ziehen** to get sb on one's side; **auf einer ~ gelähmt sein** to be paralyzed in one side; **die Hände in die ~n gestemmt** with arms akimbo, with one's hands on one's hips; **jedes Ding** *or* **alles hat zwei ~n** there are two sides to everything; **jdm zur ~ stehen** (*fig*) to stand by sb's side; **auf jds** (*dat*) **~ stehen** *or* **sein** (*fig*) to be on sb's side; **das Recht ist auf ihrer ~** she has right on her side; **etw auf die ~ legen** (*lit, fig*) to put sth on one side, to put sth aside; (*kippen*) to put sth on its side; **jdn zur ~ nehmen** to take sb aside *or* on one side; **auf der einen ~..., auf der anderen (~) ...** on the one hand ..., on the other (hand) ...; **jds starke ~** sb's forte, sb's strong point; **jds schwache ~** sb's weakness, sb's weak spot; **sich von seiner besten ~ zeigen** to show oneself at one's best; **neue ~n an jdm/etw entdecken** to discover new sides to sb/sth; **von dieser ~ kenne ich ihn gar nicht** I didn't know that side of him; **einer Sache** (*dat*) **die beste ~ abgewinnen** to make the best *or* most of sth.
(b) (*Richtung*) **von allen ~n** (*lit, fig*) from all sides; **nach allen ~n auseinandergehen** to scatter in all directions; **sich nach allen ~n umsehen/vergewissern** to look around on all sides/to check up on all sides; **das habe ich von einer anderen ~ erfahren** (*fig*) I heard it from another source *or* from elsewhere; **er erfuhr es von dritter ~** (*fig*) he heard it from a third party; **bisher wurden von keiner ~ Einwände erhoben** so far no objections have been voiced from any quarter; **die Behauptung wurde von keiner ~/von allen ~n/von beiden ~n bestritten** nobody challenged the claim/the claim was challenged by all/both parties; **von meiner ~ aus** (*fig*) on my part; **von kirchlicher ~ (aus)** on the part of the church.
(c) (*Buch~, Zeitungs~*) page ◆ **die erste/letzte ~** the first/last page; (*von Zeitung*) the front/back page.
seiten *prep +gen* **auf/von ~** on the part of.
Seiten- *in cpds* side; (*esp Tech, Sci etc*) lateral; **~altar** *m* side altar; **~angabe** *f* page reference; **~ansicht** *f* side view; (*Tech*) side elevation; **~arm** *m* branch, feeder; (*von Fluß*) branch; **~aufprallschutz** *m* (*Aut*) side impact protection system, SIPS; **~ausgang** *m* side exit; **~blick** *m* sidelong glance; **mit einem ~blick auf** (*+acc*) (*fig*) with one eye on; **~einsteiger** *m* (*fig*) person who comes in through the back door; **~fläche** *f* (*Tech*) lateral face *or* surface; **~flosse** *f* (*Aviat*) fin; **~flügel** *m* side wing; (*von Altar*) wing;

~**gang** *m (Naut)* side strake; *(Rail)* (side) corridor; ~**gasse** *f* side-street, back-street; ~**gebäude** *nt* side building; *(auf Hof)* outhouse; *(Anbau)* annex(e); ~**gewehr** *nt* bayonet; ~**halbierende** *f* **-n, -n** *(Math)* median; ~**hieb** *m (Fechten)* side cut; *(fig)* side-swipe; ~**kante** *f* lateral edge; ~**lage** *f* side position; **in ~lage schlafen** to sleep on one's side; **s~lang** *adj* several pages long, going on for pages; **etw s~lang beschreiben** to devote pages to describing sth; **sich s~lang über etw** *(acc)* **auslassen** to go on for pages about sth; ~**länge** *f* length of a/the side; **ein gleichseitiges Dreieck mit der ~länge 4,5 cm** an equilateral triangle whose sides are 4.5 cm long; ~**lehne** *f* arm(rest); ~**leitwerk** *nt (Aviat)* rudder (assembly); ~**linie** *f* **(a)** *(Rail)* branch line; **(b)** *(von Fürstengeschlecht)* collateral line; **(c)** *(Tennis)* sideline; *(Ftbl etc)* touchline; ~**moräne** *f (Geol)* lateral moraine; ~**pfad** *m* bypath; ⚠~**riß** *m (Tech)* side elevation; ~**ruder** *nt (Aviat)* rudder.

seitens *prep +gen (form)* on the part of.

Seiten-: ~**scheitel** *m* side parting *(Brit)*, side part *(US)*; ~**schiff** *nt (Archit)* (side) aisle; ~**sprung** *m (fig)* bit on the side *(inf) no pl*, (little) infidelity; **die Versuchung, ~sprünge zu machen** the temptation to have a bit on the side *(inf)*; ~**stechen** *nt* stitch; **~stechen haben/bekommen** to have/get a stitch; ~**stiche** *pl siehe* **~stechen**; ~**straße** *f* side-street, side road; ~**streifen** *m* verge; *(der Autobahn)* hard shoulder, shoulder *(US)*; „**~streifen nicht befahrbar**" "soft verges" *(Brit)*, "soft shoulder" *(US)*; ~**tal** *nt* valley; ~**tasche** *f* side pocket; ~**teil** *m or nt* side; **s~verkehrt** *adj* the wrong way round; ~**vorschub** *m (beim Drucker)* form feed; ~**wagen** *m* sidecar; ~**wand** *f* side wall; *(von Schiff)* side; ~**wände** *pl (Theat)* wings *pl*; ~**wechsel** *m (Sport)* changeover; ~**weg** *m* side road, byway, back road; **~wege gehen** *(fig)* to indulge in clandestine activities; ~**wind** *m* crosswind; ~**zahl** *f* **(a)** page number; **(b)** *(Gesamtzahl)* number of pages.

seither [zait'heːɐ] *adv* since then.

seitherig [zait'heːrɪç] *adj siehe* **bisherig**.

seitlich [1] *adj* lateral *(esp Sci, Tech)*, side *attr* ◆ **die ~e Begrenzung der Straße wird durch einen weißen Streifen markiert** the side of the road is marked by a white line; **bei starkem ~en Wind** in a strong crosswind.

[2] *adv* at the side; *(von der Seite)* from the side ◆ **~ von** at the side of; **~ stehen** to stand sideways on; **etw/sich ~ stellen** to put sth/stand sideways on; **die Kisten sind ~ grün bemalt** the sides of the boxes are painted green; **er ist mir ~ ins Auto gefahren** he crashed into the side of my car.

[3] *prep +gen* to *or* at the side of.

seitlings *adv (obs) (zur Seite)* sideways; *(auf der Seite)* on one's side.

seitwärts *adv* sideways ◆ **sich ~ halten** to keep to the side.

Sek., sek. *abbr of* **Sekunde** sec.

Sekans *m* **-, -** *or* **Sekanten, Sekante** *f* **-, -n** *(Math)* secant.

Sekond *f* **-, -en** *(Fechten)* seconde.

Sekret[1] *nt* **-(e)s, -e** *(Physiol)* secretion.

Sekret[2] *f* **-,** *no pl (Eccl)* secret (of the mass).

Sekretär *m* **(a)** secretary. **(b)** *(Schreibschrank)* bureau, secretaire. **(c)** *(Orn)* secretary-bird.

Sekretariat *nt* office.

Sekretärin *f* secretary.

Sekretion *f (Physiol)* secretion.

Sekt *m* **-(e)s, -e** sparkling wine, champagne.

Sekte *f* **-, -n** sect.

Sektenwesen *nt* sectarianism.

Sekt-: ~**frühstück** *nt* champagne breakfast; ~**glas** *nt* champagne glass.

Sektierer(in *f***)** *m* **-s, -** sectarian.

sektiererisch *adj* sectarian.

Sektierertum *nt* sectarianism.

Sektion *f* **(a)** section; *(esp DDR: Abteilung)* department. **(b)** *(Obduktion)* post-mortem (examination), autopsy.

Sektions-: ~**befund** *m* post-mortem *or* autopsy findings *pl*; ~**chef** *m (von Abteilung)* head of department; ~**saal** *m* dissection room; **s~weise** *adv* in sections.

Sektkelch *m* champagne flute.

Sektor *m* sector *(auch Comput)*; *(Sachgebiet)* field.

Sektorengrenze *f* sector boundary.

Sektschale *f* champagne glass.

Sekund *f* **-, -en** *(Mus) siehe* **Sekunde**.

Sekunda *f* **-, Sekunden** *(Sch) sixth and seventh year of German secondary school.*

Sekund|akkord *m (Mus)* third inversion (of the seventh chord).

Sekundaner(in *f***)** *m* **-s, -** *(Sch) pupil in sixth and seventh year of German secondary school.*

Sekundant *m* second.

sekundär *adj* secondary.

Sekundär- *in cpds* secondary.

Sekundarlehrer *m (Sw)* secondary *or* high *(esp US)* school teacher.

Sekundärliteratur *f* secondary literature.

Sekundar-: ~**schule** *f (Sw)* secondary school; ~**stufe** *f* secondary *or* high *(esp US)* school level.

Sekunde *f* **-, -n** *(auch Mus, Math)* second ◆ **eine ~, bitte!** just a *or* one second, please; **auf die ~ genau** to the second.

Sekunden *pl of* **Sekunda, Sekunde.**

Sekunden-: ~**bruchteil** *m* split second, fraction of a second; ~**geschwindigkeit** *f siehe* **~schnelle**; **s~lang** [1] *adj* of a few seconds; [2] *adv* for a few seconds; ~**schnelle** *f*: **in ~schnelle** in a matter of seconds; ~**zeiger** *m* second hand.

sekundieren* *vi +dat* to second; *(unterstützen auch)* to back up ◆ **jdm (bei einem Duell) ~** to act as *or* be sb's second (in a duel).

sekundlich, sekündlich [1] *adj (rare) Abstand* one-second.

[2] *adv* every second.

Sekurit ® *nt* **-s,** *no pl* Triplex ®.

sel. *abbr of* **selig.**

Sela *nt* **-s, -s** *(Bibl)* selah.

selber *dem pron siehe* **selbst 1**.

Selbermachen *nt* do-it-yourself, DIY *(inf)*; *(von Kleidern etc)* making one's own ◆ **Möbel/Spielzeug zum ~** do-it-yourself furniture/build-it-yourself toys.

selbe(r, s) *pron siehe* **derselbe, dieselbe, dasselbe.**

selbig *pron (obs, Bibl)* the same.

selbst [1] *dem pron* **(a) ich/er/sie/das Haus/die Katze ~** I myself/he himself/she herself/the house itself/the cat itself; **wir/Sie/sie/die Häuser ~** we ourselves/you yourselves/they themselves/the houses themselves; **er ist gar nicht mehr er ~** he's not himself any more; **du Esel! — ~ einer** *(inf)* you idiot! — same to you *(inf)*; **sie ist die Güte/Tugend ~** she's kindness/virtue itself; **~ ist der Mann/die Frau!** self-reliance is the name of the game *(inf)*; **er wäscht seine Wäsche ~** he does his washing himself, he does his own washing; **was man von sich ~ hält** what one thinks of oneself; **zu sich ~ kommen** to collect one's thoughts; **eine Sache um ihrer ~ willen tun** to do sth for its own sake; **sie tut mir ~ leid** I feel very sorry for her myself.

(b) *(ohne Hilfe)* alone, by oneself/himself/yourself *etc*, on one's/his/your *etc* own.

(c) von ~ by myself/yourself/himself/itself/ourselves *etc*; **das funktioniert von ~** it works by itself *or* automatically; **das regelt sich alles von ~** it'll sort itself out (by itself); **er kam ganz von ~** he came of his own accord *or* off his own bat *(inf)*; **das hat er ganz von ~ entschieden** he decided that all by himself.

[2] *adv* even ◆ **~ der Minister/Gott** even the Minister/God (himself); **~ wenn** even if.

Selbst *nt*, **-,** *no pl* self.

Selbst-: ~**abholer(in** *f***)** *m* **-s, -** **~abholer sein** to collect one's own mail; ~**achtung** *f* self-respect, self-esteem; ~**analyse** *f* self-analysis.

⚠**selbständig** *adj* independent; *(steuerlich)* self-employed; *(rare: getrennt)* separate ◆ **~ denken** to think for oneself; **~ arbeiten/handeln** to work/act independently *or* on one's own; **~ sein** *(beruflich)* to have set up on one's own; **sich ~ machen** *(beruflich)* to set up on one's own, to start one's own business; *(hum)* to go off on its own; *(verschwinden)* to grow legs *(hum)*; **das entscheidet er ~** he decides that on his own *or* by himself *or* independently.

⚠**Selbständige(r)** *mf decl as adj* independent businessman/woman; *(steuerlich)* self-employed person.

⚠**Selbständigkeit** *f* independence ◆ **in großer ~ handeln** *(beruflich)* to act on one's own (initiative) *or* independently; **~ im Denken lernen** to learn to think for oneself.

Selbst-: ~**anklage** *f* self-accusation; ⚠~**anschluß** *m (Telec)* automatic dial telephone; *(Verbindung)* automatic dialling connection; ~**anzeige** *f* **(a)** *(steuerlich)* voluntary declaration; **(b) ~anzeige erstatten** to come forward oneself; ~**aufopferung** *f* self-sacrifice; ~**auslöser** *m (Phot)* delayed-action shutter release, delay timer; ~**bedienung** *f* self-service; ~**bedienungsladen** *m* self-service shop *(esp Brit) or* store; ~**befleckung** *f (old, Rel)* self-abuse; ~**befreiung** *f* self-liberation; *(Jur)* prison escape without outside assistance; ~**befriedigung** *f* masturbation; *(fig auch)* self-gratification; ~**befruchtung** *f (Biol)* self-fertilization; ~**behauptung** *f* self-assertion; ~**beherrschung** *f* self-control; **die ~beherrschung wahren/verlieren** to keep/lose one's self-control *or* temper; ~**bekenntnis** *nt* confession; ~**beköstigung** *f (dated)* self-catering; ~**beobachtung** *f* self-observation; ~**bescheidung** *f (geh)* self-denial; ~**besinnung** *f* self-contemplation; **zur ~besinnung kommen** to reflect; **hier ist es unmöglich, zur ~besinnung zu kommen** that there is no opportunity (afforded) here for self-contemplation; ~**bespiegelung** *f (pej)* self-admiration; ~**bestätigung** *f* self-affirmation; **das empfand er als ~bestätigung** it boosted his ego; **man braucht ab und zu eine ~bestätigung** now and then you need something to boost your ego; **Lob dient der ~bestätigung der Kinder** praise boosts the children's confidence; ~**bestäubung** *f (Bot)* self-pollination; ~**bestimmung** *f* self-determination; ~**bestimmungsrecht** *nt* right of self-determination; ~**beteiligung** *f (Insur)* (percentage) excess; ~**betrug** *m* self-deception; ~**beweihräucherung** *f (pej)* self-congratulation, self-adulation, self-admiration; ~**bewunderung** *f* self-admiration; ⚠**s~bewußt** *adj* **(a)** *(s~sicher)* self-assured, self-confident; *(eingebildet)* self-important; **(b)** *(Philos)* self-aware, self-conscious; ⚠~**bewußtsein** *nt* **(a)** self-assurance, self-confidence; *(Einbildung)* self-importance; **(b)** *(Philos)* self-awareness, self-consciousness; ~**bildnis** *nt* self-portrait; ~**bucher** *m* **-s, -** *(Post) firm etc with its own franking machine*; ~**darstellung** *f* self-portrayal; **Autoren des 20. Jahrhunderts in ~darstellungen** self-portraits of 20th century writers; ~**disziplin** *f* self-discipline; ~**einschätzung** *f* self-assessment; **eine gesunde ~einschätzung** a healthy self-awareness; ~**entfaltung** *f* self-development; *(Philos)* unfolding; ~**entleibung** *f (liter)* suicide; ~**entzündung** *f* spontaneous combustion; ~**erfahrung** *f* self-awareness; ~**erfahrungsgruppe** *f* encounter group; ~**erhaltung** *f* self-preservation, survival; ~**erhaltungstrieb** *m* survival instinct, instinct of self-preservation; ~**erkenntnis** *f* self-knowledge; **~erkenntnis ist der erste Schritt zur Besserung** *(prov)* self-knowledge is the first step towards self-improvement; ⚠**s~ernannt** *adj* self-appointed; (*in bezug auf Titel*) self-styled; **~erniedrigung** *f* self-abasement; **~erziehung** *f* self-discipline; **~erziehung zur Pünktlichkeit** teaching oneself to be punctual; **~fahrer** *m* **(a)** (*Krankenfahrstuhl*) self-propelling wheelchair; **(b)** (*Aut*) *person who drives a hired car himself*; **Autovermietung für ~fahrer** self-drive car hire; **wir vermieten nur an ~fahrer** we only have self-drive; **~fahrlafette** *f* (*Mil*) self-propelled gun; **~finanzierend** *adj* self-financing; **~finanzierung** *f* self-financing; **in/durch ~finanzierung** with one's own resources *or* means; **~findung** *f* finding one's self; ⚠**s~gebacken** *adj* home-baked, home-made; ⚠**s~gebaut** *adj* home-made, self-made; *Haus* self-built; ⚠**s~gebraut** *adj Bier* home-brewed; **~gedrehte** *f decl as adj* roll-up (*inf*); **~gedrehte rauchen** to roll one's own; **s~gefällig** *adj* self-satisfied, smug, complacent; **~gefälligkeit** *f* self-satisfaction, smugness, complacency; **~gefühl** *nt* self-esteem; **ein übertriebenes ~gefühl besitzen** to have an exaggerated opinion of oneself, to have an oversized ego (*inf*); ⚠**s~gemacht** *adj Möbel etc* home-made, self-made; *Marmelade etc* home-made; **s~genügsam** *adj* **(a)** (*bescheiden*) modest (in one's demands); **(b)** (*sich selbst genug*) self-sufficient; **~genügsamkeit** *f siehe adj* **(a)** modesty (in one's demands); **(b)** self-sufficiency; **s~gerecht** *adj* self-righteous; **~gerechtigkeit** *f* self-righteousness; ⚠**s~gesponnen** *adj* homespun; **~gespräch** *nt* **~gespräche führen** *or* **halten** to talk to oneself; ⚠**s~gestrickt** *adj* **(a)** *Pullover etc* hand-knitted; **ist das s~gestrickt?** did you knit it yourself?; **(b)** (*inf*) *Hund* fluffy; *Methode etc* homespun, amateurish; ⚠**s~gezogen** *adj* **(a)** *Rosen etc* home-cultivated; **(b)** *Kerzen* home-made; ⚠**~haß** *m* self-hate, self-hatred; **~heilungskraft** *f* self-healing power; **s~herrlich** *adj* (*pej*) **(a)** (*eigenwillig*) high-handed; **(b)** (*s~gefällig, s~gerecht*) self-satisfied; **~herrlichkeit** *f* (*pej*) *siehe adj* **(a)** high-handedness; **(b)** self-satisfaction; **~herrschaft** *f* (*rare*) autocracy; **~herrscher** *m* (*rare*) autocrat; **~hilfe** *f* self-help; **zur ~hilfe greifen** to take matters into one's own hands; **~hilfegruppe** *f* self-help group; **~interpretation** *f* image of oneself, self-image; **~ironie** *f* self-mockery, self-irony.

selbstisch *adj* (*geh*) selfish.

Selbst-: ~isolierung *f* self-isolation; **~justiz** *f* arbitrary law; **~justiz üben** to take the law into one's own hands; **~klebeetikett** *nt* self-adhesive label; **s~klebend** *adj* self-adhesive; **~kontrolle** *f* check on oneself; (*von Computer*) automatic check; **zur ~kontrolle** to keep a check on oneself; **der Computer hat ~kontrolle** the computer is self-checking *or* has an automatic check.

Selbstkosten *pl* (*Econ*) prime costs *pl*.

Selbstkosten-: ~beteiligung *f* (*Insur*) excess; **~preis** *m* cost price; **zum ~preis** at cost.

Selbst-: ~kritik *f* self-criticism; **s~kritisch** *adj* self-critical; **~lader** *m* **-s, -** self-loader, semi-automatic weapon *or* firearm; **~laut** *m* vowel; **s~lautend** *adj* vocalic; **~lerner** *m* autodidact (*form*); **er ist ~lerner** he is self-taught; **dies Buch ist geeignet für ~lerner** this book is suitable for people teaching themselves; **~lob** *nt siehe* **Eigenlob**; **s~los** *adj* selfless; **~losigkeit** *f* selflessness; **~medikation** *f* - *no pl* self-medication; **~mitleid** *nt* self-pity.

Selbstmord *m* (*lit, fig*) suicide.

Selbstmörder *m* suicide ♦ **ich bin doch kein ~!** (*inf*) I have no desire to commit suicide.

selbstmörderisch *adj* (*lit, fig*) suicidal ♦ **in ~er Absicht** intending to commit suicide.

Selbstmord-: ~gedanken *pl* suicidal thoughts *pl*; **sich mit ~gedanken tragen** to contemplate suicide; **s~gefährdet** *adj* suicidal; **~kommando** *nt* suicide squad; **~versuch** *m* suicide attempt, attempted suicide.

Selbst-: ~porträt *nt siehe* **~bildnis**; **s~quälerisch** *adj* self-tormenting; **s~redend** *adv* of course, naturally; **~regierung** *f* self-government; **~reinigungskraft** *f* self-purifying power; **~schuldner** *m* (*Jur*) directly suable guarantor; **s~schuldnerisch** *adj* (*Jur*) *Bürgschaft* directly enforceable; *Bürge* directly suable; ⚠**~schuß** *m* set-gun, spring-gun; **~schutz** *m* self-protection; **s~sicher** *adj* self-assured, self-confident; **~sicherheit** *f* self-assurance, self-confidence; **~studium** *nt* private study; **etw im ~studium lernen** to learn sth by studying on one's own; **~sucht** *f* egoism; **s~süchtig** *adj* egoistic; **s~tätig** *adj* **(a)** (*automatisch*) automatic, self-acting; **damit sich nicht s~tätig ein Schuß lösen kann** so that a gun can't fire by itself; **(b)** (*eigenständig*) independent; **~tätigkeit** *f siehe adj* **(a)** automatic functioning; **(b)** independence; **~täuschung** *f* self-deception; **~test** *m* (*von Maschine*) self-test; **~tor** *nt siehe* **Eigentor**; **~tötung** *f* suicide; **~überschätzung** *f* over-estimation of one's abilities; **das ist eine ~überschätzung, wenn er meint ...** he's over-estimating himself *or* his abilities if he thinks ...; **~überwindung** *f* will-power; **das war echte ~überwindung** that shows real will-power; **selbst bei der größten ~überwindung könnte ich das nicht tun** I simply couldn't bring *or* force myself to do it; **~verachtung** *f* self-contempt; **~verbraucher** *m* **Verkauf nur an ~verbraucher** goods not for resale; **~verbrennung** *f* **sich durch ~verbrennung töten** to burn oneself to death; **„zwei ~verbrennungen in einem Monat"** "two people burn themselves to death in one month"; ⚠**s~verdient** *adj* **s~verdientes Geld** money one has earned oneself; **sein s~verdientes Motorrad** the motorbike he bought with the money he earned; ⚠**s~verfaßt** *adj* of one's own composition; **alle seine Reden sind s~verfaßt** he writes all his speeches himself; **s~vergessen** *adj* absent-minded; *Blick* faraway; **s~vergessen dasitzen** to sit there lost to the world; **~vergessenheit** *f* absent-mindedness; **in seinem Blick lag völlige ~vergessenheit** he looked totally lost to the world; **~vergötterung** *f* self-glorification; **~verlag** *m* **im ~verlag erschienen** published oneself *or* at one's own expense; **~verleugnung** *f* self-denial; **~verliebtheit** *f* self-love; **~vernichtung** *f* self-destruction; **~verschulden** *nt* one's own fault; **wenn ~verschulden vorliegt ...** if the claimant is himself at fault ...; ⚠**s~verschuldet** *adj* **wenn der Unfall/Verlust s~verschuldet ist** if the claimant is himself responsible *or* to blame for the accident/loss; **~versicherung** *f* personal insurance; **~versorger** *m* **(a) ~versorger sein** to be self-sufficient *or* self-reliant; **(b)** (*im Urlaub etc*) self-caterer; **Appartements/Urlaub für ~versorger** self-catering apartments/holiday; **~versorgung** *f* self-sufficiency, self-reliance; (*in Urlaub etc*) self-catering; ⚠**s~verständlich** [1] *adj Freundlichkeit* natural; *Wahrheit* self-evident; **das ist doch s~verständlich!** that goes without saying, that's obvious; **vielen Dank für Ihre Hilfe — aber das ist doch s~verständlich** thanks for your help — it's no more than anybody would have done; **kann ich mitkommen? — aber das ist doch s~verständlich** can I come too? — but of course; **es war für uns s~verständlich, daß Sie ...** we took it for granted that you ...; **das ist keineswegs s~verständlich** it's by no means a matter of course, it cannot be taken for granted; **etw für s~verständlich halten, etw als s~verständlich annehmen** to take sth for granted; [2] *adv* of course; **wie s~verständlich** as if it were the most natural thing in the world; **~verständlichkeit** *f* naturalness; (*Unbefangenheit*) casualness *no indef art*; (*von Wahrheit*) self-evidence; (*s~verständliche Wahrheit etc*) self-evident truth *etc*; **nichts zu danken, das war doch eine ~verständlichkeit** think nothing of it, it was no more than anyone would have done; **das war doch eine ~verständlichkeit, daß wir ...** it was only natural that we ...; **etw für eine ~verständlichkeit halten** to take sth as a matter of course; **das sind heute ~verständlichkeiten** those are things we take for granted today; **~verständnis** *nt* **jds ~verständnis** the way sb sees himself/herself; **nach seinem eigenen ~verständnis** as he sees himself; **~verstümmelung** *f* self-inflicted wound; (*das Verstümmeln*) self-mutilation; **~versuch** *m* experiment on oneself; **~verteidigung** *f* self-defence; **~vertrauen** *nt* self-confidence; **~verwaltung** *f* self-administration; (*Verwaltungskörper*) self-governing body; **~verwirklichung** *f* self-realization; **~vorwurf** *m* self-reproach; **~wählferndienst** *m* (*Telec*) automatic dialling service, subscriber trunk dialling (*Brit*), STD (*Brit*); **~wählfernverkehr** *m* (*Telec*) automatic dialling, STD system (*Brit*); **~wertgefühl** *nt* feeling of one's own worth *or* value, self-esteem; **s~zerstörerisch** *adj* self-destructive; **~zerstörung** *f* self-destruction; **s~zufrieden** *adj* self-satisfied; **~zufriedenheit** *f* self-satisfaction; **s~zündend** *adj* self-igniting; **~zweck** *m* end in itself; **als ~zweck** as an end in itself.

selchen *vti* (*S Ger, Aus*) *Fleisch* to smoke.

Selcher(in *f*) *m* **-s, -** (*S Ger, Aus*) (pork) butcher.

Selchfleisch *nt* (*S Ger, Aus*) smoked meat.

selektieren* *vt* to select.

Selektion *f* selection.

Selektions-: ~lehre, ~theorie *f* theory of natural selection.

selektiv *adj* selective.

Selektivität [zelɛktivi'tɛ:t] *f* (*Rad*) selectivity; (*fig*) selectiveness.

Selen *nt* **-s,** *no pl* (*abbr* **Se**) selenium.

Selenzelle *f* (*Phot*) selenium cell.

Selfmademan ['sɛlfme:tmɛn] *m* **-s, Selfmademen** self-made man.

selig *adj* **(a)** (*Rel*) blessed; (*old: verstorben*) late ♦ **~ die Armen im Geiste, denn ...** (*Bibl*) blessed are the poor in spirit, for ... (*Bibl*); **bis an mein ~es Ende** (*old, hum*) until the day I die; **mein Vater ~** (*old*), **mein ~er Vater** (*old*) my late father; **~ entschlafen** (*liter*) departed this life; **Gott hab ihn ~** (*old*) God rest his soul; *siehe* **Angedenken, geben, Gefilde**.
(b) (*überglücklich*) overjoyed; *Lächeln auch* beatific (*liter*); *Stunden* blissful; (*inf: beschwipst*) tipsy (*inf*), merry (*inf*).

Selige(r) *mf decl as adj* **(a)** (*Eccl*) blessed (*inf*) ♦ **die ~n** the Blessed. **(b)** (*old*) **mein/Ihr ~r** my/your late husband.

Seligkeit *f* **(a)** (*Rel*) salvation ♦ **ewige ~** eternal salvation. **(b)** (*Glück*) (supreme) happiness, bliss.

Selig-: ⚠**s~preisen** *sep irreg* [1] *vt* **(a)** (*Bibl*) to bless; **(b)** (*liter: verherrlichen*) to glorify; [2] *vr* to thank one's lucky stars; **~preisung** *f* (*Bibl*) Beatitude; (*liter*) glorification; ⚠**s~sprechen** *vt sep irreg* (*Eccl*) to beatify; **~sprechung** *f* (*Eccl*) beatification.

Sellerie *m* **-s, -(s)** *or f* **-, -** celeriac; (*Stangen~*) celery.

selten [1] *adj* rare; (*kaum vorkommend auch*) scarce ♦ **du bist ja in letzter Zeit ein ~er Gast** you're a stranger here these days; *siehe* **Erde**.
[2] *adv* (*nicht oft*) rarely, seldom; (*besonders*) exceptionally ♦ **nur/höchst ~** very/extremely rarely *or* seldom; **~ so gelacht!** (*inf*) what a laugh! (*inf*).

Seltenheit *f* **(a)** *no pl* (*seltenes Vorkommen*) rareness, rarity. **(b)** (*seltene Sache*) rarity ♦ **das ist keine ~ bei ihr** it's nothing unusual with her.

Seltenheitswert *m* rarity value.

Selters *nt* **-, -** (*inf*), **Selter(s)wasser** *nt* soda (water).

seltsam *adj* strange; (*komisch auch*) odd, peculiar ♦ **~ berührt** strangely moved.

seltsamerweise *adv* strangely enough.

Seltsamkeit *f* **(a)** *no pl* (*Sonderbarkeit*) strangeness, oddness, peculiarity. **(b)** (*seltsame Sache*) oddity.

Semantik *f* semantics *sing*.

semantisch *adj* semantic.

Semaphor [zema'fo:ɐ] *nt or m* **-s, -e** (*Naut, Rail*) semaphore.

Semasiologie *f* (*Ling*) semasiology.

Semester *nt* **-s, -** (*Univ*) semester (*US*), term (*of a half-year's duration*) ♦ **im 7./8. ~ sein** to be in one's 4th year; **die älteren ~** the older *or* senior students;

ein älteres ~ a senior student; (*hum*) an old boy/girl; **sie ist auch schon ein älteres ~** she's no chicken (*inf*).
Semester- (*Univ*): **~ferien** *pl* vacation *sing*; **s~lang** *adj* for years; ⚠**~schluß** *m* end of term, end of the semester (*US*).
-semestrig *adj suf* -term, -semester (*US*).
Semi- *in cpds* semi-; **~finale** ['ze:mi-] *nt* (*Sport*) semifinal(s); **~kolon** [zemi'ko:lɔn] *nt* **-s, -s** *or* **-kola** semicolon.
Seminar *nt* **-s, -e** *or* (*Aus*) **-ien** [-iən] **(a)** (*Univ*) department; (*~übung*) seminar. **(b)** (*Priester~*) seminary. **(c)** (*Lehrer~, Studien~*) teacher training college, college of education.
Seminar- (*Univ*): **~apparat** *m* seminar course books *pl*; **~arbeit** *f* seminar paper.
Seminarist *m* (*Eccl*) seminarist.
seminaristisch *adj* (*Eccl*) seminarian.
Seminar- (*Univ*): **~schein** *m certificate of attendance for one semester (US) or half-year*; **~übung** *f* seminar.
Semiologie *f* semiology.
Semiotik *f* semiotics *sing*.
semipermeabel *adj* semipermeable.
Semit(in *f*) *m* **-en, -en** Semite.
semitisch *adj* Semitic.
Semitist(in *f*) *m* Semitist.
Semitistik *f* Semitics *sing*.
Semivokal *m* semivowel.
Semmel *f* **-, -n** (*dial*) roll ◆ **geriebene ~** breadcrumbs *pl*.
Semmel-: s~blond *adj* (*dated*) flaxen-haired; **~brösel(n)** *pl* breadcrumbs *pl*; **~kloß, ~knödel** (*S Ger, Aus*) *m* bread dumpling; **~mehl** *nt* breadcrumbs *pl*.
sen. *abbr of* **senior** sen.
Senat *m* **-(e)s, -e (a)** (*Pol, Univ*) senate. **(b)** (*Jur*) Supreme Court.
Senator *m*, **Senatorin** *f* senator.
Senats- *in cpds* of the senate; ⚠**~ausschuß** *m* senate committee; **s~eigen** *adj* belonging to the senate; **~präsident** *m* chairman of the senate.
Send-: ~bote *m* (*Hist*) emissary, ambassador (*old*); **~brief** *m* (*liter*) circular letter.
Sende-: ~anlage *f* transmitting installation; **~antenne** *f* transmitting aerial; **~bereich** *m* transmission range; **~einrichtung** *f* transmitting facility; **~folge** *f* **(a)** (*Sendung in Fortsetzungen*) series *sing*; (*einzelne Folge*) episode; **(b)** (*Programmfolge*) programmes *pl*; **~gebiet** *nt* transmission area; **~leiter** *m* producer.
➤ **senden**[1] *pret* **sandte** *or* **sendete**, *ptp* **gesandt** *or* **gesendet** 1 *vt* to send (*an +acc* to) ◆ **jdm etw ~** to send sb sth, to send sth to sb.
2 *vi* **nach jdm ~** to send for sb.
senden[2] *vti* (*Rad, TV*) to broadcast; *Signal etc* to transmit.
Sendepause *f* interval; (*fig inf*) deathly silence ◆ **danach tritt eine ~ bis 6 Uhr ein** afterwards we shall be going off the air until 6 o'clock; **auf meine Frage hin herrschte ~** my question was met by deathly silence.
Sender *m* **-s, -** transmitter; (*~kanal*) (*Rad*) station; (*TV*) channel (*Brit*), station (*esp US*) ◆ **der ~ Prag** Radio Prague.
Sende-: ~raum *m* studio; **~reihe** *f* (radio/television) series.
Sender-: ~einstellung *f* tuning; **~-Empfänger** *m* transceiver; **~suchlauf** *m* search tuning.
Sende-: ~saal *m* studio; ⚠**~schluß** *m* (*Rad, TV*) closedown, end of broadcasts; **und nun bis ~schluß** and now until we close down; **~turm** *m* radio tower; **~zeichen** *nt* call sign; **~zeit** *f* broadcasting time; **und damit geht unsere heutige ~zeit zu Ende** and that concludes our programmes for today; **in der besten ~zeit** in prime time.
Sendschreiben *nt* (*liter*) circular letter.
Sendung *f* **(a)** *no pl* (*das Senden*) sending. **(b)** (*Post~*) letter; (*Päckchen*) packet; (*Paket*) parcel; (*Comm*) consignment. **(c)** (*Rad, TV*) programme; (*Rad auch*) broadcast; (*das Senden*) broadcasting; (*von Signal etc*) transmission ◆ **auf ~ gehen/sein** to go/be on the air. **(d)** (*liter: Aufgabe*) mission.
⚠ **Sendungsbewußtsein** *nt* sense of mission.
Senegal[1] *m* **-(s) der ~** the Senegal (River).
Senegal[2] *nt* **-s** Senegal.
Senegaler(in *f*) *m* **-s, -, Senegalese** *m* **-n, -n, Senegalesin** *f* Senegalese.
senegalesisch, senegalisch *adj* Senegalese.
Seneschall *m* **-s, -e** (*Hist*) seneschal.
Seneszenz *f* (*Med*) senescence.
Senf *m* **-(e)s, -e** mustard ◆ **seinen ~ dazugeben** (*inf*) to get one's three ha'p'orth in (*Brit inf*), to have one's say.
Senf-: s~farben, s~farbig *adj* mustard(-coloured); **~gas** *nt* (*Chem*) mustard gas; **~gurke** *f gherkin pickled with mustard seeds*; **~korn** *nt* mustard seed; **~mehl** *nt* flour of mustard; **~packung** *f* (*Med*) mustard poultice; **~pflaster** *nt* (*Med*) mustard plaster; **~soße, ~tunke** (*dial*) *f* mustard sauce; **~umschlag** *m* (*Med*) mustard poultice.
Senge *pl* (*dated inf*) **~ kriegen** to get a good hiding.
sengen 1 *vt* to singe.
2 *vi* to scorch ◆ **~d und brennend** (*old, liter*) with fire and sword.
senil *adj* (*pej*) senile.
Senilität *f*, *no pl* (*pej*) senility.
senior *adj* **Franz Schulz ~** Franz Schulz senior.
Senior *m* **(a)** (*auch ~chef*) boss, old boy (*inf*) ◆ **kann ich mal den ~ sprechen?** can I speak to Mr X senior? **(b)** (*Sport*) senior player ◆ **die ~en** the seniors, the senior team. **(c) ~en** *pl* senior citizens *pl*; (*hum*) old folk *pl*.

Senioren-: ~hotel *nt* hotel for the elderly; **~karte** *f* pensioner's *or* senior citizen's ticket; **~mannschaft** *f* senior team; ⚠**~paß** *m* senior citizen's travel pass; **~(wohn)haus, ~(wohn)heim** *nt* old people's home.
Seniorpartner *m* senior partner.
Senkblei *nt siehe* **Senklot.**
Senke *f* **-, -n** valley.
Senkel *m* **-s, - (a)** lace. **(b)** *siehe* **Senklot.**
senken 1 *vt* to lower; *Lanze, Fahne* to dip; *Kopf* to bow; *Preis, Steuern auch* to decrease; (*Tech*) *Schraube, Loch, Schacht* to sink; (*Hort*) *Schößlinge, Wurzeln etc* to plant.
2 *vr* to sink; (*Decke*) to sag; (*Grab, Haus, Boden, Straße auch*) to subside; (*Flugzeug*) to descend; (*Wasserspiegel auch*) to go down, to drop, to fall; (*Stimme*) to drop; (*liter: Nacht*) to fall, to descend (*über, auf +acc* on) ◆ **dann senkte sich ihr Blick** then she looked down, then she lowered her eyes *or* her gaze (*liter*).
Senk-: ~fuß *m* (*Med*) fallen arches *pl*; **~fußeinlage** *f* arch support; **~grube** *f* cesspit; **~kasten** *m* caisson; **~kopfschraube** *f* countersunk screw; **~lot** *nt* plumbline; (*Gewicht*) plummet.
senkrecht *adj* vertical; (*Math*) perpendicular ◆ **immer schön ~ bleiben!** (*inf*) keep your end up (*inf*); *siehe* **einzig.**
Senkrechte *f decl as adj* vertical; (*Math*) perpendicular.
Senkrechtstarter *m* (*Aviat*) vertical take-off aircraft; (*fig inf*) whizz kid (*inf*).
Senkung *f* **(a)** sinking; (*von Boden, Straße*) subsidence; (*von Wasserspiegel*) fall (*gen* in), drop (*gen* in); (*als Maßnahme*) lowering; (*von Decke*) sag(ging); (*von Stimme*) lowering; (*von Preisen*) lowering (*von* of), decrease (*von* in).
(b) (*Vertiefung*) hollow, valley.
(c) (*Poet*) thesis.
(d) (*Med*) *siehe* **Blutsenkung.**
Senkungsgeschwindigkeit *f* (*Med*) rate of sedimentation.
Senkwaage *f* hydrometer.
Senn *m* **-(e)s, -e, Senne** *m* **-n, -n** (*S Ger, Aus*) *siehe* **Senner.**
Senne *f* **-, -n** (*S Ger, Aus*) Alpine pasture.
Senner *m* **-s, -** (Alpine) dairyman.
Sennerei *f* (*Gebäude*) Alpine dairy; (*Wirtschaftsform*) Alpine dairy farming.
Sennerin *f* (Alpine) dairymaid.
Sennesblätter *pl* senna leaves *pl*.
Sennhütte *f* Alpine dairy hut.
Sensation *f* sensation.
sensationell [zɛnzatsio'nɛl] *adj* sensational.
Sensations-: ~bedürfnis *nt* need for sensation; **~blatt** *nt* sensational paper; **~gier** *f* (*pej*) sensation-seeking; **aus ~gier** for the sheer sensation; **~lust** *f* desire for sensation; **s~lüstern** *adj* sensation-seeking; **s~lustig** *adj* sensation-loving; **~mache** *f* (*inf*) sensationalism; **~meldung, ~nachricht** *f* sensational news *sing*; **eine ~nachricht** a sensation, a scoop, a sensational piece of news; **~presse** *f* sensational papers *pl*, yellow press; ⚠**~prozeß** *m* sensational trial.
Sense *f* **-, -n (a)** scythe. **(b)** (*inf*) **jetzt/dann ist ~!** that's the end!; **es ist nichts mehr da, ~!** there's none left, all gone!
Sensenmann *m* (*liter*) Death *no art*, Reaper (*liter*).
sensibel *adj* sensitive; (*heikel auch*) problematic, delicate.
Sensibilisator *m* (*Phot*) sensitizer.
sensibilisieren* *vt* to sensitize.
Sensibilisierung *f* sensitization.
Sensibilität *f* sensitivity; (*Feingefühl auch*) sensibility.
sensitiv *adj* (*geh*) sensitive.
Sensitivität *f* (*geh*) sensitivity.
Sensor *m* sensor.
sensoriell *adj siehe* **sensorisch.**
Sensorien [zɛn'zo:riən] *pl* sensoria *pl*.
sensorisch *adj* sensory.
Sensortaste *f* touch-sensitive button.
Sensualismus *m* (*Philos*) sensualism, sensationalism.
Sensualität *f* sensuality.
sensuell *adj siehe* **sensorisch.**
Sentenz *f* aphorism.
sentenziös *adj* sententious.
Sentiment [sãti'mã:] *nt* **-s, -s** (*liter*) *siehe* **Empfindung.**
sentimental, sentimentalisch (*old*) *adj* sentimental.
Sentimentalität *f* sentimentality.
separat *adj* separate; (*in sich abgeschlossen*) *Wohnung, Zimmer* self-contained.
Separat-: ~(ab)druck *m* offprint; **~friede(n)** *m* separate peace.
Separatismus *m* (*Pol*) separatism.
Separatist(in *f*) *m* (*Pol*) separatist.
separatistisch *adj* (*Pol*) separatist.
⚠ **Séparée** [zepa're:] *nt* **-s, -s** private room; (*Nische*) private booth.
separieren* *vt* (*rare*) *siehe* **absondern 1 (a).**
separiert *adj* (*esp Aus*) *Zimmer* self-contained.
sepia *adj inv* sepia.
Sepia *f* **-, Sepien** [-iən] **(a)** (*Zool*) cuttle-fish. **(b)** *no pl* (*Farbstoff*) sepia (ink).
Sepia-: ~schale *f* cuttle-fish shell; **~zeichnung** *f* sepia (drawing).
Sepien ['ze:piən] *pl of* **Sepia.**
Sepp(e)lhose *f* (*inf*) lederhosen *pl*, leather shorts *pl*.
Sepp(l) *m* **-s** (*S Ger*) *abbr of* **Josef.**
Sepsis *f* **-, Sepsen** (*Med*) sepsis.
September *m* **-(s), -** September; *siehe auch* **März.**

Septett *nt* **-(e)s, -e** *(Mus)* septet(te).
Septime *f* **-, -n, Septim** *f* **-, -en** *(Aus) (Mus)* seventh.
septisch *adj* septic.
Septuaginta *f* **-** *(Eccl)* Septuagint.
sequentiell *adj* sequential.
Sequenz *f* sequence; *(Cards auch)* flush, run.
sequestrieren* *vt (Jur)* to sequester, to sequestrate.
Sera *pl of* **Serum.**
Serail [ze'ra:j, ze'rai(l)] *nt* **-s, -s** seraglio.
Seraph ['ze:raf] *m* **-s, -e** *or* **-im** [-i:m] seraph.
Serbe *m* **-n, -n** Serbian.
Serbien ['zɛrbiən] *nt* **-s** Serbia.
Serbin *f* Serbian (woman/girl).
serbisch *adj* Serbian.
Serbokroatisch(e) *nt* Serbo-Croat; *siehe auch* **Deutsch(e).**
Seren *pl of* **Serum.**
Serenade *f* serenade.
Sergeant [zɛr'ʒant] *m* **-en, -en** *(dated Mil)* sergeant.
Serie ['ze:riə] *f* series *sing*; *(von Waren auch)* line; *(Billard)* break ◆ **in ~ gehen** to go into production, to go onto the production line; **in ~ hergestellt werden** to be mass-produced; **das Gesetz der ~** the law of averages.
seriell *adj Herstellung* series *attr*; *(Comput)* serial ◆ **~ hergestellt werden** to be mass-produced; **~e Musik** serial music.
Serien- ['ze:riən-]: **~fabrikation, ~fertigung** *f* series production; **~herstellung** *f* series production; **s~mäßig** [1] *adj Autos* production *attr*, *Ausstattung* standard; *Herstellung* series *attr*; [2] *adv herstellen* in series; **das wird s~mäßig eingebaut** it's a standard fitting; **~nummer** *f* serial number; **~produktion** *f* series production; **in ~produktion gehen** to go into production, to go onto the production line; **s~reif** *adj (Aut)* ready to go into production; **~schaltung** *f (Elec)* series connection; **s~weise** *adv produzieren* in series; *(inf: in Mengen)* wholesale.
Serigraphie *f* **(a)** *(Verfahren)* silk-screen printing, serigraphy *(spec)*. **(b)** *(Bild)* silk-screen print, serigraph *(spec)*.
seriös *adj* serious; *(anständig)* respectable; *Firma* reputable.
Seriosität *f siehe adj* seriousness; respectability; reputableness.
Sermon *m* **-s, -e** *(pej)* sermon, lecture.
Serodiagnostik *f* serodiagnosis.
Serologie *f* serology.
serologisch *adj* serological.
Serpentin *m* **-s, -e** *(Miner)* serpentine.
Serpentine *f* winding road, zigzag; *(Kurve)* double bend ◆ **die Straße führt in ~n den Berg hinauf** the road winds *or* zigzags its way up the mountain.
Serpentinenstraße *f* winding *or* serpentine road.
Serum *nt* **-s, Seren** *or* **Sera** serum.
Serum-: ~behandlung, ~therapie *f* serotherapy, serum-therapy.
Server ['zɛrvɐ] *m* **-s, -** *(Comput)* server.
Service[1] [zɛr'vi:s] *nt* **-(s), -** [*auch* zer'vi:sə] *(Geschirr)* dinner/coffee *etc* service; *(Gläser~)* set.
Service[2] ['sə:vɪs] *m or nt* **-, -s** *(Comm, Sport)* service; *(Sport auch)* serve.
Servierbrett [zɛr'vi:ɐ-] *nt* tray.
servieren* [zɛr'vi:rən] [1] *vt* to serve *(jdm etw* sb sth, sth to sb); *(inf: anbieten)* to serve up *(inf) (jdm* for sb) ◆ **jdm den Ball ~** *(Ftbl etc)* to pass the ball to sb; *(Tennis)* to hit the ball right to sb; **er bekam den Ball toll serviert** the ball was beautifully set up for him.
[2] *vi* to serve ◆ **nach 24 Uhr wird nicht mehr serviert** there is no waiter service after midnight; **es ist serviert!** lunch/dinner *etc* is served.
Serviererin [zɛr'vi:rərɪn] *f* waitress.
Servier- [zɛr'vi:ɐ-]: **~tisch** *m* serving table; **~tochter** *f (Sw)* waitress; **~wagen** *m* trolley.
Serviette [zɛr'viɛtə] *f* serviette, napkin.
Serviettenring *m* serviette *or* napkin ring.
servil [zɛr'vi:l] *adj (geh)* servile.
Servilität [zɛrvili'tɛ:t] *f (geh)* servility.
Servo- ['zɛrvo-] *(Tech)*: **~bremse** *f* power *or* servo(-assisted) brake; **~lenkung** *f* power *or* servo(-assisted) steering; **~motor** *m* servomotor.
Servus ['zɛrvʊs] *interj (Aus, S Ger) (beim Treffen)* hello; *(beim Abschied)* goodbye, so long *(inf)*, cheerio *(Brit inf)*.
Sesam *m* **-s, -s** sesame ◆ **~, öffne dich!** open Sesame!
Sessel *m* **-s, -** easy chair; *(Polstersessel)* armchair; *(Aus: Stuhl)* chair.
Sessel-: ~lehne *f* (chair) arm; **~lift** *m* chairlift.
seßhaft *adj* settled; *(ansässig)* resident ◆ **~ werden, sich ~ machen** to settle down.
Seßhaftigkeit *f, no pl* settled form of existence; *(von Lebensweise)* settledness ◆ **die sprichwörtliche ~ der Holsteiner** the proverbial sedentariness of the Holsteiners.
Session *f siehe* **Sitzungsperiode.**
Set *m or nt* **-s, -s (a)** set. **(b)** *(Deckchen)* place mat, tablemat.
Setter *m* **-s, -** setter.
Setzei *nt* fried egg.
setzen [1] *vt* **(a)** *(hintun, hinbringen)* to put, to place, to set; *(sitzen lassen)* to sit, to place, to put ◆ **etw auf die Rechnung/Speisekarte** *etc* **~** to put sth on the bill/menu *etc*; **etw an den Mund/die Lippen ~** to put sth to one's mouth/lips; **jdn an Land ~** to put *or* set sb ashore; **jdn über den Fluß ~** to take sb across the river; **Fische in einen Teich ~** to stock a pond with fish; **ein Stück auf den Spielplan ~** to put on a play; **etw auf die Tagesordnung ~** to put sth on the agenda; **etw in die Zeitung ~** to put sth in the paper; **jdn über andere/jemanden anders ~** to put *or* set sb above others/somebody else; **sich** *(dat)* **etw in den Kopf** *or* **Schädel** *(inf)* **~** to take sth into one's head; **dann setzt es was** *or* **Hiebe** *or* **Prügel** *(all inf)* there'll be trouble; **seine Hoffnung/sein Vertrauen in jdn/etw ~** to put *or* place one's hopes/trust in sb/sth; **seine Ehre in etw** *(acc)* **~** to make sth a point of honour; **seinen Ehrgeiz in etw** *(acc)* **~** to make sth one's goal; **sein Leben an etw** *(acc)* **~** *(geh)* to devote one's life to sth; *siehe* **Druck**[1].
(b) *(Hort: pflanzen)* to set, to plant; *(aufziehen) Stander, Laternen* to put up; *(Naut) Segel* to set; *(Typ)* to set; *(geh: formulieren) Worte* to choose ◆ **ein Gedicht/einen Text in Musik ~** to set a poem/words to music.
(c) *Preis, Summe* to put *(auf +acc* on); *(bei Gesellschaftsspielen: spielen, ziehen) Stein, Figur* to move ◆ **Geld auf ein Pferd ~** to put *or* place *or* stake money on a horse; **auf seinen Kopf sind 100.000 Dollar gesetzt** there's 100,000 dollars on his head.
(d) *(errichten, aufstellen)* to build; *Denkmal auch* to erect, to put *or* set up; *(fig) Norm etc* to set ◆ **jdm ein Grabmal/Denkmal ~** to put *or* set up *or* build a monument to sb.
(e) *(schreiben) Komma, Punkt* to put ◆ **seinen Namen unter etw** *(acc)* **~** to put one's signature to sth.
(f) *(bestimmen) Ziel, Grenze, Termin etc* to set; *(annehmen) Hypothese etc* to assume, to posit *(form)* ◆ **jdm/sich ein Ziel/eine Frist ~** to set sb/oneself a goal/deadline; **den Fall ~** to make the assumption; *siehe* **gesetzt.**
(g) *(Hunt: gebären)* to bear, to produce.
(h) jdm eine Spritze ~ to give sb an injection; **sich** *(dat)* **einen Schuß ~** *(sl)* to shoot up *(sl)*.
[2] *vr* **(a)** *(Platz nehmen)* to sit down; *(Vogel)* to perch, to alight ◆ **sich auf einen Stuhl/seinen Platz ~** to sit down on a chair/at one's place; **sich ins Auto ~** to get into the car; **sich in die Sonne/ins Licht ~** to sit in the sun/light; **sich jdm auf den Schoß ~** to sit on sb's lap; **sich zu jdm ~** to sit with sb; **wollen Sie sich nicht zu uns ~?** won't you join us?; **darf ich mich zu Ihnen ~?** may I join you?; **bitte ~ Sie sich** please sit down, please take a seat, please be seated *(form)*; **setz dich doch** sit yourself down *(inf)*.
(b) *(Kaffee, Tee, Lösung)* to settle.
(c) *(sich festsetzen: Staub, Geruch, Läuse)* to get *(in +acc* into).
[3] *vi* **(a)** *(bei Glücksspiel, Wetten)* to bet ◆ **auf ein Pferd ~** to bet on *or* to place a bet on *or* to back a horse; **auf jdn/etw ~** *(lit, fig)* to put one's money on sb/sth, to back sb/sth; **hoch/niedrig ~** to play for high/low stakes.
(b) *(Typ)* to set.
(c) *(springen) (Pferd, Läufer)* to jump; *(Mil)* to cross ◆ **über einen Graben/Zaun/ein Hindernis ~** to jump (over) *or* clear a ditch/fence/hurdle; **über einen Fluß ~** to cross a river.
Setzer *m* **-s, -** *(Typ)* compositor, typesetter, comp *(Typ sl)*.
Setzerei *f*, **Setzersaal** *m (Typ)* composing room, caseroom.
Setz-: ~fehler *m (Typ)* printer's error, literal; **~hase** *m (Hunt)* doe hare; **~kasten** *m* case; **~latte** *f (Surv)* aligning pole; **~ling** *m* **(a)** *(Hort)* seedling; **(b)** *(Fisch)* fry; **~maschine** *f* typesetting machine, typesetter; **~schiff** *nt (Typ)* galley; **~waage** *f* spirit level.
Seuche *f* **-, -n** epidemic; *(fig pej)* scourge.
Seuchen-: s~artig *adj* epidemic; **sich s~artig ausbreiten** to spread like the plague; **~bekämpfung** *f* epidemic control; **~gebiet** *nt* epidemic *or* infested area *or* zone; **~gefahr** *f* danger of epidemic; **~herd** *m* centre of an/the epidemic.
seufzen *vti* to sigh.
Seufzer *m* **-s, -** sigh.
Seufzerbrücke *f* Bridge of Sighs.
Sex [*auch* sɛks] *m* **-(es),** *no pl* sex ◆ **sie hat viel ~** she's very sexy.
Sex-: ~-Appeal [-ə'pi:l] *m* **-s,** *no pl* sex appeal; **~bombe** *f (inf)* sex bomb *(inf)*; **~film** *m* sex film, skin flick *(sl)*; **~foto** *nt* sexy photo.
Sexismus *m* sexism.
Sexist(in *f*) *m* sexist.
sexistisch *adj* sexist.
Sex-: ~kontrolle *f* sex check; **~magazin** *nt* sex magazine; **~muffel** *m (hum inf)* sexless person; **~objekt** *nt* sex object.
Sexologe *m*, **Sexologin** *f* sexologist.
Sexologie *f* sexology.
Sex-: ~protz *m (hum inf)* sexual athlete; **~shop** ['zɛksʃɔp] *m* sex shop.
Sexta *f* **-, Sexten** *(Sch) first year in a German secondary school; top year in an Austrian secondary school.*
Sextaner(in *f*) *m* **-s, -** *pupil in the first year of a German secondary school; pupil in the top year of an Austrian secondary school.*
Sextanerblase *f (hum inf)* weak *or* Chinese *(hum sl)* bladder.
Sextant *m (Naut)* sextant.
Sexte *f* **-, -n** *(Mus)* sixth.
Sexten *pl of* **Sexta.**
Sextett *nt* **-(e)s, -e** *(Mus)* sextet(te).
Sextillion [zɛkstɪ'lio:n] *f* sextillion *(Brit)*, undecillion *(US)*.
Sex-: ~tourismus *m* sex tourism; **~tourist** *m* sex tourist.
sexual *adj (rare)* sexual.
Sexual-: ~atlas *m* illustrated sex handbook; **~empfinden** *nt* sexual feeling; **~erziehung** *f* sex education; **~ethik** *f* sexual ethics *pl*; **~forscher** *m* sexologist; **~forschung** *f* sexology; **~hormon** *nt* sex hormone; **~hygiene** *f* sex(ual) hygiene.
sexualisieren* *vt* to eroticize.
Sexualisierung *f* eroticization.

Sexualität *f, no pl* sexuality.
Sexual-: **~kunde** *f (Sch)* sex education; **~leben** *nt* sex life; **~moral** *f* sexual morals *pl*; **~mord** *m* sex killing; **~mörder** *m* sex murderer; **~neurose** *f* sex neurosis; **~objekt** *nt* sex object; **~pädagogik** *f* sex education; **~partner** *m* sexual partner; **~praktik** *f usu pl* sexual practices *pl*; **~trieb** *m* sex(ual) drive; **~wissenschaft** *f* sexology.
sexuell *adj* sexual.
Sexus *m -, - (geh)* sexuality.
sexy ['sɛksi, 'zɛksi] *adj pred (inf)* sexy *(inf)*.
Seychellen [ze'ʃɛlən] *pl (Geog)* Seychelles *pl*.
Sezession *f* secession.
Sezessionist(in *f*) *m* secessionist.
sezessionistisch *adj* secessionist.
Sezessionskrieg *m* American Civil War.
sezieren* *vti (lit, fig)* to dissect.
Seziersaal *m* dissecting room.
SFB [ɛs|ɛf'beː] *m - abbr of* **Sender Freies Berlin**.
S-förmig ['ɛs-] *adj* S-shaped.
sfr *abbr of* **Schweizer Franken** sfr.
Sgraffito [sgra'fiːto] *nt* **-s, -s** *or* **Sgraffiti** [sgra'fiːti] *(Art)* sgraffito.
Shag [ʃɛk] *m* **-s, -s** shag.
Shakehands ['ʃeːkhɛnts] *nt -, - (inf)* handshake ◆ **~ machen** to shake hands, to press the flesh *(hum inf)*.
Shakespearebühne ['ʃeːkspiːɐ-] *f* Elizabethan stage.
⚠**Shakespearesch**, ⚠**Shakespearisch** ['ʃeːkspiːrɛʃ, -ɪʃ] *adj* Shakespearean.
Shampoo(n) [ʃam'puː(n), ʃam'poː(n), 'ʃampoː(n)] *nt* **-s, -s** shampoo.
shampoonieren* [ʃampu'niːrən, ʃampo'n-] *vt* to shampoo.
Shanty ['ʃɛnti, ʃanti] *nt* **-s, -s** *or* **Shanties** shanty.
Shareware ['ʃɛːɐwɛːɐ] *f - no pl (Comput)* shareware.
Shareware-Programm *nt* shareware program.
Sheriff ['ʃɛrɪf] *m* **-s, -s** sheriff.
Sherpa ['ʃɛrpa] *m* **-s, -s** Sherpa.
Sherry ['ʃɛri] *m* **-s, -s** sherry.
Shetland- ['ʃɛtlant-]: **~inseln** *pl* Shetland Islands *pl*, Shetlands *pl*; **~pony** *nt* Shetland pony; **~wolle** *f* Shetland wool.
Shift-Taste *f (Comput)* shift key.
Shit [ʃɪt] *nt* **-s,** *no pl (sl: Haschisch)* dope *(sl)*.
shocking ['ʃɔkɪŋ] *adj pred* shocking.
Shopping ['ʃɔpɪŋ] *nt* **-s,** *no pl* shopping ◆ **~ machen** *(inf)* to do some shopping.
Shopping-Center ['ʃɔpɪŋsɛntɐ] *nt* shopping centre.
Shorts [ʃoːɐts, ʃɔrts] *pl* (pair of) shorts *pl*.
Shorty ['ʃoːɐti, 'ʃɔrti] *nt* **-s, -s** *or* **Shorties** shorty pyjamas *pl*.
Show [ʃoː] *f* **-, -s** show ◆ **eine ~ abziehen** *(inf)* to put on a show *(inf)*.
Show-: **~down** ['ʃoːdaʊn] *m or nt* showdown; **≈geschäft** *nt* show business; **~man** ['ʃoːmən] *m* **-s, -men** showman; **~master** ['ʃoːmaːstə] *m* **-s, -** compère, emcee *(US)*.
Shredder ['ʃrɛdɐ] *m* **-s, -, Shredder|anlage** *f* shredder, shredding machine.
Siam [ziːam] *nt* **-s** Siam.
Siamese *m* **-n, -n, Siamesin** *f* Siamese.
siamesisch *adj* Siamese ◆ **~e Katze** Siamese cat; **~e Zwillinge** Siamese twins.
Siamkatze *f* Siamese (cat).
Sibirien [zi'biːriən] *nt* **-s** Siberia.
sibirisch *adj* Siberian ◆ **~e Kälte** Siberian *or* arctic conditions *pl*.
Sibylla [zi'bʏla], **Sibylle** [zi'bʏlə] *f* **-, Sibyllen** sibyl.
sibyllinisch [zibʏ'liːnɪʃ] *adj* sibylline, sibyllic.
sich *refl pron* **(a)** *(acc) (+infin, bei „man")* oneself; *(3. pers sing)* himself; herself; itself; *(Höflichkeitsform)* yourself; yourselves; *(3. pers pl)* themselves.
(b) *(dat) (+infin, bei „man")* to oneself; *(3. pers sing)* to himself; to herself; to itself; *(Höflichkeitsform)* to yourself/ yourselves; *(3. pers pl)* to themselves ◆ **~ die Haare waschen/färben** *etc* to wash/dye *etc* one's hair; **er hat ~ das Bein gebrochen** he has broken his leg; **sie hat ~ einen Pulli gekauft/gestrickt** she bought/knitted herself a pullover, she bought/knitted a pullover for herself; **wann hat sie ~ das gekauft?** when did she buy that?
(c) *acc, dat (mit prep) (+infin, bei „man")* one; *(3. pers sing)* him; her; it; *(Höflichkeitsform)* you; *(3. pers pl)* them ◆ **wenn man keinen Paß bei ~** *(dat)* **hat** if one hasn't a passport with one *or* him *(US)*, if you haven't a passport with you; **nur an ~** *(acc)* **denken** to think only of oneself; **wenn er jemanden zu ~** *(dat)* **einlädt** if he invites somebody round to his place.
(d) *(einander)* each other, one another.
(e) *(impers)* **hier sitzt/singt es ~ gut** it's good to sit/sing here; **diese Wolle strickt ~ gut/dieses Auto fährt ~ gut** this wool knits well/this car drives well.
Sichel *f* **-, -n** sickle; *(Mond~)* crescent.
▼ **sicher** [1] *adj* **(a)** *(gewiß)* certain, sure ◆ **der ~e Tod/Sieg** certain death/ victory; **(sich** *dat*) **einer Sache** *(gen)* **~ sein** to be sure *or* certain of sth; **sich** *(dat)* **jds/seiner selbst ~ sein** to be sure of sb/oneself; **(sich** *dat*) **seiner Sache** *(gen)* **~ sein** to be sure of what one is doing/saying; **soviel ist ~** that/this much is certain; **ist das ~?** is that certain?; **man weiß nichts S~es** we don't know anything certain; **das ist uns ~** that is for sure; **mit der guten Zeit ist uns der zweite Platz ~** with such a good time we're sure *or* certain of second place.
(b) *(geschützt, gefahrlos)* safe; *(geborgen)* secure; *Investition auch* secure ◆ **vor jdm/etw ~ sein** to be safe from sb/sth; **~ leben** to live *or* lead a secure life; **~ ist ~** you can't be too sure.
(c) *(zuverlässig)* reliable; *Methode auch* sure-fire *attr (inf)*; *Verhütungsmethode auch, Fahrer, Schwimmer* safe; *(fest) Gefühl, Zusage* certain, definite; *Hand, Einkommen, Job* steady; *Stellung* secure ◆ **ein ~er Schütze** a sure shot; **~ auf den Beinen sein** to be steady on one's legs; **mit ~em Instinkt** with a sure instinct.
(d) *(selbstbewußt)* (self-)confident, (self-)assured ◆ **~ wirken/auftreten** to give an impression of (self-)confidence *or* (self-)assurance.
[2] *adv* **(a)** *fahren etc* safely.
(b) *(natürlich)* of course ◆ **~!** of course, sure *(esp US)*.
(c) *(bestimmt)* **das wolltest du ~ nicht sagen** surely you didn't mean that; **du hast dich ~ verrechnet** you must have counted wrongly; **das weiß ich ganz ~** I know that for certain *or* for sure; **das ist ganz ~ das Beste** it's quite certainly the best; **aber er kommt ~ noch** I'm sure *or* certain he'll come; **das hat er ~ vergessen** I'm sure he's forgotten it; *(garantiert)* he's sure to have forgotten it; **er kommt ~ auch mit** he's bound *or* sure *or* certain to want to come too.
sichergehen *vi sep irreg aux sein* to be sure; *(sich vergewissern auch)* to make sure.
▼ **Sicherheit** *f* **(a)** *no pl (Gewißheit)* certainty ◆ **mit an ~ grenzender Wahrscheinlichkeit** almost certainly, probably if not certainly; **das ist mit ~ richtig** that is definitely right; **obwohl die These sich nicht mit ~ beweisen läßt** although the thesis cannot be proved with any degree of certainty.
(b) *no pl (Schutz, das Sichersein)* safety; *(als Aufgabe von Sicherheitsbeamten etc)* security ◆ **~ und Ordnung** law and order; **die öffentliche ~** public safety *or* security; **die ~ der Bevölkerung** the safety *or* security of the population; **soziale ~** social security; **jdn/etw in ~ bringen** to get sb/sth to safety; **sich in ~ bringen** to get (oneself) to safety; **es gelang mir in letzter Minute, mich im Keller in ~ zu bringen** at the last minute I managed to get to the safety of the cellar; **~ im Straßen-/Flugverkehr** road/air safety; **in ~ sein, sich in ~ befinden** to be safe; **sich in ~ wiegen** *or* **wähnen** to think oneself safe; **jdn in ~ wiegen/wähnen** to lull sb into a (false) sense of security/to think sb safe; **der ~** *(geh)* **halber** in the interests of safety; *(um sicherzugehen)* to be on the safe side; **schnallen Sie sich zu Ihrer ~ an** fasten your seat belt for your own safety.
(c) *no pl (Zuverlässigkeit) (von Mittel, Methode, Geschmack, Instinkt)* reliability, sureness; *(Festigkeit) (der Hand, beim Balancieren etc)* steadiness; *(von Fahrer, Schwimmer)* competence; *(von Hand, Job, Einkommen)* steadiness; *(von Stellung)* security ◆ **mit tödlicher ~** with deadly accuracy.
(d) *no pl (Selbstbewußtsein)* (self-)confidence, (self-) assurance ◆ **~ im Auftreten** self-confident *etc* manner.
(e) *no pl (Gewandtheit)* confidence, assurance, sureness.
(f) *(Comm)* security; *(Pfand)* surety ◆ **~ leisten** *(Comm)* to offer security; *(Jur)* to stand *or* go bail.
Sicherheits-: **~abstand** *m* safe distance; **~auto** *nt* safe car; **~beamte(r)** *m* security officer; *(Pol auch)* security agent *or* man; **~behälter** *m (von Atomreaktor)* containment dome; **~behörde** *f* security service; **~berater** *m* safety adviser; **~bestimmungen** *pl* safety regulations *pl*; *(betrieblich, Pol etc)* security controls *pl or* regulations *pl*; **~bindung** *f (Ski)* safety binding; **~bügel** *m (an Sessellift)* safety bar; **~faktor** *m* security factor; **~garantie** *f* safety guarantee; **~glas** *nt* safety glass; **~gurt** *m (in Flugzeug)* seat belt; *(in Auto auch)* safety belt; **s~halber** *adv* to be on the safe side; **~hülle** *f (von Atomreaktor)* shell; **~kette** *f* safety chain; **~kontrolle** *f* security check; **~kopie** *f (Comput)* backup copy; **~kräfte** *pl* security forces *pl*; **~lampe** *f (Min)* safety lamp; **~leistung** *f (Comm)* surety; *(Jur)* bail; **~maßnahme** *f* safety precaution *or* measure; *(betrieblich, Pol etc)* security measure; **~nadel** *f* safety pin; **~rat** *m* security council; **~risiko** *nt* security risk; **~schleuse** *f* security door system; ⚠**~schloß** *nt* safety *or* Yale ® lock; **~schlüssel** *m* special key *(for safety locks)*, Yale ® key; **~truppen** *pl* security troops *pl*; **~ventil** *nt* safety valve; ⚠**~verschluß** *m* safety catch; **~vorkehrung** *f* safety precaution; *(betrieblich, Pol etc)* security precaution; **die ~vorkehrungen waren sehr gut** security was *or* the security precautions were very good.
sicherlich *adv siehe* **sicher 2 (b, c)**.
sichern [1] *vt* **(a)** *(gegen, vor +dat* against) to safeguard; *(absichern)* to protect; *(Mil auch)* to protect, to cover; *(sicher machen) Tür, Wagen, Fahrrad etc* to secure; *Bergsteiger etc* to belay, to secure; *(Mil)* to protect, to cover; *(Comput) Daten* to save ◆ **eine Feuerwaffe ~** to put the safety catch of a firearm on.
(b) jdm/sich etw ~ to get *or* secure sth for sb/oneself; **diese beiden Flaschen habe ich extra für mich gesichert** I've made sure of these two bottles for myself.
[2] *vr* to protect oneself; *(Bergsteigen)* to belay *or* secure oneself ◆ **sich vor etw** *(dat) or* **gegen etw ~** to protect oneself against sth, to guard against sth.
[3] *vi (Hunt)* to scent.
sicherstellen *vt sep* **(a)** *(in Gewahrsam nehmen) Waffen, Drogen* to take possession of ◆ **das Tatfahrzeug wurde sichergestellt** the vehicle used in the crime was found (and taken in). **(b)** *(garantieren)* to guarantee.
Sicherstellung *f siehe vt* **(a)** taking possession; finding. **(b)** guarantee.
Sicherung *f* **(a)** *siehe vt (a)* safeguarding; protection; securing; belaying. **(b)** *(Schutz)* safeguard. **(c)** *(Elec)* fuse; *(von Waffe)* safety catch ◆ **da ist (bei) ihm die ~ durchgebrannt** *(fig inf)* he blew a fuse *(inf)*.
Sicherungs-: **~kopie** *f (Comput)* back-up copy; **~übereignung** *f (Jur)* transfer of ownership as security on a debt; **~verkauf** *m (Fin)* hedge selling; **~verwahrung** *f (Jur)* preventive detention.
sicherwirkend *adj attr* reliable.
Sicht *f* **-,** *no pl* **(a)** *(Sehweite)* visibility ◆ **die ~ betrug teilweise nur 20 Meter** at

times visibility was down to 20 metres; **eine ~ von 30 Metern** 30 metres' visibility; **in ~ sein/kommen** to be in/come into sight; **aus meiner/seiner** *etc* **~** (*fig*) as I see/he sees it, from my/his point of view; **auf lange/kurze ~** (*fig*) in the long/short term; *planen* for the long/short term; **auf lange ~ ausgebucht** fully booked for a long time ahead.
(b) (*Ausblick*) view.
(c) (*Comm*) **auf** *or* **bei ~** at sight; **acht Tage nach ~** one week after sight.

sichtbar *adj* (*lit, fig*) visible ♦ **~ werden** (*fig*) to become apparent; **allmählich wurden Fortschritte ~** it could gradually be seen that progress was being made.

Sichtbarkeit *f, no pl* visibility.

Sichtbarwerden *nt* (*lit, fig*) appearance ♦ **um das ~ früherer Fehler zu verhindern** to prevent earlier mistakes from becoming apparent.

Sicht-: ~beton *m* exposed concrete; **~einlage** *f* (*Fin*) sight *or* demand deposit.

sichten *vt* **(a)** (*erblicken*) to sight. **(b)** (*durchsehen*) to look through, to examine, to inspect; (*ordnen*) to sift through.

Sicht-: ~flug *m* contact flight; **~gerät** *nt* monitor; (*Comput*) VDU, visual display unit; **~grenze** *f* visibility limit; **~kartei** *f* visible card index; **~kontakt** *m* eye contact.

sichtlich [1] *adj* obvious.
[2] *adv* obviously, visibly.

Sichtung *f siehe vt* **(a)** sighting. **(b)** looking through (*einer Sache (gen)* sth), examination, inspection. **(c)** sifting.

Sicht-: ~verhältnisse *pl* visibility *sing*; **~vermerk** *m* endorsement; (*im Paß*) visa stamp; **~wechsel** *m* (*Fin*) bill payable on demand; **~weite** *f* visibility *no art*; **außer ~weite** out of sight.

Sickergrube *f* soakaway.

sickern *vi aux sein* to seep; (*dickere Flüssigkeit auch*) to ooze; (*in Tropfen*) to drip; (*fig*) to leak out ♦ **in die Presse ~** to be leaked to the press.

Sickerwasser *nt* water seeping through the ground.

Sideboard ['saidbɔːd] *nt* **-s, -s** sideboard.

siderisch *adj* (*Astron*) sidereal.

sie *pers pron 3. pers* **(a)** *sing gen* **ihrer,** *dat* **ihr,** *acc* **sie** (*von Frau, weiblichem Tier*) (*nom*) she; (*acc*) her; (*von Dingen*) it; (*von Behörde, Polizei*) (*nom*) they *pl*; (*acc*) them *pl* ♦ **wenn ich ~ wäre** ... if I were her *or* she (*form*) ...; **~ ist es** it's her, it is she (*form*); **wer hat das gemacht? — ~** who did that? — she did *or* her!; **wer ist der Täter? — ~** who is the person responsible? — she is *or* her!; **~ war es nicht, ich war's** it wasn't her, it was me; **~ und du/ich** you and she/she and I; **unser Hund ist eine ~** our dog is a she.
(b) *pl gen* **ihrer,** *dat* **ihnen,** *acc* **sie** (*nom*) they; (*acc*) them ♦ **~ sind es** it's them; **~ sind es, die** ... it's them *or* it is they (*form*) who ...; **wer hat's zuerst bemerkt? — ~** who noticed it first? — they did *or* them (*inf*).
(c) (*obs: als Anrede*) **S~** *sing* you, thee (*obs*); *pl* you.

Sie [1] *pers pron 2. pers sing or pl with 3. pers pl vb gen* **Ihrer,** *dat* **Ihnen,** *acc* **Sie** you; (*im Imperativ*) *nicht übersetzt* ♦ **beeilen ~ sich!** hurry up!; **he, ~!** (*inf*) hey, you!; **~, wissen ~ was** ... (*inf*) do you know what ...
[2] *nt* **-s,** *no pl* polite *or* "Sie" form of address ♦ **jdn per** *or* **mit ~ anreden** to use the polite form of address to sb, to call sb "Sie".

Sieb *nt* **-(e)s, -e** sieve; (*für Erde auch*) riddle; (*für Korn, Gold auch*) screen; (*Tee~*) strainer; (*Gemüse~*) colander ♦ **ein Gedächtnis wie ein ~ haben** to have a memory like a sieve.

Sieb-: ~bein *nt* (*Anat*) ethmoid (bone); **~druck** *m* (silk-)screen print; (*~druckverfahren*) (silk-)screen printing.

sieben[1] [1] *vt* to pass through a sieve; *Korn, Gold* to screen; (*Cook*) to sift, to sieve.
[2] *vi* (*fig inf*) **solche Unternehmen ~ sehr** organisations like that pick and choose very carefully *or* are very selective; **es wird stark gesiebt** they pick and choose *or* are very selective; **bei der Prüfung wird stark gesiebt** the exam will weed a lot of people out.

sieben[2] *num* seven ♦ **die S~ Weisen** the Seven Sages; **die S~ Weltwunder** the seven wonders of the world; **die S~ Weltmeere** the Seven Seas; **die S~ Freien Künste** the humanities, the (seven) liberal arts; **die ~ Todsünden** *or* **Hauptsünden** the seven deadly sins; **die ~ fetten und die ~ mageren Jahre** (*Bibl*) the seven fat and the seven lean years; *siehe auch* **vier.**

Sieben *f* **-, -** *or* **-en** seven; *siehe* **Vier, böse.**

Sieben- *in cpds siehe auch* **Vier-**; **s~armig** *adj Leuchter* seven-armed; **~bürgen** *nt* (*Geog*) Transylvania; **~eck** *nt* heptagon; **~gestirn** *nt* (*Astron*) Pleiades *pl*; **~hügelstadt** *f* city of the seven hills; **s~hundert** *num* seven hundred; **s~jährig** *adj* seven-year-old; (*sieben Jahre dauernd*) seven-year *attr*; **der ~jährige Krieg** the Seven-Years' War; **s~mal** *adv* seven times; **~meilenstiefel** *pl* (*Liter*) seven-league boots *pl*; **~meter** *m* (*Sport*) penalty; **~monatskind** *nt* seven-month baby; **~sachen** *pl* (*inf*) belongings *pl*, things *pl*; **~schläfer** *m* **(a)** (*Zool*) edible *or* fat dormouse; **(b)** *27th June, day which is said to determine the weather for the next seven weeks*; **s~tausend** *num* seven thousand.

Siebentel, Siebtel *nt* **-s, -** seventh.

siebentens, siebtens *adv* seventh(ly), in seventh place.

siebente(r, s) *adj siehe* **siebte(r, s).**

siebte(r, s) *adj* seventh; *siehe auch* **vierte(r, s).**

siebzehn *num* seventeen ♦ **S~ und Vier** (*Cards*) pontoon; *siehe auch* **vierzehn.**

siebzig *num* seventy; *siehe auch* **vierzig.**

Siebziger(in *f***)** *m* **-s, -, Siebzigjährige(r)** *mf decl as adj* seventy-year-old, septuagenarian.

siech *adj* (*old, liter*) ailing, infirm.

siechen *vi* (*rare*) *siehe* **dahinsiechen.**

Siechtum *nt, no pl* (*liter*) infirmity.

Siedelland *nt* settlement area.

siedeln *vi* to settle.

sieden *pret* **siedete** *or* **sott,** *ptp* **gesiedet** *or* **gesotten** [1] *vi* (*Wasser, Zucker etc*) to boil; (*Aus, S Ger*) to simmer ♦ **da siedet einem das Blut** it makes your blood boil.
[2] *vt Seife, Leim* to produce by boiling; (*Aus, S Ger*) to simmer ♦ **~d heiß/~de Hitze** boiling *or* scalding hot/heat; (*von Klima auch*) sweltering hot/sweltering heat; *siehe* **gesotten.**

Siede-: ~punkt *m* (*Phys, fig*) boiling-point; **~wasserreaktor** *m* boiling water reactor.

Siedler(in *f***)** *m* **-s, -** settler; (*Bauer*) smallholder.

Siedlung *f* **(a)** (*Ansiedlung*) settlement. **(b)** (*Siedlerstelle*) smallholding. **(c)** (*Wohn~*) housing scheme *or* estate.

Siedlungshaus *nt house on a housing scheme.*

Sieg *m* **-(e)s, -e** victory (*über +acc* over); (*in Wettkampf auch*) win (*über +acc* over) ♦ **um den ~ kämpfen** to fight for victory; **den ~ davontragen** *or* **erringen** to be victorious; (*in Wettkampf auch*) to be the winner/winners; **einer Sache** (*dat*) **zum ~ verhelfen** to help sth to triumph; **von ~ zu ~ schreiten** (*geh*) to heap victory upon victory.

Siegel *nt* **-s, -** seal ♦ **unter dem ~ der Verschwiegenheit** under the seal of secrecy; *siehe* **Buch, Brief.**

Siegellack *m* sealing wax.

siegeln *vt Urkunde* to affix a/one's seal to; (*ver~*) *Brief* to seal.

Siegel-: ~ring *m* signet ring; **~wachs** *nt* sealing wax.

siegen *vi* (*Mil*) to be victorious; (*fig auch*) to triumph; (*in Wettkampf*) to win ♦ **über jdn/etw ~** (*Mil*) to vanquish sb/sth; (*fig*) to triumph over sb/sth; (*in Wettkampf*) to beat sb/sth, to win against sb/sth; **ich kam, sah und siegte** I came, I saw, I conquered.

Sieger *m* **-s, -** victor; (*in Wettkampf*) winner ♦ **zweiter ~** runner-up; **~ werden** to be the winner, to win; **als ~ hervorgehen** to emerge victorious.

Sieger|ehrung *f* (*Sport*) presentation ceremony.

Siegerin *f* victress (*liter*); (*in Wettkampf*) winner.

Sieger-: ~kranz *m* victor's laurels *pl*; **im ~kranz** crowned with the victor's laurels; **~macht** *f usu pl* (*Pol*) victorious power; **~pose** *f* victory pose; **~straße** *f* road to victory; **~urkunde** *f* (*Sport*) winner's certificate.

Sieges-: ⚠s~bewußt *adj* confident of victory; **~botschaft** *f* news of victory *sing*; **~denkmal** *nt* victory monument; **~feier** *f* victory celebrations *pl*; (*Sport*) victory celebration; **~geschrei** *nt* (*pej*) shouts of victory *pl*; **⚠s~gewiß** *adj siehe* **s~sicher**; **~göttin** *f* goddess of victory; **~kranz** *m* victor's laurels *pl*; **~palme** *f* palm (of victory); **~preis** *m* winner's prize; (*Boxen*) winner's purse; **~säule** *f* victory column; **~serie** *f* series *sing* of victories/wins; **s~sicher** *adj* certain *or* sure of victory; **~taumel** *m* triumphant euphoria; **im ~taumel** euphoric with their *etc* victory *or* triumph; **s~trunken** *adj* (*liter*) drunk with victory; **~zug** *m* triumphal march.

sieg-: ~gewohnt *adj* used to victory/winning; **~haft** *adj siehe* **siegesbewußt**; **~reich** *adj* victorious, triumphant; (*in Wettkampf*) winning *attr*, successful.

sieh, siehe *imper sing of* **sehen.**

siehste (*inf*) *2. pers sing present of* **sehen** (you) see.

Siel *nt or m* **-(e)s, -e** (*Schleuse*) sluice; (*Abwasserkanal*) sewer.

Siele *f* **-, -n** trace ♦ **in den ~n sterben** (*fig*) to die in harness.

sielen *vr* (*dial*) *siehe* **suhlen.**

siena ['zieːna] *adj inv* sienna.

Sierra [si'ɛra] *f* **-, -s** *or* **Sierren** [si'ɛrən] (*Geog*) sierra.

Sievert *nt* **-, -** (*Phys*) (*abbr* **Sv**) sievert.

siezen *vt* **jdn/sich ~** to use the formal term of address to sb/each other, to address sb/each other as "Sie".

Sigel *nt* **-s, -, Sigle** ['ziːgl] *f* **-, -n** short form, grammalogue (*spec*).

Sightseeing ['saitsiːɪŋ] *nt* **-,** *no pl* sightseeing ♦ **~ machen** to do some sightseeing.

Signal *nt* **-s, -e** signal ♦ **(ein) ~ geben** to give a signal; **mit der Hupe (ein) ~ geben** to hoot (as a signal); **~e setzen** (*fig*) to blaze a trail.

Signal|anlage *f* signals *pl*, set of signals.

Signalement [zɪgnaləˈmãː, -mɛnt] *nt* **-s, -s** (*Sw*) (personal) description.

Signal-: ~flagge *f* signal flag; **~gast** *m* signalman; **~horn** *nt* (*Hunt*) (hunting) horn; (*Mil*) bugle.

signalisieren* *vt* (*lit, fig*) to signal.

Signal-: ~kelle *f* signalling disc; **~lampe, ~laterne** *f* signalling lamp; (*installiert*) signal lamp; **~mast** *m* signal mast; **~pfeife** *f* whistle; **~pistole** *f* Very pistol; **~technik** *f* signalling; **~wirkung** *f* signal; **davon ging eine ~wirkung aus** this acted as a signal.

Signatar(in *f***)** *m* (*form*) signatory (*gen* to).

Signatarmächte *pl* signatory powers *pl*.

Signatur *f* **(a)** (*Unterschrift, Buch~*) signature. **(b)** (*auf Landkarten*) symbol. **(c)** (*Bibliotheks~*) shelf mark.

Signet [zɪ'gneːt, zɪ'gnɛt, zɪn'jeː] *nt* **-s, -s** (*Typ*) publisher's mark.

signieren* *vt* to sign; (*mit Anfangsbuchstaben auch*) to initial.

Signierung *f, no pl siehe vt* signing; initialling.

signifikant *adj* (*geh*) significant.

Signifikanz *f* (*geh*) significance.

Sikh [ziːk] *m* **-(s), -s** Sikh.

Silage [ziˈlaːʒə] *f* **-,** *no pl* (*Agr*) silage.

⚠: for details of spelling reform, see supplement

Silbe *f* **-, -n** syllable ◆ **~ für ~** *(fig)* word for word; **er hat es mit keiner ~ erwähnt/verraten** he didn't say/breathe a word about it.

Silben-: ~rätsel *nt word game in which the answers are obtained by combining syllables from a given list*; **~schrift** *f* syllabary; **~trennung** *f* syllabification; *(Typ, Comput)* hyphenation; **s~weise** *adv* in syllables; **~zahl** *f* number of syllables.

-silber *m* **-, -** *in cpds (Poet)* syllable.

Silber *nt* **-s,** *no pl (abbr* **Ag***)* silver; *(Tafelbesteck auch)* silverware; *(Her)* argent ◆ **aus ~** made of silver; *siehe* **reden.**

Silber- *in cpds* silver; **~arbeit** *f* silverwork *no pl*; **~besteck** *nt* silver(ware), silver cutlery; **~blick** *m (inf)* squint; **~distel** *f* carline thistle; **s~farben, s~farbig** *adj* silver(-coloured); *(Her)* argent; **~fischchen** *nt* silverfish; **~folie** *f* silver foil; **~fuchs** *m* silver fox; **~geld** *nt* silver; **~geschirr** *nt* silver(ware); **~glanz** *m (Miner, Chem)* silver glance, argentite, silver sulphide; *(poet)* silvery gleam; **s~grau** *adj* silver(y)-grey; **~haar** *nt (poet)* silver(y) hair; *(von Mann auch)* hoary head *(poet)*; **s~haltig** *adj* silver-bearing, argentiferous *(spec)*; **s~hell** *adj Stimme, Lachen* silvery; **~hochzeit** *f* silver wedding (anniversary); **~hütte** *f* silverworks *sing or pl.*

silberig *adj siehe* **silbrig.**

Silber-: ~klang *m (poet)* silvery sound; **~ling** *m (Bibl)* piece of silver; **~löwe** *m* puma; **~medaille** *f* silver medal; **~möwe** *f* herring gull.

silbern *adj* silver; *(liter) Licht, Stimme, Haare* silvery *(liter)*, silvern *(poet)* ◆ **~e Hochzeit** silver wedding (anniversary).

Silber-: ~pappel *f* white poplar; **~schmied** *m* silversmith; **~stickerei** *f (Kunst)* silver embroidery; *(Produkt)* silver-embroidered garment/cushion *etc*; **~streif(en)** *m (fig)* **es zeichnete sich ein ~streif(en) am Horizont ab** you/they *etc* could see light at the end of the tunnel; **das war wie ein ~streif(en) am Horizont** that was a ray of sunshine; **~stück** *nt* silver coin; **~tanne** *f siehe* **Edeltanne**; **~währung** *f* currency based on the silver standard; **~waren** *pl* silver *sing*; **s~weiß** *adj* silvery white; **~zeug** *nt* silver *sing.*

-silbig *adj suf* **fünf~/zehn~ sein** to have five/ten syllables; **ein sechs~es Wort** a word with six syllables.

silbrig *adj* silvery.

Silhouette [zi'luɛtə] *f* silhouette ◆ **sich als ~ gegen etw abheben** *or* **abzeichnen** to be silhouetted against sth.

Silikat, Silicat *(spec) nt* **-(e)s, -e** silicate.

Silikon *nt* **-s, -e** silicone.

Silikose *f* **-, -n** *(Med)* silicosis.

Silizium *nt, no pl (abbr* **Si***)* silicon.

Siliziumscheibe *f* silicon chip.

Silo *m* **-s, -s** silo.

Silur *nt* **-s,** *no pl (Geog)* Silurian.

Silvaner [zɪl'vaːnɐ] *m* **-s, -** sylvaner (grape/wine).

Silvester [zɪl'vɛstɐ] *m or nt* **-s, -** New Year's Eve, Hogmanay *(esp Scot)*.

Silvester-: ~abend *m* New Year's Eve, Hogmanay *(esp Scot)*; **~feier** *f* New Year's Eve *or* New Year party; **~nacht** *f* night of New Year's Eve *or* Hogmanay *(esp Scot)*.

Simbabwe *nt* **-s** Zimbabwe.

Simonie *f* simony.

simpel *adj* simple; *Mensch auch* simple-minded; *(vereinfacht)* simplistic.

Simpel *m* **-s, -** *(inf)* simpleton.

Simplex *nt* **-, -e** *or* **Simplizia** *(Gram)* simplex.

Simplifikation *f (geh)* simplification.

simplifizieren* *vt (geh)* to simplify.

Simplizität *f (geh)* simplicity.

Sims *m or nt* **-es, -e** *(Fenster~)* (window)sill; *(außen auch)* (window)ledge; *(Gesims)* ledge; *(Kamin~)* mantlepiece.

Simulant(in *f***)** *m* malingerer.

Simulation *f* simulation.

Simulator *m (Sci)* simulator.

simulieren* [1] *vi* **(a)** to feign illness ◆ **er simuliert nur** he's shamming; *(um sich zu drücken auch)* he's malingering. **(b)** *(inf: nachdenken)* to meditate, to ruminate.
[2] *vt* **(a)** *Krankheit* to feign, to sham. **(b)** *(Sci)* to simulate.

simultan *adj* simultaneous.

Simultan-: ~dolmetschen *nt* **-s,** *no pl* simultaneous translation; **~dolmetscher** *m* simultaneous translator.

Simultaneität [zimʊltanei'tɛːt], **Simultanität** *f (geh)* simultaneity, simultaneousness.

sin. *abbr of* **Sinus.**

Sinai ['ziːnai] *m* **-(s), Sinaihalb|insel** *f* Sinai (Peninsula).

sind *1. and 3. pers pl, with Sie sing and pl present of* **sein.**

Sinekure *f* **-, -n** *(liter)* sinecure.

sine tempore *adv (abbr* **s.t.***) (Univ)* punctually.

Sinfonie *f* symphony.

Sinfonie-: ~konzert *nt* symphony concert; **~orchester** *nt* symphony orchestra.

Sinfoniker(in *f***)** *m* **-s, -** member of a symphony orchestra ◆ **die Bamberger ~** the Bamberg Symphony Orchestra.

sinfonisch *adj* symphonic.

Sing|akademie *f* choral society.

Singapur ['zɪŋgapuːɐ] *nt* **-s** Singapore.

Sing-: s~bar *adj* singable; **schwer s~bar sein** to be hard to sing; **~drossel** *f* song thrush.

singen *pret* **sang,** *ptp* **gesungen** [1] *vi* **(a)** *(lit, fig)* to sing; *(esp Eccl: eintönig, feierlich)* to chant; *(Dynamo auch)* to hum; *(Telegraphendrähte auch)* to buzz, to hum ◆ **zur Gitarre/Mandoline ~** to sing to the guitar/mandoline; **ein ~der Tonfall** a lilt, a lilting accent; **singe, wem Gesang gegeben** *(dated prov)* if God gave you a good voice you should use it; *siehe* **Alte(r).**
(b) *(sl: gestehen)* to squeal *(sl)*, to sing *(sl)*, to talk.
[2] *vt (lit, fig)* to sing; *(esp Eccl) Psalmen, Kanon* to chant ◆ **jdn in den Schlaf** *or* **Schlummer** *(liter)* **~** to sing sb to sleep; **das kann ich schon ~** *(inf)* I know it backwards.
[3] *vr* **sich heiser/in den Schlaf ~** to sing oneself hoarse/to sleep; **sich müde ~** to sing until one is tired; **das Lied singt sich leicht** it's an easy song to sing.

Singen *nt* **-s,** *no pl* **(a)** *siehe vi (a)* singing; chanting; humming; buzzing. **(b)** *(Sch)* singing.

Singerei *f (inf)* singing.

Singhalese [zɪŋga'leːzə] *m* **-n, -n, Singhalesin** *f* Sin(g)halese.

Singhalesisch(e) [zɪŋga'leːzɪʃ(ə)] *nt decl as adj* Sin(g)halese.

Single[1] ['sɪŋgl] *f* **-, -(s)** *(Schallplatte)* single.

Single[2] ['sɪŋgl] *nt* **-, -(s)** *(Tennis etc)* singles *sing.*

Single[3] ['sɪŋgl] *m* **-s, -s** *(Alleinlebender)* single ◆ **Urlaub für ~s** singles' holiday.

Singlebar ['sɪŋgl-] *f* singles' bar.

Sing-: ~sang *m* **-s, -s (a)** *(Liedchen)* ditty; **(b)** *(Gesang)* monotonous singing; **(c)** *(singende Sprechweise)* singsong; **~spiel** *nt* lyrical drama; **~stimme** *f* vocal part.

Singular *m* **-s, -e** *(Gram)* singular ◆ **im ~ stehen** to be (in the) singular; **den ~ zu etw bilden** to form the singular of sth.

singulär *adj (geh)* unique.

singularisch *adj (Gram)* singular.

Singularität *f (geh)* uniqueness.

Sing-: ~vogel *m* song-bird; **~weise** *f* way of singing.

sinister *adj (geh)* sinister.

sinken *pret* **sank,** *ptp* **gesunken** *vi aux sein* **(a)** to sink; *(Schiff auch)* to go down; *(Ballon)* to descend; *(Nebel)* to come down, to descend *(liter)* ◆ **auf den Grund ~** to sink to the bottom; **auf einen Stuhl/zu Boden ~** to sink into a chair/to the ground; **ins Bett ~** to fall into bed; **in Schlaf ~** to sink into a sleep; **an jds Brust** *(acc) or* **jdm an die Brust ~** *(liter)* to fall upon sb's breast; **in Ohnmacht ~** *(geh)* to swoon, to fall into a faint; **ich hätte in die Erde ~ mögen** I wished the earth would (open and) swallow me up; **sein Stern ist im** *or* **am S~** *(geh)* his star is waning; **die Arme/den Kopf ~ lassen** to let one's arms/head drop.
(b) *(Boden, Gebäude)* to subside, to sink; *(Fundament)* to settle ◆ **das Haus war ein Meter tiefer gesunken** the house had sunk one metre; **in Staub** *or* **Trümmer/in Schutt und Asche ~** *(geh)* to fall in ruins/be reduced to a pile of rubble.
(c) *(niedriger werden: Wasserspiegel, Temperatur, Preise etc)* to fall, to drop.
(d) *(schwinden) (Ansehen, Vertrauen)* to diminish; *(Einfluß auch)* to wane, to decline; *(Hoffnung, Stimmung)* to sink ◆ **den Mut/die Hoffnung ~ lassen** to lose courage/hope.
(e) *(moralisch)* to sink ◆ **tief gesunken sein** to have sunk low; **in jds Meinung/Achtung** *(dat)* **~** to go down in sb's estimation.

Sinn *m* **-(e)s, -e (a)** *(Wahrnehmungsfähigkeit)* sense ◆ **die ~e** *(sinnliche Begierde)* one's desires; **seiner ~e** *(gen)* **nicht mehr mächtig sein, nicht mehr Herr seiner ~e** *(gen)* **sein** to have lost all control over oneself; *siehe* **fünf, sechste(r, s).**
(b) ~e *pl (Bewußtsein)* senses *pl*, consciousness ◆ **er war von** *or* **nicht bei ~en** he was out of his senses *or* mind; **wie von ~en** like one demented; **bist du noch bei ~en?** have you taken leave of your senses?
(c) *(Gedanken, Denkweise)* mind ◆ **sich** *(dat)* **jdn/etw aus dem ~ schlagen** to put sb/(all idea of) sth out of one's mind, to forget all about sb/sth; **es kommt** *or* **will mir nicht aus dem ~** *(geh)* I can't get it out of my mind; **es kam mir plötzlich in den ~** it suddenly came to me; **das will mir einfach nicht in den ~** I just can't understand it; **etw im ~ haben** to have sth in mind; **anderen ~es werden** *(geh)* to change one's mind; **(mit jdm) eines ~es sein** *(geh)* to be of the same mind (as sb), to be of one mind.
(d) *(Wunsch)* inclination ◆ **ihr ~ ist auf ...** *(acc)* **gerichtet** *(geh)* her inclination is to ...; **danach steht ihm der ~** *(geh)* that is his wish.
(e) *(Verständnis, Empfänglichkeit)* feeling ◆ **dafür fehlt ihm der ~** he has no feeling for that sort of thing; **~ für Humor/Proportionen/Gerechtigkeit** *etc* **haben** to have a sense of humour/proportion/justice *etc*; **~ für Kunst/Literatur/das Höhere haben** to appreciate art/literature/higher things.
(f) *(Geist)* spirit ◆ **im ~e des Gesetzes** according to the spirit of the law; **in jds ~e** *(dat)* **handeln** to act as sb would have wished; **im ~e des Verstorbenen** in accordance with the wishes of the deceased; **das ist nicht in meinem/seinem ~e** that is not what I myself/he himself would have done/wished *etc*; **das wäre nicht im ~e unserer Kunden** it would not be in the interests of our customers.
(g) *(Zweck)* point ◆ **das ist nicht der ~ der Sache** that is not the point, that is not the object of the exercise; **~ und Zweck einer Sache** *(gen)* the (aim and) object of sth; **~ und Unsinn dieser Maßnahmen/des Geschichtsunterrichts** reasoning or lack of it behind these measures/behind history teaching; **der ~ des Lebens** the meaning of life; **ohne ~ und Verstand sein** to make no sense at all; **das hat keinen ~** there is no point *or* sense in that; **was hat denn das für einen ~?** what's the point of *or* in that *or* the sense in that?
(h) *(Bedeutung)* meaning; *(von Wort, Ausdruck auch)* sense ◆ **im übertragenen/weiteren ~** in the figurative/broader sense; **der Satz (er)gibt** *or* **macht keinen ~** the sentence doesn't make sense.

Sinn-: s~betörend *adj (liter)* sensuously intoxicating; **~bild** *nt* symbol; **s~bildlich** *adj* symbolic(al).

sinnen *pret* **sann**, *ptp* **gesonnen** *(geh)* [1] *vi* **(a)** *(nachdenken)* to meditate, to ponder, to muse; *(grübeln)* to brood ◆ **über etw** *(acc)* ~ to reflect on/brood over sth.
(b) *(planen)* **auf etw** *(acc)* ~ to devise sth, to think sth up, to think of sth; **auf Verrat/Rache ~** to plot treason/revenge; **all sein S~ und Trachten** all his mind and energies.
[2] *vt (old liter) Verrat, Rache* to plot.

Sinnen-: ~freude *f* enjoyment of the pleasures of life; **s~freudig, s~froh** *adj* **ein s~freudiger Mensch** a person who enjoys the pleasures of life; ⚠**~genuß** *m* sensual pleasure; **~lust** *f (liter)* sensuality; **~mensch** *m* sensuous person; **~rausch** *m (liter)* sensual passion.

sinn-: ~entleert *adj* bereft of content; **~entstellend** *adj* **~entstellend sein** to distort the meaning; **~entstellend übersetzt** translated so that the meaning is/was distorted.

Sinnenwelt *f (liter)* material world.

Sinnes-: ~änderung *f* change of mind *or* heart; **~art** *f (geh) siehe* **Gesinnung; ~eindruck** *m* sensory impression, impression on the senses; **~nerv** *m* sensory nerve; **~organ** *nt* sense organ; **~reiz** *m* sensory stimulus; **~störung** *f* sensory disorder; **~täuschung** *f* hallucination; **~wahrnehmung** *f* sensory perception *no pl*; **~wandel** *m* change of mind *or* heart.

Sinn-: s~fällig *adj* manifest, obvious; **~gebung** *f (geh)* giving meaning *(+gen* to); *(Sinn)* meaning; **~gedicht** *nt* epigram; **s~gemäß** *adj* **(a)** *(inhaltlich)* **etw s~gemäß wiedergeben** to give the gist of sth; **eine s~gemäße Zusammenfassung** a summary which gives the gist (of it); **(b)** *(esp Jur: analog)* corresponding, analogous; **etw s~gemäß anwenden** to apply sth by analogy; **s~getreu** *adj Übersetzung* faithful (to the sense *or* meaning).

sinnieren* *vi* to brood *(über +acc* over), to ruminate *(über +acc* about).

sinnig *adj* apt; *Vorrichtung* practical; *(iro: wenig sinnvoll)* clever.

sinnlich *adj* **(a)** *(Philos) Empfindung, Eindrücke* sensory, sensorial ◆ **die ~e Welt** the material world; **~e Anschauung** perception (by the senses); **~ wahrnehmbar** perceptible by the senses. **(b)** *(vital, sinnenfroh)* sensuous; *(erotisch)* sensual ◆ **~e Liebe** sensual love.

Sinnlichkeit *f* **(a)** *(Philos)* sensory *or* sensorial nature. **(b)** *(Vitalität, Sinnenfreude)* sensuousness; *(Erotik)* sensuality.

sinnlos *adj* **(a)** *(unsinnig) Redensarten, Geschwätz* meaningless; *Verhalten, Töten* senseless.
(b) *(zwecklos)* pointless, futile, senseless; *Hoffnung* forlorn ◆ **es ist/wäre ~, zu** ... it is/would be pointless *or* futile to ...; **das ist völlig ~** there's no sense in that, that's completely pointless.
(c) *Wut* blind; *Hast* desperate ◆ **~ betrunken** blind drunk.

Sinnlosigkeit *f* **(a)** *siehe adj (a) (Unsinnigkeit)* meaninglessness; senselessness. **(b)** *siehe adj (b) (Zwecklosigkeit)* pointlessness, futility, senselessness; forlornness.

Sinn-: s~reich *adj Deutung* meaningful; *(zweckdienlich) Einrichtung, Erfindung* useful; **~spruch** *m* epigram; **s~verwandt** *adj* synonymous; **s~verwandte Wörter** synonyms; **~verwandtschaft** *f* synonymity; **s~voll** *adj* **(a)** *Satz* meaningful; **(b)** *(fig) (vernünftig)* sensible; *(nützlich)* useful; **s~widrig** *adj* nonsensical, absurd; **~widrigkeit** *f* nonsensicalness, absurdity.

Sinologe *m*, **Sinologin** *f* Sinologist.

Sinologie *f* Sinology.

sintemal(en) *conj (obs, hum)* because, since.

Sinter *m* **-s, -** *(Miner)* sinter.

sintern *vti* to sinter.

Sintflut *f (Bibl)* Flood ◆ **nach mir/uns die ~** *(inf)* it doesn't matter what happens when I've/we've gone.

sintflut|artig *adj* **~e Regenfälle** torrential rain.

Sinto *m* **-, Sinti** *usu pl* Sinto (gypsy) ◆ **Sinti und Roma** Sinti and Roma.

Sinus *m* **-, -** *or* **-se** **(a)** *(Math)* sine. **(b)** *(Anat)* sinus.

Sinus-: ~kurve *f* sine curve; **~satz** *m* sine theorem.

Sioux ['ziːʊks] *m* **-, -** Sioux.

Siphon ['ziːfõ] *m* **-s, -s** siphon; *(Aus inf)* soda (water).

Sippe *f* **-, -n** (extended) family, kinship group *(spec)*; *(inf: Verwandtschaft)* family, clan *(inf)*; *(Zool)* species *sing*.

Sippen-: ~älteste(r) *mf* head of the family; **~forschung** *f* genealogy, genealogical research; **~haft** *(inf)*, **~haftung** *(Jur) f liability of all the members of a family for the crimes of one member*; **~verband** *m* kinship group.

Sippschaft *f (pej inf) (Familie)* tribe *(inf)*; *(Bande, Gesindel auch)* bunch *(inf)*.

Sire [siːr] *interj (old liter)* Sire *(old)*.

Sirene *f* **-, -n** *(Myth, Tech, fig)* siren; *(Zool)* sirenian.

Sirenen-: ~geheul *nt* wail of a/the siren/sirens; **~gesang** *m* siren song.

Sirius *m* **-** *(Astron)* Sirius.

sirren *vi siehe* **surren**.

Sirup *m* **-s, -e** syrup; *(schwarz, aus Zuckerrohr auch)* treacle.

Sisal(hanf) *m* **-s** sisal (hemp).

Sisalteppich *m* sisal mat.

sistieren* *vt (Jur) Verdächtigen* to detain; *Verfahren* to adjourn.

Sisyphus|arbeit ['ziːzyfʊs-] *f* Sisyphean task *(liter)*, never-ending task.

Sit-in [sɪt'|ɪn] *nt* **-(s), -s** sit-in ◆ **ein ~ machen** to have *or* stage *or* hold a sit-in.

Sitte *f* **-, -n** **(a)** *(Brauch)* custom; *(Mode)* practice ◆ **~ sein** to be the custom/the practice; **~n und Gebräuche** customs and traditions; **was sind denn das für ~n?** what's all this?; **hier reißen ja ~n ein!** *(inf)* the things people have started doing!
(b) *usu pl (gutes Benehmen)* manners *pl*; *(Sittlichkeit)* morals *pl* ◆ **gegen die (guten) ~n verstoßen, ~ und Anstand verletzen** to offend common decency; **gute ~n** good manners *pl*; **was sind denn das für ~n?** what sort of a way is that to behave!
(c) *(sl: Sittenpolizei)* vice squad.

Sitten-: ~apostel *m (pej)* moralizer; **~bild** *nt (Art)* genre picture; **~dezernat** *nt* vice squad; **~gemälde** *nt siehe* **~bild; ~geschichte** *f* **~geschichte Roms** history of Roman life and customs; **~gesetz** *nt* moral law; **~kodex** *m* moral code; **~lehre** *f* ethics *sing*; **s~los** *adj* immoral; **~losigkeit** *f* immorality; **~polizei** *f* vice squad; **~prediger** *m* moralist, sermonizer; **~richter** *m* judge of public morals; **s~streng** *adj* highly moral; **~strenge** *f* strict morality; **~strolch** *m (Press sl)* sex fiend; **~verfall** *m* decline *or* drop in moral standards; **~wächter** *m (iro)* guardian of public morals; **s~widrig** *adj (form)* immoral.

Sittich *m* **-s, -e** parakeet.

sittlich *adj* moral ◆ **ihm fehlt der ~e Halt/die ~e Reife** he lacks moral fibre/he's morally immature; **er verlor jeden ~en Halt** he became morally unstable; **das S~e** morality.

Sittlichkeit *f, no pl* morality.

Sittlichkeits-: ~delikt *nt* sexual offence; **~verbrechen** *nt* sex crime; **~verbrecher** *m* sex offender.

sittsam *adj* demure.

Sittsamkeit *f* demureness.

Situation *f* situation; *(persönliche Lage auch)* position.

Situations-: ~bericht *m* report on the situation; **~komik** *f* comicalness *or* comedy of the situation/situations; *(Art der Komik)* situation comedy, sitcom *(inf)*.

situiert *adj* **gut/schlecht ~ sein** to be well/poorly situated financially; *siehe* **gutsituiert**.

Sitz *m* **-es, -e** **(a)** *(~platz, Parl)* seat ◆ **~ und Stimme haben** to have a seat and a vote.
(b) *(von Regierung, Graf, Universität, fig)* seat; *(Wohn~)* residence, domicile *(form)*; *(von Firma, Verwaltung)* headquarters *pl* ◆ **diese Stadt ist der ~ der Forstverwaltung** the forestry authority has its headquarters in this town.
(c) *no pl (Tech, von Kleidungsstück)* sit; *(von der Größe her)* fit ◆ **einen guten/schlechten ~ haben** to sit/fit well/badly.
(d) *no pl (von Reiter)* seat.

Sitz-: ~bad *nt* sitz *or* hip bath; **~badewanne** *f* sitz *or* hip bath; **~bank** *f* bench; **~blockade** *f* sit-in; **~demonstrant** *m* sit-down demonstrator.

sitzen *vi pret* **saß**, *ptp* **gesessen** *aux haben or (Aus, S Ger, Sw) sein* **(a)** to sit; *(auf Mauer, Stuhllehne etc auch, Vogel)* to perch ◆ **bleiben Sie bitte ~!, bitte bleiben Sie ~!** please don't get up; **~ Sie bequem?** are you comfortable?; **hier sitzt man sehr bequem** it's very comfortable sitting here; **auf der Toilette ~** to be on *(inf) or* in the toilet; **etw im S~ tun** to do sth sitting down; **beim Frühstück/Mittagessen ~** to be having breakfast/lunch; **beim Wein/Schach ~** to sit over a glass of wine/a game of chess; **an einer Aufgabe/über den Büchern/einer Arbeit ~** to sit over a task/one's books/a piece of work.
(b) *(Modell ~)* to sit *(jdm* for sb).
(c) *(seinen Sitz haben) (Regierung, Gericht etc)* to sit; *(Firma)* to have its headquarters.
(d) *(Mitglied sein) (im Parlament)* to have a seat *(in +dat* in); *(im Vorstand, Aufsichtsrat etc)* to be *or* sit *(in +dat* on).
(e) *(inf: im Gefängnis ~)* to be inside *(inf)* ◆ **gesessen haben** to have done time *(inf)*, to have been inside *(inf)*; **er mußte zwei Jahre ~** he had to do two years *(inf)*.
(f) *(sein)* to be ◆ **er sitzt in Bulgarien/im Kultusministerium** *(inf)* he's in Bulgaria/the ministry of culture; **er sitzt in der Äußeren Mongolei (und kann nicht weg)** *(inf)* he's stuck in outer Mongolia *(inf)*; **die Verfolger saßen uns auf den Fersen** our pursuers were hard on our heels.
(g) *(angebracht sein: Deckel, Schraube etc)* to sit ◆ **der Deckel/die Schraube sitzt fest** the lid is on tightly/the screw is in tightly; **locker ~** to be loose.
(h) *(stecken)* to be (stuck) ◆ **fest ~** to be stuck tight(ly); **der Splitter saß fest in meinem Fuß** the splinter wouldn't come out of my foot.
(i) *(im Gedächtnis ~)* to have sunk in.
(j) *(seinen Herd haben) (Infektion, Schmerz)* to be; *(fig: Übel, Haß, Schmerz auch)* to lie.
(k) *(Kleid, Frisur)* to sit ◆ **deine Krawatte sitzt nicht richtig** your tie isn't straight; **sein Hut saß schief** his hat was (on) crooked.
(l) *(inf: treffen)* to hit home ◆ **das saß** *or* **hat gesessen!** that hit home.
(m) einen ~ haben *(inf)* to have had one too many.

⚠**sitzenbleiben** *vi sep irreg aux sein (inf)* **(a)** *(Sch)* to stay down (a year), to have to repeat a year. **(b) auf einer Ware ~** to be left with a product. **(c)** *(Mädchen) (beim Tanz)* to be left sitting; *(nicht heiraten)* to be left on the shelf *(inf)*.

Sitzenbleiber(in *f***)** *m* **-s, -** *(inf) pupil who has to repeat a year.*

sitzend *adj attr Lebensweise etc* sedentary.

⚠**sitzenlassen** *vt sep irreg ptp ~ or* **sitzengelassen** *(inf)* **(a)** *(Sch: nicht versetzen)* to keep down (a year).
(b) *(hinnehmen)* **eine Beleidigung** *etc* **auf sich** *(dat)* ~ to stand for *or* take an insult *etc*.
(c) jdn ~ *(im Stich lassen)* to leave sb in the lurch; *(warten lassen)* to leave sb waiting; *Freund(in) (durch Nichterscheinen)* to stand sb up.
(d) *(nicht heiraten)* to jilt, to walk out on.

-sitzer *m* **-s, -** *in cpds* -seater.

Sitzerei *f (inf)* sitting about.

⚠: for details of spelling reform, see supplement

Sitz-: **~fleisch** *nt (inf)* ability to sit still; **~fleisch haben** to be able to sit still; *(hum: Besucher)* to stay a long time; **~gelegenheit** *f* seats *pl*, seating (accommodation); **eine ~gelegenheit suchen** to look for somewhere to sit *or* for a seat; **~kissen** *nt* (floor) cushion; **~ordnung** *f* seating plan; **~platz** *m* seat; **~reihe** *f* row of seats; **~riese** *m (hum) short person with a long body who looks tall when sitting down;* **~streik** *m siehe* **Sit-in.**
Sitzung *f* **(a)** *(Konferenz)* meeting; *(Jur: Gerichtsverhandlung)* session; *(Parlaments~)* sitting. **(b)** *(Einzel~)* *(bei Künstler)* sitting; *(bei Zahnarzt)* visit; *(sl: Toilettenbesuch)* session ◆ **spiritistische ~** séance.
Sitzungs-: **~bericht** *m* minutes *pl*; **~geld** *nt (Parl)* attendance allowance; **~periode** *f (Parl)* session; *(Jur)* term; **~saal** *m* conference hall; *(Jur)* courtroom; **~zimmer** *nt* conference room.
sixtinisch *adj* Sistine.
Sizilianer(in *f***)** *m* **-s, -** Sicilian.
sizilianisch *adj* Sicilian.
Sizilien [zi'tsi:liən] *nt* **-s** Sicily.
Skai ® *nt* **-(s),** *no pl* imitation leather.
Skala *f* **-, Skalen** *or* **-s** *(Gradeinteilung, Mus)* scale; *(Reihe gleichartiger Dinge)* range; *(fig)* gamut, range.
Skalde *m* **-n, -n** skald.
Skaldendichtung *f* skaldic poetry.
Skalp *m* **-s, -e** scalp.
Skalpell *nt* **-s, -e** scalpel.
skalpieren* *vt* to scalp.
Skandal *m* **-s, -e** scandal; *(inf: Krach)* to-do *(inf)*, fuss ◆ **einen ~ machen** to create *or* cause a scandal; to make a to-do *(inf) or* fuss; **das ist ein ~!** it's scandalous *or* a scandal.
Skandal-: **~blatt** *nt (pej)* scandal sheet; **~geschichte** *f* (bit *or* piece of) scandal; **~nudel** *f (hum)* **sie ist eine richtige ~nudel** she's always involved in some scandal or other.
skandalös *adj* scandalous.
Skandal-: **~presse** *f (pej)* gutter press; ⚠**~prozeß** *m* sensational trial *or* case; **s~süchtig** *adj (pej) Publikum, Leser* fond of scandal; *Klatschtante, Presse etc auch* scandalmongering *attr*; **s~trächtig** *adj* potentially scandalous; **s~umwittert** *adj (Press sl)* surrounded by scandal.
skandieren* *vti* to scan.
Skandinavien [skandi'na:viən] *nt* **-s** Scandinavia.
Skandinavier(in *f***)** [skandi'na:viɐ, -iərın] *m* **-s, -** Scandinavian.
skandinavisch *adj* Scandinavian.
Skandium *nt, no pl (abbr* **Sc***)* scandium.
Skarabäus [skara'bɛ:ʊs] *m* **-, Skarabäen** [-'bɛ:ən] scarab.
Skat *m* **-(e)s, -e** *(Cards)* skat ◆ **~ spielen** *or* **dreschen** *(inf) or* **kloppen** *(sl)* to play skat.
Skatbrüder *pl (inf)* fellow skat players *pl.*
Skateboard ['ske:tbɔ:d] *nt* **-s, -s** skateboard.
Skateboard- ['ske:tbɔ:d-]: **~bahn** *f* skateboard rink; **~fahrer** *m* skateboarder.
skaten *vi (inf)* to play skat.
Skatspieler *m* skat player.
Skeleton ['skɛlətn, -letɔn] *m* **-s, -s** *(Sport)* skeleton.
Skelett *nt* **-(e)s, -e** *(lit, fig)* skeleton ◆ **er war bis aufs ~ abgemagert, er war nur noch ein ~** he was like a skeleton.
Skepsis *f* **-,** *no pl* scepticism ◆ **mit/voller ~** sceptically.
Skeptiker(in *f***)** *m* **-s, -** sceptic.
skeptisch *adj* sceptical.
Skeptizismus *m (esp Philos)* scepticism.
skeptizistisch *adj (esp Philos)* sceptic(al).
Sketch [skɛtʃ] *m* **-(es), -e(s)** *(Art, Theat)* sketch.
Ski [ʃi:] *m* **-s, -** *or* **-er** ['ʃi:ɐ] ski ◆ **~ laufen** *or* **fahren** to ski.
Ski- *in cpds* ski; **~anzug** *m* ski suit; **~ausrüstung** *f* skiing gear; **eine komplette ~ausrüstung** a complete set of skiing gear; **~bob** *m* skibob; **~brille** *f* ski goggles *pl.*
Skier ['ʃi:ɐ] *pl of* **Ski.**
Ski- ['ʃi:-]: **~fahrer** *m* skier; **~fliegen** *nt*, **~flug** *m* ski flying; **~gebiet** *nt* ski(ing) area; **~gelände** *nt* ski(ing) area; **~gymnastik** *f* skiing exercises *pl*; **~hase** *m*, **~haserl** *nt* **-s, -n** *(hum inf)* girl skier; **~hose** *f* (pair of) ski pants *pl*; **~hütte** *f* ski hut *or* lodge *(US)*; **~kurs** *m* skiing course; **~lauf** *m* skiing; **~läufer** *m* skier; **~lehrer** *m* ski instructor; **~lift** *m* ski-lift.
Skin *m* **-s, -s** *(inf)* skin *(sl)*.
Skinhead *m* **-s, -s** skinhead.
Ski-: ⚠**~paß** *m* ski pass; **~piste** *f* ski-run; **~schuh** *m* ski boot; **~schule** *f* ski school; **~sport** *m* skiing; **~springen** *nt* ski jumping; **~springer** *m* ski-jumper; **~stock** *m* ski stick; **~träger** *m (Aut)* ski rack, ski roof carrier *(US)*; **~zirkus** *m* ski circus.
Skizze ['skıtsə] *f* **-, -n** sketch; *(fig: Grundriß)* outline, plan.
Skizzen- ['skıtsn-]: **~buch** *nt* sketchbook; **s~haft** [1] *adj Zeichnung etc* roughly sketched; *Beschreibung etc* (given) in broad outline; [2] *adv* **etw s~haft zeichnen/beschreiben** to sketch sth roughly/describe sth in broad outline.
skizzieren* [skı'tsi:rən] *vt* to sketch; *(fig) Plan etc* to outline.
Skizzierung [skı'tsi:rʊŋ] *f* sketching; *(fig: von Plan etc)* outlining.
Sklave ['skla:və, 'skla:fə] *m* **-n, -n** slave ◆ **~ einer Sache** *(gen)* **sein** *(fig)* to be a slave to sth; **jdn zum ~n machen** to make a slave of sb; *(fig)* to enslave sb, to make sb one's slave.
Sklaven- ['skla:vn-, 'skla:fn-]: **~arbeit** *f* slavery; *(Arbeit von Sklaven)* work of slaves; **~dienst** *m* slavery; **~galeere** *f* slave galley; **~halter** *m* slave-holder; **~haltergesellschaft** *f* slave-owning society; **~handel** *m* slave trade; **~handel betreiben** to deal in slaves; **~händler** *m* slave-trader, slaver; **~markt** *m* slave market; **~treiber** *m (lit, fig)* slave-driver.
Sklaverei [skla:və'rai, -a:fə'rai] *f no pl (lit, fig)* slavery *no art* ◆ **jdn in die ~ führen** to take sb into slavery.
Sklavin ['skla:vın, 'skla:fın] *f (lit, fig)* slave.
sklavisch ['skla:vıʃ, 'skla:fıʃ] *adj* slavish.
Sklerose *f* **-, -n** sclerosis.
skontieren* *vt* **jdm etw ~** to give sb a cash discount on sth.
Skonto *nt or m* **-s, -s** *or* **Skonti** cash discount ◆ **bei Barzahlung 3% ~** 3% discount for cash; **jdm ~ geben** *or* **gewähren** *(form)* to give *or* allow sb a cash discount *or* a discount for cash.
Skorbut *m* **-(e)s,** *no pl* scurvy.
Skorpion *m* **-s, -e** *(Zool)* scorpion; *(Astrol)* Scorpio.
Skribent *m (dated pej)* hack, scribbler.
Skript *nt* **-(e)s, -en (a)** *pl usu* **-s** *(Film)* (film) script. **(b)** *(Univ)* (set of) lecture notes *pl* ◆ **ein ~ anfertigen** to take lecture notes.
Skriptgirl ['skrıptgø:ɐl, -gœrl] *nt* script girl.
Skriptum *nt* **-s, Skripten** *or* **Skripta** *(Univ, esp Aus) siehe* **Skript (b).**
Skrotum *nt* **-s, Skrota** *(Med)* scrotum.
Skrupel *m* **-s, -** *usu pl* scruple ◆ **keine ~ haben** *or* **kennen** to have no scruples; **er hatte keine ~, das zu tun** he didn't scruple to do it; **ohne (jeden) ~** without (the slightest) scruple.
Skrupel-: **s~los** *adj* unscrupulous; **~losigkeit** *f* unscrupulousness.
skrupulös *adj (geh)* scrupulous.
Skullboot ['skʊlbo:t] *nt* sculling boat.
skullen ['skʊlən] *vi (Sport)* to scull.
Skulptur *f* sculpture.
Skunk *m* **-s, -s** *or* **-e** skunk.
skurril *adj (geh)* droll, comical.
Skurrilität *f (geh)* drollery.
S-Kurve ['ɛs-] *f* S-bend.
Skyeterrier ['skaıtɛriɐ] *m* Skye terrier.
Slalom *m* **-s, -s** slalom ◆ **(im) ~ fahren** *(fig inf)* to drive a crazy zig-zag course.
Slang [slæŋ] *m* **-s,** *no pl* slang.
Slapstick ['slɛpstık] *m* **-s, -s** slapstick.
S-Laut ['ɛs-] *m (stimmlos)* 's'-sound; *(stimmhaft)* 'z'-sound.
Slawe *m* **-n, -n, Slawin** *f* Slav.
slawisch *adj* Slavonic, Slavic.
Slawist(in *f***)** *m* Slavonicist, Slavist.
Slawistik *f* Slavonic studies *sing.*
Slibowitz *m* **-(e)s, -e** slivovitz.
Slip *m* **-s, -s** (pair of) briefs *pl*; *(Damen~ auch)* (pair of) panties *pl.*
Slip|einlage *f* panty liner.
Slipper *m* **-s, -** slip-on shoe.
Slogan ['slo:gn] *m* **-s, -s** slogan.
Slowake *m* **-n, -n, Slowakin** *f* Slovak.
Slowakei *f* **- die ~** Slovakia.
slowakisch *adj* Slovakian, Slovak.
Slowene *m* **-n, -n, Slowenin** *f* Slovene.
Slowenien [slo've:niən] *nt* **-s** Slovenia.
slowenisch *adj* Slovenian.
Slowfox ['slo:fɔks] *m* **-(es), -e** slow foxtrot.
Slum [slam] *m* **-s, -s** slum.
S.M. *abbr of* **Seine(r) Majestät** HM.
sm *abbr of* **Seemeile.**
Smalltalk ['smɔ:ltɔ:k] *m* **-(s),** *no pl* small talk.
Smaragd *m* **-(e)s, -e** emerald.
smaragdgrün *adj* emerald-green.
smart [sma:ɐt, smart] *adj (inf)* smart.
Smartcard, Smart-Card *f* **-s, -s** *(inf)* smart card.
Smog *m* **-(s), -s** smog.
Smog-: **~alarm** *m* smog alert; **~alarmstufe** *f* **~alarmstufe 1** smog warning level 1; **~verordnung** *f* smog regulations *pl.*
Smok|arbeit *f (Sew)* smocking.
smoken *vti (Sew)* to smock.
Smoking ['smo:kıŋ] *m* **-s, -s** dinner-jacket, dj *(inf)*, tuxedo *(US)*, tux *(US inf)*.
Smutje *m* **-s, -s** *(Naut)* ship's cook.
Smyrnateppich *m* Smyrna (carpet).
Snack [snɛk] *m* **-s, -s** snack (meal).
Snob *m* **-s, -s** snob.
Snobismus *m* snobbery, snobbishness.
snobistisch *adj* snobbish.
Snowboard ['snoʊbo:ɐd] *nt* **-s, -s** snowboard.
Snowboarden, Snowboarding *nt* **-s** *no pl* snowboarding.
Snowboarder(in *f***)** *m* **-s, -** snowboarder.
SO *abbr of* **Südosten** SE.
s.o. *abbr of* **siehe oben.**
so [1] *adv* **(a)** *(mit adj, adv)* so; *(mit vb: ~ sehr)* so much ◆ **~ groß** *etc* so big *etc*; **eine ~ große Frau** such a big woman; **es ist gar nicht ~ einfach** it's really not so easy; **~ groß** *etc* **wie** ... as big *etc* as ...; **~ groß** *etc*, **daß** ... so big *etc* that ...; **sie hat ihn ~ geschlagen, daß** ... she hit him so hard that ...; **er ist ~ gelaufen** he ran so fast; **ich habe ~ gearbeitet** I worked so hard; **~ gut es geht** as best *or* well as I/he *etc* can; **er ist nicht ~ dumm, das zu glauben** he's not so stupid

as to believe that, he's not stupid enough to believe that; **sie hat sich ~ gefreut** she was so *or* really pleased; **das hat ihn ~ geärgert, daß ...** that annoyed him so much that ...; **ich wußte nicht, daß es ihn ~ ärgern würde** I didn't know that it would annoy him so *or* that much; **ich freue mich ~ sehr, daß du kommst** I'm so pleased you're coming.
(b) *(auf diese Weise, von dieser Art)* like this/that, this/that way, thus *(form)* ♦ **mach es nicht ~** don't do it like that *or* that way; **du sollst es ~ machen, ...** do it like this *or* this way ...; **mach es ~, wie er es vorgeschlagen hat** do it the way *or* as *or* like *(inf)* he suggested; **ist es dort tatsächlich ~?** is it really like that there?; **ist das tatsächlich ~?** is that really so?; **~ ist sie nun einmal** that's the way she is, that's what she's like; **sei doch nicht ~** don't be like that; **~ ist es nicht gewesen** it wasn't like that, that's not how it was; **es ist vielleicht besser ~** perhaps it's better like that *or* that way; **~ *ist* das!** that's the way things are, that's how it is; **(ach) ~ ist das!** I see!; **ist das ~?** is that so?; **~ oder/und ~** either way; **und ~ weiter (und ~ fort)** and so on (and so forth); **gut ~!** fine!, good!; **das ist gut ~** that's fine; **das ist auch gut~!** (and) a good thing too!; **mir ist (es) ~, als ob ...** it seems to me as if ...; **~ geht es, wenn ...** that's what happens if ...; **... und ~ ist es also geschehen ...** and so that is what happened; **das kam ~: ...** this is what happened ..., it happened like this ...; **es verhält sich ~: ...** the facts are thus *(form) or* as follows ...; **das habe ich nur ~ gesagt** I didn't really mean it.
(c) *(etwa)* about, or so ♦ **ich komme ~ um 8 Uhr** I'll come at about 8, I'll come at 8 or so *or* or thereabouts; **sie heißt doch Malitzki oder ~** she's called Malitzki or something.
(d) *(inf: umsonst)* for nothing.
(e) *(als Füllwort) nicht übersetzt* ♦ **~ dann und wann** now and then; **~ bist du also gar nicht dort gewesen?** *(geh)* so you weren't there after all?; **~ beeil dich doch!** do hurry up!; **~ mancher** a number of people *pl*, quite a few people *pl*.
(f) *(solch)* **~ ein Gebäude/Fehler** a building/mistake like that, such a building/mistake; **~ ein guter Lehrer/schlechtes Bild** *etc* such a good teacher/bad picture *etc*; **~ ein Idiot!** what an idiot!; **hast du ~ etwas schon einmal gesehen?** have you ever seen anything like it?; **~ (et)was ist noch nie vorgekommen** nothing like that has ever happened; **sie ist doch Lehrerin oder ~ was** she's a teacher or something like that; **na ~ was!** well I never!, no!; **~ etwas Schönes** something as beautiful as that, such a beautiful thing; **~ einer wie ich/er** somebody like *or* a person such as myself *or* me/him; **er ist ~ einer wie ich** he's like me; *siehe* **um 3b**.
[2] *conj* **(a) ~ daß** so that.
(b) ~ wie es jetzt ist as *or* the way things are at the moment.
(c) ~ klein er auch sein mag however small he may be; **~ wahr ich lebe** as true as I'm standing here.
(d) kaum hatte er ..., ~ ... scarcely had he ... when ...
(e) *(old: falls)* if, provided that ♦ **~ der Herrgott will, sehen wir uns wieder** God willing, we shall see one another again.
[3] *interj* so; *(wirklich)* oh, really; *(abschließend)* well, right ♦ **er ist schon da — ~** he's here already — is he? *or* oh *or* really; **ich kann nicht mitkommen — ~** I can't come with you — can't you? *or* oh!; **~, das wär's für heute** well *or* right *or* so, that's it for today; **~, jetzt habe ich die Nase voll** I've had enough; **~, ~!** well well; *siehe* **ach**.

sobald *conj* as soon as.
Söckchen *nt dim of* **Socke**.
Socke *f* **-, -n** sock ♦ **sich auf die ~n machen** *(inf)* to get going *(inf)*; **von den ~n sein** *(inf)* to be flabbergasted *(inf)*, to be knocked for six *(inf)*.
Sockel *m* **-s, -** base; *(von Denkmal, Statue)* plinth, pedestal, socle *(spec)*; *(Elec)* socket; *(für Birne)* holder.
Sockel-: ~betrag *m* basic sum; **~rente** *f* basic pension.
Socken *m* **-s, -** *(S Ger, Aus)* sock.
Sockenhalter *m* (sock) suspender *(Brit)*, garter.
Soda *f* **-,** *no pl, nt* **-s,** *no pl* soda.
sodann *adv (old)* thereupon *(old, form)*, then.
⚠ **sodaß** *conj (Aus)* = **so daß**.
Sodawasser *nt* soda water.
Sodbrennen *nt* heartburn.
Sode *f* **-, -n** *(Rasenstück, Torfscholle)* turf, sod.
Sodom ['zo:dɔm] *nt* **-s** Sodom ♦ **~ und Gomorrha** *(lit, fig)* Sodom and Gomorrah.
Sodomie *f* buggery, bestiality.
sodomitisch *adj* bestial.
so|eben *adv* just (this moment) ♦ **~ hören wir** *or* **haben wir gehört ...** we have just (this moment) heard ...; **~ erschienen** just out *or* published.
Sofa *nt* **-s, -s** sofa, settee *(esp Brit)*.
Sofa-: ~bett *nt* bed-settee *(Brit)*, sofa bed; **~ecke** *f* corner of the/a sofa; **~kissen** *nt* sofa cushion.
sofern *conj* provided (that) ♦ **~ ... nicht** if ... not.
soff *pret of* **saufen**.
Sofia ['zɔfia, 'zo:fia] *nt* **-s** *(Geog)* Sofia.
Sofioter(in *f*) *m* **-s, -** Sofian.
sofort *adv* immediately, straight *or* right away, at once ♦ **~ nach ...** immediately after ...; **komm hierher, aber** *or* **und zwar ~!** come here this instant *or* at once!; **(ich) komme ~!** (I'm) just coming!; *(Kellner etc)* I'll be right with you.
Sofort-: ~bildkamera *f* Polaroid ® camera, instant camera; **~hilfe** *f* emergency relief *or* aid.
sofortig *adj* immediate, instant.

⚠: for details of spelling reform, see supplement

Sofortmaßnahme *f* immediate measure.
Soft|eis, Soft-Eis ['sɔft-] *nt* soft ice-cream.
Softie *m* **-s, -s** *(inf)* caring type.
Software ['sɔftwɛ:ɐ] *f* **-, -s** *(Comput)* software.
Softwarepaket ['sɔftwɛ:ɐ-] *nt* software package.
sog *pret of* **saugen**.
sog. *abbr of* **sogenannt**.
Sog *m* **-(e)s, -e** *(saugende Kraft)* suction; *(bei Schiff)* wake; *(bei Flugzeug, Fahrzeug)* slipstream; *(von Strudel)* vortex; *(von Brandungswelle)* undertow; *(fig)* maelstrom.
sogar *adv* even ♦ **er kam ~** he even came; **jedes Getränk, ja ~ schon ein kleines Bier, kostet sehr viel** every drink, even a small glass of beer *or* a small glass of beer, even, costs a lot; **schön, ~ sehr schön** beautiful, in fact very beautiful; **ich kann sie gut leiden, ich finde sie ~ sehr nett** I like her, in fact I think she's very nice; **ich habe sie nicht nur gesehen, sondern ~ geküßt** I didn't just see her, I actually kissed her (as well).
sogenannt *adj attr* as it/he *etc* is called; *(angeblich)* so-called.
sogleich *adv siehe* **sofort**.
Sogwirkung *f* suction; *(fig)* knock-on effect.
Sohle *f* **-, -n (a)** *(Fuß~ etc)* sole; *(Einlage)* insole ♦ **auf leisen ~n** *(poet)* softly, noiselessly; **mit nackten ~n** barefoot; **es brennt ihm unter den ~n** he has itchy feet *(inf)*, his feet are itching *(inf)*; **eine kesse ~ aufs Parkett legen** *(inf hum)* to put up a good show on the dance floor; *siehe* **heften, Scheitel**.
(b) *(Boden)* bottom; *(Tal~ auch)* floor; *(Fluß~ auch)* bed.
(c) *(Min)* *(Grubenboden)* floor; *(Stollen)* level.
sohlen *vt* to sole.
Sohl(en)leder *nt* sole leather.
Sohn *m* **-(e)s, ¨-e** *(lit, fig)* son ♦ **Gottes ~, der ~ Gottes** *(Bibl)* the Son of God; **des Menschen ~** *(Bibl)* the Son of Man; **na, mein ~** well, son *or* sonny; *siehe* **verloren**.
Söhnchen *nt dim of* **Sohn**.
Sohnemann *m (dial inf)* son, sonny.
Söhnlein *nt dim of* **Sohn**.
soigniert [soan'ji:ɐt] *adj (geh)* elegant; *(bei Frauen auch)* soignée; *(bei Männern auch)* soigné.
Soiree [soa're:] *f* **-, -n** [-e:ən] soirée.
Soja *f* **-, Sojen** soya, soy.
Soja-: ~bohne *f* soya bean, soybean; **~bohnenkeime** *pl* bean sprouts *pl*; **~soße** *f* soya sauce.
Sokrates ['zo:kratɛs] *m* **-** Socrates.
sokratisch *adj* Socratic.
solang(e) *conj* as *or* so long as.
Solar- *in cpds* solar.
Solarenergie *f* solar energy.
Solarium *nt* **-s, Solarien** solarium.
Solarplexus *m* **-, -** *(Anat)* solar plexus.
Solarzelle *f* solar cell.
Solbad *nt (Bad)* salt-water *or* brine bath; *(Badeort)* salt-water spa.
solch *adj inv,* **solche(r, s)** *adj* such ♦ **ein ~er Mensch, ~ ein Mensch** such a person, a person like that/this; **~e Menschen** people like that, such people; **~es Wetter/Glück** such weather/luck; **wir haben ~en Durst/~e Angst** we're so thirsty/afraid; **~ langer Weg** such a long way; **der Mensch als ~er** man as such; **~es** that kind of thing; **~e** *(Leute)* such people; **Experten und ~e, die es werden wollen** experts and people who would like to be experts; **Rechtsanwälte gibt es ~e und ~e** there are lawyers and lawyers; **ich hätte gern ~e und ~e (Bonbons)** I'd like some of those (sweets) and some of those.
solcher-: ~art, ~lei *adj attr inv (geh)* such; **~gestalt** *adv (geh) siehe* **dergestalt**; **~maßen** *adv (old)* to such an extent, so.
Sold *m* **-(e)s,** *no pl (Mil)* pay ♦ **in jds ~** *(dat)* **stehen** *(old)* to be in sb's employ; *(pej)* to be in sb's pay.
Soldat *m* **-en, -en** soldier; *(old Chess)* pawn ♦ **bei den ~en sein** *(dated)* to be in the army, to be a soldier; **zu den ~en kommen** *(dated)*, **~ werden** to join the army, to join up *(inf)*, to become a soldier; **~ spielen** to play soldiers; *siehe* **Grabmal**.
Soldaten-: ~friedhof *m* military cemetery; **~gesetz** *nt* military regulations *pl, no art*; **~lied** *nt* army *or* soldier's song; **~rat** *m* soldiers' council; *(Sowjet)* soldiers' soviet; **~rock** *m (old)* military *or* soldier's uniform; **~sprache** *f* military *or* soldier's slang; **~stiefel** *m* army *or* soldier's boot; **~tum** *nt* soldiership *no art*, soldiery *no art*; *(Tradition)* military tradition.
Soldateska *f* **-, Soldatesken** *(pej)* band of soldiers.
Soldatin *f* soldier.
soldatisch *adj (militärisch)* military; *(soldatengemäß)* soldierly.
Soldbuch *nt (Hist)* military passbook.
Söldner(in *f*) *m* **-s, -** mercenary.
Söldner-: ~heer *nt* army of mercenaries, mercenary army; **~truppe** *f* mercenary force.
Sole *f* **-, -n** brine, salt water.
Solei ['zo:l|ai] *nt* pickled egg.
Soli *pl of* **Solo**.
solid *adj siehe* **solid(e)**.
Solidar-: ~beitrag *m (von Interessengemeinschaft)* donation *(to public funds, social services etc)*; **~gemeinschaft** *f* solidarity committee.
solidarisch *adj* **sich mit jdm ~ erklären** to declare one's solidarity with sb; **eine ~e Haltung zeigen** to show (one's) solidarity; **in ~er Übereinstimmung** in complete solidarity; **sich mit jdm ~ fühlen** to feel solidarity with sb; **~ mit**

jdm handeln to act in solidarity with sb.
solidarisieren* *vr* **sich ~ mit** to show (one's) solidarity with.
Solidarität *f* solidarity.
Solidaritäts-: **~adresse** *f* message of solidarity; **~gefühl** *nt* feeling of solidarity; **~streik** *m* sympathy strike; **~zuschlag** *m* (*Fin*) solidarity surcharge on income tax (*for the reconstruction of eastern Germany*).
solid(e) *adj Haus, Möbel etc* solid, sturdy; *Arbeit, Wissen, Mechaniker* sound; *Mensch, Leben, Lokal* respectable; *Firma* solid; *Preise* reasonable.
Solidität *f siehe adj* solidness, sturdiness; soundness; respectability; solidness; reasonableness.
Solipsismus *m* (*Philos*) solipsism.
Solist(in *f*) *m* (*Mus*) soloist.
solistisch *adj, adv* solo.
Solitär *m* solitaire; (*Diamant*) diamond solitaire, solitaire diamond.
Soll *nt* **-(s), -(s)** **(a)** (*Schuld*) debit; (*Schuldseite*) debit side ♦ **~ und Haben** debit and credit. **(b)** (*Comm: Planaufgabe*) target.
▼ **sollen** [1] *modal aux vb pret* **sollte**, *ptp* **~** **(a)** (*bei Befehl, Anordnung, Verpflichtung, Plan*) to be to ♦ **was soll ich/er tun?** what shall *or* should I/should he do?, what am I/is he to do?; (*was sind meine etc Aufgaben auch*) what am I/is he meant to do?; **kannst du mir helfen? — klar, was soll ich tun?** can you help me? — of course, what shall I do?; **soll ich Ihnen helfen?** shall *or* can I help you?; **soll ich dir mal sagen, wie ...?** shall I tell you how ...?; **du weißt, daß du das nicht tun sollst** you know that you shouldn't do that *or* aren't to do that; (*das ist nicht deine Aufgabe auch*) you know that you're not meant to do that; **er weiß nicht, was er tun soll** he doesn't know what to do *or* what he should do; (*kennt seine Aufgaben nicht auch*) he doesn't know what he's meant to do; **sie sagte ihm, er solle draußen warten** she told him (that he was) to wait *or* that he should wait outside; **er wurde wütend, weil er draußen warten sollte** he was livid that he was told to wait outside; **sie sagte mir, was ich tun sollte/alles tun soll** she told me what to do *or* what I should do/everything I should do *or* am meant to do; **was ich (nicht) alles tun/wissen soll!** the things I'm meant *or* supposed to do/know!; **es soll nicht wieder vorkommen** it shan't *or* won't happen again; **er soll reinkommen** let him come in, tell him to come in; **der soll nur kommen!** just let him come!; **und da soll man nicht böse werden/nicht lachen!** and then they expect you/me *etc* not to get cross/not to laugh; **niemand soll sagen, daß ...** let no-one say that ..., no-one shall say that ...; **ich soll Ihnen sagen, daß ...** I am to tell you *or* I've been asked to tell you that ...; **ich soll dir schöne Grüße von Renate bestellen** Renate asked me to give you her best wishes; **du sollst nicht töten** (*Bibl*) thou shalt not kill; **so soll es sein** that's how it should be; **das Haus soll nächste Woche gestrichen werden** the house is (meant) to be painted next week; **das Gebäude soll ein Museum werden** the building is (meant) to become a museum.
▼ **(b)** (*konjunktivisch*) **was sollte ich/er deiner Meinung nach tun?** what do you think I/he should do *or* ought to do?; **so etwas sollte man nicht tun** one shouldn't do *or* oughtn't to do that; **das hättest du nicht tun ~** you shouldn't have *or* oughtn't to have done that; **das hättest du sehen ~!** you should have seen it!; **du solltest lieber etwas früher kommen/zu Hause bleiben** it would be better if you came early/stayed at home.
(c) (*bei Vermutung, Erwartung*) to be supposed *or* meant to ♦ **er soll heute kommen** he should come today, he is supposed *or* meant to come today; **sie soll krank/verheiratet sein** I've heard she's ill/married, she's supposed to be ill/married; **Xanthippe soll zänkisch gewesen sein** Xanthippe is supposed *or* said to have been quarrelsome; **das soll gar nicht so einfach sein** they say it's not that easy; **was soll das heißen?** what's that supposed *or* meant to mean?; **wer soll das sein?** who is that supposed *or* meant to be?
(d) (*können, mögen*) **gut, Sie ~ recht haben!** all right, have it your own way (*inf*) *or* whatever you say; **mir soll es gleich sein** it's all the same to me; **so etwas soll es geben** these things happen; **man sollte glauben, daß ...** you would think that ...; **sollte das möglich sein?** is that possible?, can that be possible?
▼ **(e)** (*konditional*) **sollte das passieren, ...** if that should happen ..., should that happen ...; **sollte ich unrecht haben, tut es mir leid** I'm sorry if I should be wrong, I'm sorry should I be wrong.
(f) *subjunc* (*geh: jdm beschieden sein*) **er sollte sie nie wiedersehen** he was never to see her again; **es hat nicht ~ sein** it wasn't to be; **Jahre sollten vergehen, bevor ...** years were to pass before ...; **es sollte nicht lange dauern, bis ...** it was not to be long until ...
[2] *vi pret* **sollte**, *ptp* **gesollt** **(a)** **soll ich?** should I?; **ja, du sollst** yes, you should; **er hätte ~** he should have.
(b) **was soll das?** what's all this?; (*warum denn das*) what's that for?; **was soll's?** what the hell (*inf*) *or* heck (*inf*)?; **was soll der Quatsch/Mist** *etc*? (*inf*) what do you/they think you're/they're playing at? (*inf*); **was soll ich dort?** what would I do there?
[3] *vt pret* **sollte**, *ptp* **gesollt** **das sollst/solltest du nicht** you shouldn't do that; **das hast du nicht gesollt** you shouldn't have done that; **was man nicht alles soll** *or* **sollte!** (*inf*) the things you're meant to do!
Söller *m* **-s, -** balcony.
Soll-: **~seite** *f* (*Fin*) debit-side; **~stärke** *f* required *or* authorized strength; **~zinsen** *pl* (*Fin*) interest owing *sing*.
solo *adv* (*Mus*) solo; (*fig inf*) on one's own, alone.
Solo *nt* **-s, Soli** (*alle Bedeutungen*) solo.
Solo- *in cpds* solo; **~gesang** *m* solo; **~geschäft** *nt* (*St Ex*) outright transaction.
Solothurn *nt* (*Kanton, Stadt*) Solothurn.
solvent [zɔl'vɛnt] *adj* (*Fin*) solvent.
Solvenz [zɔl'vɛnts] *f* (*Fin*) solvency.
Somali *m* **-(s), -(s)** Somali.
Somalia *nt* **-s** Somalia.
Somalier(in *f*) [-iɐ, -iərɪn] *m* **-s, -** Somali.
Somalihalbinsel *f*, **Somaliland** *nt* Somaliland.
somalisch *adj* Somali.
somatisch *adj* (*Med*) somatic.
Sombrero *m* **-s, -s** sombrero.
somit *adv* consequently, therefore.
Sommer *m* **-s, -** summer ♦ **im ~, des ~s** (*geh*) in (the) summer; **im nächsten ~** next summer; **im ~ des Jahres 1951** in the summer of 1951; **~ wie** *or* **und Winter** all year round.
Sommer- *in cpds* summer; **~abend** *m* summer('s) evening; **~anfang** *m* beginning of summer; **~ferien** *pl* summer holidays *pl* (*Brit*) *or* vacation (*esp US*); (*Jur, Parl*) summer recess; **in die ~ferien fahren** to go away for the *or* one's summer holidays (*Brit*) *or* vacation (*US*); **in die ~ferien gehen** to begin one's summer holidays (*Brit*) *or* vacation (*US*); (*Sch auch*) to break up for the summer (holidays) (*Brit*); (*Univ*) to go down for the summer; (*Jur, Parl*) to go into the summer recess; **~frische** *f* (*dated*) **(a)** *no pl* (*~urlaub*) summer holiday *or* vacation (*US*) *or* break; **in die ~frische gehen** to go away for a summer holiday *etc*; **(b)** (*Ort*) summer resort; **~frischler(in *f*)** *m* **-s, -** (*dated*) summer holidaymaker *or* vacationist (*US*); **~gast** *m* summer guest; **~gerste** *f* spring barley; **~getreide** *nt* spring cereal; **~halbjahr** *nt* summer semester, ≃ summer term (*Brit*); **~haus** *nt* holiday home; **~kleidung** *f* summer clothing; (*esp Comm*) summerwear.
sommerlich *adj* (*sommerartig, heiter*) summery; (*Sommer-*) summer *attr* ♦ **~ gekleidet sein** to be in summer clothes.
Sommer-: **~loch** *nt* (*inf*) silly season; **~monat** *m* summer month; **~nacht** *f* summer('s) night; **~olympiade** *f* Summer Olympics *pl*; **~pause** *f* summer break; (*Jur, Parl*) summer recess; **~reifen** *m* normal tyre.
sommers *adv* (*geh*) in summer ♦ **~ wie winters** all year round.
Sommer-: **~saison** *f* summer season; ⚠**~schlußverkauf** *m* summer sale; **~semester** *nt* (*Univ*) summer semester, ≃ summer term (*Brit*); **~sitz** *m* summer residence; **~spiele** *pl* Summer Games *pl*; **die Olympischen ~spiele** the Summer Olympics *or* Olympic Games; **~sprosse** *f* freckle; **s~sprossig** *adj* freckled.
sommersüber *adv* during summer.
Sommer-: **~tag** *m* summer's day; **~theater** *nt* open-air theatre; **~weizen** *m* spring wheat; **~wetter** *nt* summer weather; **~wohnung** *f* holiday flat (*Brit*) *or* apartment; **~zeit** *f* summer time *no art*; (*geh: Sommer*) summertime, summertide (*liter*); **zur ~zeit** (*geh*) in summertime.
somnambul *adj* (*spec*) somnambulary.
Somnambule(r) *mf decl as adj* (*spec*) somnambulist.
Somnambulismus *m* (*spec*) somnambulism.
sonach *adv* (*old*) *siehe* **somit**.
Sonargerät *nt* sonar (device).
Sonate *f* **-, -n** sonata.
Sonatine *f* sonatine.
Sonde *f* **-, -n** (*Space, Med: zur Untersuchung*) probe; (*Med: zur Ernährung*) tube; (*Met*) sonde.
sonder *prep +acc* (*obs*) without.
Sonder- *in cpds* special; **~abdruck** *m* (*Typ*) offprint; **~anfertigung** *f* special model; **eine ~anfertigung sein** to have been made specially; **~angebot** *nt* special offer; **im ~angebot sein** to be on special offer; **~ausbildung** *f* specialist *or* special training; **~ausführung** *f* special model *or* version; (*Auto auch*) custom-built model; **~ausgabe** *f* **(a)** special edition; **(b)** **~ausgaben** *pl* (*Fin*) additional *or* extra expenses *pl*.
sonderbar *adj* strange, peculiar, odd.
sonderbarerweise *adv* strangely enough, strange to say.
Sonder-: **~beauftragte(r)** *mf* (*Pol*) special emissary; **~berichterstatter** *m* (*Press*) special correspondent; **~botschafter** *m* ambassador extraordinary; **~druck** *m siehe* **~abdruck**; **~einsatz** *m* special action; **~fahrt** *f* special excursion *or* trip; **„~fahrt"** (*auf Schild*) "special"; **~fall** *m* special case; (*Ausnahme*) exception; **~genehmigung** *f* special permission; (*Schein*) special permit; **~gericht** *nt* special court; **s~gleichen** *adj inv* **eine Frechheit/Geschmacklosigkeit s~gleichen** the height of cheek/bad taste; **mit einer Frechheit s~gleichen** with unparalleled cheek; **~klasse** *f* special class; (*von Obst etc*) top grade; **~kommando** *nt* special unit; **~konto** *nt* special account.
sonderlich [1] *adj attr* particular, especial, special ♦ **ohne ~e Begeisterung** without any particular enthusiasm, without much enthusiasm.
[2] *adv* particularly, especially.
Sonderling *m* eccentric.
Sonder-: **~marke** *f* special issue (stamp); **~maschine** *f* special plane *or* aircraft; **~meldung** *f* (*Rad, TV*) special announcement; **~müll** *m* hazardous waste; **~mülldeponie** *f* hazardous waste depot.
sondern[1] *conj* but ♦ **~?** where/who/what *etc* then?; **wir fahren nicht nach Spanien, ~ nach Frankreich** we're not going to Spain, we're going to France, we're not going to Spain but to France; **nicht nur ..., ~ auch** not only ... but also.
sondern[2] *vt* (*old, geh*) to separate (*von* from); *siehe* **gesondert**.
Sonder-: **~nummer** *f* (*Press*) special edition *or* issue; **~preis** *m* special reduced price; **~recht** *nt* (special) privilege; **~regelung** *f* special provision.
sonders *adv siehe* **samt**.

➤ SPRACHE AKTIV: **sollen:** **1a** → 30, 37.2, 53.2 **1b** → 28.1, 29.1, 29.2, 37.2, 41, 43.1, 53.2, 53.6 **1e** → 43.2, 47.1

Sonder-: ~schicht *f* special shift; (*zusätzlich*) extra shift; **~schule** *f* special school; **~schullehrer** *m* teacher at a special school; **~sitzung** *f* special session; (*von Vorstand*) special meeting; **~stellung** *f* special position; **~stempel** *m* (*bei der Post*) special postmark; **~urlaub** *m* (*Mil*) special leave; (*für Todesfall etc*) compassionate leave; **~wünsche** *pl* special requests *pl*; **~zeichen** *nt* (*Comput*) special character; **~ziehungsrechte** *pl* (*Fin*) special drawing rights *pl*; **~zug** *m* special train.

sondieren* [1] *vt* to sound out ♦ **das Terrain** *or* **Gelände ~** to spy out the land; **die Lage ~** to find out how the land lies.
[2] *vi* to sound things out ♦ **~, ob ...** to try to sound out whether ...

Sondierung *f* sounding out *no pl* ♦ **die ~ des Terrains** spying out the land; **ohne gründliche ~** without sounding things out thoroughly.

Sondierungsgespräch *nt* exploratory discussion *or* talk.

Sonett *nt* **-(e)s, -e** sonnet.

Song [sɔŋ] *m* **-s, -s** song.

Sonn|abend *m* Saturday; *siehe auch* **Dienstag.**

sonn|abends *adv* on Saturdays, on a Saturday.

Sonne *f* **-, -n (a)** sun; (*Sonnenlicht auch*) sunlight ♦ **die liebe ~** (*poet, inf*), **Frau ~** (*poet*) the sun; **unter der ~** (*fig geh*) under the sun; **an** *or* **in die ~ gehen** to go out in the sun(shine); **er kommt viel/wenig an die ~** he gets/doesn't get a lot of sun, he goes/doesn't go out in the sun a lot; **geh mir aus der ~!** (*inf*) stop blocking my view!, get out of the way!; (*aus dem Licht*) get out of the *or* my light!; **das Zimmer hat wenig ~** the room doesn't get much sun(light); **die ~ bringt es an den Tag** (*prov*) truth will out (*prov*).
(b) (*Heiz~*) electric fire.

sonnen [1] *vt Betten* to put out in the sun.
[2] *vr* to sun oneself ♦ **sich in etw** (*dat*) **~** (*fig*) to bask in sth.

Sonnen-: ~anbeter *m* (*lit, fig*) sun-worshipper; **~aufgang** *m* sunrise, sun-up (*inf*); **den ~aufgang abwarten** to wait for the sun to rise; **~bad** *nt* sunbathing *no pl*; **ein fünfstündiges ~bad** five hours in the sun, five hours' sunbathing; **ein ~bad nehmen** to sunbathe, to bask in the sun; **s~baden** *vi sep infin, ptp only* to sunbathe; **~bahn** *f* sun's path; **~ball** *m* (*liter*) fiery orb (*liter*); **~blende** *f* (*Phot*) lens hood.

Sonnenblume *f* sunflower.

Sonnenblumen-: ~kern *m* sunflower seed; **~öl** *nt* sunflower oil.

Sonnen-: ~brand *m* sunburn *no art*; **~bräune** *f* suntan; **~brille** *f* (pair of) sunglasses *pl*, shades *pl* (*US*); **~dach** *nt* awning, sun-blind; (*Aut dated*) sun(shine)-roof; **~deck** *nt* (*Naut*) sundeck; **s~durchflutet** *adj* (*geh*) sunny, with the sun streaming in; **~energie** *f* solar energy; **~ferne** *f* (*Astron*) aphelion; **~finsternis** *f* solar eclipse, eclipse of the sun; **~fleck** *m* (*Astron*) sunspot; **s~gebräunt** *adj* suntanned; **~geflecht** *nt* (*Physiol*) solar plexus; **~generator** *m* (*an Satellit*) solar generator; **~glanz** *m* (*poet*), **~glut** *f* (*geh*) blazing heat of the sun; **~gott** *m* sungod; **s~halb** *adv* (*Sw*) *siehe* **sonnseitig**; **s~hell** *adj* sunny, sunlit; **~hitze** *f* heat of the sun; **s~hungrig** *adj* hungry for the sun; **~hungrige** *pl* sun-seekers *pl*; **~hut** *m* sunhat; **~jahr** *nt* (*Astron*) solar year; **s~klar** *adj* (*inf*) clear as daylight, crystal-clear; **~kollektor** *m* solar panel; **~könig** *m* (*Hist*) Sun King, Roi Soleil; **~kraftwerk** *nt* solar power station; **~kult** *m* sun cult; **~licht** *nt* sunlight; **~milch** *f* suntan lotion; **~nähe** *f* (*Astron*) perihelion; **~öl** *nt* suntan oil; **~paddel** *nt* (*inf*: *~generator*) solar paddle (*inf*); **~rad** *nt* (*Hist*) (representation of the) sun; **~schein** *m* sunshine; **bei ~schein/strahlendem ~schein** in the sunshine/in brilliant sunshine; **~schirm** *m* sun-shade; (*für Frauen auch*) parasol; **~schutz** *m* protection against the sun; **~schutzfaktor** *m* protection factor; **~segel** *nt* awning; **~seite** *f* side facing the sun, sunny side (*auch fig*); **~stand** *m* position of the sun; **~stich** *m* heatstroke *no art*, sunstroke *no art*; **du hast wohl einen ~stich!** (*inf*) you must have been out in the sun too long!; **~strahl** *m* sunbeam, ray of sunshine; (*esp Astron, Phys*) sun-ray; **~system** *nt* solar system; **~tag** *m* sunny day; (*Met auch*) day of sunshine; (*Astron*) solar day; **~uhr** *f* sundial; **~untergang** *m* sunset, sundown; **den ~untergang abwarten** to wait for the sun to set; **s~verbrannt** *adj Vegetation* scorched; *Mensch* sunburnt; **~wende** *f* solstice; **~wendfeier** *f siehe* **Sonnwendfeier**; **~wind** *m* (*Phys*) solar wind.

sonnig *adj* sunny.

Sonn-: ~seite *f* (*Aus*) *siehe* **Sonnenseite**; **s~seitig** *adv* (*Aus*) **s~seitig gelegen** facing the sun.

Sonntag *m* Sunday; *siehe auch* **Dienstag.**

sonntägig *adj attr* Sunday ♦ **die gestrigen ~en Verhandlungen** ... the negotiations yesterday, Sunday, ...

sonntäglich *adj* Sunday *attr* ♦ **~ gekleidet** dressed in one's Sunday best.

sonntags *adv* on Sundays, on a Sunday; *siehe auch* **dienstags.**

Sonntags- *in cpds* Sunday; **~arbeit** *f* Sunday working; **~ausflug** *m* Sunday trip; **~beilage** *f* Sunday supplement; **~dienst** *m* (*von Polizist etc*) Sunday duty; **~dienst haben** (*Apotheke*) to be open on Sundays; **~fahrer** *m* (*pej*) Sunday driver; **~kind** *nt* (*lit*) Sunday's child; **ein ~kind sein** (*fig*) to have been born under a lucky star; **~kleidung** *f* Sunday clothes *pl*; **~maler** *m* Sunday painter; **~rede** *f* (*iro*) **~reden halten** to get up on one's soap-box from time to time; **~redner** *m* (*iro*) soap-box speaker; **~ruhe** *f* **die ~ruhe stören/einhalten** to contravene the observance of/to observe Sunday as a day of rest; **~schule** *f* Sunday school; **~staat** *m* (*hum*) Sunday best; **in vollem ~staat** in one's Sunday best; **~zeitung** *f* Sunday paper.

Sonn- und Feiertage *pl* Sundays and public holidays *pl*.

sonn- und feiertags *adv* on Sundays and public holidays.

Sonnwend-: ~feier *f* midsummer/midwinter celebrations *pl*; **~feuer** *nt* bonfire at midsummer/midwinter celebrations.

Sonographie *f* (*Med*) sonography.

sonor *adj* sonorous.

sonst [1] *adv* **(a)** (*außerdem*) (*mit pron, adv*) else; (*mit n*) other ♦ **~ keine Besucher/Zeitungen** *etc* no other visitors/papers *etc*; **~ noch Fragen?** any other questions?; **wer/wie** *etc* **(denn) ~?** who/how *etc* else?; **bringst du all deine Freunde mit? — was denn ~?** are you bringing all your friends? — of course; **~ niemand** *or* **keiner/(noch) jemand** *or* **wer** (*inf*) nobody/somebody else; **er und ~ keiner** nobody else but he, he and nobody else, he and he alone; **wenn du ~ irgend jemanden kennst** if you know somebody *or* anybody else *or* any other person; **wenn du ~ irgendwann mal kommen kannst** if you can come some *or* any other time; **er denkt, er ist ~ wer** (*inf*) he thinks he's somebody special, he thinks he's the bee's knees (*inf*) *or* the cat's whiskers (*inf*); **~ nichts/noch etwas** nothing/something else; **~ noch etwas?** is that all?, anything else?; (*in Geschäft auch*) will there be anything else?, will that be all?; **ja ~ noch was!** (*iro inf*) that'd be right! (*inf*); **~ bist du gesund** *or* **geht's dir gut?** (*iro inf*) are you feeling okay? (*inf*); **~ willst du nichts?** (*iro inf*) anything else you'd like?; **und wer weiß was ~ noch alles** and goodness knows what else; **wo warst du ~ überall?** where else were you?
(b) (*andernfalls, im übrigen*) otherwise ♦ **wie geht's ~?** how are things apart from that *or* otherwise?
(c) (*in anderer Hinsicht*) in other ways ♦ **wenn ich Ihnen ~ noch behilflich sein kann** if I can help you in any *or* some other way.
(d) (*gewöhnlich*) usually ♦ **genau wie es ~ ist** just as it usually is; **genau wie/anders als ~** the same as/different from usual; **mehr/weniger als ~** more/less than usual; **der ~ so mürrische Herr Grün war heute direkt freundlich** Mr Grün, who is usually so grumpy, was really friendly today.
(e) (*früher*) **alles war wie ~** everything was as it always used to be; **war das auch ~ der Fall?** was that always the case?; **wenn er ~ zu Besuch hier war** when he has visited us before.
[2] *conj* otherwise, or (else).

sonstig *adj attr* other; *Fragen, Auskünfte etc* further ♦ **aber ihr ~es Verhalten ist/ihre ~en Leistungen sind verhältnismäßig gut** but her behaviour/performance otherwise is quite good; **„S~es"** "other".

⚠**sonst-: ~jemand** *indef pron* (*inf*) *siehe* **~wer**; **~wann** *adv* (*inf*) some other time; **~was** *indef pron* (*inf*) **da kann ja ~was passieren** anything could happen; **von mir aus kannst du ~was machen** as far as I'm concerned you can do whatever you like; **ich habe ~was versucht** I've tried everything; **~wer** *indef pron* (*inf*) **das kannst du ~wem schenken** you can give that to some other sucker (*sl*) *or* to somebody else; **das kannst du ~wem erzählen!** tell that to the marines! (*inf*); **sei still, da kann ~wer kommen** be quiet, anybody might come; **da kann ~wer kommen, wir machen keine Ausnahmen** it doesn't matter who it is, we're not making any exceptions; **~wie** *adv* (*inf*) (in) some other way; (*sehr*) like mad (*inf*) *or* crazy (*inf*); **~wo** *adv* (*inf*) somewhere else; **~wo, nur nicht hier** anywhere (else) but here; **~wohin** *adv* (*inf*) somewhere else; **wo soll ich hingehen? — von mir aus ~wohin** where shall I go? — anywhere you like; **das kannst du dir ~wohin stecken!** (*sl*) you can stuff that! (*sl*), you know where you can put that! (*sl*).

so|oft *conj* whenever.

Soor *m* **-(e)s, -e** (*Med*) thrush *no art*.

Sophismus *m* sophism.

Sophist(in *f*) *m* sophist.

Sophisterei *f* sophistry.

Sophistik *f* sophistry.

Sophokles ['zo:foklɛs] *m* **-** Sophocles.

Sopran *m* **-s, -e** soprano; (*Knaben~, Instrumenten~ auch*) treble; (*Chorstimmen*) sopranos *pl*; trebles *pl*.

Sopranist *m* treble.

Sopranistin *f* soprano.

Sorbinsäure *f* sorbic acid.

Sore *f* **-,** *no pl* (*sl*) loot, swag (*hum*).

Sorge *f* **-, -n (a)** worry; (*Ärger auch*) trouble; (*Kummer auch*) care ♦ **frei von ~n** free of care *or* worries; **keine ~!** (*inf*) don't (you) worry!; **~ haben, ob/daß ...** to be worried whether /that ...; **wir betrachten diese Entwicklung mit ~** we view this development with concern; **~n haben** to have problems; **weniger/nichts als ~n haben** to have fewer/nothing but worries *or* headaches (*inf*); **ich habe solche ~** I'm so worried; **du hast ~n!** (*iro*) you think you've got troubles! (*inf*); **~n haben die Leute!** the worries people have!; **mit dem haben wir nichts als ~n** we've had nothing but trouble with him/that; **jdm ~n machen** (*Kummer bereiten*) to cause sb a lot of worry; (*beunruhigen*) to worry sb; **es macht mir ~n, daß ...** it worries me that ...; **in ~** (*dat*) **sein** to be worried; **sich** (*dat*) **~n machen** to worry; **wir haben uns solche ~n gemacht** we were so worried; **machen Sie sich deshalb keine ~n** don't worry about that; **seien Sie ohne ~!** (*geh*) do not fear (*liter*) *or* worry; **lassen Sie das meine ~ sein** let me worry about that; **das ist nicht meine ~** that's not my problem; **für etw ~ tragen** (*geh*) to attend *or* see to sth, to take care of sth; **dafür ~ tragen, daß ...** (*geh*) to see to it that ...
(b) (*Für~, Jur*) care.

Sorge-: s~berechtigt *adj* **s~berechtigt sein** to have custody; **~berechtigte(r)** *mf* person having custody.

sorgen [1] *vr* to worry ♦ **sich ~ um** to be worried *or* to worry about.
[2] *vi* **~ für** (*sich kümmern um*) to take care of, to look after; (*betreuen auch*) to care for; (*vorsorgen für*) to provide for; (*herbeischaffen*) *Proviant, Musik* to provide; (*bewirken*) to ensure; **dafür ~, daß ...** to see to it that ..., to make sure that ...; **für Ruhe/einen reibungslosen Ablauf ~** to make sure that things are quiet/go smoothly; **das reichlich fließende Bier sorgte für Stimmung** the plentiful supply of beer made sure that things went with a swing; **dafür ist**

⚠: for details of spelling reform, see supplement

gesorgt that's taken care of.
Sorgen-: ~falte *f* worry line; **s~frei** *adj* free of care; (*heiter, sich keine ~ machend*) carefree; **~kind** *nt* (*inf*) problem child; (*fig auch*) biggest headache (*inf*); **~last** *f* (*geh*) burden of one's cares; **s~los** *adj siehe* **s~frei**; **s~schwer** *adj Stimme, Blick* troubled; *Leben* full of cares; **s~voll** *adj* worried; *Leben* full of worries.
Sorgerecht *nt* (*Jur*) custody.
Sorgfalt *f* -, *no pl* care ♦ **ohne ~ arbeiten** to work carelessly; **viel ~ auf etw** (*acc*) **verwenden** to take a lot of care over sth.
sorgfältig *adj* careful.
Sorgfaltspflicht *f* (*Jur*) duty of care to a child ♦ **Verletzung der ~** negligence of one's duties as a parent/guardian.
sorglos *adj* (*unbekümmert*) carefree; (*leichtfertig, nachlässig*) careless ♦ **jdm ~ vertrauen** to trust sb implicitly.
Sorglosigkeit *f siehe adj* carefreeness; carelessness.
sorgsam *adj* careful.
Sorte *f* -, **-n** (**a**) sort, type, kind; (*von Waren*) variety, type; (*Qualität, Klasse*) grade; (*Marke*) brand ♦ **beste** *or* **erste ~** top quality *or* grade; **diese Psychiater sind eine ganz komische ~** these psychiatrists are quite a peculiar bunch (*inf*).
(**b**) (*Fin*) *usu pl* foreign currency.
Sorter *m* **-s**, - *siehe* **Sortiermaschine**.
sortieren* *vt* to sort (*auch Comput*); *Waren* (*nach Qualität, Größe auch*) to grade ♦ **etw in einen Schrank/ein Regal** *etc* **~** to sort sth and put it in a cupboard/ bookcase *etc*.
Sortierer(in *f*) *m* **-s**, - sorter.
Sortier-: ~lauf *m* (*Comput*) sort run; **~maschine** *f* sorting machine, sorter.
Sortiment *nt* (**a**) assortment; (*von Waren auch*) range; (*Sammlung auch*) collection. (**b**) (*Buchhandel*) retail book trade.
Sortimenter *m* **-s**, - retail bookseller, book retailer.
Sortiments-: ~buchhandel *m* retail book trade; **~buchhändler** *m siehe* **Sortimenter**; **~buchhandlung** *f* retail bookshop (*esp Brit*) *or* bookstore (*esp US*).
SOS [ɛs|oː'|ɛs] *nt* -, - SOS ♦ **~ funken** to put out an SOS.
sosehr *conj* however much, no matter how much.
Sosein *nt* (*Philos*) essence.
SOS-Kinderdorf [ɛs|oː'|ɛs-] *nt children's home organized into family units.*
soso 1 *adv* (*inf: einigermaßen*) so-so (*inf*), middling (*inf*).
2 *interj* **~!** I see!; (*erstaunt*) well well!; (*indigniert, iro auch*) really!; (*interessiert-gelassen auch*) oh yes?; (*drohend*) well!
SOS-Ruf [ɛs|oː'|ɛs-] *m* (*lit*) SOS (call), Mayday; (*fig*) SOS.
Soße *f* -, **-n** sauce; (*Braten~*) gravy; (*pej inf*) gunge (*inf*).
Soßenlöffel *m* gravy spoon.
sott *pret of* **sieden**.
Soubrette [zu'brɛtə] *f* soubrette.
⚠ **Soufflé** [zu'fleː] *nt* **-s**, **-s** (*Cook*) soufflé.
Souffleur [zu'fløːɐ] *m*, **Souffleuse** [zu'fløːzə] *f* (*Theat*) prompter.
Souffleurkasten [zu'fløːɐ-] *m* (*Theat*) prompt-box.
soufflieren* [zu'fliːrən] *vti* (*Theat*) to prompt ♦ **jdm (den Text) ~** to prompt sb.
Sound [saund] *m* **-s**, **-s** (*inf*) sound.
Soundkarte *f* (*Comput*) sound card.
so|undso *adv* **~ lange** for such and such a time; **~ groß/breit** of such and such a size/width; **~ oft** n (number of) times; **~ viele** so and so many; **Paragraph ~** article such-and-such *or* so-and-so; **er sagte, mach das ~** he said, do it in such and such a way.
So|undso *m* **-s**, **-s Herr ~** Mr So-and-so.
so|undsovielte(r, s) *adj* umpteenth ♦ **am/bis zum S~n** (*Datum*) on/by such and such a date; **er ist der S~, der** ... he's the umpteenth person who ... (*inf*).
Soundtrack *m* **-s**, **-s** (*inf*) soundtrack (music).
Souper [zu'peː] *nt* **-s**, **-s** (*geh*) dinner.
soupieren* [zu'piːrən] *vi* (*geh*) to dine.
Soutane [zu'taːnə] *f* -, **-n** (*Eccl*) cassock.
Souterrain [zutɛ'rɛ̃ː, 'zuːtɛrɛ̃] *nt* **-s**, **-s** basement.
Souvenir [zuvə'niːɐ] *nt* **-s**, **-s** souvenir.
Souvenir- [zuvə'niːɐ]: **~jäger** *m* (*inf*) souvenir-hunter; **~laden** *m* souvenir shop.
souverän [zuvə'rɛːn] *adj* sovereign *no adv*; (*fig*) supremely good; (*überlegen*) (most) superior *no adv* ♦ **das Land wurde ~** the country became a sovereign state; **~ regieren** to rule as (the) sovereign, to have sovereign power, to be sovereign; **~ siegen** to win a commanding victory; **sein Gebiet/die Lage ~ beherrschen** to have a commanding knowledge of one's field/to be in full command of a situation; **er hat die Situation ganz ~ gehandhabt** he dealt with the situation supremely well; **er ist ganz ~ darüber hinweggegangen** he blithely ignored it.
Souverän [zuvə'rɛːn] *m* **-s**, **-e** sovereign; (*Parlament, Organisation*) sovereign power.
Souveränität [zuvərɛni'tɛːt] *f* sovereignty; (*fig*) (*Überlegenheit*) superiority; (*Leichtigkeit*) supreme ease.
soviel 1 *adv* so much ♦ **halb/doppelt ~** half/twice as much; **~ als** *or* **wie** ... as much as ...; **nimm dir ~ du willst** take as much as you like; **noch einmal ~** the same again; (*doppelt ~*) twice as much; **das ist ~ wie eine Zusage** that is tantamount to *or* that amounts to a promise; **~ für heute!** that's all for today; **~**, was ihn betrifft so much for him.
2 *conj* as *or* so far as ♦ **~ ich weiß, nicht!** not as *or* so far as I know; **~ ich auch** ... however much I ...
sovielmal 1 *adv* so many times.
2 *conj* **~ ... auch** ... no matter how many times ..., however many times ...
soweit 1 *adv* (**a**) by and large, on the whole; (*bis jetzt*) up to now; (*bis zu diesem Punkt*) thus far ♦ **~ ganz gut** (*inf*) not too bad; **~ wie** *or* **als möglich** as far as possible; **ich bin ~ fertig** I'm more or less ready.
(**b**) **~ sein** to be finished *or* (*bereit*) ready; **seid ihr schon ~, daß ihr anfangen könnt?** are you ready to start?; **es ist/war bald ~** the time has/had nearly come; **wie lange dauert es noch, bis der Film anfängt? — es ist gleich ~** how long will it be before the film begins? — it'll soon be time.
2 *conj* as *or* so far as; (*insofern*) in so far as ♦ **~ ich sehe** as *or* so far as I can tell *or* see.
sowenig 1 *adv* no more, not any more (*wie* than) ♦ **sie ist mir ~ sympathisch wie dir** I don't like her any more than you do; **~ wie** *or* **als möglich** as little as possible.
2 *conj* however little, little as ♦ **~ ich auch** ... however little I ...
sowie *conj* (**a**) (*sobald*) as soon as, the moment (*inf*). (**b**) (*und auch*) as well as.
sowieso *adv* anyway, anyhow, in any case ♦ **wir sind ~ nicht gegangen** we didn't go anyway *or* anyhow *or* in any case; **das ~!** obviously!, of course!, that goes without saying.
Sowjet *m* **-s**, **-s** Soviet. **~armee** *f* Soviet Army; **~bürger** *m* Soviet citizen.
sowjetisch *adj* Soviet.
Sowjet-: ~macht *f* Soviet power *no art*; **~mensch** *m* Soviet citizen; **~republik** *f* Soviet Republic; **Union der Sozialistischen ~republiken** Union of Soviet Socialist Republics; **~russe** *m* Soviet Russian; **~staat** *m* Soviet State; **~stern** *m* Soviet star, star of the Soviets; **~union** *f* Soviet Union.
sowohl *conj* **~ ... als** *or* **wie (auch)** both ... and, ... as well as.
Sozi *m* **-s**, **-s** (*pej inf*) Socialist.
sozial *adj* social; (*~ bewußt*) socially conscious; (*an das Gemeinwohl denkend*) public-spirited ♦ **die ~en Berufe** the caring professions; **~er Wohnungsbau** ≃ council housing (*Brit*); **~es Jahr** *year spent by young person as voluntary assistant in hospitals, social services etc*; **~e Indikation** (*bei Abtreibung*) social factor; **~er Friede** social harmony; **~ denken** to be socially minded; **ich habe heute meinen ~en Tag!** (*inf*) I'm feeling charitable today.
Sozial-: ~abbau *m* cuts *pl* in social services; **~abgaben** *pl* social security contributions *pl*; **~amt** *nt* social security office; **~arbeit** *f* social work; **~arbeiter** *m* social worker; **~ausgaben** *pl* public spending *sing*; **~beiträge** *pl siehe* **~abgaben**; **~bericht** *m* (*BRD Parl*) welfare report; **~beruf** *m* caring profession; **~bindung** *f* social obligation scheme (*restricting rents etc to a socially acceptable level*); **unter die ~bindung fallen** to come under the social obligation scheme; **~demokrat** *m* social democrat; **~demokratie** *f* social democracy; **s~demokratisch** *adj* social-democratic; **~demokratismus** *m* (*pej*) social democracy; **~einrichtungen** *pl* social facilities *pl*; **~fall** *m* hardship case; **~faschismus** *m* socialist fascism; **~forschung** *f* social research; **~fürsorge** *f* (*dated*) *siehe* **~hilfe**; **~gericht** *nt* (social) welfare tribunal; **~geschichte** *f* social history; **~gesetzgebung** *f* social welfare legislation; **~hilfe** *f* income support, welfare (aid) (*US*); **~hilfeempfänger** *m* person receiving income support *or* welfare (aid) (*US*); **~hygiene** *f* public health *or* hygiene; **~imperialismus** *m* social imperialism.
Sozialisation *f* (*Psych, Sociol*) socialization.
sozialisieren* *vt* (*Psych, Sociol, Ind*) to socialize; (*Pol: verstaatlichen*) to nationalize.
Sozialisierung *f siehe vt* socialization; nationalization.
Sozialismus *m* socialism.
Sozialist(in *f*) *m* socialist.
sozialistisch *adj* socialist.
Sozial-: ~leistungen *pl* employers' contribution (*sometimes including pension scheme payments*); **s~ökonomisch** *adj* socioeconomic; **~pädagoge** *m* social education worker; **~pädagogik** *f* social education; **~partner** *pl* unions and management *pl*; **wenn einer der ~partner** ... if either unions or management ...; **~plan** *m* redundancy payments scheme; **~politik** *f* social policy; **s~politisch** *adj* socio-political; **~prestige** *nt* social standing; **~produkt** *nt* national product; **~psychologie** *f* social psychology; **~recht** *nt* social legislation; **~reform** *f* social reform; **~rente** *f* social security pension; **~staat** *m* welfare state; **~station** *f* health and advice centre; **~struktur** *f* social structure; **~tarif** *m* subsidized rate; **~versicherung** *f* national insurance (*Brit*), social security (*US*); **~versicherungsausweis** *m* national insurance card (*Brit*), social security card (*US*); **~versicherungsträger** *m* ≃ Department of Social Security; **~wissenschaften** *pl* social sciences *pl*; **~wissenschaftler** *m* social scientist; **s~wissenschaftlich** *adj attr* social science; **~wohnung** *f* council flat (*Brit*), state-subsidized apartment; **~zulage** *f* (welfare) allowance.
Sozio-: ~gramm *nt* sociogram; ⚠**~graphie** *f* sociography; **s~kulturell** *adj* socio-cultural; **~lekt** *m* (e)s, -e sociolect; **~linguistik** *f* sociolinguistics *sing*; **s~linguistisch** *adj* sociolinguistic.
Soziologe *m*, **Soziologin** *f* sociologist.
Soziologie *f* sociology.
soziologisch *adj* sociological.
Sozio-: ~metrie *f* sociometry; **s~ökonomisch** *adj* socioeconomic.
Sozius *m* -, **-se** (**a**) (*Partner*) partner. (**b**) (*Beifahrer*) pillion rider *or* passenger; (*inf: ~sitz*) pillion (seat).
Soziussitz *m* pillion (seat).
sozusagen *adv* so to speak, as it were.

Spachtel *m* **-s, -** *or f* **-, -n (a)** *(Werkzeug)* spatula. **(b)** *(spec: ~masse)* filler.
Spachtelmasse *f* filler.
spachteln [1] *vt Mauerfugen, Ritzen* to fill (in), to smooth over, to stop.
[2] *vi* to do some filling; *(inf: essen)* to tuck in.
Spagat¹ *m or nt* **-(e)s, -e** *(lit)* splits *pl*; *(fig)* balancing act ◆ **~ machen** to do the splits.
Spagat² *m* **-(e)s, -e** *(S Ger, Aus: Bindfaden)* string.
⚠ **Spaghetti¹** [ʃpa'geti] *pl* spaghetti *sing.*
⚠ **Spaghetti²** *m* **-(s), -s,** ⚠ **Spaghettifresser** *m* **-s, -** *(pej sl: Italiener)* wop *(pej sl)*, eyetie *(sl)*.
⚠ **Spaghettiträger** *m (Fashion)* shoestring strap.
spähen *vi* to peer; *(durch Löcher etc auch)* to peep; *(vorsichtig auch)* to peek; *(old Mil)* to reconnoitre, to scout ◆ **nach jdm/etw ~** to look out for sb/sth.
Späher(in *f)* *m* **-s, -** *(old Mil)* scout; *(Posten)* lookout.
Spähtrupp *m (Mil)* reconnaissance *or* scouting party *or* patrol.
spakig *adj (N Ger) Bettwäsche, Matratze* mildewed.
Spalier *nt* **-s, -e (a)** trellis; *(für Obst auch)* espalier ◆ **am ~ ziehen** to trellis/espalier, to train on a trellis/an espalier. **(b)** *(von Menschen)* row, line; *(zur Ehrenbezeigung)* guard of honour ◆ **~ stehen/ein ~ bilden** to form a guard of honour.
Spalier|obst *nt* wall fruit.
Spalt *m* **-(e)s, -e (a)** *(Öffnung)* gap, opening; *(zwischen Vorhängen etc auch)* chink; *(Riß)* crack; *(Fels~)* crevice, fissure ◆ **die Tür stand einen ~ offen** the door was slightly ajar; **die Tür/Augen einen ~ öffnen** to open the door/one's eyes slightly.
(b) *(fig: Kluft)* split.
spaltbar *adj (Phys) Material* fissile.
Spaltbarkeit *f (Phys)* fissionability.
Spaltbreit *m*: **etw einen ~ öffnen** *etc* to open *etc* sth slightly.
spaltbreit *adj* **ein ~er Schlitz** a narrow crack.
Spalte *f* **-, -n (a)** *(esp Geol)* fissure; *(Fels~ auch)* cleft, crevice; *(Gletscher~)* crevasse; *(in Wand)* crack; *(sl: Vagina)* hole *(sl)*. **(b)** *(Typ, Press)* column.
spalten *ptp auch* **gespalten** [1] *vt (lit, fig)* to split; *(Chem) Öl* to crack *(spec)*; *Holz* to chop ◆ **bei dieser Frage sind die Meinungen gespalten** opinions are divided on this question; *siehe* **gespalten, Schädel.**
[2] *vr* to split; *(Meinungen)* to be split.
Spalt-: **~material** *nt* fissile material; **~pilz** *m (old) usu pl* bacterium; **~produkt** *nt* fission product.
Spaltung *f (lit, fig)* splitting; *(von Atomkernen auch)* fission; *(von Öl)* cracking *(spec)*; *(in Partei etc)* split; *(eines Landes)* split, division ◆ **die ~ der Persönlichkeit/des Bewußtseins** the split in his *etc* personality/mind.
Span *m* **-(e)s, ¨-e** *(Hobel~)* shaving; *(Bohr~ auch)* boring; *(zum Feueranzünden)* piece of kindling; *(Metall~)* filing ◆ **arbeiten, daß die ¨-e fliegen** *(prov)* to work furiously.
spänen *vt Holzboden* to scour with steel wool.
Spanferkel *nt* sucking pig.
Spange *f* **-, -n** clasp; *(Haar~)* hair slide *(Brit)*, barrette *(US)*; *(Schuh~)* strap, bar; *(Schnalle)* buckle; *(Arm~)* bangle, bracelet.
Spangenschuh *m* bar shoe.
Spaniel ['ʃpa:niɛl] *m* **-s, -s** spaniel.
Spanien ['ʃpa:niən] *nt* **-s** Spain.
Spanier(in *f)* ['ʃpa:niɐ, -iərɪn] *m* **-s, -** Spaniard ◆ **die ~** the Spanish, the Spaniards; **stolz wie ein ~ sein** *(prov)* to be (very) proud; *siehe* **Deutsche(r).**
spanisch *adj* Spanish ◆ **S~e Fliege** Spanish fly; **~e Wand** (folding) screen; **das kommt mir ~ vor** *(inf)* that seems odd to me.
Spanisch(e) *nt* Spanish; *siehe auch* **Deutsch(e).**
Span-: **~kiste** *f* chip basket; **~korb** *m* chip basket.
Spann *m* **-(e)s, -e** instep.
spann *pret of* **spinnen.**
Spann-: **~beton** *m* prestressed concrete; **~bettuch** *nt* fitted sheet.
Spanne *f* **-, -n** *(altes Längenmaß)* span; *(geh: Zeit~)* while; *(Verdienst~)* margin ◆ **eine ~ Zeit** *(geh)* a space *or* span of time.
spannen [1] *vt* **(a)** *Saite, Seil* to tighten, to tauten; *Bogen* to draw; *Feder* to tension; *Muskeln* to tense, to flex; *Strickteile, Wolle* to stretch; *Gewehr, (Abzugs)hahn, (Kamera)verschluß* to cock ◆ **einen Tennisschläger ~** to put a tennis racket in a/the press.
(b) *(straff befestigen) Werkstück* to clamp; *Wäscheleine* to put up; *Netz, Plane, Bildleinwand* to stretch ◆ **einen Bogen in die Schreibmaschine ~** to insert *or* put a sheet in the typewriter.
(c) *(fig)* **seine Erwartungen zu hoch ~** to pitch one's expectations too high; *siehe* **Folter.**
(d) *(inf: merken)* to catch on to *(inf)*, to get wise to *(inf)*.
[2] *vr* **(a)** *(Haut)* to go *or* become taut; *(Muskeln auch)* to tense.
(b) sich über etw *(acc)* **~** *(Regenbogen, Brücke)* to span sth; *(Haut)* to stretch over sth.
[3] *vi* **(a)** *(Kleidung)* to be (too) tight; *(Haut)* to be taut.
(b) *(Gewehr ~)* to cock; *(Kamera ~)* to cock the shutter.
spannend *adj* exciting; *(stärker)* thrilling ◆ **mach's nicht so ~!** *(inf)* don't keep me/us in suspense.
Spanner *m* **-s, - (a)** *(für Tennisschläger)* press; *(Hosen~)* hanger; *(Schuh~)* shoetree; *(Stiefel~)* boot-tree. **(b)** *(Zool)* geometer moth; *(Raupe)* looper. **(c)** *(inf: Voyeur)* peeping Tom.
-spänner *m* **-s, -** *in cpds* **Vier~** *etc* four-in-hand *etc.*
-spännig *adj suf* **vier~ fahren** to drive a four-in-hand.
Spann-: **~kraft** *f (von Feder, Bremse)* tension; *(von Muskel)* tone, tonus *(spec)*; *(fig)* vigour; **s~kräftig** *adj (fig)* vigorous.
Spannung *f* **(a)** *no pl (von Seil, Feder, Muskel etc)* tension, tautness; *(Mech: innerer Druck)* stress ◆ **wegen der zu großen ~ riß das Seil** the rope broke because the strain (on it) was too great.
(b) *(Elec)* voltage, tension ◆ **unter ~ stehen** to be live.
(c) *no pl (fig)* excitement; *(Spannungsgeladenheit)* suspense, tension ◆ **mit großer/atemloser ~** with great/breathless excitement; **in erwartungsvoller ~** full of excited anticipation, full of excitement; **etw mit ~ erwarten** to await sth full of suspense; **seine mit ~ erwarteten Memoiren sind endlich erschienen** his eagerly awaited memoirs have appeared at last.
(d) *no pl (innerliche, nervliche Anspannung)* tension.
(e) *usu pl (Feindseligkeit)* tension *no pl.*
Spannungs-: **~abfall** *m* voltage drop; **~feld** *nt (lit)* electric field; *(fig)* area of conflict; **s~frei** *adj (lit) Metall, Glas* unstressed; *(fig)* relaxed; **~gebiet** *nt (Pol)* flashpoint, area of tension; **~kopfschmerz** *m usu pl* tension headache; **~messer** *m* **-s, -** *(Elec)* voltmeter; **~moment** *nt (fig)* suspense-creating factor; **~prüfer** *m* voltage detector; **~regler** *m* voltage regulator; **~stoß** *m* surge.
Spannweite *f (Math)* range; *(Archit)* span; *(Aviat)* (wing)span; *(von Vogelflügeln)* wingspread, (wing)span.
Span-: **~platte** *f* chipboard; **~schachtel** *f small box made from very thin strips of wood.*
Spant¹ *nt* **-(e)s, -en** *(Naut)* rib.
Spant² *m* **-(e)s, -en** *(Aviat)* frame.
Spar-: **~brief** *m (Fin)* savings certificate; **~buch** *nt* savings book; *(bei Bank auch)* bankbook, passbook; **~büchse, ~dose** *f* piggy bank; **~eckzins** *m* basic savings rate; **~einlage** *f* savings deposit.
sparen [1] *vt* to save; *Energie auch* to conserve ◆ **dadurch habe ich (mir) viel Geld/Zeit/Arbeit gespart** I saved (myself) a lot of money/time/work that way; **keine Kosten/Mühe ~** to spare no expense/effort; **spar dir deine guten Ratschläge!** *(inf)* you can keep your advice!; **diese Mühe/diese Kosten/das hätten Sie sich** *(dat)* **~ können** you could have saved *or* spared yourself the trouble/this expense/the bother; **diese Bemerkung hätten Sie sich** *(dat)* **~ können!** you should have kept that remark to yourself!
[2] *vi* to save; *(sparsam sein, haushalten)* to economize, to make savings ◆ **an etw** *(dat)* **~** to be sparing with sth; *(mit etw haushalten)* to economize *or* save on sth; **er hatte nicht mit Lob gespart** he was unstinting *or* lavish in his praise; **für** *or* **auf etw** *(acc)* **~** to save up for sth; **am falschen Ort ~** to make false economies, to make savings in the wrong place; **spare in der Zeit, so hast du in der Not** *(Prov)* waste not, want not *(Prov)*.
Sparer(in *f)* *m* **-s, -** *(bei Bank etc)* saver.
Sparflamme *f* low flame; *(Zündflamme)* pilot light ◆ **auf ~** *(fig inf)* just ticking over *(inf)*; **auf ~ kochen** *(fig)* to soft-pedal *(inf)*, to go easy.
Spargel *m* **-s, -,** *(Sw) f* **-, -n** asparagus.
Spargelder *pl* savings *pl.*
Spargelspitze *f* asparagus tip.
Spar-: **~groschen** *m* nest egg; **~guthaben** *nt* savings account; **~kasse** *f* savings bank; **~kassenbuch** *nt siehe* **~buch**; **~konto** *nt* savings *or* deposit account.
spärlich *adj* sparse; *Ausbeute, Reste, Einkünfte, Kenntnisse* meagre, scanty; *Beleuchtung* poor; *(Be)kleidung* scanty, skimpy; *Mahl* meagre; *Nachfrage* poor, low ◆ **~ bekleidet** scantily clad *or* dressed; **~ bevölkert** sparsely *or* thinly populated; **~ beleuchtet** poorly lit; **die Geldmittel fließen nur ~** the money is only coming slowly *or* in dribs and drabs.
Spärlichkeit *f siehe adj* sparseness; meagreness, scantiness; poorness; scantiness, skimpiness; meagreness; low level, poorness.
Spar-: **~maßnahme** *f* economy measure; **~packung** *f* economy size (pack); **~pfennig** *m* nest egg; **~politik** *f* cost-cutting policy; **~prämie** *f* savings premium; **~preis** *m* economy price; **~quote, ~rate** *f* rate of saving.
Sparren *m* **-s, -** rafter ◆ **du hast ja einen ~ (zuviel im Kopf)** *(inf)* you must have a screw loose *(inf)*.
Sparring ['ʃparɪŋ, 'sparɪŋ] *nt* **-s,** *no pl (Boxen)* sparring.
Sparrings-: **~kampf** *m* sparring bout; **~partner** *m* sparring partner.
sparsam *adj* thrifty; *(haushälterisch, wirtschaftlich)* economical ◆ **~ leben** to live economically; **~ im Verbrauch** economical; **mit etw ~ umgehen** *or* **sein** to be sparing with sth; **~ verwenden** to use sparingly; **von einer Möglichkeit nur ~(en) Gebrauch machen** to make little use of an opportunity.
Sparsamkeit *f* thrift; *(das Haushalten)* economizing ◆ **~ im Verbrauch** economicalness.
Sparschwein *nt* piggy bank.
Spartakiade [ʃparta'kia:də, sp-] *f* Spartakiad.
Spartakusbund ['ʃpartakʊs-, 'sp-] *m* Spartacus league.
Spartaner(in *f)* [ʃpar'ta:nɐ, -ərɪn, sp-] *m* **-s, -** Spartan.
spartanisch [ʃpar'ta:nɪʃ, sp-] *adj (lit)* Spartan; *(fig auch)* spartan ◆ **~ leben** to lead a Spartan *or* spartan life.
Spartarif *m* discount price ◆ **zum ~ einkaufen** to shop at discount prices.
Sparte *f* **-, -n (a)** *(Comm) (Branche)* line of business; *(Teilgebiet)* branch, area. **(b)** *(Rubrik)* column, section.
Spar-: **~vertrag** *m* savings agreement; **~zins** *m* interest *no pl* (on a savings account); **~zulage** *f* savings bonus.
spasmisch, spasmodisch *adj (Med)* spasmodic, spasmic.
Spaß *m* **-es, ¨-e** *(no pl: Vergnügen)* fun; *(Scherz)* joke; *(Streich)* prank, lark *(Brit inf)* ◆ **laß die dummen ¨-e!** stop fooling around!; **~ beiseite** joking apart; **viel ~!** have fun *(auch iro)*, have a good time!, enjoy yourself/yourselves!; **wir**

⚠: for details of spelling reform, see supplement

haben viel ~ gehabt we had a lot of fun *or* a really good time, we enjoyed ourselves a lot; **an etw** (*dat*) **~ haben** to enjoy sth; **er hat viel ~ an seinem Garten** his garden gives him a lot of pleasure; **es macht mir ~/keinen ~(, das zu tun)** it's fun/no fun (doing it), I enjoy *or* like/don't enjoy *or* like (doing) it; **wenn's dir ~ macht** if you want to, if it turns you on (*sl*); **Hauptsache, es macht ~** the main thing is to have fun *or* to enjoy yourself; **es macht ~/keinen ~** it's fun/no fun; **ich hab' doch nur ~ gemacht!** I was only joking *or* kidding (*inf*)!, it was only (in) fun; **(nur so,) zum** *or* **aus ~** (just) for fun, (just) for the fun *or* hell of it (*inf*); **etw aus** *or* **im** *or* **zum ~ sagen** to say sth as a joke *or* in fun; **das sage ich nicht bloß zum ~** I'm not saying that for the fun of it, I kid you not (*hum inf*); **da hört der ~ auf, das ist kein ~ mehr** that's going beyond a joke; **aus (dem) ~ wurde Ernst** the fun turned deadly earnest; **~ muß sein** there's no harm in a joke; (*als Aufheiterung*) all work and no play (makes Jack a dull boy) (*prov*); **es war ein ~, ihm bei der Arbeit zuzusehen** it was a joy to see him at work; **sich** (*dat*) **einen ~ daraus machen, etw zu tun** to get enjoyment *or* a kick (*inf*) out of doing sth; **seinen ~ mit jdm treiben** to make fun of sb; (*sich mit jdm vergnügen*) to have one's fun with sb; **laß/gönn ihm doch seinen** *or* **den ~!** let him enjoy himself *or* have his fun; **er versteht keinen ~** he has no sense of humour; (*er läßt nicht mit sich spaßen*) he doesn't stand for any nonsense; **da verstehe ich keinen ~!** I won't stand for any nonsense; **das war ein teurer ~** (*inf*) that was an expensive business (*inf*).

Späßchen *nt dim of* **Spaß** little joke.

spaßen *vi* (*dated*) to joke, to jest ◆ **mit Blutvergiftung/mit radioaktivem Material ist nicht zu ~** blood poisoning is no joke *or* joking matter/ radioactive material is no joke; **mit ihm ist nicht zu ~, er läßt nicht mit sich ~** he doesn't stand for any nonsense.

spaßeshalber *adv* for the fun of it, for fun.

spaßhaft, spaßig *adj* funny, droll.

Späßlein *nt siehe* **Späßchen.**

Spaß-: ~macher *m* (*~vogel*) joker; (*im Zirkus*) clown; **~verderber** *m* **-s, -** spoilsport, wet blanket, killjoy; **~vogel** *m* joker.

Spastiker(in *f*) [ˈʃpastikɐ, -ərɪn, ˈsp-] *m* **-s, -** spastic.

spastisch [ˈʃpastɪʃ, ˈsp-] *adj* spastic ◆ **~ gelähmt** suffering from spastic paralysis.

Spat *m* **-(e)s, -e (a)** (*Miner*) spar. **(b)** *no pl* (*Vet*) spavin.

spät [1] *adj* late; *Reue, Ruhm, Glück* belated ◆ **am ~en Nachmittag** in the late afternoon; **im ~en 18. Jahrhundert** in the late 18th century; **die Werke des ~en Shakespeare, die ~en Werke Shakespeares** the works of the late(r) Shakespeare, Shakespeare's late(r) works; **ein ~es Mädchen** (*inf*) an old maid.

[2] *adv* late ◆ **~ in der Nacht/am Tage** late at night/in the day; **es ist/wird schon ~** it is/is getting late; **heute abend wird es ~** it'll be a late night tonight; (*nach Hause kommen*) I/he *etc* will be late this evening; **gestern ist es (bei der Arbeit) ~ geworden** I worked late yesterday; **wir hatten gestern eine Party, und da ist es ziemlich ~ geworden** we had a party yesterday and it went on fairly late; **von früh bis ~** from morning till night; **wie ~ ist es?** what's the time?; **zu ~** too late; **er kommt morgens regelmäßig fünf Minuten zu ~** he's always five minutes late in the mornings; **der Zug ist zu ~ angekommen** the train arrived late; **wir sind ~ dran** we're late; **er hat erst ~ mit dem Schreiben angefangen** he only started writing late in life; **besser ~ als nie** (*prov*) better late than never (*prov*).

Spät- *in cpds* late; **~aussiedler** *m emigrant of German origin from Eastern European state.*

Spatel *m* **-s, -** spatula.

Spaten *m* **-s, -** spade.

Spatenstich *m* cut of the spade ◆ **den ersten ~ tun** to turn the first sod.

Spät|entwickler *m* late developer.

später *comp of* **spät** [1] *adj* later; (*zukünftig*) future ◆ **in der ~en Zukunft** further on in the future; **die S~en** (*liter*) posterity *sing.*

[2] *adv* later (on) ◆ **das werden wir ~ erledigen** we'll settle that later (on); **ein paar Minuten ~** a few minutes later; **~ als** later than; **das war viel ~ als Augustus** that was much later (on) than Augustus; **was will er denn ~ (einmal) werden?** what does he want to do later (on)?; **an ~ denken** to think of the future; **bis ~!, also dann, auf ~!** see you later!

späterhin *adv* later (on).

spätestens *adv* at the latest ◆ **~ morgen/in einer Stunde** tomorrow/in one hour at the latest; **~ um 8 Uhr** not later than 8 o'clock, by 8 o'clock at the latest; **bis ~ in einer Woche** in one week at the latest.

Spät-: ~folge *f usu pl* late effect; **~gebärende** *f* woman having her (first) child around forty, elderly prim (*inf*); **~geburt** *f* late birth; **~gotik** *f* late Gothic; **~heimkehrer** *m* late returnee (*from a prisoner-of-war camp*); **~herbst** *m* late autumn, late fall (*US*); **~jahr** *nt* (*liter*) autumn, fall (*US*); **~kapitalismus** *m* late capitalism; **~lese** *f* late vintage; **~nachmittag** *m* late afternoon; **~schaden** *m usu pl* long-term damage; **~schicht** *f* late shift; **~sommer** *m* late summer; **~vorstellung** *f* late show.

Spatz *m* **-en, -en (a)** sparrow ◆ **wie ein ~ essen** to peck at one's food; **besser ein ~ in der Hand als eine Taube auf dem Dach** (*Prov*) a bird in the hand is worth two in the bush (*Prov*); *siehe* **pfeifen. (b)** (*inf: Kind*) tot, mite; (*Anrede*) darling, honey.

Spätzchen *nt dim of* **Spatz** little sparrow; (*inf: Kind*) tot, mite; (*Anrede*) honey-bun (*inf*), sweetie pie (*inf*).

Spatzenhirn *nt* (*pej*) birdbrain (*inf*).

Spätzle *pl* (*S Ger Cook*) spaetzle (*sort of pasta*).

Spät-: ~zünder *m* (*hum inf*) **~zünder sein** (*schwer von Begriff*) to be slow on the uptake; (*spät im Leben mit etw anfangen*) to be a late starter; **~zündung** *f* retarded ignition; **~zündung haben** (*inf*) to be slow on the uptake.

spazieren* *vi aux sein* to stroll; (*stolzieren*) to strut ◆ **wir waren ~** we went for a walk *or* stroll.

⚠**spazieren-: ~fahren** *sep irreg* [1] *vi aux sein* (*im Auto*) to go for a drive *or* ride *or* run; (*mit Fahrrad, Motorrad*) to go for a ride; **ich will nur ein bißchen ~fahren** I just want to go for a little drive *or* ride *or* run; [2] *vt* **jdn ~fahren** to take sb for a drive *or* ride *or* run; **das Baby (im Kinderwagen) ~fahren** to take the baby for a walk (in the pram); **~führen** *vt sep* **jdn ~führen** to take sb for a walk; **sie hat ihr neues Kleid/ihren Fotoapparat ~geführt** (*inf*) she paraded her new dress/her camera; **~gehen** *vi sep irreg aux sein* to go for a walk *or* stroll; **ich gehe jetzt ein bißchen ~** I'm going to go for a little walk *or* stroll now.

Spazier-: ~fahrt *f* (*im Auto*) ride, drive, run; (*mit Fahrrad, Motorrad*) ride; **eine ~fahrt machen** to go for a ride *etc*; **~gang** *m* walk, stroll; (*fig*) child's play *no art*, doddle (*inf*); (*Match*) walkover; **einen ~gang machen** to go for a walk *or* stroll; **~gänger** *m* **-s, -** stroller; **~ritt** *m* ride; **~stock** *m* walking stick; **~weg** *m* path, walk.

SPD [ɛspeːˈdeː] *f* - *abbr of* **Sozialdemokratische Partei Deutschlands.**

Specht *m* **-(e)s, -e** woodpecker.

Speck *m* **-(e)s, -e** (*Schweine~*) bacon fat; (*Schinken~, durchwachsener ~*) bacon; (*Wal~*) blubber; (*inf: bei Mensch*) fat, flab (*inf*) ◆ **mit ~ fängt man Mäuse** (*Prov*) you have to throw a sprat to catch a mackerel; **~ ansetzen** (*inf*) to get fat, to put on weight, to put it on (*inf*); **~ auf den Knochen** *or* **drauf haben** (*inf*) to be fat; (*an Hüften*) to be broad in the beam (*inf*); **ran an den ~** (*inf*) let's get stuck in (*inf*).

Speck-: ~bauch *m* (*inf*) potbelly (*inf*), paunch; **s~bäuchig** *adj* (*inf*) potbellied (*inf*).

speckig *adj* greasy.

Speck-: ~nacken *m* fat neck; **s~nackig** *adj* fat-necked; **~scheibe** *f* (bacon) rasher; **~schwarte** *f* bacon rind; **wie eine ~schwarte glänzen** (*inf*) to shine greasily; **~seite** *f* side of bacon; **~stein** *m* (*Miner*) soapstone, steatite.

Spediteur [ʃpediˈtøːɐ] *m* carrier, haulier, haulage contractor; (*Zwischen~*) forwarding agent; (*von Schiffsfracht*) shipper, shipping agent; (*Umzugsfirma*) furniture remover.

Spedition *f* **(a)** (*das Spedieren*) carriage, transporting; (*auf dem Wasserweg*) shipping. **(b)** (*Firma*) haulage contractor; (*Zwischen~*) forwarding agency; (*Schiffskontor*) shipping agency; (*Umzugsfirma*) removal firm; (*Versandabteilung*) forwarding department.

Speditions-: ~branche *f* haulage business; **~firma** *f*, **~geschäft** *nt* haulage contractor; (*Zwischenspediteur*) forwarding agency; (*Schiffskontor*) shipping agency; (*Umzugsfirma*) removal firm; **~kosten** *pl* haulage (costs *pl*).

Speer *m* **-(e)s, -e** spear; (*Sport*) javelin.

Speer-: ~spitze *f* (*lit, fig*) spearhead; **~werfen** *nt* (*Sport*) **das ~werfen** the javelin, throwing the javelin; **im ~werfen** in the javelin; **~werfer** *m* (*Sport*) javelin thrower.

Speiche *f* **-, -n (a)** spoke ◆ **dem Schicksal in die ~n greifen** *or* **fallen** (*fig*) to try to stop the wheel of fate. **(b)** (*Anat*) radius.

Speichel *m* **-s,** *no pl* saliva, spittle.

Speichel-: ≈drüse *f* salivary gland; ⚠**≈fluß** *m* salivation; **≈lecker** *m* **-s, -** (*pej inf*) lickspittle, toady, bootlicker (*inf*); **~leckerei** *f* (*pej inf*) toadying, bootlicking (*inf*).

Speicher *m* **-s, -** (*Lagerhaus*) storehouse; (*im Haus*) loft, attic; (*Wasser~*) tank, reservoir; (*Comput*) memory, store ◆ **auf dem ~** in the loft *or* attic.

Speicher-: ~batterie *f* storage battery, accumulator (*Brit*); **~becken** *nt* reservoir; **~chip** *m* (*Comput*) memory chip; **~einheit** *f* (*Comput*) storage device; **~erweiterung** *f* (*Comput*) memory expansion; **~funktion** *f* (*Comput*) memory function; **~kapazität** *f* storage capacity; (*Comput*) memory capacity; **~kraftwerk** *nt* storage power station.

speichern [1] *vt Vorräte, Energie, Daten* to store; (*ab~*) to save; (*fig*) *Gefühle* to store up.

[2] *vr* to accumulate.

Speicher-: ~ofen *m* storage heater; **~platz** *m* (*Comput*) storage space; **s~resident** *adj* (*Comput*) memory-resident; **~schreibmaschine** *f* memory typewriter; **~schutz** *m* (*Tech*) memory protection.

Speicherung *f* storing, storage.

Speicherverwaltung *f* (*Comput*) memory management.

speien *pret* **spie,** *ptp* **gespie(e)n** *vti* to spit, to expectorate (*spec*); *Lava, Feuer* to spew (forth); *Wasser* to spout; *Flammen, Dämpfe* to belch (forth *or* out); (*sich übergeben*) to vomit ◆ **der Drache spie Feuer** the dragon breathed fire; *siehe* **Gift.**

Speis *m* **-es,** *no pl* (*S Ger*) mortar.

Speise *f* **-, -n (a)** (*geh: Nahrung*) food, fare (*liter*); (*Gericht*) dish; (*Süß~*) sweet (*Brit*), dessert ◆ **~n und Getränke** meals and beverages; **vielen Dank für Speis und Trank** many thanks for the meal; **kalte und warme ~n** hot and cold meals; **erlesene ~n** choice dishes.

(b) *no pl* (*Mörtel*) mortar.

(c) (*Metal*) speiss; (*Glocken~*) bell metal.

Speise-: ~brei *m* chyme; **~eis** *nt* icecream; **~fett** *nt* cooking *or* edible fat; **~kammer** *f* larder, pantry; **~karte** *f* menu; **~leitung** *f* (*Elec*) feeder, supply main; **~lokal** *nt* restaurant.

speisen (*hum*) *ptp* **gespiesen** [1] *vti* (*geh*) to eat, to dine (*form*) ◆ **zu Abend ~** to have dinner, to dine (in the evening) (*form*); **zu Mittag ~** to lunch; **wünsche wohl zu ~** I hope you enjoy your meal; **etw ~** to eat sth, to dine on sth (*form*); **was wünschen Sie zu ~?** what do you wish to eat, sir/madam?

[2] *vt (liter, Tech)* to feed; *(old) Gast* to dine.

Speisen-: ~aufzug *m* dumb waiter, service lift; **~folge** *f* order of the menu *or* the courses.

Speise-: ~öl *nt* salad oil; *(zum Braten)* cooking *or* edible oil; **~quark** *m* quark; **~reste** *pl* left-overs *pl*; *(zwischen den Zähnen)* food particles *pl*; **~röhre** *f (Anat)* gullet; **~saal** *m* dining hall; *(in Hotel etc)* dining room; *(auf Schiffen)* dining saloon; *(in Klöstern, Internaten etc auch)* refectory; **~schrank** *m* larder, pantry; **~stärke** *f* cornflour, cornstarch *(US)*; **~wagen** *m (Rail)* dining car, restaurant car, diner *(esp US)*; **~wärmer** *m* hot plate; **~zettel** *m* menu; **~zimmer** *nt* dining room.

Speisung *f (geh)* feeding; *(Tech auch)* supply ◆ **die ~ der Fünftausend** the feeding of the five thousand.

spei|übel *adj* **mir ist ~** I think I'm going to be sick *or* to throw up; **da kann einem ~ werden, wenn man das sieht** the sight of that is enough to make you feel sick.

Spektabilität [ʃpɛktabili'tɛ:t, sp-] *f (dated Univ)* (Mr) Dean.

Spektakel[1] *m* **-s, -** *(inf)* row, rumpus *(inf)*; *(Aufregung)* fuss, bother, palaver *(inf)*.

Spektakel[2] [ʃpɛk'ta:kl, sp-] *nt* **-s, -** *(old)* spectacle, show.

spektakulär [ʃpɛktaku'lɛ:ɐ, sp-] *adj* spectacular.

Spektra *pl of* **Spektrum.**

Spektral- [ʃpɛk'tra:l-, sp-]: **~analyse** *f* spectrum analysis; **~farbe** *f* colour of the spectrum.

Spektren *pl of* **Spektrum.**

Spektroskop [ʃpɛktro'sko:p, sp-] *nt* **-s, -e** spectroscope.

Spektrum ['ʃpɛktrʊm, 'sp-] *nt* **-s, Spektren** *or* **Spektra** spectrum.

Spekulant(in *f)* *m* speculator.

Spekulation *f* **(a)** *(Fin)* speculation *(mit* in) ◆ **~ mit Grundstücken** property speculation. **(b)** *(Vermutung)* speculation ◆ **~en anstellen** to make speculations; **man stellt schon ~en an, ob ...** people are already speculating as to whether ...

Spekulations-: ~geschäft *nt* speculative transaction *or* operation; **es war ein ~geschäft, aber es hat sich gelohnt** it was a gamble but it was worth it; **~gewinn** *m* speculative gains *pl or* profit; **~objekt** *nt* object of speculation.

Spekulatius [ʃpeku'la:tsiʊs] *m* **-, -** spiced biscuit *(Brit) or* cookie *(US)*.

spekulativ *adj* speculative.

spekulieren* *vi* **(a)** *(Fin)* to speculate *(mit* in); *siehe* **Baisse, Hausse. (b)** *(Vermutungen anstellen)* to speculate ◆ **auf etw** *(acc)* **~** *(inf)* to have hopes of sth.

Spellchecker *m* **-s, -** *(Comput)* spellchecker.

Spelunke *f* **-, -n** *(pej inf)* dive *(inf)*.

Spelz *m* **-es, -e** *(Agr)* spelt.

Spelze *f* **-, -n** *(Bot)* husk; *(von Gras)* glume.

spendabel *adj (inf)* generous, open-handed.

Spende *f* **-, -n** donation; *(Beitrag)* contribution ◆ **eine ~ geben** *or* **machen** to give a donation/contribution, to donate/contribute something; **bitte eine kleine ~!** please give *or* donate *or* contribute something (for charity).

spenden *vti Lebensmittel, Blut, Geld* to donate, to give; *(beitragen) Geld* to contribute; *Abendmahl, Segen* to administer; *Schatten* to afford, to offer; *Trost* to give ◆ **bitte ~ Sie für das Rote Kreuz!** please donate/contribute something to *or* for the Red Cross; *siehe* **Beifall, Lob.**

Spenden-: ~affäre *f* donations scandal; **~aufkommen** *nt* revenue from donations; **~beschaffung** *f* procuring of donations; **~konto** *nt* donations account; **~sammler** *m* fund-raiser; **~waschanlage** *f (Pol sl)* money-laundering facility.

Spender *m* **-s, -** *(Seifen~ etc)* dispenser.

Spender(in *f)* *m* **-s, -** donator; *(Beitragleistender)* contributor; *(Med)* donor ◆ **wer war der edle ~?** *(inf)* to whom am I indebted?

spendieren* *vt* to buy, to get *(jdm etw* sb sth, sth for sb) ◆ **spendierst du mir einen?** *(inf)* are you going to buy *or* stand me a drink?; **laß mal, das spendiere ich** forget it, it's on me.

Spendierhosen *pl (inf)* **seine ~ anhaben** to be in a generous mood, to be feeling generous.

Spengler(in *f)* *m* **-s, -** *(dial: Klempner)* plumber.

Spenzer *m* **-s, -** long-sleeved vest; *(kurze Jacke)* short jacket.

Sperber *m* **-s, -** sparrowhawk.

Sperenzchen, Sperenzien [-iən] *pl (inf)* **~ machen** *(inf)* to make trouble, to be difficult.

Sperling *m* sparrow.

Sperma *nt* **-s, Spermen** *or* **-ta** sperm.

spermizid *adj* spermicidal.

Spermizid *nt* **-(e)s, -e** spermicide.

⚠ **Sperrad** *nt getrennt* **Sperr-rad** ratchet wheel.

sperr|angelweit *adv (inf)* **~ offen** wide open.

Sperr-: ~ballon *m (Mil)* barrage balloon; **~bezirk** *m* no-go area, prohibited area; ⚠**~differential** *nt (Aut)* locking differential.

Sperre *f* **-, -n (a)** *(Hindernis, Schlagbaum, Bahnsteig~ etc)* barrier; *(Polizei~)* roadblock; *(Mil)* obstacle; *(Tech)* locking device.
(b) *(Verbot, Sport)* ban; *(Blockierung)* blockade; *(Comm)* embargo; *(Nachrichten~)* (news) blackout.
(c) *(Psych)* mental block ◆ **eine psychologische/emotionale ~** a mental/emotional block.

sperren [1] *vt* **(a)** *(schließen) Grenze, Hafen, Straße, Brücke, Tunnel* to close; *Platz, Gegend auch* to close off; *(Tech)* to lock ◆ **Tunnel gesperrt!** tunnel closed; **etw für jdn/etw ~** to close sth to sb/sth.
(b) *(Comm) Konto* to block, to freeze; *Scheck* to stop.
(c) *(Sport: ausschließen)* to ban, to bar.
(d) *(Sport: behindern) Gegner* to obstruct, to block.
(e) *(verbieten) Einfuhr, Ausfuhr* to ban ◆ **jdm den Urlaub/das Gehalt ~** to stop sb's holidays/salary; **jdm den Ausgang ~** *(Mil)* to confine sb to barracks.
(f) *(abstellen) Gas, Strom, Telefon* to cut off, to disconnect ◆ **jdm den Strom/das Telefon ~** to cut off *or* disconnect sb's electricity/telephone.
(g) *(einschließen)* **jdn in etw** *(acc)* **~** to shut *or* lock sb in sth.
(h) *(Typ)* to space out.
[2] *vr* **sich (gegen etw) ~** to ba(u)lk *or* jib (at sth); **jetzt laß dir doch auch einmal etwas schenken und sperr dich nicht so** accept a present for once, can't you, and don't be so ungracious.
[3] *vi* **(a)** *(nicht schließen: Tür, Fenster)* to stick, to jam; *(blockiert sein: Räder)* to lock.
(b) *(Sport)* to obstruct ◆ **S~ ist nicht zulässig** obstruction is not allowed.

Sperr-: ~feuer *nt (Mil, fig)* barrage; **sein Vorschlag geriet ins ~feuer der Kritik** his suggestion ran into a barrage of criticism; **~frist** *f* waiting period *(auch Jur)*; *(Sport)* (period of) suspension; **~gebiet** *nt* no-go area, prohibited area *or* zone; **~getriebe** *nt* locking mechanism; **~gut** *nt* bulky freight *or* goods *pl*; **~holz** *nt* plywood.

sperrig *adj* bulky; *(unhandlich)* unwieldy.

Sperr-: ~kette *f* chain; *(an Haustür)* safety chain; **~klausel** *f* exclusion clause; **~klinke** *f* pawl; **~konto** *nt* blocked account; **~kreis** *m (Rad)* wave trap; **~mauer** *f* wall; **~minorität** *f (Fin)* blocking minority; **~müll** *m* bulky refuse; **~müllabfuhr** *f* removal of bulky refuse; **~rad** *nt siehe* **Sperrad; ~schrift** *m (Typ)* spaced type; **~sitz** *m (im Kino)* back seats *pl*; *(im Zirkus)* front seats *pl*; *(old: im Theater)* stalls *pl*, orchestra; **~stück** *m (Fin)* blocked security; **~stunde** *f* closing time.

Sperrung *f* **(a)** *siehe vt* closing; closing off; locking; blocking; stopping; banning, barring; banning; stopping, stoppage; cutting off, disconnection, disconnecting; spacing. **(b)** *siehe* **Sperre (b).**

Sperr-: ~vermerk *m (in Dokumenten)* restricted notice; **~zoll** *m* prohibitive tariff; **~zone** *f siehe* **~gebiet.**

Spesen *pl (auch Fin)* expenses *pl* ◆ **auf ~ reisen/essen** to travel/eat on expenses; **außer ~ nichts gewesen** nothing doing, no joy *(Brit inf)*.

Spesen-: s~frei *adj* free of charge; **~konto** *nt* expense account; **~ritter** *m (inf)* expense-account type *(inf)*.

Spezerei *f usu pl (old)* spice; *(Delikatesse)* exotic delicacy.

Spezi *m* **-s, -s (a)** *(S Ger inf)* pal *(inf)*, mate *(inf)*. **(b)** *(Getränk)* Coca Cola ® and lemonade.

Spezial-: ~arzt *m* specialist; **~ausbildung** *f* specialized training; **~ausführung** *f* special model *or* version; **ein Modell in ~ausführung** a special version; **~disziplin** *f* special discipline; **~effekt** *m* special effect; **~fach** *nt* special subject; **~fahrzeug** *nt* special-purpose vehicle; **~fall** *m* special case; **~gebiet** *nt* special field *or* topic; **~geschäft** *nt* specialist shop; **ein ~geschäft für Sportkleidung** a sportswear specialist's.

spezialisieren* [1] *vr* **sich (auf etw** *acc)* **~** to specialize (in sth).
[2] *vt (old: spezifizieren)* to specify, to itemize.

Spezialisierung *f* specialization.

Spezialist(in *f)* *m* specialist *(für* in).

Spezialistentum *nt* specialization.

Spezialität *f* **(a)** speciality *(esp Brit)*, specialty *(esp US)*. **(b) ~en** *pl (Cook)* specialities *pl*.

Spezialitätenrestaurant *nt* speciality restaurant.

Spezial-: ~slalom *m* special slalom; **~vollmacht** *f* special authorization.

speziell [1] *adj* special; *(außerordentlich, individualisierend auch)* especial ◆ **auf Ihr (ganz) S~es!** your good health!; **er ist mein ganz ~er Freund** he's a very special friend of mine *(auch iro)*.
[2] *adv* (e)specially.

Spezies ['ʃpe:tsiɛs, 'sp-] *f* **-, -** *(Biol)* species *sing* ◆ **die ~ Mensch** the human species.

Spezifikation *f* specification; *(Aufgliederung)* classification.

spezifisch *adj* specific.

spezifizieren* *vt* to specify; *(einzeln aufführen auch)* to itemize.

Spezifizierung *f* specification, specifying; *(Einzelaufführung auch)* itemization, itemizing.

Sphäre *f* **-, -n** *(lit, fig)* sphere; *siehe* **schweben.**

Sphären-: ~harmonie *f* harmony of the spheres; **~musik** *f* music of the spheres.

sphärisch *adj* spherical; *Klänge, Musik* celestial.

Sphinx *f* **-, -e** sphinx.

Spick-: ~aal *m* smoked eel; **~braten** *m* larded roast.

spicken [1] *vt (Cook) Braten* to lard; *(inf: bestechen)* to bribe, to square *(inf)* ◆ **eine (gut) gespickte Brieftasche** a well-lined wallet; **mit Fehlern/Zitaten gespickt** peppered with mistakes/quotations, larded with quotations.
[2] *vi (Sch sl)* to copy, to crib *(inf) (bei* off, from).

Spickzettel *m* crib.

spie *pret of* **speien.**

Spiegel *m* **-s, - (a)** mirror, glass *(old)*; *(Med)* speculum; *(fig)* mirror ◆ **in den ~ schauen** *or* **sehen** to look in the mirror; **glatt wie ein ~** like glass; **im ~ der Öffentlichkeit** *or* **der öffentlichen Meinung** as seen by the public, as reflected in public opinion; **jdm den ~ vorhalten** *(fig)* to hold up a mirror to sb.
(b) *(Wasser~, Alkohol~, Zucker~)* level.
(c) *(Aufschlag)* lapel; *(Mil: Kragen~)* tab.
(d) *(Archit: von Decke, Tür)* panel.

(e) (*Hunt*) (*bei Rotwild*) escutcheon; (*bei Vögeln*) speculum.
(f) (*Liter: Sammlung von Regeln, Gesetzen etc*) code.
(g) (*Typ*) type area.

Spiegel-: ~bild *nt* (*lit, fig*) reflection; (*seitenverkehrtes Bild*) mirror image; **die Schrift im ~bild** the mirror image of the writing; **s~bildlich** *adj Zeichnung etc* mirror image; **s~bildlich schreiben** to do mirror writing; **s~blank** *adj* glossy, shining, bright as a mirror; **sie hat den Herd s~blank geputzt** she polished the cooker until it shone like a mirror.

Spiegel|ei *nt* fried egg.

Spiegel-: ~fechterei *f* (*fig*) (*Scheingefecht*) shadow-boxing; (*Heuchelei, Vortäuschung*) sham, bluff; **≈fernrohr** *nt* reflector (telescope); **≈folie** *f* mirror foil; **s≈frei** *adj Brille, Bildschirm etc* non-reflecting; **≈glas** *nt* mirror glass; **s≈glatt** *adj* like glass, glassy, as smooth as glass; **s≈gleich** *adj* symmetrical; **≈gleichheit** *f* symmetry; **≈heck** *nt* (*Naut*) square stern; **≈karpfen** *m* mirror carp.

spiegeln [1] *vi* (*reflektieren*) to reflect (the light); (*glitzern*) to gleam, to shine.
[2] *vt* to reflect, to mirror.
[3] *vr* to be mirrored *or* reflected; (*sich betrachten*) to look at one's reflection.

Spiegel-: ~reflexkamera *f* reflex camera; **~schrift** *f* mirror writing; **etw in ~schrift schreiben** to write sth backwards.

Spiegelung *f* reflection; (*Luft~*) mirage.

Spieker *m* **-s, -** **(a)** (*N Ger: Nagel*) nail; (*Naut*) spike. **(b)** (*N Ger: Speicher*) storehouse.

Spiel *nt* **-(e)s, -e** **(a)** (*Unterhaltungs~, Glücks~, Sport, Tennis*) game; (*Wettkampf~ auch*) match; (*Theat: Stück*) play; (*fig: eine Leichtigkeit*) child's play *no art* ◆ **ein ~ spielen** (*lit, fig*) to play a game; **im ~ sein** (*lit*) to be in the game; (*fig*) to be involved *or* at work; **die Kräfte, die hier mit im ~ waren** the forces which were at play here; **das Leben ist kein ~** life is not a game; **das ~ verloren geben** to give the game up for lost; (*fig*) to throw in the towel; **machen Sie ihr ~!** place your bets!, faites vos jeux; **jdn ins ~ schicken** (*Sport*) to send sb on; **jdn aus dem ~ nehmen** (*Sport*) to take sb off.
(b) (*das Spielen, Spielweise*) play(ing); (*Mus, Theat*) playing; (*Sport*) play; (*bei Glücksspielen*) gambling ◆ **das ~ ist für die Entwicklung des Kindes wichtig** play(ing) is important for children's development; **stör das Kind nicht beim ~** don't disturb the child while he's playing *or* at play; **stummes ~** miming.
(c) (*Bewegung, Zusammenspiel*) play ◆ **~ der Hände** hand movements; **das (freie) ~ der Kräfte** the (free) (inter)play of forces; **~ der Lichter** play of lights; **das ~ der Wellen** the play of the waves.
(d) ein ~ des Schicksals *or* **Zufalls** a whim of fate.
(e) (*Spielzubehör*) game; (*Karten*) deck, pack; (*Satz*) set ◆ **führen Sie auch ~e?** do you have games?; **das Monopoly-~ ist nicht mehr vollständig** the Monopoly set has something missing.
(f) (*von Stricknadeln*) set.
(g) (*Tech*) (free) play; (*~raum*) clearance.
(h) (*Hunt*) tail.
(i) (*fig*) **das ist ein ~ mit dem Feuer** that's playing with fire; **leichtes ~ (mit** *or* **bei jdm) haben** to have an easy job of it (with sb); **bei den einfachen Bauern hatten die Betrüger leichtes ~** the simple peasants were easy game for the swindlers; **das ~ ist aus** the game's up; **die Hand** *or* **Finger im ~ haben** to be involved, to have a hand in affairs; **jdn/etw aus dem ~ lassen** to leave *or* keep sb/sth out of it; **etw mit ins ~ bringen** to bring in *or* up sth; **etw aufs ~ setzen** to put sth at stake *or* on the line (*inf*), to risk sth; **auf dem ~(e) stehen** to be at stake; **sein ~ mit jdm treiben** to play games with sb.

Spiel-: ~alter *nt* playing stage; **~anzug** *m* playsuit, rompers *pl*; **~art** *f* variety; **~automat** *m* gambling *or* gaming machine; (*zum Geldgewinnen*) fruit machine, one-armed bandit (*hum inf*); **~bahn** *f* (*Golf*) fairway; **~ball** *m* (*Volleyball*) match-ball, game-ball (*US*); (*Tennis*) game point; (*Billard*) cue ball; (*fig*) plaything; **ein ~ball der Wellen sein** (*geh*) to be at the mercy of *or* be tossed about by the waves; **~bank** *f* casino; **s~bar** *adj* playable; **~beginn** *m* start of play; **gleich nach ~beginn** just after the start of play; **~bein** *nt* free leg; **s~bereit** *adj* ready to play; **~brett** *nt* board; (*Basketball*) backboard.

Spielchen *nt* (*inf*) little game.

Spieldose *f* musical box (*Brit*), music box (*US*).

spielen [1] *vt* to play ◆ **jdm einen Streich ~** to play a trick on sb; **Klavier/Flöte ~** to play the piano/the flute; **was wird heute im Theater/Kino gespielt?** what's on at the theatre/cinema today?, what's playing at the theatre/what's showing at the cinema today?; **sie ~ einen Film von ...** they're showing a film by ...; **das Stück war sehr gut gespielt** the play was very well acted *or* performed *or* done; **wir haben die Mutter Courage in Stuttgart gespielt** we played Mother Courage in Stuttgart; **den Unschuldigen ~** to play the innocent; **den Beleidigten ~** to act all offended; **sie spielt die große Dame** she's playing *or* acting the grand lady; **am Sonntag mußte ich mal wieder Klempner ~** on Sunday I had to do my plumber's act again; **was wird hier gespielt?** (*inf*) what's going on here?; *siehe* **Herr, Schicksal**.
[2] *vi* to play; (*Theat*) (*Schauspieler*) to act, to play; (*Stück*) to be on, to play; (*Film*) to be on, to show; (*beim Glücksspiel*) to gamble ◆ **die Mannschaft hat gut/schlecht** *etc* **gespielt** the team had a good/bad *etc* game, the team played well/badly *etc*; **bei ihm spielt das Radio den ganzen Tag** he has the radio on all day; **seine Beziehungen ~ lassen** to bring one's connections to bear *or* into play; **seine Muskeln ~ lassen** to ripple one's muscles; **na ja, wie das Leben so spielt** life's funny like that; **in der Hauptrolle spielt X** X is playing the lead; **das Stück spielt im 18. Jahrhundert/in Italien** the play is set in the 18th century/in Italy; **nervös spielte er mit dem Bleistift** he played *or* toyed nervously with the pencil; **mit dem Gedanken ~, etw zu tun** to toy *or* play with the idea of doing sth; **mit jdm/jds Liebe/Gefühlen ~** to play (around) with sb/sb's affections/feelings; **ein Lächeln spielte um ihre Lippen** a smile played about her lips; **ihr Haar spielt ins Rötliche** her hair has a reddish tinge.
[3] *vr* **sich müde ~** to tire oneself out playing; **sich warm ~** to warm up; **sich in den Vordergrund ~** to push oneself into the foreground; **auf nassem Boden spielt es sich schlecht** (*Sport*) wet ground isn't very good to play on.

spielend [1] *adj* playing.
[2] *adv* easily ◆ **das ist ~ leicht** that's very easy.

Spiel|ende *nt* end of play ◆ **kurz vor ~** just before the end of play.

Spieleport *m* (*Comput*) games port.

Spieler(in *f*) *m* **-s, -** player; (*Theat auch*) actor/actress; (*Glücks~*) gambler.

Spielerei *f* **(a)** *no pl* (*das Spielen*) playing; (*beim Glücksspiel*) gambling; (*das Herumspielen*) playing *or* fooling *or* fiddling (*inf*) about *or* around; (*Kinderspiel*) child's play *no art*, doddle (*inf*) ◆ **das ist nur ~** I am/he is *etc* just playing *or* fooling about; **hör mit der ~ am Fernseher auf!** stop playing *or* fooling *or* fiddling about *or* around with the TV!
(b) (*Gegenstand*) frivolity; (*Gerät auch*) gadget.

spielerisch [1] *adj* **(a)** (*verspielt*) *Geste, Katze etc* playful.
(b) mit ~er Leichtigkeit with the greatest of ease, with consummate ease.
(c) (*Sport*) playing; (*Theat*) acting ◆ **~es Können** playing/acting ability; **die ~e Leistung** the playing/acting.
[2] *adv* **(a)** (*verspielt*) playfully.
(b) (*mit Leichtigkeit*) with the greatest of ease, with consummate ease.
(c) (*Sport*) in playing terms; (*Theat*) in acting terms.

Spieler-: ~natur *f* gambler; **~wechsel** *m* substitution.

Spiel-: ~feld *nt* field, pitch (*Brit*); (*Tennis, Squash, Basketball*) court; **~figur** *f* piece; **~film** *m* feature film; **~fläche** *f* playing area; (*bei Gesellschaftsspielen*) playing surface; **~folge** *f* (*Sport*) order of play; (*Theat*) programme; **s~frei** *adj* (*Theat, Sport*) **s~freier Tag** rest-day; **die s~freie Zeit** the close season; **der Sonntag ist s~frei** (*Theat*) there is no performance on Sundays; (*Sport*) there is no game on Sundays; **s~freudig** *adj* keen, enthusiastic; **~führer** *m* (team) captain; **~gefährte** *m* playmate, playfellow; **~geld** *nt* **(a)** (*Einsatz*) stake; **(b)** (*unechtes Geld*) play money, toy money; **~genosse** *m siehe* **~gefährte**; **~geschehen** *nt* (*Sport*) play, action; **das gesamte ~geschehen** all of the play *or* action; **~gestatter** *m* (*Sport*) key player; **~halle** *f* amusement arcade; **~hölle** *f* gambling den; **~kamerad** *m siehe* **~gefährte**; **~karte** *f* playing card; **~kasino** *nt* (gambling) casino; **~klasse** *f* division; **~leidenschaft** *f* passion for gambling, gambling mania; **~leiter** *m* **(a)** *siehe* **Regisseur(in)**; **(b)** (*Sport*) organizer; **(c)** (*Conférencier*) master of ceremonies, emcee (*inf*); **~macher** *m* key player; **~mann** *m, pl* **-leute** (*Hist*) minstrel; (*Mitglied eines ~mannszuges*) bandsman; **~mannszug** *m* (brass) band; **~marke** *f* chip, counter; **~minute** *f* minute (of play); **~plan** *m* (*Theat, Film*) programme; **ein Stück vom ~plan absetzen** to drop a play (from the programme); **~platz** *m* (*für Kinder*) playground; (*Sport*) playing-field; **~raum** *m* room to move; (*fig*) scope; (*zeitlich*) time; (*bei Planung etc*) leeway; (*Tech*) clearance, (free) play; **jedes Kind braucht einen gewissen ~raum, um sich frei entwickeln zu können** all children need a certain amount of scope to be able to develop freely; **~rausch** *m* gambling fever; **~regel** *f* (*lit, fig*) rule of the game; **sich an die ~regeln halten, die ~regeln beachten** (*lit, fig*) to stick to the rules (of the game), to play the game; **gegen die ~regeln verstoßen** (*lit, fig*) to break the rules, not to play the game; **~runde** *f* round; **~saal** *m* gaming hall; **~sachen** *pl* toys *pl*, playthings *pl*; **~saison** *f* (*Theat, Sport*) season; **~schuld** *f* gambling debt; **~stand** *m* score; **bei einem ~stand von ...** with the score (standing) at ...; **~sucht** *f* compulsive gambling; **~süchtige(r)** *mf* compulsive gambler; **~tag** *m* day; **~teufel** *m* gambling urge *or* bug (*inf*); **vom ~teufel besessen sein** (*inf*) to have the gambling bug (*inf*); **~tisch** *m* games table; (*beim Glücksspiel*) gaming *or* gambling table; **~trieb** *m* play instinct; **~uhr** *f* musical box (*Brit*), music box (*US*); **~verbot** *nt* (*Sport*) ban; **~verbot haben** to be banned; **~verderber(in** *f*) *m* **-s, -** spoilsport; **~verlängerung** *f* extra time (*Brit*), overtime (*US*); (*wegen Verletzung auch*) injury time (*Brit*); **es gab eine ~verlängerung (von 30 Minuten)** (30 minutes') extra time *etc* was played; **~verlauf** *m* action, play; **~waren** *pl* toys *pl*; **~warengeschäft** *nt*, **~warenhandlung** *f* toy shop (*Brit*) *or* store (*esp US*); **~weise** *f* way of playing; **offensive/defensive/unfaire ~weise** attacking/defensive/unfair play; **~werk** *nt* musical mechanism; **~wiese** *f* playing field; (*fig*) playground; **~zeit** *f* **(a)** (*Saison*) season; **(b)** (*~dauer*) playing time; **die normale ~zeit** (*Sport*) normal time; **nach dreimonatiger ~zeit wurde das Stück abgesetzt** the play was taken off after a three-month run.

Spielzeug *nt* toy; toys *pl*, playthings *pl*; (*fig auch*) plaything ◆ **er hat viel ~** he has a lot of toys.

Spielzeug- *in cpds* toy; **~eisenbahn** *f* toy train set.

Spielzimmer *nt* playroom.

Spiere *f* **-, -n**, **Spier** *f* **-, -en** (*Naut*) spar, boom.

Spierling *m* (*Eberesche*) service tree.

Spieß *m* **-es, -e** **(a)** (*Stich- und Wurfwaffe*) spear; (*Brat~*) spit; (*kleiner*) skewer ◆ **am ~ gebraten** roasted on the spit, spit-roast(ed); **Schaschlik am ~** skewered kebab, kebab on the spit; **wie am ~(e) schreien** (*inf*), **schreien als ob man am ~ steckt** (*inf*) to squeal like a stuck pig; **den ~ umkehren** *or* **umdrehen** (*fig*) to turn the tables; *siehe* **brüllen**.
(b) (*Mil sl*) sarge (*sl*).
(c) (*Hunt*) spike.
(d) (*Typ*) work-up (*US*), spacing mark.

Spieß-: ~bock *m* (*Hunt*) brocket, spike buck; **~braten** *m* joint roasted on a spit.

Spießbürger *m* (petit) bourgeois ♦ **ihre Eltern sind richtige ~** her parents are typically middle-class.

spießbürgerlich *adj* middle-class, (petit) bourgeois.

Spießbürgertum *nt* (petit-)bourgeois conformism, middle-class values *pl*.

spießen *vt* **etw auf etw** (*acc*) **~** (*auf Pfahl etc*) to impale sth on sth; (*auf Gabel etc*) to skewer sth on sth; (*auf größeren Bratspieß*) to spit sth on sth; (*auf Nadel*) to pin sth on sth.

Spießer *m* **-s, -** (a) (*inf*) *siehe* **Spießbürger**. (b) (*Hunt*) *siehe* **Spießbock**.

Spießgeselle *m* (*old*) companion; (*hum: Komplize*) crony (*inf*).

spießig *adj* (*inf*) *siehe* **spießbürgerlich**.

Spießrute *f* switch ♦ **~n laufen** (*fig*) to run the gauntlet.

Spießrutenlauf *m* (*fig*) running the gauntlet ♦ **für ihn wird jeder Gang durch die Stadt zum ~** every time he walks through town it's like running the gauntlet.

Spikes [ʃpaiks, sp-] *pl* (*Sportschuhe, Stifte*) spikes *pl*; (*Autoreifen*) studded tyres *pl*; (*Stifte an Reifen*) studs *pl*.

Spill *nt* **-(e)s, -e** (*Naut*) capstan.

spillerig *adj* (*N Ger*) spindly.

spinal *adj* (*Med*) spinal ♦ **~e Kinderlähmung** poliomyelitis.

Spinat *m* **-(e)s**, *no pl* spinach.

Spinatwachtel *f* (*pej inf*) old cow (*inf*) *or* baggage (*inf*).

Spind *m or nt* **-(e)s, -e** (*Mil, Sport*) locker; (*old: Vorratskammer*) cupboard.

Spindel *f* **-, -n** spindle; (*Treppen~*) newel.

spindeldürr *adj* (*pej*) spindly, thin as a rake ♦ **~e Beine** spindle-shanks (*inf*), spindly legs.

spindelförmig *adj* spindle-shaped.

Spinett *nt* **-s, -e** (*Mus*) spinet.

Spinnaker [ˈʃpɪnakɐ] *m* **-s, -** (*Naut*) spinnaker.

Spinne *f* **-, -n** spider; (*Wäsche~*) rotary clothes line.

spinnefeind *adj pred* (*inf*) **sich** *or* **einander** (*dat*) **~ sein** to be deadly enemies.

spinnen *pret* **spann**, *ptp* **gesponnen** [1] *vt* to spin; (*old liter: ersinnen*) *Verrat, Ränke* to plot; *Lügen* to concoct, to invent; *Geschichte* to spin ♦ **ein Netz von Lügen** *or* **ein Lügengewebe ~** to weave a web of lies; **das ist alles gesponnen** (*inf*) it's all fairy-tales; *siehe* **Garn, Seemannsgarn**.

[2] *vi* (a) (*lit*) to spin.

(b) (*inf*) (*leicht verrückt sein*) to be crazy *or* nutty (*inf*) *or* screwy (*inf*); (*Unsinn reden*) to talk rubbish; (*Lügengeschichten erzählen*) to make it up, to tell tall stories ♦ **stimmt das, oder spinnst du?** is that true, or are you having me on? (*inf*) *or* putting me on? (*US inf*); **sag mal, spinn' ich, oder ...?** am I imagining things or ...?; **ich denk' ich spinn'** I don't believe it; **ich spinn' doch nicht** no way (*inf*); **spinn doch nicht!** come off it! (*inf*); **du spinnst wohl!, spinnst du?** you must be crazy!, are you crazy!; **ich dein Auto waschen?, du spinnst wohl!** me clean your car!, you've got to be joking *or* kidding (*inf*).

Spinnen-: **~faden** *m* spider's thread; **~gewebe** *nt siehe* **Spinngewebe**; **~netz** *nt* cobweb, spider's web.

Spinner(in *f*) *m* **-s, -** (a) spinner. (b) (*inf*) nutcase (*inf*), screwball (*esp US inf*) ♦ **du ~, das stimmt doch nicht!** are you crazy?, that's not true at all! (c) (*Zool*) silkworm moth.

Spinnerei *f* (a) (*das Spinnen*) spinning. (b) (*Spinnwerkstatt*) spinning mill. (c) (*inf*) crazy behaviour *no pl*; crazy thing; (*Unsinn*) rubbish, garbage (*inf*) ♦ **das ist doch eine ~, so was zu machen** it's crazy to do that; **deine ~en glaubt dir doch kein Mensch!** nobody's going to believe all that rubbish.

spinnert *adj* (*inf*) crazy (*inf*).

Spinn-: **~faser** *f* spinning fibre; **~gewebe** *nt* cobweb, spider's web; **~maschine** *f* spinning-machine; **~rad** *nt* spinning-wheel; **~rocken** *m* **-s, -** distaff; **~stube** *f* spinning-room; **~web** *nt or m* **-(e)s, -e** (*Aus, S Ger*), **~webe** *f* **-, -n** cobweb, spider's web.

spinös *adj* crackpot *attr* (*inf*).

spintisieren* *vi* (*inf*) to ruminate, to muse.

Spion *m* **-s, -e** spy; (*inf: Guckloch*) spy-hole, peephole; (*Fensterspiegel*) busy-body, window mirror.

Spionage [ʃpioˈnaːʒə] *f* **-**, *no pl* spying, espionage ♦ **~ treiben** to spy, to carry on espionage; **unter dem Verdacht der ~ für ...** on suspicion of spying for ...

Spionage-: **~abwehr** *f* counter-intelligence *or* counter-espionage (service); **~dienst** *m* (*inf*) secret service; **~netz** *nt* spy network; **~ring** *m* spy-ring; **~satellit** *m* spy satellite.

spionieren* *vi* to spy; (*fig inf: nachforschen*) to snoop *or* poke about (*inf*).

Spionin *f* spy.

Spirale *f* **-, -n** spiral; (*geometrisch, Sci auch*) helix; (*Med*) coil.

Spiral-: **~feder** *f* coil spring; **s~förmig** *adj* spiral.

spiralig *adj* (*rare*) spiral, helical.

Spiralnebel *m* (*Astron*) spiral nebula.

Spirans [ˈʃpiːrans, ˈsp-] *f* **-**, **Spiranten, Spirant** [ʃpiˈrant, sp-] *m* (*Ling*) fricative, spirant.

Spiritismus [ʃpiriˈtɪsmʊs, sp-] *m* spiritualism, spiritism.

Spiritist(in *f*) [ʃpiriˈtɪst(ɪn), sp-] *m* spiritualist.

spiritistisch [ʃpiriˈtɪstɪʃ, sp-] *adj* spiritualist.

Spiritual [ˈspɪrɪtjʊəl] *m or nt* **-s, -s** (negro) spiritual.

Spiritualismus [ʃpiritua'lɪsmʊs, sp-] *m* spiritualism.

spiritualistisch [ʃpiritua'lɪstɪʃ, sp-] *adj* spiritualist.

spirituell [ʃpiriˈtuel, sp-] *adj* spiritual.

Spirituosen [ʃpiriˈtuoːzn, sp-] *pl* spirits *pl*.

Spiritus *m* **-**, *no pl* (a) [ʃp-] (*Alkohol*) spirit ♦ **mit ~ kochen** to cook with a spirit stove; **etw in ~ legen** to put sth in alcohol. (b) [sp-] (*Ling*) spiritus.

Spiritus-: **~kocher** *m* spirit stove; **~lampe** *f* spirit lamp.

Spital *nt* **-s, ¨er** (*old, Aus, Sw: Krankenhaus*) hospital, spital (*obs*); (*rare: Altersheim*) old people's home.

spitz *adj* (a) (*mit einer Spitze*) pointed; (*nicht stumpf*) *Bleistift, Nadel etc* sharp; (*Math*) *Winkel* acute ♦ **die Feder dieses Füllhalters ist nicht ~ genug** the nib on this fountain pen is too broad; **~e Schuhen** pointed shoes, winkle-pickers (*hum inf*); **~e Klammern** angle brackets; **~ zulaufen** *or* **zugehen** to taper (off), to run to a point; **etw mit ~en Fingern anfassen** (*inf*) to pick sth up gingerly; **über einen ~en Stein stolpern** *to pronounce "sp" and "st" as in English*.

(b) (*gehässig*) *Bemerkung* pointed, barbed; *Zunge* sharp.

(c) (*kränklich*) *Aussehen, Gesicht* pinched, haggard, peaky.

(d) (*sl: lüstern*) randy (*Brit inf*), horny (*inf*) ♦ **~ wie Nachbars Lumpi** as randy *or* horny as (*Frau*) a bitch in heat *or* (*Mann*) an old goat (*all inf*); **jdn ~ machen** to turn sb on (*sl*).

Spitz *m* **-es, -e** (*Hunderasse*) spitz, pomeranian.

Spitz-: **~bart** *m* goatee; **s~bärtig** *adj* with a goatee, goateed; **~bauch** *m* potbelly (*inf*); **s~bekommen*** *vt sep irreg* (*inf*) **etw s~bekommen** to cotton on to sth (*inf*), to get wise to sth (*inf*); **s~bekommen, daß ...** to cotton on *or* get wise to the fact that ... (*inf*); **~bogen** *m* pointed arch, ogive (*spec*); **~bub(e)** *m* (*old*) villain, rogue; (*dial inf: Schlingel*) scamp (*inf*), scallywag (*inf*); **~bubengesicht** *nt* (*old*) villainous *or* roguish face; **~bubenstreich** *m* (*dated*) nasty *or* knavish (*old*) trick; **~bübin** *f siehe* **~bub(e)**; **s~bübisch** *adj* roguish, mischievous.

Spitze *f* **-, -n** (a) (*Schwert~, Nadel~, Pfeil~, Bleistift~, Kinn~*) point; (*Schuh~*) pointed toe; (*Finger~, Nasen~, Bart~, Spargel~*) tip; (*Zigarren~, Haar~*) end; (*Berg~, Fels~*) peak, top; (*Baum~, Turm~, Giebel~*) top; (*Pyramiden~*) top, apex (*form*); (*Dreiecks~*) top, vertex (*form*) ♦ **auf der ~ stehen** to be upside-down; **etw auf die ~ treiben** to carry sth too far *or* to extremes; **einer Sache** (*dat*) **die ~ abbrechen/nehmen** (*fig*) to take the sting out of sth.

(b) (*fig: Höchstwert*) peak; (*inf: Höchstgeschwindigkeit*) top speed ♦ **dieser Sportwagen fährt 200 ~** (*inf*) this sports car has a top speed of 200.

(c) (*Führung*) head; (*vorderes Ende*) front; (*esp Mil: von Kolonne etc*) head; (*Tabellen~*) top ♦ **die ~n der Gesellschaft** the leading lights of society; **an der ~ stehen** to be at the head; (*auf Tabelle*) to be (at the) top (of the table); **an der ~ liegen** (*Sport, fig*) to be in front *or* in the lead; **Ruritanien liegt im Lebensstandard an der ~** Ruritania has the highest standard of living; **die ~ halten** (*Sport, fig*) to keep the lead; **sich an die ~ setzen** to put oneself at the head; (*in Wettbewerb etc, Sport*) to go into *or* take the lead; (*auf Tabelle*) to go to the top (of the table); (*im Pferderennen*) to take up the running; **er wurde an die ~ des Unternehmens gestellt** he was put at the top *or* head of the company.

(d) (*Zigaretten-, Zigarrenhalter*) (cigarette/cigar) holder.

(e) (*fig: Stichelei*) dig ♦ **das ist eine ~ gegen Sie** that's a dig at you, that's directed at you; **die ~ zurückgeben** to give tit for tat.

(f) (*Comm: Überschuß*) surplus.

(g) (*Gewebe*) lace ♦ **Höschen mit ~n** panties with lace borders.

(h) (*inf: prima*) great (*inf*).

Spitzel *m* **-s, -** (*Informant*) informer; (*Spion*) spy; (*Schnüffler*) snooper; (*Polizei~*) police informer, nark (*Brit sl*).

Spitzeldienste *pl* informing *no pl* ♦ **für jdn ~ leisten** to act as an informer for sb.

spitzeln *vi* to spy; (*Spitzeldienste leisten*) to act as an informer.

spitzen [1] *vt* (*spitz machen*) *Bleistift* to sharpen; *Lippen, Mund* to purse; (*zum Küssen*) to pucker; *Ohren* (*lit, fig*) to prick up ♦ **spitzt doch die Ohren, dann versteht ihr auch, was ich sage!** open your ears and then you'll understand what I'm saying!

[2] *vir* (*inf*) **(sich) auf etw** (*acc*) **~** to look forward to sth.

[3] *vi* (*dial inf*) (*aufpassen*) to keep a look-out, to keep one's eyes skinned (*inf*); (*heimlich spähen*) to peek.

Spitzen- *in cpds* top; (*aus Spitze*) lace; **~belastung** *f* peak (load); **die Zeit der ~belastung** the peak period; **~besatz** *m* lace trimming; **~bluse** *f* lace blouse; **~deckchen** *nt*, **~decke** *f* lace doily; **~erzeugnis** *nt* top(-quality) product; **~feld** *nt* (*Sport*) leaders *pl*, leading group; **im ~feld** amongst the leaders, in the leading group; **~funktionär** *m* top official; **~garnitur** *f* set of lace underwear; **~gehalt** *nt* top salary; **~geschwindigkeit** *f* top speed; **~gremien** *pl* leading *or* top committees *pl*; **~gruppe** *f* top group; (*Sport: ~feld*) leading group; **~höschen** *nt* lace panties *pl*; **~kandidat** *m* top candidate; **~klasse** *f* top class; **Sekt/ein Auto** *etc* **der ~klasse** top-class champagne/a top-class car *etc*; **~klasse!** (*inf*) great! (*inf*); **~könner** *m* ace, first-rate *or* top-class talent; **~kragen** *m* lace collar; **~leistung** *f* top performance; (*von Maschine, Auto*) peak performance; (*bei der Herstellung von Produkten, Energie*) peak output; (*fig: ausgezeichnete Leistung*) top-class *or* first-rate performance; (*Sport: Rekord*) record (performance); **~lohn** *m* top wage(s *pl*); **~modell** *nt* top model; **~organisation** *f siehe* **~verband**; **~position** *f* leading *or* top position; **~preise** *pl* (*Comm*) top prices; **~qualität** *f* top quality; **~reiter** *m* (*Sport*) leader; (*fig*) (*Kandidat*) front-runner; (*Ware*) top seller; (*Film, Stück etc*) hit; (*Schlager*) top of the pops, number one; **~sportler** *m* top(-class) sportsman; **~stellung** *f* leading position; **~steuersatz** *m* top rate of income tax; **~stickerei** *f* lace embroidery; **~tanz** *m* dance on points, toe-dance (*US*); **~technologie** *f* state-of-the-art technology; **~tuch** *nt* lace cloth, piece of lace; (*Taschentuch*) lace handkerchief; **~verband** *m* leading organization *or* group; **~verdiener** *m* top earner; **~verkehrszeit** *f* peak period; **~wein** *m* top-quality wine; **~wert** *m* peak; **~zeit** *f* (*Sport*) record time.

Spitzer *m* **-s, -** *(inf)* (pencil-)sharpener.

Spitz-: ~feile *f* taper file; **s~findig** *adj* over-subtle, over-precise; *(haarspalterisch auch)* hairsplitting, nit-picking *(inf)*; *Unterschied auch* over-nice; **~findigkeit** *f* over-subtlety, over-precision *no pl*; *(Haarspalterei auch)* hairsplitting *no pl*, nit-picking *no pl (inf)*; *(von Unterschied auch)* over-nicety; **zu behaupten, daß das Wort hier seine Bedeutung ändert, ist eine ~findigkeit** it's splitting hairs *or* it's over-subtle *or* it's nit-picking *(inf)* to claim that the word changes its meaning here; **s~giebelig** *adj* with pointed gables; **s~haben** *vt sep irreg (inf)* **etw s~haben** to have cottoned on to sth *(inf)*, to have got wise to sth *(inf)*; **s~haben, daß ...** to have cottoned on to *or* have got wise to the fact that ... *(inf)*; **~hacke** *f* pick-axe.

spitzig *adj (old, dial) siehe* **spitz.**

Spitz-: ~kehre *f (Rail)* switchback turn; *(Ski)* kick-turn; **~kopf** *m* pointed head; **s~kriegen** *vt sep (inf) siehe* **s~bekommen**; **~kühler** *m (Aut)* pointed *or* V-shaped radiator; *(hum inf)* pot-belly; **~marke** *f (Typ)* sidehead; **~maus** *f* shrew; **du bist eine richtige ~maus geworden** *(inf)* you've gone so thin; **~name** *m* nickname; **mit dem ~namen** nicknamed; **~wegerich** *m* ribwort; **s~wink(e)lig** *adj (Math) Dreieck* acute-angled; *Gasse* sharp-cornered, angular; **s~züngig** *adj* sharp-tongued.

Spleen [ʃpliːn] *m* **-s, -s** *(inf) (Angewohnheit)* strange *or* crazy habit, eccentricity, quirk (of behaviour); *(Idee)* crazy idea *or* notion; *(Fimmel)* obsession ◆ **die Psychologen haben doch alle irgendeinen ~!** these psychologists are all cranks!; **du hast ja einen ~!** you're round the bend *(inf)* *or* off your head *(inf)*.

spleenig [ˈʃpliːnɪç] *adj (inf)* crazy, nutty *(inf)*.

spleißen *pret* **spliß**, *ptp* **gesplissen** *vt* **(a)** *(dial, old) Holz* to split. **(b)** *(Naut) Taue, Leinen* to splice.

splendid [ʃplɛnˈdiːt, sp-] *adj (geh)* generous; *Behandlung etc auch* handsome.

Splint *m* **-(e)s, -e** cotter (pin), split pin.

Splintentreiber *m* pin punch.

⚠ **spliß** *pret of* **spleißen.**

Splitt *m* **-(e)s, -e** stone chippings *pl*; *(Streumittel)* grit.

Splitter *m* **-s, -** *(Holz~, Metall~, Knochen~)* splinter; *(Glas~ auch, Granat~)* fragment ◆ **der ~ in deines Bruders Auge** *(Bibl)* the mote that is in thy brother's eye *(Bibl)*.

Splitter-: ~bombe *f (Mil)* fragmentation bomb; **s~(faser)nackt** *adj (inf)* stark-naked, starkers *pred (Brit hum inf)*; **~fraktur** *f (Med)* splintered *or* comminuted *(spec)* fracture; **s~frei** *adj Glas* shatterproof; **~graben** *m (Mil)* slit trench; **~gruppe** *f (Pol)* splinter group.

splitt(e)rig *adj* splintering.

splittern *vi aux sein or haben (Holz, Glas)* to splinter.

splitternackt *adj siehe* **splitter(faser)nackt.**

Splitterpartei *f (Pol)* splinter party.

Splittingsystem [ˈʃplɪtɪŋ-, ˈsp-] *nt (Fin) tax system in which husband and wife each pay income tax on half the total of their combined incomes.*

splittrig *adj siehe* **splitt(e)rig.**

SPÖ [ɛspeːˈ|øː] *f* **-** *abbr of* **Sozialistische Partei Österreichs** Austrian Socialist Party.

Spoiler [ˈʃpɔylɐ] *m* **-s, -** spoiler.

Spökenkieker *m* **-s, -** *(N Ger)* psychic, clairvoyant, person who has second sight.

sponsern *vt* to sponsor.

Sponsor *m*, **Sponsorin** *f* sponsor.

spontan [ʃpɔnˈtaːn, sp-] *adj* spontaneous.

Spontaneität [ʃpɔntaneiˈtɛːt, sp-] *f* spontaneity.

Sponti *m* **-s, -s** *(Pol sl) member of alternative movement rejecting traditional procedures.*

sporadisch [ʃpoˈraːdɪʃ, sp-] *adj* sporadic.

Spore *f* **-, -n** *(Biol)* spore.

Sporen *pl of* **Sporn, Spore.**

sporenklirrend *adv (old)* with a clatter of spurs.

Sporentierchen *pl (Biol)* sporozoa *pl*.

Sporn *m* **-(e)s, Sporen** *usu pl (auch Zool, Bot)* spur; *(Naut auch)* ram; *(am Geschütz)* trail spade; *(Aviat: Gleitkufe)* tail-skid; *(Rad)* tail-wheel ◆ **einem Pferd die Sporen geben** to spur a horse, to give a horse a touch of the spurs; **sich** *(dat)* **die (ersten) Sporen verdienen** *(fig)* to win one's spurs.

spornen *vt (geh)* to spur; *(fig)* to spur on; *siehe* **gestiefelt.**

spornstreichs *adv (old)* post-haste, straight away.

Sport *m* **-(e)s,** *(rare)* **-e** sport; *(Zeitvertreib)* hobby, pastime ◆ **treiben Sie ~?** do you do any sport?; **er treibt viel ~** he goes in for *or* he does a lot of sport; **etw aus** *or* **zum ~ betreiben** to do sth as a hobby *or* for fun; **sich** *(dat)* **einen ~ aus etw machen** *(inf)* to get a kick out of sth *(inf)*.

Sport-: ~abzeichen *nt* sports certificate; **~angler** *m* angler; **~anzug** *m* sports clothes *pl*; *(Trainingsanzug)* track suit; **~art** *f* (kind of) sport; **~artikel** *m* **(a) ~artikel** *pl* sports equipment *with sing vb*; **ein ~artikel** a piece of sports equipment; **(b)** *(inf: ~bericht)* sports report; **~arzt** *m* sports physician; **s~begeistert** *adj* keen on sport, sports-mad *(inf)*; **ein ~begeisterter** a sports enthusiast *or* fan; **~beilage** *f* sports section *or* page(s *pl*); **~bericht** *m* sports report; **~berichterstattung** *f* sports reporting; **~ereignis** *nt* sporting event; **~fechten** *nt* fencing; **~feld** *nt* sports ground; **~fest** *nt* sports festival; **~flieger** *m* amateur pilot; **~flugzeug** *nt* sporting aircraft; **~freund** *m* sport(s)-fan; **~geist** *m* sportsmanship; **~gerät** *nt* piece of sports equipment; **~geräte** *pl* sports equipment; **~geschäft** *nt* sports shop *(Brit)* *or* store *(esp US)*; **~halle** *f* sports hall; **~hemd** *nt* casual *or* sports *or* sport *(US)* shirt; **~hochschule** *f* college of physical education.

sportiv *adj (Fashion)* sporty; *(dated)* athletic, sporty *(inf)*.

Sport-: ~jackett *nt* sports jacket *(Brit)*, sport coat *(US)*; **~karre** *f (N Ger)* pushchair *(Brit)*, (baby-)stroller *(US)*; **~kleidung** *f* sportswear; **~klub** *m* sports club; **~lehrer** *m* sports instructor; *(Sch)* PE *or* physical education teacher; *(für Sport im Freien)* games master *(Brit)* *or* teacher *(Brit)*, sport teacher.

Sportler *m* **-s, -** sportsman, athlete.

Sportlerherz *nt* athlete's heart.

Sportlerin *f* sportswoman, (woman) athlete.

sportlich *adj* **(a)** *(den Sport betreffend) Veranstaltung, Wettkampf* sporting ◆ **~ gesehen, ...** from a sporting point of view ...
(b) *Mensch* sporty; *(durchtrainiert)* athletic.
(c) *(fair)* sporting, sportsmanlike *no adv*.
(d) *Kleidung* casual; *(~-schick)* natty *(inf)*, snazzy *(inf)*, smart but casual; *(wie Sportkleidung aussehend)* sporty ◆ **~ gekleidet** casually dressed/wearing smart but casual clothes, smartly but casually dressed; **eine ~e Note** a sporty touch.
(e) *Auto* sporty.

Sportlichkeit *f* **(a)** *(von Menschen)* sportiness; *(Durchtrainiertheit)* athletic appearance ◆ **er bewies seine ~, indem er über den Zaun sprang** he proved how athletic he was by jumping over the fence. **(b)** *(Fairneß)* sportsmanship; *(von Verhalten auch, um Entscheidung)* sporting nature. **(c)** *(von Kleidung) siehe adj (d)* casualness; nattiness *(inf)*, snazziness *(inf)*, casual smartness; sportiness ◆ **die ~ der neuen Jacke macht sie so vielseitig verwendbar** the clean, simple cut of the new jacket makes it suitable for all occasions.

Sport-: ~mantel *m* casual coat; **s~mäßig** *adj siehe* **s~smäßig**; **~medizin** *f* sports medicine; **~meldung, ~nachricht** *f* **~nachrichten** *pl* sports news *with sing vb or* reports *pl*; **eine wichtige ~meldung** *or* **~nachricht** an important piece of sports news; **~platz** *m* sports field; *(in der Schule)* playing field(s *pl*); **~rad** *nt* sports cycle *or* bike *(inf)*; **~redakteur** *m* sports editor; **~reportage** *f* sports reporting; *(Bericht)* sports report; **die ~reportage über die Weltmeisterschaft** the coverage of the world championships; **~schlitten** *m* racing toboggan; **~schuh** *m* casual shoe.

Sports-: ~freund *m (fig inf)* buddy *(inf)*; **wenn der ~freund da ...** if this guy ... *(inf)*; **~kanone** *f (inf)* sporting ace *(inf)*; **~mann** *m, pl* **-männer** *or* **-leute** *(dated)* sportsman; *(inf: als Anrede)* sport *(esp Austral inf)*, mate *(inf)*; **s~mäßig** *adj* sporty; **sich s~mäßig betätigen** to do sport; **wie sieht's denn dort s~mäßig aus?** what sort of sporting facilities are there?

Sport-: ~unfall *m* sporting accident; **~veranstaltung** *f* sporting event; **~verein** *m* sports club; **~wagen** *m* sports *(Brit)* *or* sport *(US)* car; *(für Kind)* pushchair *(Brit)*, (baby-)stroller *(US)*; **~zeitung** *f* sports paper; **~zeug** *nt (inf)* sport(s) things *pl*.

Spot [spɔt] *m* **-s, -s** commercial, advertisement, ad *(inf)*.

Spot- [ˈspɔt-]: **~geschäft** *nt (Fin)* spot transaction; **~light** [-lait] *nt* **-s, -s** spotlight; **~markt** *m (Fin)* spot market.

Spott *m* **-(e)s,** *no pl* mockery; *(höhnisch auch)* ridicule, derision ◆ **~ und Hohn ernten** to earn scorn and derision, to be laughed out of court; **jdn dem ~ preisgeben** to hold sb up to ridicule; **dem ~ preisgegeben sein** to be held up to ridicule, to be made fun of; **seinen ~ mit jdm treiben** to make fun of sb; **Gegenstand des allgemeinen ~es** object of general ridicule, laughing-stock; *siehe* **Schaden.**

Spott-: ~bild *nt (fig)* travesty, mockery; **das ~bild eines Präsidenten** a travesty *etc* of a president; **s~billig** *adj* dirt-cheap *(inf)*; **das habe ich s~billig gekauft** I bought it for a song *(inf)* *or* for practically nothing, I bought it dirt-cheap *(inf)*; **~drossel** *f* mocking-bird; *(dated fig: Spötter)* tease, mocker.

Spöttelei *f (das Spotten)* mocking; *(ironische Bemerkung)* mocking remark.

spötteln *vi* to mock *(über jdn/etw* sb/sth), to poke gentle fun *(über jdn/etw* at sb/sth).

spotten *vi* **(a)** to mock, to poke fun; *(höhnen auch)* to ridicule, to be derisive ◆ **über jdn/etw ~** to mock sb/sth, to poke fun at sb/sth, to ridicule sb/sth; *(höhnisch auch)* to deride sb/sth, to ridicule sb/sth; **du hast leicht ~!, spotte nur!** it's easy for you to mock *or* laugh!, it's all very well for you to mock.
(b) *+gen (old, liter: hohnsprechen)* to mock; *(geh: mißachten) der Gefahr* to be contemptuous of, to scorn ◆ **das spottet jeder Beschreibung** that simply defies *or* beggars description.

Spötter(in *f)* *m* **-s, -** *(satirischer Mensch)* wit, satirist; *(jd, der über etw spottet)* mocker.

Spott-: ~figur *f* joke figure, ludicrous character; **eine ~figur sein** to be a figure of fun, to be an object of ridicule; **~geburt** *f (liter)* freak, monstrosity; **~gedicht** *nt* satirical poem, squib, lampoon; **~gelächter** *nt* mocking laughter.

spöttisch *adj* mocking; *(höhnisch auch)* ridiculing, derisive.

Spott-: ~lied *nt* satirical song; **~lust** *f* love of mockery, inclination to mock; **s~lustig** *adj* given to mockery, inclined to mock; **~name** *m* derisive nickname; **~preis** *m* ridiculously *or* ludicrously low price; **für einen ~preis** for a song *(inf)*; **~rede** *f* satirical *or* lampooning speech; **~reden führen** to make satirical *or* lampooning speeches; **~sucht** *f* compulsive mocking; **s~süchtig** *adj* who/which delights in (constant) mockery; **~vers** *m* satirical verse.

sprach *pret of* **sprechen.**

Sprach-: ~atlas *m* linguistic atlas; **~autonomie** *f (Pol)* linguistic autonomy; **~barriere** *f* language barrier; **~bau** *m* linguistic structure; **s~begabt** *adj* good at languages, linguistically talented *or* gifted; **~begabung** *f* talent for languages, linguistic talent; **~computer** *m* computer with speech synthesizer; *(Taschenübersetzer)* pocket electronic dictionary; **~denkmal** *nt* linguistic monument.

Sprache *f* -, **-n** language; (*das Sprechen*) speech; (*Sprechweise*) speech, way of speaking; (*Fähigkeit, zu sprechen*) power *or* faculty of speech ◆ **eine/die ~ sprechen** to (be able to) speak a language/the language *or* lingo (*inf*); **die ~ analysieren** to analyze language; **die ~ der Musik** the language of music; **in französischer** *etc* **~** in French *etc*; **die gleiche ~ sprechen** (*lit, fig*) to speak the same language; **das spricht eine klare** *or* **deutliche ~** (*fig*) that speaks for itself, it's obvious what that means; **er spricht jetzt eine ganz andere ~** (*fig*) he's changed his tune now; **heraus mit der ~!** (*inf*) come on, out with it!; **die ~ auf etw** (*acc*) **bringen** to bring the conversation round to sth; **zur ~ kommen** to be mentioned *or* brought up, to come up; **etw zur ~ bringen** to bring sth up, to mention sth; **die ~ verlieren** to lose the power of speech; **hast du die ~ verloren?** have you lost your tongue?, has the cat got your tongue? (*inf*); **die ~ wiederfinden** to be able to speak again; **es raubt** *or* **verschlägt einem die ~** it takes your breath away; **mir blieb die ~ weg** I was speechless.

Sprach-: **~eigentümlichkeit** *f* linguistic peculiarity *or* idiosyncrasy; **~einheit** *f* **(a)** (*Ling*) linguistic unit; **(b)** (*Einheitlichkeit*) linguistic unity.

Sprachen-: **~gewirr** *nt* babel of tongues (*usu hum*), mixture *or* welter of languages; **~schule** *f* language school; **~zentrum** *nt* (*Univ*) language centre.

Sprach-: **~erkennung** *f* (*Comput*) speech recognition; **~erwerb** *m* language acquisition; **~erziehung** *f* (*form*) language education; **~familie** *f* family of languages, language family; **~fehler** *m* speech defect *or* impediment; **~forscher** *m* linguist(ic researcher); (*Philologe*) philologist; **~forschung** *f* linguistic research; (*Philologie*) philology; **~führer** *m* phrasebook; **~gebiet** *nt* language area; **ein französisches** *etc* **~gebiet** a French-speaking *etc* area; **~gebrauch** *m* (linguistic) usage; **moderner deutscher ~gebrauch** modern German usage; **~gefühl** *nt* feeling for language; **~gelehrte(r)** *mf* linguistic scholar; **~gemeinschaft** *f* speech community; **~genie** *nt* linguistic genius; **~geschichte** *f* linguistic history; **die ~geschichte des Mongolischen** the history of the Mongolian language; **~gesetze** *pl* linguistic laws *pl*; **~gewalt** *f* power of expression, eloquence; **s~gewaltig** *adj* eloquent; **ein s~gewaltiger Redner** a powerful speaker; **s~gewandt** *adj* articulate, fluent; **~grenze** *f* linguistic *or* language boundary; **~gut** *nt* linguistic heritage; **ein Wörterbuch kann nicht das gesamte ~gut widerspiegeln** a dictionary cannot reflect the whole wealth of a language.

-sprachig *adj suf* -language; (*zwei~, mehr~*) -lingual.

Sprach-: **~insel** *f* linguistic enclave *or* island; **~kenntnisse** *pl* linguistic proficiency *sing*; **mit englischen ~kenntnissen** with a knowledge of English; **haben Sie irgendwelche ~kenntnisse?** do you know any languages?; **~kenntnisse erwünscht** (knowledge of) languages desirable; **~kompetenz** *f* linguistic competence; **~kritik** *f* linguistic criticism; **s~kundig** *adj* (*in mehreren Sprachen*) proficient in *or* good at (foreign) languages; (*in einer bestimmten Sprache*) linguistically proficient; **es ist schwer, sich in diesem Land zurechtzufinden, wenn man nicht s~kundig ist** it's very difficult to get along in this country if you don't know *or* are not familiar with the language; **~kurs(us)** *m* language course; **~labor** *nt* language laboratory *or* lab (*inf*); **~lähmung** *f* paralysis of the organs of speech; **~landschaft** *f* linguistic geography; **~lehre** *f* (*Grammatik, Grammatikbuch*) grammar; **~lehrer** *m* language teacher; **~lehrgang** *m* language course.

sprachlich *adj* linguistic; *Unterricht, Schwierigkeiten* language *attr*; *Fehler* grammatical ◆ **~ hatten die Einwanderer keine Schwierigkeiten** the immigrants had no language difficulties; **~ falsch/richtig** ungrammatical/grammatical, grammatically incorrect/correct; **eine intelligente Analyse, auch ~ gut** an intelligent analysis, well written too.

sprachlos *adj* (*ohne Sprache*) speechless; (*erstaunt*) speechless, dumbfounded ◆ **ich bin ~!** I'm speechless; **da ist man (einfach) ~** (*inf*) that's quite *or* really something (*inf*).

Sprachlosigkeit *f* speechlessness.

Sprach-: **~melodie** *f* intonation, speech melody; **⚠~mißbrauch** *m* misuse of language; **~pflege** *f* concern for the purity of language; **aktive ~pflege betreiben** to be actively concerned with the purity of a language; **~philosophie** *f* philosophy of language; **~psychologie** *f* psychology of language; **~raum** *m siehe* **~gebiet**; **~regel** *f* grammatical rule, rule of grammar; (*für Aussprache*) pronunciation rule; (*Ling*) linguistic rule, rule of language; **die einfachsten ~regeln des Lateinischen** the most elementary rules of Latin; **~regelung** *f* (*Bestimmung*) linguistic ruling; (*Formulierung*) wording, phrasing; **~regler** *m* linguistic arbiter; **~reinheit** *f* linguistic purity; **~rohr** *nt* (*Megaphon*) megaphone; (*fig*) mouthpiece; **sich zum ~rohr einer Sache/Gruppe machen** to become the spokesman for *or* mouthpiece (*usu pej*) of sth/a group; **~schatz** *m* (*geh*) vocabulary; **dem englischen ~schatz fehlt ein Wort für ...** the English language has no word for ...; **~schönheit** *f* linguistic beauty, beauty of language; **die ~schönheit Rimbauds** the beauty of Rimbaud's language; **~schöpfer** *m* linguistic innovator; **s~schöpferisch** *adj* innovatory, (linguistically) creative; **~schöpfung** *f* linguistic innovation; **~schule** *f siehe* **Sprachenschule**; **~silbe** *f* syllable; **~soziologie** *f* sociology of language; **~stamm** *m* (language) stock; **~stil** *m* style, way one uses language; **~störung** *f* speech disorder; **~struktur** *f* linguistic structure; **~studium** *nt* study of languages/a language, linguistic *or* language studies *pl*; **~talent** *nt* talent *or* gift for languages; **~theorie** *f* theory of language; **~übung** *f* linguistic *or* language exercise; **~unterricht** *m* language teaching *or* instruction; **der französische ~unterricht** French teaching, the teaching of French; **~unterricht/französischen ~unterricht erteilen** to give language lessons/French lessons; **~urlaub** *m* language-learning holiday; **~verein** *m* language society; **~verfall** *m* decay of language; **~vergleichung** *f* comparative analysis (of languages); **~vermögen** *nt* faculty of language; **~verwandtschaft** *f* linguistic relationship *or* kinship; **~verwirrung** *f* confused mixture of languages, confusion of tongues (*Bibl*); *siehe* **babylonisch**; **~wissenschaft** *f* linguistics *sing*; (*Philologie*) philology; **vergleichende ~wissenschaften** comparative linguistics/philology; **~wissenschaftler** *m* linguist; (*Philologe*) philologist; **s~wissenschaftlich** *adj* linguistic; **~zentrum** *nt* (*Univ*) language centre; **~zweig** *m* (language) branch.

sprang *pret of* **springen.**

Spray [ʃpreː, spreː] *m or nt* **-s, -s** spray.

Spraydose [ˈʃpreː-, ˈspreː-] *f* aerosol (can), spray.

sprayen [ˈʃpreːən, ˈsp-] *vti* to spray.

Sprayer(in *f*) [ˈʃpreːɐ, -ərɪn, ˈsp-] sprayer.

Sprech-: **~anlage** *f* intercom; **~blase** *f* balloon; **~bühne** *f* theatre, stage; **~chor** *m* chorus; (*fig*) chorus of voices; **im ~chor rufen** to shout in unison, to chorus; **~einheit** *f* (*Telec*) unit.

▼ **sprechen** *pret* **sprach**, *ptp* **gesprochen** 1 *vi* to speak (*über +acc, von* about, of); (*reden, sich unterhalten auch*) to talk (*über +acc, von* about) ◆ **viel ~** to talk a lot; **frei ~** to extemporize, to speak off the cuff (*inf*); **er spricht wenig** he doesn't say *or* talk very much; **sprich!** (*liter*) speak! (*liter*); **~ Sie!** (*form*) speak away!; **sprich doch endlich!** say something; **also sprach ...** thus spoke ..., thus spake ... (*liter, Bibl*); **im Traum** *or* **Schlaf ~** to talk in one's sleep; **gut/schön ~** to speak well/beautifully; **im Rundfunk/Fernsehen ~** to speak on the radio/on television; **es spricht/es ~ ...** the speaker is/the speakers are ...; **die Vernunft ~ lassen** to listen to reason, to let the voice of reason be heard; **sein Herz ~ lassen** to follow the dictates of one's heart; **schlecht** *or* **nicht gut auf jdn zu ~ sein** to be on bad terms with sb; **mit jdm ~** to speak *or* talk with *or* to sb; **mit sich selbst ~** to talk to oneself; **ich muß mit dir ~** I must talk *or* speak with you; **ich habe mit dir zu ~** I want to have a word *or* a few words with you; **wie sprichst du mit mir?** who do you think you're talking to?; **so spricht man nicht mit seinem Großvater** that's no way to talk *or* speak to your grandfather; **sie spricht nicht mit jedem** she doesn't speak *or* talk to just anybody; **wir ~ nicht mehr miteinander** we are no longer on speaking terms, we're not speaking any more; **mit wem spreche ich?** to whom am I speaking, please?; **~ wir nicht mehr darüber!** let's not talk about that any more, let's drop the subject; **darüber spricht man nicht** one doesn't talk about *or* speak of such things; **ich weiß nicht, wovon Sie ~** I don't know what you're talking about; **~ wir von etwas anderem** let's talk about something else, let's change the subject; **wir haben gerade von dir gesprochen** we were just talking about you; **es wird kaum noch von ihm gesprochen** he's hardly mentioned now; **für jdn/etw ~** to speak for sb/sth, to speak on (*Brit*) *or* in (*US*) behalf of sb/sth; **es spricht für jdn/etw(, daß ...)** it says something for sb/sth (that ...), it speaks well for sb/sth (that ...); **das spricht für ihn** that's a point in his favour, that says something for him; **es spricht nicht für die Firma, daß so was passieren konnte** it doesn't say much for the firm that something like that could happen; **das spricht für sich (selbst)** that speaks for itself; **es spricht vieles dafür** there's a lot to be said for it; **es spricht vieles dafür, daß ...** there is every reason to believe that ...; **was spricht dafür/dagegen?** what is there to be said for/against it?; **aus seinen Worten sprach Verachtung/Hoffnung** his words expressed contempt/hope; **er sprach vor den Studenten/dem Ärztekongreß** he spoke to the students/the medical conference; **ganz allgemein gesprochen** generally speaking.

▼ 2 *vt* **(a)** (*sagen*) to say, to speak; *eine Sprache, Mundart* to speak; (*aufsagen*) *Gebet* to say; *Gedicht* to say, to recite ◆ **es wurde viel gesprochen** a lot of talking was done; **alles, was er sprach ...** everything he said ...; **~ Sie Japanisch?** do you speak Japanese?; **hier spricht man Spanisch** Spanish spoken, we speak Spanish; *siehe* **Sprache**.

(b) *Urteil* to pronounce; *siehe* **Recht**.

▼ **(c)** (*mit jdm reden*) to speak to ◆ **kann ich bitte Herrn Kurz ~?** may I speak to Mr Kurz, please?; **er ist nicht zu ~** he can't see anybody; **ich bin für niemanden zu ~** I can't see anybody, I'm not available; **ich hätte gern Herrn Bremer gesprochen** could I speak to Mr Bremer?; **kann ich Sie einen Augenblick** *or* **kurz ~?** can I see you for a moment?, can I have a quick word?; **für Sie bin ich jederzeit zu ~** I'm always at your disposal; **wir ~ uns noch!** you haven't heard the last of this!

sprechend *adj Augen, Gebärde* eloquent.

Sprecher(in *f*) *m* **-s, -** speaker; (*Nachrichten~*) newscaster, newsreader; (*für Dokumentarfilme, Stücke etc*) narrator; (*Ansager*) announcer; (*Wortführer*) spokesman ◆ **sich zum ~ von jdm/etw machen** to become the spokesman of sb/sth.

Sprech-: **~erziehung** *f* speech training, elocution; **s~faul** *adj* taciturn; **sei doch nicht so s~faul!** haven't you got a tongue in your head!; **morgens ist sie besonders s~faul** she's not exactly talkative in the mornings; **~fehler** *m* slip of the tongue; **~fenster** *nt* grille; **~funk** *m* radio-telephone system; **~funkgerät** *nt* radiotelephone; (*tragbar auch*) walkie-talkie; **~funkverkehr** *m* local radio traffic; **den ~funkverkehr unterbrechen** to interrupt radiotelephone communications; **~gebühr** *f* (*Telec*) call charge; **~gesang** *m* (*Mus*) speech-song, sprechgesang; **~kunde** *f* study of speech; **~melodie** *f siehe* **Sprachmelodie**; **~muschel** *f* (*Telec*) mouthpiece; **~organ** *nt* organ of speech, speech organ; **~platte** *f* spoken-word record; **~probe** *f* voice trial; **~puppe** *f* talking *or* speaking doll; **~rolle** *f* speaking part; **~schulung** *f* voice training; **~silbe** *f* (*Ling*) (phonetic) syllable; **~stimme** *f* speaking voice; (*Mus*) sprechstimme, speech voice; **~stunde** *f* consultation (hour); (*von Arzt*) surgery (*Brit*), doctor's office (*US*); **~stunden** consultation hours; (*von Arzt*) surgery (*Brit*) *or* consulting hours; **~stunde halten** to hold surgery (*Brit*); **~stundenhilfe** *f* (doctor's) receptionist; **~taste** *f* "talk" button *or* switch; **~übung** *f* speech exercise; **~unterricht** *m* elocution lessons *pl*; **~weise** *f* way of speaking; **~werkzeuge** *pl* organs of speech; **~zeit** *f* **(a)** (*~stunde*) consulting time; (*von Arzt*) surgery time (*Brit*); **(b)** (*Besuchszeit: in Gefängnis, Kloster*) visiting time; **(c)** (*Telec*) call time; **~zimmer** *nt* consulting room.

Spreißel *nt* **-s, -** (*Aus*) kindling *no pl*.

Spreite *f* **-, -n** (leaf) blade.

Spreizdübel *m* cavity plug.

Spreize *f* **-, -n (a)** (*Build*) strut. **(b)** (*Sport*) straddle.

spreizen [1] *vt Flügel, Gefieder* to spread; *Finger, Zehen auch* to splay (out); *Beine auch* to open; (*Sport*) to straddle.
[2] *vr* (*sich sträuben*) to kick up (*inf*); (*sich aufplustern*) to give oneself airs, to put on airs ◆ **sich wie ein Pfau ~** to puff oneself up, to put on airs; **sich gegen etw ~** to kick against sth.

Spreiz-: ~fuß *m* splayfoot; **~schritt** *m* (*Sport*) straddle; **im ~schritt stehen** to stand with one's legs apart.

Spreng-: ~arbeiten *pl* blasting operations *pl*; **„~arbeiten"** "blasting"; **~bombe** *f* high-explosive bomb.

Sprengel *m* **-s, -** (*Kirchspiel*) parish; (*Diözese*) diocese.

sprengen [1] *vt* **(a)** to blow up; *Fels* to blast.
(b) *Türschloß, Tor* to force (open); *Tresor* to break open; *Bande, Fesseln* to burst, to break; *Eisdecke, Versammlung* to break up; (*Spiel*)*bank* to break; *siehe* **Rahmen**.
(c) (*bespritzen*) to sprinkle; *Beete, Rasen auch* to water; *Wäsche* to sprinkle (with water); (*verspritzen*) *Wasser* to sprinkle, to spray.
[2] *vi* **(a)** to blast.
(b) *aux sein* (*liter: kraftvoll reiten*) to thunder.

Spreng-: ~kammer *f* demolition chamber; **~kapsel** *f* detonator; **~kommando** *nt* demolition squad; (*zur Bombenentschärfung*) bomb disposal squad; **~kopf** *m* warhead; **~körper** *m* explosive device; **~kraft** *f* explosive force; **~ladung** *f* explosive charge; **~meister** *m* (*in Steinbruch*) blaster; (*bei Abbrucharbeiten*) demolition expert; (*zur Bombenentschärfung*) bomb-disposal expert; **~satz** *m* explosive device.

Sprengstoff *m* explosive.

Sprengstoff-: ~anschlag *m*, **~attentat** *nt* bomb attack; (*erfolgreich auch*) bombing; **auf ihn/das Haus wurde ein ~anschlag verübt** he was the subject of a bomb attack/there was a bomb attack on the house.

Sprengung *f siehe vt* **(a)** blowing-up; blasting. **(b)** forcing (open); breaking open; bursting, breaking; breaking-up. **(c)** sprinkling; watering; sprinkling (with water); spraying.

Spreng-: ~wagen *m* water(ing)-cart, street sprinkler; **~wedel** *m* (*Eccl*) aspergellum; **~wirkung** *f* explosive effect.

Sprenkel *m* **-s, - (a)** (*Tupfen*) spot, speckle. **(b)** (*Vogelschlinge*) snare.

sprenkeln *vt Farbe* to sprinkle spots of; *siehe* **gesprenkelt**.

Spreu *f* **-,** *no pl* chaff ◆ **wie (die) ~ im Wind** (*Bibl*) like chaff in the wind (*Bibl*); **die ~ vom Weizen trennen** *or* **sondern** (*fig*) to separate the wheat from the chaff.

sprich *imper sing of* **sprechen**.

Sprichwort *nt, pl* **¨er** proverb.

sprichwörtlich *adj* (*lit, fig*) proverbial.

sprießen *pret* **sproß** *or* **sprießte**, *ptp* **gesprossen** *vi aux sein* (*aus der Erde*) to come up, to spring up; (*Knospen, Blätter*) to shoot; (*fig geh: Liebe, Zuneigung*) to burgeon (*liter*).

Spriet *nt* **-(e)s, -e** (*Naut*) sprit.

Springbrunnen *m* fountain.

springen *pret* **sprang**, *ptp* **gesprungen** [1] *vi aux sein* **(a)** (*lit, fig, Sport, bei Brettspielen*) to jump; (*mit Schwung auch*) to leap, to spring; (*beim Stabhochsprung*) to vault; (*Raubtier*) to pounce; (*sich springend fortbewegen*) to bound; (*hüpfen, seilhüpfen*) to skip; (*auf einem Bein hüpfen*) to hop; (*Ball etc*) to bounce; (*Wassersport*) to dive; (*S Ger inf: eilen*) to nip (*Brit inf*), to pop (*inf*) ◆ **singen/tanzen und ~** to sing and leap about/dance and leap about; **jdm an den Hals** *or* **die Kehle** *or* **die Gurgel** (*inf*) **~** to leap *or* fly at sb's throat; (*fig*) to fly at sb, to go for sb; **ich hätte ihm an die Kehle ~ können** I could have strangled him; **aus dem Gleis** *or* **den Schienen ~** to jump the rails; **ins Aus ~** (*Sport*) to go out (of play); *siehe* **Bresche, Klinge**.
(b) etw ~ lassen (*inf*) to fork out for sth (*inf*); *Runde* to stand sth; *Geld* to fork out sth; **für jdn etw ~ lassen** (*inf*) to treat sb to sth; *esp Getränke auch* to stand sb sth; **das hat der Chef ~ lassen!** (*inf*) that was on the boss! (*inf*).
(c) (*geh: hervorsprudeln*) to spring; (*Wasserstrahl, Quelle auch, Blutstrahl*) to spurt; (*Funken*) to leap.
(d) (*Saite, Glas, Porzellan*) to break; (*Risse bekommen*) to crack; (*sich lösen: Knopf*) to come off (*von etw* sth).
(e) (*geh: aufplatzen*) to burst (forth).
[2] *vt aux haben* **einen (neuen) Rekord ~** (*Sport*) to make a record jump.

Springen *nt* **-s, -** (*Sport*) jumping; (*Stabhoch~*) vaulting; (*Wassersport*) diving.

springend *adj* **der ~e Punkt** the crucial point.

Springer(in *f*) *m* **-s, - (a)** jumper; (*Stabhoch~*) vaulter; (*Wassersport*) diver. **(b)** (*Chess*) knight. **(c)** (*Ind*) stand-in.

Springerstiefel *m* Doc Martens ® (boot).

Spring-: ~flut *f* spring tide; **~form** *f* (*Cook*) springform.

Spring|insfeld *m* **-(e)s, -e** madcap.

Spring-: ~kraut *nt* (*Bot*) touch-me-not; **s~lebendig** *adj* lively, full of beans (*inf*); **~pferd** *nt* jumper; **~reiten** *nt* show jumping; **~rollo** *nt* roller blind; **~seil** *nt* skipping rope; **über ein ~seil springen** (*seilspringen*) to skip; **~turnier** *nt* show jumping competition.

Sprinkler *m* **-s, -** sprinkler.

Sprinkler|anlage *f* sprinkler system.

Sprint *m* **-s, -s** sprint.

sprinten *vti aux sein* to sprint.

Sprinter(in *f*) *m* **-s, -** sprinter.

Sprintstrecke *f* sprint distance.

Sprit *m* **-(e)s, -e** (*inf: Benzin*) gas (*inf*), juice (*inf*); (*Rohspiritus*) neat spirit, pure alcohol.

Spritz-: ~beutel *m* icing *or* piping bag; **~düse** *f* nozzle; (*Tech*) jet.

Spritze *f* **-, -n** syringe; (*Feuer~, Garten~*) hose; (*Injektion*) injection, jab (*inf*) ◆ **eine ~ bekommen** to have an injection *or* a jab (*inf*); **an der ~ hängen** (*sl*) to shoot up (*sl*), to be on heroin.

spritzen [1] *vti* **(a)** to spray; (*in einem Strahl auch*) *Wasser* to squirt; (*Cook*) *Zuckerguß etc* to pipe; (*verspritzen*) *Wasser, Schmutz etc* to splash; (*Fahrzeug*) to spray, to spatter ◆ **die Feuerwehr spritzte (Wasser) in das brennende Gebäude** the firemen directed their hoses into the burning building; **das vorbeifahrende Auto spritzte mir Wasser ins Gesicht** the passing car sprayed *or* spattered water in my face.
(b) (*lackieren*) *Auto* to spray.
(c) *Wein* to dilute with soda water/mineral water ◆ **er trinkt Rotwein gespritzt** he drinks red wine with soda water/mineral water; *siehe* **Gespritzte(r)**.
(d) (*injizieren*) *Serum etc* to inject; *Heroin etc auch* to shoot (*sl*); (*eine Injektion geben*) to give injections/an injection ◆ **wir müssen (dem Kranken) Morphium ~** we have to give (the patient) a morphine injection; **er spritzt seit einem Jahr** (*inf*) he has been shooting *or* mainlining for a year (*sl*); (*Diabetiker*) he has been injecting himself for a year.
[2] *vi* **(a)** *aux haben or sein* (*Wasser, Schlamm*) to spray, to splash; (*heißes Fett*) to spit; (*in einem Strahl*) to spurt; (*aus einer Tube, Wasserpistole etc*) to squirt ◆ **es spritzte gewaltig, als er ins Wasser plumpste** there was an enormous splash when he fell into the water.
(b) *aux sein* (*inf: eilen*) to dash, to nip (*Brit inf*).

Spritzen-: ~haus *nt* fire station; **~wagen** *m* (*old*) fire engine.

Spritzer *m* **-s, -** (*Farb~, Wasser~*) splash; (*von Parfüm, Mineralwasser auch*) dash.

Spritz-: ~fahrt *f* (*inf*) spin (*inf*); **eine ~fahrt machen** to go for a spin (*inf*); **~gebäck** *nt* (*Cook*) ≃ Viennese whirl/whirls *pl*; ⚠**~guß** *m* injection moulding; (*Metal*) die-casting.

spritzig [1] *adj Wein* tangy, piquant; *Auto* lively, nippy (*Brit inf*), zippy (*inf*); *Aufführung, Dialog etc* sparkling, lively; (*witzig*) witty ◆ **das Kabarett war ~ und witzig** the cabaret was full of wit and sparkle.
[2] *adv aufführen, darstellen* with sparkle; *schreiben* racily; (*witzig*) wittily.

Spritz-: ~kuchen *m* (*Cook*) cruller; **~lack** *m* spray(ing) paint; **~lackierung** *f* spraying; **~pistole** *f* spray-gun; **~schutz** *m* guard; **~tour** *f siehe* **~fahrt**; **~tülle** *f* nozzle.

spröd(e) *adj Glas, Stein, Haar* brittle; *Haut* rough; *Stimme* thin; (*fig*) *Material* obdurate, recalcitrant; (*abweisend*) aloof; *Charme* austere.

⚠**sproß** *pret of* **sprießen**.

⚠**Sproß** *m* **-sses, -sse** shoot; (*fig: Nachkomme*) scion (*liter*).

Sprosse *f* **-, -n** (*lit, fig*) rung; (*Fenster~*) (*senkrecht*) mullion; (*waagerecht*) transom; (*Geweih~*) branch, point, tine.

sprossen *vi aux sein* (*liter*) *siehe* **sprießen**.

Sprossen-: ~fenster *nt* lattice window; **~wand** *f* (*Sport*) wall bars *pl*.

⚠**Sprößling** *m* shoot; (*fig hum*) offspring.

Sprotte *f* **-, -n** sprat.

Spruch *m* **-(e)s, ¨e (a)** saying; (*Sinn~ auch*) aphorism; (*Maxime auch*) adage, maxim; (*Wahl~*) motto; (*Bibel~*) quotation, quote; (*Poet: Gedicht*) medieval lyric poem ◆ **die ¨e Salomos** (*Bibl*) (the Book of) Proverbs; **¨e** (*inf: Gerede*) patter *no pl* (*inf*); **¨e machen** (*inf*) *or* **klopfen** (*inf*) *or* **kloppen** (*sl*) to talk fancy (*inf*); (*angeben*) to talk big (*inf*); (*Verkäufer*) to give one's patter (*inf*) *or* spiel (*sl*); **mach keine ¨e!** (*inf*) come off it! (*inf*); **das sind doch nur ¨e!** that's just talk.
(b) (*Richter~*) judgement; (*Frei~/Schuld~*) verdict; (*Strafurteil*) sentence; (*Schieds~*) ruling.

Spruchband *nt* banner.

Spruchdichtung *f* (*Poet*) medieval lyric poetry.

Sprücheklopfer *m* (*inf*) patter-merchant (*inf*); (*Angeber*) big talker (*inf*).

Sprüchlein *nt dim of* **Spruch** ◆ **sein ~ hersagen** to say one's (little) piece.

spruchreif *adj* (*inf*) **die Sache ist noch nicht ~** it's not definite yet so we'd better not talk about it; **die Sache wird erst ~, wenn ...** we can only start talking about it definitely when ...

Sprudel *m* **-s, -** (*saurer ~*) mineral water; (*süßer ~*) fizzy drink.

sprudeln [1] *vi* **(a)** (*schäumen*) (*Wasser, Quelle*) to bubble; (*Sekt, Limonade*) to effervesce, to fizz; (*fig: vor Freude, guten Ideen etc*) to bubble. **(b)** *aux sein* (*hervor~*) (*Wasser etc*) to bubble; (*fig: Worte*) to pour out.
[2] *vt* (*Aus: quirlen*) to whisk.

sprudelnd *adj* (*lit*) *Getränke* fizzy, effervescent; (*fig*) *Temperament, Witz* bubbling, bubbly (*inf*), effervescent.

Sprudeltablette *f* effervescent tablet.

Sprudler *m* **-s, -** (*Aus*) whisk.

Sprüh-: ~aktion *f* slogan-spraying operation; **~dose** *f* spray (can); (*unter Druck stehend auch*) aerosol (can).

sprühen [1] *vi* **(a)** *aux haben or sein* to spray; (*Funken*) to fly.
(b) (*fig*) (*vor Witz etc*) to bubble over, to effervesce; (*Augen*) (*vor Freude etc*) to sparkle; (*vor Zorn etc*) to glitter, to flash.
[2] *vt* to spray; (*fig: Augen*) to flash ♦ **er sprühte Lack auf die beschädigte Stelle** he sprayed the damaged spot with paint.

sprühend *adj Laune, Temperament etc* bubbling, bubbly (*inf*), effervescent; *Witz* sparkling, bubbling.

Sprüh-: ~flugzeug *nt* crop-spraying plane; **~nebel** *m* mist; **~regen** *m* drizzle, fine rain.

Sprung *m* **-(e)s, ¨e (a)** jump; (*schwungvoll, fig: Gedanken~ auch*) leap; (*Hüpfer*) skip; (*auf einem Bein*) hop; (*Satz*) bound; (*von Raubtier*) pounce; (*Stabhoch~*) vault; (*Wassersport*) dive ♦ **einen ~/einen kleinen ~ machen** to jump/do a small jump; **zum ~ ansetzen** (*lit*) to get ready to jump *etc*; (*fig*) to get ready to pounce; **sie wagte den ~ nicht** (*fig*) she didn't dare (to) take the plunge; **ein großer ~ nach vorn** (*fig*) a great leap forward; **damit kann man keine großen ¨e machen** (*inf*) you can't exactly live it up (*inf*); **auf dem ~ sein** *or* **stehen, etw zu tun** to be about to do sth; **immer auf dem ~ sein** (*inf*) to be always on the go (*inf*); (*aufmerksam*) to be always on the ball (*inf*); **jdm auf die ¨e helfen** (*wohlwollend*) to give sb a (helping) hand; (*drohend*) to show sb what's what.
(b) (*inf: kurze Strecke*) stone's throw (*inf*) ♦ **bis zum Postamt ist es nur ein ~** the post office is only a stone's throw from here (*inf*); **auf einen ~ bei jdm vorbeikommen/-gehen** to drop *or* pop in to see sb (*inf*).
(c) (*Riß*) crack ♦ **einen ~ haben/bekommen** to be cracked/to crack.
(d) (*Geol*) *siehe* **Verwerfung**.
(e) (*Hunt: Rudel*) herd.
(f) (*Agr: Begattung*) mounting ♦ **dieser Hengst eignet sich nicht zum ~** this stallion isn't suitable for stud purposes; **es kam nicht zum ~** they didn't mate.

Sprung-: ~bein *nt* **(a)** (*Anat*) anklebone; **(b)** (*Sport*) takeoff leg; **s~bereit** *adj* ready to jump; *Katze* ready to pounce; (*fig hum*) ready to go; **~brett** *nt* (*lit, fig*) springboard; **~deckel** *m* spring lid; **~feder** *f* spring; **~federmatratze** *f* spring mattress; **~gelenk** *nt* ankle joint; (*von Pferd*) hock; **~grube** *f* (*Sport*) (landing) pit; **s~haft** [1] *adj* **(a)** *Mensch, Charakter* volatile; *Denken* disjointed; **(b)** (*rapide*) *Aufstieg, Entwicklung etc* rapid; *Preisanstieg auch* sharp; [2] *adv ansteigen, entwickeln* by leaps and bounds; **~haftigkeit** *f siehe adj* **(a)** volatile nature, volatility; disjointedness; **(b)** rapidity, rapidness; sharpness; **~kraft** *f* (*Sport*) takeoff power, leg power; **~lauf** *m* (*Ski*) ski-jumping; **~netz** *nt* (jumping) net, life net (*US*); **~schanze** *f* (*Ski*) ski-jump; **~stab** *m* (vaulting) pole; **~tuch** *nt* jumping sheet *or* blanket, life net (*US*); **~turm** *m* diving platform; **s~weise** *adv* in bounds *or* jumps; (*fig*) by leaps and bounds.

Spucke *f* **-,** *no pl* (*inf*) spittle, spit ♦ **da bleibt einem die ~ weg!** (*inf*) it's flabbergasting (*inf*); **als ich das hörte, blieb mir die ~ weg** when I heard that I was flabbergasted (*inf*) *or* you could have knocked me down with a feather (*inf*); **mit Geduld und ~** (*hum inf*) with blood, sweat and tears (*hum*).

spucken *vti* to spit; (*inf: sich übergeben*) to throw up (*inf*), to be sick; (*fig inf*) *Lava, Flammen* to spew (out); (*inf: Maschine, Motor etc*) to give the occasional hiccup (*inf*) ♦ **in die Hände ~** (*lit*) to spit on one's hands; (*fig*) to roll up one's sleeves.

Spucknapf *m* spittoon.

Spuk *m* **-(e)s, -e (a)** (*Geistererscheinung*) **der ~ fing um Mitternacht an** the ghosts started to walk at midnight; **ich glaube nicht an diesen ~** I don't believe the place is haunted. **(b)** (*fig*) (*Lärm*) din, racket (*inf*); (*Aufheben*) fuss, to-do (*inf*), palaver (*inf*).

spuken *vi* to haunt ♦ **an einem Ort/in einem Schloß ~** to haunt *or* walk a place/castle; **es spukt auf dem Friedhof/im alten Haus** *etc* the cemetery/old house *etc* is haunted; **hier spukt es** this place is haunted; **durch den Film spukten wunderliche Gestalten/eigenartige Ideen** the film was haunted by weird and wonderful apparitions/strange ideas; **das spukt noch immer in den Köpfen** that still has a hold on people's minds.

Spuk-: ~geschichte *f* ghost story; **s~haft** *adj* eerie; ⚠**~schloß** *nt* haunted castle.

Spül-: ~automat *m* (automatic) dishwasher; **~bad** *nt* rinse; **~becken** *nt* sink.

Spule *f* **-, -n (a)** spool, reel; (*Nähmaschinen~, Ind*) bobbin; (*Elec*) coil. **(b)** (*Federkiel*) quill.

Spüle *f* **-, -n** sink.

spulen *vt* to spool (*auch Comput*), to reel; (*auf~ auch*) to wind onto a spool *or* reel/bobbin.

spülen *vti* **(a)** (*aus~, ab~*) to rinse; *Wunde* to wash; *Darm* to irrigate; *Vagina* to douche; (*abwaschen*) *Geschirr* to wash up; (*auf der Toilette*) to flush ♦ **du spülst und ich trockne ab** you wash and I'll dry; **vergiß nicht zu ~** don't forget to flush the toilet.
(b) (*Wellen etc*) to wash ♦ **etw an Land ~** to wash sth ashore.

Spüler(in *f*) *m* **-s, -** dishwasher, washer-up.

Spülicht *nt* **-s, -e** (*old*) dishwater.

Spül-: ~kasten *m* cistern; **~klosett** *nt* flush toilet, water closet; **~lappen** *m* dishcloth; **~maschine** *f* (automatic) dishwasher; **s~maschinenfest** *adj* dishwasher-proof; **~mittel** *nt* washing-up liquid; **~programm** *nt* wash programme; (*von Waschmaschine*) rinse cycle.

Spulrad *nt* bobbin-winder.

Spül-: ~schüssel *f* washing-up bowl; **~tisch** *m* sink (unit).

Spülung *f* rinsing; (*Wasser~*) flush; (*Med*) (*Darm~*) irrigation; (*Vaginal~*) douche; (*Aut*) scavenging.

Spülwasser *nt* (*beim Abwaschen*) dishwater, washing-up water; (*beim Wäschewaschen*) rinsing water.

Spulwurm *m* roundworm, ascarid (*Med*).

Spund *m* **-(e)s, ¨e (a)** bung, spigot; (*Holztechnik*) tongue. **(b)** *pl* **-e junger ~** (*dated inf*) young pup (*dated inf*).

spunden *vt Faß* to bung.

Spund-: ~loch *nt* bunghole; **~wand** *f* (*Build*) bulkhead.

Spur *f* **-, -en (a)** (*Abdruck im Boden etc*) track; (*Hunt auch*) spoor *no pl*; (*hinterlassenes Zeichen*) trace, sign; (*Brems~*) skidmarks *pl*; (*Blut~, Schleim~ etc, Fährte zur Verfolgung*) trail ♦ **von den Tätern fehlt jede ~** there is no clue as to the whereabouts of the persons responsible; **der Täter hat keine ~en hinterlassen** the culprit left no traces *or* marks; **jds ~ aufnehmen** to take up sb's trail; **jdm auf der ~ sein** to be on sb's trail; **auf der richtigen/falschen ~ sein** (*lit, fig*) to be on the right/wrong track; **jdn auf jds ~ bringen** to put sb onto sb's trail *or* onto sb; **jdn auf die richtige ~ bringen** (*fig*) to put sb on(to) the right track; **jdm auf die ~ kommen** to get onto sb; **auf** *or* **in jds ~en wandeln** (*fig*) to follow in sb's footsteps; **(seine) ~en hinterlassen** (*fig*) to leave its mark; **ohne/nicht ohne ~(en) an jdm vorübergehen** to have no effect on sb/to leave its mark on sb.
(b) (*fig: kleine Menge, Überrest*) trace; (*von Pfeffer, Paprika etc*) touch, soupçon; (*von Vernunft, Anstand, Talent etc*) scrap, ounce ♦ **von Anstand/Takt keine ~** (*inf*) no decency/tact at all; **von Liebe keine ~** (*inf*) love doesn't/didn't come into it; **keine ~** (*inf*), **nicht die ~** (*inf*) not/nothing at all; **keine ~ davon ist wahr** (*inf*) there's not a scrap *or* an ounce of truth in it; **eine ~ zu laut/grell** a shade *or* a touch too loud/garish.
(c) (*Fahrbahn*) lane ♦ **auf der linken ~ fahren** to drive in the left-hand lane; **in der ~ bleiben** to keep in lane.
(d) (*Aut: gerade Fahrtrichtung*) tracking ♦ **~ halten** (*beim Bremsen etc*) to hold its course; (*nach Unfall*) to track properly; **aus der ~ geraten** *or* **kommen** (*durch Seitenwind etc*) to go off course; (*beim Bremsen etc*) to skid.
(e) (*~weite*) (*Rail*) gauge; (*Aut*) track.
(f) (*Comput*) track.

spürbar *adj* noticeable, perceptible.

Spurbreite *f* (*Rail*) gauge.

spuren [1] *vt* (*Ski*) *Loipe* to make, to lay.
[2] *vi* (*Ski*) to make *or* lay a track; (*Aut*) to track; (*inf*) to obey; (*sich fügen*) to toe the line; (*funktionieren: Maschine, Projekt*) to run smoothly, to go well ♦ **jetzt wird gespurt!** (*inf*) I want a little obedience; **bei dem Lehrer wird gespurt** (*inf*) he makes you obey, that teacher.

spüren [1] *vt* to feel; (*intuitiv erfassen*) *jds Haß, Zuneigung, Unwillen etc auch* to sense ♦ **sie spürte, daß der Erdboden leicht bebte** she felt the earth trembling underfoot; **sie ließ mich ihr Mißfallen ~** she made no attempt to hide her displeasure, she let me know that she was displeased; **etw in allen Gliedern ~** (*lit, fig*) to feel sth in every bone of one's body; **davon ist nichts zu ~** there is no sign of it, it's not noticeable; **etw zu ~ bekommen** (*lit*) to feel sth; (*fig*) to feel the (full) force of sth; *jds Spott, Anerkennung etc* to meet with sth; (*bereuen*) to suffer for sth, to regret sth; **es zu ~ bekommen, daß ...** to feel the effects of the fact that ...; **ihr werdet es noch zu ~ bekommen, daß ihr so faul seid** some day you'll regret being so lazy; **sie bekamen es deutlich zu ~, daß sie Weiße waren** they were made very conscious *or* aware of the fact that they were whites.
[2] *vti* (*Hunt*) **(nach) etw ~** to track sth, to follow the scent of sth.

Spuren-: ~element *nt* trace element; **~sicherung** *f* securing of evidence; **die Leute von der ~sicherung** the forensic people.

Spürhund *m* tracker dog; (*inf: Mensch*) sleuth.

spurlos *adj* without trace ♦ **~ verschwinden** to disappear *or* vanish without trace, to vanish into thin air; **~ an jdm vorübergehen** to have no effect on sb; (*Ereignis, Erfahrung etc auch*) to wash over sb; **das ist nicht ~ an ihm vorübergegangen** it left its mark on him.

Spür-: ~nase *f* (*Hunt*) nose; **eine ~nase für etw haben** (*fig inf*) to have a (good) nose for sth; **~sinn** *m* (*Hunt, fig*) nose; (*fig: Gefühl*) feel.

Spurt *m* **-s, -s** *or* **-e** spurt; (*End~, fig*) final spurt ♦ **zum ~ ansetzen** (*lit, fig*) to make a final spurt.

spurten *vi aux sein* (*Sport*) to spurt; (*zum Endspurt ansetzen*) to make a final spurt; (*inf: rennen*) to sprint, to dash.

Spurweite *f* (*Rail*) gauge; (*Aut*) track.

sputen *vr* (*old, dial*) to hurry, to make haste (*old, liter*).

Sputnik ['ʃpʊtnɪk, 'sp-] *m* **-s, -s** sputnik.

Squash [skvɔʃ] *nt* **-,** *no pl* squash.

Squash-: ~halle *f* squash courts *pl*; **~schläger** *m* squash racket.

Sri Lanka *nt* Sri Lanka.

Srilanker(in *f*) *m* Sri Lankan.

srilankisch *adj* Sri Lankan.

SS[1] [ɛs'|ɛs] *nt* **-, -** (*Univ*) *abbr of* **Sommersemester**.

SS[2] [ɛs'|ɛs] *f* **-,** *no pl* (*NS*) *abbr of* **Schutzstaffel** SS.

SSO *abbr of* **Südsüdost** SSE.

SSV [ɛs|ɛs'fau] *m* **-s, -s** *abbr of* **Sommerschlußverkauf**.

SSW *abbr of* **Südsüdwest** SSW.

st *interj* (*Aufmerksamkeit erregend*) psst; (*Ruhe gebietend*) shh.

s.t. [ɛs'teː] *adv abbr of* **sine tempore**.

St. *abbr of* **Stück; Sankt** St.

Staat *m* **-(e)s, -en (a)** state; (*Land*) country ♦ **die ~en** (*inf*) the States (*inf*); **im deutschen ~** in Germany; **ein ~ im ~e** a state within a state; **von ~s wegen**

⚠: for details of spelling reform, see supplement

on a governmental level; **im Interesse/zum Wohl des ~es** in the national interest *or* in the interests of the state/for the good of the nation; **beim ~ arbeiten** *or* **sein** (*inf*) to be employed by the government *or* state; **so wenig ~ wie möglich** minimal government; **~ ist ~** the state's the state; **der ~ bin ich** (*prov*) l'Etat, c'est moi.
(b) (*Ameisen~, Bienen~*) colony.
(c) (*fig*) (*Pracht*) pomp; (*Kleidung, Schmuck*) finery ♦ **in vollem ~** in all one's finery; (*Soldaten*) in full dress; (*Würdenträger*) in full regalia; **(großen) ~ machen** to make a show; **damit ist kein ~ zu machen, damit kann man nicht gerade ~ machen** that's nothing to write home about (*inf*); **ohne großen ~ damit zu machen** without making a big thing about it (*inf*).

Staaten-: ~bund *m* confederation (of states); **s~los** *adj* stateless; **~lose(r)** *mf decl as adj* stateless person; **~losigkeit** *f* statelessness.

staatl. gepr. *abbr of* **staatlich geprüft.**

staatlich [1] *adj* state *attr*; *Gelder, Unterstützung etc auch* government *attr*; (*staatseigen*) *Betrieb, Güter auch* state-owned; (*~ geführt*) state-run.
[2] *adv* by the state ♦ **~ subventioniert** subsidized by the state, state-subsidized; **~ anerkannt** state-approved, government-approved; **~ geprüft** state-certified.

staatlicherseits *adv* on a governmental level.

Staats-: ~abgaben *pl* (government) taxes *pl*; **~affäre** *f* **(a)** (*lit*) affair of state; **(b)** (*fig*) *siehe* **~aktion**; **~akt** *m* (*lit*) state occasion; (*fig inf*) song and dance (*inf*); **er wurde in** *or* **mit einem feierlichen ~akt verabschiedet** his farewell was a state occasion; **~aktion** *f* major operation; **~amt** *nt* public office; **~angehörige(r)** *mf decl as adj* national; (*einer Monarchie auch*) subject; **~angehörigkeit** *f* nationality; **~angehörigkeitsnachweis** *m* proof of nationality; **~anleihe** *f* government bond; **~anwalt** *m* prosecuting attorney (*US*), public prosecutor; **der ~anwalt forderte ...** the prosecution called for ...; **~anwaltschaft** *f* prosecuting attorney's office (*US*), public prosecutor's office; (*Anwälte*) prosecuting attorneys *pl* (*US*), public prosecutors *pl*; **~apparat** *m* apparatus of state; **~archiv** *nt* state archives *pl*; **~ausgaben** *pl* public spending *sing or* expenditure *sing*; **~bahn** *f* state-owned *or* national railway(s *pl*); **~bank** *f* national *or* state bank; **~bankrott** *m* national bankruptcy; **~beamte(r)** *m* public servant; **~begräbnis** *nt* state funeral; **~besitz** *m* state property; **(in) ~besitz sein** to be state-owned; **~besuch** *m* state visit; **~betrieb** *m* state-owned *or* nationalized enterprise; **~bibliothek** *f* national library; **~bürger** *m* citizen; **~bürgerkunde** *f* (*Sch*) civics *sing*; **s~bürgerlich** *adj attr* civic; *Rechte* civil; **~chef** *m* head of state; **~diener** *m* public servant; **~dienst** *m* civil service; **s~eigen** *adj* state-owned; **~eigentum** *nt* state property *no art*, property of the state; **~empfang** *m* state reception; **s~erhaltend** *adj* conducive to the well-being of the state; **~examen** *nt* state exam(ination), ≃ first degree, *university degree required for the teaching profession*; **~feiertag** *m* national holiday; **~feind** *m* enemy of the state; **s~feindlich** *adj* hostile to the state; **sich s~feindlich betätigen** to engage in activities hostile to the state; **~finanzen** *pl* public finances *pl*; **~flagge** *f* national flag; **~form** *f* type of state; **~gebiet** *nt* national territory *no art*; **s~gefährdend** *adj* threatening the security of the state; **~gefährdung** *f* threat to the security of the state; **~geheimnis** *nt* (*lit, fig hum*) state secret; **~gelder** *pl* public funds *pl*; **~gerichtshof** *m* constitutional court; **~gewalt** *f* authority of the state; **~grenze** *f* state frontier *or* border; **~haushalt** *m* national budget; **~hoheit** *f* sovereignty; **~idee** *f* conception of a state; **~interesse** *nt* interests *pl* of (the) state; **~kanzlei** *f* state chancellery; **~kapitalismus** *m* state capitalism; **~karosse** *f* state carriage; **~kasse** *f* treasury, public purse; **~kirche** *f* state church; **~klugheit** *f* (*liter*) statesmanship; **~kommissar** *m* state commissioner; **~kosten** *pl* public expenses *pl*; **auf ~kosten** at the public expense; **~kunst** *f* (*liter*) statesmanship, statecraft; **~lehre** *f* political science; **~lotterie** *f* national *or* state lottery; **~mann** *m* statesman; **s~männisch** *adj* statesmanlike; **~minister** *m* state minister; **~monopol** *nt* state monopoly; **~oberhaupt** *nt* head of state; **~ordnung** *f* system of government; **~- und Gesellschaftsordnung** social system and system of government; **~organ** *nt* organ of the state; **~partei** *f* official party; **s~politisch** *adj* political; **~polizei** *f* state police, ≃ Special Branch (*Brit*); **die Geheime ~polizei** (*Hist*) the Gestapo; **~präsident** *m* president; **~prüfung** *f* (*form*) *siehe* **~examen**; **~raison, ~räson** *f* reasons of state; **~rat** *m* **(a)** (*Kollegium*) council of state; (*Sw*) cantonal government; **(b)** (*Hist: Titel*) councillor of state; (*Sw*) member of the cantonal government; **~ratsvorsitzende(r)** *m* (*DDR*) head of state; **~recht** *nt* **(a)** national law; **(b)** (*Verfassungsrecht*) constitutional law; **s~rechtlich** *adj siehe n* **(a)** *Entscheidung, Überlegung* of national law; **s~rechtlich unterscheiden sich ...** in national law there are differences between ...; **(b)** constitutional; **~regierung** *f* state government; **~religion** *f* state religion; **~rente** *f* state *or* government pension; **~ruder** *nt* (*geh*) helm of (the) state; **~säckel** *m* (*old, hum*) national coffers *pl*; **~schatz** *m* national treasury; **~schiff** *nt* (*liter*) ship of state; **~schuld** *f* (*Fin*) national debt; **~sekretär** *m* (*BRD: Beamter*) ≃ permanent secretary (*Brit*), under-secretary (*US*); **~sicherheit** *f* national *or* state security; **~sicherheitsdienst** *m* (*DDR*) national *or* state security service; **~sozialismus** *m* state socialism; **~streich** *m* coup (d'état); **~theater** *nt* state theatre; **s~tragend** *adj Politiker* representing the interests of the state; *Partei* established; *Rede* statesmanlike; **s~tragend ausgedrückt** expressed in a statesmanlike manner; **~unternehmen** *nt* state-owned enterprise; **~verbrechen** *nt* political crime; (*fig*) major crime; **~verfassung** *f* (national) constitution; **~verleumdung** *f* slander *or* (*schriftlich*) libel of the state; **~vermögen** *nt* national *or* public assets *pl*; **~vertrag** *m* international treaty; **~verwaltung** *f* administration of the state; **~wald** *m* state-owned forest; **~wesen** *nt* state; **~wissenschaft(en** *pl*) *f* (*dated*) political science; ⚠**~zuschuß** *m* state *or* government grant.

Stab *m* **-(e)s, ¨-e (a)** rod; (*Gitter~*) bar; (*Spazierstock, Wander~*) stick; (*Bischofs~*) crosier; (*Hirten~*) crook; (*Marschall~, Dirigenten~, für Staffellauf, von Majorette etc*) baton; (*als Amtzeichen*) mace; (*für ~hochsprung, Zelt~*) pole; (*Meß~*) (measuring) rod *or* stick; (*Aut*) dipstick; (*Zauber~*) wand ♦ **den ~ über jdn brechen** (*fig*) to condemn sb; **den ~ führen** (*Mus geh*) to conduct.
(b) (*Mitarbeiter~, Mil*) staff; (*von Experten*) panel; (*Mil: Hauptquartier*) headquarters *sing or pl*.

Stäbchen *nt dim of* **Stab** (*Eß~*) chopstick; (*Kragen~*) (collar) stiffener; (*Korsett~*) bone; (*Anat: der Netzhaut*) rod; (*beim Häkeln*) treble; (*inf: Zigarette*) ciggy (*inf*).

Stab-: s~förmig *adj* rod-shaped; **~führung** *f* (*Mus*) conducting; **unter der ~führung von** conducted by *or* under the baton of; **~heuschrecke** *f* stick insect; **~hochspringer** *m* pole-vaulter; **~hochsprung** *m* pole vault.

stabil [ʃta'bi:l, st-] *adj Möbel, Schuhe, Kind* sturdy, robust; *Währung, Beziehung, Charakter* stable; *Gesundheit* sound; (*euph: korpulent*) well-built, solid.

Stabilisation [ʃtabiliza'tsio:n, st-] *f* stabilization.

Stabilisator [ʃtabili'za:to:ɐ, st-] *m* stabilizer.

stabilisieren* [ʃtabili'zi:rən, st-] [1] *vt* to stabilize.
[2] *vr* to stabilize, to become stable.

Stabilität [ʃtabili'tɛ:t, st-] *f* stability.

Stab-: ~kirche *f* stave church; **~lampe** *f* (electric) torch, flashlight (*US*); **~magnet** *m* bar magnet; **~reim** *m* alliteration.

Stabs-: ~arzt *m* (*Mil*) captain in the medical corps; **~chef** *m* (*Mil inf*) chief of staff; **~feldwebel** *m* (*Mil*) warrant officer class II (*Brit*), master sergeant (*US*); **~offizier** *m* (*Mil*) staff officer; (*Rang*) field officer.

Stabwechsel *m* (*Sport*) baton change, change-over.

Staccato [sta'ka:to] *nt* **-s, -s** *or* **Staccati** staccato.

stach *pret of* **stechen.**

Stachel *m* **-s, -n** (*von Rosen, Ginster etc*) thorn, prickle; (*von Kakteen, Stachelhäutern, Igel*) spine; (*von ~schwein*) quill, spine; (*auf ~draht*) barb; (*zum Viehantrieb*) goad; (*Gift~: von Bienen etc*) sting; (*fig liter*) (*von Ehrgeiz, Neugier etc*) spur; (*von Vorwurf, Haß*) sting ♦ **Tod, wo ist dein ~?** (*Bibl*) Death where now thy sting?; **der ~ des Fleisches** (*liter*) the urges of the body *pl*; **ein ~ im Fleisch** (*liter*) a thorn in the flesh *or* side; *siehe* **löcken.**

Stachel-: ~beere *f* gooseberry; **~beerstrauch** *m* gooseberry bush.

Stacheldraht *m* barbed wire.

Stacheldraht-: ~verhau *m* barbed-wire entanglement; **~zaun** *m* barbed-wire fence.

Stachel-: ~flosser *m* **-s, -** (*Zool*) spiny-finned fish; **s~förmig** *adj* spiky; (*Biol*) spiniform *no adv*; **~halsband** *nt* spiked (dog) collar; **~häuter** *m* **-s, -** (*Zool*) echinoderm (*spec*).

stach(e)lig *adj Rosen, Ginster etc* thorny; *Kaktus, Igel etc* spiny; (*sich ~ anfühlend*) prickly; *Kinn, Bart* bristly; *Draht* spiky, barbed.

stacheln *vti siehe* **anstacheln.**

Stachel-: ~rochen *m* stingray; **~schnecke** *f* murex; **~schwein** *nt* porcupine.

stachlig *adj siehe* **stach(e)lig.**

Stadel *m* **-s, -** (*S Ger, Aus, Sw*) barn.

Stadion *nt* **-s, Stadien** [-iən] stadium.

Stadium *nt* **-s, Stadien** [-iən] stage ♦ **im vorgerückten/letzten ~** (*Med*) at an advanced/terminal stage; **er hat Krebs im vorgerückten/letzten ~** he has advanced/terminal cancer.

städt. *abbr of* **städtisch.**

Stadt *f* **-, ¨-e (a)** town; (*Groß~*) city ♦ **die ~ Paris** the city of Paris; **~ und Land** town and country; **in ~ und Land** throughout the land, the length and breadth of the land; **die ganze ~ spricht davon** it's all over town, the whole town is talking about it, it's the talk of the town; **in die ~ gehen** to go into town.
(b) (*~verwaltung*) (town) council; (*von Groß~*) corporation ♦ **bei der ~ angestellt sein** to be working for the council/corporation; **die ~ Ulm** Ulm Corporation.

Stadt-: ~adel *m* town nobility; **~amtmann** *m siehe* **Amtmann**; **s~auswärts** *adv* out of town; **~autobahn** *f* urban motorway (*Brit*) *or* freeway (*US*); **~bad** *nt* municipal swimming pool *or* baths *pl*; **~bahn** *f* suburban railway (*Brit*), city railroad (*US*); **~behörde** *f* municipal authority; **s~bekannt** *adj* well-known, known all over town; **~bewohner** *m* town-dweller; (*von Groß~*) city-dweller; **~bewohner** *pl* townspeople; city-people; **~bezirk** *m* municipal district; **~bild** *nt* urban features *pl*, townscape; cityscape; **das ständig wechselnde ~bild Bonns** the constantly changing face of Bonn; **~bücherei** *f* municipal *or* town/city (lending) library; **~bummel** *m* stroll in the *or* through town.

Städtchen *nt dim of* **Stadt** small town.

Stadt-: ~chronik *f* town/city chronicles *pl*; **~direktor** *m* town clerk (*Brit*), town/city manager (*US*).

Städte-: ~bau *m* urban development; **s~baulich** [1] *adj* urban development *attr*; *Veränderungen* in urban development; [2] *adv* as regards urban development.

stadt|einwärts *adv* into town.

Städte-: ~partnerschaft *f* town twinning; **~planung** *f* town *or* urban planning.

Städter(in *f*) *m* **-s, -** town-dweller; (*Groß~*) city-dweller.

Städtetag *m* convention *or* congress of municipal authorities.

Stadt-: ~fahrt *f* journey within a/the town/city; **~flucht** *f* exodus from the cities; **~gas** *nt* town gas; **~gebiet** *nt* municipal area; (*von Groß~ auch*) city zone; **~gemeinde** *f* municipality; **~gespräch** *nt* **(a)** **(das) ~gespräch sein** to be the talk of the town; **(b)** (*Telec*) local call; **~grenze** *f* town/city boundary; **~gue(r)rilla** *f* urban guerrilla; **~haus** *nt* townhouse.

städtisch *adj* municipal, town/city *attr*; (*nach Art einer Stadt*) urban ◆ **die ~e Bevölkerung** the town/city *or* urban population; **die ~e Lebensweise** the urban way of life, town/city life.

Stadt-: ~kämmerer *m* town/city treasurer; **~kasse** *f* town/city treasury; **~kern** *m* town/city centre; **~kind** *nt* town/city child; **~kommandant** *m* military governor (of a town/city); **~kreis** *m* town/city borough; **~landschaft** *f* town/city landscape, townscape/cityscape; **~luft** *f* town/city air; **~luft macht frei** (*Hist*) *principle whereby a serf became a freeman if he stayed in a town/city for a year and a day*; **~magazin** *nt* listings magazine, entertainment and events guide; **~mauer** *f* city wall; **~mensch** *m* town/city person; **~mission** *f* city mission; **~mitte** *f* town/city centre; **~oberhaupt** *nt* head of a/the town/city; **~park** *m* town/city *or* municipal park; **~parlament** *nt* city council; **~plan** *m* (street) map (of a/the town); (*Archit*) town/city plan; **~planung** *f* town planning; **~rand** *m* outskirts *pl* (of a/the town/city); **am ~rand** on the outskirts (of the town/city); **~randsiedlung** *f* suburban housing scheme; **~rat** *m* **(a)** (*Behörde*) (town/city) council; **(b)** (*Mitglied*) (town/city) councillor; **~recht** *nt* (*Hist*) town charter; **~rundfahrt** *f* (sightseeing) tour of a/the town/city; **eine ~rundfahrt machen** to go on a (sightseeing) tour of a/the town/city; **~schreiber** *m* (*obs, Sw*) town clerk; **~staat** *m* city state; **~streicher(in** *f*) *m* **-s, -** town/city tramp; **~streicherei** *f* urban vagrancy; **~teil** *m* district, part of town; **~theater** *nt* municipal theatre; **~tor** *nt* town/city gate; **~väter** *pl* (*old, hum*) city fathers *pl or* elders *pl*; **~verkehr** *m* **(a)** (*Straßenverkehr*) town/city traffic; **(b)** (*örtlicher Nahverkehr*) local town/city transport; **~verordnete(r)** *mf decl as adj* town/city councillor; **~verwaltung** *f* (town/city) council; **~viertel** *nt* district, part of town; **~wappen** *nt* municipal coat of arms; **~werke** *pl* town's/city's department of works; **~wohnung** *f* town/city apartment *or* flat (*Brit*); **~zentrum** *nt* town/city centre.

Stafette *f* (*Hist*) courier, messenger.

Staffage [sta'fa:ʒə] *f* **-, -n** (*Art: Beiwerk*) staffage; (*fig*) window-dressing.

Staffel *f* **-, -n** **(a)** (*Formation*) (*Mil, Naut, Aviat*) echelon; (*Aviat: Einheit*) squadron ◆ **~ fliegen** to fly in echelon formation. **(b)** (*Sport*) relay (race); (*Mannschaft*) relay team; (*fig*) relay ◆ **~ laufen/schwimmen** to run/swim in a relay (race). **(c)** (*Stufe, Sprosse*) rung; (*S Ger: Steintreppe*) stone steps *pl*.

Staffelei *f* easel.

Staffellauf *m* relay (race).

staffeln *vt* **(a)** *Gehälter, Tarife, Fahrpreise* to grade, to graduate; *Anfangszeiten, Startplätze* to stagger ◆ **nach Dienstalter gestaffelte Gehälter** salaries graded according to years of service; **die Startplätze gestaffelt anordnen** to stagger the starting places.
(b) (*in Formation bringen*) to draw up in an echelon ◆ **gestaffelte Formation** (*Aviat*) echelon formation.

Staffel-: ~schwimmen *nt* relay swimming; **~tarif** *m* graduated *or* differential tariff.

Staff(e)lung *f siehe* **staffeln (a)** grading, graduating; staggering. **(b)** drawing up in an echelon.

Stag *nt* **-(e)s, -e(n)** (*Naut*) stay.

Stagflation [ʃtakfla'tsio:n, st-] *f* (*Econ*) stagflation.

Stagnation [ʃtagna'tsio:n, st-] *f* stagnation, stagnancy ◆ **es kam zu einer ~** there was a period of stagnation *or* stagnancy.

stagnieren* [ʃta'gni:rən, st-] *vi* to stagnate.

Stagnierung *f siehe* **Stagnation.**

stahl *pret of* **stehlen.**

Stahl *m* **-(e)s, -e** *or* **¨e** steel; (*old liter: Schwert auch*) blade ◆ **Nerven aus** *or* **wie ~** nerves of steel.

Stahl- *in cpds* steel; **~bau** *m* steel-girder construction; **~beton** *m* reinforced concrete; **s~blau** *adj* steel-blue; **~blech** *nt* sheet-steel; (*Stück*) steel sheet; **~bramme** *f* steel girder.

stählen [1] *vt Körper, Muskeln, Nerven* to harden, to toughen ◆ **seinen Mut ~** to steel oneself.
[2] *vr* to toughen *or* harden oneself; (*sich wappnen*) to steel oneself.

stählern *adj Waffen, Ketten* steel; (*fig*) *Muskeln, Wille* of iron, iron *attr*; *Nerven* of steel; *Blick* steely.

Stahl-: ~feder *f* steel nib; **~gerüst** *nt* tubular steel scaffolding; (*Gerippe*) steel-girder frame; **s~grau** *adj* steel-grey; **s~hart** *adj* (as) hard as steel; **~helm** *m* (*Mil*) steel helmet; **~helm-Fraktion** *f* (*Pol*) hawks *pl*, hardliners *pl*; **~hochstraße** *f* temporary (steel) overpass; **~kammer** *f* strongroom; **~kocher** *m* steelworker; ⚠**~mantelgeschoß** *nt* steel jacket bullet; **~rohr** *nt* tubular steel; (*Stück*) steel tube; **~rohrmöbel** *pl* tubular steel furniture *sing*; ⚠**~roß** *nt* (*hum*) bike (*inf*), velocipede (*form, hum*); **~stich** *m* (*Art*) steel engraving; **~träger** *m* steel girder; **~waren** *pl* steel goods *pl*, steelware *sing*; **~werk** *nt* steelworks *sing or pl*; **~wolle** *f* steel wool.

stak (*geh*) *pret of* **stecken 1.**

Stake *f* **-, -n Staken** *m* **-s, -** (*N Ger*) (punt/barge) pole.

staken *vti* (*vi: aux sein*) to pole; *Stocherkahn auch* to punt; (*fig*) to stalk.

Staket *nt* **-(e)s, -e, Staketenzaun** *m* paling, picket fence.

Stakkato [ʃta'ka:to, st-] *nt* **-s, -s** *or* **Stakkati** staccato.

staksen *vi aux sein* (*inf*) to stalk; (*unsicher*) to teeter; (*steif*) to hobble ◆ **mit ~den Schritten gehen** to stalk/teeter/hobble.

staksig *adj* (*unbeholfen*) gawky ◆ **~ gehen** (*steif*) to hobble; (*unsicher*) to teeter.

Stalagmit [ʃtala'gmi:t, st-, -mɪt] *m* **-en** *or* **-s, -en** stalagmite.

Stalaktit [stalak'ti:t, ʃt-, -tɪt] *m* **-en** *or* **-s, -en** stalactite.

Stalinismus [stali'nɪsmʊs] *m* Stalinism.

Stalinist(in *f*) [stali'nɪst(ɪn)] *m* Stalinist.

stalinistisch [stali'nɪstɪʃ] *adj* Stalinist.

Stalin|orgel ['sta:lin-, 'ʃt-] *f* multiple rocket launcher.

Stall *m* **-(e)s, ¨e** **(a)** (*Pferde~, Gestüt, Aut: Renn~*) stable; (*Kuh~*) cowshed, (cow) barn (*US*), byre (*Brit*); (*Hühner~*) hen-house, coop; (*Kaninchen~*) hutch; (*Schaf~*) (sheep)cote; (*Schweine~*) (pig)sty, (pig)pen (*US*) ◆ **den ~ ausmisten** to clean out the stable *etc*; (*fig*) to clean out the Augean stables; **ein (ganzer) ~ voll Kinder** (*inf*) a (whole) pack of children.
(b) (*inf: Hosenschlitz*) flies *pl*, fly (*esp US*).

⚠**Stallaterne** *f getrennt* **Stall-laterne** stable lamp.

Stall-: ~bursche *m siehe* **~knecht**; **~dung, ~dünger** *m* farmyard manure; **~hase** *m* rabbit; **~knecht** *m* farm hand; (*für Pferde*) stableman, stable lad *or* hand; (*für Kühe*) cowhand; **~laterne** *f siehe* **Stallaterne**; **~magd** *f* farm girl; (*für Pferde*) stable maid; (*Kuhmagd*) milkmaid; **~meister** *m* equerry; **~mist** *m* farmyard manure.

Stallung(en *pl*) *f* stables *pl*.

Stallwache *f* (*fig*) watchdog.

Stamm *m* **-(e)s, ¨e** **(a)** (*Baum~*) trunk; *siehe* **Apfel.**
(b) (*Ling*) stem.
(c) (*Volks~*) tribe; (*Abstammung*) line; (*Biol*) phylum; (*Bakterien~*) strain ◆ **der ~ der Bourbonen** the house of Bourbon; **aus königlichem ~** of royal blood *or* stock *or* lineage; **aus dem ~e Davids** of the line of David, of David's line; **vom ~e Nimm sein** (*hum*) to be one of the takers of this world.
(d) (*Kern, fester Bestand*) regulars *pl*; (*Kunden auch*) regular customers *pl*; (*von Mannschaft*) regular team-members *pl*; (*Arbeiter*) regular *or* permanent workforce; (*Angestellte*) permanent staff *pl* ◆ **ein fester ~ von Kunden** regular customers, regulars; **zum ~ gehören** to be one of the regulars *etc*.

Stamm-: ~aktie *f* (*St Ex*) ordinary *or* common (*US*) share; **~baum** *m* family *or* genealogical tree; (*Biol*) phylogenetic tree; (*von Zuchttieren*) pedigree; (*Ling*) tree; **einen guten ~baum haben** (*lit, hum*) to have a good pedigree; **~belegschaft** *f* permanent *or* regular workforce; (*Angestellte*) regular staff *pl*; **~buch** *nt* **(a)** *siehe* **Familienbuch**; **(b)** (*fig*) **jdm etw ins ~buch schreiben** to make sb take note of sth; **~burg** *f* ancestral castle; **~daten** *pl* (*Comput*) master data; **~einlage** *f* (*Fin*) capital investment in ordinary shares *or* common stock (*US*).

stammeln *vti* to stammer.

Stamm|eltern *pl* progenitors *pl*.

stammen *vi* to come (*von, aus* from); (*zeitlich*) to date (*von, aus* from); (*Gram auch*) to be derived (*von, aus* from) ◆ **woher ~ Sie?** where do you come from (originally)?; **die Bibliothek/Uhr stammt von seinem Großvater** the library/watch originally belonged to his grandfather.

Stammes- *in cpds* tribal; ⚠**~bewußtsein** *nt* tribal spirit; **~genosse** *m* member of a/the tribe, tribesman; **~geschichte** *f* (*Biol*) phylogeny; **s~geschichtlich** *adj* (*Biol*) phylogenetic; **~kunde** *f* (*Hist*) ethnology; **~zugehörigkeit** *f* tribal membership.

Stamm-: ~form *f* base form; **~gast** *m* regular; **~gericht** *nt* standard meal; **~gut** *nt* family estate; **~halter** *m* son and heir; **~haus** *nt* (*Comm*) parent branch; (*Gesellschaft*) parent company; (*Fabrik*) parent factory; **~holz** *nt* trunk wood.

stämmig *adj* (*gedrungen*) stocky, thickset *no adv*; (*kräftig*) sturdy.

Stämmigkeit *f siehe adj* stockiness; sturdiness.

Stamm-: ~kapital *nt* (*Fin*) ordinary share *or* common stock (*US*) capital; **~kneipe** *f* (*inf*) local (*Brit inf*); **~kunde** *m* regular (customer); **~kundschaft** *f* regulars *pl*, regular customers *pl*; **~land** *nt* place of origin.

Stammler(in *f*) *m* **-s, -** stammerer.

Stamm-: ~lokal *nt* favourite café/restaurant *etc*; (*Kneipe*) local (*Brit*); **~mutter** *f siehe* **Stammutter**; **~personal** *nt* permanent staff *pl*; **~platz** *m* usual *or* regular seat; **~rolle** *f* (*Mil*) muster roll; **~silbe** *f* radical, root syllable; **~sitz** *m* (*von Firma*) headquarters *sing or pl*; (*von Geschlecht*) ancestral seat; (*im Theater etc*) regular seat; **~tafel** *f* genealogical table; **~tisch** *m* (*Tisch in Gasthaus*) table reserved for the regulars; (*~tischrunde*) group of regulars; **er hat mittwochs seinen ~tisch** Wednesday is his night for meeting his friends at the pub; **~tischpolitiker** *m* (*pej*) armchair *or* alehouse politician; **~tischrunde** *f* group of regulars.

⚠**Stammutter** *f getrennt* **Stamm-mutter** progenitrix (*form*).

Stamm-: ~vater *m* progenitor (*form*); **s~verwandt** *adj* related; *Wörter* cognate, derived from the same root; **~vokal** *m* radical *or* root vowel; **~wähler** *m* (*Pol*) staunch supporter, loyal voter; **~würze** *f* original wort.

Stamokap ['ʃta:mokap] *m* **-s,** *no pl* (*Pol*) *abbr of* **staatsmonopolistischer Kapitalismus.**

Stamper *m* **-s, -, Stamperl** *nt* **-s, -n** (*S Ger, Aus*) *stemless schnapps glass.*

stampfen [1] *vi* **(a)** (*laut auftreten*) to stamp; (*auf und nieder gehen: Maschine*) to pound ◆ **mit dem Fuß/den Hufen ~** to stamp one's foot/to paw the ground with its hooves.
(b) *aux sein* (*gehen*) (*mit schweren Schritten*) to tramp; (*wütend*) to stamp; (*stapfen*) to trudge.
(c) *aux haben or sein* (*Schiff*) to pitch, to toss.
[2] *vt* **(a)** (*festtrampeln*) *Lehm, Sand* to stamp; *Trauben* to press; (*mit den Füßen*) to tread; *siehe* **Boden.**
(b) (*mit Stampfer*) to mash; (*im Mörser*) to pound.

Stampfer *m* **-s, -** (*Stampfgerät*) pounder; (*Saugkolben*) plunger; (*sl: Bein*) tree-trunk (*inf*).

Stampfkartoffeln *pl* (*dial*) mashed potato(es *pl*).

stand *pret of* **stehen**.

Stand *m* **-(e)s, ⸚e (a)** *no pl* (*das Stehen*) standing position; (*~fläche*) place to stand; (*für Gegenstand*) stand ◆ **aus dem ~** from a standing position; **ein Sprung/Start aus dem ~** a standing jump/start; **bei jdm** *or* **gegen jdn einen schweren ~ haben** (*fig*) to have a hard time of it with sb; **aus dem ~ (heraus)** (*inf*) off the cuff.
(b) (*Markt~ etc*) stand; (*Taxi~ auch*) rank.
(c) *no pl* (*Lage*) state; (*Niveau, Fin: Kurs*) level; (*Zähler~, Thermometer~, Barometer~ etc*) reading, level; (*Kassen~, Konto~*) balance; (*von Gestirnen*) position; (*Sport: Spiel~*) score ◆ **beim jetzigen ~ der Dinge** the way things stand *or* are at the moment; **nach letztem ~ der Dinge** from the way things stood *or* were when we *etc* last heard; **der neueste ~ der Forschung** the latest developments in research; **etw auf den neuesten ~ bringen** to bring sth up to date; **auf den neuesten ~ der Technik sein** (*Gerät*) to be state-of-the-art technology; **im ~ der Sklaverei/Knechtschaft** in a state of slavery/bondage; **~: November 1990** as at November 1990.
(d) (*soziale Stellung*) station, status; (*Klasse*) rank, class; (*Beruf, Gewerbe*) profession; (*Reichs~*) estate ◆ **Name und ~** (*old*) name and profession; **die niederen/vornehmen** *or* **höheren ⸚e** (*old*) the lower/upper classes; **ein Mann von (hohem) ~** (*old*) a man of (high) rank.

Standard ['ʃtandart, 'st-] *m* **-s, -s** standard.

Standard- *in cpds* standard.

standardisieren* [ʃtandardi'ziːrən, st-] *vt* to standardize.

Standardisierung [ʃt-, st-] *f* standardization.

Standarte *f* **-, -n (a)** (*Mil, Pol*) standard. **(b)** (*Hunt*) brush.

Stand-: ~bein *nt* (*Sport*) pivot leg; (*Art*) standing leg; (*fig*) pillar; **~bild** *nt* statue; (*TV*) freeze frame.

Standby-Ticket ['stændbaɪ-] *nt* (*inf*) standby ticket.

Ständchen *nt* serenade ◆ **jdm ein ~ bringen** to serenade sb.

Stände-: ~ordnung *f* system of estates; **~organisation** *f* professional organization; **~parlament** *nt* parliament of estates.

Stander *m* **-s, -** pennant.

Ständer *m* **-s, -** (*Hut~, Noten~, Karten~ etc*) stand; (*Pfeifen~, Schallplatten~ etc auch*) rack; (*Pfeiler*) upright; (*Elec*) stator; (*sl: Erektion*) hard-on (*sl*).

Ständerat ['ʃtɛndəraːt] *m* (*Sw Parl*) upper chamber; (*Abgeordneter*) member of the upper chamber.

Standes-: ~amt *nt* registry office (*Brit*); **auf dem ~amt** at the registry office; **s~amtlich** *adj* **s~amtliche Trauung** registry office (*Brit*) *or* civil wedding; **sich s~amtlich trauen lassen** to get married in a registry office, to have a registry office *or* civil wedding; **~beamte(r)** *m* registrar; ⚠**~bewußtsein** *nt* status consciousness; **~dünkel** *m* snobbishness, snobbery; **~ehe** *f* marriage between people of the same rank; **~ehre** *f* honour as a nobleman/officer *etc*; (*von Ärzten, Handwerkern etc*) professional honour; **s~gemäß** [1] *adj* befitting one's rank *or* station (*dated*); [2] *adv* in a manner befitting one's rank *or* station (*dated*); **~heirat** *f siehe* **~ehe**; **~herr** *m* (*Hist*) mediatized prince; **~organisation** *f* professional association; **~person** *f* (*old*) person of quality (*old*); **~privileg** *nt* class privilege.

Ständestaat *m* (*Hist*) corporate *or* corporative state.

Standes-: ~tracht *f* (official) robes *pl*; **~unterschied** *m* class difference; **s~widrig** *adj* socially degrading; (*beruflich*) unprofessional.

➤ **Stand-: s~fest** *adj Tisch, Leiter* stable, steady; (*fig*) steadfast; **~festigkeit** *f* stability (*auch Sci*); (*fig auch*) steadfastness; **~foto** *nt* still (photograph); **~geld** *nt* stallage; **~gericht** *nt* (*Mil*) drumhead court martial; **vor ein ~gericht kommen** *or* **gestellt werden** to be summarily court-martialled; **s~haft** *adj* steadfast, strong; **etw s~haft verteidigen** to defend sth staunchly; **er weigerte sich s~haft** he staunchly *or* steadfastly refused; **~haftigkeit** *f* steadfastness; staunchness, resolution; ⚠**s~halten** *vi sep irreg* (*Mensch*) to stand firm; (*Gebäude, Brücke etc*) to hold; (*+dat*) to withstand, to stand up to; **Versuchungen** (*dat*) **s~halten** to resist temptation; **einer/der Prüfung s~halten** to stand up to *or* bear close examination; **~heizung** *f* (*Aut*) stationary heating.

ständig *adj* **(a)** (*dauernd*) permanent; *Praxis, Regel* established; *Korrespondent* (*Press*) resident; *Mitglied* full; *Einkommen* regular ◆ **~er Ausschuß** standing committee.
(b) (*unaufhörlich*) constant, continual ◆ **müssen Sie mich ~ unterbrechen?** must you keep (on) interrupting me?, must you continually *or* constantly interrupt me?; **sie kommt ~ zu spät** she's constantly *or* always late; **sie beklagt sich ~** she's forever *or* always complaining; **sie ist ~ krank** she's always ill; **passiert das oft? — ~** does it happen often? — always *or* all the time.

ständisch *adj* corporate, corporative.

Standleitung *f* direct line (phone system).

Standlicht *nt* sidelights *pl* ◆ **mit ~ fahren** to drive on sidelights.

Stand|ort *m* location; (*von Schütze, Schiff etc*) position; (*Mil*) garrison; (*Bot*) habitat; (*von Pflanzungen*) site; (*fig*) position ◆ **den ~ der Schule in der Gesellschaft bestimmen** to define the position *or* place of the school in society; **die Division hat ihren ~ in ...** the division is based *or* garrisoned in ...

Stand|ort-: ~älteste(r) *m* (*Mil*) senior officer of a garrison, post senior officer (*US*); **~bestimmung** *f* (*fig*) definition of the position; **~faktor** *m usu pl* (*Econ*) locational factor; **~katalog** *m* shelf catalogue, shelf list; **~zeichen** *nt* shelf mark.

Stand-: ~pauke *f* (*inf*) lecture (*inf*), telling-off (*inf*); **jdm eine ~pauke halten** to give sb a lecture (*inf*) *or* telling-off (*inf*), to tell sb off (*inf*); **~platz** *m* stand; (*für Taxis auch*) rank; **~punkt** *m* **(a)** (*rare: Beobachtungsplatz*) vantage point, viewpoint; **(b)** (*Meinung*) point of view, standpoint; **auf dem ~punkt stehen** *or* **den ~punkt vertreten, daß ...** to take the view that ...; **jdm seinen ~punkt klarmachen** to make one's point of view clear to sb; **von seinem ~punkt aus** from his point of view; **das ist doch kein** *or* **vielleicht ein** (*iro*) **~punkt!** what kind of attitude is that!; **~quartier** *nt* (*Mil*) base; **~recht** *nt* (*Mil*) military law (*invoked in times of emergency*); **~recht verhängen** to impose military law (*über +acc* on); **s~rechtlich** *adj* **s~rechtlich erschießen** to put straight before a firing squad; **eine s~rechtliche Erschießung** an on-the-spot execution; **s~sicher** *adj* stable; *Mensch* steady (on one's feet/skis *etc*); **~sicherheit** *f siehe adj* stability; steadiness; **~spur** *f* (*Aut*) hard shoulder; **~uhr** *f* grandfather clock; **~vogel** *m* non-migratory bird.

Stange *f* **-, -n (a)** (*langer, runder Stab*) pole; (*Querstab*) bar; (*Ballett~*) barre; (*Kleider~, Teppich~*) rail; (*Gardinen~, Leiste für Treppenläufer*) rod; (*Vogel~*) perch; (*Hühner~*) perch, roost; (*Gebiß~*) bit; (*Hunt: Schwanz*) brush; (*Geweihteil*) branch (of antlers); (*fig: dünner Mensch*) beanpole (*inf*).
(b) (*länglicher Gegenstand*) stick ◆ **eine ~ Zigaretten** a carton of 200 cigarettes.
(c) (*zylinderförmiges Glas*) tall glass.
(d) (*Redewendungen*) **ein Anzug von der ~** a suit off the peg; **von der ~ kaufen** to buy off the peg; **jdn bei der ~ halten** (*inf*) to keep *or* hold sb; **bei der ~ bleiben** (*inf*) to stick at it (*inf*); **jdm die ~ halten** (*inf*) to stick up for sb (*inf*), to stand up for sb; **eine schöne ~ Geld** (*inf*) a tidy sum (*inf*); **eine ~ angeben** (*sl*) to show off like crazy (*inf*), to lay it on thick (*inf*).

Stangen-: ~bohne *f* runner bean; **~brot** *nt* French bread; (*Laib*) French loaf; **~spargel** *m* asparagus spears *pl*.

stank *pret of* **stinken**.

Stänkerei *f* (*inf*) grousing.

Stänk(er)er *m* **-s, -** (*inf*) grouser.

stänkern *vi* (*inf*) **(a)** (*Unfrieden stiften*) to stir things up (*inf*). **(b)** (*Gestank verbreiten*) to make a stink (*inf*).

Stanniol [ʃta'nioːl, st-] *nt* **-s, -e** silver foil.

Stanniolpapier *nt* silver paper.

stante pede ['stantə 'peːdə] *adv* instanter, hotfoot.

Stanze *f* **-, -n (a)** (*für Prägestempel, Bleche*) die, stamp; (*Loch~*) punch. **(b)** (*Poet*) eight-line stanza.

stanzen *vt* to press; (*prägen*) to stamp, to emboss; *Löcher* to punch.

Stanzer(in *f*) *m* **-s, -** press worker.

Stapel *m* **-s, - (a)** (*geschichteter Haufen, fig: Vorrat*) stack, pile.
(b) (*Comm*) (*~platz*) store, depot; (*Handelsplatz*) trading centre, emporium.
(c) (*Naut: Schiffs~*) stocks *pl* ◆ **auf ~ legen** to lay down; **auf ~ liegen** to be on the stocks; **vom ~ laufen** to be launched; **vom ~ lassen** to launch; (*fig*) to come out with (*inf*).
(d) (*von Wolle, Baumwolle*) staple.

Stapel-: ~kasten *m* crate; **~lauf** *m* (*Naut*) launching.

stapeln [1] *vt* to stack; (*lagern*) to store.
[2] *vr* to pile up.

Stapel-: ~platz *m siehe* **Stapel (b)**; **~stuhl** *m* stackable chair.

Stapelung *f siehe* **stapeln 1** stacking; storing.

Stapel-: ~verarbeitung *f* (*Comput*) batch processing; **~ware** *f* staple commodity.

Stapfe *f* **-, -n**, **Stapfen** *m* **-s, -** footprint.

stapfen *vi aux sein* to trudge, to plod.

Star[1] *m* **-(e)s, -e** (*Orn*) starling.

Star[2] *m* **-(e)s, -e** (*Med*) **grauer/grüner/schwarzer ~** cataract/glaucoma/amaurosis (*spec*); **jdm den ~ stechen** (*fig*) to tell sb some home truths.

Star[3] [ʃtaːɐ, staːɐ] *m* **-s, -s** (*Film etc*) star; (*fig auch*) leading light ◆ **er trat wie ein ~ auf** he put on a big star act.

Star|allüren *pl* (*inf*) airs and graces *pl* ◆ **~ an den Tag legen** to put on *or* give oneself airs and graces.

starb *pret of* **sterben**.

Star-: ~besetzung *f* star cast; **~brille** *f* pair of glasses fitted with cataract lenses.

Star(en)kasten *m* nesting box (for starlings).

Star- (*Press*): **~gage** *f* top fee; **~gast** *m* star guest.

stark [1] *adj comp* **⸚er**, *superl* **⸚ste(r, s) (a)** (*kräftig, konzentriert*) strong (*auch Gram*); (*mächtig*) *Stimme, Staat, Partei auch* powerful ◆ **~ bleiben** to be strong; (*im Glauben*) to hold firm; **sich für etw ~ machen** (*inf*) to stand up for sth; **den ~en Mann spielen** *or* **markieren** *or* **mimen** (*all inf*) to play the big guy (*inf*); **das ist seine ~e Seite** that is his strong point *or* his forte; **das ist ~** *or* **ein ~es Stück** (*inf*) *or* **~er Tobak!** that's a bit much!; (*eine Unverschämtheit auch*) that's a bit thick! (*inf*).
(b) (*dick*) thick; (*euph: korpulent*) *Dame, Herr* large, well-built (*euph*); *Arme, Beine* large, strong (*euph*) ◆ **Kostüme für ⸚ere Damen** costumes for the fuller figure.
(c) (*beträchtlich, heftig*) *Schmerzen, Kälte* severe; *Frost auch, Regen, Schneefall, Verkehr, Raucher, Trinker, Druck* heavy; *Sturm* violent; *Erkältung* bad, heavy; *Wind, Strömung, Eindruck* strong; *Appetit, Esser* hearty; *Beifall* hearty, loud; *Fieber* high; *Trauer, Schmerz* deep; *Übertreibung, Widerhall, Bedenken* considerable, great ◆ **~e Abneigung** strong dislike.
(d) (*leistungsfähig*) *Motor* powerful; *Sportler* able; *Mannschaft* strong; *Brille, Arznei* strong ◆ **er ist in Englisch nicht sehr ~** he isn't very strong in English.
(e) (*zahlreich*) *Auflage, Gefolge* large; *Nachfrage* great, big ◆ **wir hoffen auf ~e Beteiligung** we are hoping that a large number of people will take part; **zehn Mann ~** ten strong; **das Buch ist 300 Seiten ~** the book is 300 pages long.

➤ SPRACHE AKTIV: **standhalten** → 32.3, 53.3, 53.6

⚠: Informationen zur Rechtschreibreform im Anhang

(f) *(inf: hervorragend) Leistung, Werk* great *(inf)* ◆ **sein ¨~stes Buch** his best book.
[2] *adv, comp* **¨~er**, *superl* **am ¨~sten (a)** *(mit vb)* a lot; *(mit adj, ptp)* very; *regnen, rauchen etc auch* heavily; *beeindrucken auch* greatly; *übertreiben auch* greatly, grossly; *vertreten, dagegen sein* strongly; *abgenutzt, beschmutzt, beschädigt etc* badly; *vergrößert, verkleinert* greatly ◆ **~ wirken** to have a strong effect; **~ gesalzen/gewürzt** very salty/highly spiced; **~ verschuldet** heavily *or* deeply in debt; **~ behaart sein** to be very hairy, to have a lot of hair; **¨~er behaart sein** to have more hair; **¨~er befahrene Straßen** busier roads; **die Ausstellung wurde ~ besucht** there were a lot of visitors to the exhibition; **das Auto zieht ~ nach links** the car is pulling badly to the left; **er ist ~ erkältet** he has a bad *or* heavy cold; **drück ¨~er auf die Klingel** push the bell harder.
(b) *(inf: hervorragend)* really well ◆ **die singt unheimlich ~** she's a really great singer *(inf)*, she sings really well.

Starkasten *m siehe* **Star(en)kasten.**

Starkbier *nt* strong beer.

Stärke¹ *f* **-, -n (a)** strength *(auch fig)*; *(von Stimme auch)* power.
(b) *(Dicke, Durchmesser)* thickness; *(Macht)* power.
(c) *(Heftigkeit) (von Strömung, Wind, Einfluß)* strength; *(von Eindruck auch, von Leid)* intensity; *(von Regen, Frost, Verkehr, Druck)* heaviness; *(von Sturm, Abneigung)* violence; *(von Schmerzen, Kälte, Erkältung, Fieber etc)* severity; *(von Appetit)* heartiness.
(d) *(Leistungsfähigkeit) (von Motor)* power; *(von Sportmannschaft, Arznei, Brille)* strength.
(e) *(Anzahl) (von Gefolge, Heer, Mannschaft)* size, strength; *(von Beteiligung, Nachfrage)* amount; *(Auflage)* size.
(f) *(fig: starke Seite)* strength, strong point.

Stärke² *f* **-, -n** *(Chem)* starch.

Stärkemehl *nt (Cook)* thickening agent, ≃ cornflour *(Brit)*, cornstarch *(US)*.

stärken [1] *vt* **(a)** *(kräftigen) (lit, fig)* to strengthen; *Selbstbewußtsein* to boost, to increase; *Gesundheit* to improve; *siehe* **Rückgrat. (b)** *(erfrischen)* to fortify. **(c)** *Wäsche* to starch.
[2] *vi* to be fortifying ◆ **das stärkt** it fortifies you; **~des Mittel** tonic.
[3] *vr* to fortify oneself.

Stärkezucker *m* glucose.

stark-: ~gliedrig, ~knochig *adj* heavy-boned.

Starkstrom *m (Elec)* heavy current.

Starkstrom- *in cpds* power; **~kabel** *nt* power cable; **~leitung** *f* power line; *(Kabel)* power lead; **~technik** *f branches of electrical engineering not connected with telecommunications.*

Starkult *m* star-cult.

Stärkung *f* **(a)** strengthening *(auch fig)*; *(des Selbstbewußtseins)* boosting ◆ **das dient der ~ der Gesundheit** it is beneficial to the health. **(b)** *(Erfrischung)* refreshment. **eine ~ zu sich nehmen** to take *or* have some refreshment.

Stärkungsmittel *nt (Med)* tonic.

stark-: ~wandig *adj Schiff* thick-walled; **~wirkend** *adj attr Medikament, Alkohol* potent.

Starlet ['ʃtaːɐlɛt, 'st-] *nt* **-s, -s** *(Film)* starlet.

Star|operation *f* cataract operation.

starr *adj* **(a)** stiff; *(unbeweglich)* rigid ◆ **~ vor Frost** stiff with frost; **meine Finger sind vor Kälte ganz ~** my fingers are frozen stiff *or* stiff with cold; **~ miteinander verbunden** joined rigidly; **~ abstehen** to stand up stiffly.
(b) *(unbewegt) Augen* glassy; *Blick auch* fixed ◆ **jdn ~ ansehen** to look fixedly at sb, to stare at sb.
(c) *(regungslos)* paralyzed ◆ **~ vor Schrecken/Entsetzen** paralyzed with fear/horror; **~ vor Staunen** dumbfounded.
(d) *(nicht flexibel) Regelung, Prinzip* inflexible, rigid; *Haltung auch* intransigent ◆ **~ an etw** *(dat)* **festhalten** to hold rigidly to sth.

Starre *f* **-,** *no pl* stiffness, rigidity.

starren *vi* **(a)** *(starr blicken)* to stare *(auf +acc* at) ◆ **ins Leere ~** to stare *or* gaze into space; **jdm ins Gesicht ~** to stare sb in the face; **vor sich** *(acc)* **hin ~** to stare straight ahead; **was ~ Sie so?** what are you staring at?; *siehe* **Loch.**
(b) von Gewehren ~ to bristle with guns.
(c) *(steif sein)* to be stiff *(von, vor +dat* with) ◆ **Moskau starrt vor Kälte** Moscow is in the grip of the cold; **vor Dreck ~** to be thick *or* covered with dirt; *(Kleidung)* to be stiff with dirt.
(d) *(abstehen)* to jut up/out.

Starrflügler *m (Aviat)* fixed-wing aircraft.

Starrheit *f siehe adj* stiffness; rigidity; glassiness; fixedness; paralysis; inflexibility, rigidity; intransigence.

Starr-: ~kopf *m (Mensch)* stubborn *or* obstinate mule; **einen ~kopf haben** to be stubborn *or* obstinate; **s~köpfig** *adj* stubborn, obstinate; **~köpfigkeit** *f* stubbornness, obstinacy; **~krampf** *m (Med)* tetanus, lockjaw; **~sinn** *m* stubbornness, mulishness; **s~sinnig** *adj* stubborn, mulish; **~sinnigkeit** *f siehe* **~sinn; ~sucht** *f (Med)* catalepsy.

Start *m* **-s, -s (a)** *(Sport)* start; *(~platz, ~linie auch)* starting line; *(Pferderennen auch)* starting post; *(Autorennen auch)* starting grid ◆ **am~ sein** to be at the start/on *or* at the starting line/at the starting post/on the starting grid; *(Läufer)* to be on their blocks; **das Zeichen zum ~ geben** to give the starting signal; **einen guten/schlechten ~ haben** *(lit, fig)* to get (off to) a good/bad start.
(b) *(Aviat)* take-off; *(Raketen~)* launch; *(~platz)* runway ◆ **der Maschine den ~ freigeben** to clear the plane for take-off.

Start-: ~abbruch *m* aborted take-off; **~automatik** *f (Aut)* automatic choke; **~bahn** *f (Aviat)* runway; **~- und Landebahn** runway; **s~berechtigt** *adj (Sport)* eligible (to enter); **s~bereit** *adj (Sport, fig)* ready to start *or* go, ready for (the) off *(inf)*; *(Aviat)* ready for take-off; *(Space)* ready for lift-off; **~block** *m (Sport)* starting block.

starten [1] *vi aux sein* to start; *(Aviat)* to take off; *(zum Start antreten)* to take part; to run; to swim; *(Pferde- or Autorennen)* to race; *(inf: abreisen)* to set off ◆ **in die letzte Runde ~** to go into *or* enter the last lap.
[2] *vt Satelliten, Rakete* to launch; *Unternehmen, Kampagne auch, Motor* to start; *Expedition* to get under way.

Starter *m* **-s, -** *(Aut, Sport)* starter.

Starterklappe *f (Aut)* choke.

Start-: ~erlaubnis *f (Sport)* permission to take part/run/swim/race; *(Aviat)* clearance for take-off; **~flagge** *f* starting flag; **~freigabe** *f* clearance for take-off; **~geld** *nt (Sport)* entry fee; **~gerät** *nt (für Raketen)* launcher; **~hilfe** *f (Aviat)* rocket-assisted take-off; *(fig)* initial aid; **im Winter braucht mein Auto ~hilfe** my car won't start on its own in winter; **jdm ~hilfe geben** to help sb get off the ground; **~hilfekabel** *nt* jump leads *(Brit) pl*, jumper cable *(US)*; **~kapital** *nt* starting capital; **s~klar** *adj (Aviat)* clear(ed) for take-off; *(Sport)* ready to start *or* for the off; **~kommando** *nt (Sport)* starting signal; *(Aviat)* take-off command; **~linie** *f (Sport)* starting line; **~loch** *nt (Sport)* starting hole; **in den ~löchern** on their marks; **~maschine** *f (Sport)* starting gate; **~nummer** *f* number; **~platz** *m (Sport)* starting place; *(für Läufer)* marks *pl*; *(Autorennen)* starting grid; **~rampe** *f (Space)* launching pad; **~schleuder** *f (Aviat)* catapult; ⚠**~schuß** *m (Sport)* starting signal; *(fig)* signal *(zu* for); **vor dem ~schuß** before the gun; **den ~schuß geben** to fire the (starting) pistol; *(fig)* to open the door; *(Erlaubnis geben)* to give the go-ahead; **~sprung** *m* racing dive; **~verbot** *nt (Aviat)* ban on take-off; *(Sport)* ban; **~verbot bekommen** to be banned *or* barred; **~-Ziel-Sieg** *m (Sport)* runaway victory.

Stasi *m* **-,** *no pl abbr of* **Staatssicherheitsdienst** *(DDR)*.

Statement ['steːtmənt] *nt* **-s, -s** statement ◆ **ein ~ abgeben** to issue a statement.

Statik ['ʃtaːtɪk, 'st-] *f* **(a)** *(Sci)* statics *sing.* **(b)** *(Build)* structural engineering.

Statiker(in *f*) ['ʃtaːtɪkɐ, -ərɪn, 'st-] *m* **-s, -** *(Tech)* structural engineer.

Station *f* **(a)** station; *(Haltestelle)* stop; *(fig: Abschnitt) (von Reise)* stage; *(von Leben)* phase ◆ **~ machen** to stop off. **(b)** *(Kranken~)* ward ◆ **er liegt/arbeitet auf ~ drei** he is in/works on ward three.

stationär [ʃtatsio'nɛːɐ] *adj (Astron, Sociol)* stationary; *(Med)* in-patient *attr* ◆ **~er Patient** in-patient; **~ behandeln** to treat in hospital.

stationieren* [ʃtatsio'niːrən] *vt Truppen* to station; *Atomwaffen etc* to deploy.

Stationierung [ʃtatsio'niːrʊŋ] *f siehe vt* stationing; deployment.

Stationierungskosten *pl* stationing costs *pl.*

Stations-: ~arzt *m* ward doctor; **~schwester** *f* ward sister; **~vorsteher** *m (Rail)* station-master, station-agent *(US)*; **~wahltaste** *f* tuning button.

statisch ['ʃtaːtɪʃ, 'st-] *adj (lit, fig)* static; *Gesetze* of statics ◆ **das Gebäude ist ~ einwandfrei** the building is structurally sound.

Statist *m (Film)* extra; *(Theat)* supernumerary; *(fig)* cipher ◆ **er war nur ein kleiner ~** *(fig)* he only played a minor role.

Statistenrolle *f (lit, fig)* minor role; *(Film, Theat auch)* walk-on part, bit part.

Statisterie *f (Film)* extras *pl*; *(Theat)* supernumeraries *pl.*

Statistik [ʃta'tɪstɪk, st-] *f* statistics *sing* ◆ **eine ~** a set of statistics; **die ~en** the statistics *pl.*

Statistiker(in *f*) [ʃta'tɪstɪkɐ, -ərɪn, st-] *m* **-s, -** statistician.

Statistin *f siehe* **Statist.**

statistisch [ʃta'tɪstɪʃ, st-] *adj* statistical; *siehe* **erfassen.**

Stativ *nt* tripod.

statt [1] *prep +gen or (old, inf, wenn kein Artikel) +dat* instead of ◆ **~ dessen** instead; **~ meiner/seiner/ihrer** *etc* in my/his/her *etc* place, instead of me/him/her *etc*; **~ Urlaub(s)** in lieu of *or* instead of holiday; **~ Karten** *heading of an announcement expressing thanks for condolences in place of individual replies.*
[2] *conj* instead of ◆ **~ zu bleiben** instead of staying; **~ zu bleiben, wollte ich lieber ...** rather than stay I wanted to ...; **~ ein Wort zu sagen** without saying a word.

⚠**Statt** *f* **-,** *no pl (form)* stead *(form)*, place ◆ **an meiner/seiner/ihrer ~** in my/his/her stead *(form) or* place; **an Kindes ~ annehmen** *(Jur)* to adopt; **an Zahlungs ~** *(Comm)* in lieu of payment; *siehe* **Eid.**

Stätte *f* **-, -n** *(liter)* place ◆ **eine bleibende ~** a permanent home.

Statt-: s~finden *vi sep irreg* to take place; *(Veranstaltung auch)* to be held; *(Ereignis auch)* to occur; **s~geben** *vi sep irreg +dat (form)* to grant; *siehe* **Einspruch; s~haft** *adj pred* permitted, allowed; **~halter** *m* governor; **~halterschaft** *f* governorship.

stattlich *adj* **(a)** *(hochgewachsen, groß) Tier* magnificent; *Bursche* strapping, powerfully built; *(eindrucksvoll) Erscheinung, Fünfziger* imposing; *(ansehnlich) Gebäude, Anwesen, Park* magnificent, splendid ◆ **ein ~er Mann** a fine figure of a man.
(b) *(umfangreich) Sammlung* impressive; *Familie* large; *(beträchtlich) Summe, Anzahl, Einnahmen* handsome, considerable.

Stattlichkeit *f, no pl siehe adj* **(a)** magnificence; powerful build; imposingness; splendour; *(von Mann)* imposing figure. **(b)** impressiveness; largeness; handsomeness.

Statue ['ʃtaːtuə, 'st-] *f* **-, -n** statue.

statuenhaft ['ʃtaːtuən-, 'st-] *adj* statuesque; *(unbeweglich)* like a statue, statue-like.

Statuette [ʃta'tuɛtə, st-] *f* statuette.

statuieren* [ʃtatuˈiːrən, st-] *vt* **ein Exempel an jdm ~** to make an example of sb; **um ein Exempel zu ~** as an example *or* warning to others; **ein Exempel mit etw ~** to use sth as a warning; **wir müssen da ein Exempel ~** we will have to make an example of somebody.

Statur *f* build.

Status [ˈʃtaːtʊs, ˈst-] *m* **-, -** status ◆ **~ quo/~ quo ante** status quo.

Status-: ~symbol *nt* status symbol; **~zeile** *f* (*Comput*) status line.

Statut [ʃtaˈtuːt, st-] *nt* **-(e)s, -en** statute.

statutarisch [ʃtatuˈtaːrɪʃ, st-] *adj* statutory ◆ **das ist ~ nicht möglich** that is excluded by statute.

Stau *m* **-(e)s, -e** *or* **-s (a)** (*Wasserstauung*) build-up; (*Wind~*) barrier effect; (*Verkehrsstauung*) traffic jam ◆ **ein ~ von 3 km** a 3km tailback. **(b)** *siehe* **Stauung.**

Stau|anlage *f* dam.

Staub *m* **-(e)s, -e** *or* **Stäube** dust; (*Bot*) pollen ◆ **~ saugen** to vacuum, to hoover ®; **~ wischen** to dust; **zu ~ werden** (*liter*) to turn to dust; (*wieder*) to return to dust (*liter*); **sich vor jdm in den ~ werfen** to throw oneself at sb's feet; **vor jdm im ~ kriechen** (*lit, fig*) to grovel before sb *or* at sb's feet; **sich aus dem ~e machen** (*inf*) to clear off (*inf*); **den ~ (eines Ortes/Landes) von den Füßen schütteln** (*liter*) to shake the dust (of a place/country) off one's feet; *siehe* **aufwirbeln.**

Staub- *in cpds* dust; **~beutel** *m* **(a)** (*Bot*) anther; **(b)** (*von ~sauger*) dust bag; **~blatt** *nt* (*Bot*) stamen.

Stäubchen *nt* speck *or* particle of dust.

Staubecken *nt* reservoir.

stauben *vi* to be dusty; (*Staub machen, aufwirbeln*) to make *or* create a lot of dust ◆ **bei Trockenheit staubt es mehr** there's a lot more dust around when it's dry.

stäuben [1] *vt* **Mehl/Puder** *etc* **auf etw** (*acc*) **~** to dust sth with flour/powder *etc*, to sprinkle flour/powder *etc* on sth.
[2] *vi aux sein* (*rare*) (*zerstieben*) to scatter; (*Wasser*) to spray.

Staub-: ~faden *m* (*Bot*) filament; **~fänger** *m* (*inf*) dust collector; **die vielen Bücher sind bloß ~fänger** all those books just lie around collecting dust; **~fetzen** *m* (*Aus*) duster; **~flocke** *f* piece of fluff; **~geborene(r)** *mf decl as adj* (*old, liter*) mortal (being); **~gefäß** *nt* (*Bot*) stamen.

staubig *adj* dusty.

Staub-: ~kamm *m* fine-tooth comb; **~korn** *nt* speck of dust, dust particle; **~lappen** *m* duster; **~lunge** *f* (*Med*) dust on the lung; (*von Kohlen~*) black lung, silicosis; **s~saugen** *vi insep, ptp* **s~gesaugt** to vacuum, to hoover ®; **~sauger** *m* vacuum cleaner, hoover ®; **~saugervertreter** *m* vacuum cleaner salesman; (*pej*) door-to-door salesman; **~schicht** *f* layer of dust; **~tuch** *nt* duster; **~wedel** *m* feather duster; **~wolke** *f* cloud of dust.

stauchen *vt* **(a)** (*zusammendrücken*) to compress (*auch Tech*), to squash (*inf*); (*rare: ver~*) to sprain. **(b)** (*inf*) *siehe* **zusammen~.**

Staudamm *m* dam.

Staude *f* **-, -n** (*Hort*) herbaceous perennial (plant); (*Busch*) shrub; (*Bananen~, Tabak~, Rosenkohl~*) plant.

stauen [1] *vt* **(a)** *Wasser, Fluß* to dam (up); *Blut* to stop *or* stem the flow of. **(b)** (*Naut*) to stow (away).
[2] *vr* (*sich anhäufen*) to pile up; (*ins Stocken geraten*) to get jammed; (*Wasser, fig*) to build up; (*Menschen*) to crowd; (*Blut*) to accumulate; (*durch Abbinden*) to be cut off ◆ **die Menschen stauten sich in den Gängen** people were jamming the corridors; **der Verkehr staute sich über eine Strecke von 2 km** there was a 2km tailback.

Stauer *m* **-s, -** (*Naut*) stevedore.

Stau-: ~gefahr *f* risk of congestion; **„~gefahr"** "delays likely"; **~mauer** *f* dam wall.

staunen *vi* to be astonished *or* amazed (*über +acc* at) ◆ **~d** in astonishment *or* amazement; **ich staune(, ich staune)!** (*inf*) well, I never!, well well!; **man staunt, wie ...** it's amazing how ...; **da kann man nur noch** *or* **bloß ~** it's just amazing; **da staunst du, was?** (*inf*) you didn't expect that, did you!; *siehe* **Bauklotz.**

Staunen *nt* **-s,** *no pl* astonishment, amazement (*über +acc* at) ◆ **jdn in ~ versetzen** to amaze *or* astonish sb.

staunenswert *adj* astonishing, amazing.

Staupe *f* **-, -n** (*Vet*) distemper.

Stau-: ~raum *m* storage space; **~see** *m* reservoir, artificial lake.

Stauung *f* **(a)** (*Stockung*) pile-up; (*in Lieferungen, Post etc*) hold-up; (*von Menschen*) jam; (*von Verkehr*) tailback ◆ **bei einer ~ der Züge im Bahnhof/der Schiffe im Hafen** when the station/harbour gets congested; **eine ~ des Verkehrs** a traffic jam.
(b) (*von Wasser*) build-up (of water) ◆ **~en sind hier sehr häufig** the water often gets blocked here; **zur ~ eines Flusses** to block a river.
(c) (*Blut~*) congestion *no pl* ◆ **bei ~(en) (des Blutes) in den Venen** when the veins become congested, when blood becomes congested in the veins.

Std., Stde. *abbr of* **Stunde** hr.

stdl. *abbr of* **stündlich.**

Steak [steːk] *nt* **-s, -s** steak.

Stearin [ʃteaˈriːn, st-] *nt* **-s, -e** stearin.

Stech-: ~apfel *m* (*Bot*) thorn-apple; **~becken** *nt* (*Med*) bed-pan; **~beitel** *m* chisel.

stechen *pret* **stach,** *ptp* **gestochen** [1] *vi* **(a)** (*Dorn, Stachel etc*) to prick; (*Insekt mit Stachel*) to sting; (*Mücken, Moskitos*) to bite; (*mit Messer etc*) to (make a) stab (*nach* at); (*Sonne*) to beat down; (*mit Stechkarte*) (*bei Ankunft*) to clock in *or* on; (*bei Weggang*) to clock out *or* off ◆ **die Sonne sticht in die Augen** the sun hurts one's eyes; **der Geruch sticht in die Nase** the smell stings one's nose; **mit etw in etw** (*acc*) **~** to stick sth in(to) sth; **jdm durch die Ohrläppchen ~** to pierce sb's ears.
(b) (*Cards*) to take the trick.
(c) (*Sport*) to have a play-/jump-/shoot-off.
(d) (*Farbe: spielen*) **die Farbe sticht ins Rötliche** the colour has a tinge of red *or* a reddish tinge.
[2] *vt* **(a)** (*Dorn, Stachel etc*) to prick; (*Insekt mit Stachel*) to sting; (*Mücken, Moskitos*) to bite; (*mit Messer etc*) to stab; *Löcher* to pierce ◆ **die Kontrolluhr ~** to clock on *or* in/out.
(b) (*Cards*) to take.
(c) (*ausschneiden, herauslösen*) *Spargel, Torf, Rasen* to cut.
(d) (*ab~*) *Schwein, Kalb* to stick, to kill; (*Angeln*) *Aale* to spear.
(e) (*gravieren*) to engrave ◆ **wie gestochen schreiben** to write a clear hand.
[3] *vr* to prick oneself (*an +dat* on, *mit* with) ◆ **sich** (*acc or dat*) **in den Finger ~** to prick one's finger.
[4] *vti impers* **es sticht** it is prickly; **es sticht mir** *or* **mich im Rücken** I have a sharp pain in my back.

Stechen *nt* **-s, - (a)** (*Sport*) play-/jump-/shoot-off. **(b)** (*Schmerz*) sharp pain.

stechend *adj* piercing; (*jäh*) *Schmerz* sharp; (*durchdringend*) *Augen, Blick auch* penetrating; (*beißend*) *Geruch* pungent.

Stech-: ~fliege *f* stable fly; **~kahn** *m* punt; **~karte** *f* clocking-in card; **~mücke** *f* gnat, midge, mosquito; **~palme** *f* holly; **~schritt** *m* (*Mil*) goose-step; **~uhr** *f* time-clock; **~zirkel** *m* (pair of) dividers.

Steck-: ~brief *m* "wanted" poster; (*fig*) personal description; **s~brieflich** *adv* **jdn s~brieflich verfolgen** to put up "wanted" posters for sb; **s~brieflich gesucht werden** to be wanted *or* on the wanted list; **~dose** *f* (*Elec*) (wall)socket.

Stecken *m* **-s, -** stick.

stecken [1] *vi pret* **steckte** *or* **stak** (*geh*), *ptp* **gesteckt (a)** (*festsitzen*) to be stuck; (*an- or eingesteckt sein*) to be; (*Nadel, Splitter etc*) to be (sticking); (*Brosche, Abzeichen etc*) to be (pinned) ◆ **eine Blume im Knopfloch/einen Ring am Finger ~ haben** to have a flower in one's buttonhole/a ring on one's finger; **der Stecker steckt in der Dose** the plug is in the socket; **er steckte in einem neuen Anzug** (*hum*) he was all done up in a new suit (*inf*); **der Schlüssel steckt** the key is in the lock.
(b) (*verborgen sein*) to be (hiding) ◆ **wo steckt er?** where has he got to?; **wo hast du die ganze Zeit gesteckt?** where have you been (hiding) all this time?; **darin steckt viel Mühe** a lot of work *or* trouble has gone into *or* has been put into that; **da steckt etwas dahinter** (*inf*) there's something behind it; **in ihm steckt etwas** he certainly has it in him; **zeigen, was in einem steckt** to show what one is made of, to show one's mettle.
(c) (*strotzen vor*) **voll** *or* **voller Fehler/Nadeln/Witz** *etc* **~** to be full of mistakes/pins/wit *etc.*
(d) (*verwickelt sein in*) **in Schwierigkeiten/tief in Schulden ~** to be in difficulties/to be deep(ly) in debt; **in einer Krise/der Pubertät ~** to be in the throes of a crisis/to be an adolescent.
[2] *vt pret* **steckte,** *ptp* **gesteckt (a)** to put; *Haare* to put up; *Brosche* to pin (*an +acc* onto) ◆ **die Hände in die Taschen ~** to put *or* stick (*inf*) one's hands in one's pockets; **das Hemd in die Hose ~** to tuck one's shirt in (one's trousers); **jdn ins Bett ~** (*inf*) to put sb to bed (*inf*); **jdn ins Gefängnis ~** (*inf*) to stick sb in prison (*inf*), to put sb away *or* inside (*inf*); **jdn in Uniform ~** (*inf*) to put sb in uniform; **etw in den Ofen/Briefkasten ~** to put *or* stick (*inf*) sth in the oven/letter-box.
(b) (*Sew*) to pin ◆ **den Saum eines Kleides ~** to pin up the hem of a dress.
(c) (*inf: investieren*) *Geld, Mühe* to put (*in +acc* into); *Zeit* to devote (*in +acc* to).
(d) jdm etw ~ (*inf*) to tell sb sth; **es jdm ~** (*inf*) to give sb a piece of one's mind.
(e) (*pflanzen*) to set.

Stecken-: ⚠s~bleiben *vi sep irreg aux sein* to stick fast, to get stuck; (*Kugel*) to be lodged; (*in der Rede*) to falter; (*beim Gedichtaufsagen*) to get stuck; **etw bleibt jdm im Halse s~** (*lit, fig*) sth sticks in sb's throat; **⚠s~lassen** *vt sep irreg* to leave; **den Schlüssel s~lassen** to leave the key in the lock; **laß dein Geld s~!** leave your money where it is *or* in your pocket!; **~pferd** *nt* (*lit, fig*) hobby-horse; **sein ~pferd reiten** (*fig*) to be on one's hobby-horse.

Stecker *m* **-s, -** (*Elec*) plug.

Steck-: ~karte *f* (*Comput*) expansion card; **~kissen** *nt* papoose; **~kontakt** *m* (*Elec*) plug.

Steckling *m* (*Hort*) cutting.

Stecknadel *f* pin ◆ **keine ~ hätte zu Boden fallen können** there wasn't room to breathe; **man hätte eine ~ fallen hören können** you could have heard a pin drop; **jdn/etw wie eine ~ suchen** to hunt high and low for sb/sth; **eine ~ im Heuhaufen** *or* **Heuschober suchen** (*fig*) to look for a needle in a haystack.

Steck-: ~nadelkissen *nt* pincushion; **~platz** *m* (*Comput*) expansion slot; **~reis** *nt* (*Hort*) cutting; **~rübe** *f* swede (*Brit*), rutabaga (*US*); **~schach** *nt* travelling chess-set; **⚠~schloß** *nt* bicycle lock; **~schlüssel** *m* box spanner; **⚠~schuß** *m* bullet lodged in the body; **~tuch** *nt* (*esp Aus*) breast-pocket handkerchief; **~zwiebel** *f* bulb.

Stefan *m* **-** Stephen.

Steg *m* **-(e)s, -e (a)** (*Brücke*) footbridge; (*Landungs~*) landing stage; (*old: Pfad*) path. **(b)** (*Mus, Brillen~*) bridge; (*Tech: an Eisenträgern*) vertical plate, web. **(c)** (*Hosen~*) strap (*under the foot*). **(d)** (*Typ*) furniture.

Steghose *f* stirrup pants *pl.*

Stegreif *m* **aus dem ~ spielen** (*Theat*) to improvise, to ad-lib; **eine Rede aus**

dem ~ halten to make an impromptu or off-the-cuff or ad-lib speech; etw aus dem ~ tun to do sth just like that.

Stegreif-: ~dichter m extempore poet; ~komödie f improvised comedy; ~rede f impromptu speech; ~spiel nt (Theat) improvisation; ~vortrag m impromptu lecture.

Steh- in cpds stand-up.

Steh|aufmännchen nt (Spielzeug) tumbler; (fig) somebody who always bounces back ◆ er ist ein richtiges ~ he always bounces back, you can't keep a good man down (prov).

Steh|ausschank m stand-up bar.

stehen pret stand, ptp gestanden aux haben or (S Ger, Aus, Sw) sein [1] vi (a) (in aufrechter Stellung sein) to stand; (warten auch) to wait; (Penis) to be erect; (inf: fertig sein) to be finished; (inf: geregelt sein) to be settled ◆ fest/sicher ~ to stand firm(ly)/securely; (Mensch) to have a firm/safe foothold; gebückt/krumm ~ to slouch; unter der Dusche ~ to be in the shower; an der Bushaltestelle ~ to stand or wait at the bus-stop; neben jdm zu ~ kommen (Mensch) to end up beside sb; ich kann nicht mehr ~ I can't stand (up) any longer; der Weizen steht gut the wheat is growing well; der Kaffee ist so stark, daß der Löffel drin steht (hum) the coffee is so strong that the spoon will almost stand up in it; so wahr ich hier stehe as sure as I'm standing here; hier stehe ich, ich kann nicht anders! (Hist) here I stand, I can do no other; mit jdm/etw ~ und fallen to depend on sb/sth; (wesentlich sein für) to stand or fall by sb/sth; mit ihm steht und fällt die Firma he's the kingpin of the organization; seine Hose steht vor Dreck (inf) his trousers are stiff with dirt; er steht (ihm) (sl), er hat einen ~ (sl) he has a hard-on (sl); das/die Sache steht (inf) that/the whole business is finally settled.
(b) (sich befinden) to be ◆ die Vase/die Tasse steht auf dem Tisch the vase is (standing)/the cup is on the table; mein Auto steht seit Wochen vor der Tür my car has been standing or sitting (inf) outside for weeks; meine alte Schule steht noch my old school is still standing or is still there; vor der Tür stand ein Fremder there was a stranger (standing) at the door; auf der Fahrbahn stand Wasser there was water on the road; ihm steht der Schweiß auf der Stirn his forehead is covered in sweat; am Himmel ~ to be in the sky; der Mond steht am Himmel the moon is shining; die Sonne steht abends tief/im Westen the sun in the evening is deep in the sky/in the West; unter Schock ~ to be in a state of shock; unter Drogeneinwirkung/Alkohol ~ to be under the influence of drugs/alcohol; kurz vor dem Krieg ~ to be on the brink of war; vor einer Entscheidung ~ to be faced with a decision; die Frage steht vor der Entscheidung the question is about to be decided; im 83. Lebensjahr ~ to be in one's 83rd year; man muß wissen, wo man steht you have to know where you stand; ich tue, was in meinen Kräften/meiner Macht steht I'll do everything I can/in my power; das steht zu erwarten/fürchten (geh) that is to be expected/feared; siehe Leben.
(c) (geschrieben, gedruckt sein) to be; (aufgeführt sein auch) to appear ◆ wo steht das? (lit) where does it say that?; (fig) who says so?; was steht da/in dem Brief/in der Zeitung? what does it/the letter/the paper say?, what does it say there/in the letter/in the paper?; das steht im Gesetz the law says so, that is what the law says; darüber steht nichts im Gesetz the law says nothing about that; es stand im „Kurier" it was in the "Courier"; das steht bei Nietzsche it says that in Nietzsche; das steht in der Bibel (geschrieben) it says that or so in the Bible, the Bible says so; es steht geschrieben (Bibl) it is written (Bibl).
(d) (angehalten haben) to have stopped; (Maschine, Fließband auch) to be at a standstill ◆ meine Uhr steht my watch has stopped; der ganze Verkehr steht all traffic is at a complete standstill.
(e) (inf: geparkt haben) to be parked ◆ wo ~ Sie? where are or have you parked?
(f) (anzeigen) (Rekord) to stand (auf +dat at); (Mannschaft etc) to be (auf +dat in) ◆ der Pegel steht auf 3.48 m the water mark is at or is showing 3.48 m; der Zeiger steht auf 4 Uhr the clock says 4 (o'clock); die Kompaßnadel steht auf or nach Norden the compass needle is indicating or pointing north; wie steht das Spiel? what is the score?; es steht 0:0 neither side has scored, there is still no score; es steht 2:1 für München the score is or it is 2-1 to Munich; es/die Sache steht mir bis hier (oben) (inf) I'm fed up to the back-teeth with it (inf), I'm sick and tired of it (inf).
(g) (Gram) (bei Satzstellung) to come; (bei Zeit, Fall, Modus) to be; (gefolgt werden von) to take ◆ mit dem Dativ/Akkusativ ~ to take or govern the dative/accusative.
(h) (passen zu) jdm ~ to suit sb.
(i) (Belohnung, Strafe etc) auf Betrug steht eine Gefängnisstrafe the penalty for fraud is imprisonment, fraud is punishable by imprisonment; auf die Ergreifung der Täter steht eine Belohnung there is a reward for or a reward has been offered for the capture of the persons responsible.
(j) (bewertet werden: Währung, Kurs) to be or stand (auf +dat at) ◆ wie steht das Pfund? how does the pound stand?; am besten steht der Schweizerfranken the Swiss franc is strongest.
(k) (Redewendungen) zu seinem Versprechen ~ to stand by or keep one's promise; zu dem, was man gesagt hat, ~ to stick to what one has said; zu seinen Behauptungen/seiner Überzeugung ~ to stand by what one says/by one's convictions; zum Sozialismus ~ to be a staunch socialist; zu jdm ~ to stand or stick by sb; wie ~ Sie dazu? what are your views or what is your opinion on that?; für etw ~ to stand for sth; auf jdn/etw ~ (sl) to be mad about sb/sth (inf), to go for sb/sth (inf), to be into sb/sth (sl); hinter jdm/etw ~ to be behind sb/sth; das steht (ganz) bei Ihnen (form) that is (entirely) up to you.
[2] vr (a) wie ~ sich Müllers jetzt? how are things with the Müllers now?; sich gut/schlecht ~ to be well-off/badly off; sich bei or mit jdm/etw gut/schlecht ~ to be well-off/badly off with sb/sth; sich mit jdm gut/schlecht ~ (sich verstehen) to get on well/badly with sb.
(b) hier steht es sich nicht gut this isn't a very good place to stand.
[3] vi impers es steht schlecht/gut/besser um jdn (bei Aussichten) things look or it looks bad/good/better for sb; (gesundheitlich, finanziell) sb is doing badly/well/better; es steht schlecht/gut/besser um etw things look or it looks bad/good/better for sth, sth is doing badly/well/better; wie steht's? how are or how's things?; wie steht es damit? how about it?; wie steht es mit ...? what is the position regarding ...?; so steht es also! so that's how it is, so that's the way it is.
[4] vt Posten, Wache to stand ◆ sich (acc) müde ~, sich (dat) die Beine in den Bauch (inf) ~ to stand until one is ready to drop.

Stehen nt -s, no pl (a) standing ◆ das viele ~ all this standing; etw im ~ tun to do sth standing up.
(b) (Halt) stop, standstill ◆ zum ~ bringen to stop; Lokomotive, LKW, Verkehr, Produktion auch to bring to a standstill or halt or stop; Produktion, Heer, Vormarsch auch to halt; zum ~ kommen to stop; (Lokomotive, LKW, Verkehr, Produktion auch) to come to a standstill or halt or stop.

⚠ **stehenbleiben** vi sep irreg aux sein (a) (anhalten) to stop; (Zug, LKW, Verkehr, Produktion auch) to come to a standstill or halt or stop; (Aut: Motor auch) to cut out; (beim Lesen auch) to leave off ◆ ~! stop!; (Mil) halt!
(b) (nicht weitergehen) (Mensch, Tier) to stay; (Entwicklung) to stop; (Zeit) to stand still; (Auto, Zug) to stand.
(c) (vergessen or zurückgelassen werden) to be left (behind) ◆ mein Regenschirm muß im Büro stehengeblieben sein I must have left my umbrella in the office.
(d) (im Text unverändert bleiben) to be left (in) ◆ soll das so ~? should that stay or be left as it is?

stehend adj attr Fahrzeug stationary; Wasser, Gewässer stagnant; (ständig) Heer standing, regular; Start (Radfahren) standing ◆ ~e Redensart stock phrase; ~en Fußes (liter) instanter, immediately; ~es Gut (Naut) standing rigging.

⚠ **stehenlassen** ptp ~ or stehengelassen vt sep irreg to leave; (zurücklassen, vergessen auch) to leave behind; (Cook) to let stand; Essen, Getränk to leave (untouched); Fehler to leave (in) ◆ laßt das (an der Tafel) stehen leave it (on the board); alles stehen- und liegenlassen to drop everything; (Flüchtlinge etc) to leave everything behind; jdn einfach ~ to leave sb standing (there), to walk off and leave sb; sich (dat) einen Bart ~ to grow a beard; jdn vor der Tür/in der Kälte ~ to leave sb standing outside/in the cold.

Steher m -s, - (Pferderennen, fig) stayer; (Radfahren) motor-paced rider.

Steherrennen nt (Radfahren) motor-paced race.

Steh-: ~geiger m café violinist; ⚠~imbiß m stand-up snack-bar; ~kneipe f stand-up bar; ~konvent m (hum) stand-up do (inf); ~kragen m stand-up collar; (Vatermörder) wing collar; (von Geistlichen auch) dog collar; ~lampe f standard lamp; ~leiter f stepladder.

stehlen pret stahl, ptp gestohlen [1] vti to steal ◆ hier wird viel gestohlen there's a lot of stealing around here; jdm die Ruhe ~ to disturb sb; jdm die Zeit ~ to waste sb's time; siehe Elster, gestohlen.
[2] vr to steal ◆ sich in das/aus dem Haus ~ to steal into/out of the house; die Sonne stahl sich durch die Wolken (liter) the sun stole forth from behind the clouds (liter).

Stehler m -s, - siehe Hehler(in).

Steh-: ~lokal nt stand-up café; ~platz m ich bekam nur noch einen ~platz I had to stand; ein ~platz kostet 1 Mark a ticket for standing room costs 1 mark, it costs 1 mark to stand; ~plätze standing room sing; zwei ~plätze, bitte two standing, please; die Anzahl der ~plätze ist begrenzt only a limited number of people are allowed to stand; ~pult nt high desk; ~satz m (Typ) standing or line type; ~vermögen nt staying power, stamina.

Steiermark f - Styria.

steif adj (a) stiff; Grog auch strong; Penis auch hard, erect ◆ ~ vor Kälte stiff or numb with cold; eine ~e Brise a stiff breeze; ein ~er Hals a stiff neck; ein ~er Hut a homburg (hat); (Melone) a bowler (hat), a derby (US); sich ~ (wie ein Brett) machen to go rigid; das Eiweiß ~ schlagen to beat the egg white until stiff; ~ und fest auf etw (dat) beharren to insist stubbornly or obstinately on sth; ein S~er (sl) a hard-on (sl).
(b) (gestärkt) starched; Kragen auch stiff.
(c) (förmlich) stiff; Empfang, Konventionen, Begrüßung, Abend formal ◆ ~ lächeln to smile stiffly.

Steife f -, -n (a) no pl stiffness. (b) (Stärkemittel) starch.

steifen vt to stiffen; Wäsche to starch; siehe Nacken.

Steifftier ® nt soft toy (animal).

Steifheit f siehe adj (a) stiffness; strength; hardness, erectness. (b) starchedness; stiffness. (c) stiffness; formality.

Steifleinen nt buckram.

Steig m -(e)s, -e steep track.

Steigbügel m stirrup ◆ jdm den ~ halten (fig) to help sb on.

Steigbügelhalter m (esp Pol pej) jds ~ sein to help sb to come to power.

Steige f -, -n (dial) (a) siehe Steig. (b) siehe Stiege.

Steig|eisen nt climbing iron usu pl; (Bergsteigen) crampon; (an Mauer) rung (in the wall).

steigen pret stieg, ptp gestiegen aux sein [1] vi (a) (klettern) to climb ◆ auf einen Berg/Turm/Baum/eine Leiter ~ to climb (up) a mountain/tower/tree/ladder; aufs Fahrrad/Pferd ~ to get on(to) the/one's bicycle/get on(to) or mount the/one's horse; ins Bett/in die Straßenbahn ~ to get into bed/on

⚠: for details of spelling reform, see supplement

the tram; **ins Wasser/in die Badewanne ~** to climb *or* get into the bath; **in die Kleider ~** (*inf*) to put on one's clothes; **vom Fahrrad/Pferd ~** to get off *or* dismount from the/one's bicycle/horse; **aus dem Wasser/der Badewanne/dem Bett ~** to get out of the water/the bath/bed; **aus dem Zug/Bus/Flugzeug ~** to get off the train/bus/plane; **wer hoch steigt, fällt tief** (*Prov*) the bigger they come the harder they fall (*prov*).
(b) (*sich aufwärts bewegen*) to rise; (*Vogel auch*) to soar; (*Flugzeug, Straße*) to climb; (*sich aufbäumen: Pferd*) to rear; (*sich auflösen: Nebel*) to lift; (*sich erhöhen*) (*Preis, Zahl, Gehalt etc*) to increase, to go up, to rise; (*Fieber*) to go up; (*zunehmen*) (*Chancen, Mißtrauen, Ungeduld etc*) to increase; (*Spannung*) to increase, to mount ◆ **Drachen ~ lassen** to fly kites; **der Gestank/Duft stieg ihm in die Nase** the stench/smell reached his nostrils; **das Blut stieg ihm in den Kopf/das Gesicht** the blood rushed to his head/face; **in jds Achtung** (*dat*) **~** to rise in sb's estimation; **die allgemeine/meine Stimmung stieg** the general mood improved/my spirits rose.
(c) (*inf: stattfinden*) to be ◆ **steigt die Demonstration/Prüfung oder nicht?** is the demonstration/examination on or not?; **bei Helga steigt Sonnabend eine Party** Helga's having a party on Saturday.
[2] *vt Treppen, Stufen* to climb (up).

Steiger *m* **-s, -** (*Min*) pit foreman.

Steigerer *m* **-s, -** bidder.

steigern [1] *vt* (a) to increase; *Geschwindigkeit auch* to raise (*auf +acc* to); *Not, Gefahr auch* to intensify; *Wert auch* to add to; *Wirkung auch* to heighten; *Farbe* to intensify, to heighten; (*verschlimmern*) *Übel, Zorn* to aggravate.
(b) (*Gram*) to compare.
(c) (*ersteigern*) to buy at an auction.
[2] *vi* to bid (*um* for).
[3] *vr* (a) (*sich erhöhen*) to increase; (*Geschwindigkeit auch*) to rise; (*Gefahr auch*) to intensify; (*Wirkung auch*) to be heightened; (*Farben*) to be intensified; (*Zorn, Übel*) to be aggravated, to worsen ◆ **sein Ärger steigerte sich zu Zorn** his annoyance turned into rage; **seine Schmerzen steigerten sich ins Unerträgliche** his pain became unbearable.
(b) (*sich verbessern*) to improve.
(c) (*hinein~*) **sich in etw** (*acc*) **~** to work oneself (up) into sth.

Steigerung *f* (a) *siehe vt (a)* (*das Steigern*) increase (*gen* in); rise (*gen* in); intensification; heightening; intensification, heightening; aggravation. (b) (*Verbesserung*) improvement. (c) (*Gram*) comparative.

Steigerungs-: s~fähig *adj* improvable; **~form** *f* (*Gram*) comparative/superlative form; **~stufe** *f* (*Gram*) degree of comparison.

Steig-: ~fähigkeit *f* (*Aut*) hill-climbing *or* pulling capacity; (*Aviat*) climbing capacity; **~ fähigkeit beweisen** to pull well; **~flug** *m* (*Aviat*) climb, ascent; **~geschwindigkeit** *f* rate of climb *or* ascent.

Steigung *f* (*Hang*) slope; (*von Hang, Straße, Math*) gradient; (*Gewinde~*) pitch ◆ **eine ~ von 10%** a gradient of one in ten *or* of 10%.

Steigungs-: ~grad *m* gradient; **~winkel** *m* angle of gradient.

steil *adj* (a) steep ◆ **eine ~e Karriere** (*fig*) a rapid rise. (b) (*senkrecht*) upright ◆ **sich ~ aufrichten** to sit/stand up straight. (c) (*Sport*) **~e Vorlage, ~er Paß** through ball. (d) (*dated sl*) super (*inf*), smashing (*inf*) ◆ **ein ~er Zahn** (*dated sl*) a smasher (*inf*).

Steil-: ~hang *m* steep slope; **~heck** *nt* hatchback.

Steilheit *f* steepness.

Steil-: ~küste *f* steep coast; (*Klippen*) cliffs *pl*; ⚠**~paß** *m*, **~vorlage** *f* (*Sport*) through ball; **~wand** *f* steep face; **~wandfahrer** *m* wall-of-death rider; **~wandzelt** *nt* frame tent.

Stein *m* **-(e)s, -e** (a) (*auch Bot, Med*) stone; (*Feuer~*) flint; (*Edel~ auch, in Uhr*) jewel; (*Spiel~*) piece ◆ **der ~ der Weisen** (*lit, fig*) the philosophers' stone; **es blieb kein ~ auf dem anderen** everything was smashed to pieces; (*bei Gebäuden, Mauern*) not a stone was left standing; **das könnte einen ~ erweichen** that would move the hardest heart to pity; **mir fällt ein ~ vom Herzen!** (*fig*) that's a load off my mind!; **bei jdm einen ~ im Brett haben** (*fig inf*) to be well in with sb (*inf*); **den ersten ~ (auf jdn) werfen** (*prov*) to cast the first stone (at sb); *siehe* **Anstoß, rollen, Krone**.
(b) (*Bau~, Natur~*) stone; (*groß, esp Hohlblock*) block; (*kleiner, esp Ziegel~*) brick.
(c) *no pl* (*Material*) stone ◆ **ein Haus aus ~** a house made of stone, a stone house; **ein Herz aus ~** (*fig*) a heart of stone; **es friert ~ und Bein** (*fig inf*) it's freezing cold outside; **~ und Bein schwören** (*fig inf*) to swear blind (*inf*); **zu ~ erstarren** *or* **werden** to turn to stone; (*fig*) to be as if turned to stone.

Stein-: ~adler *m* golden eagle; **s~alt** *adj* ancient, as old as the hills; **~bau** *m* (a) *no pl* building in stone *no art*; (b) (*Gebäude*) stone building; **~bock** *m* (a) (*Zool*) ibex; (b) (*Astrol*) Capricorn; **~boden** *m* stone floor; **~bohrer** *m* masonry drill; (*Gesteinsbohrer*) rock drill; **~bruch** *m* quarry; **~brucharbeiter** *m* quarryman, quarry worker; **~butt** *m* (*Zool*) turbot; **~druck** *m* (*Typ*) lithography; **~drucker** *m* lithographer; **~eiche** *f* holm oak.

steinern *adj* stone; (*fig*) stony ◆ **ein ~es Herz** a heart of stone.

Stein-: ~erweichen *nt* **zum ~erweichen weinen** to cry heartbreakingly; **s~erweichend** *adj* heart-rending, heartbreaking; **~fraß** *m* stone erosion; **~frucht** *f* stone fruit; **~fußboden** *m* stone floor; **~garten** *m* rockery, rock garden; **~geiß** *f* female ibex; **s~grau** *adj* stone-grey; **~gut** *nt* stoneware; **~hagel** *m* hail of stones.

Steinhäger ® *m* **-s, -** Steinhäger, *type of schnapps.*

steinhart *adj* (as) hard as a rock, rock hard.

steinig *adj* stony ◆ **ein ~er Weg** (*fig*) a path of trial and tribulation.

steinigen *vt* to stone.

Steinigung *f* stoning.

Steinkohle *f* hard coal.

Steinkohlen-: ~bergbau *m* coal mining; **~bergwerk** *nt* coal mine, colliery; **~revier** *nt* coal-mining area.

Stein-: ~krug *m* (*aus ~gut/~zeug*) (*Kanne*) earthenware/stoneware jug; (*Becher*) earthenware/stoneware mug; (*für Bier*) stein; **~leiden** *nt* (*Nieren-/Blasen-/Gallen~e*) kidney/bladder stones *pl*; gallstones *pl*; **ein ~leiden haben** to suffer from kidney *etc* stones; **~meißel** *m* stone chisel; **~metz** *m* **-en, -en** stonemason; **~obst** *nt* stone fruit; **~pilz** *m* boletus edulis (*spec*); **~platte** *f* stone slab; (*zum Pflastern*) flagstone; **s~reich** *adj* (*inf*) stinking rich (*inf*), rolling in it (*inf*); **~salz** *nt* rock salt; **~schlag** *m* (a) rockfall; **„Achtung ~schlag"** "danger falling stones"; (b) *no pl* (*Schotter*) broken stone; (*zum Straßenbau*) (road-)metal; **~schlaggefahr** *f* danger of rockfall(s); **~schleuder** *f* catapult; **~schneider** *m* gem-cutter; **~schnitt** *m* (a) cut (gem)stone; (b) *no pl* (*Verfahren*) gem cutting; **~tafel** *f* stone tablet; **~topf** *m* (*aus ~gut/~zeug*) earthenware/stoneware pot; **~wild** *nt* (*Hunt*) ibexes *pl*; **~wurf** *m* (a) (*fig*) stone's throw; (b) (*lit*) **mit einem ~wurf** by throwing a stone; **~wüste** *f* stony desert; (*fig*) concrete jungle; **~zeit** *f* Stone Age; **s~zeitlich** *adj* Stone Age *attr*; **~zeug** *nt* stoneware.

Steirer(in *f*) *m* **-s, -** Styrian.

steirisch *adj* Styrian.

Steiß *m* **-es, -e** (*Anat*) coccyx; (*hum inf*) tail (*inf*), behind.

Steiß-: ~bein *nt* (*Anat*) coccyx; **~geburt** *f* (*Med*) breech birth *or* delivery; **~lage** *f* (*Med*) breech presentation.

Stele ['ste:lə, 'ʃte:lə] *f* **-, -n** (*Bot, Archeol*) stele.

Stellage [ʃtɛ'la:ʒə] *f* **-, -n** (*inf: Gestell*) rack, frame; (*dial inf: Beine*) legs *pl*, pins *pl* (*inf*).

stellar [ʃtɛ'la:ɐ, st-] *adj* (*Astron*) stellar.

Stelldichein *nt* **-(s), -(s)** (*dated*) rendezvous, tryst (*old*) ◆ **sich** (*dat*) **ein ~ geben** (*fig*) to come together.

▼ **Stelle** *f* **-, -n** (a) place, spot; (*Standort*) place; (*Fleck: rostend, naß, faul etc*) patch ◆ **an dieser ~** in this place, on this spot; **eine gute ~ zum Parken/Picknicken** a good place *or* spot to park/for a picnic; **legen Sie das an eine andere ~** put it in a different place; **diese ~ muß repariert werden** this bit needs repairing, it needs to be repaired here; **eine kahle ~ am Kopf** a bald patch on one's head; **eine wunde/entzündete ~ am Finger** a cut/an inflammation on one's finger, a cut/an inflamed finger; **Salbe auf die wunde/aufgeriebene ~ auftragen** apply ointment to the affected area; **eine empfindliche ~** (*lit*) a sensitive spot *or* place; (*fig*) a sensitive point; **eine schwache ~** a weak spot; (*fig auch*) a weak point; **auf der ~ laufen** to run on the spot; **auf der ~ treten** (*lit*) to mark time; (*fig*) not to make any progress *or* headway; **auf der ~** (*fig: sofort*) on the spot; *kommen, gehen* straight *or* right away; **nicht von der ~ kommen** not to make any progress *or* headway; (*fig auch*) to be bogged down; **etw nicht von der ~ kriegen** (*inf*) *or* **bekommen** to be unable to move *or* shift sth; **sich nicht von der ~ rühren** *or* **bewegen, nicht von der ~ weichen** to refuse to budge (*inf*) *or* move; **zur ~ sein** to be on the spot; (*bereit, etw zu tun*) to be at hand; **X zur ~!** (*Mil*) X reporting!; **sich bei jdm zur ~ melden** (*Mil*) to report to sb; *siehe* **Ort**[1].
▼ (b) (*in Buch etc*) place; (*Abschnitt*) passage; (*Text~, esp beim Zitieren*) reference; (*Bibel~*) verse; (*Mus*) passage ◆ **an dieser ~** here; **an anderer ~** elsewhere, in another place.
(c) (*Zeitpunkt*) point ◆ **an dieser ~** at this point *or* juncture; **an anderer ~** on another occasion; **an früherer/späterer ~** earlier/later; (*an anderem Tag auch*) on an earlier/a later occasion; **an passender ~** at an appropriate moment.
(d) (*in Reihenfolge, Ordnung, Liste*) place; (*in Tabelle, Hierarchie auch*) position ◆ **an erster ~** in the first place, first; **an erster/zweiter ~ geht es um** ... in the first instance *or* first/secondly it's a question of ...; **(bei jdm) an erster/letzter ~ kommen** to come first/last (for sb); **an erster/zweiter** *etc* **~ stehen** to be first/second *etc*, to be in first/second *etc* place; (*in bezug auf Wichtigkeit*) to come first/second *etc*; **an führender/einflußreicher ~ stehen** to be in *or* have a leading/an influential position.
(e) (*Math*) figure, digit; (*hinter Komma*) place ◆ **drei ~n hinter dem Komma** three decimal places; **eine Zahl mit drei ~n** a three-figure number.
▼ (f) (*Lage, Platz, Aufgabenbereich*) place ◆ **an ~ von** *or* (*+gen*) in place of, instead of; **an jds ~** (*acc*)**/an die ~ einer Sache** (*gen*) **treten** to take sb's place/the place of sth; **das erledige ich/ich gehe an deiner ~** I'll do that for you/I'll go in your place; **ich möchte jetzt nicht an seiner ~ sein** I wouldn't like to be in his position *or* shoes; **an deiner ~ würde ich** ... in your position *or* if I were you I would ...
▼ (g) (*Posten*) job; (*Ausbildungs~*) place ◆ **eine freie** *or* **offene ~** a vacancy; **ohne ~** without a job; **wir haben zur Zeit keine ~n zu vergeben** we haven't any vacancies at present.
(h) (*Dienst~*) office; (*Behörde*) authority ◆ **da bist du bei mir/ihm an der richtigen ~!** (*inf*) you've come/you went to the right place; **sich an höherer ~ beschweren** to complain to somebody higher up *or* to a higher authority.

stellen [1] *vt* (a) (*hin~*) to put; (*an bestimmten Platz legen auch*) to place ◆ **jdm etw auf den Tisch ~** to put sth on the table for sb; **jdn über/unter jdn ~** (*fig*) to put *or* place sb above/below sb; **auf sich** (*acc*) **selbst gestellt sein** (*fig*) to have to fend for oneself.
(b) (*in senkrechte Position bringen*) to stand ◆ **die Ohren ~** to prick up its ears; **du solltest es ~, nicht legen** you should stand it up, not lay it down.
(c) (*Platz finden für*) **etw nicht ~ können** (*unterbringen*) not to have room *or* space for sth; **etw gut ~ können** to have a good place for sth.
(d) (*anordnen*) to arrange ◆ **das sollten Sie anders ~** you should put it in a

different position.
(e) *(er~)* **(jdm) eine Diagnose ~** to provide (sb with) a diagnosis, to make a diagnosis (for sb); **jdm sein Horoskop ~** to draw up *or* cast sb's horoscope.
(f) *(arrangieren) Szene* to arrange; *Aufnahme* to pose ◆ **eine gestellte Pose** a pose.
(g) *(beschaffen, aufbieten)* to provide.
(h) *(ein~)* to set *(auf +acc* at); *Uhr etc* to set *(auf +acc* for) ◆ **das Radio lauter/leiser ~** to turn the radio up/down; **die Heizung höher/kleiner ~** to turn the heating up/down.
(i) *(finanziell)* **gut/besser/schlecht gestellt** well/better/badly off.
(j) *(erwischen)* to catch; *(fig inf)* to corner; *siehe* **Rede.**
(k) *in Verbindung mit n siehe auch dort. Aufgabe, Thema, Bedingung, Termin* to set *(jdm* sb); *Frage* to put *(jdm, an jdn* to sb); *Antrag, Forderung, Bedingung* to make.
(l) *(in Redewendungen)* **etw in jds Belieben** *or* **Ermessen** *(acc)* **~** to leave sth to sb's discretion, to leave sth up to sb; **jdn unter jds Aufsicht** *(acc)* **~** to place *or* put sb under sb's care; **jdn vor ein Problem/eine Aufgabe** *etc* **~** to confront sb with a problem/task *etc*; **jdn vor eine Entscheidung ~** to put sb in the position of having to make a decision.
[2] *vr* **(a)** to (go and) stand *(an +acc* at, by); *(sich auf~, sich einordnen)* to position oneself; *(sich aufrecht hin~)* to stand up ◆ **sich auf (die) Zehenspitzen ~** to stand on tip-toe; **sich auf den Standpunkt ~, ...** to take the view ...; **sich gegen jdn/etw ~** *(fig)* to oppose sb/sth; **sich hinter jdn/etw ~** *(fig)* to support *or* back sb/sth, to stand by sb/sth; **sich jdm in den Weg/vor die Nase ~** to stand in sb's way *(auch fig)*/right in front of sb.
(b) *(Gegenstand, Körperteil)* **sich senkrecht ~** to stand *or* come up; **sich in die Höhe ~** to stand up; *(Ohren)* to prick up.
(c) *(fig: sich verhalten)* **sich positiv/anders zu etw ~** to have a positive/different attitude towards sth; **wie stellst du dich zu ...?** how do you regard ...?, what do you think of ...?; **sich gut mit jdm ~** to put oneself on good terms with sb.
(d) *(inf: finanziell)* **sich gut/schlecht ~** to be well/badly off.
(e) *(sich ein~: Gerät etc)* to set itself *(auf +acc* at) ◆ **die Heizung stellt sich von selbst kleiner** the heating turns itself down.
(f) *(sich ausliefern, antreten)* to give oneself up, to surrender *(jdm* to sb) ◆ **sich der öffentlichen Kritik ~** to lay oneself open to public criticism; **sich den Journalisten/den Fragen der Journalisten ~** to make oneself available to the reporters/to be prepared to answer reporters' questions; **sich einer Herausforderung/einem Herausforderer ~** to take up a challenge/take on a challenger; **sich (jdm) zum Kampf ~** to be prepared to do battle (with sb), to announce one's readiness to fight (sb).
(g) *(sich ver~)* **sich krank/schlafend** *etc* **~** to pretend to be ill/asleep *etc*; *siehe* **dumm, taub.**
(h) *(fig: entstehen)* to arise *(für* for) ◆ **es stellten sich uns** *(dat)* **allerlei Probleme** we were faced *or* confronted with all sorts of problems.

Stellen-: ~angebot *nt* offer of employment, job offer; **„~angebote"** "situations vacant", "vacancies"; **~anzeige, ~ausschreibung** *f* job advertisement *or* ad *(inf)*; **~beschreibung** *f* job description; **~besetzung** *f* appointment, filling a/the post *no art*; **~gesuch** *nt* advertisement seeking employment, "employment wanted" advertisement; **„~gesuche"** "situations wanted"; **~markt** *m* employment *or* job market; *(in Zeitung)* appointments section; **~nachweis** *m*, **~vermittlung** *f* employment bureau *or* centre; *(privat auch)* employment agency; **s~weise** *adv* in places, here and there; **s~weise Schauer** scattered showers, showers in places; **~wert** *m (Math)* place value; *(fig)* status; **einen hohen ~wert haben** to play an important role.

-stellig *adj suf (bei Zahlen)* -figure, -digit; *(hinter Komma)* -place ◆ **ein drei~er Dezimalbruch** a number with three decimal places.

Stell-: ~macher *m (N Ger) (Wagenbauer)* cartwright; *(esp von Wagenrädern)* wheelwright; **~macherei** *f* cart-making; *(Werkstatt)* cartwright's/wheelwright's (work-)shop; **~platz** *m (für Auto)* parking space; **~probe** *f (Theat)* blocking rehearsal; **~schraube** *f (Tech)* adjusting *or* set screw.

Stellung *f* **(a)** *(lit, fig, Mil)* position ◆ **in ~ bringen/gehen** to bring/get into position, to place in position/take up one's position; **die ~ halten** *(Mil)* to hold one's position; *(hum)* to hold the fort; **~ beziehen** *(Mil)* to move into position; *(fig)* to declare one's position, to make it clear where one stands; **zu etw ~ nehmen** to give one's opinion on sth, to comment on sth; **ich möchte dazu nicht ~ nehmen** I would rather not comment on that; **für jdn/etw ~ nehmen** *or* **beziehen** to come out in favour of sb/sth; *(verteidigen)* to take sb's part/to defend sth; **gegen jdn/etw ~ nehmen** *or* **beziehen** to come out against sb/sth.
(b) *(Rang)* position ◆ **in führender/untergeordneter ~** in a leading/subordinate position; **in meiner ~ als ...** in my capacity as ...; **die rechtliche ~ des Mieters** the legal status of the tenant; **gesellschaftliche ~** social status *or* standing.
(c) *(Posten)* position, post, situation *(dated, form)* ◆ **bei jdm in ~ sein** to be in sb's employment *or* employ *(form)*; **ohne ~ sein** to be without employment *or* unemployed.

Stellungnahme *f* **-, -n** statement *(zu* on) ◆ **sich** *(dat)* **seine ~ vorbehalten, sich einer ~** *(gen)* **enthalten** to decline to comment; **eine ~ zu etw abgeben** to make a statement on sth; **was ist Ihre ~ dazu?** what is your position on this?

Stellungs-: ~befehl *m siehe* **Gestellungsbefehl**; **~fehler** *m (Sport)* positional error; **~krieg** *m* positional warfare *no indef art*; **s~los** *adj* without employment, unemployed; **~spiel** *nt (Sport)* positional play *no indef art*; **~suche** *f* search for employment; **auf ~suche sein** to be looking for employment *or* a position; **~wechsel** *m* change of employment.

stellv. *abbr of* **stellvertretend.**

Stell-: s~vertretend *adj (von Amts wegen)* deputy *attr*; *(vorübergehend)* acting *attr*; **s~vertretend für jdn** deputizing *or* acting for sb, on behalf of sb; **s~vertretend für jdn handeln** to deputize *or* act for sb; **s~vertretend für jdn/etw stehen** to stand in for sb/sth *or* in place of sb/sth; **~vertreter** *m* (acting) representative; *(von Amts wegen)* deputy; *(von Arzt)* locum; **der ~vertreter Christi (auf Erden)** the Vicar of Christ; **~vertretung** *f (~vertreter)* representative; *(von Amts wegen)* deputy; *(von Arzt)* locum; **die ~vertretung für jdn übernehmen** to represent sb; *(von Amts wegen)* to stand in *or* deputize for sb; **in ~vertretung** *+gen* for, on behalf of; **~wand** *f* partition wall; **~werk** *nt (Rail)* signal box *(Brit)*, signal *or* switch tower *(US)*.

stelzbeinig *adj (fig) (steif)* stiff.

Stelze *f* **-, -n (a)** stilt; *(inf: Bein)* leg, pin *(inf)* ◆ **auf ~n gehen** to walk on stilts; *(fig: Lyrik etc)* to be stilted. **(b)** *(Orn)* wagtail. **(c)** *(Aus: Schweins~)* pig's trotter.

stelzen *vi aux sein (inf)* to stalk.

Stelzenlaufen *nt* walking on stilts *no art* ◆ **~ lernen** to learn to walk on stilts.

Stelz-: ~fuß *m* wooden leg, peg *(inf)*, peg-leg; *(Mensch)* peg-leg; **~vögel** *pl (Orn)* waders *pl.*

Stemmbogen *m (Ski)* stem turn.

Stemm|eisen *nt* crowbar.

stemmen [1] *vt* **(a)** *(stützen)* to press; *Ellenbogen* to prop ◆ **die Arme in die Seiten** *or* **Hüften gestemmt** with arms akimbo; **die Arme in die Hüften ~** to put one's hands on one's hips; **er hatte die Arme in die Hüften gestemmt** he stood with arms akimbo.
(b) *(hoch~)* to lift (above one's head) ◆ **einen ~** *(inf)* to have a few *(inf)*.
(c) *(meißeln)* to chisel; *(kräftiger) Loch* to knock *(in +acc* in).
[2] *vr* **sich gegen etw ~** to brace oneself against sth; *(fig)* to set oneself against sth, to oppose sth.
[3] *vi (Ski)* to stem.

Stemmschwung *m (Ski)* stem turn.

Stempel *m* **-s, - (a)** *(Gummi~)* (rubber-)stamp.
(b) *(Abdruck)* stamp; *(Post~)* postmark; *(Vieh~)* brand, mark; *(auf Silber, Gold)* hallmark ◆ **jdm/einer Sache einen/seinen ~ aufdrücken** *(fig)* to make a/one's mark on sb/sth; **den ~** *+gen or* **von tragen** to bear the stamp of.
(c) *(Tech) (Präge~)* die; *(stangenförmig, Loch~)* punch.
(d) *(Tech: von Druckpumpe etc)* piston, plunger.
(e) *(Min)* prop.
(f) *(Bot)* pistil.

Stempel-: ~farbe *f* stamping ink; **~geld** *nt (inf)* dole (money) *(inf)*; **~karte** *f* punch card; **~kissen** *nt* ink pad.

stempeln [1] *vt* to stamp; *Brief* to postmark; *Briefmarke* to frank; *Gold, Silber* to hallmark ◆ **jdn zum Lügner ~** *(fig)* to brand sb as a liar.
[2] *vi (inf)* **(a) ~ gehen** to be/go on the dole *(inf)*. **(b)** *(Stempeluhr betätigen)* to clock on *or* in; *(beim Hinausgehen)* to clock off *or* out.

Stempel-: ~schneider *m* punch cutter; **~ständer** *m* rubber-stamp holder; **~uhr** *f* time-clock.

Stempelung *f* stamping; *(von Brief)* postmarking; *(von Briefmarke)* franking; *(von Gold, Silber)* hallmarking.

⚠ **Stengel** *m* **-s, -** stem, stalk ◆ **vom ~ fallen** *(inf) (Schwächeanfall haben)* to collapse; *(überrascht sein)* to be staggered *(inf)*; **fall nicht vom ~!** *(inf)* prepare yourself for a shock!; **er fiel fast vom ~** *(inf)* he almost fell over backwards *(inf)*.

⚠ **stengellos** *adj* stemless.

Steno *f* **-,** *no pl (inf)* shorthand.

Steno-: ~block *m* shorthand pad; **~gramm** *nt* text in shorthand; *(Diktat)* shorthand dictation; **ein ~gramm aufnehmen** to take shorthand; **~grammblock** *m* shorthand pad; ⚠**~graph(in** *f***)** *m (im Büro)* shorthand secretary; *(esp in Gericht, bei Konferenz etc)* stenographer; ⚠**~graphie** *f* shorthand, stenography *(dated, form)*; ⚠**s~graphieren*** [1] *vt* to take down in shorthand; [2] *vi* to do shorthand; **können Sie s~graphieren?** can you do shorthand?; ⚠**s~graphisch** *adj* shorthand *attr*; **etw s~graphisch notieren** to take sth down in shorthand; **~stift** *m* shorthand pencil; **~typist(in** *f***)** *m* shorthand typist.

Stentorstimme *f (geh)* stentorian voice.

Stenz *m* **-es, -e** *(dated)* dandy.

⚠ **Step** *m* **-s, -s** tap-dance ◆ **~ tanzen** to tap-dance.

⚠ **Step|eisen** *nt* tap *(on tap-dancing shoes)*.

Stephan, Stephen *m* - Stephen, Steven.

Stepp|anorak *m* quilted anorak.

Steppdecke *f* quilt.

Steppe *f* **-, -n** steppe.

steppen[1] *vti* to (machine-)stitch; *wattierten Stoff* to quilt.

steppen[2] *vi* to tap-dance.

Steppen-: ~brand *m* steppe fire; **~käse** *m low-fat (hard) cheese*; **~wolf** *m (Zool)* prairie wolf, coyote.

Stepp-: ~fuß *m* foot; **~jacke** *f* quilted jacket.

Steppke *m* **-(s), -s** *(N Ger inf)* nipper *(inf)*, (little) laddie *(inf)*.

Stepp-: ~naht *f (Sew)* backstitch seam; *(mit Maschine)* straight stitch seam; **~stich** *m (Sew)* backstitch; *(mit Maschine)* straight stitch.

⚠ **Step-: ~tanz** *m* tap-dance; **~tänzer** *m* tap-dancer.

Ster *nt* **-s, -s** *or* **-e** stere.

Sterbe-: ~alter *nt* age of death; **~bett** *nt* death-bed; **auf dem ~bett liegen** to be on one's death-bed; **~buch** *nt* register of deaths; **~datum** *nt* date of

⚠: for details of spelling reform, see supplement

death; **~fall** *m* death; **~geld** *nt* death benefit; **~glocke** *f* funeral bell; **das Läuten der ~glocke** the death knell; **~hemd** *nt* (burial) shroud; **~hilfe** *f* **(a)** death benefit; **(b)** (*Euthanasie*) euthanasia; **jdm ~hilfe geben** *or* **gewähren** to administer euthanasia to sb (*form*); **~kasse** *f* death benefit fund; **~lager** *nt* (*geh*) death-bed.

sterben *pret* **starb,** *ptp* **gestorben** *vti aux sein* to die ♦ **jung/als Christ ~** to die young/a Christian; **einen schnellen/leichten Tod/eines natürlichen Todes ~** to die quickly/to have an easy death/to die a natural death; **an einer Krankheit/Verletzung ~** to die of an illness/from an injury; **daran wirst du nicht ~!** (*hum*) it won't kill you!; **vor Angst/Durst/Hunger ~** to die of fright/thirst/starvation (*auch fig*); **er stirbt vor Angst** (*fig*) he's frightened to death, he's scared stiff (*inf*); **vor Langeweile/Neugierde ~** to die of boredom/curiosity; **tausend Tode ~** to die a thousand deaths; **so leicht stirbt man nicht!** (*hum*) you'll/he'll *etc* survive!; **gestorben sein** to be dead *or* deceased (*Jur, form*); **gestorben!** (*Film sl*) print it!, I'll buy it!; **er ist für mich gestorben** (*fig inf*) he might as well be dead *or* he doesn't exist as far as I'm concerned; **„und wenn sie nicht gestorben sind, so leben sie noch heute"** "and they lived happily ever after".

Sterben *nt* **-s,** *no pl* death ♦ **Angst vor dem ~** fear of death *or* dying; **wenn es ans ~ geht** when it comes to dying; **im ~ liegen** to be dying; **zum ~ langweilig** (*inf*) deadly boring *or* dull, deadly (*inf*).

Sterbens-: ~angst *f* (*inf*) mortal fear; **s~elend** *adj* (*inf*) wretched, ghastly; **ich fühle mich s~elend** I feel wretched *or* ghastly, I feel like death (*inf*); **s~krank** *adj* mortally ill; **s~langweilig** *adj* (*inf*) deadly boring *or* dull, deadly (*inf*); **~wort, ~wörtchen** *nt* (*inf*) **er hat kein ~wort gesagt** *or* **verraten** he didn't say a (single) word; **ich werde kein ~wort davon sagen** I won't breathe a word.

Sterbe-: ~ort *m* place of death; **~rate** *f* death rate; **~sakramente** *pl* last rites *pl or* sacraments *pl*; **~stunde** *f* last hour, dying hour; **~urkunde** *f* death certificate; **~ziffer** *f* mortality *or* death rate; **~zimmer** *nt* death chamber (*liter, form*) ♦ **Goethes ~zimmer** the room where Goethe died.

sterblich [1] *adj* mortal ♦ **jds ~e Hülle** *or* **(Über)reste** sb's mortal remains *pl*. [2] *adv* (*inf*) terribly (*inf*), dreadfully (*inf*).

Sterbliche(r) *mf decl as adj* mortal.

Sterblichkeit *f* mortality; (*Zahl*) mortality (rate), death-rate.

Stereo ['ʃteːreo, 'st-] *nt* **in ~** in stereo.

stereo ['ʃteːreo, 'st-] *adj pred* (in) stereo.

Stereo- [ʃteːreo, st-] *in cpds* stereo; (*s~skopisch*) stereoscopic; **≈anlage** *f* stereo unit *or* system, stereo (*inf*); **≈aufnahme** *f* stereo recording; **≈box** *f* speaker; **≈gerät** *nt* stereo unit; **≈kamera** *f* stereoscopic camera; **~metrie** *f* stereometry, solid geometry; **⚠s~phon** [1] *adj* stereophonic; [2] *adv* stereophonically; **⚠~phonie** *f* stereophony; **⚠s~phonisch** *adj* stereophonic; **~skop** *nt* **-s, -e** stereoscope; **~skopie** *f* stereoscopy; **s~skopisch** *adj* stereoscopic; (*dreidimensional*) 3-D, three-dimensional; **~-Turm** *m* hi-fi stack; **s~typ** [1] *adj* (*fig*) stereotyped, stock *attr*; *Lächeln* (*gezwungen*) stiff; (*unpersönlich*) impersonal; [2] *adv* in stereotyped fashion; stiffly; impersonally; **~typdruck** *m* stereotype; **~typie** *f* (*Psych*) stereotypy; (*Typ auch*) stereotype printing; (*Werkstatt*) stereotype printing shop.

steril [ʃte'riːl, st-] *adj* (*lit, fig*) sterile.

Sterilisation [ʃteriliza'tsioːn, st-] *f* sterilization.

sterilisieren* [ʃterili'ziːrən, st-] *vt* to sterilize.

Sterilität [ʃterili'tɛːt, st-] *f* (*lit, fig*) sterility.

Sterling ['ʃtɛrlɪŋ, 'st-] *m* **-s, -e** sterling ♦ **30 Pfund ~** 30 pounds sterling.

Stern[1] *m* **-(e)s, -e (a)** star ♦ **dieser ~** (*poet: die Erde*) this earth *or* orb (*poet*); **mit ~en übersät** star-spangled *attr*, *Himmel auch* starry *attr*; **unter fremden ~en sterben** (*poet*) to die in foreign climes (*liter*); **in den ~en lesen** (*Astrol*) to read the stars; **in den ~en (geschrieben) stehen** (*fig*) to be (written) in the stars; **das steht (noch) in den ~en** (*fig*) it's in the lap of the gods; **nach den ~en greifen** (*fig*) to reach for the stars; **er wollte die ~e vom Himmel holen** he wanted the moon; **für sie holt er die ~e vom Himmel** he would do anything for her, he would go to the ends of the earth and back again for her; **~e sehen** (*inf*) to see stars; **der ~ der Weisen** (*Bibl*) the Star of Bethlehem; **sein ~ geht auf** *or* **ist im Aufgehen/sinkt** *or* **ist im Sinken** his star is in the ascendant/on the decline; **mein guter ~** my lucky star; **unter einem guten** *or* **glücklichen** *or* **günstigen ~ geboren sein** to be born under a lucky star; **unter einem guten** *or* **glücklichen** *or* **günstigen/ungünstigen ~ stehen** to be blessed with good fortune/to be ill-starred *or* ill-fated; **mit ihr ging am Theaterhimmel ein neuer ~ auf** with her coming a new star was born in the theatrical world; **~e sehen** (*inf*) to see stars (*inf*).
(b) (*Abzeichen*) (*von Uniform*) star ♦ **ein Hotel/Cognac mit 3 ~en** a 3-star hotel/brandy.

Stern[2] *m* **-s, -e** (*Naut*) stern.

Stern-: s~bedeckt *adj* starry, star-spangled; **~bild** *nt* (*Astron*) constellation; (*Astrol*) sign (of the zodiac).

Sternchen *nt dim of* **Stern**[1] **(a)** little star. **(b)** (*Typ*) asterisk, star. **(c)** (*Film*) starlet.

Stern-: ~deuter *m* astrologer, star-gazer (*hum*); **~deuterei** *f, no pl*, **~deutung** *f* astrology, star-gazing (*hum*).

Sternen-: ~banner *nt* Star-Spangled Banner, Stars and Stripes *sing*; **s~bedeckt** *adj* starry, star-covered; **~gewölbe** *nt* (*poet*) starry vault (*poet*); **~glanz** *m* (*poet*) starshine (*liter*); **der Himmel erstrahlte im ~glanz** the heavens shone with the light of the stars (*liter*); **~himmel** *m* starry sky; **Veränderungen am ~himmel** changes in the star formation; **s~klar** *adj* starry *attr*, starlit; **~krieg** *m* (*Pol*) Star Wars *pl*; **s~los** *adj* starless; **~zelt** *nt* (*poet*) starry firmament (*liter*).

Stern-: ~fahrt *f* (*Mot, Pol*) rally (*where participants commence at different points*); **eine ~fahrt nach Ulan Bator** a rally converging on Ulan Bator; **s~förmig** *adj* star-shaped, stellate (*spec*); **~forscher** *m* astronomer; **~gewölbe** *nt* (*Archit*) stellar vault; **~gucker** *m* **-s, -** (*hum*) star-gazer (*hum*); **s~hagelblau, s~hagelvoll** *adj* (*inf*) rolling *or* roaring drunk (*inf*), blotto (*sl*) *pred*; **~haufen** *m* (*Astron*) star cluster; **s~hell** *adj* starlit, starry *attr*; **~jahr** *nt* sidereal year; **~karte** *f* (*Astron*) celestial chart, star *or* stellar map *or* chart; **s~klar** *adj* starry *attr*, starlit; **~konstellation** *f* (stellar) constellation; **~kunde** *f* astronomy; **~marsch** *m* (*Pol*) *protest march with marchers converging on assembly point from different directions*; **~motor** *m* radial engine; **~schnuppe** *f* shooting star; **~singer** *pl* carol singers *pl*; **~stunde** *f* great moment; **das war meine ~stunde** that was a great moment in my life; **~system** *nt* galaxy; **~tag** *m* (*Astron*) sidereal day; **~warte** *f* observatory; **~zeichen** *nt* (*Astrol*) sign of the zodiac; **im ~zeichen der Jungfrau** under the sign of Virgo; **~zeit** *f* (*Astron*) sidereal time.

Steroid *nt* **-(e)s, -e** steroid.

Stert [ʃteːɐt] *m* **-(e)s, -e** (*N Ger*), **Sterz** *m* **-es, -e (a)** (*Schwanzende*) tail; (*Cook*) parson's nose (*inf*). **(b)** (*Pflug~*) handle.

stet *adj attr* constant; *Fleiß auch* steady; *Arbeit, Wind auch* steady, continuous ♦ **~er Tropfen höhlt den Stein** (*Prov*) constant dripping wears away the stone.

Stethoskop [ʃteto'skoːp, st-] *nt* **-s, -e** stethoscope.

stetig *adj* steady; (*Math*) *Funktion* continuous ♦ **~ steigende Bedeutung** ever-increasing *or* steadily increasing importance; **~es Meckern** constant moaning.

Stetigkeit *f siehe adj* constancy, steadiness; continuity.

stets *adv* always ♦ **~ zu Ihren Diensten** (*form*) always *or* ever (*form*) at your service; **~ der Ihre** (*old form*) yours ever.

Steuer[1] *nt* **-s, -** (*Naut*) helm, tiller; (*Aut*) (steering-)wheel; (*Aviat*) control column, controls *pl* ♦ **am ~ stehen** (*Naut*) *or* **sein** (*Naut, fig*) to be at the helm; **am ~ sitzen** *or* **sein, hinter dem ~ sitzen** (*inf*) (*Aut*) to be at *or* behind the wheel, to drive; (*Aviat*) to be at the controls; **jdn ans ~ lassen** to let sb drive, to let sb take the wheel; **das ~ übernehmen** (*lit, fig*) to take over; (*lit auch*) to take (over) the helm/wheel/controls; (*fig auch*) to take the helm; **das ~ fest in der Hand haben** (*fig*) to be firmly in control, to have things firmly under control; **das ~ herumwerfen** *or* **-reißen** (*fig*) to turn the tide of events.

Steuer[2] *f* **-, -n (a)** (*Abgabe*) tax; (*Gemeinde~*) rates *pl* (*Brit*), local tax (*US*) ♦ **~n** tax; (*Arten von ~n*) taxes; **~n zahlen** to pay tax; **ich bezahle 35% ~n** I pay 35% tax; **in Schweden zahlt man hohe ~n** in Sweden tax is very high *or* people are highly taxed; **die ~n herabsetzen** to reduce taxation, to cut tax *or* taxes; **der ~ unterliegen** (*form*) to be liable *or* subject to tax, to be taxable. **(b)** (*inf: ~behörde*) **die ~** the tax people (*inf*) *or* authorities *pl*, the Inland Revenue (*Brit*), the Internal Revenue (*US*).

Steuer-: ~aufkommen *nt* tax revenue, tax yield; **s~bar** *adj* tax able, liable *or* subject to tax; **~beamte(r)** *m* tax officer *or* official; **s~begünstigt** *adj Investitionen, Hypothek* tax-deductible; *Waren* taxed at a lower rate; **s~begünstigtes Sparen** *form of saving entitling the saver to tax relief*; **Investitionen sind s~begünstigt** you get tax relief on investments; **~begünstigung** *f* tax concession (*gen* on); **~behörde** *f* tax authorities *pl*, inland (*Brit*) *or* internal (*US*) revenue authorities *pl*; **~berater** *m* tax consultant; **~bescheid** *m* tax assessment; **~betrug** *m* tax evasion *or* dodging; **~bevollmächtigte(r)** *mf* tax expert *or* consultant; **~bord** *nt* **-s,** *no pl* (*Naut*) starboard; **s~bord(s)** *adv* (*Naut*) to starboard; **s~ehrlich** *adj* **s~ehrlich sein** to be an honest tax-payer; **~einnahmen** *pl* revenue from taxation; **~einnehmer** *m* (*Hist*) tax-collector; **~erhöhung** *f* tax increase; **~erklärung** *f* tax return *or* declaration; **⚠~erlaß** *m* tax exemption; **~erstattung** *f* tax rebate; **~fahndung** *f* investigation of (suspected) tax evasion; (*Behörde*) commission for investigation of suspected tax evasion; **~flucht** *f* tax evasion (*by leaving the country*); **~flüchtling** *m* tax exile; **s~frei** *adj* tax-free, exempt from tax; **~freiheit** *f* tax exemption, exemption from tax; **~freiheit genießen** to be exempt from tax; **~gelder** *pl* tax money, taxes *pl*; **warum soll das aus ~geldern finanziert werden?** why should it be paid for with tax-payers' money?, why should the tax-payer have to pay for it?; **Veruntreuung von ~geldern** tax embezzlement; **~gerät** *nt* tuner-amplifier; (*Comput*) control unit; **~harmonisierung** *f* harmonization of taxes; **~hinterziehung** *f* tax evasion; **~hoheit** *f* right to levy tax(es); **~inspektor** *m* tax inspector; **~jahr** *nt* tax year; **~karte** *f* *notice of pay received and tax deducted*; **~kette** *f* (*an Motorrad*) tuning chain; **~kettenspanner** *m* tuning chain tightener; **~klasse** *f* tax bracket *or* group; **~knüppel** *m* control column; (*Aviat auch*) joystick; **~last** *f* tax burden.

steuerlich *adj* tax *attr* ♦ **~e Belastung** tax burden; **aus ~en Überlegungen** for tax reasons; **es ist ~ günstiger ...** for tax purposes it is better ...; **das wirkt sich ~ ganz günstig aus** tax-wise *or* from the tax point of view it works out very well.

steuerlos *adj* rudderless, out of control; (*fig*) leaderless.

Steuermann *m, pl* **-männer** *or* **-leute** helmsman; (*als Rang*) (first) mate; (*Rowing*) cox(swain) ♦ **Zweier mit/ohne ~** coxed/coxless pairs.

Steuermannspatent *nt* (*Naut*) mate's ticket (*inf*) *or* certificate.

Steuer-: ~marke *f* revenue *or* tax stamp; (*für Hunde*) dog licence disc, dog tag (*US*); **~mittel** *pl* tax revenue(s); **etw aus ~mitteln finanzieren** to finance sth out of public funds; **~moral** *f* tax-payer honesty.

steuern [1] *vt* **(a)** *Schiff* to steer, to navigate; (*lotsen auch*) to pilot; *Flugzeug* to pilot, to fly; *Auto* to steer; (*fig*) *Wirtschaft, Politik* to run, to control, to manage; (*Comput*) to control ♦ **staatlich gesteuert** state-controlled, under

state control; **einen Kurs ~** (*lit, fig*) to steer a course; (*fig auch*) to take *or* follow a line; **eine Diskussion/die Wirtschaft in eine bestimmte Richtung ~** to steer a discussion/the economy in a certain direction.
(b) (*regulieren*) to control.
2 *vi* **(a)** *aux sein* to head; (*Aut auch*) to drive; (*Naut auch*) to make, to steer ◆ **wohin steuert die Wirtschaft?** where is the economy heading *or* headed (for)?
(b) (*am Steuer sein*) (*Naut*) to be at the helm; (*Aut*) to be at the wheel; (*Aviat*) to be at the controls.

Steuer-: ~oase *f*, **~paradies** *nt* tax haven; **~pflicht** *f* liability to tax; (*von Person auch*) liability to pay tax; **der ~pflicht unterliegen** to be liable to tax, to be taxable; **s~pflichtig** *adj Einkommen* taxable, liable to tax; *Person auch* liable to (pay) tax; **~pflichtige(r)** *mf* tax-payer; **~politik** *f* tax *or* taxation policy; **s~politisch** *adj* relating to tax policy; **s~politische Maßnahmen der Regierung** government tax measures; **aus s~politischen Gründen** for tax *or* taxation reasons; **es wäre s~politisch unklug ...** it would be unwise tax policy ...; **~progression** *f* progressive taxation; **~prüfer** *m* tax inspector; **~prüfung** *f* tax inspector's investigation; **~rad** *nt* (*Aviat*) control wheel; (*Aut*) (steering-)wheel; **~recht** *nt* tax law; **s~rechtlich** *adj* relating to tax(ation) law; **s~rechtliche Änderungen** changes in the tax(ation) laws; **ein s~rechtlicher Fachmann** a tax expert; **das ist s~rechtlich unmöglich** the tax laws make that impossible; **~reform** *f* tax reform; **~ruder** *nt* rudder; **~sache** *f* tax matter; **Helfer in ~sachen** tax consultant; **~satz** *m* rate of taxation; **~schraube** *f* **die ~schraube anziehen** to put the screws on *or* to squeeze the taxpayer; **~schuld** *f* tax(es *pl*) owing *no indef art*, tax liability; **~senkung** *f* tax cut; **~sparmodell** *nt* tax relief scheme; **~sünder** *m* tax evader; **~system** *nt* tax system; **~taste** *f* (*Comput*) control key.

Steuerung *f* **(a)** *no pl* (*das Steuern*) (*von Schiff*) steering, navigation; (*von Flugzeug*) piloting, flying; (*fig*) (*von Politik, Wirtschaft*) running, control, management; (*Comput*) control; (*Regulierung*) control, regulation; (*Bekämpfung*) control.
(b) (*Steuervorrichtung*) (*Aviat*) controls *pl*; (*Tech*) steering apparatus *or* mechanism ◆ **automatische ~** (*Aviat*) automatic pilot, autopilot; (*Tech*) automatic steering (device).

Steuer-: ~veranlagung *f* tax assessment; **~vergehen** *nt* tax evasion *or* dodging *no pl*; **~vorteil** *m* tax advantage *or* benefit; **~werk** *nt* (*Comput*) control unit; **~zahler** *m* taxpayer; **~zeichen** *nt* **(a)** (*form*) *siehe* **Banderole**; **(b)** (*Comput*) control character.

Steven ['ʃte:vn] *m* **-s, -** (*Naut*) (*Vorder~*) prow; (*Achter~*) stern.

Steward ['stju:ɐt, ʃt-] *m* **-s, -s** (*Naut, Aviat*) steward.

⚠ **Stewardeß, Stewardess** ['stju:ɐdɛs, stju:ɐ'dɛs, ʃt-] *f* **-, -ssen** stewardess.

StGB [ɛste:ge:'be:] *nt* **-s** *abbr of* **Strafgesetzbuch.**

stibitzen* *vt* (*dated hum*) to swipe (*inf*), to pinch (*inf*).

stich *imper sing of* **stechen.**

Stich *m* **-(e)s, -e (a)** (*das Stechen*) (*Insekten~*) sting; (*Mücken~*) bite; (*Nadel~*) prick; (*Messer~*) stab.
(b) (*~wunde*) (*von Messer etc*) stab wound; (*von Insekten*) sting; (*von Mücken*) bite; (*Einstichloch*) prick.
(c) (*stechender Schmerz*) piercing *or* shooting *or* stabbing pain; (*Seiten~*) stitch; (*fig*) pang ◆ **~e haben** to have a stitch; **es gab mir einen ~ (ins Herz)** I was cut to the quick.
(d) (*Sew*) stitch.
(e) (*Kupfer~, Stahl~*) engraving.
(f) (*Schattierung*) tinge, shade (*in +acc* of); (*Tendenz*) hint, suggestion (*in +acc* of) ◆ **ein ~ ins Rote** a tinge of red, a reddish tinge; **ein ~ ins Gewöhnliche/Vulgäre** a hint *or* suggestion of commonness/vulgarity.
(g) (*Cards*) trick ◆ **einen ~ machen** *or* **bekommen** to get a trick.
(h) jdn im ~ lassen to let sb down; (*verlassen*) to abandon *or* desert sb, to leave sb in the lurch; **etw im ~ lassen** to abandon sth.
(i) ~ halten to hold water, to be valid *or* sound.
(j) einen ~ haben (*Eßwaren*) to be off *or* bad, to have gone off *or* bad; (*Butter auch*) to be *or* have gone rancid; (*Milch*) to be *or* have gone sour *or* off; (*sl: Mensch: verrückt sein*) to be nuts (*inf*), to be round the bend (*inf*).

Stich-: ~bahn *f* (*Rail*) branch terminal line; **~blatt** *nt* **(a)** (*von Degen*) guard; **(b)** (*Cards*) trump (card).

Stichel *m* **-s, -** (*Art*) gouge.

Stichelei *f* **(a)** (*Näherei*) sewing. **(b)** (*pej inf: boshafte Bemerkung*) snide (*inf*) *or* sneering remark, gibe, dig ◆ **deine ständigen ~en kannst du dir sparen** stop getting at me *or* making digs at me.

sticheln *vi* **(a)** to sew; (*sticken*) to embroider. **(b)** (*pej inf: boshafte Bemerkungen machen*) to make snide (*inf*) *or* sneering remarks ◆ **gegen jdn ~** to make digs at sb.

▼ **Stich-: ~entscheid** *m* (*Pol*) result of a/the run-off (*US*), final ballot; (*Sport*) result of a/the play-off; **s~fest** *adj siehe* **hiebfest**; **~flamme** *f* tongue of flame; **s~halten** *vi sep irreg* (*Aus*) *siehe* **Stich (i)**; **s~haltig, s~hältig** (*Aus*) *adj* sound, valid; *Beweis* conclusive; **sein Alibi ist nicht s~haltig** his alibi doesn't hold water; **~haltigkeit** *f, no pl* soundness, validity; **~kampf** *m* (*Sport*) play-off; **~kanal** *m* branch canal.

Stichling *m* (*Zool*) stickleback.

Stichprobe *f* spot check; (*Sociol*) (random) sample survey ◆ **~n machen** to carry out *or* make spot checks; (*Sociol*) to carry out a (random) sample survey; **bei der ~ wurde festgestellt, daß ...** the spot check/sampling revealed that ...

Stichproben-: ~erhebung *f* (*Sociol*) (random) sample survey; **s~weise** *adv* on a random basis; **es werden nur s~weise Kontrollen gemacht** only spot checks are made.

Stich-: ~säge *f* fret-saw; **~tag** *m* qualifying date; **~waffe** *f* stabbing weapon; **~wahl** *f* (*Pol*) final ballot, run-off (*US*).

Stichwort *nt* **(a)** *pl* **-wörter** (*in Nachschlagewerken*) headword. **(b)** *pl* **-worte** (*Theat, fig*) cue. **(c)** *pl* **-worte** *usu pl* notes *pl*; (*bei Nacherzählung etc*) key words *pl*.

Stichwort-: s~artig *adj* abbreviated, shorthand; **eine s~artige Gliederung** an outline; **etw s~artig zusammenfassen/wiedergeben** to summarize the main points of sth/to recount sth in a shorthand *or* an abbreviated fashion; **jdn s~artig über etw** (*acc*) **informieren** to give sb a brief outline of sth; **~katalog** *m* classified catalogue; **~verzeichnis** *nt* index.

Stichwunde *f* stab wound.

Stick|arbeit *f* embroidery ◆ **sie saß gerade an einer ~** she was sitting embroidering.

sticken *vti* to embroider.

Sticker *m* **-s, -** (*inf*) sticker.

Stickerei *f* **(a)** *no pl* (*das Sticken*) embroidery, embroidering. **(b)** (*Gegenstand*) embroidery.

Stickerin *f* embroideress, embroiderer.

Stickgarn *nt* embroidery thread *or* silk.

stickig *adj Luft, Zimmer* stuffy, close; *Klima* sticky, humid; (*fig*) *Atmosphäre* stifling, oppressive.

Stick-: ~maschine *f* embroidery machine; **~muster** *nt* embroidery pattern; **~nadel** *f* embroidery needle; **~oxid, ~oxyd** *nt* nitric oxide; **~rahmen** *m* embroidery frame.

Stickstoff *m* (*abbr* **N**) nitrogen.

Stickstoff-: ~dünger *m* nitrogen fertilizer; **s~haltig** *adj* containing nitrogen, nitrogenous (*spec*).

stieben *pret* **stob** *or* **stiebte,** *ptp* **gestoben** *or* **gestiebt** *vi* (*geh*) **(a)** *aux haben or sein* (*sprühen*) (*Funken, Staub etc*) to fly; (*Schnee*) to spray, to fly; (*Wasser*) to spray. **(b)** *aux sein* (*jagen, rennen*) to flee; *siehe* **auseinander~.**

Stiefbruder *m* stepbrother.

Stiefel *m* **-s, - (a)** boot.
(b) (*inf*) **seinen (alten) ~ arbeiten** *or* **weitermachen** to carry on as usual *or* in the same old way; **einen ~ zusammenreden** to talk a lot of nonsense *or* a load of rubbish (*inf*).
(c) (*Trinkgefäß*) *large, boot-shaped beer glass holding 2 litres* ◆ **einen (ordentlichen) ~ vertragen** (*inf*) to be able to take one's drink *or* hold one's liquor.

Stiefel-: ~absatz *m* (boot-)heel; **~anzieher** *m* **-s, -** boot-hook.

Stiefelette *f* (*Frauen~*) bootee; (*Männer~*) half-boot.

Stiefelknecht *m* boot-jack.

stiefeln *vi aux sein* (*inf*) to hoof it (*inf*); *siehe* **gestiefelt.**

Stiefelschaft *m* **-(e)s, ¨e** bootleg, leg of a/the boot.

Stief|eltern *pl* step-parents *pl*.

Stiefelwichse *f* (*dated*) boot-polish, boot-blacking.

Stief-: ~geschwister *pl* stepbrother(s) and sister(s); **~kind** *nt* stepchild; (*fig*) poor cousin; **sie fühlt sich immer als ~kind des Glücks** she always feels that fortune never smiles upon her; **~mutter** *f* stepmother; **~mütterchen** *nt* (*Bot*) pansy; **s~mütterlich** *adj* (*fig*) **jdn/etw s~mütterlich behandeln** to pay little attention to sb/sth, to put sb/sth in second place; **die Natur hat ihn s~mütterlich behandelt** Nature has not been kind to him; **~schwester** *f* stepsister; **~sohn** *m* stepson; **~tochter** *f* stepdaughter; **~vater** *m* stepfather.

stieg *pret of* **steigen.**

Stieg *m* **-(e)s, -e** *siehe* **Steig.**

Stiege *f* **-, -n (a)** (*schmale Treppe*) (narrow) flight of stairs *or* staircase. **(b)** (*old: 20 Stück*) score ◆ **eine ~ Eier** a score of eggs. **(c)** (*Lattenkiste*) crate.

Stiegenhaus *nt* (*S Ger, Aus*) staircase.

Stieglitz *m* **-es, -e** goldfinch.

stiehl *imper sing of* **stehlen.**

stiekum *adv* (*N Ger: heimlich*) on the sly *or* fly.

Stiel *m* **-(e)s, -e (a)** (*Griff*) handle; (*Besen~ auch*) broomstick; (*Pfeifen~, Glas~*) stem. **(b)** (*Stengel*) stalk; (*Blüten~*) stalk, stem, peduncle (*spec*); (*Blatt~*) leafstalk, petiole (*spec*).

Stiel|augen *pl* (*fig inf*) **~ machen** *or* **kriegen** to gape, to gawp, to goggle (*inf*); **er machte ~** his eyes (nearly) popped out of his head.

Stiel-: ~glas *nt* stemmed glass; **~kamm** *m* tail comb; **s~los** *adj Gerät* handleless, without a handle; *Blatt* stalkless; *Glas* stemless; **~pfanne** *f* frying pan with a (long) handle; **~topf** *m* long-handled pan.

stiemen *vi impers* (*dial*) to snow heavily, to blow a blizzard.

stier *adj* **(a)** (*stumpfsinnig*) *Blick* vacant, blank. **(b)** (*Aus, Sw inf*) *Geschäft* slack, slow; *Mensch* broke (*inf*).

Stier *m* **-(e)s, -e (a)** bull; (*junger ~*) bullock ◆ **wütend wie ein ~ (sein)** (to be) beside oneself with rage *or* fury; **wie ein ~ brüllen** to bawl one's head off (*inf*), to bellow like a bull; **den ~ bei den Hörnern packen** *or* **fassen** (*prov*) to take the bull by the horns (*prov*).
(b) (*Astrol*) Taurus *no art* ◆ **ich bin (ein) ~** I'm (a) Taurus.

stieren *vi* (*auf +acc* at) to stare; (*neugierig auch*) to gape ◆ **(lüstern) auf jdn ~** to ogle (*inf*) *or* eye sb; **sein Blick stierte ins Leere** he stared vacantly into space.

Stier-: ~kampf *m* bull-fight; **~kampfarena** *f* bull-ring; **~kämpfer** *m* bull-fighter; **~nacken** *m* neck like a bull, thick neck; **s~nackig** *adj* bull-necked; **~opfer** *nt* sacrifice of a bull.

Stiesel *m* **-s, -** (*inf*) boor, lout (*inf*).

sties(e)lig *adj* (*inf*) boorish, loutish (*inf*).

Sties(e)ligkeit *f (inf)* boorishness, loutishness *(inf)*.
stieß *pret of* **stoßen.**
Stift[1] *m* **-(e)s, -e (a)** *(Metall~)* pin; *(Holz~ auch)* peg; *(Nagel)* tack. **(b)** *(Blei~)* pencil; *(Bunt~ auch)* crayon; *(Filz~)* felt-tip, felt-tipped pen; *(Kugelschreiber)* ball-point (pen), biro ® *(Brit)*. **(c)** *(inf: Lehrling)* apprentice (boy).
Stift[2] *nt* **-(e)s, -e** *(Dom~)* cathedral chapter; *(Theologie~)* seminary; *(old: Heim, Anstalt)* home; *(in Namen)* foundation; *(old: Bistum)* diocese.
stiften *vt* **(a)** *(gründen) Kirche, Universität* to found, to establish; *(spenden, spendieren)* to donate; *Geld, Summe* to put up, to donate; *Universität, Stipendium etc* to endow.
(b) *Verwirrung* to cause; *Unfrieden, Unheil auch, Frieden* to bring about, to stir up; *Ehe* to arrange ◆ **Gutes/Schaden ~** to do good/damage.
⚠ **stiftengehen** *vi sep irreg aux sein (inf)* to hop it *(inf)*.
Stifte(n)kopf *m (dated inf)* crew-cut; *(Mensch)* person with a crew-cut.
Stifter(in *f***)** *m* **-s, -** *(Gründer)* founder; *(Spender)* donator.
Stifterreligion *f religion founded by a particular person eg Buddha, Jesus.*
Stifts-: ~dame *f (Eccl)* canoness; **~herr** *m (Eccl)* canon; **~hütte** *f (Bibl)* Tabernacle; **~kirche** *f* collegiate church.
Stiftung *f* **(a)** *(Gründung)* foundation, establishment; *(Schenkung)* donation; *(von Universität, Stipendium etc)* endowment. **(b)** *(Organisation)* foundation.
Stiftungs-: ~fest *nt* Founder's Day celebration; **~urkunde** *f* foundation charter.
Stiftzahn *m* post crown.
Stigma ['ʃtɪgma, st-] *nt* **-s, -ta** *(Biol, Rel, fig)* stigma.
Stigmatisierte(r) [ʃt-, st-] *mf decl as adj (Biol, Rel)* stigmatic; *(fig)* stigmatized person.
Stil [ʃti:l, sti:l] *m* **-(e)s, -e** style; *(Eigenart)* way, manner ◆ **im großen ~, großen ~s** in a big way; **schlechter ~** bad style; **das ist schlechter ~** *(fig)* that is bad form; **~ haben** *(fig)* to have style; **er fährt einen rücksichtslosen ~** he drives recklessly *or* in a reckless manner; **er schwimmt/schreibt einen sehr schwerfälligen ~** his swimming style is very awkward/his writing style is very clumsy.
Stil-: ~analyse *f (Art, Liter)* stylistic analysis; **s~bildend** *adj* **(für jdn) s~bildend sein/s~bildend wirken** to improve sb's style; **~blüte** *f (hum)* stylistic howler; **~bruch** *m* stylistic incongruity *or* inconsistency; *(in Roman etc)* abrupt change in style; **das ist ein glatter ~bruch** *(inf)* that is really incongruous; **~ebene** *f (Liter, Ling)* style level; **s~echt** *adj* period *attr*; **s~echt eingerichtet** with period furniture; **~element** *nt* stylistic element; **~empfinden** *nt siehe* **~gefühl.**
Stilett [ʃti'lɛt, st-] *nt* **-s, -e** stiletto.
Stil-: ~fehler *m* stylistic lapse; **~gefühl** *nt* feeling for *or* sense of style; **s~gerecht** *adj* appropriate to *or* in keeping with a/the style; **s~getreu** *adj* in *or* true to the original style.
stilisieren* [ʃtili'zi:rən, st-] *vt* to stylize.
Stilisierung [ʃt-, st-] *f* stylization.
Stilist(in *f***)** [ʃti'lɪst(ɪn), st-] *m* stylist.
Stilistik [ʃti'lɪstɪk, st-] *f (Liter)* stylistics *sing*; *(Handbuch)* guide to good style.
stilistisch [ʃti'lɪstɪʃ, st-] *adj* stylistic ◆ **ich muß meine Vorlesung ~ überarbeiten** I must go over my lecture to polish up the style.
Stilkunde *f siehe* **Stilistik.**
still *adj* **(a)** *(ruhig)* quiet, silent; *(lautlos) Seufzer* quiet; *Gebet* silent; *(schweigend) Vorwurf, Beobachter* silent ◆ **~ werden** to go quiet, to fall silent; **im Saal wurde es ~, der Saal wurde ~** the room fell silent; **um ihn/darum ist es ~ geworden** you don't hear anything about him/it any more; **es blieb ~** there was no sound, silence reigned; **S~e Nacht** Silent Night; **~ weinen/leiden** to cry quietly/to suffer in silence; **~ vor sich hin arbeiten** to work away quietly; **in ~em Gedenken** in silent tribute; **in ~em Schmerz/in ~er Trauer** in silent suffering/grief; **im ~en** without saying anything, quietly; **ich dachte mir im ~en** I thought to myself; **die S~en im Lande** the quiet ones; **sei doch ~!** be *or* keep quiet; **~e Messe** silent mass.
(b) *(unbewegt) Luft* still; *See auch* calm ◆ **der S~e Ozean** the Pacific (Ocean); **~ sitzen** to sit *or* keep still; **den Kopf/die Hände/Füße ~ halten** to keep one's head/hands/feet still; **ein Glas/Tablett ~ halten** to hold a glass/tray steady; **vor uns lag ~ die Ägäis** before us lay the calm waters of the Aegean; **~e Wasser sind tief** *(Prov)* still waters run deep *(Prov)*; **er ist ein ~es Wasser** he's a deep one *or* a dark horse.
(c) *(einsam, abgeschieden) Dorf, Tal, Straße* quiet ◆ **ein ~es Eckchen** a quiet corner; **ein ~es Plätzchen** a quiet spot.
(d) *(heimlich)* secret ◆ **im ~en** in secret; **er ist dem ~en Suff ergeben** *(inf)* he drinks on the quiet, he's a secret drinker.
(e) *(Comm) Gesellschafter, Teilhaber* sleeping *(Brit)*, silent *(US)*; *Reserven, Rücklagen* secret, hidden ◆ **~e Beteiligung** sleeping partnership *(Brit)*, non-active interest.
Stille *f* **-,** *no pl* **(a)** *(Ruhe)* quiet(ness), peace(fulness); *(Schweigen)* silence ◆ **in der ~ der Nacht** in the still of the night; **in aller ~** quietly, calmly; **die Beerdigung fand in aller ~ statt** it was a quiet funeral; **jdn in aller ~ begraben** to give sb a quiet burial.
(b) *(Unbewegtheit)* calm(ness); *(der Luft)* stillness.
(c) *(Einsamkeit, Abgeschiedenheit)* quiet, seclusion.
(d) *(Heimlichkeit)* secrecy ◆ **in aller ~** in secret, secretly.
stille *adj (old) siehe* **still.**
⚠ **Stilleben** ['ʃtɪlle:bn] *nt getrennt* **Still-leben** still life.
⚠ **stillegen** *vt sep getrennt* **still-legen** to close *or* shut down; *Schiff* to lay up ◆ **stillgelegtes Bergwerk** disused mine.
⚠ **Stillegung** *f getrennt* **Still-legung** *siehe vt* closure, shut-down; laying-up.
Stillehre *f* stylistics *sing.*
stillen [1] *vt* **(a)** *(zum Stillstand bringen) Tränen* to stop; *Schmerzen* to ease, to relieve, to allay; *Blutung auch* to staunch, to check. **(b)** *(befriedigen) Neugier, Begierde, Verlangen, Hunger* to satisfy, to still *(liter)*; *Durst auch* to quench. **(c)** *Säugling* to breast-feed, to nurse.
[2] *vi* to breast-feed ◆ **~de Mutter** nursing mother.
Stillgeld *nt* nursing mothers' allowance.
stillgestanden *interj (Mil)* halt.
Stillgruppe *f* mothers' group.
Stillhalte|abkommen *nt (Fin, fig)* moratorium.
⚠ **stillhalten** *vi sep irreg* to keep *or* hold still; *(fig)* to keep quiet.
Stillhalter *m (St Ex)* taker of an option.
⚠ **stilliegen** *vi sep irreg aux sein or haben getrennt* **still-liegen (a)** *(außer Betrieb sein)* to be closed *or* shut down. **(b)** *(lahmliegen)* to be at *or* have been brought to a standstill, to have come to a halt.
stillos *adj* lacking in style; *(fehl am Platze)* incongruous ◆ **eine völlig ~e Zusammenstellung von Möbelstücken** a collection of furniture completely lacking (in) any sense of style; **völlig ~ servierte sie Hummersuppe in Teetassen** showing absolutely no sense of style she served up lobster soup in tea cups.
Stillosigkeit *f siehe adj* lack of style *no pl*; incongruity ◆ **solche ~en ist man von ihr gewohnt** we're used to her having no sense of style *or* to such displays of tastelessness from her.
stillschweigen *vi sep irreg* to remain silent ◆ **zu etw ~** to stand silently by *or* remain silent in the face of sth; **schweig still!** be silent *or* quiet.
Stillschweigen *nt* silence ◆ **auf sein ~ kann man sich verlassen** one can rely on his keeping silent; **jdm ~ auferlegen** to swear sb to silence; **über etw** *(acc)* **~ bewahren** to observe *or* maintain silence about sth; **etw mit ~ übergehen** to pass over sth in silence.
stillschweigend *adj* silent; *Einverständnis* tacit ◆ **über etw** *(acc)* **~ hinweggehen** to pass over sth in silence.
⚠ **stillsitzen** *vi sep irreg aux sein or haben* to sit still.
Stillstand *m* standstill; *(von Betrieb, Produktion, Verhandlungen etc auch)* stoppage; *(vorübergehend)* interruption; *(in Entwicklung)* halt ◆ **bei ~ der Maschine ...** when the machine is stopped ...; **ein ~ des Herzens** a cardiac arrest; **Hauptsache ist, daß kein ~ in der Produktion eintritt** the main thing is that production is not interrupted; **zum ~ kommen** *(Verkehr)* to come to a standstill *or* stop; *(Produktion auch, Maschine, Motor, Herz, Blutung)* to stop; **etw zum ~ bringen** *Verkehr* to bring sth to a standstill *or* stop; *Produktion auch, Maschine, Motor* to stop sth; *Blutung* to stop *or* check sth; **~ ist Rückgang** *(prov)* if you don't go forwards, you go backwards.
stillstehen *vi sep irreg aux sein or haben* **(a)** *(Produktion, Handel etc)* to be at a standstill; *(Fabrik, Maschine auch)* to be *or* stand idle; *(Verkehr auch)* to be stopped; *(Herz)* to have stopped ◆ **die Zeit schien stillzustehen** time seemed to stand still *or* to stop.
(b) *(stehenbleiben)* to stop; *(Maschine)* to stop working ◆ **keinen Moment ~** not to stop for a moment; **mein Herz stand still vor Schreck** I was so frightened my heart stood still.
stillvergnügt *adj* contented.
Stillzeit *f* lactation period.
Stil-: ~mittel *nt* stylistic device; **~möbel** *pl* period furniture *sing*; **~probe** *f* specimen *or* sample of written work; **s~rein** *adj* stylistically correct; **~übung** *f* exercise in stylistic composition; **s~voll** *adj* stylish; **s~widrig** *adj* (stylistically) incongruous *or* inappropriate; **~wörterbuch** *nt* dictionary of correct usage.
Stimm-: ~abgabe *f* voting; **sie kommen zur ~abgabe** they come to vote *or* cast their votes; **~aufwand** *m* vocal effort; **~band** *nt usu pl* vocal chord; **seine ~bänder strapazieren** to strain one's voice; *(fig)* to talk one's head off; **s~berechtigt** *adj* entitled to vote; **~berechtigte(r)** *mf decl as adj* person entitled to vote; **~bezirk** *m* constituency; **~bildung** *f* **(a)** voice production; **(b)** *(Ausbildung)* voice training; **~bruch** *m siehe* **~wechsel**; **~bürger** *m* voter, elector.
Stimme *f* **-, -n (a)** voice; *(Mus: Part)* part; *(Orgel~)* register; *(fig) (Meinungsäußerung)* voice; *(Sprachrohr)* mouthpiece, voice; *(liter: Ruf)* call ◆ **mit leiser/lauter ~** in a soft/loud voice; **gut/nicht bei ~ sein** to be in good/bad voice; **erste/zweite/dritte ~** *(in Chor)* first/second/third part; **bei einem Lied die erste/zweite ~ singen** to sing the top part *or* melody of/descant to a song; **die ~n mehren sich, die ...** there is a growing body of (public) opinion that ..., there is a growing number of people calling for ...; **die ~(n) der Glocken/Geigen** *(liter)* the sound of the bells/violins; **die ~ der Öffentlichkeit/des Volkes** *(geh)* public opinion/the voice of the people; **die ~ der Wahrheit** the voice of truth; **eine ~ aus dem Dunkel/Exil** a voice out of the darkness/from exile; **der ~ der Natur folgen** *(euph hum) (seine Notdurft verrichten)* to answer the call of nature; *(dem Geschlechtstrieb nachgeben)* to give way to a natural urge; **der ~ des Gewissens folgen** to act on *or* according to one's conscience; **der ~ des Herzens folgen** to follow the leanings *or* dictates of one's heart; **der ~ der Vernunft folgen** to be guided by reason, to listen to the voice of reason.
(b) *(Wahl~, Votum)* vote ◆ **eine/keine ~ haben** to have the vote/not to be entitled to vote; *(Mitspracherecht)* to have a/no say *or* voice; **seine ~ abgeben** to cast one's vote, to vote; **jdm/einer Partei seine ~ geben** to vote for sb/a party; **die abgegebenen ~n** the votes cast; *siehe* **enthalten.**
▼ **stimmen** [1] *vi* **(a)** *(richtig sein)* to be right; *(zutreffen auch)* to be correct ◆ **stimmt es, daß ...?** is it true that ...?; **das stimmt** that's right; **das stimmt nicht** that's not right, that's wrong; **hier stimmt was nicht!** there's some-

thing wrong here; **mit ihr stimmt etwas nicht** there's something wrong *or* the matter with her; **das stimmt schon, aber ...** that's true, but ...; **stimmt so!** that's all right, keep the change.
(b) *(zusammenpassen)* to go (together).
(c) *(wählen, sich entscheiden)* to vote ◆ **für/gegen jdn/etw ~** to vote for/against sb/sth.
2 *vt Instrument* to tune ◆ **etw höher/niedriger ~** to raise/lower the pitch of sth, to tune sth up/down, to sharpen/flatten sth; **jdn froh/traurig ~** to make sb (feel) cheerful/sad; **jdn gegen etw ~** *(geh)* to prejudice *or* turn sb against sth; *siehe* **gestimmt**.

Stimmen-: ~auszählung *f* count (of votes); **~fang** *m (inf)* canvassing, vote-getting *(inf)*; **auf ~fang sein/gehen** to be/go canvassing; **~gewirr** *nt* babble of voices; **~gleichheit** *f* tie, tied vote; **bei ~gleichheit** in the event of a tie *or* tied vote; **~hören** *nt (Psych, Med)* hearing voices; **~kauf** *m* vote-buying, buying votes; **~mehrheit** *f* majority of votes; **~splitting** [-ʃplɪtɪŋ, -sp-] *nt* **-s,** *no pl (Pol)* splitting one's vote.

Stimm|enthaltung *f* abstention.

Stimmenwerbung *f* canvassing.

Stimmer(in *f***)** *m* **-s, -** *(Mus)* tuner.

Stimm-: ~gabel *f* tuning fork; **s~gewaltig** *adj (geh)* with a strong *or* powerful voice; **s~haft** *adj (Ling)* voiced; **s~haft ausgesprochen werden** to be voiced.

stimmig *adj Umfeld* ordered; *Argumente* coherent.

Stimmigkeit *f* coherence.

Stimmlage *f (Mus)* voice, register.

stimmlich *adj* vocal ◆ **sie hat ~ nachgelassen** the quality of her voice has declined; **ihre ~en Qualitäten** the quality of her voice; **~ hat er nicht viel zu bieten** he doesn't have much of a voice.

Stimm-: ~liste *f* voting list; **s~los** *adj (Ling)* voiceless, unvoiced; **s~los ausgesprochen werden** not to be voiced; **~recht** *nt* right to vote; **~ritze** *f* glottis; **~umfang** *m* vocal range.

Stimmung *f* **(a)** *(Gemütszustand)* mood; *(Atmosphäre auch)* atmosphere; *(bei der Truppe, unter den Arbeitern)* morale ◆ **in (guter)/gehobener/schlechter ~** in a good mood/in high spirits/in a bad mood; **wir hatten eine tolle ~** we were in a tremendous mood; **in ~ kommen/sein** to liven up/to be in a good mood; **ich bin nicht in der ~ zum Tanzen** I'm not in the mood for dancing; **sehr von ~en abhängig sein** to be moody, to be subject to changeable moods; **~!** enjoy yourselves, have a good time.
(b) *(Meinung)* opinion ◆ **~ gegen/für jdn/etw machen** to stir up (public) opinion against/in favour of sb/sth.
(c) *(St Ex)* mood.
(d) *(Mus) (das Stimmen)* tuning; *(das Gestimmtsein)* pitch.

Stimmungs-: ~barometer *nt (esp Pol)* barometer of public opinion; **~bild** *nt* atmospheric picture; **dieser Bericht gibt ein eindrucksvolles ~bild** this report conveys the general atmosphere extremely well; **s~fördernd** *adj* **s~förderndes Mittel** anti-depressant (drug); **~kanone** *f (inf)* life and soul of the party; **eine richtige ~kanone** the life and soul of the party; **~kapelle** *f* band which plays light music; **~lage** *f* atmosphere; **~mache** *f, no pl (pej)* cheap propaganda; **~mensch** *m* moody person; **~musik** *f* light music; **~umschwung** *m* change of atmosphere; *(Pol)* swing (in public opinion); *(St Ex)* change in trend; **s~voll** *adj Bild* idyllic; *Atmosphäre* tremendous; *Gedicht, Beschreibung* full of atmosphere, atmospheric; **~wandel** *m* change of atmosphere; *(Pol)* change in (public) opinion.

Stimm-: ~vieh *nt (pej)* gullible voters *pl*; **~volk** *nt* voters *pl*, electorate; **~wechsel** *m* **nach dem ~wechsel** after one's voice has broken; **er ist im ~wechsel** his voice is breaking; **~werkzeuge** *pl* vocal organs *pl*; **~zettel** *m* ballot paper.

Stimulans ['ʃti:mulans, st-] *nt* **-, Stimulantia** [ʃtimu'lantsia, st-] *or* **Stimulanzien** [ʃtimu'lantsiən, st-] *(Med, fig)* stimulant.

Stimulation [ʃtimula'tsio:n, st-] *f (Med, fig)* stimulation.

stimulieren* [ʃtimu'li:rən, st-] *vt (Med, fig)* to stimulate.

Stimulierung [ʃt-, st-] *f (Med, fig)* stimulation.

Stimulus ['ʃti:mulʊs, st-] *m* **-, Stimuli** *(Psych)* stimulus; *(fig auch)* stimulant.

Stinkadores *f* **-, -** *(inf)* smelly cigar.

Stink-: ~bombe *f* stink bomb; **~drüse** *f (Zool)* scent gland.

stinken *pret* **stank,** *ptp* **gestunken** *vi* **(a)** *(nach* of) to stink, to reek, to pong *(Brit inf)* ◆ **die Wohnung/er stinkt nach Kneipe** the flat smells like a pub/he smells of drink; **wie ein Bock** *or* **Wiedehopf** *or* **eine Wachtel** *or* **die Pest ~** *(inf)* to stink to high heaven *(inf)*.
(b) *(fig inf)* **er stinkt nach Geld** he's stinking rich *(inf)*; **er stinkt vor Faulheit** he's bone-idle; **das stinkt zum Himmel** it's an absolute scandal *or* absolutely appalling; **an der Sache stinkt etwas** there's something fishy about it *(inf)*; **das stinkt nach Verrat** that smells of treachery; **die Sache stinkt mir** *(sl)*, **mir stinkt's!** *(sl)* I'm fed up to the back teeth (with it) *(inf)*.

stinkend *adj* stinking, foul-smelling.

stinkfaul *adj (inf)* bone-idle, bone-lazy.

stinkig *adj (inf)* stinking *(inf)*; *(verärgert)* pissed off *(sl)*.

Stink-: s~langweilig *adj (inf)* deadly boring *or* dull; **~laune** *f (inf)* stinking *(inf) or* foul mood; **~morchel** *f (Bot)* stinkhorn; **s~normal** *adj (inf)* boringly normal *or* ordinary; **s~reich** *adj (inf)* stinking rich *(inf)*; **~stiebel** *(dial)*, **~stiefel** *m (inf)* stinking pig *(inf)*; *(hum: Kumpel)* mate *(inf)*; **~tier** *nt* skunk; **s~vornehm** *adj (inf)* posh *(inf)*, swanky *(inf)*; *Lokal auch* swish *(inf)*; **sie tut so s~vornehm** she acts so posh; **~wut** *f (inf)* raging temper; **eine ~wut (auf jdn) haben** to be livid (with sb).

Stint *m* **-(e)s, -e** *(Zool)* smelt, sparling ◆ **sich freuen wie ein ~** *(inf)* to be as happy as a sandboy.

Stipendiat(in *f***)** *m* **-en, -en** scholarship holder, person receiving a scholarship/grant.

Stipendium *nt (als Auszeichnung etc erhalten)* scholarship; *(zur allgemeinen Unterstützung des Studiums)* grant.

Stippe *f* **-, -n** *(dial) siehe* **Tunke**.

stippen *vti (dial) siehe* **tunken**.

Stippvisite *f (inf)* flying visit.

Stipulation [ʃtipula'tsio:n, st-] *f (Jur)* stipulation.

stipulieren* [ʃtipu'li:rən, st-] *vti* to stipulate ◆ **von Arbeitgeberseite wurden neue Verhandlungen stipuliert** the employers insisted on new talks.

stirb *imper sing of* **sterben**.

Stirn *f* **-, -en** forehead, brow *(esp liter)* ◆ **sich/jdm das Haar aus der ~ streichen** to brush one's/sb's hair out of one's/his/her face; **den Hut in die ~ drücken** to pull one's hat down over one's eyes; **es steht ihm auf der ~ geschrieben** *(geh)* it is written in his face; **die ~ haben** *or* **besitzen, zu ...** to have the effrontery *or* nerve *or* gall to ...; **jdm/einer Sache die ~ bieten** *(geh)* to stand up to sb/sth, to defy sb/sth; *siehe* **eisern**.

Stirn-: ~ader *f* vein in the/one's temple; **~auge** *nt (Zool)* ocellus; **~band** *nt* headband; **~bein** *nt* frontal bone; **~falte** *f* wrinkle (on one's forehead); **~glatze** *f* receding hair-line; **~höhle** *f* frontal sinus; **⚠~höhlenkatarrh** *m*, **~höhlenvereiterung** *f* sinusitis; **~lage** *f (Med)* brow presentation; **~locke** *f* quiff, cowlick; **~rad** *nt (Tech)* spurwheel; **~reflektor** *m (Med)* forehead mirror; **~riemen** *m* brow band; **~runzeln** *nt* **-s,** *no pl* frown; **~seite** *f* end wall, gable-end; **~spiegel** *m (Med) siehe* **~reflektor**; **~wand** *f* end wall.

Stoa ['ʃto:a, st-] *f* **-,** *no pl (Philos)* Stoics *pl*, Stoic school.

stob *pret of* **stieben**.

stöbern *vi* to rummage *(in +dat* in, *durch* through).

Stocherkahn *m* punt.

stochern *vi* to poke *(in +dat* at); *(im Essen)* to pick *(in +dat* at) ◆ **er stocherte mit einem Schürhaken im Feuer** he poked the fire; **sich** *(dat)* **in den Zähnen ~** to pick one's teeth.

Stock *m* **-(e)s, ¨-e** **(a)** stick; *(Rohr~)* cane; *(Takt~)* baton; *(Zeige~)* pointer; *(Billard~)* cue ◆ **er stand da (steif) wie ein ~** *or* **als ob er einen ~ verschluckt hätte** he stood there as stiff as a poker; **am ~ gehen** to walk with (the aid of) a stick; *(fig inf)* to be in a bad way; *(nach viel Arbeit)* to be dead-beat *(inf)*; *(finanziell)* to be in difficulties; **da gehst du am ~** *(sl)* you'll be flabbergasted *(inf)*; **~ und Hut** *(dated)* hat and stick.
(b) *(Wurzel~)* roots *pl*.
(c) *(Pflanze) (Reb~)* vine; *(Rosen~)* rose-bush; *(Bäumchen)* rose-tree; *(Blumen~)* pot-plant ◆ **über ~ und Stein** up hill and down dale.
(d) *(Bienen~)* hive.
(e) *(Geol: Gesteinsmasse)* massif, rock mass.
(f) *(Hist)* stocks *pl* ◆ **jdn in den ~ legen** to put sb in the stocks.
(g) *pl* **-** *(~werk)* floor, storey *(Brit)*, story *(US)* ◆ **das Haus hat drei ~** *or* **ist drei ~ hoch** the house is three storeys/stories high; **im ersten ~** on the first floor *(Brit)*, on the second floor *(US)*.
(h) [stɔk] *pl* **-s** *(Econ)* stock.

Stock-: ~ausschlag *m* shoot from a tree stump; **s~besoffen** *(sl)*, **s~betrunken** *(inf) adj* blind *or* dead drunk; **ein ~besoffener** a drunk; **~bett** *nt* bunk bed; **s~blind** *adj (inf)* as blind as a bat, completely blind.

Stöckchen *nt dim of* **Stock (a, c)**.

stock-: ~dumm *adj (inf)* thick (as two short planks) *(inf)*; **~dunkel** *adj (inf)* pitch-dark.

Stöckel[1] *m* **-s, -** *(inf)* stiletto.

Stöckel[2] *nt* **-s, -** *(Aus)* outhouse, outbuilding.

Stöckel|absatz *m* stiletto heel.

stöckeln *vi aux sein (inf)* to trip, to mince.

Stöckelschuh *m* stiletto, stiletto-heeled shoe.

stocken *vi* **(a)** *(Herz, Puls)* to miss *or* skip a beat; *(Gedanken, Worte)* to falter; *(nicht vorangehen) (Arbeit, Entwicklung)* to make no progress; *(Unterhaltung, Gespräch)* to flag; *(Verkehr)* to be held up *or* halted ◆ **ihm stockte das Herz/der Puls** his heart/pulse missed *or* skipped a beat; **ihm stockte der Atem** he caught his breath; **ins S~ geraten** *or* **kommen** *(Unterhaltung, Gespräch)* to begin to flag.
(b) *(stagnieren) (Verhandlungen)* to break off *or* stop (temporarily); *(Geschäfte, Handel)* to slacken *or* drop off.
(c) *(innehalten) (in der Rede)* to falter; *(im Satz)* to break off, to stop short.
(d) *(gerinnen) (Blut)* to thicken; *(S Ger, Aus: Milch)* to curdle, to go sour ◆ **das Blut stockte ihm in den Adern** *(geh)* the blood froze in his veins.
(e) *(stockig werden) (Wäsche, Papier, Bücher)* to become mildewed, to go mouldy.

stockend *adj* faltering, hesitant.

Stock|ente *f* mallard.

Stock-: s~finster *adj (inf)* pitch-dark, pitch-black; **~fisch** *m* dried cod; *(pej: Mensch)* dull old stick, stick-in-the-mud; **~fleck** *m mark caused by mould or mildew*; **s~fleckig** *adj* mouldy, mildewed; **~haus** *nt (Hist)* gaol; **~hieb** *m siehe* **~schlag**.

Stockholm *nt* **-s** Stockholm.

Stockholmer *adj* Stockholm *attr*.

Stockholmer(in *f***)** *m* native of Stockholm; *(Einwohner)* inhabitant of Stockholm.

stockig *adj Geruch, Luft* musty; *Papier, Wäsche* mildewed, mouldy.

-stöckig *adj suf* -storey *attr*, -storeyed *(Brit)*, -storied *(US)*.

stock-: ~katholisch *adj (inf)* Catholic through and through; **~konservativ** *adj (inf)* arch-conservative.

Stock-: s~nüchtern *adj (inf)* stone-cold sober *(inf)*; **s~sauer** *adj (sl)* pissed-off *(sl)*; **~schirm** *m* walking-length umbrella; **~schlag** *m* blow (from a stick); *(mit Rohr~)* stroke of the cane; **~schnupfen** *m* permanent cold; **s~steif** *adj (inf)* as stiff as a poker; **sie bewegt sich s~steif** she moves very stiffly; **s~taub** *adj (inf)* as deaf as a post.

Stockung *f* **(a)** *(vorübergehender Stillstand)* interruption, hold-up *(gen, in +dat* in); *(Verkehrs~)* congestion, traffic-jam, hold-up ◆ **der Verkehr läuft wieder ohne ~en** traffic is flowing smoothly again.
(b) *(von Verhandlungen)* breakdown *(gen* of, in); *(von Geschäften, Handel)* slackening *or* dropping off *(gen* in).
(c) *(Pause, Unterbrechung) (im Gespräch)* break, lull; *(in der Rede)* pause, hesitation.
(d) *(Gerinnung)* thickening; *(von Milch)* curdling.

stockvoll *adj (sl: betrunken)* blind *or* dead drunk *(inf)*, pissed *(sl)*.

Stockwerk *nt* floor, storey *(Brit)*, story *(US)* ◆ **im 5. ~** on the 5th *(Brit) or* 6th *(US)* floor; **ein Haus mit vier ~en** a four-storeyed *(Brit) or* four-storied *(US)* building.

Stockzahn *m (Aus)* molar (tooth).

Stoff *m* **-(e)s, -e (a)** material, fabric; *(als Materialart)* cloth.
(b) *(no pl: Materie)* matter ◆ **~ und Form** *(Philos)* matter and form.
(c) *(Substanz, Chem)* substance; *(Papier~)* pulp ◆ **tierische/pflanzliche ~e** animal substance/vegetable matter; **aus härterem ~ gemacht sein** *(fig)* to be made of sterner stuff.
(d) *(Gegenstand, Thema)* subject (matter); *(Unterhaltungs~, Diskussions~)* topic, subject; *(Material)* material ◆ **~ für ein** *or* **zu einem Buch sammeln** to collect material for a book; **der Vortrag bot reichlich ~ für eine Diskussion** the lecture provided plenty of material *or* topics for discussion; **~ zum Lesen/Nachdenken** reading matter/food for thought.
(e) *(inf: Rauschgift)* dope *(sl)*, stuff *(sl)*.

Stoff-: ~bahn *f* length of material; **~ballen** *m* roll *or* bolt of material *or* cloth; **s~bespannt** *adj* fabric-covered.

Stoffel *m* **-s, -** *(pej inf)* lout *(inf)*, boor.

stoff(e)lig *adj (pej inf)* uncouth, boorish.

⚠ **Stoffetzen** *m getrennt* **Stoff-fetzen** scrap of cloth.

Stoff-: ~fülle *f siehe* **Stofffülle**; **~handschuh** *m* fabric glove.

stofflich *adj (Philos)* material; *(den Inhalt betreffend)* as regards subject matter.

Stofflichkeit *f (Philos)* materiality.

stofflig *adj siehe* **stoff(e)lig.**

Stoff-: ~puppe *f* rag doll; **~rest** *m* remnant; **~tier** *nt* soft toy.

⚠ **Stoffülle** *f getrennt* **Stoff-fülle** wealth of material.

Stoffwahl *f* choice of subject.

Stoffwechsel *m* metabolism.

Stoffwechsel-: ~krankheit *f* metabolic disease *or* disorder; **~störung** *f* metabolic disturbance.

Stoffzugabe *f* extra material.

stöhnen *vi (alle Bedeutungen)* to groan; *(klagen auch)* to moan ◆ **~d** with a groan.

Stöhnen *nt* **-s,** *no pl (lit, fig)* groaning *no pl*; *(Stöhnlaut)* groan.

Stoiker(in *f)* [ˈʃtoːikɐ, -ərɪn, st-] *m* **-s, -** *(Philos)* Stoic (philosopher); *(fig)* stoic.

stoisch [ˈʃtoːɪʃ, st-] *adj (Philos)* Stoic; *(fig)* stoic(al).

Stoizismus [ʃtoiˈtsɪsmʊs, st-] *m (Philos)* Stoicism; *(fig)* stoicism.

Stola [ˈʃtoːla, st-] *f* **-, Stolen** stole.

Stolle *f* **-, -n** *siehe* **Stollen (b).**

Stollen *m* **-s, - (a)** *(Min, Mil)* gallery, tunnel. **(b)** *(Cook)* fruit loaf *(eaten at Christmas)*, stollen *(US)*. **(c)** *(Zapfen) (Hufeisen)* calk(in); *(Schuh~)* stud. **(d)** *(Poet)* stollen, *one of the two equal sections forming the "Aufgesang" in "Minnesang".*

Stolperdraht *m* trip-wire; *(fig)* stumbling-block.

stolp(e)rig *adj Gang* stumbling; *Weg* uneven, bumpy.

stolpern *vi aux sein* to stumble, to trip *(über +acc* over); *(fig: zu Fall kommen)* to come a cropper *(inf)*, to come unstuck *(inf)* ◆ **ins S~ kommen** *or* **geraten** *(lit)* to come a cropper *(inf)*; *(fig auch)* to slip up; **jdn zum S~ bringen** *(lit)* to trip sb up, to make sb trip; *(fig)* to be sb's downfall; **über einen Hinweis ~** *(fig)* to stumble upon a clue; **über einen Bekannten ~** *(fig)* to bump *or* run into an acquaintance; **über einen Strohhalm ~** *(fig)* to come to grief over a trifle.

stolz *adj* **(a)** proud *(auf +acc* of) ◆ **~ wie ein Pfau** as proud as a peacock; **warum so ~?** why so proud?; *(bei Begegnung)* don't you know me any more?; **darauf kannst du ~ sein** that's something to be proud of; **der ~e Besitzer** the proud owner.
(b) *(imposant) Bauwerk, Schiff* majestic, impressive; *(iro: stattlich) Preis, Summe* princely ◆ **~ erhebt sich die Burg über der kleinen Stadt** the castle rises proudly above the little town.

Stolz *m* **-es,** *no pl* pride ◆ **sein Garten/Sohn** *etc* **ist sein ganzer ~** his garden/son *etc* is his pride and joy; **voller ~ auf etw** *(acc)* **sein** to be very proud of sth; **ich habe auch meinen ~** I do have my pride; **aus falschem/verletztem ~ handeln** to act out of false/wounded pride; **seinen ~ in etw** *(acc)* **setzen** to take a pride in sth.

stolzieren* *vi aux sein* to strut, to swagger; *(hochmütig, beleidigt)* to stalk.

⚠ **stop** [ʃtɔp, stɔp] *interj* stop; *(auf Verkehrsschild auch)* halt *(Brit)*.

Stop-and-go-Verkehr [stɔpəndˈgoː-] *m* stop-go traffic, slow-moving traffic.

Stopf-: ~büchse, ~buchse *f (Tech)* stuffing box; **~ei** *nt* ≃ darning mushroom.

stopfen [1] *vt* **(a)** *(aus~, füllen)* to stuff; *Pfeife, Loch, Wurst* to fill; *(inf) Taschen auch* to cram ◆ **jdm den Mund** *(inf) or* **das Maul** *(sl)* **~** to silence sb.
(b) *(hinein~)* to stuff; *Korken auch* to ram ◆ **gierig stopfte er alles in sich hinein, was man ihm auftischte** he greedily stuffed down everything they served up.
(c) *(ver~) Trompete etc* to mute; *(mit Stöpsel)* to plug, to stop.
(d) *(ausbessern, flicken) Loch, Strümpfe etc* to darn, to mend; *siehe* **gestopft.**
[2] *vi* **(a)** *(Speisen) (ver~)* to cause constipation, to constipate; *(sättigen)* to be filling.
(b) *(inf: gierig essen)* to bolt *or* wolf (down) one's food, to stuff oneself *(inf)*.
(c) *(flicken)* to darn, to do darning.

Stopfen *m* **-s, -** *(dial)* stopper; *(Korken)* cork.

Stopfer *m* **-s, -** *(Pfeifen~)* tamper.

Stopf-: ~garn *nt* darning cotton *or* thread; **~nadel** *f* darning needle; **~pilz** *m (Sew)* darning mushroom.

stopp [ʃtɔp] *interj* stop.

Stopp [ʃtɔp] *m* **-s, -s** stop, halt; *(Lohn~)* freeze.

Stoppball *m (Tennis etc)* dropshot.

Stoppel[1] *f* **-, -n** *(Getreide~, Bart~)* stubble.

Stoppel[2] *m* **-s, -** *(Aus) siehe* **Stöpsel.**

Stoppel-: ~bart *m* stubbly beard, stubble; **~feld** *nt* stubble-field; **~haar** *nt* bristly hair.

stopp(e)lig *adj Bart* stubbly; *Kinn auch* bristly.

stoppen [1] *vt* **(a)** to stop; *Gehälter, Preise* to freeze; *(Ftbl) Ball auch* to trap. **(b)** *(Zeit abnehmen)* to time ◆ **er hat die Laufzeit/Zeit genau gestoppt** he timed exactly how long it took.
[2] *vi* **(a)** to stop. **(b) ihr beide lauft, und ich stoppe** you two run and I'll time you.

Stopper *m* **-s, - (a)** *(Ftbl)* centre half. **(b)** *(Naut)* stopper. **(c)** *(an Gardinenstange)* curtain stop, end-piece. **(d)** *(Zeitnehmer)* timekeeper.

Stopplicht *nt* stop-light, red light; *(Aut)* brake light.

stopplig *adj siehe* **stopp(e)lig.**

Stopp-: ~schild *nt* stop *or* halt *(Brit)* sign; **~straße** *f road with stop signs,* secondary road, stop street *(US)*; **~uhr** *f* stop-watch.

Stopsel *m* **-s, -** *(Aus)* stopper; *(Korken)* cork.

Stöpsel *m* **-s, -** *(von Waschbecken, Badewanne etc)* plug; *(Telec auch)* jack; *(Pfropfen)* stopper; *(Korken)* cork; *(inf: Knirps)* little fellow.

stöpseln *vti (Telec)* to connect.

Stopselzieher *m* **-s, -** *(Aus)* corkscrew.

Stör[1] *m* **-(e)s, -e** *(Zool)* sturgeon.

Stör[2] *f (Aus)*: **in** *or* **auf die ~ gehen** to work at the customer's home.

Stör-: ~aktion *f* disruptive action *no pl*; **s~anfällig** *adj* susceptible to interference.

Storch *m* **-(e)s, ¨-e** stork ◆ **wie der ~ im Salat einherstolzieren/gehen** *(inf)* to stalk about/to pick one's way carefully; **der ~ hat sie ins Bein gebissen** *(dated hum)* she's expecting a little stranger *(hum)*.

Storchennest *nt* stork's nest.

Störchin *f* female stork.

Storchschnabel *m* **(a)** *(Bot)* cranesbill, crane's-bill. **(b)** *(Tech)* pantograph.

Store [ʃtoːɐ, stoːɐ] *m* **-s, -s** *usu pl* net curtain; *(Sw)* shutters *pl.*

➤ **stören** [1] *vt* **(a)** *(beeinträchtigen) Schlaf, öffentliche Ordnung, Frieden etc* to disturb; *Verhältnis, Harmonie, Gesamteindruck etc* to spoil; *Rundfunkempfang* to interfere with; *(absichtlich)* to jam ◆ **jds Pläne ~** to interfere with sb's plans.
(b) *Handlungsablauf, Prozeß, Vorlesung, Feier* to disrupt.
➤ **(c)** *(unangenehm berühren)* to disturb, to bother ◆ **was mich an ihm/daran stört** what I don't like about him/it; **entschuldigen Sie, wenn ich Sie störe** I'm sorry to bother you, I'm sorry if I'm disturbing you; **störe mich jetzt nicht!** don't bother *or* disturb me now!; **lassen Sie sich nicht ~!** don't let me disturb you, don't mind me; **stört es Sie, wenn ich rauche?** do you mind if I smoke?, does it bother you if I smoke?; **würden Sie bitte aufhören zu rauchen, es stört mich** would you mind not smoking, I find it annoying; **das stört mich nicht** that doesn't bother me, I don't mind; **sie stört uns nicht** she doesn't bother us, we don't mind her; **sie läßt sich durch nichts ~** she doesn't let anything bother her.
[2] *vr* **sich an etw** *(dat)* **~** to be bothered about; **ich störe mich an seiner Unpünktlichkeit** I take exception to his unpunctuality.
[3] *vi* **(a)** *(lästig, im Weg sein)* to get in the way; *(unterbrechen)* to interrupt; *(Belästigung darstellen: Musik, Lärm etc)* to be disturbing ◆ **bitte nicht ~!** please do not disturb!; **ich möchte nicht ~** I don't want to be in the way *or* to be a nuisance, I don't want to interrupt; *(in Privatsphäre etc)* I don't want to intrude; **störe ich?** am I intruding?; **wenn ich nicht störe** if I'm not in the way *or* disturbing you; **stört das sehr, wenn ich jetzt fernsehe?** would it disturb you if I watch television?; **etw als ~d empfinden** to find sth bothersome; **ein ~der Lärm** a disturbing noise; **ein ~der Umstand** a nuisance, an annoyance; **eine ~de Begleiterscheinung** a troublesome side-effect; **sich ~d bemerkbar machen** to be all too noticeable *or* obvious; **ein ~der Besucher** an unwelcome visitor.
(b) *(unangenehm auffallen)* to spoil the effect, to stick out ◆ **ein hübsches Gesicht, aber die große Nase stört doch etwas** a pretty face, though the big nose does spoil the effect.

Störenfried *m* **-(e)s, -e, Störer** *m* **-s, -** trouble-maker.

Stör-: ~faktor *m* source of friction, disruptive factor; **~fall** *m (in Kernkraftwerk etc)* malfunction, accident; **s~frei** *adj* free from interference;

~geräusch *nt (Rad, TV)* interference; **~manöver** *nt* disruptive action.
Storni *pl of* **Storno.**
stornieren* [ʃtɔrˈniːrən, st-] *vti (Comm) Auftrag* to cancel; *Buchungsfehler* to reverse.
Storno [ˈʃtɔrno, ˈst-] *m or nt* **-s, Storni** *(Comm) (von Buchungsfehler)* reversal; *(von Auftrag)* cancellation.
störrisch, störrig *(rare) adj* stubborn, obstinate; *Kind, Pferd* unmanageable, disobedient, refractory; *Pferd* restive; *Haare* unmanageable; *siehe* **Esel.**
Störsender *m (Rad)* jamming transmitter, jammer.
Störung *f* **(a)** disturbance.
(b) *(von Ablauf, Verhandlungen etc)* disruption ◆ **die Demonstranten beschlossen die ~ der Parlamentssitzung** the demonstrators decided to disrupt the parliamentary session.
(c) *(Verkehrs~)* hold-up ◆ **es kam immer wieder zu ~en des Verkehrs** there were continual hold-ups (in the traffic), the traffic was continually held up.
(d) *(Tech)* fault, trouble *no indef art* ◆ **eine ~** trouble, a fault; **in der Leitung muß eine ~ sein** there must be a fault on the line.
(e) *(Astron)* perturbation.
(f) *(Met)* disturbance.
(g) *(Rad)* interference; *(absichtlich)* jamming ◆ **atmosphärische ~** atmospherics *pl.*
(h) *(Med)* disorder ◆ **gesundheitliche/geistige/nervöse ~en** physical/mental/nervous disorders, nervous trouble.
Störungs-: ~anzeige *f* fault indicator; **~feuer** *nt (Mil)* harassing fire; **s~frei** *adj* trouble-free; *(Rad)* free from interference; **der Verkehr ist/läuft wieder s~frei** the traffic is moving freely again; **~stelle** *f (Telec)* faults service.
Story [ˈstoːri, ˈstɔri] *f* **-, -s** *or* **Stories** story; *(sl: von Verkäufer etc)* spiel *(sl)*.
Stoß *m* **-es, ⸚e (a)** push, shove *(inf)*; *(leicht)* poke; *(mit Faust)* punch; *(mit Fuß)* kick; *(mit Ellbogen)* nudge, dig; *(mit Kopf, Hörnern)* butt; *(Dolch~ etc)* stab, thrust; *(Kugelstoßen)* put, throw; *(Fechten)* thrust; *(Schwimm~)* stroke; *(Atem~)* gasp; *(Koitusbewegung)* thrust ◆ **einen ~ vertragen können** *(lit, fig)* to be able to take a knock (or two); **sich** *(dat) or* **seinem Herzen einen ~ geben** to pluck up *or* take courage; **das gab ihm den letzten ~** *(fig)* that was the last straw *or* final blow (for him).
(b) *(Anprall)* impact; *(Erd~)* tremor; *(eines Wagens)* jolt, bump.
(c) *(Med)* intensive course of drugs.
(d) *(Stapel)* pile, stack.
(e) *(Rail: Schienen~)* (rail) joint.
(f) *(Sew: ~band)* selvage; *(Tech: Kante)* butt joint ◆ **auf ~** edge to edge.
(g) *(Mil: Feuer~)* volley, burst of fire; *(Trompeten~ etc)* blast, blow *(in +acc* on).
(h) *(Min)* stope, face.
(i) *(Hunt)* tail feathers *pl.*
Stoß-: s~artig *adj Bewegung, Fahrt* jerky; *Lachen* staccato; *(spasmodisch)* spasmodic; **~band** *nt (Sew)* selvage; **~dämpfer** *m (Aut)* shock absorber.
Stößel *m* **-s, -** pestle; *(Aut: Ventil~)* tappet.
stoß|empfindlich *adj* susceptible *or* sensitive to shock; *Obst* easily damaged ◆ **diese Uhr ist ~** this watch is not shock-proof.
stoßen *pret* **stieß**, *ptp* **gestoßen** [1] *vt* **(a)** *(einen Stoß versetzen)* to push, to shove *(inf)*; *(leicht)* to poke; *(mit Faust)* to punch; *(mit Fuß)* to kick; *(mit Ellbogen)* to nudge, to dig; *(mit Kopf, Hörnern)* to butt; *(stechen) Dolch* to plunge, to thrust; *(vulg)* to fuck *(vulg)*, to shag *(vulg)*, to poke *(sl)* ◆ **sich** *(dat)* **den Kopf** *etc or* **sich** *(acc)* **an den Kopf** *etc* **~** to hit one's head *etc*; **jdm** *or* **jdn in die Seite ~** to nudge sb, to dig sb in the ribs; **jdn von sich ~** to push sb away; *(fig)* to cast sb aside; **jdn/etw zur Seite ~** to push sb/sth aside; *(mit Fuß)* to kick sb/sth aside *or* to one side; **er stieß den Ball mit dem Kopf ins Tor** he headed the ball into the goal; **ein Loch ins Eis ~** to make *or* bore a hole in the ice.
(b) *(werfen)* to push; *(Sport) Kugel* to put ◆ **jdn von der Treppe/aus dem Zug ~** to push sb down the stairs/out of *or* off the train; **jdn aus dem Haus ~** *(fig)* to throw *or* turn sb out (of the house); **jdn ins Elend ~** *(liter)* to plunge sb into misery.
(c) *(zerkleinern) Zimt, Pfeffer, Zucker* to pound.
(d) *(Sw: schieben, drücken)* to push.
[2] *vr* to bump *or* bang *or* knock oneself ◆ **sich an etw** *(dat)* **~** *(lit)* to bump *etc* oneself on *or* against sth; *(fig)* to take exception to sth, to disapprove of sth; **er stößt sich daran, wenn Männer Ohrringe tragen** he takes exception to men wearing earrings.
[3] *vi* **(a)** *(mit den Hörnern)* to butt *(nach* at).
(b) *(Tech)* to butt *(an +acc* against).
(c) *(Gewichtheben)* to jerk.
(d) *aux sein (treffen, prallen)* to run *or* bump into *(auch fig)*; *(herab~: Vogel)* to swoop down *(auf +acc* on) ◆ **an etw** *(acc)* **~** to bump into *or* hit sth; *(grenzen)* to border on sth; **gegen etw ~** to run into sth; **zu jdm ~** to meet up with sb, to join sb; **auf jdn ~** to bump *or* run into sb; **auf etw** *(acc)* **~** *(Straße)* to lead into *or* onto sth; *(Schiff)* to hit sth, to run into *or* against sth; *(fig: entdecken)* to come upon *or* across sth; **auf Erdöl/Grundwasser ~** to strike oil/to discover underground water; **auf Widerstand/Ablehnung/Zustimmung ~** to meet with *or* encounter resistance/to meet with disapproval/approval.
(e) *(old: blasen)* to blow, to sound; *siehe* **Horn.**
Stoß-: s~fest *adj* shock-proof; **~gebet** *nt* quick prayer; **ein ~gebet zum Himmel schicken** to say a quick prayer; **~geschäft** *nt* business with short periods of peak activity; *(Saisonarbeit)* seasonal business; **~karrette** *f (Sw: Schubkarre)* wheelbarrow; **~kraft** *f* force; *(von Aufprall)* impact; *(Mil)* combat strength; **~seufzer** *m* deep sigh; **s~sicher** *adj* shock-proof; **~stange** *f (Aut)* bumper; **~therapie** *f (Med)* intensive course of drug treatment; **~trupp** *m (Mil)* raiding party; **~verkehr** *m* rush-hour (traffic); **~waffe** *f* thrust weapon; **s~weise** *adv* **(a)** *(ruckartig)* spasmodically, by fits and starts; **s~weise atmen** to pant; **die Autoschlange bewegte sich s~weise vorwärts** the line of cars moved forward by fits and starts; **(b)** *(stapelweise)* by the pile; **~zahl** *f (Phys)* impact coefficient; **~zahn** *m* tusk; **~zeit** *f (im Verkehr)* rush-hour; *(in Geschäft etc)* peak period, busy time.
Stotterei *f (inf)* stuttering; *(fig)* stuttering and stammering.
Stotterer *m* **-s, -, Stotterin** *f* stutterer.
stottern *vti* to stutter; *(Motor)* to splutter ◆ **leicht/stark ~** to have a slight/bad stutter, to stutter slightly/badly; **ins S~ kommen** to start stuttering; **etw auf S~ kaufen** *(inf)* to buy sth on the never-never *(Brit inf) or* on the cuff *(US inf)*.
Stotzen *m* **-s, -** *(esp S Ger)* **(a)** *(Baumstumpf)* (tree-)stump. **(b)** *(Bottich)* tub, vat.
Stövchen *nt* (teapot- *etc*) warmer.
StPO [ɛsteːpeːˈ|oː] *f* - *abbr of* **Strafprozeßordnung.**
Str. *abbr of* **Straße** St.
stracks *adv* straight, immediately.
Straf-: ~androhung *f* threat of punishment; **unter ~androhung** on *or* under threat of penalty; **~anstalt** *f* penal institution, prison; **~antrag** *m* action, legal proceedings *pl*; **~antrag stellen** to institute legal proceedings; **einen ~antrag zurückziehen** to withdraw an action; **~antritt** *m* commencement of (prison) sentence; **sein ~antritt** the commencement of his (prison) sentence; **~anzeige** *f* **~anzeige gegen jdn erstatten** to bring a charge against sb; **~arbeit** *f (Sch)* punishment; *(schriftlich)* lines *pl*; **~aufhebungsgrund** *m (Jur) siehe* **~ausschließungsgrund**; **~aufschub** *m (Jur)* suspension of sentence; *(von Todesstrafe)* reprieve; **~ausschließungsgrund** *m (Jur)* ground for exemption from punishment; **~aussetzung** *f (Jur)* suspension of sentence; **~aussetzung zur Bewährung** probation; **~bank** *f (Sport)* penalty bench, sin-bin *(inf)*.
strafbar *adj Vergehen* punishable ◆ **~e Handlung** punishable offence; **das ist ~!** that's an offence; **sich ~ machen** to commit an offence.
Strafbarkeit *f, no pl* **er war sich** *(dat)* **der ~ seines Verhaltens nicht bewußt** he didn't realize that what he was doing was against the law *or* was a punishable offence.
Straf-: ~bataillon *nt (Mil)* punishment battalion; **~befehl** *m (Jur)* order of summary punishment (from a local court, on the application of the DPP); **~befehl ergeht gegen ...** ... is being prosecuted; **~bescheid** *m (Jur)* notification of penalty for a tax offence; **~bestimmung** *f (Jur)* penal laws *pl*, legal sanction.
Strafe *f* **-, -n** punishment; *(Jur, Sport)* penalty; *(Geld~)* fine; *(Gefängnis~)* sentence ◆ **etw bei ~ verbieten** to make sth punishable by law, to prohibit sth by law; **... bei ~ verboten** ... forbidden; **es ist bei ~ verboten, ...** it is a punishable *or* prosecutable offence ...; **etw unter ~ stellen** to make sth a punishable offence; **unter ~ stehen** to be a punishable offence; **bei ~ von** on pain *or* penalty of; **seine ~ abbüßen** *or* **absitzen** *or* **abbrummen** *(inf)* to serve one's sentence, to do one's time *(inf)*; **eine ~ von drei Jahren Gefängnis** a three-year prison sentence; **~ zahlen** to pay a fine; **100 Dollar ~ zahlen** to pay a $100 fine, to be fined $100; **zur ~** as a punishment; **~ muß sein!** discipline is necessary; **seine verdiente** *or* **gerechte ~ bekommen** to get one's just deserts, to be duly punished; **die ~ folgte auf dem Fuße** punishment was swift to come; **das ist die (gerechte) ~ dafür(, daß du gelogen hast)** that's your punishment (for lying), that's what you get (for lying); **etw als ~ empfinden** *(als lästig)* to find sth a bind *(inf)*; *(als Bestrafung)* to see sth as a punishment; **es ist eine ~, ihr zuhören zu müssen** it's a pain in the neck having to listen to her *(inf)*; **dieses Kind/Wetter ist eine ~** this child/weather is a pain (in the neck) *(inf)*.
strafen [1] *vt* **(a)** *(be~)* to punish ◆ **jdn (für etw/mit etw) ~** to punish sb (for sth/with sth); **mit etw gestraft sein** to be cursed with sth; **mit seinen Kindern/dieser Arbeit ist er wirklich gestraft** his children are a real trial to him/he finds this work a real bind *(inf)*; **sie ist vom Schicksal gestraft** she is cursed by Fate, she has the curse of Fate upon her; **er ist gestraft genug** he has been punished enough; *siehe* **Verachtung.**
(b) *(old Jur)* **jdn an seinem Leben/Vermögen ~** to sentence sb to death/to fine sb; *siehe* **Lüge.**
[2] *vi* to punish ◆ **orientalische Richter ~ hart** oriental judges give severe sentences; **das S~** punishment.
strafend *adj attr* punitive; *Blick, Worte* reproachful ◆ **die ~e Gerechtigkeit** *(liter)* avenging justice.
Straf-: ~entlassene(r) *mf decl as adj* ex-convict, discharged prisoner; **~entlassung** *f* discharge, release (from prison); ⚠**~erlaß** *m* remission (of sentence); **s~erschwerend** *adj Umstand* aggravating; **(als) s~erschwerend kam hinzu, daß ...** the offence/crime was compounded by the fact that ...; **als s~erschwerend wurde gewertet, daß der Täter keine Reue gezeigt hat** the accused's lack of remorse led to the passing of a heavier sentence/imposition of a heavier fine; **s~exerzieren*** *vi insep (Mil)* to do punishment drill; **~expedition** *f* punitive expedition.
straff *adj Seil* tight, taut; *Haut* smooth; *Busen* firm; *Haltung, Gestalt* erect; *(~ sitzend) Hose etc* tight, close-fitting; *(fig: streng) Disziplin, Organisation* strict, tight ◆ **~ sitzen** to fit tightly, to be close-fitting *or* tight; **etw ~ spannen** *or* **ziehen** to tighten sth; *Decke, Laken etc* to pull sth tight; **die Leine muß ~ gespannt sein** the line has to be tight; **das Haar ~ zurückkämmen** to comb one's hair back severely.

➤ SPRACHE AKTIV: **stornieren** → 47.4, 48.3

straffällig *adj* **~ werden** to commit a criminal offence; **wenn Sie wieder ~ werden ...** if you commit a further offence ...

Straffällige(r) *mf decl as adj* offender.

straffen [1] *vt* to tighten; *(spannen) Seil, Leine auch* to tauten; *(raffen) Handlung, Darstellung* to make more taut, to tighten up ◆ **sich** *(dat)* **die Gesichtshaut/den Busen ~ lassen** to have a face-lift/to have one's breasts lifted.
[2] *vr* to tighten, to become taut; *(Haut)* to become smooth; *(Busen)* to become firm; *(sich aufrichten)* to stiffen.

Straffheit *f, no pl siehe adj* tightness, tautness; smoothness; firmness; erectness; strictness.

Straf-: s~frei *adj* **s~frei bleiben/ausgehen** to go unpunished; **s~frei ausgehen** to get off scot-free *(inf)*; **~freiheit** *f* impunity, exemption from punishment; **~gebühr** *f* surcharge; **~gefangene(r)** *mf* detainee, prisoner; **~geld** *nt* fine; **~gericht** *nt* criminal court; **ein ~gericht abhalten** to hold a trial; **das göttliche** *or* **himmlische ~gericht** divine judgement; **das ~gericht Gottes** *or* **des Himmels** *(liter)* the judgement of God; **ein ~gericht brach über ihn herein** *(fig)* the wrath of God descended upon him; **~gerichtsbarkeit** *f* jurisdiction; **~gesetz** *nt* criminal *or* penal law; **~gesetzbuch** *nt* Criminal Code; **~gesetzgebung** *f* penal legislation; **~gewalt** *f* legal *or* penal authority; **~justiz** *f* criminal justice *no art*; **~kammer** *f* division for criminal matters (of a court); **~kolonie** *f* penal colony; **~kompanie** *f (Mil)* punishment battalion; **~lager** *nt* disciplinary *or* punishment camp.

sträflich [1] *adj (lit, fig)* criminal.
[2] *adv vernachlässigen etc* criminally ◆ **sich ~ blamieren** to make a terrible fool of oneself, to make a proper charlie of oneself *(inf)*.

Sträfling *m* prisoner.

Sträflingskleidung *f* prison clothing.

Straf-: s~los *adj siehe* **s~frei**; **~mandat** *nt* ticket; **~maß** *nt* sentence; **das höchste ~maß** the maximum penalty *or* sentence; **s~mildernd** *adj* extenuating, mitigating; **~milderung** *f* mitigation *or* commutation of the/a sentence; **~minute** *f (Sport)* penalty minute; **s~mündig** *adj* of the age of criminal responsibility; **ein kleines Kind ist nicht s~mündig** a small child is under the age of criminal responsibility; **~mündigkeit** *f* age of criminal responsibility; ⚠**~nachlaß** *m* remission; **~porto** *nt* excess postage; **~predigt** *f* reprimand, dressing-down; **jdm eine ~predigt halten** to give sb a lecture *or* dressing-down; ⚠**~prozeß** *m* criminal proceedings *pl*, criminal action *or* case; ⚠**~prozeßordnung** *f* code of criminal procedure; **~punkt** *m (Sport)* penalty point; **~rahmen** *m* range of sentences; **~raum** *m (Sport)* penalty area *or (Ftbl auch)* box; **~recht** *nt* criminal law; **~rechtler(in** *f***)** *m* **-s, -** expert in criminal law, penologist; **s~rechtlich** *adj* criminal; **jdn/etw s~rechtlich verfolgen** to prosecute sb/sth; **das ist aber kein s~rechtliches Problem** but that is not a problem of criminal law; **~rechtspflege** *f* criminal justice; **~rede** *f siehe* **~predigt**; **~register** *nt* police *or* criminal records *pl*; *(hum inf)* record; **ein Eintrag im ~register** an entry in the police *or* criminal records *pl*; **einen Eintrag im ~register haben** to have a record; **er hat ein langes ~register** he has a long (criminal) record; *(hum inf)* he's got a bad record; **~richter** *m* criminal judge; **~sache** *f* criminal matter; ⚠**~schuß** *m (Sport)* penalty (shot); **~senat** *m* criminal division (of the Court of Appeal and Federal Supreme Court); **~stoß** *m (Ftbl etc)* penalty (kick); *(Hockey etc)* penalty (shot); **~tat** *f* criminal offence *or* act; **~tatbestand** *m (Jur)* **das erfüllt den ~tatbestand der Verleumdung** *etc* that constitutes calumny *or* libel *etc*; **~täter** *m* offender, criminal; **~umwandlung** *f (Jur)* commutation of a/the penalty; **~verbüßung** *f* serving of a sentence; **nach seiner ~verbüßung** after serving his sentence; **~verfahren** *nt* criminal proceedings *pl*, criminal action *or* case; **~verfolgung** *f* criminal prosecution; **~verfügung** *f (Jur) siehe* **~mandat**; **s~verschärfend** *adj siehe* **s~erschwerend**; **~verschärfung** *f* increase in the severity of the/a penalty *or* sentence; **das führte zu einer ~verschärfung** this led to the imposition of a heavier fine/the passing of a heavier sentence; **s~versetzen*** *vt insep Beamte* to transfer for disciplinary reasons; **~versetzung** *f* (disciplinary) transfer; **~verteidiger** *m* counsel for the defence, defence counsel *or* lawyer; **~vollstreckung** *f* execution of the/a sentence; **~vollzug** *m* penal system; **offener ~vollzug** non-confinement; **~vollzugsanstalt** *f (form)* penal institution; **s~würdig** *adj (form)* criminal; **~wurf** *m (Sport)* penalty throw; **~zettel** *m (inf)* ticket.

Strahl *m* **-(e)s, -en (a)** *(lit, fig)* ray; *(Licht~ auch)* shaft *or* beam of light; *(Sonnen~)* shaft of light; *(Radio~, Laser~ etc)* beam; *(poet: das Leuchten)* light ◆ **im ~ einer Taschenlampe** by the light *or* in the beam of a torch; **ein ~ der Hoffnung** *(liter)* a ray of hope.
(b) *(Wasser~, Luft~)* jet.

Strahl|antrieb *m (Aviat)* jet propulsion.

Strahlemann *m, pl* **-männer** *(inf)* golden boy *(inf)*.

strahlen *vi* **(a)** *(Sonne, Licht etc)* to shine; *(Sender)* to beam; *(glühen)* to glow *(vor +dat* with); *(Heizofen etc)* to radiate; *(radioaktiv)* to give off radioactivity.
(b) *(leuchten)* to gleam, to sparkle; *(fig: Gesicht)* to beam ◆ **der Himmel strahlte** the sky was bright; **das ganze Haus strahlte vor Sauberkeit** the whole house was sparkling clean; **was strahlst du so?** what are you beaming about?, what are you so happy about?; **er/sie strahlte vor Freude** he/she was beaming with happiness, she was radiant with happiness; **er strahlte (übers ganze Gesicht)** he was beaming all over his face; *siehe* **strahlend**.

strählen *vt (S Ger, Sw)* to comb.

Strahlen-: ~behandlung *f (Med)* ray treatment; **~belastung** *f* radiation; **~biologie** *f* radiobiology; **~brechung** *f* refraction; **~bündel** *nt* pencil of rays.

strahlend *adj* radiant; *Wetter, Tag* bright, glorious; *Gesicht auch* beaming; *(radioaktiv)* radioactive ◆ **~es Lachen** beaming smile, beam; **der Tag war ~ schön, es war ein ~ schöner** *or* **strahlendschöner Tag** it was a glorious day; **mit ~en Augen** with bright *or* shining eyes; **mit ~em Gesicht** with a beaming face; *(von Frau, Kind auch)* with a radiant face; **er sah sie ~ an** he beamed at her; **sie sah ihn ~ an** she looked at him, beaming *or* radiant with happiness.

Strahlen-: ~dosis *f* dose of radiation; **s~förmig** *adj* radial; **sich s~förmig ausbreiten** to radiate out; **s~geschädigt** *adj* suffering from radiation damage; *Organ* damaged by radiation; **die ~geschädigten** the radiation victims; **~heilkunde** *f* radiotherapy; **s~krank** *adj* radiation sick; **~kranke(r)** *mf* person with radiation sickness; **~krankheit** *f* radiation sickness; **~pilz** *m* ray-fungus; **~quelle** *f* source of radiation; **~schäden** *pl* radiation injuries *pl*; *(von Organ auch)* radiation damage *sing*; **~schutz** *m* radiation protection; **~therapie** *f* radiotherapy; **~tierchen** *nt* radiolarian; **~tod** *m* death through radiation; **s~verseucht** *adj* contaminated (with radiation); **~waffe** *f* laser weapon.

Strahler *m (Lampe)* spotlight.

strahlig *adj (Bot)* radial.

-strahlig *adj suf* **ein zwei~es/vier~es Düsenflugzeug** a two-/four-engined jet plane.

Strahl-: ~kraft *f* radiation intensity; **~material** *nt* radioactive material; **~triebwerk** *nt* jet engine; **~turbine** *f* turbo-jet.

Strahlung *f* radiation.

Strahlungs-: s~arm *adj Bildschirm, Monitor* low-radiation; **~energie** *f* radiation *or* radiant energy; **~gürtel** *m* Van Allen belt; **der ~gürtel der Erde** the Van Allen belt; **~intensität** *f* dose of radiation; **~wärme** *f* radiant heat.

Strahlverfahren *nt* (jet-)blasting.

Strähne *f* **-, -n, Strähn** *m* **-(e)s, -e** *(Aus) (Haar~)* strand; *(Längenmaß: Woll~, Garn~)* skein, hank ◆ **ich habe schon eine weiße ~** I already have a white streak.

strähnig *adj Haar* straggly ◆ **das Haar fiel ihr ~ auf die Schultern** her hair fell in strands *or* in rats' tails *(pej inf)* on her shoulders.

Stramin *m* **-s, -e** evenweave (embroidery) fabric.

stramm *adj (straff) Seil, Hose* tight; *Seil auch* taut; *(schneidig) Haltung, Soldat* erect, upright; *(kräftig, drall) Mädchen, Junge* strapping; *Junge, Beine* sturdy; *Brust* firm; *(inf) (tüchtig) Marsch, Arbeit* strenuous, tough, hard; *Tag, Programm* packed; *Leistung* solid; *(überzeugt)* staunch; *(sl: betrunken)* tight *(inf)* ◆ **~ sitzen** to be tight *or* close-fitting, to fit tightly; **~e Haltung annehmen** to stand to attention; **~ arbeiten** *(inf)* to work hard, to get down to it *(inf)*; **~ marschieren** *(inf)* to march hard; **~ konservativ** staunchly conservative, true blue *(Brit)*; **~er Max** *open sandwich of boiled ham and fried egg*.

stramm-: ~stehen *vi sep irreg (Mil inf)* to stand to attention; ⚠**~ziehen** *vt sep irreg Seil, Hose* to pull tight, to tighten; *Socken* to pull up; **jdm den Hosenboden** *or* **die Hosen ~ziehen** *(inf)* to give sb a good hiding *(inf)*.

Strampelhöschen [-'hø:sçən] *nt* rompers *pl*.

strampeln *vi* **(a)** to flail *or* thrash about; *(Baby)* to thrash about ◆ **das Baby strampelte mit Armen und Beinen** the baby was kicking its feet and waving its arms about. **(b)** *aux sein (inf: radfahren)* to pedal. **(c)** *(inf: sich abrackern)* to (sweat and) slave.

Strampelsack *m (für Säuglinge)* carry-nest.

Strand *m* **-(e)s, ¨e** *(Meeres~)* beach, strand *(poet)*; *(Seeufer)* shore; *(poet: Flußufer)* bank ◆ **am ~** on the beach; **auf ~ geraten** *or* **laufen** to run aground; **auf ~ setzen** to beach.

Strand-: ~anzug *m* beach suit; **~bad** *nt* (seawater) swimming pool; *(Badeort)* bathing resort; **~distel** *f* sea-holly.

stranden *vi aux sein* to run aground, to be stranded; *(fig)* to fail.

Strand-: ~gerste *f* sea barley; **~gut** *nt (lit, fig)* flotsam and jetsam; **~hafer** *m* marram (grass); **~haubitze** *f*: **blau** *or* **voll wie eine ~haubitze** *(inf)* as drunk as a lord *(inf)*, rolling drunk *(inf)*; **~hotel** *nt* seaside hotel; **~kiefer** *f (Bot)* maritime pine, cluster pine; **~kleidung** *f* beachwear; **~korb** *m* wicker beach chair with a hood; **~läufer** *m (Orn)* sandpiper; **~promenade** *f* promenade; **~raub** *m* beachcombing; **~räuber** *m* beachcomber; **~recht** *nt* right of salvage.

Strandung *f* running aground.

Strand-: ~vogt *m* beach warden; **~wache** *f* lifeguard; *(Dienst)* lifeguard duty; **~wächter** *m* lifeguard; **~weg** *m* beach path.

Strang *m* **-(e)s, ¨e** *(Nerven~, Muskel~)* cord; *(Strick auch)* rope; *(Woll~, Garn~)* hank, skein; *(am Pferdegeschirr)* trace, tug; *(Rail: Schienen~)* track ◆ **jdn zum Tod durch den ~ verurteilen** to sentence sb to be hanged; **der Tod durch den ~** death by hanging; **am gleichen** *or* **an demselben ~ ziehen** *(fig)* to act in concert; **über die ¨e schlagen** *or* **hauen** *(inf)* to run riot *(inf)*, to get carried away *(inf)*; *siehe* **reißen**.

Strangulation *f* strangulation.

strangulieren* *vt* to strangle.

Strapaze *f* **-, -n** strain.

strapazfähig *adj (Aus) siehe* **strapazierfähig**.

strapazieren* [1] *vt* to be a strain on, to take a lot out of; *Schuhe, Kleidung* to be hard on, to give a lot of hard wear to; *(fig inf) Redensart, Begriff* to flog (to death) *(inf)*; *Nerven* to strain, to try ◆ **er sah strapaziert aus** he looked worn out *or* exhausted.
[2] *vr* to tax oneself.

strapazierfähig *adj Schuhe, Kleidung* hard-wearing, durable; *(fig inf) Nerven* strong, tough.

strapaziös *adj (lit, fig)* wearing, exhausting.
Straps *m* **-es, -e** suspender belt *(Brit)*, garter belt *(US)*.
⚠ **Straß** *m* **-** *or* **-sses,** *no pl* paste.
straß|auf *adv:* **~, straßab** up and down the street.
Straßburg *nt* **-s** Strasbourg, Strassburg.
Sträßchen *nt dim of* **Straße.**
Straße *f* **-, -n (a)** road; *(in Stadt, Dorf)* street, road *(Brit)*; *(kleine Land~)* lane ◆ **an der ~** by the roadside; **auf die ~ gehen** *(lit)* to go out on the street; *(als Demonstrant)* to take to the streets, to go out into the streets; *(als Prostituierte)* to go on *or* walk the streets; **auf der ~ liegen** *(fig inf)* to be out of work; *(als Wohnungsloser)* to be on the streets; *(als Faulenzer, Asozialer etc)* to hang around the streets *or* around street corners; *(Kraftfahrer)* to have broken down; **auf die ~ gesetzt werden** *(inf)* to be turned out (onto the streets); *(als Arbeiter)* to be sacked *(inf)*, to get the sack *(inf)*; **über die ~ gehen** to cross (the road/street); **er wohnt drei ~n weiter** he lives three blocks further on; **mit etw auf die ~ gehen** to take to the streets about sth; **er ist aus unserer ~** he's from our street; **davon spricht die ganze ~** the whole street's talking about it; **die ~n der Großstadt** the city streets; **Verkauf über die ~** take-away *(Brit) or* take-out *(US)* sales; *(von Getränken)* off-licence sales *pl (Brit)*, package store sales *pl (US)*; **etw über die ~ verkaufen** to sell sth to take away *(Brit) or* to take out *(US)*; **das Geld liegt/liegt nicht auf der ~** money is there for the asking/money doesn't grow on trees; **ein Mädchen von der ~** a lady of pleasure; **der Mann auf der ~** *(fig)* the man in the street.
(b) *(Meerenge)* strait(s *pl*) ◆ **die ~ von Dover/Gibraltar/Messina** *etc* the Straits of Dover/Gibraltar/Messina *etc.*
(c) *(Mob, Pöbel)* **die ~** the masses *pl*, the rabble; **die Herrschaft der ~** mob-rule.
(d) *(Tech) (Fertigungs~)* (production) line; *(Walz~)* train.
Straßen-: ~anzug *m* lounge suit *(Brit)*, business suit *(US)*; **~arbeiten** *pl* roadworks *pl*; **~arbeiter** *m* roadmender.
Straßenbahn *f (Wagen)* tram *(Brit)*, streetcar *(US)*; *(Netz)* tramway(s) *(Brit)*, streetcar system *(US)* ◆ **mit der ~** by tram *or* streetcar.
Straßenbahner(in *f***)** *m* **-s, -** *(inf)* tramway *(Brit) or* streetcar *(US)* employee.
Straßenbahn-: ~fahrer, ~führer *m* tram/streetcar driver, motorman *(US)*; **~haltestelle** *f* tram/streetcar stop; **~linie** *f* tramline *(Brit)*, tram route *(Brit)*, streetcar line *(US)*; **mit der ~linie 11 fahren** to take the number 11 tram/streetcar; **~schaffner** *m* tram/streetcar conductor; **~schiene** *f* tramline *(Brit)*, tram *(Brit) or* streetcar *(US)* rail; **~wagen** *m* tram, streetcar.
Straßen-: ~bau *m* road construction; **~bauamt** *nt* highways *or (städtisch)* roads department; **~bauarbeiten** *pl* roadworks *pl*; **~bekanntschaft** *f* passing *or* nodding acquaintance; **~belag** *m* road surface; **~beleuchtung** *f* street lighting; **~benutzungsgebühr** *f* (road) toll; **~bild** *nt* street scene; **~böschung** *f* embankment; **~breite** *f* width of a/the road; **~decke** *f* road surface; **~dirne** *f (dated, form)* common prostitute, street-walker; **~dorf** *nt* linear village; **~ecke** *f* street corner; **ein paar ~ecken weiter** a few blocks further; **~einmündung** *f* road junction; **~feger(in** *f***)** *m* **-s, -** road sweeper; **~fest** *nt* street party; **~führung** *f* route; **~gabelung** *f* fork (in a/the road); **~glätte** *f* slippery road surface; **~graben** *m* ditch; **~handel** *m* street trading; **~händler** *m* street trader; *(mit Obst, Fisch etc auch)* costermonger; **~junge** *m (pej)* street urchin, street arab; **~kampf** *m* street fighting *no pl*; **ein ~kampf** a street fight *or* battle; **~kämpfer** *m* street fighter; **~karte** *f* road map; **~kehrer** *m* **-s, -** road sweeper; **~kleid** *nt* outdoor dress; **~kreuzer** *m* **-s, -** *(inf)* limousine; **~kreuzung** *f* crossroads *sing or pl*, intersection *(US)*; **~lage** *f (Aut)* road holding; **dieses Auto hat eine gute ~lage** this car holds the road well or has good road holding; **~lärm** *m* street noise; **~laterne** *f* street lamp; **~mädchen** *nt* streetwalker, prostitute; **~meisterei** *f* road maintenance department; **~musikant** *m* street musician; **~name** *m* street name; **~netz** *nt* road network *or* system; **~rand** *m* roadside; **~raub** *m* mugging *(inf)*, street robbery; *(durch Wegelagerer)* highway robbery; **~räuber** *m* mugger *(inf)*, thief, footpad *(old)*; *(Wegelagerer)* highwayman; **~reinigung** *f* street cleaning; **~rennen** *nt* road race; **~sammlung** *f* street collection; **~sänger** *m* street singer; **~schäden** *pl* damage *sing* to the road surface; **„Achtung ~schäden"** "uneven road surface"; **~schild** *nt* street sign; **~schlacht** *f* street battle; **~schuh** *m* walking shoe; **~seite** *f* side of a/the road; **~sperre** *f* roadblock; **~sperrung** *f* closing (off) of a/the road; **eine ~sperrung vornehmen** to close (off) the road; **~strich** *m (inf)* walking the streets, street-walking; *(Gegend)* red-light district; **auf den ~strich gehen** to walk the streets; **~theater** *nt* street theatre; **~tunnel** *m* (road) tunnel; **~überführung** *f* footbridge, pedestrian bridge; **~unterführung** *f* underpass, subway; **~verhältnisse** *pl* road conditions *pl*; **~verkauf** *m* street-trading; take-away *(Brit) or* take-out *(US)* sales *pl*; *(Außer-Haus-Verkauf) (von alkoholischen Getränken)* off-licence sales *pl (Brit)*, package store sales *pl (US)*; *(Verkaufsstelle)* take-away *(Brit)*, take-out *(US)*; *(für alkoholische Getränke)* off-licence *(Brit)*, package store *(US)*; **Zeitungen werden im ~verkauf angeboten** newspapers are sold on the streets; **~verkäufer** *m* street seller *or* vendor; *(von Obst, Fisch etc auch)* costermonger; **~verkehr** *m* traffic; **~verkehrsordnung** *f (Jur)* Road Traffic Act; **~verzeichnis** *nt* index of street names; *(in Buchform auch)* street directory; **~wacht** *f* road patrol; **~walze** *f* road-roller, steam roller; **~zug** *m* street; **~zustand** *m* road conditions *pl*; **~zustandsbericht** *m* road report.
Sträßlein *nt dim of* **Straße.**
Stratege *m* **-n, -n** strategist ◆ **na, alter ~** *(fig inf)* well, you old fox *(inf)*.
Strategie *f* strategy.
Strategiepapier *nt (Pol)* strategy document.
strategisch *adj* strategic.
Stratifikation *f* stratification.
stratifizieren* *vt (Geol, Agr)* to stratify.
Stratosphäre *f* **-,** *no pl* stratosphere.
stratosphärisch *adj* stratospheric.
Stratus *m* **-, Strati, Stratuswolke** *f (Met)* stratus (cloud).
sträuben [1] *vr* **(a)** *(Haare, Fell)* to stand on end; *(Gefieder)* to become ruffled ◆ **der Katze sträubt sich das Fell** *(aggressiv)* the cat raises its hackles; **da ~ sich einem die Haare** it's enough to make your hair stand on end.
(b) *(fig)* to resist *(gegen etw* sth) ◆ **die Feder/die Zunge sträubt sich, das zu schildern** *(geh)* one hesitates to put it down on paper/to say it; **es sträubt sich alles in mir, das zu tun** I am most reluctant to do it.
[2] *vt Gefieder* to ruffle.
Strauch *m* **-(e)s, Sträucher** bush, shrub.
Strauchdieb *m (old)* footpad *(old)*.
straucheln *vi aux sein* **(a)** *(geh: stolpern)* to stumble, to trip. **(b)** *(fig) (auf die schiefe Bahn geraten)* to transgress; *(Mädchen)* to go astray ◆ **an etw** *(dat)* **~** to come to grief over sth; **die Gestrauchelten** the reprobates.
Strauchritter *m (old)* footpad *(old)*.
Strauchwerk *nt, no pl (Gebüsch)* bushes *pl*, shrubs *pl*; *(Gestrüpp)* undergrowth.
Strauß¹ *m* **-es, -e** ostrich ◆ **wie der Vogel ~** like an ostrich.
Strauß² *m* **-es, Sträuße (a)** bunch; *(Blumen~)* bunch of flowers; *(als Geschenk)* bouquet, bunch of flowers; *(kleiner ~, Biedermeier~)* posy ◆ **einen ~ binden** to tie flowers/twigs *etc* into a bunch; *(Blumen~ auch)* to make up a bouquet.
(b) *(old: Kampf, fig)* struggle, battle ◆ **mit jdm einen harten ~ ausfechten** *(lit, fig)* to have a hard struggle *or* fight with sb.
Sträußchen *nt dim of* **Strauß².**
Straußenfeder *f* ostrich feather *or* plume.
Strauß(en)wirtschaft *f (Aus) place which sells home-grown wine when a broom is displayed outside.*
Straußvögel *pl* struthionidae *pl (spec)*, struthioids *pl (spec)*.
Streamer ['stri:mɐ] *m* **-s, -** *(Comput)* streamer.
Streb *m* **-(e)s, -e** *(Min)* coal face ◆ **im ~ arbeiten** to work on the coal face.
Strebe *f* **-, -n** brace, strut; *(Decken~)* joist; *(von Flugzeug)* strut.
Strebe-: ~balken *m* diagonal brace *or* strut; **~bogen** *m* flying buttress.
streben *vi (geh)* **(a)** *(den Drang haben, sich bemühen)* to strive *(nach, an +acc, zu* for); *(Sch pej)* to swot *(inf)* ◆ **danach ~, etw zu tun** to strive to do sth; **die Pflanze strebt nach Licht** the plant seeks the light; **der Fluß strebt zum Meer** the river flows towards the sea; **in die Ferne ~** to be drawn to distant parts; **sich ~d bemühen** to strive one's hardest.
(b) *aux sein (sich bewegen)* **nach** *or* **zu etw ~** to make one's way to sth; *(Armee)* to push towards sth; **aus etw ~** to make one's way out of sth.
(c) *aux sein* **in die Höhe/zum Himmel ~** to rise *or* soar aloft.
Streben *nt* **-s,** *no pl* **(a)** *(Drängen, Sinnen)* striving *(nach* for); *(nach Ruhm, Geld)* aspiration *(nach* to); *(Bemühen)* efforts *pl.* **(b)** *(Tendenz)* shift, movement.
Strebepfeiler *m* buttress.
Streber(in *f***)** *m* **-s, -** *(pej inf)* pushy person; *(Sch)* swot *(inf)*.
Streberei *f (pej inf)* pushiness *(inf)*; *(Sch)* swotting *(inf)*.
Streber-: ~natur *f (pej)* pushy nature; *(Sch)* swotting; *(Mensch)* pushy person; *(Sch)* swot *(inf)*; **~tum** *nt, no pl* pushiness; *(Sch)* swotting.
strebsam *adj* assiduous, industrious.
Strebsamkeit *f, no pl* assiduity, industriousness.
Strebung *f (esp Psych)* tendency.
Streckbett *nt (Med)* orthopaedic bed *with traction facilities.*
Strecke *f* **-, -n (a)** *(Entfernung zwischen zwei Punkten, Sport)* distance; *(Math)* line *(between two points)* ◆ **eine ~ zurücklegen** to cover a distance; **eine ziemliche** *or* **gute ~ entfernt sein** *(lit, fig)* to be a long way away; **bis zum Ende des Projekts ist es noch eine ziemliche** *or* **lange ~** there is still quite a good way to go until the end of the project.
(b) *(Abschnitt) (von Straße, Fluß)* stretch; *(von Bahnlinie)* section.
(c) *(Weg, Route)* route; *(Straße)* road; *(Bahnlinie, Sport: Bahn)* track; *(fig: Passage)* passage ◆ **welche ~ bist du gekommen?** which way *or* route did you come?; **für die ~ London-Glasgow brauchen wir 5 Stunden** the journey from London to Glasgow will take us 5 hours; **auf der ~ sein** to be in the race; **auf** *or* **an der ~ Paris-Brüssel** on the way from Paris to Brussels; **die ~ Wien-München führt durch ...** the road/track *etc* between Vienna and Munich goes through ...; **in einer ~** in one go *(inf)*, without stopping; **auf der ~ arbeiten** *(Rail)* to work on the track; **auf freier** *or* **offener ~** *(esp Rail)* on the open line, between stations; **auf weite ~n (hin)** *(lit, fig)* for long stretches; **auf der ~ bleiben** *(bei Rennen)* to drop out of the running; *(in Konkurrenzkampf)* to fall by the wayside.
(d) *(Hunt) (Jagdbeute)* bag, kill ◆ **zur ~ bringen** to bag, to kill; *(fig) Verbrecher* to hunt down.
(e) *(Min)* gallery.
strecken [1] *vt* **(a)** *Arme, Beine, Oberkörper* to stretch; *Hals* to crane; *(Sch: sich melden) Finger, Hand* to raise, to put up ◆ **die Zunge aus dem Mund ~** to stick out one's tongue; **den Kopf aus dem Fenster/durch die Tür ~** to stick one's head out of the window/through the door; **jdn zu Boden ~** to knock sb to the floor.
(b) *(im Streckverband) Bein, Arm* to straighten.
(c) *(Metal) Blech, Eisen* to hammer out.
(d) *(inf: absichtlich verlängern) Vorräte, Geld* to eke out, to stretch; *Arbeit* to drag out *(inf)*; *Essen* to make go further; *(verdünnen)* to thin down, to dilute.

⚠: for details of spelling reform, see supplement

[2] *vr* (a) (*sich recken*) to have a stretch, to stretch; (*inf: wachsen*) to shoot up (*inf*) ◆ **sich ins Gras/aufs Bett ~** to stretch out on the grass/the bed.
(b) (*sich hinziehen*) to drag on.
Strecken-: ~abschnitt *m* (*Rail*) section of the line *or* track, track section; **~arbeiter** *m* (*Rail*) plate-layer; **~begehung** *f* (*Rail*) track inspection; **~führung** *f* (*Rail*) route; **~netz** *nt* rail network; **~rekord** *m* (*Sport*) track record; **~stillegung** *f* (*Rail*) line closure; **~wärter** *m* (*Rail*) track inspector; **s~weise** *adv* in parts *or* places.
Strecker *m* **-s, -**, **Streckmuskel** *m* (*Anat*) extensor (muscle).
Streckverband *m* (*Med*) *bandage used in traction.*
Streetworker ['stri:twøɐkɐ, -wœrkɐ] *m* **-s, -** (*Sozialarbeiter*) community worker.
Streich *m* **-(e)s, -e** (a) (*Schabernack*) prank, trick ◆ **jdm einen ~ spielen** (*lit*) to play a trick on sb; (*fig: Gedächtnis etc*) to play tricks on sb; **immer zu ~en aufgelegt sein** to be always up to pranks *or* tricks.
(b) (*old, liter*) blow; (*mit Rute, Peitsche*) stroke, lash ◆ **jdm einen ~ versetzen** to strike sb; **auf einen ~** at one blow; (*fig auch*) in one go (*inf*).
Streichel|einheiten *pl* tender loving care *sing.*
streicheln *vti* to stroke; (*liebkosen*) to caress ◆ **jdm die Wange/das Haar ~** to stroke/caress sb's cheek/hair.
streichen *pret* **strich**, *ptp* **gestrichen** [1] *vt* (a) to stroke ◆ **etw glatt~** to smooth sth (out); **sich** (*dat*) **die Haare aus dem Gesicht/der Stirn ~** to push one's hair back from one's face/forehead; *siehe* **gestrichen.**
(b) (*auftragen*) *Butter, Brot etc* to spread; *Salbe, Farbe etc* to apply, to put on ◆ **sich** (*dat*) **ein Brot (mit Butter) ~** to butter oneself a slice of bread; **sich ~ lassen** to spread easily.
(c) (*an~: mit Farbe*) to paint ◆ **frisch gestrichen!** wet paint.
(d) *Geige, Cello* to bow.
(e) (*tilgen*) *Zeile, Satz* to delete, to cross out; *Auftrag, Plan, Zug etc* to cancel; *Schulden* to write off; *Zuschuß etc* to cut ◆ **etw aus dem Protokoll ~** to delete sth from the minutes; **jdn/etw von** *or* **aus der Liste ~** to take sb/sth off the list, to delete sb/sth from the list; **etw aus seinem Gedächtnis ~** (*geh*) to erase sth from one's memory.
(f) (*Naut*) *Segel, Flagge, Ruder* to strike.
[2] *vi* (a) (*über etw hinfahren*) to stroke ◆ **mit der Hand über etw** (*acc*) **~** to stroke sth (with one's hand); **sie strich ihm über die Hand/das Haar** she stroked his hand/hair.
(b) *aux sein* (*streifen*) to brush past (*an etw* (*dat*) sth); (*Wind*) to waft ◆ **um/durch etw ~** (*herum~*) to prowl around/through sth; **die Katze strich mir um die Beine** the cat rubbed against my legs; **durch den Wald/die Felder ~** (*old, geh*) to ramble *or* wander through the woods/fields.
(c) *aux sein* (*Vögel*) to sweep (*über +acc* over).
(d) (*schmieren*) to spread.
(e) (*malen*) to paint.
Streicher *pl* (*Mus*) strings *pl.*
Streich-: s~fähig *adj* easy to spread; **s~fertig** *adj* ready to use *or* apply; **~holz** *nt* match; **~holzschachtel** *f* matchbox; **~instrument** *nt* string(ed) instrument; **die ~instrumente** the strings; **~käse** *m* cheese spread; **~musik** *f* music for strings; **~orchester** *nt* string orchestra; **~quartett** *nt* string quartet; **~quintett** *nt* string quintet; **~riemen** *m* strop.
Streichung *f* (*Tilgung*) (*von Zeile, Satz*) deletion; (*Kürzung*) cut; (*von Auftrag, Plan, Zug*) cancellation; (*von Schulden*) writing off; (*von Zuschüssen etc*) cutting ◆ **die drastischen ~en bei den Subventionen** the drastic cuts in subsidies.
Streichwurst *f* sausage for spreading, ≃ meat paste.
Streifband *nt* wrapper ◆ **im** *or* **unter** (*Sw*) **~** *posted in a wrapper at reduced rate.*
Streifband-: ~depot *nt* (*Fin*) individual safe-deposit box room; **~zeitung** *f newspaper sent at printed paper rate.*
Streife *f* **-, -n** (a) (*Patrouille*) patrol ◆ **auf ~ gehen/sein** to go/be on patrol; **seine ~ machen** to do one's rounds, to patrol; **ein Polizist auf ~** a policeman on his beat. (b) (*Hunt*) *siehe* **Streifjagd.**
streifen [1] *vt* (a) (*flüchtig berühren*) to touch, to brush (against); (*Kugel*) to graze; (*Billardkugel*) to kiss; (*Auto*) to scrape ◆ **jdn an der Schulter ~** to touch sb on the shoulder; **jdn mit einem Blick ~** to glance fleetingly at sb; **ein flüchtiger Blick streifte mich** he/she glanced fleetingly at me.
(b) (*fig: flüchtig erwähnen*) to touch (up)on.
(c) (*ab~, überziehen*) **die Butter vom Messer ~** to scrape the butter off the knife; **die Schuhe von den Füßen ~** to slip one's shoes off; **den Ring vom Finger ~** to slip *or* take the ring off one's finger; **sich** (*dat*) **die Handschuhe über die Finger ~** to pull on one's gloves; **er streifte sich** (*dat*) **den Pullover über den Kopf** (*an-/ausziehen*) he slipped the pullover on/off over his head; **die Blätter von den Zweigen ~** to strip the leaves from the twigs; **die Ärmel in die Höhe ~** to pull up one's sleeves.
[2] *vi* (*geh*) (a) *aux sein* (*wandern*) to roam, to wander; (*Fuchs*) to prowl ◆ **(ziellos) durch das Land/die Wälder ~** to roam the country/the forests.
(b) *aux sein* (*flüchtig berühren: Blick etc*) **sie ließ ihren Blick über die Menge ~** she scanned the crowd; **sein Blick streifte über seine Besitztümer** he gazed at his possessions.
(c) (*fig: grenzen*) to border (*an +acc* on).
Streifen *m* **-s, -** (a) (*Stück, Band*) strip; (*Speck~*) rasher ◆ **ein ~ Land** *or* **Landes** (*geh*)**/Speck** a strip of land/bacon.
(b) (*Strich*) stripe; (*Farb~*) streak.
(c) (*Loch~, Klebe~ etc*) tape.
(d) (*Tresse*) braid; (*Mil*) stripe.
(e) (*Film*) film; (*Abschnitt*) strip of film.
(f) (*Linie*) line.
Streifen-: ~dienst *m* patrol duty; **~muster** *nt* stripy design *or* pattern; **ein Anzug mit ~muster** a striped suit; **~polizei** *f* patrol police; **~polizist** *m* policeman on patrol; **~wagen** *m* patrol car.
streifig *adj* streaky.
Streif-: ~jagd *f* walk-up, *hunt where beaters and guns walk together flushing out game*; **~licht** *nt* (*fig*) highlight; **ein ~licht auf etw** (*acc*) **werfen** to highlight sth; ⚠**~schuß** *m* graze; **~zug** *m* raid; (*Bummel*) expedition; (*fig: kurzer Überblick*) brief survey (*durch* of).
Streik *m* **-(e)s, -s** *or* (*rare*) **-e** strike ◆ **zum ~ aufrufen** to call a strike; **jdn zum ~ aufrufen** to call sb out on strike; **in den ~ treten** to come out *or* go on strike.
Streik-: ~aufruf *m* strike call; **~brecher(in** *f*) *m* **-s, -** strikebreaker, blackleg (*pej*), scab (*pej*).
streiken *vi* to be on strike, to strike; (*in den Streik treten*) to come out on *or* go on strike, to strike; (*hum inf*) (*nicht funktionieren*) to pack up (*inf*); (*Magen*) to protest; (*Gedächtnis*) to fail ◆ **der Kühlschrank streikt schon wieder** (*inf*) the fridge has packed up again (*inf*) *or* is on the blink again (*inf*); **als er noch einen Schnaps eingoß, habe ich gestreikt** (*inf*) when he poured out another schnapps I refused to drink any more; **wenn ich heute abwaschen soll, streike ich** (*inf*) if I have to do the washing up today, I'll go on strike (*inf*); **da streike ich** (*inf*) I refuse!, count me out (*inf*).
Streikende(r) *mf decl as adj* striker.
Streik-: ~geld *nt* strike pay; **~kasse** *f* strike fund; **~posten** *m* picket; **~posten aufstellen** to put up pickets; **~posten stehen** to picket; **~recht** *nt* right *or* freedom to strike; **~welle** *f* wave *or* series of strikes.
Streit *m* **-(e)s, -e** (a) argument (*über +acc* about); (*leichter*) quarrel, squabble; (*zwischen Eheleuten, Kindern auch*) fight; (*Fehde*) feud; (*Auseinandersetzung*) dispute ◆ **~ haben** to be arguing *or* quarrelling; **wegen etw mit jdm (einen) ~ haben** to argue with sb about sth, to have an argument with sb about sth; **die Nachbarn haben seit Jahren ~** the neighbours have been arguing *or* fighting for years; **wegen einer Sache ~ bekommen** to get into an argument over sth; **~ anfangen** to start an argument; **~ suchen** to be looking for an argument *or* a quarrel; **in ~ liegen** (*Gefühle*) to conflict; **mit jdm in ~ liegen** to be at loggerheads with sb.
(b) (*old, liter: Kampf*) battle ◆ **zum ~(e) rüsten** to arm oneself for battle.
Streit|axt *f* (*Hist*) battleaxe ◆ **die ~ begraben** (*fig*) to bury the hatchet.
streitbar *adj* (a) (*streitlustig*) pugnacious. (b) (*old: tapfer*) valiant.
streiten *pret* **stritt**, *ptp* **gestritten** [1] *vi* (a) to argue; (*leichter*) to quarrel, to squabble; (*Eheleute, Kinder auch*) to fight; (*Gefühle*) to conflict; (*Jur: prozessieren*) to take legal action ◆ **mit Waffen/Fäusten ~** to fight with weapons/one's fists; **Scheu und Neugier stritten in ihr** she had conflicting feelings of shyness and curiosity; **die S~den** the arguers, the people fighting; **es wird immer noch gestritten, ob ...** the argument about whether ... is still going on.
(b) **über etw** (*acc*) **~** to dispute *or* argue about *or* over sth; (*Jur*) to go to court over sth; **darüber kann man** *or* **läßt sich ~** that's a debatable *or* moot point; **die ~den Parteien** (*Jur*) the litigants.
(c) (*old, liter*) (*kämpfen*) to fight; (*in Wettbewerb*) to compete (*um* for).
[2] *vr* to argue, to quarrel, to squabble; (*Eheleute, Kinder auch*) to fight ◆ **habt ihr euch schon wieder gestritten?** have you been fighting again?; **wir wollen uns deswegen nicht ~!** don't let's fall out over that!; **man streitet sich, ob ...** there is argument as to whether ...
Streiter(in *f*) *m* **-s, -** (*geh*) fighter (*für* for); (*für Prinzip etc auch*) champion (*für* of).
Streiterei *f* (*inf*) arguing *no pl*; quarrelling *no pl*; (*zwischen Eheleuten, Kindern auch*) fighting *no pl* ◆ **eine ~** an argument.
Streit-: ~fall *m* dispute, conflict; (*Jur*) case; **im ~fall** in case of dispute *or* conflict; **im ~fall Müller gegen Braun** in the case of Müller versus Braun; **~frage** *f* dispute; **~gegenstand** *m* matter in dispute; (*strittiger Punkt*) matter of dispute; **~gespräch** *nt* debate, discussion; (*Liter, Univ auch*) disputation; **~grund** *m* cause of the/an argument; **~hahn** *m* (*inf*) squabbler; **~hammel** *m* (*inf*), **~hans(e)l** *m* **-s, -** (*S Ger, Aus inf*) quarrelsome person.
streitig *adj* **jdm das Recht auf etw** (*acc*) **~ machen** to dispute sb's right to sth; **das/seine Kompetenz kann man ihm nicht ~ machen** that/his competence is indisputable.
Streitigkeiten *pl* quarrels *pl*, squabbles *pl.*
Streit-: ~kräfte *pl* forces *pl*, troops *pl*; **~lust** *f* (*liter*) argumentative disposition; (*Aggressivität*) aggressive disposition; **s~lustig** *adj* (*geh*) argumentative; (*aggressiv*) aggressive; **~macht** *f* armed forces *pl*; **~objekt** *nt siehe* **~gegenstand**; **~punkt** *m* contentious issue; ⚠**~roß** *nt* war-horse; **~sache** *f* dispute; (*Jur*) case; **~schrift** *f* polemic; **~sucht** *f* quarrelsomeness; **s~süchtig** *adj* quarrelsome; **~wagen** *m* (*Hist*) chariot; **~wert** *m* (*Jur*) amount in dispute.
▼ **streng** *adj* (a) strict; *Regel, Kontrolle auch, Maßnahmen* stringent; *Bestrafung* severe; *Anforderungen* rigorous; *Ausdruck, Blick, Gesicht* stern; *Sitten, Disziplin auch* rigid; *Stillschweigen, Diskretion* absolute; *Mode, Schnitt* severe; *Kritik, Urteil* harsh, severe; *Richter* severe, stern; *Lebensführung, Schönheit, Form* austere; *Examen* stiff ◆ **~ gegen jdn/etw vorgehen** to deal severely with sb/sth; **~ durchgreifen** to take rigorous *or* stringent action; **~ gegen sich selbst sein** to be strict *or* severe on *or* with oneself; **~ aber gerecht** severe but just; **etw ~ befolgen, sich ~ an etw halten** to keep strictly *or* rigidly to sth, to observe sth strictly *or* rigidly; **~ geheim** top secret; **~ vertraulich/wissenschaftlich**

strictly confidential/scientific; **~ nach Vorschrift** strictly according to regulations; **~(stens) verboten!** strictly prohibited; **sie kleidet sich sehr ~** she wears very severe clothes.

(b) (*durchdringend*) *Geruch, Geschmack* pungent; *Frost, Kälte, Winter* intense, severe.

(c) (*~gläubig*) Katholik, Moslem strict.

Strenge *f* **-,** *no pl siehe adj* **(a)** strictness; stringency; severity; rigorousness; sternness; rigidity; absoluteness; severity; harshness, severity; severity, sternness; austerity; stiffness ◆ **mit ~ regieren** to rule strictly. **(b)** pungency; intensity, severity. **(c)** strictness.

Streng-: ⚠**s~genommen** *adv* strictly speaking; (*eigentlich*) actually; **s~gläubig** *adj* strict; ⚠**s~nehmen** *vt sep irreg* to take seriously; **es mit etw s~nehmen** to be strict about sth; **wenn man es s~nimmt** strictly speaking.

Streptokokken [ʃtrɛpto'kɔk(ə)n, st-] *pl* (*Med*) streptococci *pl.*

Streptomycin [ʃtrɛptomy'tsi:n, st-] *nt* **-s,** *no pl* (*Med*) streptomycin.

Stresemann *m* **-s,** *no pl formal, dark suit with striped trousers.*

⚠**Streß** [ʃtrɛs, st-] *m* **-sses, -sse** (*alle Bedeutungen*) stress ◆ **der tägliche ~ im Büro** the daily stress *or* hassle (*inf*) in the office; **im ~ sein** to be under stress; **ich bin heute im ~** I'm feeling hassled today (*inf*).

stressen *vt* to put under stress ◆ **gestreßt sein** to be under stress.

⚠**streß-:** **~frei** *adj* stress-free; **~geplagt** *adj* under stress; **~geplagte Manager** highly stressed executives, executives suffering from stress.

stressig *adj* stressful.

⚠**Streß-:** **~krankheit** *f* stress disease; **~situation** *f* stress situation.

Stretching *nt* (*Gymnastik*) stretching exercises *pl.*

Stretchstoff ['strɛtʃ-] *m* stretch fabric.

Streu *f* **-,** *no pl* straw; (*aus Sägespänen*) sawdust.

streuen 1 *vt Futter, Samen* to scatter; *Blumen auch* to strew; *Dünger, Stroh, Sand, Kies* to spread; *Gewürze, Zucker etc* to sprinkle; *Straße, Gehweg etc* to grit; to salt ◆ **die Regierung ließ ~, daß ...** the government gave reason to believe, that ...

2 *vi* **(a)** (*Streumittel anwenden*) to grit; to put down salt. **(b)** (*Salzstreuer etc*) to sprinkle. **(c)** (*Linse, Gewehr etc*) to scatter.

Streuer *m* **-s, -** shaker; (*Salz~*) cellar; (*Pfeffer~*) pot; (*Zucker~ auch*) castor; (*Mehl~ auch*) dredger.

Streufahrzeug *nt* gritter, sander.

streunen *vi* **(a)** to roam about, to wander about *or* around; (*Hund, Katze*) to stray. **(b)** *aux sein* **durch etw/in etw** (*dat*) **~** to roam *or* wander through/ around sth.

Streu-: **~pflicht** *f obligation on householder to keep area in front of house gritted in icy weather;* **~pulver** *nt* grit/salt (*for icy roads*); **~salz** *nt* salt (*for icy roads*); **~sand** *m* sand; (*für Straße*) grit.

Streusel *nt* **-s, -** (*Cook*) crumble (mixture).

Streuselkuchen *m thin sponge cake with crumble topping.*

Streuung *f* (*Statistik*) mean variation; (*Phys*) scattering.

Streu-: **~wagen** *m* (road) gritter; **~zucker** *m* (*grob*) granulated sugar; (*fein*) castor sugar.

strich *pret of* **streichen.**

Strich *m* **-(e)s, -e** **(a)** line; (*Quer~*) dash; (*Schräg~*) oblique, slash (*esp US*); (*Feder~, Pinsel~*) stroke; (*von Land*) stretch ◆ **etw mit (ein paar) knappen ~en zeichnen** (*lit, fig*) to sketch *or* outline sth with a few brief strokes; **jdm einen ~ durch die Rechnung/einen Plan machen** to thwart sb's plans/plan; **einen ~ (unter etw *acc*) machen** *or* **ziehen** (*fig*) to forget sth; **unterm ~ sein** (*inf*) not to be up to scratch; **unterm ~** at the final count; **er kann noch auf dem ~ gehen** (*inf*) he can still walk along a straight line; **dünn wie ein ~** (*inf*) as thin as a rake (*inf*); **sie ist nur noch ein ~ (in der Landschaft** *hum*) (*inf*) she's as thin as a rake now; **keinen ~ tun** (*inf*) not to do a stroke (of work).

(b) *no pl* (*Kompaß~*) point.

(c) (*von Teppich*) pile; (*von Samt auch, von Gewebe*) nap; (*von Fell, Haar*) direction of growth ◆ **gegen den ~ bürsten** (*lit*) to brush the wrong way; **es geht (mir) gegen den ~** (*inf*) it goes against the grain; **nach ~ und Faden** (*inf*) good and proper (*inf*), thoroughly; **jdn nach ~ und Faden versohlen** (*inf*) to give sb a thorough *or* good hiding.

(d) (*Mus: Bogen~*) stroke, bow ◆ **einen harten/weichen ~ haben** to bow heavily/lightly.

(e) (*inf*) (*Prostitution*) prostitution *no art;* (*Bordellgegend*) red-light district ◆ **auf den ~ gehen** to be/go on the game (*sl*), to be/become a prostitute.

(f) (*von Schwalben etc*) flight.

Strich-: **~ätzung** *f* (*Typ*) line etching; **~code** *m* bar code (*Brit*), universal product code (*US*).

stricheln 1 *vi* to sketch it in; (*schraffieren*) to hatch.

2 *vt* to sketch in; to hatch ◆ **eine gestrichelte Linie** a broken line.

Stricher *m* **-s, -** (*pej*) rent boy (*inf*).

Strich-: **~junge** *m* (*inf*) rentboy; **~mädchen** *nt* (*inf*) tart (*inf*), hooker (*esp US sl*); **~punkt** *m* semi-colon; **s~weise** *adv* (*Met*) here and there; **s~weise Regen** rain in places; **~zeichnung** *f* line drawing.

Strick[1] *m* **-(e)s, -e** **(a)** rope; (*dünner, als Gürtel*) cord ◆ **jdm aus etw einen ~ drehen** to use sth against sb; **zum ~ greifen** (*inf*) to hang oneself; **dann kann ich mir einen ~ nehmen** *or* **kaufen** (*inf*) I may as well pack it all in (*inf*); *siehe* **reißen.**

(b) (*inf: Schelm*) rascal ◆ **fauler ~** lazybones *sing* (*inf*), lazy so-and-so (*inf*).

Strick[2] *nt* (*inf*) knitwear.

Strick-: **~arbeit** *f* knitting *no pl;* **eine ~arbeit** a piece of knitting; **~beutel** *m* knitting bag.

stricken *vti* to knit.

Stricker(in *f*) *m* **-s, -** knitter.

Strickerei *f* **(a)** knitting *no indef art, no pl.* **(b)** (*Betrieb*) knitware factory.

Strick-: **~garn** *nt* knitting wool; **~handschuhe** *pl* knitted gloves *pl;* **~jacke** *f* cardigan; **~kleid** *nt* knitted dress; **~leiter** *f* rope ladder; **~maschine** *f* knitting machine; **~muster** *nt* (*lit*) knitting pattern; (*fig*) pattern; **~nadel** *f* knitting needle; **~waren** *pl* knitwear *sing;* **~weste** *f* knitted waistcoat; (*mit Ärmeln*) cardigan; **~wolle** *f* knitting wool; **~zeug** *nt* knitting.

Striegel *m* **-s, -** currycomb.

striegeln 1 *vt* **(a)** to curry(comb); (*fig inf: kämmen*) to comb. **(b)** (*inf: hart behandeln*) **jdn ~** to put sb through the hoop (*inf*).

2 *vr* (*inf*) to spruce oneself up.

Strieme *f* **-, -n, Striemen** *m* **-s, -** weal.

striemig *adj Haut* marked with weals.

Striezel *m* **-s, -** (*dial Cook*) plaited Danish pastry.

stringent *adj* (*geh*) stringent; *Handlung* tight ◆ **etw ~ nachweisen** to provide rigorous proof for sth.

strikt [ʃtrɪkt, st-] *adj* strict.

Strip [ʃtrɪp, strɪp] *m* **-s, -s** (*inf*) strip(tease).

Strippe *f* **-, -n** (*inf*) **(a)** (*Bindfaden*) string. **(b)** (*Telefonleitung*) phone, blower (*Brit inf*) ◆ **an der ~ hängen/sich an die ~ hängen** to be/get on the phone *or* blower (*Brit sl*); **jdn an der ~ haben** to have sb on the line *or* phone *or* blower (*Brit sl*).

strippen ['ʃtrɪpn, 'strɪpn] *vi* to strip, to do a striptease act.

Stripper(in *f*) ['ʃtrɪpɐ, -ərɪn, st-] *m* **-s, -** (*inf*) stripper.

Striptease ['ʃtrɪpti:s, st-] *m or nt* **-,** *no pl* striptease.

Stripteasetänzer(in *f*) ['ʃtrɪpti:s-, st-] *m* stripper.

stritt *pret of* **streiten.**

strittig *adj* contentious, controversial ◆ **noch ~** still in dispute.

Strizzi *m* **-s, -s** (*Aus inf*) pimp.

Stroboskop *nt* **-s, -e** stroboscope.

Stroboskopblitz *m* stroboscopic light.

stroboskopisch *adj* stroboscopic.

Stroboskoplampe *f* strobe light.

Stroh *nt* **-(e)s,** *no pl* straw; (*Dach~*) thatch ◆ **~ im Kopf haben** (*inf*) to have sawdust between one's ears (*inf*); *siehe* **dreschen.**

Stroh-: **~ballen** *m* bale of straw; **s~blond** *adj Mensch* flaxen-haired; *Haare* flaxen, straw-coloured; **~blume** *f* strawflower; **~bund** *nt* bundle of straw; **~dach** *nt* thatched roof; **s~dumm** *adj* thick (*inf*); **s~farben** *adj* straw-coloured; *Haare auch* flaxen; **~feuer** *nt*: **ein ~feuer sein** (*fig*) to be a passing fancy; **s~gedeckt** *adj* thatched; **s~gelb** *adj* straw-coloured; *Haare auch* flaxen; **~halm** *m* straw; **sich an einen ~halm klammern, nach einem ~halm greifen** to clutch at a straw; **~hut** *m* straw hat; **~hütte** *f* thatched hut.

strohig *adj Gemüse* tough; *Orangen etc* dry; *Haar* dull and lifeless.

Stroh-: **~kopf** *m* (*inf*) blockhead (*inf*); **~lager** *nt* pallet, straw mattress; **~mann** *m, pl* **-männer** (*~puppe*) scarecrow; (*fig*) front man; (*Cards*) dummy; **~matte** *f* straw mat; **~puppe** *f* scarecrow; **~sack** *m* palliasse; **heiliger ~sack!** (*dated inf*) good(ness) gracious (me)!; **~witwe** *f* grass widow; **~witwer** *m* grass widower.

Strolch *m* **-(e)s, -e** (*dated pej*) rogue, rascal.

strolchen *vi aux sein* to roam about ◆ **durch etw/in etw** (*dat*) **~** to roam through/around sth.

Strom *m* **-(e)s, ~̈e** **(a)** (large) river; (*Strömung*) current; (*von Schweiß, Blut*) river; (*von Besuchern, Flüchen etc*) stream ◆ **ein reißender ~** a raging torrent; **~̈e und Flüsse Europas** rivers of Europe; **ein ~ von Tränen** (*geh*) floods of tears *pl;* **in dem** *or* **im ~ der Vergessenheit versinken** (*geh*) to sink *or* pass into oblivion; **in ~̈en regnen** to be pouring with rain; **der Wein floß in ~̈en** the wine flowed like water; **der ~ seiner Rede** (*geh*) the torrent *or* flood of his words; **der ~ der Zeit/Geschichte** (*geh*) the flow of time/the course of history; **mit dem/gegen den ~ schwimmen** (*lit*) to swim with/against the current; (*fig*) to swim *or* go with/against the tide.

(b) (*Elec*) current; (*Elektrizität*) electricity ◆ **~ führen** to be live; **unter ~ stehen** (*lit*) to be live; (*fig*) to be high (*inf*); **mit ~ heizen** to have electric heating; **der ~ ist ausgefallen** the power *or* electricity is off.

Strom-: **s~ab** *adv* downstream; **≈abnehmer** *m* **(a)** (*Tech*) pantograph; **(b)** (*~verbraucher*) user *or* consumer of electricity; **s~abwärts** *adv* downstream; ⚠**≈anschluß** *m* **~anschluß haben** to be connected to the electricity mains; **s~auf(wärts)** *adv* upstream; **≈ausfall** *m* power failure; **≈bett** *nt* riverbed.

strömen *vi aux sein* to stream; (*Blut auch, Gas*) to flow; (*heraus~*) to pour (*aus* from); (*Menschen auch*) to flock (*aus* out of) ◆ **be ~dem Regen** in (the) pouring rain.

Stromer *m* **-s, -** (*inf*) rover; (*Landstreicher*) tramp, hobo (*esp US*).

stromern *vi aux sein* (*inf*) to roam *or* wander about.

Strom-: ⚠**s~führend** *adj attr* (*Elec*) *Leitung* live; **~kabel** *nt* electric *or* power cable; **~kreis** *m* (electrical) circuit; **~leitung** *f* electric cables *pl;* **~linienform** [-li:niən-] *f* streamlined design; (*von Auto auch*) streamlined body; **s~linienförmig** [-li:niən-] *adj* streamlined; **~messer** *m* **-s, -** (*Elec*) ammeter; **~netz** *nt* electricity *or* power supply system; **~quelle** *f* source of power *or* electricity; **~schiene** *f* (*Rail*) live *or* conductor rail; **~schnelle** *f* rapids *pl;* **~speicher** *m* (storage) battery; **~sperre** *f* power cut; **~stärke** *f* strength of the/an electric current; **~stoß** *m* electric shock.

Strömung *f* current; (*fig auch*) trend.

Strömungslehre *f* (*von Flüssigkeiten*) hydrodynamics *sing;* (*von Luft und Gasen*) aerodynamics *sing.*

Strom-: ~verbrauch *m* electricity *or* power consumption; **~versorgung** *f* electricity *or* power supply; **~wender** *m* **-s, -** commutator; **~zähler** *m* electricity meter.

Strontium ['ʃtrɔntsiʊm, st-] *nt, no pl* (*abbr* **Sr**) strontium.

Strophe *f* **-, -n** verse; (*in Gedicht auch*) stanza.

-strophig *adj suf* **drei~/vier~** of three/four stanzas *or* verses.

strophisch [1] *adj* stanzaic.
[2] *adv* in stanzas.

strotzen *vi* to be full (*von, vor +dat* of), to abound (*von, vor +dat* with); (*von Kraft, Gesundheit, Lebensfreude*) to be bursting (*von* with); (*vor Ungeziefer*) to be teeming *or* crawling (*vor +dat* with); (*von Waffen*) to be bristling (*von, vor +dat* with) ◆ **von Schmutz ~** to be thick *or* covered with dirt.

strubb(e)lig *adj* (*inf*) *Haar, Fell* tousled.

Strubbelkopf *m* (*inf*) tousled hair; (*Mensch*) tousle-head ◆ **einen ~ haben, ein ~ sein** to have tousled hair.

Strudel *m* **-s, - (a)** (*lit, fig*) whirlpool; (*von Ereignissen, Vergnügen*) whirl. **(b)** (*Cook*) strudel.

strudeln *vi* to whirl, to swirl.

Strudelteig *m* (*esp S Ger, Aus: Cook*) strudel pastry.

Struktur *f* structure; (*von Stoff etc*) texture; (*Webart*) weave.

Strukturalismus *m* structuralism.

strukturalistisch *adj* structuralist ◆ **etw ~ interpretieren** to interpret sth according to structuralist methods.

Struktur|analyse *f* structural analysis.

strukturell *adj* structural.

Strukturformel *f* (*Chem*) structural formula.

strukturieren* *vt* to structure.

Strukturierung *f* structuring.

Struktur-: ~krise *f* structural crisis; **~politik** *f* structural policy; **~problem** *nt* structural problem; **~reform** *f* structural reform; **s~schwach** *adj* lacking in infrastructure; **die s~schwachen Gebiete Bayerns** the parts of Bavaria with less well-developed infrastructure; **~schwäche** *f* lack of infrastructure; **~wandel** *m* structural change (*gen* in).

Strumpf *m* **-(e)s, ¨-e (a)** sock; (*Damen~*) stocking ◆ **ein Paar ¨~e** a pair of socks/stockings; **auf ¨~en** in one's stockinged feet; **sich auf die ¨~e machen** (*inf*) to get going (*inf*). **(b)** (*Spar~*) **sein Geld im ~ haben** ≃ to keep one's money under the mattress. **(c)** (*Glüh~*) mantle.

Strumpf-: ~band *nt* garter; **~fabrik** *f* hosiery factory; **~geschäft** *nt* hosiery shop (*esp Brit*) *or* store (*esp US*); **~halter** *m* **-s, -** suspender (*Brit*), garter (*US*); **~haltergürtel** *m* suspender belt (*Brit*), garter belt (*US*); **~hose** *f* tights *pl* (*esp Brit*), panty-hose; **eine ~hose** a pair of tights (*esp Brit*) *or* panty-hose; **~maske** *f* stocking mask; **~waren** *pl* hosiery *sing;* **~wirker(in** *f*) *m* **-s, -** hosiery worker.

Strunk *m* **-(e)s, ¨-e** stalk.

struppig *adj* unkempt; *Tier* shaggy.

Struwwelkopf ['ʃtrʊvl-] *m* (*inf*) *siehe* **Strubbelkopf.**

Struwwelpeter ['ʃtrʊvl-] *m* tousle-head ◆ **der ~** (*Liter*) shock-headed Peter, Struwwelpeter.

Strychnin [ʃtrʏç'niːn, st-] *nt* **-s,** *no pl* strychnine.

Stubben *m* **-s, -** (*N Ger*) tree stump.

Stübchen *nt dim of* **Stube** little room.

Stube *f* **-, -n** (*dated, dial*) room; (*dial: Wohnzimmer*) lounge; (*in Kaserne*) barrack room; (*Sch*) study; (*Schlafsaal*) dormitory ◆ **auf der ~** (*Mil*) in one's barrack room, in one's quarters; (*Sch*) in one's study/dormitory; **die gute ~** the parlour (*dated*); **(immer) herein in die gute ~!** (*hum inf*) come right in; **in der ~ hocken** (*inf*) to sit around indoors.

Stuben-: ~älteste(r) *mf* (*Mil*) senior soldier in a/the barrack room; (*Sch*) study/dormitory prefect; **~appell** *m* (*Mil*) barrack room inspection; (*Sch*) study/dormitory inspection; **~arrest** *m* confinement to one's room *or* (*Mil*) quarters; **~arrest haben** to be confined to one's room/quarters; **~dienst** *m* (*Mil*) fatigue duty, barrack room duty; (*Sch*) study/dormitory cleaning duty; **~dienst haben** to be on fatigue duty *etc;* **~fliege** *f* (common) housefly; **~gelehrte(r)** *mf* (*pej*) armchair scholar; **~hocker** *m* **-s, -** (*pej inf*) house-mouse (*inf*); **~kamerad** *m* (*esp Mil*) roommate; **~mädchen** *nt* (*dated*) chambermaid; **s~rein** *adj Katze, Hund* house-trained; (*hum*) *Witz* clean.

Stübe(r)l *nt* **-s, -** (*Aus*) small room.

Stuck *m* **-(e)s,** *no pl* stucco; (*zur Zimmerverzierung*) moulding.

Stück *nt* **-(e)s, -e** *or* (*nach Zahlenangaben*) **- (a)** piece; (*von Vieh, Wild*) head; (*von Zucker*) lump; (*Ausstellungs ~ auch*) item; (*Seife*) bar, cake; (*von abgegrenztem Land*) plot ◆ **ich nehme fünf ~** I'll take five; **12 ~ (Eier)** twelve *or* a dozen (eggs); **20 ~ Vieh** 20 head of cattle; **sechs ~ von diesen Apfelsinen** six of these oranges; **12 ~, ~er 12** (*hum*) 12 all told; **10 Pfennig das ~, pro ~ 10 Pfennig** 10 pfennigs each; **im** *or* **am ~** in one piece; *Käse, Wurst auch* unsliced; **aus einem ~** in one piece; **~ für ~** (*ein Exemplar nach dem andern*) one by one; **etw nach ~ verkaufen** to sell sth by the piece; **nach ~ bezahlt werden** to do piecework; **das größte/beste ~ (Fleisch** *etc*) the biggest/best piece (of meat *etc*); **ein ~ Garten** a patch of garden; **das ist unser bestes ~** (*hum*) that is our pride and joy.
(b) (*Teil, Abschnitt*) piece, bit; (*von Buch, Rede, Reise etc*) part; (*von Straße etc*) stretch ◆ **ich möchte nur ein kleines ~** I only want a little bit *or* a small piece; **~ für ~** (*einen Teil um den andern*) bit by bit; **in ~e gehen/zerspringen** to be broken/smashed to pieces; **etw in ~e schlagen** to smash sth to pieces *or* smithereens; **etw in ~e reißen** to tear sth to pieces *or* shreds; **sich für jdn in ~e reißen lassen** to do anything for sb; **ein ~ Heimat** a piece of home; **in allen ~en** on every matter; *übereinstimmen auch* in every detail; **ich komme ein ~ (des Weges) mit** I'll come some *or* part of the way with you.
(c) ein ~ spazierengehen to go for a walk; **ein gutes ~ weiterkommen** to make considerable progress *or* headway; **ein schweres ~ Arbeit** a tough job; **ein schönes ~ Geld** (*inf*) a tidy sum, a pretty penny (*inf*); **das ist (doch) ein starkes ~!** (*inf*) that's a bit much *or* thick (*inf*); **große ~e auf jdn halten** to think much *or* highly of sb, to have a high opinion of sb; **große ~e auf etw** (*acc*) **halten** to be very proud of sth; **aus freien ~en** of one's own free will.
(d) (*Fin*) share.
(e) (*Bühnen~*) play; (*Musik~*) piece.
(f) (*inf: Mensch*) beggar (*inf*), so-and-so (*inf*) ◆ **mein bestes ~** (*hum inf*) my pride and joy; **ein ~ Dreck** *or* **Mist** (*sl*) a bitch (*inf*), a cow (*inf*); (*Mann*) a bastard (*sl*).

Stück-: ~akkord *m,* **~arbeit** *f* piecework.

Stuck|arbeit *f* stucco work *no pl;* (*in Zimmer*) moulding.

Stückchen *nt dim of* **Stück (a, b, e).**

Stuckdecke *f* stucco(ed) ceiling.

stücke(l)n [1] *vt* to patch.
[2] *vi* to patch it together.

stucken *vi* (*Aus inf*) to swot (*inf*), to cram (*inf*).

Stückeschreiber *m* dramatist, playwright.

⚠ **Stückfaß** *nt* (*Weinmaß*) *measure of wine containing 1,200 litres.*

Stück-: ~gut *nt* (*Rail*) parcel service; **etw als ~gut schicken** to send sth as a parcel; **~leistung** *f* production capacity; **~lohn** *m* piece(work) rate; **~notierung** *f* quotation per unit; **~preis** *m* unit price; (*Comm auch*) price for one; **s~weise** *adv* bit by bit, little by little; **s~weise verkaufen** to sell individually; **~werk** *nt, no pl* incomplete *or* unfinished work; **~werk sein/bleiben** to be/remain incomplete *or* unfinished; **~zahl** *f* number of pieces *or* items; **~zeit** *f* production time per piece *or* item; **~zins** *m* (*Fin*) accrued interest.

stud. *abbr of* **studiosus** ◆ **stud. med./phil.** *etc* student of medicine/humanities *etc.*

Student *m* student; (*Aus: Schüler*) schoolboy; (*einer bestimmten Schule*) pupil.

Studenten-: ~ausweis *m* student card; **~bewegung** *f* student movement; **~blume** *f* French marigold; **~bude** *f* (*inf*) student digs *pl;* **~futter** *nt* nuts and raisins; **~gemeinde** *f* student religious society; **~heim** *nt* hall of residence, student hostel; **~leben** *nt* student life; **~liebe** *f* student romance; **~lied** *nt* student song; **~lokal** *nt* students' pub; **~pfarrer** *m* university/college chaplain; **~rabatt** *m* student discount; **~revolte** *f* student revolt; **~schaft** *f* students *pl*, student body; **~sprache** *f* student slang; **~verbindung** *f* students' society *or* association; (*für Männer auch*) fraternity (*US*); (*für Frauen auch*) sorority (*US*); **~werk** *nt* student administration; **~wohnheim** *nt* hall of residence, student hostel.

Studentin *f* student; (*Aus: Schülerin*) schoolgirl; (*einer bestimmten Schule*) pupil.

studentisch *adj attr* student *attr.*

Studie ['ʃtuːdiə] *f* study (*über +acc* of); (*Entwurf auch*) sketch; (*Abhandlung*) essay (*über +acc* on).

Studien- ['ʃtuːdiən-]: **~abbrecher(in** *f*) *m* **-s, -** *student who fails to complete his/her course of study;* ⚠**~abschluß** *m* completion of a course of study; **Volkswirtschaftler mit ~abschluß** graduate economist; **die Universität ohne ~abschluß verlassen** to leave university without graduating; **~anfänger** *m* first year student; **~assessor** *m graduate teacher who has recently completed his/her training;* **~aufenthalt** *m* study visit; **~beratung** *f* course guidance service; **~buch** *nt book in which the courses one has attended are entered;* **~direktor** *m* (*von Fachschule*) principal; (*in Gymnasium*) ≃ deputy principal; **~fach** *nt* subject; **~fahrt** *f* study trip; (*Sch*) educational trip; **~förderung** *f* study grant; (*an Universität*) university grant; **~freund** *m* university/college friend; **~gang** *m* course of studies; **~gebühren** *pl* tuition fees *pl;* **s~halber** *adv* for the purpose of study *or* studying; **~inhalte** *pl* course contents *pl;* **~jahr** *nt* academic year; **~jahre** *pl* university/college years *pl;* **~plan** *m* course of study; **~platz** *m* university/college place; **ein ~platz in Medizin** a place to study medicine; **~rat** *m,* **~rätin** *f* teacher at a secondary school; **~referendar** *m* student teacher; **~reform** *f* university/college reform; **~reise** *f siehe* **~fahrt**; **~seminar** *nt* teacher training course; **sie ist im ~seminar in Essen** she is doing her teacher training in Essen; **~zeit** *f* **(a)** student days *pl;* **(b)** (*Dauer*) duration of a/one's course of studies; **~zeitbegrenzung** *f* limitation on the length of courses of studies; **~zweck** *m* **für ~zwecke, zu ~zwecken** for the purposes of study, for study purposes.

studieren* [1] *vi* to study; (*Student sein*) to be a student, to be at university/college, to be at school (*US inf*) ◆ **ich studiere an der Universität Bonn** I am (a student) at Bonn University; **nicht jeder kann ~** not everyone can go to university/college; **wo haben Sie studiert?** what university/college did you go to?; **bei jdm ~** to study under sb; **jdn ~ lassen** to send sb to university/college.
[2] *vt* to study; (*an Uni auch*) to read; (*genau betrachten*) to scrutinize ◆ **sie hat vier Semester Jura studiert** she has studied law for two years.

Studierende(r) *mf decl as adj* student.

studiert *adj* (*inf*) educated ◆ **~ sein** to have been at university/college; **ein S~er/eine S~e** an intellectual.

Studierzimmer *nt* study.

Studio *nt* **-s, -s** studio.

Studiobühne *f* studio theatre.

Studiosus *m* **-s, Studiosi** (*old, hum*) student.

Studium *nt* study; (*Hochschul~*) studies *pl;* (*genaue Betrachtung auch*) scrutiny

◆ **sein ~ beginnen** *or* **aufnehmen** (*form*) to begin one's studies, to go to university/college; **das ~ hat fünf Jahre gedauert** the course of study lasted five years; **während seines ~s** while he is/was *etc* a student *or* at university/college; **er ist noch im ~** he is still a student; **das ~ der Mathematik, das mathematische ~** the study of mathematics, mathematical studies *pl*; **archäologische/psychologische Studien betreiben** to study archaeology/psychology; **er war gerade beim ~ des Börsenberichts, als ...** he was just studying the stock exchange report when ...; **seine Studien zu etw machen** to study sth.

Studium generale *nt* **- -,** *no pl* general course of studies ◆ **ein ~ machen** to do a general degree.

Stufe *f* **-, -n (a)** step; (*Gelände ~ auch*) terrace; (*Mus: Ton~*) degree; (*bei Rock etc*) tier; (*zum Kürzen*) tuck; (*im Haar*) layer ◆ **mehrere ~n auf einmal nehmen** to run up the stairs two or three at a time.
(b) (*fig*) stage; (*Niveau*) level; (*Rang*) grade; (*Gram: Steigerungs~*) degree ◆ **eine ~ höher als ...** a step up from ...; **die höchste/tiefste ~** the height *or* pinnacle/the depths *pl*; **mit jdm auf gleicher ~ stehen** to be on a level with sb; **jdn/sich mit jdm/etw auf die gleiche** *or* **eine ~ stellen** to put *or* place sb/oneself on a level *or* par with sb/sth.

stufen *vt Schüler, Preise* to grade; *Haare* to layer; *Land etc* to terrace.

Stufen-: ~barren *m* asymmetric bar; **~dach** *nt* stepped roof; **s~förmig** [1] *adj* (*lit*) stepped; *Landschaft* terraced; (*fig*) gradual; [2] *adv* (*lit*) in steps; *angelegt* in terraces; (*fig*) in stages, gradually; **~führerschein** *m* (graded) motorcycle licence; **~heck** *nt* **ein Auto mit ~heck** a saloon car; **~leiter** *f* (*fig*) ladder (*gen* to); **s~los** *adj Schaltung* infinitely variable; (*fig: gleitend*) smooth; **~ordnung** *f* successive order; **~plan** *m* step-by-step plan (*zu* for); **~rakete** *f* multi-stage rocket; **~schalter** *m* (*Elec*) sequence switch; **~schnitt** *m* (*von Haaren*) layered cut; **~tarif** *m* (*Econ*) graduated tariff; **s~weise** [1] *adv* step by step, gradually; [2] *adj attr* gradual.

stufig *adj* stepped; *Land etc* terraced; *Haar* layered ◆ **das Haar ~ schneiden** to layer sb's hair.

-stufig *adj suf* **drei~e Rakete** three-stage rocket.

Stufung *f* gradation.

Stuhl *m* **-(e)s, ¨-e (a)** chair ◆ **ist dieser ~ noch frei?** is this chair taken?, is this somebody's chair?; **sich zwischen zwei ¨~e setzen, zwischen zwei ¨~en sitzen** (*fig*) to fall between two stools; **ich wäre fast vom ~ gefallen** (*inf*) I nearly fell off my chair (*inf*); **das haut einen vom ~** (*sl*) it knocks you sideways (*inf*); **jdm den ~ vor die Tür setzen** (*fig*) to kick sb out (*inf*).
(b) (*Königs~*) throne ◆ **der Apostolische** *or* **Heilige** *or* **Päpstliche ~** the Apostolic *or* Holy *or* Papal See; **der ~ Petri** the See of Rome; **vor Gottes ~ gerufen werden** to be called before one's Maker.
(c) (*Lehramt*) chair (*gen* of, *für* of, in).
(d) (*~gang*) bowel movement; (*Kot*) stool ◆ **~ haben/keinen ~ haben** to have had/not to have had a bowel movement.

Stuhl-: ~bein *nt* chair leg; **~drang** *m* (*form*) urgent need to empty the bowels; **~entleerung** *f* (*form*) evacuation of the bowels; **~gang** *m, no pl* bowel movement; **regelmäßig ~gang haben** to have regular bowels; **~gang/keinen ~gang haben** to have had/not to have had a bowel movement; **~lehne** *f* back of a chair; **~verhaltung** *f* (*form*) retention of faeces.

Stuka ['ʃtuːka, 'ʃtʊka] *m* **-s, -s** *abbr of* **Sturzkampfflugzeug** stuka, dive bomber.

⚠ **Stukkateur(in** *f***)** [ʃtʊka'tøːɐ, -'tørɪn] *m* plasterer (*who works with stucco*).

⚠ **Stukkatur** *f* stucco (work), ornamental plasterwork.

Stulle *f* **-, -n** (*N Ger*) slice of bread and butter; sandwich.

Stulpe *f* **-, -n** cuff; (*von Handschuh*) gauntlet.

stülpen *vt* **den Kragen nach oben ~** to turn up one's collar; **etw auf/über etw** (*acc*) **~** to put sth on/over sth; **etw nach innen/außen ~** to turn sth to the inside/outside; **sich** (*dat*) **den Hut auf den Kopf ~** to clap *or* slap on one's hat.

Stulpen-: ~handschuh *m* gauntlet; **~stiefel** *m* top boot.

Stülpnase *f* snub *or* turned-up nose.

stumm *adj* **(a)** (*lit, fig*) dumb ◆ **die ~e Kreatur** (*geh*) the dumb creatures *pl*; **~ vor Schmerz** in silent agony; **~ vor Zorn** speechless with anger; **~er Diener** (*Servierwagen*) dumb waiter; (*Kleiderständer*) valet.
(b) (*schweigend*) mute; *Anklage, Blick, Gebet auch* silent ◆ **sie sah mich ~ an** she looked at me without speaking *or* without saying a word; **~ bleiben** to stay silent; *siehe* **Fisch**.
(c) (*Gram*) mute, silent.
(d) *Rolle* non-speaking; *Film, Szene* silent.

Stummel *m* **-s, - (a)** (*Zigaretten~, Zigarren~*) end, stub, butt; (*Kerzen~*) stub; (*von Gliedmaßen, Zahn*) stump. **(b)** (*Stummelschwanz*) dock.

Stummelpfeife *f* short-stemmed pipe.

Stumme(r) *mf decl as adj* dumb *or* mute person ◆ **die ~n** the dumb.

Stummfilm *m* silent film.

Stummfilmzeit *f* silent film era.

Stumpen *m* **-s, -** cheroot.

Stümper(in *f***)** *m* **-s, -** (*pej*) **(a)** amateur. **(b)** (*Pfuscher*) bungler.

Stümperei *f* (*pej*) **(a)** amateur work. **(b)** (*Pfuscherei*) bungling; (*stümperhafte Arbeit*) botched *or* bungled job.

stümperhaft *adj* (*pej*) (*nicht fachmännisch*) amateurish; (*schlecht auch*) botched *no adv*, bungled *no adv*.

stümpern *vi* (*auf Klavier, bei Schach etc*) to play in an amateurish way (*auf +dat* on) ◆ **bei einer Arbeit ~** to do a job in an amateur way; **er stümpert nur** he's just an amateur; (*pfuschen*) he's just a bungler.

stumpf *adj* **(a)** blunt; *Nase* snub, turned-up ◆ **Rhabarber macht die Zähne ~** rhubarb sets one's teeth on edge.
(b) (*fig*) *Haar, Farbe, Mensch* dull; *Blick, Sinne auch* dulled ◆ **~ vor sich hin brüten** to sit brooding impassively; **einer Sache gegenüber ~ sein** to remain impassive about sth.
(c) (*Math*) *Winkel* obtuse; *Kegel etc* truncated.
(d) (*Poet*) *Reim* masculine.

Stumpf *m* **-(e)s, ¨-e** stump; (*Bleistift~*) stub ◆ **etw mit ~ und Stiel ausrotten** to eradicate sth root and branch.

Stumpfheit *f* **(a)** bluntness. **(b)** (*fig*) dullness.

Stumpf-: ~sinn *m* mindlessness; (*Langweiligkeit*) monotony, tedium; **das ist doch ~sinn** that's a tedious business; **s~sinnig** *adj* mindless; (*langweilig*) monotonous, tedious; **~sinnigkeit** *f siehe* **~sinn**; **s~wink(e)lig** *adj* (*Math*) *Winkel, Dreieck* obtuse.

Stündchen *nt dim of* **Stunde** ◆ **ein paar ~** an hour or so.

Stunde *f* **-, -n (a)** hour ◆ **eine viertel/halbe/dreiviertel ~** a quarter of an hour/half an hour/three-quarters of an hour; **in einer dreiviertel ~** in three-quarters of an hour; **eine ganze/gute/knappe ~** a whole/good hour/barely an hour; **eine halbe ~ Pause** a half-hour break, a break of half an hour; **eine ~ entfernt** an hour away; **eine Reise von zwei ~n** a two-hour journey; **jede ~** every hour; **~ um ~, ~n um ~n** hour after hour; **von ~ zu ~** hourly, from hour to hour; **sein Befinden wird von ~ zu ~ schlechter** his condition is becoming worse hour by hour *or* worse every hour; **acht-~n-Tag** eight-hour day; **90 Meilen in der ~** 90 miles per *or* an hour.
(b) (*Augenblick, Zeitpunkt*) time ◆ **zu dieser ~** at this/that time; **zu jeder ~** at any time; **zu später ~** at a late hour; **bis zur ~** up to the present moment, as yet; **von Stund an** (*old*) from henceforth; **die ~ X** (*Mil*) the impending onslaught; **sich auf die ~ X vorbereiten** (*fig*) to prepare for the inevitable; **eine schwache/schwere ~** a moment of weakness/a time of difficulty; **seine ~ kommen** *or* **nahen fühlen** (*geh: Tod*) to feel one's hour (of death) approaching; **seine ~ hat geschlagen** (*fig*) his hour has come; **seine schwerste ~** his darkest hour; **die ~ der Entscheidung/Wahrheit** the moment of decision/truth.
(c) (*Unterricht*) lesson; (*Unterrichts~ auch*) class, period ◆ **sonnabends haben wir vier ~n** on Saturday we have four lessons; **in der zweiten ~ haben wir Latein** in the second period we have Latin; **~n geben/nehmen** to give/have *or* take lessons.

stunden *vt* **jdm etw ~** to give sb time to pay sth; **jdm etw zwei Wochen/bis Mittwoch ~** to give sb two weeks/until Wednesday to pay sth.

Stunden-: ~buch *nt* (*Hist Liter*) book of hours; **~gebet** *nt prayer said at any of the canonical hours eg matins, vespers*; **~geschwindigkeit** *f* speed per hour; **eine ~geschwindigkeit von 90 km** a speed of 90 km per hour; **~glas** *nt* hour-glass; **~hotel** *nt hotel where rooms are rented by the hour*; **~kilometer** *pl* kilometres per *or* an hour *pl*.

stundenlang [1] *adj* lasting several hours ◆ **eine ~e Verspätung** a delay of several hours; **nach ~em Warten** after hours of waiting.
[2] *adv* for hours.

Stunden-: ~lohn *m* hourly wage; **~lohn bekommen** to be paid by the hour; **~plan** *m* (*Sch*) time-table; **~schlag** *m* striking of the hour; **s~weise** *adv* (*pro Stunde*) by the hour; (*stündlich*) every hour; **Kellner s~weise gesucht** part-time waiters required; **der Patient darf s~weise aufstehen** the patient may get up for an hour at a time; **~zeiger** *m* hour-hand.

-stündig *adj suf* **eine halb/zwei~e Fahrt** a half-hour/two-hour journey, a journey of half an hour/two hours.

Stündlein *nt* **ein ~** a short while; **sein letztes ~ hat geschlagen** (*stirbt*) his last hour has come; (*fig inf*) he's had it (*inf*).

stündlich [1] *adj* hourly.
[2] *adv* hourly, every hour.

-stündlich *adv suf* **zwei/drei~** every two/three hours.

Stundung *f* deferment of payment.

Stunk *m* **-s,** *no pl* (*inf*) stink (*inf*), row (*inf*) ◆ **~ machen** to kick up a stink (*inf*); **dann gibt es ~** then there'll be a stink (*inf*).

Stunt [stant] *m* **-s, -s** stunt.

Stuntman [-mən] *m* **-s, -men** stunt man.

Stuntwoman *f* **-, -women** stunt woman.

stupend *adj* (*geh*) astounding, tremendous.

stupid(e) *adj* (*geh*) mindless.

Stups *m* **-es, -e** nudge.

stupsen *vt* to nudge.

Stupsnase *f* snub nose.

stur *adj* stolid; (*unnachgiebig*) obdurate; *Nein, Arbeiten* dogged; (*hartnäckig*) pig-headed, stubborn; (*querköpfig*) cussed ◆ **~ weitermachen/-reden/-gehen** *etc* to carry on regardless *or* doggedly; **er fuhr ~ geradeaus/in der Mitte der Straße** he just carried straight on/he just carried on driving in the middle of the road; **sich ~ stellen, auf ~ stellen** (*inf*) to dig one's heels in; **ein ~er Bock** (*inf*) a pig-headed fellow.

Sturheit *f siehe adj* stolidness; obdurateness; doggedness; pig-headedness, stubbornness; cussedness.

Sturm *m* **-(e)s, ¨-e (a)** (*lit, fig*) storm; (*Orkan auch*) gale ◆ **in ~ und Regen** in wind and rain; **das Barometer steht auf ~** (*lit*) the barometer is indicating stormy weather; (*fig*) there's a storm brewing; **die Ruhe** *or* **Stille vor dem ~** the calm before the storm; **ein ~ im Wasserglas** (*fig*) a storm in a teacup; **~ läuten** to keep one's finger on the doorbell; (*Alarm schlagen*) to ring *or* sound the alarm bell; **die ¨~e des Lebens** the storms *or* the ups and downs of life; **ein ~ der Begeisterung/des Gelächters** a wave of enthusiasm/roars of laughter; **im ~ der Leidenschaft** (*geh*) in the throes of passion; **~ und Drang**

(*Liter*) Storm and Stress, Sturm und Drang; (*fig*) emotion.
(b) (*Angriff*) attack; (*Mil auch*) assault; (*Sport: Stürmerreihe*) forward line ◆ **etw im ~ nehmen** (*Mil, fig*) to take sth by storm; **zum ~ blasen** (*Mil, fig*) to sound the attack; **gegen etw ~ laufen** (*fig*) to be up in arms against sth; **ein ~ auf die Banken/Aktien** a run on the banks/shares; **ein ~ auf die Karten/Plätze** a rush for tickets/seats; **der ~ auf die Festung/Bastille** the storming of the stronghold/Bastille; *siehe* **erobern.**

Sturm-: ~abteilung *f* (*NS*) Storm Troopers *pl*; **~angriff** *m* (*Mil*) assault (*auf +acc* on); **s~bewegt** *adj* stormy, storm-tossed (*liter*); **~bö** *f* squall; **~bock** *m* (*Mil*) battering-ram; **~boot** *nt* (*Mil*) assault boat; **~deck** *nt* hurricane deck.

stürmen [1] *vi* **(a)** (*Meer*) to rage; (*Wind auch*) to blow; (*Sport*) to attack; (*Mil*) to attack, to assault (*gegen etw* sth). **(b)** (*Sport*) (*als Stürmer spielen*) to play forward; (*angreifen*) to attack. **(c)** *aux sein* (*rennen*) to storm.
[2] *vi impers* to be blowing a gale.
[3] *vt* (*Mil, fig*) to storm; *Bank etc* to make a run on.

Stürmer *m* **-s, -** (*Sport*) forward; (*Ftbl auch*) striker; (*fig: Draufgänger*) go-getter (*inf*) ◆ **~ und Dränger** (*Liter*) writer of the Storm and Stress period; (*fig*) ≃ angry young man.

Stürmerreihe *f* (*Sport*) forward line.

Sturm-: ~fahne *f* warning flag; (*Mil Hist*) standard; **s~fest** *adj* (*lit*) stormproof; (*fig*) steadfast; **~flut** *f* storm tide; **s~frei** *adj* (*Mil*) unassailable; **bei mir ist heute abend s~freie Bude** (*inf*) it's open house at my place tonight; **ich habe eine s~freie Bude** (*inf*) where I live I can do as I please; **~gepäck** *nt* combat *or* light pack; **s~gepeitscht** *adj* (*geh*) storm-lashed (*liter*); **~haube** *f* **(a)** (*Hist*) helmet, morion; **(b)** (*Zool*) whelk shell; **~hut** *m* (*Bot*) aconite.

stürmisch *adj* **(a)** *Meer, Überfahrt* rough, stormy; *Wetter, Tag* blustery; (*mit Regen*) stormy. **(b)** (*fig*) tempestuous; (*aufregend*) *Zeit, Jugend* stormy, turbulent; *Entwicklung* rapid; *Liebhaber* passionate, ardent; *Jubel, Beifall* tumultuous, frenzied ◆ **nicht so ~** take it easy.

Sturm-: ~laterne *f* hurricane lamp; **~lauf** *m* trot; **im ~lauf** at a trot; **~leiter** *f* scaling ladder; **s~reif** *adj* (*Mil*) **s~reif sein** to be ripe for attack (*für* by); **~schaden** *m* storm damage *no pl*; **~schritt** *m* (*Mil, fig*) double-quick pace; **im ~schritt** at the double; **~segel** *nt* storm sail; **~spitze** *f* (*Mil, Sport*) spearhead; **s~stark** *adj* (*Sport*) **eine s~starke Mannschaft** a team with a strong forward line; **~trupp** *m* (*Mil*) assault troop; **~-und-Drang-Zeit** *f* (*Liter*) Storm and Stress *or* Sturm und Drang period; **~vogel** *m* petrel; (*Albatros*) albatross; **~warnung** *f* gale warning; **~wind** *m* whirlwind.

Sturz *m* **-es, ¨-e** **(a)** (*von* from, off, *aus* out of) fall ◆ **einen ~ tun** to have a fall. **(b)** (*in Temperatur, Preis*) drop, fall; (*von Börsenkurs*) slump. **(c)** (*von Regierung, Minister*) fall; (*durch Coup, von König*) overthrow. **(d)** (*Archit*) lintel. **(e)** (*Rad~*) camber. **(f)** (*S Ger, Aus: Glas~*) cover.

Sturz-: ~acker *m* (*Agr*) newly ploughed field; **~bach** *m* (*lit*) fast-flowing stream; (*fig*) stream, torrent; **s~besoffen, s~betrunken** *adj* (*inf*) pissed as a newt (*sl*).

stürzen [1] *vi aux sein* **(a)** to fall (*von* from, off); (*geh: steil abfallen*) to plunge; (*hervor~*) to stream ◆ **ins Wasser ~** to plunge into the water; **vom Pferd ~** to fall off a/one's horse; **er ist schwer** *or* **heftig/unglücklich gestürzt** he had a heavy/bad fall; **die Tränen stürzten ihm aus den Augen** (*geh*) tears streamed from his eyes.
(b) (*fig: abgesetzt werden*) to fall.
(c) (*rennen*) to rush, to dash ◆ **sie kam ins Zimmer gestürzt** she burst *or* came bursting into the room; **jdm in die Arme ~** to fling oneself into sb's arms.
[2] *vt* **(a)** (*werfen*) to fling, to hurl ◆ **jdn aus dem Fenster ~** to fling *or* hurl sb out of the window; **jdn ins Unglück** *or* **Verderben ~** to bring disaster to sb.
(b) (*kippen*) to turn upside down; *Pudding* to turn out ◆ **„nicht ~!"** "this side up"; **etw über etw** (*acc*) **~** to put sth over sth.
(c) (*absetzen*) *Regierung, Minister* to bring down; (*durch Coup*) to overthrow; *König* to depose.
[3] *vr* **sich zu Tode ~** to fall to one's death; (*absichtlich*) to jump to one's death; **sich auf jdn/etw ~** to pounce on sb/sth; *auf Essen* to fall on sth; *auf Zeitung etc* to grab sth; *auf den Feind* to attack sb/sth; **sich ins Wasser ~** to fling *or* hurl oneself into the water; (*sich ertränken*) to drown oneself; **sich in die Arbeit ~** to throw oneself into one's work; **sich in Schulden ~** to plunge into debt; **sich ins Unglück/Verderben ~** to plunge headlong into disaster/ruin; **sich ins Vergnügen ~** to fling oneself into a round of pleasure; **sich in Unkosten ~** to go to great expense.

Sturz-: ~flug *m* (nose)dive; **etw im ~flug angreifen** to dive and attack sth; **~geburt** *f* (*Med*) precipitate delivery; **~gut** *nt* (*form*) *goods unloaded by tipping*; **~helm** *m* crash helmet; **~kampfflugzeug** *nt* dive bomber; **~see** *f* (*Naut*) breaker.

⚠ **Stuß** *m* **-sses,** *no pl* (*inf*) nonsense, rubbish (*inf*), codswallop (*Brit inf*) ◆ **was für ein ~** what a load of nonsense *etc* (*inf*).

Stutbuch *nt* studbook.

Stute *f* **-, -n** mare.

Stuten-: ~fohlen, ~füllen *nt* filly; **~zucht** *f* studfarm; (*Züchtung*) stud farming.

Stütz-: ~apparat *m* calliper, brace; (*für Kopf*) collar; **~balken** *m* beam; (*in Decke*) joist; (*quer*) crossbeam.

Stütze *f* **-, -n** **(a)** support; (*Pfeiler*) pillar; (*für Wäscheleine etc*) prop; (*Buch~*) rest.
(b) (*Halt*) support; (*Fuß~*) foot-rest.
(c) (*fig*) (*Hilfe*) help, aid (*für* to); (*Beistand*) support; (*wichtiger Mensch*) mainstay; (*dated: Hausgehilfin*) (domestic) help ◆ **seine Tochter war die ~ seines Alters** his daughter was his support in his old age; **als ~ für seinen Kreislauf** as an aid for *or* to aid his circulation; **die ~n der Gesellschaft** the pillars of society.
(d) (*inf: Arbeitslosengeld*) dole (*Brit inf*), welfare (*US*) ◆ **~ bekommen** to be on the dole, to be on welfare.

stutzen[1] *vi* to stop short; (*zögern*) to hesitate.

stutzen[2] *vt* to trim; *Baum auch* to prune; *Flügel, Ohren, Hecke* to clip; *Schwanz* to dock.

Stutzen *m* **-s, -** **(a)** (*Gewehr*) carbine. **(b)** (*Rohrstück*) connecting piece; (*Endstück*) nozzle. **(c)** (*Strumpf*) woollen gaiter.

stützen [1] *vt* (*Halt geben*) to support; *Gebäude, Mauer* to shore up; *Währung auch* to back; (*fig: untermauern auch*) to back up ◆ **einen Verdacht durch etw ~** to back up *or* support a suspicion with sth; **einen Verdacht auf etw** (*acc*) **~** to base *or* found a suspicion on sth; **die Ellbogen auf den Tisch ~** to prop *or* rest one's elbows on the table; **den Kopf in die Hände ~** to hold one's head in one's hands.
[2] *vr* **sich auf jdn/etw ~** (*lit*) to lean on sb/sth; (*fig*) to count on sb/sth; (*Beweise, Verteidigung, Theorie*) to be based on sb/sth; **können Sie sich auf Fakten ~?** can you produce facts to bear out what you're saying?; **in seiner Dissertation stützte er sich weitgehend auf diese Theorie** he based his thesis closely on this theory.

Stutzer *m* **-s, -** **(a)** (*pej*) fop, dandy. **(b)** (*Mantel*) three-quarter length coat.

stutzerhaft *adj* foppish, dandified.

Stutzflügel *m* baby grand (piano).

Stützgewebe *nt* (*Med*) stroma (*spec*).

stutzig *adj pred* **~ werden** (*argwöhnisch*) to become *or* grow suspicious; (*verwundert*) to begin to wonder; **jdn ~ machen** to make sb suspicious; **das hat mich ~ gemacht** that made me wonder; (*argwöhnisch*) that made me suspicious.

Stütz-: ~korsett *nt* support corset; **~mauer** *f* retaining wall; **~pfeiler** *m* supporting pillar *or* column; (*von Brücke auch*) pier; **~preis** *m* (*Econ*) support price; **~punkt** *m* (*Mil, fig*) base; (*Ausbildungsstätte*) centre; **~rad** *nt* (*an Fahrrad*) stabilizer; **~stange** *f* supporting pole.

Stützung *f* support.

Stützungs-: ~käufe *pl purchases to support share prices, currency rate etc*; **~maßnahme** *f* supporting measure.

StVO *abbr of* **Straßenverkehrsordnung.**

stylen ['stail-] *vt Wagen, Wohnung* to design; *Frisur* to style; *siehe* **gestylt.**

Styling ['stailɪŋ] *nt* **-s,** *no pl* styling.

Styropor ® [st-, ʃt-] *nt* **-s** polystyrene.

Styx [ʃtʏks, st-] *m* **-** (*Myth*) Styx.

SU [ɛs'|uː] *f* **-** *abbr of* **Sowjetunion.**

s.u. *abbr of* **siehe unten.**

Suada, Suade *f* **-, Suaden** (*liter*) torrent of words.

Suaheli[1] [zua'heːli] *m* **-(s), -(s)** Swahili.

Suaheli[2] [zua'heːli] *nt* **-(s),** *no pl* (*Sprache*) Swahili; *siehe auch* **Deutsch(e).**

sub-, Sub- *in cpds* sub-.

sub|altern *adj* (*pej*) *Stellung, Beamter* subordinate; *Gesinnung* obsequious, subservient; (*unselbständig*) unselfreliant.

Subdominante *f* **-, -n** (*Mus*) subdominant.

Subjekt *nt* **-(e)s, -e** **(a)** subject. **(b)** (*pej: Mensch*) customer (*inf*), character (*inf*).

subjektiv *adj* subjective.

Subjektivismus [-'vɪsmʊs] *m, no pl* (*Philos*) subjectivism.

Subjektivität [-vɪ'tɛːt] *f* subjectivity.

Subjektsatz *m* (*Gram*) noun clause as subject.

Sub-: ~kontinent *m* subcontinent; **~kultur** *f* subculture; **s~kutan** *adj* (*Med*) subcutaneous.

sublim *adj* (*geh*) sublime, lofty; *Einfühlungsvermögen, Charakter* refined; *Interpretation* eloquent.

Sublimat *nt* (*Chem*) **(a)** (*Niederschlag*) sublimate. **(b)** (*Quecksilberverbindung*) mercuric chloride.

Sublimation *f* (*Chem*) sublimation.

sublimieren* *vt* **(a)** (*Psych*) to sublimate. **(b)** (*Chem*) to sublimate, to sublime.

Sublimierung *f* sublimation.

submarin *adj* marine.

Sub|ordination *f* subordination.

Subsidiarität *f* subsidiarity.

Subsidiaritätsprinzip *nt* subsidiarity principle.

Subskribent(in *f***)** *m* subscriber.

subskribieren* *vti* **(auf) etw** (*acc*) **~** to subscribe to sth.

Subskription *f* subscription (*gen, auf +acc* to).

Subskriptionspreis *m* subscription price.

⚠ **substantiell** [zʊpstan'tsiɛl] *adj* **(a)** (*Philos*) (*stofflich*) material; (*wesenhaft*) essential.
(b) (*fig geh: bedeutsam, inhaltlich*) fundamental.
(c) (*nahrhaft*) substantial, solid.

Substantiv ['zʊpstantiːf] *nt* **-s, -e** *or* (*rare*) **-a** noun.

substantivieren* [zʊpstanti'viːrən] *vt* to nominalize.

substantivisch ['zʊpstantiːvɪʃ] *adj* nominal.

Substanz [zʊp'stants] *f* **(a)** substance; (*Wesen*) essence ◆ **die ~ des Volkes** the (essential) character of the people; **etw in seiner ~ treffen** to affect the substance of sth. **(b)** (*Fin*) capital assets *pl* ◆ **von der ~ zehren** *or* **leben** to live on one's capital.

Substanz-: s~los *adj* insubstantial; **s~reich** *adj* solid; *Aufsatz auch* meaty

(*inf*); **~verlust** *m* loss of volume; (*Gewichtsverlust*) loss of weight; (*fig*) loss of significance *or* importance.
substituieren* [zupstitu'i:rən] *vt* (*geh*) **A durch B ~** to substitute B for A, to replace A with B.
Substitut(in *f*) [zupsti'tu:t(ɪn)] *m* **-en, -en** deputy *or* assistant departmental manager.
Substitution [zupstitu'tsio:n] *f* (*geh*) **die ~ von A durch B** the substitution of B for A, the replacement of A by B.
Substrat [zup'stra:t] *nt* substratum.
subsumieren* *vti* to subsume (*unter +dat* to).
subtil *adj* (*geh*) subtle.
Subtilität *f* (*geh*) subtlety.
Subtrahend [zuptra'hɛnt] *m* **-en, -en** (*Math*) subtrahend.
subtrahieren* [zuptra'hi:rən] *vti* to subtract.
Subtraktion *f* subtraction.
Subtraktionszeichen *nt* subtraction sign.
Subtropen ['zuptro:pn] *pl* subtropics *pl*.
subtropisch ['zuptro:pɪʃ] *adj* subtropical.
Subvention [zupvɛn'tsio:n] *f* subsidy; (*von Regierung, Behörden auch*) subvention.
subventionieren* [zupvɛntsio'ni:rən] *vt* to subsidize.
Subversion [zupvɛr'zio:n] *f* (*Pol*) subversion.
subversiv [zupvɛr'zi:f] *adj* subversive ◆ **sich ~ betätigen** to engage in subversive activities.
Such-: ~aktion *f* search operation; **~anzeige** *f* missing person/dog *etc* report; **eine ~anzeige aufgeben** to report sb/sth missing; **~begriff** *m* (*Comput*) search item; **~bild** *nt* (*form*) searching image; (*Rätsel*) picture puzzle; **~dauer** *f* (*Comput*) search time; **~dienst** *m* missing persons tracing service.
Suche *f* **-,** *no pl* search (*nach* for) ◆ **auf die ~ nach jdm/etw gehen, sich auf die ~ nach jdm/etw machen** to go in search of sb/sth; **auf der ~ nach etw sein** to be looking for sth.
-suche *f in cpds* **auf ...~ sein** to be looking for a ...
suchen [1] *vt* (**a**) to look for; (*stärker, intensiv*) to search for (*auch Comput*) ◆ **Abenteuer ~** to go out in search of adventure; **die Gefahr ~** to look for *or* seek danger; **sich** (*dat*) **einen Mann/eine Frau ~** to look for a husband/wife (for oneself); **Verkäufer(in) gesucht** sales person wanted; **gesucht!** wanted (*wegen* for); **Streit/Ärger (mit jdm) ~** to be looking for trouble/a quarrel (with sb); **Schutz vor etw** (*dat*) **~** to seek shelter from sth; **etw zu tun ~** (*geh*) to seek *or* strive to do sth; **was suchst du hier?** what are you doing here?; **du hast hier nichts zu ~** you have no business being here; **er sucht in allem etwas** he always has to see a meaning in everything; **seinesgleichen ~** to be unparalleled.
(**b**) (*wünschen, streben nach*) to seek; (*versuchen auch*) to strive, to try ◆ **er sucht, die tragischen Erlebnisse zu vergessen** he is trying to forget the tragic events; **sein Recht/seinen Vorteil ~** to be out for one's rights/one's own advantage; **ein Gespräch ~** to try to have a talk.
[2] *vi* to search, to hunt ◆ **nach etw ~** to look for sth; (*stärker*) to search *or* hunt for sth; **nach Worten ~** to search for words; (*sprachlos sein*) to be at a loss for words; **S~ und Ersetzen** (*Comput*) search and replace; **such!** (*zu Hund*) seek!, find!; **suchet, so werdet ihr finden!** (*Bibl*) seek and ye shall find (*Bibl*).
Sucher *m* **-s, -** (**a**) (*geh*) seeker. (**b**) (*Phot*) viewfinder; (*Astron*) finder.
Sucherei *f* (*inf*) searching.
Such-: ~funktion *f* (*Comput*) search function; **~lauf** *m* (*bei Hi-Fi-Geräten*) search; **~lauffunktion** *f* search function; **~mannschaft** *f* search party; **~meldung** *f* SOS message; (*von ~dienst*) missing person announcement; **~scheinwerfer** *m* searchlight.
Sucht *f* **-, ¨e** addiction (*nach* to); (*fig*) obsession (*nach* with) ◆ **eine krankhafte ~ haben, etw zu tun** (*fig*) to be obsessed with doing sth; **das kann zur ~ werden** you'll get *or* become addicted to that; **das Trinken ist bei ihm zur ~ geworden** he has become addicted to drink; **an einer ~ leiden** to be an addict.
-sucht *f in cpds* **Drogen-/Trink~** addiction to drugs/drink.
Sucht-: ~droge *f* addictive drug; ⚠**s~erzeugend** *adj* addictive; **~gefahr** *f* danger of addiction.
süchtig *adj* addicted (*nach* to) ◆ **von** *or* **nach etw ~ werden/sein** to get *or* become/be addicted to sth; **~ machen** (*Droge*) to be addictive; **davon wird man nicht ~** that's not addictive.
Süchtige(r) *mf decl as adj* addict.
Süchtigkeit *f* addiction (*nach* to).
Sucht-: ~kranke(r) *mf* addict; **~mittel** *nt* addictive drug; ⚠**~mittelmißbrauch** *m* drug abuse.
Sud *m* **-(e)s, -e** liquid; (*esp von Fleisch, für Suppe*) stock ◆ **der ~ des Gemüses/der Kartoffeln/des Fleisches** the vegetable water/potato water/meat stock.
Süd *m* **-(e)s,** (*rare*) **-e** (**a**) (*Naut, Met, liter*) south ◆ **aus** *or* **von/nach ~** from/to the south. (**b**) (*liter: Wind*) south wind, southerly (wind).
Süd- *in cpds* (*in Ländernamen, politisch*) South; (*geographisch auch*) the South of ..., Southern; **~afrika** *nt* South Africa; **~amerika** *nt* South America.
Sudan [zu'da:n, 'zu:dan] *m* **-s der ~** the Sudan.
Sudaner(in *f*) *m* **-s, -, Sudanese** *m* **-n, -n, Sudanesin** *f* Sudanese.
sudanesisch, sudanisch *adj* Sudanese.
Süd-: s~deutsch *adj* South German; *Dialekt, Spezialität, Mentalität auch* Southern German; **die ~deutschen** the South Germans; **~deutschland** *nt* South(ern) Germany, the South of Germany.
Sudelei *f* (*geschrieben*) scrawling; (*gezeichnet*) daubing; (*an Mauern etc*) graffiti.
sudeln *vti* (*schreiben*) to scrawl; (*zeichnen*) to daub.
Süden *m* **-s,** *no pl* south; (*von Land*) South ◆ **aus dem ~, vom ~ her** from the south; **gegen** *or* **gen** (*liter*) *or* **nach ~** south(wards), to the south; **nach ~ hin** to the south; **im ~ der Stadt/des Landes** in the south of the town/country; **im tiefen ~** in the deep *or* far south; **weiter** *or* **tiefer im ~** further south; **im ~ Frankreichs** in southern France.
Süd|england *nt* the South of England.
Sudeten *pl* (*Geog*) **die ~** the Sudeten(land).
Sudetenland *nt* **das ~** the Sudetenland.
Süd-: ~europa *nt* Southern Europe; **~frankreich** *nt* the South of France; **~früchte** *pl* citrus and tropical fruit(s *pl*); **~halbkugel** *f* southern hemisphere; **auf der ~halbkugel** in the southern hemisphere.
Sudhaus *nt* (*in Brauerei*) brewing room.
Süd-: ~italien *nt* Southern Italy; **~italiener** *m* southern Italian; **~jemen** *m* South Yemen; **~korea** *nt* South Korea; **~küste** *f* south(ern) coast; **die ~küste Englands** the south coast of England; **~lage** *f* southern aspect; **~länder** *m* **-s, -** southerner; (*Italiener, Spanier etc*) Mediterranean *or* Latin type; **s~ländisch** *adj* southern; (*italienisch, spanisch etc*) Mediterranean, Latin; *Temperament* Latin.
südlich [1] *adj* (**a**) southern; *Kurs, Wind, Richtung* southerly ◆ **der ~e Polarkreis** the Antarctic Circle; **der ~e Wendekreis** the Tropic of Capricorn; **52 Grad ~er Breite** 52 degrees south; **~es Eismeer** Antarctic Ocean.
(**b**) (*mediterran*) Mediterranean, Latin; *Temperament* Latin.
[2] *adv* (to the) south ◆ **~ von Wien (gelegen)** (to the) south of Vienna; **es liegt ~er** *or* **weiter ~** it is further (to the) south.
[3] *prep +gen* (to the) south of.
Süd-: ~licht *nt* southern lights *pl*, aurora australis; **~-Nord-Gefälle** *nt* North-South divide.
Süd|ost *m* (**a**) (*Met, Naut, liter*) south-east, sou'-east (*Naut*) ◆ **aus** *or* **von ~** from the south-east; **nach ~** to the south-east, south-east(wards). (**b**) (*liter: Wind*) south-east(erly) (wind), sou'-easterly (*Naut*).
Süd|ost- *in cpds* south-east; (*bei Namen*) South-East.
Süd|osten *m* south-east; (*von Land*) South East ◆ **aus** *or* **von ~** from the south-east; **nach ~** to the south-east, south-east(wards).
Süd|ost|europa *nt* South-East(ern) Europe.
süd|östlich [1] *adj Gegend* south-eastern; *Wind* south-east(erly).
[2] *adv* (to the) south-east.
[3] *prep +gen* (to the) south-east of.
Süd-: ~pol *m* South Pole; **~polargebiet** *nt* Antarctic (region), area of the South Pole; **~polarmeer** *nt* Antarctic Ocean; **~polexpedition** *f* South Pole *or* Antarctic expedition; **~see** *f* South Seas *pl*, South Pacific; **~seeinsulaner** *m* South Sea Islander; **~seite** *f* south(ern) side; (*von Berg*) south(ern) face; **~staat** *m* southern state; **die ~staaten** (*US*) the Southern States; **~staatler(in** *f*) *m* (*US*) Southerner.
Südsüd-: ~ost *m* (**a**) (*Naut, Met, liter*) south-south-east, sou'-sou'-east (*Naut*); (**b**) (*liter: Wind*) sou'-sou'-easterly; **~osten** *m* south-south-east, sou'-sou'-east (*Naut*); **s~östlich** *adj* south-south-east(erly), sou'-sou'-east(erly) (*Naut*); **~west** *m* (**a**) (*Naut, Met, liter*) south-south-west, sou'-sou'-west (*Naut*); (**b**) (*liter: Wind*) sou'-sou'-westerly; **~westen** *m* south-south-west, sou'-sou'-west (*Naut*); **s~westlich** *adj* south-south-west(erly), sou'-sou'-west(erly) (*Naut*).
Süd-: ~tirol *nt* South(ern) Tyrol; **~tiroler** *m* South Tyrolean; **~vietnam** *nt* South Vietnam; **~wand** *f* (*von Berg*) south face.
südwärts *adv* south(wards) ◆ **der Wind dreht ~** the wind is moving round to the south.
Südwein *m* Mediterranean wine.
Südwest[1] *m* (**a**) (*Naut, Met, liter*) south-west ◆ **aus ~** from the south-west. (**b**) (*liter: Wind*) south-west(erly) wind, south-wester(ly), sou'-wester (*Naut*).
Südwest[2]**, Südwestafrika** *nt* South West Africa.
Südwest- *in cpds* south-west; (*bei Namen*) South-West.
Südwesten *m* south-west; (*von Land*) South West ◆ **aus** *or* **von ~** from the south-west; **nach ~** to the south-west, south-west(wards).
Südwester *m* **-s, -** (*Hut*) sou'wester.
südwestlich [1] *adj Gegend* south-western; *Wind* south-west(erly).
[2] *adv* (to the) south-west.
[3] *prep +gen* (to the) south-west of.
Südwind *m* south wind.
Sueskanal *m* Suez Canal.
Suff *m* **-(e)s,** *no pl* (*inf*) **dem ~ verfallen** to hit the bottle (*inf*); **dem ~ ergeben** *or* **verfallen sein** to be on the bottle (*inf*); **etw im ~ sagen** to say sth when one is tight (*inf*) *or* plastered (*sl*).
süffeln *vi* (*inf*) to tipple (*inf*).
süffig *adj* light and sweet.
Süffisance [zyfi'zã:s] *f* **-,** *no pl* (*geh*) smugness, complacency.
süffisant *adj* smug, complacent.
Suffix *nt* **-es, -e** suffix.
Suffragette *f* suffragette.
suggerieren* *vt* to suggest ◆ **jdm etw ~** to influence sb by suggesting sth; **jdm ~, daß ...** to get sb to believe that ...; **jdm Zweifel an seinen Fähigkeiten ~** to get sb to doubt his own abilities.
suggestibel *adj* suggestible.
Suggestion *f* suggestion.
suggestiv *adj* suggestive.
Suggestivfrage *f* leading question.

⚠: for details of spelling reform, see supplement

Suhle *f* **-, -n** muddy pool.
suhlen *vr* (*lit, fig*) to wallow.
Sühne *f* **-, -n** (*Rel, geh*) atonement; (*von Schuld*) expiation ◆ **als ~ für etw** to atone for sth; **das Verbrechen fand seine ~** the crime was atoned for; **~ leisten** to atone (*für* for).
sühnen [1] *vt Unrecht, Verbrechen* to atone for; *Schuld* to expiate.
[2] *vi* to atone.
Sühne-: ~opfer *nt* (*Rel*) expiatory sacrifice; **~termin** *m* (*Jur*) conciliatory hearing.
Suite ['svi:tə, 'zui:tə] *f* **-, -n** suite; (*Gefolge*) retinue.
Suizid [zui'tsi:t] *m or nt* **-(e)s, -e** (*form*) suicide.
Suizid- [zui'tsi:t-]: **~gefahr** *f* risk of suicide; **s~gefährdet** *adj* suicidal; **~gefährdete(r)** *mf* suicidal person; **~täter** *m* (*form*) suicide; **~versuch** *m* suicide attempt.
Sujet [sy'ʒe:] *nt* **-s, -s** (*geh*) subject.
Sukkade *f* candied peel.
sukzessiv(e) *adj* gradual.
Sulfat *nt* sulphate.
Sulfid *nt* **-(e)s, -e** sulphide.
Sulfit *nt* **-s, -e** sulphite.
Sulfonamid *nt* **-(e)s, -e** sulphonamide.
Sulky ['zʊlki, 'zalki] *nt* **-s, -s** sulky.
Süll *m or nt* **-(e)s, -e, Süllbord, Süllrand** *m* (*Naut*) coaming.
Sultan ['zʊlta:n] *m* **-s, -e** sultan.
Sultanat *nt* sultanate.
Sultanin *f* sultana.
Sultanine *f* (*Rosine*) sultana.
Sülze *f* **-, -n, Sulz** *f* **-, -en** (*esp S Ger, Aus, Sw*) brawn.
sülzen [1] *vt* **(a)** (*dial inf*) to go on and on about (*inf*). **(b)** (*Cook*) to pickle in aspic.
[2] *vi* (*dial inf*) to go on and on (*inf*).
Sülzkotelett *nt* cutlet in aspic.
Sumatra¹ [zu'ma:tra, 'zu:matra] *nt* **-s** Sumatra.
Sumatra² *f* **-, -s** *mild cigar originally from Sumatra.*
Sumerer *m* **-s, -** (*Hist*) Sumerian.
sumerisch *adj* (*Hist*) Sumerian.
summ *interj* buzz ◆ **~ machen** to buzz.
summa cum laude *adv* (*Univ*) summa cum laude (*US*), with distinction.
Summand *m* **-en, -en** (*Math*) summand.
summarisch [1] *adj* (*auch Jur*) summary; *Zusammenfassung* summarizing.
[2] *adv* **etw ~ zusammenfassen** to summarize sth; **~ läßt sich sagen, daß** ... to summarize, we can say that ...
summa summarum *adv* all in all, on the whole.
Sümmchen *nt dim of* **Summe** ◆ **ein nettes ~** (*hum*) a tidy sum, a pretty penny (*inf*).
Summe *f* **-, -n** sum; (*Gesamt~ auch*) total; (*fig*) sum total ◆ **die ~ aus etw ziehen** to sum up *or* evaluate sth; **die ~, die ich daraus ziehe** ... my evaluation of that ...
summen [1] *vt Melodie etc* to hum.
[2] *vi* to buzz; (*Mensch, Motor*) to hum.
[3] *vi impers* **es summt** there is a buzzing/humming noise.
Summer *m* **-s, -** buzzer.
summieren* [1] *vt* to sum up.
[2] *vr* to mount up ◆ **das summiert sich** it (all) adds *or* mounts up.
Summton *m*, **Summzeichen** *nt* buzz, buzzing sound.
Sumo *nt* - *no pl* sumo.
Sumoringen *nt* sumo wrestling.
Sumoringer *n* sumo wrestler.
Sumpf *m* **-(e)s, ⸚e** marsh; (*Morast*) mud; (*in tropischen Ländern*) swamp ◆ **im ~ der Großstadt** in the squalor and corruption of the big city.
Sumpf-: ~blüte *f sb who or sth which flourishes in a decaying society*; **~boden** *m* marshy ground; **~dotterblume** *f* marsh marigold.
sumpfen *vi* (*inf*) to live it up (*inf*).
Sumpf-: ~fieber *nt* malaria; **~huhn** *nt* moorhen; (*inf: unsolider Mensch*) fast-liver (*inf*).
sumpfig *adj* marshy, swampy.
Sumpf-: ~land *nt* marshland; (*in tropischen Ländern*) swampland; **~otter** *m* mink; **~pflanze** *f* marsh plant; **~vogel** *m* wader; **~zypresse** *f* deciduous cypress.
Sund *m* **-(e)s, -e** sound, straits *pl*.
Sünde *f* **-, -n** sin ◆ **eine ~ begehen** to sin, to commit a sin; **jdm seine ~n vergeben** to forgive sb his sins; **es ist eine ~ und Schande** (*inf*) it's a crying shame.
Sünden-: ~babel *nt* hotbed of vice; **~bekenntnis** *nt* confession of one's sins; (*Gebet*) confession (of sins); **~bock** *m* (*inf*) scapegoat, whipping boy; **jdn zum ~bock machen** to make sb one's scapegoat; **~fall** *m* (*Rel*) Fall (of Man); **s~frei** *adj* free from sin, without sin; **~pfuhl** *m* den of iniquity; **~register** *nt* (*fig*) list of sins; **jds ~register** the list of sb's sins; **jdm ein langes/sein ~register vorhalten** to list all sb's sins; **~vergebung** *f* forgiveness *or* remission of sins.
Sünder *m* **-s, -** sinner ◆ **armer ~** (*Eccl*) miserable sinner; (*old*) *criminal under sentence of death*; (*fig*) poor wretch; **na, alter ~!** (*dated inf*) well, you old rogue! (*inf*).
Sünderin *f* sinner.
Sündermiene *f* shame-faced expression ◆ **jdn mit einer ~ ansehen** to look at sb shamefaced(ly).
Sündflut *f, no pl siehe* **Sintflut**.
sündhaft *adj* (*lit*) sinful; (*fig inf*) *Preise* wicked ◆ **ein ~es Geld** (*inf*) a ridiculous amount of money; **~ teuer** (*inf*) wickedly expensive.
Sündhaftigkeit *f* sinfulness.
sündig *adj* sinful ◆ **~ werden** to sin (*an +dat* against).
sündigen *vi* to sin (*an +dat* against); (*hum*) to indulge ◆ **gegen Gott/die Natur ~** to sin against God/to commit a crime against nature; **gegen seine Gesundheit ~** to jeopardize one's health.
sündteuer *adj* (*Aus*) wickedly expensive.
Super¹ *nt* **-s,** *no pl* (*Benzin*) four-star (petrol) (*Brit*), premium (*US*), super.
Super² *m* **-s, -** (*Rad*) superhet (radio set).
super (*inf*) [1] *adj inv* super, smashing, great (*all inf*).
[2] *adv* (*mit adj*) really, incredibly (*inf*); (*mit vb*) really *or* incredibly (*inf*) well.
Super- *in cpds* super-; (*sehr*) ultra-; **~-8-Film** *m* super-8 film.
superb [zu'pɛrp], **süperb** (*dated geh*) *adj* splendid, superb, superlative.
Super-: ~benzin *nt* ≃ 4-star petrol (*Brit*), premium (*US*); **~chip** *m* (*Comput*) superchip; **s~fein** *adj Qualität* top *attr*; *Eßwaren etc* top-quality; (*inf*) posh (*inf*); **~intendent** *m* (*Eccl*) superintendent.
Superior *m*, **Superiorin** *f* superior.
Superiorität *f, no pl* (*geh*) superiority.
superklug *adj* (*iro inf*) brilliant ◆ **du bist ein S~er** (*Besserwisser*) you are a (real) knowall (*inf*); (*Dummkopf*) you're brilliant, you are (*iro*); (*das ist nichts Neues*) you're not telling us anything new.
Superlativ ['zu:pɐlati:f, zupɐla'ti:f] *m* (*Gram, fig*) superlative.
superlativisch *adj* (*Gram*) superlative; (*fig*) grand ◆ **ins S~e geraten** to assume massive proportions, to snowball in a big way (*inf*); **er bedient sich einer ~en Ausdrucksweise** his speech is full of superlatives.
Super-: s~leicht *adj* (*inf*) *Zigaretten* extra mild; (*kinderleicht*) dead easy (*inf*); **~macht** *f* superpower; **~mann** *m, pl* **-männer** superman; **~markt** *m* supermarket; **s~modern** *adj* (*inf*) ultramodern; **~nova** *f* supernova; **s~schnell** *adj* (*inf*) ultrafast; **~schnellzug** *m* high-speed train; **~star** *m* (*inf*) superstar.
Süppchen *nt dim of* **Suppe** ◆ **sein ~ am Feuer anderer kochen** to exploit *or* use other people.
Suppe *f* **-, -n** soup; (*sämig mit Einlage*) broth; (*klare Brühe*) bouillon; (*fig inf: Nebel*) pea-souper (*inf*) ◆ **klare ~** consommé; **jdm ein schöne ~ einbrocken** (*inf*) to get sb into a pretty pickle (*inf*) *or* nice mess; **du mußt die ~ auslöffeln, die du dir eingebrockt hast** (*inf*) you've made your bed, now you must lie on it (*prov*); **jdm die ~ versalzen, jdm in die ~ spucken** (*inf*) to put a spoke in sb's wheel (*inf*), to queer sb's pitch (*inf*); **du siehst aus, als ob dir jemand in die ~ gespuckt hätte** you look as though you've lost a pound and found sixpence; *siehe* **Haar, Salz**.
Suppen- *in cpds* soup; **~fleisch** *nt* meat for making soup; (*gekocht*) boiled beef/pork *etc*; **~gemüse** *nt* vegetables *pl* for making soup; **~grün** *nt* herbs and vegetables *pl* for making soup; **~huhn** *nt* boiling fowl; **~kaspar, ~kasper** *m* (*inf*) poor eater; (*~freund*) soup-fan (*inf*); **~kelle** *f* soup ladle; **~küche** *f* soup kitchen; **~löffel** *m* soup spoon; **~nudel** *f* vermicelli *pl*, noodles *pl*; **~schüssel** *f* tureen; **~tasse** *f* soup bowl; **~teller** *m* soup plate; **~würfel** *m* stock cube; **~würze** *f* soup seasoning.
Supplement [zuple'mɛnt] *nt* (*geh*) supplement.
Supplement-: ~band *m* supplementary volume; **~winkel** *m* supplementary angle.
Suppositorium *nt* (*Med*) suppository.
Supra-: s≈leitend *adj* (*Phys*) superconductive; **≈leiter** *m* (*Phys*) superconductor; **≈leitung** *f* (*Phys*) superconductivity.
superanational *adj* supranational.
Supranaturalismus *m* supernaturalism.
Supremat *m or nt* **-(e)s, -e, Suprematie** *f* (*geh*) supremacy.
Sure *f* **-, -n** (*im Koran*) sura(h).
Surfbrett ['zø:ɐf-, 'zœrf-, s-] *nt* surfboard.
surfen ['zø:ɐfən, 'zœrfən, s-] *vi* to surf.
Surfer(in *f*) ['zø:ɐfɐ, 'zœrfɐ, -ərin, s-] *m* surfer.
Surfing ['zø:ɐfɪŋ, 'zœr-, s-] *nt* **-s,** *no pl* (*Sport*) surfing.
Surinam [zuri'nam] *nt* **-s** Dutch Guiana.
surreal *adj* surreal.
Surrealismus *m, no pl* surrealism.
surrealistisch *adj* surrealist(ic).
surren *vi* **(a)** to hum; (*Insekt auch*) to buzz; (*Motor auch, Kamera, Insektenflügel*) to whirr. **(b)** *aux sein* (*sich bewegen: Insekt*) to buzz.
Surrogat *nt* surrogate.
Suse, Susi *f* - *abbr of* **Susanne**.
suspekt [zʊs'pɛkt] *adj* suspicious ◆ **jdm ~ sein** to seem suspicious to sb.
suspendieren* [zʊspɛn'di:rən] *vt* to suspend (*von* from).
Suspension [zʊspɛn'zio:n] *f* (*alle Bedeutungen*) suspension.
suspensiv [zʊspɛn'zi:f] *adj* (*Jur*) suspensory.
Suspensorium [zʊspɛn'zo:riʊm] *nt* (*Med*) suspensory.
süß *adj* (*lit, fig*) sweet ◆ **etw ~ machen** to sweeten sth; *Tee, Kaffee (mit Zucker)* to sugar sth; **gern ~ essen** to have a sweet tooth, to be fond of sweet things; **sie ist eine S~e** (*inf*) (*ißt gerne ~*) she has a sweet tooth; (*ist nett*) she's a sweetie(-pie) (*inf*); **das ~e Leben** the good life; **es auf die ~e Tour** *or* **auf die S~e versuchen** (*inf*) to turn on the charm; **(mein) S~er/(meine) S~e** (*inf*) my sweetheart; (*als Anrede auch*) my sweet, sweetie(-pie) (*inf*); *siehe* **Geheimnis**.
Süße *f* **-,** *no pl* (*lit, fig*) sweetness.

süßen [1] *vt* to sweeten; (*mit Zucker*) *Tee, Kaffee* to sugar.
[2] *vi* **mit Honig** *etc* ~ to use honey *etc* as a sweetener.
Süßholz *nt* liquorice ◆ **~ raspeln** (*fig*) to turn on the blarney; **du kannst aufhören, ~ zu raspeln** you can stop soft-soaping me/him *etc* (*inf*).
Süßholzraspler *m* **-s, -** (*hum*) soft-soaper (*inf*).
Süßigkeit *f* **(a)** *no pl* (*lit, fig*) sweetness. **(b)** **~en** *pl* sweets *pl* (*Brit*), candy (*US*).
Süß-: ~kartoffel *f* sweet potato; **~kirsche** *f* sweet cherry; **~klee** *m* hedysarum (*spec*).
süßlich *adj* **(a)** (*leicht süß*) sweetish, slightly sweet; (*unangenehm süß*) sickly (sweet), cloying.
(b) (*fig*) *Töne, Miene* terribly sweet; *Lächeln auch* sugary; *Worte auch* honeyed; *Farben, Geschmack* pretty-pretty (*inf*); (*kitschig*) mawkish.
Süß-: ~most *m* unfermented fruit juice; **~rahmbutter** *f* creamery butter; **s~sauer** *adj* sweet-and-sour; *Gurken etc* pickled; (*fig: gezwungen freundlich*) *Lächeln* forced; *Miene* artificially friendly; **~speise** *f* sweet dish; **~stoff** *m* sweetener; **~waren** *pl* confectionery *sing*; **~warengeschäft** *nt* sweetshop (*Brit*), candy store (*US*), confectioner's; **~wasser** *nt* freshwater; **~wasserfisch** *m* freshwater fish; **~wein** *m* dessert wine.
Sutane *f* **-, -n** *siehe* **Soutane.**
Sütterlinschrift *f old-fashioned style of German hand-writing.*
SW *abbr of* **Südwesten** SW.
Swasiland *nt* **-s** Swaziland.
Swastika ['svastika] *f* **-, Swastiken** swastika.
Sweatshirt ['swɛtʃɜ:t] *nt* **-s, -s** sweatshirt.
Swimming-pool ['svɪmɪŋpu:l] *m* **-s, -s** swimming pool.
Swinegel *m* **-s, -** (*dial*) hedgehog.
Swing *m* **-s,** *no pl* (*Mus, Fin*) swing.
swingen *vi* (*Mus*) to swing.
syllabisch *adj* syllabic.
Syllogismus *m* (*Philos*) syllogism.
Sylphe *m* **-n, -n,** *f* **-, -n** (*Myth*) sylph.
Sylt *nt* **-s** Sylt.
Sylvaner [zʏl'va:nɐ] *m* **-s, -** Sylvaner (wine/grape).
Sylvester [zʏl'vɛstɐ] *nt* **-s, -** *siehe* **Silvester.**
Symbiose *f* **-, -n** symbiosis.
symbiotisch *adj* symbiotic.
Symbol *nt* **-s, -e** symbol.
Symbolfigur *f* symbol, symbolic figure.
symbolhaft *adj* symbolic(al).
Symbolik *f* symbolism.
symbolisch *adj* symbolic(al) (*für* of).
symbolisieren* *vt* to symbolize.
Symbolismus *m* symbolism.
Symbolist(in *f*) *m* symbolist.
symbolistisch *adj* symbolist(ic).
Symbol-: ~kraft *f* symbolic force *or* power; **s~kräftig** *adj* strongly *or* richly symbolic; **s~trächtig** *adj* heavily symbolic, full of symbolism.
Symmetrie *f* symmetry.
Symmetrieachse *f* axis of symmetry.
Symmetrieebene *f* plane of symmetry.
symmetrisch *adj* symmetric(al).
Sympathie [zʏmpa'ti:] *f* (*Zuneigung*) liking; (*Mitgefühl, Solidaritätsgefühl*) sympathy ◆ **für jdn/etw ~ haben** to have a liking for/a certain amount of sympathy with sb/sth; **diese Maßnahmen haben meine volle ~** I sympathize completely with these measures; **durch seine Unverschämtheit hat er meine ~/hat er sich** (*dat*) **alle ~(n) verscherzt** he has turned me/everyone against him with his rudeness; **seine ~n gelten nicht der extremen Rechten** he isn't sympathetic towards the extreme right.
Sympathie-: ~äußerung *f* expression of support; **~kundgebung** *f* demonstration of support; **~streik** *m* sympathy strike; **in ~streik (mit jdm) treten** to come out in sympathy (with sb); **~werte** *pl* popularity rating *sing.*
Sympathikus *m* **-,** *no pl* (*Physiol*) sympathetic nerve.
Sympathisant(in *f*) *m* sympathizer.
sympathisch *adj* **(a)** pleasant, nice, simpatico (*esp US inf*) ◆ **er/es ist mir ~** I like him/it; **er/es war mir gleich ~** I liked him/it at once, I took to him/it at once, I took an immediate liking to him/it; **das ist mir gar nicht ~** I don't like it at all.
(b) (*Anat, Physiol*) sympathetic.
sympathisieren* *vi* to sympathize (*mit* with).
Symphonie [zʏmfo'ni:] *f* symphony.
Symphonie- *in cpds siehe* **Sinfonie-.**
Symphoniker(in *f*) *m* **-s, -** *siehe* **Sinfoniker(in).**
symphonisch *adj* symphonic.
Symposion [zʏm'po:ziɔn], **Symposium** [zʏm'po:ziʊm] *nt* **-s, Symposien** [zʏm'po:ziən] symposium.
Symptom *nt* **-s, -e** symptom.
symptomatisch *adj* symptomatic (*für* of).
Synagoge *f* **-, -n** synagogue.
synchron [zʏn'kro:n] *adj* synchronous; (*Ling*) synchronic.
Synchrongetriebe [zʏn'kro:n-] *nt* (*Aut*) synchromesh gearbox.
Synchronisation [zʏnkroniza'tsio:n] *f* (*Film, TV*) synchronization; (*Übersetzung*) dubbing.
synchronisieren* [zʏnkroni'zi:rən] *vt* to synchronize; (*übersetzen*) *Film* to dub.
Synchron- [zʏn'kro:n-]: **~schwimmen** *nt* synchronized swimming; **~uhr** *f* synchronous *or* mains-synchronized clock; ⚠**~verschluß** *m* (*Phot*) flash-synchronized shutter.
Syndikalismus *m, no pl* syndicalism.
syndikalistisch *adj* syndicalist(ic).
Syndikat *nt* (*Kartell*) syndicate.
Syndikus *m* **-, Syndiken** *or* **Syndizi** (*Geschäftsführer*) syndic; (*Justitiar*) (company *etc*) lawyer.
Syndrom *nt* **-s, -e** syndrome.
Synergie *f* synergy.
Synkope *f* **-, -n** **(a)** ['zʏnkopə] syncope, syncopation. **(b)** [zʏn'ko:pə] (*Mus*) syncopation.
synkopieren* *vt* to syncopate.
synkopisch *adj* syncopic, syncopated (*esp Mus*).
Synkretismus *m, no pl* syncretism.
Synodale(r) *mf decl as adj* (*Eccl*) synod member.
Synode *f* **-, -n** (*Eccl*) synod.
Synonym [zyno'ny:m] *nt* **-s, -e** synonym.
synonym(isch) [zyno'ny:m(ɪʃ)] *adj* synonymous.
Synonymwörterbuch *nt* dictionary of synonyms, thesaurus.
Synopse *f* **-, -n, Synopsis** *f* **-, Synopsen** synopsis; (*Bibl*) synoptic Gospels *pl*, Synoptics *pl.*
Synoptiker *pl* (*Bibl*) Synoptics *pl*; (*Apostel*) Synoptists *pl.*
Syntagma *nt* **-s, Syntagmen** *or* **-ta** (*Ling*) syntactic construction.
syntaktisch *adj* syntactic(al).
Syntax *f* **-, -en** syntax.
Synthese *f* **-, -n** synthesis.
Synthesizer ['sɪntəsaizɐ] *m* synthesizer.
Synthetik *f, no pl* **(a)** (*Math*) synthesis. **(b)** (*Kunstfaser*) synthetic fibre.
synthetisch *adj* synthetic; *Stoff, Faser auch* man-made ◆ **etw ~ herstellen** to make *or* produce sth synthetically.
synthetisieren* *vt* to syntheticize.
Syphilis ['zy:filɪs] *f* **-,** *no pl* syphilis.
syphiliskrank *adj* syphilitic, suffering from syphilis ◆ **~ sein** to have syphilis.
Syphilitiker(in *f*) *m* **-s, -** syphilitic.
syphilitisch *adj* syphilitic.
Syrakus *nt* **-** Syracuse.
Syrer(in *f*) *m* **-s, -** Syrian.
Syrien ['zy:riən] *nt* **-s** Syria.
Syrier(in *f*) [-iɐ, -iərɪn] *m* **-s, -** Syrian.
syrisch *adj* Syrian.
Syrisch(e) *nt, no pl* Syriac; *siehe auch* **Deutsch(e).**
System [zʏs'te:m] *nt* **-s, -e** system (*auch Comput*); (*Ordnung, Ordnungsprinzip auch*) method ◆ **etw mit ~ machen** to do sth systematically; **etw mit einem ~ machen** to do sth according to a system; **hinter dieser Sache steckt ~** there's method behind it; **~ in etw** (*acc*) **bringen** to get *or* bring some system into sth; **Apparate verschiedener ~e** machinery of different designs; **ein ~ von Straßen/Kanälen** a road/canal system.
System-: ~absturz *m* (*Comput*) system crash ◆ **gelegentlich treten ~abstürze auf** occasionally the system crashes; **~analyse** *f* systems analysis; **~analytiker** *m* systems analyst.
Systematik *f, no pl* **(a)** (*systematisches Ordnen*) system. **(b)** (*Lehre, Klassifikation*) systematology.
Systematiker(in *f*) *m* **-s, -** systematist; (*fig*) systematic person.
systematisch *adj* systematic.
systematisieren* *vt* to systematize.
System-: s~bedingt *adj* determined by the system; **~diskette** *f* systems disk; **~fehler** *m* (*Comput*) system error; **s~gerecht** *adj* in accordance with the system; **s~immanent** *adj* inherent in the system; **dem Kapitalismus s~immanent sein** to be inherent in the capitalist system.
systemisch *adj* systemic.
System-: s~konform *adj* in conformity with the system; **~kritiker** *m* critic of the system; **s~kritisch** *adj* critical of the system; **s~los** *adj* unsystematic; **~software** *f* systems software; **~spezialist** *m* (*Comput*) systems specialist; **~treue** *f* loyalty to the system; **~veränderer** *m* (*Pol pej*) **die Partei besteht aus lauter ~veränderern** the whole party is just a bunch of people out to change the system; **~veränderung** *f* change in the system; **~zwang** *m* obligation to conform to the system.
Systole ['zʏstolə, -'to:lə] *f* **-, -n** (*Med*) systole.
Szenar *nt* **-s, -e, Szenario** *nt* **-s, -s, Szenarium** *nt* scenario.
Szene ['stse:nə] *f* **-, -n** **(a)** (*Theat, fig*) scene; (*Theat: Bühnenausstattung*) set; (*sl: Drogen~ etc*) scene; (*sl: Milieu*) subculture ◆ **Beifall auf offener ~** applause during the performance; **hinter der ~** backstage; (*fig*) behind the scenes; **in ~** (*acc*) **gehen** to be staged; **etw in ~ setzen** (*lit, fig*) to stage sth; **sich in ~ setzen** to play to the gallery; **die ~ beherrschen** (*fig*) to dominate the scene (*gen* in); (*meistern*) to control things; **sich in der ~ auskennen** (*sl*) to know the scene.
(b) (*fig: Zank, Streit*) scene ◆ **jdm eine ~ machen** to make a scene in front of sb; **mach bloß keine ~** don't go making a scene, I don't want a scene.
-szene *f in cpds* (*sl*) scene (*sl*).
Szenenfolge *f* sequence of scenes.
Szenenwechsel *m* scene change.
Szenerie *f* (*Theat, fig*) scenery.
szenisch *adj* (*Theat*) scenic.

⚠: for details of spelling reform, see supplement

Szepter ['stsɛptɐ] *nt* **-s, -** sceptre.
Szilla *f* -, **Szillen** (*Bot*) scilla.
Szinti-: **~gramm** *nt* scintigram; ⚠**~graph** *m* scintigraph; ⚠**~graphie** *f* scintigraphy.
Szylla ['stsʏla] *f* - (*Myth*) Scylla ◆ **zwischen ~ und Charybdis** (*liter*) between Scylla and Charybdis.

T, t [teː] *nt* -, - T, t.
t *abbr of* **Tonne.**
Tab *m* **-(s), -e** *or* **-s** tab.
Tabak ['taːbak, 'tabak, (*aus*) ta'bak] *m* **-s, -e** tobacco; (*Schnupf~*) snuff.
Tabak- *in cpds* tobacco; **~beutel** *m siehe* **Tabaksbeutel**; **~dose** *f siehe* **Tabaksdose**; ⚠**~genuß** *m* (tobacco) smoking; **~händler** *m* (*im Großhandel*) tobacco merchant; (*im Einzelhandel*) tobacconist; **~laden** *m* tobacconist's, tobacco shop; **~mischung** *f* blend (of tobaccos), (tobacco) mixture; **~monopol** *nt* tobacco monopoly, monopoly on tobacco; **~pfeife** *f siehe* **Tabakspfeife**; **~qualm** *m* (*pej*) fug; **~rauch** *m* tobacco smoke.
Tabaks-: ~beutel *m* tobacco pouch; **~dose** *f* tobacco tin; (*für Schnupftabak*) snuff-box; **~pfeife** *f* pipe.
Tabak-: ~steuer *f* duty on tobacco; **~trafik** [ta'bak-] *f* (*Aus*) tobacconist's, tobacco shop; **~trafikant** [ta'bak-] *m* (*Aus*) tobacconist; **~waren** *pl* tobacco; „**~waren**" tobacconist's.
Tabatiere [taba'tieːrə] *f* **-, -n** (*Aus*) tobacco tin; (*old: Schnupftabakdose*) snuff-box.
tabellarisch [1] *adj* tabular ◆ **bitte fügen Sie einen ~en Lebenslauf bei** please write out your curriculum vitae in tabular form.
[2] *adv* in tabular form, in tables/a table.
tabellarisieren* *vt* to tabulate.
Tabelle *f* table; (*Diagramm*) chart; (*Sport*) (league) table.
Tabellen-: ~form *f*: **in ~form** in tabular form, in tables/a table; as a chart, in chart form; **t~förmig** *adj* tabular, in tabular form, in the form of a table; as a chart, in chart form; **~führer** *m* (*Sport*) league leaders *pl*; **~führer sein** to be at the top of the (league) table; **~gestaltung** *f* (*an Schreibmaschine*) tabulation; **~kalkulation** *f* (*Comput*) spreadsheet; **~kalkulationsprogramm** *nt* (*Comput*) spreadsheet (program); **~platz** *m* (*Sport*) place *or* position in the league; **auf den letzten ~platz fallen** to drop to the bottom of the table; **~stand** *m* (*Sport*) league situation; **~stand auf Seite 15** league tables on page 15.
Tabelliermaschine *f* tabulator, tabulating machine.
Tabernakel *nt or m* **-s, -** tabernacle.
Tablett *nt* **-(e)s, -s** *or* **-e** tray ◆ **jdm etw auf einem silbernen ~ servieren** (*fig: einfach machen*) to hand sb sth on a plate; **muß man dir alles/die Einladung auf einem silbernen ~ servieren?** do you have to have everything done for you/do you want an official invitation?
Tablette *f* tablet, pill.
Tabletten-: ~form *f*: **in ~form** in tablet form; ⚠**~mißbrauch** *m* pill abuse; **~röhre** *f* tablet tube; tube of tablets; **~sucht** *f* addiction to pills, compulsive pill-taking; **t~süchtig** *adj* addicted to pills; **sie ist t~süchtig** she's always popping pills (*inf*); **~süchtige(r)** *mf* pill addict, pill-popper (*inf*).
Tabu *nt* **-s, -s** taboo.
tabu *adj pred* taboo.
tabuieren* *vt* to make taboo, to taboo.
Tabuierung *f* taboo(ing).
tabuisieren* *vt siehe* **tabuieren.**
Tabula rasa *f* **- -,** *no pl* (*Philos*) tabula rasa ◆ **t~ ~ machen** (*inf*) to make a clean sweep.
Tabulator *m* tabulator, tab (*inf*).
Tabu-: ~schranke *f* taboo; **~wort** *nt* taboo word *or* expression.
Tach(e)les *no art* (*sl*) **(mit jdm) ~ reden** to have a talk with sb; **nun wollen wir beide mal ~ reden** let's do some straight talking, let's talk turkey (*US inf*).
tachinieren* *vi* (*Aus inf*) to laze *or* loaf about (*inf*).
Tachinierer(in *f***)** *m* **-s, -** (*Aus inf*) layabout (*inf*), loafer (*inf*).
Tacho *m* **-s, -s** (*inf*) speedo (*Brit inf*), speedometer.
Tachometer *m or nt* **-s, -** speedometer.
Tacker *m* **-s, -** (*inf*) stapler.
Tadel *m* **-s, -** (*Verweis*) reprimand; (*Vorwurf*) reproach; (*Kritik*) criticism, censure; (*geh: Makel*) blemish, taint; (*Sch: Eintragung ins Klassenbuch*) black mark ◆ **ein Leben ohne jeden ~** (*geh*) an unblemished *or* spotless *or* blameless life; **ihn trifft kein ~** (*geh*) he is above *or* beyond reproach.
tadellos [1] *adj* perfect; *Deutsch etc auch* faultless; *Benehmen auch* faultless, irreproachable; *Leben* blameless; (*inf*) splendid, first-class.
[2] *adv* perfectly; faultlessly; irreproachably; *gekleidet* immaculately.
tadeln *vt jdn* to rebuke, to reprimand; *jds Benehmen* to criticize, to express one's disapproval of.
tadelnd *adj attr* reproachful ◆ **ein ~er Blick** a reproachful look, a look of reproach.
tadelnswert, tadelnswürdig *adj* (*geh*) reprehensible, blameworthy.
Tadels|antrag *m* (*Parl*) motion of censure, censure motion.
Tafel *f* **-, -n (a)** (*Platte*) slab; (*Holz~*) panel; (*~ Schokolade etc*) bar; (*Gedenk~*) plaque; (*Wand~*) (black)board; (*Schreib~*) slate; (*Elec: Schalt~*) control panel, console; (*Anzeige~*) board; (*Verkehrs~*) sign.
(b) (*Bildseite*) plate.
(c) (*form: festlicher Speisetisch*) table; (*Festmahl*) meal; (*mittags*) luncheon (*form*); (*abends*) dinner ◆ **jdn zur ~ bitten** to ask sb to table; **die ~ aufheben** to officially end the meal.
Tafel-: ~apfel *m* eating apple; **~aufsatz** *m* centrepiece; **~berg** *m* (*Geog*) table mountain; **~besteck** *nt* (best) silver; **~bild** *nt* panel; **t~fertig** *adj* ready to serve; **t~förmig** *adj* slab-like; *Hochplateau* table-shaped; **~freuden** *pl* delicacies *pl*, culinary delights *pl*; (*Freude am Essen*) pleasures of the table *pl*; **~geschäft** *nt* (*Fin*) counter transactions *pl*; **~geschirr** *nt* tableware; **~glas** *nt* sheet glass, plate glass; **~land** *nt* plateau, tableland; **~lappen** *m* (blackboard) duster; **~malerei** *f* panel painting; **~musik** *f* musical entertainment.
tafeln *vi* (*geh*) to feast ◆ **mit jdm ~** to dine with sb.
täfeln *vt Wand* to wainscot; *Decke* to panel, to line with wooden panels.
Tafel-: ~obst *nt* (dessert) fruit; **~öl** *nt* cooking/salad oil; **~runde** *f* company (at table); (*Liter*) Round Table; **die ganze ~runde applaudierte** the whole table applauded; **eine festliche ~runde saß beisammen** a banquet/dinner party was in progress; **~salz** *nt* table salt; **~silber** *nt* silver; **~spitz** *m* (*Cook*) soured boiled rump.
Täf(e)lung *f siehe* **täfeln** wainscoting; (wooden) panelling.
Tafel-: ~wasser *nt* mineral water; **~wein** *m* table wine.
Taft *m* **-(e)s, -e** taffeta.
taften *adj* taffeta.
Tag *m* **-(e)s, -e (a)** day ◆ **am ~(e) des/der ...** (on) the day of ...; **am ~** during the day; **alle ~e** (*inf*), **jeden ~** every day; **am vorigen ~(e), am ~(e) vorher** the day before, the previous day; **auf den ~ (genau)** to the day; **auf ein paar ~e** for a few days; **auf seine alten ~e** at his age; **bei ~ und Nacht** night and day, day and night; **bis in unsere ~e** up to the present day; **bis die ~e!** (*sl*) so long (*inf*), cheerio (*inf*); **diese** (*inf*) *or* **dieser ~e** (*bald*) in the next few days; **den ganzen ~ (lang)** (*lit, fig*) all day long, the whole day; **eines ~es** one day; **eines ~es wirst du ...** one day *or* one of these days you'll ...; **eines (schönen** *or* **guten) ~es** one (fine) day; **sich** (*dat*) **einen schönen/faulen ~ machen** to have a nice/lazy day; **~ für** *or* **um ~** day by day; **in unseren** *or* **den heutigen ~en** these days, nowadays; **unter ~s** (*dial*) during the daytime; **von ~ zu ~** from day to day, every day; **~ der Arbeit** Labour Day; **~ der Republik/Befreiung** (*DDR*) Republic/Liberation Day; **der ~ des Herrn** (*Eccl*) the Lord's Day; **welcher ~ ist heute?** what day is it today?, what's today?; **ein ~ wie jeder andere** a day like any other; **guten ~!** hello (*inf*), good day (*dated form*); (*esp bei Vorstellung*) how-do-you-do; (*vormittags auch*) good morning; (*nachmittags auch*) good afternoon; **~!** (*inf*) hello, hi (*inf*); morning (*inf*); afternoon (*inf*); **ich wollte nur guten ~ sagen** I just wanted to have a chat; **zweimal am ~(e)** *or* **pro ~** twice daily *or* a day; **von einem ~ auf den anderen** overnight; **der Lärm des ~es** the bustle of the world; **der ~ X** D-Day (*fig*); **er erzählt** *or* **redet viel, wenn der ~ lang ist** (*inf*) he'll tell you anything if you let him; **seinen guten/schlechten ~ haben** to have a good/bad *or* off day, to have one of one's good/bad *or* off days; **das war heute wieder ein ~!** (*inf*) what a day!; **das Thema/Ereignis des ~es** the talking-point/event of the day; **Sie hören jetzt die Nachrichten des ~es** and now the *or* today's news; **in den ~ hinein leben** to take each day as it comes, to live from day to day; **~ und Nacht** night and day, day and night; **das ist ein Unterschied wie ~ und Nacht** they are as different as chalk and cheese; **~ und Stunde bestimmen** to fix a precise time.
(b) (*Tageslicht*) **bei ~(e)** *ankommen* while it's light; *arbeiten, reisen* during the day; **es wird schon ~** it's getting light already; **es ist ~** it's light; **solange (es) noch ~ ist** while it's still light; **an den ~ kommen** (*fig*) to come to light; **etw**

⚠: for details of spelling reform, see supplement

an den ~ bringen to bring sth to light; **er legte großes Interesse an den ~** he showed great interest.
(c) (*inf: Menstruation*) **meine/ihre ~e** my/her period; **sie hat ihre ~e (bekommen)** it's that time of the month for her.
(d) (*Min*) **über/unter ~e arbeiten** to work above/below ground *or* underground, to work on *or* at/below the surface.

-tag *m in cpds* (*Konferenz*) convention, congress.

Tag- (*S Ger, Aus, Sw*) *in cpds siehe* **Tage-**.

tag|aus *adv* **~, tagein** day in, day out, day after day.

Tagchen ['taxçən] *interj* (*hum*) hello there, hi(ya) (*inf*).

Tagdienst *m* day duty.

Tage-: ~bau *m, pl* **-e** (*Min*) open-cast mining; **~blatt** *nt* daily (news)paper, local rag (*inf*); **Göttinger ~blatt** Göttingen Daily News; **~buch** *nt* diary, journal (*liter, form*); **(über etw** *acc*) **~buch führen** to keep a diary (of sth); **~dieb** *m* (*dated*) idler, wastrel; **~geld** *nt* daily allowance.

tag|ein *adv siehe* **tagaus**.

Tage-: t~lang *adj* lasting for days; **nach t~langer Unterbrechung** after an interruption of several days, after an interruption lasting several days; **t~lange Regenfälle** several days' rain; **er war t~lang verschwunden** he disappeared for (several) days; **~lohn** *m* (*dated*) daily wage(s); **im ~lohn arbeiten** *or* **stehen** to be paid by the day; **~löhner(in** *f*) *m* **-s, -** day labourer.

tagen [1] *vi impers* (*geh*) **es tagt** day is breaking *or* dawning; **es begann schon zu ~** day was breaking *or* dawning, (the) dawn was breaking.
[2] *vi* (*konferieren*) to sit ◆ **wir haben noch bis in den frühen Morgen getagt** (*inf*) we had an all-night sitting (*inf*).

Tagereise *f* day's journey.

Tages-: ~ablauf *m* day; **~anbruch** *m* daybreak, dawn; **~arbeit** *f* day's work; **~auftrag** *m* (*St Ex*) day order; **~ausflug** *m* day trip *or* excursion, day's outing; **~bedarf** *m* daily requirement; **~befehl** *m* (*Mil*) order of the day; **~creme** *f* day cream; **~decke** *f* bedspread; **~dienst** *m* duty day; **jeder Kollege hat monatlich sieben ~dienste** each colleague is on duty for seven days a month; **~einnahmen** *pl* day's takings *pl*; **~ereignis** *nt* event of the day; **~festpreis** *m* fixed daily rate; **~fragen** *pl* issues of the day, day-to-day matters; **~geld** *nt* (*Fin*) overnight money; **~geschehen** *nt* events *pl* of the day; **~gespräch** *nt* talk of the town; **~hälfte** *f* half of the day; **~karte** *f* **(a)** (*Speisekarte*) menu of the day; **(b)** (*Fahr-, Eintrittskarte*) day ticket; **~kasse** *f* **(a)** (*Theat*) box-office; **(b)** (*Econ*) day's takings *pl*; **~klinik** *f* day clinic; **~kurs** *m* (*St Ex*) (*von Effekten*) current price; (*von Devisen*) current rate; **~lauf** *m* day; **~leistung** *f* daily workload; (*von Maschine, Schriftsteller etc*) daily output; (*von Milchkuh auch*) daily yield; (*Sport*) performance of the day; **~licht** *nt, no pl* daylight; **ans ~licht kommen** (*fig*) to come to light; **das ~licht scheuen** to be a creature of the night, to shun the daylight; **~lichtprojektor** *m* overhead projector; **~lohn** *m* day's wages; **~losung** *f* (*Mil*) password of the day; **~marsch** *m* day's march; **zwei ~märsche entfernt** two days' march away; **~menü** *nt* menu of the day; **~mutter** *f* child-minder; **~nachrichten** *pl* (today's) news *sing*; **die wichtigsten ~nachrichten** (main) headlines; **~ordnung** *f* agenda, order of the day (*form*); **zur ~ordnung!** keep to the agenda!; **etw auf die ~ordnung setzen** to put sth on the agenda; **auf der ~ordnung stehen** to be on the agenda; **zur ~ordnung übergehen** to proceed to the agenda; (*an die Arbeit gehen*) to get down to business; (*wie üblich weitermachen*) to carry on as usual; **an der ~ordnung sein** (*fig*) to be the order of the day; **~ordnungspunkt** *m* item on the agenda; **~pauschale** *f* fixed daily amount; **~preis** *m* (*Comm*) current price; **gestern betrug der ~preis ...** yesterday's price was ...; **~- und Abendpreise** daytime and night prices; **~presse** *f* daily (news)papers *or* press; **~ration** *f* daily rations; **~raum** *m* day room; **~reise** *f* **(a)** (*Entfernung*) day's journey; **(b)** (*Ausflug*) day trip; **~satz** *m* daily rate; **~schau** *f* (*TV*) news *sing*; **~stätte** *f* (*für Kinder*) day care centre; **~suppe** *f* soup of the day; **~zeit** *f* time (of day); **zu jeder ~- und Nachtzeit** at all hours of the day and night; **zu dieser ~zeit kommst du nach Hause?!** what sort of time do you call this to come home!; **~zeitung** *f* daily (paper).

Tage-: t~weise *adv* on a daily basis; **~werk** *nt* (*geh*) day's work.

Tag-: ~fahrt *f* (*Min*) ascent; **t~hell** *adj* (as) bright as day; **es war schon t~hell** it was already broad daylight.

-tägig *adj suf* -day.

tägl. *abbr of* **täglich**.

täglich [1] *adj* daily; (*attr: gewöhnlich*) everyday ◆ **~e Gelder** (*Comm*) call-money; **~e Zinsen** (*Comm*) daily interest; **das reicht gerade fürs ~e Leben** it's just about enough to get by on; **sein ~(es) Brot verdienen** to earn a living; **das ist unser ~(es) Brot** (*fig: Ärger etc*) it is our stock-in-trade; **das ist so wichtig wie das ~e Brot** it's as important as life itself; **unser ~ Brot gib uns heute** (*Bibl*) give us this day our daily bread.
[2] *adv* every day ◆ **einmal ~** once a day *or* daily.

-täglich *adj suf* **sechs~** every six days.

Tagmem *nt* **-s, -e** (*Ling*) tagmeme.

tags *adv* **(a) ~ zuvor** the day before, the previous day; **~ darauf** *or* **danach** the next *or* following day. **(b)** (*bei Tag*) in the daytime, by day.

Tagschicht *f* day shift ◆ **~ haben** to be on (the) day shift.

tags|über *adv* during the day.

Tag-: t~täglich [1] *adj* daily;
[2] *adv* every (single) day; **~traum** *m* daydream; **~träumer** *m* daydreamer; **~undnachtgleiche** *f* equinox.

Tagung *f* conference; (*von Ausschuß*) sitting, session.

Tagungs-: ~ort *m* venue (of a/the conference); **~teilnehmer** *m* conferee, person attending a conference.

Tag-: ~wache[1] *f* (*Aus, Sw Mil*) **(a)** reveille; **(b) ~wache!** rise and shine!; **~wache**[2], **~wacht** *f* (*Aus, Sw*) day guard.

Tahiti [ta'hi:ti] *nt* **-s** Tahiti.

Tahitianer(in *f*) [tahi:'tia:nɐ, -ərɪn] *m* **-s, -**, **Tahitier(in** *f*) [ta'hi:tiɐ, -ərɪn] *m* **-s, -** Tahitian.

tahitisch [ta'hi:tɪʃ] *adj* Tahitian.

Tai Chi (Chuan) [taɪ'tʃi:(tʃwan)] *nt* **-** *no pl* t'ai chi (ch'uan).

Taifun *m* **-s, -e** typhoon.

Taiga *f* **-**, *no pl* taiga.

Taille ['taljə] *f* **-, -n** waist; (*bei Kleidungsstücken auch*) waistline ◆ **auf seine ~ achten** to watch one's waistline; **zu eng in der ~** too tight at the waist; **ein Kleid auf ~** a fitted dress.

Taillenweite ['taljən-] *f* waist measurement.

taillieren* [ta'ji:rən] *vt* to fit (at the waist).

tailliert [ta'ji:ɐt] *adj* waisted, fitted; *Hemd auch* slimfit.

Taiwan *nt* **-s** Taiwan.

Taiwanese *m* **-n, -n**, **Taiwanesin** *f* Taiwanese.

taiwanesisch *adj* Taiwan(ese).

Take [te:k] *nt or m* **-, -s** (*Film, TV*) take.

Takel *nt* **-s, -** (*Naut*) tackle.

Takelage [takə'la:ʒə] *f* **-, -n** (*Naut*) rigging, tackle.

takeln *vt* (*Naut*) to rig.

Takelung *f* rigging.

Takt *m* **-(e)s, -e (a)** (*Einheit*) (*Mus*) bar; (*Phon, Poet*) foot.
(b) (*Rhythmus*) time ◆ **den ~ schlagen** to beat time; **(den) ~ halten** to keep time; **im ~ bleiben** to stay in time; **den ~ verlieren/wechseln** to lose/change the beat, to change (the) time; **im ~ singen/tanzen** to sing/dance in time (to the music); **gegen den ~** out of time; **im/gegen den ~ marschieren** to be in/out of step; **den ~ angeben** to give the beat *or* time; **im ~ der Musik** in time to *or* with music; **das Publikum klatschte den ~ dazu** the audience clapped in time to the music; **der Zug ratterte in eintönigem ~** the train rattled along with a monotonous rhythm; **wenn alle Kolben im ~ arbeiten** if all the pistons are in phase.
(c) (*Aut*) stroke.
(d) (*Ind*) phase.
(e) *no pl* (*Taktgefühl*) tact ◆ **mit dem ihm eigenen ~** with his great tact(fulness); **er hat keinen ~ im Leibe** (*inf*) he hasn't an ounce of tact in him.

Taktbezeichnung *f* time signature.

takten *vt* (*Comput*) to clock ◆ **ein mit 60 mhz getakteter Prozessor** a processor with a clock speed of 60 mhz.

Takt-: ~fahrplan *m* (*Rail*) *timetable of departures at regular intervals*; **t~fest** *adj* (*Mus*) **(a)** able to keep time; **(b)** (*inf*) (*gesundheitlich*) fighting fit (*inf*); (*sicher*) sure of his *etc* stuff (*inf*); **~folge** *f* (*form*) sequence; **~frequenz** *f* (*Comput*) clock speed; **~gefühl** *nt* **(a)** sense of tact; **(b)** (*rare: Mus*) sense of rhythm *or* time.

taktieren* *vi* **(a)** to manoeuvre ◆ **so kann man nicht ~** you can't use those tactics. **(b)** (*rare: Mus*) to beat time.

Taktik *f* tactics *pl* ◆ **eine ~** tactics *pl*, a tactical approach; **man muß mit ~ vorgehen** you have to use tactics; **~ der verbrannten Erde** (*Mil*) scorched earth policy.

Taktiker *m* **-s, -** tactician.

taktisch *adj* tactical ◆ **~ vorgehen** to use tactics; **~ klug** good tactics.

Takt-: t~los *adj* tactless; **~losigkeit** *f* tactlessness; **es war eine ~losigkeit sondergleichen** it was a particularly tactless thing to do/say; **~maß** *nt* (*Mus*) time; **~messer** *m* **-s, -** *siehe* **Metronom**; **~stock** *m* baton; **den ~stock schwingen** (*inf*) to wield the baton; **~strich** *m* (*Mus*) bar (line); **~verkehr** *m* (*Rail etc*) regular service ◆ **die Züge fahren im ~verkehr** the trains go at regular intervals; **einstündiger ~verkehr** service at hourly intervals; **t~voll** *adj* tactful; **~wechsel** *m* (*Mus*) change of time, time change.

Tal *nt* **-(e)s, ¨er** valley, vale (*poet*) ◆ **zu ~e** into the valley.

tal|ab(wärts) *adv* **(a)** down into the valley. **(b)** (*flußabwärts*) downriver, downstream.

Talar *m* **-s, -e** (*Univ*) gown; (*Eccl auch*) cassock; (*Jur*) robe(s).

tal|aufwärts *adv* **(a)** up the valley. **(b)** (*flußaufwärts*) upriver, upstream.

Tal-: ~brücke *f* bridge over a valley; **~enge** *f* narrow part of a/the valley, gorge.

Talent *nt* **-(e)s, -e (a)** (*Begabung*) talent (*zu* for) ◆ **ein großes ~ haben** to be very talented; **sie hat viel ~ zum Singen/zur Schauspielerin** she has a great talent *or* gift for singing/acting; **da saß** *or* **stand er nun mit seinem ~** (*inf*) he was left looking a right charlie (*Brit inf*).
(b) (*begabter Mensch*) talented person ◆ **junge ~e** young talent; **er ist ein großes ~** he is very talented.
(c) (*Hist: Geld*) talent.

talentiert *adj* talented, gifted ◆ **die Mannschaft lieferte ein ~es Spiel** the team played a game of great skill *or* a brilliant game.

Talent-: t~los *adj* untalented; **~probe** *f* audition; **~suche** *f* search for talent; **wir sind auf ~suche** we are looking for new talent; **t~voll** *adj* talented; **das war nicht sehr t~voll** (*inf*) that wasn't very clever *or* bright.

Taler *m* **-s, -** (*Hist*) Thaler; (*inf*) mark, ≃ quid (*inf*), ≃ buck (*US inf*).

Talfahrt *f* (*bergabwärts*) descent; (*flußabwärts*) downriver trip; (*fig*) decline.

Talg *m* **-(e)s, -e** tallow; (*Cook*) suet; (*Hautabsonderung*) sebum.

Talgdrüse *f* (*Physiol*) sebaceous gland.

Talisman *m* **-s, -e** talisman, (lucky) charm; (*Maskottchen*) mascot.

Talje *f* **-, -n** (*Naut*) block and tackle.
Talk *m* **-(e)s,** *no pl* talc(um).
Talkessel *m* basin, hollow.
Talkpuder *m or nt* talcum powder.
Talkshow ['tɔːkʃoː] *f* **-, -s** (*TV*) talk show, chat show (*Brit*).
Talkum *nt* **(a)** *siehe* **Talk. (b)** (*Puder*) talc, talcum powder.
Tallandschaft *f* valley; valleys *pl*.
Talmi *nt* **-s,** *no pl* (*geh*) pinchbeck; (*fig*) rubbish, trash ♦ **~-Religion** sham religion.
Talmigold *nt* pinchbeck gold.
Talmud *m* **-(e)s, -e** Talmud.
Talmulde *f* basin, hollow.
Talon [ta'lõ] *m* **-s, -s** (*St Ex*) renewal coupon.
Tal-: ~schaft *f* (*Sw, Aus*) valley inhabitants *pl or* dwellers *pl or* folk; **~senke** *f* hollow (of a/the valley); **~sohle** *f* bottom of a/the valley, valley bottom; (*fig*) rock bottom; **in der ~sohle** (*fig*) at rock bottom, in the doldrums; **~sperre** *f* dam; **~station** *f* base camp; (*Skilift etc*) station at the bottom of a skilift *etc*; **t~wärts** *adv* down to the valley.
Tamarinde *f* **-, -n** tamarind.
Tamariske *f* **-, -n** tamarisk.
Tambour ['tambuːɐ] *m* **-s, -e** drummer.
Tambourmajor ['tambuːɐ-] *m* drum-major.
Tamburin *nt* **-s, -e** tambourine.
Tamile *m* **-n, -n, Tamilin** *f* Tamil.
tamilisch *adj* Tamil.
Tamp *m* **-s, -e, Tampen** *m* **-s, -** (*Naut*) rope end.
Tampon ['tampɔn, tam'poːn] *m* **-s, -s** tampon; (*für Wunde auch*) plug.
tamponieren* *vt* to plug, to tampon.
Tamtam *nt* **-s, -s (a)** (*Mus*) tomtom. **(b)** (*inf: Wirbel*) fuss, to-do (*inf*), ballyhoo (*inf*); (*Lärm*) row, din (*inf*) ♦ **der Faschingszug zog mit großem ~ durch die Straßen** the Fasching procession paraded loudly through the streets.
Tand *m* **-(e)s,** *no pl* (*liter*) trinkets *pl*, knick-knacks *pl* ♦ **alles Menschenwerk ist doch nur ~** all human works are but dross (*liter*).
Tändelei *f* (*liter*) (*Spielerei*) (dilly-)dallying, trifling; (*Liebelei*) dalliance (*liter*).
Tandelmarkt (*Aus*), **Tändelmarkt** (*dial*) *m* flea market.
tändeln *vi* (*liter*) (*liebeln*) to dally (*liter*); (*trödeln*) to (dilly-) dally, to trifle.
Tandem *nt* **-s, -s** tandem.
Tandler(in *f*) *m* **-s, -** (*Aus*) **(a)** (*Trödler*) second-hand dealer. **(b)** (*langsamer Mensch*) slowcoach (*Brit inf*), slowpoke (*US inf*).
Tang *m* **-(e)s, -e** seaweed.
Tanga *m* **-s, -s** tanga.
Tanganjika [taŋgan'jiːka] *nt* **-s** Tanganyika.
Tanga-Slip *m* tanga.
Tangens ['taŋgɛns] *m* **-, -** (*Math*) tan(gent).
Tangenskurve ['taŋgɛns-] *f* (*Math*) tan wave.
Tangente [taŋ'gɛntə] *f* **-, -n** (*Math*) tangent; (*Straße*) ring-road, expressway.
tangential [taŋgɛn'tsiaːl] *adj* tangential.
Tanger ['taŋɐ, 'tandʒɐ] *nt* **-s** Tangier(s).
tangieren* [taŋ'giːrən] *vt* **(a)** (*Math*) to be tangent to. **(b)** (*berühren*) *Problem* to touch on; *Stadt, Gebiet* to skirt ♦ **das tangiert das Problem nur** that is merely tangential *or* peripheral to the problem. **(c)** (*betreffen*) to affect; (*inf: kümmern*) to bother.
Tango ['taŋgo] *m* **-s, -s** tango.
Tank *m* **-(e)s, -s** *or* **-e** (*Behälter, Panzer*) tank.
Tank-: ~anzeige *f* fuel gauge; **~deckel** *m* filler cap.
tanken *vti* **(a)** (*bei Auto*) to tank up; (*bei Rennwagen, Flugzeug*) to refuel ♦ **wo kann man hier ~?** where can I get petrol (*Brit*) *or* gas (*US*) round here?; **ich muß noch ~** I have to get some petrol/gas; **wir hielten an, um zu ~** we stopped for petrol/gas; **ich tanke bleifrei** I use unleaded; **ich tanke nur für 10 DM** I'll just put 10 marks' worth in; **ich habe 30 l getankt** I put 30 litres in (the tank); **hast du getankt?** have you tanked up?, have you put petrol/gas in?
(b) (*inf*) (*viel trinken*) to have a few; *frische Luft* to get, to fill one's lungs with; *neue Kräfte* to get ♦ **er hat ganz schön** *or* **einiges getankt** he's had a few, he's really tanked up (*inf*).
Tanker *m* **-s, -** (*Naut*) tanker.
Tankerflotte *f* tanker fleet, fleet of tankers.
Tank-: ~fahrzeug *nt* (*Aut*) tanker; **~füllmenge** *f* tank capacity; **~inhalt** *m* contents of the tank *pl*; **der ~inhalt beträgt ...** the tank holds ..., the tank capacity is ... (*form*); **~lager** *nt* oil *or* petrol depot; **~laster, ~lastzug** *m* tanker; **~möglichkeit** *f* **letzte ~möglichkeit vor ...** last filling station before ...; **~säule** *f* petrol pump (*Brit*), gas(oline) pump (*US*); **~schiff** *nt* tanker; **~stelle** *f* filling *or* petrol (*Brit*) *or* gas(oline) (*US*) station; **~stutzen** *m* filler pipe; **~uhr** *f* fuel gauge; **⚠~verschluß** *m* petrol (*Brit*) *or* gas (*US*) cap; **~wagen** *m* tanker; (*Rail*) tank wagon *or* car; **~wart** *m* petrol pump (*Brit*) *or* gas station (*US*) attendant; **~zug** *m siehe* **~laster**.
Tann *m* **-(e)s, -e** (*poet*) pine forest.
Tännchen *nt dim of* **Tanne**.
Tanne *f* **-, -n** fir, pine; (*Holz*) pine, deal ♦ **sie ist schlank wie eine ~** she is as slender as a reed.
Tannen-: ~baum *m* **(a)** fir-tree, pine-tree; **(b)** (*Weihnachtsbaum*) Christmas tree; **~nadel** *f* (pine) needle; **~wald** *m* pine forest; **~zapfen** *m* fir cone, pine cone.

⚠: for details of spelling reform, see supplement

Tannin *nt* **-s,** *no pl* tannin.
Tannzapfen *m siehe* **Tannenzapfen**.
Tansania *nt* **-s** Tanzania.
Tansanier(in *f*) [tan'zaːniɐ, -ərɪn] *m* **-s, -** Tanzanian.
tansanisch *adj* Tanzanian.
Tantal *nt* **-s,** *no pl* (*abbr* **Ta**) tantalum.
Tantalusqualen *pl* torments of Tantalus (*liter*) ♦ **ich litt ~** it was tantalizing, I suffered torments (*liter*); **jdm ~ bereiten** to tantalize sb.
Tantchen *nt* (*inf*) **(a)** (*Verwandte*) auntie, aunty. **(b)** (*alte Dame*) old dear (*inf*).
Tante *f* **-, -n (a)** (*Verwandte*) aunt, aunty, auntie. **(b)** (*pej inf: Frau*) old girl (*inf*), old dear (*inf*). **(c)** (*baby-talk: Frau*) lady ♦ **~ Schneider/Monika** aunty *or* auntie Schneider/Monika. **(d)** (*Kindergartenschwester etc*) teacher; (*Krippenschwester*) nurse.
Tante-Emma-Laden *m* (*inf*) corner shop.
tantenhaft *adj* **(a)** (*inf*) old-maidish ♦ **sie benimmt sich so richtig ~** she acts like a real old maid *or* maiden aunt. **(b)** (*pej: betulich*) *Ausdruck(sweise)* twee.
Tantieme [tã'tieːmə, -'tieːmə] *f* **-, -n** percentage (of the profits); (*für höhere Angestellte*) director's fee; (*für Künstler*) royalty.
Tanz *m* **-es, ¨-e (a)** dance ♦ **dort ist heute abend ~** there's a dance *or* (*für Jugendliche*) disco there this evening; **im Goldenen Ochsen ist neuerdings auch ~** they now have dancing too at the Golden Ox; **zum ~ aufspielen** (*dated*) to strike up a dance (tune); **jdn zum ~ auffordern** to ask sb to dance *or* for a dance.
(b) (*fig geh: von Licht, Schatten*) play ♦ **der ~ der Boote auf den Wellen** the boats' dancing (*liter*) *or* bobbing on the waves; **ein ~ auf dem Vulkan** (*fig*) playing with fire.
(c) (*inf: Aufheben*) fuss ♦ **einen ~ um jdn machen** to make a fuss of sb.
Tanz-: ~abend *m* dance; **~bar** *f* bar with dancing; **~bär** *m* dancing bear; **~bein** *nt*: **das ~bein schwingen** (*hum*) to trip the light fantastic (*hum*), to shake a leg (*hum*); **~boden** *m* (*~fläche*) dance floor; (*Saal*) dance hall; (*dated: Veranstaltung*) dance; **~café** *nt* restaurant with dancing.
Tänzchen *nt dim of* **Tanz** (*dated hum*) dance ♦ **ein ~ wagen** to venture onto the floor.
Tanzdiele *f* (*dated*) (*Raum*) dance hall; (*~fläche*) dance floor.
tänzeln *vi aux haben or* (*bei Richtungsangabe*) *sein* to mince, to sashay (*esp US*), to trip; (*Boxer*) to skip; (*Pferd*) to step delicately.
tanzen *vti aux haben or* (*bei Richtungsangabe*) *sein* to dance; (*Boot auch*) to bob; (*Kreisel*) to spin; (*hüpfen*) to hop ♦ **~ gehen, zum T~ gehen** to go dancing; *siehe* **Pfeife**.
Tänzer(in *f*) *m* **-s, -** dancer; (*Partner*) (dancing) partner; (*Ballett~*) ballet dancer.
Tanzerei *f* **(a)** dancing; (*pej*) prancing about. **(b)** (*Aus*) dancing party.
tänzerisch *adj* dance-like ♦ **~ veranlagt sein** to have a talent for dancing; **~ ausgebildet** trained as a dancer; **eine große ~e Leistung** a tremendous piece of dancing; **~ gestaltete Gymnastik** gymnastics done in a dance-like way *or* as a dance; **~e Darbietungen** dance acts; **sein ~es Können** his dancing ability.
Tanz-: ~fläche *f* dance floor; **~gruppe** *f* dance group; (*bei Revue, TV-Show auch*) chorus; **~kapelle** *f* dance band; **~kunst** *f* art of dancing, dance; **~kurs(us)** *m* dancing course; **~lehrer** *m* dancing teacher; **~lied** *nt* dance tune; **~lokal** *nt* café with dancing; **t~lustig** *adj* fond of *or* keen on dancing; **einige t~lustige Paare blieben noch** a few couples who wanted to dance stayed on; **~musik** *f* dance music; **~orchester** *nt* dance orchestra; **~partner** *m* dancing partner; **~platte** *f* record of dance music; **~platz** *m* (open-air) dance floor; **~saal** *m* dance hall; (*in Hotel etc*) ballroom; **~schritt** *m* (dance) step; **~schuh** *m* dancing shoe; **~schule** *f* dancing school, school of dancing; **~sport** *m* competitive dancing; **~sprache** *f* (*Zool*) dance language; **~stunde** *f* dancing lesson *or* class; **sie haben sich in der ~stunde kennengelernt** they met at dancing lessons *or* classes; **~tee** *m* thé dansant, tea-dance; **~turnier** *nt* dancing contest *or* competition; **~veranstaltung** *f*, **~vergnügen** *nt* dance.
Taoismus [tao'ɪsmʊs, tau-] *m* Taoism.
Tapergreis *m* (*pej inf*) old dodderer (*pej inf*).
tap(e)rig *adj* (*pej inf*) doddering, doddery.
tapern *vi* (*inf*) to totter.
Tapet *nt*: (*inf*) **etw aufs ~ bringen** to bring sth up; **aufs ~ kommen** to be brought up, to come up.
Tapete *f* **-, -n** wallpaper ♦ **ohne ~n** without wallpaper; **die ~n wechseln** (*fig inf*) to have a change of scenery *or* surroundings.
Tapeten-: ~bahn *f* strip of wallpaper; **~rolle** *f* roll of wallpaper; **~tür** *f* concealed door; **~wechsel** *m* (*inf*) change of scenery *or* surroundings.
Tapezier *m* **-s, -e** (*esp S Ger*), **Tapezierer** *m* **-s, - (a)** paper-hanger, decorator. **(b)** (*Polsterer*) upholsterer.
Tapezier-: ~arbeit *f* wallpapering; **~bürste** *f* wallpaper brush.
tapezieren* *vt* to (wall)paper; (*inf: mit Bildern*) to plaster (*inf*) ♦ **neu ~** to repaper.
Tapezier-: ~nagel *m* tack; **~tisch** *m* trestle table.
tapfer *adj* brave, courageous; (*wacker*) steadfast; *Soldat, Versuch auch* bold ♦ **wir marschierten immer ~ weiter, ohne zu merken ...** we marched on blithely, not realizing ...; **halt dich** *or* **bleib ~!** (*inf*) be brave; **sich ~ schlagen** (*inf*) to put on a brave show.
Tapferkeit *f siehe adj* bravery, courage; steadfastness; boldness.
Tapferkeitsmedaille *f* medal for bravery.
Tapioka *f* **-,** *no pl* tapioca.
Tapir *m* **-s, -e** (*Zool*) tapir.

Tapisserie [tapısə'ri:] f (a) tapestry. (b) (old, Sw) drapery.
tapp interj tap.
tappen vi (a) aux sein (tapsen) to go/come falteringly; (Bär) to lumber, to lollop (inf); (dial: gehen) to wander ◆ ~de Schritte faltering steps; er ist in eine Pfütze getappt (inf) he walked smack into a puddle (inf).
(b) (tasten) nach etw ~ to grope for sth; im finstern or dunkeln ~ (fig) to grope in the dark.
täppisch, tappig (dial) adj awkward, clumsy.
tap(p)rig adj (dial) siehe tap(e)rig.
Taps m -es, -e (dial) clumsy oaf (inf) ◆ kleiner ~ little bundle.
tapsen vi aux sein (inf) (Kind) to toddle; (Bär) to lumber, to lollop (inf); (Kleintier) to waddle.
tapsig adj (inf) awkward, clumsy.
Tara f -, **Taren** (Comm) tare.
Tarantel f -, -n tarantula ◆ wie von der ~ gestochen as if stung by a bee, as if bitten by a snake.
Tarantella f -, -s or **Tarantellen** tarantella.
tarieren* vt to tare.
Tarif m -(e)s, -e rate; (Wasser~, Gas~, Verkehrs~ etc auch) tariff; (Gebühr auch) charge ◆ die ~e für Telefonanschlüsse telephone rental; neue ~e für Löhne/Gehälter new wage rates/salary scales; die Gewerkschaft hat die ~e für Löhne und Gehälter gekündigt the union has put in a new wage claim; nach/über/unter ~ bezahlen to pay according to/above/below the (union) rate(s).
Tarif-: ⚠~abschluß m wage settlement; ~autonomie f (right to) free collective bargaining; ~gehalt nt union rates pl; ~gruppe f grade; ~kommission f joint working party on pay.
tariflich adj agreed, union ◆ der ~e Mindestlohn the agreed minimum wage; die Gehälter sind ~ festgelegt there are fixed rates for salaries.
Tarif-: ~lohn m standard wage; t~los adj t~loser Zustand period when new rates are being negotiated; t~mäßig adj siehe t~lich; ~ordnung f wage/salary scale; ~partei f party to a wage agreement; die ~parteien unions and management; ~partner m party to the wage/salary agreement; die ~partner union and management; (Sozialpartner) both sides of industry; ~runde f pay round; ~verhandlungen pl wage/salary negotiations pl, negotiations on pay pl; ~vertrag m wage/pay agreement; ~zone f fare zone.
Tarn-: ~anstrich m camouflage; ~anzug m (Mil) camouflage battledress.
tarnen [1] vti to camouflage; (fig) Absichten, Identität etc to disguise ◆ Massagesalons sind meist getarnte Bordelle massage parlours are usually a cover for brothels; als Polizist getarnt disguised as a policeman.
[2] vr (Tier) to camouflage itself; (Mensch) to disguise oneself.
Tarn-: ~farbe f camouflage colour/paint; ~kappe f magic hat; ~kleid nt (Zool) protective camouflage; ~name m cover name; ~netz nt (Mil) camouflage netting.
Tarnung f camouflage; (von Agent etc) disguise ◆ die Arztpraxis ist nur eine ~ the doctor's practice is just a cover; er fuhr zur ~ erst eine Station mit der U-Bahn as a cover he first travelled one stop on the subway.
Tarock m or nt -s, -s tarot.
Tartanbahn f (Sport) tartan track.
Tartar m -en, -en siehe Tatar[1].
Täschchen ['tɛʃçən] nt dim of Tasche.
Tasche f -, -n (a) (Hand~) bag (Brit), purse (US); (Reise~ etc) bag; (Backen~) pouch; (Akten~) case.
(b) (bei Kleidungsstücken, Billard~) pocket ◆ sich (dat) die ~n füllen (fig) to line one's own pockets; in die eigene ~ arbeiten or wirtschaften to line one's own pockets; etw in der ~ haben (inf) to have sth in the bag (inf); die Hand auf die ~ halten (dated inf), die ~ zuhalten (dated inf) to keep a tight grip on the purse strings; jdm das Geld aus der ~ locken or ziehen or lotsen to get sb to part with his money; etw aus der eigenen ~ bezahlen to pay for sth out of one's own pocket; etw in die eigene ~ stecken (fig) to put sth in one's own pocket, to pocket sth; sich (dat) etwas in die ~ lügen (inf) to kid oneself (inf); jdm auf der ~ liegen (inf) to live off sb or at sb's expense; die Hände in die ~n stecken (lit) to put one's hands in one's pockets; (fig) to stand idly by; jdn in die ~ stecken (inf) to put sb in the shade (inf); siehe tief.
Taschen-: ~ausgabe f pocket edition; ~buch nt paperback (book); ~buchausgabe f paperback (edition); ~dieb m pickpocket; ~diebstahl m pickpocketing; ~fahrplan m (pocket) timetable; ~feitel m (Aus inf) penknife, pocket-knife; ~format nt pocket size; Transistorradio im ~format pocket-size(d) transistor; ~geld nt pocket-money; ~kalender m pocket diary; ~kamm m pocket comb; ~krebs m edible crab; ~lampe f torch, flashlight (US); ~messer nt pocket-knife, penknife; wie ein ~messer zusammenklappen (inf) to double up; ~rechner m pocket calculator; ~schirm m collapsible umbrella; ~spiegel m pocket mirror; ~spieler m conjurer; ~spielerei f sleight of hand no pl; ~spielertrick m (fig) sleight of hand no indef art, no pl; ~tuch nt handkerchief, hanky (inf); ~uhr f pocket watch; ~veitel m (Aus inf) siehe ~feitel; ~wörterbuch nt pocket dictionary.
Taschner, Täschner m -s, - bag-maker.
Tasmanien [-iən] nt -s Tasmania.
Tasmanier(in f) [tas'ma:niɐ, -ərın] m -s, - Tasmanian.
tasmanisch adj Tasmanian.
⚠**Täßchen** nt dim of Tasse (little) cup ◆ ein ~ Tee a quick cup of tea.
Tasse f -, -n cup; (mit Untertasse) cup and saucer; (Suppen~) bowl ◆ eine ~ Kaffee a cup of coffee; er hat nicht alle ~n im Schrank (inf) he's not all there (inf); eine trübe ~ (inf) a wet blanket (inf); hoch die ~n! (inf) bottoms up (inf).
Tastatur f keyboard.
tastbar adj palpable ◆ eine ~e Beule a bump you can feel.
Taste f -, -n key; (Knopf an Gerät auch) button ◆ in die ~n greifen (hum) to strike up a tune; auf die ~n hauen or hämmern (inf) to hammer away at the keyboard; „~ drücken" "push button".
Tast-: ~empfinden nt siehe ~sinn; ~empfindung f tactual sensation.
tasten [1] vi to feel ◆ nach etw ~ (lit, fig) to feel or grope for sth; vorsichtig ~d feeling or groping one's way carefully; ~de Schritte (lit, fig) tentative steps.
[2] vr to feel or grope one's way.
[3] vti (drücken) to press, to punch; Nummer auch to punch out; Telex etc to key; (Typ: setzen) to key(board).
Tasten-: ~feld nt (Comput) keypad, keys pl; ~instrument nt (Mus) keyboard instrument; ~telefon nt push-button telephone.
Taster m -s, - (a) (Zool) siehe Tastorgan. (b) (Typ: Tastatur) keyboard. (c) (Typ: Setzer) keyboard operator, keyboarder.
Tasterin f siehe Taster (c).
Tast-: ~organ nt organ of touch, tactile organ; ~sinn m sense of touch; ~werkzeug nt siehe ~organ; ~zirkel m (outside) callipers pl.
Tat f -, -en (das Handeln) action; (Einzel~ auch) act; (Helden~, Un~) deed; (Leistung) feat; (Verbrechen) crime ◆ ein Mann der ~ a man of action; keine Worte sondern ~en not words but deeds or actions; eine ~ der Verzweiflung/Nächstenliebe an act of desperation/charity; als er sah, was er mit dieser ~ angerichtet hatte when he saw what he had done by this; eine geschichtliche/verbrecherische ~ an historic/a criminal act or deed; eine gute/böse ~ a good/wicked deed; eine eindrucksvolle ~ vollbringen to do something impressive; Leben und ~en des ... the life and exploits of ...; etw in die ~ umsetzen to put sth into action; zur ~ schreiten to proceed to action; (hum) to get on with it; in der ~ indeed; (wider Erwarten, erstaunlicherweise etc) actually.
tat pret of tun.
Tatar[1] m -en, -en (Volksstamm) Tartar.
Tatar[2] nt -(s), no pl, **Tatarbeefsteak** nt steak tartare.
Tat-: ~bestand m (Jur) facts (of the case) pl; (Sachlage) facts (of the matter) pl; den ~bestand des Betrugs erfüllen (Jur) to constitute fraud; ~einheit f (Jur) commission of two or more offences in one act; in ~einheit mit concomitantly with.
Taten-: ~drang m thirst for action, energy; ~durst m (old, hum) thirst for action; t~durstig adj (old, hum) eager for action; t~froh adj (dated) enthusiastic; t~los adj idle; t~los herumstehen to stand idly by, to stand by and do nothing; wir mußten t~los zusehen we could only stand and watch.
Täter(in f) m -s, - culprit; (Jur) perpetrator (form) ◆ als ~ verdächtigt werden to be a suspect; als ~ in Frage kommen to be a possible suspect; nach dem ~ wird noch gefahndet the police are still searching for the person responsible or the person who committed the crime; wer war der ~? who did it?; unbekannte ~ person or persons unknown; jugendliche ~ young offenders.
Täterschaft f guilt ◆ die Frage (nach) der ~ (form) the question of who was responsible or of who committed the crime; die ~ leugnen/zugeben to deny/admit one's guilt; (vor Gericht) to plead innocent/guilty.
Tat-: ~form f (Gram) active (voice); t~froh adj siehe tatenfroh.
tätig adj (a) attr active ◆ dadurch hat er ~e Reue bewiesen he showed his repentance in a practical way; ~e Nächstenliebe practical charity; in einer Sache ~ werden (form) to take action in a matter.
(b) (arbeitend) ~ sein to work; als was sind Sie ~? what do you do?; er ist im Bankwesen ~ he's in banking.
tätigen vt (Comm) to conclude, to effect; Geschäft auch to transact; (geh) Einkäufe to carry out; (geh) Anruf to make.
Tätigkeit f activity; (Beschäftigung) occupation; (Arbeit) work; (Beruf) job ◆ während meiner ~ als Lehrer while I was working as a teacher; zur Zeit übt er eine andere ~ aus at present he's doing a different job; auf eine langjährige ~ zurückblicken to look back on many years of work; in ~ treten to come into operation; (Mensch) to act, to step in; in ~ sein (Maschine) to be operating or running; in/außer ~ setzen Maschine to set going or in motion/to stop; Alarmanlage to activate/to put out of action.
Tätigkeits-: ~bereich m field of activity; ~bericht m progress report; ~beschreibung f job description; ~form f (Gram) siehe Tatform; ~merkmale pl job characteristics pl; ~wort nt (Gram) verb.
Tätigung f siehe vt conclusion, effecting; transaction; carrying out; making.
Tat-: ~kraft f, no pl energy, vigour, drive; t~kräftig adj energetic; Hilfe active.
tätlich adj violent ◆ ~e Beleidigung (Jur) assault (and battery); ~ werden to become violent; gegen jdn ~ werden to assault sb; jdn ~ angreifen to attack sb physically, to assault sb.
Tätlichkeiten pl violence sing ◆ es kam zu ~ there was violence.
Tat-: ~mensch m man of action; ~motiv nt motive (for the crime); ~ort m scene of the crime.
tätowieren* vt to tattoo ◆ sich ~ lassen to have oneself tattooed.
Tätowierung f (a) no pl (das Tätowieren) tattooing. (b) (Darstellung) tattoo.
▼ **Tatsache** f fact ◆ ~ ist aber, daß ... but the fact of the matter or the truth is that ...; ~? (inf) really?, no!; das stimmt, ~! (inf) it's true, really; das ist ~ (inf) that's a fact; nackte ~n (inf) the hard facts; (hum) girlie pictures; jdn vor vollendete ~n stellen to present sb with a fait accompli; vor der vollendeten ~ stehen to be faced with a fait accompli; (unter) Vorspiegelung falscher ~n (under) false pretences.
Tatsachen-: ~bericht m documentary (report); ~material nt siehe

Faktenmaterial.
tatsächlich [1] *adj attr* real, actual.
[2] *adv* **(a)** (*in Wirklichkeit, objektiv*) actually, really, in fact ◆ **~ war es aber ganz anders** in (actual) fact *or* actually *or* really it was quite different.
(b) (*sage und schreibe*) really, actually ◆ **willst du das ~ tun?** are you really *or* actually going to do it?; **~?** really?; **~!** oh yes, so it/he *etc* is/was *etc*; **da kommt er! — ~!** he's coming! — so he is!
Tatsächlichkeit *f* (*geh*) actuality, fact.
tätscheln *vt* to pat.
tatschen *vi* (*pej inf*) **auf etw** (*acc*) **~** to paw sth.
Tattergreis *m* (*pej inf*) old dodderer, doddering old man (*pej*).
Tatterich *m* (*inf*): **den ~ haben/bekommen** to have/get the shakes (*inf*).
tatt(e)rig *adj* (*inf*) *Mensch* doddering, doddery; *Hände, Schriftzüge* shaky, quivery.
tatütata *interj* **~! die Feuerwehr ist da!** da-da-da-da! here comes the fire engine!
Tat-: ~verdacht *m* suspicion (*of having committed a crime*); **unter ~verdacht stehen** to be under suspicion; **t~verdächtig** *adj* suspected; **~verdächtige(r)** *mf* suspect; **~waffe** *f* weapon (used in the crime); (*bei Mord*) murder weapon.
Tatze *f* **-, -n** (*lit, fig*) paw ◆ **das ~ des Polizeiautos** the (wailing) siren of the police car.
Tat-: ~zeit *f* time of the incident *or* crime; **~zeuge** *m* witness (to the incident *or* crime).
Tau[1] *m* **-(e)s,** *no pl* dew ◆ **vor ~ und Tag** (*poet*) at break of day (*poet*).
Tau[2] *nt* **-(e)s, -e** (*Seil*) rope; (*Naut auch*) hawser.
taub *adj* deaf; *Glieder* numb; *Gestein* dead; *Metall* dull; *Ähre* unfruitful; *Nuß* empty ◆ **sich ~ stellen** to pretend not to hear; **gegen** *or* **für etw ~ sein** (*fig*) to be deaf to sth.
Täubchen *nt dim of* **Taube** ◆ **mein ~!** my little dove.
Taube *f* **-, -n (a)** (*Zool*) pigeon; (*Turtel~ auch*) dove ◆ **hier fliegen einem die gebratenen ~n nicht in den Mund** this isn't exactly the land of milk and honey. **(b)** (*fig, als Symbol*) dove ◆ **~n und Falken** (*Pol inf*) hawks and doves.
Tauben-: t~blau *adj* blue-grey; **~ei** *nt* pigeon's/dove's egg; **t~eigroß** *adj* the size of a golf ball/golf balls.
taubenetzt *adj* (*liter*) dewy, dew-covered.
Tauben-: t~grau *adj* dove grey; **~haus** *nt* dovecot(e); (*für Brieftauben*) pigeon loft; **~post** *f*: **mit der ~post** by pigeon post; **~schießen** *nt* (*Sport*) pigeon shooting; **~schlag** *m* **(a)** (*lit*) *siehe* **~haus**; **(b)** (*fig*) **hier geht es zu wie im ~schlag** it's like Waterloo Station here (*inf*); **~sport** *m* pigeon racing; **~zucht** *f* pigeon breeding *or* fancying.
Taube(r) *mf decl as adj* deaf person *or* man/woman *etc* ◆ **die ~n** the deaf.
Tauber, Täuber *m* **-s, -, Täuberich** *m* cock pigeon.
Taubheit *f* **(a)** deafness. **(b)** (*von Körperteil*) numbness.
Täubling *m* (*Bot*) russula (toadstool).
Taub-: ~nessel *f* deadnettle; **t~stumm** *adj* deaf and dumb, deaf-mute *attr*; **~stumme(r)** *mf* deaf-mute; **~stummheit** *f* deaf-muteness, deaf-mutism.
Tauchboot *nt siehe* **Unterseeboot.**
tauchen [1] *vi* **(a)** *aux haben or sein* to dive (*nach* for); (*als Sport auch*) to skin-dive; (*kurz ~*) to duck under; (*unter Wasser sein*) to stay under water; (*U-Boot auch*) to submerge.
(b) *aux sein* (*fig*) to disappear (*in +acc* into); (*aus etw auf~*) to emerge, to appear (*aus* out of, from); (*Boxen: abducken*) to duck ◆ **die Sonne tauchte langsam ins Meer/hinter den Horizont** the sun sank slowly into the sea/ beneath the horizon.
[2] *vt* (*kurz ~*) to dip; *Menschen, Kopf* to duck; (*ein~, bei Taufe*) to immerse ◆ **in Licht getaucht** (*geh*) bathed in light.
Tauchen *nt* **-s,** *no pl* diving; (*Sport~ auch*) skin-diving.
Taucher *m* **-s, -** diver.
Taucher-: ~anzug *m* diving suit; **~ausrüstung** *f* diving equipment *or* gear; **~brille** *f* diving goggles *pl*; **~flosse** *f* (diving) flipper; **~glocke** *f* diving bell; **~helm** *m* diving *or* diver's helmet.
Taucherin *f* diver.
Tauch-: ~maske *f* diving mask; **~sieder** *m* **-s, -** immersion coil (*for boiling water*); **~sport** *m* (skin-)diving; **~station** *f* **auf ~station gehen** (*U-Boot*) to dive; (*hum: in Schützengraben etc*) to duck, to get one's head down; (*fig: sich verstecken*) to make oneself scarce; **auf ~station sein** (*U-Boot*) to be submerged; **~tiefe** *f* depth; (*Naut: von Fluß*) navigable depth.
tauen[1] *vti* (*vi: aux haben or sein*) (*Eis, Schnee*) to melt, to thaw ◆ **es taut** it is thawing; **der Schnee taut von den Bergen/Dächern** the snow on the mountains/roofs is melting *or* thawing.
tauen[2] *vt* (*N Ger, Naut*) to tow.
Tau|ende *nt* (*Naut*) end of a piece of rope.
Tauf-: ~akt *m* baptism *or* christening (ceremony); **~becken** *nt* font; **~buch** *nt* baptismal register.
Taufe *f* **-, -n** baptism; (*christliche auch*) christening; (*Schiffs~*) launching (ceremony) ◆ **die ~ empfangen** to be baptized *or* christened; **jdm die ~ spenden** to baptize *or* christen sb; **ein Kind aus der ~ heben** (*old*) to stand sponsor to a child (*old*); **etw aus der ~ heben** (*hum*) *Verein* to start sth up; *Plan* to launch sth.
taufen *vt* to baptize; (*bei Äquatortaufe*) to duck; (*nennen*) *Kind, Schiff, Hund etc* to christen ◆ **sich ~ lassen** to be baptized; **jdn auf den Namen Rufus ~** to christen sb Rufus.
Täufer *m* **-s, -: Johannes der ~** John the Baptist; **die ~** (*Eccl*) the Baptists.
taufeucht *adj* dewy, wet with dew.

Tauf-: ~formel *f* baptism formula; **~gelübde** *nt* baptismal vows *pl*; **~kapelle** *f* baptistry; **~kleid** *nt* christening robe.
Täufling *m* child/person to be baptized.
Tauf-: ~name *m* Christian name; **~pate** *m* godfather; **~patin** *f* godmother; **~register** *nt* baptismal register.
taufrisch *adj* (*geh*) dewy; (*fig*) fresh; (*nicht müde*) sprightly.
Tauf-: ~schein *m* certificate of baptism; **~stein** *m* (baptismal) font; **~zeuge** *m* godparent.
taugen *vi* **(a)** (*geeignet sein*) to be suitable (*zu, für* for) ◆ **wozu soll denn das ~?** what is that supposed to be for?; **er taugt zu gar nichts** he is useless; **er taugt nicht zum Arzt** he wouldn't make a good doctor; **in der Schule taugt er nichts** he's useless *or* no good at school; **er taugt nicht zu harter Arbeit** he's not much good at hard work; (*wegen Faulheit*) he's not keen on hard work.
(b) (*wert sein*) **etwas/nicht viel** *or* **nichts ~** to be good *or* all right/to be not much good *or* no good *or* no use; **taugt der Neue etwas?** is the new bloke any good *or* use?; **der Bursche taugt nicht viel/gar nichts** that bloke is a (real) bad lot (*inf*); **als Mensch taugt er gar nichts** he is worthless as a person.
Taugenichts *m* **-(es), -e** (*dated*) good-for-nothing, ne'er-do-well (*old*).
tauglich *adj Kandidat, Bewerber, Material* suitable (*zu* for); (*Mil*) fit (*zu* for) ◆ **jdn für ~ erklären** (*Mil*) to declare *or* certify sb fit for service.
Tauglichkeit *f* suitability; (*Mil*) fitness (for service).
Tauglichkeitsgrad *m* (*Mil*) physical fitness rating (for military service).
Taumel *m* **-s,** *no pl* (*geh: Schwindel*) (attack of) dizziness *or* giddiness; (*liter: Rausch*) frenzy ◆ **im ~ der Ereignisse sein** (*liter*) to be caught up in the whirl of events; **im ~ des Glücks** (*liter*) in a transport of happiness (*liter*); **im ~ der Sinne** *or* **Leidenschaft** (*liter*) in the fever of his/her *etc* passion; **wie im ~** in a daze.
taum(e)lig *adj* dizzy, giddy.
taumeln *vi aux sein* to stagger; (*zur Seite*) to sway.
taumlig *adj siehe* **taum(e)lig.**
Tau-: ~perle *f* (*liter*) dewdrop; **~punkt** *m* dewpoint.
Tausch *m* **-(e)s, -e** exchange, swap; (*~ handel*) barter ◆ **im ~ gegen** *or* **für etw** in exchange for sth; **etw in ~ geben** to exchange *or* swap/barter sth; (*bei Neukauf*) to give in part-exchange; **jdm etw zum ~ für etw anbieten** to offer to exchange *or* swap sth for sth; **etw in ~ nehmen** to take sth in exchange; **einen guten/schlechten ~ machen** to get a good/bad deal.
tauschen [1] *vt* to exchange, to swap; *Güter* to barter; (*aus~*) *Briefmarken, Münzen etc* to swap; *Geld* to change (*in +acc* into); (*inf: um~*) *Gekauftes* to change ◆ **einen Blick mit jdm ~** (*geh*) to exchange glances with sb; **Küsse ~** (*geh*) to kiss; **wollen wir die Plätze ~?** shall we change *or* swap places?
[2] *vi* to swap; (*in Handel*) to barter; (*Geschenke aus~*) to exchange presents ◆ **wollen wir ~?** shall we swap (places *etc*)?; **wir haben getauscht** we swapped, we did a swap; **ich möchte nicht mit ihm ~** I wouldn't like to change places with him.
täuschen [1] *vt* to deceive; *Vertrauen* to betray ◆ **mit dieser Fälschung täuschte er sogar die Experten** he even deceived *or* fooled the experts with his forgery; **man kann ihn nicht ~** you can't fool him; **er wurde in seinen Erwartungen/Hoffnungen getäuscht** his expectations/hopes were disappointed; **wenn mich mein Gedächtnis nicht täuscht** if my memory serves me right; **wenn mich nicht alles täuscht** unless I'm completely wrong; **sie läßt sich leicht/nicht ~** she is easily/not easily fooled (*durch* by).
[2] *vr* to be wrong *or* mistaken (*in +dat, über +acc* about) ◆ **darin ~ Sie sich** you are mistaken there, that's where you're wrong; **dann hast du dich getäuscht!** then you are mistaken.
[3] *vi* **(a)** (*irreführen*) (*Aussehen etc*) to be deceptive; (*Sport*) to feint ◆ **das täuscht** that is deceptive.
(b) (*Sch form: betrügen*) to cheat.
täuschend [1] *adj Nachahmung* remarkable; *Ähnlichkeit auch* striking ◆ **eine ~e Ähnlichkeit mit jdm haben** to look remarkably like sb.
[2] *adv* **sich** (*dat*) **~ ähnlich sehen/sein** to look/be remarkably alike *or* almost identical; **jdm ~ ähnlich sehen** to look remarkably like sb, to be the spitting image of sb.
Täuscher *m* **-s, -** (*inf*) phoney (*inf*).
Tauscherei *f* (*inf*) exchanging, swapping.
Tausch-: ~geschäft *nt* exchange, swap; (*Handel*) barter (deal); **mit etw ein ~geschäft machen** to exchange/barter sth; **~gesellschaft** *f* barter society; **~handel** *m* barter; **~handel treiben** to barter; **~mittel** *nt* medium of exchange; **~objekt** *nt* barter *no pl*, barter object; **~partner** *m* **~partner für 2-Zimmer-Wohnung gesucht** exchange wanted for 2 room flat.
Täuschung *f* **(a)** (*das Täuschen*) deception ◆ **das tat er zur ~** he did that in order to deceive.
(b) (*Irrtum*) mistake, error; (*falsche Wahrnehmung*) illusion; (*Selbst~*) delusion ◆ **er gab sich einer ~** (*dat*) **hin** he was deluding himself; **darüber darf man sich keiner ~** (*dat*) **hingeben** one must not delude oneself (about that).
Täuschungs-: ~absicht *f* intention to deceive/of cheating; **~manöver** *nt* (*Sport*) feint; (*inf*) ploy; **~versuch** *m* attempted deception/cheating.
Tausch-: ~wert *m* (*Sociol*) exchange value, value in exchange; **~wirtschaft** *f* (*Sociol*) barter economy.
tausend *num* a *or* one thousand; **~ Dank/Grüße/Küsse** a thousand thanks/ greetings/kisses; *siehe auch* **hundert.**
Tausend[1] *f* **-, -en** (*Zahl*) thousand.
Tausend[2] *nt* **-s, -e** thousand ◆ **vom ~** in a *or* per thousand; **ei der ~!** (*obs*) zounds! (*obs*); *siehe auch* **Hundert**[2].
Tausend- *in cpds* a thousand; *siehe auch* **Hundert-.**
Tausender *m* **-s, - (a)** (*Zahl*) **ein ~** a figure in the thousands; **die ~** the

thousands. **(b)** *(Geldschein)* thousand (mark/dollar *etc* note *or* bill).

tausenderlei *adj inv* a thousand kinds of.

Tausend-: ~füßer *(form)*, **~füßler** *m* **-s, -** centipede; *(Zool auch)* millipede; **die ~füß(l)er** the myriapods *(spec)*; **~jahrfeier** *f* millenary; **t~jährig** *adj attr* thousand year old; *(t~ Jahre lang)* thousand year (long); **nach mehr als t~jähriger Unterdrückung** after more than a thousand years of oppression; **das t~jährige Reich** *(Bibl)* the millennium; **Hitlers „~jähriges Reich"** Hitler's "thousand-year empire"; **~künstler** *m* jack-of-all-trades; **t~mal** *adv* a thousand times; **ich bitte t~mal um Entschuldigung** a thousand pardons; **viel t~mal** *(old)* times without number; *siehe auch* **hundertmal**; **~sas(s)a** *m* **-s, -s** *(dated inf)* hell of a chap *(dated inf)*; **~schön** *nt* **-s, -e, ~schönchen** *nt* daisy.

Tausendstel *nt* **-s, -** thousandth; *siehe auch* **Hundertstel**.

tausendste(r, s) *adj* thousandth; *siehe auch* **hundertste(r, s)**.

Tausend-: t~undein(e, er, es) *adj* a thousand and one; **Märchen aus ~undeiner Nacht** Tales of the Thousand and One Nights, the Arabian Nights; **t~(und)eins** *num* one thousand and one.

Tautologie *f* tautology.

tautologisch *adj* tautological, tautologous.

Tau-: ~tropfen *m* dewdrop; **~werk** *nt, no pl (Naut)* rigging; **~wetter** *nt* thaw; *(fig auch)* relaxation; **wir haben** *or* **es ist ~wetter** it is thawing; **bei ~wetter** during a thaw, when it thaws; **es herrschte ein kulturelles/politisches ~wetter** there was a period of cultural/political relaxation; **~ziehen** *nt* **-s,** *no pl (lit, fig)* tug-of-war.

Taverne [ta'vɛrnə] *f* **-, -n** *(old)* tavern (old), inn; *(in Italien)* taverna.

Taxameter *m* **-s, -** taximeter, clock *(inf)*.

Taxator *m (Comm)* valuer.

Taxe *f* **-, -n (a)** *(Schätzung)* valuation, estimate. **(b)** *(Gebühr)* charge; *(Kur~ etc)* tax; *(Gebührenordnung)* scale of charges. **(c)** *(dial) siehe* **Taxi**.

Taxi *nt* **-s, -s** taxi, cab, taxicab *(form)* ◆ **sich** *(dat)* **ein ~ nehmen** to take a taxi, to go by taxi; **~ fahren** to drive a taxi; *(als Fahrgast)* to go by taxi.

Taxichauffeur *m* taxi *or* cab driver.

taxieren* *vt Preis, Wert* to estimate *(auf +acc* at); *Haus, Gemälde etc* to value *(auf +acc* at) ◆ **etw zu hoch ~** to overestimate/overvalue sth; **etw zu niedrig ~** to underestimate/undervalue sth; **er hat mich richtiggehend taxiert** he looked me up and down.

Taxi-: ~fahrer *m* taxi *or* cab driver, cabby *(inf)*; **~fahrt** *f* taxi ride; **~stand** *m* taxi rank.

Taxkurs *m* rate of taxation.

Taxler *m* **-s, -** *(Aus inf)* cabby *(inf)*.

Taxpreis *m* estimated price *(according to valuation)*.

Taxus *m* **-, -** yew(tree).

Taxwert *m* estimated value.

Tb(c) [te:(')be: ('tse:)] *f* **-, -s** *abbr of* **Tuberkulose** TB.

Tb(c)-krank [te:(')be:('tse:)-] *adj* **~ sein** to have TB; **die ~en Patienten** patients with TB, TB patients *or* cases.

Teakholz ['ti:k-] *nt* teak ◆ **ein Tisch aus ~** a teak table.

Team [ti:m] *nt* **-s, -s** team.

Team- ['ti:m-]: **~arbeit** *f* teamwork; **etw in ~arbeit machen** to do sth as a team *or* by teamwork; **das wird in ~arbeit gemacht** it's done by teamwork; **~leader** [-li:dɐ] *m (Sport: Aus, Sw) siehe* **Tabellenführer**; **~work** [-wə:k] *nt* **-s,** *no pl siehe* **~arbeit**.

Technetium [teç'ne:tsiʊm] *nt, no pl (abbr* **Tc**) technetium.

Technik *f* **(a)** *(no pl: Technologie)* technology; *(als Studienfach auch)* engineering ◆ **der Mensch und die ~** man and technology; **das Zeitalter der ~** the technological age, the age of technology; **verfluchte ~!** stupid technology!
(b) *(Arbeitsweise, Verfahren)* technique ◆ **jdn mit der ~ von etw vertraut machen** to familiarize sb with the techniques *or* skills of sth; **die ~ des Dramas/der Musik** dramatic/musical techniques.
(c) *(no pl: Funktionsweise und Aufbau) (von Auto, Motor etc)* mechanics *pl*.
(d) *(inf: technische Abteilung)* technical department, backroom boys *pl (inf)*.
(e) *(Aus inf: Technische Hochschule)* institute of technology.

Technika *pl of* **Technikum**.

technikbesessen *adj* obsessed with new technology.

Techniker(in *f*) *m* **-s, -** engineer; *(Beleuchtungs~, Labor~)* technician; *(fig: Fußballspieler, Künstler)* technician ◆ **ich bin kein ~, ich verstehe das nicht** I am not technically minded, I don't understand that; **er ist mehr Theoretiker als ~** he is more concerned with theoretical than practical matters.

technikfeindlich *adj* hostile to new technology, technophobic.

Technikum *nt* **-s, Technika** college of technology.

technisch *adj* **(a)** *(technologisch)* technological; *Studienfach* technical ◆ **T~e Hochschule/Universität** technological university, Institute of (Science and) Technology; **~e Chemie/Medizin** chemical/medical engineering; **er ist ~ begabt** he is technically minded; **das ~e Zeitalter** the technological age, the age of technology.
(b) *(die Ausführung betreffend) Schwierigkeiten, Gründe* technical; *(mechanisch)* mechanical ◆ **~er Zeichner** engineering draughtsman; **~er Leiter** technical director; **das ist ~ unmöglich** it is technically impossible; *(inf: das geht nicht)* it is absolutely impossible; **~e Einzelheiten** *(fig)* technicalities, technical details; **~e Daten** specifications.

technisieren* *vt* to mechanize.

Technisierung *f* mechanization.

Techno *m* **-** *no pl (Mus)* techno.

Technokrat(in *f*) *m* **-en, -en** technocrat.

Technokratie *f* technocracy.

technokratisch *adj* technocratic.

Technologe *m*, **Technologin** *f* technologist.

Technologie *f* technology.

Technologie-: ~park *m* technology park; **~transfer** *m* technology transfer; **~zentrum** *nt siehe* **~park.**

technologisch *adj* technological.

Techno-Musik *f* techno music.

Techno-Party *f* techno party.

Techtelmechtel *nt* **-s, -** *(inf)* affair, carry-on *(inf)* ◆ **ein ~ mit jdm haben** to be carrying on with sb *(inf)*.

Teckel *m* **-s, -** dachshund.

Teddy ['tɛdi] *m* **-s, -s (a)** *(auch* **~bär**) teddy (bear). **(b)** *(auch* **~stoff**) fur fabric.

Teddyfutter ['tɛdi-] *nt* fleecy *or* fur-fabric lining.

Tedeum [te'de:ʊm] *nt* **-s, -s** Te Deum.

TEE [te:|e:'|e:] *m* **-, -(s)** *(Rail) abbr of* **Trans-Europ(a)-Express.**

Tee *m* **-s, -s** tea ◆ **einen im ~ haben** *(inf)* to be tipsy *(inf)*; **einen ~ geben** *(dated)* to give a tea party.

Tee-: ~beutel *m* tea bag; **~blatt** *nt* tea-leaf; ⚠**~-Ei** *nt* (tea) infuser, tea ball *(esp US)*; **~gebäck** *nt, no pl* sweet biscuits *pl*; **~glas** *nt* tea-glass; **~haube** *f siehe* **~wärmer**; **~haus** *nt* tea-house; **~kanne** *f* teapot; **~kessel** *m* **(a)** kettle; **(b)** *(Gesellschaftsspiel) guessing-game based on puns*; **~licht** *nt* night-light; **~löffel** *m* teaspoon; *(Menge)* teaspoonful; **t~löffelweise** *adv* by the teaspoonful; **~maschine** *f* tea-urn; **~mischung** *f* blend of tea.

Teen [ti:n] *m* **-s, -s** *(Press sl)* teenager.

Teenager ['ti:ne:dʒɐ] *m* **-s, -** teenager.

Teenetz *nt* tea filter.

Teeny ['ti:ni:] *m* **-, Teenies** *(inf)* teeny bopper *(inf)*.

Teepause *f* tea break.

Teer *m* **-(e)s, -e** tar.

Teer-: ~(dach)pappe *f* (bituminous) roofing felt; **~decke** *f* tarred (road) surface.

teeren *vt* to tar ◆ **~ und federn** to tar and feather.

Teer-: ~farben, ~farbstoffe *pl* aniline dyes *pl*; **~gehalt** *m* tar content; **t~haltig** *adj* **eine wenig/stark t~haltige Zigarette** a low/high tar cigarette; **t~haltig sein** to contain tar.

Teerose *f* tea-rose.

Teer-: ~pappe *f siehe* **~(dach)pappe**; **~straße** *f* tarred road.

Teerung *f* tarring.

Tee-: ~service *nt* tea-set; **~sieb** *nt* tea-strainer; **~sorte** *f* (type *or* sort of) tea; **~strauch** *m* tea bush; **~strumpf** *m* tea filter; **~stube** *f* tea-room; **~stunde** *f* afternoon tea (time); **~tasse** *f* teacup; **~wagen** *m* tea-trolley; **~wärmer** *m* **-s, -** tea-cosy; **~wurst** *f smoked German sausage for spreading.*

Teflon ® *nt* **-s** teflon.

Teheran ['te:həra:n, tehə'ra:n] *nt* **-s** Teh(e)ran.

Teich *m* **-(e)s, -e** pond ◆ **der große ~** *(dated inf)* the (herring) pond *(hum)*.

Teich-: ~molch *m* smooth newt; **~rose** *f* yellow water-lily.

Teig *m* **-(e)s, -e** *(Hefe~, Knet~, Nudel~)* dough; *(Mürb~, Blätter~ etc)* pastry; *(Pfannkuchen~)* batter; *(esp in Rezepten auch)* mixture.

teigig *adj* doughy; *(voller Teig) Hände* covered in dough/pastry.

Teig-: ~masse *f (Cook)* dough/pastry/batter/mixture; **~waren** *pl (Nudeln)* pasta *sing*.

Teil¹ *m* **-(e)s, -e (a)** part; *(von Strecke auch)* stretch; *(von Stadt auch)* district, area; *(von Gebäude auch)* area, section; *(von Zeitung)* section ◆ **der Bau/das Projekt ist zum ~ fertig** the building/project is partly finished; **wir hörten zum ~ interessante Reden** some of the speeches we heard were interesting; **zum ~ ..., zum ~ ...** partly ..., partly ...; **zum großen/größten ~** for the most part, mostly; **er hat die Bücher darüber zum großen/größten ~ gelesen** he has read many/most of the books about that; **die Studenten wohnen zum größten ~ bei ihren Eltern** for the most part the students live with their parents; **der größere ~ ihres Einkommens** the bulk of her income; **ein großer ~ stimmte dagegen** a large number (of people) voted against it; **der dritte/vierte/fünfte** *etc* **~** a third, a quarter, a fifth *etc (von* of); **in zwei ~e zerbrechen** to break in two *or* half.
(b) *(Jur: Partei, Seite)* party.
(c) *(auch nt: An~)* share ◆ **ein gut ~ Arbeit/Frechheit/der Leute** *(dated)* quite a bit of work/cheek/many *or* a lot of people; **zu gleichen ~en erben/beitragen** to get an equal share of an inheritance/to make an equal contribution; **er hat seinen ~ dazu beigetragen** he did his bit *or* share; **er hat sein(en) ~ bekommen** *or* **weg** *(inf)* he has (already) had his due; **sich** *(dat)* **sein(en) ~ denken** *(inf)* to draw one's own conclusions.
(d) *(auch nt)* **ich für mein(en) ~** for my part, I ..., I, for my part ...

Teil² *nt* **-(e)s, -e (a)** part; *(Bestand~ auch)* component; *(Ersatz~)* spare, (spare) part; *(sl: großer Gegenstand)* thing ◆ **etw in seine ~e zerlegen** *Tier, Leiche* to cut sth up; *Motor, Möbel etc* to take sth apart *or* to bits *or* to pieces; **... das waren vielleicht ~e** *(sl)* ... they were real whoppers *(inf)*.
(b) *siehe* **Teil¹ (c, d).**

Teil-: ~abkommen *nt* partial agreement/treaty; **~ansicht** *f* partial view; **~aspekt** *m* aspect, part; **t~bar** *adj* divisible, which can be divided *(durch* by); **~barkeit** *f* divisibility; **~bereich** *m* part; *(in Abteilung)* section; **~betrag** *m* part (of an amount); *(auf Rechnung)* item; *(Rate)* instalment; *(Zwischensumme)* subtotal.

Teilchen *nt* particle; *(dial: Gebäckstück)* cake.

Teilchen-: ~beschleuniger *m (Phys)* particle accelerator; **~physik** *f* particle physics *sing*.

⚠: Informationen zur Rechtschreibreform im Anhang

Teilefertigung *f (Ind)* manufacture of parts *or* components.
teilen [1] *vt* **(a)** *(zerlegen, trennen)* to divide (up); *(Math)* to divide *(durch* by) ◆ **27 läßt sich durch 9 ~** 27 can be divided by 9; **der Fluß teilt das Land in der Mitte** the river divides the country down the middle; **(politisch) geteilter Meinung sein** to have different (political) opinions; **darüber sind die Meinungen geteilt** opinions differ on that; **darüber kann man geteilter Meinung sein** one can disagree about that; **etw in drei Teile ~** to divide sth in(to) three (parts); **das Schiff teilte die Wellen** *or* **Wogen** *(liter)* the ship forged its way through the waves.
(b) *(auf~)* to share (out) *(unter +dat* amongst) ◆ **etw mit jdm ~** to share sth with sb.
(c) *(an etw teilhaben)* to share ◆ **sie haben Freud und Leid miteinander geteilt** they shared the rough and the smooth; **geteilte Freude ist doppelte Freude** *(prov)* a joy shared is a joy doubled *(prov)*; **geteilter Schmerz ist halber Schmerz** *(prov)* a trouble shared is a trouble halved *(prov)*; **sie teilten unser Schicksal** *or* **Los** they shared the same fate as us.
[2] *vr* **(a)** *(in Gruppen)* to split up.
(b) *(Straße, Fluß)* to fork, to divide; *(Vorhang)* to part.
(c) sich *(dat)* **etw ~** to share *or* split sth; **teilt euch das!** share *or* split that between you; **sich in etw** *(acc)* **~** *(geh)* to share sth.
(d) *(fig: auseinandergehen)* **in diesem Punkt ~ sich die Meinungen** opinion is divided on this.
[3] *vi* to share ◆ **er teilt nicht gern** he doesn't like sharing.
Teiler *m* **-s, -** *(Math)* factor.
Teil-: ~erfolg *m* partial success; **~ergebnis** *nt* partial result; **einige ~ergebnisse sind schon bekannt** we already know some of the results; **~errichtungsgenehmigung** *f* restricted planning permission; **~fabrikat** *nt* component; **~frage** *f* part (of a question); **~gebiet** *nt* **(a)** *(Bereich)* branch; **(b)** *(räumlich)* area; **~genehmigung** *f* partial permission; **~habe** *f (liter)* participation, sharing *(an +dat* in); *(esp an Gott)* communion *(an +dat* with); **t~haben** *vi sep irreg (geh) (an +dat* in) *(mitwirken)* to have a part, to participate; *(liter: t~nehmen)* to share; **~haber(in** *f***)** *m* **-s, -** *(Comm)* partner; **~haberschaft** *f (Comm)* partnership; **t~haftig** *adj (old)* **eines großen Glücks/einer großen Ehre t~haftig werden** to be blessed with great good fortune/a great honour *(liter)*.
-teilig *adj suf* -piece.
Teilkasko-: t~versichert *adj insured with ~versicherung*; **~versicherung** *f* third party, fire and theft.
Teil-: ~menge *f (Math)* subset; **t~möbliert** *adj* partially furnished.
Teilnahme *f* **-,** *no pl* **(a)** *(Anwesenheit)* attendance *(an +dat* at); *(Beteiligung an Wettbewerb etc)* participation *(an +dat* in) ◆ **jdn zur ~ an etw** *(dat)* **aufrufen** to urge sb to take part *or* participate in sth; **~ am Straßenverkehr** *(form)* road use.
(b) *(Interesse)* interest *(an +dat* in); *(Mitgefühl)* sympathy ◆ **jdm seine herzliche/aufrichtige ~ aussprechen** to offer sb one's heartfelt condolences.
Teilnahme-: t~berechtigt *adj* eligible; **~berechtigung** *f* eligibility; **von der ~berechtigung ausgeschlossen sein** to be ineligible, not to be eligible.
Teilnahms-: t~los *adj (gleichgültig)* indifferent, apathetic; *(stumm leidend)* listless; **~losigkeit** *f siehe adj* indifference, apathy; listlessness; **t~voll** *adj* compassionate, sympathetic.
teilnehmen *vi sep irreg* **(a) an etw** *(dat)* **~** *(sich beteiligen)* to take part *or* participate in sth; *(anwesend sein)* to attend sth; *an Wettkampf, Preisausschreiben etc* to take part in sth, to enter sth, to go in for sth; *an Wettkampf auch* to compete in sth; *an Gespräch auch* to join in sth; **er hat nicht teilgenommen** he did not take part *etc*; **an einem Ausflug ~** to go on an outing; **am Krieg ~** to fight in the war; **am Unterricht ~** to attend school; **an einem Kurs ~** to do a course.
(b) *(Anteil nehmen)* to share *(an +dat* in).
teilnehmend *adj* compassionate, sympathetic ◆ **~e Beobachtung** *(Sociol)* participatory observation.
Teilnehmer(in *f***)** *m* **-s, - (a)** *(Beteiligter bei Kongreß etc)* participant; *(Kriegs~)* combatant; *(bei Wettbewerb, Preisausschreiben etc)* competitor, contestant; *(Kurs~)* student; *(bei Ausflug etc)* member of a party ◆ **alle ~ an dem Ausflug** all those going on the outing. **(b)** *(Telec)* subscriber ◆ **der ~ meldet sich nicht** there is no reply.
Teilnehmerzahl *f* attendance.
Teilperücke *f* toupee; *(für Damen)* hair-piece.
teils *adv* partly ◆ **~ ... ~ ...** partly ... partly ...; *(inf: sowohl ... als auch)* both ... and ...; **die Demonstranten waren ~ Arbeiter, ~ Studenten** some of the demonstrators were workers and the others were students; **~ heiter, ~ wolkig** cloudy with sunny periods; **~, ~** *(als Antwort)* half and half; *(inf)* sort of *(inf)*; **wie geht es dir? — ~, ~** how are you? — so-so.
Teil-: ~schuldverschreibung *f (Fin)* bond (forming part of a loan issue); **~staat** *m* region, state; **~strecke** *f* stretch (of road/railway *etc*); *(bei Reise)* stage; *(bei Rennen)* leg, stage; *(bei öffentlichen Verkehrsmitteln)* (fare-)stage; **~strich** *m* secondary graduation line; **~stück** *nt* part; *(~strecke auch)* stretch.
Teilung *f* division.
Teilungs|artikel *m (Gram)* partitive article.
Teilverlust *m* partial loss.
teilweise [1] *adv* partly; *(manchmal)* sometimes ◆ **nicht alle Schüler sind so faul, ~ sind sie sehr interessiert** not all the pupils are so lazy, some of them are very interested; **der Film war ~ gut** the film was good in parts; **~ bewölkt** cloudy in parts; **morgen tritt ~ eine Wetterbesserung ein** there will be a partial improvement in the weather tomorrow.
[2] *adj attr* partial.
Teil-: ~zahlung *f* hire-purchase; *(Rate)* instalment; **auf ~zahlung** on hire-purchase; **~zahlungspreis** *m* hire-purchase price.
Teilzeit-: ~arbeit *f* part-time job/work; **t~beschäftigt** *adj* employed part-time; **~beschäftigung** *f siehe* **~arbeit**; **~kraft** *f* part-time worker.
Teint [tɛ̃:] *m* **-s, -s** complexion.
T-Eisen ['te:-] *nt* t- *or* tee-iron.
Tektonik *f (Archit, Geol)* tectonics *pl*.
tektonisch *adj* tectonic.
Tel. *abbr of* **Telefon.**
Tele-: ~arbeit *f* telecommuting, teleworking; **~arbeiter(in** *f***)** *m* telecommuter, teleworker; **~arbeitsplatz** *f* job for telecommuters *or* teleworkers; **~brief** *m* telemessage, mailgram *(US)*; **~fax** *nt (Kopie, Gerät)* fax; **t~faxen** *vti insep* to fax; **~faxgerät** *nt* fax machine; **~fax-Teilnehmer** *m* fax subscriber.
Telefon [tele'fo:n, 'te:lefo:n] *nt* **-s, -e** (tele)phone ◆ **am ~ (verlangt werden)** (to be wanted) on the phone; **~ haben** to be on the phone; **jdn ans ~ rufen** to get sb (to come) to the phone; **ans ~ gehen** to answer the phone.
Telefon- *in cpds* (tele)phone; *siehe auch* **Fernsprech-**; **~anruf** *m* (tele)phone call; **~ansage** *f* telephone information service; **~apparat** *m* telephone.
Telefonat *nt* (tele)phone call.
Telefon-: ~auskunft *f* directory enquiries *pl*, information *(US)*; **~banking** *nt* **-s** telephone banking; **~buch** *nt* (tele)phone book; **~draht** *m* telephone line; **~gebühr** *f* call charge; *(Grundgebühr)* telephone rental; **~gespräch** *nt* (tele)phone call; *(Unterhaltung)* telephone conversation; ⚠**~hauptanschluß** *m* telephone line; **~häuschen** *nt (inf)* phone box *(Brit) or* booth.
telefonieren* [1] *vi* to make a (tele)phone call ◆ **wir haben stundenlang telefoniert** we talked *or* were on the phone for hours; **bei jdm ~** to use sb's phone; **es wird entschieden zuviel telefoniert** the phones are definitely used too much; **ins Ausland/nach Amerika/Hamburg ~** to make an international call/to call America/Hamburg; **er telefoniert den ganzen Tag** he is on the phone all day long; **mit jdm ~** to speak to sb on the phone.
[2] *vt (inf, Sw)* to phone, to ring (up), to call ◆ **jdm etw ~** to call *or* phone and tell sb sth.
telefonisch *adj* telephonic ◆ **~e Auskunft/Beratung** telephone information/advice service; **eine ~e Mitteilung** a (tele)phone message; **jdm etw ~ mitteilen** to tell sb sth over the phone; **er hat sich ~ entschuldigt** he phoned to apologize; **ich bin ~ erreichbar** *or* **zu erreichen** I can be contacted by phone; **die ~e Zeitangabe** the Speaking Clock.
Telefonist(in *f***)** *m* telephonist; *(in Betrieb auch)* switchboard operator.
Telefonitis *f* **-,** *no pl (hum inf)* **die ~ haben** to be telephone-mad *(inf)*.
Telefon-: ~karte *f* phonecard; **~konferenz** *f* telephone conference; **~kunde** *m* telephone customer; **~leitung** *f* telephone line; **~netz** *nt* telephone network; **~nummer** *f* (tele)phone number; **~rechnung** *f* (tele)phone bill; **~satellit** *m* telecommunications satellite; **~seelsorge** *f* ≃ Samaritans *pl*; **~sex** *n* telephone sex; **~überwachung** *f* telephone tapping; **~verbindung** *f* telephone line; *(zwischen Orten)* telephone link; *siehe auch* **Verbindung (c)**; **~verstärker** *m* telephone amplifier; **~verzeichnis** *nt* telephone directory; **~zelle** *f* (tele)phone box *(Brit) or* booth; **~zentrale** *f* (telephone) switchboard.
telegen *adj* telegenic.
Telegraf *m* **-en, -en** telegraph.
Telegrafen-: ~amt *nt* telegraph office; **~apparat** *m* telegraph; **~büro** *nt (dated)* news agency; **~mast** *m* telegraph pole.
Telegrafie *f* telegraphy.
telegrafieren* *vti* to telegram, to cable, to wire.
telegrafisch *adj* telegraphic ◆ **jdm ~ Geld überweisen** to wire sb money.
Telegramm *nt* **-s, -e** telegram; *(Auslands~ auch)* cable.
Telegramm-: ~adresse *f* telegraphic address; **~bote** *m* telegram boy; **~formular** *nt* telegram form; **~stil** *m* staccato *or* telegram style, telegraphese.
⚠**Telegraph** *m siehe* **Telegraf.**
⚠**Telegraphen-** *in cpds siehe* **Telegrafen-.**
⚠**Telegraphie** *f siehe* **Telegrafie.**
⚠**telegraphieren*** *vti siehe* **telegrafieren.**
⚠**telegraphisch** *adj siehe* **telegrafisch.**
Tele- ['tele-]: **~kinese** *f* **-,** *no pl* telekinesis; **t~kinetisch** *adj* telekinetic; **≈kolleg** *nt* ≃ Open University *(Brit)*; **≈kommunikation** *f* telecommunications *pl or (als Fachgebiet) sing.*
Telekom *f* **- die ~** *German telecommunications service.*
Tele-: ≈kopie *f* fax; **≈kopierer** *m* fax machine.
Telemark *m* **-s, -s** *(Ski)* telemark.
Tele|objektiv *nt (Phot)* telephoto lens.
Teleologie *f (Philos)* teleology.
teleologisch *adj (Philos)* teleological.
Tele|ordern *nt* **-s,** *no pl* teleordering.
Telepath(in *f***)** *m* **-en, -en** telepathist.
Telepathie *f* telepathy.
telepathisch *adj* telepathic.
Telephon *nt* **-s, -e, Telephon-** *in cpds siehe* **Telefon, Telefon-.**
Teleprompter *m* **-s, -** autocue.
Teleshopping ['teliʃɔpiŋ] *nt* teleshopping.
Teleskop *nt* **-s, -e** telescope.
Teleskop|auge *nt* telescope eye.

⚠: for details of spelling reform, see supplement

teleskopisch *adj* telescopic.
Tele-: **≈spiel** *nt* video game; **≈tex** *nt* **-,** *no pl* teletex; **~vision** [televi'zio:n] *f siehe* **Fernsehen.**
Telex *nt* **-, -e** telex.
⚠ **Telex|anschluß** *m* telex link.
telexen *vti* to telex.
Teller *m* **-s, -** **(a)** plate ♦ **ein ~ Suppe** a plate of soup. **(b)** (*sl: Platten~*) turntable. **(c)** (*Ski*) basket.
Teller-: **~eisen** *nt* (*Hunt*) steel trap; **t~förmig** *adj* plate-shaped; **~gericht** *nt* (*Cook*) one-course meal; **~mine** *f* (*Mil*) flat anti-tank mine; **~rand** *m* rim *or* edge of a/the plate; **nicht zum Blick über den ~rand fähig sein** (*fig*) to be unable to see beyond the end of one's own nose; **~wärmer** *m* **-s, -** plate warmer; **~wäscher** *m* dishwasher.
Tellur *nt* **-s,** *no pl* (*abbr* **Te**) tellurium.
Tempel *m* **-s, -** temple (*auch fig*).
Tempel-: **~bau** *m* (*Gebäude*) temple; **~herr, ~ritter** *m* (*Hist*) (Knight) Templar; **~schändung** *f* desecration of a temple; **~tanz** *m* temple dance; **~tänzerin** *f* temple dancer.
Tempera-: **~(farbe)** *f* tempera (colour); **~malerei** *f* (*Maltechnik*) painting in tempera; (*Gemälde*) tempera painting(s).
Temperament *nt* **(a)** (*Wesensart*) temperament ♦ **die vier ~e** (*old*) the four humours (*old*); **ein hitziges ~ haben** to be hot-tempered. **(b)** *no pl* (*Lebhaftigkeit*) vitality, vivacity ♦ **viel/kein ~ haben** to be very/not to be vivacious *or* lively; **sein ~ ist mit ihm durchgegangen** he lost his temper; **sie konnte ihr ~ nicht mehr zügeln** she could control herself *or* her temper no longer.
Temperament-: **t~los** *adj* lifeless, spiritless; **~losigkeit** *f* lifelessness, spiritlessness.
Temperaments|ausbruch *m* temperamental fit *or* outburst.
temperamentvoll *adj* vivacious, lively; *Aufführung auch* spirited; *Auto, Fahrer* nippy (*inf*) ♦ **ein Lied ~ vortragen** to give a spirited rendering of a song.
Temperatur *f* temperature ♦ **erhöhte ~ haben** to have a *or* be running a temperature; **die ~en sind angestiegen/gesunken** the temperature has risen/fallen; **bei diesen/solchen ~en** in these/such temperatures.
Temperatur-: **~abfall** *m* drop *or* fall in temperature; **~anstieg** *m* rise in temperature; **~regler** *m* thermostat; **~rückgang** *m* fall in temperature; **~schwankung** *f* variation in temperature; **~skala** *f* temperature scale; **~sturz** *m* sudden drop *or* fall in temperature.
Temperenzler(in *f*) *m* **-s, -** member of a/the temperance league.
temperieren* *vt* **etw ~** (*auf die richtige Temperatur bringen*) to make sth the right temperature; (*anwärmen*) to warm sth up; **der Raum ist angenehm temperiert** the room is at a pleasant temperature *or* is pleasantly warm; **Rotwein leicht temperiert trinken** to drink red wine at room temperature.
Templer *m* **-s, -** Templar.
Templer|orden *m* Order of the Knights Templar.
Tempo *nt* **-s, -s** **(a)** (*Geschwindigkeit*) speed; (*Arbeits~, Schritt~ auch*) pace ♦ **~!** (*inf*) hurry up!; **bei jdm ~ dahintermachen/hinter etw** (*acc*) **machen** (*inf*) to make sb get a move on (with sth) (*inf*); **nun mach mal ein bißchen ~!** (*inf*) get a move on! (*inf*); **~ 100** speed limit (of) 100 km/h; **mit vollem/hohem ~** at full/a high speed; **im ~ zulegen/nachlassen** to speed up/slow down.
(b) (*Mus*) *pl* **Tempi** tempo ♦ **das ~ einhalten** to keep time; **das ~ angeben** to set the tempo; (*fig*) to set the pace.
(c) ® (*inf: Taschentuch*) paper handkerchief, tissue, Kleenex ®.
Tempo-30-Zone *f area with 30kph speed limit.*
Tempolimit *nt* speed limit.
Tempora *pl of* **Tempus.**
temporal *adj* (*Gram*) temporal.
Temporalsatz *m* temporal clause.
temporär *adj* (*geh*) temporary.
Tempo-: **~sünder** *m* person caught for speeding; **~überschreitung** *f* speeding.
Tempus *nt* **-, Tempora** (*Gram*) tense.
Tendenz *f* trend (*auch St Ex*); (*Neigung*) tendency; (*Absicht*) intention; (*no pl: Parteilichkeit*) bias, slant ♦ **die ~ haben, zu ...** to tend to ..., to have a tendency to ...; **die ~ zeigen, zu ...** to show a tendency to ...; **er hat nationalistische ~en** he has nationalist leanings.
tendenziell *adj* **eine ~e Veränderung** a change in direction; **~ ist Ruritanien ein faschistischer Staat** Ruritania is a country which shows fascist tendencies; **die Ziele der beiden Parteien unterscheiden sich ~ kaum voneinander** the aims of the two parties are broadly similar (in direction).
tendenziös *adj* tendentious.
Tendenz-: **~stück** *nt* tendentious play; **~wende** *f* change of direction; (*Wendepunkt*) turning point.
Tender *m* **-s, -** (*Naut, Rail*) tender.
tendieren* *vi* **(a)** (*Fin, St Ex*) to tend.
(b) dazu ~, etw zu tun (*neigen*) to tend to do sth; (*beabsichtigen*) to be moving towards doing sth; **zum Kommunismus/Katholizismus ~** to have leanings towards communism/Catholicism, to have communist/Catholic leanings *or* tendencies; **zu Erkältungen/Wutausbrüchen ~** to tend to have colds/fits of anger; **seine Begabung tendiert mehr ins Künstlerische** his talents tend more towards the artistic.
Teneriffa *nt* **-s** Tenerife.
Tenne *f* **-, -n, Tenn** *m* **-s, -e** (*Sw*) threshing floor.
Tennis *nt* **-,** *no pl* tennis.
Tennis- *in cpds* tennis; **~halle** *f* indoor tennis centre; **~platz** *m* tennis court; **~schläger** *m* tennis racquet; **~schuh** *m* tennis shoe.
Tenno *m* **-s, -s** Emperor of Japan.
Tenor[1] *m* **-s,** *no pl* tenor.
Tenor[2] *m* **-s, ¨-e** (*Mus*) tenor.
Tenorist *m* tenor (singer).
Tenorschlüssel *m* tenor clef.
Tensid *nt* **-(e)s, -e** (*Chem*) surfactant.
Tentakel *m or nt* **-s, -** tentacle.
Tenuis ['te:nuɪs] *f* **-, Tenues** ['te:nue:s] (*Phon*) tenuis.
Teppich *m* **-s, -e** **(a)** carpet (*auch fig*); (*Gobelin*) tapestry; (*inf: Wandbehang*) wall-hanging; (*inf: Brücke auch*) rug; (*Öl~*) slick ♦ **etw unter den ~ kehren** *or* **fegen** (*lit, fig*) to sweep sth under the carpet; **bleib auf dem ~!** (*inf*) be realistic!, be reasonable!; **den roten ~ ausrollen** to bring out the red carpet.
(b) (*dial inf*) *siehe* **Decke.**
Teppich-: **~boden** *m* carpet(ing); **das Zimmer ist mit ~boden ausgelegt** the room has wall-to-wall carpeting; **~fliese** *f* carpet tile; **~kehrer** *m* **-s, -,** **~kehrmaschine** *f* carpet-sweeper; **~klopfer** *m* carpet-beater; **~reinigung** *f* carpet cleaning/cleaner's; **~schnee** *m* carpet foam; **~stange** *f frame for hanging carpets over for beating.*
Terbium *nt, no pl* (*abbr* **Tb**) terbium.
Term *m* **-s, -e** (*Math, Phys, Ling*) term.
Termin *m* **-s, -e** date; (*für Fertigstellung*) deadline; (*Comm: Liefertag*) delivery date; (*bei Arzt, Besprechung etc*) appointment; (*Sport*) fixture; (*Jur: Verhandlung*) hearing ♦ **der letzte ~** the deadline, the last date; (*bei Bewerbung etc*) the closing date; **sich** (*dat*) **einen ~ geben lassen** to make an appointment; **schon einen anderen ~ haben** to have a prior engagement.
Terminal ['tø:ɐminəl, 'tœr-] *nt or m* **-s, -s** terminal.
Termin-: **~börse** *f* futures market, forward exchange; **~einlage** *f* (*Fin*) time deposit; **~geld** *nt* fixed-term deposit; **t~gemäß, t~gerecht** *adj* on schedule, according to schedule; **~geschäft** *nt* deal on the forward market; **~geschäfte** futures.
Termini *pl of* **Terminus.**
Terminkalender *m* (appointments *or* engagements) diary.
terminlich *adj* **etw ~ einrichten** to fit sth in (to one's schedule); **~e Verpflichtungen** commitments; **ich habe schon zu viele ~e Verpflichtungen** I have too many prior commitments.
Terminmarkt *m* (*St Ex*) forward *or* futures market.
terminmäßig *adj siehe* **terminlich.**
Terminologie *f* terminology.
terminologisch *adj* terminological.
Termin-: **~planung** *f* time scheduling; **~schwierigkeiten** *pl* scheduling difficulties *pl.*
Terminus *m* **-, Termini** term ♦ **~ technicus** technical term.
Termite *f* **-, -n** termite, white ant.
Termiten-: **~hügel** *m* termites' nest, termitarium (*form*); **~staat** *m* colony of termites.
Terpene *pl* terpenes *pl.*
Terpentin *nt or* (*Aus*) *m* **-s, -e** turpentine; (*inf: ~öl*) turps (*inf*).
Terpentin|öl *nt* oil of turpentine, turps (*inf*).
Terrain [tɛ'rɛ̃:] *nt* **-s, -s** land, terrain; (*fig*) territory ♦ **das ~ sondieren** (*Mil*) to reconnoitre the terrain; (*fig*) to see how the land lies; **sich auf neuem ~ bewegen** to be exploring new ground; **sich auf unsicheres ~ begeben** to get onto shaky ground.
Terrakotta *f* **-, Terrakotten** terracotta.
Terrarium *nt* terrarium.
Terrasse *f* **-, -n** **(a)** (*Geog*) terrace. **(b)** (*Veranda*) terrace, patio; (*Dach~*) roof garden.
Terrassen-: **t~artig, t~förmig** [1] *adj* terraced; [2] *adv* in terraces; **~garten** *m* terraced garden; **~haus** *nt house built on a terraced slope;* (*modern*) split-level house.
Terrazzo *m* **-s, Terrazzi** terrazzo.
terrestrisch *adj* terrestrial.
Terrier ['tɛriɐ] *m* **-s, -** terrier.
Terrine *f* tureen.
territorial *adj* territorial.
Territorial-: **~armee** *f* territorial army; **~gewässer** *pl* territorial waters *pl*; **~hoheit** *f* territorial sovereignty.
Territorium *nt* territory.
Terror *m* **-s,** *no pl* terror; (*Terrorismus*) terrorism; (*~herrschaft*) reign of terror; (*brutale Einschüchterung*) intimidation; (*Belästigung*) menace ♦ **die Stadt steht unter dem ~ der Mafia** the town is being terrorized by the Mafia; **blutiger ~** terrorism and bloodshed; **organisierter ~** organized terrorism/intimidation; **~ machen** (*inf*) to raise hell (*inf*).
Terror-: **~akt** *m* act of terrorism, terrorist act; **~angriff** *m* terrorist raid; **~anschlag** *m* terrorist attack; **~herrschaft** *f* reign of terror.
terrorisieren* *vt* to terrorize; *Untergebene etc auch* to intimidate.
Terrorismus *m* terrorism.
Terrorismus-: **~bekämpfung** *f* counterterrorism; **~experte** *m* expert on terrorism.
Terrorist(in *f*) *m* terrorist.
terroristisch *adj* terrorist *attr.*
Terror-: **~justiz** *f* brutal, intimidatory justice; **~organisation** *f* terrorist organization.
Tertia ['tɛrtsia] *f* **-, Tertien** ['tɛrtsiən] **(a)** (*Sch*) (*Unter-/Ober~*) *fourth/fifth year*

of German secondary school. **(b)** *no pl* (*Typ*) 16 point type.

Tertianer(in *f*) [tertsi'a:nɐ, -ərɪn] *m* **-s, -** (*Sch*) *pupil in fourth/fifth year of German secondary school.*

Tertiär [tɛr'tsiɛ:ɐ] *nt* **-s,** no pl (*Geol*) tertiary period.

tertiär [tɛr'tsiɛ:ɐ] *adj* tertiary.

Tertiärbereich [tɛr'tsiɛ:ɐ-] *m* tertiary education.

Tertien *pl of* **Tertia.**

Terz *f* **-, -en** (*Mus*) third; (*Fechten*) tierce ◆ **große/kleine ~** (*Mus*) major/minor third.

Terzett *nt* **-(e)s, -e** (*Mus*) trio.

Terzine *f* (*Poet*) tercet.

Tesafilm ® *m* Sellotape ® (*Brit*), Scotch tape ® (*esp US*).

Tessin *nt* **-s das ~** Ticino.

Test *m* **-(e)s, -s** *or* **-e** test.

Testament *nt* **(a)** (*Jur*) will; (*fig*) legacy ◆ **das ~ eröffnen** to read the will; **sein ~ machen** to make one's will; **du kannst dein ~ machen!** (*inf*) you'd better make your will! (*inf*); **ohne Hinterlassung eines ~s** intestate. **(b)** (*Bibl*) Testament ◆ **Altes/Neues ~** Old/New Testament.

testamentarisch *adj* testamentary ◆ **eine ~e Verfügung** an instruction in the will; **etw ~ festlegen** to write sth in one's will; **~ festgelegt** (written) in the will.

Testaments-: ~eröffnung *f* reading of the will; **~vollstrecker** *m* executor; (*Frau auch*) executrix.

Testat *nt* (*Univ*) course attendance certificate.

Testator *m* (*Erblasser*) testator.

Test-: ~bild *nt* (*TV*) testcard; **~bogen** *m* test paper.

testen *vt* to test (*auf +acc* for) ◆ **jdn auf seine Intelligenz ~** to test sb's intelligence.

Tester(in *f*) *m* **-s, -** tester.

Test-: ~fahrer *m* test driver; **~fall** *m* test case; **~frage** *f* test question.

testieren* *vt* **(a)** (*bescheinigen*) to certify ◆ **sich** (*dat*) **etw ~ lassen** to get oneself a certificate of sth; **jdm etw ~** to certify sth for sb. **(b)** (*Jur: letztwillig verfügen*) to will.

Testikel *m* **-s, -** testicle.

Testosteron *nt* **-s** testosterone.

Test-: ~person *f* subject (of a test); **~pilot** *m* test-pilot; **~programm** *nt* (*Comput*) test program; **~reihe, ~serie** *f* series of tests; **~stopp** *m* test ban; **~stopp-Abkommen** *nt* test ban treaty *or* agreement; **~verfahren** *nt* method of testing; **~wahl** *f* (*inf*) test election; **Kommunalwahlen kann man häufig als ~wahlen ansehen** local elections can often be regarded as a test of electoral feeling.

Tetanus *m* **-,** *no pl* tetanus.

Tete ['te:tə, 'tɛ:tə] *f* **-, -n** (*Mil*) head of a column.

Tête-à-tête [tɛ:ta'tɛ:t] *nt* **-, -s** tête-à-tête.

Tetra-: ~eder [tetra'|e:dɐ] *nt* **-s, -** (*Math*) tetrahedron; **~gon** [tetra'go:n] *nt* **-s, -e** (*Math*) tetragon; **~logie** *f* tetralogy.

teuer *adj* expensive, dear *usu pred*; (*fig*) dear ◆ **etw ~ kaufen/verkaufen** to buy/sell sth for *or* at a high price; **etw zu ~ kaufen** to pay too much for sth; **etw für teures Geld kaufen** to pay good money for sth; **teurer werden** to go up (in price); **Brot wieder teurer!** bread up again; **in Tokio lebt man ~/ist das Leben ~** life is expensive in Tokyo, Tokyo is expensive; **~ aber gut** expensive but well worth the money; **das ist mir (lieb und) ~** (*liter*) that's very dear *or* precious to me; **das wird ihn ~ zu stehen kommen** (*fig*) that will cost him dear; **einen Sieg ~ erkaufen** to pay dearly for victory; **~ erkauft** dearly bought; **sich** (*dat*) **etw ~ bezahlen lassen** to charge a high price for sth; **mein Teurer** *or* **T~ster/meine Teure** *or* **T~ste** (*old, hum*) my dearest; (*von Mann zu Mann*) my dearest friend.

Teuerung *f* rise in prices, rising prices *pl*.

Teuerungs-: ~rate *f* rate of price increases; **~welle** *f* wave *or* round of price increases; **~zulage** *f* cost of living bonus *or* supplement; **~zuschlag** *m* surcharge.

Teufel *m* **-s, - (a)** (*lit, fig*) devil ◆ **den ~ durch Beelzebub austreiben** to replace one evil with another; **den ~ im Leib haben** to be possessed by the devil; **der ~ der Eifersucht** *etc* a jealous *etc* devil; **ein ~ von einem Mann/einer Frau** (*old*) a devil of a man/woman.

(b) (*inf: Redewendungen*) **~ (noch mal** *or* **aber auch)!** damn it (all)! (*sl*), confound it! (*inf*); **~ auch** (*bewundernd*) well I'll be damned (*sl*) *or* blowed (*inf*); **scher dich** *or* **geh zum ~, hol dich der ~!** go to hell (*sl*) *or* blazes (*inf*)!; **der ~ soll ihn/es holen!, hol ihn/es der ~** damn (*sl*) *or* blast (*inf*) him/it!, to hell with him/it (*sl*); **jdn zum ~ wünschen** to wish sb in hell; **jdn zum ~ jagen** *or* **schicken** to send sb packing (*inf*); **zum ~!** damn! (*sl*), blast! (*inf*); **wer zum ~?** who the devil (*inf*) *or* the hell? (*sl*); **zum ~ mit dem Ding!** damn (*sl*) *or* blast (*inf*) the thing!, to hell with the thing! (*sl*); **zum ~ sein** (*kaputt sein*) to have had it (*inf*); (*verloren sein*) to have gone west (*inf*); **den ~ an die Wand malen** (*schwarzmalen*) to think *or* imagine the worst; (*Unheil heraufbeschwören*) to tempt fate *or* providence; **wenn man vom ~ spricht(, dann ist er nicht weit)** (*prov*) talk of the devil (and he's sure to appear) (*inf*); **das müßte schon mit dem ~ zugehen** that really would be a stroke of bad luck; **ihn muß der ~ geritten haben** he must have had a devil in him; **dann kommst** *or* **gerätst du in ~s Küche** then you'll be in a hell of a mess (*sl*); **wie der ~** like hell (*sl*), like the devil (*inf*); **er ist hinter dem Geld her wie der ~ hinter der armen Seele** he's money mad (*inf*); **auf ~ komm raus** like crazy (*inf*); **ich mache das auf ~ komm raus** I'll do that come hell or high water; **da ist der ~ los** all hell's been let loose (*inf*); **bist du des ~s?** (*old*) have you taken leave of your senses?; **sich den ~ um etw kümmern** *or* **scheren** not to give a damn (*sl*) *or* a fig (*inf*) about sth; **den ~ werde ich (tun)!** I'll be damned if I will! (*sl*), like hell I will! (*sl*); **der ~ steckt im Detail** it's the small things that cause problems.

Teufelei *f* (*inf*) devilish trick; (*Streich*) piece of devilry.

Teufels-: ~arbeit *f* (*inf*) hell of a job (*sl*); **~austreibung** *f* casting out of devils *no pl*, exorcism; **~beschwörung** *f* exorcism; (*Anrufen*) invocation of/to the devil; **~braten** *m* (*old inf*) devil; **~brut** *f* (*old*) devil's *or* Satan's brood; **~kerl** *m* (*dated*) devil of a fellow (*dated*); **~kirsche** *f* (*Bot*) deadly nightshade, belladonna; **~kreis** *m* vicious circle; **~kult** *m* devil-worship; **~messe** *f* black mass; **~weib** *nt* (*dated*) devil of a woman.

teuflisch *adj* fiendish, devilish, diabolical.

Teutone *m* **-n, -n, Teutonin** *f* Teuton.

teutonisch *adj* Teutonic.

Text *m* **-(e)s, -e** text; (*einer Urkunde auch, eines Gesetzes*) wording; (*von Lied*) words *pl*; (*von Schlager*) lyrics *pl*; (*von Film, Hörspiel, Rede etc*) script; (*Mus: Opern~*) libretto; (*unter Bild*) caption; (*auf Plakat*) words *pl* ◆ **weiter im ~** (*inf*) (let's) get on with it; **ein Telegramm mit folgendem ~ ...** a telegram which said *or* read ...

Text-: ~aufgabe *f* problem; **~baustein** *m* (*Comput*) boilerplate; **~buch** *nt* script; (*für Lieder*) songbook; **~dichter** *m* (*von Liedern*) songwriter; (*bei Oper*) librettist; **~eingabe** *f* (*Comput*) text input.

texten [1] *vt* to write.

[2] *vi siehe* **Texter(in)** to write songs/copy.

Texter(in *f*) *m* **-s, -** (*für Schlager*) songwriter; (*für Werbesprüche*) copywriter.

Text|erfasser(in *f*) *m* keyboarder.

Textil- *in cpds* textile; **~arbeiter** *m* textile worker; **~branche** *f* textile trade; **~fabrik** *f* textile factory; (*für Textilien aus Naturfasern auch*) textile mill.

Textilien [-iən] *pl linen, clothing, fabrics etc*; (*Ind*) textiles *pl*.

Textil-: ~industrie *f* textile industry; **~waren** *pl siehe* **Textilien.**

Text-: ~kritik *f* textual criticism; **~linguistik** *f* (*Ling*) text linguistics *sing*; **~modus** *m* (*Comput*) text mode; **~semantik** *f* (*Ling*) textual semantics *sing*; **~speicher** *m* (*Comput*) memory; **~stelle** *f* passage; **~system** *nt* (*Comput*) *siehe* **~verarbeitungssystem.**

Textur *f* texture.

Textverarbeitung *f* word processing.

Textverarbeitungs-: ~anlage *f* word processor, word processing system; **~programm** *nt* word processor, word processing program; **~system** *nt* word processor, word processing system.

Tezett *nt* (*inf*): **jdn/etw bis ins** *or* **zum ~ kennen** to know sb/sth inside out (*inf*).

TH [te:'ha:] *f* **-, -s** *abbr of* **Technische Hochschule.**

Thailand *nt* **-s** Thailand.

Thailänder(in *f*) *m* **-s, -** Thai.

thailändisch *adj* Thai.

Thallium *nt, no pl* (*abbr* **Tl**) thallium.

Theater *nt* **-s, - (a)** theatre (*Brit*), theater (*US*); (*~kunst auch*) drama; (*Schauspielbühne*) theatre company; (*Zuschauer*) audience ◆ **beim** *or* **am/im ~ arbeiten** to be on the stage/work in the theatre; **er ist** *or* **arbeitet beim Ulmer ~** he's with the Ulm theatre company; **heute abend wird im ~ „Othello" gezeigt** *or* **gegeben** "Othello" is on *or* is playing at the theatre tonight; **das ~ fängt um 8 Uhr an** the performance begins at 8 o'clock; **zum ~ gehen** to go on the stage; **ins ~ gehen** to go to the theatre; **das französische ~** French theatre; **~ spielen** (*lit*) to act; (*Stück aufführen*) to put on a play; (*fig*) to put on an act, to play-act; **jdm ein ~ vormachen** *or* **vorspielen** (*fig*) to put on an act for sb's benefit; **das ist doch alles nur ~** (*fig*) it's all just play-acting.

(b) (*fig*) to-do (*inf*), fuss ◆ **das war vielleicht ein ~, bis ich ...** what a palaver *or* performance *or* carry-on I had to ... (*inf*); **das ist vielleicht immer ein ~, wenn er kommt** there's always a big fuss when he comes; **(ein) ~ machen** (*Umstände*) to make a (big) fuss (*mit jdm* of sb); (*Szene auch*) to make a scene *or* a song and dance (*inf*).

Theater- *in cpds* theatre (*Brit*), theater (*US*); **~abonnement** *nt* theatre subscription; **~aufführung** *f* stage production; (*Vorstellung, Darbietung*) performance; **~besuch** *m* visit to the theatre; **~besucher** *m* theatregoer; **~dichter** *m* dramatist, playwright; **~gebäude** *nt* theatre; **~karte** *f* theatre ticket; **~kasse** *f* theatre box office; **~kritiker** *m* theatre *or* drama critic; **~probe** *f* rehearsal; **~stück** *nt* (stage) play.

theatralisch *adj* theatrical, histrionic.

Theismus *m* theism.

Theke *f* **-, -n** (*Schanktisch*) bar; (*Ladentisch*) counter.

T-Helfer-Zelle [te:-] *f* T helper cell.

Thema *nt* **-s, Themen** *or* **-ta** (*Gegenstand*) subject, topic; (*Leitgedanke, Mus*) theme ◆ **interessant vom ~ her** interesting as far as the subject matter is concerned; **beim ~ bleiben/vom ~ abschweifen** to stick to/stray from *or* wander off the subject *or* point; **das ~ wechseln** to change the subject; **ein/kein ~ sein** to be/not to be an issue; **aus etw ein ~ machen** to make an issue of sth; **zum ~ werden** to become an issue; **wir wollen das ~ begraben** (*inf*) let's not talk about it any more, let's forget the whole subject; **das ~ ist (für mich) erledigt** (*inf*) as far as I'm concerned the matter's closed; **~ Nr. 1** (*hum inf*) sex.

Themata *pl of* **Thema.**

Thematik *f* topic.

thematisch *adj* thematic; (*vom Thema her*) as regards subject matter ◆ **~es Verzeichnis** subject index.

thematisieren* *vt* (*geh*) to pick out as a central theme.

Themen *pl of* **Thema.**

Themen-: ~bereich *m*, **~kreis** *m* topic; **in den ~bereich „Tiere" gehören** to come under the heading of "animals"; **~stellung** *f* subject; **~wahl** *f* choice of subject *or* topic.

Themse *f* - **die ~** the Thames.

Theologe *m*, **Theologin** *f* theologian.

Theologie *f* theology ♦ **Doktor der ~** Doctor of Divinity.

theologisch *adj* theological.

Theorem *nt* **-s, -e** theorem.

Theoretiker(in *f*) *m* **-s, -** theorist, theoretician.

theoretisch *adj* theoretical ♦ **~ gesehen** in theory, theoretically.

theoretisieren* *vi* to theorize.

Theorie *f* theory; *siehe* **grau.**

Theosophie *f* theosophy.

Therapeut(in *f*) *m* **-en, -en** therapist.

Therapeutik *f* therapeutics *sing.*

therapeutisch *adj* therapeutic(al).

Therapie *f* therapy (*auch fig*), treatment; (*Behandlungsmethode*) (method of) treatment (*gegen* for).

therapieren* *vt* to give therapy to, to treat.

Thermal-: ~bad *nt* thermal bath; (*Gebäude*) thermal baths *pl*; (*Badeort*) spa, watering-place (*old*); **jdm ~bäder verschreiben** to prescribe hydrotherapy for sb; **~quelle** *f* thermal spring.

Therme *f* **-, -n** (*Quelle*) thermal *or* hot spring ♦ **die ~n** the thermals; (*Hist*) the (thermal) baths.

thermisch *adj attr* (*Phys*) thermal.

Thermo- *in cpds* thermo-; **~chemie** *f* thermochemistry; **~drucker** *m* thermal printer; **~dynamik** *f* thermodynamics *sing*; **t~elektrisch** *adj* thermoelectric(al); **~hose** *f* quilted trousers; **~kanne** *f* thermos jug.

Thermometer *nt* **-s, -** thermometer.

Thermometerstand *m* temperature ♦ **bei ~ 60°** when the temperature reaches 60°, when the thermometer reads 60°.

thermonuklear *adj* thermonuclear.

Thermopapier *nt* thermal paper.

Thermosflasche *f* thermos (flask) ®, vacuum flask *or* bottle (*US*).

Thermostat *m* **-(e)s, -e** thermostat.

Thesaurus *m* **-, Thesauri** *or* **Thesauren** thesaurus.

▼ **These** *f* **-, -n** hypothesis, thesis; (*inf: Theorie*) theory ♦ **Luthers 95 ~n** Luther's 95 propositions.

Thing *nt* **-(e)s, -e** (*Hist*) thing.

Thingplatz *m* (*Hist*) thingstead.

Thorium *nt, no pl* (*abbr* **Th**) thorium.

Thriller ['θrɪlə] *m* **-s, -** thriller.

Thrombose *f* **-, -n** thrombosis.

thrombotisch *adj* thrombotic.

Thron *m* **-(e)s, -e** throne; (*hum inf: Nachttopf*) pot ♦ **von seinem ~ herabsteigen** (*fig*) to come down off one's high horse.

Thron-: ~anwärter *m* claimant to the throne; (*Thronfolger*) heir apparent; **~besteigung** *f* accession (to the throne).

thronen *vi* (*lit: auf dem Thron sitzen*) to sit enthroned; (*fig: in exponierter Stellung sitzen*) to sit in state; (*liter: überragen*) to stand in solitary splendour.

Thron-: ~erbe *m*, **~erbin** *f* heir to the throne; **~folge** *f* line of succession; **die ~folge antreten** to succeed to the throne; **~folger(in** *f*) *m* **-s, -** heir to the throne, heir apparent; **~himmel** *m* canopy; **~räuber** *m* usurper; **~rede** *f* King's/Queen's speech at the opening of parliament; **~saal** *m* throne room.

Thuja *f* **-, Thujen** arborvitae, thuja.

Thulium *nt, no pl* (*abbr* **Tm**) thulium.

⚠ **Thunfisch** *m* tuna (fish).

Thurgau *m* **-s der ~** the Thurgau.

Thüringen *nt* **-s** Thuringia.

Thüringer(in *f*) *m* **-s, -** Thuringian.

thüringisch *adj* Thuringian.

Thusnelda *f* **-** (*inf*) bird (*Brit inf*), chick (*inf*).

Thymian *m* **-s, -e** thyme.

Thymusdrüse *f* thymus (gland).

Tiara *f* **-, Tiaren** tiara, triple crown.

Tibet *nt* **-s** Tibet.

Tibetaner(in *f*) *m* **-s, -** Tibetan.

tibetanisch *adj* Tibetan.

tick *interj* tick ♦ **~ tack!** tick-tock!

Tick *m* **-(e)s, -s** tic; (*inf: Schrulle*) quirk (*inf*) ♦ **Uhren sind sein ~** he has a thing about clocks (*inf*); **einen ~ haben** (*inf*) to be crazy; **er hat einen ~ mit seiner Ordnung** he has this thing about tidiness (*inf*).

-tick *m in cpds* (*inf*) **ein Auto~** a thing about cars (*inf*).

ticken *vi* to tick (away) ♦ **du tickst ja nicht richtig** you're off your rocker! (*inf*).

Ticker *m* **-s, -** (*inf*) telex (machine), ticker (*US*).

tickern (*inf*) [1] *vi* **aus dem Fernschreiber ~** to come out of the telex.
[2] *vi* to telex.

Ticket *nt* **-s, -s** (plane) ticket.

Tide *f* **-, -n** (*N Ger*) tide.

Tie-break, Tiebreak ['taibre:k] *m* **-s, -s** (*Tennis*) tiebreak(er).

tief [1] *adj* **(a)** (*weit reichend*) *Tal, Wasser, Wurzeln, Schnee, Wunde, Seufzer* deep; *Verbeugung auch, Ausschnitt* low ♦ **~er Teller** soup plate; **ein ~er Eingriff in jds Rechte** (*acc*) a gross infringement of sb's rights; **die ~eren Ursachen** the underlying causes; **aus ~stem Herzen/~ster Seele** from the bottom of one's heart/the depths of one's soul.
(b) (*sehr stark, groß*) *Ohnmacht, Schlaf, Erröten, Gefühl* deep; *Haß auch, Schmerz* intense; *Not* dire; *Verlassenheit, Einsamkeit, Elend* utter ♦ **bis in den ~sten Winter/die ~ste Nacht, bis ~ in den Winter/die Nacht hinein** (till) well into winter/late into the night.
(c) *auch adv* (*mitten in etwas liegend*) **er wohnt ~ in den Bergen** he lives deep in the mountains; **~ im Wald, im ~en Wald** deep in the forest, in the depths of the forest; **~ im Winter, im ~en Winter** in the depths of winter; **~ in der Nacht, in der ~en Nacht** at dead of night; **~ in Afrika, im ~sten Afrika** in darkest Africa; **~ im Innern, im ~sten Innern** in one's heart of hearts.
(d) (*tiefgründig*) deep, profound ♦ **der ~ere Sinn** the deeper meaning.
(e) (*niedrig*) *Lage, Stand, Temperatur* low.
(f) (*dunkel*) *Farbton, Stimme* deep; (*Mus*) low; *Ton* low ♦ **in ~es Schwarz gekleidet sein** to be in deep mourning; **etw zu ~ singen** to sing sth flat; **~ sprechen** to talk in a deep voice; **~er spielen** to play in a lower key *or* lower; **~er stimmen** to tune down.
[2] *adv* **(a)** (*weit nach unten, innen, hinten*) a long way; *bohren, graben, eindringen, tauchen auch* deep; *sich bücken* low; *untersuchen* in depth ♦ **~ in etw** (*acc*) **einsinken** to sink deep into sth, to sink down a long way into sth; **3 m ~ fallen** to fall 3 metres; **~ sinken** (*fig*) to sink low; **~ fallen** (*fig*) to go downhill; **bis ~ in etw** (*acc*) **hinein** (*örtlich*) a long way down/deep into sth; **(ganz) ~ unter uns** a long way below us, far below us; **seine Augen liegen ~ in den Höhlen** his eyes are like hollows in his face; **~ verschneit** deep *or* thick with snow; **~ in Gedanken (versunken)** deep in thought; **~ in Schulden stecken** to be deep in debt; **jdm ~ in die Augen sehen** to look deep into sb's eyes; **~ in die Tasche** *or* **den Beutel greifen müssen** (*inf*) to have to reach *or* dig deep in one's pocket; **das geht bei ihm nicht sehr ~** (*inf*) it doesn't go very deep with him.
(b) (*sehr stark*) *verletzen, atmen, erröten, schockieren, erschüttern* deeply; *schlafen auch* soundly; *fühlen, empfinden auch* acutely; *bedauern auch* profoundly; *erschrecken* terribly.
(c) (*tiefgründig*) *nachdenken* deeply ♦ **etw ~er begründen** to find a deeper reason for sth.
(d) (*niedrig*) low ♦ **ein Stockwerk ~er** one floor down *or* lower, on the floor below; **Hanau liegt ~er als Schlüchtern** Hanau is lower-lying than Schlüchtern; **das Haus liegt ~er als die Straße** the house lies below (the level of) the road; **im Winter steht die Sonne ~er** the sun is lower (in the sky) in winter.

Tief *nt* **-(e)s, -e (a)** (*Met*) depression; (*im Kern, fig*) low ♦ **ein moralisches ~** (*fig*) a low. **(b)** (*Naut: Rinne*) deep (*spec*), channel.

Tief-: ~bau *m* civil engineering (*excluding the construction of building*); *siehe* **Hoch- und Tiefbau**; ⚠**t~betrübt** *adj attr* deeply distressed; ⚠**t~bewegt** *adj attr* deeply moved; **t~blau** *adj attr* deep blue; ⚠**t~blickend** *adj attr* (*fig*) perceptive, astute.

Tiefdruck *m* **(a)** (*Met*) low pressure. **(b)** (*Typ*) gravure.

Tiefdruck-: ~gebiet *nt* (*Met*) area of low pressure, depression; **~keil** *m* (*Met*) trough of low pressure; **~rinne** *f* (*Met*) depression.

Tiefe *f* **-, -n** *siehe* **tief (a)** depth; (*von Verbeugung, Ausschnitt*) lowness ♦ **unten in der ~** far below; **in die ~ blicken** to look down into the depths *or* a long way; **in der ~ versinken** to sink into the depths; **das U-Boot ging auf ~** the submarine dived; **aus der ~ meines Herzens** from the depths of my heart.
(b) deepness; intensity; direness; depths *pl.*
(c) (*von Wald*) depths *pl.*
(d) deepness, profundity.
(e) lowness.
(f) deepness; lowness.
(g) (*Art, Phot*) depth.

Tief-: ~ebene *f* lowland plain; **die Oberrheinische ~ebene** the Upper Rhine Valley; ⚠**t~empfunden** *adj attr* deep(ly)-felt.

Tiefen-: ~bestrahlung *f* deep ray therapy; **~gestein** *nt* plutonic rock, pluton; **~psychologe** *m* depth psychologist; psychoanalyst; **~psychologie** *f* depth psychology; psychoanalysis; **~schärfe** *f* (*Phot*) depth of field; **~wirkung** *f* deep action; (*Art, Phot*) effect of depth.

Tief-: ⚠**t~erschüttert** *adj attr* deeply disturbed; **~flieger** *m* low-flying aircraft, hedgehopper (*inf*); **geistiger ~flieger** (*pej inf*) numskull (*inf*), dummy (*inf*); **~flug** *m* low-level *or* low-altitude flight; **er überquerte den Kanal im ~flug** he crossed low over the Channel; **~flugübung** *f* low-flying exercise; **~gang** *m* (*Naut*) draught; (*fig inf*) depth; **~garage** *f* underground car park; **t~gefroren** *adj* frozen; ⚠**t~gehend** *adj* (*lit, fig*) deep; *Schmerz* extreme, acute; *Kränkung* extreme; **t~gekühlt** *adj* (*gefroren*) frozen; (*sehr kalt*) chilled; ⚠**t~greifend** *adj* far-reaching; **t~gründig** *adj* profound, deep; (*durchdacht*) well-grounded.

Tiefkühl-: ~fach *nt* freezer compartment; **~kost** *f* frozen food; **~truhe** *f* (chest-type) deep-freeze *or* freezer.

Tief-: ~lader *m* **-s, -, ~ladewagen** *m* low-loader; **~land** *nt* lowlands *pl*; ⚠**t~liegend** *adj attr Gegend, Häuser* low-lying; *Augen* deep-set; (*nach Krankheit*) sunken; **~punkt** *m* low; **~schlag** *m* (*Boxen, fig*) hit below the belt; **jdm einen ~schlag verpassen** (*lit, fig*) to hit sb below the belt; **das war ein ~schlag** (*lit, fig*) that was below the belt; ⚠**t~schürfend** *adj* profound.

Tiefsee *f* deep sea.

Tiefsee- *in cpds* deep-sea.

Tief-: ≈sinn *m* profundity; **t≈sinnig** *adj* profound; **≈sinnigkeit** *f* profundity; **≈stand** *m* low; **~stapelei** *f* understatement; (*auf eigene Leistung bezogen*) modesty; **t≈stapeln** *vi sep* to understate the case; to be modest; **≈start** *m* crouch start.

Tiefst-: ~preis *m* lowest price; **„~preise"** "rock bottom prices"; **~temperatur** *f* lowest temperature; **~wert** *m* lowest value.

tieftraurig *adj* very sad.

Tiegel *m* **-s, -** (*zum Kochen*) (sauce)pan; (*in der Chemie*) crucible; (*~druckpresse*) platen (press).

Tier *nt* **-(e)s, -e** animal; (*großes ~ auch*) beast; (*Haus~ auch*) pet; (*inf: Ungeziefer*) bug (*inf*); (*inf: Mensch*) (*grausam*) brute; (*grob*) animal; (*gefräßig*) pig (*inf*) ♦ **großes** *or* **hohes ~** (*inf*) big shot (*inf*); **das ~ im Menschen** the beast in man; **da wird der Mensch zum ~** it brings out man's bestiality; **sich wie die ~e benehmen** to behave like animals.

Tier- *in cpds* animal; (*Med*) veterinary; (*für Haustiere*) pet; **~arzt** *m* vet, veterinary surgeon (*form*), veterinarian (*US*); **~asyl** *nt* (animal) pound.

Tierchen *nt dim of* **Tier** little animal ♦ **ein niedliches ~** a sweet little creature; *siehe* **Pläsierchen.**

Tier-: ~freund *m* animal/pet lover; **~futter** *nt* animal food *or* fodder; (*für Haustiere*) pet food; **~garten** *m* zoo; **~halter** *m* (*von Haustieren*) pet-owner; (*von Nutztieren*) livestock owner; **~handlung** *f* pet shop; **~heilkunde** *f* veterinary medicine; **~heim** *nt* animal home.

tierisch *adj* animal *attr*; (*fig*) *Roheit, Grausamkeit* bestial; (*unzivilisiert*) *Benehmen, Sitten* animal *attr*; (*fig inf: unerträglich*) deadly *no adv* (*inf*), terrible ♦ **~er Ernst** (*inf*) deadly seriousness; **der nervt mich ~** (*sl*) he irritates me like hell (*inf*); **ich habe mich ~ geärgert** (*sl*) I got really furious.

Tier-: ≈kämpfe *pl* animal fights *pl*; **≈kreis** *m* zodiac; **≈kreiszeichen** *nt* sign of the zodiac; **im ~kreiszeichen des Skorpions geboren sein** to be born under Scorpio; **≈kunde** *f* zoology; **≈liebe** *f* love of animals; **t≈liebend** *adj* fond of animals, animal-loving *attr*, pet-loving *attr*, **≈medizin** *f* veterinary medicine; **≈mehl** *nt* animal feed; **≈park** *m* zoo; **≈pfleger** *m* zookeeper; **≈quäler** *m* **-s, -** person who is cruel to animals; **ein ~quäler sein** to be cruel to animals; **~quälerei** *f* cruelty to animals; (*fig inf*) cruelty to dumb animals; **≈reich** *nt* animal kingdom; **≈schutz** *m* protection of animals; **≈schützer(in** *f***)** *m* animal conservationist; **≈schutzverein** *m* society for the prevention of cruelty to animals; **≈versuch** *m* animal experiment; **≈welt** *f* animal kingdom; **≈zucht** *f* stockbreeding.

Tiger *m* **-s, -** tiger.

Tiger-: ~auge *nt* tiger's-eye; **~fell** *nt* tiger skin.

Tigerin *f* tigress.

tigern [1] *vt siehe* **getigert.**
[2] *vi aux sein* (*inf*) to mooch.

Tigris *m* - Tigris.

Tilde *f* **-, -n** tilde.

tilgbar *adj Schulden* repayable.

tilgen *vt* (*geh*) **(a)** *Schulden* to pay off. **(b)** (*beseitigen*) *Sünde, Unrecht, Spuren* to wipe out; *Erinnerung, Druckfehler* to erase; *Strafe* to set aside; *Posten* (*Typ, Ling*) to delete ♦ **ein Volk vom Erdboden ~** to wipe a nation off the face of the earth.

Tilgung *f siehe vt* **(a)** repayment. **(b)** wiping out; erasure; setting aside; deletion.

Tilgungs-: t~frei *adj* redemption-free; **~rate** *f* redemption.

Tilsiter *m* **-s, -** Tilsit cheese.

Timbre ['tɛ̃:bʀə] *nt* **-s, -s** (*geh*) timbre.

timen ['taimən] *vt* to time.

Timer ['taimɐ] *m* **-s, -** timer.

Timing ['taimɪŋ] *nt* **-,** *no pl* timing.

Timpani *pl* (*Mus*) timpani *pl.*

tingeln *vi* (*inf*) to appear in small night-clubs/theatres *etc.*

Tingeltangel *nt or m* **-s, -** (*dated*) (*Veranstaltung*) hop (*inf*); (*Lokal*) second-rate night-club, honky-tonk (*US inf*).

Tinktur *f* tincture.

Tinnef *m* **-s** *no pl* (*inf*) rubbish, trash (*inf*).

Tinte *f* **-, -n** ink ♦ **sich in die ~ setzen, in die ~ geraten** to get (oneself) into a pickle (*inf*); **in der ~ sitzen** (*inf*) to be in the soup (*inf*).

Tinten-: ⚠**~faß** *nt* inkpot; (*eingelassen*) inkwell; **~fisch** *m* cuttlefish; (*Kalmar*) squid; (*achtarmig*) octopus; **~fleck** *m* (*auf Kleidung*) ink stain; (*auf Papier*) ink blot; **~klecks** *m* ink blot; **~pilz** *m* ink-cap; **~stift** *m* indelible pencil; **~strahldrucker** *m* ink-jet (printer).

⚠ **Tip** *m* **-s, -s** (*Sport, St Ex*) tip; (*Andeutung*) hint; (*an Polizei*) tip-off ♦ **ich gebe dir einen ~, wie du ...** I'll give you a tip how to ...; **ich gebe dir einen ~, was du mir schenken kannst** I'll give you a hint as to what you could give me; **unser ~ für diesen Sommer: ...** this summer we recommend ...

Tippelbruder *m* (*dated inf*) gentleman of the road.

tippeln *vi aux sein* (*inf*) (*gehen*) to foot it (*inf*); (*mit kurzen Schritten*) to trip; (*auf Zehenspitzen*) to tiptoe; (*Maus, Kinder*) to patter.

tippen *vti* **(a)** (*klopfen*) to tap (*an/auf/gegen etw* (*acc*) sth); (*zeigen*) to touch (*auf or an etw* (*acc*) sth) ♦ **jdn** *or* **jdm auf die Schulter ~** to tap sb on the shoulder.
(b) (*inf: auf der Schreibmaschine*) to type (*an etw* (*dat*) sth).
(c) (*wetten*) to fill in one's coupon; (*im Toto auch*) to do the pools ♦ **im Lotto ~** to do the lottery; **eine bestimmte Zahl ~** to put a particular number on one's coupon.
(d) *nur vi* (*inf: raten*) to guess ♦ **auf jdn/etw ~** to put one's money on sb/sth (*inf*); **ich tippe darauf, daß ...** I bet (that) ...; **auf jds Sieg** (*acc*) **~** to back sb to win (*inf*).

Tipp-Ex ® *nt* **-,** *no pl* Tipp-Ex ®, whiteout (*US*) ♦ **etw mit ~ entfernen** to Tipp-Ex sth out.

Tippfehler *m* (*inf*) typing mistake *or* error.

Tippfräulein *nt* (*inf*), **Tippse** *f* **-, -n** (*pej*) typist.

tipptapp *interj* pitter-patter.

tipptopp (*inf*) [1] *adj* immaculate; (*prima*) first-class, tip-top (*dated inf*).
[2] *adv* immaculately; (*prima*) really well ♦ **~ sauber** spotless.

Tippzettel *m* (*im Toto*) football *or* pools coupon; (*im Lotto*) lottery coupon.

Tirade *f* tirade, diatribe.

Tirana *nt* **-s** Tirana.

tirilieren* *vi* (*geh*) to warble, to trill.

Tirol *nt* **-s** Tyrol.

Tiroler(in *f***)** *m* **-s, -** Tyrolese, Tyrolean.

Tirolerhut *m* Tyrolean hat.

Tisch *m* **-(e)s, -e** table; (*Schreib~*) desk; (*Werk~*) bench; (*Mahlzeit*) meal ♦ **bei ~** at (the) table; **vom ~ aufstehen** to leave the table; **sich zu** *or* **an den ~ setzen** to sit down at the table; **die Gäste zu ~ bitten** to ask the guests to take their places; **bitte zu ~!** lunch/dinner is served!; **vor/nach ~** before/after the meal; **zu ~ sein/gehen** to be having one's lunch/dinner/to go to lunch/dinner; **er zahlte bar auf den ~** he paid cash down *or* cash on the nail (*inf*); **etw auf den ~ bringen** (*inf*) to serve sth (up); **die Beine** *or* **Füße unter jds ~ strecken** (*inf*) to eat at sb's table; **unter den ~ fallen** (*inf*) to go by the board; **jdn unter den ~ trinken** *or* **saufen** (*inf*) to drink sb under the table; **es wird gegessen, was auf den ~ kommt!** you'll eat what you're given; **zwei Parteien an einen ~ bringen** (*fig*) to get two parties round the conference table; **getrennt von ~ und Bett leben** to be separated; **vom ~ sein** (*fig*) to be cleared out of the way; **etw vom ~ wischen** (*fig*) to dismiss sth; **jdn über den ~ ziehen** (*fig inf*) to take sb to the cleaners (*inf*); *siehe* **rund, grün, rein**[2]**.**

Tisch- *in cpds* table; **~besen** *m* crumb brush; **~dame** *f* dinner partner; **~decke** *f* tablecloth; **~ende** *nt* end of a/the table; **am oberen/unteren ~ende sitzen** to sit at the head/the foot of the table; **~feuerzeug** *nt* table lighter; **~fußball** *nt* table football; **~gebet** *nt* grace; **~gesellschaft** *f* dinner party; **~gespräch** *nt* table talk; **~herr** *m* dinner partner; **~karte** *f* place card; **~lampe** *f* table lamp; **~läufer** *m* table runner.

Tischleindeckdich *nt* **-(s) ein ~ gefunden haben** (*fig*) to be on to a good thing (*inf*).

Tischler *m* **-s -** joiner, carpenter; (*Möbel~*) cabinet-maker.

Tischlerei *f* **(a)** (*Werkstatt*) joiner's *or* carpenter's/cabinet-maker's workshop. **(b)** *no pl* (*inf*) *siehe* **Tischlerhandwerk.**

Tischlerhandwerk *nt* joinery, carpentry; cabinetmaking.

Tischlerin *f siehe* **Tischler.**

tischlern (*inf*) [1] *vi* to do woodwork.
[2] *vt Tisch, Regal etc* to make.

Tischlerwerkstatt *f siehe* **Tischlerei (a).**

Tisch-: ~nachbar *m* neighbour (at table); **~ordnung** *f* seating plan; **~platte** *f* tabletop; **~rechner** *m* desk calculator; **~rede** *f* after-dinner speech; (*Unterhaltung*) table talk; **~redner** *m* after-dinner speaker; **~telefon** *nt* table telephone (*in night-club*).

Tischtennis *nt* table tennis.

Tischtennis- *in cpds* table-tennis; **~platte** *f* table-tennis table; **~schläger** *m* table-tennis bat.

Tisch-: ~tuch *nt* tablecloth; **~wäsche** *f* table linen; **~wein** *m* table wine; **~zeit** *f* mealtime; **zur ~zeit** at mealtimes.

Titan[1] *m* **-en, -en** (*Myth*) Titan.

Titan[2] *nt* **-s,** *no pl* (*abbr* **Ti**) titanium.

titanenhaft, titanisch *adj* titanic.

Titel *m* **-s, - (a)** title ♦ **jdn mit ~ ansprechen** to address sb by his/her title, to give sb his/her title; **unter dem ~** under the title; (*fig: Motto*) under the slogan. **(b)** (*~blatt*) title page. **(c)** (*von Gesetz, Etat*) section.

Titel-: ~anwärter *m* (main) contender for the title; **~bild** *nt* cover (picture); **~blatt** *nt* title page.

Titelei *f* (*Typ*) prelims *pl.*

Titel-: ~held *m* eponymous hero, hero (*mentioned in the title*); **~kampf** *m* (*Sport*) finals *pl*; (*Boxen*) title fight; **~melodie** *f* (*von Film*) theme tune *or* music; **~rolle** *f* title role; **~schutz** *m* copyright (*of a title*); **~seite** *f* cover, front page; **~träger** *m* person with a title; **~verteidiger** *m* title holder; **~zeile** *f* title line.

Titte *f* **-, -n** (*vulg*) tit (*sl*), boob (*inf*), knocker (*sl*).

Titularbischof *m* titular bishop.

Titulatur *f* title, form of address.

titulieren* *vt Buch, Werk etc* to entitle (*mit etw* sth); *jdn* to call (*mit etw* sth), to address (*mit* as).

tizianrot *adj Haare* titian (red).

tja *interj* well.

Toast [to:st] *m* **-(e)s, -e (a)** (*Brot*) toast ♦ **ein ~** some toast. **(b)** (*Trinkspruch*) toast ♦ **einen ~ auf jdn ausbringen** to propose a toast to sb.

Toastbrot ['to:st-] *nt sliced white bread for toasting.*

toasten ['to:stn] [1] *vi* to drink a toast (*auf +acc* to).
[2] *vt Brot* to toast.

Toaster ['to:stɐ] *m* **-s, -** toaster.

Toastständer ['to:st-] *m* toast rack.

Tobak *m*: **das ist starker ~!** (*inf*) that's a bit thick! (*inf*); *siehe* **Anno.**

toben *vi* **(a)** (*wüten*) (*Elemente, Leidenschaften, Kämpfe etc*) to rage; (*Mensch*) to throw a fit; (*vor Wut, Begeisterung etc*) to go wild (*vor* with). **(b)** (*ausgelassen spielen*) to rollick (about); *aux sein* (*inf: laufen*) to charge about.

Toberei *f* (*inf*) rollicking about.

Tobsucht *f* (*bei Tieren*) madness; (*bei Menschen*) maniacal rage.

tobsüchtig *adj* mad; *Mensch auch* raving mad.

⚠: for details of spelling reform, see supplement

Tobsuchts|anfall *m* (*inf*) fit of rage ♦ **einen ~ bekommen** to blow one's top (*inf*), to go stark raving mad (*inf*).
Tochter *f* -, ⁻ daughter; (*~firma*) subsidiary; (*Sw: Bedienstete*) girl ♦ **die ~ des Hauses** (*form*) the daughter *or* young lady of the house; **das Fräulein ~** (*iro, form*) mademoiselle; *siehe* **höher.**
Töchterchen *nt* baby daughter.
Tochter-: **~firma** *f* subsidiary (firm); **~geschwulst** *f* secondary growth *or* tumour; **~gesellschaft** *f* subsidiary (company).
töchterlich *adj attr* daughterly; *Pflicht, Gehorsam, Liebe* filial.
▼ **Tod** *m* -(e)s, -e death ♦ **der ~ als Schnitter** Death the Reaper; **~ durch Erschießen/Ersticken** death by firing squad/suffocation; **eines natürlichen/gewaltsamen ~es sterben** to die of natural causes/a violent death; **er muß des ~es sterben** he will have to die; **sich zu ~e fallen/trinken** to fall to one's death/drink oneself to death; **des ~es/ein Kind des ~es sein** to be doomed; **sich** (*dat*) **den ~ holen** to catch one's death (of cold); **in den ~ gehen** to go to one's death; **für jdn in den ~ gehen** to die for sb; **bis in den ~** until death; **jdm in den ~ folgen** to follow sb; **~ und Teufel!** (*old*) by the devil! (*old*); **weder ~ noch Teufel werden mich davon abhalten!** I'll do it, come hell or high water!; **jdn/etw auf den ~ nicht leiden** *or* **ausstehen können** (*inf*) to be unable to abide *or* stand sb/sth; **etw zu ~e hetzen** *or* **reiten** (*fig*) to flog sth to death; **sich zu ~(e) langweilen** to be bored to death; **sich zu ~(e) schämen** to be utterly ashamed; **zu ~e betrübt sein** to be in the depths of despair; *siehe* **Leben, bleich.**
tod-: **~bringend** *adj* (*geh*) *Gift* deadly, lethal; *Krankheit* fatal; **~elend** *adj* (*inf*) as miserable as sin (*inf*), utterly miserable; **~ernst** *adj* (*inf*) deadly *or* absolutely serious; **es ist mir ~ernst (damit)** I'm deadly *or* absolutely serious (about it).
Todes-: **~angst** *f* mortal agony; **eine ~angst haben/~ängste ausstehen** (*inf*) to be scared to death (*inf*); **~anzeige** *f* (*als Brief*) letter announcing sb's death; (*Annonce*) obituary (notice); „**~anzeigen**" Deaths; **~art** *f* death, way to die; **~fall** *m* death; (*bei Unglück auch*) fatality; (*in der Familie auch*) bereavement; **~furcht** *f* fear of death; **~gefahr** *f* mortal danger; **~jahr** *nt* year of sb's death; **~kampf** *m* death throes *pl*; **~kandidat** *m* condemned man/woman *etc*; **~kommando** *nt* death squad; **t~mutig** *adj* absolutely fearless; **~nachricht** *f* news of sb's death; **~not** *f* mortal anguish; **in ~nöten sein** (*fig*) to be in a desperate situation; **~opfer** *nt* death, casualty, fatality; **~qualen** *pl* final *or* mortal agony; **~qualen ausstehen** (*fig*) to suffer agony *or* agonies; ⚠**~schuß** *m* fatal shot; **der ~schuß auf jdn** the shot which killed sb; **~schütze** *m* person who fires/fired the fatal shot; (*Attentäter*) assassin; **~schwadron** *f* death squad; **~spirale** *f* death spiral; **~stoß** *m* deathblow; **jdm/einer Sache den ~stoß geben** *or* **versetzen** (*lit, fig*) to deal sb the deathblow/deal the deathblow to sth; **~strafe** *f* death penalty; **~streifen** *m* (*an Grenze*) no-man's land; **~stunde** *f* hour of death; **~tag** *m* day of sb's death; (*Jahrestag*) anniversary of sb's death; **~trieb** *m* death wish; **~ursache** *f* cause of death; **~urteil** *nt* death sentence; **~verachtung** *f* (*inf*) **mit ~verachtung** with utter disgust *or* repugnance; **jdn mit ~verachtung strafen** to scorn to notice sb.
Tod-: **~feind** *m* deadly *or* mortal enemy; **t~geweiht** *adj* doomed; **t~krank** *adj* dangerously *or* critically ill.
tödlich *adj* fatal; *Gefahr* mortal, deadly; *Gift* deadly, lethal; *Dosis* lethal; (*inf*) *Langeweile, Ernst, Sicherheit* deadly; *Beleidigung* mortal ♦ **~ verunglücken** to be killed in an accident.
Tod-: **t~müde** *adj* (*inf*) dead tired (*inf*); **t~schick** *adj* (*inf*) dead smart (*inf*); **t~sicher** (*inf*) [1] *adj* dead certain (*inf*); *Methode, Tip* sure-fire (*inf*); **eine t~sichere Angelegenheit** *or* **Sache** a dead cert (*inf*), a cinch (*esp US inf*); **das ist doch t~sicher, daß** ... it's a dead cert that ... (*inf*); [2] *adv* for sure *or* certain; **~sünde** *f* mortal *or* deadly sin; **t~unglücklich** *adj* (*inf*) desperately unhappy.
Toe-Loop ['to:lu:p] *m* (*Eiskunstlauf*) toe loop.
Tofu *nt* -, *no pl* tofu.
Toga *f* -, **Togen** toga.
Tohuwabohu [to:huva'bo:hu] *nt* -(s), -s chaos *no pl* ♦ **das war ein ~** it was utter *or* complete chaos.
Toilette [toa'lɛtə] *f* (a) (*Abort*) toilet, lavatory (*Brit*); (*im Privathaus auch*) bathroom (*euph*) ♦ **öffentliche ~** public conveniences *pl* (*Brit*), comfort station (*US*); **auf die ~ gehen/auf der ~ sein** to go to/be in the toilet.
(b) *no pl* (*geh: Ankleiden, Körperpflege*) toilet ♦ **~ machen** to do one's toilet (*old*).
(c) (*geh: Kleidung*) outfit ♦ **in großer ~** in full dress.
Toiletten- [toa'lɛtn-] *in cpds* toilet; **~artikel** *m usu pl* toiletry; **~beutel** *m* sponge (*Brit*) *or* toilet bag; **~frau** *f* toilet *or* lavatory (*Brit*) attendant; **~garnitur** *f* (a) toilet *or* bathroom set; (b) (*für ~tisch*) dressing table set; **~papier** *nt* toilet paper; **~schrank** *m* bathroom cabinet; **~seife** *f* toilet soap; **~sitz** *m* toilet *or* lavatory (*Brit*) seat; **~tasche** *f* toilet bag; **~tisch** *m* dressing table; **~wasser** *nt* toilet water.
toi, toi, toi *interj* (*inf*) (*vor Prüfung etc*) good luck; (*unberufen*) touch wood.
Tokaier(wein) *m* -s, - Tokay.
Tokio *nt* -s Tokyo.
Tokioter *adj attr* Tokyo.
Tokioter(in *f*) *m* native of Tokyo; (*Einwohner*) inhabitant of Tokyo.
Töle *f* -, -n (*dial pej*) cur.
tolerant *adj* tolerant (*gegen* of).
Toleranz *f* tolerance (*gegen* of).
Toleranz-: **~dosis** *f* tolerance dose; **~grenze** *f* limit of tolerance; **~schwelle** *f* tolerance level *or* threshold.
tolerieren* *vt* to tolerate.
Tolerierung *f* toleration.
Tolerierungs- (*Pol*): **~abkommen** *nt* toleration agreement; **~politik** *f* policy of toleration.
toll *adj* (a) (*old: irr, tollwütig*) mad.
(b) (*wild, ausgelassen*) wild; *Streiche, Gedanken, Treiben auch* mad ♦ **es ging ~ her** *or* **zu** things were pretty wild (*inf*); **die (drei) ~en Tage** the (last three) days of Fasching.
(c) (*inf: verrückt*) mad, crazy ♦ **das war ein ~es Ding** that was mad *or* madness; **(wie) ~ regnen/fahren** *etc* to rain like mad (*inf*) *or* crazy (*inf*)/drive *etc* like a madman *or* maniac.
(d) (*inf: schlimm*) terrible ♦ **es kommt noch ~er!** there's more *or* worse to come; **es zu ~ treiben** to go too far.
(e) (*inf: großartig*) fantastic (*inf*), great (*inf*) *no adv*.
tolldreist *adj* bold, (as) bold as brass.
Tolle *f* -, -n quiff.
tollen *vi* (a) to romp *or* rollick about. (b) *aux sein* (*laufen*) to rush about.
Toll-: **~haus** *nt* (*old*) lunatic asylum; **~heit** *f* (a) *no pl* (*old*) madness; (b) (*Tat*) mad act; **~kirsche** *f* deadly nightshade, belladonna; **t~kühn** *adj* daredevil *attr*, daring; **~kühnheit** *f* daring; **in seiner ~kühnheit** daringly; **~wut** *f* rabies; **~wutgefahr** *f* danger of rabies; **t~wütig** *adj* rabid.
⚠**Tolpatsch** *m* -es, -e (*inf*) clumsy *or* awkward creature.
⚠**tolpatschig** *adj* (*inf*) awkward, ungainly, clumsy.
Tölpel *m* -s, - (*inf*) fool.
tölpelhaft *adj* foolish, silly.
Toluol *nt* -s, *no pl* toluol, toluene.
Tomahawk ['tɔmaha:k, -ho:k] *m* -s, -s tomahawk.
Tomate *f* -, -n tomato ♦ **du treulose ~!** (*inf*) you're a fine friend!
Tomaten- *in cpds* tomato; **~mark, ~püree** *nt* tomato puree.
Tombola *f* -, -s *or* **Tombolen** tombola.
Tommy ['tɔmi] *m* -s, -s (*inf*) tommy.
Tomogramm *nt* -(e)s, -e (*Med*) tomogram.
Tomograph *m* (*Med*) tomograph.
⚠**Tomographie** *f* tomography.
Ton[1] *m* -(e)s, -e (*Erdart*) clay.
Ton[2] *m* -(e)s, ⁻e (a) (*Laut*) sound (*auch Rad, Film*); (*von Zeitzeichen, im Telefon*) pip; (*Klangfarbe*) tone; (*Mus: Note*) note ♦ **halber/ganzer ~** semitone/tone; **den ~ angeben** (*lit*) to give the note; (*fig*) (*Mensch*) to set the tone; (*Thema, Farbe etc*) to be predominant; **keinen ~ heraus-** *or* **hervorbringen** not to be able to say a word; **keinen ~ sagen** *or* **von sich geben** not to make a sound; **er hat keinen ~ von sich hören lassen** (*fig*) we haven't heard a word *or* a peep (*inf*) from him; **keinen ~ (über etw** *acc*) **verlauten lassen** (*fig*) not to say a word (about sth); **hast du** *or* **hat der Mensch ⁻e!** (*inf*) did you ever! (*inf*); **dicke** *or* **große ⁻e spucken** *or* **reden** (*inf*) to talk big; **jdn in höchsten ⁻en loben** (*inf*) to praise sb to the skies *or* highly.
(b) (*Betonung*) stress; (*Tonfall*) intonation; (*im Chinesischen etc*) tone.
(c) (*Redeweise, Umgangston*) tone; (*Atmosphäre*) atmosphere ♦ **den richtigen ~ finden** to strike the right note; **ich verbitte mir diesen ~** I will not be spoken to like that; **einen anderen ~ anschlagen** to change one's tune; **der ~ macht die Musik** (*Prov*) it's not what you say but the way that you say it; **der gute ~** good form.
(d) (*Farb~*) tone; (*Nuance*) shade.
Ton|abnehmer *m* cartridge, pick-up.
tonal *adj* tonal.
Ton-: **t~angebend** *adj* who/which sets the tone; **t~angebend sein** to set the tone; **~arm** *m* pick-up arm; **~art** *f* (*Mus*) key; (*fig: Tonfall*) tone; **eine andere ~art anschlagen** to change one's tune; **~assistent** *m* sound operator; **~assistenz** *f* sound; **~atelier** *nt* recording studio.
Tonband *nt* tape (*mit* of); (*inf: Gerät*) tape recorder.
Tonband-: **~aufnahme** *f* tape recording; **~gerät** *nt* tape recorder.
Ton-: **~blende** *f* tone control; **~dichter** *m* composer; **~dichtung** *f* tone poem.
tonen *vt* (*Phot*) to tone.
tönen[1] *vi* (*lit, fig: klingen*) to sound; (*schallen auch*) to resound; (*großspurig reden*) to boast ♦ **nach etw ~** (*fig*) to contain (over)tones of sth; **von unten tönten Kinderstimmen** children's voices could be heard from below.
tönen[2] *vt* to tint ♦ **die Sonne hat ihre Haut schon goldbraun getönt** the sun has bronzed her skin; **der Herbst tönt alle Blätter** autumn makes all the leaves change colour; **etw leicht rot** *etc* **~** to tinge sth (with) red *etc*.
Toner *m* -s, - toner.
Ton|erde *f* aluminium oxide; *siehe* **essigsauer.**
tönern *adj attr* clay ♦ **auf ~en Füßen stehen** (*fig*) to be shaky.
Ton-: **~fall** *m* tone of voice; (*Intonation*) intonation; **~film** *m* sound film, talkie (*inf*); **~folge** *f* sequence of notes/sounds; (*bei Film*) sound sequence; **~frequenz** *f* audio frequency; **~gefäß** *nt* earthenware vessel; **~geschirr** *nt* earthenware; **~geschlecht** *nt* scale; **t~haltig** *adj* clayey, argillaceous (*spec*), argilliferous (*spec*); **~höhe** *f* pitch.
Tonika *f* -, **Toniken** (*Mus*) tonic.
Tonikum *nt* -s, **Tonika** tonic.
Ton-: **~ingenieur** *m* sound engineer; **~kabine** *f* sound booth; **~kamera** *f* sound camera; **~kopf** *m* recording head; **~lage** *f* pitch (level); (*~umfang*) register; **eine ~lage höher** one note higher; **~leiter** *f* scale; **t~los** *adj* toneless; *Stimme auch* flat; ... **sagte er t~los** ... he said in a flat voice; **~malerei** *f* (*Mus*) tone painting; **~meister** *m* sound mixer.
Tonnage [tɔ'na:ʒə] *f* -, -n (*Naut*) tonnage.

➤ SPRACHE AKTIV: **Tod** → 51.4

Tönnchen *nt* little barrel, tub; (*fig hum: Mensch*) roly-poly (*inf*), dumpling (*inf*).

Tonne *f* **-, -n (a)** (*Behälter*) barrel, cask; (*aus Metall*) drum; (*für Regen auch*) butt; (*Müll~*) bin (*Brit*), trash can (*US*); (*inf: Mensch*) fatty (*inf*). **(b)** (*Gewicht*) metric ton(ne). **(c)** (*Register~*) (register) ton. **(d)** (*Naut: Boje*) buoy.

Tonnen-: ~gewölbe *nt* (*Archit*) barrel vaulting; **t~weise** *adv* by the ton, in tons; **t~weise Fische fangen** (*fig*) to catch tons (and tons) of fish.

Ton-: ~setzer *m* (*geh*) composer; **~silbe** *f* tonic *or* stressed syllable; **~sprache** *f* tone language; **~spur** *f* soundtrack; **~störung** *f* sound interference; **~streifen** *m* soundtrack; **~studio** *nt* recording studio.

Tonsur *f* tonsure.

Ton-: ~taube *f* clay pigeon; **~taubenschießen** *nt* clay pigeon shooting; **~techniker** *m* sound technician; **~träger** *m* sound-carrier; **~umfang** *m* register.

Tonung *f* (*Phot*) toning.

Tönung *f* (*das Tönen*) tinting; (*Farbton*) shade, tone; (*Haar~*) hair colour.

Ton-: ~waren *pl* earthenware *sing*; **~ziegel** *m* brick; (*Dachziegel*) tile.

Top *nt* **-s, -s** (*Fashion*) top.

Top- *in cpds* top.

Topas *m* **-es, -e** topaz.

Topf *m* **-(e)s, ¨-e** pot; (*Koch~ auch*) (sauce)pan; (*Nacht~*) potty (*inf*); (*sl: Toilette*) loo (*Brit inf*), john (*US inf*) ◆ **alles in einen ~ werfen** (*fig*) to lump everything together; **jeder ~ findet seinen Deckel** (*fig inf*) every Jack will find his Jill (*prov*).

Topfblume *f* potted flower.

Töpfchen *nt dim of* **Topf.**

Topfen *m* **-s, -** (*Aus, S Ger*) *siehe* **Quark.**

Töpfer(in *f*) *m* **-s, -** potter; (*dial: Ofensetzer*) stove fitter.

Töpferei *f* pottery.

Töpferhandwerk *nt* potter's trade.

töpfern [1] *vi* to do pottery.
[2] *vt* to make (in clay) ◆ **wir sahen zu, wie er auf der Scheibe eine Vase töpferte** we watched him throwing a vase.

Töpfer-: ~ofen *m* kiln; **~scheibe** *f* potter's wheel; **~waren** *pl* pottery *sing*; (*irden*) earthenware *sing.*

Topfhandschuh *m* ovenglove.

topfit ['tɔp'fɪt] *adj pred* in top form; (*gesundheitlich*) as fit as a fiddle.

Topf-: ~kuchen *m siehe* **Gugelhupf**; **~lappen** *m* ovencloth; (*kleiner*) panholder; **~markt** *m market where pots and pans are sold*; **~pflanze** *f* potted plant.

Toplader *m* **-s, -** top loader.

⚠**Topograph(in** *f*) *m* topographer.

⚠**Topographie** *f* topography.

⚠**topographisch** *adj* topographic(al).

Topologie *f* (*Math*) topology.

Topos *m* **-, Topoi** (*Liter*) topos.

topp *interj* done, it's a deal.

Topp *m* **-s, -e** *or* **-s** (*Naut*) masthead ◆ **über die ~en geflaggt sein** *or* **haben** to be dressed overall.

Toppsegel *nt* topsail.

Tor[1] *m* **-en, -en** (*old, liter*) fool.

Tor[2] *nt* **-(e)s, -e (a)** (*lit, fig: Himmels~, Höllen~*) gate; (*Durchfahrt, fig: zum Glück etc*) gateway; (*~bogen*) archway; (*von Garage, Scheune*) door ◆ **jdm das ~ zu etw öffnen** to open sb's eyes to sth; *zu Karriere etc* to open the door to sth for sb; *siehe* **Felsentor, Gletschertor, Tür. (b)** (*Sport*) goal; (*bei Skilaufen*) gate ◆ **im ~ stehen** to be in goal, to be the goalkeeper.

Tor-: ~bogen *m* arch, archway; **~einfahrt** *f* entrance gate.

Torero *m* **-(s), -s** torero.

⚠**Toresschluß** *m siehe* **Torschluß.**

Torf *m* **-(e)s,** *no pl* peat.

Torf-: ~boden *m* peat; **~erde** *f* peat; **~feuerung** *f* peat fire(s).

torfig *adj* peaty.

Torflügel *m* gate (*of a pair of gates*).

Torf-: ~moor *nt* peat bog *or* (*trocken*) moor; **~moos** *nt* sphagnum (moss); **~mull** *m* (loose) garden peat; **~stecher** *m* **-s, -** peat-cutter; **~stich** *m* patch *or* plot of peat.

Torheit *f* foolishness, stupidity; (*törichte Handlung*) foolish *or* stupid action ◆ **er hat die ~ begangen, zu ...** he was foolish *or* stupid enough to ...

Torhüter *m siehe* **Torwart.**

töricht *adj* foolish, stupid; *Wunsch, Hoffnung* idle.

törichterweise *adv* foolishly, stupidly.

Torjäger *m siehe* **Torschütze.**

torkeln *vi aux sein* to stagger, to reel.

Tor-: ~latte *f* crossbar; **~lauf** *m* slalom; **~linie** *f* goal-line; **t~los** *adj* goalless; **das Spiel blieb t~los** *or* **ging t~los aus** it was a goalless draw, there was no score; **~mann** *m, pl* **-männer** goalkeeper, goalie (*inf*).

Törn *m* **-s, -s** (*Naut*) cruise.

Tornado *m* **-s, -s** tornado.

Tornister *m* **-s, -** (*Mil*) knapsack; (*dated: Schulranzen*) satchel.

torpedieren* *vt* (*Naut, fig*) to torpedo.

Torpedo *m* **-s, -s** torpedo.

Torpedoboot *nt* torpedo-boat.

Tor-: ~pfosten *m* gatepost; (*Sport*) goalpost; ⚠**~schluß** *m* (*fig*) **kurz vor ~schluß** at the last minute *or* the eleventh hour; **nach ~schluß** too late; ⚠**~schlußpanik** *f* (*inf*) last minute panic; (*von Unverheirateten*) fear of being left on the shelf; **~schütze** *m* (goal) scorer.

Torsion *f* torsion.

Torsions-: ~festigkeit *f* torsional strength; **~stab** *m* torsion bar.

Torso *m* **-s, -s** *or* **Torsi** torso; (*fig*) skeleton.

Torszene *f* action in the goal area *no pl.*

Tort [tɔrt] *m* **-(e)s,** *no pl* (*geh*) wrong, injustice ◆ **jdm etw zum ~ tun** to do sth to vex sb.

Törtchen *nt dim of* **Torte** (small) tart, tartlet.

Torte *f* **-, -n** gâteau; (*Obst~*) flan.

Tortelett *nt* **-s, -s, Tortelette** *f* (small) tart, tartlet.

Torten-: ~boden *m* flan case *or* (*ohne Seiten*) base; **~diagramm** *nt* pie chart; ⚠**~guß** *m* glaze; **~heber** *m* **-s, -** cake slice; **~platte** *f* cake plate; **~schaufel** *f* cake slice.

Tortur *f* torture; (*fig auch*) ordeal.

Tor-: ~verhältnis *nt* score; **~wächter, ~wart** *m* goalkeeper.

tosen *vi* **(a)** to roar, to thunder; (*Wind, Sturm*) to rage ◆ **~der Beifall** thunderous applause. **(b)** *aux sein* (*mit Ortsangabe*) to thunder.

tot *adj* **(a)** (*gestorben*) (*lit, fig*) dead; (*inf: erschöpft*) dead (beat) (*inf*), whacked (*inf*) ◆ **mehr ~ als lebendig** (*fig inf*) more dead than alive; **~ geboren werden** to be stillborn; **~ umfallen** *or* **zu Boden fallen** to drop dead; **ich will ~ umfallen, wenn das nicht wahr ist** cross my heart and hope to die (if it isn't true) (*inf*); **~ zusammenbrechen** to collapse and die; **er war auf der Stelle ~** he died instantly; **den ~en Mann machen** (*inf*) to float on one's back; **ein ~er Mann sein** (*fig inf*) to be a goner (*inf*).
(b) (*leblos*) *Ast, Pflanze, Geschäftszeit, Sprache, Leitung* dead; *Augen* sightless, blind; *Haus, Stadt* deserted; *Gegend auch, Landschaft etc* bleak; *Wissen* useless; *Vulkan auch* extinct; *Farbe* dull, drab; (*Rail*) *Gleis* disused ◆ **~er Flußarm** backwater; (*Schleife*) oxbow (lake); **ein ~er Briefkasten** a dead-letter box; **der ~e Winkel** the blind spot; (*Mil*) dead angle; **das T~e Meer** the Dead Sea; **ein ~er Punkt** (*Stillstand*) a standstill *or* halt; (*in Verhandlungen*) deadlock; (*körperliche Ermüdung*) low point (*of energy/stamina*); **ich habe im Moment meinen ~en Punkt** I'm at a low ebb just now; **den ~en Punkt überwinden** to break the deadlock; (*körperlich*) to get one's second wind.
(c) (*nutzlos*) *Last, Gewicht* dead; (*bei Fahrzeug auch*) unladen; *Kapital* dead ◆ **ein ~es Rennen** (*lit, fig*) a dead heat; **~er Gang** (*Tech*) play.
(d) (*Min*) **ein ~er Mann** *a worked-out part of a mine.*

total [1] *adj* total; *Staat* totalitarian.
[2] *adv* totally.

Total-: ~ansicht *f* complete view; **~ausverkauf** *m* clearance sale.

Totalisator *m* totalizator, tote (*inf*).

totalitär [1] *adj* totalitarian.
[2] *adv* in a totalitarian way.

Totalitarismus *m* totalitarianism.

Totalität *f* totality, entirety.

Total-: ~operation *f* extirpation; (*von Gebärmutter*) hysterectomy; (*mit Eierstöcken*) hysterosaphorectomy; **~schaden** *m* write-off; **~schaden machen** (*inf*) to write a car *etc* off.

tot-: ~arbeiten *vr sep* (*inf*) to work oneself to death; **~ärgern** *vr sep* (*inf*) to be/become livid.

Totem *nt* **-s, -s** totem.

Totemismus *m* totemism.

Totempfahl *m* totem pole.

töten *vti* (*lit, fig*) to kill; *Nerv* to deaden ◆ **er/das kann einem den Nerv ~** (*fig inf*) he/that really gets on my/one's *etc* nerves *or* wick (*inf*); *siehe* **Blick.**

Toten-: ~acker *m* (*liter*) graveyard; **~amt** *nt* requiem mass; **~bestattung** *f* burial of the dead; **~bett** *nt* deathbed; ⚠**t~blaß** *adj* deathly pale, pale as death; **~blässe** *f* deathly pallor; **t~bleich** *adj siehe* **t~blaß**; **~feier** *f* funeral *or* burial ceremony; **~flecke** *pl* post-mortem *or* cadaveric (*spec*) lividity *sing*; **~glocke** *f* (death) knell; **~gräber** *m* gravedigger; **~hemd** *nt* shroud; **~klage** *f* lamentation of the dead; (*Liter*) dirge, lament; **~kopf** *m* **(a)** skull; (*als Zeichen*) death's-head; (*auf Piratenfahne, Arzneiflasche etc*) skull and crossbones; **(b)** (*Zool*) death's-head moth; **~kult** *m* cult of the dead; **~maske** *f* death mask; **~messe** *f* requiem mass; **~reich** *nt* (*Myth*) kingdom of the dead; **~schein** *m* death certificate; **~sonntag** *m Sunday before Advent, on which the dead are commemorated*; **~stadt** *f* necropolis; **~starre** *f* rigor mortis; **t~still** *adj* deathly silent *or* quiet; **~stille** *f* deathly silence *or* quiet; **~tanz** *m* dance of death, danse macabre; **~wache** *f* wake.

Tote(r) *mf decl as adj* dead person, dead man/woman; (*bei Unfall etc*) fatality; (*Mil*) casualty ◆ **die ~n** the dead; **es gab 3 ~** 3 people died *or* were killed; **das ist ein Lärm, um ~ aufzuwecken** the noise is enough to waken the dead.

Tot-: ~erklärte(r) *mf decl as adj* person *or* man/woman *etc* declared to be dead; **t~fahren** *vt sep irreg* (*inf*) to knock down and kill; ⚠**t~geboren** *adj attr* stillborn; **ein t~geborenes Kind sein** (*fig*) to be doomed (to failure); **~geburt** *f* stillbirth; (*Kind*) stillborn child *or* baby; **~geglaubte(r)** *mf decl as adj* person *or* man/woman *etc* believed to be dead; **~gesagte(r)** *mf decl as adj* person *or* man/woman *etc* who has been declared dead; **t~kriegen** *vt sep* (*inf*) **nicht t~zukriegen sein** to go on for ever; **t~lachen** *vr sep* (*inf*) to kill oneself (laughing) (*inf*); **es ist zum ~lachen** it is killingly funny *or* killing (*inf*); **t~laufen** *vr sep irreg* (*inf*) to peter out; **t~machen** *sep* (*inf*) [1] *vt* to kill; [2] *vr* (*fig*) to kill oneself.

Toto *m or* (*inf, Aus, Sw*) *nt* **-s, -s** (football) pools ◆ **(im) ~ spielen** to do the pools; **etw im ~ gewinnen** to win sth on the pools; **im ~ gewinnen** (*Hauptgewinn*) to win the pools; **er hat vier Richtige im ~** four of his matches came up.

Toto- *in cpds* pools; **~schein, ~zettel** *m* pools coupon.

Tot-: **t~schießen** *vt sep irreg (inf)* to shoot dead; **~schlag** *m (Jur)* manslaughter; *(US)* homicide; *siehe* **Mord**; **t~schlagen** *vt sep irreg (lit, fig)* to kill; *(inf) Menschen auch* to beat to death; **du kannst mich t~schlagen, ich weiß es nicht/habe es nicht** for the life of me I don't know/haven't got it; **~schläger** *m* cudgel, club; **t~schweigen** *vt sep irreg* to hush up *(inf)*; **t~stellen** *vr sep* to pretend to be dead, to play dead; *(Mensch auch)* to play possum *(inf)*; **t~treten** *vt sep irreg* to trample to death; *Insekt etc* to tread on and kill.

Tötung *f* killing ◆ **fahrlässige ~** manslaughter through culpable negligence.

Tötungs-: **~absicht** *f* intention to kill; **~versuch** *m* attempted murder.

Touch [tatʃ] *m* **-s, -s** *(Atmosphäre)* air, tone, flavour; *(Flair)* touch; *(Tendenz)* leanings *pl*.

Toupet [tu'pe:] *nt* **-s, -s** toupée.

toupieren* [tu'pi:rən] *vt* to backcomb.

Tour [tu:ɐ] *f* **-, -en** **(a)** *(Fahrt)* trip, outing; *(Ausflugs~)* tour; *(Spritz~) (mit Auto)* drive; *(mit Rad)* ride; *(Wanderung)* walk, hike; *(Berg~)* climb ◆ **auf ~ gehen** to go on *or* for a trip *or* outing/on a tour/for a drive/ride/walk *or* hike/climb; **auf ~ sein** to be away on a trip *or* outing/tour; to be out for a drive/ride/walk; to be off climbing; **eine ~ machen** to go on a trip *or* outing/tour; to go for a drive/ride/walk/climb.
(b) *(Umdrehung)* revolution, rev *(inf)*; *(beim Tanz)* figure; *(beim Stricken)* two rows; *(mit Rundnadeln)* round ◆ **auf ~en kommen** *(Auto)* to reach top speed; *(fig inf)* to get into top gear; *(sich aufregen)* to get worked up *(inf)*; **auf vollen ~en laufen** *(lit)* to run at full *or* top speed; *(fig)* to be in full swing; **in einer ~** *(inf)* incessantly, the whole time.
(c) *(inf: Art und Weise)* ploy ◆ **mit der ~ brauchst du mir gar nicht zu kommen** don't try that one on me; **auf die krumme** *or* **schiefe** *or* **schräge ~** by dishonest means; **etw auf die weiche ~ versuchen** to try using soft soap to get sth.

Tour de force [tu:ɐdə'fɔrs] *f* **-** *no pl* tour de force.

Touren- ['tu:rən-]: **~fahrer** *m* long-distance driver; **~rad** *nt* tourer; **~ski** *m* cross country ski; **~wagen** *m (im Motorsport)* saloon (car); **~zahl** *f* number of revolutions *or* revs *pl (inf)*; **~zähler** *m* rev counter.

Tourismus [tu'rɪsmʊs] *m* tourism.

Tourist [tu'rɪst] *m* tourist.

Touristenklasse [tu'rɪst(ə)n-] *f* tourist class.

Touristik [tu'rɪstɪk] *f* tourism, tourist industry.

Touristik|unternehmen [tu'rɪstɪk-] *nt* tour company.

Touristin [tu'rɪstɪn] *f* tourist.

Tournedos [tʊrnə'do:] *nt* **-, -** [-'do:s] *usu pl (Cook)* tournedos.

Tournee [tʊr'ne:] *f* **-, -n** [-e:ən] *or* **-s** tour ◆ **auf ~ gehen/sein** to go on tour/be on tour *or* touring.

tour-retour [tu:ɐre'tu:ɐ] *adv (Aus)* return.

Tower ['tauə] *m* **-s, -** *(Aviat)* control tower.

Toxikologe *m*, **Toxikologin** *f* toxicologist.

toxikologisch *adj* toxicological.

toxisch *adj* toxic.

Toxizität *f* **-**, *no pl* toxicity.

Toxoplasmose *f* **-, -n** toxoplasmosis.

Trab *m* **-(e)s**, *no pl* trot ◆ **im ~** at a trot; **(im) ~ reiten** to trot; **sich in ~ setzen** *(inf)* to get going *or* cracking *(inf)*; **auf ~ sein** *(inf)* to be on the go *(inf)*; **jdn in ~ halten** *(inf)* to keep sb on the go; **jdn auf (den) ~ bringen** *(inf)* to make sb get a move on *(inf)*.

Trabant *m* **(a)** *(Astron)* satellite. **(b)** *(Hist)* bodyguard; *(fig)* satellite. **(c)** *usu pl (dated inf)* kiddie-wink *(inf)*.

Trabantenstadt *f* satellite town.

Trabbi *m* **-s, -s** *(inf)* East German car.

traben *vi* **(a)** *aux haben or sein* to trot ◆ **mit dem Pferd ~** to trot one's horse. **(b)** *aux sein (inf: laufen)* to trot ◆ **ich mußte noch einmal in die Stadt ~** I had to go traipsing back into town.

Traber *m* **-s, -** trotter.

Trab-: **~rennbahn** *f* trotting course; **~rennen** *nt* trotting; *(Veranstaltung)* trotting race.

Tracht *f* **-, -en** **(a)** *(Kleidung)* dress, garb; *(Volks~ etc)* costume; *(Schwestern~)* uniform. **(b)** *(obs: Traglast)* load ◆ **jdm eine ~ Prügel verabfolgen** *or* **verabreichen** *(inf)* to give sb a beating *or* thrashing.

trachten *vi (geh)* to strive *(nach* for, after) ◆ **danach ~, etw zu tun** to strive *or* endeavour to do sth; **jdm nach dem Leben ~** to be after sb's blood.

Trachten-: **~fest** *nt festive occasion where traditional/national costume is worn*; **~gruppe** *f group dressed in traditional/national costume*; **~jacke** *f traditionally styled jacket made of thick woollen material*; *(von Volkstracht) jacket worn as part of traditional/national costume*; **~kostüm** *nt suit made of thick woollen material*.

trächtig *adj (lit) Tier* pregnant; *(fig geh)* laden *(von* with); *Gedanke etc* meaningful, significant.

Trackball ['trɛkbɔ:l] *m (Comput)* trackball.

tradieren* *vt (geh)* to hand down.

Tradition [tradi'tsio:n] *f* tradition.

Traditionalismus [traditsiona'lɪsmʊs] *m* traditionalism.

Traditionalist(in *f)* [traditsiona'lɪst, -ɪn] *m* traditionalist.

traditionalistisch [traditsiona'lɪstɪʃ] *adj* traditionalistic.

traditionell [traditsio'nɛl] *adj usu attr* traditional.

Traditions-: ⚠**t~bewußt** *adj* tradition-conscious; ⚠**~bewußtsein** *nt* tradition-consciousness, consciousness of tradition; **t~gebunden** *adj* bound by tradition; **t~gemäß** *adv* traditionally, according to tradition; **t~reich** *adj* rich in tradition.

traf *pret of* **treffen**.

Trafik *f* **-, -en** *(Aus)* tobacconist's (shop).

Trafikant(in *f)* *m (Aus)* tobacconist.

Trafo *m* **-(s), -s** *(inf)* transformer.

träg *adj siehe* **träge**.

Trag-: **~bahre** *f* stretcher; **t~bar** *adj* **(a)** *Apparat, Gerät* portable; *Kleid* wearable; **(b)** *(annehmbar)* acceptable *(für* to); *(erträglich)* bearable.

Trage *f* **-, -n** *(Bahre)* litter; *(Tragkorb)* pannier.

träge *adj* **(a)** sluggish; *Mensch, Handbewegung etc auch* lethargic ◆ **geistig ~** mentally lazy. **(b)** *(Phys) Masse* inert.

tragen *pret* **trug**, *ptp* **getragen** [1] *vt* **(a)** *(durch Hochheben, befördern, dabeihaben)*, *(fig) Schall* to carry; *(an einen Ort bringen)* to take; *(Wellen etc auch)* to bear; *(fig) Gerücht etc* to pass on, to spread ◆ **etw mit** *or* **bei sich ~** to carry sth with one; **den Brief zur Post ~** to take the letter to the post office; **den Arm in der Schlinge ~** to have one's arm in a sling.
(b) *(am Körper ~) Kleid, Brille, Rot etc, Perücke* to wear; *(im Moment auch)* to have on; *Bart, Gebiß* to have; *Waffen* to carry ◆ **wie trägt sie zur Zeit ihre Haare?** how is she wearing her hair now?; **getragene Kleider** second-hand clothes; *(abgelegt)* cast-offs; *siehe* **Trauer**.
(c) *(stützen, halten, fig)* to support; *(fig: Vertrauen, Hoffnung auch)* to sustain; *siehe* **tragend, getragen**.
(d) *(aushalten, Tragfähigkeit haben)* to take (the weight of), to carry.
(e) *(hervorbringen) Zinsen* to yield; *Ernte auch* to produce; *(lit, fig) Früchte* to bear ◆ **der Baum/Acker trägt viele Früchte/viel Weizen** the tree/field produces a good crop of fruit/wheat; *(in dieser Saison)* the tree/field is full of fruit/wheat.
(f) *(trächtig sein)* to be carrying.
(g) *(ertragen) Schicksal, Leid etc* to bear, to endure; *Kreuz* to bear.
(h) *(übernehmen) Verluste* to defray; *Kosten auch* to bear, to carry; *Risiko* to take; *Folgen* to take, to bear; *(unterhalten) Verein, Organisation* to support, to back ◆ **die Verantwortung/Schuld für etw ~** to be responsible for sth/to be to blame for sth.
(i) *(haben) Titel, Namen, Aufschrift etc* to bear, to have; *Vermerk* to contain; *Etikett* to have ◆ **der Brief trägt das Datum vom ...** the letter is dated ...
[2] *vi* **(a)** *(Baum, Acker etc)* to crop, to produce a crop ◆ **gut/schlecht ~** to crop well/badly, to produce a good/bad crop; *(in dieser Saison)* to have a good/bad crop.
(b) *(schwanger sein)* to be pregnant.
(c) *(reichen: Geschütz, Stimme)* to carry.
(d) *(Eis)* to take weight ◆ **das Eis trägt noch nicht** the ice won't take anyone's weight yet.
(e) **schwer an etw** *(dat)* **~** to have a job carrying *or* to carry sth; *(fig)* to find sth hard to bear; **schwer zu ~ haben** to have a lot to carry; *(fig)* to have a heavy cross to bear.
(f) **zum T~ kommen** to come to fruition; *(nützlich werden)* to come in useful; **etw zum T~ bringen** to bring sth to bear *(in +dat* on).
[3] *vr* **(a)** **sich gut** *or* **leicht/schwer** *or* **schlecht ~** to be easy/difficult *or* hard to carry; **schwere Lasten ~ sich besser auf dem Rücken** it is better to carry heavy loads on one's back.
(b) *(Kleid, Stoff)* to wear.
(c) *(geh: gekleidet sein)* to dress.
(d) **sich mit etw ~** *(geh)* to contemplate sth.
(e) *(ohne Zuschüsse auskommen)* to be self-supporting.

tragend *adj* **(a)** *(stützend) Säule, Bauteil, Chassisteil* weight- *or* load-bearing; *(fig: bestimmend) Idee, Motiv* fundamental, basic. **(b)** *(Theat) Rolle* major, main. **(c)** *Stimme* resonant. **(d)** *(trächtig)* pregnant.

Träger *m* **-s, -** **(a)** *(an Kleidung)* strap; *(Hosen~)* braces *pl*.
(b) *(Build) (Holz~, Beton~)* (supporting) beam; *(Stahl~, Eisen~)* girder.
(c) *(Tech: Stütze von Brücken etc)* support.
(d) *(Flugzeug~)* carrier.
(e) *(Mensch) (von Lasten)* bearer, porter; *(Aus~ von Zeitungen)* delivery boy; *(von Namen)* bearer; *(rare: von Orden, Amt, Titel)* bearer, holder; *(von Kleidung)* wearer; *(eines Preises)* winner; *(von Krankheit)* carrier.
(f) *(fig) (der Kultur, Staatsgewalt etc)* representative; *(einer Bewegung, Entwicklung)* upholder, supporter; *(einer Veranstaltung)* sponsor; *(Mittel)* vehicle ◆ **~ des Vereins/der Universitäten** those who support *or* back the club/are responsible for the universities.

Träger-: **~flugzeug** *nt* carrier plane; **~hose** *f* trousers *pl* with straps.

Trägerin *f siehe* **Träger (e)**.

Träger-: **~kleid** *nt* pinafore dress *(Brit)*, jumper *(US)*; *(sommerlich)* sundress; **~lohn** *m* porterage; **~material** *nt* base material, carrier material; **~rakete** *f* booster, carrier rocket; **~rock** *m* pinafore dress *(Brit)*, jumper *(US)*; *(für Kinder)* skirt with straps; **~schürze** *f* pinafore; **~system** *nt (Mil)* carrier system; **~waffe** *f* carrier weapon.

Trage-: **~tasche** *f* carrier bag; **~zeit** *f* gestation period.

Trag-: **t~fähig** *adj* able to take a load/weight; *(fig)* serviceable, workable; **~fähigkeit** *f* load-/weight-bearing capacity; *(von Brücke)* maximum load; *(fig)* workability; **~fläche** *f* wing; *(von Boot)* hydrofoil; **~flächenboot** *nt* hydrofoil; **~flügel** *m siehe* **~fläche**; **~flügelboot** *nt siehe* **~flächenboot**.

Trägheit *f siehe adj* sluggishness; lethargy; *(Faulheit)* laziness; *(Phys)* inertia.

Trägheits-: **~gesetz** *nt* law of inertia; **~moment** *nt* moment of inertia.

Traghimmel *m* canopy, baldachin.

Tragik *f* tragedy ◆ **das ist die ~ der Sache, daß ...** what's tragic about it is that ...

⚠: Informationen zur Rechtschreibreform im Anhang

Tragiker *m* **-s, -** tragedian.

Tragi-: ~komik *f* tragicomedy; **t~komisch** *adj* tragicomical; **~komödie** *f* tragicomedy.

tragisch *adj* tragic ◆ **etw ~ nehmen** (*inf*) to take sth to heart; **das ist nicht so ~** (*inf*) it's not the end of the world.

Trag-: ~korb *m* pannier; **~kraft** *f siehe* **~fähigkeit**; **~last** *f* load; (*Gepäck*) heavy luggage (*esp Brit*) *or* baggage; **~lufthalle** *f* air hall.

Tragöde *m* **-n, -n** tragedian.

Tragödie [-iə] *f* (*Liter, fig*) tragedy ◆ **es ist eine ~ mit ihm/dieser Maschine** he/this machine is a disaster.

Tragödien- [-iən-]: **~darsteller** *m* tragedian; **~dichter** *m* tragedian.

Tragödin *f* tragedienne.

Trag-: ~pfeiler *m* weight- *or* load-bearing pillar; (*von Brücke*) support; **~riemen** *m* strap; (*von Gewehr*) sling; **~schicht** *f* base course; **~sessel** *m* sedan chair; **~weite** *f* (*von Geschütz etc*) range; (*fig*) consequences *pl*; (*von Gesetz*) scope; **sind Sie sich der ~weite dieses Schritts/Ihres Handelns bewußt?** are you aware of the possible consequences *or* of the implications of this step/of your action?, are you aware of what this step/your action could mean?; **von großer ~weite sein** to have far-reaching consequences *or* implications; **~werk** *nt* (*Aviat*) wing assembly.

Trailer ['treılɐ] *m* **-s, -** **(a)** (*Aut: Anhänger*) trailer. **(b)** (*Filmwerbung*) trailer.

Trainer(in *f*) ['trɛːnɐ, 'treː-] *m* **-s, -** coach, trainer; (*von Rennpferd*) trainer; (*von Schwimmer, Tennisspieler*) coach; (*bei Fußball*) manager; (*Sw: Trainingsanzug*) track-suit.

trainieren* [trɛ'niːrən, treː'n-] **1** *vt* to train; *Mannschaft, Sportler auch* to coach; *Sprung, Übung, Weitsprung* to practise; *Muskel* to exercise ◆ **Fußball/Tennis ~** to do some football/tennis practice; **ein (gut) trainierter Sportler** an athlete who is in training; **auf etw** (*acc*) **trainiert sein** to be trained to do sth; **jdn auf** *or* **für etw** (*acc*) **~** to train *or* coach sb for sth.

2 *vi* (*Sportler*) to train; (*Rennfahrer*) to practise; (*Übungen machen*) to exercise; (*üben*) to practise ◆ **auf** *or* **für etw** (*acc*) **~** to train/practise for sth; **da mußt du schon noch etwas ~** you'll have to practise that a bit more.

3 *vr* to train (*auf +acc* for); (*üben*) to practise; (*um fit zu werden*) to get some exercise, to get into training.

Training ['trɛːnɪŋ, 'treːn-] *nt* **-s, -s** training *no pl*; (*Fitneß~*) exercise *no pl*; (*Autorennen*) practice; (*fig: Übung*) practice ◆ **er geht jeden Abend zum ~** he goes training every evening; **ein 2-stündiges ~** a 2-hour training session *or* bout; **er übernimmt das ~ der Mannschaft** he's taking over the training *or* coaching of the team; **im ~ stehen** to be in training; **durch regelmäßiges ~ lernen die Schüler ...** by regular practice the pupils learn ...

Trainings-: ~anzug *m* track-suit; **~hose** *f* track-suit trousers *pl*; **~jacke** *f* track-suit top; **~lager** *nt* training camp; **~methode** *f* training method; **~möglichkeit** *f* training facilities *pl*; **~runde** *f* practice lap; **~schuh** *m* training shoe; **~zeit** *f* practice time.

Trakehner *m* **-s, -** *type of riding horse from Prussia.*

Trakt *m* **-(e)s, -e** (*Gebäudeteil*) section; (*Flügel*) wing; (*von Autobahn auch*) stretch.

Traktat *m or nt* **-(e)s, -e** **(a)** (*Abhandlung*) treatise; (*Flugschrift, religiöse Schrift*) tract.
(b) (*obs: Vertrag*) treaty.

Traktätchen *nt* (*pej*) tract.

traktieren* *vt* (*inf*) (*schlecht behandeln*) to maltreat; *Menschen auch* to give a rough time (to); (*quälen*) *kleine Schwester, Tier etc* to torment ◆ **jdn mit Vorwürfen ~** to keep on at sb (*inf*); **er hat ihn mit Tritten gegen das Schienbein traktiert** he kicked him on the shin.

Traktion *f* (*Aut*) traction.

Traktor *m* **-s, -en** tractor; (*Comput*) tractor feed.

Traktorist(in *f*) *m* (*DDR*) tractor-driver.

trällern *vti* to warble; (*Vogel auch*) to trill ◆ **vor sich hin ~** to warble away to oneself.

Tram *f* **-, -s** (*dial, Sw*), **Trambahn** *f* (*S Ger*) *siehe* **Straßenbahn.**

Tramp [trɛmp, tramp] *m* **-s, -s** tramp.

Trampel *m or nt* **-s, -** *or f* **-, -n** clumsy clot (*inf*), clumsy oaf (*inf*) ◆ **~ vom Land** (country) bumpkin *or* cousin.

trampeln **1** *vi* **(a)** (*mit den Füßen stampfen*) to stamp ◆ **die Zuschauer haben getrampelt** the audience stamped their feet.
(b) *aux sein* (*schwerfällig gehen*) to stamp *or* tramp along ◆ **über die Wiese/das Gras ~** to tramp across the meadow/grass.
2 *vt* **(a)** (*mit Füßen bearbeiten*) *Weg* to trample ◆ **jdn zu Tode ~** to trample sb to death.
(b) (*abschütteln*) to stamp (*von* from).

Trampel-: ~pfad *m* track, path; **~tier** *nt* **(a)** (*Zool*) (Bactrian) camel; **(b)** (*inf*) clumsy oaf (*inf*).

trampen ['trɛmpn, 'tram-] *vi aux sein* to hitch-hike, to hitch (*inf*).

Tramper(in *f*) ['trɛmpɐ, -ərın] *m* **-s, -** hitch-hiker, hitcher (*inf*).

Trampfahrt *f* **(a)** (*Naut*) tramp voyage ◆ **auf ~ sein** to be tramping. **(b)** (*Reise per Anhalter*) hitch-hiking tour ◆ **auf ~ sein** to be away hitch-hiking.

Trampolin *nt* **-s, -e** trampoline.

Trampolinspringen *nt* **-s,** *no pl* trampolining.

Tramp-: ~schiff *nt* tramp (ship); **~schiffahrt** *f* tramp shipping.

Tramway ['tramve] *f* **-, -s** (*Aus*) *siehe* **Straßenbahn.**

Tran *m* **-(e)s, -e** **(a)** (*von Fischen*) train oil. **(b)** (*inf*) **im ~** dop(e)y (*inf*); (*leicht betrunken*) tipsy, merry (*inf*); **ich lief wie im ~ durch die Gegend** I was running around in a dream *or* a daze; **das habe ich im ~ ganz vergessen** it completely slipped my mind.

Trance ['trãːs(ə)] *f* **-, -n** trance.

Trance-: t~artig *adj* trance-like; **~zustand** *m* (state of) trance.

Tranche ['trãːʃ(ə)] *f* **-, -n** (*St Ex*) tranche of a bond issue; (*Anleihe*) quota share.

Tranchierbesteck [trã'ʃiːɐ-] *nt* carving set, set of carvers.

tranchieren* [trã'ʃiːrən] *vt* to carve.

Tranchier-: ~gabel *f* carving-fork; **~messer** *nt* carving-knife.

Träne *f* **-, -n** tear; (*einzelne ~*) tear(drop); (*inf: Mensch*) drip (*inf*) ◆ **den ~n nahe sein** to be near to *or* on the verge of tears; **zu ~n rühren** to move to tears; **unter ~n lächeln** to smile through one's tears; **unter ~n gestand er seine Schuld/Liebe** in tears he confessed his fault/love; **~n lachen** to laugh till one cries *or* till the tears run down one's cheeks; **deswegen vergieße ich keine ~n** (*fig*) I'll shed no tears over that; **die Sache/der Mann ist keine ~ wert** the matter/man isn't worth crying over; **bittere ~n weinen** to shed bitter tears; **jdm/sich die ~n trocknen/abwischen** to dry sb's/one's eyes, to wipe away sb's/one's tears.

tränen *vi* to water.

Tränen-: ~drüse *f* lachrymal gland; **der Film drückt sehr auf die ~drüsen** the film is a real tear-jerker (*inf*); **im Schlußakt drückt der Autor kräftig auf die ~drüsen** (*inf*) the author has written a real tear-jerker of a final act; **t~feucht** *adj* wet with tears; *Augen* tear-filled; ⚠**~fluß** *m* flood of tears; **~gas** *nt* tear gas; **~kanal** *m* tear duct; **t~reich** *adj* tearful; **~sack** *m* lachrymal sac.

Tran-: ~funsel, ~funzel *f* (*inf*) slowcoach (*Brit inf*), slowpoke (*US inf*); **t~funzlig** *adj* (*inf*) slow, sluggish.

tranig *adj* like train oil; (*inf*) slow, sluggish.

Trank *m* **-(e)s, ¨e** (*liter*) drink, draught (*liter*), potion (*liter*).

trank *pret of* **trinken.**

Tränke *f* **-, -n** drinking trough.

tränken *vt* **(a)** *Tiere* to water. **(b)** (*durchnässen*) to soak ◆ **seine Antwort war mit Hohn getränkt** (*geh*) his answer brimmed with scorn.

Trans- *in cpds* trans-.

Trans|aktion *f* transaction.

trans|atlantisch *adj* transatlantic.

transchieren* *vt* (*Aus*) *siehe* **tranchieren.**

Trans-Europ(a)-Express *m* Trans-Europe Express.

Transfer *m* **-s, -s** transfer; (*Psych*) transference.

transferieren* *vt* to transfer.

Transformation *f* transformation.

Transformations-: ~grammatik *f* transformational grammar; **~regel** *f* transformation rule.

Transformator *m* transformer.

Transformatorenhäuschen *nt* transformer. .

transformieren* *vt* to transform.

Transfusion *f* transfusion.

Transistor *m* transistor.

Transistorradio *nt* transistor (radio).

Transit *m* **-s, -e** transit.

Transit-: ~abkommen *nt* transit agreement; **~halle** *f* (*Aviat*) transit area; **~handel** *m* transit trade.

transitiv *adj* (*Gram*) transitive.

Transit-: ~raum *m* (*Aviat*) transit lounge; **~sperre** *f*, **~verbot** *nt ban on the transit of goods, people etc through neighbouring country*; **~verkehr** *m* transit traffic; (*~handel*) transit trade; **Passagiere im ~verkehr** transit passengers *pl.*

transkribieren* *vt* to transcribe; (*Mus*) to arrange.

Transmission *f* (*Mech*) transmission.

Trans|ozean- *in cpds* transoceanic.

transparent [transpa'rɛnt] *adj* transparent; *Gewebe etc* diaphanous (*liter*); (*fig geh*) *Argument* lucid, clear.

Transparent [transpa'rɛnt] *nt* **-(e)s, -e** (*Reklameschild etc*) neon sign; (*Durchscheinbild*) transparency; (*Spruchband*) banner.

Transparentpapier *nt* waxed tissue paper; (*zum Pausen*) tracing paper.

Transparenz [transpa'rɛnts] *f siehe adj* transparency; diaphaneity (*liter*); lucidity, clarity ◆ **sie fordern mehr ~ bei allen Vorgängen in der Politik** they demand more openness in all political matters.

transpersonal *adj* (*Psych*) transpersonal.

Transpiration [transpira'tsioːn] *f* (*geh*) perspiration; (*von Pflanze*) transpiration.

transpirieren* [transpi'riːrən] *vi* (*geh*) to perspire; (*Pflanze*) to transpire.

Transplantat [transplan'taːt] *nt* (*Haut*) graft; (*Organ*) transplant.

Transplantation [transplanta'tsioːn] *f* **(a)** (*Med*) transplant; (*von Haut*) graft; (*Vorgang*) transplantation; grafting. **(b)** (*Bot*) grafting.

transplantieren* [transplan'tiːrən] *vti* **(a)** (*Med*) *Organ* to transplant; *Haut* to graft. **(b)** (*Bot*) to graft.

transponieren* [transpo'niːrən] *vt* (*Mus*) to transpose.

Transport [trans'pɔrt] *m* **-(e)s, -e** **(a)** (*das Transportieren*) transport ◆ **ein ~ auf dem Landweg** road transport; **ein ~ des Kranken ist ausgeschlossen** moving the patient is out of the question; **beim ~ beschädigte/verlorengegangene Waren** goods damaged/lost in transit.
(b) (*Fracht*) consignment, shipment; (*von Soldaten etc*) load, transport; (*von Gefangenen*) transport.

transportabel [transpɔr'taːbl] *adj* transportable.

Transport- [trans'pɔrt-]: **~arbeiter** *m* transport worker; **~band** *nt* conveyor belt; **~behälter** *m* container.

Transporter [trans'pɔrtɐ] *m* **-s, -** (*Schiff*) cargo ship; (*Flugzeug*) transport

⚠: for details of spelling reform, see supplement

plane; (*Auto*) van; (*Auto*~) transporter.

Transporteur [transpɔr'tøːɐ] *m* **(a)** (*Mensch*) removal man. **(b)** (*an Nähmaschine*) fabric guide, feed dog. **(c)** (*Winkelmesser*) protractor.

Transporteurin [transpɔr'tøːrɪn] *f siehe* **Transporteur (a)**.

Transport- [trans'pɔrt-]: **t~fähig** *adj* moveable; **~flugzeug** *nt* transport plane *or* aircraft.

transportieren* [transpɔr'tiːrən] [1] *vt* to transport; *Güter, Sauerstoff auch* to carry; *Patienten* to move; *Film* to wind on; (*Nähmaschine*) to feed.
[2] *vi* (*Förderband*) to move; (*Nähmaschine*) to feed; (*Kamera*) to wind on.

Transport- [trans'pɔrt-]: **~kosten** *pl* carriage *sing*; **~mittel** *nt* means of transport *sing*; **~schaden** *m* damage in transit; **~schiff** *nt* cargo ship; (*Mil*) transport ship; **~unternehmen** *nt* haulier, haulage firm; **~wesen** *nt* transport.

Transsexuelle(r) *mf decl as adj* transsexual.

Transuse *f* **-, -n** (*inf*) slowcoach (*Brit inf*), slowpoke (*US inf*).

Transvestismus [transvɛs'tɪsmʊs] *m* transvestism.

Transvestit [transvɛs'tiːt] *m* **-en, -en** transvestite.

transzendent *adj* transcendent(al); (*Math*) transcendental.

transzendental *adj* transcendental.

Transzendenz *f* transcendency, transcendence.

Trantüte *f* (*inf*) slowcoach (*Brit inf*), slowpoke (*US inf*).

Trapez *nt* **-es, -e (a)** (*Math*) trapezium. **(b)** (*von Artisten*) trapeze.

Trapez-: **~akt** *m* trapeze act; **t~förmig** *adj* trapeziform; **~künstler** *m* trapeze artist.

Trapezoeder *nt* **-s, -** trapezohedron.

Trapezoid *nt* **-(e)s, -e** trapezoid.

Trappist *m* (*Eccl*) trappist.

trapp, trapp *interj* (*von Kindern etc*) clitter clatter; (*von Pferd*) clip clop.

trappeln *vi aux sein* to clatter; (*Pony*) to clip-clop.

trapsen *vi aux sein* (*inf*) to galumph (*inf*); *siehe* **Nachtigall**.

Trara *nt* **-s, -s** (*von Horn*) tantara; (*fig inf*) hullabaloo (*inf*), to-do (*inf*) (*um* about).

Trassant *m* (*Fin*) drawer.

Trassat *m* **-en, -en** (*Fin*) drawee.

Trasse *f* **-, -n** (*Surv*) marked-out route.

Trassenführung *f* route.

trat *pret of* **treten**.

Tratsch *m* **-(e)s,** *no pl* (*inf*) gossip, scandal, tittle-tattle (*inf*).

tratschen *vi* (*inf*) to gossip.

Tratscherei *f* (*inf*) gossip(ing) *no pl*, scandalmongering *no pl*.

Tratsch-: **~maul** *nt*, **~tante** *f* (*pej inf*) scandalmonger, gossip.

Tratte *f* **-, -n** (*Fin*) draft.

Trau|altar *m* altar.

Traube *f* **-, -n** (*einzelne Beere*) grape; (*ganze Frucht*) bunch of grapes; (*Blütenstand*) raceme (*spec*); (*fig*) (*von Bienen*) cluster; (*Menschen~*) bunch, cluster ◆ **~n** (*Fruchtart*) grapes.

Trauben-: **~lese** *f* grape harvest; **~saft** *m* grape juice; **~zucker** *m* glucose, dextrose.

trauen [1] *vi +dat* to trust ◆ **einer Sache** (*dat*) **nicht ~** to be wary of sth; **ich traute meinen Augen/Ohren nicht** I couldn't believe my eyes/ears; **ich traue dem Frieden nicht** (I think) there must be something afoot, it's too good to be true; *siehe* **Weg**.
[2] *vr* to dare ◆ **sich** (*acc or (rare) dat*) **~, etw zu tun** to dare (to) do sth; **ich trau' mich nicht** I daren't, I dare not; **sich auf die Straße/nach Hause/zum Chef ~** to dare to go out (of doors)/home/to one's boss.
[3] *vt* to marry ◆ **sich standesamtlich/kirchlich ~ lassen** to get married in a registry office (*Brit*)/in church.

➤ **Trauer** *f* **-,** *no pl* (*das Trauern, ~zeit, ~kleidung*) mourning; (*Schmerz, Leid*) sorrow, grief ◆ **~ haben/tragen** to be in mourning; **in tiefer ~** ... (much loved and) sadly missed by ...

Trauer-: **~anzeige** *f* obituary, death notice; **~arbeit** *f, no pl* (*Psych*) grieving; **~binde** *f* black armband; **~botschaft** *f* sad news *sing, no indef art*; **~brief** *m* letter announcing sb's death; **~fall** *m* bereavement, death; **~feier** *f* funeral service; **~flor** *m* black ribbon; **~gefolge** *nt* funeral procession; **~gemeinde** *f* mourners *pl*; **~haus** *nt* house of mourning; **~jahr** *nt* year of mourning; **~karte** *f* card announcing sb's death; **~kleidung** *f* mourning; **~kloß** *m* (*inf*) wet blanket (*inf*); **~mantel** *m* (*Zool*) Camberwell beauty; **~marsch** *m* funeral march; **~miene** *f* (*inf*) long face.

trauern *vi* to mourn (*um jdn* (for) sb, *um etw* sth); (*Trauerkleidung tragen*) to be in mourning ◆ **die ~den Hinterbliebenen** his/her bereaved family.

Trauer-: **~nachricht** *f* sad news *sing, no indef art*; **~parte** *f* (*Aus*) *siehe* **~anzeige**; **~rand** *m* black edge *or* border; **~ränder** (*inf*) dirty fingernails; **~schleier** *m* black *or* mourning veil; **~spiel** *nt* tragedy; (*fig inf*) fiasco; **es ist ein ~spiel mit ihm/dem Projekt** he's really pathetic/the project is in a bad way (*inf*); **~weide** *f* weeping willow; **~zeit** *f* (period of) mourning; **~zug** *m* funeral procession.

Traufe *f* **-, -n** eaves *pl*; *siehe* **Regen**.

träufeln [1] *vt* to dribble.
[2] *vi aux haben or sein* (*old, geh: Wasser*) to trickle.

Trauformel *f* marriage vows *pl*.

traulich *adj* cosy ◆ **~ zusammenleben** to live together harmoniously *or* in harmony.

Traulichkeit *f* cosiness.

Traum *m* **-(e)s, Träume** (*lit, fig*) dream; (*Tag~ auch*) daydream, reverie ◆ **sie lebt wie im ~** she is living (as if) in a dream *or* (*nach Schock*) daze; **er fühlte sich wie im ~** he felt as if he were dreaming; **es war immer sein ~, ein großes Haus zu besitzen** he had always dreamed of owning a large house; **aus der ~!, der ~ ist aus!** it's all over; **aus der ~ vom neuen Auto** that's put paid to your/my *etc* dreams of a new car; **dieser ~ ist ausgeträumt** this dream is over; **der ~ meiner schlaflosen Nächte** (*hum inf*) the man/woman of my dreams; **Träume sind Schäume** dreams are but shadows; *siehe* **einfallen**.

Trauma *nt* **-s, Traumen** *or* **-ta** (*Med, Psych*) trauma; (*fig auch*) nightmare.

traumatisch *adj* (*Psych*) traumatic; (*fig auch*) nightmarish.

Traum-: **~arbeit** *f, no pl* (*Psych*) dreaming; **~beruf** *m* dream job, job of one's dreams; **~bild** *nt* vision; **~deuter** *m* interpreter of dreams; **~deutung** *f* dream interpretation, interpretation of dreams.

Traumen *pl of* **Trauma**.

träumen [1] *vi* to dream; (*tag~ auch*) to daydream; (*inf: nicht aufpassen*) to (day)dream, to be in a dream ◆ **von jdm/etw ~** to dream about sb/sth; (*sich ausmalen*) to dream of sb/sth; **mir träumte, daß** ... I dreamed *or* dreamt that ...; **träume süß!** sweet dreams!; **vor sich hin ~, mit offenen Augen ~** to daydream; **du träumst wohl!** (*inf*) you must be joking!; **das hätte ich mir nicht ~ lassen** I'd never have thought it possible.
[2] *vt* to dream; *Traum* to have ◆ **etwas Schönes/Schreckliches ~** to have a pleasant/an unpleasant dream.

Träumer(in *f*) *m* **-s, -** (day)dreamer; (*Phantast*) dreamer, visionary.

Träumerei *f* **(a)** *no pl* (*das Träumen*) (day)dreaming. **(b)** (*Vorstellung*) daydream, reverie.

träumerisch *adj* dreamy; (*schwärmerisch*) wistful.

Traum-: **~fabrik** *f* (*pej*) dream factory; **t~haft** *adj* (*phantastisch*) fantastic; (*wie im ~*) dreamlike.

Trauminet *m* **-s, -e** (*Aus*) coward.

Traum-: **~paar** *nt* perfect couple; **~reise** *f* trip of a lifetime, dream holiday; **~tänzer** *m* dreamer; **t~tänzerisch** *adj* dreamy, idealistic; **t~verloren** [1] *adj* dreamy; [2] *adv* dreamily, as if in a dream.

Traurede *f* marriage sermon; (*im Standesamt*) marriage address.

traurig *adj* sad; (*unglücklich*) *Verhältnisse, Leben auch* unhappy; *Blick auch* sorrowful; (*beklagenswert*) *Zustand* sad, sorry; *Leistung, Erfolg, Rekord* pathetic, sorry; *Wetter* miserable; *Berühmtheit* notorious ◆ **mit meinen Finanzen/der Wirtschaft sieht es sehr ~ aus** my finances are/the economy is in a very sorry state; **~, ~** dear, dear; **wie sieht es damit aus? — ~(, ~)** what are the prospects for that? — not at all good *or* pretty bad; **um meine Zukunft sieht es ~ aus** my future doesn't look too bright; **das ist doch ~, was er da geleistet hat** what he's done is pathetic; **das sind ja ~e Verhältnisse, wenn** ... it is a sorry *or* sad state of affairs when ...; **es ist ~, wenn** it is sad if ...; **~ weggehen** to go away sadly *or* feeling sad.

Traurigkeit *f* sadness ◆ **allgemeine ~** a general feeling of sadness.

Trau-: **~ring** *m* wedding ring; **~schein** *m* marriage certificate.

traut *adj* (*liter, hum*) (*gemütlich*) cosy; (*vertraut*) familiar; *Freund* close ◆ **im ~en Kreise** among one's family and friends; **ein Abend im ~en Heim** an evening at home; **~es Heim Glück allein** (*prov*) home sweet home.

Traute *f*: **~ haben/keine ~ haben** (*inf*) to have/not to have the guts (*inf*).

Trauung *f* wedding, wedding *or* marriage ceremony.

Trauzeuge *m* witness (*at marriage ceremony*).

Travestie [travɛs'tiː] *f* travesty.

travestieren* [travɛs'tiːrən] *vt* to travesty, to make a travesty of.

Trebe *f*: **auf ~ gehen/sein** (*sl*) to run away from home/to be a runaway.

Treber *pl* (*Bier~*) spent hops *pl*; (*Wein~*) marc *sing*; (*Frucht~*) pomace *sing*.

Treck *m* **-s, -s** trek, trail; (*Leute*) train; (*die Wagen etc*) wagon train.

Trecker *m* **-s, -** tractor.

Treff[1] *nt* **-s, -s** (*Cards*) club ◆ **die ~sieben** the seven of clubs; **das ~as** the ace of clubs.

Treff[2] *m* **-s, -s** (*inf*) (*Treffen*) meeting, get-together (*inf*); (*~punkt*) haunt, rendezvous.

treffen *pret* **traf**, *ptp* **getroffen** [1] *vt* **(a)** (*durch Schlag, Schuß etc*) to hit (*an/in +dat* on, *in +acc* in); (*Blitz, Faust auch, Unglück*) to strike ◆ **auf dem Photo bist du gut getroffen** (*inf*) that's a good photo *or* picture of you; *siehe* **Schlag**.
(b) (*fig: kränken*) to hurt.
(c) (*betreffen*) to hit, to affect ◆ **es trifft immer die Falschen** it's always the wrong people who are hit *or* affected; **ihn trifft keine Schuld** he's not to blame.
(d) (*finden*) to hit upon, to find; (*lit, fig*) *Ton* to hit ◆ **du hast's getroffen** (*mit Antwort*) you've hit the nail on the head; (*mit Geschenk*) that's the very thing.
(e) (*jdm begegnen, mit jdm zusammenkommen*) to meet; (*an~*) to find.
(f) **es gut/schlecht ~** to be fortunate *or* lucky/unlucky (*mit* with); **es mit dem Wetter/der Unterkunft gut/schlecht ~** to have good/bad weather/accommodation; **ich hätte es schlechter ~ können** it could have been worse.
(g) *Anstalten etc* to make; *Vereinbarung* to reach; *Entscheidung auch, Vorsorge, Maßnahmen* to take.
[2] *vi* **(a)** (*Schlag, Schuß etc*) to hit ◆ **der Schuß/er hat getroffen** the shot/he hit it/him *etc*; **nicht ~** to miss; **gut/schlecht ~** to aim well/badly; **getroffen!** a hit; *siehe* **Schwarze(s)**.
(b) *aux sein* (*stoßen*) **auf jdn/etw ~** to meet sb/sth.
(c) (*verletzen*) to hurt ◆ **sich getroffen fühlen** to feel hurt; (*auf sich beziehen*) to take it personally.
[3] *vr* (*zusammen~*) to meet ◆ **unsere Interessen ~ sich im Sport** we are both interested in sport.
[4] *vr impers* **es trifft sich, daß** ... it (just) happens that ...; **das trifft sich gut/schlecht, daß** ... it is convenient/inconvenient that ...

Treffen *nt* **-s, -** meeting; (*Sport, Mil*) encounter ◆ **ins ~ führen** (*Mil*) to send into battle; (*fig*) to put forward.
treffend *adj* apt; *Ähnlichkeit* striking ◆ **jdn ~ nachahmen** to do a brilliant imitation of sb.
Treffer *m* **-s, -** hit; (*Tor*) goal; (*fig: Erfolg*) hit; (*Gewinnlos*) winner ◆ **das Geschenk/das Auto war ein ~** the present/car was just the right thing; **einen ~ erzielen** to score a hit; (*Ftbl*) to shoot a goal.
Trefferquote *f* **-, -n** hit rate; (*Ftbl*) number of goals scored; (*bei Ratespiel etc*) score.
trefflich *adj* (*liter*) splendid, excellent.
Treff-: ~punkt *m* rendezvous, meeting place; **einen ~punkt ausmachen** to arrange where *or* somewhere to meet; **t~sicher** *adj* accurate; (*fig*) *Bemerkung* apt; *Urteil* sound, unerring; **~sicherheit** *f* accuracy; aptness; soundness, unerringness.
Treib-: ~anker *m* sea anchor, drag anchor; **~eis** *nt* drift ice.
treiben *pret* **trieb**, *ptp* **getrieben** [1] *vt* **(a)** (*lit, fig*) to drive; (*Tech: an~ auch*) to propel; (*auf Treibjagd*) *Wild* to beat; *Teig* to make rise; (*fig: drängen*) to rush; (*an~*) to push ◆ **jdn zum Wahnsinn/zur Verzweiflung/zum Selbstmord ~** to drive sb mad/to despair/to (commit) suicide; **jdn zur Eile/Arbeit ~** to make sb hurry (up)/work; **jdn zum Äußersten ~** to push sb too far; **die ~de Kraft bei etw sein** to be the driving force behind sth.
(b) (*Reaktion erzeugen*) to bring ◆ **jdm den Schweiß/das Blut ins Gesicht ~** to make sb sweat/blush; **der Wind/der Gedanke treibt mir Tränen in die Augen** the wind makes my eyes water/the thought brings tears to my eyes.
(c) (*einschlagen*) *Nagel, Pfahl etc* to drive.
(d) (*bearbeiten, formen*) *Metall* to beat.
(e) (*ausüben, betreiben*) *Handel, Geschäfte* to do; *Studien, Politik* to pursue; *Gewerbe* to carry on; *Sport* to do; (*machen*) to do; *Schabernack, Unfug, Unsinn* to be up to; *Spaß* to have; *Aufwand* to make, to create; *Unzucht* to commit ◆ **was treibst du?** what are you up to?; **Schiffahrt ~** to sail; **Mißbrauch mit etw ~** to abuse sth; **Handel mit etw/jdm ~** to trade in sth/with sb; **Wucher ~** to profiteer.
(f) wenn du es weiter so treibst ... if you go *or* carry on like that ...; **es toll ~** to have a wild time; **es zu toll ~** to overdo it; **es schlimm ~** to behave badly; **es zu bunt** *or* **weit ~** to go too far; **er treibt es noch so weit, daß er hinausgeworfen wird** if he goes on like that, he'll get thrown out; **es mit jdm ~** (*sl*) to have it off with sb (*Brit inf*), to have sex with sb.
(g) (*hervorbringen*) *Blüten, Knospen etc* to sprout, to put forth; (*im Treibhaus*) to force; *siehe* **Blüte**.
[2] *vi* **(a)** *aux sein* (*sich fortbewegen*) to drift ◆ **sich ~ lassen** (*lit, fig*) to drift; **sich von der Stimmung ~ lassen** to let oneself be carried along by the mood.
(b) (*wachsen*) to sprout.
(c) (*Bier, Kaffee, Medizin etc*) to have a diuretic effect; (*Hefe*) to make dough *etc* rise ◆ **~de Medikamente** diuretics.
Treiben *nt* **-s, - (a)** (*Getriebe*) hustle and bustle; (*von Schneeflocken*) swirling ◆ **ich beobachte dein ~ schon lange** I've been watching what you've been getting up to for a long time. **(b)** (*Treibjagd*) battue (*spec*).
Treiber *m* (*Comput*) driver.
Treiber(in *f*) *m* **-s, -** (*Vieh~*) drover; (*Hunt*) beater.
Treib-: ~gas *nt* (*bei Sprühdosen*) propellant; **~gut** *nt* flotsam and jetsam *pl*.
Treibhaus *nt* hothouse.
Treibhaus-: ~effekt *m* (*Met*) greenhouse effect; **~gas** *nt* greenhouse gas; **~luft** *f* **(a)** hothouse air; **(b)** (*fig*) hot, humid atmosphere; (*im Freien auch*) sultry atmosphere; **~pflanze** *f* hothouse plant; **~temperatur** *f* hothouse temperature; **hier herrscht die reinste ~temperatur!** it's like a hothouse here.
Treib-: ~holz *nt* driftwood; **~jagd** *f* battue (*spec*), shoot (*in which game is sent up by beaters*); **~mittel** *nt* (*in Sprühdosen*) propellant; (*Cook*) raising agent; **~netz** *nt* driftnet; **~sand** *m siehe* **Triebsand**; **~schlag** *m* (*Sport*) drive; **~stoff** *m* fuel; (*Raketen~ auch*) propellant.
treideln *vt* to tow.
Trema *nt* **-s, -s** *or* **-ta** dieresis.
tremolieren* *vi* to quaver.
Tremolo *nt* **-s, -s** *or* **Tremoli** tremolo.
Trenchcoat ['trentʃko:t] *m* **-(s), -s** trenchcoat.
Trend *m* **-s, -s** trend ◆ **voll im ~ liegen** to follow the trend.
Trend-: ~meldung *f* (*Pol*) report on voting trends *or* patterns; (*fig*) projection; **~setter** *m* **-s, -** trendsetter; **~wende** *f* new trend.
trennbar *adj* separable ◆ **ein nicht ~es Wort** an inseparable word.
trennen [1] *vt* **(a)** (*entfernen*) *Mensch, Tier* to separate (*von* from); (*Tod*) to take away (*von* from); (*in Teile teilen, ab~*) to separate; *Kopf, Glied etc* to sever; (*abmachen*) to detach (*von* from); *Aufgenähtes* to take off, to remove; *Saum, Naht* to unpick, to undo ◆ **zwei Teile voneinander ~** to separate two parts; **etw in zwei Hälften ~** to divide *or* split sth into two halves.
(b) (*aufspalten, scheiden*) *Bestandteile, Eier, Raufende* to separate; *Partner, Freunde* to split up; (*räumlich*) to separate; *Begriffe* to differentiate, to distinguish (between); *Ehe* to dissolve; (*nach Rasse, Geschlecht*) to segregate ◆ **voneinander getrennt werden** to be separated; **Ursache und Folge ~** to make *or* draw a distinction between cause and results; **Gut von Böse ~** to distinguish between good and evil, to differentiate *or* distinguish good from evil; **uns trennt zu vieles** we have too little in common; **jetzt kann uns nichts mehr ~** now nothing can ever come between us; **alles T~de (zwischen uns/den beiden)** all our/their differences; **das Radio trennt die Sender gut/schlecht** the radio has good/bad selectivity; *siehe* **getrennt**.
(c) (*in Bestandteile zerlegen*) *Kleid* to take to pieces; (*Ling*) *Wort* to divide, to split up; (*Chem*) *Gemisch* to separate (out).
[2] *vr* **(a)** (*auseinandergehen*) to separate; (*Partner, Eheleute etc auch*) to split up; (*Abschied nehmen*) to part ◆ **sich von jdm/der Firma ~** to leave sb/the firm; **die zwei Mannschaften trennten sich 2:0/1:1** the final score was 2-0/the two teams drew one-all; **sich im guten/bösen ~** to part on good/bad terms.
(b) (*weggeben, verkaufen etc*) **sich von etw ~** to part with sth; **er konnte sich davon nicht ~** he couldn't bear to part with it; (*von Plan*) he couldn't give it up; (*von Anblick*) he couldn't take his eyes off it; (*von Party*) he couldn't tear himself away.
(c) (*sich teilen*) (*Wege, Flüsse*) to divide ◆ **hier ~ sich unsere Wege** (*fig*) now we must go our separate ways.
[3] *vi* (*zwischen Begriffen*) to draw *or* make a distinction.
Trenn-: ~messer *nt* (*Sew*) unpicker; **~punkt** *m* (*Ling*) dieresis; **t~scharf** *adj* **t~scharf sein** to have good selectivity; **~schärfe** *f* selectivity.
Trennung *f* **(a)** (*Abschied*) parting. **(b)** (*Getrenntwerden, Getrenntsein*) separation; (*das Trennen auch*) separating; (*in Teile*) division; (*von Begriffen*) distinction; (*von Sender*) selectivity; (*von Wort*) division; (*Rassen~, Geschlechter~*) segregation ◆ **die Partner entschlossen sich zu einer ~** the partners decided to separate *or* split up.
Trennungs-: ~entschädigung *f*, **~geld** *nt* separation allowance; **~schmerz** *m* pain of parting; **~strich** *m* hyphen; **einen ~strich ziehen** (*fig*) to make a clear distinction (*zwischen* between).
Trenn(ungs)-: ~wand *f* partition (wall); **~zeichen** *nt* hyphen.
Trense *f* **-, -n** snaffle.
trepp|auf *adv*: **~, treppab** up and down stairs.
Treppe *f* **-, -n (a)** (*Aufgang*) (flight of) stairs *pl*, staircase; (*im Freien*) (flight of) steps *pl* ◆ **eine ~** a staircase, a flight of stairs/steps; **wir haben die ~** (*inf*), **wir sind mit der ~ an der Reihe** (*inf*) it's our turn to clean *or* do the stairs; **die ~ hinaufgehen/hinuntergehen** to go up/down the stairs, to go upstairs/downstairs; **du bist wohl die ~ hinuntergefallen!** (*fig inf*) what's happened to your hair?; *siehe* **hinauffallen**.
(b) (*inf: Stufe*) step.
(c) (*inf: Stockwerk*) floor.
Treppen-: ~absatz *m* half-landing; **~geländer** *nt* banister; **~haus** *nt* stairwell; **im ~haus** on the stairs; **~stufe** *f* step, stair; **~witz** *m*: **ein ~witz der Weltgeschichte** an irony of history.
Tresen *m* **-s, -** (*Theke*) bar; (*Ladentisch*) counter.
Tresor *m* **-s, -e** (*Raum*) strongroom, vault; (*Schrank*) safe.
Tresorknacker *m* **-s, -** (*inf*) safebreaker.
Tresse *f* **-, -n** gold/silver braid.
Trester *pl siehe* **Treber**.
Tret-: ~auto *nt* pedal car; **~boot** *nt* pedal boat, pedalo; **~eimer** *m* pedal bin.
treten *pret* **trat**, *ptp* **getreten** [1] *vi* **(a)** (*ausschlagen, mit Fuß anstoßen*) to kick (*gegen etw* sth, *nach* out at).
(b) *aux sein* (*mit Raumangabe*) to step ◆ **hier kann man nicht mehr ~** there is no room to move here; **vom Schatten ins Helle ~** to move out of the shadow into the light; **etwas näher an etw** (*acc*) **~** to move *or* step closer to sth; **vor die Kamera ~** to appear on TV/in a film *or* on the screen; **in den Vordergrund/Hintergrund ~** to step forward/back; (*fig*) to come to the forefront/to recede into the background; **an jds Stelle ~** to take sb's place; *siehe* **nah(e)**.
(c) *aux sein or haben* (*in Loch, Pfütze, auf Gegenstand etc*) to step, to tread ◆ **jdm auf den Fuß ~** to step on sb's foot, to tread on sb's toe; **jdm auf die Füße ~** (*fig*) to tread on sb's toes; **jdm auf den Schlips** (*inf*) *or* **Schwanz** (*sl*) **~** to offend sb; **sich auf den Schlips** (*inf*) *or* **Schwanz** (*sl*) **getreten fühlen** to feel offended; *siehe* **Stelle**.
(d) *aux sein or haben* (*betätigen*) **in die Pedale ~** to pedal hard; **aufs Gas(pedal) ~** (*Pedal betätigen*) to press the accelerator; (*schnell fahren*) to put one's foot down (*inf*), to step on it (*inf*); **auf die Bremse ~** to brake, to put one's foot on the brake.
(e) *aux sein* (*hervor~, sichtbar werden*) **Wasser trat aus allen Ritzen und Fugen** water was coming out of every crack and cranny; **der Schweiß trat ihm auf die Stirn** sweat appeared on his forehead; **Tränen traten ihr in die Augen** tears came to her eyes, her eyes filled with tears; **der Fluß trat über die Ufer** the river overflowed its banks; **der Mond trat aus den Wolken** the moon appeared from behind the clouds; **es trat plötzlich wieder in mein Bewußtsein** it suddenly came back to me.
(f) *aux sein* (*Funktionsverb*) (*beginnen*) to start, to begin; (*ein~*) to enter ◆ **in jds Leben** (*acc*) **~** to come into *or* enter sb's life; **ins Leben ~** to come into being; **in den Ruhestand ~** to retire; **in den Streik** *or* **Ausstand ~** to go on strike; **in den Staatsdienst/Stand der Ehe** *or* **Ehestand ~** to enter the civil service/into the state of matrimony; **mit jdm in Verbindung ~** to get in touch with sb; *siehe* **Erscheinung, Kraft** *etc*.
[2] *vt* **(a)** (*einen Fußtritt geben, stoßen*) to kick; (*Sport*) *Ecke, Freistoß* to take ◆ **jdn ans Bein ~** to kick sb's leg *or* sb on the leg; **jdn mit dem Fuß ~** to kick sb; **sich** (*dat*) **in den Hintern ~** (*fig inf*) to kick oneself.
(b) (*mit Fuß betätigen*) *Spinnrad, Webstuhl, Blasebalg* to operate (*using one's foot*) ◆ **die Bremse ~** to brake, to put on the brakes; **die Pedale ~** to pedal.
(c) (*trampeln*) *Pfad, Weg, Bahn* to tread ◆ **sich** (*dat*) **einen Splitter in den Fuß ~** to get a splinter in one's foot; *siehe* **Wasser**.
(d) (*fig*) (*schlecht behandeln*) to shove around (*inf*) ◆ **jdn ~** (*inf: antreiben*) to get at sb.
(e) (*begatten*) to tread, to mate with.
Treter *m* **-s, -** (*inf*) comfortable shoe.

Tret-: ~mine *f (Mil)* (anti-personnel) mine; **~mühle** *f (lit, fig)* treadmill; **in der ~mühle sein** to be in a rut *(inf)*; **die tägliche ~mühle** the daily grind; **~rad** *nt* treadmill; **~roller** *m* scooter.

treu [1] *adj Freund, Sohn, Kunde etc* loyal; *Diener auch* devoted; *Seele auch, Hund, Gatte etc* faithful; *Abbild* true; *Gedenken* respectful; *(~herzig)* trusting; *Miene* innocent ◆ **jdm in ~er Liebe verbunden sein** to be bound to sb by loyalty and love; **jdm ~ sein/bleiben** to be/remain faithful; *(nicht betrügen auch)* to be/remain true to sb; **sich** *(dat)* **selbst ~ bleiben** to be true to oneself; **seinen Grundsätzen ~ bleiben** to stick to *or* remain true to one's principles; **der Erfolg/das Glück ist ihr ~ geblieben** success kept coming her way/her luck held (out); **~ wie Gold** faithful and loyal; *(Diener etc auch)* faithful as a dog; **Dein ~er Freund** *(old)* yours truly; **jdm etw zu ~en Händen übergeben** to give sth to sb for safekeeping.
[2] *adv* faithfully; *dienen auch* loyally; *sorgen* devotedly; *(~herzig)* trustingly; *ansehen* innocently ◆ **~ und brav** *(Erwachsener)* dutifully; *(Kind)* like a good boy/girl, as good as gold; *siehe* **ergeben**.

Treu-: ~bruch *m* breach of faith; **t~brüchig** *adj* faithless, false; **(jdm) t~brüchig werden** to break faith (with sb); **t~deutsch** *adj* truly German; *(pej)* typically German; **t~doof** *adj (inf)* guileless, artless, naive.

Treue *f -, no pl siehe* **treu** loyalty; devotion, devotedness; faithfulness; *(eheliche ~)* faithfulness, fidelity ◆ **einer Flagge ~ geloben** to pledge allegiance to a flag; **sie gelobten einander ewige ~** they vowed to be eternally faithful to one another; **jdm die ~ halten** to keep faith with sb; *(Ehegatten etc)* to remain faithful to sb; **auf Treu und Glauben** in good faith; **in alter ~** for old times' sake; **in alter ~ Dein** as ever, yours; *siehe* **brechen**.

Treu|eid *m* oath of loyalty *or* allegiance.

Treu(e)pflicht *f* loyalty *(owed by employee to employer and vice versa)*.

Treueprämie *f* long-service bonus.

⚠ **treu|ergeben** *adj attr* devoted, loyal, faithful.

Treueschwur *m* oath of loyalty *or* allegiance; *(von Geliebtem etc)* vow to be faithful.

Treu-: ~hand *f -, no pl* trust; **~händer(in** *f***)** *m* **-s, -** trustee, fiduciary *(form)*; **~handgesellschaft** *f* trust company; **t~herzig** *adj* innocent, trusting; **~herzigkeit** *f* innocence; **t~los** *adj* disloyal, faithless; **t~los an jdm handeln** to fail sb; **du t~loses Stück** *(inf)* you wretch; *siehe* **Tomate**; **~losigkeit** *f* disloyalty, faithlessness; ⚠**t~sorgend** *adj attr* devoted.

Triage [tri'a:ʒə] *f* **-, -n (a)** *(Med)* triage. **(b)** *(Comm)* lower grade goods *pl*.

Triangel *m or (Aus) nt* **-s, -** triangle.

Trias *f -, no pl* Triassic (Period).

Triathlon *m* **-, -e** *(Sport)* triathlon.

Tribun *m* **-s** *or* **-en, -e(n)** tribune.

Tribunal *nt* **-s, -e** tribunal.

Tribunat *nt* **-(e)s, -e** tribunate.

Tribüne *f* **-, -n** *(Redner~)* platform, rostrum; *(Zuschauer~, Zuschauer)* stand; *(Haupt~)* grandstand.

Tribut *m* **-(e)s, -e** *(Hist)* tribute, dues *pl*; *(fig)* tribute; *(Opfer)* toll ◆ **jdm ~ entrichten** *or (fig)* **zollen** to pay tribute to sb.

tributpflichtig *adj* tributary *(rare)*, obliged to pay tribute.

Trichine *f* trichina.

Trichinen-: t~haltig *adj* trichinous; **~schau** *f* meat inspection *(to check for trichinae)*; **~schauer(in** *f***)** *m* **-s, -** meat inspector.

Trichter *m* **-s, -** funnel; *(Bomben~)* crater; *(von Grammophon)* horn; *(von Trompete, Megaphon etc)* bell; *(von Hörgerät)* trumpet; *(von Lautsprecher)* cone; *(Einfüll~)* hopper ◆ **jdn auf den ~ bringen** *(inf)*, to give sb a clue; **auf den ~ kommen** *(inf)* to catch on *(inf)*.

trichterförmig *adj* funnel-shaped, funnel-like.

Trick *m* **-s, -s** *or (rare)* **-e** trick; *(betrügerisch auch, raffiniert)* ploy, dodge; *(Tip, Rat)* tip ◆ **ein fauler/gemeiner ~** a mean *or* dirty trick; **keine faulen ~s!** no funny business! *(inf)*; **das ist der ganze ~** that's all there is to it; **den ~ raushaben, wie man etw macht** *(inf)* to have got the knack of doing sth; **der ~ dabei ist, ...** the trick is to ...; **da ist doch ein ~ dabei** there is a trick to (doing) it; **jdm einen ~ verraten** to give sb a tip.

Trick-: ~betrug *m* confidence trick; **~betrüger, ~dieb** *m* confidence trickster; **~film** *m* trick film; *(Zeichen~)* cartoon (film); **~kiste** *f (von Zauberer)* box of tricks; *(fig inf)* bag of tricks; **t~reich** *adj (inf)* tricky; *(raffiniert)* clever.

tricksen *(inf)* [1] *vi* to fiddle; *(Sport)* to feint ◆ **phantastisch, wie er mit den Karten trickst** it's amazing what he can do with cards.
[2] *vt* to trick.

Trickski *nt* trick skiing.

Tricktaste *f* trick *or* superimpose button.

trieb *pret of* **treiben**.

Trieb *m* **-(e)s, -e (a)** *(Psych, Natur~)* drive; *(Drang)* urge; *(Verlangen)* desire, urge; *(Neigung, Hang)* inclination; *(Selbsterhaltungs~, Fortpflanzungs~)* instinct ◆ **sie ist von ihren ~en beherrscht** she is guided completely by her physical urges *or* desires; **einen ~ zum Verbrechen haben** to have criminal urges.
(b) *(Bot)* shoot.
(c) *(Tech)* drive.

Trieb-: t~artig *adj attr Verhalten* instinctive; *(von Sexualverbrecher etc)* compulsive; **~befriedigung** *f* gratification of a physical urge; **~feder** *f (fig)* motivating force *(gen* behind*)*; **t~haft** *adj Handlungen* compulsive; **ein t~hafter Instinkt** an instinctive urge; **sie hat ein sehr t~haftes Wesen, sie ist ein t~hafter Mensch** she is ruled by her physical urges *or* desires; **~haftigkeit** *f* domination by one's physical urges; **~handlung** *f* act motivated by one's physical urges; **~kraft** *f (Mech)* motive power; *(Bot)* germinating power; *(fig)* driving force; **~leben** *nt* physical activities *pl*; *(Geschlechtsleben)* sex life; **~mensch** *m* creature of instinct; **~mittel** *nt siehe* **Treibmittel**; **~rad** *nt* driving wheel; **~sand** *m* quicksand; **~täter, ~verbrecher** *m* sexual offender; **~wagen** *m (Rail)* railcar; **~werk** *nt* power plant; *(in Uhr)* mechanism.

Trief-: ~auge *nt (Med)* bleary eye; **~augen** *(pej)* watery eyes; *(von Mensch)* sheep-like eyes; **t~äugig** *adj* watery-eyed; **er schaute mich t~äugig an** *(pej)* he looked at me with dumb devotion.

trief(e)lig *adj (inf) Mensch* drippy *(inf)*.

triefen *pret* **triefte** *or (geh)* **troff**, *ptp* **getrieft** *or (rare)* **getroffen** *vi* to be dripping wet; *(Nase)* to run; *(Auge)* to water ◆ **~ vor** to be dripping with; *(fig pej)* to gush with; **~d vor Nässe, ~d naß** dripping wet, wet through; **~d** soaking (wet).

Triefnase *f (inf)* runny nose *(inf)*.

triezen *vt (inf)* **jdn ~** to pester sb; *(schuften lassen)* to drive sb hard.

triff *imper sing of* **treffen**.

Trift *f* **-, -en** *(Weide)* pasture; *(Weg)* cattle/sheep track.

triftig *adj* convincing; *Entschuldigung, Grund auch* good.

Trigonometrie *f* trigonometry.

trigonometrisch *adj* trigonometric(al).

Trikolore *f* **-, -n** tricolour.

Trikot[1] [tri'ko:, 'trɪko] *m or nt* **-s**, *no pl (~stoff)* cotton jersey.

Trikot[2] [tri'ko:, 'trɪko] *nt* **-s, -s** *(Hemd)* shirt, jersey; *(dated: Turnanzug)* leotard; *(old: Badeanzug)* bathing costume ◆ **das gelbe ~** *(bei Tour de France)* the yellow jersey.

Trikotage [triko'ta:ʒə] *f* **-, -n** cotton jersey underwear *no pl*.

Trikotwerbung [tri'ko:-] *f* shirt advertising.

Triller *m* **-s, -** *(Mus)* trill; *(von Vogel auch)* warble.

trillern *vti* to warble, to trill ◆ **du trillerst wie eine Lerche** you sing like a lark.

Trillerpfeife *f* (pea-)whistle.

Trillion *f* **-, -en** trillion *(Brit)*, quintillion *(US)*.

Trilogie *f* trilogy.

Trimester *nt* **-s, -** term.

Trimm-: ~-Aktion *f* keep-fit campaign; **~-dich-Gerät** *nt* keep-fit apparatus; **~-dich-Pfad** *m* keep-fit trail.

trimmen [1] *vt Hund, Schiff, Flugzeug* to trim; *(inf) Mensch, Tier* to teach, to train; *Funkgerät* to tune ◆ **den Motor/das Auto auf Höchstleistung ~** *(inf)* to soup up the engine/car *(inf)*; **jdn auf tadelloses Benehmen ~** to teach *or* train sb to behave impeccably; **etw auf alt ~** to make sth look old; **auf alt getrimmt** done up to look old; **auf rustikal getrimmtes Restaurant** restaurant done up in rustic style; **jdn auf einen bestimmten Typ ~** to make *or* mould sb into a certain type.
[2] *vr* to do keep-fit (exercises) ◆ **trimm dich durch Sport** keep fit with sport.

Trimm-: ~gerät *nt* keep-fit apparatus; **~pfad** *m* keep-fit trail.

Trinität *f (geh)* trinity.

Trink-: t~bar *adj* drinkable; **~ei** *nt* new-laid egg.

trinken *pret* **trank**, *ptp* **getrunken** [1] *vt* to drink; *ein Bier, Tasse Tee, Flasche Wein auch* to have ◆ **alles/eine Flasche leer ~** to finish off all the drink/a bottle; **ich habe nichts zu ~ im Haus** I haven't any drink in the house; **er trinkt gern einen** *(inf)* he likes his drink; **(schnell) einen ~ gehen** *(inf)* to go for a (quick) drink; *siehe* **Tisch**.
[2] *vi* to drink ◆ **jdm zu ~ geben** to give sb a drink *or* something to drink; **laß mich mal ~** let me have a drink; **auf jds Wohl/jdn/etw ~** to drink sb's health/to sb/to sth.
[3] *vr* **sich voll/satt ~** to drink one's fill; *(mit Alkohol)* to get drunk; **sich arm ~** to drink one's money away.
[4] *vr impers* **es trinkt sich gut/schlecht daraus** it is easy/difficult to drink from; **dieser Wein trinkt sich gut** this is a pleasant *or* palatable wine.

Trinker(in *f***)** *m* **-s, -** drinker; *(Alkoholiker)* alcoholic.

Trinkerheil|anstalt *f (old)* detoxification centre.

Trink-: t~fest *adj* **so t~fest bin ich nicht** I can't hold my drink very well; **seine t~festen Freunde** his hard-drinking friends; **~festigkeit** *f* ability to hold one's drink; **t~freudig** *adj* fond of drinking; **~gefäß** *nt* drinking vessel; **~gelage** *nt* drinking session; **~geld** *nt* tip; **jdm ~geld geben** to tip sb, to give sb a tip; **~glas** *nt* (drinking) glass; **~halle** *f (in Heilbädern)* pump room; *(Kiosk)* refreshment kiosk; **~halm** *m* drinking straw; **~lied** *nt* drinking song; **~milch** *f* milk; **~schale** *f* drinking bowl; **~schokolade** *f* drinking chocolate; **~spruch** *m* toast.

Trinkwasser *nt* drinking water ◆ **„kein ~"** "not for drinking", "no drinking water".

Trinkwasser-: ~brunnen *m* drinking fountain; **~versorgung** *f* provision of drinking water.

Trio *nt* **-s, -s** trio.

Triole *f* **-, -n** *(Mus)* triplet.

Triolett *nt* **-(e)s, -e** triolet.

Trip *m* **-s, -s** *(inf)* trip.

trippeln *vi aux haben or (bei Richtungsangabe) sein* to trip; *(Kind, alte Dame)* to toddle; *(geziert)* to mince; *(Boxer)* to dance around; *(Pferd)* to frisk.

Tripper *m* **-s, -** gonorrhoea *no art* ◆ **sich** *(dat)* **den ~ holen** *(inf)* to get a dose (of the clap) *(inf)*.

trist *adj* dreary, dismal; *Farbe* dull.

Triste *f* **-, -n** *(Aus)* haystack.

Tritium *nt*, *no pl (abbr* **T***)* tritium.

tritt *imper sing of* **treten**.

Tritt *m* **-(e)s, -e (a)** (*Schritt*) step; (*Gang auch*) tread ◆ **einen falschen ~ machen** to take a wrong step; **ich hörte ~e** I heard footsteps; **(wieder) ~ fassen** to find one's feet (again).
(b) (*Gleichschritt*) step ◆ **im ~ marschieren, ~ halten** to march in step, to keep in step.
(c) (*Fuß~*) kick ◆ **jdm einen ~ geben** to give sb a kick, to kick sb; (*fig*) (*entlassen etc*) to kick sb out (*inf*); (*inf: anstacheln*) to give sb a kick in the pants (*inf*) *or* up the backside (*inf*); **einen ~ in den Hintern kriegen** (*inf*) to get a kick in the pants (*inf*) *or* up the backside (*inf*); (*fig*) to get kicked out (*inf*).
(d) (*bei ~leiter, Stufe*) step; (*Gestell*) steps *pl*; (*~brett*) step; (*an Auto*) running board.
(e) (*Fußspur*) footprint; (*von Tier*) track.
(f) (*Hunt: Fuß*) foot.
(g) (*bei Vögeln*) mating.

Tritt-: ~brett *nt* step; (*an Auto*) running board; (*an Nähmaschine*) treadle; **~brettfahrer** *m* (*inf*) fare-dodger; (*fig*) free-rider (*inf*); **~leiter** *f* stepladder; **~roller** *m siehe* **Tretroller.**

Triumph *m* **-(e)s, -e** triumph ◆ **im ~** in triumph; **~e feiern** to be a great success *or* very successful.

triumphal *adj* triumphant.

Triumph-: ~bogen *m* triumphal arch; **~geschrei** *nt* triumphant cheer, cheer of triumph.

triumphieren* *vi* (*frohlocken*) to rejoice, to exult ◆ **über jdn/etw ~** (*geh*) to triumph over *or* overcome sb/sth.

triumphierend *adj* triumphant.

Triumphzug *m* triumphal procession.

Triumvirat [triʊmvi'ra:t] *nt* triumvirate.

trivial [tri'via:l] *adj* trivial; *Gespräch auch* banal, trite.

Trivialität [triviali'tɛ:t] *f siehe adj* triviality; banality, triteness.

Trivialliteratur [tri'via:l-] *f* (*pej*) light fiction.

Trochäus [trɔ'xɛ:ʊs] *m* **-, Trochäen** [trɔ'xɛ:ən] (*Poet*) trochee.

trocken *adj* **(a)** dry; *Gebiet auch* arid; *Gedeck* without wine *etc* ◆ **~er Dunst** (*Met*) haze; **~ werden** to dry; (*Brot*) to go *or* get *or* become dry; **das Schiff liegt ~** the ship is high and dry; **noch ~ nach Hause kommen** to get home dry *or* without getting wet; **ins T~e kommen/gehen** to come/go into the dry; **im T~en sein** to be somewhere dry *or* sheltered; **da bleibt kein Auge ~** everyone is moved to tears; (*vor Lachen*) everyone laughs till they cry, everyone falls about laughing (*inf*); **~en Auges/Fußes** (*liter*) dry-eyed/without getting one's feet wet; **~ Brot essen** (*liter*) to eat dry bread; **~ aufbewahren/lagern** to keep/store in a dry place; **sich ~ rasieren** to use an electric razor; **die Haare ~ schneiden** to cut one's/sb's hair dry; **die Gäste ~ sitzen lassen** to leave one's guests without a drink; **auf dem ~en sitzen** (*inf*) to be in a tight spot (*inf*) *or* in difficulties; *siehe* **Schäfchen, Ohr.**
(b) (*langweilig*) dry.
(c) (*herb*) *Sekt, Sherry*, (*fig*) *Humor, Art etc* dry.

Trocken-: ~automat *m* tumble dryer; **~batterie** *f* dry-cell battery; **~beerenauslese** *f wine made from choice grapes left on the vine to dry out at the end of the season*; **~blume** *f* dried flower; **~boden** *m* drying room (*in attic*); **t~bügeln** *vt sep* to iron dry; **~dock** *nt* dry dock; **~ei** *nt* dried egg; **~futter** *nt* dried *or* dehydrated food; **~gebiet** *nt* arid region; **t~gefrieren*** *vt insep irreg* to freeze-dry; **~gestell** *nt* drying rack; **~haube** *f* (salon) hairdryer; **~hefe** *f* dried yeast.

Trockenheit *f* (*lit, fig*) dryness; (*von Gebiet auch*) aridness; (*Trockenperiode*) drought.

Trocken-: ~kurs *m* (*Sport, fig: beim Autofahren etc*) *course in which a beginner learns the basic techniques/skills out of the normal element*; **einen ~kurs machen** to learn the basics; **t~legen** *vt sep* **(a)** *Baby* to change; (*inf*) *Trinker* to dry out; **(b)** *Sumpf, Gewässer* to drain; **~legung** *f* draining; **~maß** *nt* dry measure; **~milch** *f* dried milk; **~platz** *m* drying area; **~rasierer** *m* **-s, -** (*inf*) user of electric shaver *or* razor; (*Rasierapparat*) electric shaver *or* razor; **~rasur** *f* dry *or* electric shave; (*das Rasieren*) shaving with an electric razor *no art*; **t~reiben** *vt sep irreg* to rub dry; **~shampoo** *nt* dry shampoo; ⚠**t~sitzen** *vi sep irreg* (*inf*) to sit there without a drink/with one's glass empty; **~spiritus** *m* solid fuel (*for camping stove etc*); **~starre** *f* aestivation; **t~stehen** *vi sep irreg* (*Kuh*) to be dry; **~wäsche** *f* dry weight (of washing); **~zeit** *f* **(a)** (*Jahreszeit*) dry season; **(b)** (*von Wäsche etc*) drying time.

trocknen 1 *vt* to dry.
2 *vi aux sein* to dry.

Troddel *f* **-, -n** tassel.

Trödel *m* **-s,** *no pl* (*inf*) junk.

Trödelei *f* (*inf*) dawdling.

Trödel-: ~kram *m siehe* **Trödel**; **~laden** *m* junk shop.

trödeln *vi* to dawdle.

Trödler *m* **-s, - (a)** (*Händler*) junk dealer. **(b)** (*inf: langsamer Mensch*) dawdler, slowcoach (*Brit inf*), slowpoke (*US inf*).

troff *pret of* **triefen.**

Trog *m* **-(e)s, ¨e** trough; (*Wasch~*) tub.

trog *pret of* **trügen.**

Trogtal *nt* glaciated *or* U-shaped valley.

Trojaner(in *f*) *m* **-s, -** Trojan.

trojanisch *adj* Trojan ◆ **das T~e Pferd** the Trojan Horse.

trölen *vi* (*Sw*) to dawdle.

Troll *m* **-s, -e** troll.

Trollblume *f* globe flower, trollius.

trollen *vr* (*inf*) to push off (*inf*).

⚠: for details of spelling reform, see supplement

Trommel *f* **-, -n (a)** (*Mus*) drum ◆ **die ~ rühren** (*fig inf*) to drum up (some) support. **(b)** (*Tech*) (*in Maschine*) drum; (*in Revolver*) revolving breech.

Trommel-: ~bremse *f* drum brake; **~fell** *nt* eardrum; **da platzt einem ja das ~fell** (*fig*) the noise is earsplitting; **~feuer** *nt* drumfire, heavy barrage.

trommeln 1 *vi* to drum; (*Regen*) to bear (down) ◆ **gegen die Brust ~** to beat one's chest; **mit den Fingern ~** to drum one's fingers.
2 *vt Marsch, Lied* to play on the drum/drums, to drum ◆ **jdn aus dem Schlaf ~** to knock sb up (*Brit inf*), to wake sb up (by hammering on the door).

Trommel-: ~revolver *m* revolver; **~schlag** *m* drum beat; (*das Trommeln*) drumming; ⚠**~schlegel** *m* drumstick; **~sprache** *f* bush telegraph; **~stöcke** *pl* drumsticks *pl*; **~waschmaschine** *f* drum washing machine; **~wirbel** *m* drum-roll.

Trommler(in *f*) *m* **-s, -** drummer.

Trompete *f* **-, -n** trumpet; *siehe* **Pauke.**

trompeten* 1 *vi* to trumpet; (*sich schneuzen*) to blow one's nose loudly.
2 *vt Marsch* to play on the trumpet.

Trompeter(in *f*) *m* **-s, -** trumpeter.

Tropen *pl* tropics *pl.*

Tropen- *in cpds* tropical; **~anzug** *m* tropical suit; **~fieber** *nt* malaria; **~helm** *m* pith-helmet, topee; **~klima** *nt* tropical climate; **~koller** *m* tropical madness; **~krankheit** *f* tropical disease; **~tag** *m* scorcher (*inf*); **~tauglichkeit** *f fitness for service in the tropics.*

Tropf *m* **-(e)s, ¨e** (*inf*) **(a)** (*Schelm*) rogue, rascal ◆ **einfältiger ~** twit (*Brit inf*), dummy (*inf*); **armer ~** poor beggar (*inf*) *or* devil. **(b)** *no pl* (*Infusion*) drip (*inf*) ◆ **am ~ hängen** to be on a/the drip.

tropf *interj* drip.

Tröpfchen-: ~infektion *f* airborne infection; **t~weise** *adv* in dribs and drabs.

tröpfeln 1 *vi* **(a)** (*Leitung, Halm*) to drip; (*Nase*) to run. **(b)** *aux sein* (*Flüssigkeit*) to drip.
2 *vi impers* **es tröpfelt** it is spitting.
3 *vt* to drip.

tropfen 1 *vi* to drip; (*Nase*) to run ◆ **es tropft durch die Decke/von den Bäumen/aus der Leitung** there is water dripping through the ceiling/the rain is dripping from the trees/the pipe is dripping.
2 *vt* to drop, to drip.

Tropfen *m* **-s, -** drop; (*Schweiß~ auch*) bead; (*einzelner ~ an Kanne, Nase etc*) drip; (*inf: kleine Menge*) drop ◆ **~** *pl* (*Medizin*) drops; **ein guter** *or* **edler ~** (*inf*) a good wine; **bis auf den letzten ~** to the last drop; **ein ~ auf den heißen Stein** (*fig inf*) a drop in the ocean.

-tropfen *pl in cpds* (*Med*) drops *pl.*

Tropfenfänger *m* **-s, -** drip-catcher.

tropfenweise *adv* drop by drop.

Tropf-: ~infusion *f* intravenous drip; ⚠**t~naß** *adj* dripping wet; **~stein** *m* dripstone; (*an der Decke*) stalactite; (*am Boden*) stalagmite; **~steinhöhle** *f* dripstone cave.

Trophäe [tro'fɛ:ə] *f* **-, -n** trophy.

tropisch *adj* tropical.

Tropo-: ~pause *f* (*Met*) tropopause; **~sphäre** *f* (*Met*) troposphere.

⚠**Troß** *m* **-sses, -sse** (*old*) baggage train ◆ **er gehört zum ~** (*fig*) he's a hanger-on; (*hat untergeordnete Rolle*) he's an underling.

Trosse *f* **-, -n** cable, hawser.

Trost *m* **-(e)s,** *no pl* consolation, comfort ◆ **jdm ~ zusprechen/bringen** to console *or* comfort sb; **das Kind war ihr einziger ~** the child was her only comfort; **~ im Alkohol/in der Religion suchen** to seek solace in alcohol/religion; **zum ~ kann ich Ihnen sagen, daß ...** it may comfort you to know that ...; **das ist ein schwacher** *or* **schlechter/schöner** (*iro*) **~** that's pretty cold comfort/some comfort that is!; **du bist wohl nicht ganz** *or* **recht bei ~(e)!** (*inf*) you must be out of your mind!

trösten *vt* to comfort; (*Trost zusprechen auch*) to console ◆ **jdn/sich mit etw ~** to console sb/oneself with sth; **sich/jdn über etw** (*acc*) **~** to get over sth/to help sb to get over sth; **~ Sie sich!** never mind.

Tröster(in *f*) *m* **-s, -** comforter.

tröstlich *adj* cheering, comforting ◆ **das ist ja sehr ~** (*iro*) that's some comfort.

trostlos *adj* hopeless; *Jugend, Verhältnisse* miserable, wretched; (*verzweifelt*) inconsolable; (*öde, trist*) dreary ◆ **~ langweilig** desperately boring.

Trostlosigkeit *f, no pl siehe adj* hopelessness; misery, wretchedness; inconsolability; dreariness.

Trost-: ~pflaster *nt* consolation; **als ~pflaster** by way of consolation; **~preis** *m* consolation prize; **t~reich** *adj* comforting; **~worte** *pl* words of consolation *pl.*

Tröstung *f* comfort; (*das Trösten*) comforting.

Trott *m* **-s,** *no pl* (slow) trot; (*fig*) routine ◆ **im ~** at a (slow) trot; **aus dem alten ~ herauskommen** to get out of one's rut.

Trottel *m* **-s, -** (*inf*) idiot, dope (*inf*).

trottelig *adj* (*inf*) stupid, dopey (*inf*).

trotten *vi aux sein* to trot along; (*Pferd*) to trot slowly.

Trotteur [trɔ'tø:ɐ] *m* **-s, -s** casual (shoe).

Trottoir [trɔ'toa:ɐ] *nt* **-s, -s** *or* **-e** (*dated, S Ger*) pavement.

trotz *prep +gen* (*geh*) *or +dat* (*inf*) in spite of, despite ◆ **~ allem** *or* **alledem** in spite of everything, for all that.

Trotz *m* **-es,** *no pl* defiance; (*trotziges Verhalten*) contrariness ◆ **jdm/einer Sache zum ~** in defiance of sb/sth; **jdm/einer Sache ~ bieten** (*geh*) to defy *or* flout sb/sth.

Trotz|alter *nt* defiant age ◆ **sich im ~ befinden, im ~ sein** to be going through a defiant phase; **ins ~ kommen** to get to *or* reach a defiant age.

trotzdem [1] *adv* nevertheless ◆ **(und) ich mache das ~!** I'll do it all the same.
[2] *conj (strictly incorrect)* even though.

trotzen *vi* **(a)** *+dat* to defy; *der Kälte, dem Klima etc* to withstand; *der Gefahr auch* to brave. **(b)** *(trotzig sein)* to be awkward *or* difficult *or* contrary.

trotzig *adj* defiant; *Kind etc* difficult, awkward; *(widerspenstig)* contrary.

Trotzkismus *m* Trotskyism.

Trotzkist(in *f*) *m* Trotskyite, Trotskyist.

Trotz-: ~kopf *m (inf) (Einstellung)* defiant streak; *(widerspenstig)* contrary streak; *(Mensch)* contrary so-and-so *(inf)*; **sei doch nicht so ein ~kopf** don't be so difficult; **seinen ~kopf haben** to be in a defiant/contrary mood; **t~köpfig** *adj* contrary; **~phase** *f* phase of defiance; **~reaktion** *f* act of defiance; **das war eine reine ~reaktion** he/she just reacted like that out of defiance.

Troubadour ['tru:badu:ɐ, truba'du:ɐ] *m* **-s, -s** *or* **-e** troubadour.

Trouble ['trabl] *m* **-s,** *no pl (sl)* trouble ◆ **~ kriegen/machen** to make trouble; **~ haben** to have problems.

trüb(e) *adj* **(a)** *(unklar) Flüssigkeit* cloudy; *(glanzlos, matt) Glas, Augen, Himmel, Tag* dull; *Sonne, Mond, Licht* dim ◆ **in ~en Wassern** *or* **im ~en fischen** *(inf)* to fish in troubled waters.
(b) *(fig: bedrückend, unerfreulich)* cheerless; *Zeiten* bleak; *Stimmung, Aussichten, Vorahnung, Miene* gloomy; *Erfahrung* grim ◆ **es sieht trüb aus** things are looking pretty bleak; **~e Tasse** *(inf)* drip *(inf)*; *(Spielverderber)* wet blanket *(inf)*.

Trubel *m* **-s,** *no pl* hurly-burly.

trüben [1] *vt* **(a)** *Flüssigkeit* to make cloudy, to cloud; *Glas, Metall* to dull; *(geh) Himmel* to overcast; *Wasseroberfläche* to ruffle; *Augen, Blick* to dull, to cloud ◆ **sie sieht aus, als könnte sie kein Wässerlein ~** *(inf)* she looks as if butter wouldn't melt in her mouth; **kein Wölkchen trübte den Himmel** there wasn't a cloud in the sky.
(b) *(fig) Glück, Freude, Verhältnis* to spoil, to mar; *Beziehungen* to strain; *Laune* to dampen; *Bewußtsein, Erinnerung* to dull, to dim; *(geh) Verstand* to dull; *Urteilsvermögen* to dim, to cloud over.
[2] *vr (Flüssigkeit)* to go cloudy; *(Spiegel, Metall)* to become dull; *(geh) (Verstand)* to become dulled; *(Augen)* to dim, to cloud; *(Himmel)* to cloud over; *(fig) (Stimmung, Laune)* to be dampened; *(Beziehungen, Verhältnis)* to become strained; *(Glück, Freude)* to be marred.

Trüb-: ~heit *f no pl* cloudiness; dullness; **~sal** *f* **-, -e** *(liter)* afflictions *pl*; *(no pl: Stimmung)* sorrow; **~sal blasen** *(inf)* to mope; **t~selig** *adj (betrübt, verzagt)* gloomy, miserable; *(öde, trostlos) Gegend, Zeiten* depressing, bleak; *Behausung, Wetter* miserable; **~seligkeit** *f siehe adj* gloom, misery; depressingness, bleakness; gloominess, miserableness; **~sinn** *m, no pl* gloom, melancholy; **t~sinnig** *adj* gloomy, melancholy.

Trübung *f siehe vt* **(a)** clouding; dulling; overcasting; ruffling. **(b)** spoiling, marring; straining; dampening; dulling.

trudeln *vi* **(a)** *aux sein or haben (Aviat)* to spin ◆ **ins T~ kommen** *or* **geraten** to go into a spin. **(b)** *(dial: würfeln)* to play dice.

Trüffel[1] *f* **-, -n** *(Pilz)* truffle.

Trüffel[2] *m* **-s, -** truffle.

Trug *m* **-(e)s,** *no pl (liter)* deception; *(der Sinne)* illusion; *(der Phantasie)* delusion; *siehe* **Lug.**

trug *pret of* **tragen.**

Trugbild *nt* delusion; *(der Sinne)* illusion.

trügen *pret* **trog,** *ptp* **getrogen** [1] *vt* to deceive ◆ **wenn mich nicht alles trügt** unless I am very much mistaken.
[2] *vi* to be deceptive.

trügerisch *adj (liter: betrügerisch)* deceitful, false; *(irreführend)* deceptive.

⚠ **Trugschluß** *m* fallacy, misapprehension ◆ **einem ~ unterliegen** to be labouring under a misapprehension.

Truhe *f* **-, -n** chest.

Trümmer *pl* rubble *sing*; *(Ruinen, fig: von Glück etc)* ruins *pl*; *(von Schiff, Flugzeug etc)* wreckage *sing*; *(Überreste)* remnants *pl*; *(inf: von Essen)* remains *pl* ◆ **in ~n liegen** to be in ruins; **in ~ gehen** to be ruined *(auch fig)*/wrecked; **etw in ~ schlagen** to smash sth to pieces *or* up.

Trümmer-: ~feld *nt* expanse of rubble/ruins; *(fig)* scene of devastation *or* destruction; **~frau** *f woman who clears away rubble after bombing;* **~haufen** *m* heap of rubble.

Trumpf *m* **-(e)s, ¨-e** *(Cards) (~karte)* trump (card); *(Farbe)* trumps *pl*; *(fig)* trump card ◆ **~ sein** to be trumps; *(fig inf: modisch sein)* to be in *(inf)*; **den ~ in der Hand haben/aus der Hand geben** *(fig)* to hold the/waste one's trump card; **noch einen ~ in der Hand haben** to have an ace up one's sleeve; **jdm den ~ aus der Hand nehmen** *(fig)* to trump sb.

Trumpf|as *nt* ace of trumps.

trumpfen [1] *vt* to trump.
[2] *vi* to play a trump (card) ◆ **mit dem König ~** to play the king of trumps.

Trumpf-: ~farbe *f* trumps *pl*; **~karte** *f* trump (card).

Trunk *m* **-(e)s, ¨-e** **(a)** *(old, liter)* draught *(old, liter)*; *(Zauber~ auch)* potion; *(das Trinken)* drink ◆ **jdm etw/das Glas zum ~ reichen** to pass sb sth to drink/a glass *or* drink. **(b)** *(~sucht)* **dem ~ ergeben** *or* **verfallen sein** to have taken to drink.

trunken *(liter)* [1] *adj* inebriated, intoxicated; *(vor Freude, Glück etc)* drunk *(vor +dat* with).
[2] *adv* drunkenly.

Trunken-: ~bold *m* **-(e)s, -e** *(pej)* drunkard; **~heit** *f* drunkenness, inebriation, intoxication; **~heit am Steuer** drunken *or* drink driving.

Trunk-: ~sucht *f* alcoholism; **t~süchtig** *adj* alcoholic; **t~süchtig werden** to become an alcoholic; **~süchtige(r)** *mf* alcoholic.

Trupp *m* **-s, -s** bunch; *(Einheit)* group; *(Mil)* squad; *(esp beritten)* troop.

Truppe *f* **-, -n** **(a)** *(Mil)* army, troops *pl*; *(Panzer~ etc)* corps *sing*. **~n** *pl* troops ◆ **zur ~ zurückkehren** to report back; **von der schnellen ~ sein** *(inf)* to be a fast mover *(inf)*; **nicht von der schnellen ~ sein** *(inf)* to be slow. **(b)** *(Künstler~)* troupe, company.

Truppen-: ~abzug *m* withdrawal of troops; **~arzt** *m* (army) medical officer; **~bewegung** *f usu pl* troop movement; **~einheit** *f* unit; *(bei der Kavallerie)* troop; **~führer** *m* unit/troop commander; **~gattung** *f* corps *sing*; **~parade** *f* military parade *or* review; **~schau** *f* troop inspection; **~stationierung** *f* stationing of troops; **~teil** *m* unit; **~übung** *f* field exercise; **~übungsplatz** *m* military training area.

truppweise *adv* in bunches/groups; *(Mil)* in squads/troops.

Trust [trast] *m* **-(e)s, -s** *or* **-e** trust.

Trut-: ~hahn *m* turkey(cock); **~henne** *f* turkey(hen).

Trutz *m* **-es,** *no pl (obs) siehe* **Schutz.**

trutzen *vi (obs)* to defy.

Tschad *m* **- der ~** Chad.

tschadisch *adj* Chad *attr*.

Tschapperl *nt* **-s, -n** *(Aus)* dolt *(inf)* ◆ **armes ~** poor devil *(inf)*.

tschau *interj (inf)* cheerio *(Brit inf)*, so long *(inf)*, ciao *(inf)*.

Tscheche *m* **-n, -n, Tschechin** *f* Czech.

Tschechei *f* **- die ~** *(dated inf)* Czechoslovakia.

Tschechien *nt* **-s** the Czech Republic.

tschechisch *adj* Czech.

Tschechisch(e) *nt* Czech; *siehe auch* **Deutsch(e).**

Tschechoslowake *m* **-n, -n, Tschechoslowakin** *f* Czechoslovak.

Tschechoslowakei *f* **- die ~** Czechoslovakia.

tschechoslowakisch *adj* Czechoslovak(ian).

Tschik *m* **-s, -** *(Aus) (inf: Stummel)* fag-end *(Brit inf)*; *(sl: Zigarette)* fag *(Brit inf)*.

tschilpen *vi* to chirp.

Tschinelle *f (Aus Mus)* cymbal.

⚠ **tschüs** *interj (inf)* cheerio *(Brit inf)*, 'bye *(inf)*, so long *(inf)*.

Tschusch *m* **-en, -en** *(Aus pej)* ≃ wog *(pej sl)*.

Tsd. *abbr of* **Tausend.**

Tsetsefliege *f* tsetse fly.

T-Shirt ['ti:ʃɜ:t] *nt* **-s, -s** T-shirt, tee-shirt.

T-Träger ['te:-] *m* T-bar, T-girder.

TU [te:'|u:] *f* **-** *abbr of* **Technische Universität.**

Tuba *f* **-, Tuben** **(a)** *(Mus)* tuba. **(b)** *(Anat)* tube.

Tube *f* **-, -n** tube ◆ **auf die ~ drücken** *(inf)* to get a move on *(inf)*; *(im Auto auch)* to put one's foot down *(inf)*.

Tuberkel *m* **-s, -** *or (Aus auch) f* **-, -n** tubercle.

Tuberkelbazillus *m* tuberculosis bacillus.

tuberkulös *adj* tubercular, tuberculous.

Tuberkulose *f* **-, -n** tuberculosis.

Tuberkulose-: t~krank *adj* tubercular, tuberculous; **~kranke(r)** *mf* TB case, TB-sufferer.

Tuch *nt* **-(e)s, ¨-er** **(a)** *pl* **-e** *(old: Stoff)* cloth, fabric.
(b) *(Stück Stoff)* cloth; *(Tisch~)* cloth; *(Hals~, Kopf~)* scarf; *(Schulter~)* shawl; *(Hand~)* towel; *(Geschirr~)* cloth, towel; *(Taschen~)* handkerchief; *(zum Abdecken von Möbeln)* dustsheet ◆ **das rote ~ (des Stierkämpfers)** the bullfighter's cape; **das wirkt wie ein rotes ~ auf ihn** it makes him see red, it's like a red rag to a bull (to him).

Tuch-: ~art *f* type of cloth *or* fabric; **~fabrik** *f* textile factory *or* mill; **~fühlung** *f* physical *or* body contact; **in ~fühlung** in physical contact; *(Mil)* shoulder to shoulder; *(fig)* cheek by jowl; **~fühlung haben** to be in physical contact (with sb); *(fig)* to be close to sb; **auf ~fühlung gehen** to move closer (to sb/together); **~händler** *m* cloth merchant; **~macher** *m* clothworker.

tüchtig [1] *adj* **(a)** *(fähig)* capable, competent *(in +dat* at); *(fleißig)* efficient; *Arbeiter* good ◆ **etwas T~es lernen/werden** *(inf)* to get a proper training/job; **~, ~!** not bad!
(b) *(inf: groß) Portion* big, huge; *Stoß, Schlag* hard; *Appetit, Esser* big ◆ **eine ~e Tracht Prügel** a good hiding; **eine ~e Portion Frechheit** *etc* a fair amount of cheek *etc*.
[2] *adv* **(a)** *(fleißig, fest)* hard; *essen* heartily ◆ **hilf ~ mit** lend *or* give us a hand. **(b)** *(inf: sehr)* good and proper *(inf)* ◆ **~ regnen** to pelt *(inf)*; **jdm ~ die Meinung sagen** to give sb a piece of one's mind; **~ ausschimpfen** to scold thoroughly; **~ zulangen** to tuck in *(inf)*; **jdn ~ anschmieren/betrügen** to take sb for a ride *(inf)*; **jdn ~ belügen** to tell sb a pack of lies; **sich ~ ausruhen** to have a good rest.

Tüchtigkeit *f (Fähigkeit)* ability, competence; *(von Arbeiter etc)* efficiency.

Tuchwaren *pl* cloth goods *pl*.

Tücke *f* **-, -n** **(a)** *(no pl: Bosheit)* malice, spite; *(böswillige Handlung)* malicious *or* spiteful action.
(b) *(Gefahr)* danger, peril; *(von Krankheit)* perniciousness ◆ **voller ~n stecken** to be difficult; *(gefährlich)* to be dangerous *or (Berg, Fluß auch)* treacherous; **das ist die ~ des Objekts** these things have a will of their own!; **seine ~n haben** *(Maschine etc)* to be temperamental; *(schwierig sein)* to be difficult; *(gefährlich sein)* to be dangerous *or (Berg, Fluß auch)* treacherous; *siehe* **List.**
(c) *(des Glücks etc)* vagary *usu pl*; *(des Schicksals auch)* fickleness *no pl*.

tuckern *vi aux haben or (bei Richtungsangabe) sein* to put-put, to chug.

tückisch *adj (boshaft) Mensch, Blick, Lächeln* malicious, spiteful; *Zufall* un-

happy; (*bösartig, gefährlich*) *Berge, Strom etc* treacherous; *Krankheit* pernicious.
tu(e) *imper sing of* **tun.**
Tuerei [tuːəˈrai] *f* (*inf*) antics *pl.*
Tuff *m* **-s, -e, Tuffstein** *m* tuff.
Tüftel|arbeit *f* (*inf*) fiddly *or* finicky job.
Tüftelei *f* (*inf*) fiddly *or* finicky job ◆ **das ist eine ~** that's fiddly *or* finicky.
tüftelig *adj* (*inf*) fiddly, finicky.
tüfteln *vi* (*inf*) to puzzle; (*basteln*) to fiddle about (*inf*) ◆ **an etw** (*dat*) **~** to fiddle about with sth; (*geistig*) to puzzle over sth; **er tüftelt gern** he likes doing fiddly *or* finicky things.
Tüftler(in *f*) *m* **-s, -** (*inf*) *person who likes doing fiddly or finicky things.*
Tugend *f* **-, -en** virtue ◆ **seine ~ bewahren** to remain virtuous; (*Unschuld auch*) to keep one's virtue; *siehe* **Not.**
Tugend-: ~bold *m* **-(e)s, -e** (*pej*) paragon of virtue; **t~haft** *adj* virtuous; **~haftigkeit** *f* virtuousness; **t~sam** *adj* virtuous; **~wächter** *m* (*iro*) guardian of his/her *etc* virtue.
Tukan *m* **-s, -e** toucan.
Tüll *m* **-s, -e** tulle; (*für Gardinen*) net.
Tülle *f* **-, -n** spout; (*Spritzdüse*) pipe.
Tüllgardine *f* net curtain.
Tulpe *f* **-, -n (a)** (*Bot*) tulip. **(b)** (*Glas*) tulip glass.
Tulpenzwiebel *f* tulip bulb.
tumb *adj* (*obs, hum*) stupid, dim.
tummeln *vr* **(a)** (*Hunde, Kinder etc*) to romp (about). **(b)** (*sich beeilen*) to hurry (up).
Tummelplatz *m* play area; (*fig*) hotbed.
Tümmler *m* **-s, -** (bottle-nosed) dolphin.
Tumor *m* **-s, -en** [tuˈmoːrən] tumour.
Tümpel *m* **-s, -** pond.
Tumult *m* **-(e)s, -e** commotion; (*Aufruhr auch*) disturbance; (*der Gefühle*) tumult, turmoil.
tun *pret* **tat,** *ptp* **getan** [1] *vt* **(a)** (*machen, ausführen*) to do ◆ **etw aus Liebe/Bosheit** *etc* **~** to do sth out of love/malice *etc;* **jdm etw zu ~ geben** to give sb sth to do; **was kann ich für Sie ~?** what can I do for you?; **was tut man in dieser Situation?** what should one do in this situation?; **wir haben getan, was wir konnten** we did what we could; **sie wußte nicht, was ~** *or* **was sie ~ sollte** she didn't know what to do; **was ~?** what can be done?, what shall we do?; **mal sehen, was sich (für Sie) ~ läßt** let's see what we can do (for you); **du kannst ~ und lassen, was du willst** you can do as you please; **er bestimmt, was wir zu ~ und zu lassen haben** he tells us what to do and what not to do; **tu, was du nicht lassen kannst** well, if you must; **... aber er tut es einfach nicht ...** but he just won't (do it); **damit ist es noch nicht getan** and that's not all; **was tut das Buch unterm Bett?** (*inf*) what is the book doing under the bed?; **etwas/nichts gegen etw ~** to do something/nothing about sth; **Sie müssen etwas für sich ~** you should treat yourself; (*sich schonen*) you should take care of yourself; **er tut nichts als faulenzen/unsere Zeit vergeuden** he does nothing but laze around/waste our time; **so etwas tut man nicht!** that is just not done; **so etwas tut man als anständige Frau nicht!** a decent woman doesn't do such things; **es mit jdm ~** (*sl*) to do it with sb (*inf*).
(b) (*Funktionsverb*) *Arbeit, Pflicht* to do; *Blick, Schritt, Gelübde* to take; *Reise* to go on ◆ **einen Schrei ~** to cry *or* shout (out).
(c) (*angehen, beteiligt sein*) **das hat etwas/nichts mit ihm/damit zu ~** that is something/nothing to do with him; **das hat doch damit gar nichts zu ~** that is nothing to do with it; **das tut nichts zur Sache** that's beside the point; **damit/mit ihm habe ich nichts zu ~/will ich nichts zu ~ haben** I have/want nothing to do with it/him; **ich habe mit mir (selbst) zu ~** I have problems (myself *or* of my own); **es mit jdm zu ~ bekommen** *or* **kriegen** (*inf*) to get into trouble with sb; **er hat es mit der Leber/dem Herzen** *etc* **zu ~** (*inf*) he has liver/heart *etc* trouble.
(d) (*ausmachen*) **was tut's?** what does it matter?, what difference does it make?; **das tut nichts** it doesn't matter; **das tut dir/ihm nichts** it won't do you/him any harm; **darum ist es mir sehr getan** *or* **zu ~** (*geh*) I am very concerned about it.
(e) (*an~, zuteil werden lassen*) **jdm etwas ~** to do something to sb; (*stärker*) to harm *or* hurt sb; **er hat mir nichts getan** he didn't do anything (to me); (*stärker*) he didn't hurt *or* harm me; **der Hund tut dir schon nichts** the dog won't hurt *or* harm you; **hat der Mann/der Lehrer/dein Chef dir was getan?** did the man/teacher/your boss do anything (to you)?; **jdm Böses** *or* **ein Leid** (*old*)**/einen Gefallen ~** to harm sb/do sb a favour; **was du nicht willst, daß man dir tu', das füg' auch keinem andern zu** (*Prov*) do as you would be done by (*prov*).
(f) (*inf: an einen bestimmten Ort legen, geben etc*) to put ◆ **jdn in eine andere Schule ~** to put sb in a different school.
(g) (*inf: ausreichen, genügen*) to do ◆ **das tut's für heute** that'll do for today; **unser Auto muß es noch ein Weilchen ~** we'll have to make do with our car a little while longer.
(h) (*inf: funktionieren*) **die Uhr/das Auto tut es nicht mehr** the watch/car has had it (*inf*).
(i) *+infin* (*inf: zur Betonung, old: zur Bildung der Vergangenheit*) **dann tat er sich waschen** then he washed *or* did wash (*obs*) himself; **sie ~ jetzt essen** (*inf*) they're eating; **und dann tut er schwimmen** (*inf*) and then he goes swimming.
[2] *vr* **(a)** (*geschehen*) **es tut sich etwas/nichts** there is something/nothing happening, something/nothing is happening; **hat sich in dieser Hinsicht schon etwas getan?** has anything been done about this?; **hat sich bei euch etwas getan?** have things changed (with you)?; **hier hat sich einiges getan** there have been some changes here.
(b) (*mit adj*) **sich (mit etw) dicke ~** (*inf*) to show off (about sth); **sich** (*acc or dat*) **mit etw schwer ~** to have difficulty *or* problems with sth.
[3] *vi* **(a) zu ~ haben** (*beschäftigt sein*) to be busy, to have work to do; **in der Stadt/auf dem Finanzamt zu ~ haben** to have things to do in town/business at the tax office; **ich hatte zu ~, das wieder in Ordnung zu bringen** I had my work cut out putting *or* to put it back in order; **mit jdm zu ~ haben** to deal with sb.
(b) (*sich benehmen*) to act ◆ **so ~, als ob ...** to pretend that ...; **tu doch nicht so** stop pretending; **tust du nur so dumm?** are you just acting stupid?; **sie tut nur so** she's only pretending.
(c) Sie täten gut daran, früh zu kommen you would do well to come early; **Sie haben recht getan** you did right.
Tun *nt* **-s,** *no pl* conduct ◆ **sein ganzes ~, sein ~ und Lassen** everything he does; **heimliches/verbrecherisches ~** secret/criminal actions.
Tünche *f* **-, -n** whitewash; (*getönt*) distemper, wash; (*fig*) veneer; (*inf: Schminke*) make-up.
tünchen *vt* to whitewash/distemper.
Tundra *f* **-, Tundren** tundra.
Tunell *nt* **-s, -e** (*dial, S Ger, Aus*) tunnel.
tunen [ˈtjuːnən] *vt* to tune.
Tuner [ˈtjuːnɐ] *m* **-s, -** tuner.
Tuning [ˈtjuːnɪŋ] *nt* **-s,** *no pl* tuning.
Tuneser(in *f*) *m*, **Tunesier(in** *f*) [-iɐ, -iərɪn] *m* **-s, -** Tunisian.
Tunesien [-iən] *nt* **-s** Tunisia.
tunesisch *adj* Tunisian.
Tunichtgut *m* **-(e)s, -e** (*dated*) ne'er-do-well (*old*), good-for-nothing.
Tunika *f* **-, Tuniken** tunic.
Tunke *f* **-, -n** sauce; (*Braten~*) gravy.
tunken *vt* to dip; (*stippen auch*) to dunk (*inf*); *jdn* to duck.
tunlich *adj* possible, feasible; (*ratsam*) advisable.
tunlichst *adv* if possible ◆ **~ bald** as soon as possible; **ich werde es ~ vermeiden, ihm meine Meinung zu sagen** I'll do my best to avoid telling him what I think; **das wirst du ~ bleiben lassen** you'll do nothing of the kind *or* sort.
Tunnel *m* **-s, -** *or* **-s** tunnel.
Tunte *f* **-, -n** (*inf*) **(a)** (*dated*) sissy (*inf*). **(b)** (*Homosexueller*) fairy (*pej inf*).
tuntenhaft *adj* (*inf*) fussy; *Homosexueller etc* effeminate.
tuntig *adj* (*inf*) **(a)** (*dated: albern, zimperlich*) sissy (*inf*). **(b)** (*weibisch*) effeminate, poofy (*sl*).
Tupf *m* **-(e)s, -e** (*Aus*) *siehe* **Tupfen.**
Tüpfel *m or nt* **-s, -, Tüpfelchen** *nt* dot.
tüpfeln *vt* to spot ◆ **getüpfelt** spotted; (*mit kleinen Tupfen*) dotted.
tupfen *vt* to dab ◆ **getupft** spotted.
Tupfen *m* **-s, -** spot; (*klein*) dot.
Tupfer *m* **-s, -** swab.
Tür *f* **-, -en** door; (*Garten~*) gate ◆ **in der ~** in the doorway; **~ an ~ mit jdm wohnen** to live next door to sb; **an die ~ gehen** to answer the door, to go/come to the door; **Weihnachten steht vor der ~** Christmas is just (a)round the corner; **jdn vor die ~ setzen** (*inf*) to throw *or* kick (*inf*) sb out; **jdm die ~ weisen** to show sb the door; **jdm die ~ vor der Nase zumachen** to shut the door in sb's face; **ein jeder kehre vor seiner ~** (*prov*) everyone should set his own house in order; **die Leute haben ihm fast die ~ eingerannt** (*nach Anzeige etc*) he was snowed under with replies; **mit der ~ ins Haus fallen** (*inf*) to blurt it/things out; **die ~ für etw offenhalten** *or* **nicht zuschlagen** (*fig*) to keep the way open for sth; **zwischen ~ und Angel** in passing; **einer Sache** (*dat*) **~ und Tor öffnen** (*fig*) to open the way to sth; **ach, du kriegst die ~ nicht zu!** (*inf*) well I never!
Tür|angel *f* (door) hinge.
Turban *m* **-s, -e** turban.
Türbeschlag *m* (ornamental) mounting (on a door).
Turbine *f* turbine.
Turbinen-: ~antrieb *m* turbine drive; (*an Flugzeug*) turbo-jet propulsion; **~flugzeug** *nt* turbo-jet; **~triebwerk** *nt* turbine engine; (*an Flugzeug*) turbo-jet, jet turbine engine.
Turbo-: ~diesel *m* (*Aut*) turbo-diesel engine; **~generator** *m* turbogenerator; **~lader** *m* **-s, -** (*Aut*) turbocharger; **~motor** *m* turbo-engine; **~-Prop-Flugzeug** *nt* turboprop aircraft.
turbulent *adj* turbulent, tempestuous ◆ **dort geht's ~ zu** things are in turmoil there.
Turbulenz *f* **(a)** *no pl* turbulence, turmoil. **(b)** (*turbulentes Ereignis*) excitement, turmoil *no pl.* **(c)** (*Wirbel, Luftstrom*) turbulence *no pl.*
Türchen *nt* small door.
Türdrücker *m* (*Knauf*) doorknob; (*inf: Öffner*) buzzer (*for opening the door*).
Türe *f* **-, -n** (*dial*) *siehe* **Tür.**
Turf [tʊrf] *m* **-s, -s (a)** (*Rennbahn*) racecourse. **(b)** (*no pl: Sportart*) turf.
Tür-: ~flügel *m* door (*of a pair of doors*); **~füllung** *f* door panel; **~griff** *m* door handle; **~hüter** *m* (*obs*) doorman.
-türig *adj suf* **ein~/zwei~** *etc* with one door/two doors *etc;* **ein vier~es Auto** a four-door car.
Türke *m* **-n, -n** Turk ◆ **einen ~n bauen** (*inf: etwas vortäuschen*) to fiddle the figures (*inf*).
Türkei *f* **-** **die ~** Turkey.

Türken *m* **-s,** *no pl (Aus inf)* maize.
türken *vt (sl) jdn* to diddle *(inf)*; *etw* to fiddle *(inf)* ◆ **die Statistik ~** to massage the figures; **Belege ~** to falsify documents.
Türkenbund *m* **-(e)s, Türkenbünde** *(Bot)* Turk's cap lily.
Türkette *f* (door) chain.
Türkin *f* Turk, Turkish woman/girl.
Türkis[1] *m* **-es, -e** *(Edelstein)* turquoise.
Türkis[2] *nt* **-,** *no pl (Farbe)* turquoise.
türkis *adj* turquoise.
türkisch *adj* Turkish ◆ **T~er Honig** nougat; **~er Weizen** maize.
Türkisch(e) *nt decl as adj* Turkish; *siehe auch* **Deutsch(e)**.
türkisfarben, türkisgrün *adj* turquoise(-coloured).
Tür-: ~klinke *f* door handle; **~klopfer** *m* doorknocker.
Turm *m* **-(e)s, ¨-e (a)** tower; *(spitzer Kirch~)* spire; *(im Schwimmbad)* diving tower. **(b)** *(Chess)* castle, rook.
Turmalin *m* **-s, -e** *(Miner)* tourmaline.
Turmbau *m (das Bauen)* building a tower ◆ **der ~ zu Babel** the building of the Tower of Babel.
Türmchen *nt dim of* **Turm** turret.
türmen [1] *vt* to pile (up).
[2] *vr* to pile up; *(Wolken)* to build up, to bank; *(Wellen)* to tower up.
[3] *vi aux sein (inf: davonlaufen)* to skedaddle *(inf)*, to take to one's heels, to run off.
Turm-: ~falke *m* kestrel; **t~hoch** *adj* towering, lofty; **~schwalbe** *f* swift; **~springen** *nt* high diving; **~uhr** *f* clock (on a/the tower); *(Kirch~)* church clock.
Turn|anzug *m* leotard.
turnen [1] *vi* **(a)** *(an Geräten)* to do gymnastics; *(Sch)* to do gym *or* PE *or* PT ◆ **am Reck/an den Ringen/auf der Matte** *etc* **~** to work on *or* do exercises on the horizontal bar/rings/mat *etc*; **sie kann gut ~** she is good at gym *or* PE *or* PT.
(b) *aux sein (herumklettern)* to climb about; *(Kind)* to romp.
[2] *vt Reck etc* to work on, to do exercises on; *Übung* to do.
Turnen *nt* **-s,** *no pl* gymnastics *sing*; *(inf: Leibeserziehung)* gym, PE *(inf)*, PT *(inf)*.
Turner(in *f***)** *m* **-s, -** gymnast.
Turnerei *f (inf)* sporting activities *pl*; *(fig)* acrobatics *pl*.
turnerisch *adj* gymnastic ◆ **~ hervorragend** *Mensch* excellent at gymnastics; *Übung* excellent gymnastically.
Turnerschaft *f* **(a)** *(die Turner)* gymnasts *pl*; *(Vereinigung der Turnvereine)* gymnastic association. **(b)** *(Studentenverbindung)* student organization.
Turn-: ~fest *nt* gymnastics display *or* festival; *(von Schule)* sports day; **~gerät** *nt (Reifen, Ball etc)* (piece of) gymnastic equipment; *(Reck, Barren etc)* (piece of) gymnastic apparatus; **~halle** *f* gym(nasium); *(Gebäude auch)* sports hall; **~hemd** *nt* gym *or* PE *or* PT shirt; **~hose** *f* gym *or* PE *or* PT shorts *pl*.
Turnier *nt* **-s, -e** *(Ritter~, sportliche Veranstaltung)* tournament; *(Tanz~)* competition; *(Reit~)* show.
Turnier-: ~pferd *nt* show *or* competition horse; **~reiter** *m* show *or* competition rider; **~tanz** *m* (competition) ballroom dance/dancing.
Turn-: ~kleidung *f* gym *or* PE *or* PT clothes *pl or* kit; **~kunst** *f* gymnastic skills *pl*; **~lehrer** *m* gym *or* PE *or* PT teacher; **~riege** *f* gymnastics team; **~schuh** *m* gym shoe, sneaker *(US)*; **~stunde** *f* gym *or* PE *or* PT lesson; *(im Verein)* gymnastics lesson; **~übung** *f* gymnastic exercise; **~unterricht** *m* gymnastic instruction; *(~stunde)* gym, PE, PT.
Turnus *m* **-, -se (a)** rota ◆ **im (regelmäßigen) ~** in rotation. **(b)** *(Aus) (Arbeitsschicht)* shift; *(Med)* housemanship *(Brit)*, internship *(US)*.
Turn-: ~vater *m*: **~vater Jahn** Jahn, the father of gymnastics; **~verein** *m* gymnastics club; **~wart** *m* gymnastics supervisor; **~zeug** *nt* gym *or* PE *or* PT things *pl or* kit.
Tür-: ~öffner *m (im Hotel)* doorman, commissionaire; **elektrischer ~öffner** buzzer (for opening the door); **~pfosten** *m* doorpost; **~rahmen** *m* doorframe; **~schild** *nt* doorplate; ⚠**~schloß** *nt* door lock; **~schnalle** *f (Aus) siehe* **~klinke**; **~schwelle** *f* threshold; **~spalt** *m* crack (of a/the door); **~sprechanlage** *f* entry phone; **~steher** *m* **-s, -** doorman, bouncer; **~sturz** *m* lintel.
turteln *vi* to bill and coo; *(fig auch)* to whisper sweet nothings.
Turteltaube *f* turtle-dove ◆ **~n** *(inf: Verliebte)* lovebirds, turtle-doves.
Türvorleger *m* doormat.
Tusch *m* **-es, -e (a)** *(Mus)* flourish; *(von Blasinstrumenten auch)* fanfare. **(b)** *(Aus) siehe* **Tusche**.
Tusche *f* **-, -n** *(Auszieh~)* Indian ink; *(~farbe)* water colour; *(Wimpern~)* mascara.
tuscheln *vti* to whisper ◆ **hinter seinem Rücken über jdn ~** to say things *(inf) or* talk behind sb's back.
tuschen *vt (mit Farbe)* to paint in water colour(s); *(mit Ausziehtusche)* to draw in Indian ink ◆ **sich** *(dat)* **die Wimpern ~** to put one's mascara on.
Tusch-: ~farbe *f* water colour; **~kasten** *m* paintbox; **ihr Gesicht sieht aus wie ein ~kasten** *(fig inf)* she's made up to the eyeballs *(inf)*; **~zeichnung** *f* pen-and-ink drawing.
Tussi *f* **-, -s** *(inf)* female *(inf)*, tart *(pej inf)*.
tut *interj* toot.
Tüte *f* **-, -n** *(aus Papier, Plastik)* bag; *(Eis~)* cornet, cone; *(von Suppenpulver etc)* packet; *(inf: für Alkoholtest)* breathalyzer; *(inf: Mensch)* drip *(inf)* ◆ **in die ~ blasen** *(inf)* to be breathalyzed, to blow in the bag *(inf)*; **~n kleben** *(inf)* to be in clink *(inf)*; **das kommt nicht in die ~!** *(inf)* no way! *(inf)*.
tuten *vti* to toot; *(Schiff)* to sound its hooter/foghorn ◆ **von T~ und Blasen keine Ahnung haben** *(inf)* not to have a clue *(inf)*.
Tutor *m*, **Tutorin** *f* tutor.
TÜV [tyf] *m* **-s, -s** *abbr of* **Technischer Überwachungs-Verein** ≃ MOT *(Brit)* ◆ **das Auto ist durch den ~ gekommen** the car got through *or* passed its MOT.
TÜV-Plakette *f disc displayed on number plate showing that a car has passed the TÜV*, ≃ MOT certificate.
Tuwort *nt, pl* **Tuwörter** doing-word.
TV [te:'fau] *abbr of* **(a) Television. (b) Turnverein.**
TV- [te:'fau-] *in cpds* TV; **~-Moderator** *m* TV presenter; **~-Programm** *nt* TV programmes *pl*; **~-Sendung** *f* TV broadcast.
Tweed [tvi:t] *m* **-s, -s** *or* **-e** tweed.
Twen *m* **-(s), -s** *person in his/her twenties.*
Twinset *nt or m* **-(s), -s** twin-set, sweater-set *(US)*.
Twist[1] *m* **-es, -e** *(Garn)* twist.
Twist[2] *m* **-s, -s** *(Tanz)* twist.
twisten *vi* to twist, to do the twist.
Tympanon *nt* **-s, Tympana** *(Archit)* tympanum.
Typ *m* **-s, -en (a)** *(Modell)* model. **(b)** *(Menschenart)* type ◆ **er ist nicht mein ~** *(inf)* he's not my type *(inf)*. **(c)** *(inf: Mensch)* person, character; *(sl: Mann, Freund)* bloke *(Brit inf)*, guy *(inf)* ◆ **dein ~ wird verlangt** *(inf)* you're wanted; **dein ~ ist nicht gefragt** *(inf)* you're not wanted round here.
Type *f* **-, -n (a)** *(Typ) (Schreibmaschinen~)* type bar; *(Druckbuchstabe)* character ◆ **~n** *(Schrift)* type *sing*; **~n gießen** to set type. **(b)** *(inf: Mensch)* character. **(c)** *(bei Mehl)* grade.
Typen *pl of* **Typus, Type**.
Typenrad *nt* daisy wheel.
Typenraddrucker *m* daisy wheel (printer).
Typhus *m* **-,** *no pl* typhoid (fever).
Typhus-: ~epidemie *f* typhoid (fever) epidemic; **~impfung** *f* typhoid inoculation; **~kranke(r)** *mf* typhoid case.
typisch *adj* typical (*für* of) ◆ **~ deutsch/Mann/Frau** typically German/male/female; **(das ist ein) ~er Fall von denkste!** *(inf)* no such luck! *(inf)*.
typisieren* *vt Charakter* to stylize; *Erzeugnisse etc* to standardize.
⚠**Typographie** *f* typography.
⚠**typographisch** *adj* typographic(al).
Typologie *f* typology.
Typus *m* **-, Typen** type.
Tyrann *m* **-en, -en** *(lit, fig)* tyrant.
Tyrannei *f* tyranny.
Tyrannen-: ~mord *m* tyrannicide; **~mörder** *m* tyrannicide.
Tyrannin *f* tyrant.
tyrannisch *adj* tyrannical.
tyrannisieren* *vt* to tyrannize.
tyrrhenisch [tʏ're:nɪʃ] *adj* **T~es Meer** Tyrrhenian Sea.
Tz ['te:tsɛt, te'tsɛt] *nt*: **bis ins** *or* **zum ~** completely, fully; *siehe auch* **Tezett**.

U, u [uː] *nt* **-, -** U, u; *siehe* **X.**
u. *abbr of* **und.**
u.a. *abbr of* **und andere(s); unter anderem/anderen.**
U.A.w.g. *abbr of* **Um Antwort wird gebeten** RSVP.
UB [uːˈbeː] *f* **-, -s** *abbr of* **Universitätsbibliothek.**
U-Bahn [ˈuː-] *f* underground, subway (*US*); (*in London*) tube.
U-Bahnhof [ˈuː-] *m* underground *etc* station.
übel [1] *adj* **(a)** (*schlimm, unangenehm*) bad; *Kopfweh, Erkältung etc auch* nasty ◆ **er war übler Laune** he was in a bad *or* nasty mood; **das ist gar nicht so ~** that's not so bad at all.
(b) (*moralisch, charakterlich schlecht*) wicked, bad; *Eindruck, Ruf* bad; *Tat auch* evil ◆ **ein übler Bursche** *or* **Kunde** (*inf*) a nasty piece of work (*inf*), a bad lot (*inf*); **das ist eine üble Sache!** it's a bad business; **ein übler Streich** a nasty trick; **auf üble** *or* **in der ~sten Weise, in übler** *or* **~ster Weise** in a most unpleasant way; **jdm Übles antun** (*geh*) to be wicked to sb, to do wicked things to sb.
(c) (*physisch schlecht, eklig*) *Geschmack, Geruch, Gefühl* nasty; (*fig*) *Geschmack auch* bad ◆ **mir wird ~** I feel ill *or* sick; **es kann einem ~ werden** it's enough to make you feel ill *or* sick.
(d) (*verkommen, ~beleumdet*) *Stadtviertel* evil, bad; *Kaschemme* evil, low.
[2] *adv* **(a)** (*schlimm, unangenehm, schlecht*) badly ◆ **etw ~ aufnehmen** to take sth badly; **das ist ihm ~ bekommen** it did him no good at all; **~ dran sein** to be in a bad way; **es steht ~ mit ihm** he's in a bad way; **das schmeckt gar nicht so ~** it doesn't taste so bad; **wie geht's? — danke, nicht ~** how's things? — not bad, thanks; **ich hätte nicht ~ Lust, jetzt nach Paris zu fahren** I wouldn't mind going to Paris now.
(b) (*moralisch, charakterlich schlecht*) badly ◆ **über jdn ~ reden** to say bad things about sb; **jdm etw ~ vermerken** to hold sth against sb, to take sth amiss; **jdm etw ~ auslegen** to take sth amiss.
(c) (*physisch schlecht*) ill, poorly ◆ **das Essen ist ihm ~ bekommen** the food disagreed with him.
Übel *nt* **-s, - (a)** (*geh: Krankheit, Leiden*) illness, malady (*old*).
(b) (*Mißstand*) ill, evil ◆ **ein notwendiges/das kleinere ~** a necessary/the lesser evil; **das alte ~** the old trouble; **der Grund allen ~s ist, daß ...** the cause *or* root of all the trouble is that ...; **die Gleichgültigkeit ist die Wurzel alles** *or* **allen ~s** indifference is the root of all evil; **das ~ bei der Sache** the trouble.
(c) (*Plage, Schaden*) evil ◆ **von ~ sein** to be a bad thing, to be bad; **zu allem ~ ...** to make matters worse ...; **ein ~ kommt selten allein** (*Prov*) misfortunes seldom come alone.
⚠**übel-: ~beleumdet** *adj attr* disreputable, of ill repute; **~beraten** *adj attr* (*geh*) ill-advised; **~gelaunt** *adj attr* ill-humoured, sullen, morose; **~gesinnt** *adj attr* (*geh*) ill-disposed.
Übelkeit *f* (*lit, fig*) nausea ◆ **eine plötzliche ~** a sudden feeling of nausea; **~ erregen** to cause nausea.
Übel-: ü~launig *adj* ill-tempered, cantankerous; ⚠**ü~nehmen** *vt sep irreg* to take amiss *or* badly *or* in bad part; **jdm etw ü~nehmen** to hold sth against sb, to take sth amiss *or* badly *or* in bad part; **bitte nehmen Sie es (mir) nicht ü~, aber ...** please don't take it amiss *or* take offence, but ...; **ich habe ihm gar nicht einmal ü~genommen, daß er gelogen hat, aber ...** I didn't even mind him lying but ..., I didn't even take it amiss that he lied but ...; **ü~nehmerisch** *adj* (*schnell beleidigt*) touchy; (*nachtragend*) resentful; ⚠**ü~riechend** *adj* foul-smelling, evil-smelling; **~sein** *nt* nausea; **~stand** *m* (social) evil *or* ill; **~tat** *f* (*dated, liter*) evil or wicked act *or* deed, misdeed; **~täter** *m* (*geh*) wrongdoer; ⚠**ü~tun** *vi sep irreg* (*dated, liter*) **jdm ü~tun** to be wicked to sb; ⚠**ü~wollen** *vi sep* (*geh*) **jdm ü~wollen** to wish sb harm *or* ill, to be ill-disposed towards sb.
üben [1] *vt* **(a)** (*praktisch erlernen*) *Aussprache, Musik, Sport* to practise; (*Mil*) to drill.
(b) (*schulen, trainieren*) *Gedächtnis, Muskeln etc* to exercise ◆ **mit geübtem Auge** with a practised eye; **geübt sein** to be experienced.
(c) (*tun, erkennen lassen*) to exercise ◆ **Gerechtigkeit ~** (*geh*) to be just (*gegen* to), to show fairness (*gegen* to); **Kritik an etw** (*dat*) **~** to criticize sth; **Geduld ~** to be patient; *siehe* **Barmherzigkeit.**
[2] *vr* **sich in etw** (*dat*) **~** to practise sth; **sich in Geduld** (*dat*) **~** (*geh*) to have patience, to possess one's soul in patience.
[3] *vi* (*praktisch lernen*) to practise.

über [1] *prep* **(a)** *+acc* (*räumlich*) over; (*quer ~ auch*) across; (*weiter als*) beyond ◆ **etw ~ etw hängen/stellen** to hang/put sth over *or* above sth; **es wurde ~ alle Sender ausgestrahlt** it was broadcast over all transmitters; **er lachte ~ das ganze Gesicht** he was beaming all over his face.
(b) *+dat* (*räumlich*) (*Lage, Standort*) over, above; (*jenseits*) over, across ◆ **zwei Grad ~ Null** two degrees (above zero); **~ der Stadt lag dichter Nebel** a thick mist hung over the town; **~ uns lachte die Sonne** the sun smiled above us; **er trug den Mantel ~ dem Arm** he was carrying his coat over his arm; **~ jdm stehen** *or* **sein** (*fig*) to be over *or* above sb; **er steht ~ der Situation** (*fig*) he is above it all.
(c) *+dat* (*zeitlich: bei, während*) over ◆ **~ der Arbeit einschlafen** to fall asleep over one's work; **etw ~ einem Glas Wein besprechen** to discuss sth over a glass of wine; **~ all der Aufregung/unserer Unterhaltung habe ich ganz vergessen, daß ...** in all the *or* what with all the excitement/what with all this chatting I quite forgot that ...; **~ Mittag geht er meist nach Hause** he usually goes home over lunch *or* at midday.
(d) *+acc* **Cäsars Sieg ~ die Gallier** Caesar's victory over the Gauls; **Gewalt ~ jdn haben** to have power over sb; **es kam plötzlich ~ ihn** it suddenly came over him; **sie liebt ihn ~ alles** she loves him more than everything; **das geht mir ~ den Verstand** that's beyond my understanding; **Fluch ~ dich!** (*obs*) a curse upon you! (*obs*).
(e) *+acc* (*vermittels, auf dem Wege ~*) via ◆ **die Nummer erfährt man ~ die Auskunft** you'll get the number from *or* through *or* via information; **wir sind ~ die Autobahn gekommen** we came by *or* via the autobahn; **nach Köln ~ Aachen** to Cologne via Aachen; **Zug nach Frankfurt ~ Wiesbaden und Mainz** train to Frankfurt via *or* stopping at *or* calling at Wiesbaden and Mainz.
(f) *+acc* (*zeitlich*) (*innerhalb eines Zeitraums, länger als*) over ◆ **~ Weihnachten** over Christmas; **bis ~ Ostern** until after Easter; **den ganzen Sommer ~** all summer long; **~ Wochen (ausgedehnt)** for weeks on end; **die ganze Zeit ~** all the time; **das ganze Jahr ~** all through the year, all year round; **~ kurz oder lang** sooner or later; **es ist ~ vierzehn Tage her, daß ...** it's over fourteen days since ...
(g) *+acc* (*bei Zahlenangaben*) (*in Höhe von*) for; (*mehr als*) over ◆ **ein Scheck ~ DM 20** a cheque for 20 DM; **eine Rechnung von ~ £ 100** a bill for over *or* of over £100; **Kinder ~ 14 Jahre/Städte ~ 50.000 Einwohner** children over 14 years *or* of 14 (years of age) and over/towns of over 50,000 inhabitants; **Pakete ~ 10 kg** parcels over 10 kgs.
(h) *+acc* (*wegen*) over; (*betreffend*) about ◆ **ein Buch/Film/Vortrag** *etc* **~ ...** a book/film/lecture *etc* about *or* on ...; **was wissen Sie ~ ihn?** what do you know about him?; **~ welches Thema schreiben Sie Ihr neues Buch?** what's the subject of your new book?, what's your new book about?; **~ Politik/Wörterbücher/Fußball** *etc* **reden** to talk (about) politics/dictionaries/football *etc*; **~ jdn/etw lachen** to laugh about *or* at sb/sth; **sich ~ etw freuen/ärgern** to be pleased/angry about *or* at sth.
(i) *+acc* (*steigernd*) upon ◆ **Fehler ~ Fehler** mistake upon *or* after mistake, one mistake after another.
[2] *adv* **~ und ~** all over; **er wurde ~ und ~ rot** he went red all over; **ich stecke ~ und ~ in Schulden** I am up to my ears in debt; **(das) Gewehr ~!** (*Mil*) shoulder arms!; **jdm in etw** (*dat*) **~ sein** (*inf*) to be better than sb at sth.
über|aktiv *adj* hyperactive, overactive.
über|all *adv* everywhere ◆ **ich habe dich schon ~ gesucht** I've been looking everywhere *or* all over (*inf*) for you; **~ herumliegen** to be lying all over the place *or* shop (*inf*); **~ in London/der Welt** everywhere in *or* all over London/the world; **~ wo** wherever; **~ Bescheid wissen** (*wissensmäßig*) to have a wide-ranging knowledge; (*an Ort*) to know one's way around; **sie ist ~ zu gebrauchen** she can do everything; **es ist ~ dasselbe** it's the same wherever you go; **so ist es ~** it's the same everywhere; **~ und nirgends zu Hause sein** to be at home everywhere and nowhere; **er ist immer ~ und nirgends, den erreichst du nie** he's always here, there and everywhere, you'll never find him.
über|all-: ~her *adv* from all over; **~hin** *adv* everywhere.
Über-: ü~altert *adj* **(a)** (*Sociol*) having a disproportionate number of *or* too high a percentage of old people; **(b)** (*rare*) *siehe* **veraltet**; **~alterung** *f* (*Sociol*) increase in the percentage of old people; **~angebot** *nt* surplus (*an +dat* of); **ü~ängstlich** *adj* overanxious; **ü~anstrengen*** *insep* [1] *vt* to overstrain, to overexert; *Kräfte* to overtax; *Augen* to strain; [2] *vr* to over-

⚠: for details of spelling reform, see supplement

strain *or* overexert oneself; **ü~anstrenge dich nicht!** (*iro*) don't strain yourself! (*iro*); **~anstrengung** *f* overexertion; **eine ~anstrengung der Nerven/Augen** a strain on the *or* one's nerves/eyes; **ü~antworten*** *vt insep* (*geh*) **jdm etw ü~antworten** to hand sth over to sb, to place sth in sb's hands; **etw dem Feuer ü~antworten** (*liter*) to commit sth to the flames; **ü~arbeiten*** *insep* [1] *vt* to rework, to go over; **in einer ü~arbeiteten Fassung** published in a revised edition; [2] *vr* to overwork; **~arbeitung** *f, no pl* (**a**) (*Vorgang*) reworking; (*Ergebnis*) revision, revised version; (**b**) (*~anstrengung*) overwork; **ü~aus** *adv* extremely, exceedingly; **ü~backen*** *vt insep irreg* to put in the oven/under the grill; **mit Käse ü~backen** au gratin; **ü~backene Käseschnitten** cheese on toast.

Überbau *m, pl* **-e** *or* (*Build auch*) **-ten** (*Build, Philos*) superstructure.

überbauen* *vt insep* to build over; (*mit einem Dach*) to roof over, to build a roof over.

Über-: ü~beanspruchen* *vt insep* (**a**) *Menschen, Körper* to overtax, to make too many demands on; **(arbeitsmäßig) ü~beansprucht sein** to be overworked; (**b**) *Einrichtungen, Dienste* to overburden; (**c**) *Maschine, Auto etc* to overtax, to overstrain; (**d**) *Werkstoffe, Materialien* to overstrain; (*durch Gewicht auch*) to overload; **~beanspruchung** *f siehe vt* (**a**) (*von Menschen*) overtaxing; (*arbeitsmäßig*) overworking; (**b**) overburdening; (**c**) overtaxing, overstraining; (**d**) overstraining; overloading; **ü~behalten*** *vt sep irreg* (*inf*) (**a**) *siehe* **übrigbehalten**; (**b**) (*nicht ausziehen*) *Mantel* to keep on; **~bein** *nt* (*an Gelenk*) ganglion; **ü~bekommen*** *vt sep irreg* (*inf*) **jdn/etw ü~bekommen** to get sick of *or* fed up with sb/sth (*inf*); **ü~belasten*** *vt insep siehe* **ü~lasten**; **~belastung** *f siehe* **~lastung**; **ü~belegen*** *vt insep usu ptp* to overcrowd; *Kursus, Fach etc* to oversubscribe; **~belegung** *f siehe vt* overcrowding; oversubscription; **ü~belichten*** *vt insep* (*Phot*) to overexpose; **~belichtung** *f* (*Phot*) overexposure; **~beschäftigung** *f* overemployment; **ü~besetzt** *adj Behörde, Abteilung* overstaffed; **ü~betonen*** *vt insep* (*fig*) to overstress, to overemphasize; *Hüften, obere Gesichtshälfte etc* to overaccentuate, to overemphasize; **ü~betrieblich** *adj* industry-wide; **~bevölkerung** *f* overpopulation; **ü~bewerten*** *vt insep* (*lit*) to overvalue; (*fig auch*) to overrate; *Schulleistung etc* to mark too high; **wollen wir doch eine so vereinzelte Äußerung nicht ü~bewerten** let's not attach too much importance to such an isolated remark; **~bewertung** *f* (*lit*) overvaluing; (*fig auch*) overrating; **die ~bewertung einer einzelnen Äußerung** attaching too much importance to an isolated statement; **diese Eins ist eine klare ~bewertung** this grade one is clearly too high; **~bezahlung** *f* overpayment.

überbietbar *adj* (*fig*) **kaum noch ~ sein** to take some beating; **ein an Vulgarität nicht mehr ~er Pornofilm** a porn film of unsurpassed *or* unsurpassable vulgarity.

überbieten* *insep irreg* [1] *vt* (*bei Auktion*) to outbid (*um* by); (*fig*) to outdo; *Leistung, Rekord* to beat ◆ **das ist kaum noch zu ~** it's outrageous.

[2] *vr* **sich in etw** (*dat*) **(gegenseitig) ~** to vie with one another *or* each other in sth; **sich (selber) ~** to surpass oneself.

Überbietung *f siehe vt* outbidding; outdoing; beating ◆ **eine ~ dieses Rekordes** to beat this record.

über-: ~binden *vt sep irreg* (*Mus*) to join up; **~blasen*** *vt insep irreg* (*Mus*) to overblow; **~blättern*** *vt insep Buch* to leaf *or* flick *or* glance through; *Stelle* to skip over *or* past, to miss; **~bleiben** *vi sep irreg aux sein* (*inf*) *siehe* **übrigbleiben**.

Überbleibsel *nt* **-s, -** remnant; (*Speiserest*) leftover *usu pl*, remains *pl*; (*Brauch, Angewohnheit etc*) survival, hangover; (*Spur*) trace.

überblenden[1] *vi sep* (*Film, Rad: Szene etc*) to fade; (*Film auch*) to dissolve; (*plötzlich*) to cut ◆ **wir blenden über zu ...** we now go over to ...

überblenden[2]* *vt insep* (*ausblenden*) to fade out; (*überlagern*) to superimpose.

Überblendung[1] *f siehe vi* fade; dissolve; cut; (*das Überblenden*) fading; dissolving; cutting.

Überblendung[2] *f siehe vt* fading out; superimposition.

Überblick *m* (*über +acc* of) (**a**) (*freie Sicht*) view.

(**b**) (*Einblick*) perspective, overall *or* broad view, overview ◆ **er hat keinen ~, es fehlt ihm an ~** (*dat*) he lacks an overview, he has no overall picture; **den ~ verlieren** to lose track (of things).

(**c**) (*Abriß*) survey; (*Übersicht, Zusammenhang*) synopsis, summary ◆ **sich** (*dat*) **einen ~ verschaffen** to get a general idea; **Weltgeschichte im ~** compendium of world history.

überblicken* *vt insep* (**a**) (*lit*) *Platz, Stadt* to overlook, to have *or* command a view of.

(**b**) (*fig*) to see; *Lage etc auch* to grasp ◆ **die Entwicklung läßt sich leicht ~** the development can be seen at a glance; **bis ich die Lage besser überblicke** until I have a better view of the situation; **das läßt sich noch nicht ~** I/we *etc* cannot tell *or* say as yet.

über-: ~borden* *vi insep aux haben or sein* (*fig geh*) to be overextravagant; **~bordende Metaphern** overextravagant metaphors; **~bordende Selbstgewißheit** excessive self-assurance; **~braten**[1]* *vt insep irreg* (*Cook*) to fry lightly; **~braten**[2] *vt sep irreg* **jdm eins ~braten** (*sl*) to land sb one (*inf*).

Überbreite *f* excess width ◆ **Vorsicht, ~!** caution, wide load.

überbringen* *vt insep irreg* **jdm etw ~** to bring sb sth, to bring sth to sb; *Brief etc auch* to deliver sth to sb.

Überbringer(in *f*) *m* **-s, -** bringer, bearer; (*von Scheck etc*) bearer.

überbrückbar *adj Gegensätze* reconcilable ◆ **schwer ~e Gegensätze** differences which are difficult to reconcile.

überbrücken* *vt insep* (**a**) (*old*) *Fluß* to bridge (over). (**b**) (*fig*) *Kluft, Zeitraum* to bridge; *Krisenzeiten* to get over *or* through; *Gegensätze* to reconcile ◆ **die Gegensätze zwischen ... ~** to bridge the gap between ...

Überbrückung *f siehe vt* (**b**) (*fig*) bridging; getting over *or* through; reconciliation ◆ **100 Mark zur ~** 100 marks to tide me/him *etc* over.

Überbrückungs-: ~beihilfe *f*, **~geld** *nt* interim aid, money to tide one over; **~kredit** *m* bridging loan.

Über-: ü~buchen* *vt insep* to overbook; **ü~bürden*** *vt insep* (*geh*) to overburden; **~dach** *nt* roof; **ü~dachen*** *vt insep* to roof over, to cover over; **ü~dachte Fahrradständer/Bushaltestelle** covered bicycle stands/bus shelter; **ü~dauern*** *vt insep* to survive; **~decke** *f* bedspread, bedcover, counterpane; **ü~decken**[1] *vt sep* to cover up *or* over; (*inf: auflegen*) *Tischtuch* to put on; **ü~decken**[2]* *insep* [1] *vt Riß, Geschmack* to cover up, to conceal; [2] *vr* (*sich ü~schneiden*) to overlap; **ü~dehnen*** *vt insep Sehne, Muskel etc* to strain; *Gummi,* (*fig*) *Begriff* to overstretch; **ü~denken*** *vt insep irreg* to think over, to consider; **etw noch einmal ü~denken** to reconsider sth; **ü~deutlich** *adj* all too obvious.

überdies *adv* (*geh*) (**a**) (*außerdem*) moreover, furthermore, what is more. (**b**) (*ohnehin*) in any case, anyway.

Über-: ü~dimensional *adj* colossal, huge, oversize(d); **ü~dosieren*** *infin auch* **ü~zudosieren** *vt insep* **dieses Mittel wird oft ü~dosiert** an excessive dose of this medicine is often given/taken; **nicht ü~dosieren** do not exceed the dose; **~dosis** *f* overdose, OD (*inf*); (*zu große Zumessung*) excessive amount; **sich** (*dat*) **eine ~dosis Heroin spritzen** to give oneself an overdose of heroin, to OD on heroin (*inf*); **ü~drehen*** *vt insep Uhr etc* to overwind; *Motor* to overrev; *Gewinde, Schraube* to strip; **ü~dreht** *adj* (*inf*) overexcited; (*ständig*) highly charged, hyped(-up) (*sl*); (*ü~kandidelt*) weird; **ein ü~drehter Typ** a weirdo (*inf*).

Überdruck[1] *m* **-s, -e** overprint.

Überdruck[2] *m* **-s, ¨-e** (*Tech*) excess pressure *no pl*.

überdrucken* *vt insep* to overprint.

Überdruck-: ~kabine *f* (*Aviat*) pressurized cabin; **~ventil** *nt* pressure relief valve, blow-off valve.

⚠**Überdruß** *m* **-sses,** *no pl* (*Übersättigung*) surfeit, satiety (*liter*) (*an +dat* of); (*Widerwille*) aversion (*an +dat* to), antipathy (*an +dat* to) ◆ **bis zum ~** ad nauseam; **er aß Kaviar bis zum ~** he ate caviar until he wearied of it *or* had had a surfeit of it; **~ am Leben** weariness of living *or* life.

überdrüssig *adj* **jds/einer Sache** (*gen*) **~ sein/werden** to be weary of sb/sth/to (grow) weary of sb/sth.

Über-: ü~düngen* *vt sep* to over-fertilize; **~düngung** *f* over-fertilization; **ü~durchschnittlich** [1] *adj* above-average; [2] *adv* exceptionally, outstandingly; **er arbeitet ü~durchschnittlich gut** he works better than average; **sie verdient ü~durchschnittlich gut** she earns more than the average, she has an above-average salary; **ü~eck** *adv* at right angles (to each other *or* one another); **~eifer** *m siehe adj* overenthusiasm, overeagerness, overzealousness; officiousness; **ü~eifrig** *adj* overenthusiastic, overeager, overzealous; (*pej: wichtigtuerisch*) officious; **ü~eignen*** *vt insep* (*geh*) **jdm etw ü~eignen** to make sth over to sb, to transfer sth to sb; **~eignung** *f* (*geh*) transference; **~eile** *f* haste; **ü~eilen*** *insep* [1] *vt* to rush; **ü~eilen Sie nichts!** don't rush things!; [2] *vr* to rush; **ü~eil dich bloß nicht!** (*iro*) don't rush yourself (*iro*); **ü~eilt** *adj* hasty, precipitate.

über|einander *adv* (**a**) (*räumlich*) on top of each other *or* one another, one on top of the other; *hängen* one above the other ◆ **wir wohnen ~** we live one above the other, we live on top of each other. (**b**) *reden etc* about each other *or* one another.

⚠**über|einander-: ~legen** *vt sep* to put *or* lay one on top of the other, to put *or* lay on top of each other *or* one another; **~liegen** *vi sep irreg* to lie one on top of the other, to lie on top of each other *or* one another; **~schlagen** *vt sep irreg* **die Beine/Arme ~schlagen** to cross one's legs/to fold one's arms.

über|einkommen *vi sep irreg aux sein* to agree ◆ **wir sind darin übereingekommen, daß ...** we have agreed that ...

Über|einkommen *nt* **-s, -, Über|einkunft** *f* **-, ¨-e** arrangement, understanding, agreement; (*Vertrag*) agreement ◆ **ein Übereinkommen** *or* **eine Übereinkunft treffen** to enter into *or* make an agreement; **ein Übereinkommen** *or* **eine Übereinkunft erzielen** to reach *or* come to an agreement, to reach agreement.

über|einstimmen *vi sep* to agree, to concur (*form*); (*Meinungen*) to tally, to concur (*form*); (*Angaben, Meßwerte, Rechnungen etc*) to correspond, to tally, to agree; (*zusammenpassen: Farben, Stile etc*) to match; (*Gram*) to agree; (*Dreiecke*) to be congruent ◆ **mit jdm in etw** (*dat*) **~** to agree with sb on sth; **wir stimmen darin überein, daß ...** we agree *or* are agreed that ...

über|einstimmend [1] *adj* corresponding; *Meinungen* concurring, concurrent; *Farben etc* matching ◆ **nach ~en Meldungen/Zeugenaussagen** according to all reports/according to mutually corroborative testimonies.

[2] *adv* **alle erklärten ~, daß ...** everybody agreed that ..., everybody unanimously stated that ...; **wir sind ~ der Meinung, daß ...** we are unanimously of the opinion that ..., we unanimously agree that ...; **~ mit** in agreement with.

Über|einstimmung *f* (**a**) (*Einklang, Gleichheit*) correspondence, agreement ◆ **sein Handeln steht nicht mit seiner Theorie in ~** there's a disparity *or* no correspondence between his actions and his theory; **bei den Zeugenaussagen gab es nur in zwei Punkten ~** the testimonies only agreed *or* corresponded *or* tallied in two particulars; **zwei Dinge in ~ bringen** to bring two things into line; **es besteht keine ~ zwischen x und y** x and y do not agree.

(**b**) (*von Meinung*) agreement ◆ **darin besteht bei allen Beteiligten ~** all

parties involved are agreed on that; **in ~ mit jdm/etw** in agreement with sb/in accordance with sth.
(c) *(Gram)* agreement.

Über-: ü~empfindlich *adj (gegen* to) oversensitive, hypersensitive *(auch Med)*; **~empfindlichkeit** *f (gegen* to) oversensitivity, hypersensitivity *(auch Med)*; **ü~erfüllen*** *vt insep infin auch* **ü~zuerfüllen** *Norm, Soll* to exceed *(um* by); **~erfüllung** *f (no pl: das ~erfüllen)* exceeding; **bei ~erfüllung des Plansolls werden Sonderprämien gezahlt** anyone who exceeds the target *or* quota is paid special premiums; **ü~ernähren*** *vt insep infin auch* **ü~zuernähren** to overfeed; **~ernährung** *f (no pl: das ~ernähren)* overfeeding; *(Krankheit)* overeating; **ü~essen¹** *vt sep irreg* **sich** *(dat)* **etw ü~essen** to grow sick of sth; **Spargel kann ich mir gar nicht ü~essen** I can't eat enough asparagus; **ü~essen²** *pret* **ü~aß,** *ptp* **ü~gessen** *vr insep* to overeat; **ich habe mich an Käse ü~gessen** I've eaten too much cheese.

überfahren¹ *sep irreg* **1** *vt (mit Boot etc)* to take *or* ferry across.
2 *vi aux sein* to cross over.

überfahren²* *vt insep irreg* **(a)** *jdn, Tier* to run over, to knock down. **(b)** *(hinwegfahren über)* to go *or* drive over; *Fluß etc auch* to cross (over). **(c)** *(übersehen und weiterfahren) Ampel etc* to go through. **(d)** *(inf: übertölpeln)* **jdn ~** to stampede sb into it. **(e)** *(plötzlich über einen kommen)* to come over.

Überfahrt *f* crossing.

Überfall *m* **(a)** *(Angriff)* attack *(auf +acc* on); *(auf jdn auch)* assault *(auf +acc* on); *(auf offener Straße auch)* mugging *(auf +acc* of); *(auf Bank etc)* raid *(auf +acc* on), holdup; *(auf Land)* invasion *(auf +acc* of) ◆ **einen ~ auf jdn/etw verüben** *or* **ausführen** to carry out an attack *etc* on sb/sth; **dies ist ein ~, keine Bewegung!** this is a holdup *or* stick-up *(inf)*, freeze!
(b) *(hum: unerwartetes Erscheinen)* invasion ◆ **er hat einen ~ auf uns vor** he's planning to descend on us.

überfallen* *vt insep irreg* **(a)** *(angreifen)* to attack; *jdn auch* to assault; *(auf offener Straße auch)* to mug; *Bank etc* to raid, to hold up, to stick up *(inf)*; *Land auch* to invade; *(Mil) Hauptquartier, Lager* to raid.
(b) *(fig geh: überkommen) (Gefühle, Schlaf, Müdigkeit, Krankheit etc)* to come over *or* upon; *(überraschen: Nacht)* to overtake, to come upon suddenly ◆ **plötzlich überfiel ihn heftiges Fieber** he suddenly had a bad attack of fever.
(c) *(fig inf) (überraschend besuchen)* to descend (up)on; *(bestürmen)* to pounce upon ◆ **jdn mit Fragen/Wünschen ~** to bombard sb with questions/ requests.

Über-: ü~fällig *adj* overdue *usu pred*; **seit einer Woche ü~fällig sein** to be a week overdue; **~fallkommando, ~fallskommando** *(Aus) nt* flying squad, riot squad; **ü~feinert** *adj* overrefined; **~feinerung** *f* overrefinement; **ü~fischen*** *vt insep* to overfish; **~fischung** *f* overfishing; **ü~fliegen*** *vt insep irreg* **(a)** *(lit)* to fly over, to overfly; **(b)** *(fig)* **ein Lächeln/eine leichte Röte ü~flog ihr Gesicht** a smile/a faint blush flitted across her face; **(c)** *(flüchtig ansehen) Buch etc* to take a quick look at, to glance through *or* at *or* over; **~flieger** *m (fig)* high-flyer; **ü~fließen¹*** *vt insep irreg (rare)* to inundate, to flood; **ü~fließen²** *vi sep irreg aux sein* **(a)** *(Gefäß)* to overflow; *(Flüssigkeit auch)* to run over; **(b) ineinander ü~fließen** *(Farben)* to run; **(c)** *(fig: vor Dank, Höflichkeit etc)* to overflow, to gush *(vor +dat* with); **~flug** *m* overflight; **einem Flugzeug den ~flug verweigern** to refuse to allow an aircraft to fly over one's territory; **ü~flügeln*** *vt insep* to outdistance, to outstrip; *(in Leistung, bei Wahl)* to outdo; *Erwartungen etc* to surpass.

⚠**Überfluß** *m* **-sses,** ⚠*no pl* **(a)** (super)abundance *(an +dat* of); *(Luxus)* affluence ◆ **Arbeit/Geld im ~** plenty of work/money, an abundance of work/money; **das Land des ~sses** the land of plenty; **im ~ leben** to live in luxury; **im ~ vorhanden sein** to be in plentiful supply; **~ an etw** *(dat)* **haben, etw im ~ haben** to have plenty *or* an abundance of sth, to have sth in abundance.
(b) zu allem *or* **zum ~** *(unnötigerweise)* superfluously; *(obendrein)* to crown it all *(inf)*, into the bargain; **zu allem** *or* **zum ~ fing es auch noch an zu regnen** and then, to crown it all, it started to rain, and then it started to rain into the bargain.

⚠**Überflußgesellschaft** *f* affluent society.

überflüssig *adj* superfluous; *(frei, entbehrlich)* spare; *(unnötig)* unnecessary; *(zwecklos)* futile, useless ◆ **~ zu sagen, daß ...** it goes without saying that ...

überflüssigerweise *adv* superfluously.

Über-: ü~fluten¹ *vi sep aux sein (ü~fließen²)* to overflow; **ü~fluten²*** *vt insep (lit, fig)* to flood; *(fig auch)* to inundate; **~flutung** *f* **(a)** *(lit)* flood; *(das ~fluten)* flooding *no pl*; **(b)** *(fig)* flooding *no pl*, inundation; **ü~fordern*** *vt insep* to overtax; *jdn auch* to ask *or* expect too much of; **damit ist er ü~fordert** that's asking *or* expecting too much of him; **als Abteilungsleiter wäre er doch etwas ü~fordert** being head of department would be too much for him *or* would stretch him too far; **~forderung** *f* excessive demand(s) *(für* on); *(no pl: das ~fordern)* overtaxing; **~fracht** *f* excess freight; **ü~frachten*** *vt insep (fig)* to overload; **ein mit Emotionen ü~frachteter Begriff** a concept fraught with emotions, an emotionally loaded concept; **ü~fragt** *adj pred* stumped (for an answer); **da bin ich ü~fragt** there you've got me, there you have me, that I don't know; **ü~fremden*** *vt insep* to infiltrate with too many foreign influences; *(Econ)* to swamp; **ü~fremdet werden** to be swamped by foreigners/foreign capital; **~fremdung** *f, no pl* foreign infiltration; *(Econ)* swamping; **ü~fressen*** *vr insep irreg (inf)* to overeat, to eat too much; **sich an etw** *(dat)* **ü~fressen** to gorge oneself on sth; **~fuhr** *f* **-, -en** *(Aus)* ferry; **ü~führen¹** *vt sep* to transfer; *Leichnam* to transport; *Wagen* to drive; **ü~führen²*** *vt insep* **(a)** *siehe* **ü~führen¹**; **(b)** *Täter* to convict *(gen* of), to find guilty *(gen* of); **ein ü~führter Verbrecher** a convicted criminal; **(c)** *(ü~bauen)* **eine Straße/einen Fluß mit einer Brücke ü~führen** to build a footbridge/bridge over a street/ river; **~führung** *f* **(a)** transportation; **(b)** *no pl (Jur)* conviction; **(c)** *(Brücke über Straße etc)* bridge *(auch Rail)*, overpass; *(Fußgängerüberführung)* footbridge; **~fülle** *f* profusion, superabundance; **ü~füllen*** *vt insep Glas* to overfill; **sich** *(dat)* **den Magen ü~füllen** to eat too much; **ü~füllt** *adj* overcrowded; *Kurs* oversubscribed; *(Comm) Lager* overstocked, overfilled; **~füllung** *f, no pl* overcrowding; *(von Kursus, Vorlesung)* oversubscription; **~funktion** *f* hyperactivity, hyperfunction(ing); **ü~füttern*** *vt insep* to overfeed; **~fütterung** *f* overfeeding.

Übergabe *f* **-,** *no pl* handing over *no pl*; *(von Neubau)* opening; *(Mil)* surrender ◆ **die ~ der Zeugnisse findet am Ende des Schuljahres statt** reports are handed out at the end of the school year; **die ~ des neuen Schwimmbads an die Öffentlichkeit wird durch den Bürgermeister vorgenommen** the mayor will open the new swimming pool to the public.

Übergang *m* **(a)** *(das Überqueren)* crossing.
(b) *(Fußgänger~)* crossing, crosswalk *(US)*; *(Brücke)* footbridge; *(Bahn~)* level crossing *(Brit)*, grade crossing *(US)*.
(c) *(Grenzübergangsstelle)* checkpoint.
(d) *(fig: Wechsel, Überleitung)* transition.

Übergangs-: ~bestimmung *f* interim *or* temporary regulation; **~erscheinung** *f* temporary phenomenon; **ü~los** *adj* without a transition; *(zeitlich auch)* without a transitional period; **~lösung** *f* interim *or* temporary solution; **~mantel** *m* between-seasons coat; **~phase** *f* transitional phase; **~regelung** *f* interim arrangement; **~regierung** *f* caretaker *or* transitional government; **~stadium** *nt* transitional stage; **~zeit** *f* **(a)** transitional period, period of transition; **(b)** *(zwischen Jahreszeiten)* in-between season/weather; **~zustand** *m* transitional state.

Übergardine *f* curtain, drape *(US)*.

übergeben* *insep irreg* **1** *vt* **(a)** to hand over; *(überreichen) Dokument, Zettel, Einschreiben* to hand *(jdm* sb); *Diplom etc* to hand over *(jdm* to sb), to present *(jdm* to sb); *(vermachen)* to bequeath *(jdm* to sb); *(Mil auch)* to surrender ◆ **ein Gebäude der Öffentlichkeit/eine Straße dem Verkehr ~** to open a building to the public/a road to traffic; **eine Angelegenheit einem Rechtsanwalt ~** to place a matter in the hands of a lawyer.
(b) *(weiterreichen, verleihen) Amt, Macht* to hand over.
(c) einen Leichnam der Erde/dem Wasser ~ *(liter)* to commit a body to the earth/water.
2 *vr (sich erbrechen)* to vomit, to be sick ◆ **ich muß mich ~** I'm going to be sick.

übergehen¹ *vi sep irreg aux sein* **(a) in etw** *(acc)* **~** *(in einen anderen Zustand)* to turn *or* change into sth; *(Farben)* to merge into sth; **in jds Besitz** *(acc)* **~** to become sb's property; **in Schreien ~** to degenerate into shouting; **in andere Hände/in Volkseigentum ~** to pass into other hands/into public ownership.
(b) auf jdn ~ *(geerbt, übernommen werden)* to pass to sb.
(c) zu etw ~ to go over to sth; **wir sind dazu übergegangen, Computer zu benutzen** we went over to (using) computers.

übergehen²* *vt insep irreg* to pass over; *Kapitel, Abschnitt etc auch* to skip; *Einwände etc auch* to ignore.

Über-: ü~genau *adj* overprecise, pernickety *(inf)*; **ü~genug** *adv* more than enough; **ü~geordnet** *adj* **(a)** *Behörde, Dienststelle* higher; **die uns ü~geordnete Behörde** the next authority above us; **(b)** *(Gram) Satz* superordinate; *(Ling, Philos) Begriff* generic; **(c)** *(fig)* **von ü~geordneter Bedeutung sein** to be of overriding importance; **~gepäck** *nt (Aviat)* excess baggage; **ü~gescheit** *adj (iro)* know-all, know-it-all *(US)*, smart-ass *(sl) all attr*; **so ein ~gescheiter** some clever dick *(inf)* or smart-ass *(sl)* or know-all; **ü~geschnappt** **1** *ptp of* **ü~schnappen**; **2** *adj (inf)* crazy; **~gewicht** *nt* overweight; *(fig)* predominance; **~gewicht haben** *(Paket etc)* to be overweight; **an ~gewicht leiden, ~gewicht haben** *(Mensch)* to be overweight; **5 Gramm ~gewicht** 5 grammes excess weight; **das ~gewicht bekommen/ haben** *(fig)* to become predominant/to predominate; **wenn sie das militärische ~gewicht bekommen** if they gain military dominance; **ü~gewichtig** *adj* overweight; **ü~gießen¹** *vt sep irreg* **jdm etw ü~gießen** to pour sth over sb; **ü~gießen²*** *vt insep irreg* to pour over; *jdn* to douse; *Braten* to baste; **jdn/sich mit etw ü~gießen** to pour sth over sb/oneself; *(absichtlich auch)* to douse sb/oneself with sth; **ü~glücklich** *adj* overjoyed; **ü~greifen** *vi sep irreg* **(a)** *(beim Klavierspiel)* to cross one's hands (over); **(b)** *(auf Rechte etc)* to encroach *or* infringe *(auf +acc* on); *(Feuer, Streik, Krankheit etc)* to spread *(auf +acc* to); **ineinander ü~greifen** to overlap; **ü~greifend** *adj (fig) Gesichtspunkte, Überlegungen* general, comprehensive; **~griff** *m (Einmischung)* infringement *(auf +acc* of), encroachment *(auf +acc* on), interference *no pl (auf +acc* with *or* in); *(Mil)* attack *(auf +acc* upon), incursion *(auf +acc* into); **ü~groß** *adj* oversize(d), huge, enormous; **~größe** *f (bei Kleidung etc)* outsize; **62 ist eine ~größe** 62 is outsize; **ü~haben** *vt sep irreg (inf)* **(a)** *(satt haben)* to be sick (and tired) of *(inf)*, to be fed up of *or* with *(inf)*; **(b)** *(übrig haben)* to have left (over); **für etw nichts ü~haben** not to like sth; **(c)** *Kleidung* to have on.

⚠**überhandnehmen** *vi sep irreg* to get out of control *or* hand; *(schlechte Sitten, massive Lohnforderungen, Laxheit etc auch)* to become rife *or* rampant; *(Meinungen, Ideen etc)* to become rife *or* rampant, to gain the upper hand.

Über-: ~hang *m* **(a)** *(Fels~)* overhang, overhanging rock; *(Baum~)* overhanging branches *pl*; **(b)** *(Vorhang)* pelmet; *(von Bettdecke etc)* valance; **(c)** *(Comm: Überschuß)* surplus *(an +dat* of); **ü~hängen** *sep* **1** *vi irreg aux haben or sein* to overhang; *(hinausragen auch)* to jut out; **2** *vt* **sich** *(dat)* **ein Gewehr ü~hängen** to sling a rifle over one's shoulder; **sich** *(dat)* **einen Mantel**

ü~hängen to put *or* hang a coat round *or* over one's shoulders; **~hangmandat** *nt (Pol) seat gained as a result of votes for a specific candidate over and above the seats to which a party is entitled by the number of votes cast for the party*; **ü~hasten*** *vt insep* to rush; **ü~hastet** *adj* overhasty, hurried; **ü~hastet sprechen** to speak too fast; **ü~häufen*** *vt insep jdn* to overwhelm, to inundate; *Schreibtisch etc* to pile high; **jdn mit Geschenken/Glückwünschen/Titeln ü~häufen** to heap presents/congratulations/titles (up)on sb; **ich bin völlig mit Arbeit ü~häuft** I'm completely snowed under *or* swamped (with work); **jdn mit Vorwürfen ü~häufen** to heap reproaches (up)on sb('s head).

überhaupt *adv* **(a)** *(sowieso, im allgemeinen)* in general; *(überdies, außerdem)* anyway, anyhow ♦ **und ~, warum nicht?** and anyway *or* after all, why not?; **er sagt ~ immer sehr wenig** he never says very much at the best of times *or* anyway *or* anyhow; **nicht nur Rotwein, sondern Wein ~ mag ich nicht** it's not only red wine I don't like, I don't like wine at all *or* full stop *(esp Brit) or* period.
(b) *(in Fragen, Verneinungen)* at all ♦ **~ nicht** not at all; **ich denke ~ nicht daran, mitzukommen** I've (absolutely) no intention whatsoever of coming along; **~ nie** never (ever), never at all; **~ kein Grund** no reason at all *or* whatsoever; **hast du denn ~ keinen Anstand?** have you no decency at all?; **das habe ich ja ~ nicht gewußt** I had no idea at all; **ich habe ~ nichts gehört** I didn't hear anything at all, I didn't hear a thing; **das steht in ~ keinem Verhältnis zu ...** that bears no relationship at all *or* whatsoever to ...
(c) *(erst, eigentlich)* **dann merkt man ~ erst, wie schön ...** then you really notice for the first time how beautiful ...; **waren Sie ~ schon in dem neuen Film?** have you actually been to the latest film?; **da fällt mir ~ ein, ...** now I remember ...; **wenn ~** if at all; **wie ist das ~ möglich?** how is that possible?; **gibt es das ~?** is there really such a thing?, is there really any such thing?; **was wollen Sie ~ von mir?** *(herausfordernd)* what do you want from me?; **wer sind Sie ~?** who do you think you are?; **wissen Sie ~, wer ich bin?** do you realize who I am?

Über-: ü~heben* *vr insep irreg (lit)* to (over)strain oneself; *(fig geh: hochmütig sein)* to be arrogant; **sich über jdn ü~heben** to consider oneself superior to sb; **ü~heblich** *adj* arrogant; **~heblichkeit** *f, no pl* arrogance; **~hebung** *f (fig geh)* presumption; **ü~heizen*** *vt insep* to overheat; **ü~hitzen*** *vt insep* to overheat; **ü~hitzt** *adj (fig) Gemüter, Diskussion* very heated *pred*; *Phantasie* wild; **ü~höhen*** *vt insep Preise* to raise *or* increase excessively; *Kurve* to bank, to superelevate *(spec)*; **ü~höht** *adj Kurve* banked, superelevated *(spec)*; *Forderungen, Preise* exorbitant, excessive.

überholen[1]* *vti insep* **(a)** *Fahrzeug* to overtake *(esp Brit)*, to pass; *(fig: übertreffen)* to overtake. **(b)** *(Tech) Maschine, Motor etc* to overhaul.

überholen[2] *sep* [1] *vti (old)* to ferry ♦ **hol über!** ferry!
[2] *vi (Naut: Schiff)* to keel over.

Überhol- (Aut): ~manöver *nt* overtaking *(esp Brit) or* passing manoeuvre; **~spur** *f* overtaking *(esp Brit) or* fast lane.

überholt *adj* out-dated.

Überhol-: ~verbot *nt* restriction on overtaking *(esp Brit) or* passing; *(als Schild etc)* no overtaking *(Brit)*, no passing; **auf dieser Strecke besteht ~verbot** no overtaking *etc* on this stretch; **nach der nächsten Kurve ist das ~verbot wieder aufgehoben** the restriction on overtaking *etc* ends after the next bend; **~vorgang** *m (form)* overtaking *(esp Brit)*, passing; **vor Beginn des ~vorganges** before starting *or* beginning to overtake *etc*; **der ~vorgang war noch nicht abgeschlossen, als das Fahrzeug ...** the vehicle had not finished overtaking *etc* when it ...

überhören[1]* *vt insep* not to hear; *(nicht hören wollen)* to ignore ♦ **das möchte ich überhört haben!** (I'll pretend) I didn't hear that!

überhören[2] *vr sep* **sich** *(dat)* **etw ~** to be tired *or* sick *(inf)* of hearing sth.

Über-Ich *nt* superego.

über|interpretieren* *vt insep infin auch* **überzuinterpretieren** to over-interpret.

Über-: ü~irdisch *adj* celestial, heavenly; **ü~kandidelt** *adj (inf)* eccentric; **~kapazität** *f* overcapacity; **ü~kauft** *adj (Comm)* saturated; **ü~kippen** *vi sep aux sein* to topple *or* keel over; *(Stimme)* to crack; **ü~kleben[1]*** *vt insep* **die Kiste ü~kleben** to stick something over the box; **etw mit Papier ü~kleben** to stick paper over sth; **ü~kleben[2]** *vt sep* **etwas ü~kleben** to stick something over it; **ü~klug** *adj (pej)* too clever by half, know-all *attr*, know-it-all *(US) attr*, smart-ass *(sl) attr*; **sei doch nicht so ü~klug!** don't be so clever *or* such a know-all; **ü~kochen** *vi sep aux sein (lit, fig)* to boil over.

überkommen[1]* *insep irreg* [1] *vt (überfallen, ergreifen)* to come over ♦ **ein Gefühl der Verlassenheit überkam ihn** a feeling of desolation came over him, he was overcome by a feeling of desolation; **Furcht** *etc* **überkam ihn** he was overcome with fear *etc*; **was überkommt dich denn?** what's come over you?
[2] *vi aux sein ptp only (überliefern)* **es ist uns** *(dat)* **~** *(old)* it has come down to us, it has been handed down to us.

überkommen[2] *vt sep irreg (Sw)* to get handed down.

Über-: ~kompensation *f* overcompensation; **ü~kompensieren*** *vt insep infin auch* **ü~zukompensieren** to overcompensate for; **ü~kreuz** *adv siehe* **Kreuz[1]**; **ü~kriegen** *vt sep (inf)* **(a)** *(ü~drüssig werden)* to get tired *or* sick (and tired) *(inf)* of, to get fed up of *or* with *(inf)*, to get browned off with *(inf)*; **(b) eins ü~kriegen** to get landed one *(inf)*; **ü~krusten*** *vt insep* to cover (with a layer *or* crust of); **ü~kühlen*** *vt insep (Aus Cook)* to cool down; **ü~laden*** [1] *vt insep irreg (zu stark belasten)* to overload; *(mit Arbeit auch)* to overburden; *(reichlich geben)* to shower; *(zu voll packen) Schreibtisch, Wand etc auch* to clutter, to cover; *(zu stark verzieren auch)* to clutter; [2] *adj Wagen* overloaded, overladen; *(fig) Stil* over-ornate, flowery; *Bild* cluttered; **ü~lagern*** *insep* [1] *vt* **(a) diese Schicht wird von einer anderen ü~lagert** another stratum overlies this one; **am Abend ist dieser Sender von einem anderen ü~lagert** in the evenings this station is blotted out by another one; **(b)** *Thema, Problem, Konflikt etc* to eclipse; [2] *vr (sich überschneiden)* to overlap; **~lagerung** *f (von Themen, Problemen etc)* eclipsing; (~*schneidung*) overlapping.

Überland-: ~bus *m* country bus, coach; **~leitung** *f (Elec)* overhead power line *or* cable; **~zentrale** *f (Elec)* rural power station.

Über-: ü~lang *adj Oper, Stück etc* overlength; *Arme, Mantel* too long; **~länge** *f* excessive length; **~länge haben** to be overlength; **ü~lappen*** *vir insep* to overlap.

überlassen[1]* *vt insep irreg* **(a)** *(haben lassen, abgeben)* **jdm etw ~** to let sb have sth.
(b) *(anheimstellen)* **es jdm ~, etw zu tun** to leave it (up) to sb to do sth; **das bleibt (ganz) Ihnen ~** that's (entirely) up to you; **das müssen Sie schon mir ~** you must leave that to me; **es bleibt Ihnen ~, zu ...** it's up to you to ...; **jdm die Initiative/Wahl ~** to leave the initiative/choice (up) to sb.
(c) *(in Obhut geben)* **jdm etw ~** to leave sth with sb *or* in sb's care, to entrust sth to sb's care; **sich** *(dat)* **selbst ~ sein** to be left to one's own devices, to be left to oneself; *(ohne Anleitung)* to be left to one's own resources; **jdn sich** *(dat)* **selbst ~** to leave sb to his/her own devices/resources.
(d) *(preisgeben)* **sich seinem Schmerz/seinen Gedanken/Gefühlen ~** to abandon oneself to one's pain/thoughts/feelings; **jdn seinem Schicksal ~** to leave *or* abandon sb to his fate; **jdn seinem Kummer ~** to offer sb no comfort in his/her grief.

überlassen[2] *vt sep irreg (inf) siehe* **übriglassen**.

Überlassung *f, no pl (von Recht, Anspruch)* surrender.

überlasten* *vt insep* to put too great a strain on; *jdn* to overtax; *(Elec) Telefonnetz*, *(durch Gewicht)* to overload ♦ **überlastet sein** to be under too great a strain; *(überfordert sein)* to be overtaxed; *(Elec etc)* to be overloaded.

Überlastung *f (von Mensch)* overtaxing; *(Überlastetsein)* strain; *(Elec, durch Gewicht)* overloading ♦ **bei ~ der Leber** when there is too much strain on the liver.

Überlauf *m* overflow.

Überlauf|anzeige *f (beim Taschenrechner)* decimal cut-off symbol.

überlaufen[1]* *vt insep irreg* **(a)** *Gegner, Abwehr* to overrun.
(b) *(fig: ergreifen: Angst etc)* to seize ♦ **es überlief ihn heiß** he felt hot under the collar; **es überlief ihn kalt** a cold shiver ran down his back *or* up and down his spine; **es überlief mich heiß und kalt** I went hot and cold all over.

überlaufen[2] *vi sep irreg aux sein* **(a)** *(Wasser, Gefäß)* to overflow; *(überkochen)* to boil over ♦ **ineinander ~** *(Farben)* to run (into one another); **zum Ü~ voll** full to overflowing; **jetzt läuft das Maß über** *(fig)* my patience is at an end; *siehe* **Galle**.
(b) *(Mil: überwechseln)* to desert ♦ **zum Feind ~** to go over *or* desert to the enemy.

überlaufen[3] *adj* overcrowded; *(mit Touristen)* overrun.

Überläufer *m (Mil)* deserter; *(Mil auch, Pol)* turncoat.

Überlaufrohr *nt* overflow pipe.

überlaut [1] *adj* **(a)** *(zu laut)* overloud. **(b)** *(aufdringlich) Mensch* obtrusive, loud; *Farben* loud, garish; *(flegelhaft) Benehmen* brash, loud.
[2] *adv* too loudly.

überleben* *insep* [1] *vti* **(a)** *Unglück, Operation etc* to survive; *die Nacht auch* to last, to live through ♦ **das überlebe ich nicht!** *(inf)* it'll be the death of me *(inf)*; **Sie werden es sicher ~** *(iro)* it won't kill you, you'll survive.
(b) *(länger leben als)* to outlive, to survive *(um* by).
[2] *vr* **das hat sich überlebt/wird sich ganz schnell überlebt haben** that's had its day/will very soon have had its day; **diese Mode überlebt sich ganz schnell** this fashion will soon be a thing of the past.

Überlebende(r) *mf decl as adj* survivor.

Überlebenschance *f* chance of survival.

überlebensgroß *adj* larger-than-life.

Überlebensgröße *f* **in ~** larger than life.

Überlebenstraining *nt* survival training.

überlebt *adj* outmoded, out-of-date.

▼ **überlegen[1]*** *insep* [1] *vi (nachdenken)* to think ♦ **überleg doch mal!** think!; **hin und her ~** to deliberate; **ich habe hin und her überlegt** I've thought about it a lot; **ohne zu ~** without thinking; *(ohne zu zögern)* without thinking twice.
▼ [2] *vt (überdenken, durchdenken)* to think over *or* about, to consider ♦ **das werde ich mir ~** I'll think it over, I'll think about it, I'll have a think about it, I'll give it some thought; **ich habe es mir anders/noch mal überlegt** I've changed my mind/I've had second thoughts about it; **wollen Sie es sich** *(dat)* **nicht noch einmal ~?** won't you think it over again?, won't you reconsider?; **das muß ich mir noch sehr ~** I'll have to think it over *or* consider it very carefully; **das hätten Sie sich** *(dat)* **vorher ~ müssen** you should have thought of *or* about that before *or* sooner; **es wäre zu ~** it should be considered.

überlegen[2] *sep* [1] *vt* **jdm etw ~** to put *or* lay sth over sb.
[2] *vr (sich zur Seite legen)* to lean over, to tilt.

überlegen[3] [1] *adj* superior; *(hochmütig auch)* supercilious ♦ **jdm ~ sein** to be superior to sb; **das war ein ~er Sieg** that was a good *or* convincing victory.
[2] *adv* in a superior manner *or* fashion ♦ **Bayern München hat ~ gesiegt** Bayern Munich won convincingly.

Überlegenheit *f, no pl* superiority; *(Hochmut auch)* superciliousness.

überlegt [1] *adj* (well-)considered.
[2] *adv* in a considered way.

➤ SPRACHE AKTIV: **überlegen[1]: 2 → 29.3**

Überlegung *f* **(a)** (*Nachdenken*) consideration, thought, reflection ◆ **bei näherer/nüchterner ~** on closer examination/on reflection; **das wäre wohl einer ~ wert** that would be worth thinking about *or* over, that would be worth considering *or* worthy of consideration; **ohne ~** without thinking.
(b) (*Bemerkung*) observation ◆ **~en anstellen** to make observations (*zu* about *or* on); **~en vortragen** to give one's views (*zu* on *or* about).

überleiten *sep* 1 *vt Thema, Abschnitt etc* to link up (*in +acc* to, with).
2 *vi* **zu etw ~** to lead up to sth; **in eine andere Tonart ~** (*Mus*) to change key.

Überleitung *f* connection; (*zur nächsten Frage, Mus*) transition ◆ **gut gegliedert, aber ~ fehlt** (*Sch*) well organized, but disjointed.

überlesen* *vt insep irreg* **(a)** (*flüchtig lesen*) to glance through *or* over *or* at. **(b)** (*übersehen*) to overlook, to miss.

überliefern* *vt insep Brauch, Tradition* to hand down ◆ **das Manuskript ist nur als Fragment überliefert** the manuscript has only come down to us in fragmentary form.

Überlieferung *f* **(a)** tradition ◆ **schriftliche ~en** (written) records. **(b)** (*Brauch*) tradition, custom ◆ **an der ~ festhalten** to hold on to tradition; **nach alter ~** according to tradition.

überlisten* *vt insep* to outwit.

überm *contr of* **über dem.**

übermachen* *vt insep* (*old: vermachen*) to make over (*dat* to).

Übermacht *f, no pl* superior strength *or* might; (*fig: von Gefühlen, Ideologie etc*) predominance ◆ **in der ~ sein** to have the greater strength.

übermächtig *adj Gewalt, Stärke* superior; *Feind, Opposition* powerful, strong; *Wunsch, Bedürfnis* overpowering; (*fig*) *Institution, Rauschgift* all-powerful.

übermalen¹ *vt sep* to paint over.

übermalen²* *vt insep* to paint over *or* on top of.

übermannen* *vt insep* (*geh*) to overcome.

Übermaß *nt, no pl* excess, excessive amount (*an +acc* of) ◆ **im ~** to *or* in excess; **er hat Zeit im ~** he has more than enough time.

übermäßig 1 *adj* **(a)** excessive; *Schmerz, Sehnsucht* violent; *Freude* intense ◆ **das war nicht ~** that was not too brilliant.
(b) (*Mus*) **~es Intervall** augmented interval.
2 *adv* excessively; *essen/trinken auch* to excess ◆ **sich ~ anstrengen** to overdo things; **er hat sich nicht ~ bemüht** he didn't exactly overexert himself.

Übermensch *m* **(a)** (*Philos*) superman. **(b)** (*fig inf*) superman; superwoman. **ich bin doch kein ~** I'm not superman/superwoman.

übermenschlich *adj* superhuman ◆ **Ü~es leisten** to perform superhuman feats.

übermitteln* *vt insep* to convey (*jdm* to sb); (*telephonisch etc*) *Meldung* to transmit, to send.

Übermitt(e)lung *f siehe vt* conveyance; transmission, sending.

übermorgen *adv* the day after tomorrow ◆ **~ abend/früh** the day after tomorrow in the evening/morning.

übermüden* *vt insep usu ptp* to overtire; (*erschöpfen auch*) to overfatigue.

Übermüdung *f* overtiredness; (*Erschöpfung auch*) overfatigue.

Übermüdungs|erscheinung *f* sign of overtiredness/fatigue.

Übermut *m* high spirits *pl* ◆ **vor lauter ~ wußten die Kinder nicht, was sie tun sollten** the children were so full of high spirits that they didn't know what to do with themselves; **~ tut selten gut** (*prov*) pride goes before a fall (*Prov*); (*zu Kindern*) it'll end in tears.

übermütig *adj* **(a)** (*ausgelassen*) high-spirited, boisterous. **(b)** (*zu mutig*) cocky (*inf*) ◆ **werd bloß nicht ~!** don't be cocky (*inf*). **(c)** (*dated: überheblich*) arrogant.

übern *contr of* **über den.**

übernächste(r, s) *adj attr* next ... but one ◆ **das ~ Haus** the next house but one; **die ~ Woche** the week after next; **am ~n Tag war er ...** two days later *or* the next day but one he was ...; **er kommt ~en Freitag** he's coming a week on Friday *or* (on) Friday week.

übernachten* *vi insep* to sleep; (*in Hotel, Privathaus etc auch*) to stay; (*eine Nacht*) to spend *or* stay the night ◆ **bei jdm ~** to stay with sb, to sleep *or* stay at sb's place; **wie viele Leute können bei dir ~?** how many people can you put up?

übernächtigt, übernächtig (*esp Aus*) *adj* bleary-eyed.

Übernachtung *f* overnight stay ◆ **~ und Frühstück** bed and breakfast.

Übernachtungsmöglichkeit *f* overnight accommodation *no pl* ◆ **sich nach einer ~ umsehen** to look around for somewhere to stay the night.

Übernahme *f* **-, -n (a)** takeover; (*das Übernehmen*) taking over; (*von Ausdruck, Ansicht*) adoption; (*von Zitat, Wort*) borrowing ◆ **seit der ~ des Geschäfts durch den Sohn** since the son took over the business.
(b) (*von Amt*) assumption; (*von Verantwortung auch*) acceptance ◆ **durch ~ dieser Aufgabe** by taking on *or* undertaking this task; **er hat sich zur ~ der Kosten/Hypothek verpflichtet** he has undertaken to pay the costs/mortgage; **bei ~ einer neuen Klasse** when taking charge of a new class; **er konnte Rechtsanwalt Mayer zur ~ seines Falles bewegen** he persuaded Mr Mayer, the barrister, to take (on) his case.

Übernahme|angebot *nt*, **Übernahme|offerte** *f* takeover bid.

Übernahmsstelle *f* (*Aus*) *siehe* **Annahmestelle.**

übernational *adj* supranational.

übernatürlich *adj* supernatural.

▼ **übernehmen¹*** *insep irreg* 1 *vt* **(a)** to take; *Aufgabe, Arbeit* to take on, to undertake; *Verantwortung* to take on, to assume, to accept; *Kosten, Hypothek* to agree to pay; (*Jur*) *Fall* to take (on); *jds Verteidigung* to take on; (*kaufen*) to buy ◆ **den Befehl** *or* **das Kommando ~** to take command *or* charge; **seit er das Amt übernommen hat** since he assumed office; **er übernimmt Ostern eine neue Klasse** he's taking charge of a new class at Easter; **lassen Sie mal, das übernehme ich!** let me take care of that; **es ~, etw zu tun** to take on the job of doing sth, to undertake to do sth.
(b) (*stellvertretend, ablösend*) to take over (*von* from); *Ausdruck, Ansicht auch* to adopt; *Zitat, Wort* to take, to borrow.
(c) *Geschäft, Praxis etc* to take over.
(d) (*Aus inf: übertölpeln*) to put one over on (*inf*).
2 *vr* to take on *or* undertake too much; (*sich überanstrengen*) to overdo it; (*beim Essen*) to overeat ◆ **~ Sie sich nur nicht!** (*iro*) don't strain yourself! (*iro*).

übernehmen² *vt sep Cape etc* to put on ◆ **das Gewehr ~** (*Mil*) to slope arms.

übernervös *adj* highly strung.

über|ordnen *vt sep* **(a) jdn jdm ~** to put *or* place *or* set sb over sb; *siehe* **übergeordnet. (b) etw einer Sache** (*dat*) **~** to give sth precedence over sth; **einer Sache** (*dat*) **übergeordnet sein** to have precedence over sth, to be superordinate to sth.

überparteilich *adj* non-party *attr*, non-partisan; (*Parl*) *Problem* all-party *attr*, crossbench *attr* (*Brit*); *Amt, Präsident etc* above party politics.

Überparteilichkeit *f* non-partisanship.

überpinseln¹ *vt sep* (*inf*) *Wand* to paint over.

überpinseln²* *vt insep Fleck* to paint over.

Überpreis *m* exorbitant price ◆ **zu ~en** at exorbitant prices.

Überproduktion *f* overproduction.

überprüfbar *adj* checkable.

überprüfen* *vt insep* (*auf +acc* for) to check; *Gepäck auch, Maschine, Waren,* (*Fin*) *Bücher* to inspect, to examine; *Entscheidung, Lage, Frage* to examine, to review; *Ergebnisse, Teilnehmer etc* to scrutinize; (*Pol*) *jdn* to screen ◆ **etw erneut ~** to re-check/re-examine sth/scrutinize sth again; **die Richtigkeit von etw ~** to check (the correctness of) sth.

Überprüfung *f* **(a)** *no pl siehe vt* checking; inspection, examination; review; scrutiny; (*Pol*) screening ◆ **nach ~ der Lage** after reviewing the situation, after a review of the situation. **(b)** (*Kontrolle*) check, inspection.

überquellen *vi sep irreg aux sein* to overflow (*von, mit* with); (*Cook*) (*Teig*) to rise over the edge; (*Reis*) to boil over ◆ **die Augen quollen ihm über** his eyes grew as big as saucers; **vor Freude/Dankbarkeit ~** to be overflowing with joy/gratitude.

überqueren* *vt insep* to cross.

überragen¹* *vt insep* **(a)** (*lit: größer sein*) to tower above. **(b)** (*fig: übertreffen*) to outshine (*an +dat, in +dat* in).

überragen² *vi sep* (*senkrecht*) to protrude; (*waagerecht*) to jut out, to project.

überragend *adj* (*fig*) outstanding; *Bedeutung auch* paramount.

▼ **überraschen*** *vt insep* to surprise; (*überrumpeln auch*) to catch *or* take unawares, to take by surprise ◆ **jdn bei etw ~** to surprise *or* catch sb doing sth; **von einem Gewitter überrascht werden** to be caught in a storm; **lassen wir uns ~!** let's wait and see!

überraschend *adj* surprising; *Besuch* surprise *attr*; *Tod, Weggang* unexpected ◆ **eine ~e Wendung nehmen** to take an unexpected turn; **das kam (für uns) völlig ~** that came as a complete surprise *or* (*Sterbefall etc*) shock (to us); **er mußte ~ nach Köln fahren** he had to go to Cologne unexpectedly.

überraschenderweise *adv* surprisingly.

überrascht *adj* surprised (*über +acc* at) ◆ **jdn ~ ansehen** to look at sb in surprise; **sich von etw (nicht) ~ zeigen** to show (no) surprise at sth; **da bin ich aber ~!** that's quite a surprise.

Überraschung *f* surprise ◆ **zu meiner (größten) ~** to my (great) surprise, much to my surprise; **Mensch, ist das eine ~!** (*inf*) well, that's a surprise (and a half *inf*)!; **jdm eine kleine ~ kaufen** to buy a little something for sb as a surprise; **für eine ~ sorgen** to have a surprise in store; **mit ~ mußte ich sehen** *or* **feststellen, daß ...** I was surprised to see that ...

Überraschungs-: ~angriff *m* surprise attack; **~effekt** *m* shock effect; **~moment** *nt* moment of surprise; **~sieger** *m* (*Sport*) surprise winner.

überreagieren* *vi insep* to overreact.

Überreaktion *f* overreaction.

überreden* *vt insep* to persuade, to talk round ◆ **jdn ~, etw zu tun** to persuade sb to do sth, to talk sb into doing sth; **jdn zu etw ~** to talk sb into sth; **ich habe mich zum Kauf ~ lassen** I let myself be talked *or* persuaded into buying it/them; **laß dich nicht ~** don't (let yourself) be talked into anything.

Überredung *f* persuasion.

Überredungskunst *f* persuasiveness ◆ **all ihre Überredungskünste** all her powers of persuasion.

überregional *adj* national; *Zeitung, Sender auch* nationwide.

überreich *adj* lavish, abundant; (*zu reich*) overabundant ◆ **~ an etw** (*dat*) overflowing with sth; **jdn ~ beschenken** to lavish presents on sb.

überreichen* *vt insep* **(jdm) etw ~** to hand sth over (to sb); (*feierlich*) to present sth (to sb).

überreichlich *adj* ample, abundant; (*zu reichlich*) overabundant ◆ **in ~em Maße** in abundance; **~ essen/trinken** to eat/drink more than ample.

Überreichung *f* presentation.

überreif *adj* overripe.

Überreife *f* overripeness.

überreizen* *insep* 1 *vt* to overtax; *Phantasie* to overexcite; *Nerven, Augen* to overstrain.
2 *vtr* (*Cards*) to overbid.

überreizt *adj* overtaxed; *Augen* overstrained; (*nervlich*) overwrought; (*zu*

erregt) overexcited.
Überreizung *f siehe vt* overtaxing; overexcitement, overstimulation; overstraining.
überrennen* *vt insep irreg* to run down; (*Mil*) to overrun; (*fig*) to overwhelm.
überrepräsentiert *adj* overrepresented.
Überrest *m* remains *pl*; (*letzte Spur: von Ruhm, Selbstachtung etc auch*) remnant, vestige ♦ **ein Häufchen Asche war der klägliche ~** the only remains were a sorry heap of ashes.
überrieseln* *vt insep Wiese* to water, to spray; (*mit Gräben*) to irrigate ♦ **ein Schauer überrieselte ihn** a shiver ran down his spine; **es überrieselt mich kalt, wenn ...** it makes my blood run cold *or* sends a shiver down my spine when ...
Überrock *m* (*dated: Mantel*) greatcoat, overcoat; (*old: Gehrock*) frock-coat.
Überrollbügel *m* (*Aut*) roll bar.
überrollen* *vt insep* to run down; (*Mil, fig*) to overrun ♦ **wir dürfen uns von ihnen nicht ~ lassen** we mustn't let them steamroller us.
überrumpeln* *vt insep* (*inf*) to take by surprise, to take *or* catch unawares; (*überwältigen*) to overpower ♦ **jdn mit einer Frage ~** to throw sb with a question.
Überrump(e)lung *f* surprise attack; (*Überwältigung*) overpowering ♦ **durch ~** with a surprise attack.
Überrump(e)lungstaktik *f* surprise tactics *pl*.
überrunden* *vt insep* (*Sport*) to lap; (*fig*) to outstrip.
übers *prep +acc* **(a)** *contr of* **über das**. **(b)** (*old*) **~ Jahr** in a year.
übersäen* *vt insep* to strew; (*mit Abfall etc auch*) to litter ♦ **übersät** strewn; (*mit Abfall etc auch*) littered; (*mit Sternen*) *Himmel* studded; (*mit Narben etc*) covered; **ein mit Fehlern übersäter Aufsatz** an essay strewn *or* littered with mistakes.
übersatt *adj* more than full *or* replete (*von* with).
übersättigen* *vt insep* to satiate; *Markt* to glut, to oversaturate; (*Chem*) to supersaturate ♦ **übersättigt sein** (*Menschen*) to be sated with luxuries; **das reizt ihn nicht mehr, er ist schon übersättigt** that doesn't hold any attraction for him any more, he has had a surfeit.
Übersättigung *f* satiety; (*des Marktes*) glut, oversaturation; (*Chem*) supersaturation.
Überschall- *in cpds* supersonic; **~flugzeug** *nt* supersonic aircraft, SST (*US*); **~geschwindigkeit** *f* supersonic speed; **mit ~geschwindigkeit fliegen** to fly supersonic *or* at supersonic speeds; **~knall** *m* sonic boom.
überschatten* *vt insep* (*geh*) (*lit, fig*) to overshadow; (*fig: trüben*) to cast a shadow *or* cloud over.
überschätzen* *vt insep* to overrate, to overestimate; *Entfernung, Zahl etc* to overestimate.
Überschätzung *f* overestimation.
Überschau *f* (*geh*) overview (*über +acc* of).
überschaubar *adj Plan, Gesetzgebung etc* easily comprehensible, clear ♦ **damit die Abteilung ~ bleibt** so that one can keep a general overview of *or* keep track of (*inf*) the department; **die Folgen sind noch nicht ~** the consequences cannot yet be clearly seen.
Überschaubarkeit *f* comprehensibility, clarity ♦ **zum Zwecke der besseren ~** to give (you) a better idea.
überschauen* *vt insep siehe* **überblicken**.
überschäumen *vi sep aux sein* to froth *or* foam over; (*fig*) to brim *or* bubble (over) (*vor +dat* with); (*vor Wut*) to seethe ♦ **~de Begeisterung** *etc* exuberant *or* effervescent *or* bubbling enthusiasm *etc*.
Überschicht *f* (*Ind*) extra shift.
überschlächtig *adj Wasserrad* overshot.
überschlafen* *vt insep irreg Problem etc* to sleep on.
Überschlag *m* **(a)** (*Berechnung*) (rough) estimate. **(b)** (*Drehung*) somersault (*auch Sport*); (*Aviat: Looping*) loop ♦ **einen ~ machen** to turn *or* do a somersault; (*Aviat*) to loop the loop.
überschlagen¹* *insep irreg* [1] *vt* **(a)** (*auslassen*) to skip, to miss.
(b) (*berechnen*) *Kosten etc* to estimate (roughly).
[2] *vr* **(a)** to somersault; (*Auto auch*) to turn over; (*Mensch: versehentlich auch*) to go head over heels; (*fig: Ereignisse*) to come thick and fast ♦ **sich vor Hilfsbereitschaft/Freundlichkeit** (*dat*) **~** to fall over oneself to be helpful/friendly; **nun überschlag dich mal nicht!** don't get carried away.
(b) (*Stimme*) to crack.
überschlagen² *sep irreg* [1] *vt Beine* to cross; *Arme* to fold; *Decke* to fold *or* turn back ♦ **mit übergeschlagenen Beinen/Armen** with one's legs crossed/arms folded.
[2] *vi aux sein* **(a)** (*Wellen*) to break. **(b)** (*Stimmung etc*) **in etw** (*acc*) **~** to turn into sth.
überschlagen³ *adj Flüssigkeit* lukewarm, tepid; *Zimmer* slightly warm.
Über-: ü~schlägig *adj siehe* **ü~schläglich**; **~schlaglaken** *nt* top sheet; **ü~schläglich** *adj* rough, approximate; **ü~schlank** *adj* too thin; **ü~schlau** *adj* (*inf*) too clever by half, clever-clever (*inf*), smart-aleck *attr* (*inf*).
überschnappen *vi sep aux sein* **(a)** (*Riegel etc*) to clip *or* snap on. **(b)** (*Stimme*) to crack, to break; (*inf: Mensch*) to crack up (*inf*); *siehe* **übergeschnappt**.
überschneiden* *vr insep irreg* (*Linien*) to intersect; (*Flächen, fig: Themen, Interessen, Ereignisse etc*) to overlap; (*völlig*) to coincide; (*unerwünscht*) to clash.
Überschneidung *f siehe vr* intersection; overlap *no pl*; coincidence; clash.
überschnell *adj* overhasty.
Überschreibemodus *m* (*Comput*) typeover mode.
überschreiben* *vt insep irreg* **(a)** (*betiteln*) to head. **(b)** (*übertragen*) **etw jdm** *or* **auf jdn ~** to make *or* sign sth over to sb. **(c)** (*Comput*) *Daten, Diskette* to overwrite.
überschreien* *vt insep irreg* to shout down.
überschreiten* *vt insep irreg* to cross; (*fig*) to exceed; *Höhepunkt, Alter* to pass ♦ **„Ü~ der Gleise verboten"** "do not cross the line"; **die Grenze des Erlaubten/des Anstands ~** to go beyond what is permissible/decent.
Überschrift *f* heading; (*Schlagzeile*) headline.
Überschuh *m* overshoe, galosh *usu pl*.
überschuldet *adj* heavily in debt; *Grundstück* heavily mortgaged.
Überschuldung *f* excessive debts *pl*; (*von Grundstück*) heavy mortgaging.
⚠ **Überschuß** *m* surplus (*an +dat* of) ♦ **seinen ~ an Kraft austoben** to work off one's surplus energy.
⚠ **Überschußbeteiligung** *f* surplus sharing.
überschüssig *adj* surplus.
⚠ **Überschuß-: ~land** *nt* country producing a surplus; **~produktion** *f* surplus production.
überschütten* *vt insep* **(a)** (*bedecken*) **jdn/etw mit etw ~** to tip sth onto sb/sth, to cover sb/sth with sth; (*mit Flüssigkeit*) to pour sth onto sb/sth.
(b) (*überhäufen*) **jdn mit etw ~** to shower sb with sth, to heap sth on sb; *mit Vorwürfen* to heap sth on sb.
Überschwang *m* **-(e)s,** *no pl* exuberance ♦ **im ~ der Freude/der Gefühle** in one's joyful exuberance/in exuberance; **im ersten ~** in the first flush of excitement.
überschwappen *vi sep aux sein* to splash over; (*aus Tasse etc auch*) to slop over; (*sich ausbreiten*) to spill over ♦ **die von Amerika nach Europa ~de Drogenwelle** the drug wave spilling over from America into Europe.
überschwemmen* *vt insep* (*lit, fig*) to flood; (*Touristen*) *Land etc auch* to overrun, to inundate *usu pass*; (*Angebote, Anträge*) *Inserenten, Behörde etc auch* to inundate *usu pass*, to deluge *usu pass*, to swamp; *Verbraucher, Leser etc* to swamp.
Überschwemmung *f* (*lit*) flood; (*das Überschwemmen*) flooding *no pl*; (*fig*) inundation; (*von Verbrauchern, Lesern*) swamping ♦ **es kam zu ~en** there was a lot of flooding *or* were a lot of floods.
Überschwemmungs-: ~gebiet *nt* (*überschwemmtes Gebiet*) flood area; (*Geog*) floodplain; **~gefahr** *f* danger of flooding; **~katastrophe** *f* flood disaster.
⚠ **überschwenglich** *adj* effusive, gushing (*pej*).
⚠ **Überschwenglichkeit** *f* effusiveness.
Übersee *no art* **in/nach ~** overseas; **aus/von ~** from overseas; **Briefe für ~** overseas letters, letters to overseas destinations; **Besitzungen in ~ haben** to have overseas territories *or* territories overseas.
Übersee-: ~dampfer *m* ocean liner; **~hafen** *m* international port; **~handel** *m* overseas trade.
überseeisch ['y:bɐze:ɪʃ] *adj* overseas *attr*.
Übersee-: ~kabel *nt* transoceanic cable; (*im Atlantik*) transatlantic cable; **~koffer** *m* trunk; **~verkehr** *m* overseas traffic.
übersehbar *adj* **(a)** (*lit*) *Gegend etc* visible ♦ **das Tal ist von hier schlecht ~** you don't get a good view of the valley from here.
(b) (*fig*) (*erkennbar*) *Folgen, Zusammenhänge etc* clear; (*abschätzbar*) *Kosten, Dauer etc* assessable ♦ **dieses Fachgebiet ist nicht mehr ~** it is no longer possible to have an overall view of this subject; **die Folgen sind klar/schlecht ~** the consequences are quite/not very clear; **der Schaden ist noch gar nicht ~** the damage cannot be assessed yet.
(c) solche Druckfehler sind leicht ~ misprints like that are easily overlooked *or* are easy to overlook *or* miss.
übersehen¹* *vt insep irreg* **(a)** (*lit*) *Gegend etc* to look over, to have a view of.
(b) (*erkennen, Bescheid wissen über*) *Folgen, Zusammenhänge, Sachlage* to see clearly; *Fachgebiet* to have an overall view of; (*abschätzen*) *Schaden, Kosten, Dauer* to assess ♦ **dieses Fach ist nicht mehr zu ~** it is no longer possible to have an overall view of this subject.
(c) (*ignorieren, nicht erkennen*) to overlook; (*nicht bemerken*) to miss, to fail to see *or* notice ♦ **~, daß** ... to overlook the fact that ...; **dieses Problem ist nicht mehr zu ~** this problem cannot be overlooked any longer; **etw stillschweigend ~** to pass over sth in silence.
übersehen² *vt sep irreg* **sich** (*dat*) **etw ~** to get *or* grow tired *or* to tire of seeing sth.
⚠ **übersein** *vi sep irreg aux sein* (*Zusammenschreibung nur bei infin und ptp*) (*inf*) **jdm ist etw über** sb is fed up with sth (*inf*); **mir ist diese Arbeit schon lange über** I've been fed up with this work for a long time (*inf*).
übersenden* *vt insep irreg* to send; *Geld auch* to remit (*form*) ♦ **hiermit ~ wir Ihnen ...** please find enclosed ...
Übersendung *f siehe vt* sending; remittance (*form*).
übersetzbar *adj* translatable ♦ **leicht/schwer ~** easy/hard to translate.
übersetzen¹* *vti insep* **(a)** to translate ♦ **aus dem** *or* **vom Englischen ins Deutsche ~** to translate from English into German; **ein Buch aus dem Englischen ~** to translate a book from (the) English; **etw falsch ~** to mistranslate sth; **sich leicht/schwer ~ lassen** to be easy/hard to translate; **sich gut/schlecht ~ lassen** to translate well/badly. **(b)** (*Tech*) (*umwandeln*) to translate; (*übertragen*) to transmit.
übersetzen² *sep* [1] *vt* **(a)** (*mit Fähre*) to take *or* ferry across. **(b) den Fuß ~** to put one's leg over.
[2] *vi aux sein* to cross (over).
Übersetzer(in *f*) *m* **-s, -** translator.
Übersetzung *f* **(a)** translation. **(b)** (*Tech*) (*Umwandlung*) translation; (*Über-*

tragung) transmission; *(Herab~, Herauf~)* change in the transmission ratio; *(~sverhältnis)* transmission *or* gear ratio.

Übersetzungs-: ~büro *nt* translation bureau *or* agency; **~fehler** *m* translation error, error in translation; **~verhältnis** *nt (Tech)* transmission *or* gear ratio.

Übersicht *f* **(a)** *no pl (Überblick)* overall view ◆ **die ~ verlieren** to lose track of things *or* of what's going on. **(b)** *(Abriß, Resümee)* survey; *(Tabelle)* table.

übersichtlich *adj Gelände etc* open; *(erfaßbar) Darstellung etc* clear ◆ **eine Bibliothek muß ~ sein** a library should be clearly laid out.

Übersichtlichkeit *f siehe adj* openness; clarity.

Übersichtskarte *f* general map.

übersiedeln *sep*, **übersiedeln*** *insep vi aux sein* to move *(von* from, *nach, in +acc* to).

Übersied(e)lung [*auch* 'y:bɐ-] *f (das Übersiedeln)* moving; *(Umzug)* move, removal *(form)*.

Übersiedler(in *f***)** *m* migrant.

übersinnlich *adj* supersensory; *(übernatürlich)* supernatural.

überspannen* *vt insep* **(a)** *(Brücke, Decke etc)* to span ◆ **etw mit Leinwand/Folie** *etc* **~** to stretch canvas/foil *etc* over sth, to cover sth with canvas/foil *etc.* **(b)** *(zu stark spannen)* to put too much strain on; *(fig) Forderungen* to push too far; *siehe* **Bogen.**

überspannt *adj Ideen, Forderungen* wild, extravagant; *(exaltiert)* eccentric; *(hysterisch)* hysterical; *Nerven* overexcited.

Überspanntheit *f siehe adj* wildness, extravagance; eccentricity; hysteria; overexcited state.

Überspannung *f (Elec)* overload.

überspielen* *vt insep* **(a)** *(verbergen)* to cover (up). **(b)** *(übertragen) Aufnahme* to transfer ◆ **ein Platte (auf Band) ~** to tape a record, to put a record on *or* transfer a record to tape. **(c)** *(Sport)* to pass; *(ausspielen, klar besiegen)* to outplay.

überspitzen* *vt insep* to carry too far, to exaggerate; *Argument* to overstate.

überspitzt [1] *adj (zu spitzfindig)* oversubtle, fiddly *(inf)*; *(übertrieben)* exaggerated; *Argument* overstated.
[2] *adv* oversubtly; in an exaggerated fashion ◆ **~ argumentieren** to overstate one's argument(s) *or* case.

übersprechen* *vt insep irreg* to speak over.

überspringen¹* *vt insep irreg* **(a)** *Hindernis, Höhe* to jump, to clear. **(b)** *(weiter springen als)* to jump more than ◆ **die 2-m-Marke ~** to jump more than 2 metres. **(c)** *(auslassen) Klasse* to miss (out), to skip; *Kapitel, Lektion auch* to leave out.

überspringen² *vi sep irreg aux sein (lit, fig)* to jump *(auf +acc* to); *(Begeisterung)* to spread quickly *(auf +acc* to); *siehe* **Funke.**

übersprudeln *vi sep aux sein (lit, fig)* to bubble over *(vor* with); *(beim Kochen)* to boil over ◆ **~d** *(fig)* bubbling, effervescent.

überspülen* *vt insep* to flood; *(Wellen auch)* to wash over ◆ **überspült sein** to be awash.

überstaatlich *adj* supranational.

überstehen¹* *vt insep irreg (durchstehen)* to come *or* get through; *(überleben)* to survive; *(überwinden)* to overcome; *Gewitter* to weather, to ride out; *Krankheit* to get over, to recover from ◆ **etw lebend ~** to survive sth, to come out of sth alive; **das Schlimmste ist jetzt überstanden** the worst is over now; **nach überstandener Gefahr** when the danger was past; **das wäre überstanden!** thank heavens that's over; **er hat es überstanden** *(euph)* he has gone to rest *(euph) or* has passed away *(euph)*.

überstehen² *vi sep irreg aux haben or sein* to jut *or* stick out, to project ◆ **um 10 cm ~** to jut out *etc* 10cm.

übersteigen* *vt insep irreg* **(a)** *(klettern über)* to climb over. **(b)** *(hinausgehen über)* to exceed, to go beyond; *(Philos, Liter: transzendieren)* to transcend; *siehe* **Fassungsvermögen.**

übersteigern* *insep* [1] *vt Preise, Tempo* to force up; *Forderungen* to push too far.
[2] *vr* to get carried away.

übersteigert *adj* excessive ◆ **an einem ~en Selbstbewußtsein leiden** to have an inflated view of oneself.

Übersteigerung *f (von Emotionen)* excess; *(von Forderungen)* pushing too far.

überstellen* *vt insep (Admin)* to hand over.

überstempeln* *vt insep* to stamp over ◆ **ein überstempeltes Paßbild** a passport photograph which has been stamped (over).

übersteuern* *insep* [1] *vi (Aut)* to oversteer.
[2] *vt (Elec)* to overmodulate.

überstimmen* *vt insep* to outvote; *Antrag* to vote down.

überstrahlen* *vt insep (lit)* to illuminate; *(fig)* to outshine.

überstrapazieren* *insep infin auch* **überzustrapazieren** [1] *vt* to wear out; *Ausrede etc* to wear thin ◆ **überstrapaziert** worn out, outworn; thin.
[2] *vr* to wear oneself out.

überstreichen* *vt insep irreg* to paint/varnish over.

überstreifen *vt sep* **(sich** *dat***) etw ~** to slip sth on.

überströmen¹* *vt insep (überfluten)* to flood ◆ **von Schweiß/Blut überströmt sein** to be streaming *or* running with sweat/blood.

überströmen² *vi sep aux sein* **(a)** *(lit, fig: überlaufen)* to overflow ◆ **er sprach mit ~der Freude/Dankbarkeit** he spoke in a voice overflowing with joy/gratitude. **(b)** *(hinüberströmen)* to spread, to communicate itself *(auf +acc* to).

überstülpen *vt sep* **sich** *(dat)* **etw ~** to put on sth; **jdm/einer Sache etw ~** to put sth on sb/sth.

Überstunde *f* hour of overtime ◆ **~n** overtime *sing*; **~n/zwei ~n machen** to do *or* work overtime/two hours overtime.

Überstundenzuschlag *m* overtime allowance ◆ **der ~ beträgt 50%** overtime is paid at time and a half.

überstürzen* *insep* [1] *vt* to rush into; *Entscheidung auch* to rush ◆ **man soll nichts ~** *(prov)* look before you leap *(Prov)*.
[2] *vr (Ereignisse etc)* to happen in a rush; *(Nachrichten)* to come fast and furious; *(Worte)* to come tumbling out ◆ **sich beim Sprechen ~** to speak all in a rush.

überstürzt *adj* overhasty, precipitate.

Überstürzung *f (das Überstürzen)* rushing *(+gen* into); *(Hast)* rush.

übersüß *adj* too sweet, oversweet; *Kuchen etc auch* sickly.

übertariflich *adj, adv* above the agreed *or* union rate.

überteuern* *vt insep Waren* to overcharge for; *Preis* to inflate, to force up.

überteuert *adj* overexpensive; *Preise* inflated, excessive.

Überteuerung *f* **(a)** *(das Überteuern)* overcharging *(+gen* for); *(von Preisen)* forcing up, (over)inflation. **(b)** *(Überteuert sein)* expensiveness; excessiveness.

übertippen* *vt insep* to type over.

übertölpeln* *vt insep* to take in, to dupe.

Übertölpelung *f* taking-in.

übertönen* *vt insep* to drown.

Übertrag *m* **-(e)s, ¨e** amount carried forward *or* over.

übertragbar *adj* transferable *(auch Jur, Comput)*; *Methode, Maßstab* applicable *(auf +acc* to); *Ausdruck* translatable *(in +acc* into); *Krankheit* communicable *(form) (auf +acc* to), infectious; *(durch Berührung)* contagious.

übertragen¹* *insep irreg* [1] *vt* **(a)** *(an eine andere Stelle bringen, an jdn übergeben)* to transfer *(auch Jur, Psych, Comput)*; *Krankheit* to pass on, to transmit, to communicate *(auf +acc* to); *(Tech) Bewegung* to transmit.
(b) *(an eine andere Stelle schreiben)* to transfer; *(kopieren)* to copy (out); *(transskribieren)* to transcribe.
(c) *(übersetzen) Text* to render *(in +acc* into).
(d) *(anwenden) Methode, Maßstab* to apply *(auf +acc* to).
(e) *(Mus: in andere Tonart)* to transpose.
(f) **etw auf Band ~** to tape sth, to record sth (on tape); **eine Platte auf Band ~** to transfer a record to tape, to tape a record.
(g) *(verleihen) Auszeichnung, Würde* to confer *(jdm* on sb); *Vollmacht, Verantwortung* to give *(jdm* sb).
(h) *(auftragen) Aufgabe, Mission* to assign *(jdm* to sb).
(i) *(TV, Rad)* to broadcast, to transmit ◆ **etw im Fernsehen ~** to televise sth, to broadcast sth on television; **durch Satelliten ~ werden** to be broadcast *or* sent by satellite.
[2] *vr (Eigenschaft, Krankheit etc)* to be passed on *or* communicated *or* transmitted *(auf +acc* to); *(Tech)* to be transmitted *(auf +acc* to); *(Heiterkeit etc)* to communicate itself, to spread *(auf +acc* to) ◆ **seine Fröhlichkeit hat sich auf uns ~** we were infected by his happiness.

übertragen² *adj* **(a)** *Bedeutung etc* figurative. **(b)** *(Aus)* worn; *(gebraucht)* secondhand, used.

Überträger *m (Med)* carrier.

Übertragung *f siehe vt* **(a)** transference, transfer *(auch Comput)*; passing on, transmission, communication.
(b) transference; copying (out); transcription.
(c) rendering.
(d) application.
(e) transposition.
(f) „**~ auf andere Tonträger verboten**" "recording forbidden in any form"; **die ~ von Platten auf Tonband** the taping of records, the transfer of records to tape.
(g) conferral; giving.
(h) assignment.
(i) broadcasting, transmission; *(Sendung)* broadcast, transmission.

Übertragungswagen *m* outside broadcast unit.

übertrainiert *adj* overtrained.

übertreffen* *insep irreg* [1] *vt* to surpass *(an +dat* in); *(mehr leisten als auch)* to do better than, to outdo, to outstrip; *(übersteigen auch)* to exceed; *Rekord* to break ◆ **jdn an Intelligenz/Schönheit** *etc* **~** to be more intelligent/beautiful *etc* than sb; **jdn um vieles** *or* **bei weitem ~** to surpass sb by far; *(bei Leistung auch)* to do far better than sb, to outstrip sb by a long way; **alle Erwartungen ~** to exceed *or* surpass all expectations; **er ist nicht zu ~** he is unsurpassable.
[2] *vr* **sich selbst ~** to surpass *or* excel oneself.

übertreiben* *vt insep irreg* **(a)** *(auch vi: aufbauschen)* to exaggerate ◆ **der „Macbeth" übertrieb stark** Macbeth overacted a lot.
(b) *(zu weit treiben)* to overdo, to carry *or* take too far *or* to extremes ◆ **es mit der Sauberkeit ~** to carry cleanliness too far; **man kann es auch ~** you can overdo things, you can go too far.

Übertreibung *f* **(a)** exaggeration; *(theatralisch)* overacting *no pl* ◆ **man kann ohne ~ sagen ...** it's no exaggeration to say ...
(b) **ihre ~ der Sparsamkeit/Sauberkeit** the way she carries economy/cleanliness too far *or* to extremes; **etw ohne ~ tun** to do sth without overdoing it *or* carrying it too far *or* to extremes.

übertreten¹ *vi sep irreg aux sein* **(a)** *(Fluß)* to break its banks, to flood. **(b)** *(zu anderer Partei etc)* to go over *(zu* to); *(in andere Schule)* to move *(in +acc* to). **(c)** *(im Sport)* to overstep.

übertreten²* *vt insep irreg Grenze etc* to cross; *(fig) Gesetz, Verbot* to break, to

infringe, to violate.
Übertretung *f (von Gesetz etc)* violation, infringement; *(Jur: strafbare Handlung)* misdemeanour.
übertrieben *adj* exaggerated; *(zu stark, übermäßig) Vorsicht, Training* excessive.
Übertriebenheit *f* exaggeratedness; *(Übermäßigkeit)* excessiveness.
Übertritt *m (über Grenze)* crossing *(über +acc* of); *(zu anderem Glauben)* conversion; *(von Abtrünnigen, esp zu anderer Partei)* defection; *(in andere Schule)* move *(in +acc* to) ◆ **die Zahl der ~e zur demokratischen Partei** the number of people going over to the democratic party.
übertrocknen* *vi insep aux sein (Aus)* to dry.
übertrumpfen* *vt insep (Cards)* to overtrump; *(fig)* to outdo.
übertun[1] *vt sep irreg* **sich** *(dat)* **einen Mantel** *etc* ~ *(inf)* to put a coat *etc* on; **jdm einen Schal** *etc* ~ to put a scarf *etc* on sb.
übertun[2]* *vr insep irreg (dial)* to overdo it *(inf)*.
übertünchen[1]* *vt insep* to whitewash; *(mit Farbton)* to distemper; *(fig)* to cover up.
übertünchen[2] *vt sep* to whitewash (over); *(mit Farbton)* to distemper (over).
über|übermorgen *adv (inf)* in three days, the day after the day after tomorrow.
Übervater *m* overlord.
überversichern* *vt insep infin auch* **überzuversichern** to overinsure.
Überversicherung *f* overinsurance.
übervölkern* *vt insep* to overpopulate.
Übervölkerung *f* overpopulation.
übervoll *adj* overfull *(von* with), too full; *(von Menschen, Sachen auch)* crammed *(von* with); *Glas* full to the brim *or* to overflowing.
übervorsichtig *adj* overcautious.
übervorteilen* *vt insep* to cheat, to do down *(inf)*.
Übervorteilung *f* cheating.
überwach *adj* (too) wide-awake; *(fig)* alert.
überwachen* *vt insep (kontrollieren)* to supervise; *(beobachten)* to keep a watch on, to observe; *Verdächtigen* to keep under surveillance, to keep a watch on, to watch; *(auf Monitor, mit Radar, fig)* to monitor.
Überwachung *f siehe vt* supervision; observation; surveillance; monitoring.
Überwachungskamera *f* surveillance camera.
Überwachungsstaat *f* police state.
überwältigen* *vt insep* **(a)** *(lit)* to overpower; *(zahlenmäßig)* to overwhelm; *(bezwingen)* to overcome. **(b)** *(fig) (Schlaf, Mitleid, Angst etc)* to overcome; *(Musik, Schönheit etc)* to overwhelm.
überwältigend *adj* overwhelming; *Schönheit* stunning; *Gestank, Gefühl auch* overpowering ◆ **nicht gerade ~** nothing to write home about *(inf)*.
Überwältigung *f siehe vt (a)* overpowering; overwhelming; overcoming.
überwälzen* *vt insep (esp Aus) siehe* **abwälzen**.
überwechseln *vi sep aux sein* to move *(in +acc* to); *(zu Partei etc)* to go over *(zu* to); *(Wild)* to cross over.
Überweg *m* ~ **für Fußgänger** pedestrian crossing.
▼ **überweisen*** *vt insep irreg Geld* to transfer *(an +acc, auf +acc* to); *(weiterleiten) Vorschlag etc, Patienten* to refer *(an +acc* to) ◆ **mein Gehalt wird direkt auf mein Bankkonto überwiesen** my salary is paid directly into my bank account.
Überweisung *f (Geld~)* (credit) transfer, remittance; *(von Patient, Vorschlag etc)* referral.
Überweisungs-: ~auftrag *m* (credit) transfer order; **~formular** *nt* (credit) transfer form; **~schein** *m (von Arzt)* letter of referral; *(für Bank)* (credit) transfer form.
überweit *adj* loose-fitting, too big.
Überweite *f* large size ◆ **Kleider in ~(n)** outsize dresses, dresses in the larger sizes.
überwerfen[1]* *vr insep irreg* **sich (mit jdm) ~** to fall out (with sb).
überwerfen[2] *vt sep irreg* to put over; *Kleidungsstück* to put on; *(sehr rasch)* to throw on.
Überwesen *nt* preterhuman being.
überwiegen* *insep irreg* [1] *vt* to outweigh.
[2] *vi (das Übergewicht haben)* to be predominant, to predominate; *(das Übergewicht gewinnen)* to prevail.
überwiegend [1] *adj* predominant; *Mehrheit* vast.
[2] *adv* predominantly, mainly.
überwindbar *adj Schwierigkeiten, Hindernis* surmountable ◆ **diese Angst ist nur schwer ~** it is hard to overcome this fear.
überwinden* *insep irreg* [1] *vt* to overcome; *Schwierigkeiten, Hindernis auch* to surmount, to get over; *Enttäuschung, Angst, Scheu auch* to get over; *(hinter sich lassen)* to outgrow; *siehe* **überwunden**.
[2] *vr* to overcome one's inclinations ◆ **sich ~, etw zu tun** to force oneself to do sth; **ich konnte mich nicht ~, das zu tun** *or* **nicht dazu ~** I couldn't bring myself to do it.
Überwindung *f* overcoming; *(von Schwierigkeiten, Hindernis auch)* surmounting; *(Selbst~)* will power ◆ **das hat mich viel ~ gekostet** that was a real effort of will for me, that took me a lot of will power; **selbst bei der größten ~ könnte ich das nicht tun** I simply couldn't bring myself to do it.
überwintern* *vi insep* to (spend the) winter; *(Pflanzen)* to overwinter; *(inf: Winterschlaf halten)* to hibernate.
Überwinterung *f* wintering, spending the winter; *(von Pflanzen)* overwintering; *(inf: Winterschlaf)* hibernation.
überwölben* *vt insep* to vault.
überwuchern* *vt insep* to overgrow, to grow over; *(fig)* to obscure.
überwunden *adj Standpunkt, Haltung etc* of the past; *Angst* conquered ◆ **ein bis heute noch nicht ~es Vorurteil** a prejudice which is still prevalent today.
Überwurf *m (Kleidungsstück)* wrap; *(Ringen)* shoulder throw; *(Aus: Bett~)* bedspread, counterpane.
Überzahl *f, no pl* **in der ~ sein** to be in the majority; *(Feind)* to be superior in number; **die Frauen waren in der ~** the women outnumbered the men *or* were in the majority.
überzahlen* *vt insep Waren* to pay too much for ◆ **das Auto ist überzahlt** you/he *etc* paid too much for the car, the car cost too much.
überzählig *adj (überschüssig)* surplus; *(überflüssig)* superfluous; *(übrig)* spare.
überzeichnen* *vt insep* **(a)** *(Fin) Anleihe* to oversubscribe. **(b)** *(fig: übertrieben darstellen)* to exaggerate, to overdraw.
Über-: ~zeit *f (Sw)* overtime; **~zelt** *nt* fly sheet.
▼ **überzeugen*** *insep* [1] *vt* to convince; *(umstimmen auch)* to persuade; *(Jur)* to satisfy ◆ **er ließ sich nicht ~** he would not be convinced *or* persuaded, there was no convincing *or* persuading him; **ich bin davon überzeugt, daß** ... I am convinced *or* certain that ...; **Sie dürfen überzeugt sein, daß** ... you may rest assured *or* be certain that ...; **er ist sehr von sich überzeugt** he is very sure of himself.
[2] *vi* to be convincing, to carry conviction ◆ **er konnte nicht ~** he wasn't convincing, he was unconvincing.
[3] *vr* **sich (selbst) ~** to convince oneself *(von* of), to satisfy oneself *(von* as to); *(mit eigenen Augen)* to see for oneself; **~ Sie sich selbst!** see for yourself!
überzeugend *adj* convincing.
überzeugt *adj attr Anhänger, Vegetarier etc* dedicated, convinced; *Christ, Moslem* devout, convinced.
Überzeugung *f* **(a)** *(das Überzeugen)* convincing.
(b) *(das Überzeugtsein)* conviction; *(Prinzipien)* convictions *pl*, beliefs *pl* ◆ **meiner ~ nach** ... I am convinced (that) ..., it is my conviction that ...; **ich bin der festen ~, daß** ... I am firmly convinced *or* of the firm conviction that ...; **zu der ~ gelangen** *or* **kommen, daß ..., die ~ gewinnen, daß** ... to become convinced that ..., to arrive at the conviction that ...; *siehe* **Brustton**.
Überzeugungs-: ~arbeit *f, no pl* convincing; **viel ~arbeit leisten** to do a lot of convincing; **~kraft** *f* persuasiveness, persuasive power; **~täter** *m* political/religious criminal.
überziehen[1]* *insep irreg* [1] *vt* **(a)** *(bedecken)* to cover; *(mit Schicht, Belag)* to coat; *(mit Metall)* to plate; *(mit Zuckerguß)* to ice, to frost *(esp US)* ◆ **Polstermöbel neu ~ lassen** to have furniture re-covered; **von Rost überzogen** covered in *or* coated with rust; **mit Gold/Silber überzogen** gold-/silver-plated.
(b) *Konto* to overdraw ◆ **er hat sein Konto (um 500 Mark) überzogen** he has overdrawn his account (by 500 marks), he is (500 marks) overdrawn.
(c) *(geh: heimsuchen)* to invade ◆ **er wurde mit einem Verfahren überzogen** a legal action was brought against him.
(d) *Redezeit etc* to overrun.
(e) *(übertreiben)* **sein Benehmen wirkte überzogen** his behaviour seemed exaggerated *or* over the top *(inf)*.
[2] *vi (Fin)* to overdraw one's account.
[3] *vr* **(a)** *(sich bedecken: Himmel)* to cloud over, to become overcast ◆ **der Himmel ist überzogen** the sky is overcast.
(b) *(mit Schicht etc)* to become covered *or* coated.
überziehen[2] *vt sep irreg* **(a) (sich** *dat***) etw ~** to put sth on. **(b) jdm eins ~** *(inf)* to give sb a clout *(inf)*, to clout *or* clobber sb *(inf)*.
Überzieher *m* **-s, -** *(dated)* **(a)** *(Mantel)* greatcoat. **(b)** *(inf: Kondom)* sheath, French letter *(inf)*.
Überziehungskredit *m* overdraft provision.
überzüchten* *vt insep* to overbreed; *Motor* to overdevelop.
überzuckern* *vt insep* **(a)** *(mit Zucker überstreuen)* to (sprinkle with) sugar. **(b)** *(zu stark zuckern)* to put too much sugar in/on.
Überzug *m* **(a)** *(Beschichtung)* coat(ing); *(aus Metall)* plating; *(für Kuchen, esp aus Zuckerguß)* icing, frosting *(esp US)*. **(b)** *(Bett~, Sessel~ etc)* cover; *(Kopfkissen~ auch)* (pillow)slip.
Üble(s) *nt decl as adj siehe* **übel**.
üblich *adj* usual; *(herkömmlich)* customary; *(typisch, normal)* normal ◆ **wie ~** as usual; **es ist bei uns/hier ~** *or* **das ~e, daß** ... it's usual for us/here to ..., it's the custom with us/here that ...; **das ist bei ihm so ~** that's usual for him; **allgemein ~ sein** to be common practice; **die allgemein ~en Bedingungen/Methoden** the usual conditions/methods.
üblicherweise *adv* usually, generally, normally.
Übliche(s) *nt decl as adj* **das ~** the usual things *pl*, the usual.
U-Bogen *m loop which some Germans write over "u".*
U-Boot *nt* submarine, sub *(inf)*; *(esp Hist: der deutschen Marine)* U-boat.
U-Boot-: ~-Ausschnitt *m (Fashion)* boatneck; **~-gestützt** *adj* submarine-based; **~-Krieg** *m* submarine warfare *no art*.
übrig *adj* **(a)** *attr (verbleibend)* rest of, remaining; *(andere auch)* other ◆ **meine/die ~en Sachen** the rest of my/the things; **alle ~en Bücher** all the rest of the books, all the other *or* remaining books; **der ~e Teil des Landes** the rest of *or* remaining part of *or* remainder of the country.
(b) *pred* left, left over, over; *(zu entbehren)* spare ◆ **etw ~ haben** to have sth left/to spare; **haben Sie vielleicht eine Zigarette (für mich) ~?** could you spare (me) a cigarette?
(c) *(mögen)* **für jdn/etw wenig/nichts ~ haben** not to have much/to have no time for sb/sth; **für jdn/etw etwas/viel ~ haben** to have a soft spot for *or* to

be fond/very fond of sb/sth, to have a liking/a great liking for sb/sth.
(d) (*substantivisch*) **das ~e** the rest, the remainder; **alles ~e** all the rest, everything else; **die/alle ~en** the/all the rest *or* others; **im ~en** incidentally, by the way; **ein ~es tun** (*geh*) to do one more thing.

⚠ **übrig-: ~behalten** *vt sep irreg* to have left over; **~bleiben** *vi sep irreg aux sein* to be left over, to remain; **wieviel ist ~geblieben?** how much is left?; **da wird ihm gar nichts anderes ~bleiben** he won't have any choice *or* any other alternative; **was blieb mir anderes ~ als ...?** what choice did I have but ...?, there was nothing left for it but to ...

übrigens *adv* incidentally, by the way.

⚠ **übriglassen** *vt sep irreg* to leave (*jdm* for sb) ◆ **(einiges)/viel zu wünschen ~** (*inf*) to leave something/a lot to be desired.

Übung *f* **(a)** *no pl* (*das Üben, Geübtsein*) practice ◆ **das macht die ~, das ist alles nur ~** it's a question of practice, it comes with practice; **aus der ~ kommen/außer ~ sein** to get/be out of practice; **in ~ bleiben** to keep in practice, to keep one's hand in (*inf*); **zur ~** for *or* as practice; **(richtig) ~ in etw** (*dat*) **haben/bekommen** to have/get (quite) a bit of practice in sth; **~ macht den Meister** (*Prov*) practice makes perfect (*Prov*).
(b) (*Veranstaltung*) practice; (*Mil, Sport, Sch*) exercise; (*Feuerwehr~*) exercise, drill; (*Univ: Kursus*) seminar.

Übungs-: ~arbeit *f* (*Sch*) practice *or* mock test; **~aufgabe** *f* (*Sch*) exercise; **~buch** *nt* (*Sch*) book of exercises; **~flug** *m* practice flight; **ü~halber** *adv* for practice; **~heft** *nt* (*Sch*) exercise book; **~munition** *f* blank ammunition; **~platz** *m* training area *or* ground; (*Exerzierplatz*) drill ground; **~stück** *nt* (*Sch, Mus*) exercise.

UdSSR [u:de:|ɛs|ɛs'|ɛr] *f* - *abbr of* **Union der Sozialistischen Sowjetrepubliken** ◆ **die ~** the USSR.

u.E. *abbr of* **unseres Erachtens.**

UEFA-Cup [u:'|e:fa:kap] *m* (*Ftbl*) UEFA cup.

U-Eisen *nt* U-iron.

Ufer *nt* **-s, -** (*Fluß~*) bank; (*See~*) shore; (*Küstenlinie*) shoreline ◆ **direkt am ~ gelegen** right on the water's edge *or* waterfront; **etw ans ~ spülen** to wash sth ashore; **der Fluß trat über die ~** the river broke *or* burst its banks; **das sichere ~ erreichen** to reach dry land *or* terra firma.

Ufer-: ~befestigung *f* bank reinforcement; **~böschung** *f* embankment; **~land(schaft** *f*) *nt* shoreland; **u~los** *adj* (*endlos*) endless; (*grenzenlos*) boundless; **ins u~lose gehen** (*Debatte etc*) to go on forever *or* interminably, to go on and on; (*Kosten*) to go up and up; **sonst geraten wir ins u~lose** otherwise things will get out of hand; **ans ~lose grenzen** (*Verleumdungen etc*) to go beyond all bounds; **~mauer** *f* sea wall; **~straße** *f* lakeside/riverside road.

uff *interj* (*inf*) phew ◆ **~, das wäre geschafft!** phew, that's that done!

Uffz. *m* **-, -e** *abbr of* **Unteroffizier** NCO.

UFO, Ufo ['u:fo] *nt* **-(s), -s** UFO, Ufo.

⚠ **U-förmig** *adj* U-shaped ◆ **~ gebogen** with a U-shaped bend, bent into a U.

Uganda *nt* **-s** Uganda.

Ugander(in *f*) *m* **-s, -** Ugandan.

ugandisch *adj* Ugandan.

uh *interj* oh; (*angeekelt*) ugh, yuck (*inf*).

U-Haft *f* (*inf*) custody.

U-Haken *m* U-shaped hook.

Uhl *f* **-, -en** (*N Ger*) *siehe* **Eule.**

Uhlenspiegel *m* (*N Ger*) *siehe* **Eulenspiegel.**

Uhr *f* **-, -en (a)** clock; (*Armband~, Taschen~*) watch; (*Anzeigeinstrument*) gauge, dial, indicator; (*Wasser~, Gas~*) meter ◆ **nach der** *or* **auf die** *or* **zur ~ sehen** to look at the clock *etc*; **Arbeiter, die ständig auf die** *or* **nach der ~ sehen** clock-watchers; **nach meiner ~** by my watch; **wie nach der ~** (*fig*) like clockwork; **rund um die ~** round the clock; **seine ~ ist abgelaufen** (*fig geh*) the sands of time have run out for him.
(b) (*bei Zeitangaben*) **um drei (~)** at three (o'clock); **ein ~ dreißig,** (*in Ziffern*) 1[30] **~** half past one, 1.30 (*ausgesprochen "one-thirty"*); **wieviel ~ ist es?** what time is it?, what's the time?; **um wieviel ~?** (at) what time?

Uhr(arm)band *nt* watch strap; (*aus Metall*) watch bracelet.

Ührchen *nt dim of* **Uhr** little clock *etc.*

Uhren-: ~industrie *f* watch-and-clock(-making) industry; **~vergleich** *m* comparison of watch/clock times; **einen ~vergleich machen** to check *or* synchronize watches.

Uhr-: ~feder *f* watch spring; **~glas** *nt* (*auch Sci*) watch-glass; **~kette** *f* watch chain, fob (chain); **~macher(in** *f*) *m* watch-maker; clock-maker, horologist (*form*); **~macherhandwerk** *nt* watch-making; clock-making, horology (*form*); **~werk** *nt* clockwork mechanism (*auch fig*), works *pl* (of a watch/clock), movements *pl*; **~zeiger** *m* (clock/watch) hand; **~zeigersinn** *m* **im ~zeigersinn** clockwise; **entgegen dem ~zeigersinn** anti- *or* counter-clockwise; **~zeit** *f* time (of day); **haben Sie die genaue ~zeit?** do you have the correct time?

Uhu ['u:hu] *m* **-s, -s** eagle-owl.

Ukas *m* **-ses, -se** (*Hist, pej*) ukase.

Ukraine [*auch* u'krainə] *f* - **die ~** the Ukraine.

Ukrainer(in *f*) [*auch* u'kraine, -ərɪn] *m* **-s, -** Ukrainian.

ukrainisch [*auch* u'krainɪʃ] *adj* Ukrainian.

Ukulele *f* **-, -n** ukulele.

UKW [u:ka:'ve:] *abbr of* **Ultrakurzwelle** ≃ FM.

Ul *f* **-, -en** (*N Ger*) *siehe* **Eule.**

Ulan *m* **-en, -en** (*Hist*) u(h)lan.

Ulensp(i)egel *m siehe* **Eulenspiegel.**

Ulk *m* **-(e)s, -e** (*inf*) lark (*inf*); (*Streich*) trick, practical joke; (*Spaß*) fun *no pl, no indef art* ◆ **~ machen** to clown *or* play about *or* around; **etw aus ~ sagen/tun** to say/do sth as a joke *or* in fun; **mit jdm seinen ~ treiben** (*Spaß machen*) to have a bit of fun with sb; (*Streiche spielen*) to play tricks on sb.

ulken *vi* (*inf*) to joke, to clown around ◆ **über ihn wurde viel geulkt** they often had a bit of fun with him.

ulkig *adj* (*inf*) funny; (*seltsam auch*) odd, peculiar.

Ulknudel *f* (*inf*) joker (*inf*).

Ulkus *nt* **-, Ulzera** (*Med*) ulcer.

Ulme *f* **-, -n** elm.

Ulmen-: ~krankheit *f*, **~sterben** *nt* Dutch elm disease.

Ultima *f* **-, Ultimä** *or* **Ultimen** (*Ling*) final syllable.

⚠ **Ultima ratio** ['ʊltima 'ra:tsio] *f* **--,** *no pl* (*geh*) final *or* last resort.

Ultimaten *pl of* **Ultimatum.**

ultimativ *adj Forderung etc* given as an ultimatum ◆ **wir fordern ~ eine Lohnerhöhung von 9%** we demand a pay rise of 9% and this is an ultimatum; **jdn ~ zu etw auffordern** to give sb an ultimatum to do sth.

Ultimatum *nt* **-s, -s** *or* **Ultimaten** ultimatum ◆ **jdm ein ~ stellen** to give sb an ultimatum.

Ultimen *pl of* **Ultima.**

Ultimo *m* **-s, -s** (*Comm*) last (day) of the month ◆ **per ~** by the end of the month; **bis ~** (*fig*) till the last minute.

Ultra *m* **-s, -s** (*pej*) extremist.

Ultra- *in cpds* ultra; **u~kurz** *adj* (*Phys*) ultra-short.

Ultrakurzwelle *f* (*Phys*) ultra-short wave; (*Rad*) ≃ very high frequency, ≃ frequency modulation.

Ultrakurzwellen-: ~empfänger *m* VHF receiver; **~sender** *m* VHF station; (*Apparat*) VHF transmitter.

Ultra-: ~marin *nt* **-s,** *no pl* ultramarine; **u~marin(blau)** *adj* ultramarine; **u~modern** *adj* ultramodern; **u~montan** *adj* (*pej geh*) papist (*pej*); **u~rot** *adj siehe* **infrarot.**

Ultraschall *m* (*Phys*) ultrasound.

Ultraschall- *in cpds* ultrasound; **~aufnahme** *f* scan (*Brit*), ultrasound (picture); **~bild** *nt* ultrasound picture; **~diagnostik** *f* ultrasound diagnosis; **~gerät** *nt* ultrasound scanner; **~untersuchung** *f* scan (*Brit*), ultrasound; **~wellen** *pl* ultrasonic waves *pl*.

Ultra-: ~strahlung *f* (*Phys*) cosmic rays *pl*; **u~violett** *adj* ultraviolet.

Ulzera *pl of* **Ulkus.**

um **1** *prep +acc* **(a) ~ ... (herum)** round (*esp Brit*), around; (*unbestimmter, in der Gegend von*) around, about; **er hat gern Freunde ~ sich** he likes to have friends around him.
(b) (*nach allen Seiten*) **~ sich schauen** to look around (one) *or* about one; **~ sich schlagen** to hit out in all directions; **etw ~ sich werfen** to throw sth around *or* about.
(c) (*zur ungefähren Zeitangabe*) **~ ... (herum)** around about; (*bei Uhrzeiten auch*) at about; **die Tage ~ die Sommersonnenwende (herum)** the days either side of the summer solstice; **~ Weihnachten/Ostern** *etc* around Christmas/Easter *etc.*
(d) (*zur genauen Angabe der Uhrzeit*) at ◆ **bitte kommen Sie (genau) ~ acht** please come at eight (sharp).
(e) (*betreffend, über*) about ◆ **es geht ~ das Prinzip** it's a question of principles, it's the principle of the thing; **es geht ~ alles** it's all or nothing; **es steht schlecht ~ seine Gesundheit** his health isn't very good.
(f) (*für, Ergebnis, Ziel bezeichnend*) for ◆ **der Kampf ~ die Stadt/den Titel** the battle for the town/the title; **~ Geld spielen** to play for money; **~ etw rufen/bitten** *etc* to cry/ask *etc* for sth.
(g) (*wegen*) **die Sorge ~ die Zukunft** concern for *or* about the future; **(es ist) schade ~ das schöne Buch** (it's a) pity *or* shame about that nice book; **sich ~ etw sorgen** to worry about sth; **es tut mir leid ~ ihn** I'm sorry for him.
(h) (*bei Differenzangaben*) by ◆ **~ 10% teurer** 10% more expensive; **er ist ~ zwei Jahre jünger als sie** he is two years younger than she is, he is younger than her by two years; **~ vieles besser** far better, better by far; **~ einiges besser** quite a bit better; **~ nichts besser/teurer** *etc* no better/dearer *etc*; **etw ~ 4 cm verkürzen** to shorten sth by 4 cm.
(i) (*bei Verlust*) **jdn ~ etw bringen** to deprive sb of sth; **~ etw kommen** to be deprived of sth, to miss out on sth.
(j) (*nach*) after, upon ◆ **Stunde ~ Stunde** hour after *or* upon hour; **einer ~ den anderen/eine ~ die andere** one after the other; **einen Tag ~ den anderen** day after day.
2 *prep +gen* **~ ... willen** for the sake of; **~ Gottes willen!** for goodness *or* (*stärker*) God's sake!
3 *conj* **(a) ~ ... zu** (*final*) (in order) to; **er spart jeden Pfennig, ~ sich später ein Haus kaufen zu können** he is saving every penny in order to be able to buy a house later; **intelligent genug/zu intelligent, ~ ... zu** intelligent enough/too intelligent to ...; **der Fluß schlängelt sich durch das enge Tal, ~ dann in der Ebene zu einem breiten Strom anzuwachsen** the stream winds through the narrow valley and then broadens out into a wide river in the plain; **er studierte jahrelang Jura, ~ dann Taxifahrer zu werden** he studied law for several years only to become a taxi-driver.
(b) (*desto*) **~ so besser/schlimmer!** so much the better/worse!, all the better/that's even worse!; **je mehr ... ~ so weniger/eher kann man ...** the more ... the less/sooner one can ...; **~ so mehr, als ...** all the more considering *or* as; **unser Urlaub ist sehr kurz, ~ so besser muß er geplant werden** as our holiday is so short, we have to plan it all the better.
4 *adv* **(a)** (*ungefähr*) **~ (die) 30 Schüler** *etc* about *or* around *or* round about

30 pupils *etc*, 30 pupils *etc* or so.
(b) (*rare*) ~ **und** ~ all around.

um|adressieren* *vt sep* to readdress; (*und nachschicken*) to redirect.

um|ändern *vt sep* to alter; (*modifizieren auch*) to modify.

um|arbeiten *vt sep* to alter; *Buch etc* to revise, to rewrite, to rework; *Metall etc* to rework ◆ **einen Roman zu einem Drama/Drehbuch ~** to adapt a novel for the stage/screen.

Um|arbeitung *f* alteration; (*von Buch etc*) revision, rewriting, reworking; (*zu Drama etc*) adaptation; (*von Metall*) reworking.

um|armen* *vt insep* to embrace (*auch euph*); (*fester*) to hug.

Um|armung *f siehe vt* embrace; hug.

um|arrangieren* ['ʊmarãʒiːrən] *vt sep or insep* to rearrange.

Umbau *m siehe vt* rebuilding, renovation; conversion; alterations *pl* (*+gen, von* to); modification; reorganization; changing ◆ **das Gebäude befindet sich im ~** the building is being rebuilt.

umbauen¹ *sep* [1] *vt Gebäude* (*gründlich renovieren*) to rebuild, to renovate; (*zu etw anderem*) to convert (*zu* into); (*umändern*) to alter; *Maschine etc* to modify; (*fig: Organisation*) to reorganize; (*Theat*) *Kulissen* to change.
[2] *vi* to rebuild.

umbauen²* *vt insep* to enclose ◆ **der Dom ist völlig umbaut** the cathedral is completely surrounded by buildings; **umbauter Raum** enclosed *or* interior area.

umbehalten* *vt sep irreg Schal etc* to keep on.

umbenennen* *vt sep irreg* to rename (*in etw* sth).

Umbenennung *f* renaming.

umbesetzen* *vt sep* (*Theat*) to recast; *Mannschaft* to change, to reorganize; *Posten, Stelle* to find someone else for, to reassign.

Umbesetzung *f siehe vt* recasting; change, reorganization; reassignment ◆ **eine ~ vornehmen** (*Theat*) to alter the cast; **~en vornehmen** (*Theat*) to recast roles; **~en im Kabinett vornehmen** to reshuffle the cabinet.

umbestellen* *sep* [1] *vi* to change one's order.
[2] *vt Patienten etc* to give another *or* a new appointment to.

umbetten *vt sep Kranken* to move *or* transfer (to another bed); *Leichnam* to rebury, to transfer; *Fluß* to rechannel.

umbiegen *sep irreg* [1] *vt* to bend.
[2] *vr* to curl.
[3] *vi aux sein* (*Weg*) to bend, to turn; (*zurückgehen*) to turn round *or* back.

umbilden *vt sep* (*fig*) to reorganize, to reconstruct; (*Pol*) *Kabinett* to reshuffle (*Brit*), to shake up (*US*).

Umbildung *f siehe vt* reorganization, reconstruction; reshuffle, shake-up.

umbinden¹ *vt sep irreg* to put on; (*mit Knoten auch*) to tie on ◆ **sich** (*dat*) **einen Schal ~** to put a scarf on.

umbinden²* *vt insep irreg siehe* **umwickeln²**.

umblasen *vt sep irreg* to blow down.

umblättern *vti sep* to turn over.

umblicken *vr sep* to look round ◆ **sich nach jdm/etw ~** to turn round to look at sb/sth.

Umbra *f -, no pl* (*Astron*) umbra; (*Farbe*) umber.

Umbralglas ® *nt* photochrom(at)ic glass.

umbranden* *vt insep* to surge around ◆ **von der See umbrandet** surrounded by the surging sea.

umbrausen* *vt insep* to surge around ◆ **vom Sturm umbraust** buffeted by the storm.

umbrechen¹ *sep irreg* [1] *vt* **(a)** (*umknicken*) to break down. **(b)** (*umpflügen*) *Erde* to break up.
[2] *vi aux sein* to break.

umbrechen²* *vti insep irreg* (*Typ*) to make up.

umbringen *sep irreg* [1] *vt* to kill (*auch fig inf*), to murder ◆ **das ist nicht umzubringen** (*fig inf*) it's indestructible; **das bringt mich noch um!** (*inf*) it'll be the death of me! (*inf*).
[2] *vr* to kill oneself ◆ **bringen Sie sich nur nicht um!** (*fig inf*) you'll kill yourself (if you go on like that)!; **er bringt sich fast um vor Höflichkeit** (*inf*) he falls over himself to be polite.

Umbruch *m* **(a)** radical change. **(b)** (*Typ*) makeup. **(c)** (*Agr*) ploughing (*Brit*) *or* plowing (*US*) up.

▼ **umbuchen** *sep* [1] *vt* **(a)** *Reise, Termin* to alter one's booking for. **(b)** (*Fin*) *Betrag* to transfer.
[2] *vi* **(a)** to alter one's booking (*auf +acc* for). **(b)** to transfer (*auf +acc* to).

Umbuchung *f siehe vb* **(a)** rebooking. **(b)** transfer.

umdenken *vi sep irreg* to change one's ideas *or* views ◆ **darin müssen wir ~** we'll have to rethink that.

umdeuten *vt sep* to change the meaning of; (*Liter*) to reinterpret, to give a new interpretation to.

umdichten *vt sep* to rework, to recast.

umdirigieren* *vt sep* to redirect.

umdisponieren* *vi sep* to change one's arrangements *or* plans.

umdrängen* *vt insep* to throng *or* crowd around; (*stärker*) to mob ◆ **sie wurde so umdrängt, daß ...** there was such a crowd around her that ...

umdrehen *sep* [1] *vt* **(a)** to turn over; (*auf den Kopf*) to turn up (the other way); (*mit der Vorderseite nach hinten*) to turn round, to turn back to front; (*von innen nach außen*) *Strumpf etc* to turn inside out; *Tasche* to turn (inside) out; (*von außen nach innen*) to turn back the right way; (*um die Achse*) to turn round; *Schlüssel* to turn; *siehe* **Pfennig, Spieß.**
(b) einem Vogel/jdm den Hals ~ to wring a bird's/sb's neck.
(c) (*verrenken*) **jdm den Arm ~** to twist sb's arm; *siehe* **Wort.**
[2] *vr* to turn round (*nach* to look at); (*im Bett etc*) to turn over ◆ **dabei drehte sich ihm der Magen um** (*inf*) it turned his stomach.
[3] *vi* to turn round *or* back.

Umdrehung *f* turn; (*Phys*) revolution, rotation; (*Mot*) revolution, rev.

Umdrehungszahl *f* (number of) revolutions *pl* per minute/second.

umdüstern* *vr insep* (*liter*) to become melancholy *or* sombre.

um|einander (*emph* **umeinander**) *adv* about each other *or* one another; (*räumlich*) (a)round each other.

um|erziehen* *vt sep irreg* (*Pol euph*) to re-educate (*zu* to become).

Um|erziehungslager *nt* (*Pol euph*) re-education centre.

umfächeln* *vt insep* (*geh*) to fan; (*Luftzug auch*) to caress (*liter*).

umfahren¹ *sep irreg* [1] *vt* to run over *or* down, to knock down.
[2] *vi aux sein* (*inf*) to go out of one's way (*by mistake*) ◆ **er ist 5 Kilometer umgefahren** he went 5 kilometres out of his way.

umfahren²* *vt insep irreg* to travel *or* go round; (*mit dem Auto*) to drive round; (*auf Umgehungsstraße*) to bypass; (*um etw zu vermeiden*) to make a detour round, to detour; *Kap* to round, to double; *die Welt* to sail round, to circumnavigate.

Umfahrung *f* **(a)** *siehe* **umfahren²** travelling round; driving round; bypassing; detour; rounding, doubling; sailing (round), circumnavigation. **(b)** (*Aus*) *siehe* **Umgehungsstraße.**

Umfahrungsstraße *f* (*Aus*) *siehe* **Umgehungsstraße.**

Umfall *m* (*Pol inf*) turnaround (*inf*).

umfallen *vi sep irreg aux sein* (*Mensch*) to fall over *or* down; (*Baum, Gegenstand*) to fall (down); (*vornüber kippen*) to fall *or* topple over; (*inf: ohnmächtig werden*) to pass out, to faint; (*fig inf: nachgeben*) to give in ◆ **vor Müdigkeit fast ~, zum U~ müde sein** to be (almost) dead on one's feet (*inf*), to be ready *or* fit to drop; **vor Schreck fast ~** (*inf*) to almost die with fright, to almost have a heart attack (*inf*); **~ wie die Fliegen** (*inf*) to drop like flies; *siehe* **tot.**

umfalzen *vt sep* to fold over.

Umfang *m* **-(e)s, Umfänge (a)** (*von Kreis etc*) perimeter, circumference (*auch Geom*); (*von Baum auch, Bauch~*) girth.
(b) (*Fläche*) area; (*Rauminhalt*) capacity; (*Größe*) size; (*von Gepäck etc*) amount ◆ **das Buch hat einen ~ von 800 Seiten** the book contains *or* has 800 pages.
(c) (*fig*) (*Ausmaß*) extent; (*Reichweite*) range; (*Stimm~*) range, compass; (*von Untersuchung, Arbeit etc*) scope; (*von Verkehr, Verkauf etc*) volume ◆ **in großem ~** on a large scale; **in vollem ~** fully, entirely, completely; **größeren/erschreckenden ~ annehmen** to assume greater/alarming proportions; **das hat einen solchen ~ angenommen, daß ...** it has assumed such proportions that ...; **etw in vollem ~ übersehen können** to be able to see the full extent of sth.

umfangen* *vt insep irreg* **(a) jdn mit seinen Blicken ~** (*fig*) to fix one's eyes upon sb. **(b)** (*fig: umgeben*) to envelop. **(c)** (*geh: umarmen*) to embrace.

umfänglich, umfangreich *adj* extensive; (*fig: breit*) *Wissen etc auch* wide; (*geräumig*) spacious; *Buch* thick.

umfärben *vt sep* to dye a different colour.

umfassen* *vt insep* **(a)** to grasp, to clasp; (*umarmen*) to embrace ◆ **ich konnte den Baum nicht mit den Armen ~** I couldn't get my arms (a)round the tree; **er hielt sie umfaßt** he held her close *or* to him, he held her in an embrace.
(b) (*Mil*) to encircle, to surround.
(c) (*fig*) (*einschließen*) *Zeitperiode* to cover; (*enthalten*) to contain, to include; *Seiten* to contain.

umfassend *adj* (*umfangreich, weitreichend*) extensive; (*vieles enthaltend*) comprehensive; *Vollmachten, Maßnahmen auch* sweeping; *Vorbereitung* thorough; *Geständnis* full, complete.

Umfassung *f* (*Mil*) encirclement.

Umfeld *nt* surroundings *pl*; (*fig*) sphere ◆ **zum ~ von etw gehören** to be associated with sth.

umfirmieren* *insep* [1] *vt Unternehmen* to change the name of.
[2] *vi* (*von Unternehmen*) to change one's name.

Umfirmierung *f* change of name.

umflechten* *vt insep irreg* **eine Flasche** *etc* **mit etw ~** to weave sth around a bottle *etc*; **eine umflochtene Flasche** a raffia-covered bottle.

umfliegen¹* *vt insep irreg* to fly (a)round.

umfliegen² *vi sep irreg aux sein* (*inf*) to go flying (*inf*).

umfließen* *vt insep irreg* (*lit, fig*) to flow around; (*fig poet: Licht*) to flood around ◆ **von einem Strom umflossen sein** to be surrounded by a river.

umflort *adj* (*liter*) *Augen* misty, misted over.

umfluten* *vt insep* to surge around.

umformen *vt sep* **(a)** to remodel, to reshape (*in +acc* into). **(b)** (*Elec*) to convert. **(c)** (*Ling*) to transform.

Umformer *m* **-s, -** (*Elec*) converter.

Umformung *f siehe vt* remodelling, reshaping; conversion; transformation.

Umfrage *f* **(a)** (*Sociol*) survey; (*esp Pol*) (opinion) poll ◆ **eine ~ halten** *or* **machen** *or* **veranstalten** to carry out *or* hold a survey/a poll *or* an opinion poll.
(b) ~ halten to ask around.

Umfrage|ergebnis *nt* survey/poll result(s *pl*).

umfried(ig)en* *vt insep* to enclose; (*mit Zaun auch*) to fence in; (*mit Mauer auch*) to wall in.

Umfried(ig)ung *f* **(a)** (*das Umfrieden*) **die ~ der Burg dauerte Jahrzehnte** enclosing/walling in the castle took years. **(b)** (*Zaun, Mauer etc*) enclosing fence/wall *etc* ◆ **als ~ für den Park dient eine Hecke** the park is enclosed by a hedge.

umfrisieren* *vt sep* (*inf*) **(a)** *Nachrichten etc* to doctor (*inf*). **(b) sich** (*dat*) **die**

Haare ~ lassen to have one's hair restyled.
umfüllen *vt sep* to transfer into another bottle/container *etc.*
umfunktionieren* *vt sep* to change *or* alter the function of ◆ **etw in** (*+acc*) *or* **zu etw ~** to change *or* turn sth into sth; **die Kinder haben das Wohnzimmer umfunktioniert** (*hum*) the children have done a conversion job on the living-room (*hum*).
Umfunktionierung *f* **die ~ einer Sache** (*gen*) changing the function of sth; **die ~ der Versammlung zu einer Protestkundgebung** changing the function of the meeting and making a protest rally out of it.
Umgang[1] *m* **-s** *no pl* **(a)** (*gesellschaftlicher Verkehr*) contact, dealings *pl*; (*Bekanntenkreis*) acquaintances *pl*, friends *pl* ◆ **schlechten ~ haben** to keep bad company; **das sieht man schon/das liegt an seinem ~** you can tell that from/that's because of the company he keeps; **~ mit jdm/einer Gruppe haben** *or* **pflegen** to associate with sb/associate *or* mix with a group; **keinen/so gut wie keinen ~ mit jdm haben** to have nothing/little to do with sb; **sie hat nur ~ mit den besten gesellschaftlichen Kreisen** she only mixes in the best social circles; **er ist kein ~ für dich** he's not fit company *or* no company for you.
(b) im ~ mit Tieren/Jugendlichen/Vorgesetzten muß man ... in dealing with animals/young people/one's superiors one must ...; **durch ständigen ~ mit Autos/Büchern/Kindern** through having a lot to do with cars/books/children; **an den ~ mit Tieren/Kindern gewöhnt sein** to be used to animals/children; **an den ~ mit Büchern/Nachschlagewerken gewöhnt sein** to be used to having books around (one)/to using reference books; **der ~ mit Tieren/Kindern muß gelernt sein** you have to learn how to handle animals/children.
Umgang[2] *m* **-(e)s, Umgänge (a)** (*Archit: Säulen~*) ambulatory. **(b)** (*Feld~, Flur~*) procession.
umgänglich *adj* (*entgegenkommend*) obliging; (*gesellig*) sociable, friendly; (*verträglich*) affable, pleasant-natured.
Umgänglichkeit *f siehe adj* obliging nature; sociability, friendliness; affability, pleasant nature.
Umgangs-: ~formen *pl* manners *pl*; **~sprache** *f* colloquial language *or* speech; **die deutsche ~sprache** colloquial German; **u~sprachlich** *adj* colloquial; **~ton** *m* tone, way of speaking; **hier herrscht ein rüder/höflicher ~ton** people talk brusquely/politely here.
umgarnen* *vt insep* to ensnare, to beguile.
umgaukeln* *vt insep* (*geh*) to flutter about *or* around; (*fig: mit Schmeicheleien etc*) to ensnare, to beguile.
umgeben* *insep irreg* [1] *vt* to surround (*auch fig*) ◆ **mit einer Mauer/einem Zaun ~ sein** to be walled/fenced in, to be surrounded by a wall/fence; **das von Weinbergen ~e Stuttgart** the town of Stuttgart, surrounded by vineyards.
[2] *vr* **sich mit jdm/etw ~** to surround oneself with sb/sth.
Umgebung *f* (*Umwelt*) surroundings *pl*; (*von Stadt auch*) environs *pl*, surrounding area; (*Nachbarschaft*) vicinity, neighbourhood; (*gesellschaftlicher Hintergrund*) background; (*Freunde, Kollegen etc*) people *pl* about one ◆ **Hamburg und ~** Hamburg and the Hamburg area, Hamburg and its environs *or* the surrounding area; **in der näheren/weiteren ~ Münchens** on the outskirts/in the environs of Munich; **zu jds (näherer) ~ gehören** (*Menschen*) to be one of the people closest to sb.
Umgegend *f* surrounding area ◆ **die ~ von London** the area around London.
umgehen[1] *vi sep irreg aux sein* **(a)** (*Gerücht etc*) to circulate, to go (a)round *or* about; (*Grippe*) to be about; (*Gespenst*) to walk ◆ **in diesem Schloß geht ein Gespenst um** this castle is haunted (by a ghost).
(b) mit jdm/etw ~ können (*behandeln, handhaben*) to know how to handle *or* treat sb/sth; *mit Geld* to know how to handle sth; (*mit jdm/etw verfahren*) to know how to deal with *or* handle sb/sth; **mit jdm grob/behutsam ~** to treat sb roughly/gently; **wie der mit seinen Sachen umgeht!** you should see how he treats his things!; **sorgsam/verschwenderisch mit etw ~** to be careful/lavish with sth; **sage mir, mit wem du umgehst, und ich sage dir, wer du bist** (*Prov*) you can tell the sort of person somebody is from *or* by the company he keeps; **mit dem Gedanken ~, etw zu tun** to be thinking about doing sth.
(c) (*inf: Umweg machen*) to go out of one's way (by mistake).
umgehen[2]* *vt insep irreg* **(a)** to go round; (*vermeiden*) to avoid; (*Straße*) to by-pass; (*Mil*) to outflank.
(b) (*fig*) to avoid; *Schwierigkeit auch, Gesetz* to circumvent, to get round, to by-pass; *Frage, Thema auch* to evade ◆ **die Antwort auf etw** (*acc*) **~** to avoid answering sth.
umgehend [1] *adj* immediate, prompt ◆ **mit ~er Post** (*dated*) by return of post (*Brit*) *or* mail (*US*).
[2] *adv* immediately.
Umgehung *f, no pl* **(a)** *siehe* **umgehen**[2] going round; avoidance; by-passing; outflanking; circumvention, getting round, evasion ◆ **die ~ des Geländes** going round the grounds; **unter ~ der Vorschriften** by getting round *or* circumventing the regulations. **(b)** (*inf: ~sstraße*) by-pass.
Umgehungsstraße *f* by-pass, beltway (*US*).
umgekehrt [1] *adj* reversed; *Reihenfolge* reverse; (*gegenteilig*) opposite, contrary; (*anders herum*) the other way around ◆ **in die ~e Richtung fahren** to go in the opposite direction; **nein, ~!** no, the other way round; **gerade** *or* **genau ~!** quite the contrary!, just the opposite!; **die Sache war genau ~ und nicht so, wie er sie erzählte** the affair was exactly the reverse of what he said; **im ~en Verhältnis zu etw stehen** *or* **sein** to be in inverse proportion to sth.
[2] *adv* (*anders herum*) the other way round; (*am Satzanfang: dagegen*) conversely; *proportional* inversely ◆ **... und/oder ~** ... and/or vice versa; **~ als** *or* **wie** (*inf*) ... the other way round to what ...; **es kam ~** (*inf*) the opposite happened.
umgestalten* *vt sep* to alter; (*reorganisieren*) to reorganize; (*umbilden*) to remodel; (*umordnen*) to rearrange ◆ **etw in etw** (*acc*) *or* **zu etw ~** to redesign sth as sth; *Werk, Buch* to rewrite *or* recast sth as sth.
Umgestaltung *f siehe vt* alteration; reorganization; remodelling; rearrangement.
umgewöhnen* *vr sep* to re-adapt.
umgießen *vt sep irreg* **(a)** to transfer (*in +acc* into); (*verschütten*) to spill. **(b)** (*Metal*) to recast.
umglänzen* *vt insep* (*poet*) (*Sonne etc*) to bathe in light ◆ **von der Morgensonne/von Ruhm umglänzt** bathed in the morning sunlight/resplendent with glory.
umgraben *vt sep irreg* to dig over; *Erde* to turn (over).
umgrenzen* *vt insep* to bound, to surround; (*umfassen auch*) to enclose; (*fig*) to delimit, to define.
Umgrenzung *f* **(a)** boundary. **(b)** (*das Umgrenzen*) (*mit Mauer etc*) enclosing; (*fig*) delimitation, definition.
umgruppieren* *vt sep Möbel etc* to rearrange; *Mitarbeiter* to redeploy; (*auf andere Gruppen verteilen*), (*Mil*) *Truppen* to regroup.
Umgruppierung *f siehe vt* rearrangement; redeployment; regrouping.
umgucken *vr sep siehe* **umsehen.**
umgürten[1] *vt sep* to fasten (*dat* around).
umgürten[2]* *vr insep* **sich mit einem Schwert ~** (*liter*) to gird on a sword (*liter*).
umhaben *vt sep irreg* (*inf*) to have on.
umhalsen* *vt sep* **jdn ~** (*inf*) to throw one's arms around sb's neck.
Umhang *m* **-(e)s, Umhänge** cape; (*länger*) cloak; (*Umhängetuch*) shawl, wrap (*esp US*).
umhängen *vt sep* **(a)** *Rucksack etc* to put on; *Jacke, Schal etc* to drape round; *Gewehr auch* to sling on ◆ **sich** (*dat*) **etw ~** to put sth on; to drape sth round one; **jdm etw ~** to put sth on sb; to drape sth around sb. **(b)** *Bild* to rehang.
Umhängetasche *f* shoulder bag.
umhauen *vt sep irreg* **(a)** to chop *or* cut down, to fell. **(b)** (*inf: umwerfen*) to knock flying (*inf*) *or* over. **(c)** (*inf*) (*erstaunen*) to bowl over (*inf*); (*Gestank etc*) to knock out.
umhegen* *vt insep* (*geh*) to look after *or* care for lovingly.
umher *adv* around, about ◆ **weit ~** all around.
umher- *pref siehe auch* **herum-, rum-** around, about; **~fahren** *sep irreg* [1] *vt* (*mit Auto*) to drive around *or* about; (*in Kinderwagen*) to walk around *or* about; [2] *vi aux sein* to travel around *or* about; (*mit Auto*) to drive around *or* about; (*mit Kinderwagen*) to walk around *or* about; **~gehen** *vi sep irreg aux sein* to walk around *or* about; **im Zimmer/Garten ~gehen** to walk (a)round the room/garden; **~getrieben** *adj* (*liter*) wandering *attr*; **U~getriebene(r)** *mf decl as adj* (*liter*) wanderer, wandering soul (*liter*); **~irren** *vi sep aux sein* (*in etw* (*dat*) sth) to wander around *or* about; (*Blick, Augen*) to roam about; **ängstlich irrte ihr Blick im Zimmer ~** her eyes anxiously scanned the room; **nach langen Jahren des U~irrens** after many years of wandering (around); **~jagen** *vti sep* (*vi: aux sein*) to chase about *or* around; **~laufen** *vi sep irreg aux sein* to walk about *or* around; (*rennen*) to run about *or* around; **im Garten ~laufen** to walk/run about *or* (a)round the garden; **~schlendern** *vi sep aux sein* to stroll about *or* around (*in etw* (*dat*) sth); **~spähen** *vi sep* to look about *or* around; **~streifen** *vi sep aux sein* to wander *or* roam about *or* around (*in etw* (*dat*) sth); **~streunen** *vi sep aux sein* (*geh*) *siehe* **herumstreunen**; **~wandern** *vi sep aux sein* to wander *or* roam about (*in etw* (*dat*) sth); **~ziehen** *sep irreg* [1] *vi aux sein* to move *or* travel around (*in etw* (*dat*) sth); [2] *vt* to pull about *or* around.
umhinkönnen *vi sep irreg* **ich/er** *etc* **kann nicht umhin, das zu tun** I/he *etc* can't avoid doing it; (*einem Zwang folgend*) I/he *etc* can't help doing it; **ich konnte nicht umhin** I couldn't avoid it; I couldn't help it; ..., **so daß sie einfach nicht umhinkonnten, mir zu glauben** ... so that they simply couldn't help but believe me.
umhören *vr sep* to ask around ◆ **sich unter seinen Kollegen ~** to ask around one's colleagues.
umhüllen* *vt insep* to wrap (up) (*mit* in) ◆ **von einem Geheimnis umhüllt** shrouded in secrecy *or* mystery.
um|interpretieren* *vt sep* to interpret differently; (*Liter*) to reinterpret.
umjubeln* *vt insep* to cheer ◆ **ein umjubelter Popstar** a wildly acclaimed pop idol.
umkämpfen* *vt insep Entscheidung, Stadt* to dispute; *Wahlkreis, Sieg* to contest.
Umkehr *f* **-,** *no pl* **(a)** (*lit*) turning back ◆ **jdn zur ~ zwingen** to force sb to turn back. **(b)** (*fig geh*) (*Änderung*) change; (*zur Religion etc*) changing one's ways ◆ **zur ~ bereit sein** to be ready to change one's ways.
Umkehranstalt *f* (*Phot*) reversal film processing laboratory.
umkehrbar *adj* reversible.
umkehren *sep* [1] *vi aux sein* to turn back; (*auf demselben Weg zurückgehen*) to retrace one's steps; (*fig*) to change one's ways.
[2] *vt Kleidungsstück* (*von innen nach außen*) to turn inside out; (*von außen nach innen*) to turn the right way out; *Tasche* to turn (inside) out; *Reihenfolge* to reverse, to invert (*auch Gram, Math, Mus*); *Verhältnisse* (*umstoßen*) to overturn; (*auf den Kopf stellen*) to turn upside down, to invert ◆ **das ganze Zimmer ~** (*inf*) to turn the whole room upside down (*inf*); *siehe auch* **umgekehrt.**
[3] *vr* (*Verhältnisse*) to become inverted *or* reversed ◆ **dabei kehrt sich mir der**

Magen um it turns my stomach, my stomach turns (over) at the sight/smell *etc* of it; **mein Inneres kehrt sich um, wenn ...** my gorge rises when ...

Umkehr- ~film *m (Phot)* reversal film; **~linse** *f* inverting lens; ⚠**~schluß** *m* inversion of an argument; **im ~schluß bedeutet das ...** to turn the argument on its head, it means ...

Umkehrung *f (von Gesagtem, Reihenfolge etc)* reversal, inversion *(auch Gram, Math, Mus)* ♦ **das ist eine ~ dessen, was ich gesagt habe** that's the opposite *or* reverse of what I said.

umkippen *sep* [1] *vt* to tip over, to upset; *Auto, Boot* to overturn, to turn over; *Leuchter, Vase* to knock over; *volles Gefäß* to upset.
[2] *vi aux sein* **(a)** to tip *or* fall over; *(Auto, Boot)* to overturn, to turn over; *(volles Gefäß, Bier)* to be spilled *or* upset.
(b) *(inf: ohnmächtig werden)* to pass out.
(c) *(es sich anders überlegen)* to come round.
(d) *(sich umwandeln)* to tip over *(in +acc* into) ♦ **plötzlich kippte seine Fröhlichkeit in Depression um** suddenly his cheerfulness turned to depression.
(e) *(Fluß, See)* to become polluted.

umklammern* *vt insep* to wrap one's arms/legs around; *(umarmen auch)* to hug, to embrace; *(mit Händen)* to clasp; *(festhalten)* to cling to; *(Ringen)* to hold, to clinch; *(Mil)* to trap in a pincer movement ♦ **sie hielt ihn/meine Hand umklammert** she held him/my hand tight, she clung (on) to him/my hand; **einander** *or* **sich ~** *(Ringen)* to go into a/be in a clinch.

Umklammerung *f* clutch; *(Umarmung)* embrace; *(Ringen)* clinch; *(Mil)* pincer movement.

umklappbar *adj* folding *attr*, collapsible.

umklappen *sep* [1] *vt* to fold down.
[2] *vi aux sein (inf)* to pass out.

Umkleidekabine *f* changing cubicle; *(in Kleidungsgeschäft auch)* changing *or* fitting room.

umkleiden[1] *vr sep* to change (one's clothes) ♦ **sie ist noch nicht umgekleidet** she isn't changed yet.

umkleiden[2]* *vt insep* to cover ♦ **die Wahrheit mit schönen Worten ~** *(fig)* to gloss over *or* varnish the truth.

Umkleideraum *m* changing room; *(esp mit Schließfächern)* locker room; *(Theat)* dressing room.

umknicken *sep* [1] *vt Ast* to snap; *Gras, Strohhalm* to bend over; *Papier* to fold (over).
[2] *vi aux sein (Ast)* to snap; *(Gras, Strohhalm)* to get bent over ♦ **mit dem Fuß ~** to twist one's ankle.

umkommen *vi sep irreg aux sein* **(a)** *(sterben)* to die, to be killed, to perish *(liter)* ♦ **vor Lange(r)weile ~** *(inf)* to be bored to death *(inf)*, to nearly die of boredom; **da kommt man ja um!** *(inf) (vor Hitze)* the heat is killing *(inf)*; *(wegen Gestank)* it's enough to knock you out *(inf)*.
(b) *(inf: verderben: Lebensmittel)* to go off *or* bad.

umkränzen* *vt insep (liter)* to wreathe, to garland.

Umkreis *m (Umgebung)* surroundings *pl*; *(Gebiet)* area; *(Nähe)* vicinity; *(Geometrie)* circumcircle ♦ **im näheren ~** in the vicinity; **im ~ von 20 Kilometern** within a radius of 20 kilometres.

umkreisen* *vt insep* to circle (around); *(Astron)* to orbit, to revolve around; *(Space)* to orbit.

Umkreisung *f (Space, Astron)* orbiting ♦ **drei ~en der Erde** three orbits of the Earth; **die ~ des Feindes** circling the enemy.

umkrempeln *vt sep* **(a)** to turn up; *(mehrmals)* to roll up. **(b)** *(umwenden)* to turn inside out; *(inf) Zimmer* to turn upside down *(inf)*; *Betrieb* to shake up *(inf)* ♦ **jdn ~** *(fig inf)* to change sb *or* sb's ways.

umkucken *vr sep (N Ger inf) siehe* **umsehen.**

umladen *vt sep irreg* to transfer, to reload; *(Naut)* to transship.

Umladung *f* transfer, reloading; *(Naut)* transshipping.

Umlage *f* **eine ~ machen** to split the cost; **sie beschlossen eine ~ der Kosten** they decided to split the costs.

umlagern[1]* *vt insep* to surround; *(sich drängen um, Mil)* to besiege, to beleaguer.

umlagern[2] *vt sep* to transfer *(in +acc* into); *(in anderes Lager bringen) Waren etc* to re-store.

Umland *nt, no pl* surrounding countryside.

Umlauf *m* **-s, Umläufe (a)** *(von Erde etc)* revolution; *(das Kursieren)* circulation *(auch fig)* ♦ **im ~ sein** to be circulating, to be in circulation; **in ~ bringen** to circulate; *Geld auch* to put in circulation; *Gerücht auch* to put about, to spread. **(b)** *(Rundschreiben)* circular. **(c)** *(Med: Fingerentzündung)* whitlow.

Umlaufbahn *f* orbit ♦ **die ~ um den Mond/die Erde** lunar/earth orbit; **auf der ~ um die Erde sein** to be orbiting the earth.

umlaufen[1] *sep irreg* [1] *vt* to (run into and) knock over.
[2] *vi aux sein* to circulate.

umlaufen[2]* *vt insep irreg* to orbit.

Umlauf-: ~schreiben *nt* circular; **~zeit** *f (Astron)* period; *(Space)* orbiting time.

Umlaut *m* **(a)** *no pl* umlaut, vowel mutation. **(b)** *(Laut)* vowel with umlaut, mutated vowel.

umlauten *vt sep* to mutate, to modify *(zu* into).

umlegen *sep* [1] *vt* **(a)** *(umhängen, umbinden)* to put round; *Verband* to put on, to apply ♦ **jdm/sich eine Stola ~** to put a stole round sb's/one's shoulders.
(b) *Mauer, Baum* to bring down; *(sl: zu Boden schlagen) Gegner* to knock down, to floor.
(c) *(umklappen)* to tilt (over); *Kragen* to turn down; *Manschetten* to turn up; *(Cards)* to turn (over); *Hebel* to turn.
(d) *(verlegen) Kranke* to transfer, to move; *Leitung* to re-lay.
(e) *Termin* to change *(auf +acc* to).
(f) *(verteilen)* **die 20 Mark wurden auf uns fünf umgelegt** the five of us each had to pay a contribution towards the 20 marks.
(g) *(sl: ermorden)* to do in *(inf)*, to bump off *(sl)*.
(h) *(sl) Mädchen* to lay *(sl)*, to screw *(sl)*.
[2] *vr* **(a)** *(Boot)* to capsize, to turn over; *(Getreide)* to be flattened.
(b) *(sl: sich umbringen)* to do oneself in *(inf)*.

umleiten *vt sep* to divert.

Umleitung *f* diversion; *(Strecke auch)* detour.

umlernen *vi sep* to retrain; *(fig)* to change one's ideas.

umliegend *adj* surrounding.

umlodern* *vt insep (liter)* to light up ♦ **von Fackeln umlodert** lighted up by blazing torches.

Umluft *f (Tech)* circulating air.

ummanteln* *vt insep (Tech)* to coat.

ummauern* *vt insep* to wall in *(mit* by).

ummelden *vtr sep* **jdn/sich ~** to notify (the police of) a change in sb's/one's address.

Ummeldung *f* notification of (one's) change of address.

ummi *adv (Aus inf) siehe* **hinüber.**

ummodeln *vt sep (inf)* to change.

umnachtet *adj (geh) Geist* clouded over *pred* ♦ **geistig ~** mentally deranged.

Umnachtung *f* **geistige ~** mental derangement; **da muß ich in geistiger ~ gewesen sein** *(iro)* I must have had a brainstorm.

umnähen *vt sep Saum* to stitch up.

umnebeln* *insep* [1] *vt (mit Tabakrauch)* to surround with smoke.
[2] *vr (Blick)* to cloud *or* mist over ♦ **mit umnebeltem Blick** with misty eyes.

umnehmen *vt sep irreg Mantel, Schal* to put on.

umnieten *vt sep (sl: töten)* to blow away *(sl)*.

⚠**umnumerieren*** *vt sep* to renumber.

um|ordnen *vt sep* to rearrange; *(in andere Reihenfolge bringen auch)* to re-order.

Um|organisation *f* reorganization.

um|organisieren* *vt sep* to reorganize.

um|orientieren* *vr sep (fig)* to reorientate oneself.

Um|orientierung *f* reorientation.

umpacken *vt sep* to repack.

umpflanzen[1] *vt sep* to transplant; *Topfpflanze* to repot.

umpflanzen[2]* *vt insep* **einen Platz mit Bäumen ~** to plant trees around a square.

umpflügen *vt sep* to plough up.

umpolen *vt sep (Elec)* to reverse the polarity of; *(inf: ändern)* to convert *(auf +acc* to).

umquartieren* *vt sep* to move; *Truppen (in andere Kaserne etc)* to re-quarter; *(in anderes Privathaus)* to rebillet.

umrahmen[1]* *vt insep* to frame ♦ **die Ansprache war von musikalischen Darbietungen umrahmt** the speech was accompanied by musical offerings (before and after).

umrahmen[2] *vt sep* to reframe.

Umrahmung *f* setting *(+gen, von* for); *(das Umrahmen)* framing ♦ **mit musikalischer ~** with music before and after.

umranden* *vt insep* to edge, to border ♦ **tragen Sie die Postleitzahl in das stark umrandete Feld ein** write the postcode in the area marked in bold outline.

umrändert *adj Augen* red-rimmed.

Umrandung *f* border, edging.

umranken* *vt insep* to climb *or* twine (a)round ♦ **von** *or* **mit Efeu umrankt** twined around with ivy.

umräumen *sep* [1] *vt (anders anordnen)* to rearrange, to change (a)round; *(an anderen Platz bringen)* to shift, to move.
[2] *vi* to change the furniture (a)round, to rearrange the furniture.

umrechnen *vt sep* to convert *(in +acc* into).

Umrechnung *f* conversion.

Umrechnungs-: ~kurs *m* exchange rate, rate of exchange; **~tabelle** *f* conversion table.

umreißen[1] *vt sep irreg* to tear down; *(umwerfen)* to knock over.

umreißen[2]* *vt insep irreg* to outline ♦ **scharf umrissen** clear-cut, well defined; *Züge auch* sharply defined.

umrennen *vt sep irreg* to (run into and) knock down.

umringen* *vt insep* to surround, to gather around; *(drängend)* to throng *or* crowd around ♦ **von neugierigen Passanten umringt** surrounded/thronged by curious passers-by.

⚠**Umriß** *m* outline; *(Kontur)* contour(s *pl)* ♦ **etw in Umrissen zeichnen/erzählen** to outline sth, to draw/tell sth in outline; **„Geschichte in Umrissen"** "History — A Brief Outline".

⚠**umrißhaft** *adj* in outline.

⚠**Umrißzeichnung** *f* outline drawing.

umrühren *vt sep* to stir ♦ **etw unter ständigem U~ kochen** to boil sth stirring constantly *or* continually.

umrüsten *vt sep* **(a)** *(Tech)* to adapt ♦ **etw auf etw** *(acc)* **~** to adapt *or* convert sth to sth. **(b)** *(Mil)* to re-equip.

ums *contr of* **um das.**

umsatteln *sep* [1] *vt Pferd* to resaddle.

[2] *vi* (*inf*) (*beruflich*) to change jobs; (*Univ*) to change courses ◆ **von etw auf etw** (*acc*) ~ to switch from sth to sth.

Umsatz *m* (*Comm*) turnover ◆ **500 Mark ~ machen** (*inf*) to do 500 marks' worth of business.

Umsatz-: ~anstieg *m* increase in turnover; **~beteiligung** *f* commission; **~plus** *nt* (*Comm*) increase in turnover; **~rückgang** *m* drop in turnover; **~steuer** *f* sales tax.

umsäumen[1] *vt sep Stoffrand* to hem.

umsäumen[2]* *vt insep* to line; (*Sew*) to edge ◆ **von Bäumen umsäumt** tree-lined.

umschalten *sep* [1] *vt* (*auf +acc* to) *Schalter* to flick; *Hebel* to turn; *Strom* to convert; *Gerät* to switch over ◆ **den Schalter auf „heiß" ~** to put the switch to "hot".
[2] *vi* to flick the/a switch; to push/pull a/the lever; (*auf anderen Sender*) to turn *or* change over (*auf +acc* to); (*im Denken, sich gewöhnen*) to change (*auf +acc* to); (*Aut*) to change (*Brit*), to shift (*in +acc* to) ◆ **„wir schalten jetzt um nach Hamburg"** "and now we go over *or* we're going over to Hamburg".

Umschalter *m* (*Elec*) (change-over) switch; (*von Schreibmaschine*) shift-key.

Umschalt-: ~pause *f* (*Rad, TV*) intermission, break (*before going over to somewhere else*); **~taste** *f* (*Comput*) shift-key.

Umschaltung *f* (*auf +acc* to) change-over; (*im Denken, Umgewöhnung*) change.

umschatten* *vt insep* (*geh*) **seine Augen waren umschattet** he had shadows *or* rings under his eyes.

Umschau *f, no pl* (*fig*) review; (*TV, Rad*) magazine programme ◆ **~ halten** to look around (*nach* for).

umschauen *vr sep siehe* **umsehen.**

umschichten *sep* [1] *vt* to restack.
[2] *vr* (*Sociol*) to restructure itself.

umschichtig *adv* on a shift basis ◆ **~ arbeiten** to work in shifts.

Umschichtung *f* (**a**) restacking. (**b**) (*Sociol*) restructuring ◆ **soziale ~** change of social stratification, social regrouping *or* restructuring.

umschießen *vt sep irreg* to (shoot at and) knock over.

umschiffen[1]* *vt insep* to sail (a)round; *Kap auch* to round, to double (*spec*); *Erde auch* to circumnavigate; *siehe* **Klippe.**

umschiffen[2] *vt sep* to transfer; *Fracht auch* to transship.

Umschiffung[1] *f siehe* **umschiffen**[1] sailing (a)round; rounding, doubling; circumnavigation ◆ **die ~ einer gefährlichen Klippe** (*fig*) getting over a dangerous obstacle.

Umschiffung[2] *f siehe* **umschiffen**[2] transfer; transshipping, transshipment.

Umschlag *m* (**a**) (*Veränderung*) (sudden) change (*+gen* in, *in +acc* into).
(**b**) (*Hülle*) cover; (*Brief~*) envelope; (*als Verpackung*) wrapping; (*Buch~*) jacket.
(**c**) (*Med*) compress; (*Packung*) poultice.
(**d**) (*Ärmel~*) cuff; (*Hosen~*) turn-up (*Brit*), cuff (*US*).
(**e**) (*umgeschlagene Gütermenge*) volume of traffic ◆ **einen hohen ~ an Baumwolle** *etc* **haben** to handle a lot of cotton *etc*.
(**f**) (*Umladung*) (*auf +acc* to) transfer, transshipment.

umschlagen *sep irreg* [1] *vt* (**a**) *Seite etc* to turn over; *Ärmel, Hosenbein, Saum* to turn up; *Teppich, Decke* to fold *or* turn back; *Kragen* to turn down.
(**b**) (*um die Schultern*) *Schal* to put on.
(**c**) (*umladen*) *Güter* to transfer, to transship ◆ **etw vom Schiff auf die Bahn ~** to unload sth from the ship onto the train.
(**d**) (*absetzen*) *Güter* to handle.
[2] *vi aux sein* (**a**) (*sich ändern*) to change (suddenly); (*Wind auch*) to veer round; (*Stimme*) to break, to crack ◆ **in etw** (*acc*) **~** to change *or* turn into sth; **ins Gegenteil ~** to become the opposite.
(**b**) (*sauer werden*) to go off; (*Milch auch*) to turn.

Umschlag-: ~entwurf *m* jacket design; **~hafen** *m* port of transshipment; **~klappe** *f* jacket flap (*of book*); **~platz** *m* trade centre; **~tuch** *nt* shawl, wrap (*esp US*).

umschleichen* *vt insep irreg* to creep *or* prowl around.

umschließen* *vt insep irreg* to surround (*auch Mil*), to enclose; (*mit den Armen*) to embrace (*mit* in); (*fig: Plan, Entwurf etc*) to include, to encompass.

umschlingen* *vt insep irreg* (**a**) (*Pflanze*) to twine (a)round. (**b**) (*geh*) **jdn** (**mit den Armen**) **~** to enfold (*liter*) *or* clasp sb in one's arms, to embrace sb.

umschlungen *adj* **eng ~** with their *etc* arms tightly round each other.

⚠ **Umschluß** *m* (*in Strafanstalt*) recreation.

umschmeicheln* *vt insep* to flatter; (*fig*) to caress.

umschmeißen *vt sep irreg* (*inf*) (**a**) *siehe* **umhauen** (**b, c**). (**b**) **das schmeißt meine Pläne um** that mucks my plans up (*inf*).

umschmelzen *vt sep irreg* to recast.

umschnallen *vt sep* to buckle on.

umschreiben[1] *vt sep irreg* (**a**) *Text etc* to rewrite; (*in andere Schrift*) to transcribe (*auch Phon*), to transliterate; (*bearbeiten*) *Theaterstück etc* to adapt (*für* for).
(**b**) (*umbuchen*) to alter, to change (*auf +acc* for).
(**c**) *Hypothek etc* to transfer ◆ **etw auf jdn ~/~ lassen** to transfer sth/have sth transferred to sb *or* sb's name.

umschreiben[2]* *vt insep irreg* (**a**) (*mit anderen Worten ausdrücken*) to paraphrase; (*darlegen*) to outline, to describe; (*abgrenzen*) to circumscribe; (*verhüllen*) *Sachverhalt* to refer to obliquely, to skate around (*inf*). (**b**) (*Ling*) *Verneinung* to construct.

Umschreibung[1] *f siehe* **umschreiben**[1] rewriting; transcription (*auch Phon*), transliteration; adaptation; altering, changing; transfer.

Umschreibung[2] *f siehe* **umschreiben**[2] (**a**) *no pl* paraphrasing; outlining, description; circumscribing, circumscription; oblique reference (*gen* to). (**b**) *no pl* construction. (**c**) (*das Umschriebene*) paraphrase; outline, description; circumscription; oblique reference (*gen* to), circumlocution.

Umschrift *f* (**a**) (*auf Münze*) inscription, circumscription. (**b**) (*Ling: Transkription*) transcription (*auch Phon*), transliteration.

umschulden *vt sep* (*Comm*) *Kredit* to convert, to fund ◆ **ein Unternehmen ~** to change the terms of a firm's debt(s).

Umschuldung *f* funding *no pl*.

umschulen *vt sep* (**a**) to retrain; (*Pol euph*) to re-educate. (**b**) (*auf andere Schule*) to transfer (to another school).

Umschüler *m* student for retraining.

Umschulung *f siehe vt* retraining; re-education; transfer.

umschütten *vt sep* to spill, to upset ◆ **etw aus einer Dose in eine Kanne ~** to pour sth from a can into a jug.

umschwärmen* *vt insep* to swarm (a)round; (*Menschen auch*) to flock (a)round; (*verehren*) to idolize ◆ **von Verehrern umschwärmt werden** (*fig*) to be besieged *or* surrounded by admirers; **eine umschwärmte Schönheit** a much-courted beauty.

Umschweife *pl* **ohne ~** straight out, plainly; **mach keine ~!** don't beat about the bush, come (straight) to the point.

umschwenken *vi sep* (**a**) *aux sein or haben* (*Anhänger, Kran*) to swing out; (*fig*) to do an about-face *or* about-turn ◆ **der Kran schwenkte nach rechts um** the crane swung to the right. (**b**) (*Wind*) to veer (round).

umschwirren* *vt insep* (*lit, fig*) to buzz (a)round.

Umschwung *m* (**a**) (*Gymnastik*) circle. (**b**) (*fig*) (*Veränderung*) drastic change; (*ins Gegenteil*) reversal, about-turn ◆ **ein ~ zum Besseren** a drastic change for the better.

umsegeln* *vt insep* to sail round; *Kap auch* to round, to double (*spec*); *Erde auch* to circumnavigate.

Umseg(e)lung *f siehe vt* sailing round; rounding, doubling (*spec*); circumnavigation.

umsehen *vr sep irreg* to look around (*nach* for); (*rückwärts*) to look round *or* back ◆ **sich in der Stadt ~** to have a look (a)round the town; **sich in der Welt ~** to see something of the world; **ich möchte mich nur mal ~** (*in Geschäft*) I'm just looking, I just wanted to have a look (around); **ohne mich wird er sich noch ~** (*inf*) he's not going to find it easy without me.

⚠ **umsein** *vi sep irreg aux sein* (*Zusammenschreibung nur bei infin und ptp*) (*Frist, Zeit*) to be up.

Umseite *f* (*Press*) page two ◆ **auf der ~** on page two.

umseitig *adj* overleaf ◆ **die ~e Abbildung** the illustration overleaf.

umsetzen *sep* [1] *vt* (**a**) *Pflanzen* to transplant; *Topfpflanze* to repot; *Schüler* to move (to another seat).
(**b**) *Waren* to turn over.
(**c**) (*Typ*) to re-set.
(**d**) **etw in etw** (*acc*) **~** to convert sth into sth; (*Mus: transponieren*) to transpose sth into sth; (*in Verse etc*) to render *or* translate sth into sth; **sein Geld in Briefmarken/Alkohol ~** to spend all one's money on stamps/alcohol; **etw in die Tat ~** to translate sth into action.
[2] *vr* (*Schüler*) to change seats *or* places ◆ **sich in etw** (*acc*) **~** to be converted into sth.

Umsichgreifen *nt* **-s,** *no pl* spread.

Umsicht *f siehe adj* circumspection, prudence; judiciousness.

umsichtig *adj* circumspect, prudent; *Handlungsweise etc auch* judicious.

umsiedeln *vti sep* (*vi: aux sein*) to resettle ◆ **von einem Ort an einen anderen ~** to move from one place and settle in another.

Umsied(e)lung *f* resettlement.

Umsiedler *m* resettler.

umsinken *vi sep irreg aux sein* (*geh*) to sink to the ground ◆ **vor Müdigkeit ~** to drop with exhaustion.

umso *conj* (*Aus*) = **um so.**

umsomehr *adv* (*Aus*) = **um so mehr.**

umsonst *adv* (**a**) (*unentgeltlich*) free, for nothing, free of charge (*esp Comm*) ◆ **~ sein** to be free (of charge); **das hast du nicht ~ getan!** you'll pay for that, I'll get even with you for that; **~ ist nur der Tod(, und der kostet das Leben)** (*Prov*) you don't get anything for nothing in this world.
(**b**) (*vergebens*) in vain, to no avail; (*erfolglos*) without success.
(**c**) (*ohne Grund*) for nothing ◆ **nicht ~** not for nothing, not without reason.

umsorgen* *vt insep* to care for, to look after.

umsoweniger *adv* (*Aus*) = **um so weniger.**

umspannen[1]* *vt insep* (**a**) **etw mit beiden Armen/der Hand ~** to get both arms/one's hand (all the way) round sth. (**b**) (*fig*) *Bereich* to encompass, to embrace.

umspannen[2] *vt sep* (**a**) *Pferde* to change. (**b**) (*Elec*) to transform.

Umspanner *m* **-s, -** (*Elec*) transformer.

Umspann-: ~station *f,* **~werk** *nt* (*Elec*) transformer (station).

umspielen* *vt insep* (**a**) (*geh*) (*Rock etc*) to swirl about; (*Lächeln*) to play about; (*Wellen*) to lap about. (**b**) (*Ftbl*) to dribble round, to take out (*inf*).

Umspringbild *nt* (*Psych*) dual-aspect picture.

umspringen[1] *vi sep irreg aux sein* (**a**) (*Wind*) to veer round (*nach* to), to change; (*Bild*) to change. (**b**) (*Ski*) to jump-turn. (**c**) **mit jdm grob** *etc* **~** (*inf*) to treat sb roughly *etc*, to be rough *etc* with sb; **so kannst du nicht mit ihr ~!** (*inf*) you can't treat her like that!

umspringen[2]* *vt insep irreg* to jump about, to leap around.

⚠: for details of spelling reform, see supplement

umspulen *vt sep* to rewind.
umspülen* *vt insep* to wash round.
Umstand *m* **-(e)s, Umstände (a)** circumstance; (*Tatsache*) fact ♦ **ein unvorhergesehener ~** something unforeseen, unforeseen circumstances; **den Umständen entsprechend** much as one would expect (under the circumstances); **es geht ihm den Umständen entsprechend (gut)** he is as well as can be expected (under the circumstances); **nähere/die näheren Umstände** further details; **in anderen Umständen sein** to be expecting, to be in the family way; **unter diesen/keinen/anderen Umständen** under these/no/any other circumstances; **unter Umständen** possibly; **unter allen Umständen** at all costs.
(b) Umstände *pl* (*Mühe, Schwierigkeiten*) bother *sing*, trouble *sing*; (*Förmlichkeit*) fuss *sing*; **ohne (große) Umstände** without (much) fuss, without a (great) fuss; **das macht gar keine Umstände** it's no bother *or* trouble at all; **jdm Umstände machen** *or* **bereiten** to cause sb bother *or* trouble, to put sb out; **machen Sie bloß keine Umstände!** please don't go to any bother *or* trouble, please don't put yourself out; **einen ~ machen** to make a fuss (*mit* over).
umständehalber *adv* owing to circumstances ♦ **„~ zu verkaufen"** "forced to sell".
umständlich *adj Arbeitsweise, Methode* (awkward and) involved; (*langsam und ungeschickt*) ponderous; *Vorbereitung* elaborate; *Erklärung, Übersetzung, Anleitung* long-winded; *Abfertigung* laborious, tedious; *Arbeit, Reise* awkward ♦ **sei doch nicht so ~!** don't make such heavy weather of everything!, don't make everything twice as hard as it really is!; **er ist fürchterlich ~** he always makes such heavy weather of everything; **etw ~ machen** to make heavy weather of doing sth; **etw ~ erzählen/erklären/beschreiben** *etc* to tell/explain/describe *etc* sth in a roundabout way; **das ist vielleicht ~** what a palaver (*inf*); **das ist mir zu ~** that's too much palaver (*inf*) *or* trouble *or* bother.
Umständlichkeit *f siehe adj* involvedness; ponderousness; elaborateness; long-windedness; laboriousness, tediousness; awkwardness ♦ **ihre ~** the way she makes such heavy weather of everything.
Umstands-: ~bestimmung *f* adverbial phrase; **~kleid** *nt* maternity dress; **~kleidung** *f* maternity wear; **~kommissar, ~krämer** *m* (*inf*) fusspot (*inf*), fussbudget (*US inf*); **~moden** *pl* maternity fashions *pl*; **~wort** *nt* adverb.
umstecken *vt sep* **(a)** (*Elec*) *Kontakt etc* to move; *Gerät etc auch* to plug into another socket. **(b)** *Kleid, Saum* to pin up. **(c)** *Pflanzen* to transplant.
umstehen* *vt insep irreg* to surround, to stand round ♦ **ein von Bäumen umstandener Teich** a pond surrounded by trees.
umstehend [1] *adj attr* **(a)** (*in der Nähe stehend*) standing round about ♦ **die U~en** the bystanders, the people standing round about. **(b)** (*umseitig*) overleaf ♦ **die ~e Erklärung** the explanation overleaf; **im ~en** overleaf.
[2] *adv* overleaf.
Umsteige-: ~bahnhof *m* interchange (station); **~berechtigung** *f* **mit diesem Fahrschein haben Sie keine ~berechtigung** you can't change (buses/trains) on this ticket; **~fahrschein** *m* transfer ticket; **~möglichkeit** *f* **dort haben Sie ~möglichkeit** you can change there (*nach* for).
umsteigen *vi sep irreg aux sein* **(a)** to change (*nach* for); (*in Bus, Zug etc*) to change (buses/trains *etc*) ♦ **bitte hier ~ nach Eppendorf** (all) change here for Eppendorf; **in einen anderen Wagen/von einem Auto ins andere ~** to change *or* switch carriages/cars; **bitte beim U~ beeilen!** will those passengers changing here please do so quickly.
(b) (*fig inf*) to change over, to switch (over) (*auf +acc* to).
Umsteiger *m* **-s, -** (*inf*) transfer (ticket).
umstellen¹ *sep* [1] *vti* **(a)** *Möbel etc* to rearrange, to change round; (*Gram*) *Wörter, Satz auch* to reorder; *Subjekt und Prädikat* to transpose.
(b) (*anders einstellen*) *Hebel, Telefon, Fernsehgerät, Betrieb* to switch over; *Radio* to tune *or* switch to another station; *Uhr* to alter, to put back/forward ♦ **auf etw** (*acc*) **~** (*Betrieb*) to go *or* switch over to sth; *auf Erdgas etc* to convert *or* be converted to sth; **etw auf Computer ~** to computerize sth; **der Betrieb wird auf die Produktion von Turbinen umgestellt** the factory is switching over to producing turbines.
[2] *vr* to move *or* shift about; (*fig*) to get used to a different lifestyle ♦ **sich auf etw** (*acc*) **~** to adapt *or* adjust to sth.
umstellen²* *vt insep* to surround.
Umstellung *f siehe* **umstellen¹ 1 (a)** rearrangement, changing round; reordering; transposition.
(b) switch-over; tuning to another station; alteration, putting back/forward ♦ **~ auf Erdgas** conversion to natural gas; **~ auf Computer** computerization.
(c) (*fig: das Sichumstellen*) adjustment (*auf +acc* to) ♦ **das wird eine große ~ für ihn sein** it will be a big change for him.
umsteuern¹ *vt sep Satelliten etc* to alter the course of.
umsteuern²* *vt insep Hindernis* to steer round.
umstimmen *vt sep* **(a)** *Instrument* to tune to a different pitch, to retune. **(b) jdn ~** to change sb's mind; **er war nicht umzustimmen, er ließ sich nicht ~** he was not to be persuaded.
umstoßen *vt sep irreg Gegenstand* to knock over; (*fig*) (*Mensch*) *Plan, Testament, Bestimmung etc* to change; (*Umstände etc*) *Plan, Berechnung* to upset.
umstrahlen* *vt insep* (*liter*) to shine around ♦ **von einem Heiligenschein umstrahlt** surrounded *or* illuminated by a halo.
umstritten *adj* (*fraglich*) controversial; (*wird noch debattiert*) disputed.
umstrukturieren* *vt sep* to restructure.
Umstrukturierung *f* restructuring.
umstülpen *vt sep* to turn upside down; *Tasche* to turn out; *Manschetten etc* to turn up *or* back; *Seite* to turn over; *Wörterbucheintrag* to reverse.
Umsturz *m* coup (d'état), putsch.
Umsturzbewegung *f* subversive movement.
umstürzen *sep* [1] *vt* to overturn; *Puddingform etc* to turn upside down; (*fig*) *Regierung, Staat, Verfassung* to overthrow; *Demokratie* to destroy ♦ **~de Veränderungen** revolutionary changes.
[2] *vi aux sein* to fall; (*Möbelstück, Wagen etc*) to overturn.
Umstürzler(in *f*) *m* **-s, -** subversive.
umstürzlerisch *adj* subversive ♦ **sich ~ betätigen** to engage in subversive activities.
Umsturzversuch *m* attempted coup *or* putsch.
umtanzen* *vt insep* to dance round.
umtaufen *vt sep* to rebaptize; (*umbenennen*) to rename, to rechristen.
Umtausch *m* exchange ♦ **diese Waren sind vom ~ ausgeschlossen** these goods cannot be exchanged; **beim ~ bitte den Kassenzettel vorlegen** please produce the receipt when exchanging goods.
umtauschen *vt sep* to (ex)change; *Geld* to change, to convert (*form*) (*in +acc* into).
umtopfen *vt sep Blumen etc* to repot.
umtost *adj* (*liter*) buffeted (*von* by).
Umtriebe *pl* machinations *pl* ♦ **umstürzlerische ~** subversive activities.
umtriebig *adj* (*betriebsam*) go-getting.
Umtrunk *m* drink.
umtun *vr sep irreg* (*inf*) to look around (*nach* for).
U-Musik *f abbr of* **Unterhaltungsmusik.**
umverteilen* *vt sep or insep* to redistribute.
Umverteilung *f* redistribution.
umwachsen* *vt insep irreg* to grow round ♦ **ein von Bäumen ~er Teich** a pond with trees growing all round it.
Umwallung *f* ramparts *pl.*
Umwälz|anlage *f* circulating plant.
umwälzen *vt sep Luft, Wasser* to circulate; (*fig*) to change radically, to revolutionize.
umwälzend *adj* (*fig*) radical; *Veränderungen auch* sweeping; *Ereignisse* revolutionary.
Umwälzpumpe *f* circulating pump.
Umwälzung *f* (*Tech*) circulation; (*fig*) radical change.
umwandelbar *adj* (*in +acc* to) convertible; *Strafe* commutable.
umwandeln¹ *sep* [1] *vt* to change (*in +acc* into); (*Comm, Fin, Sci*) to convert (*in +acc* to); (*Jur*) *Strafe* to commute (*in +acc* to); (*fig*) to transform (*in +acc* into) ♦ **er ist wie umgewandelt** he's a changed man *or* a (completely) different person.
[2] *vr* to be converted (*in +acc* into).
umwandeln*² *vt insep* (*liter*) to walk round.
Umwandlung *f siehe* **umwandeln¹** change; conversion; commutation; transformation.
umweben* *vt insep irreg* (*liter*) to envelop ♦ **viele Sagen umwoben das alte Schloß** many legends had been woven round the old castle; **ein von Sagen umwobener Ort** a place around which many legends have been woven.
umwechseln *vt sep Geld* to change (*in +acc* to, into).
Umwechslung *f* exchange (*in +acc* for).
Umweg ['umveːk] *m* detour; (*fig*) roundabout way ♦ **einen ~ machen/fahren** to go a long way round; (*absichtlich auch*) to make a detour; **wenn das für Sie kein ~ ist** if it doesn't take you out of your way; **auf ~en (ans Ziel kommen)** (to get there) by a roundabout *or* circuitous route; (*fig*) (to get there) in a rather roundabout way; **auf dem ~ über jdn** (*fig*) indirectly via sb; **etw auf ~en erfahren** (*fig*) to find sth out indirectly.
Umwegfinanzierung *f* indirect financing.
umwehen¹* *vt insep* to fan, to blow round ♦ **sich vom Wind ~ lassen** to be fanned by the breeze.
umwehen² *vt sep* to blow over.
Umwelt *f, no pl* environment.
Umwelt- *in cpds* environmental; **~alarm** *m* environmental alarm; **~auflage** *f* (*Admin*) ecological requirement; **u~bedingt** *adj* caused by the environment; **~behörde** *f* environmental authority; **~belastung** *f* ecological damage, damage to the environment; ⚠**u~bewußt** *adj* environmentally *or* ecologically aware; ⚠**~bewußtsein** *nt* environmental *or* ecological awareness; **~bundesamt** *nt* Department of the Environment; **~engel** *m* **der blaue ~engel** *symbol attached to a product guaranteeing environmental friendliness*; **~erziehung** *f* education in environmental problems; **u~feindlich** *adj* ecologically harmful, damaging to the environment; **u~freundlich** *adj* environmentally *or* ecologically friendly, eco-friendly; **~gefährdend** *adj* harmful to the environment; **~gefährdung** *f* endangering of the environment; **u~geschädigt** *adj* environmentally deprived; **u~gestört** *adj* (*Psych*) maladjusted (*due to adverse social factors*); **~gift** *nt* environmental pollutant; **~karte** *f cheap ticket to encourage use of public transport*; **~katastrophe** *f* ecological disaster; **~krankheiten** *pl* diseases *pl* caused by pollution; **~kriminalität** *f* environmental crimes *pl*; **~krise** *f* ecological crisis; **~ministerium** *nt* Ministry of the Environment; **~papier** *nt siehe* **~schutzpapier**; **~pfennig** *m* levy on petrol (*used to improve the environment*); **~planung** *f* ecological planning; **~politik** *f* ecological policy; **~qualität** *f* quality of life; **~schaden** *m* damage to the environment; **u~schädlich** *adj* ecologically harmful, harmful to the environment; **u~schonend** *adj* environmentally *or* ecologically friendly, eco-friendly.

Umweltschutz *m* environmental protection *no art.*
Umweltschützer *m* conservationist, environmentalist.
Umweltschutz-: **~organisation** *f* ecology group; **~papier** *nt* recycled paper; **~technik** *f* conservation technology.
Umwelt-: **~steuer** *f* ecology tax; **~sünder** *m* (*inf*) polluter; **~verschmutzung** *f* pollution (of the environment); **~verseuchung** *f* contamination of the environment; **~verstöße** *pl* environmental offences *pl*; **u~verträglich** *adj Produkte, Stoffe* ecologically harmless; **~wärme** *f* ambient heat; **~zerstörung** *f* destruction of the environment.
umwenden *sep irreg* [1] *vt* to turn over.
[2] *vr* to turn (round) (*nach* to).
umwerben* *vt insep irreg* to court.
umwerfen *vt sep irreg* **(a)** *Gegenstand* to knock over; *Möbelstück etc* to overturn.
(b) (*fig: ändern*) to upset, to knock on the head (*inf*).
(c) *jdn* (*körperlich*) to knock down; (*Ringen*) to throw down; (*fig inf*) to stun, to bowl over ◆ **ein Whisky wirft dich nicht gleich um** one whisky won't knock you out.
(d) **sich** (*dat*) **etw ~** to throw *or* put sth round one's shoulders.
umwerfend *adj* fantastic ◆ **von ~er Komik** hilarious, a scream (*inf*).
Umwertung *f* re-evaluation.
umwickeln[1]* *vt insep* to wrap round; (*mit Band, Verband auch*) to swathe (*liter*) (*mit* in); (*mit Schnur, Draht etc*) to wind round ◆ **etw mit Stoff/Draht ~** to wrap cloth/wind wire round sth.
umwickeln[2] *vt sep* to wrap round; (*Garn etc*) to rewind ◆ **jdm/sich etw ~** to wrap sth round sb/oneself.
umwinden* *vt insep irreg* (*geh*) to wind round (*mit* with) ◆ **etw mit Blumen ~** to entwine sth with flowers.
umwittert *adj* (*geh*) surrounded (*von* by) ◆ **von Geheimnissen ~** shrouded in mystery.
umwogen* *vt insep* (*liter*) to wash round.
umwohnend *adj* neighbouring ◆ **die U~en** the local residents.
umwölken* *vr insep* (*geh*) to cloud over; (*Sonne, Mond auch*) to become veiled in cloud (*liter*), to darken; (*Berggipfel*) to become shrouded in cloud; (*fig: Stern*) to cloud.
umzäunen* *vt insep* to fence round.
Umzäunung *f* (*das Umzäunen*) fencing round; (*Zaun*) fence, fencing.
umziehen[1] *sep irreg* [1] *vi aux sein* to move (house); (*Firma etc*) to move ◆ **nach Köln ~** to move to Cologne.
[2] *vt* **(a)** **die Kinder ~** to get the children changed. **(b)** (*hum: den Umzug für jdn durchführen*) to move.
[3] *vr* to change, to get changed.
umziehen[2]* *insep irreg* (*geh*) [1] *vt* to surround.
[2] *vr* (*Himmel*) to cloud over (*auch fig*), to become overcast *or* cloudy.
umzingeln* *vt insep* to surround, to encircle.
Umzingelung *f* encirclement.
Umzug ['ʊmtsu:k] *m* **(a)** (*Wohnungs~*) move, removal ◆ **wann soll euer ~ sein?** when are you moving? **(b)** (*Festzug*) procession; (*Demonstrationszug*) parade.
Umzugs-: **~karton** *m* packing case; **~kosten** *pl* removal costs *pl*.
UN [u:'ɛn] *pl* UN *sing*, United Nations *sing*.
un|ab|änderlich *adj* **(a)** (*unwiderruflich*) unalterable; *Entschluß, Urteil auch* irrevocable, irreversible ◆ **~ feststehen** to be absolutely certain. **(b)** (*ewig*) *Gesetze, Schicksal* immutable.
Un|ab|änderlichkeit *f siehe adj* **(a)** unalterability; irrevocability, irreversibility. **(b)** immutability.
un|abdingbar, un|abdinglich *adj Voraussetzung, Forderung* indispensable; *Recht* inalienable.
Un|abdingbarkeit *f siehe adj* indispensability; inalienability.
un-: **~abgelegt** *adj* unfiled; **~abgeschlossen** *adj* (*nicht verschlossen*) unlocked; (*nicht fertiggestellt*) unfinished.
un|abhängig *adj* independent (*von* of); *Journalist* freelance ◆ **das ist ~ davon, ob/wann** *etc* that does not depend on *or* is not dependent on whether/when *etc*; **~ davon, was Sie meinen** irrespective of *or* regardless of what you think; **sich ~ machen** to go one's own way; **sich von jdm/etw ~ machen** to become independent of sb/sth.
Un|abhängigkeit *f* independence.
Un|abhängigkeits-: **~bewegung** *f* independence movement; **~erklärung** *f* declaration of independence; **~krieg** *m* war of independence.
un|abkömmlich *adj* (*geh*) busy, engaged *pred* (*form*).
un|ablässig *adj* continual; *Regen, Lärm etc auch* incessant; *Versuche, Bemühungen auch* unremitting, unceasing ◆ **~ für den Frieden kämpfen** to fight unceasingly for peace.
un|absehbar *adj* **(a)** (*fig*) *Folgen etc* unforeseeable; *Schaden* incalculable, immeasurable ◆ **der Schaden/die Zahl der Toten ist noch ~** the amount of damage/the number of dead is not yet known; **auf ~e Zeit** for an indefinite period.
(b) (*lit*) interminable; *Weite* boundless ◆ **~ lang sein** to seem to be interminable; **in ~er Weite** boundlessly; **in ~er Ferne** in the far far distance.
Un|absehbarkeit *f siehe adj* **(a)** unforeseeability; incalculability, immeasurability. **(b)** interminability; boundlessness.
Un-: **u~absichtlich** *adj* unintentional; (*aus Versehen auch*) accidental; **u~abwählbar** *adj* **er ist u~abwählbar** he cannot be voted out of office; **u~abweisbar, u~abweislich** *adj* irrefutable; **u~abwendbar** *adj* inevitable; **~abwendbarkeit** *f* inevitability; **u~achtsam** *adj* (*unaufmerksam*) inattentive; (*nicht sorgsam*) careless; (*unbedacht*) thoughtless; **~achtsamkeit** *f siehe adj* inattentiveness; carelessness; thoughtlessness.
un|ähnlich *adj* dissimilar ◆ **einer Sache** (*dat*) **~ sein** to be unlike sth *or* dissimilar to sth; **einander ~** unlike each other, dissimilar.
Un|ähnlichkeit *f* dissimilarity.
un-: **~anfechtbar** *adj Urteil, Entscheidung, Gesetz* unchallengeable, incontestable; *Argument etc* unassailable; *Beweis* irrefutable; **~angebracht** *adj Bescheidenheit, Bemerkung* uncalled-for; *Sorge, Sparsamkeit, Bemühungen auch* misplaced; (*für Kinder, Altersstufe etc*) unsuitable; (*unzweckmäßig*) *Maßnahmen* inappropriate; **~angefochten** *adj* unchallenged *no adv*; *Testament, Wahlkandidat* uncontested; *Urteil, Entscheidung auch* undisputed, uncontested; **Liverpool führt ~angefochten die Tabelle** Liverpool are unchallenged at the top of the league; **~angemeldet** *adj* unannounced *no adv*; *Besucher* unexpected; *Patient etc* without an appointment.
un|angemessen *adj* (*zu hoch*) unreasonable, out of all proportion; (*unzulänglich*) inadequate ◆ **einer Sache** (*dat*) **~ sein** to be inappropriate to sth; **dem Ereignis ~ sein** to be unsuitable for *or* inappropriate to the occasion, to ill befit the occasion.
un|angenehm *adj* unpleasant; *Mensch, Arbeit, Geschmack, Geruch auch* disagreeable; (*peinlich*) *Situation auch* awkward, embarrassing; *Zwischenfall, Begegnung* embarrassing ◆ **das ist mir immer so ~** I never like that, I don't like that at all; **es war mir ~, das tun zu müssen** I didn't like having to do it; **es ist mir ~, daß ich Sie gestört habe** I feel bad about having disturbed you; **mein ständiges Husten war mir ~** I felt bad *or* embarrassed about coughing all the time; **~ berührt sein** to be embarrassed (*von* by); **er kann ~ werden** he can get quite nasty.
un-: ⚠**~angepaßt** *adj* non-conformist; **~angetastet** *adj* untouched; **~angetastet bleiben** (*Rechte*) not to be violated; **~angreifbar** *adj Macht, Herrscher* unassailable; *Argument auch* irrefutable, unchallengeable; *Festung, Land* impregnable; **~annehmbar** *adj* unacceptable.
Un|annehmlichkeit *f usu pl* trouble *no pl*; (*lästige Mühe auch*) bother *no pl* ◆ **~en haben/bekommen** *or* **kriegen** to be in/to get into trouble; **das macht mir nicht die geringste ~** it's no trouble *or* bother at all; **mit etw ~en haben** to have a lot of trouble with sth; **mit den Behörden ~en haben** to get into trouble with the authorities.
un|ansehnlich *adj* unsightly; *Frau etc* plain; *Tapete, Möbel* shabby; *Nahrungsmittel* unappetizing.
un|anständig *adj* **(a)** (*unkultiviert, unerzogen*) ill-mannered, bad-mannered; (*frech, unverschämt*) rude; (*charakterlich minderwertig*) unprincipled ◆ **so was U~es!** how rude!
(b) (*obszön, anstößig*) dirty; *Witz, Lied auch* rude; *Wörter auch* four-letter *attr*, rude; (*vulgär*) *Kleidung* indecent ◆ **~e Reden führen** to talk smut.
Un|anständigkeit *f siehe adj* **(a)** bad *or* ill manners *pl*; rudeness *no pl*; unprincipledness *no pl*. **(b)** dirtiness; rudeness; indecency ◆ **~en erzählen** to tell dirty jokes/stories.
Un-: **u~antastbar** *adj* (*nicht zu verletzen*) inviolable, sacrosanct; (*über Zweifel erhaben*) unimpeachable; **~antastbarkeit** *f siehe adj* inviolability; unimpeachability; **u~appetitlich** *adj* (*lit, fig*) unappetizing.
Un|art *f* bad habit; (*Ungezogenheit*) rude habit.
un|artig *adj* naughty.
Un|artigkeit *f* **(a)** *no pl* (*Unartigsein*) naughtiness. **(b)** (*Handlungsweise*) naughty behaviour *no pl or* trick.
Un-: **u~artikuliert** *adj* inarticulate; (*undeutlich*) unclear, indistinct; **u~ästhetisch** *adj* unappetizing; **u~aufdringlich** *adj* unobtrusive; *Parfüm auch* discreet; *Mensch* unassuming; **~aufdringlichkeit** *f siehe adj* unobtrusiveness; discreetness; unassuming nature.
un|auffällig [1] *adj* inconspicuous; (*unscheinbar, schlicht*) unobtrusive ◆ **die Narbe/sein Hinken ist ziemlich ~** the scar/his limp isn't very noticeable; **er ist ein ziemlich ~er junger Mann** he's not the kind of young man you notice particularly.
[2] *adv* unobtrusively, discreetly; *siehe* **folgen**.
Un|auffälligkeit *f siehe adj* inconspicuousness; unobtrusiveness.
un|auffindbar *adj* nowhere to be found; *Verbrecher, vermißte Person* untraceable.
un|aufgefordert [1] *adj* unsolicited (*esp Comm*).
[2] *adv* without being asked ◆ **~ anfallende Arbeiten erledigen können** to be able to work on one's own initiative; **jdm ~ Prospekte zuschicken** to send sb unsolicited brochures; **~ zugesandte Manuskripte** unsolicited manuscripts.
Un-: **u~aufgeklärt** *adj* **(a)** unexplained; *Verbrechen* unsolved; **(b)** *Mensch* ignorant; (*sexuell*) ignorant of the facts of life; **u~aufgeräumt** *adj* untidy; **u~aufgeregt** *adj Musik* unobtrusive; **u~aufhaltbar** *adj* unstoppable; **u~aufhaltsam** *adj* **(a)** (*unaufhaltbar*) unstoppable; **(b)** (*unerbittlich*) inexorable; **u~aufhörlich** *adj* continual, constant, incessant; **u~auflösbar, u~auflöslich** *adj* (*Math*) insoluble; (*Chem auch*), *Ehe* indissoluble; **~auflösbarkeit, ~auflöslichkeit** *f siehe adj* insolubility; indissolubility; **u~aufmerksam** *adj* inattentive; (*flüchtig*) *Leser etc* unobservant; **da war ich einen Augenblick u~aufmerksam** I didn't pay attention for a moment; **~aufmerksamkeit** *f siehe adj* inattentiveness; unobservance; **u~aufrichtig** *adj* insincere; **~aufrichtigkeit** *f* insincerity; **u~aufschiebbar** *adj* urgent; **es ist u~aufschiebbar** it can't be put off *or* delayed *or* postponed; **u~ausbleiblich** *adj* inevitable, unavoidable; **u~ausdenkbar** *adj* unimaginable, unthinkable; **u~ausführbar** *adj* impracticable, unfeasible; **u~ausgefüllt** *adj* **(a)** *Formular etc* blank; **(b)** *Leben, Mensch* unfulfilled.
un|ausgeglichen *adj* unbalanced; *Verhältnis auch, Vermögensverteilung etc*

unequal; *Stil auch* disharmonious; *Mensch* (*launisch*) moody; (*verhaltensgestört*) unstable ◆ **ein Mensch mit ~em Wesen** a person of uneven temper.

Un|ausgeglichenheit *f siehe adj* imbalance; inequality; disharmony; moodiness; instability ◆ **die ~ seines Wesens** the unevenness of his temper.

Un-: u~ausgegoren *adj* immature; *Idee, Plan auch* half-baked (*inf*); *Jüngling auch* callow; **u~ausgeschlafen** *adj* tired; **er ist u~ausgeschlafen/sieht u~ausgeschlafen aus** he hasn't had/looks as if he hasn't had enough sleep; **u~ausgesetzt** *adj* incessant, constant, continual; **u~ausgesprochen** *adj* unsaid *pred*, unspoken; **u~ausgewogen** *adj* unbalanced; **~ausgewogenheit** *f* imbalance; **u~auslöschlich** *adj* (*geh*) (*lit, fig*) indelible; **u~ausrottbar** *adj Unkraut* indestructible; (*fig*) *Vorurteile, Vorstellung etc* ineradicable.

un|aussprechlich *adj* **(a)** *Wort, Laut* unpronounceable. **(b)** *Schönheit, Leid etc* inexpressible ◆ **er verehrt sie ~** he absolutely worships her. **(c)** (*liter: ungeheuerlich*) *Tat, Verbrechen* unspeakable. **(d) die U~en** (*hum*) one's unmentionables (*inf*).

Un-: u~ausstehlich *adj* intolerable; *Mensch, Art, Eigenschaft auch* insufferable; **u~ausweichlich** *adj* unavoidable, inevitable; *Folgen auch* inescapable; **~ausweichlichkeit** *f* inevitability; (*Dilemma*) dilemma.

unbändig *adj* **(a)** (*ausgelassen, ungestüm*) *Kind* boisterous ◆ **sie freuten sich ~** they were dancing around (with joy). **(b)** (*ungezügelt*) unrestrained *no adv*; *Haß, Zorn etc auch* unbridled *no adv*; *Hunger* enormous.

Un-: u~bar *adj* (*Comm*) **etw u~bar bezahlen** not to pay sth in cash, to pay sth by cheque/credit card *etc*; **u~bare Zahlungsweise** non-cash payment; **u~barmherzig** *adj* merciless; *Mensch auch* pitiless; **~barmherzigkeit** *f siehe adj* mercilessness; pitilessness; **u~beabsichtigt** *adj* unintentional.

unbe|achtet *adj* unnoticed; *Warnung, Vorschläge* unheeded ◆ **jdn/etw ~ lassen** not to take any notice of sb/sth; **wollen wir die weniger wichtigen Punkte zunächst ~ lassen** let's leave aside the less important points for the time being; **das dürfen wir nicht ~ lassen** we mustn't overlook that, we mustn't leave that out of account.

Un-: u~beachtlich *adj* insignificant; **u~beanstandet** [1] *adj* not objected to; **etw u~beanstandet lassen** to let sth pass *or* go; [2] *adv* without objection; **das Paket wurde u~beanstandet weitergeleitet** the parcel got through without any problems; **u~beantwortet** *adj* unanswered; **u~bebaut** *adj Land* undeveloped; *Grundstück* vacant; *Feld* uncultivated; **u~bedacht** *adj* (*hastig*) rash; (*unüberlegt*) thoughtless; **~bedachtheit** *f* rashness; thoughtlessness; **u~bedachtsam** *adj siehe* **u~bedacht**; **u~bedarft** *adj* (*inf*) simple-minded; *Mensch* (*auf bestimmtem Gebiet*) green (*inf*), clueless (*inf*); (*dumm*) dumb (*inf*); **u~bedeckt** *adj* bare; **u~bedeckten Hauptes** (*geh*), **mit u~bedecktem Haupt** (*geh*) bare-headed.

unbedenklich [1] *adj* (*ungefährlich*) completely harmless, quite safe; (*sorglos*) thoughtless.

[2] *adv* (*ungefährlich*) quite safely, without coming to any harm; (*ohne zu zögern*) without thinking (twice *inf*).

Unbedenklichkeit *f siehe adj* harmlessness; thoughtlessness.

Unbedenklichkeitsbescheinigung *f* (*Jur*) *document certifying that one has no taxes, loans etc outstanding.*

unbedeutend *adj* (*unwichtig*) insignificant, unimportant; (*geringfügig*) *Rückgang, Änderung etc* minor, minimal.

➤ **unbedingt** [1] *adj attr* (*absolut*) *Ruhe, Verschwiegenheit* absolute; (*bedingungslos*) *Gehorsam, Treue auch* implicit, unconditional; *Anhänger etc* unreserved; *Reflex* unconditioned.

➤ [2] *adv* (*auf jeden Fall*) really; *nötig, erforderlich* absolutely ◆ **ich muß ~ mal wieder ins Kino gehen** I really must go to the cinema again; **ich mußte sie ~ sprechen** I really *or* absolutely had to speak to her; (*äußerst wichtig*) it was imperative that I spoke to her; **müßt ihr denn ~ in meinem Arbeitszimmer spielen?** do you *have* to play in my study?; **das ist nicht meine Schuld, du wolltest ja ~ ins Kino gehen!** it's not my fault, you *would* go to the cinema *or* you were (hell-)bent on going to the cinema; **er wollte ~ mit Renate verreisen** he was (hell-)bent on going away with Renate; **~!** of course!, I should say so!; **nicht ~** not necessarily; **nicht ~ nötig** not absolutely *or* strictly necessary.

Unbedingtheit *f* (*Bedingungslosigkeit*) unconditionalness; (*von Treue, Vertrauen auch*) absoluteness.

Un-: u~beeidigt *adj* (*Jur*) unsworn *usu attr*, not on oath; **u~beeindruckt** *adj* unimpressed; **⚠u~beeinflußbar** *adj Entwicklung* unalterable; *Mensch* unswayable, uninfluenceable; **⚠u~beeinflußt** *adj* uninfluenced (*von* by); **u~befahrbar** *adj Straße, Weg* impassable; *Gewässer* unnavigable; **u~befahren** *adj Straße, Fluß* unused; **u~befangen** *adj* **(a)** (*unparteiisch*) impartial, unbiased *no adv*, objective; **(b)** (*natürlich*) natural; (*ungehemmt*) uninhibited; **~befangenheit** *f siehe adj* **(a)** impartiality, objectiveness; **(b)** naturalness; uninhibitedness; **u~befleckt** *adj* (*liter*) spotless, unsullied, untarnished; *Jungfrau* undefiled; **die ~befleckte Empfängnis** the Immaculate Conception; **u~befriedigend** *adj* unsatisfactory; **u~befriedigt** *adj* (*frustriert*) unsatisfied; (*unerfüllt auch*) unfulfilled; (*unzufrieden*) dissatisfied; **u~befristet** *adj Arbeitsverhältnis, Vertrag* for an indefinite period; *Aufenthaltserlaubnis, Visum* permanent; **etw u~befristet verlängern** to extend sth indefinitely *or* for an indefinite period; **u~befruchtet** *adj* unfertilized; **u~befugt** *adj* unauthorized; **Eintritt für ~befugte verboten, kein Zutritt für ~befugte** no admittance to unauthorized persons; **u~begabt** *adj* untalented, ungifted; **für etw u~begabt sein** to have no talent for sth; **er ist handwerklich völlig u~begabt** he's no handyman; **~begabtheit** *f* lack of talent; **u~beglichen** *adj* unpaid, unsettled.

unbegreiflich *adj* (*unverständlich*) incomprehensible; *Leichtsinn, Irrtum, Dummheit* inconceivable; (*unergründlich*) *Menschen, Länder* inscrutable ◆ **es wird mir immer ~ bleiben, wie/daß ...** I shall never understand how/why ...; **es ist uns allen ~, wie das passieren konnte** none of us can understand how it happened; **das U~e** (*Rel*) the Unknowable.

unbegreiflicherweise *adv* inexplicably.

unbegrenzt *adj* unlimited; *Möglichkeiten, Energie, Vertrauen etc auch* limitless, boundless, infinite; *Land, Meer etc* boundless; *Zeitspanne, Frist* indefinite ◆ **zeitlich ~** indefinite; **~, auf ~e Zeit** indefinitely; **er hat ~e Zeit** he has unlimited time; **in ~er Höhe** of an unlimited *or* indefinite amount; **es ist nach oben ~** there's no upper limit (on it), the sky's the limit (*inf*); **„~ haltbar"** "will keep indefinitely".

unbegründet *adj Angst, Verdacht, Zweifel* unfounded, groundless, without foundation; *Maßnahme* unwarranted ◆ **eine Klage als ~ abweisen** to dismiss a case.

unbehaart *adj* hairless; (*auf dem Kopf*) bald.

Unbehagen *nt* (feeling of) uneasiness *or* disquiet, uneasy feeling; (*Unzufriedenheit*) discontent (*an +dat* with); (*körperlich*) discomfort.

unbehaglich *adj* uncomfortable; *Gefühl auch* uneasy ◆ **sich in jds Gesellschaft** (*dat*) **~ fühlen** to feel uncomfortable *or* ill at ease in sb's company.

Un-: u~behauen *adj* unhewn; **u~behaust** *adj* (*liter*) homeless; **u~behelligt** *adj* (*unbelästigt*) unmolested; (*unkontrolliert*) unchecked; **jdn u~behelligt lassen** to leave sb alone; (*Polizei etc*) not to stop sb; **u~beherrscht** *adj* uncontrolled; *Mensch* lacking self-control; (*gierig*) greedy; **u~beherrscht reagieren** to react in an uncontrolled way *or* without any self-control; **~beherrschtheit** *f siehe adj* lack of self-control; greediness; **u~behindert** *adj* unhindered, unimpeded; *Sicht* clear, uninterrupted.

unbeholfen *adj* clumsy, awkward; (*hilflos*) helpless; (*plump*) *Annäherungsversuch* clumsy ◆ **mit seinem verletzten Bein geht er sehr ~** he walks very awkwardly with his injured leg.

Unbeholfenheit *f, no pl siehe adj* clumsiness, awkwardness; helplessness; clumsiness.

un-: ~beirrbar *adj* unwavering; **~beirrt** *adj* **(a)** (*ohne sich irritieren zu lassen*) unflustered; **(b)** *siehe* **~beirrbar**.

unbekannt *adj* unknown; *Gesicht auch* unfamiliar; *Flugzeug, Flugobjekt etc* unidentified ◆ **eine (mir) ~e Stadt/Stimme** a town/voice I didn't know, a town/voice unknown to me; **das war mir ~** I didn't know that, I was unaware of that; **dieser Herr/diese Gegend ist mir ~** I don't know *or* I'm not acquainted with this gentleman/area; **Angst ist ihm ~** he doesn't know what fear is *or* the meaning of (the word) fear; **es wird Ihnen nicht ~ sein, daß ...** you will no doubt be aware that ...; **~e Größe** (*Math, fig*) unknown quantity; **aus ~er Ursache** for some unknown reason; **nach ~ verzogen** moved — address unknown; **ich bin hier ~** (*inf*) I'm a stranger here; **~e Täter** person or persons unknown; **Strafanzeige gegen U~e** charge against person or persons unknown.

Unbekannte *f* **-n, -n** (*Math*) unknown.

Unbekannte(r) *mf decl as adj* stranger ◆ **der große ~** (*hum*) the mystery man/person *etc*.

unbekannterweise *adv* **grüße sie/ihn ~ von mir** give her/him my regards although I don't know her/him.

unbekleidet *adj* bare ◆ **sie war ~** she had nothing *or* no clothes on, she was bare.

unbekümmert *adj* **(a)** (*unbesorgt*) unconcerned ◆ **sei ganz ~** don't worry; **das kannst du ~ tun** you needn't worry about doing that. **(b)** (*sorgenfrei*) carefree.

Unbekümmertheit *f siehe adj* **(a)** lack of concern. **(b)** carefreeness.

unbelastet *adj* **(a)** (*ohne Last*) unloaded, unladen ◆ **das linke Bein ~ lassen** to keep one's weight off one's left leg.

(b) (*ohne Schulden*) unencumbered.

(c) (*Pol: ohne Schuld*) guiltless.

(d) (*ohne Sorgen*) free from care *or* worries ◆ **von Hemmungen/Ängsten** *etc* **~** free from inhibitions/fears *etc*.

Un-: u~belebt *adj Straße, Gegend* quiet; **die u~belebte Natur** the inanimate world, inanimate nature; **u~beleckt** *adj* **u~beleckt von aller Kultur sein** (*inf*) to be completely uncultured; **u~belehrbar** *adj* fixed in one's views; *Rassist etc* dyed-in-the-wool *attr*; **er ist u~belehrbar** you can't tell him anything; **wenn du so u~belehrbar bist** if you won't be told; **~belehrbarkeit** *f* **seine ~belehrbarkeit** the fact that you just can't tell him anything; **u~belesen** *adj* unread, unlettered; **u~beleuchtet** *adj* unlit; *Fahrzeug* without lights; **u~belichtet** *adj* (*Phot*) unexposed; **u~beliebt** *adj* unpopular (*bei* with); **sich u~beliebt machen** to make oneself unpopular; **~beliebtheit** *f* unpopularity (*bei* with); **u~bemannt** *adj Raumflug, Station* unmanned; *Fahrzeug* driverless; *Flugzeug* pilotless; (*inf: ohne Mann*) without a man; **u~bemerkbar** *adj* imperceptible; **u~bemerkt** *adj* unnoticed; (*nicht gesehen auch*) unobserved; **u~bemerkt bleiben** to escape attention, to go unnoticed.

unbemittelt *adj* without means ◆ **~e Studenten erhalten vom Staat eine Beihilfe** students without (any) means of their own receive state aid.

unbenommen *adj pred* (*form*) **es bleibt** *or* **ist Ihnen ~, zu ...** you are (quite) free *or* at liberty to ...; **das bleibt** *or* **ist dir ~** you're quite free *or* at liberty to do so.

un-: ~benutzbar *adj* unusable; **~benutzt** *adj* unused.

unbe|obachtet *adj* unobserved, unnoticed ◆ **in einem ~en Moment** when nobody was looking; **wenn er sich ~ fühlt ...** when he thinks nobody is looking ...

unbequem *adj (ungemütlich)* uncomfortable, uncomfy; *(lästig) Mensch, Frage, Situation* awkward, inconvenient; *Aufgabe* unpleasant; *(mühevoll)* difficult ◆ **diese Schuhe sind mir zu ~** these shoes are too uncomfortable; **der Regierung/den Behörden** *etc* **~ sein** to be an embarrassment to the government/authorities *etc.*

Unbequemlichkeit *f siehe adj* uncomfortableness, uncomfiness; awkwardness, inconvenience; unpleasantness; difficulty.

Un-: u~berechenbar *adj* unpredictable; **~berechenbarkeit** *f* unpredictability; **u~berechtigt** *adj (ungerechtfertigt)* unwarranted; *Sorge, Kritik etc* unfounded; *(unbefugt)* unauthorized; **u~berechtigterweise** *adv siehe adj* without justification; without reason; without authority.

unberücksichtigt *adj* unconsidered ◆ **etw ~ lassen** not to consider sth, to leave sth out of consideration; **die Frage ist ~ geblieben** this question has not been considered; **ein bisher ~er Punkt** a point which has not yet been considered.

unberufen *adj* **~ (toi, toi, toi)!** touch wood!

unberührbar *adj* untouchable ◆ **die U~en** the untouchables.

unberührt *adj* **(a)** untouched; *(fig) Wald etc* virgin; *Natur* unspoiled ◆ **~ sein** *(Mädchen)* to be a virgin; **~ in die Ehe gehen** to be a virgin when one marries; **das Essen ~ stehenlassen** to leave one's food untouched.
(b) *(mitleidlos)* unmoved ◆ **das kann ihn nicht ~ lassen** he can't help but be moved by that.
(c) *(unbetroffen)* unaffected.

Unberührtheit *f (von Mädchen)* virginity ◆ **wo finden Sie sonst noch diese ~ der Natur?** where else will you find nature so completely unspoiled?

unbeschadet *prep +gen (form)* regardless of ◆ **~ dessen, daß** ... regardless of the fact that ...

unbeschädigt *adj* undamaged; *Geschirr, Glas etc auch* intact, unbroken; *Siegel* unbroken; *(inf) Mensch* intact *(inf)*, unharmed, in one piece *(inf)* ◆ **~ bleiben** not to be damaged/broken; *(seelisch etc)* to come off unscathed.

unbeschäftigt *adj (müßig)* idle; *(arbeitslos)* not working.

unbescheiden *adj* presumptuous ◆ **darf ich mir die ~e Frage erlauben, ...?** I hope you don't think me impertinent but might I ask ...?, I hope you don't mind my asking, but ...?

Unbescheidenheit *f* presumptuousness; *(von Mensch auch)* presumption.

Un-: u~bescholten *adj (geh)* respectable; *Ruf* spotless; *(Jur)* with no previous convictions; **~bescholtenheit** *f (geh) siehe adj* respectability; spotlessness; lack of previous convictions; **u~beschrankt** *adj Bahnübergang* without gates, unguarded.

unbeschränkt *adj* unrestricted; *Macht* absolute; *Geldmittel, Haftung, Zeit, Geduld* unlimited; *Vertrauen* unbounded, boundless; *Freiheit, Vollmacht auch* limitless ◆ **wieviel darf ich mitnehmen?** — **~** how much can I take? — there's no limit *or* restriction; **jdm ~e Vollmacht geben** to give sb carte blanche.

unbeschreiblich *adj* indescribable; *Frechheit* tremendous, enormous ◆ **~ zunehmen** *(zahlenmäßig)* to show a staggering increase.

un-: ~beschrieben *adj* blank; *siehe* **Blatt**; **~beschwert** *adj* **(a)** *(sorgenfrei)* carefree; *Melodien* light; *Unterhaltung, Lektüre* light-hearted; **(b)** *(ohne Gewicht)* unweighted; **~beseelt** *adj (liter) siehe* **~belebt.**

unbesehen *adv* indiscriminately; *(ohne es anzusehen)* without looking at it/them ◆ **das glaube ich dir ~** I believe it if you say so; **das glaube ich dir nicht ~** I'll believe that when I see it.

Un-: u~besetzt *adj* vacant; *Stuhl, Platz auch* unoccupied; *Bus, Zug* empty; *Schalter* closed; **u~besiegbar** *adj Armee etc* invincible; *Mannschaft, Sportler etc auch* unbeatable; **~besiegbarkeit** *f* invincibility; **~besiegt** *adj* undefeated; **u~besonnen** *adj* rash; **~besonnenheit** *f* rashness.

unbesorgt [1] *adj* unconcerned ◆ **Sie können ganz ~ sein** you can set your mind at rest *or* ease.
[2] *adv* without worrying ◆ **das können Sie ~ tun** you don't need to worry about doing that.

Un-: u~beständig *adj Wetter (immer)* changeable; *(zu bestimmtem Zeitpunkt auch)* unsettled; *Mensch* unsteady; *(in Leistungen)* erratic; *(launisch)* moody; *Liebhaber* inconstant; *Liebe* transitory; **~beständigkeit** *f siehe adj* changeableness, changeability; unsettledness; unsteadiness; erraticness; moodiness; inconstancy; transitoriness; **u~bestätigt** *adj* unconfirmed; **u~bestechlich** *adj* **(a)** *Mensch* incorruptible; **(b)** *Urteil, Blick* unerring; **~bestechlichkeit** *f siehe adj* **(a)** incorruptibility; **(b)** unerringness; **u~bestimmbar** *adj* indeterminable; **~bestimmbarkeit** *f* nondeterminability.

unbestimmt *adj* **(a)** *(ungewiß)* uncertain; *(unentschieden auch)* undecided. **(b)** *(unklar, undeutlich) Gefühl, Erinnerung etc* vague ◆ **etw ~ lassen** to leave sth open; **auf ~e Zeit** for an indefinite period, indefinitely. **(c)** *(Gram)* indefinite.

Unbestimmtheit *f, no pl siehe adj* **(a)** uncertainty. **(b)** vagueness.

▼ **unbestreitbar** *adj Tatsache* indisputable; *Verdienste, Fähigkeiten* unquestionable.

unbestritten *adj* undisputed, indisputable ◆ **es ist ja ~, daß** ... nobody denies *or* disputes that ...

unbeteiligt *adj* **(a)** *(uninteressiert)* indifferent; *(bei Diskussion)* uninterested. **(b)** *(nicht teilnehmend)* uninvolved *no adv (an +dat, bei* in); *(Jur, Comm)* disinterested ◆ **es kamen auch U~e zu Schaden** innocent bystanders were also injured.

un-: ~betont *adj* unstressed; **~beträchtlich** *adj* insignificant; *Unannehmlichkeiten etc* minor; *Aufpreis, Verbilligung* slight; **nicht ~beträchtlich** not inconsiderable; **~beugsam** *adj* uncompromising, unbending; *Wille* unshakeable; **~bewacht** *adj (lit, fig)* unguarded; *Parkplatz* unattended; **~bewaffnet** *adj* unarmed; **~bewältigt** *adj* unconquered, unmastered; **Deutschlands ~bewältigte Vergangenheit** the past with which Germany has not yet come to terms.

unbeweglich *adj* **(a)** *(nicht zu bewegen)* immovable; *(steif)* stiff; *(geistig~)* rigid, inflexible ◆ **ohne Auto ist man ziemlich ~** you're not very mobile *or* you can't get around much without a car; **~e Güter** *(Jur)* immovable property.
(b) *(bewegungslos)* motionless ◆ **~ dastehen/daliegen** to stand/lie there without moving *or* motionless.

Unbeweglichkeit *f siehe adj* **(a)** immovability; stiffness; rigidity, inflexibility. **(b)** motionlessness.

un-: ~bewegt *adj* motionless, unmoving; *Meer* unruffled; *(fig: unberührt)* unmoved; **~beweibt** *adj (inf)* unmarried, wifeless *(inf)*; **~bewiesen** *adj* unproven; **~bewohnbar** *adj* uninhabitable; **~bewohnt** *adj Gegend, Insel, Planet* uninhabited; *Wohnung, Haus* unoccupied, empty; ⚠**~bewußt** *adj* unconscious; *Reflex* involuntary; **das U~bewußte** *(Psych)* the unconscious; **~bezahlbar** *adj* **(a)** *(lit: zu teuer)* prohibitively expensive, impossibly dear; *Luxus, Artikel* which one couldn't possibly afford; *(fig: komisch)* priceless; **(b)** *(fig: praktisch, nützlich)* invaluable; **~bezahlt** *adj Urlaub* unpaid; *Rechnung, Schuld etc auch* unsettled, outstanding; **sein noch ~bezahltes Auto** the car he hasn't finished paying for yet; **~bezähmbar** *adj Optimismus, heiteres Gemüt, Neugier etc* irrepressible, indomitable; *Verlangen, Lust* uncontrollable; *Hunger* insatiable; *Durst* unquenchable; **~bezweifelbar** *adj* undeniable; *Tatsache auch* unarguable; **~bezwingbar, ~bezwinglich** *adj* unconquerable; *Gegner* invincible; *Festung* impregnable; *Drang* uncontrollable.

Unbilden *pl (liter)* **(a)** *(des Wetters)* rigours *pl.* **(b)** *(einer schweren Zeit etc)* trials *pl*, (trials and) tribulations *pl.*

Unbildung *f* lack of education.

Unbill *f -, no pl (old, liter)* injustice, wrong.

unbillig *adj (Jur: ungerecht)* unjust; *(unangemessen)* unreasonable ◆ **~e Härte** *(Jur)* undue hardship.

Unbilligkeit *f siehe adj* injustice; unreasonableness.

Un-: u~blutig [1] *adj* bloodless; *(Med)* non-operative; [2] *adv* without bloodshed; **u~botmäßig** *adj (geh) (undiszipliniert)* insubordinate; *(wild)* unruly; *(rebellisch)* rebellious; **~botmäßigkeit** *f (geh)* insubordination; unruliness; rebelliousness; **u~brauchbar** *adj (nutzlos)* useless, (of) no use *pred*; *(nicht zu verwenden)* unusable; **~brauchbarkeit** *f siehe adj* uselessness; unusability; **u~bürokratisch** [1] *adj* unbureaucratic; [2] *adv* without a lot of red tape, unbureaucratically; **u~christlich** *adj* unchristian; **eine u~christliche Zeit** *(inf)* an ungodly hour.

und *conj* **(a)** and ◆ **~?** well?; **~ dann?** (and) what then *or* then what?; *(danach)* and then?, and after that?; **~ ähnliches** and things like that, and suchlike; **~ anderes** and other things; **er kann es nicht, ~ ich auch nicht** he can't do it, (and) nor *or* neither can I; **ich ~ ihm Geld leihen?** *(inf)* me, lend him money?; **du ~ tanzen können?** *(inf)* you dance?; **immer zwei ~ zwei** two at a time; **Gruppen zu fünf ~ fünf** groups of five; **er aß ~ aß** he ate and ate, kept on (and on) eating; **er konnte ~ konnte nicht aufhören** he simply couldn't stop; **Unfälle, Staus, ~ ~ ~** accidents, tailbacks etc etc etc.
(b) *(konzessiv)* even if ◆ **..., ~ wenn ich selbst bezahlen muß** ... even if I have to pay myself; **~ ... (auch) noch** no matter how ...; **..., ~ wenn du auch noch so bettelst** ... no matter how much you beg; **~ selbst** even; **~ selbst dann** even then.

Undank *m* ingratitude ◆ **~ ernten** to get little thanks; **~ ist der Welt Lohn** *(Prov)* never expect thanks for anything.

undankbar *adj* **(a)** *Mensch* ungrateful ◆ **sich jdm gegenüber ~ zeigen** *or* **erweisen** to be ungrateful to sb. **(b)** *(unerfreulich) Aufgabe, Arbeit etc* thankless.

Undankbarkeit *f siehe adj* **(a)** ingratitude, ungratefulness. **(b)** thanklessness.

un-: ~datiert *adj* undated; **~definierbar** *adj Begriff* indefinable; **das Essen war ~definierbar** nobody could say what the food was; **~dehnbar** *adj* inelastic; **~deklinierbar** *adj* indeclinable; **~demokratisch** *adj* undemocratic.

undenkbar *adj* unthinkable, inconceivable ◆ **es/diese Möglichkeit ist nicht ~** it/the possibility is not inconceivable.

undenklich *adj*: **seit ~en Zeiten** *(geh)* since time immemorial.

undeutlich *adj* indistinct; *(wegen Nebel etc auch)* hazy; *Foto auch* blurred; *Erinnerung auch* vague, hazy; *Schrift* illegible; *Ausdrucksweise, Erklärung* unclear, muddled ◆ **~ sprechen** to speak indistinctly, to mumble; **ich konnte es nur ~ verstehen** I couldn't understand it very clearly; **bemüh dich mal, nicht so ~ zu schreiben** try to write more clearly; **sie/es war nur ~ erkennbar** *or* **zu erkennen** you couldn't see her/it at all clearly.

undeutsch *adj* un-German.

undicht *adj Dose, Gefäß* not air-/water-tight ◆ **das Rohr ist ~** the pipe leaks; **das Fenster ist ~** the window lets in a draught; **er/sie/es muß eine ~e Stelle haben** *(Rohr etc)* it must have a leak; *(Reifen etc)* it must have a hole in it; *(Flasche etc)* the seal must be broken; **im Geheimdienst muß eine ~e Stelle sein** the secret service must have a leak somewhere.

undifferenziert *adj* simplistic; *(nicht analytisch)* undifferentiated; *(gleichartig)* uniform; *Warenangebot* uncomprehensive.

Unding *nt, no pl* absurdity ◆ **es ist ein ~, zu ...** it is preposterous *or* absurd to ...

Un-: u~diplomatisch *adj* undiplomatic; **u~diszipliniert** *adj*

➤ SPRACHE AKTIV: **unbestreitbar** → 42.1, 53.6

undisciplined; **~disziplinierthei t** *f* lack of discipline; **u~dramatisch** *adj* (*fig*) undramatic, unexciting; **u~duldsam** *adj* intolerant (*gegen* of); **~duldsamkeit** *f, no pl* intolerance (*gegen* of); **u~durchdringbar, u~durchdringlich** *adj Gebüsch, Urwald* impenetrable; *Gesicht, Miene* inscrutable; **u~durchführbar** *adj* impracticable, unworkable; **~durchführbarkeit** *f* impracticability, unworkability; **u~durchlässig** *adj* impermeable, impervious (*gegen* to); **~durchlässigkeit** *f* impermeability, imperviousness; **u~durchschaubar** *adj* unfathomable; *Exot, Volk etc* inscrutable; **er ist ein u~durchschaubarer Typ** (*inf*) you never know what game he's playing (*inf*); **~durchschaubarkeit** *f siehe adj* unfathomability; inscrutability; **u~durchsichtig** *adj* **(a)** *Fenster* opaque; *Papier* non-transparent; *Stoff etc* non-transparent, not see-through (*inf*); **(b)** (*fig pej*) *Mensch, Methoden* devious; *Motive* obscure; *Vorgänge, Geschäfte* dark; **es ist eine ganze u~durchsichtige Angelegenheit** you can't tell what's going on in that business; **~durchsichtigkeit** *f, no pl siehe adj* **(a)** opacity; non-transparency; **(b)** deviousness; obscureness; darkness.

un|eben *adj* **(a)** *Oberfläche, Fußboden, Wand etc* uneven; *Straße auch* bumpy; *Gelände* rough, bumpy. **(b)** (*dial inf*) bad.

Un|ebenheit *f siehe adj (a)* unevenness; bumpiness; roughness ◆ **kleine ~en** uneven patches.

Un-: u~echt *adj* false; (*vorgetäuscht*) fake; *Schmuck, Edelstein, Blumen etc* artificial, fake (*usu pej*); *Bruch* improper; **u~edel** *adj Metalle* base; **u~egal** *adj* (*sl*) unequal; **u~ehelich** *adj* illegitimate; **u~ehelich geboren sein** to be illegitimate, to have been born out of wedlock (*old, form*); **~ehelichkeit** *f* illegitimacy; **~ehre** *f, no pl* dishonour; **jdm ~ehre machen** *or* **zur ~ehre gereichen** (*geh*) to disgrace sb; **u~ehrenhaft** *adj* dishonourable; **u~ehrenhaft (aus der Armee) entlassen werden** to be given a dishonourable discharge; **u~ehrerbietig** *adj* disrespectful; **u~ehrlich** *adj* dishonest; **u~ehrlich spielen** to cheat; **auf u~ehrliche Weise** by dishonest means; **~ehrlichkeit** *f* dishonesty; **u~eidlich** *adj* **u~eidliche Falschaussage** (*Jur*) false statement made while not under oath; **u~eigennützig** *adj* unselfish, selfless, altruistic; **~eigennützigkeit** *f* unselfishness, selflessness, altruism; **u~eigentlich** *adj* **(a)** (*Math*) improper; **(b)** (*übertragen*) figurative; **u~eingeladen** *adj* uninvited; **u~eingeladen kommen** to come uninvited *or* without an invitation; **u~eingeladen erscheinen** to gatecrash (*bei etw* sth); **u~eingelöst** *adj* unredeemed; *Wechsel* dishonoured; *Versprechen etc* unfulfilled.

un|eingeschränkt [1] *adj* absolute, total; *Freiheit, Rechte* unlimited, unrestricted; *Annahme, Zustimmung* unqualified; *Vertrauen auch, Lob* unreserved; *Handel* free, unrestricted; *Vollmachten* plenary.
[2] *adv siehe adj* absolutely, totally; without limitation *or* restriction; without qualification; without reservation, unreservedly; freely, without restriction.

Un-: u~eingeweiht *adj* uninitiated; **u~einheitlich** *adj* non-uniform; *Öffnungs-, Arbeitszeiten, Systeme, Reaktion* varied; (*nicht für alle gleich*) *Arbeitszeiten, Schulferien* different; *Qualität* inconsistent; *Börse* irregular; *Preise* unsteady; **u~einheitlich sein** to vary; **u~einig** *adj* **(a)** (*verschiedener Meinung*) in disagreement; **über etw** (*acc*) **u~einig sein** to disagree *or* to be in disagreement about sth; **ich bin mit mir selbst noch u~einig** I haven't made up my mind yet; **(b)** (*zerstritten*) divided; **~einigkeit** *f* disagreement (*gen* between); **~einigkeit in der Partei** division within the party; **u~einnehmbar** *adj* impregnable.

un|eins *adj pred* disagreed; (*zerstritten*) divided ◆ **(mit jdm) ~ sein/werden** to disagree with sb; **ich bin mit mir selbst ~** I cannot make up my mind; **die Mitglieder sind (untereinander) ~** the members are divided amongst themselves.

Un-: u~elegant *adj* inelegant; **u~empfänglich** *adj* (*für* to) insusceptible, unsusceptible; (*für Eindrücke auch, Atmosphäre*) insensitive; **~empfänglichkeit** *f siehe adj* insusceptibility, unsusceptibility; insensitiveness.

un|empfindlich *adj* (*gegen* to) insensitive; (*durch Übung, Erfahrung*) inured; *Bazillen etc* immune; *Pflanzen* hardy; *Baustoffe* which weather well; *Textilien* practical ◆ **gegen Kälte ~e Pflanzen** plants which aren't sensitive to the cold.

Un|empfindlichkeit *f siehe adj* insensitiveness, insensitivity; inurement; immunity; hardiness ◆ **dieser Baustoff ist wegen seiner ~ gegen Witterungseinflüsse besonders gut geeignet** this building material is particularly suitable because it weathers so well; **die ~ dieses Stoffs** the fact that this material is so practical.

un|endlich [1] *adj* infinite; (*zeitlich*) endless; *Universum* infinite, boundless ◆ **das U~e** infinity; **im U~en** at infinity; **(bis) ins U~e** (*lit, Math*) to infinity; **bis ins ~e** (*~ lange*) forever; **auf ~ einstellen** (*Phot*) to focus at infinity.
[2] *adv* endlessly; infinitely; (*fig: sehr*) terribly ◆ **~ lange diskutieren** to argue endlessly; **~ viele Dinge/Leute** *etc* no end of things/people *etc.*

un|endlichemal, un|endlichmal *adv* endless times.

Un|endlichkeit *f* infinity; (*zeitlich*) endlessness; (*von Universum*) boundlessness ◆ **~ von Raum und Zeit** infinity of time and space.

Un|endlichkeitszeichen *nt* (*Math*) infinity symbol.

Un-: u~entbehrlich *adj* indispensable; *Kenntnisse* essential; **~entbehrlichkeit** *f siehe adj* indispensability; essentiality; **u~entdeckt** *adj* undiscovered; **u~entgeltlich** *adj* free of charge; **etw u~entgeltlich tun** to do sth free of charge; **u~entrinnbar** *adj* (*geh*) inescapable.

un|entschieden *adj* (*nicht entschieden*) undecided; (*entschlußlos*) indecisive; (*Sport*) drawn ◆ **das Spiel steht immer noch 2:2 ~** the score is still level at 2 all; **~ enden** *or* **ausgehen** to end in a draw; **~ spielen** to draw; **ein ~es Rennen** a dead heat.

Un|entschieden *nt* **-s, -** (*Sport*) draw ◆ **mit einem ~ enden** to end in a draw.

un|entschlossen *adj* (*nicht entschieden*) undecided; (*entschlußlos*) *Mensch* indecisive, irresolute ◆ **ich bin noch ~** I haven't decided *or* made up my mind yet; **~ stand er vor dem Haus** he stood hesitating in front of the house.

Un|entschlossenheit *f siehe adj* undecidedness; indecision, irresoluteness.

un|entschuldbar *adj* inexcusable.

un|entschuldigt [1] *adj* unexcused ◆ **~es Fernbleiben von der Arbeit/Schule** absenteeism/truancy.
[2] *adv* without an excuse.

un|entwegt [1] *adj* (*mit Ausdauer*) continuous, constant; (*ohne aufzuhören auch*) incessant; *Kämpfer* untiring ◆ **einige U~e** a few stalwarts.
[2] *adv* constantly; incessantly; without tiring ◆ **~ weitermachen** to continue unceasingly.

un-: ~entwirrbar *adj* which can't be disentangled; *Zusammenhänge* involved, complex; **~entzündbar** *adj* non-inflammable, non-flammable; **~erachtet** *prep +gen* (*old*) *siehe* **~geachtet.**

un|erbittlich *adj* relentless; *Mensch auch* inexorable, pitiless ◆ **~ auf jdn einschlagen** to hit sb pitilessly *or* mercilessly.

Un|erbittlichkeit *f siehe adj* relentlessness; inexorableness, pitilessness.

Un-: u~erfahren *adj* inexperienced; **~erfahrene(r)** *mf decl as adj* inexperienced person/man/woman *etc*; **~erfahrenheit** *f* inexperience, lack of experience; **u~erfindlich** *adj* incomprehensible; *Grund* obscure; **aus u~erfindlichen Gründen** for some obscure reason; **u~erforschbar, u~erforschlich** *adj* impenetrable; *Wille* unfathomable; **u~erfreulich** *adj* unpleasant; **~erfreuliches** (*schlechte Nachrichten*) bad news *sing*; (*Übles*) bad things *pl*; **u~erfüllbar** *adj* unrealizable; *Wunsch, Ziel auch* unattainable; **u~erfüllt** *adj* unfulfilled; **u~ergiebig** *adj Quelle, Thema* unproductive; *Boden, Ernte, Nachschlagewerk* poor; *Kaffee, Trauben* uneconomical; **u~ergründbar, u~ergründlich** *adj* unfathomable; **u~erheblich** *adj* (*geringfügig*) insignificant; (*unwichtig auch*) unimportant, irrelevant; **nicht u~erheblich verbessert** considerably improved; **u~erhofft** *adj* unexpected.

un|erhört[1] [1] *adj attr* (*ungeheuer, gewaltig*) enormous; (*empörend*) outrageous; *Frechheit* incredible ◆ **das ist ja ~!** that's quite outrageous.
[2] *adv* incredibly ◆ **~ viel** a tremendous amount (of); **~ viel wissen/arbeiten** to know a tremendous amount/to work tremendously hard; **wir müssen uns ~ beeilen** we really have to hurry; **~ aufpassen** to watch very carefully.

un|erhört[2] *adj Bitte, Gebet* unanswered; *Liebe* unrequited; *Liebhaber* rejected.

un-: ~erkannt *adj* unrecognized; **~erkannt entkommen** to get away without being recognized; **~erkennbar** *adj* unrecognizable; **~erklärbar, ~erklärlich** *adj* inexplicable; **das ist mir ~erklärbar** *or* **~erklärlich** I can't understand it; **~erklärt** *adj Phänomen, Sachverhalt* unexplained; *Krieg, Liebe* undeclared; **⚠~erläßlich** *adj* imperative.

un|erlaubt *adj* forbidden; *Betreten, Parken* unauthorized; (*ungesetzlich*) illegal ◆ **etw ~ tun** to do sth without permission; **~e Handlung** (*Jur*) tort; **~er Waffenbesitz** illegal possession of firearms; *siehe* **entfernen, Entfernung.**

un|erlaubterweise *adv* without permission.

un|erledigt *adj* unfinished; *Post* unanswered; *Rechnung* outstanding; *Auftrag* unfulfilled; (*schwebend*) pending ◆ **auf dem Aktenordner stand „~"** the file was marked "pending".

un-: ⚠~ermeßlich *adj* immense; *Weite, Himmel, Ozean* vast; **~ermüdlich** *adj Bestrebungen, Fleiß* untiring, tireless; *Versuche* unceasing; **~ernst** *adj* frivolous; **~erprobt** *adj* untested, untried; **~erquicklich** *adj* (*unerfreulich*) unedifying; (*nutzlos*) unproductive, fruitless; **~erreichbar** *adj Ziel, Leistung, Qualität* unattainable; *Ort, Ferne* inaccessible; (*telefonisch*) unobtainable; **~erreicht** *adj* unequalled; *Ziel* unattained.

un|ersättlich *adj* insatiable; *Wissensdurst auch* inexhaustible.

Un|ersättlichkeit *f siehe adj* insatiability; inexhaustibility.

Un-: u~erschlossen *adj Land* undeveloped; *Boden* unexploited; *Vorkommen, Markt, Erdöllager* untapped; **u~erschöpflich** *adj* inexhaustible; **u~erschrocken** *adj* intrepid, courageous; **~erschrockenheit** *f* intrepidity, courage; **u~erschütterlich** *adj* unshakeable; *Ruhe* imperturbable.

un|erschwinglich *adj* exorbitant, prohibitive ◆ **für jdn ~ sein** to be beyond sb's means; **ein für uns ~er Luxus** a luxury beyond our means; **~ (teuer) sein** to be prohibitively expensive *or* prohibitive.

un-: ~ersetzbar, ~ersetzlich *adj* irreplaceable; *Mensch auch* indispensable; **~ersprießlich** *adj* (*unerfreulich*) unedifying; (*nutzlos*) unproductive, fruitless; **~erträglich** *adj* unbearable; **~erwähnt** *adj* unmentioned; **~erwartet** *adj* unexpected; **~erwidert** *adj Brief, Behauptung* unanswered; *Liebe* unrequited; *Sympathie* one-sided; **~erwünscht** *adj Kind* unwanted; *Besuch, Effekt* unwelcome; **du bist hier ~erwünscht** you're not welcome here; **ein ~erwünschter Ausländer** (*Pol*) an undesirable alien; **~erzogen** *adj* ill-bred, ill-mannered; *Kind auch* badly brought up.

UNESCO [u'nesko] *f* **- die ~** UNESCO.

unfachgemäß, unfachmännisch *adj* unprofessional.

▼ **unfähig** *adj* **(a)** *attr* incompetent. **(b) ~ sein, etw zu tun** to be incapable of doing sth; (*vorübergehend*) to be unable to do sth; **einer Sache** (*gen*) *or* **zu etw ~ sein** to be incapable of sth.

Unfähigkeit *f* **(a)** (*Untüchtigkeit*) incompetence. **(b)** (*Nichtkönnen*) inability.

Un-: u~fair *adj* unfair (*gegenüber* to); **⚠~fairneß, ~fairness** *f* unfairness.

Unfall *m* **-s, Unfälle** accident ◆ **er ist bei einem ~ ums Leben gekommen** he died in an accident; **gegen ~ versichert** insured against accidents.

Unfall-: ~arzt *m* specialist for accident injuries; **~beteiligte(r)** *mf* person/man/woman *etc* involved in an/the accident; **~bilanz** *f* accident figures *pl or* statistics *pl*; **~fahrer** *m* driver at fault in an/the accident;

~flucht *f* failure to stop after *or* (*nicht melden*) report an accident; (*bei Verletzung von Personen auch*) hit-and-run driving; **~flucht begehen** to fail to stop after/report an accident; to commit a hit-and-run offence; **u~flüchtig** *adj Fahrer* who fails to stop after/report an accident; hit-and-run *attr*; **u~flüchtig werden** to fail to stop after/report an accident; **~flüchtige** *pl* drivers *pl* who fail to stop after/report an accident; hit-and-run drivers *pl*; **~folge** *f* result of an/the accident; **u~frei** [1] *adj* accident-free; [2] *adv* without an accident; **~gegner** *m* plaintiff for damages; **~hilfe** *f* help at the scene of an/the accident; (*Erste Hilfe*) first aid; **~klinik** *f*, **~krankenhaus** *nt* accident hospital; **~opfer** *nt* casualty; **~ort** *m* scene of an/the accident; **~quote, ~rate** *f* accident rate; **~rente** *f* accident benefits *pl*; **~risiko** *nt* accident risk; **~schaden** *m* damages *pl*; **~schutz** *m* (*Versicherung*) accident insurance; (*Maßnahmen*) accident prevention; **~skizze** *f* diagram *or* sketch of an/the accident; **~station** *f* accident *or* emergency ward; **~statistik** *f* accident statistics *pl*; **~stelle** *f* scene of an/the accident; **~tod** *m* accidental death; **bei ~tod** in the event of death by misadventure; **~tote(r)** *mf siehe* **Verkehrstote(r)**; **u~trächtig** *adj* accident-prone; **~ursache** *f* cause of an/the accident; **~verhütung** *f* accident prevention; **~verletzte(r)** *mf* casualty; **~versicherung** *f* accident insurance; **~wagen** *m* car involved in an/the accident; (*inf: Rettungswagen*) ambulance; **der Wagen ist so billig, weil es ein ~wagen ist** the car is so cheap because it has been involved in an accident; **~zahl, ~ziffer** *f* number of accidents; **steigende ~ziffern** rising accident rates; **~zeuge** *m* witness to an/the accident.

⚠**unfaßbar,** ⚠**unfaßlich** *adj* incomprehensible ◆ **es ist mir** *or* **für mich ~, wie ...** I (simply) cannot understand how ...

Un-: u~fehlbar [1] *adj* infallible; *Instinkt* unerring; [2] *adv* without fail; **~fehlbarkeit** *f* infallibility; **u~fein** *adj* unrefined *no adv*, indelicate; **das ist u~fein/mehr als u~fein** that's bad manners/most ungentlemanly/unladylike; **u~fern** (*geh*) [1] *prep +gen* not far from, near; [2] *adv* **u~fern von** not far from, near; **u~fertig** *adj* (*unvollendet*) unfinished; (*nicht vollständig*) incomplete; (*unreif*) *Mensch* immature.

Unflat [ˈʊnflaːt] *m* **-(e)s,** *no pl* (*lit old*) feculence (*form*); (*fig geh*) vituperation ◆ **jdn mit ~ bewerfen** (*fig*) to inveigh against *or* vituperate sb.

unflätig *adj* (*geh*) offensive ◆ **sich ~ ausdrücken** to use obscene language.

Unflätigkeit *f* offensiveness; (*von Ausdrucksweise*) obscenity.

un-: ~flektiert *adj* (*Gram*) uninflected; **~flott** *adj* (*inf*) not nice; **das ist gar nicht so ~flott** that's not bad; **er/sie ist gar nicht so ~flott** he's/she's a bit of all right (*inf*); **~folgsam** *adj* disobedient; **~formatiert** *adj* (*Comput*) unformatted.

unförmig *adj* (*formlos*) shapeless; *Möbel, Auto* inelegant; (*groß*) cumbersome; *Füße, Gesicht* unshapely.

Unförmigkeit *f siehe adj* shapelessness; inelegance; cumbersomeness; unshapeliness.

un-: ~förmlich *adj* informal; **~frankiert** *adj* unstamped; **~fraulich** *adj* unfeminine.

unfrei *adj* **(a)** (*politisch, Hist: leibeigen*) not free ◆ **~ sein** (*Hist*) to be a bondman *or* in bondage *or* a serf. **(b)** (*befangen, eingeengt*) constrained, uneasy. **(c)** *Brief etc* unfranked.

Unfreie(r) *mf decl as adj* (*Hist*) serf.

Unfreiheit *f* lack of freedom; (*Hist*) bondage.

unfreiwillig *adj* **(a)** (*gezwungen*) compulsory ◆ **ich mußte ~ zuhören/war ~er Zeuge** I was forced to listen/was an unwilling witness. **(b)** (*unbeabsichtigt*) *Witz, Fehler* unintentional.

unfreundlich *adj* unfriendly (*zu, gegen* to); *Wetter* inclement; *Landschaft, Zimmer, Farbe* cheerless ◆ **jdn ~ behandeln** to be unfriendly to sb; **jdn ~ begrüßen/ansehen** to give sb an unfriendly welcome/look; **~ reagieren** to react in an unfriendly way; **ein ~er Akt** (*Pol*) a hostile act.

Unfreundlichkeit *f* **(a)** *siehe adj* unfriendliness; inclemency; cheerlessness. **(b)** (*unfreundliche Bemerkung*) unpleasant remark.

Unfriede(n) *m* strife ◆ **in ~n (mit jdm) leben** to live in conflict (with sb).

un-: ~frisiert *adj* (*lit*) *Haare* uncombed; *Mensch* with one's hair in a mess; (*fig inf*) (*nicht verfälscht*) undoctored; *Auto* not souped-up (*sl*); **~fromm** *adj* impious.

unfruchtbar *adj* infertile; *Boden auch* barren; *Frau auch* barren (*old, liter*); (*fig: Debatte etc*) fruitless; *Schaffenszeit* unproductive ◆ **~ machen** to sterilize; **die ~en Tage** (*Med*) the days of infertility.

Unfruchtbarkeit *f siehe adj* infertility; barrenness; fruitlessness.

Unfug [ˈʊnfuːk] *m* **-s,** *no pl* nonsense ◆ **~ treiben** *or* **anstellen** *or* **machen** to get up to mischief; **laß den ~!** stop that nonsense!; **wegen groben ~s** for causing a public nuisance.

un-: ~fundiert *adj* unfounded; **~galant** (*geh*) *adj* discourteous, ungentlemanly *no adv*; **~gar** *adj* underdone.

Ungar(in *f***)** [ˈʊŋgar(ɪn)] *m* **-n, -n** Hungarian.

ungarisch [ˈʊŋgarɪʃ] *adj* Hungarian.

Ungarisch(e) [ˈʊŋgarɪʃ(ə)] *nt* Hungarian; *siehe auch* **Deutsch(e)**.

Ungarn [ˈʊŋgarn] *nt* **-s** Hungary.

Un-: u~gastlich *adj* inhospitable; **~gastlichkeit** *f* inhospitableness.

ungeachtet *prep +gen* in spite of, despite ◆ **~ dessen, daß es regnet** in spite of it raining *or* of the fact that it is raining; **~ aller Ermahnungen, aller Ermahnungen ~** despite all warnings; **er ist sehr stark, ~ dessen, daß er so klein ist** he's very strong, in spite of being so small.

un-: ~geahndet *adj* (*Jur*) unpunished; **~geahnt** *adj* undreamt-of; **~gebacken** *adj* unbaked; **~gebärdig** *adj* unruly; **~gebeten** *adj* uninvited; **er kam ~gebeten** he came uninvited *or* unasked *or* without an invitation; **~gebeugt** *adj* **(a)** unbent, unbowed; **(b)** (*Gram*) uninflected; **~gebildet** *adj* uncultured; (*ohne Bildung*) uneducated; **U~gebildete** uneducated *or* ignorant people; **~gebleicht** *adj* unbleached; **~geboren** *adj* unborn; **~gebrannt** *adj Kaffee* unroasted; *Ton etc* unfired; **~gebräuchlich** *adj* uncommon; **~gebraucht** *adj* unused; **~gebrochen** *adj* unbroken; (*Phys*) *Licht* unrefracted.

Ungebühr *f, no pl* (*old, form*) impropriety ◆ **~ vor Gericht** contempt of court.

ungebührlich *adj* improper ◆ **sich ~ aufregen** to get unduly excited.

ungebunden *adj* **(a)** *Buch* unbound; *Blumen* loose. **(b) in ~er Rede** in prose. **(c)** (*unabhängig*) *Leben* (fancy-)free; (*unverheiratet*) unattached; (*Pol*) independent ◆ **frei und ~** footloose and fancy-free; **parteipolitisch ~** (politically) independent, not attached to any political party.

Ungebundenheit *f* independence.

Un-: u~gedeckt *adj* **(a)** (*schutzlos*) *Schachfigur etc* unprotected, unguarded; (*Sport*) *Tor* undefended; *Spieler* unmarked, uncovered; *Scheck, Kredit* uncovered; **(b)** *Tisch* unlaid; **u~gedient** *adj* (*dated Mil*) with no prior service; **~gediente(r)** *m decl as adj* (*dated*) person with no prior service; **u~gedruckt** *adj* unprinted; (*nicht veröffentlicht*) unpublished.

Ungeduld *f* impatience ◆ **vor ~** with impatience; **voller ~** impatiently.

ungeduldig *adj* impatient.

ungeeignet *adj* unsuitable; (*für Beruf, Stellung auch*) unsuited (*für* to, for).

ungefähr [1] *adj attr* approximate, rough ◆ **nach ~en Schätzungen** at a rough guess *or* estimate.

[2] *adv* roughly; (*bei Zahlen-, Maßangaben auch*) approximately ◆ **(so) ~ dreißig** about *or* approximately thirty; **~ 12 Uhr** about *or* approximately 12 o'clock; **von ~** from nowhere; (*zufällig*) by chance; **das kommt nicht von ~** it's no accident; **diese Bemerkung kommt doch nicht von ~** he *etc* didn't make this remark just by chance; **wo ~?** whereabouts?; **wie ~?** approximately how?; **so ~!** more or less!; **können Sie mir (so) ~ sagen, wieviel das kosten soll/wie Sie sich das vorgestellt haben?** can you give me a rough idea of *or* tell me roughly how much it will cost/how you imagined it?; **~ (so) wie** a bit like; **können Sie den Mann ~ beschreiben?** can you give me/us *etc* a rough description of the man?; **etw (so) ~ wissen** to know sth roughly *or* have a rough idea of sth; **dann weiß ich ~ Bescheid** then I've got a rough idea; **so ~ habe ich mir das gedacht** I thought it would be something like this; **so ~, als wären wir kleine Kinder** a bit as if we were little children; **das hat sich ~ so abgespielt** it happened something like this.

Un-: u~gefährdet *adj* **(a)** safe, unendangered *no adv*; **(b)** (*Sport*) not in danger; **u~gefährdet siegen** to win comfortably; **u~gefährlich** *adj* safe; *Tier, Krankheit, Arzneimittel etc* harmless; **nicht ganz u~gefährlich** not altogether safe/harmless; (*Expedition*) not altogether without its dangers; **~gefährlichkeit** *f siehe adj* safeness; harmlessness; **u~gefällig** *adj Mensch* unobliging; **u~gefärbt** *adj Haare, Stoff* undyed, natural; *Lebensmittel* without (added) colouring; **u~gefedert** *adj* springless, without springs; **u~gefiltert** *adj* unfiltered; **u~geformt** *adj* unformed; (*gestaltlos*) amorphous; **u~gefragt** *adv* unasked; **u~gefüttert[1]** *adj Tier* unfed; **u~gefüttert[2]** *adj Kleidung, Briefumschlag* unlined; **u~gegerbt** *adj* untanned; **u~gegliedert** *adj Körper, Stengel* unjointed; (*fig*) disjointed; *Satz, Aufsatz etc* unstructured.

ungehalten *adj* indignant (*über +acc* about).

Ungehaltenheit *f* indignation.

un-: ~gehärtet *adj Stahl* untempered; **~geheißen** *adv* (*geh*) voluntarily; **~geheizt** *adj* unheated; **~gehemmt** *adj* unrestrained.

Ungeheuer *nt* **-s, -** monster; (*fig auch*) ogre.

ungeheuer [1] *adj* **(a)** *siehe* **ungeheuerlich**.

(b) (*riesig*) enormous, immense; (*in bezug auf Länge, Weite*) vast ◆ **sich ins ~e steigern** to take on enormous dimensions.

(c) (*genial, kühn*) tremendous.

(d) (*frevelhaft, vermessen*) outrageous, dreadful.

[2] *adv* (*sehr*) enormously, tremendously; (*negativ*) terribly, awfully ◆ **~ groß** tremendously big; **~ viele Menschen** an enormous number of people.

ungeheuerlich *adj* monstrous; *Tat auch* atrocious; *Verleumdung* outrageous; *Verdacht, Dummheit* dreadful; *Leichtsinn* outrageous, appalling.

Ungeheuerlichkeit *f siehe adj* monstrosity; atrocity, atrociousness; outrageousness; dreadfulness ◆ **so eine ~!** how outrageous!; **~en** (*Verbrechen etc*) atrocities; (*Behauptungen etc*) outrageous claims.

Un-: u~gehindert *adj* unhindered; **u~gehobelt** *adj Brett etc* unplaned; *Mensch, Benehmen* boorish; **u~gehörig** *adj* impertinent; **~gehörigkeit** *f* impertinence; **u~gehorsam** *adj* disobedient; **~gehorsam** *m* disobedience; (*Mil*) insubordination; **ziviler ~gehorsam** civil disobedience; **u~gehört** *adv* unheard; **u~gehört verhallen** (*fig*) to fall on deaf ears.

Ungeist *m, no pl* (*geh*) demon.

un-: ~geistig *adj* unintellectual; **~gekämmt** *adj Haar* uncombed; **~gekämmt aussehen** to look unkempt; **~geklärt** *adj* **(a)** *Abwasser etc* untreated; **(b)** *Frage, Verbrechen* unsolved; *Ursache* unknown; **~gekocht** *adj* raw; *Flüssigkeit* unboiled; *Obst etc* uncooked; **~gekrönt** *adj* uncrowned; **~gekühlt** *adj* unchilled; **~gekündigt** *adj*: **in ~gekündigter Stellung** not under notice (to leave); **~gekünstelt** *adj* natural, genuine; *Sprechweise* unaffected; **~gekürzt** *adj* not shortened; *Buch* unabridged; *Film* uncut; *Ausgaben* not cut back; **~geladen** *adj* **(a)** *Kamera, Gewehr etc* unloaded; **(b)** *Gäste etc* uninvited; **~geläufig** *adj* unfamiliar.

ungelegen *adj* inconvenient ◆ **komme ich (Ihnen) ~?** is this an inconvenient time for you?; **etw kommt jdm ~** sth is inconvenient for sb; **das kam (mir) gar nicht so ~** that was really rather convenient.

Ungelegenheiten *pl* inconvenience *sing* ◆ **jdm ~ bereiten** *or* **machen** to inconvenience sb.

un-: ~gelegt *adj siehe* **Ei**; **~gelehrig** *adj* unteachable; **~gelenk** *adj* awkward; *Bewegungen auch* clumsy; **~gelenkig** *adj* not supple, stiff; *(fig inf: nicht flexibel)* inflexible, unbending; **~gelernt** *adj attr* unskilled; **~gelesen** *adj* unread; **~geliebt** *adj* unloved; **~gelogen** *adv* honestly; **~gelöst** *adj* unsolved; *(Chem)* undissolved; **~gelüftet** *adj* unaired.

Ungemach ['ʊngəmaːx] *nt* **-s**, *no pl (liter)* hardship.

un-: ~gemacht *adj Bett* unmade; **~gemahlen** *adj* unground.

ungemein *adj* immense, tremendous.

un-: ~gemildert *adj* undiminished; **~gemildert fortbestehen** to continue undiminished; **~gemustert** *adj* plain.

ungemütlich *adj* uncomfortable; *Mensch* awkward; *Land, Wetter, Wochenende* unpleasant ◆ **mir wird es hier ~** I'm getting a bit uncomfortable *or* uneasy; **er kann ~ werden** he can get nasty; **ich kann auch ~ werden** I can be very unpleasant if I choose; **hier kann es gleich sehr ~ werden** things could get very nasty here in a moment.

Ungemütlichkeit *f siehe adj* uncomfortableness; unpleasantness.

ungenannt *adj* anonymous ◆ **~ bleiben** to remain anonymous.

ungenau *adj (nicht fehlerfrei)* inaccurate; *(nicht wahrheitsgetreu)* inexact; *(vage)* vague; *(ungefähr)* rough, approximate ◆ **~ arbeiten/messen/rechnen** to work inaccurately/measure approximately/calculate roughly.

Ungenauigkeit *f siehe adj* inaccuracy; inexactness; vagueness; roughness.

ungeneigt *adj* disinclined.

ungeniert ['ʊnʒeniːɐt] [1] *adj (frei, ungehemmt)* unembarrassed, free and easy; *(bedenkenlos, taktlos)* uninhibited.
[2] *adv* openly; *(bedenkenlos, taktlos)* without any inhibition ◆ **greifen Sie bitte ~ zu** please feel free to help yourself/yourselves.

Ungeniertheit ['ʊnʒeniːɐthait] *f siehe adj* lack of embarrassment; lack of inhibition.

ungenießbar *adj (nicht zu essen)* inedible; *(nicht zu trinken)* undrinkable; *(unschmackhaft)* unpalatable; *(inf) Mensch* unbearable.

ungenügend ['ʊngənyːgnt] *adj* inadequate, insufficient; *(Sch)* unsatisfactory ◆ **ein U~** an "unsatisfactory", the lowest mark.

Un-: u~genutzt, u~genützt *adj* unused; *Energien* unexploited; **eine Chance u~genutzt** *or* **u~genützt lassen** to miss an opportunity; **u~geöffnet** *adj* unopened; **u~geordnet** *adj Bücher, Papiere etc* untidy, disordered; *(fig)* disordered; **u~geordnet herumliegen** to lie (about) in disorder *or* disarray; **u~gepflastert** *adj* unpaved; **u~gepflegt** *adj Mensch* untidy, unkempt; *Park, Rasen, Hände etc* neglected; **sich u~gepflegt ausdrücken** to talk in a common way; **u~geprüft** *adj* untested; **etw u~geprüft übernehmen** to accept sth without testing it; *Zahlen* to accept sth without checking; *(unkritisch)* to accept sth at face value; **u~geputzt** *adj* uncleaned; *Zähne* unbrushed; *Schuhe* unpolished; **u~gerächt** *adj* unavenged; **u~gerade** *adj* odd; **u~geraten** *adj Kind* ill-bred; **u~gerechnet** *prep +gen* not including, excluding; **u~gerecht** *adj* unjust, unfair; **u~gerechterweise** *adv* unjustly, unfairly; **u~gerechtfertigt** [1] *adj* unjustified; *Behauptung auch* unwarranted; [2] *adv* unjustly, unduly; **~gerechtigkeit** *f* injustice; **so eine ~gerechtigkeit!** how unjust!; **u~geregelt** *adj Zeiten* irregular; *Leben* disordered; **u~gereimt** *adj Verse* unrhymed; *(fig)* inconsistent; **u~gereimte Verse** blank verse *sing*; **~gereimtheit** *f (fig)* inconsistency.

ungern *adv* reluctantly ◆ **(höchst) ~!** if I/we really have to!; **etw höchst ~ tun** to do sth very reluctantly *or* with the greatest reluctance; **das tue ich gar nicht ~** I don't mind doing that at all.

un-: ~gerufen *adj* uncalled, without being called; **~gerührt** *adj* unmoved; **~gesagt** *adj* unsaid; **etw ~gesagt machen** to pretend sth has never been said; **~gesalzen** *adj* unsalted; **~gesattelt** *adj* unsaddled; **~gesättigt** *adj Hunger etc* unsatisfied; *(Chem)* unsaturated; **~gesäuert** *adj Brot* unleavened; **~geschält** *adj Obst, Gemüse* unpeeled; *Getreide, Reis* unhusked; *Baumstämme* unstripped; **~geschehen** *adj* undone; **etw ~geschehen machen** to undo sth.

Ungeschick *nt* **-s**, *no pl*, **Ungeschicklichkeit** *f* clumsiness.

ungeschickt *adj* clumsy, awkward; *(unbedacht)* careless, undiplomatic ◆ **U~ läßt grüßen!** *(inf)* butter-fingers!

Ungeschicktheit *f siehe* **Ungeschick**.

ungeschlacht *adj (pej)* hulking great; *Sitten* barbaric.

Un-: u~geschlechtlich *adj* asexual; **u~geschliffen** *adj Edelstein, Glas* uncut; *Messer etc* blunt; *(fig) Benehmen, Mensch* uncouth; **~geschliffenheit** *f (fig)* uncouthness; **u~geschmälert** *adj* undiminished; **u~geschmeidig** *adj Stoff, Leder* rough; *Haar* coarse; **u~geschminkt** *adj* without make-up; *(fig) Wahrheit* unvarnished; **etw u~geschminkt berichten** to give an unvarnished report of sth.

ungeschoren *adj* unshorn; *(fig)* spared ◆ **jdn ~ lassen** *(inf)* to spare sb; *(ungestraft)* to let sb off (scot-free); **~ davonkommen** *(inf)* to get off (scot-free).

Un-: u~geschrieben *adj attr* unwritten; **u~geschult** *adj* untrained; **u~geschützt** *adj* unprotected; *Schachfigur auch* unguarded; *(Mil) Einheit* exposed; *Anlagen* undefended; *(Sport) Tor* undefended; **u~gesehen** *adj* unseen; **u~gesellig** *adj* unsociable; *Tier* non-gregarious; **~geselligkeit** *f siehe adj* unsociableness; non-gregariousness; **u~gesetzlich** *adj* unlawful, illegal; **~gesetzlichkeit** *f* unlawfulness, illegality; **u~gesichert** *adj* unsecured, not secured; *Schußwaffe* cocked, with the safety catch off; **u~gesittet** *adj* uncivilized; **u~gestalt** *adj (geh) Mensch* misshapen, deformed; **u~gestempelt** *adj* unstamped; *Briefmarke* unfranked; *(für Sammler)* mint; **u~gestillt** *adj Durst* unquenched; *Hunger* unappeased; *Blutung* unstaunched; *Schmerz* unrelieved; *Verlangen* unfulfilled; *Neugier* unsatisfied; **u~gestört** *adj* undisturbed; *(Rad, TV etc)* without interference; **u~gestraft** *adv* with impunity.

ungestüm ['ʊngəʃtyːm] *adj* impetuous.

Ungestüm ['ʊngəʃtyːm] *nt* **-(e)s**, *no pl* impetuousness.

un-: ~gesühnt *adj* unexpiated, unatoned; **~gesund** *adj* unhealthy; *(schädlich)* harmful; **~gesüßt** *adj* unsweetened; **~getan** *adj* undone; **etw ~getan machen** to undo sth; **~getauft** *adj* unchristened; *(inf: unverwässert)* undiluted; **~geteilt** *adj* undivided; **~getilgt** *adj Schulden* uncleared; **~getragen** *adj Kleidung* new, unworn; **~getreu** *adj (liter)* disloyal, faithless *(liter)*; **~getrübt** *adj* clear; *Glück, Freude* perfect, unspoilt.

Ungetüm ['ʊngətyːm] *nt* **-(e)s, -e** monster.

un-: ~geübt *adj* unpractised; *Mensch* out of practice; **~gewandt** *adj* awkward; **~gewaschen** *adj* unwashed.

⚠ **ungewiß** *adj* uncertain; *(vage)* vague ◆ **ein Sprung/eine Reise ins Ungewisse** *(fig)* a leap/a journey into the unknown; **jdn (über etw** *acc***) im ungewissen lassen** to leave sb in the dark (about sth); **im ungewissen bleiben/sein** to stay/be in the dark.

⚠ **Ungewißheit** *f* uncertainty.

Ungewitter *nt (obs) siehe* **Unwetter**.

ungewöhnlich [1] *adj* unusual.
[2] *adv* unusually; *(äußerst auch)* exceptionally.

Ungewöhnlichkeit *f* unusualness.

ungewohnt *adj (fremdartig)* strange, unfamiliar; *(unüblich)* unusual ◆ **das ist mir ~** I am unaccustomed *or* not used to it.

ungewollt *adj* unintentional ◆ **er mußte ~ lachen** he couldn't help laughing.

un-: ~gewürzt *adj* unseasoned; **~gezählt** *adj (unzählbar)* countless; *(nicht gezählt)* uncounted; **~gezähmt** *adj* untamed; *(fig)* uncurbed; **~gezeichnet** *adj* unsigned.

Ungeziefer *nt* **-s**, *no pl* pests *pl*, vermin; *(old fig)* vermin.

ungezielt *adj* unaimed ◆ **~ schießen** to shoot without taking aim.

ungezogen *adj* ill-mannered.

Ungezogenheit *f* **(a)** *no pl* unmannerliness. **(b)** *(ungezogene Handlung)* bad manners *no indef art* ◆ **so eine ~ von dir!** what bad manners!; **noch mehr solche ~en, und es setzt was!** if you don't stop being naughty you'll catch it.

Un-: u~gezügelt [1] *adj (unbeherrscht)* unbridled; *(ausschweifend)* dissipated; [2] *adv* without restraint; **u~gezwungen** *adj* casual, informal; **sich u~gezwungen bewegen** to feel quite free; **~gezwungenheit** *f* casualness, informality; **u~giftig** *adj* nonpoisonous.

Unglaube *m* unbelief, lack of faith; *(esp Philos)* scepticism.

unglaubhaft *adj* incredible, unbelievable.

ungläubig [1] *adj* unbelieving; *(Rel)* infidel; *(zweifelnd)* doubting, disbelieving ◆ **~er Thomas** *(Bibl, fig)* doubting Thomas.
[2] *adv* doubtingly, doubtfully, in disbelief.

Ungläubige(r) *mf* unbeliever; *(Rel)* infidel.

unglaublich *adj* unbelievable, incredible ◆ **das grenzt ans U~e** that's almost incredible.

unglaubwürdig *adj* implausible; *Dokument* dubious; *Mensch* unreliable ◆ **diese Regierung wirkt völlig ~** this government lacks credibility; **sich ~ machen** to lose credibility.

Unglaubwürdigkeit *f siehe adj* implausibility; dubiousness; unreliability.

ungleich [1] *adj (nicht gleichartig) Charaktere* dissimilar, unalike *pred*; *Größe, Farbe* different; *(nicht gleichwertig, nicht vergleichbar) Mittel, Waffen* unequal; *(Math)* not equal ◆ **fünf plus fünf ~ neun** five plus five does not equal nine; **sie sind ein ~es Paar** they are very different; **das Zeichen für ~** the not-equals sign.
[2] *adv* much, incomparably.

Ungleich-: ~behandlung *f, no pl* discrimination; **~gewicht** *nt (fig)* imbalance.

Ungleichheit *f siehe adj* dissimilarity; difference; inequality; difference.

Ungleichheitszeichen *nt (Math)* not-equals sign.

Ungleich-: u~mäßig *adj* uneven; *Atemzüge, Gesichtszüge, Puls* irregular; **u~mäßig lang** of uneven length; **~mäßigkeit** *f siehe adj* unevenness; irregularity; **u~namig** *adj (Math)* of different denominations; *(Phys)* opposite, unlike; **u~seitig** *adj (Math) Vieleck* irregular.

Ungleichung *f (Math)* inequation.

Unglück *nt* **-(e)s, -e** *(Unfall, Vorfall)* accident; *(Mißgeschick auch)* mishap; *(Schicksalsschlag)* disaster, tragedy; *(Unheil)* misfortune; *(Pech, im Aberglauben, bei Glücksspiel)* bad luck; *(Unglücklichsein)* unhappiness ◆ **in sein ~ rennen** to head for disaster; **sich ins ~ stürzen** to rush headlong into disaster; **du stürzt mich noch ins ~!** you'll be my undoing!; **das ist auch kein ~** that is not a disaster; **so** *or* **welch ein ~!** what a disaster!; **er hat im Leben viel ~ gehabt** he has experienced a great deal of misfortune in life; **es ist ein ~, daß ...** it is bad luck that ...; **das ~ wollte es, daß ...** as (bad) luck would have it, ...; **das bringt ~** that brings bad luck, that's unlucky; **zum ~, zu allem ~** to make matters worse; **ein ~ kommt selten allein** *(Prov)* it never rains but it pours *(Prov)*; **~ im Spiel, Glück in der Liebe** *(prov)* unlucky at cards, lucky in love; *siehe* **Glück, Häufchen**.

⚠ **unglückbringend** *adj (geh)* ominous, unpropitious.

▼ **unglücklich** *adj* **(a)** *(traurig) Mensch, Gesicht etc* unhappy; *Liebe* unrequited; *Liebesgeschichte* unhappy ◆ **~ verliebt sein** to be crossed in love.
▼ **(b)** *(bedauerlich)* sad, unfortunate ◆ **~ enden** *or* **ausgehen** to turn out badly, to end in disaster; **eine ~e Figur abgeben** to cut a sorry figure.

Unglückliche(r) *mf decl as adj* unhappy person, unhappy man/woman *etc* ◆ **ich ~(r)!** poor me!; **der ~!** the poor man!

➤ SPRACHE AKTIV: **unglücklich: b** → 45.3

unglücklicherweise *adv* unfortunately.
Unglücks-: ~bote *m* bringer of bad tidings; **~botschaft** *f* bad tidings *pl.*
Unglück-: u~selig *adj (liter)* **(a)** *(Unglück habend)* unfortunate, hapless; *(armselig)* miserable; *(bedauernswert)* lamentable; **(b)** *(u~bringend)* disastrous; **~selige(r)** *mf (liter)* (poor) wretch; **ich ~selige(r)** woe is me! *(liter)*; **u~seligerweise** *adv (liter)* unfortunately.
Unglücks-: ~fahrer *m* driver who caused an/the accident; **~fall** *m* accident, mishap; **ein tragischer ~fall** a tragic accident; **~kind** *nt*, **~mensch** *m* unlucky person, unlucky man/woman *etc*; **ich war schon immer ein ~mensch/~kind** I've always been unlucky; **~rabe** *m (inf)* unlucky thing *(inf)*; **~tag** *m* fateful day; **~vogel** *m (inf)* unlucky thing *(inf)*; **~wurm** *m (inf)* poor soul; **~zahl** *f* unlucky number.
Ungnade *f* disgrace, disfavour ◆ **bei jdm in ~ fallen** to fall out of favour with sb.
ungnädig *adj* ungracious; *(hum)* unkind, harsh ◆ **etw ~ aufnehmen** to take sth with bad grace.
un-: ~grammatisch *adj* ungrammatical; **~graziös** *adj* ungraceful, inelegant.
Ungulaten [ʊŋgu'la:tn] *pl (Zool)* ungulates *pl.*
ungültig *adj (nicht gültig)* invalid; *(nicht mehr gültig)* no longer valid; *(nichtig)* void; *Stimmzettel* spoilt; *(Sport) Tor* disallowed ◆ **„~"** *(in Paß)* "cancelled"; **~ werden** *(Paß)* to expire; **~er Sprung** no-jump; **etw für ~ erklären** to declare sth null and void; **eine Ehe für ~ erklären** to annul a marriage.
Ungültigkeit *f* invalidity; *(Nichtigkeit)* voidness; *(von Ehe)* nullity; *(von Tor)* disallowing.
Ungültigmachung *f (Admin)* invalidation.
Ungunst *f (liter)* disfavour; *(von Umständen, Lage)* adversity; *(von Witterung)* inclemency ◆ **zu jds ~en** to sb's disadvantage.
ungünstig *adj* unfavourable, disadvantageous; *Termin* inconvenient; *Augenblick, Wetter* bad; *Licht* unflattering; *(nicht preiswert)* expensive.
ungünstigstenfalls *adv* if the worst comes/came to the worst.
ungut *adj* bad; *Verhältnis auch* strained ◆ **ein ~es Gefühl haben** to have an uneasy *or* bad feeling; **nichts für ~!** no offence!
un-: ~haltbar *adj Zustand* intolerable; *Vorwurf, Behauptung etc* untenable; *Torschuß* unstoppable; **~handlich** *adj* unwieldy; **~harmonisch** *adj* unharmonious.
Unheil *nt* **-s,** *no pl* disaster ◆ **~ stiften** *or* **anrichten** to do damage.
unheilbar *adj* incurable ◆ **~ krank sein** to have a terminal illness.
unheil-: ⚠~bringend *adj* fateful, ominous; **~drohend, ~schwanger** *adj (liter)* portentous.
Unheilsprophet *m* prophet of doom.
Unheilstifter *m* mischief-maker.
unheil-: ⚠~verkündend *adj (liter)* ominous, fateful; **~voll** *adj* disastrous.
unheimlich [1] *adj* **(a)** *(angsterregend)* frightening, eerie, sinister ◆ **das/er ist mir ~** it/he gives me the creeps *(inf)*; **mir ist ~ (zumute)** it is uncanny.
(b) *(inf)* tremendous *(inf)*.
[2] *adv* [*auch* ʊn'haimlɪç] *(inf: sehr)* incredibly *(inf)* ◆ **~ viel Geld/viele Menschen** a tremendous *(inf) or* an incredible *(inf)* amount of money/number of people.
Un-: u~heizbar *adj* unheatable; **u~historisch** *adj* unhistoric; **u~höflich** *adj* impolite; **~höflichkeit** *f* impoliteness.
Unhold *m* **-(e)s, -e (a)** *(old: Böser)* fiend. **(b)** *(Press sl)* monster, fiend.
un-: ~hörbar *adj* silent; *Frequenzen* inaudible; **~hygienisch** *adj* unhygienic.
Uni *f* **-, -s** *(inf)* varsity *(dated Brit inf)*, "U" *(US inf)*, university; *siehe auch* **Universität.**
uni [y'ni:] *adj pred* self-coloured, plain ◆ **in U~blau** in plain blue.
UNICEF ['u:nitsɛf] *f* **- (die) ~** UNICEF.
un-: ~idealistisch *adj* unidealistic; **~idiomatisch** *adj* unidiomatic.
uniert *adj (Eccl) Kirche* uniate.
Unierte(r) *mf decl as adj (Eccl)* member of a uniate church.
unifarben [y'ni:-] *adj siehe* **uni.**
Uniform *f* **-, -en** uniform; *siehe* **ausziehen.**
uniform *adj* uniform.
uniformieren* *vt* **(a)** *(mit Uniform ausstatten)* to uniform. **(b)** *(einheitlich machen)* to make uniform.
uniformiert *adj* uniformed.
Uniformierte(r) *mf decl as adj* person *etc* in uniform.
Uniformität *f* uniformity.
Uniformrock *m* tunic.
Unikat *nt* **-(e)s, -e** unique specimen ◆ **ein ~ sein** to be unique.
Unikum *nt* **-s, -s** *or* **Unika (a)** *(Einmaliges)* unique thing *etc* ◆ **ein ~** a curiosity; *(Seltenheit)* a rarity. **(b)** *(inf)* real character.
unilateral *adj* unilateral.
un-: ~intelligent *adj* unintelligent; **~interessant** *adj* uninteresting; **sein Angebot ist für uns ~interessant** his offer is of no interest to us; **das ist doch völlig ~interessant** that's of absolutely no interest; **~interessiert** *adj (neutral)* disinterested; *(nicht interessiert)* uninterested.
Union *f* **-, -en** union ◆ **die ~** *(BRD Pol)* the CDU and CSU.
Unionsparteien *pl (BRD Pol)* CDU and CSU parties *pl.*
Unisono *nt* **-s, -s** *or* **Unisoni** *(Mus)* unison.
unisono *adv (Mus, fig)* in unison.
Unitarier(in *f*) [-iɐ, -iərɪn] *m* **-s, -** Unitarian.
Unitarismus *m* Unitarianism.
Unität *f* **(a)** *siehe* **Einheit. (b)** *siehe* **Einzigkeit. (c)** *(hum: Universität)* varsity *(dated Brit inf)*, "U" *(US inf)*, university.
Univ. abbr of **Universität.**
universal, universell [univɛr-] *adj* universal.
Universal- [univɛr'za:l-] *in cpds* all-purpose, universal; *(Mech)* universal; *Bildung etc* general; **~entwickler** *m (Phot)* universal developer; **~erbe** *m* universal successor, sole heir; **~genie** *nt* universal genius; **~geschichte** *f* world history.
Universalien [univɛr'za:liən] *pl (Philos, Ling)* universals.
Universalität [univɛrzali'tɛ:t] *f* universality.
Universal- [univɛr'za:l-]: **~mittel** *nt* universal remedy, cure-all; **~reiniger** *m* general-purpose cleaner.
universell [univɛr-] *siehe* **universal.**
Universität [univɛrzi'tɛ:t] *f* university ◆ **die ~ Freiburg, die Freiburger ~** the university of Freiburg, Freiburg university; **auf die ~ gehen, die ~ besuchen** to go to university; **die ~ verlassen** to leave university; *(das Gebäude)* to leave the university; **an eine ~ berufen werden** to be appointed to a professorship *or* given a chair.
Universitäts- *in cpds* university; *siehe auch* **Hochschul-**; **~bibliothek** *f* university library; **~buchhandlung** *f* university bookshop *(Brit) or* bookstore *(esp US)*; **~dozent** *m* senior lecturer *(Brit)*, associate professor *(US)*; **~gelände** *nt* university campus; **~institut** *nt* university institute; **~klinik** *f* university clinic *or* hospital; **~laufbahn** *f* university career; **~stadt** *f* university town; **~studium** *nt (Ausbildung)* university training; **dazu ist ein ~studium erforderlich** you need a degree for that; **~zeit** *f* university years *pl.*
Universum [uni'vɛrzʊm] *nt* **-s,** *no pl* universe.
unkameradschaftlich *adj* uncomradely; *Schüler, Verhalten* unfriendly.
Unke *f* **-, -n** toad; *(inf: Schwarzseher)* Jeremiah.
unken *vi (inf)* to foretell gloom.
unkenntlich *adj* unrecognizable; *Inschrift etc* indecipherable.
Unkenntlichkeit *f siehe adj* unrecognizableness; indecipherability ◆ **bis zur ~** beyond recognition.
Unkenntnis *f, no pl* ignorance ◆ **jdn in ~ über etw** *(acc)* **lassen** to leave sb in ignorance about sth; **in ~ über etw** *(acc)* **sein** to be ignorant about sth; **~ schützt vor Strafe nicht** *(Prov)* ignorance is no excuse.
Unkenruf *m (fig)* prophecy of doom.
Un-: u~keusch *adj* unchaste; **~keuschheit** *f* unchastity; **u~kindlich** *adj* unchildlike.
unklar *adj (unverständlich)* unclear; *(ungeklärt)* unclarified; *(undeutlich)* blurred, indistinct; *Wetter* hazy ◆ **es ist mir völlig ~, wie das geschehen konnte** I (just) can't understand how that could happen; **ich bin mir darüber noch im ~en** I'm not quite clear about that yet; **über etw** *(acc)* **völlig im ~en sein** to be completely in the dark about sth; **jdn über etw** *(acc)* **im ~en lassen** to leave sb in the dark about sth; **nur ~ zu erkennen sein** not to be easily discernible, not to be easy to make out.
Unklarheit *f* lack of clarity; *(über Tatsachen)* uncertainty ◆ **darüber herrscht noch ~** it is still uncertain *or* unclear.
Un-: u~kleidsam *adj* unflattering; **u~klug** *adj* unwise, imprudent, ill-advised; **~klugheit** *f* imprudence; *(Handlung)* imprudent act; **u~kollegial** *adj* uncooperative; **u~kompliziert** *adj* straightforward, uncomplicated; **u~komplizierter** more straightforward, less complicated; **~kompliziertheit** *f* straightforwardness; **u~kontrollierbar** *adj* uncontrollable; **u~kontrollierbar werden** *(Mißbrauch etc)* to get out of hand; **u~kontrolliert** *adj* unchecked; **u~konventionell** *adj* unconventional; **u~konzentriert** *adj* lacking in concentration; **er ist so u~konzentriert** he can't concentrate; **u~konzentriert arbeiten** to lack concentration in one's work; **u~korrekt** *adj* **(a)** improper; **(b)** *siehe* **inkorrekt**; **~korrektheit** *f* impropriety.
Unkosten *pl* costs *pl*; *(Ausgaben)* expenses *pl* ◆ **die ~ (für etw) tragen** to bear the cost(s) (of sth); to pay the expenses (for sth); **das ist mit großen ~ verbunden** that involves a great deal of expense; **(mit etw) ~ haben** to incur expense (with sth); **sich in ~ stürzen** *(inf)* to go to a lot of expense; **sich in geistige ~ stürzen** *(hum)* to strain oneself *(hum, iro)*.
Unkosten-: ~beitrag *m* contribution towards costs/expenses; **~vergütung** *f* reimbursement of expenses.
Unkraut *nt* weed ◆ **~, Unkräuter** weeds; **~ vergeht nicht** *(Prov)* it would take more than that to finish *me/him etc* off! *(hum)*.
Unkraut-: ~bekämpfung *f* weed control; **~bekämpfungsmittel** *nt* weed killer, herbicide *(form)*; **~vernichtung, ~vertilgung** *f* weed killing; **~vertilgungsmittel** *nt* weed killer, herbicide *(form)*.
Un-: u~kriegerisch *adj* unwarlike; **u~kritisch** *adj* uncritical; **u~kultiviert** [1] *adj* uncultivated; *Mensch auch* uncultured; [2] *adv* in an uncultivated *or* uncultured manner; **~kultur** *f (geh)* lack of culture; **u~kündbar** *adj* permanent; *Vertrag* binding, not terminable; *Anleihe* irredeemable; **in u~kündbarer Stellung** in a permanent position; **~kündbarkeit** *f* permanence; binding nature; irredeemability.
unkundig *adj* ignorant (*+gen* of) ◆ **einer Sprache ~ sein** to be unacquainted with *or* to have no knowledge of a language; **des Lesens/Schreibens ~ sein** to be illiterate, not to be able to read/write.
un-: ~künstlerisch *adj* unartistic; **~längst** *adv (geh)* recently; **~lauter** *adj* dishonest; *Wettbewerb* unfair; **~leidlich** *adj* disagreeable, unpleasant; **~lenkbar** *adj* uncontrollable; *Fahrzeug* unsteerable; **~lesbar, ~leserlich** *adj* unreadable; *Handschrift etc auch* illegible; **~leugbar** *adj* undeniable, indisputable; **~lieb** *adj*: **es ist mir nicht ~lieb, daß ...** I am quite glad that ...; **~liebenswürdig** *adj* not very pleasant.

⚠: for details of spelling reform, see supplement

➤ SPRACHE AKTIV: **unhaltbar** → 53.3

ụnliebsam *adj* unpleasant ◆ **er ist dem Lehrer ~ aufgefallen** his behaviour brought him to the teacher's notice; **das ist mir noch in ~er Erinnerung** that's still an unpleasant memory.

Un-: ụ~liniert *adj Papier* unruled, unlined; **~logik** *f* illogicality, lack of logic; **ụ~logisch** *adj* illogical; **u~lösbar** *adj* **(a)** *(fig) (untrennbar)* indissoluble; *(nicht lösbar) Problem etc* insoluble; *Widerspruch* irreconcilable; **(b)** *(lit) (Chem)* insoluble; *Knoten etc* inextricable; **u~löslich** *adj (Chem)* insoluble.

Ụnlust *f, no pl* **(a)** *(Widerwille)* reluctance ◆ **etw mit ~ tun** to do sth reluctantly *or* with reluctance. **(b)** *(Lustlosigkeit, Langeweile)* listlessness; *(St Ex)* slackness.

ụnlustig *adj (gelangweilt)* bored; *(widerwillig)* reluctant ◆ **ich bin heute ausgesprochen ~** I just can't find any enthusiasm today.

ụn-: ~magnetisch *adj* non-magnetic; **~manieriert** *adj (liter)* unmannered *(liter)*, unaffected; **~manierlich** *adj (dated)* unmannerly; **~männlich** *adj* unmanly; **~maskiert** *adj Ballbesucher etc* undisguised; *Bankräuber etc* unmasked.

Ụnmasse *f (inf)* load *(inf)* ◆ **eine ~ Leute/Bücher** *or* **an Büchern, ~n von Leuten/Büchern** a load of people/books *(inf)*, loads *or* masses of people/books *(inf)*.

ụnmaßgeblich *adj (nicht entscheidend) Urteil* not authoritative; *(unwichtig) Äußerung, Mensch* inconsequential, of no consequence ◆ **nach meiner ~en Meinung** *(hum)* in my humble opinion *(hum)*.

ụnmäßig *adj* excessive, immoderate ◆ **~ essen/trinken** to eat/drink to excess; **er hat gestern ~ getrunken** he drank far too much *or* an excessive amount yesterday.

Ụnmäßigkeit *f* excessiveness, immoderateness ◆ **~ im Essen/Trinken** excessive eating/drinking.

ụn-: ~materialistisch *adj* unmaterialistic; **~melodisch** *adj* unmelodious.

Ụnmenge *f* vast number; *(bei unzählbaren Mengenbegriffen)* vast amount ◆ **~n von Leuten, eine ~ Leute** a vast number *or* vast numbers of people; **~n essen** to eat an enormous amount, to eat masses *(inf)*.

Ụnmensch *m* brute, monster ◆ **ich bin ja kein ~** I'm not an ogre.

ụnmenschlich *adj* **(a)** inhuman. **(b)** *(inf: ungeheuer)* tremendous, terrific.

Ụnmenschlichkeit *f* inhumanity.

un-: ~mẹrklich *adj* imperceptible; **⚠~meßbar** *adj* unmeasurable; **~methodisch** *adj* unmethodical; **~militärisch** *adj* unmilitary; **⚠~mißverständlich** *adj* unequivocal, unambiguous; **jdm etw ~mißverständlich zu verstehen geben** to tell sb sth in no uncertain terms.

ụnmittelbar [1] *adj Nähe, Nachbarschaft etc* immediate; *(direkt)* direct; *(Jur) Besitz, Besitzer* direct, actual ◆ **aus ~er Nähe schießen** to fire at close range.
[2] *adv* immediately; *(ohne Umweg)* directly ◆ **~ danach** *or* **darauf** immediately *or* straight afterwards; **~ vor** *(+dat) (zeitlich)* immediately before; *(räumlich)* right *or* directly in front of; **das berührt mich ~** it affects me directly.

ụn-: ~möbliert *adj* unfurnished; **~modern** *adj* old-fashioned; **~modern werden** to go out of fashion; **~modisch** *adj* unfashionable.

▼ **ụnmöglich** [1] *adj* impossible; *(pej inf: unpassend auch)* ridiculous ◆ **das ist mir ~** that is impossible for me; **U~es/das U~e** the impossible; **etw ~ machen** to make sth impossible; **jdm etw ~ machen** to make it impossible for sb to do sth; **~ aussehen** *(inf)* to look ridiculous; **jdn/sich ~ machen** to make sb/oneself (look) ridiculous, to make sb look a fool/to make a fool of oneself.
▼ [2] *adv (keinesfalls)* not possibly; *(pej inf: unpassend)* impossibly ◆ **ich kann es ~ tun** I cannot possibly do it.

Ụnmöglichkeit *f* impossibility.

Ụn-: ~moral *f* immorality; **u~moralisch** *adj* immoral; **u~motiviert** [1] *adj* unmotivated; [2] *adv* without motivation; **u~mündig** *adj* under-age; *(fig: geistig unselbständig)* sheep-like; **~mündige(r)** *mf decl as adj* minor; **~mündigkeit** *f* minority; *(fig: geistige Unselbständigkeit)* mental immaturity; **u~musikalisch** *adj* unmusical; **~musikalität** *f* lack of musicality, unmusicalness.

Ụnmut *m* ill-humour; *(Unzufriedenheit)* displeasure *(über +acc* at).

ụnmutig *adj* ill-humoured; *(unzufrieden)* displeased *(über +acc* at).

Ụnmutsfalte *f* frown.

Un-: ụ~nachahmlich *adj* inimitable; **ụ~nachgiebig** *adj Material etc* inflexible; *(fig) Haltung, Mensch auch* intransigent, unyielding; **sich u~nachgiebig verhalten** to be obstinate *or* adamant; **~nachgiebigkeit** *f* inflexibility; intransigence; **ụ~nachsichtig** [1] *adj* severe; *(stärker)* merciless, pitiless; *Strenge* unrelenting; [2] *adv hinrichten* mercilessly, pitilessly; *bestrafen* severely; **~nachsichtigkeit** *f* severity; mercilessness, pitilessness; **u~nahbar** *adj* unapproachable, inaccessible; **~nahbarkeit** *f* unapproachableness, inaccessibility; **ụ~natürlich** *adj* unnatural; *(abnorm auch)* abnormal; **er ißt u~natürlich viel** he eats an abnormal amount; **~natürlichkeit** *f* unnaturalness; abnormality; **u~nẹnnbar** *adj (liter)* unspeakable, unutterable *(liter)*; **ụ~normal** *adj* abnormal; **ụ~nötig** *adj* unnecessary, needless; **sich u~nötig aufregen** to get unnecessarily *or* needlessly excited; **u~nötigerweise** *adv* unnecessarily, needlessly.

ụnnütz *adj* useless; *Geschwätz* idle; *(umsonst auch)* pointless ◆ **~ Geld ausgeben** to spend money unnecessarily *or* needlessly.

ụnnützerweise *adv* unnecessarily, needlessly.

UNO ['u:no] *f -, no pl* **die ~** the UN *sing*.

Ụn-: u~ökonomisch *adj* uneconomic; *Fahrweise, Konsumverhalten* uneconomical; **u~ordentlich** *adj* untidy; *Lebenswandel* disorderly; **~ordentlichkeit** *f* untidiness; disorderliness.

Ụn|ordnung *f* disorder *no indef art*; *(in Zimmer etc auch)* untidiness *no indef art*; *(Durcheinander)* muddle, mess ◆ **in ~ geraten** to get into (a state of) disorder/become untidy/get into a muddle *or* mess; **etw in ~ bringen** to get sth in a mess, to mess sth up; **~ machen** *or* **schaffen** to put *or* throw everything into disorder, to turn everything upside down.

Ụn-: u~organisch *adj* inorganic; **u~organisiert** [1] *adj* **(a)** disorganized; **(b)** *siehe* **nichtorganisiert**; [2] *adv* in a disorganized fashion *or* way; **u~orthodox** *adj* unorthodox; **~paarhufer** *pl (Zool)* odd-toed ungulates *pl*; **u~paar(ig)** *adj* unpaired; *(Med)* azygous *(spec)*; **u~pädagogisch** *adj* educationally unsound; *Lehrer etc* bad (as a teacher).

ụnparlamentarisch *adj* unparliamentary.

ụnparteiisch *adj* impartial, neutral; *Meinung, Richter, Urteil* impartial, unbiased.

Ụnparteiische(r) *mf decl as adj* impartial *or* neutral person ◆ **die Meinung eines ~n einholen** to get an impartial opinion; **der ~** *(Sport)* the referee.

Ụn-: u~parteilich *adj (esp Pol)* neutral; **~parteilichkeit** *f* neutrality; **u~passend** *adj (unangebracht)* unsuitable, inappropriate; *Zeit auch* inconvenient; *Augenblick* inconvenient, inopportune; **u~passierbar** *adj* impassable.

⚠ **ụnpäßlich** *adj (geh)* indisposed *(form)*, unwell *(auch euph)* ◆ **sich ~ fühlen** to be indisposed/feel unwell.

⚠ **Ụnpäßlichkeit** *f (geh)* indisposition *(form)* ◆ **sie mußte die Vorstellung wegen ~ leider absagen** unfortunately she had to cancel the performance because she was indisposed.

Ụn-: u~patriotisch *adj* unpatriotic; **~person** *f (Pol)* unperson; **u~persönlich** *adj* impersonal *(auch Ling)*; *Mensch* distant, aloof; **~persönlichkeit** *f siehe adj* impersonality; distance, aloofness; **u~pfändbar** *adj (Jur)* unseizable; **u~poetisch** *adj* unpoetic(al); **u~politisch** *adj* unpolitical; **u~populär** *adj* unpopular; **u~praktisch** *adj Mensch* unpractical; *Maschine, Lösung* impractical; **u~prätentiös** *adj (geh)* unpretentious; **u~präzis(e)** *adj* imprecise; **u~problematisch** *adj (ohne Probleme)* unproblematic; *(einfach, leicht)* uncomplicated; **das wird nicht ganz u~problematisch sein** it won't be without its problems; **u~produktiv** *adj* unproductive; *Kapital auch* idle; **u~proportioniert** *adj* out of proportion, disproportionate; *Körper* out of proportion, ill-proportioned.

ụnpünktlich *adj Mensch* unpunctual; *Zug* not on time ◆ **~ kommen/abfahren** to come/leave late; **er ist immer ~** he's never punctual *or* on time; **die Züge dort fahren immer ~** the trains there never run to time.

Ụnpünktlichkeit *f* unpunctuality ◆ **er kommt wegen der ~ der Züge oft zu spät** he's often late because the trains don't run to time.

ụn-: ~qualifiziert *adj* unqualified; *Äußerung* incompetent; **~quittiert** *adj* unreceipted; **~rasiert** *adj* unshaven; *siehe* **fern**.

Ụnrast *f -, no pl (geh)* restlessness.

Unrat ['ʊnra:t] *m* **-(e)s,** *no pl (geh)* refuse; *(fig)* filth ◆ **~ wittern** to suspect something.

ụn-: ~rationell *adj* inefficient; **~ratsam** *adj* inadvisable, unadvisable; **~realistisch** *adj* unrealistic.

ụnrecht *adj* wrong ◆ **auf ~e Gedanken kommen** *(dated)* to get naughty *or* wicked ideas; **das ist mir gar nicht so ~** I don't really mind.

Ụnrecht *nt* **-s,** *no pl* wrong, injustice ◆ **zu ~** *verdächtigt* wrongly, unjustly; **diese Vorurteile bestehen ganz zu ~** these prejudices are quite unfounded; **nicht zu ~** not without good reason; **im ~ sein** to be wrong; **jdn/sich ins ~ setzen** to put sb/oneself in the wrong; **ihm ist im Leben viel ~ geschehen** he has suffered many injustices *or* he has often been wronged in life; **u~ bekommen** to be shown to be wrong; **u~ haben** to be wrong; **jdm u~ geben** to contradict sb; **u~ handeln, ~ tun** to do wrong; **jdm ~ tun** to do sb an injustice, to do wrong by sb; **Sie haben nicht ganz u~** you're not entirely wrong.

Ụnrecht-: u~mäßig *adj* illegitimate, unlawful, illegal; *Thronfolger* wrongful; **sich etw u~mäßig aneignen** to misappropriate sth; **u~mäßigerweise** *adv* illegitimately, unlawfully, illegally; wrongfully; **~mäßigkeit** *f* unlawfulness, illegality; wrongfulness.

Ụnrechts-: ⚠~bewußtsein *nt* awareness of wrongdoing; **~tatbestand** *m* illegality; **~vereinbarung** *f* agreement to break the law.

Ụn-: u~redlich *adj* dishonest; **~redlichkeit** *f* dishonesty; **u~reell** *adj* unfair; *(unredlich)* dishonest; *Preis, Geschäft* unreasonable; **u~reflektiert** *adj Strahlen* unreflected; *Bemerkung* spontaneous; *Mensch* who acts/speaks without thinking; **etw u~reflektiert wiedergeben** to repeat sth without thinking.

ụnregelmäßig *adj* irregular *(auch Ling)*; *Zähne, Gesicht, Handschrift auch* uneven ◆ **~ essen/schlafen** not to eat/sleep regularly.

Ụnregelmäßigkeit *f siehe adj* irregularity; unevenness ◆ **ihm wurden (finanzielle) ~en vorgeworfen** he was accused of (financial) irregularities.

Ụn-: u~reif *adj Obst* unripe; *Mensch, Plan, Gedanke, Werk* immature; **~reife** *f siehe adj* unripeness; immaturity.

ụnrein *adj (schmutzig)* not clean, dirty; *Klang, Ton* impure; *Atem, Haut* bad; *(Rel) Speise, Tier, Mensch* unclean; *Gedanken, Taten* unchaste, impure ◆ **etw ins ~e sprechen** to say sth off the record; **etw ins ~e schreiben** to write sth out in rough.

Ụnreinheit *f siehe adj* dirtiness; impurity; *(von Atem)* unpleasantness; uncleanness; unchasteness, impurity ◆ **die ~ ihrer Haut** her bad skin.

Ụn-: u~reinlich *adj* not clean; **~reinlichkeit** *f* uncleanliness; **u~rentabel** *adj* unprofitable.

unrẹttbar *adv* **~ verloren** irretrievably lost; *(wegen Krankheit)* beyond all hope; **die ~ Verdammten** those damned beyond redemption *or* salvation.

Ụn-: u~richtig *adj* incorrect; *(Admin) Angaben etc* false; **u~richtigerweise** *adv* incorrectly; falsely; **~richtigkeit** *f* incorrectness; *(Admin: von Angaben*

etc) falseness; (Fehler) error, mistake; **u~romantisch** *adj* unromantic.
Unruh *f -, -en* (*von Uhr*) balance spring.
Unruhe *f -, -n* **(a)** *no pl* restlessness; (*Nervosität*) agitation; (*Besorgnis*) agitation, disquiet ◆ **in ~ sein** to be restless; (*besorgt*) to be agitated *or* uneasy. **(b)** *no pl* (*Lärm*) noise, disturbance; (*Geschäftigkeit*) (hustle and) bustle. **(c)** *no pl* (*Unfrieden*) unrest *no pl*, trouble ◆ **~ stiften** to create unrest; (*in Familie, Schule*) to make trouble. **(d)** **(politische) ~n** (political) disturbances *or* unrest *no pl*.
Unruhe-: **~herd** *m* trouble spot; ⚠**~potential** *nt* potential (for) unrest; **~stifter(in** *f*) *m -s, -* troublemaker.
unruhig *adj* restless; (*nervös auch*) fidgety *no adv*; (*laut, belebt*) noisy; *Schlaf* troubled *no adv*, fitful, uneasy; *Zeit etc* troubled, uneasy; *Bild, Muster* busy; *Meer* troubled ◆ **ein ~er Geist** (*inf*) a restless creature.
unrühmlich *adj* inglorious ◆ **ein ~es Ende nehmen** to have an inglorious end.
uns [1] *pers pron acc, dat of* **wir** us; (*dat auch*) to/for us ◆ **bei ~** (*zu Hause, im Betrieb etc*) at our place; (*in unserer Beziehung*) between us; (*in unserem Land*) in our country; **bei ~ zu Hause/im Garten** at our house/in our garden; **einer von ~** one of us; **ein Freund von ~** a friend of ours; **das gehört ~** that is ours *or* belongs to us; **viele Grüße von ~ beiden/allen** best wishes from both/all of us.
[2] *refl pron acc, dat* ourselves; (*einander*) each other, one another ◆ **wir freuten ~** we were glad; **wir wollen ~ ein neues Auto kaufen** we want to buy (ourselves) a new car; **~ selbst** ourselves; **wann sehen wir ~ wieder?** when will we see each other again?; **unter ~ gesagt** between ourselves, between you and me; **mitten unter ~** in our midst; **hier sind wir unter ~** we are alone here; **das bleibt unter ~** it won't go any further.
unsachgemäß *adj* improper ◆ **ein Gerät ~ behandeln** to put an appliance to improper use.
unsachlich *adj* **(a)** (*nicht objektiv*) unobjective. **(b)** (*fehl am Platz*) uncalled-for. **~ werden** to become personal.
Unsachlichkeit *f* lack of objectivity, unobjectiveness ◆ **diese Bemerkung zeugt von ~** this remark is/was uncalled-for.
unsagbar, unsäglich *adj* (*liter*) unspeakable, unutterable (*liter*).
unsanft *adj* rough; *Druck* ungentle; (*unhöflich*) rude ◆ **~ aus dem Schlaf gerissen werden** to be rudely awakened.
unsauber *adj* **(a)** (*ungewaschen, schmutzig*) dirty, not clean. **(b)** (*unordentlich*) *Handschrift, Arbeit* untidy; (*nicht exakt*) *Schuß, Schlag, Schnitt* inaccurate; *Ton, Klang* impure. **(c)** (*unmoralisch*) shady, underhand; *Spielweise* dirty (*inf*), unfair.
unschädlich *adj* harmless; *Genußmittel, Medikament auch* safe, innocuous; *Bombe auch* safe ◆ **jdn/etw ~ machen** (*inf*) to take care of sb/sth (*inf*).
Unschädlichkeit *f siehe adj* harmlessness; innocuousness; safeness.
unscharf *adj* **(a)** blurred, fuzzy; *Foto auch* out of focus; *Justierung* unsharp; (*Rad*) indistinct, unclear; *Erinnerung, Vorstellung* indistinct, hazy ◆ **der Sender/das Radio ist ~ eingestellt** the station/the radio is not clearly tuned. **(b)** *Munition* blank; *Bomben etc* unprimed.
Unschärfe *f siehe adj (a)* blurredness, fuzziness; unsharpness; indistinctness; haziness ◆ **begriffliche ~** lack of conceptual clarity.
unschätzbar *adj* incalculable, inestimable; *Hilfe* invaluable ◆ **von ~em Wert** invaluable; *Schmuck etc* priceless.
unscheinbar *adj* inconspicuous; (*unattraktiv*) *Aussehen, Mensch* unprepossessing.
unschicklich *adj* unseemly, improper ◆ **es ist ~ für eine junge Dame, das zu tun** it ill becomes a young lady *or* it is unseemly *or* improper for a young lady to do that.
Unschicklichkeit *f siehe adj* unseemliness *no indef art*, impropriety.
unschlagbar *adj* unbeatable.
Unschlagbarkeit *f* unbeatability.
unschlüssig *adj* (*unentschlossen*) undecided; (*zögernd*) irresolute, hesitant ◆ **sich** (*dat*) **~ (über etw** *acc*) **sein** to be undecided (about sth); to be hesitant about sth.
Unschlüssigkeit *f siehe adj* indecision; irresoluteness, hesitancy.
unschön *adj* (*häßlich*) unsightly; (*stärker*) ugly; *Gesicht* plain; (*unangenehm*) unpleasant ◆ **~e Szenen** ugly scenes.
Unschuld *f, no pl* **(a)** (*Schuldlosigkeit*) innocence. **(b)** (*Jungfräulichkeit*) virginity. **(c)** (*Naivität, Unverdorbenheit*) innocence; (*fig: Mädchen*) innocent ◆ **die ~ vom Lande** (*inf*) a real innocent; **in aller ~** in all innocence.
unschuldig *adj* **(a)** (*nicht schuldig*) innocent ◆ **an etw** (*dat*)**~ sein** not to be guilty of sth; **er war völlig ~ an dem Unfall** he was completely without blame in the accident, he was in no way responsible for the accident; **sind Sie schuldig oder ~?** — **~** how do you plead, guilty or not guilty? — not guilty; **jdn ~ verurteilen** to convict sb when he is innocent; **er sitzt ~ im Gefängnis** he is being held, an innocent man, in prison. **(b)** (*jungfräulich*) innocent, virginal ◆ **~ in die Ehe gehen** to be married a virgin; **er/sie ist noch ~** he/she is still a virgin. **(c)** (*harmlos, unverdorben*) innocent ◆ **~ tun** to act the innocent.
Unschuldige(r) *mf decl as adj* innocent (man/child *etc*) ◆ **die ~n** the innocent.
unschuldigerweise *adv* unjustly, despite one's innocence.
Unschulds-: **~beteuerung** *f* protest of innocence; **~engel** *m* (*inf*), **~lamm** *nt* (*inf*) little innocent; **~miene** *f* innocent face *or* expression; **mit ~miene** with an air of innocence; **~vermutung** *f* presumption of innocence; **u~voll** *adj* innocent; **mit u~voller Miene** with an air of innocence.

unschwer *adv* easily, without difficulty ◆ **das dürfte ja wohl ~ zu erraten sein** that shouldn't have been too hard to guess.
Unsegen *m* (*Unglück*) misfortune; (*Fluch*) curse (*für* (up)on).
⚠**unselbständig** [1] *adj* *Denken, Handeln* lacking in independence, unindependent; *Mensch auch* dependent, unable to stand on one's own two feet ◆ **Einkünfte aus ~er Arbeit** income from (salaried) employment; **manche Menschen bleiben ihr Leben lang ~** some people never manage to stand on their own two feet; **sei doch nicht immer so ~!** show a bit of independence once in a while!
[2] *adv* (*mit fremder Hilfe*) not independently ◆ **diese Schularbeit ist ~ angefertigt worden** this exercise was not done independently.
⚠**Unselbständige(r)** *mf decl as adj* (*Fin*) employed person.
⚠**Unselbständigkeit** *f* lack of independence, dependence.
unselig *adj* (*unglücklich*) unfortunate; (*verhängnisvoll*) ill-fated ◆ **Zeiten ~en Angedenkens!** unhappy memories!; **ich U~er!** (*old liter*) oh unhappy wretch! (*old liter*), woe is me! (*old liter*); *siehe* **Angedenken**.
unser [1] *poss pron* **(a)** (*adjektivisch*) our ◆ **~e** *or* **unsre Bücher** our books. **(b)** (*old: substantivisch*) ours.
[2] *pers pron gen of* **wir** (*old, Bibl, geh*) of us ◆ **~ beider gemeinsame Zukunft** our common future; **Herr, erbarme dich ~** Lord, have mercy upon us; **~ aller heimlicher Wunsch** the secret wish of all of us.
unser|einer, unser|eins *indef pron* (*inf*) the likes of us (*inf*).
uns(e)re(r, s) *poss pron, nt auch* **unsers** (*substantivisch*) ours ◆ **der/die/das ~** (*geh*) ours; **wir tun das U~** (*geh*) we are doing our bit; **die U~n** (*geh*) our family; **das U~** (*geh: Besitz*) what is ours.
unser(er)seits *adv* (*auf unserer Seite*) for our part; (*von unserer Seite*) from *or* on our part ◆ **den Vorschlag haben wir ~ gemacht** we made the suggestion ourselves.
uns(e)resgleichen *indef pron* people like us *or* ourselves ◆ **Menschen ~** people like us *or* ourselves.
uns(e)resteils *adv siehe* **unser(er)seits**.
uns(e)rige(r, s) *poss pron* (*old, geh*) **der/die/das ~** ours; **die U~n** our families; **das ~** (*Besitz*) what is ours; **wir haben das U~ getan** we have done our part.
unseriös *adj* *Mensch* slippery, not straight; *Auftreten, Aussehen, Kleidung, Bemerkung* frivolous; *Firma, Bank* untrustworthy, shady; *Zeitung* not serious; *Verlag* low-brow; *Schriftsteller, Wissenschaftler* not to be taken seriously, not serious, frivolous ◆ **das Geschäft war keineswegs ~** the deal was strictly above board.
unserseits *adv siehe* **unser(er)seits**.
unsersgleichen *indef pron siehe* **uns(e)resgleichen**.
unserthalben, unsertwegen *adv* on our behalf.
unsertwillen *adv*: **um ~** for our sake.
Unservater *nt -s, -* (*Sw*) *siehe* **Vaterunser**.
unsicher *adj* **(a)** (*gefährlich*) dangerous, unsafe ◆ **die Gegend ~ machen** (*fig inf*) to knock about the district (*inf*); **sich ~ fühlen** to feel unsafe. **(b)** (*nicht selbstbewußt, verunsichert*) insecure, unsure (of oneself) ◆ **jdn ~ machen** to make sb feel unsure of himself/herself; **sie blickte ~ im Kreise umher** she looked round timidly. **(c)** (*ungewiß, zweifelhaft*) unsure, uncertain; (*unstabil*) uncertain, unstable, unsettled. **(d)** (*ungeübt, ungefestigt*) unsure; *Hand* unsteady; *Kenntnisse* shaky ◆ **~ auf den Beinen** unsteady on one's feet; **mit ~er Hand** with an unsteady hand.
Unsicherheit *f siehe adj (a-c)* **(a)** danger. **(b)** unsureness. **(c)** unsureness, uncertainty; instability.
Unsicherheitsfaktor *m* element of uncertainty.
unsichtbar *adj* (*lit, fig*) invisible.
Unsichtbarkeit *f, no pl* invisibility.
Unsinn *m, no pl* nonsense *no indef art*, rubbish *no indef art* ◆ **~ machen** *or* **treiben** to do silly things; **~ reden** to talk nonsense; **laß den ~!** stop fooling about!; **mach keinen ~, Hände hoch!** (*inf*) no clever stuff — put your hands up! (*inf*); **wirklich? mach keinen ~!** (*inf*) really? — stop messing about! (*inf*); *siehe* **Sinn**.
unsinnig [1] *adj* (*sinnlos*) nonsensical, foolish; (*ungerechtfertigt*) unreasonable; (*stärker*) absurd.
[2] *adv* nonsensically, foolishly; unreasonably; absurdly ◆ **~ viel** (*inf*) an incredible amount (*inf*); **~ hohe Preise** (*inf*) ridiculously high prices (*inf*).
Unsinnigkeit *f siehe adj* foolishness; unreasonableness; absurdity.
Unsitte *f* (*schlechte Gewohnheit*) bad habit; (*dummer Brauch*) silly custom.
unsittlich *adj* immoral; (*in sexueller Hinsicht*) indecent.
unsolid(e) *adj* *Mensch* free-living; (*unredlich*) *Firma, Angebot, Geschäftsmann* unreliable ◆ **~ leben** to have an unhealthy life-style; **ein ~es Leben führen** to be free-living; **an dem Angebot war nichts U~es** the offer was strictly above board.
Un-: **u~sortiert** *adj* unsorted; **u~sozial** *adj* *Verhalten, Mensch* antisocial; *Maßnahmen, Politik* unsocial; **u~spezifisch** *adj* non-specific; **u~sportlich** *adj* **(a)** (*ungelenkig*) unathletic; **(b)** (*unfair*) unsporting; **~sportlichkeit** *f* (*unfairness*) lack of sportsmanship; **und das bei seiner ~sportlichkeit!** and he being so unathletic!
unsre *pron siehe* **unser**.
unsrerseits *adv siehe* **uns(er)erseits**.
unsresgleichen *indef pron siehe* **uns(e)resgleichen**.
unsresteils *adv siehe* **uns(e)resteils**.
unsretwegen *adv siehe* **unsertwegen**.
unsretwillen *adv siehe* **unsertwillen**.

⚠: for details of spelling reform, see supplement

unsrige(r, s) *poss pron siehe* **uns(e)rige(r, s).**
un-: ~stabil *adj* unstable; **~statthaft** *adj (form)* inadmissible; *(~gesetzlich)* illegal; *(Sport)* not allowed.
unsterblich [1] *adj* immortal; *Liebe* undying ◆ **jdn ~ machen** to immortalize sb.
[2] *adv (inf)* utterly ◆ **sich ~ blamieren** to make an utter fool *or* a complete idiot of oneself; **~ verliebt sein** to be head over heels *or* madly in love *(inf)*.
Unsterbliche(r) *mf* immortal.
Unsterblichkeit *f* immortality ◆ **die ~ seiner Liebe** his undying love.
Unsterblichkeitsglaube *m* belief in immortality.
Unstern *m, no pl (liter)* unlucky star ◆ **die Liebe der beiden stand unter einem ~** their love was followed by an unlucky star.
unstet *adj Glück, Liebe* fickle; *Mensch* restless; *(wankelmütig)* changeable; *Entwicklung* unsteady; *Leben* unsettled.
Unstete *f -, no pl siehe* **Unstetigkeit.**
Unstetigkeit *f siehe adj* fickleness; restlessness; changeability; unsteadiness; unsettled nature.
Un-: u~stillbar *adj* **(a)** *Durst, Wissensdurst* unquenchable; *Verlangen, Sehnsucht, Hunger* insatiable; **(b)** *Blutstrom* uncontrollable; **u~stimmig** *adj Aussagen etc* at variance, differing *attr*; **in einem Punkt sind wir noch u~stimmig** we still disagree *or* differ on one point; **~stimmigkeit** *f (~genauigkeit, Fehler)* discrepancy, inconsistency; *(Streit)* difference; **u~stofflich** *adj* immaterial; *Seele auch* incorporeal; **u~streitig** *adv* indisputably, incontestably; **~summe** *f* vast sum; **u~symmetrisch** *adj* asymmetric(al).
unsympathisch *adj* unpleasant, disagreeable ◆ **er ist ~** he's unpleasant *or* a disagreeable type; **das/er ist mir ~** I don't like that/him; **am ~sten an diesen Leuten ist mir ...** what I find most unpleasant about *or* what I like least about these people is ...
unsystematisch *adj* unsystematic.
untad(e)lig, untadelhaft *(rare) adj* impeccable; *Verhalten auch* irreproachable; *Mensch* beyond reproach.
untalentiert *adj* untalented.
Untat *f* atrocity, atrocious deed ◆ **~en begehen** *(im Krieg etc)* to commit atrocities.
untätig *adj (müßig)* idle; *(nicht handelnd)* passive; *Vulkan* inactive, dormant.
Untätigkeit *f siehe adj* idleness; passivity; dormancy.
Un-: u~tauglich *adj (zu, für* for) unsuitable; *(für Wehrdienst)* unfit; **~tauglichkeit** *f siehe adj* unsuitability; unfitness; **u~teilbar** *adj* indivisible.
unten *adv (im unteren Teil, am unteren Ende, in Rangfolge)* at the bottom; *(tiefer, drunten)* (down) below; *(an der Unterseite)* underneath; *(in Gebäude)* (down) below, downstairs; *(inf: geographisch)* down south; *(flußab)* downstream; *(tiefer gelegen)* down there/here ◆ **von ~** from below; **die Frau von ~ war gekommen** the woman from downstairs *or* down below had come; **nach ~** down; **die Säule wird nach ~ hin breiter** the column broadens out towards the base *or* bottom; **bis ~** to the bottom; **der Schneefall kam nicht bis ~ ins Tal** the snow did not reach as far down as the valley; **~ am Berg/Fluß** at the bottom of the hill/down by the river(side); **~ im Tal/Wasser/Garten** down in the valley/water/garden; **~ im Glas** at the bottom of the glass; **~ auf dem Bild** at the bottom of the picture; **~ auf der Straße** down on the street; **dort** *or* **da/hier ~** down there/here; **weiter ~** further down; **~ bleiben** to stay down; **rechts/links ~** down on the right/left; **siehe ~** see below; **er ist bei mir ~ durch** *(inf)* I'm through *or* I've finished with him *(inf)*; **ich weiß schon nicht mehr, was oben und ~ ist** *(inf)* I don't know whether I'm coming or going *(inf) or* whether I'm on my head or my heels *(inf)*; **~ wohnen** to live downstairs.
Unten-: u~an *adv (am unteren Ende)* at the far end; *(in Reihenfolge: lit, fig)* at the bottom; **(bei jdm) u~an stehen** *(fig)* not to be a priority (with sb), to be at the bottom of sb's list; **u~drunter** *adv (inf)* underneath; **⚠u~erwähnt, ⚠u~genannt** *adj attr* mentioned below; **der/die ~erwähnte** *or* **~genannte** the undermentioned (person) *(form)*, the person mentioned below; **bitte lesen Sie auch das u~erwähnte** please also see below; **u~herum** *adv (inf)* down below *(inf)*; **⚠u~liegend** *adj attr* bottom; **⚠u~stehend** *adj* following; *(lit)* standing below; **im u~stehenden** given below; **u~stehendes** the following; **das U~stehende** what follows.
unter *prep* **(a)** *+dat (~halb von)* under; *(drunter)* underneath, below; *(U~ordnung ausdrückend)* under; *(zwischen, innerhalb)* among(st); *(weniger, geringer als)* under, below ◆ **~ 18 Jahren/DM 50** under 18 years (of age)/DM 50; **~ dem Durchschnitt** below average; **Temperaturen ~ 25 Grad** temperatures below 25 degrees; **Städte ~ 10.000 Einwohner(n)** towns with a population of under *or* below 10,000; **~ sich** *(dat)* **sein** to be by themselves; **jdn ~ sich haben** to have sb under one; **~ etw leiden** to suffer from sth; **~ Mittag** *(dial)* in the morning; **~ der Woche** *(dial)* within the (working) week; **~ anderem** inter alia, among other things.
(b) *+acc* under ◆ **bis ~ das Dach voll mit ...** full to the rafters with ...; **~ Verbrecher geraten** to fall in with criminals.
Unter-: ~abteilung *f* subdivision; **~angebot** *nt* lack *(an +dat* of); **~arm** *m* forearm; **~armtasche** *f* clutch bag; **~art** *f (esp Biol)* subspecies; **⚠~ausschuß** *m* subcommittee; **~bau** *m, pl* **-ten** *(von Gebäude)* foundations *pl*; *(von Brücke, Bahnstrecke, fig)* substructure; *(bei Straßen)* (road)bed; **~begriff** *m* member of a conceptual class, subsumable concept; **u~belegt** *adj Hotel etc* not full; *Fortbildungskurs* under-subscribed; **das Hotel ist ziemlich u~belegt** the hotel is not very full; **u~belichten*** *vti insep (Phot)* to underexpose; **u~belichtet** *adj (Phot)* underexposed; **geistig u~belichtet sein** *(hum)* to be a bit dim *(inf)*; **u~bemannt** *adj* undermanned; **u~besetzt** *adj* understaffed; **~besetzung** *f* understaffing; **~bett** *nt* feather bed; **u~bewerten*** *vt insep* to underrate, to undervalue; **~bewertung** *f* underrating *no pl*, undervaluation; **⚠u~bewußt** *adj* subconscious; **das ~bewußte** the subconscious; **⚠~bewußtsein** *nt* subconscious; **im ~bewußtsein** subconsciously; **u~bezahlen*** *vt insep* to underpay; **u~bezahlt** *adj* underpaid; **~bezahlung** *f* underpayment; **u~bieten*** *vt insep irreg Konkurrenten* to undercut; *(fig)* to surpass; **sich gegenseitig u~bieten** to undercut each other; **eine kaum noch zu u~bietende Leistung** an unsurpassable achievement *(iro)*; **~bilanz** *f* deficit balance; **u~binden[1]*** *vt insep irreg* to stop, to prevent; *(Med) Blutung* to ligature; **u~binden[2]** *vt sep irreg* to tie (on) underneath; **~bindung** *f, no pl* ending; *(Med)* ligature; **u~bleiben*** *vi insep irreg aux sein* **(a)** *(aufhören)* to cease, to stop; **das hat zu u~bleiben** that will have to cease *or* stop; **(b)** *(nicht geschehen)* not to occur *or* happen; **das wäre besser u~blieben** *(Vorfall)* it would have been better if it had never happened; *(Bemerkung)* it would have been better left unsaid; **(c)** *(versäumt werden)* to be omitted; **~bodenschutz** *m (Mot)* underseal; **u~brechen*** *insep irreg* [1] *vt* to interrupt; *Stille, Reise, Eintönigkeit, Langeweile, Gleichförmigkeit* to break; *(langfristig)* to break off; *Telefonverbindung* to disconnect; *Spiel* to suspend, to stop; **entschuldigen Sie bitte, wenn ich Sie u~breche** forgive me for interrupting; **wir sind u~brochen worden** *(am Telefon)* we've been cut off; [2] *vr* to break off; **~brecher** *m* **-s, -** *(Elec)* interrupter; *(Aut)* contact breaker; **~brecherkontakt** *m (Elec, Aut)* (contact-breaker) point; **~brechung** *f* interruption; break *(+gen* in); *(von Telefonverbindung)* disconnection; *(von Spiel)* stoppage; **bei ~brechung der Reise** when breaking the journey; **ohne ~brechung** without a break; **nach einer kurzen ~brechung** *(Rad, TV)* after a short break *or* intermission; **mit ~brechungen** with a few breaks in between; **~brechungsbefehl** *m (Comput)* break command; **u~breiten*** *vt insep Plan* to present; **(jdm) einen Vorschlag u~breiten** to make a proposal (to sb), to put a suggestion (to sb).
unterbringen *vt sep irreg* **(a)** *(verstauen, Platz geben)* to put; *(in Heim, Krankenhaus etc)* to put; *Arbeitslose etc* to fix up *(bei* with); *Zitat (in Text etc)* to get in *(in etw (acc)* sth) ◆ **ich kann in meinem Auto noch einen ~** I can get one more *or* I have room for one more in my car; **das Krankenhaus kann keine neuen Patienten ~** the hospital has room for *or* can accommodate no new patients; **etw bei jdm ~** to leave sth with sb; **ich kenne ihn, aber ich kann ihn nirgends ~** *(inf)* I know him, but I just can't place him.
(b) *(Unterkunft geben) Menschen* to accommodate; *(in Haus, Hotel, Krankenhaus etc auch)* to put up; *Ausstellung, Sammlung auch* to house ◆ **gut/schlecht untergebracht sein** to have good/bad accommodation; *(versorgt werden)* to be well/badly looked after; **wie sind Sie untergebracht?** what's your accommodation like?; how are you looked after?
Unterbringung *f* accommodation.
Unterbruch *m (Sw) siehe* **Unterbrechung.**
unterbuttern *vt sep (inf)* **(a)** to sneak in *(inf)*; *(zuschießen)* to throw in. **(b)** *(unterdrücken)* to ride roughshod over; *(opfern)* to sacrifice ◆ **er wird von ihr untergebuttert** she dominates him.
Unterdeck *nt (Naut)* lower deck ◆ **im ~** below deck.
⚠**unterderhand** *adv* secretly; *verkaufen* privately.
unterdes(sen) *adv* (in the) meantime, meanwhile.
Unterdruck *m (Phys)* below atmospheric pressure; *(Med)* low blood pressure, hypotension *(spec)*.
unterdrücken* *vt insep* **(a)** *(zurückhalten) Neugier, Gähnen, Lachen* to suppress; *Gefühle, Tränen auch* to hold back, to restrain; *Antwort, Bemerkung* to hold back. **(b)** *(beherrschen) Volk, Sklaven* to oppress, to repress; *Freiheit* to suppress; *Revolution* to suppress, to put down ◆ **die Unterdrückten** the oppressed.
Unterdrücker(in *f***)** *m* **-s, -** oppressor.
Unterdruckschleuse *f* vacuum lock.
Unterdrückung *f siehe vt* **(a)** suppression; restraining; holding back. **(b)** oppression, repression; suppression.
unterdurchschnittlich *adj* below average ◆ **er verdient ~** he has a below average income, he earns below the average.
unter|einander *adv* **(a)** *(gegenseitig)* each other; *(miteinander)* among ourselves/themselves *etc* ◆ **Familien, die ~ heiraten** families that intermarry. **(b)** *(räumlich)* one below *or* underneath the other.
⚠**unter|einander-** *pref* **(a)** *(durcheinander-)* together. **(b)** *(örtlich)* one below *or* underneath the other.
Unter-: u~entwickelt *adj* underdeveloped; *(inf: geistig u~entwickelt)* thick *(inf)*; **~entwicklung** *f* underdevelopment.
Unter-: u~ernährt *adj* undernourished, suffering from malnutrition; **~ernährung** *f* malnutrition.
untere(r, s) *adj, superl* **unterste(r, s)** lower.
unterfangen* *vr insep irreg (geh)* to dare, to venture.
Unterfangen *nt* **-s, -** *(geh)* venture, undertaking ◆ **ein schwieriges ~** a difficult undertaking.
unterfassen *vt sep* **jdn ~** to take sb's arm; **sie gingen untergefaßt** they walked along arm in arm *or* with arms linked.
Unterfranken *nt (Geog)* Lower Franconia.
unterführen* *vt insep* to pass underneath ◆ **die Autobahn wird hier von einer Landstraße unterführt** a highway passes underneath the motorway at this point.
Unterführung *f* **(a)** underpass; *(für Fußgänger auch)* subway. **(b)** *(Typ etc) siehe* **Unterführungszeichen.**
Unterführungszeichen *nt (Typ)* ditto (mark).

Unter-: ~funktion *f* insufficient function *no indef art*, hypofunction (*spec*); **(eine) ~funktion der Schilddrüse** thyroid insufficiency, hypothyroidism (*spec*); **~futter** *nt* interfacing; **u~füttern*** *vt insep* to interface.
Untergang *m* **(a)** (*von Schiff*) sinking.
(b) (*von Gestirn*) setting.
(c) (*das Zugrundegehen*) (*allmählich*) decline; (*völlig*) destruction; (*der Welt*) end; (*von Individuum*) downfall, ruin ◆ **die Propheten des ~s** the prophets of doom; **dem ~ geweiht sein** to be doomed; **du bist noch mal mein ~!** you'll be the death of me! (*inf*).
Untergangsstimmung *f* feeling of doom.
Unter-: u~gärig *adj Bier* bottom-fermented; **~gattung** *f* subgenus.
untergeben *adj* subordinate.
Untergebene(r) mf decl as adj subordinate; (*pej: Subalterner auch*) underling.
untergegangen *adj Schiff* sunken; *Gestirn* set; *Volk etc* extinct; *Zivilisation, Kultur* extinct, lost.
untergehen *vi sep irreg aux sein* **(a)** (*versinken*) to sink; (*Schiff auch*) to go down; (*fig: im Lärm etc*) to be submerged *or* drowned.
(b) (*Gestirn*) to set ◆ **sein Stern ist im U~** his star is waning *or* on the wane.
(c) (*zugrundegehen*) (*Kultur*) (*allmählich*) to decline; (*völlig*) to be destroyed; (*Welt*) to come to an end; (*Individuum*) to perish ◆ **dort muß man sich durchsetzen, sonst geht man unter** you've got to assert yourself there or you'll go under.
Unter-: u~geordnet *adj Dienststelle, Stellung* subordinate; *Rolle auch* secondary; *Bedeutung* secondary; ⚠**~geschoß** *nt* basement; **~gestell** *nt* **(a)** base; (*Mot*) subframe; **(b)** (*inf*) (*Beine*) pins *pl* (*inf*); **~gewicht** *nt* underweight; **~gewicht haben** to be underweight; **u~gewichtig** *adj* underweight; **u~gliedern*** *vt insep* to subdivide; **u~graben[1]*** *vt insep irreg* to undermine; **u~graben[2]** *vt sep irreg* to dig in.
Untergrund *m, no pl* **(a)** (*Geol*) subsoil. **(b)** (*Farbschicht*) undercoat; (*Hintergrund*) background. **(c)** (*Liter, Pol etc*) underground ◆ **er lebt seit Jahren im ~** he's been living underground for years; **in den ~ gehen** to go underground.
Untergrund- *in cpds* (*Liter, Pol*) underground; **~bahn** *f* underground, subway (*US*).
Unter-: ~gruppe *f* subgroup; **u~haben** *vt sep irreg* (*inf*) to have (on) underneath; **u~haken** *sep* [1] *vt* **jdn u~haken** to link arms with sb; [2] *vr* **sich bei jdm u~haken** to link arms with sb; **u~gehakt gehen** to walk arm in arm.
unterhalb [1] *prep +gen* below; (*bei Fluß auch*) downstream from.
[2] *adv* below; downstream ◆ **~ von** below; downstream from.
Unterhalt *m* **-(e)s,** *no pl* **(a)** (*Lebens~*) keep, maintenance (*esp Jur*) ◆ **für jds ~ aufkommen** to pay for sb's keep; **seinen ~ verdienen** to earn one's living; **seinen ~ haben** to earn enough. **(b)** (*Instandhaltung*) upkeep.
unterhalten[1]* *insep irreg* [1] *vt* **(a)** (*versorgen, ernähren*) to support; *Angestellten* to maintain.
(b) (*halten, betreiben*) *Geschäft, Gaststätte* to keep, to run; *Konto* to have; *Kfz* to run.
(c) (*instand halten*) *Gebäude, Fahrzeug etc* to maintain.
(d) (*pflegen, aufrechterhalten*) *Kontakte, Beziehungen* to maintain.
(e) *Gäste, Publikum* to entertain.
[2] *vr* **(a)** (*sprechen*) to talk (*mit* to, with) ◆ **man kann sich mit ihm gut/schlecht/glänzend ~** he's easy/not easy/really easy to talk to; **man kann sich mit ihm nicht ~** he's impossible to talk to, you can't talk to him; **sich mit jdm (über etw** *acc*) **~** to (have a) talk *or* chat with sb (about sth); **Herr Schmidt, ich hätte mich mal gerne mit Ihnen ein bißchen ~** Herr Schmidt I should like (to have) a little talk *or* chat with you; **wir ~ uns noch!** (*drohend, begütigend*) we'll talk about that later.
(b) (*sich vergnügen*) to enjoy oneself, to have a good time ◆ **habt ihr Euch gut ~?** did you enjoy yourselves *or* have a good time?; **sich mit etw ~** to amuse *or* entertain oneself with sth.
unterhalten[2] *vt sep irreg* to hold underneath ◆ **ein Tuch ~** to hold a cloth underneath.
Unterhalter(in *f*) *m* **-s, - (a)** entertainer; (*unterhaltsamer Mensch*) conversationalist. **(b)** (*Verdiener*) breadwinner.
unterhaltsam *adj* entertaining.
Unterhalts-: u~berechtigt *adj* entitled to maintenance; **~geld** *nt* maintenance; **~klage** *f* action for maintenance; **(gegen jdn) ~klage erheben** to file a suit for maintenance (against sb); **~kosten** *pl* (*von Gebäude, Anlage*) maintenance (costs *pl*); (*von Kfz*) running costs *pl*; **~leistung** *f* payment of maintenance; **~pflicht** *f* obligation to pay maintenance; **u~pflichtig** *adj* under obligation to pay maintenance; **~pflichtige(r)** *mf decl as adj* person obliged to pay maintenance.
Unterhaltung *f* **(a)** (*Gespräch*) talk, chat, conversation ◆ **eine ~ (mit jdm) führen** to have a talk *or* conversation (with sb); **hier kann man keine ~ führen** we can't talk here.
(b) (*Amüsement*) entertainment ◆ **wir wünschen gute** *or* **angenehme ~** we hope you enjoy the programme.
(c) *no pl* (*Instandhaltung*) upkeep; (*von Gebäuden auch, Kfz, Maschinen*) maintenance.
Unterhaltungs-: ~elektronik *f* (*Industrie*) consumer electronics *sing*; (*Geräte*) audio systems *pl*; **~film** *m* light entertainment film; **~kosten** *pl siehe* **Unterhaltskosten**; **~lektüre** *f* light reading; **~literatur** *f* light fiction; **~musik** *f* light music; **~programm** *nt* light entertainment programme; **~roman** *m* light novel; **~sendung** *f* light entertainment programme; **~wert** *m, no pl* entertainment value.

Unterhändler *m* negotiator.
Unterhandlung *f* negotiation.
Unterhaus *nt* Lower House, House of Commons (*Brit*), Commons *sing* (*Brit*) ◆ **Mitglied des ~es** member of parliament, MP.
Unterhaus-: ~abgeordnete(r) *mf*, **~mitglied** *nt* member of parliament, MP; **~sitzung** *f* session of the House; **~wahl** *f* Commons vote (*Brit*).
Unterhaut *f* (*Anat*) subcutis.
Unterhemd *nt* vest (*Brit*), undershirt (*US*).
unterhöhlen* *vt insep* **(a)** to hollow out. **(b)** (*fig*) to undermine.
Unterholz *nt, no pl* undergrowth.
Unterhose *f* (*Herren~*) (under)pants *pl*, pair of (under)pants, briefs *pl*; (*Damen~*) (pair of) pants *pl or* briefs *pl* ◆ **lange ~n** long johns *pl*.
unter|irdisch *adj* underground; *Fluß etc auch* subterranean ◆ **~ verlaufen** to run underground.
unterjochen* *vt insep* to subjugate.
Unterjochung *f* subjugation.
unterjubeln *vt sep* (*inf*) **(a)** (*andrehen*) **jdm etw ~** to palm sth off on sb (*inf*). **(b)** (*anlasten*) **jdm etw ~** to pin sth on sb (*inf*).
unterkellern* *vt insep* to build with a cellar ◆ **das Haus ist nicht unterkellert** the house doesn't have a cellar; **ein ganz/teilweise unterkellertes Haus** a house with a cellar underneath the whole of it/underneath part of it.
Unter-: ~kiefer *m* lower jaw; **~klasse** *f* **(a)** subclass; **(b)** (*Sociol*) lower class; **~kleid** *nt* full-length slip *or* petticoat; **~kleidung** *f* underwear, underclothes *pl*.
unterkommen *vi sep irreg aux sein* **(a)** (*Unterkunft finden*) to find accommodation; (*inf: Stelle finden*) to find a job (*als* as, *bei* with, at) ◆ **bei jdm ~** to stay at sb's (place). **(b)** (*inf*) **so etwas ist mir noch nie untergekommen!** I've never come across anything like it!
Unterkommen *nt* **-s, -** (*Obdach*) accommodation ◆ **bei jdm ein ~ finden** to be put up at sb's (place).
Unter-: ~körper *m* lower part of the body; **u~kriechen** *vi sep irreg aux sein* (*inf*) to shack up (*bei jdm* with) (*inf*); **u~kriegen** *vt sep* (*inf*) to bring down; (*deprimieren*) to get down; **sich nicht u~kriegen lassen** not to let things get one down; **laß dich von ihnen nicht u~kriegen** don't let them get you down; **u~kühlen*** *vt insep Flüssigkeit, Metalle, Gas* to supercool, to undercool; *Körper* to expose to subnormal temperatures; **u~kühlt** *adj* supercooled, undercooled; *Körper* affected by hypothermia; (*fig*) *Atmosphäre* chilly; *Mensch* cool; *Musik, Spielweise* subdued, reserved; **~kühlung** *f, no pl* (*von Flüssigkeit, Metall, Gas*) supercooling, undercooling; (*im Freien*) exposure; (*Med*) hypothermia.
Unterkunft *f* **-, Unterkünfte (a)** accommodation (*Brit*) *no pl*, accommodations *pl* (*US*), lodging ◆ **eine ~ suchen** to look for accommodation *or* lodging; **~ und Verpflegung** board and lodging. **(b)** (*von Soldaten etc*) quarters *pl*; (*esp in Privathaus*) billet.
Unterkunfts-: ~möglichkeit *f* accommodation *no pl*; **habt ihr dort eine ~möglichkeit?** have you any accommodation *or* somewhere to stay there?; **~raum** *m* quarters *pl*.
Unterlage *f* **(a)** base; (*Schreib~, Tuch, Decke zum Bügeln auch*) pad; (*für Teppich*) underlay; (*im Bett*) drawsheet ◆ **du brauchst eine ~** (*zum Schreiben*) you need something to rest on; (*zum Schlafen*) you need something to lie on. **(b)** *usu pl* (*Belege, Urkunden, Papiere*) document, paper. **(c)** (*Hort*) rootstock.
Unter-: ~land *nt, no pl* lowland; **~länder(in** *f*) *m* **-s, -** lowlander; **u~ländisch** *adj attr* lowland; **~länge** *f* tail (of letters), descender (*spec*); ⚠**~laß** *m*: **ohn(e) ~laß** (*old*) incessantly, continuously; *arbeiten auch* without respite.
unterlassen* *vt insep irreg* (*nicht tun*) to refrain from; (*nicht durchführen*) not to carry out; (*auslassen*) to omit; *Bemerkung, Zwischenrufe* to refrain from making; *etwas Dummes etc* to refrain from doing; *Trinken auch* to abstain from ◆ **keine Anstrengung** *or* **nichts ~** to spare no effort; **~ Sie das!** don't do that, stop that!; **er hat es ~, mich zu benachrichtigen** he failed *or* omitted to notify me; **warum wurde das ~?** why was it not done?; **~e Hilfeleistung** (*Jur*) failure to give assistance.
Unterlassung *f* **(a)** (*Versäumnis*) omission (of sth), failure (to do sth) ◆ **bei ~ (der Zahlung)** in case of default (of payment); **auf ~ klagen** (*Jur*) to ask for an injunction. **(b)** (*Gram*) **~ der Deklination** non-declension.
Unterlassungs-: ~delikt *nt siehe* **~straftat**; **~fall** *m* (*Admin*) case of default; **im ~falle** in case of default; **~klage** *f* (*Jur*) injunction suit; **~straftat** *f* (*Jur*) (offence of) default; **~sünde** *f* sin of omission; **~urteil** *nt* injunction.
Unterlauf *m* lower reaches (of a river).
unterlaufen[1]* *insep irreg* [1] *vi +dat aux sein* (*Fehler, Irrtum, Versehen*) to occur ◆ **mir ist ein Fehler/Fauxpas ~** I made a mistake/faux pas.
[2] *vt Bestimmungen, Maßnahmen* to get round; *Steuergesetze* to avoid; (*umgehen*) to circumvent; (*zuvorkommen*) to anticipate; (*unterminieren*) to undermine ◆ **jdn ~** (*Sport*) to slip under sb's guard.
unterlaufen[2] *adj* suffused with blood ◆ **ein mit Blut ~es Auge** a bloodshot eye.
Unterleder *nt* sole leather.
unterlegen[1] *vt sep* to put underneath; (*fig*) to attribute, to ascribe ◆ **einer Sache** (*dat*) **einen anderen Sinn ~** to put a different interpretation *or* construction on sth, to read another meaning into sth.
unterlegen[2]* *vt insep* to underlay; (*mit Stoff, Watte etc*) to line; (*mit Watte*) to pad ◆ **einer Melodie** (*dat*) **einen Text ~** to put *or* set words to a tune.
unterlegen[3] *adj* inferior; (*besiegt*) defeated ◆ **jdm ~ sein** to be inferior to sb, to be sb's inferior; **zahlenmäßig ~ sein** to be outnumbered, to be numerically inferior.
Unterlegene(r) *mf decl as adj* underdog ◆ **der ~ sein** to be in the weaker

⚠: for details of spelling reform, see supplement

position.
Unterlegenheit *f, no pl* inferiority.
Unterlegscheibe *f (Tech)* washer.
Unterleib *m* abdomen; *(im engeren Sinne: Geschlechtsorgane)* lower abdomen.
Unterleibs- *in cpds* abdominal; *(in bezug auf weibliche Geschlechtsorgane)* gynaecological; **~krebs** *m* cancer of the abdomen; cancer of the womb; **~organ** *nt* abdominal organ; **~schmerzen** *pl* abdominal pains.
Unter-: ~leutnant *m (Mil)* second lieutenant; **~lid** *nt* lower lid.
unterliegen* *vi insep irreg aux sein* **(a)** *(besiegt werden)* to be defeated (*+dat* by), to lose (*+dat* to); *(fig) einer Versuchung etc* to succumb (*+dat* to), to give away (*+dat* to).
(b) *+dat (unterworfen sein)* to be subject to; *einer Gebühr, Steuer* to be liable to ◆ **es unterliegt keinem Zweifel, daß ...** it's not open to any doubt that ...; *siehe* **unterlegen³**.
Unterlippe *f* bottom *or* lower lip.
unterm *contr of* **unter dem.**
untermalen* *vt insep* **(a)** *(Art) Bild* to prime. **(b)** *(mit Musik)* to provide with background *or* incidental music; *Film* to provide a soundtrack for; *(fig)* to underlie ◆ **eine Ansage mit leiser Musik ~** to play soft background music with an announcement.
Untermalung *f siehe vt* **(a)** preparatory *or* priming coat. **(b)** background music.
untermauern* *vt insep (Build)* to underpin; *(fig auch) Behauptung, Theorie* to back up, to substantiate, to support.
Untermauerung *f siehe vt* underpinning; support ◆ **zur ~ seiner These** in support of his thesis, to back up *or* substantiate his thesis.
Untermenge *f (Math)* subset.
untermengen *vt sep* to mix in, to add.
Untermensch *m (esp NS)* subhuman creature.
Untermenü *nt (Comput)* submenu.
Untermiete *f* subtenancy ◆ **bei jdm zur** *or* **in ~ wohnen** to be sb's tenant; *(als Zimmerherr etc auch)* to lodge with sb; **bei jdm zur** *or* **in ~ wohnen** to rent a room from sb.
Untermieter *m* lodger, subtenant.
Untermietzimmer *nt (Aus)* sublet room.
unterminieren* *vt insep (lit, fig)* to undermine.
Unterminierung *f* undermining.
untermischen *vt sep* to mix in, to add.
untern *contr of* **unter den.**
unternehmen* *vt insep irreg* to do; *(durchführen auch)* to undertake; *Versuch, Vorstoß, Reise* to make ◆ **einen Ausflug ~** to go on an outing; **Schritte ~** to take steps; **etwas/nichts gegen jdn/etw ~** to do something/nothing about sb/sth, to take some/no action against sb/sth; **zu viel ~** to do too much, to take on too much.
Unternehmen *nt* **-s, -** **(a)** *(Firma)* business, concern, enterprise. **(b)** *(Aktion, Vorhaben)* undertaking, enterprise, venture; *(Mil)* operation.
unternehmend [1] *prp of* **unternehmen.**
[2] *adj* enterprising.
Unternehmens-: ~althandel *m* trade in second-hand factory equipment; **~berater** *m* management consultant; **~form** *f* form *or* type of enterprise; **~leitung** *f* management; **die Herren in der ~leitung** management; **~planung** *f* business planning; **~spitze** *f* top management; **~vorstand** *m* board of directors.
Unternehmer(in *f*) *m* **-s, -** (business) employer; *(alten Stils)* entrepreneur; *(Industrieller auch)* industrialist ◆ **die ~** the employers.
Unternehmer-: ~geist *m* entrepreneurial spirit; **~gewinn** *m* (business) profit.
unternehmerisch *adj* entrepreneurial.
Unternehmer-: ~kreise *pl* **in/aus ~kreisen** in/from business circles; **~organisation** *f siehe* **~verband**; **~tum** *nt (die Unternehmer)* management *no art*, employers *pl*; *(~geist)* entrepreneurship; **ein freies/das freie ~tum** free enterprise; **~verband** *m* employers' association.
Unternehmung *f* **(a)** *siehe* **Unternehmen. (b)** *(Transaktion)* undertaking.
Unternehmungs-: ~geist *m, no pl* enterprise; **~lust** *f, no pl* enterprise; **u~lustig** *adj (tatendurstig)* enterprising; *(abenteuerlustig auch)* adventurous.
Unter|offizier *m* **(a)** *(Rang)* non-commissioned officer, NCO ◆ **~ vom Dienst** duty NCO. **(b)** *(Dienstgrad) (bei der Armee)* sergeant; *(bei der Luftwaffe)* corporal *(Brit)*, airman first class *(US)*.
Unter|offiziers-: ~anwärter *m* NCO candidate; **~rang** *m* non-commissioned rank.
Unter-: u~ordnen *sep* [1] *vt* to subordinate (*+dat* to); *siehe* **u~geordnet**; [2] *vr* to subordinate oneself (*+dat* to); **u~ordnend** *adj (Gram) Konjunktion* subordinating; **~ordnung** *f* **(a)** *no pl* subordination; **(b)** *(Biol)* suborder; **~organisation** *f* subsidiary organization.
Unterpfand *nt (old, liter)* pledge.
unterpflügen *vt sep* to plough under *or* in.
Unterprima *f (Sch) eighth year of German secondary school,* ≃ lower sixth *(Brit)*.
Unterprimaner *m (Sch) pupil in eighth year of German secondary school,* ≃ sixth-former *(Brit)*.
unterprivilegiert *adj* underprivileged ◆ **U~e/die U~en** underprivileged people/the underprivileged.
Unterproduktion *f* underproduction.
Unterprogramm *nt (Comput)* sub-routine.
Unterputzleitung *f (Elec)* concealed cable.
unterqueren* *vt insep* to underrun.
unterreden* *vr insep* **sich (mit jdm) ~** to confer (with sb), to have a discussion (with sb).
Unterredung *f* discussion; *(Pol auch)* talks *pl*.
unterrepräsentiert *adj* under-represented.
Unterricht *m* **-(e)s,** *no pl* lessons *pl*, classes *pl* ◆ **theoretischer/praktischer ~** theoretical/practical instruction *or* classes; **~ in Mathematik/Englisch** maths/English lessons *or* classes; **heute fällt der ~ in Englisch aus** there will be no English lesson today; **(jdm) ~ geben** *or* **erteilen** to teach (sb) *(in etw (dat)* sth); **(bei jdm) ~ nehmen** *or* **haben** to take *or* have lessons (with sb); **am ~ teilnehmen** to attend classes; **zu spät zum ~ kommen** to be late for class; **im ~ aufpassen** to pay attention in class; **den ~ vorbereiten** to prepare one's lessons; **der ~ beginnt um 8 Uhr** lessons *or* classes start at 8 o'clock; **~ in Fremdsprachen** foreign language teaching.
unterrichten* *insep* [1] *vt* **(a)** *(Unterricht geben) Schüler, Klasse, Fach* to teach ◆ **jdn in etw** *(dat)* **~** to teach sb sth.
(b) *(informieren)* to inform *(von, über +acc* about).
[2] *vi* to teach.
[3] *vr* **sich über etw** *(acc)* **~** to obtain information about sth, to inform oneself about sth; **sich von jdm über etw** *(acc)* **~ lassen** to be informed by sb about sth.
unterrichtet *adj* informed ◆ **gut ~e Kreise** well-informed circles.
Unterrichts-: ~betrieb *m, no pl* lessons *pl*, classes *pl*; *(~routine)* teaching *no art*; **~brief** *m* correspondence lesson; **~einheit** *f* teaching unit; **~fach** *nt* subject; **Geschichte ist ~fach** history is on the curriculum; **~film** *m* educational film; **u~frei** *adj Stunde, Tag* free; **der Montag ist u~frei** there are no classes on Monday; **~gegenstand** *m* **(a)** topic, subject; **(b)** *(Aus) siehe* **~fach**; **~methode** *f* teaching method; **~ministerium** *nt* Ministry of Education; **~mittel** *nt* teaching aid; **~raum** *m* teaching room; **~software** *f* educational software; **~sprache** *f* language in which lessons are conducted; **~stoff** *m* subject matter, teaching subject; **~stunde** *f* lesson, period; **während der ~stunden** during lessons; **~veranstaltung** *f* lesson; *(Univ)* lecture; **~vorbereitung** *f* teaching preparation; **~wesen** *nt* educational system; **~ziel** *nt* teaching objective; **~zwecke** *pl* **zu ~zwecken** for teaching purposes.
Unterrichtung *f, no pl (Belehrung)* instruction; *(Informierung)* information.
Unterrock *m* underskirt, slip.
unterrühren *vt sep* to stir *or* mix in.
unters *contr of* **unter das.**
untersagen* *vt insep* to forbid, to prohibit ◆ **jdm etw ~** to forbid sb sth, to prohibit sb from doing sth; **(das) Rauchen (ist hier) strengstens untersagt** smoking (is) strictly prohibited *or* forbidden (here); **jdm etw gerichtlich ~** to enjoin sb to do sth.
Untersatz *m* **(a)** mat; *(für Gläser, Flaschen etc)* coaster; *(für Blumentöpfe etc)* saucer ◆ **etw als ~ verwenden** to use sth to put underneath; *siehe* **fahrbar. (b)** *(Philos)* minor premise.
Unterschall-: ~flug *m* subsonic flight; **~geschwindigkeit** *f* subsonic speed.
unterschätzen* *vt insep* to underestimate.
Unterschätzung *f* underestimation.
unterscheidbar *adj* distinguishable.
▼ **unterscheiden*** *insep irreg* [1] *vt (einen Unterschied machen, trennen)* to distinguish; *(auseinanderhalten auch)* to tell apart ◆ **A nicht von B ~ können** to be unable to tell the difference between A and B, to be unable to tell A from B; **zwei Personen (voneinander) ~** to tell two people apart; **kannst du die beiden ~?** can you tell which is which?; **das ~de Merkmal** the distinguishing feature; **nach verschiedenen Merkmalen ~** to classify *or* divide according to various characteristics.
[2] *vi* to differentiate, to distinguish.
▼ [3] *vr* **sich von etw ~** to differ (from) sth; **worin unterscheidet sich eine Amsel von einer Drossel?** what is the difference between a blackbird and a thrush?
Unterscheidung *f* differentiation; *(Unterschied)* difference, distinction ◆ **eine ~ treffen** to make a distinction.
Unterscheidungs-: ~merkmal *nt* distinctive *or* distinguishing feature; **~vermögen** *nt* discernment; **das ~vermögen** the power of discernment.
Unterschenkel *m* lower leg.
Unterschicht *f (Sociol)* lower stratum *(Sociol)*, underclass.
unterschieben¹* *vt insep irreg (inf: unterstellen)* **jdm etw ~** to attribute sth to sb; **du unterschiebst mir immer, daß ich schwindle** you're always accusing me of cheating; **einer Äußerung einen ganz falschen Sinn ~** to twist the meaning of a statement completely.
unterschieben² *vt sep irreg* **(a)** *(lit)* to push underneath ◆ **etw unter etw** *(acc)* **~** to push sth under(neath) sth.
(b) *(fig)* **jdm etw ~** to foist sth on sb; **er wehrte sich dagegen, daß man ihm das Kind ~ wollte** he defended himself against the charge that the child was his.
(c) *siehe* **unterschieben¹.**
Unterschiebung [*auch* 'ʊntɐ-] *f* **(a)** *siehe* **unterschieben¹** imputation, attribution. **(b)** *siehe* **unterschieben² (b)** foisting.
▼ **Unterschied** *m* **-(e)s, -e** difference *(auch Math)*; *(Unterscheidung auch)* distinction ◆ **einen ~ (zwischen zwei Dingen) machen** to make a distinction (between two things); **es besteht ein ~ (zwischen ...)** there's a difference *or* distinction (between ...); **das macht keinen ~** that makes no difference; **es ist ein großer ~, ob ...** it makes a big difference whether ...; **ein feiner ~** a slight difference, a fine distinction; **zum ~ von** *(rare) or* **im ~ zu (jdm/etw)** in

➤ SPRACHE AKTIV: **unterscheiden: 3** → 32.1 **Unterschied** → 32.1, 32.4, 53.5

contrast to (sb/sth), unlike (sb/sth); **mit dem ~, daß** ... with the difference that ...; **alle ohne ~ halfen mit** everyone without exception lent a hand; **es wurden alle ohne ~ getötet** everyone was killed indiscriminately; **das ist ein gewaltiger ~!** there's a vast difference!

unterschiedlich *adj* different; (*veränderlich*) variable; (*gemischt*) varied, patchy ◆ **das ist sehr ~** it varies a lot; **~ gut/lang** of varying quality/length; **sie haben ~ reagiert** their reactions varied.

Unterschiedlichkeit *f siehe adj* difference; variability; variedness, patchiness.

unterschiedslos *adj* indiscriminate.

unterschlächtig *adj Wasserrad* undershot.

unterschlagen[1]* *vt insep irreg Geld* to embezzle, to misappropriate; *Brief, Beweise* to withhold, to suppress; (*inf*) *Neuigkeit, Nachricht, Wort etc* to keep quiet about ◆ **das hast du mir die ganze Zeit ~** and you've kept quiet about it all this time.

unterschlagen[2] *vt sep irreg* **(a)** (*verschränken*) *Beine* to cross ◆ **mit untergeschlagenen Beinen dasitzen** to sit cross-legged. **(b)** *Bettuch* to tuck in *or* under.

Unterschlagung *f* (*von Geld*) embezzlement, misappropriation; (*von Briefen, Beweisen etc*) withholding, suppression.

Unterschlupf *m* **-(e)s, Unterschlüpfe** (*Obdach, Schutz*) cover, shelter; (*Versteck*) hiding-place, hide-out.

unterschlüpfen (*dial*), **unterschlupfen** *vi sep aux sein* (*inf*) (*Obdach or Schutz finden*) to take cover *or* shelter; (*Versteck finden*) to hide out (*inf*) (*bei jdm* at sb's).

unterschreiben* *insep irreg* [1] *vt* to sign ◆ **der Brief ist mit „Müller" unterschrieben** the letter is signed "Müller"; **das kann *or* würde ich ~!** (*fig*) I'll subscribe to that!
[2] *vi* to sign ◆ **mit vollem Namen ~** to sign one's full name.

unterschreiten* *vt insep irreg* to fall short of; *Temperatur, Zahlenwert* to fall below.

Unterschrift *f* **(a)** signature ◆ **seine ~/fünf ~en leisten** to give one's signature/one's signature five times; **jdm etw zur ~ vorlegen** to give sb sth to sign; **eigenhändige ~** personal signature; **seine ~ unter etw** (*acc*) **setzen** to put one's signature to sth, to sign sth. **(b)** (*Bild~*) caption.

Unterschriften-: ~mappe *f* signature folder; **~sammlung** *f* collection of signatures.

unterschriftlich *adj, adv* by signature.

Unterschrifts-: u~berechtigt *adj* authorized to sign; **~berechtigte(r)** *mf decl as adj* authorized signatory; **~fälschung** *f* forging of a/the signature; **~leistung** *f* signing of a/the document *etc*; **~probe** *f* specimen signature; **u~reif** *adj Vertrag* ready to be signed.

unterschwellig *adj* subliminal.

Unterseeboot *nt* submarine; (*ehemaliges deutsches auch*) U-boat.

unterseeisch [-ze:ɪʃ] *adj* underwater, undersea, submarine.

Unter-: ~seite *f* underside; (*von Topf, Teller, Kuchen auch*) bottom; (*von Blatt*) undersurface; **an der ~seite** on the underside/bottom/undersurface; **~sekunda** *f* (*Sch*) *sixth year of German secondary school*; **~sekundaner** *m* (*Sch*) *pupil in sixth year of German secondary school*; **u~setzen** *vt sep* to put underneath; **~setzer** *m* **-s, -** *siehe* **Untersatz (a)**.

untersetzt *adj* stocky.

unterspülen* *vt insep* to undermine, to wash away the base of.

Unter-: ~staatssekretär *m* Undersecretary of State; **~stadt** *f* lower part of a/the town; **~stand** *m* shelter; (*Mil*) dugout.

unterständig *adj* (*Bot*) inferior, hypogynous (*spec*).

unterstandslos *adj* (*Aus*) homeless.

unterstehen[1]* *insep irreg* [1] *vi* +*dat* to be under (the control of); *jdm* to be subordinate to; *einer Behörde, dem Ministerium auch* to come under (the jurisdiction of); *dem Gesetz* to be subject to; (*in Firma*) to report to ◆ **dem Verkaufsdirektor ~ sechs Abteilungsleiter** the sales director is in charge of six department heads.
[2] *vr* to dare, to have the audacity ◆ **untersteh dich (ja nicht)!** (don't) you dare!; **was ~ Sie sich!** how dare you!

unterstehen[2] *vi sep irreg* to take shelter *or* cover.

unterstellen[1]* *insep* [1] *vt* **(a)** (*unterordnen*) to (make) subordinate (*dat* to); *Abteilung, Ministerium etc auch* to put under the control (*dat* of) ◆ **jdm unterstellt sein** to be under sb, to be answerable to sb; (*in Firma*) to report to sb; **ihm sind vier Mitarbeiter unterstellt** he is in charge of four employees, he has four employees subordinate to him; **jdm etw ~** to put sb in charge of sth; (*Mil*) to put sth under the command of sb *or* under sb's command.
(b) (*annehmen*) to assume, to suppose ◆ **einmal unterstellt, es sei so gewesen** supposing *or* let us suppose (that) it was so.
(c) (*pej: unterschieben*) **jdm etw ~** to insinuate *or* imply that sb has done/said sth; **jdm Nachlässigkeit ~** to insinuate that sb has been negligent; **ihm wurde unterstellt, gesagt zu haben, ...** he was purported to have said ...
[2] *vr* to subordinate oneself (+*dat* to).

unterstellen[2] *sep* [1] *vt* (*abstellen, unterbringen*) to keep; *Möbel auch* to store.
[2] *vr* to take shelter *or* cover.

Unterstellung *f* **(a)** (*falsche Behauptung*) misrepresentation; (*Andeutung*) insinuation; (*Annahme*) assumption, presumption. **(b)** *no pl* (*Unterordnung*) subordination (*unter* +*acc* to).

unterste(r, s) *adj superl of* **untere(r, s)** lowest; (*tiefste auch*) bottom; (*rangmäßig*) lowest; (*letzte*) last ◆ **das U~ zuoberst kehren** to turn everything upside down.

untersteuern* *vi insep* to understeer.

untersteuert *adj Auto* with understeer.

unterstreichen* *vt insep irreg* (*lit, fig*) to underline; (*fig: betonen auch*) to emphasize.

Unterstreichung *f siehe vt* underlining; emphasizing.

Unterströmung *f* (*lit, fig*) undercurrent.

Unterstufe *f* (*Sch*) lower school, lower grade (*US*).

▼ **unterstützen*** *vt insep* to support (*auch fig, Comput*); (*aus öffentlichen Mitteln auch*) to subsidize; (*finanziell fördern auch*) to back, to sponsor ◆ **jdn (moralisch) ~** to give sb (moral) support.

▼ **Unterstützung** *f* **(a)** *no pl* (*Tätigkeit, auch Comput*) support (*zu, für* for) ◆ **zur ~ seiner Behauptung** in support of his statement. **(b)** (*Zuschuß*) assistance, aid; (*inf: Arbeitslosen~*) (unemployment) benefit ◆ **staatliche ~** state aid; **~ beziehen** to be on social security *or* on welfare (*US*).

Unterstützungs-: u~bedürftig *adj* needy; **~bedürftige** the needy; **~empfänger** *m* person on relief.

Untersuch *m* **-s, -e** (*Sw*) *siehe* **Untersuchung**.

untersuchen* *vt insep* **(a)** to examine (*auf* +*acc* for); (*erforschen*) to look into, to investigate; (*genau*) *Dokumente etc* to scrutinize; (*statistisch, soziologisch etc*) to sound (out), to survey; (*chemisch, technisch etc*) to test (*auf* +*acc* for) ◆ **sich ärztlich ~ lassen** to have a medical (examination) *or* a check-up; **etw gerichtlich ~** to try sth (in court); **etw chemisch ~** to test *or* analyze sth (chemically).
(b) (*nachprüfen*) to check, to verify.

▼ **Untersuchung** *f siehe vt* **(a)** examination; investigation (*gen, über* +*acc* into); scrutiny; sounding, survey; test; (*ärztlich*) examination, check-up. **(b)** check, verification.

Untersuchungs-: ⚠**~ausschuß** *m* investigating *or* fact-finding committee; (*nach Unfall etc*) committee of inquiry; **~befund** *m* (*Med*) result of an/the examination; (*Bericht*) examination report; **~ergebnis** *nt* (*Jur*) findings *pl*; (*Med*) result of an/the examination; (*Sci*) test result; **~gefangene(r)** *mf* prisoner awaiting trial; **~gefängnis** *nt* prison (*for people awaiting trial*); **~haft** *f* custody, (period of) imprisonment *or* detention while awaiting trial; **in ~haft sein *or* sitzen** (*inf*) to be in prison *or* detention awaiting trial; **jdn in ~haft nehmen** to commit sb for trial; **~häftling** *m siehe* **~gefangene(r)**; **~kommission** *f siehe* **~ausschuß**; **~methode** *f* examination/investigation/research method; **~richter** *m* examining magistrate; **~zimmer** *nt* (*Med*) examination room; (*in Praxis*) surgery.

Untertag- *in cpds siehe* **Untertage-**.

untertage *adv siehe* **Tag**.

Untertage- *in cpds* underground; **~arbeiter** *m* (coal)face worker; **~bau** *m, no pl* underground mining; **~deponie** *f* underground dump.

untertags *adv* (*Aus, dial*) *siehe* **tagsüber**.

Untertan *m* **-en, -en** (*old: Staatsbürger*) subject; (*pej*) underling (*pej*).

untertan *adj pred* (+*dat* to) subject; (*dienstbar, hörig*) subservient ◆ **sich** (*dat*) **ein Volk ~ machen** to subjugate a nation.

Untertanen-: ~geist *m*, **~gesinnung** *f* servile *or* subservient spirit.

untertänig *adj* subservient, submissive ◆ **Ihr ~ster Diener** (*obs*) your most obedient *or* humble servant; **jdn ~st bitten** to ask sb most humbly.

Untertänigkeit *f* subservience, submissiveness.

Unter-: u~tariflich *adj Bezahlung* below an/the agreed rate; **~tasse** *f* saucer; **fliegende ~tasse** flying saucer.

untertauchen[1] *sep* [1] *vi aux sein* to dive (under); (*U-Boot auch*) to submerge; (*fig*) to disappear.
[2] *vt* to immerse; *jdn* to duck.

untertauchen[2]* *vt insep* to dive under.

Unterteil *nt or m* bottom *or* lower part.

unterteilen* *vt insep* to subdivide (*in* +*acc* into).

Unterteilung *f* subdivision (*in* +*acc* into).

Unter-: ~teller *m siehe* **~tasse**; **~temperatur** *f* low (body) temperature; **~tertia** *f* (*Sch*) *fourth year of German secondary school*; **~tertianer(in f)** *m* (*Sch*) *pupil in fourth year of German secondary school*; **~titel** *m* subtitle; (*für Bild*) caption; **u~titeln*** *vt insep Film* to subtitle; *Bild* to caption; **~ton** *m* (*Mus, fig*) undertone; **u~tourig** [-tu:rɪç] *adj* with low revs; **u~tourig fahren** to drive with low revs; **u~treiben*** *insep irreg* [1] *vt* to understate; [2] *vi* to play things down; **~treibung** *f* **(a)** understatement; **(b)** (*das ~treiben*) playing things down *no art*; **u~tunneln*** *vt insep* to tunnel under; *Berg auch* to tunnel through; **~tunnelung** *f* tunnelling; **u~vermieten*** *vti insep* to sublet, to sublease; **u~versichert** *adj* underinsured; **~versicherung** *f* underinsurance; **~versorgung** *f* inadequate provision; **~verzeichnis** *nt* (*Comput*) subdirectory.

Unterwalden *nt* **-s** Unterwalden.

Unter-: u~wandern* *vt insep* to infiltrate; **~wanderung** *f* infiltration; **u~wärts** *adv* (*dial*) underneath.

Unterwäsche *f* **(a)** *no pl* underwear *no pl*. **(b)** (*für Autos*) underbody cleaning.

Unterwasser-: ~behandlung *f* (*Med*) underwater treatment; **~fotografie** *f* underwater photography; **~gymnastik** *f* underwater exercises *pl*; **~jagd** *f* scuba *or* aqualung fishing; **~ jäger** *m* spear fisherman, underwater fisherman; **~kamera** *f* underwater camera; **~labor** *nt* underwater laboratory, sealab; **~massage** *f* (*Med*) underwater massage; ⚠**~photographie** *f siehe* **~fotografie**; **~station** *f siehe* **~labor**.

unterwegs *adv* on the *or* one's/its way (*nach, zu* to); (*auf Reisen*) away ◆ **eine Karte von ~ schicken** to send a card while one is away; **bei denen ist wieder ein Kind ~** they've got another child on the way; **bei ihr ist etwas (Kleines) ~** she's expecting.

➤ SPRACHE AKTIV: **unterstützen** → 38.1, 38.2, 39.1, 53.2, 53.6 **Unterstützung: a** → 38.2 **Untersuchung: a** → 53.2, 53.6

unterweisen* *vt insep irreg (geh)* to instruct (*in +dat* in).
Unterweisung *f (geh)* instruction.
Unterwelt *f (lit, fig)* underworld.
unterwerfen* *insep irreg* [1] *vt* (a) *Volk, Land* to subjugate, to conquer. (b) (*unterziehen*) to subject (*dat* to) ◆ **einer Sache** (*dat*) **unterworfen sein** to be subject to sth.
[2] *vr (lit, fig)* **sich jdm/einer Sache ~** to submit to sb/sth.
Unterwerfung *f siehe vtr* (a) subjugation, conquest. (b) subjection. (c) submission.
unterworfen *adj* **der Mode/dem Zeitgeschmack ~ sein** to be subject to fashion/prevailing tastes.
unterwürfig *adj (pej)* obsequious.
Unterwürfigkeit *f (pej)* obsequiousness.
unterzeichnen* *vt insep (form)* to sign.
Unterzeichner *m* **-s, -** signatory.
Unterzeichnerstaat *m* signatory state.
Unterzeichnete(r) *mf decl as adj (form)* undersigned ◆ **der rechts/links ~** the right/left signatory.
Unterzeichnung *f* signing.
Unterzeug *nt (inf)* underclothes *pl*.
unterziehen[1]* *insep irreg* [1] *vr* **sich einer Sache** (*dat*) **~ (müssen)** to (have to) undergo sth; **sich einer Operation** (*dat*) ~ to undergo *or* have an operation; **sich einer Prüfung** (*dat*) ~ to take an examination; **sich der Mühe** (*dat*) ~, etw zu tun (*geh*) to take the trouble to do sth.
[2] *vt* to subject (*dat* to) ◆ **jdn/etw einer Prüfung ~** to subject sb/sth to an examination; **jdn einer Operation ~** to perform an operation on sb.
unterziehen[2] *vt sep irreg* (a) *Unterwäsche, Kleidung* to put on underneath ◆ **sich** (*dat*) **etw ~** to put sth on underneath. (b) (*Cook*) *Eischnee, Sahne* to fold in.
Untiefe *f* (a) (*seichte Stelle*) shallow, shoal. (b) (*liter: große Tiefe*) depth.
Untier *nt* monster.
untilgbar *adj (geh)* (*nicht rückzahlbar*) irredeemable; (*fig*) indelible.
Untote(r) *mf* **die ~n** the undead.
Un-: u~tragbar *adj Zustände, Belastung* intolerable, unbearable; **~tragbarkeit** *f* intolerability, unbearableness; **u~trainiert** *adj* untrained; **u~trennbar** *adj* inseparable; **u~trennbar zusammengesetzte Verben** inseparable verbs; **mit etw u~trennbar verbunden sein** (*fig*) to be inextricably linked with sth.
untreu *adj Liebhaber etc* unfaithful; (*einem Prinzip etc*) disloyal (*dat* to) ◆ **sich** (*dat*) **selbst ~ werden** to be untrue to oneself; **jdm ~ werden** to be unfaithful to sb.
Untreue *f* (a) *siehe adj* unfaithfulness; disloyalty. (b) (*Jur*) embezzlement.
untrinkbar *adj* undrinkable.
untröstlich *adj* inconsolable (*über +acc* about) ◆ **er war ~, daß er es vergessen hatte** he was inconsolable about having forgotten it.
untrüglich *adj Gedächtnis* infallible; *Zeichen* unmistakable.
Untugend *f* (*Laster*) vice; (*schlechte Angewohnheit*) bad habit; (*Schwäche*) weakness.
untunlich *adj (dated)* (*unzweckmäßig*) impractical; (*unklug*) imprudent.
Un-: u~übel *adj*: **(gar) nicht (so) u~übel** not bad (at all); **u~überbietbar** *adj Preis, Rekord etc* unbeatable; *Frechheit, Virtuosität, Eifer* unparalleled; **u~überbrückbar** *adj (fig) Gegensätze etc* irreconcilable; *Kluft* unbridgeable; **u~überdacht** *adj* open, uncovered; **u~überlegt** *adj Mensch* rash; *Entschluß, Maßnahmen etc auch* ill-considered; **u~überlegt handeln** to act rashly; **~überlegtheit** *f* rashness; **u~übersehbar** *adj* (a) (*nicht abschätzbar*) *Schaden, Schwierigkeiten, Folgen* inestimable, incalculable; (*nicht übersehbar*) *Menge, Häusermeer etc* vast, immense; (b) (*auffällig*) *Fehler etc* obvious, conspicuous; **u~übersetzbar** *adj* untranslatable; **u~übersichtlich** *adj* (a) *Gelände* broken; *Kurve, Stelle* blind; (b) (*durcheinander*) *System, Plan* confused; **u~übertrefflich** [1] *adj* matchless, unsurpassable; *Rekord* unbeatable; [2] *adv* superbly, magnificently; **u~übertroffen** *adj* unsurpassed; **u~überwindbar** (*rare*), **u~überwindlich** *adj Gegner, Heer* invincible; *Festung* impregnable; *Hindernis, Gegensätze, Abneigung etc* insuperable, insurmountable; **u~üblich** *adj* not usual, not customary.
un|umgänglich *adj* essential, absolutely necessary; (*unvermeidlich*) inevitable ◆ **~ notwendig werden** to become absolutely essential/quite inevitable.
un|umkehrbar *adj* irreversible.
un|umschränkt *adj* unlimited; *Freiheit, Gewalt, Macht auch* absolute ◆ **~ herrschen** to have absolute rule.
un|umstößlich *adj Tatsache* irrefutable, incontrovertible; *Entschluß* irrevocable ◆ **~ feststehen** to be absolutely definite.
Un|umstößlichkeit *f siehe adj* irrefutability, incontrovertibility; irrevocability.
un-: ~umstritten *adj* indisputable, undisputed; **~umwunden** *adv* frankly; **~unterbrochen** *adj* (a) (*nicht unterbrochen*) unbroken, uninterrupted; (b) (*unaufhörlich*) incessant, continuous.
unver|änderlich *adj* (*gleichbleibend*) unchanging, invariable; (*unwandelbar*) unchangeable ◆ **eine ~e Größe, eine U~e** (*Math*) a constant, an invariable.
Unver|änderlichkeit *f siehe adj* unchangingness, invariability; unchangeableness.
unver|ändert *adj* unchanged ◆ **er ist immer ~ freundlich** he is always friendly; **du siehst ~ jung aus** you look just as young as ever; **unsere Weine sind immer von ~er Güte** our wines are always consistently good.
Un-: u~verantwortlich *adj* irresponsible; **~verantwortlichkeit** *f* irresponsibility; **u~verarbeitet** [1] *adj Material* unprocessed, raw; (*fig*) *Eindruck* raw, undigested; [2] *adv* in a raw state; **u~veräußerlich** *adj* (a) *Rechte* inalienable; (b) *Besitz* unmarketable, unsaleable; **u~verbesserlich** *adj* incorrigible; **u~verbildet** *adj Charakter, Wesen* unspoilt.
unverbindlich *adj* (a) (*nicht bindend*) *Angebot, Preisangabe* not binding; *Besichtigung* free ◆ **sich** (*dat*) **etw ~ schicken lassen** to have sth sent without obligation. (b) (*vage, allgemein*) non-committal; (*nicht entgegenkommend*) abrupt, curt.
Unverbindlichkeit *f* (a) *no pl* (*von Auskunft, Beratung etc*) freedom from obligation. (b) *no pl* (*Vagheit, Allgemeinheit*) non-commitment, vagueness; (*mangelndes Entgegenkommen*) abruptness, curtness. (c) (*unverbindliche Äußerung*) non-committal remark.
un-: ~verbleit *adj* lead-free, unleaded; **~verblümt** *adj* blunt; **das kommt einer ~verblümten Erpressung gleich!** that's downright blackmail!; **~verbraucht** *adj (fig)* unspent; **~verbrennbar** *adj* incombustible.
unverbrüchlich *adj (geh)* steadfast ◆ **~ zu etw stehen** to stand by sth unswervingly.
unverbürgt *adj* unconfirmed.
unverdächtig *adj* unsuspicious; (*nicht unter Verdacht stehend*) unsuspected, above suspicion ◆ **sich möglichst ~ benehmen** to arouse as little suspicion as possible; **das ist doch völlig ~** there's nothing suspicious about that.
Un-: u~verdaulich *adj (lit, fig)* indigestible; **u~verdaut** *adj* undigested; (*fig auch*) unassimilated; **u~verderblich** *adj* unperishable, non-perishable; **u~verdient** *adj* undeserved; **u~verdientermaßen, u~verdienterweise** *adv* undeservedly, unjustly; **u~verdorben** *adj (lit, fig)* unspoilt, pure; **~verdorbenheit** *f (fig)* purity; **u~verdrossen** *adj* undeterred; (*unermüdlich*) untiring, indefatigable; (*unverzagt*) undaunted; **~verdrossenheit** *f, no pl siehe adj* undeterredness; indefatigability; undauntedness; **u~verdünnt** *adj* undiluted; **Spirituosen u~verdünnt trinken** to drink spirits neat.
unver|ehelicht *adj (old, form)* unwedded, unwed ◆ „~" (*auf Urkunde*) (*Frau*) "spinster"; (*Mann*) "bachelor"; **die ~e Eleanor X** Eleanor X, spinster.
Un-: u~vereinbar *adj* incompatible; **miteinander u~vereinbar sein** to be incompatible; **~vereinbarkeit** *f* incompatibility; **u~verfälscht** *adj (lit, fig)* unadulterated; *Dialekt* pure; *Natürlichkeit* unaffected; *Natur* unspoilt; **~verfälschtheit** *f siehe adj* unadulterated quality *or* character; purity; unaffectedness; unspoilt quality *or* character; **u~verfänglich** *adj* harmless; **das ist u~verfänglich** it doesn't commit you to anything; **~verfänglichkeit** *f* harmlessness.
unverfroren *adj* insolent.
Unverfrorenheit *f* insolence.
unvergänglich *adj Kunstwerk, Werte, Worte, Ruhm* immortal; *Eindruck, Erinnerung, Reiz* everlasting.
Unvergänglichkeit *f siehe adj* immortality; everlastingness.
unvergessen *adj* unforgotten ◆ **August wird (uns allen) ~ bleiben** we'll (all) remember August.
⚠ **unvergeßlich** *adj* unforgettable; *Erlebnis auch* memorable ◆ **das wird mir ~ bleiben, das bleibt mir ~** I'll always remember that, I'll never forget that.
Un-: u~vergleichbar *adj* incomparable; **~vergleichbarkeit** *f* incomparability; **u~vergleichlich** [1] *adj* unique, incomparable; [2] *adv* incomparably, immeasurably; **u~vergoren** *adj* unfermented; **u~verhältnismäßig** *adv* disproportionately; (*übermäßig*) excessively; **~verhältnismäßigkeit** *f* disproportion; (*Übermäßigkeit*) excessiveness; **ihm wurde ~verhältnismäßigkeit der Strafe vorgeworfen** he was accused of imposing a disproportionate punishment; **u~verheiratet** *adj* unmarried, single; **u~verhofft** *adj* unexpected; **das kam völlig u~verhofft** it was quite unexpected, it came out of the blue; **u~verholen** *adj* open, unconcealed; **u~verhüllt** *adj* (a) *Tatsachen* undisguised, naked; *Wahrheit auch* unveiled; (b) (*liter, iro: nackt*) unclad; (c) *siehe* **u~verhohlen**; **u~verjährbar** *adj* (*Jur*) not subject to a statute of limitations; **u~verkäuflich** *adj* (*abbr* **unverk.**) unmarketable, unsaleable; **u~verkäufliches Muster** free sample; „**u~verkäuflich**" "not for sale"; **u~verkennbar** *adj* unmistak(e)able; **u~verlangt** *adj* unsolicited; **u~verlangt eingesandte Manuskripte** unsolicited manuscripts; ⚠**u~verläßlich** *adj* unreliable; **u~verletzbar** *adj siehe* **u~verwundbar**; **u~verletzlich** *adj* (a) (*fig*) *Rechte, Grenze* inviolable; (b) (*lit*) invulnerable; **~verletzlichkeit** *f* (*fig*) inviolability; (*lit*) invulnerability; **u~verletzt** *adj* uninjured, unhurt, unharmed; *Körperteil* undamaged; *Siegel* unbroken; **u~vermählt** *adj (geh)* unwedded, unwed; **u~vermeidbar** *adj* inevitable; **u~vermeidlich** *adj* inevitable; (*nicht zu umgehen*) unavoidable; **der u~vermeidliche Herr X** the inevitable Mr X; **~vermeidlichkeit** *f* inevitability; unavoidable nature; **u~vermindert** *adj* undiminished; **u~vermischt** *adj* separate, unmixed; (*rein*) pure; *Tee, Wein etc* pure, unadulterated.
unvermittelt *adj* (a) (*plötzlich*) sudden, unexpected. (b) (*Philos*) immediate.
Unvermögen *nt, no pl* inability; (*Machtlosigkeit*) powerlessness.
unvermögend *adj* (a) (*arm*) without means. (b) (*old, liter*) (*unfähig*) helpless ◆ **~ sein, etw zu tun** not to be able to do sth.
unvermutet *adj* unexpected.
Unvernunft *f* (*Torheit*) stupidity; (*mangelnder Verstand*) irrationality; (*Uneinsichtigkeit*) unreasonableness.
unvernünftig *adj siehe n* stupid; irrational; unreasonable ◆ **das war sehr ~ von ihr** it was very stupid *or* unwise of her.
un-: ~veröffentlicht *adj* unpublished; **~verpackt** *adj* unpackaged, loose; **~verputzt** *adj* unplastered.
unverrichtet *adj*: **~er Dinge** *or* **Sache** (*Aus*) without having achieved any-

⚠: Informationen zur Rechtschreibreform im Anhang

thing, empty-handed.

unverrichteterdinge, unverrichtetersache *adv* without having achieved anything.

unverrückbar *adj (fig)* unshakeable, unalterable; *Entschluß auch* firm, definite; *Gewißheit* absolute ◆ **~ feststehen** to be absolutely definite.

unverschämt *adj* outrageous; *Mensch, Frage, Benehmen etc* impudent, impertinent; *Lüge, Verleumdung etc auch* blatant, barefaced ◆ **grins/lüg nicht so ~!** take that cheeky grin off your face/don't tell such barefaced lies!

Unverschämtheit *f* **(a)** *no pl siehe adj* outrageousness; impudence, impertinence; blatancy, barefacedness ◆ **die ~ besitzen, etw zu tun** to have the impertinence *or* impudence to do sth. **(b)** *(Bemerkung)* impertinence; *(Tat)* outrageous thing ◆ **das ist eine ~!** it's outrageous!

un-: ~verschleiert *adj* **(a)** unveiled; **(b)** *(fig) Wahrheit* unvarnished; **~verschlossen** *adj* unlocked; *Briefumschlag* unsealed.

unverschuldet *adj* **(a) ein ~er Unfall** an accident which was not his/her *etc* fault *or* which happened through no fault of his/her *etc* own; **~ in eine Notlage geraten** to get into difficulties through no fault of one's own. **(b)** *(ohne Schulden)* free from *or* of debt; *Grundstück auch* unencumbered.

unverschuldetermaßen, unverschuldeterweise *adv* through no fault of one's own.

unversehens *adv* all of a sudden, suddenly; *(überraschend)* unexpectedly.

Un-: u~versehrt *adj Mensch (lit, fig)* unscathed; *(unbeschädigt)* intact *pred*; **~versehrtheit** *f (ohne Verletzung)* freedom from injury; *(ohne Beschädigung)* intactness; **körperliche ~versehrtheit** freedom from bodily harm; **seine seelische ~versehrtheit** the fact that he was mentally unscathed; **u~versiegbar, u~versieglich** *adj* inexhaustible; **u~versiegelt** *adj* unsealed; **u~versöhnlich** *adj* irreconcilable; **~versöhnlichkeit** *f* irreconcilability; **u~versorgt** *adj Familie, Kinder* unprovided-for.

Unverstand *m* lack of judgement; *(Torheit)* folly, foolishness ◆ **etw im ~ tun** to do sth to excess.

unverstanden *adj* not understood; *(mißverstanden)* misunderstood ◆ **der Arme fühlt sich ~** the poor man feels that his wife doesn't understand him/nobody understands him.

unverständig *adj* lacking understanding, ignorant.

unverständlich *adj (nicht zu hören)* inaudible; *(unbegreifbar)* incomprehensible.

Unverständnis *nt, no pl* lack of understanding; *(Nichterfassen, für Kunst etc)* lack of appreciation.

un-: ~verstellt *adj* **(a)** *Stimme* undisguised; **(b)** *(echt)* unfeigned, genuine; **~versteuert** *adj* untaxed; **~versucht** *adj*: **nichts ~versucht lassen** to try everything.

unverträglich *adj* **(a)** *(streitsüchtig)* cantankerous, quarrelsome. **(b)** *(unverdaulich)* indigestible; *(Med)* intolerable; *(Med: mit anderer Substanz etc)* incompatible.

Unverträglichkeit *f, no pl siehe adj* **(a)** cantankerousness, quarrelsomeness. **(b)** indigestibility; intolerance; incompatibility.

unverwandt [1] *adj* **~en Blickes** *(liter)* with a steadfast gaze.
[2] *adv* fixedly, steadfastly.

Un-: u~verwechselbar *adj* unmistak(e)able, distinctive; **~verwechselbarkeit** *f* unmistak(e)ableness, distinctiveness; **u~verwehrt** *adj*: **das sei dir u~verwehrt** *(old, geh)* you are at liberty to do this *(form)*; **u~verweslich** *adj* imperishable; **u~verwindbar** *adj* insurmountable; **u~verwirklicht** *adj* unrealized; **u~verwischbar** *adj (lit, fig)* indelible; **u~verwundbar** *adj (lit, fig)* invulnerable; **~verwundbarkeit** *f (lit, fig)* invulnerability.

unverwüstlich *adj* indestructible; *Stoff, Teppich etc auch* tough, durable; *Gesundheit* robust; *Humor, Mensch* irrepressible.

un-: ~verzagt *adj* undaunted; **~verzeihbar** *(rare)*, **~verzeihlich** *adj* unpardonable, unforgivable; **~verzerrt** *adj Fernsehbild etc, (fig: objektiv)* undistorted; **~verzichtbar** *adj attr Recht* inalienable; *Anspruch* undeniable, indisputable; *Bedingung* indispensable; **~verzinslich** *adj* interest-free; **~verzollt** *adj* duty-free.

unverzüglich [1] *adj* immediate, prompt.
[2] *adv* immediately, without delay, at once.

unvoll|endet *adj* unfinished ◆ **Die „U~e" von Schubert** Schubert's Unfinished (Symphony).

unvollkommen *adj (unvollständig)* incomplete; *(fehlerhaft, mangelhaft)* imperfect ◆ **er kann zwar Englisch, aber doch recht ~** he can speak English, but his knowledge is rather limited.

Unvollkommenheit *f siehe adj* incompleteness; imperfection.

unvollständig *adj* incomplete; *Hilfsverb* defective ◆ **er hat das Formular ~ ausgefüllt** he didn't fill the form out properly *or* correctly.

Unvollständigkeit *f* incompleteness; defectiveness.

unvorbereitet *adj* unprepared *(auf +acc* for) ◆ **eine ~e Rede halten** to make an impromptu speech, to speak off the cuff; **der Tod des Vaters traf sie ~** her father's death came unexpectedly.

unvordenklich *adj*: **seit ~en Zeiten** *(liter)* from time immemorial.

Un-: u~voreingenommen *adj* unbiased, unprejudiced, impartial; **~voreingenommenheit** *f, no pl* impartiality; **u~vorhergesehen** *adj* unforeseen; *Besuch* unexpected; **wir bekamen u~vorhergesehen** *or* **u~vorhergesehenen Besuch** we had visitors unexpectedly, we had unexpected visitors; **u~vorsätzlich** *adj (Jur)* unpremeditated; **u~vorschriftsmäßig** *adj* not in keeping with the regulations; **ein u~vorschriftsmäßig geparktes Fahrzeug** an improperly parked vehicle; **u~vorsichtig** *adj* careless; *(voreilig)* rash; **u~vorsichtigerweise** *adv* carelessly; *(voreilig)* rashly; **~vorsichtigkeit** *f* carelessness; rashness; **so eine ~vorsichtigkeit von dir!** how reckless *or* rash of you!; **u~vorstellbar** *adj* inconceivable; **u~vorteilhaft** *adj* unfavourable, disadvantageous; *Kleid, Frisur etc* unbecoming; **u~vorteilhaft aussehen** not to look one's best.

unwägbar *adj Umstand, Unterschied* imponderable; *Risiko auch* incalculable, inestimable.

Unwägbarkeit *f no pl siehe adj* imponderability; incalculability.

Un-: u~wahr *adj* untrue; **u~wahrhaftig** *adj* untruthful; *Gefühle* insincere; **~wahrheit** *f* untruth.

unwahrscheinlich [1] *adj (nicht zu erwarten, kaum denkbar)* unlikely, improbable; *(unglaubhaft)* implausible, improbable; *(inf: groß)* incredible *(inf)*.
[2] *adv (inf)* incredibly *(inf)* ◆ **wir haben uns ~ beeilt** we hurried as much as we possibly could; **er gab sich ~ Mühe** he took an incredible amount of trouble *(inf)*.

Unwahrscheinlichkeit *f siehe adj* unlikeliness, improbability; implausibility; incredibleness.

unwandelbar *adj (geh)* **(a)** *(unveränderlich)* unalterable, immutable. **(b)** *Treue, Liebe* unwavering, steadfast.

unwegsam *adj Gelände etc* rough.

Unwegsamkeit *f* roughness.

unweiblich *adj* unfeminine.

unweigerlich [1] *adj attr Folge* inevitable.
[2] *adv* inevitably; *(fraglos)* undoubtedly; *(grundsätzlich)* invariably.

unweit *prep +gen, adv* not far from.

unwert *adj (rare) siehe* **unwürdig**.

Unwert *m* **(a)** *siehe* **Unwürdigkeit. (b)** demerits *pl* ◆ **über Wert und ~ einer Sache diskutieren** to discuss the merits and demerits of sth.

Unwert|urteil *nt* condemnation.

Unwesen *nt, no pl (übler Zustand)* terrible state of affairs ◆ **dem ~ (der Rauschgiftsucht) steuern** *(geh)* to combat the problem (of drug addiction); **sein ~ treiben** to be up to mischief; *(Landstreicher etc)* to make trouble; *(Gespenst)* to walk abroad; *(Vampir etc)* to strike terror into people's hearts.

unwesentlich *adj (nicht zur Sache gehörig)* irrelevant; *(unwichtig)* unimportant, insignificant ◆ **sich von einer Sache nur ~ unterscheiden** to differ only negligibly *or* marginally from sth; **zu einer Sache nicht/nur ~ beitragen** to make a not insignificant/only an insignificant contribution to sth.

Unwetter *nt* (thunder)storm ◆ **ein ~ brach los** a storm broke.

Un-: u~wichtig *adj* unimportant, insignificant; *(belanglos)* irrelevant; *(verzichtbar)* non-essential; **~wichtigkeit** *f siehe adj* unimportance, insignificance; irrelevance; non-essentiality; *(unwichtige Angelegenheit)* triviality; **u~widerlegbar, u~widerleglich** *adj* irrefutable; **u~widerruflich** *adj* irrevocable; **die u~widerruflich letzte Vorstellung** positively *or* definitely the last *or* final performance; **es steht u~widerruflich fest, daß ...** it is absolutely definite that ...; **u~widersprochen** *adj* uncontradicted; *Behauptung auch* unchallenged; **das darf nicht u~widersprochen bleiben** we can't let this pass unchallenged; **u~widerstehlich** *adj* irresistible; **u~wiederbringlich** *adj (geh)* irretrievable.

Unwille(n) *m, no pl* displeasure, indignation *(über +acc* at); *(Ungeduld)* irritation ◆ **jds ~n erregen** to incur sb's displeasure; **seinem ~n Luft machen** to give vent to one's indignation.

unwillig *adj* indignant *(über +acc* about); *(widerwillig)* unwilling, reluctant.

Unwilligkeit *f siehe adj* indignation; unwillingness, reluctance.

unwillkommen *adj* unwelcome.

unwillkürlich *adj* spontaneous; *(instinktiv)* instinctive; *(Physiol, Med)* involuntary ◆ **ich mußte ~ lachen** I couldn't help laughing.

Un-: u~wirklich *adj* unreal; **~wirklichkeit** *f* unreality; **u~wirksam** *adj (wirkungslos, auch Med)* ineffective; *Vertrag, Rechtsgeschäft* inoperative; *(nichtig)* null, void; *(Chem)* inactive; **u~wirsch** *adj Mensch, Benehmen* surly, gruff; *Bewegung* brusque; **u~wirtlich** *adj* inhospitable; **~wirtlichkeit** *f* inhospitableness; **u~wirtschaftlich** *adj* uneconomic; **~wirtschaftlichkeit** *f* uneconomicalness; **~wissen** *nt* ignorance; **u~wissend** *adj* ignorant; *(ahnungslos)* unsuspecting; *(unerfahren)* inexperienced; **~wissenheit** *f, no pl siehe adj* ignorance; unsuspectingness; inexperience; **~wissenheit schützt vor Strafe nicht** ignorance is no excuse *or (Jur)* is no defence in law; **u~wissenschaftlich** *adj* unscientific; *Textausgabe* unscholarly; *Essay, Ausdrucksweise* unacademic; **~wissenschaftlichkeit** *f siehe adj* unscientific nature/character *etc*; unscholarliness; unacademic nature/character *etc*; **u~wissentlich** *adv* unwittingly, unknowingly.

unwohl *adj (unpäßlich)* unwell, indisposed *(form)*; *(unbehaglich)* uneasy ◆ **mir ist ~, ich fühle mich ~** I don't feel well; **in ihrer Gegenwart fühle ich mich ~** I'm ill at ease *or* I feel uneasy in her presence.

Unwohlsein *nt* indisposition; *(unangenehmes Gefühl)* unease ◆ **von einem (plötzlichen) ~ befallen werden** to be taken ill suddenly.

Un-: u~wohnlich *adj Zimmer etc* uncomfortable, cheerless; **~wort** *nt* taboo word; **u~würdig** *adj* unworthy *(+gen* of); *Verhalten* undignified; *(schmachvoll)* degrading, shameful; **~würdigkeit** *f siehe adj* unworthiness; lack of dignity; degradation, shame.

Unzahl *f* **eine ~ von** a host of.

unzählbar *adj* innumerable, countless; *(Ling)* uncountable ◆ **~ viele** huge numbers; **~ viele Bücher/Mädchen** innumerable books/girls.

unzählig [1] *adj* innumerable, countless ◆ **~e Male** countless times, time and again.
[2] *adv* **~ viele** huge numbers; **~ viele Bücher/Mädchen** innumerable books/

girls.
unzähligemal *adv* countless times, time and again.
un-: ~zähmbar *adj* untamable; (*fig auch*) indomitable; **~zart** *adj* ungentle.
Unze *f* **-, -n** ounce.
Unzeit *f*: **zur ~** (*geh*) at an inopportune moment, inopportunely.
un-: ~zeitgemäß *adj* (*altmodisch*) old-fashioned, outmoded; (*nicht in die Zeit passend*) untimely; **~zensiert** *adj* uncensored; (*Sch*) ungraded; **~zerbrechlich** *adj* unbreakable; **~zeremoniell** *adj* unceremonious; **~zerkaut** *adj* unchewed; **~zerreißbar** *adj* untearable; **~zerstörbar** *adj* indestructible; **~zertrennlich** *adj* inseparable.
Unziale *f* **-, -n** (*Typ*) **(a)** (*Schrift*) uncial (writing). **(b)** (*Buchstabe*) uncial (letter).
Un-: u~ziemend (*old*), **u~ziemlich** *adj* unseemly, unbecoming, indecorous; **~ziemlichkeit** *f* **(a)** *no pl* unseemliness, indecorousness; **(b)** (*Benehmen*) impropriety; **u~zivilisiert** *adj* (*lit, fig*) uncivilized.
Unzucht *f, no pl* (*esp Jur*) sexual offence ◆ **das gilt als ~** that's regarded as a sexual offence; **~ treiben** to fornicate; **~ mit Abhängigen/Kindern/Tieren** (*Jur*) illicit sexual relations with dependants/children/animals; **gewerbsmäßige ~** prostitution; **widernatürliche ~** unnatural sexual act(s *pl*); **~ mit jdm treiben** to fornicate with sb; (*Jur*) to commit a sexual offence/ sexual offences with sb; **jdn zur ~ mißbrauchen** to abuse sb (for sexual purposes).
unzüchtig *adj* (*esp Jur*) indecent; *Reden, Schriften* obscene; *Gedanken auch* unchaste ◆ **~e Handlungen** obscene acts; (*Jur*) illicit sexual acts; **~ leben** to live licentiously.
Unzüchtigkeit *f siehe adj* indecency; obscenity; unchastity; licentiousness.
Un-: u~zufrieden *adj* dissatisfied, discontent(ed); (*mißmutig*) unhappy; **manche Leute sind immer u~zufrieden** some people are never content *or* happy; **~zufriedenheit** *f, no pl siehe adj* dissatisfaction, discontent; unhappiness; discontent(ment); **u~zugänglich** *adj Gegend, Gebäude etc* inaccessible; *Charakter, Mensch* inapproachable; (*taub, unaufgeschlossen gegen*) deaf, impervious (*+dat* to); **~zugänglichkeit** *f siehe adj* inaccessibility; unapproachability; deafness, imperviousness; **u~zukömmlich** *adj* (*Aus*) insufficient, inadequate; (*nicht zukommend*) undue; **~zukömmlichkeit** *f* (*Aus*) unpleasantness; (*Unzulänglichkeit*) inadequacy; **u~zulänglich** *adj* (*nicht ausreichend*) insufficient; (*mangelhaft*) inadequate; **~zulänglichkeit** *f* **(a)** *siehe adj* insufficiency; inadequacy; **(b)** *usu pl* shortcomings *pl*; **u~zulässig** *adj* (*auch Jur*) inadmissible; *Gebrauch* improper; *Beeinflussung* undue; *Belastung, Geschwindigkeit* excessive; **für u~zulässig erklären** (*Jur*) to rule out; **u~zumutbar** *adj* unreasonable; **u~zurechnungsfähig** *adj* not responsible for one's actions, of unsound mind; **jdn für u~zurechnungsfähig erklären lassen** (*Jur*) to have sb certified (insane); **geistig u~zurechnungsfähig** non compos mentis (*Jur*), of unsound mind; **~zurechnungsfähigkeit** *f* unsoundness of mind; **~zurechnungsfähigkeit geltend machen** to enter *or* put forward a plea of insanity; **u~zureichend** *adj* insufficient, inadequate; **u~zusammenhängend** *adj* incoherent, disjointed; **u~zuständig** *adj* (*Admin, Jur*) incompetent, not competent; **sich für u~zuständig erklären** to disclaim competence; **u~zustellbar** *adj* undeliverable; *Postsendung* dead; **falls u~zustellbar bitte zurück an Absender** if undelivered, please return to sender; **~zustellbarkeit** *f* undeliverability; **u~zuträglich** *adj* unhealthy; **jdm (gesundheitlich)** *or* **jds Gesundheit u~zuträglich sein** not to agree with sb, to be bad for sb's health; **u~zutreffend** *adj* inappropriate, inapplicable; (*unwahr*) incorrect; **~zutreffendes bitte streichen** delete as applicable; **u~zuverlässig** *adj* unreliable; **~zuverlässigkeit** *f* unreliability; **u~zweckmäßig** *adj* (*nicht ratsam*) inexpedient; (*unpraktisch*) impractical; (*ungeeignet*) unsuitable, inappropriate; **~zweckmäßigkeit** *f siehe adj* inexpediency; impracticality; unsuitableness, inappropriateness; **u~zweideutig** *adj* unambiguous, unequivocal; (*fig: unanständig*) explicit; **u~zweifelhaft** [1] *adj* undoubted, indubitable, unquestionable; [2] *adv* without doubt, undoubtedly, indubitably.
Update ['ʌpdeɪt] *nt* **-s, -s** (*Comput*) update (*auf+acc or zu* to).
üppig *adj Wachstum* luxuriant; *Vegetation auch* lush; *Haar* thick; *Mahl, Ausstattung* sumptuous, opulent; *Rente, Gehalt* lavish; *Figur, Frau, Formen* voluptuous; *Busen* ample; *Leben* luxurious; *Phantasie* rich ◆ **nun werd mal nicht zu ~!** (*inf*) let's have no more of your cheek! (*inf*); **~ leben** to live in style; **~ wuchernde Vegetation** rampant vegetation.
Üppigkeit *f siehe adj* luxuriance; lushness; thickness; sumptuousness, opulence; lavishness; voluptuousness; ampleness; luxury; richness.
up to date ['aptu:'de:t] *adj pred* (*inf*) up to date; *Kleidung* modern.
Ur *m* **-(e)s, -e** (*Zool*) aurochs.
Ur- *in cpds* (*erste*) first, prime; (*ursprünglich*) original; **~abstimmung** *f* ballot; **~adel** *m* ancienne noblesse, ancient nobility; **~ahn(e)** *m* (*Vorfahr*) forefather, forebear; (*~großvater*) great-grandfather; **~ahne** *f* (*Vorfahr*) forebear; (*~großmutter*) great-grandmother.
Ural *m* **-s** (*Geog*) **(a)** (*Fluß*) Ural. **(b)** (*Gebirge*) **der ~** the Urals *pl*, the Ural mountains *pl*.
uralt *adj* ancient; *Problem, Brauch auch* age-old ◆ **seit ~en Zeiten** from time immemorial; **aus ~en Zeiten** from long (long) ago.
Uran *nt* **-s,** *no pl* (*abbr* **U**) uranium.
Uranbrenner *m* uranium pile.
Ur-: ~anfang *m* first beginning; **~angst** *f* primeval fear; **~anlage** *f* genetic predisposition; **u~aufführen** *vt ptp* **u~aufgeführt** *infin, ptp only* to give the first performance (of), to play for the first time; *Film* to premiere *usu pass.*
Uraufführung *f* premiere; (*von Theaterstück etc auch*) first night *or* performance; (*von Film auch*) first showing.
Uraufführungs-: ~(film)theater, ~kino *nt* premiere cinema.
Urausgabe *f* first edition.
urban *adj* (*geh*) urbane.
urbanisieren* *vtr* (*Sociol*) to urbanize.
Urbanisierung *f* (*Sociol*) urbanization.
Urbanität *f* (*geh*) urbanity.
urbar *adj* **einen Wald/die Wüste/Land ~ machen** to clear a forest/to reclaim the desert/to cultivate land.
urbarisieren* *vti* (*Sw*) *siehe* **urbar machen.**
Urbarisierung *f* (*Sw*), **Urbarmachung** *f siehe adj* clearing; reclamation; cultivation.
Ur-: ~bayer *m* (*inf*) typical Bavarian; **~bedeutung** *f* (*Ling*) original meaning; **~beginn** *m* very *or* first beginning; **seit ~beginn** *or* **von ~beginn an** from the beginning(s) of time; **~bevölkerung** *f* natives *pl*, original inhabitants *pl*; (*in Australien und Neuseeland*) Aborigines *pl*; **~bewohner** *m* native, original inhabitant; (*in Australien und Neuseeland*) Aborigine; **~bild** *nt* prototype, archetype; (*Philos*) idea.
urchig *adj* (*Sw*) *siehe* **urwüchsig.**
Ur-: ~christen *pl* (*Eccl Hist*) early Christians *pl*; **~christentum** *nt* early Christianity; **u~christlich** *adj* early Christian; **u~deutsch** *adj* essentially German.
Urdu *nt* **-(s)** (*Ling*) Urdu.
Ur-: u~eigen *adj* very own; **es liegt in seinem u~eigensten Interesse** it's in his own best interests; **ein dem Menschen u~eigener Hang** an inherent human quality; **~einwohner** *m* native, original inhabitant; (*in Australien und Neuseeland*) Aborigine; **~eltern** *pl* (*Vorfahren*) forebears *pl*; (*~großeltern*) great-grandparents *pl*; **~enkel** *m* great-grandchild, great-grandson; **~enkelin** *f* great-granddaughter; **~fassung** *f* original version; **~fehde** *f* (*Hist*) oath of truce; **~fehde schwören** to abjure all vengeance; **~form** *f* prototype; **~gemeinde** *f* (*Eccl Hist*) early Christian community; **u~gemütlich** *adj* (*inf*) really comfortable/cosy *etc*; *siehe* **gemütlich**; **u~germanisch** *adj* (*Ling*) Proto-Germanic; (*fig*) essentially Germanic; **das ~germanische** Proto-Germanic; **~geschichte** *f* prehistory; **~gesellschaft** *f* primitive society; **~gestalt** *f siehe* **~form**; **~gestein** *nt* prehistoric rock, primitive rocks *pl*; **politisches ~gestein** (*fig*) a dyed-in-the-wool politician; **~gewalt** *f* elemental force.
urgieren* (*Aus form*) [1] *vt* to expedite.
[2] *vi* to expedite matters.
Urgroß-: ~eltern *pl* great-grandparents *pl*; **~mutter** *f* great-grandmother; **~vater** *m* great-grandfather.
Ur-: ~grund *m* very basis, source; **~heber(in** *f***)** *m* **-s, -** originator; (*liter: Schöpfer*) creator; (*Jur: Verfasser*) author; **der geistige ~heber** the spiritual father.
Urheber-: ~gebühr *f* copyright fee; **~recht** *nt* copyright (*an +dat* on); **u~rechtlich** *adj, adv* on copyright *attr*; **u~rechtlich geschützt** copyright(ed); **~schaft** *f* authorship; **~schutz** *m* copyright.
Urheimat *f* original home(land).
Uri *nt* **-s** Uri.
urig *adj* (*inf*) *Mensch* earthy; *Lokal etc* ethnic.
Urin *m* **-s, -e** urine ◆ **etw im ~ haben** (*sl*) to have a gut feeling about sth (*inf*).
Urinal *nt* **-s, -e** (*Med*) urinal.
urinieren* *vti* to urinate.
Ur-: ~instinkt *m* primary *or* basic instinct; **~kanton** *m* (*Sw*) original canton; **~kirche** *f* early Church; **~knall** *m* (*Astron*) big bang; **u~komisch** *adj* (*inf*) screamingly funny (*inf*); **~kraft** *f* elemental force.
Urkunde *f* **-, -n** document; (*Kauf~*) deed, titledeed; (*Gründungs~ etc*) charter; (*Sieger~, Diplom~, Bescheinigung etc*) certificate ◆ **eine ~ (über etw acc) ausstellen** *or* **ausfertigen** (*Jur*) to draw up a document about sth; **eine ~ bei jdm hinterlegen** to lodge a document with sb.
Urkundenfälschung *f* forgery *or* falsification of a/the document/ documents.
urkundlich *adj* documentary ◆ **~ verbürgt** *or* **bestätigt** authenticated; **~ beweisen** *or* **belegen** to give documentary evidence; **~ erwähnt** mentioned in a document.
Urkundsbeamte(r) *m*, **Urkundsperson** *f* registrar.
Urlandschaft *f* primitive *or* primeval landscape.
Urlaub *m* **-(e)s, -e** (*Ferien*) holiday(s), vacation (*US*); (*esp Mil*) leave (of absence) ◆ **~ haben** to have a holiday *or* vacation/to have leave; **in** *or* **im** *or* **auf** (*inf*) **~ sein** to be on holiday *or* vacation/on leave; **er mach zur Zeit (in Italien) ~** he's on holiday *or* he's vacationing (*US*) (in Italy) at the moment; **in ~ fahren** to go on holiday *or* vacation/on leave; **zwei Wochen ~** two weeks' holiday *or* vacation/leave; **(sich** *dat***) einen Tag ~ nehmen** to take a day off *or* a day's holiday; **~ bis zum Wecken** (*Mil*) night leave.
urlauben *vi* (*inf*) to holiday, to vacation (*US*).
Urlauber(in *f***)** *m* **-s, -** holiday-maker, vacationist (*US*); (*Mil*) soldier on leave.
Urlaubs-: ~anspruch *m* holiday *or* vacation (*US*) entitlement; **~gebiet** *nt* holiday *or* vacation (*US*) area; **~geld** *nt* holiday pay, holiday money; **u~reif** *adj* (*inf*) ready for a holiday *or* vacation (*US*); **~reise** *f* holiday *or* vacation (*US*) trip; **eine ~reise machen** to go on a trip; **~plan** *m usu pl* holiday *or* vacation (*US*) plan; **~schein** *m* (*Mil*) pass; **~sperre** *f* (*Mil*) ban on leave; **~stimmung** *f* holiday mood; **~tag** *m* (one day of) holiday *or* vacation (*US*); **die ersten drei ~tage hat es geregnet** it rained on the first three

days of the/my/his *etc* holiday; **ich habe noch drei ~tage gut** I've still got three days' holiday to come; **~vertretung** *f* temporary replacement; **ich mache hier nur ~vertretung** I'm just filling in while someone is on holiday; **~woche** *f* (one week of) holiday *or* vacation (*US*); **~zeit** *f* holiday *or* vacation (*US*) period *or* season.

Ur-: **~laut** *m* elemental cry; **~mensch** *m* primeval man; (*inf*) caveman (*inf*); **~meter** *nt* standard metre; **~mund** *m* (*Biol*) blastopore; **~mutter** *f* first mother.

Urne *f* **-, -n** urn; (*Los~*) box; (*Wahl~*) ballot-box ◆ **zur ~ gehen** to go to the polls.

Urnen-: **~feld** *nt* (*Archeol*) urnfield, urnsite; **~friedhof** *m* urn cemetery, cinerarium; **~gang** *m* (*Pol*) going to the polls *no art*; **~grab** *nt* urn grave.

Urogenital- (*Anat*): **~system** *nt* urogenital system; **~trakt** *m* urogenital tract.

Urologe *m*, **Urologin** *f* urologist.

Urologie *f* urology.

urologisch *adj* urological.

Ur-: **~oma** *f* (*inf*) great-granny (*inf*); **~opa** *m* (*inf*) great-grandpa (*inf*); **~pflanze** *f* primordial plant; **u~plötzlich** (*inf*) [1] *adj attr* very sudden; [2] *adv* all of a sudden; **~quell** *m*, **~quelle** *f* (*geh*) primary source, fountainhead.

Ursache *f* **-, -n** cause (*auch Philos*); (*Grund*) reason; (*Beweggrund*) motive; (*Anlaß*) occasion ◆ **~ und Wirkung** cause and effect; **kleine ~, große Wirkung** (*prov*) big oaks from little acorns grow (*prov*); **keine ~!** (*auf Dank*) don't mention it, you're welcome; (*auf Entschuldigung*) that's all right; **ohne (jede) ~** for no reason (at all); **aus nichtiger ~** for a trifling reason/trifling reasons; **aus unbekannter/ungeklärter ~** for no apparent reason/for reasons unknown; **jdm ~ geben, etw zu tun** to give sb cause to do sth; **ich habe alle ~ anzunehmen, daß ...** I have every reason to suppose that ...; **alle/keine ~ zu etw haben** to have every/no reason for sth; **alle/keine ~ haben, etw zu tun** to have every/no reason to do sth; **die ~ für etw** *or* **einer Sache** (*gen*) **sein** to be the cause of/reason for sth.

ursächlich *adj* (*esp Philos*) causal ◆ **~ für etw sein** to be the cause of sth; **in ~em Zusammenhang stehen** to be causally related.

Ursächlichkeit *f* (*esp Philos*) causality.

Ur-: **~schlamm** *m* primeval mud; **~schleim** *m* protoplasm; **~schrei** *m* (*Psych*) primal scream; **~schrift** *f* original (text *or* copy); **u~schriftlich** [1] *adj* original; [2] *adv* in the original; **u~senden** *vt sep infin, ptp only* (*Rad*) to broadcast for the first time; **das wurde im April u~gesendet** that was first broadcast in April; **~sendung** *f* (*Rad*) first broadcast.

urspr. *abbr of* **ursprünglich**.

Ursprache *f* **(a)** proto-language. **(b)** (*bei Übersetzungen*) original (language), source language.

Ursprung *m* **-s, Ursprünge (a)** origin; (*Anfang auch*) beginning; (*Abstammung*) extraction ◆ **er/dieses Wort ist keltischen ~s** he is of Celtic extraction/this word is Celtic in origin *or* of Celtic origin; **seinen ~ in etw** (*dat*) **haben, einer Sache** (*dat*) **seinen ~ verdanken** to originate in *or* to have one's/its origins in sth.
(b) (*old: lit, fig: Quelle*) source.

ursprünglich [1] *adj* **(a)** *attr* original; (*anfänglich*) initial, first. **(b)** (*urwüchsig*) natural; *Natur* unspoilt.
[2] *adv* originally; (*anfänglich*) initially, at first, in the beginning.

Ursprünglichkeit *f* naturalness, simplicity.

Ursprungsland *nt* (*Comm*) country of origin.

Urständ *f*: **(fröhliche) ~ feiern** (*hum*) to come back with a vengeance, to come to life again.

Urstromtal *nt* (*Geol, Geog*) glacial valley (*in North Germany*).

Urteil *nt* **-s, -e (a)** judgement (*auch Philos*); (*Entscheidung*) decision; (*Meinung*) opinion ◆ **nach meinem ~** in my judgement/opinion; **ich kann darüber kein ~ abgeben** I am no judge of this; **sich** (*dat*) **ein ~ über etw** (*acc*) **erlauben/ein ~ über etw fällen** to pronounce *or* pass judgement on sth; **sich** (*dat*) **kein ~ über etw** (*acc*) **erlauben können** to be in no position to judge sth; **nach dem ~ von Sachverständigen** according to expert opinion; **jdn in seinem ~ bestärken** to strengthen sb in his opinion; **mit seinem ~ zurückhalten** to be reticent about giving one's opinion(s); **zu dem ~ kommen, daß ...** to come to the conclusion that ...; **sich** (*dat*) **ein ~ über jdn/etw bilden** to form an opinion about sb/sth.
(b) (*Jur: Gerichts~*) verdict; (*Richterspruch*) judgement; (*Strafmaß*) sentence; (*Schiedsspruch*) award; (*Scheidungsspruch*) decree ◆ **das ~ über jdn sprechen** (*Jur*) to pass *or* to pronounce judgement on sb; **jdm/sich selber sein ~ sprechen** (*fig*) to pronounce sb's/one's own sentence.

urteilen *vi* to judge (*nach* by) ◆ **über etw** (*acc*) **~** to judge sth; (*seine Meinung äußern*) to give one's opinion on sth; **hart/abfällig über jdn ~** to judge sb harshly/to be disparaging about sb; **nach seinem Aussehen zu ~** judging by *or* to judge by his appearance; **vorschnell ~** to make a hasty judgement.

Urteils-: **~begründung** *f* (*Jur*) opinion; **u~fähig** *adj* competent *or* able to judge; (*umsichtig*) discerning, discriminating; **dazu ist er u~fähig genug** his judgement is sound enough for that; **~fähigkeit** *f siehe adj* competence *or* ability to judge; discernment, discrimination; **~findung** *f* (*Jur*) reaching a verdict *no art*; **~kraft** *f, no pl* power *or* faculty of judgement; (*Umsichtigkeit*) discernment, discrimination; **„Kritik der ~kraft"** "Critique of Judgement"; **~schelte** *f* attack on a/the court's ruling; **~spruch** *m* (*Jur*) judgement; (*von Geschworenen*) verdict; (*von Strafgericht*) sentence; (*von Schiedsgericht*) award; **~verkündung** *f* (*Jur*) pronouncement of judgement; **~vermögen** *nt siehe* **~kraft**.

Ur-: **~text** *m* original (text); **~tiefe** *f* (*liter*) depth(s); **~tier** *nt*, **~tierchen** *nt* protozoon; (*in der Morphologie*) primordial animal; **~trieb** *m* basic drive *or* instinct; **u~tümlich** *adj siehe* **u~wüchsig**; **~tümlichkeit** *f siehe* **~wüchsigkeit**; **~typ(us)** *m* **-s, -typen** prototype.

Uruguay *nt* **-s** Uruguay.

Ur|ur- *in cpds* great-great-.

Ur-: **~vater** *m* forefather; **~väterzeit** *f* olden times *pl*; **seit ~väterzeiten** from time immemorial; **schon zur ~väterzeit** even in olden times; **u~verwandt** *adj Wörter, Sprachen* cognate; **~viech** *or* **~vieh** *nt* (*inf*) real character; **~vogel** *m* archaeopteryx; **~volk** *nt* first people; **~wahl** *f* (*Pol*) primary (election); **~wähler** *m* (*Pol*) primary elector *or* voter.

Urwald *m* primeval forest; (*in den Tropen*) jungle.

Urwaldlaute *pl* (*inf*) jungle noises *pl*.

Ur-: **~weib** *nt* (*inf*) real woman; **~welt** *f* primeval world; **u~weltlich** *adj* primeval, primordial; **u~wüchsig** *adj* (*unverbildet, naturhaft*) natural; *Natur* unspoilt; (*urweltlich*) *Flora, Fauna* primeval; (*ursprünglich*) original, native; (*bodenständig*) rooted to the soil; (*unberührt*) *Land etc* untouched; (*urgewaltig*) *Kraft* elemental; (*derb, kräftig*) sturdy; *Mensch* rugged; *Humor, Sprache* earthy; **~wüchsigkeit** *f siehe adj* naturalness, unaffectedness; primeval character; originality, nativeness; nativeness; untouched nature; elemental nature; sturdiness; ruggedness; earthiness; **~zeit** *f* primeval times *pl*; **seit ~zeiten** since primeval times; (*inf*) for donkey's years (*inf*); **vor ~zeiten** in primeval times; (*inf*) ages ago; **u~zeitlich** *adj* primeval; **~zelle** *f* (*Biol*) primordial cell; **~zeugung** *f* abiogenesis; **~zustand** *m* primordial *or* original state.

USA [u:|ɛs'|a:] *pl* **die ~** the USA *sing*; **in die ~ fahren** to travel to the USA.

Usambaraveilchen *nt* African violet.

US-amerikanisch [u:'|ɛs-] *adj* US-American.

Usance [y'zã:s] *f* **-, -n** usage, custom; (*Comm*) practice.

usf. *abbr of* **und so fort**.

Usurpation *f* (*liter*) usurpation.

Usurpator *m* (*liter*) usurper.

usurpatorisch *adj* (*liter*) usurpatory, usurpative.

usurpieren* *vt* (*liter*) to usurp.

Usus *m* **-s**, *no pl* custom ◆ **das ist hier so ~** it's the custom here.

usw. *abbr of* **und so weiter** etc.

Utensil *nt* **-s, -ien** [-iən] utensil, implement.

Uterus *m* **-, Uteri** uterus.

Utilitarismus *m* Utilitarianism.

Utilitarist(in *f*) *m* Utilitarian.

utilitaristisch *adj* utilitarian.

Utopia *nt* **-s, -s** Utopia.

Utopie *f* utopia; (*Wunschtraum*) utopian dream.

utopisch *adj* utopian; (*von Utopia*) Utopian.

Utopismus *m* utopianism.

Utopist(in *f*) *m* utopian.

utopistisch *adj* (*pej*) utopian.

u.U. *abbr of* **unter Umständen**.

UV [u:'fau] *abbr of* **ultraviolett**.

UV- [u:'fau-] *in cpds* ultraviolet.

u.v.a.(m.) *abbr of* **und vieles andere (mehr)**.

U.v.D. [u:fau'de:] *m* **-s, -s** *abbr of* **Unteroffizier vom Dienst** (*Mil*).

Ü-Wagen *m* (*Rad, TV*) outside broadcast vehicle.

uzen *vti* (*inf*) to tease, to kid (*inf*).

Uzerei *f* (*dial, inf*) teasing, kidding (*inf*).

Uzname *m* (*inf*) nickname.

V, v [fau] *nt* -, - V, v.
V *abbr of* **Volt; Volumen.**
va banque [va'bã:k]: **~ ~ spielen** (*geh*) to play vabanque; (*fig*) to put everything at stake.
Vabanquespiel [va'bã:k-] *nt* (*fig*) dangerous game.
Vaduz [fa'dʊts, va'du:ts] *nt* - Vaduz.
vag [va:k] *adj siehe* **vag(e).**
Vagabund [vaga'bʊnt] *m* **-en, -en** vagabond.
Vagabundenleben [va-] *nt* vagabond life; (*fig auch*) roving life.
vagabundieren* [vagabʊn'di:rən] *vi* **(a)** (*als Landstreicher leben*) to live as a vagabond/as vagabonds ◆ **das V~** vagabondage; **ein ~des Volk** a nomadic people. **(b)** *aux sein* (*umherziehen*) to rove around, to lead a vagabond life ◆ **durch die Welt ~** to rove *or* wander all over the world.
vag(e) [va:k, 'va:gə] *adj* vague.
Vagheit ['va:khait] *f* vagueness.
Vagina [va'gi:na] *f* **-, Vaginen** vagina.
vaginal [vagi'na:l] *adj* vaginal.
vakant [va'kant] *adj* (*old, form*) vacant.
Vakanz [va'kants] *f* (*old, form: Stelle*) vacancy; (*old, dial: Ferien*) vacation.
Vakat ['va:kat] *nt* **-(s), -s** (*Typ*) blank (page).
Vakuum ['va:kuʊm] *nt* **-s, Vakuen** ['va:kuən] *or* **Vakua** (*lit, fig*) vacuum ◆ **unter/im ~** in a vacuum.
Vakuum- ['va:kuʊm-] *in cpds* vacuum; **~pumpe** *f* vacuum pump; **~röhre** *f* vacuum tube; **v~verpackt** *adj* vacuum-packed; **~verpackung** *f* vacuum pack; (*das Verpacken*) vacuum packaging; **v~versiegelt** *adj* vacuum-sealed.
Valentinstag ['va:lɛnti:ns-] *m* (St) Valentine's Day.
Valenz [va'lɛnts] *f* valency.
valleri, vallera [falə'ri:, falə'ra:] *interj* falderal, folderol.
Valoren [va'lo:rən] *pl* (*Sw*) (*Fin*) securities *pl.*
Valuta [va'lu:ta] *f* **-, Valuten (a)** (*Währung*) foreign currency. **(b)** (*im Zahlungsverkehr*) value; (*Datum*) value date.
Vamp [vɛmp] *m* **-s, -s** vamp.
Vampir [vam'pi:ɐ] *m* **-s, -e** vampire; (*Zool*) vampire (bat).
Vampirismus [vampi'rɪsmʊs] *m* vampirism.
Vanadin [vana'di:n] **-s, Vanadium** [va'na:diʊm] *nt* (*abbr* **V**) vanadium.
Van-Allen-Gürtel [vɛn'ɛlɪn-] *m* Van Allen belt.
Vandale [van'da:lə] *m* **-n, -n** vandal; (*Hist*) Vandal.
Vandalismus [vanda'lɪsmʊs] *m, no pl* vandalism.
Vanille [va'nɪljə, va'nɪlə] *f* **-,** *no pl* vanilla.
Vanille(n)- [va'nɪljə(n)-, va'nɪlə(n)-]: **~eis** *nt* vanilla ice-cream; **~geschmack** *m* vanilla flavour; **mit ~geschmack** vanilla-flavoured; **~sauce** *f* custard; **~stange** *f* vanilla pod; **~zucker, Vanillinzucker** *m* vanilla sugar.
variabel [va'ria:bl] *adj* variable.
Variabilität [variabili'tɛ:t] *f* variability.
Variable [va'ria:blə] *f* **-n, -n** variable.
Variante [va'riantə] *f* **-, -n** variant (*zu* on).
Variation [varia'tsio:n] *f* (*alle Bedeutungen*) variation ◆ **~en zu einem Thema** variations on a theme.
Variations- [varia'tsio:ns-]: **v~fähig** *adj* capable of variation; **~möglichkeit** *f* possibility of variation.
Varietät [varie'tɛ:t] *f* (*auch Bot, Zool*) variety.
⚠ **Varieté** [varie'te:] *nt* **-s, -s (a)** variety (entertainment), vaudeville (*esp US*). **(b)** (*Theater*) variety theatre, music hall (*Brit*), vaudeville theater (*US*).
variieren* [vari'i:rən] *vti* to vary.
Vasall [va'zal] *m* **-en, -en** (*Hist, fig*) vassal.
Vasallen- [va'zalən-]: **~pflicht** *f* (*Hist*) vassalage, feudal service; **~staat** *m* (*Hist*) vassal state; (*fig*) client *or* satellite state; **~tum** *nt, no pl* vassalage.
Väschen ['vɛ:sçən] *nt* little vase.
Vase ['va:zə] *f* **-, -n** vase.
Vasektomie [vazɛkto'mi:] *f* (*spec*) vasectomy.
Vaselin [vaze'li:n] *nt* **-s,** *no pl,* **Vaseline** *f* **-,** *no pl* Vaseline ®.
vasomotorisch [vazomo'to:rɪʃ] *adj* vasomotor *attr,* vasomotory ◆ **~ gestört sein** to have a vasomotory disorder.
Vater *m* **-s, ¨** (*lit fig*) father; (*Gott, bei Namen*) Father; (*von Zuchttieren*) sire ◆ **~ von zwei Kindern sein** to be the father of two children; **~ unser** (*Rel*) Our Father; **unsere ¨** *pl* (*geh: Vorfahren*) our (fore-)fathers *or* forebears; **die ¨ der Stadt** the town/city fathers; **wie der ~, so der Sohn** (*prov*) like father, like son (*prov*); **wer war der ~ dieses Kindes?** (*fig hum*) whose idea was that?; **ach du dicker ~!** (*inf*) oh my goodness!, oh heavens!; **~ Staat** (*hum*) the State.
Väterchen *nt dim of* **Vater** (*Vater*) dad(dy) (*inf*); (*alter Mann*) grandad (*inf*) ◆ **~ Staat** (*hum*) the State.
Vater-: ~figur *f* father figure; **~freuden** *pl* joys of fatherhood *pl*; **~haus** *nt* parental home.
Vaterland *nt* native country; (*esp Deutschland*) Fatherland ◆ **dem ~ dienen/sein ~ lieben** to serve/love one's country.
vaterländisch *adj* (*national*) national; (*patriotisch*) patriotic.
Vaterlands-: ~liebe *f* patriotism, love of one's country; **v~liebend** *adj* patriotic; **v~los** *adj* without a native land (*esp poet*); (*staatenlos*) stateless; **~verräter** *m* traitor to one's country; (*in Deutschland auch*) traitor to the Fatherland.
väterlich *adj* (*vom Vater*) paternal; (*wie ein Vater auch*) fatherly ◆ **er klopfte ihm ~ auf die Schulter** he gave him a fatherly pat on the shoulder.
väterlicherseits *adv* on one's father's side ◆ **meine Großeltern ~** my paternal grandparents.
Väterlichkeit *f* fatherliness.
Vater-: ~liebe *f* paternal *or* fatherly love; **~liebe ist unersetzbar** a father's love is irreplaceable; **v~los** *adj* fatherless; **~mord** *m* patricide; **~mörder** *m* **(a)** patricide, father-killer (*inf*); **(b)** (*hum: Kragen*) stand-up collar, choker (*dated*); **~recht** *nt* patriarchy.
Vaterschaft *f* fatherhood *no art*; (*esp Jur*) paternity ◆ **gerichtliche Feststellung der ~** (*Jur*) affiliation.
Vaterschafts-: ~bestimmung *f* determination of paternity; **~klage** *f* paternity suit.
Vätersitte *f* tradition of one's forefathers.
Vater(s)name *m* (*old*) surname.
Vater-: ~stadt *f* home town; **~stelle** *f* **bei jdm ~stelle vertreten/an ~stelle stehen** to act *or* be a father to sb/take the place of sb's father; **~tag** *m* Father's Day; **~unser** *nt* **-s, -** Our Father; **das ~unser** the Lord's Prayer.
Vati *m* **-s, -s** (*inf*) dad(dy) (*inf*).
Vatikan [vati'ka:n] *m* **-s** Vatican.
vatikanisch [vati'ka:nɪʃ] *adj attr* Vatican.
Vatikanstadt [vati'ka:n-] *f* Vatican City.
V-Ausschnitt ['fau-] *m* V-neck ◆ **ein Pullover mit ~** a V-neck jumper (*Brit*) *or* sweater.
v. Chr. *abbr of* **vor Christus** BC.
VDE ['faude:'|e:] *m* **-s,** *no pl abbr of* **Verband Deutscher Elektrotechniker.**
VEB ['fau|e:'be:] *m* **-s, -s** *abbr of* **Volkseigener Betrieb.**
Vegetarier(in *f*) [vege'ta:riɐ, -iərɪn] *m* **-s, -** vegetarian.
vegetarisch [vege'ta:rɪʃ] *adj* vegetarian ◆ **sich ~ ernähren** to live on a vegetarian diet.
Vegetarismus [vegeta'rɪsmʊs] *m, no pl* vegetarianism.
Vegetation [vegeta'tsio:n] *f* vegetation.
vegetativ [vegeta'ti:f] *adj* (*pflanzlich*) vegetative; *Nervensystem* autonomic.
vegetieren* [vege'ti:rən] *vi* to vegetate; (*kärglich leben*) to eke out a bare *or* miserable existence.
vehement [vehe'mɛnt] *adj* (*geh*) vehement.
Vehemenz [vehe'mɛnts] *f* (*geh*) vehemence.
Vehikel [ve'hikl] *nt* **-s, - (a)** (*pej inf*) boneshaker (*inf*). **(b)** (*Pharm, fig geh*) vehicle.
Veilchen *nt* violet; (*inf: blaues Auge*) shiner (*inf*), black eye ◆ **sie ist bescheiden wie das ~ im Moose** *or* **wie ein ~, das im verborgenen blüht** she is modesty itself; **blau wie ein ~** (*inf*) drunk as a lord (*inf*), roaring drunk (*inf*).
veilchenblau *adj* violet; (*inf: betrunken*) roaring drunk (*inf*).
Veitstanz *m* (*Med*) St Vitus's dance ◆ **einen ~ aufführen** (*fig inf*) to jump *or* hop about like crazy (*inf*).
Vektor ['vɛktɔr] *m* vector.
Velar(laut) [ve'la:ɐ-] *m,* **-s, -e** velar (sound).
Velo ['ve:lo] *nt* **-s, -s** (*Sw*) bicycle, bike (*inf*); (*motorisiert*) moped.
Velour *nt* **-s, -s** *or* **-e, Velours** *nt* **-, -** [və'lu:ɐ, ve'lu:ɐ] (*auch* **Veloursleder**) suede.
Velours [və'lu:ɐ, ve'lu:ɐ] *m* **-, -** (*Tex*) velour(s).

⚠: Informationen zur Rechtschreibreform im Anhang

Veloursteppich [və'luːʁ-, ve'luːʁ-] *m* velvet carpet.
Vendetta [vɛn'dɛta] *f* **-, Vendetten** vendetta.
Vene ['veːnə] *f* **-, -n** vein.
Venedig [ve'neːdɪç] *nt* **-s** Venice.
Venen|entzündung ['veːnən-] *f* phlebitis.
venerisch [ve'neːrɪʃ] *adj* (*Med*) venereal.
Venezianer(in *f*) [vene'tsiaːnɐ, -ərɪn] *m* **-s, -** Venetian.
venezianisch [vene'tsiaːnɪʃ] *adj* Venetian.
Venezolaner(in *f*) [venetso'laːnɐ, -ərɪn] *m* **-s, -** Venezuelan.
venezolanisch [venetso'laːnɪʃ] *adj* Venezuelan.
Venezuela [vene'tsueːla] *nt* **-s** Venezuela.
Venia legendi ['veːnia le:gɛndi] *f* **- -**, *no pl* (*Univ*) authorization to teach at a university.
venös [ve'nøːs] *adj* venous.
Ventil [vɛn'tiːl] *nt* **-s, -e** (*Tech, Mus*) valve; (*fig*) outlet.
Ventilation [ventila'tsioːn] *f* ventilation; (*Anlage*) ventilation system.
Ventilator [vɛnti'laːtɔr] *m* ventilator.
ventilieren* [vɛnti'liːrən] *vt* (*geh*) to ventilate; (*fig*) (*äußern*) to air; (*erwägen*) to examine, to consider carefully.
Venus ['veːnʊs] *f* **-**, *no pl* (*Myth, Astron*) Venus.
ver|abfolgen* *vt* (*form*) *Medizin etc* to administer (*form*) (*jdm* to sb); (*verordnen*) to prescribe (*jdm* for sb).
ver|abreden* [1] *vt* to arrange; *Termin auch* to fix, to agree upon; *Straftat* to collude in; *Mord, Hochverrat, Meuterei* to conspire in ◆ **es war eine verabredete Sache** it was arranged beforehand; **ein vorher verabredetes Zeichen** a prearranged signal; **zum verabredeten Zeitpunkt/Ort** at the agreed time/ place, at the time/place arranged; **wir haben verabredet, daß wir uns um 5 Uhr treffen** we have arranged to meet at 5 o'clock; **wie verabredet** as arranged; **schon verabredet sein** (*für* on) to have a previous *or* prior engagement (*esp form*), to have something else on (*inf*); **mit jdm verabredet sein** to have arranged to meet sb; (*geschäftlich, formell*) to have an appointment with sb; (*esp mit Freund*) to have a date with sb.
[2] *vr* **sich mit jdm/miteinander ~** to arrange to meet sb/to meet; (*geschäftlich, formell*) to arrange an appointment with sb/an appointment; (*esp mit Freund*) to make a date with sb/a date; (*Jur*) to collude with sb/collude.
Ver|abredung *f* (*Vereinbarung*) arrangement, agreement; (*Treffen*) engagement (*form*); (*geschäftlich, formell*) appointment; (*esp mit Freund*) date; (*Jur*) collusion; (*von Mord, Hochverrat, Meuterei*) conspiracy ◆ **ich habe eine ~** I'm meeting somebody; **~ einer Straftat** (*Jur*) collusion/conspiracy to commit a criminal offence.
ver|abreichen* *vt Tracht Prügel etc* to give; *Arznei auch* to administer (*form*) (*jdm* to sb); (*verordnen*) to prescribe (*jdm* for sb); (*old*) *Speise* to serve.
Ver|abreichung *f* (*form*) *siehe vt* giving; administering; prescription; serving.
ver|absäumen* *vt* (*form*) to neglect, to omit.
ver|abscheuen* *vt* to detest, to abhor, to loathe.
ver|abscheuenswert *adj* detestable, abhorrent, loathsome.
Ver|abscheuung *f* detestation, abhorrence, loathing.
ver|abscheuungswürdig *adj siehe* **verabscheuenswert**.
ver|abschieden* [1] *vt* to say goodbye to; (*Abschiedsfeier veranstalten für*) to hold a farewell ceremony for; (*entlassen*) *Beamte, Truppen* to discharge; (*Pol*) *Haushaltsplan* to adopt; *Gesetz* to pass ◆ **wie bist du von deinen Kollegen/bei deiner Stelle verabschiedet worden?** what sort of a farewell did your colleagues arrange for you/did you receive at work?
[2] *vr* **sich (von jdm) ~** to say goodbye (to sb), to take one's leave (of sb) (*form*), to bid sb farewell (*liter*); **er ist gegangen, ohne sich zu ~** he left without saying goodbye.
Ver|abschiedung *f* (*von Beamten etc*) discharge; (*Pol*) (*von Gesetz*) passing; (*von Haushaltsplan*) adoption.
ver|absolutieren* *vt* to make absolute.
ver|achten* *vt* to despise; *jdn auch* to hold in contempt; (*liter*) *Tod, Gefahr* to scorn ◆ **nicht zu ~** (*inf*) not to be despised, not to be scoffed at, not to be sneezed at (*inf*); **einen guten Whisky hat er nie verachtet** (*inf*) but he never said no to a good drop of whisky.
ver|achtenswert *adj* despicable, contemptible.
Ver|ächter *m*: **kein ~ von etw sein** to be quite partial to sth.
ver|ächtlich *adj* contemptuous, scornful; (*verachtenswert*) despicable, contemptible ◆ **jdn/etw ~ machen** to run sb down/belittle sth.
Ver|achtung *f, no pl* contempt (*von* for) ◆ **jdn mit ~ strafen** to treat sb with contempt.
ver|albern* *vt* (*inf*) to make fun of ◆ **du willst mich wohl ~** are you pulling my leg?
ver|allgemeinern* *vti* to generalize.
Ver|allgemeinerung *f* generalization.
ver|alten* *vi aux sein* to become obsolete; (*Ansichten, Methoden*) to become antiquated; (*Mode*) to go out of date.
ver|altet *adj* obsolete; *Ansichten* antiquated; *Mode* out-of-date.
Veranda [ve'randa] *f* **-, Veranden** veranda, porch.
ver|änderbar *adj* changeable.
ver|änderlich *adj* variable; *Wetter, Mensch* changeable.
Ver|änderlichkeit *f siehe adj* variability; changeability.
ver|ändern* [1] *vt* to change.
[2] *vr* to change; (*Stellung wechseln*) to change one's job; (*Wohnung wechseln*) to move ◆ **sich zu seinem Vorteil/Nachteil ~** (*im Aussehen*) to look better/ worse; (*charakterlich*) to change for the better/worse; **verändert aussehen** to look different.
Ver|änderung *f* change ◆ **eine berufliche ~** a change of job.
ver|ängstigen* *vt* (*erschrecken*) to frighten, to scare; (*einschüchtern*) to intimidate.
ver|ankern* *vt* (*Naut, Tech*) to anchor; (*fig*) (*in +dat* in) *Rechte etc* (*in Gesetz*) to establish, to ground; *Gedanken* (*in Bewußtsein*) to embed, to fix.
Ver|ankerung *f* (*Naut, Tech*) (*das Verankern*) anchoring; (*das Verankertsein*) anchorage; (*fig*) (*von Rechten*) (firm) establishment; (*von Gedanken*) embedding, fixing.
ver|anlagen* *vt* to assess (*mit* at).
ver|anlagt *adj* **melancholisch/tuberkulös ~ sein** to have a melancholy/ tubercular disposition; **technisch/mathematisch/praktisch ~ sein** to be technically/mathematically/practically minded; **künstlerisch/musikalisch ~ sein** to have an artistic/a musical bent; **zu** *or* **für etw ~ sein** to be cut out for sth; **er ist so ~, daß ...** it's his nature to ...; **er ist eben so ~** that's just the way he is, that's just his nature.
Ver|anlagung *f* **(a)** (*körperlich, esp Med*) predisposition; (*charakterlich*) nature, disposition; (*Hang*) tendency; (*allgemeine Fähigkeiten*) natural abilities *pl*; (*künstlerisches, praktisches etc Talent*) bent ◆ **eine ~ zum Dickwerden/zur Kriminalität haben** to have a tendency to put on weight/to have criminal tendencies. **(b)** (*von Steuern*) assessment.
ver|anlassen* *vt* **(a) etw ~** to arrange for sth, to see to it that sth is done/ carried out *etc*; (*befehlen*) to order sth; **eine Maßnahme ~** to arrange for/ order a measure to be taken; **ich werde das Nötige ~** I will see (to it) that the necessary steps are taken; **wir werden alles Weitere ~** we will take care of *or* see to everything else.
(b) *auch vi* (*bewirken*) to give rise (*zu* to) ◆ **jdn zu etw ~** (*Ereignis etc*) to lead sb to sth; (*Mensch*) to cause *or* induce sb to do sth; **jdn (dazu) ~, etw zu tun** (*Ereignis etc*) to lead sb to do sth; (*Mensch*) to cause *or* induce sb to do sth; **das veranlaßt zu der Annahme, daß ...** that leads one to assume that ...; **sich (dazu) veranlaßt fühlen, etw zu tun** to feel compelled *or* obliged to do sth.
Ver|anlassung *f* cause, reason ◆ **auf ~ von** *or* *+gen* at the instigation of; **keine ~ zu etw haben/keine ~ haben, etw zu tun** to have no cause *or* reason for sth/to do sth *or* for doing sth; **~ zu etw geben** to give cause for sth.
➤ **ver|anschaulichen*** *vt* to illustrate (*+dat* to, *an +dat, mit* with) ◆ **sich** (*dat*) **etw ~** to picture sth (to oneself), to visualize sth; **sich** (*dat*) **~, daß ...** to see *or* realize that ...
Ver|anschaulichung *f* illustration ◆ **zur ~** as an illustration, to illustrate sth.
ver|anschlagen* *vt* to estimate (*auf +acc* at) ◆ **etw zu hoch/niedrig ~** to overestimate/underestimate sth.
Ver|anschlagung *f* estimate; (*das Veranschlagen*) estimation.
ver|anstalten* *vt* to organize, to arrange; *Wahlen* to hold; *Umfrage* to do; (*kommerziell*) *Wettkämpfe, Konzerte etc* to promote; *Party etc* to hold, to give; (*inf*) *Szene* to make.
Ver|anstalter(in *f*) *m* **-s, -** organizer; (*Comm: von Wettkämpfen, Konzerten etc*) promoter.
Ver|anstaltung *f* **(a)** event (*von* organized by); (*feierlich, öffentlich*) function. **(b)** *no pl* (*das Veranstalten*) organization.
Veranstaltungs-: ~kalender *m* calendar of events; **~programm** *nt* programme of events.
ver|antworten* [1] *vt* to accept (the) responsibility for; *die Folgen auch, sein Tun* to answer for (*vor +dat* to) ◆ **(es) ~, daß jd etw tut** to accept the responsibility for sb doing sth; **wie könnte ich es denn ~, ...?** it would be most irresponsible of me ...; **ein weiterer Streik/eine solche Operation wäre nicht zu ~** another strike/such an operation would be irresponsible; **eine nicht zu ~de Fahrlässigkeit/Schlamperei** inexcusable negligence/slackness; **etw sich selbst gegenüber ~** to square sth with one's own conscience.
[2] *vr* **sich für** *or* **wegen etw ~** to justify sth (*vor +dat* to); (*für Missetaten etc*) to answer for sth (*vor +dat* before); **sich vor Gericht/Gott** *etc* **~ müssen** to have to answer to the courts/God *etc* (*für, wegen* for).
ver|antwortlich *adj* responsible; (*haftbar*) liable ◆ **jdm (gegenüber) ~ sein** to be responsible *or* answerable *or* accountable to sb; **jdn für etw ~ machen** to hold sb responsible for sth; **für etw ~ zeichnen** (*form*) (*lit*) to sign for sth; (*fig*) to take responsibility for sth; **der ~e Leiter des Projekts** the person in charge of the project.
Ver|antwortliche(r) *mf decl as adj* person responsible ◆ **die ~n** *pl* those responsible.
Ver|antwortlichkeit *f, no pl* responsibility; (*Haftbarkeit*) liability.
Ver|antwortung *f* responsibility (*für* for) ◆ **auf eigene ~** on one's own responsibility; **auf deine ~!** you take the responsibility!, on your own head be it!; **die ~ übernehmen** to take *or* accept *or* assume (*esp form*) responsibility; **jdn zur ~ ziehen** to call sb to account.
Ver|antwortungs-: ⚠v~bewußt *adj* responsible; **⚠~bewußtsein** *nt* sense of responsibility; **v~freudig** *adj* willing to take responsibility; **v~los** *adj* irresponsible; **~losigkeit** *f, no pl* irresponsibility; **v~voll** *adj* responsible.
ver|äppeln* *vt* (*inf*) **jdn ~** to make fun of sb; (*auf den Arm nehmen*) to pull sb's leg (*inf*).
ver|arbeitbar *adj* workable ◆ **leicht/schwer ~** easy/hard to work.
ver|arbeiten* *vt* to use (*zu etw* to make sth); (*Tech, Biol etc*) to process; *Ton, Gold etc* to work; (*verbrauchen*) to consume; (*verdauen*) to digest; (*fig*) to use (*zu* for); *Stoff* to treat; *Daten* to process; *Erlebnis etc* to assimilate, to digest; (*bewältigen*) to overcome ◆ **~de Industrie** processing industries *pl*; **etw geistig ~** to assimilate *or* digest sth.

➤ SPRACHE AKTIV: **veranschaulichen** → 53.5

ver|arbeitet *adj* **(a)** **gut/schlecht ~** *Rock etc* well/badly finished. **(b)** (*dial:* *abgearbeitet*) worn.
Ver|arbeitung *f* **(a)** *siehe vt* use, using; processing; working; digestion; treating; assimilation, digestion; overcoming. **(b)** (*Aussehen*) finish; (*Qualität*) workmanship *no indef art*.
ver|argen* *vt* **jdm etw ~** to hold sth against sb; **jdm ~, daß ...** to hold it against sb that ...; **ich kann es ihm nicht ~, wenn er ...** I can't blame him if he ...
ver|ärgern* *vt* **jdn ~** to annoy sb; (*stärker*) to anger sb.
ver|ärgert *adj* annoyed; (*stärker*) angry.
Ver|ärgerung *f* annoyance; (*stärker*) anger.
ver|armen* *vi aux sein* (*lit, fig*) to become impoverished ◆ **verarmt** impoverished.
Ver|armung *f, no pl* impoverishment.
ver|arschen* *vt* (*sl*) to take the piss out of (*sl*); (*für dumm verkaufen*) to mess *or* muck around (*inf*).
ver|arzten* *vt* (*inf*) to fix up (*inf*); (*mit Verband*) to patch up (*inf*); (*fig hum*) to sort out (*inf*).
ver|ästeln* *vr* to branch out; (*fig*) to ramify ◆ **eine verästelte Organisation** a complex organization; **ein verästelter Baum** a branched *or* ramose (*spec*) tree.
Ver|ästelung *f* branching; (*fig*) ramifications *pl*.
ver|ausgaben* *vr* to overexert *or* overtax oneself; (*finanziell*) to overspend ◆ **ich habe mich total verausgabt** (*finanziell*) I'm completely spent out.
ver|auslagen* *vt* (*Comm*) to lay out, to disburse (*form*).
ver|äußerlich *adj* (*form: verkäuflich*) saleable, for sale.
ver|äußerlichen* [1] *vt* to trivialize.
[2] *vi aux sein* to become superficial.
ver|äußern* *vt* (*form: verkaufen*) to dispose of; *Rechte, Land* to alienate (*form*).
Ver|äußerung *f siehe vt* disposal; alienation (*form*).
Verb [vɛrp] *nt* **-s, -en** verb.
verbal [vɛr'ba:l] *adj* verbal (*auch Gram*).
Verbalinjurie [vɛr'ba:l|ɪnju:riə] *f* (*Jur*) verbal injury.
verballhornen* *vt* to parody; (*unabsichtlich*) to get wrong.
Verballhornung *f* parody; (*unabsichtlich*) ≃ spoonerism.
Verband *m* **-(e)s, ¨e** **(a)** (*Med*) dressing; (*mit Binden*) bandage. **(b)** (*Bund*) association. **(c)** (*Mil*) unit ◆ **im ~ fliegen** to fly in formation. **(d)** (*Archit*) bond.
Verband(s)-: **~kasten** *m* first-aid box; **~material** *nt* dressing material; **~päckchen** *nt* gauze bandage; **~stoff** *m* dressing; **~watte** *f* surgical cottonwool (*Brit*), absorbent cotton (*US*), cotton batting (*US*); **~zeug** *nt* dressing material.
verbannen* *vt* to banish (*auch fig*), to exile (*aus* from, *auf* to).
Verbannte(r) *mf decl as adj* exile.
Verbannung *f* banishment *no art*, exile *no art*; (*das Verbannen*) banishment, exiling.
Verbannungs|ort *m* place of exile.
verbarrikadieren* [1] *vt* to barricade.
[2] *vr* to barricade oneself in (*in etw (dat)* sth).
verbaseln* *vt* (*dial*) to mislay; *Termin, Verabredung* to forget.
verbat *pret of* **verbitten**.
verbauen* *vt* **(a)** (*versperren*) to obstruct, to block ◆ **sich** (*dat*) **alle Chancen/die Zukunft ~** to spoil one's chances/one's prospects for the future; **jdm die Möglichkeit ~, etw zu tun** to ruin *or* spoil sb's chances of doing sth.
(b) (*verbrauchen*) *Holz etc* to use in building; *Geld* to use for building.
(c) (*schlecht bauen*) to construct badly.
(d) (*inf: verderben*) *Text, Arbeit etc* to botch (*inf*).
verbe|amten* *vt* to give the status of civil servant to.
verbeißen* *irreg* [1] *vt* (*fig inf*) **sich** (*dat*) **etw ~** *Zorn etc* to stifle sth, to suppress sth; *Bemerkung* to bite back sth; *Schmerz* to hide sth; **sich** (*dat*) **das Lachen ~** to keep a straight face.
[2] *vr* **sich in etw** (*acc*) **~** (*lit*) to bite into sth; (*Hund*) to sink its teeth into sth; (*fig*) to become set *or* fixed on sth; *siehe* **verbissen**.
verbergen* *irreg* [1] *vt* (*+dat, vor +dat* from) (*lit, fig*) to hide, to conceal; (*vor der Polizei auch*) to harbour ◆ **sein Gesicht in den Händen ~** to bury one's face in one's hands; **jdm etw ~** (*verheimlichen*) to keep sth from sb; *siehe* **verborgen²**.
[2] *vr* to hide (oneself), to conceal oneself.
Verbesserer *m* **-s, -** improver; (*Welt~*) reformer.
verbessern* [1] *vt* **(a)** (*besser machen*) to improve; *Leistung, Bestzeit* to improve (up)on, to better; *die Welt* to reform ◆ **eine neue, verbesserte Auflage** a new revised edition.
(b) (*korrigieren*) to correct.
[2] *vr* (*Lage etc*) to improve, to get better; (*Mensch*) (*in Leistungen*) to improve, to do better; (*beruflich, finanziell*) to better oneself; (*sich korrigieren*) to correct oneself.
Verbesserung *f* **(a)** improvement (*von* in); (*von Leistung, Bestzeit*) improvement (*von* on); (*von Buch*) revision; (*berufliche, finanzielle ~*) betterment. **(b)** (*Berichtigung*) correction.
Verbesserungs-: **v~fähig** *adj* capable of improvement; **~vorschlag** *m* suggestion for improvement.
verbeten *ptp of* **verbitten**.
verbeugen* *vr* to bow (*vor +dat* to).
Verbeugung *f* bow ◆ **eine ~ vor jdm machen** to (make a) bow to sb.
verbeulen* *vt* to dent.

verbiegen* *irreg* [1] *vt* to bend (out of shape); *Idee, Wahrheit* to distort; *siehe* **verbogen**.
[2] *vr* to bend; (*Holz*) to warp; (*Metall*) to buckle.
verbiestern* (*inf*) [1] *vt* (*verstören*) to throw (*inf*); (*störrisch machen*) to make pig-headed (*inf*).
[2] *vr* **sich in etw** (*acc*) **~** to become fixed on sth.
verbiestert *adj* (*inf*) (*mißmutig*) crotchety (*inf*); (*verstört*) disturbed *no adv*.
verbieten *pret* **verbot**, *ptp* **verboten** *vt* to forbid; (*amtlich auch*) to prohibit; *Zeitung, Partei* to ban, to prohibit ◆ **jdm ~, etw zu tun** to forbid sb to do sth; (*amtlich auch*) to prohibit sb from doing sth; **jdm das Rauchen/den Zutritt/den Gebrauch von etw ~** to forbid sb to smoke/to enter/the use of sth; (*amtlich auch*) to prohibit sb from smoking/entering/using sth; **mein Taktgefühl/die Höflichkeit verbietet mir eine derartige Bemerkung** tact/politeness prevents me from making such a remark; **das verbietet sich von selbst** that has to be ruled out; *siehe* **verboten**.
verbilden* *vt* (*fig*) *jdn* to bring up badly, to miseducate; *Geschmack, Charakter* to spoil, to deform.
verbildlichen* *vt siehe* **veranschaulichen**.
verbilligen* [1] *vt* to reduce the cost of; *Kosten, Preis* to reduce ◆ **verbilligte Waren/Karten** reduced goods/tickets at reduced prices; **etw verbilligt abgeben** to sell sth at a reduced price.
[2] *vr* to get *or* become cheaper; (*Kosten, Preise auch*) to go down.
verbimsen* *vt* (*inf*) to bash up (*inf*).
verbinden* *irreg* [1] *vt* **(a)** (*Med*) to dress; (*mit Binden*) to bandage ◆ **jdm die Augen ~** to blindfold sb; **mit verbundenen Augen** blindfold(ed).
(b) (*verknüpfen, in Kontakt bringen*) (*lit, fig*) to connect, to link; *Punkte* to join (up).
(c) (*Telec*) **jdn (mit jdm) ~** to put sb through (to sb); **ich verbinde!** I'll put you through, I'll connect you; **(Sie sind hier leider) falsch verbunden!** (I'm sorry, you've got the) wrong number!; **mit wem bin ich verbunden?** who am I speaking to?
(d) (*gleichzeitig haben or tun, anschließen*) to combine.
(e) (*assoziieren*) to associate.
(f) (*mit sich bringen*) **mit etw verbunden sein** to involve sth, to be bound up with sth; **die damit verbundenen Kosten/Gefahren** *etc* the costs/dangers *etc* involved.
(g) (*emotional*) *Menschen* to unite, to join together ◆ **freundschaftlich/in Liebe verbunden sein** (*geh*) to be united *or* joined together in friendship/love.
[2] *vr* **(a)** to combine (*auch Chem*) (*mit* with, *zu* to form), to join (together), to join forces (*zu* in, to form) ◆ **sich ehelich/in Liebe/Freundschaft ~** (*geh*) to join together in marriage/love/friendship; **in ihrer Person ~ sich Klugheit und Schönheit** she combines both intelligence and beauty.
(b) (*assoziiert werden*) to be associated; (*hervorgerufen werden*) to be evoked (*mit* by).
[3] *vi* (*emotional*) to form a bond; *siehe* **verbunden**.
verbindlich *adj* **(a)** obliging ◆ **~sten Dank!** (*form*) thank you kindly!, I/we thank you! **(b)** (*verpflichtend*) obligatory, compulsory; *Regelung, Zusage* binding; (*verläßlich*) *Auskunft* reliable ◆ **~ zusagen** to accept definitely.
Verbindlichkeit *f siehe adj* **(a)** obligingness; (*höfliche Redensart*) civility *usu pl*, courtesy *usu pl*, polite word(s *pl*).
(b) *no pl* obligatory *or* compulsory nature, compulsoriness; binding nature *or* force; reliability.
(c) **~en** *pl* (*Comm, Jur*) obligations *pl*, commitments *pl*; (*finanziell auch*) liabilities *pl* ◆ **seine ~en erfüllen** to fulfil one's obligations *or* commitments; to meet one's liabilities; **~en gegen jdn haben** to have (financial) commitments to sb.
Verbindung *f* **(a)** connection; (*persönliche, einflußreiche Beziehung auch, Kontakt*) contact (*zu, mit* with) ◆ **in ~ mit** (*zusammen mit*) in conjunction with; (*im Zusammenhang mit*) in connection with; **jdn/etw mit etw in ~ bringen** to connect sb/sth with sth; (*assoziieren*) to associate sb/sth with sth; **er/sein Name wurde mit dem Mord/der Affäre in ~ gebracht** he/his name was mentioned in connection with the murder/the affair; **seine ~en spielen lassen** to use one's connections, to pull a few strings (*inf*); **~en anknüpfen** *or* **aufnehmen** to get contacts; **~ mit jdm aufnehmen** to contact sb; **die ~ aufrechterhalten** to maintain contact; (*esp zwischen Freunden*) to keep in touch *or* contact; **sich (mit jdm) in ~ setzen, (mit jdm) in ~ treten** to get in touch *or* contact (with sb), to contact sb; **mit jdm in ~ stehen** to be in touch *or* contact with sb; **mit etw in ~ stehen** to be connected with sth.
(b) (*Verkehrs~*) connection (*nach* to) ◆ **die ~ von Berlin nach Warschau** the connections *pl* from Berlin to Warsaw; **es besteht direkte ~ nach München** there is a direct connection to Munich.
(c) (*Telec: Anschluß*) line ◆ **telefonische ~/~ durch Funk** telephonic/radio communication; **eine ~ (zu einem Ort) bekommen** to get through (to a place); **unsere ~ wurde unterbrochen** we were cut off.
(d) (*Mil*) contact; (*durch Funk etc*) communication; (*Zusammenarbeit*) liaison ◆ **~ aufnehmen** to make contact; to establish communication.
(e) (*Kombination*) combination.
(f) (*Vereinigung, Bündnis*) association; (*ehelich*) union; (*Univ*) society; (*für Männer*) fraternity (*US*); (*für Frauen*) sorority (*US*) ◆ **eine ~ mit jdm eingehen** to join together with sb; **eine schlagende/nicht schlagende ~** (*Univ*) a duelling/non-duelling fraternity.
(g) (*Chem*) (*Prozeß*) combination; (*Ergebnis*) compound (*aus* (formed out) of) ◆ **eine ~ mit etw eingehen** to form a compound with sth, to combine with sth.

➤ SPRACHE AKTIV: **verbieten** → 36.3, 37.4 **verbinden: 1c** → 27.1, 27.3, 27.4, 27.5, 27.7 **verbindlich: b** → 47.3, 48.3 **Verbindung: a** → 46.4 **c** → 27.7

Verbindungs- *in cpds (esp Tech, Archit)* connecting; *(Univ)* fraternity; **~mann** *m, pl* **-leute** *or* **-männer** intermediary; *(Agent)* contact; **~offizier** *m* liaison officer; **~stelle** *f (von Gleisen, Kabeln)* junction (point); *(von Rohren, Geklebtem etc)* join; *(Amt)* liaison office; **~straße** *f* connecting road; **~stück** *nt* connecting piece; **~student** *m* member of a fraternity; **~tür** *f* connecting door.

⚠ **Verbiß** *m* **-sses, -sse** *(Hunt)* biting off of young shoots.

verbissen 1 *ptp of* **verbeißen.**
2 *adj* grim; *Arbeiter* dogged, determined; *Gesicht, Miene* determined.

Verbissenheit *f, no pl siehe adj* grimness; doggedness, determination.

verbitten *pret* **verbat,** *ptp* **verbeten** *vr* **sich** *(dat)* **etw (schwer/sehr** *etc)* **~** to refuse (absolutely) to tolerate sth; **das verbitte ich mir!, das will ich mir verbeten haben!** I won't have it!

verbittern* 1 *vt* to embitter, to make bitter ◆ **jdm das Leben ~** to make sb's life a misery.
2 *vi aux sein* to become embittered *or* bitter ◆ **verbittert** embittered, bitter.

Verbitterung *f* bitterness, embitterment.

verblassen* *vi aux sein (lit, fig)* to fade; *(Mond)* to pale ◆ **alles andere verblaßt daneben** *(fig)* everything else pales into insignificance beside it.

Verbleib *m* **-(e)s,** *no pl (form)* whereabouts *pl.*

verbleiben* *vi irreg aux sein* to remain ◆ **etw verbleibt jdm** sb has sth left; ... **verbleibe ich Ihr ...** *(form)* ... I remain, Yours sincerely ...; **wir sind so verblieben, daß wir ...** we agreed *or* arranged to ..., it was agreed *or* arranged that we ...; **sein V~ in dieser Position ist unmöglich geworden** it has become impossible for him to remain in this post.

verbleichen *pret* **verblich,** *ptp* **verblichen** *vi aux sein (lit, fig)* to fade; *(Mond)* to pale; *(liter: sterben)* to pass away, to expire *(liter)* ◆ **verblichen** *(lit, fig)* faded.

verbleien* *vt* **(a)** *Benzin* to lead, to put a lead additive in. **(b)** *(mit Blei überziehen)* to lead-coat, to coat with lead.

verbleit *adj Benzin* leaded.

verblenden* *vt* **(a)** *(fig)* to blind ◆ **verblendet sein** to be blind. **(b)** *(Archit)* to face.

Verblendung *f* **(a)** *(fig)* blindness. **(b)** *(Archit)* facing.

⚠ **verbleuen*** *vt (inf)* to bash up *(inf).*

verblich *pret of* **verbleichen.**

verblichen *ptp of* **verbleichen.**

Verblichene(r) *mf decl as adj (liter)* deceased.

verblöden* *vi aux sein (inf)* to become a zombi(e) *(inf).*

Verblödung *f (inf)* stupefaction ◆ **diese Arbeit führt noch zu meiner völligen ~** this job will turn me into a zombi(e) *(inf)*; **die dauernde Reklame führt noch zu unserer völligen ~** the long-term effect of advertising is to make us totally uncritical.

verblüffen* *vt (erstaunen)* to stun, to amaze; *(verwirren)* to baffle ◆ **sich durch** *or* **von etw ~ lassen** to be taken in by sth.

Verblüffung *f, no pl siehe vt* amazement; bafflement.

verblühen* *vi aux sein (lit, fig)* to fade ◆ **der Baum ist verblüht** the blossom has fallen from the tree; **sie sieht verblüht aus** her beauty has faded.

verblümt *adj* oblique ◆ **etw/sich ~ ausdrücken** to say sth/express oneself in a roundabout way.

verbluten* 1 *vi aux sein* to bleed to death.
2 *vr (fig)* to spend oneself.

Verblutung *f* fatal haemorrhage; *(das Verbluten)* bleeding to death.

verbocken* *vt (inf) (verpfuschen)* to botch *(inf)*, to bungle *(inf)*; *(anstellen)* to get up to *(inf).*

verbockt *adj (inf)* pig-headed *(inf)*; *Kind* headstrong.

verbogen 1 *ptp of* **verbiegen.**
2 *adj* bent; *Rückgrat* curved; *(fig)* twisted, warped.

verbohren* *vr (inf)* **sich in etw** *(acc)* **~** to become obsessed with sth; *(unbedingt wollen)* to become (dead) set on sth *(inf).*

verbohrt *adj Haltung* stubborn, obstinate; *Politiker auch, Meinung* inflexible.

Verbohrtheit *f* inflexibility.

verborgen[1]* *vt* to lend out *(an +acc* to).

verborgen[2] 1 *ptp of* **verbergen.**
2 *adj* hidden ◆ **etw/sich ~ halten** to hide sth/to hide; **im V~en leben** to live hidden away; **so manches große Talent blüht im ~en** great talents flourish in obscurity; **im ~en wachsen/blühen** *(lit)* to grow/bloom in places hard to find; **im ~en liegen** to be not yet known.

Verborgenheit *f, no pl* seclusion.

verbot *pret of* **verbieten.**

Verbot *nt* **-(e)s, -e** ban ◆ **er ging trotz meines ~s** he went even though I had forbidden him to do so; **trotz des ärztlichen ~es** against doctor's orders, in spite of doctor's orders; **gegen ein ~ verstoßen** to ignore a ban; **das ~ der Eltern, zu rauchen/einen Freund mitzubringen** the parents' ban on smoking/on bringing a friend; **ich bin gegen das ~ irgendeiner Partei/Zeitung** I'm opposed to a ban on *or* to banning any party/newspaper.

▼ **verboten** 1 *ptp of* **verbieten.**
▼ 2 *adj* forbidden; *(amtlich)* prohibited; *(gesetzeswidrig) Handel* illegal; *Zeitung, Partei, Buch etc* banned ◆ **jdm ist etw ~** sb is forbidden to do sth; **Rauchen/Parken ~** no smoking/parking; **er sah ~ aus** *(inf)* he looked a real sight *(inf).*

verbotenerweise *adv* against orders; *(gesetzeswidrig)* illegally ◆ **er hat ~ geraucht** he smoked even though it was forbidden *or (amtlich)* prohibited.

Verbots-: ~schild *nt,* **~tafel** *f (allgemein)* notice *or* sign (prohibiting something); *(im Verkehr)* prohibition sign.

verbrach *pret of* **verbrechen.**

verbracht *ptp of* **verbringen.**

verbrachte *pret of* **verbringen.**

verbrämen* *vt (geh) Kleidungsstück* to trim; *(fig) Rede* to pad; *Wahrheit* to gloss over; *Kritik* to veil *(mit* in).

verbrannt 1 *ptp of* **verbrennen.**
2 *adj* burnt; *(fig) Erde* scorched.

Verbrauch *m* **-(e)s,** *no pl* consumption *(von, an +dat* of); *(von Geld)* expenditure; *(von Kräften)* drain *(von, an +dat* on) ◆ **im Winter ist der ~ an Kalorien/Energie höher** we use up more calories/energy in winter; **sparsam im ~** economical; **zum baldigen ~ bestimmt** to be used immediately; **der ~ von öffentlichen Geldern** public expenditure.

verbrauchen* *vt* **(a)** *(aufbrauchen)* to use; *Vorräte* to use up; *Benzin, Wasser, Nahrungsmittel etc auch* to consume ◆ **der Wagen verbraucht 10 Liter Benzin auf 100 km** the car does 10 kms to the litre.
(b) *(abnützen) Kräfte etc* to exhaust; *Kleidung etc* to wear out ◆ **sich ~** to wear oneself out; **verbrauchte Luft/Nerven** stale *or* stuffy air/frayed *or* tattered nerves; **sie ist schon völlig verbraucht** she is already completely spent.

Verbraucher *m* **-s, -** consumer.

Verbraucher- *in cpds* consumer; **v~feindlich** *adj* anti-consumer; **v~feindlich sein** not to be in the interest of the consumer; **v~freundlich** *adj* consumer-friendly; **~genossenschaft** *f* consumer cooperative; **v~gerecht** *adj Verpackung* handy; **~markt** *m* hypermarket; **~preis** *m* consumer price; **~schutz** *m* consumer protection; **~verband** *m* consumer council; **~zentrale** *f* consumer advice centre.

Verbrauchs-: ~güter *pl* consumer goods *pl*; **~steuer** *f* excise.

Verbrechen *nt* **-s, -** *(lit, fig)* crime *(gegen, an +dat* against).

verbrechen *pret* **verbrach,** *ptp* **verbrochen** *vt* **(a)** *Straftat, Greueltat* to commit ◆ **etwas ~** to commit a crime.
(b) *(inf: anstellen)* **etwas ~** to be up to something *(inf)*; **was habe ich denn jetzt schon wieder verbrochen?** what on earth have I done now?
(c) *(hum inf) Gedicht, Kunstwerk, Übersetzung etc* to be the perpetrator of *(hum).*

Verbrechensbekämpfung *f* combating crime *no art.*

Verbrecher *m* **-s, -** criminal.

Verbrecher-: ~album *nt* rogues' gallery *(hum)*; **~bande** *f* gang of criminals; **~gesicht** *nt (pej)* criminal face.

Verbrecherin *f* criminal.

verbrecherisch *adj* criminal ◆ **in ~er Absicht** with criminal intent.

Verbrecher-: ~jagd *f* chase after a/the criminal/criminals; **~kartei** *f* criminal records *pl*; **~tum** *nt* criminality; **~viertel** *nt (pej inf)* shady part of town; **~visage** *f (pej inf)* criminal face; **~welt** *f* underworld.

verbreiten* 1 *vt* to spread; *Ideen, Lehre auch* to disseminate; *Zeitung* to distribute, to circulate; *(ausstrahlen) Wärme* to radiate; *Licht* to shed; *Ruhe* to radiate ◆ **eine (weit) verbreitete Ansicht** a widely *or* commonly held opinion; **eine verbreitete Zeitung** a newspaper with a large circulation *or* a wide distribution.
2 *vr* **(a)** to spread.
(b) sich über ein Thema ~ to expound on *or* hold forth on a subject.

verbreitern* 1 *vt* to widen.
2 *vr* to get wider, to widen out.

Verbreiterung *f* widening.

Verbreitung *f, no pl siehe vt* spreading; dissemination; distribution, circulation; radiation; shedding; radiation.

verbrennbar *adj* combustible.

verbrennen* *irreg* 1 *vt* **(a)** to burn; *Müll auch* to incinerate; *(einäschern) Tote* to cremate; *(verbrauchen) Gas, Kerzen* to burn; *Strom* to use.
(b) *(versengen)* to scorch; *Finger, Haut etc* to burn; *Haar* to singe; *(verbrühen)* to scald ◆ **sich** *(dat)* **die Zunge/den Mund** *or* **den Schnabel** *(inf)* **~** *(lit)* to burn one's tongue/mouth; *(fig)* to say too much; *siehe* **Finger.**
2 *vr* to burn oneself; *(sich verbrühen)* to scald oneself.
3 *vi aux sein* to burn; *(Mensch, Tier)* to burn (to death); *(niederbrennen: Haus etc)* to burn down; *(durch Sonne, Hitze)* to be scorched ◆ **das Fleisch ~ lassen** to burn the meat; **alles verbrannte** *or* **war verbrannt** everything was destroyed in the fire; **alle verbrannten** everyone died in the fire; *siehe auch* **verbrannt.**

Verbrennung *f* **(a)** *no pl (das Verbrennen)* burning; *(von Müll auch)* incineration; *(von Treibstoff)* combustion; *(von Leiche)* cremation. **(b)** *(Brandwunde)* burn; *(Verbrühung)* scald ◆ **starke/leichte ~en davontragen** to be badly/not seriously burned.

Verbrennungs-: ~anlage *f* incineration plant; **~kraftmaschine** *f* internal combustion vehicle; **~motor** *m* internal combustion engine; **~ofen** *m* furnace; *(für Müll)* incinerator; **~produkt** *nt* waste product (of combustion); **~wärme** *f* heat of combustion.

verbriefen* *vt* to document ◆ **verbriefte Rechte/Sicherheit** attested rights/security.

verbringen *pret* **verbrachte,** *ptp* **verbracht** *vt* **(a)** *Zeit etc* to spend. **(b)** *(obs, Jur: bringen)* to take.

verbrochen *ptp of* **verbrechen.**

verbrüdern* *vr* to swear eternal friendship *(mit* to); *(politisch)* to ally oneself *(mit* to, with) ◆ **Menschen aller Rassen sollten sich ~** people of all races should be brothers.

Verbrüderung *f* avowal of friendship; *(politisch)* alliance.

verbrühen* 1 *vt* to scald.
2 *vr* to scald oneself.

Verbrühung *f (no pl: das Verbrühen)* scalding; *(Wunde)* scald.

➤ SPRACHE AKTIV: **verboten: 2 → 36.3**

verbuchen* *vt* to enter (up) (in a/the book) ◆ **einen Betrag auf ein Konto ~** to credit a sum to an account; **Erfolge (für sich) ~** to notch up *or* chalk up successes (*inf*); **etw für sich** *or* **auf sein Konto ~ können** (*fig*) to be able to credit oneself with sth.
Verbuchung *f* entering (up).
verbuddeln* *vt* (*inf*) to bury.
Verbum ['vɛrbʊm] *nt* **-s, Verba** (*geh*) verb.
verbummeln* (*inf*) **1** *vt* (*verlieren*) to lose; (*vertrödeln, vergeuden*) *Nachmittag, Wochenende, Zeit* to waste, to fritter away; (*verpassen*) *Verabredung* to miss.
2 *vi aux sein* **(a)** (*herunterkommen*) to go to seed. **(b)** (*faul werden*) to get lazy ◆ **verbummelt sein** to be lazy.
Verbund *m* **-(e)s,** *no pl* (*Econ*) combine ◆ **im ~ arbeiten** to cooperate.
Verbundbau *m* composite (method of) building.
verbunden 1 *ptp of* **verbinden.**
2 *adj* (*form: dankbar*) **jdm (für etw) ~ sein** to be obliged to sb (for sth).
verbünden* *vr* to ally oneself (*mit* to); (*Staaten*) to form an alliance ◆ **alle haben sich gegen mich verbündet** everyone is against me *or* has sided against me; **verbündet sein** to be allies *or* allied.
Verbundenheit *f, no pl* (*von Völkern*) solidarity; (*von Menschen*) (*mit Menschen, Natur*) closeness (*mit* to); (*mit Land, Tradition*) attachment (*mit* to) ◆ **in tiefer ~,** ... very affectionately yours, ...
Verbündete(r) *mf decl as adj* ally.
Verbund-: ~fahrausweis *m* travel pass (*valid for all forms of public transport*); **~glas** *nt* laminated glass; **~(loch)karte** *f* dual(-purpose) card; **~netz** *nt* (*Elec*) (integrated) grid system; **~platte** *f* sandwich panel; **~stahl** *m* laminated steel; **~system** *nt* integrated system; **~werbung** *f* joint advertising; **~werkstoff** *m* composite material; **~wirtschaft** *f* integrated economy.
verbürgen* *vtr* to guarantee ◆ **sich für jdn/etw ~** to vouch for sb/sth; **verbürgte Nachricht** confirmed report; **ein verbürgtes Recht** an established right.
verbürgerlichen* *vi aux sein* to become bourgeois.
verbüßen* *vt* to serve.
Verbüßung *f, no pl* serving ◆ **zur ~ einer Haftstrafe von zwei Jahren verurteilt werden** to be sentenced to serve two years in prison.
verbuttern* *vt* **(a)** to make into butter. **(b)** (*inf*) *Geld* to spend.
verchromen* [fɛɐ'kro:mən] *vt* to chromium-plate.
Verchromung [fɛɐ'kro:mʊŋ] *f* chromium-plating.
Verdacht *m* **-(e)s,** *no pl* suspicion; (*hum: Vermutung*) hunch ◆ **jdn in** *or* **im ~ haben** to suspect sb; **im ~ stehen, etw getan zu haben** to be suspected of having done sth; **jdn in ~ bringen** to make sb look guilty; **den ~ auf jdn lenken** to throw *or* cast suspicion on sb; **jdn wegen ~s einer Sache** (*gen*) **festnehmen** to arrest sb on suspicion of sth; **(gegen jdn) ~ schöpfen** to become suspicious (of sb); **es besteht ~ auf Krebs** (*acc*) cancer is suspected; **bei ~ auf Krebs** in the case of suspected cancer; **etw auf ~ tun** (*inf*) to do sth on spec (*inf*).
verdächtig *adj* suspicious; (*~ aussehend*) suspicious-looking ◆ **~ aussehen** to look suspicious; **sich ~ machen** to arouse suspicion; **die drei ~en Personen** the three suspects; **einer Sache** (*gen*) **~ sein** to be suspected of sth.
verdächtigen* *vt* to suspect (*gen* of) ◆ **ich will niemanden ~, aber** ... I don't want to cast suspicion on anyone, but ...; **er wird verdächtigt, gestohlen zu haben, er wird des Diebstahls verdächtigt** he is suspected of theft.
Verdächtige(r) *mf decl as adj* suspect.
Verdächtigung *f* suspicion ◆ **die ~ eines so integren Mannes käme mir nie in den Sinn** it would never occur to me to suspect a man of his integrity.
Verdachts-: ~grund *m* grounds *pl* for suspicion; **~moment** *nt* suspicious circumstance.
verdammen* *vt* (*esp Rel: verfluchen*) to damn; (*verurteilen*) to condemn; *siehe auch* **verdammt, Scheitern.**
verdammenswert *adj* damnable, despicable.
Verdammnis *f* (*Rel*) damnation *no art.*
verdammt 1 *adj, adv* (*inf*) damned (*inf*), bloody (*Brit sl*) ◆ **~er Mist!** (*sl*) sod it! (*Brit sl*); **~e Scheiße!** (*sl*) shit! (*sl*); **~ hübsch** damned pretty (*inf*); **das tut ~ weh** that hurts like hell (*sl*); **~ viel Geld** a hell of a lot of money (*sl*); **mir geht's ~ gut/schlecht** I'm on top of the world (*inf*)/in a bad way.
2 *interj* (*sl*) **~!** damn *or* blast (it) (*inf*); **~ noch mal!** bloody hell (*Brit sl*), damn it all (*inf*); **du wirst dich ~ noch mal entschuldigen!** apologize, damn you! (*inf*).
Verdammte(r) *mf decl as adj* (*Rel*) **die ~n** the damned *pl.*
Verdammung *f* condemnation; (*Rel*) damnation.
verdampfen* *vti* (*vi: aux sein*) to vaporize; (*Cook*) to boil away.
Verdampfer *m* **-s, -** vaporizer.
Verdampfung *f* vaporization.
verdanken* *vt* **jdm etw ~** to owe sth to sb; **es ist jdm/einer Sache zu ~(, daß** ...) it is thanks *or* due to sb/sth (that ...); **das verdanke ich dir** (*iro*) I've got you to thank for that.
verdarb *pret of* **verderben.**
verdaten* *vt* **jdn ~** to store sb's details on computer.
verdattert *adj, adv* (*inf*) flabbergasted (*inf*).
verdauen* **1** *vt* (*lit, fig*) to digest.
2 *vi* (*Mensch*) to digest one's food; (*Magen etc*) to digest the food.
verdaulich *adj* digestible ◆ **leicht ~** easily digestible, easy to digest; **schwer ~** hard to digest.
Verdaulichkeit *f, no pl* digestibility.
Verdauung *f* digestion ◆ **eine gute/schlechte ~ haben** to have good/poor digestion.
Verdauungs-: ~apparat *m* digestive system; **~beschwerden** *pl* digestive trouble *sing*; **~kanal** *m* alimentary canal, digestive tract; **~organ** *nt* digestive organ; **~saft** *m* gastric juice; **~spaziergang** *m* constitutional; **~störung** *f usu pl* indigestion *no pl*; **~trakt** *m* digestive *or* alimentary tract.
Verdeck *nt* **-(e)s, -e (a)** (*Dach*) (*von Kutsche, Kinderwagen*) hood (*Brit*), canopy; (*von Auto*) soft top, hood (*Brit*); (*hart*) roof; (*von Flugzeug*) canopy. **(b)** (*von Passagierdampfer*) sundeck; (*von doppelstöckigem Bus*) open top deck.
verdecken* *vt* to hide, to conceal; (*zudecken*) to cover (up); *Sicht* to block; (*fig*) *Absichten, Widerspruch, Symptome* to conceal; *Unterschlagungen etc* to conceal, to cover up ◆ **eine Wolke verdeckte die Sonne** a cloud hid *or* covered the sun; **sie verdeckte ihr Gesicht mit den Händen** she covered her face with her hands, she hid her face in her hands; **verdeckt** concealed; *Widerspruch* hidden; *Polizeieinsatz* undercover; **verdeckt agieren** to operate undercover; *siehe* **Karte.**
verdenken* *vt irreg* **jdm etw ~** to hold sth against sb; **ich kann es ihm nicht ~(, daß er es getan hat)** I can't blame him (for doing it).
Verderb *m* **-(e)s,** *no pl* (*geh: Untergang*) ruin ◆ **sein ~** his ruin, the ruin of him; *siehe* **Gedeih.**
verderben *pret* **verdarb,** *ptp* **verdorben 1** *vt* to spoil; (*stärker*) to ruin; *Plan auch* to wreck; *Luft* to pollute; *jdn* (*moralisch*) to corrupt; (*sittlich*) to deprave, to corrupt; (*verwöhnen*) to spoil ◆ **jdm etw ~** *Abend, Urlaub* to spoil *or* ruin sth for sb; *Chancen, Leben, Witz* to ruin sth for sb; **sich** (*dat*) **das Leben ~** to ruin one's life; **sich** (*dat*) **den Magen/Appetit ~** to give oneself an upset stomach/to spoil one's appetite; **sich** (*dat*) **die Augen/Stimme/Lungen ~** to ruin *or* damage one's eyes *or* eyesight/voice/lungs; **die Preise ~** to force prices down/up; **jds Laune** *or* **jdm die Laune ~** to put sb in a bad mood; **jdm die Freude** *or* **den Spaß/die Lust an etw** (*dat*) **~** to spoil sb's enjoyment of sth; **es (sich** *dat*) **mit jdm ~** to fall out with sb.
2 *vi aux sein* (*Material*) to become spoiled/ruined; (*Nahrungsmittel*) to go bad *or* off; (*Ernte*) to be ruined; (*Mensch*) to become depraved *or* corrupted ◆ **da** *or* **daran ist nichts mehr zu ~** it *or* things couldn't get any worse; **an dem Kuchen/Hemd ist nichts mehr zu ~** the cake/shirt is absolutely ruined anyway; *siehe* **verdorben.**
Verderben *nt* **-s,** *no pl* **(a)** (*Untergang, Unglück*) undoing, ruin ◆ **in sein ~ rennen** to be heading for disaster; **jdn ins ~ stürzen** to bring ruin *or* disaster (up)on sb.
(b) (*von Material*) spoiling, ruining; (*von Nahrungsmittel*) going off; (*von Luft, Wasser*) pollution.
verderblich *adj* pernicious; *Einfluß auch* corrupting; *Lebensmittel* perishable.
Verderblichkeit *f, no pl* perniciousness; perishableness ◆ **die leichte ~ von Fisch** the extreme perishableness of fish.
Verderbnis *f* corruption, depravity; (*Verderbtheit*) corruptness, depravity.
verderbt *adj* **(a)** (*dated: moralisch*) corrupt(ed), depraved. **(b)** (*Typ*) corrupt.
Verderbtheit *f* (*dated*) corruptness, depravity.
verdeutlichen* *vt* to show clearly; (*deutlicher machen*) to clarify, to elucidate; (*erklären*) to explain ◆ **er versuchte seinen Standpunkt an einem Beispiel zu ~** he tried to clarify his position by means of an example; **sich** (*dat*) **etw ~** to think sth out for oneself; **etw besser/näher ~** to clarify sth further.
Verdeutlichung *f* clarification ◆ **zur ~ seiner Absichten** in order to show his intentions clearly.
verdeutschen* *vt* to translate into German; (*fig inf*) to translate (into normal language).
verdichten* 1 *vt* (*Phys*) to compress; (*fig: komprimieren*) to condense; *Gefühle* to intensify, to heighten.
2 *vr* to thicken; (*Schneetreiben*) to worsen; (*Gas*) to become compressed; (*fig: häufen*) to increase; (*Verdacht, Eindruck*) to deepen ◆ **die Handlung verdichtet sich** the plot thickens; **die Gerüchte ~ sich, daß** ... the rumours that ... are increasing; **mein Eindruck verdichtete sich zur Gewißheit** my impression hardened into certainty.
Verdichter *m* **-s, -** (*Tech*) compressor.
Verdichtung *f* **(a)** *siehe vt* compression; condensing; intensification, heightening. **(b)** *siehe vr* thickening; worsening; compression; increase (*gen* in); deepening; (*der Handlung*) thickening.
verdicken* 1 *vt* to thicken; *Blut* to coagulate; (*verbreitern*) to widen; (*gelieren lassen*) to make set; (*verstärken*) to strengthen.
2 *vr* to thicken; (*Gelee*) to set; (*Blut*) to coagulate; (*Milch*) to curdle; (*weiter werden*) to become thicker; (*Rohr, Flasche*) to become wider, to widen out; (*anschwellen*) to swell.
Verdickung *f* (*das Verdicken*) thickening; (*von Blut*) coagulation; (*von Gelee*) setting; (*von Milch*) curdling; (*von Rohr, Flasche*) widening; (*Schwellung*) swelling; (*Verstärkung*) strengthening; (*verdickte Stelle*) bulge.
▼ **verdienen* 1** *vt* **(a)** (*einnehmen*) (*Gewinn machen*) to make ◆ **sein Brot** *or* **seinen Unterhalt ~** to earn *or* make one's living; **er hat an dem Auto DM 200 verdient** he made DM200 on the car; **dabei ist nicht viel zu ~** there's not much money in that; **sich** (*dat*) **etw ~** to earn the money for sth; **sich** (*dat*) **das Studium ~** to pay for *or* finance one's own studies.
▼ **(b)** (*fig*) *Lob, Strafe* to deserve ◆ **sich** (*dat*) **etw (redlich) verdient haben** to deserve sth, to have earned sth; *Schläge auch* to have had sth coming to one (*inf*); **er verdient es nicht anders/besser** he doesn't deserve anything else/any bettter; *siehe* **verdient.**
2 *vi* to earn; (*Gewinn machen*) to make (a profit) (*an +dat* on) ◆ **in dieser Familie ~ drei Personen** there are three wage-earners in this family; **er verdient gut/besser** he earns a lot/more; **er verdient schlecht** he doesn't earn

much; **am Krieg ~** to profit from war.

Verdiener *m* **-s, -** wage-earner ◆ **der einzige ~** the sole breadwinner.

Verdienst[1] *m* **-(e)s, -e** *(Einkommen)* income, earnings *pl*; *(Profit)* profit ◆ **einen besseren ~ haben** to earn more.

Verdienst[2] *nt* **-(e)s, -e** **(a)** *(Anspruch auf Anerkennung)* merit; *(Dank)* credit ◆ **es ist sein ~/das ~ der Wissenschaftler(, daß ...)** it is thanks to him/the scientists (that ...); **nach ~** on merit; **das ~ gebührt ihm allein** the credit is entirely his; **sich** *(dat)* **etw als** *or* **zum** *(rare)* **~ anrechnen** to take the credit for sth.
(b) *usu pl (Leistung)* contribution; *(wissenschaftlich auch, national)* service ◆ **ihre ~e um die Wissenschaft/als Wissenschaftlerin** her services *or* contribution to science; **seine ~e um das Vaterland/die Stadt** his services to his country/town; **seine ~e um die Dichtung/den Weltfrieden** his contribution to poetry/world peace; **hohe ~e erwerben** to make a great contribution *(um* to); **er hat sich** *(dat)* **große ~e um das Vaterland erworben** he has rendered his country great service.

Verdienst-: ~adel *m* ≃ life peerage; *(Angehörige des ~adels)* ≃ life peers *pl*; **~ausfall** *m* loss of earnings; **~ausfallentschädigung** *f* compensation for loss of earnings; **~kreuz** *nt highest decoration awarded for military or other service*; **v~lich** *adj* commendable; **~möglichkeit** *f* opportunity for earning money; **~orden** *m* order of merit; **~spanne** *f* profit margin; **v~voll** *adj* commendable.

verdient [1] *ptp of* **verdienen.**
[2] *adj* **(a)** *Lohn, Strafe* rightful; *Ruhe, Lob* well-deserved. **(b)** *Wissenschaftler, Politiker, Sportler* of outstanding merit ◆ **sich um etw ~ machen** to render outstanding services to sth.

verdientermaßen, verdienterweise *adv* deservedly.

Verdikt [vɛr'dɪkt] *nt* **-(e)s, -e** *(geh)* verdict.

verdingen *pret* **verdingte,** *ptp* **verdungen** *or* **verdingt** *(old)* [1] *vt jdn* to put into service *(bei* with); *Arbeit* to give.
[2] *vr* **sich (bei jdm) ~** to enter service (with sb).

verdinglichen* *vt (konkretisieren)* to put into concrete terms, to concretize; *(Philos) Ideen* to reify; *Menschen* to objectify.

Verdinglichung *f siehe vt* concretization; reification; objectification.

verdirb *imper sing of* **verderben.**

verdolmetschen* *vt* to translate, to interpret.

verdonnern* *vt (inf) (zu Haft etc)* to sentence, to condemn *(zu* to) ◆ **jdn zu etw ~, jdn dazu ~, etw zu tun** to order sb to do sth as a punishment; **jdn zu einer Geldstrafe/Gefängnisstrafe von ... ~** to fine sb .../to sentence sb to a term of ... imprisonment.

verdoppeln* [1] *vt* to double; *(fig) Anstrengung etc* to redouble.
[2] *vr* to double.

Verdopp(e)lung *f siehe vt* doubling; redoubling.

verdorben [1] *ptp of* **verderben.**
[2] *adj* **(a)** *Lebensmittel* bad, off *pred*; *Wasser, Luft* polluted; *Magen* upset. **(b)** *Stimmung, Urlaub, Freude* spoiled, ruined. **(c)** *(moralisch)* corrupt; *(sittlich)* depraved; *(verzogen) Kind* spoiled.

Verdorbenheit *f* depravity.

verdorren* *vi aux sein* to wither.

verdösen* *vt (inf)* to doze away.

verdrahten* *vt* to wire (up).

verdrängen* *vt jdn* to drive out; *Gegner auch* to oust; *(ersetzen)* to supersede, to replace; *(Phys) Wasser, Luft* to displace; *(Met)* to drive; *(fig) Sorgen* to dispel, to drive away; *(Psych)* to repress, to suppress ◆ **er hat sie aus seinem Herzen verdrängt** he has forced himself to forget her; **jdn aus dem Amt/von der Macht ~** to oust sb; **das habe ich völlig verdrängt** *(hum: vergessen)* it completely slipped my mind *(inf)*; **jdn/etw aus dem Bewußtsein ~** to repress *or* suppress all memory of sb/sth.

Verdrängung *f siehe vt* driving out; ousting; superseding, replacing; displacement; driving; dispelling; repression, suppression.

verdrecken* *vti (vi: aux sein) (inf)* to get dirty *or* filthy ◆ **verdreckt** filthy (dirty).

verdrehen* *vt* to twist; *Gelenk auch* to wrench; *(anders einstellen) Radio, Regler, Lampe* to adjust; *(verknacksen)* to sprain; *Hals* to crick; *Augen* to roll; *jds Worte, Tatsachen* auch to distort ◆ **das Recht ~** to pervert the course of justice; **sich** *(dat)* **den Hals ~** *(fig inf)* to crane one's neck; *siehe* **Kopf.**

verdreht *adj (inf)* crazy *(inf)*; *Bericht* confused, garbled; *(psychisch durcheinander)* screwed-up *(sl)*.

Verdrehtheit *f (inf)* craziness; *(von Bericht etc)* confusion, garbledness; *(psychisch)* screwed-up behaviour *no pl (sl)*.

Verdrehung *f siehe vt* twisting; adjusting; wrenching; spraining; cricking; rolling; distortion; perversion.

verdreifachen* *vtr* to treble, to triple.

Verdreifachung *f* trebling, tripling.

verdreschen* *vt irreg (inf)* to beat up; *(als Strafe)* to thrash.

verdrießen *pret* **verdroß,** *ptp* **verdrossen** *vt jdn* to irritate, to annoy ◆ **sich** *(dat)* **den Abend/den Urlaub** *etc* **durch etw ~ lassen** to let sth spoil one's evening/holiday *etc*; **lassen Sie es sich nicht ~!** don't be put off *or* worried by it; *siehe* **verdrossen.**

verdrießlich *adj* morose; *Arbeit, Angelegenheit* irksome.

⚠ **verdroß** *pret of* **verdrießen.**

verdrossen [1] *ptp of* **verdrießen.**
[2] *adj (schlechtgelaunt)* morose; *(unlustig) Mensch, Gesicht* unwilling, reluctant.

Verdrossenheit *f (schlechte Laune)* moroseness; *(Lustlosigkeit)* unwillingness, reluctance ◆ **mit ~ arbeiten** to work unwillingly *or* reluctantly.

verdrucken* *(inf)* [1] *vr* to make a misprint.
[2] *vt* to misprint.

verdrücken* [1] *vt* **(a)** *Kleider* to crumple. **(b)** *(dial: zerdrücken)* to crush, to squash. **(c)** *(inf) Essen* to polish off *(inf)* ◆ **der kann was ~** he's got some appetite *(inf)*.
[2] *vr (inf)* to beat it *(inf)* ◆ **sich heimlich ~** to slip away (unnoticed).

Verdrückung *f (inf: Bedrängnis)* distress ◆ **in ~ geraten** *or* **kommen** to get into difficulties; **jdn in ~ bringen** to put sb under pressure.

⚠ **Verdruß** *m* **-sses, -sse** frustration ◆ **~ mit jdm haben** to get frustrated with sb; **zu jds ~** to sb's annoyance; **jdm zum ~** to spite sb.

verduften* *vi aux sein* **(a)** to lose its smell; *(Parfüm)* to lose its scent; *(Tee, Kaffee)* to lose its aroma. **(b)** *(inf: verschwinden)* to beat it *(inf)*.

verdummen* [1] *vt* **jdn ~** *(für dumm verkaufen)* to make sb out to be stupid; *(dumm machen)* to dull sb's mind.
[2] *vi aux sein* to stultify, to become stultified.

Verdummung *f* **(a)** *siehe vt* treating as stupid; dulling (of sb's mind). **(b)** *siehe vi* stultification.

verdungen *ptp of* **verdingen.**

verdunkeln* [1] *vt* to darken; *Bühne auch, (im Krieg)* to black out; *Farbe auch* to deepen, to make darker; *(fig) Zusammenhänge, Motive etc* to obscure; *jds Glück* to dim; *jds Ruf* to damage, to harm ◆ **Tatbestände ~** to suppress evidence; **die Sonne ~** *(Mond)* to eclipse the sun; *(Wolken)* to obscure the sun.
[2] *vr* to darken; *(Himmel auch)* to grow darker; *(Verstand)* to become dulled.

Verdunk(e)lung *f* **(a)** *siehe vt* darkening; blacking out; deepening; obscuring; dimming; damaging, harming ◆ **die ~ nicht einhalten** not to keep to the blackout. **(b)** *(das Dunkelwerden) siehe vr* darkening; dulling. **(c)** *(inf) (Vorhang)* curtain; *(Jalousie)* blind *usu pl.* **(d)** *(Jur)* suppression of evidence.

Verdunk(e)lungsgefahr *f (Jur) danger of suppression of evidence.*

verdünnen* [1] *vt* to thin (down); *(mit Wasser)* to water down; *Lösung* to dilute; *Gas* to rarefy ◆ **den Teig mit Wasser ~** to add water to the dough.
[2] *vr (Lösung)* to become diluted; *(Luft)* to become rarefied; *(Vegetation)* to become thinner; *(schmaler werden)* to become thinner; *(Rohr)* to become narrower ◆ **verdünnte Luft** rarefied air.

Verdünner *m* **-s, -** thinner.

verdünnisieren* *vr (hum inf)* to beat a hasty retreat.

Verdünnung *f* **(a)** thinning; *(von Lösung)* dilution; *(mit Wasser)* watering down; *(von Luft)* rarefaction *(form)*; *(Verengung)* narrowing. **(b)** *(Flüssigkeit zum Verdünnen)* thinner.

verdunsten* *vi aux sein* to evaporate.

Verdunster *m* **-s, -** humidifier.

Verdunstung *f* evaporation.

verdursten* *vi aux sein* to die of thirst.

verdusseln* *vt (inf)* **etw ~** to forget all about sth.

verdüstern* *vtr* to darken.

verdutzen* *vt (inf)* to take aback, to nonplus; *(verwirren)* to baffle.

verdutzt *adj, adv (inf)* taken aback, nonplussed; *(verwirrt)* baffled.

Verdutztheit *f (inf)* bafflement.

ver|ebben* *vi aux sein* to subside.

ver|edeln* *vt Metalle, Erdöl* to refine; *Fasern* to finish; *(Bot)* to graft; *Boden, Geschmack* to improve; *jdn, Charakter* to ennoble.

Ver|ed(e)lung *f siehe vt* refining; finishing; grafting; improving; ennoblement.

ver|ehelichen* *vr (form)* **sich (mit jdm) ~** to marry (sb).

ver|ehelicht *adj (form)* married ◆ **Eva Schmidt, ~e Meier** Eva Meier née Schmidt; **seine V~e** his wife.

Ver|ehelichung *f (form)* marriage.

ver|ehren* *vt* **(a)** *(hochachten)* to admire; *Gott, Maria, Heiligen* to honour; *(ehrerbietig lieben)* to worship, to adore; *siehe* **verehrt. (b)** *(schenken)* **jdm etw ~** to give sb sth.

Ver|ehrer(in *f) m* **-s, -** admirer.

ver|ehrt *adj (in Anrede)* **(sehr) ~e Anwesende/Gäste/~es Publikum** Ladies and Gentlemen; **(sehr) ~e gnädige Frau** *(in Brief)* (dear) Madam; **mein V~ester/meine V~este** *(iro, form)* (my) dear Sir/Madam.

Ver|ehrung *f (Hochachtung)* admiration; *(von Heiligen)* worship; *(Liebe)* adoration.

ver|ehrungs-: ~voll *adv (geh)* reverentially, in reverence; **~würdig** *adj (geh) Mensch, Güte* commendable, praiseworthy; *Künstlerin* admirable.

ver|eiden* *(dated),* **ver|eidigen*** *vt* to swear in ◆ **jdn auf etw** *(acc)* **~** to make *or* have sb swear on sth; **vereidigter Übersetzer** *etc* sworn translator *etc.*

Ver|eidigung, Ver|eidung *(dated) f* swearing in.

Ver|ein *m* **-(e)s, -e** organization; *(esp Tier~, Landschaftsschutz~ etc auch)* society; *(kulturell auch)* association; *(Sport~)* club; *(inf)* crowd ◆ **ein wohltätiger ~** a charity; **ihr seid vielleicht ein ~!** *(inf)* what a bunch you are! *(inf)*; **eingetragener ~** registered society *or (wohltätig)* charity; **im ~ mit** in conjunction with; **im ~ rufen** to shout *or* chant in unison.

ver|einbar *adj* compatible; *Aussagen* consistent ◆ **nicht (miteinander) ~** incompatible; *Aussagen* inconsistent; **eine mit meinem Gewissen nicht ~e Tat** a deed which I cannot reconcile with my conscience.

➤ **vereinbaren*** *vt* **(a)** *(miteinander absprechen)* to agree; *Zeit, Treffen, Tag* to arrange ◆ **(es) ~, daß ...** to agree/arrange that ...
➤ **(b) etw mit etw ~** to reconcile sth with sth; **sich mit etw ~ lassen** to be compatible with sth; **mit etw zu ~ sein** to be compatible with sth; *(Aussa-*

⚠: for details of spelling reform, see supplement

➤ SPRACHE AKTIV: **vereinbaren: b → 53.4**

gen) to be consistent with sth; (*Ziele, Ideale*) to be reconcilable with sth.

Ver|einbarkeit *f, no pl siehe adj* compatibility; consistency.

Ver|einbarung *f siehe vt* (*a*) (*das Vereinbaren*) agreeing; arranging; (*Abmachung*) agreement; arrangement ♦ **laut ~** as agreed; **nach ~** by arrangement.

ver|einbarungsgemäß *adv* as agreed.

ver|einen* [1] *vt* to unite; (*miteinander vereinbaren*) *Ideen, Prinzipien* to reconcile ♦ **eine Familie wieder ~** to reunite a family; **vereint rufen** to shout in unison; **vereint handeln** to act together *or* as one; **sich nicht mit etw ~ lassen** to be irreconcilable with sth; **sie vereint Tugend und Schönheit in sich** (*dat*) she combines virtue and beauty; **Vereinte Nationen** United Nations *sing*.
[2] *vr* to join together ♦ **in ihr ~ sich Schönheit und Tugend** she combines beauty and virtue.

ver|einfachen* *vt* to simplify; (*Math*) to reduce ♦ **etw vereinfacht darstellen** to portray sth in simplified terms.

Ver|einfachung *f* simplification; (*Math*) reduction.

ver|einheitlichen* *vt* to standardize.

Ver|einheitlichung *f* standardization.

ver|einigen* [1] *vt* to unite; *Kräfte auch* to combine; *Eigenschaften* to bring together; (*Comm*) *Firmen* to merge (*zu* into); *Kapital* to pool; *Aktion* to coordinate ♦ **etw mit etw ~** (*vereinbaren*) to reconcile sth with sth; **Schönheit mit Intelligenz (in sich** *dat*) **~** to combine beauty with intelligence; **die beiden Standpunkte lassen sich nicht ~** the two points of view are incompatible; **in einer Hand vereinigt sein** to be held by the same person; **Freunde um sich ~** to gather friends around one; **alle Stimmen auf sich** (*acc*) **~** to collect all the votes; **Vereinigtes Königreich** United Kingdom; **Vereinigte Staaten** United States; **Vereinigte Arabische Emirate** United Arab Emirates.
[2] *vr* to unite; (*sich verbünden auch*) to join forces; (*Firmen*) to merge; (*zusammenkommen*) to combine; (*Töne*) to blend; (*Flüsse*) to meet; (*Zellen etc*) to fuse; (*sich versammeln*) to assemble; (*geh: geschlechtlich*) to come together ♦ **sich zu einem harmonischen Ganzen ~** to merge into a harmonious whole; **sich zu einer Koalition ~** to form a coalition.

Ver|einigung *f* (**a**) *siehe vt* uniting; combining; bringing together; merging; pooling; coordination; (*Math, geh: körperliche, eheliche ~*) union. (**b**) (*Organisation*) organization.

Ver|einigungs-: ~freiheit *f* freedom of association; **~menge** *f* (*Math*) union *or* join of sets.

ver|einnahmen* *vt* (*form*) to take ♦ **jdn ~** (*fig*) to make demands on sb; (*Beruf*) to occupy sb; **sie versucht, ihn völlig zu ~** she wants him all to herself.

ver|einsamen* *vi aux sein* to become lonely *or* isolated ♦ **vereinsamt sterben** to die lonely.

Ver|einsamung *f* loneliness, isolation.

Ver|eins-: ~haus *nt* club house; **~kamerad** *m* fellow club member; **~leitung** *f* (**a**) (*Amt*) chairmanship of an organization/association/a club; (**b**) (*Personen*) club *etc* committee; **~meier** *m* **-s, -** (*inf*) club freak (*sl*); **er ist ein richtiger ~meier** all he thinks about is his club; **~meierei** *f* (*inf*) **seine ~meierei geht mir auf die Nerven** his obsession with his club is getting on my nerves; **diese ewige ~meierei!** all this club nonsense!; **~mitglied** *nt* club member; **~register** *nt* official register of societies and associations; **~wesen** *nt* clubs, organizations and societies *pl*.

ver|eint *ptp, adj siehe* **vereinen.**

ver|einzeln* *vt* (*Agr*) to thin (out).

ver|einzelt [1] *adj* occasional; (*Met auch*) isolated; *Schauer auch* scattered ♦ **die Faulheit ~er Schüler** the laziness of the occasional *or* odd pupil.
[2] *adv* occasionally; (*zeitlich auch*) now and then; (*örtlich auch*) here and there ♦ **... ~ bewölkt** ... with cloudy patches.

ver|eisen* [1] *vt* (*Med*) to freeze.
[2] *vi aux sein* to freeze; (*Straße*) to freeze *or* ice over; (*Fensterscheibe*) to ice over; (*Tragfläche auch*) to ice (up).

ver|eist *adj Straßen, Fenster* icy; *Bäche* frozen; *Türschloß, Tragfläche* iced-up; *Land* covered in ice.

Ver|eisung *f* (**a**) (*Med*) freezing. (**b**) *siehe vi* freezing; freezing *or* icing over; icing (up).

ver|eiteln* *vt Plan etc* to thwart, to foil; *Verbrechen, Attentat* to foil, to prevent; *Versuch auch* to frustrate.

Ver|eit(e)lung *f siehe vt* thwarting, foiling; prevention; frustration.

ver|eitern* *vi aux sein* to go septic; (*Wunde auch*) to fester ♦ **vereitert sein** to be septic; **vereiterte Wunde** septic wound; **vereiterter Zahn** abscess; **vereiterte Mandeln haben** to have tonsillitis.

Ver|eiterung *f* sepsis ♦ **~ der Wunde/des Zahns/der Mandeln** septic wound/dental sepsis/tonsillitis.

ver|ekeln* *vt* (*inf*) **jdm etw ~** to put sb off sth (*inf*).

ver|elenden* *vi aux sein* to become impoverished *or* (*Mensch auch*) destitute.

Ver|elendung *f* impoverishment.

ver|enden* *vi aux sein* to perish, to die.

ver|engen* [1] *vr* to narrow, to become narrow; (*Gefäße, Pupille*) to contract; (*Kleid, Taille*) to go in; (*fig: Horizont*) to narrow.
[2] *vt* to make narrower; *Pupille etc* to make contract; *Kleid* to take in; *Horizont* to narrow.

ver|engern* [1] *vt* (**a**) *Kleidung* to take in. (**b**) *siehe* **verengen 2.**
[2] *vr* (**a**) (*Ärmel, Hose*) to go in; (*spitz zulaufen*) to become narrower. (**b**) *siehe* **verengen 1.**

Ver|engung *f* (**a**) narrowing; (*von Pupille, Gefäß*) contraction. (**b**) (*verengte Stelle*) narrow part (*in +dat* of); (*in Adern*) stricture (*in +dat* of).

ver|erbbar *adj* (**a**) *Anlagen* hereditary. (**b**) *Besitz* heritable.

ver|erben* [1] *vt* (**a**) *Besitz* to leave, to bequeath (*dat, an +acc* to); (*hum*) to hand on (*jdm* to sb), to bequeath (*jdm* sb). (**b**) *Anlagen* to pass on (*dat, auf +acc* to); *Krankheit* to transmit.
[2] *vr* to be passed on/transmitted (*auf +acc* to).

ver|erblich *adj siehe* **vererbbar.**

Ver|erbung *f* (**a**) (*das Vererben*) (*von Besitz*) leaving, bequeathing; (*von Anlagen*) passing on; (*von Krankheit*) transmission. (**b**) (*Lehre*) heredity ♦ **das ist ~** (*inf*) it's hereditary.

Ver|erbungs-: ~forschung *f* genetics *sing*; **~lehre** *f* genetics *sing*.

ver|ewigen* [1] *vt* to immortalize; *Zustand, Verhältnisse* to perpetuate ♦ **seine schmutzigen Finger auf der Buchseite ~** to leave one's dirty fingermarks on the page for posterity.
[2] *vr* (*lit, fig*) to immortalize oneself.

Verf., Vf. *abbr of* **Verfasser.**

verfahren¹* *vi irreg aux sein* (*vorgehen*) to act, to proceed ♦ **mit jdm/etw streng/schlecht ~** to deal strictly/badly with sb/sth.

verfahren²* *irreg* [1] *vt Geld, Zeit* to spend in travelling; *Benzin* to use up.
[2] *vr* to lose one's way; (*fig*) (*Angelegenheit*) to get muddled; (*Mensch*) to get into a muddle.

verfahren³ *adj Angelegenheit* muddled ♦ **eine ~e Sache** a muddle.

Verfahren *nt* **-s, -** (*Vorgehen*) actions *pl*; (*~sweise*) procedure; (*Tech*) process; (*Methode*) method; (*Jur*) proceedings *pl* ♦ **ein ~ gegen jdn einleiten** *or* **anhängig machen** to take *or* initiate legal proceedings against sb.

Verfahrens-: v~rechtlich *adj* (*form*) procedural; **~technik** *f* process engineering; **~weise** *f* procedure, modus operandi.

Verfall *m* **-(e)s,** *no pl* (**a**) (*Zerfall*) decay; (*von Gebäude*) dilapidation; (*gesundheitlich, geistig*) decline ♦ **etw dem ~ preisgeben** to let sth go to (rack and) ruin; **in ~ geraten** (*Gebäude*) to become dilapidated; (*stärker*) to fall into ruins.
(**b**) (*Niedergang: von Kultur, der Sitten, sittlich*) decline; (*des Römischen Reichs auch*) fall; (*von Reichtum, Vermögen*) fall (*von* in).
(**c**) (*das Ungültigwerden*) (*von Schuldansprüchen, Rechnung etc*) lapsing; (*von Scheck, Karte*) expiry.

verfallen¹* *vi irreg aux sein* (**a**) (*zerfallen*) to decay; (*Bauwerk*) to fall into disrepair, to become dilapidated; (*Zellen*) to die; (*körperlich und geistig*) to deteriorate; (*Sitten, Kultur, Reich*) to decline ♦ **der Patient verfällt zusehends** the patient has gone into a rapid decline.
(**b**) (*ungültig werden*) (*Briefmarken, Geldscheine, Gutschein*) to become invalid; (*Scheck, Fahrkarte*) to expire; (*Strafe, Recht, Termin, Anspruch, Patent*) to lapse.
(**c**) (*in jds Besitz übergehen*) to be forfeited ♦ **jdm ~** to be forfeited to sb, to become the property of sb.
(**d**) (*abhängig werden*) **jdm/einer Sache ~/~ sein** to become/be a slave to sb/sth; *dem Alkohol etc* to become/be addicted to sth; *jds Zauber etc* to become/be enslaved by sth; **jdm völlig ~ sein** to be completely under sb's spell; **einem Irrtum ~** to make a mistake, to be mistaken.
(**e**) **auf etw** (*acc*) **~** to think of sth; (*aus Verzweiflung*) to resort to sth; **auf abstruse Gedanken ~** to start having abstruse thoughts; **wer ist denn bloß auf diesen Gedanken ~?** whoever thought this up?; **wie sind Sie bloß darauf ~?** whatever gave you that idea?
(**f**) **in etw** (*acc*) **~** to sink into sth; **in einen tiefen Schlaf ~** to fall into a deep sleep; **in einen ganz anderen Ton ~** to adopt a completely different tone; **in einen Fehler ~** to make a mistake.

verfallen² *adj Gebäude* dilapidated, ruined; *Mensch* (*körperlich*) emaciated; (*geistig*) senile; (*abgelaufen*) *Karten, Briefmarken* invalid; *Strafe* lapsed; *Scheck* expired.

Verfalls-: ~datum *nt* expiry date; (*der Haltbarkeit*) best-before date, eat-by date; **~erscheinung** *f* symptom of decline (*gen* in); **~tag** *m* expiry date; (*von Strafe etc*) date of lapsing.

verfälschen* *vt* to distort; *Wahrheit, Aussage auch, Daten* to falsify; *Lebensmittel, Wein, Geschmack* to adulterate.

Verfälschung *f siehe vt* distortion; falsification; adulteration.

verfangen* *irreg* [1] *vr* to get caught ♦ **sich in Lügen ~** to get entangled in a web of lies; **sich in Widersprüchen ~** to contradict oneself.
[2] *vi* to be accepted; (*Argument, Slogan*) to catch on ♦ **bei jdm nicht ~** not to cut any ice with sb (*inf*); **die Masche verfing** the trick worked.

verfänglich *adj Situation* awkward, embarrassing; *Aussage, Beweismaterial, Blicke, Andeutungen* incriminating; (*gefährlich*) dangerous; *Angewohnheit* insidious; *Frage* tricky.

Verfänglichkeit *f siehe adj* awkwardness; incriminating nature; dangerousness; insidiousness; trickiness.

verfärben* [1] *vt* to discolour ♦ **etw rot ~** to turn sth red; **wenn der Herbst die Blätter verfärbt** when autumn turns the leaves.
[2] *vr* to change colour; (*Blätter auch*) to turn; (*Metall, Wäsche, Stoff*) to discolour ♦ **sich grün/rot ~** to turn *or* go green/red; **sie verfärbte sich** she went red/white.

Verfärbung *f siehe vr* change in colour; turning; discolouring.

verfassen* *vt* to write; *Gesetz, Urkunde* to draw up.

Verfasser(in f) *m* **-s, -** writer; (*von Buch, Artikel etc auch*) author.

Verfasserschaft *f* authorship.

Verfassung *f* (**a**) (*Pol*) constitution ♦ **gegen die ~ handeln** to act unconstitutionally.
(**b**) (*körperlich*) state (of health); (*seelisch*) state of mind ♦ **sie ist in guter/schlechter ~** she is in good/bad shape; **seine seelische ~ ist gut/schlecht** he is

in good/poor spirits; **sie ist nicht in der ~ zu arbeiten** she is in no fit state to work.
(c) *(Zustand)* state.

verfassunggebend *adj attr* constituent.

Verfassungs-: ~änderung *f* constitutional amendment; **~beschwerde** *f complaint about infringement of the constitution*; **~feind** *m* enemy of the constitution *(being declared as such disbars sb from working in the public service)*; **v~feindlich** *adj* anticonstitutional; **~gericht** *nt* constitutional court; **v~mäßig** *adj* constitutional; **etw v~mäßig garantieren** to guarantee sth in the constitution; **eine v~mäßige Ordnung** a constitutional law; **~recht** *nt* constitutional law; **~schutz** *m (Aufgabe)* defence of the constitution; *(Organ, Amt) office responsible for defending the constitution*; **v~treu** *adj* loyal to the constitution; **~treue** *f* loyalty to the constitution; **~urkunde** *f* constitution, constitutional charter; **v~widrig** *adj* unconstitutional; **~wirklichkeit** *f* constitutional reality.

verfaulen* *vi aux sein* to decay; *(Fleisch, Gemüse auch)* to rot; *(Körper, organische Stoffe)* to decompose; *(fig)* to degenerate.

verfault *adj* decayed; *Fleisch, Obst etc* rotten; *Zähne auch* bad; *Körper* decomposed; *Mensch (innerlich)* degenerate.

verfechten* *vt irreg* to defend; *Lehre* to advocate, to champion; *Meinung auch* to maintain.

Verfechter(in *f***)** *m* **-s, -** advocate, champion.

Verfechtung *f siehe vt* defence; advocacy, championing; maintaining.

verfehlen* *vt* **(a)** *(verpassen, nicht treffen)* to miss ◆ **seine Worte hatten ihre Wirkung verfehlt/nicht verfehlt** his words had missed/hit their target; **den Zweck ~** not to achieve its purpose; **das Thema ~** to be completely off the subject.
(b) *(versäumen)* **nicht ~, etw zu tun** not to fail to do sth.

verfehlt *adj (unangebracht)* inappropriate; *(mißlungen) Leben, Angelegenheit, Planung* unsuccessful ◆ **es ist ~, das zu tun** you are mistaken in doing that.

Verfehlung *f* **(a)** *(des Ziels)* missing ◆ **bei ~ des Themas bekommt der Schüler ...** if the essay is off the subject the pupil will get ... **(b)** *(Vergehen)* misdemeanour; *(Sünde)* transgression.

verfeinden* [1] *vr* to quarrel ◆ **sich mit jdm ~** to make an enemy of sb; *mit Nachbarn* to quarrel with sb; **verfeindet sein** to have quarrelled; *(Familie etc)* to be estranged; *(Staaten)* to be on bad terms; **die verfeindeten Schwestern/ Staaten** the estranged sisters/the enemy states.
[2] *vt* **warum versucht sie, ihren Mann und seine Familie zu ~?** why is she trying to set her husband against his family?

verfeinern* [1] *vt* to improve; *Methode auch* to refine.
[2] *vr* to improve; *(Methoden auch)* to become refined.

verfeinert *adj Methode, Geräte* sophisticated.

Verfeinerung *f siehe vb* improvement; refining; *(von Geschmack auch)* refinement ◆ **die zunehmende ~ technischer Geräte** the increasing sophistication of technical equipment.

verfemen* *vt (Hist)* to outlaw; *(fig) jdn* to ostracize; *Künstler, Ideologie, Methode, Kunstrichtung* to condemn.

Verfemte(r) *mf decl as adj (Hist)* outlaw; *(fig)* persona non grata.

Verfemung *f siehe vt* outlawing; ostracizing; condemnation.

verfertigen* *vt* to manufacture, to produce; *Liste* to draw up; *(usu iro) Brief, Aufsatz* to compose.

verfestigen* [1] *vt* to harden; *Flüssigkeit* to solidify; *(verstärken)* to strengthen, to reinforce.
[2] *vr* to harden; *(Flüssigkeit)* to solidify; *(fig) (Haß, Feindschaft)* to harden; *(Kenntnisse)* to be reinforced; *(Ideen, Gewohnheiten)* to become fixed *or* set; *(Demokratie, Strukturen)* to be strengthened *or* reinforced.

verfetten* *vi aux sein (Med) (Mensch)* to become fat *or* obese; *(Herz, Leber)* to become fatty *or* adipose *(spec)*.

Verfettung *f (Med) (von Körper)* obesity; *(von Organ, Muskeln)* fatty degeneration, adiposity *(spec)*.

verfeuern* *vt* to burn; *Munition* to fire ◆ **die ganze Munition/das ganze Öl ~** to use up all the ammunition/oil.

verfilmen* *vt* to film, to make a film of; *(aufbrauchen) Film* to use up.

Verfilmung *f (das Verfilmen)* filming; *(Film)* film (version).

verfilzen* [1] *vi aux sein (Wolle, Pullover)* to become felted; *(Haare)* to become matted ◆ **verfilzt** felted/matted.
[2] *vr* to become matted.

verfinstern* [1] *vt* to darken; *Sonne, Mond* to eclipse.
[2] *vr (lit, fig)* to darken.

Verfinsterung *f* darkening; *(von Sonne etc)* eclipse.

verfitzen* *(inf)* [1] *vt* to tangle.
[2] *vr* to become tangled.

verflachen* [1] *vi aux sein* to flatten *or* level out; *(fig: Diskussion, Gespräch, Mensch)* to become superficial *or* trivial.
[2] *vr (Gelände)* to flatten *or* level out.

Verflachung *f siehe vi* flattening *or* levelling out; superficiality ◆ **um einer ~ der Diskussion vorzubeugen** to stop the conversation becoming superficial *or* trivial.

verflechten* *irreg* [1] *vt* to interweave, to intertwine; *Bänder* to interlace; *(auch fig) Methoden* to combine; *Firmen* to interlink ◆ **eng mit etw verflochten sein** *(fig)* to be closely connected *or* linked with sth; **jdn in etw** *(acc)* **~** *in Gespräch, Unternehmen* to involve sb in sth; *in dunkle Geschäfte* to entangle *or* embroil sb in sth.
[2] *vr* to interweave, to intertwine; *(Bänder)* to interlace; *(sich verwirren)* to become entangled *(mit* in); *(Themen)* to interweave; *(Methoden)* to combine ◆ **sich mit etw ~** to become linked *or* connected with sth.

Verflechtung *f* **(a)** *siehe vb* interweaving, intertwining; interlacing; entanglement; combining. **(b)** *(das Verflochtensein)* interconnection *(gen* between); *(Pol, Econ)* integration.

verfleckt *adj (inf)* stained.

verfliegen* *irreg* [1] *vi aux sein* **(a)** *(fig) (Stimmung, Zorn etc)* to blow over *(inf)*, to pass; *(Heimweh, Kummer etc)* to vanish.
(b) *(sich verflüchtigen)* to vanish; *(Alkohol)* to evaporate; *(Duft)* to fade (away); *(Zeit)* to fly.
[2] *vr* to stray; *(Pilot, Flugzeug)* to lose one's/its bearings.

verfließen* *vi irreg aux sein* **(a)** *(geh: vergehen)* to go by, to pass; *siehe* **verflossen**. **(b)** *(verschwimmen) (Farben)* to run; *(fig)* to become blurred.

verflixt *(inf)* [1] *adj* blessed *(inf)*, darned *(inf)*; *(kompliziert)* tricky ◆ **du ~er Kerl!** you devil; **das ~e siebte Jahr** ≃ the seven-year itch.
[2] *adv* darned *(inf)*.
[3] *interj* **~!** blow! *(inf)*.

Verflochtenheit *f, no pl (fig)* interconnections *pl (von* between).

verflossen [1] *ptp of* **verfließen**.
[2] *adj* **(a)** *Jahre, Tage* bygone; *(letzte)* last. **(b)** *(inf)* one-time *attr (inf)* ◆ **ihr V~er** her former *or* ex-boyfriend/-fiancé/-husband.

verfluchen* *vt* to curse ◆ **sei verflucht** curses on you.

verflucht [1] *adj (inf)* damn *(inf)*, bloody *(Brit sl)* ◆ **~ (noch mal)!** damn (it) *(inf)*; **diese ~e Tat** *(liter)* this cursed deed; **~e Tat!** *(inf)* damn! *(inf)*.
[2] *adv (sl) (bei englischem adj, n)* damn *(inf)*, bloody *(Brit sl)*; *(bei englischem vb)* like hell *(sl)* ◆ **ich habe mich ~ vertan** I made one hell of a mistake *(sl)*.

verflüchtigen* [1] *vt* to evaporate.
[2] *vr (Alkohol, Kohlensäure etc)* to evaporate; *(Duft)* to disappear; *(Gase)* to volatilize; *(fig) (Bedenken, Ärger)* to be dispelled; *(hum) (Mensch, Gegenstand, Hoffnungen etc)* to vanish; *(Geld)* to go up in smoke *(inf)*.

Verflüchtigung *f siehe vr* evaporation; disappearance; volatilization.

verflüssigen* *vtr* to liquefy.

Verflüssigung *f* liquefaction.

Verfolg *m* **-s,** *no pl (form) (Ausübung)* pursuance; *(Verlauf)* course ◆ **im ~ des Schreibens vom ...** further to our letter of ...

verfolgen* *vt Ziel, Idee, Karriere etc* to pursue; *jdn auch* to follow; *(jds Spuren folgen) jdn* to trail; *Tier* to track; *(mit Hunden etc)* to hunt; *Unterricht, Entwicklung, Geschichte, Spur* to follow; *Idee, Gedanken* to follow up; *(politisch, religiös)* to persecute; *(Gedanke, Erinnerung etc) jdn* to haunt ◆ **vom Unglück/Schicksal** *etc* **verfolgt werden** *or* **sein** to be dogged by ill fortune/by fate *etc*; **jdn politisch ~** to persecute sb for political reasons; **jdn gerichtlich ~** to prosecute sb; **jdn mit den Augen** *or* **Blicken ~** to follow sb with one's eyes; **jdn mit Bitten/Forderungen ~** to badger sb with requests/demands; **jdn mit Haß ~** to pursue sb in hate; **welche Absicht verfolgt er?** what is his intention?; *siehe* **strafrechtlich**.

Verfolger(in *f***)** *m* **-s, - (a)** pursuer. **(b)** *(politisch, wegen Gesinnung)* persecutor.

Verfolgte(r) *mf decl as adj* **(a)** quarry. **(b)** *(politisch, wegen Gesinnung)* victim of persecution.

Verfolgung *f siehe vt* pursuit; following; trailing; tracking; *(politische ~)* persecution *no pl* ◆ **die ~ aufnehmen** to take up the chase; **gerichtliche ~** court action; **strafrechtliche ~** prosecution; **bei der weiteren ~ der Frage** when this question was/is pursued further; **~ eines Ziels** pursuance of an aim.

Verfolgungs-: ~jagd *f* chase, pursuit; **~rennen** *nt (Sport)* pursuit race; **~wahn** *m* persecution mania.

verformen* [1] *vt* to make go out of shape, to distort *(zu* into); *(umformen)* to work ◆ **verformt sein** to be out of shape; *(Mensch, Gliedmaßen)* to be deformed.
[2] *vr* to go out of shape.

Verformung *f* **(a)** distortion. **(b)** *(veränderte Form)* distortion; *(von Mensch, Gliedmaßen)* deformity.

verfrachten* *vt (Comm)* to transport; *(Naut)* to ship; *(inf) jdn* to bundle off *(inf)* ◆ **etw in den Keller/eine Kiste ~** *(inf)* to dump sth in the cellar/a crate.

Verfrachter *m* **-s, -** transport agent; *(Naut)* freighter; shipper.

Verfrachtung *f* transporting; *(Naut)* shipping.

verfranzen* *vr (inf)* to lose one's way; *(Aviat sl)* to lose one's bearings; *(fig)* to get in a muddle *or* tangle.

verfremden* *vt Thema, Stoff* to make unfamiliar, to defamiliarize; *Werkstoffe* to use in an unusual way.

Verfremdung *f* defamiliarization; *(Theat, Liter)* alienation, distancing ◆ **die ~ vertrauter Formen** using familiar forms in an unfamiliar way.

Verfremdungs|effekt *m* distancing effect; *(Theat, Liter)* alienation *or* estrangement effect.

verfressen[1]***** *vt irreg (inf)* to spend *or* blow *(inf)* on food.

verfressen[2] *adj (inf)* greedy.

verfrieren* *vi irreg aux sein (dial) siehe* **erfrieren**.

verfroren *adj (inf)* sensitive to cold; *(durchgefroren)* frozen, freezing cold ◆ **~ sein** *(kälteempfindlich)* to feel the cold.

verfrühen* *vr (Winter, Entwicklung, Zug)* to come *or* arrive early; *(Gäste)* to be *or* come too early.

verfrüht *adj (zu früh)* premature; *(früh)* early ◆ **solche Aufgaben sind für dieses Alter ~** exercises like this are too advanced for this age group.

verfügbar *adj* available.

verfugen* *vt* to fit flush; *Fliesen* to grout.

verfügen* [1] *vi* **über etw** *(acc)* **~** to have sth at one's disposal; *(besitzen)* to

have sth; **über jdn/etw ~** (*bestimmen über*) to be in charge of sb/sth; **die Art und Weise wie er über seine Untergebenen/meine Zeit/mein Geld verfügt** the way in which he orders his inferiors around/tells me how to spend my time/money; **Gott verfügt über das Schicksal der Menschen** God determines man's fate; **du kannst über mein Auto ~, wenn ich in Urlaub bin** you can use my car while I'm on holiday; **du kannst doch nicht über mein Geld ~** you can't tell me how to spend my money; **du kannst doch nicht über deinen Bruder ~** you can't tell your brother what to do; **über etw** (*acc*) **frei ~ können** to be able to do as one wants with sth; **~ Sie über mich** I am at your disposal.
[2] *vt* to order; (*gesetzlich*) to decree; *siehe* **letztwillig.**
[3] *vr* (*form*) to proceed (*form*).

▼ **Verfügung** *f* **(a)** *no pl* (*das Verfügen*) possession ◆ **freie ~** (*Jur*) free disposal (*über +acc* of); **jdm etw zur ~ stellen** to put sth at sb's disposal; (*leihen*) to lend sb sth; **jdm zur ~** *or* **zu jds ~ stehen** to be at sb's disposal; **(jdm) zur ~ stehen** (*verfügbar sein*) to be available (to sb); **sich zur ~ halten** to be available (to sb); **halte dich ab 7 Uhr zur ~** be ready from 7 o'clock; **etw zur ~ haben** to have sth at one's disposal.
(b) (*behördlich*) order; (*von Gesetzgeber*) decree; (*testamentarisch*) provision; (*Anweisung*) instruction; *siehe* **letztwillig.**

Verfügungs-: ~befugnis *f* right of disposal (*über +acc* of); **~gewalt** *f* (*Jur*) right of disposal; **die ~gewalt über Atomwaffen** the power to use atomic weapons; **~recht** *nt* (*Jur*) right of disposal (*über +acc* of).

verführen* *vt* to tempt; (*esp sexuell*) to seduce; *die Jugend, das Volk etc* to lead astray ◆ **jdn zu etw ~, jdn ~, etw zu tun** to encourage sb to do sth; **ich lasse mich gern ~** you can twist my arm (*inf*); **diese offenen Kisten ~ ja direkt zum Diebstahl** these open boxes are an encouragement *or* invitation to steal.

Verführer *m* **-s, -** seducer.

Verführerin *f* seductress, temptress.

verführerisch *adj* seductive; (*verlockend*) tempting.

Verführung *f* seduction; (*von Jugend, Volk*) tempting; (*Verlockung*) enticement, temptation.

Verführungskunst *f* seductive manner; (*von Werbung*) persuasiveness ◆ **ein Meister der ~** a master of seduction *or* (*Werber*) persuasion; **Verführungskünste** seductive *or* (*von Werber*) persuasive charms *or* ways.

verfüllen* *vt* (*mit Erde, Beton etc*) to fill in.

verfünffachen* [1] *vt Zahl* to multiply by five, to quintuple (*form*).
[2] *vr* to increase fivefold *or* five times; (*Zahl auch*) to multiply by five.

verfuttern* *vt* (*inf*) to spend on food.

verfüttern* *vt* to use as animal/bird food; (*aufbrauchen*) to feed (*an +acc* to) ◆ **etw an die Schweine/Vögel ~** to feed sth to the pigs/birds.

Vergabe *f* **-, (***rare***) -n** (*von Arbeiten*) allocation; (*von Stipendium, Auftrag etc*) award.

Vergabestelle *f* (*für Studienplätze*) central universities admissions council.

vergackeiern* *vt* (*inf*) **jdn ~** to pull sb's leg (*inf*), to have sb on (*inf*).

vergaffen* *vr* (*dated inf*) **sich in jdn ~** to fall for sb (*inf*).

vergagt [fɛɐ'gɛ(:)kt] *adj* (*inf*) gimmicky (*inf*).

vergällen* *vt Alkohol* to denature; (*fig*) *jdn* to embitter, to sour; *Freude* to spoil; *Leben etc* to sour ◆ **jdm die Freude/das Leben ~** to spoil sb's fun/to sour sb's life.

vergaloppieren* *vr* (*inf*) (*sich irren*) to be on the wrong track; (*übers Ziel hinausschießen*) to go too far.

vergalt *pret of* **vergelten.**

vergammeln* (*inf*) [1] *vi aux sein* **(a)** (*verderben*) to get spoilt; (*Speisen*) to go bad. **(b)** (*verlottern*) to go to the dogs (*inf*) ◆ **vergammelt aussehen** to look scruffy; **vergammelte Studenten** scruffy(-looking) students.
[2] *vt* to waste ◆ **ich möchte mal wieder einen Tag ~** I'd like to have a day doing nothing.

vergangen [1] *ptp of* **vergehen.**
[2] *adj* **(a)** (*letzte*) last. **(b)** *Jahre* past; *Zeiten, Bräuche* bygone, former; *Größe auch* former ◆ **das V~e** the past; **das ist alles ~ und vergessen** that is all in the past now.

Vergangenheit *f* past; (*von Stadt, Staat etc auch*) history; (*Gram*) past (tense) ◆ **die erste** *or* **einfache/zweite** *or* **vollendete/dritte ~** (*Gram*) the simple past/perfect/pluperfect (tense); **eine Frau mit ~** a woman with a past; **der ~ angehören** to be a thing of the past.

Vergangenheitsbewältigung *f* process of coming to terms with the past.

vergänglich *adj* transitory.

Vergänglichkeit *f, no pl* transitoriness.

vergären* *irreg* [1] *vi aux sein* to ferment.
[2] *vt* to ferment (*zu* into).

vergasen* *vt* (*Tech: in Motor*) to carburet; (*durch Gas töten*) *jdn, Ungeziefer* to gas; *Kohle* to gasify.

Vergasen *nt, no pl* gassing.

Vergaser *m* **-s, -** (*Aut*) carburettor.

Vergaserbrand *m* fire in the carburettor.

vergaß *pret of* **vergessen.**

Vergasung *f siehe vt* carburation; gassing; gasification ◆ **etw bis zur ~ diskutieren/lernen** (*inf*) to discuss sth till one is blue in the face (*inf*)/to study sth ad nauseam.

vergattern* *vt* **(a)** *Garten etc* to fence off; *Tiere* to fence in. **(b)** (*Mil*) to instruct. **(c)** (*inf*) to punish ◆ **jdn zu etw ~** to order sb to do sth.

vergeben* *irreg* [1] *vt* **(a)** (*weggeben*) *Auftrag, Stipendium, Preis* to award (*an +acc* to); *Plätze, Studienplätze, Stellen* to allocate; *Karten* to give away; *Arbeit* to assign; (*fig*) *Chance, Möglichkeit* to throw away ◆ **ein Amt an jdn ~** to appoint sb to an office; **zu ~ sein** to be available; (*Stelle auch*) to be open; **~ sein** (*Gewinn*) to have been awarded *or* won; (*Wohnung, Karten, Plätze*) to have been taken; (*Stelle*) to have been filled; **er/sie ist schon ~** (*inf*) he/she is already spoken for (*inf*) *or* (*verheiratet auch*) married; **ich bin heute abend schon ~** (*inf*) I've got something else on this evening; **mein Herz ist schon ~** (*liter*) my heart belongs to another (*liter*); **der nächste Tanz ist schon ~** I've already promised the next dance.
(b) (*verzeihen*) to forgive; *Sünde auch* to pardon ◆ **jdm etw ~** to forgive sb (for) sth; **das ist ~ und vergessen** that is over and done with *or* forgiven and forgotten.
[2] *vr* **(a) sich** (*dat*) **etwas/nichts ~** to lose/not to lose face; **was vergibst du dir, wenn du ein bißchen netter bist?** what have you got to lose by being a bit friendlier?
(b) (*Cards*) to misdeal.

vergebens [1] *adj pred* in vain, of no avail.
[2] *adv* in vain, vainly.

vergeblich [1] *adj* futile; *Bitten, Mühe auch* vain *attr* ◆ **alle Bitten/Versuche waren ~** all requests/attempts were in vain *or* of no avail.
[2] *adv* in vain.

Vergeblichkeit *f, no pl* futility.

Vergebung *f, no pl* forgiveness.

vergegenständlichen* *vt* to concretize; (*Philos*) to reify, to hypostatize.

vergegenwärtigen* *vr* **sich** (*dat*) **etw ~** (*vor Augen rufen*) to visualize sth; (*sich vorstellen*) to imagine sth; (*erinnern*) to recall sth; **vergegenwärtige dir doch einmal die Folgen** think of the consequences.

Vergehen *nt* **-s, - (a)** (*Verstoß*) offence, misdemeanour ◆ **~ im Amt** professional misconduct *no pl*; **das ist doch kein ~, oder?** that's not a crime, is it?
(b) *no pl* (*geh: Schwinden*) passing; (*von Zeit auch*) passage; (*von Schönheit, Glück*) fading.

vergehen* *irreg* [1] *vi aux sein* **(a)** (*vorbeigehen*) to pass; (*Liebe, Leidenschaft auch*) to die; (*Zeit, Jahre etc auch*) to go by; (*Hunger, Schmerzen auch*) to wear off; (*Schönheit, Glück*) to fade; (*Duft*) to go, to wear off ◆ **wie doch die Zeit vergeht** how time flies; **mir ist die Lust/Laune dazu vergangen** I don't feel like it any more; **mir ist der Appetit vergangen** I have lost my appetite; **das vergeht wieder** that will pass; **es werden noch Monate ~, ehe ...** it will be months before ...; **damit die Zeit vergeht** in order to pass the time; *siehe* **vergangen, Hören, Lachen.**
(b) vor etw (*dat*) **~** to be dying of sth; **vor Angst ~** to be scared to death; **vor Hunger ~** to be dying of hunger, to be starving; **vor Kälte ~** to be frozen; **vor Sehnsucht ~** to pine away; **sie wollte vor Scham ~** she nearly died of shame.
[2] *vr* **sich an jdm ~** to do sb wrong; (*unsittlich*) to assault sb indecently; **sich an Gott/der Natur ~** to go against God/to defile nature; **sich gegen das Gesetz/die guten Sitten/die Moral ~** to violate the law/violate *or* outrage propriety/morality.

vergeigen* *vt* (*inf*) to lose.

vergeistigt *adj* cerebral, spiritual.

Vergeistigung *f, no pl* spiritualization.

vergelten *vt irreg* to repay ◆ **jdm etw ~** to repay sb for sth; (*lohnen auch*) to reward sb's sth; **vergelt's Gott** (*old, dial*) God bless you; *siehe* **gleich.**

Vergeltung *f* (*Rache*) retaliation ◆ **~ üben** to take revenge (*an jdm* on sb).

Vergeltungs-: ~maßnahme *f* reprisal, retaliatory measure; **~schlag** *m* act of reprisal; **~waffen** *pl* retaliatory weapons.

vergesellschaften* *vt* (*Pol*) to nationalize; *Privatbesitz* to take into public ownership; (*ins Arbeitereigentum überführen*) to hand over to the workers; (*rare: Sociol*) to socialize.

Vergesellschaftung *f, no pl siehe vt* nationalization; taking into public ownership; handing over to the workers; socialization.

▼ **vergessen** *pret* **vergaß,** *ptp* **vergessen** [1] *vti* to forget; (*liegenlassen*) to leave (behind) ◆ **... und nicht zu ~ seine Ehrlichkeit** ... and not forgetting his honesty; **daß ich es nicht vergesse** before I forget; **das werde ich dir nie ~** I will never forget that; **auf jdn/etw ~** (*Aus*) to forget sb/sth; **er vergißt noch mal seinen Kopf** (*inf*) he'd forget his head if it wasn't screwed on (*inf*).
[2] *vr* (*Mensch*) to forget oneself ◆ **Zahlen ~ sich leicht** numbers are easy to forget *or* easily forgotten.

▼ **Vergessenheit** *f, no pl* oblivion ◆ **in ~ geraten, der ~ anheimfallen** (*geh*) to be forgotten, to fall into oblivion; **etw aus der ~ hervorholen** to rescue sth from oblivion.

⚠ **vergeßlich** *adj* forgetful.

⚠ **Vergeßlichkeit** *f* forgetfulness.

vergeuden* *vt* to waste; *Geld, Talente auch* to squander.

Vergeudung *f siehe vt* wasting; squandering ◆ **das ist die reinste ~** that is (a) sheer waste; **diese ~!** what a waste!

vergewaltigen* [1] *vt* to rape; (*fig*) *Sprache etc* to murder, to mutilate; *Volkswillen* to violate.
[2] *vr* to force oneself.

Vergewaltiger *m* rapist.

Vergewaltigung *f siehe vt* rape; murder(ing), mutilation; violation.

vergewissern* *vr* to make sure ◆ **sich einer Sache** (*gen*) *or* **über etw** (*acc*) **~** to make sure of sth.

vergießen* *vt irreg Kaffee, Wasser* to spill; *Blut auch, Tränen* to shed ◆ **ich habe bei der Arbeit viel Schweiß vergossen** I sweated blood over that job.

vergiften* [1] *vt* (*lit, fig*) to poison; *Luft auch* to pollute.
[2] *vr* to poison oneself (*mit, durch, an +dat* with).

Vergiftung *f* poisoning *no pl*; *(der Luft)* pollution ◆ **bei ~en wird der Magen ausgepumpt** the stomach is pumped in cases of poisoning; **an einer ~ sterben** to die of poisoning.
Vergiftungs|erscheinung *f* symptom of poisoning.
vergilben* *vi aux sein* to go *or* become yellow ◆ **vergilbt** yellowed.
⚠ **vergiß** *imper sing of* **vergessen.**
⚠ **Vergißmeinnicht** *nt* **-(e)s, -(e)** forget-me-not.
vergittern* *vt* to put a grille on/over; *(mit Stangen)* to put bars on/over ◆ **vergitterte Fenster** barred windows/windows with grilles over them.
Vergitterung *f (Gitter)* grille, grating; *(Stangen)* bars *pl* ◆ **die ~ der Fenster** putting grilles/bars on the windows.
verglasen* *vt* to glaze.
verglast *adj Augen* glazed.
Verglasung *f* glazing.
▼ **Vergleich** *m* **-(e)s, -e (a)** comparison; *(Liter)* simile ◆ **~e ziehen** *or* **anstellen** to make *or* draw comparisons; **im ~ zu** *or* **mit** in comparison with, compared with *or* to; **das ist doch gar kein ~!** there is no comparison; **in keinem ~ zu etw stehen** to be out of all proportion to sth; *(Leistungen)* not to compare with sth; **dem ~ mit jdm standhalten/den ~ mit jdm aushalten** to stand *or* bear comparison with sb; **sie hält den ~ mit ihrer Vorgängerin nicht aus** she doesn't compare with her predecessor.
(b) *(Jur)* settlement ◆ **einen gütlichen/außergerichtlichen ~ schließen** to reach an amicable settlement/to settle out of court.
▼ **vergleichbar** *adj* comparable.
Vergleichbarkeit *f* comparability.
▼ **vergleichen*** *irreg* [1] *vt* to compare ◆ **etw mit etw ~** *(prüfend)* to compare sth with sth; *(einen Vergleich herstellen zwischen)* to compare *or* liken sth to sth; **vergleiche oben** compare above; **sie sind nicht (miteinander) zu ~** they cannot be compared (to one another); **die kann man nicht (miteinander) ~** they cannot be compared (with one another), they are not comparable.
[2] *vr* **(a) sich mit jdm ~** to compare oneself with sb; **wie könnte ich mich mit ihm ~?** how could I compare myself to him? **(b)** *(Jur)* to reach a settlement, to settle *(mit* with).
vergleichend *adj* comparative.
Vergleichs-: ~form *f (Gram)* comparative form; **~gläubiger** *m creditor in insolvency proceedings*; **~satz** *m (Gram)* comparative clause; **~schuldner** *m debtor in insolvency proceedings*; **~verfahren** *nt* insolvency proceedings *pl*; **~weg** *m (Jur)* **auf dem ~weg** by reaching a settlement; **v~weise** *adv* comparatively; **~zahl** *f usu pl* comparative figure.
vergletschern* *vi aux sein* to become glaciated.
Vergletscherung *f* glaciation.
verglimmen* *vi irreg aux sein (Zigarette)* to go out; *(Licht, Feuer auch)* to die out *or* away; *(fig liter) (Leben)* to be extinguished; *(Hoffnung, Liebe, Tageslicht)* to fade ◆ **~de Kohle** dying cinders.
verglühen* *vi aux sein (Feuer, Feuerwerk)* to die away; *(Draht)* to burn out; *(Raumkapsel, Meteor etc)* to burn up; *(liter: Leidenschaft)* to fade (away), to die down.
vergnügen* [1] *vt* to amuse.
[2] *vr* to enjoy oneself ◆ **sich mit jdm/etw ~** to amuse oneself with sb/sth; **sich mit Lesen/Tennis ~** to amuse *or* entertain oneself by reading/playing tennis; **sich an etw** *(dat)* **~** to be amused *or* entertained by sth.
▼ **Vergnügen** *nt* **-s, - (a)** *(Freude, Genuß)* pleasure; *(Spaß)* fun *no indef art*; *(Erheiterung)* amusement ◆ **~ an etw** *(dat)* **finden** to find enjoyment *or* pleasure in (doing) sth; **das macht** *or* **bereitet mir ~** I enjoy it, it gives me pleasure; **sich** *(dat)* **ein ~ aus etw machen** to get pleasure from (doing) sth; **für viele Leute ist es ein ~, den Verkehr auf der Autobahn zu beobachten** a lot of people enjoy watching the traffic on the motorway; **ich laufe jeden Tag eine halbe Stunde nur zum ~** I run for half an hour each day just for pleasure *or* for the fun of it; **das war ein teures ~** *(inf)* that was an expensive bit of fun; **ich höre ihn mit großem ~ singen** it gives me great pleasure to hear him sing; **mit ~/großem ~/größtem** *or* **dem größten ~** with pleasure/great pleasure/the greatest of pleasure; **viel ~!** enjoy yourself/yourselves *(auch iro)*; **er hat mir viel ~ gewünscht** he said he hoped I would enjoy myself; **wir wünschen Ihnen bei der Sendung viel ~** we hope you enjoy the programme; **mit wem habe ich das ~?** *(form)* with whom do I have the pleasure of speaking? *(form)*; **es ist mir ein ~** it is a pleasure for me.
(b) *(dated: Veranstaltung)* entertainment.
vergnüglich *adj* enjoyable; *Stunden auch* pleasurable; *(erheiternd)* amusing.
vergnügt *adj Abend, Stunden* enjoyable; *Mensch, Gesichter, Gesellschaft* cheerful; *Lachen, Stimmung* happy ◆ **~ aussehen/lachen** to look cheerful/laugh happily; **über etw** *(acc)* **~ sein** to be pleased *or* happy about sth.
Vergnügtheit *f (von Mensch, Gesicht)* cheerfulness; *(von Stimmung)* happiness.
Vergnügung *f* pleasure; *(Veranstaltung)* entertainment.
Vergnügungs-: ~dampfer *m* pleasure steamer; **~fahrt** *f* pleasure trip; **~industrie** *f* entertainment industry; **~park** *m* amusement park; **~reise** *f* pleasure trip; **~steuer** *f* entertainment tax; **~sucht** *f* craving for pleasure; **v~süchtig** *adj* pleasure-craving, sybaritic *(liter pej)*; **~viertel** *nt* entertainments district.
vergolden* [1] *vt (mit Gold bemalen) Nüsse etc* to paint gold; *(mit Blattgold) Statue, Buchkante* to gild; *(mit Gold überziehen) Schmuck* to gold-plate; *(liter: Sonne, Schein)* to bathe in gold, to turn golden; *(fig: verschönern) Zeit, Alter, Erinnerung* to enhance ◆ **der Herbst vergoldet die Natur** autumn turns nature golden.
[2] *vr (liter)* to turn to gold.
Vergolder(in *f)* *m* **-s, -** gilder.
vergoldet *adj Nüsse* gold-painted; *Buchseiten* gilded; *Schmuck* gold-plated; *Natur, Stadt, Erinnerung etc* golden.
Vergoldung *f (von Nüssen)* painting gold; *(von Buchseiten)* gilding; *(von Schmuck)* gold-plating; *(Überzug) (auf Nüssen)* gold paint; *(auf Buchseiten)* gilt; *(auf Schmuck)* gold plate.
vergönnen* *vt (geh)* **jdm etw ~** not to begrudge sb sth; **es war ihr noch vergönnt, das zu sehen** she was granted the privilege of seeing it; **diese Freude war ihm noch/nicht vergönnt** fate granted/did not grant him this pleasure.
vergöttern* *vt* to idolize.
Vergötterung *f* idolization.
vergraben* *irreg* [1] *vt* to bury.
[2] *vr (Maulwurf etc)* to bury oneself; *(fig: zurückgezogen leben)* to hide oneself (away) ◆ **sich hinter seinen Büchern/in Arbeit ~** to bury oneself in one's books/in work.
vergrämen* *vt* **(a)** *(verärgern, beleidigen)* to antagonize; *(vertreiben)* to alienate; *(verletzen)* to grieve ◆ **jdm das Leben ~** to make life a misery for sb.
(b) *(Hunt) Wild* to frighten, to scare.
vergrämt *adj (kummervoll, bitter) Gesicht etc* troubled; *(verärgert)* angered.
vergrätzen* *vt (inf)* to vex.
vergraulen* *vt (inf)* to put off; *(vertreiben)* to scare off.
vergreifen* *vr irreg* **(a)** *(danebengreifen)* to make a mistake; *(Musiker auch)* to play a wrong note; *(auf Schreibmaschine etc auch)* to hit the wrong key; *(Sport: bei Gerät)* to miss one's grip ◆ **sich im Ton/Ausdruck ~** *(fig)* to adopt the wrong tone/use the wrong expression; *siehe* **vergriffen.**
(b) sich an etw *(dat)* **~** *(an fremdem Eigentum)* to misappropriate sth; *(euph: stehlen)* to help oneself to sth *(euph)*; *(an Geld auch)* to embezzle sth; *(an Heiligem)* to desecrate *or* profane sth; **sich an jdm ~** *(angreifen)* to lay hands on sb; *(geschlechtlich mißbrauchen)* to assault sb (sexually); **ich vergreife mich doch nicht an kleinen Kindern** *(hum inf)* that would be baby snatching *(inf)*.
vergreisen* *vi aux sein (Bevölkerung)* to age; *(Mensch)* to become senile ◆ **vergreist** aged; senile.
Vergreisung *f (von Bevölkerung)* ageing; *(von Organismen)* senescence; *(von Mensch)* senility.
vergriffen [1] *ptp of* **vergreifen.**
[2] *adj* unavailable; *Buch* out of print.
vergröbern* [1] *vt* to coarsen.
[2] *vr* to become coarse.
vergrößern [1] *vt (räumlich) Raum, Gebäude, Fläche, Gebiet* to extend; *Abstand auch* to increase; *(größenmäßig, umfangmäßig) Maßstab, Wissen* to enlarge, to increase; *Bekanntenkreis* to enlarge, to extend; *Firma, Absatzmarkt* to expand; *Produktion* to increase; *Vollmachten* to extend; *(zahlenmäßig) Kapital, Mitgliederzahl, Anzahl* to increase; *(verstärken) Einfluß, Not, Probleme, Schmerz etc* to increase; *Fotografie* to enlarge, to blow up; *(Lupe, Brille)* to magnify.
[2] *vr (räumlich)* to be extended; *(Abstand)* to increase; *(größenmäßig, umfangmäßig) (Maßstab)* to be enlarged, to increase; *(Wissen)* to increase, to expand; *(Bekanntenkreis)* to be enlarged, to be extended; *(Firma, Absatzmarkt)* to expand; *(Produktion)* to increase; *(Vollmachten)* to be extended; *(zahlenmäßig)* to increase; *(sich verstärken)* to increase; *(Pupille, Gefäße)* to dilate; *(Organ)* to become enlarged ◆ **wir wollen uns ~** *(inf)* we want to move to a bigger place.
[3] *vi (Lupe, Brille)* to magnify; *(Mensch)* to do enlarging.
Vergrößerung *f* **(a)** *siehe vb* extension; increase; enlargement; expansion; magnification ◆ **in 1.000facher ~** magnified 1,000 times. **(b)** *(von Pupille, Gefäß)* dilation; *(von Organ)* enlargement. **(c)** *(vergrößertes Bild)* enlargement.
Vergrößerungs-: ~apparat *m* enlarger; **v~fähig** *adj Gebäude* extendable; *Firma, Absatzmarkt* expandable, able to expand; *Bekanntenkreis* able to be enlarged; *Kapital, Produktion* able to be increased; **~glas** *nt* magnifying glass.
vergucken* *vr (inf)* to see wrong *(inf)* ◆ **da hab ich mich verguckt** I didn't see it properly; **sich in jdn/etw ~** to fall for sb/sth *(inf)*.
vergülden* *vt (poet) siehe* **vergolden.**
vergünstigen* [1] *vt Lage* to improve;
[2] *vr (Lage)* to improve; *(Preise)* to come down.
vergünstigt *adj Lage* improved; *Preis* reduced ◆ **etw ~ kaufen** to buy sth at a reduced price.
Vergünstigung *f (Vorteil)* privilege; *(Preisermäßigung)* reduction ◆ **besondere ~en für Rentner** special rates for pensioners.
vergüten* *vt* **(a) jdm etw ~** *Unkosten* to reimburse sb for sth; *Preis* to refund sb sth; *Verlust, Schaden* to compensate sb for sth; *Arbeit, Leistung* to pay *or* recompense *(form)* sb for sth. **(b)** *(verbessern) Stahl* to temper; *Linse* to coat.
Vergütung *f siehe vt* **(a)** reimbursement; refunding; compensation; payment, recompense. **(b)** tempering; coating.
verh. *abbr of* **verheiratet.**
verhackstücken* *vt (inf) (kritisieren)* to tear apart, to rip to pieces *(inf)*; *Musikstück* to murder *(inf)*.
verhaften* *vt* to arrest ◆ **unschuldig verhaftet werden** to be arrested and later proved innocent; **Sie sind verhaftet!** you are under arrest!
verhaftet *adj (geh)* **einer Sache** *(dat)* *or* **mit etw ~ sein** to be (closely) attached to sth; **einem Irrtum ~ sein** to be under a misapprehension.
Verhaftete(r) *mf decl as adj* person under arrest ◆ **der ~ wurde abgeführt** the arrested man was taken away; **die zehn ~n** the ten people under arrest.
Verhaftung *f* arrest.
Verhaftungswelle *f* wave of arrests.
verhageln* *vi aux sein* to be damaged by hail ◆ **er sieht verhagelt aus** *(inf)* he looks rather the worse for wear.

➤ SPRACHE AKTIV: **Vergleich** → 32.1, 32.3, 53.5 **vergleichbar** → 32.5 **vergleichen** → 32.1, 32.3, 32.4, 32.5, 53.5 **Vergnügen** → 52.1

verhallen* *vi aux sein* (*Geräusch etc*) to die away ◆ **ihr Ruf/ihre Warnung verhallte ungehört** (*fig*) her call/her warning went unheard *or* unheeded.

verhalten[1]* *irreg* [1] *vt* (*geh: zurückhalten, unterdrücken*) *Atem* to hold; *Tränen, Urin* to hold back; *seine Schritte* to curb; *Zorn* to restrain; *Lachen* to contain; *Schmerz* to control.
[2] *vi* to stop ◆ **im Laufen/Sprechen ~** to stop running/speaking.
[3] *vr* **(a)** (*sich benehmen: Mensch, Maschine, Preise etc*) to behave; (*handeln*) to act ◆ **wie ~ Sie sich dazu?** what is your attitude to that?; **sich ruhig ~** to keep quiet; (*sich nicht bewegen*) to keep still; **sich rechtswidrig ~** to commit an offence; **wie man sich bei Hof verhält** how one conducts oneself at court.
(b) (*Sachen, Marktlage*) to be; (*Chem*) to react ◆ **wie verhält sich die Sache?** how do things stand?; **2 verhält sich zu 4 wie 1 zu 2** 2 is to 4 as 1 is to 2.
[4] *vr impers* **wie verhält es sich damit?** (*wie ist die Lage?*) how do things stand?; (*wie wird das gehandhabt?*) how do you go about it?; **damit verhält es sich anders** the situation is different; **mit den anderen verhält es sich genauso** the others feel exactly the same; **wenn sich das so verhält, ...** if that is the case ...

verhalten[2] [1] *adj* restrained; *Stimme* muted; *Atem* bated; *Wut* suppressed; *Tempo, Schritte, Rhythmus* measured.
[2] *adv sprechen* in a restrained manner; *kritisieren, sich äußern, lachen, weinen* with restraint; *laufen* at a measured pace.

Verhalten *nt* **-s,** *no pl* (*Benehmen*) behaviour; (*Vorgehen*) conduct; (*Chem*) reaction ◆ **falsches Parken ist rechtswidriges ~** unauthorized parking is an offence; **faires ~** fair conduct.

Verhaltenheit *f* restraint ◆ **die ~ des Rhythmus** the measured rhythm.

Verhaltens-: ~forscher *m* behavioural scientist; **~forschung** *f* behavioural research; **v~gestört** *adj* disturbed; **~maßregel** *f* rule of conduct; **~muster** *nt* behaviour pattern; **~psychologie** *f* behaviourism; **~störung** *f* behavioural disturbance; **~weise** *f* behaviour.

Verhältnis *nt* **(a)** (*Proportion*) proportion; (*Math, Mischungs~*) ratio ◆ **im ~ zu** in relation *or* proportion to; **im ~ zu früher** (*verglichen mit*) in comparison with earlier times; **in einem/keinem ~ zu etw stehen** to be in/out of all proportion *or* to bear no relation to sth; **das ist im ~ wenig** (*im Vergleich mit anderem*) this is proportionately very little; (*relativ wenig*) that is comparatively *or* relatively little.
(b) (*Beziehung*) relationship (*mit jdm/etw* with sb/to sth); relations *pl* (*zu* with); (*zwischen Ländern, innerhalb einer Gruppe*) relations *pl* (*zu* with); (*Einstellung*) attitude (*zu* to) ◆ **ein freundschaftliches ~ zu jdm haben, mit jdm in freundschaftlichem ~ stehen** to be on friendly terms with sb; **zu jdm/etw kein ~ finden können** not to be able to relate to sb/sth.
(c) (*Liebes~*) affair; (*inf*) (*Geliebte*) lady-friend (*inf*); (*Geliebter*) friend ◆ **ein ~ mit jdm haben** to have an affair with sb.
(d) ~se *pl* (*Umstände, Bedingungen*) conditions *pl*; (*finanzielle*) circumstances *pl* ◆ **unter** *or* **bei normalen ~sen** under normal circumstances; **so wie die ~se liegen ...** as things stand ...; **die akustischen ~se** the acoustics *pl*; **in ärmlichen ~sen leben/aus ärmlichen ~sen kommen** to live in poor conditions/come from a poor background; **über seine ~se leben** to live beyond one's means; **das geht über meine ~se** that is beyond my means; **ich bin für klare ~se** I want to know how we stand; **für klare ~se sorgen, klare ~se schaffen** to get things straight.

Verhältnis-: v~mäßig [1] *adj* **(a)** (*proportional*) proportional; (*esp Jur: angemessen*) proportionate, commensurate; **(b)** (*relativ*) comparative, relative; (*inf: ziemlich*) reasonable; [2] *adv* **(a)** (*proportional*) proportionally; **(b)** (*relativ, inf: ziemlich*) relatively; **~mäßigkeit** *f* **die ~mäßigkeit der Mittel** the appropriateness of the means; **~wahl** *f* proportional representation *no art*; **jdn durch ~wahl ermitteln** to elect sb by proportional representation; **eine ~wahl abhalten** to hold a proportional election; **~wahlrecht** *nt* (system of) proportional representation; **~wort** *nt* preposition.

verhandeln* [1] *vt* **(a)** to negotiate. **(b)** (*Jur*) *Fall* to hear.
[2] *vi* **(a)** to negotiate (*über +acc* about); (*inf: diskutieren*) to argue ◆ **da gibt's doch nichts zu ~** (*inf*) there's nothing to argue about; **über den Preis läßt sich ~** (*inf*) we can discuss the price. **(b)** (*Jur*) to hear a/the case. **gegen jdn/in einem Fall ~** to hear sb's/a case.

Verhandlung *f* **(a)** negotiations *pl*; (*das Verhandeln*) negotiation ◆ **die zur ~ stehende Frage** the question under negotiation; **mit jdm in ~(en) stehen** to be negotiating with sb, to be engaged in negotiations with sb; **(mit jdm) in ~(en) treten** to enter into negotiations (with sb); **~en führen** to negotiate; **ich lasse mich auf keine ~(en) ein** (*inf*) I don't propose to enter into any long debates.
(b) (*Jur*) hearing; (*Straf~*) trial.

Verhandlungs-: ~basis *f* basis for negotiation(s); **~basis DM 2.500** (price) DM 2,500 or near offer; **v~bereit** *adj* ready *or* prepared to negotiate; **~bereitschaft** *f* readiness to negotiate; **die mangelnde ~bereitschaft der Regierung** the government's reluctance to negotiate; **v~fähig** *adj* (*Jur*) able to stand trial; **~fähigkeit** *f* (*Jur*) ability to stand trial; **~führer** *m* chief negotiator; **~grundlage** *f* basis for negotiation(s); **~partner** *m* negotiating party; **~tisch** *m* negotiating table; **v~unfähig** *adj* (*Jur*) unable to stand trial; **~unfähigkeit** *f* (*Jur*) inability to stand trial.

verhangen *adj* overcast.

verhängen* *vt* **(a)** *Embargo, Strafe, Hausarrest etc* to impose (*über +acc* on); *Ausnahmezustand, Notstand* to declare (*über +acc* in); (*Sport*) *Elfmeter etc* to award, to give.
(b) (*zuhängen*) to cover (*mit* with); *Kruzifix, Statue* to veil; (*an den falschen Platz hängen*) to hang up in the wrong place ◆ **mit verhängtem Zügel** *or* **verhängten Zügeln** at full speed.

Verhängnis *nt* (*schlimmes Schicksal*) undoing; (*Katastrophe*) disaster ◆ **jdm zum** *or* **jds ~ werden** to prove *or* be sb's undoing; **er entging seinem ~ nicht** he could not escape his fate.

verhängnisvoll *adj* disastrous; *Irrtum, Fehler auch, Zögern, Entschlußlosigkeit* fatal; *Tag* fateful.

verharmlosen* *vt* to play down.

verhärmt *adj Mensch, Gesicht* careworn; *Ausdruck* worried.

verharren* *vi aux haben or sein* to pause; (*in einer bestimmten Stellung*) to remain ◆ **auf einem Standpunkt/in** *or* **bei einem Entschluß ~** to adhere to a viewpoint/to a decision; **in seinem Stillschweigen ~** to maintain one's silence; (*hartnäckig*) to persist in one's silence.

verharschen* *vi aux sein* (*Schnee, Piste*) to crust.

verhärten* *vtr* (*alle Bedeutungen*) to harden ◆ **sich** *or* **sein Herz gegen jdn/etw ~** to harden one's heart against sb/sth.

Verhärtung *f* **(a)** (*Verhärten*) hardening. **(b)** (*im Gewebe*) lump, knot.

verhaspeln* *vr* (*inf*) to get into a muddle *or* tangle.

⚠ **verhaßt** *adj* hated; *Arbeit auch, Pflicht* hateful ◆ **sich ~ machen** to make oneself hated (*bei* by); **das ist ihm ~** he hates that.

verhätscheln* *vt* to spoil, to pamper.

Verhau *m* **-(e)s, -e** (*zur Absperrung*) barrier; (*Käfig*) coop; (*Bretterbude etc*) shack; (*inf: Unordnung*) mess.

verhauen* *irreg* (*inf*) [1] *vt* **(a)** (*verprügeln*) to beat up; (*zur Strafe*) to beat. **(b)** *Klassenarbeit, Prüfung etc* to muff (*inf*).
[2] *vr* **(a)** (*sich verprügeln*) to have a fight. **(b)** (*beim Schreiben etc*) to make a mistake; (*beim Tippen auch*) to hit the wrong key; (*beim Klavierspielen auch*) to play a bum note (*inf*). **(c)** (*sich irren*) to slip up (*inf*).

verheben* *vr irreg* to hurt oneself lifting something; (*fig*) to overstretch oneself.

verheddern* *vr* (*inf*) to get tangled up; (*beim Sprechen*) to get in a muddle *or* tangle.

verheeren* *vt* to devastate; (*Truppen auch*) to lay waste.

verheerend [1] *adj* **(a)** *Sturm, Folgen* devastating, disastrous; *Anblick* ghastly. **(b)** (*inf: schrecklich*) frightful, fearful, ghastly (*all inf*).
[2] *adv* (*inf: schrecklich*) frightfully (*inf*).

Verheerung *f* devastation *no pl* ◆ **~(en) anrichten** to cause devastation.

verhehlen* *vt* to conceal, to hide ◆ **jdm etw ~** to conceal *or* hide sth from sb; **ich möchte Ihnen nicht ~, daß ...** I have no wish to conceal the fact that ...

verheilen* *vi aux sein* (*Wunde*) to heal (up); (*fig*) to heal.

verheimlichen* *vt* to keep secret, to conceal (*jdm* from sb) ◆ **es läßt sich nicht ~, daß ...** it is impossible to conceal the fact that ...; **ich habe nichts zu ~** I have nothing to hide.

Verheimlichung *f* concealment; (*von Tatsache*) suppression.

verheiraten* [1] *vt* to marry (*mit, an +acc* to).
[2] *vr* to get married, to marry ◆ **sich mit jdm ~** to marry sb, to get married to sb.

verheiratet *adj* married ◆ **glücklich ~ sein** to be happily married; **mit jdm/etw** (*hum inf*) **~ sein** to be married to sb/sth.

Verheiratung *f* marriage.

verheißen* *vt irreg* to promise ◆ **jdm eine große Karriere ~** to predict a great career for sb; **seine Miene verhieß nichts Gutes** his expression did not augur well; **das verheißt schönes Wetter** that heralds good weather.

Verheißung *f* promise ◆ **das Land der ~** the Promised Land.

verheißungsvoll *adj* promising; *Anfang auch* auspicious; *Blicke* alluring ◆ **wenig ~** unpromising; **mit ~en Worten** with promises.

verheizen* *vt* to burn, to use as fuel; (*fig inf*) *Sportler* to burn out; *Minister, Untergebene* to crucify ◆ **Soldaten im Kriege ~** (*inf*) to send soldiers to the slaughter.

verhelfen* *vi irreg* **jdm zu etw ~** to help sb to get sth; **jdm zu seinem Glück ~** to help to make sb happy; **jdm zum Sieg ~** to help sb to victory.

verherrlichen* *vt Gewalt, Krieg, Taten* to glorify; *Gott* to praise; *Tugenden* to extol; (*in Gedichten*) to celebrate.

Verherrlichung *f siehe vt* glorification; praising; extolment; celebration.

verhetzen* *vt* to stir up, to incite (to violence *etc*).

Verhetzung *f* incitement, stirring up.

verheult *adj Augen, Gesicht* puffy, swollen from crying ◆ **du siehst so ~ aus** you really look as if you have been crying.

verhexen* *vt* to bewitch; (*Fee, Zauberer etc auch*) to cast a spell over; (*inf*) *Maschine etc* to put a jinx on (*inf*) ◆ **jdn in etw** (*acc*) **~** to turn sb into sth (by magic); **der verhexte Prinz** the enchanted prince; **das verhexte Schloß** the bewitched castle; **heute ist alles wie verhext** (*inf*) there's a jinx on everything today (*inf*); **das ist doch wie verhext** (*inf*) it's maddening (*inf*).

verhindern* *vt* to prevent; *Unglück auch* to avert; *Versuch, Plan* to foil, to stop ◆ **ich konnte es nicht ~, daß er die Wahrheit erfuhr** I couldn't prevent him from finding out the truth; **das läßt sich leider nicht ~** it can't be helped, unfortunately; **er war an diesem Abend (dienstlich** *or* **geschäftlich) verhindert** he was unable to come that evening (for reasons of work); **ein verhinderter Politiker** (*inf*) a would-be politician.

Verhinderung *f siehe vt* prevention; avertion; foiling, stopping ◆ **im Falle seiner ~** if he is unable to come.

verhohlen *adj* concealed, secret; *Gelächter, Schadenfreude auch, Gähnen* suppressed ◆ **kaum ~** barely concealed/suppressed.

verhöhnen* *vt* to mock, to deride.

verhohnepipeln* *vt* (*inf*) (*verspotten*) to send up (*inf*); (*zum besten haben*) to have on (*inf*).

Verhohnepipelung *f* send-up (*inf*).

⚠: Informationen zur Rechtschreibreform im Anhang

Verhöhnung *f* mocking, ridiculing; (*Bemerkung*) gibe.

verhökern* *vt* (*inf*) to get rid of (*inf*).

verholen* *vt* (*Naut*) to haul away.

verholzen* *vi aux sein* (*Bot*) to lignify.

Verhör *nt* **-(e)s, -e** questioning, interrogation; (*bei Gericht*) examination ◆ **jdn ins ~ nehmen** to question *or* interrogate sb; (*bei Gericht*) to examine sb; (*inf*) to take sb to task; **jdn einem ~ unterziehen** (*form*) to subject sb to questioning *or* interrogation/examination.

verhören* [1] *vt* to question, to interrogate; (*bei Gericht*) to examine; (*inf*) to quiz (*inf*).
[2] *vr* to mishear, to hear wrongly.

verhornt *adj Haut* horny.

verhudeln* *vt* (*inf*) to botch.

verhüllen* [1] *vt* to veil; *Haupt, Körperteil* to cover; (*fig auch*) to mask, to disguise.
[2] *vr* (*Frau*) to veil oneself; (*Berge etc*) to become veiled.

verhüllend *adj Ausdruck* euphemistic.

Verhüllung *f* **(a)** *siehe vt* veiling; covering; masking, disguising. **(b)** (*die Bedeckung*) veil; cover; mask, disguise. **(c)** (*Ausdruck*) euphemism.

verhundertfachen* *vtr* to increase a hundredfold.

verhungern* *vi aux sein* to starve, to die of starvation; (*inf: Hunger haben*) to be starving (*inf*) ◆ **er sah völlig verhungert aus** he looked half-starved; (*inf*) he looked absolutely famished (*inf*); **ich bin am V~** (*inf*) I'm starving (*inf*); **jdn ~ lassen** (*lit*) to let sb starve (to death); (*beim Spielen*) to leave sb out of the game.

Verhungernde(r) *mf decl as adj* starving person/man/woman.

Verhungerte(r) *mf decl as adj* person/man/woman *etc* who has starved to death.

verhunzen* *vt* (*inf*) to ruin; *Sprache, Lied auch* to murder.

verhurt *adj* (*pej*) whorish; *Mann* loose-living.

verhuscht *adj* (*inf*) timid.

verhüten* *vt* to prevent ◆ **das verhüte Gott!** God forbid!; **möge Gott ~, daß ...** God forbid that ...; **~de Maßnahmen** preventive measures; (*zur Empfängnisverhütung*) precautions.

Verhüterli *nt* **-(s), -** (*Sw: Verhütungsmittel*) contraceptive; (*hum inf: Kondom*) johnny (*inf*), rubber (*inf*).

verhütten *vt* to smelt.

Verhüttung *f* smelting.

Verhütung *f* prevention; (*Empfängnis~*) contraception.

Verhütungsmittel *nt* contraceptive.

verhutzelt *adj Gesicht, Männlein* wizened; *Haut auch* wrinkled; *Obst* shrivelled.

Verifikation [verifika'tsio:n] *f* verification.

verifizierbar [verifi'tsi:ɐba:ɐ] *adj* verifiable.

verifizieren* [verifi'tsi:rən] *vt* to verify.

ver|innerlichen* *vt* to internalize; *jdn* to spiritualize.

ver|innerlicht *adj Wesen, Gesichtsausdruck* spiritualized.

Ver|innerlichung *f* internalization; (*von Mensch, in Literatur*) spiritualization.

ver|irren* *vr* to get lost, to lose one's way; (*fig*) to go astray; (*Tier, Kugel*) to stray ◆ **ein verirrtes Schaf** (*lit, fig*) a lost sheep.

Ver|irrung *f* losing one's way *no art*; (*fig*) aberration.

verjagen* [1] *vt* (*lit, fig*) to chase away; *trübe Gedanken, Kummer auch* to dispel.
[2] *vr* (*N Ger*) to get out of the way.

verjähren* *vi aux sein* to come under the statute of limitations; (*Anspruch*) to be in lapse ◆ **verjährtes Verbrechen** statute-barred crime; **das ist schon längst verjährt** (*inf*) that's all over and done with.

Verjährung *f* limitation; (*von Anspruch*) lapse.

Verjährungsfrist *f* limitation period.

verjazzen* [fɛɐ'dʒɛsn] *vt* to jazz up.

verjubeln* *vt* (*inf*) *Geld* to blow (*inf*).

verjüngen* [1] *vt* to rejuvenate; (*jünger aussehen lassen*) to make look younger; *Baumbestand* to regenerate ◆ **eine Mannschaft/das Personal ~** to build up a younger team/staff; **die neue Stelle hat ihn um Jahre verjüngt** the new job gave him a new lease of life; **er kam (um Jahre) verjüngt aus dem Urlaub zurück** he came back from holiday looking years younger.
[2] *vr* **(a)** to become younger; (*Haut, Erscheinung*) to become rejuvenated; (*jünger aussehen*) to look younger ◆ **du hast dich verjüngt** (*inf*) you look (much) younger. **(b)** (*dünner werden*) to taper; (*Tunnel, Rohr*) to narrow.

Verjüngung *f* **(a)** rejuvenation; (*von Baumbestand*) regeneration. **(b)** *siehe vr (b)* tapering; narrowing.

Verjüngungskur *f* rejuvenation cure.

verjuxen* *vr* (*inf*) *Geld* to blow (*inf*).

verkabeln *vt* (*Telec*) to link up to the cable network.

Verkabelung *f* (*Telec*) linking up to the cable network.

verkalken* *vi aux sein* (*Arterien*) to become hardened; (*Gewebe*) to calcify; (*Kessel, Wasserleitung etc*) to fur up, to become furred; (*inf: Mensch*) to become senile.

verkalkt *adj* (*inf*) senile.

verkalkulieren* *vr* to miscalculate.

Verkalkung *f siehe vi* hardening; calcification; furring; (*inf*) senility.

verkälten* *vr* (*dial*) *siehe* **erkälten**.

verkannt [1] *ptp of* **verkennen**.
[2] *adj* unrecognized.

verkappt *adj attr* hidden; *Lungenentzündung* undiagnosed ◆ **~er Nebensatz** (*Gram*) *subordinate clause without an introductory word*.

verkapseln* *vr* (*Med*) (*Bakterien*) to become encapsulated; (*Parasit*) to become encysted.

Verkapselung *f* (*Med*) encapsulation; encystment.

verkarsten* *vi aux sein* to develop to karst (*spec*).

Verkarstung *f* karst development (*spec*).

verkatert *adj* (*inf*) hung-over *usu pred* (*inf*) ◆ **einen ~en Eindruck machen** to look hung-over (*inf*).

Verkauf *m* **-(e)s, Verkäufe (a)** sale; (*das Verkaufen*) selling ◆ **zum ~ stehen** to be up for sale; **beim ~ des Hauses** when selling the house; *siehe* **Straße**. **(b)** (*Abteilung*) sales *sing, no art*.

verkaufen* [1] *vti* (*lit, fig*) to sell (*für, um* for) ◆ **„zu ~"** "for sale"; **jdm etw** *or* **etw an jdn ~** to sell sb sth, to sell sth to sb; **sie haben ihr Leben so teuer wie möglich verkauft** they sold their lives as dearly as possible; **er würde sogar seine Großmutter ~** he'd even sell his own grandmother; *siehe* **Straße, verraten, dumm**.
[2] *vr* **(a)** (*Ware*) to sell; (*Mensch*) to sell oneself ◆ **er hat sich ganz und gar an die Partei verkauft** he is committed body and soul to the party.
(b) (*einen schlechten Kauf machen*) to make a bad buy ◆ **damit habe ich mich verkauft** that was a bad buy.
(c) (*fig: sich anpreisen*) to sell oneself.

Verkäufer(in *f*) *m* **-s, -** seller; (*in Geschäft*) sales *or* shop assistant, salesperson; (*im Außendienst*) salesman/saleswoman/salesperson; (*Jur: von Grundbesitz etc*) vendor.

verkäuflich *adj* sal(e)able, marketable; (*zu verkaufen*) for sale ◆ **leicht** *or* **gut/schwer ~** easy/hard to sell.

Verkäuflichkeit *f, no pl* sal(e)ability, marketability.

Verkaufs- *in cpds* sales; **~abteilung** *f* sales department; **~automat** *m* vending machine; **~bedingungen** *pl* conditions of sale *pl*; **~berater** *m* sales consultant; **~büro** *nt* sales office; **~förderung** *f* sales promotion; (*Abteilung*) sales promotion department; **~genie** *nt* **ein ~genie sein** to be a genius at selling things; **~leiter** *m* sales manager; **v~offen** *adj* open for business; **v~offener Samstag** *Saturday on which the shops are open all day*; **~personal** *nt* sales personnel *or* staff; **~preis** *m* retail price; **~schlager** *m* big seller.

Verkehr *m* **-(e)s,** *no pl* **(a)** traffic; (*Beförderung, Verkehrsmittel*) transport, transportation (*US*) ◆ **für den ~ freigeben, dem ~ übergeben** *Straße etc* to open to traffic; *Transportmittel* to bring into service; **den ~ regeln** to regulate the (flow of) traffic; **aus dem ~ ziehen** to withdraw from service.
(b) (*Verbindung*) contact, communication; (*Umgang*) company; (*Geschlechts~*) intercourse ◆ **in brieflichem ~ stehen** to correspond; **in seinem ~ mit Menschen** in his dealings with people; **den ~ mit jdm pflegen** (*form*) to associate with sb; **den ~ mit jdm abbrechen** to break off relations *or* contact with sb.
(c) (*Geschäfts~, Handels~*) trade; (*Umsätze, Zahlungs~*) business; (*Post~*) service; (*Umlauf*) circulation ◆ **etw in (den) ~ bringen/aus dem ~ ziehen** to put sth into/withdraw sth from circulation; **jdn aus dem ~ ziehen** (*sl*) (*töten*) to do sb in (*sl*); (*ins Gefängnis werfen*) to put sb in jug (*sl*).

verkehren* [1] *vi* **(a)** *aux haben or sein* (*fahren*) to run; (*Flugzeug*) to fly ◆ **der Bus/das Flugzeug verkehrt regelmäßig zwischen A und B** the bus runs *or* goes *or* operates regularly/the plane goes *or* operates regularly between A and B.
(b) (*Gast sein, Kontakt pflegen*) **bei jdm ~** to frequent sb's house, to visit sb (regularly); **mit jdm ~** to associate with sb; **in einem Lokal ~** to frequent a pub; **in Künstlerkreisen ~** to move in artistic circles, to mix with artists; **mit jdm brieflich/schriftlich ~** (*form*) to correspond with sb; **mit jdm (geschlechtlich) ~** to have (sexual) intercourse with sb.
[2] *vt* to turn (*in +acc* into) ◆ **etw ins Gegenteil ~** to reverse sth.
[3] *vr* to turn (*in +acc* into) ◆ **sich ins Gegenteil ~** to become reversed.

Verkehrs- *in cpds* traffic; **~abwicklung** *f* traffic handling; **~ader** *f* artery, arterial road; **~ampel** *f* traffic lights *pl*; *siehe* **Ampel**; **~amt** *nt* divisional railway office; (*~büro*) tourist information office; **v~arm** *adj Zeit, Straße* quiet; **ein v~armes Gebiet** an area with little traffic; **~aufkommen** *nt* volume of traffic; **~behinderung** *f* (*Jur*) obstruction (of traffic); **v~beruhigt** *adj* traffic-calmed; **~beruhigung** *f* traffic calming; **~betriebe** *pl* transport services *pl*; **~büro** *nt* tourist information office; **~chaos** *nt* chaos on the roads; **~delikt** *nt* traffic offence; **~dichte** *f* volume of traffic, traffic density; **~durchsage** *f* traffic announcement; **~erziehung** *f* road safety training; **~flughafen** *m* (commercial) airport; **~flugzeug** *nt* commercial aircraft; **~funk** *m* radio traffic service; **v~gefährdend** *adj* dangerous; **~gefährdung** *f* (*Jur: v~widriges Fahren*) dangerous driving; **eine ~gefährdung darstellen** to be a hazard to other traffic; **v~günstig** *adj Lage* convenient; *Ort, Viertel* conveniently situated; **~hindernis** *nt* (traffic) obstruction; **ein ~hindernis sein** to cause an obstruction; **~hinweis** *m siehe* **~durchsage**; **~insel** *f* traffic island; **~knotenpunkt** *m* traffic junction; **~kontrolle** *f* traffic check; **bei jdm eine ~kontrolle machen** (*Polizei*) to stop sb; **verstärkte ~kontrollen machen** to increase traffic checks; **~lärm** *m* traffic noise; **~meldung** *f* traffic announcement; **~meldungen** traffic news *sing*; **~minister** *m* minister of transport; **~ministerium** *nt* ministry of transport, department of transportation (*US*); **~mittel** *nt* means of transport *sing*; **öffentliche/private ~mittel** public/private transport; **~netz** *nt* traffic network; **~opfer** *nt* road casualty; **~ordnung** *f siehe* **Straßenverkehrsordnung**; **~planung** *f* traffic engineering; **~polizei** *f* traffic police *pl*; **~polizist** *m* traffic policeman; **~regel** *f* traffic regulation; **~regelung** *f* traffic control; **v~reich** *adj Straße, Gegend* busy; **v~reiche Zeit** peak (traffic) time; **~rowdy, ~rüpel** *m* road-hog; **~schild** *nt* road sign; **~schutzmann** *m siehe* **~polizist**; **v~schwach** *adj Zeit* off-peak; *Gebiet* with little traffic; **die Nachmittagsstunden sind sehr v~schwach** there is very light traffic in the afternoons; **v~sicher** *adj Fahrzeug* roadworthy; *Straße, Brücke* safe (for traffic); **~sicherheit** *f siehe adj* roadworthiness; safety; **~sprache** *f* lingua franca; **~stau** *m*, **~stauung** *f* traffic jam; **~stockung** *f* traffic hold-up; **~straße** *f* road open to traffic; **~strom** *m* flow of traffic; **~sünder** *m* (*inf*) traffic offender; **~sünderkartei** *f* (*inf*) *central index of road traffic offenders*; **~teilnehmer** *m* road-user; **~tote(r)** *mf* road casualty; **die Zahl der ~toten** the number of deaths on the road; **v~tüchtig** *adj Fahrzeug* roadworthy; *Mensch* fit to drive; **~unfall** *m* road accident; (*hum inf*) accident; **~unternehmen** *nt* transport company; **~unterricht** *m* traffic instruction; **v~untüchtig** *adj Fahrzeug* unroadworthy; *Mensch* unfit to drive; **~verbindung** *f* link; (*Anschluß*) connection; **~verbund** *m* interconnecting transport system; **~verein** *m local organization concerned with upkeep of tourist attractions, facilities etc*; **~verhältnisse** *pl* traffic situation *sing*; (*Straßenzustand*) road conditions *pl*; **~verstoß** *m* motoring offence, traffic violation (*US*); **~vertrag** *m traffic treaty between the two Germanys*; **~volumen** *nt* volume of traffic; **~vorschrift** *f* (road) traffic regulation; **~wacht** *f* traffic patrol; **~weg** *m* highway; **~wert** *m* (*Fin*) current market value; **~wesen** *nt* transport and communications *no art*; **v~widrig** *adj* contrary to road traffic regulations; **sich v~widrig verhalten** to break the road traffic regulations; **~zählung** *f* traffic census; **~zeichen** *nt* road sign; **~zentralkartei** *f*, **~zentralregister** *nt central index of traffic offenders*.

verkehrt [1] *ptp of* **verkehren**.

[2] *adj* wrong; *Vorstellung auch, Welt* topsy-turvy.

[3] *adv* wrongly ◆ **etw ~ (herum) anhaben** (*linke Seite nach außen*) to have sth on inside out; (*vorne nach hinten*) to have sth on back to front; **etw ~ halten** to hold sth wrongly; (*falsch herum*) to hold sth the wrong way round; (*oben nach unten*) to hold sth upside down; **die Möbel alle ~ stellen** (*an den falschen Platz*) to put all the furniture in the wrong place; **er ist ~ herum** (*inf: homosexuell*) he's bent (*inf*); **das ist gar nicht (so) ~** (*inf*) that can't be bad (*inf*); **der ist gar nicht (so) ~** (*inf*) he's not such a bad sort; **das V~e** the wrong thing; **das V~este, was du tun könntest** the worst thing you could do; **der/die V~e** the wrong person; **eines Tages wirst du an den V~en geraten** one day you'll get your fingers burned; *siehe* **Kaffee**[1], **Adresse**.

Verkehrung *f* reversal; (*von Rollen auch*) switching ◆ **eine ~ ins Gegenteil** a complete reversal.

verkeilen* [1] *vt* **(a)** (*festmachen*) to wedge tight. **(b)** (*inf: verprügeln*) to thrash.

[2] *vr* to become wedged together.

verkennen* *vt irreg Lage, jdn etc* to misjudge; (*unterschätzen auch*) to underestimate ◆ **ein Dichter, der zeit seines Lebens verkannt wurde** a poet who remained unrecognized in his lifetime; **ich will nicht ~, daß** ... I would not deny that ...; **es ist nicht zu ~, daß** ... it is undeniable *or* cannot be denied that ...; **seine schlechte Laune/seine Absicht war nicht zu ~** his bad temper/his intention was unmistakable; *siehe* **verkannt**.

Verkennung *f siehe vt* misjudgement; underestimation; (*von Genie, Künstler*) failure to appreciate (*jds* sb) ◆ **in ~ der wahren Sachlage** ... misjudging the real situation ...

verketten* [1] *vt* (*lit*) to chain (up); *Tür, Kiste* to put chains/a chain on; (*fig*) to link.

[2] *vr* to become interlinked, to become bound up together ◆ **verkettet sein** (*fig*) to be interlinked *or* bound up (together).

Verkettung *f* (*das Verketten*) chaining; (*Ketten*) chains *pl*; (*fig*) interconnection.

verketzern* *vt* to denounce.

verkitschen* *vt* (*inf*) **(a)** *Gemälde, Literatur* to make kitschy; *Lied* to sentimentalize. **(b)** (*verkaufen*) to flog (*Brit inf*), to sell.

verkitten* *vt* to cement; *Fenster* to put putty round.

verklagen* *vt* to sue (*wegen* for), to take proceedings against (*wegen* for) ◆ **jdn auf etw** (*acc*) **~** to take sb to court for sth; **die verklagte Partei, der/die Verklagte** the defendant.

verklammern* [1] *vt* to staple together; (*Med*) *Wunde* to apply clips to; (*Tech*) *Bauteile* to brace, to put braces round; (*fig*) to link.

[2] *vr* (*Menschen*) to embrace; (*Hände*) to interlock.

Verklammerung *f siehe vb* **(a)** (*das Verklammern*) stapling; applying of clips (*gen* to); bracing; linking; embracing; interlocking. **(b)** (*die Klammern*) staples *pl*; clips *pl*; braces *pl*; links *pl*; embrace; clasp.

verklappen *vt Abfallstoffe* to dump.

Verklappung *f* (*von Abfallstoffen*) dumping.

verklaren *vt* (*inf*) **jdm etw ~** to spell sth out for sb.

verklären* [1] *vt* to transfigure.

[2] *vr* to become transfigured.

verklärt *adj* transfigured.

Verklarung *f* (*Naut*) ship's protest.

Verklärung *f* transfiguration.

verklatschen* *vt* (*inf*) **(a)** (*verpetzen*) to tell on (*inf*). **(b)** *Zeit* to spend chatting.

verklauseln* (*rare*), **verklausulieren*** *vt Vertrag* to hedge in *or* around with (restrictive) clauses ◆ **der Vertrag ist zu verklausuliert** the contract has too many qualifying clauses.

verkleben* [1] *vt* (*zusammenkleben*) to stick together; (*zukleben*) to cover (*mit* with); *Tapeten* to stick; *Haare, Verband* to make sticky; *Wunde* (*mit Pflaster*) to put a plaster on; (*verbrauchen*) to use up.

[2] *vi aux sein* (*Wunde, Eileiter*) to close; (*Augen*) to get gummed up; (*Mehl, Briefmarken, Bonbons*) to stick together; (*Haare*) to become matted ◆ **mit etw ~** to stick to sth.

verklebt *adj Verband, Wunde* sticky; *Augen* gummed up; *Haare* matted; *Eileiter* blocked.

verkleckern* *vt* (*inf*) to spill; (*fig*) *Zeit, Energie, Geld* to waste.

verkleiden* [1] *vt* **(a)** to disguise; (*kostümieren*) to dress up, to put into fancy dress; (*fig*) *Ideen, Absicht* to disguise, to mask ◆ **alle waren verkleidet** everyone was dressed up *or* was in fancy dress.

(b) (*verschalen*) *Wand, Schacht, Tunnel* to line; (*vertäfeln*) to panel; (*bedecken*) to cover; (*ausschlagen*) *Kiste etc* to line; (*verdecken*) *Heizkörper* to cover, to mask.

[2] *vr* to disguise oneself; (*sich kostümieren*) to dress (oneself) up ◆ **muß man sich ~?** do you have to wear fancy dress?

Verkleidung *f* **(a)** (*das Verkleiden von Menschen*) disguising; (*Kostümierung*) dressing up, putting into fancy dress; (*Kleidung*) disguise; (*Kostüm*) fancy dress. **(b)** *siehe vt (b)* (*das Verkleiden, Material*) lining; panelling; covering; masking.

verkleinern* [1] *vt* to reduce; *Raum, Gebiet, Firma,* (*Lupe, Brille*) to make smaller; *Fotografie* to reduce (in size); *Maßstab* to scale down; *Abstand* to decrease; *Not, Probleme, Schuld* to minimize; *jds Leistungen, Verdienste* to belittle; *Wort* to form the diminutive of.

[2] *vr* to be reduced; (*Raum, Gebiet, Firma*) to become smaller; (*Maßstab*) to be scaled down; (*Abstand*) to decrease; (*Not, Probleme, Schuld*) to become less ◆ **durch den großen Schrank verkleinert sich das Zimmer** the big cupboard makes the room (seem) smaller.

[3] *vi* (*Linse etc*) to make everything seem smaller.

Verkleinerung *f* **(a)** *siehe vt* reduction; making smaller; reduction (in size); scaling down; decreasing; minimizing; belittling; formation of the diminutive.

(b) *siehe vr* reduction; becoming smaller; scaling down; decreasing; lessening.

(c) (*Bild*) reduced size reproduction; (*Foto*) reduction; (*Wort*) diminutive (form); (*Mus*) diminution.

Verkleinerungsform *f* diminutive form.

verkleistern* *vt* (*zusammenkleben*) to stick together; (*zukleben*) to cover; (*inf*) (*mit Kleister beschmieren*) to get glue on; (*fig: vertuschen*) to cover up.

verklemmen* *vr* to get *or* become stuck.

verklemmt *adj* (*inf*) *Mensch* inhibited; *Beine* crossed.

verklickern* *vt* (*inf*) **jdm etw ~** to make sth clear to sb.

verklingen* *vi irreg aux sein* to die *or* fade away; (*fig: Begeisterung, Interesse*) to fade.

verklopfen*, **verkloppen*** *vt* (*inf*) **(a) jdn ~** to give sb what-for (*inf*). **(b)** (*verkaufen*) to flog (*Brit inf*), to sell.

verklumpen* *vi aux sein* to get lumpy.

verknacken* *vt* (*inf*) **jdn zu zwei Jahren/einer Geldstrafe ~** to do sb for (*inf*) *or* give sb two years/stick a fine on sb (*inf*); **verknackt werden** to be done (*inf*).

verknacksen* *vt* **(sich** *dat***) den Knöchel** *or* **Fuß ~** to twist one's ankle.

verknallen* (*inf*) [1] *vr* **sich (in jdn) ~** to fall for sb (*inf*); **ich war damals unheimlich (in ihn) verknallt** I was head over heels in love (with him) then.

[2] *vt Feuerwerkskörper* to let off; *Munition* to use up; *Geld* (*mit Feuerwerkskörpern*) to waste on fireworks.

verknappen* [1] *vt* to cut back; *Rationen* to cut down (on).

[2] *vr* to run short.

verknautschen* [1] *vt* to crush, to crumple.

[2] *vir* (*vi: aux sein*) to crease.

verkneifen* *vr irreg* (*inf*) **sich** (*dat*) **etw ~** to stop oneself (from) saying/doing *etc* sth; *Schmerzen* to hide sth; *Lächeln* to keep back sth; *Bemerkung* to bite back sth; **ich konnte mir das Lachen nicht ~** I couldn't help laughing; **das kann ich mir ~** I can manage without that (*iro*).

verkneten* *vt* to knead together.

verkniffen [1] *ptp of* **verkneifen**.

[2] *adj Gesicht, Miene* (*angestrengt*) strained; (*verbittert*) pinched; *Ansichten* narrow-minded ◆ **etw ~ sehen** to take a narrow view of sth.

verknöchern* *vi aux sein* (*lit, fig*) to ossify ◆ **verknöchert** (*fig*) ossified, fossilized.

verknorpeln* *vi aux sein* to become cartilaginous.

verknoten* [1] *vt* to tie, to knot; (*inf*) *Paket* to tie up.

[2] *vr* to become knotted.

verknüpfen* *vt* **(a)** (*verknoten*) to knot *or* tie (together); (*Comput*) to integrate.

(b) (*fig*) to combine; (*in Zusammenhang bringen*) to link, to connect; *Gedanken, Geschehnisse* to associate ◆ **mit diesem Ort sind für mich schöne Erinnerungen verknüpft** this place has happy memories for me; **so ein Umzug ist immer mit großen Ausgaben verknüpft** moving house always involves a lot of expense.

Verknüpfung *f siehe vt* knotting *or* tying (together); integration; combining, combination; linking, connecting; association.

verknusen* *vt* (*inf*) **ich kann ihn/das nicht ~** I can't stick him/that (*inf*).

verkochen* *vti* (*vi: aux sein*) (*Flüssigkeit*) to boil away; (*Kartoffeln, Gemüse*) to overboil.

verkohlen* [1] *vi aux sein* to char, to become charred; (*Braten*) to burn to a cinder.

[2] *vt* **(a)** *Holz* to char; (*Tech*) to carbonize. **(b)** (*inf*) **jdn ~** to have sb on (*inf*).

Verkohlung *f* carbonization.

verkoken* *vt* to carbonize.
Verkokung *f* carbonization.
verkommen¹* *vi irreg aux sein* **(a)** *(Mensch)* to go to the dogs, to go to pieces; *(moralisch)* to become dissolute, to go to the bad; *(Kind)* to run wild ♦ **zu etw ~** to degenerate into sth.
(b) *(Gebäude, Auto)* to become dilapidated, to fall to pieces; *(Stadt)* to become run-down; *(Gelände, Anlage etc)* to run wild.
(c) *(nicht genutzt werden: Lebensmittel, Begabung, Fähigkeiten etc)* to go to waste; *(verderben: Lebensmittel)* to go bad.
(d) *(Sw inf)* to get involved in a booze-up *(inf)*.
verkommen² *adj Mensch* depraved; *Frau auch* abandoned; *Auto, Gebäude* dilapidated; *Garten* wild ♦ **der sprachlich ~e Gewaltbegriff** the linguistically debased concept of violence.
Verkommenheit *f, no pl siehe adj* depravity; dilapidation, dilapidated state; wildness.
verkonsumieren* *vt (inf)* to get through; *Essen, Getränke auch* to consume.
verkoppeln* *vt* to connect, to couple; *Grundbesitz* to combine, to pool; *(Space)* to link (up).
Verkopp(e)lung *f siehe vt* connection, coupling; pooling; link-up.
verkorken* *vt* to cork (up).
verkorksen* *vt (inf)* to make a mess *or* cock-up *(Brit sl)* of, to mess up *(inf)*; *Kind* to screw up *(sl)* ♦ **sich** *(dat)* **den Magen ~** to upset one's stomach; **jdm etw ~** to mess sth up for sb *(inf)*, to wreck sth for sb.
verkorkst *adj (inf)* ruined; *Magen* upset; *Kind, Mensch* screwed up *(sl)* ♦ **eine völlig ~e Sache** a real mess.
verkörpern* *vt* to embody, to personify; *(Theat)* to play (the part of), to portray ♦ **jener Staat verkörperte die Idee der Demokratie** that state was the embodiment of the democratic idea.
Verkörperung *f* embodiment; *(Mensch auch)* personification; *(Theat)* playing, portrayal.
verkosten* *vt* to taste.
verköstigen* *vt* to feed.
Verköstigung *f* feeding.
verkrachen* *vr (inf)* **sich (mit jdm) ~** to fall out (with sb).
verkracht *adj (inf) Leben* ruined; *Typ, Mensch* dead-beat *(inf)*; *(zerstritten) Nachbarn, Freunde* who have fallen out with each other; *siehe* **Existenz.**
verkraften* *vt* to cope with; *(seelisch) Schock, jds Tod etc auch* to take; *(finanziell)* to afford, to manage; *(inf: essen, trinken können)* to manage ♦ **Straßen, die das Verkehrsvolumen nicht ~** streets which can't cope with the volume of traffic.
verkrallen* *vr (Katze)* to dig *or* sink its claws in; *(Hände)* to clench up ♦ **sich in etw** *(dat)* **~** *(Katze)* to dig *or* sink its claws into sth; *(Mensch)* to dig *or* sink one's fingers into sth; **sich in ein Problem ~** *(fig)* to get stuck into a problem.
verkramen* *vt (inf)* to mislay.
verkrampfen* *vr* to become cramped; *(Hände)* to clench up; *(Mensch)* to go tense, to tense up ♦ **verkrampft** *(fig)* tense.
Verkrampfung *f (lit, fig)* tenseness, tension ♦ **seelische ~** mental tension.
verkriechen* *vr irreg* to creep away; *(fig)* to hide (oneself away) ♦ **sich unter den** *or* **dem Tisch ~** to crawl *or* creep under the table; **sich ins Bett ~** *(inf)* to run off to bed, to retreat to one's bed; **vor ihm brauchst du dich nicht zu ~** *(inf)* you don't have to worry about him; **am liebsten hätte ich mich vor Scham verkrochen** I wanted the ground to open up and swallow me.
verkrümeln* [1] *vr (inf)* to disappear.
[2] *vt* to crumble.
verkrümmen* [1] *vt* to bend.
[2] *vr* to bend; *(Rückgrat)* to become curved; *(Holz)* to warp; *(Baum, Pflanze)* to grow crooked.
verkrümmt *adj* bent; *Wirbelsäule* curved; *Finger, Knochen, Bäume* crooked; *Holz* warped.
Verkrümmung *f* bend *(gen* in), distortion *(esp Tech)*; *(von Holz)* warp; *(von Fingern, Knochen, Bäumen)* crookedness *no pl* ♦ **~ der Wirbelsäule** curvature of the spine; **~ der Hornhaut** *(nach innen)* incurvation of the cornea; *(nach außen)* excurvation of the cornea.
verkrumpeln* *(dial)* [1] *vt* to crumple up.
[2] *vi aux sein* to get crumpled up.
verkrüppeln* [1] *vt* to cripple.
[2] *vi aux sein* to become crippled; *(Zehen, Füße)* to become deformed; *(Baum etc)* to grow stunted.
Verkrüpp(e)lung *f siehe vb* crippling; deformity; stunted growth.
verkrusten* *vir (vi: aux sein)* to become encrusted.
verkrustet *adj Wunde* scabby; *Strukturen, Ansichten* decrepit.
Verkrustung *f (von Wunde)* scab formation; *(von Strukturen etc)* decrepitude; *(von Partei, Organisation etc)* archaic *or* fossilized structure.
verkühlen* *vr (inf)* to catch a cold, to get a chill ♦ **sich** *(dat)* **die Nieren ~** to get a chill on the kidneys.
Verkühlung *f (inf)* chill ♦ **~ der Blase** chill on the bladder.
verkümmeln* *vt (inf)* to sell off, to flog *(Brit inf)*.
verkümmern* *vi aux sein (Glied, Organ)* to atrophy; *(ein gehen: Pflanze)* to die; *(Talent)* to go to waste; *(Schönheitssinn, Interesse etc)* to wither away; *(Mensch)* to waste away ♦ **emotionell/geistig ~** to become emotionally/intellectually stunted; **wenn die natürlichen Instinkte im Menschen ~** if man's natural instincts become stunted.
Verkümmerung *f (von Organ, Muskel, Glied etc)* atrophy; *(fig) (von Talent)* wasting away, atrophy; *(von Gerechtigkeitssinn, Instinkten etc)* atrophy.

verkünden* *vt* to announce; *Urteil* to pronounce; *Evangelium* to preach; *Gesetz* to promulgate; *nichts Gutes, Unwetter etc* to forebode, to presage *(liter)*; *Frühling, neue Zeit* to herald.
Verkünder(in *f*) *m* **-s, -** ein **~ des Evangeliums** a preacher of the gospel; **der ~ einer Friedensbotschaft** a harbinger *or* herald of peace.
verkündigen* *vt* to proclaim; *(iro)* to announce; *Evangelium auch* to preach, to propagate ♦ **ich verkündige euch große Freude** *(Bibl)* I bring you tidings of great joy *(Bibl)*.
Verkündiger *m* **-s, -** *siehe* **Verkünder(in).**
Verkündigung *f* proclamation; *(von Evangelium, von christlicher Lehre auch)* preaching, propagation ♦ **Mariä ~** the Annunciation; *(Tag auch)* Lady Day.
Verkündung *f siehe vt* announcement; pronouncement; preaching; promulgation.
verkünsteln* *vr (inf)* to overdo it, to go to town *(inf)* ♦ **sich an etw** *(dat)* **~** to go to town on sth *(inf)*, to overdo sth.
verkupfern* *vt* to copper(-plate) ♦ **verkupfert** copper-plated.
verkuppeln* *vt (pej)* to pair off, to get paired off ♦ **jdn an jdn ~** *(Zuhälter)* to procure sb for sb.
Verkupp(e)lung *f* pairing off; *(durch Zuhälter)* procuring.
verkürzen* [1] *vt* to shorten; *(Art)* to foreshorten; *Strecke, Wege etc auch* to cut; *Abstand, Vorsprung* to narrow; *Zeit auch* to reduce, to cut down; *Aufenthalt* to cut short; *Lebenserwartung auch, Haltbarkeit* to reduce; *Schmerzen, Leiden* to end, to put an end to ♦ **den Spielstand ~** to narrow the gap (between the scores); **sich** *(dat)* **die Zeit ~** to pass the time, to make the time pass more quickly; **jdm die Zeit ~** to help sb pass the time; **verkürzte Arbeitszeit** shorter working hours; **verkürzter Nebensatz** *(Gram)* elliptical subordinate clause.
[2] *vr* to be shortened; *(Art)* to become foreshortened; *(Strecke, Zeit auch)* to be cut; *(Abstand)* to be narrowed; *(Muskel)* to contract; *(Haltbarkeit)* to be reduced; *(Leiden)* to be ended; *(Urlaub, Aufenthalt)* to be cut short.
Verkürzung *f* **(a)** *siehe vb* shortening; foreshortening; narrowing; reduction; cutting short; reduction; ending. **(b)** *(abgekürztes Wort)* contraction, shortened form.
Verl. *abbr of* **Verlag; Verleger.**
verlachen* *vt* to ridicule, to deride, to laugh at.
Verladebrücke *f* loading bridge, gantry.
verladen* *vt irreg* **(a)** to load; *(Mil) (in Eisenbahn)* to entrain; *(auf Schiff)* to embark; *(in Flugzeug)* to emplane ♦ **die Güter vom Eisenbahnwaggon aufs Schiff ~** to offload the goods from the train onto the ship. **(b)** *(fig inf) Wähler* to dump.
Verladerampe *f* loading platform.
Verladung *f siehe vt (a)* loading; entrainment; embarkation; emplaning.
Verlag *m* **-(e)s, -e** **(a)** *(Buch~)* publishing house *or* company; *(Zeitungs~)* newspaper publisher's *sing* ♦ **~ Collins** Collins Publishers; **einen ~ finden** to find a publisher; **in** *or* **bei welchem ~ ist das erschienen?** who published it?; **der ~ zahlt nicht viel** the publishers do not pay much; **ein Buch in ~ nehmen** to publish a book; **ein Buch in ~ geben** to have a book published.
(b) *(Zwischenhandelsgeschäft)* (firm of) distributors *pl.*
verlagern* [1] *vt (lit, fig) Gewicht, Schwerpunkt, Betonung* to shift; *Interessen auch* to transfer; *(lit: an anderen Ort)* to move.
[2] *vr (lit, fig)* to shift; *(Met: Tief, Hoch etc)* to move; *(fig: Problem, Frage)* to change in emphasis *(auf +acc* to).
Verlagerung *f siehe vb* shift; transfer; moving, movement; change in emphasis.
Verlags-: ~anstalt *f* publishing firm; **~buchhandel** *m* publishing trade; **~buchhändler** *m* publisher; **~buchhandlung** *f* publishing firm, publisher; **~haus** *nt* publishing house; **~kaufmann** *m* publishing manager; **~leiter** *m* publishing director; **~programm** *nt* list; **~recht** *nt* publishing rights *pl*; **~redakteur** *m* (publishing) editor; **~wesen** *nt* publishing *no art.*
verlanden* *vi aux sein* to silt up; *(durch Austrocknen)* to dry up.
Verlandung *f siehe vi* silting up; drying up.
verlangen* [1] *vt* **(a)** *(fordern)* to demand; *(wollen)* to want; *Preis* to ask; *Qualifikationen, Erfahrung* to require ♦ **was verlangt der Kunde/das Volk?** what does the customer/do the people want?; **wieviel verlangst du für dein Auto?** how much are you asking for *or* do you want for your car?
(b) *(erwarten)* to ask *(von* of) ♦ **ich verlange nichts als Offenheit und Ehrlichkeit** I am asking nothing but frankness and honesty; **es wird von jdm verlangt, daß ...** it is required *or* expected of sb that ...; **das ist nicht zuviel verlangt** it's not asking too much; **das ist ein bißchen viel verlangt** that's asking rather a lot, that's rather a tall order.
(c) *(erfordern)* to require, to call for.
(d) *(fragen nach)* to ask for; *Paß, Ausweis auch* to ask to see ♦ **Sie werden am Telefon verlangt** you are wanted on the phone; **ich verlange/ich verlangte den Geschäftsführer (zu sprechen)** I want *or* demand to see the manager/I demanded *or* asked to see the manager.
[2] *vi* **~ nach** to ask for; *(sich sehnen nach)* to long for; *(stärker)* to crave.
[3] *vt impers (liter)* **es verlangt jdn nach jdm/etw** sb craves sth; *(nach der Heimat, Geliebten)* sb yearns for sb/sth.
Verlangen *nt* **-s, -** *(nach* for) desire; *(Sehnsucht)* yearning, longing; *(Begierde)* craving; *(Forderung)* request ♦ **kein ~ nach etw haben** to have no desire or wish for sth; **auf ~** on demand; **auf ~ des Gerichts** by order of the court; **auf ~ der Eltern** at the request of the parents.
verlangend *adj* longing.
verlängern* [1] *vt* **(a)** to extend; *(räumlich auch)* to lengthen, to make longer; *(Math) Strecke auch* to produce; *(zeitlich) Wartezeit, Aufenthalt auch, Leben,*

Schmerzen, Leiden etc to prolong; *Hosenbein, Ärmel etc* to lengthen; *Paß, Abonnement etc* to renew ◆ **die Suppe/Soße ~** (*fig inf*) to make the soup/gravy go further *or* stretch; **ein verlängertes Wochenende** a long weekend; *siehe* **Rücken.**
(b) (*Sport*) *Ball, Paß* to touch *or* play on (*zu jdm* to sb).
[2] *vr* to be extended; (*räumlich auch*) to be lengthened; (*zeitlich auch, Leiden etc*) to be prolonged.
[3] *vi* (*Sport*) to play on.

Verlängerung *f* **(a)** *siehe vt (a)* extension; lengthening; prolonging, prolongation; renewal.
(b) (*Gegenstand*) extension.
(c) (*Sport*) (*von Ball*) first-time pass; (*von Paß*) play-on (*zu* to); (*von Spielzeit*) extra time (*Brit*), overtime (*US*); (*nachgespielte Zeit*) injury time (*Brit*) ◆ **das Spiel geht in die ~** they're going to play extra time *etc*, they're going into extra time *etc*; **eine ~ von fünf Minuten** five minutes' extra time *etc.*

Verlängerungs-: ~kabel *nt*, **~schnur** *f* (*Elec*) extension lead.

verlangsamen* [1] *vt* to slow down *or* up; *Geschwindigkeit auch* to reduce, to decelerate; *Produktion auch* to decelerate; *Entwicklung auch* to retard ◆ **das Tempo/seine Schritte/die Fahrt ~** to slow down *or* up.
[2] *vr* to slow down *or* up; to decelerate; to be retarded.

Verlangsamung *f siehe vb* slowing down *or* up; deceleration; retarding, retardation.

verläppern* *vr* to be *or* get lost; (*Geld*) to disappear, to vanish.

⚠ **Verlaß** *m* **-sses,** *no pl* **auf jdn/etw ist kein ~, es ist kein ~ auf jdn/etw** there is no relying on sb/sth, you can't rely on sb/sth.

▼ **verlassen¹*** *irreg* [1] *vt* to leave; (*fig: Mut, Kraft, Hoffnung*) *jdn* to desert; (*im Stich lassen*) to desert, to abandon, to forsake (*liter*); (*Comput*) *Datei* to exit ◆ ... **und da verließen sie ihn** (*iro*) ... that's as far as it goes; (*bei Arbeit, Reparatur etc*) ... that's as far as I/he *etc* got; *siehe* **Geist.**
▼ [2] *vr* **sich auf jdn/etw ~** to rely *or* depend on sb/sth; **darauf können Sie sich ~** you can be sure of that, you can depend on that, take my word for it.

verlassen² *adj* **(a)** *Gegend, Ort, Straßen* deserted; (*öd*) desolate ◆ **eine Tanne, einsam und ~** a solitary fir tree. **(b)** *Mensch* (*allein gelassen*) deserted; (*einsam*) lonely, solitary ◆ **einsam und ~** so all alone. **(c)** (*ohne Besitzer*) *Haus, Fabrik* deserted; *Auto* abandoned.

Verlassenheit *f, no pl siehe adj (a)* desertedness; desolateness.

Verlassenschaft *f* (*Aus, Sw*) estate; (*literarisch*) legacy.

Verlassenschafts|abhandlung *f* (*Aus, Sw*) negotiation on inheritance.

⚠ **verläßlich, verlässig** (*old*) *adj* reliable; *Mensch auch* dependable.

⚠ **Verläßlichkeit** *f siehe adj* reliability; dependability.

verlatschen* *vt* (*inf*) to wear out.

Verlaub *m*: **mit ~** (*old*) by your leave (*old*), with your permission; **mit ~ (zu sagen)** if you will pardon *or* forgive my saying so.

Verlauf *m* **-(e)s, Verläufe** course; (*Ausgang*) end, issue ◆ **im ~ der Zeit** in the course of time; **im ~ des Tages/der Jahre/Monate** in *or* during the course of the day/over the (course of the) years/months; **im ~ der Verhandlung/Arbeit** in *or* during the course of the negotiations/work; **einen guten/schlechten ~ nehmen** to go well/badly; **den ~ einer Sache verfolgen/beobachten** to follow/observe the course (which) sth takes; **im weiteren ~ der Sache zeichnete sich folgende Tendenz ab** as things developed the following tendency became apparent.

verlaufen* *irreg* [1] *vi aux sein* **(a)** (*ablaufen*) (*Tag, Prüfung*) to go; (*Feier, Demonstration*) to go off; (*Kindheit*) to pass; (*Untersuchung*) to proceed ◆ **beschreiben Sie, wie diese Krankheit normalerweise verläuft** describe the course this illness usually takes; **die Verhandlung verlief in angespannter Atmosphäre** the negotiations took place in a tense atmosphere.
(b) (*sich erstrecken*) to run.
(c) (*auseinanderfließen, dial: schmelzen*) to run ◆ **die Spur verlief im Sand/Wald** the track disappeared in the sand/forest; **~e Farben** runny colours; *siehe* **Sand.**
[2] *vr* **(a)** (*sich verirren*) to get lost, to lose one's way.
(b) (*verschwinden*) (*Menschenmenge*) to disperse; (*Wasser auch*) to drain away; (*sich verlieren: Spur, Weg*) to disappear.

Verlaufsform *f* (*Gram*) progressive *or* continuous form.

verlaust *adj* lice-ridden.

verlautbaren* (*form*) *vti* to announce ◆ **es wird amtlich verlautbart, daß ...** it is officially announced that ..., a statement has been issued to the effect that ...; **etw ~ lassen** to let sth be announced *or* made known.

Verlautbarung *f* announcement; (*inoffiziell*) report.

verlauten* [1] *vi* **etwas/nichts ~ lassen** to give an/no indication, to say something/nothing; **er hat ~ lassen, daß ...** he indicated that ...; **er hat keinen Ton** *or* **kein Wort ~ lassen** he hasn't said a word.
[2] *vi impers aux sein or haben* **es verlautet, daß ...** it is reported that ...; **wie aus Bonn verlautet** according to reports from Bonn.

verleben* *vt* to spend ◆ **eine schöne Zeit ~** to have a nice time.

verlebt *adj* worn-out, dissipated.

verlegen¹* [1] *vt* **(a)** (*an anderen Ort*) to transfer, to move; *Schauplatz auch* to transpose, to shift.
(b) (*verschieben*) to postpone (*auf +acc* until); (*vorverlegen*) to bring forward (*auf +acc* to).
(c) (*an falschen Platz legen*) to mislay, to misplace.
(d) (*anbringen*) *Kabel, Fliesen etc* to lay.
(e) (*drucken lassen*) to publish.
[2] *vr* **sich auf etw** (*acc*) **~** to resort to sth; **er hat sich neuerdings auf Golf verlegt** he has taken to golf recently; **sich aufs Unterrichten ~** to take up teaching.

verlegen² *adj* **(a)** embarrassed *no adv* ◆ **~ sah er zu Boden** he looked at the floor in embarrassment. **(b) um Worte/eine Antwort ~ sein** to be lost *or* at a loss for words/an answer; **um Geld ~ sein** to be financially embarrassed.

Verlegenheit *f* **(a)** *no pl* (*Betretenheit, Befangenheit*) embarrassment ◆ **jdn in ~ bringen** to embarrass sb; **so ein wunderschöner Strauß, du bringst mich ja ganz in ~** such a lovely bouquet, you really shouldn't have; **in ~ kommen** *or* **geraten** to get *or* become embarrassed.
(b) (*unangenehme Lage*) embarrassing *or* awkward situation ◆ **wenn er in finanzieller ~ ist** when he's in financial difficulties, when he's financially embarrassed; **ich bin (finanziell) zur Zeit leider etwas in ~** I'm afraid I'm rather short (of funds) at the moment.

Verlegenheitslösung *f* stopgap.

Verleger(in *f*) *m* **-s, -** publisher; (*Händler*) distributor.

Verlegung *f* **(a)** (*räumlich*) *siehe* **verlegen¹ (a)** transfer, moving; transposition, shifting. **(b)** (*zeitlich*) postponement (*auf +acc* until); (*Vor~*) bringing forward (*auf +acc* to). **(c)** (*von Kabeln etc*) laying.

verleiden* *vt* **jdm etw ~** to spoil sth for sb, to put sb off sth; **das ist mir jetzt schon verleidet** you've/he's put me off it.

Verleih *m* **-(e)s, -e** **(a)** (*Unternehmen*) rental *or* hire company; (*Auto~*) car rental *or* hire; (*Film~*) distributor(s). **(b)** (*das Verleihen*) renting (out), hiring (out); (*Film~*) distribution ◆ **der ~ von Büchern** the lending *or* loan of books.

verleihen* *vt irreg* **(a)** (*verborgen*) to lend, to loan (*an jdn* to sb); (*gegen Gebühr*) to rent (out), to hire (out).
(b) (*zuerkennen*) to award (*jdm* (to) sb); *Titel, Ehrenbürgerrechte* to confer, to bestow (*jdm* on sb); *Amt* to bestow (*jdm* upon sb).
(c) (*geben, verschaffen*) to give; *Eigenschaft, Klang, Note auch* to lend ◆ **ihre Anwesenheit verlieh der Veranstaltung einen gewissen Glanz** her presence gave *or* lent a certain splendour to the occasion.

Verleiher *m* **-s, -** hire *or* rental firm; (*von Kostümen etc*) renter, hirer; (*von Filmen*) distributor, (firm of) distributors *pl*; (*von Büchern*) lender.

Verleihung *f siehe vt (a, b)* **(a)** lending, loan(ing); renting, rental, hire, hiring. **(b)** award(ing); conferment, conferring, bestowal, bestowment.

verleimen* *vt* to glue.

verleiten* *vt* **(a)** (*verlocken*) to tempt; (*verführen*) to lead astray ◆ **die Sonne hat mich verleitet, schwimmen zu gehen** the sun tempted *or* enticed me to go swimming; **jdn zur Sünde ~** to lead sb into sin; **jdn zum Stehlen/Lügen ~** to lead *or* encourage sb to steal/lie; **jdn zu einem Verbrechen ~** to lead *or* encourage sb to commit a crime; **jdn zum Ungehorsam ~** to encourage sb to be disobedient; **jdn dazu ~, die Schule zu schwänzen** to encourage sb to play truant.
(b) (*veranlassen*) **jdn zu etw ~** to lead sb to sth; **jdn zu einem Irrtum ~** to lead sb to make *or* into making a mistake.

Verleitung *f* **(a)** (*Verführung*) leading astray; (*zum Lügen, Stehlen*) encouragement ◆ **die ~ der Menschen zur Sünde** leading people into sin. **(b)** (*Veranlassung*) **die ~ zu einer vorschnellen Äußerung** leading him/one *etc* to make a hasty comment.

verlernen* *vt* to forget, to unlearn ◆ **das Tanzen ~** to forget how to dance.

verlesen* *irreg* [1] *vt* **(a)** (*vorlesen*) to read (out); *Namen auch* to call out. **(b)** *Gemüse, Linsen, Früchte etc* to sort; *Feldsalat* to clean.
[2] *vr* (*beim Vorlesen*) to make a slip ◆ **ich habe mich wohl ~** I must have read it wrong(ly), I must have misread it.

Verlesung *f siehe vt (a)* reading (out); calling out.

verletzbar *adj* (*lit, fig*) vulnerable.

Verletzbarkeit *f* (*lit, fig*) vulnerability.

verletzen* [1] *vt* **(a)** (*verwunden*) to injure; (*in Kampf etc, mit Kugel, Messer*) to wound; (*fig*) *jdn* to hurt, to wound; *jds Stolz, Gefühle* to hurt, to wound, to injure; *jds Ehrgefühl* to injure, to offend; *jds Schönheitssinn, zarte Ohren* to offend ◆ **das verletzt den guten Geschmack** it offends against good taste.
(b) *Gesetz* to break; *Pflicht, Rechte, Intimsphäre* to violate.
[2] *vr* to injure oneself.

verletzend *adj Bemerkung* hurtful.

verletzlich *adj* vulnerable.

Verletzlichkeit *f* vulnerability.

Verletzte(r) *mf decl as adj* injured person; (*Unfall~ auch*) casualty; (*bei Kampf*) wounded man ◆ **die ~n** the injured/the wounded; **es gab drei ~** three people were injured *or* hurt/wounded.

Verletzung *f* **(a)** (*Wunde*) injury. **(b)** *siehe vt* (*das Verletzen*) injuring; wounding; (*fig*) hurting, wounding; offending *etc* ◆ **zur ~ des Knies führen** to cause a knee injury.

▼ **verleugnen*** *vt* to deny; *Kind auch* to disown ◆ **ich kann es nicht ~, daß ...** I cannot deny that ...; **es läßt sich nicht ~, daß ...** there is no denying that ...; **er läßt sich immer vor ihr ~** he is never there to her, he always pretends not to be there when she calls; **sich (selbst) ~** to deny one's own self.

Verleugnung *f siehe vt* denial; disownment.

verleumden* *vt* to slander, to calumniate (*form*); (*schriftlich*) to libel.

Verleumder(in *f*) *m* **-s, -** *siehe vt* slanderer; libeller.

verleumderisch *adj siehe vt* slanderous; libellous.

Verleumdung *f* slandering; (*schriftlich*) libelling; (*Bemerkung*) slander, calumny; (*Bericht*) libel.

Verleumdungskampagne *f* smear campaign.

verlieben* *vr* to fall in love (*in +acc* with) ◆ **das Kleid ist zum V~ (schön)** I love that dress.

verliebt *adj Benehmen, Blicke, Worte* amorous ◆ **(in jdn/etw) ~ sein** to be in love (with sb/sth); **die V~en** the courting couple/couples, the lovers; *siehe*

Ohr.
Verliebtheit *f* being in love ◆ **seine ~ dauert nie lange** he is never in love for very long; **in einem Moment großer ~** feeling (all at once) tremendously in love.
verlieren *pret* **verlor**, *ptp* **verloren** [1] *vt* to lose; *Blätter auch* to shed ◆ **jdn/etw aus dem Gedächtnis ~** to lose all memory of sb/sth, to forget sb/sth; **kein Wort über jdn/etw ~** not to say a word about sb/sth; **wir brauchen kein Wort darüber zu ~** we don't need to waste any words on it; **an ihm hast du nichts verloren** he's no (great) loss; **das/er hat hier nichts verloren** (*inf*) that/he has no business to be here; **diese Bemerkung hat hier nichts verloren** (*inf*) that remark is out of place.
[2] *vi* to lose ◆ **sie hat an Schönheit/Charme verloren** she has lost some of her beauty/charm; **sie/die Altstadt** *etc* **hat sehr verloren** she/the old town *etc* is not what she/it *etc* used to be; **durch etw ~** to lose (something) by sth; **bei jdm ~** to go down in sb's eyes *or* estimation.
[3] *vr* **(a)** (*Menschen*) to lose each other; (*Mensch: sich verirren*) to get lost, to lose one's way.
(b) (*verschwinden*) to disappear; (*verhallen*) to fade away, to die ◆ **der Klang verlor sich in dem riesigen Saal/in den Bergen** the sound was lost in the enormous room/faded away *or* died among the mountains.
(c) (*fig*) (*geistesabwesend sein*) to become lost to the world; (*abschweifen*) to lose one's train of thought ◆ **sich in etw** (*acc*) **~** to become absorbed in sth; **sich in etw** (*dat*) **~** to get *or* become lost in sth; *siehe* **verloren**.
Verlierer(in *f*) *m* **-s, -** loser.
Verliererstraße *f* **auf der ~ sein** (*inf*) to be on the downward slope.
Verlies *nt* **-es, -e** dungeon.
▼ **verloben*** [1] *vr* (*mit* to) to become *or* get engaged, to become betrothed (*old*).
[2] *vt* **jdn mit jdm ~** to betroth sb to sb (*old*); **verlobt sein** to be engaged *or* betrothed (*old*) (*mit* to).
Verlöbnis *nt* (*old*) *siehe* **Verlobung**.
Verlobte(r) *mf decl as adj* **mein ~r** my fiancé, my betrothed (*old*); **meine ~** my fiancée, my betrothed (*old*); **die ~n** the engaged couple, the betrothed (*old*).
▼ **Verlobung** *f* engagement, betrothal (*old*).
Verlobungs- *in cpds* engagement; **~anzeige** *f* engagement announcement; **~zeit** *f* engagement.
verlocken* *vti* to entice, to tempt.
verlockend *adj* enticing, tempting.
Verlockung *f* enticement, temptation; (*Reiz*) allure.
verlodern* *vi aux sein* (*geh*) to flare up and die.
verlogen *adj Mensch* lying, mendacious; *Komplimente, Versprechungen* false; *Moral, Freundlichkeit, Gesellschaft* hypocritical.
Verlogenheit *f siehe adj* mendacity; falseness; hypocrisy.
verlohnen* *vir impers* (*rare*) to be worthwhile.
verlor *pret of* **verlieren**.
verloren [1] *ptp of* **verlieren**.
[2] *adj* **(a)** lost; (*einsam auch*) forlorn; (*Cook*) *Eier* poached ◆ **in den Anblick ~ sein** to be lost in contemplation.
(b) vain ◆ **der ~e Sohn** (*Bibl*) the prodigal son; **jdn/etw ~ geben** to give sb/sth up for lost; **auf ~em Posten kämpfen** *or* **stehen** to be fighting a losing battle *or* a lost cause.
⚠**verlorengehen** *vi sep irreg aux sein* to get *or* be lost; (*Zeit, Geld*) to be lost *or* wasted ◆ **an ihm ist ein Sänger verlorengegangen** he would have made a (good) singer, he ought to have been a singer.
Verlorenheit *f* forlornness.
verlöschen* [1] *pret* **verlosch**, *ptp* **verloschen** *vi aux sein* to go out; (*Inschrift, Farbe, Tinte*) to fade; (*Mond, Sterne*) to set; (*Erinnerung, Ruhm*) to fade (away) ◆ **sein Leben(slicht) ist verloschen** (*liter*) he has departed this life (*liter*).
[2] *vt reg* (*geh*) *siehe* **auslöschen**.
verlosen* *vt* to raffle (off) ◆ **wir ~ das letzte Stück Kuchen** we'll draw lots for the last piece of cake.
Verlosung *f* (*das Verlosen*) raffling; (*Lotterie*) raffle, draw; (*Ziehung*) draw.
verlöten* *vt* to solder ◆ **einen ~** (*sl: trinken*) to have a quickie (*inf*) *or* a quick one (*inf*).
verlottern* *vi aux sein* (*inf*) (*Stadt, Restaurant*) to get *or* become run down; (*Garten*) to run wild; (*Mensch*) to go to the dogs; (*moralisch*) to go to the bad ◆ **er verlottert immer mehr** he is sliding further and further downhill; **die Wohnung ist ganz verlottert** the flat is a complete shambles.
verlottert *adj* (*inf*) *Stadt* run-down; *Garten* wild; *Mensch, Aussehen* scruffy; (*moralisch*) dissolute.
verludern* (*inf*) [1] *vi aux sein* to go to the bad.
[2] *vt Geld* to squander, to fritter away.
verlumpen* (*inf*) [1] *vt Geld* to chuck away (*inf*).
[2] *vi aux sein* to go to the dogs; (*moralisch*) to go downhill.
verlumpt *adj* (*dial*) down and out; *Kleider* worn-out ◆ **~ herumlaufen** to go about in rags.
Verlust *m* **-(e)s, -e** loss ◆ **~e** *pl* losses *pl*; (*Tote auch*) casualties *pl*; (*bei Glücksspiel*) losses *pl*; **schwere ~e haben/machen** to sustain/make heavy losses; **mit ~ verkaufen** to sell at a loss; **in ~ geraten** (*form*) to be lost; *siehe* **Rücksicht**.
Verlust-: ~anzeige *f* "lost" notice; **~betrieb** *m* (*inf*) loss-making business, loss-maker, lame duck (*inf*); ⚠**v~bringend** *adj* loss-making; **v~bringend arbeiten** to work at a loss; **~geschäft** *nt* (*Firma*) loss-making business, loss-maker; **ich habe es schließlich verkauft, aber das war ein ~geschäft** I sold it eventually, but I made a loss *or* but at a loss.
verlustieren* *vr* (*hum*) to amuse oneself.
verlustig *adj* (*form*) **einer Sache** (*gen*) **~ gehen** *or* **werden** to forfeit *or* lose sth; **jdn seiner Rechte für ~ erklären** to declare sb's rights forfeit.
Verlust-: ~liste *f* (*Mil*) casualty list, list of casualties; **~meldung** *f* **(a)** report of the loss; **der Absender muß eine ~meldung machen** the sender must report the loss; **(b)** (*Mil*) casualty report, casualty figures *pl*; **v~reich** *adj* **(a)** (*Comm*) *Firma* heavily loss-making; **ein v~reiches Jahr** a year in which heavy losses were made, a year of heavy losses; **ein v~reiches Geschäft** a deal on which heavy losses were made; **(b)** (*Mil*) *Schlacht* involving heavy losses *or* casualties; **~zuweisung** *f* (*Econ*) allocation of losses.
Verm. *abbr of* **Vermerk**.
vermachen* *vt* **jdm etw ~** to leave *or* bequeath sth to sb; (*inf: gehen*) to bequeath sth to sb; **jdm etw als Schenkung ~** to bequeath sth to sb.
Vermächtnis *nt* bequest, legacy; (*fig*) legacy.
Vermächtnis- (*Jur*): **~geber** *m* legator; **~nehmer** *m* legatee.
vermahlen* *vt* to grind.
vermählen* (*form*) [1] *vt* to marry, to wed ◆ **frisch vermählt sein** to be newly married *or* wed(ded).
[2] *vr* **sich (mit jdm) ~** to marry *or* wed (sb); **„wir haben uns vermählt ..."** "the marriage is announced of ...".
Vermählte(r) *mf decl as adj* **die beiden ~n** the newly-married couple; **die/der soeben ~** the bride/(bride)groom.
▼ **Vermählung** *f* (*form*) marriage.
Vermählungs|anzeige *f* marriage announcement.
vermahnen* *vt* (*dated*) to warn.
vermaledeit *adj* (*old*) (ac)cursed (*old*), damned.
vermalen* *vt Farben* to use up.
vermännlichen* [1] *vt* to masculinize, to make masculine.
[2] *vi aux sein* (*Frauen*) to become masculine *or* like men, to adopt male characteristics; (*Gesellschaft*) to become male-dominated.
Vermännlichung *f* masculinization.
vermanschen* *vt* (*inf*) to mash up.
vermarkten* *vt* to market; (*fig*) to commercialize.
Vermarktung *f* marketing; (*fig*) commercialization.
vermasseln* *vt* (*inf*) to ruin, to mess up (*inf*); *Prüfung, Klassenarbeit* to make a mess *or* cock-up (*Brit sl*) of.
vermassen* [1] *vi aux sein* to lose one's identity *or* individuality, to become stereotyped ◆ **die Gesellschaft vermaßt immer mehr** society is becoming more and more uniform.
[2] *vt die Gesellschaft* to make uniform.
Vermassung *f* loss of identity *or* individuality, stereotyping, de-individualization ◆ **die ~ der Gesellschaft** the stereotyping of society.
vermatscht *adj* (*dial*) squashy.
vermauern* *vt* to wall *or* brick up.
vermehren* [1] *vt* to increase; (*fortpflanzen*) to breed; *Bakterien* to multiply ◆ **vermehrt** increased; **diese Fälle treten vermehrt auf** these cases are occurring with increased *or* increasing frequency *or* are happening increasingly often.
[2] *vr* to increase; (*sich fortpflanzen*) to reproduce, to breed; (*Bakterien*) to multiply; (*Pflanzen*) to propagate.
Vermehrung *f siehe vb* increase; reproduction, breeding; multiplying; propagation.
vermeidbar *adj* avoidable.
▼ **vermeiden*** *vt irreg* to avoid; *Frage auch* to evade ◆ **~, daß eine Sache an die Öffentlichkeit dringt** to avoid letting a matter become public; **es läßt sich nicht ~** it cannot be avoided *or* helped, it is inevitable *or* unavoidable; **es läßt sich nicht ~, daß ...** it is inevitable *or* unavoidable that ...; **nicht, wenn ich es ~ kann** not if I can avoid *or* help it; **er vermeidet keinen Streit** he's not one to avoid an argument.
Vermeidung *f* avoidance ◆ **die ~ eines Skandals ist nur dann möglich, wenn ...** a scandal can only be avoided if ...; **zur ~** (+*gen*) *or* **von** to avoid.
vermeil [vɛr'mɛːj] *adj* vermilion.
Vermeil [vɛr'mɛːj] *nt* **-s**, *no pl* gilded silver.
vermeinen* *vt* (*geh*) to think ◆ **ich vermeinte, eine Stimme zu hören** I thought I heard a voice.
vermeintlich *adj attr* putative, supposed; *Täter, Vater eines Kindes* putative.
vermelden* *vt* **(a)** (*liter: mitteilen*) to announce ◆ **was hast du Neues zu ~?** (*hum*) what news do you have to announce *or* report? **(b)** *Erfolg* to report.
vermengen* *vt* to mix; (*fig inf: durcheinanderbringen*) *Begriffe etc* to mix up, to confuse.
Vermengung *f* mixing.
vermenschlichen* *vt* to humanize; (*als Menschen darstellen auch*) to anthropomorphize.
Vermenschlichung *f siehe vt* humanization; anthropomorphization.
Vermerk *m* **-(e)s, -e** note, remark; (*im Kalender auch*) entry; (*in Paß*) observation; (*postalisch*) remark; (*Stempel*) stamp.
vermerken* *vt* **(a)** to make a note of, to note (down), to write down; (*in Paß, Karte*) *Namen, Datum etc* to record ◆ **alle Verkehrssünder werden in Flensburg vermerkt** a record of (the names of) all traffic offenders is kept in Flensburg; **sich** (*dat*) **etw ~** to make a note of sth, to note *or* write sth down.
(b) (*zur Kenntnis nehmen*) to note, to make a (mental) note of ◆ **jdm etw übel ~** to take sth amiss.
vermessen[1]* *irreg* [1] *vt* to measure; *Land, Gelände* to survey.

➤ SPRACHE AKTIV: **verloben: 1** → 51.2 **Verlobung** → 51.2, 52.2 **Vermählung** → 51.3 **vermeiden** → 29.2, 42.1

[2] *vr* **(a)** *(geh)* *(sich anmaßen)* to presume, to dare ◆ **wie kann er sich ~, ...?** how dare he ...? **(b)** *(falsch messen)* to measure wrongly.

vermessen[2] *adj (anmaßend)* presumptuous; *Diener* impudent; *(kühn) Unterfangen* bold.

Vermessenheit *f, no pl siehe adj* presumption, presumptuousness; impudence; boldness ◆ **es wäre eine ~, das zu tun** that would be an act of some temerity.

Vermessung *f* measurement; *(von Land, Gelände)* survey.

Vermessungs-: ~amt *nt* land survey(ing) office; **~ingenieur** *m* land surveyor; **~schiff** *nt* survey ship.

vermiesen* *vt (inf)* **jdm etw ~** to spoil sth for sb; **das hat mir den Urlaub vermiest** that spoiled my holiday.

vermietbar *adj* rentable ◆ **schlecht ~** difficult to rent (out) *or* let (out) *(esp Brit)*; **es ist nur als Büroraum ~** it can only be rented (out) *or* let (out) *(esp Brit)* as office premises.

vermieten* [1] *vt* to rent (out), to let (out) *(esp Brit)*, to lease *(Jur)*; *Boot, Auto* to rent (out), to hire (out), to lease *(Jur)* ◆ **Zimmer zu ~** room to let *(esp Brit)* *or* for rent.

[2] *vi* to rent (out) *or* let (out) *(esp Brit)* a room/rooms.

Vermieter *m* **-s, -** lessor; *(von Wohnung etc)* landlord, lessor *(Jur)*.

Vermieterin *f* lessor; *(von Wohnung etc)* landlady, lessor *(Jur)*.

Vermietung *f siehe vt* renting (out), letting (out) *(esp Brit)*; rental, hiring (out).

vermindern* [1] *vt* to reduce, to decrease; *Gefahr, Anfälligkeit, Einfluß etc auch, Ärger, Zorn* to lessen; *Widerstandsfähigkeit, Reaktionsfähigkeit* to diminish, to reduce; *Schmerzen* to ease, to lessen, to reduce; *(Mus)* to diminish ◆ **verminderte Zurechnungsfähigkeit** *(Jur)* diminished responsibility.

[2] *vr siehe vt* to decrease; to lessen; to diminish; *(Schmerzen)* to ease off, to lessen, to decrease.

Verminderung *f siehe vb* reduction *(gen* of*)*, decrease *(gen* in*)*; lessening; diminution; easing.

verminen* *vt* to mine.

Verminung *f* mining.

vermischen* [1] *vt* to mix; *Tabaksorten, Teesorten etc* to blend ◆ **vermischte Schriften** miscellaneous writings; **„Vermischtes"** "miscellaneous".

[2] *vr* to mix; *(Rassen auch)* to interbreed; *(Elemente, Klänge, Farben)* to blend, to mingle ◆ **Freude vermischt sich mit Leid** joy mingles *or* is mingled with sorrow; **wo sich Tradition und Fortschritt ~** where tradition and progress are blended (together) *or* combined.

Vermischung *f siehe vb* mixing, mixture; blending; interbreeding; blending, mingling; *(von Gefühlen, Stilebenen, Metaphern)* mixture.

vermissen* *vt* to miss ◆ **vermißt werden** to be missing; **vermißt sein, als vermißt gemeldet sein** to be reported missing; **ich vermisse zwei silberne Teelöffel** two (of my) silver teaspoons are missing, I'm missing two silver teaspoons; **ich vermisse die Blumen auf den Tischen** I see you don't have the flowers on the tables; **etw an jdm/etw ~** to find sb/sth lacking in sth; **was ich bei dieser Beschreibung vermisse, ist ...** what I miss in this description is ...; **wir haben dich bei der Party vermißt** we didn't see you at the party; **entschuldige, daß ich zu spät komme — wir hatten dich noch gar nicht vermißt** sorry I'm late — we hadn't even noticed you weren't here; **etw ~ lassen** to lack sth, to be lacking in sth.

⚠**Vermißten|anzeige** *f* missing persons report ◆ **eine ~ aufgeben** to report someone (as) missing.

⚠**Vermißte(r)** *mf decl as adj* missing person.

vermittelbar *adj Idee, Gefühl* communicable; *Arbeitsloser* placeable.

Vermittelbarkeit *f* **die hohe/niedrige ~ eines Arbeitslosen** the ease/difficulty of placing an unemployed person.

vermitteln* [1] *vt* to arrange *(jdm* for sb*)*; *Stelle, Briefpartner, Privatschüler* to find *(jdm* for sb*)*; *Aushilfskräfte, Lehrer etc* to find jobs *or* positions for, to place; *(Telec) Gespräch* to put through, to connect; *Hypotheken, Kredite, Geschäfte* to arrange, to negotiate *(jdm* for sb*)*; *Wertpapiere* to negotiate; *Lösung, Kompromiß, Waffenstillstand* to arrange, to negotiate, to mediate; *Gefühl, Bild, Idee, Einblick* to convey, to give *(jdm* to sb*)*; *Verständnis* to give *(jdm* (to) sb*)*; *Wissen* to impart *(jdm* to sb*)* ◆ **jdm etw ~** to get sth for sb; **eine Stelle, die Hotelunterkunft vermittelt** an office which finds hotel accommodation; **kennen Sie jemanden, der Wohnungen vermittelt?** do you know (anybody who acts as) an agent for renting/buying flats?; **ich kann dir eine billige Ferienwohnung ~** I can get you a cheap holiday flat; **wir ~ Wohnungen** we are agents for flats.

[2] *vi* to mediate, to act as mediator *or* a go-between ◆ **~d eingreifen** to intervene; **~de Worte** conciliatory words.

vermittels(t) *prep +gen (form)* by means of.

Vermittler(in *f***)** *m* **-s, -** **(a)** mediator, go-between. **(b)** *(Comm)* agent; *(Fin, Heirats~)* broker; *(von Anleihe)* negotiator; *(Stellen~)* clerk in/manager of/person who works in an employment agency *or* bureau.

Vermittler-: ~gebühr *f* commission; *(Fin auch)* brokerage; **~rolle** *f* role of mediator.

Vermittlung *f* **(a)** *siehe vt* arranging, arrangement; finding; finding of jobs *or* positions *(+gen* for*)*, placing; connection; negotiation; mediation; conveying; giving; imparting ◆ **sie haben sich durch die ~ einer Agentur kennengelernt** they met through an agency; **ich habe das Zimmer/die Stelle durch ~ eines Freundes bekommen** I got the room/job through (the agency of *form*) *or* via a friend; **durch seine freundliche ~** with his kind help; **zur ~ eines besseren Verständnisses** to give a better understanding; **zur ~ eines besseren Eindrucks** to give *or* convey a better impression; **heute geht die telefonische ~ automatisch vor sich** nowadays telephone calls are put through *or* connected automatically.

(b) *(Schlichtung)* mediation ◆ **eine ~ zwischen den beiden ist mir leider nicht gelungen** unfortunately I was unable to reconcile them *or* to bring about a reconciliation between them.

(c) *(Stelle, Agentur)* agency; *(Heirats~)* marriage bureau *or* agency; *(Wohnungs~)* estate agent's *or* agency *(Brit)*, realtor *(US)*; *(Arbeits~)* employment agency.

(d) *(Telec) (Amt)* exchange; *(in Firma etc)* switchboard; *(Mensch)* operator.

Vermittlungs-: ~amt *nt (Telec)* telephone exchange; ⚠**~ausschuß** *m* mediation committee; **~bemühungen** *pl* efforts to mediate *pl*; **~chance** *f usu pl* chance of being placed in a job; **~gebühr** *f* commission; **~stelle** *f* agency; *(Telec)* (telephone) exchange; *(in Firma etc)* switchboard; **~versuch** *m* attempt at mediation.

vermöbeln* *vt (inf)* to beat up; *(als Strafe)* to thrash.

vermocht *ptp of* **vermögen**.

vermodern* *vi aux sein* to moulder, to decay.

Vermod(e)rung *f* decay.

vermöge *prep +gen (liter)* by dint of.

vermögen *pret* **vermochte**, *ptp* **vermocht** *vt, v aux (geh)* **etw zu tun ~, (es) ~, etw zu tun** to be able to do sth, to be capable of doing sth; **er vermochte es nicht, sich von den Fesseln zu be freien** he was unable *or* was not able to free himself from the chains; **viel/wenig ~** to be capable of a lot/not to be capable of very much; **etwas Verständnis vermag bei den Schülern viel** a little understanding is capable of achieving a lot with students; **Geduld vermag viel bei ihm** patience works wonders with him.

Vermögen *nt* **-s, - (a)** *(Reichtum, viel Geld)* fortune ◆ **das ist ein ~ wert** it's worth a fortune; **das ist ja nicht gerade ein ~** it's not exactly a fortune; **eine Frau, die ~ hat** a woman who has money, a woman of means; **die erste Frage war, ob ich ~ hatte** the first question was whether I had private means.

(b) *(Besitz)* property ◆ **mein ganzes ~ besteht aus ...** my entire assets consist of ...; **die Verteilung des ~s in einem Land** the distribution of wealth within a country.

(c) *(Können)* ability, capacity; *(Macht)* power.

vermögend *adj (reich)* wealthy, well-off ◆ **ein ~er Mann** a man of means, a wealthy man.

Vermögens-: ~abgabe *f* property levy; **v~bildend** *adj* wealth-creating; **~bildung** *f* creation of wealth; *(durch Prämiensparen)* wealth formation by long-term saving with tax concessions; **~erklärung** *f* statement of property; *(Wertpapiere)* statement of assets; **~konzentration** *f* concentration of wealth; **~politik** *f* policy on the distribution of wealth; **~steuer** *f* wealth tax; **~verhältnisse** *pl* financial *or* pecuniary circumstances *pl*; **~verteilung** *f* distribution of wealth; **~werte** *pl* assets *pl*; **v~wirksam** *adj* profitable, profit-yielding; **Geld v~wirksam investieren** to invest money profitably; **v~wirksame Leistungen** employer's contributions to tax-deductible savings scheme; **~zuwachs** *m* increase of wealth.

vermottet *adj (lit, fig)* moth-eaten.

vermummen* [1] *vt* to wrap up (warm).

[2] *vr* **(a)** to wrap (oneself) up (warm) ◆ **vermummte Gestalten in einer Winterlandschaft** muffled-up figures in a winter landscape. **(b)** *(sich verkleiden)* to disguise. **eine vermummte Gestalt betrat den Raum** a cloaked figure entered the room; **tief vermummt** heavily disguised; **vermummte Demonstranten** masked demonstrators.

Vermummung *f* disguise; *(von Demonstranten)* covering of the face.

Vermummungsverbot *nt* **das ~ bei Demonstrationen** *the law requiring demonstrators to leave their faces uncovered.*

vermurksen* *vt (inf)* **etw ~/sich** *(dat)* **etw ~** to mess sth up *(inf)*, to make a mess of sth.

vermuten* *vt* to suspect ◆ **ich vermute es nur** that's only an assumption, I'm only assuming that, that's only what I suspect to be the case; **wir haben ihn dort nicht vermutet** we did not expect *or* think to find/see *etc* him there; **ich hatte dich nicht so früh vermutet** I didn't suspect you would be so early; **es ist zu ~, daß ...** it may be supposed that ..., we may assume *or* presume that ...; **Wissenschaftler ~ Leben auf der Venus** scientists suspect that there is life on Venus; **die Entwicklung läßt ~, daß ...** developments lead one to assume that *or* give rise to the suspicion *or* supposition that ...

vermutlich [1] *adj attr* presumable; *Täter* suspected.

[2] *adv* presumably.

Vermutung *f (Annahme)* supposition, assumption; *(Mutmaßung)* conjecture; *(Verdacht)* suspicion ◆ **die ~ liegt nahe, daß ...** there are grounds for the supposition *or* assumption that ...; **das sind alles nur ~en** that is pure conjecture, those are purely suppositions *or* assumptions; **wir sind nur auf ~en angewiesen** we have to rely on suppositions *or* assumptions *or* guesswork; **meine ~en waren doch richtig** my guess *or* suspicion was right.

vernachlässigen* [1] *vt* to neglect; *(Schicksal) jdn* to be unkind *or* harsh to ◆ **das können wir ~** *(nicht berücksichtigen)* we can ignore that.

[2] *vr* to neglect oneself *or* one's appearance.

Vernachlässigung *f siehe vt* neglect; *(Nichtberücksichtigung)* ignoring, disregarding.

vernageln* *vt* to nail up ◆ **etw mit Brettern ~** to board sth up.

vernagelt *adj (fig inf)* thick *no adv (inf)*, wooden-headed *(inf)*; *(engstirnig)* small-minded ◆ **ich war wie ~** I couldn't think straight.

vernähen* *vt* to neaten; *Wunde* to stitch (up); *(verbrauchen)* to use up.

vernarben* *vi aux sein* to heal *or* close (up).

⚠: Informationen zur Rechtschreibreform im Anhang

Vernarbung *f* healing ◆ **leichte Massagen sorgen für schöne ~en** gentle massages help the skin to scar over nicely; **eine gute ~** a good heal.
vernarren* *vr (inf)* **sich in jdn/etw ~** to fall for sb/sth, to be smitten by sb/sth; **in jdn/etw vernarrt sein** to be crazy *(inf) or* nuts *(sl)* about sb/sth, to be infatuated with sb.
Vernarrtheit *f, no pl* infatuation *(in +acc* with).
vernaschen* *vt Süßigkeiten* to eat up; *Geld* to spend on sweets; *(inf) Mädchen, Mann* to make it with *(inf)*.
vernebeln* *vt (Mil)* to cover with a smoke screen; *(fig) Tatsachen* to obscure, to obfuscate *(form)*; *(inf) Zimmer* to fug up ◆ **die Dinge ~** to confuse the issue, to muddy the waters.
Verneb(e)lung *f, no pl (Mil)* screening; *(fig: von Tatsachen)* obscuring.
vernehmbar *adj* **(a)** *(hörbar)* audible, perceptible. **(b)** *(vernehmungsfähig)* able to be questioned.
vernehmen* *vt irreg* **(a)** *(hören)* to hear.
(b) *(erfahren)* to hear, to learn ◆ **das Presseamt hat ~ lassen, daß** ... the press agency has given to understand that ...; **er hat über seine Pläne nichts ~ lassen** he has let nothing be known about his plans.
(c) *(Jur) Zeugen, Angeklagte* to examine; *(Polizei)* to question ◆ **zu diesem Fall wurden fünfzig Zeugen vernommen** fifty witnesses were heard in connection with this case.
Vernehmen *nt*: **dem ~ nach** from what I/we *etc* hear; **gutem/sicherem ~ nach** according to well-informed/reliable sources.
vernehmlich *adj* clear, audible ◆ **es tönte laut und ~** ... it sounded loud and clear ..., we heard loud and clear ...; **sich ~ räuspern** to clear one's throat audibly *or* loudly.
Vernehmung *f (Jur: von Zeugen, Angeklagten)* examination; *(durch Polizei)* questioning.
Vernehmungs-: ~beamte(r) *m* police interrogator; **v~fähig** *adj* able to be examined/questioned.
verneigen* *vr* to bow ◆ **sich vor jdm/etw ~** *(lit)* to bow to sb/sth; *(fig)* to bow down before sb/sth.
Verneigung *f* bow, obeisance *(form) (vor +dat* before) ◆ **eine ~ machen** to bow.
verneinen* *vti Frage* to answer in the negative; *(leugnen) Tatsache, Existenz Gottes etc* to deny; *These, Argument* to dispute; *(Gram, Logik)* to negate ◆ **die verneinte Form** the negative (form); **eine Seite seines Wesens, die stets verneint** a side of his nature that always denies *(liter) or* that is always negative.
verneinend *adj (auch Gram)* negative ◆ **er schüttelte ~ den Kopf** he shook his head.
Verneinung *f (Leugnung)* denial; *(von These etc)* disputing; *(Gram, Philos)* negation; *(verneinte Form)* negative ◆ **die ~ meiner Frage** the negative answer to my question.
vernetzen* *vt (esp Mot)* to link up, to integrate; *(Comput)* to network.
Vernetzung *f (esp Mot)* linking-up, integration; *(Comput)* networking.
Vernetzungskonzept *nt (Mot)* integration concept; *(Comput)* networking concept.
vernichten* *vt (lit, fig)* to destroy; *Schädlinge, Menschheit auch* to exterminate; *Menschheit, Feind auch* to annihilate.
vernichtend *adj* devastating; *Blick auch* withering; *Niederlage* crushing ◆ **~ über jdn urteilen** to make a devastating appraisal of sb; **jdn ~ schlagen** *(Mil)* to destroy sb utterly; *(Sport)* to beat sb hollow.
Vernichtung *f siehe vt* destruction; extermination; annihilation.
Vernichtungs-: ~krieg *m* war of extermination; **~lager** *nt* extermination camp; **~mittel** *nt* insecticide; *(Unkrautvernichtungsmittel)* weedkiller; **~schlag** *m* devastating blow; **das war der ~schlag für die Regierung** that was the final blow for the government; **zum ~schlag ausholen** *(Mil, fig)* to prepare to deliver the final blow; **~waffe** *f* destructive *or* doomsday weapon.
vernickeln* *vt* to nickel-plate.
Vernickelung *f, no pl* nickel plating *no pl*.
verniedlichen* *vt* to trivialize.
vernieten* *vt* to rivet.
Vernietung *f* riveting.
Vernissage [vɛrnɪ'sa:ʒə] *f* **-, -n** *(Eröffnung)* opening day.
Vernunft *f* **-,** *no pl* reason *(auch Philos)*, good sense ◆ **zur ~ kommen** to come to one's senses; **~ annehmen** to see reason; **nimm doch ~ an!** why don't you see reason?; **jdm ~ predigen** to reason with sb; **gegen alle (Regeln der) ~** against all (the laws of) reason; **~ walten lassen** *(geh)* to let reason prevail; **~ beweisen** to show (good) sense *or* common sense; **etw mit/ohne ~ tun** to do sth sensibly/foolishly; **etw mit ~ essen/trinken** to eat/drink sth with appreciation; **Kinder zur ~ erziehen** to bring children up to be sensible; *siehe* **bringen**.
Vernunft-: v~begabt *adj* rational, endowed with reason; **~begriff** *m* concept of reason; **~ehe** *f (lit, fig)* marriage of convenience; **v~geleitet** *adj* rational; **v~gemäß** *adv* rationally, from a rational point of view; **~glaube(n)** *m* rationalism; **~gründe** *pl* rational grounds *pl*; **~heirat** *f* marriage of convenience.
vernünftig [1] *adj* sensible; *(logisch denkend)* rational; *(inf) (ordentlich, anständig)* decent; *(annehmbar)* reasonable ◆ **sei doch ~!** be sensible *or* reasonable!; **ich kann keinen ~en Gedanken fassen** I can't think properly.
[2] *adv siehe adj* sensibly; rationally; decently; reasonably; *(tüchtig)* properly *(inf)* ◆ **~ reden** *(inf)* to speak properly; **er kann ganz ~ kochen** *(inf)* he can cook reasonably well.
vernünftigerweise *adv* **etw ~ tun** to have the (good) sense to do sth; **du solltest dich ~ ins Bett legen** you should be sensible and go to bed.
Vernünftigkeit *f* sensibleness; *(von Mensch auch)* sense.
Vernunft-: ~mensch *m* rational person; **v~widrig** *adj* irrational.
ver|öden* [1] *vt (Med) Krampfadern* to sclerose.
[2] *vi aux sein* to become desolate; *(sich entvölkern auch)* to become deserted; *(fig: geistig ~)* to become stultified.
Ver|ödung *f* **(a)** desolation; *(Entvölkerung)* depopulation; *(fig)* stultification. **(b)** *(Med: von Krampfadern)* sclerosis.
ver|öffentlichen* *vti* to publish.
Ver|öffentlichung *f* publication.
ver|ordnen* *vt* **(a)** to prescribe, to order; *Medikament* to prescribe *(jdm etw* sth for sb). **(b)** *(old: verfügen)* to decree, to ordain.
Ver|ordnung *f* **(a)** *(Med)* prescription ◆ **nach ~ des Arztes einzunehmen** to be taken as directed by the doctor. **(b)** *(form: Verfügung)* decree, ordinance.
verpachten* *vt* to lease, to rent out *(an +acc* to).
Verpächter *m* **-s, -** lessor.
Verpachtung *f* lease.
verpacken* *vt* to pack; *(verbrauchergerecht), (fig) Gedanken etc* to package; *(einwickeln)* to wrap.
Verpackung *f siehe vt* packing; packaging; wrapping.
Verpackungs-: ~gewicht *nt* weight of packaging, tare (weight); **~industrie** *f* packaging industry; **~müll** *m* superfluous packaging.
verpäppeln* *vt (inf)* to mollycoddle *(inf)*, to pamper *(inf)*.
verpaschen* *vt (Aus)* to sell (off), to flog *(Brit inf)*.
verpassen* *vt* **(a)** *(versäumen)* to miss; *Gelegenheit auch* to waste; *siehe* **Anschluß**.
(b) *(inf: zuteilen)* **jdm etw ~** to give sb sth; *(aufzwingen)* to make sb have sth; **jdm eins** *or* **eine** *or* **eine Ohrfeige/eine Tracht Prügel ~** to clout sb one *(inf)*/give sb a good hiding *(inf)*; **jdm einen Denkzettel ~** to give sb something to think about *(inf)*.
verpatzen* *vt (inf)* to spoil; *Vereinbarung auch* to mess up *(inf)*; *(Mensch) Vortrag auch, Examen* to make a mess of ◆ **sich** *(dat)* **etw ~** to spoil sth/mess sth up *(inf)*/make a mess of sth.
verpennen* *(inf)* [1] *vt (verpassen) Termin, Zeit* to miss by oversleeping; *(schlafend verbringen) Tag, Morgen etc* to sleep through; *Leben* to sleep away; *(fig: nicht bemerken)* to sleep through.
[2] *vir* to oversleep.
verpennt *adj (inf)* sleepy; *(trottelig: Mensch)* dozy ◆ **ein ~er Typ** *(Vielschläfer)* a sleepy-head *(inf)*; *(Trottel)* a dummy *(inf)*.
verpesten* *vt* to pollute, to contaminate ◆ **die Luft im Büro ~** *(inf)* to stink out the office.
Verpestung *f* pollution, contamination.
verpetzen* *vt (inf)* to tell *or* sneak on *(inf) (bei* to).
verpfänden* *vt* to pawn, to (put in) hock *(inf)*; *(Jur)* to mortgage ◆ **(jdm) sein Wort ~** *(obs)* to pledge one's word (to sb).
Verpfändung *f* pawning; *(Jur)* mortgage ◆ **etw zur ~ ins Leihhaus bringen** to take sth to be pawned (in a pawnshop), to put sth in pawn *or* hock *(inf)*.
verpfeifen* *vt irreg (inf)* to grass on *(bei* to) *(inf)*.
verpflanzen* *vt (Bot, Med, fig)* to transplant; *Topfpflanzen* to repot; *Haut* to graft.
Verpflanzung *f siehe vt* transplantation; repotting; grafting; *(Med)* transplant.
verpflegen* [1] *vt* to feed; *(Mil) Heer auch* to ration.
[2] *vr* **sich (selbst) ~** to feed oneself; *(selbst kochen)* to cook for oneself.
Verpflegung *f* **(a)** *(das Verpflegen)* catering; *(Mil)* rationing ◆ **die ~ von 4 Leuten** feeding 4 people, catering for 4 people. **(b)** *(Essen)* food; *(Mil)* rations *pl*, provisions *pl* ◆ **mit voller ~** including food; *(mit Vollpension)* with full board.
Verpflegungs-: ~kosten *pl* cost of food *sing*; **~mehraufwand** *m* additional meal allowance.
▼ **verpflichten*** [1] *vt* **(a)** *(moralische Pflicht auferlegen)* to oblige, to place under an obligation ◆ **verpflichtet sein, etw zu tun, zu etw verpflichtet sein** to be obliged to do sth; **sich verpflichtet fühlen, etw zu tun, sich zu etw verpflichtet fühlen** to feel obliged to do sth; **jdm verpflichtet sein** to be under an obligation to sb; **sich jdm verpflichtet fühlen** to feel under an obligation to sb.
(b) *(binden)* to commit; *(vertraglich, durch Eid, durch Handschlag etc)* to bind ◆ **verpflichtet sein, etw zu tun** to be committed to doing sth; **jdn auf die Verfassung ~** to make sb swear to uphold the constitution; **auf die Verfassung verpflichtet werden** to be sworn to uphold the constitution; **~d** *Zusage, Unterschrift, Versprechen* binding.
(c) *(einstellen)* to engage; *Sportler* to sign on; *(Mil)* to enlist.
[2] *vi (moralische Pflicht darstellen)* to carry an obligation *(zu etw* to do sth); *(bindend sein)* to be binding ◆ **das verpflichtet zu nichts** there is no obligation involved; *siehe* **Adel**.
[3] *vr (moralisch)* to make a commitment; *(eidlich, vertraglich)* to commit oneself; *(Mil)* to enlist, to sign up ◆ **sich zu etw ~** to undertake to do sth; *(vertraglich, eidlich)* to commit oneself to doing sth.
Verpflichtung *f* **(a)** *(das Verpflichten)* obligation *(zu etw* to do sth); *(Pflicht auch, finanzielle ~)* commitment *(zu etw* to do sth); *(Aufgabe)* duty ◆ **dienstliche ~en** official duties; **~en gegen jdn haben** to be in sb's debt *(auch finanziell)*, to be indebted to sb; **seinen ~en nachkommen** to fulfil one's obligations.
(b) *(Einstellung)* engaging; *(von Sportlern)* signing on; *(Mil)* enlistment.

➤ SPRACHE AKTIV: **verpflichten: 1a** → 37.1, 37.3

(c) (*das Sich-Verpflichten*) (*für, auf +acc* for) signing on; (*Mil*) signing up ◆ **ich habe meine ~ auf sechs Monate bereut** I regret having signed on *or* committed myself/signed up for six months.

verpfuschen* *vt* (*inf*) *Arbeit etc* to bungle; *Leben, Erziehung, Urlaub etc* to muck up (*inf*), to ruin; *Mensch* to ruin; *Kind* to spoil ◆ **jdm/sich den Abend** *etc* **~** to ruin sb's/one's evening *etc.*

verpiepelt, verpimpelt *adj* (*dial*) soft (*inf*) ◆ **tu nicht so ~** don't act *or* be so soft (*inf*).

verpissen* *vr* (*sl*) to piss off (*sl*).

verplanen* [1] *vt Zeit* to book up; *Geld* to budget ◆ **jdn ~** (*inf*) to fill up all sb's spare time (for him/her).
[2] *vr* to plan badly *or* wrongly; (*falsch berechnen*) to miscalculate.

verplappern* *vr* (*inf*) to open one's mouth too wide (*inf*).

verplaudern* [1] *vt Zeit* to talk *or* chat away.
[2] *vr* (*inf*) to forget the time talking *or* chatting.

verplauschen* *vr* (*Aus*) to forget the time chatting *or* talking.

verplempern* [1] *vt* (*inf*) *Zeit* to waste, to fritter away; *Geld auch* to squander.
[2] *vr* to waste oneself.

verplomben* *vt* to seal.

verpönt *adj* frowned (up)on (*bei* by).

verpoppen* *vt* to jazz up, to make a pop version of.

verprassen* *vt* to blow (*inf*) (*für* on) ◆ **etw sinnlos ~** to fritter sth away.

verprellen* *vt* to put off, to intimidate.

verproviantieren* [1] *vt* to supply with food.
[2] *vr* to get a food supply.

verprügeln* *vt* to thrash, to beat up.

verpuffen* *vi aux sein* to (go) pop; (*fig*) to fall flat.

verpulvern* *vt* (*inf*) to fritter away.

verpumpen* *vt* (*inf*) to lend out, to loan (*an +acc* to).

verpuppen* *vr* to pupate.

verpusten* *vi/r* (*inf*) to get one's breath back.

Verputz *m* **-es,** *no pl* plaster, plasterwork; (*Rauhputz*) roughcast ◆ **über/unter ~** on top of/under plaster.

verputzen* *vt* (a) *Gebäude, Wand* to plaster; (*mit Rauhputz*) to roughcast. (b) (*inf: aufessen*) to polish off (*inf*), to demolish (*inf*) ◆ **ich kann ihn/das nicht ~** (*inf*) I can't stomach him/it.

verqualmen* *vt Zimmer* to fill with smoke; (*inf*) *Zigaretten etc* to smoke; *Geld* to spend on smoking ◆ **ein verqualmtes Zimmer** a room full of smoke.

verquast *adj* (*inf: verworren*) mixed-up; *Text* garbled; *Ideen* half-baked.

verquatschen* (*inf*) [1] *vt* to chat away.
[2] *vr* (a) (*lange plaudern*) to forget the time chatting. (b) (*Geheimnis ausplaudern*) to open one's mouth too wide (*inf*).

verquellen* *vi irreg aux sein* to swell; (*Holz auch*) to warp ◆ **verquollene Augen** puffy *or* swollen eyes.

verquer *adj* squint, skew-whiff (*inf*) ◆ **das ist eine ~e Optik** that's a twisted way of looking at things; **(jdm) ~ gehen** (*schiefgehen*) to go wrong (for sb); **das kommt mir jetzt etwas ~** that could have come at a better time; **so etwas geht mir ~** that goes against the grain.

verquicken* [1] *vt* (a) (*Chem*) to amalgamate. (b) (*fig*) to bring together, to combine; (*vermischen*) to mix ◆ **eng miteinander verquickt** closely related.
[2] *vr* **sich (miteinander) ~** to combine.

Verquickung *f* (a) amalgamation. (b) (*fig*) combination.

verquirlen* *vt* to whisk.

verrammeln* *vt* to barricade.

verramschen* *vt* (*Comm*) to sell off cheap; (*inf auch*) to flog (*Brit inf*).

Verrat *m* **-(e)s,** *no pl* betrayal (*an +dat* of); (*Jur*) treason (*an +dat* against) ◆ **~ an jdm üben** to betray sb.

verraten* *irreg* [1] *vt* (a) *Geheimnis, Absicht, jdn* to betray, to give away; (*bekanntgeben, ausplaudern*) to tell; (*fig: erkennen lassen*) to reveal, to show ◆ **nichts ~!** don't say a word!; **er hat es ~** he let it out.
(b) *Freunde, Vaterland, gute Sache etc* to betray (*an +acc* to) ◆ **~ und verkauft** (*inf*) well and truly sunk (*inf*).
[2] *vr* to give oneself away, to betray oneself.

Verräter(in *f*) *m* **-s, -** traitor (*+gen* to).

verräterisch *adj* treacherous, perfidious (*liter*); (*Jur*) treasonable; (*verdächtig*) *Blick, Lächeln etc* telling, telltale *attr.*

verrauchen* [1] *vi aux sein* (*fig: Zorn*) to blow over, to subside.
[2] *vt Tabak, Zigarren etc* to smoke; *Geld* to spend on smoking.

verräuchern* *vt* to fill with smoke.

verraucht *adj* smoky, filled with smoke.

verräumen* *vt* (*S Ger, Aus, Sw*) to put away somewhere.

verrauschen* *vi aux sein* (*fig*) to die *or* fade away.

verrechnen* [1] *vt* (*begleichen*) to settle; *Scheck* to clear; *Lieferung, Leistungen, Guthaben* to credit/debit to an account; (*auszahlen*) to pay out; *Gutschein* to redeem ◆ **die Spesen von der Firma ~ lassen** to have one's expenses paid by the firm; **etw mit etw ~** (*zusammen abrechnen*) to settle sth (together) with sth; (*gegeneinander aufrechnen*) to balance sth with sth, to offset sth against sth.
[2] *vr* to miscalculate; (*Rechenfehler machen*) to make a mistake/mistakes; (*inf: sich täuschen*) to be mistaken ◆ **sich um eine Mark ~** to be out by one mark.

Verrechnung *f siehe vt* settlement; clearing; crediting/debiting to an account; paying out; redemption ◆ **„nur zur ~"** "A/C payee only".

Verrechnungs-: ~einheit *f* clearing unit; **~preise** *pl* (*Comm*) internal prices; **~scheck** *m* crossed (*Brit*) *or* non-negotiable cheque; voucher check (*US*); **~stelle** *f* clearing house.

verrecken* *vi aux sein* (*vulg*) to die; (*elend sterben*) to die a wretched death ◆ **er ist elend verreckt** he died like a dog (*inf*); **soll er doch ~!** let him bloody well die!; **jetzt ist der Alte endlich verreckt** he's finally kicked the bucket (*sl*) *or* snuffed it (*sl*); **zu Tausenden ~** to perish in their thousands; **es ist zum V~** (*sl*) it's damn awful (*inf*), it's bloody terrible (*Brit sl*); **etw nicht ums V~** *or* **ums V~ nicht tun** (*sl*) to damn well (*inf*) *or* bloody well (*Brit sl*) refuse to do sth.

verregnen *vi aux sein* to be spoilt *or* spoiled *or* ruined by rain.

verregnet *adj* rainy, wet.

verreiben* *vt irreg* to rub (*auf +dat* into); *Salbe* to massage (*auf +dat* into).

verreisen* *vi aux sein* to go away (on a trip *or* journey) ◆ **er ist verreist/geschäftlich verreist** he's away, he's out of town/away on business; **wohin ~ Sie in diesem Jahr?** where are you going (on holiday) this year?; **mit dem Auto/der Bahn ~** to go on a car/train journey; (*in Urlaub*) to go on holiday by car/train.

verreißen* *vt irreg* (a) (*kritisieren*) to tear to pieces. (b) (*dial*) *siehe* **zerreißen.** (c) (*dial*) *Schuß, Lenkrad* to jerk; *Wagen* to make swerve.

verrenken* [1] *vt* to dislocate, to put out of joint; *Hals* to crick ◆ **sich** (*dat*) **die Zunge ~** to twist one's tongue; **lieber sich den Bauch** *or* **Magen ~, als dem Wirt was schenken** (*prov*) waste not, want not (*prov*); *siehe* **Hals[1].**
[2] *vr* to contort oneself.

Verrenkung *f* (a) contortion ◆ **~en machen** to contort oneself. (b) (*Med: das Verrenken*) dislocation.

verrennen* *vr irreg* to get carried away ◆ **sich in etw** (*acc*) **~** to get stuck on sth.

Verrentung *f* retirement ◆ **frühe ~** early retirement.

verrichten* *vt Arbeit* to perform, to carry out; *Andacht* to perform; *Gebet* to say; *siehe* **Geschäft, Notdurft.**

Verrichtung *f siehe vt* performing, carrying out; performing; saying ◆ **alltägliche/häusliche ~en** routine *or* daily/domestic *or* household tasks.

verriegeln* *vt* to bolt; (*Comput*) *Tastatur* to lock.

verringern* [1] *vt* to reduce; *Leistungen* to make deteriorate.
[2] *vr* to decrease; (*Qualität auch, Leistungen*) to deteriorate; (*Abstand, Vorsprung auch*) to lessen, to diminish.

Verringerung *f siehe vb* reduction; decrease; deterioration; lessening, diminution.

verrinnen* *vi irreg aux sein* (*Wasser*) to trickle away (*in +dat* into); (*Zeit*) to elapse.

⚠ **Verriß** *m* **-sses, -sse** slating review.

verrohen* [1] *vt* to brutalize.
[2] *vi aux sein* (*Mensch, Gesellschaft*) to become brutalized; (*Sitten*) to coarsen.

Verrohung *f* brutalization.

verrosten* *vi aux sein* to rust; (*fig: steif werden*) to get rusty ◆ **verrostet** rusty.

verrotten* *vi aux sein* to rot; (*sich organisch zersetzen*) to decompose.

verrucht *adj* despicable, loathsome; *Tat auch* heinous; (*verrufen*) disreputable.

Verruchtheit *f, no pl siehe adj;* despicable nature, loathsomeness; disreputableness.

verrücken* *vt* to move, to disarrange.

verrückt *adj* (a) (*geisteskrank*) mad, insane.
(b) (*inf*) crazy, mad ◆ **~ auf** (*+acc*) *or* **nach** crazy *or* mad about (*inf*); **wie ~** like mad *or* crazy (*inf*); **die Leute kamen wie ~** loads of people came (*inf*); **so etwas V~es!** what a crazy idea!; **jdn ~ machen** to drive sb crazy *or* mad *or* wild; **~ werden** to go crazy; **bei dem Lärm kann man ja ~ werden** this noise is enough to drive you round the bend (*inf*); **ich werd' ~, (ich zieh aufs Land)!** (well,) I'll be blowed! (*inf*); **du bist wohl ~!** you must be crazy *or* mad!; **~ spielen** to play up.

Verrückte(r) *mf decl as adj* (*inf*) lunatic.

Verrücktheit *f* (*inf*) madness, craziness; (*Handlung*) mad *or* crazy thing.

Verrücktwerden *nt*: **zum ~** enough to drive one mad *or* crazy *or* round the bend (*inf*) *or* up the wall (*inf*).

Verruf *m* **-(e)s,** *no pl* **in ~ kommen** *or* **geraten** to fall into disrepute; **jdn/etw in ~ bringen** to bring sb/sth into disrepute.

verrufen *adj* disreputable.

verrühren* *vt* to mix, to stir.

verrußen* *vi aux sein* to get *or* become sooty.

verrutschen* *vi aux sein* to slip.

Vers [fɛrs] *m* **-es, -e** verse (*auch Bibl*); (*Zeile*) line ◆ **etw in ~e bringen** *or* **setzen** to put sth into verse; **~e machen** *or* **schmieden** (*inf*) to make up poems; **ich kann mir keinen ~ darauf machen** (*fig*) there's no rhyme or reason in it.

versachlichen* *vt* to objectify.

Versachlichung *f* objectification.

versacken* *vi aux sein* (a) (*lit*) to sink, to become submerged. (b) (*fig inf*) (*lange zechen*) to get involved in a booze-up (*inf*); (*nicht wegkommen*) to stay on; (*herunterkommen*) to go downhill.

versagen* [1] *vt* **jdm/sich etw ~** to deny sb/oneself sth; (*verweigern*) to refuse sb sth; **ich kann es mir nicht ~, eine Bemerkung zu machen** I can't refrain from making a comment; **sich jdm ~** (*geh*) to refuse to give oneself to sb; **etw bleibt** *or* **ist jdm versagt** sth is denied sb, sb is denied sth; *siehe* **Dienst.**
[2] *vi* to fail; (*Mensch: im Leben auch*) to be a failure; (*Gewehr*) to fail to function; (*Maschine auch*) to break down ◆ **die Beine/Nerven** *etc* **versagten ihm** his legs/nerves *etc* gave way; **da versagt diese Methode** this method doesn't work there.

Versagen *nt* **-s,** *no pl* failure; (*von Maschine*) breakdown ◆ **menschliches ~** human error.

⚠: Informationen zur Rechtschreibreform im Anhang

Versagensangst *f usu pl* fear of failure.
Versager(in *f*) *m* **-s, -** failure, flop (*inf*).
Versagung *f* denial; (*Entbehrung*) privation.
Versailler Vertrag [vɛr'zaiɐ] *m* Treaty of Versailles.
Versal [vɛr'za:l] *m* **-s, Versalien** [-'za:liən] *usu pl* (*Typ*) capital letter, cap (*Typ sl*).
versalzen[1]* *vt irreg* to put too much salt in/on, to oversalt; (*inf: verderben*) to spoil; *siehe* **Suppe.**
versalzen[2] *adj Essen* too salty.
versammeln* [1] *vt* to assemble (*auch Mil*), to gather together; *Truppen auch* to rally, to muster ◆ **Leute um sich ~** to gather people around *or* about one; **vor versammelter Mannschaft** (*inf*) in front of *or* before the assembled company.
[2] *vr* to assemble; (*Parlament*) to sit; (*Ausschuß, Verein, Mitglieder*) to meet; (*Tagung*) to convene.
versammelt *adj* (*Reitsport*) collected.
Versammlung *f* **(a)** (*Veranstaltung*) meeting; (*versammelte Menschen*) assembly ◆ **verfassunggebende ~** legislative assembly. **(b)** *siehe vt* assembly, gathering (together); rallying, mustering. **(c)** *siehe vr* assembly; sitting; meeting; convening. **(d)** (*Reitsport*) collection.
Versammlungs-: ~freiheit *f* freedom of assembly; **~lokal** *nt* meeting place; **~raum** *m* (*in Hotel etc*) conference room; (*form: allgemein*) assembly room; **~recht** *nt* right of assembly; **~verbot** *nt* prohibition of assembly.
Versand *m* **-(e)s,** *no pl* **(a)** (*das Versenden*) dispatch; (*das Vertreiben*) distribution ◆ **der ~ per Land/Schiene** shipment by land/rail. **(b)** (*Abteilung*) dispatch department. **(c)** (*inf: ~kaufhaus*) mail order firm.
Versand-: ~abteilung *f* dispatch department; **~anzeige** *f* shipping *or* dispatch advice; **~artikel** *m* article for dispatch; **~bahnhof** *m* dispatch station; **v~bereit** *adj* ready for dispatch; **~buchhandel** *m* mail order book business; **~dokument** *nt usu pl* shipping document.
versanden* *vi aux sein* to silt (up); (*fig*) to peter out, to fizzle out (*inf*).
Versand-: v~fertig *adj siehe* **v~bereit; ~geschäft** *nt* **(a)** mail order firm; **(b)** *siehe* **~handel; ~gut** *nt* goods *pl* for dispatch; **~handel** *m* mail order business; **~haus** *nt* mail order firm *or* house; **~kosten** *pl* transport(ation) costs *pl*; **~papiere** *pl* transport(ation) documents *pl*; **~tasche** *f* padded envelope, jiffy bag ®.
Versandung *f* silting (up); (*fig*) petering out, fizzling out (*inf*).
Versand-: ~unternehmen *nt* mail order business; **~weg** *m* **auf dem ~weg** by mail order.
Versatz *m* **-es,** *no pl* **(a)** (*das Versetzen*) pawning. **(b)** (*Min*) packing, stowing.
Versatz-: ~amt *nt* (*dial*) pawnshop; **~stück** *nt* **(a)** (*Theat*) set piece; **(b)** (*fig*) setting, background; **(c)** (*Aus: Pfandstück*) pledge.
versaubeuteln* *vt* (*inf*) **(a)** (*verschlampen*) to go and lose (*inf*). **(b)** (*verderben*) to mess up (*inf*).
versauen* *vt* (*sl*) to mess up (*inf*).
versauern* (*inf*) [1] *vi aux sein* to stagnate ◆ **eine versauerte alte Jungfer** an embittered old spinster.
[2] *vt* **jdm etw ~** to mess sth up (*inf*) *or* to ruin sth (for sb).
Versauerung, Versäuerung *f* (*von Gewässer, Boden*) acidification.
versaufen* *irreg* (*inf*) [1] *vt Geld* to spend on booze (*inf*) ◆ **seinen Verstand ~** to drink oneself silly; *siehe* **Fell.**
[2] *vi aux sein* (*dial*) **(a)** (*ertrinken*) to drown. **(b)** (*Motor*) to flood.
versäumen* [1] *vt* to miss; *Zeit* to lose; *Pflicht* to neglect; (*Sw: aufhalten*) *jdn* to delay, to hold up ◆ **(es) ~, etw zu tun** to fail to do sth; **nichts ~, um jdn glücklich zu machen** to do everything to make sb happy; **das Versäumte** what one has missed; **die versäumte Zeit aufholen** to make up for lost time.
[2] *vr* **sich bei jdm ~** to stay too long at sb's house.
Versäumnis *nt* (*Fehler, Nachlässigkeit*) failing; (*Unterlassung*) omission; (*versäumte Zeit, Sch*) absence (*gen* from); (*Jur*) default (*gen* in) ◆ **bei ~ rechtzeitiger Bezahlung** failing punctual payment.
Versäumnis|urteil *nt* (*Jur*) judgement by default.
Versbau *m* versification, metrical structure.
verschachern* *vt* to sell off.
verschachtelt *adj Satz* encapsulated, complex ◆ **ineinander ~** interlocking.
verschaffen* [1] *vt* **jdm etw ~** *Geld, Kapital, Arbeit, Stelle, Alibi* to provide *or* supply sb with sth *or* sth for sb; *Arbeit, Stelle auch* to find sth for sb; *Erleichterung, Genugtuung, Vergnügen* to give sb sth; *Ansehen, Respekt* to earn sb sth; *siehe* **Ehre.**
[2] *vr* **sich** (*dat*) **etw ~** to obtain sth; *Kenntnisse* to acquire sth; *Ansehen, Vorteil* to gain sth; *Ruhe, Respekt* to get sth; **sich mit Gewalt Zutritt ~** to force an entry *or* one's way in; **ich muß mir darüber Gewißheit/Klarheit ~** I must be certain about it/I must clarify the matter.
verschalen* [1] *vt Wand* to panel; *Heizung etc* to box in, to encase; (*für Beton*) to build a framework *or* mould for.
[2] *vi* (*für Beton*) to build a framework *or* mould.
Verschalung *f siehe vb* panelling; casing; building a framework *or* mould; (*Bretter*) framework, mould.
verschämt *adj* coy.
Verschämtheit *f* coyness.
verschandeln* *vt* to ruin.
Verschand(e)lung *f* ruining.
verschanzen* [1] *vt* (*Mil*) to fortify.
[2] *vr* (*Mil, fig*) to entrench oneself (*hinter +dat* behind); (*sich verbarrikadieren*) to barricade oneself in (*in etw* (*dat*) sth); (*Deckung suchen*) to take cover (*hinter +dat* behind).

Verschanzung *f* **(a)** *siehe vb* fortification; entrenchment; barricading; taking cover. **(b)** (*Mil: Befestigung*) fortification.
verschärfen* [1] *vt* (*erhöhen*) *Tempo, Aufmerksamkeit* to increase; *Gegensätze* to intensify; (*verschlimmern*) *Lage* to aggravate; *Spannungen* to heighten; (*strenger machen*) *Kontrollen, Strafe, Gesetze, Maßnahmen, Prüfungen* to tighten.
[2] *vr siehe vt* to increase; to intensify; to become aggravated; to heighten, to mount; to become tighter.
verschärft [1] *adj* **(a)** *siehe vb* increased; intensified; aggravated; heightened; tightened; *Arrest* close. **(b)** (*inf: gut*) brilliant (*inf*), wicked (*sl*).
[2] *adv* (*intensiver*) more intensively; (*strenger*) more severely; *prüfen* more closely ◆ **~ aufpassen** to keep a closer watch; **~ kontrollieren** to keep a tighter control; **~ vorgehen** to take more stringent measures.
Verschärfung *f siehe vb* increase; intensification; aggravation; heightening, mounting; tightening.
verscharren* *vt* to bury.
verschatten* *vt* to shade; (*fig: maskieren*) to mask.
verschätzen* *vr* to misjudge, to miscalculate (*in etw* (*dat*) sth) ◆ **sich um zwei Monate ~** to be out by two months.
verschauen* *vr* (*Aus*) **(a)** to make a mistake. **(b) sich in jdn ~** to fall for sb.
verschaukeln* *vt* (*inf*) to take for a ride (*inf*).
verscheiden* *vi irreg aux sein* (*geh*) to pass away, to expire.
verscheißen* *vt irreg* (*vulg*) to cover with shit (*vulg*); *siehe* **verschissen.**
verscheißern* *vt* (*sl*) **jdn ~** to take the piss out of sb (*sl*).
verschenken* [1] *vt* (*lit, fig*) to give away ◆ **sein Herz an jdn ~** (*liter*) to give sb one's heart.
[2] *vr* **sich an jdn ~** to throw oneself away on sb.
verscherbeln* *vt* (*inf*) to flog (*Brit inf*), to sell.
verscherzen* *vr* **sich** (*dat*) **etw ~** to lose *or* forfeit sth; **sich** (*dat*) **seine Chancen/jds Gunst** *or* **Wohlwollen ~** to throw away one's chances/lose *or* forfeit sb's favour; **es sich** (*dat*) **mit jdm ~** to spoil things (for oneself) with sb.
verscheuchen* *vt* to scare *or* frighten off *or* away; (*fig*) *Sorgen, Gedanken etc* to drive away.
verscheuern* *vt* (*inf*) to sell off, to flog off (*Brit inf*).
verschicken* *vt* **(a)** (*versenden*) to send out *or* off. **(b)** (*zur Kur etc*) to send away. **(c)** (*deportieren*) to deport.
verschiebbar *adj Möbel etc* movable; *Regler, Spange, Teil* sliding ◆ **leicht ~e Gegenstände** objects which are easy to move; **der Termin ist ~** this appointment can be changed.
Verschiebe- (*Rail*): **~bahnhof** *m* shunting yard; **~gleis** *nt* shunting track; **~lokomotive** *f* shunter.
verschieben* *irreg* [1] *vt* **(a)** (*verrücken*) to move (*auch Comput*), to shift; *Truppen* to displace; (*Rail*) *Eisenbahnwagen* to shunt; *Perspektive* to alter, to shift.
(b) (*aufschieben*) to change; (*auf später*) to postpone, to put off, to defer (*um* for).
(c) (*inf*) *Waren, Devisen* to traffic in.
[2] *vr* **(a)** to move out of place; (*fig: Perspektive, Schwerpunkt*) to alter, to shift.
(b) (*zeitlich*) to be postponed *or* put off *or* deferred.
(c) (*Med*) (*bei Knochenbruch*) to become displaced; (*Kniescheibe*) to slip.
(d) (*Ling: Laute*) to shift.
Verschiebung *f siehe vt* **(a)** moving, shifting; displacement; shunting; alteration.
(b) postponement, deferment.
(c) trafficking.
(d) (*Geol*) displacement, heave.
(e) (*Ling: von Lauten*) shift.
(f) (*Med*) (*bei Knochenbruch*) displacement; (*von Kniescheibe*) slip.
(g) (*Psych*) displacement.
verschieden [1] *adj* **(a)** (*unterschiedlich*) different; (*unähnlich auch*) dissimilar; *Meinungen etc auch* differing ◆ **die ~sten Sorten** many different kinds, all sorts; **das ist ganz ~** (*wird ~ gehandhabt*) that varies, that just depends; **das sind doch V~e** they are different.
(b) *attr* (*mehrere, einige*) various, several.
(c) (*substantivisch*) **~e** *pl* various *or* several people ◆ **~es** several things; **V~es** different things; (*in Zeitungen, Listen*) miscellaneous.
[2] *adv* differently ◆ **die Häuser sind ~ lang/breit/hoch** the houses vary *or* are different in length/breadth/height.
verschieden|artig *adj* different; (*mannigfaltig*) various, diverse ◆ **die ~sten Dinge** all sorts *or* manner of things.
Verschieden|artigkeit *f* different nature; (*Mannigfaltigkeit*) variety, diversity.
verschiedenemal *adv* several times.
verschiedenerlei *adj inv* **(a)** *attr* many different, various. **(b)** (*substantivisch*) many different things, various things.
verschieden-: ~farbig, ~färbig (*Aus*) *adj* different-coloured; **die Kostüme waren ~farbig** the costumes were many different colours.
Verschiedenheit *f* difference (*gen* of, in); (*Unähnlichkeit*) dissimilarity; (*Vielfalt*) variety.
verschiedentlich *adv* (*mehrmals*) on several occasions, several times; (*vereinzelt*) occasionally.
verschießen* *irreg* [1] *vt* **(a)** *Munition* to use up; *Pfeile* to shoot off; (*inf*) *Fotos, Film auch* to take; *siehe* **Pulver. (b)** (*Sport*) to miss.
[2] *vr* (*inf*) **sich in jdn ~** to fall for sb (*inf*); **in jdn verschossen sein** to be crazy about sb (*inf*).

⚠: for details of spelling reform, see supplement

3 *vi aux sein* (*Stoff, Farbe*) to fade.
verschiffen* *vt* to ship; *Sträfling* to transport.
Verschiffung *f* shipment; (*von Sträflingen*) transportation.
verschilfen* *vi aux sein* to become overgrown with reeds.
verschimmeln* *vi aux sein* (*Nahrungsmittel*) to go mouldy; (*Leder, Papier etc*) to become mildewed, to go mildewy ◆ **verschimmelt** (*lit*) mouldy; mildewed, mildewy; (*fig*) *Ansichten etc* fusty.
verschissen *adj* (*vulg*) *Unterhose* shitty (*sl*) ◆ **du hast bei mir ~** (*sl*) I'm through with you (*inf*).
verschlacken* *vi aux sein* (*Ofen*) to become clogged (up) with slag; (*Med: Gewebe*) to become clogged.
verschlafen* *irreg* 1 *vir* to oversleep.
2 *vt Termin* to miss by oversleeping; (*schlafend verbringen*) *Tag, Morgen* to sleep through; *Leben* to sleep away.
3 *adj* sleepy; (*trottelig*) *Mensch* dozy (*inf*) ◆ **~ sein** (*Vielschläfer sein*) to like one's sleep.
Verschlafenheit *f siehe adj* sleepiness; doziness (*inf*).
Verschlag *m* **-(e), ¨e** (*abgetrennter Raum*) partitioned area; (*Schuppen*) shed; (*grob gezimmert*) shack; (*esp für Kaninchen*) hutch; (*ans Haus angebaut*) lean-to; (*unter der Treppe*) glory-hole; (*elende Behausung*) hovel; (*Verpackung*) crate.
verschlagen[1]* *vt irreg* **(a)** **etw mit Brettern ~** to board sth up.
(b) (*nehmen*) *Atem* to take away ◆ **das hat mir die Sprache ~** it left me speechless.
(c) (*geraten lassen*) to bring ◆ **auf eine einsame Insel ~ werden** to be cast up on a lonely island; **an einen Ort ~ werden** to end up somewhere.
(d) (*Sport*) *Ball* to mishit.
(e) (*verblättern*) *Seite, Stelle* to lose.
(f) (*dial: verprügeln*) to wallop (*inf*), to thrash.
verschlagen[2] *adj* **(a)** *Mensch, Blick, Tier etc* sly, artful. **(b)** (*dial: lauwarm*) tepid, lukewarm.
Verschlagenheit *f siehe adj* **(a)** slyness, artfulness. **(b)** (*dial*) tepidness.
verschlammen* *vi aux sein* to silt up.
verschlampen* (*inf*) 1 *vt* **(a)** (*verlieren*) to go and lose (*inf*). **(b)** (*verkommen lassen*) to spoil.
2 *vi aux sein* (*Mensch*) to go to seed (*inf*).
verschlechtern* 1 *vt* to make worse, to worsen; *Zustand, Lage auch* to aggravate; *Qualität* to impair; *Aussicht* to diminish, to decrease.
2 *vr* to get worse, to worsen, to deteriorate; (*Leistungen auch*) to decline ◆ **sich finanziell/beruflich ~** to be worse off financially/to take a worse job.
Verschlechterung *f siehe vr* worsening, deterioration; decline ◆ **eine finanzielle/berufliche ~** a financial setback/a retrograde step professionally.
verschleiern* 1 *vt* to veil; (*fig auch*) to disguise, to cover up; *Blick* to blur ◆ **Nebel verschleiert die Aussicht/die Berge** the view is/the mountains are hidden by *or* under a veil of mist.
2 *vr* (*Frau*) to veil oneself; (*Himmel*) to become hazy; (*Blick*) to become blurred; (*träumerisch werden*) to become hazy; (*Stimme*) to become husky.
verschleiert *adj Frau* veiled; *Augen, Aussicht* misty; *Berge* misty, veiled in mist; *Stimme* husky; *Blick* blurred; (*träumerisch*) hazy; (*Phot*) foggy ◆ **etw nur ~ sehen** to see sth only hazily.
Verschleierung *f siehe vt* veiling; disguising, covering up; blurring.
Verschleierungs-: ~taktik *f* cover-up (*gen* by); **~versuch** *m* attempt at covering up.
verschleifen* *vt irreg* to slur.
verschleimen* 1 *vt* to block *or* congest with phlegm ◆ **verschleimt sein** (*Patient*) to be congested with phlegm.
2 *vi aux sein* to become blocked *or* congested with phlegm.
Verschleimung *f* mucous congestion.
Verschleiß *m* **-es, -e** **(a)** (*lit, fig*) wear and tear; (*Verbrauch*) consumption; (*Verluste*) loss ◆ **ein ~ deiner Kräfte** a drain on your strength; **eingeplanter ~** built-in obsolescence; **ihr ~ an Männern** (*hum*) the rate she gets through men. **(b)** (*Aus: Kleinverkauf*) retail trade.
verschleißen *pret* **verschliß**, *ptp* **verschlissen** 1 *vt* **(a)** to wear out; (*verbrauchen*) to use up. **(b)** (*Aus*) to retail.
2 *vi aux sein* to wear out; *siehe* **verschlissen.**
3 *vr* to wear out; (*Menschen*) to wear oneself out.
Verschleißer(in *f*) *m* **-s, -** (*Aus*) retailer.
Verschleiß-: ~erscheinung *f* sign of wear; **~krieg** *m* war of attrition; **~prüfung** *f* wear test; **~teil** *nt* part subject to wear and tear.
verschleppen* *vt* **(a)** (*entführen*) *jdn* to abduct; *Kunstschätze etc* to carry off; (*inf*) *etw* to go off with. **(b)** (*verbreiten*) *Seuche* to spread, to carry. **(c)** (*hinauszögern*) *Prozeß, Verhandlung* to draw out, to protract; (*Pol*) *Gesetzesänderung etc* to delay; *Krankheit* to protract.
Verschleppte(r) *mf decl as adj* displaced person.
Verschleppung *f siehe vt* **(a)** abduction; carrying off. **(b)** spreading, carrying. **(c)** protraction; delay; protraction.
Verschleppungstaktik *f* delaying tactics *pl*.
verschleudern* *vt* (*Comm*) to dump; (*vergeuden*) *Vermögen, Geld* to squander.
verschließbar *adj Dosen, Gläser etc* closeable, sealable; *Tür, Schublade, Zimmer etc* lockable.
verschließen* *irreg* 1 *vt* **(a)** (*abschließen*) to lock (up); (*fig*) to close, to shut; (*versperren*) to bar; (*mit Riegel*) to bolt ◆ **jdm etw ~** (*fig*) to deny sb sth; *siehe* **verschlossen.**
(b) (*wegschließen*) to lock up *or* away.
(c) (*zumachen*) to close; *Glas auch, Karton auch, Brief* to seal; (*mit Pfropfen*) *Flasche* to cork ◆ **die Augen/Ohren/sein Herz (vor etw** *dat*) **~** to shut one's eyes/ears/heart (to sth); **seine Gedanken/seinen Kummer in sich** (*dat*) ~ to keep one's thoughts/one's worries to oneself.
2 *vr* (*Reize, Sprache, Möglichkeit*) to be closed (*dat* to); (*Mensch: reserviert sein*) to shut oneself off (*dat* from) ◆ **sich vor jdm ~** to shut oneself off from sb; **sich einer Sache** (*dat*) *or* **gegen etw ~** to close one's mind to sth; **ich kann mich der Tatsache nicht ~, daß ...** I can't close my eyes to the fact that ...
verschlimmbessern* *vt insep* (*hum*) to make worse, to disimprove.
Verschlimmbesserung *f* (*hum*) worsening, disimprovement.
verschlimmern* 1 *vt* to make worse, to aggravate; *Schmerzen auch* to increase.
2 *vr* to get worse, to worsen.
Verschlimmerung *f* worsening; (*von Schmerzen auch*) increase.
verschlingen* *irreg* 1 *vt* **(a)** to entwine, to intertwine ◆ **er stand mit verschlungenen Armen da** he stood there with his arms folded; **ein verschlungener Pfad** a winding path.
(b) (*fressen, gierig essen*) to devour; (*auffressen auch*) to swallow up; (*fig*) (*Welle, Dunkelheit*) to engulf; (*verbrauchen*) *Geld, Strom etc* to eat up, to consume; (*inf*) *Buch, jds Worte* to devour ◆ **jdn mit den Augen** *or* **Blicken ~** to devour sb with one's eyes.
2 *vr* to become entwined *or* intertwined; (*zu einem Knoten etc*) to become entangled; (*Därme*) to become twisted.
Verschlingung *f* **(a)** (*von Fäden etc*) tangle; (*von Muster, Arabeske*) interlacing. **(b)** (*von Darm*) twisting.
⚠**verschliß** *pret of* **verschleißen.**
verschlissen 1 *ptp of* **verschleißen.**
2 *adj* worn (out); *Kleidung, Teppich, Material auch* threadbare.
verschlossen 1 *ptp of* **verschließen.**
2 *adj* closed; (*mit Schlüssel*) *Tür, Fach etc* locked; (*mit Riegel*) bolted; *Dose auch, Briefumschlag* sealed; (*fig*) (*unzugänglich*) reserved ◆ **gut ~ aufbewahren** keep tightly closed; **etw bleibt jdm ~** sth is (a) closed (book) to sb; **hinter ~en Türen** behind closed doors; **wir standen vor ~er Tür** we were left standing on the doorstep.
Verschlossenheit *f* (*von Mensch*) reserve, reticence.
verschlucken* 1 *vt* to swallow; (*fig auch*) *Wörter, Silben, Buchstaben* to slur; *Geld* to consume; *Schall* to deaden; *siehe* **Erdboden.**
2 *vr* to swallow the wrong way; (*fig*) to splutter.
verschludern* (*inf*) 1 *vt* to go and lose (*inf*).
2 *vi aux sein* to let oneself go.
⚠**Verschluß** *m* **-sses, ¨sse** **(a)** (*Schloß*) lock; (*luft-, wasserdicht, für Zoll*) seal; (*Deckel, Klappe*) top, lid; (*Pfropfen, Stöpsel*) stopper; (*an Kleidung*) fastener; (*an Schmuck*) catch; (*an Tasche, Buch, Schuh*) clasp ◆ **etw unter ~ halten** to keep sth under lock and key. **(b)** (*Phot*) shutter; (*an Waffe*) breechblock. **(c)** (*Med, Phon*) occlusion.
verschlüsseln* *vt* to (put into) code, to encode.
Verschlüsselung, ⚠**Verschlüßlung** *f* coding.
⚠**Verschluß-: ~laut** *m* (*Phon*) plosive; **~sache** *f* item of classified information; **~sachen** *pl* classified information *sing*.
verschmachten* *vi aux sein* to languish (*vor +dat* for) ◆ **(vor Durst/Hitze) ~** (*inf*) to be dying of thirst/heat (*inf*).
verschmähen* *vt* to spurn, to scorn; *Liebhaber* to spurn, to reject ◆ **verschmähte Liebe** unrequited love; **einen Whisky verschmähe ich nie** I never say no to a whisky.
verschmälern* 1 *vt* to make narrower.
2 *vr* to become narrower, to narrow.
verschmausen* *vt* (*inf*) to feast on.
verschmelzen* *irreg* 1 *vi aux sein* to melt together; (*Metalle*) to fuse; (*Farben*) to blend; (*Betriebe etc*) to merge; (*fig*) to blend (*zu* into).
2 *vt* **(a)** (*verbinden*) *Metalle* to fuse; *Farben* to blend; *Betriebe, Firmen* to merge. **(b)** *Bruchflächen* to smooth, to round off. **(c)** (*fig*) to unify (*zu* into).
Verschmelzung *f* **(a)** (*Verbindung*) fusion; (*von Reizen, Eindrücken*) blending; (*von Farben*) blending. **(b)** (*von Bruchflächen*) smoothing, rounding off. **(c)** (*fig*) (*von Völkern, Begriffen etc*) fusion. **(d)** (*Comm*) merger.
verschmerzen* *vt* to get over.
verschmieren* 1 *vt* **(a)** (*verstreichen*) *Salbe, Schmiere, Creme, Fett* to spread (*in +dat* over). **(b)** (*verputzen*) *Löcher* to fill in. **(c)** (*verwischen*) *Fenster, Gesicht* to smear; *Geschriebenes, Lippenstift, Schminke* to smudge.
2 *vi* to smudge.
verschmiert *adj Hände, Gesicht* smeary; *Schminke* smudged.
verschmitzt *adj* mischievous.
verschmutzen* 1 *vt* to dirty, to soil; *Luft, Wasser, Umwelt* to pollute; *Gewehr, Zündkerze* to foul; *Fahrbahn* to make muddy; (*Hund*) *Bürgersteig* to foul.
2 *vi aux sein* to get dirty; (*Luft, Wasser, Umwelt*) to become polluted.
verschmutzt *adj* dirty, soiled; *Luft etc* polluted ◆ **stark ~** very dirty, badly soiled; **„~e Fahrbahn"** "mud on road".
Verschmutzung *f* **(a)** *no pl siehe vt* dirtying, soiling; pollution; fouling; making muddy. **(b)** (*das Verschmutztsein*) dirtiness *no pl*; (*von Luft etc*) pollution ◆ **starke ~en auf der Autobahn** a great deal of mud *or* dirt on the motorway.
verschnaufen* *vir* (*inf*) to have a breather, to have a rest.
Verschnaufpause *f* breather.
verschneiden* *vt irreg* **(a)** *Wein, Rum, Essigsorten* to blend. **(b)** (*stutzen*) *Flügel* to clip; *Hecke auch* to cut. **(c)** (*falsch schneiden*) *Kleid, Stoff* to cut wrongly; *Haar* to cut badly. **(d)** *Tiere* to geld, to castrate.

verschneit *adj* snow-covered ◆ **tief ~** thick with snow.
Verschnitt *m* **(a)** (*von Rum, Wein, Essig*) blend. **(b)** (*Abfall*) waste material, clippings *pl*.
verschnörkeln* *vt* to adorn with flourishes.
verschnörkelt *adj* ornate.
Verschnörkelung *f* **(a)** (*das Verschnörkeln*) embellishing (with flourishes). **(b)** (*Schnörkel*) flourish.
verschnupft *adj* (*inf*) **(a)** (*erkältet*) *Mensch* with a cold; *Nase* bunged up (*inf*). **(b)** (*usu pred: beleidigt*) peeved (*inf*).
verschnüren* *vt* to tie up; *Schuhe auch* to lace.
Verschnürung *f* **(a)** (*das Verschnüren*) *siehe vt* tying (up); lacing. **(b)** (*Schnur*) string; (*Schnürband*) lace.
verschollen *adj Schiff, Flugzeug, Mensch etc* missing, lost without trace; *Literaturwerk* forgotten ◆ **ein lange ~er Freund** a long-lost friend; **er ist ~** (*im Krieg*) he is missing, presumed dead; **V~e(r)** missing person; (*Jur*) person presumed to be dead.
verschonen* *vt* to spare (*jdn von etw* sb sth); (*von Steuern auch*) to exempt ◆ **verschone mich mit deinen Reden!** spare me your speeches; **verschone mich damit!** spare me that!; **von etw verschont bleiben** to escape sth.
verschöne(r)n* *vt* to improve (the appearance of); *Wohnung, Haus, Zimmer* to brighten (up).
Verschönerung, Verschönung *f siehe vt* improvement; brightening up.
Verschonung *f* sparing; (*von Steuern*) exemption.
verschorfen* *vi aux sein* to (form a) scab ◆ **die verschorfte Wunde** the encrusted wound.
Verschorfung *f* encrustation, scabbing.
verschrammen* [1] *vt* to scratch.
[2] *vi aux sein* to become *or* get scratched.
verschränken* *vt* to cross over; *Arme* to fold; *Beine* to cross; *Hände* to clasp; *Hölzer* to joggle; (*Stricken*) to cable ◆ **verschränkter Reim** embracing rhyme.
Verschränkung *f* **(a)** (*das Verschränktsein*) fold. **(b)** *siehe vt* crossing over; folding; crossing; clasping; jogging; cabling.
verschrauben* *vt* to screw together.
verschrecken* *vt* to frighten *or* scare off *or* away.
verschreckt *adj* frightened, scared.
verschreiben* *irreg* [1] *vt* **(a)** (*verordnen*) to prescribe.
(b) (*old: übereignen*) to make over, to transfer ◆ **seine Seele dem Teufel ~** to sign away one's soul to the devil.
(c) *Papier* to use up; (*rare*) *Wort* to write incorrectly.
[2] *vr* **(a)** (*falsch schreiben*) to make a slip (of the pen).
(b) sich einer Sache (*dat*) **~** to devote *or* dedicate oneself to sth; **sich dem Teufel ~** to sell oneself to the devil.
Verschreibung *f* **(a)** (*Verordnung*) prescription. **(b)** (*old: Übertragung*) making over, transference. **(c)** (*Schreibfehler*) mistake, error.
verschreibungspflichtig *adj* only available on prescription, ethical.
verschrie(e)n *adj* notorious.
verschroben *adj* eccentric, odd.
Verschrobenheit *f, no pl* eccentricity.
verschroten* *vt* to grind coarsely.
verschrotten* *vt* to scrap.
Verschrottung *f* scrapping ◆ **etw zur ~ geben** to send sth to be scrapped.
verschrumpeln* *vi aux sein* to shrivel.
verschüchtern* *vt* to intimidate.
verschulden* [1] *vt* (*schuldhaft verursachen*) to be to blame for, to be responsible for; *Unfall, Unglück* to cause.
[2] *vi aux sein* (*in Schulden geraten*) to get into debt ◆ **immer mehr ~** to get deeper and deeper into debt; **verschuldet sein** to be in debt.
Verschulden *nt* **-s,** *no pl* fault ◆ **durch eigenes ~** through one's own fault; **ohne sein/mein ~** through no fault of his (own)/of my own *or* of mine.
Verschuldung *f* **(a)** (*Schulden*) indebtedness. **(b)** (*schuldhafte Verursachung*) blame (*gen* for) ◆ **bei eigener ~ eines Schadens** if one is (oneself) to blame for damage caused.
verschusseln* *vt* (*inf*) (*vermasseln*) to mess *or* muck up (*inf*); (*vergessen*) to forget; (*verlegen*) to mislay, to lose.
verschusselt *adj siehe* **schusselig**.
verschütten* *vt* **(a)** *Flüssigkeit* to spill. **(b)** (*zuschütten*) *Brunnen, Flußarm* to fill in. **(c)** (*begraben*) **verschüttet werden** (*Mensch*) to be buried (alive); (*fig*) to be submerged.
verschüttet *adj* buried (alive); (*fig*) submerged.
Verschüttete(r) *mf decl as adj* buried man/woman (*in an accident*).
⚠ **verschüttgehen** *vi sep irreg aux sein* (*inf*) to get lost.
verschwägert *adj* related (by marriage) (*mit* to).
Verschwägerung *f* relationship by marriage (*mit* to).
verschweigen* *vt irreg Tatsachen, Wahrheit etc* to hide, to conceal, to withhold (*jdm etw* sth from sb) ◆ **ich habe nichts zu ~** I've nothing to hide.
Verschweigen *nt* **-s,** *no pl* concealment, hiding, withholding ◆ **das ~ der Wahrheit** concealing *or* withholding the truth.
verschweißen* *vt* to weld (together).
verschwelen* *vti Holz* to burn; (*Tech*) *Kohle* to carbonize.
verschwenden* *vt* to waste (*auf or an +acc, für* on); (*leichtsinnig vertun*) *Geld* to squander.
Verschwender(in *f*) *m* **-s, -** spendthrift, squanderer.
verschwenderisch *adj* wasteful; *Leben* extravagant; (*üppig*) lavish, sumptuous; *Fülle* lavish ◆ **mit etw ~ umgehen** to be lavish with sth.
Verschwendung *f* wastefulness ◆ **~ von Geld/Zeit** waste of money/time.
Verschwendungs-: ~sucht *f, no pl* extravagance; **v~süchtig** *adj* (wildly) extravagant.
verschwiegen [1] *ptp of* **verschweigen.**
[2] *adj Mensch* discreet; *Ort* secluded; *siehe* **Grab.**
Verschwiegenheit *f, no pl* (*von Mensch*) discretion; (*von Ort*) seclusion ◆ **zur ~ verpflichtet** bound to secrecy; *siehe* **Siegel.**
verschwiemelt *adj* (*N Ger inf*) *siehe* **verschwollen.**
verschwimmen* *vi irreg aux sein* to become blurred *or* indistinct ◆ **es verschwamm ihr alles vor den Augen** everything went fuzzy *or* hazy; **ineinander ~** to melt into one another, to merge (into one another); *siehe* **verschwommen.**
verschwinden* *vi irreg aux sein* to disappear, to vanish ◆ **verschwinde!** clear off! (*inf*), away! (*liter*); **etw ~ lassen** (*Zauberer*) to make sth disappear *or* vanish; (*verstecken*) to dispose of sth; (*stehlen*) to steal *or* filch sth; **etw in etw** (*dat*) **~ lassen** to slip sth into sth; **neben jdm/etw ~** to pale into insignificance beside sb/sth, to be eclipsed by sb/sth; (*in bezug auf Größe*) to look minute beside sb/sth; **(mal) ~ müssen** (*euph inf*) to have to spend a penny (*inf*).
Verschwinden *nt* **-s,** *no pl* disappearance.
verschwindend *adj Anzahl, Menge* insignificant ◆ **~ wenig** very, very few; **~ klein** minute.
verschwistern* *vr* (*fig*) to form a close union; (*Städte*) to become twinned; (*liter: Seelen*) to become closely united.
verschwistert *adj* **(miteinander) ~ sein** to be brother and sister, to be siblings (*Sociol, Med etc*); (*Brüder*) to be brothers; (*Schwestern*) to be sisters; (*fig*) to be close; (*Städte*) to be twinned, to be twin towns; **~e Seelen** (*liter*) kindred spirits.
verschwitzen* *vt* **(a)** *Kleidung* to make sweaty. **(b)** (*fig inf*) to forget.
verschwitzt *adj* sweat-stained; (*feucht*) sweaty; *Mensch* sweaty.
verschwollen *adj* swollen.
verschwommen [1] *ptp of* **verschwimmen.**
[2] *adj Foto, Umrisse* blurred, fuzzy; *Berge* hazy, indistinct; *Erinnerung, Vorstellung* vague, hazy; *Argumente, Begriffe* woolly *no adv*, vague ◆ **ich sehe alles ~** everything looks hazy to me.
Verschwommenheit *f siehe adj* blurredness, fuzziness; haziness, indistinctness; vagueness; woolliness.
verschworen [1] *ptp of* **verschwören.**
[2] *adj* **(a)** *Gesellschaft* sworn. **(b) einer Sache** (*dat*) **~ sein** to have given oneself over to sth.
verschwören* *vr irreg* **(a)** to conspire, to plot (*mit* with, *gegen* against) ◆ **sich zu etw ~** to plot sth, to conspire to do sth; **sie haben sich zu einem Attentat gegen den Diktator verschworen** they are conspiring *or* plotting to assassinate the dictator; **alles hat sich gegen mich verschworen** (*fig*) there's a conspiracy against me.
(b) (*sich verschreiben*) **sich einer Sache** (*dat*) **~** to give oneself over to sth.
Verschworene(r) *mf decl as adj* conspirator, plotter; (*fig*) ally, accomplice.
Verschwörer(in *f*) *m* **-s, -** conspirator.
Verschwörung *f* conspiracy, plot.
verschwunden [1] *ptp of* **verschwinden.**
[2] *adj* missing, who/that has/had disappeared.
versechsfachen* [-'zeks-] [1] *vt* to multiply by six.
[2] *vr* to increase sixfold.
versehen* *irreg* [1] *vt* **(a)** (*ausüben*) *Amt, Stelle etc* to occupy, to hold; *Dienst* to perform, to discharge (*form*); (*sich kümmern um*) to look after, to take care of; *Küche* to see to, to do; (*Bus, Schiff etc*) *Route* to provide the/a service on; *Dienst* to provide ◆ **den Dienst eines Kollegen ~** to take a colleague's place, to perform a colleague's duties.
(b) (*ausstatten*) **jdn mit etw ~** to provide *or* supply sb with sth; (*ausrüsten auch*) to equip sb with sth; **etw mit etw ~** to put sth on/in sth; (*montieren*) to fit sth with sth; **ein Buch mit einem Umschlag ~** to provide a book with a dust-jacket; **mit etw ~ sein** to have sth; **mit Blättern/Wurzeln/Haaren** *etc* **~ sein** to have leaves/roots/hairs *etc*; **mit Etiketten/Wegweisern ~ sein** to be labelled/sign-posted; **mit allem reichlich/wohl ~ sein** to be well provided for; **die Bücherei ist gut (mit Fachliteratur) ~** the library is well stocked (with specialist literature).
(c) (*Eccl*) **jdn (mit den Sterbesakramenten) ~** to administer the last rites *or* sacraments to sb.
(d) (*geben*) to give ◆ **jdn mit einer Vollmacht ~** to invest sb with full powers; **etw mit seiner Unterschrift ~** to affix one's signature to sth (*form*), to sign sth; **etw mit einem Stempel/Siegel ~** to stamp sth/to affix a seal to sth; **etw mit Akzept ~** (*Fin*) to accept sth.
(e) (*vernachlässigen*) to omit, to overlook.
[2] *vr* **(a)** (*sich irren*) to be mistaken, to make a mistake.
(b) sich mit etw ~ (*sich versorgen*) to provide oneself with sth; (*sich ausstatten*) to equip oneself with sth.
(c) ehe man sich's versieht before you could turn round, before you could say Jack Robinson (*inf*).
➤ **Versehen** *nt* **-s, -** (*Irrtum*) mistake, error; (*Unachtsamkeit*) inadvertence, oversight ◆ **aus ~** by mistake, inadvertently.
versehentlich [1] *adj attr* inadvertent; (*irrtümlich*) erroneous.
[2] *adv* inadvertently, by mistake.
Versehgang *m* (*Eccl*) visit to a/the dying man/woman.
versehren* *vt* (*verletzen*) to injure, to hurt; (*zum Invaliden machen*) to disable; (*beschädigen*) to damage.
Versehrten-: ~rente *f* disability *or* invalidity pension; **~sport** *m* sport for

➤ SPRACHE AKTIV: Versehen → 45.4

the disabled.

Versehrte(r) *mf decl as adj* disabled person/man/woman *etc* ◆ **Platz für ~** seat for the disabled *or* for disabled persons.

verseifen* *vt* (*Chem*) to saponify.

⚠ **verselbständigen*** *vr* to become independent; (*beruflich auch*) to become self-employed.

⚠ **Verselbständigung** *f* **die ~ der Kinder** children's becoming independent; **er hatte zu einer ~ nicht genügend Startkapital** he hadn't sufficient capital to become independent.

versenden* *vt irreg or reg* to send; (*Comm auch*) to forward; *Kataloge, Heiratsanzeige etc* to send (out); (*verfrachten auch*) to ship.

Versendung *f siehe vt* sending; forwarding; sending out; shipment ◆ **die ~ der Kataloge** sending (out) the catalogues.

versengen* *vt* **(a)** (*Sonne, mit Bügeleisen*) to scorch; (*Feuer*) to singe. **(b)** (*inf: verprügeln*) to thrash, to wallop (*inf*).

versenkbar *adj* that can be lowered; *Scheinwerfer* retractable; *Nähmaschine, Tischplatte* fold-away *attr* ◆ **nicht ~** *Schiff* unsinkable.

versenken* [1] *vt* **(a)** *Schatz, Behälter* to sink; *Leiche, Sarg* to lower; *Schiff auch* to send to the bottom; *das eigene Schiff* to scuttle ◆ **die Hände in die Taschen ~** to thrust one's hands into one's pockets; **den Kopf in ein Buch ~** to bury one's head *or* to immerse oneself in a book.
(b) *Schraube* to countersink; *Tischplatte* to fold away; (*Theat*) to lower ◆ **eine Nähmaschine, die man ~ kann** a fold-away sewing-machine.
[2] *vr* **sich in etw** (*acc*) **~** to become immersed in sth; *in Gedanken auch, in Anblick* to lose oneself in sth.

Versenkung *f* **(a)** *siehe vt (a)* sinking; lowering; scuttling.
(b) (*Theat*) trap(door).
(c) (*das Sichversenken*) immersion ◆ **jdn aus seiner ~ reißen** to tear sb from (his absorption *or* immersion in) his book/work *etc*; **seine ~ in diesen Anblick** his rapt contemplation of this sight; **innere/mystische ~** inner/mystic contemplation.
(d) (*inf*) **in der ~ verschwinden** to vanish; (*berühmter Mensch, Buch etc*) to vanish *or* disappear from the scene, to sink into oblivion; **aus der ~ auftauchen** to re-appear; (*Mensch auch*) to re-emerge (on the scene).

Verseschmied *m* (*pej*) rhymester (*pej*), versifier (*pej*).

versessen [1] *ptp of* **versitzen**.
[2] *adj* (*fig*) **auf etw** (*acc*) **~ sein** to be very keen on sth, to be mad *or* crazy about sth (*inf*).

Versessenheit *f* keenness (*auf +acc* on).

versetzen* [1] *vt* **(a)** (*an andere Stelle setzen*) *Gegenstände, Möbel, Schüler* to move, to shift; *Pflanzen auch* to transplant; (*nicht geradlinig anordnen*) to stagger.
(b) (*beruflich*) to transfer, to move ◆ **jdn in einen höheren Rang ~** to promote sb, to move sb up; *siehe* **Ruhestand**.
(c) (*Sch: in höhere Klasse*) to move *or* put up.
(d) (*Typ, Mus*) to transpose.
(e) (*inf*) (*verkaufen*) to flog (*Brit inf*), to sell; (*verpfänden*) to pawn, to hock (*inf*).
(f) (*inf: nicht erscheinen*) **jdn ~** to stand sb up (*inf*).
(g) (*in bestimmten Zustand bringen*) **etw in Bewegung/Schwingung ~** to set sth in motion/to set sth swinging; **jdn in Wut/in fröhliche Stimmung ~** to send sb into a rage/to put sb in a cheerful mood; **jdn in Sorge/Unruhe ~** to worry/disturb sb; **jdn in Angst ~** to frighten sb, to make sb afraid; **jdn in die Lage ~, etw zu tun** to put sb in a position to do sth.
(h) (*geben*) *Stoß, Schlag, Tritt etc* to give ◆ **jdm eins ~** (*inf*) to belt sb (*inf*), to land sb one (*inf*); **jdm einen Stich ~** (*fig*) to cut sb to the quick, to wound sb (deeply); *siehe* **Todesstoß**.
(i) (*mischen*) to mix.
(j) (*antworten*) to retort.
[2] *vr* **(a)** (*sich an andere Stelle setzen*) to move (to another place), to change places.
(b) sich in jdn/in jds Lage/Gefühle ~ to put oneself in sb's place *or* position.
(c) sich in eine frühere Zeit/seine Jugend *etc* **~** to take oneself back to *or* imagine oneself back in an earlier period/one's youth *etc*.

Versetzung *f* **(a)** (*beruflich*) transfer ◆ **seine ~ in einen höheren Rang** his promotion (to a higher grade/rank). **(b)** (*Sch*) moving up, being put up ◆ **bei nicht erfolgter ~** when the pupil isn't moved *or* put up. **(c)** (*Mus, Typ*) transposition. **(d)** (*nicht geradlinige Anordnung*) staggering. **(e)** (*Vermischung*) mixing.

Versetzungs-: ~konferenz *f* end of year staff meeting (*to decide whether pupils should be put up to next class*); **~zeichen** *nt* (*Mus*) accidental; **~zeugnis** *nt* end-of-year report.

verseuchen* *vt* (*mit Bakterien*) to infect; (*mit Gas, Giftstoffen*) to contaminate; (*fig*) to contaminate, to poison; (*Comput*) to infect with a virus.

Verseuchung *f siehe vt* infection; contamination *no pl*; poisoning *no pl*.

Verseuchungsgrad *m* contamination level.

Vers-: ~form *f* (*Poet*) verse form; **~fuß** *m* (*Poet*) (metrical) foot.

Versicherer *m* **-s, -** insurer; (*bei Lebensversicherung auch*) assurer; (*bei Schiffen*) underwriter.

▼ **versichern*** [1] *vt* **(a)** (*bestätigen*) to assure; (*beteuern*) to affirm, to protest ◆ **jdm ~, daß ...** to assure sb that ...; **jdm etw ~** to assure sb of sth; *seine Unschuld* to affirm *or* protest sth to sb.
(b) (*geh*) **jdn einer Sache** (*gen*) **~** to assure sb of sth; **seien Sie versichert, daß** ... (you can *or* may) rest assured that ...
(c) (*gegen Betrag*) to insure; *Leben auch* to assure.

➤ SPRACHE AKTIV: **versichern: 1a** → 42.1

[2] *vr* **(a)** (*Versicherung abschließen*) to insure oneself (*mit* for); (*Lebensversicherung auch*) to take out a life insurance *or* assurance policy (*mit* of).
(b) (*sich vergewissern*) to make sure *or* certain.
(c) sich jds/einer Sache ~ (*geh*) to secure sb/sth.

Versicherte(r) *mf decl as adj* insured/assured (party).

Versicherung *f* **(a)** (*Bestätigung*) assurance; (*Beteuerung*) affirmation, protestation. **(b)** (*Feuer~ etc*) insurance; (*Lebens~ auch*) assurance.

Versicherungs-: ~agent *m* (*Aus*) insurance agent; **~anstalt** *f* insurance company; **~beitrag** *m* **(a)** (*bei staatlicher Versicherung etc*) insurance contribution; **(b)** (*bei Haftpflichtversicherung etc*) insurance premium; **~betrug** *m* insurance fraud; **~dauer** *f* period of insurance; **~fall** *m* event of loss/damage; **~gesellschaft** *f* insurance/assurance company; **~karte** *f* insurance card; **die grüne ~karte** (*Mot*) the green card; **~kaufmann** *m* insurance broker; **~mathematik** *f* actuarial theory; **~nehmer** *m* (*form*) policy holder, insurant (*form*); **~pflicht** *f* compulsory insurance; **jeder Autofahrer unterliegt der ~pflicht** insurance is compulsory for every driver; **v~pflichtig** *adj* subject to compulsory insurance; **~police** *f* insurance/assurance policy; **~prämie** *f* insurance premium; **~satz** *m* rate of insurance; **~schutz** *m* insurance cover; **~summe** *f* sum insured/assured; **~träger** *m siehe* **Versicherer**; **~vertreter** *m* insurance agent; **~wert** *m* insurance value; **~wesen** *nt* insurance (business); **~zwang** *m* compulsory insurance.

versickern* *vi aux sein* to seep away; (*fig*) (*Gespräch, Unterstützung*) to dry up; (*Interesse, Teilnahme*) to peter out.

versieben *vt* (*inf*) (*vergessen*) to forget; (*verlieren*) to lose; (*verpfuschen*) to make a mess of (*inf*).

versiebenfachen* [1] *vt* to multiply by seven.
[2] *vr* to increase sevenfold.

versiegeln* *vt Brief, Tür* to seal (up); *Parkett etc* to seal.

Versiegelung *f* (*Vorgang*) sealing; (*Siegel*) seal.

versiegen* *vi aux sein* (*Fluß, Quelle*) to dry up, to run dry; (*fig*) (*Gespräch, Unterstützung*) to dry up; (*Interesse*) to peter out; (*Tränen*) to dry up; (*gute Laune, Humor, Kräfte*) to fail ◆ **nie ~der Humor** never-failing *or* irrepressible humour; **nie ~de Hoffnung** never-failing *or* undying hope.

versiert [vɛr-] *adj* experienced, practised ◆ **in etw** (*dat*) **~ sein** to be experienced *or* (*in bezug auf Wissen*) (well) versed in sth.

Versiertheit [vɛr-] *f* experience (*in +dat* in); (*in bezug auf Wissen*) knowledge (*in +dat* of).

versilbern* *vt* (*silbern bemalen*) to paint silver; (*mit Silber überziehen*) to silver(-plate); (*fig inf: verkaufen*) to flog (*Brit inf*), to sell; (*fig liter: Mond*) to silver.

Versilberung *f* (*Vorgang*) silvering, (silver-)plating; (*Silberschicht*) silver-plate.

versimpeln* (*inf*) [1] *vt* (*vereinfachen*) to make easier *or* simpler.
[2] *vi aux sein* (*einfältig werden*) **sie ist völlig versimpelt** her mind has completely gone to seed.

versinken* *vi irreg aux sein* (*untergehen*) to sink; (*Schiff auch*) to founder ◆ **ich hätte im Boden** *or* **in der Erde/vor Scham ~ mögen** I wished the ground would (open and) swallow me up; **im Laster/Morast der Großstadt ~** to sink into vice/into the mire of the big city; **in etw** (*acc*) **~** (*fig*) *in Trauer, Melancholie* to sink into sth; *in Anblick* to lose oneself in sth; *in Gedanken, Musik* to become immersed in sth, to lose oneself in sth; **alles versinkt um ihn (herum)** (*fig*) he becomes totally oblivious to everything (around him); *siehe* **versunken**.

versinnbildlichen* *vt* to symbolize, to represent.

Versinnbildlichung *f* symbolization, representation.

Version [vɛr'zioːn] *f* version.

versippt *adj* (*pej*) interrelated.

versitzen* *vt irreg* (*inf*) *Kleidung* to crease, to crush ◆ **ich habe heute morgen meine ganze Zeit beim Arzt versessen** I sat about (waiting) the whole morning at the doctor's.

versklaven* [fɛɐ'sklaːvn, -aːfn] *vt* (*lit, fig*) to enslave.

Versklavung *f* enslavement.

Vers-: ~kunst *f* versification; **~lehre** *f* study of verse; **~maß** *nt* metre.

versnoben* *vi aux sein* (*pej*) to become snobbish *or* a snob ◆ **versnobt** snobbish, snobby (*inf*).

versoffen *adj* (*sl*) boozy (*inf*) ◆ **ein ~es Genie** a drunken genius.

versohlen* *vt* (*inf*) to belt (*inf*); (*zur Strafe auch*) to leather.

versöhnen* [1] *vt* to reconcile; (*besänftigen*) *jdn, Götter* to placate, to appease; (*fig*) *Unterschiede, jdn* to reconcile ◆ **~de Worte** conciliatory/placatory words; **das versöhnt einen dann wieder** it almost makes up for it.
[2] *vr* to be(come) reconciled; (*Streitende*) to make it up ◆ **sich mit Gott ~** to make one's peace with God; **sich mit etw ~** to reconcile oneself to sth.

versöhnlich *adj Mensch* conciliatory; *Laune, Ton auch* placatory; (*nicht nachtragend*) forgiving ◆ **die Götter ~ stimmen** to placate *or* appease the gods.

Versöhnung *f* reconciliation; (*Beschwichtigung*) appeasement ◆ **zur ~ opferte er den Göttern** ... to appease *or* placate the gods he sacrificed ...

Versöhnungs-: ~fest *nt*, **~tag** *m* (*Rel*) Day of Atonement, Yom Kippur *no def art*; **~politik** *f* policy of reconciliation.

versonnen *adj* (*in Gedanken verloren*) *Gesichtsausdruck* pensive, thoughtful; *Mensch auch* lost in thought; (*träumerisch*) *Blick* dreamy.

versorgen* [1] *vt* **(a)** *Kinder, Tiere, Pflanzen, Haushalt, finanzielle Angelegenheiten* to look after, to take care of; (*bedienen*) *Maschine, Lift, Heizung* to look after.
(b) (*beliefern*) to supply ◆ **jdn mit etw ~** (*versehen*) to provide *or* supply sb with sth.

(c) (*unterhalten*) *Familie* to provide for, to support ◆ **versorgt sein** to be provided for *or* taken care of.
(d) (*dial: wegräumen*) to put away.
2 *vr* **(a) sich mit etw ~** to provide oneself with sth.
(b) sich selbst ~ to look after *or* take care of oneself.

Versorger(in *f*) *m* **-s, - (a)** (*Ernährer*) provider, breadwinner. **(b)** (*Belieferer*) supplier.

Versorgung *f siehe vt* (*a - c*) **(a)** care ◆ **vielen Dank für die gute ~ meiner Katze/Pflanzen** many thanks for taking such good care of my cat/plants.
(b) supply ◆ **die ~ dieses Gebiets mit Bussen** the supply of buses to *or* provision of buses for this district; **die ~ der Truppen (mit Munition)** supplying the troops (with ammunition); **Probleme mit der ~ haben** to have supply problems; **auf Grund der schlechten ~ der Truppen** because the troops were being poorly supplied.
(c) (*Unterhalt*) **die ~ im Alter/einer sechsköpfigen Familie** providing for one's old age/a family of six; **der Staat übernimmt die ~ von Witwen und Waisen** the state undertakes to provide for widows and orphans.

Versorgungs-: ~ausgleich *m* (*bei Ehescheidung*) maintenance, alimony; **v~berechtigt** *adj* entitled to maintenance; (*durch Staat*) entitled to (state) benefit; **~betrieb** *m* public utility; **~empfänger** *m* recipient of state benefit; △**~engpaß** *m* supply shortage *or* bottleneck; **~fahrzeug** *nt* (*Mil*) supply vehicle; **~flugzeug** *nt* supply plane; **~güter** *pl* supplies *pl*; **~netz** *nt* (*Wasser~, Gas~ etc*) (supply) grid; (*von Waren*) supply network; **~schwierigkeiten** *pl* supply problems *pl*; **~truppen** *pl* supply troops *pl*; **~weg** *m* supply channel.

verspachteln* *vt* **(a)** to fill in. **(b)** (*fig inf: aufessen*) to put *or* tuck away (*inf*).

verspannen* **1** *vt* to brace, to stay, to guy.
2 *vr* (*Muskeln*) to tense up ◆ **verspannt** tense(d up).

Verspannung *f* **(a)** (*Seile etc*) bracing, stays *pl*. **(b)** (*von Muskeln*) tenseness *no pl*.

verspäten* *vr* **(a)** (*zu spät kommen*) to be late ◆ **der Frühling hat sich verspätet** spring is late. **(b)** (*nicht rechtzeitig wegkommen*) to be late leaving; (*aufgehalten werden*) to be delayed, to be held up.

verspätet *adj Zug, Flugzeug* delayed, late *pred*; *Ankunft, Eintreten, Frühling, Entwicklung* late; *Glückwunsch* belated; *Bewerbung* late, belated.

Verspätung *f* (*von Verkehrsmitteln*) delay; (*von Mensch*) late arrival; (*von Glückwunsch etc*) belatedness ◆ **(10 Minuten) ~ haben** to be (10 minutes) late; **eine zweistündige ~** a delay of two hours, a two-hour delay; **die ~ aufholen** to catch up lost time; **mit ~ abfahren/ankommen** to leave/arrive late; **ohne ~ ankommen** to arrive on time; **mit zwanzig Minuten ~** twenty minutes late *or* (*von Verkehrsmitteln auch*) behind schedule; **mit sechsmonatiger** *etc* **~** six months *etc* late; (*nach Ablauf der Frist auch*) six months *etc* too late.

verspeisen* *vt* (*geh*) to consume.

verspekulieren* **1** *vt* to lose through speculation.
2 *vr* to ruin oneself by speculation; (*fig*) to miscalculate, to be out in one's speculations.

versperren* *vt* **(a)** to block; *Weg auch* to bar; *Aussicht auch* to obstruct. **(b)** (*dial: verschließen*) to lock *or* close up.

verspielen* **1** *vt* (*lit, fig*) *Geld, Chancen* to gamble away; *Vorteile* to bargain away ◆ **den ganzen Abend ~** to spend the whole evening playing.
2 *vi* (*fig*) **jetzt hast du verspielt** it's all up with you now, you've had it now (*inf*); **er hatte bei ihr verspielt** he was finished *or* he had had it (*inf*) as far as she was concerned.

verspielt *adj Kind, Katze etc* playful; *Frisur* pretty; *Muster, Kleid* pretty, dainty; *Verzierung* dainty.

verspinnen* *irreg* **1** *vt* (*zu Faden*) to spin; (*verbrauchen*) to use.
2 *vr* **die Larve verspinnt sich (zur Puppe)** the larva spins itself into *or* forms a cocoon; **sich in etw** (*dat*) **~** (*fig*) *in Ideen* to become immersed in sth; *in Lügen* to become embroiled *or* enmeshed in sth.

versponnen *adj* airy-fairy; *Ideen auch* wild *attr*; *Mensch* head-in-the-clouds *pred*.

verspotten* *vt* to mock; (*höhnisch*) to jeer at, to deride.

Verspottung *f* **(a)** *siehe vt* mocking; jeering, derision *all no indef art*. **(b)** (*spöttische Rede*) mockery *no indef art, no pl*; jeer, derision *no indef art, no pl*.

versprechen* *irreg* **1** *vt* **(a)** to promise (*jdm etw* sb sth) ◆ **aber er hat es doch versprochen!** but he promised!; **jdm/einander versprochen sein** (*obs*) to be betrothed (*old*) *or* promised to sb/to be betrothed (*old*); *siehe* **hoch, Blaue**.
(b) (*erwarten lassen*) to promise ◆ **das verspricht interessant zu werden** it promises to be interesting; **das Wetter verspricht schön zu werden** the weather looks promising *or* promises to be good; **nichts Gutes ~** to be ominous, to bode ill (*liter*).
2 *vr* **(a)** (*erwarten*) **sich** (*dat*) **viel/wenig von jdm/etw ~** to have high hopes/no great hopes of sb/sth; **was versprichst du dir davon?** what do you expect to achieve *or* gain (by that)?
(b) (*falsch sagen, aussprechen*) to pronounce a word/words wrong(ly); (*etwas Nicht-Gemeintes sagen*) to make a slip (of the tongue) *or* a mistake ◆ **bei dem Wort verspreche ich mich noch immer** I still can't pronounce that word properly.

Versprechen *nt* **-s, -** promise.

Versprecher *m* **-s, -** (*inf*) slip (of the tongue) ◆ **ein Freudscher ~** a Freudian slip.

Versprechung *f* promise.

versprengen* *vt* **(a)** *Truppen, Soldaten* to disperse, to scatter ◆ **versprengte Soldaten** scattered soldiers. **(b)** *Wasser* to sprinkle.

verspritzen* **1** *vt* **(a)** (*versprühen, verteilen*) to spray; (*versprengen*) to sprinkle; *Farbe* to spray on; (*zuspritzen*) *Fugen* to seal by injection moulding; (*fig*) *Tinte* to use up; *siehe* **Gift**.
(b) (*beim Planschen*) *Wasser* to splash, to sp(l)atter; (*verkleckern*) *Farbe, Boden, Heft, Kleidung* to sp(l)atter.
(c) (*verbrauchen*) *Wasser, Farbe etc* to use.
2 *vi aux sein* (*Wasser*) to spray; (*Fett*) to sp(l)atter.

versprochenermaßen *adv* as promised.

verspröden* *vi aux sein* to go brittle.

versprühen* *vt* to spray; *Funken auch* to send up *or* out; (*verbrauchen*) to use ◆ **Witz/Geist ~** (*fig*) to scintillate.

verspüren* *vt* to feel, to be conscious of ◆ **er verspürte keine Lust, zur Arbeit zu gehen** he felt no desire to go to work.

verstaatlichen* *vt* to nationalize; *Schulen* to put under state control; *Kirchen* to secularize.

Verstaatlichung *f siehe vt* nationalization; putting under state control; secularization.

verstädtern* **1** *vt* to urbanize.
2 *vi aux sein* to become urbanized.

Verstand *m* **-(e)s,** *no pl* (*Fähigkeit zu denken*) reason; (*Intellekt*) mind, intellect; (*Vernunft*) (common) sense; (*Urteilskraft*) (powers *pl* of) judgement ◆ **das müßte dir dein ~ sagen** your common sense should tell you that; **den ~ verlieren** to lose one's mind; **hast du denn den ~ verloren?** have you taken leave of your senses?, are you out of your mind?; **jdn um den ~ bringen** to drive sb out of his mind; **nicht recht** *or* **ganz bei ~ sein** not to be in one's right mind; **zu ~ kommen** to come to one's senses; **mit seinem ~ am Ende sein** to be at one's wits' end; **das geht über meinen ~** it's beyond me, it beats me (*inf*); **da steht einem der ~ still** (*fig inf*), **da bleibt einem der ~ stehen** (*fig inf*) the mind boggles (*inf*); **etw ohne ~ tun** to do sth mindlessly; **etw ohne ~ essen/trinken** not to pay attention to what one is eating/drinking; **etw mit ~ genießen/essen/trinken** to savour *or* relish sth.

Verstandes-: ~ehe *f siehe* **Vernunftehe**; **~kraft** *f* mental *or* intellectual faculties *pl or* powers *pl*; **v~mäßig** *adj* rational; **v~mäßig leuchtet das mir ein** it makes (rational) sense to me; **~mensch** *m* rational person; **~schärfe** *f* acuteness *or* sharpness of mind *or* intellect.

verständig *adj* (*vernünftig*) sensible; (*einsichtig*) understanding.

verständigen* **1** *vt* to notify, to advise (*von* of, about).
2 *vr* to communicate (with each other); (*sich einigen*) to come to an understanding *or* agreement ◆ **sich mit jdm ~** to communicate with sb.

Verständigung *f, no pl* **(a)** (*Benachrichtigung*) notification, advising. **(b)** (*das Sichverständigen*) communication *no indef art* ◆ **die ~ am Telephon war schlecht** the (telephone) line was bad. **(c)** (*Einigung*) understanding, agreement.

Verständigungs-: ~bereitschaft *f* willingness *or* readiness to negotiate; **~schwierigkeiten** *pl* communication difficulties *pl*; **~versuch** *m* attempt at rapprochement.

verständlich *adj* (*begreiflich*) *Reaktion etc* understandable; (*intellektuell erfaßbar*) comprehensible; (*hörbar*) audible; (*klar*) *Erklärung, Ausdruck* intelligible ◆ **allgemein ~** readily comprehensible; **eine schwer ~e Unterscheidung** a distinction that is difficult to grasp *or* understand; **jdm etw ~ machen** to make sb understand sth; **sich ~ machen** to make oneself understood; (*sich klar ausdrücken*) to make oneself clear, to express oneself intelligibly; (*gegen Lärm*) to make oneself heard; **nicht ~** incomprehensible; inaudible; unintelligible.

verständlicherweise *adv* understandably (enough).

Verständlichkeit *f, no pl* comprehensibility; (*Hörbarkeit*) audibility.

Verständnis *nt, no pl* **(a)** (*das Begreifen*) understanding (*für* of), comprehension (*für* of); (*Einfühlungsvermögen, Einsicht*) understanding (*für* for); (*Mitgefühl*) sympathy (*für* for) ◆ **solche Grausamkeiten gehen über menschliches/mein ~** such cruelty is beyond human/my comprehension; **für etw kein ~ haben** to have no understanding/sympathy for sth; *für Probleme, Lage auch* to have no feeling for sth; **für so was habe ich kein ~** I have no time for that kind of thing; **dafür hast du mein vollstes ~** you have my fullest sympathy; **wir bitten um Ihr ~** we apologize for any inconvenience.
(b) (*intellektuelles Erfassen*) (*für* of) understanding, comprehension ◆ **mit ~ lesen/zuhören** to read/listen with understanding.
(c) (*Kunst~ etc*) appreciation (*für* of).
(d) (*Verständigung*) understanding.

Verständnis-: v~innig *adj* knowing *attr*, meaningful; **v~los** *adj* uncomprehending; *Gesicht, Blick auch* blank; (*ohne Mitgefühl*) unsympathetic (*für* towards); (*für Kunst*) unappreciative (*für* of); **~losigkeit** *f siehe adj* lack of understanding; blankness; lack of sympathy; lack of appreciation; **v~voll** *adj* understanding; (*mitfühlend auch*) sympathetic (*für* towards); *Blick* knowing *no pred*.

verstänkern* *vt* (*inf*) *Zimmer* to make a stink in (*inf*); *Stadt* to pollute.

verstärken* **1** *vt Eindruck, Truppen, (Sport)* to reinforce; *Argumente, Mauer auch* to strengthen; *Spannung, Zweifel* to intensify, to increase; (*Chem*) to concentrate; (*Phot*) to intensify; (*Elec*) *Signal, Strom, Spannung* to boost, to amplify; *Stimme, Musik, Musikinstrument* to amplify.
2 *vr* (*fig*) to intensify; (*sich vermehren*) to increase.

Verstärker *m* **-s, -** (*Rad, Elec*) amplifier; (*Telec*) repeater; (*von Signalen etc*) booster; (*Phot*) intensifier.

Verstärkerröhre *f* (*Elec*) amplifier valve.

Verstärkung *f siehe vt* reinforcement; strengthening; intensification, increase; concentration; boosting; amplification.

△: for details of spelling reform, see supplement

verstauben* *vi aux sein* to get dusty *or* covered in dust; (*Möbel, Bücher auch, fig*) to gather dust ◆ **verstaubt** dusty, covered in dust; (*fig*) *Ideen, Ansichten* fuddy-duddy (*inf*).
verstauchen* *vt* to sprain ◆ **sich** (*dat*) **die Hand/den Fuß** *etc* ~ to sprain one's hand/foot *etc*.
Verstauchung *f* sprain; (*das Verstauchen*) spraining.
verstauen* *vt* (*in +dat* in(to)) *Gepäck* to load, to pack; (*Naut*) to stow; (*hum*) *Menschen* to pile, to pack.
Versteck *nt* **-(e)s, -e** hiding-place; (*von Verbrechern*) hide-out ◆ **~ spielen** to play hide-and-seek.
verstecken* [1] *vt* to hide, to conceal (*vor* from).
[2] *vr* to hide, to conceal oneself ◆ **sich vor** *or* **neben jdm ~ können/müssen** (*fig*) to be no match for sb; **sich vor jdm ~** to hide from sb; **sich vor** *or* **neben jdm nicht zu ~ brauchen** (*fig*) not to need to fear comparison with sb; **sich hinter etw** (*dat*) ~ (*fig*) *hinter Pseudonym* to write under sth; *hinter falschem Namen, Maske* to hide behind sth; *hinter Andeutungen* to be behind sth; **V~ spielen** to play hide-and-seek.
Versteckspiel *nt* (*lit, fig*) hide-and-seek.
versteckt *adj* **(a)** (*lit: verborgen*) hidden; (*nicht leicht sichtbar*) *Eingang, Tür, Winkel* concealed; (*abgelegen auch*) *Ort* secret. **(b)** (*fig*) *Lächeln, Blick* furtive; *Gähnen auch* disguised; *Bemerkung, Andeutung* veiled; *Bedeutung* hidden, concealed.
▼ **verstehen*** *irreg* [1] *vti* **(a)** to understand; (*einsehen auch*) to see ◆ **jdn/etw falsch** *or* **nicht recht ~** to misunderstand sb/sth; **versteh mich recht** don't misunderstand me, don't get me wrong; **jdm zu ~ geben, daß ...** to give sb to understand that ...; **ein ~der Blick** a knowing look; **(ist das) verstanden?** (is that) understood?; *siehe* **Bahnhof, Spaß.**
(b) (*hören*) to hear, to understand; *siehe* **Wort.**
(c) (*können, beherrschen*) to know; *Sprache auch* to understand ◆ **es ~, etw zu tun** to know how to do sth; **es mit Kindern ~** to be good with *or* have a way with children; **es mit seinen Kollegen ~** to know how to get on with one's colleagues; **etwas/nichts von etw ~** to know something/nothing about sth; **etw machen, so gut man es versteht** to do sth to the best of one's ability *or* as well as one can; *siehe* **Handwerk.**
▼ **(d)** (*auslegen*) to understand, to interpret, to see ◆ **etw unter etw** (*dat*) ~ to understand sth by sth; **wie soll ich das ~?** how am I supposed to take that?; **das ist bildlich** *or* **nicht wörtlich zu ~** that isn't to be taken literally.
[2] *vr* **(a)** to understand each other.
(b) (*miteinander auskommen*) to get on *or* along (with each other *or* together) ◆ **sich mit jdm ~** to get on with sb; **wir ~ uns (schon)** (*sind einer Meinung*) we understand each other.
(c) (*klar sein*) to go without saying ◆ **versteht sich!** (*inf*) of course!, naturally!; **das versteht sich von selbst** that goes without saying.
(d) (*auffassen*) **sich als etw ~** to think of *or* see oneself as sth.
(e) **sich auf etw** (*acc*) ~ to be (an) expert at sth, to be a dab hand (*inf*) *or* very good at sth.
(f) **sich zu etw ~** (*form*) to agree to sth.
(g) (*Comm*) to be ◆ **die Preise ~ sich einschließlich Lieferung** prices are inclusive of delivery.
versteifen* [1] *vt* to strengthen, to reinforce; (*Tech*) to strut; (*Comm*) to tighten; (*Sew*) to stiffen.
[2] *vr* to stiffen up; (*fig*) (*Haltung, Gegensätze*) to harden; (*Maßnahmen*) to tighten (up) ◆ **sich auf etw** (*acc*) ~ (*fig*) to become set on sth; **er hat sich darauf versteift** he is set on it.
Versteifung *f* **(a)** *no pl siehe vt* strengthening, reinforcement; strutting; tightening; stiffening.
(b) (*Verstärkung*) stiffener.
(c) (*Med*) stiffening *no pl*.
(d) (*fig*) (*von Haltung*) hardening; (*von Maßnahmen*) tightening (up); (*von Gegensätzen*) increasing intractability.
versteigen* *vr irreg* (*lit*) to get into difficulties (while climbing) ◆ **er hat sich zu der Behauptung verstiegen, daß ...** he presumed to claim that ...; **er verstieg sich zu völlig übertriebenen Forderungen** he had the presumption to make quite excessive demands; *siehe* **verstiegen.**
versteigern* *vt* to auction (off) ◆ **etw ~ lassen** to put sth up for auction.
Versteigerung *f* (sale by) auction ◆ **zur ~ kommen** to be put up for auction.
versteinern* [1] *vi aux sein* (*Geol*) (*Pflanzen, Tiere*) to fossilize; (*Holz*) to petrify; (*fig: Miene*) to harden ◆ **versteinerte Pflanzen/Tiere** fossilized plants/animals; **wie versteinert (da)stehen** to stand there petrified.
[2] *vr* (*fig*) *Miene* to harden; (*Lächeln*) to become fixed *or* set.
Versteinerung *f* (*Vorgang*) fossilization; petrifaction, petrification; (*versteinertes Tier etc*) fossil; (*fig: von Miene*) hardening.
verstellbar *adj* adjustable ◆ **in der Höhe ~** adjustable for height.
Verstellbarkeit *f* adjustability.
verstellen* [1] *vt* **(a)** (*anders einstellen, regulieren*) to adjust; *Signal, Zahlen* to alter, to change; *Möbel, Gegenstände* to move *or* shift (out of position *or* place); (*in Unordnung bringen*) to put in the wrong place, to misplace; (*falsch einstellen*) to adjust wrongly; *Radio* to alter the tuning of; *Uhr* to put wrong.
(b) *Stimme* to disguise.
(c) (*versperren*) to block, to obstruct; (*vollstellen*) *Zimmer* to clutter up ◆ **das verstellt den Blick auf das Wesentliche** that obscures one's view of the essential.
[2] *vr* to move (out of position); (*fig*) to act *or* play a part; (*Gefühle verbergen*) to hide one's (true) feelings ◆ **er kann sich gut ~** he's good at playing *or* acting a part.
Verstellung *f siehe vt* **(a)** adjustment; alteration; moving *or* shifting (out of position) *no indef art*; misplacing *no indef art*. **(b)** disguise. **(c)** blockage, obstruction; cluttering up. **(d)** (*Vortäuschung*) pretending, feigning.
versteppen* *vti* to turn into desert.
Versteppung *f* desertification.
▼ **versterben*** *vi irreg aux sein* to die, to pass away *or* on.
versteuern* *vt* to pay tax on ◆ **versteuerte Waren/das versteuerte Einkommen** taxed goods/income; **das zu versteuernde Einkommen** taxable income.
Versteuerung *f, no pl* taxation.
verstiegen [1] *ptp of* **versteigen.**
[2] *adj* (*fig: überspannt*) extravagant, fantastic; *Pläne, Ideen auch* high-flown.
Verstiegenheit *f* extravagance.
verstimmen* *vt* (*lit*) to put out of tune; (*fig*) to put out, to disgruntle.
verstimmt *adj Klavier etc* out of tune; (*fig*) (*verdorben*) *Magen* upset; (*verärgert*) put out, disgruntled.
Verstimmung *f* disgruntlement; (*zwischen Parteien*) ill-feeling, ill-will.
verstockt *adj Kind, Wesen* obstinate, stubborn; *Sünder* unrepentant, unrepenting.
Verstocktheit *f, no pl siehe adj* obstinacy, stubbornness; unrepentance.
verstohlen *adj* furtive, surreptitious.
verstopfen* *vt* to stop up; *Ohren auch* to plug; *Ausguß auch* to block (up); *Straße* to block, to jam.
verstopft *adj* blocked; *Straßen auch* jammed; *Nase* stuffed up, blocked (up); *Mensch* constipated.
Verstopfung *f* blockage; (*Verkehrsstauung*) jam; (*Med*) constipation.
Verstorbene(r) *mf decl as adj* deceased.
verstören* *vt* to disturb.
verstört *adj* disturbed; (*vor Angst*) distraught.
Verstörtheit *f, no pl* disturbed state; (*vor Angst*) distraction; (*Verwirrung*) confusion.
Verstoß *m* **-es, ¨-e** violation (*gegen* of); (*gegen Gesetz auch*) offence.
verstoßen* *irreg* [1] *vt jdn* to disown, to repudiate ◆ **jdn aus einem Verein/einer Gruppe ~** to expel sb from *or* throw sb out of a club/group.
[2] *vi* **gegen etw ~** to offend against sth; *gegen Gesetz, Regel auch* to contravene sth.
Verstoßene(r) *mf decl as adj* outcast.
verstrahlen* *vt* **(a)** *Licht, Wärme* to give off. **(b)** *Tier, Mensch* to expose to radiation; *Gebäude, Gebiet auch* to make (highly) radioactive ◆ **lebensgefährlich verstrahlt sein** to have had a potentially lethal dose of radiation.
verstrahlt *adj* contaminated (by radiation).
Verstrahlung *f* radiation.
verstreben* *vt* to brace, to strut.
Verstrebung *f* supporting *no pl*; (*Strebebalken*) support(ing beam).
verstreichen* *irreg* [1] *vt Salbe, Farbe* to put on, to apply (*auf +dat* to); *Butter* to spread (*auf +dat* on); *Riß* to fill in; (*verbrauchen*) to use.
[2] *vi aux sein* (*Zeit*) to pass (by), to elapse; (*Frist*) to expire.
verstreuen* *vt* to scatter; (*versehentlich*) to spill ◆ **seine Kleider/Spielsachen im ganzen Zimmer ~** to scatter *or* strew one's clothes/toys over the (whole) room.
verstricken* [1] *vt* **(a)** *Wolle* to use. **(b)** (*fig*) to involve, to embroil, to mix up ◆ **in eine Angelegenheit verstrickt sein** to be mixed up *or* involved *or* embroiled in an affair.
[2] *vr* **(a)** (*Wolle*) to knit (up). **(b)** (*fig*) to become entangled, to get tangled up.
Verstrickung *f* (*fig*) entanglement.
verstromen* *vt Kohle* to convert into electricity.
verströmen* *vt* (*lit, fig*) to exude; (*liter*) *sein Blut* to shed.
Verstromung *f* (*von Kohle*) conversion into electricity.
verstümmeln* *vt* to mutilate, to maim; (*fig*) *Nachricht, Bericht* to garble, to distort; *Namen* to mutilate ◆ **sich selbst ~** to mutilate oneself.
Verstümmelung *f siehe vt* mutilation, maiming *no pl*; garbling *no pl*, distortion.
verstummen* *vi aux sein* (*Mensch*) to go *or* fall silent, to stop talking; (*Geräusch, Gespräch, Musik, Beifall*) to cease, to stop; (*Wind, Glocken, Instrumente*) to become silent *or* still (*liter*); (*langsam verklingen*) to die away; (*fig*) (*Kritik, Stimmen der Opposition*) to become silent *or* still; (*sich langsam legen*) to subside; (*Gewissen*) to become silent; (*Gerüchte*) to subside ◆ **jdn ~ lassen** (*Bemerkung, Einwurf*) to silence sb; **jdn/etw zum V~ bringen** to silence sb/sth; **vor Entsetzen ~** to be struck dumb *or* to be speechless with terror.
Versuch *m* **-(e)s, -e** attempt (*zu tun* at doing, to do); (*wissenschaftlich*) experiment, test; (*Test*) trial, test; (*Essay*) essay; (*Rugby*) try ◆ **einen ~ machen** to make an attempt; to do *or* carry out an experiment/a trial; **mit jdm/etw einen ~ machen** to give sb/sth a try *or* trial; (*Forscher*) to do a trial/an experiment with sb/sth; **das käme auf einen ~ an** we'll have to have a try; **sie unternahm den ~, ihn umzustimmen** she made an attempt at changing *or* to change his mind, she had a try at changing his mind; **wir sollten es auf einen ~ ankommen lassen** we should give it a try; **das wollen wir doch auf einen ~ ankommen lassen!** we'll see about that!
▼ **versuchen*** [1] *vt* **(a)** (*auch vi: probieren, kosten*) to try; (*sich bemühen auch*) to attempt ◆ **es mit etw ~** to try sth; **versuch's doch!** try, have a try; **es mit jdm ~** to give sb a try; **versuchter Mord/Diebstahl** attempted murder/theft.
(b) (*in Versuchung führen*) to tempt ◆ **sich versucht fühlen** to feel tempted; **versucht sein** to be tempted.

➤ SPRACHE AKTIV: **verstehen: 1a** → 53.1, 53.5 **1d** → 33.3 **versterben** → 51.4 **versuchen: 1a** → 27.3, 27.4, 45.4

[2] *vr* **sich an** *or* **in etw** (*dat*) ~ to try one's hand at sth.

Versucher(in *f*) *m* **-s, -** tempter, temptress ◆ **der ~** (*Rel*) the Tempter.

Versuchs-: ~abteilung *f* experimental department; **~anlage** *f* experimental plant; **~anstalt** *f* research institute; **~ballon** *m* sounding balloon; **einen ~ballon steigen lassen, es mit einem ~ballon probieren** (*fig*) to fly a kite; **~bedingungen** *pl* test conditions *pl*; **~bohrung** *f* experimental drilling; **~kaninchen** *nt* (*lit*) laboratory rabbit; (*fig*) guinea-pig; **~objekt** *nt* test object; (*fig: Mensch*) guinea-pig; **~person** *f* test *or* experimental subject; **~reihe** *f* series of experiments; **~stadium** *nt* experimental stage; **~strecke** *f* test track; **~tier** *nt* laboratory animal; **v~weise** *adv* as a trial, on a trial basis; *einstellen, engagieren* on probation, on trial.

Versuchung *f* temptation (*auch Rel*) ◆ **jdn in ~ führen** to lead sb into temptation; **„und führe uns nicht in ~"** "and lead us not into temptation"; **in ~ geraten** *or* **kommen** to be tempted.

versudeln* *vt* to scribble on.

versumpfen* *vi aux sein* **(a)** (*Gebiet*) to become marshy *or* boggy. **(b)** (*fig inf*) (*verwahrlosen*) to go to pot (*inf*); (*lange zechen*) to get involved in a booze-up (*inf*).

Versumpfung *f* (*lit*) increasing marshiness.

versündigen* *vr* (*geh*) **sich an jdm/etw ~** to sin against sb/sth; **sich an seiner Gesundheit ~** to abuse one's health.

Versündigung *f* sin (*an +dat* against) ◆ **eine ~ an der Gesundheit** an abuse of one's health.

versunken [1] *ptp of* **versinken**.

[2] *adj* sunken, submerged; *Kultur* submerged; (*fig*) engrossed, absorbed ◆ **in Gedanken ~** lost *or* immersed in thought; **völlig in diesen Anblick ~** completely lost in *or* caught up in this sight.

Versunkenheit *f, no pl* (*fig*) engrossment ◆ **jdn aus seiner ~ reißen** to tear sb from his (immersion in his) book/thoughts *etc*; **seine ~ in diesen Anblick** his rapt contemplation of this sight.

versüßen* *vt* (*fig*) to sweeten ◆ **jdm etw ~** to sweeten sth for sb; *siehe* **Pille**.

Vertäfelung *f* panelling *no pl, no indef art*.

vertagen* [1] *vti* to adjourn; (*verschieben*) to postpone, to defer (*auf +acc* until, till); (*Parl auch*) to prorogue (*form*).

[2] *vr* to be adjourned, to adjourn.

Vertagung *f siehe vti* adjournment; postponement; prorogation (*form*).

vertändeln* *vt* to fritter away.

vertäuen* *vt* (*Naut*) to moor.

vertauschbar *adj* exchangeable (*gegen* for); (*miteinander*) interchangeable.

vertauschen* *vt* **(a)** (*austauschen*) to exchange (*gegen or mit* for); (*miteinander*) to interchange; *Auto, Plätze* to change (*gegen or mit* for); (*Elec*) *Pole* to transpose ◆ **vertauschte Rollen** reversed roles.

(b) (*verwechseln*) *Hüte, Mäntel etc* to mix up ◆ **seinen Mantel mit einem anderen ~** to mistake another coat for one's own, to mix one's coat up with another.

Vertauschung *f* **(a)** (*Austausch*) exchange; (*von Auto, von Plätzen*) changing *no pl*; (*Elec: von Polen*) transposition. **(b)** (*Verwechslung*) mix-up; (*das Vertauschen*) mixing up.

Vertäuung *f* (*das Vertäuen*) mooring; (*die Taue*) moorings *pl*.

verteidigen* [1] *vt* to defend.

[2] *vr* to defend oneself (*auch Sport*); (*vor Gericht*) to conduct one's own defence.

[3] *vi* (*Sport*) to defend; (*als Verteidiger spielen*) to be a *or* play as a defender; (*defensiv spielen*) to play a defensive game, to play defensively.

Verteidiger(in *f*) *m* **-s, -** defender (*auch Sport*); (*Fürsprecher auch*) advocate; (*Anwalt*) defence lawyer ◆ **der ~ des Angeklagten** the counsel for the defence, the defence counsel.

Verteidigung *f* (*alle Bedeutungen*) defence, defense (*US*) ◆ **zur ~ von** *or* *gen* in defence of; **zu ihrer/seiner eigenen ~** in her/one's own defence; **er ist immer zur ~ seiner Meinung bereit** he is always ready to defend his opinion.

Verteidigungs- *in cpds* defence; **~beitrag** *m* defence contribution; **~bündnis** *nt* defence alliance; **v~fähig** *adj* able to defend itself/oneself; **~fähigkeit** *f* defensive capability; **~fall** *m* **wenn der ~fall eintritt** if defence should be necessary; **~gemeinschaft** *f* defence community; **~initiative** *f* defence initiative; **~krieg** *m* defensive war; **~minister** *m* Minister of Defence; **~ministerium** *nt* Ministry of Defence; **~rede** *f* (*Jur*) speech for the defence; (*fig*) apologia; **~schlacht** *f* defensive battle; **~schrift** *f* (*Jur*) (written) defence statement; (*fig*) apologia; **~spieler** *m* defender; **~stellung** *f* defensive position; **in ~stellung gehen** to adopt a defensive position; **~system** *nt* defence system, defences *pl*; **das ~system der Nato** the Nato defence system; **v~unfähig** *adj* defenceless; **~waffe** *f* defensive weapon; **~wille** *m* spirit of resistance; **~zustand** *m* defence alert; **im ~zustand** in a defence alert; **im ~zustand sein** on the defence alert; **~zweck** *m* **für ~zwecke, zu ~zwecken** for defence purposes, for purposes of defence.

verteilen* [1] *vt* **(a)** (*austeilen*) (*an +acc* to, *unter +acc* among) to distribute; *Flugblätter auch* to hand out; *Essen* to dish out; *Süßigkeiten etc auch* to share *or* divide out; *Preise auch* to give out; (*Theat*) *Rollen* to allot, to allocate.

(b) (*anordnen, aufteilen*) to distribute; *Investitionen, Lehrstoff* to spread (*über +acc* over); (*Mil*) to deploy; (*verstreuen*) to spread out; (*streichen*) *Aufstrich, Farbe etc* to spread; (*streuen*) *Sand, Zucker, Puder* to sprinkle ◆ **Blumen im Zimmer/auf verschiedene Vasen ~** to arrange flowers around the room/in different vases.

[2] *vr* (*Zuschauer, Polizisten etc*) to spread (themselves) out; (*Bevölkerung*) to spread (itself) out; (*Mil: Truppen auch*) to deploy; (*Farbe, Wasser*) to spread (itself) out; (*Med: Bakterien, Metastasen*) to spread; (*Reichtum etc*) to be spread *or* distributed; (*zeitlich*) to be spread (*über +acc* over) ◆ **auf dem ganzen Platz verteilt** spread out over the square; **übers ganze Land verteilt** spread throughout the country.

Verteiler *m* **-s, - (a)** (*Comm, Aut*) distributor. **(b)** *siehe* **Verteilerschlüssel**.

Verteiler-: ~deckel *m* distributor cap; **~kopf** *m* (*Aut*) distributor head; **~netz** *nt* (*Elec*) distribution system; (*Comm*) distribution network; **~schlüssel** *m* list of people to receive a copy.

Verteilung *f* distribution; (*Zuteilung*) allocation; (*Mil*) deployment; (*Theat*) casting.

vertelefonieren* *vt* (*inf*) *Geld, Zeit* to spend on the phone.

vertellen* *vt* (*N Ger inf*) to tell; *Unsinn* to talk.

verteuern* [1] *vt* to make dearer *or* more expensive, to increase *or* raise the price of.

[2] *vr* to become dearer *or* more expensive, to increase in *or* go up in price.

Verteuerung *f* rise *or* increase in price.

verteufeln* *vt* to condemn.

verteufelt (*inf*) [1] *adj Lage, Angelegenheit* devilish (*inf*), tricky, awkward ◆ **~es Glück haben** to be damned *or* darned *or* deuced (*dated*) lucky (*inf*).

[2] *adv* (*mit adj*) damned (*inf*), darned (*inf*), deuced (*dated inf*), devilish (*dated inf*); (*mit vb*) a lot.

Verteufelung *f* condemnation.

vertiefen* [1] *vt Graben, Loch etc* to deepen; (*fig*) *Eindruck auch* to heighten; *Kenntnis, Wissen auch* to extend; (*Sch*) *Unterrichtsstoff* to consolidate, to reinforce; (*Mus*) to flatten.

[2] *vr* (*lit, fig*) to deepen; (*fig: Lehrstoff*) to be consolidated *or* reinforced ◆ **sich in etw** (*acc*) ~ (*fig*) to become engrossed *or* absorbed in sth; **in etw** (*acc*) **vertieft sein** (*fig*) to be engrossed *or* absorbed in sth; *siehe* **Gedanke**.

Vertiefung *f* **(a)** *siehe vt* deepening; heightening; extension; consolidation, reinforcement; flattening. **(b)** (*in Oberfläche*) depression; (*im Boden auch*) dip, hollow. **(c)** (*vertieft sein*) engrossment, absorption.

vertikal [vɛrti'ka:l] *adj* vertical.

Vertikale [vɛrti'ka:lə] *f* **-, -n** vertical line ◆ **in der ~n** vertically, in a vertical plane.

vertilgen* *vt* **(a)** *Unkraut etc* to destroy, to eradicate, to kill off; *Ungeziefer auch* to exterminate. **(b)** (*inf: aufessen*) to demolish (*inf*), to polish off (*inf*).

Vertilgung *f siehe vt* (*a*) destruction, eradication; extermination.

Vertilgungsmittel *nt* weed-killer; (*Insekten~*) pesticide.

vertippen* (*inf*) [1] *vr* **(a)** to make a typing error. **(b)** (*beim Lotto, Toto etc*) to slip up (*inf*).

[2] *vt* to mistype, to type wrongly.

vertobacken* *vt* (*dated inf*) to thrash.

vertonen* *vt* to set to music; *Theaterstück auch* to make a musical version of; *Film etc* to add a sound-track to.

vertönen* *vi aux sein* to fade *or* die away.

Vertonung *f siehe vt* setting (to music); (*vertonte Fassung*) musical version, setting; adding a sound-track (*gen* to).

vertorfen* *vi aux sein* to turn into peat.

Vertorfung *f* conversion into peat.

vertrackt *adj* (*inf*) awkward, tricky; (*verwickelt*) complicated, complex.

Vertracktheit *f* (*inf*) awkwardness, trickiness; (*Verwickeltheit*) complexity.

Vertrag *m* **-(e)s, ¨e** contract; (*Abkommen*) agreement; (*Pol: Friedens~*) treaty ◆ **mündlicher ~** verbal *or* oral agreement; **laut ~** under the terms of the contract; **jdn unter ~ nehmen** to contract sb; **unter ~ stehen** to be under contract.

vertragen* *irreg* [1] *vt* **(a)** to take; (*aushalten auch*) to stand; (*dulden auch*) to tolerate, to endure, to stand for ◆ **Eier vertrage ich nicht** *or* **kann ich nicht ~** I can't take eggs, eggs don't agree with me; **ein Automotor, der viel verträgt** an engine that can stand (up to) a lot *or* can take a lot; **synthetische Stoffe vertrage ich nicht** *or* **kann ich nicht ~** I can't wear synthetics; **so etwas kann ich nicht ~** I can't stand that kind of thing; **er verträgt keinen Spaß** he can't take a joke; **viel ~ können** (*inf: Alkohol*) to be able to hold one's drink; **er verträgt nichts** (*inf*) he can't take his drink; **jd/etw könnte etw ~** (*inf*) sb/sth could do with sth.

(b) (*dial*) *Kleider* to wear out ◆ **~ sein** to be (well) worn.

(c) (*Sw*) to deliver.

[2] *vr* **sich (mit jdm) ~** to get on *or* along (with sb); **sich wieder ~** to be friends again; **sich mit etw ~** (*Nahrungsmittel, Farbe*) to go with sth; (*Aussage, Verhalten*) to be consistent with sth; **diese Farben/Aussagen ~ sich nicht** these colours don't go together/these statements are inconsistent *or* not consistent.

Verträger *m* (*Sw*) delivery man; (*Zeitungs~*) paper boy/man.

vertraglich [1] *adj* contractual.

[2] *adv* by contract; *festgelegt* in the/a contract ◆ **ein ~ zugesichertes Recht** a contractual right.

verträglich *adj* (*friedlich, umgänglich*) peaceable, easy-going, amicable; *Speise* digestible; (*bekömmlich*) wholesome; *Medikament* well tolerated (*für* by) ◆ **gut ~** easily digestible.

Verträglichkeit *f, no pl siehe adj* amicability; digestibility; wholesomeness ◆ **die ~ dieses Medikaments** the fact that this medicine is well tolerated.

Vertrags- *in cpds* of the/a contract/an agreement/a treaty; **~bruch** *m* breach of contract; breaking of an/the agreement; breaking of a/the treaty; **v~brüchig** *adj* who is in breach of contract; who has broken an/the agreement; who has broken a/the treaty; **v~brüchig werden** to be in breach of contract; to break an/the agreement; to break a/the treaty;

~entwurf *m* draft contract/agreement/treaty; **~gaststätte** *f* tied house; **~gegenstand** *m* object of the contract/agreement/treaty; **v~gemäß** [1] *adj* (as) stipulated in the contract/agreement/treaty; [2] *adv* as stipulated in the contract/agreement/treaty; **~hafen** *m* treaty port; **~händler** *m* concessionary, appointed retailer; **~partner** *m* party to a/the contract/treaty; **v~schließend** *adj* contracting; **~spieler** *m* player under contract; **~strafe** *f* penalty for breach of contract; **~verletzung** *f* breach of contract; infringement of the agreement/treaty; **~werk** *nt* contract; treaty; **~werkstätte** *f* authorized repair shop; **v~widrig** [1] *adj* contrary to (the terms of) the contract/agreement/treaty; [2] *adv* in breach of contract/the agreement/the treaty.

vertrauen* *vi* **jdm/einer Sache ~** to trust sb/sth, to have trust in sb/sth; **auf jdn/etw ~** to trust in sb/sth; **auf sein Glück ~** to trust to luck; **sich** (*dat*) **selbst ~** to have confidence in oneself.

Vertrauen *nt* **-s,** *no pl* trust, confidence (*zu, in +acc, auf +acc* in); (*Pol*) confidence ◆ **voll ~** full of confidence; **im ~ (gesagt)** strictly in confidence; **ich habe dir das im ~ gesagt** that's strictly in confidence, that's strictly between you and me; **im ~ darauf, daß** ... confident that ..., in the confidence that ...; **~ zu jdm fassen** to gain confidence in sb; **jdn ins ~ ziehen** to take sb into one's confidence.

⚠**vertrauen|erweckend** *adj* **ein ~er Mensch/Arzt** *etc* a person/doctor *etc* who inspires confidence; **einen ~en Eindruck machen/~ aussehen** to inspire confidence.

Vertrauens-: ~arzt *m doctor who examines patients signed off sick for a lengthy period by their private doctor;* **v~bildend** *adj* confidence-building; **~bildung** *f* confidence building; **~bruch** *m* breach of confidence *or* trust; **~frage** *f* question *or* matter of trust; **die ~frage stellen** (*Parl*) to ask for a vote of confidence; **~lehrer** *m* liaison teacher (*between pupils and staff*); **~mann** *m, pl* **~leute** *or* **-männer** intermediary agent; (*Gewerkschaft*) (union) negotiator *or* representative; **~person** *f* someone to confide in, confidant(e); **~posten** *m* position of trust; **~sache** *f* (*vertrauliche Angelegenheit*) confidential matter; (*Frage des Vertrauens*) question *or* matter of trust; **~schwund** *m* loss of confidence; **v~selig** *adj* trusting; (*leichtgläubig auch*) credulous; **~seligkeit** *f* trustfulness; credulity; **~stellung** *f* position of trust; **~verhältnis** *nt* mutual trust *no indef art*; **persönliches ~verhältnis** relationship of personal trust; **v~voll** *adj* trusting; **wende dich v~voll an mich** you know you can always turn to me (for help); ⚠**~vorschuß** *m* trust; **~votum** *nt* (*Parl*) vote of confidence; **v~würdig** *adj* trustworthy; **~würdigkeit** *f* trustworthiness.

vertrauern *vt* to spend (in) moping, to mope away.

vertraulich [1] *adj* **(a)** (*geheim*) *Angelegenheit, Ton, Gespräch* confidential. **(b)** (*freundschaftlich*) friendly, matey (*inf*), pally (*inf*); (*plump-~*) familiar ◆ **~ werden** to take liberties.
[2] *adv* **(a)** confidentially, in confidence. **(b)** in a friendly/familiar way.

Vertraulichkeit *f* confidentiality; (*vertrauliche Mitteilung*) confidence; (*Aufdringlichkeit*) familiarity ◆ **mit aller ~** in strict(est) confidence; **plumpe/dreiste ~** familiarity.

verträumen* *vt* to dream away.

verträumt *adj* dreamy; (*idyllisch*) *Städtchen etc auch* sleepy.

➤ **vertraut** *adj* intimate; *Freund auch* close; (*bekannt*) *Gesicht, Umgebung* familiar, well-known ◆ **eine ~e Person** a close *or* an intimate friend; **sich mit etw ~ machen** to familiarize *or* acquaint oneself with sth; **sich mit dem Gedanken ~ machen, daß** ... to get used to the idea that ...; **mit etw ~ sein** to be familiar *or* well acquainted with sth; **mit jdm ~ werden** to become friendly with sb; **mit jdm sehr ~ werden** to get on intimate terms with sb, to become close friends with sb.

Vertraute(r) *mf decl as adj* close *or* intimate friend, confidant(e).

Vertrautheit *f, no pl siehe adj* intimacy; closeness; familiarity.

vertreiben* *vt irreg Tiere, Wolken, Einbrecher* to drive away; (*aus Haus etc*) to drive *or* turn out (*aus* of); (*aus Land*) to drive out (*aus* of), to expel (*aus* from); (*aus Amt, von Stellung*) to oust; *Feind* to drive off, to repulse; (*fig*) *Sorgen, Schmerzen* to drive away, to banish; (*Comm*) *Waren* to sell ◆ **ich wollte Sie nicht ~, bleiben Sie doch noch ein wenig** I didn't mean to chase *or* drive you away — do stay a bit longer; **ich wollte Sie nicht von Ihrem Stuhl/Platz ~** I didn't mean to take your chair/seat; **jdn vom Thron/aus seinem Amt ~** to oust sb from the throne/his office; **jdm/sich die Zeit mit etw ~** to help sb pass the time/to pass (away) *or* while away the time with sth.

Vertreibung *f* (*aus* from) expulsion; (*aus Amt etc*) ousting; (*von Feind*) repelling.

vertretbar *adj* justifiable; *Theorie, Argument* defensible, tenable ◆ **nicht ~** unjustifiable; indefensible, untenable.

vertreten* *vt irreg* **(a)** (*jds Stelle, Dienst übernehmen*) *Kollegen, Arzt etc* to replace, to stand in for, to deputize for; *Schauspieler* to replace, to stand in for; (*fig: Funktion einer Sache übernehmen*) to replace, to take the place of.
(b) *jds Interessen, Firma, Land, Wahlkreis* to represent; *Sache* to look after, to attend to; (*Rechtsanwalt*) *Klienten auch* to appear for; *Fall* to plead.
(c) (*Comm: Waren vertreiben für*) (*Firma*) to be the agent for; (*Angestellter*) to represent.
(d) (*verfechten, angehören*) *Standpunkt, Doktrin, Theorie* to support; *Meinung* to hold, to be of; *Ansicht* to take, to hold; *Kunstrichtung* to represent; (*rechtfertigen*) to justify (*vor* to).
(e) **~ sein** to be represented.
(f) **jdm den Weg ~** to bar sb's way.
(g) **sich** (*dat*) **den Fuß ~** to twist *or* strain one's ankle; **sich** (*dat*) **die Beine** *or* **Füße ~** (*inf*) to stretch one's legs.

Vertreter(in *f*) *m* **-s, -** **(a)** (*von Land, Firma etc*) representative; (*Comm*) (*Firma*) agent; (*Angestellter*) (sales) representative, rep (*inf*) ◆ **~ für Damenkleider** (sales) representative in ladies' wear; **~ einer Versicherung** insurance representative *or* rep (*inf*); **ein übler ~** (*fig inf*) a nasty piece of work (*inf*).
(b) (*Ersatz*) replacement; (*im Amt*) deputy; (*von Arzt*) locum.
(c) (*Verfechter*) (*von Doktrin*) supporter, advocate; (*von Meinung*) holder; (*von Kunstrichtung*) representative.

Vertretung *f siehe vt* (*a-d*) **(a)** replacement ◆ **die ~ (für jdn) übernehmen** to replace sb, to stand in (for sb); **die ~ (für jdn) haben** to stand in (for sb), to deputize (for sb); **X spielt in ~** X is appearing in his/her place; **in ~** (*in Briefen*) on behalf of.
(b) representation ◆ **X übernimmt die ~ des Klienten/Falles** X is appearing for the client/pleading the case; **die ~ meiner Interessen** representing my interests.
(c) (*Comm*) agency; representation.
(d) supporting; holding; representation.
(e) *siehe* **Vertreter(in) (a, b).**

Vertretungs-: ~stunde *f* (*Sch*) *class where one stands in for another teacher,* stand-in class; **~stunden geben** to stand in for another teacher; **v~weise** *adv* as a replacement; (*bei Amtsperson*) as a deputy; **er übernimmt heute v~weise meine Deutschstunde** he's taking my German lesson for me today.

Vertrieb *m* **-(e)s, -e** **(a)** *no pl* sales *pl* ◆ **der ~ eines Produktes** the sale of a product; **den ~ für eine Firma haben** to have the (selling) agency for a firm.
(b) (*Abteilung einer Firma*) sales department.

Vertriebenen-: ~treffen *nt* reunion of exiles; **~verband** *m* association of exiles.

Vertriebene(r) *mf decl as adj* exile.

Vertriebs-: ~abteilung *f* sales department; **~erlös** *m* sales revenue; **~gesellschaft** *f* marketing company; **~kosten** *pl* marketing costs *pl*; **~leiter** *m* sales manager.

vertrimmen* *vt* (*inf*) to belt (*inf*), to wallop (*inf*).

vertrinken* *vt irreg* to drink away, to spend on drink.

vertrocknen* *vi aux sein* to dry out; (*Eßwaren*) to go dry; (*Pflanzen*) to wither, to shrivel; (*Quelle*) to dry up ◆ **er ist ein vertrockneter Mensch** he's a dry old stick (*inf*).

vertrödeln* *vt* (*inf*) to fritter away.

vertrösten* [1] *vt* to put off ◆ **jdn auf ein andermal/auf später ~** to put sb off.
[2] *vr* to be content to wait (*auf +acc* for).

vertrotteln* *vi* (*inf*) *aux sein* to vegetate.

vertrusten* [fɛɐ'trastn] *vt* (*Comm*) to form into a trust.

vertüdern* (*N Ger*) [1] *vr* to get tangled up.
[2] *vt* to tangle up, to get tangled up.

vertun* *irreg* [1] *vt* to waste.
[2] *vr* (*inf*) to make a mistake *or* slip, to slip up (*inf*).

vertuschen* *vt* to hush up ◆ **~, daß** ... to hush up the fact that ...; **etw vor jdm ~** to keep sth from sb.

Vertuschung *f* cover-up.

Vertuschungsversuch *m* attempt to hush things up.

ver|übeln* *vt* **jdm etw ~** not to be at all pleased with sb for doing sth, to take sth amiss; **ich hoffe, Sie werden mir die Frage nicht ~** I hope you won't mind my asking (this); **das kann ich dir nicht ~** I can't blame you for that.

ver|üben* *vt* to commit, to perpetrate (*form*).

ver|ulken* *vt* (*inf*) to make fun of, to take the mickey out of (*inf*).

ver|unfallen* *vi aux sein* (*Sw*) to have an accident.

ver|unglimpfen* *vt jdn* to disparage; *Ruf, Ehre, Worte auch* to decry.

Ver|unglimpfung *f* disparagement.

ver|unglücken* *vi aux sein* (*Mensch*) to have an accident; (*Fahrzeug*) to crash. (*fig inf: mißlingen*) to go wrong ◆ **mit dem Flugzeug ~** to be in a plane crash; **mit dem Auto ~** to be in a car crash, to have a car accident; *siehe* **tödlich.**

ver|unglückt *adj* (*fig*) *Versuch, Aufführung etc* unsuccessful.

Ver|unglückte(r) *mf decl as adj* casualty, victim ◆ **10 Tote, 20 ~** 10 dead, 20 injured.

ver|unreinigen* *vt Fluß, Luft, Wasser* to pollute; (*beschmutzen*) to dirty, to soil; (*euph: Hund etc*) to foul.

Ver|unreinigung *f siehe vt* pollution; dirtying, soiling; fouling; (*verunreinigter Zustand: von Wasser, Luft*) pollution ◆ **~en in der Luft/im Wasser** pollutants in the atmosphere/in the water.

ver|unsichern* *vt* to make unsure *or* uncertain (*in +dat* of) ◆ **jetzt hast du mich völlig verunsichert** I just don't know at all any more; **sie versuchten, ihn zu ~** they tried to throw him; **verunsichert** uncertain.

Ver|unsicherung *f* (*mangelnde Gewißheit*) uncertainty ◆ **das führte zur ~ der Wähler/Schüler** it put the electors/pupils into a state of uncertainty.

ver|unstalten* *vt* to disfigure; *Landschaft auch* to scar ◆ **jdn** *or* **jds Gesicht ~** to spoil *or* mar sb's looks.

Ver|unstaltung *f* disfigurement.

ver|untreuen* *vt* to embezzle, to misappropriate.

Ver|untreuung *f* embezzlement, misappropriation.

ver|unzieren* *vt Landschaft, Kunstwerk, Zimmer* to spoil ◆ **jdn** *or* **jds Gesicht ~** to spoil sb's looks.

ver|ursachen* *vt* to cause; *Schwierigkeiten auch* to create (*dat* for), to give rise to (*dat* for); *Entrüstung, Zorn auch* to provoke ◆ **jdm große Kosten ~** to cause sb a lot of expense; **jdm Umstände ~** to put sb to *or* cause sb trouble.

Ver|ursacher(in *f*) *m* **-s, -** cause ◆ **der ~ kommt für den Schaden auf** the party responsible is liable for the damages.

Ver|ursacherprinzip *nt* principle that the party responsible is liable for the damages.

Ver|ursachung *f siehe vt* causing; creation; provocation.

ver|urteilen* *vt* to condemn; (*Jur*) (*für schuldig befinden*) to convict (*für* of); (*zu Strafe*) to sentence ◆ **jdn zu einer Geldstrafe von 1.000 DM ~** to fine sb 1,000 DM, to impose a fine of 1,000 DM on sb; **jdn zum Tode ~** to condemn *or* sentence (*Jur*) sb to death; **jdn zu einer Gefängnisstrafe ~** to give sb a prison sentence.

ver|urteilt *adj* **zu etw ~ sein** (*Jur*) to be sentenced to sth; (*fig*) to be condemned to sth; **zum Tode ~** condemned *or* sentenced (*Jur*) to death; *siehe* **Scheitern.**

Ver|urteilte(r) *mf decl as adj* convicted man/woman, convict (*Jur*) ◆ **der zum Tode ~** the condemned man.

Ver|urteilung *f siehe vt* condemnation; conviction; sentencing ◆ **seine ~ zu 5 Jahren** his being sentenced to 5 years; **seine ~ zum Tode** his being condemned/sentenced to death.

Verve ['vɛrvə] *f -, no pl* (*geh*) verve, spirit.

vervielfachen* *vtr* to multiply.

Vervielfachung *f* multiplication.

vervielfältigen* *vt* to duplicate; (*hektographieren auch*) to mimeograph; (*photokopieren auch*) to photocopy.

Vervielfältigung *f* **(a)** *siehe vt* duplication; mimeographing; photocopying. **(b)** (*Abzug*) copy; mimeograph; photocopy.

Vervielfältigungs-: ~apparat *m* duplicating *or* copying machine, duplicator; **~gerät** *nt*, **~maschine** *f siehe* **~apparat**; **~recht** *nt* right of reproduction, copyright; **~verfahren** *nt* duplicating process, copying process.

vervierfachen* *vtr* to quadruple.

vervollkommnen* [1] *vt* to perfect.
[2] *vr* to perfect oneself.

Vervollkommnung *f* perfection.

vervollständigen* [1] *vt* to complete; *Kenntnisse, gutes Essen auch* to round off; *Erlebnis* to make complete.
[2] *vr* to be completed.

Vervollständigung *f siehe vt* completion; rounding off; completion.

verwachsen[1]* *vi irreg aux sein* (*zusammenwachsen*) to grow (in) together, to grow into one; (*Narbe*) to heal over; (*Knochen*) to knit; (*Wunde*) to heal, to close (over) ◆ **mit etw ~** to grow into sth.
(b) (*fig: Menschen, Gemeinschaft*) to grow closer (together) ◆ **zu etw ~** to grow into sth; **mit etw ~** *mit Arbeit, Aufgabe, Traditionen* to become caught up in sth; **mit etw ~ sein** to have very close ties with sth; **ein Volk, das mit seinen Traditionen/seiner Kultur ~ ist** a nation whose traditions are/culture is deeply rooted within it; **mit jdm ~ sein** to have become very close to sb.

verwachsen[2] *adj* **(a)** *Mensch, Tier* deformed; *Glied auch, Pflanze* malformed; (*verkümmert*) stunted. **(b)** (*überwuchert*) overgrown.

Verwachsung *f* (*Med*) deformation; malformation; (*verwachsenes Glied auch*) deformity; (*Biol, Min*) adhesion.

verwackeln* *vt* to blur.

verwählen* *vr* to misdial, to dial the wrong number.

verwahren* [1] *vt* (*aufbewahren*) to keep (safe) ◆ **jdm etw zu ~ geben** to give sth to sb for safekeeping.
[2] *vr* **sich gegen etw ~** to protest against sth.

verwahrlosen* *vi aux sein* to go to seed, to go to pot (*inf*); (*Gebäude auch*) to fall into disrepair, to become dilapidated; (*Mensch*) to let oneself go, to neglect oneself; (*verwildern*) to run wild; (*auf die schiefe Bahn geraten*) to fall into bad ways.

verwahrlost *adj* neglected; *Mensch, Äußeres auch* unkempt ◆ **sittlich ~** decadent.

Verwahrlosung *f, no pl siehe vi* neglect; dilapidation; neglect (of oneself); wildness; (*moralisch*) waywardness.

Verwahrsam *m -s, no pl* **etw in jds ~ geben** to give sth to sb for safekeeping; **etw in ~ haben/nehmen** to keep sth safe/to take sth into safekeeping.

Verwahrung *f* **(a)** *no pl* (*von Geld etc*) keeping; (*von Täter*) custody, detention ◆ **die ~ eines Menschen in einem Heim** putting/keeping a person in a home; **jdm etw in ~ geben, etw bei jdm in ~ geben** to give sth to sb for safekeeping; **etw in ~ nehmen** to take sth into safekeeping; (*Behörde*) to take possession of sth; **jdn in ~ nehmen** to take sb into custody.
(b) (*Einspruch*) protest ◆ **gegen etw ~ einlegen** to make *or* lodge a protest against sth.

verwaisen* *vi aux sein* to become an orphan, to be orphaned, to be made an orphan; (*fig*) to be deserted *or* abandoned ◆ **verwaist** orphaned; (*fig*) deserted, abandoned.

verwalken* *vt* (*inf*) to wallop (*inf*), to belt (*inf*).

verwalten* *vt* to manage; *Firma auch* to run; *Angelegenheiten auch* to conduct; *Erbe, Vermögen auch* to administer; *Treuhandsgut* to hold in trust; *Amt* to hold; (*Pol*) *Provinz etc* to govern; (*Beamte*) to administer; (*Rel*) to administer ◆ **sich selbst ~** (*Pol*) to be self-governing.

Verwalter(in f) *m -s, -* administrator; (*Treuhänder*) trustee, custodian ◆ **der Papst als ~ Gottes** the Pope as God's steward.

Verwaltung *f* **(a)** *siehe vt* management; running; conducting; administration; holding in trust; holding; government ◆ **jdm etw zur ~ übergeben** to put sb in charge of (the management/running *etc* of) sth.
(b) (*Behörde, Abteilung*) administration; (*Haus~*) management ◆ **städtische ~** municipal authorities *pl.*

Verwaltungs-: ~angestellte(r) *mf* admin(istration) employee; **~apparat** *m* administrative machinery; **~beamte(r)** *m* government (administration) official; **~behörde** *f* administration; **~bezirk** *m* administrative district; **~dienst** *m* admin(istration); **~gebäude** *nt* admin(istration) building *or* block; **~gebühr** *f* administrative charge; **~gericht** *nt* Administrative Court; **~kosten** *pl* administrative expenses *pl*; **~weg** *m* administrative channels *pl*; **auf dem ~wege** through (the) administrative channels.

verwamsen* *vt* (*inf*) to belt (*inf*), to clobber (*inf*).

verwandelbar *adj* (*Math, Econ*) convertible.

verwandeln* [1] *vt* (*umformen*) to change, to transform; *Bett, Zimmer,* (*Math, Econ, Chem*) to convert; (*Theat*) *Szene* to change; (*Jur*) *Strafe* to commute; (*Rel*) *Brot, Wein auch* to transubstantiate ◆ **jdn/etw in etw** (*acc*) **~** to turn sb/sth into sth; (*verzaubern auch*) to change *or* transform sb/sth into sth; **die Vorlage ~** (*Ftbl*) to score off the pass; **Müller verwandelte den Paß zum 2:0** Müller put the pass away to make it 2-0; **ein Gebäude in einen Trümmerhaufen ~** to reduce a building to a pile of rubble; **er ist wie verwandelt** he's a changed man.
[2] *vi* (*Sport sl*) **zum 1:0 ~** to make it 1-0.
[3] *vr* to change; (*Zool*) to metamorphose ◆ **sich in etw** (*acc*) *or* **zu etw ~** to change *or* turn into sth; **Zeus hat sich in einen Stier verwandelt** Zeus turned *or* transformed himself into a bull.

Verwandlung *f* **(a)** *siehe vt* transformation; conversion; change, changing; commuting; transubstantiation.
(b) *siehe vr* change; metamorphosis; (*von Göttern, von der Natur*) transformation ◆ **eine ~ durchmachen** to undergo a change *or* transformation; **seine erstaunliche ~** the remarkable change in him; **„die ~"** (*Liter*) "the Metamorphosis".

Verwandlungs-: ~künstler *m* quick-change artist; **~szene** *f* (*Theat*) transformation scene.

verwandt [1] *ptp of* **verwenden.**
[2] *adj* **(a)** related (*mit* to); (*Ling auch*) cognate; *siehe* **Ecke.**
(b) (*fig*) (*mit* to) *Probleme, Methoden, Fragen, Wissenschaften* related, allied; *Philosophien, Kultur, Gefühle auch* kindred *attr*; *Denker, Geister* kindred *attr* ◆ **~e Seelen** (*fig*) kindred spirits; **geistig ~ sein** (*fig*) to be kindred spirits; **wir sind uns darin ~, daß ...** we're akin to each other in that ...

verwandte *pret of* **verwenden.**

Verwandte(r) *mf decl as adj* relation, relative.

Verwandtschaft *f* relationship; (*die Verwandten*) relations *pl*, relatives *pl*; (*fig*) affinity, kinship ◆ **er leugnete die ~ zu mir** he denied being related to me, he denied any relationship with me.

verwandtschaftlich *adj* family *attr.*

Verwandtschaftsgrad *m* degree of relationship ◆ **wir kennen ihren ~ nicht** we don't know how closely they are related.

verwanzt *adj Betten, Kleider* bug-ridden, bug-infested; (*inf: mit Abhörgeräten*) bugged.

verwarnen* *vt* to caution, to warn.

Verwarnung *f* caution, warning; *siehe* **gebührenpflichtig.**

Verwarnungsgeld *nt* exemplary fine.

verwaschen *adj* faded (*in the wash*); (*verwässert*) *Farbe* watery; (*fig*) wishy-washy (*inf*), woolly (*inf*).

verwässern* *vt* to water down; (*fig auch*) to dilute.

Verwässerung *f* watering down; (*fig auch*) dilution.

verweben* *vt irreg* **(a)** *auch reg Garne* to weave; (*verbrauchen*) to use. **(b)** (*lit, fig: verflechten*) to interweave (*mit, in +acc* with).

verwechseln* *vt Gegenstände* to mix up, to get muddled *or* mixed up; *Begriffe, Menschen auch* to confuse ◆ **jdn (mit jdm) ~** to confuse sb with sb; (*für jdn halten auch*) to mistake sb for sb; **entschuldigen Sie, ich habe Sie verwechselt** sorry — I thought you were *or* I (mis)took you for someone else; **zum V~ ähnlich sein** to be the spitting image of each other, to be as like as two peas in a pod; **ich habe meinen Schirm verwechselt** I took somebody else's umbrella by mistake; **sie verwechselt mir und mich** (*lit*) she mixes up *or* confuses "mir" and "mich"; (*fig*) she doesn't know her grammar; *siehe* **mein.**

Verwechslung *f* confusion; (*Irrtum*) mistake ◆ **die Polizei ist sicher, daß eine ~ (des Täters) völlig ausgeschlossen ist** the police are certain that there can be absolutely no mistake (about the culprit); **es kam deshalb zu einer ~, weil ...** there was a mix-up *or* confusion because ...; **das muß eine ~ sein, da muß es sich um eine ~ handeln** there must be some mistake.

verwegen *adj* daring, bold; (*tollkühn*) foolhardy, rash; (*keck*) cheeky, saucy ◆ **den Hut ~ aufsetzen** to set one's hat at a jaunty *or* rakish angle.

Verwegenheit *f siehe adj* daring, boldness; foolhardiness, rashness; cheek(iness), sauciness.

verwehen* [1] *vt Blätter* to blow away, to scatter; *Spur, Pfad* to cover over, to obliterate ◆ **vom Winde verweht** gone with the wind.
[2] *vi aux sein* (*geh*) (*Worte, Musik*) to be carried away, to drift away; (*Spur, Pfad*) to be obliterated, to be covered over.

verwehren* *vt* (*geh*) **jdm etw ~** to refuse *or* deny sb sth; **die neugebauten Häuser ~ ihnen jetzt den Blick auf ...** the newly built houses now bar their view of ...; **jdm ~, etw zu tun** to bar sb from doing sth.

Verwehung *f* (*Schnee~*) (snow)drift; (*Sand~*) (sand)drift.

verweichlichen* [1] *vt* **jdn ~** to make sb soft; **ein verweichlichter Mensch** a weakling; **ein verweichlichtes Muttersöhnchen** a mollycoddled mother's boy.
[2] *vi aux sein* to get *or* grow soft.

Verweichlichung *f* softness ◆ **Zentralheizung führt zur ~** central heating makes you soft.
Verweigerer *m* refusenik (*inf*); (*Kriegsdienst~*) conscientious objector.
verweigern* *vt* to refuse; *Befehl* to refuse to obey; *Kriegsdienst* to refuse to do ◆ **jdm etw ~** to refuse *or* deny sb sth; **er kann ihr keinen Wunsch ~** he can refuse *or* deny her nothing; **es war ihr verweigert, ihren Sohn wiederzusehen** she was denied seeing her son; **die Annahme eines Briefes ~** to refuse (to accept *or* to take delivery of) a letter; **das Pferd hat (das Hindernis) verweigert** the horse refused (at the fence *or* jump); **sich jdm ~** (*euph*) to refuse (to have) intimacy with sb.
Verweigerung *f* refusal; (*von Hilfe, Auskunft etc auch*) denial ◆ **die ~ einer Aussage** (*Jur*) refusal to make a statement; **~ des Kriegsdienstes** refusal to do (one's) military service; **~ des Gehorsams** disobedience.
Verweigerungsfall *m* (*Jur*): **im ~** in case of refusal to make a statement.
verweilen* [1] *vi* (*geh*) (*Mensch*) to stay; (*Blick*) to rest; (*Gedanken*) to dwell, to linger ◆ **bei einer Sache ~** to dwell on sth; **hier laßt uns ~** let us linger *or* tarry (*liter*) here.
[2] *vr* to linger, to tarry (*liter*).
Verweilen *nt* **-s,** *no pl* (*geh*) stay ◆ **sein ~ bei dem Gedanken/Thema** his dwelling on the thought/theme; **hier ist meines ~s nicht mehr** (*liter*) I can no longer tarry here (*liter*).
verweint *adj Augen* tear-swollen; *Gesicht* tear-stained; *Mensch* with (a) tear-stained face ◆ **~ aussehen** to look as though one has (just) been crying.
Verweis *m* **-es, -e** **(a)** (*Rüge*) reprimand, rebuke, admonishment ◆ **jdm einen ~ erteilen** *or* **aussprechen** to reprimand *or* rebuke or admonish sb. **(b)** (*Hinweis*) reference (*auf +acc* to).
verweisen* *irreg* [1] *vt* **(a)** (*hinweisen*) **jdn auf etw** (*acc*)**/an jdn ~** to refer sb to sth/sb.
(b) (*von der Schule*) to expel ◆ **jdn des Landes** *or* **aus dem Lande ~** to expel sb (from the country); **jdn vom Platz** *or* **des Spielfeldes ~** to send sb off; **jdn auf den zweiten Platz ~** (*Sport*) to relegate sb to second place.
(c) (*Jur*) to refer (*an +acc* to).
(d) (*dated: rügen*) **jdn ~** to rebuke *or* reprove *or* admonish sb.
[2] *vi* **auf etw** (*acc*) **~** to refer to sth.
Verweisung *f* **(a)** expulsion. **(b)** (*Hinweis*) *siehe* **Verweis (b)**. **(c)** (*Jur*) referral (*an +acc* to).
verwelken* *vi aux sein* (*Blumen*) to wilt; (*fig*) to fade ◆ **ein verwelktes Gesicht** a worn face; **eine verwelkte Schönheit** a faded beauty.
verweltlichen* *vt* to secularize.
Verweltlichung *f* secularization.
verwendbar *adj* usable (*zu* for) ◆ **das ist nur einmal ~** it can be used once only.
Verwendbarkeit *f, no pl* usability.
verwenden *pret* **verwendete** *or* **verwandte,** *ptp* **verwendet** *or* **verwandt** [1] *vt* to use; *Methode, Mittel auch* to employ; (*verwerten auch*) to make use of, to utilize ◆ **Mühe/Fleiß auf etw** (*acc*) **~** to put effort/hard work into sth; **Zeit auf etw** (*acc*) **~** to spend time on sth, to put time into sth.
[2] *vr* **sich (bei jdm) für jdn ~** to intercede (with sb) *or* to approach sb on sb's behalf.
Verwendung *f* **(a)** use; (*von Mitteln etc auch*) employment; (*von Zeit, Geld*) expenditure (*auf +acc* on) ◆ **keine ~ für etw haben** to have no use for sth; **für alles ~ haben** (*inf*) to have a use for everything; **~ finden** to have a use, to come in handy *or* useful; **für jdn/etw ~ finden** to find a use for sb/sth; **in ~ stehen** (*Aus*) to be in use; **etw in ~ nehmen** (*Aus*) to put in service.
(b) (*old: Fürsprache*) intercession (*bei* with).
Verwendungs-: v~fähig *adj* usable; **für etw v~fähig sein** to be suitable for sth; **~möglichkeit** *f* (possible) use; **~weise** *f* manner of use; **die ~weise von etw** the way in which sth is used; **~zweck** *m* use, purpose.
verwerfen* *irreg* [1] *vt* **(a)** (*ablehnen*) to reject; *eigene Meinung, Ansicht* to discard; (*Jur*) *Klage, Antrag* to dismiss; *Urteil* to quash; (*kritisieren*) *Handlungsweise, Methode* to condemn. **(b)** *Ball* to lose.
[2] *vr* **(a)** (*Holz*) to warp; (*Geol*) to fault. **(b)** (*Cards*) to misdeal.
[3] *vi Tier* to abort.
verwerflich *adj* reprehensible.
Verwerflichkeit *f* reprehensibleness.
Verwerfung *f* **(a)** *siehe vt (a)* rejection; discarding; dismissal; quashing; condemnation. **(b)** (*Geol*) fault; (*von Holz*) warping.
verwertbar *adj* usable.
Verwertbarkeit *f* usability.
verwerten* *vt* (*verwenden*) to make use of, to utilize; *Reste* to use, to make use of; *Kenntnisse auch* to exploit, to put to (good) use; *Erfahrungen auch* to turn to (good) account; (*kommerziell*) *Erfindung, Material etc* to exploit ◆ **dieser Stoff wird sich gut für ein Kleid ~ lassen** this material will make a nice dress.
Verwertung *f siehe vt* utilization; using; exploitation.
verwesen* [1] *vi aux sein* to decay; (*Fleisch*) to rot.
[2] *vt* (*obs*) to administer ◆ **jds Amt ~** to deputize for sb.
Verweser *m* **-s, -** administrator; (*Amts~*) deputy; (*Pfarr~*) locum (tenens).
Verwesung *f, no pl* decay ◆ **in ~ übergehen** to start to decay.
verwetten* *vt* to gamble away.
verwichsen* [vɛɐ'vɪksn] *vt* (*inf*) **(a)** *siehe* **verwamsen**. **(b)** *Geld* to squander.
verwickeln* [1] *vt Fäden etc* to tangle (up), to get tangled up ◆ **jdn in etw** (*acc*) **~** to involve sb in sth; *in Kampf, in dunkle Geschäfte auch* to get sb mixed up in sth; *in Skandal auch* to get sb mixed up in sth, to embroil sb in sth.
[2] *vr* (*Fäden etc*) to tangle (up), to become tangled ◆ **sich in etw** (*acc*) **~** (*lit*) to become entangled in sth, to get caught up in sth; (*fig*) *in Widersprüche* to get oneself tangled up in sth; *in Skandal* to get mixed up *or* involved *or* embroiled in sth.
verwickelt *adj* (*fig inf*) (*schwierig*) involved, complicated, intricate; (*verwirrt*) *Mensch* fuddled, confused.
Verwick(e)lung *f* involvement (*in +acc* in); (*in Skandal auch*) embroilment; (*Komplikation*) complication; (*Verwirrung*) confusion; (*Theat, Liter*) intrigue, intricacy (of plot).
verwildern* *vi aux sein* (*Garten*) to become overgrown, to overgrow; (*Pflanzen*) to grow wild; (*Haustier*) to become wild; (*hum inf: Mensch*) to run wild.
verwildert *adj* wild; *Garten* overgrown; *Aussehen* unkempt.
Verwilderung *f* (*von Garten*) overgrowing ◆ **Zustand der ~** state of neglect; **mangelnde Sorge führte zur ~ des Tieres/der Kinder** as a result of negligence the animal became wild/the children ran wild.
verwinden* *vt irreg* to get over.
verwinkelt *adj* full of corners.
verwirken *vt* (*geh*) to forfeit.
verwirklichen* [1] *vt* to realize; *Hoffnung auch* to fulfil; *Idee, Plan auch* to put into effect, to translate into action; *Wunsch, Traum auch* to make come true, to turn into a reality.
[2] *vr* to be realized; to be fulfilled; to be put into effect, to be translated into action; to come true, to become a reality; (*Mensch*) to fulfil oneself.
Verwirklichung *f, no pl* realization; (*von Hoffnung, Selbst~*) fulfilment.
Verwirkung *f* forfeit(ure) ◆ **~ einer Strafe** (*Jur*) incurrence of a penalty.
verwirren* [1] *vt* **(a)** *Haar* to tousle; to ruffle (up); *Fäden etc* to tangle (up), to get tangled up.
(b) (*durcheinanderbringen*) to confuse; (*konfus machen*) to bewilder; (*aus der Fassung bringen auch*) to fluster; *Sinne, Verstand auch* to (be)fuddle.
[2] *vr* (*Fäden etc*) to become tangled (up) *or* snarled up; (*Haare*) to become tousled *or* dishevelled; (*fig*) to become confused.
Verwirrspiel *nt* (*fig*) confusion ◆ **ein ~ mit jdm treiben** to try to confuse sb.
Verwirrung *f* (*Durcheinander, Verlegenheit*) confusion; (*Fassungslosigkeit auch*) bewilderment ◆ **jdn in ~ bringen** to confuse/bewilder sb; (*verlegen machen*) to fluster sb.
verwirtschaften* *vt* to squander away.
verwischen* [1] *vt* (*verschmieren*) to smudge, to blur; (*lit, fig*) *Spuren* to cover over; (*fig*) *Eindrücke, Erinnerungen* to blur.
[2] *vr* (*lit, fig*) to become blurred; (*Schrift etc auch*) to become smudged; (*Erinnerung auch*) to fade.
verwittern* *vi aux sein* to weather.
verwittert *adj Gestein* weathered; *Gesicht auch* weather-beaten.
Verwitterung *f* weathering.
verwitwet *adj* widowed ◆ **Frau Meier, ~e Schulz** Mrs Meier, the widow of Mr Schulz.
verwohnen* *vt Wohnung* to run down; *Möbel* to wear out.
verwöhnen* [1] *vt* to spoil; (*Schicksal*) to smile upon, to be good to.
[2] *vr* to spoil oneself.
verwohnt *adj Wohnung* lived-in *pred*; *Möbel* battered.
verwöhnt *adj* spoilt, spoiled; *Kunde, Geschmack* discriminating ◆ **vom Schicksal/von den Göttern ~** smiled upon by fate/the gods.
Verwöhntheit *f, no pl siehe adj* spoiltness; discriminatingness.
Verwöhnung *f, no pl* spoiling.
verworfen [1] *ptp of* **verwerfen**.
[2] *adj* (*geh*) depraved, degenerate; *Blick* depraved.
verworren *adj* confused, muddled; (*verwickelt*) complicated, involved, intricate.
Verworrenheit *f, no pl siehe adj* confusion; complicatedness, intricacy.
verwundbar *adj* (*lit, fig*) vulnerable.
Verwundbarkeit *f* (*lit, fig*) vulnerability.
verwunden* *vt* to wound; (*lit auch*) to injure.
verwunderlich *adj* surprising; (*stärker*) astonishing, amazing; (*sonderbar*) strange, odd ◆ **es ist sehr ~, daß ...** it's most amazing *or* surprising that ...; **es ist nicht ~, daß ...** it is no wonder *or* not surprising that ...
verwundern* [1] *vt* to astonish, to amaze.
[2] *vr* (*über +acc* at) to be amazed *or* astonished, to wonder ◆ **sich über etw** (*acc*) **sehr ~ müssen** to be most amazed at sth.
Verwunderung *f, no pl* astonishment, amazement ◆ **zu meiner größten ~** to my great astonishment *or* amazement.
verwundet *adj* (*lit, fig*) wounded.
Verwundete(r) *mf decl as adj* casualty ◆ **die ~n** (*Mil*) the wounded.
Verwundung *f* wound.
verwunschen *adj* enchanted.
verwünschen* *vt* **(a)** (*verfluchen*) to curse ◆ **verwünscht** cursed, confounded. **(b)** (*in Märchen*) (*verzaubern*) to enchant, to put *or* cast a spell on *or* over; (*verhexen*) to bewitch.
Verwünschung *f* **(a)** (*Fluch*) curse, oath. **(b)** *no pl* (*Verzauberung*) enchantment; (*Verhexung*) bewitchment.
verwursteln* *vt* (*inf*) to mess up (*inf*), to make a mess of.
verwurzelt *adj* **~ sein** (*Pflanze*) to be rooted; **(fest) in** *or* **mit etw** (*dat*) **~ sein** (*fig*) to be deeply rooted in sth.
Verwurzelung *f* (*lit*) rooting; (*fig*) rootedness.
verwüsten* *vt* to devastate, to ravage; (*fig*) *Gesicht* to ravage.
Verwüstung *f* devastation *no pl*, ravaging *no pl*; (*von Gesicht*) ravages *pl* ◆ **die ~en durch den Sturm** the devastation caused by *or* the ravages of the storm; **~en anrichten** to inflict devastation.

⚠: Informationen zur Rechtschreibreform im Anhang

verzagen* *vi (geh)* to become disheartened, to lose heart ♦ **an etw** (*dat*) **~** to despair of sth; **nicht ~!** don't despair.

verzagt *adj* disheartened, despondent.

Verzagtheit *f, no pl* despondency.

verzählen* [1] *vr* to miscount, to count wrongly.
[2] *vti (dial inf) siehe* **erzählen.**

verzahnen* *vt Bretter* to dovetail; *Zahnräder* to cut teeth *or* cogs in, to gear; (*fig auch*) to (inter)link ♦ **ineinander verzahnt sein** to mesh.

Verzahnung *f (von Brettern) (das Verzahnen)* dovetailing; *(das Verzahntsein)* dovetail; (*von Zahnrädern*) gearing; (*fig*) dovetailing.

verzanken* *vr (inf)* to quarrel, to fall out.

verzapfen* *vt* **(a)** *Getränke* to serve *or* sell on draught. **(b)** *Holzstücke* to mortice and tenon; (*mit Dübel*) to dowel. **(c)** (*inf*) *Unsinn* to come out with; (*pej*) *Gedichte, Artikel* to concoct.

verzärteln* *vt (pej)* to mollycoddle, to pamper.

Verzärtelung *f, no pl (pej)* mollycoddling, pampering.

verzaubern* *vt (lit)* to cast a spell on *or* over, to put a spell on; (*fig*) *Mensch auch* to enchant ♦ **jdn in etw** (*acc*) **~** to turn sb into sth; **eine verzauberte Prinzessin** an enchanted princess.

Verzauberung *f (lit, fig)* enchantment; (*Verhexung*) bewitchment ♦ **die ~ des Prinzen in einen Frosch** turning the prince into a frog.

verzehnfachen* *vtr* to increase ten-fold.

Verzehr *m* **-(e)s,** *no pl* consumption.

verzehren* [1] *vt (form: lit, fig)* to consume.
[2] *vr (geh)* to languish (*liter*), to eat one's heart out ♦ **sich vor Gram/Sorgen ~** to be consumed by *or* with grief/worries; **sich nach jdm ~** to pine for sb.

verzeichnen* [1] *vt* **(a)** to record; (*aufzeichnen auch*) to note; (*in einer Liste auch*) to enter; (*St Ex*) *Kurse* to quote ♦ **gewaltige Änderungen sind zu ~** enormous changes are to be noted; **Todesfälle waren nicht zu ~** there were no fatalities; **einen Erfolg zu ~ haben** to have scored a success; **das kann die Regierung als einen Erfolg ~** the government can mark this up as a success; **in einer Liste ~** to list.
(b) (*falsch zeichnen*) to draw wrong(ly); (*fig*) to misrepresent, to distort.
[2] *vr* to make mistakes/a mistake in one's drawing.
[3] *vti (Opt)* to distort.

Verzeichnis *nt* index; (*Tabelle*) table; (*Namens~, esp amtlich*) register; (*Aufstellung*) list; (*Comput*) directory.

verzeigen* *vt (Sw)* **jdn ~** to report sb to the police.

Verzeigung *f (Sw)* reporting.

▼ **verzeihen** *pret* **verzieh,** *ptp* **verziehen** *vti* (*vergeben*) to forgive; (*Gott, Gebieter*) to pardon; (*entschuldigen*) to excuse, to pardon ♦ **jdm (etw) ~** to forgive sb (for sth); **ich kann es mir nicht ~, daß ich sie geschlagen habe** I'll never forgive myself for hitting her; **das ist nicht zu ~** that's unforgivable; (*nicht zu entschuldigen auch*) that's inexcusable *or* unpardonable; **es sei dir noch einmal verziehen** you're forgiven *or* excused!, we'll forgive you!; **~ Sie!** excuse me!; (*als Entschuldigung auch*) I beg your pardon!; **~ Sie die Störung, ~ Sie, daß ich stören muß** excuse me for disturbing you.

verzeihlich *adj* forgivable; (*zu entschuldigen*) excusable, pardonable.

Verzeihung *f, no pl* forgiveness; (*Entschuldigung*) pardon ♦ **~!** excuse me!; (*als Entschuldigung auch*) sorry!; **(jdn) um ~ bitten** (*sich entschuldigen*) to apologize (to sb); **ich bitte vielmals um ~** I do apologize (*für* for), I'm terribly sorry (*für* about).

verzerren* [1] *vt (lit, fig)* to distort; *Gesicht etc* to contort; *Sehne, Muskel* to strain, to pull ♦ **etw verzerrt darstellen** (*fig*) to present a distorted picture of sth.
[2] *vi (Lautsprecher, Spiegel etc)* to distort.
[3] *vr* to become distorted; (*Gesicht etc*) to become contorted (*zu* in.)

Verzerrung *f (lit, fig)* distortion; (*von Gesicht etc*) contortion; (*von Muskel, Sehne*) straining, pulling; (*Statistik*) bias.

verzetteln* [1] *vt* **(a)** to waste; *Geld, Zeit etc auch* to fritter away; *Energie auch* to dissipate. **(b)** *Wörter, Bücher* to catalogue.
[2] *vr* to waste a lot of time; (*bei Aufgabe, Diskussion*) to get bogged down.

Verzicht *m* **-(e)s, -e** renunciation (*auf +acc* of); (*auf Anspruch*) abandonment (*auf +acc* of); (*Opfer*) sacrifice; (*auf Recht, Eigentum, Amt*) relinquishment (*auf +acc* of); (*auf Thron*) abdication (*auf +acc* of) ♦ **der ~ auf Zigaretten fällt ihm schwer** he finds it hard to give up cigarettes; **ein ~, der mir nicht schwerfällt** that's something I can easily do without; **~ ist ein Fremdwort für sie** doing without is foreign to her; **~ leisten** *or* **üben** (*auf +acc*) (*form*) *siehe* **verzichten.**

verzichten* *vi* to do without; (*Opfer bringen*) to make sacrifices ♦ **einer muß leider ~** somebody has to do without, I'm afraid; **sie verzichtete zugunsten ihrer Schwester auf das Auto** she let her sister have the car; **der Kandidat hat zugunsten eines Jüngeren verzichtet** the candidate stepped down in favour of a younger man; **danke, ich verzichte** (*iro*) not for me, thanks; **auf jdn/etw ~** (*ohne auskommen müssen*) to do without sb/sth; *auf Alkohol, Süßigkeiten etc auch* to abstain from sth; (*aufgeben*) to give up sb/sth; *auf Erbschaft, Eigentum* to renounce sth; *auf Anspruch* to waive sth; *auf Recht* to relinquish sth; (*von etw absehen*) *auf Kommentar, Anzeige etc* to abstain from sth; *auf Kandidatur, Wiederwahl, Amt* to refuse sth; **auf den Thron ~** to abdicate; **auf jdn/etw ~ können** to be able to do without sb/sth; **auf Einzelheiten/eine förmliche Vorstellung ~ können** to be able to dispense with details/a formal introduction.

Verzicht-: ~erklärung *f* (*auf +acc* of) renunciation; (*auf finanzielle Leistungen*) disclaimer; (*auf Rechte*) waiver; **~leistung** *f (Jur)* renunciation; **~politik** *f (pej)* policy of surrender; **~politiker** *m (pej)* politician supporting a policy of surrender.

verzieh *pret of* **verzeihen.**

verziehen¹* *irreg* [1] *vt* **(a)** *Mund, Züge etc* to twist (*zu* into) ♦ **das Gesicht ~** to pull *or* make a face, to grimace; **den Mund ~** to turn up one's mouth; **keine Miene ~** not to turn a hair.
(b) *Stoff* to pull out of shape, to stretch; *Chassis, Gestell* to bend out of shape; *Holz* to warp.
(c) *Kinder* to bring up badly; (*verwöhnen*) to spoil; *Tiere* to train badly.
(d) *Pflanzen* to thin out.
[2] *vr* **(a)** (*Stoff*) to go out of shape, to stretch; (*Chassis*) to be bent out of shape; (*Holz*) to warp.
(b) (*Mund, Gesicht etc*) to twist (*zu* into), to contort.
(c) (*verschwinden*) to disappear (*auch inf*); (*Gewitter*) to pass; (*Nebel, Wolken*) to disperse; (*inf: schlafengehen*) to be off to bed (*inf*).
[3] *vi aux sein* to move (*nach* to) ♦ **verzogen** (*Vermerk*) no longer at this address; **falls Empfänger verzogen** in case of change of address.

verziehen² *ptp of* **verzeihen.**

verzieren* *vt* to decorate; (*verschönern*) to embellish; (*Mus*) to ornament.

Verzierung *f siehe vt* decoration; embellishment; ornamentation; (*Mus: verzierende Noten*) ornament; *siehe* **abbrechen.**

verzinken* *vt* **(a)** *Metalle* to galvanize. **(b)** (*sl: verraten*) to grass *or* squeal on (*sl*).

verzinsbar *adj siehe* **verzinslich.**

verzinsen* [1] *vt* to pay interest on ♦ **jdm sein Kapital (mit** *or* **zu 5%) ~** to pay sb (5%) interest on his/her capital; **das Geld wird mit 3% verzinst** 3% interest is paid on the money, the money yields *or* bears 3% interest.
[2] *vr* **sich (mit 6%) ~** to yield *or* bear (6%) interest.

verzinslich *adj* interest-bearing *attr*, yielding *or* bearing interest ♦ **~/fest ~ sein** to yield *or* bear interest/a fixed rate of interest; **zu 3%/einem hohen Satz ~** yielding *or* bearing 3% interest/a high rate of interest; **nicht ~** free of interest; **das ist ~ vom ersten Mai** the interest on that is payable from the 1st of May; **Kapital ~ anlegen** to put capital out at interest.

Verzinsung *f* (*das Verzinsen*) payment of interest (*+gen, von* on); (*Zinsertrag*) interest (yield *or* return) (*+gen, von* on); (*Zinssatz*) interest rate.

verzogen [1] *ptp of* **verziehen¹.**
[2] *adj Kind* badly brought up; (*verwöhnt*) spoilt; *Tier* badly trained.

verzögern* [1] *vt* to delay; (*verlangsamen*) to slow down.
[2] *vr* to be delayed.

Verzögerung *f* **(a)** delay, hold-up. **(b)** *no pl* (*das Verzögern*) delaying; (*Verlangsamung*) slowing down; (*Phys*) deceleration; (*Mil*) holding action.

Verzögerungstaktik *f* delaying tactics *pl*.

verzollen* *vt* to pay duty on ♦ **diese Waren müssen verzollt werden** you must pay duty on these articles; **haben Sie etwas zu ~?** have you anything to declare?; **verzollt** duty-paid.

Verzollung *f* payment of duty (*+gen* on).

verzücken* *vt* to enrapture, to send into raptures *or* ecstasies.

verzuckern* [1] *vi aux sein* (*Honig etc*) to crystallize.
[2] *vt (fig) siehe* **versüßen.**

verzückt *adj* enraptured, ecstatic ♦ **~ lauschte er der Musik** he listened enraptured to the music.

Verzückung *f, no pl* rapture, ecstasy ♦ **in ~ geraten** to go into raptures *or* ecstasies (*wegen* over).

Verzug *m* **(a)** delay; (*Rückstand von Zahlung*) arrears *pl* ♦ **ohne ~** without delay, forthwith; **bei ~ (der Zahlungen)** on default of payment; **im ~** in arrears *pl*; **mit etw in ~ geraten** to fall behind with sth; *mit Zahlungen* to fall into arrears with sth.
(b) es ist Gefahr im ~ there's danger ahead.
(c) (*form: aus Stadt*) moving away.

Verzugszinsen *pl* interest payable on arrears *sing*.

verzupfen* *vr* (*Aus inf*) to be off (*inf*).

verzwackt *adj (inf)* tricky.

verzweifeln* *vi aux sein* to despair (*an +dat* of) ♦ **am Leben ~** to despair of life; **nur nicht ~!** don't despair!, don't give up!; **es ist zum V~!** it makes you despair!, it drives you to despair!

verzweifelt *adj Blick, Stimme etc* despairing *attr*, full of despair; *Lage, Versuch, Kampf etc* desperate ♦ **ich bin (völlig) ~** I'm in (the depths of) despair; (*ratlos*) I just don't know what to do, I'm at my wits' end; **..., sagte er ~** ... he said despairingly.

Verzweiflung *f* (*Gemütszustand*) despair; (*Ratlosigkeit*) desperation ♦ **etw in seiner** *or* **aus ~ tun** to do sth in desperation; **in ~ geraten** to despair; **jdn zur** *or* **in die ~ treiben** to drive sb to despair; *siehe* **bringen.**

Verzweiflungstat *f* act of desperation.

verzweigen* *vr* (*Bäume*) to branch (out); (*Straße*) to branch (off); (*Leitung*) to branch; (*Firma*) to establish branches; (*Anat, fig*) to ramify.

verzweigt *adj Baum, Familie, Firma, Straßennetz* branched; (*Anat, fig*) ramified.

Verzweigung *f siehe vr* branching (out); branching (off); branching; establishment of branches; ramification.

verzwickt *adj (inf)* tricky.

Vesper¹ *f* **-, -n** (*Eccl*) vespers *pl*.

Vesper² *nt* **-s, -** (*dial*) (*auch* **~pause, ~zeit**) break; (*auch* **~brot**) sandwiches *pl*.

vespern (*dial*) [1] *vt* to guzzle (*inf*).
[2] *vi* (*essen*) to guzzle things (*inf*); (*Pause machen*) to have a break ♦ **er vespert gerade** he's just having his break.

Vestibül [vɛsti'by:l] *nt* **-s, -e** (*dated, geh*) vestibule.

Veteran [vete'ra:n] *m* **-en, -en** (*Mil, fig*) veteran; (*Aut*) vintage car.

➤ SPRACHE AKTIV: verzeihen → 45.1

Veterinär [veteri'nɛːɐ] *m* (*old, form*) veterinary surgeon.
Veterinärmedizin [veteri'nɛːɐ-] *f* veterinary medicine.
Veto ['veːto] *nt* **-s, -s** veto; *siehe* **einlegen.**
Vetorecht ['veːto-] *nt* right of veto.
Vettel *f* **-, -n** (*old pej*) hag.
Vetter *m* **-s, -n** cousin; (*in Märchen*) Brother, Brer.
Vetternwirtschaft *f* (*inf*) nepotism.
Vexierbild [vɛ'ksiːɐ-] *nt* picture puzzle.
vexieren* [vɛ'ksiːrən] *vt* (*old*) to vex.
V-Form ['fau-] *f* V-shape ◆ **in ~** in a V-shape, in (the shape of) a V.
v-förmig ['fau-] *adj* V-shaped, in (the shape of) a V ◆ **~ aussehen** to look like a V, to be V-shaped.
vgl. *abbr of* **vergleiche** cf.
v.H. *abbr of* **vom Hundert** per cent.
VHS [fauhaː'|ɛs] *f abbr of* **Volkshochschule.**
via ['viːa] *adv* via.
Viadukt [via'dʊkt] *m* **-(e)s, -e** viaduct.
⚠**Vibraphon** [vibra'foːn] *nt* **-s, -e** vibraphone, vibraharp (*US*).
Vibration [vibra'tsioːn] *f* vibration.
Vibrator [vi'braːtɔr] *m* vibrator.
vibrieren* [vi'briːrən] *vi* to vibrate; (*Stimme*) to quiver, to tremble; (*schwanken: Ton*) to vary, to fluctuate.
Video ['viːdeo] *nt* **-s, -s** video ◆ **etw auf ~ aufnehmen** to video sth, to record sth on video.
Video- ['viːdeo-] *in cpds* video; **~aufnahme** *f* video recording; **~band** *nt* video-tape; **~clip** *m* video clip; **~gerät** *nt* video (recorder); **~kamera** *f* video camera; **~kassette** *f* video cassette; **~konferenz** *f* video conference; **~rekorder** *m* video recorder; **~spiel** *nt* video game; **~technik** *f* video technology; **~text** *m* teletext.
Videothek [viːdeo-] *f* **-, -en** video(-tape) library.
Videoverfahren ['viːdeo-] *nt* video *no art.*
vidieren* [vi'diːrən] *vt* (*Aus, obs*) to sign.
Viech *nt* **-(e)s, -er** (*inf*) creature.
Viecherei *f* (*inf*) **(a)** (*Quälerei*) torture *no indef art* (*inf*). **(b)** (*grober Scherz*) rotten trick.
Vieh *nt* **-(e)s,** *no pl* **(a)** (*Nutztiere*) livestock; (*Rinder auch*) cattle *pl* ◆ **10 Stück ~** 10 head of livestock/cattle. **(b)** (*inf: Tier*) animal, beast (*usu hum*). **(c)** (*pej inf: Mensch*) swine.
Vieh-: ~bestand *m* livestock; **~futter** *nt* (animal) fodder *or* feed; **~handel** *m* livestock/cattle trade; **~händler** *m* livestock/cattle dealer.
viehisch *adj* brutish; *Schmerzen* beastly; (*unzivilisiert*) *Benehmen* swinish ◆ **~ essen** to eat like a pig; **~ hausen** to live like an animal/animals.
Vieh-: ~markt *m* livestock/cattle market; **~salz** *nt* (*für Tiere*) cattle salt; (*zum Streuen*) road salt; **~seuche** *f* livestock disease; **~treiber** *m* drover; **~wagen** *m* cattle truck; **~weide** *f* pasture; **~zeug** *nt* (*inf*) animals *pl*, creatures *pl*; **~zucht** *f* (live)stock/cattle breeding.
viel *indef pron, adj, comp* **mehr,** *superl* **meiste(r, s)** *or adv* **am meisten (a)** *sing* (*adjektivisch*) a lot of, a great deal of; (*fragend, verneint auch*) much; (*substantivisch*) a lot, a great deal; (*fragend, verneint auch*) much ◆ **~es** a lot of things; **~(es), was ..., ~(es) von dem, was ...** a lot *or* great deal of what ...; **in ~em, in ~er Hinsicht** *or* **Beziehung** in many respects; **mit ~em** with a lot of things; **um ~es besser** *etc* a lot *or* much *or* a great deal better *etc*; **sehr ~ (Geld** *etc***)** a lot *or* a great deal (of money *etc*); **nicht sehr ~ (Geld** *etc***)** not very much (money *etc*); **so ~ (Arbeit** *etc***)** so much *or* such a lot (of work *etc*); **noch (ein)mal so ~ (Zeit** *etc***)** as much (time *etc*) again; **zweimal so ~ (Arbeit** *etc***)** twice as much (work *etc*); **gleich ~ (Gewinn** *etc***)** the same amount (of profit *etc*); **ziemlich ~ (Schmutz** *etc***)** rather a lot (of dirt *etc*); **ein bißchen ~ (Regen** *etc***)** a bit too much (rain *etc*); **furchtbar ~ (Regen** *etc***)** an awful lot (of rain *etc*); **~ Erfolg!** good luck!, I wish you every success!; **~ Spaß!** have fun!, enjoy yourself/yourselves!; **~ Neues/Schönes** *etc* a lot of *or* many new/beautiful *etc* things; **~ Volk** a lot of people; **das ~e/sein ~es Geld** all that/all his money; **das ~e Geld/Lesen** *etc* all this money/reading *etc*; **~ zu tun haben** to have a lot to do; **er hält ~/nicht ~ von ihm/davon** he thinks a lot *or* a great deal/doesn't think much of him/it; **das will ~/nicht ~ heißen** *or* **sagen** that's saying a lot *or* a great deal/not saying much.
(b) ~e *pl* (*adjektivisch*) many, a lot of, a great number of; (*substantivisch*) many, a lot ◆ **es waren nicht ~e auf der Party/in der Schule** there weren't many (people) *or* a lot (of people) at the party/many (children) *or* a lot (of children) at school; **da wir so ~e sind** since there are so many *or* such a lot of us; **davon gibt es nicht ~e/nicht mehr ~e** there aren't many *or* a lot about/many *or* a lot left; **furchtbar ~e (Kinder/Bewerbungen** *etc***)** a tremendous number *or* an awful lot (of children/applications *etc*); **gleich ~e (Angestellte/Anteile** *etc***)** the same number (of employees/shares *etc*); **so/zu ~e (Menschen/Fehler** *etc***)** so/too many (people/mistakes *etc*); **er hat ~(e) Sorgen/Probleme** *etc* he has a lot of worries/problems *etc*; **~e hundert Menschen** many hundreds of people; **die/seine ~en Fehler** *etc* the/his many mistakes *etc*; **die ~en Leute/Bücher!** all these people/books!; **~e glauben, ...** many (people) *or* a lot of people believe ...; **und ~e andere** and many others; **es waren derer** *or* **ihrer ~e** (*liter*) there were many of them.
(c) (*adverbial: mit vb*) a lot, a great deal; (*fragend, verneint auch*) much ◆ **er arbeitet ~/nicht ~** he works a lot/doesn't work much; **er arbeitet zu/so ~** he works too/so much *or* such a lot; **sie ist ~ krank/von zu Hause weg** she's ill/away a lot; **die Straße wird (sehr/nicht) ~ befahren** this street is (very/not very) busy; **dieses Thema wird ~ diskutiert** this subject is much debated; **sich ~ einbilden** to think a lot of oneself.
(d) (*adverbial: mit adj, adv*) much, a lot ◆ **~ größer** *etc* much *or* a lot bigger *etc*; **nicht ~ anders** not very *or* much *or* a lot different; **~ zu ...** much too ...; **~ zu ~** much *or* far too much; **~ zu ~e** far too many; **ich ginge ~ lieber ins Kino** I'd much rather go *or* I'd much prefer to go to the cinema.
Viel-: v~bändig *adj* multivolumed, in many volumes; ⚠**v~beschäftigt** *adj attr* very busy; **v~deutig** *adj* ambiguous; **~deutigkeit** *f* ambiguity; ⚠**v~diskutiert** *adj attr* much discussed; **~eck** *nt* polygon; **v~eckig** *adj* polygonal (*Math*), many-sided; **~ehe** *f* polygamy.
vielen|orts *adv siehe* **vielerorts.**
vielerlei *adj inv* **(a)** various, all sorts of, many different. **(b)** (*substantivisch*) all kinds *or* sorts of things.
viel|er|örtert *adj attr* much discussed.
vieler|orts *adv* in many places.
vielfach [1] *adj* multiple *attr*, manifold ◆ **ein ~er Millionär** a multi-millionaire; **auf ~e Weise** in many various ways; **auf ~en Wunsch** at the request of many people; **um ein ~es besser** *etc* many times better *etc.*
[2] *adv* many times; (*in vielen Fällen*) in many cases; (*auf ~e Weise*) in many ways; (*inf: häufig*) frequently ◆ **~ bewährt** tried and tested many times.
Vielfache(s) *nt decl as adj* (*Math*) multiple ◆ **das kleinste gemeinsame ~** (*Math*) the least *or* lowest common multiple; **um ein ~s** many times over; **der Gewinn hat sich um ein ~s vermehrt/ist um ein ~s gestiegen** the profit has been multiplied several times; **er verdient ein ~s von dem, was ich verdiene** his salary is many times larger than mine.
Vielfalt *f* (great) variety.
vielfältig *adj* varied, diverse.
Vielfältigkeit *f, no pl* variety, diversity.
Viel-: v~farbig, v~färbig (*Aus*) *adj* multicoloured; (*Tech*) polychrome *attr*, polychromatic; **v~flächig** *adj* many-faced, polyhedral (*Math*); **~flächner** *m* **-s, -** (*Math*) polyhedron; **~flieger** *m* **-s, -** (*inf*) frequent *or* regular air traveller ◆ **Sondertarife für Vielflieger** special rates for regular air travellers; **~fraß** *m* **-es, -e** (*Zool, fig*) glutton; (*amerikanischer ~fraß auch*) wolverine; ⚠**v~gehaßt** *adj attr* much-hated; ⚠**v~gekauft** *adj attr* frequently bought, much-purchased; ⚠**v~geliebt** *adj attr* much-loved; ⚠**v~genannt** *adj attr* much-cited, frequently mentioned; ⚠**v~geprüft** *adj attr* (*hum*) sorely tried; ⚠**v~gereist** *adj attr* much-travelled; ⚠**v~geschmäht** *adj attr* much-maligned; **v~gestaltig** *adj* variously shaped, varied in shape and form, multiform (*form*); (*fig: mannigfaltig*) varied; **in v~gestaltiger Weise** in multifarious ways; **~gestaltigkeit** *f* multiformity; (*Sci*) polymorphism; (*fig*) variety; **v~glied(e)rig** *adj* having *or* with many parts; (*Math*) polynomial; **~götterei** *f* polytheism; **v~hundertmal** *adv* (*liter*) hundreds upon hundreds of times, many hundreds of times; **v~köpfig** *adj* many-headed, polycephalous (*Sci, form*); (*inf*) *Familie, Schar* large.
vielleicht *adv* **(a)** perhaps; (*in Bitten auch*) by any chance ◆ **ja, ~** yes, perhaps *or* maybe; **haben Sie ~ meinen Hund gesehen?** have you seen my dog by any chance?; **könnten Sie mir ~ sagen, wie spät es ist?** could you possibly tell me the time?; **~ könnten Sie so freundlich sein und ...?** perhaps you'd be so kind as to ...?; **~ sagst du mir mal, warum** you'd better tell me why; **~ hältst du mal den Mund!** keep your mouth shut; **hat er sich ~ verirrt/weh getan?** maybe he has got lost/hurt himself; **hast du ihm das ~ erzählt?** did you perhaps tell him that?; (*entsetzt: denn etwa*) you didn't tell him that, did you?; **~ hast du recht** perhaps you're right, you may be right, maybe you're right; **~, daß** ... it could be that ...
(b) (*wirklich, tatsächlich, inf: verstärkend*) really ◆ **soll ich ~ 24 Stunden arbeiten?!** am I supposed to work 24 hours then?; **willst du mir ~ erzählen, daß ...?!** do you really mean to tell me that ...?; **du bist ~ ein Idiot!** you really are an idiot!; **ich war ~ nervös!** I wasn't half nervous! (*inf*), was I nervous!, I was as nervous as anything (*inf*); **das ist ~ ein Haus!** that's what I call a house! (*inf*), that's some house! (*inf*).
(c) (*ungefähr*) perhaps, about.
vielmal *adv* (*Sw*) *siehe* **vielmals.**
vielmalig *adj attr* repeated.
vielmals *adv* **(a)** (*in bestimmten Wendungen*) **danke ~!** thank you very much!, many thanks!; **ich bitte ~ um Entschuldigung!** I do apologize!; **er läßt ~ grüßen** he sends his best regards. **(b)** (*liter: häufig*) many times, oft-times (*liter*).
Vielmännerei *f* polygamy, polyandry.
vielmehr *adv* rather; (*sondern, nur*) just ◆ **ich glaube ~, daß ...** rather I *or* I rather think that ...: **nicht dumm, ~ faul** lazy rather than stupid, not stupid just lazy.
Viel-: ⚠**v~sagend** *adj* meaningful, significant; **jdn v~sagend ansehen** to give sb a meaningful look; **v~schichtig** *adj* (*lit rare*) multilayered; (*fig*) complex; **~schreiber** *m* prolific writer; **er ist ein richtiger ~schreiber** (*pej*) he really churns out the stuff (*inf*); **v~seitig** *adj* (*lit*) many-sided; *Mensch, Gerät, Verwendung* versatile; *Interessen* varied; *Ausbildung* broad, all-round *attr*; **diese Beruf ist sehr v~seitig** there are many different sides to this job; **v~seitig interessiert/anwendbar** *etc* to have varied interests/many uses *etc*; **auf v~seitigen Wunsch** by popular request; **~seitigkeit** *f siehe adj* many-sidedness; versatility; variedness; broadness, all-round nature; **v~sprachig** *adj* multilingual, polyglot; **er ist v~sprachig** he is multilingual *or* a polyglot; **~staaterei** *f* particularism; **v~stimmig** *adj* many-voiced; **v~tausendmal** *adv* (*liter*) thousands upon thousands of times, many thousands of times; ⚠**v~umworben** *adj attr* much-sought-after; *Frau* much-courted; ⚠**v~verheißend** *adj* promising, full of promise; ⚠**v~versprechend** *adj* promising, encouraging; **~völkerstaat** *m* multi-

racial state; **~weiberei** *f* polygamy, polygyny; **≈zahl** *f* multitude; **eine ~zahl von Abbildungen** a wealth of illustrations.

Vielzweck- *in cpds* multipurpose.

vier *num* **(a)** four ◆ **die ersten/nächsten/letzten ~** the first/next/last four; **sie ist ~ (Jahre)** she's four (years old); **mit ~ (Jahren)** at the age of four; **~ Millionen** four million; **es ist ~ (Uhr)** it's four (o'clock); **um/gegen ~ (Uhr)** *or* **~e** (*inf*) at/around four (o'clock); **~ Uhr ~** four minutes past four; **~/fünf Minuten vor/nach ~** four minutes/five (minutes) to/past four; **halb ~** half past three; **~ Minuten vor/nach halb ~** twenty-six minutes past three/ twenty-six minutes to four; **für** *or* **auf ~ Tage** for four days; **in ~ Tagen** in four days, in four days' time; **~ zu drei** (*geschrieben* **4:3**) four-three, four to three, 4-3; **wir waren ~** *or* **zu ~t** *or* **zu ~en** *or* **unser ~** (*geh*) there were four of us, we were four in number (*form*); **wir fahren zu ~t** *or* **mit ~en in Urlaub** there are four of us going on holiday together, we are going on holiday as a foursome; **sie kamen zu ~t** *or* **~en** four of them came; **stellt euch ~ und ~** *or* **zu je ~** *or* **zu ~t** *or* **zu ~en auf** line up in fours; **eine Familie von ~en** (*inf*) a family of four; **Vater ~er Töchter** *or* **von ~ Töchtern** father of four daughters.

(b) jdn unter ~ Augen sprechen to speak to sb in private *or* privately; **ein Gespräch unter ~ Augen** a private conversation *or* talk, a tête-à-tête; **jdn um ein Gespräch unter ~ Augen bitten** to ask to speak to sb privately *or* in private; **~ Augen sehen mehr als zwei** (*prov*) two heads are better than one (*prov*); **alle ~e von sich strecken** (*inf*) (*ausgestreckt liegen*) to stretch out; (*tot sein*) to have given up the ghost; **auf allen ~en** (*inf*) on all fours; **sich auf seine ~ Buchstaben setzen** (*hum inf*) to sit oneself down; *siehe* **Wind, Wand, Hand.**

Vier *f* **-, -en** four; (*Buslinie etc*) (number) four ◆ **die ~** *pl* (*Pol*) the (Big) Four; **die Herz-~** the four of hearts.

Vier-: ≈achser *m* **-s, -** (*Aut*) four-axle vehicle; **v≈armig** *adj* with four arms; *Leuchter* with four branches; **~-Augen-Gespräch** *nt* personal *or* private discussion; **v≈bändig** *adj* four-volume *attr*, in four volumes; **≈beiner** *m* **-s, -** (*hum*) four-legged friend (*hum*); **v≈beinig** *adj* four-legged; **v≈blätt(e)rig** *adj* four-leaf *attr*, four-leaved; **v≈dimensional** *adj* four-dimensional; **≈eck** *nt* four-sided figure, quadrilateral (*Math*); (*Rechteck*) rectangle; **v≈eckig** *adj* square; (*esp Math*) four-sided, quadrangular, quadrilateral; (*rechteckig*) rectangular; **v≈einhalb** *num* four and a half.

Vierer *m* **-s, -** (*Rudern, Sch*) four; (*Golf*) foursome; (*inf: Linie*) (number) four; (*inf: Lotto*) score of 4 correct; (*Aus, S Ger*) (*Ziffer*) four.

Vierer-: ~bande *f* Gang of Four; **~bob** *m* four-man bob; **~gruppe** *f* group of four; **v~lei** *adj inv* **(a)** *attr Brot, Käse, Wein* four kinds *or* sorts of; *Möglichkeiten, Fälle, Größen* four different; **(b)** (*substantivisch*) four different things; (*vier Sorten*) four different kinds; **~pasch** *m* (all) fours *no indef art*; **~reihe** *f* row of four; **~treffen** *nt* (*Pol*) (*der vier Mächte*) four-power conference, meeting of the four powers; (*von Politikern*) meeting of four politicians.

vierfach [1] *adj* fourfold, quadruple (*esp Math*) ◆ **die ~e Größe/Menge/ Anzahl** four times the size/amount/number; **in ~er Ausfertigung** in quadruplicate; **in ~er Vergrößerung** enlarged four times.

[2] *adv* four times, fourfold ◆ **das Papier ~ legen** *or* **nehmen** to fold the paper in four; **den Faden ~ nehmen** to take four threads together; **er hat den Band ~** he has four copies of the book.

Vierfache(s) *nt decl as adj* four times the amount, quadruple (*Math*) ◆ **das ~ von jdm verdienen** to earn four times as much as sb; **das ~ von 3 ist 12** four times 3 is 12; **zwei um das ~ vermehren** to add two to the quadruple of two; **um das ~ zunehmen** to quadruple.

Vier-: ≈fachsteckdose *f* (*Elec*) 4-socket plug; **v≈fältig** *adj siehe* **vierfach; ~farbendruck** *m* (*Verfahren*) four-colour printing; (*Erzeugnis*) four-colour print; **~farb(en)stift** *m* four-colour pen; **~felderwirtschaft** *f* four-course rotation; **≈flach** *nt* **-(e)s, -e** (*Math*) tetrahedron; **v≈flächig** *adj Körper, Gebilde* tetrahedral; **≈fruchtmarmelade** *f* four-fruit jam; **≈füßer** *m* **-s, -** *siehe* **~füßler; v≈füßig** *adj* four-legged, quadruped(al) (*spec*); (*Poet*) tetrameter *attr*, with four feet; **≈füßler** *m* **-s, -** (*Zool*) quadruped, tetrapod (*spec*); **≈ganggetriebe** *nt* four-speed gearbox; **v≈geschossig** *adj* four-storey *attr*, four storeyed; **v≈geschossig bauen** to build houses/offices *etc* with four storeys; **≈gespann** *nt* (*vier Tiere, Wagen mit vier Tieren*) four-in-hand; (*Hist: Quadriga*) quadriga; (*vier Menschen*) foursome; **v≈gliedrig** *adj* (*Math*) quadrinomial; **v≈händig** *adj* (*Mus*) four-handed; **v~händig spielen** to play something for four hands; **v≈hebig** *adj* (*Poet*) tetrameter; **v~hebig sein** to be a tetrameter.

vierhundert *num* four hundred.

Vierhundertjahrfeier *f* quatercentenary, quadricentennial (*US*).

vierhundertste(r, s) *adj* four hundredth.

vierhunderttausend *num* four hundred thousand.

Vier-: ~jahresplan *m* (*Econ*) four-year plan; **v≈jährig, 4jährig** *adj* (*4 Jahre alt*) four-year-old *attr*; (*4 Jahre dauernd*) four-year *attr*, quadrennial; **ein v~jähriges Kind** a four-year-old child, a child of four; **≈jährige(r)** *mf decl as adj* four-year-old; **≈kampf** *m* (*Sport*) four-part competition; **v≈kant** *adj, adv* (*Naut*) square; **≈kant** *m or nt* **-(e)s, -e** (*Tech*) square; (*Math*) tetrahedron; **≈kanteisen** *nt* square steel bar; **≈kantholz** *nt* squared timber; **v≈kantig** *adj* square(-headed); *siehe* **achtkantig; ≈kantschlüssel** *m* square box spanner (*Brit*) *or* wrench; **v≈köpfig** *adj Ungeheuer* four-headed; **eine v~köpfige Familie** a family of four.

Vierling *m* quadruplet, quad (*inf*).

Viermächte-: ~abkommen *nt* quadripartite *or* four-power agreement; **~stadt** *f* city occupied by the four powers.

Vier-: v~mal *adv* four times; **v~mal so viele** four times as many; **v~malig** *adj* done *or* repeated four times; **v~maliges Klingeln/v~malige Vorstellungen** four rings/performances; **nach v~maligem Versuch** after the fourth attempt; **nach v~maliger Aufforderung** after the fourth time of asking, after four repeated requests; **~master** *m* **-s, -** (*Naut*) four-master; **v~monatig** *adj attr Säugling* four-month-old; *Abstände* four-monthly; *Lieferungsfrist, Aufenthalt* four months; **v~monatlich** [1] *adj attr Erscheinen* four-monthly; [2] *adv erscheinen, sich wiederholen* every four months; **v~motorig** *adj* four-engined; **~pfünder** *m* four-pounder; **v~phasig** *adj* (*Elec*) four-phase.

Vierrad- (*Aut*): **~antrieb** *m* four-wheel drive; **~bremse** *f* four-wheel braking system.

Vier-: v≈räd(e)rig *adj* four-wheel *attr*, four-wheeled; **das Auto ist v~räd(e)rig** that car is a four-wheeler; **v≈saitig** *adj* four-stringed; **v~saitig sein** to have four strings; **v≈schrötig** *adj* burly; **v≈seitig** *adj* four-sided; *Abkommen, Verhandlungen etc* quadripartite; *Brief, Broschüre* four-page *attr*; **≈silber** *m* **-s, -** (*Poet*) tetrasyllable; **v≈silbig** *adj* four-syllable *attr*, quadrisyllabic, tetrasyllabic; **≈sitzer** *m* **-s, -** four-seater; **v≈sitzig** *adj* four-seater *attr*, with four seats; **v~sitzig sein** to be a four-seater, to have four seats; **v≈spaltig** *adj* four-column *attr*; **v~spaltig sein** to have four columns; **≈spänner** *m* **-s, -** four-in-hand; **v≈spännig** *adj Wagen* four-horse *attr*; **v≈spännig fahren** to drive a team of four horses *or* a four-in-hand; **v≈sprachig** *adj Mensch, Wörterbuch* quadrilingual; *Speisekarte* in four languages; **v~sprachig aufwachsen** to grow up speaking four languages; **das Buch wird v~sprachig angeboten** the book is available in four languages; **v≈spurig** *adj* four-lane *attr*; **v~spurig sein** to have four lanes; **v≈stellig** *adj* four-figure *attr*; (*Math*) *Funktion, Dezimalbruch* four-place *attr*; **v≈stellig sein** to have four figures/places; **~sternehotel** *nt* 4-star hotel; **v≈stimmig** *adj* four-part *attr*, for four voices; **v~stimmig singen** to sing a song for four voices; **v≈stöckig** *adj Haus* four-storey *attr*, four-storeyed, four storeys high; **v≈strahlig** *adj Flugzeug* four-jet *attr*, four-engined; **v≈strophig** *adj Gedicht* four-verse *attr*, four-stanza *attr*; **v~strophig sein** to have four verses *or* stanzas; **~stufenrakete** *f* four-stage rocket; **v≈stufig** *adj* four-stage *attr*; **v≈stufig sein** to have four stages; **v≈stündig** *adj attr Reise, Vortrag* four-hour; **v≈stündlich** [1] *adj attr* four-hourly; [2] *adv* every four hours.

viert *adj* **(a) zu ~** *siehe* **vier. (b)** *siehe* **vierte(r, s).**

Vier-: ~tagewoche *f* four-day week; **v≈tägig** *adj attr* (*4 Tage dauernd*) four-day; (*4 Tage alt*) four-day old; **v≈täglich** *adj, adv* every four days; **≈takter** *m* **-s, -** (*inf*), **≈taktmotor** *m* four-stroke (engine); **v≈tausend** *num* four thousand; **≈tausender** *m* **-s, -** (*Berg*) four-thousand-metre mountain.

vierte *adj siehe* **vierte(r, s).**

vier-: ~teilen *vt* **(a)** *insep* (*Hist*) to quarter; **(b)** *sep siehe* **vierteln; ~teilig** *adj* (*mit vier einzelnen Teilen*) four-piece *attr*; *Roman* four-part *attr*, in four parts; **~teilig sein** to have four pieces/parts; **ich habe dieses Service nur ~teilig** I only have four settings of this dinner service.

Viertel[1] ['fɪrtl] *nt* (*Sw auch m*) **-s, - (a)** (*Bruchteil*) quarter; (*inf*) (*~pfund*) ≃ quarter; (*~liter*) quarter-litre ◆ **der Mond ist im ersten/letzten ~** the moon is in the first/last quarter; **ein ~ Wein/Butter** *etc* a quarter-litre of wine/ quarter of butter *etc*.

(b) (*Uhrzeit*) **(ein) ~ nach/vor sechs** (a) quarter past/to six; **(ein) ~ sechs** (a) quarter past five; **drei ~ sechs** (a) quarter to six; **es ist ~** it's (a) quarter past; **die Uhr schlug ~** the clock struck (a) quarter past *or* the quarter; *siehe* **akademisch.**

Viertel[2] ['fɪrtl] *nt* **-s, -** (*Stadtbezirk*) quarter, district.

viertel ['fɪrtl] *adj inv* quarter ◆ **ein ~ Liter/Pfund** a quarter (of a) litre/pound; **drei ~ Liter** three quarters of a litre.

Viertel- ['fɪrtl-]: **~drehung** *f* quarter-turn; **~finale** *nt* quarter-finals *pl*; **~finalspiel** *nt* quarter-final.

Vierteljahr *nt* three months *pl*, quarter (*Comm, Fin*).

Vierteljahres- *in cpds* quarterly; **~schrift** *f* quarterly.

Viertel- ['fɪrtl-]: **~jahrhundert** *nt* quarter of a century; **v~jährig** *adj attr Kind etc* three-month-old; *Aufenthalt, Frist* three months'; **v~jährlich** [1] *adj* quarterly; *Kündigung* three months' *attr*; [2] *adv* quarterly, every three months; **v~jährlich kündigen** to give three months' notice; **~kreis** *m* quadrant; **~liter** *m or nt* quarter of a litre, quarter-litre.

vierteln ['fɪrtln] *vt* (*in vier Teile teilen*) to divide into four; *Kuchen, Apfel etc auch* to divide into quarters; (*durch vier teilen*) to divide by four; *Summe, Gewinn* to quarter, to divide by four.

Viertel- ['fɪrtl-]: **~note** *f* crotchet (*Brit*), quarter note (*US*); **~pause** *f* crotchet/quarter-note rest; **~pfund** *nt* ≃ quarter of a pound, quarter(-pound); **~stunde** *f* quarter of an hour; **v~stündig** *adj attr Abstand* quarter-hour, of a quarter of an hour; *Vortrag* lasting *or* of a quarter of an hour; **v~stündlich** [1] *adj attr Abstand* quarter-hour, of a quarter of an hour; [2] *adv* every quarter of an hour, quarter-hourly; **~ton** *m* quarter tone.

viertens *adv* fourth(ly), in the fourth place.

Vierte(r) *mf decl as adj* fourth ◆ **~r werden** to be *or* come fourth; **am V~n (des Monats)** on the fourth (of the month); **Karl IV** *or* **der ~** Charles IV *or* the Fourth.

vierte(r, s) *adj* fourth ◆ **der ~ Oktober** the fourth of October; **den 4. Oktober** October 4th, October the fourth; **am ~n Oktober** on the fourth of October; **der ~ Stock** the fourth (*Brit*) *or* fifth (*US*) floor; **der ~ Stand** the Fourth Estate; **im ~n Kapitel/Akt** in the fourth chapter/act, in chapter/act four; **er war ~r im Rennen** he was *or* came fourth in the race; **als ~r durchs Ziel**

gehen to be fourth at the finish; **du bist der ~, der mich das fragt** you're the fourth person to ask me that; **jeder ~ muß** ... every fourth person/boy *etc* has to ...
viertletzte(r, s) *adj* fourth (from) last.
Vier-: ~tonner, 4tonner *m* **-s, -** ≃ four-ton truck, four-tonner; **~türer** *m* (*Aut*) four-door model; **v~türig** *adj* four-door *attr*, with four doors; **v~türig sein** to have four doors; **~uhrzug, 4-Uhr-Zug** *m* four o'clock (train); **v~undeinhalb** *num siehe* **viereinhalb**; **~undsechzigstelnote** *f* hemidemisemiquaver (*Brit*), sixty-fourth note (*US*); **~undsechzigstelpause** *f* hemidemisemiquaver/sixty-fourth note rest; **v~undzwanzig** *num* twenty-four.
Vierung *f* (*Archit*) crossing.
Vierungskuppel *f* (*Archit*) crossing cupola.
Viervierteltakt [-'fɪrtl-] *m* four-four *or* common time.
Vierwaldstätter See *m* Lake Lucerne.
vier-: ~wertig *adj* (*Chem*) quadrivalent, tetravalent; (*Ling*) four-place; **~wöchentlich** *adj, adv* every four weeks; **~wöchig** *adj* four-week *attr*, four weeks long.
vierzehn ['fɪrtse:n] *num* fourteen ◆ **~ Uhr** 2 p.m.; (*auf Fahrplan, Mil*) fourteen hundred hours, 14.00; **~ Tage** two weeks, a fortnight *sing* (*Brit*); **die V~ Punkte** (*Hist*) the Fourteen Points.
Vierzehn- ['fɪrtse:n-]: **~ender** *m* (*Hunt*) fourteen-pointer; **v~tägig** *adj* two-week *attr*, lasting two weeks; **nach v~tägiger Dauer** after two weeks *or* a fortnight (*Brit*); **v~täglich** *adj, adv* fortnightly (*Brit*), every two weeks.
Vierzehntel ['fɪrtse:ntl] *nt* **-s, -** fourteenth; *siehe* **Vierzigstel**.
vierzehnte(r, s) ['fɪrtse:ntə(r, s)] *adj* fourteenth; *siehe* **vierte(r, s)**.
Vier-: ~zeiler *m* **-s, -** four-line poem; (*Strophe*) four-line stanza, quatrain; **v~zeilig** *adj* four-line *attr*, of four lines; **v~zeilig sein** to have four lines.
vierzig ['fɪrtsɪç] *num* forty ◆ **mit ~ (km/h) fahren** to drive at forty (kilometres an hour); **etwa ~ (Jahre alt)** about forty (years old); fortyish (*inf*); **mit ~ (Jahren), mit V~** at forty (years of age); **Mitte (der) V~** in one's mid-forties; **über ~** over forty; **der Mensch über V~** *or* **~** people *pl* over forty; **im Jahre ~** in forty; (**~** *nach/vor Christi Geburt*) in (the year) forty (AD/BC).
Vierzig ['fɪrtsɪç] *f* **-, -en** forty.
vierziger, 40er ['fɪrtsɪgɐ] *adj attr inv* **die ~ Jahre** the forties; **ein ~ Jahrgang** (*Mensch*) a person born in nineteen/eighteen forty; (*Wein*) a vintage forty.
Vierziger(in *f*) ['fɪrtsɪgɐ, -ərɪn] *m* **-s, -** (*Mensch*) forty-year-old; (*Wein*) wine of vintage forty; (*Aus, S Ger: Geburtstag*) fortieth (birthday) ◆ **die ~** *pl* (*Menschen*) people in their forties; **er ist Mitte der ~** he is in his mid-forties; **er ist in den ~n** he is in his forties; **in die ~ kommen** to be getting on for forty.
Vierziger- ['fɪrtsɪgɐ-]: **~jahre** *pl* **die ~jahre** one's forties; **v~lei** *adv inv siehe* **viererlei** forty kinds *or* sorts of; forty different; forty different things; forty different kinds.
Vierzig- ['fɪrtsɪç-]: **v~fach** [1] *adj* forty-fold; [2] *adv* forty times; *siehe* **vierfach**; **v~jährig** *adj attr* (*40 Jahre alt*) forty-year-old; (*40 Jahre dauernd*) forty-year; **der v~jährige Gründungstag** the 40th anniversary (of the foundation); **ein ~jähriger** a forty-year-old; **v~mal** *adv* forty times; **~pfennigmarke, 40-Pfennig-Marke** *f* forty-pfennig stamp.
Vierzigstel ['fɪrtsɪçstl] *nt* **-s, -** fortieth ◆ **ein ~ des Kuchens/der Summe** a fortieth (part) of the cake/the amount.
vierzigstel ['fɪrtsɪçstl] *adj inv* fortieth ◆ **eine ~ Minute** a *or* one fortieth of a minute.
vierzigste(r, s) ['fɪrtsɪçstə(r, s)] *adj* fortieth.
Vierzigstundenwoche [fɪrtsɪç-] *f* forty-hour week.
Vier-: ~zimmerwohnung *f* four-room flat (*Brit*) *or* apartment; **~zylindermotor** *m* four-cylinder engine; **v~zylindrig** *adj* four-cylinder *attr*.
Vietcong, Vietkong [viɛt'kɔŋ] *m* **-, -(s)** Vietcong.
Vietnam [viɛt'nam] *nt* **-s** Vietnam.
Vietnamese [viɛtna'me:zə] *m* **-n, -n, Vietnamesin** *f* Vietnamese.
vietnamesisch [viɛtna'me:zɪʃ] *adj* Vietnamese.
vif [vi:f] *adj* (*old, dial*) bright.
Vigil [vi'gi:l] *f* **-, -ien** [-iən] vigil.
Vignette [vɪn'jɛtə] *f* vignette.
Vikar [vi'ka:ɐ] *m* curate; (*Sw Sch*) supply teacher.
Vikariat [vika'ria:t] *nt* curacy.
Viktorianisch [vɪkto'ria:nɪʃ] *adj* Victorian.
Viktualien [vɪk'tua:liən] *pl* (*obs*) victuals *pl* (*old, form*).
Viktualienmarkt [vɪk'tua:liən-] *m* food market.
Villa ['vɪla] *f* **-, Villen** villa.
Villenviertel ['vɪlən-] *nt* exclusive residential area.
Vinaigrette [vinɛ'grɛtə] *f* (*Cook*) vinaigrette (sauce).
vinkulieren* *vt* [vɪŋku'li:rən] (*Fin*) to restrict transferability of.
Vinyl [vi'ny:l] *nt* **-s,** *no pl* (*Chem*) vinyl.
Viola ['vi:ola] *f* **-, Violen (a)** (*Mus*) viola. **(b)** (*Bot*) violet.
Viola da Gamba ['vio:la da 'gamba] *f* **- - -, Viole - -** viola da gamba.
Violett [vio'lɛt] *nt* **-s, -** purple, violet; (*im Spektrum, Regenbogen*) violet.
violett [vio'lɛt] *adj siehe n* purple, violet; violet.
Violine [vio'li:nə] *f* violin; *siehe* **Geige**.
Violinist(in *f*) [violi'nɪst(ɪn)] *m* violinist.
Violin- [vio'li:n-]: **~konzert** *nt* violin concerto; (*Darbietung*) violin concert; **~schlüssel** *m* treble clef.
Violoncell *nt* **-s, -e, Violoncello** [violɔn'tʃɛl(o)] *nt* violoncello.
VIP [vɪp] (*inf*), **V.I.P.** ['vi:|ai'pi:] *m* **-, -s** (*inf*) *abbr of* **Very Important Person** VIP.
Viper ['vi:pɐ] *f* **-, -n** viper, adder.
Viren ['vi:rən] *pl of* **Virus**.
Virensuchprogramm *nt* (*Comput*) virus checker.
Virginiatabak [vɪr'gi:nia-, vɪr'dʒi:nia-] *m* Virginia tobacco.
viril [vi'ri:l] *adj* virile.
Virilität [virili'tɛ:t] *f* virility.
Virologe [viro'lo:gə] *m*, **Virologin** *f* virologist.
Virologie [virolo'gi:] *f* virology.
virologisch [viro'lo:gɪʃ] *adj* virological.
virtuell [vɪr'tuɛl] *adj* virtual.
virtuos [vɪr'tuo:s] *adj* virtuoso *attr* ◆ **~ spielen** to give a virtuoso performance, to play like a virtuoso.
Virtuose [vɪr'tuo:zə] *m* **-n, -n, Virtuosin** *f* virtuoso.
Virtuosität [vɪrtuozi'tɛ:t] *f, no pl* virtuosity.
virulent [viru'lɛnt] *adj* (*Med, fig*) virulent.
Virulenz [viru'lɛnts] *f* (*Med, fig*) virulence, virulency.
Virus ['vi:rʊs] *nt or m* **-, Viren** (*auch Comput*) virus.
Virus- ['vi:rʊs-]: **~infektion** *f* viral *or* virus infection; **~krankheit** *f* viral disease; **~programm** *nt* (*Comput*) virus (program).
Visa ['vi:za] *pl of* **Visum**.
Visage [vi'za:ʒə, (*Aus*) vi'za:ʒ] *f* **-, -n** (*pej*) face, physog (*dated inf*), (ugly) mug (*inf*); *siehe* **polieren**.
Visagist(in *f*) [viza:'ʒɪst(ɪn)] *m* make-up artist.
vis-à-vis [viza'vi:] (*dated*) [1] *adv* opposite (*von* to). [2] *prep +dat* opposite (to).
Visavis [viza'vi:] *nt* **-, -** (*dated*) person (sitting) opposite, vis-à-vis (*form*) ◆ **mein ~** the person opposite me.
Visen ['vi:zən] *pl of* **Visum**.
Visier [vi'zi:ɐ] *nt* **-s, -e (a)** (*am Helm*) visor ◆ **mit offenem ~ kämpfen** to fight with an open visor; (*fig*) to be open and above board (in one's dealings). **(b)** (*an Gewehren*) sight ◆ **jdn/etw ins ~ bekommen** to get sb/sth in one's sights; **jdn/etw ins ~ fassen** to train one's sights on sb/sth.
visieren* [vi'zi:rən] *vi* **~ auf** (*+acc*) to take aim at.
Vision [vi'zio:n] *f* vision.
visionär [vizio'nɛ:ɐ] *adj* visionary.
Visionär [vizio'nɛ:ɐ] *m* visionary.
Visitation [vizita'tsio:n] *f* (*form*) **(a)** (*Besuch*) visitation (*auch Eccl*), inspection. **(b)** (*Durchsuchung*) search, inspection.
Visite [vi'zi:tə] *f* **-, -n** (*Med*) (*im Krankenhaus*) round; (*zu Hause*) visit, house call ◆ **um 9 Uhr ist ~** the doctors do their rounds at 9 o'clock ; **~ machen** to do one's round; to do visits *or* house calls; (*dated inf*) to visit (*bei jdm* sb), to pay a visit (*bei* to); **zur ~ kommen** to come on one's round; to come on a visit *or* house call.
Visitenkarte [vi'zi:tn-] *f* (*lit, fig*) visiting *or* calling (*US*) card.
visitieren* [vizi'ti:rən] *vt* **(a)** (*form*) *Amtsbezirk etc* to visit, to inspect. **(b)** (*old*) *Gepäck* to search, to inspect.
Visitkarte [vi'zi:t-] *f* (*Aus*) *siehe* **Visitenkarte**.
viskos [vɪs'ko:s], **viskös** [vɪs'kø:s] *adj* viscous.
Viskose [vɪs'ko:zə] *f* **-,** *no pl* viscose.
Viskosität [vɪskozi'tɛ:t] *f* viscosity.
visuell [vi'zuɛl] *adj* visual.
Visum ['vi:zʊm] *nt* **-s, Visa** *or* **Visen** visa.
Visumzwang ['vi:zʊm-] *m* obligation to hold a visa ◆ **für San Serife besteht ~** it is necessary to obtain a visa for San Serife.
Vita ['vi:ta] *f* **-, Viten** ['vi:tən] *or* **Vitae** ['vi:tɛ:] (*geh*) life.
vital [vi'ta:l] *adj* vigorous, energetic; (*lebenswichtig*) vital.
Vitalität [vitali'tɛ:t] *f* vitality, vigour.
Vitamin [vita'mi:n] *nt* **-s, -e** vitamin ◆ **~ B** (*lit*) vitamin B; (*fig inf*) contacts *pl*.
Vitamin- [vitami:n-]: **v~arm** *adj* poor in vitamins; **v~arm leben/essen** to live on/have a vitamin-deficient diet; **eine v~arme Zeit** a time when there are/were few vitamins available; **~bedarf** *m* vitamin requirement; **~-C-haltig** *adj* containing vitamin C; **~-C-haltig sein** to contain vitamin C; **v~haltig, v~hältig** (*Aus*) *adj* containing vitamins; **v~haltig sein** to contain vitamins.
vitamin(is)ieren* [vitamini'zi:rən, -'ni:rən] *vt* to vitaminize, to add vitamins to.
Vitamin- [vita'mi:n-]: **~mangel** *m* vitamin deficiency; **~mangelkrankheit** *f* disease due to a vitamin deficiency; **v~reich** *adj* rich in vitamins; **~spritze** *f* vitamin injection; (*fig*) shot in the arm (*fig inf*); **~stoß** *m* (massive) dose of vitamins.
Vitrine [vi'tri:nə] *f* (*Schrank*) glass cabinet; (*Schaukasten*) showcase, display case.
Vitriol [vitri'o:l] *nt* **-s, -e** vitriol.
Vivarium [vi'va:riʊm] *nt* vivarium.
vivat ['vi:vat] *interj* (*geh*) vivat (*form*).
Vivisektion [vivizɛk'tsio:n] *f* vivisection.
vivisezieren* [vivize'tsi:rən] *vti* to vivisect.
Vize ['fi:tsə] *m* **-s, -** (*inf*) number two (*inf*), second-in-command; (**~***meister*) runner-up.
Vize- ['fi:tsə-] *in cpds* vice-; **~kanzler** *m* vice-chancellor; **~könig** *m* viceroy; **~meister** *m* runner-up; **~präsident** *m* vice-president; **~rektor** *m* (*von Schule*) deputy headmaster *or* principal (*esp US*); (*von Universität*) deputy vice-chancellor *or* rector (*US*).
Vlies [fli:s] *nt* **-es, -e** fleece.

Vlieseline ® *f* interfacing.
V-Mann ['fau-] *m siehe* **Verbindungsmann.**
VN *pl abbr of* **Vereinte Nationen** UN *sing.*
Vogel *m* **-s, ¨** (*lit, fig*) bird ◆ **ein seltener ~** (*lit, fig*) a rare bird; **ein seltsamer** *etc* **~** (*inf*) a queer bird (*inf*) *or* customer (*inf*); **ein lustiger ~** (*inf*) a lively character (*inf*); **~ friß oder stirb** (*prov*) do or die! (*prov*); **den ~ abschießen** (*inf*) to surpass everyone (*iro*); **einen ~ haben** (*inf*) to be crazy (*inf*), to have a screw loose (*inf*); **jdm den ~ zeigen** (*inf*) to tap one's forehead *to indicate to sb that he's not quite right in the head,* ≃ to give sb the V sign (*Brit*) *or* the finger (*US*).
Vogel-: ~bauer *nt* bird-cage; **~beere** *f* (*auch* **~beerbaum**) rowan(-tree), mountain ash; (*Frucht*) rowan(-berry).
Vögelchen, Vög(e)lein (*liter*) *nt* little bird ◆ **gleich kommt's Vögelchen raus** (*inf*) watch the birdie (*inf*).
Vogel-: ~dreck *m* bird droppings *pl*; **~ei** *nt* bird's egg; **~eier** *pl* (*von einem Vogel*) bird's eggs *pl*; (*verschiedene Arten*) birds' eggs *pl*; **~fänger** *m* bird-catcher, fowler; **~flug** *m* flight of birds; **~fluglinie** *f* **in der ~fluglinie** as the crow flies; **v~frei** *adj* (*Hist*) outlawed; **für v~frei erklärt werden** to be outlawed *or* declared an outlaw/outlaws; **~futter** *nt* bird food; (*Samen*) birdseed; **~haus, ~häuschen** *nt* bird house; **~käfig** *m* bird-cage; (*auch* **~haus**) aviary; **~kunde** *f* ornithology; **~männchen** *nt* cock (bird), male bird.
vögeln *vti* (*vulg*) to screw (*sl*).
Vogel-: ~nest *nt* bird's nest; **~perspektive, ~schau** *f* bird's-eye view; **(ein Bild von) Ulan Bator aus der ~perspektive** a bird's-eye view of Ulan Bator; **~scheuche** *f* (*lit, fig inf*) scarecrow; **~schutz** *m* protection of birds; **~-Strauß-Politik** *f* head-in-the-sand *or* ostrich-like policy; **~-Strauß-Politik treiben** to bury one's head in the sand; **~tränke** *f* bird bath; **~warte** *f* ornithological station; **~weibchen** *nt* hen (bird), female bird; **~zug** *m* (*Wanderung*) bird migration.
Vogerlsalat *m* (*Aus*) *siehe* **Rapunzel.**
Vogesen [vo'ge:zən] *pl* Vosges *pl.*
Vöglein *nt* (*liter*) little bird.
Vogt *m* **-(e)s, ¨e** (*Hist*) (*Kirchen~*) church advocate; (*Reichs~*) protector; (*Land~*) landvogt, governor; (*von Burg, Gut*) steward, bailiff.
Vogtei *f siehe* **Vogt** office of church advocate; protectorate; governorship; (*Gebiet*) area administered by a/the church advocate; protectorate; province; (*Residenz*) church advocate's/protector's/landvogt's *or* governor's residence.
Voice-Mail ['vɔɪsmeɪl] *f* **-** *no pl* voice mail.
Voice-Recorder ['vɔɪsrikɔrdɐ] *m* (*Aviat*) (cockpit) voice recorder.
Vokabel [vo'ka:bl] *f* **-, -n** *or* (*Aus*) *nt* **-s, -** word ◆ **~n** *pl* vocabulary *sing*, vocab *sing* (*Sch inf*).
Vokabelschatz [vo'ka:bl-] *m* vocabulary.
Vokabular [vokabu'la:ɐ] *nt* **-s, -e** vocabulary.
Vokal [vo'ka:l] *m* **-s, -e** vowel.
vokal [vo'ka:l] *adj* (*Mus*) vocal.
Vokalisation [vokaliza'tsio:n] *f* vocalization.
vokalisch [vo'ka:lɪʃ] *adj* (*Ling*) vocalic ◆ **~e Anlaute/Auslaute** initial/final vowels.
Vokalismus [voka'lɪsmʊs] *m* (*Ling*) vocalism.
Vokalist(in *f*) [voka'lɪst(ɪn)] *m* (*Mus geh*) vocalist.
Vokalmusik [vo'ka:l-] *f* vocal music.
Vokativ ['vo:kati:f, voka'ti:f] *m* vocative.
vol. *abbr of* **Volumen.**
Vol.-% *abbr of* **Volumprozent.**
Volant [vo'lã:] *m* **-s, -s (a)** (*Stoffbesatz*) valance; (*am Rock, Kleid*) flounce. **(b)** *auch nt* (*Aus, Sw, old: Lenkrad*) steering wheel.
Volk *nt* **-(e)s, ¨er (a)** *no pl* people *pl*; (*Nation auch*) nation; (*Volksmasse auch*) masses *pl*; (*inf: Gruppe*) crowd *pl*; (*pej: Pack*) rabble *pl* ◆ **alles ~** everybody; **viel ~** lots of people *pl*, crowds *pl*; **etw unters ~ bringen** *Nachricht* to spread sth; *Geld* to spend sth; **die sind ein lustiges ~** (*inf*) they are a lively lot (*inf*) *or* bunch (*inf*) *or* crowd; **da verkehrt ein ~!** there's a really strange crowd there!; *siehe* **Mann, fahrend.**
(b) (*ethnische Gemeinschaft*) people *sing* ◆ **die ¨er Afrikas** the peoples of Africa; **ein ~ für sich sein** to be a race apart.
(c) (*Zool*) colony.
Völkchen *nt* **(a)** (*kleine Nation*) small nation. **(b)** (*inf: Gruppe*) lot (*inf*), crowd ◆ **ein ~ für sich sein** to be a race apart.
Völker-: ~ball *m game for two teams where the object is to hit an opponent with a ball and thus put him out of the game*; **~bund** *m* (*Hist*) League of Nations; **~freundschaft** *f* friendship among nations; **~kunde** *f* ethnology; **~kundemuseum** *nt* museum of ethnology; **~kundler(in** *f*) *m* **-s, -** ethnologist; **v~kundlich** *adj* ethnological; **~mord** *m* genocide; **~recht** *nt* international law, law of nations; **v~rechtlich** [1] *adj Vertrag, Entscheidung, Anerkennung* under international law; *Frage, Thema, Hinsicht, Standpunkt* of international law; *Anspruch, Haftung* international; **vom v~rechtlichen Standpunkt** according to *or* under international law; **v~rechtliche Anerkennung eines Staates** recognition of a state; [2] *adv regeln, entscheiden* by international law; *klären* according to international law; *bindend sein* under international law; **~schlacht** *f* (*Hist*) Battle of the Nations; **~verständigung** *f* international understanding; **~wanderung** *f* (*Hist*) migration of the peoples; (*hum*) mass migration *or* exodus.
völkisch *adj* (*NS*) national.
volkreich *adj* populous.
Volks- *in cpds* popular; (*auf ein Land bezogen*) national; (*Pol, esp DDR*) people's; **~abstimmung** *f* plebiscite; **~armee** *f* (*DDR*) People's Army; **~armist** *m* (*DDR*) soldier in the People's Army; **~ausgabe** *f* popular edition; **~beauftragte(r)** *mf* people's representative *or* delegate; **~befragung** *f* public opinion poll; **~befreiungsarmee** *f* people's liberation army; **~begehren** *nt* petition for a referendum; **~belustigung** *f* public entertainment; **~bildung** *f* national education; (*Erwachsenenbildung*) adult education; **~brauch** *m* national custom; **~bücherei** *f* public library; **~bühne** *f* people's theatre; **~charakter** *m* national character; **~demokratie** *f* people's democracy; **~deutsche(r)** *mf* ethnic German; **~dichter** *m* poet of the people; **~dichtung** *f* folk literature/poetry; **v~eigen** *adj* (*DDR*) nationally-owned; (*in Namen*) People's Own; **~eigentum** *nt* (*DDR*) national property, property of the people; **im ~eigentum** nationally-owned, owned by the people; **~einkommen** *nt* national income; **~empfinden** *nt* public feeling; **das gesunde ~empfinden** popular sentiment; **~entscheid** *m* referendum; **~erhebung** *f* popular *or* national uprising; **~etymologie** *f* folk etymology; **~feind** *m* enemy of the people; **v~feindlich** *adj* hostile to the people; **~fest** *nt* public festival; (*Jahrmarkt*) funfair; **~front** *f* (*Pol*) popular front; **~genosse** *m* (*NS*) national comrade; **~gerichtshof** *m* (*NS*) People's Court; **~gesundheit** *f* public health; **~glaube(n)** *m* popular belief; **~gruppe** *f* ethnic group; (*Minderheit*) ethnic minority; **~held** *m* popular hero; (*Held des Landes*) national hero; **~herrschaft** *f* popular rule, rule of the people; **~hochschule** *f* adult education centre; **einen Kurs in der ~hochschule machen** to do an adult education class; (*am Abend auch*) to do an evening class; **~justiz** *f* popular justice; **~kammer** *f* (*DDR*) East German Parliament; **~krankheit** *f* widespread disease; **~küche** *f* soup kitchen; **~kunde** *f* folklore; **~kundler(in** *f*) *m* **-s, -** folklorist; **v~kundlich** *adj* folkloristic; **ein v~kundliches Institut** an institute of folklore; **~lauf** *m* (*Sport*) open cross-country race; **~lied** *nt* folk song; **~märchen** *nt* folktale; **~meinung** *f* public *or* popular opinion; **~menge** *f* crowd, mob (*pej*); **~mund** *m* vernacular; **im ~mund nennt man das ...** this is popularly called ..., in the vernacular this is called ...; **~musik** *f* folk music; **~nähe** *f* **sie ist bekannt für ihre ~nähe** she is renowned for her popular touch; **~partei** *f* people's party; **~poesie** *f* folk poetry; **~polizei** *f* (*DDR*) People's Police; **~polizist** *m* (*DDR*) member of the People's Police; **~rede** *f* (*rare: lit*) public speech; (*inf*) (long) speech; **du sollst keine ~reden halten!** (*inf*) I/we don't want any speeches!; **~republik** *f* people's republic; **~sage** *f* folk legend, folktale; **~schicht** *f* level of society, social stratum; ⚠**~schulabschluß** *m* (*dated*) elementary school-leaving certificate; **~schule** *f* (*dated*) ≃ elementary school (*Hist*), *school providing basic primary and secondary education*; **~schüler** *m* (*dated*) pupil at elementary school (*Hist*); **~schullehrer** *m* (*dated*) elementary school teacher (*Hist*); **~seele** *f* soul of the people; **die kochende ~seele** the seething *or* angry populace; **~seuche** *f* epidemic; **~souveränität** *f* (*Pol*) sovereignty of the people; **~sprache** *f* everyday language, vernacular; **~staat** *m* (*Pol*) people's state; **~stamm** *m* tribe; **~stimme** *f* voice of the people; **~stück** *nt* dialect folk play; **~sturm** *m* (*Hist*) Volkssturm, German territorial army; **~tanz** *m* folk dance; **~theater** *nt* folk theatre; (*Gattung auch*) folk drama; **~tracht** *f* traditional costume; (*eines Landes*) national costume; **~trauertag** *m* national day of mourning, ≃ Remembrance Day (*Brit*), Veterans' Day (*US*); **~tribun** *m* (*Hist*) tribune (of the people); **~tum** *nt* national traditions *pl*, folklore; **~tümelei** *f* (*inf*) folksiness (*inf*); **v~tümlich** *adj* folk *attr*, folksy (*inf*); (*traditionell, überliefert*) traditional; (*beliebt*) popular; **etw v~tümlich darstellen/ausdrücken** to popularize sth/express oneself in plain language; **ein v~tümlicher König** a king with the common touch; **~tümlichkeit** *f siehe adj* folk character, folksiness (*inf*); tradition; popularity; (*von Darstellungs-, Ausdrucksweise*) popular appeal; (*von König*) common touch; **v~verbunden** *adj* close to the people; **~verführer** *m* demagogue; **~verhetzung** *f* incitement (of the people); **~vermögen** *nt* national wealth; **~versammlung** *f* people's assembly; (*Kundgebung*) public gathering; **~vertreter** *m* representative *or* delegate of the people; **~vertretung** *f* representative body (of the people); **~wirt** *m* economist; **~wirtschaft** *f* national economy; (*Fach*) economics *sing*, political economy; **~- und Betriebswirtschaft** economics and business studies; **~wirtschaftler** *m* economist; **~wirtschaftslehre** *f* economics *sing*, political economy; **~wohl** *nt* good *or* welfare of the people, public weal; **~zählung** *f* (national) census; **~zugehörigkeit** *f* ethnic origin.
voll [1] *adj* **(a)** (*gefüllt*) full ◆ **~er** +*gen* full of; **~ (von** *or* **mit) etw** full of sth; (*bedeckt mit*) covered with sth; **~ des Lobes** full of praise; **mit ~em Mund** with one's mouth full; **aus dem ~en leben** to live a life of luxury, to live in the lap of luxury; **aus dem ~en schöpfen** to draw on unlimited resources.
(b) (*ganz*) full; *Satz, Service, Erfolg* complete; *Woche, Jahr auch, Wahrheit* whole ◆ **ein ~es Dutzend** a full *or* whole dozen; **~e drei Jahre/Tage** three whole years/days, fully three years/days; **die Uhr schlägt nur alle ~en Stunden** the clock only strikes the full hour; **die Zahl ist ~** the numbers are complete; **die ~e Summe bezahlen** to pay the full sum *or* the sum in full; **in ~er Fahrt/~em Galopp/~em Lauf** at full speed/gallop/speed; **in ~er Größe** (*Bild*) life-size; (*bei plötzlicher Erscheinung etc*) large as life; **sich zu ~er Größe aufrichten** to draw oneself up to one's full height; **im ~en Tageslicht** in full daylight; **in ~er Uniform** in full dress *or* uniform; **den Mund ~ nehmen** (*fig*) to exaggerate, to overdo it; **jdn nicht für ~ nehmen** not to take sb seriously; **aus ~em Halse** *or* **~er Kehle** *or* **Brust singen** to sing at the top of one's voice; **etw mit ~em Recht tun** to be perfectly right to do sth; **mit dem ~en Namen unterschreiben** to sign one's full name, to sign one's name in full.
(c) ~ sein (*inf*) (*satt*) to be full (up); (*betrunken*) to be plastered (*inf*) *or* tight (*inf*); **~ wie ein Sack** *or* **eine Strandhaubitze** *or* **tausend Mann** absolutely

plastered (*inf*), roaring drunk (*inf*).
(d) (*üppig*) *Gesicht, Busen etc* full; *Wangen* chubby; *Haar* thick ◆ **~er werden** to fill out.
(e) *Stimme, Ton* full, rich; *Farbton* rich.
[2] *adv* fully; (*vollkommen auch*) completely ◆ **~ und ganz** completely, wholly; **die Straße ist ~ gesperrt/wieder ~ befahrbar** the road is completely closed/completely free again; **jdn ~ ansehen** to look sb straight in the face; **eine Rechnung ~ bezahlen** to pay a bill in full; **~ hinter jdm/etw stehen** to be *or* stand fully behind sb/sth; **jdn/etw ~ treffen** (*mit Stein, Bombe etc*) to score a direct hit on sb/sth; (*ins Gesicht*) to hit sb full in the face; **etw ~ ausnützen** to take full advantage of sth; **~ zuschlagen** (*inf*) to lam out (*inf*); **~ durcharbeiten** (*inf*) to work solidly (throughout); **~ drinstecken** (*inf*) (*bei Arbeit*) to be in the middle of it; (*in unangenehmer Situation*) to be right in it; **~ (Stoff) gegen etw fahren** (*inf*) to run full tilt *or* slap-bang (*inf*) into sth; **nicht ~ dasein** (*inf*) to be not quite with it (*inf*); **~ dabeisein** (*inf*) to be totally involved.

⚠ **volladen** *vt sep irreg getrennt* **voll-laden** to load up ◆ **vollgeladen** fully-laden.

Vollakademiker *m* honours graduate.

vollauf *adv* fully, completely ◆ **~ genug** quite enough; **das genügt ~** that's quite enough; **~ zu tun haben** to have quite enough to do (*mit* with).

⚠ **vollaufen** *vi sep irreg aux sein getrennt*: **voll-laufen** to fill up ◆ **etw ~ lassen** to fill sth (up); **sich ~ lassen** (*inf*) to get tanked up (*inf*).

Voll-: v~automatisch *adj* fully automatic; **v~automatisiert** *adj* fully automated; **~bad** *nt* (proper) bath; **~bart** *m* (full) beard; ⚠**v~bekommen*** *vt sep irreg* to (manage to) fill; **v~berechtigt** *adj attr* with full rights; *Unterhändler* fully authorized; *Mitglied* full; **v~beschäftigt** *adj Arbeiter* employed full-time; (*attr: sehr beschäftigt*) fully occupied; **~beschäftigung** *f* full employment; **~besitz** *m*: **im ~besitz** *+gen* in full possession of; **~bier** *nt* beer with 11-14% original wort; **~bild** *nt* (*Med: von Krankheit*) full-blown form; **~bild-Aids** *nt* full-blown Aids.

Vollblut *nt, no pl* thoroughbred.

Vollblut- *in cpds* (*lit: Tier*) thoroughbred; (*fig*) full-blooded.

Voll-: ~blüter *m* **-s, -** thoroughbred; **v~blütig** *adj* thoroughbred; (*fig*) full-blooded.

Vollblut-: ~opportunist *m* full-blooded opportunist; **~politiker** *m* thoroughbred politician.

Voll-: ~bremsung *f* emergency stop; **eine ~bremsung machen** to slam on the brakes (*inf*), to do an emergency stop; ⚠**v~bringen**[1] *vt sep irreg* (*inf*) *siehe* **v~bekommen; v~bringen**[2]* *vt insep irreg* (*ausführen*) to accomplish, to achieve; *Wunder* to work, to perform; **es ist v~bracht** (*Bibl*) it is done (*Bibl*); **~bringung** *f* accomplishment, achievement; **v~busig** *adj* full-bosomed, bosomy (*inf*); **~busigkeit** *f* full bosom.

Volldampf *m* (*Naut*) full steam ◆ **mit ~** at full steam *or* speed; (*inf*) flat out; **mit ~ voraus** full steam *or* speed ahead; (*inf*) full tilt.

volldröhnen *sep* (*sl*) [1] *vt* **jdn volldröhnen** (*mit Drogen*) to dose sb up (*inf*); (*mit Alkohol*) to get sb tanked up (*sl*); **er war total vollgedröhnt** (*mit Drogen*) he was dosed up to his eyeballs (*inf*); (*mit Alkohol*) he was completely tanked up (*sl*) *or* loaded (*inf*).
[2] *vr* (*mit Drogen*) to dose oneself up (*inf*); (*mit Alkohol*) to tank up (*sl*); (*mit Musik*) to blow one's head off (*inf*).

Völlegefühl *nt* (unpleasant) feeling of fullness; satiety.

vollelektronisch *adj* fully electronic.

vollenden* *insep* [1] *vt* (*abschließen*) to complete; (*liter*) *Leben* to bring to an end; (*vervollkommnen*) to make complete; *Geschmack* to round off.
[2] *vr* (*zum Abschluß kommen*) to come to an end; (*vollkommen werden*) to be completed; (*Liebe*) to be fulfilled.

vollendet *adj* (*vollkommen*) completed; *Tugend, Schönheit* perfect; *Mensch* accomplished ◆ **nach ~em 18. Lebensjahr** upon completion of one's 18th year; **~ Klavier spielen** to be an accomplished piano player; *siehe* **Tatsache.**

vollends *adv* **(a)** (*völlig*) completely, altogether. **(b)** (*besonders*) especially, particularly.

Vollendung *f, no pl* completion; (*Vervollkommnung, Vollkommenheit*) perfection; (*von Liebe*) fulfilment.

voller *adj siehe* **voll.**

Völlerei *f* gluttony.

⚠ **vollessen** *vr sep irreg* (*inf*) to gorge oneself.

Volley ['vɔli] *m* **-s, -s** volley.

Volleyball ['vɔli-] *m* volleyball.

Voll-: v~fett *adj* full fat; **~fettkäse** *m* full fat cheese; ⚠**v~fressen** *vr sep irreg* (*pej inf*) to stuff oneself (*inf*).

vollführen* *vt insep* to execute, to perform; *Lärm,* (*fig*) *Theater* to create.

Voll-: ⚠**v~füllen** *vt sep* to fill (up); **~gas** *nt, no pl* full speed *or* throttle; **~gas geben** to open it right up; (*mit Auto auch*) to put one's foot hard down; **mit ~gas fahren** to drive at full throttle; **mit ~gas** (*fig inf*) full tilt; **mit ~gas arbeiten** to work flat out; **~gefühl** *nt*: **im ~gefühl** *+gen* fully aware of; **im ~gefühl der Jugend** in the full bloom of youth; **im ~gefühl der Lebensfreude** full of the joys of life; ⚠**~genuß** *m*: **im ~genuß** *+gen* in full enjoyment of; ⚠**v~gießen** *vt sep irreg* (*auffüllen*) to fill (up); **sie hat sich** (*dat*) **den Rock v~gegossen/mit Kaffee v~gegossen** (*inf*) she spilt it/coffee all over her skirt; **v~gültig** *adj attr Paß* fully valid; *Ersatz* completely satisfactory; *Beweis* conclusive; **~gummi** *nt or m* solid rubber; **~gummireifen** *m* solid rubber tyre; **~idiot** *m* (*inf*) complete idiot.

▼ **völlig** [1] *adj* complete ◆ **das ist mein ~er Ernst** I'm completely *or* absolutely serious.

▼ [2] *adv* completely ◆ **es genügt ~** that's quite enough; **er hat ~ recht** he's absolutely right.

Voll-: v~inhaltlich *adj attr* full, complete; **v~jährig** *adj* of age; **v~jährig werden/sein** to come/be of age; **sie hat drei v~jährige Kinder** she has three children who are of age; **~jährige(r)** *mf decl as adj* major; **~jährigkeit** *f* majority *no art*; **bei ~jährigkeit** on attaining one's majority; **~jurist** *m* fully qualified lawyer; **v~kaskoversichert** *adj* comprehensively insured; **v~kaskoversichert sein** to have fully comprehensive insurance; **~kasko(versicherung** *f*) *nt* fully comprehensive insurance; **v~klimatisiert** *adj* fully air-conditioned.

▼ **vollkommen** [1] *adj* perfect; (*völlig*) complete, absolute ◆ **sein Glück war ~** his happiness was complete.
▼ [2] *adv* completely.

Vollkommenheit *f, no pl siehe adj* perfection; completeness, absoluteness ◆ **die ~ der Stille wurde durch nichts gestört** nothing disturbed the perfect *or* complete silence.

Voll-: ~kornbrot *nt* coarse wholemeal bread; **~kraft** *f* (*geh*) **in der ~kraft seiner Jahre/seines Schaffens** in his prime; ⚠**v~machen** *sep* [1] *vt* **(a)** *Gefäß* to fill (up); *Zahl, Dutzend* to make up; *Sammlung, Set* to complete; *siehe* **Maß**[1]; **(b)** (*inf*) *Hosen, Windeln* to fill; **sich** (*dat*) **die Hosen v~machen** (*fig inf*) to wet oneself (*inf*); [2] *vr* (*inf*) to get messed up *or* dirty; (*in die Hosen etc machen*) to fill one's pants/nappy/diaper.

Vollmacht *f* **-, -en** (legal) power *or* authority *no pl, no indef art*; (*Urkunde*) power of attorney ◆ **jdm eine ~ erteilen** *or* **ausstellen** to give *or* grant sb power of attorney.

Vollmachtgeber *m* principal ◆ **~ und Vollmachtnehmer** principal and agent.

Vollmachtsurkunde *f* power of attorney.

Voll-: v~mast *adv* full mast; **auf v~mast** at full mast; **~matrose** *m* able-bodied seaman; **~milch** *f* full-cream milk; **~milchschokolade** *f* full-cream milk chocolate; **~mitglied** *nt* full member; **~mond** *m* full moon; **heute ist ~mond** there's a full moon today; **~mondgesicht** *nt* (*inf*) moon-face; **~mondnacht** *f* night of a full moon; **v~mundig** *adj Wein* full-bodied; *Unterstützung, Versprechen* wholehearted; **etw v~mundig gutheißen** to support sth wholeheartedly; **etw v~mundig bestreiten** to dispute sth vehemently; **~narkose** *f* general anaesthetic; ⚠**v~packen** *vt sep* (*lit, fig*) to pack full; *jdn* to load up; **~pension** *f* full board; ⚠**v~pfropfen** *vt sep* (*inf*) to cram full; ⚠**v~pumpen** *vt sep* to fill (up); **~rausch** *m* drunken stupor; **einen ~rausch haben** to be in a drunken stupor; **v~reif** *adj* fully ripe; ⚠**v~saugen** *vr sep reg or irreg* to become saturated; ⚠**v~schenken** *vt sep* to fill; ⚠**v~schlagen** *vr sep irreg* (*inf*) **sich** (*dat*) **den Bauch v~schlagen** to stuff oneself with food (*inf*); **v~schlank** *adj* plump, stout; **Mode für v~schlanke Damen** fashion for the fuller figure *or* for ladies with a fuller figure; ⚠**v~schmieren** *sep* [1] *vt* to mess up; [2] *vr* to mess oneself up; ⚠**v~schreiben** *vt sep irreg Heft, Seite* to fill (with writing); *Tafel* to cover (with writing); **~spur** *f* (*Rail*) standard gauge, standard-gauge track; **v~spurig** (*Rail*) [1] *adj* standard-gauge; [2] *adv* on standard-gauge track.

vollständig (*abbr* **vollst.**) [1] *adj* complete. *Sammlung, Satz auch* entire *attr*; *Adresse* full *attr* ◆ **nicht ~** incomplete; **etw ~ machen** to complete sth; **etw ~ haben** to have sth complete.
[2] *adv* completely, entirely.

Vollständigkeit *f, no pl* completeness ◆ **der ~ halber** to complete the picture; **keinen Anspruch auf ~ erheben** to make no claim to be exhaustive.

⚠ **vollstopfen** *vt sep* to cram full.

vollstreckbar *adj* enforceable, able to be carried out *or* executed ◆ (*Jur*) **~e Urkunde** executory deed.

vollstrecken* *vt insep* to execute; *Todesurteil* to carry out; *Pfändung* to enforce ◆ **~de Gewalt** executive (power); **ein Todesurteil an jdm ~** to execute sb.

Vollstrecker(in *f*) *m* **-s, -** executor; (*Frau auch*) executrix ◆ **~ des Todesurteils** executioner.

Vollstreckung *f siehe vt* execution; carrying out; enforcement.

Vollstreckungs-: ~beamte(r) *m* enforcement officer; **~befehl** *m* enforcement order, writ of execution; **~gericht** *nt* court of execution *or* enforcement; (*bei Konkursverfahren*) bankruptcy court.

Voll-: v~synchronisiert *adj* fully synchronized; ⚠**v~tanken** *vti sep* to fill up; **bitte v~tanken** fill her up, please; **v~tönend** *adj* resonant, sonorous; **~treffer** *m* (*lit, fig*) bull's eye; **v~trunken** *adj* completely *or* totally drunk; **in v~trunkenem Zustand Auto fahren** to drive when drunk *or* in a drunken state; **~trunkenheit** *f* total inebriation; **~versammlung** *f* general assembly; (*von Stadtrat etc*) full meeting *or* assembly; **~waise** *f* orphan; **~waschmittel** *nt* detergent; **v~wertig** *adj* full *attr*, *Stellung* equal; *Ersatz* (fully) adequate; **jdn als v~wertig behandeln/betrachten** to treat/regard sb as an equal; **~wertkost** *f* wholefoods *pl*; **~zahler** *m* (*für Fahrkarte etc*) person paying full fare; **v~zählig** *adj usu pred Satz, Anzahl, Mannschaft* complete; (*ausnahmslos anwesend*) all present *pred*; **um v~zähliges Erscheinen wird gebeten** everyone is requested to attend; **sie sind v~zählig erschienen** everyone came; **v~zählig versammelt sein** to be assembled in full force *or* strength; **~zähligkeit** *f, no pl* full number; (*ausnahmslose Anwesenheit*) full attendance.

vollziehbar *adj Strafe, Urteil* enforceable, executable.

vollziehen* *insep irreg* [1] *vt* to carry out; *Befehl auch* to execute; *Strafe, Urteil auch* to execute, to enforce; *Opferung, Trauung* to perform; *Bruch* to make; (*form*) *Ehe* to consummate ◆ **einen Gedankengang ~ können** to be capable of a train of thought; **die ~de Gewalt** the executive (power).
[2] *vr* to take place; *Trauung* to be performed; (*jds Schicksal*) to be fulfilled.

Vollziehung *f* **(a)** *siehe vt* carrying out; execution; enforcement; performance; making; consummation. **(b)** *siehe vr* completion; performance; fulfilment.

Vollzug *m, no pl* **(a)** (*Straf~*) penal system ◆ **offener ~** *daytime release for prisoners pending parole.* **(b)** *siehe* **Vollziehung.**

Vollzugs-: ~anstalt *f* (*form*) penal institution; **~beamte(r)** *m* (*form*) warder.

Volontariat [volɔnta'ria:t] *nt* **(a)** (*Zeit*) practical training. **(b)** (*Stelle*) post as a trainee.

Volontär(in *f*) [volɔn'tɛ:ɐ, -'tɛ:ərɪn] *m* trainee.

volontieren* [volɔn'ti:rən] *vi* to be training (*bei* with).

Volt [vɔlt] *nt* **-(e)s, -** volt.

Volte ['vɔltə] *f* **-, -n** **(a)** (*Fechten, Reiten*) volte. **(b)** (*Cards*) sleight of hand.

voltigieren* [vɔlti'ʒi:rən] *vi* to perform exercises on horseback; (*im Zirkus*) to do trick-riding.

Volt- ['vɔlt-]: **~meter** *nt* voltmeter; **~zahl** *f* voltage.

Volumen [vo'lu:mən] *nt* **-s, -** *or* **Volumina** **(a)** (*lit, fig: Inhalt*) volume. **(b)** (*obs: Schriftrolle, Band*) volume.

Volumgewicht [vo'lu:m-] *nt* (*Phys*) volumetric weight.

voluminös [volumi'nø:s] *adj* (*geh*) voluminous.

vom *contr of* **von dem. ~ 10. September an** from the 10th September; **Bier ~ Faß** draught beer; **das kommt ~ Rauchen/Trinken** that comes from smoking/drinking; **ich kenne ihn nur ~ Sehen** I know him only by sight; **~ Kochen hat er keine Ahnung** he has no idea about cooking.

von *prep +dat* **(a)** (*einen Ausgangspunkt angebend, räumlich, zeitlich*) from ◆ **der Wind kommt ~ Norden** the wind comes from the North; **nördlich ~** to the North of; **~ München nach Hamburg** from Munich to Hamburg; **~ weit her** from a long way away; **~ ... an** from ...; **~ Jugend/vom 10 Lebensjahr an** from early on/since he/she *etc* was ten years old; **~ diesem Tag/Punkt an** *or* **ab** from this day/point on(wards); **~ heute ab** *or* **an** from today; **Waren ~ 5 Mark an** *or* **ab** goods from 5 marks; **~ ... aus** from ...; **~ dort aus** from there; **etw ~ sich aus wissen/tun** to know sth by oneself/do sth of one's own accord; **~ ... bis** from ... to; **~ morgens bis abends** from morning till night; **Ihr Brief ~ vor 2 Wochen** your letter of two weeks ago; **~ ... zu** from ... to.

(b) (*~ ... weg*) from ◆ **etw ~ etw nehmen/abreißen** to take/tear sth off sth; **~ der Straßenbahn abspringen** to jump off the tram; **alles ~ sich werfen** to throw everything down *or* aside; **~ der Stelle weichen** to move from the spot.

(c) *in Verbindung mit adj, vb siehe auch dort.* (*Ursache, Urheberschaft ausdrückend, im Passiv*) by ◆ **das Gedicht ist ~ Schiller** the poem is by Schiller; **ein Kleid ~ Dior** a Dior dress; **ein Kind ~ jdm kriegen** to have a child by sb; **das Kind ist ~ ihm** the child is his; **~ etw müde** tired from sth; **~ etw begeistert** enthusiastic about sth; **~ etw satt** full up with sth; **~ etw beeindruckt/überrascht** impressed/surprised by sth.

(d) (*partitiv, anstelle von Genitiv*) of ◆ **jeweils zwei ~ zehn** two out of every ten; **ein Riese ~ einem Mann** (*inf*) a giant of a man; **ein Prachtstück ~ einem Hund** (*inf*) a magnificent (specimen of a) dog; **dieser Dummkopf ~ Gärtner ...!** (*inf*) that idiot of a gardener ...!

(e) *in Verbindung mit n, adj, vb siehe auch dort.* (*Beschaffenheit, Eigenschaft etc ausdrückend, bestehend aus*) of ◆ **~ 50 m Länge** 50 m in length; **im Alter ~ 50 Jahren** at the age of 50; **Kinder ~ 10 Jahren** ten-year-old children; **~ Bedeutung sein** to be of significance; **~ Dauer sein** to be lasting; **das ist sehr freundlich ~ Ihnen** that's very kind of you; **frei ~ etw sein** to be free of sth.

(f) (*in Titel*) of; (*bei deutschem Adelstitel*) von ◆ **die Königin ~ England** the queen of England; **Otto ~ Bismarck** Otto von Bismarck; **~ und zu Falkenburg** von Falkenburg; **ein „~ (und zu)" sein** to have a handle to one's name; **sich „~" schreiben** (*lit*) to have a "von" before one's name; **da kannst du dich aber „~" schreiben** (*fig*) you can be really proud yourself (there).

(g) (*über*) about ◆ **er erzählte vom Urlaub** he talked about his holiday; **Geschichten vom Weihnachtsmann/~ Feen** stories about Father Christmas/fairies.

(h) (*mit Fragepronomen*) from ◆ **~ wo/wann/was** where/when/what ... from, from where/when/what (*form*).

(i) (*inf: in aufgelösten Kontraktionen*) **~ dem halte ich gar nichts** I don't think much of him; **da weiß ich nichts ~** I don't know anything about it.

(j) (*inf*) **~ wegen** no way! (*inf*); **~ wegen der Karte/dem Buch** (*incorrect*) about the map/the book.

von|einander *adv* of each other *or* one another; from each other *or* one another ◆ **etwas/nichts ~ haben** to see something/nothing of each other *or* one another; (*Zusammensein genießen*) to be able/not to be able to enjoy each other's company; (*ähnlich aussehen*) to look/not to look like each other; (*sich im Wesen ähnlich sein*) to have a lot/nothing in common; **sie konnten die Augen nicht ~ wenden** they couldn't take their eyes off *or* away from each other *or* one another; **sich ~ trennen** to part *or* separate (from each other *or* one another); **sie hatten ~ die Nase voll** (*inf*) they were fed up with each other *or* one another.

vonnöten *adj*: **~ sein** to be necessary.

vonstatten *adv*: **~ gehen** (*stattfinden*) to take place; **wie geht so etwas ~?** what is the procedure for that?; **es ging alles gut ~** everything went well.

Vopo ['fo:po] *m* **-s, -s** *abbr of* **Volkspolizist.**

vor [1] *prep +acc or dat* **(a)** *+dat* (*räumlich*) in front of; (*außerhalb von*) outside; (*~ Hintergrund*) against; (*in Gegenwart von*) in front of; (*in jds Achtung*) in the eyes of; (*bei Reihenfolge*) before; (*bei Rangordnung*) before, ahead of ◆ **der See/die Stadt lag ~ uns** the lake/town lay before us; **~ jdm herfahren/hergehen** to drive/walk in front of *or* ahead of sb; **~ der Kirche rechts abbiegen** turn right before the church; **~ der Stadt** outside the town; **~ einer Kommission/allen Leuten** before *or* in front of a commission/everyone; **~ Gott sind alle Menschen gleich** all people are equal before God *or* in God's sight; **sich ~ jdm/etw verneigen** (*lit, fig*) to bow before *or* to sb/sth; **~ allen Dingen/allem** above all; **~ dem Fernseher sitzen** *or* **hocken** (*inf*) to sit in front of the TV.

(b) *+acc* (*Richtung angebend*) in front of; (*außerhalb von*) outside ◆ **ein Schlag ~ den Oberkörper** a blow on the chest.

(c) *+dat* (*zeitlich*) before ◆ **~ Christi Geburt** before Christ, BC; **zwanzig (Minuten) ~ drei** twenty (minutes) to three; **heute ~ acht Tagen** a week ago today; **das ist** *or* **liegt noch ~ uns** this is still to come; **ich war ~ ihm an der Reihe/da** I was in front of him/there before him; **~ einigen Tagen/langer Zeit/fünf Jahren** a few days/a long time/five years ago; **am Tage ~ der Prüfung** the day before the examination.

(d) *+acc* **~ sich hin summen/lachen/sprechen** *etc* to hum/laugh/talk *etc* to oneself; **~ sich hin schreiben/arbeiten** to write/work away; **~ sich hin wandern** to wander on.

(e) *+dat* **~ sich her** before one, in front of one; **er ließ die Schüler ~ sich her gehen** he let the pupils go in front (of him).

(f) *+dat* (*Ursache angebend*) with ◆ **~ Hunger sterben** to die of hunger; **~ Kälte zittern** to tremble with *or* from cold; **~ Schmerz laut schreien** to cry out with *or* in pain; **~ lauter Arbeit** for *or* because of work; **alles strahlt ~ Sauberkeit** everything is shining clean.

(g) *in fester Verbindung mit n, vb, adj siehe auch dort* ◆ **Schutz ~ jdm/etw suchen** to seek protection from sb/sth; **~ jdm/etw sicher sein** to be safe from sb/sth; **Achtung ~ jdm/etw haben** to have respect for sb/sth; **sich ~ jdm verstecken** to hide from sb; **wie ist das ~ sich gegangen?** how did it happen?

[2] *adv* **(a) ~ und zurück** backwards and forwards; **alle kleinen Kinder ~!** all small children to the front!; **wer Karten will, ~!** come up and get your tickets!; **Borussia ~, noch ein Tor!** come on Borussia, let's have another!

(b) *siehe* **nach.**

(c) (*N Ger inf: davor*) **da sei Gott ~** God forbid; **das wird nicht passieren, da bin ich ~** that won't happen, I'll see to it.

vor|ab *adv* to begin *or* start with ◆ **lassen Sie mich ~ erwähnen ...** first let me mention ...

Vor-: ~abdruck *m* preprint; **~abend** *m* evening before; (*mit nachfolgendem Genitiv auch*) eve (*auch fig*); **das war am ~abend** that was the evening before; **am ~abend von Weihnachten** (on) the evening before Christmas, on Christmas Eve; **am ~abend der Revolution** (*fig*) on the eve of revolution; **~ahnung** *f* presentiment, premonition; **~alpen** *pl* foothills *pl* of the Alps.

voran *adv* **(a)** (*vorn, an der Spitze*) first ◆ **ihm/ihr ~** in front of him/her; **der Festzug mit der Kapelle ~** the parade, led by the band; **mit dem Kopf ~ fallen** to fall head first.

(b) (*vorwärts*) forwards ◆ **nur** *or* **immer ~** keep going; **immer langsam ~!** gently does it!

voran- *pref siehe auch* **voraus-; ~bringen** *vt sep irreg* to make progress with; **~gehen** *vi sep irreg aux sein* **(a)** (*an der Spitze gehen*) to go first *or* in front; (*anführen auch*) to lead the way; (*fig: Einleitung etc*) to precede (*dat* sth); **jdm ~gehen** to go ahead of sb; **(b)** (*zeitlich vor jdm gehen*) to go on ahead; **sie war ihm ~gegangen** (*euph: gestorben*) she had passed on before him; **jdn ~gehen lassen** to let sb go first; **wie im ~gehenden berichtet** as reported (in the) above; *siehe* **Beispiel; (c)** (*zeitlich*) **einer Sache** (*dat*) **~gehen** to precede sth; **das V~gegangene** what has gone before; **(d)** *auch vi impers* (*Fortschritte machen*) to come on *or* along, to make progress *or* headway; **es will mit der Arbeit nicht so richtig ~gehen** the work's not coming on *or* along very well; **~gestellt** *adj* (*Gram*) preceding *attr*; **~gestellt sein** to precede; **~kommen** *vi sep irreg aux sein* to get on *or* along, to make progress *or* headway; **im Leben/beruflich ~kommen** to get on in life/in one's job; **nur langsam ~kommen** to make slow progress *or* little headway; **~machen** *vi sep* (*inf*) to hurry up, to get a move on (*inf*).

Vor-: ~anmeldung *f* appointment; (*von Telefongespräch*) booking; **ohne ~anmeldung** without an appointment/without booking; **~anschlag** *m* estimate.

voran-: ~schreiten *vi sep irreg aux sein* (*geh*) (*lit*) to stride in front *or* ahead (*jdm* of sb); (*Zeit*) to march on; (*Fortschritte machen*) to progress; **~stellen** *vt sep* to put *or* place in front (*dat* of); (*fig*) to give precedence (*dat* over); **~treiben** *vt sep irreg* to drive forward *or* on; (*fig auch*) to hurry along.

Vor-: ~anzeige *f* (*für Theaterstück*) advance notice; (*für Film*) trailer, preview (*US*); **~arbeit** *f* preparatory *or* preliminary work, groundwork; **gute ~arbeit leisten** to do good groundwork, to prepare the ground well; **v~arbeiten** *sep* [1] *vi* (*inf*) to (do) work in advance; [2] *vt* to work in advance; [3] *vr* to work one's way forward; **~arbeiter(in** *f*) *m* foreman; forewoman.

Vorarlberg *nt* **-s** Vorarlberg.

vorauf *adv* (*rare*) *siehe* **voran, voraus.**

voraus *adv* **(a)** (*voran*) in front (*+dat* of); (*Naut, fig*) ahead (*+dat* of) ◆ **er ist den anderen Schülern/seiner Zeit ~** he is ahead of the other pupils/his time. **(b)** (*vorher*) **im ~** in advance.

Voraus-: ~abteilung *f* (*Mil*) advance party; **v~ahnen** *vt sep* to anticipate; **v~berechenbar** *adj* predictable; **v~berechnen*** *vt sep* to predict; *Wahlergebnis auch* to forecast; *Kosten* to estimate; **v~bestimmen*** *vt sep* to predict, to forecast; **~bezahlung** *f* payment in advance, advance payment; **v~blicken** *vi sep* to look ahead; **v~blickend** [1] *adj* foresighted; [2] *adv* with regard to the future; **v~eilen** *vi sep aux sein* (*lit, fig*) to hurry on ahead, to rush (on) ahead (*dat* of); **einer Sache** (*dat*) **v~eilen** to be ahead of *or* in advance of sth; **v~fahren** *vi sep irreg aux sein* (*an der Spitze*) to drive/go in front (*dat* of); (*früher*) to drive/go on ahead; **v~gehen** *vi sep irreg aux sein siehe* **vorangehen (a-c)**; **v~gesetzt** *adj* **v~gesetzt, (daß)** ... provided (that) ...; **v~haben** *vt sep irreg* **jdm etw/viel v~haben** to have the advantage of sth/a great advantage over sb; **v~planen** *vti sep* to plan ahead; **v~reiten** *vi sep irreg aux sein* (*an der Spitze*) to ride in front (*dat* of); (*früher*) to ride on ahead; **~sage** *f* prediction; (*Wetter~*) forecast; **v~sagen** *vt sep* to predict (*jdm* for sb); (*prophezeien auch*) to prophesy; *Wahlergebnisse auch, Wetter* to forecast; **jdm die Zukunft v~sagen** to foretell sb's future; **v~schauend** *adj, adv siehe* **v~blickend**; **v~schicken** *vt sep* to send on ahead *or* in advance (*dat* of); (*fig: vorher sagen*) to say in advance (*dat* of); **v~sehen** *vt sep irreg* to foresee; **ich habe es ja v~gesehen, daß** ... I knew that ...; **das war v~zusehen!** that was (only) to be expected!

voraussetzen *vt sep* to presuppose; (*als selbstverständlich, sicher annehmen*) *Interesse, Zustimmung, jds Liebe, Verständnis* to take for granted; (*erfordern*) *Qualifikation, Kenntnisse, Geduld etc* to require, to demand ◆ **wenn wir einmal ~, daß** ... let us *or* if we assume that ...; **etw als selbstverständlich ~** to take sth for granted; **etw als bekannt ~** to assume that everyone knows sth.

Voraussetzung *f* prerequisite, condition, precondition; (*Qualifikation*) qualification; (*Erfordernis*) requirement; (*Annahme*) assumption, premise ◆ **unter der ~, daß** ... on condition that ...; **eine Mitarbeit hat zur ~, daß** ... a requirement of cooperation is that ...

Voraus-: **~sicht** *f* foresight; (*Erwartung*) anticipation; **aller ~sicht nach** in all probability; **in der ~sicht, daß** ... anticipating that ...; **in kluger** *or* **weiser ~sicht** with great foresight *or* forethought; **nach menschlicher ~sicht** as far as we can foresee; **v~sichtlich** [1] *adj* expected; [2] *adv* probably; **er wird v~sichtlich gewinnen** he is expected to win; **v~sichtlich wird es keine Schwierigkeiten geben** we don't anticipate *or* expect any difficulties; **~zahlung** *f* payment in advance, advance payment.

Vorbau *m* porch; (*Balkon*) balcony; (*Min*) advancing working ◆ **sie hat einen ganz schönen ~** (*hum: vollbusig*) she's well-stacked (*inf*).

vorbauen *sep* [1] *vt* (*anbauen*) to build on (in front) ◆ **Häuser bis an die Straße ~** to build houses right on the road; **ein weit vorgebauter Erker** a deep oriel window.
[2] *vi* (*Vorkehrungen treffen*) to take precautions ◆ **einer Sache** (*dat*) **~** to provide against sth; *siehe* **klug**.

Vorbedacht *m*: **mit/ohne ~** (*Überlegung*) with/without due care *or* consideration; (*Absicht*) intentionally/unintentionally; (*Jur*) with/without intent.

Vorbedeutung *f* portent, presage, prognostic.

Vorbedingung *f* precondition.

▼ **Vorbehalt** *m* **-(e)s, -e** reservation ◆ **unter dem ~, daß** ... with the reservation that ...

vorbehalten* *vt sep irreg* **sich** (*dat*) **etw ~** to reserve sth (for oneself); *Recht* to reserve sth; **jdm etw ~** to leave sth (up) to sb; **diese Entscheidung ist** *or* **bleibt ihm ~** this decision is left (up) to him; **alle Rechte ~** all rights reserved; **Änderungen (sind) ~** subject to alterations; **Irrtümer ~** errors excepted.

vorbehaltlich, vorbehältlich *prep +gen* (*form*) subject to ◆ **~ anderer Bestimmungen** unless otherwise provided (*form*); **~ Artikel 3** save as provided in paragraph 3 (*form*).

vorbehaltlos *adj* unconditional, unreserved ◆ **~ zustimmen** to agree without reservations.

vorbei *adv* **(a)** (*räumlich*) past, by ◆ **er möchte hier ~** he wants to go past *or* by; **~ an** (*+dat*) past; **~!** (*nicht getroffen*) missed!
(b) (*zeitlich*) **~ sein** to be past; (*vergangen auch, beendet*) to be over *or* finished; (*Sorgen*) to be over; (*Schmerzen*) to be gone; **es ist schon 8 Uhr ~** it's already past *or* after *or* gone 8 o'clock; **damit ist es nun ~** that's all over now; **~ die schöne Zeit!** gone are the days!; **es war schon ~ mit ihm** it was all up with him; **aus und ~** over and done; **~ ist ~** what's past is past; (*reden wir nicht mehr davon*) let bygones be bygones.

vorbei- *pref* (*vorüber*) past; (*zu Besuch*) over; **~benehmen*** *vr sep irreg* (*inf*) *siehe* **danebenbenehmen**; **~bringen** *vt sep irreg* (*inf*) to drop off *or* by *or* in; **~drücken** *vr sep* (*inf*) (*an jdm/etw* sb/sth) to squeeze past; (*fig*) to slip past; **~dürfen** *vi sep irreg* (*inf*) to be allowed past; **dürfte ich bitte ~?** could I come *or* get past *or* by, please?; **~fahren** *sep irreg* [1] *vi aux sein* (*an jdm/etw* sb/sth) to go/drive/sail past, to pass; **im V~fahren** in passing; **bei jdm ~fahren** (*inf*) to drop *or* call in on sb, to stop *or* drop by sb's house (*inf*); [2] *vt* **jdn an etw** (*dat*) **~fahren** to drive sb past sth; **ich kann dich ja schnell dort/bei ihnen ~fahren** (*inf*) I can run *or* drive you over there/to their place; **~gehen** *vi sep irreg aux sein* **(a)** (*lit, fig*) (*an jdm/etw* sb/sth) to go past *or* by, to pass; **an etw** (*dat*) **~gehen** (*fig: nicht beachten*) to overlook sth; **bei jdm ~gehen** (*inf*) to drop *or* call in on sb, to stop *or* drop by sb's house (*inf*); **eine Gelegenheit ~gehen lassen** to let an opportunity pass *or* slip by; **im V~gehen** (*lit, fig*) in passing; **(b)** (*vergehen*) to pass; (*Laune, Zorn auch*) to blow over; **(c)** (*danebengehen*) (*an etw* sth) to miss; (*fig auch*) to bypass; **das Leben geht an ihm ~** life is passing him by; **an der Wirklichkeit ~gehen** (*Bericht etc*) to miss the truth; (*Mensch*) to be unrealistic; **~kommen** *vi sep irreg aux sein* **(a)** (*an jdm/etw* sb/sth) to pass, to go past; (*an einem Hindernis*) to get past *or* by; **an einer Sache/Aufgabe nicht ~kommen** to be unable to avoid a thing/task; **wir kommen nicht an der Tatsache ~, daß** ... there's no escaping the fact that ...; **(b) bei jdm ~kommen** (*inf*) to drop *or* call in on sb, to stop *or* drop by sb's house (*inf*); **komm doch mal wieder ~!** (*inf*) drop *or* call in again sometime!, stop *or* drop by again sometime! (*inf*); **~können** *vi sep irreg* to be able to get past *or* by (*an etw* (*dat*) sth); **~lassen** *vt sep irreg* to let past (*an jdm/etw* sb/sth); **~laufen** *vi sep irreg aux sein* (*an jdm/etw* sb/sth) to run past; (*inf: ~gehen*) to go *or* walk past; (*fig*) to miss; **V~marsch** *m* march-past; **~marschieren*** *vi sep aux sein* to march past; **~müssen** *vi sep irreg* (*an jdm/etw* sb/sth) to have to go past, to have to pass; **~reden** *vi sep* **an etw** (*dat*) **~reden** to talk round sth; (*absichtlich*) to skirt sth; **aneinander ~reden** to talk at cross purposes; **~schauen** *vi sep* (*inf*) *siehe* **~kommen (b)**; **~schießen** *vi sep irreg* **(a)** *aux sein* (*an jdm/etw* sb/sth) to shoot past *or* by; (*an Kurve*) to overshoot; **(b)** (*am Ziel etc*) to shoot wide (*an +dat* of), to miss (*an etw* (*dat*) sth); **~schrammen** *vi* to scrape past (*an +dat* sth); **am Konkurs/an der Niederlage ~schrammen** to escape bankruptcy/defeat by the skin of one's teeth; **~ziehen** *sep irreg* [1] *vi aux sein* (*an jdm/etw* sb/sth) to file past; (*Truppen, Festzug etc*) to march past; (*Wolken, Rauch, Duft*) to drift past *or* by; **an jdm** *or* **vor jds innerem Auge ~ziehen** to go through sb's mind; [2] *vt* to pull past (*an jdm* sb).

vorbelastet *adj* handicapped ◆ **von den Eltern/vom Milieu her ~ sein** to be at a disadvantage because of one's parents/background; **dazu will ich mich nicht äußern, da bin ich ~** I don't want to comment on that, I'm biased; *siehe* **erblich**.

Vorbemerkung *f* introductory *or* preliminary remark; (*kurzes Vorwort*) (short) preface *or* foreword.

vorbereiten* *sep* [1] *vt* to prepare ◆ **auf etw** (*acc*) **vorbereitet sein** to be prepared for sth; **jdn (schonend) auf etw** (*acc*) **~** to prepare sb for sth.
[2] *vr* (*Mensch*) to prepare (oneself) (*auf +acc* for); (*Ereignisse*) to be in the offing (*inf*).

vorbereitend *adj attr* preparatory, preliminary.

Vorbereitung *f* preparation ◆ **~en (für** *or* **zu etw) treffen** to make preparations (for sth).

Vorbereitungs- *in cpds* preparatory; **~dienst** *m* teaching practice; **~zeit** *f* preparation time.

Vor-: **~bericht** *m* preliminary report; **~besprechung** *f* preliminary meeting *or* discussion; **v~bestellen*** *vt sep* to order in advance; *Platz, Tisch, Zimmer, Karten auch* to book (in advance); to reserve; **~bestellung** *f* advance order; (*von Platz, Tisch, Zimmer*) (advance) booking; **bei ~bestellung** when ordering/booking in advance; **v~bestraft** *adj* previously convicted; **er ist schon einmal/dreimal v~bestraft** he (already) has a previous conviction/three previous convictions; **~bestrafte(r)** *mf decl as adj* man/woman *etc* with a previous conviction *or* a record (*inf*); **v~beten** *sep* [1] *vi* to lead the prayer/prayers; [2] *vt* **jdm etw v~beten** (*lit*) to lead sb in sth; (*fig inf*) to keep spelling sth out for sb (*inf*); **~beter** *m* prayer leader.

Vorbeugehaft *f* preventive custody.

vorbeugen *sep* [1] *vi* (*einer Sache* (*dat*) sth) to prevent; *einer Möglichkeit, Fehlinterpretation, einem Fehler auch* to preclude ◆ **~ ist besser als heilen** (*Prov*) prevention is better than cure (*prov*).
[2] *vt Kopf, Oberkörper* to bend forward.
[3] *vr* to lean *or* bend forward.

vorbeugend *adj* preventive.

Vorbeugung *f* prevention (*gegen, von* of) ◆ **zur ~** (*Med*) as a prophylactic.

Vorbeugungs-: **~haft** *f* preventive custody; **~maßnahme** *f* preventive measure.

Vorbild *nt* model; (*Beispiel*) example ◆ **das diente ihm als** *or* **war das ~ für seine Skulptur** his sculpture was modelled on this; **er/sein Verhalten kann uns zum ~ dienen** he/his behaviour is an example to us; **sich** (*dat*) **jdn zum ~ nehmen** to model oneself on sb; (*sich ein Beispiel nehmen an*) to take sb as an example; **jdn/etw als ~/leuchtendes ~ hinstellen** to hold sb/sth up as an example/a shining example.

vorbildlich *adj* exemplary ◆ **sich ~ benehmen** to be on one's best behaviour.

Vorbildlichkeit *f* exemplariness.

Vor-: **~bildung** *f* previous experience; (*schulisch*) educational background; **v~binden** *vt sep irreg* (*inf*) to put *or* tie on; **jdm/sich etw v~binden** to put *or* tie sth on sb/one; **~börse** *f* before-hours market; **~bote** *m* (*fig*) harbinger, herald.

vorbringen *vt sep irreg* **(a)** (*inf: nach vorn bringen*) to take up *or* forward; (*Mil*) to take up to the front.
(b) (*äußern*) to say; *Plan* to propose; *Meinung, Wunsch, Forderung* to express, to state; *Klage, Beschwerde* to make, to lodge; *Entschuldigung* to make, to offer; *Einwand* to make, to raise; *Argument, Beweis* to produce, to bring forward; *Grund* to put forward ◆ **können Sie dagegen etwas ~?** have you anything to say against it?; **was hast du zu deiner Entschuldigung vorzubringen?** what have you to say in your defence?; **er brachte vor, er hätte** ... (*sagte*) he said that he ...; (*behauptete*) he claimed *or* alleged that he ...
(c) (*inf: hervorbekommen*) to get out (*hinter +dat* from behind) ◆ **die Katze war nicht hinter dem Ofen vorzubringen** the cat couldn't be got out from behind the stove.

Vor-: **~bühne** *f* apron; **v~christlich** *adj* pre-Christian; **das zweite v~christliche Jahrhundert** the second century before Christ; **~dach** *nt* canopy; **v~datieren*** *vt sep* to postdate; *Ereignis* to predate, to antedate, to foredate; **~datierung** *f* postdating; predating, antedating, foredating.

vordem *adv* (*old*) in days of yore (*old, liter*), in olden days.

Vordenker *m* mentor; (*Prophet*) prophet.

Vorder-: **~achse** *f* front axle; **~ansicht** *f* front view; **v~asiatisch** *adj* Near Eastern; **~asien** *nt* Near East; **in ~asien** in the Near East; **~bein** *nt* foreleg; **~deck** *nt* foredeck.

Vordere(r) *mf decl as adj* person/man/woman *etc* in front.

vordere(r, s) *adj* front ◆ **die ~ Seite des Hauses** the front of the house; **der V~ Orient** the Near East; *siehe* **vorderste(r, s)**.

Vorder-: **~front** *f* frontage; **~fuß** *m* forefoot; **~gaumenlaut** *m* palatal (sound); **~grund** *m* foreground; (*fig auch*) fore(front); **sich in den ~grund schieben** *or* **drängen** to push oneself to the fore(front); **im ~grund stehen** (*fig*) to be to the fore; **in den ~grund treten** to come to the fore; (*Mensch auch*) to step into the limelight; **v~gründig** *adj* (*fig*) (*oberflächlich*) superficial; (*vorrangig*) *Probleme, Fragen* central; **v~hand** *adv* for the time being, for the present; **~hand** *f siehe* **Vorhand**; **~haus** *nt* front-facing house, front building; **~lader** *m* **-s, -** muzzle-loader; **v~lastig** *adj Schiff, Flugzeug* front-heavy; **~lauf** *m* (*Hunt*) foreleg; **~mann** *m, pl* **-männer** person in front; **sein ~mann** the person in front of him; **jdn auf ~mann bringen** (*fig inf*) to get sb to shape up; (*gesundheitlich*) to get sb fighting fit (*inf*); **etw auf ~mann bringen** (*fig inf*) *Haushalt, Auto etc* to get sth ship-shape; *Kenntnisse, Wissen* to brush sth up; *Finanzen* to get sth straightened out; (*auf neuesten Stand bringen*) *Listen, Garderobe* to bring sth up-to-date; **~pfote** *f* front paw; **~rad** *nt* front wheel; **~radantrieb** *m* front-wheel drive; **~schinken** *m* shoulder of ham; **~seite** *f* front; (*von Münze*) head, obverse; **~sitz** *m* front seat.

vorderste(r, s) *adj superl of* **vordere(r, s)** front(most) ◆ **der/die V~ in der Schlange** the first man/woman in the queue (*Brit*) *or* line (*US*).

Vorder-: ~steven *m* (*Naut*) stem; **~teil** *m or nt* front; **~tür** *f* front door; **~zahn** *m* front tooth; **~zimmer** *nt* front room.

Vordiplom *nt* first diploma.

vordrängen *vr sep* to push to the front ◆ **sich in einer Schlange ~** to jump a queue (*Brit*), to push to the front of a line (*US*).

vordringen *vi sep irreg aux sein* to advance; (*Mil, in den Weltraum auch*) to penetrate (*in +acc* into) ◆ **bis zu jdm/etw ~** to reach sb/sth, to get as far as sb/sth.

vordringlich *adj* urgent, pressing.

Vordruck *m* form.

vor|ehelich *adj attr* premarital.

vor|eilig *adj* rash ◆ **~e Schlüsse ziehen** to jump to conclusions; **~ urteilen** to be rash in one's judgement.

vor|einander *adv* (*räumlich*) in front of *or* before one another *or* each other; (*einander gegenüber*) face to face ◆ **wir haben keine Geheimnisse ~** we have no secrets from each other; **Angst ~ haben** to be afraid of each other; **sie schämten sich ~** they were embarrassed with each other.

vor|eingenommen *adj* prejudiced, biased.

Vor|eingenommenheit *f, no pl* prejudice, bias.

vor|enthalten* *vt sep irreg* **jdm etw ~** to withhold sth from sb; *Nachricht auch* to keep sth from sb.

Vor|entscheidung *f* preliminary decision; (*Sport: auch* **~skampf, ~srunde**) preliminary round *or* heat.

vor|erst *adv* for the time being, for the moment *or* present.

vor|erwähnt *adj attr* (*form*) aforementioned, aforesaid.

Vorfahr *m* **-en, -en** forefather, ancestor.

vorfahren *sep irreg* [1] *vi aux sein* **(a)** to go *or* move forward, to move up; (*in Auto auch*) to drive forward.
(b) (*ankommen*) to drive up ◆ **den Wagen ~ lassen** to have the car brought (up), to send for *or* order the car.
(c) (*früher fahren*) to go on ahead ◆ **in den Urlaub ~** to go on holiday ahead (of the others).
(d) (*an der Spitze fahren*) to drive in front.
[2] *vt* **(a)** (*weiter nach vorn fahren*) to move up *or* forward.
(b) (*vor den Eingang fahren*) to drive up.

Vorfahrt *f* **-,** *no pl* right of way ◆ **~ haben** to have (the) right of way; **die ~ beachten/nicht beachten** to observe/ignore the right of way; **„~ (be)achten"** "give way" (*Brit*), "yield" (*US*); **(sich** *dat***) die ~ erzwingen** to insist on one's right of way; **jdm die ~ nehmen** to ignore sb's right of way.

Vorfahrts-: v~berechtigt *adj* having (the) right of way; **v~berechtigt sein** to have (the) right of way; **der/die ~berechtigte** the driver with (the) right of way; **~recht** *nt* right of way; **~regel** *f* rule on (the) right of way; **~schild** *nt* give way (*Brit*) *or* yield (*US*) sign; **~straße** *f* major road; **~zeichen** *nt* give way (*Brit*) *or* yield (*US*) sign.

Vorfall *m* **(a)** incident, occurrence. **(b)** (*Med*) prolapse.

vorfallen *vi sep irreg aux sein* **(a)** (*sich ereignen*) to occur, to happen ◆ **was ist während meiner Abwesenheit vorgefallen?** what's been happening while I've been away? **(b)** (*inf: nach vorn fallen*) to fall forward.

vorfaseln *vt sep* **jdm etw ~** (*pej inf*) to prattle on about sth to sb.

Vor-: v~feiern *vti sep* to celebrate early; **~feld** *nt* (*Mil*) territory situated in front of the main battle-line; (*Aviat*) apron; (*fig*) run-up (*+gen* to); **im ~feld der Wahlen/Verhandlungen** in the run-up to the elections/in the preliminary stages of the negotiations; **etw im ~feld klären** to clear sth up beforehand; **v~fertigen** *vt sep* to prefabricate; **~film** *m* supporting film *or* programme, short; **~finanzierung** *f* prefinancing; **v~finden** *vt sep irreg* to find, to discover; **v~flunkern** *vt sep* (*inf*) **jdm etwas v~flunkern** to tell sb a fib/fibs; **~freude** *f* anticipation; **~frühling** *m* early spring, foretaste of spring.

vorfühlen *vi sep* (*fig*) to put *or* send out (a few) feelers ◆ **bei jdm ~** to sound sb out.

vorführen *vt sep* **(a)** *Angeklagten* to bring forward; *Zeugen auch* to produce ◆ **den Patienten einem Spezialisten ~** to have the patient seen by a specialist; **den Angeklagten dem Richter ~** to bring the accused before the judge.
(b) (*zeigen*) to present; *Film* to show; *Mode* to model; *Übung, (Vertreter) Modell, Gerät* to demonstrate (*dat* to); *Theaterstück auch, Kunststücke* to perform (*dat* to *or* in front of).
(c) **er wurde vom Direktor regelrecht vorgeführt** the director really made him look small *or* silly.

Vorführer *m* projectionist.

Vorführraum *m* projection room.

Vorführung *f* presentation; (*von Angeklagten, Zeugen etc*) production *no pl*; (*von Filmen*) showing; (*von Mode*) modelling; (*von Geräten, Modellen, Übungen*) demonstration; (*von Theaterstück, Kunststücken*) performance.

Vorführwagen *m* demonstration model *or* car.

Vorgabe *f* handicap.

Vorgang *m* **(a)** (*Ereignis*) event, occurrence; (*Ablauf, Hergang*) series *or* course of events ◆ **jdm den genauen ~ eines Unfalls schildern** to tell sb exactly what happened in an accident. **(b)** (*biologischer, chemischer, technischer Prozeß*) process. **(c)** (*form: Akten*) file, dossier.

Vorgänger(in *f***)** *m* **s, -** predecessor, precursor (*form*).

Vorgarten *m* front garden.

vorgaukeln *vt sep* **jdm etw ~** to lead sb to believe in sth; **jdm ~, daß ...** to lead sb to believe that ...; **er hat ihr ein Leben im Luxus vorgegaukelt** he led her to believe that he lived in luxury.

vorgeben *vt sep irreg* **(a)** (*vortäuschen*) to pretend; (*fälschlich beteuern*) to profess ◆ **sie gab Zeitmangel vor, um ...** she pretended to be pressed for time in order to ... **(b)** (*Sport*) to give (a start of). **(c)** (*inf: nach vorn geben*) to pass forward.

Vorgebirge *nt* foothills *pl.*

vorgeblich *adj siehe* **angeblich.**

vorgeburtlich *adj attr* prenatal.

vorgedruckt *adj* pre-printed.

⚠ **vorgefaßt** *adj Meinung* preconceived.

Vorgefühl *nt* anticipation; (*böse Ahnung*) presentiment, foreboding.

vorgehen *vi sep irreg aux sein* **(a)** (*handeln*) to act, to proceed ◆ **gerichtlich/energisch gegen jdn ~** to take legal proceedings *or* action/assertive action against sb.
(b) (*geschehen, vor sich gehen*) to go on, to happen.
(c) (*Uhr*) (*spätere Zeit anzeigen*) to be fast; (*zu schnell gehen*) to gain ◆ **meine Uhr geht (zwei Minuten) vor** my watch is (two minutes) fast; **meine Uhr geht pro Tag zwei Minuten vor** my watch gains two minutes a day.
(d) (*nach vorn gehen*) to go forward *or* to the front; (*Mil*) to advance.
(e) (*als erster gehen*) to go first; (*früher gehen*) to go on ahead.
(f) (*den Vorrang haben*) to come first, to take precedence, to have priority.

Vorgehen *nt* **-s,** *no pl* action.

Vor-: v~gelagert *adj* offshore; **es ist dem Kap v~gelagert** it lies off the Cape; **v~genannt** *adj* (*form*) aforementioned, aforesaid; **~gericht** *nt* hors d'œuvre, starter (*Brit*); **v~gerückt** *adj Stunde* late; *Alter* advanced; **~geschichte** *f* **(a)** (*eines Falles*) past history; **(b)** (*Urgeschichte*) prehistory, prehistoric times *pl*; **aus der ~geschichte** from prehistoric times; **v~geschichtlich** *adj* prehistoric; **~geschmack** *m* (*fig*) foretaste; **v~geschritten** *adj* advanced; **im v~geschrittenen Alter** at an advanced age; **zu v~geschrittener Stunde** at a late hour.

Vorgesetzte(r) *mf decl as adj* superior.

vorgestern *adv* the day before yesterday ◆ **von ~** (*fig*) antiquated; *Methoden, Ansichten auch, Kleidung* old-fashioned; **~ abend/morgen** the evening/morning before last; **~ mittag** midday the day before yesterday.

vorgestrig *adj attr* of the day before yesterday.

vorgreifen *vi sep irreg* to anticipate; (*verfrüht handeln*) to act prematurely ◆ **jdm ~** to forestall sb; **einer Sache** (*dat*) **~** to anticipate sth.

Vorgriff *m* anticipation (*auf +acc* of); (*in Erzählung*) leap ahead ◆ **im ~ auf** (*+acc*) in anticipation of; **verzeihen Sie mir den ~ auf** (*+acc*) ... excuse me for leaping ahead to ...

➤ **vorhaben** *vt sep irreg* to intend; (*geplant haben*) to have planned ◆ **was haben Sie heute vor?** what are your plans for today?, what do you intend doing today?; **ich habe morgen nichts vor** I've nothing planned *or* no plans for tomorrow; **hast du heute abend schon etwas vor?** have you already got something planned *or* are you already doing something this evening?; **wenn du nichts Besseres vorhast ...** if you've nothing better *or* else to do ...; **etw mit jdm/etw ~** to intend doing sth with sb/sth; (*etw geplant haben*) to have sth planned for sb/sth; **die ehrgeizigen Eltern haben viel mit dem Kind vor** the ambitious parents have great plans for the child; **was hast du jetzt wieder vor?** what are you up to now?

Vorhaben *nt* plan; (*Absicht*) intention.

Vorhalle *f* (*von Tempel*) portico; (*Diele*) entrance hall, vestibule; (*Foyer*) foyer; (*von Parlament*) lobby.

vorhalten *sep irreg* [1] *vt* **(a)** (*vorwerfen*) **jdm etw ~** to reproach sb with *or* for sth.
(b) (*als Beispiel*) **jdm jdn/etw ~** to hold sb/sth up to sb; **man hält ihm den älteren Bruder als Vorbild vor** his elder brother is held up to him as an example; **jdm die Qualen der Hölle ~** to hold up the torments of hell before sb's eyes.
(c) (*vor den Körper halten*) to hold up; (*beim Niesen etc*) *Hand, Taschentuch* to put in front of one's mouth ◆ **mit vorgehaltener Pistole** at gunpoint; **sich** (*dat*) **ein Handtuch ~** to hold up a towel in front of oneself; *siehe* **Spiegel.**
[2] *vi* (*anhalten*) to last.

Vorhaltung *f usu pl* reproach ◆ **jdm/sich (wegen etw) ~en machen** to reproach sb/oneself (with *or* for sth).

Vorhand *f* (*Sport*) forehand; (*von Pferd*) forehand; (*Cards*) lead.

vorhanden *adj* (*verfügbar*) available; (*existierend*) in existence, existing ◆ **eine Dusche ist hier leider nicht ~** I'm afraid there isn't a shower here; **davon ist genügend/nichts mehr ~** there's plenty/no more of that.

Vorhang *m* **-s, Vorhänge** curtain ◆ **die Schauspieler bekamen 10 Vorhänge**

⚠: for details of spelling reform, see supplement

➤ SPRACHE AKTIV: **vorhaben** → 29.2, 35.1, 35.2, 35.3

the actors got *or* took 10 curtain calls *or* took 10 curtains.

⚠**Vorhängeschloß** *nt* padlock.

Vorhang-: ~stange *f* (*zum Aufhängen*) curtain pole; (*zum Ziehen*) curtain rod; **~stoff** *m* curtaining *no pl*, curtain(ing) material *or* fabric.

Vor-: ~haus *nt* (*Aus*) hall; **~haut** *f* foreskin, prepuce (*spec*).

vorher *adv* before(hand); (*früher*) before ◆ **am Tage ~** the day before, the previous day; **man weiß ~ nie, wie die Sache ausgeht** one never knows beforehand *or* in advance how things will turn out; **konntest du das nicht ~ sagen?** couldn't you have said that earlier?

Vorher-: v~bestimmen* *vt sep* to determine *or* ascertain in advance; *Schicksal, Zukunft* to predetermine; (*Gott*) to preordain; **es war ihm v~bestimmt ...** he was predestined ...; **v~gehen** *vi sep irreg aux sein* to go first *or* in front, to lead the way; (*fig*) to precede; **v~gehend** *adj Tag, Ereignisse* preceding, previous.

vorherig [foːɐ̯'heːrɪç, 'foːɐ̯heːrɪç] *adj attr* prior, previous; (*ehemalig*) former.

Vorherrschaft *f* predominance, supremacy; (*Hegemonie*) hegemony.

vorherrschen *vi sep* to predominate, to prevail ◆ **Rot herrscht in diesem Winter vor** red is predominant this winter.

vorherrschend *adj* predominant; (*weitverbreitet*) prevalent; *Ansicht, Meinung auch* prevailing.

Vorher-: ~sage *f* forecast; **v~sagen** *vt sep siehe* **voraussagen**; **v~sehen** *vt sep irreg* to foresee.

vorheucheln *vt sep* to feign, to pretend ◆ **jdm etw ~** to feign *or* pretend sth to sb; **jdm ~, daß ...** to pretend to sb that ...; **er heuchelt dir doch bloß was vor!** (*inf*) he's just putting on an act.

vorheulen *vt sep* (*inf*) **jdm etwas ~** to give sb a sob-story (*inf*).

Vorhimmel *m* first heaven.

vorhin *adv* just now, a little while ago.

⚠**vorhinein** *adv*: **im ~** in advance.

Vor-: ~hof *m* forecourt; (*Anat: von Herz, Ohr*) vestibule; **~hölle** *f* limbo; **in der ~hölle** in limbo; **~hut** *f* **-, -en** (*Mil*) vanguard, advance guard.

vorig *adj attr* (*früher*) *Besitzer, Wohnsitz* previous; (*vergangen*) *Jahr, Woche etc* last ◆ **im ~en** (in the) above, earlier; **der/die/das ~e** the above(-mentioned); **die V~en** (*Theat*) the same.

Vor-: ~jahr *nt* previous year, year before; **~jahresergebnis** *nt* previous year's result; **~jahreswert** *m* previous year's value; **v~jährig** *adj* of the previous year *or* year before; **v~jammern** *vti sep* **jdm (etwas) v~jammern** to moan to sb (*von* about); **~kammer** *f* (*Anat: von Herz*) vestibule; (*Tech*) pre-combustion chamber; **~kämpfer** *m* (*für* of) pioneer, champion; **v~kauen** *vt sep Nahrung* to chew; **jdm etw** (*acc*) **v~kauen** (*fig inf*) to spoon-feed sth to sb (*inf*); **~kaufsrecht** *nt* option of purchase *or* to buy.

Vorkehrung *f* precaution ◆ **~en treffen** to take precautions.

Vorkenntnis *f* previous knowledge *no pl*; (*Erfahrung*) previous experience *no pl* ◆ **sprachliche ~se** previous knowledge of languages/the language.

vorknöpfen *vt sep* (*fig inf*) **sich** (*dat*) **jdn ~** to take sb to task; **den hat sich die Mafia vorgeknöpft** the Mafia got him.

vorkommen *vi sep irreg aux sein* **(a)** *auch vi impers* (*sich ereignen*) to happen ◆ **so etwas ist mir noch nie vorgekommen** such a thing has never happened to me before; **daß mir das nicht noch einmal vorkommt!** don't let it happen again!; **das soll nicht wieder ~** it won't happen again; **das kann schon mal ~** it can happen, it has been known to happen; (*das ist nicht ungewöhnlich*) that happens; **so was soll ~!** that's life!
(b) (*vorhanden sein, auftreten*) to occur; (*Pflanzen, Tiere*) to be found ◆ **in dem Aufsatz dürfen keine Fehler ~** there mustn't be any mistakes in the essay.
(c) (*erscheinen*) to seem ◆ **das kommt mir bekannt/merkwürdig vor** that seems familiar/strange to me; **sich** (*dat*) **überflüssig/dumm ~** to feel superfluous/silly; **sich** (*dat*) **klug ~** to think one is clever; **das kommt dir nur so vor** it just seems that way *or* like that to you; **wie kommst du mir eigentlich vor?** (*inf*) who do you think you are?
(d) (*nach vorn kommen*) to come forward *or* to the front.
(e) (*herauskommen*) to come out.

Vorkommen *nt* **-s, -** (*no pl: das Auftreten*) occurrence, incidence; (*Min*) deposit.

Vorkommnis *nt* incident, event, occurrence.

Vorkoster *m* taster; (*fig*) guinea-pig.

Vorkriegs- *in cpds* pre-war; **~zeit** *f* pre-war period.

vorladen *vt sep irreg* (*bei Gericht*) to summons; *Zeugen auch* to subpoena.

Vorladung *f siehe vt* summons; subpoena.

Vorlage *f* **-, -n (a)** *no pl* (*das Vorlegen*) (*von Dokument*) presentation, production; (*von Scheck, Schuldschein*) presentation; (*von Beweismaterial*) submission ◆ **gegen ~ einer Sache** (*gen*) (up)on production *or* presentation of sth; **zahlbar bei ~** payable on demand.
(b) (*Muster*) (*zum Stricken, Nähen*) pattern; (*Liter*) model ◆ **etw von einer ~ abzeichnen/nach einer ~ machen** to copy sth; **hattest du dafür eine ~?** did you have a pattern for it?; did you copy it from something?
(c) (*Entwurf*) draft; (*Parl: Gesetzes~*) bill.
(d) (*Ftbl*) through-ball ◆ **jdm eine ~ machen** to lay the ball on for sb; **das war eine tolle ~** the ball was beautifully laid on.
(e) (*Ski*) vorlage, forward lean (position).
(f) *siehe* **Vorleger**.

Vorland *nt* (*der Alpen etc*) foothills *pl*; (*vor Deich*) foreshore.

vorlassen *vt sep irreg* **(a)** (*inf*) **jdn ~** (*nach vorn gehen lassen*) to let sb go in front; (*in der Schlange auch*) to let sb go first; (*vorbeigehen lassen*) to let sb (go) past, to let sb pass; **ein Auto ~** (*einbiegen lassen*) to let a car in; (*überholen lassen*) to let a car pass, to let a car (go) past.
(b) (*Empfang gewähren*) to allow in, to admit.

Vorlauf *m* **(a)** (*Sport*) qualifying *or* preliminary heat/round. **(b)** (*Chem: bei Destillation*) forerun. **(c)** (*Tech: von Rad*) offset. **(d)** (*von Film, Band*) leader; (*von Tonbandgerät*) fast-forward.

vorlaufen *vi sep irreg aux sein* (*inf*) (*vorauslaufen*) to run on ahead *or* in front; (*nach vorne laufen*) to run to the front.

Vorläufer *m* forerunner (*auch Ski*), precursor.

vorläufig [1] *adj* temporary; *Regelung auch* provisional; *Urteil* preliminary; *Verfügung des Gerichts* interim, provisional.
[2] *adv* (*einstweilig*) temporarily; (*fürs erste*) for the time being, for the present, provisionally.

Vorlaufzeit *f* (*Sport*) qualifying time; (*Ind: Entwicklungszeit*) lead time.

vorlaut *adj* cheeky, impertinent.

Vorleben *nt* past (life).

vorleben *vt sep* **jdm etw ~** to set an example of sth to sb.

Vorlege-: ~besteck *nt* serving cutlery, serving spoons *pl*; (*Tranchierbesteck*) carvers *pl*; **~gabel** *f* serving fork; (*von Tranchierbesteck*) carving fork; **~löffel** *m* serving *or* table spoon; **~messer** *nt* carving knife.

vorlegen *sep* [1] *vt* **(a)** to present; *Entwurf, Doktorarbeit auch* to submit; *Paß* to show, to produce; *Beweismaterial* to submit; *Zeugnisse, Bewerbungsunterlagen* to produce; *Schulzeugnis* to show; *Schularbeit auch* to hand in; (*Pol*) *Entwurf* to table (*Brit*), to introduce ◆ **jdm etw zur Unterschrift ~** to give *or* present sth to sb for signature *or* signing; **etw dem Parlament ~** to lay sth before the house, to table sth (*Brit*); **jdm eine Frage ~** to put a question to sb; **ein schnelles Tempo ~** to go at a fast pace; **ein schnelleres Tempo ~** to speed up, to quicken the pace.
(b) *Speisen* to serve; (*hinlegen*) *Futter* to put down (*dat* for) ◆ **jdm etw ~** to serve sth to sb, to serve sb with sth.
(c) *Riegel* to put across, to shoot (across); *Schloß, Kette* to put on; (*inf: davorlegen*) to put in front.
(d) (*Ftbl*) **jdm den Ball ~** to lay the ball on for sb.
[2] *vr* to lean forward.
[3] *vi* (*Kellner*) to serve.

Vorleger *m* **-s, -** mat; (*Bett~ auch*) (bedside) rug.

⚠**Vorlegeschloß** *nt siehe* **Vorhängeschloß**.

vorlehnen *vr sep* to lean forward.

Vorleistung *f* (*Econ*) (*Vorausbezahlung*) advance (payment); (*finanzielle Aufwendung*) outlay *no pl* (*an +dat* on); (*vorausgehende Arbeit*) preliminary work; (*Pol*) prior concession.

vorlesen *vti sep irreg* to read aloud *or* out ◆ **jdm (etw) ~** to read (sth) to sb.

Vorleser *m* reader.

Vorlesung *f* (*Univ*) lecture; (*Vorlesungsreihe*) course (of lectures), lectures *pl* ◆ **über etw** (*acc*) **~en halten** to give (a course of) lectures on sth; **~en hören** to go to lectures.

Vorlesungs-: ~betrieb *m* lectures *pl*; **v~frei** *adj* **v~freie Zeit** free period(s *pl*); **~verzeichnis** *nt* lecture timetable.

vorletzte(r, s) *adj* last but one, penultimate ◆ **im ~n Jahr** the year before last.

➤**Vorliebe** *f* predilection, special liking, preference ◆ **etw mit ~ tun** to particularly like doing sth.

⚠**vorliebnehmen** *vi sep irreg* **mit jdm/etw ~** to make do with sb/sth, to put up with sb/sth.

vorliegen *sep irreg* [1] *vi* (*zur Verfügung stehen: Beweise, Katalog, Erkenntnisse*) to be available; (*Urteil*) to be known; (*eingereicht, vorgelegt sein: Unterlagen, wissenschaftliche Arbeit*) to be in, to have come in; (*Pol*) (*Gesetzesvorlage*) to be before the house; (*Haushalt*) to be published, to be out; (*vorhanden sein*) (*Irrtum, Schuld etc*) to be; (*Symptome*) to be present; (*Gründe*) to be, to exist ◆ **jdm ~** (*Unterlagen, Akten etc*) to be with sb; **die Ergebnisse liegen der Kommission vor** the commission has the results; **das Beweismaterial liegt dem Gericht vor** the evidence is before the court; **mir liegt ein Brief vor** I have (here) a letter; **etw liegt gegen jdn vor** sth is against sb; (*gegen Angeklagten*) sb is charged with sth.
[2] *vi impers* to be ◆ **es liegen fünf Bewerbungen vor** there are *or* we have five applications; **es muß ein Irrtum ~** there must be some mistake.

vorliegend *adj attr Gründe* existing; *Akten, Unterlagen,* (*Typ*) *Auflage* on hand; *Frage* at issue; *Angelegenheit, Probleme* in hand; *Ergebnisse* available ◆ **im ~en Fall** in this *or* in the present case; **die uns ~en Ergebnisse** the results we have to hand.

vorlügen *vt sep irreg* **jdm etwas ~** to lie to sb.

vorm. *abbr of* **vormittags**.

vormachen *vt sep* **(a) jdm etw ~** (*zeigen*) to show sb how to do sth, to demonstrate sth to sb; (*fig: als Beispiel dienen*) to show sb sth.
(b) (*fig*) **jdm etwas ~** (*täuschen*) to fool *or* kid (*inf*) sb; **ich lasse mir so leicht nichts ~** you/he *etc* can't fool *or* kid (*inf*) me so easily; **er läßt sich** (*dat*) **von niemandem etwas ~** nobody can fool him, he's nobody's fool; **mach mir doch nichts vor** don't try and fool *or* kid (*inf*) me; **sich** (*dat*) **(selbst) etwas ~** to fool *or* kid (*inf*) oneself; *siehe* **Dunst**.
(c) (*inf: davorlegen, -stellen etc*) *Kette, Schürze, Riegel* to put on; *Brett* to put across.

Vormacht(stellung) *f* supremacy (*gegenüber* over) ◆ **eine ~ haben** to have supremacy.

Vormagen *m* (*von Rind*) rumen; (*von Vogel*) crop.

vormalig *adj attr* former.

vormals *adv* formerly.

Vormarsch *m* (*Mil*) advance ◆ **im ~ sein** to be on the advance, to be advanc-

ing; (*fig*) to be gaining ground.
Vormärz *m* (*Hist*) *period from 1815 to March revolution of 1848.*
Vormast *m* foremast.
vormerken *vt sep* to note down, to make a note of; (*bei Bestellung auch*) to take an order for; *Plätze* to reserve, to book ◆ **ich werde Sie für Mittwoch ~** I'll put you *or* your name down for Wednesday; **können Sie für mich 5 Exemplare ~?** can you put me down for 5 copies?, can you reserve 5 copies for me?; **sich beim Friseur ~ lassen** to make an appointment at the hairdresser's; **sich für einen Kursus ~ lassen** to put one's name *or* oneself down for a course.
Vormittag *m* morning ◆ **am ~** in the morning.
vormittag *adv* **heute/gestern/morgen ~** this/yesterday/tomorrow morning.
vormittägig *adj* morning.
vormittags *adv* in the morning; (*jeden Morgen*) in the morning(s).
Vormund *m* **-(e)s, -e** *or* **Vormünder** guardian ◆ **ich brauche keinen ~** (*fig*) I don't need anyone to tell me what to do.
Vormundschaft *f* guardianship, tutelage ◆ **jdn unter ~ stellen** to place sb under the care of a guardian.
Vormundschaftsgericht *nt court dealing with matters relating to guardianship.*
vorn *adv* **(a)** in front ◆ **von ~** from the front; **nach ~** (*ganz nach ~*) to the front; (*weiter nach ~*) forwards; **von weit ~** from the very front; **~ im Buch/in der Schlange/auf der Liste** at the front of the book/queue/at the top of the list; **sich ~ anstellen** to join the front of the queue (*Brit*) *or* line (*US*); **~ im Bild** in the front of the picture; **nach ~ abgehen** (*Theat*) to exit at the front of the stage; **nach ~ laufen** to run to the front; **~ bleiben** (*lit*) to stay in front; (*fig*) not to lag behind; **wenn es etwas umsonst gibt, ist er immer ganz ~(e)** when something's going free he's always (the) first on the scene.
(b) (*am Anfang*) von **~** from the beginning; **wie schon ~ erklärt** as explained above; **von ~ anfangen** to begin at *or* to start from the beginning; (*von neuem*) to start (all) over again, to start from scratch; (*neues Leben*) to start afresh, to make a fresh start; **etw ~ anfügen** to add sth at the beginning; **das Auto kam von ~ auf ihn zugefahren** the car came at him head on.
(c) (*am vorderen Ende*) at the front; (*Naut*) fore ◆ **von ~** from the front; **jdn von ~ sehen** to see sb's face; **~ im Auto/Bus** in the front of the car/bus; **der Blinker ~** the front indicator; **nach ~** to the front; *fallen, ziehen* forwards.
(d) (*auf der Vorderseite*) at the front ◆ **das Buch ist ~ schmutzig** the front of the book is dirty; **~ auf der Medaille** on the face of the medal; **ein nach ~ gelegenes Zimmer** a room facing the front; **ein Blick nach ~** a look to the front.
(e) (*weit entfernt*) **das Auto da ~** the car in front *or* ahead there; **sie waren ziemlich weit ~** they were quite far ahead *or* quite a long way ahead; (*Läufer auch*) they were quite a long way (out) in front *or* quite a long way in the lead.
(f) ich kann doch nicht ~ und hinten gleichzeitig sein I can't be everywhere at once; **sich von ~e bis** *or* **und hinten bedienen lassen** to be waited on hand and foot; **er betrügt sie von ~ bis hinten** he deceives her right, left and centre; *siehe auch* **hinten.**
Vornahme *f* **-, -n** (*form*) undertaking ◆ **die ~ von Änderungen am Text bleibt dem Autor überlassen** it is left to the author to undertake changes to the text.
Vorname *m* Christian name, first name.
vorne *adv siehe* **vorn.**
vornehm *adj* **(a)** (*von hohem Rang*) *Familie, Kreise* distinguished, high-ranking; (*von adliger Herkunft*) aristocratic, noble; (*kultiviert*) *Herr, Dame* distinguished, posh (*inf*); *Manieren, Art, Benehmen* genteel, refined; (*edel*) *Gesinnung, Charakter, Handeln* noble ◆ **die ~e Gesellschaft** high society; **ihr seid mir eine ~e Gesellschaft** (*iro*) you're a fine lot! (*inf*); **die ~e Welt, die V~en** fashionable society; **so was sagt/tut man nicht in ~en Kreisen** one doesn't say/do that in polite society; **ein ~er Besuch** a distinguished visitor; **~er Anstrich** (*fig*) distinguished air; **~ heiraten** to marry into high society; **~ tun** (*pej inf*) to act posh (*inf*).
(b) (*elegant, luxuriös*) *Wohngegend* fashionable, smart, posh (*inf*); *Haus* smart, posh (*inf*); *Geschäft* exclusive, posh (*inf*); *Kleid, Äußeres* elegant, stylish; *Auto* smart, posh (*inf*); *Geschmack* refined, exclusive.
(c) (*dated*) **die ~ste Pflicht/Aufgabe** the first *or* foremost duty/task.
vornehmen *vt sep irreg* **(a)** (*ausführen*) to carry out; *Test, Untersuchung auch* to do; *Umfrage, Änderungen auch* to make; *Messungen* to take.
(b) (*in Angriff nehmen*) **(sich** *dat*) **etw ~** to get to work on sth.
(c) sich (*dat*) **etw ~** (*planen, vorhaben*) to intend *or* mean to do sth; (*Vorsatz fassen*) to have resolved to do sth; **ich habe mir vorgenommen, das nächste Woche zu tun** I intend *or* mean to do that next week; **ich habe mir zuviel vorgenommen** I've taken on too much.
(d) sich (*dat*) **jdn ~** (*inf*) to have a word with sb.
(e) (*früher drannehmen*) *Kunden, Patienten* to attend to *or* see first.
(f) (*inf: vorhalten*) *Schürze, Serviette* to put on; *Hand* to put in front of one's mouth; (*vorbeugen*) *Schultern* to hunch.
Vornehmheit *f, no pl siehe adj* **(a)** high rank; nobility; distinguished ways *pl*; refinement; nobility. **(b)** smartness, poshness (*inf*); exclusiveness; elegance, stylishness; refinement.
vornehmlich 1 *adv* (*hauptsächlich, vor allem*) principally, especially, above all; (*vorzugsweise*) first and foremost.
2 *adj* principal, main, chief.
vorneigen *vtr sep* to lean forward.
Vorneverteidigung *f* (*Mil*) forward defence.

vorn(e)weg *adv* ahead, in front, first; (*als erstes*) first ◆ **er geht immer ~** he always walks on ahead *or* in front; **mit dem Kopf ~** head first; **gleich ~** straight away; **mit dem Mund ~ sein** (*inf*) to have a big mouth.
vornherein *adv*: **von ~** from the start *or* outset.
Vorniere *f* pronephros (*spec*).
vorn-: ~über *adv* forwards; **~über fallen** to fall (over) forwards; **~weg** *adv siehe* **vorn(e)weg.**
Vor|ort *m* (*Vorstadt*) suburb.
Vor-Ort- *in cpds* on-site.
Vor|ortbahn *f* suburban line; (*für Berufsverkehr*) commuter line.
Vor-Ort-Kontrolle *f* on-site supervision.
Vorort-: ~verkehr *m* suburban traffic; (*von öffentlichen Verkehrsmitteln*) suburban service; **~zug** *m* suburban train; (*im Berufsverkehr*) commuter train.
Vor-: v~österlich *adj* immediately before Easter; **~platz** *m* forecourt; **~pommern** *nt* West Pomerania; **~posten** *m* (*Mil*) outpost; **~prämie** *f* (*St Ex*) call option; **~preschen** *vi sep aux sein* (*lit, fig*) to press ahead; **~programm** *nt* supporting bill *or* programme; **im ~programm** on the supporting bill; **v~programmieren*** *vt sep* to preprogram; (*fig auch*) to precondition; **v~programmiert** *adj Erfolg, Antwort* automatic; *Verhaltensweise* preprogrammed; *Weg* predetermined, pre-ordained; **die nächste Krise ist v~programmiert** the seeds of the next crisis have been sown; **~prüfung** *f* preliminary examination; **v~quellen** *sep irreg* 1 *vt Erbsen, Linsen etc* to soak; 2 *vi aux sein* (*Augen*) to bulge; *siehe* **hervorquellen.**
Vorrang *m* **-(e)s,** *no pl* **(a) ~ haben** to have priority, to take precedence; **den ~ vor etw** (*dat*) **haben** to take precedence over sth; **jdm/einer Sache den ~ geben** *or* **einräumen** to give sb/a matter priority; **jdm/einer Sache den ~ streitig machen** to challenge sb's/sth's pre-eminence.
(b) (*Aus: Vorfahrt*) right of way.
vorrangig 1 *adj* of prime importance, priority *attr.*
2 *adv* as a matter of priority ◆ **eine Angelegenheit ~ erledigen/behandeln** to give a matter priority treatment.
Vorrangstellung *f* pre-eminence *no indef art* ◆ **er hat in der Firma eine ~** he has a position of prime importance in the firm.
Vorrat *m* **-(e)s, Vorräte** (*an +dat* of) stock, supply; (*von Waren*) stocks *pl*; (*an Lebensmitteln auch*) store, provisions *pl*; (*an Atomwaffen*) stockpile; (*Geld*) reserves *pl*; (*an Geschichten, Ideen*) stock ◆ **heimlicher ~** (secret) hoard; **etw auf ~ kaufen** to stock up with sth; **~e anlegen** *or* **anschaffen** *or* **ansammeln** to lay in a stock *or* stocks *pl*; **solange der ~ reicht** (*Comm*) while stocks last; **etw auf ~ haben** to have sth in reserve; (*Comm*) to have sth in stock.
vorrätig *adj* in stock; (*verfügbar*) available ◆ **etw nicht mehr ~ haben** to be out (of stock) of sth.
Vorrats-: ~kammer *f* store cupboard; (*für Lebensmittel*) larder; **~raum** *m* store room; (*in Geschäft*) stock room.
Vorraum *m* anteroom; (*Büro*) outer office; (*von Gericht*) lobby; (*von Kino, Theater*) foyer.
vorrechnen *vt sep* **jdm etw ~** to work out *or* reckon up *or* calculate sth for sb; **er rechnet mir dauernd vor, wieviel alles kostet** he's always pointing out to me how much everything costs; **jdm seine Fehler ~** (*fig*) to enumerate sb's mistakes.
Vorrecht *nt* prerogative; (*Vergünstigung*) privilege.
Vorrede *f* (*Vorwort*) preface; (*Theat*) prologue; (*einleitende Rede*) introductory speech.
vorreden *vt sep* (*inf*) **jdm etwas ~** to tell sb a tale; **red mir doch nichts vor** don't give me that (*inf*).
Vorredner *m* (*vorheriger Redner*) previous speaker; (*einleitender Redner*) introductory speaker ◆ **mein ~ hat gesagt ...** the previous speaker said ...
vorreiten *sep irreg* 1 *vt* **(a)** *aux sein* (*vorausreiten*) to ride on ahead. **(b)** (*zur Demonstration*) to demonstrate (*a riding exercise*).
2 *vt* (*demonstrieren*) *Übung* to demonstrate.
Vorreiter *m* **(a)** forerunner ◆ **den ~ für etw machen** to be the first to do sth.
(b) (*beim Reiten*) demonstrator.
Vorreiterrolle *f* **eine ~ für andere einnehmen** to make the running for others.
vorrennen *vi sep irreg aux sein* (*inf*) (*voraus*) to run *or* race (on) ahead; (*nach vorn*) to run forward.
vorrichten *vt sep* to prepare; *Zutaten, Gegenstände* to get ready.
Vorrichtung *f* device, gadget.
vorrücken *sep* 1 *vt* to move forward; *Schachfigur* to advance, to move on.
2 *vi aux sein* to move *or* go forward; (*Mil*) to advance; (*Sport, im Beruf etc*) to move up; (*Uhrzeiger*) to move on ◆ **mit dem Stuhl ~** to move one's chair forward; **in vorgerücktem Alter** in later life; **zu vorgerückter Stunde** at a late hour.
Vorruhestand *m* early retirement.
Vorruheständler(in *f*) *m* person taking early retirement.
Vorruhestandsregelung *f* early retirement scheme.
Vorrunde *f* (*Sport*) preliminary *or* qualifying round; (*von Saison*) first part (of the season).
vorsagen *sep* 1 *vt* **jdm etw ~** *Gedicht* to recite sth to sb; (*Sch*) *Antwort, Lösung* to tell sb sth.
2 *vi* (*Sch*) **jdm ~** to tell sb the answer.
Vorsaison *f* low season, early (part of the) season.
Vorsänger *m* (*Eccl*) precentor; (*in Chor*) choir leader; (*fig*) leading voice.
Vorsatz *m* **(a)** (firm) intention ◆ **mit ~** (*Jur*) with intent; **den ~ haben, etw zu tun** to (firmly) intend to do sth; **den ~ fassen, etw zu tun** to make up one's mind to do sth, to resolve to do sth; **bei seinen Vorsätzen bleiben, seinen**

Vorsätzen treu bleiben to keep to one's resolve *or* resolution; *siehe* **Weg.**
(b) (*von Buch*) *siehe* **Vorsatzblatt.**
Vorsatzblatt *nt* (*Typ*) endpaper.
vorsätzlich *adj* deliberate, intentional; *Lüge* deliberate; (*Jur*) wilful; *Mord* premeditated ◆ **jdn ~ töten** to kill sb intentionally.
Vorsatzlinse *f* (*Phot*) ancillary lens.
Vorschaltgesetz *nt* (*Pol*) interim law (*preparing the way for a subsequent law*).
Vorschau *f* preview; (*Film*) trailer; (*Wetter~*) forecast.
Vorschein *m*: **zum ~ bringen** (*lit: zeigen*) to produce; *Fleck* to show up; (*fig: deutlich machen*) to bring to light; **zum ~ kommen** (*lit: sichtbar werden*) to appear; (*fig: entdeckt werden*) to turn up, to come to light; (*Tatsachen*) to come to light, to come out.
vorschieben *sep irreg* 1 *vt* **(a)** (*davorschieben*) to push in front; *Riegel* to put across, to shoot (across); (*nach vorn schieben*) to push forward; *Kopf* to stick forward; *Unterlippe, Kinn* to stick out; *siehe* **Riegel.**
(b) (*Mil*) *Truppen* to move forward ◆ **vorgeschobener Posten** advance guard, advance party.
(c) (*fig: vorschützen*) to put forward as a pretext *or* excuse ◆ **vorgeschobene Gründe** pretexts *pl*, excuses *pl*.
(d) jdn ~ to put sb forward as a front man.
2 *vr* (*Wolken, Erdmassen*) to advance, to move forward; (*Menschen*) to push *or* press forward.
vorschießen *sep irreg* 1 *vt* **jdm Geld ~** to advance sb money.
2 *vi aux sein* to shoot forward; (*Schlange, Läufer auch*) to dart forward.
Vorschiff *nt* forecastle, fo'c's'le.
➤ **Vorschlag** *m* **(a)** suggestion, proposal; (*Rat*) recommendation, advice; (*Angebot*) offer, proposition; (*Pol: von Kandidaten*) proposal ◆ **auf ~ von** *or* +*gen* at *or* on the suggestion of; on the recommendation of; **das ist ein ~!** that's an idea!; **wäre das nicht ein ~?** how's that for an idea?; *siehe* **Güte.**
(b) (*Mus*) appogiatura.
(c) (*Typ*) sink.
(d) (*Sw: Gewinn*) profit.
➤ **vorschlagen** *vt sep irreg* **(a)** to suggest, to propose ◆ **jdn für ein Amt ~** to propose *or* nominate sb for a post; **jdm ~, daß er etw tut** to suggest that sb do(es) sth, to suggest to sb that he do(es) sth. **(b) den Takt ~** to beat time.
Vorschlaghammer *m* sledge-hammer.
⚠ **Vorschlußrunde** *f* (*Sport*) semi-final(s).
vorschnell *adj siehe* **voreilig.**
vorschreiben *vt sep irreg* **(a)** (*befehlen*) to stipulate; (*gesetzlich, durch Bestimmungen, vertraglich auch*) to lay down; (*Med*) *Dosis* to prescribe ◆ **jdm ~, wie/was ...** to dictate to sb how/what ...; **ich lasse mir nichts ~** I won't be dictated to; **vorgeschriebene Lektüre** (*Sch, Univ*) prescribed texts.
(b) (*lit*) to write out (*dat* for).
vorschreiten *vi sep irreg aux sein* to progress, to make progress; *siehe* **vorgeschritten.**
Vorschrift *f* **-, -en** (*gesetzliche etc Bestimmung*) regulation, rule; (*Anweisung*) instruction, order, direction ◆ **nach ~ des Arztes** according to doctor's orders *or* the doctor's instructions; **~en für den Verkehr** traffic regulations; **jdm ~en machen** to give sb orders, to dictate to sb; **ich lasse mir (von dir) keine ~en machen lassen** I won't be dictated to (by you), I won't take orders (from you); **sich an die ~en halten** to observe the regulations; to follow the instructions; **Arbeit nach ~** work to rule; **das ist ~** that's the regulation.
vorschrifts-: ~gemäß, ~mäßig 1 *adj* regulation *attr*, *Signal, Parken, Verhalten* correct, proper *attr*; (*Med*) *Dosis* prescribed; 2 *adv* (*laut Anordnung*) as instructed *or* directed; according to (the) regulations; (*Med*) as directed; **~gemäß** *or* **~mäßig gekleidet sein** to be in regulation dress; **~widrig** *adj, adv* contrary to (the) regulations; (*Med*) *Dosis* contrary to the prescription.
Vorschub *m*: **jdm ~ leisten** to encourage sb; **einer Sache** (*dat*) **~ leisten** to encourage *or* foster sth.
Vorschul|alter *nt* pre-school age.
Vorschule *f* nursery school; (*Vorschuljahr*) pre-school years *pl*.
Vorschul|erziehung *f* pre-school education.
vorschulisch *adj* pre-school *attr*.
⚠ **Vorschuß** *m* advance ◆ **jdm einen ~ leisten** to give sb an advance.
⚠ **Vorschuß-: ~lorbeeren** *pl* premature praise *sing*; **~zinsen** *pl* (*Fin*) penalty interest on early settlement.
vorschützen *vt sep* to plead as an excuse, to put forward as a pretext; *Krankheit auch* to feign; *Unwissenheit* to plead ◆ **er schützte vor, daß ...** he pretended that ...; *siehe* **Müdigkeit.**
vorschwärmen *vti sep* **jdm von jdm/etw ~** to go into raptures over sb/sth; **jdm ~, wie schön etw ist** to go into raptures over how beautiful sth is.
vorschwatzen *vt sep* (*inf*) **jdm etwas ~** to tell sb a lot of rubbish (*inf*); **schwatz mir doch nichts vor** don't give me that rubbish (*inf*).
vorschweben *vi sep* **jdm schwebt etw vor** sb has sth in mind.
vorschwindeln *vt sep* **jdm etwas ~** to lie to sb; **jdm ~, daß ...** to lie to sb that ...; **ich lasse mir doch von dir nichts ~** I won't have any of your lies.
vorsehen *sep irreg* 1 *vt* (*planen*) to plan; (*zeitlich auch*) to schedule; *Gerät* to design; (*einplanen*) *Kosten, Anschaffungen* to provide *or* allow for; *Zeit* to allow; *Fall* to provide *or* cater for; (*im Gesetz, Vertrag*) to provide for ◆ **etw für etw ~** (*bestimmen*) to intend sth for sth; *Geld* to earmark *or* destine sth for sth; **jdn für etw ~** (*beabsichtigen*) to have sb in mind for sth; (*bestimmen*) to designate sb for sth; **er ist für dieses Amt vorgesehen** we have him in mind for this post; **was haben wir für heute vorgesehen?** what is on the agenda today?, what have we planned for today?; **der Plan sieht vor, daß das Projekt bis September abgeschlossen ist** the project is scheduled to be finished by September.
2 *vr* (*sich in acht nehmen*) to be careful, to watch out, to take care ◆ **sich vor jdm/etw ~** to beware of sb/sth, to be wary of sb/sth; *vor Hund auch* to mind sth.
3 *vi* (*sichtbar sein*) to appear ◆ **hinter/unter etw** (*dat*) **~** to peep out from behind/under sth.
Vorsehung *f, no pl* Providence ◆ **die (göttliche) ~** (divine) Providence.
vorsetzen *sep* 1 *vt* **(a)** (*nach vorn*) to move forward; *Fuß* to put forward; *Schüler* to move (up) to the front.
(b) (*davorsetzen*) to put in front ◆ **etw vor etw** (*acc*) **~** to put sth in front of sth *or* before sth.
(c) jdm etw ~ (*geben*) to give sb sth, to put sth in front of sb; (*anbieten*) to offer sb sth; (*fig inf*) *Lügen, Geschichte, Erklärung* to serve *or* dish sth up to sb (*inf*).
(d) (*dated*) **jdn jdm/einer Sache ~** (*als Vorgesetzten*) to put sb in charge of sb/sth.
2 *vr* to (come/go and) sit in (the) front ◆ **sich in die erste Reihe ~** to (come/go and) sit in the front row.
Vorsicht *f* **-,** *no pl* care; (*bei Gefahr*) caution; (*Überlegtheit*) circumspection, prudence; (*Behutsamkeit*) guardedness, wariness ◆ **~ üben** to be careful; to exercise caution, to be cautious; to be circumspect *or* prudent; to be wary; **jdn zur ~ (er)mahnen** to advise sb to be careful/cautious/circumspect; **zur ~(er)mahnen** to advise sb to be careful/cautious/circumspect; **zur ~ raten** to advise caution; **~!** watch *or* look *or* mind out!; **„~ bei Einfahrt des Zuges"** "stand back when the train approaches the platform"; **„~ Bahnübergang/Gift/Kurve"** "Level crossing/Poison/Bend"; **„~ nicht stürzen/feuergefährlich/gefährliche Kreuzung"** "danger — steep drop/inflammable/crossroads"; **„~ zerbrechlich"** "fragile — with care"; **„~ Glas"** "glass — with care"; **„~ nicht knicken"** "do not bend"; **„~ Stufe"** "mind the step"; **mit ~** carefully; cautiously; prudently; guardedly, warily; **etw zur ~ tun** to do sth as a precaution, to be on the safe side; **was er sagt/dieser Artikel ist mit ~ zu genießen** (*hum inf*) you have to take what he says/this article with a pinch of salt (*inf*); **sie ist mit ~ zu genießen** (*hum inf*) she has to be handled with kid gloves; **~ ist besser als Nachsicht** (*Prov*) better safe than sorry; **~ ist die Mutter der Porzellankiste** (*inf*) better safe than sorry.
vorsichtig *adj* careful; (*besonnen*) cautious; (*überlegt*) prudent; *Äußerung auch* guarded, wary; (*mißtrauisch*) wary; *Schätzung* cautious, conservative.
Vorsichtigkeit *f siehe adj* carefulness; caution, cautiousness; prudence; guardedness; wariness.
Vorsichts-: v~halber *adv* as a precaution, to be on the safe side; **~maßnahme, ~maßregel** *f* precaution, precautionary measure; **~maßnahmen treffen** to take precautions *or* precautionary measures.
Vor-: ~signal *nt* (*Rail*) warning signal; **~silbe** *f* prefix; **v~singen** *sep irreg* 1 *vti* **(a)** (*vor Zuhören*) **jdm (etw) v~singen** to sing (sth) to sb; **ich singe nicht gern v~** I don't like singing to people *or* in front of people; **(b)** (*als erster singen*) to sing first; 2 *vi* (*zur Prüfung*) to have a singing test; (*esp Theat: vor Einstellung*) to audition; **v~sintflutlich** *adj* (*inf*) antiquated, prehistoric (*hum*), antediluvian.
Vorsitz *m* chairmanship; (*Amt eines Präsidenten*) presidency ◆ **unter dem ~ von** under the chairmanship of; **den ~ haben** *or* **führen (bei etw)** to be chairman (of sth); (*bei Sitzung*) to chair sth; **den ~ übernehmen** to take the chair.
vorsitzen *vi sep irreg* **einer Versammlung/Diskussion ~** to chair a meeting/discussion.
Vorsitzende(r) *mf decl as adj* chairman; (*von Firma auch*) president (*US*); (*von Verein*) president; (*von Partei, Gewerkschaft etc*) leader ◆ **der ~ Mao** Chairman Mao.
Vorsorge *f, no pl* (*Vorsichtsmaßnahme*) precaution; (*vorherplanende Fürsorge*) provision(s *pl*) *no def art* ◆ **zur ~** as a precaution; **~ tragen** to make provisions; **~ treffen** to take precautions; (*fürs Alter*) to make provisions.
vorsorgen *vi sep* to make provisions (*daß* so that) ◆ **für etw ~** to provide for sth, to make provisions for sth.
Vorsorge|untersuchung *f* (*Med*) medical check-up.
vorsorglich 1 *adj* precautionary; *Mensch* cautious.
2 *adv* as a precaution, to be on the safe side.
Vorspann *m* **-(e)s, -e (a)** (*Vordergespann*) extra team (of horses). **(b)** (*Vorlauf: von Film, Tonband*) leader; (*Film, TV: Titel und Namen*) opening credits *pl*; (*Press*) introductory *or* opening paragraph.
vorspannen *vt sep* *Pferde* to harness; (*Elec*) to bias ◆ **jdn ~** (*fig*) to enlist sb's help, to rope sb in (*inf*).
Vorspannung *f* (*Elec*) bias (voltage).
Vorspeise *f* hors d'œuvre, starter.
vorspiegeln *vt sep* to feign, to sham; *Krankheit, Bedürftigkeit auch* to plead ◆ **jdm ~(, daß ...)** to pretend to sb (that ...).
Vorspiegelung *f* pretence ◆ **unter ~ von etw** under the pretence of sth; **das ist nur (eine) ~ falscher Tatsachen** (*hum*) it's all sham; *siehe* **Tatsache.**
Vorspiel *nt* (*Einleitung*) prelude; (*Ouvertüre*) overture; (*Theat*) prologue; (*Sport*) preliminary match/game; (*bei Geschlechtsverkehr*) foreplay; (*von Musiker*) performance; (*bei Prüfung*) practical (exam); (*bei Einstellung*) audition ◆ **das ist erst das ~** (*hum*) that is just for starters (*inf*).
vorspielen *sep* 1 *vt* **(a) jdm etw ~** (*Mus*) to play sth to *or* for sb; (*Theat*) to act sth to *or* for sb; (*fig*) to act out a sham of sth in front of sb; **jdm eine Szene ~** to play a scene to *or* for sb; **jdm eine Komödie ~** (*fig*) to play *or* act out a farce in front of sb; **jdm ~, daß ...** to pretend to sb that ...; **spiel mir**

doch nichts vor don't try and put on an act, don't try and pretend to me. **(b)** (*zuerst spielen*) to play first.
[2] *vi* (*vor Zuhörern*) to play; (*Mus, Theat*) (*zur Prüfung*) to do one's practical (exam); (*bei Einstellung*) to audition ◆ **jdm ~** (*Mus*) to play for sb; (*Theat*) to act (a role) for *or* in front of sb; **jdn ~ lassen** (*bei Einstellung*) to audition sb.

Vorsprache *f* (*form: Besuch*) visit (*bei, auf* +*dat* to).

vorsprechen *sep irreg* [1] *vt* to say first; (*vortragen*) to recite ◆ **jdm etw ~** to pronounce sth for sb, to say sth for sb; **wiederholt, was ich euch vorspreche** repeat after me.
[2] *vi* **(a)** (*form: jdn aufsuchen*) to call (*bei jdm* on sb) ◆ **bei** *or* **auf einem Amt ~** to call at an office. **(b)** (*Theat*) to audition. **jdn ~ lassen** to audition sb.

vorspringen *vi sep irreg aux sein* to jump *or* leap out; (*vorwärts*) to jump *or* leap forward; (*herausragen*) to jut out, to project; (*Nase*) to be prominent; (*Kinn*) to be prominent, to protrude ◆ **vor etw** (*dat*) ~ to jump *or* leap (out) in front of sth.

vorspringend *adj* projecting; *Nase* prominent; *Kinn, Backenknochen* prominent, protruding.

Vorsprung *m* **(a)** (*Archit*) projection; (*Fels~*) ledge; (*von Küste*) promontory. **(b)** (*Sport, fig: Abstand*) lead (*vor* +*dat* over); (*Vorgabe*) start ◆ **jdm 2 Meter/10 Minuten ~ geben** to give sb a 2-metre/a 10-minute start, to give sb 2 metres'/10 minutes' start; **einen ~ vor jdm haben** to be ahead of sb; (*Sport auch*) to be leading sb, to be in the lead; **einen ~ vor jdm gewinnen** to gain a lead over sb, to get ahead of sb.

Vor-: ~stadt *f* suburb; **v~städtisch** *adj* suburban.

Vorstand *m* **(a)** (*leitendes Gremium*) board; (*von Firma*) board (of directors); (*von Verein*) committee; (*von Partei*) executive; (*von Akademie*) board (of governors). **(b)** (*Leiter*) chairman, managing director. **(c)** (*Aus*) *siehe* **Vorsteher(in)**.

Vorstands-: ~etage *f* boardroom; **~mitglied** *nt siehe* **Vorstand (a)** member of the board; committee member; member of the executive; member of the board; **~sitzung** *f* (*von Firma*) board meeting; (*von Partei*) executive meeting; **~vorsitzende(r)** *mf decl as adj* chairman *or* chair *or* chairperson of the board of directors; **~wahl** *f* (*in Firma*) elections *pl* to the board; (*in Partei*) elections *pl* to the executive.

vorstecken *vt sep* (*anstecken*) to put on; *Brosche auch* to pin on.

Vorstecknadel *f* (*Brosche*) brooch; (*Krawattennadel*) tie-pin.

vorstehen *vi sep irreg aux haben or sein* **(a)** (*hervorragen*) to project, to jut out; *Zähne* to stick out, to protrude; *Backenknochen, Kinn* to be prominent, to protrude; *Nase* to be prominent ◆ **~de Zähne** protruding teeth, buck-teeth.
(b) **einer Sache ~** *dem Haushalt* to preside over sth; *einer Firma, einer Partei* to be the chairman of sth; *einer Schule* to be the head(master/mistress) (*Brit*) *or* principal (*US*) of sth; *einem Geschäft* to manage sth; *einer Abteilung* to be in charge of sth; *einem Amt* to hold sth.
(c) (*form*) **wie im ~den** as above; **die ~den Erläuterungen** the above explanations.
(d) (*Hunt: Hund*) to set, to point.

Vorsteher(in *f*) *m* **-s, -** (*Kloster~*) abbot/abbess; (*Büro~*) manager; (*Gefängnis~*) governor; (*Gemeinde~*) chairman of parish council; (*dated Sch*) head(master/mistress) (*Brit*), principal (*US*); (*Bahnhofs~*) station-master.

Vorsteherdrüse *f* prostate (gland).

Vorstehhund *m* pointer; (*langhaariger*) setter.

vorstellbar *adj* conceivable, imaginable ◆ **das ist nicht ~** that is inconceivable *or* unimaginable.

vorstellen *sep* [1] *vt* **(a)** (*nach vorn*) *Tisch, Stuhl, Auto* to move forward; *Bein* to put out; *Uhr* to put forward *or* on (*um* by).
(b) (*inf: davorstellen*) **etw (vor etw** *acc*) ~ to put sth in front of sth; *Auto auch* to park sth in front of sth.
(c) (*darstellen*) to represent; (*bedeuten*) to mean, to signify ◆ **was soll das ~?** (*inf*) what is that supposed to be?; **etwas ~** (*fig*) (*gut aussehen*) to look good; (*Ansehen haben*) to count for something.
(d) (*bekannt machen*) **jdn jdm ~** to introduce sb to sb.
(e) (*bekanntmachen, vorführen*) to present; *Folgen, Gefahren* to point out (*jdm* to sb) ◆ **jdm etw ~** to show sb sth.
[2] *vr* **(a)** **sich** (*dat*) **etw ~** to imagine sth; **stell dir mal vor** just imagine; **das kann ich mir gut ~** I can imagine that well; **das muß man sich** (*dat*) **mal (bildlich** *or* **plastisch) ~** just imagine *or* picture it!; **sich** (*dat*) **etw unter etw** (*dat*) ~ *Begriff, Wort* to understand sth by sth; **darunter kann ich mir nichts ~** it doesn't mean anything to me; **das Kleid ist genau, was ich mir vorgestellt hatte** the dress is just what I had in mind; **was haben Sie sich (als Gehalt) vorgestellt?** what (salary) did you have in mind?; **ich kann sie mir gut als Lehrerin ~** I can just imagine *or* see her as a teacher; **stell dir das nicht so einfach vor** don't think it's so easy.
(b) (*sich nach vorn stellen*) to move *or* go forward; (*in Schlange*) to stand at the front.
(c) (*sich bekannt machen*) to introduce oneself (*jdm* to sb); (*bei Bewerbung*) to come/go for an interview; (*Antrittsbesuch machen*) to present oneself (*dat, bei* to).

vorstellig *adj* **bei jdm ~ werden** to go to sb; (*wegen Beschwerde*) to complain to sb, to lodge a complaint with sb.

Vorstellung *f* **(a)** (*Gedanke*) idea; (*bildlich*) picture; (*Einbildung*) illusion; (*~skraft*) imagination ◆ **in meiner ~ sah das größer aus** I imagined it bigger; **in meiner ~ ist Gott kein alter Mann** I don't picture God as an old man; **du hast falsche ~en** you are wrong (in your ideas); **es übertrifft alle ~en** it's incredible *or* unbelievable; **das entspricht ganz meiner ~** that is just how I imagined *or* saw it; **sich** (*dat*) **eine ~ von etw machen** to form an idea *or* (*Bild*) picture of sth; **du machst dir keine ~, wie schwierig das ist** you have no idea how difficult that is.
(b) (*Theat etc*) performance; (*Film auch*) showing.
(c) (*das Bekanntmachen*) (*zwischen Leuten*) introduction; (*bei Hofe*) presentation (*bei* at); (*Vorführung: von Geräten, neuem Artikel etc*) presentation; (*bei Bewerbung, Antrittsbesuch*) interview (*bei* with).
(d) (*Einwand*) objection, protest.

Vorstellungs-: ~gespräch *nt* (job) interview; **~kraft** *f* imagination; **~vermögen** *nt* powers of imagination *pl*; **~welt** *f* imagination.

Vorstopper *m* **-s, -** (*Ftbl*) centre-half.

Vorstoß *m* **(a)** (*Vordringen*) venture; (*Mil*) advance, push; (*fig: Versuch*) attempt. **(b)** (*Tech: an Rädern*) wheel rim; (*Sew*) edging; (*Litze*) braiding.

vorstoßen *sep irreg* [1] *vt* to push forward.
[2] *vi aux sein* to venture; (*Sport*) to attack; (*Mil*) to advance ◆ **ins All ~** (*Rakete, Mensch*) to venture into space.

Vorstrafe *f* previous conviction.

Vorstrafenregister *nt* criminal *or* police record; (*Kartei*) criminal *or* police records *pl*.

vorstrecken *vt sep* to stretch forward; *Arme* to stretch out; *Hand* to stretch *or* put out; *Krallen* to put out; (*fig*) *Geld* to advance (*jdm* sb).

Vorstufe *f* preliminary stage; (*von Entwicklung*) early stage.

vorstürmen *vi sep aux sein* to charge *or* rush forward (*hinter* +*dat* from behind).

Vortag *m* day before, eve ◆ **am ~ der Konferenz** (on) the day before the conference, on the eve of the conference.

Vortagesschluß *m* (*St Ex*) close of trading on the previous day.

vortanzen *sep* [1] *vt* **jdm einen Tanz/die Schritte ~** to dance a dance/the steps for sb; (*zur Demonstration*) to demonstrate a dance/the steps for sb.
[2] *vi* (*zur Demonstration*) to demonstrate a dance/step *etc* (*jdm* to sb); (*als Prüfung*) to dance (*jdm* in front of sb).

Vortänzer *m* leading dancer; (*Anführer eines Tanzes*) leader of the dance.

vortäuschen *vt sep Krankheit, Armut* to feign; *Schlag, Orgasmus* to fake ◆ **sie hat mir eine glückliche Ehe vorgetäuscht** she pretended to me that her marriage was happy.

Vortäuschung *f* pretence, fake ◆ **die ~ einer Krankheit/eines Schlags** feigning an illness/faking a blow; **~ von Tatsachen** (*Jur*) misrepresentation of the facts; **unter ~ falscher Tatsachen** under false pretences.

Vorteil *m* **-s, -e** advantage (*auch Sport*) ◆ **die Vor- und Nachteile** the pros and cons; **auf den eigenen ~ bedacht sein** to have an eye to one's own interests; **jdm gegenüber im ~ sein** to have an advantage over sb; **sich zu seinem ~ ändern** to change for the better; **ein ~ sein** to be an advantage, to be advantageous; **von ~ sein** to be advantageous; **das kann für dich nur von ~ sein** it can only be to your advantage; **ich habe dabei an deinen ~ gedacht** I was thinking of your interests; **im ~ sein** to have the advantage (*jdm gegenüber* over sb); **~e aus etw ziehen** to benefit from sth, to gain advantage from sth.

vorteilhaft *adj* advantageous; *Kleider* flattering; *Geschäft* lucrative, profitable ◆ **~ aussehen** to look one's best; **etw ~ verkaufen** (*finanziell*) to sell sth for a profit; **ein ~er Kauf** a good buy, a bargain; **der helle Teppich wirkt ~** the light carpet looks good.

Vortrag *m* **-(e)s, Vorträge (a)** (*Vorlesung*) lecture; (*Bericht, Beschreibung*) talk ◆ **einen ~ halten** to give a lecture/talk; **halt keine Vorträge** (*inf*) don't give a whole lecture.
(b) (*Darbietung*) performance; (*eines Gedichtes*) reading, recitation; (*Mus: Solo~*) recital.
(c) (*Art des Vortragens*) performance.
(d) (*Fin*) balance carried forward.

vortragen *vt sep irreg* **(a)** (*lit*) to carry forward.
(b) (*berichten*) to report; (*förmlich mitteilen*) *Fall, Angelegenheit* to present; *Forderungen* to present, to convey; *Beschwerde* to lodge; *Meinung* to express, to convey; *Wunsch* to express; (*einen Vortrag halten über*) to give a lecture/talk on.
(c) (*vorsprechen*) *Gedicht* to recite; *Rede* to give; (*Mus*) to perform, to play; *Lied* to sing, to perform.
(d) (*Fin*) to carry forward.

Vortragende(r) *mf decl as adj* lecturer; (*von Rede, Bericht*) speaker; (*von Musikstück, Lied etc*) performer.

Vortrags-: ~abend *m* lecture evening; (*mit Gedichten*) poetry evening; (*mit Musik*) recital; **~folge** *f* series of lectures; (*einzelne Sendung*) lecture in a series; **~kunst** *f* skill as a performer; (*von Redner*) skill as a speaker; **~reihe** *f* series of lectures.

vortrefflich *adj* excellent, splendid, superb.

Vortrefflichkeit *f* excellence.

vortreten *vi sep irreg aux sein* **(a)** (*lit*) to step forward, to come forward. **(b)** (*hervorragen*) to project, to jut out; (*Augen*) to protrude ◆ **~de Backenknochen** prominent cheek-bones.

Vortritt *m, no pl* precedence, priority; (*Sw: Vorfahrt*) right of way ◆ **in etw** (*dat*) **den ~ haben** (*fig*) to have precedence in sth (*vor* +*dat* over); **jdm den ~ lassen** (*lit*) to let sb go first; (*fig auch*) to let sb go ahead.

vortrocknen *vt* to dry partially.

Vortrupp *m* advance guard, advance party.

vortun *vt sep irreg* (*inf*) *Schürze, Riegel, Kette etc* to put on.

vorturnen *sep* [1] *vt* **jdm eine Übung ~** (*vormachen*) to demonstrate an exercise to sb; (*öffentlich zeigen*) to perform an exercise in front of sb.
[2] *vi* **jdm ~** (*vormachen*) to demonstrate to sb; (*öffentlich*) to perform in front

➤ SPRACHE AKTIV: **vorstellen: 2a** → 33.2, 34.3, 35.1 **Vorstellung: a** → 28.2, 53.1, 53.3 **Vorstellungsgespräch** → 46.4, 46.6 **Vorteil** → 40.2, 53.4

of sb.

Vorturner *m* demonstrator (of gymnastic exercises); (*fig sl*) front man.

vorüber *adv* ~ **sein** (*räumlich, Jugend*) to be past; (*zeitlich auch, Gewitter, Winter, Kummer*) to be over; (*Schmerz*) to have gone.

vorüber- *pref siehe auch* **vorbei-; ~gehen** *vi sep irreg aux sein* **(a)** (*räumlich*) (*an etw* (*dat*) sth) to go past, to pass (by); **an jdm/etw ~gehen** (*fig: ignorieren*) to ignore sb/sth; **(b)** (*zeitlich*) to pass; (*Gewitter*) to blow over; **eine Gelegenheit ~gehen lassen** to let an opportunity slip; **(c) an jdm ~gehen** (*sich nicht bemerkbar machen*) to pass sb by; **an jdm nicht ~gehen** (*Erlebnis etc*) to leave its/their mark on sb; **~gehend** *adj* (*flüchtig*) momentary, passing *attr*; *Krankheit* short; (*zeitweilig*) temporary; **sich ~gehend aufhalten** to stay for a short time.

Vorübung *f* preliminary exercise.

Voruntersuchung *f* preliminary examination; (*Jur*) preliminary *or* initial investigation.

Vor|urteil *nt* prejudice (*gegenüber* against) ◆ **das ist ein ~** it's prejudice; **~e haben** *or* **hegen, in ~en befangen sein** to be prejudiced.

vorurteilsfrei, vorurteilslos [1] *adj* unprejudiced; *Entscheidung, Verhalten auch* unbiased.

[2] *adv* without prejudice; without bias.

Vorurteilslosigkeit *f* freedom from prejudice.

Vor-: ~väter *pl* forefathers, ancestors, forebears *all pl*; **~vergangenheit** *f* (*Gram*) pluperfect; **~verhandlung** *f* preliminary negotiations *or* talks *pl*; (*Jur*) preliminary hearing; **~verkauf** *m* (*Theat, Sport*) advance booking; **sich** (*dat*) **Karten im ~verkauf besorgen** to buy tickets in advance; **~verkaufskasse, ~verkaufsstelle** *f* advance booking office.

vorverlegen* *vt sep* **(a)** *Termin* to bring forward. **(b)** (*Mil*) *Front, Gefechtslinie* to push forward ◆ **das Feuer ~** to increase the range.

Vor-: ~verständnis *nt* preconception; **~verstärker** *m* pre-amplifier; **~vertrag** *m* preliminary contract/treaty; **~verurteilung** *f* prejudgement; **v~vorgestern** *adv* (*inf*) three days ago; **v~vorig** *adj* (*inf*) **v~vorige Woche/v~voriges Jahr** the week/year before last; **v~vorletzte(r, s)** *adj* last but two.

vorwagen *vr sep* (*lit*) to venture forward; (*fig auch*) to venture.

Vorwahl *f* **(a)** preliminary election; (*US*) primary. **(b)** (*Telec*) dialling *or* area (*US*) code.

vorwählen *vt sep* (*Telec*) to dial first.

Vorwahlnummer, Vorwählnummer *f* dialling *or* area (*US*) code.

vorwalten *vi sep* to prevail.

Vorwand *m* **-(e)s, Vorwände** pretext, excuse ◆ **unter dem ~, daß ...** under the pretext that ...

vorwärmen *vt sep* to pre-heat; *Teller* to heat.

Vorwarnung *f* (prior *or* advance) warning; (*Mil: vor Angriff*) early warning.

vorwärts *adv* forwards, forward ◆ **~!** (*inf*) let's go (*inf*); (*Mil*) forward march!; **weiter ~** further ahead *or* on; **~ und rückwärts** backwards and forwards; **etw ~ und rückwärts kennen** (*fig inf*) to know sth backwards, to know sth inside out; **wir kamen nur langsam ~** we made slow progress; **Rolle/Salto ~** forward roll/somersault.

Vorwärts-: ~bewegung *f* forward movement; ⚠**v~bringen** *vt sep irreg* (*fig*) to advance; **jdn v~bringen** to help sb to get on; **~gang** *m* forward gear; ⚠**v~gehen** *sep irreg aux sein* (*fig*) [1] *vi* to progress, to come on; (*Gesundheit*) to improve; [2] *vi impers* **es geht wieder v~** things are looking up; **mit etw geht es v~** sth is progressing *or* going well; ⚠**v~kommen** *vi sep irreg aux sein* (*fig*) to make progress, to get on (*in, mit* with); (*beruflich, gesellschaftlich*) to get on; **im Leben/Beruf v~kommen** to get on in life/one's job; **~verteidigung** *f* (*Mil*) forward defence.

Vorwäsche *f*, **Vorwaschgang** *m* prewash.

vorwaschen *vt sep irreg* to prewash.

vorweg *adv* (*voraus, an der Spitze*) at the front; (*vorher*) before(hand); (*als erstes, von vornherein*) at the outset.

Vorwegleistung *f* (*Sw: Vorauszahlung*) advance (payment).

Vorwegnahme *f* **-, -n** anticipation.

vorwegnehmen *vt sep irreg* to anticipate; **um das Wichtigste v~zunehmen** to come to the most important point first.

Vorweihnachtszeit *f* pre-Christmas period.

vorweisen *vt sep irreg* to show, to produce; *Zeugnisse* to produce ◆ **etw ~ können** (*fig*) to have *or* possess sth.

vorwerfen *vt sep irreg* **(a)** (*fig*) **jdm etw/Unpünktlichkeit ~** (*anklagen*) to reproach sb for sth/for being unpunctual; (*beschuldigen*) to accuse sb of sth/of being unpunctual; **jdm ~, daß er etw getan hat** to reproach sb for having done sth; **jdm ~, daß er etw nicht getan hat** to accuse sb of not having done sth; **das wirft er mir heute noch vor** he still holds it against me; **ich habe mir nichts vorzuwerfen** my conscience is clear.

(b) (*lit*) **Tieren/Gefangenen etw ~** to throw sth down for the animals/prisoners.

Vorwerk *nt* (*von Gut*) outlying estate; (*von Burg*) outwork.

vorwiegend [1] *adj attr* predominant.

[2] *adv* predominantly, mainly, chiefly.

Vorwissen *nt* previous knowledge; (*Vorherwissen*) foreknowledge ◆ **ohne mein ~** without my previous knowledge.

Vorwitz *m, no pl* (*Keckheit*) cheek(iness); (*Vorlautheit*) forwardness, pertness; (*dial: Neugier*) inquisitiveness, curiosity.

vorwitzig *adj* (*keck*) cheeky; (*vorlaut*) forward, pert; (*dial: neugierig*) inquisitive, curious.

⚠**Vorwochenschluß** *m* (*St Ex*) close of trading the previous week.

Vorwort *nt* **-(e)s, -e (a)** foreword; (*esp von Autor*) preface. **(b)** *pl* **-wörter** (*Aus: Präposition*) preposition.

Vorwurf *m* **-(e)s, Vorwürfe (a)** reproach; (*Beschuldigung*) accusation ◆ **man machte ihm den ~ der Bestechlichkeit** he was accused of being open to bribery; **jdm/sich große Vorwürfe machen, daß ...** to reproach sb/oneself for ...; **ich habe mir keine Vorwürfe zu machen** my conscience is clear; **jdm etw zum ~ machen** to reproach sb with sth.

(b) (*Vorlage*) subject.

vorwurfsvoll *adj* reproachful.

vorzählen *vt sep* **jdm etw ~** to count sth out to sb; (*fig: auflisten*) to enumerate sth (to sb).

vorzaubern *vt sep* **jdm Kunststücke ~** to perform conjuring tricks for sb; **jdm etw ~** (*fig*) to conjure sth up for sb.

Vorzeichen *nt* (*Omen*) omen, sign; (*Med*) early symptom; (*Math*) sign; (*Mus*) (*Kreuz/b*) sharp/flat (sign); (*vor einzelner Note*) accidental; (*von Tonart*) key-signature ◆ **positives/negatives ~** (*Math*) plus/minus (sign); **mit umgekehrtem ~** (*fig*) the other way round; **unter dem gleichen ~** (*fig*) under the same circumstances; **dadurch haben die Verhandlungen ein negatives ~ erhalten** that put the negotiations under a cloud.

vorzeichnen *vt sep* *Linien etc* to sketch *or* draw (out) ◆ **jdm etw ~** (*zum Nachmalen*) to sketch *or* draw sth out for sb; (*fig*) to map *or* mark sth out for sb.

Vorzeige- *in cpds* token; **~frau** *f* token woman.

vorzeigen *vt sep* to show, to produce; *Zeugnisse* to produce ◆ **jdm die Hände ~** to show sb one's hands.

Vorzeige-: ~objekt, ~stück *nt* showpiece.

Vorzeit *f* prehistoric times *pl* ◆ **in der ~** in prehistoric times; (*vor langem*) in the dim and distant past; *siehe* **grau**.

vorzeiten *adv* (*liter*) in days gone by, in olden times.

vorzeitig *adj* early; *Geburt, Altern etc* premature.

Vorzeitigkeit *f* (*Gram*) anteriority.

vorzeitlich *adj* prehistoric; (*fig*) archaic.

Vorzelt *nt* awning.

vorziehen *vt sep irreg* **(a)** (*hervorziehen*) to pull out; (*nach vorne ziehen*) *Stuhl etc* to pull up; *Truppen* to move up; (*zuziehen*) *Vorhänge* to draw, to close ◆ **etw hinter/unter etw** (*dat*) **~** to pull sth out from behind/under sth.

(b) (*fig*) (*lieber mögen*) to prefer; (*bevorzugen*) *jdn* to favour ◆ **etw einer anderen Sache ~** to prefer sth to sth else; **es ~, etw zu tun** to prefer to do sth; (*allgemein gesehen*) to prefer doing sth.

(c) (*zuerst behandeln, abfertigen*) to give priority to.

(d) *Wahlen* to bring forward ◆ **vorgezogener Ruhestand** early retirement.

Vorzimmer *nt* anteroom; (*Büro*) outer office; (*Aus: Diele*) hall.

Vorzimmerdame *f* receptionist.

Vorzimmerwand *f* (*Aus*) hall stand.

Vorzug[1] *m* **-(e)s, Vorzüge (a)** preference; (*Vorteil*) advantage; (*gute Eigenschaft*) merit, asset ◆ **einer Sache** (*dat*) **den ~ geben** (*form*) to prefer sth, to give sth preference; (*Vorrang geben*) to give sth precedence; **den ~ vor etw** (*dat*) **haben** to be preferable to sth; **den ~ haben, daß ...** to have the advantage that ...

(b) (*Aus Sch*) distinction.

Vorzug[2] *m* (*Rail*) train in front; (*früher fahrend*) train before; (*Entlastungszug*) relief train.

vorzüglich [(*esp Aus*) 'fo:ɐtsy:klɪç] [1] *adj* excellent, superb; *Qualität, Arbeit auch* exquisite; *siehe* **Hochachtung**.

[2] *adv* excellently, superbly; (*vornehmlich*) especially, particularly ◆ **der Wein schmeckt ~** the wine tastes excellent *or* superb.

Vorzüglichkeit *f, no pl* excellence.

Vorzugsaktien *pl* (*St Ex*) preference shares *pl*.

Vorzugbehandlung *f* preferential treatment *no indef art*.

Vorzugsmilch *f milk with high fat content,* ≃ gold-top milk (*Brit*).

Vorzugspreis *m* special discount price.

Vorzugsschüler *m* (*Aus*) star pupil.

vorzugsweise *adv* preferably, by preference; (*hauptsächlich*) mainly, chiefly; **etw v~weise trinken** to prefer to drink *or* drinking sth.

Vorzündung *f* (*Aut*) pre-ignition.

Voten ['vo:t(ə)n], **Vota** (*geh*) *pl of* **Votum**.

votieren* [vo'ti:rən] *vi* (*geh*) to vote.

Votiv- [vo'ti:f]: **~bild** *nt* votive picture; **~kapelle** *f* votive chapel; **~tafel** *f* votive tablet.

Votum ['vo:tʊm] *nt* **-s, Voten** *or* **Vota** (*geh*) vote.

Voyeur(in *f*) [voa'jø:ɐ, -'jø:rɪn] *m* voyeur.

VP [fau'pe:] *f* - *abbr of* **Volkspolizei**.

VPS [faupe:'|ɛs] *abbr of* **Videoprogrammsystem** VPS.

V-Pullover ['fau-] *m* V-neck pullover.

v.R.w. *abbr of* **von Rechts wegen**.

v.T. *abbr of* **vom Tausend**.

vulgär [vʊl'gɛ:ɐ] *adj* vulgar.

Vulgär|ausdruck [vʊl'gɛ:ɐ-] *m* vulgar expression, vulgarity.

Vulgarität [vʊlgari'tɛ:t] *f* vulgarity.

Vulgärlatein [vʊl'gɛ:ɐ-] *nt* vulgar Latin.

Vulkan [vʊl'ka:n] *m* **-(e)s, -e** volcano ◆ **auf einem ~ leben** (*fig*) to be living on the edge of a volcano; *siehe* **Tanz**.

Vulkanausbruch *m* volcanic eruption.

Vulkanfiber *f* vulcanized fibre.

Vulkanisation [vʊlkaniza'tsio:n] *f* (*Tech*) vulcanization.
vulkanisch [vʊl'ka:nɪʃ] *adj* volcanic.
Vulkanisier|anstalt [vʊlkani'zi:r-] *f* vulcanization plant.
vulkanisieren* [vʊlkani'zi:rən] *vt* to vulcanize.
Vulkanologe *m*, **Vulkanologin** *f* volcanologist.
Vulkanologie *f* volcanology.
v.u.Z. *abbr of* **vor unserer Zeitrechnung** BC.
V-Waffen ['fau-] *pl siehe* **Vergeltungswaffen.**

W, w [ve:] *nt* **-, -** W, w.
W *abbr of* **Westen.**
WAA [ve:|a:'|a:] *f abbr of* **Wiederaufbereitungsanlage.**
Waadt *f* Vaud.
Waage *f* **-, -n (a)** (*Gerät*) scales *pl*; (*Feder~, Apotheker~*) balance; (*für Lastwagen, Autos*) weighbridge ◆ **eine ~** a pair of scales; **sich** (*dat*) **die ~ halten** (*fig*) to balance one another *or* each other; **einer Sache** (*dat*) **die ~ halten** to balance sth (out); *siehe* **Zünglein.**
(b) (*Astron, Astrol*) **die ~** Libra; **er ist (eine) ~** he's (a) Libra.
(c) (*Sport: Stand~/Knie~*) horizontal single leg/knee stand.
Waagebalken *m* (balance *or* scale) beam.
Waag(e)-: w~recht *adj* horizontal, level; *Linie, Ebene* horizontal; **~rechte** *f* horizontal; **etw in die ~rechte bringen** to make sth horizontal *or* level; **in der ~rechten transportieren** to transport sth horizontally.
Waagschale *f* (scale) pan, scale ◆ **(schwer) in die ~ fallen** (*fig*) to carry weight; **jedes Wort auf die ~ legen** to weigh every word (carefully); **jds Worte/etw auf die ~ legen** to take sb's words/sth literally; **seinen Einfluß/seine Autorität/sein ganzes Gewicht in die ~ werfen** (*fig*) to bring one's influence/one's authority/one's full weight to bear.
wabb(e)lig *adj Pudding, Gelee* wobbly; *Mensch* flabby.
wabbeln *vi* to wobble.
Wabe *f* **-, -n** honeycomb.
Waben-: w~förmig *adj* honeycombed; **~honig** *m* comb honey.
wabern *vi* (*geh*) to undulate; (*Nebel, Gerüche*) to drift, to waft; (*Gerücht*) to float; (*obs, dial: flackern*) to flicker.
wach *adj* awake *pred*; (*fig: aufgeweckt*) alert, wide-awake; *Nacht* sleepless, wakeful ◆ **in ~em Zustand** in the waking state; **sich ~ halten** to keep *or* stay awake; **~ werden** to wake up; **~ liegen** to lie awake; **jdn ~ schütteln/küssen** to shake sb awake/to wake sb with a kiss.
Wach-: ~ablösung *f* changing of the guard; (*fig: Regierungswechsel*) change of government; (*Mensch*) relief guard; **~bataillon** *nt* guard battalion, guards *pl*; **~boot** *nt* patrol boat; **~dienst** *m* look-out, guard (duty); (*Mil*) guard (duty); (*Naut*) watch; **~dienst haben/machen** to be on guard (duty); (*Naut*) to have the watch.
Wache *f* **-, -n (a)** *no pl* (*Wachdienst*) guard (duty) ◆ **auf ~** on guard (duty); **(bei jdm) ~ halten** to keep guard *or* watch (over sb); (*Kranken~*) to keep watch (at sb's bedside), to watch over sb; (*Toten~*) to watch over sb; **~ stehen** *or* **schieben** (*inf*) to be on guard (duty); (*Dieb, Schüler etc*) to keep a look-out.
(b) (*Mil*) (*Wachposten*) guard, sentry; (*Gebäude*) guard-house; (*Raum*) guard-room.
(c) (*Naut: Personen, Dauer*) watch ◆ **~ haben** to be on watch.
(d) (*Polizei~*) (police) station.
wachen *vi* **(a)** (*wach sein*) to be awake; (*nicht schlafen können*) to lie awake. **(b)** (*Wache halten*) to keep watch ◆ **bei jdm ~** to sit up with sb, to keep watch by sb's bedside; **das W~ am Krankenbett** sitting up with a/the patient *or* at a/the sickbed; **über etw** (*acc*) **~** to (keep) watch over sth; *über Verkehr* to supervise sth; **der Polizist wachte darüber, daß niemand ...** the policeman watched that no-one ...
Wach-: w~habend *adj attr* duty; **~habende(r)** *m decl as adj* (*Offizier*) duty officer; (*Naut*) watch; ⚠**w~halten** *vt sep irreg* (*fig*) *Interesse etc* to keep alive *or* up; **~heit** *f* (*fig*) alertness; **(die) ~heit des Geistes** alertness of mind, an alert *or* wide-awake mind; **~hund** *m* (*lit, fig*) watchdog; (*lit auch*) guard-dog; **~leute** *pl of* **~mann**; **~lokal** *nt* guard-room; **~macher** *m* (*Med inf*) stimulant; **~mann** *m, pl* **-leute** watchman; (*Aus*) policeman; **~mannschaft** *f* men *or* squad on guard; (*Naut*) watch; **~offizier** *m* (*Naut*) officer of the watch.
Wacholder *m* **-s, - (a)** (*Bot*) juniper (tree). **(b)** *siehe* **Wacholderschnaps.**
Wacholder-: ~beere *f* juniper berry; **~branntwein** (*form*), **~schnaps** *m* spirit made from juniper berries, ≃ gin; **~strauch** *m siehe* **Wacholder (a).**
Wach-: ~posten *m siehe* **Wachtposten**; **w~rufen** *vt sep irreg* (*fig*) *Erinnerung etc* to call to mind, to evoke; **w~rütteln** *vt sep* (*fig*) to shake up, to (a)rouse; *Gewissen* to stir, to (a)rouse; **jdn aus seiner Apathie w~rütteln** to shake sb out of his apathy.
Wachs [vaks] *nt* **-es, -e** wax ◆ **weich wie ~** as soft as butter; **meine Knie wurden weich wie ~** my knees turned to jelly; **~ in jds Händen sein** (*fig*) to be putty in sb's hands.
wachsam *adj* watchful, vigilant; (*vorsichtig*) on one's guard ◆ **ein ~es Auge auf jdn/etw haben** to keep a watchful *or* sharp eye on sb/sth.
Wachsamkeit *f, no pl* watchfulness, vigilance; (*Vorsichtigkeit*) guardedness.
Wachs- ['vaks-]: **~bild** *nt* waxen image; **w~bleich** *adj* waxen; **~bohne** *f* wax bean; **~buntstift** *m* wax crayon.
Wachschiff *nt* patrol ship.
wachseln ['vaksln] *vt* (*Aus*) *siehe* **wachsen**[2].
wachsen[1] ['vaksn] *pret* **wuchs** [vu:ks], *ptp* **gewachsen** *vi aux sein* to grow; (*Spannung, Begeisterung auch*) to mount ◆ **in die Breite/Länge ~** to broaden (out)/to lengthen, to get *or* grow broader/longer; **in die Höhe ~** to grow taller; (*Kind*) to shoot up (*inf*); **sich** (*dat*) **einen Bart/die Haare ~ lassen** to grow a beard/to let one's hair grow *or* to grow one's hair; **Sauerkraut kann ich mit ~der Begeisterung essen** I can eat sauerkraut till the cows come home (*hum inf*); **gut gewachsen** *Baum* well-grown; *Mensch* with *or* having a good figure; **wie gewachsen** with fat and gristle not removed; **er wächst mit** *or* **an seiner Verantwortung** (*fig*) he grows with his responsibility.
wachsen[2] ['vaksn] *vt* to wax.
wächsern ['vɛksɐn] *adj* (*lit, fig*) waxen.
Wachs- ['vaks-]: **~farbe** *f* **(a)** (*Farbstift*) wax crayon; **mit ~farbe(n) gemalt** drawn with *or* in wax crayons; **(b)** (*Farbstoff*) wax dye; **~farbstift** *m* wax crayon; **~figur** *f* wax figure; **~figurenkabinett** *nt* waxworks *pl*; **~kerze** *f* wax candle; **~licht** *nt* night light; **~malerei** *f* **(a)** *no pl* (*Technik*) encaustic painting; **(b)** (*Bild*) encaustic; **~malstift** *m*, **~malkreide** *f* wax crayon; **~maske** *f* wax mask; **~matrize** *f* stencil; **~papier** *nt* waxed paper; **~stift** *m* wax crayon; **~stock** *m* wax taper.
Wachstube ['vaxʃtu:bə] *f* guard-room; (*von Polizei*) duty room.
Wachstuch ['vaks-] *nt* oilcloth.
Wachstum ['vakstu:m] *nt, no pl* growth ◆ **im ~ zurückgeblieben** stunted; **eigenes ~ (des Winzers)** from *or* grown in our own vineyards.
Wachstums-: ~aktie *f* growth stock; **~branche** *f* growth industry; **~fonds** *m* growth fund; **w~hemmend** *adj* growth-inhibiting; **~hemmung** *f* inhibition of growth *no pl*; **~hormon** *nt* growth hormone; **~politik** *f* growth policy; **~rate** *f* (*Biol, Econ*) growth rate; **~schmerzen** *pl* growing pains *pl*; **~störung** *f* disturbance of growth.
Wachs- ['vaks-]: **w~weich** *adj* (as) soft as butter; *Ausrede* lame; **w~weich werden** (*Mensch*) to melt; (*Knie*) to turn to jelly; **~zieher(in** *f*) *m* **-s, -** chandler.
Wacht *f* **-, -en** (*obs, liter*) *siehe* **Wache.**
Wachtel *f* **-, -n** quail; (*fig inf: Frau*) silly goose (*inf*) ◆ **alte ~** (*inf*) (*unfreundlich*) old hen (*inf*); (*dumm*) silly old goose (*inf*).
Wächter *m* **-s, - (a)** guardian; (*Nacht~*) watchman; (*Turm~*) watch; (*Museums~, Parkplatz~*) attendant. **(b)** (*Hund*) guard-dog, watchdog.
Wächterin *f siehe* **Wächter (a).**
Wacht-: ~meister *m* **(a)** (*old Mil*) sergeant; **(b)** (*Polizist*) (police) constable (*Brit*), patrolman (*US*); **Herr ~meister** officer, constable (*Brit*); **~posten** *m* sentry, guard; (*Schüler, Dieb etc*) look-out.
Wachtraum *m* daydream.
Wach(t)turm *m* watch-tower.
Wach-: ~- und Schließgesellschaft *f* security corps; **~wechsel** *m* (*lit, fig*) changing of the guard; **~zimmer** *nt* (*Aus*) *siehe* **~lokal**; **~zustand** *m* **im ~zustand** in the waking state.
Wackelei *f* (*inf*) wobbling.
wack(e)lig *adj* wobbly; *Möbelstück auch* rickety; *Zahn, Schraube auch* loose; (*fig*) *Firma, Unternehmen* shaky ◆ **~ auf den Beinen sein** (*inf*) (*Patient*) to be wobbly on one's legs, to be shaky; (*alter Mensch*) to be doddery; **~ stehen** (*lit*) to be unsteady *or* wobbly; (*fig: Unternehmen, Schüler*) to be shaky.
Wackelkontakt *m* loose connection.
wackeln *vi* **(a)** to wobble; (*zittern*) to shake; (*Zahn, Schraube*) to be loose; (*fig*) (*Thron*) to totter; (*Position*) to be shaky ◆ **du hast gewackelt** you wobbled/shook; (*beim Fotografieren*) you moved; **mit den Ohren/Hüften/dem Kopf/Schwanz ~** to waggle one's ears/wiggle one's hips/wag one's head/its tail.
(b) *aux sein* (*langsam, unsicher gehen*) to totter; (*kleines Kind*) to toddle.
Wackelpeter *m* **-s, -** (*inf*) jelly.
wacker *adj* **(a)** (*tapfer*) brave, valiant ◆ **sich ~ halten** (*inf*) to stand *or* hold one's ground; **sich ~ schlagen** (*inf*) to put up a brave fight. **(b)** (*old: tüchtig*)

upright, honest.
Wackerstein *m* boulder.
wacklig *adj siehe* **wack(e)lig.**
Wade *f* **-, -n** calf.
Waden-: ~bein *nt* fibula; **~krampf** *m* cramp in the/one's calf; **~strumpf** *m* half stocking; **~wickel** *m* (*Med*) compress around the leg.
Waffe *f* **-, -n** (*lit, fig*) weapon; (*Schuß~*) gun; (*Mil: Waffengattung*) arm. **~n** (*Mil*) arms ◆ **~n tragen** to carry arms; **zu den ~n rufen** to call to arms; **unter ~n (stehen)** (to be) under arms; **die ~n strecken** (*lit, fig*) to lay down one's arms, to surrender; **jdn mit seinen eigenen ~n schlagen** (*fig*) to beat sb at his own game *or* with his own weapons.
Waffel *f* **-, -n** waffle; (*Keks, Eis~*) wafer; (*Eistüte*) cornet.
Waffel-: ~eisen *nt* waffle iron; **~stoff** *m* honeycomb cloth.
Waffen- *in cpds* arms; **~arsenal** *nt* arsenal; (*von Staat*) stockpile; **~besitz** *m* possession of firearms; **~bruder** *m* (*old*) comrade in arms (*old*); **~dienst** *m* (*old*) military service; **~embargo** *nt* arms embargo; **w~fähig** *adj* capable of bearing arms, able-bodied; **~gang** *m* (*old Mil*) passage at arms, armed encounter; (*Univ*) round; **~gattung** *f* (*Mil*) arm of the service; **~gewalt** *f* force of arms; **mit ~gewalt** by force of arms; **~handel** *m* arms trade *or* traffic; (*illegal auch*) gunrunning; **der ~handel ist ...** arms trade *or* traffic/gunrunning is ...; **~händler** *m* arms dealer; (*illegal auch*) gunrunner; **~hilfe** *f* military assistance; **~kammer** *f* armoury (*Brit*), armory (*US*); **~lager** *nt* (*von Armee*) ordnance depot; (*von Terroristen*) cache; **~lieferung** *f* supply of arms; **w~los** *adj* unarmed; **~rock** *m* (*old*) uniform; **~ruhe** *f* ceasefire; **~schein** *m* firearms *or* gun licence; **~schmied** *m* (*Hist*) armourer; **~schmuggel** *m* gunrunning, arms smuggling; **~-SS** *f* (*NS*) Waffen-SS; **w~starrend** *adj* bristling with weapons.
Waffenstillstand *m* armistice.
Waffenstillstands-: ~abkommen *nt* armistice agreement; **~linie** *f* armistice line.
Waffen-: ~system *nt* weapon system; **~träger** *m* (*Fahrzeug*) weapon carrier; **~träger sein** (*Mensch*) to carry arms.
waffnen *vr siehe* **wappnen.**
wägbar *adj* (*geh*) ponderable ◆ **ein nicht ~es Risiko** an imponderable risk.
Wage-: ~hals *m* daredevil; **w~halsig** *adj siehe* **waghalsig.**
Wägelchen *nt dim of* **Wagen.**
Wage-: ~mut *m, no pl* (*geh*) (heroic) daring *or* boldness; **w~mutig** *adj* daring, bold.
wagen [1] *vt* to venture; (*riskieren*) *hohen Einsatz, sein Leben* to risk; (*sich getrauen*) to dare ◆ **es ~, etw zu tun** to venture to do sth; to risk doing sth; to dare (to) do sth; **wage nicht, mir zu widersprechen!** don't you dare (to) contradict me!; **ich wag's** I'll risk it, I'll take the risk *or* plunge; **wer wagt, gewinnt** (*Prov*), **wer nichts wagt, der nichts gewinnt** (*Prov*) nothing ventured, nothing gained (*Prov*); *siehe* **gewagt, Tänzchen, frisch.**
[2] *vr* to dare ◆ **sich ~, etw zu tun** to dare (to) do sth; **sich an etw** (*acc*) **~** to venture to do sth; **ich wage mich nicht daran** I dare not do it; **sich auf ein Gebiet ~** to venture into an area; **bei dem schönen Wetter kann ich mich aus dem Haus/ins Wasser ~** in this lovely weather I can venture out of doors/into the water; **er wagt sich nicht mehr aus dem Haus** he doesn't venture out (of the house) any more, he doesn't dare leave the house any more.
Wagen *m* **-s, -** *or* (*S Ger, Aus*) **¨ (a)** (*Personen~*) car; (*Liefer~*) van; (*Plan~*) (covered) wag(g)on; (*Zirkus~, Zigeuner~*) caravan, wag(g)on; (*von Pferden gezogen*) wag(g)on, cart; (*Kutsche*) coach; (*Puppen~, Kinder~*) pram (*Brit*), baby carriage (*US*); (*Hand~*) (hand)cart; (*Kofferkuli, Einkaufs~*) trolley; (*Schreibmaschinen~*) carriage; (*Straßenbahn~, Seilbahn~*) car; (*Eisenbahn~*) coach (*Brit*), car, carriage (*Brit*); (*Omnibus*) bus ◆ **jdm an den ~ fahren** (*fig*) to pick holes in sb; **sich nicht vor jds ~ spannen lassen** (*fig*) not to allow oneself to be used *or* made use of by sb; *siehe* **Rad.**
(b) (*Astrol*) **der Große/Kleine ~** the Plough *or* (Big) Dipper/the Little Dipper.
wägen *pret* **wog** *or* **wägte,** *ptp* **gewogen** *or* **gewägt** *vt* (*old, form*) to weigh; (*geh: bedenken auch*) to ponder ◆ **erst ~, dann wagen** (*Prov*) look before you leap (*Prov*).
Wagen-: ~abteil *nt* (*Rail*) compartment; **~bauer** *m* coach builder; **~burg** *f* barricade (of wag(g)ons); **~deichsel** *f* shaft; **~folge** *f* order of cars/coaches *or* carriages *etc*; **~führer** *m* driver; **~heber** *m* jack; **~ladung** *f* (*von Lastwagen*) lorryload (*Brit*), truckload; (*von Eisenbahn*) wag(g)onload; **~lenker** *m* (*Hist*) charioteer; **~park** *m* fleet of cars/vans; **~pflege** *f* care of the/one's car; **~rad** *nt* cartwheel; (*hum: Hut*) picture hat; **~rennen** *nt* (*Hist*) chariot racing; (*einzelner Wettkampf*) chariot race; **~rücklauf** *m* (*an Schreibmaschine*) carriage return; **~schlag** *m* (*von Kutsche*) carriage door; (*von Auto*) car door; **~schmiere** *f* cart-grease; **~typ** *m* type of car; **~wäsche** *f* car wash; (*das Waschen*) car washing.
Wagestück *nt* daring deed, deed of daring.
⚠**Waggon** [va'gõ:, va'gɔŋ] *m* **-s, -s** (goods) wag(g)on (*Brit*), freight car (*US*); (*Ladung*) wag(g)onload/carload.
⚠**waggonweise** [va'gõ:-, va'gɔŋ-] *adv* by the wag(g)onload (*Brit*) *or* carload (*US*).
Wag-: ~hals *m* daredevil; **w~halsig** *adj* foolhardy, daredevil *attr*; **~halsigkeit** *f* foolhardiness.
Wagner *m* **-s, -** (*dial*) coach builder.
Wagnerianer(in *f*) *m* **-s, -** Wagnerian.
Wagnis *nt* hazardous business; (*Risiko*) risk.
Wahl *f* **-, -en (a)** (*Auswahl*) choice ◆ **die ~ fiel auf ihn/dieses Buch** he/this book was chosen; **aus freier ~** of one's own free choice; **wir hatten keine (andere) ~(, als)** we had no alternative *or* choice (but); **es gab/blieb keine andere ~(, als)** there was no alternative (but); **jdm die ~ lassen** to leave (it up to) sb to choose; **jdm etw zur ~ stellen** to give sb the choice of sth; **3 Farben stehen zur ~** there is a choice of 3 colours; **seine/eine ~ treffen** to make one's/a choice *or* selection; **du hast die ~** take your choice *or* pick; **sie hat die ~, ob sie ...** the choice is hers *or* it's up to her whether she ...; **wer die ~ hat, hat die Qual** (*Prov*) he is/you are *etc* spoilt for choice; *siehe* **eng.**
(b) (*Pol etc*) election; (*Abstimmung*) vote; (*geheim*) ballot ◆ **geheime/freie ~** secret ballot/free elections; **~ durch Handerheben** vote by (a) show of hands; **(die) ~en** (the) elections; **~ eines Präsidenten** election of a president; **seine ~ in den Vorstand/zum Präsidenten** his election to the board/as president; **die ~ gewinnen** to win the election; **zur ~ gehen** to go to vote, to go to the polls; **jdn zur ~ aufstellen** *or* **vorschlagen** to propose sb *or* put sb up as a candidate (for election); **sich zur ~ stellen** to stand (as a candidate *or* at the/an election), to run (for parliament/president *etc*); **zur ~ schreiten** to take a vote *or* (*geheim*) ballot; **die ~ annehmen** to accept the *or* one's election.
(c) (*Qualität*) quality ◆ **erste ~** top quality; *Gemüse, Eier* class *or* grade one; **zweite/dritte ~** second/third quality; *Gemüse, Eier* class *or* grade two/three; **Waren/Eier/Fleisch erster ~** top-quality goods/class- *or* grade-one eggs/prime meat; **Waren/Gemüse zweiter ~** seconds *pl*/class- *or* grade-two vegetables; **der Teller war zweite ~** the plate was a second.
Wahl-: ~akt *m* polling; **~alter** *nt* voting age; **~analytiker** *m* election analyst; **~aufruf** *m* election announcement; **~auftrag** *m* election brief; **~ausgang** *m* outcome of an/the election, election results *pl*; ⚠**~ausschuß** *m* election committee.
Wählautomatik *f* (*Telec*) automatic dialling (*Brit*) *or* dialing (*US*).
wählbar *adj* eligible (for office), able to stand at an/the election.
Wahl-: ~benachrichtigung, ~benachrichtigungskarte *f* polling card; **w~berechtigt** *adj* entitled to vote; **~berechtigte(r)** *mf decl as adj* person entitled to vote; **~berechtigung** *f* (right to) vote; **~beteiligung** *f* poll; **eine hohe ~beteiligung** a heavy poll, a high *or* good turnout (at an/the election); **~bezirk** *m* ward; **~bündnis** *nt* electoral pact; **~bürger** *m* (*form*) voter.
wählen [1] *vt* **(a)** (*von* from, out of) to choose; (*aus~ auch*) to select, to pick ◆ **seine Worte ~** to choose one's words, to select *or* pick one's words carefully; *siehe* **gewählt.**
(b) (*Telec*) *Nummer* to dial.
(c) (*durch Wahl ermitteln*) *Regierung, Sprecher etc* to elect; (*sich entscheiden für*) *Partei, Kandidaten* to vote for ◆ **jdn ins Parlament/in den Vorstand ~** to elect *or* return sb to Parliament/to elect *or* vote sb onto the board; **jdn zum Präsidenten ~** to elect sb president.
[2] *vi* **(a)** (*auswählen*) to choose.
(b) (*Telec*) to dial.
(c) (*Wahlen abhalten*) to hold elections; (*Stimme abgeben*) to vote ◆ **wann wird gewählt?** when are the elections?; **man darf ab 18 ~** you can vote at 18; **durch Handerheben ~** to vote by (a) show of hands; **~ gehen** to go to the polls, to go to vote.
Wähler *m* **-s, - (a)** (*Pol*) elector, voter ◆ **der** *or* **die ~** the electorate *sing or pl*, the electors *pl*. **(b)** (*Tech*) selector.
Wähler|auftrag *m* mandate.
Wahl|ergebnis *nt* election result; (*Stimmenverteilung auch*) election returns *pl*.
Wählerin *f siehe* **Wähler (a).**
Wähler|initiative *f* pressure from the electorate.
wählerisch *adj* particular; *Geschmack, Kunde* discriminating ◆ **sei nicht so ~!** don't be so choosy (*inf*) *or* fussy.
Wählerreservoir *nt* source of votes.
Wählerschaft *f, no pl* electorate *sing or pl*; (*eines Wahlkreises*) constituents *pl*.
Wähler-: ~schicht *f* section of the electorate; **~schwund** *m* loss of voters; **~stimme** *f* vote; **10% der ~stimmen** 10% of the vote(s) *or* poll; **~verzeichnis** *nt* electoral roll *or* register.
Wahl-: ~fach *nt* (*Sch*) option, optional subject, elective (*US*); **~feldzug** *m* election(eering) campaign; **~fieber** *nt* election fever; **~forscher** *m* electoral researcher, psephologist; **w~frei** *adj* (*Sch*) optional; **w~freier Zugriff** (*Comput*) random access; **~freiheit** *f* (*Pol*) electoral freedom; (*Sch*) freedom of choice; **~gang** *m* ballot; **~geheimnis** *nt* secrecy of the ballot; **~geschenk** *nt* pre-election promise; **~gesetz** *nt* electoral law; **~heimat** *f* country of adoption *or* of (one's) choice, adopted country; **~helfer** *m* (*im ~kampf*) electoral *or* election assistant; (*bei der Wahl*) polling officer; **~kabine** *f* polling booth; **~kampf** *m* election(eering) campaign; **einen ~kampf führen** to conduct an election campaign; **~kreis** *m* constituency; **~leiter** *m* returning officer (*Brit*); **~lokal** *nt* polling station; **~lokomotive** *f* (*inf*) vote-puller; **w~los** [1] *adj* indiscriminate; [2] *adv* at random, haphazardly; (*nicht wählerisch*) indiscriminately; **~mann** *m, pl* **-männer** delegate; **~möglichkeit** *f* choice, option; **~nacht** *f* election night; **~niederlage** *f* election defeat; **~periode** *f* lifetime of a/the parliament; **~pflicht** *f* electoral duty; **seine ~pflicht erfüllen** to use one's vote; **~pflichtfach** *nt* (*Sch*) (compulsory) optional subject; **~plakat** *nt* election poster; **~propaganda** *f* election propaganda; **~recht** *nt* **(a)** (right to) vote; **allgemeines ~recht** universal franchise *or* suffrage; **das aktive ~recht** the right to vote; **das passive ~recht** eligibility (for political office); **mit 25 bekommt man das passive ~recht** at 25 one becomes eligible for political office; **(b)** (*Gesetze*) electoral law *no def art*; **~rede** *f* election speech; **~reform** *f* electoral reform.
Wählscheibe *f* dial.

Wahl-: ~schein *m* polling card; **~sieg** *m* electoral *or* election victory; **~slogan** *m* election slogan; **~sonntag** *m* polling Sunday; **~spruch** *m* **(a)** motto, watchword; **(b)** *siehe* **~slogan**; **~system** *nt* electoral system; **~tag** *m* election *or* polling day; **~urne** *f* ballot box; **~verfahren** *nt* electoral procedure; **~vergehen** *nt* electoral misdemeanour; **~verhalten** *nt* behaviour at the polls; **~versammlung** *f* election meeting; **~versprechungen** *pl* election promises *pl*; **~verwandtschaft** *f* (*Chem*) elective attraction; (*fig*) affinity (*von* between); **„die ~verwandtschaften"** (*Liter*) "The Elective Affinities"; **w~weise** *adv* alternatively; **w~weise Kartoffeln oder Reis** (a) choice of potatoes or rice; **Sie können w~weise Wasserski fahren oder reiten** you have a choice between water-skiing and riding.

Wahlwiederholung *f* (*Telec*) **(automatische) ~** (automatic) redial.

Wählzeichen *nt* (*Telec*) dialling tone.

Wahlzelle *f* polling booth.

Wahn *m* **- (e)s,** *no pl* **(a)** illusion, delusion ◆ **in dem ~ leben, daß ...** to labour under the delusion that ... **(b)** (*Manie*) mania.

Wahnbild *nt* delusion, illusion.

wähnen (*geh*) [1] *vt* to imagine (wrongly), to believe (wrongly) ◆ **wir wähnten ihn glücklich** we (wrongly) imagined *or* believed him (to be) happy.

[2] *vr* **sich sicher/von allen verlassen ~** to imagine *or* believe oneself (to be) safe/abandoned by all.

Wahn|idee *f* delusion; (*verrückte Idee*) mad *or* crazy notion.

Wahnsinn *m, no pl* **(a)** (*old Psych*) insanity, lunacy, madness ◆ **in ~ verfallen** to go mad *or* insane.

(b) (*Unvernunft*) madness, insanity ◆ **des ~s fette Beute sein** (*inf*) to be off one's rocker (*sl*); **das ist doch (heller) ~, so ein ~!** that's sheer madness *or* idiocy!; **Mensch, ~** *or* **einfach ~!** (*sl: prima*) way *or* far out! (*sl*).

(c) religiöser ~ religious mania.

wahnsinnig [1] *adj* **(a)** (*old Psych*) insane, mad.

(b) (*inf*) (*verrückt*) mad, crazy; (*toll, super*) brilliant (*inf*), great (*inf*); (*attr: sehr groß, viel*) terrible, awful, dreadful ◆ **eine ~e Arbeit/ein ~es Geld** a crazy *or* incredible amount of work/money; **wie ~** (*inf*) like mad; **das macht mich ~** (*inf*) it's driving me mad *or* crazy *or* round the bend (*inf*); **~ werden** to go mad *or* crazy *or* round the bend (*inf*); **ich werde ~!** it's mind-blowing! (*sl*).

[2] *adv* (*inf*) incredibly (*inf*) ◆ **~ verliebt** madly in love; **~ viele/viel** an incredible number/amount (*inf*).

Wahnsinnige(r) *mf decl as adj* madman/madwoman, lunatic.

Wahnsinnigwerden *nt* **zum ~** enough to drive you round the bend (*inf*) *or* up the wall (*inf*).

Wahnsinns- *in cpds* (*inf: verrückt*) crazy; (*sl: prima*) fantastic (*inf*), incredible (*inf*); **~arbeit** *f* **eine ~arbeit** a crazy *or* an incredible amount of work (*inf*).

Wahn-: ~vorstellung *f* delusion; **~witz** *m, no pl* utter *or* sheer foolishness; **w~witzig** [1] *adj* mad, crazy, lunatic *attr*; [2] *adv* terribly, awfully.

wahr *adj* *Geschichte, Liebe, Glaube etc* true; (*echt*) *Kunst, Glück etc auch* real, genuine; *Freund, Freundschaft auch* real; (*attr: wirklich*) real, veritable ◆ **im ~sten Sinne des Wortes, in des Wortes ~ster Bedeutung** in the true sense of the word; **daran ist kein ~es Wort, davon ist kein Wort ~** there's not a word of truth in it; **da ist etwas W~es daran** there's some truth in that; **da hast du ein ~es Wort gesprochen** (*inf*) that's very true, there's a lot of truth in that; **etw ~ machen** *Pläne* to make sth a reality; *Versprechung, Drohung* to carry out; **~ werden** to come true; (*Hoffnung, Pläne auch*) to become a reality; **so ~ mir Gott helfe!** so help me God!; **so ~ ich lebe/hier stehe** as sure as I'm alive/standing here, as sure as eggs are eggs (*inf*); **das darf** *or* **kann doch nicht ~ sein!** (*inf*) it can't be true!; **das ist schon gar nicht mehr ~** (*inf*) (*verstärkend*) it's not true! (*inf*); (*schon lange her*) that was ages ago; **das ist nicht der ~e Jakob** *or* **Otto** (*inf*), **das ist nicht das W~e** (*inf*) it's no great shakes (*inf*); **die Stelle ist nicht gerade der ~e Jakob** *or* **Otto** *or* **das W~e** (*inf*) it's not exactly the greatest job (on earth); *siehe* **nicht, einzig**.

wahren *vt* **(a)** (*wahrnehmen*) *Interessen, Rechte* to look after, to protect, to safeguard.

(b) (*erhalten*) *Autorität, Ruf, Würde* to preserve, to keep; *Geheimnis* to keep; *gute Manieren* to adhere to, to observe ◆ **die Form/den Anstand ~** to adhere to correct form/to observe the proprieties; *siehe* **Schein**[1], **Gesicht**[1].

währen *vi* (*geh*) to last ◆ **es währte nicht lange, da geschah ein Unglück** it was not long before misfortune struck; **was lange währt, wird (endlich) gut** (*Prov*) a happy outcome is worth waiting for; *siehe* **ehrlich**.

während [1] *prep +gen or dat* during ◆ **~ eines Zeitraums** over a period of time; **~ der ganzen Nacht** all night long, all during the night, throughout the night.

[2] *conj* while; (*wohingegen auch*) whereas.

während-: ~dem (*inf*), **~des** (*geh*), **~dessen** *adv* meanwhile, in the meantime.

Wahr-: w~haben *vt sep irreg* **etw nicht w~haben wollen** not to want to admit sth; **w~haft** [1] *adj* (*ehrlich*) truthful; (*echt*) *Freund* true, real; *Enttäuschung* real; (*attr: wirklich*) real, veritable; [2] *adv* really, truly; **w~haftig** [1] *adj* (*geh*) (*aufrichtig*) truthful; *Gemüt* honest; *Worte etc* true; **der w~haftige Gott** the true God; **w~haftiger Gott!** (*inf*) strewth! (*inf*); [2] *adv* really; (*tatsächlich*) actually; **~haftigkeit** *f, no pl* (*geh*) truthfulness; (*von Aussage auch*) veracity.

▼ **Wahrheit** *f* truth ◆ **in ~** in reality; **die ~ sagen** to tell the truth; **um die ~ zu sagen** to tell the truth; **das schlägt der ~ ins Gesicht** that's patently untrue; **er nimmt es mit der ~ nicht so genau** (*inf*) you have to take what he says with a pinch of salt; *siehe* **Ehre**.

Wahrheits-: ~beweis *m* (*Jur*) **den ~beweis bringen** *or* **antreten** to supply proof of the truth of a/one's statement; **~findung** *f* establishment of the truth; **~gehalt** *m* substance; **w~getreu** *adj* *Bericht* truthful; *Darstellung* faithful; **ein w~getreues Bild** (*fig*) a factual *or* true picture; **~liebe** *f* love of truth; **w~liebend** *adj* truth-loving; (*ehrlich*) truthful; **w~widrig** *adj* false.

wahrlich *adv* really, indeed, verily (*Bibl*); (*garantiert*) certainly, definitely.

Wahr-: w~nehmbar *adj* perceptible, noticeable; **nicht w~nehmbar** imperceptible, not noticeable; **mit bloßem Auge w~nehmbar/nicht w~nehmbar** visible/invisible to the naked eye; **w~nehmen** *vt sep irreg* **(a)** (*mit den Sinnen erfassen*) to perceive; (*bemerken*) *Vorgänge, Veränderungen etc* to be aware of; (*entdecken, erkennen*) *Geräusch, Licht auch* to distinguish; *Geruch* to detect; (*heraushören*) *Unterton, Stimmung* to detect, to discern; **nichts mehr/alles um sich herum w~nehmen** to be no longer aware of anything/to be aware of everything around one; **(b)** (*nutzen, vertreten*) *Frist, Termin* to observe; *Gelegenheit* to take; *Interessen, Angelegenheiten, Rechte* to look after; **~nehmung** *f siehe vt* **(a)** perception; awareness; detection; **(b)** observing; taking; looking after; **~nehmungsvermögen** *nt* perceptive faculty; **w~sagen** *sep or insep* [1] *vi* to tell fortunes, to predict the future; **aus dem Kaffeesatz/aus den Teeblättern/aus den Karten w~sagen** to read coffee grounds/tea leaves/cards; **jdm w~sagen** to tell sb's fortune, to predict the future (to sb); **sich (*dat*) w~sagen lassen** to have one's fortune told; [2] *vt* **(jdm) die Zukunft w~sagen** to tell sb's fortune, to predict the future (to sb); **er hat mir w~gesagt, daß ...** he predicted (to me) that ...; **~sager(in *f*)** *m* **-s, -** fortuneteller, soothsayer (*old*); **~sagerei** *f, no pl* fortunetelling; **w~sagerisch** *adj* prophetic; **~sagung** *f* prediction.

Wahrschau *f*: **~!** (*Naut*) attention!

▼ **wahrscheinlich** [1] *adj* probable, likely; (*glaubhaft*) plausible ◆ **es liegt im Bereich des W~en** it is quite within the bounds of probability.

▼ [2] *adv* probably ◆ **er kommt ~ erst später** he probably won't come till later, he won't come till later most likely.

▼ **Wahrscheinlichkeit** *f* probability, likelihood *no pl*; (*Glaubhaftigkeit*) plausibility ◆ **mit großer ~, aller ~ nach, in aller ~** in all probability *or* likelihood.

Wahrscheinlichkeitsrechnung *f* probability calculus, theory of probabilities.

Wahrung *f, no pl* **(a)** (*Wahrnehmung*) protection, safeguarding. **(b)** (*Erhaltung*) preservation; (*von Geheimnis*) keeping ◆ **~ der guten Manieren** adherence to *or* observance of good manners.

Währung *f* currency.

Währungs- *in cpds* currency, monetary; **~ausgleich** *m* cur rency conversion compensation; **~block** *m* monetary bloc; **~einheit** *f* monetary unit; **~fonds** *m* Monetary Fund; **~krise** *f* monetary *or* currency crisis; **~parität** *f* mint par of exchange; **~reform** *f* monetary *or* currency reform; **~reserve** *f* monetary *or* currency reserve; **~schlange** *f* (currency) snake; **~system** *nt* monetary system; **~union** *f* monetary union.

Wahrzeichen *nt* (*von Stadt, Verein*) emblem; (*Gebäude, Turm etc*) symbol.

Waid- *in cpds siehe* **Weid-**.

Waise *f* **-, -n** orphan.

Waisen-: ~haus *nt* orphanage; **~kind** *nt* orphan; **~knabe** *m* (*liter*) orphan (boy); **gegen dich ist er ein ~knabe** *or* **~kind** (*inf*) he's no match for you, you would run rings round him (*inf*); **~rente** *f* orphan's allowance.

Wal *m* **-(e)s, -e** whale.

Wald *m* **-(e)s, ¨er** wood(s *pl*); (*großer*) forest; (*no pl: ~land*) woodland(s *pl*), wooded country ◆ **~ und Wiese/Feld** *or* **Flur** (*liter*) woods and meadows/fields; **ich glaub, ich steh im ~** (*inf*) I must be seeing/hearing things! (*inf*); **er sieht den ~ vor lauter Bäumen nicht** he can't see the wood for the trees (*Prov*); **wie es in den ~ hineinschallt** *or* **wie man in den ~ hineinruft, so schallt es wieder heraus** (*Prov*) you get as much as you give.

Wald-: ~ameise *f* red ant; **~arbeiter** *m* forestry worker; (*Holzfäller*) lumberjack, woodman; **~bestand** *m* forest land; **~blume** *f* woodland flower; **~boden** *m* forest soil; **~brand** *m* forest fire.

Wäldchen *nt dim of* **Wald** little wood.

Wald|erdbeere *f* wild strawberry.

Waldes- (*liter*): **~dunkel** *nt* gloom of the forest; **~rauschen** *nt* rustling *or* whispering of the woods/forest; **~saum** *m* edge of the wood(s)/forest.

Wald-: ~frevel *m* offence against the forest laws; **~geist** *m* sylvan (*poet*) *or* silvan (*poet*) *or* forest spirit; **~heini** *m* (*inf*) nitwit (*inf*); **~horn** *nt* (*Mus*) French horn.

waldig *adj* wooded, woody.

Wald-: ~land *nt* woodland(s *pl*); **~landschaft** *f* woodland/forest landscape; **~lauf** *m* cross-country running; (*einzelner Lauf*) cross-country run; **~lehrpfad** *m* nature trail; **~meister** *m* (*Bot*) woodruff.

Waldorf-: ~salat *m* (*Cook*) Waldorf salad; **~schule** *f* Rudolf Steiner School.

Wald-: w~reich *adj* densely wooded; **~reichtum** *m* abundance of woods/forests; **~schaden** *m* damage to woods/forests; **~schneise** *f* lane, aisle; **~schrat** *m* wood gnome; **~sterben** *nt* dying of the forests (*due to pollution*); **~tier** *nt* woodland/forest creature.

Wald- und Wiesen- *in cpds* (*inf*) common-or-garden (*inf*).

Waldung *f* (*geh*) woodland(s *pl*).

Wald-: ~vogel *m* woodland bird; **~weg** *m* woodland/forest path; **~wiese** *f* glade; **~wirtschaft** *f siehe* **Forstwirtschaft**.

Wales [weɪlz] *nt* **-** Wales.

Wal-: ~fang *m* whaling; **~fangboot** *nt* whaler, whaling boat; **~fänger** *m* (*Schiff, Mensch*) whaler; **~fisch** *m* (*inf*) whale; **~fischspeck** *m* blubber; **~fischtran** *m siehe* **Waltran**.

walgen, wälgern *vt* (*dial*) *Teig* to roll out.

Walhall(a) ['valhal, val'hal(a)] *f* **-,** *no pl* (*Myth*) Valhalla.

➤ SPRACHE AKTIV: **Wahrheit** → 53.4, 53.6 **wahrscheinlich: 2** → 42.2, 43.2, 53.2, 53.6 **Wahrscheinlichkeit** → 42.2

Waliser(in *f*) *m* **-s, -** Welshman; Welsh woman.
walisisch *adj* Welsh.
Walke *f* **-, -n** fulling machine.
walken *vt Felle, Leder* to drum, to tumble; *Wollgewebe* to full, to mill; *Blech* to flex ♦ **jdn ~** (*inf*) to give sb a belting (*inf*).
Walkie-talkie ['vɔ:ki:'tɔ:ki:] *nt* **-(s), -s** walkie-talkie.
Walkman ® ['vɔ:kmən] *m* **-s, -s** (*Rad*) walkman ®.
Walküre *f* **-, -n** (*Myth, fig*) Valkyrie.
Wall *m* **-(e)s, ¨e** embankment; (*Mil*) rampart; (*fig*) bulwark, rampart.
Wallach *m* **-(e)s, -e** gelding.
wallen *vi* **(a)** (*liter*) (*Meer*) (*brodeln*) to surge, to seethe; (*fließen*) to flow; (*Dämpfe, Nebel*) to surge; (*fig: Blut*) to boil; (*hum: Busen*) to heave. **(b)** (*obs*) *aux sein siehe* **wallfahren.**
wallfahren *vi insep reg aux sein* to go on a pilgrimage.
Wallfahrer *m* **-s, -** pilgrim.
Wallfahrt *f* pilgrimage.
Wallfahrts-: ~kirche *f* pilgrimage church; **~ort** *m* place of pilgrimage; **~stätte** *f* place of pilgrimage; (*Grab, Kirche etc auch*) shrine.
Wallgraben *m* moat.
Wallis *nt* **-** Valais.
Walliser(in *f*) *m* **-s, -** inhabitant of the Valais.
Walliser Alpen *pl* **die ~ ~** the Valais Alps *pl.*
walliserisch *adj* Valaisan.
Wallone *m* **-n, -n, Wallonin** *f* Walloon.
Wallung *f* **-, -en (a)** (*geh*) **das Meer war in ~** the sea was surging *or* seething; **in ~ geraten** (*See, Meer*) to begin to surge *or* seethe; (*vor Leidenschaft*) to be in a turmoil; (*vor Wut*) to fly into a rage *or* passion; **sein Blut geriet in ~** his blood began to surge through his veins; **jds Blut/jdn in ~ bringen** to make sb's blood surge through his/her veins.
(b) (*Med*) (hot) flush *usu pl.*
Walmdach *nt* (*Archit*) hipped roof.
⚠**Walnuß** *f* walnut.
⚠**Walnußbaum** *m* walnut (tree).
Walpurgisnacht *f* Walpurgis Night, Walpurgisnacht.
⚠**Walroß** *nt* **-sses, -sse** walrus; (*pej: Mensch*) baby elephant (*inf*) ♦ **schnaufen wie ein ~** (*pej*) to puff like a grampus.
Walstatt *f* (*obs*) battlefield.
walten *vi* (*geh*) to prevail, to reign (*in +dat* over); (*wirken: Mensch, Naturkräfte*) to be at work ♦ **über jdm/etw ~** to rule (over) sb/sth; **Vernunft ~ lassen** to let reason prevail; **Vorsicht/Milde/Gnade ~ lassen** to exercise caution/leniency/to show mercy; **das W~ der Naturgewalten/Gottes** the workings of the forces of nature/of God; **jdn ~ lassen** to let sb have a free rein, to let sb do as he pleases; **das walte Gott** *or* (*inf*) **Hugo** amen (to that)!; *siehe* **Amt.**
Waltran *m* sperm oil.
Walz *f* (*dated*) **auf die ~ gehen** to go off on one's travels; **auf der ~ sein** to be on the road.
Walzblech *nt* sheet metal.
Walze *f* **-, -n** roller; (*Schreibmaschinen~ auch*) platen; (*Drehorgel~*) barrel; (*von Spieluhr*) cylinder, drum.
walzen 1 *vt* to roll.
2 *vi* **(a)** *aux sein or haben* (*dated: tanzen*) to waltz. **(b)** *aux sein* (*old inf: wandern*) to tramp, to hike.
wälzen 1 *vt* **(a)** (*rollen*) to roll; (*Cook*) (*in Ei, Mehl*) to coat (*in +dat* with); (*in Butter, Petersilie*) to toss.
(b) (*inf*) *Akten, Bücher* to pore over; *Probleme, Gedanken, Pläne* to turn over in one's mind ♦ **die Schuld/Verantwortung auf jdn ~** to shift *or* shove (*inf*) the blame/responsibility onto sb.
2 *vr* to roll; (*vor Schmerzen*) to writhe (*vor +dat* with); (*schlaflos im Bett*) to toss and turn; (*fig: Menschenmenge, Wassermassen*) to surge; (*im Schlamm*) to wallow.
walzenförmig *adj* cylindrical.
Walzer *m* **-s, -** waltz ♦ **Wiener ~** Viennese waltz; **~ tanzen** to (dance the/a) waltz; **sich im ~ drehen** (*liter*) to waltz around and around.
Wälzer *m* **-s, -** (*inf*) heavy *or* weighty tome (*hum*).
Walzer-: ~musik *f* waltz music; **~schritt** *m* waltz step; **~takt** *m* waltz time.
Walz-: ~straße *f* rolling train; **~werk** *nt* rolling mill.
Wamme *f* **-, -n (a)** (*Hautfalte*) dewlap. **(b)** (*von Pelz*) belly part. **(c)** (*dial: Bauch*) paunch.
Wampe *f* **-, -n** (*dial*) paunch.
Wams *nt* **-es, ¨er** (*old, dial: Jacke*) jerkin; (*unter Rüstung*) gambeson; (*dial: Weste*) waistcoat (*Brit*), vest (*US*).
wand *pret of* **winden[1].**
Wand *f* **-, ¨e** wall (*auch Anat*); (*nicht gemauerte Trenn~*) partition (wall); (*von Gefäß, Behälter, Schiff*) side; (*Fels~*) (rock) face; (*Wolken~*) bank of clouds; (*Biol*) septum (*spec*); (*fig*) barrier, wall ♦ **spanische ~** (folding) screen; **etw an die ~ werfen** *or* **schmeißen** *or* **schleudern** (*inf*) (*lit*) to throw sth against *or* at the wall; (*fig: aus Wut, Verzweiflung*) to throw sth out of the window; **~ an ~** wall to wall; **in seinen vier ~en** (*fig*) within one's own four walls; **weiß wie die ~** as white as a sheet; **wenn die ~e reden könnten** if walls could speak; **man rennt bei denen gegen eine ~** with them you come up against a brick wall; **mit dem Kopf gegen die ~ rennen** (*fig*) to bang one's head against a brick wall; **jdn an die ~ drücken** (*fig*) to push *or* drive sb to the wall; **jdn an die ~ spielen** (*fig*) to outdo *or* outshine sb; (*Theat*) to steal the show from sb, to upstage sb; **jdn an die ~ stellen** (*fig*) to shoot sb, to send sb before the firing squad; **er lachte/tobte** *etc*, **daß die ~e wackelten** (*inf*) *or* **zitterten** (*inf*) he raised the roof (with his laughter/ranting and raving *etc*) (*inf*); **die ~** *or* **~e hochgehen** (*inf*) to go up the wall (*inf*); **das ist, um an den ~en hochzugehen** (*inf*), **es ist zum Die-~e-Hochgehen** (*inf*) it's enough to drive you up the wall (*inf*).
Wandale *m* **-n, -n** (*Hist*) Vandal; *siehe* **hausen.**
Wandalismus *m siehe* **Vandalismus.**
Wand-: ~behang *m* wall hanging; **~bekleidung** *f* wall covering; (*aus Holz*) panelling; **~bewurf** *m* plaster(ing); (*Rauhputz*) roughcast; **~bord, ~brett** *nt* (wall) shelf.
Wandel *m* **-s,** *no pl* **(a)** change ♦ **im ~ der Zeiten** throughout the ages *or* the changing times; **im ~ der Jahrhunderte** down the centuries. **(b)** (*Lebens~*) way *or* mode of life; *siehe* **Handel[1].**
Wandel-: ~altar *m* polyptych; **~anleihe** *f* convertible loan; **w~bar** *adj* changeable; **~barkeit** *f, no pl* changeability; **~gang** *m* covered walk; **~halle** *f* foyer; (*im Parlament*) lobby; (*im Kurhaus*) pump room.
wandeln[1] *vtr* (*ändern*) to change.
wandeln[2] *vi aux sein* (*geh: gehen*) to walk, to stroll ♦ **ein ~des Wörterbuch** (*hum*) a walking dictionary; **er ist die ~de Güte** he is goodness *or* kindness itself *or* personified; *siehe* **Leiche.**
Wandelstern *m* (*old*) planet.
Wander-: ~ameise *f* army ant; **~ausstellung** *f* travelling *or* touring exhibition; **~bühne** *f* touring company; (*Hist*) strolling players *pl*; **~bursche** *m* (*obs*) journeyman; **~düne** *f* shifting *or* drifting (sand) dune.
Wanderer *m* **-s, -** hiker; (*esp Angehöriger eines Wandervereins*) rambler; (*old: Reisender*) traveller, wayfarer (*old*).
Wander-: ~fahrt *f* hiking trip; (*old: Reise*) journey; **~falke** *m* peregrine (falcon); **~freund(in** *f*) *m* hiker; **~heuschrecke** *f* migratory locust.
Wanderin *f siehe* **Wanderer.**
Wander-: ~jahre *pl* years of travel; **~karte** *f* map of walks *or* trails; **~kleidung** *f* hiking outfit; **~leben** *nt* roving *or* wandering life; (*fig*) unsettled life; **~leber** *f* floating liver; **~lied** *nt* hiking song; **~lust** *f* wanderlust; **w~lustig** *adj* filled with wanderlust, with a passion for travel.
wandern *vi aux sein* **(a)** (*gehen*) to wander, to roam; (*old: reisen*) to travel, to journey; (*Wanderbühne, Zigeuner*) to travel ♦ **durchs Leben ~** (*liter*) to journey through life.
(b) (*sich bewegen*) to move, to travel; (*Wolken, Gletscher*) to drift; (*Düne*) to shift, to drift; (*Med: Leber, Niere*) to float; (*Blick*) to rove, to roam, to wander; (*Gedanken*) to roam, to wander, to stray; (*weitergegeben werden*) to be passed (on).
(c) (*Vögel, Tiere, Völker*) to migrate.
(d) (*zur Freizeitgestaltung*) to hike; (*esp in Verein*) to ramble.
(e) (*inf: ins Bett, in den Papierkorb, ins Feuer*) to go ♦ **hinter Schloß und Riegel/ins Krankenhaus/ins Leihhaus ~** to be put behind bars/to end *or* land up in hospital/at the pawnbroker's.
Wander-: ~niere *f* floating kidney; **~pokal** *m* challenge cup; **~prediger** *m* itinerant preacher; **~preis** *m* challenge trophy; **~ratte** *f* brown rat.
Wanderschaft *f, no pl* travels *pl* ♦ **auf (der) ~ sein** to be on one's travels; **auf ~ gehen** to go off on one's travels; **mein Bleistift ist auf ~ gegangen** (*inf*) my pencil seems to have walked off (*inf*).
Wander-: ~schauspieler *m* travelling actor; (*Hist*) strolling player; **~schuhe** *pl* walking shoes *pl.*
Wandersmann *m, pl* **-leute** (*liter*) *siehe* **Wanderer.**
Wander-: ~stab *m* staff; **den ~stab ergreifen** (*fig*) to take to the road; **~tag** *m day in German schools on which pupils go rambling*; **~trieb** *m* (*von Tier*) migratory instinct; (*Psych*) urge to travel, dromomania (*spec*); (*fig*) wanderlust, passion for travel; **~truppe** *f* touring company; (*Hist*) strolling players *pl.*
Wanderung *f* **(a)** (*Ausflug*) walk ♦ **eine ~ machen** to go on a walk *or* hike *or* ramble. **(b)** (*old: Reise, von Handwerksgesellen, fig liter: durchs Leben*) journey. **(c)** (*von Vögeln, Tieren, Völkern*) migration; (*Sociol: Wohnortwechsel*) shift (in the population), population shift.
Wanderungsgewinn *m* (*Sociol*) increase in population (through population shifts).
Wander-: ~verein *m* rambling club; **~vogel** *m* (*Hist*) member of the Wandervogel youth movement; (*begeisterter Wanderer*) hiker; (*fig inf*) bird of passage, rolling stone (*inf*); **~weg** *m* walk, trail, (foot)path; **~zirkus** *m* travelling circus.
Wandgemälde *nt* mural, wall-painting.
-wandig *adj suf* -walled.
Wand-: ~kalender *m* wall calendar; **~karte** *f* wall map; **~lampe** *f* wall lamp/light; **~leuchter** *m* wall bracket, sconce.
Wandlung *f* **(a)** (*Wechsel, Wandel*) change; (*völlige Um~*) transformation ♦ **~ zum Guten** change for the better; **eine ~ durchmachen** to undergo a change. **(b)** (*Eccl*) transubstantiation; (*Teil der Messe*) consecration. **(c)** (*Jur*) cancellation of sale contract.
wandlungsfähig *adj* adaptable; *Schauspieler etc* versatile.
Wand-: ~malerei *f* mural painting; (*Bild*) mural, wall-painting; **~pfeiler** *m* (*Archit*) pilaster.
Wandrer(in *f*) *m* **-s, -** *siehe* **Wanderer.**
Wand-: ~schirm *m* screen; **~schrank** *m* wall cupboard; **~tafel** *f* (black)board.
wandte *pret of* **wenden.**
Wand-: ~teller *m* wall plate; **~teppich** *m* tapestry, wall hanging; **~uhr** *f* wall clock; **~verkleidung** *f* wall covering; (*aus Holz*) panelling; **~zeitung** *f* wall news-sheet.

⚠: for details of spelling reform, see supplement

Wange *f* **-, -n** **(a)** *(geh)* cheek ♦ **~ an ~** cheek to cheek. **(b)** *(von Treppe)* stringboard.
Wank *m (Sw)*: **keinen ~ tun** not to lift a finger.
Wankelmotor *m* Wankel engine.
Wankelmut *m*, **Wankelmütigkeit** *f* fickleness, inconstancy.
wankelmütig *adj* fickle, inconstant.
wanken *vi* **(a)** *(schwanken)* *(Mensch, Gebäude)* to sway; *(Knie)* to shake, to wobble; *(Boden)* to rock; *(fig: Thron, Regierung)* to totter; *(unsicher sein/werden)* to waver, to falter; *(schwanken)* to vacillate ♦ **nicht ~ und nicht weichen** not to move *or* budge an inch; **ihm wankt der Boden unter den Füßen** *(fig)* he is on shaky ground; **ins W~ geraten** *(lit)* to begin to sway/rock; *(fig)* to begin to totter/waver *or* falter/vacillate; **etw ins W~ bringen** *(lit)* to cause sth to sway/rock; *(fig) Thron, Regierung* to cause sth to totter; *Glauben, Mut* to shake sth; *Moral* to throw doubt upon sth; **jds Entschluß ins W~ bringen** to make sb waver in his decision.
(b) *aux sein (gehen)* to stagger; *(alter Mensch)* to totter.
wann *interrog adv* when ♦ **~ ist er angekommen?** when did he arrive?; **~ kommt ihr?** when *or* (at) what time are you coming?; **~ (auch) immer** whenever; **bis ~ ist das fertig?** when will that be ready (by)?; **bis ~ gilt der Ausweis?** until when is the pass valid?, when is the pass valid until?; **seit ~ bist/hast du ...?** *(zeitlich)* how long have you been/had ...?; *(bezweifelnd, entrüstet etc)* since when are you/do you have ...?; **von ~ an bist du in Deutschland?** from when will you be in Germany?; **von ~ bis ~?** when?, during what times?
Wanne *f* **-, -n** bath; *(Bade~ auch)* (bath)tub; *(Öl~)* reservoir; *(im Auto)* sump *(Brit)*, oil pan *(US)*.
wannen *adv (obs)* **von ~** whence *(liter)*.
Wannenbad *nt* bath.
Wanst *m* **-(e)s, ⸚e** *(Zool: Pansen)* rumen; *(inf: dicker Bauch)* paunch *(inf)*, belly *(inf)* ♦ **sich** *(dat)* **den ~ vollschlagen** *(inf)* to stuff oneself *(inf)*.
Want *f* **-, -en** *(Naut)* shroud.
Wanze *f* **-, -n** *(Zool, Comput, inf: Abhörgerät)* bug ♦ **frech wie eine ~** *(inf)* (as) bold as brass, very cheeky.
Wanzen-: ~bude *f*, **~loch** *nt (inf)* hole *(inf)*, dump *(inf)*.
Wappen *nt* **-s, -** coat of arms; *(auf Münze)* heads *no art* ♦ **etw im ~ führen** to have *or* bear sth on one's coat of arms; *(fig)* to have sth as one's trademark.
Wappen-: ~kunde *f* heraldry; **~schild** *m or nt* shield; **~seite** *f* heads side; **~tier** *nt* heraldic animal.
wappnen *vr (fig)* **sich (gegen etw) ~** to prepare (oneself) (for sth); **gewappnet sein** to be prepared *or* forearmed.
war *pret of* **sein**[1].
warb *pret of* **werben**.
ward *(old, liter) pret of* **werden 1 (c)** *and* **2**.
Ware *f* **-, -n** product; *(einzelne ~)* article; *(als Sammelbegriff)* goods *pl*, merchandise. **~n** *pl* goods *pl*; *(zum Verkauf auch)* merchandise *sing*, wares *pl* *(esp old, hum)* ♦ **gute ~ hält sich** *(prov)* good-quality goods last longer.
wäre *pret subjunc of* **sein**[1].
Waren-: ~angebot *nt* range of goods for sale; **~aufzug** *m* goods hoist; **~ausfuhr** *f* export of goods *or* merchandise; **~austausch** *m* exchange *or* *(bei Tauschgeschäft)* barter of goods; **~begleitpapiere** *pl* shipping documents *pl*; **~beleihung** *f* loan against goods; **~bestand** *m* stocks *pl* of goods *or* merchandise; **~börse** *f* commodity exchange; **~einfuhr** *f* import of goods *or* merchandise; **~export** *m* export of goods *or* merchandise; **~haus** *nt* (department) store, emporium *(old)*; **~import** *m* import of goods *or* merchandise; **~korb** *m (Econ)* basket of goods; **~lager** *nt* warehouse; *(Bestand)* stocks *pl*; **~muster** *nt*, **~probe** *f* trade sample; **~sendung** *f* trade sample *(sent by post)*; **~terminbörse** *f* commodity futures exchange; **~test** *m* test of goods; **~umsatz** *m* turnover of goods *or* merchandise; **~umsatzsteuer** *f (Sw)* value added tax, VAT; **~zeichen** *nt* trademark.
warf *pret of* **werfen**.
warm *adj comp* **⸚er**, *superl* **⸚ste(r, s)** *or adv* **am ⸚sten** *(lit, fig)* warm; *Wetter auch, Getränk, Speise, (auf Wasserhahn)* hot; *(sl: homosexuell)* queer *(pej inf)* ♦ **mir ist ~** I'm warm; **aus dem W~en in die Kälte kommen** to come out of the warm(th) into the cold; **das hält ~** it keeps you warm; **das macht ~** it warms you up; **das Essen ~ machen** to warm *or* heat up the food; **das Essen ~ stellen** to keep the food hot *or* warm; **~e Miete** rent including heating; **nur einen ~en Händedruck bekommen** *(fig inf)* to get nothing for one's pains; **wie ~e Semmeln weggehen** *(inf)* to sell *or* go like hot cakes; **~ sitzen** to sit in a warm place; **sich ~ anziehen** to dress up warmly; **jdn/etw ⸚stens empfehlen** to recommend sb/sth warmly; **weder ~ noch kalt sein** *(fig)* to be indifferent; **~ werden** *(fig inf)* to thaw out *(inf)*; **mit jdm ~ werden** *(inf)* to get close to sb; **mit etw ~ werden** *mit Stelle* to get used to sth; *mit Stadt auch* to get to know sth; *siehe* **Bruder, laufen, spielen**.
Warm-: ~blut *nt, pl* **~blüter** crossbreed; **~blüter** *m* **-s, -** *(Zool)* warm-blooded animal; **w~blütig** *adj* warm-blooded.
Wärme *f* **-,** *(rare)* **-n** *(lit, fig)* warmth; *(von Wetter etc, Phys)* heat; *(Wetterlage)* warm weather ♦ **10 Grad ~** 10 degrees above zero *or* above freezing; **an dem Gerät kann man verschiedene ~n einstellen** you can adjust the appliance to different heat settings; **ist das eine ~!** isn't it warm!; **komm in die ~** come into the warm(th); **mit ~** *(fig)* warmly.
Wärme-: ~behandlung *f (Med)* heat treatment; **w~beständig** *adj* heat-resistant; **~dämmung** *f* (heat) insulation; **~einheit** *f* thermal unit, unit of heat; **~energie** *f* thermal energy; **~grad** *m* degree of heat; **~kraftwerk** *nt* thermal power station; **~lehre** *f* theory of heat; **~leiter** *m* heat conductor; **~messer** *m* **-s, -** thermometer.
wärmen [1] *vt* to warm; *Essen, Kaffee etc* to warm *or* heat up.
[2] *vi (Kleidung, Sonne)* to be warm; *(Ofen auch)* to provide warmth ♦ **Schnaps wärmt** schnapps warms you up.
[3] *vr* to warm oneself (up), to warm up ♦ **sich gegenseitig ~** to keep each other warm.
Wärmepumpe *f* heat pump.
Warme(r) *m decl as adj (sl)* queer *(inf)*, poof *(sl)*, fag *(US sl)*.
Wärme-: ~regler *m* thermostat; **~schutz** *m* heat shield; **~speicher** *m* storer of heat; *(Gerät)* heat storer *or* accumulator; **~stau** *m* build-up of heat; *(Met)* greenhouse effect; **~strahlung** *f* thermal radiation, radiant heat; **~tauscher** *m* heat exchanger; **~technik** *f* heat technology; **~verlust** *m* heat loss.
Wärmflasche *f* hot-water bottle.
Warm-: ~front *f (Met)* warm front; **w~gemäßigt** *adj (Geog)* temperate; ⚠**w~halten** *vt sep irreg* **sich** *(dat)* **jdn w~halten** *(fig inf)* to keep in with sb *(inf)*; **~halteplatte** *f* hot plate; **w~herzig** *adj* warm-hearted; **~herzigkeit** *f* warm-heartedness; ⚠**w~laufen** *vi sep irreg aux sein* to warm up; **~luft** *f* warm air; **~luftzufuhr** *f* inflow *or* influx of warm air; *(von Heizung)* warm air supply; **~miete** *f* rent including heating; **~start** *m (Aut, Comput)* warm start.
Warmwasser-: ~bereiter *m* **-s, -** water heater; **~heizung** *f* hot-water central heating; **~leitung** *f* hot-water pipe; **~speicher** *m* hot-water tank; **~versorgung** *f* hot-water supply.
Warn-: ~anlage *f* warning system; **~blinkanlage** *f* flashing warning lights *pl*; *(an Auto)* hazard warning lights *pl*; **~blinkleuchte** *f* flashing warning light; **~blinklicht** *nt* flashing warning light; *(an Auto)* hazard warning light; **~dreieck** *nt* warning triangle.
warnen *vti* to warn *(vor +dat* of) ♦ **die Polizei warnt vor Schneeglätte** the police have issued a warning of snow and ice on the roads; **jdn (davor) ~, etw zu tun** to warn sb against doing sth, to warn sb not to do sth; **vor Taschendieben wird gewarnt!** beware of pickpockets!
Warn-: ~kreuz *nt* warning cross (before level crossing); **~meldung** *f* warning (announcement); **~ruf** *m* warning cry; **~schild** *nt* warning sign; ⚠**~schuß** *m* warning shot; **~signal** *nt* warning signal; **~streik** *m* token strike.
Warnung *f* warning ♦ **~ vor etw** warning about sth; *vor Gefahr* warning of sth.
Warn-: ~vorrichtung *f* warning system; **~zeichen** *nt* warning sign; *(hörbar)* warning signal.
Warrant [*auch* 'vɔrənt] *m* **-s, -s** warrant.
Warschau *nt* **-s** Warsaw.
Warschauer *adj attr* Warsaw.
Warschauer(in *f*) *m* native of Warsaw; *(Einwohner)* inhabitant of Warsaw.
Warschauer Pakt *m* Warsaw Pact.
Warschauer-Pakt-Staaten *pl* Warsaw Pact states *pl*.
Warte *f* **-, -n** observation point; *(fig)* standpoint, viewpoint ♦ **von jds ~ (aus)** *(fig)* from sb's point of view *or* sb's standpoint; **von seiner hohen ~ aus** *(fig iro)* from his lofty standpoint *(iro)*.
Warte-: ~frist *f* waiting period; *(für Lieferung)* delivery time; **~halle** *f* waiting room; *(im Flughafen)* departure lounge; **~liste** *f* waiting list.
warten[1] *vi* to wait *(auf +acc* for) ♦ **warte mal!** hold on, wait a minute; *(überlegend)* let me see; **na warte!** *(inf)* just you wait!; **warte, wenn ich das noch mal sehe!** just let me see that again; **bitte ~** *(Telec)* hold the line please; *(Zeichen)* please wait; **du wirst ~ können** you'll have to wait; **da kannst du ~, bis du schwarz wirst** *(inf)*, **da(rauf) kannst du lange ~** *(iro)* you can wait till the cows come home; **auf Antwort/Einlaß ~** to wait for an answer/to be let in; **mit dem Essen auf jdn ~** to wait for sb (to come) before eating; to wait with lunch/dinner *etc* for sb; **ich bin gespannt, was da auf mich wartet** I wonder what's waiting for me *or* what awaits me *or* what's in store for me there; **auf sie/darauf habe ich gerade noch gewartet!** *(iro)* she/that was all I needed!; **lange auf sich ~ lassen** to be a long time (in) coming; **nicht lange auf sich ~ lassen** to be not long in coming; **das lange W~ hatte ihn müde gemacht** the long wait had made him tired.
warten[2] *vt* **(a)** *(liter: pflegen) Kinder etc* to look after; *Tiere* to tend. **(b)** *Auto* to service; *Maschine auch* to maintain.
Wärter(in *f*) *m* **-s, -** attendant; *(Leuchtturm~, Tier~)* keeper; *(Kranken~)* nurse, orderly; *(Gefängnis~)* warder/wardress *(Brit)*, guard.
Warte-: ~raum *m* waiting room; **~saal** *m* waiting room; **~schleife** *f (Aviat)* holding pattern, stack; **~schleifen ziehen** *or* **drehen** to circle; **~zeit** *f* waiting period; *(an Grenze etc)* wait; **~zimmer** *nt* waiting room; **~zyklus** *m (Comput)* wait state.
-wärts *adv suf* -wards.
Wartung *f (von Auto)* servicing; *(von Maschine auch)* maintenance.
wartungsfrei *adj* maintenance-free.
warum *interrog adv* why ♦ **~ nicht?** why not?; **~ nicht gleich so!** that's better; **nach dem W~ fragen** to ask why; **das W~ und Weshalb** the whys and wherefores.
Warze *f* **-, -n** wart; *(Brust~)* nipple.
Warzen-: ~hof *m (Anat)* areola *(spec)*; **~schwein** *nt* warthog.
was [1] *interrog pron* **(a)** what; *(wieviel auch)* how much ♦ **~ kostet das?** how much is that?, what does *or* how much does that cost?; **~ ist** *or* **gibt's?** what is it?, what's up?; **~ ist, kommst du mit?** well, are you coming?; **sie kommt nicht — ~?** she's not coming — what?; **~ hast du denn?, ~ ist denn los?** what's the matter?, what's wrong?; **~ willst** *or* **hast du denn?** what are you

talking about?; **~ denn?** *(ungehalten)* what (is it)?; *(um Vorschlag bittend)* but what?; **~ denn, bist du schon fertig?** what, are you finished already?; **das ist gut, ~?** *(inf)* that's good, isn't it *or* what *(dated)*?; **~ haben wir gelacht!** *(inf)* how we laughed!; **~ ist das doch schwierig** *(inf)* it's really difficult.
(b) *(inf: warum)* why, what ... for ◆ **~ lachst du denn so?** what are you laughing for?, why are you laughing?
(c) ~ für ... what sort *or* kind of ...; **~ für ein Haus hat er?** what sort *or* kind of (a) house does he have?; **~ für ein schönes Haus!** what a lovely house!; **und ~ für ein Haus!** and what a house!; **~ für ein Wahnsinn!** what madness!
2 *rel pron (auf ganzen Satz bezogen)* which ◆ **das, ~** ... that which ..., what ...; **ich weiß, ~ ich/er tun soll** I know what I should do *or* what to do/what he should do; **~ auch (immer)** whatever; **das ist etwas, ~ ich nicht verstehe** that is something (which) I don't understand; **alles, ~** ... everything *or* all (that) ...; **das Beste/Schönste/wenige/einzige, ~ ich** ... the best/prettiest/little/only thing (that) I ...; **schreib/iß** *etc*, **~ du kannst** *(inf)* write/eat *etc* what you can; **lauf, ~ du kannst!** *(inf)* run as fast as you can!; **~ du immer hast!** you do go on!
3 *(inf) indef pron abbr of* **etwas** something; *(fragend, bedingend auch, verneint)* anything; *(unbestimmter Teil einer Menge)* some; any ◆ **(na,) so ~!** well I never!; **so ~ von Blödheit** such stupidity; **kann ich dir ~ helfen?** *(inf)* can I give you a hand?; **ist (mit dir) ~?** is something the matter (with you)?; *siehe auch* **etwas, sehen.**

Was *nt* **-,** *no pl* **das ~ und nicht das Wo ist das Wichtigste** the most important thing is what is done, not where it is done.

Wasch-: ~anlage *f (für Autos)* car-wash; *(Scheiben~)* wipers *pl*; *(fig inf: für Geld)* laundering facility; **~anleitung** *f* washing instructions *pl*; **~anweisung** *f* washing instructions *pl*; **~automat** *m* automatic washing machine; **w~bar** *adj* washable; **~bär** *m* rac(c)oon; **~becken** *nt* wash-basin; *(Schüssel)* wash-bowl; **~benzin** *nt* benzine; **~beutel** *m* sponge bag; **~brett** *nt* wash-board; **~bütte** *f* wash-tub.

Wäsche *f* **-,** *no pl* **(a)** washing; *(Schmutz~, bei Wäscherei)* laundry ◆ **große/kleine ~ haben** *(in bezug auf Menge)* to have a large/small amount of washing (to do); *(in bezug auf Größe)* to wash the big/small things; **bei** *or* **in der ~** in the wash; **in der ~ sein** to be in the wash; *(in der Wäscherei)* to be at the laundry; **etw in die ~ geben** to put sth in the wash; *(in die Wäscherei)* to send sth to the laundry; *siehe* **schmutzig.**
(b) *(Stoffzeug) (Bett~, Tisch~, Küchen~)* linen; *(Unter~)* underwear ◆ **dumm aus der ~ gucken** *(inf)* to look stupid.

Wäschebeutel *m* dirty clothes bag; *(für Wäscherei)* laundry bag.

wasch|echt *adj Farbe* fast; *Stoff auch* colourfast; *(fig)* genuine, real, pukka *(inf)*.

Wäsche-: ~geschäft *nt* draper's (shop); **~klammer** *f* clothes-peg; **~knopf** *m* linen-covered button; **~korb** *m* dirty clothes basket; **~leine** *f* (clothes-)line; **~mangel** *f* mangle.

waschen *pret* **wusch,** *ptp* **gewaschen** **1** *vt* to wash; *Gold etc* to pan; *(fig inf) Geld, Spenden* to launder ◆ **(Wäsche) ~** to do the washing; **etw** *(acc)* **warm/kalt ~** to wash sth in hot/cold water; **sich** *(dat)* **die Hände/Haare** *etc* **~** to wash one's hands/hair *etc*; **W~ und Legen** *(beim Friseur)* shampoo and set.
2 *vr (Mensch, Tier)* to wash (oneself/itself); *(Stoff)* to wash ◆ **das hat sich gewaschen** *(inf)* that really made itself felt, that really had an effect; **eine Geldbuße/Ohrfeige/Klassenarbeit, die sich gewaschen hat** *(inf)* a really heavy fine/hard box on the ears/a real stinker of a test *(inf)*.

Wäschepuff *m* dirty clothes basket.

Wäscher *m* **-s, -** *(Gold~)* panner; *(Erz~)* washer ◆ **~ und Plätter** launderer.

Wäscherei *f* laundry.

Wäscherin *f* washerwoman; *(Berufsbezeichnung)* laundress.

Wäsche-: ~rolle *f (esp Aus)* mangle; **~sack** *m* laundry bag; **~schleuder** *f* spin-drier; **~schrank** *m* linen cupboard; **~spinne** *f* revolving *or* rotary clothes dryer; **~ständer** *m* clothes-horse; **~stärke** *f* starch; **~tinte** *f* marking ink; **~trockner** *m (Ständer)* clothes-horse; *(Trockenautomat)* drier; **~zeichen** *nt* name tape.

Wasch-: **⚠~faß** *nt* wash-tub; **~frau** *f* washerwoman; **~gang** *m* stage of the washing programme; **~gelegenheit** *f* washing facilities *pl*; **~handschuh** *m* flannel mitt; **~haus** *nt* wash-house, laundry; **~kessel** *m* (wash-)boiler, copper; **~küche** *f* wash-room, laundry; *(inf: Nebel)* pea-souper *(inf)*; **~lappen** *m* flannel; *(fürs Gesicht auch)* facecloth; *(inf: Feigling)* sissy *(inf)*, softy *(inf)*; **~lauge** *f* suds *pl*; **~leder** *nt* chamois leather; **~maschine** *f* washing-machine; **w~maschinenfest** *adj* machine-washable; **~mittel** *nt* detergent; **~pulver** *nt* washing-powder; **~raum** *m* wash-room; **~rumpel** *f* **-, -n** *(Aus) siehe* **~brett**; **~salon** *m* laundry; *(zum Selbstwaschen)* launderette; **~schüssel** *f* wash-bowl, wash-basin; **~seide** *f* washable silk; **~straße** *f (zur Autowäsche)* car wash; **~tag** *m* wash-day; **~tag haben** to have one's wash-day; **~tisch** *m*, **~toilette** *f* wash-stand; **~trog** *m* washing trough.

Waschung *f (Rel, Med)* ablution.

Wasch-: ~wasser *nt* washing water; **~weib** *nt (fig pej)* washerwoman; **~zettel** *m (Typ)* blurb; **~zeug** *nt* toilet *or* washing things *pl*; **~zuber** *m* wash-tub; **~zwang** *m (Psych)* obsession with washing oneself.

Waserl *nt* **-s, -(n)** *(Aus inf)* **armes ~** poor thing.

Wasser *nt* **-s, - (a)** *no pl* water ◆ **bei ~ und Brot** *(euph)* behind bars, in prison; **das ist ~ auf seine Mühle** *(fig)* this is all grist to his mill; **bis dahin fließt noch viel ~ den Bach** *or* **den Rhein** *or* **die Donau** *etc* **hinunter** a lot of water will have flowed under the bridge by then; **dort wird auch nur mit ~ gekocht** *(fig)* they're no different from anybody else (there); **ihr kann er nicht das ~ reichen** *(fig)* he can't hold a candle to her, he's not a patch on her; **~ lassen** *(Med)* to pass water; *siehe* **Blut, Rotz, abgraben, rein**[2].
(b) *pl* **¨** *(Flüssigkeit) (Abwasch~ etc)* water; *(medizinisch)* lotion; *(Parfüm)* cologne, scent; *(Mineral~)* mineral water; *(Schnaps)* schnapps; *(Tränen)* tears *pl*; *(Speichel)* saliva; *(Schweiß)* sweat; *(Urin)* water, urine; *(Med: in Beinen etc)* fluid; *(Ab~)* sewage *no pl* ◆ **~ mit Geschmack** *(inf)* pop *(inf)*; **das ~ läuft mir im Mund zusammen** my mouth is watering.
(c) *(~masse, im Gegensatz zu Land)* water. **die ~** *pl (geh)* the waters *pl* ◆ **etw unter ~ setzen** to flood sth; **unter ~ stehen** to be flooded, to be under water; **~ treten** *(beim Schwimmen)* to tread water; *(Med)* to paddle *(in cold water as a therapy)*; **zu ~** on the water *or (Meer)* sea; *(auf dem ~weg)* by water/sea; **ein Boot zu ~ lassen** to launch a boat; **einen Ort zu ~ erreichen** to reach a place by water; **ins ~ fallen, zu ~ werden** *(fig)* to fall through; **nahe ans ~ gebaut haben** *(inf)* to be inclined to tears; **ins ~ gehen** *(euph)* to drown oneself; **sich über ~ halten** *(fig)* to keep one's head above water; **er ist mit allen ~n gewaschen** he is a shrewd customer, he knows all the tricks; *siehe* **Schlag, Hals**[1].
(d) *(Gezeiten)* tide ◆ **das ~ kommt/läuft ab** the tide is coming in/going out; *siehe* **auflaufen.**

Wasser-: **⚠w~abstoßend, ⚠w~abweisend** *adj* water-repellent; **⚠~anschluß** *m* mains water supply; *(auf Zeltplatz)* water point; **w~arm** *adj* arid; **~armut** *f* aridity; **~aufbereitung** *f* treatment of water; **~bad** *nt* water bath; *(Cook)* double-boiler, bain-marie; **im ~bad** *(Cook)* in a double boiler *or* bain-marie; **~ball** *m* **(a)** *(no pl: Spiel)* water polo; **(b)** *(Ball)* beach-ball; *(fürs ~ballspiel)* water-polo ball; **~bau** *m*, *no pl* hydraulic engineering; **~bett** *nt* water-bed; **~blase** *f* (water) blister; **~bombe** *f (Mil)* depth charge; *(inf)* water bomb; **~bruch** *m (Med)* hydrocele; **~burg** *f* castle built in water.

Wässerchen *nt* little stream *or* brook; *(Parfüm)* scent, perfume; *(kosmetisch)* lotion, potion ◆ **ein ~ machen** *(baby-talk)* to do a wee-wee *(baby-talk)*; **er sieht aus, als ob er kein ~ trüben könnte** he looks as if butter wouldn't melt in his mouth.

Wasser-: ~dampf *m* steam; **w~dicht** *adj (lit, fig)* watertight; *Uhr, Stoff etc* waterproof; **~eimer** *m* bucket, pail; **~enthärter** *m* water-softener; **~erhitzer** *m* water-heater; **~fahrzeug** *nt* water-craft; **~fall** *m* waterfall; **wie ein ~fall reden** *(inf)* to talk nineteen to the dozen *(inf)*; **~farbe** *f* water-colour; **w~fest** *adj* waterproof; **~floh** *m* water-flea; **~flugzeug** *nt* seaplane; **~frosch** *m* aquatic frog; **~gas** *nt* water-gas; **~gehalt** *m* water content; **~geist** *m* water sprite; **w~gekühlt** *adj* water-cooled; **~glas** *nt* **(a)** *(Trinkglas)* water glass, tumbler; *siehe* **Sturm**; **(b)** *no pl (Chem)* water-glass; **~glätte** *f* slippery roads due to surface water; **~graben** *m (Sport)* water-jump; *(um Burg)* moat; **~hahn** *m* water tap, faucet *(US)*; *(Haupthahn)* stop-cock; **w~haltig** *adj (Chem)* aqueous; **w~haltig sein** to contain water; **~härte** *f* hardness of water; **~haushalt** *m (Biol etc)* water balance; **~hose** *f (Met)* waterspout; **~huhn** *nt* coot.

wässerig *adj (lit, fig)* watery; *Augen* pale-coloured; *(Chem)* aqueous ◆ **jdm den Mund ~ machen** *(inf)* to make sb's mouth water.

Wasser-: ~jungfer *f (Zool)* dragonfly; **~jungfrau** *f (Myth)* naiad; **~kante** *f siehe* **Waterkant**; **~kessel** *m* kettle; *(Tech)* boiler; **~kissen** *nt (Med)* water cushion; **~klosett** *nt* water-closet; **~kopf** *m* water on the brain *no indef art*, hydrocephalus *no indef art (spec)*; *(inf)* big head; **bürokratischer ~kopf** *(fig)* top-heavy bureaucracy; **~kraft** *f* water-power; **~kraftwerk** *nt* hydro-electric power station; **~kreislauf** *m* water cycle; **~kresse** *f* watercress; **~kühlung** *f (Aut)* water-cooling; **mit ~kühlung** water-cooled; **~kühlung haben** to be water-cooled; **~lassen** *nt (Med)* passing water, urination; **~latte** *f (vulg)* early-morning erection *or* hard-on *(sl)*; **~lauf** *m* watercourse; **~läufer** *m (Vogel)* shank, sandpiper; *(Insekt)* water-measurer *or* -skater; **dunkler ~läufer** spotted redshank; **~leiche** *f* drowned body; **~leitung** *f (Rohr)* water pipe; *(Anlagen)* plumbing *no pl*; *(inf: Hahn)* tap, faucet *(US)*; **~lilie** *f* water-lily; **~linie** *f (Naut)* water-line; **~loch** *nt* water-hole; **w~löslich** *adj* water-soluble, soluble in water; **~mangel** *m* water shortage; **~mann** *m*, *pl* **-männer (a)** *(Myth)* water sprite; **(b)** *(Astrol)* Aquarius *no art*, Water-carrier; **~mann sein** to be (an) Aquarius; **~melone** *f* water-melon; **~messer** *m* **-s, -** water-meter; **~mühle** *f* water-mill.

wassern *vi (Aviat)* to land on water *or (im Meer auch)* in the sea; *(Space)* to splash down.

wässern **1** *vt Heringe, Erbsen etc* to soak; *(Phot)* to rinse; *(bewässern) Pflanzen, Felder* to water.
2 *vi* to water ◆ **mir ~ die Augen** my eyes are watering.

Wasser-: ~nixe *f (Myth)* water-nymph; **~orgel** *f* hydraulic organ; **~pfeife** *f* hookah, hubble-bubble; **~pflanze** *f* aquatic plant; **~pistole** *f* water-pistol; **~pocken** *pl (Med)* chickenpox *sing*; **~polizei** *f siehe* **~schutzpolizei**; **~rad** *nt* water-wheel; **~ratte** *f* water-rat *or* -vole; *(inf: Kind)* water-baby; **~recht** *nt laws pertaining to water and waterways*; **w~reich** *adj Gebiet* with plenty of water, abounding in water; *Fluß* containing a lot of water; **~reservoir** *nt* reservoir; **~rohr** *nt* water-pipe; **~säule** *f* water column; **~schaden** *m* water damage; **~schaff** *nt* **-(e)s, -e** *(Aus)* water tub; **~scheide** *f* watershed; **w~scheu** *adj* scared of water; **~scheu** *f* fear of water; *(Psych)* water phobia; **~schi** *m, nt siehe* **~ski**; **~schildkröte** *f* turtle; **~schlange** *f* **(a)** *(Zool)* water-snake; *(Myth)* (sea)serpent; **(b)** *(Astron)* Hydra; **~schlauch** *m* **(a)** (water) hose; *(Behälter)* skin; **(b)** *(Bot)* bladderwort; **⚠~schloß** *nt* castle surrounded by water; **~schutzpolizei** *f (auf Flüssen, ~wegen)* river police; *(im Hafen)* harbour police; *(auf der See)* coastguard service; **~ski** **1** *m* water-ski; **2** *nt* water-skiing; **~speier** *m* **-s, -** gargoyle; **~spiegel** *m (Oberfläche)* surface of the water; *(~stand)* water-level; **~sport** *m* **der ~sport** water sports *pl*; **~sportfahrzeug** *nt* water sport craft; **~sportler** *m* water sportsman; **~spülung** *f* flush; **Klosett mit ~spülung**

⚠: for details of spelling reform, see supplement

flush toilet, water-closet; **~stand** *m* water-level; **niedriger/hoher ~stand** low/high water; **~standsanzeiger** *m* water-level indicator; **~standsmeldungen** *pl* water-level *or* (*für Gezeiten*) tide report.

Wasserstoff *m* hydrogen.

Wasserstoff-: w~blond *adj attr Haar* peroxide blonde; **ein w~blondes Mädchen** a peroxide blonde (*inf*); **~bombe** *f* hydrogen bomb, H-bomb; **~superoxid, ~superoxyd** *nt* hydrogen peroxide.

Wasser-: ~strahl *m* jet of water; **~straße** *f* waterway; **~sucht** *f* dropsy; **w~süchtig** *adj* suffering from dropsy, dropsical; **~tank** *m* water-tank; (*für WC*) cistern; **~tier** *nt* aquatic animal; **~träger** *m* water-carrier; **~treten** *nt* (*Sport*) treading water; (*Med*) paddling (*in cold water as therapy*); **~tropfen** *m* water-drop, drop of water; **~turm** *m* water-tower; **~uhr** *f* (*~zähler*) water-meter; (*Hist*) water-clock.

Wasserung *f* sea/water landing; (*Space*) splashdown.

Wässerung *f, no pl siehe* **wässern 1** soaking, steeping; rinsing, washing; watering.

Wasser-: ~verbrauch *m* water consumption *no def art*; **~versorgung** *f* water-supply; **Maßnahmen zur ~versorgung** measures to ensure the supply of water; **~verunreinigung** *f* water pollution; **~vogel** *m* waterfowl; **~waage** *f* spirit-level; **~weg** *m* waterway; **auf dem ~weg** by water *or* (*Meer*) sea; **~welle** *f* water-wave; **~werfer** *m* water-cannon; **~werk** *nt* waterworks *sing or pl*; **~wirtschaft** *f* water-supply (and distribution); **~zähler** *m* water-meter; **~zeichen** *nt* watermark.

⚠ **wäßrig** *adj siehe* **wässerig.**

waten *vi aux sein* to wade.

Waterkant *f -, no pl* coast (*esp North Sea coast of Germany*).

watschelig *adj* waddling *attr* ◆ **~ laufen** to waddle.

watscheln *vi aux sein* to waddle.

Watschen *f -, -* (*Aus, S Ger inf*) *siehe* **Ohrfeige.**

watschen *vt* (*S Ger inf*) **jdm eine ~** (*auf Backe*) to slap sb's face; (*ans Ohr*) to give sb a clip round the ear; **eine gewatscht kriegen** to get a slap in the face/clip round the ear.

Watschenmann *m, pl* **-männer** (*Aus*) (*lit*) *fairground dummy*; (*fig*) Aunt Sally (*fig*).

Watstiefel *m* wader.

Watt¹ *nt* **-s, -** (*Elec*) watt.

Watt² *nt* **-(e)s, -en** (*Geog*) mud-flats *pl*.

Watte *f -, -n* cotton wool, cotton (*US*); (*zur Polsterung*) padding, wadding ◆ **jdn in ~ packen** (*fig inf*) to wrap sb in cotton wool; **laß dich doch in ~ packen!** you're far too over-sensitive!

Wattebausch *m* cotton-wool ball.

Wattenmeer *nt* mud-flats *pl*.

Watte-: ~pad [-pɛd] *m* cotton(-wool) pad; **~stäbchen** *nt* cotton bud.

wattieren* *vt* to pad; (*füttern*) to line with padding; (*und absteppen*) *Stoff, Steppdecke* to quilt ◆ **wattierte Umschläge/Jacken** padded envelopes/quilted jackets.

Wattierung *f siehe vt* padding; lining; quilting; (*die Füllung*) padding.

Watt-: ~meter *nt* wattmeter; **~sekunde** *f* watt-second; **~stunde** *f* watt-hour; **~zahl** *f* wattage.

Watvogel *m* wader.

wau wau *interj* bow-wow, woof-woof.

Wauwau *m* **-s, -s** (*baby-talk*) bow-wow (*baby-talk*).

WC [veːˈtseː] *nt* **-s, -s** WC.

Webe *f -, -n* (*Aus*) linen.

Webekante *f siehe* **Webkante.**

weben *pret* **webte** *or* (*liter, fig*) **wob**, *ptp* **gewebt** *or* (*liter, fig*) **gewoben** *vti* (*lit, fig*) to weave; *Spinnennetz, Lügennetz* to spin.

Weber(in *f*) *m* **-s, -** weaver.

Weberei *f* **(a)** *no pl* (*das Weben*) weaving. **(b)** (*Betrieb*) weaving mill. **(c)** (*Zeug*) woven article.

Weber-: ~kamm *m* weaver's reed; **~knecht** *m* (*Zool*) daddy-long-legs; **~knoten** *m* reef knot.

Web-: ~fehler *m* weaving flaw; **einen ~fehler haben** (*fig inf*) to have a screw loose (*inf*); **~garn** *nt* weaving yarn; **~kante** *f* selvage, selvedge; **~stuhl** *m* loom; **~waren** *pl* woven goods *pl*.

Wechsel [ˈvɛksl] *m* **-s, - (a)** (*Änderung*) change; (*abwechselnd*) alternation; (*Geld~*) exchange; (*der Jahreszeiten, Agr: Frucht~*) rotation ◆ **ein ~ der Wohnung/Schule** *etc* a change of address/school *etc*; **der ~ von Tag und Nacht** the alternation of day and night; **im ~ der Zeiten** through the ages; **in buntem ~** in motley succession; **im ~** (*abwechselnd*) in turn, alternately.
(b) (*Sport*) (*Staffel~*) (baton) change, change-over; (*Ftbl etc*) substitution.
(c) (*Fin*) bill (of exchange); (*inf: Geldzuwendung*) allowance.
(d) (*Hunt*) trail used by game *or* wild animals.

Wechsel- [ˈvɛksl-]: **~bad** *nt* alternating hot and cold baths *pl*; **~bad der Gefühle** (*fig*) emotional roller-coaster; **jdn einem ~bad aussetzen** (*fig*) to blow hot and cold with sb; **~balg** *m* changeling (child); (*inf*) little monster (*inf*); **~beziehung** *f* correlation, interrelation; **in ~beziehung miteinander** *or* **zueinander stehen** to be correlated *or* interrelated; **~bürgschaft** *f* guarantee (on a bill); **~fälle** *pl* vicissitudes *pl*; **~fieber** *nt* (*old*) malaria; **~geld** *nt* change; **~gesang** *m* antiphonal singing; **~gespräch** *nt* dialogue; **~getriebe** *nt* (*Tech*) variable gears *pl*; **w~haft** *adj* changeable; *Schicksal, Mensch auch* fickle, capricious; **~jahre** *pl* menopause *sing*, change of life *sing*; **in die ~jahre kommen/in den ~jahren sein** to start the menopause/be suffering from the menopause; **~kurs** *m* rate of exchange.

wechseln [ˈvɛksln] 1 *vt* to change (*in +acc* into); (*austauschen*) to exchange; (*Ftbl etc*) to substitute (*gegen* for) ◆ **den Arzt ~** to change doctors *or* one's doctor; **den Tisch/die Schule/das Hemd ~** to change tables/schools/one's shirt; **die Farbe ~** to change colour; **den Platz mit jdm ~** to exchange one's seat with sb; **Briefe ~** to correspond *or* be in correspondence (*mit* with); **die Wohnung ~** to move house; **den Wohnsitz ~** to move to another place; **können Sie (mir) 10 Mark ~?** can you change 10 marks (for me)?; **Wäsche zum W~** a change of underwear.
2 *vi* **(a)** to change; (*Sport auch*) to change over; (*einander ablösen*) to alternate ◆ **ich kann Ihnen leider nicht ~** I'm sorry, I don't have any change.
(b) (*Hunt*) to pass by ◆ **über die Straße** *etc* **~** to cross the road *etc*; **über die Grenze ~** (*Mensch*) to cross the border.

wechselnd [ˈvɛkslnt] *adj* changing; (*einander ablösend, ab~*) alternating; *Launen, Stimmungen* changeable; *Winde* variable; *Bewölkung* variable, intermittent ◆ **mit ~em Erfolg** with varying (degrees of) success; **~ bewölkt** cloudy with sunny intervals.

Wechsel [ˈvɛksl-]: **~nehmer** *m* payee of a bill; **~platte** *f* (*Comput*) floppy disk; **~protest** *m* protest of a bill; **~rahmen** *m* clip-on picture frame; **~recht** *nt* law relating to bills of exchange; **~schalter** *m* **(a)** (*Elec*) change-over switch; **(b)** (*in Bank*) counter for foreign currency exchange; **~schuldner** *m* payer of a bill; **w~seitig** *adj* reciprocal; (*gegenseitig auch*) mutual; **~spiel** *nt* interplay; **w~ständig** *adj* (*Bot*) alternate; **~strom** *m* alternating current; **~stube** *f* bureau de change, exchange; **~tierchen** *nt* amoeba; **w~voll** *adj* varied; **~wähler** *m* floating voter; **w~weise** *adv* in turn, alternately; **~wirkung** *f* interaction; **in ~wirkung stehen** to interact.

Wechsler [ˈvɛkslɐ] *m* **-s, - (a)** (*Automat*) change machine, change dispenser. **(b)** (*Mensch*) money-changer.

Weck *m* **-(e)s, -e** (*dial*) (bread) roll; (*Aus: Brot*) loaf.

Weck-: ~apparat *m* preserving and bottling equipment; **~dienst** *m* (*Telec*) alarm call service, wake-up service, early morning call service; (*Mil*) reveille; **~dienst machen** to do reveille.

Wecke *f* **-, -n, Wecken** *m* **-s, -** (*dial*) (bread) roll.

wecken *vt* to wake (up), to waken; (*fig*) to arouse; *Bedarf* to create; *Erinnerungen* to bring back, to revive ◆ **sich ~ lassen** to have sb wake one up; (*telefonisch*) to get an alarm call.

Wecken *nt* **-s,** *no pl* waking-up time; (*Mil*) reveille ◆ **Ausgang bis zum ~** overnight leave (until reveille).

Wecker *m* **-s, -** alarm clock ◆ **jdm auf den ~ fallen** *or* **gehen** (*inf*) to get on sb's nerves *or* wick (*sl*), to drive sb up the wall (*inf*).

Weck-: ~glas ® *nt* preserving *or* Kilner ® jar; **~radio** *nt* radio-alarm clock; **~ring** ® *m* rubber ring (*for preserving jars*); **~ruf** *m* (*Telec*) alarm call; (*Mil*) reveille; **~uhr** *f* alarm clock.

Wedel *m* **-s, -** fly whisk; (*Fächer*) fan; (*Staub~ aus Federn*) feather duster; (*zum Besprengen*) sprinkler; (*Zweig*) twig; (*Eccl*) ≃ palm leaf; (*Bot: Blatt*) frond; (*Hunt*) tail.

wedeln 1 *vi* **(a)** **(mit dem Schwanz) ~** (*Hund*) to wag its tail; **mit etw ~** (*winken*) to wave sth; **mit dem Fächer ~** to wave the fan. **(b)** (*Ski*) to wedel. **das W~** wedel(l)ing.
2 *vt* to waft.

weder *conj* **~ ... noch ...** neither ... nor ...; **er ist ~ gekommen, noch hat er angerufen** he neither came nor phoned up; **~ das eine noch das andere** (*als Antwort*) neither.

weg *adv* (*fort*) **~ sein** (*fortgegangen, abgefahren, verschwunden*) to have *or* be gone; (*nicht hier, entfernt*) to be away; (*inf: geistes abwesend*) to be not quite with it (*inf*); (*inf: eingeschlafen*) to have dozed off; (*inf: tot*) to be dead; (*inf: begeistert*) to be really taken, to be bowled over (*von* by); **von zu Hause ~ sein** to be away from home; (*erwachsene Kinder*) to have left home; **über etw** (*acc*) **~ sein** (*inf*) to have got over sth; **er ist schon lange darüber ~** (*inf*) he got over it a long while ago; **über den Tisch/meinen Kopf ~** across the table/over my head; **weit ~ von hier** far (away) from here; **~ (von hier)!** get away from here!; let's get away from here; **~ mit euch!** away with you!, scram! (*inf*); **nichts wie** *or* **nur ~ von hier!** let's scram (*inf*); **~ da!** (get) out of the way!; **~ damit!** (*mit Schere etc*) put it away!; **immer ~ damit** throw *or* chuck (*inf*) it all out; **~ mit den alten Traditionen!** away with these old traditions!; **Hände ~!** hands off!; **in einem ~** (*inf*) non-stop; **~ vom Fenster sein** (*sl*) to be out of the game (*sl*).

Weg *m* **-(e)s, -e (a)** (*Pfad, Geh~, fig*) path; (*Wald~, Wander~ etc auch*) track, trail; (*Straße*) road ◆ **am ~e** by the wayside; **woher des ~(e)s?** (*old*) where have you come from?, whence comest thou? (*obs*); **wohin des ~(e)s?** (*old*) where are you going to?, whither goest thou? (*obs*); **des ~(e)s kommen** (*old*) to come walking/riding *etc* up; **in einer Gegend ~ und Steg kennen** to know an area like the back of one's hand; **jdm in den ~ treten, jdm den ~ versperren** *or* **verstellen** to block *or* bar sb's way; **jdm/einer Sache im ~ stehen** (*fig*) to stand in the way of sb/sth; **jdm Hindernisse** *or* **Steine in den ~ legen** (*fig*) to put obstructions in sb's way; **jdm nicht über den ~ trauen** (*fig*) not to trust sb an inch; **jdn aus dem ~ räumen** (*fig*) to get rid of sb; **etw aus dem ~ räumen** (*fig*) to remove sth; *Mißverständnisse* to clear sth up; **neue ~e beschreiten** (*fig*) to tread new paths; **den ~ der Sünde/Tugend gehen** to follow the path of sin/virtue; **die ~e Gottes** the ways of the Lord; **den ~ des geringsten Widerstandes gehen** to follow the line of least resistance; **der ~ zur Hölle ist mit guten Vorsätzen gepflastert** (*Prov*) the road to Hell is paved with good intentions; *siehe* **irdisch.**
(b) (*lit, fig: Route*) way; (*Entfernung*) distance; (*Reise*) journey; (*zu Fuß*) walk; (*fig: zum Erfolg auch, Bildungs~*) road ◆ **ich muß diesen ~ jeden Tag zweimal gehen/fahren** I have to walk/drive this stretch twice a day; **auf dem ~ nach London/zur Arbeit** on the way to London/work; **auf dem ~ zu jdm/nach ei-**

nem Ort sein to be on the *or* one's way to sb's/a place; **6 km ~** 6 kms away; **noch zwei Stunden/ein Stück ~ vor sich haben** to still have two hours/some distance to travel; **jdn ein Stück ~(es) begleiten** (*geh*) to accompany sb part of the way; **mein erster ~ war zur Bank** the first thing I did was go to the bank; **jdn auf seinem letzten ~ begleiten** (*euph*) to pay one's last respects to sb; **seiner ~e gehen** (*geh*) (*lit*) to go on one's way; (*fig*) to go one's own way; **welchen ~ haben sie eingeschlagen?** (*lit*) what road did they take?; **einen neuen ~ einschlagen** (*fig*) to follow a new avenue; (*beruflich*) to follow a new career; **den falschen/richtigen ~ einschlagen** (*lit*) to follow the wrong/right path *or* road *or* (*fig*) avenue; **jdm etw mit auf den ~ geben** (*lit*) to give sb sth to take with him/her *etc*; **jdm einen guten Rat mit auf den ~ geben** to give sb good advice to follow in life; **jdm/einer Sache aus dem ~ gehen** (*lit*) to get out of sb's way/the way of sth; (*fig*) to avoid sb/sth; **jdm über den ~ laufen** (*fig*) to run into sb; **seinen ~ (im Leben/Beruf) machen** (*fig*) to make one's way in life/one's career; **seinen ~ nehmen** (*fig*) to take its/their course; **etw in die ~e leiten** to arrange sth; **jdm/sich den ~ verbauen** to ruin sb's/one's chances *or* prospects (*für* of); **auf dem besten ~ sein, etw zu tun** to be well on the way to doing sth; **der gerade ~ ist der kürzeste** *or* **beste** (*Prov*) honesty is the best policy.

(c) (*Mittel, Art und Weise*) way; (*Methode*) method ◆ **auf welchem ~ kommt man am schnellsten zu Geld?** what's the fastest way of making *or* to make money?; **auf welchem ~ sind Sie zu erreichen?** how can I get in touch with you?; **auf diesem ~e** this way; **auf diplomatischem ~e** through diplomatic channels; **auf gesetzlichem** *or* **legalem ~e** legally, by legal means; **auf künstlichem ~e** artificially, by artificial means; *siehe* **schriftlich**.

(d) (*inf: Besorgung*) errand.

wẹgbekommen* *vt sep irreg* **(a)** (*entfernen, loswerden*) to get rid of (*von* from); *Klebstoff, Fleck etc* to remove (*von* from), to get off; (*von bestimmtem Ort*) *jdn, Hund* to get away (*von* from). **(b)** (*inf: erhalten*) to get; *Grippe* to catch.

Weg-: ~bereiter *m* precursor, forerunner; **~bereiter einer Sache** (*gen*) *or* **für etw sein** to pave the way for sth; **~bereiter für jdn sein** to prepare the way for sb; **~biegung** *f* turn, bend.

wẹg-: ~blasen *vt sep irreg* to blow away; **wie ~geblasen sein** (*fig*) to have vanished; **~bleiben** *vi sep irreg aux sein* to stay away; (*nicht mehr kommen*) to stop coming; (*Satz, Wort etc*) to be left out *or* omitted; (*Vergünstigung etc*) not to apply; **mir blieb die Luft ~** (*lit*) I couldn't breathe; **mir bleibt die Spucke** *or* **Luft ~!** (*inf*) I'm absolutely speechless *or* flabbergasted!; **sein W~bleiben** his absence; **~bringen** *vt sep irreg* to take away; (*zur Reparatur*) to take in; (*inf: ~bekommen*) to get rid of; **~denken** *vt sep irreg*: **sich** (*dat*) **etw ~denken** to imagine *or* picture things/the place/one's life *etc* without sth; **die Elektrizität ist aus unserem modernen Leben nicht mehr ~zudenken** we cannot imagine life today without electricity; **~diskutieren*** *vt sep* to explain away; **dieses Problem läßt sich nicht ~diskutieren** talking about it won't make the problem go away; **~dürfen** *vi sep irreg* to be allowed to go *or* leave; (*inf: ausgehen dürfen*) to be allowed to go out.

Wegegeld *nt* (*Hist*) (road) toll.

wẹg|ekeln *vt sep* (*inf*) to drive away.

Wegelagerer *m* **-s, -** highwayman; (*zu Fuß*) footpad.

wegen *prep +gen or* (*inf*) *+dat* because of, on account of; (*infolge auch*) due to ◆ **jdn ~ einer Sache bestrafen/verurteilen/entlassen** *etc* to punish/sentence/dismiss *etc* sb for sth; **von ~!** (*inf*) you've got to be kidding! (*inf*); (*Verbot auch*) no way! (*inf*), no chance! (*inf*); **... aber von ~!** (*inf*) ... but not a bit of it! (*inf*); **er ist krank — von ~ krank!** (*inf*) he's ill — since when? (*iro*), what do you mean "ill"? (*iro*); **~ mir** (*inf*) *or* **meiner** (*obs*) *siehe* **meinetwegen**; *siehe* **Amt, Recht.**

Wegerich *m* **-s, -e** (*Bot*) plantain.

wẹg|essen *vt sep irreg* **jdm den Kuchen** *etc* **~** to eat sb's cake *etc*; **er hat (mir) alles weggegessen** he's eaten all my food.

wẹgfahren *sep irreg* [1] *vi aux sein* (*abfahren*) to leave; (*Auto, Bus, Fahrer*) to drive off *or* away; (*im Boot*) to sail away; (*zum Einkaufen, als Ausflug*) to go out; (*verreisen*) to go away.

[2] *vt Menschen, Gegenstände* to take away; *Fahrzeug* to drive away; (*umstellen*) to move.

Wẹgfahrsperre *f* (*Aut*) **(elektronische) ~** (electronic) immobilizer.

Wẹgfall *m, no pl* (*Einstellung*) discontinuation; (*Aufhören*) cessation (*form*); (*Streichung*) cancellation; (*Unterbleiben*) loss; (*Auslassung*) omission ◆ **in ~ kommen** (*form*) to be discontinued; (*Bestimmung*) to cease to apply.

wẹgfallen *vi sep irreg aux sein* to be discontinued; (*Bestimmung, Regelung*) to cease to apply; (*unterbleiben*) to be lost; (*überflüssig werden*) to become no longer necessary; (*ausgelassen werden*) to be omitted ◆ **~ lassen** to discontinue; (*auslassen*) to omit; **wir haben den Nachtisch ~ lassen** we did without *or* dispensed with dessert.

wẹg-: ~fegen *vt sep* (*lit, fig*) to sweep away; (*sl: besiegen*) to wipe the floor with (*inf*); **~fischen** *vt sep* to catch; (*fig inf*) to snap up; **er hat uns alle Forellen ~gefischt** he's caught all our trout; **~fliegen** *vi sep irreg aux sein* to fly away *or* off; (*Hut*) to fly off; (*mit Flugzeug*) to fly out; **wann bist du denn in Frankfurt ~geflogen?** when did you fly out of Frankfurt?; **~fressen** *vt sep* (*inf*) *siehe* **~essen**; **~führen** *sep* [1] *vt* to lead away; [2] *vi* **das führt zu weit (vom Thema) ~** that will lead *or* take us too far off the subject.

Wẹggabelung *f* fork (in the road), bifurcation (*form*).

Wẹggang *m* departure, leaving.

wẹggeben *vt sep irreg* (*verschenken*) to give away; (*in Pflege geben*) to have looked after ◆ **eine kaputte Uhr ~** to take in a broken watch; **seine Wäsche (zum Waschen) ~** to have one's washing done.

Wegefährte *m* (*fig*) companion.

wẹggehen *vi sep irreg aux sein* to go, to leave; (*verreisen, umziehen etc*) to go away; (*ausgehen*) to go out; (*inf: Fleck*) to come off; (*inf: Ware*) to sell ◆ **über etw** (*acc*) **~** (*inf*) to ignore sth, to pass over sth; **aus Heidelberg/aus dem Büro/von der Firma ~** to leave Heidelberg/the office/the firm; **geh mir damit weg!** (*inf*) don't give me that! (*inf*); **geh mir mit dem weg!** (*inf*) don't talk to me about him!

Weggenosse *m* (*lit, fig*) companion.

Wẹggli *nt* **-s, -** (*Sw*) (bread) roll.

wẹggucken *sep* [1] *vi* to look away.

[2] *vt* **es wird dir schon niemand was ~!** (*hum*) we/they *etc* won't be seeing anything we/they *etc* haven't seen before (*hum*).

wẹghaben *vt sep irreg* (*inf*) (*erledigt haben*) to have got done; (*bekommen, verstanden haben*) to have got; (*entfernt haben*) *Fleck etc* to have got rid of (*inf*); (*umstellen, umhängen*) *Tisch, Bild* to have moved ◆ **jdn/etw ~ wollen** (*inf*) to want to get rid of sb/sth; **der hat was weg** (*inf*) he's really clever; **darin hat er was weg** (*inf*) he's pretty good at that; **du hast deine Strafe/deinen Denkzettel weg** you have had your punishment; **einen ~** (*sl*) (*verrückt sein*) to be off one's head (*inf*), to have a screw loose (*inf*); (*betrunken sein*) to be tight (*inf*); *siehe* **Fett, Ruhe, Teil.**

wẹg-: ~helfen *vi sep irreg* **jdm von irgendwo ~helfen** to help sb get away from *or* out of (*inf*) a place; **jdm über etw** (*acc*) **~helfen** (*fig*) to help sb (to) get over sth; **~holen** *vt sep* to take away; (*abholen*) to fetch; **sich** (*dat*) **was/eine Krankheit ~holen** (*inf*) to catch something/a disease; **~hören** *vi sep* not to listen; **~jagen** *vt sep* to chase away, to drive away *or* off; *Menschen auch* to send packing (*inf*); (*aus Land*) to drive out.

wẹgkommen *vi sep irreg aux sein* **(a)** (*inf*) (*entfernt werden*) to go; (*abhanden kommen*) to disappear; (*weggehen können*) to get away; (*aus dem Haus*) to get out ◆ **was ich nicht brauche, kommt weg** what I don't want can go; **das Buch ist mir weggekommen** the book has disappeared, I've lost the book; **mach, daß du wegkommst!** make yourself scarce! (*inf*), hop it! (*inf*); **gut/schlecht (bei etw) ~** to come off well/badly (with sth); **über etw** (*acc*) **~/nicht ~** to get over/be unable to get over sth; **ich komme nicht darüber weg, daß ...** (*inf*) I can't get over the fact that ...

(b) (*dial: herkommen*) to come from.

Weg-: ~kreuz *nt* **(a)** (*Kruzifix*) wayside cross; **(b)** *siehe* **~kreuzung**; **~kreuzung** *f* crossroads.

wẹgkriegen *vt sep* (*inf*) *siehe* **wegbekommen (a).**

Wegkrümmung *f* bend in the road.

wẹg-: ~lassen *vt sep irreg* (*auslassen*) to leave out; (*nicht benutzen*) not to use; (*inf: gehen lassen*) to let go; **ich lasse heute den Zucker im Kaffee ~** I won't have any sugar in my coffee today; **~laufen** *vi sep irreg aux sein* to run away (*vor +dat* from); **seine Frau ist ihm ~gelaufen** his wife has run away (from him) *or* run off (and left him); **das läuft (dir) nicht ~!** (*fig hum*) that can wait; **~legen** *vt sep* (*in Schublade etc*) to put away; (*zur Seite, zum späteren Verbrauch*) to put aside; **~leugnen** *vt sep* to deny.

wẹgmachen *sep* [1] *vt* (*inf*) to get rid of ◆ **sie ließ sich** (*dat*) **das Kind ~** (*sl*) she got rid of the baby (*inf*).

[2] *vr* (*sl*) to clear *or* shove off (*inf*).

[3] *vi aux sein or haben* (*dial, inf*) to get away (*aus* from), to get out (*aus* of).

wẹgmüssen *vi sep irreg* to have to go; (*weggehen müssen auch*) to have to leave *or* be off (*inf*); (*entfernt werden*) to have to be removed ◆ **ich muß eine Zeitlang von/aus New York weg** I must get away from/get out of New York for a while; **du mußt da weg, du behinderst ja den ganzen Verkehr** you'll have to move (from there), you're blocking all the traffic; **die paar Reste müssen weg** we/you *etc* can't leave those little bits; **wenn wir die Wand streichen wollen, muß der Schrank weg** if we're going to paint the wall, we'll have to move the cupboard *or* get the cupboard out of it (*inf*).

Wẹgnahme *f* **-,** *no pl siehe* **wegnehmen** taking; taking away; removal; absorption; blocking out; blocking.

wẹgnehmen *vt sep irreg* to take (*auch Chess*); (*fortnehmen, entfernen, entziehen*) to take away; *Fleck, Rost* to get rid of, to remove; (*absorbieren*) *Strahlen, Licht, Lärm* to absorb; (*verdecken*) *Licht, Sonne* to block out; *Aussicht, Sicht* to block; (*beanspruchen*) *Zeit, Platz* to take up ◆ **Gas ~** (*Aut*) to ease off the accelerator *or* gas (*US*); **fünf Tage vom Urlaub ~** to take five days off the holiday; **die Bässe ~** to turn down *or* reduce the bass; **jdm seine Kinder/Frau ~** to take sb's children away from him/to steal sb's wife.

wẹg-: ~packen *vt sep* to pack *or* put away; (*inf: essen*) to put away (*inf*); **~putzen** *vt sep* to wipe away *or* off; (*inf: essen*) to polish off; **er putzt ganz schön was ~** (*inf*) he doesn't half eat a lot *or* stow a lot away (*inf*); **~raffen** *vt sep* to snatch away; (*liter: durch Tod*) to carry off.

Wegrand *m* wayside, side of the path/road.

wẹg-: ~rasieren* *vt sep* to shave off; **er hat mir den vorderen Kotflügel ~rasiert** (*fig inf*) he took my front mudguard with him (*hum*); **~rationalisieren*** *vt sep Arbeitsplätze* to rationalize away; **~räumen** *vt sep* to clear away; (*in Schrank*) to put away; **~reißen** *vt sep irreg* to tear away (*jdm* from sb); *Zweige* to break off; (*inf*) *Häuser etc* to tear *or* pull down; **der Fluß hat die Brücke ~gerissen** the river swept away the bridge; **~rennen** *vi sep irreg aux sein* (*inf*) to run away; **~retuschieren*** *vt sep* to spot out; **~rücken** *vti sep* (*vi: aux sein*) to move away; **~rücker** *m* (*Pol*) *politician who gives up his/her seat in a rotation procedure*; **~rufen** *vt sep irreg* to call away; **~rutschen** *vi sep aux sein* (*aus der Hand etc*) to slip away; (*auf Eis etc*) to slide away; **mein Wagen ist mir ~gerutscht** my car went into a skid.

wẹgsam *adj* (*obs*) passable.

wẹg-: ~schaffen *vt sep* (*beseitigen, loswerden*) to get rid of; (*~räumen*) to clear away; (*~tragen, ~fahren*) to remove, to cart away (*inf*); (*erledigen*) *Arbeit* to get done; **~schauen** *vi sep siehe* **~sehen.**

Wegscheide *f* parting of the ways (*liter*).

weg-: ~schenken *vt sep* (*inf*) to give away; **~scheren** *vr sep* (*inf*) to clear out *or* shove off (*inf*); **~schicken** *vt sep Brief etc* to send off *or* away; *jdn* to send away; (*um etwas zu holen etc*) to send off; **~schießen** *vt sep irreg* **jdm den Arm** *etc* **~schießen** to shoot sb's arm *etc* off; **~schlaffen** *vi sep aux sein* (*sl*) to peg *or* poop out (*inf*); **er schlaffte ihm immer wieder ~** it kept on going limp on him (*inf*); **~schleichen** *vir sep irreg* (*vi: aux sein*) to creep *or* steal away; **~schleppen** *sep* [1] *vt* to drag *or* lug (*inf*) *or* haul away *or* off; (*tragen*) to carry off; [2] *vr* to drag *or* haul oneself away; **~schließen** *vt sep irreg* to lock away; **~schmeißen** *vt sep irreg* (*inf*) to chuck away (*inf*); **~schnappen** *vt sep* (*inf*) **jdm etw ~schnappen** to snatch sth (away) from sb; **die andere Kundin hat mir das Kleid ~geschnappt** the other customer snapped up the dress before I could; **jdm die Freundin/den Job ~schnappen** to pinch sb's girl-friend/job (*inf*).

Wegschnecke *f* slug (*of the genus Arionidae*).

weg-: ~schütten *vt sep* to tip away; **~schwemmen** *vt sep* to wash away; **~sehen** *vi sep irreg* to look away; **über etw** (*acc*) **~sehen** (*lit*) to look over sth; (*fig inf*) to overlook sth, to turn a blind eye to sth.

wegsetzen *sep* [1] *vt* to move (away); (*wegstellen*) to put away.
[2] *vr* to move away ◆ **sich über etw** (*acc*) **~** (*inf*) to ignore sth, to pay no attention to sth.
[3] *vi aux sein or haben* **über etw** (*acc*) **~** to leap *or* jump over sth, to clear sth.

weg-: ~sollen *vi sep irreg* (*inf*) **das soll ~** that is to go; **ich soll von London ~** I should leave London; **warum soll ich/mein Auto da ~?** why should I move/ my car be moved?; **~spülen** *vt sep* to wash away; (*in der Toilette*) to flush away; (*inf*) *Geschirr* to wash up; **~stecken** *vt sep* (*lit*) to put away; (*inf*) *Niederlage, Kritik* to take; *Enttäuschung, Verlust* to get over; **einen ~stecken** (*sl*) to have it off (*sl*); **~stehlen** *vr sep irreg* to steal away; **~stellen** *vt sep* to put away; (*abstellen*) to put down; **~sterben** *vi sep irreg aux sein* (*inf*) to die off; **jdm ~sterben** to die on sb (*inf*); **~stoßen** *vt sep irreg* to push *or* shove away; (*mit Fuß*) to kick away.

Weg-: ~strecke *f* (*rare*) stretch of road; **schlechte ~strecke** poor road surface; **~stunde** *f* (*old*) hour.

weg-: ~tauchen *vi sep aux sein* to disappear; (*inf: aus unangenehmer Situation*) to duck out (*inf*); **~tragen** *vt sep irreg* to carry away or off; **~treiben** *sep irreg* [1] *vt Boot etc* to carry away *or* off; (*vertreiben*) *Tier etc* to drive away *or* off; [2] *vi aux sein* to drift away; **~treten** *vi sep irreg aux sein* (*rare*) to step away *or* aside; (*Mil*) to fall out; **(lassen Sie) ~treten!** (*Mil*) dismiss!; **er ist (geistig) ~getreten** (*inf*) (*geistesabwesend*) he's miles away (*inf*); (*schwachsinnig*) he's soft in the head (*inf*), he's not all there (*inf*); **~tun** *vt sep irreg* to put away; (*sparen*) *Geld etc auch* to put by *or* aside; (*~ werfen*) to throw away; (*verstecken*) to hide away; **tu die Hände ~!** take your hands off!

Wegwarte *f* (*Bot*) chicory.

weg-: ~waschen *vt sep irreg Fleck* to wash off; (*~spülen*) *Erde etc* to wash away; **~wehen** *vti sep* (*vi: aux sein*) to blow away.

Weg-: w~weisend *adj* pioneering *attr*, revolutionary, pathbreaking (*US*); **~weiser** *m* **-s, -** sign; (*an einem Pfosten*) signpost; (*fig: Buch etc*) guide.

Wegwerf- *in cpds* disposable, throw-away.

weg-: ~werfen *sep irreg* [1] *vt* to throw away; **~geworfenes Geld** money down the drain; [2] *vr* **sich (an jdn) ~werfen** to waste oneself (on sb), to throw oneself away (on sb); **~werfend** *adj* dismissive, disdainful; **W~werfgesellschaft** *f* throwaway society; **~wischen** *vt sep* to wipe off; (*fig*) to dismiss; **~wollen** *vi sep irreg* (*verreisen*) to want to go away; (*~gehen: von Haus, Party etc*) to want to leave *or* go; (*hinausgehen*) to want to go out; **~wünschen** *vt sep* **jdn ~wünschen** to wish sb would go away; **~zählen** *vt sep* (*Aus*) to take away, to subtract; **~zaubern** *vt sep* to make disappear (*lit* by magic/*fig* as if by magic).

Wegzehrung *f* (*liter*) provisions for the journey *pl*; (*Eccl*) viaticum.

wegziehen *sep irreg* [1] *vt* to pull away (*jdm* from sb); *Vorhang* to draw back.
[2] *vi aux sein* to move away; (*Vögel*) to migrate.

Wegzug *m* move (*aus, von* (away) from).

weh [1] *adj* **(a)** (*wund*) sore; (*geh: schmerzlich*) aching *attr* ◆ **sie verspürte ein ~es Gefühl** (*geh*) her heart ached; **mir ist so ~ zumute** *or* **ums Herz** (*old, liter*) my heart is sore (*liter*), I am sore of heart (*old*).
(b) ~ tun (*lit, fig*) to hurt; **mir tut der Rücken ~** my back hurts *or* is aching; **mir tut mein verbrannter Finger ~** my finger hurts *or* is sore where I burnt it; **sich/jdm ~ tun** (*lit, fig*) to hurt oneself/sb; **was tut dir denn nun schon wieder ~?** what's the matter now?; **wo tut es denn ~?** (*fig inf*) what's your problem?, what's up? (*inf*); *siehe* **ach.**
[2] *interj* (*geh, liter*) woe (*old*); (*bedauernd*) alas (*liter*), alack (*old*) ◆ **o ~!** oh dear!, oh, my goodness!; **(über jdn) ~ schreien** to lament (sb); **~ mir!** woe is me! (*liter*); **~ mir, wenn ...** woe betide me if ...

Weh *nt* **-(e)s, -e** (*old, liter*) woe; (*dumpfes Gefühl*) ache; (*Leid, Gram*) grief ◆ **ein tiefes ~ erfüllte ihn** his heart ached.

wehe *interj* **~ (dir), wenn du das tust** you'll be sorry *or* you'll regret it if you do that; **darf ich das anfassen? — ~ (dir)!** can I touch? — you dare! (*inf*) **~ dem, der ...!** woe betide anyone who ...!

Wehe *f* **-, -n (a)** (*Schnee~ etc*) drift. **(b)** (*Geburts~*) **~n** *pl* (*lit*) (labour) pains *pl*, contractions *pl*; (*fig*) birth pangs ◆ **in den ~n liegen** to be in labour; **die ~n setzten ein** labour *or* the contractions started, she went into labour.

wehen [1] *vi* **(a)** (*Wind*) to blow; (*Fahne*) to wave, to flutter; (*Haare*) to blow about ◆ **der Geist der Aufklärung wehte durch Deutschland** (*geh*) the spirit of enlightenment was abroad *or* reigned in Germany; **es weht ein warmer Wind** there's a warm wind (blowing), a warm wind is blowing; *siehe* **Fahne, frisch, Wind.**
(b) *aux sein* (*Geruch, Klang*) to drift; (*Duft*) to waft.
[2] *vt* to blow (*von* off); (*sanft*) to waft.

Weh-: ~gefühl *nt* (*geh*) ache; **ein ~gefühl befiel ihn** his heart ached; **~geschrei** *nt* wailing, cries *pl* of woe (*liter*); **in ~geschrei ausbrechen, ein ~geschrei anstimmen** to start to wail, to give vent to one's woe (*liter*); **~klage** *f* (*liter*) lament(ation); **w~klagen** *vi insep* (*liter*) to lament, to wail; **über etw** (*acc*) **w~klagen** to lament (over) *or* bewail sth; **um jdn w~klagen** to lament the loss of sb; **~laut** *m* (*liter*) cry of pain; (*bei Kummer*) cry of woe; (*leise*) whimper; **w~leidig** *adj* over-sensitive to pain; (*jammernd*) whining *attr*, snivelling *attr*; (*voller Selbstmitleid*) sorry for oneself, self-pitying; **tu** *or* **sei nicht so w~leidig!** don't be such a sissy!; stop feeling sorry for yourself; **er ist ja so w~leidig** he whines at the least little thing; he's always feeling sorry for himself; **~mut** *f* **-,** *no pl* (*geh*) melancholy; (*Sehnsucht*) wistfulness; (*nach Vergangenem*) nostalgia; **w~mütig, w~mutsvoll** *adj siehe n* (*geh*) melancholy; wistful; nostalgic.

Wehr[1] *f* **-, -en (a)** (*Feuer~*) fire brigade *or* department (*US*). **(b)** (*old*) (*Bollwerk*) defences *pl*; (*no pl: Widerstand*) defence ◆ **mit ~ und Waffen** (*old*) in full panoply (*old*); **sich zur ~ setzen** to defend oneself.

Wehr[2] *nt* **-(e)s, -e** weir.

Wehr- *in cpds* defence, defense (*US*); **~beauftragte(r)** *m decl as adj* commissioner for the armed forces; **~bereich** *m* military district; **~dienst** *m* military service; **seinen ~dienst (ab)leisten** to do one's military service; **jdn zum ~dienst einberufen** to call sb up, to draft sb (*US*); **w~(dienst)pflichtig** *adj* liable for military service; **~(dienst)pflichtige(r)** *mf decl as adj* person liable for military service; (*der schon eingezogen ist*) conscript, draftee (*US*); **~dienstverweigerer** *m* conscientious objector.

wehren [1] *vt* (*obs*) *siehe* **verwehren.**
[2] *vr* to defend oneself; (*sich aktiv widersetzen*) to (put up a) fight ◆ **sich gegen einen Plan** *etc* **~** to fight (against) a plan *etc*; **dagegen weiß ich mich zu ~** I know how to deal with that.
[3] *vi +dat* (*geh*) to fight; (*Einhalt gebieten*) to check ◆ **wehret den Anfängen!** these things must be nipped in the bud *or* stopped before they get out of hand.

Wehr-: ~erfassung *f compilation of the call-up list for military service*; **~ersatzbehörde** *f* military recruitment board *or* agency; **~ersatzdienst** *m* alternative national service; **~etat** *m* defence budget; **~experte** *m* defence expert; **w~fähig** *adj* fit for military service, able-bodied; **~gang** *m* walk along the battlements; **w~haft** *adj* (*geh*) able to put up a fight; *Stadt etc* well-fortified; **~hoheit** *f* military sovereignty; **~kirche** *f* fortified church; **w~los** *adj* defenceless; (*fig: gegenüber Gemeinheiten etc*) helpless; **jdm w~los ausgeliefert sein** to be at sb's mercy; **~losigkeit** *f* defencelessness; helplessness; **~macht** *f* armed forces *pl*; (*Hist*) Wehrmacht; **~mann** *m, pl* **-männer** (*Sw*) soldier; ⚠**~paß** *m* service record (book); **~pflicht** *f* **(allgemeine) ~pflicht** (universal) conscription, compulsory military service; **w~pflichtig** *adj siehe* **w~(dienst)pflichtig**; **~sold** *m* (military) pay; **~sportgruppe** *f* paramilitary group; **~turm** *m* fortified tower; **~übung** *f* reserve duty training exercise.

Wehweh *nt* **-s, -s** (*baby-talk*) hurt (place).

Wehwehchen *nt* (*inf*) (minor) complaint ◆ **seine tausend ~** all his little aches and pains.

Weib *nt* **-(e)s, -er** woman, female (*pej*), broad (*US sl*); (*old, Bibl: Ehefrau*) wife; (*pej inf: Mann*) old woman ◆ **~ und Kind** (*old*) wife and children; **eine Frau zu seinem ~(e) nehmen** (*old*) to take a woman to wife (*old*); **sie ist ein tolles ~** (*inf*) she's quite a woman *or* quite a dame (*US inf*).

Weibchen *nt* (*Zool*) female; (*hum: Ehefrau*) little woman (*hum*); (*pej: nicht emanzipierte Frau*) dumb female.

Weiber-: ~art *f* (*old, pej*) woman's way; **~fastnacht** *f day during the carnival period when women assume control*; **~feind** *m* woman-hater, misogynist; **~geschichten** *pl* sexploits *pl* (*hum*); (*Affären auch*) womanizing *sing*; **~geschwätz** *nt* (*pej*) women's talk; ⚠**~haß** *m* (*inf*) misogyny; **~held** *m* (*pej*) lady-killer, womanizer; **~hengst** *m* (*sl*) womanizer (*inf*); **~herrschaft** *f* (*pej*) petticoat government (*inf*); **~kram** *m* (*pej*) women's stuff; **~volk** *nt* (*obs*) womenfolk *pl*; (*pej*) females *pl* (*pej*); **~wirtschaft** *f* (*pej*) henhouse (*inf*).

weibisch *adj* effeminate.

Weiblein *nt* little woman ◆ **ein altes ~** a little old woman, an old dear (*inf*).

weiblich *adj* (*Zool, Bot, von Frauen*) female; (*Gram, Poet, fraulich, wie Frauen*) feminine.

Weiblichkeit *f* femininity; (*Frauen*) women *pl* ◆ **die holde ~** (*hum*) the fair sex.

Weibsbild *nt* (*old*) woman; (*junges ~*) wench (*old*); (*pej auch*) female.

Weibsen *nt* **-s, -** *usu pl* (*hum inf*) woman, female.

Weibsperson *f* (*old*) woman.

Weib(s)stück *nt* (*pej*) bitch (*inf*), cow (*inf*).

weibstoll ['vaips-] *adj* woman-mad.

weich *adj* soft (*auch fig, Ling, Phot*); *Ei* soft-boiled; *Fleisch, Gemüse* tender; *Energietechnik* non-nuclear; *Währung* soft; (*geschmeidig*) *Bewegungen* smooth; *Mensch* (*nachgiebig*) soft; (*mitleidig*) soft-hearted ◆ **~er Boykott** civil disobedience; **~ landen** to land softly; (*auf ~em Untergrund*) to have a soft landing; **~ werden** (*lit, fig*) to soften; **die Knie wurden mir ~** my knees turned to jelly, I went weak at the knees; **~ machen** to soften; **ein ~es Herz haben** to be soft-hearted, to have a soft heart; **eine ~e Birne** *or* **einen ~en Keks haben** (*sl*) to be soft in the head (*inf*).

⚠: Informationen zur Rechtschreibreform im Anhang

Weich- *in cpds* soft; **~bild** *nt* **im ~bild der Stadt** within the city/town precincts.

Weiche[1] *f* **-, -n (a)** *no pl siehe* **Weichheit. (b)** (*Seite*) side; (*von Tier auch*) flank.

Weiche[2] *f* **-, -n (a)** (*Rail*) points *pl* (*Brit*), switch (*US*) ◆ **die ~n stellen** (*lit*) to switch the points; (*fig*) to set the course. **(b)** (*Ausweichstelle*) passing place.

weichen[1] *vti* (*vi: aux haben or sein*) to soak.

weichen[2] *pret* **wich,** *ptp* **gewichen** *vi aux sein* **(a)** (*Mensch, Tier, Fahrzeug: weggehen, verlassen*) to move; (*Armee, Mensch, Tier: zurück~*) to retreat (*dat, vor +dat* from); (*Platz machen, fig: nachgeben*) to give way (*dat* to) ◆ **(nicht) von jdm** *or* **jds Seite ~** (not) to leave sb's side; **er wich nicht** *or* **keinen Schritt vom Wege** he did not deviate an inch; **sie wich nicht von der Stelle** she refused to *or* wouldn't budge (an inch); **alles** *or* **das Blut/die Farbe wich aus ihren Wangen** (*liter*) the blood/colour drained from her cheeks; **die Angst ist von ihr gewichen** her fear has left her *or* disappeared; **weiche böser Geist!** (*liter*) begone evil spirit! (*liter*).
(b) (*Gefühl, Druck, Schmerz*) (*nachlassen*) to ease, to abate; (*verschwinden*) to go.

Weichen-: ~steller *m* **-s, -** pointsman (*Brit*), switchman (*US*); (*fig*) guiding spirit, moving force (*+gen* behind); **~stellung** *f* (*lit*) changing the points; (*fig*) setting the course.

⚠**weich-: ~geklopft** *adj attr Fleisch* hammered tender; **~gekocht** *adj attr Ei* soft-boiled; *Fleisch, Gemüse* boiled until tender; *Nudeln* cooked until soft.

Weichheit *f, no pl siehe* **weich** softness; softness; tenderness; smoothness; softness; soft-heartedness, kindness.

Weich-: w~herzig *adj* soft-hearted; **~herzigkeit** *f* soft-heartedness; **~holz** *nt* softwood; **~käse** *m* soft cheese; ⚠**w~klopfen,** ⚠**w~kriegen** *vt sep* (*fig inf*) to soften up.

weichlich *adj* (*lit*) soft; (*fig*) weak; (*weibisch*) effeminate; (*verhätschelt*) soft ◆ **ein Kind zu ~ erziehen** to mollycoddle a child.

Weichlichkeit *f* (*fig*) weakness; effeminacy; softness.

Weichling *m* (*pej*) weakling, softy (*inf*).

Weich-: ⚠**w~machen** *vt sep* (*fig*) to soften up; **~macher** *m* (*Chem*) softener, softening agent; **w~schalig** *adj* soft-shelled; *Apfel* soft-skinned.

Weichsel ['vaiksl] *f* **-** Vistula.

Weichselkirsche ['vaɪksl-] *f* St Lucie cherry.

Weich-: w~spülen *vt sep* to condition; *Wäsche* to use (fabric) conditioner *or* softener on; **~spüler** *m* conditioner; (*für Wäsche auch*) (fabric) softener; **~teile** *pl* soft parts *pl*; (*sl: Geschlechtsteile*) privates *pl*, private parts *pl*; **~tier** *nt* mollusc; **~zeichner** *m* (*Phot*) soft-focusing lens.

Weide[1] *f* **-, -n** (*Bot*) willow.

Weide[2] *f* **-, -n** (*Agr*) pasture; (*Wiese*) meadow ◆ **auf die** *or* **zur ~ treiben** to put out to pasture *or* to graze *or* to grass; **auf der ~ sein** to be grazing, to be out at pasture.

Weide-: ~land *nt* (*Agr*) pasture(land), grazing land, pasturage; **~monat** *m* (*old*) month of May.

weiden [1] *vi* to graze.
[2] *vt* to (put out to) graze, to put out to pasture ◆ **seine Blicke** *or* **Augen an etw** (*dat*) **~** to feast one's eyes on sth.
[3] *vr* **sich an etw** (*dat*) **~** (*fig*) to revel in; (*sadistisch auch*) to gloat over.

Weiden-: ~baum *m* willow tree; **~busch** *m* willow bush; **~gerte** *f* willow rod *or* switch; (*zum Korbflechten*) osier, wicker; **~kätzchen** *nt* (pussy) willow catkin; **~korb** *m* wicker basket; **~laubsänger** *m* (*Orn*) chiffchaff; **~rost** *m* cattle grid.

Weide-: ~platz *m* pasture; **~wirtschaft** *f* (*Econ*) pastural agriculture.

weidgerecht *adj* in accordance with hunting principles.

weidlich [1] *adv* (*mit adj*) pretty ◆ **sich über etw** (*acc*) **~ amüsieren** to be highly amused at sth; **etw ~ ausnutzen** to make full use of sth; **er hat sich ~ bemüht** he tried pretty hard.
[2] *adj* (*rare*) *siehe* **weidmännisch.**

Weid-: ~mann *m, pl* **-männer** (*liter*) huntsman, hunter; **w~männisch** [1] *adj* huntsman's *attr*; **das ist nicht w~männisch** that's not done in hunting; [2] *adv* in a huntsman's manner; *ausgebildet* as a huntsman; **~mannsdank** *interj* (*Hunt*) thank you (*as answer to ~mannsheil*); **~mannsheil** *interj* (*Hunt*) good hunting; **~werk** *nt* art of hunting; **w~wund** *adj* (*Hunt*) wounded in the belly.

Weigand *m* **-(e)s, -e** (*obs*) warrior.

➤ **weigern** [1] *vr* to refuse.
[2] *vt* (*old*) **jdm etw ~** to deny sb sth.

Weigerung *f* refusal.

Weigerungsfall *m* (*form*) **im ~** in case of refusal (*form*).

Weih *m* **-(e)s, -e** (*Orn*) *siehe* **Weihe[1].**

Weihbischof *m* suffragan bishop.

Weihe[1] *f* **-, -n** (*Orn*) harrier.

Weihe[2] *f* **-, -n (a)** (*Eccl*) consecration; (*Priester~*) ordination ◆ **die niederen/höheren ~n** minor/major orders. **(b)** (*Einweihung*) (*eines Gebäudes*) inauguration; (*einer Brücke*) (ceremonial) opening; (*eines Denkmals*) unveiling. **(c)** (*Feierlichkeit*) solemnity. **(d)** (*Ehre*) **höhere ~n** (*fig*) greater glory, greater things.

weihen [1] *vt* **(a)** (*Eccl*) *Altar, Glocke, Kirche, Bischof* to consecrate; *Priester* to ordain ◆ **jdn zum Bischof/Priester ~** to consecrate sb bishop/ordain sb priest.
(b) *Gebäude* to inaugurate; *Brücke* to open; *Denkmal* to unveil.
(c) (*widmen*) **etw jdm/einer Sache ~** to dedicate sth to sb/sth; (*Eccl auch*), (*sehr feierlich*) to consecrate sth to sb/sth; **dem Tod(e)/Untergang geweiht** (*liter*) doomed (to die/fall).
[2] *vr +dat* (*liter*) to devote *or* dedicate oneself to.

Weiher *m* **-s, -** pond.

Weihe-: ~stätte *f* holy place; **w~voll** *adj* (*liter*) solemn.

Weih-: ~gabe *f* (*Rel*) (votive) offering, oblation (*form*); **~gefäß** *nt* (*Rel*) votive vessel.

Weihnacht *f* **-,** *no pl siehe* **Weihnachten.**

➤ **Weihnachten** *nt* **-, -** Christmas; (*geschrieben auch*) Xmas (*inf*) ◆ **fröhliche** *or* **gesegnete** *or* **schöne** *or* **frohe(s)** *or* **ein fröhliches ~!** happy *or* merry Christmas!; **(an) ~** at Christmas; **(zu** *or* **an) ~ nach Hause fahren** to go home for Christmas; **etw zu ~ bekommen/schenken** to get sth for Christmas/to give sth as a Christmas present; **weiße/grüne ~** (a) white Christmas/(a) Christmas without snow; **das ist ein Gefühl wie ~(, nur nicht so feierlich)** (*iro inf*) it's an odd feeling.

weihnachten *vi impers* (*poet, iro*) **es weihnachtet sehr** Christmas is very much in evidence.

weihnachtlich *adj* Christmassy (*inf*), festive.

Weihnachts- *in cpds* Christmas; **~abend** *m* Christmas Eve; **~bäckerei** *f* Christmas baking; **~baum** *m* Christmas tree; **~butter** *f reduced-price butter at Christmas time*; **~einkäufe** *pl* Christmas shopping *sing*; **~feier** *f* Christmas celebration(s *pl*); **~(feier)tag** *m* (*erster*) Christmas Day; (*zweiter*) Boxing Day; **~fest** *nt* Christmas; **~freibetrag** *m* Christmas tax allowance; **~gans** *f* Christmas goose; **jdn ausnehmen wie eine ~gans** (*sl*) to fleece sb (*inf*), to take sb to the cleaners (*sl*); **~geld** *nt* Christmas money; (*~gratifikation*) Christmas bonus; (*für Briefträger etc*) Christmas box; **~geschenk** *nt* Christmas present *or* gift; **~geschichte** *f* Christmas story; **~gruß** *m* Christmas greeting; **~insel** *f* Christmas Island; **~kaktus** *m* (*Bot*) Christmas cactus; **~karte** *f* Christmas card; **~lied** *nt* (Christmas) carol; **~mann** *m, pl* **-männer** Father Christmas, Santa Claus; (*pej inf*) clown (*pej inf*); **~märchen** *nt* (Christmas) pantomime; **~markt** *m* Christmas fair; **~spiel** *nt* nativity play; **~stern** *m* **(a)** (*Bot*) poinsettia; **(b)** (*Rel*) star of Bethlehem; **~tag** *m siehe* **~(feier)tag**; **~teller** *m plate of biscuits, chocolates etc*; **~tisch** *m* table for Christmas presents; **~zeit** *f* Christmas (time), Yuletide (*old, liter*), Christmas season (*esp Comm*).

Weih-: ~rauch *m* incense; **jdm ~rauch streuen** (*fig*) to praise *or* laud sb to the skies; ⚠**~rauchfaß** *nt* censer, thurible (*form*); **~rauchschiffchen** *nt* incense boat; **~wasser** *nt* holy water; **~wasserbecken** *nt* stoup, holy-water font.

weil *conj* because.

weiland *adv* (*obs, hum*) formerly ◆ **Botho von Schmettwitz, ~ Leutnant der Kürassiere** Botho von Schmettwitz, formerly *or* erstwhile *or* one-time lieutenant of the cuirassiers; **er hat eine Frisur, wie ~ Napoleon** he has a haircut like Napoleon's in former times.

Weilchen *nt* **ein ~** a (little) while, a bit.

Weile *f* **-,** *no pl* while ◆ **wir können eine ~ Karten spielen** we could play cards for a while; **vor einer (ganzen) ~, eine (ganze) ~ her** quite a while ago; **damit hat es noch (gute) ~, das hat noch (gute) ~** there's no hurry.

weilen *vi* (*geh*) to be; (*bleiben*) to stay, to tarry (*poet*) ◆ **er weilt nicht mehr unter uns** he is no longer with *or* among us.

Weiler *m* **-s, -** hamlet.

Weimarer Republik *f* Weimar Republic.

Wein *m* **-(e)s, -e** wine; (*no pl: ~stöcke*) vines *pl*; (*no pl: ~trauben*) grapes *pl* ◆ **in Frankreich wächst viel ~** there is a lot of wine-growing in France; **wilder ~** Virginia creeper; **jungen ~ in alte Schläuche füllen** (*Prov*) to pour new wine into old bottles (*Prov*); **jdm reinen** *or* **klaren ~ einschenken** to tell sb the truth, to come clean with sb (*inf*); **im ~ ist Wahrheit** (*Prov*) in vino veritas (*Prov*); **heimlich ~ trinken und öffentlich Wasser predigen** (*geh*) not to practise what one preaches; **voll des süßen ~es sein** (*liter, hum*) to be heavy with wine.

Wein- *in cpds* (*auf Getränk bezogen*) wine; (*auf Pflanze bezogen*) vine; **~bau** *m* wine-growing, viniculture (*form*); **~bauer** *m* wine-grower; **~beere** *f* grape; (*Rosine*) raisin; **~beißer** *m* **-s, -** (*Aus: ~kenner*) wine connoisseur; (*Aus: Lebkuchenart*) sugar-coated ginger biscuit; (*~prüfer*) wine taster; **~berg** *m* vineyard; **~bergschnecke** *f* snail; (*auf Speisekarte*) escargot; **~brand** *m* brandy; **~brennerei** *f* brandy distillery.

Weinchen *nt dim of* **Wein** (*inf*) **ein ~** (*etwas Wein*) a little wine; **das ist vielleicht ein ~!** that's a really beautiful wine!

weinen *vti* to cry; (*aus Trauer, Kummer auch*) to weep (*um* for, *über +acc* over, *aus, vor +dat* with) ◆ **etw naß ~** to make sth wet with one's tears; **sich** (*dat*) **die Augen rot** *or* **aus dem Kopf ~** to cry one's eyes *or* heart out; **sich in den Schlaf ~** to cry oneself to sleep; **sich müde ~** to tire oneself out crying; **es ist zum W~!, man könnte ~!** it's enough to make you weep!, it makes you want to weep *or* cry!; **es ist zum W~ mit dieser Frau** that woman is enough to make you want to weep *or* cry; **leise ~d** weeping *or* crying softly; (*inf: kleinlaut*) rather crestfallen *or* subdued; (*inf: resigniert*) resignedly; (*iro inf: mir nichts, dir nichts*) with a shrug of the shoulders.

Weinerei *f* (*inf*) crying, howling.

weinerlich *adj* whining, whiny (*inf*).

Wein-: ~ernte *f* grape harvest; **~essig** *m* wine vinegar; ⚠**~faß** *nt* wine cask; **~garten** *m* vineyard; **~gärtner** *m* wine-grower; **~gegend** *f* wine-growing area; **~geist** *m* spirits of wine (*old*), (ethyl) alcohol; **~gummi** *nt or m* winegum; **~gut** *nt* wine-growing estate; **~händler** *m* wine dealer; (*für Großhandel auch*) vintner; **~handlung** *f* wine shop (*Brit*) *or* store; **~hauer** *m* **-s, -** (*esp Aus*) wine-grower; **~haus** *nt* wine tavern, wine bar; (*Geschäft*) wine shop; **~heber** *m* **-s, -** wine cradle *or* basket.

weinig *adj* winy, vinous (*form*).

⚠: for details of spelling reform, see supplement

➤ SPRACHE AKTIV: **weigern: 1** → 39.3 **Weihnachten** → 50.2

Wein-: **~jahr** *nt* **ein gutes/schlechtes ~jahr** a good/bad year for wine; **~karte** *f* wine list; **~keller** *m* wine-cellar; (*Lokal*) wine bar *or* tavern; **~kelter** *f* wine press; **~kenner** *m* connoisseur of wine, wine connoisseur.

Weinkrampf *m* crying fit; (*Med*) uncontrollable fit of crying.

Wein-: **~kraut** *nt* sauerkraut; **~küfer** *m* cellarman; **~kultur** *f* wine culture; (*~bau*) wine-growing, viniculture (*form*); **~lage** *f* vineyard location; **~land** *nt* wine-growing *or* -producing country; **~laub** *nt* vine leaves *pl*; **~laube** *f* vine arbour *or* bower; **~laune** *f* **in einer ~laune beschlossen sie ...** after a few glasses of wine they decided ...; **~lese** *f* grape harvest, vintage; **~lokal** *nt* wine bar; **~monat, ~mond** (*old*) *m* grape-harvesting month; (*Oktober*) (month of) October; **~panscher** *m* wine-adulterator, wine-doctorer (*inf*); **~panscherei** *f* wine-adulterating, wine-doctoring (*inf*); **~probe** *f* wine-tasting; **~prüfer** *m* wine taster; **~rebe** *f* (grape)vine; **w~rot** *adj* wine-red, claret; **~säure** *f* (*Chem*) tartaric acid; **~schlauch** *m* wineskin; **w~selig** *adj* merry with wine; **~sorte** *f* sort *or* type of wine; **~stein** *m* tartar; **~stock** *m* vine; **~straße** *f* wine trail *or* route; **~stube** *f* wine tavern *or* bar; **~traube** *f* grape; **~zierl** *m* **-s, -(n)** (*Aus*) wine-grower; **~zwang** *m* obligation to order wine; **in diesem Restaurant ist ~zwang** you have to order wine in this restaurant.

weise *adj* (*geh*) wise ◆ **die ~ Frau** (*old*) the midwife.

Weise *f* **-, -n** **(a)** (*Verfahren etc*) way, manner, fashion ◆ **auf diese ~** in this way; **auf geheimnisvolle** *etc* **~** in a mysterious *etc* way *or* manner *or* fashion, mysteriously *etc*; **auf jede (erdenkliche) ~** in every conceivable way; **in gewisser/keiner** *or* **keinster** (*inf*) **~** in a/no way; **in der ~, daß ...** in such a way that ...; **jeder nach seiner ~** each in his own way, each after his own fashion; *siehe* **Art**.
(b) (*liter: Melodie*) tune, melody.

-weise *adv suf* (*an Substantiv*) as a ...; (*bei Maßangabe*) by the ...; (*an Adjektiv*) -ly ◆ **ausnahms~** as an exception; **meter~** by the metre; **bedauerlicher~** regrettably; **er hat mir netter~ ...** it was kind of him to ...

Weisel *m* **-s, -** queen bee.

weisen *pret* **wies**, *ptp* **gewiesen** (*geh*) **1** *vt* **jdm etw ~** (*lit, fig*) to show sb sth; **jdn aus dem Lande ~** to expel sb; **jdn aus dem Saal ~** to eject sb (from the hall); **jdn vom Feld** *or* **Platz ~** (*Sport*) to order sb off (the field); (*als Strafe*) to send sb off; **jdn von der Schule ~** to expel sb (from school); **etw (weit) von sich ~** (*fig*) to reject sth (emphatically); **jdn zur Ruhe/Ordnung ~** (*form*) to order sb to be quiet/to behave himself; *siehe* **Hand**.
2 *vi* to point (*nach* to(wards), *auf +acc* at); *siehe* **Finger**.

Weise(r) *m decl as adj* wise man; (*Denker auch*) sage ◆ **die drei ~n aus dem Morgenland** the three Wise Men from the East; **die Fünf ~n** (*BRD Pol*) *panel of five experts advising government on economic policy*.

Weiser *m* **-s, -** *siehe* **Weisel**.

Weisheit *f* **(a)** *no pl* wisdom ◆ **das war der ~ letzter Schluß** that was all they/we *etc* came up with; **das ist auch nicht der ~ letzter Schluß** that's not exactly the ideal solution; **er glaubt, er hat die ~ mit Löffeln gegessen** *or* **gefressen** he thinks he knows it all; **er hat die ~ nicht mit Löffeln gegessen** *or* **gefressen** he's not so bright; *siehe* **Ende**.
(b) (*weiser Spruch*) wise saying, pearl of wisdom (*usu iro*) ◆ **eine alte ~** a wise old saying; **behalte deine ~(en) für dich!** keep your pearls of wisdom to yourself!

Weisheitszahn *m* wisdom tooth.

weismachen *vt sep* **jdm etw ~** to make sb believe sth; **er wollte uns ~, daß ...** he would have us believe that ...; **wie konnten sie ihm ~, daß ...?** how could they fool him into believing that ...?; **das kannst du mir nicht ~!** you can't expect me to believe that; **das kannst du (einem) andern ~!** (go) tell that to the marines! (*inf*), pull the other one(, it's got bells on)! (*hum inf*).

weiß *adj* white ◆ **ein ~es (Blatt) Papier** a blank *or* clean sheet of paper; **ein ~er Fleck (auf der Landkarte)** a blank area (on the map); **das W~e Haus** the White House; **das W~e Meer** the White Sea; **der W~e Nil** the White Nile; **W~er Sonntag** Low Sunday; **der ~e Sport** tennis; skiing; **der W~e Tod** death in the snow; **~ werden** to go *or* turn white; (*Sachen auch*) to whiten; **~ wie Kreide** *or* **die Wand** white as chalk *or* a sheet *or* a ghost; **das W~e des Eis** *or* **vom Ei/von drei Eiern** eggwhite/the white(s) of three eggs; **das W~e im Auge** the whites of one's/the eyes.

Weiß *nt* **-(es), -** white.

Weiß|afrika *nt* White Africa.

Weis-: **w~sagen** *vt insep* to prophesy, to foretell; **~sager(in** *f*) *m* **-s, -** (*liter*) seer, prophet; **~sagung** *f* prophecy.

Weiß-: **~bier** *nt* weissbier (*light, fizzy beer made using top-fermentation yeast*); **~binder** *m* (*dial*) (*Böttcher*) cooper; (*Anstreicher*) house-painter; **w~blau** *adj* (*inf: bayrisch*) Bavarian; **~blech** *nt* tinplate; **w~blond** *adj* ash-blond(e); **~bluten** *nt*: **jdn bis zum ~bluten ausbeuten** to bleed sb white; **bis zum ~bluten zahlen müssen** to be bled white; **~brot** *nt* white bread; (*Laib*) loaf of white bread, white loaf; **~buch** *nt* (*Pol*) white paper; **~buche** *f* (*Bot*) hornbeam; **~dorn** *m* (*Bot*) whitehorn.

Weiße *f* **-, -n** **(a)** (*Weißheit*) whiteness. **(b)** *siehe* **Berliner**[2].

weißeln *vti* (*S Ger, Aus*) whitewash.

weißen *vt* to whiten; (*weiß tünchen*) to whitewash.

Weiße(r) *mf decl as adj* white, white man/woman ◆ **die ~n** the whites, white people *pl*.

Weiß-: **~fisch** *m* whitefish; **~fuchs** *m* white fox; **~gardist** *m* (*Hist*) member of the White Guard; ⚠**w~glühend** *adj* white-hot, incandescent; **~glut** *f* white heat, incandescence; **jdn zur ~glut bringen, jdn bis zur ~glut reizen** to make sb livid (with rage), to make sb see red (*inf*); **~gold** *nt* white gold; ⚠**w~haarig** *adj* white-haired.

Weißheit *f* whiteness.

Weiß-: **~herbst** *m* ≃ rosé; **~käse** *m* (*dial*) *siehe* **Quark**; **~kohl** *m*, **~kraut** *nt* (*S Ger, Aus*) white cabbage.

weißlich *adj* whitish.

Weiß-: **~metall** *nt* white metal; **~näherin** *f* (plain) seamstress; **~russe** *m*, **w~russisch** *adj* White Russian; **~rußland** *nt* White Russia; **~sucht** *f* albinism; **~tanne** *f* (*Bot*) silver fir; **~wal** *m* white whale; **~wandreifen** *m* (*Aut*) whitewall (tyre); **~waren** *pl* linen *sing*; **w~waschen** *vtr sep irreg* (*fig, usu pej*) **sich/jdn w~waschen** to whitewash one's/sb's reputation; **~wein** *m* white wine; **~wurst** *f* veal sausage; **~zeug** *nt* linen.

Weisung *f* directive, instruction, direction; (*Jur*) ruling ◆ **auf ~** on instructions; **ich habe ~, keine Auskünfte zu geben** I have instructions not to give any details.

Weisungs-: **~befugnis** *f* authority to issue directives; **w~berechtigt** *adj* (*Jur*) authorized to issue directives; **w~gebunden** *adj* subject to directives; **w~gemäß** *adj* according to *or* as per instructions, as instructed *or* directed; **~recht** *nt siehe* **~befugnis**.

weit *siehe auch* **weiter** **1** *adj* **(a)** wide; (*fig*) *Begriff, Horizont etc* broad; *Pupille* dilated; *Meer* open; *Gewissen* elastic; *Herz* big ◆ **~e Kreise** *or* **Teile (der Bevölkerung)** large sections *or* parts (of the population); **im ~eren Sinne** in the broader *or* wider sense; **das Herz wurde mir ~** (*liter*) my heart swelled (with emotion); **das ist ein ~es Feld** (*fig*) that is a big subject.
(b) (*lang*) *Weg, Reise, Wurf etc* long ◆ **in ~en Abständen** widely spaced; (*zeitlich*) at long intervals; **man hat hier einen ~en Blick** *or* **eine ~e Sicht** you can see a long way from here; **in ~er Ferne** far in the distance, in the far distance; **das liegt (noch) in ~er Ferne** it's still a long way away; (*zeitlich auch*) it's still in the distant future.
(c) (*groß*) *Unterschied* great, big.
2 *adv* **(a)** far ◆ **~er** further, farther; **am ~esten** (the) furthest, (the) farthest; **wie ~ ist Bremen?** how far is Bremen?; **Bremen ist 10 km ~** Bremen is 10 kms away *or* off; **es ist noch ~ bis Bremen** it's still a long way to Bremen, there's still a long way to go till Bremen; **3,60 m ~ springen** to jump 3m 60; **wie ~ bist du gesprungen?** how far did you jump?; **(sehr) ~ springen/fahren** to jump/drive a (very) long way; **~ und breit** for miles around; **~ ab** *or* **weg (von)** far away (from); **~ am Anfang/Ende/Rand** right at the beginning/end/edge; **ziemlich ~ am Ende** fairly near the end; **hast du es noch ~ (nach Hause)?** have you got a long way *or* far to go (to get home)?; **von ~em** from a long way away *or* off, from afar (*liter*); **von ~ her** from a long way away.
(b) (*breit*) *verzweigt, herumkommen, bekannt* widely; *offen, öffnen* wide ◆ **10 cm ~** 10cm wide; **~ verbreitet** widespread.
(c) **~ entfernt** far away *or* off, a long way away *or* off; **~er entfernt** further *or* farther away *or* off; **ich bin ~ davon entfernt, das zu tun** I have no intention of doing that; **der Film ist ~ davon entfernt, fertig zu sein** the film is far from (being) finished; **~ entfernt** *or* **gefehlt!** far from it!
(d) (*in Entwicklung*) **~ fortgeschritten** far *or* well advanced; **der Junge/der Frühling/die Krankheit ist schon ziemlich ~** the boy/spring/the disease is already quite (far) advanced; **wie ~ bist du?** how far have you got?; **wie ~ ist das Essen?** how far have you/they *etc* got with the food?; **so ~, so gut** so far so good; **er wird es ~ bringen** he will go far; **er hat es ~ gebracht** he has come a long way, he has got on in the world; **es so ~ bringen, daß ...** to bring it about that ...; **sie hat es so ~ gebracht, daß man sie entließ** she drove them to the point of dismissing her; **jdn so ~ bringen, daß ...** to bring sb to the point where ...; **~ kommen** to get far.
(e) (*zeitlich*) **es ist noch ~ bis Ostern** there's still a long way to go till Easter, Easter is still a long way off; **(bis) ~ in die Nacht** (till) well *or* far into the night; **~ zurückliegen** to be a long way back, to be far back in the past; **~ nach Mitternacht** well *or* long after midnight.
(f) (*fig: erheblich*) (*mit adj, adv*) far; (*mit vb*) by far ◆ **das hat unsere Erwartungen ~ übertroffen** that far exceeded our expectations; **~ über 60** well over 60; **bei ~em besser** *etc* **als** far better *etc* than, better *etc* by far than; **bei ~em der beste** far and away *or* by far the best; **bei ~em nicht so gut** *etc* **(wie ...)** not nearly as good *etc* (as ...), nowhere near as good *etc* (as ...); **bei ~em nicht!** not by a long shot (*inf*) *or* chalk (*inf*) *or* way!
(g) (*fig: andere Wendungen*) **das ist nicht ~ her** (*inf*) that's not up to much (*inf*), that's nothing to write home about (*inf*); **damit/mit ihm ist es nicht ~ her** (*inf*) this/he isn't up to much (*inf*), this/he isn't much use; **~/~er vom Thema** well off the subject/further away from the subject; **das würde zu ~ führen** that would be taking things too far; **zu ~ gehen** to go too far; **das geht zu ~!** that's going too far; **das Geld reicht nicht ~** the money won't go far; **sein Einfluß reicht sehr ~** his influence is far-reaching; **etw zu ~ treiben** to carry sth too far.

Weit-: **w~ab** *adv* **w~ab von** far (away) from; **w~aus** *adv* (*vor comp*) far; (*vor superl*) (by) far, far and away; **w~ausholend** *adj Geste etc* expansive; (*fig*) *Erzählung etc* long-drawn-out, long-winded; **etw w~ausholend erzählen** to tell sth at great length; **w~bekannt** *adj attr* widely known; **~blick** *m* (*fig*) vision, far-sightedness; **w~blickend** *adj* (*fig*) far-sighted.

Weite[1] *f* **-, -n** (*Entfernung, Ferne*) distance; (*Länge*) length; (*Größe*) expanse; (*Durchmesser, Breite*) width ◆ **in die ~ blicken** to look into the distance; **etw in der ~ ändern** to alter the width of sth; **in der ~ paßt das Hemd** the shirt fits as regards width; **etw in die ~ ziehen** to pull sth out; *Pullover* to stretch out.

Weite[2] *nt* **-n**, *no pl* distance ◆ **ins ~ gehen** to go out into the dis tance; **das ~ suchen/gewinnen** (*liter*) to take to one's heels/to reach freedom.

weiten **1** *vt* to widen; (*durch Ziehen auch*) to stretch.
2 *vr* to widen, to broaden (*auch fig*); (*Pupille, Gefäße*) to dilate; (*fig liter: Herz*) to swell.

weiter [1] *comp of* **weit.**
[2] *adj (fig)* further; (*zusätzlich auch*) additional; (*andere*) other ◆ **~e Auskünfte** further information.
[3] *adv* (*noch hinzu*) further; (*außerdem*) furthermore; (*sonst*) otherwise; (*nachher*) afterwards ◆ **nichts ~, ~ nichts** (*darüber hinaus nichts*) nothing further *or* more *or* else; **~ nichts?** is that all?; **nichts ~** *or* **~ nichts als ...** nothing more than ..., nothing but ...; **ich brauche ~ nichts** that's all I need, I don't need anything else; **ich brauche nichts ~ als ...** all I need is ...; **er wollte ~ nichts, als nach Hause gehen** all he wanted was to go home; **wenn es ~ nichts ist, ...** well, if that's all (it is), ...; **außer uns war ~ niemand** *or* **niemand ~ da** there was nobody else there besides us; **nicht ~, ~ nicht** (*eigentlich*) not really; **das stört ~ keinen** that doesn't really bother anybody; **das hat ~ nichts zu sagen** that doesn't really matter, that's neither here nor there; **das macht ~ nichts** it's not that *or* really important; **etw ~ tun** to continue to do *or* continue doing sth, to go *or* carry on doing sth; **immer ~** on and on; (*Anweisung*) keep on (going); **er hat sich immer ~ verbessert** he kept on improving; **(nur) immer ~!** keep at it!; **und ~?** and then?; **was geschah (dann) ~?** what happened then *or* next?; **und so ~** and so on *or* forth, et cetera; **und so ~ und so fort** and so on and so forth, et cetera et cetera; **kein Wort ~!** not another word!; *siehe* **Weitere(s).**

weiter- *pref* (*~machen mit*) to carry on *or* go on *or* continue *+prp*, to continue to *+infin*; (*nicht aufhören mit*) to keep on *or* go on *+prp*; (*bei Bewegung, Beförderung, Reise etc*) *vb+* on.

Weiter- *pref mit n* further; (*bei Bewegung, Beförderung, Reise etc*) continuation of.

Weiter-: w~arbeiten *vi sep siehe* **weiter-** to carry on *etc* working, to work on; **an einer Sache** (*dat*) **w~arbeiten** to do some more work on sth; **w~befördern*** *vt sep* to send on; *jdn* (*in Firma etc*) to promote further; **w~behandeln*** *vt sep siehe* **weiter-** to carry on *etc* treating; **~behandlung** *f* further treatment; ⚠**w~bestehen*** *vi sep irreg* to continue to exist, to survive; **~bestehen** *nt* continued existence; ⚠**w~bewegen*** *sep* [1] *vt* to move further; [2] *vr* to move further; (*w~hin*) to carry on *etc* moving; **w~bilden** *sep* [1] *vt* **jdn w~bilden** to give sb further education, to educate sb further; [2] *vr* to continue one's education; **~bildung** *f* continuation of one's education; (*an Hochschule*) further education; **w~bringen** *vt sep irreg* to take further, to advance; **das bringt uns auch nicht w~** that's not much help (to us), that doesn't get us any further; **w~denken** *sep irreg* [1] *vt* to think out (further); [2] *vi* to think it out; (*an Zukünftiges*) to think ahead; **w~empfehlen*** *vt sep irreg* to recommend (to one's friends *etc*); **w~entwickeln*** *sep* [1] *vt* to develop; *Idee* to develop (further); [2] *vr* to develop (*zu* into); **~entwicklung** *f* development; **w~erzählen*** *vt sep siehe* **weiter-** to carry on *etc* telling; *Geheimnis etc* to repeat, to pass on; **das hat er der ganzen Klasse w~erzählt** he told the whole class.

Weitere(s) *nt decl as adj* further details *pl* ◆ **ich habe nichts ~s zu sagen** I have nothing further to say; **das ~** the rest; **alles ~** everything else, all the rest; **des w~n** in addition, furthermore; **bis auf w~s** for the time being; (*amtlich, auf Schildern etc*) until further notice; **im w~n** subsequently, afterwards; **zum w~n** furthermore, in addition, on top of that; *siehe* **ohne.**

Weiter-: w~fahren *sep irreg* [1] *vt siehe* **weiter-** to carry on *etc* driving, to keep on driving; [2] *vi aux sein* **(a)** (*Fahrt fortsetzen*) to go on, to continue; (*durchfahren*) to drive on; (*w~ reisen*) to travel on; **(b)** (*dial*) *siehe* **fortfahren (b)**; **~fahrt** *f* continuation of the/one's journey; **vor der ~fahrt sahen wir ...** before continuing our journey we saw ...; **w~fliegen** *vi sep irreg aux sein* to fly on; **die Maschine fliegt in 10 Minuten w~** the plane will take off again in 10 minutes; **~flug** *m* continuation of the/one's flight; **auf dem ~flug** after we'd taken off again; **Passagiere zum ~flug nach ...** passengers continuing their flight to ...; **w~führen** *sep* [1] *vt* to continue; *Gespräch auch* to carry on (with); [2] *vi* to continue, to lead on; **das führt nicht w~** (*fig*) that doesn't lead *or* get us anywhere; **w~führend** *adj Schule* secondary; **~gabe** *f* passing on; (*von Informationen, Erbfaktoren auch*) transmission; **w~geben** *vt sep irreg* to pass on; to transmit; **w~gehen** *vi sep irreg aux sein* to go on; **bitte w~gehen!** (*Polizist etc*) move along *or* on (there), please!; **so kann es nicht w~gehen** (*fig*) things can't go on like this; **wie soll es nun w~gehen?** what's going to happen now?; **w~gehend** *adj, adv* (*Aus*) *comp of* **weitgehend**; **w~helfen** *vi sep irreg* to help (along) (*jdm* sb); **w~hin** *adv* (*außerdem*) furthermore, on top of that; **etw w~hin tun** to carry on *etc* doing sth; **w~kämpfen** *vi sep* to fight on; **w~kommen** *vi sep irreg aux sein* to get further; (*fig auch*) to make progress *or* headway; **nicht w~kommen** (*fig*) to be stuck *or* bogged down; **wir kommen einfach nicht w~** we're just not getting anywhere; **~kommen** *nt* advancement; **w~können** *vi sep irreg* to be able to carry on *or* go on *or* continue; **ich kann nicht w~** I can't go on; (*bei Rätsel, Prüfung etc*) I'm stuck; **w~laufen** *vi sep irreg aux sein* to run/walk on; (*Film*) to go on; (*Betrieb, Produktion*) to go on, to continue; (*Gehalt*) to continue to be paid; (*Motor*) to keep on running; **ich kann nicht w~laufen** I can't walk any further; **den Motor w~laufen lassen** to leave the engine running; **w~leben** *vi sep* to live on, to continue to live; **w~leiten** *vt sep* to pass on (*an +acc* to); (*w~befördern, senden*) to forward; **w~machen** *vti sep* to carry on (*etw* with sth), to continue; **w~machen!** (*Mil*) carry on!; **~marsch** *m* **zum ~marsch bereit** ready to march on; **auf dem ~marsch waren sie ...** as they marched on they were ...; **w~reichen** *vt sep* to pass on; **w~reichend** *adj* further-reaching; **~reise** *f* continuation of the/one's journey; **ich wünsche Ihnen eine gute ~reise** I hope the rest of the journey goes well; **auf der ~reise nach ...** when I *etc* was travelling on to ...; **w~rücken** *sep* [1] *vt* to move further along; [2] *vi aux sein* to move up, to move further along.

⚠: for details of spelling reform, see supplement

weiters *adv* (*Aus*) *siehe* **ferner.**

weiter-: ~sagen *vt sep* to repeat, to pass on; **~sagen!** pass it on!; **nicht ~sagen!** don't tell anyone!; **~schenken** *vt sep* to give away (to somebody else); **~schlafen** *vi sep irreg* to sleep on, to go on sleeping; (*wieder einschlafen*) to go back to sleep; **~schleppen** *sep* [1] *vt* to haul *or* drag further; [2] *vr* to drag *or* haul oneself on; **~senden** *sep irreg* [1] *vti* (*Rad, TV*) *siehe* **weiter-** to carry on *etc* broadcasting; [2] *vt* (*form*) to forward; **~spinnen** *vt sep irreg* (*fig*) *Gedanken etc* to develop further; **~tragend** *adj* (*Mil*) longer-range *attr*; (*fig*) further-reaching.

Weiterungen *pl* (*old, form*) complications *pl*, difficulties *pl* ◆ **unangenehme ~ zur Folge haben** to have unpleasant consequences.

Weiter-: w~verarbeiten* *vt sep* to process; **w~verbreiten*** *sep* [1] *vt* to spread (further), to repeat, to propagate (*form*); [2] *vr* to spread (further); **w~verfolgen*** *vt sep siehe* **weiter-** *Entwicklung, Straße* to carry on *etc* following; *Verbrecher* to continue to pursue; *Idee* to pursue further; **~verkauf** *m* resale; **nicht zum ~verkauf bestimmt** not for resale; **w~verkaufen*** *vti sep* to resell; **w~vermieten*** *vt sep* to sublet; **~versand** *m* redispatch; **w~wissen** *vi sep irreg* **nicht (mehr) w~wissen** not to know how to go on; (*bei Rätsel, Prüfung*) to be stuck; (*verzweifelt sein*) to be at one's wits' end; **w~wollen** *vi sep irreg* to want to go on; **der Esel wollte einfach nicht w~** the donkey simply wouldn't go any further; **w~zahlen** *vti sep* to continue paying *or* to pay.

weitestgehend [1] *adj superl of* **weitgehend.**
[2] *adv* to the greatest possible extent.

weit-: ~gehend *comp* **~gehender** *or* (*Aus*) **weitergehend**, *superl* **weitestgehend** *or* **~gehendst** [1] *adj Vollmachten etc* far-reaching, extensive, wide; *Übereinstimmung etc* a large degree of; **er hatte viel ~gehendere Befürchtungen** his fears went a lot further than that; [2] *adv* to a great *or* large extent, largely; ⚠**~gereist** *adj attr, comp* **weiter gereist,** *superl* **am weitesten gereist** widely travelled; ⚠**~gesteckt** *adj attr* ambitious; ⚠**~greifend** *adj attr* far-reaching; **~her** *adv* (*auch* **von ~her**) from a long way away, from far away, from afar (*liter*); ⚠**~hergeholt** *adj attr* far-fetched; **~herzig** *adj* understanding, charitable; **~hin** *adv* over a long distance, for a long way; (*fig*) *bekannt, beliebt* widely; *unbekannt* largely; (*weitgehend*) to a large *or* great extent.

weitläufig *adj* **(a)** *Park, Gebäude* spacious; (*verzweigt*) rambling; *Dorf* covering a wide area, sprawling *attr*; (*fig*) *Erzählung* lengthy, long-drawn-out, long-winded ◆ **etw ~ erzählen** to tell sth at (great) length. **(b)** *Verwandte* distant.

Weitläufigkeit *f siehe adj* (*a*) spaciousness; rambling nature; sprawling nature; length, long-windedness.

Weit-: w~maschig *adj Netz* coarse-meshed, wide-meshed, broad-meshed; *Gestricktes* loosely knitted, loose-knit; **w~räumig** *adj* wide-ranging; **ein Gelände w~räumig absperren** to cordon off a wide area around a site; **die Unfallstelle w~räumig umfahren** to keep well away from the scene of the accident; ⚠**w~reichend** *adj, comp* **w~reichender** *or* (*Aus*) **weiterreichend,** *superl* **weitestreichend** (*fig*) far-reaching; (*Mil*) long-range *attr*; ⚠**w~schauend** *adj* (*fig*) far-sighted; **w~schweifig** *adj* long-winded, circumlocutory, prolix (*form*); **~sicht** *f* (*fig*) far-sightedness; **w~sichtig** *adj* (*Med*) long-sighted, far-sighted (*esp US*); (*fig*) far-sighted; **~sichtigkeit** *f* (*Med*) long-sightedness, far-sightedness (*esp US*); **w~springen** *vi sep* (*infin only*) (*Sport*) to do the long jump *or* broad jump (*US*); **~springen** *nt* (*Sport*) long-jumping, broad-jumping (*US*); **~springer** *m* (*Sport*) long-jumper, broad-jumper (*US*); **~sprung** *m* (*Sport*) the long jump *or* broad jump (*US*); ⚠**w~tragend** *adj, comp* **w~tragender** *or* (*Aus*) **weitertragend,** *superl* **weitesttragend** (*Mil*) long-range *attr*; (*fig*) far-reaching, far-ranging; **w~um** *adv* for miles around.

Weitung *f* (*geh*) widening.

Weit-: ⚠**w~verbreitet** *adj attr* widespread, common; *Ansicht auch* widely held; *Zeitung* with a wide circulation; ⚠**w~verzweigt** *adj attr Straßensystem* branching out in all directions; *Konzern* with many branches; **~winkelobjektiv** *nt* wide-angle lens.

Weizen *m* **-s,** *no pl* wheat; *siehe* **Spreu.**

Weizen-: ~bier *nt light, very fizzy beer made by using wheat, malt and top-fermentation yeast*; **~brot** *nt* wheat(en) bread; **~keime** *pl* (*Cook*) wheatgerm *sing*; **~keimöl** *nt* (*Cook*) wheatgerm oil; **~mehl** *nt* wheat(en) flour; **~schrot** *m or nt* wheatmeal.

welch [1] *interrog pron inv* **(a)** (*geh: in Ausrufen*) what ◆ **~ friedliches Bild!** what a peaceful scene!
(b) (*in indirekten Fragesätzen*) **~ (ein)** what.
[2] *rel pron inv* **X, Y und Z, ~ letztere(r, s) ...** (*obs, form*) X, Y and Z, the last of which/whom ...

welche(r, s) [1] *interrog pron* **(a)** (*adjektivisch*) what; (*bei Wahl aus einer begrenzten Menge*) which ◆ **~r Mensch könnte behaupten ...?** what person could claim ...?; **~s Kleid soll ich anziehen, das rote oder das grüne?** which dress shall I wear, the red one or the green one?
(b) (*substantivisch*) which (one) ◆ **~r von den beiden?** which (one) of the two?; **~s sind die Symptome dieser Krankheit?** what are the symptoms of this illness?; **es gibt viele schöne Frauen, aber ~ könnte sich mit Isabella vergleichen?** there are many beautiful women, but which of them could compare with Isabella?
(c) (*in Ausrufen*) **~ Schande/Freude** *etc***!** what a disgrace/what joy *etc*!
[2] *indef pron* some; (*in Fragen, konditional auch, verneint*) any ◆ **es gibt ~, die glauben ...** there are some (people) who think ...; **ich habe keine Tinte/Äpfel, haben Sie ~?** I don't have any ink/apples, do you have some *or* any?
[3] *rel pron* (*rare*) (*Mensch*) who; (*Sache*) which, that ◆ **~(r, s) auch immer**

whoever/whichever/whatever.

welcher|art [1] *interrog adj inv* (*geh*) (*attributiv*) what kind of; (*substantivisch*) of what kind ◆ **sagen Sie mir, ~ Ihre Erfahrungen sind** tell me what sort of experiences you (have) had; **~ Ihre Erfahrungen auch sein mögen** whatever your experiences may have been like.
[2] *interrog adv* in what way.

welcherlei *interrog adj inv* (*geh*) what kind *or* sort of.

welches *pron siehe* **welche(r, s)**.

Welfe *m* **-n, -n** (*Hist*) Guelph.

welfisch *adj* (*Hist*) Guelphic.

welk *adj Blume, Pflanze* wilted, faded; *Blatt* dead; (*fig*) *Schönheit* fading, wilting; *Haut, Gesicht* tired-looking; (*schlaff*) flaccid; *Hände* withered ◆ **wie ein ~es Pflänzchen** (*inf*) like a wet rag (*inf*).

welken *vi aux sein* (*lit, fig*) to fade, to wilt; (*Haut, Gesicht*) to grow tired-looking; (*schlaff werden*) to sag.

Welkheit *f* wilted state; (*von Haut, Gesicht*) tired look.

Wellblech *nt* corrugated iron.

Welle *f* **-, -n** **(a)** wave (*auch fig, Phys, im Haar etc*); (*Rad: Frequenz*) wavelength ◆ **sein Grab in den ~n finden** (*geh*) to go to a watery grave; **weiche ~** (*inf*) soft line; **mach keine ~n!** (*inf*) don't make such a fuss; **(hohe) ~n schlagen** (*fig*) to create (quite) a stir.
(b) (*fig: Mode*) craze ◆ **die Neue ~** (*Film*) the nouvelle vague; (*Mus*) the New Wave.
(c) (*Tech*) shaft.
(d) (*Sport*) circle.

wellen [1] *vt Haar* to wave; *Blech etc* to corrugate.
[2] *vr* to be/become wavy ◆ **gewelltes Haar** wavy hair.

Wellen-: w~artig *adj* wave-like; *Linie etc* wavy; **~bad** *nt swimming-pool with artificially induced waves*; **~bereich** *m* (*Phys, Telec*) frequency range; (*Rad*) waveband; **~berg** *m* mountainous *or* giant wave; **~brecher** *m* breakwater, groyne; **w~förmig** [1] *adj* wave-like; *Linie* wavy; [2] *adv* in the form of waves; **~gang** *m, no pl* waves *pl*, swell; **starker ~gang** heavy sea(s) *or* swell; **leichter ~gang** light swell; **~kamm** *m* crest (of a wave); **~länge** *f* (*Phys, Telec*) wavelength; **sich auf jds ~länge** (*acc*) **einstellen** (*inf*) to get on sb's wavelength (*inf*); **auf der gleichen ~länge sein** *or* **liegen, die gleiche ~länge haben** (*inf*) to be on the same wavelength (*inf*); **~linie** *f* wavy line; **~mechanik** *f* (*Phys*) wave mechanics *sing*; **~reiten** *nt* (*Sport*) surfing; (*auf Fluß*) *sport of balancing on a board attached by a rope to the riverbank*; **~salat** *m* (*Rad inf*) jumble of frequencies; **~schlag** *m* breaking of the waves; (*sanft auch*) lapping of the waves; (*heftig auch*) pounding of the waves; **~schliff** *m* (*am Messer*) serrated edge; **~sittich** *m* budgerigar, budgie (*inf*).

Well-: ~fleisch *nt* boiled pork; **~hornschnecke** *f* whelk.

wellig *adj Haar etc* wavy; *Oberfläche, Fahrbahn* uneven; *Hügelland* rolling, undulating.

Wellpappe *f* corrugated cardboard.

Welpe *m* **-n, -n** pup, whelp; (*von Wolf, Fuchs*) cub, whelp.

Wels *m* **-es, -e** catfish.

welsch *adj* **(a)** (*old*) Latin, Southern European; (*~sprachig*) Romance-speaking ◆ **~e Sitten und Gebräuche** dubious morals and practices. **(b)** (*Aus pej: italienisch*) Eyetie (*pej sl*) ◆ **die W~en** the Eyeties (*pej sl*). **(c)** (*Sw*) (Swiss-) French ◆ **die ~e Schweiz** French Switzerland.

Welsch-: ~land *nt* (*Sw*) French Switzerland; **~schweizer** *m* (*Sw*) French Swiss; **w~schweizerisch** *adj* (*Sw*) Swiss-French.

Welt *f* **-, -en** (*lit, fig*) world ◆ **die ~ im Kleinen/Großen** the microcosm/macrocosm; **die (große) weite ~** the big wide world; **der höchste Berg der ~** the highest mountain in the world, the world's highest mountain; **die ~ von heute/morgen** the world of today/tomorrow, today's/tomorrow's world; **die ~ des Theaters/Kindes** the world of the theatre/child, the theatre/child's world; **die Alte/Neue/Freie/Dritte ~** the Old/New/Free/Third World; **die große** *or* **vornehme ~** high society; **alle ~, Gott und die ~** everybody, the whole world, the world and his wife (*hum*); **eine ~ brach für ihn zusammen** his whole world collapsed about him *or* his ears, the bottom fell out of his world; **das ist doch nicht die ~** it isn't as important as all that; **davon** *or* **deswegen geht die ~ nicht unter** (*inf*) it isn't the end of the world; **das kostet doch nicht die ~** it won't cost the earth; **uns/sie trennen ~en, zwischen uns/ihnen liegen ~en** (*fig*) we/they are worlds apart; **auf der ~** in the world; **davon gibt es noch mehr auf der ~** there are plenty of those around; **etw mit auf die ~ bringen** to be born with sth; **aus aller ~** from all over the world; **aus der ~ schaffen** to eliminate; **aus der ~ scheiden** (*geh*) to depart this life (*liter*); (*Selbstmord begehen*) to put an end to one's life; **in aller ~** all over the world; **in alle ~ zerstreut** scattered all over the world *or* globe; **warum/wer in aller ~ ...?** why/who on earth *or* in the world ...?; **so geht es nun mal in der ~** that's the way of the world, that's the way things go; **in einer anderen ~ leben** to live in a different world; **in seiner eigenen ~ leben** to live in a world of one's own; **um nichts in der ~, nicht um alles in der ~, um keinen Preis der ~** not for love (n)or money, not at any price, not for all the tea in China (*inf*); **ein Kind in die ~ setzen** to bring a child into the world; **ein Gerücht in die ~ setzen** to put about *or* spread a rumour; **ein Mann/eine Dame von ~** a man/woman of the world; **die beste Frau** *etc* **(von) der ~** the best woman *etc* in the world; **vor aller ~** publicly, in front of everybody, openly; **zur ~ bringen** to give birth to, to bring into the world; **auf die** *or* **zur ~ kommen** to come into the world, to be born; *siehe* **Brett, Ende**.

Welt- *in cpds* world; **w~abgewandt** *adj* withdrawn; **~all** *nt, no pl* universe, cosmos; **~alter** *nt* age, epoch; **w~anschaulich** *adj* ideological; **~anschauung** *f* philosophy of life; (*Philos, Pol*) world view, weltanschauung; **~ausstellung** *f* world exhibition, world's fair; **~bank** *f* World Bank; **w~bekannt** *adj* world-famous; **w~berühmt** *adj* world-famous; *Schriftsteller, Künstler etc auch* world-renowned; **~beste(r)** *mf* world's best; **w~beste(r, s)** *adj attr* world's best; **~bestleistung** *f* world's best performance, world best (*inf*); **~bevölkerung** *f* world population; **w~bewegend** *adj* world-shattering; **~bild** *nt* conception of the world; (*jds Ansichten*) philosophy, view of life; **~blatt** *nt* (*Press*) international (news)paper; **~brand** *m* global conflagration; **~bürger** *m* citizen of the world, cosmopolitan; **~bürgertum** *nt* cosmopolitanism; **~chronik** *f* world chronicle.

Welten-: ~bummler *m* globetrotter; **~raum** *m siehe* **Weltraum**.

welt|entrückt *adj* remote, isolated.

Weltergewicht *nt* (*Boxen*) welterweight.

Welt-: w~erschütternd *adj* world-shattering; **w~fern** *adj* unrealistic, naïve; **~flucht** *f* flight from reality, escapism; **w~fremd** *adj* unworldly; **~fremdheit** *f* unworldliness; **~friede(n)** *m* world peace; **~friedenstag** *m* (*esp DDR*) World Peace Day; **~gefüge** *nt* universe, world system, scheme of things; **~geist** *m* (*Philos*) world spirit; **~geistliche(r)** *m* secular priest; **~geltung** *f* international standing, world-wide recognition; **~gericht** *nt* Last Judgement; **~gerichtshof** *m* International Court; **~geschichte** *f* world history; **in der ~geschichte herumfahren** (*inf*) to travel around all over the place; **w~geschichtlich** *adj* **ein w~geschichtliches Ereignis** an important event in the history of the world; **von w~geschichtlicher Bedeutung** of great significance in world history; **w~geschichtlich gesehen, aus w~geschichtlicher Sicht** looked at from the point of view of world history; **~gesundheitsorganisation** *f* World Health Organization; **~getriebe** *nt* (*liter*) (hustle and) bustle of the world; **w~gewandt** *adj* sophisticated, well-versed in the ways of the world; **~gewandtheit** *f* sophistication, experience in the ways of the world; **~handel** *m* world trade; **~herrschaft** *f* world domination; **~hilfssprache** *f* international auxiliary language; **~karte** *f* map of the world; **~kirchenrat** *m* World Council of Churches; **~klasse** *f* **ein Hochspringer der ~klasse** a world-class high-jumper; **~klasse sein** to be world-class; (*inf*) to be great (*inf*) *or* fantastic (*inf*); **w~klug** *adj* worldly-wise; **~körper** *m* (*old*) *siehe* **Himmelskörper**; **~krieg** *m* world war; **der erste** *or* **Erste** (*abbr* **I.**)/**zweite** *or* **Zweite** (*abbr* **II.**) **~krieg** World War One/Two (*abbr* I/II), the First/Second World War; **~kugel** *f* globe; **~lauf** *m* way of the world; **w~läufig** *adj* cosmopolitan; **w~lich** *adj* worldly, mundane; (*nicht kirchlich, geistlich*) secular; *Macht* temporal; **~literatur** *f* world literature; **~macht** *f* world power; **~mann** *m, pl* **-männer** man of the world; **w~männisch** *adj* urbane, sophisticated; **~marke** *f* name known all over the world; **~markt** *m* world market; **~marktpreis** *m* world (market) price; **~meer** *nt* ocean; **die sieben ~meere** the seven seas; **~meister** *m* world *or* world's (*US*) champion; **England/die englische Mannschaft ist ~meister** England/the English team are (the) world or world's (*US*) champions; **~meisterschaft** *f* world *or* world's (*US*) championship; (*Ftbl*) World Cup; **w~offen** *adj* liberal-minded, cosmopolitan; **~offenheit** *f* cosmopolitan attitudes *pl*; **~öffentlichkeit** *f* general public; **was meint die ~öffentlichkeit dazu?** what is world opinion on this?, what does the world think about this?; **etw der ~öffentlichkeit zugänglich machen** to make sth accessible to the world at large; **~ordnung** *f* world order; **~politik** *f* world politics *pl*; **w~politisch** *adj* **eine/die w~politische Entwicklung** a development in/the development of world politics; **eine w~politische Entscheidung** a decision affecting world politics; **von w~politischer Bedeutung** of importance in world politics; **w~politisch gesehen, aus w~politischer Sicht** seen from the standpoint of world politics; **~rang** *m* **von ~rang** world-famous; **~rang genießen** to have world status; **~rangliste** *f* world rankings *pl*.

Weltraum *m* (outer) space.

Weltraum- *in cpds* space; **~abwehr** *f* space defence; **~bahnhof** *m* (*inf*) space mission launch centre; **~behörde** *f* space agency; **~fahrer** *m* space traveller; **~fahrt** *f* space travel; **~fahrzeug** *nt* spacecraft, spaceship; **~forschung** *f* space research; **w~gestützt** *adj* space-based; **~labor** *nt* space laboratory; **~rüstung** *f* space weaponry; **~station** *f* space station; **~waffe** *f* space weapon.

Welt-: ~reich *nt* empire; **~reise** *f* world tour, journey round the world; **eine ~reise machen** to go round the world; **das ist doch schließlich keine ~reise** (*inf*) it's not the other end of the world; **~reisende(r)** *mf* globetrotter; **~rekord** *m* world *or* world's (*US*) record; **~rekordinhaber, ~rekordler(in *f*)** *m* **-s, -** world *or* world's (*US*) record holder; **~religion** *f* world religion; **~revolution** *f* world revolution; **~ruf** *m* world(-wide) reputation; **~ruf haben** to have a world(-wide) reputation; **~ruhm** *m* world fame; **~schmerz** *m* world-weariness, weltschmerz (*liter*); **~sicherheitsrat** *m* (*Pol*) (United Nations) Security Council; **~sprache** *f* world language; **~stadt** *f* international *or* cosmopolitan city, metropolis; **w~städtisch** *adj* cosmopolitan; **~umrundung** *f* (*Space*) orbit of the earth; (*Naut*) circumnavigation of the earth; **~umsegler** *m* **-s, -** circumnavigator (of the globe); (*Sport*) round-the-world yachtsman; **w~umspannend** *adj* world-wide, global; **~untergang** *m* (*lit, fig*) end of the world; **~untergangsstimmung** *f* apocalyptic mood; **~verbesserer** *m* starry-eyed idealist; **w~weit** *adj* world-wide, global; **~wirtschaft** *f* world economy; **~wirtschaftskrise** *f* world economic crisis; **~wunder** *nt* **die sieben ~wunder** the Seven Wonders of the World; **er starrte mich an wie ein ~wunder** (*fig*) he stared at me as if I were from another planet *or* as if I were some kind of freak; **~zeituhr** *f* world clock.

wem *dat of* **wer** [1] *interrog pron* who ... to, to whom ◆ **mit/von** *etc* **~** ... who ... with/from *etc*, with/from *etc* whom; **~ von euch soll ich den Schlüssel geben?** which (one) of you should I give the key to?, to which (one) of you should I give the key?
[2] *rel pron (derjenige, dem)* the person (who ...) to, the person to whom ...; *(jeder, dem)* anyone to whom ..., anyone ... to ◆ **~ ... auch (immer)** whoever ... to, no matter who ... to.
[3] *indef pron (inf: jemandem)* to/for somebody; *(mit prep, bestimmten Verben)* somebody; *(in Fragen, konditionalen Sätzen auch)* (to/for) anybody.

Wemfall *m* dative (case).

wen *acc of* **wer** [1] *interrog pron* who, whom ◆ **an ~ hast du geschrieben?** who did you write to?, to whom did you write?; **~ von den Schülern kennst du?** which (one) of these pupils do you know?
[2] *rel pron (derjenige, den)* the person (who *or* whom); *(jeder, den)* anybody (who *or* whom) ◆ **~ ... auch immer** whoever ...
[3] *indef pron (inf: jemanden) (inf)* somebody; *(in Fragen, konditionalen Sätzen auch)* anybody.

Wende[1] *f* **-, -n** turn; *(Veränderung)* change; *(~punkt)* turning point; *(Turnen: am Pferd)* face *or* front vault ◆ **die ~ vom 19. zum 20. Jahrhundert** the transition from the 19th to the 20th century; **nach dem Tod seines Vaters nahm seine Entwicklung eine ~** after the death of his father his development changed direction *or* started to take a different direction.

Wende[2] *m* **-n, -n** Wend.

Wende-: ~fläche *f (Mot)* turning area; **~hals** *m (Orn)* wryneck; *(fig inf)* turncoat *(pej)*; **er ist einer der ~hälse** he's one of those who have done a (complete) U-turn; **~jacke** *f* reversible jacket.

Wendekreis *m* **(a)** tropic ◆ **der nördliche ~** *(Geog)*, **der ~ des Krebses** *(Astrol)* the Tropic of Cancer; **der südliche ~** *(Geog)*, **der ~ des Steinbocks** *(Astrol)* the Tropic of Capricorn. **(b)** *(Aut)* turning circle.

Wendel *f* **-, -n** spiral, helix; *(in Glühbirne etc)* coil.

Wendel-: ~bohrer *m* twist drill; **~rutsche** *f* spiral chute; **~treppe** *f* spiral staircase.

Wende-: ~mantel *m* reversible coat; **~marke** *f (Sport)* turning mark.

wenden *pret* **wendete** *or (liter)* **wandte,** *ptp* **gewendet** *or (liter)* **gewandt** [1] *vt* **(a)** to turn *(auch Sew)*; *(auf die andere Seite)* to turn (over); *(in die entgegengesetzte Richtung)* to turn (round); *(Cook)* to toss ◆ **bitte ~!** please turn over; **seinen Blick nach Norden ~** *(geh)* to turn *or* bend one's eyes *or* to look to(wards) the north; **seinen Schritt gen Süden ~** *(liter)* to turn *or* bend one's steps southwards *(liter)*; **sie wandte kein Auge von ihm** *(geh)* she did not take her eyes off him; **wie man es auch wendet ..., man kann die Sache** *or* **es drehen und ~, wie man will ...** *(fig)* whichever way you (care to) look at it ...
(b) *(aufbringen)* **Geld/Zeit an etw** *(acc)* **~** *(geh)* to spend money/time on sth; **viel Mühe/Sorgfalt** *etc* **an etw** *(acc)* **~** *(geh)* to devote a lot of effort/care *etc* to sth.
[2] *vr* **(a)** to turn (round); *(Wetter, Glück)* to change, to turn ◆ **sich nach links/zum Gehen/zur Tür ~** to turn to the left/to go/to the door; **sich ins Gegenteil ~** to become the opposite; **das Gespräch wendete sich** the conversation took another turn; **seine Liebe/Freude** *etc* **wendete sich ins Gegenteil** his love/joy turned to hate/despair; **sich von jdm ~** *(esp Bibl)* to turn from sb *(liter)*; **sich zu jdm/etw ~** to turn to face sb/sth, to turn towards sb/sth; **sich zum Guten** *or* **Besseren/Schlimmeren ~** to take a turn for the better/worse; **sich zum besten ~** to turn out for the best.
(b) sich an jdn ~ *(um Auskunft)* to consult sb; *(um Hilfe)* to turn to sb; *(Buch, Fernsehserie etc)* to be directed at sb, to be (intended) for sb; **sich gegen jdn/etw ~** to come out against sb/sth, to oppose sb/sth.
[3] *vi* to turn *(auch Sport)*; *(umkehren)* to turn round ◆ **„~ verboten"** "no U-turns".

Wende-: ~platz *m* turning area *or* place; **~punkt** *m* turning point; *(Geometrie)* point of inflection.

wendig *adj* agile, nimble; *Auto etc* manoeuvrable; *(fig) Mensch* agile.

Wendigkeit *f siehe adj* agility, nimbleness; manoeuvrability; agility.

Wendin *f* Wendish woman, Wend.

wendisch *adj* Wendish.

Wendung *f* **(a)** turn *(auch Mil)*; *(Veränderung)* change ◆ **eine interessante/unerwartete ~ nehmen** *(fig)* to take an interesting/unexpected turn; **eine ~ zum Besseren** *or* **Guten/Schlechten nehmen** to take a turn for the better/worse, to change for the better/worse; **einer Sache** *(dat)* **eine unerwartete/neue ~ geben** to give sth an unexpected/new turn; **das gab seinem Leben eine neue ~** that changed the direction of his life; **eine interessante** *etc* **~ trat ein** there was an interesting *etc* turn of events.
(b) *(Rede~)* expression, phrase.

Wenfall *m* accusative (case).

wenig *siehe auch* **weniger, wenigste(r, s)** [1] *adj, indef pron* **(a)** *sing* little; *(unverändert alleinstehend)* not much ◆ **ich habe ~** I have only a little; **(nur) ~ Geld** (only a) little money; **ich besitze nur ~** I only own a few things, I don't own much, I own little; **hast du Zeit? — ~!** have you got time? — not much; **das ist ~** that isn't much; **so ~** so little; **du sagst so ~** you're not saying much; **darüber weiß ich ~** I don't know much about that, I know little about that; **mein ~es Geld** what little money I have; **das ~e, was er übrig hatte** the little he had left; **das ~e Geld muß ausreichen** we'll have to make do with this small amount of money; **um ein ~es jünger (als)** *(geh)* a little younger (than); **es fehlte (nur) ~, und er wäre überfahren worden** he was very nearly run over; **wir haben nicht ~ Mühe damit gehabt** we had more than a little *or* no little difficulty with that; **er gibt sich mit ~(em) zufrieden** *(verlangt nicht viel)* he is satisfied with a little; *(ist selten zufrieden)* he isn't satisfied with much; **sie hat zu ~ Geld** *etc* she doesn't have enough money *etc*; **ein Exemplar zu ~ haben** to have one copy too few; **ich habe ihm £ 20 zu ~ geboten** I offered him £20 too little.
(b) ~e *pl (ein paar)* a few; *(einschränkend: nicht viele)* few ◆ **da wir nur ~e sind** as there are only a few of us, as we are only a few; **er ist ein Freund, wie es nur ~e gibt** there are few friends like him; **in ~en Tagen** in (just) a few days; **es sind nur noch ~e Stunden, bis ...** there are only a few hours to go until ...; **nicht ~e (waren da)** quite a few people (were there); **einige ~e Leute** a few people.
(c) *(auch adv)* **ein ~** a little; **ein ~ Salz/besser** a little salt/better.
[2] *adv* little ◆ **sie kommt (nur) ~ raus** she doesn't get out very often; **er hat sich nicht ~ geärgert** he was not a little annoyed; **das überraschte ihn nicht ~** he was more than a little surprised; **~ besser** little better; **~ bekannt** little-known *attr*, little known *pred*; **~ mehr** little more, not much more; **~ erfreulich** not very pleasant.

Wenig *nt*: **viele ~ machen ein Viel** *(Prov)* it all adds up, many a mickle makes a muckle *(Scot Prov)*.

weniger *comp of* **wenig** [1] *adj, indef pron* less; *pl* fewer ◆ **~ werden** to get less and less; **mein Geld wird immer ~** my money is dwindling away; **er wird immer ~** *(inf)* he's getting thinner and thinner; **~ wäre mehr gewesen** it's quality not quantity that counts.
[2] *adv* less ◆ **ihr kommt es ~ auf die Liebe als (vielmehr) auf das Geld an** she's less interested in love than in money; **die Vorlesung war ~ lehrreich als belustigend** the lecture was not so much instructive as amusing; **das finde ich ~ schön!** that's not so nice!; **ich kann seinen Brief kaum lesen, noch viel ~ verstehen** I can hardly read his letter much less *or* let alone understand it; **je mehr ... desto** *or* **um so ~ ...** the more ... the less ...; **ich glaube ihm um so ~, weil ...** I believe him all the less because ...; **ich möchte nichts ~, als ihn (zu) beleidigen** the last thing I'd want to do is insult him.
[3] *conj, prep +acc or gen* less ◆ **sieben ~ drei ist vier** seven less three is four.

Wenigkeit *f (dated: Kleinigkeit)* little, small amount ◆ **meine ~** *(hum inf)* yours truly *(inf)*; **und meine ~ hat er vergessen** and he forgot little me *(hum inf)*.

wenigstens *adv* at least.

wenigste(r, s) *superl of* **wenig** *adj, indef pron, adv* **am ~n** least; *pl* fewest ◆ **er hat von uns allen das ~** *or* **am ~n Geld** he has the least money of any of us; **sie hat von uns allen die ~n** *or* **am ~n Sorgen** she has the fewest worries of any of us; **von den vier Farben finde ich diese am ~n schön** of the four colours I think this one is the least attractive; **das konnte er am ~n vertragen** he could tolerate that least of all; **die ~n (Leute) glauben das** very few (people) believe that; **das ist (doch) das ~, was du tun könntest** that's the (very) least you could do; **das ist noch das ~!** *(inf)* that's the least of it!; **das am ~n!** that least of all!

▼ **wenn** *conj* **(a)** *(konditional, konzessiv bei Wünschen)* if ◆ **~ er nicht gewesen wäre, hätte ich meine Stelle verloren** if it had not been *or* had it not been for him, I'd have lost my job; **selbst** *or* **und ~** even if; **~ das Wörtchen ~ nicht wär' (, wär' mein Vater Millionär)** *(Prov)* if ifs and ans were pots and pans (there'd be no need for tinkers) *(Prov)*; **~ ... auch ...** even though *or* if ...; **~ ... gleich ...** *(geh)* although ..., even though ...; **~ er auch noch so dumm sein mag, ...** however stupid he may be, ...; **~ auch!** *(inf)* even so!, all the same!; **~ schon!** *(inf)* what of it?, so what? *(inf)*; **~ es denn gar nicht anders geht** well, if there's no other way; **~ es schon sein muß** well, if that's the way it's got to be; **es ist nicht gut, ~ man mit vollem Magen schwimmt** it's not good to swim on a full stomach; **~ man bedenkt, daß ...** when you consider that ..., considering ...; **~ wir erst die neue Wohnung haben** once we get the new flat; **~ ich doch** *or* **nur** *or* **bloß ...** if only I ...; **~ er nur da wäre!** if only he were *or* was here!; **es ist, als** *or* **wie** *(inf)* **~ ...** it's as if ...; **außer ~** except if, unless; **~ du das schon machen willst, (dann) mache es wenigstens richtig** if you want to do it at least do it properly.
(b) *(zeitlich)* when ◆ **jedesmal** *or* **immer ~** whenever; **außer ~** except when, unless.

Wenn *nt*: **(die** *pl or* **das) ~ und Aber** (the) ifs and buts; **ohne ~ und Aber** without any ifs and buts.

wenngleich *conj (geh)* although, even though; *(mit adj auch)* albeit *(form)*.

wennschon *adv (inf)* **(na,) ~!** what of it?, so what? *(inf)*; **~, dennschon!** in for a penny, in for a pound!, if you're going to do something at all, you might as well do it properly!

Wenzel *m* **-s, -** *(Cards)* jack, knave *(form, dated)*.

wer [1] *interrog pron* who ◆ **~ von ...** which (one) of ...; **~ da?** *(Mil)* who goes there?
[2] *rel pron (derjenige, der)* the person who; *(jeder, der)* anyone *or* anybody who; *(esp in Sprichwörtern)* he who ◆ **~ ... auch (immer)** whoever ...
[3] *indef pron (inf: jemand)* somebody, someone; *(in Fragen, konditionalen Sätzen auch)* anybody, anyone ◆ **ist da ~?** is somebody *or* anybody there?; **~ sein** to be somebody *(inf)*.

Werbe- *in cpds* advertising; **~abteilung** *f* publicity department; **~agentur** *f* advertising agency; **~aktion** *f* advertising campaign; **~antwort** *f* business reply card; **~block** *m, pl* **-blocks** *or* **-blöcke** *(TV)* commercial break; **~chef** *m* advertising *or* publicity manager; **~etat** *m* advertising budget; **~fachmann** *m* advertising man; **~feldzug** *m* advertising campaign; **~fernsehen** *nt* commercial television; *(Sendung)* TV advertisements *pl or* commercials *pl*; **~film** *m* advertising *or* promotional film; *(Spot)* (filmed) commercial; **~fritze** *m (inf)* PR man; **~funk** *m* (programme of) radio commercials *pl*; **~gag** *m* publicity stunt *or* gimmick; **~gemeinschaft** *f* joint advertising arrangement; **~geschenk** *nt* gift *(from company)*; *(zu*

Gekauftem) free gift; **~grafiker** *m* commercial artist; **~kampagne** *f* publicity campaign; (*für Verbrauchsgüter*) advertising campaign; **w~kräftig** *adj Aufmachung etc* catchy; **ein w~kräftiger Slogan** an effective publicity slogan; **ein w~kräftiger Faktor** a good advertising point; **~leiter** *m* advertising *or* publicity manager, head of advertising *or* promotions; **~material** *nt* advertising material; **~mittel** *nt* means of advertising; **~muster** *nt* advertising sample.

wẹrben *pret* **wạrb,** *ptp* **gewọrben** [1] *vt Mitglieder, Mitarbeiter* to recruit; *Kunden, Abonnenten, Stimmen* to attract, to win; *Soldaten* to recruit, to enlist.
[2] *vi* to advertise ◆ **für etw ~** to advertise sth, to promote sth; **für eine Partei ~** to try to get support for a party; **Plakate, die für den linken Kandidaten ~** placards supporting the left-wing candidate; **um etw ~** to solicit sth, to court sth; **um Unterstützung ~** to try to enlist support; **um junge Wähler/neue Leser ~** to try to attract *or* woo young voters/new readers; **um ein Mädchen ~** to court *or* woo (*old*) a girl; **er hat bei ihren Eltern um sie geworben** he asked her parents for permission to marry her.

Wẹrbe|offizier *m* recruiting officer.

Wẹrber *m* **-s, -** (*um Kunden, Wähler*) canvasser; (*um Mädchen*) suitor; (*für Mitglieder etc, Mil Hist*) recruiter, recruiting officer; (*inf: Werbefachmann*) advertising man, adman (*inf*).

Wẹrberin *f* (*um Kunden, Wähler*) canvasser; (*für Mitglieder*) recruiter; (*inf: Werbefachfrau*) adwoman.

wẹrberisch [1] *adj* advertising *attr*, promotional.
[2] *adv* publicity-wise.

Wẹrbe-: ~schrift *f* publicity leaflet; (*für Verbrauchsgüter*) advertising leaflet; **~schriften** promotional literature *sing*; **~slogan** *m* publicity slogan; (*für Verbrauchsgüter*) advertising slogan; **~spot** *m* commercial; **~spruch** *m siehe* **~slogan**; **~text** *m* advertising copy *no pl*; **zwei ~texte** two pieces of advertising copy; **~texte verfassen** to write (advertising) copy; **~texter** *m* (advertising) copywriter; **~träger** *m* advertising medium; **~trommel** *f*: **die ~trommel (für etw) rühren** (*inf*) to beat the big drum (for sth) (*inf*), to push sth (*inf*); **w~wirksam** *adj* effective (for advertising purposes); **der Skandal erwies sich als äußerst w~wirksam** the scandal proved to be excellent publicity *or* to have excellent publicity value; **~wirksamkeit** *f* publicity value.

wẹrblich *adj* advertising *attr*, promotional ◆ **~ gesehen** from an advertising point of view.

Wẹrbung *f* (*esp Comm*) advertising; (*Werbeabteilung*) publicity department; (*Pol: Propaganda*) pre-election publicity; (*von Kunden, Stimmen*) winning, attracting; (*von Mitgliedern, Soldaten etc*) recruitment, recruiting; (*um Mädchen*) courting (*um* of) ◆ **~ für etw machen** to advertise sth.

Wẹrbungskosten *pl* (*von Mensch*) professional outlay *sing or* expenses *pl*; (*von Firma*) business expenses *pl*.

Wẹrdaruf *m* (*Mil*) call of "who goes there?", challenge.

Wẹrdegang *m, no pl* development; (*beruflich*) career.

wẹrden *pret* **wụrde,** *ptp* **gewọrden** *aux sein* [1] *v aux* **(a)** (*zur Bildung des Futurs und Konjunktivs*) **ich werde/wir ~ es tun** I/we will *or* shall do it, I'll/we'll do it; **er wird/du wirst/ihr werdet es tun** he/you will do it, he'll/you'll do it; **ich werde das nicht tun** I shall not *or* shan't *or* will not *or* won't do that; **er wird das nicht tun** he will not *or* won't do that; **du wirst heute schön zu Hause bleiben!** you'll *or* you will stay at home today!; **es wird gleich regnen** it's going to rain; **wer wird denn gleich weinen!** you're not going to cry now, are you?; **wer wird denn gleich!** (*inf*) come on, now!; **er hat gesagt, er werde/würde kommen** he said he would *or* he'd come; **das würde ich gerne tun** I would *or* I'd gladly do that.
(b) (*Ausdruck der Vermutung*) **sie wird wohl in der Küche sein** she will *or* she'll probably be in the kitchen; **er wird (wohl) ausgegangen sein** he will *or* he'll (probably) have gone out; **das wird etwa 20 Mark kosten** it will cost roughly 20 marks.
(c) (*zur Bildung des Passivs*) *pret auch* **wạrd** (*old, liter*), *ptp* **wọrden geschlagen ~** to be beaten; **er ist erschossen worden** he was shot/he has been shot; **das Haus wird (gerade) renoviert** the house is being redecorated (just now); **es wurde gesungen** there was singing; **hier wird nicht geraucht!** there's no smoking here; **in England wird links gefahren** in England people drive on the left; **mir wurde gesagt, daß ...** I was told ...
[2] *vi pret auch* **wạrd** (*old, liter*), *ptp* **gewọrden (a)** (*mit adj*) to become, to get; (*allmählich*) to grow ◆ **verrückt/blind ~** to go crazy/blind; **rot/sauer/blaß/kalt ~** to turn *or* go red/sour/pale/cold; **es wird kalt/dunkel/spät** it's getting cold/dark/late; **mir wird kalt/warm** I'm getting cold/warm; **mir wird schlecht/wohl/besser** I feel bad/good/better; **anders ~** to change; **die Fotos sind gut geworden** the photos have turned *or* come out nicely; **es wird schon wieder (gut) ~** it'll turn out all right.
(b) (*mit Gleichsetzungsnominativen, Pronomen*) to become; (*sich verwandeln in auch*) to turn into; (*sein werden*) to be going to be ◆ **Lehrer ~** to become a teacher; **was willst du einmal ~?** what do you want to be when you grow up?; **ich will Lehrer ~** I want to be *or* become a teacher; **Erster ~** to come *or* be first; **er ist nichts (Rechtes)/etwas geworden** he hasn't got anywhere/he's got somewhere in life, he hasn't made anything/he has made something of himself; **das ist nichts geworden** it came to nothing; **das Eis wird Wasser** the ice is turning (in)to water; **das wird bestimmt ein guter Eintopf** the stew is going to turn out nicely; **was soll das ~? — das wird ein Pullover** what's that going to be? — it's going to be a pullover; **es wird sicher ein Junge (~)** it's bound to be a boy; **das wird ein guter Urlaub (~)** it's going to be a good holiday; **... es werde Licht! und es ward Licht** (*Bibl*) ... let there be light, and there was light (*Bibl*).
(c) (*mit Zeitangaben*) **es wird bald ein Jahr, daß ...** it's almost a year since ...; **es wird Zeit, daß er kommt** it's time (that) he came *or* (that) he was coming; **es wird Nacht** it's getting dark, night is falling; **es wird Tag** it's getting light, day is dawning; **es wird Winter** winter is coming; **es wurde 10 Uhr, und ...** 10 o'clock came, and ...; **es wird jetzt 13 Uhr** in a moment it will be 1 o'clock; **er wird am 8. Mai 36** he is *or* will be 36 on the 8th of May; **er ist gerade 40 geworden** he has just turned 40.
(d) (*mit prep*) **was ist aus ihm geworden?** what has become of him?; **aus ihm ist ein großer Komponist geworden** he has become a great composer; **aus ihm ist nichts (Rechtes)/etwas geworden** he hasn't got anywhere/has got somewhere in life; **daraus wird nichts** that won't come to anything, nothing will come of that; **daraus wird bestimmt nichts Gutes/kann nichts Gutes ~** no good will/can come of it; **was wird daraus (~)?** what will come of it?; **zu etw ~** to turn into sth, to become sth; **zu Staub ~** to turn to dust; *siehe* **nichts**.
(e) (*andere Wendungen*) **alles Leben wird und vergeht** (*liter*) life comes into being and then passes away (*liter*); **was nicht ist, kann noch ~** (*Prov inf*) my/your *etc* day will come; **was soll nun ~?** so what's going to happen now?, so what do we do now?; **es wird schon ~** (*inf*) it'll come out okay (*inf*) *or* all right in the end, everything'll turn out okay (*inf*) *or* all right; **es will einfach nicht ~** (*inf*) it's simply not working; **ich denke, ich werde nicht wieder!** (*sl*) I was flabbergasted (*inf*), I got the shock of my life; **er wird mal wie sein Vater** he's going to be like his father; **wie sind die Fotos geworden?** how did the photos turn *or* come out?; **wie soll der Pullover ~?** what's the pullover going to be like?; **ihm ist ein großes Glück geworden** (*old, liter*) he has been favoured with great fortune (*liter*).

Wẹrden *nt* **-s,** *no pl* **(a)** (*Entstehung*) development ◆ **im ~ sein** to be in the making; **die lebenden Sprachen sind immer im ~ begriffen** living languages are in a state of continual development. **(b)** (*Philos*) Becoming.

wẹrdend *adj* nascent, emergent ◆ **~e Mutter** expectant mother, mother-to-be.

Wẹrfall *m* nominative (case).

wẹrfen *pret* **wạrf,** *ptp* **gewọrfen** [1] *vt* **(a)** to throw (*auch beim Ringkampf*) (*nach* at), to cast (*liter, Bibl*); *Tor, Korb* to score ◆ **Bomben ~** (*von Flugzeug*) to drop bombs; **eine Münze ~** to toss a coin; **„nicht ~"** "handle with care"; **Bilder an die Wand ~** to project pictures onto the wall; **etw auf jdn/etw ~** to throw sth at sb/sth; **etw auf den Boden/das Dach ~** to throw sth to the ground, to throw sth on(to) the ground/roof; **die Sonne warf ihre Strahlen auf den See** the sun cast its rays on the lake; **die Tischlampe wirft ihr Licht auf ...** the table-lamp throws its light on ...; **die Laterne wirft ein helles Licht** the lantern gives off a bright light; **billige Waren auf den Markt ~** to dump cheap goods on the market; **jdn aus der Firma/dem Haus** *etc* **~** to throw *or* kick sb out (of the firm/house *etc*); **jdn ins Gefängnis** *etc* **~** to throw sb into prison *etc*; **alle Sorgen hinter** *or* **von sich ~** (*fig*) to cast aside all one's worries; **etw in den Briefkasten ~** to put sth in the letter box; **etw ins Gespräch/in die Debatte ~** to throw sth into the conversation/debate *etc*; **etw aufs Papier ~** (*geh*) to jot sth down; **die Kleider von sich ~** to throw *or* cast off one's clothes; *siehe* **Blick, Licht** *etc*.
(b) (*Junge kriegen*) to have, to throw (*spec*).
[2] *vi* **(a)** to throw ◆ **mit etw (auf jdn/etw) ~** to throw sth (at sb/sth); **mit Geld um sich ~** (*inf*) to throw *or* chuck (*inf*) one's money about; **mit Komplimenten um sich ~** to be free and easy *or* be lavish with one's compliments; **mit Fremdwörtern um sich ~** to bandy foreign words about.
(b) (*Tier*) to have its young; (*Katze, Hund etc auch*) to have a litter, to litter; (*bei einzelnen Jungen*) to have a pup *etc*.
[3] *vr* to throw oneself (*auf +acc* (up)on, at); (*Holz*) to warp; (*Metall, Asphalt etc*) to buckle ◆ **sich auf eine Aufgabe** *etc* **~** to throw oneself into a task *etc*; **sich in die Kleider ~** to throw on one's clothes; *siehe* **Brust, Hals[1]**.

Wẹrfer *m* **-s, -** thrower; (*Cricket*) bowler; (*Baseball*) pitcher.

Wẹrft *f* **-, -en** shipyard; (*für Flugzeuge*) hangar.

Wẹrft|arbeiter *m* shipyard worker.

Wẹrg *nt* **-(e)s,** *no pl* tow.

Wẹrgeld *nt* (*Hist Jur*) wer(e)gild.

Wẹrk *nt* **-(e)s, -e (a)** (*Arbeit, Tätigkeit*) work *no indef art*; (*geh: Tat*) deed, act; (*Schöpfung, Kunst~, Buch*) work; (*Gesamt~*) works *pl* ◆ **Schweitzer hat in Afrika ein bedeutendes ~ vollbracht** Schweitzer has done (some) important work in Africa; **ein ~ wie das verdient unsere Förderung** work such as that deserves our support; **das ~ eines Augenblicks** the work of a moment; **das ist sein ~** this is his doing; **das ~ vieler Jahrzehnte** the work of many decades; **das ~ jahrelanger Arbeit/seines Fleißes** the product of many years of work/of his industry; **die ~e Gottes** the works of God; **gute ~e tun** to do good works; **ein gutes ~ (an jdm) tun** to do a good deed (for sb); **du tätest ein gutes ~, wenn ...** (*auch hum*) you'd be doing me/him *etc* a good turn if ..., you'd be doing your good deed for the day if ... (*hum*); **ein ~ der Nächstenliebe** an act of charity; **ans ~ gehen, sich ans ~ machen, zu ~e gehen** (*geh*) to set to *or* go to work; **(frisch) ans ~!** (*old, liter*) to work!; **am ~ sein** to be at work; **etw ins ~ setzen** (*geh*) to set sth in motion; **wir müssen vorsichtig zu ~e gehen** we must proceed cautiously.
(b) (*Betrieb, Fabrik*) works *sing or pl*, factory, plant ◆ **ab ~** (*Comm*) ex works.
(c) (*Trieb~*) works *pl*, mechanism.
(d) *usu pl* (*Festungswerke*) works *pl*.

Wẹrk- *in cpds* works, factory; *siehe auch* **Werk(s)-**; **~bank** *f* workbench.

Wẹrkel *nt* **-s, -(n)** (*Aus*) hurdy-gurdy, street organ.

Wẹrkelmann *m, pl* **-männer** (*Aus*) organ grinder.

wẹrkeln *vi* (*dated inf*) to potter about *or* around ◆ **daran ist noch einiges zu ~**

⚠: Informationen zur Rechtschreibreform im Anhang

it still needs a bit of fixing.

werken [1] *vi* to work, to be busy; (*handwerklich*) to do handicrafts ◆ **W~** (*Sch*) handicrafts.
[2] *vt* to make.

Werk-: w~getreu *adj* true *or* faithful to the original; **~halle** *f* factory building; **w~immanent** *adj* (*Liter*) text-based; **etw w~immanent interpretieren** to make a text-based interpretation of sth; **~kunstschule** *f* arts and crafts school; **~lehrer** *m* woodwork/metalwork *etc* teacher, handicrafts teacher; **~leute** *pl* (*old, liter*) craftsmen *pl*, artisans *pl*; **~meister** *m* foreman.

Werk(s)-: ~angehörige(r) *mf* works *or* factory employee; **~arzt** *m* works *or* company doctor.

Werkschutz *m* works *or* factory security service.

Werks-: w~eigen *adj* company *attr*; **w~eigen sein** to be company-owned, to belong to the company; **~fahrer** *m* company *or* factory driver; **~feuerwehr** *f* works *or* factory fire service; **~gelände** *nt* works *or* factory premises *pl*; **~kantine** *f* works *or* factory canteen; **~küche** *f* works kitchen; **~leiter** *m* works *or* factory director *or* manager; **~leitung** *f* works *or* factory management; **~schließung** *f* plant closure; **~spionage** *f* industrial espionage.

Werkstatt, Werkstätte *f* workshop (*auch fig*); (*für Autoreparaturen*) garage; (*von Künstler*) studio.

Werkstattwagen *m* breakdown truck, wrecker (*US*).

Werkstoff *m* material.

Werkstoff-: ~prüfer *m* materials tester; **~prüfung** *f* testing of materials.

Werk-: ~stück *nt* (*Tech*) workpiece; **~student** *m* working student; **~student sein** to work one's way through college.

Werk(s)-: ~verkehr *m* company transport; **~vertrag** *m* contract of manufacture; **~wohnung** *f* company flat (*Brit*) *or* apartment.

Werktag *m* working day, workday.

werktäglich [1] *adj attr Kleidung etc* workaday ◆ **~e Öffnung** opening on workdays *or* working days.
[2] *adv* (*werktags*) on workdays *or* working days.

werktags *adv* on workdays *or* working days.

werktätig *adj* working.

Werktätige(r) *mf decl as adj* working man/woman ◆ **die ~n** the working people *pl*.

Werk-: ~tisch *m* work-table; **~treue** *f* faithfulness to the original; **~unterricht** *m* handicraft lessons *pl*, woodwork/metalwork *etc* instruction.

Werkzeug *nt* (*lit, fig*) tool.

Werkzeug-: ~kasten *m* toolbox; **~macher** *m* toolmaker; **~maschine** *f* machine tool; **~stahl** *m* (*Tech*) tool steel.

Wermut *m* **-(e)s,** *no pl* **(a)** (*Bot*) wormwood ◆ **ein Tropfen ~** (*fig geh*) a drop of bitterness. **(b)** (*~wein*) vermouth.

Wermut-: ~bruder (*inf*), **~penner** (*sl*) *m* wino (*sl*).

Wermutstropfen *m* (*fig geh*) drop of bitterness.

Werst *f* **-, -e** (*Maß*) verst.

wert *adj* **(a)** (*old, form: Anrede*) dear ◆ **Ihr ~es Schreiben** (*form*) your esteemed letter (*form*); **wie war doch gleich Ihr ~er Name?** (*form*) what was the name, sir/madam?
(b) etw ~ sein to be worth sth; **nichts ~ sein** to be worthless *or* worth nothing; (*untauglich*) to be no good; **sie war ihm offenbar nicht viel ~** she obviously didn't mean all that much to him; **er ist £ 100.000 ~** (*Press sl*) he is worth £100,000; **Glasgow ist eine Reise ~** Glasgow is worth a visit; **einer Sache** (*gen*) **~ sein** (*geh*) to be worthy of sth; **es ist der Mühe ~** it's worth the trouble *or* it; **es ist nicht der Rede ~** it's not worth mentioning; **er ist es nicht ~, daß man ihm vertraut** he doesn't deserve to be trusted; **er ist (es) nicht ~, daß wir ihn unterstützen** he is not worthy of *or* he does not deserve our support; **dieser Film ist es durchaus ~, daß man sich ihn ansieht** this film is definitely worth seeing.
(c) (*nützlich*) useful ◆ **ein Auto ist viel ~** a car is very useful; **das ist schon viel ~** (*erfreulich*) that's very encouraging.

Wert *m* **-(e)s, -e** value; (*esp menschlicher*) worth; (*von Banknoten, Briefmarken*) denomination; (*~sache*) article of value, valuable object. **~e** *pl* (*von Test, Analyse*) results *pl* ◆ **einen ~ von DM 5 haben** to be worth DM 5, to have a value of DM 5; **im ~e von** to the value of, worth; **an ~ verlieren/zunehmen, im ~ sinken/steigen** to decrease/increase in value, to depreciate/appreciate (*esp Econ*); **eine Sache unter/über (ihrem wirklichen) ~ verkaufen** to sell sth for less/more than its true value; **sie hat innere ~e** she has certain inner qualities; **~ auf etw** (*acc*) **legen** (*fig*) to set great store by sth, to attach importance to sth; **ich lege ~ darauf, festzustellen, daß ...** I think it important to establish that ...; **das hat keinen ~** (*inf*) there's no point.

Wert-: ~angabe *f* declaration of value; **~arbeit** *f* craftsmanship, workmanship; **~berichtigung** *f* (*Comm*) valuation adjustment; **w~beständig** *adj* stable in value; **~beständigkeit** *f* stability of value; **~brief** *m* registered letter (*containing sth of value*).

⚠**Wertebewußtsein** *nt* sense of right and wrong.

werten *vti* (*einstufen*) to rate (*als* as); *Klassenarbeit etc* to grade; (*beurteilen*) to judge (*als* to be); (*Sport*) (*als gültig ~*) to allow; (*Punkte geben*) to give a score ◆ **ein Tor** *etc* **nicht ~** (*Ftbl etc*) to disallow a goal; **der Punktrichter aus Polen wertete besonders hoch** the Polish judge gave particularly high marks; **je nachdem, wie gewertet wird** according to how the scoring is done; **ohne (es) ~ zu wollen ...** without wanting to make any judgement (on it) ...

Werte-: ~system *nt* system of values; **~wandel** *m* change in values.

wertfrei *adj* unbias(s)ed, without prejudice ◆ **etw völlig ~ beurteilen** to give a completely unbias(s)ed assessment of sth.

Wertgegenstand *m* object of value. **¨e** *pl* valuables *pl*.

-wertig *adj suf* **(a)** -valued. **(b)** (*Chem, Ling*) -valent.

Wertigkeit *f* (*Chem, Ling*) valency.

Wert-: ~karte *f* (*Aus Telec*) phonecard; **~kartentelefon** *nt* (*Aus*) card telephone; **w~los** *adj* worthless, valueless; **~losigkeit** *f* worthlessness; **~marke** *f* ticket; (*zum Aufkleben*) stamp; **~maß** *nt*, **~maßstab** *m*, **~messer** *m* **-s, -** standard, yardstick; **~minderung** *f* reduction in value; **w~neutral** *adj* non-normative, value-free; **~objekt** *nt siehe* **~gegenstand**; **~ordnung** *f* system of values; **~paket** *nt* registered parcel (*containing sth of value*); **~papier** *nt* security, bond; **~papiere** *pl* stocks and shares *pl*; **~papierbörse** *f* stock exchange; **~philosophie** *f* (*analytische ~*) axiology; (*allgemeine Ethik*) moral philosophy; **~sache** *f siehe* **~gegenstand**; **w~schätzen** *vt sep* (*liter*) to (hold in high) esteem; **~schätzung** *f* (*liter*) esteem, high regard; **~schöpfung** *f* (*Econ*) net product; **~schrift** *f* (*Sw*) *siehe* **~papier**; **~sendung** *f* registered consignment; **~setzung** *f* scale of values; (*das Festsetzen*) fixing of values; **~steigerung** *f* increase in value; **~stellung** *f* (*Fin*) value; **~stoff** *m* reusable material; **das Recyceln von ~stoffen** the recycling of reusable materials; **~system** *nt* system of values, value system.

Wertung *f* **(a)** evaluation, assessment; (*von Jury etc*) judging, scoring; (*Punkte*) score ◆ **aus der ~ fallen** to be disqualified. **(b)** (*das Werten*) *siehe vti* rating; grading; judging; allowing; scoring.

Wertungs- (*Sport etc*): **~gericht** *nt* jury; **~richter** *m* judge.

Wert|urteil *nt* value judgement.

Wert|urteils-: w~frei *adj* free from value judgements; **~freiheit** *f* non-normativity.

wertvoll *adj* valuable; (*moralisch*) *Mensch* worthy, estimable.

Wert-: ~vorstellung *f* moral concept; **~zeichen** *nt* (*form*) postage stamp; **~zuwachssteuer** *f* capital gains tax.

werweißen *vi insep* (*Sw*) to guess.

Werwolf *m* werewolf.

wes *pron* (*old*) [1] *gen of* **wer** whose.
[2] *gen of* **was** of which.

Wesen *nt* **-s, - (a)** *no pl* nature; (*Wesentliches*) essence ◆ **am ~ unserer Beziehung hat sich nichts geändert** the basic nature of our relationship remains unchanged; **es liegt im ~ einer Sache ...** it's in the nature of a thing ...; **das gehört zum ~ der Demokratie** it is of the essence of democracy.
(b) *no pl* **sein ~ treiben** (*geh*) (*Dieb etc*) to be at work; (*Schalk etc*) to be up to one's tricks; (*Gespenst*) to be abroad; **viel ~s machen (um** *or* **von)** to make a lot of fuss (about).
(c) (*Geschöpf*) being; (*tierisches ~ auch*) creature; (*Mensch*) person, creature ◆ **armes ~** poor thing *or* creature; **das höchste ~** the Supreme Being; **das kleine ~** the little thing; **ein weibliches/männliches ~** a female/male.

wesen *vi* (*liter*) to be present.

Wesen-: w~haft *adj* intrinsic, essential; **~heit** *f* (*Philos*) being; **w~los** *adj* insubstantial, unreal.

Wesens-: w~ähnlich *adj* similar in nature; **~art** *f* nature, character; **es ist griechische ~art, zu ...** it's a Greek characteristic to ...; **w~eigen** *adj* intrinsic; **w~fremd** *adj* (*im Wesen verschieden*) different *or* dissimilar in nature; **das Lügen ist ihm völlig w~fremd** lying is completely foreign *or* alien to his nature; **w~gemäß** *adj* **das ist ihm nicht w~gemäß** it's not in accordance with his nature; **w~gleich** *adj* essentially alike, identical in character *or* nature; **w~verwandt** *adj* related in character; **~verwandtschaft** *f* relatedness of character; **~zug** *m* characteristic, trait.

wesentlich [1] *adj* (*den Kern der Sache betreffend, sehr wichtig*) essential; (*grundlegend*) fundamental; (*erheblich*) substantial, considerable, appreciable; (*wichtig*) important ◆ **das W~e** the essential part *or* thing; (*von dem, was gesagt wurde*) the gist; **im ~en** in essence, basically, essentially; (*im großen*) in the main.
[2] *adv* (*grundlegend*) fundamentally; (*erheblich*) considerably ◆ **es ist mir ~ lieber, wenn wir ...** I would much rather we ...; **sie hat sich nicht ~ verändert** she hasn't changed much.

Wesfall *m* genitive case.

weshalb [1] *interrog adv* why.
[2] *rel adv* which is why, for which reason ◆ **der Grund, ...** the reason why ...; **das ist es ja, ~ ...** that is why ...

Wesir *m* **-s, -e** vizi(e)r.

Wespe *f* **-, -n** wasp.

Wespen-: ~nest *nt* wasp's nest; **in ein ~nest stechen** (*fig*) to stir up a hornets' nest; **das war ein Stich ins ~nest** (*fig*) that stirred up a hornets' nest; **~stich** *m* wasp sting; **~taille** *f* (*fig*) wasp waist.

wessen *pron* [1] *gen of* **wer (a)** *interrog* whose.
(b) *rel, indef* **~ Handschrift das auch (immer) sein mag, ...** no matter whose handwriting it may be, ...
[2] *gen of* **was** (*liter*) **(a)** *interrog* **~ hat man dich angeklagt?** of what have you been accused?
(b) *rel, indef* **~ man dich auch (immer) anklagt, ...** whatever they *or* no matter what they accuse you of ...

wessentwegen *interrog adv* (*geh*) on whose/what account.

wessentwillen *interrog adv* (*geh*): **um ~** for whose sake.

Wessi *m* **-s, -s** (*inf*) Westerner, West German.

West *m* **-s,** *no pl* **(a)** (*Naut, Met, liter*) west; *siehe* **Nord. (b)** (*liter: ~wind*) west wind.

West- *in cpds* (*in Ländernamen*) (*politisch*) West; (*geographisch auch*) the West of

⚠: for details of spelling reform, see supplement

..., Western; **~afrika** *nt* West Africa; **~australien** *nt* Western Australia; **~-Berlin, ~berlin** *nt* West Berlin; **w~deutsch** *adj* (*Pol*) West German; (*Geog*) Western German; **~deutsche(r)** *mf* West German; **~deutschland** *nt* (*Pol*) West Germany, Western Germany; (*Geog*) the West of Germany.

Weste *f* -, -n waistcoat, vest (*US*) ♦ **eine reine** *or* **saubere** *or* **weiße ~ haben** (*fig*) to have a clean slate.

Westen *m* -s, *no pl* west; (*von Land*) West ♦ **der ~** (*Pol*) the West; (*im Gegensatz zum Orient auch*) the Occident; **aus dem ~, von ~ (her)** from the west; **gegen** *or* **gen** (*liter*) *or* **nach ~** west(wards), to the west; **nach ~ (hin)** to the west; **im ~ der Stadt/des Landes** in the west of the town/country; **weiter im ~** further west; **im ~ Frankreichs** in the west of France, in Western France.

Westentasche *f* waistcoat *or* vest (*US*) pocket ♦ **etw wie seine ~ kennen** (*inf*) to know sth like the back of one's hand (*inf*).

Westentaschenformat *nt* (*hum*) **ein X im ~** a miniature X.

Western *m* -(s), - western.

West-: ~europa *nt* Western Europe; **w~europäisch** *adj* West(ern) European; **w~europäische Zeit** Greenwich Mean Time, Western European Time (*rare*); **die w~europäische Union** the Western European Union.

Westfale *m* -n, -n Westphalian.

Westfalen *nt* -s Westphalia.

Westfälin *f* Westphalian (woman).

westfälisch *adj* Westphalian ♦ **der W~e Friede** (*Hist*) The Treaty of Westphalia.

Westfriesische Inseln *pl* West Frisians *pl*, West Frisian Islands *pl*.

West-: ~geld *nt* (*inf*) Western currency; **~germanen** *pl* (*Hist*) West Germanic peoples *pl or* tribes *pl*; **w~germanisch** *adj* (*Hist, Ling*) West Germanic; **~goten** *pl* (*Hist*) Visigoths *pl*, West Goths *pl*; **w~griechisch** *adj* Western Greek; **~indien** *nt* the West Indies *pl*; **w~indisch** *adj* West Indian; **die ~indischen Inseln** the West Indies *pl*; **~küste** *f* west coast.

Westler *m* -s, - (*DDR inf*) westerner; (*Hist*) westernist.

westlerisch *adj* (*DDR inf*) western; (*Hist*) westernist.

westlich [1] *adj* western; *Kurs, Wind, Richtung* westerly; (*Pol*) Western ♦ **der ~ste Ort** the westernmost place.
[2] *adv* (to the) west (*von* of).
[3] *prep +gen* (to the) west of.

West-: ~mächte *pl* (*Pol*) **die ~mächte** the western powers *pl*; **~mark** *f* (*inf*) West German mark; **w~mitteldeutsch** *adj* West Middle German; **~nordwest** *m* **(a)** (*Naut, Met, liter*) west-north-west; **(b)** (*liter: Wind*) west-north-west wind; **w~östlich** *adj* west-to-east; **in w~östlicher Richtung** from west to east; **~politik** *f* policy towards the west, western policy; **~preußen** *nt* West Prussia; **~rom** *nt* (*Hist*) Western Roman Empire; **w~römisch** *adj* (*Hist*) Western Roman; **~russen** *pl* White Russians *pl*; **~schweiz** *f* **die ~schweiz** Western Switzerland; **~sektor** *m* western sector; **~südwest** *m* **(a)** (*Naut, Met, liter*) west-south-west; **(b)** (*liter: Wind*) west-south-west wind; **~wall** *m* (*Hist*) Siegfried Line; **w~wärts** *adv* westward(s), (to the) west; **~wind** *m* west wind.

weswegen *interrog adv* why.

wett *adj pred* **~ sein** to be quits.

Wett|annahme(stelle) *f* betting office.

Wettbewerb *m* competition ♦ **mit jdm in ~ stehen/treten** to be in/enter into competition with sb, to be competing/to compete with sb; **außer ~ teilnehmen** *or* **laufen** to take part hors concours *or* as a non-competitor.

Wettbewerber *m* competitor.

Wettbewerbs-: ~bedingungen *pl* terms of a/the competition *pl*; **~beschränkung** *f* restraint of trade; **w~fähig** *adj* competitive; **~fähigkeit** *f* competitiveness; **~nachteil** *m* competitive disadvantage; **~recht** *nt* fair trading law; **~teilnehmer** *m* competitor; **~verzerrung** *f* distortion of competition; **~vorteil** *m* competitive advantage *or* edge; **~wirtschaft** *f* competitive economy.

Wettbüro *nt* betting office.

Wette *f* -, -n bet (*auch Sport*); wager ♦ **eine ~ machen** *or* **abschließen/annehmen** to make/take up *or* accept a bet; **eine ~ auf ein Pferd abschließen** to place a bet on a horse; **darauf gehe ich jede ~ ein** I'll bet you anything you like; **was gilt die ~?** what will you bet me?, what are you betting?; **die ~ gilt!** done!, you're on! (*inf*); **um die ~ laufen/schwimmen** to run/swim a race (with each other); **mit jdm um die ~ laufen** *or* **rennen** to race sb; **sie arbeiten/singen/schreien um die ~** they're working as hard as they can/singing at the tops of their voices/having a screaming competition.

Wett|eifer *m* competitive zeal, competitiveness.

wett|eifern *vi insep* **mit jdm um etw ~** to compete *or* contend *or* vie with sb for sth.

wetten *vti* to bet (*auch Sport*); to wager ♦ **(wollen wir) ~?** (do you) want to bet?; **~, daß ich recht habe?** (I) bet you I'm right!; **so haben wir nicht gewettet!** that's not part of the deal *or* bargain!; **auf etw** (*acc*) **~** to bet on sth; **mit jdm ~** to bet with sb; **(mit jdm) (darauf) ~, daß ...** to bet (sb) that ...; **(mit jdm) um 5 Mark/eine Flasche Bier** *etc* **~** to bet (sb) 5 marks/a bottle of beer *etc*; **wir wetteten um einen Kasten Sekt** we bet each other a case of champagne; **ich habe mit ihm um 10 Mark auf/gegen den Sieg der Sozialisten gewettet** I bet him 10 marks that the Socialists would win/wouldn't win *or* would lose; **gegen etw ~** to bet against sth; **da wette ich gegen** (*inf*) *or* **dagegen** I bet you that isn't so/won't happen *etc*; **ich wette 100 gegen 1 (darauf)(, daß ...)** I'll bet *or* lay (you) 100 to 1 (that ...); **ich wette meinen Kopf (darauf)(, daß ...)** I'll bet you anything (you like) (that ...).

Wetter[1] *m* -s, - better.

Wetter[2] *nt* -s, - **(a)** weather *no indef art* ♦ **bei jedem ~** in all weathers; **bei so einem ~** in weather like this/that, in such weather; **das ist vielleicht ein ~!** (*inf*) what weather!; **was haben wir heute für ~?** what's the weather like today?; **wir haben herrliches ~** the weather's marvellous; **ein ~ zum Eierlegen** (*inf*) *or* **Heldenzeugen** (*inf*) fantastic weather (*inf*); **übers** *or* **vom ~ sprechen** to talk about the weather; **(bei jdm) gut ~ machen** (*inf*) to make up to sb; **(jdn) um gutes ~ bitten** (*inf*) to try to smooth things over (with sb); **alle ~!** (*inf*) my goodness!, by Jove! (*dated*).
(b) (*Un~*) storm.
(c) *usu pl* (*Min*) air ♦ **matte ~** *pl* chokedamp *sing*, blackdamp *sing*; **giftige** *or* **böse ~** *pl* whitedamp *sing*; **schlagende ~** *pl* firedamp *sing*.

Wetter-: ~amt *nt* weather *or* met(eorological) office; **~aussichten** *pl* weather outlook *sing or* prospects *pl*; **~ballon** *m* weather *or* meteorological balloon; **~beobachtung** *f* meteorological observation; **~bericht** *m* weather report; **~besserung** *f* improvement in the weather; **w~beständig** *adj* weatherproof; **w~bestimmend** *adj* weather-determining; **w~bestimmend sein** to determine the weather.

Wetterchen *nt* (*inf*) **das ist ja heute ein ~!** the weather's really great *or* fantastic today! (*inf*).

Wetter-: ~dienst *m* weather *or* meteorological service; **w~empfindlich** *adj* sensitive to (changes in) the weather; **~fahne** *f* weather vane; **w~fest** *adj* weatherproof; **~fleck** *m* (*Aus*) weatherproof cape; **~front** *f* front; **~frosch** *m* **(a)** *type of barometer using a frog*; **(b)** (*hum inf*) weatherman (*inf*); **w~fühlig** *adj* sensitive to (changes in) the weather; **~führung** *f* (*Min*) ventilation; **w~geschützt** *adj* sheltered; **~glas** *nt* (*old*) weatherglass; **~gott** *m* weather god; **der ~gott** (*hum*) the person up there who controls the weather (*hum*); **~hahn** *m* weathercock; **~häuschen** *nt* weather house *or* box; **~kanal** *m* (*Min*) fan drift; **~karte** *f* weather map *or* chart; **~kunde** *f* meteorology; **w~kundlich** *adj* meteorological; **~lage** *f* weather situation, state of the weather; **~lampe** *f* (*Min*) safety lamp; **~leiden** *nt* ailment *or* complaint caused by the weather; **w~leuchten** *vi impers insep* **es w~leuchtet** there's sheet lightning; (*fig*) there's a storm brewing; **~leuchten** *nt* -s, *no pl* sheet lightning; (*fig*) storm clouds *pl*; **~meldung** *f* weather *or* meteorological report.

wettern [1] *vi impers* **es wettert** it's thundering and lightening, there's a thunderstorm.
[2] *vi* to curse and swear ♦ **gegen** *or* **auf etw** (*acc*) **~** to rail against sth.

Wetter-: ~prognose *f* (*Aus*) weather forecast; **~prophet** *m* (*hum*) weatherman (*inf*); **~regel** *f* weather maxim *or* saying; **~satellit** *m* weather satellite; **~schacht** *m* (*Min*) ventilation shaft; **~scheide** *f* weather *or* meteorological divide; **~schiff** *nt* weather ship; **~seite** *f* windward side, side exposed to the weather; **~station** *f* weather *or* meteorological station; **~störung** *f* weather *or* meteorological disturbance; **~sturz** *m* sudden fall in temperature and atmospheric pressure; **~umbruch** (*esp Sw*), **~umschlag, ~umschwung** *m* sudden change in the weather; **~verhältnisse** *pl* weather conditions *pl*; **~verschlechterung** *f* deterioration in *or* worsening of the weather; **~voraussage, ~vorhersage** *f* weather forecast; **~warte** *f* weather station; **~wechsel** *m* change in the weather; **w~wendisch** *adj* (*fig*) changeable, moody; **~wolke** *f* storm cloud.

Wetteufel *m getrennt:* **Wett-teufel** (*inf*) betting bug (*inf*) ♦ **ihn hat der ~ gepackt** he's got the betting bug (*inf*).

Wett-: ~fahrt *f* race; **~kampf** *m* competition; **~kämpfer** *m* competitor; **~lauf** *m* race; **einen ~lauf machen** to run a race; **ein ~lauf mit der Zeit** a race against time; **w~laufen** *vi* (*infin only*) to run a race/races; **~läufer** *m* runner (in a/the race).

wettmachen *vt sep* to make up for; *Verlust etc* to make good; *Rückstand* to make up.

Wett-: w~rennen *vi* (*infin only*) to run a race; **~rennen** *nt* (*lit, fig*) race; **ein ~rennen machen** to run a race; **~rudern** *nt* boat race; **~rüsten** *nt* arms race; **~schein** *m* betting slip; **~schießen** *nt* shooting competition *or* contest; **~schuld** *f* betting debt; **~schwimmen** *nt* swimming competition *or* contest; **~singen** *nt* singing competition *or* contest; **~streit** *m* competition (*auch fig*), contest; **mit jdm im ~streit liegen** to compete with sb; **mit jdm in ~streit treten** to enter into competition with sb; ⚠**~teufel** *m siehe* **Wetteufel**.

⚠**Wetturnen** *nt getrennt:* **Wett-turnen** gymnastics competition.

Wettzettel *m* betting slip *or* ticket.

wetzen [1] *vt* to whet.
[2] *vi aux sein* (*inf*) to scoot (*inf*).

Wetz-: ~stahl *m* steel; **~stein** *m* whetstone.

WEU [veːǀeːˈǀuː] *abbr of* **Westeuropäische Union** WEU.

WEZ [veːǀeːˈtsɛt] *abbr of* **Westeuropäische Zeit** GMT.

WG [veːˈgeː] *f* -, -s *abbr of* **Wohngemeinschaft**.

WG-: ~-Bewohner *m* flat (*Brit*) *or* apartment (*US*) *or* house sharer; **~-Zimmer** *nt* room in a shared flat *etc*.

WGB [veːgeːˈbeː] *abbr of* **Weltgewerkschaftsbund** WFTU.

Whirlpool [ˈvøːɐlpuːl] *m* -s, -s jacuzzi.

Whisky [ˈvɪski] *m* -s, -s whisky, whiskey (*US*); (*schottischer auch*) Scotch; (*irischer*) whiskey; (*amerikanischer Mais~ auch*) bourbon (whisk(e)y); (*amerikanischer Roggen~ auch*) rye (whisk(e)y) ♦ **~ mit Eis/(mit) Soda** whisky and ice *or* on the rocks/and soda.

Whist [vɪst] *nt* -(e)s, *no pl* whist.

wich *pret of* **weichen**[2].

Wichs [vɪks] *m* -es, -e, (*Aus*) *f* -, -en **in vollem** *or* (*Aus*) **voller ~** (*Univ*) in full dress, in full regalia; **sich in ~ werfen** (*Univ, fig*) to dress up.

Wichse [ˈvɪksə] *f* -, -n **(a)** (*dated: Schuh~*) shoe polish ♦ **schwarze ~** blacking (*dated*), black shoe polish. **(b)** *no pl* (*inf: Prügel*) **~ bekommen** to get a hiding (*inf*).

wichsen ['vɪksn] 1 *vt* **(a)** *auch vi* (*dated*) *Schuhe* to polish; (*mit schwarzer Wichse*) to black (*dated*); *Schnurrbart, Boden etc* to wax; *siehe* **gewichst. (b)** (*inf: prügeln*) **jdn (ganz schön) ~** to give sb a (good) hiding (*inf*).
2 *vi* (*sl: onanieren*) to jerk *or* toss off (*sl*), to (have a) wank (*Brit vulg*).

Wichser ['vɪksɐ] *m* **-s, -** (*sl*) wanker (*Brit sl*), jerk-off (*US sl*).

Wichsleinwand ['vɪks-] *f* (*Aus*) *siehe* **Wachstuch.**

Wicht *m* **-(e)s, -e** (*Kobold*) goblin, wight (*obs*); (*kleiner Mensch*) titch (*inf*); (*Kind*) (little) creature; (*fig: verachtenswerter Mensch*) scoundrel ♦ **ein armer ~** a poor devil (*inf*) *or* wretch; (*Kind*) a poor little thing *or* creature.

Wichte *f* **-, -n** (*Phys*) density.

Wichtel *m* **-s, - (a)** (*auch* **~männchen**) gnome; (*Kobold*) goblin, imp; (*Heinzelmännchen*) brownie. **(b)** (*bei Pfadfinderinnen*) brownie.

wichtig *adj* important ♦ **eine ~e Miene machen** to put on an air of importance; **sich ~ machen** *or* **tun** to be full of one's own importance, to be self-important *or* pompous; **er will sich nur ~ machen** he just wants to get attention; **sich mit etw ~ machen** *or* **tun** to go on and on about sth; **sich selbst/etw (zu) ~ nehmen** to take oneself/sth (too) seriously; **es mit etw ~ haben** (*inf*) to take sth (very) seriously; **du hast's aber ~!** (*inf*) what's all the fuss about?; **~ tun** (*inf*), **sich** (*dat*) **~ vorkommen** to be full of oneself; **alles W~e** everything of importance; **W~eres zu tun haben** to have more important things *or* better things to do; **nichts W~eres zu tun haben** to have nothing better to do; **das W~ste** (*die ~ste Sache*) the most important thing; (*die ~sten Einzelheiten*) the most important details.

Wichtigkeit *f* importance ♦ **einer Sache** (*dat*) **große** *etc* **~ beimessen** *or* **beilegen** to place great *etc* importance on sth.

Wichtigmacher(in *f*) (*Aus*), **Wichtigtuer(in** *f*) [-tuɐ, -ərɪn] *m* **-s, -** (*pej*) pompous ass (*inf*), stuffed shirt (*inf*).

Wichtigtuerei [-tuːə'rai] *f* (*pej*) pomposity, pompousness.

wichtigtuerisch [-tuːərɪʃ] *adj* pompous.

Wicke *f* **-, -n** (*Bot*) vetch; (*Garten~*) sweet pea.

Wickel *m* **-s, - (a)** (*Med*) compress. **(b)** (*Rolle*) reel, spool; (*Locken~*) roller, curler. **(c)** (*inf*) **jdn am** *or* **beim ~ packen** *or* **nehmen** *or* **kriegen/haben** to grab/have sb by the scruff of the neck; (*fig*) to give sb a good talking to (*inf*); (*stärker*) to have sb's guts for garters (*inf*).

Wickel-: ~bluse *f* wrap-around blouse; **~gamasche** *f* puttee; **~kind** *nt* babe-in-arms; (*fig auch*) baby; **~kleid** *nt* wrap-around dress; **~kommode** *f* baby's changing unit.

wickeln 1 *vt* **(a)** (*schlingen*) to wind (*um* round); (*Tech*) *Spule, Transformator etc auch* to coil; *Verband etc* to bind; *Haare, Locken* to put in rollers *or* curlers; *Zigarren* to roll; (*umschlagen*) to wrap ♦ **sich** (*dat*) **eine Decke um die Beine ~** to wrap a blanket around one's legs; **wenn du das denkst, bist du schief gewickelt!** (*fig inf*) if you think that, you're very much mistaken; *siehe* **Finger.**
(b) (*einwickeln*) to wrap (*in +acc* in); (*mit Verband*) to dress, to bandage ♦ **einen Säugling ~** to put on a baby's nappy (*Brit*) *or* diaper (*US*); (*frisch ~*) to change a baby's nappy/diaper.
2 *vr* to wrap oneself (*in +acc* in) ♦ **sich um etw ~** to wrap itself around sth; *Schlange, Pflanze* to wind itself around sth.

Wickel-: ~raum *m* (*in Kaufhaus etc*) mothers' (and babies') room, nursing room. **~rock** *m* wrap-around skirt; **~tisch** *m* baby's changing table.

Widder *m* **-s, -** (*Zool*) ram; (*Astrol*) Aries; (*Mil, Hist*) battering ram ♦ **er/sie ist (ein) ~** (*Astrol*) he's/she's an Arian *or* (an) Aries; **der ~** (*Astron, Astrol*) Aries, the Ram.

Widder-: ~frau *f* (*Astrol, inf*) (female) Arian, Aries (woman); **~mann** *m, pl* **-männer** (*Astrol, inf*) (male) Arian, Aries (man).

wider *prep +acc* (*geh*) against; (*entgegen auch*) contrary to ♦ **~ Erwarten** contrary to expectations; **~ alles Erwarten** against all *or* contrary to all expectations; *siehe* **Für, löcken, Wille.**

widerborstig *adj* contrary, perverse.

Wider-: ~borstigkeit *f* contrariness, perversity; **~druck** *m* (*Typ*) perfecting.

widerfahren* *vi, vi impers insep irreg aux sein +dat* (*geh*) to happen (*jdm* to sb); (*Unglück etc*) to befall (*jdm* sb) (*liter*) ♦ **mir ist in meinem Leben schon viel Gutes ~** life has given me many good things.

Wider-: ~haken *m* barb; (*an größerer Harpune*) fluke; **~hall** *m* echo, reverberation; **(bei jdm) keinen ~hall finden** (*Interesse*) to meet with no response (from sb); (*Gegenliebe etc*) not to be reciprocated (by sb); **w~hallen** *vi sep or* (*rare*) *insep* to echo *or* reverberate (*von* with); **~handlung** *f* (*Sw*) *siehe* **Zuwiderhandlung; ~klage** *f* counterclaim; **w~klingen** *vi sep irreg* to resound *or* ring (*von* with).

widerlegbar *adj* refutable, disprovable ♦ **nicht ~** irrefutable.

widerlegen* *vt insep Behauptung etc* to refute, to disprove; *jdn* to prove wrong.

Widerlegung *f* refutation, disproving.

widerlich *adj* disgusting, revolting; *Mensch* repulsive; *Kopfschmerzen* nasty.

Widerlichkeit *f* (*widerliche Sache*) disgusting *or* revolting thing; (*von Mensch*) repulsiveness; (*von Kopfschmerzen*) nastiness ♦ **die ~ des Anblicks/seines Benehmens** the disgusting *or* revolting sight/his disgusting *or* revolting behaviour.

Widerling *m* (*pej inf*) repulsive creep (*inf*).

widern *vt, vt impers* **es/etw widert jdn** sb finds it/sth disgusting *or* revolting.

Wider-: w~natürlich *adj* unnatural; (*pervers auch*) perverted; **~natürlichkeit** *f* unnaturalness; perversion; **~part** *m* (*old, geh: Gegner*) adversary, opponent; **jdm ~part bieten** *or* **geben** (*geh*) to oppose sb.

widerraten* *vi insep irreg* (*old*) **jdm ~, etw zu tun** to advise *or* counsel sb against doing sth.

Wider-: w~rechtlich *adj* unlawful, illegal; **etw w~rechtlich betreten** *Gelände* to trespass (up)on sth; *Gebäude* to enter sth unlawfully *or* illegally; **sich** (*dat*) **etw w~rechtlich aneignen** to misappropriate sth; **w~rechtlich geparkte Fahrzeuge** illegally parked vehicles; **~rede** *f* **(a)** *siehe* **Gegenrede; (b)** (*Widerspruch*) contradiction, argument; **keine ~rede!** no arguing!, don't argue!; **er duldet keine ~rede** he will not have any arguments about it; **ohne ~rede** without protest *or* demur.

Widerruf *m siehe vb* revocation, withdrawal, cancellation; retraction; withdrawal; cancellation, countermand; recantation ♦ **~ leisten** to recant; **bis auf ~** until revoked *or* withdrawn *or* cancelled.

widerrufen* *insep irreg* 1 *vt Erlaubnis, Anordnung etc* to revoke (*auch Jur*), to withdraw, to cancel; *Aussage, Geständnis, Behauptung* to retract (*auch Jur*), to withdraw; *Befehl* to cancel, to countermand.
2 *vi* (*bei Verleumdung etc*) to withdraw; (*esp bei ketzerischen Behauptungen*) to recant.

widerruflich (*form*) 1 *adj* revocable, revokable.
2 *adv* until revoked *or* withdrawn.

Wider-: ≈sacher(in *f*) *m* **-s, -** adversary, antagonist, opponent; **w~schallen** *vi sep* (*old*) *siehe* **w~hallen; ≈schein** *m* (*liter*) reflection; **w~setzen*** *vr insep* **sich jdm/einer Sache w~setzen** to oppose sb/sth; *einem Polizisten, der Festnahme* to resist sb/sth; *einem Befehl, einer Aufforderung* to refuse to comply with sth; **w~setzlich** *adj* contrary, obstreperous; *Befehlsempfänger* insubordinate; **≈sinn** *m, no pl* absurdity, illogicality; **w≈sinnig** *adj* absurd, nonsensical; **w≈spenstig** *adj* unruly, wilful; (*störrisch*) stubborn; (*fig*) unmanageable; *Haar* unruly, unmanageable; **„der ~spenstigen Zähmung"** "The Taming of the Shrew"; **≈spenstigkeit** *f siehe adj* unruliness, wilfulness; stubbornness; unmanageableness; **w≈spiegeln** *sep* 1 *vt* (*lit, fig*) to reflect; *Gegenstand auch* to mirror; 2 *vr* (*lit, fig*) to be reflected/mirrored; **≈spieg(e)lung** *f* reflection; **≈spiel** *nt* **das ~spiel der Kräfte** the play of forces.

widersprechen* *insep irreg* 1 *vi* **jdm/einer Sache ~** to contradict sb/sth; (*nicht übereinstimmen mit*) *den Tatsachen etc auch* to be inconsistent with sth; **da muß ich aber ~** I've got to contradict you there; **das widerspricht meinen Grundsätzen** that goes *or* is against my principles.
2 *vr* (*einander*) to contradict each other *or* one another; (*nicht übereinstimmen: Aussagen etc auch*) to be inconsistent, to conflict ♦ **sich (selbst) ~** to contradict oneself.

widersprechend *adj* **(sich** *or* **einander) ~** contradictory, conflicting, inconsistent.

Widerspruch *m* **(a)** (*Gegensätzlichkeit*) contradiction (*auch Philos*); (*Unvereinbarkeit auch*) inconsistency ♦ **ein ~ in sich selbst** a contradiction in terms; **in** *or* **im ~ zu** contrary to; **in ~ zu** *or* **mit etw geraten** to come into conflict with sth, to contradict sth; **sich in ~ zu jdm/etw setzen** to go against sb/sth; **in** *or* **im ~ zu** *or* **mit etw stehen** to conflict with sth, to stand in contradiction to sth, to be contrary to sth.
(b) (*Widerrede*) contradiction, dissent; (*Protest*) protest; (*Ablehnung*) opposition ♦ **kein ~!** don't argue!; **er duldet keinen ~** he won't have any argument; **es erhob sich ~** there was opposition (*gegen* to), there were protests (*gegen* against); **~ erheben** to protest; **~ erfahren, auf ~ stoßen** to meet with opposition (*bei* from).

widersprüchlich *adj* contradictory; *Erzählung, Theorie auch, Verhalten* inconsistent.

Widersprüchlichkeit *f siehe adj* contradiction, contradictoriness; inconsistency.

Widerspruchs-: w~frei *adj Theorie* consistent; **~geist** *m* spirit of opposition; **w~los** 1 *adj* (*unangefochten*) *Zustimmung, Annahme* unopposed; (*ohne Einwände*) *Zuhören, Befolgen von Anordnung* without contradiction; (*folgsam*) *Kind, Gehorchen* unprotesting; (*nicht widersprüchlich*) *Theorie, Mensch, Verhalten* consistent; 2 *adv siehe adj* without opposition; without contradiction; without protest; consistently; **w~voll** *adj* full of contradictions; (*voller Unvereinbarkeiten*) full of inconsistencies.

Widerstand *m* **-(e)s, ¨e** resistance (*auch Pol, Elec etc*); (*im 2. Weltkrieg*) Resistance; (*Ablehnung*) opposition; (*Elec: Bauelement*) resistor ♦ **zum ~ aufrufen** to call upon people to resist; **es erhebt sich ~** there is resistance; **jdm/einer Sache** *or* **gegen jdn/etw ~ leisten** to resist sb/sth, to put up *or* offer (*form*) resistance to sb/sth; **seine inneren ¨e überwinden** to overcome one's inhibitions; **~ gegen die Staatsgewalt** obstructing an officer in the performance of his duties; *siehe* **Weg.**

Widerstands-: ~beiwert *m* drag factor; **~bewegung** *f* resistance movement; (*im 2. Weltkrieg*) Resistance movement; **w~fähig** *adj* robust; *Pflanze* hardy; (*Med, Tech etc*) resistant (*gegen* to); **~fähigkeit** *f siehe adj* robustness; hardiness; resistance (*gegen* to); **~kämpfer** *m* member of the resistance; (*im 2. Weltkrieg*) member of the Resistance, Resistance fighter; **~kraft** *f* (power of) resistance; **w~los** *adj, adv* without resistance; **~messer** *m* **-s, -** (*Elec*) ohmmeter; **~nest** *nt* (*Mil*) pocket of resistance.

widerstehen* *vi insep irreg +dat* **(a)** to resist; (*standhalten*) to withstand ♦ **einer Versuchung/einem Erdbeben ~ können** to be able to resist a temptation/withstand an earthquake. **(b)** (*anekeln*) **etw widersteht jdm** sb loathes sth.

widerstreben* *vi insep +dat* **jdm/einer Sache ~** (*Mensch*) to oppose sb/sth; **etw widerstrebt einer Sache** sth conflicts with sth; **jds sittlichem Empfinden/jds Interessen** *etc* **~** to go against sb's moral sense/sb's interests *etc*; **das**

widerstrebt mir *(das möchte ich nicht tun)* I can't do things like that, I can't be like that; **so eine Handlungsweise widerstrebt mir** *(lehne ich ab)* I find such behaviour repugnant; **es widerstrebt mir, so etwas zu tun** *(lehne ich ab)* it goes against the grain to do anything like that; *(möchte ich nicht)* I am reluctant to do anything like that.

Widerstreben *nt* **-s,** *no pl* reluctance ◆ **nach anfänglichem ~** after some initial reluctance.

widerstrebend *adj (gegensätzlich) Interessen* conflicting; *(widerwillig, zögernd)* reluctant ◆ **mit ~en Gefühlen** with (some) reluctance.

Widerstreit *m (geh)* conflict ◆ **im** *or* **in ~ zu etw stehen** to be in conflict with sth.

widerstreitend *adj (geh)* **(einander)** ~ conflicting.

widertönen *vi sep* to echo ◆ **seine Worte tönten ihr noch im Ohr wider** his words were still ringing in her ears.

widerwärtig *adj* offensive; *(ekelhaft auch)* disgusting; *Aufgabe, Arbeit, Verhalten* objectionable ◆ **etw ist jdm ~** sb finds sth offensive/disgusting/objectionable.

Widerwärtigkeit *f siehe adj* offensiveness; disgusting nature; objectionable nature.

Widerwille *m (Abscheu, Ekel)* disgust *(gegen* for), revulsion; *(Abneigung)* distaste *(gegen* for), aversion *(gegen* to); *(Widerstreben)* reluctance ◆ **etw mit größtem ~n tun/trinken** to do sth with the greatest reluctance/drink sth with intense distaste.

widerwillig *adj* reluctant, unwilling.

Widerworte *pl* answering back *sing* ◆ **~ geben** *or* **machen** to answer back; **er tat es ohne ~** he did it without protest.

widmen [1] *vt* **jdm etw ~** to dedicate sth to sb; *(schenken, verwenden auf)* to devote sth to sb.
[2] *vr +dat* to devote oneself to; *(sich kümmern um) den Gästen etc* to attend to; *einem Problem, einer Aufgabe* to apply oneself to, to attend to ◆ **nun kann ich mich dir/dieser Aufgabe ganz ~** I can now give you/this task my undivided attention.

Widmung *f (in Buch etc)* dedication *(an +acc* to).

widrig *adj* adverse; *Winde, Umstände auch* unfavourable.

widrigenfalls *adv (form)* if this is not the case, otherwise; *(Nebensatz einleitend)* failing which.

Widrigkeit *f siehe adj* adversity; unfavourability.

wie [1] *interrog adv* **(a)** how ◆ **~ anders ...?** how else ...?; **~ schwer/oft** *etc*? how heavy/often *etc*?; **~ viele?** how many?; **~ das?** how come?; **~ ist dir (zumute)?** how do you feel?; **aber frag (mich) nicht ~!** but don't ask me how!; **~ wär's (mit uns beiden** *etc***)** *(inf)* how about it? *(inf)*; **wie wär's mit einem Whisky?** *(inf)* how about a whisky?; **~ wäre es, wenn du mir ein Bier bezahlen würdest?** how *or* how's *(inf)* about (you) buying me a beer?
(b) *(welcher Art)* **~ war's bei der Party/in Italien?** what was it like at the party/in Italy?, what was the party/Italy like?, how was the party/Italy?; **~ ist er (denn)?** what's he like?; **~ war das Wetter?** what was the weather like?, how was the weather?; **~ ist es eigentlich, wenn ...?** what's the situation if ...?, what happens if ...?; **~ war das (noch mal genau) mit dem Unfall?** what (exactly) happened in the accident?; **und ~ ist es mit deinem Job?** and what about your job?; **Sie wissen ja, ~ das so ist** well, you know how it is.
(c) *(was)* **~ heißt er/das?** what's he/it called?; **~ nennt man das?** what is that called?; **~?** what?; **~ bitte?, ~ war das?** *(inf)*, **~ meinen** *or* **belieben?** *(inf)* sorry?, pardon?, come again? *(inf)*; **~ bitte?!** *(entrüstet)* I beg your pardon!
(d) *(in Ausrufen)* how ◆ **und ~!, aber ~!** and how! *(inf)*; **~ groß er ist!** how big he is!, isn't he big!; **~ schrecklich!** how terrible!; **~ haben wir gelacht, als ...** how we laughed when ...
(e) *(nicht wahr)* eh ◆ **das macht dir Spaß, ~?** you like that, don't you?; **das macht dir keinen Spaß, ~?** you don't like that, do you?
[2] *adv* **(a)** *(relativ)* **die Art, ~ sie geht** the way (in which) she walks; **in dem Maße, ~ ...** to the same extent that ...; **in dem Stil, ~ er jetzt Mode ist** in the style which *or* that is now fashionable; **es war ein Sonnenuntergang, ~ er noch nie einen gesehen hatte** it was a sunset the like of which he had never seen before.
(b) *(in Verbindung mit auch)* **~ stark du auch sein magst** however strong you may be; **~ auch immer du das machen wirst** however you *or* whatever way you are going to do it; **~ sie auch alle heißen** whatever they're called.
[3] *conj* **(a)** *(vergleichend) (wenn sich Vergleich auf adj, adv bezieht)* as; *(wenn sich Vergleich auf n bezieht, bei Apposition)* like ◆ **so ... ~** as ... as; **so lang ~ breit** the same length and width, as long as it *etc* is wide; **weiß ~ Schnee** (as) white as snow; **mutig ~ ein Löwe** as brave as a lion; **eine Nase ~ eine Kartoffel** a nose like a potato; **ein Mann ~ er** a man like him, a man such as he *(form)*; **in einer Lage ~ diese(r)** in a situation like this *or* such as this; **er ist Lehrer, ~ sein Vater es war** he is a teacher like his father was *(inf) or* as was his father; **T ~ Theodor** "t" as in "Tommy"; *(bei Rundfunk etc)* t for Tommy; **er ist intelligent, ~ wir** he is intelligent like us; **~ gewöhnlich/immer** as usual/always *or* ever; **ich fühlte mich ~ betrunken/im Traum** I felt (as if I were *or* was) drunk/as if I were *or* was *or* like I *(inf)* was dreaming; **~ sie nun (ein)mal ist, mußte sie ...** the way she is she just had to ...; **~ du weißt/man sagt** as you know/they say; **~ noch nie** as never before.
(b) *(zum Beispiel)* **~ (zum Beispiel** *or* **etwa)** such as (for example).
(c) *(incorrect: als)* **größer/schöner ~** bigger/more beautiful than; **nichts ~ Ärger** *etc* nothing but trouble *etc.*
(d) *(und)* as well as ◆ **Alte ~ Junge** old and young alike.
(e) *(inf)* **~ wenn** as if *or* though.
(f) *(bei Verben der Gefühlsempfindung)* **er sah, ~ es geschah** he saw it happen; **sie spürte, ~ es kalt wurde** she felt it getting cold; **er hörte, ~ der Regen fiel** he heard the rain falling.
(g) *(zeitlich: als)* **~ ich mich umdrehte, sah ich ...** as I turned round, I saw ..., turning round, I saw ...; **~ ich mit der Schule fertig war, ...** *(inf)* when I was finished with school, ...

Wie *nt* **-s,** *no pl* **das ~ spielt dabei keine Rolle** how (it'll happen/it'll be done *etc*) is unimportant; **daß es geschehen muß, ist klar, nur das ~ ist noch ein Problem** it's clear that it has to happen, the only problem is how; **das ~ und Wann werden wir später besprechen** we'll talk about how and when later.

Wiedehopf *m* **-(e)s, -e** hoopoe.

wieder *adv* **(a)** again ◆ **~ nüchtern/glücklich** *etc* sober/happy *etc* again; **immer ~, ~ und ~** again and again; **~ mal, (ein)mal ~** (once) again; **komm doch ~ mal vorbei** come and see me/us again; **~ ist ein Jahr vorbei** another year has passed; **~ was anderes** *or* **Neues** something else again, something quite different; **wie, schon ~?** what, again?; **~ da** back (again); **da bin ich ~!** I'm back!, here I am again!; **das ist auch ~ wahr** that's true; **da sieht man mal ~, ...** it just shows ...
(b) *(in Verbindung mit vb)* again ◆ **das fällt mir schon ~ ein** I'll remember it again; **das Boot tauchte ~ auf** the boat resurfaced; **wenn die Wunde ~ aufbricht** if the wound reopens.

Wieder- *pref* re; *(bei Verben) (erneut, noch einmal)* again; *(zurück)* back; **~abdruck** *m* reprint; ⚠**w~aufarbeiten*** *vt sep siehe* **w~aufbereiten**; **~aufarbeitung** *f siehe* **~aufbereitung**; **~aufarbeitungsanlage** *f siehe* **~aufbereitungsanlage**; **~aufbau** *m (lit, fig)* reconstruction, rebuilding; **der ~aufbau nach dem Krieg/des Hauses** post-war reconstruction/the rebuilding of the house; ⚠**w~aufbauen** *vti sep, ptp* **w~aufgebaut** to reconstruct, to rebuild; **w~aufbereiten*** *vt sep* to recycle; *Atommüll* to reprocess; **~aufbereitung** *f* recycling; *(von Atommüll)* reprocessing; **~aufbereitungsanlage** *f* recycling plant; *(für Atommüll)* reprocessing plant; ⚠**w~auferstehen*** *vi sep irreg aux sein* to rise from the dead, to be resurrected; **~auferstehung** *f* resurrection; ⚠**w~aufforsten** *vti sep, ptp* **w~aufgeforstet** to reforest; ⚠**w~aufführen** *vt sep, ptp* **w~aufgeführt** *Theaterstück* to revive; *Film* to reshow, to rerun; *Musikwerk* to reperform; ⚠**w~aufladen** *vt sep irreg, ptp* **w~aufgeladen** to recharge; **w~aufleben** *vi sep, ptp* **w~aufgelebt** *aux sein* to revive; ⚠**~aufleben** *nt* revival; *(von Nationalismus etc auch)* resurgence; ⚠**w~auflegen** *vt sep, ptp* **w~aufgelegt** to republish; **~aufnahme** *f* **(a)** *(von Tätigkeit, Gespräch etc)* resumption; *(von Beziehungen auch)* re-establishment; *(von Gedanken, Idee)* readoption; *(von Thema)* reversion *(gen* to); **die ~aufnahme des Verfahrens** *(Jur)* the reopening of proceedings; **(b)** *(von verstoßenem Menschen)* taking back; *(im Verein etc)* readmittance, reacceptance; *(von Patienten)* readmission; **~aufnahmeverfahren** *nt (Jur) (im Zivilrecht)* rehearing; *(im Strafrecht)* retrial; ⚠**w~aufnehmen** *vt sep irreg, ptp* **w~aufgenommen (a)** to resume; *Beziehungen auch* to re-establish; *Gespräch auch, Gedanken, Idee, Hobby* to take up again; *Thema* to revert to; *(Jur) Verfahren* to reopen; **(b)** *verstoßenen Menschen* to take back; *(in Verein etc)* to readmit, to reaccept; *Patienten* to readmit; ⚠**w~aufrichten** *vt sep, ptp* **w~aufgerichtet** *(fig) jdn* to give new heart to; ⚠**w~aufrüsten** *vti sep, ptp* **w~aufgerüstet** to rearm; **jdn moralisch w~aufrüsten** to raise sb's morale; **~aufrüstung** *f* rearmament; **jds moralische ~aufrüstung** the raising of sb's morale; **~ausfuhr** *f* re-export; ⚠**w~ausführen** *vt sep, ptp* **w~ausgeführt** to re-export; **≈beginn** *m* recommencement, restart; *(von Schule)* reopening; **w≈bekommen*** *vt sep irreg* to get back; **das bekommst du w~, du gemeines Stück!** I'll get my own back, you bastard *(sl)*!; ⚠**w≈beleben*** *vt sep* to revive, to resuscitate; *(fig) Brauch etc* to revive, to resurrect; **≈belebung** *f* resuscitation, revival; *(fig)* revival, resurrection; **≈belebungsversuch** *m* attempt at resuscitation; *(fig)* attempt at revival; **~belebungsversuche bei jdm anstellen** to attempt to revive *or* resuscitate sb.

wiederbeschaffen* *vt sep* to replace; *(zurückbekommen)* to recover.

Wiederbeschaffung *f siehe vt* replacement; recovery.

Wiederbeschaffungs- *(Comm)*: **~kosten** *pl* replacement cost *sing*; **~wert** *m* replacement value.

Wieder-: ⚠**w≈bewaffnen*** *vr sep* to rearm; **≈bewaffnung** *f* rearmament; **w≈bringen** *vt sep irreg* to bring back; ⚠**w~einbürgern** *vt sep, ptp* **w~eingebürgert** to renaturalize; ⚠**w~einfinden** *vr sep irreg, ptp* **w~eingefunden** to turn up again; **~einfuhr** *f* reimport(ation); ⚠**w~einführen** *vt sep, ptp* **w~eingeführt** to reintroduce; *Todesstrafe auch* to bring back; *(Comm) Waren* to reimport; **~einführung** *f* reintroduction; ⚠**w~eingliedern** *vt sep, ptp* **w~eingegliedert** to reintegrate *(in +acc* into); **einen Straftäter in die Gesellschaft w~eingliedern** to rehabilitate a criminal offender; **~eingliederung** *f* reintegration; **die ~eingliederung eines Straftäters in die Gesellschaft** the rehabilitation of a criminal offender; **w~einliefern** *vt sep, ptp* **w~eingeliefert** *Kranken* to readmit *(in +acc* to); *Häftling* to reimprison; **~einnahme** *f (Mil)* recapture, retaking; ⚠**w~einnehmen** *vt sep irreg, ptp* **w~eingenommen** *(Mil)* to retake, to recapture; ⚠**w~einsetzen** *sep, ptp* **w~eingesetzt** [1] *vt* to reinstate *(in +acc* in); **jdn als König w~einsetzen** to restore sb to the throne; [2] *vi (Regen)* to start up again; *(Med: Fieber, Schmerzen, Wehen)* to recur; **~einsetzung** *f* reinstatement; *(von König)* restoration; ⚠**w~einstellen** *vt sep, ptp* **w~eingestellt** to re-employ, to re-engage; *(nach ungerechtfertigter Entlassung)* to reinstate; **~einstellung** *f siehe vt* re-employment, re-engagement; reinstatement; **~einstellungsklausel** *f* reinstatement clause; **~eintritt** *m* re-entry *(auch Space) (in +acc* into); ⚠**w≈entdecken*** *vt sep (lit, fig)* to rediscover; **≈entdeckung** *f* rediscovery; **w≈ergreifen*** *vt* *sep irreg* to recapture; **≈ergreifung** *f* recapture; **w≈erhalten*** *vt sep irreg* to recover; **⚠w≈erkennen*** *vt sep irreg* to recognize; **das/er war nicht w~zuerkennen** it/he was unrecognizable; **w≈erlangen*** *vt sep* to regain; *Eigentum* to recover; **≈erlangung** *f siehe vt* regaining; recovery; **⚠w≈ernennen*** *vt sep irreg* to reappoint (*zu etw* (as) sth); **≈ernennung** *f* reappointment (*zu* as); **⚠w≈eröffnen*** *vti sep* to reopen; **≈eröffnung** *f* reopening; **⚠w≈erscheinen*** *vi sep irreg aux sein* to reappear; (*Buch etc*) to be republished; **w≈erstatten*** *vt sep Unkosten etc* to refund, to reimburse (*jdm etw* sb for sth); **≈erstattung** *f siehe vt* refund(ing), reimbursement; **⚠w≈erstehen*** *vi sep irreg aux sein* to rise again; **⚠w≈erwachen*** *vi sep aux sein* to reawake(n); **⚠w≈erwecken*** *vt sep* to bring back to life, to revive (*auch fig*); **⚠w≈finden** *sep irreg* [1] *vt* to find again; (*fig*) *Selbstachtung, Mut etc* to regain; **die Sprache w~finden** (*fig*) to find one's tongue again; [2] *vr* (*nach Schock*) to recover; **sich irgendwo w~finden** to find oneself somewhere; **sich** *or* **einander w~finden** to find each other again.

Wiedergabe *f* **-, -n** **(a)** (*von Rede, Ereignis, Vorgang*) account, report; (*Beschreibung*) description; (*Wiederholung: von Äußerung etc*) repetition.
(b) (*Darbietung: von Stück etc*) rendering, rendition.
(c) (*Übersetzung*) translation.
(d) (*Darstellung*) representation.
(e) (*Reproduktion*) (*von Gemälde, Farben, akustisch*) reproduction ◆ **bei der ~** in reproduction.
(f) (*Rückgabe*) return; (*von Rechten, Freiheit etc*) restitution.

Wiedergabe-: **~gerät** *nt* playback unit; **~treue** *f* fidelity of sound reproduction; **hohe ~treue** high fidelity.

wiedergeben *vt sep irreg* **(a)** *Gegenstand, Geld* to give back; (*fig*) *Rechte, Mut etc auch* to restore ◆ **jdm ein Buch ~** to give a book back to sb, to give sb his/her book back; **jdm die Freiheit ~** to restore sb's freedom, to give sb back his freedom.
(b) (*erzählen*) to give an account of; (*beschreiben*) to describe; (*wiederholen*) to repeat ◆ **seine Worte sind nicht wiederzugeben** his words are unrepeatable.
(c) *Gedicht* to recite; *Theaterstück, Musik* to perform.
(d) (*übersetzen*) to translate.
(e) (*darstellen, porträtieren*) to represent.
(f) (*reproduzieren*) *Gemälde, Farbe, Ton* to reproduce.
(g) (*vermitteln*) *Bedeutung, Gefühl, Erlebnis* to convey.

Wieder-: **⚠w≈geboren** *adj* (*lit, fig*) reborn; **w~geboren werden** to be reborn; to be reincarnated; **≈geburt** *f* (*lit, fig*) rebirth; reincarnation; **≈genesung** *f* recovery; **w≈gewinnen*** *vt sep irreg* (*lit, fig*) to regain; *jdn* to win back; *Land, Rohstoffe etc* to reclaim; *Geld, Selbstvertrauen* to recover; **w≈grüßen** *vti sep* **(jdn) w~grüßen** to return sb's greeting; (*einen ausgerichteten Gruß erwidern*) to send sb one's regards in return; (*Mil*) to return the/sb's salute; **⚠w~gutmachen** *vt sep, ptp* **w~gutgemacht** to make good; *Schaden* to compensate for; *Fehler* to rectify; *Beleidigung* to put right; (*sühnen*) to atone for; (*Pol*) to make reparations for; (*Jur*) to redress; **das ist nie w~gutzumachen** that can never be put right; **~gutmachung** *f* compensation; (*Sühne*) atonement; (*Pol*) reparations *pl*; (*Jur*) redress; **als ~gutmachung für mein Benehmen/den Schaden/den Fehler/die Beleidigung** to make up for my behaviour/compensate for the damage/rectify the fault/put right the insult; **w≈haben** *vt sep irreg* (*inf*) to have (got) back; **etw w~haben wollen** to want sth back; **⚠w~herrichten** *vt sep, ptp* **w~hergerichtet** to repair; *Zimmer* to redecorate; **⚠w~herstellen** *vt sep, ptp* **w~hergestellt** *Gebäude, Ordnung, Frieden, jds Gesundheit* to restore; *Beziehungen* to re-establish; *Patienten* to restore to health; **von einer Krankheit w~hergestellt sein** to have recovered from an illness; **~herstellung** *f siehe vt* restoration; re-establishment; restoration of sb's health; **~herstellungskosten** *pl* restoration costs *pl*.

wiederholbar *adj* repeatable ◆ **leicht/schwer ~** easy/hard to repeat; **das ist nicht ~** that can't be repeated.

wiederholen[1]* *insep* [1] *vti* to repeat; (*zum zweiten Mal, mehrmals*) *Forderung etc* to reiterate; (*zusammenfassend*) to recapitulate; *Lernstoff* to revise, to review (*US*); (*Film*) *Szene auch* to retake; (*Sport*) *Elfmeter etc* to retake, to take again; *Spiel* to replay ◆ **wiederholt, was ich euch vorsage** repeat after me; **(eine Klasse** *or* **ein Jahr) ~** (*Sch*) to repeat a year.
[2] *vr* (*Mensch*) to repeat oneself; (*Thema, Ereignis*) to recur, to be repeated; (*Dezimalstelle*) to recur ◆ **es wiederholt sich doch alles im Leben** life has a habit of repeating itself.

wiederholen[2] *vt sep* to get back.

wiederholt *adj* repeated ◆ **zu ~en Malen** repeatedly, on repeated occasions; **zum ~en Male** once again.

Wiederholung *f* repetition; (*von Aufführung*) repeat performance; (*von Sendung*) repeat; (*in Zeitlupe*) replay; (*von Lernstoff*) revision; (*zum zweiten Mal, mehrmals: von Forderung etc*) reiteration; (*zusammenfassend*) recapitulation; (*von Filmszene*) retaking; (*Sport*) (*von Elfmeter*) retaking, retake; (*von Spiel*) replay ◆ **trotz zweimaliger ~ derselben Klasse** in spite of repeating the year twice.

Wiederholungs-: **~kurs** *m* refresher course; **~spiel** *nt* (*Sport*) replay; **~taste** *f* repeat key; **~täter** *m* (*Jur*) (*bei erster Wiederholung*) second offender; (*bei ständiger Wiederholung*) persistent offender, recidivist (*Psych*); **~zeichen** *nt* (*Mus*) repeat (mark); **~zwang** *m* (*Psych*) recidivism; (*Sprachfehler*) palilalia (*spec*).

Wieder-: **≈hören** *nt* **(auf) ~hören!** (*am Telefon*) goodbye!; (*im Hörfunk*) goodbye for now!; **≈impfung** *f* revaccination; **~inbesitznahme** *f* (*form*) resumption of possession; **~inbetriebnahme** *f* (*form*) putting into operation again; (*von U-Bahnlinie*) reopening; **~instandsetzung** *f* (*form*) repair, repairs *pl* (*+gen* to); **w≈käuen** *sep* [1] *vt* to ruminate, to chew again; (*fig inf*) to go over again and again; [2] *vi* to ruminate, to chew the cud; (*fig inf*) to harp on; **≈käuer** *m* **-s, -** ruminant.

Wiederkehr *f* **-,** *no pl* (*geh*) (*Rückkehr*) return; (*zweites, ständiges Vorkommen*) recurrence; (*esp langweilig*) repetition; (*von Datum, Ereignis*) anniversary ◆ **die ewige ~** the eternal recurrence.

wiederkehren *vi sep aux sein* (*zurückkehren*) to return; (*sich wiederholen, wieder vorkommen*) to recur, to be repeated.

wiederkehrend *adj* recurring ◆ **regelmäßig/oft ~** recurrent; **ein jährlich ~es Fest** an annual festival.

Wieder-: **⚠w~kennen** *vt sep irreg* (*inf*) to recognize; **w~kommen** *vi sep irreg aux sein* (*lit, fig*) to come back, to return; **komm doch mal w~!** you must come again!; **w~kriegen** *vt sep* (*inf*) to get back; **warte nur, das kriegst du (von mir) w~!** just you wait, I'll get my own back (on you)!; **~kunft** *f* **-,** *no pl* (*liter*) return; **die ~kunft Christi** the Second Coming; **⚠w~lieben** *vt sep* to love back; **~schauen** *nt* **(auf) ~schauen!** goodbye!, good day! (*form*); **w~schenken** *vt sep* **jdm etw w~schenken** to give sth back to sb; **er wurde dem Leben w~geschenkt** he was restored to life; **⚠w~sehen** *vt sep irreg* to see again; (*wieder zusammentreffen mit auch*) to meet again; **wann sehen wir uns w~?** when will we see each other *or* meet again?; **~sehen** *nt* **-s, -** (*nach kürzerer Zeit*) (another) meeting; (*nach längerer Zeit*) reunion; **ich freue mich auf das ~sehen mit meinen Freunden/mit der Heimat** I'm looking forward to seeing my friends/being back home again; **sie hofften auf ein baldiges ~sehen** they hoped to see each other *or* meet again soon; **irgendwo, irgendwann gibt es ein ~sehen** we'll meet again, don't know where, don't know when; **(auf) ~sehen!** goodbye!; **(auf) ~sehen sagen** to say goodbye; **~sehen macht Freude!** (*hum*) I hope that's not the last I see of it!, I wouldn't mind having it back again!; **~sehensfreude** *f* **unsere ~sehensfreude war groß** we were very pleased to see each other again; **meine ~sehensfreude war groß** I was very pleased to see him/her etc again; **~taufe** *f* (*Rel*) rebaptism; **~täufer** *m* (*Rel, Hist*) Anabaptist; **⚠w~tun** *vt sep irreg* to do again.

wiederum *adv* **(a)** (*andererseits*) on the other hand; (*allerdings*) though ◆ **das ist ~ richtig, daran habe ich nicht gedacht** that's quite correct, I didn't think of that. **(b)** (*geh: nochmals*) again, anew (*liter*). **(c)** (*seinerseits etc*) in turn. **er ~ wollte ...** he, for his part, wanted ...

Wieder-: **⚠≈vereinigen*** *sep* [1] *vt Menschen, Fraktionen* to reunite; *Kirche auch, Land* to reunify; [2] *vr* to reunite, to come together again; **≈vereinigung** *f* reunification; **⚠w≈verheiraten*** *vr sep* to remarry; **≈verheiratung** *f* remarriage; **≈verkauf** *m* resale; (*durch Einzelhandel*) retail; **⚠w≈verkaufen*** *vt sep* to resell; (*Einzelhändler*) to retail; **≈verkäufer** *m* reseller; (*Einzelhändler*) retailer; **≈verkaufswert** *m* resale value; **⚠w≈verpflichten*** *vr sep* (*Mil*) to re-enlist; **w≈verwendbar** *adj* reusable; **⚠w≈verwenden*** *vt sep* to reuse; **≈verwendung** *f* reuse; **w≈verwertbar** *adj* recyclable; **⚠w≈verwerten*** *vt sep* to recycle; **≈verwertung** *f* recycling; **≈wahl** *f* re-election; **eine ~wahl ablehnen** to decline to run for re-election; **wenn es zu einer ~wahl der Partei kommt** if the party is returned again; **⚠w≈wählen** *vt sep* to re-elect; **⚠w~zulassen** *vt sep irreg, ptp* **w~zugelassen** *Auto* to relicense; **~zulassung** *f* relicensing.

wiefern *adv siehe* **inwiefern**.

Wiege *f* **-, -n** (*lit, fig, Tech*) cradle ◆ **seine ~ stand in Schwaben** (*geh*) his birthplace was Swabia; **es ist mir/ihm auch nicht an der ~ gesungen worden, daß ...** no-one could have foreseen that ...; **das ist ihm (schon** *or* **gleich) in die ~ gelegt worden** he inherited it; **damals lagst du noch in der ~** at that time you were still a babe-in-arms; **von der ~ bis zur Bahre** (*geh*) from the cradle to the grave.

Wiegemesser *nt* chopper, chopping knife.

wiegen[1] [1] *vt* **(a)** to rock; *Kopf* to shake (slowly); *Hüften*, (*Wind*) *Äste etc* to sway ◆ **~de Bewegung** swaying motion; **einen ~den Gang haben** to sway one's hips when one walks.
(b) (*zerkleinern*) to chop up.
[2] *vr* (*Boot etc*) to rock (gently); (*Mensch, Äste etc*) to sway ◆ **sich im Tanz ~** to do an undulating dance; **sich in trügerischen Hoffnungen ~** to nurture false hopes; *siehe* **gewiegt**.

wiegen[2] *pret* **wog**, *ptp* **gewogen** *vti* to weigh ◆ **ein knapp gewogenes Kilo** something short of a kilo; **wieviel wiegst du?** what weight are you?, what do you weigh?; **schwer ~** (*fig*) to carry a lot of weight; (*Irrtum*) to be serious; **gewogen und zu leicht befunden** (*Bibl, fig*) weighed and found wanting; *siehe* **gewogen**.

Wiegen-: **~druck** *m* incunabulum; (*Verfahren*) early printing; **~fest** *nt* (*geh*) birthday; **~kind** *nt* (*liter*) infant, babe-in-arms; **~lied** *nt* lullaby, cradle-song.

wiehern *vi* to neigh; (*leiser*) to whinny ◆ **(vor Lachen) ~** to bray with laughter; **das ist ja zum W~** (*inf*) that's dead funny (*inf*).

Wien *nt* **-s** Vienna.

Wiener *adj attr* Viennese ◆ **~ Würstchen** frankfurter, wiener (sausage) (*esp US*); **~ Schnitzel** Wiener schnitzel.

Wiener(in *f***)** *m* **-s, -** Viennese.

wienerisch *adj* Viennese ◆ **das W~e** Viennese, the Viennese accent/dialect.

wiener(l)n *vti* (*inf*) to speak Viennese.

wienern *vti* (*usu pej*) to polish, to shine (*vt only*).

wies *pret of* **weisen**.

Wiese *f* **-, -n** meadow; (*inf: Rasen*) grass, lawn ◆ **auf der grünen ~** (*fig*) in the open countryside.

wiesehr *conj* (*Aus*) **~ ... auch** however much.

⚠: for details of spelling reform, see supplement

Wiesel *nt* **-s, -** weasel ◆ **schnell** *or* **flink wie ein ~** quick as a flash; **laufen** *or* **rennen wie ein ~** to run like a hare.

wieselflink [1] *adj* quick, quicksilver *attr.* [2] *adv* quick as a flash.

wieseln *vi aux sein* to scurry, to scuttle.

Wiesen-: **~blume** *f* meadow flower; **~grund** *m* (*poet*) meadow, mead (*poet*); **~rain** *m* (*liter*) meadow's edge; **~schaumkraut** *nt* lady's smock.

Wiesn *f* **-, -** (*dial*) fair.

wieso *interrog adv* why; (*aus welchem Grund auch*) how come (*inf*) ◆ **~ gehst du nicht?** how come you're not going? (*inf*), why aren't you going?; **~ nicht** why not; **~ sagst du das?** why do you say that?; **~ weißt du das?** how do you know that?

⚠**wieviel** *interrog adv* how much; (*bei Mehrzahl*) how many ◆ **(um) ~ größer** how much bigger.

wievielerlei *interrog adj inv* how many sorts *or* kinds of ◆ **~ verschiedene (Whiskys** *etc***)?** how many different sorts *or* kinds (of whisky *etc*)?

wievielmal *interrog adv* how many times.

Wievielte(r) *m decl as adj* (*bei Datum*) **den ~n haben wir** *or* **der ~ ist heute?** what's the date today?; **am ~n (des Monats)?** what date?, what day of the month?; **der ~ ist Donnerstag?** what's the date on Thursday?

wievielte(r, s) *interrog adj* **das ~ Kind ist das jetzt?** how many children is that now?; **das ~ Kind bist du? — das zweite** which child are you? — the second; **der ~ Band fehlt?** which volume is missing?; **den ~n Platz hat er im Wettkampf belegt?** where did he come in the competition?; **als ~r ging er durchs Ziel?** what place did he come?; **das ~ Mal** *or* **zum ~n Mal bist du schon in England?** how often *or* how many times have you been to England?; **am ~n September hast du Geburtstag?** when *or* what date in September is your birthday?; **das ~ Jahr bist du jetzt in Schottland?** how many years have you lived in Scotland now?; **ich habe morgen Geburtstag! — der ~ ist es denn?** it's my birthday tomorrow! — how old will you be?

wieweit *conj siehe* **inwieweit.**

wiewohl *conj* (*old*) **(a)** *siehe* **obwohl. (b)** (*dafür aber auch*) and at the same time, as well as.

Wigwam *m or nt* **-s, -s** wigwam.

Wikinger *m* **-s, -** Viking.

Wikinger-: **~schiff** *nt* longboat, Viking ship; **~zeit** *f* age of the Vikings, Viking age.

wikingisch *adj* Viking *attr.*

wild *adj* wild; *Stamm* savage; *Schönheit auch* rugged; *Kind auch, Haar* unruly; (*laut, ausgelassen*) boisterous; (*heftig*) *Kampf,* (*zornig*) *Blick* fierce, furious; (*ungesetzlich*) *Parken, Zelten etc* illegal; *Streik* wildcat *attr,* unofficial ◆ **~es Fleisch** proud flesh; **der W~e Jäger** the Wild Huntsman; **den ~en Mann spielen** (*inf*) *or* **machen** (*inf*) to come the heavy (*inf*); **der W~e Westen** the Wild West; **~ leben** to live in the wild; **~ wachsen** to grow wild; **~ ins Gesicht hängende Haare** wild, tousled hair hanging over one's face; **~ durcheinanderliegen** to be strewn all over the place; **dann ging alles ~ durcheinander** there was chaos then; **wie ~ rennen/arbeiten** *etc* to run/work *etc* like mad; **~ drauflosreden/drauflosschreiben** to talk nineteen to the dozen/to write furiously; **seid nicht so ~!** calm down a bit!; **jdn ~ machen** to make sb furious *or* mad (*inf*); (*esp vor Vergnügen etc*) to drive sb wild; **einen Hund ~ machen** to drive a dog wild; **~ werden** to go wild (*auch inf*); (*Kinder: ausgelassen werden*) to run wild; **der Bulle wurde ~** (*inf*) the bull was enraged; **ich könnte ~ werden** (*inf*) I could scream (*inf*); **~ auf jdn/etw sein** (*inf*) to be wild *or* crazy *or* mad about sb/sth (*inf*); **das ist nicht so** *or* **halb so ~** (*inf*) never mind; **~ entschlossen** (*inf*) really *or* dead (*inf*) determined; *siehe* **Ehe, Wein.**

Wild *nt* **-(e)s,** *no pl* (*Tiere, Fleisch*) game; (*Rot~*) deer; (*Fleisch von Rot~*) venison ◆ **ein Stück ~** a head of game.

Wild-: **~bach** *m* torrent; **~bahn** *f* hunting ground *or* preserve; **auf** *or* **in freier ~bahn** in the wild; **~bestand** *m* game population, stock of game; **~braten** *m* roast venison; **ein ~braten** a roast of venison; **~bret** *nt* **-s,** *no pl* game; (*von Rotwild*) venison; **~dieb** *m* poacher; **~diebstahl** *m* poaching; **~ente** *f* wild duck.

Wilde(r) *mf decl as adj* savage, wild man/woman; (*fig*) madman, maniac ◆ **die ~n** the savages.

Wilderei *f* poaching.

Wilderer *m* **-s, -** poacher.

wildern *vi* (*Mensch*) to poach; (*Hund etc*) to kill game ◆ **~der Hund** dog which kills game.

Wildern *nt* **-s,** *no pl* poaching; (*von Hund etc*) killing game.

Wild-: **~esel** *m* wild ass; **~falle** *f* trap set for game; **~fang** *m* **(a)** (*Hunt*) (*Falke*) passage *or* wild-caught hawk; (*Tier*) animal captured in the wild; **(b)** (*dated inf*) little rascal *or* devil, scamp; (*Mädchen*) tomboy; **~fleisch** *nt* game; (*von Rotwild*) venison; **~fraß** *m* damage caused by game; **w~fremd** *adj* (*inf*) completely strange; **w~fremde Leute** complete strangers; **ein ~fremder, ein w~fremder Mensch** a complete stranger; **~fütterung** *f* feeding of game animals; **~gans** *f* wild goose; **~gehege** *nt* game enclosure *or* preserve; **~geschmack** *m* gam(e)y taste.

Wildheit *f* wildness; (*von Stamm etc*) savagery; (*von Kind auch, von Haar*) unruliness; (*von Kampf, Blick*) fierceness; (*Leidenschaft*) wild passion.

Wild-: **~hüter** *m* gamekeeper; **~kaninchen** *nt* wild rabbit; **~katze** *f* wildcat; ⚠**w~lebend** *adj attr* wild, living in the wild; **~leder** *nt* suede; **w~ledern** *adj* suede.

Wildnis *f* (*lit, fig*) wilderness ◆ **Tiere der ~** wild animals; **in der ~ leben/geboren werden** to live/be born in the wild.

Wild-: **~park** *m* game park; (*für Rotwild*) deer park; **~reichtum** *m* abundance of game; **~reservat** *nt* game reserve; **w~romantisch** *adj* (*iro*) terribly romantic; **~sau** *f* wild sow; (*fig sl*) pig (*inf*); **~schaden** *m* damage caused by game; **~schütz(e)** *m* (*obs*) poacher; **~schutzgebiet** *nt* game preserve; **~schwein** *nt* wild boar *or* pig; ⚠**w~wachsend** *adj attr* wild(-growing); **~wasser** *nt* white water; **~wasserboot** *nt* fast-water canoe; **~wasserfahren** *nt* white-water canoeing; **~wasserrennen** *nt* fast-water canoe race; **~wechsel** *m* path used by game *or* wild animals; (*bei Rotwild*) deer path; **„~wechsel"** "wild animals"; **~west** *no art* the wild west; **~westfilm** *m* western; **~westroman** *m* western; **~wuchs** *m* (*geh*) rank growth; (*fig*) proliferation.

Wilhelm ['vɪlhɛlm] *m* **-s** William ◆ **falscher ~** (*inf*) toupee; **seinen (Friedrich) ~ unter etw** (*dat*) **setzen** (*inf*) to put one's signature *or* moniker (*inf*) to sth.

Wilhelminisch [vɪlhɛl'miːnɪʃ] *adj* (*Hist*) Wilhelminian (*pertaining to the reign of William II of Germany 1888 — 1918*).

will *1. pers present of* **wollen**[2]**.**

Wille *m* **-ns,** *no pl* will; (*Absicht, Entschluß*) intention ◆ **nach jds ~n** as sb wanted/wants; (*von Architekt etc*) as sb intended/intends; **wenn es nach ihrem ~n ginge** if she had her way; **etw mit ~n tun** to do sth on purpose *or* deliberately; **das geschah gegen** *or* **wider meinen ~n** (*meinen Wünschen*) that was done against my will; (*unabsichtlich*) I didn't intend that to happen; **er mußte wider ~n** *or* **gegen seinen ~n lachen** he couldn't help laughing; **jds ~n tun** to do sb's will; **es steht (nicht) in unserem ~n, das zu tun** (*geh*) it is (not) our intention to do that; **seinen ~n durchsetzen** to get one's (own) way; **auf seinem ~n bestehen** to insist on having one's way; **jdm seinen ~n lassen** to let sb have his own way; **er soll seinen ~n haben** let him have his (own) way; **seinen eigenen ~n haben** to be self-willed, to have a mind of one's own; **beim besten ~n nicht** not with all the will *or* with the best will in the world; **ich hätte das beim besten ~n nicht machen können** I couldn't have done that for the life of me; **es war kein** *or* **nicht böser ~** there was no ill-will intended; **etw aus freiem ~n tun** to do sth of one's own free will; **der gute ~** good will; **guten ~ns sein** to be full of good intentions; **alle Menschen, die guten ~ns sind** all people of good will; **den guten ~n für die Tat nehmen** to take the thought for the deed; **jdm zu ~n sein** to comply with sb's wishes; (*Mädchen: sich hingeben*) to yield to sb, to let sb have his way with one; **sich** (*dat*) **jdn zu ~n machen** to bend sb to one's will, to force sb to do one's will; *Mädchen* to have one's way with sb; **wo ein ~ ist, ist auch ein Weg** (*Prov*) where there's a will there's a way (*Prov*); *siehe* **letzte(r, s).**

willen *prep siehe* **um 2.**

Willen-: **w~los** *adj* weak-willed, spineless; **völlig w~los sein** to have no will of one's own; **sich jdm w~los unterwerfen** to submit totally to sb; **jds w~loses Werkzeug sein** to be sb's mere tool; **~losigkeit** *f* weakness of will, spinelessness.

willens *adj* (*geh*) **~ sein** to be willing *or* prepared.

Willens-: **~akt** *m* act of will; **~anstrengung** *f* effort of will; **~äußerung** *f* expression of will; **~bildung** *f* development of an informed opinion; **~erklärung** *f* professed intention; **~freiheit** *f* freedom of will; **~kraft** *f* willpower, strength of mind; **~mensch** *m* (*inf*) very determined person; **w~schwach** *adj* weak-willed; **~schwäche** *f* weakness of will; **w~stark** *adj* strong-willed, determined; **~stärke** *f* will-power; **~vollstrecker** *m* (*Sw*) *siehe* **Testamentsvollstrecker.**

willentlich *adj* wilful, deliberate.

willfahren *pret* **willfahrte,** *ptp* **willfahrt** *vi* +*dat* (*old, liter*) to please, to satisfy, to obey (*jdm* sb).

willfährig *adj* (*old, liter*) submissive, compliant ◆ **jdm ~ sein** to submit to sb.

Willfährigkeit *f* (*old, liter*) submissiveness, compliance.

willig *adj* willing.

willigen *vi* (*old, liter*) **in etw** (*acc*) **~** to agree to sth.

Willigkeit *f* willingness.

Willkomm *m* **-s, -e** (*old, liter*) **(a)** welcome. **(b)** (*auch* **~becher**) cup of welcome (*old*).

willkommen *adj* welcome ◆ **du bist (mir) immer ~** you are always welcome; **jdn ~ heißen** to welcome *or* greet sb; **seid (herzlich) ~!** welcome, welcome!; **herzlich ~** welcome (*in* +*dat* to); **es ist mir ganz ~, daß ...** I quite welcome the fact that ...; **die Gelegenheit, das zu sagen/zu tun, ist mir ~** I welcome the opportunity of saying/doing this.

Willkommen *nt* **-s, -** welcome ◆ **jdm ein ~ bieten** (*liter*) to bid sb welcome; **ein herzliches ~!** welcome indeed!

Willkommens-: **~gruß** *m* greeting, welcome; **~trunk** *m* welcoming drink, cup of welcome (*old*).

Willkür *f* **-,** *no pl* capriciousness; (*politisch*) despotism; (*bei Entscheidungen, Handlungen*) arbitrariness ◆ **sie sind seiner ~ schutzlos preisgegeben** *or* **ausgeliefert** they are completely at his mercy; **das ist reinste ~** that is purely arbitrary *or* just a whim; **ein Akt der ~** an act of caprice/a despotic act/an arbitrary act.

Willkür-: **~akt** *m siehe* **Willkür** act of caprice; despotic act; arbitrary act; **~herrschaft** *f* tyranny, despotic rule.

willkürlich *adj* **(a)** arbitrary; *Herrscher* autocratic ◆ **sie kann ~ Tränen produzieren** she can produce tears at will. **(b)** *Muskulatur* voluntary.

Willkürlichkeit *f siehe adj* **(a)** arbitrariness; autocracy. **(b)** voluntariness. **(c)** *siehe* **Willkürakt.**

Willkürmaßnahme *f* arbitrary measure.

wimmeln *vi* **(a)** *auch vi impers* (*in Mengen vorhanden sein*) **der See wimmelt von Fischen, in dem See wimmelt es von Fischen** the lake is teeming with fish; **hier wimmelt es von Mücken/Pilzen/Menschen/Fehlern** this place is swarming with midges/overrun with mushrooms/teeming with people/this is

teeming with mistakes; **der Käse wimmelt von Maden** the cheese is crawling with maggots.
(b) *aux sein* (*sich bewegen*) to teem; (*Menschen, Mücken, Ameisen auch*) to swarm.

wimmen (*Sw*) [1] *vt* to harvest, to gather.
[2] *vi* to harvest *or* gather (the) grapes.

Wimmer(in *f*) *m* **-s, -** (*Sw*) *siehe* **Winzer(in).**

Wimmerl *nt* **-(s), -n** (*Aus*) **(a)** (*Pickel*) spot, pimple. **(b)** (*Skiläufertasche*) pouch.

wimmern *vi* to whimper.

Wimmet *m or f* **-,** *no pl* (*esp Sw, Aus*) grape harvest.

Wimpel *m* **-s, -** pennant.

Wimper *f* **-, -n (a)** (eye)lash ♦ **ohne mit der ~ zu zucken** (*fig*) without batting an eyelid. **(b)** (*Bot, Zool*) cilium.

Wimperntusche *f* mascara.

Wimpertierchen *nt* ciliate.

Wind *m* **-(e)s, -e (a)** wind ♦ **bei** *or* **in ~ und Wetter** in all weathers; **~ und Wetter ausgesetzt sein** to be exposed to the elements; **laufen/sich verbreiten wie der ~** to run like the wind/to spread like wildfire; **der ~ dreht sich** the wind is changing direction; (*fig*) the climate is changing; **wissen/merken, woher der ~ weht** *or* **bläst** (*fig*) to know/notice the way the wind is blowing; **daher weht der ~!** (*fig*) so that's the way the wind is blowing; **seither weht** *or* **bläst ein anderer/frischer ~** (*fig*) things have changed since then; **ein neuer ~ weht durch das Land** (*fig*) the wind of change is blowing in the country; **frischen** *or* **neuen ~ in etw** (*acc*) **bringen** (*fig*) to breathe new life into sth; **mach doch nicht so einen ~** (*inf*) don't make such a to-do (*inf*); **viel ~ um etw machen** (*inf*) to make a lot of fuss *or* to-do (*inf*) about sth; **vor dem/gegen den ~ segeln** (*lit*) to sail with the wind (behind one)/into the wind; **mit dem ~ zu segeln verstehen** (*fig*) to know how to bend with the wind; **den Mantel** *or* **das Mäntelchen** *or* **die Fahne** *or* **das Fähnchen nach dem ~ hängen** *or* **drehen** *or* **richten** to trim one's sails to the wind, to swim with the tide; **jdm den ~ aus den Segeln nehmen** (*fig*) to take the wind out of sb's sails; **sich** (*dat*) **den ~ um die Nase** *or* **Ohren wehen lassen** to see a bit of the world; **etw in den ~ schlagen** *Warnungen, Rat* to turn a deaf ear to sth; *Vorsicht, Vernunft* to throw *or* cast sth to the winds; **in den ~ reden** to waste one's breath; **wer ~ sät, wird Sturm ernten** (*Prov*) sow the wind and reap the whirlwind (*prov*).
(b) (*Himmelsrichtung*) wind (direction) ♦ **in alle (vier) ~e** to the four winds.
(c) (*Med: Blähung*) wind ♦ **einen ~ fahren** *or* **streichen lassen** to break wind.
(d) (*Hunt*) wind ♦ **von jdm/etw ~ nehmen** *or* **bekommen** to take *or* get the wind of sb/sth; **von etw ~ bekommen** *or* **kriegen/haben** (*fig inf*) to get/have wind of sth.

wind *adj* (*S Ger, Sw*) **jdm wird es ~ und weh** (*übel*) sb feels really ill; (*traurig*) sb feels really sad; (*angst*) sb feels really afraid.

Wind-: ~beutel *m* **(a)** cream puff; **(b)** (*inf: Mensch*) rake; **~bluse** *f* windcheater; **~bö(e)** *f* gust of wind; **~büchse** *f* (*inf*) air rifle.

Winde[1] *f* **-, -n** (*Tech*) winch, windlass.

Winde[2] *f* **-, -n** (*Bot*) bindweed, convulvulus.

Wind|ei *nt* (*fig*) non-starter.

Windel *f* **-, -n** nappy (*Brit*), diaper (*US*) ♦ **damals lagst du noch in den ~n** you were still in nappies/diapers then; **noch in den ~n stecken** *or* **liegen** (*fig*) to be still in its infancy.

Windel-: ~einlage, ~folie *f* nappy (*Brit*) *or* diaper (*US*) liner; **~höschen** *nt* plastic pants *pl*.

windeln [1] *vt* **ein Baby ~** to put a baby's nappy (*Brit*) *or* diaper (*US*) on; (*neu ~*) to change a baby *or* a baby's nappy/diaper.
[2] *vi* to put on nappies/a nappy (*Brit*) *or* diapers/a diaper (*US*).

windelweich *adj* **(a) jdn ~ schlagen** *or* **hauen** (*inf*) to beat sb black and blue, to beat the living daylights out of sb. **(b)** (*nachgiebig*) softly-softly.

winden[1] *pret* **wand,** *ptp* **gewunden** [1] *vt* to wind; *Kranz* to bind; (*hoch~*) *Eimer, Last* to winch ♦ **jdm etw aus der Hand ~** to wrest sth out of sb's hand.
[2] *vr* (*Pflanze, Schlange*) to wind (itself); (*Bach*) to wind, to meander; (*Mensch*) (*durch Menge, Gestrüpp etc*) to wind (one's way); (*vor Schmerzen*) to writhe (*vor* with, in); (*vor Scham, Verlegenheit*) to squirm (*vor* with, in); (*fig: ausweichen*) to try to wriggle out ♦ **sich ~ wie ein (getretener) Wurm** to squirm.

winden[2] *vi impers* **es windet (sehr)** the wind is blowing (hard).

winden[3] *vti* (*Hunt*) *siehe* **wittern.**

Wind|energie *f* wind energy.

Wind|energie|anlage *f* wind energy plant.

Windes-: ~eile *f* **etw in** *or* **mit ~eile tun** to do sth in no time (at all); **sich in** *or* **mit ~eile verbreiten** to spread like wildfire; **~flügel** *pl* (*liter*) **auf ~flügeln** like the wind.

Wind-: ~fahne *f* (*Met*) windvane; **~fang** *m* draught-excluder; (*Raum*) porch; **~fangtür** *f* porch door; **~farm** *f* wind farm; **~generator** *m* wind generator; **w~geschützt** [1] *adj* sheltered (from the wind); [2] *adv* in a sheltered place; **~geschwindigkeit** *f* wind speed; **~hafer** *m* wild oat; **~harfe** *f* wind harp; **~hauch** *m* breath of wind; **~hose** *f* vortex.

Windhuk *nt* **-s** Windhoek.

Windhund *m* **(a)** (*Hund*) greyhound; (*afghanischer Windhund*) Afghan (hound). **(b)** (*fig pej*) rake.

windig *adj* windy; (*fig*) *Bursche, Sache* dubious, dodgy (*inf*).

windisch *adj* (*Aus usu pej*) Slovene.

Wind-: ~jacke *f* windcheater; **~jammer** *m* **-s, -** (*Naut*) windjammer; **~kanal** *m* wind-tunnel; (*an Orgel*) wind-trunk; **~kraft** *f* wind power; **~kraftanlage** *f*, **~kraftwerk** *nt* wind power station; **~licht** *nt* lantern; **~loch** *nt* (*Aviat*) air-pocket; **~mühle** *f* windmill; **gegen ~mühlen (an)kämpfen** (*fig*) to tilt at windmills; **~mühlenflügel** *m* windmill sail *or* vane; **~pocken** *pl* chickenpox *sing*; **~rad** *nt* (*Tech*) wind turbine; **~richtung** *f* wind direction; **~röschen** *nt* anemone; **~rose** *f* (*Naut*) compass card; (*Met*) wind rose; **~sack** *m* (*Aviat*) windsock, airsock; (*an Dudelsack etc*) (pipe)bag.

Windsbraut *f* (*old, liter*) storm, tempest (*liter*); (*Wirbelwind*) whirlwind ♦ **wie eine** *or* **die ~** (*fig geh*) like a whirlwind.

Wind-: ~schatten *m* lee; (*von Fahrzeugen*) slipstream; **~scheibe** *f* (*Sw*) *siehe* **~schutzscheibe; w~schief** *adj* crooked; *Dach auch* askew *pred*; *Haus* crooked; **~schirm** *m* windbreak; **w~schlüpf(r)ig, w~schnittig** *adj* streamlined; **~schutzscheibe** *f* windscreen; (*Brit*), windshield (*US*) **~seite** *f* windward side; **~skala** *f* wind scale; **~spiel** *nt* greyhound; **~stärke** *f* strength of the wind; (*Met*) wind-force; **w~still** *adj* still, windless; *Platz, Ecke etc* sheltered; **wenn es völlig w~still ist** when there is no wind at all; **~stille** *f* calm; **~stoß** *m* gust of wind; **~surfbrett** *nt* sailboard, windsurfer; **~surfen** *nt* sailboarding, windsurfing; **w~surfen** *vi insep* to sailboard, to windsurf; **w~surfen gehen** to go sailboarding *or* windsurfing; **~surfer** *m* sailboarder, windsurfer; **~turbine** *f* wind turbine.

Windung *f* (*von Weg, Fluß etc*) meander; (*von Schlange*) coil; (*Anat: von Darm*) convolution; (*Tech: von Schraube*) thread; (*eine Umdrehung*) revolution; (*Elec: von Spule*) coil.

Wingert *m* **-s, -e** (*dial, Sw*) *siehe* **Weinberg.**

Wink *m* **-(e)s, -e** (*Zeichen*) sign; (*mit der Hand*) wave (*mit* of); (*mit dem Kopf*) nod (*mit* of); (*Hinweis, Tip*) hint, tip ♦ **er gab mir einen ~, daß ich still sein sollte** he gave me a sign to be quiet.

Winkel *m* **-s, - (a)** (*Math*) angle; *siehe* **tot.**
(b) (*Tech*) square.
(c) (*Mil: Rangabzeichen*) stripe.
(d) (*fig: Stelle, Ecke*) corner; (*Plätzchen: esp von Land, Wald etc*) place, spot ♦ **jdn/etw in allen (Ecken und) ~n suchen** to look high and low for sb/sth; **in einem verborgenen ~ seines Herzens** in a hidden corner of his heart.

Winkel-: ~advokat *m* (*pej*) incompetent lawyer; **~eisen** *nt* angle iron; **w~förmig** *adj* angled; **w~förmig gebogen** bent at an angle; **~funktion** *f* (*Math*) trigonometrical function; **~halbierende** *f* **-n, -n** bisector of an/the angle.

wink(e)lig *adj siehe* **winklig.**

Winkel-: ~maß *nt* **(a)** (*Astron*) Norma, the Level; **(b)** (*Winkel*) square; **~messer** *m* **-s, -** protractor; **~zug** *m* (*Trick*) dodge, trick; (*Ausflucht*) evasion; **mach keine ~züge** stop evading the issue.

winken *ptp* **gewinkt** *or* (*dial*) **gewunken** [1] *vi* to wave (*jdm* to sb) ♦ **jdm ~, etw zu tun** to signal sb to do sth; **sie winkte mit einem Fähnchen/den Armen** she waved a flag/her arms; **einem Taxi ~** to hail a taxi; **jdm winkt etw** (*fig: steht in Aussicht*) sb can expect sth; **bei der Verlosung ~ wertvolle Preise** valuable prizes are being offered in the draw; **dem Sieger winkt eine Reise nach Italien** the winner will receive (the attractive prize of) a trip to Italy; **ihm winkt das Glück** fortune *or* luck is smiling on him, luck is on his side.
[2] *vt* to wave; (*esp Sport: anzeigen*) to signal; *Taxi* to hail; *Kellner* to call ♦ **jdn zu sich ~** to beckon sb over to one.

Winker *m* **-s, -** (*Aut*) indicator, trafficator.

Winker|alphabet *nt* semaphore alphabet.

winke-winke machen *vi* (*baby-talk*) to wave.

winklig *adj Haus, Altstadt* full of nooks and crannies; *Gasse* twisty, windy.

Winkzeichen *nt* signal; (*Mot*) hand signal; (*mit Fahne*) semaphore signal.

Winsch *f* **-, -en** (*Naut*) windlass, winch.

winseln *vti* to whimper; (*pej: um Gnade etc*) to grovel.

Winter *m* **-s, -** winter ♦ **es ist/wird ~** winter is here *or* has come/is coming; **im/über den ~** in (the)/over the winter; **über den ~ kommen** to get through the winter; **der nächste ~ kommt bestimmt** (*inf*) you never know how long the good times are going to last; **der nukleare ~** nuclear winter.

Winter- *in cpds* winter; **~anfang** *m* beginning of winter; **vor/seit ~anfang** before/since the beginning of winter; **~dienst** *m* (*Mot*) winter road clearance; **~einbruch** *m* onset of winter; **~fell** *nt* winter coat; **w~fest** *adj* hardy; *Saat* winter *attr*; **ein Auto w~fest machen** to winterize a car (*US*); **~garten** *m* winter garden; **~getreide** *nt* winter crop; **~halbjahr** *nt* winter; **im ~halbjahr** from September to March; **im ~halbjahr 1976/77** in the winter of 1976/77; **w~hart** *adj Pflanzen* hardy; **~kälte** *f* cold winter weather; **in der größten ~kälte** in the depths of winter; **~kartoffeln** *pl* (old) potatoes *pl*; **~kleid** *nt* winter dress; (*Zool*) winter coat; (*liter: von Landschaft etc*) winter covering (of snow); **~kleider** *pl* winter clothes *pl*; **~kleidung** *f* winter clothing; **~landschaft** *f* winter landscape; **w~lich** *adj* wintry; *Wetter auch, Kleidung, Beschäftigung* winter *attr*, **w~lich gekleidet** dressed for winter; **~monat** *m* winter month.

wintern *vi impers* (*liter*) **es winterte schon** winter was coming.

Winter-: ~nacht *f* winter night; **~obst** *nt* winter fruit; **~olympiade** *f* Winter Olympics *pl*; **~pause** *f* winter break; **~quartier** *nt* (*Mil*) winter quarters *pl*; **~reifen** *m* winter tyre.

winters *adv* in winter, in the wintertime.

Winter-: ~saat *f* winter seed; **~sachen** *pl* winter clothes *pl*; **~schlaf** *m* (*Zool*) hibernation; **(den) ~schlaf halten** to hibernate; ⚠**~schlußverkauf** *m* winter sale; **~semester** *nt* winter semester; **~sonnenwende** *f* winter solstice; **~spiele** *pl* **(Olympische) ~spiele** Winter Olympic Games *or* Olympics *pl*; **~sport** *m* winter sports *pl*; (*Sportart*) winter sport; **in den ~sport fahren** to go on a winter sports holiday.

⚠: for details of spelling reform, see supplement

Winters-: w~über *adv* in winter; **~zeit** *f (liter)* wintertime.
Winter-: ~tag *m* winter('s) day; **~wetter** *nt* winter weather; **~zeit** *f* winter time; *(Jahreszeit)* wintertime.
Winzer(in *f*) *m* **-s, -** wine-grower; *(Weinleser)* grape-picker.
Winzergenossenschaft *f* wine-growers' organization.
winzig *adj* tiny ◆ **ein ~es bißchen** a tiny little bit; **~ klein** minute, tiny little *attr.*
Winzigkeit *f* tininess.
Winzling *m (inf)* mite.
Wipfel *m* **-s, -** treetop ◆ **in den ~n der Bäume** in the treetops *or* tops of the trees.
Wippe *f* **-, -n** *(zum Schaukeln)* seesaw.
wippen *vi (auf und ab)* to bob up and down; *(hin und her)* to teeter; *(Schwanz)* to wag; *(mit Wippe schaukeln)* to seesaw ◆ **mit dem Schwanz ~** to wag its tail; **mit dem Fuß ~** to jiggle one's foot; **in den Knien ~** to give at the knees; **~der Gang** bouncing gait.
wir *pers pron gen* **unser,** *dat* **uns,** *acc* **uns** we ◆ **~ alle/beide/drei** all/both *or* the two/the three of us; **~ als Betroffene/Kollegen ...** as those affected/as colleagues, we ...; **~ Armen/Kommunisten** we poor people/we Communists; **~ (selbst) sind/waren es, die ...** we are/were the ones who ..., it is/was we *(form) or* us who ...; **nicht nur ~ sind der Ansicht ...** it is not only we who are of the opinion ...; **immer sollen ~'s gewesen sein** everyone always blames us; **wer war das? — ~ nicht** who was that? — it wasn't us; **wer kommt noch mit? — ~/~ nicht** who's coming along? — we are/not us; **wer ist da? — ~ (sind's)** who's there? — (it's) us; **trinken ~ erst mal einen** let's have a drink first; **da haben ~ wohl nicht aufgepaßt?** *(iro)* we weren't paying attention, were we?; **~, Wilhelm, Kaiser von ...** we, William, Emperor of ...
wirb *imper sing of* **werben.**
Wirbel *m* **-s, - (a)** *(lit, fig)* whirl; *(in Fluß etc)* whirlpool, eddy; *(von Wind auch)* eddy; *(Drehung beim Tanz etc)* pirouette; *(der Gefühle, Ereignisse)* turmoil; *(Aufsehen)* to-do ◆ **im ~ des Festes** in the whirl *or* hurly-burly of the party; **(viel/großen) ~ machen/verursachen** to make/cause (a lot of/a big) commotion.
(b) *(Haar~)* crown; *(nicht am Hinterkopf)* cowlick; *(auf Fingerkuppe, in Stein)* whorl.
(c) *(Trommel~)* (drum) roll.
(d) *(Anat)* vertebra.
(e) *(an Saiteninstrument)* peg; *(an Fenster)* catch.
Wirbeldüse *f* water nozzle *or* jet.
wirb(e)lig *adj (temperamentvoll)* vivacious, lively; *(wirr)* dizzy.
wirbellos *adj (Zool)* invertebrate ◆ **die W~en** the invertebrates.
wirbeln [1] *vi* **(a)** *aux sein (Mensch, Wasser etc)* to whirl; *(Laub, Staub, Rauch etc auch)* to swirl. **(b) mir wirbelt der Kopf** *(inf)* my head is spinning *or* reeling. **(c)** *(Trommeln etc)* to roll.
[2] *vt jdn, Wasser* to whirl; *Staub, Laub etc auch* to swirl.
Wirbel-: ~säule *f (Anat)* spinal column; **~sturm** *m* whirlwind; **~tier** *nt* vertebrate; **~wind** *m* whirlwind; **wie der/ein ~wind** like a whirlwind.
wirblig *adj siehe* **wirb(e)lig.**
wird *3. pers sing present of* **werden.**
wirf *imper sing of* **werfen.**
Wirform, Wir-Form *f* first person plural.
wirken[1] [1] *vi* **(a)** *(geh: tätig sein) (Mensch)* to work; *(Einflüsse, Kräfte etc)* to be at work ◆ **ich werde dahin ~, daß man ihn befördert** I will work for his promotion.
(b) *(Wirkung haben)* to have an effect; *(erfolgreich sein)* to work ◆ **als Gegengift/Katalysator ~** to work as an antidote/to act as a catalyst; **schalldämpfend/abführend ~** to have a soundproofing/laxative effect; **das wirkt auf viele als Provokation** many people see that as a provocation; **die Frau wirkt abstoßend auf mich** I find this woman repulsive; **die Pillen ~ gut gegen Bauchschmerzen** the pills are good for stomach-ache; **eine stark ~de Droge** a strong drug.
(c) *(einwirken)* **auf etw** *(acc)* **~** *(esp Chem)* to act on sth; **etw auf sich** *(acc)* **~ lassen** to take sth in.
(d) *(erscheinen)* to seem, to appear ◆ **nervös/ruhig (auf jdn) ~** to give (sb) the impression of being nervous/calm, to seem nervous/calm (to sb).
(e) *(zur Geltung kommen)* to be effective ◆ **neben diesen Gardinen wirkt das Muster nicht (richtig)** the pattern loses its effect next to those curtains; **ich finde, das Bild wirkt** I think the picture has something; **die Musik wirkt erst bei einer gewissen Lautstärke** you only get the full effect of the music when it's played loud.
[2] *vt (geh: tun) Gutes* to do; *Wunder* to work; *siehe* **Wunder.**
wirken[2] *vt* **(a)** *(liter) Teppiche, Stoffe* to weave. **(b)** *(spec) Maschinentextilien* to knit ◆ **Goldfäden durch etw ~** to work gold threads into sth.
wirken[3] *vt (rare: kneten) Teig* to knead, to work.
Wirken *nt* **-s,** *no pl* work.
Wirker(in *f*) *m* **-s, -** knitter.
Wirkerei *f* **(a)** knitting. **(b)** *(Fabrik)* knitwear factory.
Wirkkraft *f* effect.
wirklich [1] *adj* **(a)** *(zur Wirklichkeit gehörig)* real; *(tatsächlich auch) Sachverhalt, Aussage, Meinung etc* actual ◆ **im ~en Leben** in real life.
(b) *(echt)* real; *Freund auch* true.
[2] *adv* really ◆ **ich wüßte gern, wie es ~ war** I would like to know what really happened; **das meinst du doch nicht ~** you don't really mean that; **ich war das ~ nicht** it really was not me; **~?/nein, ~?** *(als Antwort)* really?/what, really?; **er ist es ~** it really is him; **~ und wahrhaftig** really and truly.

▼ **Wirklichkeit** *f* reality ◆ **~ werden** to come true; **die Literatur spiegelt die ~ wider** literature reflects reality; **in ~** in reality; **in ~ heißt er anders** his real name is different; *siehe* **Boden.**
Wirklichkeits-: ~form *f (Gram)* indicative; **w~fremd** *adj* unrealistic; **w~getreu, w~nah** *adj* realistic; **etw w~getreu** *or* **w~nah abbilden/erzählen** to paint a realistic picture/give a realistic account of sth; **~sinn** *m* realism.
Wirkmaschine *f* knitting machine.
wirksam *adj* effective ◆ **~ bleiben** to remain in effect; **mit (dem)/am 1. Januar ~ werden** *(form: Gesetz)* to take effect on *or* from January 1st.
Wirksamkeit *f* effectiveness.
Wirkstoff *m (esp Physiol)* active substance.
Wirkung *f* effect *(bei* on); *(von Tabletten etc)* effects *pl* ◆ **seine ~ tun** to have an effect; *(Droge)* to take effect; **ohne ~ bleiben** to have no effect; **an ~ verlieren** to lose its effect; **seine ~ verfehlen** not to have the desired effect; **zur ~ kommen** *(Medikament)* to take effect; *(fig: zur Geltung)* to come into effect; **mit ~ vom 1. Januar** *(form)* with effect from January 1st.
Wirkungs-: ~bereich *m (eines Menschen)* domain; *(einer Tageszeitung)* area of influence; *(von Atombombe, Golfstrom)* affected area; **der ~bereich des atlantischen Tiefs** the area affected by the Atlantic depression; **~dauer** *f* period over which sth is effective; **~feld** *nt* field (of activity/interest *etc*); **~grad** *m* (degree of) effectiveness; **~kreis** *m* sphere of activity; **w~los** *adj* ineffective; **~losigkeit** *f* ineffectiveness; **~stätte** *f (geh)* domain; **w~voll** *adj* effective; **~weise** *f (von Medikament)* action; **die ~weise eines Kondensators** the way a condenser works.
Wirkwaren *pl* knitwear *sing*; *(Strümpfe etc auch)* hosiery *sing.*
wirr *adj* confused; *Blick* crazed; *(unordentlich) Haare, Fäden* tangled; *Gedanken, Vorstellungen* weird; *(unrealistisch, verstiegen)* wild ◆ **er ist ~ im Kopf** *(geistig gestört)* he is confused in his mind; *(konfus)* he is confused *or* muddled; *(benommen: esp von Lärm)* his head is reeling *or* swimming; **mach mich nicht ~** don't confuse me; **alles lag ~ durcheinander** everything was in chaos; **das Haar hängt ihm ~ ins Gesicht** his hair is hanging all in tangles over his face; **er ist ein ~er Kopf** he has crazy ideas; **sich ~ ausdrücken** to express oneself in a confused way.
Wirren *pl* confusion *sing*, turmoil *sing.*
Wirrkopf *m (pej)* muddle-head ◆ **das sind alles ~̈e** they've all got crazy ideas.
Wirrnis *f*, **Wirrsal** *nt* **-(e)s, -e** *(liter)* confusion.
Wirrung *f (liter)* confusion.
Wirrwarr *m* **-s,** *no pl* confusion; *(von Stimmen)* hubbub; *(von Verkehr)* chaos *no indef art*; *(von Fäden, Haaren etc)* tangle.
Wirsing *m* **-s,** *no pl*, **Wirsingkohl** *m* savoy cabbage.
Wirt *m* **-(e)s, -e** *(Gastwirt, Untervermieter)* landlord; *(Biol, rare: Gastgeber)* host ◆ **den ~ machen** to play the host, to do the honours; *siehe* **Rechnung.**
wirten *vi (Sw)* to be a/the landlord.
Wirtin *f* landlady; *(Gastgeberin)* hostess; *(Frau des Wirts)* landlord's wife.
Wirtschaft *f* **(a)** *(Volks~)* economy; *(Handel, Geschäftsleben)* industry and commerce; *(Finanzwelt)* business world ◆ **freie ~** free market economy; **er ist in der ~ tätig** he works in industry; he's a businessman; **ein Mann der ~** a man of industry and commerce; **seitens der ~ können wir keine Unterstützung erwarten** we can expect no support from the business world.
(b) *(Gast~)* ≃ pub *(Brit)*, public house *(Brit form)*, saloon *(US)* ◆ **~!** *(inf)* waiter!; **Frau ~!** *(hum inf)* waitress!
(c) *(dated: Haushalt)* household ◆ **jdm die ~ führen** to keep house for sb; **er gründete eine eigene ~** he set up house on his own.
(d) *(dated: landwirtschaftlicher Betrieb)* farm ◆ **in einer ~ arbeiten** to work on a farm.
(e) *(inf: Zustände)* state of affairs ◆ **du hast vielleicht eine ~ in deinem Haus/auf deinem Schreibtisch** a fine mess *or* state your house/desk is in; **eine schöne/saubere ~** *(iro)* a fine state of affairs; **jetzt werden wir hier erst mal reine ~ machen** *(dial)* first of all we'll put this house in order.
(f) *(inf: Umstände)* trouble, bother ◆ **eine ~ haben/sich** *(dat)* **eine ~ machen** to have/go to a lot of trouble *or* bother.
wirtschaften [1] *vi* **(a)** *(sparsam sein)* to economize ◆ **gut ~ können** to be economical; ◆ **sparsam ~** to economize, to budget carefully; **ins Blaue hinein ~** not to budget at all; *siehe* **Tasche.**
(b) *(den Haushalt führen)* to keep house.
(c) *(inf: sich betätigen)* to busy oneself; *(gemütlich)* to potter about; *(herumfummeln)* to rummage about.
[2] *vt* **jdn/etw zugrunde ~** to ruin sb/sth financially.
Wirtschafter(in *f*) *m* **-s, - (a)** *(Verwalter)* manager. **(b)** *(im Haushalt, Heim etc)* housekeeper. **(c)** *(dial: Wirtschaftler)* economist.
Wirtschaftler *m* **-s, - (a)** *(Wissenschaftler)* economist. **(b)** *(Mann der Wirtschaft)* business man.
wirtschaftlich *adj* **(a)** *(die Wirtschaft betreffend)* economic ◆ **jdm geht es ~ gut/schlecht** sb is in a good/bad financial *or* economic position. **(b)** *(sparsam)* economical; *Hausfrau* careful.
Wirtschaftlichkeit *f* economy; *(mit Genitiv)* economicalness.
Wirtschaftlichkeitsberechnung *f* evaluation of economic efficiency.
Wirtschafts- *in cpds* economic; **~aufschwung** *m* economic upswing *or* upturn; **~auskünfte** *pl* financial information *sing*; **~auskunftei** *f* credit investigation agency; ⚠**~ausschuß** *m* economic committee; **~berater** *m* business consultant; **~beziehungen** *pl* business relations *pl*; **~block** *m (Pol)* economic bloc; **~demokratie** *f* industrial democracy; **~flüchtling** *m* tax refugee; **~form** *f* economic system; **gemischte ~form** mixed economy; **~führer** *m* leading businessman/industrialist; **~führung** *f*

management; **~gebäude** *nt* working quarters *pl*; **~gefüge** *nt* economic framework; **~geld** *nt* housekeeping (money); **~gemeinschaft** *f* economic community; ⚠**~geographie** *f* economic geography; **~güter** *pl* economic goods *pl*; **~gymnasium** *nt grammar school which places emphasis on economics, law, management studies etc*; **~hilfe** *f* economic aid; **~hochschule** *f* business school; **~kapitän** *m* (*inf*) captain of industry; **~kraft** *f* economic power; **~krieg** *m* economic war/warfare; **~kriminalität** *f* white collar crime; **~krise** *f* economic crisis; **~lage** *f* economic situation; **~leben** *nt* business life; **er ist im ~leben zu Hause** he is at home in the business world; **Persönlichkeiten des ~lebens** business personalities; **~macht** *f* economic power; **~minister** *m* minister of trade and commerce; **~ministerium** *nt* ministry of trade and commerce; **~ordnung** *f* economic order *or* system; **~politik** *f* economic policy; **w~politisch** *adj* political-economic; **w~politisch ist es unmöglich ...** in terms of economic policy it is impossible ...; **~prüfer** *m* accountant; (*zum Überprüfen der Bücher*) auditor; **~raum** *m* **(a)** (*Agr*) working area; **(b)** (*Econ*) economic area; **~recht** *nt* commercial *or* business law; **~spionage** *f* industrial espionage; **~system** *nt* economic system; **~teil** *m* business *or* financial section; **~theorie** *f* economic theory; **~treibende(r)** *mf decl as adj* (*Aus*) *siehe* **Gewerbetreibende(r)**; **~union** *f* economic union; **~verband** *m* business *or* commercial association; **~wachstum** *nt* economic growth; **~wissenschaft** *f* economics *sing*; **~wissenschaftler** *m* economist; **~wunder** *nt* economic miracle; **~zeitung** *f* financial *or* business (news)paper; **~zweig** *m* branch of industry.

Wirts-: ~haus *nt* ≃ pub (*Brit*), saloon (*US*); (*esp auf dem Land*) inn; **~hausschlägerei** *f* pub brawl; **~leute** *pl* landlord and landlady; **~pflanze** *f* host (plant); **~programm** *nt* (*Comput*) host program; **~stube** *f* lounge; **~tier** *nt* host (animal).

Wisch *m* **-(e)s, -e** (*pej inf*) piece of paper; (*mit Gedrucktem, Dokument*) piece of bumph (*inf*); (*Zettel mit Notiz*) note.

wischen 1 *vti* to wipe; (*mit Lappen reinigen*) to wipe clean ◆ **mit einem Tuch über eine Schallplatte ~** to wipe a record with a cloth; **jdm über den Ärmel ~** to wipe sb's sleeve; **mit dem Ärmel über die feuchte Tinte ~** to get one's sleeve in the wet ink; **sie wischte ihm/sich den Schweiß mit einem Handtuch von der Stirn** she wiped the sweat from his/her brow with a towel; **Bedenken/Einwände (einfach) vom Tisch ~** (*fig*) to sweep aside thoughts/objections.
2 *vi aux sein* (*sich schnell bewegen*) to whisk.
3 *vt* (*inf*) **jdm eine ~** to clout sb one (*inf*); **einen gewischt bekommen** (*elektrischen Schlag*) to get a shock.

Wischer *m* **-s, -** (*Aut*) (windscreen) wiper.

Wischerblatt *nt* (*Aut*) wiper blade.

Wischiwaschi *nt* **-s,** *no pl* (*pej inf*) drivel (*inf*).

Wisch-: ~lappen *m* cloth; (*für Fußboden*) floorcloth; (*dial: für Geschirr*) dishcloth; **~tuch** *nt* cloth; (*dial: für Geschirr*) dishcloth; **~-Wasch-Automatik** *f* (*Aut*) wash-wipe.

Wisent *m* **-s, -e** bison.

Wismut *nt or* (*Aus*) *m* **-(e)s,** *no pl* (*abbr* **Bi**) bismuth.

wispern *vti* to whisper; (*unverständlich auch*) to mumble.

⚠**Wißbegier(de)** *f* thirst for knowledge.

⚠**wißbegierig** *adj Kind* eager to learn.

wisse *imper sing of* **wissen.**

▼ **wissen** *pret* **wußte,** *ptp* **gewußt** 1 *vti* **(a)** (*informiert sein*) to know (*über +acc, von* about) ◆ **ich weiß (es) (schon)/nicht** I know/don't know; **weißt du schon das Neuste?** have you heard the latest?; **das weiß alle Welt/jedes Kind** (absolutely) everybody/any fool knows that; **was ich alles ~ soll!, als ob ich das wüßte!** how should I know?; **ich weiß von ihr** *or* **über sie nur, daß sie ...** all I know about her is that she ..., I only know that she ...; **von ihr weiß ich das Alter** I know her age *or* how old she is; **von jdm/etw nichts ~ wollen** not to be interested in sb/sth; **er weiß es nicht anders/besser** he doesn't know any different/better; **er weiß zu genießen/schönen Urlaub zu machen** he knows how to enjoy himself/how to have a nice holiday; **jdn/etw zu schätzen ~** to appreciate sb/sth; **das mußt du (selbst) ~** it's your decision; **das solltest du selber ~** you ought to know; **das hättest du ja ~ müssen!** you ought to have realized that; **man kann nie ~** you never know; **man weiß nie, wozu das (noch mal) gut ist** you never know when it will come in handy; **das ~ die Götter** (*inf*), **das weiß der Henker** (*inf*) God only knows; **weiß Gott** (*inf*) God knows (*inf*); **sich für weiß Gott was halten** (*inf*) to think one is somebody really special; **sie hält sich für wer weiß wie klug** (*inf*) she doesn't half think she's clever (*inf*); **... oder was weiß ich** (*inf*) ... or something; **... und was weiß ich noch alles** (*inf*) ... and whatever (*inf*); **er ist wieder wer weiß wo** (*inf*) goodness knows where he's got to again (*inf*); **(ja) wenn ich das wüßte!** goodness knows!; **wenn ich nur wüßte ...** if only I knew ...; **nicht, daß ich wüßte** not to my knowledge, not as far as I know; **gewußt wie/wo!** *etc* sheer brilliance!; **weißt du was?** (do) you know what?; **weißt du, ...** you know ...; **ja, weißt du** well, you see; **daß du es (nur) (gleich) weißt** just so you know; **ich weiß sie in Sicherheit/glücklich** I know that she is safe/happy; **was ich/er nicht weiß, macht mich/ihn nicht heiß** (*Prov*) what the eye does not see the heart cannot grieve over (*Prov*).
(b) (*kennen*) to know ◆ **ich weiß keinen größeren Genuß, als ...** I know (of) no greater delight than ...
(c) (*erfahren*) **jdn etw ~ lassen** to let sb know sth, to tell sb sth.
(d) (*sich erinnern*) to remember; (*sich vor Augen führen*) to realize ◆ **ich weiß seine Adresse nicht mehr** I can't remember his address; **weißt du noch, wie schön es damals war?** do you remember how lovely things were then?; **weißt du noch, damals im Mai/in Stone?** do you remember that May/the times in Stone?; **du mußt ~, daß ...** you must realize that ...
2 *vi* **um etw** (*acc*) **~** (*geh*), **von etw ~** to know of *or* about sth; **ich/er weiß von nichts** I don't/he doesn't know anything about it; **... als ob er von nichts wüßte** ... as if he didn't know a thing.

Wissen *nt* **-s,** *no pl* knowledge ◆ **meines ~s** to my knowledge; **etw ohne jds ~ tun** to do sth without sb's knowledge; **etw gegen** *or* **wider** (*geh*) **(sein) besseres ~ tun** to do sth against one's better judgement; **nach bestem ~ und Gewissen** to the best of one's knowledge and belief; **mit jds ~ und Willen** with sb's knowledge and consent; **~ ist Macht** knowledge is power.

wissend *adj Blick etc* knowing.

Wissende(r) *mf decl as adj* (*Eingeweihter*) initiate ◆ **die ~n schwiegen** those who knew kept silent.

Wissenschaft *f* science.

Wissenschaftler(in *f***), Wissenschafter(in** *f***)** (*old, Sw, Aus form*) *m* **-s, -** scientist; (*Geistes~*) academic.

wissenschaftlich *adj* scientific; (*geistes~*) academic ◆ **W~er Assistent** assistant lecturer; **W~er Rat** lecturer, assistant professor (*US*); **~ arbeiten** to work scientifically.

Wissenschaftlichkeit *f* scientific nature *or* character; (*in bezug auf Geisteswissenschaften*) academic nature *or* character ◆ **der Arbeit mangelt es an ~** this thesis lacks a scientific approach.

Wissenschafts-: ~betrieb *m* academic life; **~lehre** *f* epistemology.

Wissens-: ~drang *m*, **~durst** *m* (*geh*) urge *or* thirst for knowledge; **~gebiet** *nt* field (of knowledge); **~schatz** *m* (*geh*) store of knowledge; **~stoff** *m* material; **das ist ~stoff der 3. Klasse** that's material learned in the 3rd form; **ein enormer ~stoff** an enormous amount of material; **w~wert** *adj* worth knowing; *Information auch* valuable; **das Buch enthält viel ~wertes** the book contains much valuable information.

wissentlich 1 *adj* deliberate, intentional.
2 *adv* knowingly, deliberately, intentionally.

wisset, ⚠**wißt** *imper pl of* **wissen.**

Witfrau *f* (*old*), **Witib** *f* **-, -e** (*obs*) widow.

Witmann *m* (*old*) widower.

wittern 1 *vi* (*Wild*) to sniff the air.
2 *vt* (*Wild*) to scent, to get wind of; (*Riese, Teufel*) to smell; (*fig: ahnen*) *Gefahr etc* to sense, to scent ◆ **wenn er eine Klassenarbeit witterte ...** whenever he suspected that a test was in the offing ...

Witterung *f* **(a)** (*Wetter*) weather ◆ **bei günstiger/guter ~** if the weather is good. **(b)** (*Hunt*) (*Geruch*) scent (*von* of); (*Geruchssinn*) sense of smell.

Witterungs-: w~beständig *adj* weather-proof; **~einflüsse** *pl* effects *pl* of the weather; **~lage** *f* weather; **~umschlag** *m* change in the weather; **~verhältnisse** *pl* weather conditions *pl*.

Wittib *f* **-, -e, Wittiber** *m* **-s, -** (*Aus*) *siehe* **Witwe, Witwer.**

Witwe *f* **-, -n** widow ◆ **~ werden** to be widowed.

Witwen-: ~geld *nt* widow's allowance; **~jahr** *nt* year of mourning; **~rente** *f* widow's pension; **~schaft** *f* widowhood; **~schleier** *m* widow's veil; **~stand** *m* widowhood; **~tröster** *m* (*pej inf*) widow chaser (*inf*); **~verbrennung** *f* suttee.

Witwer *m* **-s, -** widower.

Witz *m* **-es, -e (a)** (*Geist*) wit.
(b) (*Äußerung*) joke (*über +acc* about) ◆ **einen ~ machen** *or* **reißen** (*inf*) to make *or* crack a joke; **mach keine ~e!** don't be funny; **ich mach' keine ~e** I'm not being funny; **das soll doch wohl ein ~ sein, das ist doch wohl ein ~** that must be a joke, he/you *etc* must be joking; **die Prüfung/der Preis war ein ~** (*inf*) the exam/price was a joke.
(c) der ~ an der Sache ist, daß ... the great thing about it is that ...; **das ist der ganze ~** that's the thing.

Witz-: ~blatt *nt* joke book; **~blattfigur** *f* (*fig inf*) joke figure; **sich** (*dat*) **wie eine ~blattfigur vorkommen** to feel ridiculous; **~bold** *m* **-(e)s, -e** joker; (*unterhaltsamer Mensch*) comic; **du bist vielleicht ein ~bold!** (*iro*) you're a great one! (*iro*).

Witzelei *f* teasing *no pl* ◆ **laß doch diese blöde ~** stop teasing.

witzeln *vi* to joke (*über +acc* about).

Witzfigur *f* (*lit*) joke character; (*fig inf*) figure of fun.

witzig *adj* funny.

Witzigkeit *f* humour.

witzlos *adj* (*inf: unsinnig*) pointless, futile.

w.L. *abbr of* **westlicher Länge.**

Wladiwostok *nt* **-s** Vladivostok.

WM [veːˈ|ɛm] *f* **-, -s** *abbr of* **Weltmeisterschaft.**

WNW *abbr of* **Westnordwest** WNW.

w.o. *abbr of* **wie oben.**

wo 1 *interrog, rel adv* where; (*irgendwo*) somewhere ◆ **überall, ~** wherever; **~ könnte er anders** *or* **~ anders könnte er sein als in der Kneipe?** where else could he be but in the pub?; **~ immer ...** wherever ...; **der Tag/eine Zeit ~ ...** (*inf*) the day/a time when ...; **ach** *or* **i ~!** (*inf*) nonsense!
2 *conj* **~ nicht/möglich** if not/possible; **~ er doch wußte, daß ich nicht kommen konnte** when he knew I couldn't come; **~ du doch in die Stadt gehst, könntest du ...?** (*inf*) seeing that you're going into town, could you ...?; **~ ich gerade daran denke** (*inf*) while I'm thinking about it; **und das jetzt, ~ ich doch dazu keine Lust habe** (*inf*) and that now when I'm just not in the mood.

wo-: ~anders *adv* somewhere else, elsewhere; **~andersher** *adv* from somewhere else *or* elsewhere; **~andershin** *adv* somewhere else, elsewhere.

⚠: for details of spelling reform, see supplement

➤ SPRACHE AKTIV: **wissen: 1a** → 28.2, 30, 33.1, 43.1, 43.4, 49, 52.5, 53.6

wob *pret of* **weben.**
wobei *adv siehe auch* **bei (a)** *interrog* **~ ist das passiert?** how did that happen?; **~ hast du ihn erwischt?** what did you catch him at *or* doing?; **~ seid ihr gerade?** what are you doing just now?; *(im Buch)* where are you at just now?
(b) *rel* in which ◆ **ich erzähle mal, was passiert ist, ~ ich allerdings das Unwichtige auslasse** I will tell you what happened but I will leave out all the unimportant details; **~ man sehr aufpassen muß, daß man nicht betrogen wird/keinen Sonnenstich bekommt** and you have to be very careful that you don't get cheated/don't get sunburnt; **~ mir gerade einfällt** which reminds me; **das Auto prallte gegen einen Baum, ~ der Fahrer schwer verletzt wurde** the car hit a tree severely injuring the driver.
Woche *f* **-, -n** week ◆ **zweimal in der ~** twice a week; **in dieser ~** this week; **in die ~n kommen** *(old)* to be near one's time *(old)*.
Wochen-: ~arbeitszeit *f* working week; **welche ~arbeitszeit haben Sie?** what is your working week?, how many hours a week do you work?; **~bericht** *m* weekly report; **~bett** *nt* **im ~bett liegen** to be lying in *(old)*; **im ~bett sterben** to die in the weeks following childbirth; **~bettfieber** *nt* puerperal fever.
Wochen|end- *in cpds* weekend; **~ausgabe** *f* weekend edition; **~beilage** *f* weekend supplement.
Wochen|ende *nt* weekend ◆ **schönes ~!** have a nice weekend; **langes** *or* **verlängertes ~** long weekend.
Wochen|endler(in *f***)** *m* **-s, -** *(inf)* weekend tripper.
Wochen-: ⚠~fluß *m (Med)* lochia *(spec)*; **~kalender** *m* week-by-week calendar; **~karte** *f* weekly season ticket; **w~lang** *adj, adv* for weeks; **nach w~langem Warten** after waiting for weeks, after weeks of waiting; **~lohn** *m* weekly wage; **~markt** *m* weekly market; **~schau** *f* newsreel; **~schrift** *f* weekly (periodical); **~tag** *m* weekday *(including Saturday)*; **was ist heute für ein ~tag?** what day (of the week) is it today?; **w~tags** *adv* on weekdays.
wöchentlich [1] *adj* weekly.
[2] *adv* weekly; *(einmal pro Woche)* once a week ◆ **zwei Vormittage ~ kommen** to come two mornings a week; **~ zweimal** twice a week; **sich ~ abwechseln** to take turns every week.
Wochen-: w~weise *adv* week by week; *(einmal pro Woche)* once a week; *(für eine Woche)* by the week; **~zeitschrift** *f* weekly (magazine *or* periodical); **~zeitung** *f* weekly (paper).
Wöchnerin *f woman who has recently given birth*, woman in childbed *(old)*, puerpera *(spec)*.
Wöchnerinnenstation *f* maternity ward.
Wodan *m* **-s** *(Myth) siehe* **Wotan.**
Wodka *m* **-s, -s** vodka.
wodurch *adv siehe auch* **durch (a)** *interrog* how. **(b)** *rel* which ◆ **alles, ~ sie glücklich geworden war ...** everything which had made her happy ...
wofern *conj (old)* if.
wofür *adv siehe auch* **für (a)** *interrog* for what, what ... for; *(warum auch)* why. **(b)** *rel* for which, which ... for.
wog *pret of* **wägen, wiegen**[2].
Woge *f* **-, -n** wave; *(fig auch)* surge ◆ **wenn sich die Wogen geglättet haben** *(fig)* when things have calmed down.
wogegen *adv siehe auch* **gegen (a)** *interrog* against what, what ... against ◆ **~ ist dieses Mittel?** what's this medicine for? **(b)** *rel* against which, which ... against.
wogen *vi (liter)* to surge *(auch fig)*; *(Kornfeld)* to wave, to undulate; *(fig: Kampf)* to rage; *(Busen)* to heave.
Wogenschlag *m* pounding (of the waves).
woher *adv* **(a)** *interrog* where ... from ◆ **~ weißt du das?** how do you (come to) know that?; **~ kommt es eigentlich, daß ...** how is it that ...?, how come ... *(inf)*; **ach ~!** *(dial inf)* nonsense! **(b)** *rel* from which, where ... from.
wohin *adv* **(a)** *interrog* where ◆ **~, bitte?, ~ soll's gehen?** where to?, where do you want to go?; **~ so eilig?** where are you off to so fast *or* rushing off to?; **~ damit?** where shall I/we put it?; **ich muß mal ~** *(euph inf)* I've got to go somewhere *(euph inf)*. **(b)** *rel* where. **~ man auch schaut** wherever you look.
wohinein *adv siehe* **worein.**
wohingegen *conj* whereas, while.
wohinter *adv siehe auch* **hinter (a)** *interrog* what *or* where ... behind ◆ **~ kann ich in Deckung gehen?** what can I take cover behind?, behind what can I take cover?
(b) *rel* behind which ◆ **~ man sich auch versteckt** whatever you hide behind.
wohl [1] *adv* **(a)** *comp* **-er,** *superl* **am -sten** *(angenehm zumute)* happy; *(gesund)* well ◆ **sich ~/~er fühlen** to feel happy/happier; *(wie zu Hause)* to feel at home/more at home; *(gesundheitlich)* to feel well/better; **bei dem Gedanken ist mir nicht ~** I'm not very happy at the thought; **am ~sten wäre mir, wenn ...** I'd feel happier if ...; **jdm ist ~ ums Herz** sb feels light of heart; **~ oder übel** whether one likes it or not, willy-nilly; **~ dem, der ...** happy the man who ...; **~ ihm, daß ...** it's a good thing for him that ...; **es sich** *(dat)* **~ gehen/sein/ergehen lassen** to enjoy oneself.
(b) *(gut) comp* **besser,** *superl* **bestens** *or* **am besten** well ◆ **nun ~!** now then!; **ich wünsche ~ gespeist/geruht zu haben** *(dated)* I do hope you have enjoyed your meal/had a pleasant sleep; **laßt es euch ~ schmecken!** I hope you like *or* enjoy it; *siehe* **bekommen.**
(c) *(wahrscheinlich)* probably, no doubt; *(iro: bestimmt)* surely ◆ **er ist ~ schon zu Hause** he's probably at home by now, no doubt he's at home by now; **das ist ~ nicht gut möglich** I should think it's unlikely; **es ist ~ anzunehmen, daß ...** it is to be expected that ...; **du bist ~ verrückt** you must be crazy!; **das ist doch ~ nicht dein Ernst!** surely you're not serious!, you can't be serious!
(d) *(vielleicht)* perhaps, possibly; *(etwa)* about ◆ **ob ~ noch jemand kommt?** I wonder if anybody else is coming?; **das kann man sich ~ vorstellen, nicht wahr?** you can just imagine something like that, can't you?; **das mag ~ sein** that may well be; **willst du das ~ lassen!** I wish you'd stop (doing) that.
(e) *(durchaus)* well ◆ **das kann ~ mal vorkommen** that might well happen; **ich denke, ich verstehe dich sehr ~!** I think I understand you very *or* perfectly well; **doch, das glaube ich ~** I certainly do believe it; **sehr ~ (der Herr)!** *(old)* very good (sir); **~!** *(doch)* yes!; *(S Ger, Sw: selbstverständlich)* of course!
[2] *conj (zwar)* **er hat es ~ versprochen, aber ...** he may have promised, but ...; **~, aber ...** that may well be, but ...
Wohl *nt* **-(e)s,** *no pl* welfare, well-being ◆ **das öffentliche ~ und das ~ des Individuums** the public good *or* common weal and the welfare of the individual; **der Menschheit zum ~e** for the benefit of mankind; **das ~ und Weh(e)** the weal and woe; **zu eurem ~** for your benefit *or* good; **zum ~!** cheers!; **auf dein ~!** your health!; **auf jds ~ trinken** to drink sb's health.
Wohl-: w~an *interj (old, poet)* come *or* well now; **w~anständig** *adj* respectable; *Benehmen* proper, correct; **w~auf** [1] *adj pred* well, in good health; [2] *interj siehe* **w~an; ⚠w~ausgewogen** *adj, comp* **besser ausgewogen,** *superl* **bestausgewogen** (well) balanced; **⚠w~bedacht** *adj, comp* **besser bedacht,** *superl* **bestbedacht** well considered; **~befinden** *nt* well-being; **⚠w~begründet** *adj, comp* **besser begründet,** *superl* **bestbegründet** well-founded; *Maßnahme, Strafe* well-justified; **~behagen** *nt* feeling of well-being; **w~behalten** *adj Mensch* safe and sound; *Gegenstand* intact; **⚠w~bekannt** *adj, comp* **besser bekannt,** *superl* **bestbekannt** well-known; **sie ist mir w~bekannt** I know her well; **w~beleibt** *adj (hum)* stout, portly; **⚠w~beraten** *adj, comp* **besser beraten,** *superl* **bestberaten** well-advised; **w~bestallt** *adj attr (form)* well-established; **⚠w~durchdacht** *adj, comp* **besser durchdacht,** *superl* **bestdurchdacht** well *or* carefully thought out; **~ergehen** *nt* **-s,** *no pl* welfare; **⚠w~erprobt** *adj, comp* **besser erprobt,** *superl* **besterprobt** well-tested, well-tried; *Mitarbeiter* experienced; **w~erwogen** *adj, comp* **besser erwogen,** *superl* **besterwogen** well *or* carefully considered; **w~erzogen** *adj, comp* **besser erzogen,** *superl* **besterzogen** *(geh)* well-bred; *Kind* well-mannered; **w~erzogen sein/sich w~erzogen benehmen** to be well-bred/well-mannered.
Wohlfahrt *f* **-,** *no pl* **(a)** *(old geh: Wohlergehen)* welfare. **(b)** *(Fürsorge)* welfare ◆ **bei der ~ arbeiten** to do welfare work.
Wohlfahrts-: ~amt *nt (dated, inf) siehe* **Sozialamt; ⚠~ausschuß** *m (Hist)* Committee of Public Safety; **~einrichtung** *f* social service; **~marke** *f* charity stamp; **~organisation** *f* charity, charitable institution *or* organization; **~pflege** *f* social *or* welfare work; **freie ~pflege** voluntary social *or* welfare work; **~rente** *f* benefit pension; **~staat** *m* welfare state; **~unterstützung** *f (dated) siehe* **Sozialhilfe.**
Wohl-: w~feil *adj, comp* **w~feiler,** *superl* **w~feilste(r, s)** *(old, liter)* inexpensive; **w~geboren** *adj (obs)* **Eure** *or* **Euer ~geboren** Sir; **Seiner ~geboren Herr XY** XY Esq; **~gefallen** *nt* **-s,** *no pl* satisfaction, pleasure; **sein ~gefallen an etw** *(dat)* **haben** to take pleasure in sth; **sich in ~gefallen auflösen** *(hum) (Freundschaft, Argument)* to peter out; *(Plan, Problem)* to vanish into thin air; *(Auto, Kleidung)* to fall apart; **w~gefällig** *adj (gefallend)* pleasing; *(zufrieden, erfreut)* well-pleased; **Gott w~gefällig** well-pleasing to God; **w~geformt** *adj, comp* **besser geformt,** *superl* **bestgeformt** well-shaped; *Körperteil* shapely; *Satz* well-formed; **~gefühl** *nt* feeling *or* sense of well-being; **w~gelitten** *adj, comp* **w~gelittener,** *superl* **w~gelittenste(r, s)** *(geh)* well-liked; **⚠w~gemeint** *adj, comp* **besser gemeint,** *superl* **bestgemeint** well-meant, well-intentioned; **w~gemerkt** *adv* mark you, mind (you); **das waren w~gemerkt englische Pfund** that was English pounds, mark *or* mind you; **w~gemut** *adj, comp* **w~gemuter,** *superl* **w~gemuteste(r, s)** *(old, liter)* cheerful; **w~genährt** *adj, comp* **w~genährter,** *superl* **w~genährteste(r, s)** well-fed; **⚠w~geordnet** *adj, comp* **besser geordnet,** *superl* **bestgeordnet** *(geh)* well-ordered; *Leben auch* well-regulated; **w~geraten** *adj, comp* **w~geratener,** *superl* **w~geratenste(r, s)** *(geh) Kind* fine; *Werk* successful; **~geruch** *m (geh)* pleasant smell; *(von Garten, Blumen etc auch)* fragrance; **~geschmack** *m (geh)* flavour, pleasant taste; **w~gesinnt** *adj, comp* **w~gesinnter,** *superl* **w~gesinnteste(r, s)** *(geh)* well-disposed *(dat* towards); *Worte* well-meaning; **w~gestalt** *adj (geh) Gegenstand* well-shaped; *Körperteil, Frau* shapely; *Mann* well-proportioned; **w~gestaltet** *adj, comp* **w~gestalteter,** *superl* **w~gestaltetste(r, s)** well-shaped, well-proportioned; **w~getan** *adj (old, liter)* well done *pred*; **w~habend** *adj, comp* **w~habender,** *superl* **w~habendste(r, s)** well-to-do, prosperous; **~habenheit** *f* prosperity, affluence.
wohlig *adj* pleasant; *(gemütlich)* cosy; *Ruhe* blissful ◆ **~ rekelte er sich in der Sonne** he stretched luxuriously in the sun.
Wohl-: ~klang *m (geh)* melodious sound; **w~klingend** *adj, comp* **w~klingender,** *superl* **w~klingendste(r, s)** pleasant(-sounding), melodious; **~leben** *nt (geh)* life of luxury; **w~meinend** *adj, comp* **w~meinender,** *superl* **w~meinendste(r, s)** well-meaning; **w~proportioniert** *adj, comp* **besser proportioniert,** *superl* **bestproportioniert** well-proportioned; **w~riechend** *adj, comp* **w~riechender,** *superl* **w~riechendste(r, s)** *(geh)* fragrant; **w~schmeckend** *adj, comp* **w~schmeckender,** *superl* **w~schmeckendste(r, s)** *(geh)* palatable; **~sein** *nt*: **zum/auf Ihr ~sein!**

your health!

Wohlstand *m* **-(e)s,** *no pl* affluence, prosperity; *siehe* **ausbrechen.**

Wohlstands-: ~bürger *m (pej)* member of the affluent society; **~gesellschaft** *f* affluent society; **~kriminalität** *f crimes typical of the affluent society;* **~müll** *m* refuse of the affluent society.

Wohltat *f* **(a)** *(Genuß)* relief. **(b)** *(Dienst, Gefallen)* favour; *(gute Tat)* good deed ♦ **jdm eine ~ erweisen** to do sb a favour *or* a good turn.

Wohltäter(in *f*) *m* benefactor; benefactress.

wohltätig *adj* **(a)** charitable. **(b)** *(dial) siehe* **wohltuend.**

Wohltätigkeit *f* charity, charitableness.

Wohltätigkeits-: ~basar *m* charity bazaar; **~konzert** *nt* charity concert; **~verein** *m* charitable organization, charity; **~zweck** *m* charitable cause, good cause.

Wohl-: ⚠**w~temperiert** *adj, comp* **besser temperiert,** *superl* **besttemperiert** *Wein, Bad, Zimmer* at the right temperature *no comp;* **das „~temperierte Klavier"** "The Well-Tempered Clavier"; **w~tuend** *adj, comp* **w~tuender,** *superl* **w~tuendste(r, s)** (most) agreeable; ⚠**w~tun** *vi sep irreg* **(a)** *(angenehm sein)* to do good *(jdm* sb), to be beneficial *(jdm* to sb); **das tut w~** that's good; **(b)** *(old, liter: Gutes tun)* to benefit *(jdm* sb); ⚠**w~überlegt** *adj, comp* **besser überlegt,** *superl* **bestüberlegt** well thought out; **etw w~überlegt machen** to do sth after careful consideration; ⚠**w~unterrichtet** *adj attr* well-informed; **w~verdient** *adj Strafe* well-deserved; *Belohnung, Ruhe etc auch* well-earned; **~verhalten** *nt (usu iro)* good conduct *or* behaviour; ⚠**w~versorgt** *adj, comp* **besser versorgt,** *superl* **bestversorgt** well-provided; **w~verstanden** [1] *adj attr (geh)* well-understood; [2] *adv* mark *or* mind you; **w~weislich** *adv* very wisely; **ich habe das w~weislich nicht gemacht** I was careful not to do that; ⚠**w~wollen** *vi sep irreg (geh)* **jdm w~wollen** to wish sb well; **~wollen** *nt* **-s,** *no pl* goodwill; **selbst bei dem größten ~wollen** with the best will in the world; **jdn mit ~wollen betrachten** to regard sb benevolently; **sich** *(dat)* **jds ~wollen erwerben** to win sb's favour; **w~wollend** *adj, comp* **w~wollender,** *superl* **w~wollendste(r, s)** benevolent; **jdm w~wollend geneigt** *or* **gesonnen sein, jdm gegenüber w~wollend sein** to be kindly disposed towards sb.

Wohn-: ~anhänger *m* caravan; **~bau** *m, pl* **-ten** residential building; **~bevölkerung** *f* residential population; **~block** *m, pl* **-s** block of flats, apartment house *(US);* **~container** *m* Portakabin ®; **~dichte** *f (Sociol)* occupant density; **~diele** *f* hall-cum-living-room; **~einheit** *f* accommodation unit.

wohnen *vi* **(a)** to live; *(vorübergehend)* to stay ♦ **wo ~ Sie?** where do you live/are you staying?; **er wohnt (in der) Friedrichstraße 11** he lives at (number) 11 Friedrichstraße; **wir ~ sehr schön** we have a very nice flat/house *etc;* **wir ~ da sehr schön** it's very nice where we live; **hier wohnt es sich gut, hier läßt es sich gut ~** it's a nice place to live/stay.
(b) *(fig liter)* to dwell *(liter),* to live.

Wohn-: ~fläche *f* living space; **50m² ~fläche** living room(, dining room) and bedroom(s) totalling 50 sq m; **~gebäude** *nt siehe* **~bau; ~gebiet** *nt* residential area; **~gegend** *f* residential area; **~geld** *nt* housing benefit; **~gemeinschaft** *f (Menschen)* people sharing a/the flat *(Brit) or* apartment/house; **unsere ~gemeinschaft** the people I share a flat *etc* with; **in einer ~gemeinschaft leben** to share a flat *etc;* **~gift** *nt* poisonous substance found in the home; **w~haft** *adj (form)* resident; **~haus** *nt* residential building; **~heim** *nt (esp für Arbeiter)* hostel; *(für Studenten)* hall (of residence), dormitory *(US); (für alte Menschen)* home; **~komfort** *m* comfort of one's home; **ein Appartement mit sämtlichem ~komfort** an apartment with every modern convenience *or* all mod cons; **~komplex** *m* housing estate; **~küche** *f* kitchen-cum-living-room; **~kultur** *f* style of home décor; **keine ~kultur haben** to have no taste in home décor; **~lage** *f* residential area; **unsere ~lage ist schön/ungünstig** our house/apartment is nicely/awkwardly situated; **~landschaft** *f* landscaped interior; **w~lich** *adj* homely, cosy; **es sich** *(dat)* **w~lich machen** to make oneself comfortable; **~lichkeit** *f* homeliness, cosiness; **~mobil** dormobile ®, camper, motor caravan, RV *(US);* **~objekt** *nt (Aus form)* accommodation unit; **~ort** *m* place of residence; **~partei** *f (esp Aus)* tenant; *(mehrere Personen)* tenants *pl;* **~qualität** *f* quality of housing; **~raum** *m* living-room; *(no pl: ~fläche)* living space; **~-Schlafzimmer** *nt* bed-sitting-room; **~siedlung** *f* housing estate *(Brit) or* scheme *or* development; **~silo** *m (pej)* concrete block; **~sitz** *m* domicile; **ohne festen ~sitz** of no fixed abode; **~stadt** *f* residential town; **~stube** *f siehe* **~zimmer; ~turm** *m* tower block.

Wohnung *f* flat *(Brit),* apartment; *(liter: von Tieren etc)* habitation; *(Wohneinheit)* dwelling *(form); (Unterkunft)* lodging ♦ **1.000 neue ~en** 1,000 new homes; **~ nehmen** *(form)* to take up residence *(form);* **freie ~ haben** to have free lodging.

Wohnungs-: ~amt *nt* housing office; **~bau** *m, no pl* house building *no def art;* **~bauprogramm** *nt* housing programme; **~bedarf** *m* housing requirements *pl;* **~besetzer(in** *f*) *m* **-s,** squatter; **~inhaber** *m* householder, occupant; *(Eigentümer auch)* owner-occupier; **w~los** *adj (form)* homeless; **~makler** *m* estate agent, real estate agent *(US);* **~mangel** *m* housing shortage; **~markt** *m* housing market; **~nachweis** *m* accommodation registry; **~not** *f* serious housing shortage *or* lack of housing; **~suche** *f* flat-hunting *(Brit);* **auf ~suche sein** to be looking for a flat *(Brit) or* apartment, to be flat-hunting *(Brit);* **w~suchend** *adj attr* looking for accommodation; **~tausch** *m* exchange (of flats/houses); **~tür** *f* door (to the flat *(Brit) or* apartment); **~wechsel** *m* change of address; **~wesen** *nt* housing.

Wohn-: ~verhältnisse *pl (von Familie)* living conditions *pl; (in Stadt)* housing conditions *pl;* **~viertel** *nt* residential area *or* district; **~wagen** *m* caravan *(Brit),* trailer *(US);* **~wert** *m* **einen hohen ~wert haben** to be an attractive place to live in; **~zimmer** *nt* living-room; **~zwecke** *pl* residential purposes *pl.*

Wok *m* **-s, -s** *(Cook)* wok.

wölben [1] *vt* to curve; *Blech etc* to bend; *Dach etc* to vault.
[2] *vr* to curve; *(Asphalt)* to bend *or* buckle; *(Tapete)* to bulge out; *(Brust)* to swell; *(Stirn)* to be domed; *(Decke, Brücke)* to arch ♦ **ein klarer Sternenhimmel wölbte sich über uns** the clear sky formed a star-studded dome above us *(liter).*

Wölbung *f* curvature; *(kuppelförmig)* dome; *(bogenförmig)* arch; *(von Körperteil)* curve; *(von Straße)* camber; *(von Tapete)* bulge.

Wolf *m* **-(e)s, ⸚e (a)** wolf ♦ **ein ~ im Schafspelz** a wolf in sheep's clothing; **mit den ⸚en heulen** *(fig)* to run with the pack.
(b) *(Tech)* shredder; *(Fleisch~)* mincer *(Brit),* grinder *(US)* ♦ **jdn durch den ~ drehen** *(fig)* to put sb through his paces; **ich fühle mich wie durch den ~ gedreht** I feel as if I've been on the rack.
(c) *(Med)* intertrigo *no art (spec) (inflammation of the skin between the buttocks).*

Wölfchen *nt dim of* **Wolf** wolf-cub.

Wölfin *f* she-wolf.

wölfisch *adj* wolfish.

Wölfling *m (Pfadfinder)* cub (scout).

Wolfram *nt* **-s,** *no pl (abbr* **W)** tungsten, wolfram.

Wolfs-: ~hund *m* Alsatian *(Brit),* German shepherd *(US);* **irischer ~hund** Irish wolfhound; **~hunger** *m (fig inf)* ravenous hunger; **ich hatte einen ~hunger** I was ravenous; **~mensch** *m* **(a)** wolf child; **er war ein ~mensch** he had been reared by wolves; **(b)** *(Werwolf)* werewolf; **~milch** *f (Bot)* spurge; **~rachen** *m (Med)* cleft palate; **~rudel** *nt* pack of wolves; **~spinne** *f* wolf spider.

Wolga *f* - Volga.

Wölkchen *nt dim of* **Wolke.**

Wolke *f* **-, -n** *(lit, fig)* cloud; *(in Edelstein)* flaw ♦ **aus allen ~n fallen** *(fig)* to be flabbergasted *(inf);* **das ist 'ne ~** *(inf)* it's fantastic *(inf); siehe* **schweben.**

Wolken-: ~bank *f* cloudbank; **~bildung** *f* cloud formation; **es kann zu ~bildung kommen** it may become cloudy *or* overcast; **~bruch** *m* cloudburst; **w~bruchartig** *adj* torrential; **~decke** *f* cloud cover; **die Stadt liegt unter einer dichten ~decke** the town lies under a heavy layer of cloud; **~himmel** *m* cloudy *or* overcast sky; **~kratzer** *m* skyscraper; **~kuckucksheim** *nt* cloud-cuckoo-land; **in einem ~kuckucksheim leben** to live in cloud-cuckoo-land; **~landschaft** *f (liter)* clouds *pl;* **w~los** *adj* cloudless; **~meer** *nt (liter)* sea of clouds; **~schicht** *f* layer of cloud, cloud layer; **~schleier** *m (liter)* veil of cloud *(liter);* **von einem ~schleier eingehüllt** veiled in cloud; **~streifen** *m* streak of cloud; **w~verhangen** *adj* overcast; **~wand** *f* cloudbank.

wolkig *adj* cloudy; *(fig)* obscure.

Wolldecke *f* (woollen) blanket.

Wolle *f* **-, -n** wool ♦ **in der ~ gefärbt** *(fig)* dyed-in-the-wool; **mit jdm in die ~ kommen** *or* **geraten, sich mit jdm in die ~ kriegen** *(fig inf)* to start squabbling with sb; **sich mit jdm in der ~ haben** *(fig inf)* to be at loggerheads with sb.

wollen¹ *adj attr* woollen.

▼ **wollen²** *1. pers present* **will,** *pret* **wollte,** *ptp* **gewollt** [1] *vi* **(a)** *(Willen zeigen, haben)* **er kann schon, wenn er nur will** he can (do it) if he really wants (to); **man muß nur ~** you simply have to have the will; **man muß sich nur sagen: ich will** you only have to say: I will do it; **da ist nichts zu ~** there is nothing we/you can do (about it).
(b) *(bereit, gewillt sein)* **wenn er will** if he wants to; **er will nicht so recht** he doesn't seem all that willing, he seems rather unwilling; **so Gott will** God willing.
(c) *(mögen)* to want to, to like ♦ **wenn man so will, wenn du so willst** if you like, as it were; **ganz wie du willst** just as you like; **wenn du willst, machen wir das so** if you want to *or* if you like, we'll do it that way; **wer nicht will, der hat schon** if you don't/he doesn't like it, you/he can lump it *(inf);* **ob du willst oder nicht** whether you like it or not.
(d) *(an bestimmten Ort gehen etc)* to want to go ♦ **ich will nach Hause/hier raus/weg** I want to go home/to get out of here/to get away; **er will unbedingt ins Kino** he is set on going *or* determined to go to the cinema; **wo willst du hin?** where do you want to go?; **zu wem ~ Sie?** whom do you want to see?
[2] *vt* **(a)** to want ♦ **er will doch nur dein Bestes** he only wants the best for you; **~, daß jd etw tut** to want sb to do sth; **was wollten sie denn von dir?** what did they want then?; **was willst du (noch) mehr!** what more do you want!; **ich weiß nicht, was du willst, das ist doch ausgezeichnet** I don't know what you're on about, it's excellent; **er hat gar nichts zu ~** he has no say at all; **ohne es zu ~** without wanting to; **das wollte ich nicht** *(war unbeabsichtigt)* I didn't mean to (do that); **was ~ sie?** what do they want?; *siehe* **gewollt.**
(b) etw lieber ~ to prefer sth; **etw unbedingt ~** to want sth desperately.
(c) *(bezwecken)* **etw mit etw ~** to want sth with sth, to want sth for sth; **was willst du mit dem Messer?** what are you doing with that knife?; **was willst du mit der Frage?** why are you asking that?; **was ~ die Leute mit solchen Filmen?** what do people hope to achieve with films like that?
(d) *(brauchen)* to want, to need.
▼ [3] *modal aux vb ptp* **~ (a) etw haben ~** to want (to have) sth; **ich will so einen Fehler nie wieder machen** I won't make a mistake like that again; **er will immer alles besser wissen** he thinks he knows it all; **was will man da schon machen/sagen?** what can you do/say?; **wenn man darauf noch Rücksicht**

⚠: for details of spelling reform, see supplement

➤ SPRACHE AKTIV: **wollen: 3a** → 52.2, 53.5

nehmen wollte if one were to take that into account too.
▼(b) (*beabsichtigen*) **etw gerade tun ~** to be going to do sth; **wolltest du gerade weggehen?** were you just leaving?; **ich wollte schon gehen/gerade aufhören, als ...** I was just going to leave/just about to stop when ...
(c) (*werden*) **das ~ wir doch erst mal sehen!** we'll have to see about that!
(d) (*Anschein haben*) **es sieht aus, als wollte es regnen** it looks as if it's going to rain; **es will nicht besser/wärmer werden** it just won't get better/warmer; **es will und will nicht aufhören** it just goes on and on; **er will und will sich nicht ändern** he just will not change.
(e) (*in bezug auf Behauptung*) **keiner wollte etwas gehört/gesehen haben** nobody will admit to having heard/seen anything; **keiner will es gewesen sein** nobody will admit to it; **der Zeuge will den Dieb beobachtet haben** the witness claims to have seen the thief; **und so jemand will Lehrer sein!** and he calls himself a teacher.
(f) (*in Wunsch, Aufforderung*) **ich wollte, ich wäre ...** I wish I were ...; **das wolle Gott verhüten** heaven forbid; **~ wir uns nicht setzen?** why don't we sit down?; **wir ~ beten!** let us pray; **man wolle bitte ...** would you kindly ...; **wenn Sie bitte Platz nehmen ~** if you would care to sit down please; **wenn er mir das doch ersparen wollte!** if only he would spare me that!; **na, ~ wir gehen?** well, shall we go?; **darauf ~ wir mal anstoßen!** let's drink to that; **wir ~ mal nicht übertreiben/in Ruhe überlegen** let's not exaggerate/let's think about it calmly.
(g) **komme, was da wolle** come what may; **sei er, wer er wolle** whoever he may be.
(h) *impers* **es will mir nicht einleuchten, warum** I really can't see why; **es will mir scheinen, daß ...** it seems to me that ...
(i) (*müssen*) **das will alles genauestens überlegt sein/werden** it all has to be most carefully considered; **die Pflanzen ~ oft gegossen werden** the plants have to be watered frequently.

Woll-: ~faser *f* wool fibre; **~fett** *nt* wool-fat, lanolin; **~garn** *nt* woollen yarn; **~gras** *nt* (*Bot*) cotton grass.

wollig *adj* woolly.

Woll-: ~jacke *f* cardigan; **~kämmerei** *f* (a) (*Fabrik*) wool-carding shop; (b) (*Tätigkeit*) wool-carding; **~knäuel** *nt* ball of wool; **~sachen** *pl* woollens *pl*; **~siegel** *nt* Woolmark ®; **~spinnerei** *f* (a) (*Fabrik*) woolmill; (b) (*Tätigkeit*) wool-spinning; **~stoff** *m* woollen material; **~strumpf** *m* woollen stocking.

Wollust *f* -, *no pl* (*liter*) (*Sinnlichkeit*) sensuality, voluptuousness; (*Lüsternheit*) lust, lewdness, lasciviousness ◆ **~ empfinden** to be in ecstasy; **etw mit wahrer ~ tun** (*fig*) to delight in doing sth.

wollüstig *adj* (*geh*) (*sinnlich*) sensual; *Frau auch* voluptuous; (*lüstern*) lascivious, lusty; (*verzückt, ekstatisch*) ecstatic ◆ **seine ~e Freude an etw** (*dat*) **haben** (*fig*) to go into ecstasies over sth; **jdn ~ anblicken** to give sb a lascivious look; **sich ~ im warmen Bad rekeln** to luxuriate in a warm bath.

Wollüstling *m* (*hum inf*) sensualist.

Woll-: ~waren *pl* woollen goods *pl*, woollens *pl*; **~wäsche** *f* washing woollens *no art*; (*Artikel*) woollens *pl*; **~waschmittel** *nt* detergent for woollens.

womit *adv siehe auch* **mit** (a) *interrog* with what, what ... with ◆ **~ kann ich dienen?** what can I do for you?
(b) *rel* with which; (*auf ganzen Satz bezüglich*) by which ◆ **ein Gerät, ~ man auch bohren kann** an appliance you can drill with too; **das ist es, ~ ich nicht einverstanden bin** that's what I don't agree with; **~ ich nicht sagen will, daß ...** by which I don't mean *or* which doesn't mean to say that ...; **~ man es auch versuchte ...** whatever they tried to do it with ...

womöglich *adv* possibly; *siehe* **wo**.

wonach *adv siehe auch* **nach** (a) *interrog* after what, what ... after ◆ **~ sehnst du dich?** what do you long for?; **~ riecht das?** what does it smell of?; **~ sollen wir uns richten?** what should we go by?
(b) *rel* **das Land, ~ du dich sehnst** the land for which you are longing *or* (which) you are longing for; **das war es, ~ ich mich erkundigen wollte** that was what I wanted to ask about; **die Nachricht, ~ er ...** the news that he ...

Wonne *f* -, -n (*geh*) (*Glückseligkeit*) bliss *no pl*; (*Vergnügen*) joy, delight ◆ **mit ~** with great delight; **(aber) mit ~!** with great pleasure!; **das ist ihre ganze ~** that's all her joy; **in eitel ~ schwimmen** to be lost in rapture; **die ~n der Liebe/~(n) des Paradieses** the joys *or* delights of love/delights of paradise; **es ist eine wahre ~** it's a sheer delight.

Wonne-: ~gefühl *nt* blissful feeling; **~monat, ~mond** (*poet*) *m* May; **im ~monat Mai** in the merry month of May; **~proppen** *m* (*hum inf*) bundle of joy; **~schauer** *m* thrill of joy; **~schrei** *m* cry of delight; **w~voll** *adj Gefühl* blissful; *Kind, Anblick* delightful; *Gesichtsausdruck* delighted.

wonnig *adj* delightful; *Gefühl, Ruhe* blissful.

wonniglich *adj* (*poet*) *Gefühl, Stunden* blissful; *Kind, Anblick* delightful.

woran *adv siehe auch* **an** (a) *interrog* **~ soll ich den Kleiderbügel hängen?** what shall I hang the coat-hanger on?; **~ denkst du?** what are you thinking about?; **man weiß bei ihm nie, ~ man ist** you never know where you are with him; **~ liegt das?** what's the reason for it?; **~ ist er gestorben?** what did he die of?
(b) *rel* (*auf vorausgehenden Satz bezogen*) by which ◆ **das, ~ ich mich gerne erinnere** what I like to recall; **die Wand, ~ sie immer die Plakate kleben** the wall on which they are always sticking posters, the wall they're always sticking posters on; **..., ~ ich schon gedacht hatte** ... which I'd already thought of; **~ ich merkte, daß ...** which made me realize that ...; **~ er auch immer gestorben ist ...** whatever he died of ...

worauf *adv siehe auch* **auf** (a) *interrog* (*räumlich*) on what, what ... on ◆ **~ wartest du?** what are you waiting for?; **~ sollte ich mich freuen?** what do I have to look forward to?
(b) *rel* (*zeitlich*) whereupon ◆ **~ du dich verlassen kannst** of that you can be sure; **das ist etwas, ~ ich mich freue** that's something I'm looking forward to; **das, ~ er sich vorbereitet hatte** what he was prepared for; **~ er einen Wutanfall bekam** whereupon he flew into a rage; **~ er sich auch beruft ...** whatever his arguments are ...

woraufhin *rel adv* whereupon.

woraus *adv siehe auch* **aus** (a) *interrog* out of what, what ... out of ◆ **~ ist der Pullover?** what is the pullover made (out) of?; **~ schließt du das?** from what do you deduce that?
(b) *rel* out of which, which ... out of ◆ **das Buch, ~ ich gestern vorgelesen habe** the book I was reading from yesterday; **~ ich schließe/gelernt habe, daß ...** from which I conclude/have learned that ...; **~ man das Öl auch gewinnt ...** whatever oil is obtained from ...

worden *ptp of* **werden 1 (c)**.

worein *adv siehe auch* **hinein** (a) *interrog* in what, what ... in. (b) *rel* in which, which ... in ◆ **das ist etwas, ~ ich mich nie fügen werde** that's something I shall never submit to *or* put up with.

worfeln *vti* (*Agr*) to winnow.

worin *adv siehe auch* **in** (a) *interrog* in what, what ... in ◆ **~ war das eingewickelt?** what was it wrapped in?; **~ liegt der Unterschied/Vorteil?** what is the difference/advantage?
(b) *rel* in which, which ... in, wherein (*form*) ◆ **das ist etwas, ~ wir nicht übereinstimmen** that's something we don't agree on; **dann sagte er ..., ~ ich mit ihm übereinstimme** then he said ..., which is where I agree with him; **~ du es auch einwickelst ...** whatever you wrap it in ...

Workshop ['vøːɐkʃɔp] *m* -s, -s workshop.

Workstation ['vøːɐksteɪʃn] *f* -, -s (*Comput*) work station.

Wort *nt* -(e)s, -e (a) *pl usu* ¨er (*Vokabel*) word ◆ **ein ~ mit sechs Buchstaben** a word with six letters, a six-letter word; **~ für ~** word for word; *siehe* **wahr**.
(b) (*Äußerung*) word ◆ **nichts als ~e** nothing but words *or* talk; **genug der ~e!** enough talk!; **das ist ein ~!** wonderful!; **in ~ und Schrift** in speech and writing; **er beherrscht die Sprache in ~ und Schrift** he has a command of the written and spoken language; **in ~ und Tat** in word and deed; **in ~en und Werken sündigen** to sin in words and deeds; **~en Taten folgen lassen** to suit the action to the word(s); **mit einem ~** in a word; **mit anderen/wenigen ~en** in other/a few words; **hast du/hat der Mensch (da noch) ~e!** it leaves you speechless; **kein ~ mehr** not another word; **kein ~ von etw sagen/erwähnen/fallenlassen** not to say one word *or* a thing about sth; **kein ~ von etw wissen/verstehen** not to know/understand a thing about sth; **ich verstehe kein ~!** I don't understand a word (of it); (*hören*) I can't hear a word (that's being said); **er sagte** *or* **sprach kein einziges ~** he didn't say a single word; **ein ~ mit jdm sprechen** *or* **reden** to have a word with sb; **mit dir habe ich noch ein ~ zu reden!** I want a word with you!; **ein ernstes ~ mit jdm reden** to have a serious talk with sb; **kein ~ miteinander/mit jdm sprechen** *or* **reden** not to say a word to each other/to sb; **hättest du doch ein ~ gesagt** if only you had said something; **davon hat man mir kein ~ gesagt** they didn't tell me anything about it; **man kann sein eigenes ~ nicht (mehr) verstehen** *or* **hören** you can't hear yourself speak; **er brach in die ~e aus: ...** he burst out: ...; **um nicht viel(e) ~e zu machen** to make it brief; **ich konnte kein ~ anbringen** I couldn't get a word in edgeways; **ein ~ gab das andere** one thing led to another; **jdm das ~** *or* **die ~e im Mund (her)umdrehen** to twist sb's words; **du sprichst ein großes** *or* **wahres ~ gelassen aus** how true, too true; **die passenden/keine ~e für etw finden** to find the right/no words for sth; **das rechte ~ zur rechten Zeit** the right word at the right time; **jdn mit schönen ~en abspeisen** to fob sb off; **er hat nur schöne ~e gemacht** it was just talk; **auf ein ~!** a word!; **jdm aufs ~ glauben** to believe sb implicitly; **das glaub ich dir aufs ~** I can well believe it; **ohne ein ~ (zu sagen)** without (saying) a word; **dein ~ in Gottes Ohr** let us hope so; **seine ~e galten dir** he meant you, he was talking about you; *siehe* **verlieren**.
(c) *no pl* (*Rede, Recht zu sprechen*) **das ~ nehmen** to speak; (*bei Debatte auch*) to take the floor; **das große ~ haben** *or* **führen** (*inf*) to shoot one's mouth off (*inf*); **einer Sache** (*dat*) **das ~ reden** to put the case for sth; **das ~ an jdn richten** to address (oneself to) sb; **jdm ins ~ fallen** to interrupt sb; **jdm das ~ abschneiden** to cut sb short; **zu ~ kommen** to get a chance to speak; **ums ~ bitten, sich zu ~ melden** to ask to speak; **er hat das ~** it's his turn to speak; (*bei Debatte auch*) he has the floor; **jdm das ~ erteilen** *or* **geben** to allow sb to speak; (*in Debatte auch*) to allow sb to take the floor; **er hat mir das ~ verboten** he forbade me to speak; **(bei jdm) im ~ stehen** *or* **sein** to have given one's word (to sb), to have made a commitment (to sb).
(d) (*Ausspruch*) saying; (*Zitat*) quotation; (*Rel*) Word ◆ **ein ~, das er immer im Munde führt** one of his favourite sayings; **ein ~ Goethes/aus der Bibel** a quotation from Goethe/the Bible; **das ~ zum Sonntag** *short religious broadcast on Saturday night*, ≃ late call (*Brit*); **nach dem ~ des Evangeliums** according to the Gospel.
(e) (*Text, Sprache*) words *pl* ◆ **in ~en** in words; **in ~ und Bild** in words and pictures; **etw in ~e fassen** to put sth into words; **das geschriebene/gedruckte/gesprochene ~** the written/printed/spoken word; **das ~ als Kommunikationsmittel** language as a means of communication.
(f) (*Befehl, Entschluß*) **das ~ des Vaters ist ausschlaggebend** the father's word is law; **das ~ des Königs** the king's command; **jdm aufs ~ gehorchen** *or* **folgen** to obey sb's every word; **dabei habe ich auch (noch) ein ~ mitzureden** *or* **mitzusprechen** I (still) have something to say about that too; **das letzte ~ ist noch nicht gesprochen** the final decision hasn't been taken yet.

(g) *no pl* (*Versprechen*) word ◆ **auf mein ~** I give (you) my word; **jdn beim ~ nehmen** to take sb at his word; **ich gebe mein ~ darauf** I give you my word on it; **sein ~ halten** to keep one's word.

Wort-: ~akzent *m* word stress; **~art** *f* (*Gram*) part of speech; **~aufwand** *m* verbosity; **~auswahl** *f* choice of words; **~bedeutung** *f* meaning of a/the word; **~bildung** *f* (*Ling*) morphology; **~bruch** *m* **das wäre ein ~bruch** that would be breaking your/my *etc* promise; **w~brüchig** *adj* false; **w~brüchig werden** to break one's word.

Wörtchen *nt dim of* **Wort** little word ◆ **da habe ich wohl ein ~ mitzureden** (*inf*) I think I have some say in that; **mit ihm habe ich noch ein ~ zu reden** (*inf*) I want a word with him.

Wörter-: ~buch *nt* dictionary; **~verzeichnis** *nt* vocabulary; (*von Spezialbegriffen*) glossary.

Wort-: ~familie *f* word family; **~feld** *nt* semantic field; **~folge** *f* (*Gram*) word order; **~führer** *m* spokesman; **~gebühr** *f* (*Telec*) rate per word; **~gefecht** *nt* battle of words; **~geklingel** *nt* (*pej*) verbiage; ⚠**~geographie** *f* word geography; **~geplänkel** *nt* banter; **w~getreu** *adj, adv* verbatim; **w~gewandt** *adj* eloquent; **~gut** *nt* vocabulary; **~hülse** *f* (*pej*) hollow word; **w~karg** *adj* taciturn; **~kargheit** *f* taciturnity; **~klauber** *m* **-s, -** caviller, quibbler; **~klauberei** *f* cavilling, quibbling; **~kunde** *f* lexicology; (*Vokabelsammlung*) vocabulary; **~laut** *m* wording; **im ~laut** verbatim; **folgenden ~laut haben** to read as follows.

Wörtlein *nt dim of* **Wort**; *siehe* **Wörtchen**.

wörtlich *adj Bedeutung* literal; *Übersetzung, Wiedergabe etc auch* word-for-word; *Rede* direct ◆ **etw ~ wiedergeben/abschreiben** to repeat/copy sth verbatim *or* word for word; **etw ~ übersetzen** to translate sth literally *or* word for word; **das darf man nicht so ~ nehmen** you mustn't take it literally; **das hat er ~ gesagt** those were his very *or* actual words.

Wort-: w~los [1] *adj* silent; [2] *adv* without saying a word; **~meldung** *f* request to speak; **wenn es keine weiteren ~meldungen gibt** if nobody else wishes to speak; **~prägung** *f* (*auch* **~neubildung**) neologism; **ein Meister der ~prägung** a master at coining words; **~rätsel** *nt* word puzzle; **w~reich** *adj Rede, Erklärung etc* verbose, wordy; *Sprache* rich in vocabulary *or* words; **sich w~reich entschuldigen** to apologize profusely; **~reichtum** *m siehe adj* verbosity, wordiness; richness in vocabulary *or* words; **~schatz** *m* vocabulary; **~schöpfung** *f* neologism; **~schwall** *m* torrent of words; **~sinn** *m* meaning of a/the word; **~spiel** *nt* pun, play on words; **~stamm** *m* (*Ling*) root (of a/the word); **~stellung** *f* (*Gram*) word order; **~verdrehung** *f* twisting of words; **~wahl** *f* choice of words; **~wechsel** *m* exchange (of words), verbal exchange; **w~weise** *adj* word for word; **~witz** *m* pun; **w~wörtlich** [1] *adj* word-for-word; [2] *adv* word for word, quite literally.

worüber *adv siehe auch* **über (a)** *interrog* about what, what ... about; (*örtlich*) over what, what ... over.
(b) *rel* about which, which ... about; (*örtlich*) over which, which ... over; (*auf vorausgehenden Satz bezogen*) which ◆ **das Thema, ~ ich gerade einen Artikel gelesen habe** the subject I have just read an article about; **~ sie sich auch unterhalten, sie ...** whatever they talk about they ...

worum *adv siehe auch* **um (a)** *interrog* about what, what ... about ◆ **~ handelt es sich?** what's it about? **(b)** *rel* about which, which ... about ◆ **der Ast, ~ ich die Schnur gebunden hatte** the branch I tied the rope (a)round; **~ die Diskussion auch geht, ...** whatever the discussion is about ...

worunter *adv siehe auch* **unter (a)** *interrog* under what, what ... under ◆ **ich weiß nicht, ~ er leidet** I don't know what he is suffering from. **(b)** *rel* under which, which ... under.

woselbst *rel adv* (*obs*) where.

Wotan *m* **-s** (*Myth*) Wotan.

wovon *adv siehe auch* **von (a)** *interrog* from what, what ... from ◆ **~ hat er das abgeleitet?** what did he derive that from?
(b) *rel* from which, which ... from; (*auf vorausgehenden Satz bezogen*) about which, which ... about ◆ **das ist ein Gebiet, ~ er viel versteht** that is a subject he knows a lot about; **~ du dich auch ernährst, ...** whatever you eat ...

wovor *adv siehe auch* **vor (a)** *interrog* (*örtlich*) before what, what ... before ◆ **~ fürchtest du dich?** what are you afraid of?
(b) *rel* before which, which ... before ◆ **das Ereignis, ~ ich schon immer gewarnt habe** the event I have always warned you about; **~ du dich auch fürchtest, ...** whatever you're afraid of ...

wozu *adv siehe auch* **zu (a)** *interrog* to what, what ... to; (*warum*) why ◆ **~ soll ich das legen?** where shall I put it?; **~ hast du dich entschlossen?** what have you decided on?; **~ soll das gut sein?** what's the point of that?; **~ denn das?** what for?; **~ denn?** why should I/you? *etc.*
(b) *rel* to which, which ... to ◆ **das, ~ ich am meisten neige** what I'm most inclined to do; **das Verfahren, ~ ich raten würde** the procedure I would advise; **..., ~ ich mich jetzt auch entschlossen habe** ... which I have now decided to do; **sie haben geheiratet, ~ ich nichts weiter sagen möchte** they have got married, and I shall say no more about that; **~ du dich auch entschließt, ...** whatever you decide (on) ...

Wrack *nt* **-s, -s** *or* (*rare*) **-e** wreck; (*fig*) (physical) wreck.

Wrackboje, Wracktonne *f* (*Naut*) wreck buoy.

wrang *pret of* **wringen.**

Wrasen *m* **-s, -** (*esp N Ger*) vapour.

wringen, *pret* **wrang,** *ptp* **gewrungen** *vti* to wring.

WS [veːˈ|ɛs] *nt* (*Univ*) *abbr of* **Wintersemester.**

WSW *abbr of* **Westsüdwest** WSW.

Wucher *m* **-s,** *no pl* profiteering; (*bei Geldverleih*) usury ◆ **das ist doch ~!** that's daylight robbery!

Wucherer *m* **-s, -** profiteer; (*Geldverleiher*) usurer.

Wuchergeschäft *nt* profiteering *no pl*; usury *no pl.*

Wucherin *f siehe* **Wucherer.**

wucherisch *adj* profiteering; *Geldverleih, Zinsen* usurious; *Bedingungen, Preis, Miete etc* exorbitant, extortionate.

Wuchermiete *f* exorbitant *or* extortionate rent.

wuchern *vi* **(a)** *aux sein or haben* (*Pflanzen*) to grow rampant, to proliferate; (*wildes Fleisch*) to proliferate; (*Bart, Haare*) to grow profusely ◆ **in die Höhe ~** to shoot up(wards).
(b) (*fig: sich verbreiten*) to be rampant ◆ **sein Haß wuchert im verborgenen** his hatred is quietly intensifying.
(c) (*Kaufmann etc*) to profiteer; (*Geldverleiher*) to practise usury ◆ **mit seinen Talenten ~** (*fig*) to make the most of one's talents.

wuchernd *adj Pflanzen* rampant, proliferous; *Bart, wildes Fleisch* proliferous.

Wucherpreis *m* exorbitant price ◆ **~e bezahlen** to pay through the nose.

Wucherung *f* rank growth, proliferation; (*Med*) growth; (*wildes Fleisch*) proud flesh.

Wucherzins *m* exorbitant *or* usurious interest.

wuchs [vuːks] *pret of* **wachsen**[1].

Wuchs [vuːks] *m* **-es,** *no pl* (*Wachstum*) growth; (*Gestalt, Form*) stature; (*von Mensch*) build, stature.

Wucht *f* **-,** *no pl* **(a)** force; (*von Angriff auch*) brunt; (*Stoßkraft auch*) momentum; (*fig auch*) power ◆ **mit aller ~** with all one's force *or* might; **mit voller ~** with full force.
(b) (*inf: Menge*) load (*inf*) ◆ **eine ~ (Prügel)** a good hiding.
(c) (*inf*) **er/das ist die** *or* **eine ~!** he's/that's smashing! (*inf*).

wuchten *vti* **(a)** to heave. **(b)** *siehe* **auswuchten.**

⚠**Wuchtgeschoß** *nt* stun bullet.

wuchtig *adj* massive, solid; *Schlag* heavy, powerful; *Wein,* (*fig*) heavy.

Wuchtigkeit *f* massiveness, solidness; power; heaviness.

Wühl|arbeit *f* (*fig pej*) subversive activities *pl.*

wühlen [1] *vi* **(a)** (*nach* for) to dig; (*Maulwurf etc*) to burrow; (*Schwein, Vogel*) to root ◆ **im Bett ~** to toss and turn; **im Schmutz ~** (*fig*) to wallow in the mire.
(b) (*suchen*) to rummage, to root (*nach etw* for sth) ◆ **in den Schubladen ~** to rummage *or* root through the drawers.
(c) (*fig*) to gnaw (*in +dat* at).
(d) (*inf: schwer arbeiten*) to slog (*inf*).
(e) (*Untergrundarbeit leisten*) to stir things up.
[2] *vt* to dig, to burrow ◆ **er wühlte seinen Kopf in die Kissen** he buried his face in the pillows.
[3] *vr* **sich durch die Menge/das Gestrüpp/die Akten ~** to burrow one's way through the crowd/the undergrowth/the files.

Wühler *m* **-s, - (a)** (*pej: Aufrührer*) agitator, subversive. **(b)** (*inf: schwer Arbeitender*) slogger (*inf*). **(c)** (*inf: unruhig Schlafender*) wriggler.

Wühlerei *f siehe vi (a, b, d, e)* **(a)** digging; burrowing; rooting. **(b)** rummaging *or* rooting (about). **(c)** (*inf: Arbeiten*) slogging. **(d)** (*Pol inf*) agitation.

Wühl-: ~maus *f* vole; (*fig pej*) subversive; **~tisch** *m* (*inf*) bargain counter.

Wulst *m* **-es, ¨e** *or f* **-, ¨e** bulge; (*an Reifen*) bead; (*an Flasche, Glas*) lip; (*Archit*) torus; (*Her*) wreath; (*Naut*) bulb ◆ **ein ~ von Fett** a roll of fat; **die dicken ¨e seiner Lippen** his thick lips.

wulstig *adj* bulging; *Rand, Lippen* thick.

Wulst-: ~lippen *pl* thick lips *pl*; **~reifen** *m* bead tyre.

wummern *vi* (*inf*) **(a)** (*dröhnen*) to rumble; (*pochen*) to drum ◆ **an** *or* **gegen die Tür ~** to hammer at the door. **(b)** *aux sein* (*dröhnend fahren*) to rumble along.

wund *adj* sore ◆ **etw ~ kratzen/scheuern** to make sth sore by scratching/chafing it; **das Pferd/ich war vom Reiten ~ gescheuert** the horse/I was saddle-sore; **ein Tier ~ schießen** to wound an animal; **sich** (*dat*) **die Füße/Fersen ~ laufen** (*lit*) to get sore feet/heels from walking; (*fig*) to walk one's legs off; **sich** (*dat*) **die Finger ~ schreiben** (*fig*) to write one's fingers to the bone; **sich** (*dat*) **den Mund ~ reden** (*fig*) to talk till one is blue in the face; **ein ~er Punkt, eine ~e Stelle** a sore point; **ein ~es Herz** (*liter*) a wounded heart.

Wund-: ~arzt *m* (*old*) surgeon; **~benzin** *nt* surgical spirit; **~brand** *m* gangrene.

Wunde *f* **-, -n** (*lit, fig*) wound ◆ **alte ~n/eine alte ~ wieder aufreißen** (*fig*) to open up old sores; **an eine alte ~ rühren** (*fig geh*) to touch on a sore point; **(bei jdm) tiefe ~n schlagen** (*fig*) to scar sb; **den Finger auf die (brennende) ~ legen** (*fig*) to bring up a painful subject; **Salz in eine/jds ~ streuen** (*fig*) to turn the knife in the wound; **Balsam** *or* **Öl in eine/jds ~ gießen** *or* **träufeln** (*fig geh*) to comfort sb.

Wunder *nt* **-s, - (a)** (*übernatürliches Ereignis, Rel*) miracle; (*wunderbare Erscheinung*) wonder; (*Leistung auch*) marvel; (*erstaunlicher Mensch*) marvel ◆ **~ tun** *or* **wirken** (*Rel*) to work miracles; **das grenzt an ein ~** it verges on the miraculous, it's almost a miracle; **durch ein ~** by a miracle; **nur durch ein ~ können sie noch gerettet werden** only a miracle can save them now; **die ~ der Natur/dieser Welt** the wonders of nature/this world; **ein architektonisches ~** an architectural miracle.
(b) (*überraschendes Ereignis*) **~ tun** *or* **wirken** to do wonders; **es ist ein/kein ~, daß ...** it's a wonder/no wonder *or* small wonder that ...; **ist es ein ~, daß er dick ist?** is it any wonder that he's fat?; **kein ~** no wonder; **was ~, wenn ...** it's no wonder *or* surprise if ...; *siehe* **blau.**

wunder *adv inv* **meine Eltern denken ~ was passiert ist/~ was über mein Privatleben** my parents think goodness knows what has happened/goodness knows what about my private life; **das hat er sich ~ wie einfach**

⚠: for details of spelling reform, see supplement

vorgestellt he imagined it would be ever so easy; er glaubt, ~ wer zu sein/~ was geleistet zu haben he thinks he's marvellous/done something marvellous; er meint, ~ wie schön das sei he thinks it's fantastic; er bildet sich ~ was ein he thinks he's too wonderful for words.

wunderbar *adj* (a) (*schön*) wonderful, marvellous. (b) (*übernatürlich, wie durch ein Wunder*) miraculous.

wunderbarerweise *adv* miraculously.

Wunder-: ~ding *nt* marvellous thing; daß er überlebt hat, ist ein ~ding that he survived is a miracle; ~doktor *m* wonder doctor; (*pej: Quacksalber*) quack; ~droge *f* (*von Zauberer, Fee etc*) miracle drug; (*fig auch*) wonder drug; ~glaube *m* belief in miracles; w~gläubig *adj* w~gläubig sein to believe in miracles; ein w~gläubiger Mensch a person who believes in miracles; ~heiler *m* wonder doctor; (*pej*) faith-healer; ~horn *nt* (*liter, Myth*) magic horn; w~hübsch *adj* wonderfully pretty, wondrously beautiful (*liter*); ~kerze *f* sparkler; ~kind *nt* child prodigy; ~knabe *m* (*usu iro*) wonder boy *or* child; ~kur *f* (*iro*) miracle cure; ~lampe *f* magic lamp *or* lantern; ~land *nt* wonderland; w~lich *adj* (a) (*merkwürdig*) strange, odd; (b) (*w~sam*) wondrous; ~lichkeit *f siehe adj* (a) strangeness, oddness; (b) wondrousness; ~mittel *nt* miracle cure; (*von Fee etc*) magic potion.

wundern [1] *vt, vt impers* to surprise ◆ es wundert mich *or* mich wundert, daß er noch nicht hier ist I'm surprised *or* it surprises me that he is not here yet; das wundert mich nicht I'm not surprised, that doesn't surprise me; das würde mich nicht ~ I shouldn't be surprised; mich wundert gar nichts mehr nothing surprises me any more.

[2] *vr* to be surprised (*über +acc* at) ◆ du wirst dich ~! you'll be amazed!; ich wunderte mich über seine schnelle Rückkehr I was surprised at *or* about his quick return; du wirst dich noch einmal ~! you're in for a shock *or* surprise!; da wirst du dich aber ~! you're in for a surprise; ich muß mich doch sehr ~! well, I am surprised (at you/him *etc*); ich wundere mich über gar nichts mehr nothing surprises me any more; dann darfst/brauchst du dich nicht ~, wenn ... then don't be surprised if ...

Wunder-: w~nehmen *sep irreg* [1] *vi impers* (*geh*) to be surprising; [2] *vt impers* to surprise; w~sam *adj* (*liter*) wondrous (*liter*); w~schön *adj* beautiful, lovely; (*herrlich auch*) wonderful; einen w~schönen guten Morgen/Tag *etc* a very good morning/day *etc* to you; ~tat *f* miracle; ~täter *m* miracle worker; w~tätig *adj* magic, miraculous; *Leben, Heilige* miracle-working; w~tätig wirken to perform miracles; ~tier *nt* (*hum*) weird and wonderful animal (*hum*); ~tüte *f* surprise packet; w~voll *adj* wonderful, marvellous; ~waffe *f* wonder weapon; ~welt *f* (*im Märchen etc*) magic world; (*zauberhafte Umgebung*) world of wonders; die ~welt der Mineralien the wonderful world of minerals; ~werk *nt* miracle, marvel; ~zeichen *nt* miraculous sign.

Wund-: ~fieber *nt* traumatic fever; ⚠w~gelegen *adj* ein w~gelegener Patient a patient with bedsores; eine w~gelegene Stelle a bedsore; w~gelegen sein to have bedsores; ~heit *f* soreness; ~infektion *f* wound infection; ⚠w~liegen *vr sep irreg* to get bedsores; ~mal *nt* (a) (*Rel*) stigma; (b) (*liter*) scar; ~pflaster *nt* adhesive plaster; ~rand *m* edge (of a/the wound); ~rose *f* (*Med*) erysipelas (*spec*), St Anthony's fire; ~salbe *f* ointment; ~sein *nt* soreness; ~sekret *nt* secretion of a/the wound; ~starrkrampf *m* tetanus; ~versorgung *f* dressing a/the wound/wounds; ~watte *f* surgical wool.

▼ **Wunsch** *m* -(e)s, ¨e (a) wish; (*sehnliches Verlangen*) desire; (*Bitte*) request ◆ ein Pferd war schon immer mein ~ I've always wanted a horse; nach ~ just as he/she *etc* wants/wanted; (*wie geplant*) according to plan, as planned; (*nach Bedarf*) as required; auf *or* nach ~ der Eltern as his/her *etc* parents wish/wished; alles geht nach ~ everything is going smoothly; von dem ~ beseelt sein, ... to be filled with the desire ...; hier ist der ~ der Vater des Gedankens (*prov*) the wish is father to the thought (*prov*); ich habe einen ~ an dich I've a request to make of you; haben Sie (sonst) noch einen ~? (*beim Einkauf etc*) is there anything else you would like *or* I can do for you?; was haben Sie für einen ~? what can I do for you?; auf ~ by *or* on request; auf jds (besonderen/ausdrücklichen) ~ hin at sb's (special/express) request; auf allgemeinen/vielfachen ~ hin by popular request *or* demand; jdm jeden ~ von *or* an den Augen ablesen to anticipate sb's every wish; *siehe* fromm.

▼ (b) *usu pl* (*Glückwunsch*) wish ◆ beste ¨e zum Fest the compliments of the season.

wünschbar *adj* (*Sw*) *siehe* wünschenswert.

Wunsch-: ~bild *nt* ideal; ~denken *nt* wishful thinking.

Wünschelrute *f* divining *or* dowsing rod.

Wünschelrutengänger(in *f*) *m* -s, - diviner, dowser.

▼ **wünschen** [1] *vt* (a) sich (*dat*) etw ~ to want sth; (*den Wunsch äußern*) to ask for sth; (*im stillen: bei Sternschnuppe etc*) to wish for sth; ich wünsche mir das I would like that, I want that; ich wünsche mir, daß du ... I would like you to ...; ... wie ich mir das gewünscht habe ... as I wanted; das habe ich mir von meinen Eltern zu Weihnachten gewünscht I asked my parents to give me that for Christmas, I asked for that for Christmas from my parents; ich wünsche mir einen Mantel von dir I'd like a coat from you; er wünscht sich (*dat*), daß es erfolgreich wird he so wants it to be *or* he hopes it will be successful; er wünscht sich (*dat*) ein glückliches Leben für seine Kinder he would like his children to have a happy life; er wünscht sich (*dat*) diesen Mann als Lehrer/Vater/als *or* zum Freund he wishes that this man was his teacher/father/friend; was wünschst du dir? what do you want?, what would you like?; (*im Märchen*) what is your wish?; du darfst dir was (zum Essen) ~ you can say what you'd like (to eat); du darfst dir etwas ~ (*Wunsch frei haben*) you can make a wish; (*im Märchen auch*) I'll give you a wish; sie haben alles, was man sich (*dat*) nur ~ kann they have everything you could possibly wish for; man hätte es sich (*dat*) nicht besser ~ können you couldn't have wished for anything better.

▼ (b) jdm etw ~ to wish sb sth; jdm einen guten Morgen ~ to wish sb good morning; wir ~ dir gute Besserung/eine gute Reise we hope you get well soon/have a pleasant journey; wir ~ gute Fahrt we hope you have *or* we wish you a good journey; jdm den Tod/die Pest an den Hals ~ (*fig inf*) to wish sb would die/drop dead (*inf*); das würde ich meinem schlimmsten Feind nicht ~ (*prov*) I wouldn't wish that on my worst enemy.

▼ (c) (*ersehnen, hoffen*) to wish ◆ jdn fort/weit weg ~ to wish sb would go away/were far away; es bleibt/wäre zu ~, daß ... it is to be hoped that ...; ich wünschte, ich hätte dich nie gesehen I wish I'd never seen you.

▼ (d) (*begehren, verlangen*) to want ◆ was ~ Sie? (*Diener*) yes, Sir/Madam?; (*in Geschäft*) what can I do for you?, can I help you?; (*in Restaurant*) what would you like?; wen ~ Sie zu sprechen? to whom would you like to speak?; ich wünsche, daß du das machst I want you to do that.

[2] *vi* (*begehren*) to wish ◆ Sie ~? what can I do for you?; (*in Restaurant*) what would you like?; ganz wie Sie ~ (just) as you wish *or* please *or* like; zu ~/viel zu ~ übrig lassen to leave something/a great deal to be desired.

[3] *vr* sich in eine andere Lage/weit weg ~ to wish one were in a different situation/far away.

wünschenswert *adj* desirable.

Wunsch-: ~form *f* (*Gram*) optative (mood); w~gemäß [1] *adj* requested; (*erwünscht*) desired; (*geplant*) planned; [2] *adv siehe adj* as requested; as desired; as planned; ~kandidat *m* ideal candidate; ~kind *nt* planned child; unser Töchterchen war ein ~kind our little daughter was planned; ~kindpille *f* (*DDR*) birth control pill; ~konzert *nt* (*Rad*) musical request programme; ~liste *f siehe* ~zettel; w~los *adj Mensch* content(ed); *Glück* perfect; w~los glücklich perfectly happy; ~partner *m* ideal partner; ~satz *m* (*Gram*) optative clause; ~sendung *f* (*Rad*) request programme; ~traum *m* dream; (*Illusion*) illusion; das ist doch bloß ein ~traum that's just a pipe-dream; ~zettel *m* wish list; das steht schon lange auf meinem ~zettel (*fig*) I've wanted that for a long time.

wupp (dich), wupps *interj* whoomph.

Wupp(dich) *m* -s, *no pl* (*inf*) mit einem ~ in a flash.

wurde *pret of* werden.

Würde *f* -, -n (a) *no pl* dignity ◆ ~ bewahren to preserve one's dignity; unter aller ~ sein to be beneath contempt; unter jds ~ sein to be beneath sb *or* sb's dignity; etw mit ~ tragen to bear sth with dignity. (b) (*Auszeichnung*) honour; (*Titel*) title; (*Amt*) rank ◆ ~ bringt Bürde (*Prov*) the burdens of office.

würdelos *adj* undignified.

Würdelosigkeit *f* lack of dignity.

Würdenträger *m* -s, - dignitary.

würdevoll *adj siehe* würdig (a).

würdig *adj* (a) (*würdevoll*) dignified ◆ sich ~ verhalten to behave with dignity.

(b) (*wert*) worthy ◆ jds/einer Sache ~/nicht ~ sein to be worthy/unworthy of sb/sth; eine ihm ~e Verabschiedung a farewell worthy of him; sich jds/einer Sache ~ erweisen *or* zeigen to prove oneself to be worthy of sb/sth; jdn einer Sache (*gen*) für ~ halten *or* befinden (*geh*) to find sb worthy of sth.

würdigen *vt* (a) to appreciate; (*lobend erwähnen*) to acknowledge; (*respektieren*) to respect; (*ehren*) to pay tribute to ◆ etw gebührend *or* nach Gebühr/richtig ~ to appreciate sth properly/fully; etw zu ~ wissen to appreciate sth.

(b) (*geh: für würdig befinden*) jdn einer Sache (*gen*) ~ to deem sb worthy of sth; jdn eines/keines Blickes/Grußes *etc* ~ to deign/not to deign to look at/greet *etc* sb.

Würdigkeit *f, no pl* (a) *siehe* Würde. (b) (*Wertsein*) merit.

Würdigung *f* (a) *siehe vt* appreciation; acknowledgement; respect. (b) (*lobende Worte, Artikel*) appreciation. (c) (*Ehrung*) honour ◆ die zahlreichen ~en der Gäste the numerous tributes paid to the guests.

Wurf *m* -(e)s, ¨e (a) throw; (*beim Kegeln etc*) bowl; (*gezielter ~, beim Handball etc auch*) shot; (*beim Baseball*) pitch ◆ drei ~ *or* ¨e zwei Mark three goes *or* throws for two marks.

(b) *no pl* (*das Werfen*) throwing ◆ beim ~ when throwing; zum ~ ansetzen/ausholen to get ready to throw; sich auf den ~ konzentrieren to concentrate on throwing.

(c) (*fig: Erfolg*) success, hit (*inf*) ◆ mit dem Film ist ihm ein großer ~ gelungen this film is a great success *or* big hit (*inf*) for him; einen großen/glücklichen ~ tun (*Erfolg haben*) to be very successful *or* have great success; (*Glück haben*) to have a stroke of luck.

(d) (*Zool*) litter; (*das Gebären*) birth.

(e) (*Falten~*) fall ◆ einen eleganten ~ haben to hang elegantly.

(f) (*Mil*) *siehe* Abwurf.

Wurf-: ~arm *m* (*Sport*) throwing arm; ~bahn *f* trajectory; ~disziplin *f* (*Sport*) throwing discipline *or* event.

Würfel *m* -s, - (a) (*auch Math*) cube ◆ etw in ~ schneiden to dice sth, to cut sth into cubes. (b) (*Spiel~*) dice, die (*form*) ◆ die ~ sind gefallen the die is cast; ~ spielen to play at dice.

Würfel-: ~becher *m* shaker; ~brett *nt* dice board; ~form *f* cube shape; ~form haben to be cube-shaped; w~förmig *adj* cube-shaped, cubic (*esp Math*).

würf(e)lig *adj* cubic ◆ etw ~ schneiden to cut sth into cubes.

würfeln [1] *vi* to throw, to have a throw; (*Würfel spielen*) to play at dice ◆ hast du schon gewürfelt? have you had your throw *or* go?; um etw ~ to throw dice for sth.

➤ SPRACHE AKTIV: Wunsch: b → 50.1, 50.2, 50.4, 50.6 wünschen: 1b → 50.1., 50.5 1c → 52.4 1d → 27.3

[2] *vt* **(a)** to throw. **(b)** (*in Würfel schneiden*) to dice, to cut into cubes.

Würfel-: ~spiel *nt* (*Partie*) game of dice; (*Spielart*) dice; **beim ~spiel** at dice; **~spieler** *m* dice player; **~zucker** *m* cube sugar.

Wurf-: ⚠~geschoß *nt* projectile, missile; **~hammer** *m* (*Sport*) hammer; **~hand** *f* (*Sport*) throwing hand; **~körper** *m* (*Phys*) projectile; **~kraft** *f* (*Phys*) projectile force; (*Sport*) throwing strength; **w~kräftig** *adj* (*Sport*) strong-armed.

würflig *adj siehe* **würf(e)lig.**

Wurf-: ~mal *nt* (*Baseball*) pitcher's mound; **~maschine** *f* (*Mil, Hist*) catapult; (*beim Tontaubenschießen*) trap; **~messer** *nt* throwing knife; **~parabel** *f* (*Phys*) trajectory (parabola); **~pfeil** *m* dart; **~ring** *m* quoit; **~sendung** *f* circular; **Reklame durch ~sendungen** direct advertising; **~speer, ~spieß** *m* javelin; **~stern** *m* spiked metal disc; **~taube** *f* (*Sport*) clay pigeon; **~taubenschießen** *nt* (*Sport*) clay pigeon shooting; **~waffe** *f* missile; (*Speer*) throwing spear; **~weite** *f* throwing range; (*von Geschütz*) mortar range; **~winkel** *m* (*Sport*) throwing angle.

Würge-: ~engel *m siehe* **Würgengel**; **~griff** *m* (*lit, fig*) stranglehold; **~mal** *nt* strangulation mark.

würgen [1] *vt jdn* to strangle, to throttle; (*fig: Angst*) to choke.
[2] *vi* **(a)** (*mühsam schlucken*) to choke; (*Schlange*) to gulp ♦ **an etw** (*dat*) **~** (*lit*) to choke on sth; (*fig*) (*an Kritik*) to find sth hard to swallow; (*an Arbeit*) to struggle over sth.
(b) (*beim Erbrechen*) to retch ♦ **ein W~ im Hals spüren** to feel one is going to be sick.
[3] *vt impers* **es würgte sie (im Hals** *etc*) she felt she was going to be sick; **mit Hängen und W~** by the skin of one's teeth.

Würg|engel *m* Angel of Death.

Würger *m* **-s, - (a)** strangler; (*poet: der Tod*) death *no art.* **(b)** (*Orn*) shrike.

Würgschraube *f siehe* **Garotte.**

Wurm *m* **-(e)s, ¨er (a)** worm; (*Made*) maggot; (*poet: Schlange*) snake; (*Myth: Lind~*) dragon ♦ **der (nagende) ~ des schlechten Gewissens** the (gnawing) pangs of a guilty conscience; **da ist** *or* **steckt** *or* **sitzt der ~ drin** (*fig inf*) there's something wrong somewhere; (*seltsam*) there's something odd about it; (*verdächtig*) there's something fishy about it (*inf*); *siehe* **winden.**
(b) *auch nt* (*inf: Kind*) (little) mite.

Würmchen *nt dim of* **Wurm** little worm; (*inf: Kind*) (poor) little mite *or* thing.

wurmen *vt, vt impers* (*inf*) to rankle with.

Wurm-: ~fortsatz *m* (*Anat*) vermiform appendix; **~fraß** *m, no pl* worm damage.

wurmig *adj* wormeaten; (*madig*) *Obst* maggoty.

Wurm-: ~krankheit *f* worm disorder, helminthiasis (*spec*); **~kur** *f* worming treatment; **die Katze braucht eine ~kur** the cat needs to be wormed; **eine ~kur machen** to have worm treatment; **~loch** *nt* worm-hole; **~mittel** *nt* vermicide, vermifuge; **w~stichig** *adj Holz* full of worm-holes; (*madig auch*) *Obst* maggoty.

Wurscht *etc* (*inf*) *siehe* **Wurst** *etc.*

Wurst *f* **-, ¨e** sausage; (*Salami*) salami; (*wurstförmiges Gebilde auch*) roll; (*inf: Kot von Hund*) dog's mess (*inf*) ♦ **jetzt geht es um die ~** (*fig inf*) the moment of truth has come (*inf*); **mit der ~ nach der Speckseite** *or* **dem Schinken werfen** (*fig inf*) to cast a sprat to catch a mackerel; **es ist jdm ~** *or* **Wurscht** (*inf*) it's all the same to sb.

Wurst-: ~aufschnitt *m* assortment of sliced sausage/salami; **~brot** *nt* open sausage/salami sandwich; (*zusammengeklappt*) sausage/salami sandwich; **~brühe** *f* sausage stock.

Würstchen *nt* **(a)** *dim of* **Wurst** small sausage ♦ **heiße** *or* **warme ~** hot sausages; (*in Brötchen*) ≃ hot dogs; **Frankfurter/Wiener ~** frankfurters/wienerwursts. **(b)** (*pej: Mensch*) squirt (*inf*), nobody ♦ **ein armes ~** (*fig*) a poor soul.

Würstchen-: ~bude *f*, **~stand** *m* sausage stand; hot-dog stand.

wurst|egal *adj* (*inf*) **das ist mir ~** I couldn't care less (about that).

Wurstel *m* **-s, -** (*Aus*) *siehe* **Hanswurst.**

Würstel *nt* **-s, -** (*dial*) *siehe* **Würstchen.**

Wurstelei *f* (*inf*) muddle.

wursteln *vi* (*inf*) to muddle along ♦ **sich durchs Leben/die Schule ~** to muddle (one's way) through life/school.

wursten *vi* to make sausages.

Wurster *m* **-s, -** (*dial*) *siehe* **Fleischer.**

Wursterei *f* (*dial*) *siehe* **Fleischerei.**

Wurstfinger *pl* (*pej inf*) podgy fingers *pl.*

wurstig *adj* (*inf*) devil-may-care *attr*, couldn't-care-less *attr* (*inf*) ♦ **sei doch nicht so ~!** don't be such a wet blanket! (*inf*).

Wurstigkeit *f* (*inf*) devil-may-care *or* couldn't-care-less (*inf*) attitude.

Wurst-: ~konserve *f* tinned (*Brit*) *or* canned sausages; **~maxe** *m* **-n, -n** (*inf*) ≃ man who sells sausages, hot-dog man (*inf*); **~ring** *m* sausage ring; **~salat** *m* sausage salad; **~vergiftung** *f* sausage poisoning; **~waren** *pl* sausages *pl*; **~zipfel** *m* sausage-end.

Württemberg *nt* **-s** Württemberg.

Württemberger *m* (*Wein*) Württemberg wine.

Württemberger(in *f*) *m* native of Württemberg; (*Einwohner*) inhabitant of Württemberg.

württembergisch *adj* Württembergian.

Würze *f* **-, -n (a)** (*Gewürz*) seasoning, spice; (*Aroma*) aroma; (*fig: Reiz*) spice ♦ **das gibt dem Leben die ~** that adds spice to life; *siehe* **Kürze. (b)** (*von Bier*) wort.

Wurzel *f* **-, -n (a)** (*lit, fig*) root; (*Hand~*) wrist; (*Fuß~*) ankle ♦ **etw mit der ~ ausreißen** to pull sth out by the root; **etw mit der ~ ausrotten** (*fig*) to eradicate sth; **~n schlagen** (*lit*) to root; (*fig: sich einleben*) to put down roots; (*an einem Ort hängenbleiben*) to grow roots; **die ~ Jesse** (*Bibl*) the stem of Jesse.
(b) (*Math*) root ♦ **~n ziehen** to find the roots; **die ~ aus einer Größe ziehen** to find the root of a number; **(die) ~ aus 4 ist 2** the square root of 4 is 2; **die vierte ~ aus 16 ist 2** the fourth root of 16 is 2; **unter/außerhalb der ~ stehen** to be inside/outside the radical sign.
(c) (*N Ger*) *siehe* **Möhre.**

Wurzel-: ~ballen *m* (*Hort*) bale of roots, root bale; **~behandlung** *f* (*von Zahn*) root treatment; **~bildung** *f* rooting; **~bürste** *f* (coarse) scrubbing brush.

Würzelchen *nt dim of* **Wurzel** little root, rootlet.

Wurzel-: ~entzündung *f* (*an Zahn*) inflammation of the root/roots; **~exponent** *m* (*Math*) radical index; **~gemüse** *nt* root vegetables *pl*; **w~los** *adj Pflanze* without roots; (*fig auch*) rootless; **~mann** *m*, **~männchen** *nt* (*Alraune*) mandrake; (*Figur aus Wurzel*) *small figure carved out of a root*; (*Kräutersucher*) herb man.

wurzeln *vi* **(a)** (*lit, fig*) to be rooted ♦ **in etw** (*dat*) **~** (*fig*) to be rooted in sth; (*verursacht sein*) to have its/their roots in sth. **(b)** (*rare: Wurzeln schlagen*) to (take) root.

Wurzel-: ~resektion *f* (*Zahnmedizin*) root resection; **~sepp** *m* (*inf*) country bumpkin (*inf*); **~silbe** *f* (*Ling*) root syllable; **~stock** *m* (*Bot*) rhizome; **~verzeichnis** *nt* (*Comput*) root directory; **~werk** *nt, no pl* **(a)** root system, roots *pl*; **(b)** (*Cook*) flavouring greens *pl*; **~zeichen** *nt* (*Math*) radical sign; **~ziehen** *nt* **-s,** *no pl* (*Math*) root extraction.

wurzen *vti* (*Aus inf*) to get everything one can (*jdn* out of sb).

würzen *vt* to season; (*fig*) to add spice to ♦ **eine Geschichte mit etw ~** to season a story with sth.

Wurzerei *f* (*Aus inf*) robbery (*inf*).

würzig *adj Speise* tasty; (*scharf*) spicy; *Zigaretten, Tabak, Geruch etc* aromatic; *Luft* fragrant, tangy; *Wein, Bier* full-bodied.

Würz-: ~nelke *f siehe* **Gewürznelke**; **~stoff** *m* flavouring.

wusch[1] *pret of* **waschen.**

wusch[2] *interj* (*Aus*) (*erstaunt*) whoops; (*schnell*) zoom.

Wuschelhaar *nt* (*inf*) mop of curly hair.

wusch(e)lig *adj* (*inf*) *Tier* shaggy; *Haare* fuzzy (*inf*).

Wuschelkopf *m* **(a)** (*Haare*) mop of curly hair, fuzz (*inf*). **(b)** (*Mensch*) fuzzy-head (*inf*).

wuselig *adj* (*dial*) (*lebhaft*) lively; (*unruhig*) fidgety; (*bewegt*) busy, bustling; *Ameisenhaufen* teeming ♦ **das ~e Treiben** the hustle and bustle.

wuseln *vi* (*dial*) **(a)** (*belebt sein*) to be teeming. **(b)** *aux sein* (*sich schnell bewegen*) to scurry.

⚠**wußte** *pret of* **wissen.**

Wust *m* **-(e)s,** *no pl* (*inf*) (*Durcheinander*) jumble; (*Menge*) pile; (*unordentlicher Haufen*) heap; (*Kram, Gerümpel*) junk (*inf*) ♦ **dieser ~ von Kleidern** this pile of clothes.

wüst *adj* **(a)** (*öde*) desert *attr*, waste, desolate ♦ **die Erde war ~ und leer** (*Bibl*) the earth was without form, and void (*Bibl*).
(b) (*unordentlich*) wild, chaotic; *Aussehen, Haar* wild ♦ **~ aussehen** to look a real mess.
(c) (*ausschweifend*) wild ♦ **~ feiern** to have a wild party.
(d) (*rüde*) *Beschimpfung, Beleidigung etc* vile ♦ **jdn ~ beschimpfen** to use vile language to sb.
(e) (*arg*) terrible, awful; *Übertreibung auch* wild.

Wüste *f* **-, -n** (*Geog*) desert; (*Ödland*) waste, wilderness (*liter*); (*fig*) waste(land), wilderness, desert ♦ **die ~ Gobi** the Gobi Desert; **jdn in die ~ schicken** (*fig*) to send sb packing (*inf*).

wüsten *vi* (*inf*) **mit etw ~** to squander *or* waste sth; **mit seiner Gesundheit/seinen Kräften ~** to ruin one's health/strength.

Wüstenei *f* **(a)** (*öde Gegend*) wasteland, desert. **(b)** (*fig: wildes Durcheinander*) chaos.

Wüsten-: ~fuchs *m* desert fox; **~klima** *nt* desert climate; **~könig** *m* (*poet*) king of the desert (*poet*); **~landschaft** *f* desert landscape; **~sand** *m* desert sand; **~schiff** *nt* (*poet*) ship of the desert (*poet*), camel; **~steppe** *f* steppe.

Wüstling *m* (*dated, iro*) lecher.

Wüstung *f* deserted settlement.

Wut *f* **-,** *no pl* **(a)** (*Zorn, Raserei*) rage, fury; (*fig: der Elemente*) fury ♦ **(auf jdn/etw) eine ~ haben** to be furious (with sb/sth), to be mad (at sb/sth); **eine ~ im Bauch haben** (*inf*) to be seething, to be hopping mad (*inf*); **eine ~ haben/kriegen** *or* **bekommen** to be in/get into a rage; **in ~ geraten, von der ~ gepackt werden** to fly into a rage; **jdn in ~ bringen** *or* **versetzen** to infuriate sb.
(b) (*Verbissenheit*) frenzy ♦ **mit einer wahren ~** as if possessed, like crazy (*inf*).

-wut *f* (*inf*) *in cpds* bug (*inf*).

Wut-: ~anfall *m* fit of rage; (*esp von Kind*) tantrum; **~ausbruch** *m* outburst of rage *or* fury; (*esp von Kind*) tantrum.

wüten *vi* (*lit, fig*) (*toben*) to rage; (*zerstörerisch hausen*) to cause havoc; (*verbal*) to storm (*gegen* at); (*Menge*) to riot.

wütend *adj* furious, enraged; *Tier* enraged; *Menge* angry; *Kampf, Elemente* raging; (*fig*) *Schmerz, Haß etc* fierce ♦ **~ raste der Stier auf ihn zu** the enraged bull raced towards him; **auf jdn/etw** (*acc*) **~ sein** to be mad at sb/sth; **über jdn/etw** (*acc*) **~ sein** to be furious about sb/sth.

wut-: ~entbrannt *adj* furious, enraged; **~entbrannt hinausgehen** to leave in a fury *or* rage; **~erfüllt** *adj* filled *or* seething with rage, furious.

Wüterich *m* brute.

Wut-: ~geheul *nt* howl of fury; **~geschrei** *nt* cries *pl* of rage.

⚠: for details of spelling reform, see supplement

-wütig *adj suf* (*inf*) bitten by the ... bug (*inf*).
wutsch *interj* whoosh.
wutschäumend *adj* foaming with rage.
wutschen *vi aux sein* (*inf*) to whoosh (*inf*); (*schnell verschwinden*) to whiz (*inf*), to zoom (*inf*).
Wut-: w~schnaubend *adj* snorting with rage; **~schrei** *m* yell of rage; **w~verzerrt** *adj* distorted with rage.
Wutz *f* **-, -en** (*pej dial*) pig (*inf*).
Wuzerl *nt* **-s, -(n)** (*Aus*) **(a)** (*Kind*) porker (*inf*). **(b)** (*Fussel*) piece of fluff.
wuzerldick *adj* (*Aus*) porky (*inf*).
Wwe. *abbr of* **Witwe.**
Wz *abbr of* **Warenzeichen.**

X, x [ɪks] *nt* -, - X, x ◆ **Herr X** Mr X; **jdm ein X für ein U vormachen** to put one over on sb (*inf*); **er läßt sich kein X für ein U vormachen** he's not easily fooled.
x-Achse ['ɪks-] *f* x-axis.
Xanthippe [ksan'tɪpə] *f* -, **-n** (*fig inf*) shrew.
X-Beine ['ɪks-] *pl* knock-knees *pl* ◆ **~ haben** to be knock-kneed.
X-beinig ['ɪks-] *adj* knock-kneed.
x-beliebig [ɪks-] *adj* any old (*inf*) ◆ **wir können uns an einem ~en Ort treffen** we can meet anywhere you like.
X-Chromosom ['ɪks-] *nt* X-chromosome.
Xenon *nt* **-s**, *no pl* (*abbr* **Xe**) xenon.
⚠ **Xerographie** [kserogra'fi:] *f* Xerox (copy).
⚠ **xerographieren*** [kserogra'fi:rən] *vti insep* to Xerox.
Xerokopie [kseroko'pi:] *f* Xerox (copy).
xerokopieren* [kseroko'pi:rən] *vti insep* to Xerox.
x-fach ['ɪks-] *adj* **die ~e Menge** (*Math*) n times the amount; **trotz ~er Ermahnungen** (*inf*) in spite of umpteen *or* n warnings (*inf*).
X-förmig ['ɪks-] *adj* X-shaped.
x-mal ['ɪks-] *adv* (*inf*) n (number of) times (*inf*), umpteen times (*inf*).
x-malig ['ɪks-] *adj* (*inf*) n number of (*inf*), umpteen (*inf*) ◆ **wenn ein ~er Weltmeister ...** when somebody who has been world champion n (number of) times *or* umpteen times ...
X-Strahlen ['ɪks-] *pl* (*dated*) X-rays *pl*.
x-te ['ɪkstə] *adj* (*Math*) nth; (*inf*) nth (*inf*), umpteenth (*inf*) ◆ **zum ~n Male, zum ~nmal** for the nth *or* umpteenth time (*inf*).
⚠ **Xylophon** [ksylo'fo:n] *nt* **-s, -e** xylophone.

⚠: for details of spelling reform, see supplement

Y, y ['ʏpsilɔn] *nt* **-, -** Y, y.
y-Achse ['ʏpsilɔn-] *f* y-axis.
Yacht [jaxt] *f* **-, -en** *siehe* **Jacht**.
Yankee ['jɛŋki] *m* **-s, -s** (*pej*) Yankee, Yank.
Yard [jaːɐt] *nt* **-s, -s** yard.
Y-Chromosom ['ʏpsilɔn-] *nt* Y-chromosome.
Yen [jɛn] *m* **-(s), -(s)** yen.
Yeti ['jeːti] *m* **-s, -s** Yeti, Abominable Snowman.
Yoga ['joːga] *m or nt* **-(s)** *siehe* **Joga**.
Yogi ['joːgi] *m* **-s, -s** *siehe* **Jogi**.
⚠ **Yoghurt** ['joːgʊrt] *m or nt* **-s, -s** *siehe* **Joghurt**.
Ypsilon ['ʏpsilɔn] *nt* **-(s), -s** y; (*griechischer Buchstabe*) upsilon.
Ysop ['iːzɔp] *m* **-s, -e** (*Bot*) hyssop.
Ytong ® ['yːtɔŋ] *m* **-s, -s** breezeblock.
Ytterbium [ʏ'tɛrbiʊm] *nt, no pl* (*abbr* **Yb**) ytterbium.
Yttrium ['ʏtrium] *nt, no pl* (*abbr* **Y**) yttrium.
Yucca ['jʊka] *f* **-, -s** yucca.
Yuppie ['jʊpiː, 'japiː] *m* **-s, -s** yuppie.

⚠: Informationen zur Rechtschreibreform im Anhang

Z

Z, z [tsɛt] *nt* -, - Z, z.

z.A. *abbr of* **zur Ansicht; zur Anstellung** on probation.

Zack *m* **-s,** *no pl* (*inf*) **auf ~ bringen** to knock into shape (*inf*); **auf ~ sein** to be on the ball (*inf*).

zack *interj* (*inf*) pow, zap (*inf*) ◆ **~, ~!** chop-chop! (*inf*); **sei nicht so langsam, mach mal ein bißchen ~, ~** don't be so slow, get a move on (*inf*); **bei uns muß alles ~, ~ gehen** we have to do everything chop-chop (*inf*); **die Leute waren so gut gedrillt, die ganze Sache lief ~, ~** the people were drilled so well that the whole thing went off just like that (*inf*).

Zacke *f* **-, -n, Zacken** *m* **-s, -** point; (*von Gabel*) prong; (*von Kamm*) tooth; (*Berg~*) jagged peak; (*Auszackung*) indentation; (*von Fieberkurve etc*) peak; (*inf: Nase*) conk (*inf*), beak (*inf*).

zacken *vt* to serrate; *Kleid, Saum, Papier* to pink; *siehe* **gezackt.**

Zacken-: ~linie *f* jagged line; (*Zickzack*) zig-zag (line); **~litze** *f* ric-rac braid.

zackig *adj* **(a)** (*gezackt*) jagged; *Stern* pointed ◆ **~ schreiben** to write a very angular hand.
(b) (*inf*) *Soldat, Bursche* smart; *Tempo, Musik* brisk; *Team, Manager etc* dynamic, zippy (*inf*) ◆ **bring mir meine Hausschuhe, aber ein bißchen ~!** fetch me my slippers, and make it snappy (*inf*)!

zag *adj* (*liter*) *siehe* **zaghaft.**

zagen *vi* (*liter*) to be apprehensive, to hesitate; *siehe* **Zittern.**

zaghaft *adj* timid.

Zaghaftigkeit *f* timidity.

zäh *adj* tough; (*dickflüssig*) glutinous; (*schleppend*) *Verkehr etc* slow-moving; (*ausdauernd*) dogged, tenacious ◆ **ein ~es Leben haben** (*lit: Mensch, Tier*) to have a tenacious hold on life; (*fig*) to die hard; **mit ~em Fleiß** doggedly, with dogged application.

⚠ **Zäheit** ['tsɛ:hait] *f, no pl* toughness.

zähflüssig *adj* thick, viscous; *Verkehr, Verhandlung* slow-moving.

Zähflüssigkeit *f* thickness, viscosity ◆ **die ~ des Verkehrs** the slow-moving traffic.

Zähigkeit *f siehe* **zäh** toughness; glutinousness; doggedness, tenacity ◆ **die ~ der Verhandlungen** the fact that the negotiations were so slow-moving.

Zahl *f* **-, -en** (*Math, Gram*) number; (*Verkaufs~, Maßangabe, bei Geldmengen etc auch*) figure; (*Ziffer auch*) numeral, figure ◆ **~en nennen** to give figures; **wie waren die ~en im letzten Jahr?** what did the figures look like last year?; **sie hat ein gutes Gedächtnis für ~en** she has a good memory for figures *or* numbers; **eine fünfstellige ~** a five-figure number; **der ~ nach** numerically; **gut mit ~en umgehen können** to be good with figures, to be numerate; **die ~en stimmen nicht** the figures don't add up *or* tally; **~ oder Wappen** heads or tails; **100 an der ~** (*old*) 100 in number; **in großer ~** in large *or* great numbers; **die ~ ist voll** the numbers are complete; **in voller ~** in full number; **der Aufsichtsrat war in voller ~ versammelt** there was a full turn-out for the meeting of the board; **ohne ~** (*geh*) without number; **Leiden/Wonnen ohne ~** (*poet*) countless tribulations/joys.

zahlbar *adj* payable (*an +acc* to) ◆ **~ bei Lieferung** *or* **nach Erhalt** payable on *or* to be paid for on delivery *or* receipt.

zählbar *adj* countable.

Zählbrett, Zahlbrett *nt* money tray.

zählebig *adj* hardy, tough; (*fig*) *Gerücht, Vorurteil* persistent.

zahlen [1] *vi* to pay ◆ **Herr Ober, (bitte) ~!** waiter, the bill (*Brit*) *or* check (*US*) please; **dort zahlt man gut/schlecht** the pay there is good/bad, they pay well/badly; **wenn er nicht bald zahlt, dann ...** if he doesn't pay up soon, then ...
[2] *vt* (*bezahlen*) to pay ◆ **was habe ich (Ihnen) zu ~?** what do I owe you?; **einen hohen Preis ~** (*lit, fig*) to pay a high price; **ich zahle dir ein Bier** I'll buy you a beer; **ich zahle dir den Flug/das Kino** I'll pay for your flight/for you (to go to the cinema); **laß mal, ich zahl's** no no, I'll pay *or* it's on me *or* it's my treat (*inf*).

zählen [1] *vi* **(a)** to count ◆ **bis hundert ~** to count (up) to a hundred; **seine Verbrechen ~ nach Hunderten** (*geh*) his crimes run into hundreds.
(b) (*gehören*) **zu einer Gruppe/Menge ~** to be one of a group/set; **er zählt zu den besten Schriftstellern unserer Zeit** he ranks as one of the best authors of our time; **dieses Gebiet zählt immer noch zu Österreich** this region still counts as part of Austria; **zu welcher Sprachengruppe zählt Gälisch?** to which language group does Gaelic belong?
(c) (*sich verlassen*) **auf jdn/etw ~** to count *or* rely on sb/sth.
(d) (*gelten*) to count.
[2] *vt* to count ◆ **jdn/etw zu einer Gruppe/Menge ~** to regard sb/sth as one of a group/set, to number *or* count sb/sth among a group/set; **etw zu einem Gebiet ~** to count *or* regard sth as part of a region; **seine Tage sind gezählt** his days are numbered; **sie zählt 27 Jahre** (*liter*) she is 27 years old; **Stanford zählt 12 000 Studenten** Stanford numbers *or* has 12,000 students; **bei diesem Spiel zählt der König 5 Punkte** in this game the King counts as 5 points.

Zahlen-: ~akrobatik *f* (*inf*) juggling with statistics *or* figures, statistical sleight of hand; **~angabe** *f* figure; **ich kann keine genauen ~angaben machen** I can't give *or* quote any precise figures; **~beispiel** *nt* numerical example; **~folge** *f* order of numbers; **~gedächtnis** *nt* memory for numbers; **~lehre** *f* arithmetic; **~lotterie** *f*, **~lotto** *nt siehe* **Lotto; z~mäßig** *adj* numerical; **etw z~mäßig ausdrücken** to express sth in figures; **~material** *nt* figures *pl*; **~mystik** *f* number mysticism; (*Astrol*) numerology; **~rätsel** *nt* number *or* numerical puzzle; **~reihe** *f* sequence of numbers; ⚠**~schloß** *nt* combination lock; **~sinn** *m* head for figures; **~symbolik** *f* number symbolism; **~theorie** *f* (*Math*) theory of numbers, number theory; **~toto** *m siehe* **Toto; ~verhältnis** *nt* (numerical) ratio; **~verriegelung** *f* (*Comput*) numbers lock; **~wert** *m* numerical value; (*auf Meßgeräten*) (numerical) reading; **welche ~werte hat die Analyse ergeben?** what figures did the analysis give?; **die ~werte der beiden Versuche** the figures yielded by the two experiments.

Zahler *m* **-s, -** payer.

Zähler *m* **-s, - (a)** (*Math*) numerator. **(b)** (*Meßgerät*) meter.

Zähler-: ~ablesung *f* meter reading; **~stand** *m* meter reading.

Zahl-: ~grenze *f* fare stage; **~karte** *f* giro transfer form; **~kellner** *m waiter who presents the bill and collects payment.*

zahllos *adj* countless, innumerable.

Zählmaß *nt* numerical measure, unit of measurement.

Zahl-: ~meister *m* (*Naut*) purser; (*Mil*) paymaster; **~mutter** *f* mother supporting a child.

zahlreich *adj* numerous ◆ **wir hatten mit einer ~eren Beteiligung gerechnet** we had expected more participants; **die Veranstaltung war ~ besucht** the event was (very) well attended.

Zählrohr *nt* (*Phys*) Geiger counter.

Zahl-: ~stelle *f* payments office; **~tag** *m* payday.

Zahlung *f* payment ◆ **eine einmalige ~ leisten** to make a lump-sum payment; **in ~ nehmen** to take in part-exchange *or* as a trade-in; **in ~ geben** to trade in, to give in part-exchange; **gegen eine ~ von $ 500 erhalten Sie ...** on payment of $500 you will receive ...

Zählung *f* count; (*Volks~*) census.

Zahlungs-: ~abkommen *nt* payments agreement; **~anweisung** *f* giro transfer order; **~art** *f* method *or* mode of payment; **~aufforderung** *f* request for payment; **~aufschub** *m* extension (of credit), moratorium (*Jur*); **~bedingungen** *pl* terms (of payment) *pl*; **erleichterte ~bedingungen** easy terms; **~befehl** *m* order to pay; **~bilanz** *f* balance of payments; **~empfänger** *m* payee; **~erleichterung** *f* more convenient method of payment; **~erleichterungen** easy terms; **z~fähig** *adj* able to pay; *Firma* solvent; **~fähigkeit** *f* ability to pay; solvency; **~frist** *f* time *or* period allowed for payment; **z~kräftig** *adj* wealthy; **~mittel** *nt* means *sing* of payment; (*Münzen, Banknoten*) currency; **gesetzliches ~mittel** legal tender; **z~pflichtig** *adj* obliged to pay; **~schwierigkeiten** *pl* financial difficulties *pl*; **~system** *nt* method of payment; **~termin** *m* date for payment; **z~unfähig** *adj* unable to pay; *Firma* insolvent; **~unfähigkeit** *f* inability to pay; insolvency; **z~unwillig** *adj* unwilling to pay; **~verkehr** *m* payments *pl*, payment transactions *pl*; **~verpflichtung** *f* obligation *or* liability to pay; **~verzug** *m* default, arrears *pl*; **~weise** *f* mode *or* method of payment; **~ziel** *nt* (*Comm*) period allowed for payment.

Zahlvater *m* father supporting a child.

Zählwerk *nt* counter.

Zahl-: ~wort *nt* numeral; **~zeichen** *nt* numerical symbol.

zahm *adj* (*lit, fig*) tame ◆ **er ist schon ~er geworden** (*inf*) he has calmed down a bit (*inf*), he's a bit tamer now (*inf*).

zähmbar *adj* tam(e)able.

⚠: for details of spelling reform, see supplement

zähmen *vt* to tame; (*fig*) *Leidenschaft, Bedürfnisse* to control.

Zähmung *f* taming.

Zahn *m* **-(e)s, ¨e** (**a**) (*Anat, Zacke*) tooth; (*von Briefmarke*) perforation; (*Rad~ auch*) cog ♦ **künstliche** *or* **falsche ¨e** false teeth *pl*; **¨e bekommen** *or* **kriegen** (*inf*) to cut one's teeth; **die ersten/zweiten ¨e** one's milk teeth/second set of teeth; **die dritten ¨e** (*hum*) false teeth; **diese Portion reicht** *or* **ist für den hohlen ~** (*inf*) that's hardly enough to satisfy a mouse (*inf*); **der ~ der Zeit** the ravages *pl* of time; **ihm tut kein ~ mehr weh** (*inf*) he's gone to join his ancestors; **die ¨e zeigen** (*Tier*) to bare one's teeth; (*fig inf*) to show one's teeth; **jdm einen ~ ziehen** (*lit*) to pull a tooth out, to extract a tooth; (*fig*) to put an idea out of sb's head; **ich muß mir einen ~ ziehen lassen** I've got to have a tooth out *or* extracted; **den ~ kannst du dir ruhig ziehen lassen!** you can put that idea right out of your head!; **jdm auf den ~ fühlen** (*aushorchen*) to sound sb out; (*streng befragen*) to grill sb, to give sb a grilling; **etw mit ¨en und Klauen verteidigen** to defend sth tooth and nail; *siehe* **bewaffnet, ausbeißen.**
(**b**) (*sl: Geschwindigkeit*) **einen ~ draufhaben** to be going like the clappers (*inf*); **mit einem unheimlichen ~** at an incredible lick (*inf*); *siehe* **zulegen.**

Zahn-: **~arzt** *m* dentist; **~arzthelferin** *f* dental nurse; **z~ärztlich** *adj* dental; **sich in z~ärztliche Behandlung begeben** (*form*) to have dental treatment; **z~ärztliche Helferin** (*form*) dental nurse; **~behandlung** *f* dental treatment; **~belag** *m* film on the teeth; **~bett** *nt* socket (of a/the tooth); **~bürste** *f* tooth brush; **~creme** *f* toothpaste.

Zähne-: **~fletschen** *nt* baring of teeth, snarling; **z~fletschend** *adj attr, adv* snarling; **~klappern** *nt* chattering of teeth; *siehe* **Heulen**; **z~klappernd** *adj attr, adv* with teeth chattering; **~knirschen** *nt* grinding one's teeth; (*fig*) gnashing of teeth; **z~knirschend** *adj attr, adv* grinding one's teeth; (*fig*) gnashing one's teeth; **er fand sich z~knirschend damit ab** he agreed with (a) bad grace.

zahnen *vi* to teethe, to cut one's teeth/a tooth ♦ **das Z~** teething.

zähnen *vt* to tooth; *Briefmarken* to perforate.

Zahn-: **~ersatz** *m* dentures *pl*, set of dentures; **~fäule** *f* tooth decay, caries *sing*; **~fleisch** *nt* gum(s *pl*); **(nur noch) auf dem ~fleisch gehen** *or* **kriechen** (*inf*) to be all-in (*inf*), to be on one's last legs (*inf*); **~fleischbluten** *nt* bleeding of the gums; **~füllung** *f* filling; **~hals** *m* neck of a tooth; **~heilkunde** *f* dentistry; **~höhle** *f* pulp cavity; **~klammer** *f siehe* **~spange**; **~klempner** *m* (*hum*) dentist; **~klinik** *f* dental clinic *or* hospital; **~kranz** *m* (*Tech*) gear rim; **~krone** *f* crown; **~laut** *m* (*Ling*) dental (consonant); **z~los** *adj* toothless; **~losigkeit** *f* toothlessness; **~lücke** *f* gap between one's teeth; **~mark** *nt* dental pulp; **~medizin** *f* dentistry; **~pasta, ~paste** *f* toothpaste; **~pflege** *f* dental hygiene; **~prothese** *f* set of dentures; **~pulver** *nt* tooth powder; **~putzglas** *nt* toothbrush glass; **~rad** *nt* cogwheel, gear (wheel); **~radbahn** *f* rack-railway (*Brit*), rack-railroad (*US*); **~radgetriebe** *nt* gear mechanism; **~reihe** *f* row of teeth; **~scheibe** *f* (*Tech*) cog; **~schein** *m* (*inf*) *form for free dental treatment*; **~schmelz** *m* (tooth) enamel; **~schmerz** *m usu pl* toothache *no pl*; **~seide** *f* dental floss; **~spange** *f* brace; **~stein** *m* tartar; **~stocher** *m* **-s, -** toothpick; **~stummel** *m* stump; **~techniker** *m* dental technician.

Zähnung *f* (*Zähne, Gezahntsein*) teeth *pl*; (*von Briefmarken*) perforations *pl*; (*das Zähnen*) toothing; perforation.

Zahn-: **~wal** *m* toothed whale; **~wechsel** *m* second dentition (*form*); **~weh** *nt* toothache; **~wurzel** *f* root (of a/the tooth); **~zement** *m* (dental) cement.

Zähre *f* **-, -n** (*old, poet*) tear.

Zaire [za'i:r] *nt* **-s** Zaire.

Zairer(in *f*) [za'i:rɐ, -ərɪn] *m* **-s, -** Zairean.

Zampano *m* **-s, -s** (*inf*) **der große ~** the big cheese (*inf*).

Zander *m* **-s, -** (*Zool*) pike-perch.

Zange *f* **-, -n** (*Flach~, Rund~*) (pair of) pliers *pl*; (*Beiß~*) (pair of) pincers *pl*; (*Greif~, Kohlen~, Zucker~*) (pair of) tongs *pl*; (*von Tier*) pincers *pl*; (*Med*) forceps *pl*; (*inf: Ringen*) double lock ♦ **jdn in die ~ nehmen** (*Ringen*) to put a double lock on sb; (*Ftbl etc*) to sandwich sb; (*fig*) to put the screws on sb (*inf*); **jetzt haben wir ihn in der ~** (*fig*) we've got him now; **ihn/das möchte ich nicht mit der ~ anfassen** (*inf*) I wouldn't touch him/it with a barge-pole (*Brit inf*) *or* a ten-foot pole (*US inf*).

Zangen-: **~bewegung** *f* (*Mil*) pincer movement; **z~förmig** *adj* pincer-shaped; **~geburt** *f* forceps delivery; **~griff** *m* (*Ringen*) double lock.

Zank *m* **-(e)s,** *no pl* squabble, quarrel, row ♦ **zwischen ihnen gab es dauernd ~** they were continually squabbling *or* quarrelling *or* rowing; **~ und Streit** trouble and strife.

Zank|apfel *m* (*fig*) bone of contention.

zanken *vir* to quarrel, to squabble, to row ♦ **wir haben uns gezankt** we've had a row, we've quarrelled; **(sich) um etw ~** to quarrel over sth.

Zänker *m* **-s, -** quarreller, squabbler.

Zankerei *f* quarrelling, squabbling.

zänkisch *adj* (*streitsüchtig*) quarrelsome; (*tadelsüchtig*) *Frau* nagging *attr*, shrewish.

Zanksucht *f* quarrelsomeness; (*Tadelsucht: von Frau*) nagging, shrewishness.

zanksüchtig *adj siehe* **zänkisch.**

Zäpfchen *nt dim of* **Zapfen** small plug *etc*; (*Gaumen~*) uvula; (*Suppositorium*) suppository ♦ **~-R** (*Ling*) uvular "r".

Zapfen *m* **-s, -** (*Spund*) bung, spigot; (*Pfropfen*) stopper, bung; (*Tannen~ etc, von Auge*) cone; (*Eis~*) icicle; (*Mech: von Welle, Lager etc*) journal; (*Holzverbindung*) tenon.

zapfen *vt* to tap, to draw ♦ **dort wird das Pils frisch gezapft** they have draught Pilsener *or* Pilsener on draught *or* tap there.

Zapfenstreich *m* (*Mil*) tattoo, last post (*Brit*), taps *sing* (*US*) ♦ **den ~ blasen** to sound the tattoo; **der Große ~** the Ceremonial Tattoo; **um 12 Uhr ist ~** (*fig inf*) lights out is at 12 o'clock.

Zapfer *m* **-s, -** (*dial*) barman, tapster (*old*).

Zapf-: **~hahn** *m* tap; **~pistole** *f* (petrol (*Brit*) *or* gas (*US*) pump) nozzle; **~säule** *f* petrol pump (*Brit*), gas pump (*US*); **~stelle** *f* tap; (*Elec*) (power) point; (*Tankstelle*) petrol (*Brit*) *or* gas (*US*) station.

Zaponlack ® *m* cellulose lacquer.

zapp(e)lig *adj* wriggly; (*unruhig*) fidgety.

zappeln *vi* to wriggle; (*Hampelmann*) to jiggle; (*unruhig sein*) to fidget ♦ **er zappelte mit Armen und Beinen** he was all of a fidget, he couldn't sit still; **jdn ~ lassen** (*fig inf*) to keep sb in suspense; **in der Schlinge ~** (*fig*) to be caught in the net.

Zappelphilipp *m* **-s, -e** *or* **-s** fidget(er).

zappen *vi* (*inf*) to zap (*inf*) ♦ **in den Konkurrenzkanal ~** to zap over to the other channel (*inf*); **Z~ macht Spaß** zapping is fun (*inf*).

zappenduster *adj* (*inf*) pitch-black, pitch-dark ♦ **wie sieht es denn mit euren Plänen aus? — ~** how are your plans working out? — grim; **dann ist es ~** you'll/we'll *etc* be in trouble *or* (dead) shtook (*sl*).

Zapper(in) *m(f)* **-s, -** (*inf*) zapper (*inf*) ♦ **er ist ein leidenschaftlicher ~** he's dead keen on zapping (*inf*).

zapplig *adj siehe* **zapp(e)lig.**

Zar *m* **-en, -en** tsar, czar.

Zarewitsch *m* **-(e)s, -e** tsarevitch.

Zarge *f* **-, -n** frame; (*von Geige etc*) rib; (*von Plattenspieler*) plinth.

Zarin *f* tsarina, czarina.

Zarismus *m* tsarism.

zaristisch *adj* tsarist *no adv.*

zart *adj* (*weich*) *Haut, Flaum,* (*leise*) *Töne, Stimme* soft; *Braten, Gemüse* tender; *Porzellan, Blüte, Gebäck, Farben, Teint,* (*schwächlich*) *Gesundheit, Kind* delicate; (*feinfühlig*) *Gemüt, Gefühle* sensitive, tender, delicate; (*sanft*) *Wind, Berührung* gentle, soft ♦ **mit jdm/etw ~ umgehen** to treat *or* handle sb/sth gently; **etw nur ~ andeuten** to hint at sth only gently; **nichts für ~e Ohren** not for tender *or* sensitive ears; **im ~en Alter von ...** at the tender age of ...; **das ~e Geschlecht** the gentle sex; **~ besaitet sein** to be very sensitive.

Zart-: ⚠**z~besaitet** *adj attr* highly sensitive; **z~bitter** *adj Schokolade* plain; **z~blau** *adj* pale blue; **z~fühlend** *adj* sensitive; **~gefühl** *nt* delicacy of feeling, sensitivity; **z~gliedrig** *adj* dainty; **z~grün** *adj* pale green.

Zartheit *f siehe adj* softness; tenderness; delicacy, delicateness; sensitivity; gentleness.

zärtlich *adj* tender, affectionate, loving.

Zärtlichkeit *f* (**a**) *no pl* affection, tenderness. (**b**) (*Liebkosung*) caress ♦ **~en** (*Worte*) tender *or* loving words, words of love; **jdm ~en ins Ohr flüstern** to whisper sweet nothings in sb's ear.

Zaster *m* **-s,** *no pl* (*sl*) lolly (*inf*), loot (*inf*).

Zäsur *f* caesura; (*fig*) break.

Zauber *m* **-s, -** (*Magie*) magic; (*~bann*) (magic) spell; (*fig: Reiz*) magic, charm ♦ **den ~ lösen** to break the spell; **fauler ~** (*inf*) humbug *no indef art*; **der ganze ~** (*inf*) the whole lot (*inf*); **warum der ganze ~?** (*inf: Getue*) why all the fuss?

Zauber-: **~bann** *m* (magic) spell; **unter einem ~bann stehen** to be under a spell; **~buch** *nt* book of spells; (*für ~kunststücke*) conjuring book.

Zauberei *f* (**a**) *no pl* (*das Zaubern*) magic. (**b**) (*Zauberkunststück*) conjuring trick.

Zauberer *m* **-s, -** magician; (*in Märchen etc auch*) sorcerer, wizard; (*Zauberkünstler auch*) conjurer.

Zauber-: **~flöte** *f* magic flute; **~formel** *f* magic formula; **z~haft** *adj* enchanting; **~hand** *f*: **wie von** *or* **durch ~hand** as if by magic.

Zauberin *f* (female) magician; (*in Märchen etc auch*) enchantress, sorceress; (*Zauberkünstlerin auch*) (female) conjurer.

zauberisch *adj siehe* **zauberhaft.**

Zauber-: **~kraft** *f* magic power; **~kunst** *f* magic, conjuring; **~künstler** *m* conjurer, magician; **~kunststück** *nt* conjuring trick; **~landschaft** *f* fairy-tale scene; **~macht** *f* magical powers *pl*; **~mittel** *nt* magical cure; (*Trank*) magic potion, philtre.

zaubern 1 *vi* to do *or* perform magic; (*Kunststück vorführen*) to do conjuring tricks ♦ **ich kann doch nicht ~!** (*inf*) I'm not a magician!, I can't perform miracles!
2 *vt* (**a**) **etw aus etw ~** to conjure sth out of sth. (**b**) (*fig*) *Lösung, Essen* to produce as if by magic, to conjure up.

Zauber-: ⚠**~nuß** *f* wych-hazel, witch-hazel; **~reich** *nt* enchanted *or* magic realm; ⚠**~schloß** *nt* enchanted castle; **~spruch** *m* (magic) spell; **~stab** *m* (magic) wand; **~trank** *m* magic potion, philtre; **~trick** *m* conjuring trick; **~werk** *nt* sorcery, wizardry; **~wesen** *nt* magical being; **~wort** *nt* magic word; **~würfel** *m* Rubik's cube; **~wurzel** *f* mandrake root.

Zauderer *m* **-s, -** vacillator, irresolute person.

zaudern *vi* to hesitate, to vacillate ♦ **etw ohne zu ~ tun** to do sth without hesitating *or* any hesitation.

Zaum *m* **-(e)s, Zäume** bridle ♦ **einem Pferd den ~ anlegen** to put a bridle on a horse; **jdn/etw im ~(e) halten** (*fig*) to keep a tight rein on sb/sth, to keep sb/sth in check; **sich im ~(e) halten** (*fig*) to control oneself, to keep oneself in check; **seine Ungeduld/seinen Zorn im ~e halten** (*fig*) to control *or* curb one's impatience/anger.

zäumen *vt* to bridle.

Zaumzeug *nt* bridle.

Zaun *m* **-(e)s, Zäune** fence ◆ **einen Streit vom ~(e) brechen** to pick a quarrel, to start a fight.
Zaun-: ~eidechse *f* sand lizard; **~gast** *m sb who manages to get a free view of an event*; **~könig** *m (Orn)* wren; **~pfahl** *m* (fencing) post; **jdm einen Wink mit dem ~pfahl geben** to give *or* drop sb a broad hint; **~rebe** *f* climbing plant; **~winde** *f (Bot)* great bindweed.
Zausel *m* **-s, -s** *(inf)* codger *(inf)*.
zausen [1] *vt* to ruffle; *Haare* to tousle.
[2] *vi* **in etw** *(dat)* **~** *(Wind)* to ruffle sth.
z.B. [tsɛt'beː] *abbr of* **zum Beispiel** eg.
z.b.V. *abbr of* **zur besonderen Verwendung.**
ZDF [tsɛtdeː'|ɛf] *nt* **-s** *abbr of* **Zweites Deutsches Fernsehen.**
ZDLer [tsɛtdeː'|ɛlɐ] *m* **-s, -** *(inf) abbr of* **Zivildienstleistende(r).**
Zebaoth *m*: **der Herr ~** *(Bibl)* Jehovah.
Zebra *nt* **-s, -s** zebra.
Zebrastreifen *m* zebra crossing *(Brit)*, pedestrian crossing *or* crosswalk *(US)*.
Zebu *nt* **-s, -s** zebu.
Zechbruder *m* boozer *(inf)*; *(Kumpan)* drinking-mate *(inf)*, drinking-buddy *(inf)*.
Zeche *f* **-, -n (a)** *(Rechnung)* bill *(Brit)*, check *(US)* ◆ **die (ganze) ~ (be)zahlen** *(lit, fig)* to foot the bill; **(den Wirt um) die ~ prellen** to leave without paying (the bill); **eine (hohe) ~ machen** to run up a (large) bill. **(b)** *(Bergwerk)* (coal-)mine, pit, colliery.
zechen *vi* to booze *(inf)*; *(Zechgelage abhalten)* to carouse.
Zecher(in *f*) *m* **-s, -** boozer *(inf)*; *(bei einem Zechgelage)* carouser, reveller.
Zecherei *f* booze-up *(inf)*; *(Zechgelage)* carousal; *(das Zechen)* boozing; carousing.
Zech-: ~gelage *nt* carousal *(old, hum)*; **~kumpan** *m* drinking-mate *(inf)*, drinking-buddy *(inf)*; **~preller** *m* **-s, -** *person who leaves without paying the bill at a restaurant, bar etc*; **~prellerei** *f leaving without paying the bill for drink or food consumed at a restaurant, bar etc*; **~schwester** *f* drinking-mate *(inf)*; **~stein** *m (Geol)* Zechstein (period), Upper Permian; **~tour** *f (inf)* pub-crawl *(esp Brit inf)*.
Zeck[1] *nt or m* **-(e)s, -e** *(dial: Fangspiel)* tag.
Zeck[2] *m* **-(e)s, -en** *(Aus)*, **Zecke** *f* **-, -n** tick.
Zedent *m (Jur)* assignor.
Zeder *f* **-, -n** cedar.
zedern *adj* cedar.
Zedern|öl *nt* cedarwood oil.
zedieren* *vt (Jur)* to cede, to assign, to transfer.
Zeh *m* **-s, -en, Zehe** *f* **-, -n** toe; *(Knoblauch~)* clove ◆ **auf (den) ~en gehen/schleichen** to tiptoe, to walk/creep on tiptoe; **sich auf die ~en stellen** to stand on tiptoe; **jdm auf die ~en treten** *(fig inf)* to tread on sb's toes.
Zehen-: ~nagel *m* toenail; **~spitze** *f* tip of the toe; **auf (den) ~spitzen** on tiptoe, on tippy-toes *(US inf)*; **auf (den) ~spitzen gehen** to tiptoe, to walk on tiptoe; **auf den ~spitzen tanzen** to dance on one's toes.
zehn *num* ten ◆ **(ich wette) ~ zu** *or* **gegen eins** (I bet) ten to one; *siehe auch* **vier.**
Zehn *f* **-, -en** ten; *siehe auch* **Vier.**
Zehn-: ~eck *nt* decagon; **z~eckig** *adj* ten-sided, decagonal.
Zehner *m* **-s, - (a)** *(Math)* ten; *siehe auch* **Vierer. (b)** *(inf) (Zehnpfennigstück)* ten-pfennig piece, ten; *(Zehnmarkschein)* tenner *(inf)*.
Zehner-: ~bruch *m* decimal (fraction); **~karte** *f (für Bus etc)* 10-journey ticket; *(für Schwimmbad etc)* 10-visit ticket; **~packung** *f* packet of ten; **~stelle** *f* ten's (place); **~system** *nt* decimal system; **~tastatur** *f (Comput)* numeric keypad.
Zehn-: ~fingersystem *nt* touch-typing method; **~kampf** *m (Sport)* decathlon; **~kämpfer** *m* decathlete; **z~mal** *adv* ten times; *siehe auch* **viermal**; **~markschein** *m* ten-mark note; **~meterbrett** *nt* ten-metre board.
Zehnt *m* **-en, -en, Zehnte(r)** *m decl as adj (Hist)* tithe.
zehntausend *num* ten thousand ◆ **Z~e von Menschen** tens of thousands of people; *siehe* **obere(r, s).**
Zehntel *nt* **-s, -** tenth.
zehntel *adj* tenth.
zehntens *adv* tenth(ly), in the tenth place.
Zehnte(r) *m siehe* **Zehnt.**
zehnte(r, s) *adj* tenth; *siehe auch* **vierte(r, s).**
zehren *vi* **(a) von etw ~** *(lit)* to live off *or* on sth; *(fig)* to feed on sth. **(b) an jdm/etw ~** *an Menschen, Kraft* to wear sb/sth out; *an Kraft auch* to sap sth; *an Nerven* to ruin sth; *(Anstrengung) am Herzen* to weaken sth; *(Kummer)* to gnaw at sth; *an Gesundheit* to undermine sth.
Zehrgeld *nt*, **Zehrpfennig** *m (old)* travelling monies *pl (old)*.
Zehrung *f* **-,** *no pl (old)* provisions *pl*.
Zeichen *nt* **-s, -** sign; *(Sci, algebraisch, auf Landkarte)* symbol; *(Schrift~, Comput)* character; *(An~: von Krankheit, Winter, Beweis: von Friedfertigkeit)* sign, indication; *(Hinweis, Signal)* signal; *(Erkennungs~)* identification; *(Lese~)* bookmark, marker; *(Vermerk)* mark; *(auf Briefköpfen)* reference; *(Satz~)* punctuation mark; *(Waren~)* trade mark ◆ **wenn nicht alle ~ trügen** if I'm/we're *etc* not completely mistaken; **es ist ein ~ unserer Zeit, daß ...** it is a sign of the times that ...; **die ~ erkennen** to see the writing on the wall; **die ~ der Zeit erkennen** to recognize the mood of the times; **es geschehen noch ~ und Wunder!** *(hum)* wonders will never cease! *(hum)*; **als/zum ~** as a sign; **ein ~ des Himmels** a sign from heaven; **als ~ von etw** as a sign *or* indication of sth; **zum ~, daß ...** as a sign that ..., to show that ...; **als ~ der Verehrung** as a mark *or* token of respect; **jdm ein ~ geben** *or* **machen** to give sb a signal *or* sign, to signal to sb; **etw zum ~ tun** to do sth as a signal, to signal by doing sth; **das ~ zum Aufbruch geben** to give the signal to leave; **unser/Ihr ~** *(form)* our/your reference; **seines ~s** *(old, hum)* by trade; **er ist im ~** *or* **unter dem ~ des Widders geboren** he was born under the sign of Aries; **unter dem ~ von etw stehen** *(fig: Konferenz etc)* to take place against a background of sth; **das Jahr 1979 stand unter dem ~ des Kindes** 1979 was the year of the child.
Zeichen-: ~block *m* drawing *or* sketch pad; **~brett** *nt* drawing-board; **~dreieck** *nt* set-square; **~erklärung** *f (auf Fahrplänen etc)* key (to the symbols); *(auf Landkarte)* legend; **~feder** *f* drawing-pen; **z~haft** *adj* symbolic; **~heft** *nt* drawing-book; **~karte** *f (Comput)* graphics card; **~kette** *f (Comput)* character string; **~kohle** *f* charcoal; **~kunst** *f* (art of) drawing; **~lehrer** *m* art teacher; **~papier** *nt* drawing paper; **~saal** *m* art-room; **~satz** *m (Comput)* character set, font; **~schutz** *m* protection of registered trademarks; **~setzung** *f* punctuation; **~sprache** *f* sign language; **~stift** *m* drawing pencil; **~stunde** *f* art *or* drawing lesson; **~system** *nt* notation; *(Ling)* system of signs; **~tisch** *m* drawing table; **~trickfilm** *m* (animated) cartoon; **~unterricht** *m* art; *(Unterrichtsstunde)* drawing *or* art lesson; **~vorlage** *f* original, model *(for a drawing or trademark)*.
zeichnen [1] *vi* to draw; *(form: unter~)* to sign ◆ **an dem Entwurf hat er lange gezeichnet** he has spent a long time drawing the blueprint; **gezeichnet: XY** signed, XY.
[2] *vt* **(a)** *(abzeichnen)* to draw; *(entwerfen) Plan, Grundriß* to draw up, to draft; *(fig: porträtieren)* to portray, to depict.
(b) *(kennzeichnen)* to mark ◆ **das Gefieder des Vogels ist hübsch gezeichnet** the bird's plumage has attractive markings.
(c) *(Fin) Betrag* to subscribe; *Aktien* to subscribe (for); *Anleihe* to subscribe to.
Zeichner(in *f*) *m* **-s, - (a)** artist ◆ **muß ein Maler auch immer ein guter ~ sein?** must a painter always be a good draughtsman too?; *siehe* **technisch.**
(b) *(Fin)* subscriber *(von* to*)*.
zeichnerisch [1] *adj Darstellung, Gestaltung* graphic(al) ◆ **sein ~es Können** his drawing ability.
[2] *adv* **~ begabt sein** to have a talent for drawing; **etw ~ erklären** to explain sth with a drawing.
Zeichnung *f* **(a)** *(Darstellung)* drawing; *(Entwurf)* draft, drawing; *(fig: Schilderung)* portrayal, depiction. **(b)** *(Muster)* patterning; *(von Gefieder, Fell)* markings *pl*. **(c)** *(Fin)* subscription ◆ **eine Anleihe zur ~ auflegen** to invite subscriptions for a loan.
Zeichnungs-: z~berechtigt *adj* authorized to sign; **~vollmacht** *f* authority to sign.
Zeigefinger *m* index finger, forefinger.
▼ **zeigen** [1] *vi* to point ◆ **nach Norden/rechts ~** to point north *or* to the north/to the right; **auf jdn/etw ~** to point at sb/sth; *(hinweisen auch)* to point to sb/sth.
▼ [2] *vt* to show; *(Thermometer auch)* to be at *or* on, to indicate ◆ **jdm etw ~** to show sb sth *or* sth to sb; **ich muß mir mal von jemandem ~ lassen, wie man das macht** I'll have to get someone to show me how to do it; **dem werd' ich's (aber) ~!** *(inf)* I'll show him!; **zeig mal, was du kannst!** let's see what you can do!, show us what you can do!
[3] *vr* to appear; *(Gefühle)* to show ◆ **sich mit jdm ~** to let oneself be seen with sb; **in dem Kleid kann ich mich doch nicht ~** I can't be seen in a dress like that; **er zeigt sich nicht gern in der Öffentlichkeit** he doesn't like showing himself *or* being seen in public; **sich ~ als ...** to show *or* prove oneself to be ...; **er zeigte sich befriedigt** he was satisfied; **es zeigt sich, daß ...** it turns out that ...; **es zeigt sich (doch) wieder einmal, daß ...** it just goes to show; **es wird sich ~, wer recht hat** time will tell who is right, we shall see who's right; **daran zeigt sich, daß ...** that shows (that) ...; **das zeigt sich jetzt** it's beginning to show.
Zeiger *m* **-s, -** indicator, pointer; *(Uhr~)* hand ◆ **der große/kleine ~** the big/little hand.
Zeiger|ausschlag *m* pointer *or* indicator deflection.
Zeigestock *m* pointer.
zeihen *pret* **zieh,** *ptp* **geziehen** *vt (old)* **jdn einer Sache** *(gen)* **~** to accuse sb of sth.
Zeile *f* **-, -n** line; *(Häuser~, Baum~ etc auch)* row ◆ **davon habe ich keine ~ gelesen** I haven't read a single word of it; **zwischen den ~n lesen** to read between the lines; **vielen Dank für Deine ~n** many thanks for your letter; **jdm ein paar ~n schreiben** to write sb a few lines; *(Brief schreiben auch)* to drop sb a line.
Zeilen-: ~abstand *m* line spacing; **~abtastung** *f (TV)* line scan(ning); **~bauweise** *f* ribbon development; **~befehl** *(Comput)* line command; **~fang** *m (TV)* horizontal hold; **~honorar** *nt* payment per line; **~honorar bekommen** to be paid by the line; **~länge** *f* length (of a/the line); **~norm** *f (TV)* line standard; **~schalter** *m* line spacer; **~schaltung** *f* line spacing; **~setzmaschine** *f* Linotype ® machine; **~umbruch** *f* **(automatischer) ~umbruch** *(Comput)* wordwrap; **~vorschub** *m (Comput)* line feed; **z~weise** *adv* in lines; *(nach Zeilen)* by the line; **etw z~weise vorlesen** to read sth out line by line.
-zeilig *adj suf* -line ◆ **es ist vier~** it has four lines.
Zeisig *m* **-s, -en** *(Orn)* siskin; *siehe* **locker.**
Zeit *f* **-, -en (a)** time; *(Epoche)* age ◆ **die gute alte ~** the good old days; **das waren noch ~en!** those were the days; **die ~en sind schlecht** times are bad; **die ~en haben sich geändert** times have changed; **die ~ Goethes** the age of Goethe; **die damalige ~ machte die Einführung neuer Methoden erforderlich**

△: for details of spelling reform, see supplement

➤ SPRACHE AKTIV: **zeigen: 2** → 53.3, 53.4

the situation at the time required the introduction of new methods; **wenn ~ und Umstände es erfordern** if circumstances demand it, if the situation requires it; **die jetzigen ~en erfordern, ...** the present situation requires ...; **für alle ~en** for ever, for all time (*liter*); **etw für alle ~en entscheiden** to decide sth once and for all; **in seiner/ihrer besten ~** at his/her/its peak; **mit der ~ gehen** to move with the times; **vor der ~ alt werden** to get old before one's time; **vor jds** (*dat*) **~** before sb's time; **die ~ ist knapp bemessen** time is short; **die ~ wurde mir lang** time hung heavy on my hands; **eine lange ~ her sein** *or* **zurückliegen, daß ...** to be a long time (ago *or* back) since ...; **eine Stunde ~ haben** to have an hour (to spare); **Fräulein Glück, haben Sie vielleicht einen Augenblick ~?** Miss Glück, do you have a moment?; **sich** (*dat*) **für jdn/etw ~ nehmen** to devote time to sb/sth; **dafür muß ich mir mehr ~ nehmen** I need more time for that; **sich** (*dat*) **die ~ nehmen, etw zu tun** to take the time to do sth; **du hast dir aber reichlich ~ gelassen** you certainly took your time; **hier bin ich die längste ~ gewesen** it's about time *or* high time I was going; **keine ~ verlieren** to lose no time; **damit hat es noch ~** there's no rush *or* hurry, there's plenty of time; **das hat ~ bis morgen** that can wait until tomorrow; **laß dir ~** take your time; **... aller ~en ...** of all time, ... ever; **auf bestimmte ~** for a certain length of time; **auf unbestimmte ~** for an indefinite period; **in letzter ~** recently; **die ganze ~ über** the whole time; **mit der ~** gradually, in time; **nach ~ bezahlt werden** to be paid by the hour; **die ~ heilt alle Wunden** (*Prov*) time is a great healer (*prov*); **auf ~ spielen** (*Sport, fig*) to play for time; **es wird langsam ~, daß ...** it's about time that ...; **für dich wird es langsam ~, daß ...** it's about time that you ...; **seine ~ ist gekommen** his time has come; **hast du (die) genaue ~?** do you have the exact time?; **in der ~ von 10 bis 12** between 10 and 12 (o'clock); **es ist an der ~ , daß ...** it is about time *or* high time (that) ...; **Vertrag auf ~** fixed-term contract; **Beamter auf ~** ≃ non-permanent civil servant; **Soldat auf ~** soldier serving for a set time; **seit dieser ~** since then; **zur ~** *or* **zu ~en Königin Viktorias** in Queen Victoria's times; **zu der ~, als ...** (at the time) when ...; **alles zu seiner ~** (*Prov*) all in good time; **von ~ zu ~** from time to time; **zur ~** at the moment.
(b) (*Ling*) tense ◆ **in welcher ~ steht das Verb?** what tense is the verb in?

zeit *prep +gen* **~ meines/seines Lebens** in my/his lifetime.

-zeit *f in cpds* time.

Zeit-: ~abschnitt *m* period (of time); **~alter** *nt* age; **das goldene ~alter** the golden age; **in unserem ~alter** nowadays, in this day and age; **~angabe** *f* (*Datum*) date; (*Uhrzeit*) time (of day); **die ~angabe kommt vor der Ortsangabe** (*Gram*) time is given before place; **~ansage** *f* (*Rad*) time check; (*Telec*) speaking clock; **~arbeit** *f* temporary work/job; **~aufnahme** *f* (*Phot*) time exposure; **~aufwand** *m* time (*needed to complete a task*); **mit möglichst wenig ~aufwand** taking as little time as possible; **dieses Dokument wurde unter großen ~aufwand erstellt** it took an enormous amount of time to produce this document; **mit großem ~aufwand verbunden sein** to be extremely time-consuming; **~begriff** *m* conception of time; **~bestimmung** *f* (*Gram*) designation of the tense of a verb; **~bombe** *f* time bomb; **~dokument** *nt* contemporary document; **~druck** *m* pressure of time; **unter ~druck** under pressure; **~einheit** *f* time unit.

Zeiten-: ~folge *f* (*Gram*) sequence of tenses; **~wende** *f* **nach/vor der ~wende** anno Domini/before Christ.

Zeit-: ~ersparnis *f* saving of time; **~fahren** *nt* (*Sport*) time trial; **~form** *f* (*Gram*) tense; **~frage** *f* question of time; **z~gebunden** *adj* tied to *or* dependent on a particular time; *Mode* temporary; **~geist** *m* Zeitgeist, spirit of the times; **z~gemäß** *adj* up-to-date; **z~gemäß sein** to be in keeping with the times; **~genosse** *m* contemporary; **ein seltsamer ~genosse** (*iro*) an odd bod (*inf*), an oddball (*esp US inf*); **z~genössisch** *adj* contemporary; **~geschäft** *nt* (*Comm*) *siehe* **Termingeschäft**; **~geschehen** *nt* events *pl* of the day; **~geschichte** *f* contemporary history; **~geschmack** *m* prevailing taste; **~gewinn** *m* gain in time; **sich um einen ~gewinn bemühen** to try to gain time; **z~gleich** [1] *adj Erscheinungen* contemporaneous; *Läufer* with the same time; (*Film*) synchronized, in sync(h) (*inf*); [2] *adv* at the same time; **z~gleich den ersten Platz belegen** to tie for first place; **~historiker** *m* contemporary historian.

zeitig *adj, adv* early.

zeitigen *vt* (*geh*) *Ergebnis, Wirkung* to bring about; *Erfolg auch* to lead to ◆ **Früchte ~** to bear fruit.

Zeit-: ≈karte *f* season ticket; (*Wochenkarte*) weekly ticket; **≈karteninhaber** *m* season-ticket holder; weekly ticket holder; **≈kontrolle** *f* time study; **z≈kritisch** *adj Aufsatz, Artikel* full of comment on contemporary issues; **seine z~kritischen Bemerkungen** his thoughtful remarks on contemporary issues; **seine z~kritische Haltung** his awareness of contemporary issues; ⚠**≈lang** *f* **eine ~lang** a while, a time; **wir sind eine ~lang dort geblieben** we stayed there (for) a while *or* for a time; **eine ~lang ist das ganz schön** for a while *or* time it's quite nice; **z~lebens** *adv* all one's life.

zeitlich [1] *adj* temporal; (*vergänglich auch*) transitory; (*chronologisch*) *Reihenfolge* chronological ◆ **in kurzem/großem ~em Abstand** at short/long intervals (of time); **das Z~e segnen** (*euph: Mensch*) to depart this life; (*Sache*) to bite the dust (*inf*).
[2] *adv* timewise (*inf*), from the point of view of time; (*chronologisch*) chronologically ◆ **das kann sie ~ nicht einrichten** she can't fit that in (timewise *inf*), she can't find (the) time for that; **das paßt ihr ~ nicht** the time isn't convenient for her; **~ zusammenfallen** to coincide; **die Uhren/Pläne ~ aufeinander abstimmen** to synchronize one's watches/plans.

Zeitlichkeit *f* temporality, transitoriness.

Zeit-: ~limit *nt* time limit; **~lohn** *m* hourly rate; **~lohn bekommen** to be paid by the hour; **z~los** *adj* timeless; *Stil auch* which doesn't date; *Kleidung auch* classic; **~lupe** *f* slow motion *no art*; **etw in (der) ~lupe zeigen** to show sth in slow motion; **Wiederholung in (der) ~lupe** slow-motion replay; **~lupenaufnahme** *f* slow-motion shot; **~lupentempo** *nt* slow speed; **im ~lupentempo** (*lit*) in slow motion; (*fig*) at a snail's pace; **~mangel** *m* lack of time; **aus ~mangel** for lack of time; **~maschine** *f* time machine; **~maß** *nt* tempo; **~messer** *m* **-s, -** timekeeper; **~messung** *f* timekeeping (*auch Sport*), measurement of time; **z~nah** *adj* contemporary; *Problem auch* of our age; *Gottesdienst, Übersetzung auch* modern; *Bücher, Unterricht* relevant to present times; **~nähe** *f siehe adj* contemporary nature; modernness; relevance to present times; **~nahme** *f* **-, -n** (*Sport*) timekeeping *no pl*; **~nehmer** *m* (*Sport, Ind*) timekeeper; **~not** *f* shortage of time; **in ~not sein** to be pressed for *or* short of time; **~plan** *m* schedule, timetable; **~punkt** *m* (*Termin*) time; (*Augenblick auch*) moment; **zu diesem ~punkt** at that time; **den ~punkt für etw festlegen** to set a time for sth; **~raffer** *m* **-s,** *no pl* time-lapse photography; **einen Film im ~raffer zeigen** to show a time-lapse film; **z~raubend** *adj* time-consuming; **~raum** *m* period of time; **in einem ~raum von ...** over a period of ...; **~rechnung** *f* calendar; **nach christlicher/jüdischer ~rechnung** according to the Christian/Jewish calendar; **vor/nach unserer ~rechnung** (*abbr* **v.u.Z./n.u.Z.**) before Christ/anno Domini (*abbr* BC/AD); **~schrift** *f* (*Illustrierte*) magazine; (*wissenschaftlich*) periodical, journal; **~schriftenkatalog** *m* periodicals catalogue; **~sinn** *m* sense of time; **~soldat** *m* regular soldier (*who has signed up for a fixed period of time*); **~spanne** *f* period of time; **z~sparend** *adj* timesaving; **~studie** *f* (*Ind*) time (and motion) study; **z~synchron** *adj* synchronized *no adv*, at the same time; **~tafel** *f* chronological table; **~takt** *m* **(a)** (*Telec*) unit length; **(b)** timing; **im 10-minütigen ~takt** every 10 minutes; **~umstellung** *f* **(a)** (*Zeitänderung*) changing the clocks, putting the clocks back/forward; **(b)** (*Zeitunterschied*) time difference.

Zeitung *f* (news)paper ◆ **er hat bei der ~ gearbeitet** he worked for a newspaper.

Zeitungs- *in cpds* newspaper; **~abonnement** *nt* subscription to a newspaper; **~anzeige** *f* newspaper advertisement; (*Familienanzeige*) announcement in the (news)paper; **~ausschnitt** *m* newspaper cutting; **~austräger** *m* ≃ paperboy/girl; **~beilage** *f* newspaper supplement; **~druckpapier** *nt* newsprint; **~ente** *f* (*inf*) canard, false newspaper report; **~frau** *f* (*inf*) newspaper carrier; **~händler** *m* newsagent, newsdealer (*US*); **~inserat** *nt* newspaper advertisement; **~jargon** *m* journalese; **~junge** *m* paperboy; **~kiosk** *m* newspaper kiosk; **~korrespondent** *m* newspaper correspondent; **~laden** *m* paper shop; **~lesen** *nt* reading the (news)paper *no art*; **er war gerade beim ~lesen** he was just reading the paper/papers; **~leser** *m* newspaper reader; **~papier** *nt* newsprint; (*als Altpapier*) newspaper; **~redakteur** *m* newspaper editor; **~ständer** *m* magazine *or* newspaper rack; **~verleger** *m* newspaper publisher; **~wesen** *nt* press, newspaper world; **das ~wesen in Deutschland** the German press; **im ~wesen tätig sein** to be in the newspaper business; (*Journalist*) to be in journalism; **~wissenschaft** *f* journalism; **~zar** *m* press baron.

Zeit-: ~unterschied *m* time difference; **~vergeudung** *f* waste of time; **~verlust** *m* loss of time; **das bedeutet mehrere Stunden ~verlust** this will mean wasting several hours; **ohne ~verlust** without losing any time; **~verschiebung** *f* **(a)** (*Zeitunterschied*) time difference; **(b)** (*von Termin etc*) rescheduling, change in timing; **~verschwendung** *f* waste of time; **das wäre ~verschwendung** that would be a waste of time; **~vertreib** *m* way of passing the time; (*Hobby*) pastime; **zum ~vertreib** to pass the time, as a way of passing the time; **~vorgabe** *f* **(a)** (*Zeitbestimmung*) time setting; **(b)** (*Vorsprung*) head start; **z~weilig** *adj* temporary; **z~weise** *adv* at times; **und z~weise Regen** with rain at times; **~wende** *f siehe* **Zeitenwende**; **~wert** *m* (*Fin*) current value; (*Meßergebnis*) time; **~wort** *nt* verb; **~zeichen** *nt* time signal; **~zeuge** *m* contemporary witness; **~zünder** *m* time fuse.

zelebrieren* *vt* to celebrate.

Zelebrität *f* (*rare*) celebrity.

Zell|atmung *f* cellular respiration.

Zelle *f* **-, -n** cell (*auch Sci, Pol*); (*Kabine*) cabin; (*Telefon~*) (phone) box (*Brit*) *or* booth; (*bei Flugzeug*) airframe.

Zell-: ~gewebe *nt* cell tissue; **~kern** *m* nucleus (of a/the cell); **~kernteilung** *f* cell division, mitosis; **~membran** *f* cell membrane.

Zellophan *nt* **-s,** *no pl* cellophane.

Zell-: ~präparat *nt* cell culture; **~stoff** *m* cellulose; **~stoffwindel** *f* disposable nappy (*Brit*) *or* diaper (*US*); **~teilung** *f* cell division.

zellular *adj* cellular.

Zellulartherapie *f* cell therapy.

Zelluloid [*auch* -'lɔyt] *nt* **-s,** *no pl* celluloid.

Zellulose *f* **-, -n** cellulose.

Zell-: ~verschmelzung *f* cell fusion; **~wand** *f* cell wall; **~wolle** *f* spun rayon.

Zelt *nt* **-(e)s, -e** tent; (*Bier~, Fest~ etc auch*) marquee; (*Indianer~*) wigwam, te(e)pee; (*Zirkus~*) big top; (*liter: des Himmels*) canopy ◆ **seine ~e aufschlagen/abbrechen** (*fig*) to settle down/to pack one's bags.

Zelt-: ~bahn *f* strip of canvas; **~dach** *nt* tent-roof; (*Dachform*) pyramid roof.

zelten *vi* to camp ◆ **Z~ verboten** no camping.

Zelter *m* **-s, -** (*Hist: Pferd*) palfrey.

Zelter(in *f*) *m* **-s, -** camper.

Zelt-: ~hering *m* tent peg; **~lager** *nt* camp; **wann fahrt ihr ins ~lager?** when are you going to camp?; **~mast** *m* tent pole; **~mission** *f evangelistic*

mission with a tent as its base; **~pflock** *m* tent peg; **~plane** *f* tarpaulin; **~platz** *m* camp site; **~stange** *f* tentpole.
Zement *m* **-(e)s, -e** cement.
zementieren* *vt* to cement; (*verputzen*) to cement over; *Stahl* to carburize (*spec*); (*fig*) to reinforce; *Freundschaft* to cement.
Zementierung *f* (*fig*) reinforcement; (*von Freundschaft*) cementing.
Zement(misch)maschine *f* cement mixer.
Zen *nt* **-s,** *no pl* Zen (Buddhism).
Zenit *m* **-(e)s,** *no pl* (*lit, fig*) zenith ◆ **die Sonne steht im ~** the sun is at its zenith; **im ~ des Lebens stehen** (*liter*) to be at one's peak.
Zenotaph *m* **-s, -e** cenotaph.
zensieren* *vt* **(a)** *auch vi* (*benoten*) to mark ◆ **einen Aufsatz mit einer Drei ~** to give an essay a three. **(b)** (*Bücher etc*) to censor.
Zensor *m* censor.
Zensur *f* **(a)** (*no pl: Kontrolle*) censorship *no indef art*; (*Prüfstelle*) censors *pl*; (*esp bei Film*) board of censors ◆ **eine ~ findet nicht statt** there is no censorship, it is/they are not censored; **durch die ~ gehen/einer ~ unterliegen** to be censored.
(b) (*Note*) mark ◆ **der Plan erhielt von der Presse schlechte ~en** the plan got the thumbs-down from the press (*inf*).
(c) ~en *pl* (*Zeugnis*) report *sing* ◆ **wenn es auf die ~en zugeht** when report time approaches.
zensurieren* *vt* (*Aus*) to censor.
Zensus *m* **-, -** (*Volkszählung*) census.
Zentaur *m* **-en, -en** centaur.
Zenti-: ~grad *m* hundredth of a degree; **~gramm** *nt* centigram(me); **~liter** *m or nt* centilitre; **~meter** *m or nt* centimetre; **~metermaß** *nt* (metric) tape measure.
Zentner *m* **-s, -** (metric) hundredweight; (*Aus, Sw*) 100kg.
Zentner-: ~last *f* (*fig*) heavy burden; **mir fiel eine ~last vom Herzen** it was a great weight *or* load off my mind; **z~schwer** *adj* (*fig*) heavy; **z~schwer auf jdm** *or* **jds Seele lasten** to weigh sb down; **z~weise** *adv* by the hundredweight.
zentral *adj* (*lit, fig*) central.
Zentral- *in cpds* central; **~bank** *f* central bank; **~bankrat** *m council of the German central bank.*
Zentrale *f* **-, -n** (*von Firma etc, Mil*) head office; (*für Taxis*) headquarters *sing or pl*; (*für Busse etc*) depot; (*Schalt~*) central control (office); (*Telefon~*) exchange; (*von Firma etc*) switchboard.
Zentral-: ~einheit *f* (*Comput*) CPU, central processing unit; **~heizung** *f* central heating.
Zentralisation *f* centralization.
zentralisieren* *vt* to centralize.
Zentralisierung *f* centralization.
Zentralismus *m* centralism.
zentralistisch *adj* centralist.
Zentral-: ~komitee *nt* central committee; **~nervensystem** *nt* central nervous system; **~rechner** *m* (*Comput*) mainframe; **~speicher** *m* (*Comput*) central memory; **~verriegelung** *f* (*Aut*) central (door) locking; ⚠**~verschluß** *m* leaf shutter.
Zentren *pl of* **Zentrum.**
Zentrier|automatik *f* (*Comput*) automatic centering.
zentrieren* *vt* (*auch Comput*) to centre.
zentrifugal *adj* centrifugal.
Zentrifugalkraft *f* centrifugal force.
Zentrifuge *f* **-, -n** centrifuge.
zentripetal *adj* centripetal.
Zentripetalkraft *f* centripetal force.
zentrisch *adj* concentric; *Anziehung* centric.
Zentrum *nt* **-s, Zentren** (*lit, fig*) centre (*Brit*), center (*US*); (*Innenstadt*) (town) centre; (*von Großstadt*) (city) centre ◆ **sie wohnt im ~ (der Stadt)/von Chicago** she lives in the (town/city) centre/in the centre of Chicago, she lives downtown/in downtown Chicago (*US*); **im ~ des Interesses stehen** to be the centre of attention.
Zentrumspartei *f* (*Hist*) Centre party, *German Catholic party representing the centre politically.*
Zephir (*esp Aus*), **Zephyr** *m* **-s, -e** (*liter*) zephyr.
Zeppelin *m* **-s, -e** zeppelin.
Zepter *nt* **-s, -** sceptre ◆ **das ~ führen** *or* **schwingen** (*inf*) to wield the sceptre; (*esp Ehefrau*) to rule the roost.
Zer *nt* **-s,** *no pl* (*abbr* **Ce**) cerium.
zerbeißen* *vt irreg* to chew; *Knochen, Bonbon, Keks etc* to crunch; (*beschädigen*) *Pantoffel etc* to chew to pieces; (*auseinanderbeißen*) *Kette, Leine* to chew through.
zerbersten* *vi irreg aux sein* to burst; (*Glas*) to shatter.
Zerberus *m* **-, -se (a)** *no pl* (*Myth*) Cerberus. **(b)** (*fig hum*) watchdog.
zerbeulen* *vt* to dent ◆ **zerbeult** battered.
zerbomben* *vt* to flatten with bombs, to bomb to smithereens (*inf*); *Gebäude auch* to bomb out ◆ **zerbombt** *Stadt, Gebäude* bombed out; **zerbombt werden** to be flattened by bombs.
zerbrechen* *irreg* [1] *vt* (*lit*) to break into pieces; *Glas, Porzellan etc* to smash, to shatter; *Ketten* (*lit, fig*) to break, to sever; (*fig*) *Widerstand* to break down; *Lebenswille* to destroy; *siehe* **Kopf.**
[2] *vi aux sein* to break into pieces; (*Glas, Porzellan etc*) to smash, to shatter; (*fig*) to be destroyed (*an +dat* by); (*Widerstand*) to collapse (*an +dat* in the face of) ◆ **er ist am Leben zerbrochen** he has been broken *or* destroyed by life.
zerbrechlich *adj* fragile; *Mensch auch* frail ◆ **„Vorsicht ~!"** "fragile, handle with care".
Zerbrechlichkeit *f* fragility; (*von Mensch auch*) frailness.
zerbröckeln* *vti* to crumble.
zerdätschen* *vt* (*inf*) to squash, to crush.
zerdeppern* *vt* (*inf*) to smash.
zerdrücken* *vt* to squash, to crush; *Gemüse* to mash; (*zerknittern*) to crush, to crease, to crumple; (*inf*) *Träne* to squeeze out.
Zeremonie [tseremo'ni:, -'mo:niə] *f* ceremony.
Zeremoniell *nt* **-s, -e** ceremonial.
zeremoniell *adj* ceremonial.
Zeremonienmeister [-'mo:niən-] *m* master of ceremonies.
zerfahren *adj* scatty; (*unkonzentriert*) distracted.
Zerfall *m* **-(e)s,** *no pl* disintegration; (*von Gebäude auch, von Atom*) decay; (*von Leiche, Holz etc*) decomposition; (*von Land, Kultur*) decline, decay, fall; (*von Gesundheit*) decline.
zerfallen* [1] *vi irreg aux sein* **(a)** to disintegrate; (*Gebäude auch*) to decay, to fall into ruin; (*Atomkern*) to decay; (*auseinanderfallen auch*) to fall apart; (*Leiche, Holz etc*) to decompose; (*Reich, Kultur, Moral*) to decay, to decline; (*Gesundheit*) to decline ◆ **zu Staub ~** to crumble (in)to dust.
(b) (*sich gliedern*) to fall (*in +acc* into).
[2] *adj* **(a)** *Haus* tumble-down; *Gemäuer auch* crumbling.
(b) (*verfeindet*) **mit jdm ~ sein** to have fallen out with sb; **mit sich** (*dat*) **und der Welt/mit sich** (*dat*) **selbst ~ sein** to be at odds with the world/oneself.
Zerfalls-: ~erscheinung *f* sign of decay; **~geschwindigkeit** *f* rate of decay; **~produkt** *nt* daughter product.
zerfetzen* *vt* to tear *or* rip to pieces *or* shreds; *Brief etc* to rip up, to tear up (into little pieces); (*Geschoß*) *Arm etc* to mangle, to tear to pieces; (*fig*) to pull *or* tear to pieces.
zerfetzt *adj Hose* ragged, tattered; *Arm* lacerated.
zerfleddern*, zerfledern* *vt* (*inf*) to tatter, to get tatty (*inf*).
zerfleischen* [1] *vt* to tear limb from limb, to tear to pieces.
[2] *vt* (*fig*) **er zerfleischt sich in (Selbst)vorwürfen** he torments *or* tortures himself with self-reproaches; **sich gegenseitig ~, einander ~** to tear each other apart.
zerfließen* *vi irreg aux sein* (*Tinte, Makeup etc*) to run; (*Eis etc, fig: Reichtum etc*) to melt away ◆ **in Tränen ~** to dissolve into tears; **seine Hoffnungen zerflossen in nichts** his hopes melted away; **vor Mitleid ~** to be overcome with pity.
zerfranst *adj* frayed.
zerfressen* *vt irreg* to eat away; (*Motten, Mäuse etc*) to eat; (*Säure, Rost auch*) to corrode; (*fig*) to consume ◆ **die Säure hat ihr das Gesicht ~** the acid burnt into her face; **(von Motten/Würmern) ~ sein** to be moth-/worm-eaten.
zerfurchen* *vt* to furrow.
zergehen* *vi irreg aux sein* to dissolve; (*schmelzen*) to melt ◆ **auf der Zunge ~** (*Gebäck etc*) to melt in the mouth; (*Fleisch*) to fall apart; **vor Mitleid ~** to be overcome with pity.
zergliedern* *vt* (*Biol*) to dissect; *Satz* to parse; (*fig*) to analyse.
Zergliederung *f siehe vt* dissection; parsing; analysis.
zerhacken* *vt* to chop up.
zerhauen* *vt irreg* to chop in two; (*in viele Stücke*) to chop up; *Knoten* (*lit, fig*) to cut; (*inf: kaputtschlagen*) to smash.
zerkauen* *vt* to chew; (*Hund*) *Leine* to chew up.
zerkleinern* *vt* to cut up; (*zerhacken*) to chop (up); (*zerbrechen*) to break up; (*zermahlen*) to crush.
zerklüftet *adj* rugged; *Mandeln* fissured ◆ **tief ~es Gestein** rock with deep fissures, deeply fissured rock.
zerknautschen* *vt* (*inf*) to crease, to crumple.
zerknautscht *adj* (*inf*) *Kleidung* creased, crumpled; *Gesicht* (*faltig*) wizened ◆ **du siehst heute fürchterlich ~ aus** you're looking somewhat the worse for wear today.
zerknirscht *adj* remorseful, overcome with remorse.
Zerknirschtheit, Zerknirschung *f* remorse.
zerknittern* *vt* to crease, to crumple.
zerknittert *adj* **(a)** *Kleid, Stoff* creased. **(b)** (*inf*) (*schuldbewußt*) overcome with remorse; (*unausgeschlafen*) washed-out (*inf*).
zerknüllen* *vt* to crumple up, to scrunch up (*inf*).
zerkochen* *vti* (*vi: aux sein*) to cook to a pulp; (*zu lange kochen auch*) to overcook.
zerkratzen* *vt* to scratch.
zerkrümeln* *vt* to crumble; *Boden* to loosen.
zerlassen* *vt irreg* to melt.
zerlaufen* *vi irreg aux sein* to melt.
zerlegbar *adj* able to be taken apart; *Maschine, Gerüst auch* able to be dismantled; (*Gram*) analysable; (*Math*) reducible ◆ **die Möbel waren leicht ~** the furniture could easily be taken apart *or* was easily taken apart.
zerlegen* *vt* (*auseinandernehmen*) to take apart *or* to pieces; *Gerüst, Maschine auch* to dismantle; *Motor, Getriebe auch* to strip down; *Theorie, Argumente* to break down; (*Gram*) to analyse; (*Math*) to reduce (*in +acc* to); (*zerschneiden*) to cut up; *Geflügel, Wild* to carve up; (*Biol*) to dissect ◆ **etw in seine Einzelteile ~** to take sth to pieces; to dismantle sth completely; to strip sth down; to break sth down into its (individual) constituents; *Satz* to parse sth; **eine Zahl in ihre Faktoren ~** to factorize a number.

Zerlegung *f, no pl siehe vt* taking apart; dismantling; stripping down; breaking down; analysis; reduction; cutting up; carving up; dissection.
zerlesen *adj* well-thumbed.
zerlumpt *adj* ragged, tattered *no adv.*
zermahlen* *vt* to grind; (*in Mörser*) to crush.
zermalmen* *vt* (*lit, fig*) to crush; (*mit den Zähnen*) to crunch, to grind.
zermanschen* *vt* (*inf*) to squash; (*mit Gabel*) to mash.
zermartern* *vt* **sich** (*dat*) **den Kopf** *or* **das Hirn ~** to rack *or* cudgel one's brains.
zermatschen* *vt* (*inf*) *siehe* **zermanschen.**
zermürben* *vt* **(a)** (*fig*) **jdn ~** to wear sb down; **~d** wearing, trying. **(b)** (*rare: brüchig machen*) to make brittle.
Zermürbung *f* (*eines Gegners etc*) wearing down *no pl*, attrition.
Zermürbungs-: ~krieg *m* war of attrition; **~taktik** *f* tactics of attrition *pl.*
zernagen* *vt* to chew to pieces; (*Nagetiere*) to gnaw to pieces.
Zero ['ze:ro] *f* **-, -s** *or nt* **-s, -s** zero.
zerpflücken* *vt* (*lit, fig*) to pick to pieces.
zerplatzen* *vi aux sein* to burst; (*Glas*) to shatter.
zerquält *adj* tortured.
zerquetschen* *vt* to squash, to crush; (*mit Gabel*) *Kartoffeln etc* to mash; (*inf*) *Träne* to squeeze out.
Zerquetschte *pl* (*inf*) **10 Mark und ein paar ~** 10 marks something (or other), 10 marks odd; **Hundert und ein paar ~** a hundred odd; **elf Uhr und ein paar ~** eleven something (or other).
zerraufen* *vt* to ruffle ◆ **zerrauft** dishevelled.
Zerrbild *nt* (*lit: in Spiegel*) distorted picture *or* image; (*fig auch*) caricature; (*von Verhältnissen, System, Gesellschaft etc auch*) travesty.
zerreden* *vt* to flog to death (*inf*).
zerreiben* *vt irreg* to crumble, to crush; (*in Mörser etc*) to grind; (*fig*) to crush.
zerreißen* *irreg* 1 *vt* (*aus Versehen*) to tear; (*in Stücke*) to tear to pieces *or* shreds; *Faden, Seil etc* to break; (*absichtlich*) *Brief etc* to tear up; (*zerfleischen*) to tear apart *or* limb from limb; (*plötzlich aufreißen, durchbrechen*) *Wolkendecke, Stille etc* to rend (*liter*); (*fig*) *Land* to tear apart *or* in two; *Bindungen* to break ◆ **es zerreißt mir das Herz** (*liter*) it is heart-rending *or* heartbreaking, it breaks my heart.
2 *vi aux sein* (*Stoff*) to tear; (*Band, Seil etc*) to break.
3 *vr* (*fig*) **ich könnte mich vor Wut ~** I'm hopping (mad) (*inf*); **ich kann mich doch nicht ~!** I can't be in two places at once; **sich ~, (um) etw zu tun** to go to no end of trouble to do sth.
Zerreiß-: z~fest *adj* tear-resistant; **~probe** *f* (*lit*) pull test; (*fig*) real test; **eine ~probe für ihre Ehe** *etc* a crucial test of their marriage *etc*; **eine ~probe für meine Geduld** a real test of my patience.
zerren 1 *vt* to drag; *Sehne* to pull, to strain ◆ **jdm/sich die Kleider vom Leib ~** to tear the clothes from sb's body/to tear one's clothes off; **etw an die Öffentlichkeit ~** to drag sth into the public eye.
2 *vi* **an etw** (*dat*) **~** to tug *or* pull at sth; **an den Nerven ~** to be nerve-racking.
zerrinnen* *vi irreg aux sein* to melt (away); (*fig*) (*Träume, Pläne*) to melt *or* fade away; (*Geld, Vermögen*) to disappear ◆ **jdm unter den Händen** *or* **zwischen den Fingern ~** (*Geld*) to run through sb's hands like water; **die Zeit zerrinnt mir unter den Händen** the time just goes without me knowing where.
zerrissen 1 *ptp of* **zerreißen.**
2 *adj* (*fig*) *Volk, Partei* strife-torn, disunited; *Mensch* (inwardly) torn.
Zerrissenheit *f siehe adj* disunity *no pl*; (inner) conflict.
Zerrspiegel *m* (*lit*) distorting mirror; (*fig*) travesty.
Zerrung *f* (*das Zerren: von Sehne, Muskel*) pulling ◆ **eine ~** a pulled ligament/muscle.
zerrupfen* *vt* to pick *or* pull to pieces.
zerrütten* *vt* to destroy, to ruin, to wreck; *Ehe* to break up, to destroy; *Geist* to destroy; *Nerven* to shatter ◆ **eine zerrüttete Ehe/Familie** a broken marriage/home; **sich in einem zerrütteten Zustand befinden** to be in a very bad way.
Zerrüttung *f* destruction; (*von Ehe*) breakdown; (*von Nerven*) shattering; (*Zustand*) shattered state ◆ **der Staat/ihre Ehe befindet sich im Zustand der ~** the state is in a bad way/their marriage is breaking down.
Zerrüttungsprinzip *nt* principle of irretrievable breakdown.
zersägen* *vt* to saw up.
zerschellen* *vi aux sein* (*Schiff, Flugzeug*) to be dashed *or* smashed to pieces; (*Vase etc*) to smash (to pieces *or* smithereens) ◆ **das zerschellte Schiff** the wrecked ship.
zerschießen* *vt irreg* to shoot to pieces; (*durchlöchern*) to riddle with bullets ◆ **er hatte ein zerschossenes Bein** his leg had been shot to pieces/was riddled with bullets.
zerschlagen* *irreg* 1 *vt* **(a)** (*Mensch*) to smash (to pieces *or* smithereens); (*Stein etc auch*) to shatter; (*Hagel*) *Ernte, Wein* to crush; (*auseinanderschlagen*) to break up.
(b) (*fig*) *Angriff, Widerstand, Opposition* to crush; *Hoffnungen, Pläne* to shatter; *Spionagering, Vereinigung* to break.
2 *vr* (*nicht zustande kommen*) to fall through; (*Hoffnung, Aussichten*) to be shattered.
3 *adj pred* washed out (*inf*); (*nach Anstrengung, langer Reise etc*) shattered (*inf*), worn out ◆ **ich wachte wie ~ auf** I woke up feeling washed out (*inf*).
Zerschlagenheit *f* exhaustion.
Zerschlagung *f* (*fig*) suppression; (*von Hoffnungen, Plänen*) shattering.
zerschleißen *pret* ⚠**zerschliß,** *ptp* **zerschlissen** *vti* (*usu ptp*) to wear out ◆ **zerschlissene Kleider** worn-out *or* threadbare clothes.
zerschmeißen* *vt* (*inf*) *irreg* to shatter, to smash (to pieces).
zerschmelzen* *vi irreg aux sein* (*lit, fig*) to melt ◆ **vor Rührung/Mitleid** (*dat*) **~** (*iro*) to brim (over) with emotion/pity.
zerschmettern* 1 *vt* (*lit, fig*) to shatter; *Feind* to crush; (*Sport*) *Gegner* to smash.
2 *vi aux sein* to shatter.
zerschneiden* *vt irreg* to cut; (*in zwei Teile*) to cut in two; (*in Stücke*) to cut up; (*verschneiden*) *Stoff* to cut wrongly; (*fig*) *Stille* to pierce ◆ **jdm das Herz ~** to cut sb to the quick.
zerschnippeln* *vt* (*inf*) to snip to pieces.
zerschrammen* *vt Haut, Möbel* to scratch to pieces.
zersetzen* 1 *vt* to decompose; (*Säure*) to corrode; (*fig*) to undermine, to subvert.
2 *vr* to decompose; (*durch Säure*) to corrode; (*fig*) to become undermined *or* subverted.
zersetzend *adj* (*fig*) subversive.
Zersetzung *f* (*Chem*) decomposition; (*durch Säure*) corrosion; (*fig: Untergrabung*) undermining, subversion; (*von Gesellschaft*) decline (*von* in), decay.
Zersetzungs-: ~erscheinung *f* (*fig*) sign of decline *or* decay; **~produkt** *nt* substance produced by decomposition; ⚠**~prozeß** *m siehe* **Zersetzung** (process of) decomposition/corrosion/subversion; decline (*von* in), decay.
zersiedeln* *vt* to spoil (by development).
Zersied(e)lung *f* overdevelopment.
zerspalten* *vt* to split; *Gemeinschaft* to split up.
zersplittern* 1 *vt* to shatter; *Holz* to splinter; (*fig*) *Kräfte, Zeit* to dissipate, to squander; *Gruppe, Partei* to fragment.
2 *vi aux sein* to shatter; (*Holz, Knochen*) to splinter; (*fig*) to split up.
3 *vr* to shatter; (*Holz*) to splinter; (*fig*) to dissipate *or* squander one's energies; (*Gruppe, Partei*) to fragment, to become fragmented ◆ **der Widerstand ist zu zersplittert** the opposition is too fragmented.
Zersplitterung *f siehe vb* shattering; splintering; dissipation, squandering; fragmentation.
zersprengen* *vt* to burst; (*fig*) *Volksmenge* to disperse, to scatter.
zerspringen* *vi irreg aux sein* to shatter; (*Saite*) to break; (*einen Sprung bekommen*) to crack ◆ **in tausend Stücke ~** to shatter in(to) a thousand pieces; **das Herz wollte ihr vor Freude/Ungeduld fast ~** (*liter*) her heart was bursting with joy/impatience.
zerstampfen* *vt* (*zertreten*) to stamp *or* trample on; (*zerkleinern*) to crush; (*im Mörser*) to grind, to pound; *Kartoffeln etc* to mash.
zerstäuben* *vt* to spray.
Zerstäuber *m* **-s, -** spray; (*Parfüm~ auch*) atomizer.
zerstechen* *vt irreg* **(a)** (*Mücken*) to bite (all over); (*Bienen etc*) to sting (all over) ◆ **wir sind von den Mücken ganz zerstochen worden** we've been bitten all over by the midges. **(b)** *Material, Haut* to puncture; *Finger* to prick.
zerstieben* *vi irreg aux sein* to scatter; (*Wasser*) to spray.
zerstörbar *adj* destructible ◆ **nicht ~** indestructible.
zerstören* 1 *vt* (*lit, fig*) to destroy; *Gebäude, Ehe, Glück auch* to wreck; (*verwüsten auch*) to ruin; (*Rowdys*) to vandalize; *Gesundheit* to wreck, to ruin.
2 *vi* to destroy; *siehe* **Boden.**
Zerstörer *m* **-s, -** (*old Aviat*) fighter; (*Naut*) destroyer.
Zerstörer(in *f*) *m* **-s, -** destroyer.
zerstörerisch *adj* destructive.
Zerstörung *f* **(a)** *no pl siehe vt* destruction; wrecking; ruining; vandalizing. **(b)** (*von Krieg, Katastrophe etc*) destruction *no pl*, devastation *no pl.*
Zerstörungs-: ~drang *m* destructive urge *or* impulse; **~lust** *f* delight in destruction; **~trieb** *m* destructive urge *or* impulse; **~werk** *nt* work of destruction; **~wut** *f* destructive mania.
zerstoßen* *vt irreg* **(a)** (*zerkleinern*) to crush; (*im Mörser*) to pound, to grind. **(b)** (*durch Stoßen beschädigen*) to damage; *Leder, Schuh* to scuff.
zerstreiten* *vr irreg* to quarrel, to fall out.
zerstreuen* 1 *vt* **(a)** to scatter (*in +dat* over); *Volksmenge etc auch* to disperse; *Licht* to diffuse; (*fig*) to dispel, to allay.
(b) jdn ~ to take sb's mind off things, to divert sb.
2 *vr* **(a)** (*sich verteilen*) to scatter; (*Menge auch*) to disperse; (*fig*) to be dispelled *or* allayed.
(b) (*sich ablenken*) to take one's mind off things; (*sich amüsieren*) to amuse oneself.
zerstreut *adj* (*fig*) *Mensch* absent-minded ◆ **sie ist heute sehr ~** her mind is elsewhere today.
Zerstreutheit *f, no pl* absent-mindedness.
Zerstreuung *f* **(a)** *no pl siehe vt* scattering; dispersal; diffusion; dispelling, allaying. **(b)** (*Ablenkung*) diversion ◆ **zur ~** as a diversion. **(c)** (*Zerstreutheit*) absent-mindedness.
zerstritten 1 *ptp of* **zerstreiten.**
2 *adj* estranged ◆ **mit jdm ~ sein** to be on very bad terms with sb.
zerstückeln* *vt* (*lit*) to cut up; *Leiche* to dismember; *Land* to divide *or* carve up; (*fig*) *Tag, Semester etc* to break up.
zertalt *adj* (*Geog*) dissected.
zerteilen* *vt* to split up; (*in zwei Teile auch*) to divide; (*zerschneiden*) to cut up; *Wogen, Wolken* to part ◆ **ich kann mich nicht ~!** I can't be in two places at once.
Zertifikat *nt* certificate.
zertrampeln* *vt* to trample on.

zertrennen* *vt* to sever, to cut through; (*auftrennen*) *Nähte* to undo; *Kleid* to undo the seams of.
zertreten* *vt irreg* to crush (underfoot); *Rasen* to ruin ◆ **jdn wie einen Wurm ~** to grind sb into the ground.
zertrümmern* *vt* to smash; *Einrichtung* to smash up; *Gebäude auch, Hoffnungen, Ordnung* to wreck, to destroy; (*dated*) *Atom* to split.
Zertrümmerung *f, no pl siehe vt* smashing; smashing up; wrecking, destruction; splitting.
Zervelatwurst [tsɛrvə'la:t-] *f* cervelat, German salami.
zervikal [tsɛrvi'ka:l] *adj* (*spec*) cervical.
zerwerfen* *vr irreg* (*fig*) to fall out (*mit jdm* with sb).
zerwühlen* *vt* to ruffle up, to tousle; *Bett, Kopfkissen* to rumple (up); (*aufwühlen*) *Erdboden* to churn up; (*Wildschwein etc*) to churn *or* root up.
Zerwürfnis *nt* row, disagreement.
zerzausen* *vt* to ruffle; *Haar* to tousle.
zerzaust *adj* windswept; *Haare auch* dishevelled, tousled.
Zeter *nt*: **~ und Mord(io) schreien** (*lit*) to scream blue murder (*inf*); (*fig*) to raise a hue and cry.
Zeter-: **≈geschrei** *nt* (*lit*) hullabaloo; (*fig*) hue and cry; **z~mordio:** **z~mordio schreien** to scream blue murder (*inf*).
zetern *vi* (*pej*) to clamour; (*keifen*) to scold, to nag; (*jammern*) to moan.
Zett *nt* **-s,** *no pl* (*sl*) gaol, jail ◆ **jdn zu 10 Jahren ~ verurteilen** to send sb down for 10 years (*inf*).
Zettel *m* **-s, -** piece of paper; (*Notiz~*) note; (*Kartei~*) card; (*Anhänge~*) label; (*mit Angabe über Inhalt, Anschrift etc*) chit (*inf*), ticket; (*Bekanntmachung*) notice; (*Hand~*) leaflet, handbill (*esp US*); (*Formular*) form; (*Stimm~*) ballot paper; (*Bestell~*) coupon; (*Kassen~, Beleg*) receipt ◆ **„~ ankleben verboten"** "stick no bills".
Zettel-: **~kartei** *f* card index; **~kasten** *m* file-card box; (*~kartei*) card index; **~katalog** *m* card index; **~verteiler** *m* person who hands out leaflets; **~wirtschaft** *f* (*pej*) **eine ~wirtschaft haben** to have bits of paper everywhere; **du mit deiner ~wirtschaft** you and all your bits of paper.
Zeug *nt* **-(e)s,** *no pl* **(a)** (*inf*) stuff *no indef art, no pl*; (*Ausrüstung auch*) gear (*inf*); (*Kleidung*) clothes *pl*, things *pl* (*inf*); (*mehrere Gegenstände auch, Getier*) things *pl* ◆ **altes ~** junk, trash; ... **und solches ~** ... and such things.
(b) (*inf: Unsinn*) nonsense, rubbish ◆ **ein/dieses ~** a/this load of nonsense *or* rubbish; **dummes** *or* **ungereimtes ~ reden** to talk a lot of nonsense *or* drivel (*inf*) *or* twaddle (*inf*); **rede kein dummes ~** don't talk nonsense; **dummes ~ treiben** to be stupid.
(c) (*Fähigkeit, Können*) **das ~ zu etw haben** to have (got) what it takes to be sth (*inf*); **er hat nicht das ~ dazu** he hasn't got what it takes (*inf*).
(d) (*old*) (*Stoff*) material; (*Wäsche*) linen ◆ **jdm etwas am ~ flicken** (*inf*) to tell sb what to do; **was das ~ hält** (*inf*) for all one is worth; *laufen* like mad; *fahren* like the blazes (*inf*); **lügen, was das ~ hält** (*inf*) to lie one's head off (*inf*); **sich für jdn ins ~ legen** (*inf*) to stand up for sb; **sich ins ~ legen** to go flat out; (*bei Arbeit auch*) to work flat out.
Zeug|amt *nt* (*obs Mil*) arsenal.
Zeuge *m* **-n, -n** (*Jur, fig*) witness (*gen* to) ◆ **~ eines Unfalls/Gesprächs sein** to be a witness to an accident/a conversation; **sich als ~ zur Verfügung stellen** to come forward as a witness; **vor/unter ~n** in front of witnesses; **Gott ist mein ~** as God is my witness; **die ~n Jehovas** Jehovah's witnesses.
zeugen[1] *vt Kind* to father; (*Bibl*) to beget; (*fig geh*) to generate, to give rise to.
zeugen[2] *vi* **(a)** (*vor +dat* to) (*aussagen*) to testify; (*vor Gericht auch*) to give evidence ◆ **für/gegen jdn ~** to testify *or* give evidence for/against sb. **(b)** **von etw ~** to show sth.
Zeugen-: **~aussage** *f* testimony; **~bank** *f* witness box, witness stand (*US*); **er sitzt auf der ~bank** he's in the witness box *or* witness stand (*US*); **~beeinflussung** *f* subornation of a witness/witnesses; **~ladung** *f* summoning of a witness/witnesses; **~stand** *m* witness box, witness stand (*US*); **in den ~stand treten** to go into the witness box, to take the (witness) stand; **~vereidigung** *f* swearing in of a witness/witnesses; **~vernehmung** *f* examination of the witness(es).
Zeughaus *nt* (*obs Mil*) arsenal, armoury.
Zeugin *f* witness.
Zeugnis *nt* **(a)** (*esp liter: Zeugenaussage*) evidence ◆ **für/gegen jdn ~ ablegen** to give evidence *or* to testify for/against sb; **für jds Ehrlichkeit** *etc* **~ ablegen** to bear witness to sb's honesty *etc*; **falsches ~ ablegen, falsch ~ reden** (*Bibl*) to bear false witness.
(b) (*fig: Beweis*) evidence.
(c) (*Schul~*) report; (*Note*) mark, grade (*esp US*).
(d) (*Bescheinigung*) certificate; (*von Arbeitgeber*) testimonial, reference ◆ **gute ~se haben** to have good qualifications; (*von Arbeitgeber*) to have good references; **jdm ein ~ ausstellen** to give sb a reference *or* testimonial; **ich kann ihm nur das beste ~ ausstellen** (*fig*) I cannot speak too highly of him.
Zeugnis-: **~abschrift** *f* copy of one's report/certificate/testimonial; **~heft** *nt* (*Sch*) report book; **~konferenz** *f* (*Sch*) *staff meeting to decide on marks etc*; **~papiere** *pl* certificates *pl*; testimonials *pl*; **~verweigerungsrecht** *nt* right of a witness to refuse to give evidence.
Zeugs *nt* **-,** *no pl* (*pej inf*) *siehe* **Zeug (a, b).**
Zeugung *f siehe* **zeugen**[1] fathering; begetting; generating.
Zeugungs-: **~akt** *m* act of procreation; (*fig*) creative act; **z~fähig** *adj* fertile; **~fähigkeit, ~kraft** (*geh*) *f* fertility; **~organ** *nt* (*spec*) male reproductive organ; **z~unfähig** *adj* sterile; **~unfähigkeit** *f* sterility.
Zeus *m* **-** (*Myth*) Zeus.
zeuseln *vi* (*Sw: zündeln*) to play with matches.

ZEVIS ['tse:vɪs] *nt abbr of* **Zentrales Verkehrsinformationssystem.**
z.H(d). *abbr of* **zu Händen** attn.
Zibebe *f* **-, -n** (*S Ger, Aus*) sultana.
Zichorie [tsɪ'ço:riə] *f* chicory.
Zicke *f* **-, -n** **(a)** nanny goat. **(b)** (*pej inf: Frau*) cow (*sl*), bitch (*sl*); (*prüde*) prude; (*albern*) silly thing.
Zickel *nt* **-s, -(n)** *siehe* **Zicklein.**
Zicken *pl* (*inf*) nonsense *no pl* ◆ **mach bloß keine ~!** no nonsense now!; **~ machen** to make trouble.
zickig *adj* (*albern*) silly; (*prüde*) prudish.
Zicklein *nt* (*junge Ziege*) kid; (*junges Reh*) fawn.
Zickzack *m* **-(e)s, -e** zigzag ◆ **z~** *or* **im ~ laufen** to zigzag; **~ nähen** to zigzag.
Zickzack-: **z~förmig** *adj* zigzag; **z~förmig verlaufen** to zigzag; **~kurs** *m* zigzag course; (*von Hase etc*) zigzag path; **im ~kurs fahren/laufen** to zigzag; **~linie** *f* zigzag; **~schere** *f* pinking shears; **~stich** *m* zigzag stitch.
Ziege *f* **-, -n** **(a)** goat; (*weiblich auch*) nanny-goat. **(b)** (*pej inf: Frau*) cow (*sl*), bitch (*sl*).
Ziegel *m* **-s, -** (*Backstein*) brick; (*Dach~*) tile ◆ **ein Dach mit ~n decken** to tile a roof.
Ziegel-: **≈bau** *m, pl* **-ten** brick building; **≈brenner** *m* brickmaker; (*von Dachziegeln*) tilemaker; **~brennerei** *f siehe* **Ziegelei**; **≈dach** *nt* tiled roof.
Ziegelei *f* brickworks *sing or pl*; (*für Dachziegel*) tile-making works *sing or pl.*
Ziegel-: **z~rot** *adj* brick-red; **~stein** *m* brick.
Ziegen-: **~bart** *m* **(a)** (*an Hut*) shaving brush (*hum*); (*hum: Bart*) goatee (beard); **(b)** (*Bot*) goat's-beard mushroom; **~bock** *m* billy goat; **~fell** *nt* goatskin; **~herde** *f* herd of goats; **~hirt(e)** *m* goatherd; **~käse** *m* goat's milk cheese; **~leder** *nt* kid (-leather), kidskin; **~milch** *f* goat's milk; **~peter** *m* **-s, -** mumps *sing.*
zieh *pret of* **zeihen.**
Zieh-: **~brücke** *f* drawbridge; **~brunnen** *m* well; **~eltern** *pl* foster parents *pl.*
ziehen *pret* **zog,** *ptp* **gezogen** **1** *vt* **(a)** to pull; (*heftig auch*) to tug; (*schleppen*) to drag; (*dehnen auch*) to stretch; (*vom Kopf*) *Hut* to raise; *Handbremse* to put on; *Choke, Starter* to pull out ◆ **der Hund zog die Tischdecke vom Tisch** the dog pulled the cloth off the table; **den Ring vom Finger ~** to pull one's ring off (one's finger); **die Knie/Schultern in die Höhe ~** to raise one's knees/shoulders; **das Flugzeug nach oben/unten ~** to put the plane into a climb/descent; **etw durch etw ~** to pull sth through sth; **jdn nach unten ~** to pull *or* (*fig*) drag sb down; **die Stirn kraus** *or* **in Falten ~** to knit one's brow; **Wein auf Flaschen ~** to bottle wine; **(neue) Saiten auf ein Instrument ~** to (re)string an instrument; **etw ins Komische ~** to ridicule sth; **mußt du immer alles ins Ironische ~?** must you always be so ironical?; **unangenehme Folgen nach sich ~** to have unpleasant consequences.
(b) (*heraus~*) to pull out (*aus* of); *Zahn auch* to take out, to extract; *Fäden* to take out, to remove; *Korken, Schwert, Revolver auch* to draw; *Los, Spielkarte, (fig) Schlüsse* to draw; *Vergleich* to draw, to make; (*Math*) *Wurzel* to work out; *Wasserproben* to take ◆ **die Pflanze zieht ihre Nahrung aus dem Boden** the plant gets *or* draws its nourishment from the soil; **Zigaretten (aus dem Automaten) ~** to get *or* buy cigarettes from the machine.
(c) (*zeichnen*) *Kreis, Linie* to draw.
(d) (*verlegen, anlegen*) *Kabel, Leitung etc* to lay; *Graben, Furchen* to dig; *Grenze, Mauer* to erect, to build ◆ **Perlen auf eine Schnur ~** to thread pearls.
(e) (*herstellen*) *Draht, Kerzen, Kopien* to make; (*züchten*) *Blumen* to grow; *Tiere* to breed ◆ **Computerprogramme schwarz ~** to pirate computer programs; **sie haben die Kinder gut gezogen** (*inf*) they brought the children up well.
(f) **die Mütze tiefer ins Gesicht ~** to pull one's hat further down over one's face; **den Mantel fest um sich ~** to pull one's coat tight around one; **die Vorhänge vors Fenster ~** to pull the curtains; **den Mantel übers Kleid ~** to put one's coat on over one's dress.
(g) *in Verbindungen mit n siehe auch dort* ◆ **die Aufmerksamkeit** *or* **die Blicke auf sich** (*acc*) **~** to attract attention; **jds Haß auf sich** (*acc*) **~** to incur sb's hatred; **jdn ins Gespräch/in die Unterhaltung ~** to bring sb into the conversation.
2 *vi* **(a)** (*zerren*) to pull ◆ **an etw** (*dat*) **~** to pull (on *or* at) sth; **ein ~der Schmerz** an ache, an aching pain.
(b) *aux sein* (*sich bewegen*) to move, to go; (*Soldaten, Volksmassen*) to march; (*durchstreifen*) to wander, to roam; (*Wolken, Rauch*) to drift; (*Gewitter*) to move; (*Vögel*) to fly; (*während des Vogelzugs*) to migrate ◆ **durch die Welt/die Stadt ~** to wander through the world/town; **in den Krieg/die Schlacht ~** to go to war/battle; **heimwärts ~** to make one's way home; **laß mich ~** (*old, liter*) let me go; **die Jahre zogen ins Land** (*liter*) the years passed.
(c) *aux sein* (*um~*) to move ◆ **nach Bayern/München ~** to move to Bavaria/Munich; **zu jdm ~** to move in with sb.
(d) (*Feuer, Ofen, Pfeife*) to draw ◆ **an der Pfeife/Zigarette ~** to pull *or* puff on one's pipe/cigarette.
(e) *aux sein* (*eindringen*) to penetrate (*in etw* (*acc*) sth).
(f) (*mit Spielfigur*) to move; (*Cards*) to play; (*abheben*) to draw ◆ **mit dem Turm ~** to move the rook; **wer zieht?** whose move is it?
(g) (*Cook*) (*Tee, Kaffee*) to draw; (*in Marinade*) to marinade; (*in Kochwasser*) to simmer.
(h) (*Auto*) to pull.
(i) (*inf: Eindruck machen*) **so was zieht beim Publikum/bei mir nicht** the public/I don't like that sort of thing; **der Film zieht immer noch** the film is still popular; **so was zieht immer** that sort of thing always goes down well.
3 *vi impers* **(a)** **es zieht** there's a draught; **wenn es dir zieht** if you're in a draught, if you find it draughty; **mir zieht's im Nacken** there is *or* I can feel a

draught round my neck; **in diesem Haus zieht es aus allen Ritzen** there are draughts everywhere in this house.
(b) (*Schmerzen verursachen*) **mir zieht's im Rücken** my back hurts.
[4] *vt impers* **mich zieht nichts in die Heimat** there is nothing to draw me home; **was zieht dich denn nach Hause?** what is drawing you home?; **es zog ihn in die weite Welt** he felt drawn towards the big wide world.
[5] *vr* **(a)** (*sich erstrecken*) to stretch; (*zeitlich*) to drag on (*in +acc* into) ◆ **dieses Thema zieht sich durch das ganze Buch** this theme runs throughout the whole book.
(b) (*verlaufen*) **sich zickzackförmig durchs Land ~** to zigzag through the countryside; **sich in Schlingen/Serpentinen durch etw ~** to twist *or* wind its way through sth.
(c) (*sich dehnen*) to stretch; (*Klebstoff*) to be tacky; (*Käse*) to form strings; (*Holz*) to warp; (*Metall*) to bend.
(d) sich an etw (*dat*) **aus dem Schlamm/in die Höhe ~** to pull oneself out of the mud/up on sth; *siehe* **Affäre, Patsche.**

Ziehen *nt* **-s,** *no pl* (*Schmerz*) ache; (*im Unterleib*) dragging pain.

Zieh-: ~harmonika *f* concertina; (*mit Tastatur*) accordion; **~kind** *nt* (*old*) foster-child; **~mutter** *f* (*old*) foster-mother.

Ziehung *f* draw.

Ziehvater *m* (*old*) foster-father.

Ziel *nt* **-(e)s, -e (a)** (*Reise~*) destination; (*von Expedition auch*) goal; (*Absicht, Zweck*) goal, aim, objective; (*von Wünschen, Spott*) object ◆ **mit dem ~** with the aim *or* intention; **etw zum ~ haben** to have sth as one's goal *or* aim; **jdm/sich ein ~ stecken** *or* **setzen** to set sb/oneself a goal; **er hatte sich sein ~ zu hoch gesteckt** he had set his sights too high; **sich** (*dat*) **etw zum ~ setzen** to set sth as one's goal *etc*; **einer Sache** (*dat*) **ein ~ setzen** to put a limit on sth; (*eindämmen*) to limit sth; **zum ~ kommen** *or* **gelangen** (*fig*) to reach *or* attain one's goal *etc*; **am ~ sein** to be at *or* to have reached one's destination; (*fig*) to have reached *or* achieved one's goal; **dieser Weg führte (ihn) nicht zum ~** (*fig*) this avenue did not lead (him) to his goal.
(b) (*Sport*) finish; (*bei Pferderennen auch*) finishing-post, winning-post; (*bei Rennen auch*) finishing-line ◆ **durchs ~ gehen** to pass the winning- *or* finishing-post; to cross the finishing line.
(c) (*Mil, Schießsport, fig*) target ◆ **ins ~ treffen** to hit the target; **über das ~ hinausschießen** (*fig*) to overshoot the mark.
(d) (*Comm: Frist*) credit period ◆ **mit drei Monaten ~** with a three-month credit period.

Ziel-: ~bahnhof *m* destination; **~band** *nt* finishing-tape; ⚠**z~bewußt** *adj* purposeful, decisive; ⚠**~bewußtsein** *nt* purposefulness, decisiveness; **mangelndes ~bewußtsein** lack of purpose.

zielen *vi* **(a)** (*Mensch*) to aim (*auf +acc, nach* at); (*Waffe, Schuß*) to be aimed (*auf +acc* at).
(b) (*fig: Bemerkung, Tat*) to be aimed *or* directed (*auf +acc* at) ◆ **ich weiß, worauf deine Bemerkungen ~** I know what you're driving at; **das zielt auf uns** that's aimed at *or* meant for us, that's for our benefit.

zielend *adj* (*Gram*) *Zeitwort* transitive.

Ziel-: ~fernrohr *nt* telescopic sight; **~fluggerät** *nt* homing indicator; **~foto** *nt*, **~fotografie** *f* photograph of the finish; **Ermittlung des Siegers durch ~foto** photo-finish; **z~genau** *adj* accurate; **~genauigkeit** *f* accuracy; **~gerade** *f* home *or* finishing straight; **~gerät** *nt* (*Mil*) bomb-sight; **~gruppe** *f* target group; **~hafen** *m* port of destination; **~kauf** *m* (*Comm*) credit purchase; **~konflikt** *m* conflict of aims; **~kurve** *f* final bend; **~linie** *f* (*Sport*) finishing-line; **z~los** *adj* aimless, purposeless; **~losigkeit** *f* lack of purpose, purposelessness; **~ort** *m* destination; **~richter** *m* (*Sport*) finishing-line judge; **~scheibe** *f* target; (*von Spott auch*) object; **~setzung** *f* target, objective; **z~sicher** *adj* unerring; *Handeln, Planen* purposeful; **z~sicher auf jdn/etw zugehen** to go straight up to sb/sth; **~sprache** *f* target language; **z~strebig** [1] *adj Mensch, Handlungsweise* determined, single-minded; [2] *adv* full of determination; **~strebigkeit** *f* determination, single-mindedness; **z~suchend** *adj* target-seeking; **~vorstellung** *f* objective; **~wasser** *nt* (*hum inf*) schnapps (*drunk at a shooting match*).

ziemen [1] *vr, vr impers* (*geh*) **es ziemt sich nicht** it is not proper *or* seemly; **das ziemt sich nicht (für dich)** it is not proper (for you).
[2] *vi* (*old*) **jdm ~** to become sb.

Ziemer *m* **-s, - (a)** (*Wildrücken*) saddle. **(b)** (*Peitsche*) whip.

ziemlich [1] *adj* **(a)** (*old: geziemend*) proper, fitting.
(b) *attr* (*beträchtlich*) *Anzahl, Strecke* considerable, fair; *Vermögen* sizable; *Genugtuung* reasonable ◆ **das ist eine ~e Frechheit** that's a real cheek; **eine ~e Zeit/Anstrengung/Arbeit** quite a time/an effort/a lot of work; **sie unterhielten sich mit ~er Lautstärke** they were talking quite loudly; **mit ~er Sicherheit** pretty (*inf*) *or* fairly certainly; *sagen, behaupten* with a reasonable *or* fair degree of certainty, with reasonable certainty.
[2] *adv* **(a)** (*beträchtlich*) rather, quite, pretty (*inf*); *sicher, genau* reasonably ◆ **sie hat sich ~ anstrengen müssen** she had to make quite an effort; **wir haben uns ~ beeilt** we've hurried quite a bit; **~ lange** quite a long time, a fair time; **~ viel** quite a lot.
(b) (*inf: beinahe*) almost, nearly ◆ **so ~** more or less; **so ~ alles** just about everything, more or less everything; **so ~ dasselbe** pretty well (*inf*) *or* much the same; **~ fertig** almost *or* nearly ready/finished; **sie ist so ~ in meinem Alter** she is about the same age as me.

ziepen [1] *vi* to chirp, to tweet, to cheep.
[2] *vi impers* (*inf: weh tun*) **es ziept** it hurts.
[3] *vt* (*inf: ziehen*) to pull, to tweak ◆ **jdn an den Haaren ~** to pull *or* tug sb's hair.

Zier *f* **-,** *no pl* (*old, poet*) *siehe* **Zierde.**

⚠**Zierat** *m* **-(e)s, -e** (*geh*) decoration.

Zierde *f* **-, -n** ornament, decoration; (*Schmuckstück*) adornment; (*fig: Tugend*) virtue ◆ **zur ~** for decoration; **das alte Haus ist eine ~ der Stadt** the old house is one of the beauties of the town; **eine Eins im Betragen war die einzige ~ seines Zeugnisses** a one for behaviour was the only bright spot on his report; **eine ~ des männlichen/weiblichen Geschlechts** a fine specimen of the male sex/a flower of the female sex; **die ~ der Familie** (*fig*) a credit to the family.

zieren [1] *vt* to adorn; *Speisen* to garnish; *Kuchen* to decorate; (*fig: auszeichnen*) to grace ◆ **deine Eifersucht ziert dich nicht gerade** your envy does not exactly do you credit.
[2] *vr* (*sich bitten lassen*) to make a fuss, to need a lot of pressing; (*Mädchen*) to act coyly; (*sich gekünstelt benehmen*) to be affected ◆ **du brauchst dich nicht zu ~, es ist genügend da** there's no need to be polite, there's plenty there; **er zierte sich nicht lange und sagte ja** he didn't need much pressing before he agreed; **ohne sich zu ~** without having to be pressed; **zier dich nicht!** don't be shy *or* silly (*inf*); *siehe* **geziert.**

Ziererei *f* **-,** *no pl siehe vr* pretended hesitance; coyness; affectedness.

Zier-: ~farn *m* decorative fern; **~fisch** *m* ornamental fish; **~garten** *m* ornamental garden; **~gewächs** *nt* ornamental plant; **~gras** *nt* ornamental grass; **~leiste** *f* border; (*an Auto*) trim; (*an Möbelstück*) edging; (*an Wand*) moulding.

zierlich *adj* dainty; *Frau auch* petite; *Porzellanfigur etc* delicate.

Zierlichkeit *f siehe adj* daintiness; petiteness; delicateness.

Zier-: ~pflanze *f* ornamental plant; **~rat** *m siehe* **Zierat**; **~schrift** *f* ornamental lettering; **~stich** *m* embroidery stitch; **~strauch** *m* ornamental shrub.

Ziesel *m* **-s, -** ground-squirrel, suslik.

Ziffer *f* **-, -n (a)** (*abbr* **Ziff.**) (*Zahlzeichen*) digit; (*Zahl*) figure, number ◆ **römische/arabische ~n** roman/arabic numerals; **eine Zahl mit drei ~n** a three-figure number; **etw in ~n schreiben** to write sth in figures *or* numbers.
(b) (*eines Paragraphen*) clause.

Zifferblatt *nt* (*an Uhr*) dial, (clock) face; (*von Armbanduhr*) (watch)face; (*inf: Gesicht*) face, phiz (*sl*).

zig *adj* (*inf*) umpteen (*inf*).

zig- *pref* (*inf*) umpteen (*inf*) ◆ **~hundert** umpteen hundred (*inf*).

Zigarette *f* cigarette ◆ **~ mit Filter** filter cigarette.

Zigaretten- *in cpds* cigarette; **~anzünder** *m* (*in Auto*) cigar lighter; **~automat** *m* cigarette machine; **~dose** *f* cigarette box; **~etui** *nt* cigarette case; **~kippe** *f* cigarette end, fag-end (*Brit inf*); **~länge** *f* **auf** *or* **für eine ~länge hinausgehen** to go out for a cigarette *or* smoke; **~papier** *nt* cigarette paper; **~pause** *f* break for a cigarette *or* a smoke; **~raucher** *m* cigarette smoker; **~schachtel** *f* cigarette packet *or* (*US*) pack; **~spitze** *f* cigarette-holder; **~stummel** *m* cigarette end, fag-end (*Brit inf*).

Zigarillo *m or nt* **-s, -s** cigarillo.

Zigarre *f* **-, -n (a)** cigar. **(b)** (*inf: Verweis*) dressing-down ◆ **jdm eine ~ verpassen** to give sb a dressing-down.

Zigarren- *in cpds* cigar; **~abschneider** *m* **-s, -** cigar-cutter; **~kiste** *f* cigar-box; **~raucher** *m* cigar smoker; **~spitze** *f* cigar-holder; **~stummel** *m* cigar butt.

Zigeuner(in *f***)** *m* **-s, -** gypsy, gipsy; (*Rasse auch*) Romany; (*pej inf*) vagabond; (*Streuner*) gypsy, gipsy.

zigeunerhaft, zigeunerisch *adj* gypsylike, gipsylike.

Zigeuner-: ~lager *nt* gypsy camp *or* encampment; **~leben** *nt* gypsy life; (*fig*) vagabond *or* rootless life.

zigeunern* *vi aux haben or* (*bei Richtungsangabe*) *sein* (*inf*) to rove, to roam.

Zigeuner-: ~primas *m* leader of a gypsy band; **~schnitzel** *nt* (*Cook*) *cutlet served in a spicy sauce with green and red peppers*; **~sprache** *f* Romany, Romany *or* Gypsy language; **~steak** *nt* (*Cook*) *steak served in a spicy sauce with green and red peppers*; **~wagen** *m* gypsy caravan.

zigmal *adv* (*inf*) umpteen times (*inf*).

Zikade *f* cicada.

ziliar *adj* (*Anat*) ciliary.

Zille *f* **-, -n** barge.

Zimbabwe [tsım'babve] *nt* **-s** Zimbabwe.

Zimbabwer(in *f***)** *m* Zimbabwean.

zimbabwisch *adj* Zimbabwean.

Zimbal *nt* **-s, -e** *or* **-s** cymbals.

Zimbel *f* **-, -n** (*Mus*)) cymbal; (*Hackbrett*) cymbalon.

zimbrisch *adj* Cimbrian.

Zimmer *nt* **-s, -** room ◆ **~ frei** vacancies.

Zimmer-: ~antenne *f* indoor aerial; **~arbeit** *f* carpentry job, piece of carpentry; **~arrest** *m siehe* **Stubenarrest**; **~brand** *m* fire in a/the room; **~decke** *f* ceiling.

Zimmerei *f* **(a)** (*Handwerk*) carpentry. **(b)** (*Werkstatt*) carpenter's shop.

Zimmer|einrichtung *f* furniture.

Zimmerer *m* **-s, -** carpenter.

Zimmer-: ~flucht *f* suite of rooms; **~geselle** *m* journeyman carpenter; **~handwerk** *nt* carpentry, carpenter's trade; **~herr** *m* (gentleman) lodger.

-zimm(e)rig *adj suf* -roomed, with ... rooms.

Zimmer-: ~kellner *m* room-waiter; **~kellner bitte 5 wählen** dial 5 for room-service; **~lautstärke** *f* low volume; **~lehre** *f* apprenticeship in carpentry; **~lehrling** *m* carpenter's apprentice, apprentice carpenter; **~linde** *f* African hemp; **~mädchen** *nt* chambermaid.

Zimmermann *m, pl* **-leute** carpenter ◆ **jdm zeigen, wo der ~ das Loch gelassen hat** *(inf)* to show sb the door.
Zimmermanns-: ~beil *nt* carpenter's hatchet; **~knoten, ~stek** *m* timber-hitch.
Zimmermeister *m* master carpenter.
zimmern [1] *vt* to make *or* build *or* construct from wood; *(fig) Alibi* to construct; *Ausrede* to make up.
[2] *vi* to do woodwork *or* carpentry ◆ **an etw** *(dat)* **~** *(lit)* to make sth from wood; *(fig)* to work on sth.
Zimmer-: ~nachweis *m* accommodation service; **~pflanze** *f* house plant; **~suche** *f* room hunting, hunting for rooms/a room; **auf ~suche sein** to be looking for rooms/a room; **~temperatur** *f* room temperature; **~theater** *nt* small theatre; **~vermittlung** *f* accommodation service.
Zimmet *m* **-s,** *no pl (obs)* cinnamon.
-zimmrig *adj suf siehe* **-zimm(e)rig.**
zimperlich *adj (überempfindlich)* nervous *(gegen* about); *(beim Anblick von Blut etc)* squeamish; *(prüde)* prissy; *(wehleidig)* soft ◆ **sei doch nicht so ~** don't be so silly; **du behandelst ihn viel zu ~** you're much too soft with him; **da ist er gar nicht (so) ~** he doesn't have any qualms about that; **da darf man nicht so ~ sein** you can't afford to be soft.
Zimperliese *f* **-, -n** *(pej inf)* cissy *(inf)*.
Zimt *m* **-(e)s, -e (a)** *(Gewürz)* cinnamon. **(b)** *(fig inf: Kram)* rubbish, garbage; *(Unsinn auch)* nonsense.
Zimt-: z~farben, z~farbig *adj* cinnamon-coloured; **~stange** *f* stick of cinnamon; **~stern** *m (Cook)* cinnamon-flavoured star-shaped biscuit; **~zicke, ~ziege** *f (inf)* stupid cow *(sl)*.
Zink¹ *nt* **-(e)s,** *no pl (abbr* **Zn)** zinc.
Zink² *m* **-(e)s, -e(n)** *(Mus)* cornet.
Zink-: ~blech *nt* sheet-zinc; **~blende** *f* zinc-blende; **~dach** *nt* zinc roof.
Zinke *f* **-, -n** *(von Gabel)* prong; *(von Kamm, Rechen)* tooth; *(Holzzapfen)* tenon.
Zinken *m* **-s, - (a)** *(sl: Gaunerzeichen)* secret mark. **(b)** *(inf: Nase)* hooter *(inf)*. **(c)** *siehe* **Zinke. (d)** *siehe* **Zink².**
zinken¹ *vt* **(a)** *Karten* to mark. **(b)** *Holz etc* to tenon.
zinken² *adj* zinc *attr*, made of zinc.
Zink-: ~farbe *f* zinc(-based) paint; **z~haltig** *adj* containing zinc; **z~haltig sein** to contain zinc.
-zinkig *adj suf Gabel* -pronged; *Kamm, Rechen* -toothed.
Zink-: ~leim *m* Unna's paste; **~salbe** *f* zinc ointment; **~weiß** *nt* Chinese white.
Zinn *nt* **-(e)s,** *no pl* **(a)** *(abbr* **Sn)** tin. **(b)** *(Legierung)* pewter. **(c)** *(~produkte)* pewter, pewterware.
Zinnbecher *m* pewter tankard.
Zinne *f* **-, -n** *(Hist)* merlon ◆ **~n** *(von Burg)* battlements; *(von Stadt)* towers; *(von Gebirgsmassiv)* peaks, pinnacles.
zinne(r)n *adj* pewter.
Zinn-: ~figur *f* pewter figure *or* statuette; **~geschirr** *nt* pewterware; **~gießer** *m* pewterer.
Zinnie [-iə] *f* zinnia.
Zinnkraut *nt* horsetail.
Zinnober *m* **-s,** *no pl* **(a)** *(Farbe)* vermilion, cinnabar. **(b)** *(inf) (Getue)* fuss, commotion; *(Kram)* stuff *(inf)*; *(Unsinn)* nonsense *no indef art*, rubbish *no indef art* ◆ **macht keinen (solchen) ~** stop making such a fuss *or* commotion.
Zinnober-: ~rot *nt* vermilion; **z~rot** *adj* vermilion.
Zinn-: ~pest *f* tin disease; **~soldat** *m* tin soldier; **~verbindung** *f* tin compound.
Zins¹ *m* **-es, -e** *(Hist: Abgabe)* tax; *(S Ger, Aus, Sw) (Pacht~, Miet~)* rent; *(Wasser~)* water rates *pl*.
Zins² *m* **-es, -en** *usu pl (Geld~)* interest *no pl* ◆ **~en bringen** to earn interest; **~en tragen** *(lit)* to earn interest; *(fig)* to pay dividends; **Darlehen zu 10% ~en** loan at 10% interest; **Kapital auf ~en legen** to invest capital at interest; **jdm etw mit ~en** *or* **mit ~ und Zinseszins heimzahlen** *or* **zurückgeben** *(fig)* to pay sb back for sth with interest.
Zins-: ~abschlagsteuer *f* tax on interest payments; **~bauer** *m (Hist)* tenant farmer; **~bindung** *f* pegging of interest rates; **~bogen** *m (Fin)* interest sheet.
zinsen *vi (Hist: Abgaben zahlen)* to pay one's tax; *(Sw: Pacht zahlen)* to pay one's rent.
Zinsenkonto *nt* interest account.
Zinseszins *m* compound interest; *siehe* **Zins².**
Zinseszinsrechnung *f* calculation of compound interest.
Zins-: z~frei *adj* **(a)** *(frei von Abgaben)* tax-free; *(S Ger, Aus, Sw) (pachtfrei, mietfrei)* rent-free; *Wasser* rate-free; **(b)** *Darlehen* interest-free; **~fuß** *m* interest rate, rate of interest; **~gefälle** *nt* difference between interest levels; **z~günstig** *adj* at a favourable rate of interest; **~gut** *nt (Hist)* tenant farm; **~herr** *m (Hist)* landlord, lord of the manor; **~knechtschaft** *f (Hist) system of holding land in tenancy to a landlord;* **z~los** *adj* interest free; **~niveau** *nt* level of interest rates; **~pflicht** *f (Hist)* obligation to pay tax; **z~pflichtig** *adj (Hist)* tax-paying; **z~pflichtig sein** to be obliged to pay tax; **~politik** *f* interest policies *pl*; **~rechnung** *f* calculation of interest; **~satz** *m* interest rate, rate of interest; *(bei Darlehen)* lending rate; **~schein** *m siehe* **~bogen; ~senkung** *f* reduction in the interest rate; **~spanne** *f* margin between interest rates paid by borrowers and to investors; **~termin** *m* interest due date; **~verbilligung** *f* reduction in the interest rate; **~wucher** *m* usury.
Zionismus *m* Zionism.
Zionist(in *f***)** *m* Zionist.
zionistisch *adj* Zionist.
Zipfel *m* **-s, - (a)** *(von Tuch, Decke, Stoff)* corner; *(von Mütze)* point; *(von Hemd, Jacke)* tail; *(am Saum)* dip *(an +dat* in); *(von Wurst)* end; *(von Land)* tip ◆ **etw am** *or* **beim rechten ~ packen** *(fig inf)* to go about *or* tackle sth the right way; **jdn (gerade noch) am (letzten) ~ erwischen** *(fig inf)* to catch sb (just) at the last minute.
(b) *(inf: Mensch)* silly *(inf)*.
zipf(e)lig *adj* **(a)** *Saum* uneven. **(b)** *(inf: nervös)* fidgety *(inf)*.
Zipfelmütze *f* pointed cap *or* hat.
zipfeln *vi (Rock)* to be uneven.
Zipperlein *nt* **-s,** *no pl (old, hum)* gout.
⚠ **Zipp(verschluß)** *m (Aus)* zip (fastener).
Zirbeldrüse *f* pineal body.
Zirbelkiefer *f* Swiss *or* stone pine.
zirka *adv* about, approximately; *(bei Datumsangaben)* circa, about.
Zirkel *m* **-s, - (a)** *(Gerät)* pair of compasses, compasses *pl*; *(Stech~)* pair of dividers, dividers *pl*. **(b)** *(lit, fig: Kreis)* circle. **(c)** *(studentischer ~) monogram of a student organization.*
Zirkel-: ~definition *f* circular definition; **~kasten** *m* compasses case.
zirkeln *vi (genau abmessen)* to measure exactly.
⚠ **Zirkelschluß** *m* circular argument.
Zirkon *m* **-s,** *no pl* zircon.
Zirkonium *nt, no pl (abbr* **Zr)** zirconium.
Zirkular *nt* **-s, -e** *(old)* circular.
Zirkulation *f* circulation.
Zirkulations-: ~pumpe *f* circulation pump; **~störung** *f* circulation *or* circulatory problem.
zirkulieren* *vi* to circulate.
Zirkumflex *m* **-es, -e** *(Ling)* circumflex.
Zirkumpolarstern *m* circumpolar star.
Zirkus *m* **-, -se (a)** circus ◆ **in den ~ gehen** to go to the circus. **(b)** *(inf: Getue, Theater)* fuss, to-do *(inf)*.
Zirkus- *in cpds* circus; **~artist** *m* circus performer *or* artiste; **~wagen** *m* circus caravan; **~zelt** *nt* big top.
Zirpe *f* **-, -n** cicada.
zirpen *vi* to chirp, to cheep.
Zirrhose [tsɪ'ro:zə] *f* **-, -n** cirrhosis.
Zirrus *m* **-, -** *or* **Zirren, Zirruswolke** *f* cirrus (cloud).
zirzensisch *adj* circus *attr*.
zis|alpin(isch) *adj* cisalpine.
zisch *interj* hiss; *(Rakete, Schnellzug etc)* whoosh.
zischeln *vi* to whisper.
zischen [1] *vi* **(a)** to hiss; *(Limonade)* to fizz; *(Fett, Wasser)* to sizzle. **(b)** *aux sein (inf: ab~)* to whizz.
[2] *vt* **(a)** *(~d sagen)* to hiss. **(b)** *(inf: trinken)* **einen ~** to have a quick one *(inf)*. **(c)** *(inf: ohrfeigen)* **jdm eine ~** to belt *or* clout sb one *(inf)*; **eine gezischt bekommen** to get belted *or* clouted *(inf)*.
Zischer *m* **-s, -** hisser.
Zischlaut *m (Ling)* sibilant.
ziselieren* *vti* to chase.
Ziselierer(in *f***)** *m* **-s, -** engraver.
Zisterne *f* **-, -n** well.
Zisterzienser(in *f***)** [tsɪstɛr'tsiɛnzɐ, -ərɪn] *m* **-s, -** Cistercian (monk/nun).
Zisterzienser|orden [-'tsiɛnzər-] *m* Cistercian order.
Zitadelle *f* citadel.
Zitat *nt* **-(e)s, -e** quotation ◆ **ein falsches ~** a misquotation; **~ ... Ende des ~s** quote ... unquote.
Zitaten-: ~lexikon *nt* dictionary of quotations; **~sammlung** *f* collection of quotations; **~schatz** *m* store of quotations; *(Buch)* treasury of quotations.
Zither *f* **-, -n** zither.
Zither-: ~spiel *nt* zither-playing; **~spieler** *m* zither-player.
zitieren* *vt* **(a)** to quote; *Beispiel auch* to cite. **(b)** *(vorladen, rufen)* to summon *(vor +acc* before, *an +acc, zu* to).
Zitronat *nt* candied lemon peel.
Zitrone *f* **-, -n** lemon; *(Getränk)* lemon drink; *(Baum)* lemon tree ◆ **jdn wie eine ~ auspressen** *or* **ausquetschen** to squeeze sb dry.
Zitronen-: ~falter *m* brimstone (butterfly); **z~gelb** *adj* lemon yellow; **~limonade** *f* lemonade; **~melisse** *f* (lemon) balm; **~presse** *f* lemon squeezer; **~saft** *m* lemon juice; **~säure** *f* citric acid; **~schale** *f* lemon peel; **~wasser** *nt* fresh lemon squash.
Zitrusfrucht *f* citrus fruit.
Zitter-: ~aal *m* electric eel; **~gras** *nt* quaking grass; **~greis** *m (inf)* old dodderer *(inf)*, doddering old man.
zitt(e)rig *adj* shaky.
zittern *vi* **(a)** *(vor +dat* with) to shake, to tremble; *(vor Kälte auch)* to shiver; *(vor Angst auch)* to quake; *(Stimme auch)* to quaver; *(Lippen, Blätter, Gräser)* to tremble, to quiver; *(Pfeil)* to quiver ◆ **an allen Gliedern** *or* **am ganzen Körper ~** to shake *or* tremble all over; **mir ~ die Knie** my knees are shaking *or* trembling.
(b) *(erschüttert werden)* to shake.
(c) *(inf: Angst haben)* to tremble *or* shake with fear ◆ **vor jdm ~** to be terrified of sb; **sie zittert jetzt schon vor der nächsten Englischarbeit** she's already trembling *or* terrified at the thought of the next English test.
Zittern *nt* **-s,** *no pl siehe vi* **(a)** shaking, trembling; shivering; quaking;

⚠: for details of spelling reform, see supplement

quavering; trembling, quivering; quivering ◆ **ein ~ ging durch seinen Körper** a shiver ran through his body; **mit ~ und Zagen** in fear and trembling; **da hilft kein ~ und Zagen** it's no use being afraid. **(b)** shaking ◆ **ein ~** a tremor.

Zitter-: ~pappel *f* aspen (tree); **~partie** *f* (*fig*) nail-biting event, nail-biter (*inf*); **~rochen** *m* electric ray.

zittrig *adj siehe* **zitt(e)rig.**

Zitze *f* **-, -n** teat, dug; (*sl: Brustwarze*) tit (*sl*).

Zivi ['tsi:vi] *m* **-(s), -s** (*inf*) *abbr of* **Zivildienstleistende(r).**

zivil [tsi'vi:l] *adj* **(a)** (*nicht militärisch*) civilian; *Schaden* non-military ◆ **im ~en Leben** in civilian life, in civvy street (*inf*); **~er Ersatzdienst** community service (*as alternative to military service*); **~er Bevölkerungsschutz** civil defence. **(b)** (*inf: angemessen, anständig*) civil, friendly; *Bedingungen, Forderungen, Preise* reasonable.

Zivil [tsi'vi:l] *nt* **-s,** *no pl* **(a)** (*nicht Uniform*) civilian clothes *pl*, civvies *pl* (*inf*) ◆ **in ~** *Soldat* in civilian clothes *or* civvies; (*inf*) *Arzt etc* in mufti (*inf*); **Polizist in ~** plain-clothes policeman. **(b)** (*old: Bürgerstand*) civilian populace *no pl*.

Zivil-: ~beruf *m* civilian profession/trade; **~beschäftigte(r)** *mf decl as adj* civilian employee; **~bevölkerung** *f* civilian population; **~courage** *f* courage (*to stand up for one's beliefs*); **der Mann hat ~courage** that man has the courage to stand up for his beliefs; **~dienst** *m* community service (*as alternative to military service*); **~dienstleistende(r)** *m decl as adj* person doing community service *or* work (*instead of military service*); **z~dienstpflichtig** *adj* liable for community work (*instead of military service*); **~ehe** *f* civil marriage.

Zivile(r) [tsi'vi:lə, tsi'vi:lɐ] *mf decl as adj* (*inf*) plainclothes policeman/policewoman.

Zivil-: ~fahnder *m* plain-clothes policeman; **~flughafen** *m* civil airport; **~gericht** *nt* civil court; **~gesetzbuch** *nt* (*Sw*) code of civil law.

Zivilisation [tsiviliza'tsio:n] *f* civilization (*especially its technological aspects*).

Zivilisations- [tsiviliza'tsio:nz-]: **z~krank** *adj* **z~krank sein** to suffer from an illness produced by a civilized society; **~krankheit** *f* illness produced by a civilized society *or* caused by civilization.

zivilisatorisch [tsiviliza'to:rɪʃ] **1** *adj* of civilization. **2** *adv* in terms of civilization.

zivilisierbar [tsivili'zi:rba:ɐ] *adj* civilizable.

zivilisieren* [tsivili'zi:rən] *vt* to civilize.

zivilisiert [tsivili'zi:ɐt] *adj* civilized.

Zivilist [tsivi'lɪst] *m* civilian.

Zivil-: ~kammer *f* civil division; **~kleidung** *f siehe* **Zivil (a)**; **~leben** *nt* civilian life, civvy street (*inf*); **~liste** *f* civil list; **~person** *f* civilian; ⚠**~prozeß** *m* civil action; ⚠**~prozeßordnung** *f* (*Jur*) code of civil procedure; **~recht** *nt* civil law; **z~rechtlich** *adj* civil law *attr*, of civil law; **etw z~rechtlich klären** to settle sth in a civil court; **jdn z~rechtlich verfolgen/belangen** to bring a civil action against sb; **~richter** *m* civil court judge; **~sache** *f* matter for a civil court.

Zivilschutz *m* civil defence.

Zivilschutz-: ~behörde *f* Federal Emergency Agency, FEMA (*US*), Civil Defence Corps (*Brit*); **~raum** *m* civilian airraid shelter.

Zivil-: ~senat *m* (*Jur*) civil court of appeal; **~stand** *m* civilian status; **~standsamt** *nt* (*Sw*) registry office; **~trauung** *f* civil marriage; **~verfahren** *nt* civil proceedings *pl*.

ZK [tsɛt'ka:] *nt* **-s, -s** *abbr of* **Zentralkomitee.**

Zmittag *m* **-, -** (*Sw*) lunch.

Zmorge *m* **-, -** (*Sw*) breakfast.

Znacht *m* **-s, -** (*Sw*) supper.

Znüni *m* **-, -** (*Sw*) morning break, ≃ elevenses (*Brit*).

Zobel *m* **-s, - (a)** (*Zool*) sable. **(b)** (*auch* **~pelz**) sable (fur).

zockeln *vi aux sein* (*inf*) *siehe* **zuckeln.**

zocken *vi* (*inf*) to gamble.

Zocker(in *f***)** *m* **-s, -** (*inf*) gambler.

Zofe *f* **-, -n** lady's maid; (*von Königin*) lady-in-waiting.

Zoff *m* **-s,** *no pl* (*inf: Ärger*) trouble ◆ **dann gibt's ~** then there'll be trouble.

zog *pret of* **ziehen.**

zögerlich *adj* hesitant.

➤ **zögern** *vi* to hesitate ◆ **er tat es ohne zu ~** he did it without hesitating *or* hesitation; **er zögerte lange mit der Antwort** he hesitated (for) a long time before replying; **sie zögerte nicht lange mit ihrer Zustimmung** she lost little time in agreeing.

Zögern *nt* **-s,** *no pl* hesitation ◆ **ohne ~** without hesitation, unhesitatingly; **nach langem ~** after hesitating a long time.

zögernd *adj* hesitant, hesitating.

Zögling *m* (*old, hum*) pupil.

Zölibat *nt or m* **-(e)s,** *no pl* celibacy; (*Gelübde*) vow of celibacy ◆ **im ~ leben** to be celibate, to practise celibacy.

Zoll[1] *m* **-(e)s, -** (*old: Längenmaß*) inch ◆ **jeder ~ ein König, ~ für ~ ein König** every inch a king.

Zoll[2] *m* **-(e)s, ¨-e (a)** (*Waren~*) customs duty; (*Brücken~, Straßen~*) toll ◆ **für etw ~ bezahlen** to pay (customs) duty on sth; **einem ~ unterliegen** to carry duty; **darauf liegt (ein) ~, darauf wird ~ erhoben** there is duty to pay on that. **(b)** (*Stelle*) **der ~** customs *pl*.

Zoll|abfertigung *f* **(a)** (*Vorgang*) customs clearance. **(b)** (*Dienststelle*) customs post *or* checkpoint.

⚠ **Zollager** *nt getrennt* **Zoll-lager** bonded warehouse.

Zoll-: ~amt *nt* customs house *or* office; **z~amtlich** *adj* customs *attr*; **z~amtlich geöffnet** opened by the customs; **~ausland** *nt foreign country which one has to go through customs to enter*; **~beamte(r)** *m* customs officer *or* official; **~begleitpapiere** *pl* customs documents *pl*; **~behörde** *f* customs authorities *pl*, customs *pl*; **~bestimmung** *f usu pl* customs regulation; **z~breit** *adj* one inch wide, inch-wide *attr*; **~breit** *m* **-, -** inch; **keinen ~breit zurückweichen** not to give *or* yield an inch; **~deklaration** *f* (*form*) customs declaration; **~einnahmen** *pl* customs revenue *sing*; **~einnehmer** *m* **-s, -** (*old*) *siehe* **Zöllner.**

zollen *vt* **jdm Anerkennung/Achtung/Bewunderung ~** to acknowledge/respect/admire sb; **jdm Beifall ~** to applaud sb, to give sb applause; **jdm Dank ~** to extend *or* offer one's thanks to sb; **jdm seinen Tribut ~** to pay tribute to sb.

Zoller *m* **-s, -** (*Sw*) customs officer *or* official.

Zoll-: ~erklärung *f* customs declaration; **~fahnder** *m* customs investigator; **~fahndung** *f* customs investigation department; **z~frei** *adj* duty-free; **etw z~frei einführen** to import sth free of duty; *siehe* **Gedanke**; **~gebiet** *nt* customs area *or* territory; **~gebühr** *f* (customs) duty, excise; **~grenzbezirk** *m* customs and border district; **~grenze** *f* customs border *or* frontier; **~inhaltserklärung** *f* customs declaration; **~kontrolle** *f* customs check; **~lager** *nt siehe* **Zollager.**

Zöllner *m* **-s, -** (*old, Bibl*) tax collector; (*inf: Zollbeamter*) customs officer *or* official.

Zoll-: ~niederlage *f siehe* **Zollager**; **~papiere** *pl* customs documents *pl*; **z~pflichtig** *adj* dutiable; **~recht** *nt* **(a)** (*Hist*) right to levy tolls; **(b)** (*Jur*) customs law; **~schranke** *f* customs barrier; **~stock** *m* ruler, inch rule; **~tarif** *m* customs tariff; **~union** *f* customs union; **~verein** *m* (*Hist*) **Deutscher ~verein** German Customs Union (of 1844).

Zombie *m* **-(s), -s** (*lit, fig*) zombie.

zombig *adj* (*inf*) brilliant (*inf*), wicked (*sl*).

Zone *f* **-, -n** zone; (*von Fahrkarte*) fare stage; (*fig: von Mißtrauen etc*) area ◆ **blaue ~** (*in Straßenverkehr*) restricted parking area; **die ~** (*dated inf*) the Eastern Zone, East Germany.

Zonen-: ~grenzbezirk *m* border district (with East Germany); **~grenze** *f* zonal border; **die ~grenze** (*inf*) the border (with East Germany); **~randgebiet** *nt* border area (with East Germany); **~tarif** *m* (*Fahrgeld*) fare for a journey within a fare stage; (*Post, Telec*) zonal charge; **~zeit** *f* zonal time.

Zönobit *m* **-en, -en** coenobite.

Zönobium *nt* coenobium.

Zoo [tso:] *m* **-s, -s** zoo ◆ **gestern waren wir im ~** we went to the zoo yesterday.

Zoologe [tsoo'lo:gə] *m* **-n, -n, Zoologin** *f* zoologist.

Zoologie [tsoolo'gi:] *f* zoology.

zoologisch [tsoo'lo:gɪʃ] *adj* zoological.

Zoom [zu:m] *nt* **-s, -s** zoom shot; (*Objektiv*) zoom lens.

zoomen ['zu:mən] **1** *vt* to zoom in on. **2** *vi* to zoom (in).

Zoom|objektiv ['zu:m-] *nt* zoom lens.

Zoon-politikon ['tso:ɔn-] *nt* **-,** *no pl* political animal.

Zoowärter *m* zoo keeper.

Zopf *m* **-(e)s, ¨-e (a)** (*Haartracht*) pigtail; (*von Mädchen auch*) plait, braid (*esp US*) ◆ **das Haar in ¨-e flechten** to plait one's hair; **ein alter ~(, der abgeschnitten erden müßte)** (*fig*) an antiquated custom (that should be done away with). **(b)** (*Gebäck*) plait, plaited loaf. **(c)** (*Baumwipfel*) tree-top.

Zopf-: ~band *nt* hair ribbon; **~muster** *nt* cable stitch; **~spange** *f* clip.

Zorn *m* **-(e)s,** *no pl* anger, rage, wrath (*liter*) ◆ **der ~ Gottes** the wrath of God; **jds ~ fürchten** to fear sb's anger *or* wrath; **jds ~ heraufbeschwören** to incur sb's wrath; **jdn in ~ bringen** to anger *or* enrage sb; **wenn ihn der ~ überkommt** when he becomes angry *or* loses his temper; **in ~ geraten** *or* **ausbrechen** to fly into a rage, to lose one's temper; **der ~ packte ihn** he became angry, he flew into a rage; **im ~** in a rage, in anger; **in gerechtem ~** in righteous anger; **einen ~ auf jdn haben** to be furious with sb.

Zorn-: ~ader *f siehe* **Zornesader**; **~ausbruch** *m siehe* **Zornesausbruch.**

Zornes-: ~ader *f* **auf seiner Stirn schwoll eine ~ader** he was so angry you could see the veins standing out on his forehead; **~ausbruch** *m* fit of anger *or* rage; **~röte** *f* flush of anger; **~tränen** *pl* tears *pl* of rage.

zornig *adj* angry, furious ◆ **(leicht) ~ werden** to lose one's temper (easily); **auf jdn ~ sein** to be angry *or* furious with sb; **ein ~er junger Mann** (*fig*) an angry young man.

zoroastrisch *adj* zoroastrian.

Zote *f* **-, -n** dirty joke.

zotig *adj* dirty, filthy, smutty.

Zotte *f* **-, -n (a)** (*Anat*) villus. **(b)** (*Haarsträhne*) rat's tail (*inf*).

Zottel *f* **-, -n** (*inf*) rat's tail (*inf*); (*an Mütze*) pom-pom.

Zottelhaar *nt* (*inf*) shaggy hair.

zottelig *adj* (*inf*) *Haar* shaggy.

zotteln *vi aux sein* (*inf*) to amble.

Zotteltrab *m* gentle trot.

zottig *adj* **(a)** *Fell* shaggy. **(b)** (*Anat*) villous, villose.

ZPO [tsetpe:'|o:] *abbr of* **Zivilprozeßordnung.**

z.T. *abbr of* **zum Teil.**

Ztr. *abbr of* **Zentner.**

zu **1** *prep +dat* **(a)** (*örtlich: Bewegung, Ziel*) to ◆ **~m Bahnhof** to the station; **~r Stadt/Stadtmitte gehen** to go to town/the town centre; **~m Bäcker/Arzt**

gehen to go to the baker's/doctor's; **bis ~** as far as; **(bis) ~m Bahnhof sind es 5 km** it's 5 kms to the station; **etw ~ sich stecken** to take sth; **~m Theater gehen** to go on the stage *or* into the theatre; **~m Militär** *or* **~ den Soldaten gehen** to join the army, to join up.
(b) (*örtlich: Richtung bezeichnend*) **~m Fenster herein/hinaus** in (at)/out of the window; **~r Tür hinaus/herein** out of/in the door; **~m Himmel weisen** to point heavenwards *or* up at the heavens; **~r Decke sehen** to look (up) at the ceiling; **~ jdm/etw hinaufsehen** to look up at sb/sth; **~ jdm herüber/hinübersehen** to look across at sb; **sie wandte sich/sah ~ ihm hin** she turned to(wards) him/looked towards him; **das Zimmer liegt ~r Straße hin** the room looks out onto the street; **~m Meer hin** towards the sea; **~r Stadtmitte hin** towards the town/city centre.
(c) (*örtlich: Lage*) at; (*bei Stadt*) in ♦ **~ Frankfurt** (*old*) in Frankfurt; **der Dom ~ Köln** the cathedral in Cologne, Cologne cathedral; **der Reichstag ~ Worms** (*Hist*) the Diet of Worms; **~ Hause** at home; **~ seiner Linken saß ...** (*geh*) on his left sat ...; **~ beiden Seiten (des Hauses)** on both sides (of the house); **~ Lande und ~ Wasser** on land and sea; **jdm ~r Seite sitzen** (*geh*) to sit at sb's side; **sich ~ Tisch setzen** (*geh*) to sit down to dinner.
(d) (*bei Namen*) **der Graf ~ Ehrenstein** the Count of Ehrenstein; **Gasthof ~m goldenen Löwen** the Golden Lion (Inn).
(e) (*Zusatz, Zusammengehörigkeit, Begleitung*) with ♦ **Wein ~m Essen trinken** to drink wine with one's meal; **der Deckel ~ diesem Topf** the lid for this pan; **~r Gitarre singen** to sing to a/the guitar; **Lieder ~r Laute** songs accompanied by the lute; **die Melodie ~ dem Lied** the tune of the song; **Vorwort/Anmerkungen ~ etw** preface/notes to sth; **~ dem kommt noch, daß ich ...** on top of that I ...; **etw ~ etw legen** to put sth with sth; **sich ~ jdm setzen** to sit down next to *or* beside sb; **setz dich doch ~ uns** (come and) sit with us; **etw ~ etw tragen** (*Kleidung*) to wear sth with sth.
(f) (*zeitlich*) at ♦ **~ früher/später Stunde** at an early/late hour; **~ Mittag** (*am Mittag*) at midday *or* noon; (*bis Mittag*) by midday *or* noon; **~ Ostern** at Easter; **letztes Jahr ~ Weihnachten** last Christmas; **(bis) ~m 15. April/Donnerstag/Abend** until 15th April/Thursday/(this) evening; (*nicht später als*) by 15th April/Thursday/(this) evening; **~m Wochenende hat sich Besuch angesagt** we're having visitors at the weekend; **der Wechsel ist ~m 15. April fällig** the allowance is due on 15th April; **~m 31. Mai kündigen** to give in one's notice for May 31st; *siehe* **Anfang, Schluß, Zeit.**
(g) (*Bestimmung*) for ♦ **Stoff ~ einem Kleid** material for a dress; **die Tür ~m Keller** the door to the cellar; **Milch ~m Kaffee** milk for coffee.
(h) (*Zweck*) for ♦ **Wasser ~m Waschen** water for washing; **Papier ~m Schreiben** paper to write on, writing paper; **ein Bett ~m Schlafen** a bed to sleep in; **der Knopf ~m Abstellen** the off-button; **die Luke ~m Einsteigen** the entrance-hatch; **das Zeichen ~m Aufbruch** the signal to leave; **etw ~r Antwort geben** to say sth in reply; **~r Einführung ...** by way of (an) introduction ...; **~ seiner Entschuldigung/~r Erklärung** in apology/explanation, by way of apology/explanation; **er sagte das nur ~ ihrer Beruhigung** he said that just to set her mind at rest; **~ nichts taugen, ~ nichts zu gebrauchen sein** to be no use at all, to be no earthly use (*inf*).
(i) (*Anlaß*) **etw ~m Geburtstag/~ Weihnachten bekommen** to get sth for one's birthday/for Christmas; **ein Geschenk ~m Hochzeitstag** a wedding anniversary present; **~ Ihrem 60. Geburtstag** on the occasion of your 60th birthday (*form*); **jdm ~ etw gratulieren** to congratulate sb on sth; **jdn ~m Essen einladen** to invite sb for a meal; **~ Ihrem schweren Verlust** on your sad loss; **Ausstellung ~m Jahrestag der Revolution** exhibition to mark the anniversary of the revolution; **~ dieser Frage möchte ich folgendes sagen** I should like to say the following to this question, on this I would like to say the following; **was sagen Sie ~ diesen Preisen?** what do you say to these prices?; **~m Thema Gleichberechtigung** on the subject of equal rights; **eine Rede ~m Schillerjahr** a speech (up)on the anniversary of Schiller's death/birth; **„Zum Realismusbegriff"** "On the Concept of Realism"; **jdn ~ etw vernehmen** to question *or* examine sb about sth.
(j) (*Folge, Umstand*) **~ seinem Besten** for his own good; **~m Glück** luckily; **~ meiner Schande/Freude** *etc* to my shame/joy *etc*; **~/~m Tode** to death; **es ist ~m Lachen** it's really funny; **es ist ~m Weinen** it's enough to make you (want to) weep.
(k) (*Mittel, Art und Weise*) **~ Fuß/Pferd** on foot/horseback; **~ Schiff** by ship *or* sea; **~ deutsch** in German; **etw ~ einem hohen Preis verkaufen/versteigern** to sell sth at a high price/to bid up the price of sth.
(l) *in festen Verbindungen mit n siehe auch dort* ♦ **~m Beispiel** for example; **~ Hilfe!** help!; **jdm ~ Hilfe kommen** to come to sb's aid; **~ jds Gedächtnis, ~m Gedächtnis von jdm** in memory of sb, in sb's memory; **~m Lobe von jdm/etw** in praise of sb/sth; **~r Strafe** as a punishment; **~r Belohnung** as a reward; **~r Warnung** as a warning; **~r Beurteilung/Einsicht** for inspec tion; **~r Probe/Ansicht** on trial *or* test/approval; **~r Unterschrift** for signature *or* signing.
(m) (*Veränderung*) into ♦ **~ etw werden** to turn into sth; (*Mensch auch*) to become sth; **Leder ~ Handtaschen verarbeiten** to make handbags out of leather; **jdn/etw ~ etw machen** to make sb/sth (into) sth; **jdn ~m Manne machen** to make a man of sb; **~ Asche verbrennen** to burn to ashes; **(wieder) ~ Staub werden** to (re)turn to dust; **etw ~ Pulver zermahlen** to grind sth (in)to powder; **~ etw heranwachsen** to grow up into sth; **jdn ~m Major befördern** to promote sb to (the rank of) major.
(n) (*als*) as ♦ **jdn ~m König wählen** to choose sb as king; **jdn ~ etw ernennen** to nominate sb sth; **er machte mich ~ seinem Stellvertreter** he made me his deputy; **jdn ~m Freund haben** to have sb as a friend; **er machte sie ~ seiner Frau, er nahm sie ~r Frau** he made her his wife, he took her as his wife; **sich** (*dat*) **jdn/etw ~m Vorbild nehmen** to take sb/sth as one's example, to model oneself on sb/sth; **~m Künstler geboren sein** to be born to be an artist.
(o) (*Verhältnis, Beziehung*) **Liebe ~ jdm** love for sb; **aus Freundschaft ~ jdm** because of one's friendship with sb; **Vertrauen ~ jdm/etw** trust in sb/sth; **meine Beziehung ~ ihm** my relationship with him.
(p) **im Vergleich ~** in comparison with, compared with; **im Verhältnis ~** in relation to, in proportion to; **im Verhältnis drei ~ zwei** (*Math*) in the ratio (of) three to two; **drei ~ zwei** (*Sport*) three-two; **das Spiel steht 3 ~ 2** (*geschrieben* **3:2**) the score is 3-2 (*gesprochen* three-two); **wir haben 4 ~ 3** (*geschrieben* **4:3**) **gewonnen** we won 4-3 *or* by 4 goals/games *etc* to 3.
(q) (*bei Zahlenangaben*) **~ zwei Prozent** at two per cent; **wir verkaufen die Äpfel jetzt das Stück ~ 5 Pfennig** we're selling the apples now at *or* for 5 pfennigs each; **fünf (Stück) ~ 30 Pfennig** five for 30 pfennigs; **~ zwei Dritteln (gefüllt)** two-thirds (full); **~m halben Preis** at half price; **die Arbeit ist schon ~r Hälfte getan** the work is already half done; **~m ersten Male** for the first time; **~m ersten ..., ~m zweiten ...** (*Aufzählung*) first ..., second ...; **~m ersten, ~m zweiten, ~m dritten** (*bei Auktionen*) for the first time, for the second time, for the third time; *siehe* **vier, bis**[2].
(r) (*mit Fragepronomen*) **~ wem wollen/gehen/sprechen Sie?** who do you want/who are you going to see/who are you talking to?; **~ was** (*inf*) (*Zweck*) for what; (*warum*) why.
(s) (*inf: getrenntes „dazu"*) **da komme ich nicht ~** I can't get round to it; *siehe* **da, dazu.**
[2] *adv* **(a)** (*allzu*) too ♦ **~ sehr** too much; **sie liebte ihn ~ sehr, als daß sie ihn verraten hätte** she loved him too much to betray him; **~ verliebt** too much *or* too deeply in love; **das war einfach ~ dumm!** (*inf*) it was so stupid!; **ich wäre ~ gern mitgekommen** I should have been only too pleased to come.
(b) (*geschlossen*) shut, closed ♦ **auf, ~** (*an Hähnen etc*) on, off; **Tür ~!** (*inf*) shut the door; **die Geschäfte haben jetzt ~** the shops are shut *or* closed now.
(c) (*inf: los, weiter*) **dann mal ~!** right, off we go!; **du wolltest mir was vorsingen, dann mal ~** you wanted to sing me something? right then, go ahead; **immer** *or* **nur ~!** just keep on!; **ihr seid auf dem richtigen Wege, nur ~!** you're on the right track, just keep going; **schreie nur ~, es hilft doch nichts!** go on, scream then, but it won't do any good!; **mach ~!** hurry up!, get a move on!, come on!; **lauft schon ~, ich komme nach** you go on, I'll catch you up.
(d) (*zeitlich*) *siehe* **ab.**
(e) (*örtlich*) towards ♦ **nach hinten ~** towards the back; **auf den Wald ~** towards the forest; **dem Ausgang ~** towards the exit.
[3] *conj* **(a)** (*mit Infinitiv*) to ♦ **etw ~ essen** sth to eat; **der Fußboden ist noch ~ fegen** the floor still has to be swept; **er hat ~ gehorchen** he has to do as he's told, he has to obey; **jdm befehlen** *or* **den Auftrag erteilen, etw ~ tun** to order sb to do sth; **das Material ist noch/nicht mehr ~ gebrauchen** the material is still/is no longer usable; **diese Rechnung ist bis Montag ~ bezahlen** this bill has to be paid by Monday; **~ stehen kommen** to come to a stop; **~ liegen kommen** to come to rest; **ich habe ~ arbeiten** I have to do some work, I have some work to do; **ohne es ~ wissen** without knowing it; **um besser sehen ~ können** in order to see better; **ich komme, um mich ~ verabschieden** I've come to say goodbye.
(b) (*mit Partizip*) **noch ~ bezahlende Rechnungen** outstanding bills; **nicht ~ unterschätzende Probleme** problems (that are) not to be underestimated; **nur winzige, leicht ~ übersehende Punkte** only very small points (that are) easily overlooked; **der ~ prüfende Kandidat, der ~ Prüfende** the candidate to be examined.
[4] *adj* (*inf*) **~ sein** (*Tür, Geschäft, Kiste etc*) to be shut; (*Kleid, Verschluß*) to be done up; **die ~(n)e Tür** (*strictly incorrect*) the shut door; *siehe* **~sein.**

zu|aller-: ~allerletzt *adv* (*inf*) very last of all; **~erst** *adv* first of all; **~letzt** *adv* last of all.

zu|arbeiten *vi sep* **jdm ~** to do sb's groundwork.

zubauen *vt sep Lücke* to fill in; *Platz, Gelände* to build up; *Blick* to block with buildings/a building.

Zubehör *nt or m* **-(e)s,** (*rare*) **-e** equipment *no pl*; (*Zusatzgeräte, Auto~*) accessories *pl*; (*~teil*) attachments *pl*, accessories *pl*; (*zur Kleidung*) accessories *pl* ♦ **Küche mit allem ~** fully equipped kitchen.

Zubehör-: ~handel *m* accessories trade; **~teil** *nt* accessory, attachment.

zubeißen *vi sep irreg* to bite; (*beim Zahnarzt*) to bite (one's teeth) together ♦ **der Hund faßte mich am Bein und biß zu** the dog got hold of my leg and sank his teeth into me.

zubekommen* *vt sep irreg* (*inf*) *Kleidung* to get done up; *Koffer auch, Tür, Fenster* to get shut *or* closed.

zubenannt *adj* (*liter*) also called.

Zuber *m* **-s, -** (wash)tub.

zubereiten* *vt sep Essen* to prepare; *Arznei auch* to make up; *Cocktail* to mix.

Zubereitung *f* **(a)** *siehe vt* preparation; making up; mixing ♦ **eine neue ~ für Blumenkohl** a new way of preparing cauliflower.
(b) (*Präparat*) preparation.

Zubettgehen *nt* **vor dem/beim/nach dem ~** before (going to) bed/on going to bed/after going to bed.

zubiegen *vt sep irreg* to bend shut.

zubilligen *vt sep* **jdm etw ~** to grant sb sth, to allow sb sth; **jdm mildernde Umstände ~** to recognize that there are/were mitigating circumstances for sb; **ich will ihm gerne ~, daß er sich bemüht hat** he certainly made an effort, I'll grant *or* allow him that.

zubinden *vt sep irreg* to tie up, to do up; *Schuhe auch* to lace up ♦ **jdm die Augen ~** to blindfold sb.

zubleiben *vi sep irreg aux sein* (*inf*) to stay shut.
zublinzeln *vi sep* **jdm ~** to wink at sb.
zubringen *vt sep irreg* **(a)** (*verbringen*) to spend.
(b) (*herbeibringen*) to bring to, to take to ◆ **jdm ~, daß ...** (*fig*) to inform sb that ...; **es ist mir zugebracht worden** (*fig*) it has been brought to my notice *or* attention, I have been informed.
(c) (*inf: zumachen können*) *Knöpfe, Reißverschluß, Kleidung* to get done up; *Kiste, Koffer auch, Tür, Fenster* to get shut *or* closed.
Zubringer *m* **-s, - (a)** (*Tech*) conveyor. **(b)** *siehe* **Zubringerstraße. (c) ~(bus)** shuttle (bus); (*zum Flughafen*) airport bus; **~(flugzeug)** feeder plane.
Zubringer-: ~dienst *m* shuttle service; **~linie** *f* feeder route; **~straße** *f* feeder road.
Zubrot *nt* (*zusätzlicher Verdienst*) extra income ◆ **ein kleines ~ verdienen** to earn *or* make a bit on the side (*inf*).
zubuttern *vt sep* (*inf*) (*zuschießen*) to contribute, to add on; (*zuzüglich bezahlen*) to pay out (on top); (*dazuverdienen*) to add on ◆ **zu seinem Gehalt etwas ~** to boost *or* up (*inf*) one's salary a bit.
Zucchini [tsʊ'kiːniː] *f* **-, -** courgette (*Brit*), zucchini (*US*).
Zucht *f* **-, -en (a)** (*Disziplin*) discipline ◆ **~ und Ordnung** discipline; **jdn in strenge ~ nehmen** (*liter*) to take sb firmly in hand; **jdn in ~ halten** to keep a tight rein on sb.
(b) *no pl* (*Aufzucht, das Züchten*) (*von Tieren*) breeding; (*von Pflanzen*) growing, cultivation; (*von Bakterien, Perlen*) culture; (*von Bienen*) keeping ◆ **Tiere zur ~ halten** to keep animals for breeding; **die ~ von Bienen/Pferden** beekeeping/horse breeding.
(c) (*~generation*) (*von Tieren*) breed, stock; (*von Pflanzen*) stock, variety; (*von Bakterien, Perlen*) culture.
Zucht-: ~buch *nt* studbook; **~bulle** *m* breeding bull; **~eber** *m* breeding boar.
züchten *vt Tiere* to breed; *Bienen* to keep; *Pflanzen* to grow, to cultivate; *Perlen, Bakterien* to cultivate; *Kristalle* to grow, to synthesize; (*fig*) *Haß* to breed.
Züchter(in *f*) *m* **-s, -** (*von Tieren*) breeder; (*von Pflanzen*) grower, cultivator; (*von Bienen*) keeper; (*von Perlen, Bakterien*) culturist.
Zuchthaus *nt* (*Gebäude*) prison (*for capital offenders*), penitentiary (*US*) ◆ **zu 7 Jahren ~ verurteilt werden** to be sentenced to 7 years' in prison *or* 7 years' imprisonment; **dafür bekommt man ~, darauf steht ~** you'll go to prison for that.
Zuchthäusler(in *f*) *m* **-s, -** (*inf*) convict, con (*sl*).
Zuchthausstrafe *f* prison sentence.
Zuchthengst *m* stud horse, breeding stallion.
züchtig *adj* (*liter*) (*keusch, anständig*) *Mädchen* modest, chaste; *Wangen* innocent; *Augen, Benehmen* modest; (*tugendhaft*) virtuous.
züchtigen *vt* (*geh*) to beat; (*stärker, Jur*) to flog; *Schüler* to use corporal punishment on (*form*), ≃ to cane.
Züchtigkeit *f* (*liter*) modesty, chasteness.
Züchtigung *f siehe vt* beating; flogging; caning ◆ **körperliche ~** corporal punishment.
Züchtigungsrecht *nt* right to use corporal punishment.
Zucht-: z~los *adj* (*dated*) undisciplined; **~meister** *m* (*liter*) disciplinarian; **~mittel** *nt* (*old*) disciplinary measure; **~perle** *f* cultured pearl; **~rute** *f* (*fig*) rod; **unter jds ~rute** (*dat*) **stehen** to be under sb's rod; **~stier** *m siehe* **~bulle**; **~stute** *f* broodmare, breeding mare; **~tier** *nt* breeding animal, animal for breeding.
Züchtung *f* **(a)** *siehe vt* breeding; keeping; growing; cultivation; culture; synthesis. **(b)** (*Zuchtart*) (*Pflanzen*) strain, variety; (*Tiere*) breed.
Zucht-: ~vieh *nt* breeding cattle; **~wahl** *f* selective breeding; **natürliche ~wahl** natural selection.
zuck *interj siehe* **ruck, zuck.**
Zuck *m* **-s,** *no pl* (*Körperbewegung*) sudden movement; (*mit Augenlidern*) flutter; (*beim Reißen*) jerk, tug, yank; (*beim Ziehen*) jerk, tug.
zuckeln *vi aux sein* (*inf*) to jog ◆ **er zuckelte müde hinter den anderen drein** he trotted wearily along behind the others.
Zuckeltrab *m* jog trot ◆ **im ~** at a jog trot.
zucken [1] *vi* **(a)** (*nervös, krampfhaft*) to twitch; (*Augenlider auch*) to flutter; (*vor Schreck*) to start; (*vor Schmerzen*) to flinch; (*Fisch, verwundetes Tier*) to thrash about ◆ **er zuckte ständig mit dem Mund** his mouth kept twitching; **mit den Schultern** *or* **Achseln ~** to shrug (one's shoulders); **es zuckte um ihre Mundwinkel** the corner of her mouth twitched; **ein Lächeln zuckte um ihren Mund** a smile played around her lips; **es zuckte mir in den Fingern, das zu tun** (*fig*) I was itching to do that; **es zuckte mir in der Hand** (*fig*) I was itching to hit him/her; *siehe* **Wimper.**
(b) (*aufleuchten*) (*Blitz*) to flash; (*Flammen*) to flare up ◆ **die ~den Flammen** the flames flaring up.
(c) (*weh tun*) **der Schmerz zuckte (mir) durch den ganzen Körper** the pain shot right through my body *or* me; **es zuckte mir im Knie** (*inf*) I had a twinge in my knee.
[2] *vt* **die Achseln** *or* **Schultern ~** to shrug (one's shoulders).
zücken *vt Degen, Schwert* to draw; (*inf: hervorziehen*) *Notizbuch, Bleistift, Brieftasche* to pull *or* take out.
Zucker *m* **-s,** *no pl* **(a)** sugar ◆ **ein Stück ~** a lump of sugar, a sugar lump; **du bist doch nicht aus** *or* **von ~!** (*inf*) don't be such a softie! (*inf*).
(b) (*Med*) (*~gehalt*) sugar; (*Krankheit*) diabetes *sing* ◆ **~ haben** (*inf*) to be a diabetic; **bei ~ muß Insulin gespritzt werden** diabetics need insulin injections.
Zucker-: ~bäcker *m* (*old, S Ger, Aus*) confectioner; **~bäckerei** *f* (*old, S Ger, Aus*) confectioner's (shop); **~bäckerstil** *m* wedding-cake style; **~brot** *nt* (*obs*) sweetmeat (*old*); **mit ~brot und Peitsche** (*prov*) with a stick and a carrot.
Zuckerchen, Zückerchen *nt* (*dial: Bonbon*) sweet (*Brit*), candy (*US*).
Zucker-: ~couleur *f* (*Cook*) caramel; **~dose** *f* sugar basin *or* bowl; **~erbse** *f* mange-tout (pea); **z~frei** *adj* sugar-free; **~früchte** *pl* crystallized fruits *pl*; **~gehalt** *m* sugar content; ⚠**~guß** *m* icing, frosting (*esp US*); **mit ~guß überziehen** to ice, to frost; **ein Kuchen mit ~guß** an iced *or* a frosted cake; **~hut** *m* sugarloaf; **der ~hut in Rio** the Sugar Loaf Mountain in Rio.
zuck(e)rig *adj* sugary.
Zucker-: ~kand(is) *m siehe* **Kandis(zucker); z~krank** *adj* diabetic; **~kranke(r)** *mf decl as adj* diabetic; **~krankheit** *f* diabetes *sing.*
Zuckerl *nt* **-s, -(n)** (*S Ger, Aus*) sweet (*Brit*), candy (*US*).
Zucker-: ~lecken *nt*: **das ist kein ~lecken** (*inf*) it's no picnic (*inf*); **~melone** *f* muskmelon.
zuckern *vt* to sugar, to put sugar in ◆ **zu stark gezuckert sein** to have too much sugar in it.
Zucker-: ~plantage *f* sugar plantation; **~plätzchen** *nt* (*Bonbon*) sweet (*Brit*), candy (*US*); (*Keks*) sugar-coated biscuit (*Brit*) *or* cookie (*US*); **~puppe** *f* (*dated inf*) sweetie (*inf*); (*als Anrede auch*) sugar (*inf*), sweetie-pie (*inf*); **~raffinade** *f* refined sugar; **~raffinerie** *f* sugar refinery; **~rohr** *nt* sugar-cane; **~rübe** *f* sugar beet; **~schlecken** *nt siehe* **~lecken; ~spiegel** *m* (*Med*) (blood) sugar level; **~stange** *f* stick of rock (*Brit*) *or* candy (*US*); **~streuer** *m* sugar sprinkler; **z~süß** *adj* (*lit, fig*) sugar-sweet, as sweet as sugar; **~tüte** *f siehe* **Schultüte; ~wasser** *nt* sugar(ed) water; **~watte** *f* candy floss; **~werk** *nt* sweets *pl* (*Brit*), candies *pl* (*US*); **~zange** *f* sugar tongs *pl*; **~zeug** *nt, no pl* (*pej*) sweet stuff.
zuckrig *adj siehe* **zuck(e)rig.**
Zuckung *f* (*nervöse ~*) twitch; (*stärker: krampfhaft*) convulsion; (*von Muskeln auch*) spasm; (*von Augenlidern auch*) flutter; (*von sterbendem Tier*) convulsive movement ◆ **die letzten ~en** (*lit, fig*) the death throes.
Zudecke *f* (*dial*) cover (*on bed*).
zudecken *vt sep* to cover; *jdn, Beine auch* to cover up; (*im Bett*) to tuck up *or* in; *Gestorbenen, Grube, Fleck auch* to cover up *or* over ◆ **jdn/sich (mit etw) ~** to cover sb/oneself up (with sth); to tuck sb/oneself up (in sth).
zudem *adv* (*geh*) moreover, furthermore, in addition.
zudenken *vt sep irreg* (*geh*) **jdm etw ~** to intend *or* destine sth for sb; **dieses Glück war uns aber offenbar nicht zugedacht** but we were evidently not destined to be so lucky; **das Schicksal hatte mir schwere Schläge zugedacht** Fate had some cruel blows in store for me.
zudiktieren* *vt sep* (*inf*) *Strafe* to hand out.
Zudrang *m, no pl* (*rare*) *siehe* **Andrang.**
zudrehen *sep* [1] *vt Wasserhahn etc* to turn off; (*zuwenden*) to turn (*dat* to).
[2] *vr* to turn (*dat* to).
zudringlich *adj Mensch, Art* pushing, pushy (*inf*); *Nachbarn* intrusive ◆ **~ werden** (*zu einer Frau*) to make advances (*zu* to), to act improperly (*zu* towards).
Zudringlichkeit *f* pushiness (*inf*); intrusiveness; (*einer Frau gegenüber*) advances *pl.*
zudröhnen *vtr* (*sl*) *siehe* **volldröhen.**
zudrücken *vt sep* to press shut; *Tür auch* to push shut ◆ **jdm die Kehle ~** to throttle sb; **einem Toten die Augen ~** to close a dead person's eyes; *siehe* **Auge.**
zu|eignen *vt sep* (*geh*) *Buch, Gedicht* to dedicate (*jdm* to sb).
Zu|eignung *f* (*geh*) (*von Gedicht, Buch*) dedication.
zu|eilen *vi sep aux sein* **auf jdn ~** to rush *or* hurry towards sb *or* (*bis zu jdm*) up to sb; **auf etw** (*acc*) **~** to hurry *or* rush towards/up to sth.
zu|einander *adv* (*gegenseitig*) to each other, to one another; *Vertrauen* in each other, in one another; (*zusammen*) together ◆ **~ passen** to go together; (*Menschen*) to suit each other *or* one another, to be suited; **Braun und Grün passen gut ~** brown and green go together well *or* go well together.
⚠ **zu|einander-: ~finden** *vi sep irreg* to find common ground; (*sich versöhnen*) to be reconciled; **~gesellen*** *vr sep* (*geh*) to join each other; (*fig*) to be combined; **~stehen** *vi sep irreg* (*geh*) *siehe* **zusammenhalten.**
zu|erkennen* *vt sep irreg Preis* to award (*jdm* to sb); *Würde, Auszeichnung, Orden auch* to confer, to bestow (*jdm* on sb); *Sieg auch, Recht* to grant, to accord (*jdm etw* sb sth); (*vor Gericht*) *Entschädigung, Rente etc* to award (*jdm etw* sb sth); *Strafe* to impose, to inflict (*jdm* (up)on sb) ◆ **das Gemälde wurde dem höchsten Bieter zuerkannt** the painting went to the highest bidder; **ihm wurde der Preis zuerkannt** he was awarded the prize.
Zu|erkennung *f siehe vt* awarding; conferring, bestowing; granting, accordance; imposition.
zu|erst *adv* **(a)** (*als erster*) first ◆ **ich kam ~ an** I was (the) first to arrive, I arrived first; **wollen wir ~ essen?** shall we eat first?; **~ an die Reihe kommen** to be first; **~ bin ich Geschäftsmann, dann Privatmann** I am first and foremost a businessman, and only then a private individual; **das muß ich morgen früh ~ machen** I must do that first thing tomorrow (morning) *or* first thing in the morning; *siehe* **kommen (p).**
(b) (*zum ersten Mal*) first, for the first time.
(c) (*anfangs*) at first ◆ **er sprach ~ gar nicht** at first he didn't speak at all; **~ muß man ...** to begin *or* start with you have to ...; first (of all) you have to ...
zu|erteilen* *vt sep siehe* **zuerkennen.**
zufächeln *vt sep* (*geh*) to fan ◆ **sich/jdm Kühlung ~** to fan oneself/sb.
zufahren *vi sep irreg aux sein* **(a) auf jdn ~** to drive/ride towards sb; (*direkt*) to drive/ride up to sb; **auf etw** (*acc*) **~** to drive/ride towards sth, to head for

sth; er kam genau auf mich zugefahren he drove/rode straight at or for me.
(b) (weiterfahren, losfahren) fahren Sie doch zu! go on then!, get a move on then! (inf).
(c) (Tür) (plötzlich schließen) to slide shut.

Zufahrt f approach (road); (Einfahrt) entrance; (zu einem Haus) drive(way) ♦ „keine ~ zum Krankenhaus" "no access to hospital".

Zufahrtsstraße f access road; (zur Autobahn) approach road.

Zufall m chance, accident; (Zusammentreffen) coincidence ♦ das ist ~ it's pure chance; durch ~ (quite) by chance or accident; ich habe durch ~ gesehen, wie er das Geld in die Tasche gesteckt hat I happened to see him putting the money in his pocket; per ~ (inf) by a (pure) fluke; per ~ trafen wir uns im Bus we happened to meet on the bus; ein merkwürdiger ~ a remarkable or strange coincidence; es war reiner or purer ~, daß ... it was pure chance that ...; es ist kein ~, daß ... it's no accident that ...; es war ein glücklicher ~, daß ... it was lucky that ..., it was a stroke or bit of luck that ...; welch ein ~! what a coincidence!; etw dem ~ überlassen to leave sth to chance; etw dem ~ verdanken to owe sth to chance; es hängt vom ~ ab, ob ... it's a matter of chance whether ...

zufallen vi sep irreg aux sein (a) (sich schließen) (Fenster etc) to close, to shut ♦ die Tür fiel laut zu the door slammed or banged shut; ihm fielen beinahe die Augen zu he could hardly or scarcely keep his eyes open.
(b) jdm ~ (zuteil werden: Erbe) to pass to or devolve upon (Jur) sb; (Preis etc) to go to sb, to be awarded to sb; (Aufgabe, Rolle) to fall to or upon sb.
(c) (zukommen) diesem Treffen fällt große Bedeutung zu this meeting is of the utmost importance.

zufällig [1] adj chance attr; Ergebnis auch accidental; Zusammentreffen auch coincidental, accidental ♦ das war rein ~ it was pure chance or purely by chance; es ist nicht ~, daß er ... it's no accident that he ...; das kann doch nicht ~ gewesen sein that can't have happened by chance; „Ähnlichkeiten mit lebenden Personen sind rein ~" "any similarities with persons living or dead are purely coincidental".
[2] adv (a) by chance; (bei Zusammentreffen von Ereignissen auch) coincidentally ♦ er ging ~ vorüber he happened to be passing; ich traf ihn ~ im Bus I happened to meet him or I bumped or ran into him on the bus; das habe ich ganz ~ gesehen I just happened to see it, I saw it quite by chance or accident; wir haben gestern darüber gesprochen, und heute habe ich ~ einen Artikel darüber gefunden we were talking about it yesterday, and quite coincidentally I found an article on it; wenn Sie das ~ wissen sollten if you (should) happen to know; ~ auf ein Zitat stoßen to chance upon or happen to find a quotation.
(b) (in Fragen) by any chance ♦ kannst du mir ~ 10 Mark leihen? can you lend me 10 marks by any chance?

zufälligerweise adv siehe zufällig 2.

Zufälligkeit f (a) siehe adj chance nature; accidental nature; coincidence. (b) (Statistik) chance; (Philos auch) contingency.

Zufalls- in cpds chance; **~auswahl** f random selection; **~bekanntschaft** f chance acquaintance; **~glaube** m fortuitism; **~treffer** m fluke; einen ~treffer machen to make a lucky choice; **~tor** nt (Sport) lucky or fluke (inf) goal.

zufassen vi sep (a) (zugreifen) to take hold of it/them; (Hund) to make a grab; (fig: schnell handeln) to seize or grab an/the opportunity. (b) (helfen) to lend a hand, to muck in (inf).

zufliegen vi sep irreg aux sein (a) auf etw (acc) ~ to fly towards or (direkt) into sth; auf etw (acc) zugeflogen kommen to come flying towards sth.
(b) +dat to fly to ♦ der Vogel ist uns zugeflogen the bird flew into our house/flat etc; „grüner Wellensittich zugeflogen" "green budgerigar found"; alle Herzen flogen ihr zu she won the heart(s) of everyone; ihm fliegt alles nur so zu (fig) everything comes so easily to him.
(c) (inf: Fenster, Tür) to bang or slam shut.

zufließen vi sep irreg aux sein +dat to flow to(wards); (Süßwasser etc, fig: Geld) to flow into ♦ das Wasser wird nie warm, weil immer kaltes zufließt the water never gets warm because cold water is constantly flowing into it; jdm Geld ~ lassen to pour money into sb's coffers.

Zuflucht f refuge (auch fig), shelter (vor +dat from) ♦ du bist meine letzte ~ (fig) you are my last hope or resort; zu etw ~ nehmen (fig) to resort to sth; zu Lügen ~ nehmen to take refuge in lying; er findet ~ in seiner Musik (liter) he finds refuge in his music.

Zufluchts|ort m, **Zufluchtsstätte** f place of refuge; (fig auch) sanctuary.

⚠**Zufluß** m (a) no pl (lit, fig: Zufließen) influx, inflow; (Mech: Zufuhr) supply ♦ ~ kalter Meeresluft a stream of cold air from the sea. (b) (Nebenfluß) affluent, tributary; (zu Binnensee) inlet.

zuflüstern vti sep jdm (etw) ~ to whisper (sth) to sb; (Theat) to prompt sb (with sth).

zufolge prep +dat or gen (form) (gemäß) according to; (auf Grund) as a consequence or result of ♦ dem Bericht ~, ~ des Berichtes according to the report.

zufrieden adj contented, content pred ♦ ein ~es Gesicht machen to look pleased; ~ lächeln to smile contentedly; mit jdm/etw ~ sein to be satisfied or happy with sb/sth; wie geht es? — man ist ~ (inf) how are things? — can't complain, mustn't grumble (inf); er ist nie ~ he's never content or satisfied; er ist mit nichts ~ nothing pleases him, there's no pleasing him (inf); es ~ sein (old) to be well pleased.

Zufrieden-: ⚠**z~geben** vr sep irreg sich mit etw z~geben to be content or satisfied with sth; gib dich endlich z~! can't you be content with what you have?; **~heit** f contentedness; (Befriedigtsein) satisfaction; zu meiner ~heit to my satisfaction; zur allgemeinen ~heit to everyone's satisfaction; ⚠**z~lassen** vt sep irreg to leave alone or in peace; laß mich damit z~! (inf) shut up about it! (inf); ⚠**z~stellen** vt sep to satisfy; Wünsche, Ehrgeiz auch to gratify; Kunden etc auch to give satisfaction to; schwer z~zustellen sein to be hard or difficult to please; eine z~stellende Note a satisfactory mark; eine wenig z~stellende Antwort a less than satisfactory answer.

zufrieren vi sep irreg aux sein to freeze (over).

zufügen vt sep (a) Kummer, Leid to cause; Verlust auch to inflict ♦ jdm Schaden ~ to harm sb; jdm etw ~ to cause sb sth; to inflict sth on sb; jdm eine Verletzung (mit einem Messer etc) ~ to injure sb (with a knife etc); was du nicht willst, daß man dir tu, das füg auch keinem andern zu (Prov) do as you would be done by (Prov). (b) (inf) siehe hinzufügen.

Zufuhr f -, -en (Versorgung) supply (in +acc, nach to); (Mil: Nachschub, von Stadt) supplies pl; (Met: von Luftstrom) influx ♦ die ~ von Lebensmitteln the supply of provisions, supplies of provisions; jdm die ~ abschneiden to cut off sb's supplies, to cut off supplies to sb.

zuführen sep [1] vt +dat (a) (versorgen mit, beliefern) to supply; (Comput) Papier to feed (dat to) ♦ jdm etw ~ to supply sb with sth; einem Gerät Elektrizität ~ to supply an appliance with electricity; etw seiner Bestimmung (dat) ~ to put sth to its intended use.
(b) (bringen, zur Verfügung stellen) to bring ♦ einem Geschäft Kunden ~ to bring customers to a business; er führte ihm junge Mädchen zu he supplied him with young girls; dem Magen Nahrung ~ to supply food to the stomach; jdn der gerechten Strafe ~ to give sb the punishment he/she deserves; jdn dem Verderben ~ to lead sb on the road to ruin.
[2] vi sep auf etw (acc) ~ (lit, fig) to lead to.

Zuführung f (a) no pl (Versorgen, Beliefern) supplying; (Versorgung) supply; (Comput: von Papier) feed. (b) (Zuführungsleitung) feed-pipe; (Comput: Einzelblatt~) sheetfeed.

Zufußgehen nt, no pl walking no art.

Zug[1] m -(e)s, ⸚e (a) no pl (Ziehen) (an +dat on, at) pull, tug; (~kraft, Spannung) tension.
(b) no pl (Fortziehen: von Zugvögeln, Menschen) migration; (der Wolken) drifting ♦ im ~e (im Verlauf) in the course (gen of); einen ~ durch die Kneipen machen to do the rounds of the pubs/bars; im besten ~e sein to be going great guns (inf); das ist der or liegt im ~ der Zeit it's a sign of the times, that's the way things are today; dem ~ seines Herzens folgen to follow the dictates of one's heart.
(c) (Luft~) draught (Brit), draft (US); (Atem~) breath; (an Zigarette, Pfeife) pull, puff, drag; (Schluck) gulp, mouthful, swig (inf) ♦ einen ~ machen (an Zigarette etc) to take a pull etc; das Glas in einem ~ leeren to empty the glass with one gulp or in one go, to down the glass in one (inf); da ist kein ~ drin (fig inf) there's no go in it (inf); etw in vollen ⸚en genießen to enjoy sth to the full; er genoß sein Leben in vollen ⸚en he enjoyed life to the full; in den letzten ⸚en liegen (inf) to be at one's last gasp (inf) or on one's last legs; er hat einen guten ~ (inf) he can really put it away (inf); er hat ~ abbekommen or gekriegt (inf) he got a stiff neck etc from sitting in a draught.
(d) (beim Schwimmen) stroke; (beim Rudern) pull (mit at); (Feder~) stroke (of the pen); (bei Brettspiel) move ♦ einen ~ machen (beim Schwimmen) to do a stroke; ~ um ~ (fig) step by step, stage by stage; (nicht) zum ~e kommen (inf) (not) to get a look-in (inf); du bist am ~ (bei Brettspiel, fig)it's your move or turn; etw in großen ⸚en darstellen/umreißen to outline sth, to describe/outline sth in broad or general terms.
(e) (~vorrichtung) (Klingel~) bell-pull; (Schnur am Anorak) draw-string; (bei Feuerwaffen) groove; (Orgel~) stop.
(f) (Gruppe) (von Fischen) shoal; (Gespann von Ochsen etc) team; (von Vögeln) flock, flight; (von Menschen) procession; (Mil) platoon; (Abteilung) section.
(g) (Feld~) expedition, campaign; (Fisch~) catch, haul.

Zug[2] m -(e)s, ⸚e (Eisenbahn~) train; (Last~) truck and trailer ♦ mit dem ~ fahren to go/travel by train; jdn zum ~ bringen to take sb to the station or train, to see sb off at the station; im falschen ~ sitzen (fig inf) to be on the wrong track, to be barking up the wrong tree (inf); siehe abfahren.

Zug[3] m -(e)s, ⸚e (Gesichts~) feature; (Charakter~ auch) characteristic, trait; (sadistisch, brutal etc) streak; (Anflug) touch ♦ das ist ein/kein schöner ~ von ihm that's one of the nice things about him/that's not one of his nicer characteristics; das war kein schöner ~ von dir that wasn't nice of you; die Sache hat einen ~ ins Lächerliche (fig) the affair has something (of the) ridiculous about it or verges on the ridiculous.

Zug[4] nt -s (Kanton) Zug.

Zugabe f extra, bonus; (Comm: Werbegeschenk etc) free gift; (Mus, Theat) encore ♦ ~! ~! encore! encore!, more! more!

Zug-: **~abstand** m interval between trains; **~abteil** nt railway or train compartment.

Zugang m (a) (Eingang, Einfahrt) entrance; (auf Schild auch) way in; (Zutritt) admittance, access; (fig) access ♦ ~ zu einem Tresor/Informationen etc haben to have access to a safe/information etc; das Tal gab freien ~ zum Meer the valley gave direct access to the sea; er hat/findet keinen ~ zur Musik/Kunst etc music/art etc doesn't mean anything to him; „kein ~" "no admittance or entry".
(b) (von Patienten) admission; (von Schülern) intake; (von Soldaten) recruitment; (von Waren) receipt; (von Büchern) acquisition; (von Abonnements) new subscription ♦ in dieser Schule haben wir die meisten Zugänge im Herbst our largest intake at school is in autumn.

zugange adj pred (esp N Ger) ~ sein (beschäftigt) to be busy; (aufgestanden) to be up and about; (euph: in Nebenzimmer etc) to be carrying on (inf).

⚠: for details of spelling reform, see supplement

zugänglich *adj* (*dat, für* to) (*erreichbar*) *Gelände, Ort* accessible; (*verfügbar auch*) *Bücher, Dokumente* available; *öffentliche Einrichtungen* open; (*fig: umgänglich auch*) *Mensch, Vorgesetzter* approachable ◆ **eine private Sammlung der Allgemeinheit ~ machen** to open a private collection to the public; **der Allgemeinheit ~** open to the public; **sein Charakter ist mir nur wenig ~** his character is more or less a closed book to me; **er ist nur schwer ~, er ist ein schwer ~er Mensch** (*fig*) he's not very approachable; **für etw leicht/nicht ~ sein** to respond/not to respond to sth; *für Komplimente, Annäherungsversuche, guten Rat etc auch* to be/not to be amenable to sth.

Zugänglichkeit *f* (*Erreichbarkeit*) accessibility; (*Verfügbarkeit*) availability; (*Umgänglichkeit*) approachability ◆ **die leichte ~ dieser Dokumente** the availability of these documents.

Zug-: ~begleiter *m* (*Rail*) **(a)** guard (*Brit*), conductor (*US*); **(b)** (*~fahrplan*) train time-table; **~begleitpersonal** *nt* (*Rail*) train crew; **~brücke** *f* drawbridge.

zugeben *vt sep irreg* **(a)** (*zusätzlich geben*) to give as an extra *or* bonus; (*bei Verkauf auch*) to throw in (*inf*) ◆ **jdm etw ~** to give sb sth extra *or* as a bonus, to throw sth in for sb (*inf*).
(b) (*hinzufügen*) (*Cook*) to add; (*Mus, Theat*) to do *or* perform as an encore.
(c) (*zugestehen, einräumen*) to admit, to acknowledge; (*eingestehen*) to admit (to), to own up to ◆ **er gab zu, es getan zu haben** he admitted (to) having done it, he confessed *or* owned up to having done it; **jdm gegenüber etw ~** to confess sth to sb; **zugegeben** admittedly, granted; **gib's zu!** admit it!

zugedacht [1] *ptp of* **zudenken**.
[2] *adj* **jdm ~ sein** to be intended *or* destined *or* earmarked for sb; (*Geschenk*) to be intended *or* meant for sb.

zugegebenermaßen *adv* admittedly.

zugegen *adv* (*geh*) **~ sein** to be present; (*bei Versammlung, Konferenz etc auch*) to be in attendance (*form*).

zugehen *sep irreg aux sein* [1] *vi* **(a)** (*Tür, Deckel*) to shut, to close ◆ **der Koffer geht nicht zu** the case won't shut *or* close.
(b) auf jdn/etw ~ to approach sb/sth, to go towards sb/sth; **direkt auf jdn/etw ~** to go straight *or* right up to sb/sth; **geradewegs auf etw** (*acc*) **~** (*fig*) to get straight *or* right down to sth; **es geht nun dem Winter** *or* **auf den Winter zu** winter is drawing in *or* near; **er geht schon auf die Siebzig zu** he's getting on for *or* nearing *or* approaching seventy; **dem Ende ~** to draw to a close, to near its end; (*Vorräte*) to be running out.
(c) *+dat* (*Nachricht, Brief etc*) to reach ◆ **der Brief ist uns noch nicht zugegangen** the letter hasn't reached us yet, we haven't received the letter yet; **mir ist gestern ein Brief zugegangen** I received a letter yesterday; **die Nachricht, die ich Ihnen gestern habe ~ lassen** the news I sent you yesterday; **der Polizei sind schon mehrere Hinweise zugegangen** the police have already received several clues.
(d) (*inf: weiter-, losgehen*) to get a move on (*inf*).
[2] *vi impers* **(a) dort geht es ... zu** things are ... there; **es ging sehr lustig/fröhlich** *etc* **zu** (*inf*) we/they *etc* had a great time (*inf*); **du kannst dir nicht vorstellen, wie es dort zugeht** you can't imagine what a carry-on it is there (*inf*); **hier geht's ja zu wie in einem Affenhaus!** it's like a bear-garden here!
(b) (*geschehen*) to happen ◆ **hier geht es nicht mit rechten Dingen zu** there's something odd going on here; **so geht es nun einmal zu in der Welt** that's the way of the world; **es müßte mit dem Teufel ~, wenn ...** it'll be very bad luck if ...

Zugeherin, Zugehfrau, Zugehhilfe *f* (*S Ger, Aus*) char(-woman) (*Brit*), cleaning woman.

Zugehör *nt* **-(e)s**, *no pl* (*Sw*) *siehe* **Zubehör**.

zugehören* *vi sep irreg +dat* (*liter*) to belong to.

zugehörig *adj attr* **(a)** (*geh*) (*dazugehörend*) accompanying; (*verbunden*) affiliated (*dat* to).
(b) (*old: gehörend*) belonging to ◆ **die einst dem britischen Weltreich ~e Insel** the island that once belonged to the British Empire.

Zugehörigkeit *f* **(a)** (*zu Land, Glauben*) affiliation; (*Mitgliedschaft*) membership (*zu* of). **(b)** (*Zugehörigkeitsgefühl*) sense of belonging.

zugeknöpft *adj* (*fig inf*) *Mensch* close, reserved.

Zügel *m* **-s, -** rein (*auch fig*) ◆ **einem Pferd in die ~ fallen** to seize a horse by the reins, to seize a horse's reins; **die ~ anziehen** (*lit*) to draw in the reins; (*fig*) to keep a tighter rein (*bei* on); **die ~ fest in der Hand haben/behalten** (*fig*) to have/keep things firmly in hand *or* under control; **die ~ locker lassen** (*lit*) to slacken one's hold on the reins; (*fig*) to give free rein (*bei* to); **die ~ an sich** (*acc*) **reißen** (*fig*) to seize the reins; **seiner Wut/seinen Gefühlen** *etc* **die ~ schießen lassen** (*fig*) to give full vent *or* free rein to one's rage/feelings *etc*; **jds Übermut/seinen Begierden ~ anlegen** (*liter*) to curb sb's over-exuberance/to curb *or* bridle one's desires; *siehe* **anlegen, schleifen**[1].

zugelassen *adj* authorized; *Heilpraktiker* licensed, registered; *Kfz* licensed ◆ **amtlich/staatlich ~ sein** to be authorized/to be state-registered; **er ist an allen/für alle Gerichte ~** he is authorized to practise in any court; **eine nicht ~e Partei** an illegal party; **als Kassenarzt ~ sein** ≃ to be registered as a GP; **als Heilpraktiker ~ sein** to be a licensed *or* registered non-medical practitioner; **für Personenbeförderung nicht ~** not licensed to carry passengers.

Zügel-: z~los *adj* (*fig*) unbridled *no adv*, unrestrained; **~losigkeit** *f* (*fig*) lack of restraint, unrestraint; (*in sexueller Hinsicht*) promiscuity; (*esp Pol*) anarchy.

zügeln [1] *vt Pferd* to rein in; (*fig*) to curb, to check.
[2] *vr* to restrain oneself.
[3] *vi aux sein* (*Sw: umziehen*) to move (house).

Zügelung *f* **(a)** *siehe vt* reining in; curbing, checking. **(b)** *siehe vr* self-restraint.

zugenäht *adj*: **verflixt** *or* **verflucht und ~!** (*inf*) damn and blast! (*inf*).

Zügenglöcklein *nt* (*S Ger, Aus*) *siehe* **Sterbeglocke**.

Zugereiste(r) *mf decl as adj* (*S Ger*) newcomer.

zugesellen* *sep* [1] *vt* (*rare*) to give as a companion.
[2] *vr* **sich jdm ~** (*Mensch*) to join sb; **seinem Bankrott gesellten sich dann noch familiäre Probleme zu** on top of his bankruptcy he had family problems.

zugestandenermaßen *adv* admittedly, granted.

Zugeständnis *nt* concession (*dat, an +acc* to) ◆ **er war zu keinem ~ bereit** he would make no concession(s).

zugestehen* *vt sep irreg* (*einräumen*) *Recht, Erlaß etc* to concede, to grant; (*zugeben*) to admit, to acknowledge ◆ **jdm etw ~** (*einräumen*) to grant sb sth; **man gestand ihm zu, daß ...** it was admitted *or* acknowledged that ...; **man gestand ihm zu, nicht aus Habgier gehandelt zu haben** it was acknowledged that he had not acted out of greed; **zugestanden, Sie haben recht** you're right, I grant you (that), I admit you're right.

zugetan *adj* **jdm/einer Sache ~ sein** to be fond of sb/sth; **der dem Alkohol sehr ~e Major X** Major X who was very fond of alcohol; **der Hund war seinem Herrn sehr ~** the dog was very attached *or* devoted to his master.

Zugewanderte(r) *mf decl as adj* (*Admin*) newcomer.

zugewandt *adj* facing, overlooking ◆ **der Zukunft** (*dat*) **~ sein** to be turned toward(s) the future.

Zugewinn *m* (*Jur*) *increase in value of a married couple's property during the years of joint ownership through marriage*.

Zugewinngemeinschaft *f* (*Jur*) *joint ownership of property by a married couple*.

Zugezogene(r) *mf decl as adj* newcomer.

Zug-: z~fest *adj* (*Mech*) tension-proof; *Stahl* high-tensile; **~festigkeit** *f* (*Mech*) tensile strength; **~folge** *f* (*Rail*) succession of trains; **z~frei** *adj Raum* draught-free (*Brit*), draft-free (*US*); **~führer** *m* **(a)** (*Rail*) chief guard (*Brit*) *or* conductor (*US*); **(b)** (*Aus Mil*) platoon leader; **~funk** *m* (*Rail*) train radio.

zugießen *vt sep irreg* **(a)** (*hin~*) to add ◆ **darf ich Ihnen noch (etwas Kaffee) ~?** may I pour you a little more (coffee)?; **er goß sich** (*dat*) **ständig wieder zu** he kept topping up his glass/cup. **(b)** (*mit Beton etc*) to fill (in).

zugig *adj* draughty (*Brit*), drafty (*US*).

zügig *adj* swift, speedy; *Tempo, Bedienung auch* brisk, rapid, smart; *Handschrift* smooth.

zugipsen *vt sep Loch* to plaster up, to fill (in).

Zug-: ~kraft *f* (*Mech*) tractive power; (*fig*) attraction, appeal; **z~kräftig** *adj* (*fig*) *Werbetext, Titel, Plakat* catchy, eye-catching; *Schauspieler* crowd-pulling *attr*, of wide appeal.

zugleich *adv* (*zur gleichen Zeit*) at the same time; (*ebenso auch*) both ◆ **er ist ~ Gitarrist und Komponist** he is both a guitarist and a composer; **die älteste und ~ modernste Stadt des Landes** the country's oldest and at the same time most modern town.

Zug-: ~loch *nt* (*bei Ofen*) airhole, air vent; **~luft** *f* draught (*Brit*), draft (*US*); **zuviel ~luft bekommen** to be in too much of a draught; **~maschine** *f* towing vehicle; (*von Sattelschlepper*) traction engine, tractor; **~nummer** *f* **(a)** (*Rail*) train number; **(b)** (*fig*) crowd puller, drawing card (*US*); **~ochse** *m* draught (*Brit*) *or* draft (*US*) ox; **~personal** *nt* (*Rail*) train personnel; **~pferd** *nt* carthorse, draught (*Brit*) *or* draft (*US*) horse; (*fig*) crowd puller; **~pflaster** *nt* (*Med*) poultice; **~regler** *m* (*bei Ofen*) damper, draught (*Brit*) *or* draft (*US*) regulator.

zugreifen *vi sep irreg* **(a)** (*schnell nehmen*) to grab it/them; (*fig*) to act fast *or* quickly, to get in quickly (*inf*); (*bei Tisch*) to help oneself ◆ **greifen Sie bitte zu!** please help yourself!
(b) (*fig: einschreiten*) to step in quickly, to act fast *or* quickly.
(c) (*schwer arbeiten*) to put one's back into it *or* one's work, to get down to it *or* to work.
(d) (*Comput*) **auf etw** (*acc*) **~** to access sth.

Zugrestaurant *nt* dining car.

Zugriff *m* **(a) durch raschen ~** by stepping in *or* acting quickly, by acting fast; **sich dem ~ der Polizei/Gerichte entziehen** to evade justice. **(b)** (*Comput*) access.

Zugriffszeit *f* access time.

⚠ **zugrunde** *adv* **(a) ~ gehen** to perish; **jdn/etw ~ richten** to destroy sb/sth; (*finanziell*) to ruin sb/sth; **er wird daran nicht ~ gehen** he'll survive; (*finanziell*) it won't ruin him.
(b) einer Sache (*dat*) **~ liegen** to form the basis of sth, to underlie sth; **diesem Lied liegt ein Gedicht von Heine ~** this song is based on a poem by Heine; **etw einer Sache** (*dat*) **~ legen** to take sth as a basis for sth, to base sth on sth; **und welche Überlegungen haben Sie diesen Ihren Behauptungen ~ gelegt?** and on what considerations do you base these claims of yours?

Zugrunde-: ~legung *f, no pl* **unter/bei ~legung dieser Daten** taking this data as a basis; **z~liegend** *adj attr* underlying.

Zugs- *in cpds* (*Aus*) *siehe* **Zug-**.

Zug-: ~salbe *f* (*Med*) poultice; **~tier** *nt* draught animal.

zugucken *vi sep siehe* **zusehen**.

Zug|unglück *nt* train accident.

⚠ **zugunsten** *prep +gen* (*bei Voranstellung*) *or dat* (*bei Nachstellung*) in favour of ◆ **~ von** in favour of; **~ seines Bruders, seinem Bruder ~** in favour of his brother.

zugute *adv* **jdm etw ~ halten** to grant sb sth; (*Verständnis haben*) to make allowances for sth; **Sie waren monatelang krank, das haben wir Ihnen ~ gehalten** you were ill for some months and we've made allowances for that; **einer Sache/jdm ~ kommen** to come in useful for sth/to sb, to be of benefit to sth/sb; (*Geld, Erlös*) to benefit sth/sb; **das ist seiner Gesundheit ~ gekommen** his health benefited by *or* from it; **jdm etw ~ kommen lassen** to let sb have sth; **sich** (*dat*) **auf etw** (*acc*) **etwas ~ halten** *or* **tun** (*geh*) to pride *or* preen oneself on sth.

Zug-: ~verbindung *f* train connection; **~verkehr** *m* (*Rail*) rail *or* train services *pl*; **starker ~verkehr** heavy rail traffic; **~vieh** *nt, no pl* draught (*Brit*) *or* draft (*US*) cattle; **~vogel** *m* migratory bird; (*fig*) bird of passage; **~wagen** *m* towing vehicle; **~wind** *m siehe* **~luft**; **~zwang** *m* (*Chess*) zugzwang; (*fig*) tight spot; **jdn in ~zwang bringen** to put sb in zugzwang/on the spot; **in ~zwang geraten** to get into zugzwang/to be put on the spot; **unter ~zwang stehen** to be in zugzwang/in a tight spot; **die Gegenseite steht jetzt unter ~zwang** the other side is now forced to move.

zuhaben *sep irreg* (*inf*) [1] *vi* (*Geschäft, Museum, Behörde etc*) to be closed *or* shut.
[2] *vt irreg Geschäft, Tür etc* to keep closed *or* shut; *Kleid, Mantel etc* to have done up ◆ **jetzt habe ich den Koffer endlich zu** I've finally got the case shut.

zuhaken *vt sep* to hook up.

zuhalten *sep irreg* [1] *vt* to hold closed *or* shut *or* to ◆ **sich** (*dat*) **die Nase ~** to hold one's nose; **sich** (*dat*) **die Augen/Ohren/den Mund ~** to put one's hands over one's eyes/ears/mouth, to cover one's eyes/ears/mouth with one's hands; **er hielt ihr beide Augen zu** he put his hands over her eyes.
[2] *vi* **auf etw** (*acc*) **~** to head *or* make straight for.

Zuhälter(in *f*) *m* **-s, -** pimp, procurer.

Zuhälterei *f* procuring, pimping.

Zuhälter-: ~typ *m* (*pej*) **mit so einem ~typ** with someone who looks like a pimp; **~unwesen** *nt* (*pej*) procuring.

zuhanden *adv* (*form: Sw, Aus*) **(a)** (*auch old*) to hand ◆ **es ist mir ~ gekommen** it came to hand, it came into my hands. **(b)** for the attention of ◆ **~ (von) Herrn Braun** *or* **des Herrn Braun** (*rare*) for the attention of Mr Braun, attention Mr Braun.

zuhängen *vt sep* to cover up *or* over ◆ **etw mit einem Tuch ~** to cover sth (up *or* over) with a cloth, to hang a cloth over sth.

zuhauen *sep irreg* [1] *vt* **(a)** *Baumstamm* to hew; *Stein* to trim, to pare. **(b)** (*inf*) *Tür etc* to slam *or* bang (shut).
[2] *vi* **(a)** (*mit Axt*) to strike; (*mit Fäusten, Schwert*) to strike out ◆ **hau zu!** let him *etc* have it! **(b)** (*inf: Tür, Fenster*) to slam *or* bang (shut).

zuhauf *adv* (*old*) in throngs, in droves ◆ **~ liegen/legen** to lie/put in a heap *or* pile, to be piled up/to pile up.

zuhause *adv*, **zu Hause** *siehe* **Haus**.

Zuhause *nt* **-s,** *no pl* home.

Zuhausegebliebene(r) *mf decl as adj* he/she/those who stay/stayed at home.

zuheilen *vi sep aux sein* to heal up *or* over.

Zuhilfenahme *f*: **unter ~ von** *or* **+gen** with the aid *or* help of.

zuhinterst *adv* right at the back, at the very back.

zuhöchst *adv* **(a)** (*ganz oben*) right at the top, at the very top. **(b)** (*sehr*) highly, extremely.

zuhören *vi sep* to listen (*dat* to); (*lauschen, abhören auch*) to listen in (*dat* on *or* to), to eavesdrop (*dat* on) ◆ **hör mal zu!** (*drohend*) now (just) listen (to me)!; **gut ~ können** to be a good listener; **hör mir mal genau zu!** now listen carefully to me.

Zuhörer *m* listener ◆ **die ~** (*das Publikum*) the audience *sing*; (*Radio~ auch*) the listeners.

Zuhörerschaft *f* **(a)** audience. **(b)** (*Rad*) *siehe* **Hörerschaft**.

zu|innerst *adv* deeply ◆ **tief ~** in his/her *etc* heart of hearts, deep down.

zujubeln *vi sep* **jdm ~** to cheer sb.

zukaufen *vt sep* **etw ~** to buy more (of) sth; **Einzelstücke ~** to buy extra separate parts.

zukehren *vt sep* (*zuwenden*) to turn ◆ **jdm das Gesicht ~** to turn to face sb, to turn one's face to *or* towards sb; **jdm den Rücken ~** (*lit, fig*) to turn one's back on sb.

zuklappen *vti sep* (*vi aux sein*) to snap shut; (*Tür, Fenster*) to click shut.

zukleben *vt sep Loch etc* to stick over *or* up; *Briefumschlag* to stick down; *Brief* to seal (up); (*mit Klebstoff, Klebeband*) to stick up.

zukleistern *vt sep* (*inf: lit, fig*) to patch up.

zuklinken *sep* [1] *vt Tür* to latch.
[2] *vi aux sein* **die Tür klinkte zu** the latch fell shut.

zuknallen *vti sep* (*vi aux sein*) (*inf*) to slam *or* bang (shut).

zukneifen *vti sep irreg* to pinch hard; *Augen* to screw up; *Mund* to shut tight(ly).

zuknöpfen *vt sep* to button (up) ◆ **sich** (*dat*) **die Jacke/Hose ~** to button (up) one's jacket/trousers; *siehe* **zugeknöpft**.

zuknoten *vt sep* to knot up.

zukommen *vi sep irreg aux sein* **(a) auf jdn/etw ~** to come towards *or* (*direkt*) up to sb/sth; **das Gewitter kam genau auf uns zu** the storm was heading straight for us *or* coming right at us; **die Aufgabe, die nun auf uns zukommt** the task which is now in store for us, the task which now stands before *or* confronts us; **die Dinge/alles auf sich** (*acc*) **~ lassen** to take things as they come/to let everything take its course.
(b) jdm etw ~ lassen *Brief etc* to send sb sth; (*schenken auch*), *Hilfe* to give sb sth.
(c) *+dat* (*geziemen, gebühren*) to befit, to become ◆ **ein solches Verhalten kommt dir nicht zu** such behaviour doesn't become *or* befit you *or* ill becomes you; **es kommt Ihnen nicht zu, darüber zu entscheiden** it isn't up to you to decide this; **dieser Titel kommt ihm nicht zu** he has no right to this title; **diesem Treffen kommt große Bedeutung zu** this meeting is of (the) utmost importance.

zukorken *vt sep* to cork (up).

zukriegen *vt sep* (*inf*) *siehe* **zubekommen**.

Zukunft *f* **-,** *no pl* **(a) die ~** the future; **in ~** in future; **in ferner/naher ~** in the remote *or* distant/near future; **das hat keine ~** it has no future, there's no future in it; **unsere gemeinsame ~** our future together; **in die ~ blicken** *or* **sehen** to look *or* see into the future; **wir müssen abwarten, was die ~ bringt** we must wait and see what the future holds *or* has in store; **das gilt für alle ~** that applies without exception from now on; **das bleibt der ~** (*dat*) **überlassen** *or* **vorbehalten** that remains to be seen; **viel Glück für Ihre ~!** best wishes for the future!
(b) (*Gram*) future (tense).

zukünftig [1] *adj* future ◆ **der ~e Präsident/Bischof** the president/bishop elect *or* designate; **meine Z~e** (*inf*)/**mein Z~er** (*inf*) my future wife/husband, my wife-/husband-to-be, my intended (*hum*).
[2] *adv* in future, from now on.

Zukunfts-: ~angst *f* (*vor der Zukunft*) fear of the future; (*um die Zukunft*) fear for the future; **~aussichten** *pl* future prospects *pl*; **~beruf** *m* job for the future; **~branche** *f* new *or* sunrise (*inf*) industry; **~chancen** *pl* chances *pl* for the future, future chances *pl*; **~fach** *nt* (*Univ*) new science; **~forscher** *m* futurologist; **~forschung** *f* futurology; **~frage** *f* question about the future; **z~froh** *adj* optimistic (about the future); **~gestaltung** *f* planning for the future; **~glaube** *m* belief in the future; **z~gläubig** *adj* believing in the future; **~musik** *f* (*fig inf*) pie in the sky (*inf*), Zukunftsmusik; **~optimismus** *m* optimism about the future; **z~orientiert** *adj* forward looking, looking to the future, future-oriented; **~perspektive** *f* future prospects *pl*; **~pläne** *pl* plans *pl* for the future; **z~reich** *adj* (*geh*) *siehe* **z~trächtig**; **~roman** *m* (*naturwissenschaftlich*) science fiction novel; (*gesellschaftspolitisch*) utopian novel; **z~sicher** *adj* with a guaranteed future; **~sicherung** *f* safeguarding the future; **~szenario** *nt* vision of the future; **~technik, ~technologie** *f* new *or* sunrise (*inf*) technology; **z~trächtig** *adj* with a promising future; **z~weisend** *adj* forward-looking.

Zukurzgekommene(r) *mf decl as adj* loser ◆ **die ~n in unserer Gesellschaft** those who have lost out in *or* the losers in our society.

zulächeln *vi sep* **jdm ~** to smile at sb.

zulachen *vi sep* **jdm ~** to give sb a friendly laugh.

zuladen *vti sep irreg* to load more on/in.

Zuladung *f* (*bei Kfz*) useful load; (*Naut*) deadweight.

Zulage *f* **(a)** (*Geld~*) extra *or* additional pay *no indef art*; (*Sonder~ auch*) bonus (payment); (*Gefahren~*) danger-money *no indef art* ◆ **eine ~ von 100 Mark** an extra 100 marks pay; a bonus (payment) of 100 marks; 100 marks danger-money. **(b)** (*Gehaltserhöhung*) rise (*Brit*), raise (*US*); (*regelmäßig*) increment.

⚠ **zulande** *adv* **bei uns/euch ~** back home, where we/you come from *or* live, in our/your country.

zulangen *vi sep* **(a)** (*inf*) (*Dieb, beim Essen*) to help oneself (*auch fig*). **(b)** (*dial: reichen*) to do (*inf*) ◆ **es langt nicht zu** there's not enough.

zulänglich *adj* (*geh*) adequate.

Zulänglichkeit *f* (*geh*) adequacy.

➤ **zulassen** *vt sep irreg* **(a)** (*Zugang gewähren*) to admit.
(b) (*amtlich*) to authorize; *Arzt* to register; *Heilpraktiker* to register, to license; *Kraftfahrzeug* to license; *Rechtsanwalt* to call (to the bar), to admit (as a barrister *or* to the bar); *Prüfling* to admit ◆ **zugelassene Aktien** listed securities.
➤ **(c)** (*dulden, gestatten*) to allow, to permit ◆ **das läßt nur den Schluß zu, daß ...** that leaves *or* allows only one conclusion: that ...; **eine Ausnahme ~** (*Vorschriften*) to allow (of) *or* admit (of) *or* permit an exception; (*Mensch*) to allow *or* permit an exception; **sein Verhalten läßt keine andere Erklärung zu(, als daß)** there is no other explanation for his behaviour (but that); **ich lasse nicht zu, daß mein Bruder benachteiligt wird** I shan't allow *or* permit my brother to be discriminated against; **das läßt mein Pflichtbewußtsein nicht zu** my sense of duty won't allow *or* permit *or* countenance that.
(d) (*geschlossen lassen*) to leave *or* keep shut *or* closed.

zulässig *adj* permissible, permitted, allowed; (*amtlich auch*) authorized ◆ **~e Abweichung** (*Tech*) tolerance, permissible variation; **~es Gesamtgewicht** (*Mot*) maximum laden weight; **~e Höchstgeschwindigkeit** (upper) speed limit; **~e Höchstbelastung** weight limit; **es ist nicht ~, hier zu parken** parking is prohibited *or* not permitted here.

Zulassung *f* **(a)** *no pl* (*Gewährung von Zugang*) admittance, admission.
(b) *no pl* (*amtlich*) authorization; (*von Kfz*) licensing; (*als Rechtsanwalt*) call to the bar; (*von Prüfling*) admittance (*form*); (*als praktizierender Arzt*) registration ◆ **Antrag auf ~ zu einer Prüfung** application to enter an examination; **seine ~ als Rechtsanwalt bekommen** to be called to the bar; **~ (von Aktien) zur Börse** listing on the Stock Exchange.
(c) (*Dokument*) papers *pl*; (*von Kfz auch*) vehicle registration document; (*Lizenz*) licence.

Zulassungs-: ~beschränkung *f* (*esp Univ*) restriction on admissions; **~sperre** *f* (*esp Univ*) bar on admissions; **~stelle** *f* registration office; **~stopp** *m* (*esp Univ*) block on admissions.

Zulauf *m, no pl* **großen ~ haben** (*Geschäft, Restaurant*) to be very popular; (*Arzt etc auch*) to be much sought after *or* in great demand; **die Aufführung hat sehr großen ~ gehabt** the performance drew large crowds.

zulaufen *vi sep irreg aux sein* **(a) auf jdn/etw ~** *or* **zugelaufen kommen** to run towards sb/sth, to come running towards sb/sth; (*direkt*) to run up to sb/

sth, to come running up to sb/sth.
(b) *siehe* **spitz.**
(c) (*Wasser etc*) to run in, to add ♦ **laß noch etwas kaltes Wasser ~** run in *or* add some more cold water.
(d) (*inf: sich beeilen*) to hurry (up) ♦ **lauf zu!** hurry up!
(e) (*Hund etc*) **jdm ~** to stray into sb's house/place; **eine zugelaufene Katze** a stray (cat).

zulegen *sep* [1] *vt* **(a)** (*dazulegen*) to put on ♦ **legen Sie noch zwei Scheiben zu, bitte** please put on another two slices.
(b) *Geld* to add; (*bei Verlustgeschäft*) to lose ♦ **der Chef hat mir 200 DM im Monat zugelegt** the boss has given me DM 200 a month extra, the boss has given me an extra DM 200 a month; **die fehlenden 20 DM legte meine Mutter zu** my mother made up the remaining DM 20.
(c) etwas Tempo *or* **einen Zahn** (*sl*) **~** (*inf*) to get a move on (*inf*), to step on it (*inf*); (*sich anstrengen*) to get one's finger out (*sl*).
(d) (*inf: an Gewicht*) to put on ♦ **er hat schon wieder 5 kg zugelegt** he's put on another 5 kg; **die SPD konnte 5% ~** the SPD managed to put on *or* gain 5%.
[2] *vi* (*inf*) **(a)** (*an Gewicht*) to put on weight.
(b) (*inf*) (*sich mehr anstrengen*) to pull one's finger out (*sl*); (*sich steigern*) to do better; (*Sport*) to step up the pace (*inf*).
[3] *vr* **sich** (*dat*) **etw ~** (*inf*) to get oneself sth; **er hat sich** (*dat*) **eine teure Pfeife zugelegt** he has treated himself to an expensive pipe; **er hat sich eine Braut/Freundin zugelegt** (*hum*) he has got himself *or* has acquired a fiancée/girlfriend.

⚠ **zuleide** *adv* (*old*): **jdm etwas ~ tun** to do sb harm, to harm sb; **was hat er dir ~ getan?** what (harm) has he done to you?; **wer hat dir etwas ~ getan?** who has harmed you?; *siehe* **Fliege.**

zuleiten *vt sep Wasser, Strom* to supply; *Schreiben, Waren* to send on, to forward.

Zuleitung *f* (*Tech*) supply.

zuletzt *adv* **(a)** (*schließlich, endlich, zum Schluß*) in the end ♦ **~ kam sie doch** she came in the end; **~ kam auch Gaston** in the end *or* finally Gaston came too; **wir blieben bis ~** we stayed to the very *or* bitter end; **ganz ~** right at the last moment, at the very last moment.
(b) (*als letzte(r, s), an letzter Stelle, zum letzten Mal*) last ♦ **ich kam ~** I came last, I was last to come; **wann haben Sie ihn ~ gesehen?** when did you last see him?; **ganz ~** last of all; **nicht ~ dank/wegen** not least thanks to/because of.

zuliebe *adv* **etw jdm ~ tun** to do sth for sb's sake *or* for sb; **das geschah nur ihr ~** it was done just for her.

Zulieferbetrieb, Zulieferer *m* (*Econ*) supplier.

Zuliefer|industrie *f* (*Econ*) supply industry.

zulöten *vt sep* to solder.

Zulu[1] ['tsu:lu] *mf* **-(s), -(s)** Zulu.

Zulu[2] ['tsu:lu] *nt* **-(s)** (*Sprache*) Zulu.

zum *contr of* **zu dem (a)** (*räumlich*) **geht es hier ~ Bahnhof?** is this the way to the station?; **Z~ Löwen** The Lion Inn.
(b) (*mit Infinitiv*) **~ Schwimmen/Essen gehen** to go swimming/to go and eat.
(c) (*Folge*) **es ist ~ Verrücktwerden/Weinen** it's enough to drive you mad/make you weep.
(d) (*Zweck*) **dies Gerät ist ~ Messen des Blutdrucks** this apparatus is for measuring (the) blood pressure.
(e) *in Verbindung mit vb siehe auch dort* ♦ **~ Spießbürger/Verräter werden** to become bourgeois/a traitor.

zumachen *sep* [1] *vt* (*schließen*) to shut, to close; *Flasche* to close; *Brief* to seal; (*inf: auflösen*) *Laden etc* to close (down).
[2] *vi* (*inf*) **(a)** (*den Laden ~*) to close (down), to shut up shop; (*fig*) to pack *or* jack it in (*inf*), to call it a day. **(b)** (*sich beeilen*) to get a move on (*inf*), to step on it (*inf*).

zumal [1] *conj* **~ (da)** especially *or* particularly as *or* since.
[2] *adv* **(a)** (*besonders*) especially, particularly. **(b)** (*obs: zugleich*) at the same time.

zumauern *vt sep* to brick up, to wall up.

zumeist *adv* mostly, in the main, for the most part.

zumessen *vt sep irreg* (*geh*) to measure out (*jdm* for sb), to apportion (*jdm* to sb); *Essen* to dish out (*jdm* to sb); *Zeit* to allocate (*dat* for); *Schuld* to attribute (*jdm* to sb) ♦ **ihm wurde eine hohe Strafe zugemessen** he was dealt a stiff punishment; **dem darf man keine große Bedeutung ~** one can't attach too much importance to that.

zumindest *adv* at least ♦ **er hätte mich ~ anrufen können** he could at least have phoned me, he could have phoned me at least, at least he could have phoned me.

zumutbar *adj* reasonable ♦ **jdm** *or* **für jdn ~ sein** to be reasonable for sb; **es ist ihm (durchaus) ~, daß er das tut** he can reasonably be expected to do that.

Zumutbarkeit *f* reasonableness.

⚠ **zumute** *adv* **wie ist Ihnen ~?** how do you feel?; **mir ist traurig/seltsam** *etc* **~** I feel sad/strange *etc*; **mir ist lächerlich/gar nicht lächerlich ~** I'm in a silly mood/I'm not in a laughing mood; **ihm war recht wohl ~** he felt wonderful *or* good; **mir war dabei gar nicht wohl ~** I didn't feel right about it, I felt uneasy about it.

zumuten *vt sep* **jdm etw ~** to expect *or* ask sth of sb; **Sie wollen mir doch wohl nicht ~, diesen Unsinn zu lesen** you surely don't expect me *or* aren't asking me to read this nonsense; **das können Sie niemandem ~** you can't ask *or* expect that of anyone; **Sie muten mir doch wohl nicht zu, das zu glauben!** you surely don't expect me to *or* aren't asking me to believe that; **sich** (*dat*) **zuviel ~** to take on too much, to overdo things, to overtax oneself; **seinem Körper zuviel ~** to overtax oneself.

Zumutung *f* unreasonable demand; (*Unverschämtheit*) cheek, nerve (*inf*) ♦ **das ist eine ~!** that's a bit much!

➤ **zunächst** [1] *adv* **(a)** (*zuerst*) first (of all) ♦ **~ einmal** first of all. **(b)** (*vorläufig*) for the time being, for the moment.
[2] *prep +dat* (*rare*) (*neben*) next to.

zunageln *vt sep Fenster etc* to nail up; (*mit Brettern, Pappe etc*) to board up; *Sarg, Kiste etc* to nail down.

zunähen *vt sep* to sew up.

Zunahme *f* **-, -n** (*gen, an +dat* in) increase; (*Anstieg auch*) rise.

Zuname *m* surname, last name.

⚠ **Zünd|anlaß-** (*Aut*): **~schalter** *m* ignition switch; **~schloß** *nt* ignition lock.

Zündblättchen *nt siehe* **Zündplättchen.**

zündeln *vi* to play (about) with fire ♦ **mit Streichhölzern ~** to play (about) with matches.

zünden [1] *vi* to catch light *or* fire, to ignite; (*Pulver*) to ignite; (*Streichholz*) to light; (*Motor*) to fire; (*Sprengkörper*) to go off; (*fig*) to kindle enthusiasm ♦ **dieses Streichholz zündet nicht** this match won't light; **hat es endlich bei dir gezündet?** (*inf*) has the penny finally dropped?, have you finally cottoned on? (*inf*).
[2] *vt* to ignite, to set alight; *Rakete* to fire; *Sprengkörper* to set off, to detonate; *Feuerwerkskörper* to let off.

zündend *adj* (*fig*) stirring, rousing; *Vorschlag* exciting.

Zunder *m* **-s, -** tinder; (*Schicht auf Metall*) scale (oxide); (*inf: Prügel*) good hiding (*inf*), thrashing ♦ **wie ~ brennen** to burn like tinder; **~ kriegen/jdm ~ geben** (*inf*) to get/to give sb a good hiding (*inf*) *or* thrashing.

Zünder *m* **-s, - (a)** igniter; (*für Sprengstoff, Bombe, Torpedo etc*) fuse; (*für Mine*) detonator. **(b)** (*Aus, inf: Zündholz*) match.

Zunderschwamm *m* (*Bot*) touchwood.

Zünd-: ~flamme *f* pilot light; **~folge** *f* (*Tech*) ignition sequence, firing order; **~funke** *m* (*Aut*) ignition spark; **~holz** *nt* match(stick); **ein ~holz anreißen** to strike a match; **~hütchen** *nt* percussion cap; **~kabel** *nt* (*Aut*) plug lead; **~kapsel** *f* detonator; **~kerze** *f* (*Aut*) spark(ing) plug; **~plättchen** *nt* (*für Spielzeugpistole*) cap; ⚠**~schloß** *nt* (*Aut*) ignition lock; **~schlüssel** *m* (*Aut*) ignition key; **~schnur** *f* fuse; **~spule** *f* ignition *or* spark coil; **~stoff** *m* inflammable *or* flammable (*esp US*) matter; (*Sprengstoff*) explosives *pl*, explosive material; (*fig*) inflammatory *or* explosive stuff.

Zündung *f* ignition; (*Zündvorrichtung bei Sprengkörpern*) detonator, detonating device ♦ **die ~ ist nicht richtig eingestellt** (*Aut*) the timing is out *or* wrongly set; **die ~ einstellen** (*Aut*) to adjust the timing.

Zünd-: ~verteiler *m* (*Aut*) distributor; **~vorrichtung** *f* igniting device, detonator; **~warensteuer** *f* tax on matches; **~willigkeit** *f* (*Tech*) ignition quality, combustibility; **~zeitpunkt** *m* moment of ignition.

zunehmen *vi sep irreg* [1] *vi* (*an Zahl etc, beim Stricken*) to increase; (*anwachsen auch*) to grow; (*Tage*) to draw out; (*an Weisheit, Erfahrung etc*) to gain (*an +dat* in); (*Mensch: an Gewicht*) to put on *or* gain weight; (*Mond*) to wax ♦ **im Z~ sein** to be on the increase; (*Mond*) to be waxing; **der Wind nimmt (an Stärke) zu** the wind is increasing *or* getting up.
[2] *vt* (*Mensch: an Gewicht*) to gain, to put on ♦ **ich habe 2 kg/viel zugenommen** I've gained *or* put on 2 kg/a lot of weight.

zunehmend [1] *adj* increasing, growing; *Mond* crescent ♦ **mit ~en Jahren glaubte er ...** as he advanced in years he believed ...; **bei** *or* **mit ~em Alter** with advancing age; **wir haben ~en Mond** there is a crescent moon; **in ~em Maße** to an increasing degree.
[2] *adv* increasingly ♦ **~ an Einfluß gewinnen** to gain increasing influence.

zuneigen *sep +dat* [1] *vi* to be inclined towards ♦ **ich neige der Ansicht zu, daß ...** I am inclined to think that ...; **jdm zugeneigt sein** (*geh*) to be well disposed towards sb.
[2] *vr* to lean towards; (*fig: Glück etc*) to favour ♦ **sich dem Ende ~** (*geh*) (*Tag etc*) to be drawing to a close; (*knapp werden: Vorräte etc*) to be running out.

Zuneigung *f* affection ♦ **eine starke ~ zu jdm empfinden** to feel strong affection towards sb; **~ zu jdm fassen** to take a liking to sb, to grow fond of sb.

Zunft *f* **-, ¨e** (*Hist*) guild; (*hum inf*) brotherhood ♦ **die ~ der Bäcker/Fleischer** *etc* the bakers'/butchers' *etc* guild.

Zunft-: ~brief *m* (*Hist*) guild charter; **~genosse** *m* guildsman; (*fig pej*) crony (*pej*).

zünftig *adj* **(a)** (*Hist*) belonging to a guild. **(b)** (*fachmännisch*) *Arbeit etc* expert, professional; *Kleidung* professional (-looking); (*inf: ordentlich, regelrecht*) proper; (*inf: gut, prima*) great ♦ **eine ~e Ohrfeige** a hefty box on the ears.

Zunft- (*Hist*): ~meister *m* master of a/the guild, guild master; **~wesen** *nt* guild system, system of guilds; **~zwang** *m* compulsory membership of a guild.

Zunge *f* **-, -n** tongue; (*Mus: von Fagott, Akkordeon*) reed; (*von Waage*) pointer; (*geh: Sprache*) tongue; (*Zool: See~*) sole ♦ **mit der ~ anstoßen** to lisp; **das brennt auf der ~** that burns the tongue; **jdm die ~ herausstrecken** to put *or* stick one's tongue out at sb; **die ~ herausstrecken** (*beim Arzt*) to put out one's tongue; **eine böse** *or* **giftige/scharfe** *or* **spitze/lose ~ haben** to have an evil/a sharp/a loose tongue; **lose/böse ~n behaupten, ...** rumour/malicious gossip has it ...; **eine feine ~ haben** to be a gourmet, to have a discriminating palate; **sich** (*dat*) **die ~ abbrechen** (*fig*) to tie one's tongue in knots; **eher beißt er sich** (*dat*) **die ~ ab, als ...** he'd do anything rather than ...; **das Wort liegt** *or* **schwebt mir auf der ~, ich habe das Wort auf der ~** the word is on the tip of my tongue; **der Wein löste ihm die ~** the wine loosened his tongue; **mir hängt die ~ zum Hals heraus** (*inf*) my tongue is hanging out; **ein Lyriker polnischer** (*gen*) **~** a poet of the Polish tongue; **alle Länder arabischer** (*gen*) **~** all Arabic-speaking countries; **in fremden ~n reden** to speak in tongues.

züngeln *vi* (*Schlange*) to dart its tongue in and out; (*Flamme*) to lick.

Zungen-: ~bein *nt* tongue-bone, hyoid bone; **~belag** *m* coating of the tongue; **~brecher** *m* tongue-twister; **z~fertig** *adj* (*geh*) eloquent, fluent; (*pej*) glib; **~fertigkeit** *f siehe adj* eloquence, fluency; glibness; ⚠**~kuß** *m* French kiss; **~laut** *m* (*Ling*) lingual (sound); **~pfeife** *f* (*Mus*) reed pipe; **~-R** *nt* (*Ling*) trilled *or* rolled "r"; **~rücken** *m* back of the tongue; **~schlag** *m* (*durch Alkohol*) slur; (*Mus*) tonguing; **ein falscher ~schlag** an unfortunate turn of phrase; **zwei Töne mit ~schlag spielen** to tongue two notes; **~spitze** *f* tip of the tongue; **~wurst** *f* (*Cook*) tongue sausage; **~wurzel** *f* root of the tongue.

Zünglein *nt dim of* **Zunge** tongue; (*rare: der Waage*) pointer ♦ **das ~ an der Waage sein** (*fig*) to tip the scales; (*Pol*) to hold the balance of power.

zunichte *adv* **~ machen/werden** (*geh*) to wreck, to ruin/to be wrecked, to be ruined; *Hoffnungen auch* to shatter, to destroy/to be shattered, to be destroyed.

zunicken *vi sep* **jdm ~** to nod to *or* at sb; **jdm freundlich/aufmunternd ~** to give sb a friendly/encouraging nod.

⚠**zunutze** *adv* **sich** (*dat*) **etw ~ machen** (*verwenden*) to make use of, to utilize; (*ausnutzen*) to capitalize on, to take advantage of.

zu|oberst *adv* on *or* at the (very) top, right on *or* at the top; *siehe* **unterste(r, s)**.

zu|ordnen *vt sep +dat* to assign to ♦ **ein Tier einer Gattung ~** to assign an animal to a species; **jdn/etw jdm ~** to assign sb/sth to sb; **diesen Dichter ordnet man der Romantik zu** this poet is classified as a Romantic(ist); **wie sind diese Begriffe einander zugeordnet?** how are these concepts related (to each other)?

Zu|ordnung *f siehe vt* assignment; classification, relation.

zupacken *vi sep* (*inf*) **(a)** (*zugreifen*) to make a grab for it *etc.* **(b)** (*bei der Arbeit*) to knuckle down (to it), to get down to it. **(c)** (*helfen*) **mit ~** to give me/them *etc* a hand.

zupackend [1] *adj Film, Theaterstück, Steuersystem* hard-hitting; (*forsch*) straightforward, direct; (*aggressiv*) vigorous; (*schnörkellos*) straightforward. [2] *adv* purposefully.

⚠**zupaß, zupasse** *adv* **jdm ~ kommen** (*Mensch, Hilfe*) to have come at the right time; **dieser Holzblock kommt mir ~** this block of wood is just what I needed.

zupfen *vti* to pick; *Saite auch* to pluck; *Unkraut* to pull (up); (*auseinanderziehen*) *Fäden, Maschen* to pull, to stretch ♦ **jdn am Ärmel** *etc* **~** to tug at sb's sleeve *etc*; **sich** (*dat or acc*) **am Bart/Ohr** *etc* **~** to pull at one's beard/ear *etc.*

Zupf-: ~geige *f* (*dated*) guitar; **~instrument** *nt* (*Mus*) plucked string instrument.

zupfropfen *vt sep* to cork, to stopper.

zupressen *vt sep Tür etc* to press shut ♦ **ein Loch/Leck (mit der Hand** *etc*) **~** to press one's hand *etc* over a hole/leak.

zuprosten *vi sep* **jdm ~** to raise one's glass to sb, to drink sb's health.

zur *contr of* **zu der. ~ Schule gehen** to go to school; **jdn ~ Tür bringen** to see sb to the door; **~ See fahren** to go to sea; **Gasthof „Z~ Post"** The Post Inn; **~ Zeit** at the moment; **~ Weihnachtszeit** at Christmas time; **~ Orientierung** for orientation; **~ Abschreckung** as a deterrent.

zuraten *vi sep irreg* **jdm ~, etw zu tun** to advise sb to do sth; **er hat mich gefragt, ob er ins Ausland gehen soll, und ich habe ihm zugeraten** he asked me whether he should go abroad and I said he should; **ich will weder ~ noch abraten** I won't advise you one way or the other; **auf sein Z~ (hin)** on his advice.

zuraunen *vt sep* (*liter*) **jdm etw ~** to whisper sth to sb.

Zürcher(in *f*) *m* **-s, -** native of Zurich.

zürcherisch *adj* of Zurich.

zurechnen *vt sep* **(a)** (*inf: dazurechnen*) to add to. **(b)** (*fig: zuordnen*) (*dat* with) to class, to include; *Kunstwerk etc* (*dat* to) to attribute, to ascribe.

Zurechnung *f* **(a) unter ~ aller Kosten** inclusive of all charges. **(b)** (*Zuordnung*) assignment (to), inclusion (with).

Zurechnungs-: z~fähig *adj* of sound mind; (*esp Jur, fig inf*) compos mentis *pred*; **~fähigkeit** *f* soundness of mind; **verminderte ~fähigkeit** diminished responsibility; **ich muß doch schon manchmal an seiner ~fähigkeit zweifeln!** (*inf*) I sometimes wonder if he's quite compos mentis (*inf*).

zurecht-: ~basteln *vt sep* **sich** (*dat*) **etw ~basteln** (*auch fig, iro*) to construct sth; **~biegen** *vt sep irreg* to bend into shape; (*fig*) to twist; **er hat alles wieder ~gebogen** (*inf*) he has straightened *or* smoothed everything out again; **~feilen** *vt sep* to file into shape; **~finden** *vr sep irreg* to find one's way (*in +dat* around); **sich in der Welt nicht mehr ~finden** not to be able to cope with the world any longer; **ich finde mich in dieser Tabelle nicht ~** I can't make head nor tail of this table; **sich mit etw ~finden** to get the hang of sth (*inf*); (*durch Gewöhnung*) to get used to sth; **~kommen** *vi sep irreg aux sein* **(a)** (*rechtzeitig kommen*) to come in time; **(b)** (*fig*) to get on; (*schaffen, bewältigen*) to cope; (*genug haben*) to have enough; **kommen Sie ohne das ~?** (*inf*) can you manage without it?; **er kam nie ~ im Leben** he was never able to cope with life; **(c)** (*finanziell*) to manage; **mit 20 Mark am Tag kann man gut ~kommen** you can manage easily on 20 marks a day; **~legen** *vt sep irreg* to lay *or* get out ready; **sich** (*dat*) **etw ~legen** to lay *or* get sth out ready; (*fig*) to work sth out; **sich** (*dat*) **alle Argumente ~legen** to marshal all one's arguments; **das hast du dir (bloß) ~gelegt!** (*gedeutet*) that's just your interpretation; (*erfunden*) you just made that up!; **~machen** *vt sep* (*inf*) **(a)** *Zimmer, Essen etc* to prepare, to get ready; *Bett* to make up; **(b)** (*anziehen*) to dress; (*schminken*) to make up; **sich ~machen** to get dressed *or* ready; to put on one's make-up; **auf etw** (*acc*) **~gemacht sein** (*inf*) to be done up as sth (*inf*); **~rücken** *vt sep Brille, Hut etc* to adjust; *Stühle etc* to straighten (up), to put straight; (*fig*) to straighten out, to put straight; *siehe* **Kopf**; **~schneiden** *vt sep irreg* to cut to shape; *Haar, Nagel, Hecke* to trim, to cut; **~schustern** *vt sep* (*inf*) to knock together; **~setzen** *sep* [1] *vt* **sich** (*dat*) **den Hut/die Brille ~setzen** to adjust *or* straighten one's hat/glass; *siehe* **Kopf**; [2] *vr* to settle oneself; **~stellen** *sep* [1] *vt* to set out ready; [2] *vr* to pose, to arrange oneself; **~stutzen** *vt sep* to trim, to cut; *Hecke auch* to clip; (*fig*) to lick into shape; **~weisen** *vt sep irreg* (*form*) to rebuke; *Schüler etc* to reprimand; **Z~weisung** *f siehe vt* rebuke; reprimand; **~zimmern** *vt sep* to knock together; (*fig*) to construct.

zureden *vi sep* **jdm ~** (*ermutigen*) to encourage sb; (*überreden*) to persuade sb; **wenn du ihm gut zuredest, hilft er dir** if you talk to him nicely, he'll help you; **sie hat ihrem Vater so lange zugeredet, bis er ihr das Auto kaufte** she kept on at her father till he bought her the car; **auf mein Z~ (hin)** with my encouragement; (*Überreden*) with my persuasion; **freundliches Z~** friendly persuasion.

zureichen *sep* [1] *vt* **jdm etw ~** to hand *or* pass sth to sb. [2] *vi* to be enough *or* sufficient ♦ **ein ~der Grund** a sufficient *or* adequate reason.

zureiten *sep irreg* [1] *vt Pferd* to break in. [2] *vi aux sein* (*weiterreiten*) to ride on; (*schneller*) to ride faster ♦ **auf jdn/etw ~** *or* **zugeritten kommen** to ride toward(s) *or* (*direkt*) up to sb/sth.

Zureiter(in *f*) *m* **-s, -** roughrider; (*für Wildpferde auch*) broncobuster (*US*).

Zürich *nt* **-s** Zurich.

Züricher(in *f*) *m* **-s, -** *siehe* **Zürcher(in)**.

Zürichsee *m* Lake Zurich.

zurichten *vt sep* **(a)** *Essen etc* to prepare; *Stein, Holz* to square; *Leder, Pelz, Stoff* to finish, to dress; (*Typ*) to justify. **(b)** (*beschädigen, verunstalten*) to make a mess of; (*verletzen*) to injure ♦ **jdn übel ~** to knock sb about, to beat sb up.

Zurichter(in *f*) *m* **-s, -** (*Typ*) justifier; (*von Stoffen, Pelzen*) dresser, finisher.

Zurichtung *f* (*Typ*) justifying, justification; (*von Geweben, Pelzen*) dressing, finishing.

zuriegeln *vt sep* to bolt (shut).

zürnen *vi* (*geh*) **jdm ~** to be angry with sb; **dem Schicksal ~** to rage against fate.

zurollen *vti sep* (*vi aux sein*) to roll ♦ **auf jdn/etw ~** *or* **zugerollt kommen** to roll toward(s) *or* (*direkt*) up to sb/sth.

zurren *vt* (*Naut*) to lash; *Deckladung, Beiboot etc* to lash down.

Zurschaustellung *f* display, exhibition.

zurück *adv* back; (*mit Zahlungen*) behind; (*fig: zurückgeblieben*) (*von Kind*) backward ♦ **in Mathematik (sehr) ~ sein** (*fig*) to be (really) behind in maths; **fünf Punkte ~** (*Sport*) five points behind; **~ nach** *etc* back to *etc*; **~!** get back!; **~ an Absender** return to sender; **einmal München und ~** a return (*Brit*) *or* a round-trip ticket (*US*) to Munich; **seit wann ist Trevor ~?** since when has Trevor been back?; **ich bin in zehn Minuten wieder ~** I will be back (again) in 10 minutes; **ein paar Jahre ~** a few years back *or* ago; **hinter jdm ~ sein** (*fig*) to lie behind sb; **es gibt kein Z~ (mehr)** there's no going back.

Zurück-: z~begeben* *vr irreg* (*geh*) to return, to go back; **z~behalten*** *vt sep irreg* to keep (back); **er hat Schäden/einen Schock z~behalten** he suffered lasting damage/lasting shock; **~behaltungsrecht** *nt* (*Jur*) right of retention; **z~bekommen*** *vt sep irreg* **(a)** to get back; **(b)** (*inf: heimgezahlt bekommen*) **das wirst du (von mir) z~bekommen!** I'll get my own back on you for that!; **z~beordern*** *vt sep* to recall, to order back; **z~berufen*** *vt sep irreg* to recall; **z~beugen** *sep* [1] *vt* to bend back; [2] *vr* to lean *or* bend back; **z~bewegen*** *vtr sep* to move back(wards); (*drehend*) to turn backwards; **z~bilden** *vr sep* (*Geschwür*) to recede; (*Muskel*) to become wasted, to atrophy; (*Biol*) to regress.

zurückbleiben *vi sep irreg aux sein* **(a)** (*an einem Ort*) to stay *or* remain behind; (*weiter hinten gehen*) to stay (back) behind.
(b) (*übrigbleiben: Rest, Rückstand*) to be left; (*als Folge von Krankheit etc: Schaden, Behinderung*) to remain ♦ **er blieb als Waise/Witwer zurück** he was left an orphan/a widower.
(c) (*nicht Schritt halten, auch fig: mit Arbeitsleistung etc*) to fall behind; (*Uhr*) to lose; (*in Entwicklung*) to be retarded *or* backward; (*Sport*) to be behind ♦ **20 Meter ~** to be 20 metres behind; **ihre Leistung blieb hinter meinen Erwartungen zurück** her performance did not come up to my expectations; *siehe* **zurückgeblieben**.

zurück-: ~blenden *vi sep* (*lit, fig*) to flash back (*auf +acc* to); **~blicken** *vi sep* to look back (*auf +acc* at); (*fig*) to look back (*auf +acc* on); **~bringen** *vt sep irreg* (*wieder herbringen*) to bring back (*lit, fig*); (*wieder wegbringen*) to take back; **jdn ins Leben ~bringen** to bring sb back to life, to revive sb; **~datieren*** *vt sep* to backdate; **~denken** *vi sep irreg* to think back (*an +acc* to); **so weit ich ~denken kann** as far as I can recall *or* remember; **wenn man so ~denkt** when I think back; **~drängen** *vt sep* to force *or* push back; (*Mil*) to drive back, to repel; (*fig: eindämmen*) to repress, to restrain; **~drehen** *vt sep* to turn back; *Uhr* to put back; **die Uhr** *or* **Zeit ~drehen** to turn *or* put back the clock; **~dürfen** *vi sep irreg* (*inf*) to be allowed back; **~eilen** *vi sep aux sein* (*geh*) to hurry back; **~erhalten*** *vt sep irreg* to have returned; **~erinnern*** *vr sep* to remember, to recall (*an +acc* sth); **sich bis zu seinem 5. Lebensjahr/bis 1945 ~erinnern können** to be able to remember being 5 years old/as far back as 1945; **~erobern*** *vt sep* (*Mil*) to recapture, to retake, to reconquer;

⚠: for details of spelling reform, see supplement

(*fig*) *Freund etc* to win back; **~erstatten*** *vt sep siehe* **rückerstatten**; **~erwarten*** *vt sep* **jdn ~erwarten** to expect sb back; **~fahren** *sep irreg* [1] *vi aux sein* **(a)** to go back, to return; (*als Fahrer auch*) to drive back; **(b)** (*~weichen*) to start back; [2] *vt* **(a)** to drive back; **(b)** *Produktion* to cut back.

zurückfallen *vi sep irreg aux sein* to fall back; (*Sport*) to drop back; (*fig: Umsätze etc*) to fall, to drop (back); (*fig: an Besitzer*) to revert (*an +acc* to); (*in Leistungen*) to fall behind; (*Schande, Vorwurf etc*) to reflect (*auf +acc* on) ◆ **er fällt immer wieder in den alten Fehler zurück** he always lapses back into his old mistake; **das würde bloß auf deine armen Eltern ~** that would only reflect (badly) on your poor parents.

zurück-: ~finden *vi sep irreg* to find the *or* one's way back; **findest du allein ~?** can you find your own way back?; **er fand zu sich selbst/zu Gott/zum Sozialismus ~** he found himself again/he found his way back to God/to Socialism; **~fliegen** *vti sep irreg* (*vi aux sein*) to fly back; **~fließen** *vi sep irreg aux sein* (*lit, fig*) to flow back; **~fluten** *vi sep aux sein* (*Wellen*) to flow back; (*fig*) to stream back; **~fordern** *vt sep* **etw ~fordern** to ask for sth back; (*stärker*) to demand sth back; **~fragen** *sep* [1] *vt* **etw ~fragen** to ask sth back *or* in return; [2] *vi* to ask something *or* a question back; (*wegen einer Auskunft*) to check back; **~führbar** *adj* traceable (*auf +acc* to); **auf eine Formel ~führbar** reducible to a formula.

▼ **zurückführen** *sep* [1] *vt* **(a)** (*zurückbringen*) to lead back.
▼ **(b)** (*ableiten aus*) to put down to ◆ **etw auf seine Ursache ~** to put sth down to its cause; **etw auf eine Formel/Regel ~** to reduce sth to a formula/rule; **das ist darauf zurückzuführen, daß ...** that can be put down to the fact that ...
(c) (*bis zum Ursprung zurückverfolgen*) to trace back.
[2] *vi* to lead back ◆ **es führt kein Weg zurück** there's no way back; (*fig*) there's no going back.

zurückgeben *vt sep irreg* to give back, to return; *Wechselgeld* to give back; *Ball, Kompliment, Beleidigung* to return; (*erwidern*) to retort, to rejoin ◆ **er gab mir/der Bibliothek das Buch zurück** he gave the book back *or* returned the book to me/returned the book to the library; **das Geld kannst du dir von der Firma ~ lassen** you can ask the firm to give you the money back; **dieser Erfolg gab ihm seine Zuversicht wieder zurück** this success gave him back *or* restored his confidence; **jdm sein Wort ~** to release sb from his/her *etc* word; (*sich entloben*) to break off one's engagement.

zurückgeblieben *adj* **geistig/körperlich ~** mentally/physically retarded.

▼ **zurückgehen** *vi sep irreg aux sein* **(a)** to go back, to return (*nach, in +acc* to); (*fig: in der Geschichte etc*) to go back (*auf +acc, in +acc* to); (*seinen Ursprung haben*) to go back to (*auf +acc* to) ◆ **er ging zwei Schritte zurück** he stepped back two paces, he took two steps back; **Waren/Essen** *etc* **~ lassen** to send back goods/food *etc*; **der Brief ging ungeöffnet zurück** the letter was returned unopened.
(b) (*zurückweichen*) to retreat, to fall back; (*fig: abnehmen*) (*Hochwasser, Schwellung, Vorräte, Preise etc*) to go down; (*Geschäft, Umsatz*) to fall off; (*Seuche, Schmerz, Sturm*) to die down ◆ **im Preis ~** to fall *or* drop in price.

Zurück-: z~gesetzt *adj* neglected; (*dial*) *Waren* reduced, marked down; **z~gezogen** [1] *adj Mensch* withdrawn, retiring; *Lebensweise* secluded; [2] *adv* in seclusion; **er lebt sehr z~gezogen** he lives a very secluded life; **~gezogenheit** *f* seclusion; **z~greifen** *vi sep irreg* (*fig*) to fall back (*auf +acc* upon); (*zeitlich*) to go back (*auf +acc* to); **da müßte ich weit z~greifen** I would have to go back a long way; **z~haben** *vt sep irreg* (*inf*) to have (got *Brit*) back; **ich will mein Geld z~haben** I want my money back; **hast du das Buch schon z~?** have you got (*Brit*) *or* gotten (*US*) the book back yet?

zurückhalten *sep irreg* [1] *vt* (*daran hindern, sich zu entfernen*) to hold back; (*nicht durchlassen, aufhalten*) *jdn* to hold up, to detain; (*nicht freigeben*) *Manuskript, Film, Informationen* to withhold; (*eindämmen*) *Gefühle, Ärger etc* to restrain, to suppress; (*unterdrücken*) *Tränen, Orgasmus* to keep *or* hold back ◆ **jdn von etw** (*dat*) **~** to keep sb from sth.
[2] *vr* (*sich beherrschen*) to contain *or* restrain oneself, to control oneself; (*reserviert sein*) to be retiring *or* withdrawn; (*im Hintergrund bleiben*) to keep in the background; (*bei Verhandlung, Demonstration etc*) to keep a low profile ◆ **ich mußte mich schwer ~** I had to take a firm grip on myself; **Sie müssen sich beim Essen sehr ~** you must cut down a lot on what you eat.
[3] *vi* **mit etw ~** (*verheimlichen*) to hold sth back.

zurückhaltend *adj* **(a)** (*beherrscht, kühl*) restrained; (*reserviert*) reserved; (*vorsichtig*) cautious, guarded; *Börse* dull ◆ **sich ~ über etw** (*acc*) **äußern** to be restrained in one's comments about sth; **das Publikum reagierte ~** the audience's response was restrained.
(b) (*nicht großzügig*) sparing ◆ **mit Tadel** *or* **Kritik nicht ~ sein** to be unsparing in one's criticism.

Zurück-: ~haltung *f siehe adj (a)* restraint; reserve; caution; dullness; **sich** (*dat*) **~haltung auferlegen** to exercise restraint; **z~holen** *vt sep* to fetch back; *Geld* to get back; **jdn z~holen** (*fig*) to ask sb to come back; **z~jagen** *sep* [1] *vt* to chase back; [2] *vi aux sein* to chase *or* dash back; **z~kämmen** *vt sep* to comb back; **z~kaufen** *vt sep* to buy back, to repurchase; **z~kehren** *vi sep aux sein* to return *or* come back (*von, aus* from); to return *or* go back (*nach, zu* to); **z~kommen** *vi sep irreg aux sein* (*lit, fig*) to come back, to return; (*Bezug nehmen*) to refer (*auf +acc* to); **der Brief kam z~** the letter was returned *or* came back; **ich werde später auf deinen Vorschlag/dieses Angebot z~kommen** I'll come back to your suggestion/this offer later; **z~können** *vi sep irreg* (*inf*) to be able to go back; **ich kann nicht mehr z~** (*fig*) there's no going back!; **z~kriegen** *vt sep* (*inf*) *siehe* **z~bekommen**; **z~lassen** *vt sep irreg* **(a)** (*hinterlassen*) to leave; (*liegenlassen*) to leave behind; (*fig: übertreffen*) to leave behind, to outstrip; (*Leichtathletik*) to leave behind, to outdistance; **(b)** (*inf: z~kehren lassen*) to allow back, to allow to come/go back *or* to return; **~lassung** *f*: **unter ~lassung all seiner Habseligkeiten** *etc* leaving behind all one's possessions *etc*; **z~laufen** *vi sep irreg aux sein* to run back; (*z~gehen*) to walk *or* go back.

zurücklegen *sep* [1] *vt* **(a)** (*an seinen Platz*) to put back.
(b) *Kopf* to lay *or* lean back.
(c) (*aufbewahren, reservieren*) to put aside *or* to one side; (*sparen*) to put away, to lay aside ◆ **jdm etw ~** to keep sth for sb.
(d) *Strecke* to cover, to do ◆ **er hat schon ein ganzes Stück auf seinem Weg zum Diplomaten zurückgelegt** he has already gone a long way towards becoming a diplomat.
[2] *vr* to lie back.

Zurück-: z~lehnen *vtr sep* to lean back; **z~leiten** *vt sep* to lead back; *Postsendung* to return; *Wasser etc* to feed back, to run back; **z~liegen** *vi sep irreg* (*örtlich*) to be behind; **der Unfall liegt etwa eine Woche z~** the accident was about a week ago, it is about a week since the accident; **das liegt schon so weit z~, daß ...** that is so long ago now that ...; **es liegt zwanzig Jahre z~, daß ...** it is twenty years since ...; **z~melden** *vtr sep* to report back; **z~müssen** *vi sep irreg* (*inf*) to have to go back; **~nahme** *f -, -n* withdrawal (*auch Jur, Mil*); (*von Entscheidung*) reversal; (*von Aussage auch*) retraction; **wir bitten um ~nahme dieser Sendung** we ask you to accept the return of this consignment.

zurücknehmen *vt sep irreg* to take back; (*Mil*) to withdraw; *Verordnung etc* to revoke; *Entscheidung* to reverse; *Angebot* to withdraw; *Auftrag, Bestellung* to cancel; (*Sport*) *Spieler* to bring *or* call back; *Schachzug* to go back on ◆ **sein Wort/Versprechen ~** to go back on *or* break one's word/promise; **ich nehme alles zurück und behaupte das Gegenteil** I take it all back.

▼ **zurück-: ~pfeifen** *vt sep irreg Hund etc* to whistle back; **jdn ~pfeifen** (*fig inf*) to bring sb back into line; **~prallen** *vi sep aux sein* to rebound, to bounce back; (*Geschoß*) to ricochet; (*Strahlen, Hitze*) to be reflected; **von etw ~prallen** to bounce/ricochet/be reflected off sth; **vor Schreck ~prallen** to recoil in horror; **~rechnen** *vti sep* to count back; **~reichen** *sep* [1] *vt Gegenstand* to hand *or* pass back; [2] *vi Erinnerung, Tradition etc* to go back (*in +acc* to); **~reisen** *vi sep aux sein* to travel back, to return; **~reißen** *vt sep irreg* to pull ▼ back; **~rollen** *vti sep* (*vi: aux sein*) to roll back; **~rufen** *vti sep irreg* to call back; (*am Telefon auch*) to ring back; (*aus Urlaub, Botschafter, fehlerhafte Autos*) to recall; **jdn ins Leben ~rufen** to bring sb back to life; **jdm etw in die Erinnerung/ins Gedächtnis ~rufen** to conjure sth up for sb; **sich** (*dat*) **etw in die Erinnerung/ins Gedächtnis ~rufen** to recall sth, to call sth to mind; **~schallen** *vi sep* to re-echo, to resound; **~schalten** *vi sep* to change back; **~schaudern** *vi sep aux sein* to shrink back *or* recoil (*vor +dat* from); **~schauen** *vi sep* (*lit, fig*) to look back (*auf +acc* (*lit*) at, (*fig*) on); **~scheuchen** *vt sep* to chase back; **~scheuen** *vi sep aux sein* to shy away (*vor +dat* from); **vor nichts ~scheuen** to stop at nothing; **~schicken** *vt sep* to send back; **jdm etw ~schicken** to send sth back to sb, to send sb sth back; **~schieben** *vt sep irreg* to push back.

zurückschlagen *sep irreg* [1] *vt* **(a)** to knock away; (*mit Schläger*) *Ball* to return, to hit back; *Feind, Angriff etc* to beat back, to beat off, to repulse.
(b) (*umschlagen*) *Gardinen* to pull back; *Decke* to fold back; *Kragen* to turn down; *Schleier* to lift; *Buchseiten* to leaf back.
[2] *vi* (*lit, fig*) to hit back; (*Mil, fig*) to retaliate, to strike back; (*Flamme*) to flare back; (*Pendel*) to swing back.

zurück-: ~schnellen *vi sep aux sein* to spring back; **~schrauben** *vt sep* to screw back; (*fig inf*) *Erwartungen* to lower; **seine Ansprüche ~schrauben** to lower one's sights; **~schrecken** *vi sep irreg aux sein or haben* to shrink back, to start back, to recoil; (*fig*) to shy away (*vor +dat* from); **vor nichts ~schrekken** to stop at nothing; **~sehen** *vi sep irreg* to look back; **auf etw** (*acc*) **~sehen** (*fig*) to look back on sth; **~sehnen** *sep* [1] *vr* to long to return (*nach* to); **sich nach der guten alten Zeit ~sehnen** to long for the good old days; [2] *vt* (*liter*) **jdn/etw ~sehnen** to long for the return of sb/sth; **~senden** *vt sep irreg* to send back, to return.

zurücksetzen *sep* [1] *vt* **(a)** (*nach hinten*) to move back; *Auto* to reverse, to back.
(b) (*an früheren Platz*) to put back.
(c) (*dial*) *Preis, Waren* to reduce, to mark down.
(d) (*fig: benachteiligen*) to neglect; *siehe* **zurückgesetzt**.
[2] *vr* to sit back ◆ **er setzte sich zwei Reihen zurück** he went to sit *or* he sat two rows back.
[3] *vi* (*mit Fahrzeug*) to reverse, to back.

Zurück-: ~setzung *f* (*fig: Benachteiligung*) neglect; **von ~setzung der Mädchen kann keine Rede sein** there's no question of the girls being neglected; **z~sinken** *vi sep irreg aux sein* (*lit, fig*) to sink back (*in +acc* into); **z~spielen** *sep* [1] *vt* (*Sport*) to play back; (*Ftbl auch*) to pass back; [2] *vi* to play the ball *etc* back; (*Ftbl auch*) to pass back; **z~springen** *vi sep irreg aux sein* to leap *or* jump back; (*fig: Häuserfront*) to be set back; **z~stecken** *sep* [1] *vt* to put back; [2] *vi* **(a)** (*weniger Ansprüche stellen*) to lower one's expectations; (*weniger ausgeben*) to cut back; **(b)** (*nachgeben, einlenken*) to backtrack.

zurückstehen *vi sep irreg* **(a)** (*Haus etc*) to stand back.
(b) (*an Leistung etc*) to be behind (*hinter jdm* sb).
(c) (*verzichten*) to miss out; (*ausgelassen werden*) to be left out.
(d) (*hintangesetzt werden*) to take second place ◆ **hinter etw** (*dat*) **~** to take second place to sth; **sie muß immer hinter ihm ~** she always comes off worse than he does.

zurückstellen *vt sep* **(a)** (*an seinen Platz, Uhr*) to put back; (*nach hinten*) to move back.

➤ SPRACHE AKTIV: **zurückführen: 1b** → 44.2 **zurückgehen: a** → 44.2 **zurückrufen : 2** → 27.4, 27.6

(b) *Waren* to put aside *or* by.
(c) *(Aus: zurücksenden)* to send back, to return.
(d) *(fig) Schüler* to keep down; *(Mil: vom Wehrdienst)* to defer ◆ **jdn vom Wehrdienst ~** to defer sb's military service.
(e) *(fig: verschieben)* to defer; *Pläne auch* to shelve; *Bedenken etc* to put aside; *Sport, Privatleben, Hobbys etc* to spend less time on ◆ **persönliche Interessen hinter etw** *(dat)* **~** to put one's personal interests after sth, to subordinate one's personal interests to sth; **persönliche Interessen ~** to put one's own interests last.

Zurück-: ~stellung *f* **(a)** *(Aus: ~sendung)* return; **(b)** *(Aufschub, Mil)* deferment; **(c)** *(Hintanstellung)* **unter ~stellung seiner eigenen Interessen** putting his own interests last *or* aside; **z~stoßen** *sep irreg* 1 *vt* **(a)** *(wegstoßen)* to push back; *(fig)* to reject; **(b)** *(fig: abstoßen)* to put off; 2 *vti (Aut: z~setzen)* to reverse, to back; **z~strahlen** *sep* 1 *vt* to reflect; 2 *vi* to be reflected; **z~streichen** *vt sep irreg Haar* to smooth back; **sich** *(dat)* **das Haar z~streichen** to smooth one's hair back; **z~streifen** *vt sep Ärmel etc* to pull up; **z~strömen** *vi sep aux sein* to flow back; *(Menschen)* to stream back; **z~stufen** *vt sep* to downgrade; **z~taumeln** *vi sep aux sein* to reel back; **z~tragen** *vt sep irreg* **(a)** to carry *or* take back; **(b)** *(inf) siehe* **z~bringen**; **z~treiben** *vt sep irreg* to drive back; *(Mil auch)* to repel, to repulse.

zurücktreten *sep irreg* 1 *vi aux sein* **(a)** *(zurückgehen)* to step back; *(Mil: ins Glied auch)* to fall back; *(fig: Fluß, Hochwasser etc)* to go down, to subside ◆ **bitte ~!** stand back, please!; **einen Schritt ~** to take a step back.
(b) *(Regierung)* to resign; *(von einem Amt)* to step down.
(c) *(von einem Vertrag etc)* to withdraw *(von* from), to back out *(von* of) ◆ **von einem Anspruch/einem Recht ~** to renounce a claim/a right.
(d) *(fig: geringer werden)* to decline, to diminish; *(Wald)* to recede; *(an Wichtigkeit verlieren)* to fade (in importance); *(im Hintergrund bleiben)* to come second *(hinter jdm/etw* to sb/sth).
2 *vti (mit Fuß)* to kick back.

Zurück-: z~tun *vt sep irreg (inf)* to put back; **z~übersetzen*** *vt sep* to translate back; **z~verfolgen*** *vt sep (fig)* to trace back, to retrace; **z~verlangen*** *sep* 1 *vt* to demand back; 2 *vi* **nach etw z~verlangen** *(geh)* to yearn for the return of sth; **z~verlegen*** *vt sep* **(a)** *(zeitlich)* to set back; **(b)** *(Mil) Front etc* to move back, to withdraw; **(c)** *Wohn-, Firmensitz* to move back; **z~versetzen*** *sep* 1 *vt* **(a)** *(in seinen alten Zustand)* to restore *(in +acc* to); *(in eine andere Zeit)* to take back *(in +acc* to); **wir fühlten uns in 18. Jahrhundert z~versetzt** we felt as if we had been taken back *or* transported to the 18th century; **(b)** *Beamte etc* to transfer back; *Schüler* to move down *(in +acc* into); 2 *vr* to think oneself back *(in +acc* to); **z~verwandeln*** *vtr sep* to turn *or* change back *(in +acc, zu* to); **z~verweisen*** *vt sep irreg (auch Jur)* to refer back; *jdn auch* to direct back; *(Parl) Gesetzentwurf* to recommit; **z~weichen** *vi sep irreg aux sein (vor +dat* from) *(erschrocken)* to shrink back; *(ehrfürchtig)* to stand back; *(nachgeben)* to retreat; *(vor Verantwortung, Hindernis)* to shy away; *(Mil)* to withdraw, to fall back; *(Hochwasser)* to recede, to subside; **z~weisen** *vt sep irreg* to reject; *Geschenk, Angebot etc auch* to refuse; *Gäste, Bittsteller* to turn away; *Angriff* to repel, to repulse; *(Jur) Klage, Berufung auch* to dismiss; *(an der Grenze)* to turn back; **~weisung** *f siehe vt* rejection; refusal; turning away; repulsion; dismissal; turning back; **er protestierte gegen seine ~weisung an der Grenze** he protested against being turned away at the border; **z~wenden** *vtr sep irreg* to turn back; **z~werfen** *vt sep irreg Ball, Kopf* to throw back; *Feind* to repulse, to repel; *Strahlen, Schall* to reflect; *(fig: wirtschaftlich, gesundheitlich)* to set back *(um* by); **z~wirken** *vi sep* to react *(auf +acc* upon); **z~wollen** *vi sep (inf)* to want to go back; **z~wünschen** *vt sep* **sich** *(dat)* **jdn/etw z~wünschen** to wish sb/sth back, to wish that sb/sth were back; **z~zahlen** *vt sep* to repay, to pay back; *Schulden auch* to pay off; *Spesen etc* to refund; **das werde ich ihm noch z~zahlen!** *(fig)* I'll pay him back for that!

zurückziehen *sep irreg* 1 *vt* to pull *or* draw back; *Hand, Fuß* to pull *or* draw away *or* back; *Truppen* to pull back; *(rückgängig machen) Antrag, Bemerkung, Klage etc* to withdraw.
2 *vr* to retire, to withdraw; *(sich zur Ruhe begeben)* to retire; *(Mil)* to withdraw, to retreat; *(vom Geschäft, von der Politik etc)* to retire *(von, aus* from) ◆ **sich von jdm ~** to withdraw from sb; **sich von der Welt/in sich** *(acc)* **~** to retire from the world/into oneself; *siehe* **zurückgezogen**.
3 *vi aux sein* to move back; *(Truppen)* to march back; *(Vögel)* to fly back.

Zurück-: ~ziehung *f* withdrawal, retraction; **z~zucken** *vi sep aux sein* to recoil, to start back; *(Hand, Fuß)* to jerk back.

Zuruf *m* shout, call; *(aufmunternd)* cheer ◆ **durch ~ abstimmen** *or* **wählen** to vote by acclamation; **~e** shouts; *(Zwischenrufe)* heckling.

zurufen *vti sep irreg* **jdm etw ~** to shout sth to *or* at sb; *(feierlich)* to call sth out to sb; **jdm anfeuernd ~** to cheer sb.

zurüsten *sep* 1 *vt* to set up, to get ready, to prepare.
2 *vi* to get everything set up *or* ready.

Zurüstung *f* setting-up, preparation.

zurzeit *adv (Aus, Sw)* at present, at the moment; *siehe* **Zeit**.

Zusage *f* **-, -n** **(a)** *(Zustimmung)* assent, consent. **(b)** *(Verpflichtung)* undertaking, commitment. **(c)** *(Annahme)* acceptance; *(Bestätigung)* confirmation. **(d)** *(Versprechen)* promise, pledge ◆ **ich kann Ihnen keine ~n machen** I can't make you any promises.

zusagen *sep* 1 *vt* **(a)** *(versprechen)* to promise; *(bestätigen)* to confirm ◆ **er hat sein Kommen fest zugesagt** he has promised firmly that he will come.
(b) **jdm etw auf den Kopf ~** *(inf)* to tell sb sth outright; **ich kann ihm auf den Kopf ~, wenn er mich belügt** I can tell by his face when he's lying; **eine ~de Antwort** a favourable reply.
2 *vi* **(a)** *(annehmen)* **(jdm) ~** to accept.
(b) *(gefallen)* **jdm ~** to appeal to sb; **das will mir gar nicht ~** I don't like it one little bit.

zusammen *adv* together ◆ **alle/alles ~** all together; **wir haben das Buch ~ geschrieben** we have written the book together *or* between us; **wir hatten ~ 100 Mark zum Ausgeben** between us we had 100 marks to spend; **wir bestellten uns ~ eine Portion** we ordered one portion between us; **~ mit** together *or* along with; **das macht ~ 50 Mark** that comes to *or* makes 50 marks all together *or* in all; **er zahlt mehr als wir alle ~** he pays more than all of us *or* the rest of us put together.

Zusammen-: ~arbeit *f* co-operation; *(mit dem Feind)* collaboration; **in ~arbeit mit** in co-operation with; **z~arbeiten** *vi sep* to co-operate, to work together; *(mit dem Feind)* to collaborate; **z~backen** *vi sep aux sein (inf) siehe* **z~kleben**.

zusammenballen *sep* 1 *vt Schnee, Lehm* to make into a ball; *Papier* to screw up into a ball.
2 *vr (sich ansammeln)* to accumulate; *(Menge)* to mass (together); *(Mil)* to be concentrated *or* massed ◆ **das Unheil ballte sich über seinem Haupt zusammen** *(liter)* disaster loomed over him; **zusammengeballt leben** to live crammed together.

Zusammen-: ~ballung *f* accumulation; **~bau** *m, no pl* assembly; **z~bauen** *vt sep* to assemble, to put together; **etw wieder z~bauen** to reassemble sth; **z~beißen** *vt sep irreg* **die Zähne z~beißen** *(lit)* to clench one's teeth; *(fig)* to grit one's teeth; **z~bekommen*** *vt sep irreg siehe* **z~kriegen**; **z~betteln** *vt sep* **sich** *(dat)* **etw z~betteln** to raise the money for sth; *Geld* to get sth together; **z~binden** *vt sep irreg* to tie *or* bind together; **z~bleiben** *vi sep irreg aux sein* to stay together; **z~borgen** *vt sep* **sich** *(dat)* **Geld z~borgen** to raise money; **sich** *(dat)* **etw z~borgen** to borrow sth; **z~brauen** *sep* 1 *vt (inf)* to concoct, to brew (up); 2 *vr (Gewitter, Unheil etc)* to be brewing.

zusammenbrechen *vi sep irreg aux sein (Gebäude)* to cave in; *(Brücke auch)* to give way; *(Wirtschaft)* to collapse; *(Widerstand)* to crumble; *(zum Stillstand kommen) (Verkehr etc)* to come to a standstill *or* halt; *(Verhandlungen, Telefonverbindung, Mil: Angriff)* to break down; *(Elec: Spannung)* to fail; *(Comput: Rechner)* to crash; *(Mensch)* to break down; *(vor Erschöpfung)* to collapse.

zusammenbringen *vt sep irreg* **(a)** *(sammeln)* to bring together, to collect; *Geld* to raise.
(b) *(inf: zustande bringen)* to manage; *Gedanken* to collect; *Worte, Sätze* to put together; *(ins Gedächtnis zurückrufen)* to remember; *(zusammenkriegen, -bauen)* to get together.
(c) *(in Kontakt bringen) Stoffe* to bring into contact with each other; *(bekannt machen) Menschen* to bring together ◆ **wieder ~** *(versöhnen)* to reconcile, to bring back together; **die beiden Katzen darfst du nicht ~** you must not let the two cats get near each other.

Zusammenbruch *m (von Beziehungen, Kommunikation)* breakdown; *(Comput)* crash; *(fig)* collapse; *(Nerven~)* breakdown.

zusammendrängen *sep* 1 *vt Menschen* to crowd *or* herd together; *(fig) Ereignisse, Fakten* to condense.
2 *vr (Menschen)* to crowd (together); *(Mil: Truppen)* to be concentrated *or* massed ◆ **die ganze Handlung des Stücks drängt sich im letzten Akt zusammen** all the action of the play is concentrated into the last act.

Zusammen-: z~drücken *sep* 1 *vt* to press together; *(verdichten)* to compress; 2 *vr* to be compressed; **z~fahren** *sep irreg* 1 *vi aux sein* **(a)** *(z~stoßen)* to collide; **(b)** *(erschrecken)* to start; *(vor Schmerz)* to flinch; 2 *vt (inf)* **(a)** *(überfahren)* to run over; **(b)** *Fahrzeug* to crash, to wreck; **~fall** *m (von Ereignissen)* coincidence.

zusammenfallen *vi sep irreg aux sein* **(a)** *(einstürzen)* to collapse; *(Hoffnungen)* to be shattered ◆ **in sich** *(acc)* **~** *(lit, fig)* to collapse; *(Hoffnungen)* to be shattered; *(Lügengebäude auch)* to fall apart. **(b)** *(niedriger werden, sich senken)* to go down ◆ **die Glut war (in sich) zusammengefallen** the fire had died down. **(c)** *(durch Krankheit etc)* to wither away ◆ **er sah ganz zusammengefallen aus** he looked very decrepit. **(d)** *(Ereignisse)* to coincide.

zusammenfalten *vt sep* to fold up.

zusammenfassen *sep* 1 *vt* **(a)** to combine *(zu* in); *(vereinigen)* to unite; *(Math)* to sum; *(Mil) Truppen* to concentrate. **(b)** *Bericht etc* to summarize.
2 *vi (das Fazit ziehen)* to summarize, to sum up ◆ **ein ~der Bericht** a summary, a résumé; **~d kann man sagen, ...** to sum up *or* in summary, one can say ...; **wenn ich kurz ~ darf** just to sum up.

Zusammen-: ~fassung *f* **(a)** *siehe vt (a)* combination; union; summing; concentration; **(b)** *(Überblick)* summary, synopsis, résumé; *(von Abhandlung)* abstract; **z~fegen** *vt sep* to sweep together; **z~finden** *vr sep irreg* to meet; *(sich versammeln)* to congregate; **z~flicken** *vt sep* to patch together; *(inf) Verletzten* to patch up *(inf)*; *(fig) Aufsatz etc* to throw together; **z~fließen** *vi sep irreg aux sein* to flow together, to meet; *(Farben)* to run together; △**~fluß** *m* confluence; **z~fügen** *sep* 1 *vt* to join together; *(Tech)* to fit together; **etw zu etw z~fügen** to join/fit sth together to make sth; 2 *vr* to fit together; **sich gut z~fügen** *(fig)* to turn out well; **z~führen** *vt sep* to bring together; *Familie* to reunite; **z~geben** *vt sep irreg (dial) Zutaten* to mix together; **z~gehen** *vi sep irreg aux sein* **(a)** *(sich vereinen)* to unite; *(Linien etc)* to meet; **(b)** *(einlaufen: Wäsche)* to shrink; **(c)** *(inf: sich verbinden lassen)* to go together; **z~gehören*** *vi sep (Menschen, Städte, Firmen etc)* to belong together; *(Gegenstände)* to go together, to match; *(als Paar)* to form a pair; *(Themen etc)* to go together; **z~gehörig** *adj Kleidungsstücke etc* matching; *(verwandt)* related, connected; **z~gehörig sein** to match; to be related *or* connected; **~gehörigkeit** *f (Einheit)* unity, identity; **~gehörigkeitsgefühl** *nt (in Gemeinschaft)*

➤ SPRACHE AKTIV: **zurückweisen: 2→41** **zusagen: 2a→52.4** **zuasmmenarbeiten →47.5** **zusammenfassen: 2→53.1, 53.4**

communal spirit; (esp Pol) feeling of solidarity; (in Mannschaft) team spirit; (in Familie) sense of a common bond; **z~geraten*** vi sep irreg aux sein (a) mit jdm z~geraten to get together with sb; (b) (fig) siehe aneinandergeraten.

zusammengesetzt adj aus etw ~ sein to consist of sth, to be composed of sth; ~es Wort/Verb compound (word)/verb; ~e Zahl compound or complex number; ~er Satz complex sentence.

Zusammen-: z~gewürfelt adj oddly assorted, motley; Mannschaft scratch attr; ein bunt z~gewürfelter Haufen a motley crowd; **z~gießen** vt sep irreg to pour together; **z~haben** vt sep irreg (inf) etw z~haben to have got sth together; Geld auch to have raised sth; **~halt** m, no pl (Tech) (cohesive) strength; (einer Erzählung) coherence, cohesion; (fig: in einer Gruppe) cohesion; (esp Pol) solidarity; (fig: einer Mannschaft) team spirit.

zusammenhalten sep irreg [1] vt (a) to hold together; (inf) Geld etc to hold on to ♦ seine fünf Sinne ~ to keep one's wits about one. (b) (nebeneinanderhalten) to hold side by side.
[2] vi to hold together; (fig: Freunde, Gruppe etc) to stick or stay together; siehe Pech.

Zusammenhang m (Beziehung) connection (von, zwischen +dat between); (Wechselbeziehung) correlation (von, zwischen +dat between); (Verflechtung) interrelation (von, zwischen +dat between); (von Ideen auch, von Geschichte) coherence; (im Text) context ♦ etw mit etw in ~ bringen to connect sth with sth; im or in ~ mit etw stehen to be connected with sth; etw aus dem ~ reißen to take sth out of its context; nicht im ~ mit etw stehen to have no connection with sth; ich habe seinen Namen im ~ mit dieser Sache gehört I've heard his name mentioned in connection with this.

zusammenhängen sep [1] vt Kleider in Schrank etc to hang (up) together.
[2] vi irreg to be joined (together); (fig) to be connected ♦ ~d Rede, Erzählung coherent; das hängt damit zusammen, daß ... that is connected with the fact that ...

Zusammenhang(s)-: z~los [1] adj incoherent, disjointed; (weitschweifig auch) rambling; [2] adv incoherently; Sachen z~los anordnen to arrange things haphazardly; **~losigkeit** f incoherence, disjointedness.

Zusammen-: z~harken vt sep to rake together; **z~hauen** vt sep irreg (inf) (a) (zerstören) to smash to pieces; jdn z~hauen to beat sb up (inf); (b) (fig: pfuschen) to knock together; Geschriebenes to scribble (down); **z~heften** vt sep (mit Heftklammern) to staple together; (Sew) to tack together; **z~heilen** vi sep aux sein (Wunde) to heal (up); (Knochen) to knit (together); **z~holen** vt sep Sachen to gather together; Menschen to bring together; **z~kauern** vr sep (vor Kälte) to huddle together; (vor Angst) to cower; **z~kaufen** vt sep to buy (up); **z~kehren** vt sep to sweep together; **z~ketten** vt sep to chain together; (fig) to bind together; **~klang** m (Mus, fig geh) harmony, accord; **z~klappbar** adj folding; Stuhl, Tisch auch collapsible.

zusammenklappen sep [1] vt Messer, Stuhl etc to fold up; Schirm to shut ♦ die Hacken ~ to click one's heels.
[2] vi aux sein (a) (Stuhl etc) to collapse. (b) (fig inf) to flake out (inf); (nach vorne) to double up.

Zusammen-: z~klauben vt sep to gather (together), to collect; **z~klauen** vt sep (inf) sich (dat) etw z~klauen to collect sth (by stealing); **z~kleben** vti sep (vi: aux haben or sein) to stick together; **z~kleistern** vt sep (inf) (a) to paste together; (b) (fig) to patch up or together; **z~klingen** vi sep irreg to sound together; (fig: Farben etc) to harmonize; **z~kneifen** vt sep irreg Lippen etc to press together; Augen to screw up; **z~gekniffen** Augen screwed-up; Mund pinched; **z~knoten** vt sep to knot or tie together; **z~knüllen** vt sep to screw or crumple up.

zusammenkommen vi sep irreg aux sein to meet (together), to come together; (Umstände) to combine; (fig: sich einigen) to agree, to come to an agreement; (fig: sich ansammeln) (Schulden etc) to mount up, to accumulate; (Geld bei einer Sammlung) to be collected ♦ er kommt viel mit Menschen zusammen he meets a lot of people; wir kommen zweimal jährlich zusammen we meet or we get together twice a year; heute kommt wieder mal alles zusammen (inf) it's all happening at once today.

Zusammen-: z~koppeln vt sep Anhänger, Wagen to couple together; (Space) to dock; **z~krachen** vi sep aux sein (inf) (a) (einstürzen) to crash down; (fig: Börse, Wirtschaft) to crash; (b) (z~stoßen: Fahrzeuge) to crash (into each other); **z~krampfen** vr (Hände) to clench; (Muskel) to tense up; da krampfte sich mein Herz z~ my heart nearly stopped; **z~kratzen** vt sep to scrape or scratch together; (fig inf) Geld etc to scrape together; **z~kriegen** vt sep (inf) to get together; Wortlaut etc to remember; Geld, Spenden to collect; **~kunft** f -, -künfte meeting; (von mehreren auch) gathering; (zwanglos) get-together; **z~läppern** vr sep (inf) to add or mount up; **z~lassen** vt sep irreg to leave together.

zusammenlaufen vi sep irreg aux sein (a) (an eine Stelle laufen) to gather; (Flüssigkeit) to collect. (b) (Flüsse etc) to flow together, to meet; (Farben) to run together; (Math) to intersect, to meet; (Straßen) to converge; (fig: Fäden etc) to meet. (c) (Stoff) to shrink. (d) (Milch) to curdle, to coagulate.

zusammenleben sep [1] vi to live together.
[2] vr to learn to live with each other.

Zusammenleben nt living together no art; (von Ländern etc) co-existence ♦ das ~ der Menschen the social life of man; mein ~ mit ihm war ... living with him was ...; das menschliche ~ social existence; eheliches ~ married life; außereheliches ~ cohabitation.

zusammenlegen sep [1] vt (a) (falten) to fold (up). (b) (stapeln) to pile or heap together. (c) (vereinigen) to combine, to merge; Aktien to amalgamate, to consolidate; Grundstücke to join; Termine, Veranstaltungen to hold together or at the same time; Häftlinge, Patienten to put together; Termine to combine; (zentralisieren) to centralize ♦ sie legten ihr Geld zusammen they pooled their money, they clubbed together.
[2] vi (Geld gemeinsam aufbringen) to club together, to pool one's money ♦ für ein Geschenk ~ to club together for a present.

Zusammen-: ~legung f (Vereinigung) amalgamation, merging; (von Aktien) amalgamation, consolidation; (von Grundstücken) joining; (Zentralisierung) centralization; (von Terminen) combining; die ~legung aller Patienten auf eine Station putting all the patients together in one ward; **z~leihen** vt sep irreg sich (dat) etw z~leihen to borrow sth; **z~leimen** vt sep to glue together; **z~löten** vt sep to solder together; **z~lügen** vt sep irreg (inf) to make up, to concoct; was der (sich dat) wieder z~lügt! the stories he makes up!; **z~nageln** vt sep to nail together; **z~nähen** vt sep to sew or stitch together.

zusammennehmen sep irreg [1] vt to gather up or together; Mut to summon up, to muster up; Gedanken to collect ♦ alles zusammengenommen all together, all in all; wenn wir alle Ereignisse ~ if we consider everything that happened.
[2] vr (sich zusammen reißen) to pull oneself together, to get a grip on oneself; (sich beherrschen) to control oneself, to take a grip on oneself.

Zusammen-: z~packen sep [1] vt to pack up together; pack (deine Sachen) z~! get packed!; [2] vi siehe einpacken 2; **z~passen** vi sep (Menschen) to suit each other, to be suited to each other; (Farben, Stile) to go together; gut/überhaupt nicht z~passen to go well together/not to go together at all; **z~pferchen** vt sep to herd together; (fig) to pack together; ⚠**z~phantasieren*** vt sep (sich dat) etw z~phantasieren to dream sth up; (inf: lügen) to make sth up; **~prall** m collision; (fig) clash; **z~prallen** vi sep aux sein to collide; (fig) to clash; **z~pressen** vt sep to press or squeeze together; (verdichten) to compress; **z~raffen** sep [1] vt (a) to bundle together; Röcke to gather up; (b) (fig) Mut to summon up, to muster (up); (c) (fig pej: anhäufen) to amass, to pile up; [2] vr to pull oneself together; **z~rasseln** vi sep aux sein (inf) to collide; (fig) to have a row or set-to (inf); **z~raufen** vr sep to get it all together (sl), to achieve a viable working relationship; **z~rechnen** vt sep to add or total up; alles z~gerechnet all together; (fig) all in all.

zusammenreimen sep [1] vt (inf) sich (dat) den Rest ~ to put two and two together; das kann ich mir nicht ~ I can't make head or tail of this, I can't figure it out at all; das kann ich mir jetzt ~, warum ... I can see now why ...
[2] vr to make sense ♦ wie reimt sich das zusammen? it doesn't make sense.

Zusammen-: z~reißen sep irreg [1] vr to pull oneself together; [2] vt die Hacken z~reißen to click one's heels; **z~rollen** sep [1] vt to roll up; [2] vr to curl up; (Igel) to roll or curl (itself) up (into a ball); (Schlange) to coil up; **z~rotten** vr sep (pej) (esp Jugendliche) to gang up (gegen against); (esp heimlich) to band together (gegen against); (in aufrührerischer Absicht) to form a mob; **~rottung** f (a) siehe vr ganging up; banding together, formation of a mob; (b) (Gruppe) (esp von Jugendlichen) gang; (in aufrührerischer Absicht) mob; (Jur) riotous assembly; **z~rücken** sep [1] vt Möbel etc to move closer together; (schreiben) Wörter etc to close up; [2] vi aux sein to move up closer, to move closer together; **z~rufen** vt sep irreg to call together; **z~sacken** vi sep aux sein siehe z~sinken; in sich (acc) z~sacken (lit) to collapse; (fig) (bei Nachricht etc) to seem to crumble; (Schwung verlieren) to have lost all interest; **z~scharen** vr sep to gather; (Menschen auch) to congregate; **~schau** f overall view; erst in der ~schau ... only when you view everything as a whole ...; **z~scheißen** vt sep irreg (sl) jdn z~scheißen to give sb a bollocking (sl); **z~schießen** sep irreg vt to shoot up, to riddle with bullets, to shoot to pieces; (mit Artillerie) to pound to pieces.

zusammenschlagen sep irreg [1] vt (a) (aneinanderschlagen) to knock or bang or strike together; Becken to clash; Hacken to click; Hände to clap. (b) (falten) to fold up. (c) (verprügeln) to beat up; (zerschlagen) Einrichtung to smash up, to wreck.
[2] vi aux sein über jdm/etw ~ (Wellen etc) to close over sb/sth; (stärker) to engulf sb/sth; (fig: Unheil etc) to descend upon sb/sth, to engulf sb/sth.

Zusammen-: z~schließen vr sep irreg to join together, to combine; (Comm) to amalgamate, to merge; sich gegen jdn z~schließen to band together against sb; ⚠**~schluß** m siehe vr joining together, combining; amalgamation, merger; (von politischen Gruppen) amalgamation; **z~schmelzen** sep irreg [1] vt (verschmelzen) to fuse; [2] vi aux sein (a) (verschmelzen) to fuse, to melt together; (b) (zerschmelzen) to melt (away); (Widerstand) to melt away; (Anzahl, Vermögen) to dwindle; **z~schnüren** vt sep to tie up; dieser traurige Anblick schnürte mir das Herz z~ this pitiful sight made my heart bleed; **z~schrecken** vi sep irreg aux sein to start.

zusammenschreiben vt sep irreg (a) Wörter (orthographisch) to write together; (im Schriftbild) to join up. (b) (pej: verfassen) to scribble down ♦ was der für einen Mist zusammenschreibt what a load of rubbish he writes. (c) (inf: durch Schreiben verdienen) sich (dat) ein Vermögen ~ to make a fortune with one's writing.

Zusammen-: z~schrumpfen vi sep aux sein to shrivel up; (fig) to dwindle (auf +acc to); **z~schustern** vt sep to throw together; **z~schweißen** vt sep (lit, fig) to weld together; ⚠**z~sein** vi sep irreg aux sein mit jdm z~sein to be with sb; (inf: befreundet) to be going out with sb; (euph: mit jdm schlafen) to sleep with sb; **~sein** nt being together no art; (von Gruppe) get-together.

zusammensetzen sep [1] vt (a) Schüler etc to put or seat together. (b) Gerät, Gewehr to put together, to assemble (zu to make).
[2] vr (a) to sit together; (um etwas zu besprechen, zu trinken etc) to get together ♦ sich mit jdm (am Tisch) ~ to join sb (at their table); sich gemütlich ~ to have a cosy get-together; sich auf ein Glas Wein ~ to get together

over a glass of wine.
(b) sich ~ aus to consist of, to be composed *or* made up of.

Zusammen-: ~setzspiel *nt* puzzle; (*Puzzle*) jigsaw (puzzle); **~setzung** *f* putting together; (*von Gerät auch*) assembly; (*Struktur*) composition, make-up; (*Mischung*) mixture, combination (*aus* of); (*Gram*) compound; **das Team in dieser ~setzung** the team, in this line-up; **z~sinken** *vi sep irreg aux sein* **(in sich) z~sinken** to slump; (*Gebäude*) to cave in; **z~gesunken** (*vor Kummer etc*) bowed; **z~sparen** *vt sep* to save up; **~spiel** *nt* (*Mus*) ensemble playing; (*Theat*) ensemble acting; (*Sport*) teamwork; (*fig auch*) co-operation, teamwork; (*von Kräften etc*) interaction; **z~stauchen** *vt sep* (*inf*) to give a dressing-down (*inf*); **z~stecken** *sep* [1] *vt Einzelteile* to fit together; (*mit Nadeln etc*) to pin together; **die Köpfe z~stecken** (*inf*) to put their/our *etc* heads together; (*flüstern*) to whisper to each other; [2] *vi* (*inf*) to be together; **immer z~stecken** to be inseparable, to be as thick as thieves (*pej inf*); **z~stehen** *vi sep irreg* to stand together *or* side by side; (*Gegenstände*) to be together *or* side by side; (*fig*) to stand by each other.

zusammenstellen *vt sep* to put together; (*nach einem Muster, System*) to arrange; *Bericht, Programm auch, (sammeln) Daten* to compile; *Liste, Fahrplan* to draw up; *Rede* to draft; *Sammlung auch, Gruppe* to assemble; (*Sport*) *Mannschaft* to pick ♦ **etw nach Gruppen** *etc* **~** to arrange sth in groups *etc*.

Zusammenstellung *f* **(a)** *siehe vt* putting together; arranging; compiling; drawing up; drafting; assembling; picking. **(b)** (*nach Muster, System*) arrangement; (*von Daten, Programm*) compilation; (*Liste*) list; (*Zusammensetzung*) composition; (*Übersicht*) survey; (*Gruppierung*) assembly, group; (*von Farben*) combination.

Zusammen-: z~stimmen *vi sep* (*farblich*) to match; (*musikalisch*) to harmonize; (*übereinstimmen*) to agree, to tally (*mit* with); **z~stoppeln** *vt sep* (*inf*) to throw together; **sich** (*dat*) **eine Rede** *etc* **z~stoppeln** to throw a speech *etc* together; **~stoß** *m* collision, crash; (*Mil, fig: Streit*) clash.

zusammenstoßen *sep irreg* [1] *vi aux sein* (*z~prallen*) to collide; (*Mil, fig: sich streiten*) to clash; (*sich treffen*) to meet; (*gemeinsame Grenze haben*) to adjoin ♦ **mit jdm ~** to collide with sb, to bump into sb; (*fig*) to clash with sb; **sie stießen mit den Köpfen zusammen** they banged *or* bumped their heads together; **mit der Polizei ~** to clash with the police.
[2] *vt* to knock together ♦ **er stieß sie mit den Köpfen zusammen** he banged *or* knocked their heads together.

Zusammen-: z~streichen *vt sep irreg* to cut (down) (*auf +acc* to); **z~strömen** *vi sep aux sein* (*Flüsse*) to flow into one another, to flow together; (*Menschen*) to flock *or* swarm together; **z~stückeln** *vt sep* to patch together; **z~stürzen** *vi sep aux sein* **(a)** (*einstürzen*) to collapse, to tumble down; **(b)** (*z~laufen*) to rush to gather round; **z~suchen** *vt sep* to collect (together); **sich** (*dat*) **etw z~suchen** to find sth; **z~tragen** *vt sep irreg* (*lit, fig*) to collect; (*Typ*) *Bögen* to collate; **z~treffen** *vi sep irreg aux sein* (*Menschen*) to meet; (*Ereignisse*) to coincide; **mit jdm z~treffen** to meet sb; **~treffen** *nt* meeting; (*esp zufällig*) encounter; (*zeitlich*) coincidence; **z~treten** *sep irreg* [1] *vt* (*zertrampeln*) to trample *or* crush underfoot; [2] *vi aux sein* (*Verein etc*) to meet; (*Parlament auch*) to assemble; (*Gericht*) to sit; **~tritt** *m siehe* **~treten 2** meeting; assembly; session; **z~trommeln** *vt sep* (*inf*) to round up (*inf*); **z~tun** *sep irreg* [1] *vt* (*inf*) to put together; (*vermischen*) to mix; [2] *vr* to get together; **z~wachsen** *vi sep irreg aux sein* to grow together; (*zuheilen: Wunde*) to heal (up), to close; (*Knochen*) to knit; (*fig*) to grow close; **z~gewachsen sein** (*Knochen*) to be joined *or* fused; **z~werfen** *vt sep irreg* **(a)** to throw together; (*fig*) (*durcheinanderbringen*) to mix *or* jumble up; (*in einen Topf werfen*) to lump together; **(b)** (*umwerfen*) to throw down; **z~wirken** *vi sep* to combine, to act in combination; **z~zählen** *vt sep* to add up; **alles z~gezählt macht es 50 Mark** that makes 50 marks altogether *or* all told *or* in all.

zusammenziehen *sep irreg* [1] *vt* **(a)** to draw *or* pull together; (*verengen*) to narrow; *Augenbrauen* to knit ♦ **ein Loch in einem Strumpf ~** to mend a hole in a stocking (*by pulling the sides together and sewing it up*); **der saure Geschmack zog ihm den Mund zusammen** he screwed up his mouth at the bitter taste; **das zieht einem das Herz zusammen** it really pulls at the heart-strings; **~de Mittel** (*Med*) astringents.
(b) (*fig*) *Truppen, Polizei* to assemble.
(c) (*kürzen*) *Wörter etc* to contract, to shorten; (*Math*) *Zahlen* to add together; *mathematischen Ausdruck* to reduce.
[2] *vr* (*esp Biol, Sci*) to contract; (*enger werden*) to narrow; (*Wunde*) to close (up); (*Gewitter, Unheil*) to be brewing.
[3] *vi aux sein* to move in together ♦ **mit jdm ~** to move in (together) with sb.

zusammenzucken *vi sep aux sein* to start.

Zusatz *m* addition; (*Bemerkung*) additional remark; (*zu Gesetz, Vertrag etc*) rider; (*zu Testament*) codicil; (*Gram*) expression in opposition; (*Verb~*) separable element; (*Beimischung auch*) admixture, additive ♦ **durch/nach ~ von etw** by/after adding sth, with *or* by/after the addition of sth.

Zusatz- *in cpds* additional, supplementary; **~abkommen** *nt* supplementary agreement; **~aktie** *f* bonus share; **~antrag** *m* (*Parl etc*) amendment; **~artikel** *m* additional *or* supplementary article; **~bestimmung** *f* supplementary provision; **~gerät** *nt* attachment; (*Comput*) peripheral (device), add-on.

zusätzlich [1] *adj* additional; (*weiter auch*) added *attr*, further *attr*; (*ergänzend auch*) supplementary.
[2] *adv* in addition.

Zusatz-: ~mittel *nt* additive; **~platine** *f* (*Comput*) daughterboard; **~stoff** *m* additive; **~versicherung** *f* additional *or* supplementary insurance; **~zahl** *f* additional number, *seventh number in Lotto*.

zuschalten *sep* [1] *vt* to switch on (in addition); *Rundfunk-, Fernsehanstalt* to link up with.
[2] *vr* to come on; (*Rundfunk-, Fernsehanstalt*) to link into the network.

zuschaltbar *adj* connectible.

⚠ **zuschanden** *adv* (*geh*) **~ machen** (*fig*) to ruin, to wreck; **ein Auto ~ fahren** to wreck a car; **ein Pferd ~ reiten** to ruin a horse; **~ werden** (*fig*) to be wrecked *or* ruined.

zuschanzen *vt sep* (*inf*) **jdm etw ~** to make sure sb gets sth.

zuscharren *vt sep* to cover over *or* up.

zuschauen *vi sep siehe* **zusehen**.

Zuschauer *m* **-s, -** spectator (*auch Sport*); (*TV*) viewer; (*Theat*) member of the audience; (*Beistehender*) onlooker ♦ **die ~** *pl* the spectators *pl*; (*esp Ftbl auch*) the crowd *sing*; (*TV*) the (television) audience *sing*, the viewers; (*Theat*) the audience *sing*; **einer der ~** (*Theat*) one of the audience, a member of the audience; **wieviele ~ waren da?** (*Sport*) how many spectators were there?; (*esp Ftbl auch*) how large was the crowd?

Zuschauer-: ~befragung *f* (*TV*) (television) audience survey; **~kulisse** *f* (*Sport*) crowd; **~rang** *m* (*Sport*) stand; **~raum** *m* auditorium; **~terrasse** *f* (*Sport*) (spectators') stand; **~tribüne** *f* (*esp Sport*) stand; **~umfrage** *f* (*TV*) *siehe* **~befragung**; **~zahl** *f* attendance figure; (*Sport auch*) gate.

zuschaufeln *vt sep* to fill up.

zuschicken *vt sep* **jdm etw ~** to send sth to sb *or* sb sth; (*mit der Post auch*) to mail sth to sb; **sich** (*dat*) **etw ~ lassen** to send for sth; **etw zugeschickt bekommen** to receive sth (by post), to get sth sent to one.

zuschieben *vt sep irreg* **(a) jdm etw ~** to push sth over to sb; (*heimlich*) to slip sb sth; (*fig: zuschanzen*) to make sure sb gets sth; **jdm die Verantwortung/ Schuld ~** to put the responsibility/blame on sb; *siehe* **schwarz**. **(b)** (*schließen*) *Tür, Fenster* to slide shut; *Schublade* to push shut.

zuschießen *sep irreg* [1] *vt* **(a) jdm den Ball ~** to kick the ball (over) to sb; **jdm wütende Blicke ~** to dart angry glances at sb, to look daggers at sb.
(b) *Geld etc* to contribute ♦ **Geld für etw ~** to put money towards sth; **jdm 100 Mark ~** to give sb 100 marks towards it/sth.
[2] *vi aux sein* (*inf*) **auf jdn ~** *or* **zugeschossen kommen** to rush *or* shoot up to sb.

Zuschlag *m* **(a)** (*Erhöhung*) extra charge, surcharge (*esp Comm, Econ*); (*auf Briefmarke*) supplement; (*Rail*) supplement, supplementary charge ♦ **für diese Züge muß man ~ bezahlen** you have to pay a supplement *or* a supplementary charge on these trains.
(b) (*Tech*) addition.
(c) (*bei Versteigerung*) acceptance of a bid; (*Auftragserteilung*) acceptance of a/the tender ♦ **mit dem ~ des Versteigerers ...** when the auctioneer concluded the bidding; **jdm den ~ erteilen** (*form*) *or* **geben** to knock down the lot *or* item to sb; (*nach Ausschreibung*) to award the contract to sb; **er erhielt den ~** the lot went to him; (*nach Ausschreibung*) he obtained *or* was awarded the contract.

zuschlagen *sep irreg* [1] *vt* **(a)** *Tür, Fenster* to slam (shut), to bang shut ♦ **die Tür hinter sich** (*dat*) **~** to slam the door behind one.
(b) (*Sport: zuspielen*) **jdm den Ball ~** to hit the ball to sb; (*Ftbl inf*) to kick the ball to sb.
(c) (*rare: zufügen*) to add (on) (*dat, zu* to).
(d) (*bei Versteigerung*) **jdm etw ~** to knock sth down to sb; **einer Firma einen Vertrag ~** to award a contract to a firm.
(e) *Gebiet* to annex (*dat* to).
[2] *vi* **(a)** (*kräftig schlagen*) to strike (*auch fig*); (*losschlagen*) to hit out ♦ **schlag zu!** hit me/him/it *etc*!; **das Schicksal hat entsetzlich zugeschlagen** (*geh*) fate has struck a terrible blow.
(b) *aux sein* (*Tür*) to slam (shut), to bang shut.

Zuschlag(s)- (*Rail*): **z~frei** *adj Zug* not subject to a supplement; **~karte** *f* (*Rail*) supplementary ticket (*for trains on which a supplement is payable*); **z~pflichtig** *adj Zug* subject to a supplement.

zuschließen *sep irreg* [1] *vt* to lock; *Laden* to lock up.
[2] *vi* to lock up.

zuschmeißen *vt sep irreg* (*inf*) *Tür etc* to slam (shut), to bang shut.

zuschmieren *vt sep* (*inf*) to smear over; *Löcher* to fill in.

zuschnallen *vt sep* to fasten, to buckle; *Koffer* to strap up.

zuschnappen *vi sep* **(a)** (*zubeißen*) **der Hund schnappte zu** the dog snapped at me/him *etc*. **(b)** *aux sein* (*Schloß*) to snap *or* click shut.

zuschneiden *vt sep irreg* to cut to size; (*Sew*) to cut out ♦ **auf etw** (*acc*) **zugeschnitten sein** (*fig*) to be geared to sth; **auf jdn/etw genau zugeschnitten sein** (*lit, fig*) to be tailor-made for sb/sth.

Zuschneider *m* cutter.

zuschneien *vi sep aux sein* to snow in *or* up.

Zuschnitt *m* **(a)** *no pl* (*Zuschneiden*) cutting. **(b)** (*Form*) cut; (*fig*) calibre.

zuschnüren *vt sep* to tie up; *Schuhe, Mieder* to lace up ♦ **die Angst/innere Bewegung** *etc* **schnürte ihm die Kehle zu** he was choked with fear/emotion *etc*; **der Hals** *or* **die Kehle** (*geh*) **war ihm wie zugeschnürt** (*fig*) he felt choked (with emotion/grief *etc*); **jdm das Herz ~** to make sb's heart bleed.

zuschrauben *vt sep Hahn etc* to screw shut; *Deckel etc* to screw on ♦ **eine Flasche ~** to screw on the top of a bottle.

zuschreiben *vt sep irreg* **(a)** (*inf: hin~*) to add.
(b) (*übertragen*) to transfer, to sign over (*dat* to).
(c) (*fig*) to ascribe, to attribute (*dat* to) ♦ **das hast du dir selbst zuzuschreiben** you've only got yourself to blame; **das ist nur seiner Dummheit/ihrem Geiz zuzuschreiben** that can only be put down to his stupidity/her meanness.

zuschreiten *vi sep irreg aux sein (geh)* **tüchtig ~** to walk briskly; **auf jdn/etw ~** to stride *or* walk towards *or (bis zu)* up to sb/sth.

Zuschrift *f* letter; *(auf Anzeige)* reply; *(amtlich auch)* communication.

⚠ **zuschulden** *adv*: **sich** *(dat)* **etwas ~ kommen lassen** to do something wrong; **solange man sich nichts ~ kommen läßt** as long as you don't do anything wrong.

⚠ **Zuschuß** *m* subsidy, grant; *(nicht amtlich)* something towards it, contribution; *(esp regelmäßig von Eltern)* allowance ♦ **einen ~ zu einer Sache gewähren** *or* **geben** to give a subsidy for sth; to make a contribution towards sth; **mit einem kleinen ~ von meinen Eltern kann ich ...** if my parents give me something towards it I can ...

⚠ **Zuschuß-: ~betrieb** *m* loss-making concern; **~geschäft** *nt* loss-making deal; *(inf: ~unternehmen)* loss-making business.

zuschustern *vt sep (inf)* **jdm etw ~** to make sure sb gets sth.

zuschütten *vt sep* to fill in *or* up; *(hin~)* to add.

zusehen *vi sep irreg* **(a)** to watch; *(unbeteiligter Zuschauer sein)* to look on; *(etw dulden)* to sit back *or* stand by (and watch) ♦ **jdm/einer Sache ~** to watch sb/sth; **bei etw ~** to watch sth; *(etw dulden)* to sit back *or* stand by and watch sth; **jdm bei der Arbeit ~** to watch sb working; **er sah zu, wie ich das machte** he watched me doing it; **ich kann doch nicht ~, wie er ...** *(dulden)* I can't sit back *or* stand by and watch him ...; **ich habe nur zugesehen** I was only a spectator *or* an onlooker; **durch bloßes Z~** just by watching; **bei näherem Z~** when you watch/I watched *etc* more closely.
(b) *(dafür sorgen)* **~, daß ...** to see to it that ..., to make sure (that) ...; **sieh mal zu!** *(inf)* see what you can do.

zusehends *adv* visibly; *(merklich auch)* noticeably, appreciably; *(rasch)* rapidly ♦ **~ im Verfall begriffen sein** to be in rapid decline.

Zuseher(in *f) m* **-s, -** *(Aus TV)* viewer.

⚠ **zusein** *vi sep irreg aux sein (Zusammenschreibung nur bei infin und ptp) (inf)* to be shut *or* closed; *(sl: betrunken sein)* to have had a skinful *(inf)*.

➤ **zusenden** *vt sep irreg* to send, to forward; *Geld auch* to remit *(form)*.

zusetzen *sep* [1] *vt (hinzufügen)* to add; *(inf: verlieren) Geld* to shell out *(inf)*, to pay out ♦ **er setzt immer (Geld) zu** *(inf)* he's always having to shell out *(inf)* *or* pay out; **er hat nichts mehr zuzusetzen** *(inf)* he has nothing in reserve.
[2] *vi* **jdm ~** *(unter Druck setzen)* to lean on sb *(inf)*; *dem Gegner, Feind* to harass sb, to press sb hard; *(drängen)* to badger *or* pester sb; *(schwer treffen)* to hit sb hard, to affect sb (badly); *(Kälte, Krankheit etc)* to take a lot out of sb.

zusichern *vt sep* **jdm etw ~** to assure sb of sth, to promise sb sth; **mir wurde zugesichert, daß ...** I was assured *or* promised that ...

Zusicherung *f* assurance, promise.

Zuspätkommende(r) *mf decl as adj* latecomer.

zusperren *vt sep (S Ger, Aus, Sw) (zuschließen)* to lock; *Haus, Laden* to lock up; *(verriegeln)* to bolt.

Zuspiel *nt (Sport)* passing.

zuspielen *vt sep Ball* to pass *(dat* to) ♦ **jdm etw ~** *(fig)* to pass sth on to sb; *(der Presse)* to leak sth to sb.

zuspitzen *sep* [1] *vt Stock etc* to sharpen ♦ **zugespitzt** sharpened; *Turm, Schuhe etc* pointed; *(fig)* exaggerated.
[2] *vr* to be pointed; *(fig: Lage, Konflikt)* to intensify ♦ **die Lage spitzt sich immer mehr zu** the situation is worsening.

Zuspitzung *f (von Turm, Schuhen etc)* pointing; *(fig: von Lage, Konflikt)* worsening.

zusprechen *sep irreg* [1] *vt (Jur), Preis, Gewinn etc* to award; *Kind* to award *or* grant custody of ♦ **das Kind wurde dem Vater zugesprochen** the father was granted custody (of the child); **jdm Mut/Trost ~** *(fig)* to encourage/comfort sb.
[2] *vi* **(a) jdm (gut/besänftigend) ~** to talk *or* speak (nicely/gently) to sb.
(b) dem Essen/Wein *etc* **tüchtig** *or* **kräftig ~** to tuck into the food/wine *etc.*

zuspringen *vi sep irreg aux sein* **(a)** *(Schloß, Tür)* to spring *or* snap shut. **(b) auf jdn ~** *or* **zugesprungen kommen** to spring *or* leap towards sb; *(Ball)* to bounce towards sb.

Zuspruch *m, no pl* **(a)** *(Worte)* words *pl*; *(Aufmunterung)* (words *pl* of) encouragement; *(Rat)* advice; *(tröstlich)* (words *pl* of) comfort.
(b) *(Anklang)* **(großen) ~ finden** *or* **haben, sich großen ~s erfreuen** to be (very) popular; *(Stück, Film)* to meet with general acclaim; *(Anwalt, Arzt)* to be (very) much in demand.

Zustand *m* state; *(von Haus, Ware, Auto, Med)* condition; *(Lage)* state of affairs, situation ♦ **Zustände** *pl* conditions; *(von Mensch)* fits; **in gutem/schlechtem ~** in good/poor condition; *(Mensch auch)* in good/bad shape; *(Haus)* in good/bad repair; **in ungepflegtem/baufälligem ~** in a state of neglect/disrepair; **in angetrunkenem ~** under the influence of alcohol; **Wasser in flüssigem ~** water in its fluid state; **eine Frau in ihrem ~ ...** a woman in her condition ...; **er war wirklich in einem üblen ~** he really was in a bad way; *(seelisch)* he really was in a state; **Zustände bekommen** *or* **kriegen** *(inf)* to have a fit *(inf)*, to hit the roof *(inf)*; **das ist doch kein ~** that's not right; **das sind ja schöne** *or* **nette Zustände!** *(iro)* that's a fine state of affairs! *(iro)*; **das sind ja Zustände!** *(inf)* it's terrible; **das sind doch keine Zustände!** *(inf)* it's just dreadful *or* terrible!

⚠ **zustande** *adv* **(a) ~ bringen** to manage; *Arbeit* to get done; *Ereignis, Frieden etc* to bring about, to achieve; **es ~ bringen, daß jd etw tut** to (manage to) get sb to do sth; **ein Gespräch ~ bringen** *(am Fernsprecher)* to (manage to) put a call through *(nach* to). **(b) ~ kommen** *(erreicht werden)* to be achieved; *(geschehen)* to come about; *(stattfinden)* to take place; *(Plan etc)* to materialize; *(Gewagtes, Schwieriges)* to come off.

Zustandekommen *nt siehe* **zustande (b)**, *gebrauche Verbalkonstruktion.*

zuständig *adj (verantwortlich)* responsible; *(entsprechend) Amt etc* appropriate, relevant; *(Kompetenz habend)* competent *(form, Jur)* ♦ **dafür ist er ~** that's his responsibility; **der dafür ~e Beamte** the official responsible for *or* in charge of such matters; **~ sein** *(Jur)* to have jurisdiction; **in erster Instanz ~ sein** *(Jur)* to have original jurisdiction; **nach einer Stadt ~ sein** *(Aus form) (wohnhaft sein)* to be domiciled in a town; *(Wohnrecht haben)* to have the right of domicile in a town.

Zuständigkeit *f* **(a)** *(Kompetenz)* competence; *(Jur auch)* jurisdiction; *(Verantwortlichkeit)* responsibility. **(b)** *siehe* **Zuständigkeitsbereich.**

Zuständigkeits-: ~bereich *m* area of responsibility; *(Jur)* jurisdiction, competence; **das fällt/fällt nicht in unseren ~bereich** that is/isn't our responsibility; *(Jur)* that is within/outside our jurisdiction *(Jur)*; **z~halber** *adv (Admin, form)* for reasons of competence.

zustatten *adj* **jdm ~ kommen** *(geh)* to come in useful for sb.

zustecken *vt sep* **(a)** *Kleid etc* to pin up *or* together. **(b) jdm etw ~** to slip sb sth.

zustehen *vi sep irreg* **etw steht jdm zu** sb is entitled to sth; **darüber steht mir kein Urteil zu** it's not for me *or* up to me to judge that; **es steht ihr nicht zu, das zu tun** it's not for her *or* up to her to do that.

zusteigen *vi sep irreg aux sein* to get on, to board; to join *or* board the train/flight/ship ♦ **noch jemand zugestiegen?** *(in Bus)* any more fares, please?; *(in Zug)* tickets please!

Zustell-: ~bereich *m* postal district; **~dienst** *m* delivery service.

zustellen *vt sep* **(a)** *Brief* to deliver; *(Jur)* to serve *(jdm etw* sb with sth). **(b)** *Tür etc* to block.

Zusteller(in *f) m* **-s, -** deliverer; *(Jur)* server; *(Briefträger)* postman; *(Zustellfirma)* delivery agent.

Zustellgebühr *f* delivery charge.

Zustellung *f* delivery; *(Jur)* service (of a writ).

Zustellungs|urkunde *f (Jur)* writ of summons.

zusteuern *sep* [1] *vi aux sein* **auf etw** *(acc)* **~, einer Sache** *(dat)* **~** *(geh) (lit, fig)* to head for sth; *(beim Gespräch)* to steer towards sth.
[2] *vt (beitragen)* to contribute *(zu* to).

➤ **zustimmen** *vi sep* **(einer Sache** *dat*) **~** to agree (to sth); *(einwilligen)* to consent (to sth); *(billigen)* to approve (of sth); **jdm (in einem Punkt) ~** to agree with sb (on a point); **einer Politik ~** to endorse a policy; **dem kann man nur ~** I/we *etc* quite agree with you/him *etc*; **er nickte ~d** he nodded in agreement; **eine ~de Antwort** an affirmative answer.

➤ **Zustimmung** *f (Einverständnis)* agreement, assent; *(Einwilligung)* consent; *(Beifall)* approval ♦ **seine ~ geben/verweigern** *or* **versagen** *(geh)* to give/refuse one's consent *or* assent; **allgemeine ~ finden** to meet with general approval; **das fand meine ~** I agreed with it completely.

zustopfen *vt sep* to stop up, to plug; *(mit Faden)* to darn.

zustoßen *sep irreg* [1] *vt Tür etc* to push shut.
[2] *vi* **(a)** to plunge a/the knife/sword *etc* in; *(Stier, Schlange)* to strike ♦ **stoß zu!** go on, stab him/her *etc* !; **der Mörder hatte (mit dem Messer) dreimal zugestoßen** the murderer had stabbed him/her *etc* three times.
(b) *(passieren) aux sein* **jdm ~** to happen to sb; **wenn mir einmal etwas zustößt ...** *(euph)* if anything should happen to me ...; **ihm muß etwas zugestoßen sein** he must have had an accident, something must have happened to him.

zustreben *vi sep aux sein* **~ auf** *(+acc)* to make *or* head for; *(fig)* to strive for.

Zustrom *m, no pl (fig: Menschenmenge) (hineinströmend)* influx; *(herbeiströmend)* stream (of visitors *etc*); *(Andrang)* crowd, throng; *(Met)* inflow ♦ **großen ~ haben** to be very popular, to have crowds of people coming to it/them *etc.*

zuströmen *vi sep aux sein +dat (Fluß)* to flow toward(s); *(fig) (Menschen)* to stream toward(s); *(Aufträge etc)* to pour in to.

zustürzen *vi sep aux sein* **auf jdn/etw ~** *or* **zugestürzt kommen** to rush up to sb/sth.

⚠ **zutage** *adj* **etw ~ fördern** to unearth sth *(auch hum)*; *(aus Wasser)* to bring sth up; **etw ~ bringen** *(fig)* to bring sth to light, to reveal sth; **(offen) ~ liegen** to be clear *or* evident; **~ kommen** *or* **treten** *(lit, fig)* to come to light, to be revealed.

Zutaten *pl (Cook)* ingredients *pl*; *(fig)* accessories *pl*, extras *pl.*

zuteil *adv (geh)* **jdm wird etw ~** sb is granted sth, sth is granted to sb; **mir wurde die Ehre ~, zu ...** I was given *or* had the honour of ...; **jdm etw/große Ehren ~ werden lassen** to give sb sth/bestow great honours upon sb; **da ward ihm großes Glück ~** *(old)* he was favoured with great fortune.

zuteilen *vt sep (jdm* to sb) *(als Anteil) Wohnung, Aktien* to allocate; *Rolle, Aufgabe auch* to allot; *Arbeitskraft* to assign ♦ **etw zugeteilt bekommen** to be allocated sth; *Aufgabe etc auch* to be assigned sth; *Lebensmittel* to be apportioned sth.

Zuteilung *f siehe vt* allocation; allotment; assignment; apportionment ♦ **Fleisch gab es nur auf ~** meat was only available on rations.

zutiefst *adv* deeply ♦ **er war ~ betrübt** he was greatly saddened.

zutragen *sep irreg* [1] *vt* to carry *(jdm* to sb); *(fig: weitersagen)* to report *(jdm* to sb).
[2] *vr (liter)* to take place.

Zuträger *m* informer.

zuträglich *adj* good *(dat* for), beneficial *(dat* to); *(förderlich auch)* conducive *(dat* to) ♦ **ein der Gesundheit ~es Klima** a salubrious climate, a climate conducive to good health.

Zuträglichkeit *f (geh)* beneficial effect; *(von Klima auch)* salubrity *(liter, form)*.

zutrauen *vt sep* **jdm etw ~** *(Aufgabe, Tat)* to believe *or* think sb (is) capable of (doing) sth; **sich** *(dat)* **~, etw zu tun** to think one can do sth *or* is capable of doing sth; **sich** *(dat)* **zuviel ~** to overrate one's own abilities; *(sich überneh-*

➤ SPRACHE AKTIV: **zusenden** → 46.1, 47.1 **zustimmen** → 36.2, 38.1, 38.3, 39.1, 39.3, 40.1, 40.3, 41, 53.6 **Zustimmung** → 38.2, 40.2

men) to take on too much; **sich** (*dat*) **nichts ~** to have no confidence in oneself; **der traut sich was zu!** (*inf*) he's pretty confident, isn't he?; **den Mut/die Intelligenz (dazu) traue ich ihr nicht zu** I don't believe she has the courage/intelligence to do it; **das hätte ich ihm nie zugetraut!** I would never have thought him capable of it!; (*bewundernd auch*) I never thought he had it in him!; **jdm viel/wenig ~** to think/not to think a lot of sb, to have/not to have a high opinion of sb; **ich traue ihnen viel** *or* **einiges/alles zu** (*Negatives*) I wouldn't put much/anything past them; **das ist ihm zuzutrauen!** (*iro*) I can well believe it (of him)!; (*esp als Antwort auf Frage*) I wouldn't put it past him!

Zutrauen *nt* **-s,** *no pl* confidence (*zu* in) ◆ **zu jdm ~ fassen** to begin to trust sb.

zutraulich *adj Kind* trusting; *Tier* friendly.

Zutraulichkeit *f siehe adj* trusting nature; friendliness.

➤ **zutreffen** *vi sep irreg* (*gelten*) to apply (*auf +acc, für* to); (*richtig sein*) to be accurate *or* correct; (*wahr sein*) to be true, to be the case ◆ **es trifft nicht immer zu, daß ...** it doesn't always follow that ...; **seine Beschreibung traf überhaupt nicht zu** his description was completely inaccurate; **das trifft zu** that is so.

zutreffend *adj* (*richtig*) accurate; (*auf etw ~*) applicable ◆ **Z~es bitte unterstreichen** underline where applicable *or* appropriate.

zutreffendenfalls *adv* (*form*) if applicable *or* appropriate.

zutreten *vi sep irreg* **(a)** to kick him/it *etc.* **(b)** *aux sein* **auf jdn/etw ~** to step up to sb/sth.

zutrinken *vi sep irreg* **jdm ~** to drink to sb; (*mit Trinkspruch*) to toast sb.

Zutritt *m, no pl* (*Einlaß*) admission, admittance, entry; (*Zugang*) access ◆ **kein ~, ~ verboten** no admittance *or* entry; **freien ~ zu einer Veranstaltung haben** to be admitted to an event free of charge; **~ bekommen** *or* **erhalten, sich ~ verschaffen** to gain admission *or* admittance (*zu* to); **jdm ~ gewähren** (*geh*) to admit sb; **jdm den ~ verwehren** *or* **verweigern** to refuse sb admission *or* admittance.

zutun *vt sep irreg* **(a) ich habe die ganze Nacht kein Auge zugetan** I didn't sleep a wink all night. **(b)** (*inf: hinzufügen*) to add (*dat* to).

Zutun *nt, no pl* assistance, help ◆ **es geschah ohne mein ~** I did not have a hand in the matter.

⚠ **zu|ungunsten** *prep* (*vor n*) *+gen*, (*nach n*) *+dat* to the disadvantage of.

zu|unterst *adv* right at the bottom.

zuverlässig *adj* reliable; (*verläßlich*) *Mensch auch* dependable; (*vertrauenswürdig auch*) trustworthy ◆ **aus ~er Quelle** from a reliable source; **etw ~ wissen** to know sth for sure *or* for certain.

Zuverlässigkeit *f siehe adj* reliability; dependability; trustworthiness.

Zuversicht *f, no pl* confidence; (*religiös*) faith, trust ◆ **die feste ~ haben, daß ...** to be quite confident that ..., to have every confidence that ...; **in der festen ~, daß ...** confident that ...

zuversichtlich *adj* confident.

Zuversichtlichkeit *f* confidence.

⚠ **zuviel** *adj, adv* too much; (*inf: zu viele*) too many ◆ **viel ~** much *or* far too much; **besser ~ als zuwenig** better too much than too little; **wenn's dir ~ wird, sag Bescheid** say if it gets too much for you; **ihm ist alles ~** (*inf*) it's all too much for him; **da krieg' ich ~** (*inf*) I blow my top (*inf*); **einer/zwei** *etc* **~** one/two *etc* too many; **einen/ein paar ~ trinken** (*inf*) to drink *or* have (*inf*) one/a few too many; **was ~ ist, ist ~** that's just too much, there's a limit to everything; **ein Z~ an etw** (*dat*) an excess of sth.

zuvor *adv* before; (*zuerst*) beforehand ◆ **im Jahr ~** the year before, in the previous year; **am Tage ~** the day before, on the previous day.

zuvorderst *adv* right at the front.

zuvörderst *adv* (*old*) first and foremost.

zuvorkommen *vi sep irreg aux sein +dat* to anticipate; (*verhindern*) *einer Gefahr, unangenehmen Fragen etc* to forestall ◆ **jemand ist uns zuvorgekommen** somebody beat us to it.

zuvorkommend *adj* courteous; (*gefällig*) obliging; (*hilfsbereit*) helpful.

Zuvorkommenheit *f, no pl siehe adj* courtesy, courteousness; obligingness; helpfulness.

Zuwachs ['tsu:vaks] *m* **-es, Zuwächse (a)** *no pl* (*Wachstum*) growth (*an +dat* of). **(b)** (*Höhe, Menge des Wachstums*) increase (*an +dat* in) ◆ **~ bekommen** (*inf: ein Baby*) to have an addition to the family; **ein Kleid auf ~ kaufen** (*inf*) to buy a dress big enough to last.

zuwachsen ['tsu:vaksən] *vi sep irreg aux sein* **(a)** (*Öffnung, Loch*) to grow over; (*Garten etc, hum: Gesicht*) to become overgrown; (*Aussicht*) to become blocked (by trees *etc*); (*Wunde*) to heal. **(b)** (*esp Econ, Gewinn etc*) to accrue (*jdm* to sb) ◆ **jdm wächst Autorität/Macht/Popularität zu** sb gains authority/power/popularity.

Zuwachs- ['tsu:vaks-]: **~quote, ~rate** *f* rate of increase.

Zuwanderer *m* immigrant.

zuwandern *vi sep aux sein* to immigrate.

Zuwanderung *f* immigration.

zuwarten *vi sep* to wait.

⚠ **zuwege** *adv* **etw ~ bringen** to manage sth; (*erreichen*) to achieve *or* accomplish sth; **mit etw ~ kommen** to (be able to) cope with sth; **mit jdm ~ kommen** to get on with sb all right; **es ~ bringen, daß jd etw tut** to (manage to) get sb to do sth; **gut/schlecht ~ sein** (*inf*) to be in good/bad *or* poor health; **er ist ganz schön ~** (*dial*) he's a bit on the heavy side (*inf*).

zuwehen *sep* [1] *vt* **(a)** (*zutreiben*) to waft (*dat* towards, over to) ◆ **jdm (kalte** *etc*) **Luft ~** to fan sb (with cold *etc* air).
(b) (*zudecken*) to block (up) ◆ **mit Schnee zugeweht werden** to become snowed up.
[2] *vi aux sein* **auf jdn/etw ~** to blow towards sb/sth; (*sachte*) to waft towards sb/sth.

zuweilen *adv* (*geh*) (every) now and then, occasionally, from time to time.

zuweisen *vt sep irreg* to assign, to allocate (*jdm etw* sth to sb).

Zuweisung *f* allocation, assignment.

zuwenden *sep irreg* [1] *vt* **(a)** (*lit, fig*) to turn (*dat* to, towards); (*fig: völlig widmen*) to devote (*dat* to) ◆ **jdm das Gesicht ~** to turn to face sb, to turn one's face towards sb; **jdm seine ganze Liebe ~** to bestow all one's affections on sb; **die dem Park zugewandten Fenster** the windows facing the park.
(b) jdm Geld *etc* **~** to give sb money *etc.*
[2] *vr* **sich jdm/einer Sache ~** to turn to (face) sb/sth; (*fig*) to turn to sb/sth; (*sich widmen, liebevoll*) to devote oneself to sb/sth; **wann wird das Glück sich uns wieder ~?** when will luck smile on us again?

Zuwendung *f* **(a)** (*fig: das Sichzuwenden*) turning (*zu* to); (*Liebe*) care. **(b)** (*Geldsumme*) sum (of money); (*Beitrag*) financial contribution; (*Schenkung*) donation.

⚠ **zuwenig** *adj* too little, not enough; (*inf: zu wenige*) too few, not enough ◆ **du schläfst ~** you don't get enough sleep; **einer/zwei** *etc* **~** one/two *etc* too few; **ein Z~ an etw** a lack of sth.

zuwerfen *vt sep irreg* **(a)** (*schließen*) *Tür* to slam (shut). **(b)** (*auffüllen*) *Graben* to fill up. **(c)** (*hinwerfen*) **jdm etw ~** to throw sth to sb; **jdm einen Blick ~** to cast a glance at sb; **jdm einen bösen** *or* **giftigen/feurigen** *etc* **Blick ~** to look daggers at sb/to flash a fiery *etc* glance at sb; **jdm Blicke ~** to make eyes at sb; **jdm eine Kußhand ~** to blow sb a kiss.

zuwider *adj* **(a) er/das ist mir ~** I find him/that unpleasant; (*stärker*) I detest *or* loathe him/that; (*ekelerregend*) I find him/that revolting.
(b) (*liter: entgegen*) **dem Gesetz ~** contrary to *or* against the law; **etw einem Befehl ~ tun** to do sth in defiance of an order.
(c) (*old: ungünstig*) **unseren Plänen** *etc* **~** unfavourable to our plans *etc*; **das Glück war ihm ~** luck was against him.

Zuwider-: z~handeln *vi sep +dat* (*geh*) to go against; *einem Verbot, Befehl auch* to defy; *dem Gesetz* to contravene, to violate; *einem Prinzip auch* to violate; **~handelnde(r)** *mf decl as adj* (*form*) offender, transgressor, violator (*esp US*); **~handlung** *f* (*form*) contravention, violation; **z~laufen** *vi sep irreg aux sein +dat* to run counter to, to go directly against.

zuwinken *vi sep* **jdm ~** to wave to sb; (*Zeichen geben*) to signal to sb.

zuzahlen *sep* [1] *vt* **10 Mark ~** to pay another 10 marks.
[2] *vi* to pay extra.

zuzählen *vt sep* (*inf*) (*addieren*) to add; (*einbeziehen*) to include (*zu* in).

zuzeiten *adv* (*old*) at times.

zuziehen *sep irreg* [1] *vt* **(a)** *Vorhang* to draw; *Tür* to pull shut; *Knoten, Schlinge* to pull tight, to tighten; *Arzt etc* to call in, to consult ◆ **einen weiteren Fachmann ~** to get a second opinion.
(b) sich (*dat*) **jds Zorn/Haß** *etc* **~** to incur sb's anger/hatred *etc*; **sich** (*dat*) **eine Krankheit ~** (*form*) to contract an illness; **sich** (*dat*) **eine Verletzung ~** (*form*) to sustain an injury.
[2] *vr* (*Schlinge etc*) to tighten, to pull tight ◆ **es hat sich zugezogen** (*Wetter*) it has clouded over.
[3] *vi aux sein* to move in, to move into the area ◆ **er ist kürzlich aus Berlin zugezogen** he has recently moved here from Berlin; **auf die Stadt** *etc* **~** to move towards the town *etc.*

Zuzug *m* (*Zustrom*) influx; (*von Familie etc*) arrival (*nach* in), move (*nach* to).

zuzüglich *prep +gen* plus.

zuzwinkern *vi sep* **jdm ~** to wink at sb, to give sb a wink.

Zvieri ['tsfi:ri] *m or nt* **-s,** *no pl* (*Sw*) afternoon snack.

ZVS [tsetfau'|ɛs] *f abbr of* **Zentralstelle für die Vergabe von Studienplätzen** ≃ UCCA (*Brit*), SAT center (*US*).

zw. *abbr of* **zwischen.**

zwang *pret of* **zwingen.**

Zwang *m* **-(e)s, ¨-e** (*Notwendigkeit*) compulsion; (*Gewalt*) force; (*Verpflichtung*) obligation; (*hemmender ~*) constraint ◆ **einem inneren ~ folgen** to follow an inner compulsion; **das ist ~** that is compulsory; **der ~ der Ereignisse** the pressure of events; **gesellschaftliche ¨-e** social constraints; **unter ~** (*dat*) **stehen/handeln** to be/act under duress; **etw aus ~ tun** to do sth under duress, to be forced to do sth; **etw ohne ~ tun** to do sth without being forced to; **auf jdn ~ ausüben** to exert pressure on sb; **sich** (*dat*) **~ antun** to force oneself to be something one isn't; (*sich zurückhalten*) to restrain oneself (*etw nicht zu tun* from doing sth); **tu dir keinen ~ an** don't feel you have to be polite; (*iro*) don't force yourself; **darf ich rauchen? — ja, tu dir keinen ~ an** may I smoke? — feel free; **seinen Gefühlen ~ antun** to force oneself to ignore one's true feelings; **sie tut ihren Gefühlen keinen ~ an** she doesn't hide her feelings; **dem Gesetz ~ antun** to stretch the law; **der ~ des Gesetzes/der Verhältnisse/Konvention** the force of the law/of circumstances/of convention; **allen ~ ablegen** to dispense with all formalities; **er brauchte sich** (*dat*) **keinen ~ aufzuerlegen** he didn't need to make a big effort.

zwängen *vt* to force; *mehrere Sachen* (*in Koffer etc*) to cram ◆ **sich in/durch etw** (*acc*) **~** to squeeze into/through sth.

Zwang-: z~haft *adj* (*Psych*) compulsive; **z~los** *adj* (*ohne Förmlichkeit*) informal; (*locker, unbekümmert*) casual, free and easy; (*frei*) free; **in z~loser Folge, z~los** at irregular intervals; **da geht es recht z~los zu** (*im Hotel, Club*) things are very informal there; (*bei der Arbeit auch*) things are very relaxed there; **~losigkeit** *f siehe adj* informality; casualness; freeness.

Zwangs-: ~abgabe *f* (*Econ*) compulsory levy *or* charge; **~ablieferung** *f* compulsory delivery; ~**abtretung** *f* compulsory cession; ~**anleihe** *f* compulsory *or* forced loan; ~**arbeit** *f* hard labour; (*von Kriegsgefangenen*) forced labour; ~**beitreibung** *f siehe* ~**vollstreckung**; **z~bewirtschaftet** *adj* controlled; *Wohnraum* rent-controlled; ~**bewirtschaftung** *f* (economic) control; (*von Wohnraum*) rent control; **die ~bewirtschaftung aufheben** to decontrol the economy/rents; ~**einweisung** *f* compulsory hospitalization; ~**enteignung** *f* compulsory expropriation; **z~ernähren*** *vt insep* to force-feed; ~**ernährung** *f* force feeding; ~**erscheinung** *f* (*Psych*) compulsion; ~**geld** *nt* (*Jur*) coercive fine *or* penalty; ~**handlung** *f* (*Psych*) compulsive act; ~**hypothek** *f compulsory mortgage to enforce payment of debt(s)*; ~**jacke** *f* (*lit, fig*) straitjacket; **jdn in eine ~jacke stecken** to put sb in a straitjacket, to straitjacket sb; ~**kurs** *m* (*Fin*) compulsory rate; ~**lage** *f* predicament, dilemma; **z~läufig** *adj* inevitable, unavoidable; **das mußte ja z~läufig so kommen** that had to happen, it was inevitable that that would happen; ~**läufigkeit** *f* inevitability, unavoidability; **z~mäßig** *adj* (*form*) compulsory; ~**maßnahme** *f* compulsory measure; (*Pol*) sanction; ~**mittel** *nt* means of coercion; (*Pol*) sanction; ~**neurose** *f* obsessional neurosis; ~**pensionierung** *f* compulsory retirement; ~**räumung** *f* compulsory evacuation; **z~umsiedeln** *vt, ptp* **z~umgesiedelt**, *infin, ptp only* to displace (by force); ~**verkauf** *m* (en)forced sale; **z~verpflichtet** *adj* drafted (*zu* into); ~**verschickung** *f* deportation; ~**versicherung** *f siehe* **Pflichtversicherung**; **z~versteigern*** *vt infin, ptp only* to put (sth) up for compulsory auction; ~**versteigerung** *f* compulsory auction; ~**vollstreckung** *f* execution; ~**vorführung** *f* (*Jur*) enforced appearance in court; ~**vorstellung** *f* (*Psych*) obsession, obsessive idea; **z~weise** [1] *adv* compulsorily; [2] *adj* compulsory; ~**wirtschaft** *f* Government *or* State control.

zwanzig *num* twenty; *siehe auch* **vierzig, vier.**

Zwanzig *f* -, -**en** twenty; *siehe auch* **Vierzig, Vier.**

Zwanziger *m* -**s**, - (*Mann*) twenty-year-old; (*zwischen 20 und 30*) man in his twenties; (*inf: Geldschein*) twenty mark *etc* note; *siehe auch* **Vierziger(in).**

Zwanzigerpackung *f* packet *or* pack (*US*) of twenty.

Zwanzigmarkschein *m* twenty mark note.

zwanzigste(r, s) *adj* twentieth; *siehe auch* **vierzigste(r, s).**

zwar *adv* **(a)** (*wohl*) **er war ~ Zeuge des Unfalls, kann sich aber nicht mehr so genau erinnern** he did witness the accident *or* it's true he witnessed the accident but he can't remember much about it any more; **sie ist ~ sehr schön/krank, aber ...** it's true she's very beautiful/ill but ..., she may be very beautiful/ill but ...; **ich weiß ~, daß es schädlich ist, aber ...** I do know it's harmful but ...

(b) (*erklärend, betont*) **und ~** in fact, actually; **er ist tatsächlich gekommen, und ~ um 4 Uhr** he really did come, at 4 o'clock actually *or* in fact; **er hat mir das anders erklärt, und ~ so: ...** he explained it differently to me(, like this) ...; **ich mache das, und ~ so, wie ich es für richtig halte** I'll do it and I'll do it just as I see fit; **und ~ einschließlich ...** inclusive of ...; **die Schulen, und ~ vor allem die Volksschulen** the schools, (and more) especially the primary schools; **das hat er gemacht, und ~ so gründlich, daß ...** he did it and (he did it) so thoroughly that ...; **ich werde ihm schreiben, und ~ noch heute** I'll write to him and I'll do it today *or* this very day.

Zweck *m* -**(e)s, -e (a)** (*Ziel, Verwendung*) purpose ◆ **einem ~ dienen** to serve a purpose; **einem guten ~ dienen** to be for *or* in a good cause; **Spenden für wohltätige ~e** donations to charity; **seinen ~ erfüllen** to serve its/one's purpose; **seinem ~ entsprechen** to serve its purpose; **das entspricht nicht meinen ~en** that won't serve my purpose.

(b) (*Sinn*) point ◆ **was soll das für einen ~ haben?** what's the point of that?; **das hat keinen ~** there is no point in it, it's pointless; **es hat keinen ~, darüber zu reden** there is no point (in) talking about it, it's pointless talking about it; **es hat ja doch alles keinen ~ mehr** there is no point (in) *or* it's pointless going on any more; **das ist ja der ~ der Übung** that's the point of the exercise, that's what it's all about (*inf*).

(c) (*Absicht*) aim ◆ **zum ~ der Völkerverständigung** (in order) to promote understanding between nations; **zu welchem ~?** for what purpose?, to what end?; **zu diesem ~** to this end, with this aim in view; **einen ~ verfolgen** to have a specific aim.

Zweck-: ~**bau** *m, pl* -**ten** functional building; **z~bedingt** *adj* determined by its function; **z~dienlich** *adj* (*z~entsprechend*) appropriate; (*nützlich*) useful; **z~dienliche Hinweise** (any) relevant information; **es wäre z~dienlich, das zu tun** it would be expedient to do that.

Zwecke *f* -, -**n** tack; (*Schuh~*) nail; (*Reiß~*) drawing-pin (*Brit*), thumbtack (*US*).

Zweck-: **z~entfremden*** *vt insep* to use sth in a way in which it wasn't intended to be used; **etw als etw z~entfremden** to use sth as sth; ~**entfremdung** *f* misuse; **z~entsprechend** *adj* appropriate; **etw z~entsprechend benutzen** to use sth properly *or* correctly, to put sth to its proper *or* correct use; **z~frei** *adj Forschung etc* pure; **z~gebunden** *adj* for a specific purpose, appropriated (*spec*) *no adv*; **z~gemäß** *adj siehe* **z~entsprechend**; ~**gemeinschaft** *f* partnership of convenience; **z~los** *adj* pointless, useless, futile, of no use; **es ist z~los, hier zu bleiben** it's pointless *etc* staying here, there's no point (in) staying here; ~**losigkeit** *f, no pl* pointlessness, uselessness, futility; **z~mäßig** *adj* (*nützlich*) useful; (*wirksam*) effective; (*ratsam*) advisable, expedient (*form*); (*z~entsprechend*) *Arbeitskleider etc* suitable; ~**mäßigkeit** *f siehe adj* usefulness; effectiveness, efficacy; advisability, expediency (*form*); suitability; ~**mäßigkeitserwägung** *f* consideration of expediency; ~**optimismus** *m* calculated optimism; ~**pessimismus** *m* calculated pessimism; ~**propaganda** *f* calculated propaganda.

zwecks *prep +gen* (*form*) for the purpose of ◆ **~ Wiederverwendung** for re-use.

Zweck-: ~**satz** *m* (*Gram*) final clause; ~**steuer** *f* regulatory tax; **z~voll** *adj siehe* **z~mäßig**; **z~widrig** *adj* inappropriate.

zween *num* (*obs*) twain (*obs*).

zwei *num* two ◆ **wir ~ (beiden** *inf*) the two of us, we two, us two (*inf*); **das ist so sicher wie ~ mal ~ vier ist** (*inf*) you can bet on that (*inf*); **dazu gehören ~** (*inf*) it takes two; **da kann man ~ draus machen** (*fig inf*) it's quite incredible; **~ Gesichter haben** (*fig*) to be two-faced; *siehe* **vier, Dritte(r).**

Zwei *f* -, -**en** two; *siehe auch* **Vier.**

Zwei- *in cpds siehe auch* **Vier-**; ≈**achser** *m* -**s**, - two-axle vehicle; **z≈achsig** *adj* two-axled; ≈**akter** *m* -**s**, - (*Theat*) two-act play *or* piece; **z≈armig** *adj* (*Physiol*) with two arms; (*Tech*) with two branches; **z≈atomig** *adj* (*Phys*) diatomic; ≈**beiner** *m* -**s**, - (*hum inf*) human being; **die ~beiner** human beings, the bipeds (*hum*); **z≈beinig** *adj* two-legged, biped(al) (*spec*); ≈**bettzimmer** *nt* twin room; ≈**bund** *m* (*Hist*) dual alliance; ≈**decker** *m* -**s**, - (*Aviat*) biplane; **z≈deutig** *adj* ambiguous, equivocal; (*schlüpfrig*) suggestive; **z~deutige Reden führen** to use a lot of doubles entendres; ≈**deutigkeit** *f* **(a)** *siehe adj* ambiguity, equivocalness; suggestiveness; risqué nature; **(b)** (*Bemerkung*) ambiguous *or* equivocal remark, double entendre; (*Witz*) risqué joke; **z≈dimensional** *adj* two-dimensional; ~**drittelmehrheit** *f* (*Parl*) two-thirds majority; **der Streikbeschluß wurde mit ~drittelmehrheit gefaßt** the decision to strike was taken with a two-thirds majority; **z≈eiig** *adj Zwillinge* non-identical, fraternal (*spec*).

Zweier *m* -**s**, - two; (*Sch dial*) good; (*Zweipfennigstück*) two pfennig piece; *siehe auch* **Vierer.**

Zweier-: ~**beziehung** *f* relationship; ~**bob** *m* two-man bob; ~**kajak** *m or nt* (*Kanu*) double kayak; (*Disziplin*) kayak pairs; ~**kanadier** *m* Canadian pair; (*Disziplin*) Canadian pairs; ~**kiste** *f* (*sl*) relationship.

zweierlei *adj inv* **(a)** *attr Brot, Käse, Wein* two kinds *or* sorts of; *Möglichkeiten, Größen, Fälle* two different ◆ **auf ~ Art** in two different ways; **~ Handschuhe/Strümpfe** *etc* odd gloves/socks *etc*; **~ Meinung sein** to be of (two) different opinions; *siehe* **Maß.**

(b) (*substantivisch*) two different things; (*2 Sorten*) two different kinds.

Zweierreihe *f* two rows *pl* ◆ **~n** rows of twos; **in ~n marschieren** to march two abreast *or* in twos.

zweifach *adj* double; (*zweimal*) twice ◆ **in ~er Ausfertigung** in duplicate; **~ gesichert** doubly secure; **ein Tuch ~ legen** to lay a cloth double.

Zwei-: ~**familienhaus** *nt* two family house; ~**farbendruck** *m* (*Typ*) two-colour print; (*Verfahren*) two-colour printing; **z≈farbig** *adj* two-colour, two-tone; **etw z~farbig anstreichen** to paint sth in two (different) colours.

Zweifel *m* -**s**, - doubt ◆ **außer ~** beyond doubt; **im ~** in doubt; **ohne ~** without doubt, doubtless; **über allen ~ erhaben** beyond all (shadow of a) doubt; **da kann es gar keinen ~ geben** there can be no doubt about it; **es besteht kein ~, daß ...** there is no doubt that ...; **~ an etw** (*dat*) **haben** to have one's doubts about sth; **da habe ich meine ~** I have my doubts, I'm doubtful; **etw in ~ ziehen** to call sth into question, to challenge sth; **ich bin mir im ~, ob ich das tun soll** I'm in two minds *or* I'm doubtful whether I should do that.

zweifelhaft *adj* doubtful; (*verdächtig auch*) dubious ◆ **von ~em Wert** of doubtful *or* debatable value; **es ist ~, ob ...** it is doubtful *or* questionable *or* debatable whether ...

zweifellos [1] *adv* without (a) doubt, undoubtedly, unquestionably; (*als Antwort*) undoubtedly ◆ **er hat ~ recht** he is undoubtedly *or* unquestionably right, without (a) doubt he is right.

[2] *adj Sieger etc* undisputed.

zweifeln *vi* to doubt ◆ **an etw /jdm ~** to doubt sth/sb; (*skeptisch sein auch*) to be sceptical about sth/sb; **daran ist nicht zu ~** there's no doubt about it; **ich zweifle nicht, daß ...** I do not doubt *or* I have no doubt that ...; **ich zweifle noch, wie ich mich entscheiden soll** I am still in two minds about it.

Zweifels-: ≈**fall** *m* doubtful *or* borderline case; **im ~fall** in case of doubt, when in doubt; (*inf: gegebenenfalls*) if need be, if necessary; **z≈frei** [1] *adj* unequivocal; [2] *adv* beyond (all) doubt; **z~ohne** *adv* undoubtedly, without (a) doubt.

Zweifingersuchsystem *nt* (*hum: beim Schreibmaschineschreiben*) peer and peck method (*hum*) ◆ **ich tippe im ~** I use two fingers, I type with two fingers.

Zweifler(in *f*) *m* -**s**, - sceptic.

zweiflerisch *adj* sceptical.

Zwei-: **z~flüg(e)lig** *adj Tür, Tor* double; *Insekt* two-winged, dipterous (*spec*); ≈**flügler** *m* -**s**, - (*Zool*) dipteran (*spec*); ~**frontenkrieg** *m* war/warfare on two fronts.

Zweig *m* -**(e)s, -e (a)** (*Ast*) branch, bough (*liter*); (*dünner, kleiner*) twig. **(b)** (*fig*) (*von Wissenschaft, Familie etc, Rail*) branch; (*Abteilung*) department; *siehe* **grün.**

Zweig-: ~**bahn** *f* branch-line; ~**betrieb** *m* branch.

Zwei-: **z~geschlechtig** *adj* (*Biol*) hermaphroditic; ~**geschlechtigkeit** *f* (*Biol*) hermaphroditism; ~**gespann** *nt* carriage and pair; (*fig inf*) duo, two-man band (*hum inf*); **z~gestrichen** *adj* (*Mus*) **das z~gestrichene C/A** the C (an octave) above middle C/the A an octave above middle C.

Zweig-: ~**geschäft** *nt* branch; ~**gesellschaft** *f* subsidiary (company).

zwei-: ~**gleisig** *adj* double tracked, double-track *attr*; **~gleisig fahren** (*lit*) to be double-tracked; (*fig inf*) to have two strings to one's bow; **~gleisig argumentieren** to argue along two different lines; ~**gliedrig** *adj* (*fig*) bipartite; (*Admin*) *System* two-tier; (*Math*) binominal.

Zweig-: ~**linie** *f* branch line; ~**niederlassung** *f* subsidiary; ~**postamt** *nt* sub-post office; **~stelle** *f* branch (office); **~stellenleiter** *m* (branch) manager; **~werk**[1] *nt* (*Fabrik*) branch; **~werk**[2] *nt* (*von Baum, Gesträuch*) branches *pl.*

Zwei-: **~händer** *m* **-s, -** **(a)** (*Schwert*) two-handed sword; **(b)** (*Zool*) two-handed *or* bimanous (*spec*) animal; **z~händig** *adj* with two hands, two-handed; (*Mus*) for two hands; **z~häusig** *adj* (*Bot*) dioecian; **~heit** *f, no pl* (*Philos, Liter etc*) duality; **z~höck(e)rig** *adj Kamel* two-humped.

zweihundert *num* two hundred.

Zweihundert-: **~jahrfeier** *f* bicentenary, bicentennial; **z≈jährig** *adj Dauer* two-hundred-year *attr*, *Tradition, Geschichte* two-hundred-year-old *attr*; **nach über z~jähriger Knechtschaft** after more than two hundred years of servitude.

zweijährig *adj* **(a)** *attr Kind etc* two-year-old *attr*, two years old; (*Dauer*) two-year *attr*, of two years ◆ **mit ~er Verspätung** two years late. **(b)** (*Bot*) *Pflanze* biennial.

zweijährlich [1] *adj* two-yearly *attr*, biennial, every two years.
[2] *adv* biennially, every two years; every other year.

Zwei-: **~kammersystem** *nt* (*Pol*) two-chamber system; **≈kampf** *m* single combat; (*Duell*) duel; **jdn zum ~kampf (heraus)fordern** to challenge sb to a duel; **≈keimblätt(e)rige** *pl* (*Bot*) dicotyledons *pl.*

Zweiklang-: **~horn** *nt*, **~hupe** *f* two-tone horn.

Zwei-: **z~köpfig** *adj* two-headed; **~kreisbremse** *f* dual-circuit brake.

zweimal *adv* twice ◆ **~ jährlich** *or* **im Jahr/täglich** *or* **am Tag** twice yearly *or* a year/twice daily *or* a day; **sich** (*dat*) **etw ~ überlegen** to think twice about sth; **das lasse ich mir nicht ~ sagen** I don't have to be told twice; **das mache ich bestimmt nicht ~** I certainly shan't do that/it again.

zweimalig *adj attr* twice repeated ◆ **nach ~er Aufforderung** after being told twice; **nach ~er Wiederholung konnte er den Text auswendig** after twice repeating the text he knew it (off) by heart.

Zwei-: **≈mannboot** *nt* two-man boat; **~markstück** *nt* two-mark piece; **≈master** *m* **-s, -** two-master; **z≈monatig** *adj attr* **(a)** (*Dauer*) two-month *attr*, of two months; **(b)** *Säugling etc* two-month-old *attr*, two months old; **z≈monatlich** [1] *adj* every two months, bimonthly (*esp Comm, Admin*); [2] *adv* every two months, bimonthly (*esp Comm, Admin*), every other month; **~monatsschrift** *f* bimonthly; **z≈motorig** *adj* twin-engined; **~parteiensystem** *nt* two-party system; **~pfennigstück** *nt* two-pfennig piece; **~phasenstrom** *m* two-phase current; **z≈polig** *adj* (*Elec*) double-pole, bipolar; **≈rad** *nt* (*form*) two-wheeled vehicle, two-wheeler; (*Fahrrad*) (bi)cycle; (*für Kinder*) two-wheeler, bicycle; **z≈räd(e)rig** *adj* two-wheeled; **~reiher** *m* **-s, -** double-breasted suit *etc*; **z≈reihig** [1] *adj* double-row *attr*, in two rows; *Anzug* double-breasted; [2] *adv* in two rows; **≈samkeit** *f* (*liter, hum*) togetherness; **z≈schläfig, z≈schläf(e)rig** *adj* double; **z≈schneidig** *adj* two-edged, double-edged (*auch fig*); **das ist ein z~schneidiges Schwert** (*fig*) it cuts both ways; **z≈seitig** [1] *adj Vertrag etc* bilateral, bipartite; *Kleidungsstück* reversible; (*Comput*) *Diskette* double-sided; [2] *adv* on two sides; **ein z~seitig tragbarer Anorak** a reversible anorak; **z≈silbig** *adj* disyllabic; **ein z~silbiges Wort** a disyllable (*spec*), a disyllabic word; **≈sitzer** *m* **-s, -** (*Aut, Aviat*) two-seater; **z≈sitzig** *adj* two-seater *attr*; **z≈spaltig** *adj* double-columned, in two columns; **der Artikel ist z~spaltig (abgedruckt)** the article is printed in two columns; **≈spänner** *m* **-s, -** carriage and pair; **z≈spännig** *adj* drawn by two horses; **z~spännig fahren** to drive (in) a carriage and pair; **z≈sprachig** *adj Mensch, Wörterbuch* bilingual; *Land auch* two-language *attr*; *Dokument* in two languages; **≈sprachigkeit** *f* bilingualism; **z≈spurig** *adj* double-tracked, double-track *attr*; *Autobahn* two-laned, two-lane *attr*; **ein Band z~spurig bespielen** to record a tape on both/two tracks; **≈spur(tonband)gerät** *nt* twin-track (tape) recorder; **z≈stellig** *adj Zahl* two-digit *attr*, with two digits; **z~stelliger Dezimalbruch** number with two decimal places; **z≈stimmig** *adj* (*Mus*) for two voices, two-part *attr*; **z~stimmig singen** to sing in two parts; **z≈stöckig** *adj* two-storey *attr*, two-storeyed; **ein z~stöckiges Bett** bunk bed; **z~stöckig bauen** to build houses/offices *etc* with two storeys; *siehe auch* **doppelstöckig**; **z≈strahlig** *adj Flugzeug* twin-jet *attr*; **~stromland** *nt*: **das ~stromland** Mesopotamia; **~stufenscheibenwischer** *m* (*Aut*) two-speed windscreen wiper; **z≈stufig** *adj* two-stage; *System auch* two-tier; *Plan auch* two-phase; *Scheibenwischer, Schaltgetriebe* two-speed; **z≈stündig** *adj* two-hour *attr*, of two hours; **z≈stündlich** *adj, adv* every two hours, two-hourly.

zweit *adv*: **zu ~** (*in Paaren*) in twos; **wir gingen zu ~ spazieren** the two of us went for a walk; **ich gehe lieber zu ~ ins Kino** I prefer going to the cinema with somebody *or* in a twosome; **das Leben zu ~ ist billiger** two people can live more cheaply than one; **das Leben zu ~** living with someone; *siehe auch* **vier.**

Zwei-: **z~tägig** *adj* two-day *attr*, of two days; **~takter** *m* **-s, -** (*inf*) two-stroke (*inf*); **~taktergemisch** *nt* two-stroke mixture; **~taktmotor** *m* two-stroke engine.

zweit|älteste(r, s) *adj* second eldest *or* oldest ◆ **unser Z~r** our second (child *or* son).

Zwei-: **z≈tausend** *num* two thousand; **das Jahr z~tausend** the year two thousand; **~tausendjahrfeier** *f* bimillenary.

Zweit-: **~ausfertigung** *f* (*form*) copy, duplicate; **es liegt nur in ~ausfertigung vor** we/I have only a copy *or* duplicate; **~auto** *nt* second car; **z~beste(r, s)** *adj* second best; **er ist der Z~beste** he is the second best; **~druck** *m* reprint.

Zwei-: **z~teilen** *vt sep, infin, ptp only* to divide (into two); **~teiler** *m* (*Fashion*) two-piece; **z~teilig** *adj Roman* two-part *attr*, in two parts; *Plan* two-stage; *Kleidungsstück* two-piece; *Formular etc* two-part *attr*, in two sections; **~teilung** *f* division; (*Math: von Winkel*) bisection.

zweitens *adv* secondly; (*bei Aufzählungen auch*) second.

zweite(r, s) *adj* second ◆ **~ Klasse** (*Rail etc*) second class; **~r Klasse fahren** to travel second(-class); **Bürger ~r Klasse** second-class citizen(s); **jeden ~n Tag** every other *or* second day; **jeder ~** (*lit, inf: sehr viele*) every other; **zum ~n** secondly; **ein ~r Caruso** another Caruso; **in ~r Linie** secondly; *siehe* **Garnitur, Hand, Ich, Wahl** *etc*; *siehe auch* **erste(r, s), vierte(r, s).**

Zweite(r) *mf decl as adj* second; (*Sport etc*) runner-up ◆ **wie kein z~r** as no-one else can, like nobody else.

Zweit-: **~erkrankung** *f* secondary illness/disease; **~frisur** *f* wig; **z~geboren** *adj attr* second-born; **~gerät** *nt* (*Rad, TV*) second set; **z~größte(r, s)** *adj* second biggest/largest; *Stadt auch* second; **z~höchste(r, s)** *adj* second highest/tallest; (*fig: im Rang*) second most senior; **z~klassig** *adj* (*fig*) second-class, second-rate (*esp pej*); **z~letzte(r, s)** *adj* last but one *attr, pred*; (*in Reihenfolge auch*) penultimate; **z~rangig** *adj siehe* **z~klassig**; **~schlüssel** *m* duplicate key; **~schrift** *f* copy; **~stimme** *f* second vote.

Zwei- (*Aut*): **~türer** *m* **-s, -** two-door; **z~türig** *adj* two-door.

Zweit-: **~wagen** *m* second car; **~wohnung** *f* second home.

Zwei|unddreißigstel *nt*, **Zwei|unddreißigstelnote** *f* (*Mus*) demisemiquaver (*Brit*), thirty-second note (*US*).

Zwei|unddreißigstelpause *f* (*Mus*) demisemiquaver rest (*Brit*), thirty-second note rest (*US*).

Zwei-: **~vierteltakt** *m* (*Mus*) two-four time; **z≈wertig** *adj* (*Chem*) bivalent, divalent; (*Ling*) two-place; **z≈wöchentlich** [1] *adj* two-weekly, fortnightly (*Brit*); [2] *adv* every two weeks, fortnightly (*Brit*); **z≈wöchig** *adj* two-week *attr*, of two weeks; **z≈zackig** *adj* two-pronged; **≈zeiler** *m* **-s, -** (*Liter*) couplet; **z≈zeilig** *adj* two-lined; (*Typ*) *Abstand* double-spaced; **z~zeilig schreiben** to double-space; **~zimmerwohnung** *f* two-room(ed) flat (*Brit*) *or* apartment; **≈züger** *m* (*Chess*) **-s, -** two-mover; **≈zylinder** *m* two-cylinder; **≈zylindermotor** *m* two-cylinder engine; **z≈zylindrig** *adj* two-cylinder *attr.*

Zwerchfell *nt* (*Anat*) diaphragm ◆ **jdm das ~ massieren** (*hum inf*) to make sb split his/her sides (laughing) (*inf*).

Zwerchfell-: **z~erschütternd** *adj* side-splitting (*inf*); **~massage** *f* (*hum inf*) **es war die reinste ~massage** it was an absolute scream (*inf*) *or* hoot (*inf*).

Zwerg(in *f*) *m* **-(e)s, -e** dwarf; (*Garten~*) gnome; (*fig: Knirps*) midget; (*pej: unbedeutender Mensch*) squirt (*inf*).

zwergenhaft *adj* dwarfish; (*fig*) diminutive, minute; (*pej: minderwertig*) insignificant.

Zwerg-: **~huhn** *nt* bantam; **~pinscher** *m* pet terrier; **~pudel** *m* toy poodle; **~schule** *f* (*Sch inf*) village school; **~staat** *m* miniature state; **~stamm** *m*, **~volk** *nt* pygmy tribe; **~wuchs** *m* stunted growth, dwarfism; **z~wüchsig** *adj attr* dwarfish.

Zwetschge *f* **-, -n** plum.

Zwetschgen-: **~datschi** *m* **-s, -s** (*S Ger*) (*type of*) plum cake; **~knödel** *m* (*S Ger*) plum dumpling; **~schnaps** *m*, **~wasser** *nt* plum brandy.

Zwetschke *f* **-, -n** (*Aus*) **(a)** *siehe* **Zwetschge. (b) seine/die sieben ~n (ein)packen** (*inf*) to pack one's bags (and go).

Zwickel *m* **-s, -** (*Sew*) gusset; (*am Segel*) gore; (*Archit*) spandrel.

zwicken [1] *vt* (*inf, Aus*) (*kneifen*) to pinch; (*leicht schmerzen*) to hurt; (*esp S Ger: ärgern*) to bother.
[2] *vi* to pinch; (*leicht schmerzen*) to hurt.

Zwicker *m* **-s, -** pince-nez.

Zwickmühle *f* (*beim Mühlespiel*) double mill ◆ **in der ~ sitzen** (*fig*) to be in a catch-22 situation (*inf*), to be in a dilemma.

Zwieback *m* **-(e)s, -e** *or* **≈e** rusk.

Zwiebel *f* **-, -n** onion; (*Blumen~*) bulb; (*hum inf: Uhr*) watch; (*Haarknoten*) tight bun.

Zwiebel-: **~fisch** *m* (*Typ*) literal (*character typed in wrong face*); **z~förmig** *adj* onion-shaped; **~kuchen** *m* onion tart; **~kuppel** *f* (*Archit*) imperial roof; **~muster** *nt* onion pattern.

zwiebeln *vt* (*inf*) **jdn ~** to drive *or* push sb hard; (*schikanieren*) to harass sb; **er hat uns so lange gezwiebelt, bis wir das Gedicht konnten** he kept (on) at us until we knew the poem.

Zwiebel-: **~ring** *m* onion ring; **~schale** *f* onion-skin; **~suppe** *f* onion soup; **~turm** *m* onion dome.

Zwie-: **z~fach, z~fältig** *adj* (*old*) *siehe* **zweifach**; **~gespräch** *nt* dialogue; **ein ~gespräch mit sich selbst** an internal dialogue; (*laut*) a soliloquy; **~laut** *m* (*Ling*) *siehe* **Diphthong**; **~licht** *nt, no pl* twilight; (*abends auch*) dusk; (*morgens*) half-light; **ins ~licht geraten sein** (*fig*) to appear in an unfavourable light; **z~lichtig** *adj* (*fig*) shady.

Zwiesel *m* **-s, -** *or f* **-, -n** (*Bot*) fork, bifurcation.

Zwie-: **~spalt** *m* (*pl rare*) (*der Natur, der Gefühle etc*) conflict; (*zwischen Menschen, Parteien etc*) rift, gulf; **ich bin im ~spalt mit mir, ob ich ...** I'm in conflict with myself whether to ...; **in ~spalt mit jdm geraten** to come into conflict with sb; **in einen fürchterlichen ~spalt geraten** to get into a terrible conflict; **z~spältig** *adj Gefühle* mixed, conflicting *attr*; **mein Eindruck war z~spältig** my impressions were very mixed; **ein z~spältiger Mensch** a man/woman of contradictions; **~sprache** *f* dialogue; **~sprache mit jdm/etw halten** to commune with sb/sth; **~tracht** *f* **-,** *no pl* discord; **~tracht säen** to sow (the seeds of) discord.

Zwille *f* **-, -n** (*N Ger*) catapult (*Brit*), slingshot (*US*).

Zwil(li)ch *m* **-s, -e** (*Tex*) *siehe* **Drillich.**

Zwilling *m* **-s, -e** twin; (*Gewehr*) double-barrelled gun; (*Chem: Doppelkristall*) twin crystal ◆ **die ~e** (*Astrol*) Gemini, the Twins; (*Astron*) Gemini; **~ sein** (*Astrol*) to be (a) Gemini.

Zwillings-: ~bruder *m* twin brother; **~formel** *f* (*Ling*) dual expression, set phrase with two elements; **~geburt** *f* twin birth; **~paar** *nt* twins *pl*; **~reifen** *m* (*Aut*) double *or* twin tyres; **~schwester** *f* twin sister.

Zwingburg *f* (*Hist, fig*) stronghold, fortress.

Zwinge *f* **-, -n** (*Tech*) (screw) clamp; (*am Stock*) tip, ferrule; (*an Schirm*) tip; (*an Werkzeuggriff*) ferrule.

➤ **zwingen** *pret* **zwang,** *ptp* **gezwungen** [1] *vt* **(a)** to force, to compel ◆ **jdn ~, etw zu tun** to force *or* compel sb to do sth; (*Mensch auch*) to make sb do sth; **jdn zu etw ~** to force sb to do sth; **sie ist dazu gezwungen worden** she was forced *or* compelled *or* made to do it; **ich lasse mich nicht (dazu) ~** I shan't be forced (to do it *or* into it), I don't/shan't respond to force; **jdn an den Verhandlungstisch ~** to force sb to the bargaining table; **jdn zum Handeln ~** to force sb into action *or* to act; **jdn zum Gehorsam ~** to force *or* compel sb to obey, to make sb obey; **die Regierung wurde zum Rücktritt gezwungen** the government was forced *or* compelled to step down; **man kann niemanden zu seinem Glück ~** you can't force people; *siehe* **gezwungen.**
(b) (*inf: bewältigen*) *Essen, Arbeit* to manage; *siehe* **Knie.**
[2] *vr* to force oneself ◆ **sich ~, etw zu tun** to force oneself to do sth, to make oneself do sth; **sich zur Ruhe ~** to force oneself to be calm.
[3] *vi* **zum Handeln/Umdenken ~** to force *or* compel us/them *etc* to act/rethink; **diese Tatsachen ~ zu der Annahme, daß ...** these facts force *or* compel one to assume that ...

zwingend *adj Notwendigkeit* urgent; (*logisch notwendig*) necessary; *Schluß, Beweis, Argumente* conclusive; *Argument* cogent; *Gründe* compelling ◆ **daß B aus A resultiert, ist nicht ~** it isn't necessarily so *or* the case that B results from A; **etwas ~ darlegen** to present sth conclusively.

Zwinger *m* **-s, -** (*Käfig*) cage; (*Bären~*) bear-pit; (*Hunde~*) kennels *pl*; (*von Burg*) (outer) ward.

Zwing-: ~herr *m* (*Hist, fig*) oppressor, tyrant; **~herrschaft** *f* (*Hist, fig*) oppression, tyranny.

Zwinglianer(in *f*) *m* **-s, -** (*Hist, Rel*) Zwinglian.

zwinkern *vi* to blink; (*um jdm etw zu bedeuten*) to wink; (*lustig*) to twinkle ◆ **mit den Augen ~** to blink (one's eyes)/wink/twinkle.

Zwirbelbart *m* handlebar moustache.

zwirbeln *vt Bart* to twirl; *Schnur* to twist.

Zwirn *m* **-s, -e** (strong) thread, yarn; *siehe* **Himmel.**

zwirnen *vti* to twist ◆ **dieses Handtuch ist gezwirnt** this towel is made of strong thread.

Zwirnerei *f* mill.

Zwirnsfaden *m* thread.

zwischen *prep +dat or (mit Bewegungsverben) +acc* between; (*in bezug auf mehrere auch*) among ◆ **mitten ~** right in the middle *or* midst of; **die Liebe ~ den beiden** the love between the two of them; **die Kirche stand ~ Bäumen** the church stood among(st) trees; *siehe* **Stuhl, Tür, Zeile** *etc.*

Zwischen-: ~akt *m* (*Theat*) interval, intermission; **im ~akt** during the interval *or* intermission; **~akt(s)musik** *f* interlude; **~ansage** *f* (*Rad etc*) announcement (*interrupting a programme*); (*Kurznachricht*) newsflash; **~applaus** *m* (*Theat*) spontaneous applause (*during the performance*); **~aufenthalt** *m* stopover; **~bemerkung** *f* interjection; (*Unterbrechung*) interruption; **wenn Sie mir eine kurze ~bemerkung erlauben** if I may just interrupt; **~bericht** *m* interim report; **~bescheid** *m* provisional notification *no indef art*; **~bilanz** *f* (*Comm*) interim balance; (*fig*) provisional appraisal; **eine ~bilanz/~bilanzen ziehen** (*fig*) to take stock provisionally; **z~blenden** *vt sep* to blend in; (*Film, Rad etc*) to insert; (*nachträglich*) *Musik etc* to dub on; **~blutung** *f* (*Med*) breakthrough *or* intermenstrual (*spec*) bleeding; **~boden** *m siehe* **~decke**; **~buchhandel** *m* intermediate book trade; **~deck** *nt* (*Naut*) 'tween deck; **im ~deck** 'tween decks, between the decks; **~decke** *f* false ceiling; **~ding** *nt* cross (between the two), hybrid; **was er schreibt, ist ein ~ding zwischen Lyrik und Prosa** his writing is a cross between *or* is halfway between poetry and prose; **z~drin** *adv* (*dial*) **(a)** *siehe* **z~durch**; **(b)** *siehe* **dazwischen**; **z~durch** *adv* **(a)** (*zeitlich*) in between times; (*inzwischen*) (in the) meantime; (*nebenbei*) on the side; **er macht z~durch mal Pausen** he keeps stopping for a break in between times; **das mache ich so z~durch** I'll do that on the side; **Schokolade für z~durch** chocolate for between meals; **(b)** (*örtlich*) in between; **~eiszeit** *f* (*Geol*) interglacial period; **~ergebnis** *nt* interim result; (*von Untersuchung auch*) interim findings; (*Sport*) latest score; **~fall** *m* incident; **ohne ~fall** without incident, smoothly; **es kam zu schweren ~fällen** there were serious incidents, there were clashes; **~finanzierung** *f* bridging *or* interim finance; **~frage** *f* question; **~frequenz** *f* (*Rad*) intermediate frequency; **~fruchtbau** *m* (*Agr*) intercropping; **~futter** *nt* (*Sew*) interlining; **~gang** *m* (*Cook*) *siehe* **~gericht**; **~gas** *nt, no pl* (*Aut*) **~gas geben** to double-declutch; **~gericht** *nt* (*Cook*) entrée; **z~geschlechtlich** *adj* between the sexes; ⚠**~geschoß** *nt* mezzanine (floor); **~glied** *nt* (*lit, fig*) link; **~größe** *f* in-between size; **~halt** *m* (*Sw*) *siehe* **~aufenthalt**; **~handel** *m* intermediate trade; **~händler** *m* middleman; **z~hinein** *adv* (*Sw*) *siehe* **z~durch**; **~hirn** *nt* (*Anat*) interbrain, diencephalon (*spec*); **~hoch** *nt* (*Met*) ridge of high pressure; **~kiefer(knochen)** *m* (*Anat*) intermaxillary (bone); **~lager** *nt* temporary store; **z~lagern** *vt insep inf and ptp only* to store (temporarily); **~lagerung** *f* temporary storage; **z~landen** *vi sep aux sein* (*Aviat*) to stop over *or* off; **~landung** *f* (*Aviat*) stopover; **ohne ~landung** without a stopover; **~lauf** *m* (*Sport*) intermediate heat; **~lösung** *f* temporary *or* interim *or* provisional solution; **~mahlzeit** *f* snack (between meals); **z~menschlich** *adj attr* interhuman; **~musik** *f* interlude; **~produkt** *nt* intermediate product; **~prüfung** *f* intermediate examination; **~raum** *m* gap, space; (*Wort-, Zeilenabstand*) space; (*zeitlich*) interval; **ein ~raum von 5 m, 5 m ~raum** a gap/space of 5m, a 5m gap/space; **~ring** *m* (*Phot*) adapter; **~ruf** *m* interruption; **~rufe** heckling; **einen Redner durch ~rufe stören** to heckle a speaker; **~rufer(in** *f*) *m* **-s, -** heckler; **~runde** *f* (*esp Sport*) intermediate round; **~saison** *f* low season; **~satz** *m* (*Gram*) inserted *or* parenthetic clause, parenthesis; **z~schalten** *vt sep* (*Elec*) to insert; (*fig*) to interpose, to put in between; **~schalter** *m* (*Elec*) interruptor; **~schaltung** *f* (*Elec*) insertion; (*fig*) interposition; **z~schieben** *vt sep irreg Termin etc* to fit *or* squeeze in; **~sohle** *f* midsole; **~speicher** *m* (*Comput*) cache (memory); **z~speichern** *vt sep* (*Comput*) to store in a/the cache (memory); **~spiel** *nt* (*Mus*) intermezzo; (*Theat, fig*) interlude; **~spurt** *m* (*Sport*) short burst (of speed); **einen ~spurt einlegen** to put in a burst of speed; **z~staatlich** *adj attr* international; (*zwischen Bundesstaaten*) interstate; **~stadium** *nt* intermediate stage; **~station** *f* (intermediate) stop; **in London machten wir ~station** we stopped off in London; **~stecker** *m* (*Elec*) adaptor (plug); **~stellung** *f* intermediate position; **~stock** *m*, **~stockwerk** *nt* mezzanine (floor); **~stück** *nt* connection, connecting piece; **~stufe** *f* (*fig*) *siehe* **~stadium**; **~stunde** *f* (*Sch*) hour's break, break of an hour; **~summe** *f* subtotal; **~text** *m* inserted text; **~titel** *m* (*Film etc*) title link; **~ton** *m* (*Farbe*) shade; **~töne** (*fig*) nuances; **~träger(in** *f*) *m* informer, telltale; **~urteil** *nt* (*Jur*) interlocutory decree; **~vorhang** *m* (*Theat*) drop scene; **~wand** *f* dividing wall; (*Stellwand*) partition; **~wirt** *m* (*Biol*) intermediate host; **~zähler** *m* (*Elec*) intermediate meter; **~zeit** *f* **(a)** (*Zeitraum*) interval; **in der ~zeit** (in the) meantime, in the interim; **(b)** (*Sport*) intermediate time; **z~zeitlich** *adv* (*rare*) in between; (*inzwischen*) (in the) meantime; **~zeugnis** *nt* (*Sch*) end of term report; **~zins** *m* (*Fin*) interim interest.

Zwist *m* **-es,** (*rare*) **-e** (*geh*) discord, discordance; (*Fehde, Streit*) dispute, strife *no indef art* ◆ **den alten ~ begraben** to bury the hatchet; **mit jdm über etw** (*acc*) **in ~** (*acc*) **geraten** to become involved in a dispute with sb about *or* over sth.

Zwistigkeit *f usu pl* dispute.

zwitschern *vti* to twitter, to chir(ru)p; (*Lerche*) to warble ◆ **~d sprechen** to twitter; **bei dir zwitschert's wohl!** (*inf*) you must be batty (*inf*) *or* barmy (*Brit inf*); **Z~** twittering, chir(ru)ping; warbling; **einen ~** (*inf*) to have a drink.

Zwitter *m* **-s, -** hermaphrodite; (*fig*) cross (*aus* between).

Zwitter-: ~bildung *f* hermaphroditism; **~blüte** *f* (*Bot*) hermaphrodite; **~ding** *nt* (*fig*) hybrid, cross-breed; **~form** *f* (*Biol*) hermaphroditic stage; (*fig*) hybrid form; **z~haft** *adj* hermaphroditic.

zwitt(e)rig *adj* hermaphroditic; (*Bot auch*) androgynous.

Zwitter-: ~tum *nt* hermaphroditism; (*Bot auch*) androgyny; **~wesen** *nt siehe* **Zwitter.**

zwo *num* (*Telec, inf*) two.

zwölf *num* twelve ◆ **die ~ Apostel** the twelve apostles; **die Z~ Nächte** the Twelve Days of Christmas; **~ Uhr mittags/nachts** (12 o'clock) noon *or* midday/midnight; **fünf Minuten vor ~** (*fig*) at the eleventh hour; **davon gehen ~ aufs Dutzend** they're ten a penny (*inf*); *siehe auch* **vier.**

Zwölf- *in cpds siehe auch* **Vier-**; **~eck** *nt* (*Math*) dodecagon; **z~eckig** *adj* dodecagonal; **~ender** *m* **-s, -** (*Hunt*) royal; **z~fach** *adj* twelve-fold; *siehe auch* **vierfach**; **~fingerdarm** *m* duodenum; **ein Geschwür am ~fingerdarm** a duodenal ulcer; **~flach** *nt* **-(e)s, -e, ~flächner** *m* **-s, -** (*Math*) dodecahedron; **~kampf** *m* (*Sport*) twelve-exercise event; **~meilenzone** *f* twelve-mile zone.

Zwölftel *nt* **-s, -** twelfth; *siehe auch* **Viertel**[1].

zwölftens *adv* twelfth(ly), in twelfth place.

zwölfte(r, s) *adj* twelfth; *siehe auch* **vierte(r, s).**

Zwölftöner *m* **-s, -** (*Mus*) twelve-tone composer.

Zwölfton-: ~lehre *f* twelve-tone system; **~musik** *f* twelve-tone music; **~reihe** *f* twelve-tone row *or* series.

zwote(r, s) *adj* (*Telec, inf*) *siehe* **zweite(r, s).**

Zyan [tsya:n] *nt* **-s,** *no pl* (*Chem*) cyanogen.

Zyanid [tsya'ni:t] *nt* **-s, -e** cyanide.

Zyankali [tsya:n'ka:li] *nt* **-s,** *no pl* (*Chem*) potassium cyanide.

Zygote *f* **-, -n** (*Biol*) zygote.

Zykladen *pl* (*Geog*) Cyclades *pl.*

Zyklame *f* **-, -n** (*Aus*), **Zyklamen** *nt* **-s, -** (*spec*) cyclamen.

zyklisch [1] *adj* cyclic(al).
[2] *adv* cyclically.

Zyklon[1] *m* **-s, -e** cyclone.

Zyklon[2] *nt* **-s,** *no pl* (*Chem*) cyanide-based poison, cyanide.

Zyklone *f* **-, -n** (*Met*) depression, low(-pressure area).

Zyklop *m* **-en, -en** (*Myth*) Cyclops.

Zyklopenmauer *f* (*Archeol*) cyclopean wall.

zyklopisch *adj* (*Myth*) Cyclopean; (*liter: gewaltig*) gigantic.

Zyklotron ['tsy:klotro:n, 'tsʏk-] *nt* **-s, -e** (*Phys*) cyclotron.

Zyklus ['tsy:klʊs] *m* **-, Zyklen** ['tsy:klən] cycle.

Zykluszeit ['tsy:klʊs-] *f* (*Comput*) cycle time.

Zylinder *m* **-s, - (a)** (*Math, Tech*) cylinder; (*Lampen~*) chimney. **(b)** (*Hut*) top-hat, topper (*inf*).

Zylinder-: ~block *m* (*Aut*) engine *or* cylinder block; **~dichtungsring** *m* (*Aut*) cylinder ring; **z~förmig** *adj siehe* **zylindrisch**; **~hut** *m siehe* **Zylinder (b)**; **~kopf** *m* (*Aut*) cylinder head; **~kopfdichtung** *f* cylinder head gasket; **~mantel** *m* (*Tech*) cylinder jacket; ⚠**~schloß** *nt* cylinder lock.

-zylindrig *adj suf* -cylinder.

zylindrisch *adj* cylindrical.
Zymbal ['tsʏmbal] *nt* **-s, -e** (*Mus*) cymbal.
Zyniker(in *f*) ['tsy:nikɐ, -ərɪn] *m* **-s, -** cynic.
zynisch ['tsy:nɪʃ] *adj* cynical.
Zynismus *m* cynicism.
Zypern ['tsy:pɐn] *nt* **-s** Cyprus.
Zypresse *f* (*Bot*) cypress.
Zypr(i)er(in *f*) ['tsy:prɐ, -ərɪn, 'tsy:priɐ, -iərɪn] *m* **-s, -** (*rare*), **Zypriot(in *f*)** *m* **-en, -en** Cypriot.
zypriotisch, zyprisch ['tsy:prɪʃ] *adj* Cyprian, Cypriot.
Zyste ['tsʏstə] *f* **-, -n** cyst.
zystisch *adj* cystic ◆ **~ Fibrose** cystic fibrosis.
Zytologie *f* (*Biol*) cytology.
Zyto-: ~plasma *nt* (*Biol*) cytoplasm; **~statikum** *nt* **-s, -statika** cytostatic drug.
z.Z(t). *abbr of* **zur Zeit.**

LANGUAGE IN USE

SPRACHE AKTIV

First Edition

by

Ulrike Seeberger and Roswitha Morris

New Edition

by

Elspeth Anderson **Horst Kopleck** **Christine Bahr**

Language in Use

Contents

German-English

Sprache Aktiv

Inhalt

Englisch-Deutsch

Corpus Acknowledgements

We would like to acknowledge the assistance of the many hundreds of individuals and companies who have kindly given permission for copyright material to be used in the Bank of English. The written sources include many national and regional newspapers in Britain and overseas; magazine and periodical publishers in Britain, the United States and Australia. Extensive spoken data has been provided by radio and television broadcasting companies; research workers at many universities and other institutions; and individual numerous contributors. We are grateful to them all.

Korpusmaterial

Für ihre Unterstützung danken wir den vielen Einzelpersonen und Firmen, die freundlicherweise urheberrechtlich geschütztes Textmaterial zur Verwendung in unseren deutschen Korpora bereitgestellt haben. Dazu zählen eine Vielzahl von Zeitungs-, Zeitschriften- und Buchverlagen in Deutschland, Österreich und der Schweiz. Ihnen allen gilt unser Dank.

Introduction to Language in Use – New Edition

Our aim in writing Language in Use has been to help non-native speakers find fluent, natural ways of expressing themselves in the foreign language, without risk of the native-language distortion that sometimes results from literal translation. To achieve this, we have identified a number of essential language functions, such as *agreement*, *suggestions* and *apologies*, and provided a wealth of examples to show typical ways of expressing them. Users can select phrases to meet their needs using either their knowledge of the foreign language alone or by looking at the translations of the key elements.

In this completely revised and updated edition of Language in Use, the authentic examples are taken from Collins vast computerized language databases of modern English and German. These databases consist of around 320 million English and German words from a variety of modern written and spoken sources: literature, magazines, newspapers, letters, radio and television. The fresh new layout is designed to make consultation even easier. Clear headings and subdivisions enable you to find the topic of your choice at a glance. We have given guidance, where appropriate, so that you can be confident that the phrase you have chosen is as assertive, tentative, direct or indirect as you want it to be.

Also new is the linking of the main dictionary text to the Language in Use section. Certain words, *suggestion*, for example, have been marked in the main dictionary to show that additional material is given in Language in Use. In these cases an arrow symbol appears in the margin beside the headword and beside any relevant categories, and a footnote (**suggestion** (**a**) 1.1, 1.2) tells you which Language in Use section(s) to go to – in this case, sections 1.1 and 1.2 for examples relating to category (a). As all cross-referred words are underlined in the relevant Language in Use section, you will quickly be able to locate them there.

Since German forms of address corresponding to the English *you* vary according to the formality of the relationship, we have tried to reflect this in a consistent manner. As a general rule, the *Sie* form has been used, with the exception of such idioms and translations which are either spoken or by their nature demand the use of the *du* form.

Sprache aktiv – Einleitung zur Neubearbeitung

Bei der Zusammenstellung von "Sprache aktiv" ging es darum, Nichtmuttersprachlern eine Hilfestellung zur idiomatischen Ausdrucksweise in der Fremdsprache zu geben, so daß Verzerrungen, wie sie manchmal bei wörtlichen Übersetzungen auftreten, vermieden werden können.

Um dies zu erreichen, wurde eine Reihe grundlegender sprachlicher Funktionen, wie *Zustimmung*, *Ablehnung* und *Entschuldigungen*, identifiziert und eine Vielzahl von Beispielen zusammengestellt, die typische Ausdrucksweisen für die jeweilige Situation zeigen. Der Wörterbuchbenutzer hat die Möglichkeit, Wendungen auszuwählen und dabei entweder nur auf die fremdsprachlichen Muster zurückzugreifen, also seine eigenen Sprachkenntnisse anzuwenden, oder die Übersetzungen der Schlüsselelemente in den Beispielsätzen heranzuziehen.

Die vorliegende aktualisierte Neubearbeitung von "Sprache aktiv" basiert auf authentischen Beispielen aus den von Collins unterhaltenen, umfassenden Datenbanken des heutigen Englisch und Deutsch, in der etwa 320 Millionen Wörter beider Sprachen aus einer Vielzahl von modernen schriftlichen und mündlichen Quellen gespeichert sind: Bücher, Zeitschriften, Zeitungen, Briefe, Rundfunk- und Fernsehsendungen.

Durch das neugestaltete grafische Erscheinungsbild soll die Benutzung von "Sprache aktiv" noch leichter gemacht werden. Klare Überschriften und Unterteilungen ermöglichen das schnelle Auffinden eines gesuchten Abschnitts. Wo es sich als angebracht erwies, wurden stilistische Angaben hinzugefügt, mit deren Hilfe man feststellen kann, ob die gewählte Wendung auch genauso direkt, indirekt, bestimmt oder zögernd ist wie der entsprechende Ausgangstext.

Ebenfalls neu ist die Verknüpfung von "Sprache aktiv" mit dem Wörterbuchtext. Bestimmte Wörter, zum Beispiel *Vorschlag*, wurden im Wörterbuchtext gekennzeichnet, um darauf hinzuweisen, daß "Sprache aktiv" hierzu weiteres Material enthält. Dabei ist das jeweilige Stichwort mit einem Pfeil am Rand neben dem Wort und jeder relevanten Kategorie markiert. Eine Fußnote (**Vorschlag** (**a**) 28.1, 28.2) zeigt, in welchem Abschnitt von "Sprache aktiv" nachgeschlagen werden kann. Im angeführten Beispiel finden sich in den Abschnitten 28.1 und 28.2 Beispielsätze, die sich auf die Kategorie (a) des Stichworts *Vorschlag* beziehen. Da alle Wörter, die so kenntlich gemacht wurden, in "Sprache aktiv" unterstrichen sind, können die Querverweise dort schnell aufgefunden werden. Bezüglich der deutschen Anrede mit *du* oder *Sie* wurde generell die *Sie*-Form verwendet, mit Ausnahme solcher Wendungen und Übersetzungen, deren situatives Umfeld und sprachliche Ebene das *Du* verlangen.

1 Suggestions

1.1 Making suggestions

Tentatively

Wenn ich vielleicht einen Vorschlag machen dürfte: Wir sollten den Altbau besser abreißen	*if I might make a suggestion*
Wir möchten Ihnen gerne einige Vorschläge zu Ihrer Altersversorgung **unterbreiten**	*we would be pleased to suggest a few ideas*
Ich würde vorschlagen, Sie sprechen persönlich mit Ihrem Chef	*I would suggest*
Angenommen, Sie würden mit ihr noch einmal über alles sprechen. Vielleicht ändert sie dann ihre Meinung	*suppose*
Sie sollten sich für eine solche Einladung **vielleicht besser** schriftlich bedanken	*perhaps you ought to*

More assertively

An Ihrer Stelle würde ich dieses Angebot zurückweisen	*if I were you, I would*
Ich schlage vor, die Sitzung auf morgen zu vertagen	*I suggest*
Ich denke, wir sollten für heute Schluß machen	*I think*
Am besten sollten wir wohl einen Spezialisten zu Rate ziehen	*the best thing would be to*
Wenn Sie nächste Woche in Bonn sind, **könnten Sie doch** mal bei uns vorbeischauen	*if you ..., you could*
Wenn Sie meine Meinung hören wollen: sagen Sie zu	*if you want my opinion*
Eigentlich brauchten Sie Ihren Abfall **nur** ein bißchen vorzusortieren	*you only need to*
In diesem Falle bleibt uns wohl nichts anderes übrig, als unser gutes Recht über das Gericht ein**zu**klagen	*in that case, we have no choice but to*

Using direct questions

Was würden Sie von einer neuen Büroausstattung **halten?**	*how about*
Was würden Sie sagen, wenn wir Ihnen weitere 10 Prozent Rabatt bieten?	*what would you say if*
Warum sprechen Sie **nicht** einfach mit Ihrem Chef über diese Angelegenheit?	*why don't you*
Haben Sie schon einmal daran gedacht, sich um den Posten der Kulturreferentin **zu** bewerben?	*have you ever thought of*
Was hältst du von einer kleinen Spritztour mit dem neuen Auto?	*how about*

In an impersonal way

Tentatively

Vielleicht wäre es angebracht, in dieser heiklen Angelegenheit etwas mehr Diskretion **zu** üben	*perhaps it would be appropriate*
Vielleicht wäre es besser, die Polizei **zu** benachrichtigen	*it might be better*
Es wäre ja immerhin möglich, daß wir das Programm noch einmal ändern	*we could always*
Wäre es nicht eine mögliche Lösung, einerseits die Selbstbeschränkung **zu** lockern und andererseits Sozialklauseln durch**zu**setzen?	*one possible solution might be*

More assertively

Es wäre eine gute Idee, am Wochenende aufs Land **zu** fahren	*I think it would be a good idea*
Es wäre ratsam, eine Sicherheitskopie an**zu**legen	*you would certainly be advised to*
Man sollte diesen Versuch noch einmal bei einer anderen Temperatur durchführen	*... should be*
Wie wäre es mit einer Tasse Kaffee?	*how about*
Noch ein Bier **gefällig?**	*would you like another*

1.2 Asking for suggestions

Haben Sie vielleicht eine Idee, wie wir die Außenfassade gestalten könnten?	*do you have any suggestions about how*
Hat vielleicht noch jemand einen besseren Vorschlag?	*does anyone have a better suggestion*
Was würden Sie an meiner Stelle tun?	*what would you do if you were me*
Was könnten wir am Wochenende **unternehmen?**	*what could we do*
Was würden Sie vorschlagen?	*what would you suggest*

2 Advice

2.1 Asking for advice

Was würden Sie mir in dieser Sache **raten?**	*what would you advise*
Was würden Sie an meiner Stelle tun?	*what would you do if you were me*
Welchen Zahnarzt **würden Sie mir empfehlen?**	*would you recommend*
Meinen Sie, ich sollte lieber nicht nach Hongkong fliegen?	*do you think it would be better if I didn't*
Meinen Sie, ich sollte mich in dieser Sache mit meinem Anwalt absprechen?	*do you think I should*
Ich hätte in dieser Sache **gern Ihren Rat**	*I'd like your advice*
Ich wäre Ihnen wirklich sehr dankbar, wenn Sie mir in dieser delikaten Angelegenheit **mit Ihrem Rat zur Seite stehen könnten**	*I should be very grateful if you would help me out with some advice*
Ich möchte mich in diesem schwierigen Fall **von Ihnen in Ihrer Eigenschaft als** Rechtsanwalt **beraten lassen**	*I'd like your opinion as ... on*

2.2 Giving advice

Ich würde Ihnen raten, so schnell wie möglich einen Arzt auf**zu**suchen	*I would advise you to*
Ich würde Ihnen dringend anraten, sich in dieser Sache mit Ihrem Anwalt ab**zu**sprechen.	*I would strongly advise you to*
An Ihrer Stelle würde ich mich beschweren	*if I were you, I would*
Sie wären gut beraten, die Konditionen des Vertrages vorerst geheim**zu**halten	*you would be well advised to*
Sie wären schlecht beraten, jetzt klein bei**zu**geben	*you would be ill-advised to*
Sie sollten unbedingt die Packungsbeilage lesen	*you really ought to*
Es liegt ganz in Ihrem Interesse, wenn die Konkurrenz ein wenig eingeschüchtert wird	*it is entirely in your interest*
Es empfiehlt sich nicht, bei der Ersatzteilsuche auf ältere Fahrzeugtypen zurück**zu**greifen	*it is inadvisable to*

More tentatively

Wenn ich dir raten darf, laß sie besser in Ruhe	*can I give you some advice*
Wenn ich Ihnen einen Hinweis geben darf: meiden Sie lawinengefährdete Skigebiete	*can I give you some advice*
Es scheint mir ratsam, den Vertrag genaustens unter die Lupe **zu** nehmen	*I think it would be advisable to*
Am besten sollten Sie vielleicht mit der Bahn fahren	*you might be best to*
Haben Sie schon einmal über eine Gehaltserhöhung **nachgedacht?**	*have you ever thought of*
Könntest du mir das **vielleicht** selbst erklären?	*could you maybe*

2.3 Giving warnings

Ich kann Sie nur warnen, am langen Samstag ist in der Stadt die Hölle los	*a word of warning*
Ich rate Ihnen dringend davon ab, diese Vereinbarung **zu** unterschreiben.	*I strongly advise you not to*
Ich würde mich vor übereilten Schlußfolgerungen **hüten**	*beware of*
Sie sollten noch einmal alle Einzelheiten überprüfen, **sonst** geht am Ende noch etwas schief	*you'd better ..., otherwise*
Sie laufen Gefahr, in diesen undurchsichtigen Geschäften viel Geld **zu** verlieren	*you run the risk of*
Versuchen Sie bloß nicht, mit ihm über seine letzten Geschäfte **zu** reden	*do not try to*
Es wäre reiner Wahnsinn, ausgerechnet jetzt nach Berlin **zu** fahren	*it would be sheer madness to*
Du wirst noch in ernstliche Schwierigkeiten geraten, wenn du den Umgang mit Geld nicht bald lernst	*you'll get yourself into serious trouble if*
Du riskierst Kopf und Kragen, wenn du diesen holprigen Feldweg benutzt	*you're risking life and limb if*
Paß auf, daß du nicht ins Wasser fällst	*be careful (that)*

3 Offers

3.1 Direct offers

Wir möchten unsere Mitarbeit in diesem Projekt **anbieten**	*we should like to offer*
Ich könnte Ihnen eine zuverlässige Bürokraft vermitteln, **wenn Sie das möchten**	*I could ..., if you like*
Lassen Sie mich zumindest die Getränke bezahlen, **bitte**	*please allow me to*
Ich kümmere mich gerne um die Sache, **wenn** sich sonst niemand dafür findet	*I would be glad to take care of ... if*
Ich bin gerne bereit, Sie zum Flughafen **zu** fahren	*I'd be happy to*
Wenden Sie sich bitte jederzeit an mich, wenn Sie noch zusätzliche Informationen benötigen	*please feel free to contact me at any time*

3.2 Indirect offers

Es würde mir sehr viel Freude machen, Ihnen die Stadt **zu** zeigen	*it would be a great pleasure to*
Es wäre uns ein Vergnügen, Sie in unserem Sommerhaus begrüßen **zu** können	*we would be delighted to*
Ich würde wirklich gerne mit Ihnen nach Weimar fahren	*I would be more than happy to*

3.3 Using direct questions

Möchten Sie mit uns in die Oper gehen?	*would you like to*
Kann ich Ihnen behilflich sein?	*can I*
Soll ich für Sie bei der Zimmervermittlung anrufen?	*shall I*
Darf ich Ihnen etwas zu trinken **anbieten?**	*may I offer*
Was würden Sie zu einem kleinen Wochenendausflug **sagen?**	*what would you say to*
Wie wäre es, wenn **ich** nächste Woche mal vorbeikommen würde?	*what if I were to*
Und wenn ich dir einfach ein bißchen im Haushalt helfe?	*what if*

4 Requests

Tentatively

Würde es Ihnen etwas ausmachen, mir Ihr Programmheft **zu** leihen?	*would you mind*
Mir wäre sehr geholfen, wenn Sie mir einen Teil meiner Auslagen vorstrecken könnten	*it would be very helpful if*
Ich wäre Ihnen sehr dankbar, wenn Sie mein Anliegen noch in dieser Woche klären könnten	*I would be very grateful if*
Dürfte ich Sie vielleicht bitten, sich um die Zimmerreservierung **zu** kümmern	*could I ask you to*
Wenn Sie vielleicht etwas zur Seite rücken **würden?**	*could you maybe*
Es wäre schön, wenn Sie am Freitag zum Abendessen zu uns kommen würden	*it would be nice if*

More assertively

Ich möchte Sie bitten, das Telefon nicht für Privatgespräche **zu** benutzen	*I must ask you*
Könnten Sie mir während meines Aufenthaltes einen Wagen mit Fahrer zur Verfügung stellen?	*could you*
Würden Sie bitte in diesem Zimmer nicht rauchen?	*please*
Wären Sie bitte so freundlich, mir die Tür auf**zu**halten?	*would you be so kind as to*

More formally

Ich wäre Ihnen sehr zu Dank verpflichtet, wenn Sie in dieser sehr persönlichen Sache äußerste Diskretion walten lassen könnten	*I would be obliged if*
Ich wäre Ihnen sehr verbunden, wenn Sie mich baldmöglichst persönlich empfangen könnten	*I would be most obliged if*
Wir möchten Sie dringend auffordern, die ausgeliehenen Bücher so schnell wie möglich zurück**zu**bringen	*you are urgently requested to*
Wir danken im voraus für Ihre sofortige Antwort	*we would be grateful for*

5 Comparisons

5.1 Objective comparisons

Im Vergleich zu anderen Mittelgebirgen ist die Rhön arm an Bodenschätzen	*compared to/with*
Singapur hat, **verglichen mit** ähnlich großen Städten in den USA, eine niedrige Kriminalitätsrate	*if you compare it to/with*
Wenn man Hans **und** Paul **vergleicht**, ist Paul doch der angenehmere Charakter	*if you compare ... and*
Der Anteil stark geschädigter Bäume ist in Nordwestdeutschland mit 16 Prozent **vergleichsweise** gering	*comparatively*
Im Gegensatz zu den drückenden Außentemperaturen ist es in deiner Wohnung angenehm kühl	*in contrast with*
Es wird **immer schwieriger**, Museen zu Leihgaben zu überreden, weil die alten Kunstwerke Ortsveränderungen nicht ohne Schaden überstehen	*increasingly difficult*
Die Mitgliedsstaaten zeigen **immer weniger** Neigung, die Weltorganisation mit der Lösung neuer Konflikte zu beauftragen	*less and less*
Die neue Wohnung ist **so** groß **wie** die alte, **allerdings** etwas besser gelegen	*as ... as ..., but*
Es **sieht so aus wie** ein U-Boot, **nur** etwas kleiner	*is like ... but*
Das Design dieser Lampe **erinnert in gewisser Weise an** die Automodelle der 50er Jahre	*is reminiscent of*
Das neue Haus hat einen großen Garten, **während** unsere alte Wohnung nur einen kleinen Balkon hatte	*whereas*
Was ihn **von** vielen anderen Schriftstellern **unterscheidet**, ist sein Sprachwitz und seine positive Lebenshaltung	*what differentiates ... from*

5.2 Making favourable comparisons

Die Mitbewerber sind ihm aufgrund ihrer Qualifikation **weit überlegen**	*far superior*
Das Gulasch, das seine Mutter kocht, **ist eine Klasse für sich**	*is in a class of its own*
Ein Pianist **ist um mehrere Klassen besser** für den Ruf eines Restaurants in Wien **als** eine Zigeunerkapelle	*is very much better ... than*
Was das Klima angeht, **ist mir** Südfrankreich natürlich **lieber als** die Bretagne	*I prefer ... to*
Das **ist** noch **gar nichts im Vergleich zu** den Scherereien, die die FDP mit ihrer Figaro-Affäre hat.	*is nothing in comparison to*

5.3 Making unfavourable comparisons

Die Filmversion des Stoffes ist **bei weitem nicht so** interessant **wie** das Buch	*far less ... than*
Die Tonqualität ist **viel schlechter als** bei einem CD-Player	*much worse than*
Die heutigen Eßgewohnheiten **ähneln kaum mehr** denen vor 100 Jahren	*bear little resemblance to*
Man kann seinen ersten Roman **nicht mit** seinen Kurzgeschichten **vergleichen**	*does not compare with*
Seine Gedichte **können sich nicht mit** seiner Prosa **messen**	*cannot compare with*
Auf fachlichem Niveau **können** die Aushilfskräfte **nicht mit** den Facharbeitern **mithalten**	*cannot match*
Er **kann** seinem Bruder **nicht das Wasser reichen**	*can't hold a candle to*
Die Verteidigung **war** dem Ansturm der gegnerischen Mannschaft **in keiner Hinsicht gewachsen**	*were no match for*

5.4 Great similarity

Vieles in dem Roman **entspricht** der Wirklichkeit	*corresponds to*
Er behandelt Frauen **genauso** schlecht **wie** Männer	*just as ... as*
Ich **kann keinen Unterschied zwischen** diesen beiden Methoden **feststellen**	*I can see no difference between*
Mit seinem Sieg hat er bewiesen, **daß** sein Leistungsvermögen **an** das der Spitzenspieler **heranreicht**	*that ... match(es)*
Die Steuern dürfen nicht mehr erhöht werden, **das gleiche gilt für** die Staatsverschuldung	*the same goes for*
Rein äußerlich **sehen sich** die beiden Herren **sehr ähnlich**	*are very alike*
Das nimmt sich zeitlich **nichts, ob** wir über die Autobahn oder über die Landstraße fahren	*it makes no difference ... whether*

5.5 Great difference

Sie **sind** in ihrer Lebenseinstellung **nicht miteinander zu vergleichen**	*there is no comparison between*
Unsere Ansichten zu diesem Thema sind **grundverschieden**	*totally different*
Auf den ersten Blick **haben** die beiden **gar nichts gemein**	*have absolutely nothing in common*
Er **hat mit** dem normalen Bürger **nichts gemein**	*has nothing in common with*
Beide haben rote Haare, **aber da hört die Ähnlichkeit auch schon auf**	*but there the likeness ends*

6 Opinion

6.1 Asking for opinions

Was halten Sie (persönlich) von einer Anhebung der Benzinpreise?	*what do you (personally) think of*
Wie denken Sie über eine Reform des Schulwesens?	*what do you think about*
Wie sehen Sie die weitere Entwicklung?	*how do you see*
Wie schätzen Sie den Erfolg unserer Maßnahmen **ein?**	*how do you see*
Wie stehen Sie zu einer möglichen Mehrwertsteuererhöhung?	*what is your attitude to*
Mir wäre sehr an Ihrer fachlichen **Meinung zu** diesem Problem **gelegen**	*I would be very interested in your ... opinion on*
Es würde mich interessieren, was Ihre persönliche Meinung zu dieser Erbschaftsangelegenheit **ist**	*I would be interested to know your opinion on*

6.2 Expressing opinions

Ich meine, es ist höchste Zeit für Reformen	*I think*
Ich nehme (stark) an, daß wir alle mehr Steuern zahlen müssen	*I (fully) expect that*
Ich fürchte, wir haben keine andere Wahl	*I'm afraid*
Ich finde, der Bundeskanzler muß in der Hauptstadt präsent sein	*I feel*
Mir scheint, besser und knapper kann man sich über dieses Thema gar nicht auslassen	*it seems to me that*
Ich bin (fest) davon überzeugt, daß der Forschungsbedarf langfristig steigen wird	*I am convinced that*
Ich kann nicht umhin, darin einen weiteren Beweis für die geschwächte Stellung des Staates **zu** sehen	*I can't help*
Meiner Meinung nach ist die Wiederverwertung von Metallen nach wie vor sinnvoll	*in my opinion*
Ich bin der Meinung, daß es sich hierbei um ein Mißverständnis handelt	*I'm of the opinion that*
Ich kann mir (gut) vorstellen, daß unser Vorschlag die Zustimmung des Aufsichtsrates findet	*I have a (good) idea that*
Wenn Sie meine Meinung hören wollen: ich rechne fest mit einer Umsatzsteigerung	*if you want my opinion*
Wenn ich mich auch einmal zu diesem Problem äußern darf: Ich halte Ihren Vorschlag für keine gute Lösung	*if I could just say one thing about this problem*
Ich werde den Eindruck nicht los, daß mir hier etwas angehängt werden soll	*I can't help feeling that*
Ich habe den Eindruck, daß der Feminismus sich vor allem auf die weibliche Opferrolle konzentriert.	*I get the impression that*
So wie ich die Sache sehe, ist der Streit noch lange nicht beigelegt	*as I see it*
Wenn du mich fragst, geht es mit ihr bergab	*if you ask me*

6.3 Avoiding expressing one's opinion

Ich habe eigentlich keine besondere Meinung zu diesem Thema	*I have no particular opinion about*
Ich möchte mich zu dieser Angelegenheit **nicht äußern**	*I would rather not comment on*
Ich möchte mir darüber besser kein Urteil erlauben	*I'd rather not express an opinion on that*
Es ist schwer zu sagen, wie sich die Situation entwickeln wird	*it is hard to say*
Es scheint mir schwierig, die Lage objektiv **zu beurteilen**	*I find it hard to judge*
Darüber habe ich mir ehrlich gesagt noch keine Gedanken gemacht	*I've honestly never thought about it*
Ich habe keine Ahnung, ob sich der ganze Aufwand lohnt	*I have no idea whether*
Das kommt darauf an, was Sie unter Kunst **verstehen**	*it depends on what you mean by*

7 Likes, dislikes and preferences

7.1 Asking what someone likes

Würden Sie gerne zu den Salzburger Festspielen fahren?	*would you <u>like</u> to*
Würde es Ihnen Freude machen, am Sonntag mit in ein Konzert **zu** kommen?	*how would you <u>like</u> to*
Hätten Sie Lust auf eine Partie Schach?	*do you <u>feel</u> <u>like</u>*
Was würden Sie bevorzugen - ein neues Auto oder das Geld?	*which would you <u>prefer</u>*
Was mögen Sie lieber - Pop oder Klassik?	*which do you <u>prefer</u>*
Ich wüßte gern, was Ihre Lieblingsbeschäftigung **ist?**	*I would like to know what your <u>favourite</u> ... is*
Was machst du in den Ferien **am liebsten?**	*what do you <u>like</u> doing <u>best</u>*

7.2 Saying what you like

Ich gehe gern ins Kino	*I <u>like</u> going*
Die Führung durch den Dom **hat mir sehr gut gefallen**	*I really <u>enjoyed</u>*
Kreuzworträtsel **machen mir sehr viel Spaß**	*I really <u>enjoy</u> ... a lot*
Ich schätze es sehr, wenn Leute ihre Versprechungen halten	*I really <u>appreciate</u> it when*
Es geht doch nichts über ein gemütliches Frühstück am Sonntagmorgen	*there's nothing <u>like</u>*
Nichts mag ich lieber als eine heiße Tasse Kakao in der Dämmerung am Kamin zu trinken	*there's nothing I <u>like</u> better than*
Ich habe eine Schwäche für Schokoladenkuchen	*I have a <u>weakness</u> for*
Kaßlerbraten **ist mein Leib- und Magengericht**	*is my absolute <u>favourite</u> dish*

7.3 Saying what you dislike

Mir gefällt seine ganze Art **nicht**	*I don't <u>like</u>*
Ich mag keine langen Abendkleider	*I don't <u>like</u>*
Ich finde es schrecklich, immer auf der Flucht sein zu müssen	*I think it's <u>dreadful</u>*
Ich kann rechthaberische Leute **nicht ausstehen**	*I can't <u>stand</u>*
Ich habe die ewigen Tennisübertragungen **satt**	*I'm <u>fed</u> <u>up</u> <u>with</u>*
Die Schauspielerei **ist nichts für mich**	*isn't my cup of tea*
Die heutige Mode **ist nicht mein Fall**	*isn't my cup of tea*
Abwaschen **ist nicht gerade meine Lieblings**beschäftigung	*isn't exactly my <u>favourite</u>*
Mir graust vor dem eklig süßen Tee, den sie uns immer vorsetzt	*... makes me <u>sick</u>*
Ich bin nicht gerade begeistert von deinen Kommentaren	*I'm not wildly <u>enthusiastic</u> about*
Der neueste Hormonskandal **hat mir den Appetit auf** Rindfleisch **gründlich verleidet**	*has <u>put</u> me <u>off</u> ... completely*
Am meisten hasse ich seine ewigen Nörgeleien	*the thing I <u>hate</u> most is*
Nichts hasse ich mehr als stundenlang im Regen auf den Bus **zu** warten	*there's nothing I <u>hate</u> more than*

7.4 Saying what you prefer

Die roten Vorhänge **gefallen mir besser als** die blauen	*I <u>like</u> ... <u>better</u> than*
Ich mag Pfirsiche **lieber als** Aprikosen	*I <u>prefer</u> ... to*
Ich würde lieber ins Kino gehen, **als** zu Hause vor der Glotze **zu** hocken	*I would <u>rather</u> ... than*
Es wäre mir lieber, wenn ihr jetzt gehen würdet	*I'd <u>rather</u>*
Ich halte es für besser, wenn wir vorerst Stillschweigen bewahren	*I think it would be <u>better</u> if*
Lesen **ist eine meiner Lieblings**beschäftigungen	*is one of my <u>favourite</u>*
Sie hat eine ausgeprägte Vorliebe für Goldschmuck	*she has a marked <u>preference</u> for*
14 Uhr **würde mir besser passen**	*would <u>suit</u> me <u>better</u>*

7.5 Expressing indifference

Ich habe keine spezielle Vorliebe	*I don't have any <u>particular</u> <u>preference</u>*
Diese Art von Filmen **interessiert mich überhaupt nicht**	*doesn't <u>interest</u> me in the slightest*
Die Frage, ob die Romanfiguren wirklich existiert haben, **ist** dabei **völlig belanglos**	*of no <u>importance</u> whatsoever*
Dem Kunden **ist es völlig gleichgültig**, welche Technik im Hintergrund arbeitet	*doesn't really <u>care</u>*
Die Bilder blutiger Massaker **lassen ihn kalt**	*leave him <u>cold</u>*
Es ist mir egal, was die Leute von mir denken	*I don't <u>care</u>*
Ganz wie du willst, **mir ist alles recht**	*I'm not <u>bothered</u>*
Wofür er sein Geld zum Fenster rausschmeißt, **ist mir doch schnuppe**	*<u>I couldn't</u> <u>care</u> <u>less</u>*

8 Intentions and desires

8.1 Asking what someone intends to do

Was beabsichtigen Sie zu tun?	*what do you intend to do*
Was haben Sie am Wochenende **vor?**	*what plans do you have for*
Wie hatten Sie sich Ihr weiteres Vorgehen in dieser Sache **vorgestellt?**	*how had you envisaged*
Was versprechen Sie sich von derlei drastischen Maßnahmen?	*what do you expect to achieve by*
Welche Vorsätze haben Sie für das neue Jahr?	*what resolutions have you made*
Was bezwecken Sie damit?	*what do you expect to gain by that*
Ich wüßte gerne, was Sie nächste Woche **machen wollen**	*I would like to know what you want to do*
Haben Sie schon einen bestimmten Bewerber **ins Auge gefaßt?**	*have you already got your eye on*
Wir wären Ihnen dankbar, wenn Sie uns bis zum Monatsende mitteilen könnten, **was Sie** in dieser Sache **zu unternehmen gedenken**	*what you propose to do*
Habt ihr schon Pläne für die Ferien **geschmiedet?**	*have you made any plans*
Was führst du wieder im Schilde?	*what are you up to this time*

8.2 Saying what someone intends or wants to do

Tentatively

Er spielt mit dem Gedanken, noch dieses Jahr zurück**zu**treten	*he's toying with the idea of*
Eines Tages kaufe ich mir doch noch ein Ferienhaus in Südfrankreich	*one day I'm going to buy*
Sie hatte eigentlich nur vor, kurz bei euch vorbei**zu**schauen	*she just wanted to*
Ich wollte schon vorhin mit Ihnen darüber sprechen	*I meant to*

More assertively

Der Aufsichtsrat **hat die Absicht**, in der Innenstadt ein neues Hotel bauen **zu** lassen.	*intends to*
Unsere Absicht besteht darin, das gesamte Gewerbegebiet neu **zu** erschließen	*it is our intention to*
Wir haben uns fest vorgenommen, den Titel erfolgreich **zu** verteidigen	*we have every intention of*
Sie hat den Entschluß gefaßt, das Rauchen auf**zu**geben	*she has made up her mind to*
Ich habe beschlossen, schon morgen ab**zu**reisen	*I have decided to*
Ich gehe **ganz bestimmt** morgen zum Zahnarzt	*definitely*
Ich möchte wirklich ein paar Kilo abnehmen	*I'd really like to*
Ich plane eine Reise nach Ungarn	*I'm planning*
Er ist (wild) entschlossen, sein ganzes Leben auf den Kopf **zu** stellen	*he is (really) determined to*

8.3 Saying what someone does not intend or want to do

Ich möchte mich **nicht** zu diesem Thema äußern	*I would rather not*
Ich hatte eigentlich nicht vor, an diesem Seminar teil**zu**nehmen	*I didn't really intend to*
Ich habe nicht die (geringste) Absicht, den ganzen Abend Buchungsberichte durch**zu**sehen	*I have no (not the slightest) intention of*
Ich habe nicht das Verlangen nach neuen Abenteuern	*I have no desire for*
Ich gedenke nicht, mich noch einmal auf so ein Unternehmen ein**zu**lassen	*I don't propose to*
Ich bin nicht geneigt, mit Ihnen auch noch das Hotelzimmer **zu** teilen	*I have no intention of*
Ich bin nicht darauf erpicht, am Ende wieder als einziger den Kopf hinhalten **zu** müssen	*I'm not keen on the idea of*
Es kommt überhaupt nicht in Frage, daß ich morgen schon wieder die Spätschicht übernehme	*there's absolutely no question of*
Spätabends noch Gruselfilme angucken wollen, **kommt gar nicht in die Tüte**	*no way!*

8.4 Saying what you would like to do

Ich hätte jetzt Lust auf eine Partie Schach	*I feel like*
Ich möchte gerne die Kunstsammlung besuchen	*I would like to*
Ich hätte ihm **gerne** selbst zu seinem Erfolg gratuliert	*I would have liked to*
Wenn ich bloß mehr Zeit hätte!	*if only I*
Es wäre wünschenswert, daß die Bahn ihr Güterzentrum neben unserem Frachtpostamt baut	*it is to be hoped that*
Mein innigster Wunsch ist es, vor dem Ende meiner Tage noch einmal nach Paris **zu** fahren	*my dearest wish is to*
Ich würde jetzt **wahnsinnig gerne** eine Riesenportion Eis verschlingen	*what I'd really love*

9 Permission

9.1 Asking for permission

Könnte ich (vielleicht) in eine andere Arbeitsgruppe wechseln? — *could I*
Wäre es möglich, daß ich der Gerichtsverhandlung beiwohne? — *would it be possible to*
Darf ich mich zu Ihnen setzen? — *may I*
Macht es Ihnen etwas aus, wenn ich rauche? — *do you mind if*
Hätten Sie etwas dagegen, wenn ich das Fenster öffne? — *would you mind if*
Mit Ihrer Erlaubnis würde ich gern einige Änderungen am Grundriß vornehmen — *with your permission I'd like to*
Wenn es geht, möchte ich morgen frei nehmen — *if possible*
Ist hier Rauchen **gestattet?** — *is ... permitted*
Sind Ballspiele in diesem Park **erlaubt?** — *are ... permitted*

9.2 Giving permission

Ich habe nichts dagegen, wenn mein Name unter dem Artikel erscheint — *I don't object to*
Selbstverständlich können Sie die Arbeitsgruppe wechseln — *of course you can*
Gerne gestatten wir Ihnen Einsicht in unsere Steuerunterlagen — *we are pleased to allow you*
Rauchen **ist** hier ausdrücklich **gestattet** — *is permitted*
Sie dürfen ihm **gerne** berichten, was wir besprochen haben — *you can ... if you wish*
Ich erlaube Ihnen gerne, morgen einen Tag freizunehmen — *I'll happily give you permission to*

9.3 Refusing permission

Ich möchte nicht, daß mein Foto in diesem Zusammenhang veröffentlicht wird — *I do not want*
Sie können sich für dieses Seminar **nicht** mehr einschreiben — *you can't*
Sie sind nicht zu einer Hausdurchsuchung **befugt** — *you do not have authorization for*
Ich untersage Ihnen (in aller Form) die Teilnahme an dieser Veranstaltung — *I (absolutely) forbid you to*
Ich verbiete Ihnen, mein Grundstück **zu** betreten — *I forbid you to*
Leider muß ich diesem Plan **meine Zustimmung verweigern** — *unfortunately I cannot consent to*
Ich weigere mich, diesem waghalsigen Projekt zu**zu**stimmen — *I refuse to*
Ich kann dir beim besten Willen nicht erlauben, bei diesem Wetter mit dem Fahrrad in die Stadt **zu** fahren — *with the best will in the world I can't let you*

9.4 Saying that permission has been granted

Wir brauchen unseren Bericht **erst** nächste Woche ab**zu**geben — *we don't need to ... until*
Ich bin bevollmächtigt, während der Abwesenheit des Chefs Anweisungen **zu** erteilen — *I am authorized to*
Ich darf morgen freinehmen — *I can*
In dieser Prüfung **ist** die Benutzung von Wörterbüchern **gestattet** — *is permitted*

9.5 Saying that permission has been refused

Mein Arzt **hat mir** das Rauchen strengstens **untersagt** — *has forbidden me to*
Ich darf zur Zeit **nicht** arbeiten — *I mustn't*
Es ist nicht gestattet, Gefahrenstoffe einfach in den Hausmüll **zu** geben — *it is forbidden to*
Es ist gesetzlich **verboten**, rassistische Äußerungen **zu** publizieren — *... is prohibited*
Ich bin nicht berechtigt, Ihnen Auskünfte über unsere Klienten **zu** erteilen — *I am not authorized to*
Mein Chef **ist dagegen, daß** ich nächste Woche Urlaub nehme — *does not want*

10 Obligation

10.1 Saying what someone must do

Sie müssen sie **unbedingt** um Erlaubnis fragen, ehe Sie renovieren	*you really must*
Ich bin verpflichtet, Sie auf Ihre Rechte aus diesem Kaufvertrag hin**zu**weisen	*it is my duty to*
Ich kann nicht umhin, der Behörde die Einzelheiten mit**zu**teilen	*I cannot avoid*
Die Zulieferfirmen **sehen sich zu** weiteren Umstrukturierungen **gezwungen**	*find themselves forced into*
Die Neuregelung der Tierschutzverordnung **ist ein unbedingtes Erfordernis**	*is absolutely essential*
Es ist gesetzlich vorgeschrieben, alle Inhaltsstoffe auf der Verpackung an**zu**geben	*the law demands*
Alle Einwohner **sind aufgefordert**, den Anweisungen der Rettungsdienste Folge **zu** leisten	*are requested to*
Der Mieter **hat** pünktlich am 1. des Monats den fälligen Betrag **zu** überweisen	*must*
Ohne Hits **kann man** im Musikgeschäft **nicht** überleben	*no-one can ... without*
Es bleibt mir wohl nichts anderes übrig, als die unangenehme Aufgabe selbst **zu** übernehmen	*the only thing left for me to do is*
Ich habe keine andere Wahl, als gute Miene zum bösen Spiel **zu** machen	*I have no choice but to*

10.2 Enquiring if one is obliged to do something

Muß ich (wirklich) zu Hause bleiben?	*do I (really) have to*
Brauche ich eine Einladung?	*do I need*
Ist es (wirklich) nötig, noch heute abend ab**zu**reisen?	*do I/we (really) have to*
Erwartet man wirklich allen Ernstes von mir, daß ich diesen Unsinn gutheiße?	*am I really expected to*

10.3 Saying what someone is not obliged to do

Es ist nicht nötig, vorher noch einmal an**zu**rufen	*you don't have to*
Es ist Ihnen freigestellt, ob Sie den gesamten Betrag sofort oder in Raten zahlen	*you can choose whether*
Es zwingt Sie niemand, an diesem Treffen teil**zu**nehmen	*no-one is forcing you to*
Ich kann Sie nicht zu einem Geständnis **zwingen**, aber früher oder später finde ich doch die Wahrheit heraus	*I can't force you into*
Sie sind nicht verpflichtet, den Unfall **zu** melden	*it is not compulsory to*
Sie müssen ja nicht in der Kantine essen, **wenn** es Ihnen dort nicht schmeckt	*you don't have to ... if*

10.4 Saying what someone must not do

Unbefugten betreten **verboten!**	*prohibited*
Es ist nicht gestattet, hier **zu** parken	*it is forbidden to*
Sie können nicht einfach die Mittagspause für private Erledigungen nutzen	*you can't simply*
Sie dürfen nicht von vornherein mit einer Gehaltserhöhung rechnen	*you can't automatically*
Auf gar keinen Fall dürfen Sie einer Verfassungsänderung zustimmen	*whatever you do, don't*
Ich verbiete Ihnen, mein Büro je wieder **zu** betreten	*I forbid you to*
Wir können nicht zulassen, daß die Sozialausgaben noch weiter gekürzt werden.	*we cannot allow ... to*

11 Agreement

11.1 Agreeing with a statement

Ich bin ganz Ihrer Meinung — *I entirely agree*

Das Museum ist ein Ort der Inspiration. - **Ich kann Ihnen da nur beipflichten** — *I entirely agree (with you)*

Ich teile Ihre Meinung zum Verhältniswahlrecht **uneingeschränkt** — *I agree wholeheartedly with your opinion on*

Ich schließe mich den Worten des Vorredners **an** — *I entirely endorse*

Ich stehe voll hinter dieser Erklärung — *I entirely agree with*

Ich muß gestehen, daß er recht hat — *I must admit he's right*

Sie haben natürlich recht, wenn Sie ihn einen Verbrecher nennen, aber sagen Sie das lieber nicht laut — *you are quite right to*

Wie Sie schon richtig bemerkt haben, muß die Produktivität des neuen Standortes noch deutlich gesteigert werden — *as you so rightly say*

Im großen und ganzen stimme ich Ihnen zu, wenn Sie gegen diese unseriösen Praktiken protestieren — *broadly speaking, I agree with you*

Ich neige sehr zu Ihrer Ansicht, daß die Anklage eine unverhältnismäßig hohe Haftstrafe gefordert hat — *I am very much inclined to agree with you*

Der Baum hinter dem Haus muß weg. - **Meine Rede!** — *hear! hear!*

11.2 Agreeing to a proposal

Ich bin mit Ihrem Vorschlag **(voll und ganz) einverstanden** — *I am in (complete) agreement with*

Ich gehe auf Ihren Vorschlag ein und werde mich um alles weitere kümmern — *I agree with your proposal*

Wir schließen uns Ihrem Vorschlag **gerne an** — *we are happy to agree to/with*

Er hat Ihrem Vorschlag **zugestimmt, ich bin auch dafür** — *he agrees with ... and I am in favour (of it) as well*

Er ist in diesem Falle zwar nicht sachkundig, **geht** aber **mit unserer Entscheidung konform** — *agrees with our decision*

Ich werde dieses interessante Projekt **nach Kräften unterstützen** — *I will give my full support to*

Ich gebe gern meine Einwilligung zu den neuen Vorhaben — *I am happy to agree to*

Hiermit gebe ich mein Einverständnis zur gewerblichen Nutzung der Räume im Erdgeschoß des Hauses Augustusplatz 9 — *I hereby give my consent to*

Wir könnten ins Kino gehen. - **Gute Idee!** — *good idea!*

11.3 Agreeing to a request

Ich nehme Ihre freundliche Einladung **mit großem Vergnügen an** — *I have much pleasure in accepting*

Gerne komme ich Ihrer Bitte nach und begleiche die offenstehenden Rechnungen noch diese Woche — *I am happy to comply with your request*

Ich werde mich selbstverständlich an Ihre Anweisungen **halten** — *I will, of course, follow*

Ich werde mich bei der Auswahl der Stoffe **ganz nach Ihren Wünschen richten** — *I will respect your wishes completely in the matter of*

Es wird mir ein besonderes Vergnügen sein, Sie persönlich vom Bahnhof ab**zu**holen — *I shall be delighted to*

Der vorgeschlagene Termin **paßt mir sehr gut** — *suits me perfectly*

Die Verschiebung der Sitzung **kommt mir sehr gelegen** — *suits me perfectly*

12 Disagreement

12.1 Disagreeing with a statement

Ich bin nicht damit einverstanden, daß wir ihm allein die Schuld geben	*I don't agree that*
Ich teile Ihre Meinung zu dieser Frage **nicht**	*I don't share your views on*
Ich kann Ihren Standpunkt unmöglich akzeptieren	*I really cannot accept your point of view*
Ich muß Ihnen widersprechen: sein Kunstbegriff ist sehr vage gefaßt	*I disagree*
Ich kann mich Ihrer Interpretation von Goethes Spätwerk **nicht anschließen**	*I cannot subscribe to your interpretation*
Ich möchte bestreiten, daß dies das Ende seiner Karriere ist	*I don't agree that*
Ihren Schlußfolgerungen kann ich nicht zustimmen	*I disagree with your conclusions*
Ich verstehe nicht, wie Sie zu dieser Schlußfolgerung kommen	*I don't understand how*
Das mag ja Ihre Ansicht sein, **ich sehe die Sache anders**	*I see things differently*
Sie gehen fehl in der Annahme, der Roman habe keinen Bezug zur Wirklichkeit	*your assumption that ... is mistaken*
Sie liegen falsch, wenn Sie behaupten, die Verkehrsprobleme ließen sich durch höhere Benzinpreise lösen	*you are wrong to*
Sie irren sich, wenn Sie meinen, man könne diese Affäre so einfach unter den Teppich kehren	*you are mistaken if*
Sie täuschen sich in ihr: sie ist gar nicht so unschuldig, wie sie uns glauben machen will	*you are wrong about her*
Wie können Sie behaupten, daß ausgerechnet die Rentner die Gewinner der Einheit sind?	*how can you say that*
Ich verwahre mich gegen solche Vorwürfe	*I object to*
Ich bin völlig gegen diese hinterhältigen Machenschaften	*I am completely opposed to*

12.2 Disagreeing with a proposal

Ich kann Ihren Vorschlag nicht gutheißen	*I cannot agree to your proposal*
Ich kann Ihren Vorschlag **nicht uneingeschränkt billigen**	*I can't give ... my unqualified support*
Ich halte nicht viel von dieser Variante	*I don't think much of*
Vielen Dank für Ihr freundliches Angebot, aber ich komme allein zurecht	*thank you very much for your kind offer, but*
Es tut mir leid, aber ich kann Ihren Vorschlag **nicht annehmen**	*I am sorry but I cannot accept*
Sie können Ihr Programm jetzt **wirklich nicht** mehr ändern	*you really cannot*
Wir protestieren in aller Schärfe gegen den geplanten Autobahnneubau	*we wish to protest in the strongest possible terms against*
Von solchen Tagträumen **will ich nichts mehr hören**	*I don't want to hear any more about*
Du glaubst doch nicht im Ernst, daß ich mich auf solchen Unsinn einlasse	*you don't seriously think that*
Ich weigere mich, damit meine kostbare Zeit **zu** vertun	*I refuse to*

12.3 Refusing a request

Leider kann ich Ihrer Bitte nicht nachkommen	*I am afraid I cannot fulfil your request*
Ich kann Ihre Wünsche **leider nicht erfüllen**	*I am afraid I cannot comply with*
Es ist mir leider nicht möglich, Sie am Dienstag in meinem Büro **zu** empfangen	*I am afraid I will not be able to*
Ich bin nicht in der Lage, Ihnen Auskünfte **zu** erteilen	*I am not in a position to*
Ich kann das unmöglich bis Freitag **schaffen**	*I can't possibly manage it*
Sie können unmöglich von mir verlangen, daß ich die ganze Woche Überstunden mache	*you cannot expect me to*
Es kommt überhaupt nicht in Frage, daß Sie meine Sekretärin für Ihre Schreibarbeiten in Anspruch nehmen	*it is out of the question for ... to*
Es fällt mir nicht im Traum ein, Ihrer Bitte um Gehaltserhöhung nach**zu**kommen	*I wouldn't dream of*

In writing

Ich danke Ihnen vielmals für Ihre freundliche Einladung, **muß aber leider ablehnen**, da ich schon eine Verabredung habe	*but I am afraid I must decline*
Leider müssen wir Ihnen mitteilen, daß die bestellten Artikel zur Zeit nicht auf Lager sind	*we regret to have to inform you that*

13 Approval

Wirklich eine gute or **tolle Idee!** — *what a great idea!*
Gut, daß Sie uns so bald Bescheid gegeben haben — *(this context): thank you for*
Sie haben recht, wenn Sie sich über diese Arbeitsbedingungen beschweren — *you are right to ...*
Wir sind mit Ihrer Entscheidung, heute nicht mehr nach Paris abzureisen, **einverstanden** — *we agree with your decision*
Ich schätze Ihre Offenheit in dieser Frage **sehr** — *I greatly appreciate*
Ich finde es gut, daß Sie sich auf die wesentlichen Punkte beschränkt haben — *I think you were right to ...*
Es hat mir gut gefallen, daß die Diskussion sachlich verlaufen ist — *I liked the way*
Es spricht sehr für ihn, daß er sich erst jetzt mit dieser Bitte an Sie gewandt hat — *it says a lot for him that*
Dieser neue Vorschlag **verdient unsere Aufmerksamkeit** — *deserves our attention*
Der Entwurf des Bühnenbildes **ist** ihm **sehr gelungen** — *turned out really well*
Ich hätte es selbst nicht besser machen können — *I couldn't have made a better job of it myself*

More formally

Wir stimmen im großen und ganzen Ihren Vorschlägen **zu**, würden aber gern einige Details verändern — *we are in broad agreement with*
Der Autor **betont** diesen Aspekt **(völlig) zu Recht** — *(quite) rightly emphasizes*
Man kann ihren klaren Stil und ihre Eleganz **nur bewundern** — *one can only admire*
Wir sind von ihrer Arbeitsweise **sehr beeindruckt** — *we are very impressed with*
Wir begrüßen Ihre Eigeninitiative auf diesem Gebiet — *we welcome*
Wir sind hoch erfreut über diese positive Entwicklung — *we are delighted about*
Sein Vortrag **hat auf uns einen hervorragenden Eindruck gemacht** — *we were enormously impressed by*
Ich möchte meine Unterstützung für diese gute Sache **betonen** — *I would like to express my complete support for*

Ich habe eine hohe Meinung von seiner Forschungsarbeit — *I have a high opinion of*
Der Vorschlag, die Gewerbesteuer abzuschaffen, **wurde mit Wohlwollen zur Kenntnis genommen** — *was given a favourable reception*

14 Disapproval

Ich bin mit Ihrem Umgangston **gar nicht einverstanden** — *I really don't approve of*
Ich bin gar nicht glücklich über seine Wahl zum Parteivorsitzenden — *I am far from happy about*
Ich halte nicht viel von seiner Interpretation des Mephisto — *I don't think much of*
Ich bin von den Leistungen dieses Schülers **sehr enttäuscht** — *I am very disappointed with*
Ich muß energisch gegen diese Vorwürfe **protestieren** — *I must protest in the strongest possible terms against*

Die Kunden **sind nicht gerade begeistert von** unserer neuen Marketingstrategie — *are not particularly enthusiastic about*
Wir sind gegen eine totale Preiskontrolle — *we are opposed to*
Das hätte Ihnen **wirklich nicht** passieren **dürfen** — *that really should not have*
Er hätte besser die Polizei verständigt — *he would have been wiser to ...*
Ich finde, es war falsch, gleich so ausfällig **zu** werden — *I think it was wrong to*
Es gefällt mir überhaupt nicht, daß ausgerechnet diese Firma mit dem Bau beauftragt wurde — *I'm not at all happy that*
Es ist wirklich schade, daß die Stadt diese Truppe nicht mehr finanziell unterstützt — *it is a real shame that*
Es ist zu bedauern, daß dieses verantwortungslose Vorgehen wieder zu Gewaltausbrüchen geführt hat — *it is regrettable that*
Es paßt mir gar nicht, daß wir morgen schon wieder Besuch bekommen — *it is really inconvenient that*
Alle Parteien **verurteilten** diesen Anschlag **einstimmig** — *were united in their condemnation of*
Man darf diese undemokratischen Umtriebe **nicht tolerieren** — *we must not tolerate*
Ich bin eine erklärte Gegnerin jeglicher Tierversuche — *I am an avowed opponent of*
Was fällt dir ein, mich so anzuschreien — *how dare you*

15 Certainty, probability, possibility and capability

15.1 Expressing certainty

In an impersonal way

Es gibt nicht den geringsten Zweifel, daß dieses Gesetz morgen verabschiedet wird	*there is absolutely no doubt that*
Es läßt sich kaum bestreiten, daß die Arbeitslosenzahlen in dieser Region sehr hoch sind	*no-one can deny that*
Es steht völlig außer Frage, daß die Flüchtlinge in ihre Heimat zurückgeschickt werden	*there is no doubt that*
Es versteht sich von selbst, daß alle Abgeordneten zur ersten Sitzung erscheinen	*it goes without saying that*
Es hat sich deutlich gezeigt, daß man auf dem glatten Parkett der Börse auch ausrutschen kann	*it has been clearly established that*
Es läßt sich nicht leugnen, daß das Waldsterben weiter um sich greift	*no-one can deny that*
Man muß sich darüber im klaren sein, daß diese Friedensmission erhebliche Risiken birgt	*it must be realized that*
Zweifellos wird sich die wirtschaftliche Lage noch weiter verschlechtern	*undoubtedly*
Tatsache ist, daß sich das ökonomische Klima deutlich verbessert hat	*the fact is that*
Eine Neuregelung **läßt sich nicht vermeiden**	*is inevitable*

More directly

Wir können mit Sicherheit sagen, daß wichtige Informationen ohne unsere Zustimmung weitergegeben wurden	*we know for certain that*
Ich versichere Ihnen, daß wir das Problem bis morgen gelöst haben	*I can assure you that*
Ich bin mir sicher, daß ich den Brief gestern abgeschickt habe	*I am sure that*
Er ist davon überzeugt, daß er die Goldmedaille gewinnen wird	*he is convinced that*
Sie hören von meinem Anwalt. **Verlassen Sie sich darauf!**	*you can be sure of that*

15.2 Expressing probability

Höchstwahrscheinlich ist dieses Verfahren rechtswidrig	*it is highly probable that*
Wahrscheinlich wird die Sitzung vertagt	*probably*
Aller Wahrscheinlichkeit nach schlägt die Therapie an	*in all probability*
Anscheinend kann er nie genug kriegen	*it looks as if*
Es besteht Grund zu der Annahme, daß er von seinen Zielen abgerückt ist	*there are grounds for believing that*
Es deutet alles darauf hin, daß er zu schnell gefahren ist	*everything points to the fact that*
Es sieht fast so aus, als hätten die Spieler alles verlernt	*it looks as though*
Es könnte gut sein, daß ich heute abend kurz vorbeischaue	*... might well*
Es dürfte zu spät für eine Sanierung der maroden Finanzen **sein**	*it may well be too late for*
Es muß ihm etwas passiert sein	*must have happened*
Das Päckchen **müßte** morgen bei Ihnen ankommen	*should*
Es sollte mich nicht überraschen, wenn er jeden Moment wie ein Unschuldslamm hier hereinspaziert kommt	*it wouldn't surprise me if*
Es würde mich überhaupt nicht wundern, wenn er wieder zu spät kommt	*I wouldn't be at all surprised if*
Ich werde wohl nächste Woche nicht da sein	*I probably*
Ich sehe es schon kommen, daß ich noch einmal von ganz vorne anfangen muß	*I can see it coming*

15.3 Expressing possibility

Vielleicht ist das der neue Deutschlehrer	*perhaps*
Es könnte unter Umständen schon zu spät sein, um sich noch einzuschreiben	*it might already be too late*
Die Lage **kann sich** von einem Tag zum anderen schlagartig **ändern**	*could change*
Es ist immerhin möglich, daß man Ihnen nicht die Wahrheit gesagt hat	*after all, it is possible that*
Es besteht die Möglichkeit, daß uns die Konkurrenz zuvorgekommen ist	*there is a possibility that*
Es sieht so aus, als könnten wir den Bericht doch noch bis morgen fertigstellen	*it looks as though we should be able to ...*
Sehen Sie sich das Haus gut an: **es käme eventuell als** Bürogebäude **für uns in Frage**	*we might think about it for our*
Es ist durchaus im Rahmen des Möglichen, daß das Parlament einer Verfasssungsänderung zustimmt	*it is quite within the bounds of possibility that*
Vier Fünftel aller Maschinenbaubetriebe sind **potentiell** bankrott	*potentially*

15.4 Expressing capability

Können Sie mit einem Computer umgehen?	*do you know how*
Er kann hervorragend Gitarre spielen	*he can*
Alle Bewerber sollten **in der Lage sein**, einfache technische Texte zu übersetzen	*be able to*
Wissen Sie, wie diese neue Maschine bedient wird?	*do you know how*

16 Doubt, improbability, impossibility and incapability

16.1 Expressing doubt

In an impersonal way

Es ist zweifelhaft, ob der Außenminister dem Druck der Verhandlungspartner gewachsen ist	*it is doubtful whether*
Es besteht immer noch Ungewißheit über die Zahl der Todesopfer	*there is still some uncertainty about*
Es ist immer noch nicht sicher, ob er krank ist oder nur simuliert	*it is still not certain whether*
Es läßt sich noch nicht mit Sicherheit sagen, ob das Opfer den Anschlag überleben wird	*it is still impossible to say with any certainty whether*
Es gibt keinen Grund zu der Annahme, daß diese Methode umweltfreundlicher ist	*there is no reason to assume that*
Das muß nicht unbedingt bedeuten, daß sich die wirtschaftliche Lage schlagartig verbessern wird	*that does not necessarily mean that*

More directly

Ich bezweifele, daß ich das Pensum bis heute abend schaffe	*I doubt if*
Ich glaube nicht, daß wir je einen derart waghalsigen Plan hatten	*I don't think we ever*
Ich bin nicht sicher, ob ich Ihnen die richtige Zahl genannt habe	*I'm not sure whether*
Ich bin nicht überzeugt, daß diese Methode funktioniert	*I'm not sure whether*
Ich frage mich, ob es sich überhaupt lohnt, sich soviel Mühe zu machen	*I wonder if*
Es würde mich sehr wundern, wenn er noch einmal wiederkäme	*I would be very surprised if*
Wir wissen noch immer nicht genau, wie wir das Wohnzimmer streichen wollen	*we still don't know exactly how*
Sie tappen immer noch im Dunkeln, was das Motiv für die Tat **angeht**	*they are still in the dark about*

16.2 Expressing improbability

Einen Sieger wird es am Sonntag **wahrscheinlich nicht** geben	*probably not*
Es ist höchst unwahrscheinlich, daß die Regierung auf Atomenergie verzichtet	*it is highly unlikely that*
Es besteht die Gefahr, daß Sie Ihren Paß nicht mehr rechtzeitig bekommen	*there is a risk that*
Es ist fraglich, ob der Verein sich in der Bundesliga halten kann	*it is doubtful whether*
Es würde mich wirklich überraschen, wenn er diese Prüfung besteht	*I would be very surprised if*
Allem Anschein nach ist sie **nicht** wirklich krank	*to all appearances ... is not*
Die Chancen, diesen Winter ohne Grippe **zu** überstehen, **sind äußerst gering**	*the chances of ... are very slim*
Ich fürchte, daß es uns nicht gelingen wird, ihn **zu** überzeugen	*I am afraid that we will not succeed in*
Sollte wider Erwarten doch etwas Passendes dabei sein, gebe ich Ihnen Bescheid	*in the unlikely event that*
Ein Umschwung der öffentlichen Meinung **steht nicht zu erwarten**	*is not to be expected*

16.3 Expressing impossibility

Es ist unmöglich, daß diese Schäden beim Verladen entstanden sind	*... cannot possibly*
Es ist ausgeschlossen, daß wir Ihnen schon nächste Woche fertige Skizzen zeigen können	*there is no way we can*
Es kann sich einfach nicht um ein und dieselbe Person **handeln**	*it can't possibly be*
Ich kann mir unmöglich nächste Woche schon wieder freinehmen	*I can't possibly*
Auf gar keinen Fall wird diese Übersetzung noch vor Weihnachten fertig	*there is no way that*
Leider **ist es mir nicht möglich**, diese Einladung an**zu**nehmen	*I am unable to*
Eine Zusammenarbeit mit dieser Firma **kommt nicht in Frage**	*is out of the question*
Der Staatsstreich **macht** jede Verhandlung fürs erste **unmöglich**	*has ruled out*
Es besteht nicht die geringste Möglichkeit einer friedlichen Lösung	*there is not the remotest chance of*

16.4 Expressing incapability

Ich kann nicht schwimmen	*I can't*
Ich kann kein Französisch	*I don't speak*
Er ist nicht in der Lage *or* **imstande**, selbständig Entscheidungen **zu** fällen	*he is totally incapable of*
Ich weiß nicht, wie man Topfkuchen bäckt	*I don't know how*
Er hat einfach kein Talent für Sprachen	*he has simply no gift for*
Er ist zu einer solchen Tat **nicht fähig**	*he is incapable of*
Ich bin nicht sehr gut in Mathematik	*I am not very good at*
Sie waren dieser schweren Aufgabe **nicht gewachsen**	*they were not up to*

17 Explanations

17.1 Emphasizing the reason for something

Angesichts der schwierigen Finanzlage müssen wir das Projekt vorerst auf Eis legen	*in view of*
In Anbetracht der Tatsache, daß die Wahlen über die Macht entscheiden, ist es logisch, daß die Siegerparteien Einfluß auf die Medien gewinnen	*in view of the fact that*
Dank steigender Auftragszahlen wird sich der Umsatz erhöhen	*thanks to*
Die U-Bahn-Station wurde **aus** Sicherheits**gründen** geschlossen	*for ... reasons*
Er wurde **aus Mangel an** Beweisen freigesprochen	*for lack of*
Kurzsichtigkeit läßt sich **mittels** Lasertherapie behandeln	*by means of*
Bei solchen Windverhältnissen sollte man sich besser nicht aufs offene Meer wagen	*in*
Durch seine Popularität hat er einen gewissen Einfluß auf die Medien	*through*
Aufgrund der schlechten Sichtverhältnisse verschiebt sich der Abflug auf unbestimmte Zeit	*owing to*
Wegen des erhöhten Koffeingehaltes sollte dieses Produkt nur in geringen Mengen verzehrt werden	*because of*
Infolge des Konsums berauschender Mittel war der Angeklagte nicht zurechnungsfähig	*as a result of*
Mehrere Bauarbeiter fanden den Tod, **weil** die Gerüste nur unzureichend gesichert waren	*because*
Wir haben Ihren Roman nicht lesen können, **denn** wir sind ein Verlag und kein Lektürezirkel	*because*
Fruchtsäfte sollten nicht eiskalt getrunken werden, **da** sonst leicht eine Magenreizung entstehen kann	*as*
Er ist ohnmächtig geworden, und **deswegen** erinnert er sich an nichts mehr	*therefore*
Sie hat die Angestellten **nur aus dem einen Grund** zusammengerufen, **um** mit ihnen ein Machtwort **zu** reden	*simply (in order) to*
Der Präsident verurteilte den Bericht **mit der Begründung**, er enthalte nicht zu rechtfertigende Schlußfolgerungen	*claiming*
Wenn ihm keine überzeugende Erklärung für sein Handeln einfällt, wird er sich schon bald vor dem Militärgericht wiederfinden	*if*
Solange keine Besserung eintritt, dürfen Sie das Haus nicht verlassen	*as long as*

17.2 Other useful vocabulary

Die Unfall**ursache war** überhöhte Geschwindigkeit bei schlechter Sicht	*the ... was caused by*
Das war so: ich stand auf der Leiter, als es an der Tür klingelte ...	*it was like this:*
Es geht um folgendes: ich möchte gerne meine Wohnung renovieren	*it's like this:*
Das Problem ist, daß wir ziemlich weit weg vom Bahnhof wohnen	*the trouble is,*
Die Sache ist die: ich habe ihm den Kredit schon versprochen	*the thing is,*
Es läßt sich alles auf diese Versorgungsprobleme **zurückführen**	*it is all due/down to*
Das **läßt sich alles aus** seiner Weltanschauung **herleiten**	*all stems from*
Der Börsenkrach **hat** diese Katastrophe **ausgelöst**	*triggered off*
Das **läßt sich** alles **durch** die Zerstörung der Regenwälder **erklären**	*can be attributed to*
Woran liegt es, daß der Neubau nicht vorankommt?	*why is it that*
Das **hat** natürlich wieder **mit** dem Treibhauseffekt **zu tun**	*is connected with*
Es hat sich dann **herausgestellt, daß** er gar kein Kapital hatte	*it emerged that*
Ich schreibe das alles seinem krankhaften Ehrgeiz **zu**	*I put it all down to*
Und aus genau diesem Grund möchte ich nicht, daß Sie mir helfen	*that is exactly why*
Der Grund für ihren kometenhaften Aufstieg ist wohl nicht nur in ihrer unbestrittenen Begabung, sondern auch in ihrem Fleiß zu suchen	*the reason for ...*
Sein plötzliches Verschwinden **gab Anlaß zu** wüsten Spekulationen	*gave rise to*

18 Apologies

18.1 Apologizing for one's actions

Entschuldigen Sie bitte, ich habe mich verwählt	*I'm sorry*
Bitte verzeihen Sie, daß ich nicht früher angerufen habe	*please forgive me for not*
Es tut mir schrecklich leid, daß ich gestern nicht kommen konnte	*I'm terribly sorry that*
Ich möchte Sie wirklich wegen dieses Mißverständnisses **um Entschuldigung bitten**	*I really must apologize for*
Können Sie mir noch einmal **verzeihen, daß ich** die Karten nicht besorgt habe?	*can you forgive me for*
Es ist einfach unverzeihlich, daß ich ihren Geburtstag vergessen **habe**	*it was unforgivable of me to ...*
Ich bitte tausendmal um Entschuldigung! Ich wollte Ihnen nicht zu nahe treten	*I really am most terribly sorry*
Wir möchten Sie wegen des bedauerlichen Zwischenfalls **in aller Form um Verzeihung bitten**	*we should like to offer our most sincere apologies for*
Dürfen wir Sie wegen der gestrigen Störung **um Nachsicht bitten**	*we hope that you will forgive us for*
Ich bedaure zutiefst, daß Sie sich durch meine Ausführungen in Ihrer persönlichen Ehre gekränkt sehen	*I greatly regret that*

18.2 Apologizing for being unable to do something

Es ist wirklich schade, aber wir können euch nicht begleiten	*it is a real shame, but*
Bedauerlicherweise können wir Ihren Artikel in der Märzausgabe nicht mehr veröffentlichen	*regrettably*
Zu unserem größten Bedauern können wir Ihrer Einladung nicht nachkommen	*much to our regret*
Ich bin untröstlich darüber, daß ich Ihren Vortrag versäumen muß	*I am deeply sorry that*
Wir müssen Ihnen leider mitteilen, daß Ihr Antrag abgelehnt wurde	*we regret to inform you that*
Ich kann es mir nicht verzeihen, daß ich Ihnen in dieser für Sie so schweren Zeit nicht beistehen konnte	*I cannot forgive myself for*

18.3 Admitting responsibility

Es ist ganz allein meine Schuld, ich hätte sie **nicht** allein lassen **dürfen**	*it's entirely my fault: I shouldn't have*
Ich übernehme die volle Verantwortung für diesen Irrtum	*I take full responsibility for*
Wir hatten keine andere Wahl, als die Polizei zu informieren	*we had no choice but to*
Wir waren der irrigen Meinung, daß wir Ihnen damit helfen würden	*we mistakenly believed that*
Es war ein Fehler unserer Buchhaltung, daß Sie zwei Rechnungen über den gleichen Betrag bekommen haben	*because of an error in our Accounts Department*
Das **hätte ich nie** sagen **sollen**	*I should never have*
Ich weiß, daß es nicht richtig war, ihm das Auto **zu** leihen, aber ...	*I know I was wrong to*
Ich gebe zu, daß ich vielleicht nicht gut vorbereitet war, **aber** ...	*I admit that ... but*
Hätte ich doch nie ein Sterbenswörtchen gesagt!	*I wish I had never*
Dummerweise habe ich dann gleich bei ihnen angerufen	*foolishly*

18.4 Disclaiming responsibility

Ich hoffe, daß Sie Verständnis für diese Verzögerung **haben**, die sich ohne unsere Schuld ergeben hat	*I hope that you will pardon*
Sicher können Sie verstehen, daß wir in dieser Situation gar nicht anders reagieren konnten	*I am sure that you will appreciate that*
Ich habe diese Vase **ganz bestimmt nicht mit Absicht** fallen lassen, sie ist mir aus der Hand gerutscht	*I certainly didn't ... deliberately*
Es war doch nur meine Absicht, Sie nicht mit solchen Kleinigkeiten **zu belästigen**	*I simply wanted to avoid bothering you*
Ich weiß (auch) nicht, wie das passieren konnte	*I don't know how it happened (either)*

19 Job Applications

LEBENSLAUF

Persönliche Daten:	Müller, Dorothea Hinter dem Sausee 25 60388 Frankfurt/Main Tel.: 069/324 754 Fax: 069/324 755 geb. am 21.04.1964 in Nürnberg ledig
Schulausbildung:[1]	
1970 - 1974	Grundschule Nürnberg
1974 - 1983	Humboldt-Gymnasium Nürnberg
Hochschulausbildung:[2]	
10/1983 - 4/1989	Goethe-Universität Frankfurt/Main Studium der Psychologie Schwerpunkte: Betriebs- und Arbeitspsychologie
Praktika:	
1985	Personalabteilung Volkswagen, Wolfsburg
1987	Marketingabteilung Siemens, München
Berufspraxis:	
6/89 - 6/92	Wissenschaftliche Assistentin Lehrstuhl für Arbeitspsychologie Goethe-Universität Frankfurt/Main
7/92 - 6/94	Tutor für Organisationspsychologie Universität Birmingham/Großbritannien
seit 7/94	Referentin für Arbeitspsychologie bei der IHK Frankfurt/Main
Besondere Kenntnisse:	
EDV	Textverarbeitung (Word für Windows) Tabellenkalkulation (Excel) Präsentationsprogramme (PowerPoint)
Fremdsprachen	Englisch sehr gut Russisch Grundkenntnisse

Frankfurt/Main,
31. Juli 1997

Dorothea Müller
Hinter dem Sausee 25
60388 Frankfurt/Main
Tel.: 069/324 754
Fax: 069/324 755

Frankfurt, 31. Juli 1997

Infocomp International AG[3]
Personalabteilung
Postfach 70
40489 Düsseldorf

Ihre Anzeige vom 21.6.97 in der „Frankfurter Allgemeinen Zeitung"

Sehr geehrte Damen und Herren,

Für die von Ihnen ausgeschriebene Stelle als Personalreferentin im Bereich Personalentwicklung erfülle ich alle Voraussetzungen.

Ich bin Diplompsychologin und arbeite als Referentin bei der IHK Frankfurt. Mein Tätigkeitsbereich umfaßt dabei die Konzeption, Organisation und Durchführung von Weiterbildungsseminaren für Fach- und Führungskräfte in Handel und Management sowie die psychologische Beratertätigkeit in Fragen der beruflichen Weiterbildung.

Für die Stelle bringe ich eine breite fächerübergreifende Ausbildung und eine umfassende Allgemeinbildung mit. Hinzu kommen Spezialkenntnisse der Arbeits- und Betriebspsychologie. Ich verfüge über mehrjährige Erfahrung im Umgang mit der EDV und bin selbständiges Arbeiten gewöhnt.

Ich möchte mein Können gerne in Ihrem Unternehmen beweisen. Über eine persönliche Vorstellung würde ich mich sehr freuen.

Mit freundlichen Grüßen

Dorothea Müller

Anlagen
Lebenslauf mit Foto
Zeugniskopien

---

1 People with British or American etc qualifications applying for jobs in a German-speaking country might use some form of wording like "entspricht Abitur (3 A-levels)", "entspricht Staatsprüfung (MA Hons)" etc.

2 Note that when applying for a job in Germany you must send photocopies of certificates for all qualifications gained as well as your CV.

3 This address is appropriate when writing to a firm or institution. However, when writing to the holder of a particular post, you should put:

An den
Personaldirektor
„Mensch und Maschine" GmbH etc.

In this case, you should begin your letter with "Sehr geehrter Herr Personaldirektor" and end with "mit freundlichen Grüßen".

If you know the name of the person you should write:

An Herrn
Josef Schmidthuber
Personaldirektor
„Mensch und Maschine" GmbH

OR

An Frau
Dr. Christine Meier
Leiterin der Personalabteilung
„Mensch und Maschine" GmbH

Your letter should then begin "Sehr geehrter Herr Schmidthuber" or "Sehr geehrte Frau Dr. Meier".

19.1 Opening the letter

Ich beziehe mich auf Ihre Stellenanzeige in der heutigen Ausgabe der „Süddeutschen Zeitung" **und möchte Sie bitten, mir nähere Angaben über** die Stelle **zuzusenden**

in reply to ... I should be grateful if you would please send me further details of

Ich möchte mich um die Stelle einer Reiseleiterin **bewerben, die Sie** im „Globus" vom Mai **ausgeschrieben haben**

I wish to apply for the post of ... which you advertised

Ich bewerbe mich auf Ihr Stellenangebot in der heutigen Ausgabe der „Sächsischen Zeitung", **weil ich sicher bin,** Ihren Anforderungen an einen Betriebswirt zu entsprechen

I refer to your advertisement ... I am sure

Auf das von Ihnen ausgeschriebene Stellenangebot bewerbe ich mich gern, weil es meiner beruflichen Qualifikation und meinen Erwartungen entspricht

I have pleasure in applying for the advertised position, as

Ich möchte sehr gern während meiner Sommersemesterferien in Österreich **arbeiten** (möglichst im Hotelbereich) **und würde mich freuen, wenn Sie eine entsprechende Arbeit für mich hätten**

I am anxious to find a job in ... during my summer vacation from University ..., and wonder whether you are able to offer me work in any capacity

19.2 Detailing your experience and giving your reasons for applying

Englisch **ist meine Muttersprache. Ich verfüge über sehr gute** Deutsch**kenntnisse** in Wort und Schrift. **Außerdem besitze ich solide Grundkenntnisse** des Russischen

my first language is ... I have an excellent command of ... I also have a working knowledge of

Ich habe drei Jahre Büro**erfahrung**

I have ... experience of

Ich arbeite seit 3 Jahren in der Maschinenbaufirma Komplex in Hannover. **Meine Aufgabe besteht im** Anfertigen von technischen Zeichnungen aller Art sowie von elektronischen Schaltplänen

I have been working for ... My duties consist of

Ich besitze gute Kenntnisse im Umgang mit Tabellenkalkulationen und Textverarbeitungen

I am an experienced user of

Ich habe zwar keine Erfahrung auf diesem speziellen Arbeitsgebiet, **habe aber** verschiedene Ferienjobs ausgeübt

although I have no previous experience ..., I have had

Auf Verlangen kann ich Ihnen jederzeit **Zeugnisse** meiner früheren Arbeitgeber **vorlegen**

I can supply references from ..., if you would like them

Zur Zeit verdiene ich ... im Jahr **und habe einen jährlichen Anspruch auf** 25 Tage bezahlten **Urlaub**

my present salary is ..., and I have ... holiday per year

Ich interessiere mich ganz besonders für diese Stelle, weil ich sehr gerne im Verlagswesen arbeiten möchte

I am particularly interested in this job, as

Ich möchte in der Schweiz arbeiten, **um meine Sprachkenntnisse zu verbessern und Erfahrungen** in der Hotelbranche **zu sammeln**

I would like to ... in order to improve my languages and to gain experience

19.3 Closing the letter

Ich bin seit 5 Jahren in ungekündigter Stellung als Leiterin der Fertigung in einem Spitzenunternehmen der Halbleiterbranche **tätig und möchte mich verändern**

for the past five years I have been working ... but I would welcome a change

Ich könnte Ihnen ab April 1998 **zur Verfügung stehen**

I shall be available from

Die Tätigkeit könnte ich zum frühestmöglichen Termin **aufnehmen**

I am available to commence duties at

Ich würde mich freuen, in Ihrem Unternehmen **meine Fähigkeiten beweisen zu können**

I would be pleased to use my skills for

Über eine persönliche Vorstellung würde ich mich sehr freuen

I would be happy to attend for interview

Wenn Sie an meiner Bewerbung interessiert sind, **sende ich Ihnen gerne meine vollständigen Bewerbungsunterlagen zu**

I shall be pleased to forward my full application pack

19.4 Asking for and giving references

Ich habe mich um eine Stelle als Privatsekretärin beworben und bin in die engere Wahl gezogen worden. Man hat mich nun gebeten, Zeugnisse meiner früheren Arbeitgeber vorzulegen. **Ich wäre Ihnen sehr dankbar, wenn Sie mir so bald wie möglich ein Zeugnis über meine Tätigkeit in Ihrer Kanzlei zuschicken könnten.**

I should be very grateful if you would send me a reference relating to my time in your office as soon as possible

Wir wären Ihnen sehr dankbar, wenn Sie uns mitteilen könnten, ob er Ihrer Meinung nach **für diesen Posten geeignet ist**

I should be grateful if you would kindly let me know whether ... is suitable for this post

Ihre Antwort wird selbstverständlich streng vertraulich behandelt

your answer will be treated in strict confidence

Könnten Sie uns bitte in Ihrer Antwort mitteilen, wie lange und in welcher Eigenschaft Sie Frau Heinisch kennen und **ob Sie sie für diese Tätigkeit empfehlen können**

would you be kind enough to mention in your reply ... whether you can recommend her for this type of employment

19.5 Accepting and refusing

Ich komme gern am Donnerstag, dem 24. März, um 10.30 Uhr **zu einem Vorstellungsgespräch** in Ihr Büro

I shall be delighted to attend for interview

Ich nehme das Angebot, in Ihrer Klinik als Krankengymnastin arbeiten zu können, **gerne an und werde den Dienst am vorgesehenen Eintrittsdatum antreten**

I am pleased to accept your offer of ... and will take up my duties on the stated date

Es hat mich sehr gefreut, daß Sie an meiner Mitarbeit interessiert sind, **ich habe mich jedoch zwischenzeitlich für ein anderes Angebot entschieden**

however, in the interim, I have accepted another offer

20 Commercial correspondence

Architekturbüro Mittermayer & Partner
Bürogebäude, Hotels, Villen
Eschenallee 67
52078 Aachen
Tel.: 0241/453 2376 Durchwahl: 0241/453 23
Fax: 0241/453 2312 email: mittermayer@aachen.co.de

City Datenservice GmbH
Alexanderstr. 43
52062 Aachen

Ihr Zeichen	Unser Zeichen	Ihr Schreiben vom	Datum
	EDV 25/97	23. Mai 1997	31. Mai 1997

Sehr geehrte Frau Ackermann,

bezugnehmend auf Ihr Schreiben vom 23. Mai 1997 bestätigen wir den von Ihnen vorgeschlagenen Termin für eine Vorführung Ihres Programmes "Draw Help". Für die notwendigen Absprachen wenden Sie sich bitte an Frau Dembinski (Apparat 51).

Des weiteren möchten wir Sie bitten, uns einen Kostenvoranschlag für eine Schulung unserer Mitarbeiter an diesem System zu unterbreiten. Wir sind auch an einem Programm zur statischen Berechnung von Dachkonstruktionen interessiert und bitten um ein diesbezügliches Angebot.

Mit freundlichen Grüßen

Jürgen Schneider

Jürgen Schneider
Leiter Datenverarbeitung

Eduard Papenbrock & Sohn
Glas und Porzellan
Genthiner Str. 20
39114 Magdeburg
Tel.: 0391/857 902 Fax: 0391/857 903

Eschebach Porzellan
Verkaufsabteilung
z. Hd. Frau Klein
Erfurter Str. 105
98693 Ilmenau/Thüringen

Magdeburg, 24. Juni 1997

Sehr geehrte Frau Klein,

vielen Dank für die Zusendung Ihres neuesten Kataloges.

Hiermit bestellen wir 100 Exemplare des Speiseservice „Thüringen" sowie 75 Exemplare des Kaffeegedeckes „Junior".

Mehrere Kunden möchten von Ihrer Nachkaufgarantie Gebrauch machen. Daher bitten wir zusätzlich um die Lieferung folgender Posten:

2 Speiseteller aus der Serie „Inselberg"
1 Untertasse aus der Serie „Oberhof"
1 Sauciere aus der Serie „Schmalkalden"

Wir erwarten Ihre Lieferung fristgerecht innerhalb der nächsten 14 Tage und verbleiben

mit freundlichen Grüßen

Herbert Papenbrock

Herbert Papenbrock
Inhaber

20.1 Making an enquiry

Ihrer Anzeige in der Mai-Ausgabe von „Sport und Freizeit" **entnehmen wir, daß** Sie eine neue Sportartikelserie anbieten	*we see from your advertisement in the May edition of ... that*
Wir bitten Sie, uns nähere Angaben über das neue Sortiment **zukommen zu lassen und uns auch über** Preise, Rabatte und Lieferzeiten **zu informieren**	*we should be grateful if you would send us full details of ..., including*

20.2 Replying to an enquiry

Wir beziehen uns auf Ihre Anfrage vom 3. März **und senden Ihnen in der Anlage Einzelheiten zu** unserem derzeitigen Warenangebot **sowie** unsere Preisliste	*in response to your enquiry of ..., we enclose details of ... and*
Wir danken Ihnen für Ihre Anfrage vom 6. Juni **und erlauben uns, Ihnen folgendes Angebot zu machen:**	*we thank you for your enquiry of ..., and are pleased to submit the following offer:*
Dieses Angebot gilt bei verbindlicher **Bestellung** vor dem 31. Januar des nächsten Jahres	*this offer is subject to acceptance*

20.3 Placing an order

Bitte senden Sie uns umgehend die folgenden Posten in den angegebenen Größen und Stückzahlen zu: ...	*please send us the following items by return*
Diese Bestellung bezieht sich auf Ihre aktuelle Preisliste, und **wir gehen von Ihrem normalen Mengenrabatt** von 10% **aus**	*this order is based on ..., assuming your usual discount of ... on bulk orders*
Anbei unsere Bestellung Nr. 12-556 **über** 3000 Paar feuerfeste Handschuhe	*please find enclosed our order No ... for*

20.4 Replying to an order

Wir danken Ihnen für Ihre Bestellung vom 9. Mai und werden sie so bald wie möglich ausführen	*we thank you for your order of*
Wir brauchen etwa drei Wochen, **um Ihren Auftrag auszuführen**	*we shall require ... to complete this order*
Leider wird sich wegen eines Engpasses in der Versorgung mit Rohmaterialien **der Beginn der Produktion** bis zum 1. April **verzögern**	*unfortunately, because of ..., we cannot start manufacture*

20.5 Delivery

Unsere Lieferzeit beträgt 2 Monate, vom Eingang einer verbindlichen Bestellung aus gerechnet	*our delivery time is*
Wir erwarten ihre Lieferanweisungen	*we await your instructions with regard to delivery*
Diese Waren sind am 4. Juli per Bahn an Sie **abgegangen**	*these goods were sent ... on*
Die bestellte Ware **ist bei uns noch nicht eingegangen**	*we have not yet received*
Sollten wir die bestellten Waren nicht bis zum Ende des Monats erhalten, **sehen wir uns gezwungen, unsere Bestellung zu stornieren**	*the order will be formally cancelled*
Wir bestätigen den Erhalt der beiden von Ihnen am 3. März versandten Lieferungen	*we acknowledge receipt of*

20.6 Complaining and replying to a complaint

Wir möchten Sie auf einen Fehler in der hier am 3. Februar eingegangen Lieferung **hinweisen**	*we wish to draw your attention to an error in*
Wir bedauern sehr, daß die Lieferung nicht einwandfrei war, und sind bereit, die entsprechenden Waren zu ersetzen	*we regret that the consignment was unsatisfactory*
Für diesen Schaden **können wir keine Haftung übernehmen**	*we cannot accept responsibility for*

20.7 Payment

Anbei unsere Rechnung Nr. 64321	*please find enclosed our invoice No.*
Der zu zahlende Gesamtbetrag ist ...	*the total amount payable is ...*
Wir wären Ihnen dankbar, **wenn Sie diese Rechnung umgehend begleichen könnten**	*if you would attend to this account immediately*
In der Anlage übersenden wir Ihnen einen Scheck über ... zur Begleichung Ihrer Rechnung Nr. 67813/31	*we have pleasure in enclosing our cheque for ... in settlement of your invoice*
Wir müssen Sie leider auf einen Fehler in Ihrer Rechnung Nr. 12-556 **aufmerksam machen.** Wir wären Ihnen dankbar, wenn Sie die Rechnung entsprechend berichtigen könnten	*we must point out an error in*
In der Anlage erhalten Sie eine Gutschrift über diesen Betrag	*we enclose a credit note for*

21 General correspondence

Hamburg, 22. Mai 1997

Liebe Thekla und Andreas,

vielen Dank für Euren Brief, der schon vor einiger Zeit hier ankam. Es tut mir leid, daß ich so lange nicht geantwortet habe, aber seit meinem Umzug hierher bleibt mir kaum ein ruhiger Augenblick, um ein paar Briefe zu beantworten. Das soll aber nicht heißen, daß ich Euch vergessen habe. Im Gegenteil, ich denke oft an die gemeinsame Zeit in Berlin zurück.

Mittlerweile habe ich mich hier schon recht gut eingelebt. Meine Wohnung muß noch ein bißchen renoviert werden, aber ich hoffe, damit bald fertig zu sein. Die neue Arbeitsstelle gefällt mir sehr gut, so daß ich den Wechsel hierher keinesfalls bedaure.

Wenn Ihr im Sommer etwas Zeit habt, seid Ihr natürlich ganz herzlich eingeladen, ein paar Tage bei mir in Hamburg zu verbringen. Ich hoffe, es läßt sich einrichten, denn ich würde mich über ein Wiedersehen mit Euch sehr freuen.

Viele liebe Grüße auch an Beate und Jens
von Eurer

Christine

Elke Linke
Hertzstr. 10
13158 Berlin

Berlin, 13. Juli 1997

Edition Peters
Versandabteilung
Nürnberger Str. 35
04103 Leipzig

Sehr geehrte Damen und Herren,

einem bereits 23 Jahre alten Katalog Ihres Verlages entnahm ich, daß Sie damals verschiedene Nachdrucke der Erstausgaben von Wagners Sopranarien angeboten hatten.

Ich möchte nachfragen, ob noch Exemplare der damaligen Ausgabe der Arien in „Tannhäuser" und „Rienzi" vorhanden sind und zu welchem Preis und Versandkosten diese bei Ihnen bestellt werden können.

Ich danke Ihnen im voraus für Ihre Bemühungen.

Mit freundlichen Grüßen

Elke Linke

Elke Linke
Kammersängerin

STANDARD OPENING AND CLOSING FORMULAE

Used when you do not know the person's name	
Sehr geehrte Damen und Herren, Sehr geehrte Herren, Sehr geehrte gnädige Frau,	Mit freundlichen Grüßen Hochachtungsvoll
Used if you know the person's name	
Sehr geehrter Herr Wagner, Sehr geehrte Frau Professor Müller, Sehr geehrte Frau Kühn, Sehr geehrter Herr Kühn,	*As above, plus:* Ich verbleibe, sehr geehrte Frau Professor, mit vorzüglicher Hochachtung Ihr/Ihre

TO ACQUAINTANCES AND FRIENDS

More formal		
Sehr geehrter Herr Dr. Braun, Liebe Freunde,	Mit freundlichen Grüßen Mit besten Grüßen[1]	*If the letter is fairly formal, "Sie" should be used*
Fairly informal: "Du" or "Sie" forms may be used		
Lieber Peter, Liebe Ingrid, Liebe Ingrid, lieber Peter,	Es grüßt Sie Herzliche Grüße von Ihrem Viele Grüße an Euch beide	

TO CLOSE FRIENDS AND FAMILY

Lieber Frank, Lieber Onkel Hans, Liebe Oma, lieber Opa, Liebe Mutti, Lieber Vati,	Liebe Grüße von Bis bald. Viele liebe Grüße Viele Grüße und Küsse von Eurem Viele liebe Grüße und Küsse	*"Du" and "Ihr" are used in all these expressions*

WRITING TO A FIRM OR AN INSTITUTION (see also page 838)

Sehr geehrte Damen und Herren, Sehr geehrte Herren, Sehr geehrte Damen,	Mit freundlichen Grüßen[1] *or* Mit besten Empfehlungen (*in business letters*)	[1] *The first is more common and should generally be used*
To someone in the same profession		
Sehr geehrter Herr Kollege, Lieber Kollege, Liebe Kollegin,	Mit freundlichen kollegialen Grüßen	

TO A PERSON IN AN IMPORTANT POSITION

Very formal		
Sehr geehrter Herr Bundesminister, Sehr geehrte Frau Präsidentin, Sehr verehrter, lieber Herr Professor,	Hochachtungsvoll	

21.1 Starting a letter

To a friend or acquaintance

Vielen Dank für Deinen Brief, der hier gestern angekommen ist — *thank you for your letter*

Ich habe mich gefreut, wieder von Dir zu hören — *it was good to hear from you again*

Es tut mir sehr leid, daß ich so lange nicht geschrieben habe. Hoffentlich bist Du mir nicht böse, aber ich hatte in letzter Zeit viel zu tun und ... — *I am very sorry I haven't written for so long*

Wir haben so lange nichts voneinander gehört. Da dachte ich, ich muß einfach schnell ein paar Zeilen schreiben ... — *it's such a long time since we had any contact*

In formal correspondence

Ich möchte Sie bitten, mir mitzuteilen, ob Sie ein Buch mit dem Titel ... vorrätig haben — *I am writing to ask whether*

Schicken Sie mir bitte ... In der Anlage sende ich Ihnen einen Scheck über DM 129,95 — *would you please send me ... I enclose*

Ich habe nähere Angaben über Ihre Sommerkurse **erhalten und möchte mich erkundigen, ob** Sie für ... noch Plätze frei haben — *I have seen the details of ... and wish to know whether*

21.2 Ending a letter *(before the closing formulae)*

Viele herzliche Grüße an Euch alle, **auch von Peter** — *Peter joins me in sending very best wishes to*

Viele liebe Grüße an Matthias — *give my love to Matthias*

Barbara **läßt ganz herzlich grüßen** — *Barbara sends her kindest regards* (oder *her love)*

Catherine **läßt auch grüßen** — *... asks me to give you ... best wishes*

Bitte grüße auch Deine Mutter **von mir.** Ich hoffe, es geht ihr gut — *please remember me to*

Ganz liebe Grüße an Miriam und Tom, **sage ihnen, wie sehr sie mir fehlen** — *give my love to ... and tell them how much I miss them*

Mary läßt Euch beide **recht herzlich grüßen** — *Mary sends her love to you both*

Und grüße David **schön von mir** — *say hello to David for me*

Ich würde mich sehr freuen, bald von Ihnen zu hören — *I look forward to hearing from you soon*

Ich hoffe, daß ich recht bald eine Antwort von Dir **bekomme** — *I hope ... will write back very soon*

Schreib mal wieder, wenn Du Zeit hast — *do write when*

Laßt ab und zu **wieder von Euch hören** — *send me* (oder *us) your news*

21.3 Enquiring about and booking accommodation

Bitte schicken Sie mir nähere Informationen zu Ihren Preisen — *please give me details of*

Ich möchte bei Ihnen Übernachtungen mit Frühstück **buchen** — *I would like to book*

Ich würde gerne ein Doppelzimmer für meine Frau und mich **sowie** ein Zweibettzimmer für unsere beiden Söhne (beide unter 12 Jahren) **reservieren** — *I wish to book ... and*

Bitte teilen Sie mir umgehend mit, ob Sie für die Woche nach dem 24. Juni noch ein Einzelzimmer mit Dusche und Vollpension haben — *please let me know by return of post if*

Ich möchte für Frau Klein ein Einzelzimmer mit Bad für die Woche nach dem 8. Juni **buchen.** Frau Klein **bezahlt ihre Rechnung selbst** — *I want to reserve ... in the name of ... will settle the bill herself*

Bitte senden Sie die Rechnung an die obige Adresse — *please send the bill to*

21.4 Confirming and cancelling a booking

Bitte betrachten Sie diese Reservierung als verbindlich, und halten Sie mir das Zimmer frei, auch wenn ich sehr spät am Abend ankommen sollte — *please consider this a firm booking*

Wir wollen gegen Abend eintreffen, falls nichts dazwischenkommt — *we expect to arrive in the early evening, unless*

Leider muß ich Sie bitten, meine Reservierung vom 24. August **auf den** 3. September **umzubuchen** — *I am afraid I must ask you to alter my booking from ... to*

Ich muß Ihnen leider mitteilen, daß ich aufgrund unvorhersehbarer Umstände **meine Zimmerreservierung** für die Woche ab dem 5. September **stornieren muß** — *owing to ..., I am afraid that I must cancel my booking*

22 Thanks

Herzlichen Dank für das schöne Geschenk und deinen lieben Brief	*many thanks for*
Ich möchte Ihnen, auch im Namen meines Mannes, unseren Dank für den schönen Abend **übermitteln**	*I would like to thank you on behalf of my husband and myself for*
Ich weiß gar nicht, wie ich Ihnen für Ihre Hilfe **danken soll**	*I really don't know how to thank you for*
Als kleines Dankeschön für deine Hilfe möchten wir dich nächste Woche einmal zum Abendessen einladen	*as a small token of our gratitude for*
Für die vielen Glückwünsche und Geschenke zu unserer Verlobung **möchten wir uns** bei allen Freunden und Bekannten **herzlich bedanken**	*we would like to extend our warmest thanks to ... for*
Bitte leiten Sie unseren aufrichtigen Dank auch an Ihre Mitarbeiterin, Frau Wagner, **weiter**	*please pass on our sincere thanks to*
Keine Ursache. Ganz im Gegenteil: wir haben Ihnen zu danken	*don't mention it. On the contrary: we must thank you*
Wir sind Ihnen für diesen Beitrag **äußerst dankbar**	*we are very grateful to you for*
Der Vorsitzende **hat mir die ehrenvolle Aufgabe übertragen, Ihnen im Namen** des Forschungskomitees **unseren herzlichen Dank für** die bereitgestellten Spendenmittel **auszusprechen**	*I have the honour of conveying, on behalf of ..., our sincere thanks for*

23 Best wishes

23.1 General expressions *(used on special occasions only)*

Mit den besten Wünschen [...] **von** (+ *signature*). [...] *will be expressions like "für Ihren Ruhestand", "für die neue Stelle", "für Glück im neuen Heim", "für eine baldige Genesung" etc.*	*with best wishes for/on ... from*
Erlauben Sie mir, daß ich Ihnen meine besten Wünsche [...] **übermittle**	*please accept my best wishes for*
Bitte richten Sie Edgar **meine besten Wünsche aus**	*please give ... my best wishes*
Viele herzliche Grüße und Wünsche	*best wishes*
Alle Liebe	*love*
Unsere besten Wünsche [...]	*best wishes from both/all of us*
Alles Gute [...]!	*all the best*

23.2 Season's greetings

Fröhliche Weihnachten und ein glückliches neues Jahr wünscht Ihnen/Euch (+ *signature*)	*Merry Christmas and a Happy New Year from*
Mit den besten Wünschen für ein gesegnetes Weihnachtsfest und ein glückliches und erfolgreiches neues Jahr	*(often on company Christmas card sent to clients, suppliers etc.)*
Frohe Weihnachten und einen guten Rutsch!	*(more informal, only to friends)*

23.3 Birthday greetings

Alles Gute zum Geburtstag!	*birthday greetings (on cards)*
Herzlichen Glückwunsch zum Geburtstag von (+ *signature*)	*many happy returns of the day from*
Herzlichen Glückwunsch zum Namenstag von (+ *signature*)	*(on cards) best wishes on your saint's day*
Zu Ihrem Geburtstag unsere herzlichen Glückwünsche und alles Gute für das neue Lebensjahr	*(more formal) many happy returns of the day and best wishes for the year ahead*

23.4 Get well wishes

Gute Besserung!	*(on card) get well soon*

23.5 Wishing someone luck

Ich möchte Ihnen für Ihre Unternehmungen **viel Glück und Erfolg wünschen**	*I wish you the best of luck and every success in ...*
Viel Erfolg an Ihrer neuen Arbeitsstätte	*I wish you every success in ...*
Wir möchten Dir viel Erfolg beim Examen **wünschen**	*we'd like to wish you every success in*
Wir drücken Dir am Freitag alle **die Daumen**	*we're keeping our fingers crossed*
Viel Glück für die Fahrprüfung!	*good luck in*

23.6 Congratulations

Herzlichen Glückwunsch zum bestandenen Examen	*congratulations on*
Zu Ihrer Beförderung **möchten wir Ihnen unsere herzlichsten Glückwünsche aussprechen**	*(more formal) we would like to send you our congratulations on*
Ich gratuliere zur bestandenen Fahrprüfung. **Gut gemacht!**	*congratulations on ... Well done!*

24 Announcements

24.1 Announcing a birth and responding

Wir freuen uns über die Geburt unserer Tochter Julia am 15. Juli. Katharina und Hans Graf, Schönberg	*are happy to announce the birth of*
Unsere Annika **hat ein Brüderchen bekommen. Am** 7. September **wurde** unser Sohn Christoph-Johannes **geboren. Es freuen sich** Katja und Uwe Braun	*are happy to announce the birth of*
Karin und Rainer **haben** am 7. September **eine kleine Tochter** Sabine **bekommen.** Karin **geht es schon wieder ganz gut. Die beiden sind natürlich überglücklich**	*I'm happy to tell you that ... now have a little daughter ... is fully recovered. They are both delighted, of course*
Herzlichen Glückwunsch zum freudigen Ereignis	*congratulations on the happy event*
Herzlichen Glückwunsch zur Geburt Ihrer/Eurer Tochter	*congratulations on the birth of*
Andreas und ich **freuen uns mit Euch über die Geburt** Eures Sohnes. **Wir gratulieren von ganzem Herzen und wünschen Euch und ihm alles Gute**	*we were delighted to hear of the birth of ... Many congratulations. We wish all three of you all the best*

24.2 Announcing an engagement and responding

Wir haben uns verlobt. Judith Winter und Christian Schütte	*are engaged*
Professor Wolfgang Schwarz und Frau Gabriele **beehren sich, die Verlobung** ihrer Tochter Erika mit Herrn Ulrich von Schlieffenberg **anzuzeigen**	*are happy to announce the engagement of*
Herzlichen Glückwunsch zur Verlobung und alles Gute für die gemeinsame Zukunft	*congratulations on your engagement and best wishes for*
Wir freuen uns mit Euch über die Verlobung Eures Sohnes und wünschen dem jungen Paar viel Glück für die Zukunft	*we were very happy to hear of the engagement*

24.3 Announcing a marriage and responding

Wir heiraten am 27. April. Heinz Müller und Jutta Müller geb. Heinisch. **Die kirchliche Trauung findet** um 10 Uhr in der Dorfkirche **statt.** Tagesadresse: Hotel Weißer Schwan, Oberammergau	*... are getting married on 27 April. The ceremony will take place*
Mit großer Freude geben wir die Vermählung unserer Kinder **bekannt** (+ *names of both sets of parents*)	*we are happy to announce the wedding/marriage of*
Wir haben geheiratet. Fred Heine und Maria Heine-Obermann	*... have got married*
Zur Vermählung Ihrer Tochter mit Herrn Dr. Friedhelm Klöbner **möchten wir Ihnen unsere herzlichen Glückwünsche aussprechen**	*may we offer our congratulations on the marriage of*
Zu Eurer Hochzeit unseren herzlichen Glückwunsch und alles Gute für Eure gemeinsame Zukunft	*congratulations on your marriage*
Wir freuen uns mit Euch über die Heirat von Anne und Stefan **und möchten dem jungen Paar alles Gute wünschen**	*we are delighted to hear of ...'s wedding. Best wishes to the newly-weds*
Für die vielen Glückwünsche und Geschenke von Familie, Freunden und Bekannten **anläßlich unserer Hochzeit möchten wir uns herzlich bedanken**	*we would like to thank all our ... for the many gifts and good wishes on the occasion of our marriage*

24.4 Announcing a death and responding

Plötzlich und unerwartet ist mein geliebter Mann, unser lieber Vater, Onkel und Großvater Hans Meier **aus unserer Mitte gerissen worden. In tiefer Trauer:** Susanne Meier geb. Blume und die Kinder und Enkel	*it is with deep sorrow that I must announce the sudden and unexpected departure from this life of*
Nach schwerer Krankheit verstarb am 15. März unsere liebe Schwester, Tante und Schwägerin Hanna Pietsch, geb. Lehmann im Alter von 85 Jahren	*after a long and painful illness*
In tiefer Trauer muß ich Ihnen mitteilen, daß mein Vater vergangene Woche nach kurzer schwerer Krankheit verstorben ist *or* für immer von uns gegangen ist	*it is with deep sorrow that I have to inform you that*
Mit tiefer Bestürzung haben wir die Nachricht vom Tod Ihres Gatten **erhalten. Wir möchten Ihnen unser tiefempfundenes Beileid aussprechen**	*it is with great sorrow that we learnt of the death of ... we would like to offer our deepest sympathy*
Wir sind alle sehr bestürzt über den plötzlichen Tod Deines Bruders **und möchten Dir unser aufrichtiges Beileid aussprechen.** Wir sind in Gedanken bei Dir und wünschen Dir in dieser schweren Zeit viel Kraft und Liebe	*we are all deeply shocked to hear of the sudden death of ... and we would like to offer our deepest sympathy*
Für die zahlreichen Beweise des Mitgefühls und der aufrichtigen Anteilnahme sowie für das ehrende Geleit zur letzten Ruhestätte unseres lieben Verstorbenen **danken wir allen herzlich**	*we would like to express our deep gratitude for the numerous expressions of sympathy*

24.5 Announcing a change of address

Wir sind umgezogen! *or* **Wir ziehen um!** Ab 1. April ist unsere Adresse:	*we have moved! we're moving!*

25 Invitations

25.1 Formal invitations

Wir würden uns freuen, Sie beim Sektfrühstück im Anschluß an die Trauung im Hotel Goldener Schwan **als unseren Gast begrüßen zu dürfen**	*we would be delighted if you would join us*
Der Verlag „Mensch und Technik" **gibt sich die Ehre, Sie** am 12. Oktober um 11 Uhr **zu** einem Sektfrühstück an Stand 15 **einzuladen** u.A.w.g.	*will be pleased to welcome you at*
Karl und Greta Dauderstädt **geben sich die Ehre**, Herrn Günther Henrich **aus Anlaß** ihrer silbernen Hochzeit am 14. Mai **zu einem festlichen Abendessen** im Hotel „Zum Goldenen Hirsch" **einzuladen**	*request the pleasure of your company at a dinner to celebrate*

... and responding

Meine Frau und ich **möchten Ihnen unseren Dank für die freundliche Einladung zum Abendessen anläßlich** Ihrer Silberhochzeit **aussprechen, die wir mit Freuden annehmen/die wir leider nicht wahrnehmen können, da ...**	*would like to thank you for your kind invitation to dinner on the occasion of ... which we have pleasure in accepting/but we regret that we cannot attend, because*
Ich möchte mich herzlich für Ihre Einladung zum Abendessen am 12. Oktober **bedanken, die ich mit größtem Vergnügen annehme/der ich aber leider nicht nachkommen kann**	*I would like to thank you very much for your invitation to ... which I have much pleasure in accepting/I am unfortunately unable to accept*

25.2 Informal invitations

Unsere Verlobung **möchten wir** am 15. März um 19 Uhr im kleinen Saal des Restaurants „Stadtkrone" **mit Freunden feiern. Wir würden uns freuen, wenn Ihr** zu unserem Fest **kommen könntet**	*we are having a party amongst friends to celebrate ... and we would be very glad if you could come*
Nächsten Sonntag **möchten wir** für Ruth und Daniel Torberg, die zur Zeit bei uns zu Gast sind, **ein kleines Abendessen geben, zu dem wir auch Sie herzlich einladen möchten**	*we are giving a small dinner for ... and we would very much like you to come*
Hätten Sie Lust, am Donnerstag mit mir in die Oper zu gehen?	*would you like*
Könntest Du Dir, wenn Du nächste Woche in Bonn bist, einen Abend freihalten? **Wir würden Dich gerne einmal zum Abendessen einladen**	*we would very much like you to come to dinner*
Wir wollen den ganzen Mai in unserem Ferienhaus auf Amrum verbringen und **würden uns freuen, wenn ihr uns einmal dort besuchen könntet**	*we would be very happy if you could come and visit us there*

Accepting

Vielen Dank für die freundliche Einladung. **Ich komme gerne**	*thanks very much for ... I will be pleased to come*
Ich habe mich über Ihre freundliche Einladung zur Konfirmationsfeier Ihrer Tochter **sehr gefreut und nehme gerne an**	*thank you very much for ... I shall be happy to accept*
Ich hatte vor, am nächsten Montag in Bonn anzukommen, und **werde mich dann telefonisch bei Euch melden**	*I was planning to ... and I will phone you when I arrive*
Wir haben uns riesig über Eure Einladung nach Amrum **gefreut und würden gerne** das Wochenende nach Himmelfahrt **kommen**	*thank you so much for your invitation ... we would love to come*
Natürlich gehe ich gerne mit Ihnen in die „Zauberflöte". **Es hat mich sehr gefreut, daß Sie an mich gedacht haben**	*I would love to go with you to ... it was very kind of you to think of me*

Declining

Vielen Dank für Ihre Einladung zum Abendessen mit den Torbergs. **Ich wäre wirklich gerne gekommen, habe ich leider schon eine andere Verabredung,** die ich nicht mehr rückgängig machen kann	*many thanks for your invitation ... I would very much have liked to come, but I'm afraid I have a previous engagement*
Wir würden wirklich gern einmal für ein Wochende zu Euch zu Besuch kommen, aber **leider paßt uns keiner der vorgeschlagenen Termine**	*we would very much like to ... but I'm afraid we can't make any of the dates you suggest*
Leider kann ich mich am kommenden Dienstag **nicht frei machen. Könnten wir vielleicht** schon jetzt **etwas für** Oktober **ausmachen?**	*I'm afraid I'm not free ... perhaps we can arrange something for ...*

26 Essay writing

26.1 The broad outline of the essay

Introductory remarks

Welche Auswirkungen die neue Kommunikations- und Medientechnik auf die Zukunft des Menschen hat, **darüber wird sehr viel geschrieben und gesprochen**	*a great deal is being written and said about*
Die Frage, ob bakterielle Sporen auf geeigneten Himmelskörpern Fuß fassen können, **beschäftigt die Experten schon seit längerem**	*the question, whether ... has been preoccupying the experts for some time*
Es ist allgemein bekannt, daß bestimmte Grundsätze sich immer durchsetzen	*it is a well-known fact that*
Heute gilt allgemein als bewiesen, daß Kernkraftwerke eine Gefahr für den Menschen darstellen. **Trotzdem fragt sich**, wie man im Falle einer Schließung die Energieversorgung sichern kann. **Das läßt vermuten, daß** die Lösung des Problems so einfach nicht sein kann	*it is generally agreed today that ... however, one wonders ... this leads one to assume that*
Man muß sich verstärkt fragen, ob Fernsehen nicht eine echte Gefahr für unsere Kinder darstellt	*one must seriously ask oneself whether*
Beinahe täglich hört man neue Katastrophenmeldungen zum Wärmehaushalt der Erde. **Manche** Experten sagen den Hitzetod unseres Planeten voraus, **während andere** die gleichen Daten dazu benutzen, das Nahen der nächsten Eiszeit anzukündigen	*almost every day ... some ... while others*
Man würde zu Recht jeden auslachen, der die Aussagen der Politiker im Wahlkampf für bare Münze nähme. Aber ...	*one would be justified in*
Es ist wohl kaum übertrieben, wenn man sagt, daß sich die Rolle der Gewerkschaften grundlegend gewandelt hat	*it would hardly be an exaggeration to say*
Heutzutage kann man keine Zeitung mehr aufschlagen, ohne daß einem alarmierende Meldungen über Mafiamethoden ins Auge springen	*nowadays it is scarcely possible to open a newspaper without*
Es gibt in der Geschichte unzählige Beispiele für kluge Frauen, die im Schatten ihrer berühmten Männer standen. Ein Beispiel dafür ist ...	*history offers us numerous examples of*

Explaining the aim of the essay

„Arbeitslose sind in Wirklichkeit nur zu faul zum Arbeiten." **Bemerkungen dieser Art hört man oft**, auch in sogenannten gebildeten Kreisen. **Deshalb sollen** hier die Statistiken der Bundesanstalt für Arbeit einmal genauer **untersucht werden**	*such remarks are often heard ... we will therefore examine*
„Streß macht krank". Diese Feststellung veranschaulicht eines der drängendsten Probleme unserer Gesellschaft. **Es scheint deshalb angebracht, sich einmal näher mit** dem Phänomen Streß unter seinen medizinischen und sozialen Aspekten zu **befassen**	*it therefore seems appropriate to look more closely into*
Diese Einstellung **verdient es, genauer untersucht zu werden** und soll hier in einen größeren Gesamtzusammenhang eingeordnet werden	*deserves closer attention*
Kafka hat einmal geschrieben: „Wirkliche Realität ist immer unrealistisch". **Aus dieser Aussage ergibt sich eine grundlegende Fragestellung**: was ist Wirklichkeit, was ist Vorstellung?	*this assertion raises a fundamental question*
Heute werden wir immer wieder mit dem Problem der zunehmenden Umweltverschmutzung **konfrontiert**	*today we are repeatedly confronted with the problem of*

Developing the argument

Ich möchte mit einer kurzen Erläuterung einiger grundlegender physikalischer Prinzipien **beginnen**	*I should like to begin by*
Ich möchte zu Anfang versuchen, die medizinische Definition von Streß einzugrenzen	*I should like to begin by*
Zunächst einmal muß man darauf aufmerksam machen, daß der Autor selber lange Jahre im Exil verbracht hat	*the first thing to point out is that*
Betrachten wir zunächst die Software als Arbeitsmittel	*firstly let us look at*
Bevor ich näher auf die Frage des Bewußtseins bei Primaten eingehe, **möchte ich zunächst** verschiedene Meinungen über die Hirnstruktur von Menschenaffen zusammenfassen	*before ... I should like to*
Es wäre an dieser Stelle **angebracht, einen Blick auf** die Familienverhältnisse des Komponisten **zu werfen**	*it would be appropriate to consider*
Als erstes sollte man sich ein wenig **mit** der Geschichte der Gewerkschaftsbewegung **beschäftigen**	*let us start by considering*
Ehe wir das Umfrageergebnis **analysieren, müssen wir uns darüber klar werden**, daß nur Langzeitarbeitslose befragt wurden	*before analysing the ... it must be made clear that*
Als ersten überzeugenden Beweis für diese Behauptung kann man anführen, daß die Orientierungslosigkeit heute eines der größten Probleme der Jugendlichen ist	*the first convincing argument to support this statement is that*
Es stellt sich zunächst die Frage nach dem Motiv, das die Hauptfigur des Romans bewegt, ihre Familie so plötzlich zu verlassen	*let us first consider*

Wenn wir uns erinnern: im Vorjahr hatte sich Goethe gerade als Student der Rechte an der Universität von Straßburg aufgehalten *let us cast our minds back:*

Es ergibt sich die Frage, ob unsere Interpretation der spätantiken Prosa in dieser Form noch haltbar ist *this raises the question whether*

Connecting elements

Wir kommen nun zur Analyse der einzelnen Charaktere *let us now analyse*

Nachdem wir uns eingehend mit dem Verlauf der Handlung befaßt haben, **wollen wir uns nun** dem Sprachstil **zuwenden** *let us now turn to*

Wir haben gesehen, daß Strahlenbelastung eine Ursache für diese Krankheit sein kann, und **wollen nun andere Faktoren untersuchen**, die für ihre Verbreitung von Bedeutung sein könnten *let us now examine other factors*

Es ist nun klar, daß es eine Lösung im Bereich der Schulmedizin allein nicht geben kann, und **wir wollen** nun Lösungsansätze aus den sogenannten Grenzbereichen **betrachten** *it is now clear that ... let us turn our attention to*

Es wäre jetzt interessant, auch die soziologischen Aspekte näher **zu** beleuchten *it would also be interesting to ...*

Es drängt sich hier allerdings auch ein Gegenargument auf: nämlich wie und vor allem von wem soll diese Zensur ausgeübt werden *moreover, one argument against this cannot be ignored:*

Man kann das Problem aber auch von der rein praktischen Seite **her betrachten** *the problem can also be looked at from*

The other side of the argument

Aber sind diese traumatischen Jugenderlebnisse **wirklich der einzige Grund für** ihr Scheitern? *but are ... really the only explanation for*

Wären diese Argumente schon ein ausreichender Grund für die Wiedereinführung der Todesstrafe, **oder** sprechen nicht weitaus mehr und schwerwiegendere Argumente dagegen? *do these arguments give sufficient grounds for ... or*

Der Autor argumentiert, daß die Form wichtiger sei als der Inhalt, **es ließe sich aber mit gleichem Recht auch das Gegenteil behaupten** *the author argues that ... but the opposite may be equally true*

Es kann freilich nicht darum gehen, die ganze Branche zu akademisieren *there is certainly no question of*

Mit gleichem Recht läßt sich das Problem natürlich auch dem Bereich der Psychoanalyse **zuordnen** *this problem belongs equally in*

The balanced view

Nach eingehender Betrachtung muß man zu dem Ergebnis kommen, daß eine verantwortliche Kontrollinstanz dringend nötig wäre *on reflection, one is forced to conclude that*

Man sollte sich allerdings immer darüber im klaren sein, daß absolute Aussagen zwar eingängig, aber im Prinzip äußerst zweifelhaft sind *one should always remember that*

Man sollte auch den psychologischen Aspekt einer Währungsunion **nicht außer acht lassen** *... should also be taken into consideration*

Auch wenn der Einfluß des Fernsehens auf die jugendliche Psyche unbestritten ist, **sollte man** ihn doch **nicht überschätzen** *even if ... one must not overestimate*

Trotzdem sollte man auch einen weiteren Faktor nicht vergessen *there is however another factor which should not be ignored*

Schließlich müßte man sich fragen, ob eine berufliche Karriere wirklich der einzig mögliche Lebensinhalt ist *finally, we must ask ourselves whether*

Vielleicht sollte man noch einen Schritt weiter gehen und sich fragen, ob Städte kategorisch für Autos gesperrt werden sollten *we should perhaps go further and ask ourselves whether*

In conclusion

Welche Schlußfolgerungen lassen sich aus der Analyse **ziehen**? *what conclusions may be drawn from*

Die aufgeführten Argumente beweisen, daß der naturwissenschaftliche Unterricht an unseren Schulen in vielen Punkten mangelhaft ist *the arguments given above prove that*

Wir sehen also, daß dem Autor in seiner Erzählung wenig an stimmigen Handlungsabläufen und glaubhaften Personenbeschreibungen liegt. **Vielmehr** konzentriert er sich ganz auf Sprachartistik *we can see then, that ... rather,*

Es spricht also alles dafür, daß Frauen heute wie früher mit anderen Leistungsmaßstäben gemessen werden als Männer *all of this points to the fact that*

Aus all dem läßt sich nur folgern, daß sich hinter Argumenten für die Kernkraft erhebliche wirtschaftliche Interessen verbergen *from this one must conclude that*

Alles in allem ist der Drogenmißbrauch eines der schwierigsten und wohl dringendsten Probleme unserer Zeit *all in all*

Jedenfalls verdienen gerade die sogenannten Randgruppen unserer ruppigen Leistungsgesellschaft mehr Einfühlsamkeit und Hilfe *in any case*

Sein Lebenslauf **läßt den Schluß zu, daß** der Dichter durchaus in das Gemeinschaftsleben des Dorfes eingebunden war
leads us to the conclusion that

26.2 Constructing a paragraph

Assessing an idea

Hier lassen sich verschiedene Argumente **anführen**
at this point, various ... may be given/cited

Ehe ich mich einer ausführlichen Stilanalyse zuwende, **möchte ich noch kurz auf** die Verwendung des Tiroler Dialektes **zu sprechen kommen**
before I ... I would just like to say a few words about

Wie ich im folgenden noch zeigen werde, kann von einer genauen psychoanalytischen Bewertung hier keine Rede sein
as I will show later

Und hiermit greifen wir einen Gedanken auf, der schon einleitend erwähnt wurde
here we pick up an idea

Um aber wieder auf unser Hauptthema zurückzukommen, die Vollwertküche muß keineswegs langweilig und bieder sein
but to return to our main theme

Von dieser Reise **wird später noch ausführlich die Rede sein**, es soll hier nur kurz erwähnt werden, daß sie einen tiefen Eindruck bei ihr hinterließ
we will return to a more detailed discussion of ... later

Zum Thema Schwefelausstoß der Kohlekraftwerke **läßt sich sagen, daß** die neuen Filteranlagen ihn um mehr als 60% reduzieren
on the subject of ... it must be said that

Establishing parallels

Sowohl im Inntal **als auch** in Trostberg lag die Kohlenmonoxidkonzentration bei 0,5 Milligramm
both ... and

In diesem Zusammenhang muß auch die sogenannte Technologiefeindlichkeit der deutschen Gesellschaft **erwähnt werden**
in this context we should also mention

In gleicher Weise sorgt das Programm selbständig für die notwendigen Datei- und Satzsperren
equally

Die Bodenversiegelung führt **einerseits** zu Hochwasser, **andererseits** zu Grundwasserabsenkungen und damit zu Wassernotstand im Sommer
on (the) one hand ... and on the other (hand)

Eine Zeitung gewinnt Glanz durch exzentrische Schreiber, leben aber tut sie von guten Redakteuren. **Erstere** kommen und gehen, **letztere** aber sind da und halten die Maschine am Laufen
the former ... the latter

Das Strafrecht untersagt es den Fernsehanstalten, Filme auszustrahlen, die bei der Jugend Aggressionsbereitschaft fördern, und **das gleiche gilt für** Sendungen, die offensichtlich die Menschenwürde verletzen
and the same goes for

In dem Maße wie die Privatisierung fortschreitet, werden auch immer mehr Investitions- und Finanzierungsmöglichkeiten gefunden
as

Untrennbar hiermit verbunden ist die Tatsache, daß Chopin bereits schwer erkrankt war, als er seine Schottlandreise antrat
this cannot be dissociated from the fact that

Von den Kommunisten **bis zu** den extremen rechten Gruppen sind sich **alle** in der Verurteilung des Terrorismus einig
everyone, from ... to

Gleichermaßen sollte ein Zeitungsartikel den Leser nicht wie einen unmündigen Ignoranten von oben herab belehren
equally

Adding

In diesem Zusammenhang muß man auch ein merkliches Nachlassen der schulischen Leistungen erwähnen
in this context

Nebenbei bemerkt hielt der junge Friedrich II. Luther und Calvin für recht triste Figuren
incidentally

Außerdem muß man die ökologischen Folgen bedenken
furthermore

Man sollte auch nicht vergessen, daß durch das Spülen von Mehrwegflaschen die Gewässer erheblich belastet werden
one must also remember that

Hinzu kommt noch seine liebevolle Schilderung der englischen Landschaft
in addition to this there is

Detailing

Hiervon sind verschiedene Berufsgruppen betroffen, **besonders** Berufe, die viel Bildschirmarbeit erfordern
in particular

Es treten hier **vorzugsweise** Probleme mit den Augen, der Wirbelsäule und im Bereich des Unterarms und Handgelenks auf, **die noch** durch schlechte Sitzhaltung **verstärkt werden**
chiefly ... which may be made still worse

Was nun die Bürgerinitiativen **betrifft**, so sind sie ihrerseits keineswegs einer Meinung zum heißen Eisen Müllverbrennung
as far as ... are concerned

Was die Zigarettenwerbung **angeht**, ist der Zuschauer heute bedeutend kritischer
as far as ... is concerned

Enumerating

Zum Erfolg dieser Fernsehserie tragen verschiedene Faktoren bei. **Erstens** *or* **Zum ersten** spielt die Hauptrolle ein beliebter Star, **zweitens** liegt das Thema in der Luft und **schließlich** wurde ein erstklassiger Drehbuchautor gefunden — *first(ly) ... secondly ... finally*

Das hat drei Hauptgründe: **erstens ..., zweitens ..., drittens** — *first(ly) ... secondly ... thirdly*

Es werden dem Kunden mehrere Möglichkeiten angeboten: er könnte **entweder** bar **oder** mit Scheck- oder Kreditkarte bezahlen **oder schließlich** ein Kundenkonto einrichten — *either ... or ... or alternatively/finally*

Sollte man in diese Statistik alle Erkrankten aufnehmen? **Oder etwa** nur die chronisch Kranken? **Oder sollte man am Ende** sogar nach Art der Erkrankung getrennt analysieren? — *or else ... or should one simply*

Opposing

Entgegen einem landläufigen Vorurteil hatten wohl auch die schrecklichen Wikinger Angst vor anderen Völkern — *contrary to*

Ungeachtet ihrer Greueltaten werden die Helden zu Märtyrern erhoben — *in spite of*

Trotz harter Arbeit konnten die Eltern die Kinder kaum ernähren — *in spite of*

Obwohl es einen umfangreichen zivilen Apparat zur Verfolgung von Menschenrechtsverletzungen gibt, werden die Verantwortlichen nur selten bestraft — *although*

Wenngleich die Schwierigkeiten des Balanceakts zwischen menschlicher Tragödie und politischem Verbrechen nicht immer zu übersehen sind, löst der Autor das Problem mit viel Mut und Geschick — *although*

Schwellungen und Rötungen werden fast bei jedem Fall beobachtet, **trotzdem** stehen diese Nebenwirkungen in keinem Verhältnis zu den Folgen einer Infektion — *nevertheless*

Introducing one's own point of view

Meiner Meinung nach ist dies sein bei weitem bestes Buch — *in my opinion*

Ich für mein(en) Teil bedaure diese Entwicklung im Schulwesen sehr — *I for my part*

Was ich hier am interessantesten finde, ist die großartige Verflechtung der verschiedenen Charaktere — *what I find most interesting here*

Nach meinem Dafürhalten scheint die Autorin sich hier auf das gewagte Terrain der Vermutung zu begeben — *it seems to me that*

Ich bin hingegen der Ansicht, daß man Statistik nicht auf diese Weise zu seinem eigenen Zwecken umlügen darf — *my own point of view is that*

Wie der Verfasser, **für meine Begriffe übrigens völlig zu Recht**, bemerkt, geht es hier um mehr als nur unsere Schulen — *quite rightly in my opinion*

Introducing somebody else's point of view

Laut Verfasser or **Dem Verfasser zufolge** ist der Neid eine der Haupttriebfedern unseres Handelns — *in the author's view*

Nach Meinung einiger Experten lassen sich diese Abweichungen durch unterschiedliche Ernährungsgewohnheiten erklären — *according to some experts*

Die Ausgaben für den Umweltschutz bewegen sich **seiner Aussage zufolge** im Rahmen des Vertretbaren — *in his opinion*

Er **glaubt/meint/erklärt dagegen**, daß dieses System unzählige Vorteile besitzt — *on the other hand, he thinks/believes/declares*

Der Autor **lenkt nun unsere Aufmerksamkeit wieder auf** die verschiedenen vorangegangenen Krisensituationen — *once again draws our attention to*

Er **weist** nun **auf** die unterschiedlichen Persönlichkeiten der Hauptakteure **hin** — *points out*

Sie **behauptet, daß** die Mehrheit aller Jugendlichen sich heute nicht mehr für Bücher interessiert — *maintains that*

Die offizielle Lesart ist, daß die Probleme für die Bevölkerung bei weitem durch die Vorteile aufgewogen werden — *the official version is that*

Hier **möchte uns** ein sogenannter Experte **glauben machen** *or* **davon überzeugen, daß** dieses Problem überhaupt nicht existiert — *would have us believe/would like to convince us that*

Introducing an example, quotation or source

Nehmen wir zum Beispiel *or* **Da wäre zum Beispiel** Gretchen im „Faust" — *take for example*

Eines der interessantesten Beispiele findet sich gleich im ersten Kapitel des Buches — *one of the most interesting examples occurs*

Als Beispiel braucht man nur die problematische Lage der kleinen landwirtschaftlichen Betriebe **anzuführen** — *to illustrate this, one need only refer to*

Die Verfasser meinen dagegen, daß „die zentrale Bedeutung der Hehlerei für die organisierte Kriminalität lange Zeit nicht deutlich genug gesehen worden ist" — *however, the authors are of the opinion that*

In seinen „Xenien" **sagte/bemerkte** schon Goethe: „Amerika, du hast es besser"	*said/observed*
Was der Minister **bereits sagte** *or* **gesagt hat, sei hier zitiert**: „es hängt jetzt alles von der Einsatzbereitschaft und Toleranz unserer Mitbürger ab." **Zitat Ende**	*as ... said, and I quote ... end of quote*
Schlegel **hat** in einem historischen Aufsatz **das Wort von** der „Revolution von oben" **geprägt, das später von** vielen kritischen Historikern **aufgenommen wurde**	*coined the phrase ... which was later taken up by*
Nach den Worten von Börne fallen „Minister wie Butterbrote: gewöhnlich auf die gute Seite"	*in the words of*
In ihrer eindrucksvollen Studie zum Leben der Insekten **weist** Maria Sybilla Merian bereits im 17. Jahrhundert **darauf hin, daß** ...	*in her remarkable study of ... (she) points out that*
In einem kürzlich erschienenen Artikel in der Zeitschrift „Der Kreis" **finden wir folgende** treffende **Bemerkung von** Hans Meier:	*in a recent article in ... there is the following remark by*
„Das größer gewordene Deutschland wird nicht regiert, Machterhalt ist alles." **So steht es in** der Zeit **aus der Feder von** Nina Grunenberg	*writes ... in*
Zitat Raddatz: „Ähnlich einer Steinberg-Kontur setzt dieser Künstler sich selber aus Kunststücken zusammen." **Zitat Ende**	*to quote Raddatz ... end of quote*

26.3 The mechanics of the argument

Stating facts

Es ist richtig, daß so manches Substitut eines Umweltgiftes sich im Nachhinein nicht als die erhoffte ökologische Alternative entpuppt	*it is true that*
Hierbei wäre zu bemerken, daß die Experten zu diesem Thema gespaltener Auffassung sind	*one should note here that*
Es handelt sich um den Versuch, durch Fiktionen etwas Realität zu erfahren	*this is a*
Dieses Bauprogramm **zog die heftige Kritik** der Opposition **auf sich**	*attracted strong criticism from*
Erinnern wir uns: nach jahrzehntelangen Rangeleien war endlich eine Entscheidung gefallen. Das Steuerrecht würde grundlegend reformiert werden	*let us not forget:*
Beim Weiterlesen ergeben sich völlig neue Perspektiven: ...	*as one reads on, entirely new perspectives open up*
Es sollte erwähnt werden, daß Tschaikowski nicht der einzige Komponist ist, der in dieser Zeit historische Ereignisse in seinen Werken umsetzt	*mention should be made of the fact that*

Indicating a supposition

Es ist anzunehmen, daß der wirtschaftliche Kurs sich zunehmend nach der liberalen Mitte hin einordnen wird	*it is to be expected that*
Es läßt sich hier vermuten, daß ein Teil der Befragten den Begriff „Heimat" völlig anders verstanden hat	*one may suppose that*
Es kann gut sein, daß Schiller dieses Gedicht im Konzept schon sehr viel früher verfaßt hat	*... may well (have ...)*
Man spricht in diesem Zusammenhang von der Möglichkeit, daß die Visumpflicht bereits in den nächsten Monaten entfallen könnte	*in this context, the possibility that ... has been mentioned*
Hierfür könnte es allerdings auch eine andere Erklärung **geben**	*there could well be*
Es ist durchaus möglich, daß er mit dieser Kandidatur politisches Kapital aus seiner Beliebtheit als Schauspieler schlagen wollte	*it is very possible that*
Es steht zu vermuten, daß auch die Produktmanager in Japan in ihrem Sortiment nicht mehr so ganz durchblicken	*it must be supposed that*

Expressing a certainty

Die wenigen Akten, die die Regierung bisher herausgerückt hat, **lassen nur den einen Schluß zu:** Bonn hat über das kriminelle Imperium Schalk fast alles gewußt	*leave us with only one conclusion*
Es steht fest, daß Albrecht seinen späteren Mörder selbst eingelassen hat	*it is clear that*
Aber **es ist sicher, daß** nicht alle Sprachen, die in Europa anerkannt sind, eine Ausgabe des EU-Amtsblattes haben werden	*it is certain that*
Seine zweite Behauptung ist dagegen **unbestritten** *or* **unzweifelhaft** *or* **ohne Zweifel** den Argumenten seiner Gegner vorzuziehen	*indisputably/undeniably*
Unbestritten ist, daß die Bundesrepublik im internationalen Umweltschutz eine Vorreiterrolle einnimmt	*what cannot be denied is that*
Eine Limousine mit Chauffeur ist **zweifellos** besser gegen Diebstahl geschützt als ein Drahtesel	*doubtless*
Es deutet alles darauf hin, daß es dem SC Freiburg so ergeht wie vielen seiner Vorgänger als Aufsteiger: am Ende steht der Neuanfang in der zweiten Liga	*all the indications are that*
Wie man weiß, kann man auch in Bayern durchaus in den Genuß fiskalischer Milde gelangen	*as everyone knows*

Es ist völlig klar, daß solchen innovativen Produkten die Märkte der Zukunft gehören — *it is very clear that*

Es läßt sich nicht leugnen, daß die demographische Entwicklung das Zahlenverhältnis zwischen Beitragszahlern und Rentnern verschlechtern wird — *it cannot be denied that*

Indicating doubt or uncertainty

Es scheint wohl, daß die Liebe zu antiken Modellen der Uhrmacherkunst wieder auflebt — *it would seem that*

Es könnte immerhin sein, daß die Dauer der Studie zu kurz war — *all the same, it is possible that*

Vielleicht wäre es besser, wenn die Städtebauer einen Teil ihrer Großgrundstücke nachträglich wieder parzellieren — *perhaps it would be better*

Es könnte sich bei dem Streit **um** eine juristische Posse **handeln** — *we might be dealing with*

Dies könnte unter Umständen erklären, warum man so lange auf den zweiten Band warten mußte — *this might explain why*

Es fällt schwer, in diesem Zusammenhang **an** die Objektivität der Wissenschaft **zu glauben** — *it is difficult to believe in*

Diese Ergebnisse **stellen** erneut **die allgemeine Gültigkeit** statistischer Aussagen **in Frage** — *cast doubt upon the general validity of*

Conceding a point

In Berlin hat die Oper heute weniger Abonnenten als noch vor 10 Jahren, **trotzdem** sind sehr viele Aufführungen ausverkauft — *nonetheless*

Obwohl seine Studien sehr sorgfältig waren, muß man ihm vorwerfen, daß er die Ergebnisse der sowjetischen Gruppe außer acht ließ — *although*

Ihr Stil ist sehr ausgefeilt, **allerdings** manchmal etwas langatmig — *although*

Bis zu einem gewissen Punkt muß man ihm recht geben, wenn man sich auch nicht mit allen Rückschlüssen einverstanden erklären kann — *up to a point*

Ich stimme mit der Verfasserin im Prinzip **überein, möchte aber zu bedenken geben, daß** manche Folgerungen sehr extrem sind — *I agree with ... but I would like to raise the point that*

Im Grunde bin ich mit dem Autor **einer Meinung, möchte aber** einwenden, daß einige wichtige Punkte nicht berücksichtigt wurden — *basically, I agree with ... but I would like to*

Fischer hält die Untersuchungen für abgeschlossen. **Es bleibt aber nach wie vor die Tatsache bestehen**, daß viele Versuche noch laufen — *but the fact remains that*

Gewiß hat der Regisseur Talent und Mut. **Es stellt sich trotzdem die Frage, ob** man wirklich den „Ring" an einem Abend aufführen kann — *certainly ... but I would still question whether*

Mit der Entwicklung des Laser-TV hat die Forschungsgruppe **zwar** Beachtliches geleistet, **ob es aber** wirklich ein Meilenstein in der Fernsehtechnik ist, bleibt umstritten — *certainly ... but whether it*

Ohne den ästhetischen Reiz der Darstellung **schmälern zu wollen**, hätte ich es **doch** begrüßt, wenn ihre Quellen offengelegt worden wären — *without wishing to belittle ... I would have preferred*

Man muß zwar zugeben, daß die Verbesserung des Lebensstandards ein vorrangiges Ziel ihrer Politik ist, **muß aber gleichzeitig sagen, daß** sie noch sehr weit von diesem Ziel entfernt ist — *one must admit that ... but one must also say that*

Zweifellos ist ein hoher gesellschaftlicher Bedarf an Nervenkitzel vorhanden, **aber** das normale Leben ist keineswegs so langweilig, wie es scheint — *doubtless ... but*

Zumindest kann man sagen, daß das Thema durch die Untersuchung einmal ins Bewußtsein der Öffentlichkeit gekommen ist — *at least one can say that*

Emphasizing particular points

Um die Problematik **zu unterstreichen**, hat der Verfasser uns eine Reihe der häufigsten Nebenwirkungen genannt — *in order to emphasize*

Die Verfasserin **betont wiederholt, daß** sie neutrale Zurückhaltung nicht für eine angemessene Reaktion auf dieses Problem hält — *repeatedly stresses that*

Wir müssen klarstellen, daß wir es hier nicht mit einem Schüleraufsatz, sondern mit einem wissenschaftlichen Thesenpapier zu tun haben — *let us make it clear that*

Diese Untersuchung **wirft ein bezeichnendes Licht auf** die gegenwärtige Situation am Arbeitsmarkt — *highlights*

Man sollte auf keinen Fall vergessen, daß zu diesem Zeitpunkt niemand etwas von dem Unfall in Tschernobyl wußte — *let us not forget that*

Besonders an den Universitäten lassen sich diese politischen Strömungen erkennen — *it is particularly ... that*

Wenn er sich bisher noch nicht zu diesem Thema geäußert hat, **so liegt das an** politischen Erwägungen **und nicht an** mangelndem Interesse — *it is ... and not ... that have prevented him*

Er spricht sich **nicht nur** gegen die Etaterhöhung aus, **sondern** fordert **auch** strenge Sparmaßnahmen in allen Ministerien — *not only ... but also*

Er ist kein Dummkopf - **genau das** unterscheidet ihn von den meisten Argans der Theatergeschichte — *that is what*

26

Er fällt **nicht** auf die Artistik stürmischer Läufe herein**, im Gegenteil**, er konzentriert sich auf die leisen, lyrischen Passagen — *he doesn't ..., on the contrary*

Es wird wirtschaftlich weiter bergab gehen, **um so mehr, als** im Winter die Arbeitslosenzahlen ohnehin zunehmen — *all the more so because*

Ich möchte sogar behaupten, daß Albrecht Schwarz eine lästige Person ist, die vielleicht früher einmal einen Zweck erfüllt haben mochte — *I would even go so far as to say that*

Tritium kann die Transmutation von Thymin zu Cytosin bewirken, **und dazu kommt noch, daß** Schaden an der DNS verursacht wird — *and, furthermore*

Die Inselbewohner brauchen keine Berührungsängste zu haben, **um so weniger, als** das Fischereiabkommen weit günstiger ausgefallen ist, als angenommen — *even less so now that*

Moderating a statement

Ohne den Verfasser kritisieren zu wollen, scheint es doch, daß er mit einer anderen Methode bessere Meßergebnisse erzielt hätte — *without wishing to criticize the author*

Das soll nicht heißen, daß Exportgeschäfte groß und Menschenrechte kleingeschrieben werden, **sondern vielmehr, daß** eine wertorientierte Außenpolitik der Wirtschaft den Weg ebnen muß — *this does not mean that ..., but rather that*

Dieses Verfahren ist **keineswegs** altruistischen Überlegungen des britischen Staates zu verdanken, **sondern vielmehr** als Instrument zur Sicherung des sozialen Friedens gedacht — *in no way ... but rather*

An sich hat die Autorin **im großen und ganzen** recht, es ließe sich jedoch einwenden, daß sich inzwischen einige Details geändert haben — *by and large*

Ohne Kleinigkeiten zu viel Gewicht beimessen zu wollen, muß man doch sagen, daß ihre Zeitangaben sehr unpräzise sind — *without laying too much emphasis on details*

Es wäre ungerecht *or* **unfair**, von einem solchen Kompendium eine Art konzeptionelle Geschlossenheit zu erwarten — *it would be unfair to*

Indicating agreement

Man muß zugeben, daß gerade dieser Aspekt faszinierend ist — *one must admit that*

Seine Beschreibung der Situation **trifft in allen Punkten genau (zu)** *or* **ist bis ins Detail präzise** — *is correct in every detail*

Dieses Argument **ist völlig überzeugend** *or* **überzeugt völlig** — *is completely convincing*

Wir können uns diesen Schlußfolgerungen **nicht verschließen** — *we cannot ignore*

Wie die Verfasserin **so richtig sagt**, kommt es auch auf Details an — *as ... so rightly says*

Es ist klar, daß hier Geschichte geschrieben wurde — *it is clear that*

Ich **kann mich der Meinung** des Verfassers nur **uneingeschränkt anschließen** — *support (his) view wholeheartedly*

Indicating disagreement

Diese Sichtweise **kann man unmöglich** unwidersprochen **akzeptieren** — *one cannot possibly accept*

Dieses Argument **ist keiner Beachtung wert** *or* **verdient keine Beachtung** — *is not worthy of our attention*

Diesen Standpunkt **kann man** heute **nicht mehr vertreten** — *(this view) is no longer tenable*

Die Äußerungen des Innenministers **stehen in völligem Widerspruch zur** Haltung des Verteidigungsministers — *completely contradict*

Ich muß hier jedoch einige schwerwiegende **Bedenken gegen** diese Beweisführung **anmelden** — *express misgivings about*

Die Untersuchung von Professor Sommerfeld **widerlegt** klar diese Behauptung — *disproves*

Gegen alle diese Kritikpunkte **kann man** allerdings **einwenden** *or* **zu bedenken geben**, daß es hier um eine neue Kunstform geht — *one can object/one can argue*

Diese Behauptung **scheint mir sehr zweifelhaft** *or* **fragwürdig** — *seems to me to be questionable*

Der Autor irrt sich, wenn er uns zu verstehen gibt, daß das Ergebnis schon vor Beginn der Verhandlungen feststand — *the author is wrong to imply that*

Die Beweisführung ist bestechend, **trotzdem kann ich die Meinung** *or* **den Standpunkt der Verfasser nicht teilen** — *however I cannot share the author's view*

Ich kann seine pessimistische Weltsicht **nicht gutheißen** — *I cannot embrace*

Indicating approval

Es ist leicht zu verstehen, daß er mit dieser Meinung gut ankommt — *it is easy to understand how*

Gewiß wäre die beste Lösung, einen lockeren Staatenbund zu bilden — *the best solution would certainly be*

Die Bundesbank **hat gut daran getan**, an der Zielvorgabe für die Geldmenge festzuhalten — *did well to*

Der Student kritisiert **völlig zu Recht** die verbeamtete Mittelmäßigkeit der Professoren — *very rightly*

Es war wirklich an der Zeit, daß man sich wieder an gewisse Grundwerte der Gesellschaft erinnert — *it was high time that*

Endlich einmal ein Artikel, in dem ich mich als Lehrer wiederfinden kann	*at last*
Dieses Buch **ist besonders willkommen, weil** alle bisherigen Biographien Clara Schumanns romantisch verklärt oder feministisch überzogen waren	*is especially welcome, because*

Indicating disapproval

Es ist schade, daß diese Poesie heute weitgehend verloren ist	*it is a pity that*
Leider hat sich die Autorin mit der Zeichnung der Personen keine große Mühe gegeben	*unfortunately*
Es ist schwer einzusehen, wie das Aktionsprogramm zusätzliche Arbeitsplätze schaffen soll	*it is hard to see*
Ich möchte diese zynische Sichtweise aufs schärfste **verurteilen**	*condemn*
Man muß seine Haltung zur Geburtenkontrolle **scharf kritisieren**	*criticize ... very strongly*
Man kann dem Bürgermeister **vorwerfen, daß** er zu sehr auf die nächsten Wahlen und zu wenig auf das Wohl der Bürger bedacht war	*one may reproach ... for*

Making a correction

Möglicherweise habe ich mich mißverständlich ausgedrückt, deshalb **möchte ich** das Gesagte **an dieser Stelle richtigstellen**	*I would like to put ... right here*
Tatsächlich *or* **In Wirklichkeit** geht es um ganz etwas anderes	*in (actual) fact/in reality*
Es geht hier **nicht um** Prinzipien, **sondern um** Menschenleben	*it is not a question of ... but of*
Diese Schilderung **entspricht nicht den Tatsachen: in Wahrheit** ...	*is not in accordance with the facts: the truth is that*
Diese Befürchtungen **sind völlig grundlos**	*are completely groundless*
Es wäre eine kleine Korrektur zu dieser Behauptung **anzubringen**	*I would point out one small error in*
Die Äußerungen des Pressesprechers **muß ich energisch dementieren**	*I emphatically deny*

Indicating the reason for something

Die hohe Konzentration des Hormons **läßt sich auf** eine intravenöse Behandlung **zurückführen**	*arises from*
Dieses Haus ist die Mühen und Ausgaben wert, **es handelt sich nämlich um** eines der wenigen erhaltenen gotischen Privathäuser	*for you see it is/because it is actually*
Angesichts der Tatsache, daß die Berechnungen nur Richtwerte geben, muß man den weiteren Ergebnissen wirklich mißtrauen	*in view of the fact that*
Das läßt sich sicher durch die persönliche Vergangenheit des Autors **erklären**	*the reason for this doubtless lies in*

Setting out the consequences of something

Diese Entscheidung sollte **unangenehme Folgen** haben	*unpleasant consequences*
Das Verhandlungsergebnis wird langfristig **positive Auswirkungen** für die gesamte Region haben	*beneficial effects*
Er war offensichtlich mit den angebotenen Bedingungen nicht zufrieden, **weshalb** er auch dem Ruf an die Universität Ulm nicht folgte	*which is why*
Und deshalb spielt die Familie in allen seinen Romanen eine herausragende Rolle	*and that is why*
Die Schließung der Fabrik **wird dazu führen, daß** ein großer Teil der Einwohner in andere Industriestädte abwandert	*will cause ... to*
Die Flugpreise sind stark angestiegen, **was** zunächst eine rapide abnehmende Passagierzahl **zur Folge haben wird**	*and that will cause*
Bei der heutigen Lebensweise kommen die evolutionär ausgebildeten Grundfähigkeiten des Menschen zu kurz, **folglich** sind seine Krankheiten biopsychosozialer Natur	*and consequently*
Die Persönlichkeit der Anna ist **also doch** viel komplexer, als es auf den ersten Blick scheint	*thus/therefore*

Contrasting or comparing

Einerseits sollen die Produktionsmengen erhöht werden, **andererseits** jedoch wird die damit verbundene Zunahme der Abfallmenge nicht einkalkuliert	*on (the) one hand ... on the other (hand)*
Einige Kritiker **halten dies für** seine beste Inszenierung, **andere sind der Meinung, daß** er zu große Zugeständnisse an den Publikumsgeschmack gemacht hat	*some ... consider this ... while others believe*
Manche Experten reden heute vom Versagen der Schule. **Andere dagegen** bejubeln den Fortschritt im Bildungswesen	*some ... whereas others*
Die Hirnfunktionen von Alkoholikern regenerieren sich **weitaus besser als** angenommen	*far better than (is)*
Mit den Recherchewerkzeugen der spezialisierten Systeme **kann sich** eine einfache Textverarbeitung **nicht messen**	*is no match for*
Verglichen mit seinen früheren Werken ist dieses Buch nur ein schwacher Abglanz	*compared to*
Diese beiden Inszenierungen **lassen sich einfach nicht vergleichen**	*there is simply no comparison between*

27 Telefonieren

27.1 Nach einer Nummer fragen | Getting a number

Could you get me Newhaven 465786, please? (*four-six-five-seven-eight-six*)	Können Sie mich bitte mit Köln 465786 verbinden? (*vier-sechs-fünf-sieben-acht-sechs)*
Could you give me directory enquiries (*Brit*) *oder* directory assistance (*US*), please?	Können Sie mich bitte mit der Auskunft verbinden?
Can you give me the number of Europost of 54 Broad Street, Newham?	Ich hätte gern eine Nummer in Köln, Firma Europost, Breite Straße 54
It's not in the book	Ich kann die Nummer nicht finden
They're ex-directory (*Brit*) *oder* They're unlisted (*US*)	Das ist eine Geheimnummer
What is the code for Exeter?	Wie lautet die Vorwahl von Leipzig?
Can I dial direct to Peru?	Kann ich nach Peru durchwählen?
How do I make an outside call? *oder* What do I dial for an outside line?	Wie bekomme ich den Amtston?
What do I dial to get the speaking clock?	Wie lautet die Nummer der Zeitansage?
You'll have to look up the number in the directory	Sie müssen die Nummer im Telefonbuch nachschlagen
You should get the number from International Directory Enquiries	Sie können die Nummer bei der internationalen Auskunft erfragen
You omit the '0' when dialling England from Germany	Wenn Sie von Deutschland nach England anrufen, lassen Sie die Null weg

27.2 Verschiedene Arten von Anrufen | Different types of call

It's a local call	Es ist ein Ortsgespräch
It's a long-distance call from Worthing	Es ist ein Ferngespräch aus Hamburg
I want to make an international call	Ich möchte ins Ausland anrufen
I want to make a reverse charge call to a London number (*Brit*) *oder* I want to call a London number collect (*US*)	Ich möchte ein R-Gespräch nach London anmelden
I'd like to make a credit card call to Berlin	Ich möchte auf Kreditkarte nach Berlin anrufen
I'd like an alarm call for 7.30 tomorrow morning	Ich hätte gern einen Weckruf fü: morgen früh 7.30 Uhr

27.3 Vermittlung | The operator speaks

Number, please	Welche Nummer möchten Sie?
What number do you want? *oder* What number are you calling?	Welche Nummer wünschen Sie?
Where are you calling from?	Woher rufen Sie an?
Would you repeat the number, please?	Können Sie die Nummer bitte wiederholen?
You can dial the number direct	Sie können durchwählen
Replace the receiver and dial again	Legen Sie auf und wählen Sie noch einmal
There's a Mr Campbell calling you from Canberra and wishes you to pay for the call. Will you accept it?	Ich habe Herrn Campbell mit einem R-Gespräch aus Canberra für Sie. Nehmen Sie das Gespräch an?
Go ahead, caller	Ich verbinde
There's no listing under that name	Ich habe keine Eintragung unter diesem Namen
There's no reply from 45 77 57 84	Der Teilnehmer 45 77 57 84 antwortet nicht
I'll try to reconnect you	Ich versuche es noch einmal
Hold the line, caller	Bitte bleiben Sie am Apparat
All lines to Bristol are engaged - please try later	Alle Leitungen nach Bonn sind besetzt, bitte rufen Sie später noch einmal an
I'm trying it for you now	Ich versuche, Sie jetzt zu verbinden
It's ringing *oder* Ringing for you now	Wir haben ein Rufzeichen
The line is engaged (*Brit*) *oder* busy (*US*)	Die Leitung ist besetzt

27.4 Der Teilnehmer antwortet | When your number answers

Could I have extension 516? *oder* Can you give me extension 516?	Können Sie mich bitte mit Apparat 516 verbinden?
Is that Mr Lambert's phone?	Bin ich mit dem Apparat von Herrn Lambert verbunden?
Could I speak to Mr Swinton, please? *oder* I'd like to speak to Mr Swinton, please *oder* Is Mr Swinton there?	Kann ich bitte mit Herrn Schmiedel sprechen?
Could you put me through to Dr Henderson, please?	Können Sie mich bitte zu Herrn Dr. Graupner durchstellen?
Who's speaking?	Wer ist am Apparat?
I'll try again later	Ich versuche es später noch einmal
I'll call back in half an hour	Ich rufe in einer halben Stunde zurück
Could I leave my number for her to call me back?	Könnte ich bitte meine Nummer hinterlassen, damit sie mich zurückrufen kann?

I'm ringing from a callbox (*Brit*) *oder* I'm calling from a pay station (*US*)
I'm phoning from England
Would you ask him to ring me when he gets back?

Ich rufe aus einer Telefonzelle an

Ich rufe aus England an
Könnten Sie ihn bitten, mich zurückzurufen, wenn er wiederkommt?

27.5 Die Zentrale antwortet

Queen's Hotel, can I help you?
Who is calling, please?
Who shall I say is calling?
Do you know his extension number?
I am connecting you now *oder* I'm putting you through now
I have a call from Tokyo for Mrs Thomas
I've got Miss Trotter on the line for you
Miss Paxton is calling you from Paris
Dr Craig is talking on the other line
Sorry to keep you waiting
There's no reply
You're through to our Sales Department

The switchboard operator speaks

Hotel Maritim, guten Tag
Wer ist am Apparat, bitte?
Wen darf ich melden?
Wissen Sie, welchen Apparat er hat?
Ich verbinde Sie
Ein Gespräch aus Tokio für Frau Böhme
Frau Fehrmann für Sie
Frau Neubert aus Paris für Sie
Herr Dr. Schwendt spricht gerade auf der anderen Leitung
Bitte bleiben Sie am Apparat
Es meldet sich niemand
Sie sind mit unserer Verkaufsabteilung verbunden

27.6 Sich am Telefon melden

Hello, this is Anne speaking
(*Is that Anne?*) Speaking
Would you like to leave a message?
Can I take a message for him?
Don't hang up yet
Put the phone down and I'll call you back
This is a recorded message
Please speak after the tone

Answering the telephone

Hallo, Anne hier
(Kann ich mit Anne sprechen?) Am Apparat
Möchten Sie eine Nachricht hinterlassen?
Kann ich ihm etwas ausrichten?
Bitte bleiben Sie am Apparat
Legen Sie bitte auf, ich rufe Sie zurück
Hier spricht der automatische Anrufbeantworter
Bitte sprechen Sie nach dem Tonzeichen

27.7 Bei Schwierigkeiten

I can't get through
The number is not ringing
I'm getting "number unobtainable" *oder* I'm getting the "number unobtainable" signal
Their phone is out of order
We were cut off
I must have dialled the wrong number
We've got a crossed line
I've called them several times with no reply

You gave me a wrong number
I got the wrong extension
This is a very bad line

In case of difficulty

Ich komme nicht durch
Ich bekomme kein Rufzeichen
Ich bekomme immer nur „Kein Anschluß unter dieser Nummer"

Das Telefon ist gestört
Wir sind unterbrochen worden
Ich muß mich verwählt haben
Da ist noch jemand in der Leitung
Ich habe mehrmals angerufen, aber es hat sich niemand gemeldet
Sie haben mir die falsche Nummer gegeben
Ich bin mit dem falschen Apparat verbunden worden
Die Verbindung ist sehr schlecht

28 Vorschläge

28.1 Vorschläge machen

You might like to think it over before giving me your decision	*vielleicht möchten Sie*
If you were to give me the negative, **I could** get copies made	*wenn Sie ..., könnte ich*
You could help me clear out my office, **if you don't mind**	*Sie könnten ..., wenn es Ihnen nichts ausmacht*
We could stop off in Venice for a day or two, **if you like**	*wir könnten ..., wenn Sie möchten*
I've got an idea - **let's organize** a sùrprise birthday party for Hannah!	*laßt uns doch ... organisieren*
If you've no objection(s), I'll speak to them personally	*wenn Sie keine Einwände haben, werde ich*
If I were you, I'd go	*an Ihrer Stelle würde ich*
If you ask me, you'd better take some extra cash	*wenn Sie mich fragen, Sie sollten besser*
I'd be very careful not to commit myself at this stage	*ich würde mich hüten*
I would recommend (that) you discuss it with him before making a decision	*ich würde vorschlagen, (daß) Sie*
It could be in your interest to have a word with the owner first	*es könnte in Ihrem Interesse sein*
There's a lot to be said for living alone	*es spricht vieles dafür*
Go and see Pompeii - **it's a must!**	*das muß man gesehen haben*

Unschlüssiger

I suggest that you go to bed and try to sleep	*ich schlage vor, daß Sie*
I'd like to suggest that you seriously consider taking a long holiday	*ich würde vorschlagen, daß Sie*
We propose that half the fee be paid in advance, and half on completion	*wir schlagen vor, daß*
It is very important that you take an interest in what he is trying to do	*es ist sehr wichtig, daß*
I am convinced that this would be a dangerous step to take	*ich bin überzeugt, daß*
I cannot put it too strongly: **you really must** see a doctor	*Sie müssen wirklich*

Weniger direkt

Say you were to approach the problem from a different angle	*wenn Sie nun*
In these circumstances, **it might be better to** wait	*es wäre vielleicht besser*
Perhaps it would be as well to change the locks	*vielleicht wäre es besser*
It might be a good thing *oder* **a good idea to** warn her about this	*es wäre vielleicht gut*
Perhaps you should take up a sport	*vielleicht sollten Sie*
If I may make a suggestion, a longer hemline might suit you better	*wenn ich einen Vorschlag machen dürfte*
If I might be permitted to suggest something, installing bigger windows would make the office much brighter	*wenn ich vielleicht einen Vorschlag machen dürfte*
Might I be allowed to offer a little advice? - talk it over with a solicitor before you go any further	*dürfte ich Ihnen einen Rat geben*

Als Frage

How do you fancy a holiday in Australia?	*was hältst du von*
How would you feel about tak**ing** calcium supplements?	*was halten Sie von*
I was thinking of going for a drink later. **How about it?**	*wie wäre das*
What would you say to a trip up to town next week?	*was würden Sie zu ... sagen*
Would you like to stay in Paris for a couple of nights?	*möchten Sie*
Would you care to have lunch with me?	*möchten Sie*
What if you try ignoring her and see if that stops her complaining?	*und wenn*
What you need is a change of scene. **Why not** go on a cruise?	*warum nicht*
Suppose *oder* **Supposing** you left the kids with your mother for a few days?	*angenommen*
Have you ever thought of start**ing** up a magazine of your own?	*haben Sie schon mal daran gedacht*

28.2 Vorschläge erbitten

What would you do if you were me?	*was würden Sie an meiner Stelle tun*
Have you any idea how I should go about it to get the best results?	*haben Sie vielleicht eine Vorstellung, wie ich ... könnte*
I've no idea what to call our new puppy: **have you any suggestions?**	*haben Sie vielleicht einen Vorschlag*
I wonder if you could suggest where we might go for a few days?	*haben Sie vielleicht einen Vorschlag*
I can only afford to buy one of them: **which do you suggest?**	*welchen würden Sie vorschlagen*
I'm a bit doubtful about where to start	*ich weiß nicht genau*

29 Ratschläge

29.1 Ratschläge erbitten

What would you do **if you were me?**	*an meiner Stelle*
Would a pear tree grow in this spot? If not, **what would you recommend?**	*was würden Sie empfehlen*
Do you think I ought to tell the truth if he asks me where I've been?	*denken Sie, ich sollte*
Would you advise me to seek promotion within this firm or apply for another job?	*meinen Sie, ich sollte*
What would you advise me to do in the circumstances?	*was würden Sie mir raten*
I'd like *oder* **I'd appreciate your advice on** personal pensions	*ich würde Sie gern um Rat fragen*
I'd be grateful if you could advise me on how to treat this problem	*ich wäre Ihnen sehr dankbar, wenn Sie mir raten könnten*

29.2 Rat geben

It might be wise *oder* **sensible to** consult a specialist	*es wäre vielleicht das Vernünftigste*
It might be a good idea to seek professional advice	*es wäre vielleicht gut*
It might be better to think the whole thing over before taking any decisions	*es wäre vielleicht besser*
It would certainly be advisable to book a table	*es wäre sicherlich besser*
You'd be as well to state your position at the outset, so there is no mistake	*am besten sollten Sie vielleicht*
You would be well-advised to invest in a pair of sunglasses if you're going to Spain	*Sie wären gut beraten, wenn Sie*
You'd be ill-advised to have any dealings with this firm	*Sie wären schlecht beraten, wenn Sie*
It is in your interest *oder* **your best interests to** keep your dog under control if you don't want it to be reported	*es wäre ganz in Ihrem Interesse*
Do be sure to read the small print before you sign anything	*auf jeden Fall sollten Sie*
Try to avoid upsetting her; she'll only make your life a misery	*vermeiden Sie*
Whatever you do, don't drink the local schnapps	*was auch immer Sie vorhaben, Sie sollten nie*
If you ask me, you'd better take some extra cash	*wenn Sie mich fragen, Sie sollten besser*
If you want my advice, you should steer well clear of them	*wenn Sie mich um Rat fragen, Sie sollten*
If you want my opinion, I'd go by air to save time	*meiner Meinung nach sollten Sie*
In your shoes *oder* **If I were you, I'd** be thinking about moving on	*an Ihrer Stelle würde ich*
Might I be allowed to offer a little advice? - talk it over with a solicitor before going any further	*dürfte ich Ihnen einen Rat geben*
Take my advice and don't rush into anything	*nehmen Sie meinen Ratschlag an*
I'd be very careful not to commit myself at this stage	*ich würde mich davor hüten*
I think you ought to *oder* **should** seek professional advice	*ich denke, Sie sollten*
My advice would be to have nothing to do with them	*ich würde Ihnen raten*
I would advise you to pay up promptly before they take you to court	*ich würde Ihnen raten*
I would advise against calling in the police unless he threatens you	*ich würde Ihnen davon abraten, zu*
I would strongly advise you to reconsider this decision	*ich würde Ihnen dringend anraten*
I would urge you to reconsider selling the property	*Sie sollten unbedingt*

29.3 Warnende Hinweise

It's really none of my business but **I don't think you should** get involved	*ich denke, Sie sollten nicht*
A word of caution: watch what you say to him if you want it to remain a secret	*ein warnender Hinweis*
I should warn you that he's not an easy customer to deal with	*ich sollte Sie vielleicht warnen, daß*
Take care not to lose the vaccination certificate	*achten Sie darauf, daß Sie nicht*
Watch you don't trip over your shoelaces	*paß auf, daß du nicht*
Make sure that *oder* **Mind that** *oder* **See that you don't** say anything they might find offensive	*auf keinen Fall sollten Sie*
I'd think twice about sharing a flat with him	*ich würde es mir gut überlegen, ob*
It would be sheer madness to attempt to drive without your glasses	*es wäre reiner Wahnsinn*
You risk a long delay in Amsterdam **if** you come back by that route	*Sie riskieren ..., wenn*

30 Angebote

I would be delighted to help out, if I may	*ich würde sehr gerne*
It would give me great pleasure to show you round the city	*ich würde sehr gerne*
We would like to offer you the post of Sales Director	*wir möchten Ihnen ... anbieten*
I hope you will not be offended if I offer a contribution towards your expenses	*ich hoffe, Sie nehmen es mir nicht übel, wenn ich*
Do let me know if I can help in any way	*lassen Sie es mich wissen, wenn ich ... kann*
If we can be of any further assistance, **please do not hesitate to** contact us	*falls wir ... können, zögern Sie bitte nicht*
Say we were to offer you a 5% rise, **how would that sound?**	*und wenn wir ..., wie wäre das*
What if I were to call for you in the car?	*was halten Sie davon, wenn ich*
Could I give you a hand with your luggage?	*kann ich vielleicht*
Shall I do the photocopies for you?	*soll ich*
Would you like me to find out more about it for you?	*soll ich*
Is there anything I can do to help you find suitable accommodation?	*kann ich irgendetwas tun, um*
May *oder* **Can I offer you** a drink?	*darf ich Ihnen ... anbieten*
Would you allow me to pay for dinner, at least?	*würden Sie mir gestatten*
You will let me show you around Glasgow, **won't you**?	*Sie werden es mir doch nicht abschlagen*

31 Bitten

Please would you drop by on your way home and pick up the papers you left here?	*würden Sie bitte*
Could you please try to keep the noise down while I'm studying?	*könnten Sie bitte*
Could I ask you to watch out for anything suspicious in my absence?	*könnte ich Sie bitten*
Would you mind look**ing** after Hannah for a couple of hours tomorrow?	*würde es Ihnen etwas ausmachen*

Förmlicher

I should be grateful if you could confirm whether it would be possible to increase my credit limit to £5000	*ich wäre Ihnen dankbar, wenn Sie ... könnten*
We would ask you not to use the telephone for long-distance calls	*wir möchten Sie darum bitten*
You are requested to park at the rear of the building	*wir möchten Sie bitten*
We look forward to receiv**ing** confirmation of your order within 14 days	*wir freuen uns darauf*
Kindly inform us if you require alternative arrangements to be made	*bitte teilen Sie uns mit, wenn*

Weniger direkt

I would rather you didn't breathe a word to anyone about this	*es wäre mir lieber, wenn Sie nicht*
I would appreciate it if you could let me have copies of the best photos	*es wäre schön, wenn Sie ... könnten*
I was hoping that you might have time to visit your grandmother	*ich hatte gehofft, du würdest vielleicht*
I wonder whether you could spare a few pounds till I get to the bank?	*könntest du vielleicht*
I hope you don't mind if I borrow your exercise bike for half an hour	*hoffentlich macht es dir nichts aus, wenn ich*
It would be very helpful *oder* **useful if you could** have everything ready beforehand	*es wäre sehr zu begrüßen, wenn Sie ... könnten*
If it's not too much trouble, would you pop my suit into the dry cleaners on your way past?	*wenn es nicht zu viel Umstände macht, würden Sie*
You won't forget to lock up before you leave, **will you?**	*vergiß nicht ..., ja*

32 Vergleiche

32.1 Objektive Vergleiche

The streets, though wide for China, are narrow **compared with** English ones	*verglichen mit*
The bomb used to blow the car up was small **in** *oder* **by comparison with** those often used nowadays	*im Vergleich zu*
The quality of the paintings is disappointing **beside** that of the sculpture section	*im Vergleich zu*
If you compare the facilities we have here **with** those in other towns, you soon realize how lucky we are	*wenn man ... mit ... vergleicht*
It is interesting to note **the similarities and the differences between** the two approaches	*die Gemeinsamkeiten und Unterschiede zwischen*
In contrast to the opulence of the Kirov, the Northern Ballet Theatre is a modest company	*im Gegensatz zu*
Only 30% of the females died **as opposed to** 57% of the males	*im Gegensatz zu*
Unlike other loan repayments, those to the IMF cannot simply be rescheduled	*im Gegensatz zu*
Whereas burglars often used to make off only with video recorders, they now also tend to empty the fridge	*während*
What differentiates these wines **from** a good champagne is their price	*was ... von ... unterscheidet*

32.2 Positive Vergleiche

Orwell was, indeed, **far superior to** him intellectually	*wesentlich besser als*
Personally I think high-speed trains **have the edge over** both cars and aircraft for sheer convenience	*sind ... überlegen*
Emma was astute beyond her years and altogether **in a class of her own**	*einzigartig*

32.3 Negative Vergleiche

Andrew's piano playing **is not a patch on** his sister's	*ist gar nichts verglichen mit*
My old chair **was nowhere near as** comfortable **as** my new one	*in keiner Hinsicht so ... wie*
The parliamentary opposition **is no match for** the government, which has a massive majority	*ist ... nicht gewachsen*
Commercially-made ice-cream **is far inferior to** the home-made variety	*ist viel schlechter als*
The sad truth was that **he was never in the same class as** his friend	*er war einfach nicht mit ... zu vergleichen*
Ella doesn't rate anything **that doesn't measure up to** Shakespeare	*das nicht an ... heranreicht*
Her brash charms **don't bear comparison with** Marlene's sultry sex appeal	*halten einem Vergleich mit ... nicht stand*
The Australians are far bigger and stronger than us - **we can't compete with** their robot-like style of play	*wir können mit ... nicht mithalten*

32.4 Vergleichbar

The new computerized system costs **much the same as** a more conventional one	*fast dasselbe*
When it comes to performance, **there's not much to choose between** them	*gibt es fast kaum Unterschiede*
The impact **was equivalent to** 250 hydrogen bombs exploding	*entsprach*
In Kleinian analysis, the psychoanalyst's role **corresponds to** that of mother	*entspricht*
English literature written by people of the ex-colonies **is on a par with** the writings of native-born British people	*ist genauso gut wie*
The immune system **can be likened to** *oder* **compared to** a complicated electronic network	*kann mit ... verglichen werden*
There was a close resemblance between her **and** her son	*... und ... waren sich sehr ähnlich*
It's swings and roundabouts - what you win in one round, you lose in another	*das ist gehupft wie gesprungen*

32.5 Nicht vergleichbar

You cannot compare a small local library **with** a large city one	*man kann ... nicht mit ... vergleichen*
There's no comparison between the sort of photos I take **and** those a professional could give you	*... und ... kann man einfach nicht miteinander vergleichen*
Homemade clothes **just cannot compare with** bought ones	*sind eben nicht mit ... vergleichbar*
His books **have little in common with** those approved by the Party	*haben wenig mit ... gemein*
We might be twins, but **we have nothing in common**	*wir haben nichts gemein*
The modern army **bears little resemblance to** the army of 1940	*hat kaum mehr Ähnlichkeit mit*

33 Meinungen

33.1 Meinungen erfragen

What do you think of the new Managing Director? — *was halten Sie von*

What is your opinion on women's rights? — *wie denken Sie über*

What are your thoughts on the way forward? — *wie ist Ihre Meinung zu*

What is your attitude to people who say there is no such thing as sexual inequality? — *wie stehen Sie zu*

What are your own feelings about the way the case was handled? — *was halten Sie persönlich von*

How do you see the next stage developing? — *wie sehen Sie*

How do you view an event like the Birmingham show in terms of the cultural life of the city? — *wie schätzen Sie ... ein*

I would value your opinion on how best to set this all up — *mir wäre sehr an Ihrer Meinung über ... gelegen*

I'd be interested to know what your reaction is to the latest report on food additives — *ich wüßte gern, was Sie von ... halten*

33.2 Seine Meinung sagen

In my opinion, eight years as President is quite enough for anyone — *meiner Meinung nach*

We're prepared to prosecute the company, which **to my mind** has committed a criminal offence — *meiner Meinung nach*

From my point of view activities like these should not be illegal — *aus meiner Sicht*

I am of the opinion that the rules should be looked at and refined — *ich bin der Meinung, daß*

As I see it, everything depended on Karlov being permitted to go to Finland — *so wie ich die Sache sehe*

I feel that there is an epidemic of fear about cancer which is not helped by all the publicity about the people who die of it — *ich persönlich denke, daß*

Personally, I believe the best way to change a government is through the electoral process — *persönlich glaube ich*

It seems to me that the successful designer leads the public — *mir scheint, (daß)*

I am under the impression that he is essentially a man of peace — *ich habe den Eindruck, daß*

I have an idea that you are going to be very successful — *ich kann mir vorstellen, daß*

I'm convinced that we all need a new vision of the future — *ich bin überzeugt, daß*

I daresay there are so many names that you get them mixed up once in a while — *ich würde sagen*

As far as I'm concerned, Barnes had it coming to him — *was mich betrifft*

It's a matter of common sense, nothing more. **That's my view of the matter** — *so sehe ich die Sache*

It is our belief that to be proactive is more positive than being reactive — *wir glauben, daß*

If you ask me, there's something a bit strange going on — *wenn Sie mich fragen*

If you want my opinion, if you don't do it soon you'll lose the opportunity altogether — *wenn Sie meine Meinung hören wollen*

33.3 Keine Meinung zum Ausdruck bringen

Would I say she had been a help? **It depends what you mean by** help — *das hängt davon ab, was Sie unter ... verstehen*

It could be seen as a triumph for capitalism but **it depends on your point of view** — *das hängt von Ihrer Meinung ab*

It's hard *oder* **difficult to say whether** she has benefited from the treatment or not — *es ist schwer zu sagen, ob*

I'm not in a position to comment on whether the director's accusations are well-founded — *ich kann mich nicht dazu äußern, ob*

I'd prefer not to comment on operational decisions taken by the service in the past — *ich möchte mich lieber nicht zu ... äußern*

I'd rather not commit myself at this stage — *ich möchte mich lieber nicht festlegen*

I don't have any strong feelings about which of the two companies we decide to use for the job — *ich habe eigentlich keine besondere Meinung über*

This isn't something I've given much thought to — *damit habe ich mich noch nicht eingehend beschäftigt*

I know nothing about fine wine — *ich habe keine Ahnung von*

34 Vorlieben und Abneigungen

34.1 Vorlieben erfragen

Would you like to visit the castle while you are here? — *möchten Sie*
How would you feel about Simon join**ing** us? — *was halten Sie davon, wenn*
What do you like doing **best** when you're on holiday? — *was machen Sie am liebsten*
What's your favourite film? — *was ist Ihr Lieblings...*
Which of the two proposed options **do you prefer?** — *welche der beiden ... ist Ihnen lieber*
We could either go to Rome or stay in Florence - **which would you rather do?** — *was würden Sie lieber tun*

34.2 Vorlieben ausdrücken

I'm very keen on garden**ing** — *ich ... sehr gerne*
I'm very fond of white geraniums and blue petunias — *ich mag ... sehr*
I really enjoy a good game of squash after work — *... macht mir sehr viel Spaß*
There's nothing I like more than a quiet night in with a good book — *nichts mag ich lieber als*
I have a weakness for rich chocolate gateaux — *ich habe eine Schwäche für*
I've always had a soft spot for the Dutch — *ich habe schon immer eine Schwäche für ... gehabt*

34.3 Abneigung ausdrücken

Acting **isn't really my thing** - I'm better at singing — *ist nichts für mich*
I enjoy playing golf, although this type of course **is not my cup of tea** — *ist nicht mein Fall*
Watching football on television **isn't my favourite** pastime — *ist nicht gerade meine Lieblings...*
Some people might find it funny but **it's not my kind of** humour — *ist nicht meine Art von*
Sitting for hours on motorways **is not my idea of** fun — *ist nicht gerade das, was ich mir unter ... vorstelle*

The idea of walking home at 10 or 11 o'clock at night **doesn't appeal to me** — *gefällt mir nicht*
I've gone off the idea of cycl**ing** round Holland — *ich habe das Interesse daran verloren*
I can't stand *oder* **can't bear** the thought of seeing him — *ich kann ... nicht ertragen*
I am not enthusiastic about shopp**ing** in large supermarkets — *ich bin nicht gerade begeistert von*
I'm not keen on seafood — *ich mag ... nicht*
I dislike laziness since I'm such an energetic person myself — *ich mag ... nicht*
I don't like the fact that he always gets away with not helping out in the kitchen — *mir gefällt nicht, daß*
What I hate most is waiting in queues for buses — *am meisten hasse ich*
There's nothing I dislike more than having to go to work in the dark — *nichts hasse ich mehr als*
I have a particular aversion to the religious indoctrination of schoolchildren — *besonders abstoßend finde ich*
I find it intolerable that people like him should have so much power — *ich finde es unerträglich, daß*

34.4 Ausdrücken, was man bevorzugt

I'd prefer to *oder* **I'd rather** wait until I have enough money to go by air — *ich würde lieber*
I'd prefer not to *oder* **I'd rather not** talk about it just now — *ich würde lieber nicht*
I'd prefer you to give *oder* **I'd rather you** gave me your comments in writing — *es wäre mir lieber, wenn Sie*
I'd prefer you not to *oder* **I'd rather you didn't** invite him — *es wäre mir lieber, wenn Sie nicht*
I like the blue curtains **better than** the red ones — *... gefallen mir besser als*
I prefer red wine **to** white wine — *ich mag lieber ... als ...*

34.5 Keine Vorliebe ausdrücken

It makes no odds whether you have a million pounds or nothing, we won't judge you on your wealth — *es ist ganz egal, ob*
It doesn't matter which method you choose to use — *es ist egal, welche*
It's all the same to me whether he comes **or** not — *es ist mir vollkommen egal, ob ... oder*
I really don't care what you tell her as long as you tell her something — *es kümmert mich wirklich nicht, was*
I don't mind at all - let's do whatever is easiest — *das macht mir gar nichts aus*
I don't feel strongly about the issue of privatization — *ich habe keine besondere Meinung über*
I have no particular preference — *ich habe keine spezielle Vorliebe*

35 Absichten und Vorhaben

35.1 Nach Absichten fragen

Will you take the job? — *haben Sie vor*
What do you intend to do? — *was beabsichtigen Sie zu tun*
Did you mean to *oder* **intend to** tell him about it, or did it just slip out? — *hatten Sie die Absicht*
What do you propose to do with the money? — *was wollen Sie ... machen*
What did you have in mind for the rest of the programme? — *wie hatten Sie sich ... vorgestellt*
Have you anyone in mind for the job? — *haben Sie jemanden bestimmten ins Auge gefaßt*

35.2 Absichten ausdrücken

We're toying with the idea of releas**ing** a compilation album — *wir spielen mit dem Gedanken*
I'm thinking of retir**ing** next year — *ich trage mich mit dem Gedanken*
I'm hoping to go and see her when I'm in Paris — *ich habe eigentlich vor*
I studied history, **with a view to** becom**ing** a politician — *mit der Absicht*
We bought the land **in order to** farm it — *um zu*
We do not penetrate foreign companies **for the purpose of** collecting business information — *um zu*
We plan to move *oder* **We are planning on** mov**ing** next year — *wir planen*
Our aim *oder* **Our object in** buy**ing** the company **is to** provide work for the villagers — *unsere Absicht bei ... besteht darin*
I aim to reach Africa in three months — *ich habe mir vorgenommen*

Bestimmter

I am going to sell the car as soon as possible — *ich habe vor*
I intend to put the house on the market — *ich beabsichtige*
I went to Rome **with the intention of** visit**ing** her, but she had gone away — *mit der Absicht*
I have made up my mind to *oder* **I have decided to** go to Japan — *ich habe mich entschieden*
We have every intention of winn**ing** a sixth successive championship — *wir sind fest entschlossen*
I have set my sights on recaptur**ing** the title — *ich habe mir das Ziel gesteckt*
My overriding ambition is to get into politics — *mein allergrößter Ehrgeiz ist es*
I resolve to do everything in my power to help you — *ich habe beschlossen*

35.3 Ausdrücken, was man nicht beabsichtigt

I don't mean to offend you, but I think you're wrong — *ich möchte nicht*
I don't intend to pay unless he completes the job — *ich habe nicht vor*
We are not thinking of tak**ing** on more staff — *wir haben nicht vor*
I have no intention of accept**ing** the post — *ich habe nicht die Absicht*
We do not envisage making changes at this late stage — *wir gedenken nicht*

35.4 Wünsche ausdrücken

I'd like to see the Sistine Chapel some day — *ich würde gerne*
I want to work abroad when I leave college — *ich möchte*
We want her to be an architect when she grows up — *wir möchten, daß sie*
I'm keen to develop the business — *ich möchte gerne*

Enthusiastisch

I'm dying to leave home — *ich kann es kaum erwarten*
I long to go to Australia but I can't afford it — *ich würde wahnsinnig gerne*
My ambition is to become an opera singer — *mein Ehrgeiz geht dahin*
I insist on speak**ing** to the manager — *ich bestehe darauf*

35.5 Ausdrücken, was man nicht wünscht

I would prefer not to *oder* **I would rather not** have to speak to her about this — *ich würde lieber nicht*
I wouldn't want to have to change my plans just because of her — *ich möchte nicht*
I don't want to take the credit for something I didn't do — *ich möchte nicht*
I have no wish *oder* **desire to** become rich and famous — *ich habe nicht das Verlangen*
I refuse to be patronized by the likes of her — *ich lehne es ab*

36 Erlaubnis

36.1 Um Erlaubnis bitten

Can I *oder* **Could** I borrow your car this afternoon?	*kann ich vielleicht*
Can I use the telephone, please?	*könnte ich*
Are we allowed to say what we're up to or is it top secret at the moment?	*dürfen wir*
Would it be all right if I arrived on Monday instead of Tuesday?	*wäre es in Ordnung, wenn*
Would it be possible for us to leave the car in your garage for a week?	*wäre es möglich, daß wir*
We leave tomorrow. **Is that all right by you**?	*ist das in Ordnung*
Do you mind if I come to the meeting next week?	*haben Sie etwas dagegen, wenn*
Would it bother you if I invited him?	*würde es Sie stören, wenn*
Would you let me come into partnership with you?	*würden Sie mir gestatten*
Would you have any objection to sailing at once?	*haben Sie irgendwelche Einwände dagegen*
With your permission, I'd like to ask some questions	*mit Ihrer Erlaubnis würde ich gerne*
Can I have the go-ahead to order the supplies?	*kann ich grünes Licht bekommen*

Zögernder

Is there any chance of borrowing your boat while we're at the lake?	*wäre es vielleicht möglich*
I wonder if I could possibly use your telephone?	*könnte ich vielleicht*
Might I be permitted to suggest the following ideas?	*dürfte ich vielleicht*
May I be allowed to set the record straight?	*dürfte ich vielleicht*

36.2 Erlaubnis erteilen

You can have anything you want	*Sie können*
You are allowed to visit the museum, as long as you apply in writing to the Curator first	*Sie haben die Erlaubnis*
You have my permission to be absent for that week	*Sie haben meine Erlaubnis*
It's all right by me if you want to skip the Cathedral visit	*es ist mir recht, wenn*
I've nothing against her going there with us	*ich habe nichts dagegen, wenn sie*
The Crown **was agreeable to** having the case called on March 23	*hat zugestimmt*
I do not mind if my letter is forwarded to the lady concerned	*ich habe nichts dagegen, wenn*
You have been authorized to use all necessary force to protect relief supply routes	*Sie sind bevollmächtigt*
We should be happy to allow you to inspect the papers here	*gerne gestatten wir Ihnen*
If you need to keep your secret, **of course you must** keep it	*müssen Sie selbstverständlich*
By all means charge a reasonable consultation fee	*auf jeden Fall*
I have no objection at all to your quoting me in your article	*ich erhebe keinerlei Einwände dagegen, daß Sie*
We would be delighted to have you	*wir würden sehr gerne*

36.3 Erlaubnis verweigern

You can't *oder* **you mustn't** go anywhere near the research lab	*Sie dürfen nicht*
You're not allowed to leave the ship until relieved	*Sie dürfen nicht*
You must not enter the premises without the owners' authority	*Sie dürfen auf keinen Fall*
I don't want you to see that man again	*ich möchte nicht, daß Sie*
I'd rather you didn't give them my name	*es wäre mir lieber, wenn Sie nicht*
I've been forbidden to swim for the moment	*ich darf nicht*
I've been forbidden alcohol **by** my doctor	*... hat mir verboten*
I couldn't possibly allow you to pay for all this	*ich kann Ihnen beim besten Willen nicht erlauben*
We cannot allow the marriage **to** take place	*wir können nicht zulassen, daß*

Bestimmter

You are forbidden to contact my children	*ich verbiete es Ihnen*
I absolutely forbid you to take part in any further search	*ich verbiete Ihnen strengstens*
Smoking **is strictly forbidden** at all times	*ist streng verboten*
It is strictly forbidden to carry weapons in this country	*es ist streng verboten*
We regret that it is not possible for you to visit the castle at the moment, owing to the building works	*leider können Sie nicht*

37 Verpflichtung

37.1 Verpflichtung ausdrücken

You've got to *oder* **You have to** be back before midnight	*du mußt*
You must have an address in Prague before you can apply for the job	*Sie müssen*
You need to have a valid passport if you want to leave the country	*Sie müssen*
I have no choice: this is how **I must** live and I cannot do otherwise	*ich muß*
He was forced to ask his family for a loan	*er war gezwungen*
Jews **are obliged to** accept the divine origin of the Law	*sind verpflichtet*
A degree **is indispensable** for future entrants to the profession	*ist unentbehrlich*
Party membership **is an essential prerequisite of** a successful career	*ist eine unbedingte Voraussetzung für*
It is essential to know what the career options are before choosing a course of study	*man muß unbedingt*
Wearing the kilt **is compulsory for** all those taking part	*ist obligatorisch*
One cannot admit defeat, **one is driven to** keep on trying	*man wird dazu gezwungen*
We have no alternative but to fight	*es bleibt uns nichts anderes übrig als zu*
Three passport photos **are required**	*werden benötigt*
Club members **must not fail to** observe the regulations about proper behaviour	*müssen unbedingt*
You will go directly to the headmaster's office and wait for me there	*du wirst*

37.2 Erfragen, ob man etwas tun muß

Do I have to *oder* **Have I got to** be home by midnight?	*muß ich*
Does one have to *oder* **need to** book in advance?	*muß man*
Is it necessary to go into so much detail?	*ist es nötig*
Ought I to tell my colleagues?	*sollte ich*
Should I call the police?	*soll ich*
Am I meant to *oder* **Am I expected to** *oder* **Am I supposed to** fill in this bit of the form?	*soll ich*

37.3 Ausdrücken, was keine Verpflichtung ist

I don't have to *oder* **I haven't got to** be home so early now the nights are lighter	*ich muß nicht unbedingt*
You don't have to *oder* **You needn't** go there if you don't want to	*Sie müssen nicht*
You are not obliged to *oder* **You are under no obligation to** invite him	*Sie sind nicht verpflichtet*
It is not compulsory *oder* **obligatory to** have a letter of acceptance but it does help	*es ist nicht unbedingt notwendig*
The Council **does not expect you to** pay all of your bill at once	*erwartet nicht von Ihnen, daß*

37.4 Verbote ausdrücken

On no account must you be persuaded to give up the cause	*auf gar keinen Fall dürfen Sie*
You are not allowed to sit the exam more than three times	*Sie dürfen nicht*
You mustn't show this document to any unauthorized person	*Sie dürfen nicht*
You're not supposed to *oder* **meant to** use this room unless you are a club member	*Sie dürfen nicht*
Smoking **is not allowed** in the dining room	*ist nicht gestattet*
These are tasks **you cannot** ignore, delegate or bungle	*Sie können nicht*
I forbid you to return there	*ich verbiete Ihnen*
It is forbidden to bring cameras into the gallery	*es ist nicht gestattet*
You are forbidden to talk to anyone while the case is being heard	*es ist Ihnen nicht gestattet*
Smoking **is prohibited** *oder* **is not permitted** in the dining room	*ist nicht gestattet*

38 Zustimmung

38.1 Zustimmung zu Aussagen

I fully agree with you *oder* **I totally agree with you** on this point — *ich bin ganz Ihrer Meinung*
We are in complete agreement on this — *wir sind uns völlig einig*
I entirely take your point about the extra vehicles needed — *ich akzeptiere Ihre Meinung vollkommen, was ... betrifft*

I think **we see completely eye to eye** on this issue — *wir sind uns einig*
I talked it over with the chairman and **we are both of the same mind** — *wir sind beide der gleichen Meinung*
You're quite right in pointing at distribution as the main problem — *Sie haben recht, wenn Sie*
We share your views on the proposed expansion of the site — *wir teilen Ihre Ansichten*
My own experience certainly **bears out** *oder* **confirms** what you say — *meine eigene Erfahrung bestätigt*
It's true that you had the original idea but many other people worked on it — *es stimmt, daß*
As you have quite rightly pointed out, this will not be easy — *wie Sie bereits richtig bemerkten*
I have to concede that the results are quite eye-catching — *ich muß gestehen, daß*
I have no objection to this being done — *ich habe keine Einwände gegen*
I agree in theory, but in practice it's never quite that simple — *theoretisch stimme ich zu*
I agree up to a point — *bis zu einem gewissen Punkt stimme ich zu*

Go for a drink instead of working late? **Sounds good to me!** — *klingt gut*
That's a lovely idea — *das ist eine sehr gute Idee*
I'm all for encouraging a youth section in video clubs such as ours — *ich bin ganz dafür*
I couldn't agree with you more — *ich bin völlig Ihrer Meinung*
I am delighted to wholeheartedly endorse your campaign — *es ist mir eine Freude, ... von ganzem Herzen zu unterstützen*

Our conclusions are entirely consistent with your findings — *unsere Schlußfolgerungen entsprechen vollkommen*

Independent statistics **corroborate** those of your researcher — *bestätigen*
We applaud the group's decision to stand firm on this point — *wir begrüßen*

38.2 Zustimmung zu Vorschlägen

This certainly **seems the right way to go about it** — *scheint der richtige Verfahrensweg*
I will certainly give my backing to such a scheme — *ich werde ... selbstverständlich unterstützen*

It makes sense to enlist helping hands for the final stages — *es macht Sinn*
We certainly welcome this development — *selbstverständlich begrüßen wir*
It's a great idea — *das ist eine großartige Idee*
Cruise control? **I like the sound of that** — *klingt wirklich gut*
I'll go along with Ted's proposal that we open the club up to women — *ich schließe mich ... an*

Weniger direkt

This solution **is most acceptable** to us — *ist sehr annehmbar*
The proposed scheme **meets with our approval** — *trifft auf unsere Zustimmung*
This is a proposal which **deserves our wholehearted support** — *verdient unsere uneingeschränkte Unterstützung*

38.3 Zustimmung zu Forderungen

Of course **I'll be happy to** organize it for you — *werde ich gerne*
I'll do as you suggest and send him the documents — *ich befolge Ihren Rat*
There's no problem about getting tickets for him — *es ist kein Problem*

Weniger direkt

Reputable builders **will not object to** this reasonable request — *werden ... nicht ablehnen*
We should be delighted to cooperate with you in this enterprise — *wir würden uns freuen*
An army statement said it **would comply with** the ceasefire — *sich an ... halten*
I consent to the performance of such procedures as are considered necessary — *ich stimme ... zu*

39 Widerspruch

39.1 Widerspruch zu Gesagtem

There must be some mistake - **it can't possibly** cost as much as that	*es kann auf gar keinen Fall*
I'm afraid he **is quite wrong** if he has told you that	*irrt sich*
You're wrong in thinking that I haven't understood	*Sie irren sich, wenn Sie denken*
The article **is mistaken in** claiming that debating the subject is a waste of public money	*geht falsch in der Annahme*
Surveys **do not bear out** Mrs Fraser's assumption that these people will return to church at a later date	*bestätigen nicht*
I cannot agree with you on this point	*ich kann Ihnen nicht zustimmen*
We cannot accept the view that the lack of research and development explains the decline of Britain	*wir können die Ansicht, daß ..., nicht akzeptieren*
To say we should forget about it, no **I cannot go along with that**	*ich kann mich dem nicht anschließen*
We must agree to differ on this one	*darüber sind wir wohl unterschiedlicher Meinung*

Bestimmter

This is most emphatically not the case	*das ist auf gar keinen Fall so*
I entirely reject his contentions	*ich lehne ... vollständig ab*
I totally disagree with the previous two callers	*ich bin völlig anderer Meinung als*
This is your view of the events: **it is certainly not mine**	*meine Ansicht ist das nicht*
I cannot support you on this matter	*ich kann Sie ... nicht unterstützen*
Surely you can't believe that he'd do such a thing?	*du kannst doch nicht wirklich glauben, daß*

39.2 Ablehnung von Vorschlägen

Bestimmt

I'm dead against this idea	*ich bin völlig dagegen*
Right idea, wrong approach	*ein guter Gedanke, aber er geht in die falsche Richtung*
I will not hear of such a thing	*ich will von ... nichts hören*
It is not feasible to change the schedule at this late stage	*es ist nicht möglich*
This **is not a viable alternative**	*keine praktisch durchführbare Möglichkeit*
Trade sanctions will have an immediate effect but it **is the wrong approach**	*ist die falsche Herangehensweise*

Weniger direkt

I'm not too keen on this idea	*ich halte nicht viel von*
I don't think much of this idea	*ich halte nicht viel von*
This doesn't seem to be the right way of dealing with the problem	*dies scheint mir die falsche Methode zu sein*
While we are grateful for the suggestion, **we are unfortunately unable to** implement this change	*leider ist es uns unmöglich*
I regret that I am not in a position to accept your kind offer	*ich bedaure, daß ich nicht in der Lage bin*

39.3 Ablehnung von Forderungen

I wouldn't dream of doing a thing like that	*es würde mir nicht im Traum einfallen*
I'm sorry but **I just can't** do it	*ich kann das einfach nicht*
I cannot in all conscience leave those kids in that atmosphere	*ich kann nicht guten Gewissens*

Bestimmt

This is quite out of the question for the time being	*das steht ja wohl außer Frage*
I won't agree to any plan that involves your brother	*ich werde ... nicht zustimmen*
I refuse point blank to have anything to do with this affair	*ich weigere mich kategorisch*

Weniger direkt

I am afraid I must refuse	*es tut mir leid, ich muß das ablehnen*
I cannot possibly comply with this request	*ich kann ... wirklich nicht nachkommen*
It is unfortunately impracticable for us to commit ourselves at this stage	*leider ist es uns unmöglich*
In view of the proposed timescale, **I must reluctantly decline to** take part	*muß ich leider ablehnen*

40 Übereinstimmung

40.1 Übereinstimmung mit Gesagtem

I couldn't agree (with you) **more**	*ich stimme vollkommen zu*
I couldn't have put it better myself	*ich hätte es selbst nicht besser sagen können*
We must oppose terrorism, whatever its source. - **Hear, hear!**	*ganz meine Meinung*
I endorse his feelings regarding the condition of the Simpson memorial	*ich befürworte*

40.2 Übereinstimmung mit Vorschlägen

It's just the job!	*das ist genau das Richtige*
This is just the sort of thing I wanted	*das ist genau das, was ich wollte*
This is exactly what I had in mind	*das ist genau das, was ich wollte*
Thank you for sending the draft agenda: **I like the look of it very much**	*es gefällt mir sehr gut*
We are all very enthusiastic about *oder* **very keen on** his latest set of proposals	*wir sind alle sehr begeistert von*
I shall certainly give it my backing	*ich werde es auf jeden Fall befürworten*
Any game which is as clearly enjoyable as this **meets with my approval**	*findet meine Zustimmung*
Skinner's plan **deserves our total support** *oder* **our wholehearted approval**	*verdient unsere uneingeschränkte Zustimmung*
There are considerable advantages in the alternative method you propose	*bietet entscheidende Vorteile*
We recognize the merits of this scheme	*wir sehen die Vorzüge*
We view your proposal to extend the site **favourably**	*wir betrachten ... mit Wohlwollen*
This project **is worthy of our attention**	*verdient unsere Aufmerksamkeit*

40.3 Übereinstimmung mit einer Idee

You're quite right to wait before making such an important decision	*Sie haben ganz recht, wenn Sie*
I entirely approve of the idea	*ich finde ... sehr gut*
I'd certainly go along with that!	*ich stimme dem auf jeden Fall zu*
I'm very much in favour of that sort of thing	*ich bin sehr für*
What an excellent idea!	*was für eine ausgezeichnete Idee*

40.4 Übereinstimmung mit einer Handlung

I applaud Noble's perceptive analysis of the problems	*ich muß ... loben*
I have a very high opinion of their new teaching methods	*ich habe eine sehr hohe Meinung von*
I think very highly of the people who have been leading thus far	*ich habe eine sehr hohe Meinung von*
I have a very high regard for the work of the Crown Prosecution Service	*ich habe großen Respekt vor*
I certainly admire his courage in telling her what he thought of her	*ich bin voller Bewunderung für*
I must congratulate you on the professional way you handled the situation	*ich muß Ihnen zu ... gratulieren*
I greatly appreciate the enormous risk that they had all taken	*ich schätze ... sehr*
I can thoroughly recommend the event to field sports enthusiasts	*ich kann ... von ganzem Herzen empfehlen*

41 Ablehnung

This doesn't seem to be the right way of going about it	*dies scheint nicht der richtige Weg zu sein*
I don't think much of what this government has done so far	*ich halte nicht viel von*
The police **took a dim view of** her attempt to help her son break out of jail	*hielt nicht viel von*
I can't say I'm pleased about what has happened	*ich bin nicht gerade begeistert von*
We have a low *oder* **poor opinion of** opportunists like him	*wir haben keine sehr hohe Meinung von*
They **should not have refused to** give her the money	*hätten es nicht ablehnen sollen*

Bestimmter

I'm fed up with having to wait so long for payments to be made	*ich habe es satt*
I've had (just) about enough of this whole supermodel thing	*langsam reicht es mir mit*
I can't bear *oder* **stand** people who smoke in restaurants	*ich kann ... nicht ausstehen*
How dare he say that!	*was fällt ihm ein*
He was quite wrong to repeat what I said about her	*es war nicht richtig von ihm*
I cannot approve of *oder* **support** any sort of testing on live animals	*ich kann ... nicht zustimmen*
We are opposed to all forms of professional malpractice	*wir sind gegen*
We condemn any intervention which could damage race relations	*wir verurteilen*
I must object to the tag "soft porn actress"	*ich muß ... zurückweisen*
I'm very unhappy about your (idea of) going off to Turkey on your own	*ich bin gar nicht glücklich über*
I strongly disapprove of such behaviour	*ich bin mit ... überhaupt nicht einverstanden*

42 Gewißheit, Wahrscheinlichkeit, Möglichkeit und Fähigkeit

42.1 Gewißheit

She was bound to discover that you and I had talked	*sie mußte einfach*
It is inevitable that they will get to know of our meeting	*es läßt sich nicht vermeiden, daß sie*
I'm sure *oder* **certain (that)** he'll keep his word	*ich bin sicher, daß*
I'm positive *oder* **convinced (that)** it was your mother I saw	*ich bin überzeugt, (daß)*
We now know for certain *oder* **for sure that** the exam papers were seen by several students before the day of the exam	*wir können jetzt mit Sicherheit sagen, daß*
I made sure *oder* **certain that** no one was listening to our conversation	*ich habe darauf geachtet, daß*
From all the evidence **it is clear that** they were planning to sell up	*es ist klar, daß*
What is indisputable is that a diet of fruit and vegetables is healthier	*es ist unbestreitbar, daß*
It is undeniable that racial tensions in Britain have been increasing	*es läßt sich nicht leugnen, daß*
There is no doubt that the talks will be long and difficult	*es steht außer Zweifel, daß*
There can be no doubt about the objective of the animal liberationists	*... steht außer Zweifel*
This crisis has demonstrated **beyond all (possible) doubt** that effective political control must be in place before the creation of such structures	*ohne (jeglichen) Zweifel*
Her pedigree **is beyond dispute** *oder* **question**	*steht außer Frage*
You have my absolute assurance that this is the case	*ich versichere Ihnen, daß*
I can assure you that I have had nothing to do with any dishonest trading	*ich kann Ihnen versichern, daß*
Make no mistake about it - I will return when I have proof of your involvement	*verlassen Sie sich darauf*

42.2 Wahrscheinlichkeit

It is quite likely that you will get withdrawal symptoms at first	*wahrscheinlich*
There is a good *oder* **strong chance that** they will agree to the deal	*höchstwahrscheinlich*
It seems highly likely that it was Bert who told Peter what had happened	*höchstwahrscheinlich*
You will **very probably** be met at the airport by one of our men	*höchstwahrscheinlich*
It is highly probable that American companies will face retaliation abroad	*höchstwahrscheinlich*
The probability is that your investment will be worth more in two years' time	*aller Wahrscheinlichkeit nach*
The child's hearing will, **in all probability,** be severely affected	*aller Wahrscheinlichkeit nach*
The person indicted is, **in all likelihood**, going to be guilty as charged	*aller Wahrscheinlichkeit nach*
The likelihood is that the mood of mistrust and recrimination will intensify	*aller Wahrscheinlichkeit nach*
The chances *oder* **the odds are that** he will play safe in the short term	*es könnte sehr wohl sein, daß*
There is reason to believe that the books were stolen from the library	*es besteht Grund zu der Annahme, daß*
He must know of the paintings' existence	*er muß*
The talks **could very well** spill over into tomorrow	*können gut und gerne*
The cheque **should** reach you by Saturday	*müßte*
It wouldn't surprise me *oder* **I wouldn't be surprised if** he was working for the Americans	*es sollte mich nicht überraschen, wenn*

42.3 Möglichkeit

The situation **could** change from day to day	*kann*
Britain **could perhaps** play a more positive role in developing policy	*könnte vielleicht*
It may be (the case) that they got your name from the voters' roll	*möglicherweise*
It is possible that psychological factors play some unknown role in the healing process	*es könnte sein, daß*
It may be that the whole battle will have to be fought over again	*es könnte sein, daß*
It is conceivable that the economy is already in recession	*es ist denkbar, daß*
It is well within the bounds of possibility that England could be beaten	*es ist durchaus im Rahmen des Möglichen, daß*
I venture to suggest (that) a lot of it is to do with his political ambitions	*ich wage zu behaupten, daß*
There is an outside chance that the locomotive may appear in the Gala	*es könnte eventuell möglich sein, daß*
There is a small chance that your body could reject the implants	*es besteht eine geringe Möglichkeit, daß*

42.4 Ausdruck von Fähigkeiten

Our Design and Print Service **can** supply envelopes and package your existing literature	*kann*
Applicants **must be able to** use a word processor	*müssen in der Lage sein*
He **is qualified to** teach physics	*ist qualifiziert*

43 Zweifel, Unwahrscheinlichkeit, Unmöglichkeit und Unfähigkeit

43.1 Zweifel

I doubt if *oder* **It is doubtful whether** he knows where it came from	*ich bezweifle, daß*
There is still some doubt surrounding his exact whereabouts	*man weiß immer noch nichts Genaues über*
I have my doubts about replacing private donations with taxpayers' cash	*ich habe da so meine Zweifel an*
It isn't known for sure *oder* **It isn't certain** where she is	*man weiß nicht genau*
No one can say for sure how any child will develop	*niemand kann mit Sicherheit sagen*
It's all still up in the air - **we won't know for certain** until next week	*wir werden keine Gewißheit haben*
You're asking why I should do such an extraordinary thing and **I'm not sure** *oder* **certain that** I really know the answer	*ich bin mir nicht sicher, daß*
I'm not convinced that you can really teach people who don't want to learn	*ich bin nicht überzeugt, daß*
We are still in the dark about where the letter came from	*wir tappen immer noch im Dunkeln über*
How long this muddle can last **is anyone's guess**	*weiß niemand so recht*
Sterling is going to come under further pressure. **It is touch and go whether** base rates will have to go up	*es steht auf des Messers Schneide, ob*
I'm wondering if I should offer to help?	*vielleicht sollte ich*

43.2 Unwahrscheinlichkeit

You have **probably not** yet seen the document I am referring to	*wahrscheinlich nicht*
It is highly improbable that there will be a challenge for the party leadership in the near future	*es ist höchst unwahrscheinlich, daß*
It is very doubtful whether the expedition will reach the summit	*es bestehen starke Zweifel, ob*
In the unlikely event that the room was bugged, the music would drown out their conversation	*sollte ... wider Erwarten doch*
It was hardly to be expected that democratization would be easy	*es stand kaum zu erwarten, daß*

43.3 Unmöglichkeit

There can be no changes in the schedule	*... sind nicht möglich*
Nowadays Carnival **cannot** happen **without** the police tell**ing** us where to walk and what direction to walk in	*kann unmöglich ..., ohne daß*
People said prices would inevitably rise; **this cannot be the case**	*das kann nicht sein*
I couldn't possibly invite George and not his wife	*ich kann unmöglich*
The report **rules out any possibility of** exceptions, and amounts to little more than a statement of the obvious	*schließt jede Möglichkeit ... aus*
There is no question of us gett**ing** this finished on time	*es gibt keine Chance, daß*
A West German spokesman said **it was out of the question that** these weapons would be based in Germany	*es steht außer Frage, daß*
There is not (even) the remotest chance that *oder* **There is absolutely no chance that** he will succeed	*es besteht nicht die geringste Möglichkeit, daß*
The idea of trying to govern twelve nations from one centre **is unthinkable**	*ist unvorstellbar*
Since we had over 500 applicants, **it would be quite impossible to** interview them all	*wir können unmöglich*

43.4 Unfähigkeit

I can't drive, I'm afraid	*ich kann nicht*
I don't know how to use a word processor	*ich weiß nicht, wie*
The army **has been unable to** suppress the political violence in the area	*war nicht in der Lage*
The congress had shown itself **incapable of** real reform	*unfähig zu*
His fellow-directors **were not up** to runn**ing** the business without him	*waren nicht imstande zu*
We hoped the sales team would be able to think up new marketing strategies, but they **were** unfortunately **not equal to the task**	*waren der Aufgabe nicht gewachsen*
He simply couldn't cope with the stresses of family life	*er war ... einfach nicht gewachsen*
I'm afraid the task **proved** (to be) **beyond his capabilities**	*ging über seine Kräfte*
I'd like to leave him but sometimes I feel that such a step **is beyond me**	*geht über meine Kräfte*
Far too many women accept that they are **hopeless at** *oder* **no good at** manag**ing** money	*sind unfähig zu*
I'm not in a position to say now how much substance there is in the reports	*ich bin nicht in der Lage zu*
It is quite impossible for me to describe the confusion and horror of the scene	*ich kann unmöglich*

44 Erklärungen

44.1 Präpositionen und Konjunktionen

He was sacked **for the simple reason that** he just wasn't up to it any more	*aus dem einfachen Grunde, daß*
The reason that we admire him is that he knows what he is doing	*der Grund dafür, daß*
He said he could not be more specific **for** security **reasons**	*aus ...gründen*
I am absolutely in favour of civil disobedience **on** moral **grounds**	*aus ... Gründen*
The court had ordered his release, **on the grounds that** he had already been acquitted of most of the charges against him	*mit der Begründung, daß*
The students were arrested **because of** suspected dissident activities	*wegen*
Teachers in the eastern part of Germany are assailed by fears of mass unemployment **on account of** their communist past	*wegen*
They are facing higher costs **owing to** rising inflation	*wegen*
Parliament has prevaricated, **largely because of** the unwillingness of the main opposition party to support the changes	*hauptsächlich wegen*
Morocco has announced details of the austerity package it is adopting **as a result of** pressure from the International Monetary Fund	*infolge*
The full effects will be delayed **due to** factors beyond our control	*aufgrund*
What also had to go was the notion that some people were born superior to others **by virtue of** their skin colour	*aufgrund*
He shot to fame **on the strength of** a letter he had written to the papers	*aufgrund*
Thanks to their generosity, the charity can afford to buy new equipment	*dank*
Both companies became profitable again **by means of** severe cost-cutting	*mittels*
The King and Queen's defence of old-fashioned family values has acquired a poignancy **in view of** their inability to have children	*in Anbetracht*
In the face of this continued disagreement, the parties have asked for the polling to be postponed	*in Anbetracht*
It is unclear why they initiated this week's attack, **given that** negotiations were underway	*in Anbetracht der Tatsache, daß*
The police have put considerable pressure on the Government to toughen its stance **in the light of** recent events	*mit Blick auf*
His soldiers had been restraining themselves **for fear of** harm**ing** civilians	*aus Furcht davor*
A survey by the World Health Organization says that two out of every five people are dying prematurely **for lack of** food or health care	*aus Mangel an*
Babies have died **for want of** *oder* **for lack of** proper medical attention	*aus Mangel an*
I refused her a divorce, **out of** spite I suppose	*aus*
Seeing that he had a police escort, the only time he could have switched containers was on the way to the airport	*angesichts der Tatsache, daß*
As he had been up since 4 a.m., he was doubtless very tired	*da*
International intervention was appropriate **since** tensions had reached the point where there was talk of war	*da*
She could not have been deaf, **for** she started at the sound of a bell	*weil*
I cannot accept this decision. **So** I confirm it is my intention to appeal to a higher authority	*daher*
What the Party said was taken to be right, **therefore** anyone who disagreed must be wrong	*daher*
The thing is that once you've retired there's no going back	*das Problem ist, daß*

44.2 Andere nützliche Ausdrücke

The serious dangers to your health **caused by** *oder* **brought about by** cigarettes are now better understood	*hervorgerufen durch*
When the picture was published recently, **it gave rise to** *oder* **led to** speculation that the three were still alive and being held captive	*gab Anlaß zu*
The army argues that security concerns **necessitated** the demolitions	*erforderten*
This lack of recognition **was at the root of** the dispute	*war der eigentliche Grund für*
I attribute all this mismanagement **to** the fact that the General Staff in London is practically non-existent	*ich führe ... auf ... zurück*
This unrest **dates from** colonial times	*geht zurück auf*
The custom **goes back to** pre-Christian days	*geht zurück auf*

45 Entschuldigungen

45.1 Entschuldigungen

I'm really sorry, Steve, **but** we won't be able to come on Saturday	*es tut mir wirklich leid, aber*
I'm sorry that your time has been wasted	*es tut mir leid, daß*
I am sorry to have to say this to you but you're no good	*es tut mir leid, ... zu müssen*
Apologies if I wasn't very good company last night	*Entschuldigung, wenn*
I must apologize for what happened. Quite unforgivable, and the man responsible has been disciplined	*ich muß mich für ... entschuldigen*
I owe you an apology. I didn't think you knew what you were talking about	*ich muß mich bei Ihnen entschuldigen*
The general back-pedalled, saying that **he had not meant to** offend the German government	*es lag nicht in seiner Absicht*
Do forgive me for being a little abrupt	*verzeihen Sie mir, wenn ich*
Please forgive me for behaving so badly	*bitte entschuldigen Sie, daß ich*
Please accept our apologies if this has caused you any inconvenience	*bitte entschuldigen Sie vielmals*

45.2 Verantwortung eingestehen

I admit I overreacted, but someone needed to speak out against her	*ich gebe zu*
I have no excuse for what happened	*ich kann keine Entschuldigung für ... vorbringen*
It is my fault that our marriage is on the rocks	*es ist mein Fehler, daß*
The Government **is not entirely to blame for** the crisis	*trägt nicht die alleinige Schuld an*
I should never have let him rush out of the house in anger	*ich hätte nie ... dürfen*
Oh, but **if only I hadn't** lost the keys	*wenn ich nur nicht ... hätte*
I hate to admit that the old man was right, but **I made a stupid mistake**	*ich habe einen dummen Fehler gemacht*
My mistake was in failing to push my concerns and convictions as hard as I could have done	*mein Fehler war, daß*
My mistake was to arrive wearing a jacket and polo-neck jumper	*mein Fehler war, zu*
In December and January the markets raced ahead, and I missed out on that. **That was my mistake**	*das war mein Fehler*

45.3 Mit Bedauern

I'm very upset about her decision but I accept she needs to move on to new challenges	*ich bin sehr mitgenommen von*
It's a shame that the press gives so little coverage to these events	*schade, daß*
I feel awful about saying this but you really ought to spend more time with your children	*es tut mir sehr leid, daß*
I'm afraid I can't help you very much	*ich kann leider nicht*
It is a pity that my profession can make a lot of money out of the misfortunes of others	*schade, daß*
It is unfortunate that the matter should have come to a head just now	*es ist etwas unglücklich, daß*
David and **I very much regret that** we have been unable to reach an agreement	*bedauern sehr, daß*
The accused **bitterly regrets** this incident and it won't happen again	*bedauert zutiefst*
We regret to inform you that the post of Editor has now been filled	*zu unserem Bedauern müssen wir Ihnen mitteilen, daß*

45.4 Zur Erklärung

I didn't do it on purpose, it just happened	*ich habe es nicht absichtlich getan*
Sorry, Nanna. **I didn't mean to** upset you	*ich hatte nicht die Absicht*
Sorry about not coming to the meeting. **I was under the impression that** it was just for managers	*ich hatte den Eindruck, daß*
We are simply trying to protect the interests of local householders	*wir versuchen nur*
I know how this hurt you but **I had no choice**. I had to put David's life above all else	*ich hatte keine Wahl*
We are unhappy with 1.5%, but under the circumstances **we have no alternative but to** accept	*wir haben keine andere Wahl als zu*
We were obliged to accept their conditions	*wir sahen uns gezwungen*
I had nothing to do with the placing of any advertisement	*ich hatte nichts mit ... zu tun*
A spokesman for the club assured supporters that **it was a genuine error** and **there was no intention to** mislead them	*es war ein reines Versehen ... es war nicht beabsichtigt*

Garrion Orchard
Middletown
MD8 1NP

18th August 1997

The Managing Director
Messrs. J.M. Thomson Ltd,
Leeside Works
Barnton, MC45 6RB

Dear Sir or Madam,[1]

With reference to your advertisement in today's Guardian, I wish to apply for the post of Human Resources Manager.

I enclose my curriculum vitae. Please do not hesitate to contact me if you require any further details.

Yours faithfully,

A. Ferrier

CURRICULUM VITAE

NAME:	Andrew Iain FERRIER
ADDRESS:	Garrion Orchard, Middletown
TELEPHONE:	(01234) 861483
DATE OF BIRTH:	6.5.1972
MARITAL STATUS:	Married (no children)
NATIONALITY:	British
QUALIFICATIONS:[2]	M.A. First class Honours Degree in German with French, University of Texas, USA (June 1993) Masters Diploma in Human Resources, Glasgow University (June 1994) A-levels (1990): German (A), French (A), English (B) O-levels: 9 subjects
PRESENT POST:	Assistant Human Resources Manager, Abbots Art Metal Company plc., Middletown (since July 1995)
PREVIOUS EMPLOYMENT:	Sept. 1994 - June 1995: Human resources trainee, Abbots Art Metal Company plc. Oct. 1993 - June 1994: Student, Glasgow University

SKILLS, INTERESTS AND EXPERIENCE: fluent German & French; adequate Italian; some Russian; car owner and driver (clean licence); riding and sailing.

The following have agreed to provide references:

Ms Jocelyn Meiklejohn
Human Resources Manager
Abbots Art Metal Company plc
Middletown MD1 4CU

Dr. Garth Tritt
Department of German
University of Texas
Arizona, USA

[1] Diese Form der Adresse wird verwendet, wenn der Name des Empfängers nicht bekannt ist. Wenn der Name bekannt ist, wird folgende Schreibung benutzt:

Mr Eric Swanson

ODER

Mrs. Anna Carter,
Personnel Director,
Messrs. J.M. Kenyon Ltd, usw.

Als Anrede benutzen Sie „Dear Sir" bzw. „Dear Madam".

Alle Briefe, die mit dieser Anrede beginnen, werden mit der Grußformel „Yours faithfully" und Unterschrift beendet. Eine ausführlichere Darstellung finden Sie auf den Seiten 876 und 877.

[2] Wenn Sie sich um eine Stelle im Ausland bewerben, sollten Sie auf die Entsprechungen Ihrer Qualifikationen im englischen Sprachraum hinweisen. Etwa „Abitur – German equivalent of A-levels" usw.

46.1 Nützliche Redewendungen

In reply to your advertisement for a Trainee Manager in today's *Guardian*, **I would be grateful if you would send me further details of** the post	*mit Bezug auf Ihre Anzeige ... möchte ich Sie bitten, mir nähere Informationen über ... zuzusenden*
I wish to apply for the post of bilingual correspondent, as advertised in this week's *Euronews*	*ich möchte mich um die Stelle ... bewerben*
I am writing to ask if there is any possibility of work in your company	*ich möchte nachfragen, ob*
I am writing to enquire about the possibility of joining your company on work placement for a period of 3 months	*ich möchte mich erkundigen, ob die Möglichkeit besteht, in Ihrem Unternehmen ein Praktikum zu absolvieren*

46.2 Berufserfahrung

I have three years' **experience of** office work	*ich verfüge über ... Erfahrung*
I am familiar with word processors	*ich bin mit ... vertraut*
As well as speaking fluent English, **I have a working knowledge of** German	*ich spreche fließend ... und habe ausreichende ...kenntnisse*
As you will see from my CV, I have worked in Belgium before	*wie Sie meinem Lebenslauf entnehmen können*
Although I have no experience of this type of work, I have had other holiday jobs and can supply references from my employers, if you wish	*ich habe zwar keine Erfahrung auf diesem Arbeitsgebiet*
My current salary is ... per annum and I have four weeks' paid leave	*zur Zeit verdiene ich*

46.3 Motivationen ausdrücken

I would like to make better use of my languages	*ich möchte meine ... kenntnisse besser einsetzen*
I am keen to work in public relations	*ich möchte gerne auf dem Gebiet ... arbeiten*

46.4 Briefschluß

I will be available from the end of April	*ich stehe ab ... zur Verfügung*
I am available for interview at any time	*über ein Vorstellungsgespräch würde ich mich freuen*
Please do not hesitate to contact me for further information	*für weitere Informationen stehe ich Ihnen gerne jederzeit zur Verfügung*
Please do not contact my current employers	*ich möchte Sie bitten, sich nicht mit ... in Verbindung zu setzen*
I enclose a stamped addressed envelope for your reply	*ich lege ... bei*

46.5 Referenzen erbitten und erteilen

In my application for the position of lecturer, I have been asked to provide the names of two referees and **I wondered whether you would mind if I gave your name** as one of them	*ich möchte Sie um Ihr Einverständnis bitten, Ihren Namen angeben zu dürfen*
Ms Lee has applied for the post of Marketing Executive with our company and has given us your name as a reference. **We would be grateful if you would let us know whether you would recommend her for this position**	*wir wären Ihnen sehr dankbar, wenn Sie uns mitteilen könnten, ob Sie sie für diesen Posten empfehlen können*
Your reply will be treated in the strictest confidence	*Ihre Antwort wird selbstverständlich streng vertraulich behandelt*
I have known Mr Chambers for four years in his capacity as Sales Manager and **can warmly recommend him for the position**	*ich kann ihn für die Stelle wärmstens empfehlen*

46.6 Ein Angebot annehmen oder ablehnen

Thank you for your letter of 20 March. **I will be pleased to attend for interview** at your Manchester offices on Thursday 7 April at 10am	*ich finde mich gern ... zu einem Vorstellungsgespräch ein*
I would like to confirm my acceptance of the post of Marketing Executive	*ich nehme Ihr Angebot an*
I would be delighted to accept this post. However, would it be possible to postpone my starting date until 8 May?	*ich würde das Angebot sehr gerne annehmen. Wäre es jedoch möglich*
I would be glad to accept your offer; however, the salary stated is somewhat lower than what I had hoped for	*ich würde Ihr Angebot gerne annehmen, ich hatte jedoch*
Having given your offer careful thought, **I regret that I am unable to accept**	*bedauerlicherweise ist es mir nicht möglich, Ihr Angebot anzunehmen*

47 Geschäftsbriefe

Crosby Stills

PHOTOGRAPHIC LIBRARY
141 Academy Street
Glossop
Derby K9 4JP

22nd May 1997

Mr David Cooper
18 Crossdyke Road
Overdale
Lancs
LB3 WOD

Dear Mr Cooper,

Thank you for your recent enquiry about our limited edition photographs of classic cars. We have pleasure in enclosing our latest catalogue and current price list and would draw your attention to our free postage and packing on orders over £30. We are prepared to hold last year's prices on our range of frames and look forward to receiving your order.

Yours faithfully,

JAMES NASH
Managing Director

FABBY FABRICS LTD
Greenknowe Industrial Estate
Barbridge, Denholm
DT4 8HF

Our ref: WED/35/40
Your ref: HDF/JL

9th October, 1997

Moonshine Inn
3 Main Street
Newtown, NW1 4BB

For the attention of Ms H Boyle

Dear Madam,

Thank you for your letter of 21st September. We do stock a wide range of materials which are suitable for seating and would be delighted to send one of our representatives round at your earliest convenience. Please note that we also provide a made-to-measure service at very competitive prices and will be happy to supply you with a free quotation.

Yours faithfully,

Garry Scott
Sales Manager

47.1 Informationen erbitten

We see from your advertisement in the Healthy Holiday Guide that you are offering cut-price holidays in Scotland, and **would be grateful if you would send us** details	*wir ... wären Ihnen dankbar, wenn Sie uns nähere Informationen zusenden könnten*
I read about the Happy Pet Society in the NCT newsletter and would be very interested to learn more about it. **Please send me details of** membership	*bitte senden Sie mir Einzelheiten über ... zu*

... und darauf antworten

In response to your enquiry of 8 March, **we have pleasure in enclosing** full details on our activity holidays in Cumbria, **together with** our price list, valid until May 1997	*wir beziehen uns auf Ihre Anfrage vom ... und senden Ihnen gerne ... sowie ... zu*
Thank you for your enquiry about the Society for Wildlife Protection. **I enclose** a leaflet explaining our beliefs and the issues we campaign on. **Should you wish** to join, a membership application form is also enclosed	*ich danke für Ihre Anfrage bezüglich ... Ich lege ... bei ... Sollten Sie Interesse an ... haben*

47.2 Bestellungen und Antwort auf Bestellungen

We would like to place an order for the following items, in the sizes and quantities specified below	*wir möchten eine Bestellung über ... aufgeben*
Please find enclosed our order no. 3011 for ...	*anbei unsere Bestellung Nr.*
The enclosed order is based on your current price list, assuming our usual discount	*der beigefügten Bestellung liegt ... zugrunde*
I wish to order a can of "Buzz off!" wasp repellent, as advertised in the July issue of Gardeners' Monthly, **and enclose a cheque for** £19.50	*ich möchte ... bestellen. Ich füge einen Scheck über ... bei*
Thank you for your order of 3 May, which will be dispatched within 30 days	*wir danken Ihnen für Ihre Bestellung vom*
We acknowledge receipt of your order no. 3570 and advise that the goods will be dispatched within 7 working days	*wir bestätigen den Eingang Ihrer Bestellung Nr.*
We regret that the goods you ordered are temporarily out of stock	*leider sind die von Ihnen bestellten Waren zur Zeit nicht auf Lager*
Please allow 28 days **for delivery**	*die Lieferung erfolgt innerhalb von*

47.3 Lieferungen

Our delivery time is 60 days from receipt of order	*unsere Lieferzeit beträgt*
We await confirmation of your order	*wir erwarten Ihre verbindliche Bestellung*
We confirm that the goods were dispatched on 4 September	*wir bestätigen den Abgang der Waren am*
We cannot accept responsibility for goods damaged in transit	*wir übernehmen keine Haftung für*

47.4 Sich beschweren

We have not yet received the items ordered on 6 May (ref. order no. 541)	*... sind noch nicht bei uns eingegangen*
Unfortunately, the goods were damaged in transit	*leider wurden die Waren ... beschädigt*
The goods received differ significantly from the description in your catalogue	*die eingegangenen Waren weichen wesentlich von ... ab*
If the goods are not received by 20 October, **we shall have to cancel our order**	*sehen wir uns leider gezwungen, unsere Bestellung zu stornieren*

47.5 Bezahlung

The total amount outstanding is ...	*der zu zahlende Gesamtbetrag beläuft sich auf*
We would be grateful if you would attend to this account immediately	*wir wären Ihnen dankbar, wenn Sie diese Rechnung ... begleichen würden*
Please remit payment by return	*bitte überweisen Sie den Betrag unverzüglich*
Full payment **is due within** 14 working days from receipt of goods	*ist fällig innerhalb von*
We enclose a cheque for ... **in settlement of your invoice no.** 2003L/58	*anbei übersenden wir Ihnen ... zur Begleichung Ihrer Rechnung Nr.*
We must point out an error in your account and **would be grateful if you would adjust your invoice** accordingly	*wir ... wären Ihnen dankbar, wenn Sie die Rechnung berichtigen würden*
This mistake was due to an accounting error, and **we enclose a credit note for** the sum involved	*in der Anlage erhalten Sie eine Gutschrift über*
Thank you for your cheque for ... in settlement of our invoice	*wir bedanken uns für Ihren Scheck über ...*
We look forward to doing further business with you in the near future	*wir würden uns freuen, schon bald wieder mit Ihnen zusammenarbeiten zu können*

48 Allgemeine Korrespondenz

8. South Farmway
BARCOME
BN7 2BT

9th May, 1997

Dear Jenny,

I'm so sorry that I haven't written sooner, things were pretty hectic leading up to the wedding. I've never been so busy! Happily everything ran like clockwork and we all had a perfect day. The house is very quiet now with David away but I must admit I am enjoying it! Eric and I finally have the chance to take a short break at our cottage in the Lake District. Why don't you and James join us? There's plenty of room and I know how you love the lakes. We will be there on Saturday of the week beginning 16th of July for ten days. Give me a call soon if you're coming and we'll meet you at the station. Do say you'll come!

With love,

Kerry

11 South Street
BARCOME
BN7 2BT

5th June 1997

Mr. J. Sharpe
Sharpe Knives Ltd.,
Cromwell Place
ADDENBOROUGH
AG3 9LL

Dear Mr Sharpe,

Some years ago I bought a HANDYMAN penknife from you, and, as you suggested, it has been invaluable to me. Unfortunately, however, I have now lost it, and wonder if you still stock this range? If so, I should be grateful if you would let me have details of the various types of penknife you make, and of their prices.

Yours sincerely,

Thomas Thomson

In der untenstehenden Tabelle sind die üblichen Anreden und Schlußformeln für Privat- und Geschäftsbriefe aufgeführt.

DER EMPFÄNGER (DIE EMPFÄNGERIN) IST IHNEN PERSÖNLICH BEKANNT

Dear Mr Brown, Dear Mrs Hughes, Dear Mr and Mrs Boyle, Dear Miss Roberts, Dear Ms Jones, Dear Dr Armstrong, Dear Professor Ferrier, Dear Sir John, Dear Lady McLeod, Dear Andrew, Dear Jenny,	Yours sincerely With all good wishes, Yours sincerely With kindest regards, Yours sincerely	*persönlicher*

DER EMPFÄNGER (DIE EMPFÄNGERIN) IST VERWANDT ODER BEFREUNDET

Dear Grace, My dear Andrew, Dear Aunt Hazel, Dear Granny and Grandad, Dear Mum and Dad, My dear Caroline, Dearest Stephen, My dearest Mother, My dearest Heather, My darling Garry,	With love from Love from	
	Love to all Love from us all Yours All the best	*vertrauter*
	With much love from Lots of love from Much love as always, All my love	*herzlicher*

GESCHÄFTSBRIEFE (siehe auch Seite 874)

Dear Sirs,[1] Dear Sir,[2] Dear Madam,[3] Dear Sir or Madam,[4]	Yours faithfully	1 *Wenn Sie an eine Firma oder Behörde schreiben* 2 *Empfänger ist ein Mann* 3 *Empfänger ist eine Frau* 4 *Sie wissen nicht, ob der Empfänger ein Mann oder eine Frau ist*

AN BEKANNTE UND FREUNDE

Formeln, die Sie immer verwenden können		
Dear Alison, Dear Ann and Bob, Dear Uncle Alex, Dear Mrs Andrews, Dear Mr and Mrs Hope,	Yours sincerely	
	With best wishes, Yours sincerely With kindest regards, Yours sincerely All good wishes, Yours sincerely	*persönlicher*
	With best wishes, Yours ever Kindest regards, Best wishes With best wishes, As always	*vertrauter*

48.1 Briefanfänge

An Bekannte

Thank you *oder* **Thanks for your letter** which arrived yesterday	*vielen Dank für Deinen Brief*
It was good *oder* **nice** *oder* **lovely to hear from you**	*ich habe mich sehr gefreut, von Dir zu hören*
It's such a long time since we were last in touch that **I felt I must write a few lines** just to say hello	*und da dachte ich, ich muß einfach ein paar Zeilen schreiben*
I'm sorry I haven't written for so long, and hope you'll forgive me; I've had a lot of work recently and ...	*es tut mir sehr leid, daß ich so lange nicht geschrieben habe*

An eine Firma oder Organisation

I am writing to ask whether you have in stock a book entitled ...	*ich möchte mich erkundigen, ob*
Please send me ... I enclose a cheque for ...	*würden Sie mir bitte ... schicken*
When I left your hotel last week, I think I may have left a red coat in my room. **Would you be so kind as to** let me know whether it has been found?	*würden Sie bitte so freundlich sein und*
I have seen the details of your summer courses, and **wish to know whether** you still have any vacancies on the Beginners' Swedish course	*ich möchte nachfragen, ob*

48.2 Briefschlüsse

An Bekannte

Gerald joins me in sending very best wishes to you all	*viele herzliche Grüße an Euch alle, auch von Gerald*
Please remember me to your wife - I hope she is well	*bitte grüßen Sie auch ... von mir*
I look forward to hearing from you	*ich würde mich sehr freuen, bald von Ihnen zu hören*

An Freunde

Say hello to Martin for me	*grüß' Martin von mir*
Give my love to Daniel and Laura, and tell them how much I miss them	*grüß' ... von mir*
Give my warmest regards to Vincent	*grüße bitte Vincent ganz herzlich von mir*
Do write when you have a minute	*schreib mal wieder*
Hoping to hear from you before too long	*ich hoffe, daß ich schon bald von Dir höre*

An enge Freunde

Rhona **sends her love**/Ray **sends his love**	*läßt herzlich grüßen*
Jodie and Carla **send you a big hug**	*umarmen Dich*

48.3 Reiseplanung

Zimmerreservierung

Please send me details of your prices	*bitte schicken Sie mir nähere Informationen über ... zu*
Please let me know by return of post if you have one single room with bath, half board, for the week commencing 3 October	*bitte teilen Sie mir umgehend mit, ob*
I would like to book bed-and-breakfast accommodation with you	*ich möchte ... buchen*

Eine Buchung bestätigen oder stornieren

Please consider this a firm booking and hold the room until I arrive, however late in the evening	*bitte betrachten Sie diese Reservierung als verbindlich*
Please confirm the following by fax: one single room with shower for the nights of 20-23 April 1998	*bitte bestätigen Sie folgendes per Fax*
We expect to arrive in the early evening, unless something unforeseen happens	*wir werden ... eintreffen*
I am afraid I must ask you to alter my booking from 25 August **to** 3 September. I hope this will not cause too much inconvenience	*leider muß ich Sie bitten, meine Reservierung vom ... auf den ... umzubuchen*
Owing to unforseen circumstances, **I am afraid (that) I must cancel the booking** made with you for the week beginning 5 September	*muß ich meine Reservierung leider stornieren*

49 Danksagungen

Just a line to say thanks for the lovely book which arrived today	*danke für*
I can't thank you enough for finding my watch	*ich weiß gar nicht, wie ich Ihnen für ... danken kann*
(Would you) please thank him from me	*Richten Sie ihm bitte meinen Dank aus*
We greatly appreciated your support during our recent difficulties	*wir sind Ihnen wirklich sehr dankbar für*
Please accept our sincere thanks for all your help and support	*wir möchten uns herzlich bei Ihnen für ... bedanken*
A big thank you to everyone involved in the show this year	*ein herzliches Dankeschön an alle*
We would like to express our appreciation to the University of Durham Research Committee for providing a grant	*wir möchten unserer Dankbarkeit gegenüber ... Ausdruck verleihen*

Im Namen einer Gruppe

Thank you on behalf of the Manx Operatic Society **for** all your support	*wir danken Ihnen im Namen ... für*
I am instructed by our committee **to convey our sincere thanks for** your assistance at our recent Valentine Social	*... hat mir die Aufgabe übertragen, unseren herzlichen Dank für ... zu übermitteln*

50 Glückwünsche

50.1 Spezielle Anlässe

I hope you have a lovely holiday	*hoffentlich hast Du*
With love and best wishes for your wedding anniversary	*mit den besten Wünschen für*
(Do) give my best wishes to your mother **for** a happy and healthy retirement	*grüße ... von mir und wünsche ... alles Gute für*
Len **joins me in sending you our very best wishes for** your future career	*... schließt sich meinen besten Wünschen für ... an*

50.2 Zu Weihnachten und Neujahr

Merry Christmas and a happy New Year	*frohe Weihnachten und ein glückliches neues Jahr*
With season's greetings and very best wishes from	*mit den besten Wünschen für ein gesegnetes Weihnachtsfest und ein glückliches neues Jahr*
May I send you all our very best wishes for 1998	*ich sende Euch allen die besten Wünsche für*

50.3 Zum Geburtstag

All our love and best wishes on your 21st **birthday**, from Simon, Liz, Kerry and the cats	*alles Liebe und Gute zu Deinem ... Geburtstag*
I am writing to wish you **many happy returns (of the day)**. Hope your birthday brings you everything you wished for	*alles Gute zum Geburtstag*

50.4 Gute Besserung

Sorry (to hear) you're ill - **get well soon!**	*gute Besserung*
I was very sorry to learn that you were ill, and send you **my best wishes for a speedy recovery**	*meine besten Wünsche für eine baldige Genesung*

50.5 Erfolg wünschen

Good luck in your driving test. I hope things go well for you on Friday	*viel Glück bei*
Sorry to hear you didn't get the job - **better luck next time!**	*vielleicht klappt es beim nächsten Mal*
We all wish you the best of luck in your new job	*wir alle wünschen Dir viel Glück in*

50.6 Gratulationen

You're expecting a baby? **Congratulations!** When is the baby due?	*herzlichen Glückwunsch*
You've finished the job already? **Well done!**	*gut gemacht*
We all send you our love and congratulations on such an excellent result	*wir gratulieren alle zu*
This is to send you our warmest congratulations and best wishes on your engagement	*herzlichen Glückwunsch und die besten Wünsche anläßlich*

51 Anzeigen

51.1 Geburtsanzeigen

Julia Archer **gave birth to** a 6lb 5oz **baby daughter,** Amy, last Monday. **Mother and baby are doing well**
hat ... eine Tochter bekommen. Mutter und Kind sind wohlauf

Ian and Zoë Pitt **are delighted to announce the birth of a son**, Garry, on 9th May, 1997, at Minehead Hospital
freuen sich, die Geburt ihres Sohnes ... anzuzeigen

At the Southern General Hospital, on 1st December, 1997, **to Paul and Diane Kelly (née Smith) a son, John Alexander,** a brother for Helen
Paul und Diane Kelly, geb. Smith, freuen sich, die Geburt ihres Sohnes John Alexander ... anzuzeigen

... und darauf antworten

Congratulations on the birth of your son
herzliche Glückwünsche zur Geburt

We were delighted to hear about the birth of Stephanie, and send our very best wishes to all of you
wir freuen uns mit Euch über die Geburt von

51.2 Verlobungsanzeigen

I'm sure you'll be pleased to hear that Jim and I **got engaged** yesterday
haben uns verlobt

It is with much pleasure that the engagement is announced between Michael, younger son of Professor and Mrs Perkins, York, **and** Jennifer, only daughter of Dr and Mrs Campbell, Hucknall
... freuen sich, die Verlobung zwischen ... und ... bekanntzugeben

... und darauf antworten

Congratulations to you both on your engagement, and very best wishes for a long and happy life together
herzliche Glückwünsche anläßlich Eurer Verlobung für Euch beide

I was delighted to hear of your engagement, and wish you both all the best for your future together
ich freue mich mit Euch über Eure Verlobung

51.3 Heiratsanzeigen

I'm getting married in June, to a wonderful man named Lester Thompson
ich werde heiraten

At Jurby Church, on 1st June, 1998, Eve, daughter of Ian and Mary Jones, Jurby, to John, son of Ray and Myra Watt, Ayr
die Vermählung wird bekanntgegeben zwischen Eve, Tochter von Ian und Mary Jones, Jurby, und John, Sohn von Ray und Myra Watt, Ayr, am 1. Juni 1998 in der Kirche von Jurby

... und darauf antworten

Congratulations on your marriage, and best wishes to you both for your future happiness
zu Eurer Hochzeit herzliche Glückwünsche und alles Gute für Eure gemeinsame Zukunft

We were delighted to hear about your daughter's marriage to Iain, and wish them both all the best for their future life together
mit großer Freude haben wir die Nachricht von der Vermählung Eurer Tochter mit ... zur Kenntnis genommen

51.4 Todesanzeigen

My husband **died suddenly** in March
plötzlich und unerwartet verstarb

It is with great sadness that I have to tell you that Joe's father **passed away** three weeks ago
in tiefer Trauer muß ich Ihnen mitteilen, daß ... für immer von uns gegangen ist

Suddenly, at home, in Newcastle-upon-Tyne, on Saturday 2nd July, 1997, Alan, aged 77 years, **the beloved husband of** Helen and **loving father of** Matthew
plötzlich und unerwartet verstarb mein geliebter Mann, unser lieber Vater

... und darauf antworten

My husband and I **were greatly saddened to learn of the passing of** Dr Smith, and send (*oder* offer) you and your family our most sincere condolences
mit tiefem Bedauern haben wir die Nachricht vom Tode ... erhalten

We wish to extend our deepest sympathy for your sad loss to you and your wife
wir möchten Ihnen zum Tode ... unser tiefempfundenes Beileid aussprechen

51.5 Umzugsanzeigen

We are moving house next week. **Our new address** as of 4 May 1998 **will be ...**
unsere neue Adresse ... ist

52 Einladungen

52.1 Offizielle Einladungen

Mr and Mrs James Waller **request the pleasure of your company at the marriage of** their daughter Mary Elizabeth to Mr Richard Hanbury at St Mary's Church, Frampton on Saturday, 21st August, 1997 at 2 o'clock and afterwards at Moor House, Frampton

geben sich die Ehre, Sie zur Hochzeit ... einzuladen

The Chairman and Governors of Hertford College, Oxford **request the pleasure of the company of** Miss Charlotte Young and partner **at a dinner** to mark the anniversary of the founding of the College

geben sich die Ehre, ... anläßlich ... zu einem festlichen Abendessen einzuladen

... und darauf antworten

We thank you for your kind invitation to the marriage of your daughter Annabel on 20th November, **and have much pleasure in accepting**

wir möchten uns sehr herzlich für die freundliche Einladung zu ... bedanken, die wir mit großem Vergnügen annehmen

Mr and Mrs Ian Low **thank** Dr and Mrs Green for **their kind invitation to** the marriage of their daughter Ann on 21st July **and are delighted to accept**

möchten uns herzlich bei Ihnen für die freundliche Einladung zu ... bedanken, die wir mit großem Vergnügen annehmen

We regret that we are unable to accept your invitation to the marriage of your daughter on 6th May

zu unserem Bedauern können wir Ihre Einladung zu ... nicht annehmen

52.2 Einladungen zu Feierlichkeiten

We are celebrating Rosemary's engagement to David by holding a dinner dance at the Central Hotel on Friday 11th February, 1997, **and very much hope that you will be able to join us**

wir würden uns sehr freuen, wenn wir Sie anläßlich der Verlobung von Rosemary und David zu ... begrüßen dürften

We are giving a dinner party next Saturday, **and would be delighted if you and your wife could come**

wir möchten ... ein Abendessen geben und laden Sie und Ihre Frau herzlich dazu ein

I'm having a party next week for my 18th - **come along, and bring a friend**

ich gebe eine Party ... komm doch vorbei und bring noch jemanden mit

Would you and Gordon like to come to dinner next Saturday? — *wollt Gordon und du ... kommen*

Would you be free for lunch next Tuesday? — *können wir uns zum ... treffen*

Perhaps we could meet for coffee some time next week? — *vielleicht könnten wir*

52.3 Eine Einladung annehmen

Yes, I'd love to meet up with you tomorrow — *ja, ich würde mich gern mit dir treffen*

It was good of you to invite me, I've been longing to do something like this for ages — *es war sehr freundlich von dir, mich einzuladen*

Thank you for your invitation to dinner - **I look forward to it very much** — *herzlichen Dank für Ihre Einladung zu ... ich freue mich sehr darauf*

52.4 Eine Einladung ablehnen

I'd love to come, but I'm afraid I'm already going out that night — *ich würde gern kommen, aber leider*

I wish I could come, but unfortunately I have something else on — *ich wünschte, ich könnte kommen, aber leider*

It was very kind of you to invite me to your dinner party next Saturday. **Unfortunately I will not be able to accept** — *zu meinem Bedauern kann ich nicht zusagen*

Much to our regret, we are unable to accept — *zu unserem größten Bedauern können wir nicht zusagen*

52.5 Keine feste Zusage geben

I'm not sure what I'm doing that night, but I'll let you know later — *ich weiß nicht genau*

It all depends on whether I can get a sitter for Rosie at short notice — *es hängt alles davon ab, ob*

I'm afraid I can't really make any definite plans until I know when Alex will be able to take her holidays — *leider kann ich nichts Festes planen*

53 Erörterungen

53.1 Beweisführung

Ein Thema einführen

It is often said *oder* **claimed that** teenagers get pregnant in order to get council accommodation	*es wird oft behauptet, daß*
It is a truism *oder* **a commonplace (to say) that** American accents are infinitely more glamorous than their British counterparts	*es ist eine Binsenweisheit, daß*
It is undeniably true that Gormley helped to turn his union members into far more sophisticated workers	*es steht außer Zweifel, daß*
It is a well-known fact that in this age of technology, it is computer screens which are responsible for many illnesses	*es ist allgemein bekannt, daß*
It is sometimes forgotten that much Christian doctrine comes from Judaism	*es gerät manchmal in Vergessenheit, daß*
It would be naïve to suppose that in a radically changing world these 50-year-old arrangements can survive	*es wäre naiv anzunehmen, daß*
It would hardly be an exaggeration to say that the friendship of both of them with Britten was among the most creative in the composer's life	*man kann ohne große Übertreibung sagen, daß*
It is hard to open a newspaper nowadays without reading that electronic technology has made the written word obsolete	*man kann heutzutage schon keine Zeitung mehr aufschlagen, ohne zu lesen, daß*
First of all, it is important to try to understand some of the systems and processes involved in order to create a healthier body	*zunächst einmal ist es wichtig, ... zu verstehen*
It is in the nature of sociological theory **to** make broad generalizations about such things as the evolution of society	*es liegt in der Natur der ..., zu*
It is often the case that early interests lead on to a career	*oftmals ist*
By way of introduction, let me summarize the background to this question	*zur Einführung möchte ich*
I would like to start with a very sweeping statement which can be easily challenged	*ich möchte mit ... beginnen*
Before going specifically into the issue of criminal law, **I wish first to summarize** how Gewirth derives his principles of morality and justice	*bevor ich die Frage des ... näher erörtere, möchte ich zunächst zusammenfassen*
Let us look at what self-respect in your job actually means	*betrachten wir*
We commonly think of people **as** isolated individuals but, in fact, few of us ever spend more than an hour or two of our waking hours alone	*wir betrachten ... im allgemeinen als*
What we are mainly concerned with here is the conflict between what the hero says and what he actually does	*es geht uns hier hauptsächlich um*
We live in a world in which the word "equality" is liberally bandied about	*in unserer Welt*

Vorstellungen und Probleme einführen

The concept of controll**ing** harmful insects by genetic means isn't new	*die Vorstellung, zu*
The idea of gett**ing** rich without too much effort has universal appeal	*die Idee, zu*
The question of whether Hamlet was really insane has long occupied critics	*die Frage, ob*
Why they were successful where their predecessors had failed **is a question that has been much debated**	*über die Frage ... ist schon viel debattiert worden*
One of the most striking aspects of this issue is the way (in which) it arouses strong emotions	*einer der interessantesten Aspekte dieses Problems ist*
There are a number of issues on which China and Britain openly disagree	*es gibt einige Fragen*

Verallgemeinerungen

People who work outside the home **tend to believe that** parenting is an easy option	*diejenigen, die ..., nehmen oft an, daß*
There's always **a tendency for people to** exaggerate their place in the world	*der Mensch neigt immer dazu*
Many gardeners **have a tendency to** treat plants like humans	*neigen dazu*
Viewed psychologically, it would seem that **we all have the propensity for** such traits	*wir alle neigen zu*
For the (vast) majority of people, literature is a subject which is studied at school but which has no relevance to life as they know it	*für die (aller)meisten Menschen*
For most of us, housework is a necessary but boring task	*für die meisten von uns*
History **provides numerous examples** *oder* **instances of** misguided national heroes who did more harm than good in the long run	*bietet zahllose Beispiele für*

Genauere Angaben machen

The impact of these theories on the social sciences, and economics **in particular**, was extremely significant	*im besonderen*

One particular issue raised by Butt was, suppose Hughes at the time of his conviction had been old enough to be hanged, what would have happened?	*eine spezielle Frage*
A more specific point relates to using this insight as a way of challenging our hidden assumptions about reality	*eine genauere Aussage*
More specifically, he accuses Western governments of continuing to supply weapons and training to the rebels	*genauer gesagt*

53.2 Die These

Einführung

First of all, let us consider the advantages of urban life	*zunächst sollen ... betrachtet werden*
Let us begin with an examination of the social aspects of this question	*beginnen wir mit einer Untersuchung*
The first thing that needs to be said is that the author is presenting a one-sided view	*zunächst muß erwähnt werden, daß*
What should be established at the very outset is that we are dealing here with a practical issue rather than a philosophical one	*gleich zu Anfang sollte klargestellt werden, daß*

Die Diskussion eingrenzen

In the next section, I will pursue the question of whether the expansion of the Dutch prison system can be explained by Box's theory	*im nächsten Abschnitt werde ich auf die Frage eingehen, ob*
I will then deal with the question of whether or not the requirements for practical discourse are compatible with criminal procedure	*danach werde ich das Problem ... behandeln*
We must distinguish between the psychic and the spiritual, and **we shall see how** the subtle level of consciousness is the basis for the spiritual level	*wir werden sehen, wie*
I will confine myself to giving an account of certain decisive facts in my militant career with Sartre	*ich möchte mich darauf beschränken*
In this chapter, **I shall largely confine myself to** a consideration of those therapeutic methods that use visualization as a part of their procedures	*ich werde mich im großen und ganzen auf ... beschränken*
We will not concern ourselves here with the Christian legend of St James	*an dieser Stelle soll nicht auf ... eingegangen werden*
Let us now consider to what extent the present municipal tribunals differ from the former popular tribunals in the above-mentioned points	*betrachten wir nun*
Let us now look at the ideal types of corporatism that neo-corporatist theorists developed to clarify the concept	*betrachten wir nun*

Einzelaspekte umreißen

The main issue under discussion is how the party should re-define itself if it is to play any future role in Hungarian politics	*die Hauptfrage ist*
A second, related problem is that business ethics has mostly concerned itself with grand theorizing	*ein weiteres Problem in diesem Zusammenhang ist*
The basic issue at stake is this: is research to be judged by its value in generating new ideas?	*das zur Debatte stehende Grundproblem ist*
An important aspect of Milton's imagery **is** the play of light and shade	*ein wichtiger Aspekt von ... ist*
It is worth mentioning here that when this was first translated, the opening reference to Heidegger was entirely deleted	*an dieser Stelle sollte man erwähnen, daß*
Finally, there is the argument that watching too much television may stunt a child's imagination	*und schließlich wäre da noch die These, daß*

Ein Argument in Frage stellen

World leaders appear to be taking a tough stand, but **is there any real substance in** what has been agreed?	*hat ... Substanz*
This is a question which **merits close(r) examination**	*verdient nähere Betrachtung*
The unity of the two separate German states **has raised fundamental questions** for Germany's neighbours	*hat grundlegende Fragen ... aufgeworfen*
The failure to protect our fellow Europeans in Bosnia **raises fundamental questions on** the role of the armed forces	*wirft grundlegende Fragen über ... auf*
This raises once again the question of whether a government's right to secrecy should override the public's right to know	*dies wirft erneut die Frage ... auf*
This poses the question of whether these measures are really helping the people they were intended to help	*dies wirft die Frage auf*

Analysen anbieten

It is interesting to consider why this scheme has been so successful	*es ist interessant zu betrachten, warum*

On the question of whether civil disobedience is likely to help end the war, Chomsky is deliberately diffident	*was die Frage nach ... betrifft*
We are often faced with the choice between our sense of duty **and** our own personal inclinations	*man steht oft vor der Wahl zwischen ... und ...*
When we speak of realism in music, **we do not at all have in mind** the illustrative bases of music	*wenn wir von ... sprechen, meinen wir damit ganz bestimmt nicht*
It is reasonable to assume that most people living in industrialized societies are to some extent contaminated by environmental poisons	*es ist als wahrscheinlich anzunehmen, daß*

Ein Argument unterstützen

An argument in support of this approach **is that** it produces ...	*ein Argument zur Bestätigung ... ist, daß*
In support of his theory, Dr Gold notes that most oil contains higher-than-atmospheric concentrations of helium-3	*um seine Theorie zu bestätigen*
This is the most telling argument in favour of an extension of the right to vote	*dies ist das wichtigste Argument, daß für ... spricht*
The second reason for advocating this course of action **is that** it benefits the community at large	*ein weiterer Grund, ... zu unterstützen, besteht darin, daß*
The third, more fundamental, reason for looking to the future **is that** even the angriest investors realize they need a successful market	*ein dritter, noch wichtigerer Grund für ... ist, daß*
Despite communism's demise, confidence in capitalism seems to be at an all-time low. **The fundamental reason for** this contradiction seems to me quite simple	*der wesentliche Grund für*

53.3 Ein Gegenargument vorstellen

Etwas kritisieren oder ablehnen

In actual fact, the idea of there being a rupture between a so-called old criminology and an emergent new criminology **is somewhat misleading**	*tatsächlich ist die Vorstellung davon, daß ..., etwas irreführend*
In order to argue this, **I will show that** Wyeth**'s position is**, in actual fact, **untenable**	*ich werde zeigen, daß ... Position unhaltbar ist*
It is claimed, however, that the strict Leboyer method is not essential for a less traumatic birth experience	*es wird jedoch behauptet*
This need not mean that we are destined to suffer for ever. **Indeed, the opposite may be true**	*das muß nicht unbedingt bedeuten, daß ... Es könnte auch das genaue Gegenteil zutreffen*
Many observers, though, **find it difficult to share his opinion that** it could mean the end of the Tamil Tigers	*tun sich schwer damit, seine Meinung zu teilen, daß*
On the other hand, there are more important factors that should be taken into consideration	*andererseits*
The judgement made **may well be true but** the evidence given to sustain it is unlikely to convince the sceptical	*kann zwar zutreffen, aber*
Reform **is all very well, but** it is pointless if the rules are not enforced	*ist ja schön und gut, aber*
The case against the use of drugs in sport rests primarily on the argument that ... . **This argument is weak,** for two reasons	*dieses Argument ist schwach*
According to one theory, the ancestors of vampire bats were fruit-eating bats. But **this idea does not hold water**	*diese Vorstellung ist nicht stichhaltig*
Their claim to be a separate race **does not stand up to** historical scrutiny	*hält ... nicht stand*
This view does not stand up if we examine the known facts about John	*diese Ansicht ist nicht haltbar*
The trouble with this idea is not that it is wrong, **but rather that** it is uninformative	*das Problem mit dieser Idee ist nicht so sehr ..., sondern vielmehr*
The difficulty with this view is that he bases the principle on a false premise	*die Schwierigkeit bei dieser Betrachtungsweise liegt darin, daß*
The snag with such speculations **is that** too much turns on one man or event	*der Nachteil von ... ist, daß*
But removing healthy ovaries **is entirely unjustified in my opinion**	*ist meiner Meinung nach völlig ungerechtfertigt*

Eine Alternative vorschlagen

Another approach may be to develop substances capable of blocking the effects of the insect's immune system	*eine andere Herangehensweise könnte sein, zu*
Another way to reduce failure is to improve vocational education	*ein anderer Weg, um*
However, the other side of the coin is the fact that an improved self-image really can lead to prosperity	*die Kehrseite der Medaille ist jedoch*
It is more accurate to speak of a plurality of new criminologies rather than of a single new criminology	*es ist präziser, von ... zu sprechen*

Paradoxical as it may seem, computer models of mind can be positively humanizing	*so paradox, wie es auch erscheinen mag*

53.4 Die Synthese der Beweisführung

How can we reconcile these two apparently contradictory viewpoints?	*wie lassen sich ... vereinbaren?*
On balance, making money honestly is more profitable than making it dishonestly	*alles in allem*
Since such vitamins are more expensive, **one has to weigh up the pros and cons**	*man muß das Für und Wider abwägen*
We need to look at the pros and cons of normative theory as employed by Gewirth and Phillips	*Wir müssen die Vor- und Nachteile der ... betrachten*
The benefits of partnership in a giant trading market **will** almost certainly **outweigh the disadvantages**	*die Vorteile der ... werden ... die Nachteile überwiegen*
The two perspectives are not mutually exclusive	*die beiden Betrachtungsweisen schließen sich nicht gegenseitig aus*

Eines von mehreren Argumenten unterstützen

Dr Meaden's theory **is the most convincing explanation**	*die einleuchtendste Erklärung*
The truth *oder* **fact of the matter is that** in a free society you can't turn every home into a fortress	*die Wahrheit ist, daß*
But **the truth is that** Father Christmas has a rather mixed origin	*die Wahrheit ist, daß*
Although this operation sounds extremely dangerous, **in actual fact** it is extremely safe	*in Wirklichkeit*
When all is said and done, it must be acknowledged that a purely theoretical approach to social issues is sterile	*letzten Endes muß man erkennen, daß*

Zusammenfassen

In this chapter, **I have demonstrated** *oder* **shown that** the Cuban alternative has been undergoing considerable transformations	*ich habe nachgewiesen, daß*
This shows how, in the final analysis, adhering to a particular theory on crime is at best a matter of reasoned choice	*dies beweist, wie*
The overall picture shows that prison sentences were relatively frequent, but not particularly severe	*der Gesamteindruck zeigt, daß*
To recap *oder* **To sum up, then, (we may conclude that)** there are in effect two possible solutions to this problem	*zusammenfassend (können wir schlußfolgern, daß)*
To sum up this chapter I will offer two examples ...	*um dieses Kapitel zusammenzufassen*
To summarize, we have seen that the old staple industries in Britain had been hit after the First World War by a deteriorating international competitive position	*um noch einmal zusammenzufassen*
Habermas's argument, **in a nutshell**, is as follows	*kurz gesagt*
But **the key to the whole argument is** a single extraordinary paragraph	*der Schlüssel zur gesamten Beweisführung liegt in*
To round off this section on slugs, gardeners may be interested to hear that there are three species of predatory slugs in the British Isles	*um diesen Abschnitt über ... abzurunden*

Schlußfolgerungen ziehen

From all this, it follows that it is impossible to extend those kinds of security measures to all potential targets of terrorism	*aus alledem geht hervor, daß*
This, of course, **leads to the logical conclusion that** those who actually produce do have a claim to the results of their efforts	*führt zu der logischen Schlußfolgerung, daß*
There is only one logical conclusion we can reach, which is that we ask our customers what is the Strategic Reality that they perceive in our marketing programme	*wir können hier nur zu einer logischen Schlußfolgerung gelangen*
The inescapable conclusion is that the criminal justice system does not simply reflect the reality of crime; it helps create it	*die unweigerliche Schlußfolgerung ist, daß*
We must conclude that there is no solution to the problem of defining crime	*wir müssen schlußfolgern, daß*
In conclusion, because interpersonal relationships are so complex, there can be no easy way of preventing conflict	*die Schlußfolgerung ist, daß*
The upshot of all this is that treatment is unlikely to be available	*all das läuft darauf hinaus, daß*
So it would appear that butter is not significantly associated with heart disease after all	*es scheint also, daß*
This only goes to show that a good man is hard to find	*all dies zeigt nur, daß*
The lesson to be learned from this **is that** you cannot hope to please everyone all of the time	*aus ... kann man die Lehre ziehen, daß*
At the end of the day, the only way the drug problem will be beaten is when people are encouraged not to take them	*letzten Endes*
Ultimately, then, while we may have some sympathy for these young criminals, we must do our utmost to protect society from them	*letzten Endes*

53.5 Aufbau eines Absatzes

In addition, the author does not really empathize with his hero	*darüber hinaus*
Also, there is the question of language	*des weiteren*
This award-winning writer, **in addition to** being a critic, biographer and poet, has written 26 crime novels	*... ist nicht nur ..., sondern*
But this is only part of the picture. **Added to this are** fears that a major price increase would cause riots	*hinzu kommen noch*
An added complication **is** that the characters are not aware of their relationship to one another	*eine zusätzliche ... ist*
But, **over and above that**, each list contains fictitious names and addresses	*darüber hinaus*
Furthermore, ozone is, like carbon dioxide, a greenhouse gas	*des weiteren*
The question also arises as to how this idea can be put into practice	*es stellt sich auch die Frage*
Politicians, **as well as** academics and educationalists, tend to feel strongly about the way history is taught	*sowie*

Vergleiche

Compared with the heroine, Alison is an insipid character	*verglichen mit*
In comparison with the Czech Republic, the culture of Bulgaria is less westernized	*im Vergleich zu*
This is a high percentage for the English Midlands but low **by comparison with** some other parts of Britain	*im Vergleich zu*
On the one hand, there is no longer a Warsaw Pact threat. **On the other (hand)**, the positive changes could have negative side-effects	*einerseits ... andererseits*
Similarly, a good historian is not obsessed by dates	*in ähnlicher Weise*
There can only be one total at the bottom of a column of figures and **likewise** only one solution to any problem	*in ähnlicher Weise*
What others say of us will translate into reality. **Equally**, what we affirm as true of ourselves will likewise come true	*gleichermaßen*
There will now be a change in the way we are regarded by our partners, and, **by the same token**, the way we regard them	*gleichermaßen*
There is a fundamental difference between adequate nutrient intake **and** optimum nutrient intake	*es gibt einen wesentlichen Unterschied zwischen ... und*

Synthese der einzelnen Elemente

First of all *oder* **Firstly**, I would like to outline the benefits of the system	*zunächst*
In music we are concerned **first and foremost** with the practical application of controlled sounds relating to the human psyche	*in erster Linie*
In order to understand the conflict between the two nations, **it is first of all necessary to** know something of the history of the area	*um ... zu verstehen, ist es zunächst notwendig*
Secondly, it might be simpler to develop chemical or even nuclear warheads for a large shell than for a missile	*zweitens*
In the first/second/third place, the objectives of privatization were contradictory	*erstens/zweitens/drittens*
Finally, there is the argument that watching too much television may stunt a child's imagination	*schließlich*

Eine persönliche Meinung ausdrücken

In my opinion, the government is underestimating the scale of the epidemic	*meiner Meinung nach*
My personal opinion is that the argument lacks depth	*ich persönlich bin der Meinung, daß*
This is a popular viewpoint, but **speaking personally**, I cannot understand it	*persönlich*
Personally, I think that no one can appreciate ethnicity more than black or African people themselves	*ich persönlich glaube, daß*
My own view is that what largely determines the use of non-national workers are economic factors rather than political ones	*ich persönlich bin der Ansicht, daß*
In my view, it only perpetuates the very problem that it sets out to address	*meiner Ansicht nach*
For my part, I cannot agree with the leadership on this question	*was mich angeht*
Although the author argues the case for patriotism, **I feel that** he does not do it with any great personal conviction	*ich denke, daß*
I believe that people do understand that there can be no quick fix for Britain's economic problems	*ich glaube, daß*
It seems to me that what we have is a political problem that needs to be solved at a political level	*es scheint mir, daß*
I would maintain that we have made a significant effort to ensure that the results are made public	*ich möchte behaupten, daß*

Die Meinung anderer ausdrücken

He claims *oder* **maintains that** intelligence is conditioned by upbringing	*er behauptet, daß*
Bukharin **asserts that** all great revolutions are accompanied by destructive internal conflict	*stellt fest, daß*
The communiqué **states that** some form of nuclear deterrent will continue to be needed for the foreseeable future	*stellt fest, daß*
What he is saying is that the time of the old, highly structured political party is over	*er will damit sagen, daß*
His admirers **would have us believe that** watching this film is more like attending a church service than having a night at the pictures	*wollen uns glauben machen, daß*
According to the report, poverty creates a climate favourable to violence	*laut*

Beispiele geben

To take another example: many thousands of people have been condemned to a life of sickness and pain because ...	*um noch ein weiteres Beispiel anzuführen:*
Let us consider, **for example** *oder* **for instance**, the problems faced by immigrants arriving in a strange country	*zum Beispiel*
His meteoric rise **is the most striking example yet of** voters' disillusionment with the record of the previous government	*ist das bisher beste Beispiel*
The case of Henry Howey Robson **serves to illustrate** the courage exhibited by young men in the face of battle	*veranschaulicht*
Just consider, **by way of illustration**, the difference in amounts accumulated if interest is paid gross, rather than having tax deducted	*um dies einmal zu veranschaulichen*
A case in point is the decision to lift the ban on contacts with the republic	*ein positives Beispiel ist*
Take the case of the soldier returning from war	*nehmen wir zum Beispiel*
As the Prime Minister **remarked** recently, the Channel Tunnel will greatly benefit the whole of the European Community	*wie ... sagte*

53.6 Die Diskussion

Eine Annahme darlegen

They have telephoned the president to put pressure on him. And **that could be interpreted as** trying to gain an unconstitutional political advantage	*dies könnte man als ... interpretieren*
Retail sales rose sharply last month. This was higher than expected and **could be taken to mean that** inflationary pressures remain strong	*könnte als Zeichen dafür aufgefaßt werden, daß*
In such circumstances, **it might well be prudent** to diversify your investments	*könnte es weise sein*
These substances do not remain effective for very long. **This is possibly because** they work against the insects' natural instinct to feed	*dies rührt wahrscheinlich daher, daß*
His wife had become an embarrassment to him and therefore **it is not beyond the bounds of possibility that** he may have contemplated murdering her	*es kann nicht ausgeschlossen werden, daß*
Mr Fraser's assertion **leads one to suppose that** he is in full agreement with Catholic teaching as regards marriage	*läßt vermuten, daß*
It is probably the case that all long heavy ships are vulnerable	*wahrscheinlich*
After hearing nothing from the taxman for so long, most people **might reasonably assume that** their tax affairs were in order	*könnten durchaus annehmen, daß*
One could be forgiven for thinking that because the substances are chemicals they'd be easy to study	*man könnte fast annehmen, daß*
I venture to suggest that very often when people like him talk about love, they actually mean lust	*ich wage zu behaupten, daß*

Gewißheit ausdrücken

It is clear that any risk to the human foetus is very low	*es ist klar, daß*
Benn is **indisputably** a fine orator, one of the most compelling speakers in politics today	*zweifelsohne*
British universities are **undeniably** good, but they are not turning out enough top scientists	*unbestreitbar*
There can be no doubt that the Earth underwent a dramatic cooling which destroyed the environment and lifestyle of these creatures	*es läßt sich nicht bezweifeln, daß*
It is undoubtedly true that over the years there has been a much greater emphasis on safer sex	*es ist unbestreitbar, daß*
As we all know, adultery is far from uncommon, particularly in springtime	*wie wir alle wissen*
One thing is certain: the party is far from united	*eins ist sicher*
It is (quite) certain that unless peace can be brought to this troubled land no amount of aid will solve the long-term problems of the people	*es ist sicher, daß*

Zweifel ausdrücken

It is doubtful whether, in the present repressive climate, anyone would be brave or foolish enough to demonstrate publicly	*es ist fraglich, ob*
It remains to be seen whether the security forces will try to intervene	*es bleibt abzuwarten, ob*
I have a few reservations about the book	*ich habe einige Vorbehalte gegen*
The judges are expected to endorse the recommendation, but **it is by no means certain that** they will make up their minds today	*es ist keineswegs sicher, daß*
It is questionable whether media coverage of terrorist organizations actually affects terrorism	*es ist fraglich, ob*
This raises the whole question of exactly when men and women should retire	*dies wirft die Frage nach ... auf*
The crisis **puts a question mark against** the Prime Minister's stated commitment to intervention	*stellt ... in Frage*
Both these claims are true up to a point and they need to be made. But they are limited in their significance	*beide Behauptungen sind bis zu einem gewissen Punkt richtig*

Zustimmung ausdrücken

I agree wholeheartedly with the opinion that smacking should be outlawed	*ich stimme ... voll und ganz zu*
One must acknowledge that their history will make change more painful	*man muß eingestehen, daß*
It cannot be denied that there are similarities between the two approaches	*es läßt sich nicht verleugnen, daß*
Courtney - **rightly in my view** - is strongly critical of the snobbery and élitism that is all too evident in these circles	*für meine Begriffe zu Recht*
Preaching was considered an important activity, **and rightly so** in a country with a high illiteracy rate	*und das zu Recht*
You may dispute the Pope's right to tell people how to live their lives, **but it is hard to disagree with** his picture of modern society	*aber man kann ... nur schwer widersprechen*

Widerspruch ausdrücken

I must disagree with Gordon's article on criminality: it is dangerous to suggest that to be a criminal one must look like a criminal	*ich kann ... nicht zustimmen*
As a former teacher **I find it hard to believe that** there is no link at all between screen violence and violence on the streets	*ich kann nur schwer glauben, daß*
The strength of their feelings **is scarcely credible**	*ist kaum glaubhaft*
Her claim to have been the first to discover the phenomenon **lacks credibility**	*ist unglaubwürdig*
Nevertheless, **I remain unconvinced by** Milton	*... überzeugt mich nicht*
Many do not believe that water contains anything remotely dangerous. Sadly, **this is far from the truth**	*dies entspricht ganz und gar nicht der Wahrheit*
To say that everyone requires the same amount of a vitamin is as stupid as saying we all have blonde hair and blue eyes. **It simply isn't true**	*es ist einfach nicht wahr*
His remarks **were** not only highly offensive to black and other ethnic minorities but **totally inaccurate**	*waren vollkommen falsch*
Stomach ulcers are often associated with good living and a fast-moving lifestyle. **(But) in reality** there is no evidence to support this theory	*in Wirklichkeit (jedoch)*
This version of a political economy **does not stand up to close scrutiny**	*hält einer genaueren Untersuchung nicht stand*

Ein Argument betonen

Nowadays, there is clearly less stigma attached to unmarried mothers	*heutzutage ist ganz offensichtlich*
Evidence shows that ..., so once again **the facts speak for themselves**	*die Fakten sprechen für sich*
Few will argue with the principle that such a fund should be set up	*der Ansicht, daß ..., stimmen im Prinzip fast alle zu*
Hyams **supports this claim** by looking at sentences produced by young children learning German	*unterstützt diese Behauptung*
The most important thing is to reach agreement from all sides	*am wichtigsten ist es, zu*
Perhaps **the most important aspect of** cognition is the ability to manipulate symbols	*der wichtigste Aspekt*
It would be impossible to exaggerate the importance of these two volumes for anyone with a serious interest in the development of black gospel music	*man kann die Wichtigkeit ... gar nicht genug betonen*
The symbolic importance of Jerusalem for both Palestinians and Jews **is almost impossible to overemphasize**	*kann gar nicht genug betont werden*
It is important to be clear that Jesus does not identify himself with Yahweh	*vor allem muß man sich klar machen, daß*

It is significant that Mandalay seems to have become the central focus in this debate	*es ist bezeichnend, daß*
It should not be forgotten that many of those now in exile were close to the centre of power until only one year ago	*man sollte nicht vergessen, daß*
It should be stressed that the only way pet owners could possibly contract such a condition from their pets is by eating them	*es sollte betont werden, daß*
There is a very important point here and that is that the accused claims that he was with Ms Martins all evening on the night of the crime	*hierbei ist es äußerst wichtig festzustellen, daß*
At the beginning of his book Mr Stone **makes a telling point**. The Balkan peoples, he notes, are for the first time ...	*gibt ein aufschlußreiches Argument*
Suspicion is **the chief feature of** Britain's attitude to European theatre	*das Hauptmerkmal*
In order to focus attention on Hobson's distinctive contributions to macroeconomics, these wider issues are neglected here	*um die Aufmerksamkeit auf ... zu lenken*
These statements are interesting in that they illustrate different views	*diese Äußerungen sind dahingehend interessant, daß*

Language in Use

Contents

German-English

Sprache Aktiv

Inhalt

Englisch-Deutsch

ENGLISH~GERMAN DICTIONARY

WÖRTERBUCH ENGLISCH~DEUTSCH

A, a [eɪ] *n* A, a *nt*; *(Sch: as a mark)* eins, sehr gut; *(Mus)* A, a *nt* ◆ **from A to Z** von A bis Z; **to get from A to B** von A nach B kommen; **A-1** *(dated inf)* Ia *(inf)*, eins a *(inf)*; **A sharp/flat** *(Mus)* Ais, ais *nt*/As, as *nt*; *see also* **major, minor, natural.**

a [eɪ, ə] *indef art, before vowel* **an (a)** ein(e) ◆ **so large ~ country** so ein großes *or* ein so großes Land; **~ Mr X/~ certain young man** ein Herr X/ein gewisser junger Mann.
(b) *(in negative constructions)* **not ~** kein(e); **not ~ single man/woman** kein einziger *or* nicht ein einziger Mann/keine einzige *or* nicht eine einzige Frau; **he didn't want ~ present** er wollte kein Geschenk.
(c) *(with profession, nationality etc)* **he's ~ doctor/Frenchman** er ist Arzt/Franzose; **he's ~ famous doctor/Frenchman** er ist ein berühmter Arzt/Franzose; **as ~ young girl** als junges Mädchen; **~ Washington would have ...** ein Washington hätte ...
(d) *(the same)* **to be of ~n age/~ size** gleich alt/groß sein, in einem Alter sein/eine Größe haben; *see* **kind.**
(e) *(per)* pro ◆ **50p ~ kilo** 50 Pence das *or* pro Kilo; **twice ~ month** zweimal im *or* pro Monat; **50 km ~n hour** 50 Stundenkilometer, 50 Kilometer pro Stunde.
(f) in ~ good/bad mood gut/schlecht gelaunt; **to come/to have come to ~n end** zu Ende gehen/sein; **in ~ loud voice** mit lauter Stimme, laut; **to have ~ headache/temperature** Kopfschmerzen/erhöhte Temperatur haben.

A *abbr of* **(a) answer** Antw. **(b)** *(dated Brit Film) von der Filmkontrolle als nicht ganz jugendfrei gekennzeichneter Film* ◆ **~ certificate** *Filmkennzeichnung, die Eltern vor dem nicht ganz jugendfreien Inhalt eines Films warnt.*

a- *pref* **(a)** *(privative)* **~moral/~typical** amoralisch/atypisch. **(b)** *(old, dial)* **they came ~-running** sie kamen angerannt; **the bells were ~-ringing** die Glocken läuteten.

AA *abbr of* **(a) Automobile Association** Britischer Automobilclub. **(b) Alcoholics Anonymous. (c)** *(dated Brit Film) für Jugendliche ab 14 freigegebener Film.*

AAIB *(Brit) abbr of* **Air Accident Investigation Branch.**

aardvark ['ɑːdvɑːk] *n* Erdferkel *nt.*

Aaron's beard ['eərnz'bɪəd] *n* Hartheu *nt.*

AB *abbr of* **(a)** *(Naut)* **able-bodied seaman. (b)** *(US Univ) see* **BA.**

aback [ə'bæk] *adv*: **to be taken ~** erstaunt sein; *(upset)* betroffen sein.

abacus ['æbəkəs] *n, pl* **abaci** ['æbəsiː] Abakus *m.*

abaft [ə'bɑːft] *adv (Naut)* achtern.

abalone [æbə'ləʊnɪ] *n* Seeohr *nt.*

abandon [ə'bændən] [1] *vt* **(a)** *(leave, forsake)* verlassen; *woman also* sitzenlassen; *baby* aussetzen; *car also* (einfach) stehenlassen ◆ **they ~ed the city to the enemy** sie flohen und überließen dem Feind die Stadt; **to ~ ship** das Schiff verlassen.
(b) *(give up) project, hope, attempt* aufgeben ◆ **to ~ play** das Spiel abbrechen.
(c) *(fig)* **to ~ oneself to sth** sich einer Sache *(dat)* hingeben.
[2] *n, no pl* Hingabe, Selbstvergessenheit *f* ◆ **with ~** mit ganzer Seele, mit Leib und Seele.

abandoned [ə'bændənd] *adj* **(a)** *(dissolute)* verkommen. **(b)** *(unrestrained) dancing* selbstvergessen, hingebungsvoll, hemmungslos *(pej)*; *joy* unbändig.

abandonment [ə'bændənmənt] *n* **(a)** *(forsaking, desertion)* Verlassen *nt.* **(b)** *(giving-up)* Aufgabe *f.* **(c)** *(abandon)* Hingabe, Selbstvergessenheit, Hemmungslosigkeit *(pej) f.*

abase [ə'beɪs] *vt person* erniedrigen; *morals* verderben ◆ **to ~ oneself** sich (selbst) erniedrigen.

abasement [ə'beɪsmənt] *n* Erniedrigung *f*; *(of concept of love etc)* Abwertung *f*; *(lowering of standards)* Verfall, Niedergang *m* ◆ **~ of morality** Verfall der Moral.

abashed [ə'bæʃt] *adj* beschämt ◆ **to feel ~** sich schämen.

abate [ə'beɪt] [1] *vi* nachlassen; *(storm, eagerness, interest, noise also)* abflauen; *(pain, fever also)* abklingen; *(flood)* zurückgehen.
[2] *vt (form) noise, sb's interest* dämpfen; *rent, tax, fever* senken; *pain* lindern.

abatement [ə'beɪtmənt] *n* **(a)** *see vi* Nachlassen *nt*; Abflauen *nt*; Abklingen *nt*; Rückgang *m.* **(b)** *(form: reducing) see vt* Dämpfung *f*, Senkung *f*, Linderung *f* ◆ **the noise ~ society** die Gesellschaft zur Bekämpfung von Lärm.

abattoir ['æbətwɑːʳ] *n* Schlachthof *m.*

abbess ['æbɪs] *n* Äbtissin *f.*

abbey ['æbɪ] *n* Abtei *f*; *(church in ~)* Klosterkirche *f.*

abbot ['æbət] *n* Abt *m.*

abbreviate [ə'briːvɪeɪt] *vt word, title* abkürzen (*to* mit); *book, speech* verkürzen ◆ **an ~d skirt** *(hum inf)* ein kurzes Röckchen.

abbreviation [əˌbriːvɪ'eɪʃən] *n* *(of word, title)* Abkürzung *f*; *(of book, speech)* Verkürzung *f.*

ABC[1] ['eɪbiː'siː] *n (lit, fig)* Abc *nt* ◆ **it's as easy as ~** das ist doch kinderleicht.

ABC[2] *abbr of* **American Broadcasting Company** *amerikanische Rundfunkgesellschaft.*

abdicate ['æbdɪkeɪt] [1] *vt* verzichten auf (*+acc*).
[2] *vi (monarch)* abdanken, abdizieren *(dated geh)*; *(pope)* zurücktreten.

abdication [ˌæbdɪ'keɪʃən] *n (of monarch)* Abdankung, Abdikation *(dated geh) f*; *(of pope)* Verzicht *m* ◆ **his ~ of the throne** sein Verzicht auf den Thron.

abdomen ['æbdəmen, *(Med)* æb'dəʊmen] *n* Abdomen *nt (form)*; *(of man, mammals also)* Unterleib *m*; *(of insects also)* Hinterleib *m.*

abdominal [æb'dɒmɪnl] *adj see n* abdominal *(form)*; Unterleibs-; Hinterleibs- ◆ **~ segments** Abdominalsegmente *pl*; **~ wall** Bauchdecke *f.*

abduct [æb'dʌkt] *vt* entführen.

abduction [æb'dʌkʃən] *n* Entführung *f.*

abductor [æb'dʌktəʳ] *n* Entführer(in *f*) *m.*

abeam [ə'biːm] *adv (Naut)* querab.

abed [ə'bed] *adv (old)* im Bett ◆ **to be ~** (im Bette) ruhen *(geh).*

Aberdonian [ˌæbə'dəʊnjən] [1] *n* Aberdeener(in *f*) *m.*
[2] *adj* Aberdeener *inv.*

aberrant [ə'berənt] *adj* anomal.

aberration [ˌæbə'reɪʃən] *n* Anomalie *f*; *(Astron, Opt)* Aberration *f*; *(in statistics, from course)* Abweichung *f*; *(mistake)* Irrtum *m*; *(moral)* Verirrung *f* ◆ **in a moment of (mental) ~** *(inf)* in einem Augenblick geistiger Verwirrung; **I must have had an ~** *(inf)* da war ich wohl (geistig) weggetreten *(inf)*; **the housing scheme/this translation is something of an ~** *(inf)* die Wohnsiedlung/diese Übersetzung ist (ja) eine Krankheit *(inf).*

abet [ə'bet] [1] *vt crime, criminal* begünstigen, Vorschub leisten (*+dat*); *(fig)* unterstützen.
[2] *vi see* **aid 2.**

abetter, abettor [ə'betəʳ] *n* Helfershelfer (in *f*) *m.*

abeyance [ə'beɪəns] *n, no pl* **to be in ~** *(law, rule, issue)* ruhen; *(custom, office)* nicht mehr ausgeübt werden; **to fall into ~** außer Gebrauch kommen, nicht mehr wirksam sein; **to hold sth in ~** etw ruhenlassen.

abhor [əb'hɔːʳ] *vt* verabscheuen.

abhorrence [əb'hɒrəns] *n* Abscheu *f (of* vor *+dat)* ◆ **to hold sb/sth in ~** eine Abscheu vor jdm/etw haben.

abhorrent [əb'hɒrənt] *adj* abscheulich ◆ **the very idea is ~ to me** schon der Gedanke daran ist mir zuwider; **the notion is ~ to the rational mind** der Verstand widersetzt sich einer solchen Idee.

abidance [ə'baɪdəns] *n (form)* **~ by the rules/laws** die Einhaltung der Regeln/Gesetze.

abide [ə'baɪd] [1] *vt* **(a)** *(usu neg, interrog: tolerate)* ausstehen; *(endure)* aushalten ◆ **I cannot ~ living here** ich kann es nicht aushalten, hier zu leben.
(b) *(liter: wait for)* harren (*+gen*) *(liter).*
[2] *vi (old: remain, live)* weilen *(geh).*

◆**abide by** *vi +prep obj rule, law, decision, promise, results* sich halten an (*+acc*); *consequences* tragen ◆ **I ~ ~ what I said** ich bleibe bei dem, was ich gesagt habe.

abiding [ə'baɪdɪŋ] *adj (liter: lasting)* unvergänglich; *desire also* bleibend.

ability [ə'bɪlɪtɪ] *n* Fähigkeit *f* ◆ **~ to pay/hear** Zahlungs-/Hörfähigkeit *f*; **to the best of my ~** nach (besten) Kräften; *(with mental activities)* so gut ich es kann; **a pianist/man of great ~** ein ausgesprochen fähiger *or* begabter Pianist/ein sehr fähiger Mann; **his ~ in German** seine Fähigkeiten im Deutschen; **she has great ~** sie ist ausgesprochen fähig.

abject ['æbdʒekt] *adj* **(a)** *(wretched) state, liar, thief* elend, erbärmlich; *poverty* bitter. **(b)** *(servile) submission, apology* demütig; *person, gesture also* unterwürfig.

abjectly ['æbdʒektlɪ] *adv see adj* erbärmlich; demütig; unterwürfig.

abjectness ['æbdʒektnɪs] *n see adj* Erbärmlichkeit *f*; Demut *f*; Unterwürfigkeit *f* ◆ **such was the ~ of their poverty ...** so bitter war ihre Armut ...

abjuration [ˌæbdʒʊə'reɪʃən] *n* Abschwören *nt.*

abjure [əb'dʒʊəʳ] *vt* abschwören (*+dat*).

ablative ['æblətɪv] [1] *n* Ablativ *m* ♦ **~ absolute** Ablativus absolutus.
[2] *adj ending, case* Ablativ-; *noun* im Ablativ.

ablaut ['æblaʊt] *n* Ablaut *m.*

ablaze [ə'bleɪz] *adv, adj pred* in Flammen ♦ **to be ~** in Flammen stehen; **to set sth ~** etw in Brand stecken; **the paraffin really set the fire ~** das Paraffin ließ das Feuer wirklich auflodern; **his face was ~ with joy/anger** sein Gesicht glühte vor Freude/brannte vor Ärger; **to be ~ with light/colour** hell erleuchtet sein/in leuchtenden Farben erstrahlen.

able ['eɪbl] *adj* **(a)** (*skilled, talented*) *person* fähig, kompetent; *piece of work, exam paper, speech* gekonnt.
(b) to be ~ to do sth etw tun können; **if you're not ~ to understand that** wenn Sie nicht fähig sind, das zu verstehen; **I'm afraid I am not ~ to give you that information** ich bin leider nicht in der Lage, Ihnen diese Informationen zu geben; **you are better ~ to do it than he** Sie sind eher dazu in der Lage als er; **yes, if I'm ~** ja, wenn es mir möglich ist.

-able [-əbl] *adj suf* -bar, -lich.

able-bodied [ˌeɪbl'bɒdɪd] *adj* (gesund und) kräftig; (*Mil*) tauglich.

able(-bodied) seaman *n* Vollmatrose *m.*

ablution [ə'bluːʃən] *n* Waschung *f.* **~s** *pl* (*lavatory*) sanitäre Einrichtungen *pl* ♦ **to perform one's ~s** (*esp hum*) seine Waschungen vornehmen; (*go to lavatory*) seine Notdurft verrichten.

ably ['eɪblɪ] *adv* gekonnt, fähig.

ABM *abbr of* **anti-ballistic missile.**

abnegate ['æbnɪgeɪt] *vt* entsagen (*+dat*).

abnegation [ˌæbnɪ'geɪʃən] *n* Verzicht *m* (*of* auf *+acc*), Entsagung *f* ♦ **self-~** Selbstverleugnung *f.*

abnormal [æb'nɔːməl] *adj* anormal; (*deviant, Med*) abnorm ♦ **~ psychology** Psychologie *f* des Abnormen.

abnormality [ˌæbnɔː'mælɪtɪ] *n* Anormale(s) *nt*; (*deviancy, Med*) Abnormität *f.*

abnormally [æb'nɔːməlɪ] *adv see adj.*

Abo ['æbəʊ] *n* (*Austral inf*) (australischer) Ureinwohner.

aboard [ə'bɔːd] [1] *adv* (*on plane, ship*) an Bord; (*on train*) im Zug; (*on bus*) im Bus ♦ **all ~!** alle an Bord!; (*on train, bus*) alles einsteigen!; **to go ~** an Bord gehen; **they were no sooner ~ than the train/bus moved off** sie waren kaum eingestiegen, als der Zug/Bus auch schon abfuhr.
[2] *prep* **~ the ship/train/bus** an Bord des Schiffes/im Zug/Bus.

abode [ə'bəʊd] [1] *pret, ptp of* **abide.**
[2] *n* (*liter: dwelling place*) Behausung *f*, Aufenthalt *m* (*liter*); (*Jur: also* **place of ~**) Wohnsitz *m* ♦ **a humble ~** (*iro*) eine bescheidene Hütte (*iro*); **of no fixed ~** ohne festen Wohnsitz.

abolish [ə'bɒlɪʃ] *vt* abschaffen; *law also* aufheben.

abolishment [ə'bɒlɪʃmənt], **abolition** [ˌæbəʊ'lɪʃən] *n* Abschaffung *f*; (*of law also*) Aufhebung *f.*

abolitionist [ˌæbəʊ'lɪʃənɪst] *n Befürworter(in f) m der Abschaffung eines Gesetzes etc,* Abolitionist *m* (*form*).

A-bomb ['eɪbɒm] *n* Atombombe *f.*

abominable [ə'bɒmɪnəbl] *adj* gräßlich, abscheulich; *spelling* gräßlich, entsetzlich ♦ **A~ Snowman** Schneemensch *m.*

abominably [ə'bɒmɪnəblɪ] *adv* gräßlich, abscheulich ♦ **~ rude** furchtbar unhöflich.

abominate [ə'bɒmɪneɪt] *vt* verabscheuen.

abomination [əˌbɒmɪ'neɪʃən] *n* **(a)** *no pl* Verabscheuung *f* ♦ **to be held in ~ by sb** von jdm verabscheut werden. **(b)** (*loathsome act*) Abscheulichkeit *f*; (*loathsome thing*) Scheußlichkeit *f.*

aboriginal [ˌæbə'rɪdʒənl] [1] *adj* der (australischen) Ureinwohner, australid; *tribe also* australisch.
[2] *n see* **aborigine.**

aborigine [ˌæbə'rɪdʒɪnɪ] *n* Ureinwohner(in *f*) *m* (Australiens), Australide *m*, Australidin *f.*

abort [ə'bɔːt] [1] *vi* (*Med*) (*mother*) eine Fehlgeburt haben, abortieren (*form*); (*foetus*) abgehen; (*perform abortion*) die Schwangerschaft abbrechen, einen Abort herbeiführen (*form*); (*fig: go wrong*) scheitern; (*Comput*) abbrechen.
[2] *vt* (*Med*) *foetus* (durch Abort) entfernen, abtreiben (*pej*); (*Space*) *mission* abbrechen; (*Comput*) abbrechen.
[3] *n* (*Space*) Abort *m* (*form*).

abortion [ə'bɔːʃən] *n* Schwangerschaftsabbruch *m*, Abtreibung *f* (*pej*); (*miscarriage*) Fehlgeburt *f*, Abort *m* (*form*); (*fig: plan, project etc*) Fehlschlag, Reinfall (*inf*) *m*; (*pej: person*) Mißgeburt *f* (*pej*) ♦ **to get** *or* **have an ~** abtreiben lassen, eine Abtreibung vornehmen lassen.

abortionist [ə'bɔːʃənɪst] *n* Abtreibungshelfer(in *f*) *m*; (*doctor also*) Abtreibungsarzt *m*/-ärztin *f*; *see* **back-street.**

abortive [ə'bɔːtɪv] *adj* **(a)** (*unsuccessful*) *attempt, plan* gescheitert, fehlgeschlagen ♦ **to be ~** scheitern, fehlschlagen. **(b)** (*Med*) *drug* abortiv (*form*), abtreibend.

abortively [ə'bɔːtɪvlɪ] *adv end* ergebnislos.

abound [ə'baʊnd] *vi* (*exist in great numbers*) im Überfluß vorhanden sein; (*persons*) sehr zahlreich sein; (*have in great numbers*) reich sein (*in* an *+dat*)/ wimmeln (*with* von) ♦ **students/rabbits/berries ~ in ...** es wimmelt von Studenten/Kaninchen/Beeren in ...

about [ə'baʊt] [1] *adv* **(a)** herum, umher; (*present*) in der Nähe ♦ **to run/walk ~** herum- *or* umherrennen/-gehen; **I looked all ~** ich sah ringsumher; **the castle walls are half a mile ~** die Mauer (rings) um das Schloß ist eine halbe Meile lang; **to leave things (lying) ~** Sachen herumliegen lassen; **to be (up and) ~ again** wieder auf den Beinen sein; **we were ~ early** wir waren früh auf den Beinen; **there's a thief/a lot of measles/plenty of money ~** ein Dieb geht um/die Masern gehen um/es ist Geld in Mengen vorhanden; **there was nobody ~ who could help** es war niemand in der Nähe, der hätte helfen können; **at night when there's nobody ~** nachts, wenn niemand unterwegs ist; **where is he/it? — he's/it's ~ somewhere** wo ist er/es? — (er/es ist) irgendwo in der Nähe; **it's the other way ~** es ist gerade umgekehrt; **day and day ~** (täglich) abwechselnd; *see* **out, turn, up.**
(b) to be ~ to im Begriff sein zu; (*esp US inf: intending*) vorhaben, zu ...; **I was ~ to go out** ich wollte gerade ausgehen; **it's ~ to rain** es regnet gleich *or* demnächst; **he's ~/almost ~ to start school** er kommt demnächst in die Schule; **we are ~ to run out of petrol** uns geht demnächst das Benzin aus, uns geht gleich das Benzin aus; **are you ~ to tell me ...?** willst du mir etwa erzählen ...?
(c) (*approximately*) ungefähr, (so) um ... (herum) ♦ **he's ~ 40** er ist ungefähr 40 *or* (so) um (die) 40 (herum); **~ 2 o'clock** ungefähr *or* so um 2 Uhr; **he is ~ the same, doctor** sein Zustand hat sich kaum geändert, Herr Doktor; **that's ~ it** das ist so ziemlich alles, das wär's (so ziemlich) (*inf*); **that's ~ right** das stimmt (so) ungefähr; **I've had ~ enough (of this nonsense)** jetzt reicht es mir aber allmählich (mit diesem Unsinn) (*inf*); **he was ~ dead from exhaustion** er war halb tot vor Erschöpfung; *see* **just, round, time.**
[2] *prep* **(a)** um (... herum); (*in*) in (*+dat*) (... herum) ♦ **the fields ~ the house** die Felder ums Haus (herum); **scattered ~ the room** im ganzen *or* über das ganze Zimmer verstreut; **somewhere ~ here** irgendwo hier herum; **all ~ the house** im ganzen Haus (herum); **to sit/do jobs ~ the house** im Haus herumsitzen/sich im Haus (herum) nützlich machen; **he looked ~ him** er schaute sich um; **I have no money ~ me** ich habe kein Geld bei mir; **there's something ~ him/~ the way he speaks** er/seine Art zu reden hat so etwas an sich; **while you're ~ it** wenn du gerade *or* schon dabei bist; **you've been a long time ~ it** du hast lange dazu gebraucht; **and be quick ~ it!** und beeil dich damit!, aber ein bißchen dalli! (*inf*).
(b) (*concerning*) über (*+acc*) ♦ **tell me all ~ it** erzähl doch mal; **he knows ~ it** er weiß darüber Bescheid, er weiß davon; **what's it all ~?** worum *or* um was (*inf*) handelt es sich *or* geht es (eigentlich)?; **he knows what it's all ~** er weiß Bescheid; **he's promised to do something ~ it** er hat versprochen, (in der Sache) etwas zu unternehmen; **they fell out ~ money** sie haben sich wegen Geld zerstritten; **how** *or* **what ~ me?** und ich, was ist mit mir? (*inf*); **how** *or* **what ~ it/going to the pictures?** wie wär's damit/mit (dem) Kino?; **what ~ that book? have you brought it back?** was ist mit dem Buch? hast du es zurückgebracht?; **(yes,) what ~ it/him?** ja *or* na und(, was ist damit/mit ihm)?; **he doesn't know what he's ~** er weiß nicht, was er (eigentlich) tut.

about-face [əˌbaʊt'feɪs], **about-turn** [əˌbaʊt'tɜːn] [1] *n* (*Mil*) Kehrtwendung *f*; (*fig also*) Wendung *f* um hundertachtzig Grad ♦ **to do an ~** kehrtmachen; (*fig*) sich um hundertachtzig Grad drehen.
[2] *vi* (*Mil*) eine Kehrtwendung ausführen *or* machen.
[3] *interj* **about face** *or* **turn!** (und) kehrt!

above [ə'bʌv] [1] *adv* **(a)** (*overhead*) oben; (*in heaven also*) in der Höhe; (*in a higher position*) darüber ♦ **from ~** von oben; (*from heaven also*) aus der Höhe; **look straight ~** schau genau nach oben; **the flat ~** die Wohnung oben *or* (*~ that one*) darüber.
(b) (*in text*) oben.
[2] *prep* über (*+dat*); (*with motion*) über (*+acc*); (*upstream of*) oberhalb (*+gen*) ♦ **~ all** vor allem, vor allen Dingen; **I couldn't hear ~ the din** ich konnte bei dem Lärm nichts hören; **he valued money ~ his family** er schätzte Geld mehr als seine Familie; **to be ~ sb/sth** über jdm/etw stehen; **~ criticism/praise** über jede Kritik/jedes Lob erhaben; **he's ~ that sort of thing** er ist über so etwas erhaben; **he's not ~ a bit of blackmail** er ist sich (*dat*) nicht zu gut für eine kleine Erpressung; **it's ~ my head** *or* **me** das ist mir zu hoch; **to be/get ~ oneself** (*inf*) größenwahnsinnig werden (*inf*).
[3] *adj attr* **the ~ persons/figures** die obengenannten *or* -erwähnten Personen/Zahlen; **the ~ paragraph** der vorher- *or* vorangehende *or* obige Abschnitt.
[4] *n*: **the ~** (*statement etc*) Obiges *nt* (*form*); (*person*) der/die Obengenannte/ die Obengenannten *pl.*

above: ~ board *adj pred* korrekt; **open and ~ board** offen und ehrlich; **~-mentioned** *adj* obenerwähnt; **~-named** *adj* obengenannt.

abracadabra [ˌæbrəkə'dæbrə] *n* Abrakadabra *nt.*

abrade [ə'breɪd] *vt* (*form*) *skin* aufschürfen, abschürfen; (*Geol*) abtragen.

Abraham ['eɪbrəhæm] *n* Abraham *m* ♦ **in ~'s bosom** in Abrahams Schoß.

abrasion [ə'breɪʒən] *n* (*Med*) (Haut)abschürfung *f*; (*Geol*) Abtragung *f*; (*by the sea also*) Abrasion *f* (*form*).

abrasive [ə'breɪsɪv] [1] *adj* **(a)** *cleanser* Scheuer-, scharf; *surface* rauh ♦ **~ paper** Schmirgel- *or* Schleifpapier *nt.* **(b)** (*fig*) *personality, person* aggressiv; *tongue, voice* scharf.
[2] *n* (*cleanser*) Scheuermittel *nt*; (*~ substance*) Schleifmittel *nt.*

abrasiveness [ə'breɪsɪvnɪs] *n see adj* **(a)** Schärfe *f*; Rauheit *f.* **(b)** Aggressivität *f*; Schärfe *f.*

abreact [ˌæbrɪ'ækt] *vt* (*Psych*) abreagieren.

abreaction [ˌæbrɪ'ækʃən] *n* (*Psych*) Abreaktion *f.*

abreast [ə'brest] *adv* Seite an Seite; (*Naut also*) Bug an Bug ♦ **to march four ~** im Viererglied *or* zu viert nebeneinander marschieren; **~ of sb/sth** neben jdm/etw, auf gleicher Höhe mit jdm/etw; **to come ~ (of sb/sth)** mit jdm/ etw gleichziehen, auf gleiche Höhe mit jdm/etw kommen; **to keep ~ of the times/news** *etc* mit seiner Zeit/den Nachrichten *etc* auf dem laufenden bleiben.

abridge [ə'brɪdʒ] *vt book* kürzen.
abridgement [ə'brɪdʒmənt] *n* (*act*) Kürzen *nt*; (*abridged work*) gekürzte Ausgabe.
abroad [ə'brɔːd] *adv* **(a)** im Ausland ◆ **to go/be sent ~** ins Ausland gehen/geschickt werden; **from ~** aus dem Ausland.
(b) (*esp liter: out of doors*) draußen ◆ **to venture ~** sich nach draußen *or* ins Freie wagen; **he was ~ very early** er war schon sehr früh unterwegs.
(c) there is a rumour ~ that ... ein Gerücht geht um *or* kursiert, daß ...; **to get ~** an die Öffentlichkeit dringen; *see* **publish.**
(d) (*liter: far and wide*) *scatter* weit.
abrogate ['æbrəʊgeɪt] *vt law, treaty* außer Kraft setzen; *responsibility* ablehnen.
abrogation [,æbrəʊ'geɪʃən] *n see vt* Außerkraftsetzung, Ungültigkeitserklärung *f*; Ablehnung *f*.
abrupt [ə'brʌpt] *adj* abrupt; *descent, drop* unvermittelt, jäh; *bend* plötzlich; *manner, reply* schroff, brüsk.
abruptly [ə'brʌptlɪ] *adv see adj* abrupt; unvermittelt, jäh; plötzlich; schroff, brüsk.
abruptness [ə'brʌptnɪs] *n* abrupte Art; (*of person*) schroffe *or* brüske Art; (*of descent, drop, bend*) Plötzlichkeit, Jäheit *f*; (*of style, writing also*) Abgerissenheit *f*; (*of reply*) Schroffheit *f*.
ABS *abbr of* **anti-lock braking system** ◆ **~ brakes** ABS-Bremsen *pl*.
abscess ['æbsɪs] *n* Abszeß *m*.
abscond [əb'skɒnd] *vi* sich (heimlich) davonmachen, türmen (*inf*); (*schoolboys also*) durchbrennen.
abseil ['æpsaɪl] **1** *vi* (*Mountaineering: also* **~ down**) sich abseilen.
2 *n* Abstieg *m* (am Seil).
absence ['æbsəns] *n* **(a)** Abwesenheit *f*; (*from school, work etc also*) Fehlen *nt*; (*from meetings etc also*) Nichterscheinen *nt* (*from* bei) ◆ **in the ~ of the chairman** in Abwesenheit des Vorsitzenden; **sentenced in one's ~** in Abwesenheit verurteilt; **it's not fair to criticize him in his ~** es ist nicht fair, ihn in seiner Abwesenheit zu kritisieren; **her many ~s on business** ihre häufige Abwesenheit aus geschäftlichen Gründen; **~ makes the heart grow fonder** (*Prov*) die Liebe wächst mit der Entfernung (*Prov*).
(b) (*lack*) Fehlen *nt* ◆ **~ of enthusiasm** Mangel *m* an Enthusiasmus; **in the ~ of further evidence/qualified staff** in Ermangelung weiterer Beweise/von Fachkräften.
(c) (*person absent*) **he counted the ~s** er stellte die Zahl der Abwesenden fest; **how many ~s do we have today?** wie viele fehlen heute *or* sind heute nicht da *or* anwesend?
(d) ~ of mind Geistesabwesenheit *f*.
absent ['æbsənt] **1** *adj* **(a)** (*not present*) *person* abwesend, nicht da ◆ **to be ~ from school/work** in der Schule/am Arbeitsplatz fehlen; **~!** (*Sch*) fehlt!; **why were you ~ from class?** warum warst du nicht in der Stunde?, warum hast du gefehlt?; **to be** *or* **go ~ without leave** (*Mil*) sich unerlaubt von der Truppe entfernen; **to ~ friends!** auf unsere abwesenden Freunde!
(b) (*~-minded*) *expression, look* (geistes)abwesend ◆ **in an ~ moment** in einem Augenblick geistiger Abwesenheit.
(c) (*lacking*) **to be ~** fehlen.
2 [æb'sent] *vr* **to ~ oneself (from)** (*not go, not appear*) fernbleiben (+*dat*, von); (*leave temporarily*) sich zurückziehen *or* absentieren (*hum, geh*).
absentee [,æbsən'tiː] *n* Abwesende(r) *mf* ◆ **there were a lot of ~s** es fehlten viele; (*pej*) es haben viele krank gefeiert.
absentee ballot *n* (*esp US*) ≃ Briefwahl *f*.
absenteeism [,æbsən'tiːɪzəm] *n* häufige Abwesenheit; (*of workers also*) Nichterscheinen *nt* am Arbeitsplatz; (*pej*) Krankfeiern *nt*; (*Sch*) Schwänzen *nt* ◆ **the rate of ~ among workers** die Abwesenheitsquote bei Arbeitern.
absentee: ~ landlord *n* nicht ortsansässiger Haus-/Grundbesitzer; **~ voter** *n* (*esp US*) ≃ Briefwähler(in *f*) *m*.
absently ['æbsəntlɪ] *adv* (geistes)abwesend.
absent-minded [,æbsənt'maɪndɪd] *adj* (*lost in thought*) geistesabwesend; (*habitually forgetful*) zerstreut.
absent-mindedly [,æbsənt'maɪndɪdlɪ] *adv behave* zerstreut; *look* (geistes)abwesend ◆ **he ~ forgot it** in seiner Zerstreutheit hat er es vergessen.
absent-mindedness [,æbsənt'maɪndɪdnɪs] *n see adj* Geistesabwesenheit *f*; Zerstreutheit *f*.
absinth(e) ['æbsɪnθ] *n* Absinth *m*.
absolute ['æbsəluːt] *adj* absolut; *power, monopoly, liberty, support also, command* uneingeschränkt; *monarch also* unumschränkt; *lie, idiot* ausgemacht ◆ **the ~** das Absolute; **~ majority** absolute Mehrheit; **~ pitch** absolute Tonhöhe; (*of person*) absolutes Gehör; **~ zero** absoluter Nullpunkt.
absolutely ['æbsəluːtlɪ] *adv* absolut; *prove* eindeutig; *agree, trust also, true* vollkommen, völlig; *deny, refuse also* strikt; *forbidden also* streng; *stupid also* völlig; *necessary also* unbedingt ◆ **~!** durchaus; (*I agree*) genau!; **do you/don't you agree? — ~** sind Sie einverstanden? — vollkommen/sind Sie nicht einverstanden? — doch, vollkommen; **do you ~ insist?** muß das unbedingt *or* durchaus sein?; **he ~ refused to do that** er wollte das absolut *or* durchaus nicht tun; **it's ~ amazing** es ist wirklich erstaunlich; **you look ~ stunning/awful** du siehst wirklich großartig/schrecklich aus; **you're ~ right** Sie haben völlig recht.
absolution [,æbsə'luːʃən] *n* (*Eccl*) Absolution, Lossprechung *f* ◆ **to say the ~** die Absolution erteilen.
absolutism ['æbsəluːtɪzəm] *n* Absolutismus *m*.
absolve [əb'zɒlv] *vt person* (*from sins*) lossprechen (*from* von); (*from blame*) freisprechen (*from* von); (*from vow, oath etc*) entbinden (*from* von, *gen*).
absorb [əb'sɔːb] *vt* absorbieren, aufnehmen; *liquid also* aufsaugen; *knowledge, news also* in sich (*acc*) aufnehmen; *vibration* auffangen, absorbieren; *shock* dämpfen; *light, sound* absorbieren, schlucken; *people, firm also* integrieren (*into* in +*acc*); *costs etc* tragen; *one's time* in Anspruch nehmen ◆ **she ~s things quickly** sie hat eine rasche Auffassungsgabe; **to be/get ~ed in a book** *etc* in ein Buch *etc* vertieft *or* versunken sein/sich in ein Buch *etc* vertiefen; **she was completely ~ed in her family/job** sie ging völlig in ihrer Familie/Arbeit auf.
absorbency [əb'sɔːbənsɪ] *n* Saug- *or* Absorptionsfähigkeit *f*.
absorbent [əb'sɔːbənt] *adj* saugfähig, absorbierend.
absorbent cotton *n* (*US*) Watte *f*.
absorbing [əb'sɔːbɪŋ] *adj* fesselnd.
absorption [əb'sɔːpʃən] *n see* **absorb** Absorption, Aufnahme *f*; Aufsaugung *f*; Auffangen *nt*; Dämpfung *f*; Integration *f* ◆ **her total ~ in her family/studies/book** ihr vollkommenes Aufgehen in ihrer Familie/ihrem Studium/ihre völlige Versunkenheit in dem Buch; **to watch with ~** gefesselt *or* gebannt beobachten.
abstain [əb'steɪn] *vi* **(a)** sich enthalten (*from gen*) ◆ **to ~ from alcohol/drinking** sich des Alkohols/Trinkens enthalten (*geh*). **(b)** (*in voting*) sich der Stimme enthalten.
abstainer [əb'steɪnə^r] *n* **(a)** (*from alcohol*) Abstinenzler(in *f*) *m*. **(b)** *see* **abstention (b).**
abstemious [əb'stiːmɪəs] *adj person, life* enthaltsam; *meal, diet* bescheiden.
abstemiousness [əb'stiːmɪəsnɪs] *n see adj* Enthaltsamkeit *f*; Bescheidenheit *f*.
abstention [əb'stenʃən] *n* **(a)** *no pl* Enthaltung *f*; (*from alcohol also*) Abstinenz *f*. **(b)** (*in voting*) (Stimm)enthaltung *f* ◆ **were you one of the ~s?** waren Sie einer von denen, die sich der Stimme enthalten haben?
abstinence ['æbstɪnəns] *n* Abstinenz, Enthaltung *f* (*from* von); (*self-restraint*) Enthaltsamkeit *f* ◆ **total ~** völlige Abstinenz; **day of ~** Abstinenztag, Fasttag *m*.
abstract[1] ['æbstrækt] **1** *adj* (*all senses*) abstrakt ◆ **in the ~** abstrakt; **~ noun** Abstraktum *nt*, abstraktes Substantiv.
2 *n* (kurze) Zusammenfassung.
abstract[2] [æb'strækt] *vt* abstrahieren; *information* entnehmen (*from* aus); *metal etc* trennen; (*inf: steal*) entwenden.
abstracted [æb'stræktɪd] *adj* abwesend, entrückt (*geh*).
abstraction [æb'strækʃən] *n* Abstraktion *f*; (*abstract term also*) Abstraktum *nt*; (*mental separation also*) Abstrahieren *nt*; (*extraction: of information etc*) Entnahme *f*; (*absent-mindedness*) Entrücktheit *f* (*geh*) ◆ **to argue in ~s** in abstrakten Begriffen *or* Abstraktionen argumentieren.
abstractness ['æbstræktnɪs] *n* Abstraktheit *f*.
abstruse [æb'struːs] *adj* abstrus.
abstruseness [æb'struːsnɪs] *n* abstruse Unklarheit.
absurd [əb'sɜːd] *adj* absurd ◆ **don't be ~!** sei nicht albern; **if you think that, you're just being ~** du bist ja nicht recht bei Trost, wenn du das glaubst; **what an ~ waste of time!** so eine blödsinnige Zeitverschwendung!; **the management is being ~ again** das Management spielt mal wieder verrückt (*inf*); **theatre of the ~** absurdes Theater.
absurdity [əb'sɜːdɪtɪ] *n* Absurde(s) *nt no pl* (*of an* +*dat*); (*thing etc also*) Absurdität *f*.
absurdly [əb'sɜːdlɪ] *adv behave, react* absurd; *fast,* (*inf*) *rich, expensive etc* unsinnig ◆ **he talked/suggested very ~ ...** er redete großen Unsinn/er machte absurderweise den Vorschlag ...
abundance [ə'bʌndəns] *n* (großer) Reichtum (*of* an +*dat*); (*of hair, vegetation, details, illustrations, information, ideas, colours also, proof*) Fülle *f* (*of* von, *gen*) ◆ **in ~** in Hülle und Fülle; **a country with an ~ of oil/raw materials** ein Land mit reichen Ölvorkommen/großem Reichtum an Rohstoffen; **with his ~ of energy** mit seiner ungeheuren Energie; **such an ~ of open space** so unermeßlich viel freies Land.
abundant [ə'bʌndənt] *adj* reich; *growth, hair* üppig; *time, proof* reichlich; *energy, self-confidence etc* ungeheuer ◆ **to be ~ in sth** reich an etw (*dat*) sein; **apples are in ~ supply** es gibt reichlich Äpfel, es gibt Äpfel in Hülle und Fülle.
abundantly [ə'bʌndəntlɪ] *adv* reichlich; *grow* in Hülle und Fülle, üppig ◆ **to make it ~ clear that ...** mehr als deutlich zu verstehen geben, daß ...; **it was ~ clear (to me) that ...** es war (mir) mehr als klar, daß ...; **that is ~ obvious** das ist mehr als offensichtlich.
abuse [ə'bjuːs] **1** *n* **(a)** *no pl* (*insults*) Beschimpfungen *pl* ◆ **a term of ~** ein Schimpfwort *nt*; **to shout ~ at sb** jdm Beschimpfungen an den Kopf werfen; **to heap ~ on sb** jdn mit Beschimpfungen über schütten; *see* **shower, stream.**
(b) (*misuse*) Mißbrauch *m*; (*unjust practice*) Mißstand *m* ◆ **~ of confidence/authority** Vertrauens-/Amtsmißbrauch *m*; **the system is open to ~** das System läßt sich leicht mißbrauchen.
2 [ə'bjuːz] *vt* **(a)** (*revile*) beschimpfen, schmähen (*geh*).
(b) (*misuse*) mißbrauchen; *one's health* Raubbau treiben mit.
abusive [əb'juːsɪv] *adj* beleidigend ◆ **~ language** Beschimpfungen, Beleidigungen *pl*; **to be ~ (to sb)** (jdm gegenüber) beleidigend *or* ausfallend sein; **he muttered something ~** er murmelte etwas Beleidigendes; **to become/get ~ (with sb)** (jdm gegenüber) beleidigend *or* ausfallend werden.
abusiveness [əb'juːsɪvnɪs] *n* (*of person*) ausfallende Art ◆ **a critic should not descend to mere ~** ein Kritiker sollte sich nicht in reinen Ausfälligkeiten ergehen.

abut [ə'bʌt] *vi* stoßen (*on(to)* an + *acc*); (*land also*) grenzen (*on(to)* an +*acc*); (*two houses, fields etc*) aneinanderstoßen/-grenzen.

abutment [ə'bʌtmənt] *n* (*Archit*) Flügel- *or* Wangenmauer *f*.

abutter [ə'bʌtə[r]] *n* (*US*) Anlieger *m*; (*to one's own land*) (Grenz)nachbar(in *f*) *m*.

abutting [ə'bʌtɪŋ] *adj* (daran) anstoßend *attr*; (*fields also*) (daran) angrenzend *attr* ◆ **the two ~ houses** die zwei aneinanderstoßenden Häuser.

abysmal [ə'bɪzməl] *adj* (*fig*) entsetzlich; *performance, work, taste etc* miserabel.

abysmally [ə'bɪzməlɪ] *adv* entsetzlich; *perform, work etc also* miserabel ◆ **our team did ~ in the competition** unsere Mannschaft schnitt bei dem Wettkampf entsetzlich (schlecht) *or* miserabel ab.

abyss [ə'bɪs] *n* (*lit, fig*) Abgrund *m* ◆ **the ~ of space** die Weite des Alls.

Abyssinia [,æbɪ'sɪnɪə] *n* Abessinien *nt*.

Abyssinian [,æbɪ'sɪnɪən] [1] *adj attr* abessinisch.
[2] *n* Abessinier(in *f*) *m*.

A/C *abbr of* **account** Kto.

AC *abbr of* **alternating current; aircraftman.**

acacia [ə'keɪʃə] *n* (*also* **~ tree**) Akazie *f*.

academic [,ækə'demɪk] [1] *adj* **(a)** akademisch; *publisher, reputation* wissenschaftlich.
(b) (*intellectual*) *approach, quality, interest* wissenschaftlich; *interests* geistig; *person, appearance* intellektuell; *style, book also* akademisch.
(c) (*theoretical*) akademisch ◆ **out of ~ interest** aus rein akademischem Interesse; **since the decision has already been made the discussion is purely ~** da die Entscheidung schon getroffen wurde, ist das eine (rein) akademische Diskussion.
[2] *n* Akademiker(in *f*) *m*; (*Univ*) Universitätslehrkraft *f*.

academically [,ækə'demɪkəlɪ] *adv* **(a)** wissenschaftlich ◆ **to be ~ inclined/minded** geistige Interessen haben/wissenschaftlich denken; **~ respectable** wissenschaftlich akzeptabel; **~ gifted** intellektuell begabt.
(b) she is not doing well ~ sie ist in der Schule nicht gut/mit ihrem Studium nicht sehr erfolgreich; **she's good at handicraft but is not doing so well ~** im Werken ist sie gut, aber in den wissenschaftlichen Fächern hapert es.

academicals [,ækə'demɪkəlz] *npl* akademische Tracht.

academician [ə,kædə'mɪʃən] *n* Akademiemitglied *nt*.

academy [ə'kædəmɪ] *n* Akademie *f* ◆ **naval/military ~** Marine/Militärakademie *f*; **~ for young ladies** ≃ höhere Töchterschule.

acanthus [ə'kænθəs] *n* (*plant*) Bärenklau *f*, Akanthus *m* (*also Archit*).

ACAS, Acas ['eɪkæs] *abbr of* **Advisory Conciliation and Arbitration Service** *Schlichtungsstelle f für Arbeitskonflikte.*

acc *abbr of* **account; accommodation** Übern.

accede [æk'si:d] *vi* **(a) to ~ to the throne** den Thron besteigen; **to ~ to the Premiership/office of President** die Nachfolge als Premierminister/Präsident antreten. **(b)** (*agree*) zustimmen (*to dat*); (*yield*) einwilligen (*to* in +*acc*). **(c) to ~ to a treaty** einem Pakt beitreten.

accelerate [æk'seləreɪt] [1] *vt* beschleunigen; *speed also* erhöhen.
[2] *vi* beschleunigen; (*driver also*) Gas geben; (*work-rate, speed, change*) sich beschleunigen, zunehmen; (*growth, inflation etc*) zunehmen ◆ **he ~d away** er gab Gas und fuhr davon; **he ~d out of the bend** er hat in der Kurve beschleunigt *or* Gas gegeben; **to ~ away** (*runner etc*) lossprurten; (*car etc*) losfahren.

acceleration [æk,selə'reɪʃən] *n* Beschleunigung *f*; (*of speed also*) Erhöhung *f* ◆ **to have good/poor ~** eine gute/schlechte Beschleunigung haben, gut/schlecht beschleunigen.

acceleration ratio *n* Beschleunigungswert *m*.

accelerator [æk'seləreɪtə[r]] *n* **(a)** (*also* **~ pedal**) Gaspedal, Gas (*inf*) *nt* ◆ **to step on the ~** aufs Gas treten *or* drücken (*inf*). **(b)** (*Phys*) Beschleuniger *m*.

accent ['æksənt] [1] *n* (*all senses*) Akzent *m*; (*stress also*) Betonung *f*; (*mark on letter also*) Akzentzeichen *nt*; (*pl liter: tones*) Töne *pl*, Tonfall *m* ◆ **to speak without/with an ~** akzentfrei *or* ohne/mit Akzent sprechen; **to put the ~ on sth** (*fig*) den Akzent auf etw (*acc*) legen; **the ~ is on bright colours** der Akzent *or* die Betonung liegt auf leuchtenden Farben.
[2] [æk'sent] *vt* betonen.

accentuate [æk'sentjʊeɪt] *vt* betonen; (*in speaking, Mus*) akzentuieren; (*Ling: give accent to*) mit einem Akzent versehen ◆ **to ~ the need for sth** die Notwendigkeit einer Sache (*gen*) betonen *or* hervorheben.

accentuation [æk,sentjʊ'eɪʃən] *n* Betonung *f*; (*in speaking, Mus*) Akzentuierung *f*.

▼ **accept** [ək'sept] [1] *vt* **(a)** *offer, gift* annehmen; *suggestion, work also, report, findings* akzeptieren; *responsibility* übernehmen; *person* akzeptieren; (*believe*) *story* glauben; *excuse* akzeptieren, gelten lassen ◆ **a photograph of the President ~ing the award** ein Bild von dem Präsidenten, wie er die Auszeichnung entgegennimmt; **we will not ~ anything but the best** wir werden nur das Allerbeste akzeptieren *or* annehmen; **to ~ sb into society** jdn in die Gesellschaft aufnehmen.
▼ **(b)** (*recognize*) *need* einsehen, anerkennen; *person, duty* akzeptieren, anerkennen ◆ **it is generally ~ed that ...** es ist allgemein anerkannt, daß ...; **we must ~ the fact that ...** wir müssen uns damit abfinden, daß ...; **I ~ that it might take a little longer** ich sehe ein, daß es etwas länger dauern könnte; **the government ~ed that the treaty would on occasions have to be infringed** die Regierung akzeptierte, daß der Vertrag gelegentlich verletzt werden würde; **to ~ that sth is one's responsibility/duty** etw als seine Verantwortung/Pflicht akzeptieren.
(c) (*allow, put up with*) *behaviour, fate, conditions* hinnehmen ◆ **we'll just have to ~ things as they are** wir müssen die Dinge eben so (hin)nehmen, wie sie sind.
(d) (*Comm*) *cheque, orders* annehmen; *delivery also* abnehmen.
[2] *vi* annehmen; (*with offers also*) akzeptieren; (*with invitations also*) zusagen.

acceptability [ək,septə'bɪlətɪ] *n see adj* Annehmbarkeit, Akzeptierbarkeit *f*; Zulässigkeit *f*; Passendheit *f* ◆ **social ~** (*of person*) gesellschaftliche Akzeptabilität; (*of behaviour*) gesellschaftliche Zulässigkeit.

acceptable [ək'septəbl] *adj* annehmbar (*to* für), akzeptabel (*to* für); *behaviour* zulässig; (*suitable*) *gift* passend ◆ **tea is always ~** Tee ist immer gut *or* willkommen; **that would be most ~** das wäre sehr *or* höchst willkommen; **any job would be ~ to him** ihm wäre jede Stelle recht; **nothing less than the best is ~** nur das Beste kann angenommen werden.

▼ **acceptance** [ək'septəns] *n see vt* **(a)** Annahme *f*; Akzeptierung *f*; Übernahme *f*; (*believing*) Glauben *nt*; Akzeptierung *f*; (*receiving: of award*) Entgegennahme *f* ◆ **his ~ into the family** seine Aufnahme in der *or* die Familie; **to find** *or* **win** *or* **gain ~** (*theories, people*) anerkannt werden, Anerkennung finden; **to meet with general ~** allgemeine Anerkennung finden.
(b) Anerkennung *f*.
(c) Hinnahme *f*.
(d) Annahme *f*; Abnahme *f*.

acceptance: ~ house *n* (*Fin*) Akzept- *or* Wechselbank *f*; **~ trials** *npl* Abnahmeprüfung *f*.

acceptation [,æksep'teɪʃən] *n* (*old, form: of word*) Bedeutung *f*.

accepted [ək'septɪd] *adj truth, fact* (allgemein) anerkannt ◆ **it's the ~ thing** es ist üblich *or* der Brauch; **to do sth because it is the ~ thing** etw tun, weil es (eben) so üblich ist.

access ['ækses] [1] *n* **(a)** Zugang *m* (*to* zu); (*to room, private grounds etc also*) Zutritt *m* (*to* zu) ◆ **to be easy of ~** leicht zugänglich sein; **to give sb ~** jdm Zugang gewähren (*to sb/sth* zu jdm/etw); jdm Zutritt gewähren (*to sth* zu etw); **to refuse sb ~** jdm den Zugang verwehren (*to sb/sth* zu jdm/etw); jdm den Zutritt verwehren (*to sth* zu etw); **this door gives ~ to the garden** diese Tür führt in den Garten; **this location offers easy ~ to shops and transport facilities** von hier sind Läden und Verkehrsmittel leicht zu erreichen; **to have/gain ~ to sb/sth** Zugang zu jdm/etw haben/sich (*dat*) Zugang zu jdm/etw verschaffen; **the thieves gained ~ through the window** die Diebe gelangten durch das Fenster hinein; **~ road** Zufahrt(sstraße) *f*; **"~ only"** „nur für Anlieger", „Anlieger frei"; **right of ~ to one's children/a house** Besuchsrecht für seine Kinder/Wegerecht zu einem Haus.
(b) (*liter: attack, fit*) Anfall *m* ◆ **in an ~ of rage** *etc* in einem Zornesausbruch *etc*.
(c) (*Comput*) Zugriff *m* ◆ **~ time** Zugriffszeit *f*; **~ code** Zugangscode *m*.
[2] *vt* (*Comput*) *file, data* zugreifen auf (+ *acc*).

accessary [æk'sesərɪ] *n see* **accessory (b).**

accessibility [æk,sesɪ'bɪlɪtɪ] *n* (*of place, information*) Zugänglichkeit *f*.

accessible [æk'sesəbl] *adj information, person* zugänglich (*to dat*); *place also* (leicht) zu erreichen (*to* für).

accession [æk'seʃən] *n* **(a)** (*to an office*) Antritt *m* (*to gen*); (*also* **~ to the throne**) Thronbesteigung *f*; (*to estate, power*) Übernahme *f* (*to gen*) ◆ **since his ~ to power** seit seiner Machtübernahme. **(b)** (*consent: to treaty, demand*) Zustimmung (*to* zu), Annahme (*to gen*) *f*. **(c)** (*addition*) (*to property*) Zukauf *m*; (*to library also*) (Neu)anschaffung *f* ◆ **a sudden ~ of strength** (*liter*) eine plötzliche Anwandlung von Kraft.

accessorize [æk'sesəraɪz] *vt dress* mit Accessoires versehen; *room* dekorieren.

accessory [æk'sesərɪ] *n* **(a)** Extra *nt*; (*in fashion*) Accessoire *nt* ◆ **accessories** *pl* Zubehör *nt*; **toilet accessories** Toilettenartikel *pl*.
(b) (*Jur*) Helfershelfer(in *f*) *m*; (*actively involved*) Mitschuldige(r) *mf* (*to an* +*dat*) ◆ **to be an ~ after/before the fact** sich der Begünstigung/Beihilfe schuldig machen; **this made him an ~ to the crime** dadurch wurde er an dem Verbrechen mitschuldig.

accidence ['æksɪdəns] *n* (*Gram*) Formenlehre *f*.

accident ['æksɪdənt] *n* (*Mot, in home, at work*) Unfall *m*; (*Rail, Aviat, disaster*) Unglück *nt*; (*mishap*) Mißgeschick *nt*; (*chance occurrence*) Zufall *m*; (*inf: unplanned child*) (Verkehrs)unfall *m* (*inf*) ◆ **~ insurance** Unfallversicherung *f*; **~ prevention** Unfallverhütung *f*; **~ and emergency unit** Notfallstation *f*; **she has had an ~** sie hat einen Unfall gehabt *or* (*caused it*) gebaut (*inf*); (*by car, train etc also*) sie ist verunglückt; (*in kitchen etc*) ihr ist etwas *or* ein Mißgeschick *or* ein Malheur passiert; **little Jimmy has had an ~** (*euph*) dem kleinen Jimmy ist ein Malheur passiert (*inf*); **by ~** (*by chance*) durch Zufall, zufällig; (*unintentionally*) aus Versehen; **who by some ~ of birth possessed riches** der zufälligerweise reich geboren wurde; **~s will happen** (*prov*) so was kann vorkommen, so was kommt in den besten Familien vor (*inf*); **it was an ~** es war ein Versehen; **it was pure ~ that ...** es war reiner Zufall, daß ...; **it's no ~ that ...** es ist kein Zufall, daß ...; (*not surprisingly*) es kommt nicht von ungefähr, daß ...

accidental [,æksɪ'dentl] [1] *adj* **(a)** (*unplanned*) *meeting, benefit* zufällig, Zufalls-; (*unintentional*) *blow, shooting* versehentlich ◆ **one of the ~ effects of this scheme was ...** eine der Wirkungen, die dieser Plan unbeabsichtigterweise mit sich brachte, war ...
(b) (*resulting from accident*) *injury, death* durch Unfall.
[2] *n* (*Mus*) (*sign*) Versetzungszeichen *nt*, Akzidentale *f* (*form*); (*note*) erhöhter/erniedrigter Ton.

accidentally [,æksɪ'dentəlɪ] *adv* (*by chance*) zufällig; (*unintentionally*) versehentlich ◆ **~ on purpose** (*hum*) versehentlich-absichtlich (*hum*).

accident-prone ['æksɪdənt,prəʊn] *adj* vom Pech verfolgt ◆ **she is very ~** sie

➤ LANGUAGE IN USE: **accept: 1a** → 11.3, 19.5, 20.6, 25.1, 25.2, 27.3 **1b** → 12.1, 12.2, 26.3 **acceptance: a** → 20.2

ist vom Pech verfolgt, sie ist ein richtiger Pechvogel; (*more serious*) ihr passieren ständig Unfälle.

acclaim [ə'kleɪm] 1 *vt* (a) (*applaud*) feiern (*as* als); (*critics*) anerkennen. (b) (*proclaim*) **to ~ sb king/winner** jdn zum König/als Sieger ausrufen.
2 *n* Beifall *m*; (*of critics*) Anerkennung *f*.

acclamation [ˌæklə'meɪʃən] *n* Beifall *m*, *no pl*; (*of audience etc also*) Beifallskundgebung, Beifallsbezeigung *f*; (*of critics also*) Anerkennung *f* ♦ **by ~** durch Akklamation.

acclimate [ə'klaɪmət] *vt* (*US*) *see* **acclimatize**.

acclimatization [əˌklaɪmətaɪ'zeɪʃən], (*US*) **acclimation** [ˌæklaɪ'meɪʃən] *n* Akklimatisierung, Akklimatisation *f* (*to* an +*acc*); (*to new surroundings etc also*) Gewöhnung *f* (*to* an +*acc*).

acclimatize [ə'klaɪmətaɪz], (*US*) **acclimate** [ə'klaɪmət] 1 *vt* gewöhnen (*to* an +*acc*) ♦ **to become ~d** sich akklimatisieren; (*person also*) sich eingewöhnen.
2 *vi* (*also vr* **~ oneself**) sich akklimatisieren (*to* an +*acc*, *to a country etc* in einem Land *etc*).

acclivity [ə'klɪvɪtɪ] *n* (*form*) Hang *m*.

accolade ['ækəʊleɪd] *n* (*award*) Auszeichnung *f*; (*praise*) Lob *nt*, *no pl*; (*Hist, Mus*) Akkolade *f*.

accommodate [ə'kɒmədeɪt] 1 *vt* (a) (*provide lodging for*) unterbringen.
(b) (*hold, have room for*) Platz haben für; (*contain*) *machine part etc* enthalten ♦ **the car can ~ five people** das Auto bietet fünf Personen Platz *or* hat Platz für fünf Personen.
(c) (*be able to cope with: theory, plan, forecasts*) Rechnung *f* tragen (+*dat*).
(d) (*form: oblige*) dienen (+*dat*); *wishes* entgegenkommen (+*dat*) ♦ **I think we might be able to ~ you** ich glaube, wir können Ihnen entgegenkommen.
2 *vi* (*eye*) sich einstellen (*to* auf +*acc*).
3 *vr* **to ~ oneself to sth** sich einer Sache (*dat*) anpassen.

accommodating [ə'kɒmədeɪtɪŋ] *adj* entgegenkommend.

accommodation [əˌkɒmə'deɪʃən] *n* (a) (*US also* **~s** *pl: lodging*) Unterkunft *f*; (*room also*) Zimmer *nt*; (*flat also*) Wohnung *f*; (*holiday ~ also*) Quartier *nt* ♦ **"~"** „Fremdenzimmer"; **hotel ~ is scarce** Hotelzimmer sind knapp; **~ wanted** Zimmer/Wohnung gesucht; **they found ~ in a youth hostel** sie fanden in einer Jugendherberge Unterkunft, sie kamen in einer Jugendherberge unter.
(b) (*space: US also* **~s**) Platz *m* ♦ **seating/library ~** Sitz-/Bibliotheksplätze *pl*; **there is ~ for twenty passengers in the plane** das Flugzeug bietet zwanzig Passagieren Platz *or* hat für zwanzig Passagiere Platz; **sleeping ~ for six** Schlafgelegenheit *f* für sechs Personen; **~ in the hospital is inadequate** die Unterbringungsmöglichkeiten im Krankenhaus sind unzureichend.
(c) (*form: agreement*) **to reach an ~** eine Übereinkunft *or* ein Übereinkommen erzielen.
(d) (*of eye*) Einstellung *f* (*to* auf +*acc*).

accommodation: ~ address *n* Briefkastenadresse *f*; **~ bill** *n* Gefälligkeitswechsel *m*; **~ bureau** *n* Wohnungsvermittlung *f*; (*Univ*) Zimmervermittlung *f*; **~ ladder** *n* (*Naut*) Fallreep *nt*; **~ train** *n* (*US*) Personenzug, Bummelzug (*inf*) *m*; **~ service** *n* Zimmernachweis *m*.

accompaniment [ə'kʌmpənɪmənt] *n* Begleitung *f* (*also Mus*) ♦ **with piano ~** mit Klavierbegleitung.

accompanist [ə'kʌmpənɪst] *n* Begleiter(in *f*) *m*.

accompany [ə'kʌmpənɪ] *vt* begleiten (*also Mus*) ♦ **pork is often accompanied by apple sauce** Schweinefleisch wird oft mit Apfelmus (als Beilage) serviert; **to ~ oneself** (*Mus*) sich selbst begleiten.

accomplice [ə'kʌmplɪs] *n* Komplize *m*, Komplizin *f*, Mittäter(in *f*) *m* ♦ **to be an ~ to a crime** Komplize bei einem Verbrechen *or* Mittäter eines Verbrechens sein.

accomplish [ə'kʌmplɪʃ] *vt* schaffen ♦ **he ~ed a great deal in his short career** er hat in der kurzen Zeit seines Wirkens Großes geleistet; **that didn't ~ anything** damit war nichts erreicht.

accomplished [ə'kʌmplɪʃt] *adj* (a) (*skilled*) *player, carpenter* fähig; *performance* vollendet; *young lady* vielseitig ♦ **to be ~ in the art of ...** die Kunst ... (*gen*) beherrschen. (b) *fact* vollendet.

accomplishment [ə'kʌmplɪʃmənt] *n* (a) *no pl* (*completion*) Bewältigung *f*.
(b) (*skill*) Fertigkeit *f*; (*achievement*) Leistung *f* ♦ **social ~s** gesellschaftliche Gewandtheit.

accord [ə'kɔːd] 1 *n* (*agreement*) Übereinstimmung, Einigkeit *f*; (*esp US Pol*) Abkommen *nt* ♦ **I'm not in ~ with him/his views** ich stimme mit ihm/seinen Ansichten nicht überein; **of one's/its own ~** von selbst; (*of persons also*) aus freien Stücken; **with one ~** geschlossen; *sing, cheer, say etc* wie aus einem Mund(e); **to be in ~ with sth** mit etw in Einklang stehen.
2 *vt* (*sb sth* jdm etw) gewähren; *praise* erteilen; *courtesy* erweisen; *honorary title* verleihen; *welcome* bieten.
3 *vi* sich *or* einander entsprechen ♦ **to ~ with sth** einer Sache (*dat*) entsprechen.

accordance [ə'kɔːdəns] *n* **in ~ with** entsprechend (+*dat*), gemäß (+*dat*).

accordingly [ə'kɔːdɪŋlɪ] *adv* (*correspondingly*) (dem)entsprechend; (*so, therefore also*) folglich.

▼ **according to** [ə'kɔːdɪŋ'tuː] *prep* (*as stated or shown by*) zufolge (+*dat*), nach; *person, book, letter also* laut; (*in agreement with, in proportion to*) entsprechend (+*dat*), nach ♦ **~ the map** der Karte nach *or* zufolge; **~ Peter** laut Peter, Peter zufolge; **we did it ~ the rules** wir haben uns an die Regeln gehalten.

accordion [ə'kɔːdɪən] *n* Akkordeon *nt*, Ziehharmonika *f*.

accordionist [ə'kɔːdɪənɪst] *n* Akkordeonspieler(in *f*), Akkordeonist(in *f*) *m*.

accost [ə'kɒst] *vt* ansprechen, anpöbeln (*pej*).

▼ **account** [ə'kaʊnt] 1 *n* (a) Darstellung *f*; (*written also*) Aufzeichnung *f*; (*report also*) Bericht *m* ♦ **to keep an ~ of one's expenses/experiences** über seine Ausgaben Buch führen/seine Erlebnisse schriftlich festhalten; **by all ~s** nach allem, was man hört; **by your own ~** nach Ihrer eigenen Darstellung, nach Ihren eigenen Angaben; **to give an ~ of sth** über etw (*acc*) Bericht erstatten; **to give an ~ of oneself** Rede und Antwort stehen; **to give a good/bad ~ of oneself** sich gut/schlecht schlagen; **to call** *or* **hold sb to ~** jdn zur Rechenschaft ziehen; **to be held to ~ for sth** über etw (*acc*) Rechenschaft ablegen müssen.
(b) (*consideration*) **to take ~ of sb/sth, to take sb/sth into ~** jdn/etw in Betracht ziehen; **to take no ~ of sb/sth, to leave sb/sth out of ~** jdn/etw außer Betracht lassen; **on no ~, not on any ~** auf (gar) keinen Fall; **on this/that ~** deshalb, deswegen; **on ~ of him/his mother/the weather** seinetwegen/wegen seiner Mutter/wegen *or* aufgrund des Wetters; **on my/his/their ~** meinet-/seinet-/ihretwegen; **on one's own ~** für sich (selbst).
(c) (*benefit*) Nutzen *m* ♦ **to turn** *or* **put sth to (good) ~** (guten) Gebrauch von etw machen, etw (gut) nützen.
(d) (*importance*) **of no/small/great ~** ohne/von geringer/großer Bedeutung.
▼ (e) (*Fin, Comm*) (*at bank, shop*) Konto *nt* (*with* bei); (*client*) Kunde *m*; (*bill*) Rechnung *f* ♦ **~ number** Kontonummer *f*; **to win sb's ~** jdn als Kunden gewinnen; **to buy sth on ~** etw auf (Kunden)kredit kaufen; **please put it down to** *or* **charge it to my ~** stellen Sie es mir bitte in Rechnung; **£50 on ~** £ 50 als Anzahlung; **~(s) department** (*of shop*) Kreditbüro *nt*; **to settle** *or* **square ~s** *or* **one's ~ with sb** (*fig*) mit jdm abrechnen; **the duel squared all ~s between them** das Duell bereinigte alles zwischen ihnen; **~ executive** Kundenbetreuer(in *f*) *m*; **~ payee only** (*Brit*) nur zur Verrechnung.
(f) **~s** *pl* (*of company, club*) (Geschäfts)bücher *pl*; (*of household*) Einnahmen und Ausgaben *pl* ♦ **to keep the ~s** die Bücher führen, die Buchführung machen; **~(s) book** Geschäftsbuch *nt*; **~s department** Buchhaltung *f*.
2 *vt* (*form: consider*) erachten als ♦ **to be ~ed innocent** als unschuldig gelten; **to ~ oneself lucky** sich glücklich schätzen.

♦**account for** *vi* +*prep obj* (a) (*explain*) erklären; (*give account of*) *actions, expenditure* Rechenschaft ablegen über (+*acc*) ♦ **how do you ~ ~ it?** wie erklären Sie sich (*dat*) das?; **he wasn't able to ~ ~ the missing money** er konnte den Verbleib des fehlenden Geldes nicht erklären; **all the children were/money was ~ed ~** der Verbleib aller Kinder/des (ganzen) Geldes war bekannt, man wußte, wo die Kinder alle waren/wo das Geld (geblieben) war; **there's no ~ing ~ taste** über Geschmack läßt sich (nicht) streiten.
(b) (*be the source of*) der Grund sein für ♦ **this area ~s ~ most of the country's mineral wealth** aus dieser Gegend stammen die meisten Bodenschätze des Landes; **this area alone ~s ~ some 25% of the population** diese Gegend allein macht etwa 25% der Bevölkerung aus *or* stellt etwa 25% der Bevölkerung; **he ~s ~ most of the accidents** die meisten Unfälle gehen auf sein Konto (*inf*).
(c) (*be the cause of defeat, destruction etc*) zur Strecke bringen; (*illness*) dahinraffen; *chances* zunichte machen ♦ **Proctor ~ed ~ five Australian batsmen** Proctor hat fünf australische Schlagmänner ausgeschlagen; **John ~ed ~ most of the sandwiches** die meisten Brote hat John vertilgt.

accountability [əˌkaʊntə'bɪlətɪ] *n* Verantwortlichkeit *f* (*to sb* jdm gegenüber).

accountable [ə'kaʊntəbl] *adj* verantwortlich (*to sb* jdm) ♦ **to hold sb ~ (for sth)** jdn (für etw) verantwortlich machen.

accountancy [ə'kaʊntənsɪ] *n* Buchführung, Buchhaltung *f*; (*tax ~*) Steuerberatung *f*.

accountant [ə'kaʊntənt] *n* Buchhalter(in *f*) *m*; (*external financial adviser*) Wirtschaftsprüfer(in *f*) *m*; (*auditor*) Rechnungsprüfer(in *f*) *m*; (*tax ~*) Steuerberater(in *f*) *m*.

accounting [ə'kaʊntɪŋ] *n* Buchhaltung, Buchführung *f* ♦ **~ method** Buchhaltungsverfahren *nt*; **~ period** Abrechnungszeitraum *m*; **~ policy** Bilanzierungspolitik *f*.

accoutrements [ə'kuːtrəmənts], (*US also*) **accouterments** [ə'kuːtərmənts] *npl* Ausrüstung *f* ♦ **the ~ of knighthood/the trade** die Ritterrüstung/das Handwerkszeug.

accredit [ə'kredɪt] *vt* (a) *ambassador, representative* akkreditieren (*form*), beglaubigen.
(b) (*approve officially*) zulassen, genehmigen; *herd* staatlich überwachen; (*US*) *educational institution* anerkennen; (*establish*) *belief, custom* anerkennen ♦ **~ed agent** bevollmächtigter Vertreter; **~ed herd** staatlich überwachter Viehbestand.
(c) (*ascribe, attribute*) zuschreiben (*to sb* jdm).

accretion [ə'kriːʃən] *n* (*process*) Anlagerung *f*; (*sth accumulated*) Ablagerung *f*.

accrual [ə'kruːəl] *n see vi (a)* Ansammlung *f*, Auflaufen *nt*; Hinzukommen *nt* ♦ **~s** (*Fin: liabilities*) Verbindlichkeiten *pl*.

accrue [ə'kruː] *vi* (a) (*accumulate*) sich ansammeln, zusammenkommen (*to* für); (*Fin: interest*) auflaufen; (*be added to*) hinzukommen (*to* zu). (b) **to ~ to sb** (*honour, costs etc*) jdm erwachsen (*geh*) (*from* aus).

accumulate [ə'kjuːmjʊleɪt] 1 *vt* ansammeln, anhäufen, akkumulieren (*form*); *evidence* sammeln; (*Fin*) *interest* akkumulieren *or* zusammenkommen lassen.
2 *vi* sich ansammeln *or* akkumulieren (*form*); (*possessions, wealth also*) sich anhäufen; (*evidence*) sich häufen.

accumulation [əˌkjuːmjʊ'leɪʃən] *n see vi* Ansammlung, Akkumulation (*form*) *f*; Anhäufung *f*; Häufung *f*.

accumulative [ə'kjuːmjʊlətɪv] *adj see* **cumulative**.

accumulator [ə'kjuːmjʊleɪtə^r] *n* Akkumulator *m*.

➤ LANGUAGE IN USE: **according to** → 26.2 **account: 1e** → 20.7

accuracy ['ækjʊrəsɪ] *n* Genauigkeit *f*; (*of missile*) Zielgenauigkeit *f*.

accurate ['ækjʊrɪt] *adj worker, observation, translation, copy, instrument* genau, akkurat (*rare*); *missile* zielgenau ◆ **the clock is ~** die Uhr geht genau; **his aim/shot was ~** er hat genau gezielt/getroffen; **her work is slow but ~** sie arbeitet langsam, aber genau; **to be strictly ~** um ganz genau zu sein.

accurately ['ækjʊrɪtlɪ] *adv* genau.

accursed, accurst [ə'kɜːst] *adj* **(a)** (*old, liter: under a curse*) unter einem Fluch *or* bösen Zauber *pred*. **(b)** (*inf: hateful*) verwünscht.

accusation [ˌækjʊ'zeɪʃən] *n* Beschuldigung, Anschuldigung *f*; (*Jur*) Anklage *f*; (*reproach*) Vorwurf *m* ◆ **he denied her ~ of dishonesty** er wehrte sich gegen ihren Vorwurf, daß er unehrlich sei; **a look of ~** ein anklagender Blick.

accusative [ə'kjuːzətɪv] [1] *n* Akkusativ *m* ◆ **in the ~** im Akkusativ.
[2] *adj ending* Akkusativ- ◆ **~ case** Akkusativ *m*.

accusatorial [əˌkjuːzə'tɔːrɪəl] *adj* (*Jur*) Anklage-.

accuse [ə'kjuːz] *vt* **(a)** (*Jur*) anklagen (*of* wegen, *gen*) ◆ **he is** *or* **stands ~d of murder/theft** er ist des Mordes/Diebstahls angeklagt, er steht unter Anklage des Mordes/Diebstahls (*form*).
(b) *sb* beschuldigen, bezichtigen ◆ **to ~ sb of doing sth** jdn beschuldigen *or* bezichtigen, etw getan zu haben; **are you accusing me? I didn't take it!** ich bin unschuldig, ich habe es nicht genommen; **are you accusing me of lying/not having checked the brakes?** willst du (damit) vielleicht sagen, daß ich lüge/die Bremsen nicht nachgesehen habe?; **to ~ sb of being untidy** jdm vorwerfen, unordentlich zu sein; **who are you accusing, the police or society?** wen klagen Sie an, die Polizei oder die Gesellschaft?; **I ~ the government of neglect** ich mache der Regierung Nachlässigkeit zum Vorwurf; **a generation stands ~d of hypocrisy** eine Generation wird der Scheinheiligkeit beschuldigt *or* angeklagt *or* geziehen (*geh*); **we all stand ~d** uns alle trifft eine Schuld.

accused [ə'kjuːzd] *n* **the ~** der/die Angeklagte/die Angeklagten *pl*.

accuser [ə'kjuːzəʳ] *n* Ankläger *m*.

accusing [ə'kjuːzɪŋ] *adj* anklagend ◆ **he had an ~ look on his face** sein Blick klagte an.

accusingly [ə'kjuːzɪŋlɪ] *adv see adj*.

accustom [ə'kʌstəm] *vt* **to ~ sb/oneself to sth/to doing sth** jdn/sich an etw (*acc*) gewöhnen/daran gewöhnen, etw zu tun; **to be ~ed to sth/to doing sth** an etw (*acc*) gewöhnt sein/gewöhnt sein, etw zu tun; **it is not what I am ~ed to** ich bin so etwas nicht gewöhnt; **to become** *or* **get ~ed to sth/to doing sth** sich an etw (*acc*) gewöhnen/sich daran gewöhnen, etw zu tun.

accustomed [ə'kʌstəmd] *adj attr* (*usual*) gewohnt.

AC/DC *adj* **(a)** *abbr of* **alternating current/direct current** Allstrom(-). **(b) ac/dc** (*sl*) bi (*sl*).

ace [eɪs] [1] *n* **(a)** (*Cards*) As *nt* ◆ **the ~ of clubs** das Kreuz-As; **to have an ~ up one's sleeve** noch einen Trumpf in der Hand haben; **he was/came within an ~ of success/of winning** es wäre ihm um ein Haar gelungen/er hätte um ein Haar gesiegt.
(b) (*inf: expert*) As *nt* (*at* in +*dat*) ◆ **tennis ~** Tennisas *nt*.
(c) (*Tennis: serve*) As *nt* ◆ **to serve an ~** ein As servieren.
[2] *adj attr swimmer, pilot, reporter* Star-.

acerbity [ə'sɜːbɪtɪ] *n* Schärfe *f*.

acetate ['æsɪteɪt] *n* Acetat *nt*.

acetic [ə'siːtɪk] *adj* essigsauer ◆ **~ acid** Essigsäure *f*.

acetone ['æsɪtəʊn] *n* Aceton *nt*.

acetylene [ə'setɪliːn] *n* Acetylen *nt*.

ache [eɪk] [1] *n* (dumpfer) Schmerz *m* ◆ **I have an ~ in my side** ich habe Schmerzen in der Seite; **her body was a mass of ~s and pains** es tat ihr am ganzen Körper weh; **a few little ~s and pains** ein paar Wehwehchen (*inf*); **with an ~ in one's heart** (*fig*) mit wehem Herzen (*liter*).
[2] *vi* **(a)** weh tun, schmerzen ◆ **my head/stomach ~s** mir tut der Kopf/Magen weh; **it makes my head/eyes ~** davon bekomme ich Kopfschmerzen/tun mir die Augen weh; **I'm aching all over** mir tut alles weh; **it makes my heart ~ to see him** (*fig*) es tut mir in der Seele weh, wenn ich ihn sehe; **my heart ~s for you** mir bricht fast das Herz (*also iro*).
(b) (*fig: yearn*) **to ~ for sb/sth** sich nach jdm/etw sehnen; **to ~ to do sth** sich danach sehnen, etw zu tun; **I ~d to help him** es drängte mich, ihm zu helfen.

▼ **achieve** [ə'tʃiːv] [1] *vt* erreichen, schaffen; *success* erzielen; *victory* erringen; *rank also, title* erlangen ◆ **she ~d a great deal** (*did a lot of work*) sie hat eine Menge geleistet; (*was quite successful*) sie hat viel erreicht; **he will never ~ anything** er wird es nie zu etwas bringen.
[2] *vi* (*Psych, Sociol*) leisten ◆ **the achieving society** die Leistungsgesellschaft.

achievement [ə'tʃiːvmənt] *n* **(a)** (*act*) *see vt* Erreichen *nt*; Erzielen *nt*; Erringen *nt*; Erlangen *nt* ◆ **~-oriented** leistungsorientiert; **~-oriented society** Leistungsgesellschaft *f*.
(b) (*thing achieved*) (*of individual*) Leistung *f*; (*of society, civilization, technology*) Errungenschaft *f* ◆ **that's quite an ~!** das ist schon eine Leistung! (*also iro*); **for his many ~s** für seine zahlreichen Verdienste; **~ quotient/test** Leistungsquotient *m*/-test *m*.

achiever [ə'tʃiːvəʳ] *n* Leistungstyp *m* (*inf*) ◆ **to be an ~** leistungsorientiert sein; **high ~** (*Sch*) leistungsstarkes Kind.

Achilles [ə'kɪliːz] *n* Achill(es) *m* ◆ **~' heel** (*fig*) Achillesferse *f*; **~' tendon** Achillessehne *f*.

aching ['eɪkɪŋ] *adj attr bones, head* schmerzend; (*fig*) *heart* wund, weh (*liter*).

acid ['æsɪd] [1] *adj* (*sour, Chem*) sauer; (*fig*) ätzend, beißend ◆ **~ drop** saurer *or* saures Drops; **~ rain** saurer Regen; **~ test** (*fig*) Feuerprobe *f*.
[2] *n* **(a)** (*Chem*) Säure *f*. **(b)** (*sl: LSD*) Acid *nt* (*sl*).

acidhead ['æsɪdˌhed] *n* (*sl*) Säurekopf *m* (*sl*).

acidic [ə'sɪdɪk] *adj* sauer.

acidity [ə'sɪdɪtɪ] *n* Säure *f*; (*Chem also*) Säuregehalt *m*; (*of stomach*) Magensäure *f*.

acidly ['æsɪdlɪ] *adv* (*fig*) ätzend, beißend.

ack-ack ['æk'æk] *n* (*fire*) Flakfeuer *nt*; (*gun*) Flak *f*.

▼ **acknowledge** [ək'nɒlɪdʒ] *vt* anerkennen; *quotation* angeben; (*admit*) *truth, fault, defeat etc* eingestehen, zugeben; (*note receipt of*) *letter etc* bestätigen; *present* den Empfang bestätigen von; (*respond to*) *greetings, cheers etc* erwidern ◆ **to ~ oneself beaten** sich geschlagen geben; **to ~ sb's presence** jds Anwesenheit zur Kenntnis nehmen.

acknowledged [ək'nɒlɪdʒd] *adj attr* anerkannt.

acknowledgement [ək'nɒlɪdʒmənt] *n see vt* Anerkennung *f*; Angabe *f*; Eingeständnis *nt*; Bestätigung *f*; Empfangsbestätigung *f*; Erwiderung *f* ◆ **he waved in ~** er winkte zurück; **in ~ of** in Anerkennung (+*gen*); **to make ~ of sth** (*form*) seinen Dank für etw zum Ausdruck bringen; **to quote without ~** ohne Quellenangabe zitieren; **I received no ~** ich erhielt keine Antwort; **as an ~ of my gratitude/your kindness** zum Zeichen meiner Dankbarkeit/zum Dank für Ihre Freundlichkeit; **~s are due to ...** ich habe/wir haben ... zu danken; (*in book*) mein/unser Dank gilt ...

acme ['ækmɪ] *n* Höhepunkt, Gipfel *m*; (*of elegance etc*) Inbegriff *m* ◆ **at the ~ of his powers** auf dem Gipfel seiner (Schaffens)kraft.

acne ['æknɪ] *n* Akne *f*.

acolyte ['ækəʊlaɪt] *n* (*Eccl*) (*Catholic*) Akoluth *m*; (*Protestant: server*) Meßdiener, Ministrant *m*; (*fig*) Gefolgsmann *m*.

aconite ['ækənaɪt] *n* (*Bot*) Eisenhut *m*, Aconitum *nt*; (*drug*) Aconitin *nt*.

acorn ['eɪkɔːn] *n* Eichel *f*.

acoustic [ə'kuːstɪk] *adj* akustisch; (*soundproof*) *tiles, panel* Dämm- ◆ **~ guitar** Akustikgitarre *f*; **~ coupler** (*Comput*) Akustikkoppler *m*; **~ screen** Trennwand *f zur Schalldämpfung*.

acoustically [ə'kuːstɪkəlɪ] *adv* akustisch.

acoustics [ə'kuːstɪks] *n* **(a)** *sing* (*subject*) Akustik *f*. **(b)** *pl* (*of room etc*) Akustik *f*.

acquaint [ə'kweɪnt] *vt* **(a)** (*make familiar*) bekannt machen ◆ **to be ~ed/thoroughly ~ed with sth** mit etw bekannt/vertraut sein; **to be ~ed with grief** mit Leid vertraut sein; **he's ~ed/well ~ed with the situation** die Situation ist ihm bekannt/er ist mit der Situation vertraut; **to become ~ed with sth** etw kennenlernen; *facts, truth* etw erfahren; **to ~ oneself** *or* **make oneself ~ed with sth** sich mit etw vertraut machen.
(b) (*with person*) **to be ~ed with sb** mit jdm bekannt sein; **we're not ~ed** wir kennen einander *or* uns nicht; **to become** *or* **get ~ed** sich (näher) kennenlernen.

acquaintance [ə'kweɪntəns] *n* **(a)** (*person*) Bekannte(r) *mf* ◆ **we're just ~s** wir kennen uns bloß flüchtig; **a wide circle of ~s** ein großer Bekanntenkreis.
(b) (*with person*) Bekanntschaft *f*; (*with subject etc*) Kenntnis *f* (*with gen*); (*intimate, with sorrow etc*) Vertrautheit *f* ◆ **to make sb's ~, to make the ~ of sb** jds Bekanntschaft *or* die Bekanntschaft jds machen; **I have some ~ with Italian wines** ich kenne mich mit italienischen Weinen einigermaßen aus; **he/it improves on ~** er gewinnt bei näherer Bekanntschaft/man kommt mit der Zeit auf den Geschmack (davon); *see* **nodding**.

acquiesce [ˌækwɪ'es] *vi* einwilligen (*in* in +*acc*); (*submissively*) sich fügen (*in dat*).

acquiescence [ˌækwɪ'esns] *n see vi* Einwilligung *f* (*in* in +*acc*); Fügung *f* (*in* in +*acc*) ◆ **with an air of ~** mit zustimmender Miene.

acquiescent [ˌækwɪ'esnt] *adj* fügsam; *smile* ergeben; *attitude* zustimmend.

acquire [ə'kwaɪəʳ] *vt* erwerben; (*by dubious means*) sich (*dat*) aneignen; *habit* annehmen ◆ **I see he has ~d a secretary/wife** wie ich sehe, hat er sich eine Sekretärin/Frau angeschafft (*inf*); **he ~d a fine tan** er hat eine gute Farbe bekommen; **where did you ~ that?** woher hast du das?; **to ~ a taste/liking for sth** Geschmack/Gefallen an etw (*dat*) finden; **once you've ~d a taste for it** wenn du erst mal auf den Geschmack gekommen bist; **caviar is an ~d taste** Kaviar ist (nur) für Kenner; **~d** (*Psych*) erworben; **~d characteristics** (*Biol*) erworbene Eigenschaften *pl*.

acquirement [ə'kwaɪəmənt] *n* **(a)** (*act*) *see* **acquisition (a)**. **(b)** (*skill etc acquired*) Fertigkeit *f*.

acquisition [ˌækwɪ'zɪʃən] *n* **(a)** (*act*) Erwerb *m*; (*by dubious means*) Aneignung *f*; (*of habit*) Annahme *f*. **(b)** (*thing acquired*) Anschaffung *f*; (*hum: secretary, girlfriend etc*) Errungenschaft *f* ◆ **he's a useful ~ to the department** er ist ein Gewinn für die Abteilung.

acquisitive [ə'kwɪzɪtɪv] *adj* auf Erwerb aus, habgierig (*pej*), raffgierig (*pej*) ◆ **the ~ society** die Erwerbsgesellschaft; **magpies are ~ birds** Elstern sind Vögel mit ausgeprägtem Sammeltrieb.

acquisitiveness [ə'kwɪzɪtɪvnɪs] *n* Habgier *f* (*pej*).

acquit [ə'kwɪt] [1] *vt* freisprechen ◆ **to be ~ted of a crime/on a charge** von einem Verbrechen/einer Anklage freigesprochen werden.
[2] *vr* (*conduct oneself*) sich verhalten; (*perform*) seine Sache machen ◆ **he ~ted himself well** er hat seine Sache gut gemacht; (*stood up well*) er hat sich gut aus der Affäre gezogen.

acquittal [ə'kwɪtl] *n* Freispruch *m* (*on* von).

acre ['eɪkəʳ] *n* ≃ Morgen *m* ◆ **~s** (*old, liter: land*) Fluren *pl* (*old, liter*); **~s (and ~s) of garden/open land** hektarweise Garten/meilenweise freies Land.

acreage ['eɪkərɪdʒ] *n* Land *nt*; (*Agr*) Anbaufläche *f* ◆ **what ~ do they have?** wieviel Land *or* wie viele Morgen (*Agr*) haben sie?

acrid ['ækrɪd] *adj taste* bitter; (*of wine*) sauer; *comment, smoke* beißend.

Acrilan ® ['ækrɪlæn] *n* Acryl *nt*.

➤ LANGUAGE IN USE: **achieve: 1** → 8.1 **acknowledge** → 20.5

acrimonious [ˌækrɪ'məʊnɪəs] *adj discussion, argument* erbittert; *person, words* bissig.

acrimoniously [ˌækrɪ'məʊnɪəslɪ] *adv see adj.*

acrimony ['ækrɪmənɪ] *n see* **acrimonious** erbitterte Schärfe; Bissigkeit *f.*

acrobat ['ækrəbæt] *n* Akrobat(in *f*) *m.*

acrobatic [ˌækrəʊ'bætɪk] *adj* akrobatisch.

acrobatics [ˌækrəʊ'bætɪks] *npl* Akrobatik *f* ◆ **mental ~** *(fig)* Gedankenakrobatik *f,* geistige Klimmzüge *pl (inf).*

acronym ['ækrənɪm] *n* Akronym *nt.*

acropolis [ə'krɒpəlɪs] *n* Akropolis *f.*

across [ə'krɒs] [1] *adv* **(a)** *(direction) (to the other side)* hinüber; *(from the other side)* herüber; *(crosswise)* (quer)durch ◆ **shall I go ~ first?** soll ich zuerst hinüber(gehen/-schwimmen *etc*)?; **to throw/row ~/help sb ~** hinüberwerfen/hinüberrudern/jdm hinüberhelfen; herüberwerfen/herüberrudern/jdm herüberhelfen; **to cut sth ~** etw (quer) durchschneiden; **he was already ~** er war schon drüben; **~ from your house** gegenüber von eurem Haus, eurem Haus gegenüber; **the stripes go ~** es ist quer gestreift; **draw a line ~** machen Sie einen Strich; *(diagonal)* machen Sie einen Strich querdurch.
(b) *(measurement)* breit; *(of round object)* im Durchmesser.
(c) *(in crosswords)* waagerecht.
[2] *prep* **(a)** *(direction)* über (+*acc*); *(diagonally ~)* quer durch (+*acc*) ◆ **to run ~ the road** über die Straße laufen; **to wade ~ a river** durch einen Fluß waten; **a tree fell ~ the path** ein Baum fiel quer über den Weg; **~ country** querfeldein; *(over long distance)* quer durch das Land; **to draw a line ~ the page** einen Strich durch die Seite machen; **the stripes go ~ the material** der Stoff ist quer gestreift.
(b) *(position)* über (+*dat*) ◆ **a tree lay ~ the path** ein Baum lag quer über dem Weg; **he was sprawled ~ the bed** er lag quer auf dem Bett; **with his arms (folded) ~ his chest** die Arme vor der Brust verschränkt; **from ~ the sea** von jenseits des Meeres *(geh),* von der anderen Seite des Meeres; **he lives ~ the street from us** er wohnt uns gegenüber; **you could hear him (from) ~ the hall** man konnte ihn von der anderen Seite der Halle hören; *see vbs.*

across-the-board [ə'krɒsðə'bɔːd] *adj attr* allgemein; *see also* **board.**

acrostic [ə'krɒstɪk] *n* Akrostichon *nt.*

acrylic [ə'krɪlɪk] [1] *n* Acryl *nt.*
[2] *adj* Acryl-; *dress* aus Acryl.

act [ækt] [1] *n* **(a)** *(deed, thing done)* Tat *f; (official, ceremonial)* Akt *m* ◆ **my first ~ was to phone him** meine erste Tat *or* mein erstes war, ihn anzurufen; **an ~ of mercy/judgement** ein Gnadenakt *m*/eine (wohl)überlegte Tat; **an ~ of God** höhere Gewalt *no pl;* **an ~ of folly/madness** reine Dummheit/reiner Wahnsinn, ein Akt *m* der Dummheit/des Wahnsinns; **a small/great ~ of kindness** eine Freundlichkeit/ein Akt der Freundlichkeit; **A~s, the A~s of the Apostles** *(Bibl)* die Apostelgeschichte; *see* **faith.**
(b) *(process of doing)* **to be in the ~ of doing sth** (gerade) dabei sein, etw zu tun; **to catch sb in the ~** jdn auf frischer Tat *or (sexually)* in flagranti ertappen; **to catch/watch sb in the ~ of doing sth** jdn dabei ertappen/beobachten, wie er etw tut.
(c) *(Parl)* Gesetz *nt* ◆ **under an ~ of Parliament passed in 1976 this is illegal** nach einem 1976 vom Parlament verabschiedeten Gesetz ist das verboten.
(d) *(Theat) (of play, opera)* Akt *m; (turn)* Nummer *f* ◆ **a one-~ play/opera** ein Einakter *m*/eine Oper in einem Akt; **to get into** *or* **in on the ~** *(fig inf)* mit von der Partie sein; **how did he get in on the ~?** *(inf)* wie kommt es, daß er da mitmischt? *(inf);* **he's really got his ~ together** *(inf) (is organized, efficient with sth)* er hat die Sache wirklich im Griff; *(in lifestyle etc)* er hat im Leben erreicht, was er wollte; **get your ~ together!** reiß dich doch mal zusammen!
(e) *(fig: pretence)* Theater *nt,* Schau *f (inf)* ◆ **it's all an ~** das ist alles nur Theater *or* Schau *(inf);* **to put on an ~** Theater spielen.
[2] *vt part* spielen; *play also* aufführen ◆ **to ~ the fool/injured innocent** herumalbern/die gekränkte Unschuld spielen.
[3] *vi* **(a)** *(Theat) (perform)* spielen; *(to be an actor)* schauspielern, Theater spielen; *(fig)* Theater spielen, schauspielern, markieren ◆ **to ~ on TV/on the radio** fürs Fernsehen/in Hörspielen auftreten *or* spielen; **who's ~ing in it?** wer spielt darin?; **he learned to ~** er nahm Schauspielunterricht; **he should learn to ~!** er sollte erst mal richtig schauspielern lernen; **... but she can't ~** ... aber sie kann nicht spielen *or* ist keine Schauspielerin; **he's only ~ing** er tut (doch) nur so, er markiert *or* spielt (doch) nur; **to ~ stupid/innocent** *etc* sich dumm/unschuldig *etc* stellen, den Dummen/Unschuldigen *etc* spielen.
(b) *(function) (brakes etc)* funktionieren; *(drug)* wirken ◆ **to ~ as ...** wirken als ...; *(have function)* fungieren als ...; *(person)* das Amt des/der ... übernehmen, fungieren als ...; **~ing in my capacity as chairman** in meiner Eigenschaft als Vorsitzender; **it ~s as a deterrent** das wirkt abschreckend; **to ~ for sb** jdn vertreten.
(c) *(behave)* sich verhalten ◆ **~ like a man!** sei ein Mann!; **she ~ed as if** *or* **as though she was hurt/surprised** *etc* sie tat so, als ob sie verletzt/überrascht *etc* wäre; **he ~s as though** *or* **like he owns the place** *(inf)* er tut so, als ob der Laden ihm gehört *(inf).*
(d) *(take action)* handeln ◆ **he ~ed to stop it** er unternahm etwas *or* Schritte, um dem ein Ende zu machen; **the police couldn't ~** die Polizei konnte nichts unternehmen.

◆**act on** *or* **upon** *vi +prep obj* **(a)** *(affect)* wirken auf (+*acc*) ◆ **the yeast ~s ~ the sugar to produce alcohol** die Hefe wirkt auf den Zucker ein und führt zur Alkoholbildung.
(b) *(take action on) warning, report, evidence* handeln auf (+*acc*) ... hin; *suggestion, advice* folgen (+*dat*) ◆ **~ing ~ information received, the police ...** die Polizei handelte aufgrund der ihr zugegangenen Information und ...; **~ing ~ an impulse** einer plötzlichen Eingebung gehorchend *or* folgend; **did you ~ ~ the letter?** haben Sie auf den Brief hin etwas unternommen?

◆**act out** *vt sep fantasies, problems etc* durchspielen ◆ **the drama/affair was ~ed ~ at ...** das Drama/die Affäre spielte sich in ... ab.

◆**act up** *vi (inf)* jdm Ärger machen; *(person also)* Theater machen *(inf);* *(to attract attention)* sich aufspielen; *(machine also)* verrückt spielen *(inf).*

◆**act upon** *vi +prep obj see* **act on.**

actable ['æktəbl] *adj play* spielbar ◆ **it is very ~** es läßt sich gut spielen *or* aufführen.

acting ['æktɪŋ] [1] *adj* **(a)** stellvertretend *attr,* in Stellvertretung *pred.* **(b)** *attr (Theat)* schauspielerisch.
[2] *n (Theat) (performance)* Darstellung *f; (activity)* Spielen *nt; (profession)* Schauspielerei *f* ◆ **what was the/his ~ like?** wie waren die Schauspieler/wie hat er gespielt? **I didn't like his ~** ich mochte seine Art zu spielen nicht; **he's done some ~** er hat schon Theater gespielt; *(professionally also)* er hat schon etwas Schauspielerfahrung.

actinic [æk'tɪnɪk] *adj* aktinisch.

action ['ækʃən] *n* **(a)** *no pl (activity)* Handeln *nt; (of play, novel etc)* Handlung *f* ◆ **now is the time for ~** die Zeit zum Handeln ist gekommen; **a man of ~** ein Mann der Tat; **to take ~** etwas *or* Schritte unternehmen; **have you taken any ~ on his letter?** haben Sie auf seinen Brief hin irgend etwas *or* irgendwelche Schritte unternommen?; **course of ~** Vorgehen *nt;* **"~"** *(on office tray)* „zur Bearbeitung"; **no further ~** keine weiteren Maßnahmen; *(label on file etc)* abgeschlossen; **the ~ of the play/novel takes place ...** das Stück/der Roman spielt ...; **~!** *(Film)* Achtung, Aufnahme!
(b) *(deed)* Tat *f* ◆ **his first ~ was to phone me** als erstes rief er mich an; **to suit the ~ to the word** dem Wort die Tat folgen lassen, sein Wort in die Tat umsetzen; **~s speak louder than words** *(Prov)* die Tat wirkt mächtiger als das Wort *(prov).*
(c) *(motion, operation)* **in/out of ~** in/nicht in Aktion; *(machine)* in/außer Betrieb; *(operational)* einsatzfähig/nicht einsatzfähig; **to go into ~** in Aktion treten; **to put a plan into ~** einen Plan in die Tat umsetzen; **to put out of ~** außer Gefecht setzen; **he's been out of ~ since he broke his leg** er ist nicht mehr in Aktion gewesen *or* war nicht mehr einsatzfähig, seit er sich das Bein gebrochen hat; **he needs prodding into ~** man muß ihm immer erst einen Stoß geben.
(d) *(exciting events)* Action *f (sl)* ◆ **there's no ~ in this film** in dem Film passiert nichts, dem Film fehlt (die) Action *(sl);* **a novel full of ~** ein handlungsreicher Roman; **let's have some ~!** *(inf)* machen wir mal was los! *(inf);* **to go where the ~ is** *(inf)* hingehen, wo was los ist *(inf);* **that's where the ~ is** *(inf)* da ist was los *(inf);* **where's the ~, man?** *(sl)* he, wo ist hier was los? *(inf);* **he was out looking for ~** *(inf)* er wollte was erleben *(inf) or* was losmachen *(sl).*
(e) *(Mil) (fighting)* Aktionen *pl; (battle)* Kampf *m,* Gefecht *nt* ◆ **enemy ~** feindliche Handlungen *or* Aktionen *pl;* **killed in ~** gefallen; **he saw ~ in the desert** er war in der Wüste im Einsatz; **the first time they went into ~** bei ihrem ersten Einsatz; **they never once went into ~** sie kamen nie zum Einsatz.
(f) *(way of operating) (of machine)* Arbeitsweise *f; (of piano etc)* Mechanik *f; (of watch, gun)* Mechanismus *m; (way of moving) (of athlete etc)* Bewegung *f; (of horse)* Aktion *f* ◆ **the piano/typewriter has a stiff ~** das Klavier/die Schreibmaschine hat einen harten Anschlag; **to move/hit with an easy/a smooth ~** *(Sport)* sich ganz locker und leicht bewegen/ganz weich schlagen.
(g) *(esp Chem, Phys: effect)* Wirkung *f (on* auf +*acc).*
(h) *(Jur)* Klage *f* ◆ **to bring an ~ (against sb)** eine Klage (gegen jdn) anstrengen.
(i) *(Fin sl)* **a piece of the ~** ein Stück aus dem Kuchen *(sl).*

actionable ['ækʃnəbl] *adj* verfolgbar; *statement* klagbar.

action: ~ group *n* Bürger-/Studenten-/Elterninitiative *etc f;* **~-packed** *adj film, book* aktions- *or* handlungsgeladen; **~ painting** *n* Aktion *f;* **~ replay** *n* Wiederholung *f;* **~ stations** *npl* Stellung *f;* **~ stations!** Stellung!; *(fig)* an die Plätze!

activate ['æktɪveɪt] *vt mechanism (person)* betätigen; *(heat)* auslösen; *(switch, lever)* in Gang setzen; *alarm* auslösen; *bomb* zünden; *(Chem, Phys)* aktivieren; *(US Mil)* mobilisieren ◆ **~d sludge** Belebtschlamm *m.*

active ['æktɪv] [1] *adj* aktiv *(also Gram, Comput); mind, social life* rege; *volcano also* tätig; *dislike* offen, unverhohlen; *file* im Gebrauch; *(radio~)* radioaktiv ◆ **to be ~ in politics** politisch aktiv *or* tätig sein; **they should be more ~ in improving safety standards** sie sollten die Verbesserung der Sicherheitsvorschriften etwas tatkräftiger vorantreiben; **to be under ~ consideration** ernsthaft erwogen werden; **on ~ service** *(Mil)* im Einsatz; **to see ~ service** *(Mil)* im Einsatz sein; **to be on the ~ list** *(Mil)* zur ständigen Verfügung stehen; **he played an ~ part in it** er war aktiv daran beteiligt; **~ partner** *(Comm)* persönlich haftender Gesellschafter.
[2] *n (Gram)* Aktiv *nt* ◆ **in the ~** im Aktiv.

actively ['æktɪvlɪ] *adv* aktiv; *dislike* offen, unverhohlen.

active suspension *n (Aut)* aktive Aufhängung.

activism ['æktɪvɪzm] *n* Aktivismus *m.*

activist ['æktɪvɪst] *n* Aktivist(in *f*) *m.*

activity [æk'tɪvɪtɪ] *n* **(a)** *no pl* Aktivität *f; (in classroom, station, on beach etc also)* reges Leben; *(in market, town, office)* Geschäftigkeit *f,* geschäftiges Treiben; *(mental)* Betätigung *f* ◆ **a scene of great ~** ein Bild geschäftigen Treibens; **a**

new sphere of ~ ein neues Betätigungsfeld, ein neuer Wirkungskreis.
(b) (*pastime*) Betätigung *f* ◆ **classroom activities** schulische Tätigkeiten *pl*; **the church organizes many activities** die Kirche organisiert viele Veranstaltungen; **business/social activities** geschäftliche/gesellschaftliche Unternehmungen *pl*; **criminal activities** kriminelle Tätigkeiten *or* Aktivität en *pl*; **a programme of activities** ein Veranstaltungsprogramm *nt*.
(c) (*radio~*) Radioaktivität *f*.

activity holiday *n* Aktivurlaub *m*.

actor ['æktəʳ] *n* (*lit, fig*) Schauspieler *m*.

actress ['æktrɪs] *n* (*lit, fig*) Schauspielerin *f*.

actual ['æktjʊəl] *adj* eigentlich; *reason, price also, result* tatsächlich; *case, example* konkret ◆ **in ~ fact** eigentlich; **what were his ~ words?** was genau hat er gesagt?; **this is the ~ house** das ist hier das Haus; **there is no ~ contract** es besteht kein eigentlicher Vertrag; **your ~ ...** (*inf*) ein echter/eine echte/ein echtes ...; der/die/das echte ...

actuality [,æktjʊ'ælɪtɪ] *n* (*reality*) Wirklichkeit, Realität *f*; (*realism*) Aktualität *f* ◆ **the actualities of the situation** die tatsächlichen Gegebenheiten.

actualize ['æktjʊəlaɪz] *vt* verwirklichen.

actually ['æktjʊəlɪ] *adv* **(a)** (*used as a filler*) *usually not translated* ◆ **~ I haven't started yet** ich habe noch (gar) nicht damit angefangen; **~ we were just talking about you** wir haben eben von Ihnen geredet; **~ his name is Smith** er heißt (übrigens) Smith; **I'm going too ~** ich gehe (übrigens) auch; **~ what we could do is to ...** (wissen Sie,) wir könnten doch ...
(b) (*to tell the truth, in actual fact*) eigentlich; (*by the way*) übrigens ◆ **as you said before — and ~ you were quite right** wie Sie schon sagten — und eigentlich hatten Sie völlig recht; **~ you were quite right, it was a bad idea** Sie hatten übrigens völlig recht, es war eine schlechte Idee; **I don't ~ feel like going there** ich habe eigentlich keine Lust, da hinzugehen; **do you want that/know him? — ~ I do/don't** möchten Sie das/kennen Sie ihn? — ja, durchaus *or* schon/nein, eigentlich nicht; **you don't want that/know him, do you? — ~ I do** Sie möchten das/kennen ihn (doch) nicht, oder? — doch, eigentlich schon; **do you know her? — ~ I'm her husband** kennen Sie sie? — ja, ich bin nämlich ihr Mann; **I thought I could give you a lift but I won't be going ~** ich dachte, ich könnte Sie mitnehmen, aber ich gehe nun doch nicht; **I bet you haven't done that! — ~ I have** Sie haben das bestimmt nicht gemacht! — doch; **I'm going soon, tomorrow ~** ich gehe bald, nämlich morgen; **it won't be easy, it'll be very difficult ~** es wird nicht leicht, ja es wird sogar sehr schwierig sein.
(c) (*truly, in reality, showing surprise*) tatsächlich ◆ **if you ~ own a flat** wenn Sie tatsächlich eine Wohnung besitzen; **don't tell me you're ~ going now!** sag bloß, du gehst jetzt tatsächlich *or* wirklich!; **oh, you're ~ in/dressed/ready!** oh, du bist sogar da/angezogen/fertig!; **... but ~ I could do it ...** aber ich konnte es doch; **I haven't ~ started/done it/met him yet** ich habe noch nicht angefangen/es noch nicht gemacht/ihn noch nicht kennengelernt; **not ~ ..., but ...** zwar nicht ..., aber ...; **I wasn't ~ there, but/so ...** ich war zwar selbst nicht dabei, aber .../ich war selbst nicht dabei, deshalb ...; **did he ~ say that?** hat er das tatsächlich *or* wirklich gesagt?; **what did he ~ say?** was genau hat er gesagt?, was hat er tatsächlich gesagt?; **what do you ~ want?** was möchten Sie eigentlich?; **does that ~ exist/happen?** gibt es das denn überhaupt *or* tatsächlich/kommt das denn überhaupt *or* tatsächlich vor?; **as for ~ working ...** was die Arbeit selbst betrifft ...; **as for ~ doing it** wenn es dann daran geht, es auch zu tun; **it's the first time that I've ~ seen him/that I've ~ been home in time for the news** das ist das erste Mal, daß ich ihn mal gesehen habe/daß ich mal rechtzeitig zu den Nachrichten zu Hause bin.
(d) it's ~ taking place this very moment das findet genau in diesem Augenblick statt; **it was ~ taking place when he ...** es fand genau zu der Zeit statt, als er ...

actuarial [,æktjʊ'eərɪəl] *adj* (*Insur*) versicherungsmathematisch, versicherungsstatistisch.

actuary ['æktjʊərɪ] *n* (*Insur*) Aktuar *m*.

actuate ['æktjʊeɪt] *vt* (*lit*) auslösen; (*fig*) treiben.

acuity [ə'kju:ɪtɪ] *n* Scharfsinn *m*, Klugheit *f*; (*of mind*) Schärfe *f*.

acumen ['ækjʊmen] *n* Scharfsinn *m* ◆ **to show (great) ~** großen Scharfsinn beweisen; **business/political ~** Geschäftssinn *m*/politische Klugheit.

acupuncture ['ækjʊ,pʌŋktʃəʳ] *n* Akupunktur *f*.

acute [ə'kju:t] **1** *adj* **(a)** (*intense, serious, Med*) *pain, shortage, appendicitis* akut; *pleasure* intensiv. **(b)** (*keen*) *eyesight* scharf; *hearing also, sense of smell* fein. **(c)** (*shrewd*) scharf; *person* scharfsinnig; *child* aufgeweckt. **(d)** (*Math*) *angle* spitz. **(e)** (*Ling*) **~ accent** Akut *m*.
2 *n* (*Ling*) Akut *m*.

acutely [ə'kju:tlɪ] *adv* **(a)** (*intensely*) akut; *feel* intensiv; *embarrassed, sensitive, uncomfortable* äußerst ◆ **to be ~ aware of sth** sich (*dat*) einer Sache (*gen*) genau *or* sehr bewußt sein; (*painfully*) sich (*dat*) einer Sache (*gen*) schmerzlich bewußt sein. **(b)** (*shrewdly*) scharfsinnig; *criticize, observe* scharf.

acuteness [ə'kju:tnɪs] *n see adj* **(a)** Intensität *f* ◆ **due to the ~ of the drought** da die Trockenheit so akut ist/wurde. **(b)** Schärfe *f*; Feinheit *f*. **(c)** Schärfe *f*; Scharfsinn *m*; Aufgewecktheit *f*.

AD *abbr of* **Anno Domini** n. Chr., A.D.

ad [æd] *n abbr of* **advertisement** Anzeige *f*, Inserat *nt* ◆ **small ~s** Kleinanzeigen *pl*.

adage ['ædɪdʒ] *n* Sprichwort *nt*.

adagio [ə'dɑ:dʒɪəʊ] **1** *adv* adagio.
2 *n* Adagio *nt*.

Adam ['ædəm] *n* Adam *m* ◆ **~'s apple** Adamsapfel *m*; **I don't know him from ~** (*inf*) ich habe keine Ahnung, wer er ist (*inf*).

adamant ['ædəmənt] *adj* hart; *refusal also* hartnäckig ◆ **an ~ no** ein unerbittliches Nein; **to be ~** unnachgiebig sein, darauf bestehen; **since you're ~** da Sie darauf bestehen; **he was ~ about going** er bestand hartnäckig darauf zu gehen; **he was ~ in his refusal** er weigerte sich hartnäckig.

adamantine [,ædə'mæntaɪn] *adj* (*liter*) (*lit*) diamanten (*liter*); (*fig*) hartnäckig.

adapt [ə'dæpt] **1** *vt* anpassen (*to dat*); *machine* umstellen (*to, for* auf +*acc*); *vehicle, building* umbauen (*to, for* für); *text, book* adaptieren, bearbeiten (*for* für) ◆ **~ed to your requirements** nach Ihren Wünschen abgeändert; **~ed for Arctic conditions** arktischen Verhältnissen angepaßt; **~ed for children/television** für Kinder/für das Fernsehen adaptiert *or* bearbeitet; **~ed from the Spanish** aus dem Spanischen übertragen und bearbeitet.
2 *vi* sich anpassen (*to dat*); (*Sci also*) sich adaptieren (*to* an +*acc*).

adaptability [ə,dæptə'bɪlɪtɪ] *n see adj* Anpassungsfähigkeit *f*; Vielseitigkeit *f*; Flexibilität *f*; Eignung *f* zur Adaption.

adaptable [ə'dæptəbl] *adj plant, animal, person* anpassungsfähig; *vehicle, hairstyle* vielseitig; *schedule* flexibel; *book* zur Adaption *or* Bearbeitung geeignet ◆ **to be ~ to sth** (*person, animal, plant*) sich an etw (*acc*) anpassen können; (*vehicle*) sich in etw (*dat*) verwenden lassen.

adaptation [,ædæp'teɪʃən] *n* **(a)** (*process*) Adaptation *f* (*to* an +*acc*); (*of person, plant, animal also*) Anpassung *f* (*to* an +*acc*); (*of machine*) Umstellung *f* (*to* auf +*acc*); (*of vehicle, building*) Umbau *m*; (*of text also*) Bearbeitung *f* ◆ **the ~ of space technology to medical ends** die Nutzung der Raumfahrttechnik für medizinische Zwecke.
(b) (*of book, play etc*) Adaption, Bearbeitung *f*.

adapter, adaptor [ə'dæptəʳ] *n* **(a)** (*of book etc*) Bearbeiter(in *f*) *m*. **(b)** (*for connecting pipes etc*) Verbindungs- *or* Zwischenstück *nt*; (*to convert machine etc*) Adapter *m*. **(c)** (*Elec*) Adapter *m*; (*for several plugs*) Doppel-/Dreifachstecker, Mehrfachstecker *m*; (*on appliance*) Zwischenstecker *m* ◆ **~ card** (*Comput*) Adapterkarte *f*.

adaption [ə'dæpʃən] *n see* **adaptation**.

ADC *abbr of* **aide-de-camp**.

add [æd] **1** *vt* **(a)** (*Math*) addieren; (*~ on*) *one number also* hinzu- *or* dazuzählen (*to* zu); (*~ up*) *several numbers also* zusammenzählen ◆ **to ~ 8 and/to 5** 8 und 5 zusammenzählen *or* addieren/8 zu 5 hinzuzählen.
(b) hinzufügen (*to* zu); *ingredients, money also* dazugeben, dazutun (*to* zu); *name also* dazusetzen (*to* auf +*acc*); (*say in addition also*) dazusagen; (*build on*) anbauen ◆ **~ed to which** ... hinzu kommt, daß ...; **it ~s nothing to our knowledge** unser Wissen wird dadurch nicht erweitert; **transport/VAT ~s 10% to the cost** es kommen 10% Transportkosten hinzu/zu den Kosten kommen noch 10% Mehrwertsteuer; **they ~ 10% for service** sie rechnen *or* schlagen 10% für Bedienung dazu; **~ed together the books weigh several tons** zusammengenommen wiegen die Bücher mehrere Tonnen; **if we ~ all the money together we can get them a really nice gift** wenn wir das ganze Geld zusammenlegen, können wir ihnen ein wirklich hübsches Geschenk besorgen; *see* **insult**.
2 *vi* **(a)** (*Math*) zusammenzählen, addieren ◆ **she just can't ~** sie kann einfach nicht rechnen.
(b) to ~ to sth zu etw beitragen; **to ~ to one's income** sein Einkommen aufbessern; **it will ~ to the time the job takes** es wird die Arbeitszeit verlängern; **the house had been ~ed to** an das Haus war (etwas) angebaut worden.

◆**add on** *vt sep number, amount* dazurechnen; *two weeks* mehr rechnen; *room* anbauen; *storey* aufstocken; (*append*) *comments etc* anfügen.

◆**add up** **1** *vt sep* zusammenzählen *or* -rechnen.
2 *vi* **(a)** (*figures etc*) stimmen; (*fig: make sense*) sich reimen ◆ **it's beginning to ~ ~** jetzt wird so manches klar; **it all ~s ~** (*lit*) es summiert sich; (*fig*) es paßt alles zusammen.
(b) to ~ ~ to (*figures*) ergeben; (*expenses also*) sich belaufen auf (+*acc*); **that all ~s ~ to a rather unusual state of affairs** alles in allem ergibt das eine recht ungewöhnliche Situation; **it doesn't ~ ~ to much** (*fig*) das ist nicht berühmt (*inf*).

added ['ædɪd] *adj attr* zusätzlich ◆ **~ value** Mehrwert *m*.

addend ['ædend] *n* (*US*) Summand *m*.

addendum [ə'dendəm] *n, pl* **addenda** [ə'dendə] Nachtrag *m*.

adder ['ædəʳ] *n* Viper, Natter *f*.

addict ['ædɪkt] *n* (*lit, fig*) Süchtige(r), Suchtkranke(r) *mf* ◆ **he's a television/heroin/real ~** er ist fernseh-/heroinsüchtig/richtig süchtig; **to become an ~** süchtig werden.

addicted [ə'dɪktɪd] *adj* süchtig ◆ **to be/become ~ to heroin/drugs/drink** heroin-/rauschgift-/trunksüchtig sein/werden; **he's ~ to smoking** er ist nikotinsüchtig; **he is ~ to sport/films** Sport ist/Filme sind bei ihm zur Sucht geworden; **you might get ~ to it** das kann zur Sucht werden; (*Med*) davon kann man süchtig werden.

addiction [ə'dɪkʃən] *n* Sucht *f* (*to* nach); (*no pl: state of dependence also*) Süchtigkeit *f* ◆ **~ to drugs/alcohol/pleasure/sport** Rauschgift-/Trunk-/Vergnügungssucht/übermäßige Sportbegeisterung; **to become an ~** zur Sucht werden.

addictive [ə'dɪktɪv] *adj* **to be ~** (*lit*) süchtig machen; (*fig*) zu einer Sucht werden können; **these drugs/watching TV can become ~** diese Drogen können/Fernsehen kann zur Sucht werden; **~ drug** Suchtdroge *f*.

adding machine *n* Addiermaschine *f*.

Addis Ababa [,ædɪs'æbəbə] *n* Addis Abeba *nt*.

addition [ə'dɪʃən] *n* **(a)** (*Math*) Addition *f*; (*act also*) Zusammenzählen *nt* ◆ ~

sign Pluszeichen *nt.*
(b) (*adding*) Zusatz *m* ◆ **the ~ of one more person would make the team too large** eine zusätzliche *or* weitere Person würde das Team zu groß machen; **the ~ of one more country to the EEC/of a native speaker to the language department** die Erweiterung der EG um ein weiteres Land/der Sprachabteilung um einen Muttersprachler.
(c) (*thing added*) Zusatz *m* (*to* zu); (*to list*) Ergänzung *f* (*to* zu); (*to building*) Anbau *m* (*to* an *+acc*); (*to income*) Aufbesserung *f* (*to gen*); (*to bill*) Zuschlag (*to* zu), Aufschlag (*to* auf *+acc*) *m* ◆ **they are expecting an ~ to their family** (*inf*) sie erwarten (Familien)zuwachs (*inf*).
▼ **(d) in ~** außerdem, obendrein; **in ~ (to this) he said ...** und außerdem sagte er ...; **in ~ to sth** zusätzlich zu etw; **in ~ to her other pursuits** zusätzlich zu ihren anderen Tätigkeiten; **in ~ to being unjustified his demand was also ...** seine Forderung war nicht nur ungerechtfertigt, sondern außerdem noch ...
additional [əˈdɪʃənl] *adj* zusätzlich ◆ **~ charge** Aufpreis *m*; **any ~ expenditure beyond this limit** alle weiteren Ausgaben über diese Grenze hinaus; **any ~ suggestions will have to be raised at the next meeting** irgendwelche weiteren Vorschläge müssen bei der nächsten Sitzung vorgebracht werden; **the author has inserted an ~ chapter** der Autor hat ein weiteres Kapitel eingefügt.
additionally [əˈdɪʃənlɪ] *adv* außerdem; *say* ergänzend ◆ **~ there is ...** außerdem ist da noch ..., dazu kommt noch ...; **~ difficult/complicated** (nur) noch schwieriger/komplizierter.
additive [ˈædɪtɪv] *n* Zusatz *m.*
addle [ˈædl] **1** *vt* **(a)** verdummen. **(b)** *egg* faul werden lassen, verderben lassen.
2 *vi* (*egg*) verderben, faul werden.
addled [ˈædld] *adj* **(a)** *brain, person* benebelt; (*permanently*) verdummt. **(b)** *egg* verdorben, faul.
addle-headed [ˈædlˈhedɪd], **addle-pated** [ˈædlˈpeɪtɪd] *adj* (*inf*) trottelig (*inf*), dußlig (*inf*).
add-on [ˈædɒn] *n* (*Comput*) Zusatz *m.*
address [əˈdres] **1** *n* **(a)** (*of person, on letter etc*) Adresse, Anschrift *f* ◆ **home ~** Privatadresse *f*; (*when travelling*) Heimatanschrift *f*; **what's your ~?** wo wohnen Sie?; **I've come to the wrong ~** ich bin hier falsch *or* an der falschen Adresse; **at this ~** unter dieser Adresse; **who else lives at this ~?** wer wohnt noch in dem Haus?; **"not known at this ~"** „Empfänger unbekannt".
(b) (*speech*) Ansprache *f* ◆ **the A~** (*Parl*) die Adresse (*die Erwiderung auf die Thronrede*).
(c) (*bearing, way of behaving*) Auftreten *nt*; (*way of speaking*) Art *f* zu reden.
(d) (*form: skill, tact*) Gewandtheit *f.*
(e) form of ~ (Form *f* der) Anrede *f.*
(f) to pay one's ~es to a lady (*liter*) einer Dame die Cour machen (*liter*).
(g) (*Comput*) Adresse *f.*
2 *vt* **(a)** *letter, parcel* adressieren (*to* an *+acc*).
(b) (*direct*) *complaints* richten (*to* an *+acc*); *speech, remarks also* adressieren (*to* an *+acc*).
(c) (*speak to*) *meeting* sprechen zu; *jury* sich wenden an (*+acc*); *person* anreden ◆ **don't ~ me as "Colonel"** nennen Sie mich nicht „Colonel"; **how should one ~ an earl?** wie redet man einen Grafen an?
(d) *problem etc* angehen.
3 *vr* **(a) to ~ oneself to sb** (*speak to*) jdn ansprechen; (*apply to*) sich an jdn wenden.
(b) (*form*) **to ~ oneself to a task** sich einer Aufgabe widmen.
address: ~ book *n* Adreßbuch *nt*; **~ bus** *n* (*Comput*) Adreßbus *m.*
addressee [ˌædreˈsiː] *n* Empfänger(in *f*), Adressat(in *f*) *m.*
address label *n* Adressenaufkleber *m.*
addressograph [əˈdresəʊgrɑːf] *n* Adressiermaschine, Adrema ® *f.*
adduce [əˈdjuːs] *vt* (*form*) anführen; *proof* erbringen.
adduction [æˈdʌkʃən] *n* (*form*) *see vt* Anführung *f*; Erbringung *f.*
Aden [ˈeɪdn] *n* Aden *nt* ◆ **Gulf of ~** Golf *m* von Aden.
adenoidal [ˈædɪnɔɪdl] *adj* adenoid; *voice, adolescent* näselnd ◆ **~ infection** Infektion *f* der Rachenmandeln.
adenoids [ˈædɪnɔɪdz] *npl* Rachenmandeln, Polypen (*inf*) *pl.*
adept [ˈædept] **1** *n* (*form*) Meister(in *f*) *m*, Experte *m*, Expertin *f* (*in, at* in *+dat*).
2 *adj* geschickt (*in, at* in *+dat*) ◆ **she's quite ~ at that sort of thing** sie hat ein Talent dafür.
adequacy [ˈædɪkwəsɪ] *n* Adäquatheit, Angemessenheit *f* ◆ **we doubt the ~ of his explanation/theory/this heating system** wir bezweifeln, daß seine Erklärung/Theorie/diese Heizung angemessen *or* adäquat *or* ausreichend ist; **he's beginning to doubt his ~ as a father/for the job** er zweifelt langsam an seiner Eignung als Vater/für diese Stelle.
adequate [ˈædɪkwɪt] *adj* adäquat; (*sufficient also*) *supply, heating system* ausreichend; *time* genügend *inv*; (*good enough also*) zulänglich; *excuse* angemessen ◆ **to be ~** (*sufficient*) (aus)reichen, genug sein; (*good enough*) zulänglich *or* adäquat sein; **this is just not ~** das ist einfach unzureich end *or* (*not good enough also*) nicht gut genug; **more than ~** mehr als genug; (*heating*) mehr als ausreichend.
adequately [ˈædɪkwɪtlɪ] *adv see adj.*
adhere [ədˈhɪəʳ] *vi* (*to* an *+dat*) (*stick*) haften; (*more firmly*) kleben.
◆**adhere to** *vi +prep obj* (*support, be faithful*) bleiben bei; *to plan, belief, principle, determination also* festhalten an (*+dat*); *to rule* sich halten an (*+acc*).
adherence [ədˈhɪərəns] *n* Festhalten *nt* (*to* an *+dat*); (*to rule*) Befolgung *f* (*to gen*).
adherent [ədˈhɪərənt] *n* Anhänger(in *f*) *m.*
adhesion [ədˈhiːʒən] *n* **(a)** (*of particles etc*) Adhäsion, Haftfähigkeit *f*; (*more firmly: of glue*) Klebefestigkeit *f* ◆ **powers of ~** Adhäsionskraft *f*; (*of glue*) Klebekraft *f.* **(b)** *see* **adherence.**
adhesive [ədˈhiːzɪv] **1** *n* Klebstoff *m.*
2 *adj* haftend; (*more firmly*) klebend ◆ **to be highly/not very ~** sehr/nicht gut haften/kleben; **~ label** Haftetikett *nt*; **~ plaster** Heftpflaster *nt*; **~ tape** Klebstreifen *m*; **~ strength/powers** Adhäsionskraft *f*; (*of glue*) Klebekraft *f.*
ad hoc [ˌædˈhɒk] *adj, adv* ad hoc *inv.*
adieu [əˈdjuː] (*old, liter*) **1** *n* Adieu, Lebewohl *nt* (*old*) ◆ **to make one's ~s** adieu sagen (*old*), Abschied nehmen.
2 *interj* adieu (*old*) ◆ **to bid sb ~** jdm adieu *or* Lebewohl sagen (*old*).
ad infinitum [ˌædɪnfɪˈnaɪtəm] *adv* ad infinitum (*geh*), für immer.
adipose [ˈædɪpəʊs] *adj* (*form*) adipös (*form*), Fett- ◆ **~ tissue** Fettgewebe *nt*; (*hum*) Fettpölsterchen *pl.*
adjacent [əˈdʒeɪsənt] *adj* angrenzend; *room also, angles* Neben- ◆ **to be ~ to sth** an etw (*acc*) angrenzen, neben etw (*dat*) liegen.
adjectival *adj,* **~ly** *adv* [ˌædʒekˈtaɪvəl, -ɪ] adjektivisch.
adjective [ˈædʒektɪv] *n* Adjektiv, Eigenschaftswort *nt.*
adjoin [əˈdʒɔɪn] **1** *vt* grenzen an (*+acc*).
2 *vi* nebeneinander liegen, aneinander grenzen.
adjoining [əˈdʒɔɪnɪŋ] *adj room* Neben-, Nachbar-; (*esp Archit etc*) anstoßend; *field* Nachbar-, angrenzend; (*of two things*) nebeneinanderliegend ◆ **in the ~ office** im Büro daneben *or* nebenan.
adjourn [əˈdʒɜːn] **1** *vt* **(a)** vertagen (*until* auf *+acc*) ◆ **he ~ed the meeting for three hours** er unterbrach die Konferenz für drei Stunden. **(b)** (*US: end*) beenden.
2 *vi* **(a)** sich vertagen (*until* auf *+acc*) ◆ **to ~ for lunch/one hour** zur Mittagspause/für eine Stunde unterbrechen.
(b) (*go to another place*) **to ~ to the sitting room** sich ins Wohnzimmer begeben.
adjournment [əˈdʒɜːnmənt] *n* (*to another day*) Vertagung *f* (*until* auf *+acc*); (*within a day*) Unterbrechung *f.*
adjudge [əˈdʒʌdʒ] *vt* **(a)** (*Jur*) **the court ~d that ...** das Gericht entschied *or* befand, daß ...; **to ~ sb guilty/insane** jdn für schuldig/unzurechnungsfähig erklären *or* befinden; **the estate was ~d to the second son** der Besitz wurde dem zweiten Sohn zugesprochen.
(b) (*award*) *prize* zuerkennen, zusprechen (*to sb* jdm) ◆ **he was ~d the winner** er wurde zum Sieger *or* Gewinner erklärt.
(c) (*form: consider*) erachten für *or* als (*geh*).
adjudicate [əˈdʒuːdɪkeɪt] **1** *vt* **(a)** (*judge*) *claim* entscheiden; *competition* Preisrichter sein bei. **(b)** (*Jur: declare*) **to ~ sb bankrupt** jdn für bankrott erklären.
2 *vi* entscheiden, urteilen (*on, in* bei); (*in dispute*) Schiedsrichter sein (*on* bei, in *+dat*); (*in competition, dog-show etc*) als Preisrichter fungieren.
adjudication [əˌdʒuːdɪˈkeɪʃən] *n* Entscheidung, Beurteilung *f*; (*result also*) Urteil *nt* ◆ **~ of bankruptcy** Bankrotterklärung *f.*
adjudicator [əˈdʒuːdɪkeɪtəʳ] *n* (*in competition etc*) Preisrichter(in *f*) *m*; (*in dispute*) Schiedsrichter(in *f*)*m.*
adjunct [ˈædʒʌŋkt] *n* Anhängsel *nt* ◆ **a dictionary is an indispensable ~ to language learning** ein Wörterbuch ist unerläßlich fürs Sprachenlernen.
adjuration [ˌædʒʊəˈreɪʃən] *n* (*liter*) Beschwörung *f.*
adjure [əˈdʒʊəʳ] *vt* (*liter*) beschwören.
adjust [əˈdʒʌst] **1** *vt* **(a)** (*set*) *machine, engine, carburettor, brakes, height, speed, flow etc* einstellen; *knob, lever* (richtig) stellen; (*alter*) *height, speed* verstellen; *length of clothes* ändern; (*correct, re-adjust*) nachstellen; *height, speed, flow* regulieren; *formula, plan, production, exchange rates, terms* (entsprechend) ändern; *salaries* angleichen (*to* an *+acc*); *hat, tie* zurechtrücken ◆ **you can ~ the record-player to three different speeds** Sie können den Plattenspieler auf drei verschiedene Geschwindigkeiten (ein)stellen; **to ~ the lever upwards/downwards** den Hebel nach oben/unten stellen; **you have to ~ this knob to regulate the ventilation** Sie müssen an diesem Knopf drehen, um die Ventilation zu regulieren, die Ventilation läßt sich an diesem Knopf regulieren; **he ~ed the knobs on the TV set** er hat die Knöpfe am Fernsehapparat richtig gestellt; **do not ~ your set** ändern Sie nichts an der Einstellung Ihres Geräts; **to ~ sth to new requirements/conditions** *etc* etw neuen Erfordernissen/Umständen *etc* anpassen; **because of increased demand production will have to be appropriately ~ed** die Produktion muß auf die verstärkte Nachfrage abgestimmt werden *or* der verstärkten Nachfrage angepaßt werden; **the terms have been ~ed slightly in your favour** die Bedingungen sind zu Ihren Gunsten leicht abgeändert worden; **the layout can be ~ed to meet different needs** die Anordnung läßt sich je nach Bedarf ändern; **we ~ed all salaries upwards/downwards** wir haben alle Gehälter nach oben/unten angeglichen; **would you please ~ your dress, sir** (*euph*) ich glaube, Sie haben vergessen, etwas *or* Ihre Hose zuzumachen; **if you could ~ the price slightly** (*hum*) wenn wir uns vielleicht noch über den Preis unterhalten könnten.
(b) to ~ oneself to sth (*to new country, circumstances etc*) sich einer Sache (*dat*) anpassen; (*to new requirements, demands etc*) sich auf etw (*acc*) einstellen.
(c) (*settle*) *differences* beilegen, schlichten; (*Insur*) *claim* regulieren.
2 *vi* **(a)** (*to new country, circumstances etc*) sich anpassen (*to dat*); (*to new requirements, demands etc*) sich einstellen (*to* auf *+acc*). **(b)** (*machine etc*) sich einstellen lassen ◆ **the chair ~s to various heights** der Stuhl läßt sich in der

➤ LANGUAGE IN USE: **addition: d → 26.2**

Höhe verstellen.

adjustability [əˌdʒʌstəˈbɪlɪtɪ] *n see adj* Verstellbarkeit *f*; Veränderlichkeit, Variabilität *f*; Regulierbarkeit *f*; Beweglichkeit, Flexibilität *f*; Anpassungsfähigkeit *f*.

adjustable [əˈdʒʌstəbl] *adj tool, height, angle* verstellbar; *shape* veränderlich, variabel; *height also, speed, temperature* regulierbar; *tax, deadline, rate of production/repayment* beweglich, flexibel; *person, animal, plant* anpassungsfähig ◆ **partitions make the shape of the office ~** durch Trennwände läßt sich die Form des Büros verändern; **~ spanner** Engländer *m*.

adjustable-pitch [əˈdʒʌstəblˈpɪtʃ] *adj* **~ propeller** Verstell-Luftschraube *f*.

adjuster [əˈdʒʌstə[r]] *n* (*Insur*) (Schadens)sachverständige(r) *mf*.

adjustment [əˈdʒʌstmənt] *n* **(a)** (*setting*) (*of machine, engine, carburettor, brakes, height, speed, flow etc*) Einstellung *f*; (*of knob, lever*) (richtige) Stellung; (*alteration*) (*of height, speed*) Verstellung *f*; (*of length of clothes*) Änderung *f*; (*correction, re-adjustment*) Nachstellung *f*; (*of height, speed, flow*) Regulierung *f*; (*of formula, plan, production, exchange rate, terms*) (entsprechende) Änderung; (*of hat, tie*) Zurechtrücken *nt* ◆ **if you could make a slight ~ to my salary** (*hum inf*) wenn Sie eine leichte Korrektur meines Gehalts vornehmen könnten (*hum*); **a certain ~ of our traditional outlook** eine gewisse Änderung unserer traditionellen Haltung; **to make ~s** Änderungen vornehmen; **to make ~s to the manuscript/play/one's plans** Änderungen am Manuskript/Stück vornehmen/seine Pläne ändern; **brakes require regular ~** Bremsen müssen regelmäßig nachgestellt werden.
(b) (*socially etc*) Anpassung *f*.
(c) (*settlement*) Beilegung, Schlichtung *f*; (*Insur*) Regulierung *f*.

adjutant [ˈædʒətənt] *n* **(a)** (*Mil*) Adjutant *m* ◆ **~ general** Generaladjutant *m*. **(b)** (*Orn: also* **~ bird**) Indischer Marabu.

ad-lib [ædˈlɪb] **1** *adv* aus dem Stegreif.
2 *n* Improvisation *f*.
3 *adj* improvisiert, Stegreif-.
4 *vti* improvisieren.

Adm *abbr of* **admiral** Adm.

adman [ˈædmæn] *n* (*inf*) Werbefachmann *m* ◆ **admen** Werbeleute *pl*.

admass [ˈædmæs] *n durch Werbung leicht beeinflußbares Publikum.*

admin [ˈædmɪn] *abbr of* **administration** ◆ **it involves a lot of ~** damit ist viel Verwaltung verbunden; **~ building** Verwaltungsgebäude *nt*.

administer [ədˈmɪnɪstə[r]] **1** *vt* **(a)** *institution, funds* verwalten; *business, affairs* führen; (*run*) *company, department* die Verwaltungsangelegenheiten regeln von ◆ **the civil service ~s the country** die Beamtenschaft verwaltet das Land.
(b) (*dispense*) *relief, alms* gewähren; *law* ausführen, vollstrecken, vollziehen; *punishment* verhängen (*to* über *+acc*) ◆ **to ~ justice** Recht sprechen; **to ~ a severe blow to sb** (*fig*) jdm einen schweren Schlag versetzen.
(c) (*cause to take*) (*to sb* jdm) *medicine, drugs* verabreichen; *sacraments* spenden; *last rites* geben ◆ **to ~ an oath to sb** jdm einen Eid abnehmen.
2 *vi* **(a)** (*act as administrator*) die Verwaltungsangelegenheiten regeln. **(b)** (*form*) **to ~ to the sick/sb's needs** *etc* sich der Kranken/sich jds annehmen (*geh*).

administrate [ædˈmɪnɪstreɪt] *see* **administer 1, 2 (a)**.

administration [ədˌmɪnɪsˈtreɪʃən] *n* **(a)** *no pl* Verwaltung *f*; (*of an election, a project etc*) Organisation *f* ◆ **to spend a lot of time on ~** viel Zeit auf Verwaltungsangelegenheiten *or* -sachen verwenden.
(b) (*government*) Regierung *f* ◆ **the Schmidt ~** die Regierung Schmidt.
(c) *no pl* (*of remedy*) Verabreichung *f*; (*of sacrament*) Spenden *nt* ◆ **the ~ of an oath** die Vereidigung; **the ~ of justice** die Rechtsprechung.

administrative [ədˈmɪnɪstrətɪv] *adj* administrativ ◆ **~ body** Verwaltungsbehörde *f*.

administrator [ədˈmɪnɪstreɪtə[r]] *n* Verwalter *m*; (*Jur*) Verwaltungsbeamte(r), Administrator *m*.

admirable *adj*, **-bly** *adv* [ˈædmərəbl, -ɪ] (*praiseworthy, laudable*) bewundernswert, erstaunlich; (*excellent*) vortrefflich, ausgezeichnet.

admiral [ˈædmərəl] *n* Admiral *m* ◆ **A~ of the Fleet** (*Brit*) Großadmiral *m*; *see* **red ~**.

Admiralty [ˈædmərəltɪ] *n* (*Brit*) Admiralität *f*; (*department, building*) britisches Marineministerium ◆ **First Lord of the ~** britischer Marineminister.

admiration [ˌædməˈreɪʃən] *n* **(a)** Bewunderung *f*. **(b)** (*person, object*) **to be the ~ of all/of the world** von allen/von aller Welt bewundert werden.

▼ **admire** [ədˈmaɪə[r]] *vt* bewundern.

admirer [ədˈmaɪərə[r]] *n* Bewund(e)rer (in *f*), Verehrer(in *f*) *m*; (*dated, hum: suitor*) Verehrer *m* (*hum*).

admiring *adj*, **~ly** *adv* [ədˈmaɪərɪŋ, -lɪ] bewundernd.

admissibility [ədˌmɪsəˈbɪlɪtɪ] *n* Zulässigkeit *f*.

admissible [ədˈmɪsəbl] *adj* zulässig.

admission [ədˈmɪʃən] *n* **(a)** (*entry*) Zutritt *m*; (*to club also, university*) Zulassung *f*; (*to hospital*) Einlieferung *f* (*to* in *+acc*); (*price*) Eintritt *m* ◆ **no ~ to minors** Zutritt für Minderjährige verboten; **to gain ~ to a building** Zutritt zu einem Ort erhalten; **he had gained ~ to a whole new world** er hatte Zugang zu einer ganz neuen Welt gefunden; **a visa is necessary for ~ to the country** für die Einreise ist ein Visum nötig; **unrestricted ~ to a country** unbegrenzte Einreiseerlaubnis.
(b) (*Jur: of evidence etc*) Zulassung *f*.
(c) (*confession*) Eingeständnis *nt* ◆ **on** *or* **by his own ~** nach eigenem Eingeständnis; **that would be an ~ of failure** das hieße, sein Versagen eingestehen.

▼ **admit** [ədˈmɪt] *vt* **(a)** (*let in*) hinein-/hereinlassen; (*permit to join*) zulassen (*to* zu), aufnehmen (*to* in *+acc*) ◆ **children not ~ted** kein Zutritt für Kinder; **he was not ~ted to the cinema/to college** er wurde nicht ins Kino hineingelassen/zur Universität zugelassen *or* in der Universität aufgenommen; **to be ~ted to hospital** ins Krankenhaus eingeliefert werden; **to be ~ted to the Bar** bei Gericht zugelassen werden; **this ticket ~s two** die Karte ist für zwei (Personen).
(b) (*have space for: halls, harbours etc*) Platz bieten für.
▼ **(c)** (*acknowledge*) zugeben ◆ **do you ~ stealing his hat?** geben Sie zu, seinen Hut gestohlen zu haben?; **he ~ted himself beaten** er gab sich geschlagen; **it is generally ~ted that ...** es wird allgemein zugegeben, daß ...; **to ~ the truth of sth** zugeben, daß etw wahr ist.

◆**admit of** *vi +prep obj* (*form*) zulassen (*+acc*).

◆**admit to** *vi +prep obj* eingestehen ◆ **I have to ~ ~ a certain feeling of admiration** ich muß gestehen, daß mir das Bewunderung abnötigt.

admittance [ədˈmɪtəns] *n* (*to building*) Zutritt (*to* zu), Einlaß (*to* in *+acc*) *m*; (*to club*) Zulassung (*to* zu), Aufnahme (*to* in *+acc*) *f* ◆ **I gained ~ to the hall** mir wurde der Zutritt zum Saal gestattet; **I was denied ~** mir wurde der Zutritt verwehrt *or* verweigert; **no ~ except on business** Zutritt für Unbefugte verboten.

admittedly [ədˈmɪtɪdlɪ] *adv* zugegebenermaßen ◆ **~ this is true** zugegeben, das stimmt.

admixture [ədˈmɪkstʃə[r]] *n* (*thing added*) Zusatz *m*, Beigabe *f*.

admonish [ədˈmɒnɪʃ] *vt* ermahnen (*for* wegen).

admonishment [ədˈmɒnɪʃmənt], **admonition** [ˌædməʊˈnɪʃən] *n* (*rebuke*) Ermahnung *f*.

admonitory [ədˈmɒnɪtərɪ] *adj* (er)mahnend.

ad nauseam [ˌædˈnɔːsɪæm] *adv* bis zum Überdruß, bis zum Geht-nicht-mehr (*inf*) ◆ **and so on ~** undsoweiter, undsoweiter.

ado [əˈduː] *n* Aufheben, Trara (*inf*) *nt* ◆ **much ~ about nothing** viel Lärm um nichts; **without more** *or* **further ~** ohne weiteres.

adobe [əˈdəʊbɪ] *n* (*brick*) (ungebrannter) Lehmziegel, Adobe *m*; (*house*) *Haus nt aus Adobeziegeln* ◆ **~ wall** *Mauer f aus Adobeziegeln.*

adolescence [ˌædəʊˈlesns] *n* Jugend *f*; (*puberty*) Pubertät, Adoleszenz (*form*) *f* ◆ **the problems of ~** Pubertätsprobleme *pl*; **in his late ~** in seiner späteren Jugend.

adolescent [ˌædəʊˈlesnt] **1** *n* Jugendliche(r) *mf* ◆ **he's still an ~** er ist noch im Heranwachsen/in der Pubertät.
2 *adj* Jugend-; (*in puberty*) Pubertäts-, pubertär; (*immature*) unreif ◆ **he is so ~** er steckt noch in der Pubertät; **~ phase** Pubertätsphase *f*; **~ spots** Pubertätspickel *pl*; **~ love** jugendliche Liebe.

Adonis [əˈdəʊnɪs] *n* (*Myth, fig*) Adonis *m*.

adopt [əˈdɒpt] *vt* **(a)** *child* adoptieren, an Kindes Statt annehmen (*form*); *child in a different country, family, city also* die Patenschaft übernehmen für ◆ **the waif was ~ed into the family** der/die Waise wurde in die Familie aufgenommen; **the London court ~ed the young musician as its own** der Londoner Hof nahm den jungen Musiker als einen der ihren auf; **your cat has ~ed me** (*inf*) deine Katze hat sich mir angeschlossen.
(b) *idea, suggestion, attitude, method* übernehmen; *mannerisms* annehmen; *career* einschlagen, sich (*dat*) wählen.
(c) (*Pol*) *motion* annehmen; *candidate* nehmen.

adopted [əˈdɒptɪd] *adj son, daughter* Adoptiv-, adoptiert; *country* Wahl-.

adoption [əˈdɒpʃən] *n* **(a)** (*of child*) Adoption *f*, Annahme *f* an Kindes Statt (*form*); (*of city, of child in other country*) Übernahme *f* der Patenschaft; (*into the family*) Aufnahme *f* ◆ **parents/Japanese by ~** Adoptiveltern *pl*/Japaner(in *f*) *m* durch Adoption.
(b) (*of method, idea*) Übernahme *f*; (*of mannerisms*) Annahme *f*; (*of career*) Wahl *f* ◆ **his country of ~** die Heimat seiner Wahl; **this custom is Japanese only by ~** dieser Brauch ist von den Japanern nur übernommen worden.
(c) (*of motion, law, candidate*) Annahme *f*.

adoptive [əˈdɒptɪv] *adj parent, child* Adoptiv- ◆ **~ country** Wahlheimat *f*.

adorable [əˈdɔːrəbl] *adj* bezaubernd, hinreißend ◆ **you are ~** du bist ein Schatz.

adorably [əˈdɔːrəblɪ] *adv* bezaubernd, hinreißend.

adoration [ˌædəˈreɪʃən] *n see vt* **(a)** Anbetung *f*. **(b)** grenzenlose Liebe (*of* für). **(c)** Liebe *f* (*of* für).

adore [əˈdɔː[r]] *vt* **(a)** *God* anbeten. **(b)** (*love very much*) *family, wife* über alles lieben. **(c)** (*inf: like very much*) *French, whisky etc* (über alles) lieben; *Mozart also* schwärmen für.

adoring [əˈdɔːrɪŋ] *adj* bewundernd ◆ **his ~ fans** seine bewundernden *or* ihn anbetenden Fans.

adoringly [əˈdɔːrɪŋlɪ] *adv* bewundernd, voller Verehrung.

adorn [əˈdɔːn] *vt* schmücken, zieren (*geh*); *oneself* schmücken.

adornment [əˈdɔːnmənt] *n* Schmuck *m no pl*; (*act*) Schmücken *nt*; (*on dress, cake, design*) Verzierung *f* (*also act*); (*on manuscript*) Ornament *nt*; (*in prose style*) Ausschmückung *f*.

adrenal [əˈdriːnl] *adj* Adrenal-, Nebennieren- ◆ **~ glands** Nebennieren *pl*.

adrenalin(e) [əˈdrenəlɪn] *n* **(a)** (*Med*) Adrenalin *nt*.
(b) (*phrases*) **I could feel the ~ rising** ich fühlte, wie mein Blutdruck stieg; **to build up sb's ~** jdn in Stimmung bringen; **you burn up a lot of ~** Sie verbrauchen eine Menge Energie; **it's impossible to relax now the ~'s going** es ist unmöglich abzuschalten, wenn man so aufgedreht ist; **in a combat situation the ~ just takes over** in einer Kampfsituation leistet man einfach mehr; **working under pressure gets the ~ going** Arbeiten unter Druck weckt ungeahnte Kräfte.

Adriatic (Sea) [ˌeɪdrɪˈætɪk(ˈsiː)] *n* Adria *f*, Adriatisches Meer.

➤ LANGUAGE IN USE: **admire** → 13 **admit: c** → 11.1, 18.3, 26.3

adrift [ə'drɪft] *adv, adj pred* **(a)** *(Naut)* treibend ◆ **to be ~** treiben; **to go ~** sich losmachen *or* loslösen; **to set** *or* **cut a boat ~** ein Boot losmachen.
(b) *(fig)* **to come ~** *(wire, hair etc)* sich lösen; *(plans)* fehlschlagen; *(theory)* zusammenbrechen ◆ **we are ~ on the sea of life** wir treiben dahin auf dem Meer des Lebens; **he wandered through the city, lost and ~** (ziellos und) verloren irrte er in der Stadt umher; **you're all ~** *(inf)* da liegst du völlig verkehrt *or* falsch; **after a month's philosophy I felt all ~** nach einem Monat Philosophie war ich vollkommen durcheinander; **to cast** *or* **turn sb ~** jdn auf die Straße setzen.
adroit [ə'drɔɪt] *adj lawyer, reply, reasoning* gewandt, geschickt; *mind* scharf ◆ **to be ~ at sth/doing sth** gewandt *or* geschickt in etw *(dat)* sein/gewandt *or* geschickt darin sein, etw zu tun.
adroitly [ə'drɔɪtlɪ] *adv* gewandt, geschickt.
adroitness [ə'drɔɪtnɪs] *n see adj* Gewandtheit, Geschicklichkeit *f*; Schärfe *f*.
adsorb [æd'sɔːb] *vt* adsorbieren.
adsorption [æd'sɔːpʃən] *n* Adsorption *f*.
adulation [ˌædjʊ'leɪʃən] *n* Verherrlichung *f*.
adult ['ædʌlt, *(US)* ə'dʌlt] [1] *n* Erwachsene(r) *mf* ◆ **~s only** nur für Erwachsene.
[2] *adj* **(a)** *person* erwachsen; *animal* ausgewachsen. **(b)** *(for adults) book, film* für Erwachsene; *(mature) decision* reif ◆ **~ classes** Kurse *pl* für Erwachsene; **~ education** Erwachsenenbildung *f*.
adulterate [ə'dʌltəreɪt] *vt* **(a)** *wine, whisky etc* panschen; *food* abwandeln ◆ **some ~d Scottish version of Italian cooking** ein schottischer Abklatsch italienischer Küche. **(b)** *(fig) text, original version* verfälschen, Gewalt antun *(+dat)* ◆ **an ~d version of the original** eine verhunzte Fassung des Originals *(inf)*.
adulteration [əˌdʌltə'reɪʃən] *n* **(a)** *(of wine)* Panschen *nt*; *(of food)* Abwandlung *f*. **(b)** *(fig)* Vergewaltigung, Verhunzung *(inf) f*.
adulterer [ə'dʌltərəʳ] *n* Ehebrecher *m*.
adulteress [ə'dʌltərɪs] *n* Ehebrecherin *f*.
adulterous [ə'dʌltərəs] *adj* ehebrecherisch.
adultery [ə'dʌltərɪ] *n* Ehebruch *m* ◆ **to commit ~** Ehebruch begehen; **because of his ~ with three actresses** weil er mit drei Schauspielerinnen Ehebruch begangen hatte.
adulthood ['ædʌlthʊd, *(US)* ə'dʌlthʊd] *n* Erwachsenenalter *nt* ◆ **to reach ~** erwachsen werden.
adumbrate ['ædʌmbreɪt] *vt (liter)* **(a)** *(outline) theory* umreißen. **(b)** *(foreshadow) coming event* ankündigen.
adumbration [ˌædʌm'breɪʃən] *n (liter)* **(a)** *(of theory)* Umriß *m*. **(b)** *(of event)* Ankündigung *f*, Anzeichen *nt*.
advance [əd'vɑːns] [1] *n* **(a)** *(progress)* Fortschritt *m*.
(b) *(movement forward) (of old age)* Voranschreiten *nt*; *(of science)* Weiterentwicklung *f*; *(of sea, ideas)* Vordringen *nt* ◆ **with the ~ of old age** mit fortschreitendem Alter.
(c) *(Mil)* Vormarsch *m*, Vorrücken *nt*.
(d) *(money)* Vorschuß *m (on* auf *+acc)*.
(e) *(amorous, fig)* **~s** *pl* Annäherungsversuche *pl*.
(f) in ~ im voraus; *(temporal also)* vorher; **to send sb on in ~** jdn vorausschicken; **£10 in ~** £ 10 als Vorschuß; **thanking you in ~** mit bestem Dank im voraus; **to arrive in ~ of the others** vor den anderen ankommen; **to be (well) in ~ of sb/one's time** jdm/seiner Zeit (weit) voraussein.
[2] *vt* **(a)** *(move forward) date, time* vorverlegen ◆ **the dancer slowly ~s one foot** die Tänzerin setzt langsam einen Fuß vor.
(b) *(Mil) troops* vorrücken lassen.
(c) *(further) work, project* voran- *or* weiterbringen, förderlich sein für; *cause, interests* fördern; *knowledge* vergrößern; *(accelerate) growth* vorantreiben; *(promote) employee etc* befördern.
(d) *(put forward) reason, opinion, plan* vorbringen.
(e) *(pay beforehand) (sb* jdm) (als) Vorschuß geben, vorschießen *(inf)*; *(lend)* als Kredit geben.
(f) *(raise) prices* anheben.
[3] *vi* **(a)** *(Mil)* vorrücken.
(b) *(move forward)* vorankommen ◆ **to ~ towards sb/sth** auf jdn/etw zugehen/-kommen; **to ~ upon sb** drohend auf jdn zukommen; **as the sea ~s over the rocks** während die See über die Felsen vordringt; **old age is advancing on all of us** wir alle nähern uns dem Alter; **the forces of evil are advancing against us** die Mächte des Bösen nahen sich uns drohend.
(c) *(fig: progress)* Fortschritte machen ◆ **we've ~d a long way since those days** wir sind seither ein gutes Stück voran- *or* weitergekommen; **the work is advancing well** die Arbeit macht gute Fortschritte *pl*; **is civilization advancing towards some level of perfection?** geht die Zivilisation in irgendeiner Weise der Perfektion entgegen?; **as mankind ~s in knowledge** während die Menschheit an Wissen gewinnt.
(d) *(prices)* anziehen; *(costs)* hochgehen, ansteigen.
advance: ~ booking *n* Reservierung *f*; *(Theat)* Vorverkauf *m*; **~ booking opens on ...** der Vorverkauf beginnt am ...; **have you an ~ booking, sir?** *(Theat)* haben Sie (die Karten) vorbestellt?; *(in hotel)* haben Sie reservieren lassen?; **~ booking office** *n (Theat)* Vorverkauf(sstelle *f*) *m*; **~ copy** *n* Vorausexemplar *nt*, Vorabdruck *m*.
advanced [əd'vɑːnst] *adj student, level, age* fortgeschritten; *studies, mathematics etc* höher; *technology also, ideas* fortschrittlich; *version, model* anspruchsvoll, weiterentwickelt; *level of civilization* hoch; *position, observation post etc* vorgeschoben ◆ **~ work** anspruchsvolle Arbeit; **~ in years** in fortgeschrittenem Alter; **she is more/less ~ in years than ...** sie hat mehr/weniger Jahre auf dem Rücken als ... *(inf)*; **the summer was well ~** der Sommer war schon weit vorangeschritten; *see* **A level**.
advance: ~ guard *n* Vorhut *f*; **~ man** *n (US Pol)* Wahlhelfer *m*.
advancement [əd'vɑːnsmənt] *n* **(a)** *(furtherance)* Förderung *f*. **(b)** *(promotion in rank)* Vorwärtskommen *nt*, Aufstieg *m*.
advance: ~ notice *n* frühzeitiger Bescheid; *(of sth bad)* Vorwarnung *f*; **to give/receive ~ notice** frühzeitig Bescheid/eine Vorwarnung geben/erhalten; **~ party** *n (Mil, fig)* Vorhut *f*; **~ payment** *n* Vorauszahlung *f*; **~ warning** *n see* **~ notice**.
advantage [əd'vɑːntɪdʒ] [1] *n* **(a)** Vorteil *m* ◆ **to have an ~ (over sb)** (jdm gegenüber) im Vorteil sein; **to have the ~ of sb** jdm überlegen sein; **you have the ~ of me** *(form)* ich kenne leider Ihren werten Namen nicht *(form)*; **he had the ~ of youth/greater experience** er hatte den Vorzug der Jugend/er war durch seine größere Erfahrung im Vorteil; **that gives you an ~ over me** damit sind Sie mir gegenüber im Vorteil, das verschafft Ihnen mir gegenüber einen Vorteil; **to get the ~ of sb (by doing sth)** sich *(dat)* (durch etw) jdm gegenüber einen Vorteil verschaffen; **don't let him get the ~ of us** er darf uns gegenüber keine Vorteile bekommen; **to have the ~ of numbers** zahlenmäßig überlegen sein.
(b) *(use, profit)* Vorteil *m* ◆ **to take ~ of sb/sth** jdn ausnutzen/etw ausnutzen *or* sich *(dat)* zunutze machen; **to take ~ of sb** *(euph)* jdn mißbrauchen; **he took ~ of her while she was drunk** er machte sich *(dat)* ihre Trunkenheit zunutze; **to turn sth to (good) ~** Nutzen aus etw ziehen; **he turned it to his own ~** er machte es sich *(dat)* zunutze; **of what ~ is that to us?** welchen Nutzen haben wir davon?; **I find it to my ~ to ..., it is to my ~ to ...** es ist vorteilhaft für mich ..., es ist für mich von Vorteil ...; **to use sth to the best ~** das Beste aus etw machen; **the dress shows her off to ~** das Kleid ist vorteilhaft für sie.
(c) *(Tennis)* Vorteil *m*.
[2] *vt (old, liter)* zum Vorteil *or* Nutzen gereichen *(+dat) (geh)*.
advantageous [ˌædvən'teɪdʒəs] *adj* von Vorteil, vorteilhaft ◆ **to be ~ to sb** für jdn von Vorteil sein.
advantageously [ˌædvən'teidʒəslɪ] *adv* vorteilhaft.
advent ['ædvənt] *n* **(a)** *(of age, era)* Beginn, Anbruch *m*; *(of jet plane etc)* Aufkommen *nt*. **(b)** *(Eccl)* **A~** Advent *m* ◆ **~ calendar** Adventskalender *m*.
adventitious [ˌædven'tɪʃəs] *adj (form)* zufällig.
adventure [əd'ventʃəʳ] [1] *n* **(a)** Abenteuer, Erlebnis *nt* ◆ **an ~ into the unknown** ein Vorstoß ins Unbekannte. **(b)** *no pl* **love/spirit of ~** Abenteuerlust *f*; **to look for ~** (das) Abenteuer suchen; **a life of ~** ein abenteuerliches Leben.
[2] *vi see* **venture**.
[3] *attr story, film, holiday* Abenteuer- ◆ **~ playground** Abenteuerspielplatz *m*.
adventurer [əd'ventʃərəʳ] *n* Abenteurer(in *f*) *m*; *(pej also)* Windhund *m*.
adventuresome [əd'ventʃəsəm] *adj see* **adventurous**.
adventuress [əd'ventʃərɪs] *n (pej)* Abenteurerin *f*.
adventurous [əd'ventʃərəs] *adj* **(a)** *person* abenteuerlustig; *journey* abenteuerlich. **(b)** *(bold)* gewagt.
adventurousness [əd'ventʃərəsnɪs] *n see adj* **(a)** Abenteuerlust *f*; Abenteuerlichkeit *f*. **(b)** Gewagte(s) *nt* ◆ **the ~ of his style** sein gewagter Stil.
adverb ['ædvɜːb] *n* Adverb, Umstandswort *nt*.
adverbial *adj*, **~ly** *adv* [əd'vɜːbɪ əl, -ɪ] adverbial.
adversary ['ædvəsərɪ] *n* Widersacher(in *f*) *m*; *(in contest)* Gegner (in *f*) *m*.
adverse ['ædvɜːs] *adj* ungünstig; *criticism, comment also, reaction* negativ, ablehnend; *wind, conditions also* widrig; *effect also* nachteilig.
adversely [əd'vɜːslɪ] *adv comment, criticize, react* negativ; *affect also* nachteilig.
adversity [əd'vɜːsɪtɪ] *n* **(a)** *no pl* Not *f* ◆ **a period of ~** eine Zeit der Not; **in ~** im Unglück, in der Not. **(b)** *(misfortune)* Widrigkeit *f (geh)* ◆ **the adversities of war** die Härten des Krieges.
advert[1] [əd'vɜːt] *vi (form)* hinweisen, aufmerksam machen *(to* auf *+acc)*.
advert[2] ['ædvɜːt] *n (Brit inf) abbr of* **advertisement** Anzeige, Annonce *f*, Inserat *nt*; *(on TV, radio)* Werbespot *m*.
advertise ['ædvətaɪz] [1] *vt* **(a)** *(publicize)* Werbung *or* Reklame machen für, werben für ◆ **I've seen that soap ~d on television** ich habe die Werbung *or* Reklame für diese Seife im Fernsehen gesehen; **as ~d on television** wie durch das Fernsehen bekannt.
(b) *(in paper etc) flat, table etc* inserieren, annoncieren; *job, post also* ausschreiben ◆ **to ~ sth in a shop window/on local radio** etw durch eine Schaufensteranzeige/im Regionalsender anbieten; **I saw it ~d in a shop window** ich habe die Anzeige dafür in einem Schaufenster gesehen.
(c) *(make conspicuous) fact* publik machen; *ignorance also* offen zeigen.
[2] *vi* **(a)** *(Comm)* Werbung *or* Reklame machen, werben.
(b) *(in paper)* inserieren, annoncieren *(for* für) ◆ **to ~ for sb/sth** jdn/etw (per Anzeige) suchen; **to ~ for sth on local radio/in a shop window** etw per Regionalsender/durch Anzeige im Schaufenster suchen.
▼ **advertisement** [əd'vɜːtɪsmənt, (US) ædvə'taɪzmənt] *n* **(a)** *(Comm)* Werbung, Reklame *f no pl*; *(in paper also)* Anzeige *f* ◆ **the TV ~s** die Werbung *or* Reklame im Fernsehen; **70% of the magazine is ~s** die Zeitschrift besteht zu 70% aus Anzeigen *or* Werbung *or* Reklame; **he is not a good ~ for his school** er ist nicht gerade ein Aushängeschild für seine Schule.
(b) *(announcement)* Anzeige *f*; *(in paper also)* Annonce *f*, Inserat *nt* ◆ **to put an ~ in the paper (for sb/sth)** eine Anzeige (für jdn/etw) in die Zeitung setzen, (für jdn/etw) in der Zeitung inserieren; **~ column** Anzeigenspalte *f*.
advertiser ['ædvətaɪzəʳ] *n (in paper)* Inserent(in *f*) *m* ◆ **this company never was a very big ~** diese Firma hat nie viel Werbung *or* Reklame gemacht; **TV ~s** Firmen, die im Fernsehen werben.

➤ LANGUAGE IN USE: **advertisement: a** → 19.1, 20.1

advertising ['ædvətaɪzɪŋ] *n* Werbung, Reklame *f* ◆ **he is in ~** er ist in der Werbung (tätig).

advertising *in cpds* Werbe-; **~ agency** *n* Werbeagentur *f or* -büro *nt*; **~ campaign** *n* Werbekampagne *f or* -feldzug *m*; **~ rates** *npl* Anzeigenpreise *pl*; *(for TV, radio)* Preise *pl* für Werbespots; **~ space** *n* Platz *m* für Anzeigen.

▼ **advice** [əd'vaɪs] *n* **(a)** *no pl* Rat *m no pl* ◆ **a piece of** *or* **some ~** ein Rat(schlag) *m*; **let me give you a piece of** *or* **some ~** ich will Ihnen einen guten Rat geben; **you're a fine one to give ~** du hast gut raten, ausgerechnet du willst hier Ratschläge geben; **his ~ was always useful** er gab immer guten Rat *or* gute Ratschläge; **that's good ~** das ist ein guter Rat; **I didn't ask for your ~** ich habe dich nicht um (deinen) Rat gebeten *or* gefragt; **to take sb's ~** jds Rat (be)folgen; **take my ~** höre auf mich; **to seek (sb's) ~** (jdn) um Rat fragen; *(from doctor, lawyer etc)* Rat (bei jdm) einholen; **to take medical/legal ~** einen Arzt/Rechtsanwalt zu Rate ziehen; **my ~ to him would be ...** ich würde ihm raten ...; **it's not ~ we need** wir brauchen keine guten Ratschläge.
(b) *(Comm: notification)* Mitteilung *f*, Avis *m or nt* ◆ **~ note** Benachrichtigung *f*, Avis *m or nt*.

advisability [əd,vaɪzə'bɪlɪtɪ] *n* Ratsamkeit *f* ◆ **he questioned the ~ of going on strike** er bezweifelte, ob es ratsam wäre zu streiken.

▼ **advisable** [əd'vaɪzəbl] *adj* ratsam, empfehlenswert.

advisably [əd'vaɪzəblɪ] *adv* zu Recht.

▼ **advise** [əd'vaɪz] **1** *vt* **(a)** *(give advice to) person* raten (+*dat*); *(professionally)* beraten ◆ **to ~ discretion/caution** zur Diskretion/Vorsicht raten, Diskretion/Vorsicht empfehlen; **I wouldn't ~ it** ich würde es nicht raten *or* empfehlen; **I would ~ you to do it/not to do it** ich würde dir zuraten/abraten; **to ~ sb against sth/doing sth** jdm von etw abraten/jdm abraten, etw zu tun; **what would you ~ me to do?** was *or* wozu würden Sie mir raten?
(b) *(Comm: inform)* verständigen, avisieren ◆ **to ~ sb of sth** jdn von etw in Kenntnis setzen; **our agent keeps us ~d of developments** unser Vertreter unterrichtet uns ständig über neue Entwicklungen.
2 *vi* **(a)** raten ◆ **I shall do as you ~** ich werde tun, was Sie mir raten; **his function is merely to ~** er hat nur beratende Funktion. **(b)** *(US)* **to ~ with sb** sich mit jdm beraten.

advisedly [əd'vaɪzɪdlɪ] *adv* richtig ◆ **and I use the word ~** ich verwende bewußt dieses Wort.

advisedness [əd'vaɪzɪdnɪs] *n* Klugheit, Ratsamkeit *f*.

advisement [əd'vaɪzmənt] *n* *(US)* **to keep sth under ~** etw im Auge behalten; **to take sth under ~** etw ins Auge fassen.

adviser [əd'vaɪzə^r] *n* Ratgeber(in *f*) *m*; *(professional)* Berater(in *f*) *m* ◆ **legal ~** Rechtsberater (in *f*) *m*; **spiritual ~** geistlicher Berater.

advising bank [əd'vaɪzɪŋ,bæŋk] *n (Fin)* avisierende Bank.

advisory [əd'vaɪzərɪ] *adj* beratend ◆ **to act in a purely ~ capacity** rein beratende Funktion haben.

advocacy ['ædvəkəsɪ] *n* Eintreten *nt* *(of* für), Fürsprache *f* *(of* für); *(of plan)* Befürwortung *f* ◆ **the skills of legal ~** juristische Wortgewandtheit.

advocate ['ædvəkɪt] **1** *n* **(a)** *(upholder: of cause etc)* Verfechter, Befürworter *m*. **(b)** *(esp Scot: Jur)* (Rechts)anwalt *m*/-anwältin *f*, Advokat(in *f*) *m (old, dial)*.
2 ['ædvəkeɪt] *vt* eintreten für; *plan etc* befürworten ◆ **those who ~ extending the licensing laws** die, die eine Verlängerung der Öffnungszeiten befürworten; **what course of action would you ~?** welche Maßnahmen würden Sie empfehlen?

advocator ['ædvəkeɪtə^r] *n see* **advocate 1**.

advt *abbr of* **advertisement**.

adz(e) [ædz] *n* Dechsel *f*.

A & E *abbr of* **accident and emergency**.

Aegean [iː'dʒiːən] *adj* ägäisch; *islands* in der Ägäis ◆ **the ~ (Sea)** die Ägäis, das Ägäische Meer.

aegis ['iːdʒɪs] *n* Ägide *f (geh)* ◆ **under the ~ of** unter der Ägide *(geh) or* Schirmherrschaft von.

aegrotat ['aɪgrəʊ,tæt] *n Examen, an dem der Prüfling aus Krankheitsgründen nicht teilnimmt, und das bei Vorlage eines ärztlichen Attestes für bestanden erklärt wird.*

Aeneas [ɪ'niːəs] *n* Äneas *m*.

Aeneid [ɪ'niːɪd] *n* Äneide *f*.

Aeolian [iː'əʊlɪən] *adj* äolisch.

aeon ['iːən] *n* Äon *m (geh)*, Ewigkeit *f* ◆ **through ~s of time** äonenlang *(geh)*.

aerate ['ɛəreɪt] *vt liquid* mit Kohlensäure anreichern; *blood* Sauerstoff zuführen (+*dat*); *soil* auflockern ◆ **~d water** kohlensaures Wasser.

aerial ['ɛərɪəl] **1** *n (esp Brit)* Antenne *f* ◆ **~ input** *(TV)* Antennenanschluß *m*.
2 *adj* Luft-.

aerial: ~ barrage *n (air to ground)* Bombardement *nt*; *(ground to air)* Flakfeuer *nt*; **~ cableway** *n* Seilbahn *f*; **~ camera** *n* Luftbildkamera *f*.

aerialist ['ɛərɪəlɪst] *n (US) (on trapeze)* Trapezkünstler(in *f*) *m*; *(on highwire)* Seiltänzer(in *f*) *m*.

aerial: ~ ladder *n* Drehleiter *f*; **~ map** *n* Luftbildkarte *f*; **~ navigation** *n* Luftfahrt *f*; **~ photograph** *n* Luftbild *nt*, Luftaufnahme *f*; **~ photography** *n* Luftaufnahmen *pl*; **~ railway** *n* Schwebebahn *f*; **~ reconnaissance** *n* Luftaufklärung *f*; **~ view** *n* Luftbild *nt*, Luftansicht *f*; **in order to obtain an ~ view of the site** um das Gelände von der Luft aus zu betrachten; **~ warfare** *n* Luftkrieg *m*.

aero- ['ɛərəʊ] *pref* aero- *(form)*, Luft-.

aerobatic ['ɛərəʊ'bætɪk] *adj display, skills* kunstfliegerisch, Kunstflug-.

aerobatics ['ɛərəʊ'bætɪks] *npl* Kunstfliegen *nt*, Aerobatik *f (form)*.

aerobics [ɛər'əʊbɪks] *n sing* Aerobic *nt*.

aerodrome ['ɛərədrəʊm] *n (Brit)* Flugplatz *m*, Aerodrom *nt (old)*.

aerodynamic ['ɛərəʊdaɪ'næmɪk] *adj* aerodynamisch.

aerodynamics ['ɛərəʊdaɪ'næmɪks] *n* **(a)** *sing (subject)* Aerodynamik *f*. **(b)** *pl (of plane etc)* Aerodynamik *f*.

aero-engine ['ɛərəʊ,endʒɪn] *n* Flugzeugmotor *m*.

aerofoil ['ɛərəʊfɔɪl] *n* Tragflügel *m*; *(on racing cars)* Spoiler *m*.

aerogramme ['ɛərəʊgræm] *n* Aerogramm *nt*, Luftpost(leicht)brief *m*.

aeromodelling ['ɛərəʊ'mɒdlɪŋ] *n* Modellflugzeugbau *m*.

aeronaut ['ɛərənɔːt] *n* Aeronaut(in *f*), Luftschiffer *m (old)*.

aeronautic(al) [,ɛərə'nɔːtɪk(əl)] *adj* aeronautisch, Luftfahrt- ◆ **~ engineering** Flugzeugbau *m*.

aeronautics [,ɛərə'nɔːtɪks] *n sing* Luftfahrt, Aeronautik *f*.

aeroplane ['ɛərəpleɪn] *n (Brit)* Flugzeug *nt*.

aerosol ['ɛərəsɒl] *n (can)* Spraydose *f*; *(mixture)* Aerosol *nt* ◆ **~ paint** Spray- *or* Sprühfarbe *f*; **~ spray** Aerosolspray *nt*.

aerospace *in cpds* Raumfahrt-; **~ industry** *n* Raumfahrtindustrie *f*; **~ research** *n* Raumforschung *f*.

Aertex ® ['ɛərteks] *n Baumwolltrikotstoff mit Lochmuster.*

Aeschylus ['iːskələs] *n* Aischylos, Äschylus *m*.

Aesop ['iːsɒp] *n* Äsop *m* ◆ **~'s fables** die Äsopischen Fabeln.

aesthete, *(US)* **esthete** ['iːsθiːt] *n* Ästhet(in *f*) *m*.

aesthetic(al), *(US)* **esthetic(al)** [iːs'θetɪk(əl)] *adj* ästhetisch ◆ **an ~ discussion/argument** eine Diskussion über Ästhetik/ein Argument der Ästhetik.

aesthetically, *(US)* **esthetically** [iːs'θetɪkəlɪ] *adv* in ästhetischer Hinsicht ◆ **~ decorated** ästhetisch schön dekoriert; **~ pleasing** ästhetisch schön.

aestheticism, *(US)* **estheticism** [iːs'θetɪsɪzəm] *n* Ästhetizismus *m*.

aesthetics, *(US)* **esthetics** [iːs'θetɪks] *n sing* Ästhetik *f*.

aestival, *(US)* **estival** [iː'staɪvəl] *adj (form)* sommerlich, Sommer-.

aestivate, *(US)* **estivate** ['iːstɪveɪt] *vi (form) (animals)* Sommerschlaf halten; *(person)* den Sommer verbringen.

aetiological, *(US)* **etiological** [,iːtɪə'lɒdʒɪkəl] *adj (Med, fig)* ätiologisch.

aetiology, *(US)* **etiology** [,iːtɪ'ɒlədʒɪ] *n (Med, fig)* Ätiologie *f*.

afar [ə'fɑː^r] *adv (liter)* weit ◆ **from ~** aus der Ferne, von weit her.

affability [,æfə'bɪlɪtɪ] *n* Umgänglichkeit, Freundlichkeit *f*.

affable *adj*, **-bly** *adv* ['æfəbl, -ɪ] umgänglich, freundlich.

affair [ə'fɛə^r] *n* **(a)** *(event, concern, matter, business)* Sache, Angelegenheit *f* ◆ **it was an odd ~ altogether, that investigation** die Untersuchung war schon eine seltsame Sache *or* Angelegenheit; **a scandalous ~** ein Skandal *m*; **a novel entitled "The ~ of the golden glove"** ein Roman mit dem Titel „Der goldene Handschuh" *or* „Die Affäre mit dem goldenen Handschuh"; **the Watergate/Profumo ~** die Watergate-/Profumo-Affäre; **the state of ~s with the economy** die Lage der Wirtschaft; **in the present state of ~s** bei *or* in der gegenwärtigen Lage *or* Situation, beim gegenwärtigen Stand der Dinge; **a state of ~s I don't approve of** ein Zustand, den ich nicht billige; **what's the state of ~s with your forthcoming marriage?** wie steht's eigentlich mit deiner geplanten Hochzeit?; **there's a fine state of ~s!** das sind ja schöne Zustände!; **your private ~s don't concern me** deine Privatangelegenheiten sind mir egal; **financial ~s have never interested me** Finanzfragen haben mich nie interessiert; **I never interfere with his business ~s** ich mische mich nie in seine geschäftlichen Angelegenheiten ein; **man of ~s** *(liter, form)* Geschäftsmann *m*; **~s of state** Staatsangelegenheiten *pl*; **~s of the heart** Herzensangelegenheiten *pl*; **it's not your ~ what I do in the evenings** was ich abends tue, geht dich nichts an; **that's my/his ~!** das ist meine/seine Sache!; *see also* **current, foreign ~s**.
(b) *(love ~)* Verhältnis *nt*, Affäre *f (dated)* ◆ **to have an ~ with sb** ein Verhältnis mit jdm haben.
(c) *(duel)* **~ of honour** Ehrenhandel *m*.
(d) *(inf: object, thing)* Ding *nt* ◆ **what's this funny aerial ~?** was soll dieses komische Antennendings? *(inf)*; **the committee was an odd ~** das Komitee war eine seltsame Sache.

affect[1] [ə'fekt] *vt* **(a)** *(have effect on)* sich auswirken auf (+*acc*); *decision, sb's life also* beeinflussen; *(detrimentally) nerves, material also* angreifen; *health, person* schaden (+*dat*).
(b) *(concern)* betreffen.
(c) *(emotionally, move)* berühren, treffen ◆ **he was obviously ~ed by the news** er war von der Nachricht offensichtlich sehr betroffen, die Nachricht hatte ihn sichtlich mitgenommen.
(d) *(diseases: attack)* befallen.

affect[2] *vt* **(a)** *(feign) indifference* vortäuschen, vorgeben. **(b)** *(liter: like to use etc) clothes, colours* eine Vorliebe *or* Schwäche haben für; *accent* sich befleißigen (+*gen*) *(geh)*.

affectation [,æfek'teɪʃən] *n* **(a)** *(pretence)* Vortäuschung, Vorgabe *f*. **(b)** *(artificiality)* Affektiertheit *f no pl* ◆ **her ~s annoy me** ihr affektiertes Benehmen ärgert mich; **an ~** eine affektierte Angewohnheit.

affected [ə'fektɪd] *adj person, clothes* affektiert; *behaviour, style, accent also* gekünstelt; *behaviour also* geziert.

affectedly [ə'fektɪdlɪ] *adv see adj*.

affecting [ə'fektɪŋ] *adj* rührend.

affection [ə'fekʃən] *n* **(a)** *(fondness)* Zuneigung *f no pl (for, towards* zu) ◆ **to win sb's ~s** *(dated, hum)* jds Zuneigung gewinnen; **I have** *or* **feel a great ~ for her** ich mag sie sehr gerne; **don't you even feel any ~ for her at all?** fühlst du denn gar nichts für sie?; **you could show a little more ~ towards me** du könntest mir gegenüber etwas mehr Gefühl zeigen; **children who lacked ~** Kinder, denen die Liebe fehlte; **everybody needs a little ~** jeder braucht ein

➤ LANGUAGE IN USE: **advice: a** → 2.1, 2.2 **advisable** → 2.2 **advise: 1a** → 1.1, 2.1, 2.2, 2.3

bißchen Liebe; **he has a special place in her ~s** er nimmt einen besonderen Platz in ihrem Herzen ein; **display of ~** Ausdruck von Zärtlichkeit.
(b) *(form: Med)* Erkrankung, Affektion *(spec) f.*

affectionate [ə'fekʃənɪt] *adj* liebevoll, zärtlich ◆ **your ~ daughter** *(letter-ending)* Deine Dich liebende Tochter; **to feel ~ towards sb** jdm sehr zugetan sein, jdn sehr gern haben.

affectionately [ə'fekʃənɪtlɪ] *adv* liebevoll, zärtlich ◆ **yours ~, Wendy** *(letter-ending)* in Liebe, Deine Wendy.

affective [ə'fektɪv] *adj (Psych)* affektiv.

affidavit [,æfɪ'deɪvɪt] *n (Jur)* eidesstattliche Erklärung; *(to guarantee support of immigrant)* Affidavit *nt* ◆ **to swear an ~ (to the effect that)** eine eidesstattliche Erklärung abgeben(, daß).

affiliate [ə'fɪlɪeɪt] [1] *vt* angliedern *(to dat)* ◆ **the two banks are ~d** die zwei Banken sind aneinander angeschlossen; **~d** angeschlossen, Schwester-.
[2] *vi* sich angliedern *(with* an *+acc)*.
[3] *n* Schwestergesellschaft *f*; *(union)* angegliederte Gewerkschaft.

affiliation [ə,fɪlɪ'eɪʃən] *n* **(a)** Angliederung *f (to, with* an *+acc)*; *(state)* Verbund *m* ◆ **what are his political ~s?** was ist seine politische Zugehörigkeit?
(b) *(Brit Jur)* **~ order** Verurteilung *f* zur Leistung des Regelunterhalts; **~ proceedings** gerichtliche Feststellung der Vaterschaft, Vaterschaftsklage *f.*

affinity [ə'fɪnɪtɪ] *n* **(a)** *(liking)* Neigung *f (for, to* zu); *(for person)* Verbundenheit *f (for, to* mit). **(b)** *(resemblance, connection)* Verwandtschaft, Affinität *(form) f.* **(c)** *(Chem)* Affinität *f.*

affirm [ə'fɜːm] [1] *vt* **(a)** versichern; *(very forcefully)* beteuern ◆ **he ~ed his innocence** er versicherte, daß er unschuldig sei; er beteuerte seine Unschuld. **(b)** *(ratify)* bestätigen.
[2] *vi (Jur)* eidesstattlich *or* an Eidesstatt versichern *or* erklären.

affirmation [,æfə'meɪʃən] *n* **(a)** *see vt (a)* Versicherung *f*; Beteuerung *f.* **(b)** *(Jur)* eidesstattliche Versicherung *or* Erklärung.

affirmative [ə'fɜːmətɪv] [1] *n (Gram)* Bejahung *f*; *(sentence)* bejahender *or* positiver Satz ◆ **to answer in the ~** bejahend *or* mit „ja" antworten; **put these sentences into the ~** drücken Sie diese Sätze bejahend aus.
[2] *adj* bejahend, positiv; *(Gram)* affirmativ *(form)*, bejahend ◆ **the answer is ~** die Antwort ist bejahend *or* „ja".
[3] *interj* richtig.

affirmatively [ə'fɜːmətɪvlɪ] *adv* bejahend, positiv.

affix¹ [ə'fɪks] *vt* anbringen *(to* auf *+dat)*; *seal* setzen *(to* auf *+acc)*; *signature* setzen *(to* unter *+acc)*.

affix² ['æfɪks] *n (Gram)* Affix *nt.*

afflatus [ə'fleɪtəs] *n* Inspiration *f.*

afflict [ə'flɪkt] *vt* plagen, zusetzen *(+dat)*; *(emotionally, mentally also)* belasten; *(troubles, inflation, injuries)* heimsuchen ◆ **to be ~ed by a disease** an einer Krankheit leiden; **~ed with gout** von (der) Gicht geplagt; **to be ~ed with a tiresome child** mit einem anstrengenden Kind gestraft *or* geschlagen sein; **to be ~ed by doubts** von Zweifeln gequält werden; **the ~ed** die Leidenden *pl.*

affliction [ə'flɪkʃən] *n* **(a)** *(distress)* Not, Bedrängnis *f*; *(pain)* Leiden, Schmerzen *pl.*
(b) *(cause of suffering) (blindness etc)* Gebrechen *nt*; *(illness)* Beschwerde *f*; *(worry)* Sorge *f* ◆ **the ~s of old age** Altersbeschwerden *pl*; **a delinquent son was not the least of his ~s** er war nicht zuletzt mit einem kriminellen Sohn geschlagen; **the government is itself the greatest ~ the nation has** die Regierung ist selbst die größte Last für das Volk.

affluence ['æfluəns] *n* Reichtum, Wohlstand *m* ◆ **to live in ~** im Wohlstand leben; **to rise to ~** zu großem Wohlstand kommen.

affluent¹ ['æfluənt] *adj* reich, wohlhabend ◆ **the ~ society** die Wohlstandsgesellschaft; **you ~ so-and-so!** du reicher Sack! *(inf)*, du Großkapitalist!

affluent² *n (Geog spec)* Nebenfluß *m.*

afford [ə'fɔːd] *vt* **(a)** sich *(dat)* leisten ◆ **I can't ~ to buy both of them** ich kann es mir nicht leisten, beide zu kaufen; **he can't ~ to make a mistake** er kann es sich nicht leisten, einen Fehler zu machen; **you can't ~ to miss the chance** Sie können es sich nicht leisten, die Gelegenheit zu verpassen; **I can't ~ the time (to do it)** ich habe einfach nicht die Zeit(, das zu tun); **an offer you can't ~ to miss** ein Angebot, das Sie sich *(dat)* nicht entgehen lassen können; **can you ~ to go? — I can't ~ not to!** können Sie gehen? — ich kann gar nicht anders.
(b) *(liter: provide) (sb sth* jdm etw) gewähren, bieten; *shade also* spenden; *pleasure* bereiten.

afforest [æ'fɒrɪst] *vt* aufforsten.

afforestation [æ,fɒrɪs'teɪʃən] *n* Aufforstung *f.*

affranchise [æ'frænʧaɪz] *vt* befreien.

affray [ə'freɪ] *n (esp Jur)* Schlägerei *f.*

affright [ə'fraɪt] *vt (old, liter)* erschrecken.

affront [ə'frʌnt] [1] *vt* beleidigen.
[2] *n* Beleidigung *f (to sb* jds, *to sth* für etw), Affront *m (to* gegen) ◆ **such poverty is an ~ to our national pride** solche Armut verletzt unseren Nationalstolz.

Afghan ['æfgæn] [1] *n* **(a)** Afghane *m*, Afghanin *f.* **(b)** *(language)* Afghanisch *nt.* **(c)** *(also* **~ hound)** Afghane *m*, afghanischer Windhund. **(d) a~** *(coat)* Afghan *m.*
[2] *adj* afghanisch.

Afghanistan [æf'gænɪstæn] *n* Afghanistan *nt.*

aficionado [ə,fɪʃjə'nɑːdəʊ] *n, pl* **-s** Liebhaber(in *f*) *m.*

afield [ə'fiːld] *adv* **countries further ~** weiter entfernte Länder; **too/very far ~** zu/sehr weit weg *or* entfernt; **to venture further ~** *(lit, fig)* sich etwas weiter (vor)wagen; **to explore farther ~** die weitere Umgebung erforschen; **to go farther ~ for help** *(fig)* in der weiteren Umgebung Hilfe suchen; **his studies took him farther ~ into new areas of knowledge** seine Forschungen führten ihn immer weiter in neue Wissensbereiche.

afire [ə'faɪəʳ] *adj pred, adv* in Brand ◆ **to set sth ~** etw in Brand stecken, etw anzünden; *(fig)* etw entzünden; **~ with anger** wutentbrannt, flammend vor Zorn *(geh)*; **this set his imagination ~** das entzündete seine Phantasie.

aflame [ə'fleɪm] *adj pred, adv* in Flammen ◆ **to set sth ~** etw in Brand stecken, etw anzünden; **to be ~** in Flammen stehen; **to be ~ with colour** in roter Glut leuchten; **~ with anger/passion** flammend *or* glühend vor Zorn/ Leidenschaft.

AFL-CIO *abbr of* **American Federation of Labor and Congress of Industrial Organizations** *amerikanischer Gewerkschafts-Dachverband.*

afloat [ə'fləʊt] *adj pred, adv* **(a)** *(Naut)* **to be ~** schwimmen; **to stay ~** sich über Wasser halten; *(thing)* schwimmen, nicht untergehen; **to set a ship ~** ein Schiff zu Wasser lassen; **at last we were ~ again** endlich waren wir wieder flott; **cargo ~** schwimmende Ladung; **the largest navy ~** die größte Flotte auf See; **service ~** Dienst *m* auf See; **to serve ~** auf See dienen.
(b) *(awash)* überschwemmt, unter Wasser ◆ **to be ~** unter Wasser stehen, überschwemmt sein.
(c) *(fig)* **to get a business ~** ein Geschäft auf die Beine stellen; **those who stayed ~ during the slump** die, die sich auch während der Krise über Wasser gehalten haben.
(d) *(fig: rumour etc)* **there is a rumour ~ that ...** es geht das Gerücht um, daß ...

aflutter [ə'flʌtə] *adj pred, adv* aufgeregt ◆ **to be ~ with anticipation** vor Erwartung zittern; **her heart was/nerves were all ~** ihr Herz flatterte/sie war fürchterlich aufgeregt.

afoot [ə'fʊt] *adv* im Gange ◆ **there is something ~** da ist etwas im Gange; **what's ~?** was geht hier vor?

afore [ə'fɔː] *(obs, dial)* [1] *conj* bevor.
[2] *adv* zuvor.

aforementioned [ə,fɔː'menʃənd], **aforesaid** [ə,fɔː'sed] *adj attr (form)* obengenannt, obenerwähnt.

aforethought [ə'fɔːθɔːt] *adj see* **malice.**

a fortiori [eɪ,fɔːtɪ'ɔːraɪ] *adv* aufgrund des Vorhergehenden.

afoul [ə'faʊl] *adj pred, adv lines, ropes* verheddert, verwirrt ◆ **to run ~ of the law** mit dem Gesetz in Konflikt geraten.

▼ **afraid** [ə'freɪd] *adj pred* **(a)** *(frightened)* **to be ~ (of sb/sth)** (vor jdm/etw) Angst haben, sich (vor jdm/etw) fürchten; **don't be ~!** keine Angst!; **it's quite safe, there's nothing to be ~ of** es ist ganz sicher, Sie brauchen keine Angst zu haben; **go and talk to him then, there's nothing to be ~ of** geh und sprich mit ihm, da ist doch nichts dabei; **I am ~ of hurting him** *or* **that I might hurt him** ich fürchte, ihm weh zu tun *or* ich könnte ihm weh tun; **I am ~ he will** *or* **might hurt me, I am ~ lest he (might) hurt me** *(liter)* ich fürchte, er könnte mir weh tun; **to make sb ~** jdm Angst machen *or* einjagen, jdn ängstigen; **I am ~ to leave her alone** ich habe Angst davor, sie allein zu lassen; **I was ~ of not being precise enough** ich fürchtete, daß ich mich nicht genau genug ausdrückte; **I was ~ of waking the children** ich wollte die Kinder nicht wecken; **to be ~ of work** arbeitsscheu sein; **he's not ~ of hard work** er scheut schwere Arbeit nicht, er hat keine Angst vor schwerer Arbeit; **he's not ~ to say what he thinks** er scheut sich nicht, zu sagen, was er denkt; **that's what I was ~ of, I was ~ that would happen** das habe ich befürchtet; **go on, do it, what are you ~ of?** tu's doch, wovor hast du denn Angst?; **I was ~ you'd ask that** ich habe diese Frage befürchtet.
▼ **(b)** *(expressing polite regret)* **I'm ~ I can't do it** leider kann ich es nicht machen; **there's nothing I can do, I'm ~** ich kann da leider gar nichts machen; **I'm ~ to say that ...** ich muß Ihnen leider sagen, daß ...; **I'm ~ you'll have to wait** Sie müssen leider warten; **are you going? — I'm ~ not/I'm ~ so** gehst du? — leider nicht/ja, leider; **well, I'm ~ you're wrong** so leid es mir tut, aber Sie haben unrecht; **can I go now? — no, I'm ~ you can't** kann ich jetzt gehen? — nein, tut mir leid, noch nicht.

afresh [ə'freʃ] *adv* noch einmal von vorn *or* neuem.

Africa ['æfrɪkə] *n* Afrika *nt.*

African ['æfrɪkən] [1] *n* Afrikaner(in *f*) *m.*
[2] *adj* afrikanisch ◆ **~ violet** Usambara-Veilchen *nt.*

African-American [1] *adj* afroamerikanisch.
[2] *n* Afroamerikaner(in *f*) *m.*

Afrika(a)ner [,æfrɪ'kɑːnəʳ] *n* Afrika(a)nder(in *f*) *m.*

Afrikaans [,æfrɪ'kɑːns] *n* Afrikaans *nt.*

Afro ['æfrəʊ] [1] *pref* afro-.
[2] *n (hairstyle)* Afro-Frisur *f*, Afro-Look *m.*

Afro-: ~-American [1] *adj* afro-amerikanisch; [2] *n* Afro-Amerikaner(in *f*) *m*; **~-Asian** [1] *adj* afro-asiatisch; [2] *n* Asiat(in *f*) *m* in Afrika; **~-Caribbean** [1] *adj* afrokaribisch; [2] *n* Afrokaribe *m*, Afrokaribin *f.*

aft [ɑːft] *(Naut)* [1] *adv sit* achtern; *go* nach achtern.
[2] *adj* Achter-, achter.

after¹ ['ɑːftəʳ] *adj attr (Naut)* Achter-.

after² [1] *prep* **(a)** *(time)* nach *(+dat)* ◆ **~ dinner** nach dem Essen; **~ that** danach; **the day ~ tomorrow** übermorgen; **the week ~ next** die übernächste Woche; **I'll be back the week ~ next** ich bin übernächste Woche wieder da; **it was ~ two o'clock** es war nach zwei; **ten ~ eight** *(US)* zehn nach acht.
(b) *(order)* nach *(+dat)*, hinter *(+dat)*; *(in priorities etc)* nach *(+dat)* ◆ **the noun comes ~ the verb** das Substantiv steht nach *or* hinter dem Verb; **I would put**

➤ LANGUAGE IN USE: **afraid: a → 16.2 b → 6.2, 12.3, 21.4, 25.2**

Keats ~ Shelley für mich rangiert Keats unter Shelley; **~ you** nach Ihnen; **I was ~ him** (*in queue etc*) ich war nach ihm dran; **~ you with the salt** kann ich das Salz nach dir haben?
(c) (*place*) hinter (+*dat*) ◆ **he shut the door ~ him** er machte die Tür hinter ihm zu; **to shout ~ sb** hinter jdm herrufen *or* -schreien; **to shout sth ~ sb** jdm etw nachrufen.
(d) (*as a result of*) nach (+*dat*) ◆ **~ what has happened** nach allem, was geschehen ist; **~ this you might believe me** jetzt wirst du mir vielleicht endlich glauben.
(e) (*in spite of*) **to do sth ~ all** etw schließlich doch tun; **~ all our efforts!** und das, nachdem *or* wo (*inf*) wir uns soviel Mühe gegeben haben!; **~ all I've done for you!** und das nach allem, was ich für dich getan habe!; **~ all, he is your brother** er ist immerhin *or* schließlich dein Bruder; **... ~ I had warned him ...** und das, nachdem ich ihn gewarnt hatte.
(f) (*succession*) nach (+*dat*) ◆ **you tell me lie ~ lie** du erzählst mir eine Lüge nach der anderen, du belügst mich am laufenden Band; **it's just one complaint ~ the other** es kommen Beschwerden über Beschwerden *or* am laufenden Band Beschwerden; **one ~ the other** eine(r, s) nach der/dem anderen; **one ~ the other she rejected all the offers** sie schlug ein Angebot nach dem anderen aus; **day ~ day** Tag für *or* um Tag; **we marched on mile ~ mile** wir marschierten Meile um *or* für Meile weiter; **before us lay mile ~ mile of barren desert** vor uns erstreckte sich meilenweit trostlose Wüste.
(g) (*manner: according to*) nach (+*dat*) ◆ **~ El Greco** in der Art von El Greco, nach El Greco; **she takes ~ her mother** sie schlägt ihrer Mutter nach; *see* **name**.
(h) (*pursuit, inquiry*) **to be ~ sb/sth** hinter jdm/etw hersein; **she asked** *or* **inquired ~ you** sie hat sich nach dir erkundigt; **what are you ~?** was willst du?; (*looking for*) was suchst du?; **he's just ~ a free meal/a bit of excitement** er ist nur auf ein kostenloses Essen/ein bißchen Abwechslung aus; *see vbs*.
2 *adv* (*time, order*) danach; (*place, pursuit*) hinterher ◆ **for years/weeks ~** noch Jahre/Wochen *or* jahrelang/wochenlang danach; **the year/week ~** das Jahr/die Woche danach *or* darauf; **I'll be back sometime the year ~** ich komme irgendwann im Jahr danach *or* im darauffolgenden Jahr wieder; **soon ~** kurz danach *or* darauf; **what comes ~?** was kommt danach *or* nachher?; **the car drove off with the dog running ~** das Auto fuhr los, und der Hund rannte hinterher.
3 *conj* nachdem ◆ **~ he had closed the door he began to speak** nachdem er die Tür geschlossen hatte, begann er zu sprechen; **what will you do ~ he's gone?** was machst du, wenn er weg ist?; **~ finishing it I will/I went ...** wenn ich das fertig habe, werde ich .../als ich das fertig hatte, ging ich ...; **~ arriving they went ...** nachdem sie angekommen waren, gingen sie ...
4 *adj* **in ~ years** in späteren Jahren.
5 *n* **~s** *pl* (*Brit inf*) Nachtisch *m* ◆ **what's for ~s?** was gibt's hinterher *or* als *or* zum Nachtisch?

after: ~birth *n* Nachgeburt *f*; **~burner** *n* Nachbrenner *m*; **~burning** *n* Nachverbrennung *f*; **~-care** *n* (*of convalescent*) Nachbehandlung *f*; (*of ex-prisoner*) Resozialisierungshilfe *f*; **~deck** *n* Achterdeck *nt*; **~-dinner** *adj speech, speaker* Tisch-; *walk, rest etc* Verdauungs-; **~-effect** *n* (*of illness, Psych*) Nachwirkung *f*; (*of events etc also*) Folge *f*; **~glow** *n* (*of sun*) Abendrot, Abendleuchten *nt*; (*fig*) angenehme Erinnerung; **~-image** *n* (*Psych*) Nachempfindung *f*, Nachbild *nt*; **~life** *n* Leben *nt* nach dem Tode; **~-lunch** *adj* **to have an ~-lunch nap** ein Mittagsschläfchen halten; **~math** *n* Nachwirkungen *pl*; **in the ~math of sth** nach etw; **the country was still suffering the ~math of war** das Land litt immer noch an den Folgen *or* Auswirkungen des Krieges; **~most** *adj* (*Naut*) Achter-, Heck-.

afternoon ['ɑːftə'nuːn] **1** *n* Nachmittag *m* ◆ **in the ~, ~s** (*esp US*) am Nachmittag, nachmittags; **at three o'clock in the ~** (um) drei Uhr nachmittags; **on Sunday ~** (am) Sonntag nachmittag; **on Sunday ~s** Sonntag *or* sonntags nachmittags, am Sonntagnachmittag; **on the ~ of December 2nd** am Nachmittag des 2. Dezember, am 2. Dezember nachmittags; **this/tomorrow/yesterday ~** heute/morgen/gestern nachmittag; **good ~!** Guten Tag!; **~!** Tag! (*inf*).
2 *adj attr* Nachmittags- ◆ **~ tea** Tee *m*.

after: ~-pains *npl* Nachwehen *pl*; **~-sales service** *n* Kundendienst *m*; **~ shave (lotion)** *n* After-shave, Rasierwasser *nt*; **~shock** *n* (*of earthquake*) Nachbeben *nt*; **~-tax** *adj profits etc* nach Steuern, nach Steuerabzug; **~thought** *n* nachträgliche *or* zusätzliche Idee; **if you have any ~thoughts about ...** wenn Ihnen noch irgend etwas zu ... einfällt; **he added as an ~thought** fügte er hinzu, schickte er nach; **I just mentioned that as an ~thought** das fiel mir noch dazu *or* nachträglich ein; **the window was added as an ~thought** das Fenster kam erst später dazu.

afterwards ['ɑːftəwədz] *adv* nachher; (*after that, after some event etc*) danach ◆ **and ~ we could go to a disco** und anschließend *or* nachher *or* danach gehen wir in eine Disko; **can I have mine now? — no, ~** kann ich meins jetzt haben? — nein, nachher; **this was added ~** das kam nachträglich dazu.

afterword ['ɑːftəˌwɜːd] *n* Nachwort *nt*.

afterworld ['ɑːftəˌwɜːld] *n* Jenseits *nt*.

again [ə'gen] *adv* **(a)** wieder ◆ **~ and ~, time and ~** immer wieder; **to do sth ~** etw noch (ein)mal tun; **not to do sth ~** etw nicht wieder tun; **I'll ring ~ tomorrow** ich rufe morgen noch einmal an; **never** *or* **not ever ~** nie wieder; **if that happens ~** wenn das noch einmal passiert; **all over ~** noch (ein)mal von vorn; **what's his name ~?** wie heißt er noch gleich?; **to begin ~** von neuem *or* noch einmal anfangen; **~!/not ~!** schon wieder!; **not mince ~!** schon wieder Hackfleisch!; **it's me ~** (*arriving*) da bin ich wieder; (*phoning*) ich bin's noch (ein)mal; (*my fault*) wieder mal ich; **not you ~!** du schon wieder!?; **he was soon well ~** er war bald wieder gesund; **and these are different ~** und diese sind wieder anders; **here we are ~!** da wären wir wieder!; (*finding another example etc*) oh, schon wieder!; **~ we find that ...** und wieder einmal *or* wiederum stellen wir fest, daß ...
(b) (*in quantity*) **as much ~** doppelt soviel, noch (ein)mal soviel; **he's as old ~ as Mary** er ist doppelt so alt wie Mary.
(c) (*on the other hand*) wiederum; (*besides, moreover*) außerdem ◆ **but then ~, it may not be true** vielleicht ist es auch gar nicht wahr.

▼ **against** [ə'genst] *prep* **(a)** (*opposition, protest*) gegen (+*acc*) ◆ **he's ~ her going** er ist dagegen, daß sie geht; **everybody's ~ me!** alle sind gegen mich!; **to have something ~ sb/sth** etwas gegen jdn/etw haben; **~ that you have to consider ...** Sie müssen aber auch bedenken ...; **~ my will, I decided ...** wider Willen habe ich beschlossen ...; **~ their wish** entgegen ihrem Wunsch; **to fight ~ sb** gegen *or* wider (*liter*) jdn kämpfen.
(b) (*indicating impact, support, proximity*) an (+*acc*), gegen (+*acc*) ◆ **to hit one's head ~ the mantelpiece** mit dem Kopf gegen *or* an das Kaminsims stoßen; **push all the chairs right back ~ the wall** stellen Sie alle Stühle direkt an die Wand.
(c) (*in the opposite direction to*) gegen (+*acc*).
(d) (*in front of, in juxtaposition to*) gegen (+*acc*) ◆ **~ the light** gegen das Licht.
(e) (*in preparation for*) *sb's arrival, departure, one's old age* für (+*acc*); *misfortune, bad weather etc* im Hinblick auf (+*acc*) ◆ **~ the possibility of a bad winter** für den Fall, daß es einen schlechten Winter gibt.
(f) (*compared with*) **(as) ~** gegenüber (+*dat*); **she had three prizes (as) ~ his six** sie hatte drei Preise, er hingegen sechs; **the advantages of flying (as) ~ going by boat** die Vorteile von Flugreisen gegenüber Schiffsreisen; **~ the German mark** gegenüber der D-Mark.
(g) (*Fin: in return for*) gegen ◆ **the visa will be issued ~ payment of ...** das Visum wird gegen Zahlung von ... ausgestellt; **to draw money ~ security** gegen Sicherheit(sleistung) *or* Deckung Geld abheben.

agape [ə'geɪp] *adj pred person* mit (vor Staunen) offenem Mund, baß erstaunt (*geh*).

agaric ['ægərɪk] *n* Blätterpilz *m*.

agate ['ægət] *n* Achat *m*.

agave [ə'geɪvɪ] *n* Agave *f*.

age [eɪdʒ] **1** *n* **(a)** (*of person, star, building etc*) Alter *nt* ◆ **what is her ~, what ~ is she?** wie alt ist sie?; **he is ten years of ~** er ist zehn Jahre alt; **trees of such great ~** Bäume von so hohem Alter; **~ doesn't matter** das Alter spielt keine Rolle; **at the ~ of 15** im Alter von 15 Jahren, mit 15 Jahren; **at your ~** in deinem Alter; **when I was your ~** als ich in deinem Alter war, als ich so alt war wie du; **when you're my ~** wenn du erst in mein Alter kommst, wenn du erst mal so alt bist wie ich; **I have a daughter your ~** ich habe eine Tochter in Ihrem Alter; **but he's twice your ~** aber er ist ja doppelt so alt wie du; **we're of an ~** wir sind gleichaltrig; **he is now of an ~ to understand these things** er ist jetzt alt genug, um das zu verstehen; **over ~** zu alt; **she doesn't look her ~** man sieht ihr ihr Alter nicht an, sie sieht jünger aus, als sie ist; **be** *or* **act your ~!** sei nicht kindisch!
(b) (*length of life*) (*of star, neutron etc*) Lebensdauer *f*; (*of human, animal, object also*) Lebenserwartung *f* ◆ **the ~ of a star can be millions of years** ein Stern kann viele Millionen Jahre existieren.
(c) (*Jur*) **to be of ~** volljährig *or* mündig sein; **to come of ~** volljährig *or* mündig werden, die Volljährigkeit erlangen; (*fig*) den Kinderschuhen entwachsen; **under ~** minderjährig, unmündig; **~ of consent** Ehemündigkeitsalter *nt*; **intercourse with girls under the ~ of consent** Unzucht *f* mit Minderjährigen.
(d) (*old ~*) Alter *nt* ◆ **bent with ~** vom Alter gebeugt; **~ before beauty** (*hum*) Alter vor Schönheit.
(e) (*period, epoch*) Zeit(alter *nt*) *f* ◆ **the atomic ~** das Atomzeitalter; **the ~ of technology** das technologische Zeitalter; **in this ~ of inflation** in dieser inflationären Zeit; **the Stone ~** die Steinzeit; **the Edwardian ~** die Zeit *or* Ära Edwards VII; **the ~ of Socrates** das Zeitalter Sokrates; **down the ~s** durch alle Zeiten; **what will future ~s think of us?** was werden kommende Generationen von uns halten?
(f) (*inf: long time*) **~s, an ~** eine Ewigkeit, Ewigkeiten *pl*, ewig (lang) (*all inf*); **I haven't seen him for ~s** *or* **for an ~** ich habe ihn eine Ewigkeit *or* Ewigkeiten *or* ewig (lang) nicht gesehen (*inf*); **it's been ~s since we met** wir haben uns ja eine Ewigkeit *etc* nicht mehr gesehen (*inf*); **to take ~s** eine Ewigkeit dauern (*inf*); (*person*) ewig brauchen (*inf*).
2 *vi* alt werden, altern; (*wine, cheese*) reifen ◆ **you have ~d** du bist alt geworden; **she seems to have ~d ten years** sie scheint um zehn Jahre gealtert zu sein.
3 *vt* **(a)** (*dress, hairstyle etc*) alt machen; (*worry etc*) alt werden lassen, altern lassen. **(b)** *wine, cheese* lagern, reifen lassen.

aged [eɪdʒd] **1** *adj* **(a)** im Alter von, ... Jahre alt, -jährig ◆ **a boy ~ ten** ein zehnjähriger Junge. **(b)** ['eɪdʒɪd] *person* bejahrt, betagt; *animal, car, building etc* alt, betagt (*hum*).
2 ['eɪdʒɪd] *npl* **the ~** die alten Menschen, die Alten *pl*.

age: ~ difference *or* **gap** *n* Altersunterschied *m*; **~-group** *n* Altersgruppe *f*; **the forty to fifty ~-group** die (Alters)gruppe der Vierzig- bis Fünfzigjährigen.

ag(e)ing ['eɪdʒɪŋ] **1** *adj person* alternd *attr*; *animal, thing* älter werdend *attr*.
2 *n* Altern *nt*.

ageism ['eɪdʒɪzəm] *n* Altersdiskriminierung *f*, Seniorenfeindlichkeit *f*.

ageist ['eɪdʒɪst] *adj* altersdiskriminierend, seniorenfeindlich.

age: ~less *adj* zeitlos; **she seems to be one of those ~less people** sie scheint

➤ LANGUAGE IN USE: **against: a → 26.1**

zu den Menschen zu gehören, die nie alt werden; ~ **limit** *n* Altersgrenze *f*; ~**-long** *adj* sehr lange, ewig (*inf*).

agency ['eɪdʒənsɪ] *n* **(a)** (*Comm*) Agentur *f*; (*subsidiary of a company*) Geschäftsstelle *f* ◆ **translation/tourist ~** Übersetzungs-/Reisebüro *nt*; **this garage is** *or* **has the Citroën ~** dies ist eine Citroën-Vertragswerkstätte, diese Werkstatt ist eine *or* hat die Citroën-Vertretung.
(b) (*instrumentality*) **through** *or* **by the ~ of friends** durch die Vermittlung von Freunden, durch Freunde; **through the ~ of water** mit Hilfe von Wasser, durch Wasser; **to put sth down to the ~ of Providence** etw der Vorsehung zuschreiben.

agenda [ə'dʒendə] *n* Tagesordnung *f* ◆ **a full ~** (*lit*) eine umfangreiche Tagesordnung; (*fig*) ein volles Programm; **on the ~** auf dem Programm.

agent ['eɪdʒənt] *n* **(a)** (*Comm*) (*person*) Vertreter(in *f*) *m*; (*organization*) Vertretung *f* ◆ **who is the ~ for this car in Scotland?** wer hat die schottische Vertretung für dieses Auto?
(b) (*literary, press ~ etc*) Agent(in *f*) *m*; (*Pol*) Wahlkampfleiter(in *f*) *m* ◆ **business ~** Agent(in *f*) *m*.
(c) (*secret ~, FBI etc*) Agent(in *f*) *m* ◆ **~ extraordinary** Spezialagent(in *f*) *m*.
(d) (*person having power to act*) **man must be regarded as a moral ~** der Mensch muß als moralisch verantwortlich handelndes Wesen angesehen werden; **determinism states that we are not free ~s** der Determinismus behauptet, daß wir nicht frei entscheiden können; **you're a free ~, do what you want** du bist dein eigener Herr, tu was du willst.
(e) (*means by which sth is achieved*) Mittel *nt* ◆ **she became the unwitting ~ of his wicked plot** unwissentlich wurde sie zum Werkzeug für seinen niederträchtigen Plan; **bees as ~s of pollination play a very important role in nature** durch ihre Funktion bei der Bestäubung spielen Bienen eine wichtige Rolle in der Natur.
(f) (*Chem*) **cleansing ~** Reinigungsmittel *nt*; **special protective ~** Spezialschutzmittel *nt*.

agent provocateur ['æʒɑ̃ːŋprəˌvɒkə'tɜːʳ] *n, pl* **-s -s** Agent provocateur, Lockspitzel *m*.

age: ~**-old** *adj* uralt; ~ **range** *n* Altersgruppe *f*.

agglomerate [ə'glɒməreɪt] **1** *vti* agglomerieren.
2 [ə'glɒmərət] *adj* agglomeriert.
3 [ə'glɒmərət] *n* Agglomerat *nt*.

agglomeration [əˌglɒmə'reɪʃən] *n* Anhäufung *f*, Konglomerat *nt*; (*Sci*) Agglomeration *f*.

agglutinate [ə'gluːtɪneɪt] **1** *vi* agglutinieren (*also Ling*), verklumpen, verkleben.
2 [ə'gluːtɪnət] *adj* agglutiniert (*also Ling*), verklumpt, verklebt.

agglutinating [ə'gluːtɪneɪtɪŋ] *adj* (*Ling*) agglutinierend.

agglutination [əˌgluːtɪ'neɪʃən] *n* Agglutination (*also Ling*), Verklumpung, Verklebung *f*.

agglutinative [ə'gluːtɪnətɪv] *adj* agglutinierend.

aggrandize [ə'grændaɪz] *vt one's power, empire* vergrößern, erweitern; *person, one's family* befördern ◆ **to ~ oneself** sich befördern; (*be self-important*) sich wichtig machen.

aggrandizement [ə'grændɪzmənt] *n see vt* Vergrößerung, Erweiterung *f*; Beförderung *f*.

aggravate ['ægrəveɪt] *vt* **(a)** verschlimmern. **(b)** (*annoy*) aufregen; (*deliberately*) reizen ◆ **don't get ~d** regen Sie sich nicht auf.

aggravating ['ægrəveɪtɪŋ] *adj* ärgerlich, enervierend (*geh*); *noise, child* lästig, enervierend (*geh*) ◆ **how ~ for you** wie ärgerlich für Sie!

aggravation [ˌægrə'veɪʃən] *n* **(a)** (*worsening*) Verschlimmerung *f*. **(b)** (*annoyance*) Ärger *m* ◆ **her constant ~ made him ...** sie reizte ihn so, daß er ...

aggregate ['ægrɪgɪt] **1** *n* **(a)** Gesamtmenge, Summe, Gesamtheit *f* ◆ **considered in the ~** insgesamt betrachtet.
(b) (*Build*) Zuschlagstoffe *pl*; (*Geol*) Gemenge *nt*.
2 *adj* gesamt, Gesamt- ◆ **~ value** Gesamtwert *m*.
3 ['ægrɪgeɪt] *vt* **(a)** (*gather together*) anhäufen, ansammeln.
(b) (*amount to*) sich belaufen auf (+*acc*).
4 ['ægrɪgeɪt] *vi* sich anhäufen, sich ansammeln.

aggression [ə'greʃən] *n* **(a)** (*attack*) Aggression *f*, Angriff *m* ◆ **an act of ~** ein Angriff *m*, eine aggressive Handlung. **(b)** *no pl* Aggression *f*; (*aggressiveness*) Aggressivität *f* ◆ **to get rid of one's ~s** seine Aggressionen loswerden.

aggressive [ə'gresɪv] *adj* **(a)** aggressiv; (*physically also*) angriffslustig; (*Sport*) *play also* hart; *lover* draufgängerisch, ungestüm. **(b)** *salesman, businessman etc* dynamisch, aufdringlich (*pej*).

aggressively [ə'gresɪvlɪ] *adv see adj*.

aggressiveness [ə'gresɪvnɪs] *n see adj* **(a)** Aggressivität *f*; Härte *f*; Draufgängertum, Ungestüm *nt*. **(b)** Dynamik, Aufdringlichkeit (*pej*) *f*.

aggressor [ə'gresəʳ] *n* Angreifer(in *f*), Aggressor(in *f*) *m*.

aggrieved [ə'griːvd] *adj* betrübt (*at, by* über +*acc*); (*offended*) verletzt (*at, by* durch); *voice, look also* gekränkt ◆ **the ~ (party)** (*Jur*) der Beschwerte, die beschwerte Partei.

aggro ['ægrəʊ] *n* (*Brit inf*) **(a)** (*aggression, bother*) Aggressionen *pl* ◆ **don't give me any ~** mach keinen Ärger (*inf*) *or* Stunk (*inf*); **I get so much ~ from my mother if ...** ich kriege Ärger mit meiner Mutter, wenn ... (*inf*); **she didn't want all the ~ of moving house** sie wollte das ganze Theater mit dem Umziehen vermeiden; **motorways are too much ~** Autobahnen sind zu anstrengend.
(b) (*fight*) Schlägerei *f* ◆ **football fans looking for ~** Fußballfans, die auf Schlägereien aus sind.

aghast [ə'gɑːst] *adj pred* entgeistert (*at* über +*acc*).

agile ['ædʒaɪl] *adj person, thinker* beweglich, wendig; *person also* agil; *body also, movements* gelenkig, geschmeidig; *animal* flink, behende ◆ **he has an ~ mind** er ist geistig sehr wendig *or* beweglich *or* flexibel.

agilely ['ædʒaɪllɪ] *adv move, jump etc* geschickt, behende; *argue* geschickt, gewandt; *think* flink, beweglich.

agility [ə'dʒɪlɪtɪ] *n see adj* Beweglichkeit, Wendigkeit *f*; Agilität *f*; Gelenkigkeit, Geschmeidigkeit *f*; Flinkheit, Behendigkeit *f*.

aging *adj, n see* **ag(e)ing**.

agitate ['ædʒɪteɪt] **1** *vt* **(a)** (*lit*) *liquid* aufrühren; *surface of water* aufwühlen; *washing* hin- und herbewegen. **(b)** (*fig: excite, upset*) aufregen, aus der Fassung bringen ◆ **don't let him ~ you** laß dich von ihm nicht aufregen.
2 *vi* agitieren ◆ **to ~ for sth** sich für etw stark machen.

agitated *adj*, ~**ly** *adv* ['ædʒɪteɪtɪd, -lɪ] aufgeregt, erregt.

agitation [ˌædʒɪ'teɪʃən] *n* **(a)** *see vt (a)* Aufrühren *nt*; Aufwühlen *nt*; Hin- und Herbewegung *f*. **(b)** (*anxiety, worry*) Erregung *f*, Aufruhr *m*; (*on stock market*) Bewegung *f*. **(c)** (*incitement*) Agitation *f*.

agitator ['ædʒɪteɪtəʳ] *n* **(a)** (*person*) Agitator(in *f*) *m*. **(b)** (*device*) Rührwerk *nt*, Rührapparat *m*.

agleam [ə'gliːm] *adj pred* erleuchtet ◆ **his eyes were ~ with mischief** seine Augen blitzten *or* funkelten schelmisch.

aglitter [ə'glɪtəʳ] *adj pred* **to be ~** funkeln, glitzern.

aglow [ə'gləʊ] *adj pred* **to be ~** (*sky, fire, face*) glühen; **the sun set the mountains/sky ~** die Sonne ließ die Berge/den Himmel erglühen *or* brachte die Berge/den Himmel zum Glühen; **to be ~ with happiness/health** vor Glück strahlen/vor Gesundheit strotzen.

AGM *abbr of* **Annual General Meeting** JHV *f*.

agnail ['ægneɪl] *n* Niednagel *m*.

agnostic [æg'nɒstɪk] **1** *adj* agnostisch.
2 *n* Agnostiker(in *f*) *m*.

agnosticism [æg'nɒstɪsɪzəm] *n* Agnostizismus *m*.

ago [ə'gəʊ] *adv* vor ◆ **years/a week/a little while ~** vor Jahren/einer Woche/kurzem; **that was years/a week ~** das ist schon Jahre/eine Woche her; **ah, that's a long long time ~** o, lang, lang ist's her; **he was here less than a minute ~** er war noch vor einer Minute hier; **how long ~ is it since you last saw him?** wie lange haben Sie ihn schon nicht mehr gesehen?, wann haben Sie ihn das letzte Mal gesehen?; **how long ~ did it happen?** wie lange ist das her?; **he left 10 minutes ~** er ist vor 10 Minuten gegangen; **long, long ~** vor langer, langer Zeit; **how long ~?** wie lange ist das her?; **that was long ~** das ist schon lange her; **as long ~ as 1950** schon 1950; **no longer ~ than yesterday** erst gestern (noch).

agog [ə'gɒg] *adj pred* gespannt ◆ **the children sat there ~ with excitement** die Kinder sperrten Augen und Ohren auf; **the whole village was ~ (with curiosity)** das ganze Dorf platzte fast vor Neugierde; **~ for news** wild nach Neuigkeiten; **we're all ~ to hear your news** wir warten gespannt auf deine Nachrichten.

agonize ['ægənaɪz] *vi* sich (*dat*) den Kopf zermartern (*over* über +*acc*) ◆ **after weeks of agonizing he finally made a decision** nach wochenlangem Ringen traf er endlich eine Entscheidung.

agonized ['ægənaɪzd] *adj* gequält.

agonizing ['ægənaɪzɪŋ] *adj* qualvoll, quälend; *cry, experience* qualvoll.

agonizingly ['ægənaɪzɪŋlɪ] *adv* qualvoll ◆ **~ slow** aufreizend langsam.

agony ['ægənɪ] *n* **(a)** Qual *f*; (*mental also*) Leid *nt* ◆ **that's ~** das ist eine Qual; **it's ~ doing that** es ist eine Qual, das zu tun; **to be in ~** Schmerzen *or* Qualen leiden; **in an ~ of indecision/suspense** *etc* in qualvoller Unentschlossenheit/Ungewißheit *etc*; **to go through** *or* **suffer agonies** Qualen ausstehen.
(b) (*death ~*) Todeskampf *m*, Agonie *f*; (*of Christ*) Todesangst *f* ◆ **put him out of his ~** (*lit*) mach seiner Qual ein Ende; (*fig*) nun spann ihn doch nicht länger auf die Folter.

agony (*Brit inf*): ~ **aunt** *n* Briefkastentante *f* (*inf*); ~ **column** *n* Kummerkasten *m*; ~ **columnist** *n* Briefkastenonkel *m*/-tante *f* (*inf*).

agoraphobia [ˌægərə'fəʊbjə] *n* Agoraphobie (*spec*), Platzangst *f*.

agoraphobic [ˌægərə'fəʊbɪk] (*Med*) **1** *adj* agoraphobisch.
2 *n* an Agoraphobie *or* Platzangst Leidende(r) *mf*.

agrarian [ə'greərɪən] *adj* Agrar-.

▼ **agree** [ə'griː] *pret, ptp* ~**d** **1** *vt* **(a)** *price, date etc* vereinbaren, abmachen.
(b) (*consent*) **to ~ to do sth** sich einverstanden *or* bereit erklären, etw zu tun.
(c) (*admit*) zugeben ◆ **I ~ (that) I was wrong** ich gebe zu, daß ich mich geirrt habe.
▼ **(d)** (*come to or be in agreement about*) zustimmen (+*dat*) ◆ **we all ~ that ...** wir sind alle der Meinung, daß ...; **it was ~d that ...** man kam überein, daß ..., man einigte sich darauf *or* es wurde beschlossen, daß ...; **we ~d to do it** wir haben beschlossen, das zu tun; **to ~ to differ** sich (*dat*) verschiedene Meinungen zugestehen; **is that ~d then, gentlemen?** sind alle einverstanden?; *see also* **agreed**.
▼ **2** *vi* **(a)** (*hold same opinion*) (*two or more people*) sich einig sein, übereinstimmen, einer Meinung sein; (*one person*) der gleichen Meinung sein ◆ **to ~ with sb** jdm zustimmen; **I ~!** der Meinung bin ich auch; **we all ~, it's a silly suggestion** wir sind uns alle einig, das ist ein alberner Vorschlag; **I couldn't ~ more/less** ich bin völlig/überhaupt nicht dieser Meinung, ich stimme dem völlig/überhaupt nicht zu; **it's too late now, don't** *or* **wouldn't you ~?** finden *or* meinen Sie nicht auch, daß es jetzt zu spät ist?
(b) to ~ with a theory/the figures *etc* (*accept*) eine Theorie/die Zahlen akzeptieren *or* für richtig halten.

➤ LANGUAGE IN USE: **agree: 1d** → 11.1, 11.2, 12.1, 12.2, 13 **2a** → 11.1, 11.2, 26.1, 26.3

(c) (*come to an agreement*) sich einigen (*about* über *+acc*).
(d) (*people: get on together*) sich vertragen, miteinander auskommen.
(e) (*statements, figures etc: tally*) übereinstimmen.
(f) **to ~ with sth** (*approve of*) etw befürworten, mit etw einverstanden sein; **I don't ~ with children drinking wine** ich bin dagegen *or* ich befürworte es nicht *or* ich bin nicht damit einverstanden, daß Kinder Wein trinken.
(g) (*food, climate etc*) **sth ~s with sb** jdm bekommt etw; **whisky doesn't ~ with me** ich vertrage Whisky nicht, Whisky bekommt mir nicht.
(h) (*Gram*) übereinstimmen.

◆**agree on** *vi +prep obj solution* sich einigen auf (*+acc*), Einigkeit erzielen über (*+acc*); *price, policy also* vereinbaren ◆ **a price/policy/solution has been ~d ~** man hat sich auf einen Preis/eine Linie/eine Lösung geeinigt; **we ~d ~ the need to save** wir waren uns darüber einig, daß gespart werden muß.

◆ **agree to** *vi +prep obj* zustimmen (*+dat*); *marriage also* einwilligen in (*+acc*), seine Einwilligung geben zu; *conditions, terms also* annehmen, akzeptieren; *increase, payment also* sich einverstanden erklären mit ◆ **I cannot ~ ~ your marrying her** ich kann einer Ehe nicht zustimmen.

agreeable [ə'gri:əbl] *adj* **(a)** (*pleasant*) angenehm; *decor, behaviour* nett. **(b)** *pred* (*willing to agree*) einverstanden ◆ **are you ~ to that?** sind Sie damit einverstanden?

agreeably [ə'gri:əblı] *adv* angenehm; *decorated* nett ◆ **she behaved ~ for once** sie benahm sich ausnahmsweise nett.

agreed [ə'gri:d] *adj* **(a)** *pred* (*in agreement*) einig ◆ **to be ~ on sth/doing sth** sich über etw einig sein/sich darüber einig sein, etw zu tun; **are we all ~?** sind wir uns da einig?; (*on course of action*) sind alle einverstanden?
(b) (*arranged*) vereinbart; *price also* festgesetzt; *time also* verabredet, abgesprochen ◆ **it's all ~** es ist alles abgesprochen; **~?** einverstanden?; **~!** (*regarding price etc*) abgemacht, in Ordnung; (*I agree*) stimmt, genau.

agreement [ə'gri:mənt] *n* **(a)** (*understanding, arrangement*) Abmachung, Übereinkunft *f*; (*treaty, contract*) Abkommen *nt*, Vertrag *m* ◆ **to break the terms of an ~** die Vertragsbestimmungen verletzen; **to enter into an ~ (with sb)** (mit jdm) einen Vertrag eingehen *or* (ab)schließen; **to reach an ~ (with sb)** (mit jdm) zu einer Einigung kommen, (mit jdm) Übereinstimmung erzielen; **there's a tacit ~ in the office that ...** im Büro besteht die stillschweigende Übereinkunft, daß ...; **we have an ~ whereby if I'm home first ...** wir haben abgemacht, daß, wenn ich zuerst nach Hause komme, ...
(b) (*sharing of opinion*) Einigkeit *f* ◆ **unanimous ~** Einmütigkeit *f*; **by mutual ~** in gegenseitigem Einverständnis *or* Einvernehmen; **to be in ~ with sb** mit jdm einer Meinung sein; **to be in ~ with/about sth** mit etw übereinstimmen/über etw (*acc*) einig sein; **for once we were both in ~ on that point** ausnahmsweise waren wir uns in diesem Punkt einig *or* waren wir in diesem Punkt einer Meinung; **to find oneself in ~ with sb** mit jdm übereinstimmen *or* einiggehen.
(c) (*consent*) Einwilligung, Zustimmung *f* (*to* zu).
(d) (*between figures, accounts etc*) Übereinstimmung *f*.
(e) (*Gram*) Übereinstimmung *f*.

agribusiness ['ægrıbıznıs] *n* die Landwirtschaft.

agricultural [,ægrı'kʌltʃərəl] *adj produce, expert, tool etc* landwirtschaftlich; *ministry, science etc* Landwirtschafts- ◆ **~ worker** Landarbeiter(in *f*) *m*; **~ nation** Agrarstaat *m*, Agrarland *nt*; **the ~ country in the north** das landwirtschaftliche Gebiet im Norden; **~ college** Landwirtschaftsschule *f*; **~ show** Landwirtschaftsausstellung *f*.

agricultur(al)ist [,ægrı'kʌltʃər(əl)ıst] *n* Landwirtschaftsexperte *m*/-expertin *f*; (*farmer*) Landwirt(in *f*) *m*.

agriculturally [,ægrı'kʌltʃərəlı] *adv* landwirtschaftlich.

agriculture ['ægrıkʌltʃəʳ] *n* Landwirtschaft *f* ◆ **Minister of A~** (*Brit*) Landwirtschaftsminister(in *f*) *m*.

agronomist [ə'grɒnəmıst] *n* Agronom(in *f*) *m*.

agronomy [ə'grɒnəmı] *n* Agronomie *f*.

aground [ə'graʊnd] [1] *adj pred ship* gestrandet, aufgelaufen, auf Grund gelaufen.
[2] *adv* **to go** *or* **run ~** auflaufen, auf Grund laufen, stranden.

ague ['eıgju:] *n* Schüttelfrost *m no art*.

ah [ɑ:] *interj* ah; (*pain*) au, autsch; (*pity*) o, ach.

aha [ɑ:'hɑ:] *interj* aha.

ahead [ə'hed] *adv* **(a) there's some thick cloud ~** vor uns *or* da vorne ist eine große Wolke; **the mountains lay ~** vor uns/ihnen *etc* lagen die Berge; **the German runner was/drew ~** der deutsche Läufer lag vorn/zog nach vorne; **he is ~ by about two minutes** er hat etwa zwei Minuten Vorsprung; **keep straight ~** immer geradeaus; **full speed ~** (*Naut, fig*) volle Kraft voraus; **we sent him on ~** wir schickten ihn voraus; **in the months ~** in den bevorstehenden Monaten; **I see problems ~** ich sehe Probleme auf mich/uns *etc* zukommen; **we've a busy time ~** vor uns liegt eine Menge Arbeit; **to plan ~** vorausplanen; *see vbs*.
(b) ~ of sb/sth vor jdm/etw; **walk ~ of me** geh voran; **the leader is two laps ~ of the others** der Führende hat zwei Runden Vorsprung *or* liegt zwei Runden vor den anderen; **we arrived ten minutes ~ of time** wir kamen zehn Minuten vorher an; **to be/get ~ of schedule** schneller als geplant vorankommen; **the dollar is still ~ of the mark** der Dollar führt immer noch vor der Mark; **to be ~ of one's time** (*fig*) seiner Zeit voraus sein.

ahem [ə'həm] *interj* hm.

ahoy [ə'hɔı] *interj* (*Naut*) ahoi ◆ **ship ~!** Schiff ahoi!

AI *abbr of* **artificial intelligence** KI *f*.

aid [eıd] [1] *n* **(a)** *no pl* (*help*) Hilfe *f* ◆ **(foreign) ~** Entwicklungshilfe *f*; **with the ~ of his uncle/a screwdriver** mit Hilfe seines Onkels/eines Schraubenziehers; **to come to sb's ~** jdm zu Hilfe kommen; **a sale in ~ of the blind** ein Verkauf zugunsten der Blinden; **what's all this wiring in ~ of?** (*inf*) wozu sind all diese Drähte da *or* gut?; **what's all this in ~ of?** (*inf*) wozu soll das gut sein?
(b) (*useful person, thing*) Hilfe *f* (*to* für); (*piece of equipment, audio-visual ~ etc*) Hilfsmittel *nt*; (*hearing ~*) Hörgerät *nt*; (*teaching ~*) Lehrmittel *nt*.
(c) (*esp US*) *see* **aide**.
[2] *vt* unterstützen, helfen (*+dat*) ◆ **to ~ one another** sich gegenseitig helfen *or* unterstützen; **to ~ sb's recovery** jds Heilung fördern; **to ~ and abet sb** (*Jur*) jdm Beihilfe leisten; (*after crime*) jdn begünstigen; **he was accused of ~ing and abetting** ihm wurde Beihilfe/Begünstigung vorgeworfen.

aide [eıd] *n* Helfer(in *f*) *m*; (*adviser*) (persönlicher) Berater.

aide-de-camp ['eıddəkɒŋ] *n, pl* **aides-de-camp (a)** (*Mil*) Adjutant *m*. **(b)** *see* **aide**.

aide-memoire ['eıdmem'wɑ:] *n* Gedächtnisstütze *f*; (*official memorandum*) Aide-memoire *nt*.

aiding and abetting ['eıdıŋəndə'betıŋ] *n* (*Jur*) Beihilfe *f*; (*after crime*) Begünstigung *f*.

AIDS, Aids [eıdz] *abbr of* **acquired immune deficiency syndrome** AIDS, Aids *nt* ◆ **~ victim** Aids-Kranke(r) *mf*.

AIDS-related [,eıdzrı'leıtıd] *adj illness, death* aidsbedingt.

aigrette ['eıgret] *n* Reiherfeder *f*, Reiherbusch *m* (*old*).

ail [eıl] [1] *vt* (*old*) plagen ◆ **what's ~ing you?** (*inf*) was hast du?, was ist mit dir?
[2] *vi* (*inf*) kränklich sein, kränkeln.

aileron ['eılərɒn] *n* (*Aviat*) Querruder *nt*.

ailing ['eılıŋ] *adj* (*lit*) kränklich, kränkelnd; (*fig*) *industry, economy etc* krankend, krank.

ailment ['eılmənt] *n* Gebrechen, Leiden *nt* ◆ **minor ~s** leichte Beschwerden *pl*; **inflation, a national ~** die Inflation, eine nationale Krankheit; **all his little ~s** all seine Wehwehchen.

aim [eım] [1] *n* **(a)** Zielen *nt* ◆ **to take ~** zielen (*at* auf *+acc*); **to miss one's ~** sein Ziel verfehlen; **his ~ was bad/good** *etc* er zielte schlecht/gut *etc*.
(b) (*purpose*) Ziel *nt*, Absicht *f* ◆ **with the ~ of doing sth** mit dem Ziel *or* der Absicht, etw zu tun; **what is your ~ in life?** was ist Ihr Lebensziel?; **to achieve one's ~** sein Ziel erreichen; **what is your ~ in saying/doing that?** warum sagen Sie das?/was wollen Sie damit bezwecken?
[2] *vt* **(a)** (*direct*) *guided missile, camera* richten (*at* auf *+acc*); *stone etc* zielen mit (*at* auf *+acc*) ◆ **to teach sb how to ~ a gun** jdm zeigen, wie man zielt; **to ~ a pistol at sb/sth** eine Pistole auf jdn/etw richten, mit einer Pistole auf jdn/etw zielen, die Pistole auf jdn anlegen; **he ~ed his pistol at my heart** er zielte auf mein Herz; **the guns were ~ed directly at the city walls** die Kanonen waren direkt auf die Stadtmauer gerichtet; **you didn't ~ the camera properly** du hast die Kamera nicht richtig gehalten.
(b) (*fig*) *remark, insult, criticism* richten (*at* gegen) ◆ **this book/programme is ~ed at the general public** dieses Buch/Programm wendet sich an die Öffentlichkeit; **to be ~ed at sth** (*cuts, measure, new law etc*) auf etw (*acc*) abgezielt sein; **I think that was ~ed at me** ich glaube, das war auf mich gemünzt *or* gegen mich gerichtet.
[3] *vi* **(a)** (*with gun, punch etc*) zielen (*at, for* auf *+acc*).
(b) (*try, strive for*) **to ~ high** sich (*dat*) hohe Ziele setzen *or* stecken; **isn't that ~ing a bit high?** wollen Sie nicht etwas hoch hinaus?; **to ~ at** *or* **for sth** etw anstreben, auf etw (*acc*) abzielen; **with this TV programme we're ~ing at a much wider audience** mit diesem Fernsehprogramm wollen wir einen größeren Teilnehmerkreis ansprechen; **we ~ to please** bei uns ist der Kunde König; **he always ~s for perfection** er strebt immer nach Perfektion; **he ~s at only spending £10 per week** er hat sich zum Ziel gesetzt, mit £ 10 pro Woche auszukommen.
(c) (*inf: intend*) **to ~ to do sth** vorhaben, etw zu tun, etw tun wollen.

aimless *adj*, **~ly** *adv* ['eımlıs, -lı] ziellos; *talk, act* planlos.

aimlessness ['eımlısnıs] *n see adj* Ziellosigkeit *f*; Planlosigkeit *f*.

ain't [eınt] (*incorrect*) = **am not; is not; are not; has not; have not.**

air [ɛəʳ] [1] *n* **(a)** Luft *f* ◆ **a change of ~** eine Luftveränderung; **war in the ~** Luftkrieg *m*; **perfumes drifting in on the ~** vom Windhauch hereingetragene Düfte; **to go out for a breath of (fresh) ~** frische Luft schöpfen (gehen); **to take the ~** (*old*) frische Luft schöpfen; **to take to the ~** sich in die Lüfte schwingen (*geh*); **by ~** per *or* mit dem Flugzeug; **to transport sth by ~** etw auf dem Luftweg transportieren; **to go by ~** (*person*) fliegen, mit dem Flugzeug reisen; (*goods*) per Flugzeug *or* auf dem Luftwege transportiert werden.
(b) (*fig phrases*) **there's something in the ~** es liegt etwas in der Luft; **there's a rumour in the ~ that ...** es geht ein Gerücht um, daß ...; **it's still all up in the ~** (*inf*) es hängt noch alles in der Luft, es ist noch alles offen; **all her plans were up in the ~** (*inf*) all ihre Pläne hingen in der Luft; **to give sb the ~** (*US inf*) jdn abblitzen *or* abfahren lassen (*inf*); **to clear the ~** die Atmosphäre reinigen; **he went up in the ~ when he heard that** (*inf*) (*in anger*) als er das hörte, ist er in die Luft *or* an die Decke gegangen; (*in excitement*) als er das hörte, hat er einen Luftsprung gemacht; **to be up in the ~ about sth** (*inf*) wegen etw aus dem Häuschen sein (*inf*); **to be walking** *or* **treading on ~** wie auf Wolken gehen; *see* **castle, thin.**
(c) (*Rad, TV*) **to be on the ~** (*programme*) gesendet werden; (*station*) senden; **you're on the ~** Sie sind auf Sendung; **he's on the ~ every day** er ist jeden Tag im Radio zu hören; **the programme goes** *or* **is put on the ~ every week** das Programm wird jede Woche gesendet; **we come on the ~ at 6 o'clock** unsere Sendezeit beginnt um 6 Uhr; **to go off the ~** (*broadcaster*) die Sen-

➤ LANGUAGE IN USE: **agree to:** → 12.2 **agreed: a** → 26.1 **agreement: b** → 11.2, 13

dung beenden; (*station*) das Programm beenden.
(d) (*demeanour, manner*) Auftreten *nt*; (*facial expression*) Miene *f*; (*of building, town etc*) Atmosphäre *f* ◆ **with an ~ of bewilderment** mit bestürzter Miene; **an unpleasant ~ of self-satisfaction** ein unangenehm selbstzufriedenes Gehabe; **there is a certain military ~ about him** er hat etwas Militärisches an sich; **there was** *or* **she had an ~ of mystery about her** sie hatte etwas Geheimnisvolles an sich; **it gives** *or* **lends her an ~ of affluence** das gibt ihr einen wohlhabenden Anstrich; **she has a certain ~ about her** sie hat so etwas an sich.
(e) **~s** *pl* Getue, Gehabe *nt* ◆ **to put on ~s, to give oneself ~s** sich zieren, vornehm tun; **~s and graces** Allüren *pl*; **to put on ~s and graces** den Vornehmen/die Vornehme herauskehren.
(f) (*liter, Naut: breeze*) leichte Brise, Lüftchen *nt* (*liter*).
(g) (*Mus*) Weise *f* (*old*); (*tune also*) Melodie *f*.
[2] *vt* (a) *clothes, bed, room* (aus)lüften.
(b) *anger, grievance* Luft machen (+*dat*); *opinion* darlegen.
[3] *vi* (*clothes etc*) (*after washing*) nachtrocknen; (*after storage*) (aus)lüften ◆ **to put clothes out to ~** Kleidung zum Lüften raushängen.

air *in cpds* Luft-; **~ base** *n* Luftwaffenstützpunkt *m*; **~-bed** *n* Luftmatratze *f*; **~borne** *adj troops* Luftlande-; **to be ~borne** sich in der Luft befinden; **~ brake** *n* (*on truck*) Druckluftbremse *f*; (*Aviat*) Brems- *or* Landeklappe *f*; **~brick** *n* Entlüftungsziegel *m*; **~-bridge** *n* Luftbrücke *f*; **~brush** *m* (*Art*) Spritzpistole, Airbrush *f*; **~ bubble** *n* Luftblase *f*; **~bus** *n* Airbus *m*; **~ cargo** *n* Luftfracht *f*; **A~ Chief Marshal** *n* (*Brit*) General *m*; **A~ Commodore** *n* (*Brit*) Brigadegeneral *m*; **~-conditioned** *adj* klimatisiert; **~-conditioning** *n* (*plant*) Klimaanlage *f*; (*process*) Klimatisierung *f*; **~-conditioning plant** *n* Klimaanlage *f*; **~-cooled** *adj engine* luftgekühlt; **~ corridor** *n* Luftkorridor *m*; **~ cover** *n* Luftunterstützung *f*; **~craft** *n*, *pl* **~craft** Flugzeug *nt*, Maschine *f*; **various types of ~craft** verschiedene Luftfahrzeuge *pl*; **~craft carrier** *n* Flugzeugträger *m*; **~craft(s)man** *n* Gefreite(r) *m*; **~crew** *n* Flugpersonal *nt*; **~ current** *n* Luftströmung *f*; **~-cushion** *n* Luftkissen *nt*; **~ display** *n* Flugschau *f*; **~drome** *n* (*US*) Flugplatz *m*, Aerodrom *nt* (*old*); **~drop** [1] *n* Fallschirmabwurf *m*; [2] *vt* mit Fallschirmen abwerfen; **~-dry** *vt* lufttrocknen; **~-duct** *n* Luftkanal *m*.

Airedale ['ɛədeɪl] *n* Airedale-Terrier *m*.

airer ['ɛərəʳ] *n* Trockenständer *m*.

air: ~field *n* Flugplatz *m*; **~flow** *n* Luftstrom *m*; (*in air-conditioning*) Luftzufuhr *f*; **~foil** *n* (*US*) Tragflügel *m*; (*on racing cars*) Spoiler *m*; **~ force** *n* Luftwaffe *f*; **A~ Force One** *n* Air Force One *f*, *Dienstflugzeug des US-Präsidenten*; **~ force pilot** *n* Luftwaffenpilot *m*; **~frame** *n* (*Aviat*) Flugwerk *nt*, Zelle *f*; **~-freight** [1] *n* Luftfracht *f*; (*charge*) Luftfrachtgebühr *f*; **to send sth by ~-freight** etw als Luftfracht verschicken; [2] *vt* per Luftfracht senden; **~gun** *n* Luftgewehr *nt*; **~hole** *n* Luftloch *nt*; **~ hostess** *n* Stewardeß *f*.

airily ['ɛərɪlɪ] *adv* (*casually*) *say, reply etc* leichthin, lässig; (*vaguely*) vage; (*flippantly*) blasiert, erhaben.

airiness ['ɛərɪnɪs] *n see adj (a, b)* (a) **she liked the ~ of the rooms** ihr gefiel, daß die Zimmer so luftig waren. (b) Lässigkeit, Nonchalance *f*; Vagheit *f*; Versponnenheit *f*; Blasiertheit, Erhabenheit *f*.

airing ['ɛərɪŋ] *n* (*of linen, room etc*) (Aus- *or* Durch)lüften *nt* ◆ **to give sth a good ~** etw gut durch- *or* auslüften lassen; **to give an idea an ~** (*fig inf*) eine Idee darlegen.

airing cupboard *n* (*Brit*) (Wäsche)trockenschrank *m*.

air: ~ intake *n* Lufteinlaß *or* -eintritt *m*; (*for engine*) Luftansaugstutzen *m*; (*quantity*) Luftmenge *f*; **~lane** *n* Flugroute *f*; **~less** *adj* (*lit*) *space* luftleer; (*stuffy*) *room* stickig; (*with no wind*) *day* windstill; **~ letter** *n* Luftpostbrief *m*, Aerogramm *nt*; **~lift** [1] *n* Luftbrücke *f*; [2] *vt* **to ~lift sth into a place** etw über eine Luftbrücke herein-/hineinbringen; **~line** *n* (a) Fluggesellschaft, Luftverkehrsgesellschaft, Fluglinie *f*; (b) (*diver's tube*) Luftschlauch *m*; **~liner** *n* Verkehrsflugzeug *nt*; **~lock** *n* (*in spacecraft etc*) Luftschleuse *f*; (*in pipe*) Luftsack *m*.

airmail ['ɛəmeɪl] [1] *n* Luftpost *f* ◆ **to send sth (by) ~** etw per *or* mit Luftpost schicken.
[2] *vt* mit *or* per Luftpost schicken.

airmail: ~ edition *n* (*of newspaper*) Luftpostausgabe *f*; **~ letter** *n* Luftpostbrief *m*; **~ stamp** *or* **sticker** *n* Luftpostaufkleber *m*.

air: ~man *n* (*flier*) Flieger *m*; (*US: in ~ force*) Gefreite(r) *m*; **A~ Marshal** *n* (*Brit*) Generalleutnant *m*; **~ mass** *n* Luftmasse *f*; **~ mattress** *n* Luftmatratze *f*; **~mile** *n* ≃ Flugkilometer *m*; **~ miles** Flugmeilen *pl* (*collected by passenger*); **~ miss** *n* (*Aviat*) Beinahezusammenstoß *m*; **~ passenger** *n* Fluggast *m*; **~plane** *n* (*US*) Flugzeug *nt*; **~play** *n* (*Rad*) Sendezeit *f*; **the song received extensive ~play** das Lied wurde sehr oft im Radio gespielt; **~ pocket** *n* Luftloch *nt*; **~port** *n* Flughafen *m*; **~port bus** *n* Flughafenbus *m*; **~port tax** *n* Flughafengebühr *f*; **~ pressure** *n* Luftdruck *m*; **~ pump** *n* Luftpumpe *f*.

air raid *n* Luftangriff *m*.

air-raid: ~ shelter *n* Luftschutzkeller *m*; **~ warden** *n* Luftschutzwart *m*; **~ warning** *n* Fliegeralarm *m*.

air: ~ rescue service *n* Luftrettungsdienst *m*; **~ rifle** *n* Luftgewehr *nt*; **~ route** *n* Flugroute *f*; **~screw** *n* Luftschraube *f*; **~-sea rescue** *n* Rettung *f* durch Seenotflugzeuge; **~-sea rescue service** *n* Seenotrettungsdienst *m*; **~shaft** *n* (*Min*) Wetterschacht *m*; **~ship** *n* Luftschiff *nt*; **~ show** *n* Luftfahrtausstellung *f*; **~sick** *adj* luftkrank; **~sickness** *n* Luftkrankheit *f*; **~ sleeve** *or* **sock** *n* Windsack *m*; **~space** *n* Luftraum *m*; **~speed** *n* Eigen- *or* Fluggeschwindigkeit *f*; **~stream** *n* (*of vehicle*) Luftsog *m*; (*Met*) Luftstrom *m*; **~strip** *n* Start- und Lande-Bahn *f*; **~ supremacy** *n* Luftüberlegenheit *f*; **~ terminal** *n* (Air) Terminal *m or nt*; **~tight** *adj* (*lit*) luftdicht; (*fig*) *argument, case* hieb- und stichfest; **~ time** *n* (*Rad, TV*) Sendezeit *f*; **~-to-~** *adj* (*Mil*) Luft-Luft-; **~-to-ground** *adj* (*Mil*) Luft-Boden-; **~-to-sea** *adj* (*Mil*) Luft-See-; **~-to-surface** *adj* (*Mil*) Luft-Boden-; **~-traffic control** *n* Flugleitung *f*; **~-traffic controller** *n* Fluglotse *m*; **~ vent** *n* Ventilator *m*; (*shaft*) Belüftungsschacht *m*; **A~ Vice Marshal** *n* (*Brit*) Generalmajor *m*; **~waves** *npl* Radiowellen *pl*; **~way** *n* (*route*) Flugroute *f*; (*airline company*) Fluggesellschaft, Luftverkehrsgesellschaft *f*; **~ waybill** *n* Luftfrachtbrief *m*; **~woman** *n* Fliegerin *f*; **~worthiness** *n* Flugtüchtigkeit *f*; **~worthy** *adj* flugtüchtig.

airy ['ɛərɪ] *adj* (+*er*) (a) *room* luftig; (b) (*casual*) *manner, gesture* lässig, nonchalant; (*vague*) *promise* vage; *theory* versponnen; (*superior, flippant*) blasiert, erhaben. (c) (*liter: immaterial*) *phantom* körperlos.

airy-fairy ['ɛərɪ'fɛərɪ] *adj* (*inf*) versponnen; *excuse* windig; *talk also* larifari *inv* (*inf*) ◆ **you seem rather ~ about your plans** deine Pläne scheinen ziemlich unausgegoren; **he just muddles through in this ~ way** er wurstelt sich so aufs Geratewohl durch (*inf*).

aisle [aɪl] *n* Gang *m*; (*in church*) Seitenschiff *nt*; (*central ~*) Mittelgang *m* ◆ **~ seat** Sitz *m* am Gang; **to lead a girl up the ~** ein Mädchen zum Altar führen; **he had them rolling in the ~s** er brachte sie soweit, daß sie sich vor Lachen kugelten (*inf*) *or* wälzten (*inf*).

aitch [eɪtʃ] *n* h, H *nt* ◆ **to drop one's ~es** *den Buchstaben „h" nicht aussprechen*; (*be lower class*) ≃ „mir" und „mich" verwechseln.

ajar [ə'dʒɑːʳ] *adj, adv* angelehnt, einen Spalt offen stehend.

aka *abbr of* **also known as** alias, anderweitig bekannt als.

akela [ɑː'keɪlə] *n* Wölflingsführer *m*.

akimbo [ə'kɪmbəʊ] *adv*: **with arms ~** die Arme in die Hüften gestemmt.

akin [ə'kɪn] *adj pred* ähnlich (*to dat*), verwandt (*to* mit).

à la [ɑːlɑː] *prep* à la.

alabaster ['æləbɑːstəʳ] [1] *n* Alabaster *m*.
[2] *adj* (*lit*) alabastern, Alabaster-; (*fig liter*) *skin, neck* Alabaster-, wie Alabaster.

à la carte [ɑːlɑː'kɑːt] [1] *adv eat* à la carte, nach der (Speise)karte.
[2] *adj menu* à la carte.

alack [ə'læk] *interj* (*obs*) wehe ◆ **~ the day** wehe dem Tag.

alacrity [ə'lækrɪtɪ] *n* (*willingness*) Bereitwilligkeit *f*; (*eagerness*) Eifer *m*, Eilfertigkeit *f* ◆ **to accept with ~** ohne zu zögern annehmen.

à la mode [ɑːlɑː'məʊd] *adj* (*US*) mit Eis.

alarm [ə'lɑːm] [1] *n* (a) *no pl* (*fear*) Sorge, Besorgnis, Beunruhigung *f* ◆ **to be in a state of ~** (*worried*) besorgt *or* beunruhigt sein; (*frightened*) erschreckt sein; **to cause a good deal of ~** große Unruhe auslösen; **to cause sb ~** jdn beunruhigen.
(b) (*warning*) Alarm *m* ◆ **to raise** *or* **give/sound the ~** Alarm geben *or* (*fig*) schlagen.
(c) (*device*) Alarmanlage *f* ◆ **~ (clock)** Wecker *m*.
[2] *vt* (a) (*worry*) beunruhigen; (*frighten*) erschrecken ◆ **don't be ~ed** erschrecken Sie nicht; **the news ~ed the whole country** die Nachricht alarmierte das ganze Land *or* versetzte das ganze Land in Aufregung.
(b) (*warn of danger*) warnen; *fire brigade etc* alarmieren.

alarm *in cpds* Alarm-; **~ bell** *n* Alarmglocke *f*; **~ call** *n* (*Telec*) Weckruf *m*; **~ clock** *n* Wecker *m*.

alarming [ə'lɑːmɪŋ] *adj* (*worrying*) beunruhigend; (*frightening*) erschreckend; *news* alarmierend.

alarmingly [ə'lɑːmɪŋlɪ] *adv* erschreckend.

alarmist [ə'lɑːmɪst] [1] *n* Unheilsprophet *m*, Kassandra *f* (*geh*).
[2] *adj speech* Unheil prophezeiend *attr*.

alarum [ə'lærəm] *n* (*old*) *see* **alarm**.

alas [ə'læs] *interj* leider ◆ **~, he didn't come** leider kam er nicht.

Alaska [ə'læskə] *n* Alaska *nt*.

Alaskan [ə'læskən] [1] *n* Einwohner(in *f*) *m* von Alaska.
[2] *adj* Alaska-; *customs, winter* in Alaska; *fish, produce* aus Alaska.

alb [ælb] *n* (*Eccl*) Alba *f*.

Albania [æl'beɪnɪə] *n* Albanien *nt*.

Albanian [æl'beɪnɪən] [1] *adj* albanisch.
[2] *n* (a) Albaner(in *f*) *m*. (b) (*language*) Albanisch *nt*.

albatross ['ælbətrɒs] *n* Albatros *m*.

albeit [ɔːl'biːɪt] *conj* (*esp liter*) obgleich, wenn auch.

albinism ['ælbɪnɪzəm] *n* Albinismus *m*.

albino [æl'biːnəʊ] [1] *n* Albino *m*.
[2] *adj* Albino-.

Albion ['ælbɪən] *n* (*poet*) Albion *nt*.

album ['ælbəm] *n* Album *nt*.

albumen ['ælbjʊmɪn] *n* Albumin *nt*.

albuminous [æl'bjuːmɪnəs] *adj* albuminös.

alchemist ['ælkɪmɪst] *n* Alchemist *m*.

alchemy ['ælkɪmɪ] *n* Alchemie, Alchimie *f*.

alcohol ['ælkəhɒl] *n* Alkohol *m*.

alcohol-free ['ælkəhɒl'friː] *adj* alkoholfrei.

alcoholic [ˌælkə'hɒlɪk] [1] *adj drink* alkoholisch; *person* alkoholsüchtig, trunksüchtig.
[2] *n* (*person*) Alkoholiker(in *f*) *m*, Trinker(in *f*) *m* ◆ **to be an ~** Alkoholiker(in) *or* Trinker(in) sein; **A~s Anonymous** Anonyme Alkoholiker *pl*.

alcoholism ['ælkəhɒlɪzəm] *n* Alkoholismus *m*, Trunksucht *f*.

alcove ['ælkəʊv] *n* Alkoven *m*, Nische *f*; (*in wall*) Nische *f*.

alder ['ɔːldəʳ] *n* Erle *f*.

alderman ['ɔːldəmən] *n, pl* **-men** [-mən] Alderman *m* (*Ratsherr*).
ale [eɪl] *n* (*old*) Ale *nt*; *see* **real.**
aleck ['ælɪk] *n see* **smart ~.**
alehouse ['eɪl,haʊs] *n* (*old*) Wirtshaus *nt*, Schenke *f*.
alert [ə'lɜːt] [1] *adj* aufmerksam; (*as character trait*) aufgeweckt; *mind* scharf, hell; *dog* wachsam ◆ **to be ~ to sth** vor etw (*dat*) auf der Hut sein.
[2] *vt* warnen (*to* vor *+dat*); *troops* in Gefechtsbereitschaft versetzen; *fire brigade etc* alarmieren.
[3] *n* Alarm *m* ◆ **to give the ~** (*Mil*) Gefechtsbereitschaft befehlen; (*in the fire brigade etc*) den Alarm auslösen; (*fig*) warnen; **to put on the ~** in Gefechts-/Alarmbereitschaft versetzen; **to be on (the) ~** einsatzbereit sein; (*be on lookout*) auf der Hut sein (*for* vor *+dat*).
alertness [ə'lɜːtnɪs] *n see adj* Aufmerksamkeit *f*; Aufgewecktheit *f*; Schärfe *f*; Wachsamkeit *f*.
Aleutian Islands [ə'luːʃən] *npl* Aleuten *pl*.
A level ['eɪ,levl] *n* (*Brit*) Abschluß *m* der Sekundarstufe 2 ◆ **to take one's ~s** ≃ das Abitur machen; **~s** das Abitur in drei Fächern.
Alexander [,ælɪg'zɑːndə^r] *n* Alexander *m* ◆ **~ the Great** Alexander der Große.
alexandrine [,ælɪg'zændraɪn] [1] *n* Alexandriner *m*.
[2] *adj* alexandrinisch.
alfalfa [æl'fælfə] *n* Luzerne, Alfalfa *f*.
alfresco [æl'freskəʊ] *adj, adv* im Freien ◆ **an ~ lunch** ein Mittagessen im Freien.
alga ['ælgə] *n, pl* **-e** ['ælgɪ] Alge *f*.
algebra ['ældʒɪbrə] *n* Algebra *f*.
algebraic [,ældʒɪ'breɪɪk] *adj* algebraisch.
Algeria [æl'dʒɪərɪə] *n* Algerien *nt*.
Algerian [æl'dʒɪərɪən] [1] *n* Algerier(in *f*) *m*.
[2] *adj* algerisch.
Algiers [æl'dʒɪəz] *n* Algier *nt*.
algorithm ['ælgə,rɪðəm] *n* Algorithmus *m*.
algorithmic [,ælgə'rɪθmɪk] *adj* algorithmisch.
alias ['eɪlɪæs] [1] *adv* alias.
[2] *n* Deckname *m*.
alibi ['ælɪbaɪ] [1] *n* Alibi *nt*.
[2] *vt* ein Alibi liefern für.
alien ['eɪlɪən] [1] *n* (*esp Pol*) Ausländer(in *f*) *m*; (*Sci-Fi*) außerirdisches Wesen.
[2] *adj* **(a)** (*foreign*) ausländisch; (*Sci-Fi*) außerirdisch. **(b)** (*different*) fremd ◆ **to be ~ to sb/sb's nature/sth** jdm/jds Wesen/einer Sache fremd sein. **(c)** (*Comput*) fremd.
alienate ['eɪlɪəneɪt] *vt* **(a)** *people* befremden; *affections* zerstören, sich (*dat*) verscherzen ◆ **to ~ oneself from sb/sth** sich jdm/einer Sache entfremden; **Brecht set out to ~ his audience** Brecht wollte, daß sich die Zuschauer distanzieren. **(b)** (*Jur*) *property, money* übertragen.
alienation [,eɪlɪə'neɪʃən] *n* **(a)** Entfremdung *f* (*from* von); (*Theat*) Distanzierung *f* ◆ **~ effect** Verfremdungseffekt *m*; **~ of affections** (*Jur*) Entfremdung *f*. **(b)** (*Jur: property*) Übertragung *f*. **(c)** (*Psych*) Alienation *f*.
alight[1] [ə'laɪt] *vi* **(a)** (*form: person*) aussteigen (*from* aus); (*from horse*) absitzen (*from* von). **(b)** (*bird*) sich niederlassen (*on* auf *+dat*); (*form: aircraft etc*) niedergehen (*on* auf *+dat*) ◆ **his eyes ~ed on the ring** sein Blick fiel auf den Ring. **(c)** (*form*) **to ~ on a fact/an idea** *etc* auf ein Faktum/eine Idee *etc* stoßen.
alight[2] *adj pred* **to be ~** (*fire*) brennen; (*building also*) in Flammen stehen; **to keep the fire ~** das Feuer in Gang halten; **to set sth ~** etw in Brand setzen *or* stecken; **her face was ~ with pleasure** ihr Gesicht *or* sie glühte vor Freude.
align [ə'laɪn] [1] *vt* **(a)** *wheels of car, gun sights etc* ausrichten; (*bring into line also*) in eine Linie bringen. **(b)** (*Fin, Pol*) *currencies, policies* aufeinander ausrichten ◆ **to ~ sth with sth** etw auf etw (*acc*) ausrichten; **to ~ oneself with a party** (*follow policy of*) sich nach einer Partei ausrichten; (*join forces with*) sich einer Partei anschließen; **they have ~ed themselves against him/it** sie haben sich gegen ihn/dagegen zusammengeschlossen.
[2] *vi* **(a)** (*lit*) ausgerichtet sein (*with* nach); (*come into line*) eine Linie bilden. **(b)** (*side*) *see vt* (*b*).
alignment [ə'laɪnmənt] *n* **(a)** *see vt* (*a*) Ausrichtung *f* ◆ **to be out of ~** nicht richtig ausgerichtet sein (*with* nach).
(b) (*of currencies, policies etc*) Ausrichtung (*with* auf *+acc*), Orientierung (*with* nach) *f* ◆ **to be out of ~ with one another** nicht übereinstimmen, sich nicht aneinander orientieren; **to bring sb back into ~ with the party** jdn zwingen, wieder auf die Parteilinie einzuschwenken; **his unexpected ~ with the Socialists** seine unerwartete Parteinahme für die Sozialisten; **he argued for a new ~ of the governing parties** er war für eine Neuordnung der Regierungsparteien; **the new ~ of world powers** die Neugruppierung der Weltmächte.
▼ **alike** [ə'laɪk] *adj pred, adv* gleich ◆ **they're/they look very ~** sie sind/sehen sich (*dat*) sehr ähnlich; **they all look ~ to me** für mich sehen sie alle gleich aus; **you men are all ~!** ihr Männer seid doch alle gleich!; **it's all ~ to me** mir ist das gleich *or* einerlei; **they always think ~** sie sind immer einer Meinung; **winter and summer ~** Sommer wie Winter.
alimentary [,ælɪ'mentərɪ] *adj* (*Anat*) Verdauungs- ◆ **~ canal** Verdauungskanal *m*.
alimony ['ælɪmənɪ] *n* Unterhaltszahlung *f* ◆ **to pay ~** Unterhalt zahlen.
alive [ə'laɪv] *adj* **(a)** *pred* (*living*) lebendig, lebend *attr* ◆ **dead or ~** tot oder lebendig; **to be ~** leben; **the greatest musician ~** der größte lebende Musiker; **while ~ he was always ...** zu seinen Lebzeiten war er immer ...; **it's good to be ~** das Leben ist schön; **no man ~** niemand auf der ganzen Welt; **the wickedest man ~** der schlechteste Mensch auf der ganzen Welt; **to stay** *or* **keep ~** am Leben bleiben; **to keep sb/sth ~** (*lit, fig*) jdn am Leben erhalten/etw am Leben *or* lebendig erhalten; **to do sth as well as anyone ~** etw so gut wie jeder andere können; **to be ~ and kicking** (*hum inf*) *or* **~ and well** gesund und munter sein; **he's very much ~** er ist ausgesprochen lebendig.
(b) (*lively*) lebendig ◆ **to keep one's mind ~** geistig rege bleiben; **to come ~** (*liven up*) lebendig werden; (*prick up ears etc*) wach werden.
(c) *pred* (*aware*) **to be ~ to sth** sich (*dat*) einer Sache (*gen*) bewußt sein; **to be ~ to certain possibilities/sb's interests** gewisse Möglichkeiten/jds Interessen im Auge haben.
(d) ~ with (*full of*) erfüllt von; **to be ~ with tourists/fish/insects** *etc* von Touristen/Fischen/Insekten *etc* wimmeln.
alkali ['ælkəlaɪ] *n, pl* **-(e)s** Base, Lauge *f*; (*metal, Agr*) Alkali *nt*.
alkaline ['ælkəlaɪn] *adj* basisch, alkalisch ◆ **~ solution** Lauge *f*.
alkalinity [,ælkə'lɪnɪtɪ] *n* Alkalität *f*.
alkaloid ['ælkəlɔɪd] *n* Alkaloid *nt*.
▼ **all** [ɔːl] [1] *adj* **(a)** (*with pl n*) alle *no art*; (*every single one also*) sämtliche *no art*; (*with sing n*) ganze(r, s), alle(r, s) *no art*; (*preceding poss art also*) all ◆ **~ the books/people** alle Bücher/Leute, die ganzen Bücher/Leute; **she brought ~ the children** sie brachte alle *or* sämtliche Kinder mit; **~ the tobacco/milk/fruit** der ganze Tabak/die ganze Milch/das ganze Obst, all der *or* aller Tabak/all die *or* alle Milch/all das *or* alles Obst; **~ my strength/books/friends** all meine Kraft/all(e) meine Bücher/Freunde, meine ganze Kraft/ganzen Bücher/Freunde; **~ my life** mein ganzes Leben (lang); **~ Spain** ganz Spanien; **we ~ sat down** wir setzten uns alle; **~ you boys can come with me** ihr Jungen könnt alle mit mir kommen; **I invited them ~** ich habe sie alle eingeladen; **they ~ came** sie sind alle gekommen; **~ the time** die ganze Zeit; **~ day (long)** den ganzen Tag (lang); **to dislike ~ sport** jeglichen Sport ablehnen; **I don't understand ~ that** ich verstehe das alles nicht; **what's ~ that water?** wo kommt das ganze *or* all das Wasser her?; **what's ~ this/that about?** was soll das Ganze?; **what's ~ this/that?** was ist denn das?; (*annoyed*) was soll denn das!; **what's ~ this mess?** was ist das denn für eine Unordnung?; **what's ~ this I hear about you leaving?** was höre ich da! Sie wollen gehen?; **he took/spent it ~** er hat alles genommen/ausgegeben; **the money was ~ there** alles Geld *or* das ganze Geld war da; **~ kinds** *or* **sorts** *or* **manner of people** alle möglichen Leute; **to be ~ things to ~ men** (*person: be on good terms with*) sich mit jedem gut stellen; (*thing, invention, new software etc*) das Ideale sein; **a book that is ~ things to ~ men** ein Buch, das jedem etwas bietet; **it is beyond ~ doubt/question** es steht außer Zweifel/Frage; **in ~ respects** in jeder Hinsicht; **why me of ~ people?** warum ausgerechnet ich?; **of ~ the idiots/stupid things!** so ein Idiot/so was Dummes!
(b) (*utmost*) **with ~ possible speed** so schnell wie möglich; **with ~ due care/speed** mit angemessener Sorgfalt/in angemessenem Tempo; **they will take ~ possible care of it** sie werden sich so gut wie möglich darum kümmern.
(c) (*US inf*) **you ~** ihr (alle).
(d) for ~ his wealth trotz (all) seines Reichtums; **for ~ that** trotz allem, trotzdem; **for ~ I know she could be ill** was weiß ich, vielleicht ist sie krank; **is he in Paris? — for ~ I know he could be** ist er in Paris? — schon möglich, was weiß ich!
[2] *pron* **(a)** (*everything*) alles; (*everybody*) alle *pl* ◆ **~ who knew him** alle, die ihn kannten; **~ of them/of it** (sie) alle/alles; **~ of Paris/of the house** ganz Paris/das ganze Haus; **that is ~ I can tell you** mehr kann ich Ihnen nicht sagen; **he was ~ to her** er bedeutete ihr alles; **it was ~ I could do not to laugh** ich mußte an mich halten, um nicht zu lachen; **and I don't know what ~** (*dial inf*) und was weiß ich noch alles; **~ of 5 kms/£5** ganze 5 km/£ 5; **he ate the orange, peel and ~** er hat die ganze Orange gegessen, samt der Schale; **what with the snow and ~** (*inf*) mit dem ganzen Schnee und so (*inf*); **the whole family came, children and ~** (*inf*) die Familie kam mit Kind und Kegel; **the score was/the teams were two ~** es stand zwei zu zwei; **~ found** insgesamt, alles in allem.
(b) at ~ überhaupt; **nothing at ~** überhaupt *or* gar nichts; **did/didn't you say anything at ~?** haben Sie überhaupt etwas gesagt/gar *or* überhaupt nichts gesagt?; **it's not bad at ~** das ist gar nicht schlecht.
▼ **(c) in ~** insgesamt; **ten people in ~** *or* **~ told** insgesamt zehn Personen; **~ in ~** alles in allem.
(d) (*with superl*) **happiest/earliest/clearest** *etc* **of ~** am glücklichsten/frühsten/klarsten *etc*; **that would be best of ~** das wäre am besten; **I like him best of ~** von allen mag ich ihn am liebsten; **most of ~** am meisten; **most of ~ I'd like to be ...** am liebsten wäre ich ...; **the best car of ~** das allerbeste Auto.
[3] *adv* **(a)** (*quite, entirely*) ganz ◆ **dressed ~ in white, ~ dressed in white** ganz in Weiß (gekleidet); **~ woman** ganz Frau; **~ dirty/excited** *etc* ganz schmutzig/aufgeregt *etc*; **~ wool** reine Wolle; **an ~ wool carpet** ein reinwollener Teppich, ein Teppich aus reiner Wolle; **it was red ~ over** es war ganz rot; **~ up the side of the building** auf der ganzen Seite des Gebäudes; **~ along the road** die ganze Straße entlang; **I feared that ~ along** das habe ich schon die ganze Zeit befürchtet; **there were chairs ~ round the room** rundum im Zimmer standen Stühle; **he ordered whiskies/drinks ~ round** er hat für alle Whisky/Getränke bestellt; **~ the same** trotzdem, trotz allem; **it's ~ the same** *or* **~ one to me** das ist mir (ganz) egal *or* einerlei; **~ too soon** viel zu schnell, viel zu früh; **what's the film ~ about?** wovon handelt der Film überhaupt?; **I'll tell you ~ about it** ich erzähl dir alles; **it was ~ about a little girl** es handelte von einem kleinen Mädchen; **that's ~ very fine**

➤ LANGUAGE IN USE: **alike** → 5.4 **all: 2c** → 26.1

or **well** das ist alles ganz schön und gut; **it's not as bad as ~ that** so schlimm ist es nun auch wieder nicht; **it isn't ~ *that* expensive!** so teuer ist es nun wieder auch nicht; **if at ~ possible** wenn irgend möglich; **I'm not at ~ sure/angry** *etc*, **I'm not sure/angry** *etc* **at ~** ich bin mir ganz und gar nicht sicher, ich bin gar nicht ganz sicher/ich bin ganz und gar nicht wütend *etc*; **I don't know at ~** ich weiß es überhaupt nicht; **I'm ~ for it!** ich bin ganz dafür; **to be** *or* **feel ~ in** (*inf*) total erledigt sein (*inf*); **he's ~/not ~ there** (*inf*) er ist voll/nicht ganz da (*inf*).
(b) **~ but** fast; **he ~ but died** er wäre fast gestorben; **he ~ but lost it** er hätte es fast verloren.
(c) (*with comp*) **~ the hotter/prettier/happier** *etc* noch heißer/hübscher/glücklicher *etc*; **~ the funnier because ...** um so lustiger, weil ...; **I feel ~ the better for my holiday** jetzt, wo ich Urlaub gemacht habe, geht's mir viel besser; **~ the more so since ...** besonders weil ...; **~ the better to see you with** damit ich dich besser sehen kann.
[4] *n* **one's ~** alles; **he staked his ~ on this race/venture** er setzte alles auf dieses Rennen/Unternehmen; **the horses were giving their ~** die Pferde gaben ihr Letztes.

Allah ['ælə] *n* Allah *m*.

all: ~-American *adj team, player* amerikanische(r, s) National-; **an ~-American boy** ein richtiger amerikanischer Junge; **~-around** *adj* (*US*) *see* **~-round**.

allay [ə'leɪ] *vt* verringern; *doubt, fears, suspicion* (weitgehend) zerstreuen.

all: ~-clear *n* Entwarnung *f*; **to give/sound the ~-clear** Entwarnung geben, entwarnen; **~-day** *adj* ganztägig; **it was an ~-day meeting** die Sitzung dauerte den ganzen Tag.

allegation [,ælɪ'geɪʃən] *n* Behauptung *f*.

allege [ə'ledʒ] *vt* behaupten ◆ **the remarks ~d to have been made by him** die Bemerkungen, die er gemacht haben soll *or* angeblich gemacht hat; **he is ~d to have said that ...** er soll angeblich gesagt haben, daß ...

alleged *adj*, **~ly** *adv* [ə'ledʒd, ə'ledʒɪdlɪ] angeblich.

allegiance [ə'li:dʒəns] *n* Treue *f* (*to dat*) ◆ **oath of ~** Fahnen- *or* Treueeid *m*.

allegoric(al) [,ælɪ'gɒrɪk(əl)] *adj*, **allegorically** [,ælɪ'gɒrɪkəlɪ] *adv* allegorisch.

allegory ['ælɪgərɪ] *n* Allegorie *f*.

allegro [ə'legrəʊ] [1] *adj, adv* allegro.
[2] *n* Allegro *nt*.

all-electric [,ɔ:lɪ'lektrɪk] *adj* **an ~ house** ein Haus, in dem alles elektrisch ist; **we're ~** bei uns ist alles elektrisch.

alleluia [,ælɪ'lu:jə] [1] *interj* (h)alleluja.
[2] *n* (H)alleluja *nt*.

all-embracing [,ɔ:lɪm'breɪsɪŋ] *adj* (all)umfassend.

Allen ® ['ælən]: **~ key** *n* Inbusschlüssel ® *m*; **~ screw** *n* Inbusschraube ® *f*.

allergen ['ælə,dʒən] *n* (*Med*) Allergen *nt*.

allergic [ə'lɜ:dʒɪk] *adj* (*lit, fig*) allergisch (*to* gegen).

allergist ['ælədʒɪst] *n* Allergologe *m*, Allergologin *f*.

allergy ['ælədʒɪ] *n* Allergie *f* (*to* gegen) ◆ **he seems to have an ~ to work** (*hum*) er scheint gegen Arbeit allergisch zu sein.

alleviate [ə'li:vɪeɪt] *vt* lindern.

alleviation [ə,li:vɪ'eɪʃən] *n* Linderung *f*.

alley ['ælɪ] *n* **(a)** (*between buildings*) (enge) Gasse; (*between gardens*) Weg, Pfad *m*; (*in garden*) Laubengang *m*. **(b)** (*bowling ~, skittle ~*) Bahn *f*.

alley: ~ cat *n* streunende Katze; **to fight like ~ cats** sich in den Haaren liegen; **to yell like ~ cats** kreischen; **she's got the morals of an ~ cat** (*inf*) sie treibt's mit jedem; **~way** *n* Durchgang *m*.

all: ~-fired *adj* (*US inf*) furchtbar (*inf*), schrecklich (*inf*); **A~ Fools' Day** *n der erste April*; **A~ Hallows' (Day)** *n see* **A~ Saints' Day**.

alliance [ə'laɪəns] *n* Verbindung *f*; (*institutions also, of states*) Bündnis *nt*; (*in historical contexts*) Allianz *f* ◆ **partners in an ~** Bündnispartner *pl*.

allied ['ælaɪd] *adj* **(a)** verbunden; (*for attack, defence etc*) verbündet, aliiert. **(b)** (*Biol, fig*) verwandt. **(c) the A~ forces** die Alliierten; **an A~ attack** eine Offensive der Alliierten.

alligator ['ælɪgeɪtə^r] *n* Alligator *m* ◆ **~(-skin) bag** Alligatorledertasche *f*.

all: ~-important *adj* außerordentlich wichtig; **the ~-important question** die Frage, auf die es ankommt; **~-in** *adj* **(a)** (*inclusive*) Inklusiv-; **(b)** (*Sport*) **~-in wrestling** Freistilringen *nt*; *see also* **all 3 (a)**.

alliterate [ə'lɪtəreɪt] *vi* einen Stabreim bilden, alliterieren.

alliteration [ə,lɪtə'reɪʃən] *n* Alliteration *f*, Stabreim *m*.

alliterative [ə'lɪtərətɪv] *adj* Stabreim-, stabend, alliterierend.

all: ~-merciful *adj God* allbarmherzig, allgütig; **~-night** *adj attr café* (die ganze Nacht) durchgehend geöffnet; **an ~-night party** eine Party, die die ganze Nacht durchgeht; **we had an~-night party** wir haben die ganze Nacht durchgemacht; **it was an ~-night journey** wir/sie *etc* sind die ganze Nacht durchgefahren; **we have ~-night opening** wir haben (die ganze Nacht) durchgehend geöffnet; **~-night opening is allowed in some countries** in manchen Ländern sind 24stündige Öffnungszeiten erlaubt; **we have an ~-night service** wir haben einen durchgehenden Nachtdienst; **there is an ~-night bus service** die Busse verkehren die ganze Nacht über; **~-nighter** *n* (*inf*) *Musik-/Filmveranstaltung f etc, die die ganze Nacht hindurch andauert*.

allocate ['æləʊkeɪt] *vt* (*allot*) zuteilen, zuweisen (*to sb* jdm); (*apportion*) verteilen (*to* auf +*acc*); *tasks* vergeben (*to* an +*acc*) ◆ **to ~ money to** *or* **for a project** Geld für ein Projekt bestimmen.

allocation [,æləʊ'keɪʃən] *n see vt* Zuteilung, Zuweisung *f*; Verteilung *f*; (*sum allocated*) Zuwendung *f*.

allopathy [ə'lɒpəθɪ] *n* (*Med*) Allopathie *f*.

allophone ['æləfəʊn] *n* (*Ling*) Allophon *nt*.

allot [ə'lɒt] *vt* zuteilen, zuweisen (*to sb/sth* jdm/etw); *time* vorsehen (*to* für); *money* bestimmen (*to* für).

allotment [ə'lɒtmənt] *n* **(a)** *see vt* Zuteilung, Zuweisung *f*; Vorsehen *nt*; Bestimmung *f*; (*amount of money allotted*) Zuwendung *f*. **(b)** (*Brit: plot of ground*) Schrebergarten *m*.

all: ~-out [1] *adj strike* total; *attack* massiv; *effort, attempt* äußerste(r, s); *support* uneingeschränkt; [2] *adv* mit aller Kraft; **to go ~-out** sein Letztes *or* Äußerstes geben; **to go ~-out to do sth** alles daransetzen, etw zu tun; **to go ~-out for victory** alles daransetzen, (um) zu siegen; **~-over** *adj* ganzflächig.

▼ **allow** [ə'laʊ] [1] *vt* **(a)** (*permit*) *sth* erlauben, gestatten; *behaviour etc also* zulassen ◆ **to ~ sb sth/to do sth** jdm etw erlauben *or* gestatten/jdm erlauben *or* gestatten, etw zu tun; **to be ~ed to do sth** etw tun dürfen; **smoking is not ~ed** Rauchen ist nicht gestattet; **"no dogs ~ed"** „Hunde müssen draußen bleiben"; **we were ~ed one drink** uns wurde ein Drink erlaubt *or* gestattet; **we're not ~ed much freedom** wir haben nicht viel Freiheit; **will you be ~ed to?** darfst du denn?; **will you ~ him to?** erlauben Sie es ihm?, lassen Sie ihn denn? (*inf*); **to ~ oneself sth** sich (*dat*) etw erlauben; (*treat oneself*) sich (*dat*) etw gönnen; **to ~ oneself to be persuaded/waited on** *etc* sich überreden/bedienen *etc* lassen; **~ me!** gestatten Sie (*form*); **~ me to help you** gestatten Sie, daß ich Ihnen helfe (*form*); **to ~ sth to happen** etw zulassen, zulassen, daß etw geschieht; **to ~ sb in/out/past** *etc* jdn hinein-/hinaus-/vorbeilassen; **to be ~ed in/out/past** hinein-/hinaus-/vorbeidürfen.
(b) (*recognize, accept*) *claim, appeal* anerkennen; *goal also* geben.
(c) (*allocate, grant*) *discount* geben; *space* lassen; *time* einplanen, einberechnen; *money* geben, zugestehen; (*in tax, Jur*) zugestehen ◆ **~ (yourself) an hour to cross the city** rechnen Sie mit einer Stunde, um durch die Stadt zu kommen; **he ~ed me two hours for that** er gab mir zwei Stunden dafür; **~ 5 cms extra** geben Sie 5 cm zu.
(d) (*concede*) annehmen ◆ **~ing** *or* **if we ~ that ...** angenommen, (daß) ...
[2] *vi* **if time ~s** falls es zeitlich möglich ist.

◆**allow for** *vi +prep obj* berücksichtigen; *factor, cost, shrinkage, error also* einrechnen, einkalkulieren ◆ **~ing ~ the circumstances** unter Berücksichtigung der gegebenen Umstände; **after ~ing ~** nach Berücksichtigung (+*gen*).

◆**allow of** *vi +prep obj* zulassen.

allowable [ə'laʊəbl] *adj* zulässig; (*Fin: in tax*) absetzbar, abzugsfähig ◆ **~ expenses** (*Fin*) abzugsfähige Kosten.

allowance [ə'laʊəns] *n* **(a)** finanzielle Unterstützung; (*paid by state*) Beihilfe *f*; (*father to son*) Unterhaltsgeld *nt*; (*as compensation: for unsociable hours, overseas ~ etc*) Zulage *f*; (*on business trip*) Spesen *pl*; (*spending money*) Taschengeld *nt* ◆ **clothing ~** Kleidungsgeld *nt*; **petrol ~** Benzingeld *nt*; **travelling ~** Fahrtkostenzuschuß *m*; **his father still gives him an ~** sein Vater unterstützt ihn noch immer finanziell; **he gives his wife a dress ~** er gibt seiner Frau einen Zuschuß zu den Kleidungskosten; **he made her an ~ of £100 a month** er stellte ihr monatlich £ 100 zur Verfügung.
(b) (*Fin: tax ~*) Freibetrag *m*.
(c) (*Fin, Comm: discount*) (Preis)nachlaß *m* (*on* für); (*quantity allowed: for shrinkage etc*) Zugabe *f*.
(d) (*acceptance: of goal, claim, appeal*) Anerkennung *f*.
(e) Zugeständnisse *pl* ◆ **to make ~(s) for sth** etw berücksichtigen; **you have to make ~s** Sie müssen (gewisse) Zugeständnisse machen.

allowedly [ə'laʊɪdlɪ] *adv* gewiß, zugegeben.

alloy ['ælɔɪ] [1] *n* Legierung *f*.
[2] *vt* legieren; (*fig liter*) (ver)mischen ◆ **pleasure ~ed with suffering** von Leid getrübte Freude.

all: ~-powerful *adj* allmächtig; **~-purpose** *adj* Allzweck-.

all right ['ɔ:l'raɪt] [1] *adj pred* **(a)** (*satisfactory*) in Ordnung, okay (*inf*) ◆ **it's ~** (*not too bad*) es geht; (*working properly*) es ist in Ordnung; **that's** *or* **it's ~** (*after thanks*) schon gut, gern geschehen; (*after apology*) schon gut, das macht nichts; **it's ~, you don't have to** schon gut, du mußt nicht unbedingt; **to taste/look/smell ~** ganz gut schmecken/aussehen/riechen; **is it ~ for me to leave early?** kann ich früher gehen?; **it's ~ by me** ich habe nichts dagegen, von mir aus gern; **it's ~ for you** du hast's gut; **it's ~ for you (to talk)** du hast gut reden; **it's ~ for him to laugh** er hat gut lachen; **I made it ~ with him** ich habe das (mit ihm) wieder eingerenkt; **I saw him ~** (*inf*) (*for petrol, money etc*) ich hab ihn (dafür) entschädigt; **it'll be ~ on the night** es wird schon klappen, wenn es darauf ankommt; **he's ~** (*inf: is a good guy*) der ist in Ordnung (*inf*).
(b) (*safe, unharmed*) *person, machine* in Ordnung, okay (*inf*); *object, building, tree etc* heil, ganz, okay (*inf*) ◆ **are you ~?** (*healthy*) geht es Ihnen gut?; (*unharmed*) ist Ihnen etwas passiert?; **are you feeling ~?** fehlt Ihnen was?; (*iro*) sag mal, fehlt dir was?; **he's ~ again** es geht ihm wieder gut, er ist wieder in Ordnung (*inf*); **are you ~ (in there)?** ist alles in Ordnung (da drin)?; **that bomb damaged half the street but our house was ~** die Bombe hat die halbe Straße zerstört, aber unserem Haus ist nichts passiert; **can we come out? is it ~?** können wir rauskommen? ist es sicher?; **is it ~ for us to come out now?** können wir jetzt rauskommen?; **it's ~ now, Mummy's here** jetzt ist alles wieder gut, Mutti ist ja da; **it's ~, don't worry** keine Angst, machen Sie sich keine Sorgen; **we're ~ for the rest of our lives** wir haben für den Rest des Lebens ausgesorgt.
[2] *adv* **(a)** (*satisfactorily*) ganz gut, ganz ordentlich; (*safely*) gut ◆ **did I do it ~?** habe ich es recht gemacht?; **did you get home ~?** bist du gut nach Hause gekommen?; **did you get/find it ~?** haben Sie es denn bekommen/gefunden?

➤ LANGUAGE IN USE: **allow: 1a** → 3.1, 9.2, 10.4

(b) (*certainly*) schon ◆ **he'll come ~** er wird schon kommen; **that's the boy ~** das ist der Junge; **he's a clever man ~** er ist schon intelligent; **oh yes, we heard you ~** o ja, und ob wir dich gehört haben.
[3] *interj* gut, schön, okay (*inf*); (*in agreement also*) in Ordnung ◆ **may I leave early? — ~** kann ich früher gehen? — ja; **~ that's enough!** okay *or* komm, jetzt reicht's (aber)!; **~, ~! I'm coming** schon gut, schon gut, ich komme ja!

all: ~-round *adj athlete* Allround-; *student* vielseitig begabt; *improvement* in jeder Beziehung *or* Hinsicht; **~-rounder** *n* Allroundmann *m*; (*Sport*) Allroundsportler(in *f*) *m*; **A~ Saints' Day** *n* Allerheiligen *nt*; **A~ Souls' Day** *n* Allerseelen *nt*; **~spice** *n* Piment *m or nt*; **~-star** *adj* Star-; **~-terrain vehicle** *n* Geländefahrzeug *nt*; **~-time** *adj* aller Zeiten; **an ~-time record** der Rekord aller Zeiten; **an ~-time high/low** der höchste/niedrigste Stand aller Zeiten; **~-time great** Unvergeßliche(r), Unvergessene(r) *mf*; **to be an ~-time favourite** seit eh und je beliebt sein.

◆**allude to** [ə'lu:d] *vi +prep obj* anspielen auf (*+acc*).

allure [ə'ljʊəʳ] [1] *vt* locken, anziehen.
[2] *n* Reiz *m*.

allurement [ə'ljʊəmənt] *n* Anziehungskraft *f*, Reiz *m*.

alluring [ə'ljʊərɪŋ] *adj* verführerisch.

alluringly [ə'ljʊərɪŋlɪ] *adv see adj*.

allusion [ə'lu:ʒən] *n* Anspielung *f* (*to* auf *+acc*).

allusive [ə'lu:sɪv] *adj* voller Anspielungen.

allusively [ə'lu:sɪvlɪ] *adv* indirekt.

alluvial [ə'lu:vɪəl] *adj* angeschwemmt.

alluvium [ə'lu:vɪəm] *n* Anschwemmung *f*.

all-weather ['ɔ:l'weðəʳ] *adj* Allwetter-.

all-wheel drive ['ɔ:lwi:l'draɪv] *n* Allradantrieb *m*.

ally ['ælaɪ] [1] *n* Verbündete(r) *mf*, Bundesgenosse *m*; (*Hist*) Alliierte(r) *m*.
[2] [ə'laɪ] *vt* verbinden (*with, to* mit); (*for attack, defence etc*) verbünden, alliieren (*with, to* mit) ◆ **to ~ oneself with** *or* **to sb** sich mit jdm zusammentun/verbünden *or* alliieren.

alma mater ['ælmə'meɪtəʳ] *n* Alma Mater *f*.

almanac ['ɔ:lmənæk] *n* Almanach *m*; *see* **nautical**.

almighty [ɔ:l'maɪtɪ] [1] *adj* (a) *god, person* allmächtig; *power* unumschränkt ◆ **A~ God, God A~** (*Eccl*) der Allmächtige; (*address in prayer*) allmächtiger Gott; **God A~!** (*inf*) Allmächtiger! (*inf*), allmächtiger Gott! (*inf*). (b) (*inf*) *fool, idiot* mordsmäßig (*inf*); *blow* mächtig (*inf*) ◆ **to make an ~ fool of oneself** sich mordsmäßig blamieren (*inf*).
[2] *n* **the A~** der Allmächtige.

almond ['ɑ:mənd] *n* Mandel *f*; (*tree*) Mandelbaum *m*.

almond *in cpds* Mandel-; **~-eyed** *adj* mandeläugig; **~ oil** *n* Mandelöl *nt*; **~ paste** *n* Marzipanmasse *f*; **~-shaped** *adj* mandelförmig.

almoner ['ɑ:mənəʳ] *n* (a) (*dated Brit: in hospital*) Krankenhausfürsorger(in *f*) *m*. (b) (*old: distributor of alms*) Almosenpfleger *m*.

almost ['ɔ:lməʊst] *adv* fast, beinahe ◆ **he ~ fell** er wäre fast gefallen.

alms [ɑ:mz] *npl* Almosen *pl*.

alms: ~ box *n* Almosenstock *m*; **~ house** *n* Armenhaus *nt*.

aloe ['æləʊ] *n* (*Bot, Med*) Aloe *f*.

aloft [ə'lɒft] *adv* (*into the air*) empor; (*in the air*) hoch droben; (*Naut*) oben in der Takelung ◆ **to go ~** (*Naut*) in die Takelung hinaufklettern.

alone [ə'ləʊn] [1] *adj pred* allein(e) ◆ **we're not ~ in thinking that** wir stehen mit dieser Meinung nicht allein; **there is one man who, ~ in the world, knows** ... es gibt einen, der als einziger auf der Welt weiß ...; *see* **leave, let**³.
[2] *adv* allein(e) ◆ **to live on bread ~** von Brot allein leben; **it's mine ~** das gehört mir (ganz) allein(e); **that charm which is hers ~** der ihr ganz eigene Charme; **the hotel ~ cost £95** das Hotel allein kostete (schon) £ 95, (allein) schon das Hotel kostete £ 95; **to stand ~** (*fig*) einzig dastehen.

along [ə'lɒŋ] [1] *prep* (*direction*) entlang (*+acc*), lang (*+acc*) (*inf*); (*position*) entlang (*+dat*) ◆ **he walked ~ the river** er ging den/(an) dem Fluß entlang; **somewhere ~ the way** irgendwo unterwegs *or* auf dem Weg; (*fig*) irgendwann einmal; **somewhere ~ here/there** irgendwo hier/dort (herum); (*in this/that direction*) irgendwo in dieser Richtung/der Richtung; **the Red Lion? isn't that somewhere ~ your way?** der Rote Löwe? ist der nicht irgendwo in Ihrer Nähe *or* Gegend?; *see* **all**.
[2] *adv* (a) (*onwards*) weiter-, vorwärts- ◆ **to move ~** weitergehen; **he was just strolling ~** er ist bloß so dahingeschlendert; **run ~** nun lauf!; **he'll be ~ soon** er muß gleich da sein; **I'll be ~ about eight** ich komme ungefähr um acht; **are you coming now? — yes, I'll be ~** kommst du? — ja, (ich komme) gleich; *see vbs*.
(b) (*together*) **~ with** zusammen mit; **to come/sing ~ with sb** mit jdm mitkommen/mitsingen; **take an umbrella ~** nimm einen Schirm mit.

alongside [ə'lɒŋ'saɪd] [1] *prep* neben (*+dat*) ◆ **he parked ~ the kerb** er parkte am Bordstein; **we were moored ~ the pier/the other boats** wir lagen am Pier vor Anker/lagen Bord an Bord mit den anderen Schiffen; **the houses ~ the river** die Häuser am Fluß entlang; **he works ~ me** (*with*) er ist ein Kollege von mir; (*next to*) er arbeitet neben mir.
[2] *adv* daneben ◆ **is the launch still ~?** liegt die Barkasse immer noch längsseits?; **a police car drew up ~** ein Polizeiauto fuhr neben mich/ihn *etc* heran; **she was driving ~** sie fuhr nebenher; **they brought their dinghy ~** sie brachten ihr Dingi heran.

aloof [ə'lu:f] [1] *adv* (*lit, fig*) abseits ◆ **to remain ~** sich abseits halten; **buyers held ~** (*Comm*) die Käufer verhielten sich zurückhaltend.
[2] *adj* unnahbar.

aloofness [ə'lu:fnɪs] *n* Unnahbarkeit *f*.

aloud [ə'laʊd] *adv* laut.

alp [ælp] *n* Berg *m* in den Alpen.

alpaca [æl'pækə] [1] *n* Alpaka *nt*.
[2] *attr* Alpaka-.

alpenhorn ['ælpɪn,hɔ:n] *n* Alphorn *nt*.

alpenstock ['ælpɪnstɒk] *n* Bergstock *m*.

alpha ['ælfə] *n* (a) (*letter*) Alpha *nt*. (b) (*Brit: Sch, Univ*) Eins *f* ◆ **~ plus** Eins (plus *hum*); (*Sch also*) Eins (mit Stern *hum*).

alphabet ['ælfəbet] *n* Alphabet *nt* ◆ **does he know the** *or* **his ~?** kann er schon das Abc?

alphabetic(al) [,ælfə'betɪk(əl)] *adj* alphabetisch ◆ **in ~ order** in alphabetischer Reihenfolge.

alphabetically [,ælfə'betɪkəlɪ] *adv* alphabetisch, nach dem Alphabet.

alphabetization [,ælfəbətaɪ'zeɪʃən] *n* Alphabetisierung *f*.

alphabetize ['ælfəbətaɪz] *vt* alphabetisieren, alphabetisch ordnen.

alphanumeric ['ælfənju:'merɪk] *adj* alphanumerisch.

alpha: ~ particle *n* Alphateilchen *nt*; **~ ray** *n* Alphastrahl *m*.

alpine ['ælpaɪn] *adj* (a) **A~** alpin, Alpen-; *dialects* der Alpen. (b) (*general*) alpin; *flowers* Alpen-, Gebirgs-; (*Geol*) alpinisch; *scenery* Gebirgs-; *hut* Berg-; *club* Alpen-.

alpinism ['ælpɪnɪzəm] *n* Alpinistik *f*, Alpinismus *m*.

alpinist ['ælpɪnɪst] *n* Alpinist(in *f*) *m*.

Alps [ælps] *npl* Alpen *pl*.

already [ɔ:l'redɪ] *adv* schon ◆ **I've ~ seen it, I've seen it ~** ich habe es schon gesehen.

alright ['ɔ:l,raɪt] *adj, adv see* **all right**.

Alsace ['ælsæs] *n* das Elsaß.

Alsace-Lorraine ['ælsæslə'reɪn] *n* Elsaß-Lothringen *nt*.

alsatian [æl'seɪʃən] *n* (*Brit: also* **~ dog**) (deutscher) Schäferhund.

Alsatian [æl'seɪʃən] [1] *adj* elsässisch ◆ **the ~ people** die Elsässer *pl*.
[2] *n* (*dialect*) Elsässisch *nt*.

▼ **also** ['ɔ:lsəʊ] *adv* (a) auch ◆ **her cousin ~ came** *or* **came ~** ihre Kusine kam auch; **he has ~ been there** er ist auch (schon) dort gewesen; **not only ... but ~** nicht nur ... sondern auch; **~ present were** ... außerdem waren anwesend ... (b) (*moreover*) außerdem, ferner ◆ **~, I must explain that** ... außerdem muß ich erklären, daß ...

also-ran [,ɔ:lsəʊ'ræn] *n* **to be among the ~s, to be an ~** (*Sport, fig*) unter „ferner liefen" kommen.

alt [ɒlt] *n* (*Comput*) Alt *no art* ◆ **~ key** Alt-Taste *f*.

altar ['ɒltəʳ] *n* Altar *m* ◆ **to lead sb to the ~** jdn zum Altar führen; **she was left standing at the ~** sie wurde in letzter Minute sitzengelassen (*inf*); **to be sacrificed on the ~ of pride** *etc* auf dem Altar des Stolzes *etc* geopfert werden.

altar: ~ boy *n* Ministrant *m*; **~ cloth** *n* Altartuch *nt*, Altardecke *f*; **~piece** *n* Altarbild *nt*; **~ rail(s)** *n(pl)* Kommunionbank *f*.

alter ['ɒltəʳ] [1] *vt* (a) ändern; (*modify also*) abändern ◆ **to ~ sth completely** etw vollkommen verändern; **that ~s things** das ändert die Sache; **it does not ~ the fact that** ... das ändert nichts an der Tatsache, daß ... (b) (*US: castrate, spay*) kastrieren.
[2] *vi* sich (ver)ändern ◆ **to ~ for the better/worse** sich zu seinem Vorteil/Nachteil (ver)ändern; (*things, situation*) sich zum Besseren/Schlechteren wenden.

alterable ['ɒltərəbl] *adj* veränderbar ◆ **to be ~** sich ändern lassen.

alteration [,ɒltə'reɪʃən] *n* Änderung *f*; (*modification also*) Abänderung *f*; (*of appearance*) Veränderung *f* ◆ **a complete ~** eine vollständige Veränderung; **to make ~s in sth** Änderungen an etw (*dat*) vornehmen; **(this timetable is) subject to ~** Änderungen (im Fahrplan sind) vorbehalten; **closed for ~s** wegen Umbau geschlossen.

altercation [,ɒltə'keɪʃən] *n* Auseinandersetzung *f*.

alter ego ['æltər'i:gəʊ] *n* Alter ego *nt*.

alternate [ɒl'tɜ:nɪt] [1] *adj* (a) **I go there on ~ days** ich gehe jeden zweiten Tag *or* alle zwei Tage hin; **they do their shopping on ~ days** (*every other day*) sie machen ihre Einkäufe jeden zweiten Tag; (*taking turns*) sie wechseln sich täglich mit dem Einkaufen ab; **to go through ~ periods of happiness and despair** abwechselnd Zeiten des Glücks und der Verzweiflung durchmachen; **they put down ~ layers of brick and mortar** sie schichteten (immer) abwechselnd Ziegel und Mörtel aufeinander.
(b) (*alternative*) Alternativ- ◆ **~ route** Ausweichstrecke *f*.
[2] *n* (*US*) Vertreter(in *f*) *m*; (*Sport*) Ersatzspieler(in *f*) *m*.
[3] ['ɔ:ltəneɪt] *vt* abwechseln lassen; *crops* im Wechsel anbauen ◆ **to ~ one thing with another** zwischen einer Sache und einer anderen (ab)wechseln; **the chairs were ~d with benches** Stühle und Bänke waren abwechselnd aufgestellt.
[4] ['ɔ:ltəneɪt] *vi* (sich) abwechseln; (*Elec*) alternieren ◆ **to ~ between one thing and another** zwischen einer Sache und einer anderen (ab)wechseln; **the two actors ~d in the part** die beiden Schauspieler wechselten sich in der Rolle ab.

alternately [ɒl'tɜ:nɪtlɪ] *adv* (a) (*in turn*) im Wechsel, wechselweise, (immer) abwechselnd. (b) *see* **alternatively**.

alternating ['ɒltɜ:neɪtɪŋ] *adj* wechselnd ◆ **a pattern with ~ stripes of red and white** ein Muster mit abwechselnd roten und weißen Streifen; **~ current** Wechselstrom *m*.

alternation [,ɒltɜ:'neɪʃən] *n* Wechsel *m* ◆ **the ~ of crops** der Fruchtwechsel.

alternative [ɒl'tɜ:nətɪv] [1] *adj* Alternativ-; *route* Ausweich- ◆ **the only ~ way/possibility** die einzige Alternative; **~ theatre** Alternativtheater *nt*; **~ society** Alternativgesellschaft *f*; **for him, other than London, the only possible**

➤ LANGUAGE IN USE: **also: a** → 26.1, 26.2, 26.3

~ place to live is ... außer London kommt für ihn als Wohnort nur ... in Frage, ... ist für ihn als Wohnort die einzige Alternative zu London.
[2] *n* Alternative *f* ◆ **I had no ~ (but ...)** ich hatte keine andere Wahl *or* keine Alternative (als ...).

▼ **alternatively** [ɒl'tɜ:nətɪvlɪ] *adv* als Alternative, als andere Möglichkeit ◆ **or ~, he could come with us** oder aber, er kommt mit uns mit; **a prison sentence of three months or ~ a fine of £500** eine Gefängnisstrafe von drei Monaten oder wahlweise eine Geldstrafe von £ 500.

alternator ['ɒltɜ:neɪtə^r] *n* (*Elec*) Wechselstromgenerator *m*; (*Aut*) Lichtmaschine *f*.

althorn ['ælt,hɔ:n] *n* B-Horn *nt*.

▼ **although** [ɔ:l'ðəʊ] *conj* obwohl, obgleich ◆ **the house, ~ small ...** wenn das Haus auch klein ist, obwohl das Haus klein ist.

altimeter ['æltɪmi:tə^r] *n* Höhenmesser *m*.

altitude ['æltɪtju:d] *n* Höhe *f* ◆ **what is our ~?** in welcher Höhe befinden wir uns?; **we are flying at an ~ of ...** wir fliegen in einer Höhe von ...; **at this ~** in dieser Höhe.

alto ['æltəʊ] [1] *n* **(a)** (*voice*) Alt *m*, Altstimme *f*; (*person*) Alt *m*. **(b)** (*also* **~ saxophone**) Altsaxophon *nt*.
[2] *adj* Alt- ◆ **an ~ voice** eine Altstimme.
[3] *adv* **to sing ~** Alt singen.

alto clef *n* Altschlüssel, C-Schlüssel *m*.

altogether [,ɔ:ltə'geðə^r] [1] *adv* **(a)** (*including everything*) im ganzen, insgesamt ◆ **taken ~**, *or* **~ it was very pleasant** alles in allem war es sehr nett, es war im ganzen sehr nett.
(b) (*wholly*) vollkommen, ganz und gar ◆ **he wasn't ~ wrong/pleased/surprised** er hatte nicht ganz unrecht/war nicht übermäßig *or* besonders zufrieden/überrascht; **it was ~ a waste of time** es war vollkommene Zeitverschwendung.
[2] *n* **in the ~** (*hum inf*) hüllenlos, im Adams-/Evaskostüm; **the King is in the ~** der König hat ja gar nichts an.

alto part *n* Altpartie *f*.

alto sax(ophone) *n* Altsaxophon *nt*.

altruism ['æltrʊɪzəm] *n* Altruismus *m*.

altruist ['æltrʊɪst] *n* Altruist(in *f*) *m*.

altruistic *adj*, **~ally** *adv* [,æltrʊ'ɪstɪk, -əlɪ] altruistisch.

alum ['æləm] *n* Alaun *m*.

aluminium [,æljʊ'mɪnɪəm], (*US*) **aluminum** [ə'lu:mɪnəm] *n* Aluminium *nt* ◆ **~ foil** Alu(minium)folie *f*.

alumna [ə'lʌmnə] *n*, *pl* **-e** [ə'lʌmni:] (*US*) ehemalige Schülerin/Studentin, Ehemalige *f*.

alumnus [ə'lʌmnəs] *n*, *pl* **alumni** [ə'lʌmnaɪ] (*US*) ehemaliger Schüler/Student, Ehemalige(r) *m*.

alveolar [æl'vɪələ^r] [1] *adj* alveolar, Alveolar-.
[2] *n* (*Phon*) Alveolar *m*.

always ['ɔ:lweɪz] *adv* **(a)** immer; (*constantly, repeatedly also*) ständig ◆ **he is ~ forgetting** er vergißt das immer *or* ständig; **you can't ~ expect to be forgiven** du kannst nicht immer (wieder) erwarten, daß man dir vergibt.
(b) we could ~ go by train/sell the house wir könnten doch auch den Zug nehmen/könnten ja auch das Haus verkaufen; **there's ~ the possibility that ...** es besteht immer noch die Möglichkeit, daß ...; **there's ~ that to fall back on** wir können ja immer noch darauf zurückgreifen; **you can ~ come later** Sie können ja auch noch später kommen.

Alzheimer's disease ['ælts,haɪmədzɪ,zi:z] *n* Alzheimer-Krankheit *f*.

am [æm] *1st pers sing present of* **be**.

am, a.m. *abbr of* **ante meridiem** ◆ **2 ~** 2 Uhr morgens; **10 ~** 10 Uhr morgens *or* vormittags; **12 ~** 0 Uhr, Mitternacht; **do you mean ~ or pm?** meinen Sie morgens oder nachmittags/vormittags oder abends?

amalgam [ə'mælgəm] *n* Amalgam *nt*; (*fig also*) Gemisch *nt*, Mischung *f*.

amalgamate [ə'mælgəmeɪt] [1] *vt companies, unions* fusionieren, verschmelzen; *departments* zusammenlegen; *metals* amalgamieren.
[2] *vi* (*companies etc*) fusionieren; (*metals*) amalgamieren.

amalgamation [ə,mælgə'meɪʃən] *n* (*of companies etc*) Fusion *f*; (*of metals*) Amalgamation *f*.

amanuensis [ə,mænjʊ'ensɪs] *n*, *pl* **amanuenses** [ə,mænjʊ'ensi:z] Sekretär *m*; (*Hist*) Amanuensis *m*.

amaryllis [,æmə'rɪlɪs] *n* Amaryllis *f*.

amass [ə'mæs] *vt* anhäufen; *money also* scheffeln; *fortune, material, evidence also* zusammentragen.

amateur ['æmətə^r] [1] *n* **(a)** Amateur *m*. **(b)** (*pej*) Dilettant(in *f*) *m*.
[2] *adj* **(a)** *attr* Amateur-; *photographer also, painter, painting* Hobby-; *dramatics, work also* Laien-. **(b)** (*pej*) *see* **amateurish**.

amateurish ['æmətərɪʃ] *adj* (*pej*) dilettantisch; *performance, work also* laienhaft.

amateurishly ['æmətərɪʃlɪ] *adv* (*pej*) dilettantisch.

amateurishness ['æmətərɪʃnɪs] *n* (*pej*) Dilettantismus *m*; (*of performance, work*) Laienhaftigkeit *f*.

amateurism ['æmətərɪzəm] *n* **(a)** Amateursport *m*. **(b)** (*pej*) Dilettantentum *nt*, Dilettantismus *m*.

amatory ['æmətərɪ] *adj poem, letter* Liebes-; *adventure also* amourös; *glance, look, remark, feelings* verliebt.

amaze [ə'meɪz] [1] *vt* erstaunen, in Erstaunen (ver)setzen ◆ **I was ~d to learn that ...** ich war erstaunt zu hören, daß ..., mit Erstaunen hörte ich, daß ...; **to be ~d at sth** über etw (*acc*) erstaunt *or* verblüfft sein, sich über etw (*acc*) wundern; **you don't know that, you ~ me!** Sie wissen das nicht, das wundert mich aber; **no, really? you ~ me** (*iro*) nein wirklich? da bin ich aber erstaunt *or* Sie setzen mich in Erstaunen; **it ~s me to think that only two years ago ...** es ist erstaunlich, wenn ich denke, daß erst vor zwei Jahren ...; **it ~s me that** *or* **how he doesn't fall** ich finde es erstaunlich, daß er nicht fällt.
[2] *vi* **his virtuosity never fails to ~** seine Virtuosität versetzt einen immer wieder in Erstaunen.

amazed [ə'meɪzd] *adj look, expression* erstaunt.

amazement [ə'meɪzmənt] *n* Erstaunen *nt*, Verwunderung *f* ◆ **much to my ~** zu meinem großen Erstaunen.

amazing [ə'meɪzɪŋ] *adj* erstaunlich ◆ **he's the most ~ lawyer/idiot I've ever met** er ist der erstaunlichste Rechtsanwalt/der größte Trottel, den ich je gesehen habe; **darling, you're ~, such a super meal from two tins** wie machst du das bloß, mein Schatz, ein so tolles Essen aus zwei Büchsen!

amazingly [ə'meɪzɪŋlɪ] *adv* erstaunlich; *simple, obvious also* verblüffend ◆ **~, he got it right first time** erstaunlicherweise hat er es gleich beim ersten Male richtig gemacht.

Amazon ['æməzən] *n* Amazonas *m*; (*Myth, fig*) Amazone *f*.

ambassador [æm'bæsədə^r] *n* Botschafter *m*; (*fig*) Repräsentant, Vertreter *m* ◆ **~ extraordinary, ~-at-large** (*esp US*) Sonderbotschafter(in *f*) *m*, Sonderbeauftragte(r) *mf*.

ambassadorial [æm,bæsə'dɔ:rɪəl] *adj* Botschafter-; *rank, dignity* eines Botschafters.

ambassadress [æm'bæsɪdrɪs] *n* (*female ambassador*) Botschafterin *f*; (*ambassador's wife*) Frau *f* des Botschafters.

amber ['æmbə^r] [1] *n* Bernstein *m*; (*colour*) Bernsteingelb *nt*; (*Brit: in traffic lights*) Gelb *nt*.
[2] *adj* Bernstein-, aus Bernstein; (*~-coloured*) bernsteinfarben; *traffic light* gelb.

ambergris ['æmbəgri:s] *n* Amber *m*, Ambra *f*.

ambidextrous [,æmbɪ'dekstrəs] *adj* mit beiden Händen gleich geschickt, beidhändig.

ambidextrousness [,æmbɪ'dekstrəsnɪs] *n* Beidhändigkeit *f*.

ambience ['æmbɪəns] *n* Atmosphäre *f*, Ambiente *nt* (*geh*).

ambient ['æmbɪənt] *adj* (*liter*) *air* umgebend; (*Tech*) *temperature* Umgebungs-.

ambiguity [,æmbɪ'gjʊɪtɪ] *n see* **ambiguous** Zwei- *or* Doppeldeutigkeit *f*; Zweideutigkeit *f*; Mehr- *or* Vieldeutigkeit *f*.

ambiguous *adj*, **~ly** *adv* [æm'bɪgjʊəs, -lɪ] zwei- *or* doppeldeutig; *joke, comment etc* zweideutig; (*with many possible meanings*) mehr- *or* vieldeutig.

ambiguousness [æm'bɪgjʊəsnɪs] *n* Zwei- *or* Doppeldeutigkeit *f*; (*with many possible meanings*) Mehr- *or* Vieldeutigkeit *f*.

ambit ['æmbɪt] *n* Bereich *m*.

ambition [æm'bɪʃən] *n* **(a)** (*desire*) Ambition *f* ◆ **she has ~s in that direction/for her son** sie hat Ambitionen in dieser Richtung/ehrgeizige Pläne für ihren Sohn; **my one** *or* **big ~ in life is ...** meine große Ambition ist es, ...; **it is my ~ to become Prime Minister/to travel to the moon** es ist mein Ehrgeiz *or* Ziel *or* meine Ambition, Premierminister zu werden/zum Mond zu reisen; **it was never my ~ to take over your job** es war nie mein Bestreben *or* meine Absicht, Ihre Stelle zu übernehmen.
(b) (*ambitious nature*) Ehrgeiz *m*.

ambitious [æm'bɪʃəs] *adj* ehrgeizig, ambitiös (*pej*); *person also* ambitioniert (*geh*); *idea, undertaking also* kühn ◆ **he is ~ to ...** er setzt seinen ganzen Ehrgeiz daran, zu ...; **she is ~ for her husband** sie hat ehrgeizige Pläne für ihren Mann.

ambitiously [æm'bɪʃəslɪ] *adv* voll(er) Ehrgeiz, ehrgeizig ◆ **rather ~, we set out to prove the following** wir hatten uns das ehrgeizige Ziel gesteckt, das Folgende zu beweisen.

ambitiousness [æm'bɪʃəsnɪs] *n see adj* Ehrgeiz *m*; Kühnheit *f*.

ambivalence [æm'bɪvələns] *n* Ambivalenz *f*.

ambivalent [æm'bɪvələnt] *adj* ambivalent.

amble ['æmbl] [1] *vi* (*person*) schlendern; (*horse*) im Paßgang gehen.
[2] *n* Schlendern *nt*; (*of horse*) Paßgang *m* ◆ **he went for an ~ along the riverside** er machte einen gemütlichen Spaziergang am Fluß entlang.

ambrosia [æm'brəʊzɪə] *n* (*Myth, fig*) Ambrosia *f*.

ambulance ['æmbjʊləns] *n* Krankenwagen *m*, Krankenauto *nt*, Ambulanz *f*.

ambulance: ~-chaser *n* (*US sl*) *Rechtsanwalt, der Unfallopfer als Klienten zu gewinnen sucht*; **~ driver** *n* Krankenwagenfahrer(in *f*) *m*; **~man** *n* Sanitäter *m*; **~ service** *n* Rettungs- *or* Ambulanzdienst *m*; (*system*) Rettungswesen *nt*.

ambulant ['æmbjʊlənt] *adj* **~ patients** gehfähige Patienten.

ambulatory ['æmbjʊlətərɪ] *adj* (*US*) *patient* gehfähig.

ambush ['æmbʊʃ] [1] *n* (*place*) Hinterhalt *m*; (*troops etc*) im Hinterhalt liegende Truppe/Guerillas *etc*; (*attack*) Überfall *m* (aus dem Hinterhalt) ◆ **to lay an ~ (for sb)** (jdm) einen Hinterhalt legen; **to lie** *or* **wait in ~** (*Mil, fig*) im Hinterhalt liegen; **to lie** *or* **wait in ~ for sb** (*Mil, fig*) jdm im Hinterhalt auflauern; **to fall into an ~** in einen Hinterhalt geraten.
[2] *vt* (aus dem Hinterhalt) überfallen.

ameba *n* (*US*) *see* **amoeba**.

ameliorate [ə'mi:lɪəreɪt] (*form*) [1] *vt* verbessern.
[2] *vi* sich verbessern, besser werden.

amelioration [ə,mi:lɪə'reɪʃən] *n* (*form*) Verbesserung *f*.

amen [,ɑ:'men] [1] *interj* amen ◆ **~ to that!** (*fig inf*) ja, wahrlich *or* fürwahr! (*hum*).
[2] *n* Amen *nt* ◆ **we'll all say ~ to that** (*fig inf*) wir befürworten das alle, wir sind alle dafür.

amenability [ə,mi:nə'bɪlɪtɪ] *n* (*responsiveness: of people*) Zugänglichkeit *f* ◆ **the ~ of these data to the theory** die Möglichkeit, diese Daten in die

➤ LANGUAGE IN USE: **alternatively** → 26.2 **although** → 26.2, 26.3

Theorie einzuordnen.

amenable [ə'mi:nəbl] *adj* **(a)** (*responsive*) zugänglich (*to dat*) ◆ **he is ~ to reasonable suggestions** er ist vernünftigen Vorschlägen zugänglich; **it is not ~ to this method of classification** es läßt sich in dieses Klassifikationssystem nicht einordnen. **(b)** (*Jur: answerable*) verantwortlich ◆ **~ to the law** dem Gesetz verantwortlich.

amend [ə'mend] *vt* **(a)** *law, bill, constitution, text* ändern, amendieren (*form*), ein Amendement einbringen zu (*form*); (*by addition*) ergänzen ◆ **I'd better ~ that to "most people"** ich werde das lieber in „die meisten Leute" (ab)ändern. **(b)** (*improve*) *habits, behaviour* bessern. **(c)** *see* **emend**.

amendment [ə'mendmənt] *n* **(a)** (*to bill, in text*) Änderung *f* (*to gen*), Amendement *nt* (*form*) (*to gen*); (*addition*) Amendement *nt* (*form*) (*to* zu), Zusatz *m* (*to* zu) ◆ **the First/Second** *etc* **A~** (*US Pol*) das Erste/Zweite *etc* Amendement, Zusatz 1/2 *etc.* **(b)** (*in behaviour*) Besserung *f.*

amends [ə'mendz] *npl* **to make ~ (for sth)** etw wiedergutmachen; **to make ~ to sb for sth** jdn für etw entschädigen; **I'll try to make ~** ich werde versuchen, das wiedergutzumachen.

amenity [ə'mi:nɪtɪ] *n* **(a)** (*aid to pleasant living*) **(public) ~** öffentliche Einrichtung; **the lack of amenities in many parts of the city** der Mangel an Einkaufs-, Unterhaltungs- und Transport möglichkeiten in vielen Teilen der Stadt; **close to all amenities** in günstiger (Einkaufs- und Verkehrs)lage; **this house has every ~** dieses Haus bietet jeden Komfort; **a high/low ~ district** eine Gegend mit hoher/geringer Wohnqualität.
(b) (*pleasantness: of place*) angenehme Lage ◆ **the ~ of the climate** das angenehme Klima.

amenorrhoea, (*US*) **amenorrhea** [æ,menə'rɪə] *n* (*Med*) Amenorrhöe *f.*

Amerasian [æme'reɪʃn] *n Mensch m amerikanisch-asiatischer Herkunft*.

America [ə'merɪkə] *n* Amerika *nt* ◆ **the ~s** Amerika *nt*, der amerikanische Kontinent.

American [ə'merɪkən] 1 *adj* amerikanisch ◆ **~ English** amerikanisches Englisch; **~ Indian** Indianer(in *f*) *m*; **~ plan** Vollpension *f.*
2 *n* **(a)** Amerikaner(in *f*) *m.* **(b)** (*language*) Amerikanisch *nt.*

americanism [ə'merɪkənɪzəm] *n* **(a)** (*Ling*) Amerikanismus *m.* **(b)** (*quality*) Amerikanertum *nt.*

americanization [ə,merɪkənaɪ'zeɪʃən] *n* Amerikanisierung *f.*

americanize [ə'merɪkənaɪz] 1 *vt* amerikanisieren.
2 *vi* sich amerikanisieren.

Amerindian [æmə'rɪndɪən] 1 *n* Indianer(in *f*) *m.*
2 *adj* indianisch.

amethyst ['æmɪθɪst] 1 *n* Amethyst *m*; (*colour*) Amethystblau *nt.*
2 *adj jewellery* Amethyst-; (*~-coloured*) amethystfarben.

amiability [,eɪmɪə'bɪlɪtɪ] *n* Liebenswürdigkeit *f.*

amiable ['eɪmɪəbl] *adj* liebenswürdig.

amiably ['eɪmɪəblɪ] *adv* liebenswürdig ◆ **he very ~ offered to help** er hat sich liebenswürdigerweise angeboten zu helfen.

amicable ['æmɪkəbl] *adj person* freundlich; *relations* freundschaftlich; *discussion* friedlich; (*Jur*) *settlement* gütlich.

amicably ['æmɪkəblɪ] *adv* freundlich; *discuss* friedlich, in aller Freundschaft; (*Jur*) *settle* gütlich ◆ **they got on quite ~** sie kamen ganz gut miteinander aus.

amidships [ə'mɪdʃɪps] *adv* (*Naut*) mittschiffs.

amid(st) [ə'mɪd(st)] *prep* inmitten (*+gen*).

amino acid [ə'mi:nəʊ'æsɪd] *n* Aminosäure *f.*

amiss [ə'mɪs] 1 *adj pred* **there's something ~** da stimmt irgend etwas nicht; **what's ~ with you?** (*liter*) was fehlt Ihnen (denn)?
2 *adv* **to take sth ~** (jdm) etw übelnehmen; **to speak ~ of sb** schlecht über jdn sprechen; **to say something ~** etwas Falsches *or* Verkehrtes sagen; **a drink would not come** *or* **go ~** etwas zu trinken wäre gar nicht verkehrt; **nothing comes ~ to him** ihm kommt alles recht.

amity ['æmɪtɪ] *n* Freundschaftlichkeit *f.*

ammeter ['æmɪtəʳ] *n* Amperemeter *nt.*

ammo ['æməʊ] *n* (*inf*) Munition, Mun (*sl*) *f.*

ammonia [ə'məʊnɪə] *n* Ammoniak *nt.*

ammunition [,æmjʊ'nɪʃən] *n* (*lit, fig*) Munition *f.*

ammunition: ~ belt *n* Patronengurt *m*; **~ dump** *n* Munitionslager *nt*; **~ pouch** *n* Munitionsbeutel *m.*

amnesia [æm'ni:zɪə] *n* Amnesie *f*, Gedächtnisschwund *m.*

amnesty ['æmnɪstɪ] *n* Amnestie *f* ◆ **during** *or* **under the ~** unter der Amnestie; **a general ~** eine Generalamnestie; **A~ International** Amnesty International *no art.*

amniocentesis [,æmnɪəʊsen'ti:sɪs] *n* (*Med*) Fruchtwasseruntersuchung, Amniozentese (*spec*) *f.*

amoeba, (*US*) **ameba** [ə'mi:bə] *n* Amöbe *f.*

amoebic, (*US*) **amebic** [ə'mi:bɪk] *adj* amöbisch ◆ **~ dysentery** Amöbenruhr *f.*

amok [ə'mɒk] *adv see* **amuck**.

among(st) [ə'mʌŋ(st)] *prep* unter (*+acc or dat*) ◆ **~ other things** unter anderem; **~ the crowd** unter die/der Menge; **they shared it out ~ themselves** sie teilten es unter sich *or* untereinander auf; **he's ~ our best players** er gehört zu unseren besten Spielern; **Manchester is ~ the largest of our cities** Manchester gehört zu unseren größten Städten; **to count sb ~ one's friends** jdn zu seinen Freunden zählen; **this habit is widespread ~ the French** diese Sitte ist bei den Franzosen weitverbreitet; **there were ferns ~ the trees** zwischen den Bäumen wuchs Farnkraut; **to hide ~ the bushes** sich in den Büschen verstecken.

> LANGUAGE IN USE: **amount: 2a → 20.7**

amoral [æ'mɒrəl] *adj* amoralisch.

amorous ['æmərəs] *adj* amourös; *look also* verliebt ◆ **to make ~ advances** Annäherungsversuche *pl* machen.

amorously ['æmərəslɪ] *adv* verliebt, voller Verliebtheit.

amorphous [ə'mɔ:fəs] *adj* amorph, strukturlos, formlos; *style, ideas, play, novel* strukturlos, ungegliedert; (*Geol*) amorph.

amorphousness [ə'mɔ:fəsnɪs] *n* Strukturlosigkeit *f.*

amortization [ə,mɔ:taɪ'zeɪʃən] *n* Amortisation *f.*

amortize [ə'mɔ:taɪz] *vt debt* amortisieren, tilgen.

▼ **amount** [ə'maʊnt] 1 *vi* **(a)** (*total*) sich belaufen (*to* auf *+acc*).
(b) (*be equivalent*) gleichkommen (*to +dat*) ◆ **it ~s to the same thing** das läuft *or* kommt (doch) aufs gleiche hinaus *or* raus (*inf*); **he will never ~ to much** aus ihm wird nie etwas *or* viel werden, der wird es nie zu etwas *or* zu viel bringen; **their promises don't ~ to very much** ihre Versprechungen sind recht nichtssagend; **so what this ~s to is that ...** worauf es also hinausläuft ist, daß ...
▼ 2 *n* **(a)** (*of money*) Betrag *m* ◆ **total ~** Gesamtsumme *f*, Endbetrag *m*; **debts to** *or* (*US*) **in the ~ of £20** Schulden in Höhe von £ 20; **I was shocked at the ~ of the bill** ich war über die Höhe der Rechnung erschrocken; **in 12 equal ~s** in 12 gleichen Teilen, in 12 gleichen Beträgen; **an unlimited/a large/a small ~ of money** eine unbeschränkte *or* unbegrenzte/große/geringe Summe (Geldes); **a modest ~ of money** ein bescheidener Betrag; **any/quite an ~ of money** beliebig viel/ziemlich viel Geld, ein ziemlicher Betrag; **large ~s of money** Unsummen *pl* (Geldes); **it's not the ~ of the donation that counts** nicht die Höhe der Spende ist maßgeblich.
(b) (*quantity*) Menge *f*; (*of luck, intelligence, skill etc*) Maß *nt* (*of* an *+dat*) ◆ **an enormous/a modest ~ of work/time** sehr viel/verhältnismäßig wenig Arbeit/Zeit; **any/quite an ~ of time/food** beliebig viel/ziemlich viel Zeit/Essen, eine ziemliche Menge Essen; **no ~ of talking would persuade him** kein Reden würde ihn überzeugen; **no ~ of paint can hide the rust** keine noch so dicke Farbschicht kann den Rost verdecken; **if we increase the ~ of the loan/noise factor** wenn wir die Anleihe *or* die Höhe der Anleihe/den Lärmfaktor erhöhen.

amour [ə'mʊəʳ] *n* (*dated, liter*) Liebschaft *f*; (*person*) Liebe *f.*

amour-propre [,æmʊə'prɒprə] *n* Eigenliebe *f.*

amp(ère) ['æmp(εəʳ)] *n* Ampere *nt.*

ampersand ['æmpəsænd] *n* Et-Zeichen, Und-Zeichen *nt.*

amphetamine [æm'fetəmi:n] *n* Amphetamin *nt.*

amphibian [æm'fɪbɪən] *n* (*animal, plant*) Amphibie *f*; (*vehicle*) Amphibienfahrzeug *nt*; (*aircraft*) Amphibienflugzeug, Wasser-Land-Flugzeug *nt* ◆ **~ tank** Amphibienpanzer *m.*

amphibious [æm'fɪbɪəs] *adj animal, plant,* (*Mil*) amphibisch; *vehicle, aircraft* Amphibien-.

amphitheatre, (*US*) **amphitheater** ['æmfɪ,θɪətəʳ] *n* **(a)** Amphitheater *nt*; (*lecture-hall*) Hörsaal *m* (*Halbrund mit ansteigenden Sitzreihen*). **(b)** (*Geog*) Halbkessel *m* ◆ **a natural ~** ein natürliches Amphitheater.

amphora ['æmfərə] *n, pl* **-s** *or* **-e** ['æmfəri:] (*form*) Amphora, Amphore *f.*

ample ['æmpl] *adj* (*+er*) **(a)** (*plentiful*) reichlich ◆ **that will be ~** das ist reichlich; **more than ~** überreichlich. **(b)** (*large*) *figure, proportions* üppig; *boot of car etc* geräumig; *garden* weitläufig, ausgedehnt.

amplification [,æmplɪfɪ'keɪʃən] *n* weitere Ausführungen *pl*, Erläuterungen *pl*; (*Rad*) Verstärkung *f* ◆ **in ~ of this ...** dies weiter ausführend ...

amplifier ['æmplɪfaɪəʳ] *n* (*Rad*) Verstärker *m.*

amplify ['æmplɪfaɪ] 1 *vt* **(a)** (*Rad*) verstärken. **(b)** (*expand*) *statement, idea* näher *or* ausführlicher erläutern, genauer ausführen. **(c)** (*inf: exaggerate*) übertreiben.
2 *vi* **would you care to ~ a little?** würden Sie das bitte näher *or* ausführlicher erläutern?, würden Sie bitte auf diesen Punkt näher eingehen?; **to ~ on sth** etw näher erläutern, einen Punkt ausführen.

amplitude ['æmplɪtju:d] *n* (*of knowledge*) Weite, Breite *f*; (*of bosom*) Üppigkeit, Fülle *f*; (*Phys*) Amplitude *f.*

amply ['æmplɪ] *adv* reichlich; *proportioned figure* üppig; *proportioned rooms* geräumig, großzügig.

ampoule, (*US*) **ampull(e)** ['æmpu:l] *n* Ampulle *f.*

ampulla [æm'pʊlə] *n, pl* **-e** [æm'pʊli:] (*Hist, Eccl*) Ampulla *f.*

amputate ['æmpjʊteɪt] *vti* amputieren.

amputation [,æmpjʊ'teɪʃən] *n* Amputation *f.*

amputee [,æmpjʊ'ti:] *n* Amputierte(r) *mf.*

amuck [ə'mʌk] *adv*: **to run ~** (*lit, fig*) Amok laufen.

amulet ['æmjʊlɪt] *n* Amulett *nt.*

amuse [ə'mju:z] 1 *vt* **(a)** (*cause mirth*) amüsieren, belustigen ◆ **I was ~d to hear ...** es hat mich amüsiert *or* belustigt zu hören ...; **we are not ~d** das ist nicht spaßig (*dated*), das ist durchaus nicht zum Lachen *or* nicht komisch; **he was anything but ~d to find the door locked** er fand es keineswegs *or* durchaus nicht komisch, daß die Tür verschlossen war; **the teacher shouldn't appear to be ~d by the pupils' mistakes** der Lehrer sollte es sich nicht anmerken lassen, daß ihn die Fehler der Schüler amüsieren; **you ~ me, how can anyone ...?** daß ich nicht lache *or* da muß ich ja (mal) lachen, wie kann man nur ...?
(b) (*entertain*) unterhalten ◆ **let the children do it if it ~s them** laß die Kinder doch, wenn es ihnen Spaß macht; **give him his toys, that'll keep him ~d** gib ihm sein Spielzeug, dann ist er friedlich; **I have no problem keeping myself ~d now I'm retired** ich habe keinerlei Schwierigkeiten, mir die Zeit zu vertreiben, jetzt wo ich im Ruhestand bin.
2 *vr* **the children can ~ themselves for a while** die Kinder können sich eine

Zeitlang selbst beschäftigen; **could you ~ yourself with the magazines in the meantime?** könntest du dir derweil ein bißchen die Zeitschriften ansehen *or* dich derweil mit den Zeitschriften beschäftigen?; **to ~ oneself (by) doing sth** etw zu seinem Vergnügen *or* aus Spaß tun; **how do you ~ yourself now you're retired?** wie vertreiben Sie sich (*dat*) die Zeit, wo Sie jetzt im Ruhestand sind?; **he ~s himself with crossword puzzles** er löst zum Zeitvertreib Kreuzworträtsel; **he's just amusing himself with her** er amüsiert sich nur mit ihr.

amusement [əˈmjuːzmənt] *n* **(a)** (*enjoyment, fun*) Vergnügen *nt*; (*state of being entertained*) Belustigung *f*, Amüsement *nt* ◆ **the toys were a great source of ~** das Spielzeug bereitete großen Spaß; **he gets no ~ out of life** er kann dem Leben kein Vergnügen abgewinnen; **what do you do for ~?** was machst du als Freizeitbeschäftigung?; (*retired people*) was machen Sie zu Ihrer Unterhaltung *or* als Zeitvertreib?; **what do you do for ~ in a town like this!** was kann man denn schon in so einer Stadt zu seiner Unterhaltung machen *or* tun!; **I see no cause for ~** ich sehe keinen Grund zur Heiterkeit; **to do sth for one's own ~** etw zu seinem Vergnügen *or* Amüsement tun; **to my great ~/to everyone's ~** zu meiner großen/zur allgemeinen Belustigung.
(b) (*entertainment: of guests*) Belustigung, Unterhaltung *f*.
(c) **~s** *pl* (*place of entertainment*) Vergnügungsstätte *f usu pl*; (*at fair*) Attraktionen *pl*; (*stand, booth*) Buden *pl*; (*at the seaside*) Spielautomaten und Spiegelkabinett *etc* ◆ **what sort of ~s do you have around here?** was für Vergnügungs- und Unterhaltungsmöglichkeiten gibt es hier?

amusement: ~ arcade *n* Spielhalle *f*; **~ park** *n* Vergnügungspark, Lunapark (*dated*) *m*.

amusing [əˈmjuːzɪŋ] *adj* **(a)** amüsant ◆ **how ~** wie lustig *or* witzig!, das ist aber lustig *or* witzig!; **I've just had an ~ thought** mir ist gerade etwas Lustiges *or* Amüsantes eingefallen; **I don't find that very ~** das finde ich nicht gerade *or* gar nicht lustig *or* zum Lachen. **(b)** (*inf*) *hat, little dress etc* charmant, apart ◆ **an ~ little wine** ein nettes Weinchen (*hum*).

amusingly [əˈmjuːzɪŋlɪ] *adv* amüsant.

an [æn, ən, n] **1** *indef art see* **a**.
2 *conj* (*obs: if*) so (*old*).

Anabaptism [ˌænəˈbæptɪzəm] *n* Anabaptismus *m*.

Anabaptist [ˌænəˈbæptɪst] *n* Anabaptist, Wiedertäufer(in *f*) *m*.

anabolic steroid [ˌænəˈbɒlɪkˈstɪərɔɪd] *n* Anabolikum *nt*.

anachronism [əˈnækrənɪzəm] *n* Anachronismus *m*.

anachronistic [əˌnækrəˈnɪstɪk] *adj* anachronistisch; (*not fitting modern times*) nicht zeitgemäß, unzeitgemäß.

anaconda [ˌænəˈkɒndə] *n* Anakonda *f*.

anaemia, (*US*) **anemia** [əˈniːmɪə] *n* Anämie, Blutarmut *f*.

anaemic, (*US*) **anemic** [əˈniːmɪk] *adj* **(a)** anämisch, blutarm. **(b)** (*fig*) anämisch, saft- und kraftlos; *colour, appearance also* bleichsüchtig.

anaesthesia, (*US*) **anesthesia** [ˌænɪsˈθiːzɪə] *n* Betäubung *f*.

anaesthetic, (*US*) **anesthetic** [ˌænɪsˈθetɪk] **1** *n* Narkose, Anästhesie (*spec*) *f*; (*substance*) Narkosemittel, Anästhetikum (*spec*) *nt* ◆ **general ~** Vollnarkose *f*; **local ~** örtliche Betäubung, Lokalanästhesie (*spec*) *f*; **the nurse gave him a local ~** die Schwester gab ihm eine Spritze zur örtlichen Betäubung; **the patient is still under the ~** der Patient ist noch in der Narkose; **when he comes out of the ~** wenn er aus der Narkose aufwacht.
2 *adj effect* betäubend, anästhetisch; *drug* Betäubungs-.

anaesthetist, (*US*) **anesthetist** [æˈniːsθɪtɪst] *n* Anästhesist(in *f*) *m*, Narkose(fach)arzt *m*/-(fach) ärztin *f*.

anaesthetize, (*US*) **anesthetize** [æˈniːsθɪtaɪz] *vt* (*Med*) betäuben; (*generally also*) narkotisieren.

Anaglypta ® [ˌænəˈglɪptə] *n* Prägetapete *f*.

anagram [ˈænəgræm] *n* Anagramm *nt*.

anal [ˈeɪnəl] *adj* anal, Anal-, After- (*Med*) ◆ **~ eroticism** Analerotik *f*.

analgesia [ˌænælˈdʒiːzɪə] *n* Schmerzlosigkeit, Analgesie (*spec*) *f*.

analgesic [ˌænælˈdʒiːsɪk] **1** *n* schmerzstillendes Mittel, Schmerzmittel, Analgetikum (*spec*) *nt*.
2 *adj* schmerzstillend.

analog [ˈænəlɒg] *adj* (*Tech*) analog ◆ **~ computer** Analogrechner *m*.

analogic(al) [ˌænəˈlɒdʒɪk(əl)] *adj*, **analogically** [ˌænəˈlɒdʒɪkəlɪ] *adv* analog.

analogous *adj*, **~ly** *adv* [əˈnæləgəs, -lɪ] analog (*to, with* zu).

analogue [ˈænəlɒg] *n* Gegenstück *nt*, Parallele *f*.

analogy [əˈnælədʒɪ] *n* Analogie *f* ◆ **to argue from** *or* **by ~** analog argumentieren, Analogieschlüsse/einen Analogieschluß ziehen; **arguing from ~ one could claim that ...** analog könnte man behaupten ...; **to draw an ~** eine Analogie herstellen, einen analogen Vergleich ziehen; **on the ~ of** analog zu, nach dem Muster (*+gen*); **it's an argument by ~** es ist ein Analogiebeweis, es ist eine analoge Argumentation.

▼ **analyse,** (*US*) **analyze** [ˈænəlaɪz] *vt* **(a)** analysieren; (*Chem also*) untersuchen; (*in literary criticism also*) kritisch untersuchen; (*Gram*) *sentence also* (zer)gliedern ◆ **to ~ the situation** (*fig*) die Situation analysieren *or* (*to others*) erläutern; **to ~ sth into its parts** etw in seine Bestandteile zerlegen.
(b) (*psycho~*) psychoanalytisch behandeln, analysieren (*inf*) ◆ **stop analysing me!** hör auf, mich zu analysieren!

analysis [əˈnæləsɪs] *n, pl* **analyses** [əˈnæləsiːz] **(a)** *see vt* Analyse *f*; (Zer)gliederung *f* ◆ **what's your ~ of the situation?** wie beurteilen Sie die Situation?; **in the last** *or* **final ~** letzten Endes; **on (closer) ~** bei genauerer Untersuchung. **(b)** (*psycho~*) Psychoanalyse, Analyse (*inf*) *f*.

analyst [ˈænəlɪst] *n* Analytiker(in *f*) *m*; (*psycho~ also*) Psychoanalytiker(in *f*) *m*; (*Chem*) Chemiker(in *f*) *m* ◆ **food ~** Lebensmittelchemiker(in *f*) *m*; **he gave it to the ~ in the lab** er ließ im Labor eine Analyse davon machen.

analytic [ˌænəˈlɪtɪk] *adj* analytisch.

analytical [ˌænəˈlɪtɪkəl] *adj* analytisch ◆ **you should try to be more ~** Sie sollten versuchen, etwas analytischer vorzugehen; **he hasn't got a very ~ mind** er kann nicht analytisch denken.

analytically [ˌænəˈlɪtɪkəlɪ] *adv* analytisch.

analyze [ˈænəlaɪz] *vt see* **analyse**.

anapaest, (*US*) **anapest** [ˈænəpiːst] *n* (*Poet*) Anapäst *m*.

anarchic(al) [æˈnɑːkɪk(əl)] *adj* anarchisch.

anarchism [ˈænəkɪzəm] *n* Anarchismus *m*.

anarchist [ˈænəkɪst] *n* Anarchist(in *f*) *m*.

anarchist(ic) [ˌænəˈkɪst(ɪk)] *adj* anarchistisch.

anarchy [ˈænəkɪ] *n* Anarchie *f*.

anathema [əˈnæθɪmə] *n* (*Eccl*) Anathema (*form*) *nt*, Kirchenbann *m*; (*fig: no art*) ein Greuel *m* ◆ **voting Labour was ~ to them** der Gedanke, Labour zu wählen, war ihnen ein Greuel.

anathematize [əˈnæθɪmətaɪz] *vt* (*Eccl*) mit dem Bann belegen.

anatomical [ˌænəˈtɒmɪkəl] *adj* anatomisch.

anatomist [əˈnætəmɪst] *n* Anatom *m*.

anatomy [əˈnætəmɪ] *n* Anatomie *f*; (*structure also*) Körperbau *m*; (*fig*) Struktur *f* und Aufbau *m* ◆ **on a certain part/certain parts of her ~** (*euph*) an einer gewissen Stelle/an gewissen Stellen *or* Körperteilen (*euph*).

ANC *abbr of* **African National Congress** ANC *m*, *südafrikanische nationalistische Bewegung*.

ancestor [ˈænsɪstə^r] *n* Vorfahr, Ahne *m*; (*progenitor*) Stammvater *m* ◆ **~ worship** Ahnenkult *m*.

ancestral [ænˈsestrəl] *adj* Ahnen-, seiner/ihrer Vorfahren ◆ **~ home** Stammsitz *m*.

ancestress [ˈænsɪstrɪs] *n* Vorfahrin, Ahne *f*; (*progenitor*) Ahnfrau, Stammutter *f*.

ancestry [ˈænsɪstrɪ] *n* (*descent*) Abstammung, Herkunft *f*; (*ancestors*) Ahnenreihe, Familie *f* ◆ **to trace one's ~** seine Abstammung zurückverfolgen; **of noble ~** vornehmer Abstammung *or* Herkunft.

anchor [ˈæŋkə^r] **1** *n* (*Naut*) Anker *m*; (*fig: hope, love, person etc*) Zuflucht *f*, Rettungsanker *m* ◆ **to cast** *or* **drop ~** Anker werfen, vor Anker gehen; **to weigh ~** den Anker lichten; **to be** *or* **lie** *or* **ride at ~** vor Anker liegen; **to come to ~** vor Anker gehen; **the stone served as an ~ for the tent** der Stein diente dazu, das Zelt zu beschweren *or* am Boden festzuhalten.
2 *vt* (*Naut, fig*) verankern ◆ **we ~ed the tablecloth (down) with stones** wir beschwerten das Tischtuch mit Steinen.
3 *vi* (*Naut*) ankern, vor Anker gehen.

anchorage [ˈæŋkərɪdʒ] *n* (*Naut*) **(a)** Ankerplatz *m*. **(b)** (*also* **~ dues**) Anker- *or* Liegegebühren *pl*.

anchor buoy *n* Ankerboje *f*.

anchorite [ˈæŋkəraɪt] *n* Einsiedler, Eremit *m*.

anchorman [ˈæŋkə^rˌmæn] *n* (*TV etc*) Koordinator(in *f*) *m*; (*last person in relay race etc*) Letzte(r) *mf*; (*in tug-of-war*) hinterster Mann; (*fig*) eiserne Stütze *f*, Eckpfeiler *m*.

anchovy [ˈæntʃəvɪ] *n* Sardelle, An(s)chovis *f* ◆ **~ paste** Sardellen- *or* An(s)chovispaste *f*.

ancient [ˈeɪnʃənt] **1** *adj* **(a)** alt ◆ **in ~ times** im Altertum; (*Greek, Roman also*) in der Antike; **~ Rome** das alte Rom; **the ~ Romans** die alten Römer; **~ monument** (*Brit*) historisches Denkmal, historische Stätte; **~ history** (*lit*) Alte Geschichte; (*fig*) graue Vorzeit; **that's ~ history** (*fig*) das ist schon längst Geschichte; **he's well-known in the field of ~ history** er ist ein sehr bekannter Altertumsforscher.
(b) (*inf*) *person, clothes etc* uralt.
2 *n* **the ~s** die Völker *or* Menschen des Altertums *or* im Altertum; (*writers*) die Schriftsteller des Altertums.

ancillary [ænˈsɪlərɪ] *adj* (*subordinate*) *roads*, (*Univ*) *subject* Neben-; (*auxiliary*) *service, troops* Hilfs- ◆ **~ course** (*Univ*) Begleitkurs *m*; **~ industry** Zulieferindustrie *f*.

and [ænd, ənd, nd, ən] *conj* **(a)** und ◆ **nice ~ early/warm** schön früh/warm; **when I'm good ~ ready** wenn es mir paßt, wenn ich soweit bin; **you ~ you alone** du, nur du allein; **try ~ come** versuch zu kommen; **wait ~ see!** abwarten!, wart's ab!; **don't go ~ spoil it!** nun verdirb nicht alles!; **come ~ get it!** komm und hol's!; **one more ~ I'm finished** noch eins, dann bin ich fertig; **there are dictionaries ~ dictionaries** es gibt Wörterbücher und Wörterbücher, es gibt so'ne Wörterbücher und solche (*inf*); **~/or** und/oder; **~ so on, ~ so forth, ~ so on ~ so forth** und so weiter, und so fort, und so weiter und so fort.
(b) (*in repetition, continuation*) und; (*between comps also*) immer ◆ **better ~ better** immer besser; **for hours ~ hours/days ~ days/weeks ~ weeks** stundenlang, Stunde um Stunde (*geh*)/tagelang/wochenlang; **for miles ~ miles** meilenweit; **I rang ~ rang** ich klingelte und klingelte, ich klingelte immer wieder; **I tried ~ tried** ich habe es immer wieder versucht; **~ he pulled ~ he pulled** und er zog und zog.
(c) (*with numbers*) **three hundred ~ ten** dreihundertzehn; (*when the number is said more slowly*) dreihundertundzehn; **one ~ a half** anderthalb, eineinhalb; **two ~ twenty** (*old, form*) zweiundzwanzig.

Andean [ˈændɪən] *adj* Anden-.

Andes [ˈændiːz] *npl* Anden *pl*.

andiron [ˈændaɪrən] *n* Kaminbock *m*.

Andorra [ænˈdɔːrə] *n* Andorra *nt*.

➤ LANGUAGE IN USE: **analyse: a → 26.1**

Andorran [æn'dɔrən] [1] *n* Andorraner(in *f*) *m*.
[2] *adj* andorranisch.
Andrew ['ændru:] *n* Andreas *m*.
androgynous [æn'drɒdʒɪnəs] *adj* zweigeschlechtig, zwittrig.
android ['ændrɔɪd] *n* Androide *m*.
anecdotal [,ænɪk'dəʊtəl] *adj* anekdotenhaft, anekdotisch.
anecdote ['ænɪkdəʊt] *n* Anekdote *f*.
anemia [ə'ni:mɪə] *n* (*US*) *see* **anaemia**.
anemic [ə'ni:mɪk] *adj* (*US*) *see* **anaemic**.
anemometer [,ænɪ'mɒmɪtə^r] *n* Windmesser *m*.
anemone [ə'nemənɪ] *n* (*Bot*) Anemone *f*, Buschwindröschen *nt*; (*sea* ~) Seeanemone *f*.
aneroid barometer ['ænərɔɪdbə'rɒmɪtə^r] *n* Aneroidbarometer *nt*.
anesthesia *n* (*US*), **anesthetic** *adj, n* (*US*), **anesthetize** *vt* (*US*) *etc see* **anaesthesia** *etc*.
anew [ə'nju:] *adv* **(a)** (*again*) aufs neue ◆ **let's start** ~ fangen wir wieder von vorn *or* von neuem an. **(b)** (*in a new way*) auf eine neue Art und Weise.
angel ['eɪndʒəl] *n* (*lit, fig*) Engel *m*; (*US inf: backer*) finanzkräftiger Hintermann.
angel cake *n* ≈ Biskuitkuchen *m*.
Angeleno [,ændʒə'li:nəʊ] *n* Einwohner(in *f*) *m* von Los Angeles.
angel: ~ **face** *interj* (*hum inf*) mein Engel; ~ **fish** *n* (*shark*) Meerengel, Engelhai *m*; (*tropical fish*) Großer Segelflosser.
angelic [æn'dʒelɪk] *adj* **(a)** (*of an angel*) Engels-; *hosts* himmlisch; *salutation* Englisch. **(b)** (*like an angel*) engelhaft, engelgleich (*liter*).
angelica [æn'dʒelɪkə] *n* (*Bot*) Angelika, Brustwurz *f*; (*Cook*) kandierte Angelika.
angelically [æn'dʒelɪkəlɪ] *adv* wie ein Engel, engelgleich.
angelus ['ændʒɪləs] *n* Angelusläuten *nt*; (*prayer*) Angelus *nt*.
anger ['æŋgə^r] [1] *n* Ärger *m*; (*wrath: of gods etc*) Zorn *m* ◆ **a fit of** ~ ein Wutanfall *m*, ein Zorn(es)ausbruch *m*; **red with** ~ rot vor Wut; **public** ~ öffentliche Entrüstung; **to speak/act in** ~ im Zorn sprechen/handeln; **words spoken in** ~ was man in seiner Wut *or* im Zorn sagt; **to be filled with** ~ zornig *or* wütend sein; **to provoke sb's** ~ jdn reizen; **to rouse sb to** ~ (*liter*) jdn in Wut *or* Rage bringen; **to make one's** ~ **felt** seinem Ärger *or* Unmut Luft machen; **in great** ~ in großem Zorn.
[2] *vt* (*stressing action*) ärgern; (*stressing result*) verärgern; *gods* erzürnen (*liter*) ◆ **what** ~**s me is ...** was mich ärgert, ist ...; **to be easily** ~**ed** sich schnell *or* leicht ärgern; (*quick to take offence*) schnell verärgert sein.
angina [æn'dʒaɪnə] *n* Angina, Halsentzündung *f* ◆ ~ **pectoris** Angina pectoris *f*.
angiogram ['ændʒɪəgræm] *n* Angiogramm *nt*.
angle[1] ['æŋgl] [1] *n* **(a)** Winkel *m* ◆ **at an** ~ **of 40°** in einem Winkel von 40°; **at an** ~ schräg; **at an** ~ **to the street** schräg *or* im Winkel zur Straße; **he was wearing his hat at an** ~ er hatte seinen Hut schief aufgesetzt; ~ **of climb** (*Aviat*) Steigwinkel *m*; ~ **of elevation** (*Math*) Steigungswinkel *m*; ~ **of incidence** (*Opt*) Einfallswinkel *m*.
(b) (*projecting corner*) Ecke *f*; (*angular recess*) Winkel *m* ◆ **the building/her figure was all** ~**s** das Gebäude bestand bloß aus Ecken/sie hatte eine sehr eckige Figur.
(c) (*position*) Winkel *m* ◆ **if you take the photograph from this** ~ wenn du die Aufnahme aus *or* von diesem (Blick)winkel machst.
(d) (*of problem etc: aspect*) Seite *f*.
(e) (*point of view*) Standpunkt *m*, Position *f*; (*when used with adj also*) Warte *f* ◆ **a journalist usually has an** ~ **on a story** ein Journalist schreibt seine Berichte gewöhnlich von einer gewissen Warte aus; **an inside** ~ **on the story** die Geschichte vom Standpunkt eines Insiders *or* eines Direktbeteiligten; **what's your** ~**?** (*what are you getting at?*) worauf wollen Sie hinaus?
[2] *vt lamp etc* (aus)richten, einstellen; (*Sport*) *shot* im Winkel schießen/schlagen; (*fig*) *information, report* färben ◆ **the question was** ~**d at getting one particular answer** es war eine Suggestivfrage.
angle[2] *vi* (*Fishing*) angeln.
◆**angle for** *vi +prep obj* **(a)** (*lit*) *trout* angeln. **(b)** (*fig*) *compliments* fischen nach ◆ **to** ~ ~ **sth** auf etw (*acc*) aus sein; **to** ~ ~ **sb's attention** jds Aufmerksamkeit auf sich (*acc*) zu lenken versuchen.
angle: ~ **bracket** *n* **(a)** (*for shelves*) Winkelband *nt*, Winkelkonsole *f*; **(b)** (*Typ*) spitze Klammer; ~ **iron** *n* Winkeleisen *nt*; ~ **parking** *n* Schrägparken *nt*; **A~poise (lamp)** ® *n* Architekten- *or* Gelenkleuchte *f*.
angler ['æŋglə^r] *n* Angler(in *f*) *m*.
Angles ['æŋglz] *npl* (*Hist*) Angeln *pl*.
Anglican ['æŋglɪkən] [1] *n* Anglikaner(in *f*) *m*.
[2] *adj* anglikanisch.
Anglicanism ['æŋglɪkənɪzəm] *n* Anglikanismus *m*.
anglicism ['æŋglɪsɪzəm] *n* Anglizismus *m*.
anglicist ['æŋglɪsɪst] *n* Anglist(in *f*) *m*.
anglicize ['æŋglɪsaɪz] *vt* anglisieren.
angling ['æŋglɪŋ] *n* Angeln *nt*.
Anglo- ['æŋgləʊ] *pref* Anglo-; (*between two countries*) Englisch-; ~**-German** *adj* deutsch-englisch; ~**-Catholic** [1] *n* Anglokatholik(in *f*) *m*; [2] *adj* hochkirchlich, anglokatholisch; ~**-Indian** [1] *n* (*of British origin*) in Indien lebende(r) Engländer(in *f*) *m*; (*Eurasian*) Anglo-Inder(in *f*) *m*; [2] *adj* anglo-indisch; *relations* englisch-indisch.
anglomania [,æŋgləʊ'meɪnɪə] *n* Anglomanie *f*.
anglophile ['æŋgləʊfaɪl] [1] *n* Anglophile(r) *mf* (*form*), Englandfreund *m*.
[2] *adj* anglophil (*form*), englandfreundlich.
anglophobe ['æŋgləʊfəʊb] *n* Anglophobe(r) *mf* (*form*), Englandhasser, Englandfeind *m*.
anglophobia [,æŋgləʊ'fəʊbɪə] *n* Anglophobie *f* (*form*), Englandhaß *m*.
anglophobic [,æŋgləʊ'fəʊbɪk] *adj* anglophob (*form*), anti-englisch, englandfeindlich.
Anglo-Saxon ['æŋgləʊ'sæksən] [1] *n* **(a)** (*person, Hist*) Angelsachse *m*, Angelsächsin *f*. **(b)** (*language*) Angelsächsisch *nt*.
[2] *adj* angelsächsisch.
Angola [æŋ'gəʊlə] *n* Angola *nt*.
Angolan [æŋ'gəʊlən] [1] *n* Angolaner (in *f*) *m*.
[2] *adj* angolanisch.
angora [æŋ'gɔ:rə] [1] *adj* Angora-.
[2] *n* Angora(wolle *f*) *nt*; (*Tex*) Angoragewebe *nt*; (~ *rabbit*, ~ *cat*, ~ *goat*) Angorakaninchen *nt*/-katze/-ziege *f*.
angostura [æŋgə'stjʊərə] *n* (*bark*) Angosturarinde *f*; (*also* ® ~ **bitters**) Angosturabitter *m*.
angrily ['æŋgrɪlɪ] *adv* wütend.
angry ['æŋgrɪ] *adj* (*+er*) **(a)** zornig, ungehalten (*geh*); *letter, look also, animal* wütend ◆ **to be** ~ wütend *or* böse *or* verärgert sein; **to be** ~ **with** *or* **at sb** jdm *or* auf jdn *or* mit jdm böse sein, über jdn verärgert sein; **to be** ~ **at** *or* **about sth** sich über etw (*acc*) ärgern; **to get** ~ **(with** *or* **at sb/about sth)** (mit jdm/über etw *acc*) böse werden; **you're not** ~**, are you?** du bist (mir) doch nicht böse(, oder)?; **to be** ~ **with oneself** sich über sich (*acc*) selbst ärgern, sich (*dat*) selbst böse sein, über sich (*acc*) selbst verärgert sein; **to make sb** ~ (*stressing action*) jdn ärgern; (*stressing result*) jdn verärgern; **it makes me so** ~ es ärgert mich furchtbar, es macht mich so wütend *or* böse; ~ **young man** Rebell, Angry young man *m* (*geh*).
(b) (*fig*) *sea* aufgewühlt; *sky, clouds* bedrohlich, finster ◆ **the sky was an** ~ **purple** der Himmel war bedrohlich violett.
(c) (*inflamed*) *wound* entzündet, böse ◆ **an** ~ **red** hochrot.
angst [æŋst] *n* (Existenz)angst *f*.
anguish ['æŋgwɪʃ] *n* Qual, Pein (*old*) *f* ◆ **to be in** ~ Qualen leiden; **the look of** ~ **on the faces of the waiting wives** der angsterfüllte Blick in den Gesichtern der wartenden Frauen; **he wrung his hands in** ~ er rang die Hände in Verzweiflung; **those who suffer the** ~ **of indecision** wer die Qual der Entschlußlosigkeit erleidet; **writhing in** ~ **on the ground** sich in Qualen auf dem Boden windend; **her children/the news/the decision caused her great** ~ ihre Kinder bereiteten ihr großen Kummer *or* großes Leid/die Nachricht bereitete ihr großen Schmerz/die Entscheidung bereitete ihr große Qual(en).
anguished ['æŋgwɪʃt] *adj* qualvoll.
angular ['æŋgjʊlə^r] *adj* **(a)** *shape* eckig; *face, features, prose* kantig. **(b)** (*bony*) knochig. **(c)** (*awkward*) linkisch, steif.
angularity [,æŋgjʊ'lærɪtɪ] *n see adj* **(a)** Eckigkeit *f*; Kantigkeit *f*. **(b)** Knochigkeit *f*.
aniline ['ænɪli:n] *n* Anilin *nt* ◆ ~ **dye** Anilinfarbstoff *m*.
anima ['ænɪmə] *n* (*Psych*) Anima *f*.
animadversion [,ænɪmæd'vɜ:ʃən] *n* (*form*) kritische Äußerung.
animal ['ænɪməl] [1] *n* Tier *nt*; (*as opposed to insects etc*) Vierbeiner *m*; (*brutal person also*) Bestie *f* ◆ **man is a social** ~ der Mensch ist ein soziales Wesen; **a political** ~ ein politisches Wesen, ein Zoon politikon (*geh*) *nt*; **there's no such** ~ (*fig*) so was gibt es nicht! (*inf*); **the** ~ **in him** das Tier(ische) *or* Animalische in ihm; **he's nothing but a little** ~ er ist nicht besser als ein Tier.
[2] *adj attr story, picture* Tier-; *products, cruelty, lust* tierisch ◆ ~ **behaviour** (*lit*) das Verhalten der Tiere, tierisches Verhalten; (*fig: brutal*) tierisches Verhalten; ~ **desire** animalischer Trieb; ~ **husbandry** Viehwirtschaft *f*; ~ **kingdom** Tierreich *nt*, Tierwelt *f*; ~ **lover** Tierfreund *m*; ~ **magnetism** rein körperliche Anziehungskraft; ~ **needs** (*fig*) animalische Bedürfnisse *pl*; ~ **rights** der Tierschutz; ~ **rights activist/campaigner** Tierschützer(in *f*), Tierrechtler(in *f*) *m*; ~ **spirits** Vitalität *f*.
animalcule [,ænɪ'mælkju:l] *n* mikroskopisch kleines Tierchen.
animality [,ænɪ'mælɪtɪ] *n* Tierhaftigkeit *f* ◆ **the** ~ **of their actions** das Tierische ihrer Handlungen.
animate ['ænɪmɪt] [1] *adj* belebt; *creation, creatures* lebend.
[2] ['ænɪmeɪt] *vt* (*lit: God*) mit Leben erfüllen; (*fig*) (*enliven*) beleben; (*move to action*) anregen, animieren; (*Film*) animieren ◆ **Disney was the first to** ~ **cartoons** Disney machte als erster Zeichentrickfilme.
animated ['ænɪmeɪtɪd] *adj* **(a)** (*lively*) lebhaft, rege; *discussion, talk also* angeregt. **(b)** (*Film*) ~ **cartoon** Zeichentrickfilm *m*.
animatedly ['ænɪmeɪtɪdlɪ] *adv* rege; *talk also* angeregt.
animation [,ænɪ'meɪʃən] *n* Lebhaftigkeit *f*; (*Film*) Animation *f* ◆ **she loved the** ~ **of Parisian life** sie liebte das Getriebe des Pariser Lebens.
animator ['ænɪmeɪtə^r] *n* Animator(in *f*) *m*.
animatronics [ænɪmə'trɒnɪks] *n sing* (*Film*) Computer-Animation *f*.
animism ['ænɪmɪzəm] *n* Animismus *m*.
animosity [,ænɪ'mɒsɪtɪ] *n* Animosität (*geh*), Feindseligkeit *f* (*towards* gegenüber, gegen, *between* zwischen *+dat*).
animus ['ænɪməs] *n, no pl* **(a)** Feindseligkeit *f*. **(b)** (*Psych*) Animus *m*.
anise ['ænɪs] *n* Anis *m*.
aniseed ['ænɪsi:d] *n* (*seed*) Anis(samen) *m*; (*flavouring*) Anis *m*; (*liqueur*) Anislikör *m* ◆ ~ **ball** Anisbonbon *m or nt*.
ankle ['æŋkl] *n* Knöchel *m*.
ankle: ~**bone** *n* Sprungbein *nt*; ~**-deep** [1] *adj* knöcheltief; [2] *adv* **he was** ~**-deep in water** er stand bis an die Knöchel im Wasser; **the field was** ~**-deep in mud** auf dem Feld stand der Schlamm knöcheltief; ~ **sock** *n* Söckchen

nt; ~ **strap** *n* Schuhriemchen *nt*.

anklet ['æŋklɪt] *n* **(a)** Fußring *m*, Fußspange *f*. **(b)** (*US: sock*) Söckchen *nt*.

annalist ['ænəlɪst] *n* Chronist, Geschichtsschreiber *m*.

annals ['ænəlz] *npl* Annalen *pl*; (*of society etc*) Bericht *m* ◆ **in all the ~ of recorded history** in der gesamten bisherigen Geschichte.

anneal [ə'ni:l] *vt glass* kühlen; *metal* ausglühen; *earthenware* brennen; (*fig*) stählen.

annex [ə'neks] **1** *vt* annektieren.
2 ['æneks] *n* **(a)** (*to document etc*) Anhang, Nachtrag *m*. **(b)** (*building*) Nebengebäude *nt*, Annex *m*; (*extension*) Anbau *m*.

annexation [,ænek'seɪʃən] *n* Annexion *f*.

annexe ['æneks] *n see* **annex 2 (b)**.

annihilate [ə'naɪəleɪt] *vt* vernichten; *army also* aufreiben, auslöschen (*geh*); (*fig*) *hope* zerschlagen; *theory* vernichten, zerschlagen; (*inf*) *person, opponent, team* fertigmachen (*inf*), in die Pfanne hauen (*inf*) ◆ **I felt completely ~d** ich war völlig am Boden zerstört (*inf*).

annihilation [ə,naɪə'leɪʃən] *n* Vernichtung, Auslöschung (*geh*) *f*; (*fig: of theory*) Vernichtung, Zerschlagung *f* ◆ **our team's ~** die vollständige Niederlage unserer Mannschaft; **her ~ of her opponents** die Art, wie sie ihre Gegner fertigmachte (*inf*).

anniversary [,ænɪ'vɜ:sərɪ] *n* Jahrestag *m*; (*wedding ~*) Hochzeitstag *m* ◆ **~ celebrations** Feiern *pl* anläßlich eines Jahrestages/Hochzeitstages; **~ dinner/gift** (Fest)essen *nt*/Geschenk *nt* zum Jahrestag/Hochzeitstag; **the ~ of his death** sein Todestag *m*.

anno Domini ['ænəʊ'dɒmɪnaɪ] *n* **(a)** (*abbr* **AD**) nach Christus, anno *or* Anno Domini ◆ **in 53 ~** im Jahre 53 nach Christus. **(b)** (*inf: age*) Alter *nt*.

annotate ['ænəʊteɪt] *vt* mit Anmerkungen versehen, kommentieren ◆ **~d text** kommentierter Text.

annotation [,ænəʊ'teɪʃən] *n* (*no pl: commentary, act*) Kommentar *m*; (*comment*) Anmerkung *f*.

announce [ə'naʊns] *vt* (*lit, fig: person*) bekanntgeben, verkünden; *arrival, departure, radio programme* ansagen; (*over intercom*) durchsagen; (*signal*) anzeigen; (*formally*) *birth, marriage etc* anzeigen; *coming of spring etc* ankündigen ◆ **to ~ sb** jdn melden; **the arrival of flight BA 742 has just been ~d** soeben ist die Ankunft des Fluges BA 742 gemeldet worden.

announcement [ə'naʊnsmənt] *n* (*public declaration*) Bekanntgabe, Bekanntmachung *f*; (*of impending event, speaker*) Ankündigung *f*; (*over intercom etc*) Durchsage *f*; (*giving information: on radio etc*) Ansage *f*; (*written: of birth, marriage etc*) Anzeige *f* ◆ **after they had made the ~** nach der Bekanntgabe *etc*.

announcer [ə'naʊnsə^r] *n* (*Rad, TV*) Ansager(in *f*), Radio-/Fernsehsprecher(in *f*) *m*.

annoy [ə'nɔɪ] *vt* (*make angry, irritate*) ärgern; (*get worked up: noise, questions etc*) aufregen; (*pester*) belästigen ◆ **to be ~ed that ...** ärgerlich *or* verärgert sein, weil ...; **to be ~ed with sb/about sth** sich über jdn/etw ärgern, (mit) jdm/über etw (*acc*) böse sein; **to get ~ed** sich ärgern, sich aufregen, böse werden; **don't get ~ed** reg dich nicht auf, nur keine Aufregung; **don't let it ~ you** ärgere dich nicht darüber.

annoyance [ə'nɔɪəns] *n* **(a)** *no pl* (*irritation*) Ärger, Verdruß (*geh*) *m* ◆ **to cause (great) ~** (großes) Ärgernis erregen; **smoking can cause ~ to others** Rauchen kann eine Belästigung für andere sein; **to his ~** zu seinem Ärger *or* Verdruß. **(b)** (*nuisance*) Plage, Belästigung *f*, Ärgernis *nt*.

annoying [ə'nɔɪɪŋ] *adj* ärgerlich; *habit* lästig ◆ **the ~ thing (about it) is that ...** das Ärgerliche (daran *or* bei der Sache) ist, daß ...; **it's so ~!** das kann einen ärgern, das ist derart ärgerlich; **he has an ~ way of speaking slowly** er hat eine Art, langsam zu sprechen, die einen ärgern *or* aufregen kann.

annoyingly [ə'nɔɪɪŋlɪ] *adv* aufreizend ◆ **the bus didn't turn up, rather ~** ärgerlicherweise kam der Bus nicht.

annual ['ænjʊəl] **1** *n* **(a)** (*Bot*) einjährige Pflanze. **(b)** (*book*) Jahresalbum *nt*.
2 *adj* (*happening once a year*) jährlich; (*of or for the year*) *salary etc* Jahres- ◆ **~ accounts** Jahresbilanz *f*; **~ general meeting** Jahreshauptversammlung *f*; **~ report** Geschäftsbericht *m*; **~ ring** (*of tree*) Jahresring *m*.

annually ['ænjʊəlɪ] *adv* jährlich.

annuity [ə'nju:ɪtɪ] *n* (Leib)rente *f* ◆ **to invest money in an ~** Geld in einer Rentenversicherung anlegen; **to buy an ~** eine Rentenversicherung abschließen.

annul [ə'nʌl] *vt* annullieren; *law, decree, judgement also* aufheben; *contract, marriage also* auflösen, für ungültig erklären; *will also* für ungültig erklären.

annulment [ə'nʌlmənt] *n see vt* Annullierung *f*; Aufhebung *f*; Auflösung *f*; Ungültigkeitserklärung *f*.

Annunciation [ə,nʌnsɪ'eɪʃən] *n* (*Bibl*) Mariä Verkündigung *f* ◆ **the feast of the ~** das Fest Maria *or* Mariä Verkündigung.

anode ['ænəʊd] *n* Anode *f*.

anodize ['ænə,daɪz] *vt* anodisch behandeln, anodisieren.

anodyne ['ænəʊdaɪn] **1** *n* (*Med*) schmerzstillendes Mittel, Schmerzmittel *nt*; (*fig*) Wohltat *f*.
2 *adj* (*Med*) schmerzstillend; (*fig*) wohltuend, beruhigend.

anoint [ə'nɔɪnt] *vt* salben ◆ **to ~ sb king** jdn zum König salben.

anomalous [ə'nɒmələs] *adj* anomal, ungewöhnlich.

anomaly [ə'nɒməlɪ] *n* Anomalie *f*; (*in law etc*) Besonderheit *f*.

anon[1] [ə'nɒn] *adv* (*old*) alsbald (*dial, old*), bald ◆ **ever and ~** (*old*) dann und wann; **see you ~** (*hum*) bis demnächst.

anon[2] [ə'nɒn] *adj abbr of* **anonymous** (*at end of text*) **"A~"** Anonymus (*liter*), Verfasser unbekannt.

anonymity [,ænə'nɪmɪtɪ] *n* Anonymität *f*.

anonymous *adj*, **~ly** *adv* [ə'nɒnɪməs, -lɪ] anonym.

anorak ['ænəræk] *n* (*Brit*) Anorak *m*.

anorectic [ænə'rektɪk] *adj see* **anorexic**.

anorexia (nervosa) [ænə'reksɪə(nɜ:'vəʊsə)] *n* Appetitlosigkeit, Magersucht, Anorexie (*spec*) *f*.

anorexic [ænə'reksɪk] *adj* magersüchtig.

another [ə'nʌðə^r] **1** *adj* **(a)** (*additional*) noch eine(r, s) ◆ **~ one** noch eine(r, s); **take ~ ten** nehmen Sie noch (weitere) zehn; **I won't give you ~ chance** ich werde dir nicht noch eine *or* keine weitere Chance geben; **I don't want ~ drink!** ich möchte nichts mehr trinken; **in ~ 20 years he ...** noch 20 Jahre, und er ...; **without ~ word** ohne ein weiteres Wort; **and (there's) ~ thing** und noch eins, und (da ist) noch (et)was (anderes).
(b) (*similar, fig: second*) ein zweiter, eine zweite, ein zweites ◆ **there is not ~ such man** so einen Mann gibt es nicht noch einmal *or* gibt es nur einmal; **~ Shakespeare** ein zweiter Shakespeare; **there will never be ~ you** für mich wird es nie jemand geben wie dich *or* du.
(c) (*different*) ein anderer, eine andere, ein anderes ◆ **that's quite ~ matter** das ist etwas ganz anderes; **~ time** ein andermal; **but maybe there won't be ~ time** aber vielleicht gibt es keine andere Gelegenheit *or* gibt es das nicht noch einmal.
2 *pron* ein anderer, eine andere, ein anderes ◆ **have ~!** nehmen Sie (doch) noch einen!; **he has found ~** (*dated, liter*) er hat eine andere gefunden; **many ~** manch anderer; **such ~** noch so einer; **taking one with ~** alles zusammengenommen, im großen (und) ganzen; **tell me ~!** (*inf*) Sie können mir sonst was erzählen (*inf*), das können Sie mir nicht weismachen; **what with one thing and ~** bei all dem Trubel; **is this ~ of your brilliant ideas!** ist das wieder so eine deiner Glanzideen!; **she's ~ of his girlfriends** sie ist (auch) eine seiner Freundinnen; **yes, I'm ~ of his fans** ja, ich bin auch einer seiner Fans.

Ansaphone ® ['ɑ:nsəfəʊn] *n* Anrufbeantworter *m*.

ANSI *abbr of* **American National Standards Institute** *amerikanischer Normenausschuß*.

answer ['ɑ:nsə^r] **1** *n* **(a)** (*to auf +acc*) Antwort, Entgegnung (*geh*), Erwiderung (*geh*) *f*; (*in exam*) Antwort *f* ◆ **to get an/no ~** Antwort/keine Antwort bekommen; **there was no ~** (*to telephone, doorbell*) es hat sich niemand gemeldet; **the ~ to our prayers** ein Geschenk des Himmels; **the ~ to a maiden's prayer** (*hum*) ein Traummann *m* (*inf*), der ideale Mann; **there's no ~ to that** (*inf*) was soll man da groß machen/sagen! (*inf*); **Germany's ~ to Concorde** Deutschlands Antwort auf die Concorde; **they had no ~ to this new striker** (*Ftbl*) sie hatten dem neuen Stürmer nichts *or* niemanden entgegenzusetzen; **in ~ to your letter/my question** in Beantwortung Ihres Briefes (*form*)/auf meine Frage hin; **she's always got an ~** sie hat immer eine Antwort parat.
(b) (*solution*) Lösung *f* (*to gen*) ◆ **his ~ to any difficulty is to ignore it** seine Reaktion auf jedwede Schwierigkeit ist: einfach nicht wahrhaben wollen; **there's no easy ~** es gibt dafür keine Patentlösung; **there's only one ~ for depression ...** es gibt nur ein Mittel gegen Depression ...; **his one ~ for all ailments is ...** sein Allheilmittel für alle *or* bei allen Beschwerden ist ...
(c) (*Jur*) Einlassung (*form*), Stellungnahme *f* ◆ **the defendant's ~ to the charge was ...** laut Einlassung des Beklagten ...(*form*); **what is your ~ to the charge?** was haben Sie dazu zu sagen?
2 *vt* **(a)** antworten auf (*+acc*), erwidern auf (*+acc*) (*geh*); *person* antworten (*+dat*); *exam questions* beantworten, antworten auf (*+acc*); *objections, criticism also* beantworten ◆ **will you ~ that?** (*phone, door*) gehst du ran/hin?; **to ~ the telephone** das Telefon abnehmen, rangehen (*inf*); **to answer the bell** *or* **door** die Tür öffnen *or* aufmachen, hingehen (*inf*); **who ~ed the phone?** wer war dran (*inf*) *or* am Apparat?; (*here at this end*) wer hat den Anruf entgegengenommen?; **shall I ~ it?** (*phone*) soll ich rangehen?; (*door*) soll ich hingehen?; **to ~ the call of nature** (*also hum*)/**of duty** dem Ruf der Natur/der Pflicht folgen; **5,000 men ~ed the call for volunteers** 5.000 Männer meldeten sich auf den Freiwilligenaufruf hin; **the fire brigade ~ed the alarm call** die Feuerwehr rückte auf den Alarm hin aus; **..., he ~ed ...**, antwortete er; **~ me this** sagen *or* beantworten Sie mir eins; **~ me!** antworte (mir)!, antworten Sie!; **to anyone who claims ... I would ~ this** jemandem, der ... behauptet, würde ich folgendes erwidern *or* entgegen.
(b) (*fulfil*) *description* entsprechen (*+dat*); *hope, expectation also* erfüllen; *prayer* (*God*) erhören; *need* befriedigen ◆ **people who ~ that description** Leute, auf die diese Beschreibung paßt *or* zutrifft; **this ~ed our prayers** das war (wie) ein Geschenk des Himmels; **it ~s the/our purpose** es erfüllt seinen Zweck/es erfüllt für uns seinen Zweck.
(c) (*Jur*) *charge* sich verantworten wegen (*+gen*).
3 *vi* **(a)** (*also react*) antworten ◆ **if the phone rings, don't ~** wenn das Telefon läutet, geh nicht ran *or* nimm nicht ab.
(b) (*suffice*) geeignet *or* brauchbar sein, taugen.

◆**answer back** **1** *vi* widersprechen; (*children also*) patzige *or* freche Antworten geben ◆ **don't ~ ~!** keine Widerrede!; **it's not fair to criticize him because he can't ~ ~** es ist unfair, ihn zu kritisieren, weil er sich nicht verteidigen kann.
2 *vt sep* **to ~ sb ~** jdm widersprechen; (*children also*) jdm patzige *or* freche Antworten geben.

◆**answer for** *vi +prep obj* **(a)** (*be responsible for*) verantwortlich sein für; (*person also*) verantworten; *mistakes also* einstehen für ◆ **he has a lot to ~ ~** er hat eine Menge auf dem Gewissen; **I won't ~ ~ the consequences** ich will für die Folgen nicht verantwortlich gemacht werden.
(b) (*guarantee*) sich verbürgen für; (*speak for also*) sprechen für ◆ **to ~ ~ the**

truth of sth für die Wahrheit von etw einstehen.

◆**answer to** *vi +prep obj* **(a)** (*be accountable to*) **to ~ ~ sb for sth** jdm für etw *or* wegen einer Sache (*gen*) Rechenschaft schuldig sein; **if anything goes wrong you'll have me to ~ ~** wenn etwas nicht klappt, dann stehen Sie mir dafür ein *or* gerade *or* dann müssen Sie sich vor mir dafür verantworten.
(b) **to ~ ~ a description** einer Beschreibung entsprechen.
(c) **to ~ ~ the name of ...** auf den Namen ... hören.
(d) **to ~ ~ the wheel/helm/controls** auf das Steuer/das Ruder/die Steuerung ansprechen.

answerable ['ɑːnsərəbl] *adj* **(a)** *question* beantwortbar,zu beantworten *pred*; *charge, argument* widerlegbar.
(b) (*responsible*) verantwortlich ◆ **to be ~ to sb (for sth)** jdm gegenüber für etw verantwortlich sein; **to be held ~** verantwortlich gemacht werden; **parents are ~ for their children's behaviour** Eltern haften für ihre Kinder.

answer-back (code) ['ɑːnsəbæk(ˌkəʊd)] *n* (*for telex*) Kennung *f*.

answerer ['ɑːnsərəʳ] *n* Antwortende(r) *mf*.

answering machine ['ɑːnsərɪŋmə'ʃiːn] *n* (automatischer) Anrufbeantworter.

answer paper *n* (*in exam*) Lösung *f*, Antwortbogen *m*.

answerphone ['ɑːnsəfəʊn] *n* Anrufbeantworter *m*.

ant [ænt] *n* Ameise *f* ◆ **to have ~s in one's pants** (*inf*) Pfeffer *or* Hummeln im Hintern haben (*sl*), kein Sitzfleisch haben.

antacid ['ænt'æsɪd] *n* säurebindendes Mittel.

antagonism [æn'tægənɪzəm] *n* (*between people, theories etc*) Antagonismus *m*; (*towards sb, ideas, a suggestion, change etc*) Feindseligkeit, Feindlichkeit *f* (*to(wards)* gegenüber) ◆ **to arouse sb's ~** jdn gegen sich aufbringen.

antagonist [æn'tægənɪst] *n* Kontrahent, Gegner, Antagonist *m*; (*esp Pol*) Gegenspieler *m*.

antagonistic [ænˌtægə'nɪstɪk] *adj reaction, attitude* feindselig; *force* gegnerisch, feindlich; *interests* widerstreitend, antagonistisch ◆ **to be ~ to** *or* **towards sb/sth** jdm/gegen etw feindselig gesinnt sein.

antagonize [æn'tægənaɪz] *vt person* gegen sich aufbringen *or* stimmen; (*annoy*) verärgern.

antarctic [ænt'ɑːktɪk] [1] *adj* antarktisch, der Antarktis ◆ **A~ Circle** südlicher Polarkreis; **A~ Ocean** Südpolarmeer *nt*.
[2] *n*: **the A~** die Antarktis.

Antarctica [ænt'ɑːktɪkə] *n* die Antarktis.

ante ['æntɪ] [1] *n* (*Cards*) Einsatz *m* ◆ **to up the ~** (*fig inf*) den Einsatz erhöhen.
[2] *vt* (*also* **~ up**) einsetzen.
[3] *vi* setzen, seinen Einsatz machen ◆ **his father ~d up as usual** (*fig inf*) sein Vater blechte wie gewöhnlich (*inf*).

ante- *pref* vor-.

anteater ['æntˌiːtəʳ] *n* Ameisenbär, Ameisenfresser *m*.

antecedent [ˌæntɪ'siːdənt] [1] *adj* früher ◆ **the crisis and its ~ events** die Krise und die ihr vorangehenden *or* vorausgehenden Ereignisse; **to be ~ to sth** einer Sache (*dat*) voran- *or* vorausgehen.
[2] *n* **(a) ~s** (*of person*) (*past history*) Vorleben *nt*; (*ancestry*) Abstammung *f*; (*of event*) Vorgeschichte *f*. **(b)** (*Gram*) Bezugswort *nt*.

ante: ~chamber *n* Vorzimmer *nt*; **~date** *vt document, cheque* vordatieren (*to* auf *+acc*); *event* vorausgehen (*+dat*) (*by* um); **~diluvian** [ˌæntɪdɪ'luːvɪən] *adj* (*lit, fig inf*) vorsintflutlich.

antelope ['æntɪləʊp] *n* Antilope *f*.

ante meridiem [ˌæntɪmə'rɪdɪəm] *adv* (*abbr* **am**) vormittags.

antenatal ['æntɪ'neɪtl] *adj* vor der Geburt, pränatal (*form*) ◆ **~ care/exercises** Schwangerschaftsfürsorge *f*/-übungen *pl*; **~ clinic** Sprechstunde *f* für Schwangere *or* für werdende Mütter.

antenna [æn'tenə] *n* **(a)** *pl* **-e** [æn'teniː] (*Zool*) Fühler *m*. **(b)** *pl* **-e** *or* **-s** (*Rad, TV*) Antenne *f*.

antepenultimate ['æntɪpɪ'nʌltɪmɪt] *adj* vorvorletzte(r, s).

anterior [æn'tɪərɪəʳ] *adj* **(a)** (*prior*) früher (*to* als) ◆ **to be ~ to** vorangehen (*+dat*), vorausgehen (*+dat*). **(b)** (*Anat etc*) vordere(r, s) ◆ **~ brain** Vorderhirn *nt*.

anteroom ['æntɪruːm] *n* Vorzimmer *nt*.

anthem ['ænθəm] *n* Hymne *f*; (*by choir*) Chorgesang *m*.

anther ['ænθəʳ] *n* (*Bot*) Staubbeutel *m*, Anthere *f* (*spec*).

anthill ['æntˌhɪl] *n* Ameisenhaufen *m*.

anthology [æn'θɒlədʒɪ] *n* Anthologie *f*.

anthracite ['ænθrəsaɪt] *n* Anthrazit *m*.

anthrax ['ænθræks] *n* (*Med, Vet*) Anthrax (*spec*), Milzbrand *m*.

anthropocentric [ˌænθrəpəʊ'sentrɪk] *adj* anthropozentrisch.

anthropoid ['ænθrəʊpɔɪd] [1] *n* Anthropoid *m* (*spec*); (*ape*) Menschenaffe *m*.
[2] *adj* anthropoid (*spec*).

anthropological [ˌænθrəpə'lɒdʒɪkəl] *adj* anthropologisch.

anthropologist [ˌænθrə'pɒlədʒɪst] *n* Anthropologe *m*, Anthropologin *f*.

anthropology [ˌænθrə'pɒlədʒɪ] *n* Anthropologie *f*.

anthropomorphic [ˌænθrəʊpə'mɔːfɪk] *adj* anthropomorphisch.

anthropomorphism [ˌænθrəʊpə'mɔːfɪzəm] *n* Anthropomorphismus *m*.

anti ['æntɪ] (*inf*) [1] *adj pred* in Opposition (*inf*) ◆ **are you in favour? — no, I'm ~** bist du dafür? — nein, ich bin dagegen.
[2] *prep* gegen (*+acc*) ◆ **~ everything** grundsätzlich gegen alles.

anti- *in cpds* Anti-, anti-; **~-abortion** *adj* Anti-Abtreibungs-; **~-abortionist** *n* Abtreibungsgegner(in *f*) *m*; **~-aircraft** *adj gun, rocket* Flugabwehr-; **~-aircraft defence** Luftverteidigung *f*; **~-aircraft gun/fire** Flak(geschütz *nt*) *f*/ Flakfeuer *nt*; **~ballistic** *adj*: **~ballistic missile** Anti-Raketen-Rakete *f*; **~biotic** [ˌæntɪbaɪ'ɒtɪk] [1] *n* Antibiotikum *nt*; [2] *adj* antibiotisch; **~body** *n* Antikörper *m*.

antic ['æntɪk] *n see* **antics**.

Antichrist ['æntɪkraɪst] *n* Antichrist *m*.

anticipate [æn'tɪsɪpeɪt] [1] *vt* **(a)** (*expect*) erwarten ◆ **as ~d** wie vorausgesehen *or* erwartet.
(b) (*see in advance*) vorausberechnen, vorhersehen; (*see in advance and cater for*) *objection, need etc* zuvorkommen (*+dat*) ◆ **he always has to ~ what his opponent will do next** er muß immer vorhersehen können *or* vorausahnen, was sein Gegner als nächstes tun wird; **don't ~ what I'm going to say** nimm nicht vorweg, was ich noch sagen wollte.
(c) (*do before sb else*) zuvorkommen (*+dat*) ◆ **in his discovery he was ~d by others** bei seiner Entdeckung sind ihm andere zuvorgekommen; **a phrase which ~s a later theme** eine Melodie, die auf ein späteres Thema vor(aus)greift.
(d) (*do, use, act on prematurely*) *income* im voraus ausgeben; *inheritance* im voraus in Anspruch nehmen.
[2] *vi* (*manager, driver, chess-player etc*) vorauskalkulieren.

anticipation [ænˌtɪsɪ'peɪʃən] *n* **(a)** (*expectation*) Erwartung *f* ◆ **thanking you in ~** herzlichen Dank im voraus; **to wait in ~** gespannt warten; **we took our umbrellas in ~ of rain** wir nahmen unsere Schirme mit, weil wir mit Regen rechneten.
(b) (*seeing in advance*) Vorausberechnung *f* ◆ **impressed by the hotel's ~ of our wishes** beeindruckt, wie man im Hotel unseren Wünschen zuvorkommt/zuvorkam; **his uncanny ~ of every objection** die verblüffende Art, in der *or* wie er jedem Einwand zuvorkam; **the driver showed good ~** der Fahrer zeigte *or* bewies gute Voraussicht.
(c) (*of discovery, discoverer*) Vorwegnahme *f*; (*Mus: of theme etc*) Vorgriff *m* (*of* auf *+acc*).

anticipatory [æn'tɪsɪˌpeɪtərɪ] *adj* vorwegnehmend.

anti: ~clerical *adj* antiklerikal, kirchenfeindlich; **~climactic** *adj* enttäuschend; **~climax** *n* Enttäuschung *f*; (*no pl: Liter*) Antiklimax *f*; **~clockwise** [1] *adj movement, direction* Links-; [2] *adv* nach links, gegen den Uhrzeigersinn *or* die Uhrzeigerrichtung; **~coagulant** [ˌæntɪkəʊ'ægjʊlənt] [1] *n* Antikoagulans *nt* (*spec*); [2] *adj* antikoagulierend (*spec*), blutgerinnungshemmend; **~corrosive** *adj paint* Korrosionsschutz-.

antics ['æntɪks] *npl* Eskapaden *pl*; (*tricks*) Possen, Streiche *pl*; (*irritating behaviour*) Mätzchen *pl* (*inf*) ◆ **he's up to his old ~ again** er macht wieder seine Mätzchen (*inf*); **the photocopier is up to its old ~ again** der Fotokopierer hat wieder seine Mucken (*inf*).

anti: ~cyclone *n* Antizyklone *f*, Hoch(druckgebiet) *nt*; **~-dandruff** *adj shampoo* gegen Schuppen; **~-dazzle** *adj* blendfrei; **~depressant** [1] *n* Antidepressivum *nt*; [2] *adj* antidepressiv; **~dote** ['æntɪdəʊt] *n* (*Med, fig*) Gegenmittel, Antidot (*spec*) *nt* (*against, to, for* gegen); **~freeze** *n* Frostschutz(mittel *nt*) *m*.

antigen ['æntɪdʒən] *n* Antigen *nt*.

anti: ~-hero *n* Antiheld *m*; **~histamine** *n* Antihistamin(ikum) *nt*; **~-inflammatory** *adj drug* entzündungshemmend; **~knock** [1] *adj* Antiklopf-; [2] *n* Antiklopfmittel *nt*; **~-lock** *adj brakes, mechanism* Blockierschutz-; **~-lock braking system** *n* Blockierschutz-Bremssystem *nt*; **~log (arithm)** *n* Antilogarithmus, Numerus *m*; **~macassar** *n* (Sessel-/Sofa)schoner *m*; **~malarial** [1] *adj* gegen Malaria; [2] *n* Malariamittel *nt*; **~-marketeer** *n* EG-Gegner(in *f*) *m*; **~matter** *n* Antimaterie *f*; **~missile** *adj* Raketenabwehr-.

antimony ['æntɪmənɪ] *n* Antimon *nt*.

anti-nuclear *adj* (*against nuclear energy*) Anti-Atom(kraft)-; (*against nuclear weapons*) Anti-Atomwaffen- ◆ **the ~ lobby/protesters** die Atomkraftgegner *pl*; die Atomwaffengegner *pl*.

antioxidant [ˌæntɪ'ɒksɪdənt] *n* Antioxidans *nt* ◆ **~s** Antioxidantien *pl*.

antipasto [ˌæntɪ'pæstəʊ] *n* italienische Vorspeise.

antipathetic [ˌæntɪpə'θetɪk] *adj* **to be ~ to sb/sth** eine Antipathie *or* Abneigung gegen jdn/etw haben; **sb/sth is ~ to sb** (*arouses antipathy in*) jd/etw ist jdm unsympathisch.

antipathy [æn'tɪpəθɪ] *n* Antipathie, Abneigung *f* (*towards* gegen, *between* zwischen *+dat*).

anti: ~-personnel *adj* gegen Menschen gerichtet; **~-personnel bomb/mine** Splitterbombe *f*/Schützenmine *f*; **~perspirant** *n* Antitranspirant *nt*.

antiphony [æn'tɪfənɪ] *n* (*Eccl, Mus*) Antiphon *f*.

antipodean [ænˌtɪpə'diːən], (*US*) **antipodal** [æn'tɪpədəl] *adj* antipodisch; (*Brit*) australisch und neuseeländisch.

antipodes [æn'tɪpədiːz] *npl* (diametral) entgegengesetzte Teile der Erde ◆ **A~** (*Brit*) Australien und Neuseeland; (*Geog*) Antipoden-Inseln *pl*.

antipope ['æntɪˌpəʊp] *n* Gegenpapst *m*.

antiquarian [ˌæntɪ'kweərɪən] [1] *adj books* antiquarisch; *coins also* alt; *studies* des Altertums, der Antike ◆ **~ bookshop** Antiquariat *nt*.
[2] *n see* **antiquary**.

antiquary ['æntɪkwərɪ] *n* (*collector*) Antiquitätensammler(in *f*) *m*; (*seller*) Antiquitätenhändler(in *f*) *m*.

antiquated ['æntɪkweɪtɪd] *adj* antiquiert; *machines, ideas also* überholt; *institutions also* veraltet.

antique [æn'tiːk] [1] *adj* antik.
[2] *n* Antiquität *f*.

antique: ~ dealer *n* Antiquitätenhändler(in *f*) *m*; **~ shop** *n* Antiquitätengeschäft *nt or* -laden *m*.

antiquity [æn'tɪkwɪtɪ] *n* **(a)** (*ancient times*) das Altertum; (*Roman, Greek ~*) die

Antike. **(b)** *(great age)* großes Alter. **(c) antiquities** *pl (old things)* Altertümer *pl.*
anti: ~-riot *adj police* Bereitschafts-; **~-roll bar** *n (Brit Aut)* Stabilisator *m.*
antirrhinum [,æntɪ'raɪnəm] *n* Löwenmaul *nt.*
anti: ~-rust *adj* Rostschutz-; **~scorbutic** *adj* antiskorbutisch; **~-Semite** *n* Antisemit(in *f*) *m*; **~-Semitic** *adj* antisemitisch; **~-Semitism** *n* Antisemitismus *m*; **~septic** [1] *n* Antiseptikum *nt*; [2] *adj (lit, fig)* antiseptisch; **~-skid** *adj* rutschsicher; **~slavery** *adj attr* Antisklaverei-; *speech* gegen die Sklaverei; *politician, groups* Abolitions-; **~-smoking** *adj campaign, group* Antiraucher-; **~social** *adj person, behaviour etc* unsozial; *(Psych, Sociol)* asozial; **to be in an ~social mood** nicht in Gesellschaftslaune sein; **don't be ~social** *(don't be a spoilsport)* sei kein Spielverderber; *(don't be aloof etc)* mach doch mit; **may I smoke or would that be ~social?** darf ich rauchen oder stört das?; **~static** *adj* antistatisch; **~tank** *adj gun, fire* Panzerabwehr-; **~tank ditch/obstacle** Panzersperre *f*; **~-terrorist** *adj squad, measures* zur Terrorismusbekämpfung; *bill* Anti-Terrorismus-; **~-theft device** *n* Diebstahlsicherung *f.*
antithesis [æn'tɪθɪsɪs] *n, pl* **antitheses** [æn'tɪθɪsiːz] *(direct opposite)* genaues Gegenteil *(to, of gen)*; *(of idea, in rhetoric)* Antithese *f (to, of zu) (form)*; *(contrast)* Gegensatz *m.*
antithetic(al) [,æntɪ'θetɪk(əl)] *adj (contrasting)* gegensätzlich; *ideas also, phrases* antithetisch *(form)*; *idea* entgegengesetzt.
anti: ~toxin *n* Gegengift, Antitoxin *nt*; **~trade (wind)** *n* Anti-Passat(wind) *m*; **~trust** *adj (US)* Antitrust-; **~-trust legislation** Kartellgesetzgebung *f*; **~vivisectionism** *n* Ablehnung *f* der Vivisektion; **~vivisectionist** [1] *n* Gegner(in *f*) *m* der Vivisektion; [2] *adj* **his ~vivisectionist views** seine ablehnende Haltung der Vivisektion gegenüber; **~-wrinkle** *adj cream etc* Antifalten-.
antler ['æntləʳ] *n* Geweihstange *f* ◆ **(set** *or* **pair of) ~s** Geweih *nt.*
antonym ['æntənɪm] *n* Antonym, Gegenwort *(geh) nt.*
Antwerp ['æntwɜːp] *n* Antwerpen *nt.*
anus ['eɪnəs] *n* After, Anus *(spec) m.*
anvil ['ænvɪl] *n* Amboß *m (also Anat).*
anxiety [æŋ'zaɪətɪ] *n* **(a)** Sorge *f* ◆ **to feel ~** sich *(dat)* Sorgen machen *(about* um, *at* wegen); **no cause for ~** kein Grund zur Sorge *or* Besorgnis; **to cause sb ~** jdm Sorgen machen; **~ neurosis** *(Psych)* Angstneurose *f.*
(b) *(keen desire)* Verlangen *nt* ◆ **in his ~ to get away** weil er unbedingt wegkommen wollte.
anxious ['æŋkʃəs] *adj* **(a)** *(worried)* besorgt; *person (as character trait), thoughts* ängstlich ◆ **to be ~ about sb/sth** sich *(dat)* um jdn/etw Sorgen machen, um jdn/etw besorgt sein.
(b) *(worrying) moment, minutes* der Angst, bang *(geh)* ◆ **it's been an ~ time for us all** wir alle haben uns (in dieser Zeit) große Sorgen gemacht; **he had an ~ time waiting for ...** es war für ihn eine Zeit voll bangen Wartens auf *(+acc)* ...
(c) *(strongly desirous)* **to be ~ for sth** auf etw *(acc)* aussein; **we are ~ for all the assistance we can get** uns geht es darum, jede nur mögliche Hilfe zu bekommen; **to be ~ to do sth** bestrebt sein *or* darauf aussein, etw zu tun; **they were ~ to start/for his return** sie warteten sehr darauf abzufahren/auf seine Rückkehr; **I am ~ that he should do it** *or* **for him to do it** mir liegt viel daran, daß er es tut.
anxiously ['æŋkʃəslɪ] *adv* **(a)** besorgt. **(b)** *(keenly)* gespannt.
anxiousness ['æŋkʃəsnɪs] *n, no pl see* **anxiety.**
any ['enɪ] [1] *adj* **(a)** *(in interrog, conditional, neg sentences) not translated*; *(emph: ~ at all) (with sing n)* irgendein(e); *(with pl n)* irgendwelche; *(with uncountable n)* etwas ◆ **not ~** kein/keine; **not** *any* **... at all** überhaupt kein/keine ...; **if I had ~ plan/ideas/money** wenn ich einen Plan/Ideen/Geld hätte; **if I had** *any* **plan/ideas/money (at all)** wenn ich irgendeinen Plan/irgendwelche Ideen/(auch nur) etwas Geld hätte; **if you think it'll do ~ good/***any* **good (at all)** wenn du glaubst, daß es etwas/irgend etwas nützt; **if it's ~ help (at all)** wenn das (irgendwie) hilft; **it won't do ~ good** es wird nichts nützen; **it wasn't ~ good** *or* **use (at all)** es nützte (überhaupt *or* gar) nichts; **you mustn't do that on ~ account** das darfst du auf gar keinen Fall tun; **without ~ difficulty (at all)** ohne jede Schwierigkeit.
(b) *(no matter which)* jede(r, s) (beliebige); *(with pl or uncountable n)* alle ◆ **~ one will do** es ist jede(r, s) recht; **~ excuse will do** jede Entschuldigung ist recht; **you can have ~ book/books you can find** du kannst jedes Buch/alle Bücher haben, das/die du finden kannst; **take ~ two points** wähle zwei beliebige Punkte; **~ one you like** was du willst; **~ one of us would have done the same** jeder von uns hätte dasselbe getan; **you can't just/can come at ~ time** du kannst nicht einfach zu jeder beliebigen Zeit kommen/du kannst jederzeit kommen; **~ fool could do that** das kann jedes Kind; **~ old ...** *(inf)* jede(r, s) x-beliebige ... *(inf)*; *see* **old.**
[2] *pron* **(a)** *(in interrog, conditional, neg sentences) (replacing sing n)* ein(e), welche(r, s); *(replacing pl n)* einige, welche; *(replacing uncountable n)* etwas, welche ◆ **I want to meet psychologists/a psychologist, do you know ~?** ich würde gerne Psychologen/einen Psychologen kennenlernen, kennen Sie welche/einen?; **I need some butter/stamps, do you have ~?** ich brauche Butter/Briefmarken, haben Sie welche?; **have you seen ~ of my ties?** haben Sie eine von meinen Krawatten gesehen?; **haven't you ~ (at all)?** haben Sie (denn) (gar *or* überhaupt) keinen/keine/keines?; **he wasn't having ~ (of it/that)** *(inf)* er wollte nichts davon hören; **the profits, if ~** die eventuellen Gewinne; **I'd like some tea/tomatoes if you have ~** ich hätte gerne Tee, wenn Sie welchen haben/Tomaten, wenn Sie welche haben; **if ~ of you can sing** wenn (irgend) jemand *or* (irgend)einer/-eine von euch singen kann; **few, if ~, will come** wenn überhaupt, werden nur wenige kommen.
(b) *(no matter which)* alle ◆ **~ who do come ...** alle, die kommen ...; **~ I have ...** alle, die ich habe ...
[3] *adv* **(a)** *colder, bigger etc* noch ◆ **not ~ colder/bigger** *etc* nicht kälter/größer *etc*; **it won't get ~ colder** es wird nicht mehr kälter; **we can't go ~ further** wir können nicht mehr weitergehen; **should he grow ~ bigger he'll ...** wenn er noch mehr wächst, wird er ...; **are you feeling ~ better?** geht es dir etwas besser?; **he wasn't ~ too pleased** er war nicht allzu begeistert; **do you want ~ more soup?** willst du noch etwas Suppe?; **don't you want ~ more tea?** willst du keinen Teemehr?; **~ more offers?** noch weitere Angebote?; **I don't want ~ more (at all)** ich möchte (überhaupt *or* gar) nichts mehr.
(b) *(esp US inf: at all)* überhaupt ◆ **you can't improve it ~** du kannst es überhaupt nicht mehr verbessern; **it didn't help them ~** es hat ihnen gar *or* überhaupt nichts genützt.
anybody ['enɪ,bɒdɪ] [1] *pron* **(a)** (irgend) jemand, (irgend)eine(r) ◆ **not ... ~** niemand, keine(r); **is ~ there?** ist (irgend) jemand da?; **(does) ~ want my book?** will jemand *or* einer mein Buch?; **I can't see ~** ich kann niemand *or* keinen sehen; **don't tell ~** erzähl das niemand(em) *or* keinem.
(b) *(no matter who)* jede(r) ◆ **~ will tell you the same** jeder wird dir dasselbe sagen; **~ with any sense** jeder halbwegs vernünftige Mensch; **it's ~'s game/race** das Spiel/Rennen kann von jedem gewonnen werden; **~ but he, ~ else** jeder außer ihm, jeder andere; **is there ~ else I can talk to?** gibt es sonst jemand(en), mit dem ich sprechen kann?; **I don't want to see ~ else** ich möchte niemand anderen sehen.
[2] *n (person of importance)* jemand, wer *(inf)* ◆ **she'll never be ~** sie wird nie wer sein *(inf)*; **he's not just ~** er ist nicht einfach irgendwer *or* irgend jemand; **everybody who is ~ was there** alles, was Rang und Namen hat, war dort; **she wasn't ~ before he married her** sie war niemand, bevor er sie geheiratet hat.
anyhow ['enɪhaʊ] *adv* **(a)** *(at any rate)* jedenfalls; *(regardless)* trotzdem ◆ **~, that's what I think** das ist jedenfalls meine Meinung; **~, I went to see him** (also) jedenfalls, ich habe ihn besucht; **~, you're here now** jetzt bist du jedenfalls da; **he agrees ~, so it doesn't matter** er ist sowieso einverstanden, es spielt also keine Rolle; **it's no trouble, I'm going there ~** es ist keine Mühe, ich gehe sowieso hin; **I told him not to, but he did it ~** ich habe es ihm verboten, aber er hat es trotzdem gemacht; **who cares, ~?** überhaupt, wen kümmert es denn schon?; **~!** gut!, na ja!
(b) *(carelessly)* irgendwie; *(at random also)* aufs Geratewohl ◆ **the papers were scattered ~ on his desk** die Papiere lagen bunt durcheinander auf seinem Schreibtisch; **things are all ~** alles ist durcheinander.
anyone ['enɪwʌn] *pron, n see* **anybody.**
anyplace ['enɪpleɪs] *adv (US inf) see* **anywhere.**
anyroad ['enɪrəʊd] *adv (N Engl) see* **anyhow (a).**
anything ['enɪθɪŋ] [1] *pron* **(a)** (irgend) etwas ◆ **not ~** nichts; *(emph)* gar *or* überhaupt nichts; **is it/isn't it worth ~?** ist es etwas/gar nichts wert?; **did/didn't he say ~ else?** hat er (sonst) noch etwas/sonst (gar) nichts gesagt?; **did/didn't they give you ~ at all?** haben sie euch überhaupt etwas/überhaupt nichts gegeben?; **are you doing ~ tonight?** hast du heute abend schon etwas vor?; **is there ~ more tiring than ...?** gibt es etwas Ermüdenderes als ...?; **hardly ~** kaum etwas.
(b) *(no matter what)* alles ◆ **~ you like** (alles,) was du willst; **they eat ~** sie essen alles; **not just ~** nicht bloß irgend etwas; **I wouldn't do it for ~** ich würde es um keinen Preis tun; **~ else is impossible** alles andere ist unmöglich; **this is ~ but pleasant** das ist alles andere als angenehm; **~ but that!** alles, nur das nicht!; **~ but!** von wegen!; *see* **if, go, like[1] 2.**
[2] *adv (inf)* **it isn't ~ like him** das sieht ihm überhaupt nicht ähnlich *or* gleich; **if it looked ~ like him ...** wenn es ihm gleichsehen würde ...; **it didn't cost ~ like £100** es kostete bei weitem keine £ 100; **if it costs ~ like as much as before ...** wenn es auch nur annähernd so viel kostet wie früher ...; **~/not ~ like as wet as ...** auch nur annähernd/nicht annähernd so naß wie ...
anyway ['enɪweɪ], *(US dial)* **anyways** *adv see* **anyhow (a)**; *see also* **way.**
anywhere ['enɪweəʳ] *adv* **(a)** *be, stay, live* irgendwo; *go, travel* irgendwohin ◆ **not ~** nirgends/nirgendwohin; **too late to go ~** zu spät, um (noch) irgendwohin zu gehen; **we never go ~** wir gehen nie (irgend)wohin; **I haven't found ~ to live/to put my books yet** ich habe noch nichts gefunden, wo ich wohnen/meine Bücher unterbringen kann; **he'll never get ~** er wird es zu nichts bringen; **I wasn't getting ~** ich kam (einfach) nicht weiter; **there could be ~ between 50 and 100 people** es könnten (schätzungsweise) 50 bis 100 Leute sein.
(b) *(no matter where) be, stay, live* überall; *go, travel* überallhin ◆ **they could be ~** sie könnten überall sein; **~ you like** wo/wohin du willst; **ready to go ~** bereit, überallhin zu gehen.
Anzac ['ænzæk] *n australischer/neuseeländischer Soldat.*
AOCB *abbr of* **any other competent business** Sonstiges.
AONB *abbr of* **Area of Outstanding Natural Beauty.**
aorist ['ɛərɪst] *n* Aorist *m.*
aorta [eɪ'ɔːtə] *n* Aorta *f.*
apace [ə'peɪs] *adv* geschwind *(geh).*
Apache [ə'pætʃɪ] [1] *n* **(a)** Apache *m*, Apachin *f.* **(b)** *(language)* Apache *nt.*
[2] *adj* Apachen-, der Apachen.
apart [ə'pɑːt] *adv* **(a)** auseinander ◆ **to stand with one's feet ~/to sit with one's legs ~** mit gespreizten Beinen dastehen/dasitzen; **I can't tell them ~** ich kann sie nicht auseinanderhalten; **to live ~** getrennt leben; **they're still far** *or* **miles ~** *(fig)* ihre Meinungen klaffen *or* gehen immer noch weit auseinander; **to come** *or* **fall ~** entzweigehen, auseinanderfallen; **it came ~ in**

my hands! es fiel mir in der Hand auseinander; **to take sth ~** etw auseinandernehmen.
(b) (*to one side*) zur Seite, beiseite; (*on one side*) abseits (*from gen*) ♦ **he stood ~ from the group** er stand abseits von der Gruppe; **to hold oneself ~** sich abseits halten; **a class/thing ~** eine Klasse/Sache für sich.
(c) (*excepted*) abgesehen von, bis auf (*+acc*) ♦ **these problems ~** abgesehen von *or* außer diesen Problemen; **~ from that there's nothing else wrong with it** abgesehen davon *or* bis auf das ist alles in Ordnung; **~ from that, the gearbox is also faulty** darüber hinaus *or* außerdem ist (auch) das Getriebe schadhaft.

apartheid [ə'pɑːteɪt] *n* Apartheid *f*.

apartment [ə'pɑːtmənt] *n* **(a)** (*Brit: room*) Raum *m*. **(b)** **~s** *pl* (*Brit: suite of rooms*) Appartement *nt*. **(c)** (*esp US: flat*) Wohnung *f* ♦ **~ house** *or* (*US*) **block** *or* (*US*) **building** Wohnblock *m*.

apathetic [,æpə'θetɪk] *adj* apathisch, teilnahmslos ♦ **they are completely ~ about politics/their future** sie sind in politischen Dingen vollkommen apathisch/sie sind vollkommen apathisch, was ihre Zukunft angeht.

apathetically [,æpə'θetɪkəlɪ] *adv see adj.*

apathy ['æpəθɪ] *n* Apathie, Teilnahmslosigkeit *f*.

APB (*US*) *abbr of* **all points bulletin** ♦ **to put out an ~ on sb** nach jdm eine Fahndung einleiten.

ape [eɪp] [1] *n* (*lit, fig*) Affe *m* ♦ **to go ~** (*inf*) verrückt werden (*inf*), aus der Haut fahren.
[2] *vt* nachäffen (*pej*), nachmachen.

aperient [ə'pɪərɪənt] [1] *n* Abführmittel *nt*.
[2] *adj* abführend.

apéritif [ə,perɪ'tiːf], **aperitive** [ə'perɪtɪv] *n* Aperitif *m*.

aperture ['æpətʃjʊəʳ] *n* Öffnung *f*; (*Phot*) Blende *f*.

apeshit ['eɪpʃɪt] *adj* (*esp US sl*) **to go ~** (*lose one's temper*) an die Decke gehen (*inf*); (*go wild*) ausflippen (*sl*).

apex ['eɪpeks] *n, pl* **-es** *or* **apices** Spitze *f*; (*fig*) Höhepunkt *m*.

aphasia [ə'feɪzɪə] *n* Aphasie *f*.

aphasic [ə'feɪzɪk] [1] *adj* aphasisch.
[2] *n* Aphasiker(in *f*) *m*.

aphid ['eɪfɪd] *n* Blattlaus *f*.

aphorism ['æfərɪzəm] *n* Aphorismus *m*.

aphoristic [,æfə'rɪstɪk] *adj* aphoristisch.

aphrodisiac [,æfrəʊ'dɪzɪæk] [1] *n* Aphrodisiakum *nt*.
[2] *adj* aphrodisisch.

apian ['eɪpɪən] *adj* Bienen-.

apiarist ['eɪpɪə,rɪst] *n* Bienenzüchter(in *f*), Imker(in *f*) *m*.

apiary ['eɪpɪərɪ] *n* Bienenhaus *nt*.

apices ['eɪpɪsiːz] *pl of* **apex**.

apiculture ['eɪpɪ,kʌltʃəʳ] *n* (*form*) Bienenzucht, Imkerei *f*.

apiece [ə'piːs] *adv* pro Stück; (*per person*) pro Person ♦ **I gave them two ~** ich gab ihnen je zwei; **they had two cakes ~** sie hatten jeder zwei Kuchen.

aplomb [ə'plɒm] *n* Gelassenheit *f*.

Apocalypse [ə'pɒkəlɪps] *n* Apokalypse *f*.

apocalyptic [ə,pɒkə'lɪptɪk] *adj* apokalyptisch.

Apocrypha [ə'pɒkrɪfə] *n*: **the ~** die Apokryphen *pl*.

apocryphal [ə'pɒkrɪfəl] *adj* apokryph; (*of unknown authorship*) anonym ♦ **this story, which is almost certainly ~** ... diese Geschichte, die höchstwahrscheinlich jeder Wahrheit entbehrt ...

apogee ['æpəʊdʒiː] *n* (*Astron*) Apogäum *nt*, Erdferne *f*; (*fig: apex*) Höhepunkt *m*.

apolitical [,eɪpə'lɪtɪkəl] *adj* apolitisch.

Apollo [ə'pɒləʊ] *n* (*Myth*) Apollo *m*; (*fig also*) Apoll *m*.

apologetic [ə,pɒlə'dʒetɪk] *adj* (*making an apology*) *gesture, look* entschuldigend *attr*; (*sorry, regretful*) bedauernd *attr* ♦ **a very ~ Mr Smith rang back** Herr Smith rief zurück und entschuldigte sich sehr; **I'm afraid you didn't win, he said with an ~ look** es tut mir leid, aber Sie haben nicht gewonnen, sagte er mit bedauernder Miene; **he was most ~ (about it)** er entschuldigte sich vielmals (dafür); **his tone/expression was very ~** sein Ton war sehr bedauernd/seine Miene drückte deutlich sein Bedauern aus.

apologetically [ə,pɒlə'dʒetɪkəlɪ] *adv see adj.*

apologia [,æpə'ləʊdʒɪə] *n* Rechtfertigung, Apologie (*also Philos*) *f*.

apologist [ə'pɒlədʒɪst] *n* Apologet *m*.

▼ **apologize** [ə'pɒlədʒaɪz] *vi* sich entschuldigen (*to* bei) ♦ **to ~ for sb/sth** sich für jdn/etw entschuldigen.

apology [ə'pɒlədʒɪ] *n* **(a)** (*expression of regret*) Entschuldigung *f* ♦ **to make** *or* **offer sb an ~** jdn um Verzeihung bitten; **to make one's apologies** sich entschuldigen; **Mr Jones sends his apologies** Herr Jones läßt sich entschuldigen; **I owe you an ~** ich muß dich um Verzeihung bitten; **are there any apologies?** läßt sich jemand entschuldigen?; **I make no ~ for it, we must** ... wir müssen ..., ohne mich dafür zu entschuldigen; **I make no ~ for the fact that** ... ich entschuldige mich nicht dafür, daß ...
(b) (*defence*) Rechtfertigung, Apologie *f*.
(c) (*poor substitute*) trauriges *or* armseliges Exemplar (*for gen*) ♦ **an ~ for a breakfast/a car** ein armseliges Frühstück/Vehikel.

apoplectic [,æpə'plektɪk] *adj* (*Med*) apoplektisch; *person also* zu Schlaganfällen neigend; (*inf*) cholerisch ♦ **~ fit** *or* **attack** (*Med*) Schlaganfall *m*; **he was ~ with rage** (*inf*) er platzte fast vor Wut (*inf*).

apoplexy ['æpəpleksɪ] *n* Apoplexie *f* (*spec*), Schlaganfall *m*.

apostasy [ə'pɒstəsɪ] *n* Abfall *m*; (*Rel also*) Apostasie *f* (*form*).

apostate [ə'pɒstɪt] [1] *n* Renegat, Abtrünnige(r) *m*; (*Rel also*) Apostat *m* ♦ **an ~ from the party** ein Parteirenegat *m*.
[2] *adj* abtrünnig, abgefallen.

apostatize [ə'pɒstətaɪz] *vi* (*from church, faith, party*) abfallen, sich lossagen (*from* von).

a posteriori ['eɪpɒs,terɪ'ɔːraɪ] *adv* a posteriori.

apostle [ə'pɒsl] *n* (*lit, fig*) Apostel *m* ♦ **the A~s' Creed** das Apostolische Glaubensbekenntnis.

apostolic [,æpəs'tɒlɪk] *adj* apostolisch ♦ **~ succession** apostolische Nachfolge; **the A~ See** der Apostolische Stuhl.

apostrophe [ə'pɒstrəfɪ] *n* **(a)** (*Gram*) Apostroph *m*. **(b)** (*Liter*) Apostrophe *f*.

apostrophize [ə'pɒstrəfaɪz] [1] *vt* apostrophieren (*form*).
[2] *vi* sich in feierlichen Reden ergehen.

apothecary [ə'pɒθɪkərɪ] *n* (*old*) Apotheker(in *f*) *m* ♦ **apothecaries' weights and measures** Apothekergewichte und -maße.

apotheosis [ə,pɒθɪ'əʊsɪs] *n* Apotheose *f* (*liter*) (*into* zu).

appal, (*US also*) **appall** [ə'pɔːl] *vt* entsetzen ♦ **to be ~led (at** *or* **by sth)** (über etw *acc*) entsetzt sein.

Appalachian Mountains [,æpə'leɪtʃɪən'maʊntɪnz], **Appalachians** [,æpə'leɪtʃɪənz] *npl* Appalachen *pl*.

appalling *adj*, **~ly** *adv* [ə'pɔːlɪŋ, -lɪ] entsetzlich.

apparatus [,æpə'reɪtəs] *n* (*lit, fig*) Apparat *m*; (*equipment also*) Ausrüstung *f*; (*in gym*) Geräte *pl* ♦ **a piece of ~** ein Gerät *nt*; **the ~ of government** der Regierungsapparat.

apparel [ə'pærəl] [1] *n, no pl* (*liter, US Comm*) Gewand *nt* (*old, liter*), Kleidung *f*.
[2] *vt usu pass* (*old*) gewanden (*old*).

apparent [ə'pærənt] *adj* **(a)** (*clear, obvious*) offensichtlich, offenbar ♦ **to be ~ to sb** jdm klar sein, für jdn offensichtlich sein; **it must be ~ to everyone** es muß jedem klar sein; **to become ~** sich (deutlich) zeigen. **(b)** (*seeming*) scheinbar ♦ **more ~ than real** mehr Schein als Wirklichkeit.

apparently [ə'pærəntlɪ] *adv* anscheinend.

apparition [,æpə'rɪʃən] *n* **(a)** (*ghost, hum: person*) Erscheinung *f*. **(b)** (*appearance*) Erscheinen *nt*.

appeal [ə'piːl] [1] *n* **(a)** (*request: for help, money etc*) Aufruf, Appell *m*, (dringende) Bitte (*for* um); (*for mercy*) Gesuch *nt* (*for* um) ♦ **~ for funds** Spendenappell *or* -aufruf *m or* -aktion *f*; **to make an ~ to sb (to do sth)/to sb for sth** an jdn appellieren(, etw zu tun)/jdn um etw bitten; (*charity, organization etc*) einen Appell *or* Aufruf an jdn richten/jdn zu etw aufrufen; **to make an ~ for mercy** (*officially*) ein Gnadengesuch einreichen.
(b) (*supplication*) Flehen *nt*.
(c) (*against decision*) Einspruch *m*; (*Jur: against sentence*) Berufung *f*; (*actual trial*) Revision *f*, Revisionsverfahren *nt* ♦ **he lost his ~** er verlor in der Berufung; **to lodge an ~** Einspruch erheben; (*Jur*) Berufung einlegen (*with* bei); **right of ~** Einspruchsrecht *nt*; (*Jur*) Berufungsrecht *nt*; **Court of A~** Berufungsgericht *nt*; **A~ judge** Richter *m* am Berufungsgericht.
(d) (*for decision, support*) Appell, Aufruf *m* ♦ **the captain made an ~ against the light** der Mannschaftskapitän erhob Einspruch *or* Beschwerde wegen der Lichtverhältnisse.
(e) (*power of attraction*) Reiz *m* (*to* für), Anziehungs kraft *f* (*to* auf *+acc*) ♦ **his music has a wide ~** seine Musik spricht viele Leute *or* weite Kreise an *or* findet großen Anklang; **skiing has lost its ~ (for me)** Skifahren hat seinen Reiz (für mich) verloren; **I just don't understand the ~ of it** ich verstehe nicht, was daran so reizvoll sein soll.
[2] *vi* **(a)** (*make request*) (dringend) bitten, ersuchen (*geh*) ♦ **to ~ to sb for sth** jdn um etw bitten *or* ersuchen (*geh*); **to ~ to the public to do sth** die Öffentlichkeit (dazu) aufrufen, etw zu tun.
(b) (*against decision: to authority etc*) Einspruch erheben (*to* bei); (*Jur*) Berufung einlegen (*to* bei) ♦ **he was given leave to ~** (*Jur*) es wurde ihm anheimgestellt, Berufung einzulegen.
(c) (*apply: for support, decision*) sich wenden, appellieren (*to* an *+acc*); (*to sb's feelings etc*) appellieren (*to* an *+acc*); (*Sport*) Einspruch erheben (*to* bei), Beschwerde einlegen ♦ **to ~ to sb's better nature** an jds besseres Ich appellieren.
(d) (*be attractive*) reizen (*to sb* jdn), zusagen (*to sb* jdm); (*plan, candidate, idea*) zusagen (*to sb* jdm); (*book, magazine*) ansprechen (*to sb* jdn) ♦ **it simply doesn't ~** es findet einfach keinen Anklang; **how does that ~?** wie gefällt dir/Ihnen das?; **the story ~ed to his sense of humour** die Geschichte sprach seinen Sinn für Humor an.
[3] *vt* **to ~ a case/verdict** (*Jur*) mit einem Fall/gegen ein Urteil in die Berufung gehen; **to ~ a decision** Einspruch gegen eine Entscheidung einlegen *or* erheben.

appealing [ə'piːlɪŋ] *adj* **(a)** (*attractive*) attraktiv; *person, character also* ansprechend, gewinnend; *smile, eyes also* reizvoll; *kitten, child* süß, niedlich; *cottage, house also* reizvoll, reizend. **(b)** (*supplicating*) *look, voice* flehend.

appealingly [ə'piːlɪŋlɪ] *adv* **(a)** (*in supplication*) bittend; *look, speak* flehentlich, inbrünstig (*geh*). **(b)** (*attractively*) reizvoll.

appear [ə'pɪəʳ] *vi* **(a)** erscheinen, auftauchen; (*person, sun also*) sich zeigen ♦ **to ~ from behind/through sth** hinter etw (*dat*) hervorkommen *or* auftauchen/sich zwischen *or* durch etw hindurch zeigen; **as will presently ~** (*fig*) wie sich gleich zeigen wird.
(b) (*arrive*) erscheinen, auftauchen.
(c) (*in public*) (*Jur*) erscheinen; (*personality, ghost also*) sich zeigen; (*Theat*) auftreten ♦ **to ~ in public** sich in der Öffentlichkeit zeigen; (*Theat*) vor Publikum auftreten; **to ~ in court** vor Gericht erscheinen; (*lawyer*) bei einer Gerichtsverhandlung (dabei)sein; **to ~ for sb** jdn vertreten; **to ~ as a witness** als Zeuge auftreten.

➤ LANGUAGE IN USE: apologize → 18.1

(d) (*be published*) erscheinen ◆ **to ~ in print** gedruckt werden/sein.
(e) (*seem*) scheinen ◆ **he ~ed (to be) tired/drunk** er wirkte müde/betrunken, er schien müde/betrunken zu sein; **it ~s that ...** es hat den Anschein, daß ..., anscheinend ...; **so it ~s, so it would ~** so will es scheinen, so hat es den Anschein; **it ~s not** anscheinend nicht, es sieht nicht so aus; **there ~s** *or* **there would ~ to be a mistake** anscheinend liegt (da) ein Irrtum vor, da scheint ein Irrtum vorzuliegen; **how does it ~ to you?** welchen Eindruck haben Sie?, wie wirkt das auf Sie?; **it ~s to me that ...** mir scheint, daß ...; **it ~s from his statement that ...** aus seiner Bemerkung geht hervor *or* ergibt sich, daß ...

▼ **appearance** [ə'pɪərəns] *n* **(a)** Erscheinen *nt*; (*unexpected*) Auftauchen *nt no pl*; (*Theat*) Auftritt *m* ◆ **many successful court ~s** viele erfolgreiche Auftritte vor Gericht; **to put in** *or* **make an ~** sich sehen lassen; **to make one's ~** sich zeigen; (*Theat*) seinen Auftritt haben; **cast in order of ~** Darsteller in der Reihenfolge ihres Auftritts *or* Auftretens; **~ money** (*for TV show etc*) Honorar *nt*; (*attendance fee*) Sitzungsgeld *nt*.
▼ **(b)** (*look, aspect*) Aussehen *nt*; (*of person also*) Äußere(s) *nt*, äußere Erscheinung ◆ **~s** (*outward signs*) der äußere (An)schein; **good ~ essential** gepflegtes Äußeres *or* gepflegte Erscheinung wichtig; **in ~** dem Aussehen nach, vom Äußeren her; **at first ~** auf den ersten Blick; **he/it has the ~ of being ...** er/es erweckt den Anschein, ... zu sein; **for ~s' sake, for the sake of ~s** um den Schein zu wahren, um des Schein(e)s willen; (*as good manners*) der Form halber; **to keep up** *or* **save ~s** den (äußeren) Schein wahren; **to put on an ~ of being ...** sich (*dat*) den Anschein geben, ... zu sein; **~s are often deceptive** der Schein trügt oft; **~s were against him** der Schein sprach gegen ihn; **to all ~s** allem Anschein nach; *see* **judge**.

appease [ə'pi:z] *vt* (*calm*) *person, anger* beschwichtigen, besänftigen; (*Pol*) (durch Zugeständnisse) beschwichtigen; (*satisfy*) *hunger, thirst* stillen; *curiosity* stillen, befriedigen.

appeasement [ə'pi:zmənt] *n see vt* Beschwichtigung, Besänftigung *f*; Beschwichtigung *f* (durch Zugeständnisse); Stillung, Befriedigung *f*.

appellant [ə'pelənt] *n* (*Jur*) Berufungskläger *m*.

appellation [ˌæpe'leɪʃən] *n* Bezeichnung, Benennung *f*.

append [ə'pend] *vt notes etc* anhängen (*to* an *+acc*) (*also Comput*), hinzufügen; *seal* drücken (*to* auf *+acc*); *signature* setzen (*to* unter *+acc*) ◆ **the seal/signature ~ed to this document** das Siegel/die Unterschrift, mit dem/der das Dokument versehen ist.

appendage [ə'pendɪdʒ] *n* (*limb*) Gliedmaße *f*; (*fig*) Anhängsel *nt*.

appendectomy [ˌæpen'dektəmɪ], **appendicectomy** [ˌæpendɪ'sektəmɪ] *n* Blinddarmoperation, Appendektomie (*spec*) *f*.

appendices [ə'pendɪsi:z] *pl of* **appendix**.

appendicitis [əˌpendɪ'saɪtɪs] *n* (eine) Blinddarmentzündung, Appendizitis (*spec*) *f*.

appendix [ə'pendɪks] *n, pl* **appendices** *or* **-es** **(a)** (*Anat*) Blinddarm, Appendix (*spec*) *m* ◆ **to have one's ~ out** sich (*dat*) den Blinddarm herausnehmen lassen. **(b)** (*to book etc*) Anhang, Appendix *m*.

apperception [ˌæpə'sepʃən] *n* (*Philos, Psych*) bewußte Wahrnehmung.

appertain [ˌæpə'teɪn] *vi* (*form*) (*belong*) gehören (*to* zu), eignen (*+dat*) (*geh*); (*relate*) betreffen (*to sb/sth* jdn/etw) ◆ **this does not ~ to the argument** das gehört nicht zur Sache.

appetite ['æpɪtaɪt] *n* (*for food etc*) Appetit *m*, (Eß)lust *f*; (*fig: desire*) Verlangen, Bedürfnis *nt*, Lust *f*; (*sexual ~*) Lust, Begierde *f* ◆ **to have an/no ~ for sth** Appetit *or* Lust/keinen Appetit *or* keine Lust auf etw (*acc*) haben; (*fig*) Verlangen *or* Bedürfnis/kein Verlangen *or* Bedürfnis nach etw haben; **to have a good/bad ~** einen guten *or* gesunden/schlechten Appetit haben; **I hope you've got an ~** ich hoffe, ihr habt Appetit!; **to take away** *or* **spoil one's ~** sich (*dat*) den Appetit verderben.

appetizer ['æpɪtaɪzə^r] *n* (*food*) Appetitanreger *m*; (*hors d'oeuvres also*) Vorspeise *f*, Appetithappen *m*; (*drink*) appetitanregendes Getränk.

appetizing ['æpɪtaɪzɪŋ] *adj* appetitlich (*also fig*); *food also* appetitanregend, lecker; *smell* lecker; *description* verlockend.

appetizingly ['æpɪtaɪzɪŋlɪ] *adv see adj*.

Appian ['æpɪən] *adj* Appisch ◆ **~ Way** Appische Straße.

applaud [ə'plɔ:d] **1** *vt* (*lit, fig*) applaudieren, Beifall spenden *or* klatschen (*+dat*); (*fig*) *efforts, courage* loben; *decision* gutheißen, begrüßen ◆ **the play was vigorously ~ed** das Stück erhielt stürmischen Beifall *or* wurde lebhaft beklatscht.
2 *vi* applaudieren, klatschen, Beifall spenden.

applause [ə'plɔ:z] *n, no pl* Applaus, Beifall (*also fig*) *m*, Klatschen *nt* ◆ **to be greeted with ~** mit Applaus *or* Beifall (*also fig*) begrüßt werden; **to win sb's ~** bei jdm Beifall finden.

apple ['æpl] *n* Apfel *m* ◆ **an ~ a day keeps the doctor away** (*Prov*) eßt Obst, und ihr bleibt gesund; **to be the ~ of sb's eye** jds Liebling sein.

apple *in cpds* Apfel-; **~cart** *n* (*fig*): **to upset the ~cart** alles über den Haufen werfen (*inf*); **~ dumpling** *n* ≃ Apfel *m* im Schlafrock; **~-green** *adj* apfelgrün; **~jack** *n* (*US*) Apfelschnaps *m*; **~-pie** *n* ≃ gedeckter Apfelkuchen, Apfelpastete *f*; **~-pie bed** *Bett nt, bei dem Laken und Decken aus Scherz so gefaltet sind, daß man sich nicht ausstrecken kann*; **in ~-pie order** (*inf*) pikobello (*inf*); **~ sauce** *n* **(a)** (*Cook*) Apfelmus *nt*; **(b)** (*US inf: nonsense*) Schmus *m* (*inf*); **~-tree** *n* Apfelbaum *m*; **~ turnover** *n* Apfeltasche *f*.

appliance [ə'plaɪəns] *n* **(a)** Vorrichtung *f*; (*household ~*) Gerät *nt*; (*fire-engine*) Feuerwehrwagen *m*. **(b)** (*rare*) *see* **application (b)**.

applicability [ˌæplɪkə'bɪlɪtɪ] *n* Anwendbarkeit *f* (*to* auf *+acc*).

applicable [ə'plɪkəbl] *adj* anwendbar (*to* auf *+acc*); (*on forms*) zutreffend (*to* für) ◆ **delete as ~** Nichtzutreffendes streichen; **that isn't ~ to you** das trifft auf Sie nicht zu, das gilt nicht für Sie; **not ~** (*on forms*) entfällt, nicht zutreffend.

applicant ['æplɪkənt] *n* (*for job*) Bewerber(in *f*) *m* (*for* um, für); (*for grant, loan etc*) Antragsteller(in *f*) *m* (*for* für, auf *+acc*); (*for patent*) Anmelder(in *f*) *m* (*for gen*).

▼ **application** [ˌæplɪ'keɪʃən] *n* **(a)** (*for job etc*) Bewerbung *f* (*for* um, für); (*for grant, loan etc*) Antrag *m* (*for* auf *+acc*), Gesuch *nt* (*for* für); (*for patent*) Anmeldung *f* (*for gen*) ◆ **available on ~** auf Anforderung *or* (*written*) Antrag erhältlich; **~ form** Bewerbung(sformular *nt*) *f*; Antrag(sformular *nt*) *m*; Anmeldeformular *nt*; **to make ~ to sb for sth** (*form*) bei jdm etw anfordern; (*written*) einen Antrag auf etw (*acc*) an jdn richten.
(b) (*act of applying*) *see* **apply 1** Auftragen *nt*; Anlegen, Applizieren *nt*, Applikation *f* (*form*); Anwenden *nt*, Anwendung *f*, Verwendung *f*, Gebrauch *m*; Betätigung *f*; Verwertung *f*; Zuwendung *f*, (Aus)richten *nt*; Verhängen *nt*, Verhängung *f* ◆ **the ~ of a dressing to a head wound** das Anlegen eines Kopfverbandes; **"for external ~ only"** (*Med*) „nur zur äußerlichen Anwendung"; **~ program** (*Comput*) Anwendungsprogramm *nt*; **~ software** (*Comput*) Anwendersoftware *f*.
(c) (*form, esp Med*) Mittel *nt*; (*ointment also*) Salbe *f*.
(d) (*diligence, effort*) Fleiß, Eifer *m*.
(e) *see* **applicability**.

applicator ['æplɪkeɪtə^r] *n* Aufträger *m*.

applied [ə'plaɪd] *adj attr maths, linguistics etc* angewandt.

appliqué [æ'pli:keɪ] (*Sew*) **1** *n* Applikationen *pl* ◆ **to do ~** applizieren.
2 *vt* applizieren.
3 *adj attr* **~ work** Stickerei *f*.

▼ **apply** [ə'plaɪ] **1** *vt paint, ointment, lotion etc* auftragen (*to* auf *+acc*), applizieren (*spec*); *dressing, plaster* anlegen, applizieren (*spec*); *force, pressure, theory, rules, knowledge, skills* anwenden (*to* auf *+acc*); *knowledge, skills, funds* verwenden (*to* für), gebrauchen (*to* für); *brakes* betätigen; *results, findings* verwerten (*to* für); *one's attention, efforts* zuwenden (*to dat*), richten (*to* auf *+acc*); *embargo, sanctions* verhängen (*to* über *+acc*) ◆ **to ~ oneself/one's mind** *or* **intelligence (to sth)** sich/seinen Kopf (*inf*) (bei etw) anstrengen; **that term can be applied to many things** dieser Begriff kann auf viele Dinge angewendet werden *or* trifft auf viele Dinge zu.
▼ **2** *vi* **(a)** sich bewerben (*for* um, für) ◆ **to ~ to sb for sth** sich an jdn wegen etw wenden; (*for job, grant also*) sich bei jdm für *or* um etw bewerben; (*for loan, grant also*) bei jdm etw beantragen; **no-one applied for the reward** keiner hat sich für die Belohnung gemeldet; **~ at the office/next door/within** Anfragen im Büro/nebenan/im Laden; **she has applied for university** sie hat sich um einen Studienplatz beworben.
(b) (*be applicable*) gelten (*to* für); (*warning, threat, regulation also*) betreffen (*to acc*); (*description*) zutreffen (*to* auf *+acc*, für).

appoint [ə'pɔɪnt] *vt* **(a)** (*to a job*) einstellen; (*to a post*) ernennen ◆ **to ~ sb to an office** jdn in ein Amt berufen; **to ~ sb sth** jdn zu etw ernennen *or* bestellen (*geh*) *or* als etw (*acc*) berufen; **to ~ sb to do sth** jdn dazu bestimmen, etw zu tun; **they ~ed him to the vacant post** sie gaben ihm die (freie) Stelle; (*professorship*) sie haben ihn auf den Lehrstuhl berufen.
(b) (*designate, ordain*) bestimmen; (*agree*) festlegen *or* -setzen, verabreden, ausmachen ◆ **at the ~ed time** *or* **the time ~ed** zur festgelegten *or* -gesetzten *or* verabredeten Zeit; **his ~ed task** die ihm übertragene Aufgabe; **the date ~ed for that meeting** (*form*) der angesetzte Tagungstermin (*form*).

-appointed [-ə'pɔɪntɪd] *adj suf* **well-/poorly-~** gut/dürftig ausgestattet.

appointee [əpɔɪn'ti:] *n* Ernannte(r) *mf* ◆ **he was a Wilson/political ~** er war von Wilson/aus politischen Gründen ernannt worden; **the ~ to the ambassadorship** der neubestellte Botschafter.

appointment [ə'pɔɪntmənt] *n* **(a)** (*pre-arranged meeting*) Verabredung *f*; (*business ~, with doctor, lawyer etc*) Termin *m* (*with* bei) ◆ **to make** *or* **fix an ~ with sb** mit jdm eine Verabredung treffen; einen Termin mit jdm vereinbaren; **I made an ~ to see the doctor** ich habe mich beim Arzt angemeldet *or* mir beim Arzt einen Termin geben lassen; **do you have an ~?** sind Sie angemeldet?; **by ~** auf Verabredung; (*on business, to see doctor, lawyer etc*) mit (Vor)anmeldung, nach Vereinbarung; **~(s) book** Terminkalender *m*.
(b) (*act of appointing*) *see vt (a)* Einstellung *f*; Ernennung *f*; Berufung *f* (*to* zu); Bestellung *f* ◆ **this office is not filled by ~ but by election** für dieses Amt wird man nicht bestellt *or* berufen, sondern gewählt; **"by ~ (to Her Majesty)"** (*on goods*) „königlicher Hoflieferant".
(c) (*post*) Stelle *f* ◆ **~s (vacant)** Stellenangebote *pl*; **~s bureau** Stellenvermittlung *f*.
(d) **~s** *pl* (*furniture etc*) Ausstattung, Einrichtung *f*.

apportion [ə'pɔ:ʃən] *vt money, food, land* aufteilen; *duties* zuteilen ◆ **to ~ sth to sb** jdm etw zuteilen; **to ~ sth among** *or* **between several people** etw zwischen mehreren Leuten aufteilen, etw unter mehrere Leute (gleichmäßig) verteilen; **the blame must be ~ed equally** die Schuld muß allen in gleicher Weise *or* zu gleichen Teilen angelastet werden.

apposite ['æpəzɪt] *adj comment, phrase* treffend, passend; *question* angebracht.

apposition [ˌæpə'zɪʃən] *n* Apposition, Beifügung *f* ◆ **A is in ~ to B, A and B are in ~** A ist eine Apposition zu B.

appraisal [ə'preɪzəl] *n see vt* Abschätzung *f*, Beurteilung *f* ◆ **to make an ~ of the situation** die Lage abschätzen; **his false/accurate ~** seine falsche/genaue Einschätzung.

appraise [ə'preɪz] *vt* (*estimate*) *value, damage* (ab)schätzen; (*weigh up*) *character, ability* (richtig) einschätzen, beurteilen; *situation* abschätzen; *poem etc*

➤ LANGUAGE IN USE: **appearance: b** → 16.2 **application: a** → 19.3 **apply: 2a** → 19.1

beurteilen ◆ **an appraising look** ein prüfender Blick; **he ~d the situation accurately/falsely** er hat die Lage genau/falsch eingeschätzt.

appreciable [ə'pri:ʃəbl] *adj* beträchtlich, deutlich; *difference, change also* nennenswert, merklich.

appreciably [ə'pri:ʃəblɪ] *adv see adj.*

▼ **appreciate** [ə'pri:ʃɪeɪt] 1 *vt* **(a)** *(be aware of) dangers, problems, value etc* sich *(dat)* bewußt sein (+*gen*); *(understand) sb's wishes, reluctance etc also* Verständnis haben für ◆ **I ~ that you cannot come** ich verstehe, daß ihr nicht kommen könnt.
▼ **(b)** *(value, be grateful for)* zu schätzen wissen ◆ **nobody ~s me!** niemand weiß mich zu schätzen!; **thank you, I ~ it** vielen Dank, sehr nett von Ihnen; **my liver would ~ a rest** meine Leber könnte eine kleine Erholung gebrauchen; **I would really ~ that** das wäre mir wirklich sehr lieb; **I would ~ it if you could do this by tomorrow** können Sie das bitte bis morgen erledigen?; **I would ~ it if you could be a little quieter** könnten Sie nicht vielleicht etwas leiser sein?; **the boss would really ~ it if you would pay up** der Chef hätte nichts dagegen, wenn du bezahlst.
(c) *(enjoy) art, music, poetry* schätzen.
2 *vi (Fin)* **to ~ (in value)** im Wert steigen, an Wert gewinnen.

appreciation [ə,pri:ʃɪ'eɪʃən] *n* **(a)** *(awareness: of problems, dangers, advantages, value)* Erkennen *nt.*
(b) *(esteem, respect)* Anerkennung *f*; *(of abilities, efforts also)* Würdigung *f*; *(of person also)* Wertschätzung *f* ◆ **in ~ of sth** in Anerkennung (+*gen*), zum Dank für etw; **to show** *or* **acknowledge one's ~** seine Dankbarkeit (be)zeigen; **to smile one's ~** zum Dank lächeln.
(c) *(enjoyment, understanding)* Verständnis *nt*; *(of art)* Sinn *m (of* für) ◆ **to show (great) ~ of Mozart/art** großes Mozart-/Kunstverständnis zeigen; **to write an ~ of sb/sth** einen Bericht über jdn/etw schreiben.
(d) *(comprehension)* Verständnis *nt.*
(e) *(increase)* (Wert)steigerung *f (in* bei).

appreciative [ə'pri:ʃɪətɪv] *adj* anerkennend; *audience* dankbar; *(prepared to accept)* bereitwillig; *(grateful)* dankbar ◆ **to be ~ of sth** etw zu schätzen wissen; *(of music, art etc)* Sinn für etw haben.

appreciatively [ə'pri:ʃɪətɪvlɪ] *adv* anerkennend; *(gratefully)* dankbar.

apprehend [,æprɪ'hend] *vt* **(a)** *(arrest)* festnehmen; *escapee also* aufgreifen. **(b)** *(old, form: understand)* verstehen. **(c)** *(form: anticipate)* befürchten.

apprehension [,æprɪ'henʃən] *n* **(a)** *(fear)* Besorgnis, Befürchtung *f* ◆ **a feeling of ~** eine dunkle Ahnung *or* Befürchtung; **she knew a moment of ~** sie war einen Moment lang beklommen *or* voller Befürchtungen; **to feel ~ for sth** sich *(dat)* Gedanken *or* Sorgen um etw machen. **(b)** *(arrest)* Festnahme *f.* **(c)** *(old, form: understanding)* Erkennen *nt.*

apprehensive [,æprɪ'hensɪv] *adj* ängstlich ◆ **to be ~ of sth/that ...** etw befürchten/fürchten, daß ...; **he was ~ about the future** er schaute mit ängstlicher Sorge *or* verzagt in die Zukunft; **to be ~ for sb/sb's safety** sich *(dat)* Sorgen um jdn/jds Sicherheit machen.

apprehensively [,æprɪ'hensɪvlɪ] *adv see adj.*

apprentice [ə'prentɪs] 1 *n* Lehrling, Lehrjunge *(dated)*, Auszubildende(r) *(form) m* ◆ **to be an ~** Lehrling sein, in der Lehre sein; **~ plumber/electrician** Klempner-/Elektrikerlehrling *m*; **~ jockey** angehender Jockey.
2 *vt* in die Lehre geben *or* schicken *(to* zu, bei) ◆ **to be ~d to sb** bei jdm in die Lehre gehen *or* in der Lehre sein.

apprenticeship [ə'prentɪʃɪp] *n* Lehre, Lehrzeit *f* ◆ **to serve one's ~** seine Lehre *or* Lehrzeit absolvieren *or* machen.

apprise [ə'praɪz] *vt (form)* in Kenntnis setzen *(geh)*, Kenntnis geben (+*dat*) *(geh)* ◆ **I am ~d that ...** man hat mich davon in Kenntnis gesetzt *or* mir davon Kenntnis gegeben, daß ... *(geh)*.

appro ['æprəʊ] *n abbr of* **approval: on ~** *(Comm) (to try out)* zur Probe; *(to look at)* zur Ansicht.

approach [ə'prəʊtʃ] 1 *vi (physically)* sich nähern, näherkommen; *(date, summer etc)* nahen.
2 *vt* **(a)** *(come near)* sich nähern (+*dat*); *person, building also* zukommen auf (+*acc*); *(Aviat)* anfliegen; *(in figures, temperature, time also)* zugehen auf (+*acc*); *(in quality, stature)* herankommen an (+*acc*); *(fig)* heranreichen an (+*acc*) ◆ **to ~ thirty/adolescence/manhood** auf die Dreißig zugehen/ins Pubertätsalter/Mannesalter kommen; **the train is now ~ing platform 3** der Zug hat Einfahrt auf Gleis 3; **something ~ing a festive atmosphere** eine annähernd festliche Stimmung.
(b) *(make an ~ to) person, committee, organization* herantreten an (+*acc*) *(about* wegen), angehen *(about* um), ansprechen *(about* wegen, auf +*acc* hin) ◆ **I haven't ~ed him yet** ich habe ihn daraufhin noch nicht angesprochen, ich bin damit noch nicht an ihn herangetreten; **he is easy/difficult to ~** er ist leicht/nicht leicht ansprechbar.
(c) *(tackle) question, problem, task* angehen, herangehen an (+*acc*), anpacken.
3 *n* **(a)** *(drawing near)* (Heran)nahen *nt*; *(of troops, in time also)* Heranrücken *nt*; *(of night)* Einbruch *m*; *(Aviat)* Anflug *m (to* an +*acc)* ◆ **at the ~ of Easter** als das Osterfest nahte/wenn das Osterfest naht.
(b) *(to person, committee, organization)* Herantreten *nt* ◆ **to make ~es/an ~ to sb** *(with request)* an jdn herantreten; *(man to woman)* Annäherungsversuche machen.
(c) *(way of tackling, attitude)* Ansatz *m (to* zu) ◆ **an easy ~ to maths/teaching** ein einfacher Weg, Mathematik zu lernen/eine einfache Lehrmethode; **his ~ to the problem** seine Art *or* Methode, an das Problem heranzugehen, sein Problemansatz *m*; **you've got the wrong ~** du machst das verkehrt; **try a different ~** versuch's doch mal anders; **new ~es in psychology** neue Ansätze in der Psychologie.
(d) *(approximation)* Annäherung *f (to* an +*acc)* ◆ **this book is his nearest ~ to greatness** mit diesem Werk erreicht er fast dichterische Größe.
(e) *(access)* Zugang, Weg *m*; *(road also)* Zufahrt(sstraße) *f.*

approachable [ə'prəʊtʃəbl] *adj* **(a)** *person* umgänglich, leicht zugänglich ◆ **he's still ~/not ~ today** man kann immer noch mit ihm reden/er ist heute nicht ansprechbar. **(b)** *place* zugänglich ◆ **it's ~ from above** man kommt von oben (heran).

approaching [ə'prəʊtʃɪŋ] *adj attr* näherkommend; *date, occasion* herannahend, bevorstehend.

approach: ~ lights *npl (Aviat)* Lichter *pl* der Einflugschneise; **~ path** *n (Aviat)* Einflugschneise *f*; **~ road** *n (to city etc)* Zufahrtsstraße *f*; *(to motorway)* (Autobahn)zubringer *m*; *(slip-road)* Auf- *or* Einfahrt *f*; **~ shot** *n (Golf)* Schlag *m* zwischen Abschlag und Grün.

approbation [,æprə'beɪʃən] *n* Zustimmung *f*; *(of decision also)* Billigung *f*; *(from critics)* Beifall *m.*

▼ **appropriate**[1] [ə'prəʊprɪɪt] *adj* **(a)** *(suitable, fitting)* passend, geeignet *(for, to* für), angebracht *(for, to* für); *(to a situation, occasion)* angemessen *(to dat)*; *name, remark also* treffend ◆ **it was ~ that he came at that moment** es traf sich gut, daß er da gerade kam; **clothing ~ for** *or* **to the weather conditions** wettergemäße Kleidung; **a style ~ to one's subject** ein dem Thema entsprechender *or* angemessener Stil.
(b) *(relevant)* entsprechend; *body, authority also* zuständig ◆ **where ~** wo es angebracht ist/war, an gegebener Stelle; **put a tick where ~** Zutreffendes bitte ankreuzen; **delete as ~** Nichtzutreffendes streichen.

appropriate[2] [ə'prəʊprɪeɪt] *vt* **(a)** *(assume possession or control of)* beschlagnahmen; *(take for oneself)* sich *(dat)* aneignen, mit Beschlag belegen; *sb's ideas* sich *(dat)* zu eigen machen.
(b) *(allocate) funds* zuteilen, zuweisen.

appropriately [ə'prəʊprɪɪtlɪ] *adv* treffend; *dressed* passend *(for, to* für), entsprechend *(for, to dat)*; *(to fit particular needs) designed, equipped* entsprechend *(for, to dat)*, zweckmäßig *(for, to* für) ◆ **~ enough the letter arrived at that very moment** passenderweise kam der Brief genau in dem Augenblick; **rather ~ she was called Goldilocks** der Name Goldköpfchen paßte sehr gut zu ihr.

appropriateness [ə'prəʊprɪɪtnɪs] *n (suitability, fittingness)* Eignung *f*; *(of dress, remark, name, for a particular occasion)* Angemessenheit *f.*

appropriation [ə,prəʊprɪ'eɪʃən] *n see vt* **(a)** Beschlagnahme, Beschlagnahmung *f*; Aneignung *f.* **(b)** Zuteilung, Zuweisung *f* ◆ **to make an ~ for sth** Mittel für etw zuteilen *or* zuweisen.

approval [ə'pru:vəl] *n* **(a)** Beifall *m*, Anerkennung *f*; *(consent)* Zustimmung *(of* zu), Billigung *f*, Einverständnis *nt (of* mit) ◆ **to meet with sb's ~** jds Zustimmung *or* Beifall finden; **to seek sb's ~ for sth** jds Zustimmung zu etw suchen; **to have sb's ~** jds Zustimmung haben; **to show one's ~ of sth** zeigen, daß man einer Sache *(dat)* zustimmt *or* etw billigt; **submitted for the Queen's ~** der Königin zur Genehmigung vorgelegt.
(b) *(Comm)* **on ~** auf Probe; *(to look at)* zur Ansicht.

▼ **approve** [ə'pru:v] 1 *vt (consent to) decision* billigen, gutheißen; *minutes, motion* annehmen; *project* genehmigen; *(recommend) hotel, campsite etc* empfehlen ◆ **an ~d campsite** ein empfohlener Campingplatz.
▼ 2 *vi* **to ~ of sb/sth** von jdm/etw etwas halten, etw billigen *or* gutheißen; **I don't ~ of him/it** ich halte nichts von ihm/davon; **do you ~ of him/that?** hältst du etwas von ihm/davon?; **I don't ~ of children smoking** ich billige nicht *or* kann es nicht gutheißen, daß Kinder rauchen; **she doesn't ~** sie mißbilligt das; **how's this shirt, do you ~?** gefällt dir dies Hemd?

approved school [ə'pru:vd'sku:l] *n (Brit)* Erziehungsheim *nt.*

approving [ə'pru:vɪŋ] *adj (satisfied, pleased)* anerkennend, beifällig; *(consenting)* zustimmend.

approvingly [ə'pru:vɪŋlɪ] *adv see adj.*

approx. *abbr of* **approximately** ca.

approximate [ə'prɒksɪmɪt] 1 *adj* ungefähr ◆ **these figures are only ~** dies sind nur ungefähre Werte; **three hours is the ~ time needed** man braucht ungefähr drei Stunden.
2 [ə'prɒksəmeɪt] *vti* **to ~ (to) sth** einer Sache *(dat)* in etwa entsprechen; **they ~ (to one another)** sie entsprechen einander in etwa.

approximately [ə'prɒksɪmətlɪ] *adv* ungefähr, etwa, circa; *correct* in etwa, annähernd.

approximation [ə,prɒksɪ'meɪʃən] *n* Annäherung *f (of, to* an +*acc)*; *(figure, sum etc)* (An)näherungswert *m* ◆ **his story was an ~ of** *or* **to the truth** seine Geschichte entsprach in etwa *or* ungefähr der Wahrheit.

appurtenances [ə'pɜ:tɪnənsɪz] *npl (equipment)* Zubehör *nt*; *(accessories)* Attribute *pl*; *(Jur: rights etc)* Rechte *pl* ◆ **with all the ~ of affluence** mit allen Attributen des Wohlstands.

APR *abbr of* **annual percentage rate** Jahreszinssatz *m.*

après-ski [,æpreɪ'ski:] 1 *n* Après-Ski *nt.*
2 *adj attr* Après-Ski-.

apricot ['eɪprɪkɒt] 1 *n* Aprikose *f.*
2 *adj (also* **~-coloured)** aprikosenfarben.
3 *attr* Aprikosen-.

April ['eɪprəl] *n* April *m* ◆ **~ shower** Aprilschauer *m*; **~ fool!** ≃ April, April!; **~ Fool's Day** der Erste April; **to make an ~ fool of sb** jdn in den April schicken; *see also* **September.**

a priori [eɪpraɪ'ɔ:raɪ] 1 *adv* a priori.
2 *adj* apriorisch.

apron ['eɪprən] *n* Schürze *f*; *(of workman also)* Schurz *m*; *(Aviat)* Vorfeld *nt*; *(Theat)* Vorbühne *f.*

➤ LANGUAGE IN USE: **appreciate: 1a** → 18.4 **1b** → 7.2, 13 **appropriate**[1]**: a** → 1.1, 26.1 **approve: 2** → 14

apron: ~ stage *n* Bühne *f* mit Vorbühne; **~-strings** *npl* Schürzenbänder *pl*; **to be tied to one's mother's ~-strings** seiner Mutter (*dat*) am Schürzenzipfel hängen (*inf*).

apropos [ˌæprəˈpəʊ] 1 *prep* (*also* ~ **of**) apropos (+*nom*) ◆ **~ of nothing** ganz nebenbei.
2 *adj pred remark* passend, treffend.

apse [æps] *n* Apsis *f*.

APT *abbr of* **advanced passenger train** Hochgeschwindigkeitszug *m*.

Apt. *abbr of* **apartment** Z., Zi.

apt [æpt] *adj* (+*er*) **(a)** (*suitable, fitting*) passend; *description, comparison, remark also* treffend.
(b) (*able, intelligent*) begabt (*at* für).
(c) (*liable, likely*) **to be ~ to do sth** leicht etw tun, dazu neigen, etw zu tun; **he is always ~ to be late** er kommt gern (*inf*) zu spät, er neigt dazu, stets zu spät zu kommen; **it is ~ to rain in Glasgow** es regnet oft in Glasgow; **we are ~ to forget that ...** wir vergessen leicht *or* gern (*inf*), daß ...; **I was ~ to believe him until ...** ich war geneigt, ihm zu glauben, bis ...

aptitude [ˈæptɪtjuːd] *n* Begabung *f* ◆ **she has a great ~ for saying the wrong thing** (*hum*) sie hat ein besonderes Talent dafür, immer das Falsche zu sagen; **~ test** Eignungsprüfung *f*.

aptly [ˈæptlɪ] *adv* passend ◆ **it did not fit ~ into the context** es paßte nicht richtig in den Zusammenhang.

aptness [ˈæptnɪs] *n see adj* **(a) the ~ of the name was obvious** der Name war offensichtlich passend. **(b)** Begabung *f*. **(c)** Neigung *f*.

aqualung [ˈækwəlʌŋ] *n* Tauchgerät *nt*.

aquamarine [ˌækwəməˈriːn] 1 *n* Aquamarin *m*; (*colour*) Aquamarin *nt*.
2 *adj* aquamarin.

aquanaut [ˈækwənɔːt] *n* Aquanaut(in *f*) *m*.

aquanautics [ˌækwəˈnɔːtɪks] *n* Aquanautik *f*.

aquaplane [ˈækwəpleɪn] 1 *n* Monoski *m*.
2 *vi* **(a)** Wasserski laufen. **(b)** (*car etc*) (auf nasser Straße) ins Rutschen geraten ◆ **aquaplaning** Aquaplaning *nt*; **in order to prevent the car from aquaplaning** um ein Aquaplaning zu verhindern.

aquarium [əˈkwɛərɪəm] *n* Aquarium *nt*.

Aquarius [əˈkwɛərɪəs] *n* Wassermann *m*.

aquatic [əˈkwætɪk] *adj sports, pastimes* Wasser-, im Wasser; *plants, animals, organisms etc* Wasser-, im Wasser lebend, aquatisch (*spec*).

aquatint [ˈækwətɪnt] *n* Aquatinta *f*.

aqueduct [ˈækwɪdʌkt] *n* Aquädukt *m or nt*.

aqueous [ˈeɪkwɪəs] *adj* (*form*) Wasser-; *rocks* wasserhaltig ◆ **~ humour** (*Med*) Kammerwasser *nt*, Humor aquosus *m* (*spec*).

aquiline [ˈækwɪlaɪn] *adj nose* Adler-, gebogen; *profile* mit Adlernase, dinarisch (*geh*).

Aquinas [əˈkwaɪnəs] *n* Thomas von Aquin.

Arab [ˈærəb] 1 *n* Araber *m* (*also horse*), Araberin *f* ◆ **the ~s** die Araber.
2 *adj attr* arabisch; *policies, ideas also* der Araber; *horse* Araber-.

arabesque [ˌærəˈbesk] *n* Arabeske *f*.

Arabia [əˈreɪbɪə] *n* Arabien *nt*.

Arabian [əˈreɪbɪən] *adj* arabisch ◆ **tales of the ~ Nights** Märchen aus Tausendundeiner Nacht.

Arabic [ˈærəbɪk] 1 *n* Arabisch *nt*.
2 *adj* arabisch ◆ **~ numerals** arabische Ziffern *or* Zahlen; **~ studies** Arabistik *f*.

arable [ˈærəbl] *adj land* bebaubar; (*being used*) Acker-.

arachnid [əˈræknɪd] *n* Spinnentier *nt*.

Aragon [ˈærəgən] *n* Aragon, Aragonien *nt*.

arbiter [ˈɑːbɪtəʳ] *n* **(a)** (*of fate etc*) Herr, Gebieter *m* (*of* über +*acc*) ◆ **to be the ~ of** Herr sein über (+*acc*); **they were the ~s of fashion** sie haben die Mode bestimmt. **(b)** *see* **arbitrator**.

arbitrarily [ˈɑːbɪtrərəlɪ] *adv see adj*.

arbitrariness [ˈɑːbɪtrərɪnɪs] *n* Willkürlichkeit *f*.

arbitrary [ˈɑːbɪtrərɪ] *adj* willkürlich, arbiträr (*geh*).

arbitrate [ˈɑːbɪtreɪt] 1 *vt dispute* schlichten.
2 *vi* **(a)** vermitteln. **(b)** (*go to arbitration*) vor eine Schlichtungskommission gehen.

arbitration [ˌɑːbɪˈtreɪʃən] *n* Schlichtung *f* ◆ **to submit a dispute to ~** einen Streit vor ein Schiedsgericht *or* (*esp Ind*) eine Schlichtungskommission bringen; **to go to ~** vor eine Schlichtungskommission gehen; (*dispute*) vor eine Schlichtungskommission gebracht werden.

arbitrator [ˈɑːbɪtreɪtəʳ] *n* Vermittler *m*; (*esp Ind*) Schlichter *m*.

arbor *n* (*US*) *see* **arbour**.

arboreal [ɑːˈbɔːrɪəl] *adj* Baum-; *habitat* auf Bäumen.

arboretum [ˌɑːbəˈriːtəm] *n* Arboretum *nt* (*spec*), Baumschule *f*.

arbour, (*US***) arbor** [ˈɑːbəʳ] *n* Laube *f*.

arbutus [ɑːˈbjuːtəs] *n* Arbutus *m*.

arc [ɑːk] *n* Bogen *m*.

arcade [ɑːˈkeɪd] *n* (*Archit*) Arkade *f*; (*shopping* ~) Passage *f*.

Arcadia [ɑːˈkeɪdɪə] *n* Arkadien *nt*.

Arcadian [ɑːˈkeɪdɪən] *adj* (*lit, fig*) arkadisch.

arcane [ɑːˈkeɪn] *adj* obskur.

arch¹ [ɑːtʃ] 1 *n* **(a)** Bogen *m* ◆ **~ of the heavens** Himmelsbogen *m*, Himmelsgewölbe *nt*. **(b)** (*Anat: of foot*) Gewölbe *nt* (*spec*) ◆ **high/fallen ~es** hoher Spann/Senkfuß *m*; **~ support** Senkfußeinlage *f*.
2 *vi* sich wölben; (*arrow etc*) einen Bogen machen.
3 *vt back* krümmen; (*cat also*) krumm machen; *eyebrows* hochziehen ◆ **the cat ~ed his back** die Katze machte einen Buckel.

arch² *adj* (*wicked, mischievous*) neckisch, schelmisch.

arch³ *adj attr* Erz- ◆ **~ traitor** Hochverräter *m*.

archaeological, (*US***) archeological** [ˌɑːkɪəˈlɒdʒɪkəl] *adj* archäologisch.

archaeologist, (*US***) archeologist** [ˌɑːkɪˈɒlədʒɪst] *n* Archäologe *m*, Archäologin *f*.

archaeology, (*US***) archeology** [ˌɑːkɪˈɒlədʒɪ] *n* Archäologie *f*.

archaic [ɑːˈkeɪɪk] *adj word etc* veraltet, archaisch (*spec*); (*inf*) vorsintflutlich ◆ **my car is getting rather ~** mein Auto wird allmählich museumsreif.

archaism [ˈɑːkeɪɪzəm] *n* veralteter Ausdruck, Archaismus *m*.

arch: ~angel [ˈɑːkˌeɪndʒl] *n* Erzengel *m*; **~bishop** *n* Erzbischof *m*; **~-bishopric** *n* (*district*) Erzbistum *nt*, Erzdiözese *f*; (*office*) Amt *nt* des Erzbischofs; **~deacon** *n* Archidiakon, Erzdiakon *m*; **~diocese** *n* Erzdiözese *f*, Erzbistum *nt*; **~ducal** *adj* erzherzoglich; **~duchess** *n* Erzherzogin *f*; **~-duchy** *n* Erzherzogtum *nt*; **~duke** *n* Erzherzog *m*.

arched [ɑːtʃt] *adj* gewölbt; *window* (Rund)bogen- ◆ **the ~ curve of the temple roof** die Wölbung des Tempeldachs.

arch enemy *n* Erzfeind *m*.

archeological *etc* (*US*) *see* **archaeological** *etc*.

archer [ˈɑːtʃəʳ] *n* Bogenschütze *m*; (*Astron, Astrol*) Schütze *m*.

archery [ˈɑːtʃərɪ] *n* Bogenschießen *nt*.

archetypal [ˈɑːkɪtaɪpəl] *adj* archetypisch (*geh*); (*typical*) typisch ◆ **he is the ~ millionaire** er ist ein Millionär, wie er im Buche steht; **an ~ Scot** ein Urschotte (*inf*).

archetype [ˈɑːkɪtaɪp] *n* Archetyp(us) *m* (*form*); (*original, epitome also*) Urbild *nt*, Urtyp *m*.

arch-fiend [ɑːtʃˈfiːnd] *n* **the ~** der Erzfeind.

archiepiscopal [ˌɑːkɪɪˈpɪskəpəl] *adj* erzbischöflich.

Archimedes [ˌɑːkɪˈmiːdiːz] *n* Archimedes *m*.

archipelago [ˌɑːkɪˈpelɪgəʊ] *n, pl* **-(e)s** Archipel *m* ◆ **the A~** der Archipel(agos); (*sea*) die Ägäis.

architect [ˈɑːkɪtekt] *n* (*lit, fig*) Architekt(in *f*) *m* ◆ **~-designed** von (einem) Architekten entworfen; **he was/everybody is the ~ of his own fate** er hat sein Schicksal selbst verursacht/jeder ist seines (eigenen) Glückes Schmied (*prov*).

architectural *adj*, **~ly** *adv* [ˌɑːkɪˈtektʃərəl, -lɪ] architektonisch.

architecture [ˈɑːkɪtektʃəʳ] *n* Architektur *f* (*also Comput*); (*of building also*) Baustil *m*.

archive [ˈɑːkaɪv] 1 *n* Archiv *nt* (*also Comput*) ◆ **~ file** Archivdatei *f*.
2 *vt* archivieren.

archives [ˈɑːkaɪvz] *npl* Archiv *nt*.

archivist [ˈɑːkɪvɪst] *n* Archivar(in *f*) *m*.

archly [ˈɑːtʃlɪ] *adv* neckisch, schelmisch.

archness [ˈɑːtʃnɪs] *n* neckische *or* schelmische Art.

archpriest [ˈɑːtʃˈpriːst] *n* (*lit, fig*) Hohepriester *m*.

archway [ˈɑːtʃˌweɪ] *n* Torbogen *m*.

arc: ~lamp, ~light *n* Bogenlampe *f*, Bogenlicht *nt*.

arctic [ˈɑːktɪk] 1 *adj* (*lit, fig*) arktisch ◆ **A~ Circle** nördlicher Polarkreis; **A~ Ocean** Nordpolarmeer *nt*.
2 *n* **(a) the A~** die Arktis. **(b)** (*US: shoe*) *gefütterter, wasserundurchlässiger Überschuh*.

arc welding *n* (Licht)bogenschweißung *f*.

ardent [ˈɑːdənt] *adj* leidenschaftlich; *supporter, admirer also* begeistert; *admirer, love also* glühend; *desire, longing also* brennend, glühend; *request, imprecations* inständig.

ardently [ˈɑːdəntlɪ] *adv* leidenschaftlich; *love* heiß; *desire, admire* glühend.

ardour, (*US***) ardor** [ˈɑːdəʳ] *n* (*of person*) Begeisterung, Leidenschaft *f*; (*of voice also*) Überschwang *m*; (*of feelings also*) Heftigkeit *f*; (*of passions*) Glut *f* (*liter*), Feuer *nt*; (*of poems, letters*) Leidenschaftlichkeit *f* ◆ **the ~s of youth** die Leidenschaft der Jugend.

arduous [ˈɑːdjʊəs] *adj* beschwerlich, mühsam; *course, work* anstrengend; *task* mühselig.

arduousness [ˈɑːdjʊəsnɪs] *n see adj* Beschwerlichkeit *f*; Mühseligkeit *f* ◆ **because of the ~ of the work** weil die Arbeit so anstrengend war/ist.

are¹ [ɑːʳ] *n* Ar *nt*.

are² *2nd pers sing, 1st, 2nd, 3rd pers pl present of* **be**.

area [ˈɛərɪə] *n* **(a)** (*measure*) Fläche *f* ◆ **20 sq metres in ~** eine Fläche von 20 Quadratmetern.
(b) (*region, district*) Gebiet *nt*; (*neighbourhood, vicinity*) Gegend *f*; (*separated off, piece of ground etc*) Areal, Gelände *nt*; (*on plan, diagram etc*) Bereich *m*; (*slum ~, residential ~, commercial ~ also*) Viertel *nt* ◆ **this is not a very nice ~ to live in** dies ist keine besonders gute Wohngegend; **in the ~** in der Nähe; **do you live in the ~?** wohnen Sie hier (in der Gegend)?; **protected/prohibited/industrial ~** Schutz-/Sperr-/Industriegebiet *nt*; **drying/packaging/despatch ~** Trocken-/Pack-/Verteilerzone *f*; **dining/sleeping ~** Eß-/Schlafbereich *or* -platz *m*; **no smoking/relaxation/recreation ~** Nichtraucher-/Erholungs-/Freizeitzone *f*; **we use this corner as a discussion ~** wir benutzen diese Ecke für Diskussionen; **the goal ~** der Torraum; **this ~ is for directors' cars** dieser Platz ist für Direktorenwagen vorgesehen; **you must keep out of this ~** dies Gebiet darf nicht betreten werden; **this ~ must be kept clear** diesen Platz freihalten; **the public were told to keep well away from the ~** die Öffentlichkeit wurde aufgefordert, das Gebiet unbedingt zu meiden; **a mountainous ~/mountainous ~s** eine bergige Gegend/Bergland *nt*; **a wooded ~** ein Waldstück *nt*; (*larger*) ein Waldgebiet *nt*; **desert ~s** Wüstengebiete *pl*; **the infected ~s of the lungs** die befallenen Teile *or* (*smaller*) Stellen der Lunge; **the patchy**

~s on the wall die fleckigen Stellen an der Wand; **the additional message ~ on an airletter** der Raum für zusätzliche Mitteilungen auf einem Luftpostbrief; **in the ~ of the station** in der Bahnhofsgegend; **the thief is believed to be still in the ~** man nimmt an, daß sich der Dieb noch in der Umgebung aufhält; **in the London ~** im Raum London, im Londoner Raum; **the sterling ~** die Sterlingzone; **~ bombing** Flächenbombardierungen *pl*; **~ code** (*Telec*) Vorwahl(nummer), Ortskennzahl *f*; **postal ~** Zustellbereich (*form*), Postbezirk *m*; **~ command** Gebiets- *or* Abschnittskommandantur *f*; **~ manager** Bezirks- *or* Gebietsleiter *m*; **~ office** Bezirksbüro *nt*.

(c) (*fig*) Bereich *m* ◆ **~s of uncertainty/agreement** Bereiche, in denen Unklarheit/Übereinstimmung besteht; **his ~ of responsibility** sein Verantwortungsbereich *m*; **~ of interest/study** Interessen-/Studiengebiet *nt*; **a sum in the ~ of £100** eine Summe um die hundert Pfund.

(d) (*Brit: basement courtyard*) Vorplatz *m*.

areaway [ˈɛərɪəˌweɪ] *n* (*US*) **(a)** Vorplatz *m*. **(b)** (*passage*) Durchgang *m*, Passage *f*.

arena [əˈriːnə] *n* (*lit, fig*) Arena *f* ◆ **~ of war** Kriegsschauplatz *m*; **to enter the ~** (*fig*) die Arena betreten, auf den Plan treten.

aren't [ɑːnt] = **are not; am not**; *see* **be**.

argent [ˈɑːdʒənt] (*obs, poet, Her*) 1 *n* Silber *nt*.

2 *adj* silbern.

Argentina [ˌɑːdʒənˈtiːnə] *n* Argentinien *nt*.

Argentine [ˈɑːdʒəntaɪn] *n*: **the ~** Argentinien *nt*.

Argentinian [ˌɑːdʒənˈtɪnɪən] 1 *n* (*person*) Argentinier(in *f*) *m*.

2 *adj* argentinisch.

argon [ˈɑːgɒn] *n* Argon *nt*.

Argonaut [ˈɑːgənɔːt] *n* Argonaut *m*.

argot [ˈɑːgəʊ] *n* Argot *nt or m*; (*criminal also*) Rotwelsch *nt*.

arguable [ˈɑːgjʊəbl] *adj* **(a)** (*capable of being maintained*) vertretbar ◆ **it is ~ that ...** es läßt sich der Standpunkt vertreten, daß ..., man kann behaupten, daß ... **(b)** (*open to discussion*) **it is ~ whether ...** es ist (noch) die Frage, ob ...

arguably [ˈɑːgjʊəblɪ] *adv* wohl ◆ **this is ~ his best book** dies dürfte (wohl) sein bestes Buch sein.

▼ **argue** [ˈɑːgjuː] 1 *vi* **(a)** (*dispute*) streiten; (*quarrel*) sich streiten; (*about trivial things*) sich zanken ◆ **he is always arguing** er widerspricht ständig, er muß immer streiten; **there's no arguing with him** mit ihm kann man nicht reden; **don't ~ (with me)!** keine Widerrede!; **don't ~ with your mother!** du sollst deiner Mutter nicht widersprechen!; **I don't want to ~, if you don't want to ...** ich will mich nicht streiten, wenn Sie nicht wollen ...; **there is no point in arguing** da erübrigt sich jede (weitere) Diskussion; **you can't ~ with a line of tanks** mit Panzern kann man nicht diskutieren; **a 25% increase, you can't ~ with that** (*inf*) eine 25%ige Erhöhung, da kann man nichts sagen (*inf*) *or* nicht meckern (*inf*); **he wasn't used to employees arguing** Angestellte, die ihre Meinung sagten, war er nicht gewöhnt.

▼ **(b)** (*present reasons*) **he ~s that ...** er vertritt den Standpunkt, daß ..., er behauptet, daß ...; **I'm not arguing that ...** ich will nicht behaupten, daß ...; **to ~ for** *or* **in favour of sth** für etw sprechen; (*in book*) sich für etw aussprechen; **to ~ against sth** gegen etw sprechen; (*in book*) sich gegen etw aussprechen; **to ~ from a position of ...** von einem *or* dem Standpunkt (+*gen*) aus argumentieren; **this ~s in his favour** das spricht zu seinen Gunsten; **it ~s well for him** es spricht für ihn; **just one thing ~s against him/it** nur eins spricht gegen ihn/dagegen.

2 *vt* **(a)** (*debate*) *case, matter* diskutieren, erörtern; (*Jur*) vertreten ◆ **a well ~d case** ein gut begründeter *or* dargelegter Fall; **to ~ a case for reform** die Sache der Reform vertreten; **to ~ one's way out of sth** sich aus etw herausreden.

(b) (*maintain*) behaupten.

(c) (*persuade*) **to ~ sb out of/into sth** jdm etw aus-/einreden.

(d) (*indicate*) erkennen lassen, verraten.

◆**argue away** 1 *vi* diskutieren.

2 *vt sep facts* wegdiskutieren.

◆**argue out** *vt sep problem, issue* ausdiskutieren ◆ **to ~ sth ~ with sb** etw mit jdm durchsprechen.

▼ **argument** [ˈɑːgjʊmənt] *n* **(a)** (*discussion*) Diskussion *f* ◆ **to spend hours in ~ about how to do sth** stundenlang darüber diskutieren, wie man etw macht; **for the sake of ~** rein theoretisch; **he just said that for the sake of ~** das hat er nur gesagt, um etwas (dagegen) zu sagen; **it is beyond ~** das ist unbestreitbar; **he is open to ~** er läßt mit sich reden; **this is open to ~** darüber läßt sich streiten.

(b) (*quarrel*) Auseinandersetzung *f* ◆ **to have an ~** sich streiten; (*over sth trivial*) sich zanken.

▼ **(c)** (*reason*) Beweis(grund) *m*, Argument *nt*; (*line of reasoning*) Argumentation, Beweisführung *f* ◆ **first state your theory, then list the ~s for and against** stellen Sie erst Ihre These auf, und nennen Sie dann die Gründe und Gegengründe; **one of the best ~s I have heard in favour of private education** eines der besten Argumente zugunsten der Privatschule, die ich gehört habe; **there's an even stronger ~ than that** es gibt ein noch stärkeres Argument; **that's not a rational ~, it's just a dogmatic assertion** das ist kein rationales Argument, das ist bloß eine dogmatische Behauptung.

(d) (*theme: of play, book etc*) Aussage, These (*esp Philos*) *f*; (*claim*) These *f*.

▼ **(e)** (*statement of proof*) Beweis *m* ◆ **the two main types of ~** die beiden wichtigsten Beweisarten; **Professor Ayer's ~ is that ...** Professor Ayers These lautet, daß ...; **the Ontological/Teleological A~** der ontologische/teleologische Gottesbeweis; **all the various ~s for the existence of a god** all die verschiedenen Gottesbeweise; **I don't think that's a valid ~** ich glaube, das ist kein gültiger Beweis/Gegenbeweis; **an interesting ~** eine interessante These.

(f) (*Math*) Argument *nt*.

argumentation [ˌɑːgjʊmənˈteɪʃən] *n* Argumentation, Beweisführung *f*; (*discussion*) Diskussion *f* ◆ **an ingenious piece of ~** eine geniale Beweisführung.

argumentative [ˌɑːgjʊˈmentətɪv] *adj person* streitsüchtig.

argy-bargy [ˈɑːdʒɪˈbɑːdʒɪ] (*inf*) 1 *n* Hin und Her *nt* (*inf*), Hickhack *m or nt* (*inf*).

2 *vi* hin und her reden, endlos debattieren.

aria [ˈɑːrɪə] *n* Arie *f*.

Arian[1] [ˈɛərɪən] *n, adj see* **Aryan**.

Arian[2] (*Astrol*) 1 *n* Widder *m* ◆ **to be an ~** Widder sein.

2 *adj* Widder-.

ARIBA [əˈriːbə] *abbr of* **Associate of the Royal British Institute of Architects** *Mitglied nt des britischen Architektenverbandes*.

arid [ˈærɪd] *adj* (*lit*) *countryside, soil* dürr; *climate* trocken, arid (*spec*); (*fig*) *subject* trocken, nüchtern; *existence* freudlos, öd.

aridity [əˈrɪdɪtɪ] *n see adj* Dürre *f*; Trockenheit, Aridität (*spec*) *f*; (*fig*) Trockenheit, Nüchternheit *f*; Freudlosigkeit, Öde *f*.

Aries [ˈɛəriːz] *n* (*Astrol*) Widder *m* ◆ **she is an ~** sie ist Widder.

aright [əˈraɪt] *adv* recht, wohl (*old*) ◆ **if I understand you ~** wenn ich Sie recht verstehe.

arise [əˈraɪz] *pret* **arose** [əˈrəʊz], *ptp* **arisen** [əˈrɪzn] *vi* **(a)** (*occur*) sich ergeben, entstehen; (*misunderstanding, argument also*) aufkommen; (*problem*) aufkommen, sich ergeben; (*clouds of dust*) entstehen, sich bilden; (*protest, cry*) sich erheben; (*question, wind*) aufkommen, sich erheben (*geh*); (*question*) sich stellen ◆ **should the need ~** falls sich die Notwendigkeit ergibt.

(b) (*result*) **to ~ out of** *or* **from sth** sich aus etw ergeben.

(c) (*old, liter: get up*) sich erheben (*liter*) ◆ **~ Sir Humphrey** erhebt Euch, Sir Humphrey!

aristocracy [ˌærɪsˈtɒkrəsɪ] *n* (*system, state*) Aristokratie *f*; (*class also*) Adel *m* ◆ **~ of wealth** Geldadel *m*, Geldaristokratie *f*.

aristocrat [ˈærɪstəkræt] *n* Aristokrat(in *f*) *m*, Adlige(r) *mf* ◆ **he is too much of an ~ to ...** (*fig*) er ist sich (*dat*) zu fein, um ... zu ...; **the ~ of the dog/cat family** der edelste Vertreter der Hunde-/Katzenfamilie.

aristocratic [ˌærɪstəˈkrætɪk] *adj* (*lit, fig*) aristokratisch, adlig; (*fig also*) vornehm.

Aristotelian [ˌærɪstəˈtiːlɪən] 1 *adj* aristotelisch.

2 *n* Aristoteliker *m*.

Aristotle [ˈærɪstɒtl] *n* Aristoteles *m*.

arithmetic [əˈrɪθmətɪk] *n* Rechnen *nt*; (*calculation*) Rechnung *f* ◆ **could you check my ~?** kannst du mal gucken, ob ich richtig gerechnet habe?; **your ~ is wrong** du hast dich verrechnet; **~ book** Rechenfibel *f or* -buch *nt*; (*exercise book*) Rechenheft *nt*.

arithmetical [ˌærɪθˈmetɪkəl] *adj* Rechen-, rechnerisch ◆ **~ genius** Rechenkünstler(in *f*) *m*; **the basic ~ skills** Grundwissen *nt* im Rechnen; **~ progression** arithmetische Reihe.

arithmetician [əˌrɪθməˈtɪʃən] *n* Rechner(in *f*) *m*.

arithmetic mean *n* arithmetisches Mittel.

ark [ɑːk] *n* **(a)** Arche *f* ◆ **Noah's ~** die Arche Noah; **it looks as though it's come out of the ~** (*inf*) das sieht aus wie von Anno Tobak (*inf*). **(b) A~ of the Covenant** Bundeslade *f*.

arm[1] [ɑːm] *n* **(a)** (*Anat*) Arm *m* ◆ **in one's ~s** im Arm; **under one's ~** unter dem *or* unterm Arm; **he had a bandage on his ~** er hatte einen Verband am Arm *or* um den Arm; **to give one's ~ to sb** jdm den Arm geben *or* reichen (*geh*); **with his ~s full of books** den Arm *or* die Arme voller Bücher; **to have sb/sth on one's ~** jdn/etw am Arm haben; **to take sb in one's ~s** jdn in die Arme nehmen *or* schließen (*geh*); **to hold sb in one's ~s** jdn umarmen, jdn in den *or* seinen Armen halten (*geh*); **to put** *or* **throw one's ~s round sb** jdn umarmen, die Arme um jdn schlingen (*geh*); **to put an ~ round sb's shoulders** jdm den Arm um die Schulter legen; **~ in ~** Arm in Arm; (*~s linked*) eingehakt, untergehakt; **at ~'s length** auf Armeslänge; **to keep sb at ~'s length** (*fig*) jdn auf Distanz halten; **to receive** *or* **welcome sb/sth with open ~s** jdn mit offenen Armen empfangen/etw mit Kußhand nehmen (*inf*); **within ~'s reach** in Reichweite; **the long ~ of the law** der lange Arm des Gesetzes; **a list as long as your ~** eine ellenlange Liste; **a criminal with a record as long as your ~** ein Verbrecher mit einer langen Latte von Vorstrafen (*inf*); **it cost him an ~ and a leg** (*inf*) es kostete ihn ein Vermögen; **to put the ~ on sb** (*US inf*) jdn unter Druck setzen.

(b) (*sleeve*) Arm, Ärmel *m*.

(c) (*of river*) (Fluß)arm *m*; (*of sea*) Meeresarm *m*; (*of armchair*) (Arm)lehne *f*; (*of record player*) Tonarm *m*; (*of balance etc*) Balken *m*; (*of railway signal*) (Signal)arm *m*; (*Naut: yard~*) Rahnock *f*.

(d) (*branch*) Zweig *m*; (*Mil*) Truppengattung *f*.

arm[2] 1 *n* (*Mil, Her*) *see* **arms**.

2 *vt person, nation, ship etc* bewaffnen ◆ **to ~ sth with sth** etw mit etw ausrüsten; **to ~ oneself with sth** (*lit, fig*) sich mit etw bewaffnen; (*fig: non-aggressively*) sich mit etw wappnen; **he came ~ed with an excuse** er hatte eine Ausrede parat; **~ed only with her beauty, she ...** ihre Schönheit war die einzige Waffe, mit der sie ...

3 *vi* aufrüsten ◆ **to ~ for war** zum Krieg rüsten.

armada [ɑːˈmɑːdə] *n* Armada *f* ◆ **the A~** die Armada; (*battle*) die Armadaschlacht.

armadillo [ˌɑːməˈdɪləʊ] *n* Gürteltier *nt*.

Armageddon [ˌɑːməˈgedn] *n* (*Bibl*) Armageddon *nt*; (*fig also*) weltweite *or*

globale Katastrophe.
armament ['ɑːməmənt] *n* **(a)** **~s** *pl* *(weapons)* Ausrüstung *f.* **(b)** *(preparation)* Aufrüstung *f no pl* ◆ **much of the national budget is devoted to ~** ein großer Teil des Staatshaushalts geht in die Rüstung.
armature ['ɑːmətjʊəʳ] *n (Elec)* Anker *m.*
armband ['ɑːmbænd] *n* Armbinde *f.*
armchair [ˌɑːm'tʃɛəʳ] **1** *n* Sessel, Lehnstuhl *m.*
2 *adj* **~ philosopher/philosophy** Stubengelehrte(r) *m*/Stubengelehrsamkeit *f;* **~ politician** Stammtischpolitiker *m;* **~ strategist** Stammtisch- *or* Salonstratege *m;* **he is an ~ traveller** er reist nur mit dem Finger auf der Landkarte *(inf).*
-armed [-ɑːmd] *adj suf* -armig.
armed [ɑːmd] *adj* bewaffnet.
armed: ~ forces *or* **services** *pl* Streitkräfte *pl;* **~ robbery** *n* bewaffneter Raubüberfall.
Armenia [ɑː'miːnɪə] *n* Armenien *nt.*
Armenian [ɑː'miːnɪən] **1** *adj* armenisch.
2 *n* **(a)** *(person)* Armenier(in *f*) *m.* **(b)** *(language)* Armenisch *nt.*
arm: ~ful *n* Armvoll *m no pl,* Ladung *f (inf);* **she's quite an ~ful!** *(inf)* sie ist eine ganz schöne Handvoll *(inf) or* Portion *(inf);* **~hole** *n* Armloch *nt.*
armistice ['ɑːmɪstɪs] *n* Waffenstillstand *m* ◆ **A~ Day** 11.11., *Tag des Waffenstillstands (1918).*
arm: ~let *n* **(a)** *see* **~band; (b)** *(liter: of sea)* kleiner Meeresarm; **~lock** *n* Armschlüssel *m; (of police etc)* Polizeigriff *m.*
armor *etc (US) see* **armour** *etc.*
armorial [ɑː'mɔːrɪəl] **1** *adj* Wappen-.
2 *n* Wappenbuch *nt.*
armour, *(US)* **armor** ['ɑːməʳ] **1** *n* **(a)** Rüstung *f; (of animal)* Panzer *m* ◆ **suit of ~** Rüstung *f; (fig)* Panzer *m,* Rüstung *f;* **to wear ~** eine Rüstung tragen. **(b)** *(no pl: steel plates)* Panzerplatte(n *pl*) *f.* **(c)** *(vehicles)* Panzerfahrzeuge *pl; (forces)* Panzertruppen *pl.*
2 *vt* panzern; *(fig)* wappnen ◆ **~ed** *division, cruiser* Panzer-; **~ed car** Panzerwagen *m;* **~ed personnel carrier** Schützenpanzer(wagen) *m.*
armour-clad, *(US)* **armor-clad** ['ɑːmə'klæd] *adj (Mil, Naut)* gepanzert.
armourer, *(US)* **armorer** ['ɑːmərəʳ] *n (maker)* Waffenschmied *m; (keeper)* Waffenmeister, Feldzeugmeister *(old) m.*
armour: ~-piercing *adj* panzerbrechend; **~-plated** *adj* gepanzert; **~-plating** *n* Panzerung *f;* **a sheet of ~-plating** eine Panzerplatte.
armoury, *(US)* **armory** ['ɑːmərɪ] *n* **(a)** Arsenal, Waffenlager *nt.* **(b)** *(US: factory)* Munitionsfabrik *f.*
arm: ~pit *n* Achselhöhle *f; (of garments)* Achsel *f;* **~rest** *n* Armlehne *f.*
arms [ɑːmz] *npl* **(a)** *(weapons)* Waffen *pl* ◆ **to ~!** zu den Waffen!; **to carry ~** Waffen tragen; **to be under ~** unter Waffen stehen; **to take up ~ (against sb/sth)** (gegen jdn/etw) zu den Waffen greifen; *(fig)* gegen jdn/etw zum Angriff übergehen; **to be up in ~ (about sth)** *(fig inf),* (über etw *acc*) empört sein; **~ control** Rüstungskontrolle *f;* **~ control/limitation talks** Rüstungskontroll-/-begrenzungsverhandlungen *pl;* **~ race** Wettrüsten *nt,* Rüstungswettlauf *m.* **(b)** *(Her)* Wappen *nt.*
arm-twisting ['ɑːm'twɪstɪŋ] *n (inf)* Überredungskunst *f* ◆ **with a bit of ~ ...** wenn man etwas nachhilft ...; **it took a lot of/didn't take much ~ to get him to agree** er ließ sich nicht schnell/schnell breitschlagen *(inf).*
arm wrestling *n* Armdrücken *nt.*
army ['ɑːmɪ] **1** *n* **(a)** Armee *f,* Heer *nt* ◆ **~ of occupation** Besatzungsarmee *f;* **to be in the ~** beim Militär sein; *(BRD)* bei der Bundeswehr sein; *(DDR)* bei der NVA sein; *(Aus)* beim Bundesheer sein; **to join the ~** zum Militär gehen. **(b)** *(fig)* Heer *nt.* **(c)** *(division)* Armee(korps *nt*) *f.*
2 *attr* Militär-; *doctor also* Stabs-; *discipline* militärisch; *life, slang* Soldaten- ◆ **~ issue** Armee-; **~ list** *(Brit)* Rangliste *f;* **~ officer** Offizier *m* in der Armee; **an ~ type** *(inf)* einer vom Barras *(inf) or* Bund *(BRD inf).*
A-road ['eɪrəʊd] *n (Brit)* ≃ Bundesstraße *f.*
aroma [ə'rəʊmə] *n* Duft *m,* Aroma *nt.*
aromatherapist [əˌrəʊmə'θerəpɪst] *n* Aromatherapeut(in) *m(f).*
aromatherapy [əˌrəʊmə'θerəpɪ] *n* Aromatherapie *f.*
aromatic [ˌærəʊ'mætɪk] *adj* aromatisch, wohlriechend.
arose [ə'rəʊz] *pret of* **arise.**
around [ə'raʊnd] **1** *adv* herum, rum *(inf)* ◆ **a house with gardens all ~** ein von Gärten umgebenes Haus, ein Haus mit Gärten ringsherum; **I looked all ~** ich sah mich nach allen Seiten um; **books lying all ~** überall herumliegende Bücher; **they appeared from all ~** sie kamen aus allen Richtungen *or* von überallher; **slowly, he turned ~** er drehte sich langsam um; **for miles ~** meilenweit im Umkreis; **to stroll/travel ~** herumschlendern/-reisen; **is he ~?** ist er da?; **if you want me I'll be ~** ich bin da, falls du mich brauchst; **he must be ~ somewhere** er muß hier irgendwo sein *or* stecken *(inf);* **I didn't know you were ~** ich wußte nicht, daß du hier bist; **he's been ~!** der kennt sich aus!; **it's been ~ for ages** das ist schon uralt; **he's been ~ for ages** *(inf)* der ist schon ewig hier *(inf);* **see you ~!** *(inf)* also, bis demnächst!, bis bald!; **where have you been? — ~** wo warst du? — weg!
2 *prep* **(a)** *(right round) (movement, position)* um *(+acc); (in a circle)* um *(+acc)* ... herum.
(b) *(in, through)* **to wander ~ the city** durch die Stadt spazieren; **to travel ~ Scotland** durch Schottland reisen; **to talk ~ a subject** um ein Thema herumreden; **to be** *or* **stay ~ the house** zu Hause bleiben; **I left it ~ your office somewhere** ich habe es irgendwo in deinem Büro gelassen; **the paper/church must be ~ here somewhere** die Zeitung muß hier irgendwo (he)rumliegen/die Kirche muß hier irgendwo sein.
(c) *(approximately) (with date)* um *(+acc); (with time of day)* gegen *(+acc); (with weight, price)* etwa, um die *(inf); see also* **round.**
arousal [ə'raʊsəl] *n (sexual)* Erregung *f.*
arouse [ə'raʊz] *vt* **(a)** *(lit liter)* aufwecken, erwecken *(liter).*
(b) *(fig: excite)* erregen; *interest, suspicion etc also* erwecken ◆ **to ~ sb from his slumbers** *(fig)* jdn aus dem Schlaf wachrütteln; **to ~ sb to action** jdn zum Handeln anspornen.
arpeggio [ɑː'pedʒɪəʊ] *n* Arpeggio *nt.*
arr *abbr of* **arrival; arrives** Ank.
arrack ['ærək] *n* Arrak *m.*
arraign [ə'reɪn] *vt (Jur) person* Anklage erheben gegen; *(liter: denounce)* rügen ◆ **to be ~ed on a charge** wegen etw angeklagt werden.
arraignment [ə'reɪnmənt] *n (Jur)* Anklageerhebung *f.*
arrange [ə'reɪndʒ] *vt* **(a)** *(order)* ordnen; *furniture, objects* aufstellen, hinstellen; *items in a collection, books in library etc* anordnen; *flowers* arrangieren; *room* einrichten; *(fig) thoughts* ordnen ◆ **I don't want you arranging my life for me** ich will nicht, daß du mein Leben planst.
(b) *(fix, see to)* vereinbaren, ausmachen; *details* regeln; *party* arrangieren ◆ **to ~ a mortgage for sb** jdm eine Hypothek beschaffen; **I'll ~ for you to meet him** ich arrangiere für Sie ein Treffen mit ihm; **I have ~d for a car to pick you up** ich habe Ihnen einen Wagen besorgt, der Sie mitnimmt; **can you ~ an interview with the President for me?** können Sie mir ein Interview mit dem Präsidenten besorgen?; **there aren't enough glasses — I'll ~ that** es sind nicht genug Gläser da — das mache *or* reg(e)le *(inf)* ich; **his manager wants to ~ another fight next month** sein Manager will nächsten Monat noch einen Kampf ansetzen; **to ~ a sale/marriage** einen Verkauf/die Ehe vereinbaren; **I'll ~ the drinks, you get the food** ich besorge die Getränke, und du kümmerst dich um das Essen; **if you could ~ to be ill that morning/there at five** wenn du es so einrichten kannst, daß du an dem Morgen krank/um fünf Uhr da bist; **I think I could ~ that** ich glaube, das läßt sich machen *or* einrichten; **that's easily ~d** das läßt sich leicht einrichten *or* arrangieren *(inf);* **how can we ~ it so it looks like an accident?** wie können wir es machen *or* drehen *(inf),* daß es wie ein Unfall aussieht?; **they'd obviously ~d things between themselves before the meeting started** sie hatten die Dinge offenbar vor Beginn des Treffens untereinander abgesprochen.
(c) *(settle, decide on)* vereinbaren, abmachen ◆ **nothing definite has been ~d yet** es ist noch nichts Verbindliches vereinbart worden; **a meeting has been ~d for next month** nächsten Monat ist ein Treffen angesetzt; **good, that's ~d then** gut, das ist abgemacht!; **I don't like having things ~d for me** ich habe es nicht gern, wenn man Dinge für mich entscheidet; **but you ~d to meet me!** aber du wolltest dich doch mit mir treffen!
(d) *(Mus)* bearbeiten, arrangieren.
arrangement [ə'reɪndʒmənt] *n* **(a)** Anordnung *f; (of room)* Einrichtung *f; (inf: contrivance)* Gerät *nt (inf)* ◆ **a floral ~** ein Blumenarrangement *nt;* **the very unusual ~ of her hair** ihre sehr ungewöhnliche Haartracht.
(b) *(agreement)* Vereinbarung *f; (to meet)* Verabredung *f; (esp shifty)* Arrangement *nt* ◆ **by ~** laut *or* nach Vereinbarung *or* Absprache; **by ~ with** mit freundlicher Genehmigung *(+gen);* **salary by ~** Gehalt nach Vereinbarung; **a special ~** eine Sonderregelung; **to have an ~ with sb** eine Regelung mit jdm getroffen haben; **he has an ~ with his wife ...** er hat mit seiner Frau ein Arrangement ...; **I've got a nice little ~ going** ich habe da so eine Abmachung *or* Absprache getroffen; **to make an ~ with sb** eine Vereinbarung *or* Absprache mit jdm treffen; **to come to an ~** eine Regelung finden; **to come to an ~ with sb** eine Regelung mit jdm treffen.
(c) *(usu pl: plans)* Pläne *pl; (preparations)* Vorbereitungen *pl* ◆ **to make ~s for sb/sth** für jdn/etw Vorbereitungen treffen; **to make ~s for sth to be done** veranlassen, daß etw getan wird; **to make one's own ~s** selber zusehen(, wie ...), es selber arrangieren(, daß ...); **who's in charge of transport ~s?** wer regelt die Transportfrage?; **the new fire drill ~s** die neuen Feuerschutzmaßnahmen; **seating ~s** Sitzordnung *f;* **"funeral ~s"** „Ausführung von Bestattungen"; **who will look after the funeral ~s?** wer kümmert sich um die Beerdigung?
(d) *(Mus)* Bearbeitung *f; (light music)* Arrangement *nt.*
arranger [ə'reɪndʒəʳ] *n (Mus)* Arrangeur *m.*
arrant ['ærənt] *adj* Erz- ◆ **~ coward** Erzfeigling *m;* **~ nonsense** barer Unsinn.
arras ['ærəs] *n (old)* (Arazzo)wandteppich *m.*
array [ə'reɪ] **1** *vt* **(a)** *(line up)* aufstellen; *(Mil)* in Aufstellung bringen. **(b)** *(dress)* schmücken *(geh),* herausputzen *(hum).*
2 *n* **(a)** *(Mil: arrangement)* Aufstellung *f* ◆ **in ~** in Aufstellung; **in battle ~** in Kampfaufstellung, in Schlachtordnung.
(b) *(collection)* Ansammlung *f,* Aufgebot *nt (hum); (of objects)* stattliche *or* ansehnliche Reihe.
(c) *(Comput)* (Daten)feld, Array *nt.*
(d) *(liter)* Schmuck *m (geh); (dress)* Staat *m* ◆ **the trees in all their spring ~** die Bäume im Frühlingskleid *(poet).*
arrears [ə'rɪəz] *npl* Rückstände *pl* ◆ **to be in ~ with sth** im Rückstand mit etw sein; **to get** *or* **fall into ~** in Rückstand kommen; **to have ~ of £5000** mit £ 5000 im Rückstand sein.
arrest [ə'rest] **1** *vt* **(a)** *(apprehend)* festnehmen; *(with warrant)* verhaften; *ship* aufbringen; *(fig) attention* erregen, erheischen *(liter)* ◆ **I am ~ing you** ich muß Sie festnehmen/verhaften.
(b) *(check)* hemmen; *sth unwanted* (Ein)halt gebieten *(+dat) (geh)* ◆ **~ed development** Entwicklungshemmung *f.*
2 *n (of suspect)* Festnahme *f; (with warrant)* Verhaftung *f; (of ship)* Auf-

bringen *nt* ◆ **to be under ~** festgenommen/verhaftet sein; **you are under ~** Sie sind festgenommen/verhaftet; **to put sb under ~** jdn festnehmen/verhaften; **to make an ~** jdn festnehmen/verhaften; **they hope to make an ~ soon** man hofft, daß es bald zu einer Festnahme/Verhaftung kommt.

arresting [ə'restɪŋ] *adj* **(a)** (*striking*) atemberaubend; *features* markant. **(b) the ~ officer** der festnehmende Beamte.

arrhythmia [ə'rɪðmɪə] *n* (*Med*) Arrhythmie *f*.

arrival [ə'raɪvəl] *n* **(a)** Ankunft *f no pl*; (*of person also*) Kommen, Eintreffen *nt no pl*; (*of train also, of goods, news*) Eintreffen *nt no pl* ◆ **our eventual ~ at a decision ...** daß wir endlich zu einer Entscheidung kamen ...; **on ~** bei Ankunft; **~ time, time of ~** Ankunftszeit *f*; **~ lounge** Ankunftshalle *f*; **~s and departures** (*Rail*) Ankunft/Abfahrt *f*; (*Aviat*) Ankunft *f*/Abflug *m*; **~s board** (*Rail*) Ankunftstafel *f*; (*Aviat*) Ankunftsanzeige *f*.
(b) (*person*) Ankömmling *m* ◆ **new ~** Neuankömmling *m*; (*at school also*) Neue(r) *mf*; (*in hotel, boarding house*) neuangekommener Gast; (*in firm, office*) neuer Mitarbeiter, neue Mitarbeiterin ◆ **a new ~ on the pop scene** ein neues Gesicht auf der Popszene; **when our firm was still a new ~ in the publishing world** als unsere Firma noch ein Neuling im Verlagswesen war; **the new ~ is a little girl** der neue Erdenbürger ist ein kleines Mädchen; **he was the latest ~** er kam als letzter.

arrive [ə'raɪv] *vi* **(a)** (*come*) ankommen, eintreffen (*geh*); (*be born*) ankommen ◆ **to ~ home** nach Hause kommen; (*stressing after journey etc*) zu Hause ankommen; **I'll wait for him to ~ before ... to ~ at a town/the airport** in einer Stadt/am Flughafen ankommen *or* eintreffen (*geh*); **the train will ~ at platform 10** der Zug läuft auf Gleis 10 ein; **the great day ~d** der große Tag kam; **a new era has ~d!** ein neues Zeitalter ist angebrochen!; **the time has ~d for sth/to do sth** die Zeit für etw ist gekommen, die Zeit ist reif für etw/, etw zu tun; **television has not ~d here yet** das Fernsehen ist noch nicht bis hier durchgedrungen; **to ~ at a decision** zu einer Entscheidung kommen *or* gelangen; **to ~ at the age of ...** das Alter von ... Jahren erreichen; **to ~ at an answer/a conclusion/result** zu einer Antwort/einem Schluß/Ergebnis kommen; **to ~ at a price** auf einen Preis kommen; (*agree on*) sich auf einen Preis einigen.
(b) (*inf: succeed*) **then you know you've really ~d** dann weiß man, daß man es geschafft hat.

arriviste [,æriː'viːst] *n* Emporkömmling, Parvenü (*geh*) *m*.

arrogance ['ærəgəns] *n* Arroganz, Überheblichkeit *f*.

arrogant *adj*, **~ly** *adv* ['ærəgənt, -lɪ] arrogant, überheblich.

arrogate ['ærəʊgeɪt] *vt* **to ~ sth to oneself** etw für sich in Anspruch nehmen; *title* sich (*dat*) etw anmaßen.

arrow ['ærəʊ] [1] *n* (*weapon, sign*) Pfeil *m*.
[2] *vt way, direction* durch Pfeile/einen Pfeil markieren.

◆**arrow in** *vt sep* (*in text*) durch Pfeil einzeichnen.

arrow: ~ bracket *n* spitze Klammer; **~head** *n* Pfeilspitze *f*; **~ key** *n* (*Comput*) Pfeiltaste *f*; **~root** *n* (*plant*) Pfeilwurz *f*; (*flour*) Arrowroot *nt*.

arse [ɑːs] *n* **(a)** (*sl*) Arsch *m* (*sl*) ◆ **move** *or* **shift your ~!** sei nicht so lahmarschig! (*sl*); **get your ~ in gear!** setz mal deinen Arsch in Bewegung! (*sl*); **tell him to get his ~ into my office** sag ihm, er soll mal in meinem Büro antanzen (*inf*); **get your ~ out of here!** verpiß dich hier! (*sl*); **contribution? my ~!** Beitrag? das soll wohl ein Witz sein! (*inf*).
(b) (*sl: fool: also* **silly ~**) Armleuchter *m* (*inf*).

◆**arse about** *or* **around** *vi* (*sl*) rumblödeln (*inf*).

arse: ~hole *n* (*vulg*) Arschloch *nt* (*vulg*); **~licker** *n* (*vulg*) Arschlecker *m* (*vulg*).

arsenal ['ɑːsɪnl] *n* (*Mil*) (*store*) Arsenal, Zeughaus (*old*) *nt*; (*factory*) Waffen-/Munitionsfabrik *f*; (*fig*) Waffenlager *nt*.

arsenic ['ɑːsnɪk] *n* Arsen, Arsenik *nt* ◆ **~ poisoning** Arsenvergiftung *f*.

arson ['ɑːsn] *n* Brandstiftung *f*.

arsonist ['ɑːsənɪst] *n* Brandstifter(in *f*) *m*.

art[1] [ɑːt] [1] *n* **(a)** (*painting etc*) Kunst *f* ◆ **the ~s** die schönen Künste; **~ for ~'s sake** Kunst um der Kunst willen, Kunst als Selbstzweck; (*slogan*) L'art pour l'art; *see* **work**.
(b) (*skill*) Kunst *f*; (*physical technique also*) Geschick *nt* ◆ **there's an ~ to driving this car** es gehört ein gewisses Geschick dazu, mit diesem Auto zu fahren; **there's an ~ to it** das ist eine Kunst; **the ~ of war/government** die Kriegs-/Staatskunst; **the ~ of conversation/translation** die Kunst der Unterhaltung/Übersetzung; **~s and crafts** Kunsthandwerk, Kunstgewerbe *nt*.
(c) (*human endeavour*) Künstlichkeit *f* ◆ **unspoiled by ~** unverbildet; **are they the products of ~ or nature?** sind sie natürlich oder von Menschenhand geschaffen?; **her beauty owes more to ~ than nature** sie verdankt ihre Schönheit mehr der Kunst als der Natur.
(d) ~s (*Univ*) Geisteswissenschaften *pl* ◆ **A~s Council** Kulturausschuß *m der britischen Regierung*; **~s degree** Abschlußexamen *nt* der philosophischen Fakultät; **A~s Faculty, Faculty of A~s** Philosophische Fakultät; **A~s minister** Kulturminister *m*; **~s subject** geisteswissenschaftliches Fach; *see* **bachelor, liberal**.
(e) (*usu pl: trick*) List *f*, Kunstgriff *m*.
[2] *adj attr* Kunst-.

art[2] (*old*) *2nd pers sing present of* **be**.

art college *n see* **art school**.

Art Deco ['ɑːt'dekəʊ] [1] *n* Art deco *f*.
[2] *adj attr* Art-deco-.

artefact (*Brit*), **artifact** ['ɑːtɪfækt] *n* Artefakt *nt* ◆ **are these human ~s?** sind das Schöpfungen von Menschenhand?

arterial [ɑː'tɪərɪəl] *adj* **(a)** (*Anat*) arteriell. **(b) ~ road** (*Aut*) Fernverkehrsstraße *f*; **~ line** (*Rail*) Hauptstrecke *f*.

arteriosclerosis [ɑː'tɪərɪəʊsklɪ'rəʊsɪs] *n* (*Med*) Arteriosklerose, Arterienverkalkung *f*.

artery ['ɑːtərɪ] *n* **(a)** (*Anat*) Arterie *f*, Schlag- *or* Pulsader *f*. **(b)** (*also* **traffic ~**) Verkehrsader *f*.

Artesian well [ɑː'tiːzɪən'wel] *n* artesischer Brunnen.

art form *n* (Kunst)gattung *or* -form *f*.

artful ['ɑːtfʊl] *adj person, trick* raffiniert, schlau ◆ **~ dodger** Schlawiner *m* (*inf*).

artfully ['ɑːtfəlɪ] *adv* raffiniert.

artfulness ['ɑːtfʊlnɪs] *n* Raffinesse *f*.

art gallery *n* Kunstgalerie *f*.

art-house ['ɑːt,haʊs] *adj attr film* Experimental- ◆ **~ cinema** ≃ Filmkunsttheater *nt*.

arthritic [ɑː'θrɪtɪk] *adj* arthritisch ◆ **she is ~** sie hat Arthritis.

arthritis [ɑː'θraɪtɪs] *n* Arthritis, Gelenkentzündung *f*.

arthropod ['ɑːθrə'pɒd] *n* Gliederfüßer *m* ◆ **the ~s** die Arthropoden *pl*.

Arthur ['ɑːθə^r] *n* Art(h)ur *m* ◆ **King ~** König Artus.

Arthurian [ɑː'θjʊərɪən] *adj* Artus-.

artic [ɑː'tɪk] *n* (*Brit sl*) (Sattel)schlepper *m*.

artichoke ['ɑːtɪtʃəʊk] *n* Artischocke *f*; *see* **Jerusalem**.

article ['ɑːtɪkl] [1] *n* **(a)** (*item*) Gegenstand *m*; (*in list*) Posten *m*; (*Comm*) Ware *f*, Artikel *m* ◆ **~ of value** Wertgegenstand *m*; **~ of furniture** Möbelstück *nt*; **~s of clothing** Kleidungsstücke *pl*; **toilet ~s** Toilettenartikel *pl*; *see* **genuine**.
(b) (*in newspaper etc*) Artikel, Beitrag *m*; (*encyclopedia entry*) Eintrag *m*.
(c) (*of constitution*) Artikel *m*; (*of treaty, contract*) Paragraph *m* ◆ **~s of association** Gesellschaftsvertrag *m*; **~s of apprenticeship** Lehrvertrag *m*; **~ of faith** Glaubensartikel *m*; (*fig*) Kredo *nt*; **~s of war** (*Hist*) Kriegsartikel *pl*.
(d) (*Gram*) Artikel *m*, Geschlechtswort *nt* ◆ **definite/indefinite ~** bestimmter/unbestimmter Artikel.
(e) (*of articled clerk*) **to be under ~s** (Rechts)referendar sein; **to take one's ~s** seine Referendarprüfung machen.
[2] *vt apprentice* in die Lehre geben (*to* bei) ◆ **to be ~d to sb** bei jdm eine Lehre machen, bei jdm in die Lehre gehen; **~d clerk** (*Brit Jur*) Rechtsreferendar(in *f*) *m*.

articulate [ɑː'tɪkjʊlɪt] [1] *adj* **(a)** *sentence, book* klar ◆ **to be ~** sich gut *or* klar ausdrücken können; **clear and ~** klar und deutlich; **that is amazingly ~ for a five-year old** das ist erstaunlich gut ausgedrückt für einen Fünfjährigen. **(b)** (*Anat*) gegliedert; *limb* Glieder-.
[2] [ɑː'tɪkjʊleɪt] *vt* **(a)** (*pronounce*) artikulieren. **(b)** (*state*) *reasons, views etc* darlegen. **(c)** (*Anat*) **to be ~d** zusammenhängen (*to, with* mit); **~d lorry** *or* **truck** Sattelschlepper *m*; **~d bus** Gelenk(omni)bus, Großraumbus *m*.
[3] [ɑː'tɪkjʊleɪt] *vi* artikulieren.

articulately [ɑː'tɪkjʊlɪtlɪ] *adv pronounce* artikuliert; *write, express oneself* klar, flüssig ◆ **an ~ presented argument** eine klar verständlich vorgetragene These.

articulateness [ɑː'tɪkjʊlɪtnɪs] *n* Fähigkeit *f*, sich gut auszudrücken.

articulation [ɑː,tɪkjʊ'leɪʃən] *n* **(a)** Artikulation *f*. **(b)** (*Anat*) Gelenkverbindung *f*.

articulatory [ɑː'tɪkjʊlə,tərɪ] *adj* (*Phon*) Artikulations-.

artifact *n see* **artefact**.

artifice ['ɑːtɪfɪs] *n* **(a)** (*guile*) List *f no pl*. **(b)** (*stratagem*) (Kriegs)list *f*.

artificial [,ɑːtɪ'fɪʃəl] *adj* **(a)** (*synthetic*) künstlich ◆ **~ manure** Kunstdünger *m*; **~ hair** Kunsthaar *nt*; **~ limb** Prothese *f*, Kunstglied *nt*.
(b) (*fig*) (*not genuine*) künstlich; (*pej: not sincere*) *smile, manner* gekünstelt, unecht ◆ **you're so ~** du bist nicht echt; **if you say it that way it sounds ~** wenn du es so sagst, klingt das unecht; **roses can be so ~** Rosen können so etwas Künstliches *or* Artifizielles (*geh*) haben.

artificial: ~ horizon *n* künstlicher Horizont; **~ insemination** *n* künstliche Befruchtung; **~ intelligence** *n* künstliche Intelligenz.

artificiality [,ɑːtɪfɪʃɪ'ælɪtɪ] *n* **(a)** Künstlichkeit *f*. **(b)** (*insincerity, unnaturalness*) Gekünsteltheit *f*.

artificially [,ɑːtɪ'fɪʃəlɪ] *adv* künstlich; (*insincerely*) gekünstelt.

artificial: ~ respiration *n* künstliche Beatmung *f*; **~ silk** *n* Kunstseide *f*.

artillery [ɑː'tɪlərɪ] *n* (*weapons, troops*) Artillerie *f*.

artilleryman [ɑː'tɪlərɪmən] *n*, *pl* **-men** [-mən] Artillerist *m*.

artisan ['ɑːtɪzæn] *n* Handwerker *m*.

artist ['ɑːtɪst] *n* Künstler(in *f*) *m*; (*fig also*) Könner *m* ◆ **an ~ in words** ein Wortkünstler *m*; **~'s impression** Zeichnung *f*; (*of sth planned also*) Entwurf(zeichnung *f*) *m*.

artiste [ɑː'tiːst] *n* Künstler(in *f*) *m*; (*circus ~*) Artist(in *f*) *m* ◆ **~'s entrance** Bühneneingang *m*.

artistic [ɑː'tɪstɪk] *adj* künstlerisch; (*tasteful*) *arrangements* kunstvoll; (*appreciative of art*) *person* kunstverständig *or* -sinnig (*geh*) ◆ **the café has an ~ clientele** in dem Café verkehren Künstler; **~ temperament** Künstlertemperament *nt*; **an ~ life** ein Künstlerleben *nt*; **to look ~** wie ein Künstler aussehen; **she's very ~** sie ist künstlerisch veranlagt *or* begabt/sehr kunstverständig.

artistically [ɑː'tɪstɪkəlɪ] *adv* künstlerisch; (*tastefully*) kunstvoll.

artistry ['ɑːtɪstrɪ] *n* (*lit, fig*) Kunst *f*.

artless *adj*, **~ly** *adv* ['ɑːtlɪs, -lɪ] unschuldig.

artlessness ['ɑːtlɪsnɪs] *n* Unschuld *f*.

art lover *n* Kunstliebhaber(in *f*) *or* -freund *m*.

Art Nouveau ['ɑːnuː'vəʊ] [1] *n* Jugendstil *m*.
[2] *adj attr* Jugendstil-.

art: ~ paper *n* Kunstdruckpapier *nt*; **~ school** *n* Kunstakademie *or* -hochschule *f*; **~ student** *n* Kunststudent(in *f*) *m*; **~work** *n* **(a)** (*in book*) Bildmaterial *nt*; **this will have to be done as ~work** das muß grafisch ge-

➤ LANGUAGE IN USE: **arrive: a** → 21.4, 25.2

staltet werden; **(b)** *(for advert etc, material ready for printing)* Druckvorlage *f.*

arty ['ɑːtɪ] *adj (+er) (inf)* Künstler-; *type also, tie, clothes* verrückt *(inf)*; *person* auf Künstler machend *(pej)*; *decoration, style* auf Kunst gemacht *(inf)*; *film, novel* geschmäcklerisch ◆ **he was more of an ~ type than his brother** er war mehr ein Künstlertyp als sein Bruder; **she's in publishing/the theatre — oh yes, I knew it was something ~** sie arbeitet im Verlag/Theater — ach ja, ich wußte doch, daß es etwas Geistiges/Künstlerisches war.

arty-crafty ['ɑːtɪ'krɑːftɪ], *(US)* **artsy-craftsy** ['ɑːtsiː'krɑːftsiː] *adj (inf)* **(a)** *see* **arty.** **(b)** *object* kunstgewerblerisch.

arty-farty ['ɑːtɪ'fɑːtɪ] *adj (hum inf) see* **arty.**

Aryan ['ɛərɪən] [1] *n* Arier(in *f*) *m.*
[2] *adj* arisch.

▼ **as** [æz, əz] [1] *conj* **(a)** *(when, while)* als; *(two parallel actions)* während, als, indem *(geh)* ◆ **he got deafer ~ he got older** mit zunehmendem Alter nahm seine Schwerhörigkeit zu; **~ a child he would** ... als Kind hat er immer ...
▼ **(b)** *(since)* da.
(c) *(although)* **rich ~ he is I won't marry him** obwohl er reich ist, werde ich ihn nicht heiraten; **stupid ~ he is, he** ... so dumm er auch sein mag, ... er; **big ~ he is I'll** ... so groß, wie er ist, ich ...; **much ~ I admire her,** ... so sehr ich sie auch bewundere, ...; **be that ~ it may** wie dem auch sei *or* sein mag; **try ~ he might** so sehr er sich auch bemüht/bemühte.
▼ **(d)** *(manner)* wie ◆ **do ~ you like** machen Sie, was Sie wollen; **leave it ~ it is** laß das so; **I did it ~ he did** ich habe es wie er gemacht; **the first door ~ you go upstairs/ ~ you go in** die erste Tür oben/, wenn Sie hereinkommen; **knowing him ~ I do** so wie ich ihn kenne; **~ you yourself said** ... wie Sie selbst gesagt haben ...; **he drinks enough ~ it is** er trinkt sowieso schon genug; **it is bad enough ~ it is** es ist schon schlimm genug; **~ it is, I'm heavily in debt** ich bin schon tief verschuldet; **~ it were** sozusagen, gleichsam; **~ you were!** *(Mil)* weitermachen!; *(fig)* lassen Sie sich nicht stören; *(in dictation, speaking)* streichen Sie das; **my husband ~ was** *(inf)* mein verflossener *or (late)* verstorbener Mann.
(e) *(phrases)* **~ if** *or* **though** als ob, wie wenn; **he rose ~ if to go** er erhob sich, als wollte er gehen; **it isn't ~ if he didn't see me** schließlich hat er mich ja gesehen; **~ for him/you** (und) was ihn/dich anbetrifft *or* angeht; **~ from** *or* **of the 5th/now** vom Fünften an/von jetzt an, ab dem Fünften/jetzt; **so ~ to** *(in order to)* um zu *+infin*; *(in such a way)* so, daß; **be so good ~ to** ... *(form)* hätten Sie die Freundlichkeit *or* Güte, ... zu ... *(form)*; **he's not so silly ~ to do that** er ist nicht so dumm, das zu tun, so dumm ist er nicht.
▼ [2] *adv* **~ ... ~** so ... wie; **not ~ ... ~** nicht so ... wie; **twice ~ old** doppelt so alt; **just ~ nice** genauso nett; **late ~ usual!** wie immer, zu spät!; **is it ~ difficult ~ that?** ist das denn so schwierig?; **if he eats ~ quickly ~ that** wenn er so schnell ißt; **it is not ~ good ~ all that** so gut ist es auch wieder nicht; **you hate it ~ much ~ I do** du magst das doch genausowenig wie ich; **~ recently ~ yesterday** erst gestern; **she is very clever, ~ is her brother** sie ist sehr intelligent, genau(so) wie ihr Bruder; **she was ~ nice ~ could be** *(inf)* sie war so freundlich wie nur was *(inf)*; **~ many/much ~ I could** so viele/soviel ich (nur) konnte; **there were ~ many ~ 100** es waren mindestens *or* bestimmt 100 da; **this one is ~ good** diese(r, s) ist genauso gut; **~ often happens, he was** ... wie so oft, war er ...
[3] *rel pron* **(a)** *(with same, such)* der/die/das; *pl* die ◆ **the same man ~ was here yesterday** derselbe Mann, der gestern hier war; *see* **such.** **(b)** *(dial)* der/die/das; *pl* die ◆ **those ~ knew him** die ihn kannten.
[4] *prep* **(a)** *(in the capacity of)* als ◆ **to treat sb ~ a child** jdn als Kind *or* wie ein Kind behandeln; **he appeared ~ three different characters** er trat in drei verschiedenen Rollen auf. **(b)** *(esp: such as)* wie, zum Beispiel ◆ **animals such ~ cats and dogs** Tiere wie (zum Beispiel) Katzen und Hunde.

asap ['eɪzæp] *abbr of* **as soon as possible** baldmöglichst, baldmögl.

asbestos [æz'bestəs] *n* Asbest *m.*

asbestosis [,æzbes'təʊsɪs] *n (Med)* Asbestose, Asbeststaublunge *f.*

ascend [ə'send] [1] *vi (rise)* aufsteigen; *(Christ)* auffahren; *(slope upwards)* ansteigen *(to* auf *+acc)* ◆ **in ~ing order** in aufsteigender Reihenfolge.
[2] *vt stairs* hinaufsteigen; *mountain, heights of knowledge* erklimmen *(geh)*; *throne* besteigen ◆ **to ~ the scale** *(Mus)* die Tonleiter aufwärts singen.

ascendancy, ascendency [ə'sendənsɪ] *n* Vormachtstellung *f* ◆ **to gain/have (the) ~ over sb** die Vorherrschaft über jdn gewinnen/haben; **to gain (the) ~ over one's fears/interviewer** die Oberhand über seine Ängste/jdn, der einen befragt, gewinnen.

ascendant, ascendent [ə'sendənt] *n* **to be in the ~** *(Astrol)* im Aszendenten stehen, aszendieren *(spec)*; *(fig)* im Aufstieg begriffen sein; **his star is in the ~** *(fig)* sein Stern ist im Aufgehen.

ascender [ə'sendəʳ] *n (Typ)* Oberlänge *f.*

ascension [ə'senʃən] *n* **the ~** (Christi) Himmelfahrt *f*; **~ Day** Himmelfahrt (stag *m*) *nt.*

ascent [ə'sent] *n* Aufstieg *m* ◆ **the ~ of Ben Nevis** der Aufstieg auf den Ben Nevis; **it was his first ~ in an aeroplane** er ist das erstemal in einem Flugzeug geflogen.

ascertain [,æsə'teɪn] *vt* ermitteln, feststellen.

ascertainable [,æsə'teɪnəbl] *adj* feststellbar ◆ **~ quantities** nachweisbare Mengen.

ascetic [ə'setɪk] [1] *adj* asketisch.
[2] *n* Asket *m* ◆ **she's something of an ~** sie lebt ziemlich asketisch.

asceticism [ə'setɪsɪzəm] *n* Askese *f* ◆ **a life of ~** ein Leben in Askese.

ASCII ['æskiː] *abbr of* **American Standard Code for Information Interchange** ◆ **~ file** ASCII-Datei *f.*

ascorbic acid [ə'skɔːbɪk'æsɪd] *n* Askorbinsäure *f.*

ascribable [ə'skraɪbəbl] *adj* **to be ~ to sth** einer Sache *(dat)* zuzuschreiben sein.

ascribe [ə'skraɪb] *vt* zuschreiben *(sth to sb* jdm etw); *importance, weight* beimessen *(to sth* einer Sache *dat).*

ascription [ə'skrɪpʃən] *n* Zuschreibung *f* ◆ **difficulties arising from the ~ of emotions to animals** Schwierigkeiten, die sich ergeben, wenn man Tieren Gefühle zuschreibt.

asdic ['æzdɪk] *n* Echo(tiefen)lot *nt.*

aseptic [eɪ'septɪk] *adj* aseptisch, keimfrei; *(fig) atmosphere* steril, klinisch.

asexual [eɪ'seksjʊəl] *adj* ungeschlechtlich, geschlechtslos; *person* asexuell; *reproduction* ungeschlechtlich.

ash¹ [æʃ] *n (also* **~ tree)** Esche *f.*

ash² *n* **(a)** Asche *f* ◆ **~es** Asche *f*; **to reduce sth to ~es** etw total *or* völlig niederbrennen; *(in war etc)* etw in Schutt und Asche legen; **to rise from the ~es** *(fig)* aus den Trümmern wieder auferstehen; **~es to ~es** Erde zu Erde; *see* **sackcloth.**
(b) **~es** *pl (of the dead)* Asche *f.*
(c) *(Cricket)* **the A~es** *Testmatch zwischen Australien und England.*

ashamed [ə'ʃeɪmd] *adj* beschämt ◆ **to be** *or* **feel ~ (of sb/sth)** sich schämen (für jdn/etw, jds/einer Sache *geh*); **it's nothing to be ~ of** deswegen braucht man sich nicht zu genieren *or* schämen; **I felt ~ for him** ich habe mich für ihn geschämt; **he is ~ to do it** es ist ihm peinlich, das zu tun, er schämt sich, das zu tun; ... **I'm ~ to say** ..., muß ich leider zugeben; **you ought to be ~ (of yourself)** du solltest dich (was) schämen!, schäm dich!; **you may well look ~** schäm dich ruhig!

A shares ['eɪʃɛəz] *npl* stimmrechtslose Aktien *pl.*

ash: ~ bin *n* Asch(en)eimer *m*, Aschentonne *f*; **~ blonde** *adj* aschblond; **~can** *n (US) see* **~ bin.**

ashen ['æʃn] *adj colour* aschgrau, aschfarbig; *face* aschfahl *(geh)*, kreidebleich.

ashen-faced [,æʃn'feɪst] *adj* kreidebleich.

ashlar ['æʃləʳ] *n* Quaderstein *m.*

ashore [ə'ʃɔːʳ] *adv* an Land ◆ **to run ~** stranden, auf den Strand auflaufen; **to put ~** an Land gehen.

ash: ~pan *n* Aschenkasten *m*; **~tray** *n* Aschenbecher *m*; **A~ Wednesday** *n* Aschermittwoch *m.*

ashy ['æʃɪ] *adj* **(a)** *see* **ashen.** **(b)** *(covered with ashes)* mit Asche bedeckt.

Asia ['eɪʃə] *n* Asien *nt* ◆ **~ Minor** Kleinasien *nt.*

Asian ['eɪʃn], **Asiatic** [,eɪʃɪ'ætɪk] [1] *adj* asiatisch ◆ **Asian flu** asiatische Grippe.
[2] *n* Asiat(in *f*) *m.*

A-side *n (of record)* A-Seite *f.*

aside [ə'saɪd] [1] *adv* **(a)** *(with verbal element)* zur Seite, beiseite ◆ **to keep sth ~ for sb** für jdn etw beiseite legen; **to turn ~** sich zur Seite drehen, sich abwenden *(esp fig).*
(b) *(Theat etc)* beiseite.
(c) *(esp US)* **~ from** außer; **~ from demanding an extra 10%** ... außer einer Zusatzforderung von 10% ...; **~ from being chairman of this committee he is** ... außer Vorsitzender dieses Ausschusses ist er auch ...; **this criticism, ~ from being wrong, is** ... diese Kritik ist nicht nur falsch, sondern ...
[2] *n (Theat)* Aparte *nt (rare)* ◆ **to say sth in an ~** etw beiseite sprechen; **there are too many ~s to the audience** es wird zuviel zum Publikum gesprochen.

asinine ['æsɪnaɪn] *adj* idiotisch ◆ **what an ~ thing to do!** wie kann man bloß so ein Esel sein!

▼ **ask** [ɑːsk] [1] *vt* **(a)** *(inquire)* fragen; *question* stellen ◆ **to ~ sb the way/the time/his opinion** jdn nach dem Weg/der Uhrzeit/seiner Meinung fragen; **to ~ if** ... (nach)fragen, ob ...; **he ~ed me where I'd been** er fragte mich, wo ich gewesen sei *or* wäre *(inf)* *or* bin *(inf)*; **if you ~ me** wenn du mich fragst; **don't ~ me!** *(inf)*, **~ me another!** *(inf)* frag mich nicht, was weiß ich! *(inf)*; **I ~ you!** *(inf)* ich muß schon sagen!
(b) *(invite)* einladen; *(in dancing)* auffordern ◆ **to ~ sb for** *or* **to lunch** jdn zum (Mittag)essen einladen.
▼ **(c)** *(request)* bitten *(sb for sth* jdn um etw); *(require, demand)* verlangen *(sth of sb* etw von jdm) ◆ **to ~ sb to do sth** jdn darum bitten, etw zu tun; **are you ~ing me to believe that?** und das soll ich glauben?; **all I ~ is** ... ich will ja nur ...; **you don't ~ for much, do you?** *(iro)* sonst noch was? *(iro)*, sonst *or* weiter nichts? *(iro)*; **could I ~ your advice?** darf ich Sie um Rat bitten?; **he ~ed to be excused** er bat, ihn zu entschuldigen, er entschuldigte sich; **that's ~ing the impossible** das ist ein Ding der Unmöglichkeit; **he ~s too much of me** er verlangt zuviel von mir; **that's ~ing too much** das ist zuviel verlangt.
(d) *(Comm) price* verlangen, fordern ◆ **~ing price** Verkaufspreis *m*; *(for car, house etc also)* Verhandlungsbasis *f*; **what's your ~ing price?** was verlangen Sie (dafür)?
[2] *vi* **(a)** *(inquire)* fragen ◆ **to ~ about sb/sth** sich nach jdm/etw erkundigen; **~ away!** frag nur!; **I only ~ed** ich habe doch nur gefragt; **and what does that mean, may I ~?** und was soll das bedeuten, wenn ich mal fragen darf?; **well may you ~** das fragt man sich mit Recht.
(b) *(request)* bitten *(for sth* um etw) ◆ **you just have to ~** du mußt nur was sagen *(inf)*, du brauchst nur zu fragen; **I'm not ~ing for sympathy** ich will kein Mitleid; **there's no harm in ~ing** Fragen kostet nichts!; **it's yours for the ~ing** du kannst es haben; **you are ~ing for trouble** du willst wohl Ärger haben; **if you ... you're ~ing for trouble** wenn du ..., dann kriegst du Ärger; **that's ~ing for trouble** das kann ja nicht gutgehen; **you ~ed for it** *(inf)* du hast es ja so gewollt; **he's ~ing for it** *(inf)* er will es ja so, er will es ja nicht anders; **to ~ for Mr X** Herrn X verlangen; **she was ~ing for you** *(Scot)* sie hat sich nach dir erkundigt; **to ~ for sth back** etw wiederhaben wollen.

◆**ask after** *vi +prep obj* sich erkundigen nach ◆ **tell her I was ~ing ~ her** grüß sie schön von mir.
◆**ask around** [1] *vi* herumfragen.
[2] *vt sep* (*invite*) einladen.
◆**ask back** *vt sep* (**a**) (*invite*) zu sich einladen ◆ **he ~ed us ~ for a drink** er lud uns zu sich auf einen Drink ein. (**b**) **they never ~ed me ~ again** sie haben mich nie wieder eingeladen. (**c**) **let me ~ you something ~** lassen Sie mich eine Gegenfrage stellen.
◆**ask in** *vt sep* (*to house*) hereinbitten ◆ **she ~ed her boyfriend ~** sie hat ihren Freund mit reingenommen.
◆**ask out** *vt sep* einladen.
◆**ask up** *vt sep* heraufbitten; *boyfriend* mit raufnehmen.
askance [ə'skɑ:ns] *adv* **to look ~ at sb** jdn entsetzt ansehen; **to look ~ at a suggestion/sb's methods** *etc* über einen Vorschlag/jds Methoden *etc* die Nase rümpfen.
askew [ə'skju:] *adv* schief.
aslant [ə'slɑ:nt] (*liter*) [1] *adv* quer, schräg.
[2] *prep* quer *or* schräg über.
asleep [ə'sli:p] *adj pred* (**a**) (*sleeping*) schlafend ◆ **to be (fast** *or* **sound) ~** (fest) schlafen; **he was sitting there, ~** er saß da und schlief; **to fall ~** einschlafen (*also euph*); **to lie ~** schlafen; **he is not dead, only ~** er ist nicht tot, er schläft nur *or* liegt nur im Schlaf (*geh*). (**b**) (*inf: numb*) eingeschlafen.
ASLEF ['æzlef] (*Brit*) *abbr of* **Associated Society of Locomotive Engineers and Firemen** *Eisenbahnergewerkschaft f.*
asocial [eɪ'səʊʃəl] *adj* ungesellig.
asp [æsp] *n* (*Zool*) Natter *f.*
asparagus [əs'pærəgəs] *n, no pl* Spargel *m* ◆ **~ tips** Spargelspitzen *pl*; **~ fern** Spargelkraut *nt*, Asparagus *m.*
aspect ['æspekt] *n* (**a**) (*liter: appearance*) Anblick *m*, Erscheinung *f*; (*face also*) Antlitz *nt* (*geh*); (*of thing*) Aussehen *nt.* (**b**) (*of question, subject etc*) Aspekt *m*, Seite *f* ◆ **under the ~ of town planning** aus stadtplanerischer Sicht; **the political ~ of his novel** der politische Aspekt seines Romans; **what about the security/heating ~?** was ist mit der Sicherheit/Heizung?, und die Sicherheits-/Heizungsfrage? (*inf*). (**c**) (*of building*) **to have a southerly ~** Südlage haben. (**d**) (*Gram*) Aspekt *m.*
aspectual [æ'spektjʊəl] *adj* (*Gram*) im Aspekt.
aspen ['æspən] *n* (*Bot*) Espe, Zitterpappel *f* ◆ **to tremble like an ~** (*liter*) zittern wie Espenlaub.
aspergillum [ˌæspə'dʒɪləm] *n* Weih(wasser)wedel *m.*
asperity [æs'perɪtɪ] *n* Schroffheit, Schärfe *f no pl* ◆ **the asperities of the winter** (*liter*) der rauhe Winter (*geh*).
aspersion [əs'pɜ:ʃən] *n*: **to cast ~s upon sb/sth** abfällige Bemerkungen über jdn/etw machen; **without wishing to cast any ~s** ohne mich abfällig äußern zu wollen.
asphalt ['æsfælt] [1] *n* Asphalt *m.*
[2] *vt* asphaltieren.
[3] *adj attr* Asphalt-, asphaltiert ◆ **~ jungle** Asphaltdschungel *m.*
asphodel ['æsfəˌdel] *n* Asphodelus, Affodill *m.*
asphyxia [æs'fɪksɪə] *n* Erstickung, Asphyxie (*spec*) *f.*
asphyxiate [æs'fɪksɪeɪt] *vti* ersticken ◆ **to be ~d** ersticken.
asphyxiation [æsˌfɪksɪ'eɪʃən] *n* Erstickung *f.*
aspic ['æspɪk] *n* (*Cook*) Aspik *m or nt*, Gelee *nt.*
aspidistra [ˌæspɪ'dɪstrə] *n* Aspidistra *f.*
aspirant ['æspɪrənt] *n* Anwärter(in *f*) *m* (*to, for* auf *+acc*); (*for job*) Kandidat(in *f*) (für), Aspirant(in *f*) (*hum*) *m*; (*for sb's hand in marriage*) Bewerber *m* (um) ◆ **~ to the throne** Thronanwärter(in *f*) *m.*
aspirate ['æspərɪt] [1] *n* Aspirata *f* (*spec*), Hauchlaut *m.*
[2] *vt* ['æspəreɪt] aspirieren, behauchen.
aspiration [ˌæspə'reɪʃən] *n* (**a**) (hohes) Ziel, Aspiration *f* (*geh*) ◆ **his ~ towards Lady Sarah's hand** (*liter*) seine Hoffnung auf Lady Sarahs Hand. (**b**) (*Phon*) Aspiration, Behauchung *f.*
aspirational [ˌæspə'reɪʃənəl] *adj person* auf sozialen Aufstieg bedacht; *product* den sozialen Aufstieg verkörpernd.
aspire [ə'spaɪəʳ] *vi* **to ~ to sth** nach etw streben, etw erstreben; **to ~ to do sth** danach streben, etw zu tun.
aspirin ['æsprɪn] *n* Kopfschmerztablette *f*, Aspirin ® *nt.*
aspiring [ə'spaɪərɪŋ] *adj* aufstrebend.
ass[1] [æs] *n* (*lit, fig inf*) Esel *m* ◆ **silly ~!** blöder Esel!; **don't be an ~!** sei kein Esel!, sei nicht blöd!; **to make an ~ of oneself** sich lächerlich machen, sich blamieren.
ass[2] *n* (*US sl*) **a nice piece of ~** ein dufter Arsch (*sl*); **he was looking for a piece of ~** er wollte eine Frau aufreißen (*sl*); **this place is just full of ~** hier laufen unwahrscheinlich viele Miezen rum (*inf*); **to kick ~** (*get tough*) mit der Faust auf den Tisch hauen (*inf*); *see also* **arse**.
assagai *n see* **assegai**.
assail [ə'seɪl] *vt* (*lit, fig*) angreifen; (*fig: with questions etc*) überschütten, bombardieren ◆ **a harsh sound ~ed my ears** ein scharfes Geräusch drang an mein Ohr; **to be ~ed by doubts** von Zweifeln befallen sein *or* geplagt werden.
assailant [ə'seɪlənt] *n* Angreifer(in *f*) *m.*
assassin [ə'sæsɪn] *n* Attentäter(in *f*), Mörder(in *f*) *m.*
assassinate [ə'sæsɪneɪt] *vt* ein Attentat *or* einen Mordanschlag verüben auf (*+acc*) ◆ **JFK was ~d in Dallas** JFK fiel in Dallas einem Attentat *or* Mordanschlag zum Opfer, JFK wurde in Dallas ermordet; **they ~d him** sie haben ihn ermordet.

➤ LANGUAGE IN USE: **assertion: a → 26.1**

assassination [əˌsæsɪ'neɪʃən] *n* (geglücktes) Attentat, (geglückter) Mordanschlag (*of* auf *+acc*) ◆ **~ attempt** Attentat *nt*; **to plan an ~** ein Attentat planen; **before/after the ~** vor dem Attentat/nach dem (geglückten) Attentat.
assault [ə'sɔ:lt] [1] *n* (**a**) (*Mil*) Sturm(angriff) *m* (*on* auf *+acc*); (*fig*) Angriff *m* (*on* gegen) ◆ **to make an ~ on sth** einen (Sturm)angriff gegen etw führen; **to take sth by ~** etw im Sturm nehmen, etw erstürmen.
(**b**) (*Jur*) Körperverletzung *f* ◆ **~ and battery** Körperverletzung *f*; **indecent/sexual ~** Notzucht *f.*
[2] *vt* (**a**) (*Jur: attack*) tätlich werden gegen; (*sexually*) herfallen über (*+acc*); (*rape*) sich vergehen an (*+dat*) ◆ **to ~ sb with a stick** jdn mit einem Stock angreifen. (**b**) (*Mil*) angreifen.
assault: ~ course *n* Übungsgelände *nt*; **getting to the bathroom is like an ~ course** der Weg zum Badezimmer ist ein wahres Hindernisrennen; **~ craft** *n* Sturmlandefahrzeug *nt*; **~ troops** *npl* Sturmtruppen *pl.*
assay [ə'seɪ] [1] *n* Prüfung *f* ◆ **~ mark** Prüfzeichen *nt.*
[2] *vt* (**a**) *mineral, ore,* (*fig*) *value, sb's worth* prüfen. (**b**) (*liter*) (*try*) sich versuchen an (*+dat*); (*put to the test*) *troops* prüfen.
assegai ['æsəˌgaɪ] *n* Assagai *m.*
assemblage [ə'semblɪdʒ] *n* (**a**) (*assembling*) Zusammensetzen *nt*, Zusammenbau *m*; (*of car, machine also*) Montage *f.* (**b**) (*collection*) (*of things*) Sammlung *f*; (*of facts*) Anhäufung *f*; (*of people*) Versammlung *f.*
assemble [ə'sembl] [1] *vt* zusammensetzen, zusammenbauen; *car, machine etc also* montieren; *facts* zusammentragen; *Parliament* einberufen, versammeln; *people* zusammenrufen; *team* zusammenstellen.
[2] *vi* sich versammeln ◆ **we are ~d here today to ...** wir haben uns *or* sind heute versammelt, um ...
assembler [ə'sembləʳ] *n* (*Comput*) Assembler *m.*
assembly [ə'semblɪ] *n* (**a**) (*gathering of people, Parl*) Versammlung *f* ◆ **to meet in open ~** sich öffentlich versammeln. (**b**) (*Sch*) Morgenandacht *f*; *tägliche Versammlung.* (**c**) (*putting together*) Zusammensetzen *nt*, Zusammenbau *m*; (*of machine, cars also*) Montage *f*; (*of facts*) Zusammentragen *nt.* (**d**) (*thing assembled*) Konstruktion *f.*
assembly: ~ hall *n* (*Sch*) Aula *f*; **~ language** *n* (*Comput*) Assemblersprache *f*; **~ line** *n* Montageband *nt*; **~man** *pl* **-men** *n* (*US*) Abgeordnete(r) *m*; **~ plant** *n* Montagewerk *nt*; **~ point** *n* Sammelplatz *m*; **~ shop** *n* Montagehalle *f*; **~woman** *pl* **-women** *n* (*US*) Abgeordnete *f*; **~ worker** *n* Montagearbeiter(in *f*) *m.*
assent [ə'sent] [1] *n* Zustimmung *f* ◆ **to give one's ~ to sth** seine Zustimmung zu etw geben; **by common ~** mit allgemeiner Zustimmung; **royal ~** königliche Genehmigung.
[2] *vi* zustimmen ◆ **to ~ to sth** einer Sache (*dat*) zustimmen.
assert [ə'sɜ:t] *vt* (**a**) (*declare*) behaupten; *one's innocence* beteuern.
(**b**) (*insist on*) **to ~ one's authority** seine Autorität geltend machen; **to ~ one's rights** sein Recht behaupten; **to ~ oneself** sich behaupten *or* durchsetzen (*over* gegenüber); **if you ~ yourself too much you will lose their support** wenn Sie zu bestimmt auftreten, verlieren Sie ihre Unterstützung.
➤ **assertion** [ə'sɜ:ʃən] *n* (**a**) (*statement*) Behauptung *f*; (*of innocence*) Beteuerung *f* ◆ **to make ~s/an ~** Behauptungen/eine Behauptung aufstellen. (**b**) *no pl* (*insistence*) Behauptung *f.*
assertive *adj*, **~ly** *adv* [ə'sɜ:tɪv, -lɪ] bestimmt.
assertiveness [ə'sɜ:tɪvnɪs] *n* Bestimmtheit *f.*
assess [ə'ses] *vt* (**a**) *person, chances, abilities* einschätzen; *problem, situation, prospects also* beurteilen; *proposal, advantages also* abwägen.
(**b**) *property* schätzen, taxieren; *person* (*for tax purposes*) veranlagen (*at* mit) ◆ **to ~ sth at its true worth** einer Sache (*dat*) den richtigen Wert beimessen.
(**c**) *fine, tax* festsetzen, bemessen (*at* auf *+acc*); *damages* schätzen (*at* auf *+acc*).
assessment [ə'sesmənt] *n see vt* (**a**) Einschätzung *f*; Beurteilung *f*; Abwägen *nt* ◆ **in my ~** meines Erachtens; **what's your ~ of the situation** wie sehen *or* beurteilen Sie die Lage? (**b**) Schätzung, Taxierung *f*; Veranlagung *f.* (**c**) Festsetzung, Bemessung *f*; Schätzung *f.*
assessor [ə'sesəʳ] *n* Schätzer, Taxator (*form*) *m*; (*Insur*) (Schadens)gutachter *m*; (*Univ*) Prüfer(in *f*) *m.*
asset ['æset] *n* (**a**) *usu pl* Vermögenswert *m*; (*on balance sheet*) Aktivposten *m* ◆ **~s** Vermögen *nt*; (*on balance sheet*) Aktiva *pl*; **personal ~s** persönlicher Besitz; **~ stripping** *Aufkauf von finanziell gefährdeten Firmen und anschließender Verkauf ihrer Vermögenswerte.*
(**b**) (*fig*) **it would be an ~ ...** es wäre von Vorteil ...; **he is one of our great ~s** er ist einer unserer besten Leute; **this player, the club's newest ~** dieser Spieler, die neueste Errungenschaft des Clubs; **good health is a real ~** Gesundheit ist ein großes Kapital; **his appearance is not an ~ to him** aus seinem Aussehen kann er kein Kapital schlagen; **he's hardly an ~ to the company** er ist nicht gerade ein Gewinn für die Firma.
asseverate [ə'sevəreɪt] *vt* (*form*) beteuern.
asseveration [əˌsevə'reɪʃən] *n* (*form*) Beteuerung *f.*
asshole ['æshəʊl] *n* (*US vulg*) Arschloch *nt* (*vulg*).
assiduity [ˌæsɪ'djʊɪtɪ] *n* gewissenhafter Eifer.
assiduous *adj*, **~ly** *adv* [ə'sɪdjʊəs, -lɪ] gewissenhaft.
assiduousness [ə'sɪdjʊəsnɪs] *n* Gewissenhaftigkeit *f.*
assign [ə'saɪn] [1] *vt* (**a**) (*allot*) zuweisen, zuteilen (*to sb* jdm); *task etc also* übertragen (*to sb* jdm); (*to a purpose*) *room* bestimmen (*to* für); (*to a word*) *meaning* zuordnen (*to dat*); (*fix*) *date, time* bestimmen, festsetzen; (*attribute*) *cause, novel, play, music* zuschreiben (*to dat*) ◆ **at the time ~ed** zur festgesetzten Zeit; **which class have you been ~ed?** welche Klasse wurde Ihnen zugewiesen?

(b) (*appoint*) berufen; (*to a mission, case, task etc*) betrauen (*to* mit), beauftragen (*to* mit) ◆ **she was ~ed to this school** sie wurde an diese Schule berufen; **he was ~ed to the post of ambassador** er wurde zum Botschafter berufen; **I was ~ed to speak to the boss** ich wurde damit beauftragt *or* betraut, mit dem Chef zu sprechen.
(c) (*Jur*) übertragen, übereignen (*to sb* jdm).
[2] *n* (*Jur*) (*also* **~ee**) Abtretungsempfänger *m*.

assignation [,æsɪg'neɪʃən] *n* (a) Stelldichein, Rendezvous *nt*. (b) *see* **assignment (b-d)**.

assignment [ə'saɪnmənt] *n* (a) (*task*) Aufgabe *f*; (*mission also*) Auftrag *m*, Mission *f*.
(b) (*appointment*) Berufung *f*; (*to case, task etc*) Betrauung, Beauftragung *f* (*to* mit) ◆ **his ~ to the post of ambassador/to this school** seine Berufung zum Botschafter/an diese Schule.
(c) (*allotment*) *see vt* (*a*) Zuweisung, Zuteilung *f*; Übertragung *f*; Bestimmung *f* (*to* für); Zuordnung *f* (*to* zu).
(d) (*Jur*) Übertragung, Übereignung *f*.

assimilate [ə'sɪmɪleɪt] *vt food, knowledge* aufnehmen; (*fig: into society etc also*) integrieren ◆ **newcomers are easily ~d** Neuankömmlinge können leicht integriert werden.

assimilation [ə,sɪmɪ'leɪʃən] *n see vt* Aufnahme *f*; Integration *f* ◆ **his powers of mental ~** seine geistige Aufnahmefähigkeit.

assist [ə'sɪst] [1] *vt* helfen (*+dat*); (*act as an assistant to*) assistieren (*+dat*); *growth, progress, development* fördern, begünstigen ◆ **to ~ sb with sth** jdm bei etw helfen *or* behilflich sein; **to ~ sb in doing** *or* **to do sth** jdm helfen, etw zu tun; **... who was ~ing the surgeon ...**, der dem Chirurgen assistierte; **in a wind-~ed time of 10.01 seconds** mit Rückenwind in einer Zeit von 10,01 Sekunden; **a man is ~ing the police (with their enquiries)** (*euph*) ein Mann wird von der Polizei vernommen.
[2] *vi* (a) (*help*) helfen ◆ **to ~ with sth** bei etw helfen; **to ~ in doing sth** helfen, etw zu tun. (b) (*be present in order to help, doctor*) assistieren (*at* bei); (*in church*) ministrieren.

assistance [ə'sɪstəns] *n* Hilfe *f* ◆ **to give ~ to sb** (*come to aid of*) jdm Hilfe leisten; **my secretary will give you every ~** meine Sekretärin wird Ihnen in jeder Hinsicht behilflich sein; **to come to sb's ~** jdm zu Hilfe kommen; **to be of ~ (to sb)** jdm helfen *or* behilflich sein; **can I be of any ~?** kann ich irgendwie helfen *or* behilflich sein?

assistant [ə'sɪstənt] [1] *n* Assistent(in *f*) *m*; (*shop ~*) Verkäufer(in *f*) *m* ◆ **are you in charge here? — no, I am just an ~** sind Sie hier der Chef? — nein, ich bin bloß Mitarbeiter.
[2] *adj attr manager etc* stellvertretend ◆ **~ master/mistress** Lehrer(in *f*) *m* (*ohne besondere zusätzliche Verantwortung*); **~ priest** Hilfspriester *m*; **~ professor** (*US*) Assistenz-Professor(in *f*) *m*.

assistantship [ə'sɪstəntʃɪp] *n* (*Brit: at school*) Stelle *f* als Fremdsprachenassistent(in); (*US: at college*) Assistentenstelle *f*.

assizes [ə'saɪzɪz] *npl* (*Brit dated*) Gerichtstage, Assisen (*old*) *pl* ◆ **at the county ~** während der Bezirksgerichtstage.

assn *abbr of* **association**.

associate [ə'səʊʃɪɪt] [1] *n* (a) (*colleague*) Kollege *m*, Kollegin *f*; (*Comm: partner*) Partner, Kompagnon, Teilhaber(in *f*) *m*; (*accomplice*) Komplize *m*, Komplizin *f*. (b) (*of a society*) außerordentliches *or* assoziiertes Mitglied.
[2] [ə'səʊʃɪeɪt] *vt* in Verbindung bringen, assoziieren (*also Psych*) ◆ **to ~ oneself with sb/sth** sich jdm/einer Sache anschließen, sich mit jdm/einer Sache assoziieren; **to be ~d with sb/sth** mit jdm/einer Sache in Verbindung gebracht *or* assoziiert werden; **it is ~d in their minds with ...** sie denken dabei gleich an (*+acc*) ...; **I don't ~ him with sport** ich assoziiere ihn nicht mit Sport, ich denke bei ihm nicht an Sport; **the A~d Union of ...** der Gewerkschaftsverband der ...; **~(d) company** Partnerfirma *f*.
[3] [ə'səʊʃɪeɪt] *vi* **to ~ with** verkehren mit.

associate: ~ director *n Direktor einer Firma, der jedoch nicht offiziell als solcher ernannt wurde*; **~ member** *n* außerordentliches *or* assoziiertes Mitglied; **~ partner** *n* (Geschäfts)partner(in *f*) *m*; **~ professor** *n* (*US*) außerordentlicher Professor.

association [ə,səʊsɪ'eɪʃən] *n* (a) *no pl* (*associating: with people*) Verkehr, Umgang *m*; (*co-operation*) Zusammenarbeit *f* ◆ **he has benefited from his ~ with us** er hat von seiner Beziehung zu uns profitiert; **he has had a long ~ with the party** er hat seit langem Verbindung mit der Partei.
(b) (*organization*) Verband *m*.
(c) (*connexion in the mind*) Assoziation *f* (*with* an *+acc*) (*also Psych*) ◆ **~ of ideas** Gedankenassoziation *f*; **to have unpleasant ~s for sb** unangenehme Assoziationen bei jdm hervorrufen; **I always think of that in ~ with ...** daran denke ich immer im Zusammenhang mit ...; **free ~** (*Psych*) freie Assoziation.

association football *n* (*Brit*) Fußball *m*, Soccer *nt*.

associative [ə'səʊʃɪətɪv] *adj* assoziativ.

assonance ['æsənəns] *n* Assonanz *f*.

assort [ə'sɔːt] *vi* (*form*) (a) (*agree, match*) passen (*with* zu). (b) (*consort*) Umgang pflegen (*with* mit).

assorted [ə'sɔːtɪd] *adj* (a) (*mixed*) gemischt. (b) (*matched*) zusammengestellt; *see* **ill-assorted**.

assortment [ə'sɔːtmənt] *n* Mischung *f*; (*of goods*) Auswahl *f* (*of* an *+dat*), Sortiment *nt* (*of* von); (*of ideas*) Sammlung *f* ◆ **a whole ~ of boyfriends** ein ganzes Sortiment von Freunden.

asst *abbr of* **assistant**.

assuage [ə'sweɪdʒ] *vt hunger, thirst, desire* stillen, befriedigen; *anger, fears etc* beschwichtigen; *pain, grief* lindern.

▼ **assume** [ə'sjuːm] *vt* (a) (*take for granted, suppose*) annehmen; (*presuppose*) voraussetzen ◆ **let us ~ that you are right** nehmen wir an *or* gehen wir davon aus, Sie hätten recht; **assuming this to be true ...** angenommen *or* vorausgesetzt, (daß) das stimmt ...; **assuming (that) ...** angenommen(, daß) ...; **Professor X ~s as his basic premise that ...** Professor X geht von der Grundvoraussetzung aus, daß ...
(b) *power, control* übernehmen; (*forcefully*) ergreifen.
(c) (*take on*) *name, title* annehmen, sich (*dat*) zulegen; *guise, shape, attitude* annehmen ◆ **to ~ a look of innocence/surprise** eine unschuldige/überraschte Miene aufsetzen; **the problem has ~d a new importance** das Problem hat neue Bedeutung gewonnen; **the sky ~d a reddish glow** (*liter*) der Himmel nahm rötliche Glut an (*poet*).

assumed [ə'sjuːmd] *adj* (a) *name* angenommen; (*for secrecy etc also*) Deck-. (b) (*pretended*) *surprise, humility* gespielt, vorgetäuscht ◆ **in the ~ guise of a beggar** als Bettler verkleidet.

assumption [ə'sʌmpʃən] *n* (a) Annahme *f*; (*presupposition*) Voraussetzung *f* ◆ **to go on the ~ that ...** von der Voraussetzung ausgehen, daß ...; **the basic ~s of this theory are ...** diese Theorie geht grundsätzlich davon aus, daß ...
(b) (*of power, role etc*) Übernahme *f*; (*of office also*) Aufnahme *f*; (*forcefully*) Ergreifen *nt*.
(c) (*of guise, false name etc*) Annahme *f*; (*insincere: of look of innocence etc*) Vortäuschung *f*, Aufsetzen *nt*.
(d) (*Eccl*) **the A~** Mariä Himmelfahrt *f*.

assurance [ə'ʃʊərəns] *n* (a) Versicherung *f*; (*promise also*) Zusicherung *f* ◆ **he gave me his ~ that it would be done** er versicherte mir, daß es getan (werden) würde; **do I have your ~ that ...?** garantieren Sie mir, daß ...?; **you have my ~ that ...** Sie können versichert sein, daß ... (b) (*self-confidence*) Sicherheit *f*. (c) (*confidence*) Zuversicht *f*; (*in*) Vertrauen *nt* (*in* in *+acc*) ◆ **in the ~ that ...** (*liter*) im Vertrauen darauf, daß ..., in der Zuversicht, daß ... (d) (*esp Brit: life ~*) Versicherung *f*.

▼ **assure** [ə'ʃʊər] *vt* (a) (*say with confidence*) versichern (*+dat*); (*promise*) zusichern (*+dat*) ◆ **to ~ sb of sth** (*of love, willingness etc*) jdn einer Sache (*gen*) versichern; (*of service, support, help*) jdm etw zusichern; **to ~ sb that ...** jdm versichern/zusichern, daß ...; **... I ~ you ...** versichere ich Ihnen.
(b) (*make certain of*) *success, happiness, future* sichern ◆ **he is ~d of a warm welcome wherever he goes** er kann sich überall eines herzlichen Empfanges sicher sein.
(c) (*esp Brit: insure*) *life* versichern ◆ **she ~d her life for £10,000** sie schloß eine Lebensversicherung über £ 10.000 ab.

assured [ə'ʃʊəd] [1] *n* (*esp Brit*) Versicherte(r) *mf*.
[2] *adj* sicher; *income, future also* gesichert; (*self-confident*) sicher ◆ **to rest ~ that ...** sicher sein, daß ...; **to rest ~ of sth** einer Sache (*gen*) sicher sein.

assuredly [ə'ʃʊərɪdlɪ] *adv* mit Sicherheit ◆ **yes, most ~** ganz sicher.

Assyria [ə'sɪrɪə] *n* Assyrien *nt*.

Assyrian [ə'sɪrɪən] [1] *adj* assyrisch.
[2] *n* (a) Assyrer(in *f*) *m*. (b) (*language*) Assyrisch *nt*.

aster ['æstər] *n* Aster *f*.

asterisk ['æstərɪsk] [1] *n* Sternchen *nt*.
[2] *vt* mit Sternchen versehen.

astern [ə'stɜːn] (*Naut*) [1] *adv* achtern; (*towards the stern*) nach achtern; (*backwards*) achteraus.
[2] *prep* **~ (of) the ship/of us** achteraus.

asteroid ['æstərɔɪd] *n* Asteroid *m*.

asthma ['æsmə] *n* Asthma *nt*.

asthmatic [æs'mætɪk] [1] *n* Asthmatiker(in *f*) *m*.
[2] *adj* asthmatisch.

asthmatically [æs'mætɪkəlɪ] *adv* asthmatisch.

astigmatic [,æstɪg'mætɪk] *adj* astigmatisch.

astigmatism [æs'tɪgmətɪzəm] *n* Astigmatismus *m*.

astir [ə'stɜːr] *adj pred* (a) (*in motion, excited*) voller *or* in Aufregung. (b) (*old, liter: up and about*) auf den Beinen, auf.

ASTM (*US*) *abbr of* **American Society for Testing Materials** *amerikanischer Normenausschuß*, ≃ DNA *m*.

ASTMS ['æztəmz] *abbr of* **Association of Scientific, Technical and Managerial Staffs** *Gewerkschaft f der Wissenschaftler, Techniker und leitenden Angestellten*.

astonish [ə'stɒnɪʃ] *vt* erstaunen, überraschen ◆ **you ~ me!** (*iro*) das wundert mich aber! (*iro*), was du nicht sagst! (*iro*); **to be ~ed** erstaunt *or* überrascht sein; **I am ~ed** *or* **it ~es me that ...** ich bin erstaunt *or* es wundert mich, daß ...; **I am ~ed to learn that ...** ich höre mit Erstaunen *or* Befremden (*geh*), daß ...

astonishing [ə'stɒnɪʃɪŋ] *adj* erstaunlich.

astonishingly [ə'stɒnɪʃɪŋlɪ] *adv* erstaunlich ◆ **~ (enough)** erstaunlicherweise.

astonishment [ə'stɒnɪʃmənt] *n* Erstaunen *nt*, Überraschung *f* (*at* über *+acc*) ◆ **look of ~** erstaunter *or* überraschter Blick; **she looked at me in (complete) ~** sie sah mich (ganz) erstaunt *or* überrascht an; **to my ~** zu meinem Erstaunen.

astound [ə'staʊnd] *vt* sehr erstaunen, in Erstaunen (ver)setzen ◆ **to be ~ed (at)** höchst erstaunt sein (über *+acc*).

astounding [ə'staʊndɪŋ] *adj* erstaunlich.

astrakhan [,æstrə'kæn] [1] *n* Astrachan *m*.
[2] *attr* Astrachan-.

astral ['æstrəl] *adj* Sternen-; (*in theosophy*) Astral-.

astray [ə'streɪ] *adj* verloren ◆ **to go ~** (*person*) (*lit*) vom Weg abkommen; (*fig:*

➤ LANGUAGE IN USE: **assume: a** → 20.3, 26.1 **assure: a** → 15.1

morally) vom rechten Weg abkommen, auf Abwege geraten; (*letter, object*) verlorengehen; (*go wrong: in argument etc*) irregehen; **to lead sb ~** (*fig*) jdn vom rechten Weg abbringen; (*mislead*) jdn irreführen.

astride [əˈstraɪd] [1] *prep* rittlings auf (+*dat*).
[2] *adv* rittlings; *ride* im Herrensitz.

astringency [əsˈtrɪndʒənsɪ] *n* (*fig*) Ätzende(s) *nt*.

astringent [əsˈtrɪndʒənt] [1] *adj* adstringierend; (*fig*) *remark, humour* ätzend, beißend.
[2] *n* Adstringens *nt*.

astro- [ˈæstrəʊ] *pref* Astro-.

astrolabe [ˈæstrəˌleɪb] *n* Astrolab(ium) *nt*.

astrologer [əsˈtrɒlədʒəʳ] *n* Astrologe *m*, Astrologin *f*.

astrological [ˌæstrəˈlɒdʒɪkəl] *adj* astrologisch; *sign also* Tierkreis-.

astrology [əsˈtrɒlədʒɪ] *n* Astrologie *f*.

astronaut [ˈæstrənɔːt] *n* Astronaut(in *f*) *m*.

astronautics [ˌæstrəʊˈnɔːtɪks] *n sing* Raumfahrt, Astronautik *f*.

astronomer [əsˈtrɒnəməʳ] *n* Astronom(in *f*) *m*.

astronomical [ˌæstrəˈnɒmɪkəl] *adj* (*lit, fig also* **astronomic**) astronomisch ◆ **~ year** Sternjahr *nt*.

astronomically [ˌæstrəˈnɒmɪkəlɪ] *adv* (*lit, fig*) astronomisch.

astronomy [əsˈtrɒnəmɪ] *n* Astronomie *f*.

astrophysics [ˌæstrəʊˈfɪzɪks] *n sing* Astrophysik *f*.

astute [əˈstjuːt] *adj* schlau; *remark also* scharfsinnig; *businessman also* clever (*inf*); *child* aufgeweckt; *mind* scharf ◆ **he's very ~ for one so old** er ist für sein Alter geistig sehr rege.

astutely [əˈstjuːtlɪ] *adv see adj*.

astuteness [əsˈtjuːtnɪs] *n see adj* Schlauheit *f*; Scharfsinnigkeit *f*; Cleverneß *f* (*inf*); Aufgewecktheit *f*; Schärfe *f*.

asunder [əˈsʌndəʳ] *adv* (*liter*) (*apart*) auseinander; (*in pieces*) entzwei, in Stücke ◆ **to cleave/split ~** spalten; **her heart was rent ~** ihr brach das Herz; ... **let no man put ~** ..., soll der Mensch nicht trennen *or* scheiden.

asylum [əˈsaɪləm] *n* (**a**) Asyl *nt* ◆ **to ask for (political) ~** um (politisches) Asyl bitten. (**b**) (*lunatic* ~) (Irren)anstalt *f*.

asymmetric(al) [ˌeɪsɪˈmetrɪk(əl)] *adj* asymmetrisch ◆ **asymmetric bars** Stufenbarren *m*.

asymmetry [æˈsɪmɪtrɪ] *n* Asymmetrie *f*.

asynchronous [æˈsɪŋkrənəs] *adj* (*also Comput*) asynchron.

at [æt] *prep* (**a**) (*position*) an (+*dat*), bei (+*dat*); (*with place*) in (+*dat*) ◆ **~ the window/corner/top** am *or* beim Fenster/an der Ecke/Spitze; **~ university/school/a hotel/the zoo** an *or* auf der Universität/in der Schule/im Hotel/im Zoo; **~ my brother's** bei meinem Bruder; **~ a party** auf *or* bei einer Party; **to arrive ~ the station** am Bahnhof ankommen; **he/the rain came in ~ the window** er ist durch das Fenster hereingekommen/es hat durchs Fenster hineingeregnet.
(**b**) (*direction*) **to aim/shoot/point** *etc* **~ sb/sth** auf jdn/etw zielen/schießen/zeigen *etc*; **to look/growl/swear** *etc* **~ sb/sth** jdn/etw ansehen/anknurren/beschimpfen *etc*; **~ him!** auf ihn!
(**c**) (*time, frequency, order*) **~ ten o'clock** um zehn Uhr; **~ night/dawn** bei Nacht/beim *or* im Morgengrauen; **~ Christmas/Easter** *etc* zu Weihnachten/Ostern *etc*; **~ your age/16 (years of age)** in deinem Alter/mit 16 (Jahren); **three ~ a time** drei auf einmal; **~ the start/end of sth** am Anfang/am Ende einer Sache (*gen*).
(**d**) (*activity*) **~ play/work** beim Spiel/bei der Arbeit; **good/bad/an expert ~ sth** gut/schlecht/ein Experte in etw (*dat*); **his employees/creditors are ~ him** seine Angestellten/Gläubiger setzen ihm zu; **while we are ~ it** (*inf*) wenn wir schon mal dabei sind; **the couple in the next room were ~ it all night** (*inf*) die beiden im Zimmer nebenan haben es die ganze Nacht getrieben (*inf*); **the brakes are ~ it again** (*inf*) die Bremsen mucken schon wieder (*inf*); **he doesn't know what he's ~** (*inf*) der weiß ja nicht, was er tut (*inf*); *see vbs*.
(**e**) (*state, condition*) **to be ~ an advantage** im Vorteil sein; **~ a loss/profit** mit Verlust/Gewinn; **I'd leave it ~ that** ich würde es dabei belassen; *see* **best, worst, that**[1].
(**f**) (*as a result of, upon*) auf (+*acc*) ... (hin) ◆ **~ his request** auf seine Bitte (hin); **~ her death** bei ihrem Tod; **~ that/this he left the room** daraufhin verließ er das Zimmer.
(**g**) (*cause: with*) *angry, annoyed, delighted etc* über (+*acc*).
(**h**) (*rate, value, degree*) **~ full speed/50 km/h** mit voller Geschwindigkeit/50 km/h; **~ 50p a pound** für *or* zu 50 Pence pro *or* das Pfund; **~ 5% interest** zu 5% Zinsen; **~ a high/low price** zu einem hohen/niedrigen Preis; **when the temperature is ~ 90** wenn die Temperatur bei *or* auf 90° ist; **with prices ~ this level** bei solchen Preisen; *see* **all, cost, rate**[1].

atavism [ˈætəvɪzəm] *n* Atavismus *m*.

atavistic [ˌætəˈvɪstɪk] *adj* atavistisch.

ataxia [əˈtæksɪə] *n* Ataxie *f*.

ataxic [əˈtæksɪk] *adj* ataktisch.

ate [et, (*US*) eɪt] *pret of* **eat**.

atheism [ˈeɪθɪɪzəm] *n* Atheismus *m*.

atheist [ˈeɪθɪɪst] [1] *n* Atheist *m*.
[2] *adj attr* atheistisch.

atheistic [ˌeɪθɪˈɪstɪk] *adj* atheistisch.

Athenian [əˈθiːnɪən] [1] *n* Athener(in *f*) *m*.
[2] *adj* athenisch; (*esp modern*) Athener.

Athens [ˈæθɪnz] *n* Athen *nt*.

athirst [əˈθɜːst] *adj* (*fig liter*) **to be ~ for sth** nach etw (*dat*) dürsten (*liter*).

athlete [ˈæθliːt] *n* Athlet(in *f*) *m*; (*specialist in track and field events*) Leichtathlet(in *f*) *m* ◆ **he is a natural ~** er ist der geborene Sportler; **~'s foot** Fußpilz *m*.

athletic [æθˈletɪk] *adj* sportlich; (*referring to athletics, build*) athletisch.

athletically [æθˈletɪkəlɪ] *adv* sportlich; *built* athletisch.

athleticism [æθˈletɪsɪzəm] *n* Athletentum *nt*.

athletics [æθˈletɪks] *n sing or pl* Leichtathletik *f* ◆ **~ meeting** Leichtathletikwettkampf *m*; **sexual ~** Sexualakrobatik *f*.

at-home [ˈætˈhəʊm] *n* Empfang *m* bei sich (*dat*) zu Hause.

athwart [əˈθwɔːt] [1] *adv* quer; (*Naut*) dwars.
[2] *prep* quer über; (*Naut*) dwars, quer.

Atlantic [ətˈlæntɪk] [1] *n* (*also* **~ Ocean**) Atlantik *m*, Atlantischer Ozean.
[2] *adj attr* atlantisch ◆ **~ crossing** Atlantiküberquerung *f*; **~ Charter** Atlantik-Charta *f*; **~ liner** Ozeandampfer *m*; **~ wall** Atlantikwall *m*.

atlas [ˈætləs] *n* Atlas *m*.

Atlas Mountains *npl* Atlas(-Gebirge *nt*) *m*.

ATM *abbr of* **automated teller machine**.

atmosphere [ˈætməsfɪəʳ] *n* (*lit, fig*) Atmosphäre *f*; (*fig: of novel also*) Stimmung *f*.

atmospheric [ˌætməsˈferɪk] *adj* atmosphärisch; (*full of atmosphere*) *description* stimmungsvoll.

atmospherics [ˌætməsˈferɪks] *npl* (*Rad*) atmosphärische Störungen *pl*.

atoll [ˈætɒl] *n* Atoll *nt*.

atom [ˈætəm] *n* (**a**) Atom *nt*. (**b**) (*fig*) **to smash sth to ~s** etw völlig zertrümmern; **not an ~ of truth** kein Körnchen Wahrheit.

atom bomb *n* Atombombe *f*.

atomic [əˈtɒmɪk] *adj* atomar.

atomic *in cpds* Atom-; **~ age** *n* Atomzeitalter *nt*; **~ bomb** *n* Atombombe *f*; **~ clock** *n* Atomuhr *f*; **~ energy** *n* Atom- *or* Kernenergie *f*; **~ energy authority** (*Brit*) *or* (*US*) **commission** *n* Atomkommission *f*; **~ number** *n* Ordnungszahl *f*; **~ power** *n* Atomkraft *f*; (*propulsion*) Atomantrieb *m*; **~ powered** *adj* atomgetrieben, Atom-; **~ structure** *n* Atombau *m*; **~ weight** *n* Atomgewicht *nt*.

atomism [ˈætəmɪzəm] *n* (*Philos*) Atomismus *m*.

atomistic [ˌætəˈmɪstɪk] *adj* (*Philos*) atomistisch.

atomize [ˈætəmaɪz] *vt liquid* zerstäuben.

atomizer [ˈætəmaɪzəʳ] *n* Zerstäuber *m*.

atonal [æˈtəʊnl] *adj* atonal.

atone [əˈtəʊn] *vi* **to ~ for sth** (für) etw sühnen *or* büßen.

atonement [əˈtəʊnmənt] *n* Sühne, Buße *f* ◆ **to make ~ for sth** für etw Sühne *or* Buße tun; **in ~ for sth** als Sühne *or* Buße für etw; **the A~** (*Eccl*) das Sühneopfer (Christi).

atop [əˈtɒp] *prep* (*liter*) (oben) auf (+*dat*).

A to Z ® [ˌeɪtəˈzed] *n* Stadtplan *m* (*mit Straßenverzeichnis, meist in Buchform*).

atrocious *adj*, **~ly** *adv* [əˈtrəʊʃəs, -lɪ] grauenhaft.

atrocity [əˈtrɒsɪtɪ] *n* Grausamkeit *f*; (*act also*) Greueltat *f*.

atrophy [ˈætrəfɪ] [1] *n* Atrophie *f* (*geh*), Schwund *m*.
[2] *vt* schwinden lassen.
[3] *vi* verkümmern, schwinden.

Att, Atty *abbr of* **Attorney** (*US*).

attach [əˈtætʃ] [1] *vt* (**a**) (*join*) festmachen, befestigen (*to* an +*dat*); *document to a letter etc* an- *or* beiheften ◆ **please find ~ed** ... beigeheftet ...; **to ~ oneself to sb/a group** sich jdm/einer Gruppe anschließen; **is he/she ~ed?** ist er/sie schon vergeben?
(**b**) **to be ~ed to sb/sth** (*be fond of*) an jdm/etw hängen.
(**c**) (*attribute*) *importance* beimessen, zuschreiben (*to dat*).
(**d**) (*Mil etc*) *personnel* angliedern, zuteilen (*to dat*).
[2] *vi* **no blame ~es** *or* **can ~ to him** ihm haftet keine Schuld an, ihn trifft keine Schuld; **salary/responsibility ~ing** *or* **~ed to this post** Gehalt, das mit diesem Posten verbunden ist/Verantwortung, die dieser Posten mit sich bringt; **great importance ~es to this** dem haftet größte Bedeutung an.

attachable [əˈtætʃəbl] *adj* **to be ~** sich befestigen lassen.

attaché [əˈtæʃeɪ] *n* Attaché *m*.

attaché case *n* Aktenkoffer *m*.

attachment [əˈtætʃmənt] *n* (**a**) (*act of attaching*) *see vt (a)* Festmachen, Befestigen *nt*; An- *or* Beiheften *nt*.
(**b**) (*accessory*) Zusatzteil, Zubehörteil *nt*.
(**c**) (*fig: affection*) Zuneigung *f* (*to* zu).
(**d**) (*Mil etc: temporary transfer*) Zuordnung, Angliederung *f* ◆ **to be on ~** angegliedert *or* zugeteilt sein (*to dat*).

attack [əˈtæk] [1] *n* (**a**) (*Mil, Sport, fig*) Angriff *m* (*on* auf +*acc*) ◆ **there have been two ~s on his life** es wurden bereits zwei Anschläge auf sein Leben gemacht *or* verübt; **to be under ~** angegriffen werden; (*fig also*) unter Beschuß stehen; **to go over to the ~** zum Angriff übergehen; **to return to the ~** wieder zum Angriff übergehen; **to launch/make an ~** zum Angriff ansetzen/einen Angriff vortragen *or* machen (*on* auf +*acc*); (*on sb's character*) angreifen (*on acc*); **~ is the best form of defence** Angriff ist die beste Verteidigung; **to leave oneself open to ~** Angriffsflächen bieten; **she played the sonata with ~** sie nahm die Sonate kraftvoll *or* mit Schwung in Angriff.
(**b**) (*Med etc*) Anfall *m* ◆ **an ~ of fever/hay fever** ein Fieberanfall/ein Anfall von Heuschnupfen; **to have an ~ of nerves** plötzlich Nerven bekommen.
[2] *vt* (**a**) (*Mil, Sport, fig*) angreifen; (*from ambush, in robbery etc*) überfallen ◆ **he was ~ed by doubts** Zweifel befielen ihn.
(**b**) (*tackle*) *task, problem, sonata* in Angriff nehmen.
(**c**) (*Med: illness*) befallen.
[3] *vi* angreifen ◆ **an ~ing side** eine angriffsfreudige *or* offensive Mann-

➤ LANGUAGE IN USE: **attend: 2a** → 19.3, 19.5, 25.1

schaft; **ready to ~** zum Angriff bereit.

attacker [ə'tækəʳ] *n* Angreifer(in *f*) *m*.

attain [ə'teɪn] 1 *vt aim, rank, age, perfection* erreichen; *knowledge* erlangen; *happiness, prosperity, power* gelangen zu ◆ **he has ~ed his hopes** seine Hoffnungen haben sich erfüllt.
2 *vi* **to ~ to sth** *to perfection* etw erreichen; *to prosperity, power* zu etw gelangen; **to ~ to man's estate** *(form)* das Mannesalter erreichen *(form)*.

attainable [ə'teɪnəbl] *adj* erreichbar, zu erreichen; *knowledge, happiness, power* zu erlangen.

attainder [ə'teɪndəʳ] *n see* **bill**³ **(h)**.

attainment [ə'teɪnmənt] *n* **(a)** *(act of attaining)* Erreichung *f*, Erreichen *nt*; *(of knowledge, happiness, prosperity, power)* Erlangen *nt* ◆ **difficult/easy** *etc* **of ~** *(form)* schwierig/leicht zu erreichen *or* erlangen.
(b) *(usu pl: accomplishment)* Fertigkeit *f* ◆ **a low/high standard of ~** ein niedriger/hoher Leistungsstandard.

attempt [ə'tempt] 1 *vt* versuchen; *smile, conversation* den Versuch machen *or* unternehmen zu; *task, job* sich versuchen an (+*dat*) ◆ **~ed murder** Mordversuch *m*.
2 *n* Versuch *m*; *(on sb's life)* (Mord)anschlag *m* (*on* auf +*acc*) ◆ **an ~ on Mount Everest/the record** ein Versuch, Mount Everest zu bezwingen/den Rekord zu brechen; **an ~ at a joke/at doing sth** ein Versuch, einen Witz zu machen/etw zu tun; **to make an ~ on sb's life** einen Anschlag auf jdn *or* jds Leben verüben; **to make an ~ at doing sth** versuchen, etw zu tun; **he made no ~ to help us** er unternahm keinen Versuch, uns zu helfen; **at the first ~** auf Anhieb, beim ersten Versuch; **in the ~** dabei.

▼ **attend** [ə'tend] 1 *vt* **(a)** *classes, church, meeting etc* besuchen; *wedding, funeral* anwesend *or* zugegen sein bei, beiwohnen (+*dat*) *(geh)* ◆ **the wedding was well ~ed/was ~ed by fifty people** die Hochzeit war gut besucht/fünfzig Leute waren bei der Hochzeit anwesend *or* wohnten der Hochzeit bei *(geh)*.
(b) *(accompany)* begleiten; *(wait on) queen etc* bedienen, aufwarten (+*dat*) ◆ **which doctor is ~ing you?** von welchem Arzt werden Sie behandelt?, wer ist Ihr behandelnder Arzt?
▼ 2 *vi* **(a)** *(be present)* anwesend sein ◆ **are you going to ~?** gehen Sie hin?; **to ~ at a birth** bei einer Geburt helfen *or* assistieren; **to ~ upon sb** *(old)* jdm aufwarten *(old)*.
(b) *(pay attention)* aufpassen.

◆ **attend to** *vi +prep obj (see to)* sich kümmern um; *(pay attention to) work etc*
▼ Aufmerksamkeit schenken *or* widmen (+*dat*); *(listen to) teacher, sb's remark* zuhören (+*dat*); *(heed) advice, warning* hören auf (+*acc*), Beachtung schenken (+*dat*); *(serve) customers etc* bedienen ◆ **are you being ~ed ~?** werden Sie schon bedient?; **that's being ~ed ~** das wird (bereits) erledigt.

attendance [ə'tendəns] *n* **(a) to be in ~ at sth** bei etw anwesend sein; **to be in ~ on sb** jdm aufwarten, jdn bedienen; **to be in ~ on a patient** einen Patienten behandeln; **she came in with her maids in ~** sie kam von ihren Hofdamen begleitet herein; **the police are in ~** *(form)* die Polizei ist vor Ort *(form)*.
(b) *(being present)* Anwesenheit *f* (*at* bei) ◆ **~ officer** *Beamter, der sich um Fälle häufigen unentschuldigten Fehlens in der Schule kümmert*; **~ record** *(school register etc)* Anwesenheitsliste *f*; **he doesn't have a very good ~ record** er fehlt oft; **regular ~ at school** regelmäßiger Schulbesuch; **~ centre** Heim *nt* für jugendliche Straftäter.
(c) *(number of people present)* Teilnehmerzahl *f* ◆ **record ~** eine Rekordteilnehmerzahl, Rekordteilnehmerzahlen *pl*.

attendant [ə'tendənt] 1 *n* *(in retinue)* Begleiter(in *f*) *m*; *(in public toilets)* Toilettenwart *m*, Toilettenfrau *f*; *(in swimming baths)* Bademeister(in *f*) *m*; *(in art galleries, museums)* Aufseher(in *f*), Wärter(in *f*) *m*; *(medical ~)* Krankenpfleger(in *f*) *m*; *(of royalty)* Kammerherr *m*/-frau *f* ◆ **her ~s** ihr Gefolge *nt*.
2 *adj* **(a)** *problems etc* (da)zugehörig, damit verbunden; *circumstances, factors* Begleit- ◆ **old age and its ~ ills** Alter und die damit verbundenen Beschwerden; **to be ~ (up)on sth** mit etw zusammenhängen, etw begleiten.
(b) *(form: serving)* **to be ~ on sb** *(lady-in-waiting etc)* jdm aufwarten; **there were two ~ nurses** es waren zwei Krankenschwestern anwesend.

▼ **attention** [ə'tenʃən] *n* **(a)** *no pl (consideration, observation, notice)* Aufmerksamkeit *f* ◆ **to call ~ to sth** auf etw (*acc*) aufmerksam machen; **to call** *or* **draw sb's ~ to sth, to call sth to sb's ~** jds Aufmerksamkeit auf etw (*acc*) lenken, jdn auf etw (*acc*) aufmerksam machen; **to attract sb's ~** jds Aufmerksamkeit erregen, jdn auf sich (*acc*) aufmerksam machen; **to turn one's ~ to sb/sth** jdm/einer Sache seine Aufmerksamkeit zuwenden, seine Aufmerksamkeit auf jdn/etw richten; **to pay ~/no ~ to sb/sth** jdn/etw beachten/nicht beachten; **to pay ~ to the teacher** dem Lehrer zuhören; **to hold sb's ~** jdn fesseln; **can I have your ~ for a moment?** dürfte ich Sie einen Augenblick um (Ihre) Aufmerksamkeit bitten?; **~!** Achtung!; **your ~, please** ich bitte um Aufmerksamkeit; *(official announcement)* Achtung, Achtung!; **it has come to my ~ that ...** ich bin darauf aufmerksam geworden, daß ...; **it has been brought to my ~ that ...** es ist mir zu Ohren gekommen, daß ...
(b) ~s *pl (kindnesses)* Aufmerksamkeiten *pl* ◆ **to pay one's ~s to sb** *(dated: court)* jdm den Hof machen.
(c) *(Mil)* **to stand to** *or* **at ~, to come to ~** stillstehen; **~!** stillgestanden!
(d) *(Comm)* **~ Miss Smith, for the ~ of Miss Smith** zu Händen von Frau Smith; **your letter will receive our earliest ~** Ihr Brief wird baldmöglichst *or* umgehend bearbeitet; **for your ~** zur gefälligen Beachtung.

attention-seeking [ə'tenʃənsi:kɪŋ] 1 *n* Beachtungsbedürfnis *nt*.
2 *adj* **to show ~ behaviour** beachtet werden wollen.

attentive [ə'tentɪv] *adj* aufmerksam ◆ **to be ~ to sb/sth** sich jdm gegenüber aufmerksam verhalten/einer Sache (*dat*) Beachtung schenken; **to be ~ to sb's interests/advice** sich um jds Interessen kümmern/jds Rat (*acc*) beachten.

attentively [ə'tentɪvlɪ] *adv* aufmerksam.

attentiveness [ə'tentɪvnɪs] *n* Aufmerksamkeit *f*.

attenuate [ə'tenjʊeɪt] 1 *vt* *(weaken)* abschwächen; *statement also* abmildern; *gas* verdünnen; *(make thinner)* dünn machen ◆ **attenuating circumstances** mildernde Umstände.
2 *vi* *(get weaker)* schwächer *or* abgeschwächt werden; *(gas)* sich verdünnen; *(get thinner)* dünner werden.
3 *adj (Bot)* **~ leaf** lanzettförmiges Blatt.

attenuation [ə,tenjʊ'eɪʃən] *n see vt* Abschwächen *nt*, Abschwächung *f*; Abmildern *nt*, Abmilderung *f*; Verdünnen *nt*, Verdünnung *f*; *(making thinner)* Verdünnung *f*.

attest [ə'test] *vt* **(a)** *(certify, testify to) sb's innocence, authenticity* bestätigen, bescheinigen; *signature also* beglaubigen; *(on oath)* beschwören ◆ **~ed herd** *(Brit)* tuberkulosefreier Bestand. **(b)** *(be proof of)* beweisen, bezeugen.

◆ **attest to** *vi +prep obj* bezeugen.

attestation [,ætes'teɪʃən] *n* **(a)** *(certifying)* Bestätigung *f*; *(of signature also)* Beglaubigung *f*; *(document)* Bescheinigung *f*. **(b)** *(proof: of ability etc)* Beweis *m*.

attestor [ə'testəʳ] *n* Beglaubiger *m*.

attic ['ætɪk] *n* Dachboden, Speicher *m*; *(lived-in)* Mansarde *f* ◆ **~ room** Dachstube, Dachkammer *f*; Mansardenzimmer, Dachzimmer *nt*; **in the ~** auf dem (Dach)boden *or* Speicher.

Attic ['ætɪk] *adj* attisch.

Attica ['ætɪkə] *n* Attika *nt*.

Attila ['ætɪlə] *n* Attila *m* ◆ **~ the Hun** Attila, der Hunnenkönig.

attire [ə'taɪəʳ] 1 *vt* kleiden (*in* in +*acc*).
2 *n, no pl* Kleidung *f* ◆ **ceremonial ~** Festtracht *f*, volles Ornat.

▼ **attitude** ['ætɪtju:d] *n* **(a)** *(way of thinking)* Einstellung *f* (*to, towards* zu); *(way of acting, manner)* Haltung *f* (*to, towards* gegenüber) ◆ **~ of mind** Geisteshaltung *f*; **I don't like your ~** ich bin mit dieser Einstellung überhaupt nicht einverstanden; *(manner)* ich bin mit Ihrem Benehmen überhaupt nicht einverstanden; **well, if that's your ~** ja, wenn du *so* denkst ...
(b) *(way of standing)* Haltung *f* ◆ **to strike an ~/a defensive ~** eine Pose einnehmen/in Verteidigungsstellung gehen.
(c) *(in ballet)* Attitüde *f*.
(d) *(Aviat, Space)* Lage *f*.

attitudinize [,ætɪ'tju:dɪnaɪz] *vi* so tun, als ob, posieren *(geh)*.

attn *abbr of* **attention** z. Hd(n) von.

attorney [ə'tɜ:nɪ] *n* **(a)** *(Comm, Jur: representative)* Bevollmächtigte(r) *mf*, Stellvertreter *m* ◆ **letter of ~** (schriftliche) Vollmacht; *see* **power**. **(b)** *(US: lawyer)* (Rechts)anwalt *m*. **(c) ~ general** *(US) (public prosecutor) (of state government)* ≃ Generalstaatsanwalt *m*; *(of federal government)* ≃ Generalbundesanwalt *m*; *(Brit)* ≃ Justizminister *m*.

attract [ə'trækt] *vt* **(a)** *(Phys: magnet etc)* anziehen.
(b) *(fig: appeal to) (person)* anziehen; *(idea, music, place etc)* ansprechen ◆ **she feels ~ed to him/to the idea** sie fühlt sich von ihm angezogen *or* zu ihm hingezogen/die Idee reizt sie; **I am not ~ed to her/by it** sie zieht mich nicht an/es reizt mich nicht.
(c) *(fig: win, gain) interest, attention etc* auf sich (*acc*) ziehen *or* lenken; *new members, investors etc* anziehen, anlocken ◆ **to ~ publicity/notoriety** (öffentliches) Aufsehen erregen.

attraction [ə'trækʃən] *n* **(a)** *(Phys, fig)* Anziehungskraft *f*; *(of big city etc also)* Reiz *m* ◆ **to lose one's/its ~** seinen Reiz verlieren; **I still feel a certain ~ towards him** ich fühle mich noch immer von ihm angezogen; **to have an ~ for sb** Anziehungskraft *or* einen Reiz auf jdn ausüben; **what are the ~s of this subject?** was ist an diesem Fach reizvoll?
(b) *(attractive thing)* Attraktion *f*.

attractive [ə'træktɪv] *adj* **(a)** attraktiv; *personality, smile* anziehend; *house, view, furnishings, picture, dress, location* reizvoll; *story, music* nett, ansprechend; *price, idea, offer also* verlockend, reizvoll. **(b)** *(Phys)* Anziehungs-.

attractively [ə'træktɪvlɪ] *adv* attraktiv; *smile* anziehend; *dress, furnish, paint* reizvoll ◆ **~ priced** zum attraktiven *or* verlockenden Preis (*at* von).

attractiveness [ə'træktɪvnɪs] *n* Attraktivität *f*; *(of house, furnishing, view etc)* Reiz *m* ◆ **the ~ of her appearance** ihr reizvolles *or* ansprechendes *or* anziehendes Äußeres; **the ~ of the melody** die ansprechende Melodie.

attributable [ə'trɪbjʊtəbl] *adj* **to be ~ to sb/sth** jdm/einer Sache zuzuschreiben sein.

▼ **attribute** [ə'trɪbju:t] 1 *vt* **to ~ sth to sb** *play, remark etc* jdm etw zuschreiben; *(credit sb with sth) intelligence, feelings etc also* jdm etw beimessen; **to ~ sth to sth** *success, accident etc* etw auf etw (*acc*) zurückführen; *(attach) importance etc* einer Sache (*dat*) etw beimessen.
2 ['ætrɪbju:t] *n* Attribut *nt*; *(quality also)* Merkmal *nt*.

attribution [,ætrɪ'bju:ʃən] *n* **(a)** *no pl* **the ~ of this play to Shakespeare** (die Tatsache,) daß man Shakespeare dieses Schauspiel zuschreibt; **the ~ of the accident to mechanical failure** (die Tatsache,) daß man den Unfall auf mechanisches Versagen zurückführt. **(b)** *(attribute)* Attribut *nt*, Eigenschaft *f*.

attributive [ə'trɪbjʊtɪv] *(Gram)* 1 *adj* attributiv, Attributiv-.
2 *n* Attributiv *nt*.

attrition [ə'trɪʃən] *n (lit, form)* Abrieb *m*, Zerreibung *f*; *(fig)* Zermürbung *f*; *(Rel)* unvollkommene Reue, Attrition *f (spec)* ◆ **war of ~** *(Mil)* Zermürbungskrieg *m*.

attune [ə'tju:n] *vt (fig)* abstimmen (*to* auf +*acc*) ◆ **to ~ oneself to sth** sich auf

➤ LANGUAGE IN USE: **attend to** → 20.7 **attention: a** → 13, 20.6, 26.1, 26.2, 26.3 **attitude: a** → 6.1 **attribute: 1** → 17.2

etw (*acc*) einstellen; **to become ~d to sth** sich an etw (*acc*) gewöhnen; **the two of them are well ~d to each other** die beiden sind gut aufeinander eingespielt.

Atty Gen *abbr of* **Attorney General.**

atwitter [ə'twɪtə^r] *adj pred (fig)* in heller Aufregung.

atypical [,eɪ'tɪpɪkəl] *adj* atypisch.

aubergine ['əʊbəʒiːn] [1] *n* Aubergine *f*; (*colour*) Aubergine *nt*.
[2] *adj* aubergine(farben).

auburn ['ɔːbən] *adj hair* rotbraun, rostrot.

auction ['ɔːkʃən] [1] *n* Auktion, Versteigerung *f* ♦ **to sell sth by ~** etw versteigern; **to put sth up for ~** etw zum Versteigern *or* zur Versteigerung anbieten; **~ bridge** (*Cards*) Auktionsbridge *nt*.
[2] *vt* (*also* **~ off**) versteigern.

auctioneer [,ɔːkʃə'nɪə^r] *n* Auktionator *m*.

auction: ~ room *n* Auktionshalle *f*, Auktionssaal *m*; **~ rooms** *npl* Auktionshalle *f*; **~ sale** *n* Auktion, Versteigerung *f*.

audacious *adj*, **~ly** *adv* [ɔː'deɪʃəs, -lɪ] **(a)** (*impudent*) dreist, unverfroren. **(b)** (*bold*) kühn, wagemutig, verwegen.

audacity [ɔː'dæsɪtɪ], **audaciousness** [ɔː'deɪʃəsnɪs] *n* **(a)** (*impudence*) Dreistigkeit, Unverfrorenheit *f* ♦ **to have the ~ to do sth** die Dreistigkeit *or* Unverfrorenheit besitzen, etw zu tun. **(b)** (*boldness*) Kühnheit, Verwegenheit *f*.

audibility [,ɔːdɪ'bɪlɪtɪ] *n* Hörbarkeit, Vernehmbarkeit *f*.

audible ['ɔːdɪbl] *adj* hörbar, (deutlich) vernehmbar ♦ **she was hardly ~** man konnte sie kaum hören.

audibly ['ɔːdɪblɪ] *adv* hörbar, vernehmlich.

audience ['ɔːdɪəns] *n* **(a)** Publikum *nt no pl*; (*Theat, TV also*) Zuschauer *pl*; (*of speaker also*) Zuhörer *pl*; (*of writer, book also*) Leserkreis *m*, Leserschaft *f*; (*Rad, Mus also*) Zuhörerschaft *f* ♦ **to have a large ~** ein großes Publikum haben *or* ansprechen (*also Rad, TV etc*); **to have ~ appeal** publikumswirksam sein; **I prefer London ~s** ich ziehe das Publikum in London vor.
(b) (*formal interview*) Audienz *f* (*with* bei).

audio ['ɔːdɪəʊ] *in cpds* Audio-; **~ book** *n* Hörbuch *nt*; **~ cassette** *n* Kassette, Cassette *f*; **~ equipment** *n* (*in recording studio*) Tonaufzeichnungsgeräte *pl*; (*hi-fi*) Stereoanlage *f*.

audio-frequency [,ɔːdɪəʊ'friːkwənsɪ] *n* Hörfrequenz *f*.

audiometer [,ɔːdɪ'ɒmɪtə^r] *n* Audiometer *nt*, Gehörmesser *m*.

audio: ~ typist *n* Phonotypistin *f*; **~-visual** *adj* audiovisuell.

audit ['ɔːdɪt] [1] *n* Bücherrevision, Buchprüfung *f*.
[2] *vt* **(a)** *accounts* prüfen. **(b)** (*US Univ*) belegen, ohne einen Schein zu machen, Gasthörer sein bei.

audition [ɔː'dɪʃən] [1] *n* (*Theat*) Vorsprechprobe *f*; (*of musician*) Probespiel *nt*; (*of singer*) Vorsingen *nt* ♦ **she was asked for ~** sie wurde zum Vorsprechen/Probespiel/Vorsingen eingeladen.
[2] *vt* vorsprechen/vorspielen/vorsingen lassen.
[3] *vi* vorsprechen; vorspielen; vorsingen.

auditor ['ɔːdɪtə^r] *n* **(a)** (*listener*) Zuhörer(in *f*) *m*. **(b)** (*Comm*) Rechnungsprüfer, Buchprüfer *m*. **(c)** (*US Univ*) Gasthörer *m*.

auditorium [,ɔːdɪ'tɔːrɪəm] *n* Auditorium *nt*; (*in theatre, cinema also*) Zuschauerraum *m*; (*in concert hall also*) Zuhörersaal *m*.

auditory ['ɔːdɪtərɪ] *adj ability* Hör-; *nerve, centre* Gehör-.

au fait [,əʊ'feɪ] *adj* vertraut.

Aug *abbr of* **August** Aug.

Augean stables [ɔː'dʒiːən'steɪblz] *npl* Augiasstall *m* ♦ **to clean out the ~** (*Myth, fig*) den Augiasstall ausmisten.

auger ['ɔːgə^r] *n* Stangenbohrer *m*; (*Agr*) Schnecke *f*.

aught [ɔːt] *n* (*old, liter*) irgend etwas ♦ **he might have moved for ~ I know** was weiß ich, vielleicht ist er umgezogen; **for ~ I care** das ist mir einerlei.

augment [ɔːg'ment] [1] *vt* vermehren; *income also* vergrößern.
[2] *vi* zunehmen; (*income etc also*) sich vergrößern.

augmentation [,ɔːgmən'teɪʃən] *n see vti* Vermehrung *f*, Vergrößerung *f*, Zunahme *f*; (*Mus*) Augmentation *f*.

augmented [ɔːg'mentɪd] *adj* (*Mus*) *fourth, fifth* übermäßig.

au gratin [,əʊ'grætæŋ] *adv* überbacken, au gratin ♦ **cauliflower ~** überbackener Blumenkohl, Blumenkohl *m* au gratin.

augur ['ɔːgə^r] [1] *n* (*person*) Augur *m*.
[2] *vi* **to ~ well/ill** etwas Gutes/nichts Gutes verheißen.
[3] *vt* verheißen ♦ **it ~s no good** das verheißt nichts Gutes.

augury ['ɔːgjʊrɪ] *n* (*sign*) Anzeichen, Omen *nt*.

august [ɔː'gʌst] *adj* illuster; *occasion, spectacle* erhaben.

August ['ɔːgəst] *n* August *m*; *see* **September.**

Augustan [ɔː'gʌstən] *adj* Augusteisch.

Augustine [ɔː'gʌstɪn] *n* Augustinus *m*.

Augustinian [,ɔːgəs'tɪnɪən] [1] *adj* Augustiner-.
[2] *n* Augustiner *m*.

auk [ɔːk] *n* (*Zool*) Alk *m* ♦ **great ~** Toralk *m*; **little ~** Krabbentaucher *m*.

auld [ɔːld] *adj* (*+er*) (*Scot*) alt ♦ **A~ Lang Syne** (*song*) Nehmt Abschied, Brüder; **for ~ lang syne** um der alten Zeiten willen.

aunt [ɑːnt] *n* Tante *f*.

auntie, aunty ['ɑːntɪ] *n* (*inf*) Tante *f* ♦ **~!** Tantchen!; **A~** (*Brit hum*) die BBC, *britische Rundfunk- und Fernsehanstalt*.

Aunt Sally [,ɑːnt'sælɪ] *n* (*Brit*) (*lit*) Schießbudenfigur *f*; (*stall*) Schieß- *or* Wurfbude *f*; (*fig*) Zielscheibe *f*.

au pair ['əʊ'pɛə] [1] *n, pl* **- -s** (*also* **~ girl**) Au-pair(-Mädchen) *nt*.
[2] *adv* au pair.

aura ['ɔːrə] *n* Aura *f* (*geh*), Fluidum *nt* (*geh*) ♦ **he has an ~ of saintliness about him** ihn umgibt eine Aura der Heiligkeit (*geh*), er steht im Nimbus der Heiligkeit; **she has a mysterious ~ about her** eine geheimnisvolle Aura (*geh*) *or* ein geheimnisvoller Nimbus umgibt sie; **an ~ of prosperity/culture** ein Flair von Wohlstand/Kultur (*geh*); **he has an ~ of calm** er strömt *or* strahlt Ruhe aus; **the castle has an ~ of evil** vom Schloß strömt etwas Böses aus; **it gives the hotel an ~ of respectability** es verleiht dem Hotel einen Anstrich von Achtbarkeit.

aural ['ɔːrəl] *adj* Gehör-, aural (*spec*); *examination* Hör-.

aureole ['ɔːrɪ,əʊl] *n* (*Astron*) Korona *f*; (*because of haze*) Hof *m*, Aureole *f*; (*Art*) Aureole *f*.

auricle ['ɔːrɪkl] *n* (*Anat*) Ohrmuschel, Auricula (*spec*) *f*; (*of heart*) Vorhof *m*, Atrium *nt* (*spec*).

auricular [ɔː'rɪkjʊlə^r] *adj* (*Anat*) **(a)** (*of ear*) aurikular (*spec*), Ohren-, Gehör- ♦ **~ nerve** Hörnerv *m*; **~ confession** Ohrenbeichte *f*, geheime Beichte. **(b)** (*of heart*) aurikular (*spec*), Aurikular- (*spec*) ♦ **~ flutter** (Herz)vorhofflattern *nt*.

aurochs ['ɔːrɒks] *n* Auerochse, Ur *m*.

aurora [ɔː'rɔːrə] *n* (*Astron*) Polarlicht *nt* ♦ **~ australis/borealis** südliches/nördliches Polarlicht, Süd-/Nordlicht *nt*.

auscultate ['ɔːskəlteɪt] *vt* abhören, auskultieren (*spec*).

auscultation [,ɔːskəl'teɪʃən] *n* Abhören *nt*.

auspices ['ɔːspɪsɪz] *npl* **(a)** (*sponsorship*) Schirmherrschaft *f* ♦ **under the ~ of** unter der Schirmherrschaft (*+gen*), unter den Auspizien (*+gen*) (*geh*). **(b)** (*auguries*) Vorzeichen, Auspizien (*geh*) *pl* ♦ **under favourable ~** unter günstigen Vorzeichen *or* Auspizien (*geh*).

auspicious [ɔːs'pɪʃəs] *adj* günstig; *start* vielverheißend, vielversprechend ♦ **an ~ occasion** ein feierlicher Anlaß.

auspiciously [ɔːs'pɪʃəslɪ] *adv* verheißungsvoll, vielversprechend.

Aussie ['ɒzɪ] (*inf*) [1] *n* **(a)** (*person*) Australier(in *f*) *m*. **(b)** (*Austral*) (*country*) Australien *nt*; (*dialect*) australisches Englisch.
[2] *adj* australisch.

austere [ɒs'tɪə^r] *adj* streng; *way of life also* asketisch, entsagend; *style also* schmucklos; *room* schmucklos, karg.

austerely [ɒs'tɪəlɪ] *adv* streng; *furnish* karg, schmucklos; *live* asketisch, entsagend.

austerity [ɒs'terɪtɪ] *n* **(a)** (*severity*) Strenge *f*; (*simplicity*) strenge Einfachheit, Schmucklosigkeit *f*; (*of landscape*) Härte *f*. **(b)** (*hardship, shortage*) Entbehrung *f* ♦ **after the ~ of the war years** nach den Entbehrungen der Kriegsjahre; **a life of ~** ein Leben der Entsagung; **~ budget** Sparhaushalt *m*; **~ measures** Sparmaßnahmen *pl*.

Australasia [,ɔːstrə'leɪsjə] *n* Australien und Ozeanien *nt*.

Australasian [,ɔːstrə'leɪsjən] [1] *n* Ozeanier(in *f*) *m*.
[2] *adj* ozeanisch, südwestpazifisch, Südwestpazifik-.

Australia [ɒs'treɪlɪə] *n* Australien *nt*.

Australian [ɒs'treɪlɪən] [1] *n* Australier(in *f*) *m*; (*accent*) australisches Englisch.
[2] *adj* australisch.

Austria ['ɒstrɪə] *n* Österreich *nt*.

Austria-Hungary ['ɒstrɪə'hʌŋgərɪ] *n* Österreich-Ungarn *nt*.

Austrian ['ɒstrɪən] [1] *n* Österreicher(in *f*) *m*; (*dialect*) Österreichisch *nt*.
[2] *adj* österreichisch.

Austro- ['ɒstrəʊ] *pref* Austro- ♦ **~-Hungarian** österreichisch-ungarisch.

aut *abbr of* **automatic.**

autarchy ['ɔːtɑːkɪ] *n* **(a)** Selbstregierung *f*. **(b)** *see* **autarky.**

autarky ['ɔːtɑːkɪ] *n* Autarkie *f*.

authentic [ɔː'θentɪk] *adj signature, manuscript* authentisch; *accent, antique, tears* echt; *claim to title etc* berechtigt.

authenticate [ɔː'θentɪkeɪt] *vt* bestätigen, authentifizieren (*geh*); *signature, document* beglaubigen; *manuscript, work of art* für echt befinden *or* erklären; *claim* bestätigen ♦ **it was ~d as being ...** es wurde bestätigt, daß es ... war.

authentication [ɔː'θentɪ'keɪʃən] *n see vt* Bestätigung, Authentifizierung (*geh*) *f*; Beglaubigung *f*; Echtheitserklärung *f*.

authenticity [,ɔːθen'tɪsɪtɪ] *n* Echtheit, Authentizität (*geh*) *f*; (*of claim to title etc*) Berechtigung *f*.

author ['ɔːθə^r] *n* (*profession*) Autor(in *f*), Schriftsteller(in *f*) *m*; (*of report, pamphlet*) Verfasser(in *f*) *m*; (*fig*) Urheber(in *f*) *m*; (*of plan*) Initiator(in *f*) *m*; (*of invention*) Vater *m* ♦ **the ~ of the book** der Autor (des Buches); **~'s copy** Autorenexemplar *nt*.

authoress ['ɔːθərɪs] *n* Schriftstellerin *f*.

authorial [ɔː'θɔːrɪəl] *adj* (*liter*) eines/des Autors.

authoritarian [,ɔːθɒrɪ'tɛərɪən] [1] *adj* autoritär.
[2] *n* autoritärer Mensch/Vater/Politiker *etc* ♦ **to be an ~** autoritär sein.

authoritarianism [,ɔːθɒrɪ'tɛərɪənɪzəm] *n* Autoritarismus *m*.

authoritative [ɔː'θɒrɪtətɪv] *adj* **(a)** (*commanding*) bestimmt, entschieden; *manner also* respekteinflößend ♦ **to sound ~** Respekt einflößen, bestimmt auftreten.
(b) (*reliable*) verläßlich, zuverlässig; (*definitive*) maßgeblich, maßgebend ♦ **I won't accept his opinion as ~** seine Meinung ist für mich nicht maßgeblich *or* maßgebend.

authoritatively [ɔː'θɒrɪtətɪvlɪ] *adv* (*with authority*) bestimmt, mit Autorität; (*definitively*) maßgeblich *or* maßgebend; (*reliably*) zuverlässig.

authority [ɔː'θɒrɪtɪ] *n* **(a)** (*power*) Autorität *f*; (*right, entitlement*) Befugnis *f*; (*specifically delegated power*) Vollmacht *f*; (*Mil*) Befehlsgewalt *f* ♦ **people who are in ~** Menschen, die Autorität haben; **the person in ~** der Zuständige *or* Verantwortliche; **who's in ~ here?** wer ist hier der Verantwortliche?; **I'm in**

~ here! hier bestimme ich!; **parental ~** Autorität der Eltern; (*Jur*) elterliche Gewalt; **to be in** *or* **have ~ over sb** Weisungsbefugnis gegenüber jdm haben (*form*); (*describing hierarchy*) jdm übergeordnet sein; **those who are placed in ~ over us** diejenigen, deren Aufsicht wir unterstehen; **the Queen and those in ~ under her** die Königin und die ihr untergebenen Verantwortlichen; **to place sb in ~ over sb** jdm die Verantwortung für jdn übertragen; **to be under the ~ of sb** unter jds Aufsicht (*dat*) stehen; (*in hierarchy*) jdm unterstehen; (*Mil*) jds Befehlsgewalt (*dat*) unterstehen; **on one's own ~** auf eigene Verantwortung; **you'll have to ask a teacher for the ~ to take the key** du brauchst die Erlaubnis *or* Genehmigung des Lehrers, wenn du den Schlüssel haben willst; **under** *or* **by what ~ do you claim the right to ...?** mit welcher Berechtigung verlangen Sie, daß ...?; **to have the ~ to do sth** berechtigt *or* befugt sein, etw zu tun; **to have no ~ to do sth** nicht befugt *or* berechtigt sein, etw zu tun; **he was exceeding his area of ~** er hat seinen Kompetenzbereich *or* seine Befugnisse überschritten; **to give sb the ~ to do sth** jdn ermächtigen (*form*) *or* jdm die Vollmacht erteilen, etw zu tun; **he had my ~ to do it** ich habe es ihm gestattet *or* erlaubt; **to have full ~ to act** volle Handlungsvollmacht haben; **to do sth on sb's ~** etw in jds Auftrag (*dat*) tun; **who gave you the ~ to do that?** wer hat Sie dazu berechtigt?; **who gave you the ~ to treat people like that?** mit welchem Recht glaubst du, Leute so behandeln zu können?
(b) (*also pl: ruling body*) Behörde *f*, Amt *nt*; (*body of people*) Verwaltung *f*; (*power of ruler*) (Staats)gewalt, Obrigkeit *f* ◆ **the university authorities** die Universitätsverwaltung; **the water ~** die Wasserbehörde; **the local ~** *or* **authorities** die Gemeindeverwaltung; **the Prussian respect for ~** das preußische Obrigkeitsdenken; **the concept of ~ in a state** der Autoritätsgedanke im Staat; **they appealed to the supreme ~ of the House of Lords** sie wandten sich an die höchste Autorität *or* Instanz, das Oberhaus; **this will have to be decided by a higher ~** das muß an höherer Stelle entschieden werden; **to represent ~** die Staatsgewalt verkörpern; **the father represents ~** der Vater verkörpert die Autorität; **you must have respect for ~** du mußt Achtung gegenüber Respektspersonen haben.
(c) (*weight, influence*) Autorität *f* ◆ **to have** *or* **carry (great) ~** viel gelten (*with* bei); (*person also*) (große *or* viel) Autorität haben (*with* bei); **to speak/write with ~** mit Sachkunde *or* mit der Autorität des Sachkundigen sprechen/schreiben; **I/he can speak with ~ on this matter** darüber kann ich mich/kann er sich kompetent äußern; **to give an order with ~** einen Befehl mit der nötigen Autorität geben; **to appeal to the ~ of precedent** auf einen Präzedenzfall zurückgreifen.
(d) (*expert*) Autorität *f*, Fachmann *m* ◆ **I'm no ~ but ...** ich bin kein Fachmann, aber ...; **he is an ~ on art** er ist eine Autorität *or* ein Fachmann auf dem Gebiet der Kunst.
(e) (*definitive book etc*) (anerkannte) Autorität *f*; (*source*) Quelle *f* ◆ **to have sth on good ~** etw aus zuverlässiger Quelle wissen; **on the best ~** aus bester Quelle; **what is his ~ for that assertion?** worauf stützt er diese Behauptung?; **on whose ~ do you have that?** aus welcher Quelle haben Sie das?

▼ **authorization** [ˌɔːθəraɪˈzeɪʃən] *n* Genehmigung *f*; (*delegation of authority*) Bevollmächtigung, Autorisation (*geh*) *f*; (*right*) Recht *nt*.

▼ **authorize** [ˈɔːθəraɪz] *vt* **(a)** (*empower*) berechtigen, ermächtigen, autorisieren (*geh*); (*delegate authority*) bevollmächtigen ◆ **to be ~d to do sth** (*have right*) berechtigt sein *or* das Recht haben, etw zu tun; **he was specially ~d to ...** er hatte eine Sondervollmacht, zu ...; **this licence ~s you to drive ...** dieser Führerschein berechtigt Sie zum Fahren von ...
(b) (*permit*) genehmigen; *money, claim etc also* bewilligen; *translation, biography etc* autorisieren ◆ **the A~d Version** *engl. Bibelfassung von 1611*; **to be/become ~d by custom** zum Gewohnheitsrecht geworden sein/werden; **~d capital** Nominalkapital *nt*; **~d representative** bevollmächtigter Vertreter; **~d signatory** Zeichnungsberechtigte(r) *mf*.

authorship [ˈɔːθəʃɪp] *n* **(a)** Autorschaft, Verfasserschaft *f* ◆ **of unknown ~** eines unbekannten Autors *or* Verfassers; **he admitted ~ of the article** er bekannte, den Artikel verfaßt *or* geschrieben zu haben; **there are disagreements as to the ~ of the play** der Autor des Stückes ist umstritten.
(b) (*occupation*) Schriftstellerberuf *m*.

autism [ˈɔːtɪzəm] *n* Autismus *m*.

autistic [ɔːˈtɪstɪk] *adj* autistisch.

auto [ˈɔːtəʊ] *n* (*US*) Auto *nt*, PKW *m*.

auto- [ˈɔːtəʊ] *pref* auto-, Auto-.

autobank [ˈɔːtəʊbæŋk] *n* Geldautomat *m*.

autobiographical [ˈɔːtəʊˌbaɪəʊˈgræfɪkəl] *adj* autobiographisch.

autobiography [ˌɔːtəʊbaɪˈɒgrəfɪ] *n* Autobiographie *f*.

autocade [ˈɔːtəʊkeɪd] *n* (*US*) Wagenkolonne *f* *or* -konvoi *m*.

autochanger [ˈɔːtəʊˌtʃeɪndʒə^r] *n* (automatischer) Plattenwechsler.

autocracy [ɔːˈtɒkrəsɪ] *n* Autokratie *f*.

autocrat [ˈɔːtəʊkræt] *n* Autokrat(in *f*) *m*.

autocratic [ˌɔːtəʊˈkrætɪk] *adj* autokratisch.

autocross [ˈɔːtəʊkrɒs] *n* Auto-Cross *nt*.

autocue [ˈɔːtəʊkjuː] *n* (*Brit TV*) Teleprompter *m*.

auto-da-fé [ˈɔːtəʊdɑːˈfeɪ] *n, pl* **autos-da-fé** Autodafé *nt*.

auto-eroticism [ˌɔːtəʊɪˈrɒtɪˌsɪzəm] *n* Autoerotik *f*.

autofocus [ˈɔːtəʊfəʊkəs] *n* (*Phot*) Autofocus, Autofokus *m*; (*camera*) Autofocus, Autofokus *f*.

autograph [ˈɔːtəgrɑːf] [1] *n* (*signature*) Autogramm *nt*; (*manuscript*) Originalmanuskript *nt* ◆ **~ album** *or* **book** Autogrammalbum *or* -buch *nt*; **~ copy/letter** handgeschriebenes Manuskript/handgeschriebener Brief.
[2] *vt* signieren ◆ **he ~ed my album** er hat mir ein Autogramm fürs Album gegeben.

autoimmune [ˌɔːtəʊɪˈmjuːn] *adj* autoimmun ◆ **~ disease** Autoimmunkrankheit *f*.

automat [ˈɔːtəmæt] *n* (*US*) Automatenrestaurant *nt*.

automata [ɔːˈtɒmətə] *pl of* **automaton.**

automate [ˈɔːtəmeɪt] *vt* automatisieren ◆ **~d teller** Geldautomat *m*.

automatic [ˌɔːtəˈmætɪk] [1] *adj* (*lit, fig*) automatisch; *weapon also* Maschinen- ◆ **~ choke** Startautomatik *f*; **~ gearbox** Getriebeautomatik *f*; **the ~ model** das Modell mit Automatik; **~ pilot** Autopilot *m*; **the refund is not ~** Rückerstattung erfolgt nicht automatisch; **he has the ~ right ...** er hat automatisch das Recht ...; **the film star's ~ smile** das Routinelächeln des Filmstars; **you shouldn't need telling, it should be ~** das sollte man dir nicht erst sagen müssen, das solltest du automatisch tun; **~ data processing** automatische Datenverarbeitung.
[2] *n* (*car*) Automatikwagen *m*; (*gun*) automatische Waffe, Maschinenwaffe *f*; (*washing machine*) Waschautomat *m*.

automatically [ˌɔːtəˈmætɪkəlɪ] *adv* automatisch.

automation [ˌɔːtəˈmeɪʃən] *n* Automatisierung *f*.

automaton [ɔːˈtɒmətən] *n, pl* **-s** *or* **automata** [-ətə] (*robot*) Roboter *m*; (*fig also*) Automat *m*.

automobile [ˈɔːtəməbiːl] *n* Auto(mobil) *nt*, Kraftwagen *m* (*form*).

automotive [ˌɔːtəˈməʊtɪv] *adj vehicle* selbstfahrend, mit Selbstantrieb; *engineering, mechanic* Kfz- ◆ **~ power** Selbstantrieb *m*.

autonomous [ɔːˈtɒnəməs] *adj* autonom.

autonomy [ɔːˈtɒnəmɪ] *n* Autonomie *f*.

autopilot [ˌɔːtəʊˈpaɪlət] *n* Autopilot *m* ◆ **to switch onto ~** (*lit, fig inf*) auf Automatik umschalten; **I'm so shattered, I just do everything on ~** ich bin so geschafft, daß ich alles nur noch ganz automatisch mache.

autopsy [ˈɔːtɒpsɪ] *n* Autopsie, Leichenöffnung *f*.

autoreverse [ˌɔːtəʊrɪˈvɜːs] *n* Autoreverse-Funktion *f*.

autosuggestion [ˈɔːtəʊsəˈdʒestʃən] *n* Autosuggestion *f*.

autotimer [ˈɔːtəʊˌtaɪmə^r] *n* (*on cooker etc*) Ein-/Abschaltautomatik *f*.

autumn [ˈɔːtəm] (*esp Brit*) [1] *n* (*lit, fig*) Herbst *m* ◆ **in (the) ~** im Herbst; **two ~s ago** im Herbst vor zwei Jahren.
[2] *adj attr* Herbst-, herbstlich ◆ **~ leaves** bunte (Herbst)blätter *pl*.

autumnal [ɔːˈtʌmnəl] *adj* herbstlich, Herbst- ◆ **~ equinox** Herbst-Tagundnachtgleiche *f*.

auxiliary [ɔːgˈzɪlɪərɪ] [1] *adj* Hilfs- (*also Comput*); (*emergency also*) Not-; (*additional*) *engine, generator etc* Zusatz- ◆ **~ note** (*Mus*) Nebennote *f*; **~ nurse** Schwesternhelferin *f*.
[2] *n* **(a)** (*Mil: esp pl*) Soldat *m* der Hilfstruppe ◆ **auxiliaries** *pl* Hilfstruppe(n *pl*) *f*. **(b)** (*general: assistant*) Hilfskraft *f*, Helfer(in *f*) *m* ◆ **teaching/nursing ~** (Aus)hilfslehrer(in *f*) *m*/Schwesternhelferin *f*. **(c)** (*~ verb*) Hilfsverb *or* -zeitwort *nt*.

AV *abbr of* **Authorized Version** (*of Bible*).

av *abbr of* **average** Durchschn.

Av, Ave *abbr of* **avenue.**

avail[1] *abbr of* **available.**

avail[2] [əˈveɪl] [1] *vr* **to ~ oneself of sth** von etw Gebrauch machen; **to ~ oneself of the opportunity of doing sth** die Gelegenheit wahrnehmen *or* nutzen, etw zu tun.
[2] *vi* (*form*) helfen ◆ **nothing could ~ against their superior strength** gegen ihre Überlegenheit war nichts auszurichten.
[3] *n* **of no ~** erfolglos, ohne Erfolg, vergeblich; **of little ~** wenig erfolgreich, mit wenig *or* geringem Erfolg; **his advice was/his pleas were of no/little ~** seine Ratschläge/Bitten haben nicht(s)/wenig gefruchtet; **to no ~** vergebens, vergeblich; **of what ~ is it to ...?** (*liter*) was nützt es, zu ...?; **and to what ~?** (*liter*) und zu welchem Behuf? (*old form*).

availability [əˌveɪləˈbɪlɪtɪ] *n see adj* Erhältlichkeit *f*; Lieferbarkeit *f*; Vorrätigkeit *f*; Verfügbarkeit *f*; (*presence: of secretarial staff, mineral ore etc*) Vorhandensein *nt* ◆ **the market price is determined by ~** der Marktpreis richtet sich nach dem vorhandenen Angebot; **because of the greater ~ of their product ...** weil ihr Produkt leichter erhältlich/lieferbar ist ...; **we'd like to sell you one, but it's a question of ~** wir würden Ihnen gern eines verkaufen, das hängt aber davon ab, ob es erhältlich/lieferbar ist; **offer subject to ~ while stocks last** (das Angebot gilt) nur solange der Vorrat reicht; **greater ~ of jobs** größeres Stellenangebot; **because of the limited ~ of seats** weil nur eine begrenzte Anzahl an Plätzen zur Verfügung steht; **to increase the ~ of culture to the masses** breiteren Bevölkerungsschichten den Zugang zu Kultur erleichtern; **his ~ for discussion is, I'm afraid, determined by ...** ob er Zeit für eine Besprechung hat, hängt leider von ... ab; **the Swedish au-pair gained a reputation for "~"** das schwedische Au-pair-Mädchen hatte bald den Ruf, „leicht zu haben" zu sein.

▼ **available** [əˈveɪləbl] *adj* **(a)** *object* erhältlich; (*Comm*) (*from supplier also*) lieferbar; (*in stock*) vorrätig; (*free*) *time, post* frei; *theatre seats etc* frei, zu haben *pred*; (*at one's disposal*) *worker, means, resources etc* verfügbar, zur Verfügung stehend ◆ **to be ~** (*at one's disposal*) zur Verfügung stehen; (*person: not otherwise occupied*) frei *or* abkömmlich (*form*) sein; (*can be reached*) erreichbar sein; (*for discussion*) zu sprechen sein; **to make sth ~ to sb** jdm etw zur Verfügung stellen; (*accessible*) *culture, knowledge, information* jdm etw zugänglich machen; **to make oneself ~ to sb** sich jdm zur Verfügung stellen; **could you make yourself ~ for discussion between 2 and 3?** könnten Sie sich zwischen 2 und 3 für eine Besprechung freihalten *or* zur Verfügung halten?; **the best dictionary ~, the best ~ dictionary** das beste Wörterbuch, das es gibt; **he caught the next ~ flight home** er nahm den näch-

➤ LANGUAGE IN USE: **authorization** → 9.3 **authorize: a** → 9.4, 9.5 **available: a** → 19.3

sten *or* nächstmöglichen Flug nach Hause; **to try every ~ means (to achieve sth)** nichts unversucht lassen(, um etw zu erreichen); **reference books/consultants are ~** Nachschlagewerke/Berater stehen einem/Ihnen *etc* zur Verfügung; **all ~ staff were asked to help out** das abkömmliche *or* verfügbare *or* zur Verfügung stehende Personal wurde gebeten auszuhelfen; **are you ~ for tennis/a discussion tonight?** können Sie heute abend Tennis spielen/an einer Diskussion teilnehmen?; **when will you be ~ to start in the new job?** wann können Sie die Stelle antreten?; **I'm not ~ until October** ich bin vor Oktober nicht frei; **a professor should always be ~ to his students** ein Professor sollte stets für seine Studenten da sein *or* seinen Studenten stets zur Verfügung stehen; **he's ~ for consultation on Mondays** er hat montags Sprechzeit; **you shouldn't make yourself so ~ to him** du solltest es ihm nicht so leicht machen; **she's what is known as "~"** es ist bekannt, daß sie „leicht zu haben" ist.

(b) *(form) ticket* gültig.

avalanche ['ævəlɑːnʃ] *n (lit, fig)* Lawine *f.*

avant-garde ['ævɑ̃ŋ'gɑːd] **1** *n* Avantgarde *f.* **2** *adj* avantgardistisch.

avarice ['ævərɪs] *n* Habgier, Habsucht *f.*

avaricious [ˌævə'rɪʃəs] *adj* habgierig, habsüchtig.

avariciously [ˌævə'rɪʃəslɪ] *adv* (hab)gierig.

avdp *abbr of* **avoirdupois.**

Ave (Maria) ['ɑːveɪ(mə'rɪə)] *n* Ave(-Maria) *nt.*

avenge [ə'vendʒ] *vt* rächen ♦ **to ~ oneself on sb (for sth)** sich an jdm (für etw) rächen; **an avenging angel** ein Racheengel *m.*

avenger [ə'vendʒəʳ] *n* Rächer(in *f*) *m.*

avenue ['ævənjuː] *n* **(a)** *(tree-lined)* Allee *f*; *(broad street)* Boulevard *m.* **(b)** *(fig) (method)* Weg *m* ♦ **~s of approach** Verfahrensweisen; **an ~ of approach to the problem** ein Weg, das Problem anzugehen; **~ of escape** Ausweg *m*; **to explore every ~** alle sich bietenden Wege prüfen.

aver [ə'vɜːʳ] *vt (form)* mit Nachdruck betonen; *love, innocence* beteuern.

average ['ævərɪdʒ] **1** *n* (Durch)schnitt *m*; *(Math also)* Mittelwert *m* ♦ **to do an ~ of 50 miles a day/3% a week** durchschnittlich *or* im (Durch)schnitt 50 Meilen pro Tag fahren/3% pro Woche erledigen; **what's your ~ over the last six months?** was haben Sie im letzten halben Jahr durchschnittlich geleistet/verdient *etc*?; **on ~** durchschnittlich, im (Durch)schnitt; *(normally)* normalerweise; **if you take the ~** *(Math)* wenn Sie den (Durch)schnitt *or* Mittelwert nehmen; *(general)* wenn Sie den durchschnittlichen Fall nehmen; **above/below ~** überdurchschnittlich, über dem Durchschnitt/unterdurchschnittlich, unter dem Durchschnitt; **the law of ~s** das Gesetz der Serie; **by the law of ~s** aller Wahrscheinlichkeit nach.

2 *adj* durchschnittlich; *(ordinary)* Durchschnitts-; *(not good or bad)* mittelmäßig ♦ **above/below ~** über-/unterdurchschnittlich; **the ~ man, Mr A~** der Durchschnittsbürger; **the ~ Scot** der Durchschnittsschotte; **he's a man of ~ height** er ist von mittlerer Größe.

3 *vt* **(a)** *(find the ~ of)* den Durchschnitt ermitteln von.

(b) *(do etc on ~)* auf einen Schnitt von ... kommen ♦ **we ~d 80 km/h** wir kamen auf einen Schnitt von 80 km/h, wir sind durchschnittlich 80 km/h gefahren; **the factory ~s 500 cars a week** die Fabrik produziert durchschnittlich *or* im (Durch)schnitt 500 Autos pro Woche.

(c) *(~ out at)* **sales are averaging 10,000 copies per day** der Absatz beläuft sich auf *or* beträgt durchschnittlich *or* im (Durch)schnitt 10.000 Exemplare pro Tag.

♦**average out** **1** *vt sep* **we have to ~ ~ our weekly output over a six-month period** wir müssen unsere durchschnittliche Arbeitsleistung pro Woche über einen Zeitraum von sechs Monaten ermitteln; **if you ~ it ~** im Durchschnitt; **it'll ~ itself ~** es wird sich ausgleichen.

2 *vi* durchschnittlich ausmachen *(at acc)*; *(balance out)* sich ausgleichen ♦ **how does it ~ ~ on a weekly basis?** wieviel ist das durchschnittlich *or* im Schnitt pro Woche?

averse [ə'vɜːs] *adj pred* abgeneigt ♦ **I am not ~ to a glass of wine** einem Glas Wein bin ich nicht abgeneigt; **I am rather ~ to doing that** es ist mir ziemlich zuwider, das zu tun; **I feel ~ to doing it** es widerstrebt mir, das zu tun.

aversion [ə'vɜːʃən] *n* **(a)** *(strong dislike)* Abneigung, Aversion *(geh, Psych) f (to* gegen) ♦ **he has an ~ to getting wet** er hat eine Abscheu davor, naß zu werden; **~ therapy** *(Psych)* Aversionstherapie *f.* **(b)** *(object of ~)* Greuel *m* ♦ **smoking is his pet ~** Rauchen ist ihm ein besonderer Greuel.

avert [ə'vɜːt] *vt* **(a)** *(turn away) eyes, gaze* abwenden, abkehren *(geh)* ♦ **to ~ one's mind** *or* **thoughts from sth** seine Gedanken von etw abwenden. **(b)** *(prevent)* verhindern, abwenden; *suspicion* ablenken; *blow etc* abwehren; *accident* verhindern, verhüten.

aviary ['eɪvɪərɪ] *n* Vogelhaus, Aviarium *(geh) nt*, Voliere *f (geh).*

aviation [ˌeɪvɪ'eɪʃən] *n* die Luftfahrt ♦ **the art of ~** die Kunst des Fliegens.

aviator ['eɪvɪeɪtəʳ] *n* Flieger(in *f*) *m.*

aviculture ['eɪvɪˌkʌltʃəʳ] *n (form)* Vogelzucht *f.*

avid ['ævɪd] *adj* **(a)** *(desirous)* gierig *(for* nach); *(for fame, praise also)* süchtig *(for* nach) ♦ **~ for fame** ruhmsüchtig.

(b) *(keen)* begeistert, passioniert; *supporter also* eifrig; *interest* lebhaft, stark ♦ **he is an ~ follower of this series** er verfolgt diese Serie mit lebhaftem Interesse; **as an ~ reader of your column** als eifriger Leser Ihrer Spalte; **I am an ~ reader** ich lese leidenschaftlich gern.

avidity [ə'vɪdɪtɪ] *n, no pl (liter) see adj* **(a)** Begierde *f (for* nach); *(pej)* Gier *f (for* nach) ♦ **with ~** begierig; gierig. **(b)** Begeisterung *f*; Eifer *m.*

avidly ['ævɪdlɪ] *adv see adj* **(a)** begierig; *(pej)* gierig. **(b)** eifrig; *read* leidenschaftlich gern.

➤ LANGUAGE IN USE: **avoid** → 10.1 **await: a** → 20.5

avionics [ˌeɪvɪ'ɒnɪks] *n sing* Avionik *f.*

avocado [ˌævə'kɑːdəʊ] *n, pl* **-s** *(also* **~ pear)** Avocato(birne), Avocado(birne) *f*; *(tree)* Avocato- *or* Avocadobaum *m.*

avocation [ˌævəʊ'keɪʃən] *n (form) (calling)* Berufung *f.*

▼ **avoid** [ə'vɔɪd] *vt* vermeiden; *damage, accident also* verhüten; *person, danger* meiden, aus dem Weg gehen *(+dat)*; *obstacle* ausweichen *(+dat)*; *difficulty, duty, truth* umgehen ♦ **we've managed to ~ the danger** wir konnten der Gefahr entgehen; **in order to ~ being seen** um nicht gesehen zu werden; **he'd do anything to ~ the washing-up** er würde alles tun, um nur nicht abwaschen zu müssen; **I'm not going if I can possibly ~ it** wenn es sich irgendwie vermeiden läßt, gehe ich nicht; **... you can hardly ~ visiting them** ... dann kommst du wohl kaum darum herum *or* kannst du es wohl schlecht vermeiden, sie zu besuchen; **I can't ~ leaving now** ich muß jetzt unbedingt gehen; **to ~ sb's eye** jds Blick *(dat)* ausweichen, es vermeiden, jdn anzusehen; **to ~ notice** unbemerkt bleiben.

avoidable [ə'vɔɪdəbl] *adj* vermeidbar ♦ **if it's (at all) ~** wenn es sich (irgend) vermeiden läßt.

avoidance [ə'vɔɪdəns] *n* Vermeidung *f* ♦ **he advised us on the ~ of death duties** er hat uns beraten, wie wir die Erbschaftssteuer umgehen können; **the ~ of death duties** die Umgehung der Erbschaftssteuer; **his persistent ~ of the truth** sein ständiges Umgehen der Wahrheit; **thanks only to her steady ~ of bad company** nur weil sie konsequent schlechte Gesellschaft mied.

avoirdupois [ˌævwɑːdjuː'pwɑː] *n* Avoirdupois *nt*; *(hum: excess weight)* Fülligkeit, Üppigkeit *f* ♦ **she's been putting on the ~ a bit** sie ist ziemlich in die Breite gegangen.

avow [ə'vaʊ] *vt (liter)* erklären; *belief, faith* bekennen ♦ **to ~ one's love (to sb)** (jdm) seine Liebe erklären *or* gestehen, sich (jdm) erklären; **he ~ed himself to be a royalist** er bekannte (offen), Royalist zu sein.

avowal [ə'vaʊəl] *n* Erklärung *f*; *(of faith)* Bekenntnis *nt*; *(of love also)* Geständnis *nt*; *(of belief, interest)* Bekundung *f* ♦ **he is on his own ~ a ...** er ist erklärtermaßen ...

avowed [ə'vaʊd] *adj* erklärt.

avowedly [ə'vaʊɪdlɪ] *adv* erklärtermaßen.

avuncular [ə'vʌŋkjʊləʳ] *adj* onkelhaft; *figure* Onkel-.

aw *abbr of* **atomic weight.**

AWACS, Awacs ['eɪwæks] *abbr of* **airborne warning and control system** *mit Frühwarnsystem ausgestattetes Aufklärungsflugzeug der US-Luftwaffe.*

▼ **await** [ə'weɪt] *vt* **(a)** *(wait for)* erwarten; *future events, decision etc* entgegensehen *(+dat)* ♦ **the long ~ed day** der langersehnte Tag; **parcels ~ing despatch** zum Versand bestimmte Pakete; **we ~ your reply with interest** wir sehen Ihrer Antwort mit Interesse entgegen. **(b)** *(be in store for)* erwarten.

awake [ə'weɪk] *pret* **awoke**, *ptp* **awoken** *or* **awaked** [ə'weɪkt] **1** *vi (lit, fig)* erwachen ♦ **to ~ from sleep/one's dreams** aus dem Schlaf/seinen Träumen erwachen; **to ~ to sth** *(fig) (realize)* sich *(dat)* einer Sache *(gen)* bewußt werden; *(become interested)* beginnen, sich für etw zu interessieren; **to ~ to the joys of sth** (plötzlich) Vergnügen an etw *(dat)* finden; **his interest was slow to ~** sein Interesse ist erst spät erwacht.

2 *vt* wecken; *(fig) suspicion, interest etc also* erwecken ♦ **to ~ sb to sth** *(make realize)* jdm etw bewußt machen; *(make interested)* jds Interesse für etw wecken.

3 *adj pred (lit, fig)* wach; *(alert also)* aufmerksam ♦ **to be/lie/stay ~** wach sein/liegen/bleiben; **to keep sb ~** jdn wachhalten; **wide ~** *(lit, fig)* hellwach; **to be ~ to sth** *(fig)* sich *(dat)* einer Sache *(gen)* bewußt sein.

awaken [ə'weɪkən] *vti see* **awake.**

awakening [ə'weɪknɪŋ] **1** *n (lit, fig)* Erwachen *nt* ♦ **a rude ~** *(lit, fig)* ein böses Erwachen.

2 *adj (fig)* erwachend.

award [ə'wɔːd] **1** *vt prize, penalty, free kick etc* zusprechen *(to sb* jdm), zuerkennen *(to sb* jdm); *(present) prize, degree, medal etc* verleihen *(to sb* jdm) ♦ **to be ~ed damages** Schadenersatz zugesprochen bekommen; **to ~ sb first prize** jdm den ersten Preis zuerkennen.

2 *n* **(a)** *(prize)* Preis *m*; *(for bravery etc)* Auszeichnung *f*; *(Jur)* Zuerkennung *f* ♦ **to make an ~ (to sb)** einen Preis (an jdn) vergeben. **(b)** *(Univ)* Stipendium *nt.*

aware [ə'weəʳ] *adj esp pred* bewußt ♦ **to be/become ~ of sb/sth** sich *(dat)* jds/einer Sache bewußt sein/werden; *(notice also)* jdn bemerken/etw merken; **I was not ~ (of the fact) that ...** es war mir nicht klar *or* bewußt, daß ...; **you will be ~ of the importance of this** es muß Ihnen bewußt sein, wie wichtig das ist; **are you ~ that ...?** ist dir eigentlich klar, daß ...?; **not that I am ~ (of)** nicht daß ich wüßte; **as far as I am ~** soviel ich weiß; **we try to remain ~ of what is going on in other companies/the world** wir versuchen, uns auf dem laufenden darüber zu halten, was in anderen Firmen/auf der Welt vor sich geht; **to make sb ~ of sth** jdm etw bewußt machen *or* zum Bewußtsein bringen; **to make sb more ~/~ of sth** jds Bewußtsein wecken/jdm etw bewußt machen; **for a three-year-old he's very ~** für einen Dreijährigen ist er sehr aufgeweckt; **she's very ~ of language** sie ist sehr sprachbewußt.

awareness [ə'weənɪs] *n* Bewußtsein *nt* ♦ **he showed no ~ of the urgency of the problem** er schien sich der Dringlichkeit des Problems nicht bewußt zu sein; **her tremendous ~ of the shades of meaning in the language/of other people's feelings** ihr außerordentlich waches Gespür für die Bedeutungsnuancen der Sprache/für die Empfindungen anderer; **drugs which increase one's ~ of the outer world** bewußtseinserweiternde Drogen *pl.*

awash [ə'wɒʃ] *adj pred decks, rocks etc* überspült; *cellar* unter Wasser.

away [ə'weɪ] **1** *adv* **(a)** *(to or at a distance)* weg ♦ **three miles ~ (from here)**

drei Meilen (entfernt) von hier; **lunch seemed a long time ~** es schien noch lange bis zum Mittagessen zu sein; **~ back in the distance/past** weit in der Ferne/vor sehr langer Zeit; **they're ~ behind/out in front/off course** sie sind weit zurück/voraus/ab vom Kurs.
(b) *(motion)* **~!** *(old, liter)* fort!, hinweg! *(old, liter)*; **~ with the old philosophy, in with the new!** fort mit der alten Philosophie, her mit der neuen!; **come, let us ~!** *(liter)* kommt, laßt uns fort von hier *(old)*; **~ with him!** fort mit ihm!; **but he was ~ before I could say a word** aber er war fort *or* weg, bevor ich den Mund auftun konnte; **to look ~** wegsehen; **~ we go!** los (geht's)!; **they're ~!** *(horses, runners etc)* sie sind gestartet; **they're ~ first time** gleich der erste Start hat geklappt.
(c) *(absent)* fort, weg ◆ **he's ~ from work (with a cold)** er fehlt (wegen einer Erkältung); **he's ~ in London** er ist in London; **when I have to be ~** wenn ich nicht da sein kann.
(d) *(Sport)* **to play ~** auswärts spielen; **they're ~ to Arsenal** sie haben ein Auswärtsspiel bei Arsenal.
(e) *(out of existence, possession etc)* **to put/give ~** weglegen/weggeben; **to boil/gamble/die ~** verkochen/verspielen/verhallen; **we talked the evening ~** wir haben den Abend verplaudert.
(f) *(continuously)* unablässig ◆ **to work/knit** *etc* **~** vor sich *(acc)* hin arbeiten/stricken *etc.*
(g) *(forthwith)* **ask ~!** frag nur!, schieß los *(inf)*; **pull/heave ~!** und los(, zieht/hebt an)!; **right** *or* **straight ~** sofort.
(h) *(inf)* **he's ~ again** *(talking, giggling, drunk etc)* es geht wieder los; **he's ~ with the idea that ...** er hat den Fimmel, daß ...; **~ with you!** ach wo!
[2] *adj attr (Sport) team* auswärtig, Gast-; *match, win* Auswärts-.
[3] *n (in Ftbl pools: ~ win)* Auswärtssieg *m.*

awe [ɔː] [1] *n* Ehrfurcht *f*, ehrfürchtige Scheu ◆ **to be** *or* **stand in ~ of sb** Ehrfurcht vor jdm haben; *(feel fear)* große Furcht vor jdm haben; **to hold sb in ~** Ehrfurcht *or* großen Respekt vor jdm haben; **to strike sb with ~, to strike ~ into sb's heart** jdm Ehrfurcht einflößen; *(make fearful)* jdm Furcht einflößen; **the sight filled me with ~** der Anblick erfüllte mich mit ehrfurchtsvoller Scheu.
[2] *vt* Ehrfurcht *or* ehrfürchtige Scheu einflößen *(+dat)* ◆ **~d by the beauty/silence** von der Schönheit/der Stille ergriffen; **in an ~d voice** mit ehrfürchtiger Stimme.

awe-inspiring ['ɔːɪn,spaɪərɪŋ], **awesome** ['ɔːsəm] *adj* ehrfurchtgebietend.

awe-stricken ['ɔː,strɪkən], **awe-struck** ['ɔː,strʌk] *adj* von Ehrfurcht ergriffen; *voice, expression also* ehrfurchtsvoll; *(frightened)* von Schrecken ergriffen ◆ **I was quite ~ by its beauty** ich war von seiner Schönheit ergriffen.

awful ['ɔːfəl] [1] *adj* **(a)** *(inf)* schrecklich, furchtbar ◆ **how ~!** das ist wirklich schlimm!; **you are ~!** du bist wirklich schrecklich!; **the film was just too ~ for words** der Film war unbeschreiblich schlecht; **it's not an ~ lot better** das ist nicht arg viel besser.
(b) *(old: awe-inspiring)* ehrfurchtgebietend.
[2] *adv (strictly incorrect) see* **awfully** ◆ **he was crying something ~** er weinte ganz schrecklich *or* furchtbar.

awfully ['ɔːflɪ] *adv (inf)* furchtbar *(inf)*, schrecklich *(inf)* ◆ **thanks ~** vielen, vielen Dank!; **it's not ~ important** es ist nicht so schrecklich *or* furchtbar wichtig *(inf)*; **she is rather ~ ~** *(Brit hum)* sie ist furchtbar vornehm *(inf)*.

awfulness ['ɔːfʊlnɪs] *n (of situation)* Schrecklichkeit, Furchtbarkeit *f*; *(of person)* abscheuliche Art, Abscheulichkeit *f* ◆ **we were shocked by the ~ of it all** wir waren von der Schrecklichkeit *or* Furchtbarkeit des Ganzen überwältigt.

awhile [ə'waɪl] *adv (liter)* eine Weile ◆ **not yet ~!** noch eine ganze Weile nicht!

awkward ['ɔːkwəd] *adj* **(a)** *(difficult)* schwierig; *time, moment, angle, shape* ungünstig ◆ **4 o'clock is a bit ~ (for me)** 4 Uhr ist ein bißchen ungünstig *or* schlecht *(inf)* (für mich).
(b) *(embarrassing)* peinlich.
(c) *(embarrassed)* verlegen; *(shamefaced)* betreten; *silence* betreten ◆ **the ~ age** das schwierige Alter; **to feel ~ in sb's company** sich in jds Gesellschaft *(dat)* nicht wohl fühlen; **I felt ~ when I had to ...** es war mir peinlich, als ich ... mußte.
(d) *(clumsy) person, movement, style* unbeholfen.

awkwardly ['ɔːkwədlɪ] *adv see adj* **(a)** schwierig; ungünstig. **(b)** peinlich. **(c)** verlegen; betreten. **(d)** unbeholfen.

awkwardness ['ɔːkwədnɪs] *n see adj* **(a)** Schwierigkeit *f*; Ungünstigkeit *f*. **(b)** Peinlichkeit *f*. **(c)** Verlegenheit *f*; Betretenheit *f*. **(d)** Unbeholfenheit *f*.

awl [ɔːl] *n* Ahle *f*, Pfriem *m.*

awning ['ɔːnɪŋ] *n (on window, of shop)* Markise *f*; *(on boat)* Sonnensegel *nt*; *(of wagon)* Plane *f*; *(caravan ~)* Vordach *nt.*

awoke [ə'wəʊk] *pret of* **awake.**

awoken [ə'wəʊkən] *ptp of* **awake.**

AWOL *(Mil) abbr of* **absent without leave.**

awry [ə'raɪ] *adj pred, adv (askew)* schief ◆ **the picture/hat is ~** das Bild hängt/der Hut sitzt schief; **to go ~** *(plans etc)* schiefgehen.

axe, *(US)* **ax** [æks] [1] *n* Axt *f*, Beil *nt*; *(fig)* (radikale) Kürzung ◆ **to wield the ~ on sth** *(fig)* etw radikal kürzen; **the ~ has fallen on the project** das Projekt ist dem Rotstift zum Opfer gefallen; **to have an/no ~ to grind** *(fig)* ein/kein persönliches Interesse haben.
[2] *vt plans, projects, jobs* streichen; *person* entlassen.

axiom ['æksɪəm] *n* Axiom *nt.*

axiomatic [,æksɪəʊ'mætɪk] *adj* axiomatisch ◆ **we can take it as ~ that ...** wir können von dem Grundsatz ausgehen, daß ...

axis ['æksɪs] *n, pl* **axes** ['æksiːz] Achse *f* ◆ **the A~ (powers)** *(Hist)* die Achse, die Achsenmächte *pl.*

axle ['æksl] *n* Achse *f.*

axle: ~ bearing *n* Achslager *nt*; **~ box** *n* Achsgehäuse *nt*; **~ grease** *n* Achs(en)fett *nt*; **~ housing** *n* Achsgehäuse *nt*; **~ pin** *n* Achs(en)nagel *m*; **~ tree** *n* Achswelle *f.*

ayatollah [,aɪə'tɒlə] *n* Ajatollah *m.*

ay(e) [aɪ] [1] *interj (esp Scot, dial)* ja ◆ **aye, aye, Sir** *(Naut)* jawohl, Herr Kapitänleutnant/Admiral *etc.*
[2] *n (esp Parl)* Jastimme *f*, Ja *nt* ◆ **the ~s** diejenigen, die dafür sind, die dafür; **the ~s have it** die Mehrheit ist dafür.

aye [eɪ] *adv (old, Scot)* immer.

azalea [ə'zeɪlɪə] *n* Azalee *f.*

Azerbaijani [æzəbaɪ'dʒɑːnɪ], **Azeri** [æ'zɛərɪ] [1] *adj* aserbaidschanisch.
[2] *n* Aserbaidschaner(in) *m(f).*

azimuth ['æzɪməθ] *n (Astron)* Azimut *nt or m.*

Azores [ə'zɔːz] *npl* Azoren *pl.*

AZT *abbr of* **azidothymidine** AZT *nt.*

Aztec ['æztek] [1] *n* Azteke *m*, Aztekin *f.*
[2] *adj* aztekisch.

azure ['æʒəʳ] [1] *n* Azur(blau *nt*) *m.*
[2] *adj sky* azurblau; *eyes also* tiefblau ◆ **~ blue** azurblau.

B

B, b [biː] *n* B, b *nt*; (*Sch: as a mark*) zwei, gut; (*Mus*) H, h *nt* ◆ **~ flat/sharp** B, b *nt*/His, his *nt*; *see also* **major, minor, natural**.
B *adj* (*on pencil*) B.
b *abbr of* **born** geb.
BA *abbr of* **Bachelor of Arts**.
baa [bɑː] 1 *n* Mähen *nt no pl* ◆ **~!** mäh!; **~lamb** (*baby-talk*) Bählamm, Mähschäfchen *nt* (*baby-talk*).
2 *vi* mähen, mäh machen (*baby-talk*).
babble [ˈbæbl] 1 *n* **(a)** Gemurmel *nt*; (*of baby, excited person etc*) Geplapper *nt* ◆ **~ (of voices)** Stimmengewirr *nt*.
(b) (*of stream*) Murmeln (*liter*), Plätschern *nt no pl*.
2 *vi* **(a)** (*person*) plappern, quasseln (*inf*); (*baby*) plappern, lallen ◆ **don't ~, speak slowly** nicht so schnell, rede langsam; **the other actress tended to ~** die andere Schauspielerin neigte dazu, ihren Text herunterzurasseln.
(b) (*stream*) murmeln (*liter*), plätschern.
◆**babble away** *or* **on** *vi* quatschen (*inf*) (*about* über +*acc*), quasseln (*inf*) (*about* von) ◆ **she ~d ~ excitedly** sie quasselte *or* plapperte aufgeregt drauflos (*inf*).
◆**babble out** *vt sep* brabbeln; *secret* ausplaudern.
babbler [ˈbæbləʳ] *n* Plaudertasche *f* (*inf*) ◆ **don't tell him, he's a ~** sag ihm nichts, er quatscht (*inf*).
babbling [ˈbæblɪŋ] *adj brook* murmelnd (*liter*), plätschernd.
babe [beɪb] *n* **(a)** (*liter*) Kindlein *nt* (*liter*) ◆ **~ in arms** Säugling *m*. **(b)** (*esp US inf*) Baby *nt* (*inf*), Puppe *f* (*inf*) ◆ **hey Susie/Mike ~!** he du, Susie!/Mike!; *see also* **baby (e)**.
Babel [ˈbeɪbəl] *n* **(a) the Tower of ~** (*story*) der Turmbau zu Babel *or* Babylon; (*edifice*) der Babylonische Turm. **(b)** (*also* **b~**) (*confusion*) Durcheinander *nt*; (*several languages also*) babylonisches Sprachengewirr.
baboon [bəˈbuːn] *n* Pavian *m*.
babuschka [bəˈbuːʃkə] *n* Kopftuch *nt*.
baby [ˈbeɪbɪ] 1 *n* **(a)** Kind, Baby *nt*; (*in weeks after birth also*) Säugling *m*; (*of animal*) Junge(s) *nt* ◆ **to have a ~** ein Kind *or* Baby bekommen; **she's going to have a ~** sie bekommt ein Kind *or* Baby; **I've known him since he was a ~** ich kenne ihn von klein auf *or* von Kindesbeinen an; **the ~ of the family** der/die Kleinste *or* Jüngste, das Nesthäkchen; (*boy also*) der Benjamin; **he's a big ~** er ist ein großes Kind; **don't be such a ~!** sei nicht so ein Baby! (*inf*), stell dich nicht so an! (*inf*); **to be left holding the ~** der Dumme sein (*inf*), die Sache ausbaden müssen (*inf*); **the bank cancelled the loan and I was left holding a very expensive ~** als die Bank das Darlehen rückgängig machte, hatte ich eine teure Suppe auszulöffeln; **to throw out the ~ with the bathwater** das Kind mit dem Bade ausschütten; **that encyclopedia is his first ~** (*inf*) das Lexikon ist sein Erstling (*hum*) *or* erstes Kind; **this little ~ cost me a fortune** (*inf*) das (Ding) hat mich ein Vermögen gekostet.
(b) (*small object of its type*) Pikkolo *m* (*hum*).
(c) (*sl: thing for which one is responsible*) **that's a costing problem, that's Harrison's ~** das ist eine Kostenfrage, das ist Harrisons Problem; **I think this problem's your ~** das ist wohl dein Bier (*inf*).
(d) (*inf: girlfriend, boyfriend*) Schatz *m*, Schätzchen *nt*.
(e) (*esp US inf: as address*) Schätzchen *nt* (*inf*); (*man to man*) mein Freund, mein Junge ◆ **that's my ~** jawohl, so ist's prima (*inf*); **that's great, ~** Mensch, das ist dufte (*inf*); **Mike/Susie ~, listen** du, Mike/Susie, hör mal her!
2 *vt* (*inf*) wie einen Säugling behandeln.
baby *in cpds* **(a)** (*for baby*) Baby-, Säuglings-. **(b)** (*little*) Klein-. **(c)** (*of animal*) **~ crocodile/giraffe** Krokodil-/Giraffenjunge(s) *nt*.
baby: ~-batterer *n jd, der Kleinkinder mißhandelt*; **~-battering** *n* Kindesmißhandlung *f*; **~ boom** *n* Baby-Boom *m*; **B~ bouncer** ® *n* Baby-Schaukel *f*; **~ boy** *n* Sohn *m*, kleiner Junge; **~ buggy** *n* Sportwagen *m*; **~ car** *n* Kleinwagen *m*, Autochen *nt* (*hum*); **~ carriage** *n* (*US*) Kinderwagen *m*; **~ clothes** *npl* Kindersachen *pl*, Babywäsche *f*; **~-doll face** *n* Puppengesicht *nt*; **~-doll pyjamas** *npl* Babydoll *nt*; **~ elephant** *n* Elefantenjunge(s) *or* -baby *nt*; **~ face** *n* Kindergesicht *nt*; (*of adult male*) Milchgesicht *nt*; **~ food** *n* Babynahrung *f*; **~ girl** *n* Töchterchen *nt*; **~ grand (piano)** *n* Stutzflügel *m*.
babyhood [ˈbeɪbɪhʊd] *n* frühe Kindheit, Säuglingsalter *nt*.
babyish [ˈbeɪbɪɪʃ] *adj* kindisch.
baby linen *n* Babywäsche *f no pl*.
Babylon [ˈbæbɪlən] *n* Babylon *nt*.
Babylonian [ˌbæbɪˈləʊnɪən] 1 *adj* babylonisch.
2 *n* Babylonier(in *f*) *m*.
baby: ~-minder *n* Tagesmutter *f*, Kinderpfleger(in *f*) *m*; **~ scales** *npl* Baby- *or* Säuglingswaage *f*; **~ seat** *n* (*in car*) Baby(sicherheits)sitz *m*; **~-sit** *pret, ptp* **~-sat** *vi* babysitten, einhüten (*dial*); **she ~-sits for them** sie geht bei ihnen babysitten *or* einhüten (*dial*); **~-sitter** *n* Babysitter(in *f*) *m*; **~-sitting** *n* Babysitten, Babysitting, (Ein)hüten (*dial*) *nt*; **~-snatcher** *n* Kindesentführer(in *f*) *m*; (*fig inf*) **what a ~-snatcher** der könnte ja ihr Vater sein/sie könnte ja seine Mutter sein!; **~-snatching** *n* Kindesentführung *f*; (*fig inf*) **not her, that's ~-snatching** sie nicht, ich vergreife mich doch nicht an kleinen Kindern!; **~-stroller** *n* (*US*) Sportwagen *m*; **~ tooth** *n* Milchzahn *m*; **~-walker** *n* Laufstuhl *m*.
baccara(t) [ˈbækərɑː] *n* Bakkarat *nt*.
bacchanalia [ˌbækəˈneɪlɪə] *n* (*Hist, fig*) Bacchanal *nt* (*geh*).
bacchanalian [ˌbækəˈneɪlɪən] *adj* bacchantisch (*geh*).
Bacchus [ˈbækəs] *n* Bacchus *m*.
baccy [ˈbækɪ] *n* (*inf*) Tabak, Knaster (*inf*) *m*.
bachelor [ˈbætʃələʳ] *n* **(a)** Junggeselle *m* ◆ **still a ~** immer noch Junggeselle. **(b)** (*Univ*) **B~ of Arts/Science** ≃ Magister *m* (der philosophischen/naturwissenschaftlichen Fakultät).
bachelordom [ˈbætʃələdəm] *n see* **bachelorhood**.
bachelor: ~ flat *n* Junggesellenwohnung *f*; **~ girl** *n* Junggesellin *f*.
bachelorhood [ˈbætʃələhʊd] *n* Junggesellentum *nt*.
bacillary [bəˈsɪlərɪ] *adj* (*Med*) Bazillen-, bazillär; *form* stäbchenförmig.
bacillus [bəˈsɪləs] *n, pl* **bacilli** [bəˈsɪlaɪ] Bazillus *m*.
back [bæk] 1 *n* **(a)** (*of person, animal, book*) Rücken *m*; (*of chair also*) (Rücken)lehne *f* ◆ **with one's ~ to the engine** mit dem Rücken zur Fahrtrichtung, rückwärts; **to be on one's ~** (*be ill*) auf der Nase liegen (*inf*), krank sein; **to wear one's hair down one's ~** überschulterlange Haare haben; **to break one's ~** (*fig*) sich abrackern, sich abmühen; **we've broken the ~ of the job** wir sind mit der Arbeit über den Berg (*inf*); **behind sb's ~** (*fig*) hinter jds Rücken (*dat*); **to put one's ~ into sth** (*fig*) sich bei etw anstrengen, bei etw Einsatz zeigen; **to put** *or* **get sb's ~ up** jdn gegen sich aufbringen; **to turn one's ~ on sb** (*lit*) jdm den Rücken zuwenden; (*fig*) sich von jdm abwenden; **when I needed him he turned his ~ on me** als ich ihn brauchte, ließ er mich im Stich; **he's at the ~ of all the trouble** er steckt hinter dem ganzen Ärger; **get these people off my ~** (*inf*) schaff mir diese Leute vom Hals! (*inf*); **get off my ~!** (*inf*) laß mich endlich in Ruhe!; **he's got the boss on his ~ all the time** er hat dauernd seinen Chef auf dem Hals; **to have one's ~ to the wall** (*fig*) in die Enge getrieben sein/werden; **I was pleased to see the ~ of them** (*inf*) ich war froh, sie endlich los zu sein (*inf*).
(b) (*as opposed to front*) Rück- *or* Hinterseite *f*; (*of hand, dress*) Rücken *m*; (*of house, page, coin, cheque*) Rückseite *f*; (*of material*) linke Seite ◆ **I know London like the ~ of my hand** ich kenne London wie meine Westentasche; **the index is at the ~ of the book** das Verzeichnis ist hinten im Buch; **he drove into the ~ of me** er ist mir hinten reingefahren (*inf*); **on the ~ of his hand** auf dem Handrücken; **the ~ of one's head** der Hinterkopf; **at/on the ~ of the bus** hinten im/am Bus; **in the ~ (of a car)** hinten (im Auto); **one consideration was at the ~ of my mind** ich hatte dabei eine Überlegung im Hinterkopf; **there's one other worry at the ~ of my mind** da ist noch etwas, das mich beschäftigt; **the ~ of the cupboard is empty** hinten im Schrank ist nichts; **at the ~ of the stage** im Hintergrund der Bühne; **at the ~ of the garage** (*inside*) hinten in der Garage; (*outside*) hinter der Garage; **at the ~ of beyond** am Ende der Welt, j.w.d. (*hum*); **in ~** (*US*) hinten.
(c) (*Ftbl*) Verteidiger *m*; (*Rugby*) Hinterspieler *m*.
2 *adj wheel, yard* Hinter-; *rent* ausstehend, rückständig.
3 *adv* **(a)** (*to the rear*) **(stand) ~!** zurück(treten)!, (treten Sie) zurück!; **~ and forth** hin und her.
(b) (*in return*) zurück ◆ **to pay sth ~** etw zurückzahlen.
(c) (*returning*) zurück ◆ **to come/go ~** zurückkommen/-gehen; **to fly to London and ~** nach London und zurück fliegen; **there and ~** hin und zurück.
(d) (*again*) wieder ◆ **he went ~ several times** er fuhr noch öfters wieder hin; **I'll never go ~** da gehe ich nie wieder hin.
(e) (*ago: in time phrases*) **a week ~** vor einer Woche; **as far ~ as the 18th**

century (*dating back*) bis ins 18. Jahrhundert zurück; (*point in time*) schon im 18. Jahrhundert; **far ~ in the past** vor langer, langer Zeit, vor Urzeiten.
[4] *prep* (*US*) **~ of** hinter.
[5] *vt* **(a)** (*support*) unterstützen ♦ **I will ~ you whatever you do** egal, was du tust, ich stehe hinter dir; **if the bank won't ~ us** wenn die Bank nicht mitmacht; **to ~ a bill** (*Fin*) einen Wechsel indossieren.
(b) (*Betting*) setzen *or* wetten auf (+*acc*) ♦ **the horse was heavily ~ed** auf das Pferd wurden viele Wetten abgeschlossen.
(c) (*cause to move*) *car* zurückfahren *or* -setzen; *cart* zurückfahren; *horse* rückwärts gehen lassen ♦ **he ~ed his car into the tree/garage** er fuhr rückwärts gegen den Baum/in die Garage; **to ~ water** (*Naut*) rückwärts rudern.
(d) (*Mus*) *singer* begleiten.
(e) (*put sth behind*) *picture* mit einem Rücken versehen, unterlegen; (*stick on*) aufziehen.
[6] *vi* **(a)** (*move backwards*) (*car, train*) zurücksetzen *or* -fahren ♦ **the car ~ed into the garage** das Auto fuhr rückwärts in die Garage; **she ~ed into me** sie fuhr rückwärts in mein Auto.
(b) (*Naut: wind*) drehen.
♦**back away** *vi* zurückweichen (*from* vor +*dat*).
♦**back down** *vi* (*fig*) nachgeben, klein beigeben.
♦**back off** *vi* **(a)** (*vehicle*) zurücksetzen. **(b)** (*step back*) zurückweichen; (*crowd*) zurücktreten; (*withdraw from deal etc*) aussteigen (*inf*); (*stop harrassing*) sich zurückhalten ♦ **~ ~!** (*get out of my way*) verschwinde!
♦**back on to** *vi* +*prep obj* hinten angrenzen an (+*acc*).
♦**back out** [1] *vi* **(a)** (*car etc*) rückwärts herausfahren *or* -setzen. **(b)** (*fig: of contract, deal etc*) aussteigen (*of, from* aus) (*inf*).
[2] *vt sep vehicle* rückwärts herausfahren *or* -setzen.
♦**back up** [1] *vi* **(a)** (*car etc*) zurücksetzen ♦ **to ~ ~ to sth** rückwärts an etw (*acc*) heranfahren. **(b)** (*US*) (*drain*) verstopfen; (*traffic*) sich stauen. **(c)** (*Comput*) sichern.
[2] *vt sep* **(a)** (*support*) unterstützen; (*confirm*) *story* bestätigen; *knowledge* fundieren; *claim, theory* untermauern ♦ **he ~ed ~ the boy's story that ...** er bestätigte den Bericht des Jungen, wonach ...; **he can ~ me ~ in this** er kann das bestätigen.
(b) *car etc* zurückfahren.
(c) (*Comput*) sichern, sicherstellen.
back: ~ache *n* Rückenschmerzen *pl*; **~ bench** *n* (*esp Brit*) Abgeordnetensitz *m*; **the ~ benches** das Plenum; **~bencher** *n* (*esp Brit*) Abgeordnete(r) *mf* (*auf den hinteren Reihen im britischen Parlament*); **~-biting** *n* Lästern *nt*; **~board** *n* (*Basketball*) Korbbrett *nt*; **~ boiler** *n* Warmwasserboiler *m* (*hinter der Heizung angebracht*); **to put sth on the ~ boiler** (*fig inf*) etw zurückstellen; **this project's been on the ~ boiler for years** an diesem Projekt wird seit Jahren nur so nebenbei gearbeitet; **~bone** *n* (*lit, fig*) Rückgrat *nt*; **~-breaking** *adj* erschöpfend, ermüdend; **~ burner** *n* (*lit*) hintere Kochplatte; **to put sth on the ~ burner** (*fig inf*) etw zurückstellen; **this project's been on the ~ burner for years** an diesem Projekt wird seit Jahren nur so nebenbei gearbeitet; **~ catalogue** *n* (*Mus*) ältere Aufnahmen *pl*, Back-Katalog *m*; **~chat** *n, no pl* (*inf*) Widerrede *f*; **none of your ~chat!** keine Widerrede!; **~cloth** *n* Prospekt, Hintergrund *m*; **~comb** *vt hair* toupieren; **~ copy** *n* alte Ausgabe *or* Nummer; **~date** *vt* (zu)rückdatieren; **salary increase ~dated to May** Gehaltserhöhung rückwirkend ab Mai; **~ door** *n* (*lit*) Hintertür *f*; (*fig*) Hintertürchen *nt*; **if you use the ~-door method** wenn Sie das durchs Hintertürchen machen; **~drop** *n* Prospekt, Hintergrund (*auch fig*) *m*.
backed [bækt] *adj* **low-/high-~** mit niedriger/hoher Rückenlehne; **a low-~ dress** ein Kleid mit tiefem Rückenausschnitt; **straight-~** *chair* mit gerader Rückenlehne; *person* mit geradem Rücken.
back end *n* (*rear*) hinteres Ende ♦ **at the ~ of the year** gegen Ende des Jahres, in den letzten Monaten des Jahres; **she looks like the ~ of a bus** (*sl*) sie ist potthäßlich (*inf*).
backer ['bækəʳ] *n* **(a)** (*supporter*) **his ~s** (diejenigen,) die ihn unterstützen. **(b)** (*Betting*) Wettende(r) *mf*. **(c)** (*Comm*) Geldgeber *m*.
back: ~ file *n* alte Akte; **~fire** [1] *n* **(a)** (*Aut*) Fehlzündung *f*; **(b)** (*US*) Gegenfeuer *nt*; [2] *vi* **(a)** (*Aut*) Fehlzündungen haben; **(b)** (*inf: plan etc*) ins Auge gehen (*inf*); **it ~fired on us** der Schuß ging nach hinten los (*inf*); **~ formation** *n* (*Ling*) Rückbildung *f*; **~gammon** *n* Backgammon *nt*; **~ garden** *n* Garten *m* (hinterm Haus).
background ['bækgraʊnd] [1] *n* **(a)** (*of painting etc, fig*) Hintergrund *m* ♦ **to stay in the ~** im Hintergrund bleiben, sich im Hintergrund halten; **to keep sb in the ~** jdn nicht in den Vordergrund treten lassen; **against a ~ of poverty and disease** vor dem Hintergrund von Armut und Krankheit.
(b) (*of person*) (*educational etc*) Werdegang *m*; (*social*) Verhältnisse *pl*; (*family ~*) Herkunft *f no pl*; (*Sociol*) Background *m* ♦ **he comes from a ~ of poverty** er kommt aus ärmlichen Verhältnissen; **comprehensive schools take children from all ~s** Gesamtschulen nehmen Kinder aus allen Schichten auf; **given the right sort of ~** wenn man (nur) aus den richtigen Kreisen kommt; **what do we know about the main character's ~?** was wissen wir über das Vorleben der Hauptperson?; **what's your educational ~?** was für eine Ausbildung haben Sie?
(c) (*of case, problem etc*) Zusammenhänge, Hintergründe *pl*, Hintergrund *m* ♦ **he filled in the ~ to the crisis** er erläuterte die Zusammenhänge *or* Hintergründe der Krise.
[2] *adj reading* vertiefend ♦ **~ music** Hintergrundmusik, Musikuntermalung *f*; **~ noises** *pl* Geräuschkulisse *f*, Geräusch *nt* im Hintergrund; **~ information** Hintergrundinformationen *pl*; **what's the ~ information on this?** welche Hintergründe *or* Zusammenhänge bestehen hierfür?; **~ program** (*Comput*) Hintergrundprogramm *nt*.
back: ~hand [1] *n* (*Sport*) Rückhand, Backhand *f no pl*; (*one stroke*) Rückhandschlag *m*; [2] *adj stroke, shot* Rückhand-; [3] *adv* mit der Rückhand; **~handed** *adj compliment* zweifelhaft; *shot* Rückhand-; *writing* nach links geneigt; **~hander** *n* **(a)** (*Sport*) Rückhandschlag *m*; **(b)** (*inf: bribe*) Schmiergeld *nt*; **to give sb a ~hander** jdn schmieren (*inf*).
backing ['bækɪŋ] *n* **(a)** (*support*) Unterstützung *f*. **(b)** (*Mus*) Begleitung *f* ♦ **~ group** Begleitband, Begleitung *f*. **(c)** (*for picture frame, for strengthening*) Rücken(verstärkung *f*) *m*; (*for carpet, wallpaper etc*) Rücken(beschichtung *f*) *m*.
back: ~lash *n* **(a)** (*Tech*) (*jarring reaction*) Gegenschlag *m*; (*play*) zuviel Spiel; **(b)** (*fig*) Gegenreaktion *f*; **~less** *adj dress* rückenfrei; **~-lit** *adj screen* hinterleuchtet, mit Hintergrundbeleuchtung; **~log** *n* Rückstände *pl*; **I have a ~log of work** ich bin mit der Arbeit im Rückstand; **look at this ~log of typing** sehen Sie sich diesen Berg unerledigter Schreibarbeiten an; **~marker** *n* (*Sport*) Nachzügler *m*, Schlußlicht *nt*; **the ~markers** die Nachhut; **~ number** *n* (*of paper*) alte Ausgabe *or* Nummer; (*fig*) (*person*) altmodischer Mensch; (*thing*) veraltetes Ding; **that/he is a ~ number** das ist überholt/er ist altmodisch; **~pack** *n* Rucksack *m*; **~packer** *n* Wanderer *m*, Wanderin *f*; (*hitch-hiker*) Rucksacktourist(in *f*) *m*; **~packing** *n* Wandern *nt*; (*hitch-hiking*) Trampen *nt*; **to go ~packing** auf (Berg)tour gehen; trampen; **~ pay** *n* Nachzahlung *f*; **~-pedal** *vi* (*lit*) rückwärts treten; (*fig inf*) einen Rückzieher machen (*inf*) (*on* bei); **~-pedal brake** *n* Rücktrittbremse *f*; **~ projection** *n* (*Film*) Rückprojektion *f*; **~ rest** *n* Rückenstütze *f*; **~ room** *n* Hinterzimmer *nt*; **~-room boy** *n* (*inf*) Experte *m* im Hintergrund; **~ seat** *n* Rücksitz *m*; **to take a ~ seat** (*fig*) sich zurückhalten *or* raushalten (*inf*); **~seat driver** *n* Beifahrer, der dem Fahrer dazwischenredet; **she is a terrible ~seat driver** sie redet beim Fahren immer rein; **~shift** *n* Spätschicht *f*; **~side** *n* (*inf*) Hintern *m* (*inf*), Hinterteil *nt* (*inf*); **~ sight** *n* (*on rifle*) Visier *nt*, Kimme *f*; **~-slapping** *n* (*inf*) Schulterklopfen *nt*; **~slash** *n* (*Comput*) Backslash *m*; **~slide** *vi* (*fig*) rückfällig werden; (*Eccl*) abtrünnig werden; **~slider** *n* Rückfällige(r) *mf*; Abtrünnige(r) *mf*; **~-space** *vti* (*Typing*) zurücksetzen; **~-space key** *n* Rücktaste *f*; **~-spacer** *n* (*Typing*) Rücktaste *f*; **~stage** *adv, adj* hinter den Kulissen; (*in dressing-room area*) in die/der Garderobe; **~stage people** Leute hinter den Kulissen; **~stairs** *n sing* Hintertreppe *f*; **~stitch** *n* Steppstich *m*; **~ straight** *n* (*Sport*) Gegengerade *f*; **~ street** *n* Seitensträßchen *nt*; **he comes from the ~ streets of Liverpool** er kommt aus dem ärmeren Teil von Liverpool; **~-street abortion** *n* illegale Abtreibung; **~-street abortions** Engelmacherei *f* (*inf*); **she had a ~-street abortion** sie war bei einem Engelmacher (*inf*); **~-street abortionist** *n* Engelmacher(in *f*) *m* (*inf*); **~stroke** *n* (*Swimming*) Rückenschwimmen *nt*; **can you do the ~stroke?** können Sie rückenschwimmen?; **~talk** *n* Widerrede, Frechheit *f*; **~ to ~** [1] *adv* Rücken an Rücken; (*things*) mit den Rückseiten aneinander; [2] *adj* **~-to-~ credit** Gegenakkreditiv *nt*; **~ to front** *adv* verkehrt herum; *read* von hinten nach vorne; **~ tooth** *n* Backenzahn *m*; **~track** *vi* (*over ground*) denselben Weg zurückgehen *or* zurückverfolgen; (*on policy etc*) einen Rückzieher machen (*on sth* bei etw); **~up** [1] *n* **(a)** Unterstützung *f*; **(b)** (*Comput*) Sicherungskopie *f*, Backup *nt*; [2] *adj* **(a)** *troops* Unterstützungs-, Hilfs-; *train, plane* Entlastungs-; *staff* Reserve-; *services* zur Unterstützung; **~up service** (*for customer*) Kundendienst *m*; **(b)** (*Comput*) *copy, file, disk* Sicherungs-, Backup-; **~ vowel** *n* (*Phon*) hinterer Vokal, Rachenvokal *m*.
backward ['bækwəd] [1] *adj* **(a) ~ and forward movement** Vor-und Zurückbewegung *f*; **~ flow of information** Rückfluß *m* von Daten; **a ~ glance** ein Blick zurück.
(b) (*fig*) **a ~ step/move** ein Schritt *m* zurück/eine (Zu)rückentwicklung.
(c) (*retarded*) *child* zurückgeblieben; *region* rückständig.
[2] *adv see* **backwards**.
backwardness ['bækwədnɪs] *n* (*mental*) Zurückgebliebenheit *f*; (*of region*) Rückständigkeit *f*.
backwards ['bækwədz] *adv* **(a)** rückwärts ♦ **to fall ~** nach hinten fallen; **to walk ~ and forwards** hin und her gehen; **to stroke a cat ~** eine Katze gegen den Strich streicheln; **to lean** *or* **bend over ~ to do sth** (*inf*) sich fast umbringen *or* sich (*dat*) ein Bein ausreißen, um etw zu tun (*inf*); **I know it ~** das kenne ich in- und auswendig.
(b) (*towards the past*) zurück ♦ **to look ~** zurückblicken.
back: ~wash *n* (*Naut*) Rückströmung *f*; (*fig*) Nachwirkung *f usu pl*; **those caught up in the ~wash of the scandal** diejenigen, die in den Skandal mit hineingezogen wurden; **~water** *n* (*lit*) Stauwasser *nt*, totes Wasser; (*fig*) rückständiges Nest; **this town is a cultural ~water** kulturell (gesehen) ist diese Stadt tiefste Provinz; **~woods** *npl* unerschlossene (Wald)gebiete *pl*; **~woodsman** *n* Waldsiedler *m*; (*US inf*) Hinterwälder *m*; **~yard** *n* Hinterhof *m*; **they found one in their own ~yard** (*fig*) sie haben einen vor der eigenen Haustür gefunden.
bacon ['beɪkən] *n* durchwachsener Speck ♦ **~ and eggs** Eier mit Speck; **to save sb's ~** (*inf*) jds Rettung sein; **to bring home the ~** (*inf: earn a living*) die Brötchen verdienen (*inf*).
bacteria [bæk'tɪərɪə] *pl of* **bacterium**.
bacterial [bæk'tɪərɪəl] *adj* Bakterien-, bakteriell.
bacteriological [bæk,tɪərɪə'lɒdʒɪkəl] *adj* bakteriologisch.
bacteriologist [bæk,tɪərɪ'ɒlədʒɪst] *n* Bakteriologe *m*, Bakteriologin *f*.
bacteriology [bæk,tɪərɪ'ɒlədʒɪ] *n* Bakteriologie *f*.
bacterium [bæk'tɪərɪəm] *n, pl* **bacteria** [bæk'tɪərɪə] Bakterie *f*, Bakterium *nt* (*old*).
bad[1] [bæd] [1] *adj, comp* **worse**, *superl* **worst** **(a)** schlecht; *smell, habit also*

übel; *insurance risk* hoch; *word* unanständig, schlimm; (*immoral, wicked also*) böse; (*naughty, misbehaved*) unartig, ungezogen; *dog* böse ◆ **it was a ~ thing to do** das hättest du nicht tun sollen; **he went through a ~ time** er hat eine schlimme Zeit durchgemacht; **you ~ boy!** du ungezogener Junge!, du Lümmel! (*also iro*); **he's been a ~ boy** er war unartig *or* böse; **I didn't mean that word in a ~ sense** ich habe mir bei dem Wort nichts Böses gedacht; **it's a ~ business** das ist eine üble Sache; **things are going from ~ to worse** es wird immer schlimmer; **to go ~** schlecht werden, verderben; **to be ~ for sb/sth** schlecht *or* nicht gut für jdn/etw sein; **he's ~ at tennis** er spielt schlecht Tennis; **he's ~ at sport** im Sport ist er schlecht *or* nicht gut, er ist unsportlich; **I'm very ~ at telling lies** ich kann schlecht *or* nicht gut lügen; **he speaks ~ English** er spricht schlecht(es) Englisch; **to be ~ to sb** jdn schlecht behandeln; **there's nothing ~ about living together** es ist doch nichts dabei, wenn man zusammen lebt; **this is a ~ town for violence** in dieser Stadt ist es wirklich schlimm mit der Gewalttätigkeit; **this is a ~ district for wheat** dies ist eine schlechte *or* keine gute Gegend für Weizen; **it would not be a ~ thing** *or* **plan** das wäre nicht schlecht *or* keine schlechte Idee; **(that's) too ~!** (*indignant*) so was!; (*~ luck*) Pech!; **it's too ~ of you** das ist wirklich nicht nett von dir; **too ~ you couldn't make it** (es ist) wirklich schade, daß Sie nicht kommen konnten; **to be in ~ with sb** (*US*) bei jdm schlecht angeschrieben sein.

(b) (*serious*) *wound, sprain* schlimm; *accident, mistake, cold also* schwer; *headache also, deterioration* stark ◆ **he's got it ~** (*inf*) ihn hat's schwer erwischt (*inf*); **to have it ~ for sb** (*inf*) in jdn schwer *or* unheimlich verknallt sein (*inf*).

(c) (*unfavourable*) *time, day* ungünstig, schlecht ◆ **Thursday's ~, can you make it Friday?** Donnerstag ist ungünstig *or* schlecht, geht's nicht Freitag?

(d) (*in poor health, sick*) *stomach* krank; *leg, knee, hand* schlimm; *tooth* (*generally*) schlecht; (*now*) schlimm ◆ **he/the economy is in a ~ way** es geht ihm schlecht/es steht schlecht um die *or* mit der Wirtschaft; **I've got a ~ head** ich habe einen dicken Kopf (*inf*); **to feel ~** sich nicht wohl fühlen; **I feel ~** mir geht es nicht gut, mir ist nicht gut; **to be taken ~** (*inf*) plötzlich krank werden; **how is he? — he's not so ~** wie geht es ihm? — nicht schlecht; **I didn't know she was so ~** ich wußte nicht, daß es ihr so schlecht geht *or* daß sie so schlimm dran ist (*inf*).

(e) (*regretful*) **I feel really ~ about not having told him** es tut mir wirklich leid *or* ich habe ein schlechtes Gewissen, daß ich ihm das nicht gesagt habe; **don't feel ~ about it** machen Sie sich (*dat*) keine Gedanken *or* Sorgen (darüber).

(f) *debt* uneinbringlich; *voting slip, coin* ungültig; *cheque* ungültig; (*uncovered*) ungedeckt; (*damaged*) *copies etc* beschädigt.

[2] *n, no pl* **(a) to take the good with the ~** (auch) die schlechten Seiten in Kauf nehmen; **there is good and ~ in everything/everybody** alles/jeder hat seine guten und schlechten Seiten.

(b) he's gone to the ~ er ist auf die schiefe Bahn geraten.

bad² *pret of* **bid**.

baddie ['bædɪ] *n* (*inf*) Schurke, Bösewicht *m*.

baddish ['bædɪʃ] *adj* (*inf*) ziemlich schlecht.

bade [beɪd] *pret of* **bid**.

badge [bædʒ] *n* **(a)** Abzeichen *nt*; (*made of metal*) (*women's lib, joke ~*) Button *m*; (*on car etc*) Plakette *f*; (*sticker*) Aufkleber *m* ◆ **~ of office** Dienstmarke *f*. **(b)** (*fig: symbol*) Merkmal *nt*.

badger ['bædʒəʳ] [1] *n* Dachs *m*.

[2] *vt* zusetzen (*+dat*), bearbeiten (*inf*), keine Ruhe lassen (*+dat*) ◆ **don't ~ me** laß mich in Ruhe *or* Frieden; **to ~ sb for sth** jdm mit etw in den Ohren liegen.

badlands ['bædlændz] *npl* Ödland *nt*.

badly ['bædlɪ] *adv* **(a)** schlecht. **(b)** *wounded, mistaken* schwer ◆ **~ beaten** (*Sport*) vernichtend geschlagen; *person* schwer *or* schlimm verprügelt; **the ~ disabled** die Schwerstbeschädigten. **(c)** (*very much*) sehr; *in debt, overdrawn* hoch ◆ **to want sth ~** etw unbedingt wollen; **I need it ~** ich brauche es dringend; **he ~ needs** *or* **wants a haircut** er muß dringend zum Friseur.

bad-mannered [,bæd'mænəd] *adj* ungezogen, unhöflich.

badminton ['bædmɪntən] *n* Federball *nt*; (*on court*) Badminton *nt*.

bad-mouth ['bædmaʊθ] *vt* (*US inf*) herziehen über (*+acc*) (*inf*).

badness ['bædnɪs] *n, no pl* **(a)** Schlechtheit *f*; (*moral*) Schlechtigkeit *f*; (*naughtiness*) Unartigkeit, Ungezogenheit *f*. **(b)** (*seriousness*) Schwere *f*; (*of mistake also*) Ernst *m*; (*of headache*) Stärke *f*.

bad-tempered [,bæd'tempəd] *adj* schlechtgelaunt *attr*, übellaunig ◆ **to be ~** schlechte Laune haben; (*as characteristic*) ein übellauniger Mensch sein.

baffle ['bæfl] [1] *vt* **(a)** (*confound, amaze*) verblüffen; (*cause incomprehension*) vor ein Rätsel stellen ◆ **a ~d look** ein verdutzter Blick; **the police are ~d** die Polizei steht vor einem Rätsel; **it really ~s me how ...** es ist mir wirklich ein Rätsel, wie ...; **a case that ~d all the experts** ein Fall, der den Experten Rätsel aufgab; **this one's got me ~d** ich stehe vor einem Rätsel.

(b) (*Tech*) *sound* dämpfen.

[2] *n* (*also* **~-plate**) (*Aut*) Umlenkblech *nt*.

baffling ['bæflɪŋ] *adj case* rätselhaft; *complexity* verwirrend; *mystery* unergründlich ◆ **I find it ~** es ist mir ein Rätsel.

BAFTA ['bæftə] *n* (*Brit*) *abbr of* **British Academy of Film and Television Arts** *britische Film-und Fernsehakademie*.

bag [bæg] [1] *n* **(a)** Tasche *f*; (*with drawstrings, pouch*) Beutel *m*; (*for school*) Schultasche *f*; (*made of paper, plastic*) Tüte *f*; (*sack*) Sack *m*; (*suitcase*) Reisetasche *f* ◆ **~s** (Reise)gepäck *nt*; **with ~ and baggage** mit Sack und Pack; **to be a ~ of bones** (*fig inf*) nur Haut und Knochen sein (*inf*); **the whole ~ of tricks** (*inf*) die ganze Trickkiste (*inf*).

(b) (*Hunt*) **the ~** die (Jagd)beute; **to get a good ~** (eine) fette Beute machen *or* heimbringen; **it's in the ~** (*fig inf*) das habe ich *etc* schon in der Tasche (*inf*), das ist gelaufen (*inf*).

(c) ~s under the eyes (*black*) Ringe *pl* unter den Augen; (*of skin*) (hervortretende) Tränensäcke *pl*.

(d) ~s *pl* (*Oxford* **~s**) weite Hose; (*dated inf: trousers*) Buxe *f* (*dated inf*).

(e) (*inf: a lot*) **~s of** jede Menge (*inf*).

(f) (*pej sl: woman*) **(old) ~** (alte) Ziege (*pej sl*), Weibsstück *nt* (*pej*); **ugly old ~** Schreckschraube *f* (*inf*).

[2] *vt* **(a)** in Tüten/Säcke verpacken. **(b)** (*Hunt*) erlegen, erbeuten. **(c)** (*Brit sl: get*) (sich *dat*) schnappen (*inf*) ◆ **~s I have first go!** will anfangen!; **I ~s that ice-cream!** will das Eis!

[3] *vi* (*garment*) sich (aus)beulen.

bagatelle [,bægə'tel] *n* **(a)** (*liter: trifle*) Bagatelle, Nichtigkeit (*geh*) *f*. **(b)** (*game*) Tivoli *nt*.

bagel ['beɪgəl] *n kleines, rundes Brötchen*.

bagful ['bægfʊl] *n* **a ~ of groceries** eine Tasche voll Lebensmittel; **20 ~s of wheat** 20 Sack Weizen.

baggage ['bægɪdʒ] *n* **(a)** (*luggage*) (Reise)gepäck *nt*. **(b)** (*Mil*) Gepäck *nt*. **(c)** (*pej inf: woman*) Stück *nt* (*inf*).

baggage (*esp US*): **~ allowance** *n* Freigepäck *nt*; **~ car** *n* Gepäckwagen *m*; **~ check** *n* Gepäckkontrolle *f*; **~ checkroom** *n* Gepäckaufbewahrung *f*; **~ claim** *n* Gepäckausgabe *f*; **~ locker** *n* Gepäckschließfach *nt*; **~ master** *n* Beamte(r) *m* am Gepäckschalter; **~ reclaim** *n* Gepäckausgabe *f*; **~ room** *n* Gepäckaufbewahrung *f*; **~ wagon** *n* Gepäckwagen *m*.

bagging ['bægɪŋ] *n* (*material*) Sack- *or* Packleinen *nt*.

baggy ['bægɪ] *adj* (*+er*) (*ill-fitting*) zu weit; *dress* sackartig; *skin* schlaff (hängend); (*out of shape*) *trousers, suit* ausgebeult; *jumper* ausgeleiert ◆ **~ trousers are fashionable again** weite (Flatter)hosen sind wieder modern.

Baghdad [,bæg'dæd] *n* Bagdad *nt*.

bag lady *n* Stadtstreicherin *f* (*die ihre gesamte Habe in Einkaufstaschen mit sich führt*).

bagpiper ['bægpaɪpəʳ] *n* Dudelsackpfeifer *or* -bläser *m*.

bagpipe(s *pl*) ['bægpaɪp(s)] *n* Dudelsack *m*.

bags [bægz] *npl see* **bag 1 (d, e)**.

bag-snatcher ['bæg,snætʃəʳ] *n* Handtaschendieb *m*.

Bahamas [bə'hɑːməz] *npl*: **the ~** die Bahamas *pl*.

Bahrain, Bahrein [bɑːreɪn] *n* Bahrain *nt*.

bail¹ [beɪl] *n* (*Jur*) Kaution, Sicherheitsleistung (*form*) *f* ◆ **to go** *or* **stand** *or* **put in ~ for sb** für jdn (die) Kaution stellen *or* leisten; **to grant/refuse ~** die Freilassung gegen Kaution bewilligen/verweigern; **he was refused ~** sein Antrag auf Freilassung gegen Kaution wurde abgelehnt; **to be (out) on ~** gegen Kaution freigelassen sein; **to let sb out on ~** jdn gegen Kaution freilassen.

◆**bail out** *vt sep* **(a)** (*Jur*) gegen Kaution *or* Sicherheitsleistung freibekommen, die Kaution stellen für. **(b)** (*fig*) aus der Patsche helfen (*+dat*) (*inf*). **(c)** *boat see* **bale out**.

bail² *n* **(a)** (*Cricket*) Querholz *nt*. **(b)** (*in stable*) Trennstange *f*.

bail³ *vti see* **bale²**.

bail bandit *n* (*Brit inf*) *jd, der eine Straftat begeht, während er gegen Kaution freigelassen ist*.

Bailey bridge ['beɪlɪ'brɪdʒ] *n* Behelfsbrücke *f*.

bailiff ['beɪlɪf] *n* **(a)** (*Jur*) **(sheriff's) ~** Amtsdiener *m*; (*for property*) Gerichtsvollzieher *m*; (*in court*) Gerichtsdiener *m*. **(b)** (*on estate*) (Guts)verwalter, Landvogt (*obs*) *m*.

bairn [bɛən] *n* (*Scot*) Kind *nt*.

bait [beɪt] [1] *n* (*lit, fig*) Köder *m* ◆ **to take** *or* **swallow** *or* **rise to the ~** (*lit, fig*) anbeißen; (*fig: be trapped*) sich ködern lassen.

[2] *vt* **(a)** *hook, trap* mit einem Köder versehen, beködern. **(b)** (*torment*) *animal* (mit Hunden) hetzen; *person* quälen.

baize [beɪz] *n* Fries, Flaus *m* ◆ **green ~** Billardtuch *nt*.

bake [beɪk] [1] *vt* **(a)** (*Cook*) backen ◆ **~d apples** *pl* Bratäpfel *pl*; **~d potatoes** *pl* in der Schale gebackene Kartoffeln *pl*.

(b) *pottery, bricks* brennen; (*sun*) *earth* ausdörren.

[2] *vi* **(a)** backen; (*cake*) im (Back)ofen sein.

(b) (*pottery etc*) gebrannt werden, im (Brenn)ofen sein.

(c) (*inf*) **I'm baking** ich komme um vor Hitze; **it's baking (hot) today** es ist eine Affenhitze heute (*inf*); **I just want to lie in the sun and ~** ich möchte mich in der Sonne braten lassen.

bakehouse ['beɪkhaʊs] *n* Backhaus *nt*.

bakelite ® ['beɪkəlaɪt] *n* Bakelit ® *nt*.

baker ['beɪkəʳ] *n* Bäcker(in *f*) *m* ◆ **~'s man** *or* **boy** Bäckerjunge *m*; **~'s (shop)** Bäckerei *f*, Bäckerladen *m*; **~'s dozen** 13 (Stück).

bakery ['beɪkərɪ] *n* Bäckerei *f*.

Bakewell tart ['beɪkwel'tɑːt] *n* (*Brit*) *Törtchen nt mit Mandel- und Marmeladenfüllung*.

baking ['beɪkɪŋ] *n* **(a)** (*act*) (*Cook*) Backen *nt*; (*of earthenware*) Brennen *nt* ◆ **it's our own ~** das ist selbstgebacken. **(b)** (*batch: of bread, of bricks etc*) Ofenladung *f*, Schub *m*.

baking: ~ day *n* Backtag *m*; **~ dish** *n* Backform *f*; **~ powder** *n* Backpulver *nt*; **~ sheet** *n* Back- *or* Plätzchenblech *nt*; **~ soda** *n* Backpulver *nt*; **~ tin** *n* Backform *f*; **~ tray** *n* Kuchenblech *nt*.

baksheesh ['bækʃiːʃ] *n* Bakschisch *nt*.

Balaclava [,bælə'klɑːvə] *n* (*also* **~ helmet**) Kapuzenmütze *f*.

balalaika [,bælə'laɪkə] *n* Balalaika *f*.

balance ['bæləns] [1] *n* **(a)** (*apparatus*) Waage *f* ◆ **to be** *or* **hang in the ~** (*fig*) in der Schwebe sein; **his life hung in the ~** sein Leben hing an einem dünnen *or* seidenen Faden; **to put sth in the ~** (*risk*) etw in die Waagschale werfen.
(b) (*counterpoise*) Gegengewicht *nt* (*to* zu); (*fig also*) Ausgleich *m* (*to* für).
(c) (*lit, fig: equilibrium*) Gleichgewicht *nt* ◆ **sense of ~** Gleichgewichtssinn *m*; **to keep one's ~** das Gleichgewicht (be)halten; **to lose one's ~** aus dem Gleichgewicht kommen, das Gleichgewicht verlieren; **to recover one's ~** wieder ins Gleichgewicht kommen, das Gleichgewicht wiedererlangen; **off ~** aus dem Gleichgewicht; **to throw sb off (his) ~** jdn aus dem Gleichgewicht bringen; **the right ~ of personalities in the team** eine ausgewogene Mischung verschiedener Charaktere in der Mannschaft; **the ~ of probabilities is such that ...** wenn man die Möglichkeiten gegeneinander abwägt, dann ...; **the ~ of power** das Gleichgewicht der Kräfte; **~ of terror** Gleichgewicht *nt* des Schreckens; **to strike the right ~ between old and new/import and export** den goldenen Mittelweg zwischen Alt und Neu finden/das richtige Verhältnis von Import zu Export finden; **on ~** (*fig*) alles in allem.
(d) (*Art*) Ausgewogenheit *f*.
(e) (*preponderant weight*) Hauptgewicht *nt* ◆ **the ~ of advantage lies with you** der Hauptvorteil ist auf Ihrer Seite.
(f) (*Comm, Fin: state of account*) Saldo *m*; (*with bank also*) Konto(be)stand *m*; (*of company*) Bilanz *f* ◆ **~ in hand** (*Comm*) Kassen(be)stand *m*; **~ carried forward** Saldovortrag *or* -übertrag *m*; **~ due** (*banking*) Debetsaldo *m*, Soll *nt*; (*Comm*) Rechnungsbetrag *m*; **~ in your favour** Saldoguthaben, Haben *nt*; **to pay off the ~** den Rest bezahlen; (*banking*) den Saldo begleichen; **my father has promised to make up the ~** mein Vater hat versprochen, die Differenz zu (be)zahlen; **~ of payments/trade** Zahlungs-/Handelsbilanz *f*.
(g) (*fig: remainder*) Rest *m*.
[2] *vt* **(a)** (*keep level, in equilibrium*) im Gleichgewicht halten; (*bring into equilibrium*) ins Gleichgewicht bringen, ausbalancieren ◆ **to ~ oneself on one foot** auf einem Bein balancieren; **the seal ~s a ball on its nose** der Seehund balanciert einen Ball auf der Nase.
(b) (*in the mind*) *two arguments* (gegeneinander) abwägen ◆ **to ~ sth against sth** etw einer Sache (*dat*) gegenüberstellen.
(c) (*equal, make up for*) ausgleichen.
(d) (*Comm, Fin*) *account* (*add up*) saldieren, abschließen; (*make equal*) ausgleichen; (*pay off*) begleichen; *budget* ausgleichen ◆ **to ~ the books** die Bilanz ziehen *or* machen.
(e) (*Aut*) *wheel* auswuchten.
[3] *vi* **(a)** (*be in equilibrium*) Gleichgewicht halten; (*scales*) sich ausbalancieren; (*painting*) ausgewogen sein ◆ **he ~d on one foot** er balancierte auf einem Bein; **with a ball balancing on its nose** mit einem Ball, den er auf der Nase balancierte.
(b) (*Comm, Fin: of accounts*) ausgeglichen sein ◆ **the books don't ~** die Abrechnung stimmt nicht; **to make the books ~** die Abrechnung ausgleichen.

◆**balance out** [1] *vt sep* aufwiegen, ausgleichen ◆ **they ~ each other ~** sie wiegen sich auf, sie halten sich die Waage; (*personalities*) sie gleichen sich aus.
[2] *vi* sich ausgleichen.

balanced ['bælənst] *adj personality* ausgeglichen; *diet also, painting, photography, mixture* ausgewogen.

balance: ~ sheet *n* (*Fin*) Bilanz *f*; (*document*) Bilanzaufstellung *f*; **~ wheel** *n* (*in watch*) Unruh *f*.

balancing: ~ act *n* (*lit, fig*) Balanceakt *m*; **~ trick** *n* Balancekunststück *nt*.

balcony ['bælkənɪ] *n* **(a)** Balkon *m*. **(b)** (*Theat*) oberster Rang.

bald [bɔːld] *adj* (*+er*) **(a)** *person* kahl, glatzköpfig; *bird* federlos; *tree* kahl ◆ **he is ~** er hat eine Glatze; **to go ~** eine Glatze bekommen, kahl werden; **he is going ~ at the temples** er hat Geheimratsecken; **~ patch** kahle Stelle.
(b) *style, statement* knapp.

bald eagle *n* weißköpfiger Seeadler.

balderdash ['bɔːldədæʃ] *n* (*dated inf*) Kokolores *m* (*dated inf*).

bald-headed ['bɔːld,hedɪd] *adj* kahl- *or* glatzköpfig.

balding ['bɔːldɪŋ] [1] *adj* **his ~ head** sein schütter werdendes Haar; **a ~ gentleman** ein Herr mit schütterem Haar; **he is ~** er bekommt langsam eine Glatze.
[2] *n* Haarausfall *m*.

baldly ['bɔːldlɪ] *adv* (*fig*) (*bluntly*) unverblümt, unumwunden; (*roughly*) grob, knapp ◆ **to state the facts quite ~** die Dinge beim Namen nennen.

baldness ['bɔːldnɪs] *n* **(a)** Kahlheit *f*. **(b)** (*of style, statement*) Knappheit *f*.

baldy ['bɔːldɪ] *n* (*inf*) Glatzkopf *m*.

bale[1] [beɪl] [1] *n* (*of hay etc*) Bündel *nt*; (*out of combine harvester, of cotton*) Ballen *m*; (*of paper etc*) Pack *m*.
[2] *vt* bündeln; zu Ballen verarbeiten.

bale[2] *vti* (*Naut*) schöpfen.

◆**bale out** [1] *vi* **(a)** (*Aviat*) abspringen, aussteigen (*inf*) (*of* aus). **(b)** (*Naut*) schöpfen.
[2] *vt sep* (*Naut*) *water* schöpfen; *ship* ausschöpfen, leer schöpfen.

Balearic [,bælɪ'ærɪk] *adj*: **the ~ Islands** die Balearen *pl*.

baleful ['beɪlfʊl] *adj* **(a)** (*evil*) böse; *look* (*of bull etc*) stier. **(b)** (*sad*) traurig.

balefully ['beɪlfəlɪ] *adv see adj*.

balk, baulk [bɔːk] [1] *n* **(a)** (*beam*) Balken *m*. **(b)** (*obstacle*) Hindernis *nt*, Hemmschuh *m* (*to* für).
[2] *vt person* hemmen; *plan* vereiteln.
[3] *vi* (*person*) zurückschrecken (*at* vor *+dat*); (*horse*) scheuen, bocken (*at* bei).

Balkan ['bɔːlkən] [1] *adj* Balkan- ◆ **the ~ Mountains** der Balkan; **the ~ States** die Balkanländer *pl*.
[2] *n*: **the ~s** der Balkan, die Balkanländer *pl*.

ball[1] [bɔːl] [1] *n* **(a)** Ball *m*; (*sphere*) Kugel *f*; (*of wool, string*) Knäuel *m* ◆ **the cat lay curled up in a ~** die Katze hatte sich zusammengerollt; **~ and chain** Fußfessel *f* (mit Gewicht).
(b) (*Sport*) Ball *m*; (*Billiards, Croquet*) Kugel *f*.
(c) (*delivery of a ~*) Ball *m*; (*Tennis, Golf also*) Schlag *m*; (*Ftbl, Hockey also*) Schuß *m*; (*Cricket*) Wurf *m* ◆ **the backs were giving their strikers a lot of good ~(s)** die Verteidiger spielten den Stürmern gute Bälle zu; **no ~** (*Cricket*) falsch ausgeführter Wurf.
(d) (*game*) Ball *m*; (*US: baseball*) Baseball *nt* ◆ **to play ~** Ball/Baseball spielen.
(e) (*fig phrases*) **to keep the ~ rolling** das Gespräch in Gang halten; **to start** *or* **set the ~ rolling** den Stein ins Rollen bringen; **to have the ~ at one's feet** seine große Chance haben; **the ~ is with you** *or* **in your court** Sie sind am Ball (*inf*); **that puts the ~ back in his court** damit ist er wieder am Ball; **to be on the ~** (*inf*) am Ball sein (*inf*), auf Zack *or* Draht sein (*inf*); **to run with the ~** (*US inf*) die Sache mit Volldampf vorantreiben (*inf*); *see* **play**.
(f) (*old: for gun*) Kugel *f*; *see* **cannon ball**.
(g) (*Anat*) **~ of the foot/thumb** Fuß-/Handballen *m*.
(h) (*Cook: of meat, fish*) Klößchen *nt*, Klops *m*.
(i) (*sl: testicle*) Ei *nt usu pl* (*sl*); *pl also* Sack *m* (*sl*) ◆ **~s!** (*nonsense*) red keinen Scheiß (*sl*); **~s to him/the regulations** der kann mich am Arsch lecken (*vulg*)/ich scheiß' doch auf die Bestimmungen (*vulg*); **~s** (*courage*) Schneid (*inf*), Mumm (*inf*) *m*; **his first novel had ~s** sein erster Roman war knallhart; **he's got us by the ~s** er hat uns in der Zange (*inf*).
[2] *vti* (*US sl*) bumsen (*inf*).

ball[2] *n* **(a)** (*dance*) Ball *m*. **(b)** (*inf: good time*) Spaß *m* ◆ **to have a ~** sich prima amüsieren (*inf*).

ballad ['bæləd] *n* (*Mus, Liter*) Ballade *f*.

ball-and-socket joint *n* Kugelgelenk *nt*.

ballast ['bæləst] [1] *n* **(a)** (*Naut, Aviat, fig*) Ballast *m* ◆ **to take in/discharge ~** Ballast aufnehmen/abwerfen. **(b)** (*stone, clinker*) Schotter *m*; (*Rail*) Bettung(sschotter *m*) *f*.
[2] *vt* (*Naut, Aviat*) mit Ballast beladen.

ball: ~-bearing *n* Kugellager *nt*; (*ball*) Kugellagerkugel *f*; **~ boy** *n* (*Tennis*) Balljunge *m*; **~cock** *n* Schwimmerhahn *m*; **~ control** *n* Ballführung *f*.

ballerina [,bælə'riːnə] *n* Ballerina, Ballerine *f*; (*principal*) Primaballerina *f*.

ballet ['bæleɪ] *n* Ballett *nt*.

ballet: ~-dancer *n* Balletttänzer(in *f*) *m*, Balletteuse *f*; **~ pump, ~ shoe** *n* Ballettschuh *m*; **~ skirt** *n* Ballettröckchen *nt*.

ball: ~ game *n* Ballspiel *nt*; **it's a whole new/different ~ game** (*fig inf*) das ist 'ne ganz andere Chose (*inf*); **~ girl** *n* (*Tennis*) Ballmädchen *nt*.

ballistic [bə'lɪstɪk] *adj* ballistisch ◆ **to go ~** (*inf*) ausrasten (*inf*), an die Decke gehen (*inf*); **~ missile** Raketengeschoß *nt*.

ballistics [bə'lɪstɪks] *n sing* Ballistik *f* ◆ **~ expert** Schußwaffenfachmann *m*.

balloon [bə'luːn] [1] *n* **(a)** (*Aviat*) (Frei)ballon *m*; (*toy*) (Luft)ballon *m*; (*Met*) (Wetter)ballon *m* ◆ **the ~ went up** (*fig inf*) da ist die Bombe geplatzt (*inf*); **that went down like a lead ~** (*inf*) das kam überhaupt nicht an. **(b)** (*in cartoons*) Sprechblase *f*. **(c)** (*Chem: also* **~ flask**) (Rund)kolben *m*.
[2] *vi* **(a) to go ~ing** auf Ballonfahrt gehen. **(b)** (*swell out*) sich blähen.

balloon glass *n* Kognakglas *nt or* -schwenker *m*.

balloonist [bə'luːnɪst] *n* Ballonfahrer(in *f*) *m*.

balloon-tyre [bə'luːn,taɪə[r]] *n* Ballonreifen *m*.

ballot ['bælət] [1] *n* **(a)** (*method of voting*) (geheime) Abstimmung; (*election*) Geheimwahl *f* ◆ **voting is by ~** die Wahl/Abstimmung ist geheim; **to decide sth by ~** über etw (*acc*) (geheim) abstimmen.
(b) (*vote*) Abstimmung *f*; (*election*) Wahl *f* ◆ **first/second ~** erster/zweiter Wahlgang; **to take** *or* **hold a ~** abstimmen; eine Wahl abhalten, wählen; **they demanded a ~** sie verlangten eine (geheime) Wahl.
(c) (*numbers*) abgegebene Stimmen ◆ **a large ~** eine hohe Wahlbeteiligung.
[2] *vi* abstimmen; (*elect*) eine (geheime) Wahl abhalten.
[3] *vt members* abstimmen lassen.

ballot: ~-box *n* Wahlurne *f*; **~-paper** *n* Stimm- *or* Wahlzettel *m*.

ball: ~park *n* **(a)** (*US*) Baseballstadion *nt*; **(b) ~park figure** Richtzahl *f*; **in that ~park** in dieser Größenordnung; **am I in the right ~park?** bewege ich mich in der richtigen Größenordnung?; **~point (pen)** *n* Kugelschreiber *m*; **~room** *n* Ball- *or* Tanzsaal *m*; **~room dancing** *n* klassische Tänze, Gesellschaftstänze *pl*.

balls-up ['bɔːlzʌp], (*esp US*) **ball up** ['bɔːlʌp] *n* (*sl*) Durcheinander *nt* ◆ **he made a complete ~ of the job** er hat bei der Arbeit totale Scheiße gebaut (*sl*); **the meeting was a complete ~** die Konferenz ist total in die Hose gegangen (*sl*); **what a ~ of a repair!** so 'ne Scheißreparatur! (*sl*).

◆**balls up**, (*esp US*) **ball up** *vt sep* (*sl*) verhunzen (*inf*).

bally ['bælɪ] *adj* (*dated Brit inf*) verflixt (*inf*).

ballyhoo [,bælɪ'huː] (*inf*) [1] *n* Trara (*inf*), Tamtam (*inf*) *nt* ◆ **to make a lot of ~ about sth** ein großes Trara *or* Tamtam um etw machen (*inf*).
[2] *vt* (*US*) marktschreierisch anpreisen.

balm [bɑːm] *n* **(a)** (*lit, fig*) Balsam *m*. **(b)** (*Bot*) Melisse *f*.

balmy ['bɑːmɪ] *adj* (*+er*) (*fragrant*) wohlriechend; (*mild*) sanft, lind (*geh*) ◆ **~ breezes** sanfte Brisen, linde Lüfte (*geh*).

baloney [bə'ləʊnɪ] *n* **(a)** (*sl*) Stuß (*sl*), Quatsch (*inf*) *m* ◆ **she gave me some ~ about having had a flat tyre** sie faselte was von einem Platten (*inf*). **(b)** (*US: sausage*) Mortadella *f*.

balsa ['bɔːlsə] *n* (*also* **~ wood**) Balsa(holz) *nt*.
balsam ['bɔːlsəm] *n* **(a)** Balsam *m* ◆ **~ fir** Balsamtanne *f*. **(b)** (*Bot*) Springkraut *nt*.
Baltic ['bɔːltɪk] [1] *adj* Ostsee-; *language*, (*of* ~ *States*) baltisch ◆ **~ Sea** Ostsee *f*; **the ~ States** (*Hist*) die baltischen Staaten, das Baltikum.
[2] *n*: **the ~** die Ostsee.
baluster ['bæləstəʳ] *n* Baluster *m*, Balustersäule *f*.
balustrade [ˌbælə'streɪd] *n* Balustrade *f*.
bamboo [bæm'buː] [1] *n* Bambus *m*.
[2] *attr* Bambus- ◆ **~ shoots** *pl* Bambussprossen *pl*; **the B~ Curtain** (*Pol*) der Bambusvorhang.
bamboozle [bæm'buːzl] *vt* (*inf*) (*baffle*) verblüffen, baff machen (*inf*); (*trick*) hereinlegen (*inf*), tricksen (*inf*) ◆ **he was ~d into signing the contract** sie haben ihn so getrickst, daß er den Vertrag unterschrieben hat (*inf*).
ban [bæn] [1] *n* Verbot *nt*; (*Eccl*) (Kirchen)bann *m* ◆ **to put a ~ on sth** etw verbieten, etw mit einem Verbot belegen (*form*); **a ~ on smoking** Rauchverbot *nt*.
[2] *vt* (*prohibit*) verbieten; (*Eccl*) auf den Index setzen; *footballer etc* sperren ◆ **to ~ sb from doing sth** jdm verbieten, etw zu tun; **he is ~ned from this pub** er hat hier Lokalverbot; **she was ~ned from driving** ihr wurde Fahrverbot erteilt.
banal [bə'nɑːl] *adj* banal.
banality [bə'nælɪtɪ] *n* Banalität *f*.
banana [bə'nɑːnə] *n* Banane *f*.
banana *in cpds* Bananen-; **~ plantation** *n* Bananenplantage *f*; **~ republic** *n* Bananenrepublik *f*.
bananas [bə'nɑːnəz] *adj pred* (*sl*: *crazy*) bekloppt (*inf*), bescheuert (*sl*), beknackt (*sl*) ◆ **this is driving me ~** dabei dreh' ich noch durch (*inf*); **he's ~ about her** er steht unheimlich auf sie (*sl*); **the whole place went ~** der ganze Saal drehte durch (*inf*).
banana: ~ skin *n* Bananenschale *f*; **~ tree** *n* Bananenstaude *f*.
band¹ [bænd] [1] *n* **(a)** (*of cloth, iron*) Band *nt*; (*on barrel*) Faßband *nt*, Reifen *m*; (*over book jacket*) (Einband)streifen *m*; (*of leather*) Band *nt*, Riemen *m*; (*waist-~*) Bund *m*; (*on cigar*) Banderole, Bauchbinde *f*; (*ring: on bird, US: wedding ~*) Ring *m*; (*on machine*) Riemen *m*.
(b) (*stripe*) Streifen *m*.
(c) (*Eccl, Univ: collar*) **~s** *pl* Beffchen *pl*.
(d) (*Rad*) Band *nt*; *see* **frequency ~**, **wave~**.
[2] *vt bird* beringen.
band² *n* **(a)** Schar *f*; (*of robbers etc*) Bande *f*; (*of workers*) Trupp *m*, Kolonne *f*. **(b)** (*Mus*) Band *f*; (*dance ~*) Tanzkapelle *f*; (*in circus, brass ~, Mil etc*) (Musik)kapelle *f*.
◆**band together** *vi* sich zusammenschließen.
bandage ['bændɪdʒ] [1] *n* Verband *m*; (*strip of cloth*) Binde *f*.
[2] *vt* (*also* **~ up**) *cut* verbinden; *broken limb* bandagieren ◆ **with his heavily ~d wrist** mit einem dick verbundenen Handgelenk.
Band-Aid ['bændeɪd] (*US*) [1] ® *n* Heftpflaster *nt*.
[2] *adj* (*also* **band-aid**) (*inf*: *makeshift*) *solution etc* Not-, behelfsmäßig.
bandan(n)a [bæn'dænə] *n* großes Schnupftuch; (*round neck*) Halstuch *nt*.
B & B [ˌbiːən'biː] *n abbr of* **bed and breakfast**.
bandbox ['bændbɒks] *n* Hutschachtel *f*.
banderol(e) ['bændərəʊl] *n* (*Naut*) Wimpel *m*, Fähnlein *nt*; (*Her*) Fähnchen *nt*; (*Archit*) Inschriftenband *nt*.
bandit ['bændɪt] *n* Bandit, Räuber *m*.
banditry ['bændɪtrɪ] *n* Banditentum *or* -unwesen *nt*.
band: ~ leader *n* Bandleader *m*; **~master** *n* Kapellmeister *m*.
bandolier [ˌbændə'lɪəʳ] *n* Schulterpatronengurt *m*.
band saw *n* Bandsäge *f*.
bandsman ['bændzmən] *n*, *pl* **-men** [-mən] Musiker, Musikant (*old*) *m* ◆ **military ~** Mitglied *nt* eines Musikkorps.
band: ~stand *n* Musikpavillon *m or* -podium *nt*; **~wagon** *n* (*US*) Musikwagen *m*, (Fest)wagen der Musikkapelle; **to jump** *or* **climb on the ~wagon** (*fig inf*) sich dranhängen, auf den fahrenden Zug aufspringen; **~width** *n* (*Rad*) Bandbreite *f*.
bandy¹ ['bændɪ] *adj* krumm ◆ **~ legs** (*of people*) O-Beine.
bandy² *vt jokes* sich (*dat*) erzählen; (*old*) *ball* hin- und herspielen ◆ **to ~ words (with sb)** sich (mit jdm) herumstreiten.
◆**bandy about** *or* **around** *vt sep story, secret* herumerzählen, herumtragen; *ideas* verbreiten; *words, technical expressions* um sich werfen mit; *sb's name* immer wieder nennen ◆ **the press have been ~ing his name/these words ~ a lot** die Presse hat seinen Namen/diese Wörter stark strapaziert; **I'd rather you didn't ~ my nickname ~ the office** es wäre mir lieber, wenn Sie meinen Spitznamen nicht im Büro herumposaunen würden (*inf*).
bandy-legged [ˌbændɪ'legd] *adj* mit krummen Beinen; *person* krummbeinig, O-beinig.
bane [beɪn] *n* **(a)** (*cause of distress*) Fluch *m* ◆ **he's/it's the ~ of my life** er/das ist noch mal mein Ende (*inf*). **(b)** (*old: poison*) Gift *nt*.
baneful ['beɪnfʊl] *adj* verhängnisvoll.
bang¹ [bæŋ] [1] *n* **(a)** (*noise*) Knall *m*; (*of sth falling*) Plumps *m* ◆ **there was a ~ outside** draußen hat es geknallt; **to go off with a ~** mit lautem Knall losgehen; (*inf: be a success*) ein Bombenerfolg sein (*inf*). **(b)** (*violent blow*) Schlag *m*. **he gave himself a ~ on the shins** er hat sich (*dat*) die Schienbeine angeschlagen. **(c)** (*sl: sex*) Fick *m* (*vulg*) ◆ **to have a ~ with sb** mit jdm bumsen (*inf*).
[2] *adv* **(a) to go ~** knallen; (*gun also, balloon*) peng machen (*inf*); (*balloon*) zerplatzen.
(b) (*inf: exactly, directly etc*) voll (*inf*), genau ◆ **his answer was ~ on** seine Antwort war genau richtig; **is that right? — ~ on** stimmt das? — haargenau; **she came ~ on time** sie war auf die Sekunde pünktlich; **they came ~ up against fierce opposition** sie stießen auf heftige Gegenwehr; **the whole ~ shoot** das ganze Zeug (*inf*); (*people*) die ganze Bande (*inf*).
[3] *interj* peng; (*of hammer*) klopf ◆ **~ went a £10 note** (*inf*) und schon war ein 10-Pfund-Schein futsch (*inf*).
[4] *vt* **(a)** (*thump*) schlagen, knallen (*inf*) ◆ **he ~ed his fist on the table** er schlug *or* haute mit der Faust auf den Tisch; **I'll ~ your heads together if you don't shut up!** (*inf*) wenn ihr nicht ruhig seid, knallt's (*inf*); **I felt like ~ing their heads together** (*inf*) ich hätte ihnen am liebsten ein paar links und rechts geknallt (*inf*).
(b) (*shut noisily*) *door* zuschlagen, zuknallen (*inf*) ◆ **you have to ~ the door to close it** Sie müssen die Tür richtig zuschlagen.
(c) (*hit, knock*) *head, shin* sich (*dat*) anschlagen (*on* an +*dat*) ◆ **to ~ one's head** *etc* **on sth** sich (*dat*) den Kopf *etc* an etw (*dat*) anschlagen, mit dem Kopf *etc* gegen etw knallen (*inf*).
[5] *vi* **(a)** (*door: shut*) zuschlagen, zuknallen (*inf*); (*fireworks, gun*) knallen; (*engine*) schlagen, krachen; (*hammer*) klopfen ◆ **the door was ~ing in the wind** die Tür schlug im Wind.
(b) to ~ on *or* **at sth** gegen *or* an etw (*acc*) schlagen.
◆**bang about** [1] *vi* Krach machen; (*heavy noise*) herumpoltern.
[2] *vt sep* Krach machen mit; *chairs also* herumstoßen.
◆**bang away** *vi* **(a)** (*guns*) knallen; (*persons: keep firing*) wild (drauflos)feuern (*at* auf +*acc*), wild (drauflos)ballern (*inf*) (*at* auf +*acc*); (*workman etc*) herumklopfen *or* -hämmern (*at* an +*dat*) ◆ **to ~ ~ at the typewriter** auf der Schreibmaschine herumhauen *or* -hämmern (*inf*). **(b)** (*inf: work industriously*) **to ~ ~ (at sth)** sich hinter etw (*acc*) klemmen (*inf*). **(c)** (*sl: have sexual intercourse*) bumsen (*inf*).
◆**bang down** *vt sep* (hin)knallen (*inf*); *nail* einschlagen; (*flatten*) flachschlagen; *lid* zuschlagen, zuknallen (*inf*) ◆ **to ~ ~ the receiver** den Hörer aufknallen (*inf*).
◆**bang in** *vt sep nail* einschlagen.
◆**bang into** *vi* +*prep obj* **(a)** (*collide with*) knallen (*inf*) *or* prallen auf (+*acc*). **(b)** (*inf: meet*) zufällig treffen.
◆**bang out** *vt sep* **(a)** *nail, brick* herausschlagen, heraushauen (*inf*). **(b) to ~ ~ a tune on the piano/a letter on the typewriter** eine Melodie auf dem Klavier hämmern (*inf*)/einen Brief auf der Schreibmaschine herunterhauen (*inf*).
bang² *n* (*fringe*) Pony *m*, Ponyfransen *pl* ◆ **~s** Ponyfrisur *f*.
banger ['bæŋəʳ] *n* **(a)** (*inf: sausage*) Wurst *f*. **(b)** (*inf: old car*) Klapperkiste *f* (*inf*). **(c)** (*Brit: firework*) Knallkörper *m*.
Bangladesh ['bæŋglə'deʃ] *n* Bangladesh *nt*.
Bangladeshi [ˌbæŋglə'deʃɪ] [1] *n* Einwohner(in *f*) *m* von Bangladesh, Bangladeshi *mf*.
[2] *adj* aus Bangladesh.
bangle ['bæŋgl] *n* Armreif(en) *m*; (*for ankle*) Fußreif *or* -ring *m*.
bang-up ['bæŋʌp] *adj* (*US sl*) bombig (*inf*), prima (*inf*).
banish ['bænɪʃ] *vt person* verbannen; *cares, fear* vertreiben.
banishment ['bænɪʃmənt] *n* Verbannung *f*.
banister, bannister ['bænɪstəʳ] *n* (*also* **~s**) Geländer *nt*.
banjo ['bændʒəʊ] *n*, *pl* **-es** *or* (*US*) **-s** Banjo *nt*.
bank¹ [bæŋk] [1] *n* **(a)** (*of earth, sand*) Wall, Damm *m*; (*Rail*) (Bahn)damm *m*; (*slope*) Böschung *f*, Abhang *m*; (*on racetrack*) Kurvenüberhöhung *f* ◆ **~ of snow** Schneeverwehung *f*.
(b) (*of river, lake*) Ufer *nt* ◆ **we sat on the ~s of a river/lake** wir saßen an einem Fluß/See *or* Fluß-/Seeufer.
(c) (*in sea, river*) (Sand)bank *f*.
(d) (*of clouds*) Wand, Bank *f*.
(e) (*Aviat*) Querlage *f* ◆ **to go into a ~** in den Kurvenflug gehen.
[2] *vt* **(a)** *road* überhöhen. **(b)** *river* mit einer Böschung versehen, einfassen. **(c)** *plane* in die Querlage bringen.
[3] *vi* (*Aviat*) den Kurvenflug einleiten, in die Querlage gehen.
◆**bank up** [1] *vt sep earth etc* aufhäufen, aufschütten; (*support*) mit einer Böschung stützen; *fire* mit Kohlestaub ab- *or* bedecken (*damit es langsam brennt*).
[2] *vi* (*snow etc*) sich anhäufen; (*clouds also*) sich zusammenballen.
bank² [1] *n* **(a)** Bank *f*. **(b)** (*Gambling*) Bank *f* ◆ **to keep** *or* **be the ~** die Bank halten *or* haben. **(c)** (*Med*) Bank *f*. **(d)** (*fig*) Vorrat *m* (*of* an +*dat*).
[2] *vt money* zur Bank bringen, einzahlen.
[3] *vi* **where do you ~?** bei welcher Bank haben Sie Ihr Konto?; **I ~ with Lloyds** ich habe ein Konto *or* ich bin bei Lloyds.
◆**bank (up)on** *vi* +*prep obj* sich verlassen auf (+*acc*), rechnen mit; *sb, sb's help also* zählen *or* bauen auf (+*acc*) ◆ **you mustn't ~ ~ it** darauf würde ich mich nicht verlassen; **I was ~ing ~ your coming** ich hatte fest damit gerechnet, daß du kommst.
bank³ *n* **(a)** (*Naut: rower's bench*) Ruderbank *f*. **(b)** (*row of objects, oars*) Reihe *f*; (*on organ, typewriter*) (Tasten)reihe *f*.
bankable ['bæŋkəbl] *adj cheque etc* einzahlbar ◆ **a very ~ filmstar** (*fig inf*) ein Filmstar, der viel Geld einbringt.
bank: ~ account *n* Bankkonto *nt*; **~ balance** *n* Kontostand *m*; **~book** *n* Sparbuch *nt*; **~ charge** *n* Kontoführungsgebühr *f*; **~ clerk** *n* Bankangestellte(r) *mf*; **~ code number** *n* Bankleitzahl *f*.
banker ['bæŋkəʳ] *n* (*Fin*) Bankier, Bankfachmann, Banker (*inf*) *m*; (*gambling*) Bankhalter *m*.

banker's: ~ card *n* Scheckkarte *f*; **~ order** *n* (*standing order*) Dauerauftrag *m*; **by ~ order** durch Dauerauftrag.

bank: ~ giro *n* Banküberweisung *f*; **~ holiday** *n* (*Brit*) öffentlicher Feiertag; (*US*) Bankfeiertag *m*.

banking¹ ['bæŋkɪŋ] *n* **(a)** (*on road, racetrack*) Überhöhung *f*. **(b)** (*Aviat*) Kurvenflug *m*.

banking² [1] *n* Bankwesen *nt* ◆ **the world of ~** die Bankwelt; **he wants to go into ~** er will ins Bankfach *or* Bankgewerbe gehen.
[2] *attr matter, systems* Bank- ◆ **the ~ side of the business** die Bankangelegenheiten der Firma.

banking: ~ hours *npl* Schalterstunden *pl*; **~ house** *n* Bankhaus *nt*.

bank: ~ loan *n* Bankkredit *m*; **~ manager** *n* Filialleiter *m* (*einer Bank*); **my ~ manager** der Filialleiter meiner Bank; **~note** *n* Banknote *f*, Geldschein *m*; **~ rate** *n* Diskontsatz *m*; **~ reference** *n* (*for new customer etc*) Bankauskunft *f*.

bankrupt ['bæŋkrʌpt] [1] *n* **(a)** Gemein- *or* Konkursschuldner *m* (*Jur*), Bankrotteur *m* ◆ **~'s certificate** Eröffnungsbeschluß *m*; **~'s estate** Konkursmasse *f*. **(b)** (*fig*) **to be a moral/political ~** moralisch/politisch bankrott sein.
[2] *adj* **(a)** (*Jur*) bankrott ◆ **to go ~** Bankrott machen, in Konkurs gehen; **to be ~** bankrott *or* pleite (*inf*) sein. **(b)** (*fig*) bankrott ◆ **they are totally ~ of ideas** sie haben keinerlei Ideen.
[3] *vt person* zugrunde richten, ruinieren; *firm also* in den Konkurs treiben.

bankruptcy ['bæŋkrəptsɪ] *n* **(a)** (*Jur*) Bankrott, Konkurs *m*; (*instance*) Konkurs *m* ◆ **the possibility of ~** die Möglichkeit eines *or* des Bankrotts *or* Konkurses. **(b)** (*fig*) Bankrott *m*.

bankruptcy: B~ Court *n* Konkursgericht *nt*; **~ proceedings** *npl* Konkursverfahren *nt*.

bank: ~ statement *n* Kontoauszug *m*; **~ transfer** *n* Banküberweisung *f*.

banner ['bænəʳ] *n* Banner *nt* (*also fig*); (*in processions*) Transparent, Spruchband *nt* ◆ **~ headlines** Schlagzeilen *pl*.

bannister ['bænɪstəʳ] *n see* **banister**.

banns [bænz] *npl* (*Eccl*) Aufgebot *nt* ◆ **to read the ~** das Aufgebot verlesen; **where are you having your ~ called?** wo haben Sie das Aufgebot bestellt?

banquet ['bæŋkwɪt] [1] *n* (*lavish feast*) Festessen *nt*; (*ceremonial dinner also*) Bankett *nt*.
[2] *vt* üppig *or* festlich bewirten (*on* mit); (*ceremoniously*) ein Bankett abhalten für.
[3] *vi* speisen, tafeln (*geh*) ◆ **to ~ on sth** etw speisen.

banquet(ing)-hall ['bæŋkwɪt(ɪŋ)'hɔːl] *n* Festsaal, Bankettsaal *m*.

banshee [bæn'ʃiː] *n* (*Ir Myth*) Banshee, Todesfee *f* ◆ **to howl like a ~** gespenstisch heulen.

bantam ['bæntəm] *n* Bantamhuhn *nt*.

bantamweight ['bæntəm,weɪt] *n* Bantamgewicht *nt*.

banter ['bæntəʳ] [1] *n* Geplänkel *nt* ◆ **enough of this foolish ~** lassen wir das alberne Gerede!
[2] *vt* (*old*) verulken, necken.

bantering ['bæntərɪŋ] *adj* (*joking*) scherzhaft; (*teasing*) neckend, flachsig (*dial*).

Bantu [,bæn'tuː] [1] *n* (*language*) Bantu *nt*; (*pl: tribes*) Bantu *pl*; (*person*) Bantu *mf*, Bantuneger(in *f*) *m*.
[2] *adj* Bantu-.

banyan (tree) ['bænɪən(,triː)] *n* bengalische Feige, Banyan *m*.

BAOR *abbr of* **British Army of the Rhine**.

bap (bun) ['bæp(bʌn)] *n* (*Brit*) weiches Brötchen.

baptism ['bæptɪzəm] *n* Taufe *f* ◆ **~ of fire** (*fig*) Feuertaufe *f*.

baptismal [bæp'tɪzməl] *adj* Tauf-.

Baptist ['bæptɪst] *n* Baptist(in *f*) *m* ◆ **the ~ Church** (*people*) die Baptistengemeinde; (*teaching*) der Baptismus; *see* **John**.

baptize [bæp'taɪz] *vt* taufen.

bar¹ [bɑːʳ] [1] *n* **(a)** (*of metal, wood*) Stange *f*; (*of toffee etc*) Riegel *m*; (*of electric fire*) Element *nt* ◆ **~ of gold/silver** Gold-/Silberbarren *m*; **a ~ of chocolate, a chocolate ~** (*slab*) eine Tafel Schokolade; (*Mars* ® *~ etc*) ein Schokoladenriegel *m*; **a ~ of soap** ein Stück *nt* Seife.
(b) (*of window, grate, cage*) (Gitter)stab *m*; (*of door*) Stange *f* ◆ **the window has ~s** das Fenster ist vergittert; **behind ~s** hinter Gittern; **to put sb behind ~s** jdn hinter Gitter *or* hinter Schloß und Riegel bringen.
(c) (*Sport*) (*horizontal*) Reck *nt*; (*for high jump etc*) Latte *f*; (*one of parallel ~s*) Holm *m* ◆ **~s** (*parallel*) Barren *m*; **(wall) ~s** Sprossenwand *f*; **to exercise on the ~s** am Barren turnen.
(d) (*Ballet*) Stange *f* ◆ **at the ~** an der Stange.
(e) (*in river, harbour*) Barre *f*.
(f) (*fig: obstacle*) Hindernis (*to* für), Hemmnis (*to* für) *nt* ◆ **to be *or* present a ~ to sth** einer Sache (*dat*) im Wege stehen.
(g) (*of light, colour*) Streifen *m*; (*of light also*) Strahl *m*.
(h) (*Jur*) **the B~** die Anwaltschaft; **to be a member of the B~** Anwalt vor Gericht sein; **to be called *or* admitted** (*US*) **to the B~** als Anwalt (vor Gericht) *or* Verteidiger zugelassen werden; **to read for the B~** Jura studieren; **at the ~ of public opinion** (*fig*) vor dem Forum der Öffentlichkeit.
(i) (*for prisoners*) Anklagebank *f* ◆ **to stand at the ~** auf der Anklagebank sitzen; **prisoner at the ~** „Angeklagter!"
(j) (*for drinks*) Lokal *nt*; (*esp expensive*) Bar *f*; (*part of pub*) Gaststube *f*; (*counter*) Theke *f*, Tresen *m*; (*at railway station*) Ausschank *m*.
(k) (*Mus*) Takt *m*; (*~ line also*) Taktstrich *m*.
(l) (*on medal*) **DSO and ~** *zweimal verliehener DSO*.
(m) (*Her*) Balken *m* ◆ **~ sinister** Bastardfaden *m*.
(n) (*Met*) Bar *nt*.
[2] *vt* **(a)** (*obstruct*) *road* blockieren, versperren ◆ **to ~ sb's way** jdm den Weg versperren *or* verstellen; **to ~ the way to progress** dem Fortschritt im Wege stehen.
(b) (*fasten*) *window, door* versperren ◆ **to ~ the door against sb** jdm die Tür versperren.
(c) (*exclude, prohibit*) *person, possibility* ausschließen; *action, thing* untersagen, verbieten ◆ **to ~ sb from a competition** jdn von (der Teilnahme an) einem Wettbewerb ausschließen; **to ~ sb from a career** jdm eine Karriere unmöglich machen; **they've been ~red (from the club)** sie haben Clubverbot; **minors are ~red from this club** Minderjährige haben keinen Zutritt zu diesem Club.

bar², barring ['bɑːrɪŋ] *prep* **barring accidents** falls nichts passiert; **bar none** ohne Ausnahme, ausnahmslos; **bar one** außer einem; **~ these few mistakes it is a good essay** abgesehen von diesen paar Fehlern ist der Aufsatz gut.

barb [bɑːb] [1] *n* **(a)** (*of hook, arrow*) Widerhaken *m*; (*of barbed wire*) Stachel *m*, Spitze *f*; (*of feather*) Fahne *f*; (*Bot, Zool*) Bart *m*. **(b)** (*fig: of wit etc*) Spitze *f*; (*liter: of remorse*) Stachel *m*.
[2] *vt* (*lit*) mit Widerhaken versehen.

Barbados [bɑː'beɪdɒs] *n* Barbados *nt*.

barbarian [bɑː'beərɪən] [1] *n* (*Hist, fig*) Barbar(in *f*) *m*.
[2] *adj* (*Hist, fig*) barbarisch.

barbaric [bɑː'bærɪk] *adj* barbarisch; (*Hist also*) Barbaren-; *guard etc* grausam, roh; (*fig inf*) *conditions* grauenhaft.

barbarically [bɑː'bærɪkəlɪ] *adv* barbarisch.

barbarism ['bɑːbərɪzəm] *n* **(a)** (*Hist*) Barbarei *f*; (*fig also*) Unkultur *f*. **(b)** (*Ling*) Barbarismus *m*.

barbarity [bɑː'bærɪtɪ] *n* Barbarei *f*; (*fig*) Primitivität *f*; (*cruelty: of guard etc*) Grausamkeit, Roheit *f* ◆ **the barbarities of modern warfare** die Barbarei *or* die Greuel *pl* des modernen Krieges.

barbarous ['bɑːbərəs] *adj* (*Hist, fig*) barbarisch; (*cruel*) grausam; *guard etc* roh; *accent also* grauenhaft.

barbarously ['bɑːbərəslɪ] *adv see adj* barbarisch, wie ein Barbar/die Barbaren; grausam; grauenhaft (*inf*).

Barbary ['bɑːbərɪ] *n* Berberei *f*.

Barbary *in cpds* Berber-; **~ ape** *n* Berberaffe *m*; **~ coast** *n* Barbareskenküste *f*; **~ states** *npl* Barbareskenstaaten *pl*.

barbecue ['bɑːbɪkjuː] [1] *n* **(a)** (*Cook: grid*) Grill *m*. **(b)** (*occasion*) Grillparty *f*, Barbecue *nt*. **(c)** (*meat*) Grillfleisch *nt*/-wurst *f etc*.
[2] *vt steak etc* grillen, auf dem Rost braten; *animal* am Spieß braten.

barbed [bɑːbd] *adj* **(a)** *arrow* mit Widerhaken. **(b)** (*fig*) *wit* beißend; *remark also* spitz, bissig.

barbed: ~ wire *n* Stacheldraht *m*; **~-wire fence** *n* Stacheldrahtzaun *m*.

barbel ['bɑːbəl] *n* (*fish*) Barbe *f*; (*filament on fish*) Bartel *f*, Bartfaden *m*.

barbell [bɑː'bel] *n* Hantel *f*.

barber ['bɑːbəʳ] *n* (Herren)friseur, Barbier (*old*) *m* ◆ **the ~'s** der Friseur(laden), das (Herren)friseurgeschäft; **at/to the ~'s** beim/zum Friseur; **~'s pole** *Ladenzeichen nt der Friseure: Stange mit rot-weißer Spirale*.

barbershop [,bɑːbə'ʃɒp] (*US*) [1] *n* (Herren)friseurgeschäft *nt or* -laden *m*.
[2] *adj* **~ quartet** Barbershop-Quartett *nt*.

barbican ['bɑːbɪkən] *n* Außen- *or* Vorwerk *nt*; (*tower*) Wachtturm *m*.

Barbie doll ® ['bɑːbɪ,dɒl] *n* Barbie-Puppe ® *f*.

bar billiards *n sing: in Lokalen gespielte Form des Billard*.

barbitone ['bɑːbɪtəʊn] *n* (*Med*) barbiturathaltiges Mittel.

barbiturate [bɑː'bɪtjʊrɪt] *n* Schlafmittel, Barbiturat *nt* ◆ **~ poisoning** Schlafmittelvergiftung, Barbiturvergiftung *f*.

barbs [bɑːbz] *npl* (*sl*) *abbr of* **barbiturates**.

bar: ~ chart *n* Balkendiagramm *nt*; **~ code** *n* Strichkodierung *f*, Bar-Code *m*; **~ code reader** *n* Bar-Code-Leser *m*; **~-coded** *adj* mit Strichkodierung *or* Bar-Code.

bard [bɑːd] *n* **(a)** (*minstrel*) (*esp Celtic*) Barde *m*; (*in Ancient Greece*) (Helden)sänger *m*. **(b)** (*old Liter, hum: poet*) Barde *m* ◆ **the B~ of Avon** Shakespeare.

bardic ['bɑːdɪk] *adj poetry etc* bardisch.

bare [beəʳ] [1] *adj* (+*er*) **(a)** (*naked, uncovered*) *skin, boards, floor* nackt, bloß; *summit, tree, countryside* kahl, nackt; *room, garden* leer; *sword* blank; *wire* blank; *style* nüchtern ◆ **he stood there ~ to the waist** er stand mit nacktem Oberkörper da; **~ patch** kahle Stelle; **to sleep on ~ boards** auf blanken Brettern schlafen; **to lay ~ one's heart** sein Innerstes bloßlegen; **the ~ facts** die nackten Tatsachen; **the ~ fact that he ...** allein die Tatsache, daß er ...; **with his ~ hands** mit bloßen Händen; **a ~ statement of the facts** eine reine Tatsachenfeststellung.
(b) (*scanty, mere*) knapp ◆ **a ~ majority** eine knappe Mehrheit; **a ~ thank you** kaum ein Dankeschön; **a ~ subsistence wage** gerade das Existenzminimum; **a ~ ten centimetres** knappe *or* kaum zehn Zentimeter; **he shuddered at the ~ idea** es schauderte ihn beim bloßen Gedanken (daran); **with just the ~st hint of garlic** nur mit einer winzigen Spur Knoblauch.
[2] *vt breast, leg* entblößen; (*at doctor's*) freimachen; *teeth also* blecken; (*in anger*) fletschen; *end of a wire* freilegen ◆ **she ~d her teeth in a forced smile** sie grinste gezwungen; **to ~ one's head** den Hut *etc* ziehen, das Haupt entblößen (*liter*); **to ~ one's heart to sb** jdm sein Herz ausschütten.

bare: ~back *adv, adj* ohne Sattel; **~faced** *adj* (*fig: shameless*) *liar* unverfroren, unverschämt, schamlos; **it is ~faced robbery** das ist der reine Wucher (*inf*); **~foot** *adv* barfuß; **~footed** [1] *adj* barfüßig, barfuß *pred*; [2] *adv* barfuß; **~headed** [1] *adj* barhäuptig (*geh*), ohne Kopfbedeckung; [2] *adv* ohne

Kopfbedeckung, barhaupt (*geh*); **~legged** *adj* mit bloßen Beinen.

barely ['bɛəlɪ] *adv* **(a)** (*scarcely*) kaum; (*with figures also*) knapp ◆ **we ~ know him** wir kennen ihn kaum; **~ had he started when** ... kaum hatte er angefangen, als ... **(b)** *furnished* dürftig, spärlich.

bareness ['bɛənɪs] *n* Nacktheit *f*; (*of person also*) Blöße *f*; (*of trees, countryside*) Kahlheit *f*; (*of room, garden*) Leere *f*; (*of style*) Nüchternheit *f*.

Barents Sea ['bærənts'siː] *n* Barentssee *f*.

bargain ['bɑːgɪn] [1] *n* **(a)** (*transaction*) Handel *m*, Geschäft *nt* ◆ **to make** *or* **strike a ~** sich einigen; **they are not prepared to make a ~** sie wollen nicht mit sich handeln lassen; **I'll make a ~ with you, if you** ... ich mache Ihnen ein Angebot, wenn Sie ...; **it's a ~!** abgemacht!, einverstanden!; **you drive a hard ~** Sie stellen ja harte Forderungen!; **to offer sb a good ~** jdm ein gutes Angebot machen; **then it started raining into the ~** dann hat es (obendrein) auch noch angefangen zu regnen; **and she was rich into the ~** und außerdem war sie reich; **to get the worst/best of the ~** den schlechteren/besseren Teil erwischen.

(b) (*cheap offer*) günstiges Angebot, Sonderangebot *nt*; (*thing bought*) Gelegenheitskauf *m* ◆ **this jacket is a good ~** diese Jacke ist wirklich günstig; **what a ~!** das ist aber günstig!

[2] *vi* handeln (*for* um); (*in negotiations*) verhandeln ◆ **the traders are not prepared to ~** die Ladenbesitzer lassen nicht mit sich handeln.

◆**bargain away** *vt sep rights, advantage etc* sich (*dat*) abhandeln lassen; *freedom, independence also* veräußern.

◆**bargain for** *vi +prep obj* (*inf: expect*) rechnen mit, erwarten ◆ **I hadn't ~ed ~ that** damit hatte ich nicht gerechnet; **I got more than I ~ed ~** ich habe vielleicht mein blaues Wunder erlebt! (*inf*); (*in argument also*) ich habe vielleicht eins draufbekommen! (*inf*).

◆**bargain on** *vi +prep obj* zählen auf (*+acc*), sich verlassen auf (*+acc*).

bargain: ~ basement *n Untergeschoß nt eines Kaufhauses mit Sonderangeboten*; **~ buy** *n* Preisschlager *m* (*inf*); **that's a real ~ buy** das ist wirklich günstig; **~ counter** *n* Sonder(angebots)tisch *m*.

bargainer ['bɑːgɪnəʳ] *n* **to be a good/poor ~** handeln/nicht handeln können; (*in negotiations*) gut/nicht gut verhandeln können; **as a ~ he** ... beim Handeln/bei Verhandlungen ... er.

bargain: ~-hunter *n* **the ~-hunters** Leute *pl* auf der Jagd nach Sonderangeboten; **~ hunting** *n* Jagd *f* nach Sonderangeboten; **to go ~ hunting** auf Jagd nach Sonderangeboten gehen.

bargaining ['bɑːgənɪŋ] *n* Handeln *nt*; (*negotiating*) Verhandeln *nt* ◆ **~ position** Verhandlungsposition *f*.

bargain: ~ offer *n* Sonderangebot *nt*, günstiges Angebot; **~ price** *n* Sonderpreis *m*; **at a ~ price** zum Sonderpreis; **~ rates** *npl* Sonderpreise *pl*; **~ sale** *n* Ausverkauf *m*.

barge [bɑːdʒ] [1] *n* **(a)** (*for freight*) Last- *or* Frachtkahn *m*; (*unpowered*) Schleppkahn *m*; (*lighter*) Leichter *m*; (*ship's boat*) Barkasse *f*; (*houseboat*) Hausboot *nt* ◆ **the Royal/state ~** die königliche Barkasse/die Staatsbarkasse; (*unpowered*) das königliche Boot/das Staatsboot.

(b) (*shove*) Stoß, Rempler (*inf*) *m*.

[2] *vt* **(a) he ~d me out of the way** er hat mich weggestoßen; **he ~d his way into the room/through the crowd** er ist (ins Zimmer) hereingeplatzt (*inf*)/er hat sich durch die Menge geboxt (*inf*).

(b) (*Sport*) rempeln ◆ **he ~d him off the ball** er hat ihn vom Ball weggestoßen.

[3] *vi* **(a) to ~ into/out of a room** (in ein Zimmer) herein-/hineinplatzen (*inf*)/aus einem Zimmer heraus-/hinausstürmen; **he ~d through the crowd** er drängte *or* boxte (*inf*) sich durch die Menge; **will you boys stop barging!** hört auf zu drängeln, Jungs! **(b)** (*Sport*) rempeln.

◆**barge about** *or* **around** *vi* (*inf*) herumpoltern (*inf*).

◆**barge in** *vi* (*inf*) **(a)** hinein-/hereinplatzen (*inf*) *or* -stürzen. **(b)** (*interrupt*) dazwischenplatzen (*inf*) (*on* bei); (*interfere also*) sich einmischen (*on* in *+acc*).

◆**barge into** *vi +prep obj* **(a)** (*knock against*) *person* (hinein)rennen in (*+acc*) (*inf*); (*shove*) (an)rempeln; *thing* rennen gegen (*inf*). **(b)** (*inf*) *room, party, conversation* (hinein-/herein)platzen in (*+acc*) (*inf*).

bargee [bɑː'dʒiː] *n* Lastschiffer *m*; (*master*) Kahnführer *m*.

barge pole *n* Bootsstange *f* ◆ **I wouldn't touch it/him with a (ten-foot) ~** (*Brit inf*) von so etwas/so jemandem lasse ich die Finger (*inf*); (*because disgusting, unpleasant*) das/den würde ich noch nicht mal mit der Kneifzange anfassen (*inf*).

baritone ['bærɪtəʊn] [1] *n* Bariton *m*.

[2] *adj* Bariton-.

barium ['bɛərɪəm] *n* Barium *nt* ◆ **~ meal** Bariumbrei *m*.

bark[1] [bɑːk] [1] *n* (*of tree*) Rinde, Borke *f* ◆ **to strip the ~ off a tree** einen Baumstamm schälen.

[2] *vt* (*rub off skin*) aufschürfen; (*knock against*) anstoßen, anschlagen ◆ **to ~ one's shin against the table** sich (*dat*) das Schienbein am Tisch anschlagen.

bark[2] [1] *n* (*of dog, seal, gun, cough*) Bellen *nt* ◆ **his ~ is worse than his bite** (*Prov*) Hunde, die bellen, beißen nicht (*Prov*); **next! came the sudden ~ from the surgery** der Nächste! bellte es plötzlich aus dem Behandlungszimmer.

[2] *vi* bellen ◆ **to ~ at sb** jdn anbellen; (*person also*) jdn anfahren; **to be ~ing up the wrong tree** (*fig inf*) auf dem Holzweg sein (*inf*).

◆**bark out** *vt sep orders* bellen.

bark[3], **barque** *n* **(a)** (*poet*) Barke *f* (*liter*). **(b)** (*Naut*) Bark *f*.

barkeep(er) ['bɑːkiːp(əʳ)] *n* (*US*) Barbesitzer(in *f*), Gastwirt *m*; (*bartender*) Barkeeper, Barmann *m*.

barker ['bɑːkəʳ] *n* (*outside shop, club*) Anreißer *m* (*inf*); (*at fair*) Marktschreier *m* (*inf*).

barley ['bɑːlɪ] *n* Gerste *f* ◆ **pearl ~** (Gersten- *or* Perl)graupen *pl*.

barley: ~corn *n* Gerstenkorn *nt*; *see* **John**; **~ sugar** *n* Gersten- *or* Malzzucker *m*; (*sweet*) *hartes Zuckerbonbon*; **~ water** *n Art Gerstenextrakt*; **lemon/orange ~ water** konzentriertes Zitronen-/Orangegetränk; **~ wine** *n* (*Brit*) *Art Starkbier nt*.

bar line *n* (*Mus*) Taktstrich *m*.

barm [bɑːm] *n* (Bier)hefe, Bärme *f*.

bar: ~maid *n* Bardame *f*; **~man** *n* Barkeeper, Barmann *m*.

bar mitzvah [bɑː'mɪtsvə] *n* (*ceremony*) Bar Mizwa *nt*; (*boy*) *Junge, der Bar Mizwa feiert*.

barmy ['bɑːmɪ] *adj* (*Brit sl*) bekloppt (*inf*), plemplem *pred* (*inf*); *idea etc* blödsinnig (*inf*).

barn [bɑːn] *n* **(a)** Scheune, Scheuer *f*; (*in field*) Schober *m* (*S Ger, Aus*) ◆ **a great ~ of a house** eine große Scheune (*inf*). **(b)** (*US: for streetcars, trucks*) Depot *nt*, Hof *m*.

barnacle ['bɑːnəkl] *n* **(a)** (*shellfish*) (Rankenfuß)krebs, Rankenfüßer *m*. **(b)** (*fig: person*) Klette *f* (*inf*).

barnacle goose *n* Nonnengans *f*.

barn-dance ['bɑːndɑːns] *n* Bauerntanz *m*.

barney ['bɑːnɪ] *n* (*sl: noisy quarrel*) Krach *m* (*inf*); (*punch-up*) Schlägerei, Keilerei (*inf*) *f*.

barn: ~ owl *n* Schleiereule *f*; **~storm** *vi* (*esp US*) (*Theat*) in der Provinz spielen; (*Pol*) in der Provinz Wahlreden halten; **~stormer** *n* (*US Pol*) Wahlredner(in *f*) *m* in der Provinz; (*Theat*) Wanderschauspieler(in *f*) *m*; **~yard** *n* (Bauern)hof *m*; **~yard fowl(s)** *npl* (Haus)geflügel *nt*.

barometer [bə'rɒmɪtəʳ] *n* (*lit, fig*) Barometer *nt*.

barometric [ˌbærəʊ'metrɪk] *adj* barometrisch, Barometer- ◆ **~ pressure** Atmosphären- *or* Luftdruck *m*.

baron ['bærən] *n* **(a)** Baron *m*. **(b)** (*fig*) Baron, Magnat *m* ◆ **industrial/oil ~** Industriebaron/Ölmagnat *m*; **press ~** Pressezar *m*. **(c)** (*of beef*) doppeltes Lendenstück.

baroness ['bærənɪs] *n* Baronin *f*; (*unmarried*) Baronesse *f*.

baronet ['bærənɪt] *n* Baronet *m*.

baronetcy ['bærənɪtsɪ] *n* (*rank*) Baronetstand *m*; (*title*) Baronetswürde *f*.

baronial [bə'rəʊnɪəl] *adj* (*lit*) Barons-; (*fig*) fürstlich, feudal.

barony ['bærənɪ] *n* Baronie *f*.

baroque [bə'rɒk] [1] *adj* barock, Barock-.

[2] *n* (*style*) Barock *m or nt* ◆ **the ~ period** das *or* der Barock, die Barockzeit.

barouche [bə'ruːʃ] *n* Landauer *m*.

barque [bɑːk] *n see* **bark**[3].

barrack[1] ['bærək] *vt soldiers* kasernieren.

barrack[2] [1] *vt actor etc* auspfeifen; auszischen.

[2] *vi* pfeifen; zischen.

barracking[1] ['bærəkɪŋ] *n* (*Mil*) Kasernierung *f*.

barracking[2] *n* Pfeifen *nt*; Zischen *nt*; Buhrufe *pl* ◆ **to get a ~** ausgepfiffen/ausgezischt werden.

barrack-room ['bærəkˌruːm] *adj attr* rauh, roh ◆ **~ language** Landsersprache *f*; **~ lawyer** (*pej*) Paragraphenreiter *m* (*inf*).

barracks ['bærəks] [1] *npl* (*often with sing vb*) (*Mil*) Kaserne *f*; (*fig pej also*) Mietskaserne *f* ◆ **to live in ~** in der Kaserne wohnen; **houses like ~** Häuser wie Kasernen.

[2] *attr* **~ life** Kasernenleben *nt*; **~ square** Kasernenhof *m*.

barracuda [ˌbærə'kjuːdə] *n* Barrakuda, Pfeilhecht *m*.

barrage ['bærɑːʒ] *n* **(a)** (*across river*) Wehr *nt*; (*larger*) Staustufe *f*. **(b)** (*Mil*) Sperrfeuer *nt* ◆ **under this ~ of stones** ... unter diesem Steinhagel ...; **they kept up a ~ of stones** sie bedeckten die Polizei/uns *etc* mit einem Steinhagel. **(c)** (*fig: of words, questions etc*) Hagel *m*. **he was attacked with a ~ of questions** er wurde mit Fragen beschossen.

barrage balloon *n* Sperrballon *m*.

barre [bɑːʳ] *n* (*Ballet*) Stange *f* ◆ **at the ~** an der Stange.

barred [bɑːd] *adj* **(a)** *suf* **five-~ gate** Weidengatter *nt* (mit fünf Querbalken). **(b) ~ window** Gitterfenster *nt*.

barrel ['bærəl] [1] *n* **(a)** Faß *nt*; (*for oil, tar, rainwater etc*) Tonne *f*; (*measure: of oil*) Barrel *nt* ◆ **they've got us over a ~** (*inf*) sie haben uns in der Zange (*inf*); *see* **biscuit, scrape**.

(b) (*of handgun*) Lauf *m*; (*of cannon etc*) Rohr *nt* ◆ **to give sb both ~s** auf jdn aus beiden Läufen feuern; **I found myself looking down the ~ of a gun** ich hatte plötzlich eine Kanone *or* ein Schießeisen vor der Nase (*sl*); *see* **lock**[2].

(c) (*of fountain pen*) Tank *m*.

[2] *vt wine etc* (in Fässer) (ab)füllen; *herring* (in Fässer) einlegen ◆ **~led beer** Faßbier *nt*.

◆**barrel along** *vi* (*inf*) entlangbrausen (*inf*).

barrel: ~-chested *adj* breitbrüstig, mit gewölbter Brust; **to be ~-chested** einen gewölbten Brustkasten haben; **~ful** *n* Faß *nt*; (*of oil*) Barrel *nt*; **two ~fuls of beer/herrings** zwei Faß Bier/Fässer Heringe; **~house** (*US*) [1] *n* Kneipe *f*; (*jazz*) Kneipenjazz *m*; [2] *adj* **~house blues** *alte, in Kneipen gespielte Form des Blues*; **~ organ** *n* Drehorgel *f*, Leierkasten *m*; **~-shaped** *adj* faß- *or* tonnenförmig; **~-shaped man/woman** Faß *nt* (*inf*)/Tonne *f* (*inf*); **~ vault** *n* Tonnengewölbe *nt*.

barren ['bærən] [1] *adj* **(a)** unfruchtbar; *land also* karg.

(b) (*fig*) *years* unfruchtbar, unproduktiv; *discussion also* fruchtlos; *atmosphere also* steril; *style, subject, study* trocken; *topic* unergiebig ◆ **the house looks ~ without any furniture** das Haus wirkt ohne Möbel leer.

[2] *n* (*esp US*) **~s** *pl* Ödland *nt*.

barrenness ['bærənnıs] *n see adj* **(a)** Unfruchtbarkeit *f*; Kargheit *f*. **(b)** Unfruchtbarkeit, Unproduktivität *f*; Fruchtlosigkeit *f*; Sterilität *f*; Trockenheit *f*; Unergiebigkeit *f*.

barrette [bə'ret] *n (US)* (Haar)spange *f*.

barricade [,bærı'keıd] [1] *n* Barrikade *f*.
[2] *vt* verbarrikadieren.

◆**barricade in** *vt sep* verbarrikadieren.

◆**barricade off** *vt sep* (mit Barrikaden) absperren.

barrier ['bærıə^r] *n* **(a)** *(natural)* Barriere *f*; *(man-made, erected also)* Sperre *f*; *(railing etc)* Schranke *f*; *(crash ~)* (Leit)planke *f* ◆ **ticket ~** Sperre *f*.
(b) *(fig) (obstacle)* Hindernis *nt*, Barriere *f (to* für); *(of class, background, education, between people)* Schranke, Barriere *f* ◆ **trade ~s** Handelsschranken *pl*; **~ of language** Sprachbarriere *f*; **a ~ to success/progress** *etc* ein Hindernis für den Erfolg/Fortschritt *etc*; **because of the ~ of her shyness** auf Grund ihrer Schüchternheit, die ein Hemmnis ist/war *etc*.

barrier cream *n* Haut(schutz)creme *f*.

barring ['bɑ:rıŋ] *prep see* **bar**[2].

barrister ['bærıstə^r] *n (Brit)* Rechtsanwalt *m*/-anwältin *f* (bei Gericht), Barrister *m*.

barrow[1] ['bærəʊ] *n* Karre(n *m*) *f*; *(wheel~)* Schubkarre(n *m*) *f*; *(Rail: luggage)* Gepäckkarre(n *m*) *f*; *(costermonger's)* (handgezogener) Obst-/Gemüse-/Fischkarren *etc m*.

barrow[2] *n (Archeol)* Hügelgrab *nt*.

barrow boy *n* Straßenhändler *m (mit Karren)*.

Bart. *abbr of* **baronet**.

bartender ['bɑ:tendə^r] *n (US)* Barkeeper *m* ◆ **~!** hallo!

barter ['bɑ:tə^r] [1] *vt* tauschen *(for* gegen).
[2] *vi* tauschen; *(as general practice also)* Tauschhandel treiben ◆ **to ~ for sth** um etw handeln; **to ~ for peace** über einen Frieden verhandeln.
[3] *n* (Tausch)handel *m*.

◆**barter away** *vt sep one's rights* verspielen ◆ **to ~ sth ~ for sth** etw für etw verschachern.

barter: ~ economy *n* Tauschwirtschaft *f*; **~ society** *n* Tauschgesellschaft *f*.

basal ['beısl] *adj* **(a)** *(lit, fig)* Grund-, fundamental. **(b)** *(Med)* **~ metabolism** Grundumsatz *m*.

basalt ['bæsɔ:lt] *n* Basalt *m*.

bascule ['bæskju:l] *n* Brückenklappe *f* ◆ **~ bridge** Klappbrücke *f*.

base[1] [beıs] [1] *n* **(a)** *(lowest part)* Basis *f*; *(that on which sth stands also)* Unterlage *f*; *(Archit: of column also)* Fuß *m*; *(support for statue etc)* Sockel *m*; *(of lamp, tree, mountain)* Fuß *m*; *(undercoat also)* Grundierung *f* ◆ **at the ~ (of)** unten (an +*dat*).
(b) *(main ingredient)* Basis *f*, Haupt- *or* Grundbestandteil *m*.
(c) *(of theory)* Basis *f*; *(starting point also)* Ausgangspunkt *m*; *(foundation also)* Grundlage *f*.
(d) *(Mil etc, fig: for holidays, climbing etc)* Standort, Stützpunkt *m* ◆ **to return to ~** zur Basis *or* zum Stützpunkt zurückkehren; **~ of operations** Operationsbasis *f*.
(e) *(Chem)* Lauge, Base *f*.
(f) *(Math)* Basis, Grundzahl *f*.
(g) *(Geometry)* Basis *f*; *(of plane figure also)* Grundlinie *f*; *(of solid also)* Grundfläche *f*.
(h) *(Gram)* Wortstamm *m*, Wortwurzel *f*.
(i) *(Baseball)* Mal, Base *nt* ◆ **at** *or* **on second ~** auf Mal *or* Base 2, auf dem zweiten Mal *or* Base; **to touch ~** *(US inf)* sich melden *(with* bei).
[2] *vt* **(a)** stellen ◆ **to be ~d on** ruhen auf (+*dat*); *(statue)* stehen auf (+*dat*); **the supports are firmly ~d in concrete** die Stützen sind fest in Beton eingelassen; **you need something to ~ it on** Sie brauchen dafür eine feste *or* stabile Unterlage.
(b) *(fig) opinion, theory* gründen, basieren *(on* auf +*acc*); *hopes also* setzen *(on* auf +*acc*); *relationship also* bauen *(on* auf +*acc*) ◆ **to be ~d on sb/sth** auf jdm/etw basieren; *(hopes, theory also)* sich auf jdn/etw stützen; **to ~ one's technique/morality on sb/sth** in seiner Technik/seinem Moralverständnis von jdm/etw ausgehen; **he tried to ~ his life on this theory** er versuchte, nach dieser Theorie zu leben.
(c) *(Mil)* stationieren ◆ **the company/my job is ~d in London** die Firma hat ihren Sitz in London/ich arbeite in London; **I am ~d in Glasgow but cover all Scotland** mein Büro ist in Glasgow, aber ich bereise ganz Schottland.

base[2] *adj* (+*er*) **(a)** *motive, character* niedrig; *person, thoughts, action, lie, slander* gemein, niederträchtig. **(b)** *(inferior) task, level* niedrig; *coin* falsch, unecht; *metal* unedel. **(c)** *(obs) birth (low)* niedrig *(old)*; *(illegitimate)* unehelich.

baseball ['beısbɔ:l] *n* Baseball *m or nt*.

base: ~board *n (US)* Fußleiste, Lambrie *(S Ger) f*; **~ camp** *n* Basislager, Versorgungslager *nt*.

-based [beıst] *adj suf* **London-~** mit Sitz in London; **to be computer-~** auf Computerbasis arbeiten.

base: ~ form *n (Ling)* Stammform *f*; **~ hit** *n (Baseball) Treffer, durch den der Schlagmann sicher das Mal erreichen kann*.

baseless ['beıslıs] *adj accusations etc* ohne Grundlage, aus der Luft gegriffen; *fears, suspicion also* unbegründet, grundlos.

base line *n (Baseball) Verbindungslinie f zwischen zwei Malen*; *(Surv)* Basis, Grundlinie *f*; *(of a diagram, Tennis)* Grundlinie *f*; *(Art)* Schnittlinie *f* von Grundebene und Bildebene.

basely ['beıslı] *adv* gemein, niederträchtig; *act also* niedrig.

baseman ['beısmən] *n, pl* **-men** [-mən] *(Baseball)* Spieler *m* an einem Mal.

basement ['beısmənt] *n* **(a)** *(in building)* Untergeschoß, Souterrain *nt*; *(in house also)* Keller *m*, Kellergeschoß *nt* ◆ **~ flat** Souterrainwohnung *f*. **(b)** *(Archit: foundations)* Fundament *nt*.

baseness ['beısnıs] *n see adj* **(a)** Niedrigkeit *f*; Gemeinheit, Niederträchtigkeit *f*. **(b)** Niedrigkeit *f*; Falschheit *f*. **(c)** Niedrigkeit *f (old)*; Unehelichkeit *f*.

base: ~ rate *n* Leitzins *m*; **~ wallah** *n (Mil sl)* Etappenhengst *m (Mil sl)*.

bash [bæʃ] *(inf)* [1] *n* **(a)** Schlag *m* ◆ **to give sb a ~ on the nose** jdm (eine) auf die Nase hauen *(inf)*; **he gave himself a ~ on the shin** er hat sich *(dat)* das Schienbein angeschlagen; **the bumper has had a ~** die Stoßstange hat eine Delle abgekriegt *(inf)*.
(b) I'll have a ~ (at it) ich probier's mal *(inf)*; **have a ~** probier mal! *(inf)*.
(c) *(dated inf: party)* Party *f*.
[2] *vt person* (ver)hauen *(inf)*, verprügeln; *ball* knallen *(inf)*, dreschen *(inf)*; *car, wing* eindellen *(inf)* ◆ **to ~ one's head/shin (against** *or* **on sth)** sich *(dat)* den Kopf/das Schienbein (an etw *dat*) anschlagen; **I ~ed my shin against the table** ich bin mit dem Schienbein gegen den Tisch geknallt *(inf)*; **to ~ sb on/round the head with sth** jdm etw auf den Kopf hauen *(inf)*/jdm etw um die Ohren schlagen.

◆**bash about** *vt sep (inf) person* durchprügeln *(inf)*, verdreschen *(inf)*; *objects* demolieren *(inf)* ◆ **he/his luggage got rather ~ed ~ in the accident** er/sein Gepäck ist bei dem Unfall ziemlich lädiert worden *(inf)*.

◆**bash down** *vt sep (inf) door* einschlagen.

◆**bash in** *vt sep (inf) door* einschlagen; *hat, car* eindellen *(inf)* ◆ **to ~ sb's head ~** jdm den Schädel einschlagen *(inf)*.

◆**bash up** *vt sep (Brit inf) person* vermöbeln *(inf)*, verkloppen *(inf)*; *car* demolieren *(inf)*, kaputtfahren *(inf)*.

bashful ['bæʃfʊl] *adj* schüchtern; *(on particular occasion)* verlegen ◆ **give us a song! ah, he's ~** sing was! och, er geniert sich!

bashfully ['bæʃfəlı] *adv see adj* schüchtern; verlegen.

bashfulness ['bæʃfʊlnıs] *n see adj* Schüchternheit *f*; Verlegenheit *f*.

bashing ['bæʃıŋ] *n (inf)* Prügel *pl* ◆ **he/his luggage got a nasty ~** er/sein Gepäck hat ganz schön was abgekriegt *(inf)*.

-bashing *suf (inf)* **Paki-/queer-~** *(physical)* Überfälle *pl* auf Pakistaner/Schwule; **Tory-~** *(verbal)* das Schlechtmachen *or* Heruntermachen *(inf)* der Konservativen; *see* **bible**.

Basic ['beısık] *(Comput) abbr of* **beginner's all-purpose symbolic instruction code** BASIC *nt*.

basic ['beısık] [1] *adj* **(a)** *(fundamental)* Grund-; *problem also, reason, issue* Haupt-; *points, issues* wesentlich; *(rudimentary) knowledge, necessities, equipment also* elementar; *character, intention, purpose also* eigentlich; *incompatibility, misconception, indifference, problem* grundsätzlich ◆ **there's no ~ difference** es besteht kein grundlegender Unterschied; **he has a ~ mistrust of women** er mißtraut Frauen grundsätzlich; **a certain ~ innocence** eine gewisse elementare Unschuld; **he is, in a very ~ sense, ...** er ist, im wahrsten Sinne des Wortes, ...; **the ~ thing to remember is ...** woran man vor allem denken muß, ist ...; **must you be so ~!** müssen Sie sich denn so direkt ausdrücken?; **his knowledge/the furniture is rather ~** er hat nur ziemlich elementare Kenntnisse/die Möbel sind ziemlich primitiv; **the pub is rather ~** es ist eine recht einfache Kneipe; **you should know that, that's ~** das müßten Sie aber wissen, das ist doch elementar; **this is ~ to the whole subject** das liegt dem Fach zu Grunde; **~ salary/working hours** Grundgehalt *nt*/-arbeitszeit *f*; **the four ~ operations** *(Math)* die vier Grundrechenarten; **~ English** englischer Grundwortschatz, Basic English *nt*; **~ rate** *(of wage)* Grundgehalt *nt*; *(of tax)* Eingangssteuersatz *m*; **~ vocabulary** Grundwortschatz *m*.
(b) *(original)* zu Grunde liegend; *theory also, assumption* ursprünglich.
(c) *(essential)* notwendig ◆ **knowledge of French is/good boots are absolutely ~** Französischkenntnisse/gute Stiefel sind unbedingt nötig *or* sind eine Voraussetzung.
(d) *(Chem)* basisch ◆ **~ slag** Thomasschlacke *f*.
[2] *npl* **the ~s** das Wesentliche; **to get down to (the) ~s** zum Kern der Sache *or* zum Wesentlichen kommen.

▼ **basically** ['beısıkəlı] *adv* im Grunde; *(mainly)* im wesentlichen, hauptsächlich ◆ **is that correct? — ~ yes** stimmt das? — im Prinzip, ja, im Grunde schon; **it's ~ finished** es ist praktisch *or* im Grunde fertig; **that's ~ it** das wär's im wesentlichen.

basil ['bæzl] *n (Bot)* Basilikum, Basilienkraut *nt*.

basilica [bə'zılıkə] *n* Basilika *f*.

basilisk ['bæzılısk] *n (Myth, Zool)* Basilisk *m*.

basin ['beısn] *n* **(a)** *(vessel)* Schüssel *f*; *(wash~)* (Wasch)becken *nt*; *(of fountain)* Becken *nt*. **(b)** *(Geog)* Becken *nt*; *(harbour ~)* Hafenbecken *nt*; *(yacht~)* Jachthafen *m*; *(hollow between mountains also)* Kessel *m*.

basinful ['beısnfʊl] *n* Schüssel(voll) *f*.

basis ['beısıs] *n* **(a)** *(of food, mixture etc)* Basis, Grundlage *f*.
(b) *(fig: foundation)* Basis *f*; *(for assumption)* Grund *m* ◆ **we're working on the ~ that ...** wir gehen von der Annahme aus, daß ...; **to be on a firm ~** *(business)* auf festen Füßen stehen; *(theory)* auf einer soliden Basis ruhen; **to put sth on a firmer ~** einer Sache *(dat)* eine solidere Basis geben, etw auf eine solidere Basis stellen; **on the ~ of this evidence** aufgrund dieses Beweismaterials; **to approach a problem on a scientific ~** an ein Problem wissenschaftlich herangehen.

bask [bɑ:sk] *vi (in sun)* sich aalen *(in* in +*dat)*; *(in sb's favour etc)* sich sonnen *(in* in +*dat)*.

basket ['bɑ:skıt] *n* **(a)** Korb *m*; *(for rolls, fruit etc)* Körbchen *nt* ◆ **a ~ of eggs** ein Korb/Körbchen (voll) Eier; **a ~ of currencies** ausgewählte Währungen. **(b)** *(Basketball)* Korb *m*. **(c)** *(euph sl: bastard)* Idiot, Blödmann *m (inf)*.

basket: ~ball *n* Basketball *m*; **~ chair** *n* Korbsessel *m*; **~ maker** *n* Korbma-

➤ LANGUAGE IN USE: **basically** → 26.3

cher(in *f*), Korbflechter(in *f*) *m*.
basketry ['bɑːskɪtrɪ] *n* Korbflechterei *f*.
basket: ~weave *n* Leinenbindung *f*; **~work** *n* Korbflechterei *f*; (*articles*) Korbarbeiten *pl*; **a ~work chair** ein Korbstuhl *m*.
basking shark ['bɑːskɪŋˌʃɑːk] *n* Riesenhai *m*.
Basle [bɑːl] *n* Basel *nt*.
Basque [bæsk] 1 *n* **(a)** (*person*) Baske *m*, Baskin *f*. **(b)** (*language*) Baskisch *nt*. 2 *adj* baskisch.
bas-relief ['bæsrɪˌliːf] *n* Basrelief *nt*.
bass¹ [beɪs] (*Mus*) 1 *n* Baß *m*. 2 *adj* Baß- ◆ **~ clef** Baßschlüssel *m*; **~ drum** große Trommel; **~ viol** Gambe *f*.
bass² [bæs] *n*, *pl* **-(es)** (*fish*) Barsch *m*.
basset hound ['bæsɪthaʊnd] *n* Basset *m*.
bassinet [ˌbæsɪ'net] *n* Babykorb *m*; (*old: pram*) Kinderwagen *m*.
bassoon [bə'suːn] *n* Fagott *nt*.
bassoonist [bə'suːnɪst] *n* Fagottbläser(in *f*), Fagottist(in *f*) *m*.
basso profundo [ˌbæsəʊprə'fʊndəʊ] *n* tiefer Baß.
bastard ['bɑːstəd] 1 *n* **(a)** (*lit*) uneheliches Kind, Bastard *m* (*old*); (*fig: hybrid*) Bastard *m*, Kreuzung *f*.
(b) (*sl: person*) Scheißkerl *m* (*sl*) ◆ **stupid ~** Arschloch *nt* (*sl*); **poor ~** armes Schwein (*sl*), armer Hund (*inf*).
(c) (*sl: difficult job etc*) **this question is really a ~** diese Frage ist wirklich hundsgemein (*inf*); **a ~ of a word/job** *etc* ein Scheißwort *nt*/eine Scheißarbeit *etc* (*sl*).
2 *adj* **(a)** (*lit*) *child* unehelich. **(b)** (*fig: hybrid*) *dog, plant* Bastard-; *language* Misch-. **(c)** (*Tech*) **~ file** Bastardfeile *f*. **(d)** (*Typ*) **~ title** Schmutztitel *m*.
bastardize ['bɑːstədaɪz] *vt* (*fig*) verfälschen.
bastardy ['bɑːstədɪ] *n* (*form*) Unehelichkeit *f*.
baste¹ [beɪst] *vt* (*Sew*) heften.
baste² *vt* (*Cook*) (mit Fett) beträufeln *or* begießen.
basting¹ ['beɪstɪŋ] *n* (*Sew*) (*act*) Heften *nt*; (*stitches*) Heftnaht *f* ◆ **to take out the ~** die Heftfäden herausziehen.
basting² *n* (*inf*) (*beating*) Prügel *pl* ◆ **to give sb a ~** (*team, critics*) jdn fertigmachen (*inf*).
bastion ['bæstɪən] *n* (*lit, fig*) Bastion *f*; (*person*) Stütze, Säule *f*.
bat¹ [bæt] *n* (*Zool*) Fledermaus *f* ◆ **to have ~s in the belfry** (*inf*) eine Meise *or* einen Sparren haben (*inf*); **he fled like a ~ out of hell** er lief *or* rannte, wie wenn der Teufel hinter ihm her wäre; **(as) blind as a ~** stockblind (*inf*); **silly old ~** (*pej inf*) alte Schrulle (*pej inf*).
bat² (*Sport*) 1 *n* **(a)** (*Baseball, Cricket*) Schlagholz *nt*, Keule *f*; (*Table-tennis*) Schläger *m* ◆ **to go to ~ for sb** (*fig*) sich für jdn einsetzen; **off one's own ~** (*fig*) auf eigene Faust (*inf*); **right off the ~** (*US*) prompt. **(b)** (*batsman*) **he is a good ~** er schlägt gut. **(c)** (*inf: blow*) Schlag *m*.
2 *vt* (*Baseball, Cricket*) schlagen ◆ **to ~ sth around** (*US inf: discuss*) etw bekakeln (*inf*).
bat³ *vt* **not to ~ an eyelid** nicht mal mit der Wimper zucken.
bat⁴ *n* **(a)** (*Brit sl: speed*) **at a fair old ~** mit 'nem ganz schönen Zahn drauf (*sl*). **(b)** (*US sl: binge*) Sauftour *f* (*sl*) ◆ **to go on a ~** auf Sauftour gehen (*sl*).
batch [bætʃ] *n* (*of people*) Schwung (*inf*) *m*; (*of loaves*) Schub *m*; (*of prisoners, recruits also*) Trupp *m*; (*of things dispatched also*) Sendung, Ladung *f*; (*of letters, books, work also*) Stoß, Stapel *m*; (*of dough, concrete etc*) Ladung *f*.
batch (*Comput*): **~ command** *n* Batch-Befehl *m*; **~ file** *n* Batch-Datei *f*; **~ processing** *n* Stapelverarbeitung *f*, Batch-Betrieb *m*.
bated ['beɪtɪd] *adj*: **with ~ breath** mit angehaltenem Atem.
bath [bɑːθ] 1 *n* **(a)** Bad *nt* ◆ **to have** *or* **take a ~** baden, ein Bad nehmen (*geh*); **to give sb a ~** jdn baden; **I was just in my** *or* **the ~** ich war *or* saß gerade im Bad *or* in der Wanne (*inf*); **a room with ~** ein Zimmer mit Bad; *see* **bloodbath, Turkish** *etc*.
(b) (*bathtub*) (Bade)wanne *f* ◆ **to empty the ~** das Badewasser ablassen; *see* **eyebath, footbath** *etc*.
(c) (swimming) ~s *pl*, **swimming ~** (Schwimm)bad *nt*; **(public) ~s** *pl* Badeanstalt *f*, öffentliches Bad; (*Hist*) Bäder, Badeanlagen *pl*.
(d) (*Tech, Chem, Phot*) Bad *nt*; (*container*) Behälter *m*.
(e) (*Brit*) **the Order of the B~** der Orden vom Bade.
2 *vt* (*Brit*) baden.
3 *vi* (*Brit*) (sich) baden.
bath: B~ bun *n Hefebrötchen nt mit Zitronat und Orangeat*; **~chair** *n* Kranken- *or* Rollstuhl *m*; **~cube** *n* Würfel *m* Badesalz.
bathe [beɪð] 1 *vt* **(a)** *person, feet, eyes, wound etc* baden; (*with cottonwool etc*) waschen ◆ **to ~ one's eyes** ein Augenbad machen; **~d in tears** tränenüberströmt; **to be ~d in light/sweat** in Licht/Schweiß gebadet sein, schweißgebadet sein.
(b) (*US*) *see* **bath 2**.
2 *vi* baden.
3 *n* Bad *nt* ◆ **to have** *or* **take a ~** baden.
bather ['beɪðəʳ] *n* Badende(r) *mf*.
bathhouse ['bɑːθhaʊs] *n* (*old*) Bad(e)haus *nt* (*old*).
bathing ['beɪðɪŋ] *n* Baden *nt*.
bathing: ~-beauty *n* Badeschönheit *f*; **~-cap** *n* Bademütze, Badekappe *f*; **~-costume** *n* Badeanzug *m*; **~-hut** *n* Badehäuschen *nt*; **~ machine** *n* transportable Umkleidekabine; **~-suit** *n* (*dated*) *see* **~-costume**; **~-trunks** *npl* Badehose *f*.
bathmat ['bɑːθmæt] *n* Badematte *f or* -vorleger *m*.
bathos ['beɪθɒs] *n* (*anticlimax*) Abfall *or* Umschlag *m* ins Lächerliche; (*sentimentality*) falsches Pathos.
bathrobe ['bɑːθrəʊb] *n* Bademantel *m*.
bathroom ['bɑːθruːm] *n* Bad(ezimmer) *nt*; (*euph: lavatory*) Toilette *f*.
bathroom: ~ cabinet *n* Toilettenschrank *m*; **~ fittings** *npl* Badezimmerausstattung *f*; **~ scales** *npl* Personenwaage *f*.
bath: ~salts *npl* Badesalz *nt*; **~ sheet** *n* großes Badetuch; **~towel** *n* Badetuch *nt*; **~tub** *n* Badewanne *f*.
bathysphere ['bæθɪsfɪəʳ] *n* Tauchkugel, Bathysphäre *f*.
batik ['bætɪk] *n* Batik *m*; (*cloth*) Batikdruck *m*.
batiste [bæ'tiːst] *n* Batist *m*.
batman ['bætmən] *n*, *pl* **-men** [-mən] (*Mil*) (Offiziers)bursche *m*.
baton ['bætən, (US) bæ'ton] *n* **(a)** (*Mus*) Taktstock, Stab *m*; (*Mil*) (Kommando)stab *m* ◆ **under the ~ of** (*Mus*) unter der Stabführung von. **(b)** (*of policeman*) Schlagstock *m*; (*for directing traffic*) Stab *m* ◆ **~ charge** Schlagstockeinsatz *m*; **to make a ~ charge** Schlagstöcke einsetzen. **(c)** (*in relay race*) Staffelholz *nt*, Stab *m*.
baton round *n* (*Mil*) Plastikgeschosse *pl*.
bats [bæts] *adj pred* (*inf*) bekloppt (*inf*) ◆ **you must be ~** du spinnst wohl! (*inf*).
batsman ['bætsmən] *n*, *pl* **-men** [-mən] (*Sport*) Schlagmann *m*.
battalion [bə'tælɪən] *n* (*Mil, fig*) Bataillon *nt*.
batten ['bætn] 1 *n* **(a)** Leiste, Latte *f*; (*for roofing*) Dachlatte *f*; (*for flooring*) (Trag)latte *f*. **(b)** (*Naut*) (*for sail*) Segellatte *f*; (*for hatch*) Schalklatte *f*.
2 *vt* **(a)** *roof, floor* mit Latten versehen. **(b)** (*Naut*) *sail* mit Latten verstärken; *hatch* (ver)schalken.
◆**batten down** *vt sep* **to ~ ~ the hatches** die Luken schalken (*spec*) *or* dicht machen; (*fig*) (*close doors, windows*) alles dicht machen; (*prepare oneself*) sich auf etwas gefaßt machen.
◆**batten on** *vi +prep obj* schmarotzen bei.
◆**batten onto** *vi +prep obj idea* sich (*dat*) aneignen.
batter¹ ['bætəʳ] *n* (*Cook*) (*for frying*) (Ausback)teig *m*; (*for pancakes, waffles etc*) Teig *m*.
batter² *n* (*Sport*) Schlagmann *m*.
batter³ 1 *vt* **(a)** einschlagen auf (*+acc*); (*strike repeatedly*) *wife, baby* schlagen, (ver)prügeln; (*with* **~ing** *ram*) berennen ◆ **he ~ed him about the head with an iron bar** er schlug mit einer Eisenstange auf seinen Kopf ein; **the ship/house was ~ed by the waves/wind** die Wellen krachten unentwegt gegen das Schiff/der Wind rüttelte unentwegt am Haus.
(b) (*damage*) böse *or* übel zurichten; *car also, metal* zer- *or* verbeulen ◆ **the town was badly ~ed during the war** die Stadt wurde während des Krieges schwer zerbombt.
(c) (*inf*) *opponent* eins *or* eine draufgeben (*+dat*) (*inf*) ◆ **to get ~ed** eins *or* eine draufbekommen (*inf*).
2 *vi* schlagen, trommeln (*inf*) ◆ **to ~ at/against the door** an/gegen die Tür hämmern (*inf*) *or* trommeln (*inf*).
◆**batter about** *vt sep sb* schlagen, verprügeln; *sth* grob umgehen mit, ramponieren (*inf*).
◆**batter down** *vt sep wall* zertrümmern; *door also* einschlagen; *resistance* zerschlagen.
◆**batter in** *vt sep door* einschlagen; (*with ram*) einrennen.
battered ['bætəd] *adj* böse *or* übel zugerichtet, lädiert (*inf*); *wife, baby* mißhandelt; *hat, car, teapot also* verbeult; *city* zerbombt; *house, furniture* mitgenommen, ramponiert (*inf*); *nerves* zerrüttet ◆ **~ baby syndrome** Phänomen *nt* der Kindesmißhandlung.
battering ['bætərɪŋ] *n* (*lit*) Schläge, Prügel *pl*; (*of baby, wife*) Mißhandlung *f* ◆ **he/it got** *or* **took a real ~** er/es hat ganz schön was abgekriegt (*inf*), es hat schwer gelitten; **to give sb/sth a ~** jdn verprügeln/etw ramponieren (*inf*) *or* demolieren (*inf*); **he'll give his opponent a ~** er wird es seinem Gegner geben (*inf*).
battering ram *n* Rammbock, Sturmbock *m*.
battery ['bætərɪ] *n* (*all senses*) Batterie *f*; (*fig: of arguments etc*) Reihe *f*; *see* **assault**.
battery: ~-charger *n* Ladegerät *nt*; **~ farming** *n* (Hühner- *etc*)batterien *pl*; **~ fire** *n* (*Mil*) Geschützfeuer *nt*; **~ hen** *n* (*Agr*) Batteriehuhn *nt*; **~-powered** *adj* batteriebetrieben; **~ set** *n* (*radio*) Batteriegerät *nt*.
battle ['bætl] 1 *n* (*lit*) Schlacht *f*; (*fig*) Kampf *m* ◆ **to give/offer/refuse ~** sich zum Kampf *or* zur Schlacht stellen/bereit erklären/den Kampf *or* die Schlacht verweigern; **to fight a ~** eine Schlacht schlagen (*also fig*), einen Kampf führen; **I don't need you to fight my ~s for me** ich kann mich schon alleine durchsetzen; **to do ~ for sb/sth** sich für jdn schlagen, sich für jdn/etw einsetzen; **killed in ~** (im Kampf) gefallen; **~ of words/wits** Wortgefecht *nt*/geistiger Wettstreit; **to have a ~ of wits** sich geistig messen; **we are fighting the same ~** wir ziehen am selben Strang; **that's half the ~** damit ist schon viel gewonnen; **~ of the giants** Kampf *m* der Giganten; **~ of the sexes** Geschlechterkampf *m*.
2 *vi* sich schlagen; (*fig also*) kämpfen, streiten ◆ **to ~ for breath** um Atem ringen; **to ~ through a book** *etc* sich durch ein Buch *etc* (durch)kämpfen.
3 *vt* (*fig*) **to ~ one's way through difficulties/a book** sich (durch Schwierigkeiten) durchschlagen/sich durch ein Buch (durch)kämpfen.
◆**battle on** *vi* (*fig*) weiterkämpfen.
battle: ~-axe *n* (*weapon*) Streitaxt *f*; (*inf: woman*) Drachen *m* (*inf*); **~ cruiser** *n* Schlachtkreuzer *m*; **~ cry** *n* Schlachtruf *m*.
battledore ['bætldɔːʳ] *n* (Federball)schläger *m* ◆ **~ and shuttlecock** Federball *nt*.
battle: ~ dress *m* Kampfanzug *m*; **~field, ~ground** *n* Schlachtfeld *nt*.
battlements ['bætlmənts] *npl* Zinnen *pl*.
battle: ~ order *n* Schlachtordnung *f*; **~ royal** *n* (*fig: quarrel*) heftige Aus-

einandersetzung; **~-scarred** *adj person, country* vom Krieg gezeichnet; *furniture* schwer mitgenommen, ramponiert (*inf*); (*inf*) *person* schwer mitgenommen, angeschlagen; **~ship** *n* Kriegs- *or* Schlachtschiff *nt*; **~-song** *n* Kampf- *or* Kriegslied *nt*; **~ zone** *n* Kriegs- *or* Kampfgebiet *nt*.

batty ['bætı] *adj* (+*er*) (*inf*) verrückt; *person also* plemplem *pred* (*inf*) ◆ **to go ~** überschnappen (*inf*).

bauble ['bɔːbl] *n* Flitter *m no pl* ◆ **~s** Flitterzeug *nt*; **jester's ~** Narrenzepter *nt*.

baud [bɔːd] *n* (*Comput*) Baud *nt* ◆ **at 1200 ~** bei 1200 Baud; **~ rate** Baudrate *f*.

baulk [bɔːk] *n see* **balk**.

bauxite ['bɔːksaıt] *n* Bauxit *m*.

Bavaria [bə'vɛərıə] *n* Bayern *nt*.

Bavarian [bə'vɛərıən] [1] *n* **(a)** (*person*) Bayer(in *f*) *m*. **(b)** (*dialect*) Bayrisch *nt*.
[2] *adj* bay(e)risch.

bawd [bɔːd] *n* (*brothel-keeper*) Bordellwirtin, Puffmutter (*inf*) *f*.

bawdiness ['bɔːdınıs] *n* Derbheit *f*.

bawdy ['bɔːdı] *adj* (+*er*) derb ◆ **~ talk** derbes Gerede.

bawl [bɔːl] [1] *vi* **(a)** (*shout*) brüllen, schreien; (*sing*) grölen (*inf*) ◆ **to ~ for help** um Hilfe schreien. **(b)** (*inf: weep*) plärren (*inf*), heulen (*inf*).
[2] *vt order* brüllen, schreien; *song* grölen (*inf*).

◆**bawl out** *vt sep* **(a)** *order* brüllen; *song* schmettern, grölen (*pej inf*). **(b)** (*inf: scold*) ausschimpfen.

bawling-out ['bɔːlıŋ'aʊt] *n* (*inf*) Schimpfkanonade *f* (*inf*) ◆ **to give sb a ~** jdn zur Schnecke machen (*inf*).

bay[1] [beı] *n* Bucht *f*; (*of sea also*) Bai *f* ◆ **the Hudson B~** die Hudsonbai.

bay[2] *n* (*Bot*) Lorbeer(baum) *m*.

bay[3] *n* **(a)** (*Archit*) Erker *m*. **(b)** (*loading ~*) Ladeplatz *m*; (*parking ~*) Parkbucht *f*; (*Rail*) Abstellgleis *nt*. **(c)** (*Aviat: bomb ~*) Bombenschacht *m*. **(d)** (*sick ~*) (Kranken)revier *nt*.

bay[4] [1] *n* (*of dogs*) Bellen *nt no pl*; (*Hunt*) Melden *nt no pl* ◆ **to bring to/be at ~** (*Hunt*) stellen/gestellt sein; (*fig*) in die Enge treiben/getrieben sein; **to have sb at ~** (*fig*) jdn in der Zange haben (*inf*); **to keep** *or* **hold sb/sth at ~** jdn/etw in Schach halten.
[2] *vi* bellen; (*Hunt also*) melden ◆ **to ~ at the moon** den Mond anbellen *or* anheulen.

bay[5] [1] *adj horse* (kastanien)braun.
[2] *n* Braune(r) *m* ◆ **red ~** (*horse*) rötlicher Brauner.

bayleaf ['beıliːf] *n* Lorbeerblatt *nt*.

bayonet ['beıənıt] [1] *n* Bajonett, Seitengewehr *nt* ◆ **with ~s fixed/at the ready** mit aufgepflanzten/gefällten Bajonetten.
[2] *vt* mit dem Bajonett *or* Seitengewehr aufspießen.

bayonet fitting *n* (*Elec*) Bajonettfassung *f*.

bay: ~ rum *n* Pimentöl *nt*; **~ tree** *n* Lorbeerbaum *m*; **~ window** *n* Erkerfenster *nt*.

bazaar [bə'zɑː[r]] *n* Basar *m*.

bazooka [bə'zuːkə] *n* Bazooka, Panzerfaust *f*, Panzerschreck *m*.

BB [1] *n* (*Brit*) *abbr of* **Boys' Brigade**.
[2] *adj* (*on pencil*) 2B.

BBC *abbr of* **British Broadcasting Corporation** BBC *f*.

BC[1] *abbr of* **before Christ** v. Chr.

BC[2] *abbr of* **British Columbia**.

BCG *abbr of* **Bacille Calmette Guérin** BCG.

BD *abbr of* **Bachelor of Divinity**.

B/E *abbr of* **bill of exchange**.

be [biː] *present* **am, is, are,** *pret* **was, were,** *ptp* **been** [1] *copulative vb* **(a)** (*with adj, n*) sein ◆ **he is a soldier/a German** er ist Soldat/Deutscher; **he wants to ~ a doctor** er möchte Arzt werden; **who is that? — it's me/that's Mary** wer ist das? — ich bin's/das ist Mary; **to ~ critical/disparaging** sich kritisch/verächtlich äußern, kritisch sein; **if I were you** wenn ich Sie *or* an Ihrer Stelle wäre; **~ sensible!** sei vernünftig.
(b) (*health*) **how are you?** wie geht's?; **I'm better now** es geht mir jetzt besser; **she's none too well** es geht ihr gar nicht gut.
(c) (*physical, mental state*) **to ~ hungry/thirsty** Hunger/Durst haben, hungrig/durstig sein; **I am hot/cold/frozen** ich schwitze/friere/bin halb erfroren, mir ist heiß/kalt/eiskalt; **they were horrified** sie waren entsetzt.
(d) (*age*) sein ◆ **he'll ~ three** er wird drei (Jahre alt).
(e) (*cost*) kosten ◆ **how much is that?** wieviel *or* was kostet das?; (*altogether also*) wieviel *or* was macht das?
(f) (*Math*) sein ◆ **two times two is** *or* **are four** zwei mal zwei ist *or* sind *or* gibt vier.
(g) (*with poss*) gehören (+*dat*) ◆ **that book is your brother's/his** das Buch gehört Ihrem Bruder/ihm, das ist das Buch Ihres Bruders/das ist sein Buch.
(h) (*in exclamations*) **was he pleased to hear it!** er war vielleicht froh, das zu hören!; **but wasn't she glad when ...** hat sie sich vielleicht gefreut, als ...
[2] *v aux* **(a)** (+*prp: continuous tenses*) **what are you doing?** was machst du da?; **she is always complaining** sie beklagt sich dauernd; **they're coming tomorrow** sie kommen morgen; **you will ~ hearing from us** Sie werden von uns hören; **will you ~ seeing her tomorrow?** sehen *or* treffen Sie sie morgen?; **I've just been packing my case** ich war gerade beim Kofferpacken, ich war gerade dabei, den Koffer zu packen; **I was packing my case when ...** ich war gerade beim Kofferpacken, als ...; **I have been waiting for you for half an hour** ich warte schon seit einer halben Stunde auf Sie.
(b) (+*ptp: passive*) werden ◆ **he was run over** er ist überfahren worden, er wurde überfahren; **the box had been opened** die Schachtel war geöffnet worden; **it is/was ~ing repaired** es wird/wurde gerade repariert; **the car is to ~ sold** das Auto soll verkauft werden; **they are shortly to ~ married** sie werden bald heiraten; **they were to have been married last week** sie hätten letzte Woche heiraten sollen; **she was to ~/was to have been dismissed but ...** sie sollte entlassen werden, aber .../sie hätte entlassen werden sollen, aber ...
(c) he is to ~ pitied/not to ~ envied er ist zu bedauern/nicht zu beneiden; **not to ~ confused with** nicht zu verwechseln mit; **he was not to ~ persuaded** er war nicht zu überreden, er ließ sich nicht überreden; **I will not ~/am not to ~ intimidated** ich lasse mich nicht einschüchtern.
(d) (*intention, obligation, command*) sollen ◆ **I am to look after her** ich soll mich um sie kümmern; **he is not to open it** er soll es nicht öffnen; **I wasn't to tell you his name** ich sollte *or* durfte Ihnen nicht sagen, wie er heißt; (*but I did*) ich hätte Ihnen eigentlich nicht sagen sollen *or* dürfen, wie er heißt.
(e) (*~ destined*) sollen ◆ **she was never to return** sie sollte nie zurückkehren.
(f) (*suppositions, wishes*) **if it were** *or* **was to snow** falls *or* wenn es schneien sollte; **and were I** *or* **if I were to tell him?** und wenn ich es ihm sagen würde?; **would I were able to** (*liter*) ich wünschte, ich könnte (es) (*geh*).
(g) (*in tag questions, short answers*) **he's always late, isn't he? — yes he is** er kommt doch immer zu spät, nicht? — ja, das stimmt; **he's never late, is he? — yes he is** er kommt nie zu spät, oder? — o, doch; **you are not ill, are you? — yes I am/no I'm not** Sie sind doch nicht (etwa) krank? — doch!/nein; **it's all done, is it? — yes it is/no it isn't** es ist also alles erledigt? — ja/nein.
[3] *vi* **(a)** sein; (*remain*) bleiben ◆ **to ~ or not to ~** Sein oder Nichtsein; **the powers that ~** die zuständigen Stellen; **let me/him ~** laß mich/ihn (in Ruhe); **~ that as it may** wie dem auch sei; **he is there at the moment but he won't ~ much longer** im Augenblick ist er dort, aber nicht mehr lange; **we've been here a long time** wir sind schon lange hier.
(b) (*be situated*) sein; (*town, country, forest etc also*) liegen; (*car, tower, crate, bottle, chair also*) stehen; (*ashtray, papers, carpet also*) liegen.
(c) (*visit, call*) **I've been to Paris** ich war schon (ein)mal in Paris; **the postman has already been** der Briefträger war schon da; **he has been and gone** er war da und ist wieder gegangen.
(d) now you've been and (gone and) done it (*inf*) jetzt hast du aber was angerichtet! (*inf*); **I've just been and (gone and) broken it!** jetzt hab' ich's tatsächlich kaputtgemacht (*inf*).
(e) (*used to present, point out*) **here is a book/are two books** hier ist ein Buch/sind zwei Bücher; **over there are two churches** da drüben sind *or* stehen zwei Kirchen; **here/there you are** (*you've arrived*) da sind Sie ja; (*take this*) hier/da, bitte; (*here/there it is*) hier/da ist es/sind sie doch; **there he was sitting at the table** da saß er nun am Tisch.
[4] *vb impers* **(a)** sein ◆ **it is dark/morning** es ist dunkel/Morgen; **tomorrow is Friday/the 14th of June** morgen ist Freitag/der 14. Juni, morgen haben wir Freitag/den 14. Juni; **it is 5 km to the nearest town** es sind 5 km bis zur nächsten Stadt.
(b) (*emphatic*) **it was us** *or* **we** (*form*) **who found it** *wir* haben das gefunden, wir waren diejenigen, die das gefunden haben.
(c) (*wishes, suppositions, probability*) **were it not that I am a teacher, I would ...** wenn ich ja kein Lehrer wäre, dann würde ich ...; **were it not for my friendship with him** wenn ich ja nicht mit ihm befreundet wäre; **were it not for him, if it weren't** *or* **wasn't for him** wenn er nicht wäre; **had it not been** *or* **if it hadn't been for him** wenn er nicht gewesen wäre; **and even if it were not so** und selbst wenn das *or* dem nicht so wäre.

beach [biːtʃ] [1] *n* Strand *m* ◆ **on the ~** am Strand.
[2] *vt boat* auf Strand setzen.

beach: ~ball *n* Wasserball *m*; **~ buggy** *n* Strandbuggy *m*; **~comber** *n* Strandgutsammler *m*; (*living rough*) am Strand lebender Einsiedler; **~head** *n* (*Mil*) Landkopf *m*; **~ hut** *n* Strandhäuschen *nt*; **~ umbrella** *n* Sonnenschirm *m*; **~ volleyball** *n* Beachvolleyball *m*; **~wear** *n* Badesachen *pl*, Badezeug *nt* (*inf*); (*Fashion*) Strandmode *f*.

beacon ['biːkən] *n* (*fire, light*) Leuchtfeuer *nt*; (*radio ~*) Funkfeuer *nt*; (*one of a series of lights, radio ~s*) Bake *f*.

bead [biːd] *n* **(a)** Perle *f* ◆ **(string of) ~s** Perlenschnur *f*; (*necklace*) Perlenkette *f*; **to tell** *or* **say one's ~s** den Rosenkranz beten. **(b)** (*drop: of dew, sweat*) Perle *f*, Tropfen *m*. **(c)** (*of gun*) Korn *nt* ◆ **to draw a ~ on sb** auf jdn zielen.

beading ['biːdıŋ] *n* Perlstab *m*, Perlschnur *f*.

beadle ['biːdl] *n* (*old Eccl*) Kirchendiener *m*; (*Univ*) *Angestellter, der bei Prozessionen den Amtsstab trägt.*

beady ['biːdı] *adj* **~ eye** waches Auge; **I've got my ~ eye on you** (*inf*) ich beobachte Sie genau!; **cast your ~ eyes over this** (*hum inf*) wirf mal einen Blick darauf.

beagle ['biːgl] *n* Beagle *m* (*englischer Spürhund*).

beak [biːk] *n* **(a)** (*of bird, turtle*) Schnabel *m*. **(b)** (*inf: of person*) Zinken, Rüssel *m* (*inf*). **(c)** (*Brit inf: judge etc*) Kadi *m* (*inf*); (*Brit Sch sl*) (Di)rex *m* (*sl*).

beaker ['biːkə[r]] *n* Becher *m*; (*Chem etc*) Becherglas *nt*.

be-all and end-all ['biːɔːlənd'endɔːl] *n* **the ~** das A und O; **it's not the ~** das ist auch nicht alles.

beam [biːm] [1] *n* **(a)** (*Build, of scales*) Balken *m*.
(b) (*Naut*) (*side*) Seite *f*; (*width*) Breite *f* ◆ **on the ~** querschiffs; **on the port ~** backbords; **the ~ of a ship** die Schiffsbreite; **to be broad in the ~** (*ship*) sehr breit sein; (*person*) breit gebaut sein.
(c) (*of light etc*) Strahl *m* ◆ **to drive/be on full** *or* **high** *or* **main ~** mit Fernlicht fahren/Fernlicht eingestellt haben.
(d) (*radio ~*) Leitstrahl *m* ◆ **to be on/off ~** auf Kurs sein/vom Kurs abgekommen sein; (*fig*) (*person*) richtig liegen (*inf*)/danebenliegen (*inf*); (*figures*) stimmen/nicht stimmen; **you're/your guess is way off ~** Sie haben total danebengehauen (*inf*)/danebengeraten.

(e) (*smile*) Strahlen *nt* ♦ **a ~ of delight** ein freudiges Strahlen.

[2] *vi* **(a)** strahlen ♦ **to ~ down** (*sun*) niederstrahlen.

(b) (*fig: person, face*) strahlen ♦ **her face was ~ing with joy** sie strahlte übers ganze Gesicht.

[3] *vt* (*Rad, TV*) ausstrahlen, senden (*to* in *or* an +*acc*).

beam-ends ['bi:mendz] *npl*: **to be on one's ~** (*Naut*) stark Schlagseite haben; (*fig*) auf dem letzten Loch pfeifen (*inf*).

beaming ['bi:mɪŋ] *adj sun* strahlend; *smile, face* (freude)strahlend.

bean [bi:n] *n* **(a)** Bohne *f* ♦ **he hasn't a ~** (*Brit inf*) er hat keinen roten *or* lumpigen Heller (*inf*); **hallo, old ~!** (*dated Brit inf*) hallo, altes Haus! (*dated inf*). **(b)** (*fig*) **to be full of ~s** (*inf*) putzmunter sein (*inf*).

bean: ~bag *n* **(a)** (*seat*) Sitzsack *m*; **(b)** (*toy*) *mit Bohnen gefülltes Säckchen, das zum Spielen verwendet wird*; **~ curd** *n* Tofu *nt*; **~feast** *n* (*inf*) Schmaus *m* (*inf*).

beano ['bi:nəʊ] *n* (*dated inf*) Schmaus *m* (*inf*).

bean: ~pole *n* (*lit, fig*) Bohnenstange *f*; **~sprout** *n* Sojabohnensprosse *f*; **~stalk** *n* Bohnenstengel *m*.

▼ **bear**[1] [bɛəʳ] *pret* **bore,** *ptp* **borne** [1] *vt* **(a)** (*carry*) *burden, arms* tragen; *gift, message* bei sich tragen, mit sich führen ♦ **to ~ away/back** mitnehmen/mit (sich) zurücknehmen; (*through the air*) fort- *or* wegtragen/zurücktragen; **the music was borne/borne away on the wind** (*liter*) die Musik wurde vom Wind weiter-/weggetragen; **he was borne along by the crowd** die Menge trug ihn mit (sich).

▼ **(b)** (*show*) *inscription, signature* tragen; *mark, traces also, likeness, relation* aufweisen, zeigen; *see* **witness.**

(c) (*be known by*) *name, title* tragen, führen.

(d) (*have in heart or mind*) *love* empfinden, in sich (*dat*) tragen; *hatred, grudge also* hegen (*geh*) ♦ **the love/hatred he bore her** die Liebe, die er für sie empfand/der Haß, den er gegen sie hegte (*geh*) *or* empfand; *see* **mind.**

(e) (*lit, fig: support, sustain*) *weight, expense, responsibility* tragen ♦ **to ~ examination/comparison** einer Prüfung/einem Vergleich standhalten; **it doesn't ~ thinking about** man darf gar nicht daran denken; **his language doesn't ~ repeating** seine Ausdrucksweise läßt sich nicht wiederholen.

(f) (*endure, tolerate*) ertragen; (*with neg also*) ausstehen, leiden; *pain, smell, noise etc also* aushalten; *criticism, joking, smell, noise etc also* vertragen ♦ **she can't ~ flying/doing nothing/being laughed at** sie kann einfach nicht fliegen/untätig sein/sie kann es nicht vertragen, wenn man über sie lacht; **could you ~ to stay a little longer?** können Sie es noch ein bißchen länger hier aushalten?

(g) (*produce, yield*) *fruit etc* tragen; *see* **interest.**

(h) (*give birth to*) gebären; *see* **born.**

[2] *vi* **(a)** (*move*) **to ~ right/left/north** sich rechts/links/nach Norden halten; **to ~ away** *or* **off** (*Naut*) abdrehen.

(b) (*fruit-tree etc*) tragen.

(c) **to bring one's energies/powers of persuasion to ~** seine Energie/Überzeugungskraft aufwenden (*on* für); **to bring one's mind to ~ on sth** seinen Verstand *or* Geist für etw anstrengen; **to bring pressure to ~ on sb/sth** Druck auf jdn/etw ausüben.

[3] *vr* sich halten ♦ **he bore himself with dignity** er hat Würde gezeigt.

♦**bear down** [1] *vi* **(a)** sich nahen (*geh*); (*hawk etc*) herabstoßen ♦ **to ~ ~ on sb/sth** (*driver etc*) auf jdn/etw zuhalten. **(b)** (*woman in labour*) drücken.

[2] *vt sep* niederdrücken ♦ **he was borne ~ by poverty** seine Armut lastete schwer auf ihm; **to be borne ~ by the weight of ...** von der Last (+*gen*) gebeugt sein.

♦**bear in (up)on** *vt* +*prep obj*: **to be borne ~ ~ sb** jdm zu(m) Bewußtsein kommen.

♦**bear on** *vi* +*prep obj see* **bear (up)on.**

♦**bear out** *vt sep* bestätigen ♦ **to ~ sb ~ in sth** jdn in etw bestätigen; **you will ~ me ~ that ...** Sie werden bestätigen, daß ...

♦**bear up** *vi* sich halten ♦ **he bore ~ well under the death of his father** er trug den Tod seines Vaters mit Fassung; **~ ~!** Kopf hoch!; **how are you? — ~ing ~!** wie geht's? — man lebt!

♦**bear (up)on** *vi* +*prep obj* **(a)** (*relate to*) betreffen ♦ **does this ~ ~ what you were saying?** hat das einen Bezug zu dem, was Sie sagten? **(b)** **to ~ hard ~ sb** sich hart auf jdn auswirken.

♦**bear with** *vi* +*prep obj* tolerieren ♦ **if you would just ~ ~ me for a couple of minutes** wenn Sie sich vielleicht zwei Minuten gedulden wollen.

bear[2] [1] *n* **(a)** Bär *m*; (*fig: person*) Brummbär *m* (*inf*) ♦ **he is like a ~ with a sore head** er ist ein richtiger Brummbär (*inf*). **(b)** (*Astron*) **the Great/Little B~** der Große/Kleine Bär *or* Wagen. **(c)** (*St Ex*) Baissespekulant, Baissier *m*. **~ market** Baisse *f*.

[2] *vi* (*St Ex*) auf Baisse spekulieren.

bearable ['bɛərəbl] *adj* erträglich, zum Aushalten.

bear: ~-baiting *n* Bärenhatz *f*; **~-cub** *n* Bärenjunge(s) *nt*.

beard [bɪəd] [1] *n* **(a)** Bart *m*; (*full-face*) Vollbart *m* ♦ **a man with a ~** ein Mann mit Bart; **a week's (growth of) ~** ein eine Woche alter Bart; **small pointed ~** Spitzbart *m*. **(b)** (*of goat, bird*) Bart *m*; (*of fish also*) Barthaare *pl*; (*of grain*) Grannen *pl*.

[2] *vt* (*confront*) ansprechen ♦ **to ~ sb about sth** jdn auf etw (*acc*) hin ansprechen; **to ~ the lion in his den** (*fig*) sich in die Höhle des Löwen wagen.

bearded ['bɪədɪd] *adj man, animal* bärtig ♦ **the ~ woman** *or* **lady** die Dame mit dem Bart.

beardless ['bɪədlɪs] *adj* bartlos ♦ **~ youth** Milchbart *m* (*pej inf*), Milchgesicht *nt* (*pej inf*).

bearer ['bɛərəʳ] *n* **(a)** (*carrier*) Träger(in *f*) *m*; (*of news, letter, cheque, banknote*) Überbringer *m*; (*of name, title also, of passport, bond, cheque*) Inhaber(in *f*) *m* ♦ **~ bond** Inhaberschuldverschreibung *f*.

(b) (*tree etc*) **a good ~** ein Baum/Busch *etc*, der gut trägt.

bear: ~ garden *n* Tollhaus *nt*; **~ hug** *n* ungestüme Umarmung; (*Wrestling*) Klammer, Umklammerung *f*.

bearing ['bɛərɪŋ] *n* **(a)** (*posture*) Haltung *f*; (*behaviour*) Verhalten, Auftreten, Gebaren *nt*.

(b) (*relevance, influence*) Auswirkung *f* (*on* auf +*acc*); (*connection*) Bezug *m* (*on* zu) ♦ **to have some/no ~ on sth** von Belang/belanglos für etw sein; (*be/not be connected with*) einen gewissen/keinen Bezug zu etw haben.

(c) (*endurance*) **to be beyond (all) ~** unerträglich *or* nicht zum Aushalten sein.

(d) (*direction*) **to take/get a ~ on sth** sich an etw (*dat*) orientieren; **to take a compass ~** den Kompaßkurs feststellen; **to get one's ~s** sich zurechtfinden, sich orientieren; **to lose one's ~s** die Orientierung verlieren.

(e) (*Tech*) Lager *nt*.

bear: ~pit *n* Bärengehege *nt*; **~skin** *n* (*Mil*) Bärenfellmütze *f*.

beast [bi:st] *n* **(a)** Tier *nt*; *see* **burden, prey.**

(b) (*inf*) (*person*) Biest, Ekel *nt* ♦ **don't be a ~!** sei nicht so eklig! (*inf*); **that ~ of a brother-in-law** dieser fiese Schwager (*inf*); **this (problem) is a ~, it's a ~ (of a problem)** das (Problem) hat's in sich (*inf*); **have you finished it yet? — no, it's a ~** sind Sie fertig damit? — nein, es ist verflixt schwierig (*inf*).

beastliness ['bi:stlɪnɪs] *n* (*inf*) *see adj* Scheußlichkeit, Garstigkeit *f*; Gemeinheit, Ekligkeit (*inf*) *f*.

beastly ['bi:stlɪ] (*inf*) [1] *adj* scheußlich, garstig (*inf*); *person, conduct also* gemein, eklig (*inf*) ♦ **what ~ weather** so ein Hundewetter; **it's a ~ business** das ist eine üble Angelegenheit; **what a ~ shame!** (*dated*) so ein Jammer!

[2] *adv* (*dated*) scheußlich ♦ **it's ~ difficult** es ist verteufelt schwierig (*inf*).

beat [bi:t] (*vb: pret* **~**, *ptp* **~en**) [1] *n* **(a)** (*of heart, pulse, drum*) (*single* ~) Schlag *m*; (*repeated beating*) Schlagen *nt* ♦ **the ~ of her heart grew weaker** ihr Herzschlag wurde schwächer; **to the ~ of the drum** zum Schlag der Trommeln.

(b) (*of policeman, sentry*) Runde *f*, Rundgang *m*; (*district*) Revier *nt* ♦ **to be on** *or* **to patrol one's ~** seine Runde machen.

(c) (*Mus, Poet*) Takt *m*; (*of metronome, baton*) Taktschlag *m* ♦ **to have a strong ~** einen ausgeprägten Rhythmus haben; **on/off the ~** auf dem betonten/unbetonten Taktteil.

(d) (*~music*) Beat(musik *f*) *m*.

(e) (*Hunt*) Treibjagd *f*.

[2] *vt* **(a)** (*hit*) schlagen; *person, animal also* (ver)prügeln, hauen (*inf*); *carpet* klopfen; (*search*) *countryside, woods* absuchen, abkämmen ♦ **the crocodile ~ the ground with its tail** das Krokodil schlug mit dem Schwanz auf den Boden; **to ~ a/one's way through sth** einen/sich (*dat*) einen Weg durch etw bahnen; **to ~ a path to sb's door** (*fig*) jdm die Bude einrennen (*inf*); **to ~ a/the drum** trommeln, die Trommel schlagen; **to ~ the air** um sich schlagen, herumfuchteln; **to ~ one's breast** sich (*dat*) an die Brust schlagen; (*ape*) sich (*dat*) gegen die Brust trommeln; **~ it!** (*fig inf*) hau ab! (*inf*), verschwinde!

(b) (*hammer*) *metal* hämmern; (*shape also*) treiben ♦ **to ~ sth flat** etw flach- *or* platthämmern.

(c) (*defeat*) schlagen; *record* brechen; *inflation* in den Griff bekommen ♦ **to ~ sb at chess/tennis** jdn im Schach/Tennis schlagen; **his shot/forehand ~ me** ich war dem Schuß/Vorhandschlag nicht gewachsen; **you can't ~ these prices** diese Preise sind nicht zu unterbieten; **you can't ~ central heating/real wool** es geht doch nichts über Zentralheizung/reine Wolle; **he ~s the rest of them any day** er steckt sie alle (jederzeit) in die Tasche (*inf*); **coffee ~s tea any day** Kaffee ist allemal besser als Tee; **that ~s everything** das ist doch wirklich der Gipfel *or* die Höhe, das schlägt dem Faß den Boden aus (*all inf*); (*is very good*) darüber geht nichts; **that ~s me** (*inf*) das ist mir ein Rätsel (*inf*); **well can you ~ it!** (*inf*) ist das denn zu fassen? (*inf*); **that problem ~s me** (*inf*) das Problem geht über meinen Verstand; **he managed to ~ the charge** (*inf*) er wurde (von der Anklage) freigesprochen.

(d) (*be before*) *budget, crowds* zuvorkommen (+*dat*) ♦ **to ~ sb to the top of a hill** vor jdm oben auf dem Berg sein *or* ankommen; **I'll ~ you down to the beach** ich bin vor dir am Strand; **to ~ sb home** vor jdm zu Hause sein; **to ~ the deadline** vor Ablauf der Frist fertig sein; **to ~ sb to the draw** schneller ziehen als jd; **to ~ sb to it** jdm zuvorkommen.

(e) (*move up and down regularly*) schlagen ♦ **the bird ~s its wings** der Vogel schlägt mit den Flügeln.

(f) (*Mus*) **to ~ time (to the music)** den Takt schlagen.

(g) *cream, eggs* schlagen.

[3] *vi* **(a)** (*heart, pulse, drum*) schlagen ♦ **to ~ on the door (with one's fists)** (mit den Fäusten) gegen die Tür hämmern *or* schlagen; **with ~ing heart** mit pochendem *or* klopfendem Herzen; **her heart was ~ing with joy** ihr Herz schlug vor Freude höher; *see* **bush**[1]. **(b)** (*wind, waves*) schlagen; (*rain also*) trommeln; (*sun*) brennen. **(c)** (*cream*) sich schlagen lassen.

[4] *adj* **(a)** (*inf: exhausted*) **to be (dead) ~** total kaputt *or* geschafft *or* erledigt sein (*inf*).

(b) (*inf: defeated*) **to be ~(en)** aufgeben müssen (*inf*), sich geschlagen geben müssen; **I'm ~** ich gebe mich geschlagen; **he doesn't know when he's ~(en)** er gibt nicht auf (*inf*); **we've got him ~** wir haben ihn schachmatt gesetzt; **this problem's got me ~** mit dem Problem komme ich nicht klar (*inf*).

♦**beat back** *vt sep flames, enemy* zurückschlagen.

♦**beat down** [1] *vi* (*rain*) herunterprasseln; (*sun*) herunterbrennen.

[2] *vt sep* **(a)** (*reduce*) *prices* herunterhandeln; *opposition* kleinkriegen (*inf*) ♦ **I managed to ~ him/the price ~** ich konnte den Preis herunterhandeln; **I ~ him ~ to £2 for the chair** ich habe den Stuhl auf £ 2 heruntergehandelt. **(b)**

➤ LANGUAGE IN USE: **bear**[1]**: 1b** → 5.3

(*flatten*) *door* einrennen; *wheat, crop* niederwerfen.
◆**beat in** *vt sep door* einschlagen ◆ **to ~ sb's brains ~** (*inf*) jdm den Schädel einschlagen (*inf*).
◆**beat off** *vt sep attack, attacker* abwehren.
◆**beat out** *vt sep fire* ausschlagen; *metal, dent, wing* aushämmern; *tune, rhythm* schlagen; (*on drum*) trommeln; *plan* ausarbeiten, ausklamüsern (*inf*), austüfteln (*inf*) ◆ **to ~ sb's brains ~** (*inf: kill*) jdm den Schädel einschlagen (*inf*).
◆**beat up** *vt sep* **(a)** *person* zusammenschlagen. **(b)** (*Cook*) *eggs, cream* schlagen.
beaten ['bi:tn] 1 *ptp of* **beat.**
2 *adj* **(a)** *metal* gehämmert. **(b)** *earth* festgetreten; *path also* ausgetreten ◆ **a well-~ path** ein Trampelpfad *m*; **to be off the ~ track** (*fig*) abgelegen sein. **(c)** (*defeated*) **a ~ man** ein geschlagener Mann.
beater ['bi:tər] *n* **(a)** (*carpet* ~) Klopfer *m*; (*egg* ~) Schneebesen *m*. **(b)** (*Hunt*) Treiber(in *f*) *m*.
beat *in cpds* Beat-; ~ **generation** *n* Beatgeneration *f*; ~ **group** *n* Beatgruppe *or* -band *f*.
beatific [ˌbi:ə'tɪfɪk] *adj* glückselig; *vision* himmlisch.
beatification [bi:ˌætɪfɪ'keɪʃən] *n* Seligsprechung *f*.
beatify [bi:'ætɪfaɪ] *vt* seligsprechen, beatifizieren (*spec*).
beating ['bi:tɪŋ] *n* **(a)** (*series of blows*) Schläge, Prügel *pl* ◆ **to give sb a ~** jdn verprügeln; (*as punishment also*) jdm eine Tracht Prügel verabreichen (*inf*); **to get a ~** verprügelt werden; (*as punishment also*) Schläge *or* Prügel bekommen.
(b) (*of drums, heart, wings*) Schlagen *nt*.
(c) (*defeat*) Niederlage *f* ◆ **to take a ~** eine Schlappe einstecken (*inf*); **to take a ~ (at the hands of sb)** (von jdm) nach allen Regeln der Kunst geschlagen werden.
(d) to take some ~ nicht leicht zu übertreffen sein; (*idea, insolence etc*) seines-/ihresgleichen suchen.
(e) (*Hunt*) Treiben *nt*.
beating-up [ˌbi:tɪŋ'ʌp] *n* Abreibung *f* (*inf*) ◆ **to give sb a ~** jdn zusammenschlagen; **to get a ~** zusammengeschlagen werden.
beatitude [bi:'ætɪtju:d] *n* Glückseligkeit *f* ◆ **the B~s** (*Bibl*) die Seligpreisungen *pl*.
beatnik ['bi:tnɪk] *n* Beatnik *m*.
beat poetry *n* Beatlyrik *f*.
beat-up ['bi:tʌp] *adj* (*inf*) zerbeult, ramponiert (*inf*).
beau [bəʊ] *n* (*old*) **(a)** (*dandy*) Beau *m* (*dated*). **(b)** (*suitor*) Galan (*dated*), Kavalier *m*.
Beaufort scale ['bəʊfət'skeɪl] *n* Beaufortskala *f*.
beaut [bju:t] *n* (*esp Austral sl*) (*thing*) Prachtexemplar *nt* ◆ **to be a (real) ~** einsame Klasse sein (*sl*).
beauteous ['bju:tɪəs] *adj* (*poet*) wunderschön, prachtvoll.
beautician [bju:'tɪʃən] *n* Kosmetiker(in *f*) *m*.
beautiful ['bju:tɪfʊl] 1 *adj* schön; *weather, morning also, idea, meal* herrlich, wunderbar; (*good*) *swimmer, swimming, organization, piece of work* hervorragend, wunderbar ◆ **that's a ~ specimen** das ist ein Prachtexemplar; **the ~ people** die Schickeria; **~!** prima! (*inf*), toll! (*inf*).
2 *n* **(a) the ~** das Schöne. **(b)** (*inf*) **hello, ~** hallo, schönes Kind.
beautifully ['bju:tɪfəlɪ] *adv* schön; *warm, prepared, shine, simple* herrlich, wunderbar; (*well*) *sew, cook, sing, swim* hervorragend, sehr gut, prima (*inf*) ◆ **that will do ~** das ist ganz ausgezeichnet.
beautify ['bju:tɪfaɪ] *vt* verschönern ◆ **to ~ oneself** (*hum*) sich schönmachen (*hum*).
beauty ['bju:tɪ] *n* **(a)** Schönheit *f* ◆ **~ is only skin-deep** (*prov*) der äußere Schein kann trügen; **~ is in the eye of the beholder** (*Prov*) schön ist, was (einem) gefällt.
(b) (*beautiful person*) Schönheit *f* ◆ **B~ and the Beast** die Schöne und das Tier.
(c) (*good example*) Prachtexemplar *nt* ◆ **isn't it a ~!** ist das nicht ein Prachtstück *or* Prachtexemplar?
(d) (*pleasing feature*) **the ~ of it is that ...** das Schöne *or* Schönste daran ist, daß ...; **that's the ~ of it** das ist das Schöne daran; **one of the beauties of this job is ...** eine der schönen Seiten dieser Arbeit ist ...
beauty *in cpds* Schönheits-; ~ **competition** *or* **contest** *n* Schönheitswettbewerb *m*; ~ **parlour** *n* Schönheits- *or* Kosmetiksalon *m*; ~ **queen** *n* Schönheitskönigin *f*; ~ **sleep** *n* (*hum*) Schlaf *m*; ~ **specialist** *n* Kosmetiker(in *f*) *m*; ~ **spot** *n* **(a)** Schönheitsfleck *m*; (*patch also*) Schönheitspflästerchen *nt*; **(b)** (*place*) schönes *or* hübsches Fleckchen (Erde), schöner *or* hübscher Fleck; ~ **treatment** *n* kosmetische Behandlung.
beaver[1] ['bi:vər] *n* **(a)** Biber *m* ◆ **to work like a ~** wie ein Wilder/eine Wilde arbeiten; *see* **eager. (b)** (*fur*) Biber(pelz) *m*. **(c)** (*hat*) Biber- *or* Kastorhut *m*.
◆**beaver away** *vi* (*inf*) schuften (*inf*) (*at* an +*dat*).
beaver[2] *n* (*of helmet*) Kinnreff *nt*.
becalm [bɪ'kɑ:m] *vt* (*Naut*) **to be ~ed** in eine Flaute geraten; **the ship lay** *or* **was ~ed for three weeks** das Schiff war *or* befand sich drei Wochen lang in einer Flaute.
became [bɪ'keɪm] *pret of* **become.**
▼ **because** [bɪ'kɒz] 1 *conj* weil; (*since also*) da ◆ **it was the more surprising ~ we were not expecting it** es war um so überraschender, als wir es nicht erwartet hatten; **if I did it, it was ~ it had to be done** ich habe es nur getan, weil es getan werden mußte; **why did you do it? — ~** (*inf*) warum *or* weshalb hast du das getan? — darum *or* deshalb.
▼ 2 *prep* **~ of** wegen (+*gen or* (*inf*) *dat*); **I only did it ~ of you** ich habe es nur deinetwegen/Ihretwegen getan.
beck [bek] *n* **to be (completely) at sb's ~ and call** jdm voll und ganz zur Verfügung stehen; **I'm not at your ~ and call** du kannst doch nicht so einfach über mich verfügen; **his wife is completely at his ~ and call** seine Frau muß nach seiner Pfeife tanzen; **to have sb at one's ~ and call** jdn zur ständigen Verfügung haben, ganz über jdn verfügen können.
beckon ['bekən] *vti* winken ◆ **he ~ed (to) her to follow (him)** er gab ihr ein Zeichen *or* winkte ihr, ihm zu folgen; **he ~ed me in/back/over** er winkte mich herein/zurück/herüber.
become [bɪ'kʌm] *pret* **became,** *ptp* ~ 1 *vi* **(a)** (*grow to be*) werden ◆ **it has ~ a rule/habit/duty/custom/nuisance** es ist jetzt Vorschrift/es ist zur Gewohnheit geworden/es ist Pflicht/üblich/lästig geworden; **he's becoming a problem** er wird zum Problem; **to ~ interested in sb/sth** anfangen, sich für jdn/etw zu interessieren.
(b) (*acquire position of*) werden ◆ **to ~ king/a doctor** König/Arzt werden.
(c) what has ~ of him? was ist aus ihm geworden?; **what's to ~ of him?** was soll aus ihm werden?; **I don't know what will ~ of him** ich weiß nicht, was aus ihm noch werden soll.
2 *vt* **(a)** (*suit*) stehen (+*dat*).
(b) (*befit*) sich schicken für, sich ziemen für (*geh*).
becoming [bɪ'kʌmɪŋ] *adj* **(a)** (*suitable, fitting*) schicklich ◆ **it's not ~ (for a lady) to sit like that** es schickt sich (für eine Dame) nicht, so zu sitzen. **(b)** (*flattering*) vorteilhaft, kleidsam ◆ **that dress/colour is very ~** das Kleid/die Farbe steht ihr/dir *etc* sehr gut.
becquerel [ˌbekə'rel] *n* Becquerel *nt*.
B Ed *abbr of* **Bachelor of Education.**
bed [bed] 1 *n* **(a)** Bett *nt* ◆ **to go to ~** zu *or* ins Bett gehen; **to put** *or* **get sb to ~** jdn ins *or* zu Bett bringen; **to get into ~** sich ins Bett legen; **he couldn't get her into ~ with him** er hat sie nicht ins Bett gekriegt (*inf*); **to go to** *or* **jump into** (*inf*) **~ with sb** mit jdm ins Bett gehen *or* steigen (*inf*); **he must have got out of ~ on the wrong side** (*inf*) er ist wohl mit dem linken Fuß zuerst aufgestanden; **to be in ~** im Bett sein; (*through illness also*) das Bett hüten müssen; **a ~ of nails** ein Nagelbrett *nt*; **life isn't always a ~ of roses** (*prov*) man ist im Leben nicht immer auf Rosen gebettet; **his life is not exactly a ~ of roses** er ist nicht gerade auf Rosen gebettet; **as you make your ~ so you must lie on it** (*Prov*) wie man sich bettet, so liegt man (*Prov*); **a ~ for the night** eine Übernachtungsmöglichkeit; **can I have a ~ for the night?** kann ich hier/bei euch *etc* übernachten?; **to put a newspaper to ~** (*Press*) eine Zeitung in Druck geben; **the paper has gone to ~** (*Press*) die Zeitung ist im Druck.
(b) (*of ore*) Lager *nt*; (*of coal also*) Flöz *nt*; (*of building, road etc*) Unterbau *m* ◆ **a ~ of clay** Lehmboden *m*.
(c) (*base: of engine, lathe, machine*) Bett *nt*.
(d) (*bottom*) (*sea* ~) Grund, Boden *m*; (*river* ~) Bett *nt*.
(e) (*oyster* ~, *coral* ~) Bank *f*.
(f) (*flower* ~, *vegetable* ~) Beet *nt*.
2 *vt* **(a)** *plant* setzen, pflanzen.
(b) (*old, hum: have sex with*) beschlafen (*old, hum*).
◆**bed down** 1 *vi* sein Lager aufschlagen ◆ **to ~ ~ for the night** sein Nachtlager aufschlagen.
2 *vt sep* **(a)** *person* das Bett machen (+*dat*); *child* schlafen legen ◆ **the soldiers were ~ed ~ in the shed** die Soldaten hatten ihr (Nacht) quartier im Schuppen. **(b)** *animals* einstreuen (+*dat*).
◆**bed in** 1 *vt sep foundations* einlassen; *machine* betten; *brakes* einfahren.
2 *vi* (*brakes*) eingefahren werden.
bed and breakfast *n* Übernachtung *f* mit Frühstück; (*also* **~ place**) Frühstückspension *f* ◆ **"~"** „Fremdenzimmer".
bedaub [bɪ'dɔ:b] *vt* beschmieren; *face* anmalen, anschmieren.
bedazzle [bɪ'dæzl] *vt* blenden.
bed *in cpds* Bett-; **~-bath** *n* (Kranken)wäsche *f* im Bett; **to give sb a ~-bath** jdn im Bett waschen; **~-bug** *n* Wanze *f*; ~ **chamber** *n* (*old*) Schlafgemach *nt* (*old*); **~-clothes** *npl* Bettzeug *nt*; **to turn down the ~-clothes** das Bett aufdecken; **~cover** *n* Bettdecke *f*.
bedding ['bedɪŋ] *n* **(a)** Bettzeug *nt*. **(b)** (*for horses*) Streu *f*.
bedding plant *n* Setzling *m*.
bedeck [bɪ'dek] *vt* schmücken.
bedevil [bɪ'devl] *vt* komplizieren, erschweren ◆ **~led by misfortune/bad luck** vom Schicksal/Pech verfolgt; **~led by injuries** von Verletzungen heimgesucht; **the tour/machine seemed to be ~led** die Tour/Maschine schien wie verhext.
bed: ~fellow *n* **to be** *or* **make strange ~fellows** (*fig*) eine eigenartige Kombination *or* ein merkwürdiges Gespann sein; **~-head** *n* Kopfteil *m* des Bettes; **~-jacket** *n* Bettjäckchen *nt*.
bedlam ['bedləm] *n* (*fig: uproar*) Chaos *nt* ◆ **the class was absolute ~** in der Klasse ging es zu wie im Irrenhaus.
bed-linen ['bedlɪnɪn] *n* Bettwäsche *f*.
Bedouin ['bedʊɪn] 1 *n* Beduine *m*, Beduinin *f*.
2 *adj* beduinisch.
bed: ~-pan *n* Bettpfanne *or* -schüssel *f*; **~post** *n* Bettpfosten *m*.
bedraggled [bɪ'drægld] *adj* (*wet*) trief- *or* tropfnaß; (*dirty*) verdreckt; (*untidy*) *person, appearance* ungepflegt, schlampig.
bed-ridden ['bedrɪdn] *adj* bettlägerig.
bedrock ['bedrɒk] *n* **(a)** (*Geol*) Grundgebirge *or* -gestein *nt*. **(b)** (*fig*) **to get down to** *or* **to reach ~** zum Kern der Sache kommen.

➤ LANGUAGE IN USE: **because: 1** → 17.1, 26.3 **2** → 17.1, 20.4

bedroom ['bedru:m] *n* Schlafzimmer *nt.*

bedroom *in cpds* Schlafzimmer-; ~ **slipper** *n* Hausschuh *m.*

Beds *abbr of* **Bedfordshire.**

beds *abbr of* **bedrooms** Zi.

bed-settee ['bedse'ti:] *n* Sofabett *nt.*

bedside ['bedsaɪd] *n* **to be/sit at sb's ~** an jds Bett (*dat*) sein/sitzen.

bedside: ~ lamp *n* Nachttischlampe *f;* **~ manner** *n* Art *f* mit Kranken umzugehen; **he has a good/bad ~ manner** er kann gut/nicht gut mit den Kranken umgehen; **~ rug** *n* Bettvorleger *m;* **~ table** *n* Nachttisch *m.*

bed: ~-sit(ter) (*inf*), **~-sitting room** *n* (*Brit*) **(a)** (*rented*) möbliertes Zimmer; **(b)** Wohnschlafzimmer *nt;* (*for teenager etc*) Jugendzimmer *nt;* **~sock** *n* Bettschuh *m;* **~sore** *n* aufgelegene *or* wundgelegene Stelle; **to get ~sores** sich wund- *or* aufliegen; **~spread** *n* Tagesdecke *f;* **~stead** *n* Bettgestell *nt;* **~straw** *n* (*Bot*) Labkraut *nt;* **~time** *n* Schlafenszeit *f;* **it's ~time** es ist Schlafenszeit; **his ~time is 10 o'clock** er geht um 10 Uhr schlafen; **it's past your ~time** du müßtest schon lange im Bett sein; **~time story** *n* Gutenachtgeschichte *f;* **~-wetter** *n* Bettnässer(in *f*) *m;* **~-wetting** *n* Bettnässen *nt.*

bee [bi:] *n* **(a)** Biene *f* ◆ **like ~s round a honeypot** wie die Motten ums Licht; **to have a ~ in one's bonnet** (*inf*) einen Fimmel *or* Tick haben (*inf*); **he's got a ~ in his bonnet about cleanliness** er hat einen Sauberkeitsfimmel (*inf*) *or* -tick (*inf*); **it's something of a ~ in his bonnet** das ist so ein Fimmel *or* Tick von ihm (*inf*).
(b) (*sewing ~*) Kränzchen *nt;* (*competition*) Wettbewerb *m.*

Beeb [bi:b] *n:* **the ~** (*Brit inf*) die BBC.

beech [bi:tʃ] *n* **(a)** (*tree*) Buche *f.* **(b)** (*wood*) Buche(nholz *nt*) *f.*

beech: ~ mast *n* Bucheckern *pl;* **~nut** *n* Buchecker *f;* **~ tree** *n* Buche *f;* **~wood** *n* **(a)** (*material*) Buchenholz *nt;* **(b)** (*trees*) Buchenwald *m.*

bee-eater ['bi:,i:təʳ] *n* (*Orn*) Bienenfresser *m.*

beef [bi:f] [1] *n* **(a)** (*meat*) Rindfleisch *nt* ◆ **roast ~** Roastbeef *nt.*
(b) (*inf*) (*flesh*) Speck *m* (*pej*); (*muscles*) Muskeln *pl* ◆ **there's too much ~ on him** er ist zu massig; **to have plenty of ~** jede Menge Bizeps haben (*inf*); **you'd better get rid of some of this ~** du mußt ein bißchen abspecken (*inf*).
(c) what's his ~? (*inf*) was hat er zu meckern? (*inf*).
[2] *vi* (*inf: complain*) meckern (*inf*) (*about* über +*acc*) ◆ **what are you ~ing about?** was hast du zu meckern? (*inf*).

◆**beef up** *vt sep* (*make more powerful etc*) aufmotzen (*inf*).

beef: ~burger *n* Hamburger *m;* **~cake** *n, no pl* (*inf: male photos*) Männerfleisch *nt* (*hum*), Muskelprotze *pl;* **~ cattle** *npl* Schlachtrinder *pl;* **~eater** *n* **(a)** Beefeater *m;* **(b)** (*US inf*) Engländer(in *f*) *m;* **~ olive** *n* Rinderroulade *f;* **~ sausage** *n* Rindswürstchen *nt;* **~steak** *n* Beefsteak *nt;* **~ tea** *n* Kraft- *or* Fleischbrühe *f.*

beefy ['bi:fɪ] *adj* (+*er*) fleischig.

bee: ~hive [1] *n* **(a)** Bienenstock *m;* (*dome-shaped*) Bienenkorb *m;* **(b)** (*hairstyle*) toupierte Hochfrisur; [2] *adj* **~hive hairdo** toupierte Hochfrisur; **~keeper** *n* Bienenzüchter(in *f*), Imker(in *f*) *m;* **~-line** *n* **to make a ~-line for sb/sth** schnurstracks auf jdn/etw zugehen.

been [bi:n] *ptp of* **be.**

beep [bi:p] (*inf*) [1] *n* Tut(tut) *nt* (*inf*).
[2] *vt* **to ~ one's horn** hupen.
[3] *vi* tuten (*inf*). **~ ~!** tut, tut (*inf*).

beer [bɪəʳ] *n* Bier *nt* ◆ **two ~s, please** zwei Bier, bitte; **life is not all ~ and skittles** das Leben ist nicht nur eitel Sonnenschein.

beer *in cpds* Bier-; **~ belly** *n* (*inf*) Bierbauch *m* (*inf*); **~-bottle** *n* Bierflasche *f;* **~ cellar** *n* Bierkeller *m;* **~ glass** *n* Bierglas *nt;* **~ gut** *n* (*inf*) Bierbauch *m* (*inf*); **~mat** *n* Bierfilz, Bierdeckel *m;* **~ money** *n* (*inf*) Geld *nt* für Getränke; **~-pull** *n* Zapfhahn *m.*

beery ['bɪərɪ] *adj* Bier-; *person* mit einer Bierfahne (*inf*); (*tipsy*) bierselig; *face* biergerötet ◆ **to have ~ breath, to smell ~** eine Bierfahne haben (*inf*), nach Bier riechen.

beeswax ['bi:zwæks] *n* Bienenwachs *nt.*

beet [bi:t] *n* Rübe, Bete (*form*) *f.*

beetle¹ ['bi:tl] *n* Käfer *m.*

◆**beetle along** *vi* (*inf*) entlangpesen (*inf*); (*on foot also*) entlanghasten (*inf*).

◆**beetle off** *vi* (*inf*) abschwirren (*inf*).

beetle² *n* (*tool*) Stampfer *m;* (*for paving, pile-driving also*) Ramme *f.*

beetle: ~-browed *adj* mit buschigen, zusammengewachsenen Augenbrauen; **~ brows** *npl* buschige, zusammengewachsene Augenbrauen *pl;* **~-crushers** *npl* (*inf*) Elbkähne (*inf*), Kindersärge (*inf*) *pl.*

beetling ['bi:tlɪŋ] *adj cliffs* überhängend.

beet: ~root *n* rote Bete *or* Rübe; **~ sugar** *n* Rübenzucker *m.*

befall [bɪ'fɔ:l] *pret* **befell** [bɪ'fel], *ptp* **~en** [bɪ'fɔ:lən] (*old, liter*) [1] *vi* sich zutragen.
[2] *vt* widerfahren (+*dat*) (*geh*).

befit [bɪ'fɪt] *vt* (*form*) *sb* anstehen (+*dat*) (*geh*), sich ziemen für (*geh*); *occasion* angemessen sein (+*dat*), entsprechen (+*dat*) ◆ **it ill ~s him to speak thus** es steht ihm schlecht an *or* ziemt sich nicht für ihn, so zu reden (*geh*).

befitting [bɪ'fɪtɪŋ] *adj* gebührend, geziemend (*dated*) ◆ **~ for a lady** einer Dame geziemend (*dated*), für eine Dame schicklich.

befog [bɪ'fɒg] *vt* (*fig*) *issue* vernebeln; *person, mind* verwirren; (*alcohol, blow*) benebeln ◆ **to be ~ged** (*person*) benebelt sein; (*issue*) verwirrt sein.

before [bɪ'fɔ:ʳ] [1] *prep* **(a)** (*earlier than*) vor (+*dat*) ◆ **the year ~ last/this** vorletztes/letztes Jahr, das vorletzte/letzte Jahr; **the day ~ yesterday** vorgestern; **the day/time ~ that** der Tag/die Zeit davor; **~ Christ** (*abbr* **BC**) vor Christi Geburt (*abbr* v. Chr.); **I got/was here ~ you** ich war vor dir da; **that was ~ my time** das war vor meiner Zeit; **he died ~ his time** er ist früh gestorben; **to be ~ sb/sth** vor jdm/etw liegen; **~ then** vorher; **~ now** früher, eher, vorher; **you should have done it ~ now** das hättest du schon (eher) gemacht haben sollen; **~ long** bald; **~ everything else** zuallererst.
(b) (*in order, rank*) vor (+*dat*) ◆ **to come ~ sb/sth** vor jdm/etw kommen; **I believe in honour ~ everything** die Ehre geht mir über alles, für mich ist die Ehre das Wichtigste; **ladies ~ gentlemen** Damen haben den Vortritt.
(c) (*in position*) vor (+*dat*); (*with movement*) vor (+*acc*) ◆ **~ my (very) eyes** vor meinen Augen; **the task ~ us** (*with which we are dealing*) die uns vorliegende Aufgabe; (*with which we are confronted*) die Aufgabe, vor der wir stehen; (*which lies ahead of us*) die uns bevorstehende Aufgabe; **to sail ~ the wind** (*Naut*) vor dem Wind segeln.
(d) (*in the presence of*) vor (+*dat*) ◆ **he said it ~ us all** er sagte das vor uns allen; **~ God/a lawyer** vor Gott/einem Anwalt; **to appear ~ a court/judge** vor Gericht/einem Richter erscheinen.
(e) (*rather than*) **death ~ surrender** eher *or* lieber tot als sich ergeben; **he would die ~ betraying his country** er würde eher sterben als sein Land verraten.
[2] *adv* **(a)** (*in time*) (*~ that*) davor; (*at an earlier time, ~ now*) vorher ◆ **have you been to Scotland ~?** waren Sie schon einmal in Schottland?; **I have seen/read** *etc* **this ~** ich habe das schon einmal gesehen/gelesen *etc;* **never ~** noch nie; **(on) the evening/day ~** am Abend/Tag davor *or* zuvor *or* vorher; **(in) the month/year ~** im Monat/Jahr davor; **two hours ~** zwei Stunden vorher; **two days ~** zwei Tage davor *or* zuvor; **to continue as ~** (*person*) (so) wie vorher weitermachen; **things/life continued as ~** alles war wie gehabt/das Leben ging seinen gewohnten Gang.
(b) (*ahead*) **to march on ~** vorausmarschieren.
(c) (*indicating order*) davor ◆ **that chapter and the one ~** dieses Kapitel und das davor.
[3] *conj* **(a)** (*in time*) bevor ◆ **~ doing sth** bevor man etw tut; **you can't go ~ this is done** du kannst erst gehen, wenn das gemacht ist; **it will be six weeks ~ the boat comes again** das Boot wird erst in sechs Wochen wieder kommen; **it will be a long time ~ he comes back** es wird lange dauern, bis er zurückkommt.
(b) (*rather than*) **he will die ~ he surrenders** eher will er sterben als sich geschlagen geben.

beforehand [bɪ'fɔ:hænd] *adv* im voraus ◆ **you must tell me ~** Sie müssen mir vorher Bescheid sagen.

before-tax [bɪ'fɔ:tæks] *adj income, profits* vor Steuern.

befoul [bɪ'faʊl] *vt* (*liter: lit, fig*) besudeln; *atmosphere* verpesten.

befriend [bɪ'frend] *vt* (*help*) sich annehmen (+*gen*); (*be friend to*) Umgang pflegen mit ◆ **she seems to have ~ed them** sie scheint sich mit ihnen angefreundet zu haben.

befuddle [bɪ'fʌdl] *vt* **(a)** (*make tipsy*) benebeln. **(b)** (*confuse*) durcheinanderbringen ◆ **he is completely ~d** er ist völlig durcheinander (*inf*) *or* verwirrt; **I became ~d** ich war verwirrt.

beg [beg] [1] *vt* **(a)** *money, alms* betteln um.
(b) (*crave, ask for*) *forgiveness, mercy, a favour* bitten um ◆ **to ~ sth of sb** jdn um etw bitten; **he ~ged to be allowed to ...** er bat darum, ... zu dürfen; **the children ~ged me to let them go to the circus** die Kinder bettelten, ich solle sie in den Zirkus gehen lassen; **to ~ leave to do sth** um Erlaubnis bitten, etw tun zu dürfen; **I ~ leave to be dismissed** (*form*) gestatten Sie, daß ich mich entferne? (*form*); **I ~ to inform you ...** (*form*) ich erlaube mir, Sie davon in Kenntnis zu setzen ...; **I ~ to differ** ich erlaube mir, anderer Meinung zu sein; *see* **pardon.**
(c) (*entreat*) *sb* anflehen, inständig bitten ◆ **I ~ you!** ich flehe dich an!
(d) to ~ the question an der eigentlichen Frage vorbeigehen.
[2] *vi* **(a)** (*beggar*) betteln; (*dog*) Männchen machen.
(b) (*for help, time etc*) bitten (*for* um).
(c) (*entreat*) **to ~ of sb to do sth** jdn anflehen *or* inständig bitten, etw zu tun; **I ~ of you** ich bitte Sie.
(d) to go ~ging (*inf*) noch zu haben sein; (*to be unwanted*) keine Abnehmer finden.

began [bɪ'gæn] *pret of* **begin.**

beget [bɪ'get] *pret* **begot** *or* (*obs*) **begat** [bɪ'gæt], *ptp* **begotten** *or* **begot** *vt* **(a)** (*obs, Bibl*) zeugen; *see* **begotten. (b)** (*fig*) *difficulties etc* zeugen (*geh*).

beggar ['begəʳ] [1] *n* **(a)** Bettler(in *f*) *m* ◆ **~s can't be choosers** (*prov*) wer arm dran ist, kann nicht wählerisch sein; **oh well, ~s can't be choosers!** na ja, in der Not frißt der Teufel Fliegen (*prov*). **(b)** (*inf*) Kerl *m* (*inf*) ◆ **poor ~!** armer Tropf *or* Kerl! (*inf*), armes Schwein! (*sl*); **a lucky ~** ein Glückspilz *m;* **a funny little ~** ein drolliges Kerlchen; (*girl*) ein drolliger Fratz.
[2] *vt* **(a)** an den Bettelstab bringen.
(b) (*fig*) **to ~ description** jeder Beschreibung (*gen*) spotten.

beggarly ['begəlɪ] *adj* kümmerlich.

beggar: ~man *n* (*old*) Bettler, Bettelmann (*old*) *m;* **~-my- *or* -your-neighbour** *n* (*Cards*) *Kartenspiel nt, bei dem der gewinnt, der zum Schluß alle Karten hat;* **~woman** *n* (*old*) Bettlerin, Bettelfrau (*old*) *f.*

beggary ['begərɪ] *n* Bettelarmut *f;* (*beggars*) Bettler *pl,* Bettelvolk *nt* ◆ **to have been reduced to ~** bettelarm sein.

begging letter ['begɪŋ,letəʳ] *n* Bittbrief *m.*

▼ **begin** [bɪ'gɪn] *pret* **began,** *ptp* **begun** [1] *vt* **(a)** (*start*) beginnen, anfangen; *conversation also* anknüpfen; *song also* anstimmen; *bottle* anbrechen, anfangen; *book, letter, new cheque book, new page* anfangen; *rehearsals, work* anfangen mit; *task* in Angriff nehmen, sich machen an (+*acc*) ◆ **to ~ to do sth** *or* **doing sth** anfangen *or* beginnen, etw zu tun; **to ~ working** *or* **to work on**

sth mit der Arbeit an etw (*dat*) anfangen *or* beginnen; **to ~ an attack** zum Angriff schreiten; **when did you ~ (learning** *or* **to learn) English?** wann haben Sie angefangen, Englisch zu lernen?; **she ~s the job next week** sie fängt nächste Woche (bei der Stelle) an; **he began his speech by saying that** ... er leitete seine Rede damit *or* mit den Worten ein, daß ...; **to ~ school** eingeschult werden, in die Schule kommen; **to ~ life as a** ... als ... anfangen *or* beginnen; **she began to feel tired** sie wurde allmählich *or* langsam müde; **she's ~ning to understand** sie fängt langsam an zu verstehen, sie versteht so langsam; **his mother began to fear the worst** seine Mutter befürchtete schon das Schlimmste; **I'd begun to think you weren't coming** ich habe schon gedacht, du kommst nicht mehr; **that doesn't even ~ to compare with** ... das läßt sich nicht mal annähernd mit ... vergleichen; **they didn't even ~ to solve the problem** sie haben das Problem nicht mal annähernd gelöst; **I couldn't even ~ to count the mistakes** ich konnte die Fehler überhaupt nicht zählen; **I can't ~ to thank you for what you've done** ich kann Ihnen gar nicht genug dafür danken, was Sie getan haben.

(b) (*initiate, originate*) anfangen; *fashion, custom, policy* einführen; *society, firm, movement* gründen; (*cause*) *war* auslösen ◆ **he/that began the rumour** er hat das Gerücht in die Welt gesetzt/dadurch entstand das Gerücht.

(c) (*start to speak*) beginnen, anfangen ◆ **it's late, he began** es ist spät, begann er *or* fing *or* hub (*old*) er an.

▼ [2] *vi* **(a)** (*start*) anfangen, beginnen; (*new play etc*) anlaufen ◆ **to ~ by doing sth** etw zuerst (einmal) tun; **he began by saying that** ... er sagte eingangs *or* einleitend, daß ...; **where the hair ~s** am Haaransatz; **before October ~s** vor Anfang Oktober; **to ~ in business/teaching** ins Geschäftsleben eintreten/zu unterrichten anfangen *or* beginnen; **~ning from Monday** ab Montag, von Montag an; **~ning from page 10** von Seite 10 an; **say your names ~ning from the back** nennen Sie Ihre Namen von hinten nach vorn; **it all/the trouble began when** ... es fing alles/der Ärger fing damit an, daß ...; **to ~ with sb/sth** mit jdm/etw anfangen; **~ with me** fangen Sie bei *or* mit mir an; **he began with the intention of writing a thesis** anfänglich wollte er eine Doktorarbeit schreiben; **to ~ with there were only three** anfänglich waren es nur drei; **this is wrong to ~ with** das ist schon einmal falsch; **to ~ with, this is wrong, and** ... erstens einmal ist das falsch, dann ...; **to ~ on sth** mit etw anfangen *or* beginnen; **to ~ on a new venture/project** ein neues Unternehmen/Projekt in Angriff nehmen.

(b) (*come into being*) beginnen, anfangen; (*custom*) entstehen; (*river*) entspringen ◆ **since the world began** seit (An)beginn *or* Anfang der Welt; **when did this movement ~?** seit wann gibt es diese Bewegung?

beginner [bɪ'gɪnəʳ] *n* Anfänger(in *f*) *m* ◆ **~'s luck** Anfängerglück *nt*.

beginning [bɪ'gɪnɪŋ] *n* **(a)** (*act of starting*) Anfang *m* ◆ **to make a ~** einen Anfang machen; **a false ~** (*of project etc*) ein falscher Ansatz.

(b) (*place, of book etc*) Anfang *m*; (*temporal also*) Beginn *m*; (*of river*) Ursprung *m* ◆ **at the ~** anfänglich, zuerst; **at the ~ of sth** am Anfang *or* (*temporal also*) zu Beginn einer Sache (*gen*); **the ~ of time/the world** der Anbeginn *or* Anfang der Welt; **in the ~** (*Bibl*) am Anfang; **from the ~** von Anfang an; **from the ~ of the week/poem** seit Anfang *or* Beginn der Woche/vom Anfang des Gedichtes an; **read the paragraph from the ~** lesen Sie den Paragraphen von (ganz) vorne; **from ~ to end** von vorn bis hinten; (*temporal*) von Anfang bis Ende; **to start again at** *or* **from the ~** noch einmal von vorn anfangen; **to begin at the ~** ganz vorn anfangen; **the ~ of negotiations** der Beginn der Verhandlungen, der Verhandlungsbeginn.

(c) (*origin*) Anfang *m*; (*of custom, movement*) Entstehen *nt no pl* ◆ **the shooting was the ~ of the rebellion** die Schießerei bedeutete den Beginn *or* Anfang der Rebellion; **it was the ~ of the end for him** das war der Anfang vom Ende für ihn; **Nazism had its ~s in Germany** der Nazismus hatte seine Anfänge *or* seinen Ursprung in Deutschland; **the ~s of science** die Anfangsgründe der Naturwissenschaft.

begone [bɪ'gɒn] *vi imper and infin only* (*old*) **~!** fort (mit dir/Ihnen); (*esp Rel*) weiche; **they bade him ~** sie befahlen ihm, sich fortzuscheren.

begonia [bɪ'gəʊnɪə] *n* Begonie *f*.

begot [bɪ'gɒt] *pret, ptp of* **beget**.

begotten [bɪ'gɒtn] *ptp of* **beget** ◆ **the only ~ son** der eingeborene Sohn.

begrime [bɪ'graɪm] *vt* beschmutzen.

begrudge [bɪ'grʌdʒ] *vt* **(a)** (*be reluctant*) **to ~ doing sth** etw widerwillig tun.

(b) (*envy*) mißgönnen (*sb sth* jdm etw) ◆ **no one ~s you your good fortune** wir gönnen dir ja dein Glück; **he ~s him the air he breathes** er gönnt ihm das Salz in der Suppe nicht.

(c) (*give unwillingly*) nicht gönnen (*sb sth* jdm etw) ◆ **I wouldn't ~ you the money** ich würde dir das Geld ja gönnen; **I shan't ~ you £5** du sollst die £ 5 haben.

begrudging *adj*, **~ly** *adv* [bɪ'grʌdʒɪŋ, -lɪ] widerwillig.

beguile [bɪ'gaɪl] *vt* **(a)** (*deceive*) betören (*geh*) ◆ **to ~ sb into doing sth** jdn dazu verführen, etw zu tun. **(b)** (*charm*) *person* betören; (*liter*) *time* sich (*dat*) angenehm vertreiben.

beguiling [bɪ'gaɪlɪŋ] *adj* betörend, verführerisch.

begun [bɪ'gʌn] *ptp of* **begin**.

▼ **behalf** [bɪ'hɑːf] *n* **on** *or* (*US also*) **in ~ of** für, im Interesse von; (*as spokesman*) im Namen von; (*as authorized representative*) im Auftrag von; **I'm not asking on my own ~** ich bitte nicht für mich selbst *or* in meinem eigenen Interesse darum.

behave [bɪ'heɪv] [1] *vi* sich verhalten; (*people also*) sich benehmen; (*children also*) sich betragen, sich benehmen; (*be good*) sich benehmen ◆ **to ~ well/badly** sich gut/schlecht benehmen; **what a way to ~!** was für ein Benehmen!; **to ~ shamefully/badly/well towards sb** jdn schändlich/schlecht/gut behandeln; **to ~ like an honest man** wie ein ehrlicher Mensch handeln; **to ~ very wisely** sich sehr klug verhalten; **~!** benimm dich!; **can't you make your son/dog ~?** kannst du deinem Sohn/Hund keine Manieren beibringen?; **he knows how to ~ at a cocktail party** er weiß sich bei Cocktailpartys zu benehmen; **the car ~s well/badly at high speeds** das Auto zeigt bei hoher Geschwindigkeit ein gutes/schlechtes Fahrverhalten; **how is your car behaving these days?** wie fährt dein Auto zur Zeit?

[2] *vr* **to ~ oneself** sich benehmen; **~ yourself!** benimm dich!; **can't you make your son/dog ~ himself/itself?** kannst du deinem Sohn/Hund keine Manieren beibringen?

behaviour, (*US*) **behavior** [bɪ'heɪvjəʳ] *n* **(a)** (*manner, bearing*) Benehmen *nt*; (*esp of children also*) Betragen *nt* ◆ **to be on one's best ~** sich von seiner besten Seite zeigen, sein bestes Benehmen an den Tag legen.

(b) (*towards others*) Verhalten *nt* (*to(wards)* gegenüber).

(c) (*of car, machine*) Verhalten *nt*.

behavioural, (*US*) **behavioral** [bɪ'heɪvjərəl] *adj* Verhaltens- ◆ **~ science/scientist** Verhaltensforschung *f*/-forscher *m*.

behaviourism, (*US*) **behaviorism** [bɪ'heɪvjərɪzəm] *n* Behaviorismus *m*.

behaviourist, (*US*) **behaviorist** [bɪ'heɪvjərɪst] [1] *n* Behaviorist *m*.

[2] *adj* behavioristisch.

behead [bɪ'hed] *vt* enthaupten, köpfen.

beheld [bɪ'held] *prep, ptp of* **behold**.

behest [bɪ'hest] *n* (*liter*) Geheiß *nt* (*liter*) ◆ **at his ~/the ~ of his uncle** auf sein Geheiß (*liter*)/auf Geheiß seines Onkels (*liter*).

behind [bɪ'haɪnd] [1] *prep* **(a)** (*in or at the rear of*) (*stationary*) hinter (+*dat*); (*with motion*) hinter (+*acc*) ◆ **come out from ~ the door** komm hinter der Tür (her)vor; **he came up ~ me** er trat von hinten an mich heran; **walk close ~ me** gehen Sie dicht hinter mir; **put it ~ the books** stellen Sie es hinter die Bücher; **he has the Communists ~ him** er hat die Kommunisten hinter sich (*dat*); **to be ~ an idea** eine Idee unterstützen; **what is ~ this/this incident?** was steckt dahinter/steckt hinter diesem Vorfall?;

(b) (*more backward than*) **to be ~ sb** hinter jdm zurücksein.

(c) (*in time*) **to be ~ time** (*train etc*) Verspätung haben; (*with work etc*) im Rückstand sein; **to be ~ schedule** im Verzug sein; **to be three hours ~ time** drei Stunden Verspätung haben; **to be ~ the times** (*fig*) hinter seiner Zeit zurück(geblieben) sein; **you must put the past ~ you** Sie müssen Vergangenes vergangen sein lassen, Sie müssen die Vergangenheit begraben; **their youth is far ~ them** ihre Jugend liegt weit zurück.

[2] *adv* **(a)** (*in or at rear*) hinten; (~ *this, sb etc*) dahinter ◆ **the runner was (lying) a long way ~** der Läufer lag weit hinten *or* zurück; **from ~** von hinten; **to look ~** zurückblicken; **to stand ~** (*be standing*) dahinter stehen; (*position oneself*) sich dahinter stellen; *see vbs*.

(b) (*late*) **to be ~ with one's studies/payments** mit seinen Studien/Zahlungen im Rückstand sein; **we are three days ~ with the schedule** wir sind drei Tage im Rückstand *or* Verzug.

[3] *n* (*inf*) Hinterteil *nt* (*inf*), Hintern *m* (*inf*).

behindhand [bɪ'haɪndhænd] *adv, adj* **(a)** (*late*) **to be ~** Verspätung haben. **(b)** (*in arrears*) **to be ~ with sth** mit etw im Rückstand *or* Verzug sein.

behold [bɪ'həʊld] *pret, ptp* **beheld** *vt* (*liter*) sehen, erblicken (*liter*) ◆ **~!** und siehe (da); (*Rel*) siehe; **~ thy servant** siehe deinen Diener.

beholden [bɪ'həʊldən] *adj* (*liter*): **to be ~ to sb for sth** jdm für etw verpflichtet sein (*geh*).

behove, (*US*) **behoove** [bɪ'həʊv] *vt impers* (*form*) sich geziemen (*geh*) (*sb to do sth* für jdn, etw zu tun).

beige [beɪʒ] [1] *adj* beige.

[2] *n* Beige *nt*.

being ['biːɪŋ] *n* **(a)** (*existence*) Dasein, Leben *nt* ◆ **to come into ~** entstehen; (*club etc also*) ins Leben gerufen werden; **to bring into ~** ins Leben rufen, (er)schaffen; **then in ~** damals bestehend. **(b)** (*that which exists*) (Lebe)wesen, Geschöpf *nt*. **(c)** (*essence*) Wesen *nt*.

Beirut [beɪ'ruːt] *n* Beirut *nt*.

bejewelled, (*US*) **bejeweled** [bɪ'dʒuːəld] *adj* mit Edelsteinen geschmückt ◆ **~ with sequins** mit Pailletten besetzt; **~ with dew/stars** (*poet*) mit glitzernden Tautropfen besät/sternenbesät (*poet*).

belabour, (*US*) **belabor** [bɪ'leɪbəʳ] *vt* **(a)** einschlagen auf (+*acc*). **(b)** (*fig: with insults etc*) überhäufen; (*with questions*) beschießen, bearbeiten.

Belarus [belə'rʊs] *n* Weißrußland *nt*.

belated *adj*, **~ly** *adv* [bɪ'leɪtɪd, -lɪ] verspätet.

belay [bɪ'leɪ] (*Naut*) [1] *vt* belegen, festmachen; (*Mountaineering*) sichern.

[2] *interj* **~ there** aufhören.

belaying pin [bɪ'leɪɪŋ,pɪn] *n* (*Naut*) Belegklampe *f*; (*Mountaineering*) (Kletter)haken *m*.

belch [beltʃ] [1] *vi* (*person*) rülpsen, aufstoßen; (*volcano*) Lava speien *or* ausstoßen; (*smoke, fire*) herausquellen.

[2] *vt* (*also* **~ forth** *or* **out**) *smoke, flames* (aus)speien, ausstoßen.

[3] *n* **(a)** Rülpser *m* (*inf*). **(b)** (*of smoke etc*) Stoß *m*.

beleaguer [bɪ'liːgəʳ] *vt* belagern; (*fig*) umgeben.

belfry ['belfrɪ] *n* Glockenstube *f*; *see* **bat**[1].

Belgian ['beldʒən] [1] *n* Belgier(in *f*) *m*.

[2] *adj* belgisch.

Belgium ['beldʒəm] *n* Belgien *nt*.

Belgrade [bel'greɪd] *n* Belgrad *nt*.

belie [bɪ'laɪ] *vt* **(a)** (*prove false*) *words, proverb* Lügen strafen, widerlegen. **(b)** (*give false impression of*) hinwegtäuschen über (+*acc*). **(c)** (*fail to justify*) *hopes* enttäuschen.

➤ LANGUAGE IN USE: **begin: 2a** → 26.1 **behalf** → 22

belief [bɪ'li:f] *n* (a) Glaube *m* (*in* an +*acc*) ◆ **it is beyond ~** es ist unglaublich *or* nicht zu glauben; **a statement unworthy of your ~** (*form*) eine Aussage, der Sie keinen Glauben schenken sollten.
(b) (*Rel: faith*) Glaube *m*; (*doctrine*) (Glaubens)lehre *f*.
(c) (*convinced opinion*) Überzeugung *f*, Glaube *m no pl* ◆ **what are the ~s of the average citizen today?** woran glaubt der heutige Durchschnittsbürger?; **in the ~ that ...** im Glauben, daß ...; **acting in this ~** in gutem Glauben, im guten Glauben; **it is my ~ that ...** ich bin der Überzeugung, daß ...; **it is one of my ~s that ...** es ist meine Überzeugung, daß ...; **yes, that is my ~** ich glaube schon; **to the best of my ~** meines Wissens.
(d) *no pl* (*trust*) Glaube *m* (*in* an +*acc*) ◆ **to have ~ in** glauben an (+*acc*).

believable [bɪ'li:vəbl] *adj* glaubhaft, glaubwürdig ◆ **hardly ~** wenig glaubhaft.

▼ **believe** [bɪ'li:v] [1] *vt* (a) *sth* glauben; *sb* glauben (+*dat*) ◆ **I don't ~ you** das glaube ich (Ihnen) nicht; **don't you ~ it** wer's glaubt, wird selig (*inf*); **it's true, please ~ me** es stimmt, bitte glauben Sie mir das; **~ me, I mean it** glauben Sie mir, es ist mir ernst; **~ you me!** (*inf*) das können Sie mir glauben!; **~ it or not** ob Sie's glauben oder nicht; **would you ~ it!** (*inf*) ist das (denn) die Möglichkeit (*inf*); **I would never have ~d it of him** das hätte ich nie von ihm geglaubt; **he could hardly ~ his eyes/ears** er traute seinen Augen/Ohren nicht; **if he is to be ~d** wenn man ihm glauben darf *or* Glauben schenken kann.
(b) (*think*) glauben ◆ **he is ~d to be ill** es heißt, daß er krank ist; **I ~ so/not** ich glaube schon/nicht; *see* **make-~**.
[2] *vi* (*have a religous faith*) an Gott glauben ◆ **you must ~!** Sie müssen glauben!

◆**believe in** *vi* +*prep obj* (a) *God, ghosts* glauben an (+*acc*).
(b) (*have trust in*) *promises* glauben an (+*acc*); *method also* Vertrauen haben zu ◆ **the boss/his mother still ~s ~ him** der Chef/seine Mutter glaubt immer noch an ihn; **please trust me, ~ ~ me** bitte haben Sie Vertrauen zu mir; **he doesn't ~ ~ medicine/doctors** er hält nicht viel von Medikamenten/Ärzten.
(c) (*support idea of*) **to ~ ~ sth** (prinzipiell) für etw sein; **he ~s ~ getting up early/giving people a second chance** er ist überzeugter Frühaufsteher/er gibt prinzipiell jedem noch einmal eine Chance; **I don't ~ ~ compromises** ich halte nichts von Kompromissen, ich bin gegen Kompromisse.

believer [bɪ'li:vəʳ] *n* (a) (*Rel*) Gläubige(r) *mf*. (b) **to be a (firm) ~ in sth** (grundsätzlich) für etw sein; **I'm a ~ in doing things properly** ich bin grundsätzlich der Meinung, daß man, was man macht, richtig machen sollte; **he's a (firm)/not much of a ~ in getting up early** er ist überzeugter Frühaufsteher/er hält nicht viel vom Frühaufstehen.

Belisha beacon [bɪ'li:ʃə'bi:kən] *n gelbes Blinklicht an Zebrastreifen.*

▼ **belittle** [bɪ'lɪtl] *vt* herabsetzen, heruntermachen (*inf*); *achievement also* schmälern ◆ **to ~ oneself** sich schlechter machen, als man ist.

belittlement [bɪ'lɪtlmənt] *n see vt* Herabsetzung *f*; Schmälerung *f*.

Belize [be'li:z] *n* Belize *nt*.

bell[1] [bel] [1] *n* (a) Glocke *f*; (*small: on toys, pet's collar etc*) Glöckchen *nt*, Schelle *f*; (*school ~, door~, of cycle*) Klingel, Glocke (*dated*) *f*; (*hand~ also*) Schelle *f*; (*of typewriter, Telec*) Klingel *f* ◆ **as sound as a ~** kerngesund.
(b) (*sound of ~*) Läuten *nt*; (*of door~, school ~, telephone etc*) Klingeln *nt*; (*in athletics*) Glocke *f* zur letzten Runde ◆ **there's the ~** es klingelt *or* läutet; **was that the ~?** hat es gerade geklingelt *or* geläutet?; **the teacher came in on the ~** der Lehrer kam mit dem Klingeln *or* Läuten herein; **he's coming up to the ~** er geht nun in die letzte Runde; **it was 3.02 at the ~** zu Beginn der letzten Runde hatte er eine Zeit von 3.02.
(c) (*Naut*) Schiffsglocke *f*; (*ringing*) Läuten *nt* (der Schiffsglocke); (*for time also*) Glasen *nt* (*spec*) ◆ **it is eight ~s** es ist acht Glas (*spec*); **to ring one ~** einmal glasen (*spec*).
(d) (*of flower*) Glocke *f*, Kelch *m*; (*of trumpet*) Stürze *f*; (*of loudspeaker*) (Schall)trichter *m*.
[2] *vt* eine Glocke/ein Glöckchen umhängen (+*dat*) ◆ **to ~ the cat** (*fig*) der Katze die Schelle umhängen.

bell[2] [1] *n* (*of stag*) Röhren *nt*.
[2] *vi* röhren.

belladonna [ˌbelə'dɒnə] *n* (*Bot*) Tollkirsche, Belladonna *f*; (*Med*) Belladonin *nt*.

bell: ~-bottomed trousers, ~-bottoms *npl* ausgestellte Hosen; **~-boy** *n* (*esp US*) Page, Hoteljunge *m*.

belle [bel] *n* Schöne, Schönheit *f* ◆ **the ~ of the ball** die Ballkönigin.

bell: ~ heather *n* Glockenheide *f*; **~ hop** *n* (*US*) *see* **~-boy**.

bellicose ['belɪkəʊs] *adj nation, mood* kriegerisch, kriegslustig; (*pugnacious*) kampflustig, streitsüchtig.

bellicosity [ˌbelɪ'kɒsɪtɪ] *n see adj* Kriegslust *f*; Kampf(es)lust, Streitsüchtigkeit *f*.

belligerence, belligerency [bɪ'lɪdʒərəns, -sɪ] *n see adj (a)* Kriegslust, Kampf(es)lust *f*; Streitlust *f*; Aggressivität *f*.

belligerent [bɪ'lɪdʒərənt] [1] *adj* (a) *nation* kriegslustig, kampflustig, kriegerisch; *person, attitude* streitlustig, kampflustig; *speech* aggressiv. (b) (*waging war*) kriegführend, streitend ◆ **~ power** Streitmacht *f*.
[2] *n* (*nation*) kriegführendes Land; (*person*) Streitende(r) *mf*.

bell-jar ['beldʒɑ:ʳ] *n* (Glas)glocke *f*.

bellow ['beləʊ] [1] *vi* (*animal, person*) brüllen; (*singing also*) grölen (*inf*) ◆ **to ~ at sb** jdn anbrüllen.
[2] *vt* (*also* **~ out**) brüllen; *song also* grölen (*inf*).
[3] *n* Brüllen *nt*.

bellows ['beləʊz] *npl* Blasebalg *m* ◆ **a pair of ~** ein Blasebalg.

bell: ~pull *n* Klingelzug *m*; **~push** *n* Klingel *f*; **~-ringer** *n* Glöckner *m*; **~-ringing** *n* Glockenläuten *nt*; **~-rope** *n* (*in church*) Glockenstrang *m*; (*in house*) Klingelzug *m*; **~s and whistles** *npl* (*esp Comput inf: additional features*) Extras *pl*; **~-shaped** *adj* glockenförmig, kelchförmig; **~-tent** *n* Rundzelt *nt*; **~-wether** *n* Leithammel *m*.

belly ['belɪ] *n* (*general*) Bauch *m*; (*of violin etc*) Decke *f*.

◆**belly out** [1] *vt sep sails* blähen, schwellen lassen.
[2] *vi* (*sails*) sich blähen, schwellen.

belly: ~-ache [1] *n* (*inf*) Bauchweh *nt* (*inf*), Bauchschmerzen *pl*; [2] *vi* (*inf: complain*) murren (*about* über +*acc*); **~-aching** *n* (*inf*) Murren, Gemurre *nt*; **~ button** *n* (*inf*) Bauchnabel *m*; **~ dance** *n* Bauchtanz *m*; **~ dancer** *n* Bauchtänzerin *f*; **~-flop** *n* Bauchklatscher *m* (*inf*); **to do a ~-flop** einen Bauchklatscher machen (*inf*).

bellyful ['belɪfʊl] *n* (a) (*sl: more than enough*) **I've had a ~ of him/writing these letters** ich habe die Nase voll von ihm/davon, immer diese Briefe zu schreiben (*inf*).
(b) (*inf: of food*) **after a good ~ of beans** nachdem ich mir/er sich *etc* den Bauch mit Bohnen vollgeschlagen hatte (*inf*).

belly: ~-land *vi* bauchlanden; **~-landing** *n* Bauchlandung *f*; **~ laugh** *n* dröhnendes Lachen; **he gave a great ~ laugh** er lachte lauthals los.

belong [bɪ'lɒŋ] *vi* (a) (*be the property of*) gehören (*to sb* jdm) ◆ **who does it ~ to?** wem gehört es?; **the parks ~ to everybody** die Parkanlagen sind für alle da.
(b) (*be part of*) gehören (*to* zu); (*to town: person*) gehören (*to* nach), sich zuhause fühlen (*to* in +*dat*) ◆ **to ~ together** zusammengehören; **the lid ~s to this box** der Deckel gehört zu dieser Schachtel; **to ~ to a club** einem Club angehören; **why don't you ~?** warum sind Sie nicht Mitglied?; **attributes which ~ to people** Attribute, die sich auf Personen beziehen; **concepts that ~ to physics** Begriffe, die in die Physik gehören.
(c) (*be in right place*) gehören ◆ **I don't ~ here** ich gehöre nicht hierher, ich bin hier fehl am Platze; **to feel that one doesn't ~** das Gefühl haben, daß man fehl am Platze ist *or* daß man nicht dazugehört; **you don't ~ here, so scram** Sie haben hier nichts zu suchen, also verschwinden Sie; **the vase ~s on the mantelpiece** die Vase gehört auf den Sims; **where does this one ~?** wo gehört das hin?; **that doesn't ~ to my area of responsibility** das gehört nicht in meinen Verantwortungsbereich; **it ~s under the heading of ...** das gehört *or* fällt in die Rubrik der ...
(d) **this case ~s to the Appeal Court** dieser Fall gehört vor das Appellationsgericht; **that doesn't ~ to this department** das gehört nicht in diese Abteilung.

belongings [bɪ'lɒŋɪŋz] *npl* Sachen *pl*, Besitz *m*, Habe *f* (*geh*) ◆ **personal ~** persönliches Eigentum, persönlicher Besitz; **all his ~** sein ganzes Hab und Gut.

beloved [bɪ'lʌvɪd] [1] *adj* geliebt; *memory* lieb, teuer.
[2] *n* Geliebte(r) *mf* ◆ **dearly ~** (*Rel*) liebe Brüder und Schwestern im Herrn.

below [bɪ'ləʊ] [1] *prep* (a) (*under*) unterhalb (+*gen*); (*with line, level etc also*) unter (+*dat or with motion* +*acc*) ◆ **on it and ~ it** darauf und darunter; **her skirt comes well ~ her knees** ihr Rock geht bis weit unters Knie; **Naples is ~ Rome** (*on the map*) Neapel liegt unterhalb Roms; **the ship/sun disappeared ~ the horizon** das Schiff/die Sonne verschwand hinter dem Horizont; **to be ~ sb** (*in rank*) (rangmäßig) unter jdm stehen.
(b) (*downstream from*) unterhalb (+*gen*), nach.
(c) (*unworthy of*) **or is that ~ you?** oder ist das unter Ihrer Würde?
[2] *adv* (a) (*lower down*) unten ◆ **the cows in the valley ~** die Kühe drunten im Tal; **they live one floor ~** sie wohnen ein Stockwerk tiefer; **the tenants/flat ~** die Mieter/die Wohnung darunter; (*below us*) die Mieter/Wohnung unter uns; **write the name here with the address ~** schreiben Sie den Namen hierher und die Adresse darunter; **in the class ~** in der Klasse darunter; (*below me*) in der Klasse unter mir; **what's the next rank ~?** was ist der nächstniedere Rang?
(b) (*Naut*) unter Deck ◆ **to go ~** unter Deck gehen.
(c) (*in documents*) (weiter) unten ◆ **see ~** siehe unten.
(d) **15 degrees ~** 15 Grad unter Null, 15 Grad minus.
(e) (*on earth*) **here ~** hier unten; **and on earth ~** (*Bibl*) und unten auf der Erde; **down ~** (*in hell*) dort drunten.

Belshazzar [bel'ʃæzəʳ] *n* **~'s Feast** Belsazars Gastmahl.

belt [belt] [1] *n* (a) (*on clothes*) Gürtel *m*; (*for holding, carrying etc, seat~*) Gurt *m*; (*Mil etc: on uniform*) Koppel *nt*; (*Mil: for cartridges*) Patronengurt *m*; (*shoulder-gun~*) (Gewehr)riemen *m* ◆ **a blow below the ~** (*lit, fig*) ein Schlag *m* unterhalb der Gürtellinie, ein Tiefschlag *m*; **to hit below the ~** (*lit, fig*) (*person*) jdm einen Schlag unter die Gürtellinie versetzen; **that was below the ~** das war ein Schlag unter die Gürtellinie; **to be a Black B~** den Schwarzen Gürtel haben; **to get the ~** (mit dem Lederriemen) eine auf die Finger bekommen; **to tighten one's ~** (*fig*) den Gürtel *or* Riemen enger schnallen; **under one's ~** (*fig inf*) auf dem Rücken (*inf*).
(b) (*Tech*) (Treib)riemen *m*; (*conveyor ~*) Band *nt* ◆ **~ drive** Riemenantrieb *m*.
(c) (*tract of land*) Gürtel *m* ◆ **~ of trees** Waldstreifen *m*; (*around house etc*) Baumgürtel *m*; **industrial ~** Industriegürtel *m*; *see* **commuter**.
(d) (*inf: hit*) Schlag *m* ◆ **to give sb/the ball a ~** jdm eine knallen (*inf*)/den Ball knallen (*inf*).
(e) (*US: ringroad*) Umgehungsstraße *f*.
(f) (*US sl: drink*) Schluck *m* aus der Pulle (*inf*).
[2] *vt* (a) (*fasten*) den Gürtel zumachen (*sth gen*).
(b) (*Sch etc: thrash*) (mit dem Lederriemen) schlagen.
(c) (*inf: hit*) knallen (*inf*) ◆ **she ~ed him one in the eye** sie verpaßte *or* haute

➤ LANGUAGE IN USE: **believe: 1a** → 26.2, 26.3 **belittle** → 26.3

or knallte ihm eins aufs Auge (*inf*).
[3] *vi* (*inf: rush*) rasen (*inf*) ◆ **to ~ out** hinaus-/herausrasen (*inf*); **to ~ across** hinüber-/herüberrasen (*inf*); **we were really ~ing along** wir sind wirklich gerast (*inf*); **he ~ed off down the street** er raste davon die Straße hinunter (*inf*); **this novel really ~s along** dieser Roman ist wirklich tempogeladen (*inf*).

◆**belt down** *vt sep* (*inf: drink quickly*) hinunterschütten, hinunterkippen (*inf*).

◆**belt on** *vt sep sword* umschnallen, sich umgürten mit (*geh*); *raincoat* anziehen.

◆**belt out** *vt sep* (*inf*) *tune* schmettern (*inf*); *rhythm* voll herausbringen (*inf*); (*on piano*) hämmern (*inf*).

◆**belt up** [1] *vt sep jacket* den Gürtel (+*gen*) zumachen.
[2] *vi* **(a)** (*inf*) die Klappe (*inf*) *or* Schnauze (*sl*) halten; (*stop making noise*) mit dem Krach aufhören (*inf*). **(b)** (*esp hum: put seat-belt on*) sich anschnallen.

belting ['beltɪŋ] *n* (*inf*) Dresche *f* (*inf*) ◆ **to give sb a good ~** jdn ganz schön verdreschen (*inf*).

beltway ['beltweɪ] *n* (*US*) Umgehungsstraße *f*.

bemoan [bɪ'məʊn] *vt* beklagen.

bemused [bɪ'mju:zd] *adj* (*puzzled*) verwirrt; (*preoccupied*) *look* abwesend.

bench [bentʃ] [1] *n* **(a)** (*seat*) Bank *f* ◆ **laughter from the government ~es** Gelächter von der Regierungsbank.
(b) (*Jur: office of a judge*) Richteramt *nt*; (*judges generally*) Richter *pl*; (*court*) Gericht *nt* ◆ **member of the ~** Richter *m*; **to be raised to the ~** zum Richter bestellt werden; **to be on the ~** (*permanent office*) Richter sein; (*when in court*) der Richter sein, auf dem Richterstuhl sitzen (*geh*).
(c) (*work~*) Werkbank *f*; (*in lab*) Experimentiertisch *m*.
[2] *vt* (*US Sport*) auf die Strafbank schicken; (*keep as substitute*) auf die Reservebank setzen.

benchmark ['bentʃmɑ:k] [1] *n* (*Surv*) Höhenfestpunkt *m*; (*fig*) Maßstab *m*.
[2] *adj attr price* Richt- ◆ **the ~ machine** die Maschine, die Maßstäbe setzt.

bend [bend] (*vb: pret, ptp* **bent**) [1] *n* **(a)** (*in river, tube, etc*) Krümmung, Biegung *f*; (*90°*) Knie *nt*; (*in road also*) Kurve *f* ◆ **there is a ~ in the road** die Straße macht (da) eine Kurve; **~s for 3 miles** 3 Meilen kurvenreiche Strecke; **don't park on the ~** parken Sie nicht in der Kurve; **to go/be round the ~** (*inf*)durchdrehen (*inf*), verrückt werden/sein (*inf*); **to drive sb round the ~** (*inf*) jdn verrückt *or* wahnsinnig machen (*inf*).
(b) (*knot*) Stek *m*.
(c) (*Her*) **~ sinister** Schräglinksbalken *m*.
[2] *vt* **(a)** (*curve, make angular*) biegen; *rod, rail, pipe also* krümmen; *bow* spannen; *arm, knee also* beugen; *leg, arm also* anwinkeln; (*forwards*) *back also* beugen, krümmen; *head* beugen, neigen ◆ **he can ~ an iron bar with his teeth** er kann mit den Zähnen eine Eisenstange verbiegen; **to ~ sth at right angles** etw rechtwinklig abbiegen *or* abknicken; **to ~ sth out of shape** etw verbiegen; **the bumper got bent in the crash** die Stoßstange hat sich bei dem Zusammenstoß verbogen; **on ~ed knees** auf Knien; (*fig also*) kniefällig; **to go down on ~ed knees** auf die Knie fallen; (*fig also*) einen Kniefall machen.
(b) (*fig*) *rules* frei auslegen ◆ **to ~ the law** das Gesetz beugen; **to ~ sb to one's will** sich (*dat*) jdn gefügig machen.
(c) (*direct*) *one's steps, efforts* lenken, richten.
(d) (*Naut*) *sail* befestigen.
[3] *vi* **(a)** sich biegen; (*pipe, rail also*) sich krümmen; (*forwards also*) (*tree, corn etc*) sich neigen; (*person*) sich beugen ◆ **this metal ~s easily** (*a bad thing*) dieses Metall verbiegt sich leicht; (*a good thing*) dieses Metall läßt sich leicht biegen; **my arm won't ~** ich kann den Arm nicht biegen; **~ing strain, ~ stress** Biegespannung *f*.
(b) (*river*) eine Biegung machen; (*at right angles*) ein Knie machen; (*road also*) eine Kurve machen ◆ **the road/river ~s to the left** die Straße/der Fluß macht eine Linkskurve/-biegung.
(c) (*fig: submit*) sich beugen, sich fügen (*to dat*).

◆**bend back** [1] *vi* sich zurückbiegen; (*over backwards*) sich nach hinten biegen; (*road, river*) in einer Schleife zurückkommen.
[2] *vt sep* zurückbiegen.

◆**bend down** [1] *vi* (*person*) sich bücken; (*branch, tree*) sich neigen, sich nach unten biegen ◆ **she bent ~ to look at the baby** sie beugte sich hinunter, um das Baby anzusehen.
[2] *vt sep edges* nach unten biegen.

◆**bend over** [1] *vi* (*person*) sich bücken ◆ **to ~ ~ to look at sth** sich nach vorn beugen, um etw anzusehen.
[2] *vt sep* umbiegen.

bender ['bendəʳ] *n* (*inf*) Kneipkur *f* (*hum inf*) ◆ **to go on a ~** sich besaufen (*inf*); (*do pubcrawl*) auf eine Sauftour gehen (*inf*).

bends [bendz] *n* **the ~** die Taucherkrankheit.

beneath [bɪ'ni:θ] [1] *prep* **(a)** unter (+*dat or with motion* +*acc*); (*with line, level etc also*) unterhalb (+*gen*) ◆ **to marry ~ one** unter seinem Stand heiraten; *see also* **below 1 (a)**. **(b)** (*unworthy of*) **it is ~ him** das ist unter seiner Würde.
[2] *adv* unten; *see also* **below 2 (a)**.

Benedictine [,benɪ'dɪktɪn] [1] *n* **(a)** (*Eccl*) Benediktiner(in *f*) *m*. **(b)** (*liqueur*) Benediktiner *m*.
[2] *adj* Benediktiner-.

benediction [,benɪ'dɪkʃən] *n* **(a)** (*blessing*) Segen *m*; (*act of blessing*) Segnung *f*. **(b)** (*consecration*) Einsegnung *f*.

benefaction [,benɪ'fækʃən] *n* **(a)** (*good deed*) Wohltat *f*, gute Tat. **(b)** (*gift*) Spende *f*.

benefactor ['benɪfæktəʳ] *n* Wohltäter *m*; (*giver of money also*) Gönner *m*.

benefactress ['benɪfæktrɪs] *n* Wohltäterin *f*, Gönnerin *f*.

benefice ['benɪfɪs] *n* Pfründe *f*, kirchliches Benefizium (*spec*).

beneficence [bɪ'nefɪsəns] *n* (*liter*) Wohltätigkeit *f*.

beneficent [bɪ'nefɪsənt] *adj* (*liter*) wohltätig.

beneficial [,benɪ'fɪʃəl] *adj* **(a)** gut (*to* für); *climate also* zuträglich (*geh*) (*to dat*); *influence also* vorteilhaft; *advice, lesson* nützlich (*to* für); (*advantageous*) günstig, von Vorteil ◆ **the change will be ~ to you** die Veränderung wird Ihnen guttun. **(b)** (*Jur*) **~ owner** Nutznießer(in *f*) *m*.

beneficiary [,benɪ'fɪʃərɪ] *n* **(a)** Nutznießer(in *f*) *m*; (*of will, insurance etc*) Begünstigte(r) *mf*. **(b)** (*Eccl*) Pfründner *m*.

benefit ['benɪfɪt] [1] *n* **(a)** (*advantage*) Vorteil *m*; (*profit*) Nutzen, Gewinn *m* ◆ **to derive** *or* **get ~ from sth** aus etw Nutzen ziehen; **for the ~ of his family/the poor** zum Wohl *or* für das Wohl seiner Familie/der Armen; **for the ~ of your health** Ihrer Gesundheit zuliebe, um Ihrer Gesundheit willen; **for your ~** Ihretwegen, um Ihretwillen (*geh*); **this money is for the ~ of the blind** dieses Geld kommt den Blinden zugute; **it is for his ~ that this was done** das ist seinetwegen geschehen; **to give sb the ~ of the doubt** im Zweifelsfall zu jds Gunsten entscheiden; **we should give him the ~ of the doubt** wir sollten das zu seinen Gunsten auslegen.
(b) (*allowance*) Unterstützung *f*; (*sickness ~*) Krankengeld *nt*; (*family ~*) Kindergeld *nt*; (*social security ~*) Sozialhilfe *f*; (*maternity ~*) Wochengeld *nt*; (*insurance ~*) Versicherungsleistung *f* ◆ **old age ~** Altersrente *f*; *see* **fringe ~s**.
(c) (*special performance*) Benefizveranstaltung *f*; (*Theat also*) Benefiz(vorstellung *f*) *nt*; (*Sport also*) Benefizspiel *nt* ◆ **it's his ~** es ist eine Benefizvorstellung für ihn.
(d) without ~ of clergy ohne kirchlichen Segen.
[2] *vt* guttun (+*dat*), nützen (+*dat*), zugute kommen (+dat); (*healthwise*) guttun (+*dat*).
[3] *vi* profitieren (*from, by* von); (*from experience also*) Nutzen ziehen (*from* aus) ◆ **who will ~ from that?** wem wird das nützen?; **but how do we ~?** aber was nützt das uns?; **he would ~ from a holiday** Ferien würden ihm guttun; **I think you'll ~ from the experience** ich glaube, diese Erfahrung wird Ihnen nützlich sein *or* von Nutzen sein; **a cure from which many have ~ted** eine Behandlung, die schon manchem geholfen hat.

benefit: ~ concert *n* Benefizkonzert *nt*; **~ match** *n* Benefizspiel *nt*; **~ performance** *n* Benefizveranstaltung *f*.

Benelux ['benɪlʌks] *n* Benelux-Wirtschaftsunion *f* ◆ **~ countries** Beneluxstaaten *or* -länder *pl*.

benevolence [bɪ'nevələns] *n see adj (a)* Wohlwollen *nt*; Gutmütigkeit *f*; Güte *f*; Milde *f*.

benevolent [bɪ'nevələnt] *adj* **(a)** wohlwollend; *pat, smile, twinkle* gutmütig; (*as character trait*) gütig; *emperor, judge* mild ◆ **B~ Despotism** der Aufgeklärte Absolutismus. **(b)** (*charitable*) **~ institution** Wohltätigkeitseinrichtung *f*; **~ society** Wohltätigkeitsverein *m*.

benevolently [bɪ'nevələntlɪ] *adv see adj (a)*.

Bengal [beŋ'gɔ:l] *n* Bengalen *nt* ◆ **~ light** *or* **match** bengalisches Feuer *or* Hölzchen; **~ tiger** bengalischer Tiger, Königstiger *m*.

Bengalese [beŋgə'li:z] [1] *n* Bengale *m*, Bengalin *f*.
[2] *adj* bengalisch.

Bengali [beŋ'gɔ:lɪ] [1] *n* (*language*) Bengali *nt*; (*person*) Bengale *m*, Bengalin *f*.
[2] *adj* bengalisch.

benighted [bɪ'naɪtɪd] *adj* **(a)** (*fig*) *person* unbedarft; *country* gottverlassen; *policy etc* hirnrissig. **(b)** (*lit*) von der Dunkelheit *or* Nacht überfallen *or* überrascht.

benign [bɪ'naɪn], **benignant** (*rare*) [bɪ'nɪgnənt] *adj* **(a)** gütig; *planet, influence* günstig; *climate* mild. **(b)** (*Med*) *tumour* gutartig.

benny ['benɪ] *n* (*sl*) *dim of* **Benzedrine**.

bent [bent] [1] *pret, ptp of* **bend**.
[2] *adj* **(a)** *metal etc* gebogen; (*out of shape*) verbogen.
(b) (*Brit sl: dishonest*) *person* korrupt; *affair* unsauber (*inf*) ◆ **he's ~** er ist ein krummer Hund (*sl*).
(c) (*sl: homosexual*) andersrum *pred* (*inf*).
(d) to be ~ on sth/doing sth etw unbedingt *or* partout wollen/tun wollen; **he seemed ~ on self-destruction** er schien von einem Selbstzerstörungstrieb besessen zu sein.
[3] *n* (*aptitude*) Neigung *f* (*for* zu); (*type of mind, character*) Schlag *m* ◆ **to follow one's ~** seiner Neigung folgen; **people with** *or* **of a musical ~** Menschen mit einer musikalischen Veranlagung; **people of his ~** Leute seines Schlags.

benumb [bɪ'nʌm] *vt* **(a)** *limb* gefühllos machen; *person* betäuben; (*with cold also*) erstarren lassen ◆ **he was/his fingers were ~ed with cold** er war starr vor Kälte/seine Finger waren starr *or* taub vor Kälte. **(b)** (*fig*) *mind* betäuben; (*panic, experience etc*) lähmen ◆ **~ed by alcohol** vom Alkohol benommen.

Benzedrine ® ['benzɪdri:n] *n* Benzedrin *nt*.

benzene ['benzi:n] *n* Benzol *nt*.

benzine ['benzi:n] *n* Leichtbenzin *nt*.

bequeath [bɪ'kwi:ð] *vt* **(a)** (*in will*) vermachen, hinterlassen (*to sb* jdm). **(b)** (*fig*) *tradition* hinterlassen, vererben (*to sb* jdm).

bequest [bɪ'kwest] *n* (*act of bequeathing*) Vermachen *nt* (*to* an +*acc*); (*legacy*) Nachlaß *m*.

berate [bɪ'reɪt] *vt* (*liter*) schelten, auszanken.

Berber ['bɜ:bəʳ] [1] *n* **(a)** Berber *m*, Berberfrau *f*. **(b)** (*language*) die Berbersprache.
[2] *adj* berberisch.

bereave [bɪ'ri:v] *vt* **(a)** *pret, ptp* **bereft** (*liter*) (*deprive*) berauben (*geh*) (*of gen*). **(b)** *pret, ptp* **~d** (*cause loss by death: illness*) (*sb of sb* jdm jdn) rauben (*geh*), nehmen ◆ **he was ~d of his son** sein Sohn ist ihm genommen worden (*geh*).

bereaved [bɪ'riːvd] *adj* leidtragend ◆ **the ~** die Hinterbliebenen.

bereavement [bɪ'riːvmənt] *n* **(a)** *(death in family)* Trauerfall *m* ◆ **owing to a/his recent ~** wegen *or* auf Grund eines Trauerfalls/dieses für ihn so schmerzlichen Verlusts; **to sympathize with sb in his ~** jds Leid teilen.
(b) *(feeling of loss)* schmerzlicher Verlust ◆ **to feel a sense of ~ at sth** etw als schmerzlichen Verlust empfinden.

bereft [bɪ'reft] [1] *ptp of* **bereave.**
[2] *adj* **to be ~ of sth** einer Sache *(gen)* bar sein *(geh)*; **his life was ~ of happiness** seinem Leben fehlte jegliches Glück; **he is ~ of reason** es mangelt ihm vollkommen an Vernunft.

beret ['bereɪ] *n* Baskenmütze *f.*

berg [bɜːg] *n see* **ice~.**

beribboned [bɪ'rɪbənd] *adj* mit Bändern geschmückt, bebändert; *general* mit Ordensbändern geschmückt.

beri-beri ['berɪ'berɪ] *n* Beriberi *f.*

Bering ['berɪŋ]: **~ Sea** *n* Beringmeer *nt*; **~ Straits** *npl* Beringstraße *f.*

berk [bɜːk] *n (Brit sl)* Dussel *m (inf)*.

Berks [bɑːks] *abbr of* **Berkshire.**

Berlin [bɜː'lɪn] *n* Berlin *nt* ◆ **the ~ wall** die Mauer.

Bermuda [bɜː'mjuːdə] *n* Bermuda *nt (form rare)* ◆ **the ~s** die Bermudas, die Bermudainseln *pl*; **to go to ~** auf die Bermudas fahren; **~ shorts** Bermudashorts *pl*; **~ triangle** Bermuda-Dreieck *nt.*

Bernard ['bɜːnəd] *n* Bernhard *m.*

Berne [bɜːn] *n* Bern *nt.*

Bernese [bɜː'niːz] *adj* Berner; *village* im Berner Oberland.

berry ['berɪ] *n* **(a)** *(fruit)* Beere *f* ◆ **as brown as a ~** ganz braungebrannt. **(b)** *(Bot)* Beerenfrucht *f.*

berrying ['berɪɪŋ] *n* Beerensammeln *nt* ◆ **to go ~** Beeren sammeln gehen.

berserk [bə'sɜːk] *adj* wild ◆ **to go ~** wild werden; *(audience)* aus dem Häuschen geraten *(inf)*, zu toben anfangen; *(go mad)* überschnappen *(inf)*, verrückt werden.

berth [bɜːθ] [1] *n* **(a)** *(on ship)* Koje *f*; *(on train)* Schlafwagenplatz *m.* **(b)** *(Naut: for ship)* Liegeplatz *m.* **(c)** *(Naut: sea-room)* Raum *m* ◆ **to give a wide ~ to a ship** Abstand zu einem Schiff halten; **to give sb/sth a wide ~** *(fig)* einen (weiten) Bogen um jdn/etw machen.
[2] *vi* anlegen.
[3] *vt* **to ~ a ship** mit einem Schiff (am Kai) anlegen; *(assign ~ to)* einem Schiff einen Liegeplatz zuweisen; **where is she ~ed?** wo liegt es?; wo hat es angelegt?

beryl ['berɪl] *n* Beryll *m.*

beseech [bɪ'siːtʃ] *pret, ptp* **~ed** *or (liter)* **besought** *vt person* anflehen, beschwören; *forgiveness* flehen um, erflehen *(geh)*.

beseeching *adj*, **~ly** *adv* [bɪ'siːtʃɪŋ, -lɪ] flehentlich *(geh)*, flehend.

beset [bɪ'set] *pret, ptp* **~** *vt (difficulties, dangers)* (von allen Seiten) bedrängen; *(doubts)* befallen; *(temptations, trials)* heimsuchen ◆ **to be ~ with difficulties/danger** *(problem, journey etc)* reich an *or* voller Schwierigkeiten/Gefahren sein; *(person)* von Schwierigkeiten heimgesucht werden/von Gefahren bedrängt werden; **~ by doubts** von Zweifeln befallen.

besetting [bɪ'setɪŋ] *adj* **his ~ sin** eine ständige Untugend von ihm; **his one ~ worry/idea** *etc* die Sorge/Vorstellung *etc*, die ihn nicht losläßt.

beside [bɪ'saɪd] *prep* **(a)** *(at the side of)* neben (+*dat or with motion* +*acc*); *(at the edge of) road, river* an (+*dat or with motion* +*acc*) ◆ **~ the road** am Straßenrand.
(b) *(compared with)* neben (+*dat*) ◆ **if you put it ~ the original** wenn man es neben dem Original sieht.
(c) *(irrelevant to)* **to be ~ the question** *or* **point** damit nichts zu tun haben.
(d) **to be ~ oneself** *(with anger)* außer sich sein *(with* vor*)*; *(with joy also)* sich nicht mehr zu lassen wissen *(with* vor*)*.

besides [bɪ'saɪdz] [1] *adv* **(a)** *(in addition)* außerdem, obendrein ◆ **he wrote a novel and several short stories ~** er hat einen Roman und außerdem noch mehrere Kurzgeschichten geschrieben; **many more ~** noch viele mehr; **have you got any others ~?** haben Sie noch andere *or* noch welche?
(b) *(anyway, moreover)* außerdem.
[2] *prep* **(a)** *(in addition to)* außer ◆ **others ~ ourselves** außer uns noch andere; **there were three of us ~ Mary** Mary nicht mitgerechnet, waren wir zu dritt; **~ which he was unwell** überdies *or* außerdem fühlte er sich nicht wohl.
(b) *(except)* außer, abgesehen von.

besiege [bɪ'siːdʒ] *vt* **(a)** *(Mil) town* belagern. **(b)** *(fig)* belagern; *(with information, offers)* überschütten, überhäufen; *(pester: with letters, questions)* bestürmen, bedrängen.

besieger [bɪ'siːdʒə^r] *n (Mil)* Belagerer *m.*

besmirch [bɪ'smɜːtʃ] *vt (lit, fig)* beschmutzen, besudeln.

besom ['biːzəm] *n* **(a)** (Reisig)besen *m.* **(b)** *(pej inf: woman)* Besen *m (pej inf)*.

besotted [bɪ'sɒtɪd] *adj* **(a)** *(drunk)* berauscht *(with* von*)*. **(b)** *(infatuated)* völlig vernarrt *(with* in +*acc)*; *(with idea)* berauscht *(with* von*)*.

besought [bɪ'sɔːt] *(liter) pret, ptp of* **beseech.**

bespake [bɪ'speɪk] *(old) pret of* **bespeak.**

bespangle [bɪ'spæŋgl] *vt* besetzen ◆ **~d costume** mit Pailletten besetztes Kostüm; **the sky ~d with ...** *(liter)* der mit ... übersäte Himmel.

bespatter [bɪ'spætə^r] *vt* bespritzen.

bespeak [bɪ'spiːk] *pret* **bespoke** *or (old)* **bespake,** *ptp* **bespoken** *or* **bespoke** *vt* **(a)** *(indicate)* verraten, erkennen lassen. **(b)** *(old: reserve)* reservieren lassen, bestellen.

bespectacled [bɪ'spektɪkld] *adj* bebrillt.

bespoke [bɪ'spəʊk] [1] *prep, ptp of* **bespeak.**
[2] *adj goods* nach Maß; *garment also* Maß- ◆ **a ~ tailor** ein Maßschneider *m.*

bespoken [bɪ'spəʊkən] *ptp of* **bespeak.**

besprinkle [bɪ'sprɪŋkl] *vt (with liquid)* besprengen, bespritzen; *(with powder)* bestäuben.

Bess [bes] *n dim of* **Elizabeth** ◆ **good Queen ~** *Elisabeth I.*

Bessemer ['besɪmə^r] *in cpds* Bessemer- ◆ **~ converter** Bessemerbirne *f.*

▼ **best** [best] [1] *adj, superl of* **good** beste(r, s) *attr*; *(most favourable) route, price also* günstigste(r, s) *attr* ◆ **to be ~** am besten/günstigsten sein; **to be ~ of all** am allerbesten/allergünstigsten sein; **that was the ~ thing about her/that could happen** das war das Beste an ihr/, was geschehen konnte; **that would be ~** *or* **the ~ thing for everybody** das wäre für alle das beste; **the ~ thing to do is** *or* **it's ~ to wait** das beste ist zu warten; **may the ~ man win!** dem Besten der Sieg!; **to put one's ~ foot forward** *(lit)* seinen schnellsten Gang anschlagen; *(fig)* sein Bestes geben *or* tun; **the ~ part of the year/my money** fast das ganze Jahr/fast all mein Geld.
▼ [2] *adv, superl of* **well** **(a)** am besten; *like* am liebsten *or* meisten; *enjoy* am meisten ◆ **the ~ fitting dress** das am besten passende Kleid; **the ~ known title** der bekannteste Titel; **he was ~ known for ...** er war vor allem bekannt für ...; **~ of all** am allerbesten/-liebsten/-meisten; **I helped him as ~ I could** ich half ihm, so gut ich konnte; **I thought it ~ to go** ich hielt es für das beste, zu gehen; **do as you think ~** tun Sie, was Sie für richtig halten; **you know ~** Sie müssen es (am besten) wissen.
▼ **(b)** *(better)* **you had ~ go now** am besten gehen Sie jetzt.
[3] *n* **(a)** *(person, thing)* **the ~** der/die/das beste; **the ~ of the bunch** *(inf)* (noch) der/die/das Beste; **his last book was his ~** sein letztes Buch war sein bestes; **with the ~ of intentions** mit den besten Absichten; **he can sing with the ~ of them** er kann sich im Singen mit den Besten messen.
(b) *(clothes)* beste Sachen, Sonntagskleider *(inf) pl* ◆ **to be in one's (Sunday) ~** in Schale sein *(inf)*, im Sonntagsstaat sein.
▼ **(c)** **to do one's (level) ~** sein Bestes *or* möglichstes tun; **that's the ~ you can expect** Sie können nichts Besseres erwarten; **do the ~ you can!** machen Sie es so gut Sie können!; **it's not perfect but it's the ~ I can do** es ist nicht perfekt, aber mehr kann ich nicht tun; **what a lame excuse, is that the ~ you can do?** so eine lahme Ausrede, fällt Ihnen nichts Besseres ein?; **to get** *or* **have the ~ of sb** jdn unterkriegen; **to get the ~ out of sb/sth** das Beste aus jdm/etw herausholen; **to get the ~ of the bargain** *or* **of it** am besten dabei wegkommen; **to play the ~ of three/five** nur so lange spielen, bis eine Partei zweimal/dreimal gewonnen hat; **to make the ~ of it/a bad job** das Beste daraus machen; **to make the ~ of one's opportunities** seine Chancen voll nützen; **the ~ of it is that ...** das beste daran ist, daß ...; **we've had the ~ of the day** der Tag ist so gut wie vorbei; *(the weather's getting worse)* das schöne Wetter wäre für heute vorbei; **it's all for the ~** es ist nur zum Guten; **I meant it for the ~** ich habe es doch nur gut gemeint; **to do sth for the ~** etw in bester Absicht tun; **to the ~ of my ability** so gut ich kann/konnte; **to the ~ of my knowledge** meines Wissens; **to the ~ of my recollection** *or* **memory** soviel ich mich erinnern kann; **to look one's ~** besonders gut aussehen; **to be at one's ~** *(on form)* in Hochform sein; **he is at his ~ at about 8 in the evening** so gegen 8 abends ist seine beste Zeit; **roses are at their ~ just now** jetzt ist die beste Zeit für Rosen; **that is Goethe at his ~** das ist Goethe, wie er besser nicht sein könnte; **it's not enough (even) at the ~ of times** das ist schon normalerweise nicht genug; **at ~** bestenfalls; **to wish sb all the ~** jdm alles Gute wünschen; **all the ~ (to you)** alles Gute!
[4] *vt* schlagen.

best-before date [,bestbɪ'fɔː,deɪt] *n* Haltbarkeitsdatum *nt.*

best-dressed ['best,drest] *adj* bestgekleidet *attr.*

bestial ['bestɪəl] *adj acts, cruelty* bestialisch, tierisch; *person, look, appearance (cruel)* brutal; *(carnal)* tierisch.

bestiality [,bestɪ'ælɪtɪ] *n* **(a)** *see adj* Bestialität *f*, Tierische(s) *nt*; Brutalität *f.* **(b)** *(act)* Greueltat *f.* **(c)** *(buggery)* Sodomie *f.*

bestiary ['bestɪərɪ] *n* Bestiaire, Bestiarium *nt.*

bestir [bɪ'stɜː^r] *vr (hum, liter)* sich regen, sich rühren ◆ **to ~ oneself to do sth** sich dazu aufraffen, etw zu tun.

best man *n* Trauzeuge *m* (des Bräutigams).

bestow [bɪ'stəʊ] *vt* **(a)** *(on or upon sb* jdm*)* *(grant, give) gift, attention* schenken; *favour, friendship, kiss also* gewähren *(geh)*; *honour* erweisen, zuteil werden lassen *(geh)*; *title, medal* verleihen. **(b)** *(old: place)* verstauen, unterbringen.

bestowal [bɪ'stəʊəl] *n see vt (a)* Schenken *nt*; Gewähren *nt*; Erweisung *f*; Verleihung *f* ((*up*)*on* an +*acc*).

bestraddle [bɪ'strædl] *vt see* **bestride.**

bestride [bɪ'straɪd] *pret* **bestrode** [bɪ'strəʊd] *or* **bestrid** [bɪ'strɪd], *ptp* **bestridden** [bɪ'strɪdn] *vt (sit astride)* rittlings sitzen auf (+*dat*); *(stand astride)* (mit gespreizten Beinen) stehen über (+*dat*); *(mount)* sich schwingen auf (+*acc*) ◆ **to ~ the world like a Colossus** die Welt beherrschen.

best: **~-seller** *n* Verkaufs- *or* Kassenschlager *m*; *(book)* Bestseller *m*; *(author)* Erfolgsautor(in *f*) *m*; **~-selling** *adj article* absatzstark, der/die/das am besten geht; *author* Erfolgs-; **a ~-selling novel** ein Bestseller *m*; **this month's ~-selling books** die Bestsellerliste dieses Monats.

bet [bet] *(vb: pret, ptp* **~***)* [1] *n* Wette *f (on* auf +*acc)*; *(money etc staked)* Wetteinsatz *m* ◆ **to make** *or* **have a ~ with sb** mit jdm wetten, mit jdm eine Wette eingehen; **I have a ~ (on) with him that ...** ich habe mit ihm gewettet, daß ...; **it's a safe/bad ~** das ist ein sicherer/schlechter Tip; **it's a safe ~ he'll be in the pub** er ist bestimmt *or* garantiert in der Kneipe; **he's a bad ~ for the job** er ist nichts für diese Arbeit *(inf)*.
[2] *vt* **(a)** wetten, setzen *(against* gegen, *on* auf +*acc)* ◆ **I ~ him £5** ich habe mit ihm (um) £ 5 gewettet; **to ~ ten to one** zehn gegen eins wetten.
(b) *(inf)* wetten ◆ **I ~ he'll come!** wetten, daß er kommt! *(inf)*; **I'll ~ you any-**

➤ LANGUAGE IN USE: **best:** **1** → 1.1, 21.2, 23.1, 23.3, 24.2, 24.3 **2a** → 7.1 **2b** → 2.2 **3c** → 23.1, 23.5

thing (you like) ich gehe mit dir jede Wette (darauf) ein; **~ you!** wetten! (*inf*); **you can ~ your boots** *or* **your bottom dollar that ...** Sie können Gift darauf nehmen, daß ... (*inf*); **~ you I can!** (*inf*) wetten, daß ich das kann! (*inf*).
[3] *vi* wetten ◆ **to ~ on a horse/horses** auf ein Pferd/Pferde setzen *or* wetten, Pferdewetten abschließen; **you ~!** (*inf*) und ob! (*inf*); **(do you) want to ~?** (wollen wir) wetten?

beta ['bi:tə] *n* Beta *nt*; (*Brit Sch*) gut ◆ **~ ray** Betastrahl *m*.

beta-blocker ['bi:tə,blɒkə^r] *n* Betablocker *m*.

betake [bɪ'teɪk] *pret* **betook**, *ptp* **~n** [bɪ'teɪkn] *vr* (*old, hum*) sich begeben.

betcha ['betʃə] *interj* (*sl*) wetten(, daß) (*inf*).

betel ['bi:təl] *n* Betel *m* ◆ **~ nut** Betelnuß *f*.

bête noire [bet'nwa:^r] *n* **to be a ~ to sb** jdm ein Greuel sein.

bethink [bɪ'θɪŋk] *pret, ptp* **bethought** *vr* (*liter, obs*) **to ~ oneself of sth/that ...** etw bedenken/bedenken, daß ...

Bethlehem ['beθlɪhem] *n* Bethlehem *nt*.

bethought [bɪ'θɔ:t] *pret, ptp of* **bethink**.

betide [bɪ'taɪd] *vti* geschehen (*sb* jdm) ◆ **whatever (may) ~** was immer auch geschehen mag (*geh*); *see* **woe**.

betimes [bɪ'taɪmz] *adv* (*old, liter*) beizeiten (*geh*).

betoken [bɪ'təʊkən] *vt* (*old*) bedeuten, hindeuten auf (+*acc*).

betook [bɪ'tʊk] *pret of* **betake**.

betray [bɪ'treɪ] *vt* verraten (*also Pol*) (*to dat or (Pol)* an +*acc*); *trust* enttäuschen, brechen; (*be disloyal to also*) im Stich lassen; (*be unfaithful to*) untreu werden (+*dat*) ◆ **to ~ oneself** sich verraten; **his accent ~ed him as a foreigner** sein Akzent verriet, daß er Ausländer war.

betrayal [bɪ'treɪəl] *n* (*act*) Verrat *m* (*of gen*); (*instance*) Verrat *m* (*of* an +*dat*); (*of trust*) Enttäuschung *f*; (*of friends also*) Untreue *f* (*of* gegenüber) ◆ **the ~ of Christ** der Verrat an Christus; **a ~ of trust** ein Vertrauensbruch *m*.

betrayer [bɪ'treɪə^r] *n* Verräter(in *f*) *m* (*of gen or (Pol)* an +*dat*).

betroth [bɪ'trəʊð] *vt* (*obs, liter*) angeloben (*obs, liter*) (*to sb* jdm), versprechen (*liter*) (*to sb* jdm), verloben (*to sb* mit jdm).

betrothal [bɪ'trəʊðəl] *n* (*obs, liter, hum*) Verlobung *f*.

betrothed [bɪ'trəʊðd] *n* (*obs, liter, hum*) Anverlobte(r) *mf* (*obs*).

better[1] ['betə^r] *n* Wetter(in *f*) *m*.

▼ **better**[2] [1] *adj, comp of* **good** besser; *route, way also* günstiger ◆ **he's ~** (*recovered*) es geht ihm wieder besser; **he's much ~** es geht ihm viel besser; **the patient/his foot is getting ~** dem Patienten/seinem Fuß geht es schon viel besser; **I hope you get ~ soon** hoffentlich sind Sie bald wieder gesund; **~ and ~** immer besser; **that's ~!** (*approval*) so ist es besser!; (*relief etc*) so!; **to be ~ than one's word** mehr tun, als man versprochen hat; **it couldn't be ~** es könnte gar nicht besser sein; **I am none the ~ for it** das hilft mir auch nicht; **she is no ~ than she should be** sie ist auch keine Heilige; **the ~ part of an hour/my money/our holidays** fast eine Stunde/fast mein ganzes Geld/fast die ganzen Ferien; **it/you would be ~ to go early** es wäre besser, früh zu gehen/Sie gehen besser früh; **to go one ~** einen Schritt weiter gehen; (*in offer*) höher gehen; **this hat has seen ~ days** dieser Hut hat auch schon bessere Tage gesehen (*inf*).
▼ [2] *adv, comp of* **well (a)** besser; *like* lieber, mehr; *enjoy* mehr ◆ **they are ~ off than we are** sie sind besser dran als wir; **you would do ~** *or* **be ~ advised to go early** Sie sollten lieber früh gehen; **to think ~ of it** es sich (*dat*) noch einmal überlegen; **I didn't think any ~ of him for that** deswegen hielt ich auch nicht mehr von ihm; *see* **know, late**.
▼ **(b) I had ~ go** ich gehe jetzt wohl besser; **you'd ~ do what he says** tun Sie lieber, was er sagt; **I'd ~ answer that letter soon** ich beantworte den Brief lieber *or* besser bald; **I won't touch it Mummy — you'd ~ not!** ich fasse es nicht an, Mutti — das will ich dir auch geraten haben.
[3] *n* **(a) one's ~s** Leute, die über einem stehen; (*socially also*) Höhergestellte; **that's no way to talk to your ~s** man muß immer wissen, wen man vor sich (*dat*) hat; **respect for one's ~s** Achtung Respektspersonen gegenüber.
(b) (*person, object*) **the ~** der/die/das Bessere.
(c) it's a change for the ~ es ist eine Wendung zum Guten; **to think (all) the ~ of sb** (um so) mehr von jdm halten; **all the ~, so much the ~** um so besser; **it would be all the ~ for a drop of paint** ein bißchen Farbe würde Wunder wirken; **it's done now, for ~ or worse** so oder so, es ist geschehen; **for ~, for worse** (*in marriage ceremony*) in Freud und Leid; **to get the ~ of sb** (*person*) jdn unterkriegen (*inf*); (*illness*) jdn erwischen (*inf*); (*problem etc*) jdm schwer zu schaffen machen.
[4] *vt* (*improve on*) verbessern; (*surpass*) übertreffen.
[5] *vr* (*increase one's knowledge*) sich weiterbilden; (*in social scale*) sich verbessern.

better half *n* (*inf*) bessere Hälfte (*inf*).

betterment ['betəmənt] *n* **(a)** Verbesserung *f*; (*educational*) Weiterbildung *f*. **(b)** (*Jur*) Wertsteigerung *f*; (*of land*) Melioration *f*.

betting ['betɪŋ] *n* Wetten *nt* ◆ **the ~ was brisk** das Wettgeschäft war rege; **what is the ~ on his horse?** wie stehen die Wetten auf sein Pferd?

betting: ~ man *n* (regelmäßiger) Wetter; **I'm not a ~ man** ich wette eigentlich nicht; **if I were a ~ man I'd say ...** wenn ich ja wetten würde, würde ich sagen ...; **~ news** *n* Wettnachrichten *pl*; **~ shop** *n* Wettannahme *f*; **~ slip** *n* Wettschein *m*.

Betty ['betɪ] *n dim of* **Elizabeth**.

between [bɪ'twi:n] [1] *prep* **(a)** zwischen (+*dat*); (*with movement*) zwischen (+*acc*) ◆ **I was sitting ~ them** ich saß zwischen ihnen; **sit down ~ those two boys** setzen Sie sich zwischen diese beiden Jungen; **in ~** zwischen (+*dat/acc*); **~ now and next week we must ...** bis nächste Woche müssen wir ...; **there's nothing ~ them** (*they're equal*) sie sind gleich gut; (*no feelings, relationship*) zwischen ihnen ist nichts.
(b) (*amongst*) unter (+*dat/acc*) ◆ **divide the sweets ~ the two children/the children** teilen Sie die Süßigkeiten zwischen den beiden Kindern auf/verteilen Sie die Süßigkeiten unter die Kinder; **we shared an apple ~ us** wir teilten uns (*dat*) einen Apfel; **~ ourselves** *or* **~ you and me he is not very clever** unter uns (*dat*) (gesagt), er ist nicht besonders gescheit; **that's just ~ ourselves** das bleibt aber unter uns.
(c) (*jointly, showing combined effort*) **~ us/them** zusammen; **we have a car ~ the two/three of us** wir haben zu zweit/dritt ein Auto, wir zwei/drei haben zusammen ein Auto; **~ the two/three of us we have enough** zusammen haben wir (zwei/drei) genug; **we got the letter written ~ us** wir haben den Brief zusammen *or* gemeinsam *or* mit vereinten Kräften geschrieben.
(d) (*what with, showing combined effect*) neben (+*dat*) ◆ **~ housework and study I have no time for that** neben *or* zwischen Haushalt und Studium bleibt mir keine Zeit dazu.
[2] *adv* (*place*) dazwischen; (*time also*) zwischendurch ◆ **in ~** dazwischen; **the space/time ~** der Zwischenraum/die Zwischenzeit, der Raum/die Zeit dazwischen.

between: ~time, ~whiles *adv* in der Zwischenzeit.

betwixt [bɪ'twɪkst] [1] *prep* (*obs, liter, dial*) *see* **between**.
[2] *adv*: **~ and between** dazwischen.

bevel ['bevəl] [1] *n* Schräge, Schrägfläche, Abschrägung *f*; (*also* **~ edge**) abgeschrägte Kante, Schrägkante *f*; (*tool: also* **~ square**) Schrägmaß *nt*, Stellwinkel *m*.
[2] *vt* abschrägen, schräg abflachen ◆ **~led edge** Schrägkante *f*, abgeschrägte Kante; **~led mirror** Spiegel *m* mit schräggeschliffenen Kanten.

bevel gear *n* Kegelradgetriebe *nt*.

beverage ['bevərɪdʒ] *n* Getränk *nt*.

bevy ['bevɪ] *n* (*of birds*) Schwarm *m*; (*of girls also*) Schar *f*.

bewail [bɪ'weɪl] *vt* (*deplore*) beklagen; (*lament also*) bejammern; *sb's death also* betrauern.

▼ **beware** [bɪ'wɛə^r] *vti imper and infin only* **to ~ (of) sb/sth** sich vor jdm/etw hüten, sich vor jdm/etw in acht nehmen; **to ~ (of) doing sth** sich davor hüten, etw zu tun; **~ of falling** passen Sie auf *or* sehen Sie sich vor, daß Sie nicht fallen; **~ of being deceived, ~ lest you are deceived** (*old*) geben Sie acht *or* sehen Sie sich vor, daß Sie nicht betrogen werden; **~ (of) how you speak** geben Sie acht *or* sehen Sie sich vor, was Sie sagen; **~!** (*old, liter*) gib acht!; **"~ of the dog"** „Vorsicht, bissiger Hund"; **"~ of pickpockets"** „vor Taschendieben wird gewarnt".

bewigged [bɪ'wɪgd] *adj* mit Perücke, perücketragend *attr*.

bewilder [bɪ'wɪldə^r] *vt* (*confuse*) verwirren, irremachen; (*baffle*) verblüffen, verwundern.

bewildered [bɪ'wɪldəd] *adj see vt* verwirrt, durcheinander *pred* (*inf*); verblüfft, perplex (*inf*), verwundert.

bewildering [bɪ'wɪldərɪŋ] *adj see vt* verwirrend; verblüffend.

bewilderment [bɪ'wɪldəmənt] *n see vt* Verwirrung *f*; Verblüffung *f*, Erstaunen *nt* ◆ **in ~** verwundert; **his ~ was obvious** er war offensichtlich verwirrt/verblüfft.

bewitch [bɪ'wɪtʃ] *vt* verhexen, verzaubern; (*fig*) bezaubern.

bewitching *adj*, **~ly** *adv* [bɪ'wɪtʃɪŋ, -lɪ] bezaubernd, hinreißend.

beyond [bɪ'jɒnd] [1] *prep* **(a)** (*in space*) (*on the other side of*) über (+*dat*), jenseits (+*gen*) (*geh*); (*further than*) über (+*acc*) ... hinaus, weiter als ◆ **~ the Alps** jenseits der Alpen; **I saw peak ~ snow-capped peak** ich sah schneebedeckte Gipfel bis weit in die Ferne; **~ the convent walls** außerhalb der Klostermauern.
(b) (*in time*) **~ 6 o'clock/next week/the 17th century** nach 6 Uhr/nächster Woche/dem 17. Jahrhundert; **until ~ 6 o'clock/next week/the 17th century** bis nach 6 Uhr/bis über nächste Woche/das 17. Jahrhundert hinaus; **~ the middle of June/the week** über Mitte Juni/der Woche hinaus; **it's ~ your bedtime** es ist längst Zeit, daß du ins Bett kommst.
(c) (*surpassing, exceeding*) **a task ~ her abilities** eine Aufgabe, die über ihre Fähigkeiten geht, **it's ~ your authority** das liegt außerhalb Ihrer Befugnis; **that is ~ human understanding** das übersteigt menschliches Verständnis; **~ repair** nicht mehr zu reparieren; **it was ~ her to pass the exam** sie schaffte es nicht, das Examen zu bestehen; **that's ~ me** (*I don't understand*) das geht über meinen Verstand, das kapiere ich nicht (*inf*); *see* **compare, grave**[1], **help** *etc*.
(d) (*with neg, interrog*) außer ◆ **have you any money ~ what you have in the bank?** haben Sie außer dem, was Sie auf der Bank haben, noch Geld?; **~ this/that** sonst; **I've got nothing to suggest ~ this** sonst habe ich keine Vorschläge.
[2] *adv* (*on the other side of*) jenseits davon (*geh*); (*after that*) danach; (*further than that*) darüber hinaus, weiter ◆ **India and the lands ~** Indien und die Gegenden jenseits davon; **... a river, and ~ is a small field** ... ein Fluß, und danach kommt ein kleines Feld; **the world ~** das Jenseits.
[3] *n* **the great B~** das Jenseits; (*space*) der weite Raum.

BF (*euph*) *abbr of* **bloody fool**.

B/F, b/f *abbr of* **brought forward** Übertrag.

BFPO *abbr of* **British Forces Post Office**.

bhp *abbr of* **brake horsepower**.

bi- [baɪ] *pref* bi, Bi-.

Biafra [bɪ'æfrə] *n* Biafra *nt*.

Biafran [bɪ'æfrən] [1] *n* Biafraner(in *f*) *m*.
[2] *adj* Biafra-.

➤ LANGUAGE IN USE: **better**[2]: **1** → 1.1, 5.2, 7.4, 13 **2a** → 7.2, 7.4, 26.3 **2b** → 2.3 **beware** → 2.3

biannual *adj*, **~ly** *adv* [baɪ'ænjʊəl, -ɪ] zweimal jährlich; (*half-yearly*) halbjährlich.

bias ['baɪəs] (*vb: pret, ptp* **~(s)ed**) 1 *n* **(a)** (*inclination*) (*of course, newspaper etc*) (einseitige) Ausrichtung *f* (*towards* auf +*acc*); (*of person*) Vorliebe *f* (*towards* für) ◆ **to have a ~ against sth** (*course, newspaper etc*) gegen etw eingestellt sein; (*person*) eine Abneigung gegen etw haben; **to have a left-wing/right-wing ~** *or* **a ~ to the left/right** nach links/rechts ausgerichtet sein, einen Links-/Rechtsdrall haben (*inf*); **to be without ~** unvoreingenommen sein, ohne Vorurteile sein.
(b) (*Sew*) **on the ~** schräg zum Fadenlauf; **~ binding** Schrägband *nt or* -streifen *m*.
(c) (*Sport*) (*shape of bowl*) Überhang *m*.
2 *vt report, article etc* (einseitig) färben; (*towards sth*) ausrichten (*towards* auf +*acc*); *person* beeinflussen ◆ **he ~ed his article in favour of a historical approach to the problem** in seinem Artikel ging er das Problem eher aus historischer Sicht an; **to ~ sb towards/against sth** jdn für/gegen etw einnehmen.

bias(s)ed ['baɪəst] *adj* voreingenommen, befangen ◆ **... but then I'm ~** ... aber ich bin natürlich voreingenommen *or* befangen.

biathlon [baɪ'æθlən] *n* Biathlon *nt*.

bib [bɪb] *n* **(a)** (*for baby*) Latz *m*, Lätzchen *nt*. **(b)** (*on garment*) Latz *m*. **(c)** (*inf*) **in one's best ~ and tucker** in Schale (*inf*); **she put on her best ~ and tucker** sie warf sich in Schale (*inf*).

Bible ['baɪbl] *n* Bibel *f*; (*fig also*) Evangelium *nt*.

Bible: ~ basher *n* (*inf*) Jesusjünger(in *f*) *m* (*sl*); **~-bashing** *adj* (*inf*) **her ~-bashing father** ihr Vater, der fanatisch auf die Bibel schwört/schwörte; **~ class** *n* Bibelstunde *f*; **~ school** *n* (*US*) Bibelschule *f*; **~ story** *n* biblische Geschichte; **~ thumper** *n* (*inf*) Halleluja-Billy *m* (*sl*).

biblical ['bɪblɪkəl] *adj* biblisch, Bibel-.

bibliographer [,bɪblɪ'ɒgrəfəʳ] *n* Bibliograph *m*.

bibliographic(al) [,bɪblɪəʊ'græfɪk(əl)] *adj* bibliographisch.

bibliography [,bɪblɪ'ɒgrəfɪ] *n* Bibliographie *f*.

bibliomania [,bɪblɪəʊ'meɪnɪə] *n* Bibliomanie *f*.

bibliophile ['bɪblɪəʊfaɪl] *n* Bibliophile(r) *mf*, Büchernarr *m*.

bibulous ['bɪbjʊləs] *adj* (*form*) *person* trunksüchtig.

bicameral [baɪ'kæmərəl] *adj* (*Pol*) Zweikammer-.

bicarbonate of soda [baɪ,kɑːbənɪtəv'səʊdə] *n* (*Cook*) Natron *nt*; (*Chem*) doppelt kohlensaures Natrium.

bicentenary *or* (*US*) **~centennial** 1 *n* zweihundertjähriges Jubiläum, Zweihundertjahrfeier *f* (*of gen*); **the ~ of Beethoven's birth/death** Beethovens zweihundertster Geburts-/Todestag.
2 *adj* Zweihundertjahr-, zweihundertjährig; *celebrations* Zweihundertjahr-.

bicephalous [baɪ'sefələs] *adj* (*spec*) dizephal (*spec*), bikephalisch (*spec*).

biceps ['baɪseps] *n* Bizeps *m*.

bichromate [baɪ'krəʊmɪt] *n* Bichromat *nt*.

bicker ['bɪkəʳ] *vi* (*quarrel*) sich zanken, aneinandergeraten ◆ **they are always ~ing** sie liegen sich dauernd in den Haaren.

bickering ['bɪkərɪŋ] *n* Gezänk *nt*.

bicuspid [baɪ'kʌspɪd] 1 *adj* mit zwei Spitzen, zweihöckrig, bikuspidal (*spec*).
2 *n* (*Anat*) vorderer Backenzahn.

bicycle ['baɪsɪkl] 1 *n* Fahrrad *nt* ◆ **to ride a ~** Fahrrad fahren, radfahren; **~ kick** (*Ftbl*) Fallrückzieher *m*.
2 *vi* mit dem (Fahr)rad fahren.

bicycle *in cpds see* **cycle** *in cpds*.

bid [bɪd] 1 *vt* **(a)** *pret, ptp* ~ (*at auction*) bieten (*for* auf +*acc*).
(b) *pret, ptp* ~ (*Cards*) reizen, bieten.
(c) *pret* **bade** *or* **bad**, *ptp* **~den** (*say*) **to ~ sb good-morning** jdm einen guten Morgen wünschen; **to ~ farewell to sb, to ~ sb farewell** von jdm Abschied nehmen, jdm Lebewohl sagen (*geh*); **to ~ sb welcome** jdn willkommen heißen.
(d) *pret* **bade** *or* **bad**, *ptp* **~den to ~ sb to do sth** (*old, liter*) jdn etw tun heißen (*old*).
2 *vi* **(a)** *pret, ptp* ~ (*at auction*) bieten. **(b)** *pret, ptp* ~ (*Cards*) bieten, reizen. **(c)** *pret* **bad**, *ptp* **~den to ~ fair to** ... versprechen zu ...; **everything ~s fair to be successful** es sieht alles recht erfolgversprechend aus.
3 *n* **(a)** (*at auction*) Gebot *nt* (*for* auf +*acc*); (*Comm*) Angebot *nt* (*for* für).
(b) (*Cards*) Ansage *f*, Gebot *nt* ◆ **to raise the ~** höher bieten *or* reizen, überrufen; **to make no ~** passen; **no ~!** passe!
(c) (*attempt*) Versuch *m* ◆ **to make a ~ for power** nach der Macht greifen; **to make a ~ for fame/freedom** versuchen, Ruhm/die Freiheit zu erlangen; **his ~ for fame/freedom failed** sein Versuch, Ruhm/die Freiheit zu erlangen, scheiterte; **rescue ~ fails** Rettungsversuch erfolglos; **the ~ for the summit** der Griff nach dem Gipfel.

biddable ['bɪdəbl] *adj* (*liter*) fügsam, willfährig (*geh*).

bidden ['bɪdn] *ptp of* **bid**.

bidder ['bɪdəʳ] *n* Bietende(r) *mf*, Steigerer *m* ◆ **to sell to the highest ~** an den Höchst- *or* Meistbietenden verkaufen; **there were no ~s** niemand hat geboten *or* ein Gebot gemacht.

bidding ['bɪdɪŋ] *n* **(a)** (*at auction*) Steigern, Bieten *nt* ◆ **how high did the ~ go?** wie hoch wurde gesteigert?; **to raise the ~** den Preis in die Höhe treiben; **the ~ is closed** es werden keine Gebote mehr angenommen, keine Gebote mehr.
(b) (*Cards*) Bieten, Reizen *nt*.
(c) (*order*) Geheiß (*old*), Gebot *nt* ◆ **at whose ~?** auf wessen Geheiß? (*old*); **the slave does his master's ~** der Sklave tut, was sein Herr ihn heißt (*old*) *or* ihm befiehlt; **he needed no second ~** man mußte es ihm nicht zweimal sagen.

biddy ['bɪdɪ] *n* (*inf*) (*hen*) Huhn *nt*, Henne *f*; (*old lady*) Muttchen (*inf*), Tantchen (*inf*) *nt*.

bide [baɪd] *vt* **to ~ one's time** den rechten Augenblick abwarten *or* abpassen; **to ~ awhile** (*old*) verweilen (*geh*).

bidet ['biːdeɪ] *n* Bidet *nt*.

bidirectional [,baɪdɪ'rekʃənəl] *adj* (*Comput*) *printing* bidirektional.

biennial [baɪ'enɪəl] 1 *adj* (*every two years*) zweijährlich; (*rare: lasting two years*) zweijährig.
2 *n* (*Bot*) zweijährige Pflanze.

biennially [baɪ'enɪəlɪ] *adv* zweijährlich, alle zwei Jahre; (*Bot*) bienn.

bier [bɪəʳ] *n* Bahre *f*.

biff [bɪf] 1 *n* (*inf*) Stoß, Puff (*inf*) *m* ◆ **a ~ on the nose** eins auf die Nase (*inf*); **my car got a bit of a ~** mein Auto hat ein bißchen was abgekriegt (*inf*).
2 *interj* bums.
3 *vt* (*inf*) *car* eine Beule fahren in (+*acc*); *door* anschlagen; *lamppost* bumsen an (+*acc*) *or* gegen (*inf*) ◆ **he ~ed the door against the wall** er hat die Tür gegen die Wand geschlagen; **to ~ sb on the nose** jdm eins auf die Nase geben (*inf*).

bifocal [baɪ'fəʊkəl] 1 *adj* Bifokal-.
2 *n* **~s** *pl* Bifokalbrille *f*.

bifurcate ['baɪfɜːkeɪt] 1 *vi* (*form*) sich gabeln.
2 *adj* gegabelt.

bifurcation [,baɪfɜː'keɪʃən] *n* Gabelung *f*.

big [bɪg] 1 *adj* (+*er*) **(a)** (*in size, amount*) groß; *lie also* faustdick (*inf*) ◆ **a ~ man** ein großer, schwerer Mann; **she's a ~ girl** (*inf*) sie hat einen ganz schönen Vorbau (*inf*); **5 ~ ones** (*sl*) 5 Riesen (*sl*); **~ with child/young** hochschwanger/trächtig.
(b) (*of age*) groß ◆ **my ~ brother** mein großer Bruder; **you're ~ enough to know better** du bist groß *or* alt genug und solltest es besser wissen.
(c) (*important*) groß, wichtig ◆ **the B~ Four/Five** die Großen Vier/Fünf; **to look ~** (*inf*) ein bedeutendes Gesicht machen.
(d) (*conceited*) **~ talk** Angeberei (*inf*), Großspurigkeit *f*; **~ talker** Angeber (*inf*), Maulheld (*inf*) *m*, eingebildeter Schwätzer; **he's getting too ~ for his boots** (*inf*) (*child*) er wird ein bißchen zu aufmüpfig (*inf*); (*employee*) er wird langsam größenwahnsinnig; **to have a ~ head** (*inf*) eingebildet sein.
(e) (*generous, iro*) großzügig, nobel (*inf*); (*forgiving*) großmütig, nobel (*inf*); *heart* groß ◆ **few people have a heart as ~ as his** es sind nur wenige so großzügig/großmütig wie er; **that's really ~ of you** (*iro*) wirklich nobel von dir (*iro*).
(f) (*inf: fashionable*) in (*inf*).
(g) (*fig phrases*) **to earn ~ money** das große Geld verdienen (*inf*); **to have ~ ideas** große Pläne haben, Rosinen im Kopf haben (*pej inf*); **to have a ~ mouth** (*inf*) eine große Klappe haben (*inf*); **to do things in a ~ way** alles im großen (Stil) tun *or* betreiben; **to live in a ~ way** auf großem Fuß *or* in großem Stil leben; **what's the ~ idea?** (*inf*) was soll denn das? (*inf*); **~ deal!** (*iro inf*) na und? (*inf*); (*that's not much etc*) das ist ja ergreifend! (*iro*); **what's the ~ hurry?** warum denn so eilig?; **our company is ~ on service** (*inf*) unsere Firma ist ganz groß in puncto Kundendienst.
2 *adv* **to talk ~** groß daherreden (*inf*), große Töne spucken (*sl*); **to act ~** sich aufspielen, großtun; **to think ~** im großen (Maßstab) planen; **to go over** *or* **down ~** (*inf*) ganz groß ankommen (*inf*), großen Anklang finden (*with* bei).

bigamist ['bɪgəmɪst] *n* Bigamist *m*.

bigamous ['bɪgəməs] *adj* bigamistisch.

bigamy ['bɪgəmɪ] *n* Bigamie *f*.

big: B~ Apple *n*: **the B~ Apple** (*inf*) New York *nt*; **~ band** 1 *n* Big Band *f*; 2 *adj attr* Big-Band-; **~ bang** *n* (*Astron*) Urknall *m*; **~ bang theory** Urknalltheorie *f*; **B~ Bang** *n* (*Brit St Ex*) Big Bang *m*, *Tag der Umstellung der Londoner Börse auf Computerbetrieb*; **B~ Ben** *n* Big Ben *m*; **B~ Bertha** *n* die Dicke Berta; **~-boned** *adj* breit- *or* grobknochig; **B~ Brother** *n* der Große Bruder; **~ bug** *n* (*inf*) hohes Tier (*inf*); **~ business** *n* **(a)** (*high finance*) Großkapital *nt*, Hochfinanz *f*; **to be ~ business** das große Geschäft sein; **(b)** (*baby-talk*) großes Geschäft (*baby-talk*); **~ dipper** *n* **(a)** (*Brit: at fair*) Achterbahn, Berg-und-Talbahn *f*; **(b)** (*US Astron*) **B~ Dipper** Großer Bär *or* Wagen; **~ end** *n* (*Tech*) Pleuelfuß, Schubstangenkopf *m*; **~ game** *n* (*Hunt*) Großwild *nt*; **~ game hunter** *n* Großwildjäger *m*; **~head** *n* (*inf: person*) Angeber *m* (*inf*), eingebildeter Fatzke (*sl*); **~-headed** *adj* (*inf*) eingebildet, angeberisch (*inf*); **~-hearted** *adj* großherzig, großmütig; (*forgiving*) weitherzig.

bight [baɪt] *n* (*Geog*) Bucht *f*.

big: ~mouth *n* (*inf*) Großmaul *nt* (*sl*), Angeber *m* (*inf*); (*blabbermouth*) Schwätzer *m* (*pej*), Klatschbase *f* (*inf*); **~ name** *n* (*inf: person*) Größe *f* (*in gen*); **all the ~ names were there** alles, was Rang und Namen hat, war da; **~ noise** *n* (*inf*) hohes Tier (*inf*).

bigot ['bɪgət] *n* Eiferer *m*; (*Rel also*) bigotter Mensch.

bigoted *adj*, **~ly** *adv* ['bɪgətɪd, -lɪ] eifernd; (*Rel*) bigott.

bigotry ['bɪgətrɪ] *n* eifernde Borniertheit; (*Rel*) Bigotterie *f*.

big: ~ shot *n* hohes Tier (*inf*); **he thinks he is a ~ shot in his new Jag** (*inf*) er hält sich mit seinem neuen Jaguar für den Größten (*inf*); **~-ticket** *adj attr* (*US*) **-ticket item** teure Anschaffung; **~-time** 1 *adj* (*inf*) **one of the ~-time boys** eine ganz große Nummer (*inf*); **a ~-time politician** eine große Nummer (*inf*) in der Politik; 2 *n* (*inf*) **to make** *or* **hit the ~-time** groß einsteigen (*inf*); **once he'd had a taste of the ~-time** nachdem er einmal ganz oben *or* groß gewesen war; ~ **toe** *n* große Zehe; ~ **top** *n* (*circus*) Zirkus *m*; (*main tent*) Hauptzelt *nt*; ~ **wheel** *n* **(a)** (*US inf*) *see* ~ **shot; (b)** (*Brit: at fair*) Riesenrad *nt*; **~wig** *n* (*inf*) hohes Tier (*inf*); **the local ~wigs** die Honoratioren des Ortes.

bijou [biːˈʒuː] *adj* (*esp in advertising*) ~ **residence** nettes kleines Haus/nette kleine Wohnung.

bike [baɪk] (*inf*) [1] *n* (Fahr)rad *nt*; (*motor~*) Motorrad *nt*, Maschine (*inf*) *f* ◆ **on your ~!** (*Brit sl: clear off*) verschwinde! (*inf*), mach (ʼne) Mücke! (*sl*). [2] *vi* radeln (*inf*).

bike *in cpds see* **cycle** *in cpds.*

biker [ˈbaɪkəʳ] *n* (*inf*) Motorradfahrer *m*; (*gang member*) Rocker *m*.

bikeway [ˈbaɪkweɪ] *n* (*US*) (Fahr)radweg *m*.

bikini [bɪˈkiːnɪ] *n* Bikini *m*.

bi-: ~labial [1] *n* Bilabial *m*; [2] *adj* bilabial; **~lateral** *adj*, **~laterally** *adv* bilateral.

bilberry [ˈbɪlbərɪ] *n* Heidelbeere, Blaubeere *f*.

bile [baɪl] *n* **(a)** (*Med*) Galle *f* ◆ ~ **stone** Gallenstein *m*. **(b)** (*fig: anger*) Übellaunigkeit *f* ◆ **a man full of** ~ ein Griesgram *m*.

bilge [bɪldʒ] *n* **(a)** (*Naut*) Bilge *f*. **(b)** (*also* ~ **water**) Leckwasser *nt*. **(c)** (*of cask*) (Faß)bauch *m*. **(d)** (*Brit inf: nonsense*) Quatsch (*inf*), Mumpitz (*dated inf*) *m* ◆ **to talk** ~ Unsinn verzapfen (*inf*). **(e)** (*Sch sl: biology*) Bio *no art*.

bilharzia [bɪlˈhɑːzɪə] *n* Bilharziose *f*.

bi-: ~linear *adj* bilinear; **~lingual** *adj*, **~lingually** *adv* zweisprachig; **~lingualism** *n* Zweisprachigkeit *f*; **~lingual secretary** *n* Fremdsprachensekretärin *f*.

bilious [ˈbɪlɪəs] *adj* **(a)** (*Med*) Gallen- ◆ ~ **attack** Gallenkolik *f*. **(b)** (*irritable*) reizbar ◆ **he is very** ~ ihm läuft immer gleich die Galle über (*inf*). **(c)** (*sickly*) *colour* widerlich ◆ **you're looking a bit** ~ Sie sind ein bißchen grün um die Nase (*inf*).

biliousness [ˈbɪlɪəsnɪs] *n see adj* Gallenkrankheit *f*, Gallenleiden *nt*; Reizbarkeit *f*; Widerlichkeit *f*.

bilk [bɪlk] *vt creditor* prellen (*of* um); *debt* nicht bezahlen.

bill[1] [bɪl] [1] *n* **(a)** (*of bird, turtle*) Schnabel *m*. **(b)** (*Geog*) Landzunge *f*. [2] *vi* (*bird*) schnäbeln ◆ **to ~ and coo** (*birds*) schnäbeln und gurren; (*fig: people*) (miteinander) turteln.

bill[2] *n* (*tool*) *see* **~hook**.

bill[3] [1] *n* **(a)** (*esp Brit: statement of charges*) Rechnung *f* ◆ **could we have the ~ please** zahlen bitte!, wir möchten bitte zahlen.

(b) (*US: banknote*) Banknote *f*, Schein *m* ◆ **five-dollar** ~ Fünfdollarschein *m* *or* -note *f*.

(c) (*poster*) Plakat *nt*; (*on notice board*) Anschlag *m*; (*public announcement*) Aushang *m* ◆ **"stick no ~s"** „Plakate ankleben verboten".

(d) (*Theat: programme*) Programm *nt* ◆ **to head** *or* **top the ~, to be top of the ~** Star *m* des Abends/der Saison sein; (*act*) die Hauptattraktion sein.

(e) ~ **of fare** Speisekarte *f*.

(f) (*Parl*) (Gesetz)entwurf *m*, (Gesetzes)vorlage *f* ◆ **the ~ was passed** das Gesetz wurde verabschiedet.

(g) (*esp Comm, Fin: certificate, statement*) ~ **of health** (*Naut*) Gesundheitsattest *nt*; **to give sb a clean ~ of health** (*lit, fig*) jdm (gute) Gesundheit bescheinigen; ~ **of lading** (*Naut*) Seefrachtbrief *m*, Konnossement *nt*; ~ **of exchange** Wechsel *m*, Tratte *f*; ~ **of sale** Verkaufsurkunde *f*; **to fit** *or* **fill the ~** (*fig*) der/die/das richtige sein, passen; **B~ of Rights** (*Brit*) Bill *f* of Rights; (*US*) *Zusatzklauseln 1-10 zu den Grundrechten*.

(h) (*Jur*) ~ **of attainder** (*Brit Hist*) *Anklage und Urteil gegen politische Persönlichkeiten in Form eines Gesetzes*; (*US*) *unmittelbare Bestrafung einer Person durch den Gesetzgeber*; ~ **of indictment** Anklageschrift *f*.

[2] *vt* **(a)** *customers* eine Rechnung ausstellen (+*dat*) ◆ **we won't ~ you for that, sir** (*give free*) wir werden Ihnen das nicht berechnen *or* in Rechnung stellen (*form*). **(b)** *play, actor* ankündigen. **he's ~ed at the King's Theatre** er soll im King's Theatre auftreten.

Bill [bɪl] *n dim of* **William**.

billboard [ˈbɪlbɔːd] *n* Reklametafel *f*.

billet [ˈbɪlɪt] [1] *n* **(a)** (*Mil*) (*document*) Quartierschein *m*; (*accommodation*) Quartier *nt*, Unterkunft *f*. **(b)** (*fig inf*) **to have a soft** *or* **cushy** ~ einen schlauen Posten haben.

[2] *vt* (*Mil*) *soldier* einquartieren (*on sb* bei jdm) ◆ **troops were ~ed on** *or* **in our town** in unserer Stadt wurden/waren Truppen einquartiert.

billet-doux [bɪleɪˈduː] *n* Liebesbrief *m*, Billetdoux *nt* (*old*).

billeting [ˈbɪlɪtɪŋ] *n* (*Mil*) Einquartierung *f* ◆ ~ **officer** Quartiermeister *m*.

bill: ~fold *n* (*US*) Brieftasche *f*; **~head** *n* (*heading*) Rechnungskopf *m*; (*sheet*) Rechnungsformular *nt*; **~hook** *n* Hippe *f*.

billiard [ˈbɪljəd] *adj attr* Billard- ◆ ~ **ball** Billardkugel *f*; ~ **cue** Queue *nt*, Billardstock *m*.

billiards [ˈbɪljədz] *n* Billard *nt* ◆ **to have a game of** ~ Billard spielen.

billing [ˈbɪlɪŋ] *n* (*Theat*) **to get top/second** ~ an erster/zweiter Stelle auf dem Programm stehen.

billion [ˈbɪljən] *n* (*Brit*) Billion *f*; (*esp US*) Milliarde *f* ◆ **~s of ...** (*inf*) Tausende von ...

billionaire [ˈbɪljənɛəʳ] *n* (*esp US*) Milliardär(in *f*) *m*.

billionth [ˈbɪljənθ] [1] *adj* (*Brit*) billionste(r, s); (*esp US*) milliardste(r, s). [2] *n* (*Brit*) Billionstel *nt*; (*esp US*) Milliardstel *nt*.

billow [ˈbɪləʊ] [1] *n* **(a)** (*liter: of sea*) Woge *f* (*geh*). **(b)** (*fig: of dress etc*) Bauschen *nt no pl*; (*of sail*) Blähen *nt no pl*; (*of smoke*) Schwaden *m*.

[2] *vi* **(a)** (*liter: sea*) wogen (*geh*). **(b)** (*fig: sail*) sich blähen; (*dress etc*) sich bauschen.

◆**billow out** *vi* (*sail etc*) sich blähen; (*dress etc*) sich bauschen.

billowy [ˈbɪləʊɪ] *adj* **(a)** (*liter*) *sea* wogend (*geh*). **(b)** *sails, curtains etc* gebläht; *smoke* in Schwaden ziehend.

bill: ~ poster, ~sticker *n* Plakat(an)kleber *m*.

Billy [ˈbɪlɪ] *n dim of* **William**.

billy(-can) [ˈbɪlɪ(kæn)] *n* Kochgeschirr *nt*.

billy(-goat) [ˈbɪlɪ(gəʊt)] *n* Ziegenbock *m*.

billy-(h)o [ˈbɪlɪhəʊ] *n* (*inf*) **like** ~ wie verrückt (*inf*).

bimbo [ˈbɪmbəʊ] *n* (*pej inf: attractive brainless female*) Puppe *f* (*inf*), Häschen *nt* (*inf*).

bi-: ~metallic *adj* **(a)** *rod, bar* Bimetall-; **(b)** (*Fin*) **~metallic currency** Doppelwährung *f*; **~metallism** *n* (*Fin*) Doppelwährung *f*; **~monthly** [1] *adj* **(a)** (*twice a month*) vierzehntäglich; **(b)** (*every two months*) zweimonatlich; [2] *adv* **(a)** zweimal monatlich *or* im Monat; **(b)** alle zwei Monate, jeden zweiten Monat.

bin [bɪn] *n* **(a)** (*esp Brit*) (*for bread*) Brotkasten *m*; (*for coal*) (Kohlen)kasten *m*; (*rubbish ~*) Mülleimer *m*; (*dust~*) Mülltonne *f*; (*litter-~*) Abfallbehälter *m*. **(b)** (*for grain*) Tonne *f*.

binary [ˈbaɪnərɪ] *adj* binär; (*Mus*) *form* zweiteilig ◆ ~ **code** (*Comput*) Binärcode *m*; ~ **fission** Zellteilung *f*; ~ **number** (*Math*) Dualzahl *f*, binäre Zahl; ~ **system** (*Math*) Dualsystem, binäres System; ~ **star/~ star system** (*Astron*) Doppelstern *m*/Doppelsternsystem *nt*.

bind [baɪnd] *pret, ptp* **bound** [1] *vt* **(a)** (*make fast, tie together*) binden (*to* an +*acc*); *person* fesseln; (*fig*) verbinden (*to* mit) ◆ **bound hand and foot** an Händen und Füßen gefesselt *or* gebunden; **the emotions which ~ her to him** ihre emotionale Bindung an ihn.

(b) (*tie round*) *wound, arm etc* verbinden; *bandage* wickeln, binden; *artery* abbinden; (*for beauty*) *waist* einschnüren; *feet* einbinden *or* -schnüren; *hair* binden.

(c) (*secure edge of*) *material, hem* einfassen.

(d) *book* binden.

(e) (*oblige: by contract, promise*) **to ~ sb to sth/to do sth** jdn an etw (*acc*) binden, jdn zu etw verpflichten/jdn verpflichten, etw zu tun; **to ~ sb as an apprentice** jdn in die Lehre geben (*to* zu); *see* **bound**[3].

(f) (*Med*) *bowels* verstopfen.

(g) (*make cohere, Cook*) binden.

[2] *vi* **(a)** (*cohere: cement etc*) binden ◆ **stop the soil ~ing by adding some compost** lockern Sie den Boden mit Kompost; **the clay soil tended to** ~ der Lehmboden war ziemlich schwer *or* klebte ziemlich; **the grass should help the soil** ~ das Gras sollte den Boden festigen.

(b) (*Med: food*) stopfen.

(c) (*stick: brake, sliding part etc*) blockieren.

[3] *n* (*inf*) **in a** ~ in der Klemme (*inf*); **to be (a bit of) a** ~ recht lästig sein.

◆**bind on** *vt sep* anbinden (+*prep obj*, -*to* an +*acc*); (+*prep obj: on top of*) binden auf (+*acc*).

◆**bind over** *vt sep* (*Jur*) **to ~ sb ~ (to keep the peace)** jdn verwarnen; **he was bound ~ for six months** er bekam eine sechsmonatige Bewährungsfrist.

◆**bind together** *vt sep* (*lit*) zusammenbinden; (*fig*) verbinden.

◆**bind up** *vt sep* **(a)** *wound* verbinden; *hair* hochbinden. **(b)** *prisoner* fesseln. **(c)** (*fig*) verknüpfen, verbinden ◆ **to be bound** ~ (*with one another*) verbunden *or* verknüpft sein.

binder [ˈbaɪndəʳ] *n* **(a)** (*Agr*) (*machine*) (Mäh)binder, Bindemäher *m*; (*person*) (Garben)binder(in *f*) *m*. **(b)** (*Typ*) (*person*) Buchbinder(in *f*) *m*; (*machine*) Bindemaschine *f*. **(c)** (*for papers*) Hefter *m*; (*for magazines also*) Mappe *f*.

bindery [ˈbaɪndərɪ] *n* Buchbinderei *f*.

binding [ˈbaɪndɪŋ] [1] *n* **(a)** (*of book*) Einband *m*; (*act*) Binden *nt*. **(b)** (*Sew*) Band *nt*. **(c)** (*on skis*) Bindung *f*.

[2] *adj* **(a)** *agreement, promise* bindend, verbindlich (*on* für). **(b)** (*Tech*) bindend, Binde-. **(c)** (*Med*) *food etc* stopfend.

bindweed [ˈbaɪndwiːd] *n* Winde *f*.

binge [bɪndʒ] (*inf*) [1] *n* Gelage, Sauf-/Freßgelage (*sl*) *nt* ◆ **to go on a** ~ auf eine Sauftour (*sl*) gehen/eine Freßtour (*sl*) machen.

[2] *vi* auf eine Sauf-/Freßtour (*sl*) gehen ◆ **you'll have to stop ~ing** du mußt mit diesen Sauf-/Freßgelagen (*sl*) aufhören.

bingo [ˈbɪŋgəʊ] *n* Bingo *nt*.

bin liner *n* Mülltüte *f*.

binnacle [ˈbɪnəkl] *n* Kompaßhaus *nt*.

binoculars [bɪˈnɒkjʊləz] *npl* Fernglas *nt* ◆ **a pair of** ~ ein Fernglas *nt*.

bi-: ~nominal [1] *adj* (*Math*) binomisch; [2] *n* Binom *nt*; **~nuclear** *adj* binuklear, zweikernig.

bio- [baɪəʊ-]: **~chemical** *adj* biochemisch; **~chemist** *n* Biochemiker(in *f*) *m*; **~chemistry** *n* Biochemie *f*; **~degradable** *adj* biologisch abbaubar; **~diversity** *n* Biodiversität *f*, Artenvielfalt *f*; **~engineering** *n* Biotechnik *f*; **~feedback** *n* Biofeedback *nt*; **~genesis** *n* Biogenese *f*.

biographer [baɪˈɒgrəfəʳ] *n* Biograph(in *f*) *m*.

biographic(al) [ˌbaɪəʊˈgræfɪk(əl)] *adj* biographisch.

biography [baɪˈɒgrəfɪ] *n* Biographie, Lebensbeschreibung *f*.

biological [ˌbaɪəˈlɒdʒɪkəl] *adj* biologisch ◆ ~ **clock** biologische Uhr; ~ **detergent** Bio-Waschmittel *nt*; ~ **diversity** *see* **biodiversity**.

biologist [baɪˈɒlədʒɪst] *n* Biologe *m*, Biologin *f*.

biology [baɪˈɒlədʒɪ] *n* Biologie *f*.

biometrics [baɪəˈmetrɪks], **biometry** [baɪˈɒmətrɪ] *n* Biometrie *f*.

bionic [baɪˈɒnɪk] *adj* bionisch.

bio: ~physical *adj* biophysikalisch; **~physics** *n* Biophysik *f*.

biopic [ˈbaɪəʊˌpɪk] *n* (*inf*) Filmbiographie *f*.

biopsy [ˈbaɪɒpsɪ] *n* Biopsie *f*.

bio-: ~rhythm *n usu pl* Biorhythmus *m usu sing;* **~sphere** *n* Biosphäre *f;* **~synthesis** *n* Biosynthese *f;* **~technology** *n* Biotechnik *f.*
bipartisan [ˌbaɪpɑːtɪˈzæn] *adj* Zweiparteien-.
bi-: ~partite *adj* zweiteilig; (*affecting two parties*) zweiseitig; **~ped** [1] *n* Zweifüßer *m;* (*hum: human*) Zweibeiner *m;* [2] *adj* zweifüßig; **~plane** *n* Doppeldecker *m;* **~polar** *adj* zwei- *or* doppelpolig.
birch [bɜːtʃ] [1] *n* **(a)** Birke *f.* **(b)** (*for whipping*) Rute *f.*
[2] *attr* Birken-.
[3] *vt* (mit Ruten) schlagen.
birching [ˈbɜːtʃɪŋ] *n* (*act*) Prügeln *nt;* (*Jur*) Prügelstrafe *f* ◆ **to get a ~** mit der Rute geschlagen werden.
bird [bɜːd] *n* **(a)** Vogel *m* ◆ **~ of paradise/passage** (*lit, fig*) Paradies-/Zugvogel *m;* **the ~ has flown** (*fig*) der Vogel ist ausgeflogen; **a little ~ told me** (*inf*) das sagt mir mein kleiner Finger; **strictly for the ~s** (*sl*) das ist geschenkt (*inf*); **a ~ in the hand is worth two in the bush** (*Prov*) der Spatz in der Hand ist besser als die Taube auf dem Dach (*Prov*); **to tell sb about the ~s and the bees** jdm erzählen, wo die kleinen Kinder herkommen; *see* **feather, kill.**
(b) (*Cook*) Vogel *m* (*hum inf*).
(c) (*Brit inf: girl*) Biene *f* (*inf*).
(d) (*inf: person*) Vogel *m* (*inf*) ◆ **he's a cunning old ~** er ist ein alter Fuchs.
(e) (*inf*) **to give sb the ~** jdn auspfeifen; **to get the ~** ausgepfiffen werden.
(f) (*Brit sl: prison term*) Knast *m* (*inf*) ◆ **to do ~** sitzen (*inf*).
bird: ~ bath *n* Vogelbad *nt;* **~ box** *n* Vogelhäuschen *nt;* **~ brain** *n* (*inf*) **to be a ~ brain** ein Spatzenhirn haben (*inf*); **~-cage** *n* Vogelbauer *nt or* -käfig *m;* **~ call** *n* Vogelruf *m;* **~ dog** (*US*) [1] *n* (*lit, fig*) Spürhund *m;* [2] *vt* (*inf*) beschatten (*inf*); **~ fancier** *n* Vogelzüchter *m;* **~ house** *n* Vogelhäuschen *nt.*
birdie [ˈbɜːdɪ] *n* **(a)** (*inf*) Vögelchen *nt* ◆ **watch the ~** gleich kommt's Vögelchen raus! **(b)** (*Golf*) Birdie *nt.*
bird: ~-like *adj* vogelartig; **~lime** *n* Vogelleim *m;* **~ sanctuary** *n* Vogelschutzgebiet *nt;* **~seed** *n* Vogelfutter *nt.*
bird's: ~-eye view *n* Vogelperspektive *f;* **to get a ~-eye view of the town** die Stadt aus der Vogelperspektive sehen; **~ foot** *n* Vogelfuß *m.*
birdshot [ˈbɜːdʃɒt] *n* feiner Schrot.
bird's: ~ nest *n* Vogelnest *nt;* **~-nest** *vi* **to go ~-nesting** Vogelnester ausnehmen; **~ nest soup** *n* Schwalben- *or* Vogelnestersuppe *f.*
bird: ~ table *n* Futterplatz *m* (*für Vögel*); **~ watcher** *n* Vogelbeobachter(in *f*) *m.*
biretta [bɪˈretə] *n* Birett *nt.*
Biro ® [ˈbaɪərəʊ] *n* (*Brit*) Kugelschreiber, Kuli (*inf*) *m.*
▼ **birth** [bɜːθ] *n* **(a)** Geburt *f* ◆ **the town/country of his ~** seine Geburtsstadt/sein Geburtsland *nt;* **deaf from** *or* **since ~** von Geburt an taub; **within a few minutes of ~** einige Minuten nach der Geburt; **the rights which are ours by ~** unsere angeborenen Rechte; **to give ~ to** gebären; (*woman also*) entbunden werden von; **to give ~** entbinden; (*animal*) jungen; **she's going to give ~!** sie bekommt ihr Kind!
(b) (*parentage*) Abstammung, Herkunft *f* ◆ **Scottish by ~** Schotte von Geburt, gebürtiger Schotte; **of good/low** *or* **humble ~** aus gutem Hause *or* guter Familie/von niedriger Geburt.
(c) (*fig*) Geburt *f;* (*of movement, fashion etc*) Aufkommen *nt;* (*of nation, party, company also*) Gründung *f,* Entstehen *nt;* (*of new era*) Anbruch *m,* Geburt *f* (*geh*); (*of star*) Entstehung *f* ◆ **to give ~ to sth** etw schaffen/aufkommen lassen/gründen/anbrechen lassen.
birth: ~ certificate *n* Geburtsurkunde *f;* **~ control** *n* Geburtenkontrolle *or* -regelung *f;* **~-control clinic** *n* Familienberatungsstelle *f;* **~date** *n* Geburtsdatum *nt.*
▼ **birthday** [ˈbɜːθdeɪ] *n* Geburtstag *m* ◆ **what did you get for your ~?** was hast du zum Geburtstag bekommen?; **on my ~** an meinem Geburtstag; *see* **happy.**
birthday: ~ cake *n* Geburtstagskuchen *m or* -torte *f;* **~ card** *n* Geburtstagskarte *f;* **~ celebrations** *npl* Geburtstagsfeierlichkeiten *pl;* **~ honours** *npl* Titel- und Ordensverleihungen *pl am offiziellen Geburtstag des britischen Monarchen;* **~ party** *n* Geburtstagsfeier *f;* (*with dancing etc*) Geburtstagsparty *f;* (*for child*) Kindergeburtstag *m;* **~ present** *n* Geburtstagsgeschenk *nt;* **~ suit** *n* (*inf*) Adams-/Evaskostüm *nt* (*inf*); **the little boy in his ~ suit** der kleine Nackedei; **in one's ~ suit** im Adams-/Evaskostüm (*inf*).
birthing [ˈbɜːθɪŋ]: **~ centre,** (*US*) **~ center** *n* Geburtshaus *nt;* **~ pool** *n* Entbindungsbadewanne *f;* **~ stool** *n* Gebärstuhl *m.*
birth: ~mark *n* Muttermal *nt;* **~ mother** *n* (*biological mother*) biologische Mutter; (*surrogate mother*) Leihmutter *f;* **~place** *n* Geburtsort *m;* **~rate** *n* Geburtenrate *or* -ziffer *f;* **~right** *n* **(a)** Geburtsrecht *nt;* **(b)** (*right of firstborn*) Erstgeburtsrecht *nt;* **~stone** *n* Monatsstein *m;* **~ trauma** *n* Geburtstrauma *nt.*
biryani [bɪrɪˈɑːnɪ] *n indisches Reisgericht.*
Biscay [ˈbɪskeɪ] *n* **the Bay of ~** der Golf von Biskaya *or* Biscaya.
biscuit [ˈbɪskɪt] [1] *n* **(a)** (*Brit*) Keks *m;* (*dog ~*) Hundekuchen *m* ◆ **that takes/you take the ~!** (*inf*) das übertrifft alles *or* (*negatively*) schlägt dem Faß den Boden aus; **~ barrel** Keksdose *f.* **(b)** (*US*) Brötchen *nt.* **(c)** (*porcelain:* **~-ware**) Biskuitporzellan *nt.* **(d)** (*colour*) Beige *nt.*
[2] *adj* (*colour*) beige.
biscuity [ˈbɪskɪtɪ] *adj texture* keksartig; *colour* beige.
bisect [baɪˈsekt] [1] *vt* in zwei Teile *or* (*equal parts*) Hälften teilen; (*Math*) halbieren.
[2] *vi* sich teilen.
bisection [baɪˈsekʃən] *n* (*Math*) Halbierung *f.*
bisector [baɪˈsektəʳ] *n* (*Math*) Halbierende *f.*

➤ LANGUAGE IN USE: **birth: a** → 24.1 **birthday** → 23.3

bisexual [ˌbaɪˈseksjʊəl] [1] *adj* bisexuell; (*Biol*) zwittrig, doppelgeschlechtig.
[2] *n* (*person*) Bisexuelle(r) *mf.*
bisexuality [ˌbaɪˌseksjʊˈælɪtɪ] *n* Bisexualität *f;* (*Biol*) Zwittrigkeit, Doppelgeschlechtigkeit *f.*
bishop [ˈbɪʃəp] *n* **(a)** (*Eccl*) Bischof *m* ◆ **thank you, ~** vielen Dank, Herr Bischof. **(b)** (*Chess*) Läufer *m.*
bishopric [ˈbɪʃəprɪk] *n* (*diocese*) Bistum *nt;* (*function*) Bischofsamt *nt.*
bismuth [ˈbɪzməθ] *n* Wismut *nt.*
bison [ˈbaɪsn] *n* (*American*) Bison *m;* (*European*) Wisent *m.*
bisque [bɪsk] *n* **(a)** (*pottery*) Biskuitporzellan *nt.* **(b)** (*soup*) Fischcremesuppe *f.*
bissextile [bɪˈsekstaɪl] (*form*) [1] *n* Schaltjahr *nt.*
[2] *adj* Schalt-.
bistable [baɪˈsteɪbl] *adj* (*Tech*) bistabil.
bistro [ˈbiːstrəʊ] *n* Bistro *nt.*
bit[1] [bɪt] *n* **(a)** (*for horse*) Gebiß(stange *f*) *nt* ◆ **to take the ~ between one's teeth** (*fig*) sich ins Zeug legen; *see* **champ**[1]. **(b)** (*of drill*) (Bohr)einsatz, Bohrer *m;* (*of plane*) (Hobel)messer *nt.* **(c)** (*of key*) (Schlüssel)bart *m.*
bit[2] [1] *n* **(a)** (*piece*) Stück *nt;* (*smaller*) Stückchen *nt;* (*of glass also*) Scherbe *f;* (*section: of book, film, symphony*) Teil *m;* (*part or place in book, drama, text, symphony etc*) Stelle *f* ◆ **a few ~s of furniture** ein paar Möbelstücke; **a ~ of bread** ein Stück Brot; **I gave my ~ to my sister** ich habe meiner Schwester meinen Teil gegeben; **this is the ~ I hate, he said, taking out his wallet** das tue ich gar nicht gern, sagte er und zückte seine Brieftasche; **a ~** (*not much, small amount*) ein bißchen, etwas; **would you like a ~ of ice cream?** möchten Sie etwas *or* ein bißchen Eis?; **there's a ~ of truth in what he says** daran ist schon etwas Wahres; **a ~ of advice/luck/news** ein Rat *m*/ein Glück *nt*/eine Neuigkeit; **we had a ~ of trouble/excitement** wir hatten ein wenig Ärger/Aufregung; **I only read a ~ of the novel** ich habe nur ein bißchen *or* Stückchen von dem Roman gelesen; **don't you feel the slightest ~ of remorse?** hast du denn nicht die geringsten Gewissensbisse?; **it might be a ~ of help** das könnte eine kleine Hilfe sein; **it did me a ~ of good** das hat mir geholfen; **it wasn't a ~ of help/use** das war überhaupt keine Hilfe/hat überhaupt nichts genützt; **quite a ~** einiges; **there's quite a ~ of work/bread left** es ist noch eine ganze Menge Arbeit/Brot da; **I've experienced quite a ~ in my life** ich habe in meinem Leben schon (so) einiges erlebt; **in ~s and pieces** (*broken*) in tausend Stücken; (*lit, fig: come apart*) in die Brüche gegangen; **to do the work in ~s and pieces** die Arbeit stückchenweise machen; **the ~s and pieces** die einzelnen Teile; (*broken ~s*) die Scherben *pl;* **bring all your ~s and pieces** bring deine Siebensachen; **to pick up the ~s and pieces** (*fig*) retten, was zu retten ist; **to come** *or* **fall to ~s** kaputtgehen, aus dem Leim gehen; **to pull** *or* **tear sth to ~s** (*lit*) etw in (tausend) Stücke reißen; (*fig*) keinen guten Faden an etw (*dat*) lassen; **to go to ~s** (*fig inf*) durchdrehen (*inf*).
(b) (*with time*) **a ~** ein Weilchen *nt;* **he's gone out for a ~** er ist ein Weilchen *or* mal kurz weggegangen.
(c) (*with cost*) **a ~** eine ganze Menge; **it cost quite a ~** das hat ganz schön (viel) gekostet (*inf*).
(d) to do one's ~ sein(en) Teil tun; (*fair share also*) das Seine tun; **look, you're not doing your ~** hör mal zu, du setzt dich nicht genügend ein.
(e) a ~ of a crack/bruise *etc* ein kleiner Riß/Fleck *etc;* **he's a ~ of a rogue/musician/expert/connoisseur** er ist ein ziemlicher Schlingel/er ist gar kein schlechter Musiker/er versteht einiges davon/er ist ein Kenner; **you're a ~ of an idiot, aren't you?** du bist ganz schön dumm; **he's got a ~ of a nerve!** der hat vielleicht Nerven!; **it's a ~ of a nuisance** das ist schon etwas ärgerlich; **now that's a ~ of an improvement** das ist schon besser.
(f) ~ by ~ Stück für Stück; (*gradually*) nach und nach; **he's every ~ a soldier/Frenchman** er ist durch und durch Soldat/Franzose; **it/he is every ~ as good as ...** es/er ist genauso gut, wie ...; **not a ~ of it** keineswegs, keine Spur (*inf*).
(g) when it comes to the ~ wenn es drauf ankommt.
(h) (*coin*) (*Brit*) Münze *f* ◆ **2/4/6 ~s** (*US*) 25/50/75 Cent(s).
(i) (*Brit sl*) Weib *nt* (*sl*) ◆ **cheeky little ~** freches Stück (*sl*).
[2] *adv* **a ~** ein bißchen, etwas; **were you angry? — a ~** haben Sie sich geärgert? — ja, schon etwas *or* ein bißchen; **wasn't she a little ~ surprised?** war sie nicht etwas erstaunt?; **I'm not a (little) ~ surprised** das wundert mich überhaupt nicht *or* kein bißchen (*inf*) *or* keineswegs; **he wasn't a ~ the wiser for it** danach war er auch nicht viel klüger *or* schlauer; **quite a ~** ziemlich viel; **that's quite a ~ better** das ist schon besser; **he's improved quite a ~** er hat sich ziemlich gebessert.
bit[3] *n* (*Comput*) Bit *nt.*
bit[4] *pret of* **bite.**
bitch [bɪtʃ] [1] *n* **(a)** (*of dog*) Hündin *f;* (*of canines generally*) Weibchen *nt;* (*of fox*) Füchsin *f;* (*of wolf*) Wölfin *f* ◆ **terrier ~** weiblicher Terrier.
(b) (*inf: woman*) Miststück *nt* (*sl*); (*spiteful*) Hexe *f* ◆ **silly ~** doofe Ziege (*inf*); **don't be a ~** sei nicht so gemein *or* gehässig; **she's a mean ~** sie ist ein gemeines Stück (*sl*).
(c) (*sl: complaint*) **he has to have his little ~** er muß natürlich meckern (*inf*); **what's your ~ this time?** was hast du diesmal zu meckern? (*inf*).
[2] *vi* (*sl: complain*) meckern (*inf*) (*about* über +*acc*).
◆**bitch up** *vt sep* (*sl*) versauen (*sl*).
bitchiness [ˈbɪtʃɪnɪs] *n* Gehässigkeit, Gemeinheit *f;* (*of remark also*) Bissigkeit *f.*
bitchy [ˈbɪtʃɪ] *adj* (+*er*) (*inf*) *woman* gehässig, gemein; *remark also* bissig ◆ **that was a ~ thing to do/say** das war gehässig *or* gemein; **she started getting ~ about her** sie fing an, bissige *or* gehässige Bemerkungen über sie zu ma-

chen.

bite [baɪt] (*vb: pret* **bit**, *ptp* **bitten**) 1 *n* **(a)** Biß *m* ◆ **in two ~s** mit zwei Bissen; **he took a ~ (out) of the apple** er biß in den Apfel.
(b) (*wound etc*) (*dog, snake, flea ~ etc*) Biß *m*; (*insect ~*) Stich *m*; (*love ~*) (Knutsch)fleck *m* (*inf*).
(c) (*Fishing*) **I think I've got a ~** ich glaube, es hat einer angebissen.
(d) (*of food*) Happen *m* ◆ **there's not a ~ to eat** es ist überhaupt nichts zu essen da; **come and have a ~** komm und iß 'ne Kleinigkeit; **do you fancy a ~ (to eat)?** möchten Sie etwas essen?
(e) there's a ~ in the air es ist beißend kalt; **the ~ of the wind** der beißend-kalte Wind.
(f) (*of file, saw*) **the file has lost its ~** die Feile ist stumpf geworden; **these screws don't have enough ~** diese Schrauben greifen *or* fassen nicht richtig.
(g) (*of sauce etc*) Schärfe *f*.
2 *vt* **(a)** (*person, dog*) beißen; (*insect*) stechen ◆ **to ~ one's nails** an seinen Nägeln kauen; **to ~ one's tongue/lip** sich (*dat*) auf die Zunge/Lippen beißen; **the trapeze artist ~s the rope between her teeth** die Trapezkünstlerin hält das Seil mit den Zähnen fest; **don't worry, he won't ~ you** (*fig inf*) keine Angst, er wird dich schon nicht beißen (*inf*); **to ~ the dust** (*inf*) dran glauben müssen (*inf*); **he had been bitten by the urge to ...** der Drang, zu ..., hatte ihn erfaßt *or* gepackt; **once bitten twice shy** (*Prov*) (ein) gebranntes Kind scheut das Feuer (*Prov*); **what's biting you?** (*fig inf*) was ist mit dir los? (*inf*), was hast du denn?
(b) (*cold, frost, wind*) schneiden in (+*dat*).
(c) (*file, saw*) schneiden in (+*acc*); (*acid*) ätzen.
(d) (*inf: swindle*) **I've been bitten** ich bin reingelegt worden (*inf*).
3 *vi* **(a)** (*dog etc*) beißen; (*insects*) stechen. **(b)** (*fish, fig inf*) anbeißen. **(c)** (*cold, frost, wind*) beißen, schneiden. **(d)** (*wheels*) fassen, greifen; (*saw, anchor*) fassen; (*screw*) greifen.

◆**bite into** *vi +prep obj* (*person*) (hinein)beißen in (+*acc*); (*teeth*) (tief) eindringen in (+*acc*); (*acid, saw*) sich hineinfressen in (+*acc*); (*screw, drill*) sich hineinbohren in (+*acc*).

◆**bite off** *vt sep* abbeißen ◆ **he won't ~ your head ~** er wird dir schon nicht den Kopf abreißen; **to ~ ~ more than one can chew** (*prov*) sich (*dat*) zuviel zumuten.

◆**bite on** *vi +prep obj* beißen auf (+*acc*) ◆ **give the baby something to ~ ~** gib dem Kind etwas zum Beißen.

◆**bite through** *vt insep* durchbeißen.

biter ['baɪtə^r] *n* **the ~ bitten!** mit den eigenen Waffen geschlagen!; (*in deception also*) der betrogene Betrüger!

bite-size(d) ['baɪtsaɪz(d)] *adj* **(a)** *food* mundgerecht. **(b)** (*fig*) *information etc* leichtverdaulich.

biting ['baɪtɪŋ] *adj* beißend; *cold, wind also* schneidend.

bit-mapped ['bɪtmæpt] *adj* (*Comput*) Bit-mapped-, bit-mapped *pred*.

bit part *n* kleine Nebenrolle.

bit-part player *n* Schauspieler(in *f*) *m* in kleinen Nebenrollen.

bitten ['bɪtn] *ptp of* **bite**.

bitter ['bɪtə^r] 1 *adj* (+*er*) **(a)** *taste* bitter ◆ **~ lemon** Bitter Lemon *nt*; **it was a ~ pill to swallow** es war eine bittere Pille.
(b) *cold, winter* bitter; *weather, wind* bitterkalt *attr*, eisig ◆ **it's ~ today** es ist heute bitter kalt.
(c) *enemy, struggle, opposition* erbittert.
(d) *disappointment, hatred, reproach, remorse, tears* bitter; *criticism* scharf, heftig ◆ **to the ~ end** bis zum bitteren Ende.
(e) (*embittered*) bitter; *person also* verbittert ◆ **to be** *or* **feel ~ at sth** über etw (*acc*) bitter *or* verbittert sein.
2 *adv*: **~ cold** bitterkalt *attr*, bitter kalt *pred*.
3 *n* **(a)** (*Brit: beer*) *halbdunkles obergäriges Bier*. **(b) ~s** *pl* Magenbitter *m* ◆ **gin and ~s** Gin mit Bitterlikör.

bitterly ['bɪtəlɪ] *adv* **(a)** *reproach, disappointed* bitter; *complain also, weep* bitterlich; *oppose* erbittert; *criticize* scharf; *jealous* sehr. **(b)** *cold* bitter. **(c)** (*showing embitteredness*) verbittert; *criticize* erbittert.

bittern ['bɪtɜːn] *n* Rohrdommel *f*.

bitterness ['bɪtənɪs] *n see adj* **(a)** Bitterkeit *f*. **(b)** Bitterkeit *f*; bittere Kälte. **(c)** Erbittertheit *f*. **(d)** Bitterkeit *f*; Schärfe, Heftigkeit *f* ◆ **such was the ~ of his disappointment/jealousy** er war so bitter enttäuscht/derart eifersüchtig. **(e)** Bitterkeit *f*; Verbitterung *f*.

bitter-sweet ['bɪtə,swiːt] 1 *adj* (*lit, fig*) bittersüß.
2 *n* (*Bot*) Kletternder Baumwürger; (*nightshade*) Bittersüßer Nachtschatten.

bitty ['bɪtɪ] *adj* (+*er*) (*Brit inf: scrappy*) zusammengestoppelt (*pej inf*) *or* -gestückelt (*inf*).

bitumen ['bɪtjʊmɪn] *n* Bitumen *nt*.

bituminous [bɪ'tjuːmɪnəs] *adj* bituminös ◆ **~ coal** Stein- *or* Fettkohle *f*.

bivalent ['baɪ'veɪlənt] *adj* bivalent, zweiwertig.

bivalve ['baɪvælv] (*Zool*) 1 *n* zweischalige Muschel.
2 *adj* zweischalig.

bivouac ['bɪvʊæk] (*vb: pret, ptp* **~ked**) 1 *n* Biwak *nt*.
2 *vi* biwakieren.

bi-weekly ['baɪ'wiːklɪ] 1 *adj* **(a)** (*twice a week*) **~ meetings/editions** Konferenzen/Ausgaben, die zweimal wöchentlich *or* in der Woche stattfinden/erscheinen. **(b)** (*fortnightly*) zweiwöchentlich, vierzehntäglich.
2 *adv* **(a)** (*twice a week*) zweimal wöchentlich, zweimal in der Woche. **(b)** (*fortnightly*) alle vierzehn Tage, vierzehntäglich.

biz [bɪz] (*inf*) *abbr of* **business**.

bizarre [bɪ'zɑː^r] *adj* bizarr.

BL *abbr of* **Bachelor of Law.**

blab [blæb] 1 *vi* quatschen (*inf*); (*talk fast, tell secret*) plappern; (*criminal*) singen (*sl*).
2 *vt* (*also* **~ out**) *secret* ausplaudern.

blabbermouth ['blæbə,maʊθ] *n* (*inf*) Klatschmaul *nt* (*inf*).

black [blæk] 1 *adj* (+*er*) **(a)** schwarz ◆ **~ man/woman** Schwarze(r) *mf*; **~ and blue** grün und blau; **~ and white photography/film** Schwarzweißfotografie *f*/-film *m*; **to swear that ~ is white** schwören, daß zwei mal zwei fünf ist; **the situation isn't so ~ and white as that** die Situation ist nicht so eindeutig schwarz-weiß; **a western makes things ~ and white** ein Western stellt alles in Schwarzweißmalerei dar.
(b) (*dirty*) schwarz.
(c) (*wicked*) *thought, plan, deed* schwarz ◆ **he's not so ~ as he's painted** (*prov*) er ist nicht so schlecht wie sein Ruf.
(d) *future, prospects, mood* düster, finster ◆ **he painted their conduct in the ~est colours** er malte ihr Betragen in den schwärzesten Farben; **things are looking ~ for our project** es sieht für unser Vorhaben ziemlich schwarz *or* düster aus; **maybe things aren't as ~ as they seem** vielleicht ist alles gar nicht so schlimm, wie es aussieht; **in ~ despair** in tiefster Verzweiflung; **this was a ~ day for ...** das war ein schwarzer Tag für ...
(e) (*fig: angry*) *looks* böse ◆ **he looked as ~ as thunder** er machte ein bitterböses Gesicht; **his face went ~** er wurde rot vor Zorn.
(f) (*during strike*) **to declare a cargo** *etc* **~** eine Ladung *etc* für bestreikt erklären; **~ goods** bestreikte Waren.
2 *n* **(a)** (*colour*) Schwarz *nt* ◆ **he is dressed in ~** er trägt Schwarz; **to wear ~ for sb** für jdn Trauer tragen; **it's written down in ~ and white** es steht schwarz auf weiß geschrieben; **a ~ and white** (*Art*) eine Schwarzweißzeichnung; (*film*) ein Schwarzweißfilm *m*; **a film which oversimplifies and presents everything in ~ and white** ein Film, der durch seine Schwarzweißmalerei alles vereinfacht darstellt.
(b) (*negro*) Schwarze(r) *mf*.
(c) (*of night*) Schwärze *f*.
(d) (*Chess etc*) Schwarz *nt*; (*Billiards*) schwarzer Ball; (*Roulette*) Schwarz, Noir *nt*.
(e) in the ~ (*Fin*) in den schwarzen Zahlen.
3 *vt* **(a)** schwärzen ◆ **to ~ one's face** sich (*dat*) das Gesicht schwarz machen; **to ~ sb's eye** jdm ein blaues Auge schlagen *or* verpassen (*inf*). **(b)** *shoes* wichsen. **(c)** (*trade union*) bestreiken; *goods* boykottieren.

◆**black out** 1 *vi* das Bewußtsein verlieren, ohnmächtig werden.
2 *vt sep* **(a)** *building, stage* verdunkeln. **(b)** (*not broadcast*) **the technicians have ~ed ~ tonight's programmes** durch einen Streik des technischen Personals kann das heutige Abendprogramm nicht ausgestrahlt werden. **(c)** (*with ink, paint*) schwärzen.

◆**black up** *vi* (*Theat inf*) sich schwarz anmalen.

blackamoor ['blækəmʊə^r] *n* (*obs*) Mohr *m* (*obs*).

black: ~ball *vt* (*vote against*) stimmen gegen; (*inf: exclude*) ausschließen; **~ beetle** *n* Küchenschabe *f*; **~berry** *n* Brombeere *f*; **to go ~berrying** Brombeeren pflücken gehen, in die Brombeeren gehen (*inf*); **~bird** *n* Amsel *f*; **~board** *n* Tafel *f*; **to write sth on the ~board** etw an die Tafel schreiben; **~ book** *n* **to be in sb's ~ books** bei jdm schlecht angeschrieben sein (*inf*); **little ~ book** Notizbuch *nt* (*mit Adressen der Mädchenbekanntschaften*); **~ box** *n* (*Aviat*) Flugschreiber *m*; **~ bread** *n* Schwarzbrot *nt*; **~cap** *n* (*bird*) Mönchsgrasmücke *f*; (*US: berry*) Barett *nt*; **~ cap** *n* schwarze Kappe (*des Richters bei Todesurteilen*); **~ comedy** *n* schwarze Komödie; **B~ Country** *n Industriegebiet nt in den englischen Midlands*; **~currant** *n* schwarze Johannisbeere; **B~ Death** *n* (*Hist*) Schwarzer Tod; **~ economy** *n* Schattenwirtschaft *f*.

blacken ['blækən] 1 *vt* **(a)** schwarz machen; *one's face* schwarz anmalen ◆ **the walls were ~ed by the fire** die Wände waren vom Feuer schwarz. **(b)** (*fig*) *character* verunglimpfen ◆ **to ~ sb's name** *or* **reputation** jdn schlechtmachen.
2 *vi* schwarz werden.

black: B~ English *n* Englisch *nt* der Schwarzen; **~ eye** *n* blaues Auge; **to give sb a ~ eye** jdm ein blaues Auge schlagen *or* verpassen (*inf*); **~-eyed** *adj* schwarzäugig; **B~ Forest** *n* Schwarzwald *m*; **B~ Forest gateau** *n* Schwarzwälder Kirschtorte *f*; **~ friar** *n* Dominikaner *m*; Benediktiner *m*; **~ grouse** *n* Birkhuhn *nt*.

blackguard ['blægɑːd] *n* (*old*) Bösewicht, (Spitz)bube *m* (*old*).

blackguardly ['blægɑːdlɪ] *adj deed, person* niederträchtig.

black: ~head *n* Mitesser *m*; **~-headed gull** *n* Schwarzkopfmöwe *f*; **~-hearted** *adj* böse; **~ hole** *n* (*Astron*) schwarzes Loch; **B~ Hole of Calcutta** *n* (*cramped*) Affenstall *m*; (*dirty, dark*) scheußliches Verlies; **~ humour** *n* schwarzer Humor; **~ ice** *n* Glatteis *nt*.

blacking ['blækɪŋ] *n* **(a)** (*for shoes*) schwarze (Schuh)wichse; (*for stoves*) Ofenschwärze *f*. **(b)** (*by trade union*) Bestreikung *f*; (*of goods*) Boykottierung *f*.

blackish ['blækɪʃ] *adj* schwärzlich.

black: ~jack 1 *n* **(a)** (*flag*) schwarze (Piraten)flagge; **(b)** (*Hist: drinking vessel*) (lederner) Becher; **(c)** (*US: weapon*) Totschläger *m*; **(d)** (*Cards: pontoon*) Siebzehnundvier *nt*; 2 *vt* (*US: hit*) prügeln; **~ lead** *n* Graphit *m*; (*for stoves*) Schwärze *f*; **~-lead** *vt stove* schwärzen; **~leg** (*Brit: Ind*) 1 *n* Streikbrecher(in *f*) *m*; 2 *vi* Streikbrecher sein, sich als Streikbrecher betätigen; 3 *vt one's fellow workers* sich unsolidarisch verhalten gegen; **~ list** *n* schwarze Liste; **~-list** *vt* auf die schwarze Liste setzen.

blackly ['blæklɪ] *adv* (*gloomily*) düster, finster.

black: ~ magic *n* Schwarze Kunst *or* Magie *f*; **~mail** 1 *n* Erpressung *f*; **to**

use emotional ~mail on sb jds Gefühle brutal ausnutzen; **that's emotional ~mail!** das ist die reinste Erpressung!; [2] *vt* erpressen; **to ~mail sb into doing sth** jdn durch Erpressung dazu zwingen, etw zu tun; **he had ~mailed £500 out of her** er hatte £ 500 von ihr erpreßt; **~mailer** *n* Erpresser(in *f*) *m*; **B~ Maria** [ˌblækməˈraɪə] *n* grüne Minna (*inf*); **~ mark** *n* Tadel *m*; (*in school register also*) Eintrag *m*; **that's a ~ mark for him** das ist ein Minuspunkt für ihn; **~ market** [1] *n* Schwarzmarkt *m*; [2] *adj attr* Schwarzmarkt-; **~ marketeer** *n* Schwarzhändler *m*; **~ mass** *n* Schwarze Messe; **B~ Muslim** *n* Black Moslem *m*; **B~ Nationalism** *n* (*US*) schwarzer Nationalismus.

blackness [ˈblæknɪs] *n* Schwärze *f* ♦ **the ~ of his mood** seine düstere Laune.

black: ~out *n* **(a)** (*Med*) Ohnmacht(sanfall *m*) *f no pl*; **I must have had a ~out** ich muß wohl in Ohnmacht gefallen sein; **he had a ~out** ihm wurde schwarz vor Augen; **(b)** (*light failure*) Stromausfall *m*; (*Theat*) Blackout *nt*; (*during war*) Verdunkelung *f*; (*TV*) Ausfall *m*; **(c)** (*news ~out*) (Nachrichten)sperre *f*; **B~ Panther** *n* Black Panther *m*; **B~ Power** *n* Black Power *f*; **~ pudding** *n* ≃ Blutwurst *f*; **B~ Rod** *n Zeremonienmeister m des britischen Oberhauses*; **B~ Sea** *n* Schwarzes Meer; **~ sheep** *n* (*fig*) schwarzes Schaf; **B~shirt** *n* Schwarzhemd *nt*; **~smith** *n* (Grob- *or* Huf)schmied *m*; **at/to the ~smith's** beim/zum Schmied; **~ spot** *n* (*also* **accident ~ spot**) Gefahrenstelle *f*; **~thorn** *n* (*Bot*) Schwarzdorn *m*; **~ tie** [1] *n* (*on invitation*) Abendanzug *m*; [2] *adj dinner, function* mit Smokingzwang; **is it ~ tie?** ist da Smokingzwang?; **~top** *n* (*US*) (*substance*) schwarzer Straßenbelag; (*road*) geteerte Straße; (*paved with asphalt*) Asphaltstraße *f*; **~ velvet** *n Sekt m mit Starkbier*; **~ widow** *n* Schwarze Witwe *f*.

bladder [ˈblædəʳ] *n* **(a)** (*Anat, Bot*) Blase *f* ♦ **with all that beer in your ~** mit dem vielen Bier im Bauch. **(b)** (*Ftbl*) Blase *f*.

bladderwrack [ˈblædəræk] *n* Blasentang *m*.

blade [bleɪd] *n* **(a)** (*of knife, tool, weapon, razor*) Klinge *f*; (*of pencil sharpener*) Messerchen *nt*; (*of guillotine*) Beil *nt*.
(b) (*of tongue*) vorderer Zungenrücken; (*of oar, spade, saw, windscreen wiper*) Blatt *nt*; (*of plough*) Schar *f*; (*of turbine, paddle wheel*) Schaufel *f*; (*of propeller*) Blatt *nt*, Flügel *m*.
(c) (*of leaf*) Blatt *nt*, Spreite *f* (*spec*); (*of grass, corn*) Halm *m*, Spreite *f* (*spec*) ♦ **wheat in the ~** Weizen auf dem Halm.
(d) (*liter: sword*) Klinge *f* (*liter*).
(e) (*old: dashing fellow*) schmucker Bursch (*old*).
(f) (*Anat*) *see* **shoulder ~**.

-bladed [ˈbleɪdɪd] *adj suf* **a twin~ propeller** ein Zweiblattpropeller *m*; **a two~ knife** ein Messer *nt* mit zwei Klingen.

blaeberry [ˈbleɪbərɪ] *n* (*Scot, N Engl*) *see* **bilberry**.

blah [blɑː] (*inf*) [1] *n* (*dated: nonsense*) Blabla (*inf*), Geschwafel (*inf*) *nt*.
[2] *interj* **~, ~, ~** blabla (*inf*).

blame [bleɪm] [1] *vt* **(a)** (*hold responsible*) die Schuld geben (+*dat*), beschuldigen ♦ **to ~ sb for sth/sth on sb** jdm die Schuld an etw (*dat*) geben, die Schuld an etw (*dat*) auf jdn schieben; **to ~ sth on sth** die Schuld an etw (*dat*) auf etw (*acc*) schieben, einer Sache (*dat*) die Schuld an etw (*dat*) geben; **you only have yourself to ~** das hast du dir selbst zuzuschreiben; **I'm to ~ for this** daran bin ich schuld; **whom/what are we to ~** *or* **who/what is to ~ for this accident?** wer/was ist schuld an diesem Unfall?; **I ~ him for leaving the door open** er ist schuld, daß die Tür aufblieb; **to ~ oneself for sth** sich (*dat*) etw selbst zuzuschreiben haben, selbst an etw (*dat*) schuld sein; (*feel responsible*) sich für etw verantwortlich fühlen, sich selbst bezichtigen; **he ~s himself for starting the fire** er gibt sich selbst die Schuld daran, daß das Feuer ausgebrochen ist.
(b) (*reproach*) Vorwürfe machen (*sb for* jdm für *or* wegen) ♦ **nobody is blaming you** es macht Ihnen ja niemand einen Vorwurf.
(c) he decided to turn down the offer — well, I can't say I ~ him er entschloß sich, das Angebot abzulehnen — das kann man ihm wahrhaftig nicht verdenken; **so I told her to get lost — (I) don't ~ you** da habe ich ihr gesagt, sie soll zum Teufel gehen — da hattest du ganz recht; **so I told him what I really thought, do you ~ me?** da habe ich ihm gründlich meine Meinung gesagt, und doch wohl nicht zu unrecht, oder?
[2] *n* **(a)** (*responsibility*) Schuld *f* ♦ **to put the ~ for sth on sb** jdm die Schuld an etw (*dat*) geben; **to take the ~** die Schuld auf sich (*acc*) nehmen; (*for sb's mistakes also*) den Kopf hinhalten; **why do I always have to take the ~?** warum muß denn immer ich an allem schuld sein?; **parents must take the ~ for their children's failings** Eltern haben die Verantwortung für die Fehler ihrer Kinder zu tragen; **we share the ~** wir haben beide/alle schuld; **the ~ lies with him** er hat *or* ist schuld (daran).
(b) (*censure*) Tadel *m* ♦ **without ~** ohne Schuld; (*irreproachable*) *life etc* untadelig.

blameless [ˈbleɪmlɪs] *adj* schuldlos; *life* untadelig.

blamelessly [ˈbleɪmlɪslɪ] *adv* unschuldig.

blameworthy [ˈbleɪmwɜːðɪ] *adj* schuldig; *neglect* tadelnswert ♦ **he is to be held ~** er hat sich schuldig gemacht.

blanch [blɑːntʃ] [1] *vt* (*Hort*) bleichen; (*illness*) *face* bleich machen; (*fear*) erbleichen lassen; (*Cook*) *vegetables* blanchieren; *almonds* brühen.
[2] *vi* (*with* vor +*dat*) (*person*) blaß werden; (*with fear also*) bleich werden, erbleichen (*geh*).

blancmange [bləˈmɒnʒ] *n* Pudding *m*.

bland [blænd] *adj* (+*er*) **(a)** (*suave*) *expression, look, manner* verbindlich; *face* ausdruckslos-höflich, glatt (*pej*); *person* verbindlich; (*trying to avoid trouble*) konziliant. **(b)** (*mild*) *air, weather* mild; *taste also* nüchtern, fade (*pej*). **(c)** (*harmless, lacking distinction*) nichtssagend.

blandish [ˈblændɪʃ] *vt* schönreden (+*dat*).

blandishment [ˈblændɪʃmənt] *n* Schmeichelei *f*.

blandly [ˈblændlɪ] *adv see adj*.

blandness [ˈblændnɪs] *n see adj* **(a)** Verbindlichkeit *f*; ausdruckslose Höflichkeit; Konzilianz *f*. **(b)** Milde *f*; Fadheit *f*. **(c)** nichtssagende Art.

blank [blæŋk] [1] *adj* (+*er*) **(a)** *piece of paper, page, wall* leer; *silence, darkness* tief; *coin* ungeprägt ♦ **~ cheque** Blankoscheck *m*; (*fig*) Freibrief *m*; **to give sb a ~ cheque** (*fig*) jdm Carte blanche geben (*geh*), jdm freie Hand geben; **a ~ space** eine Lücke, ein freier Platz; (*on form*) ein freies Feld; **~ form** Formular(blatt) *nt*, Vordruck *m*; **please leave ~** (*on form*) bitte frei lassen *or* nicht ausfüllen.
(b) (*empty*) *life etc* unausgefüllt, leer ♦ **these ~ and characterless house fronts** diese nackten, charakterlosen Fassaden.
(c) (*expressionless*) *face, look* ausdruckslos; (*stupid*) verständnislos; (*puzzled*) verdutzt, verblüfft ♦ **he looked at me with ~ stupidity** er sah mich völlig verständnislos an; **to look ~** (*expressionless*) eine ausdruckslose Miene aufsetzen; (*stupid*) verständnislos dreinschauen; (*puzzled*) ein verdutztes Gesicht machen; **he just looked ~** *or* **gave me a ~ look** er guckte mich nur groß an (*inf*); **my mind went ~** ich hatte Mattscheibe (*inf*), ich hatte ein Brett vor dem Kopf (*inf*); **sorry, I've gone ~** (*inf*) tut mir leid, aber ich habe totale Mattscheibe (*inf*).
(d) ~ (cartridge) Platzpatrone *f*.
(e) ~ verse Blankvers *m*.
[2] *n* **(a)** (*in document*) freier Raum, leere Stelle; (*~ document*) Vordruck *m*, Formular *nt*; (*gap*) Lücke *f*.
(b) (*void*) Leere *f* ♦ **my mind was/went a complete ~** ich hatte totale Mattscheibe (*inf*).
(c) (*in lottery*) Niete *f* ♦ **to draw a ~** (*fig*) kein Glück haben.
(d) (*in a target*) Scheibenmittelpunkt *m*.
(e) (*cartridge*) Platzpatrone *f*.
(f) (*domino*) Blank *nt*.
(g) (*coin*) Schrötling *m* (*spec*); (*key*) Rohling *m*.

blanket [ˈblæŋkɪt] [1] *n* (*lit, fig*) Decke *f* ♦ **a ~ of snow/fog** eine Schnee-/Nebeldecke; **born on the wrong side of the ~** (*hum inf*) unehelich (geboren) sein.
[2] *adj attr statement* pauschal; *insurance etc* umfassend.
[3] *vt* **(a)** (*snow, smoke*) zudecken ♦ **fog ~ed the town** Nebel hüllte die Stadt ein. **(b)** (*Naut*) *ship* den Wind abhalten von.

blanket: ~ bath *n* Waschen *nt* im Bett; **to give sb a ~ bath** jdn im Bett waschen; **~ stitch** *n* Langettenstich *m*.

blankly [ˈblæŋklɪ] *adv see adj* (c) ausdruckslos; verständnislos; verdutzt, verblüfft ♦ **she just looked at me ~** sie sah mich nur groß an (*inf*).

blankness [ˈblæŋknɪs] *n* (*emptiness*) Leere *f*; (*of expression*) Ausdruckslosigkeit *f*; (*not understanding*) Verständnislosigkeit *f*; (*puzzlement*) Verdutztheit, Verblüffung *f*.

blare [blɛəʳ] [1] *n* Plärren, Geplärr *nt*; (*of car horn etc*) lautes Hupen; (*of trumpets etc*) Schmettern *nt*.
[2] *vi see n* plärren; laut hupen; schmettern ♦ **the orchestra tends to ~ a bit** das Orchester wird gern etwas laut; **the music/his voice ~d through the hall** die Musik/seine Stimme schallte durch den Saal.
[3] *vt* **be quiet! he ~d** Ruhe!, brüllte er.

♦**blare out** [1] *vi* (*loud voice, music*) schallen; (*trumpets*) schmettern; (*radio, music also*) plärren; (*car horn*) laut hupen; (*person*) brüllen.
[2] *vt sep* (*trumpets*) *tune* schmettern; (*radio*) *music* plärren; (*person*) *order, warning etc* brüllen.

blarney [ˈblɑːnɪ] [1] *n* Schmeichelei *f*, Schmus *m* (*inf*) ♦ **he has kissed the ~ stone** der kann einen beschwatzen (*inf*).
[2] *vt sb* schmeicheln (+*dat*) ♦ **he could ~ his way out of trouble** er könnte sich aus allem herausreden.
[3] *vi* schmeicheln.

blaspheme [blæsˈfiːm] [1] *vt* lästern, schmähen (*geh*).
[2] *vi* Gott lästern ♦ **to ~ against sb/sth** (*lit, fig*) jdn/etw schmähen (*geh*).

blasphemer [blæsˈfiːməʳ] *n* Gotteslästerer *m*.

blasphemous [ˈblæsfɪməs] *adj* (*lit, fig*) blasphemisch; *words also* lästerlich, frevelhaft.

blasphemously [ˈblæsfɪməslɪ] *adv* blasphemisch; *speak also* lästerlich, frevlerisch.

blasphemy [ˈblæsfɪmɪ] *n* Blasphemie *f*; (*Rel also*) (Gottes)lästerung *f*; (*words also*) Schmähung *f* (*geh*).

blast [blɑːst] [1] *n* **(a)** Windstoß *m*; (*of hot air*) Schwall *m* ♦ **a ~ of wind** ein Windstoß; **an icy ~** ein eisiger Wind.
(b) (*sound: of trumpets*) Geschmetter, Schmettern *nt*; (*of foghorn*) Tuten *nt* ♦ **the ship gave a long ~ on its foghorn** das Schiff ließ sein Nebelhorn ertönen; **to blow a ~ on the bugle** auf dem Horn blasen.
(c) (*noise, explosion*) Explosion *f*; (*shock wave*) Druckwelle *f* ♦ **to get the full ~ of sb's anger** jds Wut in voller Wucht abkriegen.
(d) (*in quarrying etc*) Sprengladung *f*.
(e) (*of furnace*) (Blas)wind *m* ♦ **(to go) at full ~** (*lit, fig*) auf Hochtouren (laufen); **with the radio turned up (at) full ~** mit dem Radio voll aufgedreht.
[2] *vt* **(a)** (*lightning*) schlagen in (+*acc*); (*with powder*) sprengen. **(b)** (*send*) *rocket* schießen. **(c)** (*blight*) *plant* vernichten, zerstören; *reputation also, future* ruinieren. **(d)** (*inf: criticize*) verreißen; *person* herunterputzen (*inf*).
[3] *vi* (*in quarry*) sprengen.
[4] *interj* (*inf*) **~ (it)!** verdammt! (*inf*), so ein Mist! (*inf*); **~ what he wants!** das ist doch wurscht, was der will! (*inf*); **~ him for coming so late** Herrgott, daß er aber auch so spät kommen muß! (*inf*); **~ that work, I'm going out**

tonight/I'd rather go out die Arbeit kann mich mal (*inf*), ich geh heut abend weg/diese verdammte Arbeit (*inf*), ich würde viel lieber weggehen; **~ this car!** dieses verdammte Auto! (*inf*).

◆**blast off** *vi* (*rocket, astronaut*) abheben, starten.

blasted ['blɑːstɪd] 1 *adj* (a) öde. (b) (*inf*) verdammt (*inf*), Mist- (*inf*) ◆ **he was talking all the ~ time** verdammt, er hat die ganze Zeit geredet (*inf*).

2 *adv* (*inf*) verdammt (*inf*).

blast furnace *n* Hochofen *m*.

blasting ['blɑːstɪŋ] *n* (*Tech*) Sprengen *nt* ◆ **"danger ~ in progress"** „Achtung! Sprengarbeiten!"; *see* **sand~**.

blast-off ['blɑːstɒf] *n* Abschuß *m*.

blatancy ['bleɪtənsɪ] *n see* **blatant** Offensichtlichkeit *f*; Eklatanz *f*; Kraßheit *f*; Unverfrorenheit *f* ◆ **the ~ of their disregard for ...** ihre unverhohlene *or* offene Mißachtung der ...

blatant ['bleɪtənt] *adj* (*very obvious*) offensichtlich; *injustice, lie, error, lack also* eklatant; *error also* kraß; *liar, social climber* unverfroren; *colour* schreiend; *disregard* offen, unverhohlen ◆ **there's no need (for you) to be quite so ~ about it** (*in talking*) Sie brauchen das nicht so herumzuposaunen (*inf*); (*in doing sth*) Sie brauchen das nicht so deutlich zu tun.

blatantly ['bleɪtəntlɪ] *adv* offensichtlich; (*openly*) offen; (*without respect*) unverfroren ◆ **you don't have to make it quite so ~ obvious** Sie brauchen es nicht so überdeutlich zu zeigen; **she ~ ignored it** sie hat das schlicht und einfach ignoriert.

blather ['blæðəʳ] (*inf*) *n, vi see* **blether**.

blaze[1] [bleɪz] 1 *n* (a) (*fire*) Feuer *nt*; (*of building etc also*) Brand *m* ◆ **"~ at factory"** „Brand in Fabrik"; **six people died in the ~** sechs Menschen kamen in den Flammen um.

(b) (*of guns etc*) Feuer, Funkeln *nt* ◆ **a ~ of lights/colour** ein Lichtermeer *nt*/ Meer *nt* von Farben; **a sudden ~ of light from the watchtower** ein plötzlicher Lichtstrahl vom Wachturm; **he went out in a ~ of glory** er trat mit Glanz und Gloria ab.

(c) (*of fire, sun*) Glut *f*; (*fig: of rage*) Anfall *m*.

(d) (*inf*) **go to ~s** scher dich zum Teufel! (*inf*); **it can go to ~s** das kann mir gestohlen bleiben (*inf*); **what/how the ~s ...?** was/wie zum Teufel ...? (*inf*); **like ~s** wie verrückt (*inf*).

2 *vi* (a) (*sun*) brennen; (*fire also*) lodern ◆ **to ~ with anger** vor Zorn glühen. (b) (*guns*) feuern. **with all guns blazing** aus allen Rohren feuernd.

◆**blaze abroad** *vt sep* (*liter*) verbreiten (*throughout* in +*dat*).

◆**blaze away** *vi* (a) (*soldiers, guns*) drauflos feuern (*at* auf +*acc*). (b) (*fire etc*) lodern.

◆**blaze down** *vi* (*sun*) niederbrennen (*on* auf +*acc*).

◆**blaze up** *vi* aufflammen, auflodern.

blaze[2] 1 *n* (*of horse etc*) Blesse *f*; (*on tree*) Anreißung *f*.

2 *vt tree* anreißen ◆ **to ~ a trail** (*lit*) einen Weg markieren; (*fig*) den Weg bahnen.

blazer ['bleɪzəʳ] *n* Blazer *m* (*also Sch*), Klubjacke *f*.

blazing ['bleɪzɪŋ] *adj* (a) *building etc* brennend; *fire, torch* lodernd; *sun, light* grell; *sun* (*hot*) brennend. (b) (*fig*) *eyes* funkelnd (*with* vor +*dat*); *red* knall-, leuchtend ◆ **he is ~** (*inf*) er kocht vor Wut (*inf*), er ist fuchsteufelswild (*inf*).

blazon ['bleɪzn] 1 *n* (*Her*) Wappen *nt*.

2 *vt* (*liter: also* **~ abroad**) *news* verbreiten (*throughout* in +*dat*).

bldg *abbr of* **building**.

bleach [bliːtʃ] 1 *n* (a) Bleichmittel *nt*; (*household* ~) Reinigungsmittel *nt*. (b) (*act*) Bleichen *nt* ◆ **to give sth a ~** etw bleichen.

2 *vt linen, bones, hair* bleichen.

3 *vi* (*bones*) (ver)bleichen.

◆**bleach out** *vt sep* ausbleichen.

bleachers ['bliːtʃəz] *npl* (*US*) unüberdachte Zuschauertribüne.

bleaching ['bliːtʃɪŋ] *n* Bleichen *nt* ◆ **they need a good ~** sie müßten richtig gebleicht werden; **~ agent** Bleichmittel *nt*; **~ powder** Bleichkalk *m*.

bleak [bliːk] *adj* (+*er*) (a) öde, trostlos. (b) *weather, wind* rauh, kalt. (c) (*fig*) trostlos; *prospects also* trüb ◆ **things look rather ~ for him** es sieht ziemlich trostlos für ihn aus.

bleakly ['bliːklɪ] *adv see adj* (a) öde, trostlos. (b) rauh, kalt.

bleakness ['bliːknɪs] *n see adj* (a) Öde, Trostlosigkeit *f*. (b) Rauheit, Kälte *f*. (c) Trostlosigkeit *f*; Trübheit *f*.

bleary ['blɪərɪ] *adj* (+*er*) (a) *eyes* trübe; (*after sleep*) verschlafen. (b) (*blurred*) verschwommen.

bleary-eyed ['blɪərɪ,aɪd] *adj* (*after sleep*) verschlafen ◆ **~ after proof reading** mit ganz trüben Augen nach dem Korrekturlesen.

bleat [bliːt] 1 *vi* (a) (*sheep, calf*) blöken; (*goat*) meckern.

(b) (*fig inf: complain, moan*) meckern (*inf*).

2 *n* (a) (*of sheep, calf*) Blöken, Geblök *nt*; (*of goat*) Meckern *nt*. (b) (*inf: moan*) Meckern (*inf*), Gemecker (*inf*) *nt* ◆ **they'll have to have their little ~ about ...** sie müssen natürlich ein bißchen über (+*acc*) ... meckern (*inf*).

bleed [bliːd] *pret, ptp* **bled** [bled] 1 *vi* (a) bluten ◆ **to ~ to death** verbluten; **my heart ~s for you** (*iro*) ich fang' gleich an zu weinen; **our hearts ~ for the oppressed** (*liter*) wir leiden mit den Unterdrückten (*geh*).

(b) (*plant*) bluten, schwitzen; (*wall*) schwitzen.

2 *vt* (a) *person* zur Ader lassen. (b) (*fig inf*) schröpfen (*inf*) (*for* um), bluten lassen (*inf*) ◆ **to ~ sb white** jdn total ausnehmen (*inf*). (c) (*Aut*) *brakes* lüften.

◆**bleed away** *vi* (*lit, fig*) ausströmen, verströmen (*geh*).

bleeder ['bliːdəʳ] *n* (a) (*Med inf*) Bluter *m*. (b) (*Brit sl*) (*person*) Arschloch *nt* (*vulg*); (*thing*) Scheißding *nt* (*sl*) ◆ **you're a cheeky little ~** du bist ein frecher Hund (*inf*).

bleeding ['bliːdɪŋ] 1 *n* (a) (*loss of blood*) Blutung *f* ◆ **internal ~** innere Blutungen *pl*. (b) (*taking blood*) Aderlaß *m*. (c) (*of plant*) Blutung *f*, Schwitzen *nt*. (d) (*of brakes*) Lüftung *f*.

2 *adj* (a) *wound* blutend; (*fig*) *heart* gebrochen ◆ **he is a ~ heart** sein Herz ist gebrochen, ihm blutet das Herz (*geh*).

(b) (*Brit sl*) verdammt (*inf*), Scheiß- (*sl*); (*in positive sense*) *miracle etc* verdammt (*inf*) ◆ **get your ~ hands off** nimm deine Dreckpfoten weg (*inf*); **just a ~ minute** nu mal sachte (*inf*).

3 *adv* (*Brit sl*) verdammt (*inf*) ◆ **that's ~ marvellous** das ist sauber! (*inf*); **who does he/she think he/she ~ well is?** für was hält sich der Kerl/die Kuh eigentlich? (*sl*); **not ~ likely** da ist nichts drin (*sl*), glaube kaum (*inf*).

bleep [bliːp] 1 *n* (*Rad, TV*) Piepton *m*.

2 *vi* (*transmitter*) piepen.

3 *vt* (*in hospital*) *doctor* rufen.

bleeper ['bliːpəʳ] *n* Funkrufempfänger, Piepser (*inf*) *m*.

blemish ['blemɪʃ] 1 *n* (*lit, fig*) Makel *m* ◆ **without (a) ~** makellos, ohne Makel.

2 *vt object* beschädigen; *work, beauty* beeinträchtigen; *reputation, honour* beflecken ◆ **slightly ~ed pottery** leicht fehlerhafte Keramik.

blench [blentʃ] *vi* bleich werden, erbleichen (*geh*).

blend [blend] 1 *n* Mischung *f*; (*of whiskies also*) Blend *m* ◆ **a ~ of tea** eine Teemischung.

2 *vt* (a) *teas, colours etc* (ver)mischen; *cultures* vermischen, miteinander verbinden ◆ **to ~ a building (in) with its surroundings** ein Gebäude seiner Umgebung anpassen.

(b) (*Cook*) (*stir*) einrühren; (*in blender*) *liquids* mixen; *semi-solids* pürieren.

3 *vi* (a) (*mix together*) (*teas, whiskies*) sich vermischen, sich mischen lassen; (*voices, colours*) verschmelzen ◆ **sea and sky seemed to ~ together** Meer und Himmel schienen ineinander überzugehen *or* miteinander zu verschmelzen.

(b) (*also* **~ in**: *go together, harmonize*) harmonieren (*with* mit), passen (*with* zu).

◆**blend in** 1 *vt sep flavouring* einrühren; *colour, tea* daruntermischen; *building* anpassen (*with dat*).

2 *vi see* **blend 3 (b)**.

blended ['blendɪd] *adj* **~ whisky** Blended *m*.

blender ['blendəʳ] *n* Mixer *m*, Mixgerät *nt*.

bless [bles] *vt* (a) (*God, priest*) segnen ◆ **~ you, my son** Gott segne dich, mein Sohn; **did you buy that for me, ~ you** (*inf*) hast du das für mich gekauft? das ist aber lieb von dir! (*inf*); **~ you, darling, you're an angel** (*inf*) du bist wirklich lieb, du bist ein Engel (*inf*); **~ your little cotton socks** (*inf*) du bist ja ein Schatz (*inf*); **~ you!** (*to sneezer*) Gesundheit!; **~ me!** (*inf*), **~ my soul!** (*inf*) du mein Güte! (*inf*); **he's lost it again, ~ him** (*iro*) prima, er hat es wieder mal verloren! (*iro*); **I'll be ~ed** *or* **blest if I'm going to do that!** (*inf*) das fällt mir ja nicht im Traum ein! (*inf*); **well, I'll be ~ed!** (*inf*) so was!

(b) **to ~ sb with sth** jdn mit etw segnen; **to be ~ed with** gesegnet sein mit.

(c) (*Eccl: adore*) preisen.

blessed ['blesɪd] 1 *adj* (a) (*Rel*) heilig ◆ **B~ Virgin** Heilige Jungfrau (Maria); **the B~ X** der selige X; **~ be God!** gepriesen sei Gott!; **of ~ memory** seligen Angedenkens.

(b) (*fortunate*) selig ◆ **~ are the pure in heart** (*Bibl*) selig sind, die reinen Herzens sind.

(c) (*liter: giving joy*) willkommen.

(d) (*euph inf: cursed*) verflixt (*inf*) ◆ **I couldn't remember a ~ thing** ich konnte mich an rein gar nichts mehr erinnern (*inf*); **the whole ~ day** den lieben langen Tag (*inf*); **every ~ evening** aber auch *jeden* Abend.

2 *adv* verflixt (*inf*) ◆ **he's too ~ lazy** er ist einfach zu faul.

3 *n* **the B~, the Blest** die Seligen *pl*.

blessing ['blesɪŋ] *n* (*Rel, fig*) Segen *m* ◆ **he can count his ~s** da kann er von Glück sagen; **you can count your ~s you didn't get caught** du kannst von Glück sagen, daß du nicht geschnappt worden bist; **the ~s of civilization** die Segnungen der Zivilisation; **it was a ~ in disguise** es war schließlich doch ein Segen.

blest [blest] 1 *adj* (*liter*) *see* **blessed 1 (b, c)**.

2 *n see* **blessed 2**.

blether ['bleðəʳ] (*inf*) 1 *vi* quatschen (*inf*), schwätzen (*S Ger inf*).

2 *n* (*Scot*) (a) **to have a good ~** einen ordentlichen Schwatz halten (*inf*). (b) (*person*) Quasselstrippe *f* (*inf*).

blethering ['bleðərɪŋ] *n* (*inf*) Gequatsche *nt* (*inf*).

blew [bluː] *pret of* **blow**[2].

blight [blaɪt] 1 *n* (a) (*on plants*) Braunfäule *f*.

(b) (*fig*) **to be a ~ on** *or* **upon sb's life/happiness** jdm das Leben/jds Glück vergällen; **these slums are a ~ upon the city** diese Slums sind ein Schandfleck für die Stadt; **scenes of urban ~** verfallene Stadtteile; **this poverty which is a ~ upon our nation** die Armut, mit der unser Volk geschlagen ist.

2 *vt* (a) *plants* zerstören. (b) (*fig*) *hopes* vereiteln; *sb's career, future also, life* verderben ◆ **to ~ sb's life** jdm das Leben verderben.

blighter ['blaɪtəʳ] *n* (*Brit inf*) Kerl *m* (*inf*); (*boy*) ungezogener Bengel; (*girl*) Luder *nt* (*inf*) ◆ **a poor ~** ein armer Hund (*inf*); **you ~** du Idiot! (*inf*); **what a lucky ~!** so ein Glückspilz!; **this question/window's a real ~** diese Frage ist sauschwer (*inf*)/das Fenster ist ein Mistding (*inf*).

Blighty ['blaɪtɪ] *n* (*Brit Mil sl*) (*leave*) Heimaturlaub *m*; (*England*) die Heimat ◆ **he's going back to ~** er geht nach Hause; **a ~ one** (*wound*) ein Heimatschuß *m*.

blimey ['blaɪmɪ] *interj (Brit sl)* verflucht *(inf)*, Mensch *(inf)*.
blimp [blɪmp] *n* **(a)** *(Brit inf)* **(Colonel) B~** Stockkonservativer *m*, alter Oberst *(inf)*. **(b)** *(Aviat)* Kleinluftschiff *nt*. **(c)** *(Film)* Blimp *m*, Schallschutzgehäuse *nt*.
blind [blaɪnd] 1 *adj (+er)* **(a)** blind • **a ~ man/woman** ein Blinder/eine Blinde; **~ in one eye** auf einem Auge blind.
(b) *(fig) (to faults, beauty, charm etc)* blind *(to* für, gegen) • **to be ~ to the possibilities** die Möglichkeiten nicht sehen; **to turn a ~ eye to sth** bei etw ein Auge zudrücken; **she remained ~ to the fact that ...** sie sah einfach nicht, daß ...
(c) *(fig: lacking judgement) obedience, passion* blind; *fury, panic also* hell • **in a ~ fury** in heller Wut; **~ with passion/rage** blind vor Leidenschaft/Wut; **he came home in a ~ stupor** er kam sinnlos betrunken nach Hause; **~ forces** blinde Kräfte.
(d) *(vision obscured) corner* unübersichtlich; *see* **~ spot**.
(e) *(inf)* **it's not a ~ bit of use trying to persuade him** es hat überhaupt keinen Zweck, ihn überreden zu wollen; **he hasn't done a ~ bit of work** er hat keinen Strich *or* Schlag getan *(inf)*; **but he didn't take a ~ bit of notice** aber er hat sich nicht die Spur darum gekümmert *(inf)*.
(f) *(false) door, window* blind.
(g) *(without exit) passage* ohne Ausgang, blind endend *attr*.
2 *vt* **(a)** blenden • **the explosion ~ed him** er ist durch die Explosion blind geworden; **he was ~ed in the war** er ist kriegsblind; **the war-~ed** die Kriegsblinden *pl*.
(b) *(sun, light)* blenden.
(c) *(fig) (love, hate etc)* blind machen *(to* für, gegen); *(wealth, beauty)* blenden • **to ~ sb with science** jdn mit Fachjargon beeindrucken (wollen).
3 *n* **(a) the ~** die Blinden *pl*; **it's the ~ leading the ~** *(fig)* das hieße, einen Lahmen einen Blinden führen lassen.
(b) *(window shade) (cloth)* Rollo, Rouleau *nt*; *(slats)* Jalousie *f*; *(outside)* Rolladen *m*.
(c) *(cover)* Tarnung *f* • **to be a ~** zur Tarnung dienen.
(d) *(fig sl: booze-up)* Sauferei *f (inf)*.
(e) *(US: hide)* Versteck *nt*.
4 *adv* **(a)** *(Aviat) fly* blind.
(b) ~ drunk *(inf)* sinnlos betrunken.
blind: ~ alley *n (lit, fig)* Sackgasse *f*; **to be up a ~ alley** *(fig)* in einer Sackgasse stecken; **~ date** *n* Rendezvous *nt* mit einem/einer Unbekannten; *(person)* unbekannter (Rendezvous)partner; unbekannte (Rendezvous)partnerin.
blinder ['blaɪndəʳ] *n* **(a)** *(US: blinker)* Scheuklappe *f*. **(b)** *(sl: drinking spree)* Kneipkur *f (inf)*.
blind flying *n (Aviat)* Blindflug *m*.
blindfold ['blaɪndfəʊld] 1 *vt* die Augen verbinden (+*dat*).
2 *n* Augenbinde *f*.
3 *adj* mit verbundenen Augen • **I could do it ~** *(inf)* das mach' ich mit links *(inf)*.
blinding ['blaɪndɪŋ] *adj light* blendend; *truth* ins Auge stechend • **in the ~ light of day** im grellen Tageslicht; **as ~ tears filled her eyes** von Tränen geblendet.
blindingly ['blaɪndɪŋlɪ] *adv* **it is ~ obvious** das sieht doch ein Blinder *(inf)*.
blind landing *n (Aviat)* Blindlandung *f*.
blindly ['blaɪndlɪ] *adv (lit, fig)* blind(lings).
blind man's buff *n* Blindekuh *no art*, Blindekuhspiel *nt*.
blindness ['blaɪndnɪs] *n (lit, fig)* Blindheit *f (to* gegenüber).
blind: ~ side *n (Sport)* ungedeckte Seite; **~ spot** *n (Med)* blinder Fleck; *(Aut, Aviat)* toter Winkel; *(Rad)* tote Zone; **trigonometry was his ~ spot** Trigonometrie war sein schwacher Punkt; **~ staggers** *n sing* Taumelsucht *f*; **~worm** *n* Blindschleiche *f*.
blink [blɪŋk] 1 *n* Blinzeln *nt* • **to be on the ~** *(inf)* kaputt sein *(inf)*.
2 *vi* **(a)** blinzeln, zwinkern. **(b)** *(light)* blinken.
3 *vt* **to ~ one's eyes** mit den Augen zwinkern.
◆**blink at** *vi +prep obj (ignore)* hinwegsehen über (+*acc*).
◆**blink away** *vt sep tears* wegblinzeln *(inf)*.
blinker ['blɪŋkəʳ] *n* **(a)** *(light)* Blinker *m*. **(b) ~s** *pl* Scheuklappen *pl*.
blinkered ['blɪŋkəd] *adj (fig)* engstirnig • **they are all so ~** sie laufen alle mit Scheuklappen herum.
blinking ['blɪŋkɪŋ] 1 *adj (Brit inf)* verflixt *(inf)*, blöd *(inf)* • **what a ~ cheek!** so eine bodenlose Frechheit! *(inf)*; **it's about ~ time too!** das wird aber auch Zeit! *(inf)*.
2 *adv* verflixt *(inf)*.
3 *n* **(a)** *(of eyes)* Blinzeln, Zwinkern *nt*. **(b)** *(of light)* Blinken *nt*.
blip [blɪp] *n* leuchtender Punkt (auf dem Radarschirm).
bliss [blɪs] *n* Glück *nt*; *(Rel)* (Glück)seligkeit *f* • **a feeling of ~** ein Gefühl der Wonne; **this is ~!** das ist herrlich *or* eine Wohltat!; **a beach, a drink, the sun, ah sheer ~** Strand, Sonne, ein Drink - ah, das wahre Paradies; **ah ~, she sighed** herrlich, seufzte sie; **a life of marital/academic ~** ein glückliches Eheleben/Leben an der Universität; **ignorance is ~** *(prov)* Unwissenheit ist ein Geschenk des Himmels.
blissful ['blɪsfʊl] *adj time* herrlich, paradiesisch; *respite also* wohltuend; *feeling also* wonnig; *happiness* höchste(s); *state, look, smile* (glück)selig; *moments* selig • **in ~ ignorance of the facts** *(iro)* in herrlicher Ahnungslosigkeit; **in ~ ignorance of the fact that ...** *(iro)* in keinster Weise ahnend, daß ...
blissfully ['blɪsfəlɪ] *adv stretch* wohlig; *peaceful* paradiesisch, herrlich; *smile* selig • **~ happy** überglücklich; **to be ~ ignorant/unaware** so herrlich ahnungslos/arglos sein; **he remained ~ ignorant of what was going on** er ahnte in keinster Weise, was eigentlich vor sich ging.
blister ['blɪstəʳ] 1 *n (on skin, paint)* Blase *f*; *(Aviat: for gun)* Bordwaffenstand *m*.
2 *vi (skin)* Blasen bekommen; *(paintwork, metal)* Blasen werfen.
3 *vt skin, paint* Blasen hervorrufen auf (+*dat*) • **to be ~ed** Blasen haben.
blistering ['blɪstərɪŋ] *adj heat, sun* glühend; *pace* mörderisch.
blister pack *n* (Klar)sichtpackung *f*.
blister-packed ['blɪstə,pækt] *adj* klarsichtverpackt.
blithe [blaɪð] *adj (+er)* fröhlich, munter.
blithely ['blaɪðlɪ] *adv* **(a)** *see adj*. **(b)** *ignore, carry on* munter • **he ~ ignored the problem** er setzte sich ungeniert über das Problem hinweg.
blithering ['blɪðərɪŋ] *adj (inf)* **a ~ idiot** ein Trottel *m (inf)*; **don't be such a ~ idiot** du bist ja total bescheuert *(sl)*.
B Litt *abbr of* **Bachelor of Letters**.
blitz [blɪts] 1 *n* **(a)** Blitzkrieg *m*; *(aerial)* Luftangriff *m* • **the B~** *deutscher Luftangriff auf britische Städte 1940-41*. **(b)** *(fig inf)* Blitzaktion *f* • **he had a ~ on his room** er machte gründlich in seinem Zimmer sauber.
2 *vt* heftig bombardieren.
blitzed [blɪtst] *adj* **(a)** *area* zerbombt. **(b)** *(inf: drunk)* voll *(inf)*, zu *(sl)*.
blizzard ['blɪzəd] *n* Schneesturm, Blizzard *m*.
bloated ['bləʊtɪd] *adj* **(a)** aufgedunsen • **I feel absolutely ~** *(inf)* ich bin zum Platzen voll *(inf)*. **(b)** *(fig: with pride, self-importance)* aufgeblasen *(with* vor +*dat*).
bloater ['bləʊtəʳ] *n* Räucherhering *m*.
blob [blɒb] *n (of water, honey, wax)* Tropfen *m*; *(of ink)* Klecks *m*; *(of paint)* Tupfer *m*; *(of ice-cream, mashed potatoes)* Klacks *m* • **until he was just a ~ on the horizon** bis er nur noch ein Punkt am Horizont war.
bloc [blɒk] *n* **(a)** *(Pol)* Block *m*. **(b) en ~** en bloc.
block [blɒk] 1 *n* **(a)** Block, Klotz *m*; *(executioner's ~)* Richtblock *m*; *(engine ~)* Motorblock *m* • **~s** *(toys)* (Bau)klötze *pl*; **huge ugly ~s of concrete** riesige, häßliche Betonklötze; **to be sent to** *or* **to go to the ~** dem Henker überantwortet werden/vor den Henker treten.
(b) *(building)* Block *m* • **~ of flats** Wohnblock *m*; **to take a stroll round the ~** einen Spaziergang um den Block machen; **she lived in the next ~/three ~s from us** *(esp US)* sie wohnte im nächsten Block/drei Blocks *or* Straßen weiter.
(c) *(division of seats)* Block *m*.
(d) *(obstruction) (in pipe, Med)* Verstopfung *f*; *(mental)* geistige Sperre *(about* in bezug auf +*acc*), Mattscheibe *f (inf)* • **I've a mental ~ about it** da habe ich totale Mattscheibe *(inf)*.
(e) *(Typ)* Druckstock *m*.
(f) *(of tickets, shares)* Block *m*.
(g) *(inf: head)* **to knock sb's ~ off** jdm eins überziehen *(inf)*.
(h) *(also* **writing ~)** Block *m*.
(i) *(usu pl: also* **starting ~)** Startblock *m*.
(j) *(in ballet shoe)* Spitzenverstärkung *f*; *(ballet shoe)* spitzenverstärkter Ballettschuh.
(k) *(Comput)* Block *m*.
2 *vt* **(a)** *road, harbour, wheel* blockieren; *plans also* im Wege stehen (+*dat*); *traffic also, progress* aufhalten; *pipe* verstopfen; *(Ftbl) one's opponent* blocken; *ball* stoppen • **to ~ sb's way/view** jdm den Weg/die Sicht versperren. **(b)** *credit* sperren. **(c)** *(Comput)* blocken.
3 *vi (Sport)* blocken.
◆**block in** *vt sep* **(a)** *(Art)* andeuten. **(b)** *(hem in)* einkeilen.
◆**block off** *vt sep street* absperren; *fireplace* abdecken.
◆**block out** *vt sep* **(a)** *(obscure) light* nicht durchlassen; *sun also* verdecken • **the trees are ~ing ~ all the light** die Bäume nehmen das ganze Licht weg. **(b)** *(sketch roughly)* andeuten. **(c)** *(obliterate) part of picture, photograph* wegretuschieren.
◆**block up** *vt sep* **(a)** *(obstruct) gangway* blockieren, versperren; *pipe* verstopfen • **my nose is** *or* **I'm all ~ed ~** meine Nase ist völlig verstopft. **(b)** *(close, fill in) window, entrance* zumauern; *hole* zustopfen.
blockade [blɒ'keɪd] 1 *n* **(a)** *(Mil)* Blockade *f* • **under ~** im Blockadezustand; **to break** *or* **run the ~** die Blockade brechen; **~ runner** Blockadebrecher *m*. **(b)** *(barrier, obstruction)* Sperre, Barrikade *f*.
2 *vt* blockieren, sperren.
blockage ['blɒkɪdʒ] *n* Verstopfung *f*; *(in windpipe etc)* Blockade *f*; *(act)* Blockierung *f*.
block: ~ and tackle *n* Flaschenzug *m*; **~ booking** *n (travel booking)* Gruppenbuchung *f*; *(Theat)* Gruppenbestellung *f*; **~buster** *n* **(a)** *(inf)* Knüller *m (inf)*; *(film also)* Kinohit *m (inf)*; **(b)** *(Mil)* große Bombe; **~ capitals** *npl* Blockschrift *f*; **~ grant** *n* Pauschal subvention *f*; **~head** *n (inf)* Dummkopf *m*; **~house** *n* Blockhaus *nt*; **~ish** *adj (inf)* dumm, doof *(inf)*; **~ letters** *npl* Blockschrift *f*; **~ vote** *n* Stimmenblock *m*.
bloke [bləʊk] *n (Brit inf)* Kerl *(inf)*, Typ *(inf) m*.
blond [blɒnd] *adj man, hair, beard* blond.
blonde [blɒnd] 1 *adj* blond; *skin* hell.
2 *n (woman)* Blondine *f*.
blood [blʌd] 1 *n* **(a)** Blut *nt* • **to give ~** Blut spenden; **it makes my ~ boil** das macht mich rasend; **his ~ is up** er ist wütend; **she's after** *or* **out for his ~** sie will ihm an den Kragen *(inf)*; **his ~ ran cold** es lief ihm eiskalt über den Rücken; **this firm needs new ~** diese Firma braucht frisches Blut; **it is like trying to get ~ from a stone** *(prov)* das ist verlorene Liebesmüh; **bad ~** böses Blut; **there is bad ~ between them** sie haben ein gestörtes Verhältnis.
(b) *(fig) (lineage)* Blut, Geblüt *(geh) nt*, Abstammung *f* • **a prince of the ~** ein Prinz von edlem Geblüt *(geh)*; **it's in his ~** das liegt ihm im Blut; **~ is thicker**

than water *(prov)* Blut ist dicker als Wasser *(prov)*.
(c) *(old: dandy)* Geck *(old)*, Stutzer *(dated)* *m*.
[2] *attr (pure-bred)* reinrassig.
[3] *vt hounds* an Blut gewöhnen.

blood *in cpds* Blut-; **~ and thunder** *n* Mord und Totschlag *m*; **~-and-thunder novel** *n* Reißer *m*; **~ bank** *n* Blutbank *f*; **~bath** *n* Blutbad *nt*; **~ blister** *n* Blutblase *f*; **~ brother** *n* Blutsbruder *m*; **~ clot** *n* Blutgerinnsel *nt*; **~ count** *n (Med)* Blutbild *nt*; **~curdling** *adj* grauenerregend; **they heard a ~curdling cry** sie hörten einen Schrei, der ihnen das Blut in den Adern erstarren ließ *(geh)*; **~ donor** *n* Blutspender(in *f*) *m*; **~ feud** *n* Blutfehde *f*; **~ group** *n* Blutgruppe *f*; **~ heat** *n* Körpertemperatur *f*; **~hound** *n* **(a)** *(Zool)* Bluthund *m*; **(b)** *(fig: detective)* Schnüffler *(inf)*, Detektiv *m*.

bloodiness ['blʌdɪnɪs] *n* **(a)** *(of sight, war etc)* Blutigkeit *f* ◆ **the ~ of his face/suit** das Blut in seinem Gesicht/auf seinem Anzug. **(b)** *(inf: horribleness)* Gräßlichkeit, Abscheulichkeit *f*.

bloodless ['blʌdlɪs] *adj (rare: without blood)* blutlos; *(without bloodshed) victory, coup* unblutig; *(pallid)* blutleer, bleich.

bloodlessly ['blʌdlɪslɪ] *adv* unblutig.

bloodlessness ['blʌdlɪsnɪs] *n see adj* Blutlosigkeit *f*; Unblutigkeit *f*; Blutleere, Bleichheit *f*.

blood: ~-letting *n* Aderlaß *m*; **~ lust** *n* Blutrünstigkeit *f*; **~mobile** *n (US)* Blutspendewagen *m*; **~ money** *n* Mordgeld *nt*; **~ orange** *n* Blutorange *f*; **~-poisoning** *n* Blutvergiftung *f*; **~ pressure** *n* Blutdruck *m*; **to have (high) ~ pressure** hohen Blutdruck haben; **~ pudding** *n* ≃ Blutwurst *f*; **~-red** *adj* blutrot; **~ relation** *n* Blutsverwandte(r) *mf*; **~shed** *n* Blutvergießen *nt*; **~shot** *adj* blutunterlaufen; **~ sports** *npl Jagdsport, Hahnenkampf m etc*; **~stain** *n* Blutfleck *m*; **~stained** *adj* blutig, blutbefleckt; **~ stock** *n* reinrassige Zucht; **~stone** *n* Blutjaspis, Heliotrop *m*; **~stream** *n* Blut *nt*, Blutkreislauf *m*; **~sucker** *n (Zool, fig)* Blutsauger *m*; **~ sugar** *n* Blutzucker *m*; **~ sugar level** *n* Blutzuckerspiegel *m*; **~ test** *n* Blutprobe *f*; **~thirstiness** *n see adj* Blutrünstigkeit *f*, Blutgier *f*; **~thirsty** *adj tale* blutrünstig; *person, animal, disposition also* blutgierig; **~ transfusion** *n* Blutübertragung, (Blut)transfusion *f*; **~ vessel** *n* Blutgefäß *nt*; **he almost burst a ~ vessel** *(lit)* ihm wäre beinahe eine Ader geplatzt; *(fig inf)* ihn traf fast der Schlag.

bloody ['blʌdɪ] [1] *adj (+er)* **(a)** *(lit) nose, bandage, battle* blutig.
(b) *(Brit sl: damned)* verdammt *(inf)*, Scheiß- *(sl)*; *(in positive sense) genius, wonder* echt *(inf)*, verdammt *(inf)* ◆ **it was a ~ nuisance/waste of time** Mann *or* Mensch, das war vielleicht ein Quatsch *(inf) or* Scheiß *(sl)*/das war reine Zeitverschwendung; **it was there all the ~ time** Mann *(inf) or* Mensch *(inf) or* Scheiße *(sl)*, das war schon die ganze Zeit da; **I haven't got any ~ time** verdammt noch mal, ich hab' keine Zeit *(inf)*; **he hasn't got a ~ hope** Mensch *or* Mann, der hat doch überhaupt keine Chance *(inf)*; **~ hell!** verdammt! *(inf)*, Scheiße! *(sl)*; *(in indignation)* verdammt noch mal! *(inf)*; *(in amazement)* Menschenskind! *(inf)*, meine Fresse! *(sl)*; **he is a ~ marvel** er ist echt *or* verdammt gut *(inf)*; **just a ~ minute** nu mal sachte! *(inf)*.
(c) *(inf: awful)* greulich *(inf)*; *person, behaviour* abscheulich.
[2] *adv (Brit sl)* verdammt *(inf)*, saumäßig *(sl)*; *hot, cold, stupid* sau- *(sl)*; *(in positive sense) good, brilliant* echt *(inf)*, verdammt *(inf)* ◆ **that's ~ useless/no ~ good** Mensch, das taugt doch überhaupt nichts *(inf)*/das ist Scheiße *(sl)*; **not ~ likely** da ist überhaupt nichts drin *(inf)*; **he can ~ well do it himself** das soll er schön alleine machen, verdammt noch mal! *(inf)*.
[3] *vt* blutig machen.

Bloody Mary *n Cocktail m aus Tomatensaft und Wodka.*

bloody-minded [blʌdɪ'maɪndɪd] *adj (Brit inf)* stur *(inf)*.

bloom [bluːm] [1] *n* **(a)** Blüte *f* ◆ **to be in (full) ~** in (voller) Blüte stehen; **to come/burst into ~** aufblühen/plötzlich erblühen.
(b) *(fig)* **in the ~ of youth** in der Blüte der Jugend; **she has lost the ~ of youth/her ~** sie hat den Schmelz der Jugend *(geh)*/ihre Frische verloren; **in the first ~ of love** in der ersten Begeisterung ihrer Liebe.
(c) *(on fruit)* satter Schimmer; *(on peaches)* Flaum *m*.
[2] *vi (lit fig)* blühen.

bloomer ['bluːmə^r] *n (inf)* grober Fehler ◆ **to make a ~** einen Bock schießen *(inf)*.

bloomers ['bluːməz] *npl* Pumphose *f*.

blooming ['bluːmɪŋ] [1] *prp of* **bloom**.
[2] *adj (inf)* verflixt *(inf)* ◆ **it was there all the ~ time** verflixt, das war schon die ganze Zeit da! *(inf)*.
[3] *adv* verflixt *(inf)*.

blooper ['bluːpə^r] *n (US inf)* Schnitzer *m (inf)*.

blossom ['blɒsəm] [1] *n* Blüte *f* ◆ **in ~** in Blüte.
[2] *vi* **(a)** blühen. **(b)** *(fig) (relationship)* blühen; *(person, trade etc also)* aufblühen ◆ **to ~ into sth** zu etw aufblühen; *(person also)* zu etw erblühen *(geh)*; *(relationship)* zu etw wachsen.

◆**blossom out** *vi (fig)* aufblühen *(into* zu).

blot [blɒt] [1] *n* **(a)** *(of ink)* (Tinten)klecks *m*.
(b) *(fig: on honour, reputation)* Fleck *m (on* auf *+dat)* ◆ **a ~ on his character** ein Fleck auf seiner weißen Weste; **a ~ on the landscape** ein Schandfleck in der Landschaft.
[2] *vt* **(a)** *(make ink spots on)* beklecksen ◆ **to ~ one's copybook** *(fig)* sich unmöglich machen; *(with sb)* es sich *(dat)* verderben.
(b) *(dry) ink, page* ablöschen; *skin, face etc* abtupfen.

◆**blot out** *vt sep* **(a)** *(lit) words* unleserlich machen, verschmieren. **(b)** *(fig) (hide from view) landscape* verdecken; *(obliterate) memories* auslöschen.

blotch [blɒtʃ] [1] *n (on skin)* Fleck *m*; *(of ink, colour also)* Klecks *m*.
[2] *vt paper, written work* beklecksen, Flecken machen auf *(+acc)*; *skin* fleckig werden lassen.

blotchy ['blɒtʃɪ] *adj (+er) skin* fleckig; *drawing, paint* klecksig ◆ **~ splashes of colour** Farbkleckse *pl*; **a rather ~ drawing** ein richtiges Kleckbild.

blotter ['blɒtə^r] *n* **(a)** (Tinten)löscher *m*. **(b)** *(US) (record book)* Kladde *f*; *(police ~)* Polizeiregister *nt*.

blotting ['blɒtɪŋ-]: **~ pad** *n* Schreibunterlage *f*; **~ paper** *n* Löschpapier *nt*.

blotto ['blɒtəʊ] *adj pred (sl: drunk)* sternhagelvoll *(inf)*.

blouse [blaʊz] *n* **(a)** Bluse *f*. **(b)** *(US Mil)* (Feld)bluse *f*.

bloused [blaʊzd] *adj* blusig, wie eine Bluse.

blouson ['bluːzɒn] *n* Blouson *m or nt*.

blow¹ [bləʊ] *n (lit, fig)* Schlag *m*; *(fig: sudden misfortune also)* Schicksalsschlag *m (for, to* für) ◆ **to come to ~s** handgreiflich werden; **it came to ~s** es gab Handgreiflichkeiten; **at a (single)** *or* **one ~** *(fig)* mit einem Schlag *(inf)*; **to give sb/sth a ~** jdn/etw schlagen; **to deal sb/sth a ~** *(lit, fig)* jdm/einer Sache einen Schlag versetzen; **to strike a ~ for sth** *(fig)* einer Sache *(dat)* einen großen Dienst erweisen; **without striking a ~** ohne jede Gewalt; **he returned ~ for ~** er gab Schlag um Schlag zurück.

blow² *(vb: pret* **blew**, *ptp* **~n)** [1] *vi* **(a)** *(wind)* wehen, blasen ◆ **there was a draught ~ing from the window** es zog vom Fenster her; **the wind was ~ing hard** es wehte ein starker Wind.
(b) *(person)* blasen, pusten *(on* auf *+acc)* ◆ **to ~ on one's soup** auf die Suppe pusten.
(c) *(move with the wind)* fliegen; *(leaves, hat, papers also)* geweht werden ◆ **the door blew open/shut** die Tür flog auf/zu.
(d) *(make sound: bugle horn)* blasen; *(whistle)* pfeifen ◆ **then the whistle blew** *(Sport)* da kam der Pfiff.
(e) *(pant)* pusten *(inf)*, schnaufen *(inf)*; *(animal)* schnaufen.
(f) *(whale)* spritzen ◆ **there she ~s!** Wal in Sicht!
(g) *(fuse, light bulb)* durchbrennen; *(gasket)* platzen.
(h) *(inf: leave)* abhauen *(inf)*.
[2] *vt* **(a)** *(move by ~ing) (breeze)* wehen; *(strong wind, draught)* blasen; *(gale etc)* treiben; *(person)* blasen, pusten *(inf)* ◆ **the wind blew the ship off course** der Wind trieb das Schiff vom Kurs ab; **to ~ sb a kiss** jdm eine Kußhand zuwerfen.
(b) *(drive air into) fire* anblasen; *eggs* ausblasen ◆ **to ~ one's nose** sich *(dat)* die Nase putzen.
(c) *(make by ~ing) glass* blasen; *bubbles* machen.
(d) *trumpet* blasen; *(Hunt, Mil) horn* blasen in *(+acc)* ◆ **the referee blew his whistle** der Schiedsrichter pfiff; **to ~ one's own trumpet** *(fig)* sein eigenes Lob singen.
(e) *(burn out, ~ up) safe, bridge etc* sprengen; *valve, gasket* platzen lassen; *transistor* zerstören ◆ **I've ~n a fuse/light bulb** mir ist eine Sicherung/Birne durchgebrannt; **to be ~n to pieces** *(bridge, car)* in die Luft gesprengt werden; *(person)* zerfetzt werden.
(f) *(sl: spend extravagantly) money* verpulvern *(inf)*.
(g) *(inf: reveal) secret* verraten; *see* **gaff²**.
(h) *(inf: damn)* **~!** Mist! *(inf)*; **~ this rain!** dieser mistige Regen! *(inf)*; **~ the expense/what he likes!** das ist doch wurscht, was es kostet/was er will *(inf)*; **well, I'm ~ed** Mensch(enskind)! *(inf)*; **I'll be ~ed if I'll do it** ich denke nicht im Traum dran(, das zu tun) *(inf)*; **... and ~ me if he still didn't forget** und er hat es doch glatt trotzdem vergessen *(inf)*.
(i) *(inf)* **to ~ one's chances of doing sth** es sich *(dat)* verscherzen, etw zu tun.
(j) *(sl) see* **mind 1**.
[3] *n* **(a)** *(expulsion of breath)* Blasen, Pusten *(inf) nt* ◆ **to give a ~** blasen, pusten *(inf)*; *(when ~ing nose)* sich schneuzen.
(b) *(breath of air)* **to go for a ~** sich durchlüften lassen.

◆**blow away** [1] *vi (hat, paper etc)* wegfliegen.
[2] **(a)** *vt sep* wegblasen; *(breeze also)* wegwehen. **(b)** *(sl: kill)* abknallen *(sl)*. **(c)** *(sl: defeat)* fertigmachen *(inf)*, in die Pfanne hauen *(sl)*.

◆**blow down** [1] *vi (tree etc)* umfallen, umgeweht werden.
[2] *vt sep (lit)* umwehen ◆ **~ me ~!** *(inf)* Mensch(enskind)! *(inf)*.

◆**blow in** [1] *vi* **(a)** *(lit) (be blown down: window etc)* eingedrückt werden; *(be ~n ~side: dust etc)* hinein-/hereinfliegen, hinein-/hereingeweht *or* -geblasen werden; *(wind)* hereinwehen, hereinblasen ◆ **there was a draught ~ing ~** es zog herein.
(b) *(inf: arrive unexpectedly)* hereinschneien *(inf) (+prep obj, -to* in *+acc)*.
[2] *vt sep window, door etc* eindrücken; *dust etc* hinein-/hereinblasen *or* -wehen *(+prep obj, -to* in *+acc)*.

◆**blow off** [1] *vi* wegfliegen.
[2] *vt sep* wegblasen; *(+prep obj)* blasen von; *(breeze also)* wegwehen; *(+prep obj)* wehen von.
[3] *vt insep (fig) steam* ablassen *(inf)*.

◆**blow out** [1] *vi* **(a)** *(candle etc)* ausgehen. **(b)** *(Aut: tyre)* platzen; *(Elec: fuse)* durchbrennen. **(c)** *(gas, oil)* ausbrechen; *(oil well)* einen Ausbruch haben.
[2] *vt sep* **(a)** *candle* ausblasen, löschen. **(b)** *(fill with air) one's cheeks* aufblasen.
(c) **to ~ one's brains ~** sich *(dat)* eine Kugel durch den Kopf jagen.
[3] *vr (wind, storm)* sich legen; *(fig: passion)* verpuffen *(inf)*.

◆**blow over** [1] *vi* **(a)** *(tree etc)* umfallen. **(b)** *(lit, fig: storm, dispute)* sich legen.
[2] *vt sep tree etc* umstürzen.

◆**blow up** [1] *vi* **(a)** *(be exploded)* in die Luft fliegen; *(bomb)* explodieren. **(b)** *(lit, fig: gale, crisis, row)* ausbrechen. **(c)** *(fig inf: person)* explodieren *(inf)*.
[2] *vt sep* **(a)** *mine, bridge, person* in die Luft jagen, hochjagen. **(b)** *tyre, balloon* aufblasen ◆ **he was all ~n ~ with pride** er platzte fast vor Stolz. **(c)** *photo* vergrößern. **(d)** *(fig: magnify, exaggerate) event* aufbauschen *(into* zu).

blow: ~-by-~ *adj account* detailliert; **~-dry** [1] *n* **to have a ~-dry** sich fönen lassen; [2] *vt* fönen.

blower ['bləʊə^r] *n* **(a)** (*device*) Gebläse *nt*. **(b)** (*glass~*) Glasbläser *m*. **(c)** (*Brit inf: telephone*) Telefon *nt* ◆ **to be on the ~** an der Strippe hängen (*inf*); **to get on the ~ to sb** jdn anrufen.

blow: ~fly *n* Schmeißfliege *f*; **~gun** *n* (*weapon*) Blasrohr *nt*; **~hole** *n* **(a)** (*of whale*) Atemloch *nt*; **(b)** (*Min*) Abzugsloch *nt*; **~-job** *n* (*vulg*) **to give sb a ~-job** jdm einen blasen (*vulg*); **~lamp** *n* Lötlampe *f*.

blown [bləʊn] [1] *ptp of* **blow²**.
[2] *adj flower* voll aufgeblüht.

blow: ~out *n* **(a)** (*inf: meal*) Schlemmerei *f*; **to go for a ~out** tüchtig schlemmen gehen (*inf*); **to have a ~out** schlemmen (*inf*); **(b)** (*burst tyre*) **he had a ~out** ihm ist ein Reifen geplatzt; **in the case of a ~out** wenn ein Reifen platzt; **(c)** (*Elec*) **there's been a ~out** die Sicherung ist durchgebrannt; **(d)** (*Min*) Ausbruch *m*; (*on oil-rig*) Ölausbruch *m* ; **~ pipe** *n* **(a)** (*weapon*) Blasrohr *nt*; **(b)** (*Tech*) Gebläsebrenner *m*, Lötrohr *nt*; **(c)** (*for glassmaking*) Glasbläserpfeife *f*; **~ torch** *n* Lötlampe *f*; **~-up** *n* **(a)** (*inf: outburst of temper*) Wutausbruch *m*; **(b)** (*inf: row*) Krach *m*; **they've had a ~-up** sie hatten Krach; **(c)** (*Phot*) Vergrößerung *f*.

blowy ['bləʊɪ] *adj* (*+er*) windig.

blowzy ['blaʊzɪ] *adj* (*+er*) *woman* schlampig.

blubber ['blʌbə^r] [1] *n* **(a)** Walfischspeck *m*; (*inf: on person*) Wabbelspeck *m* (*inf*). **(b)** (*inf: weep*) **to have a ~** flennen (*inf*), heulen (*inf*).
[2] *vti* (*inf*) flennen (*inf*), heulen (*inf*).

◆**blubber out** *vt sep* (*inf*) flennen (*inf*), heulen (*inf*).

blubberer ['blʌbərə^r] *n* (*inf*) Heulsuse *f* (*inf*).

blubbery ['blʌbərɪ] *adj* **(a)** wabb(e)lig (*inf*). **(b)** (*inf: weepy*) verheult (*inf*).

bludgeon ['blʌdʒən] [1] *n* Knüppel *m*, Keule *f*.
[2] *vt* **(a)** verprügeln ◆ **to ~ sb to death** jdn zu Tode prügeln. **(b)** (*fig*) bearbeiten (*inf*) ◆ **he ~ed me into doing it** er hat mich so lange bearbeitet, bis ich es getan habe (*inf*); **I don't want to ~ you** ich möchte dich nicht dazu zwingen.

blue [bluː] [1] *adj* (*+er*) **(a)** blau ◆ **~ with cold** blau vor Kälte; **until you're ~ in the face** (*inf*) bis zur Vergasung (*inf*), bis zum Gehtnichtmehr (*inf*); **once in a ~ moon** alle Jubeljahre (einmal); **like a ~ streak** (*inf*) wie ein geölter Blitz (*inf*).
(b) (*inf: miserable*) melancholisch, trübsinnig ◆ **to feel/look ~** den Moralischen haben (*inf*)/traurig aussehen.
(c) (*inf: obscene*) *language* derb, nicht salonfähig; *joke* schlüpfrig; *film* Porno-, Sex- ◆ **the air was ~ (with oaths)** da habe ich/hat er *etc* vielleicht geflucht (*inf*).
(d) (*Pol*) konservativ.
[2] *n* **(a)** Blau *nt* ◆ **the boys in ~** (*Brit inf: police*) die Polizei, die Grünen *pl* (*dated inf*).
(b) (*Univ Sport*) *Student von Oxford oder Cambridge, der bei Wettkämpfen seine Universität vertritt* (*oder vertreten hat*); (*colours*) *blaue Mütze, als Symbol dafür, daß man seine Universität in Wettkämpfen vertreten hat.*
(c) (*liter: sky*) Himmel *m* ◆ **out of the ~** (*fig inf*) aus heiterem Himmel (*inf*).
(d) (*Pol*) Konservative(r) *mf*.
(e) (*inf*) **the ~s** *pl* (*depression*) der Moralische (*inf*) ◆ **to have (a fit of) the ~s** den Moralischen haben (*inf*).
(f) (*Mus*) **the ~s** *pl* der Blues ◆ **a ~s** *sing* ein Blues.
[3] *vt* (*inf: spend*) auf den Kopf hauen (*inf*) (*on* für).

blue: ~ baby *n* Baby *nt* mit angeborenem Herzfehler; **B~beard** *n* Ritter Blaubart *m*; **~bell** *n* Sternhyazinthe *f*; (*Scot: harebell*) Glockenblume *f*; **~ beret** *n* Blauhelm *m*; **~berry** *n* Blau- *or* Heidelbeere *f*; **~bird** *n* Rotkehlhüttensänger *m*; **~ blood** *n* blaues Blut; **~-blooded** *adj* blaublütig; **~ book** *n* **(a)** (*Brit Parl*) Blaubuch *nt*; **(b)** (*US*) ≃ Who's Who *nt*; **~bottle** *n* Schmeißfliege *f*; **~ cheese** *n* Blauschimmelkäse *m*; **~-chip** *adj company, shares* erstklassig; *shares also* Blue-chip-; *investment* sicher; **~-collar** *adj* **~-collar worker/union/jobs** Arbeiter *m*/Arbeitergewerkschaft *f*/Stellen *pl* für Arbeiter; **~-eyed** *adj* blauäugig; **sb's ~-eyed boy** (*fig*) jds Liebling(sjunge) *m*; **~ helmet** *n* Blauhelm *m*; **~jacket** *n* (*dated inf*) Matrose *m*; **to join the ~jackets** zu den blauen Jungs gehen (*dated*); **~ jeans** *npl* Blue jeans *pl*.

blueness ['bluːnɪs] *n* **(a)** (*lit*) Bläue *f*. **(b)** *see adj* (*c*) Derbheit *f*, Schlüpfrigkeit *f*, Sexgeladenheit *f* (*inf*).

blue: B~ Nile *n* Blauer Nil; **~-pencil** *vt* (*edit, revise*) korrigieren; (*delete*) ausstreichen; **B~ Peter** *n* (*Naut*) Blauer Peter; **~print** *n* Blaupause *f*; (*fig*) Plan, Entwurf *m*; **do I have to draw you a ~print?** (*inf*) muß ich dir erst 'ne Zeichnung machen? (*inf*); **~ rib(b)and** *n* Blaues Band; **~ rinse** *n* **with her ~ rinse** mit ihrem silberblau getönten Haar; **~ stocking** *n* (*fig*) Blaustrumpf *m*; **~tit** *n* Blaumeise *f*; **~ whale** *n* Blauwal *m*.

bluff¹ [blʌf] [1] *n* (*headland*) Kliff *nt*; (*inland*) Felsvorsprung *m*.
[2] *adj* rauh aber herzlich (*inf*); *honesty, answer* aufrichtig.

bluff² [1] *vti* bluffen.
[2] *n* Bluff *m* ◆ **to call sb's ~** es darauf ankommen lassen; (*make prove*) jdn auf die Probe stellen.

◆**bluff out** *vt sep* **to ~ it ~** sich rausreden (*inf*); **to ~ one's way ~ of sth** sich aus etw rausreden (*inf*).

bluffer ['blʌfə^r] *n* Bluffer *m*.

bluish ['bluːɪʃ] *adj* bläulich.

blunder ['blʌndə^r] [1] *n* (dummer) Fehler, Schnitzer *m* (*inf*); (*socially also*) Fauxpas *m* ◆ **to make a ~** einen Bock schießen (*inf*); (*socially*) einen Fauxpas begehen.
[2] *vi* **(a)** einen Bock schießen (*inf*), Mist bauen (*sl*); (*socially*) sich blamieren. **(b)** (*move clumsily*) tappen (*into* gegen) ◆ **to ~ in/out** hinein-/herein-/hinaus-/heraustappen; **to ~ into a trap** (*lit, fig*) in eine Falle tappen; **he ~ed through the poem** er kämpfte sich mühsam durch das Gedicht.

blunderbuss ['blʌndəbʌs] *n* Donnerbüchse *f*.

blunderer ['blʌndərə^r] *n* Schussel *m* (*inf*); (*socially*) Elefant *m* (*inf*).

blundering ['blʌndərɪŋ] [1] *adj* **(a)** *person* (*making mistakes*) schusselig (*inf*); (*socially*) ohne jedes Feingefühl ◆ **~ idiot** Erztrottel *m* (*inf*). **(b)** (*clumsy*) tolpatschig; *reading* holp(e)rig.
[2] *n* Schußligkeit *f* (*inf*); gesellschaftliche Schnitzer *pl*.

blunt [blʌnt] [1] *adj* (*+er*) **(a)** stumpf ◆ **with a ~ instrument** mit einem stumpfen Gegenstand.
(b) (*outspoken*) *person* geradeheraus *pred*; *speech* unverblümt; *fact* nackt, unbeschönigt ◆ **he's rather a ~ sort of person** er drückt sich ziemlich unverblümt *or* deutlich aus; **to be ~ about sth** sich unverblümt zu etw äußern; **he was very ~ about it** er hat sich sehr deutlich ausgedrückt; **let me be ~ about this** lassen Sie mich das ganz ohne Umschweife sagen.
[2] *vt knife etc* stumpf machen; (*fig*) *palate, senses* abstumpfen ◆ **his wits had been ~ed** er war geistig abgestumpft.

bluntly ['blʌntlɪ] *adv speak* freiheraus, geradeheraus ◆ **he told us quite ~ what he thought** er sagte uns ganz unverblümt seine Meinung.

bluntness ['blʌntnɪs] *n* **(a)** (*of blade, needle*) Stumpfheit *f*. **(b)** (*outspokenness*) Unverblümtheit *f*.

blur [blɜː^r] [1] *n* verschwommener Fleck ◆ **the ~ of their faces** ihre verschwommenen Gesichter; **the trees became just a ~** er *etc* konnte die Bäume nur noch verschwommen erkennen.
[2] *vt* **(a)** *inscription* verwischen; *writing also* verschmieren; *view* verschleiern; *outline, photograph* unscharf *or* verschwommen machen; *sound* verzerren ◆ **to be/become ~red** undeutlich sein/werden; (*image etc also*) verschwommen sein/verschwimmen; **her eyes were ~red with tears** ihre Augen schwammen in Tränen; **the tape is ~red here** an dieser Stelle ist die Aufnahme verzerrt.
(b) (*fig*) *senses, mind, judgement* trüben; *memory also, meaning* verwischen; *intention* in den Hintergrund drängen.

blurb [blɜːb] *n* Material *nt*, Informationen *pl*; (*on book cover*) Klappentext, Waschzettel *m*.

blurt (out) [blɜːt('aʊt)] *vt sep* herausplatzen mit (*inf*).

blush [blʌʃ] [1] *vi* **(a)** rot werden, erröten (*with* vor *+dat*).
(b) (*fig: be ashamed*) sich schämen (*for* für) ◆ **I ~ to say so** es ist mir peinlich, das zu sagen.
[2] *n* Erröten *nt no pl* ◆ **with a ~/a slight ~** errötend/mit leichtem Erröten; **without a ~** ohne rot zu werden; **spare my ~es!** bring mich nicht in Verlegenheit; **to put sb to the ~** (*dated*) jdn in Verlegenheit bringen; **the first ~ of dawn** (*fig*) der zarte Schimmer der Morgenröte; **at first ~** auf den ersten Blick.

blusher ['blʌʃə^r] *n* Rouge *nt*.

blushing ['blʌʃɪŋ] *adj* errötend ◆ **the ~ bride** die sittsame Braut.

bluster ['blʌstə^r] [1] *vi* **(a)** (*wind*) tosen, toben. **(b)** (*fig: person*) ein großes Geschrei machen; (*angrily also*) toben.
[2] *vt* **to ~ one's way out of it/sth** es/etw lautstark abstreiten.
[3] *n see vi* **(a)** Tosen, Toben *nt*. **(b)** großes Geschrei; Toben *nt*.

blustering ['blʌstərɪŋ] *adj person* polternd; *manner* stürmisch.

blustery ['blʌstərɪ] *adj wind, day* stürmisch.

Blvd. *abbr of* **boulevard.**

BM *abbr of* **British Museum; Bachelor of Medicine.**

BMA *abbr of* **British Medical Association** *britischer Ärzteverband.*

B-movie ['biː,muːvɪ] *n als Beiprogramm gezeigter Kinofilm*, B-movie *nt* (*spec*).

B Mus *abbr of* **Bachelor of Music.**

BO (*inf*) *abbr of* **body odour** Körpergeruch *m*.

boa ['bəʊə] *n* Boa *f* ◆ **~ constrictor** Boa constrictor *f*.

boar [bɔː^r] *n* (*male pig*) Eber *m*; (*wild*) Keiler *m* ◆ **~'s head** Schweinskopf *m*.

board [bɔːd] [1] *n* **(a)** Brett *nt*; (*black~*) Tafel *f*; (*notice~*) Schwarzes Brett; (*sign~*) Schild *nt*; (*floor~*) Diele(nbrett *nt*) *f* ◆ **the ~s** (*Theat*) die Bretter.
(b) (*provision of meals*) Kost, Verpflegung *f* ◆ **~ and lodging** Kost und Logis; **full/half ~** Voll-/Halbpension *f*.
(c) (*group of officials*) Ausschuß *m*; (*~ of inquiry, examiners also*) Kommission *f*; (*with advisory function, ~ of trustees*) Beirat *m*; (*permanent official institution: gas ~, harbour ~ etc*) Behörde *f*; (*of company: also* **~ of directors**) Vorstand *m*; (*of British/American company*) Verwaltungsrat *m*; (*including shareholders, advisers*) Aufsichtsrat *m* ◆ **to be on the ~, to have a seat on the ~** im Vorstand/Aufsichtsrat sein *or* sitzen; **b~ of governors** (*Brit Sch*) Verwaltungsrat *m*; **B~ of Trade** (*Brit*) Handelsministerium *nt*; (*US*) Handelskammer *f*.
(d) (*Naut, Aviat*) **on ~** an Bord; **to go on ~** an Bord gehen; **on ~ the ship/plane** an Bord des Schiffes/Flugzeugs; **on ~ the bus** im Bus; **he held a party on ~ his yacht** er veranstaltete eine Party auf seiner Jacht.
(e) (*cardboard*) Pappe *f*; (*Typ*) Deckel *m*.
(f) (*~ of interviewers*) Gremium *nt* (zur Auswahl von Bewerbern); (*interview*) Vorstellungsgespräch *nt* (vor einem Gremium) ◆ **to be on a ~** einem Gremium zur Auswahl von Bewerbern angehören; **to go on a ~** (*as interviewer*) eine Gremiumssitzung zur Bewerberauswahl haben; (*as candidate*) sich einem Gremium vorstellen.
(g) (*US St Ex*) Notierung *f*; (*inf: stock exchange*) Börse *f*.
(h) (*fig phrases*) **across the ~** allgemein, generell; *criticize, agree, reject* pauschal; **an increase of £10 per week across the ~** eine allgemeine *or* generelle Lohnerhöhung von £ 10 pro Woche; **to go by the ~** (*work, plans, ideas*)

unter den Tisch fallen; (*dreams, hopes*) zunichte werden; (*principles*) über Bord geworfen werden; (*business*) zugrunde gehen; **that's all gone by the ~** daraus ist nichts geworden.

[2] *vt* **(a)** (*cover with ~s*) mit Brettern verkleiden. **(b)** *ship, plane* besteigen, an Bord (+*gen*) gehen/kommen; *train, bus* einsteigen in (+*acc*); (*Naut: in attack*) entern.

[3] *vi* **(a)** in Pension sein (*with* bei). **(b)** (*Sch*) Internatsschüler(in *f*) *m* sein. **(c)** (*Aviat*) die Maschine besteigen ♦ **flight ZA173 now ~ing through gate 13** Aufruf für Passagiere des Fluges ZA173, sich zum Flugsteig 13 zu begeben.

♦**board in** *or* **up** *vt sep door, window* mit Brettern vernageln.

♦**board out** [1] *vt sep person* in Pension schicken (*with* bei).
[2] *vi* in Pension wohnen (*with* bei).

boarder ['bɔːdəʳ] *n* **(a)** Pensionsgast *m* ♦ **to take in ~s** Leute in Pension nehmen. **(b)** (*Sch*) Internatsschüler(in *f*) *m*; (*weekly ~*) *während der Woche im Internat wohnender Schüler*; (*dated: day ~*) *Tagesschüler, der in der Schule zu Mittag ißt*. **(c)** (*Naut*) Mitglied *nt* eines Enterkommandos.

board game *n* Brettspiel *nt*.

boarding ['bɔːdɪŋ]: **~ card** *n* Bordkarte *f*; **~ house** *n* **(a)** Pension *f*; **(b)** (*Sch*) Wohngebäude *nt* eines Internats; **~ party** *n* (*Naut*) Enterkommando *nt*; **~ pass** *n* Bordkarte *f*; **~ school** *n* Internat *nt*.

board: **~ meeting** *n* Vorstandssitzung *f*; **~room** *n* Sitzungssaal *m* (*des Vorstands*); **he's ~room material** er hat Führungspotential; **~room floor** *n* Vorstandsetage *f*; **~room politics** *npl* Firmenklüngel *m* (*inf*); **~ school** *n* (*Brit Hist*) staatliche Schule; **~walk** *n* (*US*) Holzsteg *m*; (*on beach*) hölzerne Uferpromenade.

boast [bəʊst] [1] *n* **(a)** Prahlerei *f*. **(b)** (*source of pride*) Stolz *m*. **it is their ~ that** ... sie rühmen sich, daß ...

[2] *vi* prahlen (*about, of* mit, *to sb* jdm gegenüber) ♦ **without ~ing, without wishing to ~** ohne zu prahlen.

[3] *vt* **(a)** (*possess*) sich rühmen (+*gen*) (*geh*). **(b)** (*say boastfully*) prahlen.

boaster ['bəʊstəʳ] *n* Aufschneider(in *f*) *m*, Prahlhans *m* (*inf*).

boastful ['bəʊstfʊl] *adj*, **~ly** ['bəʊstfəlɪ] *adv* prahlerisch.

boastfulness ['bəʊstfʊlnɪs] *n* Prahlerei *f*.

boasting ['bəʊstɪŋ] *n* Prahlerei *f* (*about, of* mit).

boat [bəʊt] *n* **(a)** (*small vessel*) Boot *nt*; (*wooden: on lake, river etc also*) Kahn *m*; (*sea-going, passenger ~*) Schiff *nt*; (*pleasure steamer etc*) Dampfer *m* ♦ **by ~** mit dem Schiff; **to miss the ~** (*fig inf*) den Anschluß verpassen; **we're all in the same ~** (*fig inf*) wir sitzen alle in einem *or* im gleichen Boot.
(b) (*gravy ~*) Sauciere *f*.

boat: **~-builder** *n* Bootsbauer *m*; **~-building** *n* Bootsbau *m*; **~-deck** *n* Bootsdeck *nt*.

boater ['bəʊtəʳ] *n* **(a)** (*hat*) steifer Strohhut, Kreissäge *f* (*inf*). **(b)** (*person*) Bootsfahrer(in *f*), Kahnfahrer(in *f*) *m*.

boat: **~ful** *n* Schiffs-/Bootsladung *f*; **~ hire** *n* Bootsverleih *m*; (*company*) Bootsverleiher *m*; **~hook** *n* Bootshaken *m*; **~house** *n* Bootshaus *nt* or -schuppen *m*.

boating ['bəʊtɪŋ] *n* Bootfahren *nt* ♦ **to go ~** Bootsfahrten/eine Bootsfahrt machen.

boating *in cpds* Boots-; **~ holiday** *n* Bootsferien *pl*; **~ trip** *n* Bootsfahrt *f*.

boat: **~load** *n* Bootsladung *f*; **~man** *n* (*handling boat*) Segler *m*; Ruderer *m*; Paddler *m*; (*working with boats*) Bootsbauer *m*; (*hirer*) Bootsverleiher *m*; **~ people** *npl* Bootsflüchtlinge *pl*; **~ race** *n* Regatta *f*; **~-shaped** *adj* kahnförmig.

boatswain, bosun, bo's'n ['bəʊsn] *n* Bootsmann *m* ♦ **~'s mate** Bootsmanngehilfe *m*.

boat: **~ train** *n* Zug *m* mit Fährenanschluß; **~yard** *n* Bootshandlung *f*; (*as dry dock*) Liegeplatz *m*.

Bob [bɒb] *n dim of* **Robert** ♦ **... and ~'s your uncle!** (*inf*) ... und fertig ist der Lack! (*inf*).

bob[1] [bɒb] [1] *vi* **(a)** sich auf und ab bewegen; (*rabbit*) hoppeln; (*bird's tail*) wippen; (*boxer*) tänzeln ♦ **to ~ (up and down) in** *or* **on the water** auf dem Wasser schaukeln; (*cork, piece of wood etc*) sich im Wasser auf und ab bewegen; **he ~bed out of sight** er duckte sich. **(b)** (*curtsey*) knicksen (*to sb* vor jdm).

[2] *vt* **(a)** (*move jerkily*) *head* nicken mit; (*bird*) *tail* wippen mit.
(b) *curtsey* machen ♦ **to ~ a greeting** zum Gruß kurz nicken.

[3] *n* **(a)** (*curtsey*) Knicks(chen *nt*) *m*.
(b) (*of head*) Nicken *nt no pl*; (*of bird's tail*) Wippen *nt no pl*.

♦**bob down** [1] *vi* sich ducken.
[2] *vt sep one's head* ducken.

♦**bob up** [1] *vi* (*lit, fig*) auftauchen.
[2] *vt sep* **he ~bed his head ~** sein Kopf schnellte hoch.

bob[2] *n, pl* **~** (*dated Brit inf*) Shilling *m* ♦ **that must have cost a ~ or two** das muß schon ein paar Mark gekostet haben (*inf*).

bob[3] [1] *n* **(a)** (*haircut*) Bubikopf *m*. **(b)** (*horse's tail*) gestutzter Schwanz. **(c)** (*weight: on pendulum, plumbline*) Gewicht *nt*. **(d)** (*Fishing: float*) Schwimmer *m*.
[2] *vt* **to have one's hair ~bed** sich (*dat*) einen Bubikopf schneiden lassen.

bob[4] *n* (*sleigh*) Bob *m*; (*runner*) Kufe *f* ♦ **two-/four-man ~** Zweier-/Viererbob *m*.

bobbin ['bɒbɪn] *n* Spule *f*; (*cotton reel*) Rolle *f*.

bobble ['bɒbl] *n* **(a)** Bommel *f*, Pompon *m*. **(b)** (*US inf: mistake*) Schnitzer *m* (*inf*).

Bobby ['bɒbɪ] *n dim of* **Robert** ♦ **b~** (*dated Brit inf*) Bobby, Schupo (*dated*) *m*.

bobby: **~ pin** *n* Haarklemme *f*; **~ socks** *npl* (*US*) kurze Söckchen *pl*; **~soxer** *n* (*US inf*) Teenager *m*, junges Mädchen.

bob: **~cap** *n* Pudelmütze *f*; **~cat** *n* (*US*) Luchs *m*; **~sled, ~sleigh** [1] *n* Bob *m*; [2] *vi* Bob fahren; **~tail** *n* gestutzter Schwanz; **~tail cap** *or* **hat** *n* Bommelmütze *f*; **~tailed** *adj horse, dog* mit gestutztem Schwanz.

Boche [bɒʃ] *n* (*pej inf*) Boche *m*.

bod [bɒd] *n* (*Brit inf*) Mensch *m* ♦ **odd ~** komischer Kerl.

bode [bəʊd] [1] *vi*: **to ~ well/ill** ein gutes/schlechtes Zeichen sein.
[2] *vt* bedeuten, ahnen lassen ♦ **that ~s no good** das bedeutet nichts Gutes, das läßt Böses ahnen.

bodge [bɒdʒ] *n, vt see* **botch**.

bodice ['bɒdɪs] *n* **(a)** Mieder *nt*; (*of dress also*) Oberteil *nt*. **(b)** (*vest*) Leibchen *nt*.

-bodied ['bɒdɪd] *adj suf* -gebaut, von ... Körperbau.

bodiless ['bɒdɪlɪs] *adj* körperlos.

bodily ['bɒdɪlɪ] [1] *adj* (*physical*) körperlich ♦ **~ illness** Krankheit *f* des Körpers; **~ needs/wants** leibliche Bedürfnisse *pl*; **~ harm** Körperverletzung *f*.
[2] *adv* **(a)** (*forcibly*) gewaltsam. **(b)** (*in person*) leibhaftig. **(c)** (*all together*) geschlossen; (*in one piece*) ganz.

bodkin ['bɒdkɪn] *n* **(a)** (*Sew*) Durchziehnadel *f*. **(b)** (*Hist: hairpin*) lange Haarnadel; (*obs: dagger*) Dolch *m*.

body ['bɒdɪ] *n* **(a)** (*of man, animal*) Körper *m*; (*of human also*) Leib *m* (*geh*) ♦ **the ~ of Christ** der Leib des Herrn; **just enough to keep ~ and soul together** gerade genug, um Leib und Seele zusammenzuhalten.
(b) (*corpse*) Leiche *f*, Leichnam *m* (*geh*); *see* **dead**.
(c) (*main part of structure*) (*of plane, ship*) Rumpf, Körper *m*; (*of string instrument*) Korpus, Schallkörper *m*; (*of church, speech, army: also* **main ~**) Hauptteil *m* ♦ **the main ~ of his readers/the students** das Gros seiner Leser/der Studenten; **in the ~ of the House** (*Brit Parl*) im Plenum.
(d) (*coachwork: of car*) Karosserie *f*.
(e) (*group of people*) Gruppe *f* ♦ **the student ~** die Studentenschaft; **a ~ of troops** ein Truppenverband *m*; **a great ~ of followers/readers** eine große Anhängerschaft/Leserschaft; **the great ~ of readers who buy his books** die große Anzahl von Lesern, die seine Bücher kaufen; **a large ~ of people** eine große Menschenmenge; **in a ~** geschlossen; **taken in a ~** geschlossen *or* als Ganzes betrachtet.
(f) (*organization*) Organ *nt*; (*committee*) Gremium *nt*; (*corporation*) Körperschaft *f*; *see* **corporate, politic**.
(g) (*quantity*) **a ~ of facts/evidence/data** Tatsachen-/Beweis-/Datenmaterial *nt*; **a ~ of laws/legislation** ein Gesetzeskomplex *m*; **a large ~ of water** eine große Wassermasse.
(h) (*inf: person*) Mensch *m*.
(i) (*Math, Phys, Chem*) Körper *m*.
(j) (*substance, thickness*) (*of wine*) Körper *m*; (*of soup*) Substanz *f*; (*of paper, cloth*) Festigkeit, Stärke *f* ♦ **the material hasn't enough ~** der Stoff ist nicht fest *or* stark genug; **this soup hasn't enough ~** diese Suppe ist zu dünn.
(k) (*also* **~ stocking**) Body *m*.

body: **~ blow** *n* Körperschlag *m*; (*fig*) Schlag *m* ins Kontor (*to, for* für); **~builder** *n* **(a)** (*food*) Kraftnahrung *f*; **(b)** (*apparatus*) Heimtrainer *m*; **(c)** (*person*) Bodybuilder *m*; **~building** [1] *n* Bodybuilding *nt*; [2] *adj exercise* muskelkräftigend; *food* stärkend, kräftigend; **~check** *n* Bodycheck *m*; **~ clock** *n* innere Uhr; **~ count** *n* (*Mil*) Zählung *f* der Toten; **~ double** *n* (*Film, TV*) Körperdouble *nt*; **~guard** *n* (*one person*) Leibwächter *m*; (*group*) Leibwache *f*; **~ language** *n* Körpersprache *f*; **~ lotion** *n* Körperlotion *f*; **~ mike** *n* Umhängemikrofon *nt*; **~ popping** *n* Breakdance *m*; **~ (repair) shop** *n* Karosseriewerkstatt *f*; **~ scanner** *n* Scanner *m*; **~ scissors** *n sing* (*Wrestling*) über den Körper angelegte Schere; **~ search** *n* Leibesvisitation *f*; **~ shop** *n* **(a)** *see* **~ (repair) shop**; **(b)** (*in factory*) Karosseriewerk *nt*; **~slam** *n* (*Wrestling*) Wurf *m*; **~-snatcher** *n* Leichenräuber *m*; **~ stocking** *n* Body(stocking) *m*; **~ warmer** *n* Thermoweste *f*; **~work** *n* (*Aut*) Karosserie *f*.

Boer ['bəʊəʳ] [1] *n* Bure *m*, Burin *f*.
[2] *adj* burisch ♦ **the ~ War** der Burenkrieg.

B of E *abbr of* **Bank of England**.

boffin ['bɒfɪn] *n* (*Brit inf*) Eierkopf (*inf*), Egghead (*inf*) *m*.

bog [bɒg] *n* **(a)** Sumpf *m*; (*peat ~*) (Torf)moor *nt*. **(b)** (*Brit inf: toilet*) Lokus *m* (*inf*), Klo *nt* (*inf*) ♦ **~ paper** Klopapier *nt* (*inf*).

♦**bog down** *vt sep* **to be ~ged ~** (*lit*), steckenbleiben; (*fig*) steckengeblieben sein, sich festgefahren haben; (*in details*) sich verzettelt haben; **to get ~ged ~** (*lit*) steckenbleiben; (*fig also*) sich festfahren; (*in details*) sich verzetteln.

bogey[1], **bogy** ['bəʊgɪ] *n, pl* **bogeys, bogies** **(a)** (*spectre, goblin*) Kobold, Butzemann *m* ♦ **~ man** Butzemann *m*, Schwarzer Mann. **(b)** (*fig: bugbear*) Popanz *m*, Schreckgespenst *nt*. **(c)** (*baby-talk*) Popel *m* (*inf*).

bogey[2] *n* (*Golf*) Bogey *nt*.

boggle ['bɒgl] *vi* (*inf*) glotzen (*inf*), völlig sprachlos sein ♦ **he ~d at the sight** als er das sah, war er völlig sprachlos; **the mind** *or* **imagination ~s** das ist nicht *or* kaum auszumalen (*inf*).

boggy ['bɒgɪ] *adj* (+*er*) *ground* sumpfig, morastig.

bogie ['bəʊgɪ] *n* (*Rail*) Drehgestell *nt*; (*trolley*) Draisine *f*.

bog-standard ['bɒg'stændəd] *adj* (*Brit inf*) stinknormal (*inf*).

bogus ['bəʊgəs] *adj doctor, lawyer* falsch; *money, pearls also* gefälscht; *company, transaction* Schwindel-; *claim* erfunden.

bogy ['bəʊgɪ] *n see* **bogey**[1].

Bohemia [bəʊ'hiːmɪə] *n* (*Geog*) Böhmen *nt*; (*fig*) Boheme *f*.

Bohemian [bəʊ'hiːmɪən] [1] *n* **(a)** Böhme *m*, Böhmin *f*. **(b)** (*fig*) **b~** Bohemien *m*.
[2] *adj* **(a)** böhmisch. **(b)** (*fig*) **b~** *lifestyle* unkonventionell, unbürgerlich; *circles, quarter* Künstler-.

bohemianism [bəʊ'hi:mɪənɪzəm] *n* unkonventionelle *or* unbürgerliche Lebensweise.

boil[1] [bɔɪl] *n (Med)* Furunkel *m.*

boil[2] [1] *vi* **(a)** kochen; *(water also, Phys)* sieden ◆ **the kettle was ~ing** das Wasser im Kessel kochte; **~ing oil** siedendes Öl; **allow to ~ gently** *(Cook)* langsam kochen; **to let the kettle ~ dry** das Wasser im Kessel verkochen lassen.
(b) *(fig: sea, river)* brodeln, tosen.
(c) *(fig inf: be angry)* kochen, schäumen *(with* vor *+dat).*
(d) *(fig inf: be hot)* **~ing hot water** kochendheißes Wasser; **it was ~ing (hot) in the office** es war ein Affenhitze im Büro *(inf)*; **I was ~ing (hot)** mir war fürchterlich heiß; **you'll ~ in that sweater** in dem Pullover schwitzt du dich ja tot *(inf).*
[2] *vt* kochen ◆ **~ed shirt** *(inf)* weißes Hemd; **~ed/hard ~ed egg** weich-/hartgekochtes Ei; **~ed potatoes** Salzkartoffeln *pl*; **~ed sweet** Bonbon *nt.*
[3] *n* **to bring sth to the ~** etw aufkochen lassen; **to keep sth on the ~** etw kochen *or* sieden lassen; **to keep sb on the ~** *(fig inf)* jdn hinhalten; **to be on/come to/go off the ~** kochen/zu kochen anfangen/aufhören.

◆**boil away** *vi* **(a)** *(go on boiling)* weiterkochen. **(b)** *(evaporate completely)* verdampfen.

◆**boil down** [1] *vt sep* einkochen.
[2] *vi* **(a)** *(jam etc)* dickflüssig werden. **(b)** *(fig)* **to ~ ~ to sth** auf etw *(acc)* hinauslaufen; **what it ~s ~ to is that ...** das läuft darauf hinaus, daß ...

◆**boil over** *vi* **(a)** *(lit)* überkochen. **(b)** *(fig) (situation, quarrel)* den Siedepunkt erreichen ◆ **he just ~ed ~** ihm platzte der Kragen *(inf).*

◆**boil up** *vi* **(a)** *(lit)* aufkochen. **(b) he could feel the anger ~ing ~ in him** er fühlte, wie die Wut in ihm aufstieg.

boiler ['bɔɪləʳ] *n* **(a)** *(domestic)* Boiler, Warmwasserbereiter *m*; *(in ship, engine)* (Dampf)kessel *m*; *(old: for washing)* Waschkessel *m.* **(b)** *(chicken)* Suppenhuhn *nt.*

boiler: ~ house *n* Kesselhaus *nt*; **~maker** *n* Kesselschmied *m*; **~making** *n* Kesselbau *m*; **~man** *n* Heizer *m*; **~plate letter** *n (US)* (Brief)rumpf *m*; **~ room** *n* Kesselraum *m*; **~suit** *n* Overall, blauer Anton *(inf)*, Blaumann *(inf) m.*

boiling ['bɔɪlɪŋ-]: **~ fowl** *n* Suppenhuhn *nt*; **~ point** *n (lit, fig)* Siedepunkt *m*; **at ~ point** *(lit, fig)* auf dem Siedepunkt; **to reach ~ point** *(lit, fig)* den Siedepunkt erreichen; *(feelings also, person)* auf dem Siedepunkt anlangen.

boisterous ['bɔɪstərəs] *adj* **(a)** *(exuberant, noisy) person* ausgelassen; *game, party, dance also* wild. **(b)** *(rough) wind* tosend; *sea also* aufgewühlt.

boisterously ['bɔɪstərəslɪ] *adv see adj.*

bold [bəʊld] *adj (+er)* **(a)** *(valiant)* kühn *(geh)*; *(brave)* mutig; *deed, plan also* verwegen.
(b) *(impudent, forward)* unverfroren, dreist ◆ **to be** *or* **make so ~ as to ...** sich erlauben *or* erkühnen *(geh)*, zu ...; **might I be so ~ as to ...?** wenn ich es mir erlauben darf, zu ...?; **might I make so ~ as to help myself?** darf ich so frei sein und mich bedienen?; **to make ~ with sth** sich *(dat)* die Freiheit herausnehmen, sich bei etw einfach zu bedienen.
(c) *(striking) colours, pattern, stripes* kräftig; *checks also* grob; *strokes also* kühn *(geh)*; *handwriting* kraftvoll, kühn *(geh)*; *style* kraftvoll, ausdrucksvoll ◆ **to bring out in ~ relief** stark hervortreten lassen.
(d) *(Typ)* fett; *(secondary ~)* halbfett ◆ **~ type** Fettdruck *m*; **to set sth in ~ (type)** etw fett/halbfett drucken.

boldness ['bəʊldnɪs] *n see adj* **(a)** Kühnheit *(geh) f*; Mut *m*; Verwegenheit *f.* **(b)** Unverfrorenheit, Dreistigkeit *f.* **(c)** Kräftigkeit *f*; Grobheit *f*; Kühnheit *(geh) f*; Ausdruckskraft *f.*

bole [bəʊl] *n* Baumstamm *m.*

bolero [bə'lɛərəʊ] *n (all senses)* Bolero *m.*

Bolivia [bə'lɪvɪə] *n* Bolivien *nt.*

Bolivian [bə'lɪvɪən] [1] *n* Bolivianer(in *f*), Bolivier(in *f*) *m.*
[2] *adj* bolivianisch, bolivisch.

boll [bəʊl] *n* Samenkapsel *f* ◆ **~ weevil** Baumwollkapselkäfer *m.*

bollard ['bɒləd] *n (on quay, road)* Poller *m.*

bollocking ['bɒləkɪŋ] *n (Brit sl)* Schimpfkanonade *f (inf)* ◆ **to give sb a ~** jdn zur Sau machen *(sl).*

bollocks ['bɒləks] *npl (vulg)* **(a)** Eier *pl (sl).* **(b)** *(nonsense)* **(that's) ~!** Quatsch mit Soße! *(sl)*; **he was talking ~** der hat einen Scheiß geredet *(sl).*

boloney [bə'ləʊnɪ] *n see* **baloney.**

Bolshevik ['bɒlʃəvɪk] [1] *n* Bolschewik *m.*
[2] *adj* bolschewistisch.

Bolshevism ['bɒlʃəvɪzəm] *n* Bolschewismus *m.*

Bolshevist ['bɒlʃəvɪst] *n, adj see* **Bolshevik.**

bolshie, bolshy ['bɒlʃɪ] *(inf)* [1] *n* Bolschewik *m.*
[2] *adj (+er)* **(a)** *(fig) (uncooperative)* stur; *(aggressive)* pampig *(inf)*, rotzig *(sl).* **(b)** *(pej)* bolschewistisch.

bolster ['bəʊlstəʳ] [1] *n (on bed)* Nackenrolle *f.*
[2] *vt (also* **~ up***) (fig) person* Mut machen *(+dat)*; *status* aufbessern; *currency* stützen ◆ **to ~ up sb's morale** jdm Mut machen.

bolt [bəʊlt] [1] *n* **(a)** *(on door etc)* Riegel *m.*
(b) *(Tech)* Schraube *f* (ohne Spitze), Bolzen *m.*
(c) *(of lightning)* Blitzstrahl *m* ◆ **it came/was like a ~ from the blue** *(fig)* das schlug ein/war wie ein Blitz aus heiterem Himmel.
(d) *(of cloth)* Ballen *m.*
(e) *(of crossbow)* Bolzen *m*; *see* **shoot.**
(f) *(of rifle)* Kammer *f.*
(g) *(sudden dash)* Satz *m (inf)* ◆ **his ~ for freedom** sein Fluchtversuch *m*; **he made a ~ for the door** er machte einen Satz zur Tür; **to make a ~ for it** losrennen.
[2] *adv*: **~ upright** kerzengerade.
[3] *vi* **(a)** *(horse)* durchgehen; *(person)* Reißaus nehmen *(inf)* ◆ **too late now, the horse has ~ed** *(fig)* zu spät, der Zug ist schon abgefahren.
(b) *(move quickly)* sausen, rasen, pesen *(inf).*
[4] *vt* **(a)** *door, window* zu- *or* verriegeln.
(b) *(Tech) parts* verschrauben *(to* mit*)*, mit Schraubenbolzen befestigen *(to* an *+dat)* ◆ **to ~ together** verschrauben.
(c) *(also* **~ down***) one's food* hinunterschlingen.

◆**bolt in** [1] *vi (rush in)* herein-/hineinplatzen *or* -stürzen.
[2] *vt sep (lock in)* einsperren.

◆**bolt on** *vt sep (Tech)* festschrauben *(prep obj, -to* an *+dat).*

◆**bolt out** [1] *vi (rush out)* hinaus-/herausstürzen.
[2] *vt sep (lock out)* aussperren.

bolthole ['bəʊlthəʊl] *n* Schlupfloch *nt.*

bolus ['bəʊləs] *n, pl* **-es** *(Med)* große Pille.

bomb [bɒm] [1] *n* **(a)** Bombe *f.*
(b) *(inf)* **his party went like a ~** seine Party war ein Bombenerfolg *(inf)*; **the car goes like a ~** das ist die reinste Rakete von Wagen *(inf)*; **the car cost a ~** das Auto hat ein Bombengeld gekostet *(inf)*; **to go down a ~** Riesenanklang finden *(with* bei*) (inf)*; **to do a ~** *(US: fail)* durchfallen *(inf)*; **the play was a real ~** *(US sl)* das Stück war ein totaler Reinfall.
[2] *vt* **(a)** bombardieren; *(not from the air)* ein Bombenattentat verüben auf *(+acc).* **(b)** *(US inf: fail)* durchfallen bei.
[3] *vi* **(a)** *(inf: go fast)* fegen *(inf)*, zischen *(inf).*
(b) *(US inf: fail)* durchfallen *(inf).*

◆**bomb along** *vi (inf: drive fast)* dahinrasen *(inf).*

◆**bomb out** *vt sep* ausbomben.

bombard [bɒm'bɑ:d] *vt (Mil, fig)* bombardieren *(with* mit*)*; *(Phys)* beschießen.

bombardier [,bɒmbə'dɪəʳ] *n (Mil)* Artillerieunteroffizier *m*; *(Aviat)* Bombenschütze *m.*

bombardment [bɒm'bɑ:dmənt] *n (Mil)* Bombardierung *f (also fig)*, Bombardement *nt*; *(Phys)* Beschießen *nt.*

bombast ['bɒmbæst] *n* Schwulst, Bombast *m.*

bombastic *adj*, **~ally** *adv* [bɒm'bæstɪk, -əlɪ] schwülstig, bombastisch.

bomb attack *n* Bombenangriff *m.*

Bombay [bɒm'beɪ] *n* Bombay *nt* ◆ **~ duck** *kleiner getrockneter Fisch als Beigabe zur indischen Reistafel.*

bomb: ~ bay *n* Bombenschacht *m*; **~ crater** *n* Bombentrichter *m*; **~ disposal** *n* Bombenräumung *f*; **~ disposal expert** *n* Bombenräumexperte *m*; **~ disposal squad** *or* **unit** *n* Bombenräumtrupp *m or* -kommando *nt.*

bombed [bɒmd] *adj (sl) (drunk)* knülle *(sl)*; *(on drugs)* high *(sl).*

bombed out [,bɒm'daʊt] *adj (sl)* **(a)** *(exhausted)* völlig fertig *(inf)*, total alle *(sl).* **(b)** *(drunk)* voll *(inf)*, zu *(sl)*; *(on drugs)* high *(sl).* **(c) our team's ~** *(has no chance)* unsere Mannschaft hat keine Chance. **(d)** *(very busy) pub etc* gerammelt voll *(inf)* ◆ **we're absolutely ~ with work** wir stecken bis über den Hals in Arbeit *(inf).*

bomber ['bɒməʳ] *n* **(a)** *(aircraft)* Bomber *m*, Bombenflugzeug *nt.* **(b)** *(person) (Aviat)* Bombenschütze *m*; *(terrorist)* Bombenattentäter(in *f*) *m.*

bomber: ~ command *n* Bombenverband *m or* -geschwader *nt*; **~ jacket** *n* Fliegerjacke *f*; **~ pilot** *n* Bomberpilot *m.*

bombing ['bɒmɪŋ] [1] *n* Bombenangriff *m (of* auf *+acc)*; *(of target also)* Bombardierung *f.*
[2] *adj raid, mission* Bomben-.

bomb: ~proof *adj* bombensicher; **~ scare** *n* Bombenalarm *m*; **~shell** *n* **(a)** *(Mil)* Bombe *f*; **(b)** *(fig)* Bombe *f*, plötzliche Überraschung; **this news was a ~shell** die Nachricht schlug wie eine Bombe ein; **a blonde ~shell** ein blonder Superbomber *(inf)*; **~ shelter** *n* Luftschutzkeller *m*; *(specially built)* (Luftschutz)bunker *m*; **~ sight** *n* Fliegerbombenzielgerät *nt*; **~ site** *n* Trümmergrundstück *nt.*

bona fide ['bəʊnə'faɪdɪ] *adj* bona fide; *traveller, word, antique* echt ◆ **it's a ~ offer** es ist ein Angebot auf Treu und Glauben.

bona fides ['bəʊnə'faɪdɪz] *n* Echtheit *f.*

bonanza [bə'nænzə] [1] *n* **(a)** *(US Min)* reiche Erzader. **(b)** *(fig)* Goldgrube *f* ◆ **the oil ~** der Ölboom.
[2] *adj attr year* Boom-.

bonce [bɒns] *n (Brit sl: head)* Birne *f (sl)* ◆ **curly ~** Krauskopf *m (inf).*

bond [bɒnd] [1] *n* **(a)** *(agreement)* Übereinkommen *nt* ◆ **to enter into a ~ with sb** ein Übereinkommen mit jdm treffen.
(b) *(fig: link)* Band *nt (geh)*, Bindung *f.*
(c) ~s *pl (lit: chains)* Fesseln, Bande *(liter) pl*; *(fig: ties)* Bande *pl (geh)*; *(burdensome)* Fesseln *pl* ◆ **marriage ~s** das Band/die Fesseln der Ehe.
(d) *(Comm, Fin)* Obligation *f*, Pfandbrief *m*; *(Brit, US)* festverzinsliches Wertpapier, Bond *m* ◆ **government ~** Staatsanleihe *f or* -papiere *pl.*
(e) *(Comm: custody of goods)* Zollverschluß *m* ◆ **to put sth into ~** etw unter Zollverschluß geben; **goods in ~** Zollgut *nt.*
(f) *(adhesion between surfaces)* Haftfestigkeit, Haftwirkung *f* ◆ **nothing can break the ~ between the two surfaces** die beiden Flächen haften *or* kleben fest und unlösbar aneinander.
(g) *(Build)* Verband *m.*
(h) *(Chem)* Bindung *f.*
[2] *vt* **(a)** *(Comm) goods* unter Zollverschluß legen *or* nehmen.
(b) *(Build) bricks* im Verband verlegen.

[3] *vi* (*glue*) binden; (*bricks*) einen Verband bilden.

bondage ['bɒndɪdʒ] *n* (**a**) (*lit*) Sklaverei *f*; (*in Middle Ages*) Leibeigenschaft *f* ♦ **in ~ to sb** in Sklaverei/Leibeigenschaft bei jdm, jdm hörig.
(**b**) (*fig liter*) vollständige Unterjochung ♦ **we are held in ~ by our desires/economic system** wir sind Gefangene unserer Begierden/unseres Wirtschaftssystems; **her stronger will kept him in ~** ihr stärkerer Wille hielt ihn vollständig unterdrückt.
(**c**) (*sexual*) Fesseln *nt*.

bonded ['bɒndɪd] *adj goods* unter Zollverschluß ♦ **~ warehouse** Zollager, Zolldepot *nt*.

bond: ~ holder *n* Pfandbrief- *or* Obligationsinhaber(in *f*) *m*; **~man, ~sman** *n* Sklave *m*; (*medieval*) Leibeigene(r) *mf*.

bone [bəʊn] [1] *n* (**a**) Knochen *m*; (*of fish*) Gräte *f* ♦ **~s** *pl* (*of the dead*) Gebeine *pl*; **ham off the ~** Schinken *m* vom Knochen; **meat on the ~** Fleisch *m* am Knochen; **chilled to the ~** völlig durchgefroren; **to work one's fingers to the ~** sich (*dat*) die Finger abarbeiten; **~ of contention** Zankapfel *m*; **to have a ~ to pick with sb** (*inf*) mit jdm ein Hühnchen zu rupfen haben (*inf*); **I'll make no ~s about it, you're/this is ...** (*inf*) du bist/das ist, offen gestanden *or* ehrlich gesagt, ...; **he made no ~s about saying what he thought** (*inf*) er hat mit seiner Meinung nicht hinterm Berg gehalten; **I can feel it in my ~s** das spüre ich in den Knochen; **my old ~s** (*inf*) meine alten Knochen (*inf*).
(**b**) (*substance*) Knochen *m*.
(**c**) (*of corset*) Stange *f*; (*smaller*) Stäbchen *nt*.
(**d**) (*Mus*) **~s** *pl* Klangstäbe *pl*.
(**e**) (*dice*) **~s** *pl* (*inf*) Würfel, Knöchel (*old*) *pl*.
[2] *adj attr* (*made of ~*) Bein-, beinern.
[3] *vt* die Knochen lösen aus, ausbeinen (*dial*); *fish* entgräten.

♦**bone up on** *vi* +*prep obj* (*esp US inf*) *subject* pauken (*inf*).

bone china *n* feines Porzellan.

boned [bəʊnd] *adj meat* ohne Knochen; *fish* entgrätet.

-boned *adj suf* -knochig.

bone: ~-dry *adj* (*inf*) knochentrocken; **~head** *n* (*inf*) Dummkopf, Armleuchter (*inf*) *m*; **~headed** *adj* (*inf*) blöd(e) (*inf*), doof (*inf*); **~-idle** *adj* (*inf*) stinkfaul (*inf*); **~less** *adj meat* ohne Knochen; *fish* ohne Gräten; **~ meal** *n* Knochenmehl *nt*.

boner ['bəʊnəʳ] *n* (*US sl*) Schnitzer, Hammer (*sl*) *m*.

boneshaker ['bəʊnʃeɪkəʳ] *n* (**a**) (*inf*) Klapperkiste (*inf*), Mühle (*inf*) *f*. (**b**) (*old: cycle*) Fahrrad *nt* ohne Gummireifen.

bonfire ['bɒnfaɪəʳ] *n* (*for burning rubbish*) Feuer *nt*; (*as beacon*) Leucht- *or* Signalfeuer *nt*; (*Guy Fawkes*) Guy-Fawkes-Feuer *nt*; (*for celebration*) Freudenfeuer *nt* ♦ **~ night** 5. November (*Jahrestag m der Pulververschwörung*).

bongo ['bɒŋgəʊ] *n* Bongo *nt or f*.

bonhomie ['bɒnɒmi:] *n* Bonhomie (*geh*), Jovialität *f*.

boniness ['bəʊnɪnɪs] *n* Knochigkeit *f*.

bonk [bɒŋk] (*inf*) [1] *vt* (**a**) (*have sex with*) bumsen (*inf*). (**b**) (*knock*) **he ~ed his head against the doorframe** er knallte mit dem Kopf gegen den Türrahmen (*inf*).
[2] *vi* bumsen (*inf*).
[3] *n* (**a**) (*sex*) **to have a ~** bumsen (*inf*).
(**b**) (*knock*) **to give sth a ~** *head, kneecap* sich (*dat*) etw stoßen.

bonkers ['bɒŋkəz] *adj* (*Brit sl*) meschugge (*inf*) ♦ **to be ~** spinnen (*inf*); **to go ~** überschnappen (*inf*); **he's ~ about her** er ist völlig verrückt nach ihr (*inf*).

bonking ['bɒŋkɪŋ] *n* (*inf*) Bumsen *nt* (*inf*).

bon mot ['bɒn'məʊ] *n* Bonmot *nt* (*geh*).

Bonn [bɒn] [1] *n* Bonn *nt*.
[2] *adj* Bonner.

bonnet ['bɒnɪt] *n* (**a**) (*woman's*) Haube *f*; (*baby's*) Häubchen *nt*; (*esp Scot: man's*) Mütze *f*. (**b**) (*Brit Aut*) Motor- *or* Kühlerhaube *f*. (**c**) (*of chimney*) Schornsteinkappe *f*.

bonnie, bonny ['bɒnɪ] *adj* (*esp Scot*) schön; *lassie also* hübsch; *baby* prächtig.

bonsai ['bɒnsaɪ] *n, pl* - Bonsai *nt*.

bonus ['bəʊnəs] *n* (**a**) Prämie *f*; (*output, production also*) Zulage *f*; (*cost-of-living ~*) Zuschlag *m*; (*Christmas ~*) Gratifikation *f* ♦ **~ scheme** Prämiensystem *nt*. (**b**) (*Fin: on shares*) Extradividende, Sonderausschüttung *f*. (**c**) (*inf: sth extra*) Zugabe *f*.

bony ['bəʊnɪ] *adj* (+*er*) (*of bone*) knöchern; (*like bone*) knochenartig; *person, knee, hips* knochig; *fish* grätig, mit viel Gräten; *meat* mit viel Knochen.

bonze [bɒnz] *n* Bonze *m*.

bonzer ['bɒnzəʳ] *adj* (*Austral inf*) klasse (*inf*).

boo [bu:] [1] *interj* buh ♦ **he wouldn't say ~ to a goose** (*inf*) er ist ein schüchternes Pflänzchen.
[2] *vt actor, play, speaker, referee* auspfeifen, ausbuhen ♦ **to be ~ed off the stage** ausgepfiffen *or* ausgebuht werden.
[3] *vi* buhen.
[4] *n* Buhruf *m*.

boob [bu:b] [1] *n* (**a**) (*Brit inf: mistake*) Schnitzer *m* (*inf*) ♦ **a common ~** ein häufig gemachter Fehler.
(**b**) (*inf: woman's breast*) Brust *f* ♦ **big ~s** große Dinger *pl* (*sl*).
[2] *vi* (*Brit inf*) einen Schnitzer machen; (*fail*) Mist bauen (*sl*) ♦ **somebody ~ed, I didn't get the letter** da hat jemand was verbockt (*inf*), ich habe den Brief überhaupt nicht gekriegt.

booboo ['bu:bu:] *n* (*inf*) Schnitzer *m* (*inf*).

boob tube *n* (**a**) (*Tex*) Bustier *nt*. (**b**) (*esp US inf: television*) Röhre (*inf*), Glotze (*inf*) *f*.

booby ['bu:bɪ] *n* (*inf*) (**a**) (*fool*) Trottel *m*. (**b**) *see* **boob 1 (b)**.

booby: ~ hatch *n* (*US sl*) Klapsmühle *f* (*sl*); **~ prize** *n Scherzpreis m für den schlechtesten Teilnehmer*; **~ trap** [1] *n* (**a**) (*als Schabernack versteckt angebrachte*) Falle *f*; (**b**) (*Mil etc*) versteckte Bombe; **don't open that box, it's a ~ trap** machen Sie die Schachtel nicht auf, da ist eine Bombe drin; [2] *vt* **the suitcase was ~-trapped** in dem Koffer war eine Bombe versteckt.

boogie-woogie ['bu:gɪ,wu:gɪ] *n* Boogie-Woogie *m*.

boo-hoo ['bu:'hu:] *interj* (*to indicate crying*) huh-huh; (*to mock crying*) schluchz-schluchz.

booing ['bu:ɪŋ] *n* Buhrufen *nt*.

▼ **book** [bʊk] [1] *n* (**a**) Buch *nt*; (*exercise ~*) Heft *nt*; (*division: in Bible, poem etc*) Buch *nt* ♦ **the (good) B~** das Buch der Bücher; **the B~ of Genesis** die Genesis, das 1. Buch Mose; **to bring sb to ~** jdn zur Rechenschaft ziehen; **to throw the ~ at sb** (*inf*) jdn nach allen Regeln der Kunst fertigmachen (*inf*); **to go by** *or* **stick to the ~** sich an die Vorschriften halten; **according to** *or* **by the ~** nach dem Buchstaben; **he does everything according to** *or* **by the ~** er hält sich bei allem strikt an die Vorschriften; **to be in sb's good/bad ~s** bei jdm gut/schlecht angeschrieben sein (*inf*); **I can read him like a ~** ich kann in ihm lesen wie in einem Buch; **it's a closed ~ to me** das ist ein Buch mit sieben Siegeln für mich; **he/my life is an open ~** er/mein Leben ist ein offenes Buch; **he knows/used every trick in the ~** (*inf*) er ist/war mit allen Wassern gewaschen (*inf*); **that counts as cheating in my ~** (*inf*) für mich ist das Betrug; **I'm in the ~** (*Telec*) ich stehe im Telefonbuch.
(**b**) (*of tickets*) Heft *nt*; (*thicker*) Block *m* ♦ **~ of stamps/matches** Briefmarken-/Streichholzheftchen *nt*.
(**c**) (*Comm, Fin*) **~s** *pl* Bücher *pl* ♦ **to keep the ~s of a firm** die Bücher einer Firma führen; **to do** *or* **look after the ~s for sb** jdm die Bücher führen; **I've been doing the ~s** ich habe die Abrechnung gemacht.
(**d**) (*of club, society*) (Mitglieder)verzeichnis *nt*, Mitgliedsliste *f* ♦ **to be on the ~s of an organization** im Mitgliederverzeichnis *or* auf der Mitgliedsliste einer Organisation stehen.
(**e**) (*Gambling*) Wettbuch *nt* ♦ **to make** *or* **keep a ~** (*Horseracing*) Buch machen; (*generally*) Wetten abschließen.
(**f**) (*libretto: of opera etc*) Textbuch *nt*.
(**g**) (*Comm*) **~ of samples** Musterbuch *nt*.
▼[2] *vt* (**a**) bestellen; *seat, room also* buchen, reservieren lassen; *artiste* engagieren, verpflichten; *cabaret act* nehmen; (*privately*) sorgen für ♦ **this performance/flight/hotel is fully ~ed** diese Vorstellung ist ausverkauft/dieser Flug ist ausgebucht/das Hotel ist voll belegt; **can I ~ a time to see him?** kann ich einen Termin bei ihm bekommen?; **to ~ sb through to Hull** (*Rail*) jdn bis Hull durchbuchen.
(**b**) (*Fin, Comm*) *order* aufnehmen ♦ **to ~ goods to sb's account** jdm Waren in Rechnung stellen.
(**c**) (*inf*) *driver etc* aufschreiben (*inf*), einen Strafzettel verpassen (+*dat*) (*inf*); *football player* verwarnen ♦ **to be ~ed for speeding** wegen zu schnellen Fahrens aufgeschrieben werden; **let's ~ him** (*said by policeman etc*) den schnappen wir uns (*inf*).
[3] *vi see vt* (*a*) bestellen; buchen ♦ **to ~ through to Hull** bis Hull durchlösen.

♦**book in** [1] *vi* (*in hotel etc*) sich eintragen ♦ **we ~ed ~ at the Hilton** wir sind im Hilton abgestiegen.
[2] *vt sep* (**a**) (*register*) eintragen. (**b**) (*make reservation for*) **to ~ sb ~ to a hotel** jdm ein Hotelzimmer reservieren lassen; **we're ~ed ~ at the Hilton** unsere Zimmer sind im Hilton bestellt *or* reserviert.

♦**book up** [1] *vi* buchen.
[2] *vt sep* (*usu pass*) reservieren lassen ♦ **to be (fully) ~ed ~** (ganz) ausgebucht sein; (*evening performance, theatre*) (bis auf den letzten Platz) ausverkauft sein.

bookable ['bʊkəbl] *adj* im Vorverkauf erhältlich.

book: ~binder *n* Buchbinder *m*; **~binding** *n* Buchbinderei *f*; **~case** *n* Bücherregal *nt*; (*with doors*) Bücherschrank *m*; **~ club** *n* Buchgemeinschaft *f*; **~end** *n* Bücherstütze *f*; **~ fair** *n* Buchmesse *f*.

bookie ['bʊkɪ] *n* (*inf*) Buchmacher *m*.

▼ **booking** ['bʊkɪŋ] *n* Buchung, Bestellung, Reservierung *f*; (*of artiste, performer*) Engagement *nt*, Verpflichtung *f* ♦ **to make a ~** buchen; **to cancel a ~** den Tisch/die Karte *etc* abbestellen; die Reise/den Flug *etc* stornieren; **to change one's ~** umbuchen; **have you got a ~ in the name of Higgins?** ist bei Ihnen etwas auf den Namen Higgins gebucht?

booking: ~ clerk *n* Fahrkartenverkäufer(in *f*) *m*; (*official also*) Schalterbeamte(r) *m*, Schalterbeamtin *f*; **~ office** *n* (*Rail*) Fahrkartenschalter *m*; (*Theat*) Vorverkaufsstelle *or* -kasse *f*.

bookish ['bʊkɪʃ] *adj* gelehrt (*pej, hum*); (*given to reading*) lesewütig; (*not worldly*) lebensfremd; *language, expression* buchsprachlich; (*pej*) trocken, papieren ♦ **a ~ word** ein Wort *m* der Schriftsprache; **he is a very ~ person** er hat die Nase dauernd in einem Buch; (*not worldly*) er ist ein richtiger Stubengelehrter (*pej*); **~ woman** Blaustrumpf *m* (*pej*); **~ style** Buchstil *m*; (*pej*) papierener Stil.

book: ~ jacket *n* Schutzumschlag *m*, Buchhülle *f*; **~-keeper** *n* Buchhalter(in *f*) *m*; **~-keeping** *n* Buchhaltung *or* -führung *f*; **~ knowledge** *or* **learning** *n* Bücherweisheit *f*.

booklet ['bʊklɪt] *n* Broschüre *f*.

book: ~ lover *n* Bücherfreund *m*; **~maker** *n* Buchmacher *m*; **~mark** *n* Lesezeichen *nt*; **~mobile** *n* (*US*) Fahrbücherei *f*; **~plate** *n* Exlibris *nt*; **~ post** *n* Büchersendung *f*; **to send sth by ~ post** etw als Büchersendung schicken; **~ post is ...** Büchersendungen sind ...; **~rest** *n* Lesepult *nt*; **~seller** *n* Buchhändler *m*; **~shelf** *n* Bücherbord *or* -brett *nt*; **~shelves** *npl*

➤ LANGUAGE IN USE: **book: 2a** → 21.3 **booking** → 21.4

(*~case*) Bücherregal *nt*; **~shop** (*Brit*), **~store** (*US*) *n* Buchhandlung *f or* -laden *m*; **~stall** *n* Bücherstand *m*; **~ token** *n* Buchgutschein *m*; **~ trade** *n* Buchhandel *m*; **~ value** *n* (*Fin*) Buchwert, Bilanzwert *m*; **~worm** *n* (*fig*) Bücherwurm *m*.

Boolean ['bu:lɪən] *adj algebra, logic* boolesch *attr*.

boom[1] [bu:m] *n* **(a)** (*barrier, across river etc*) Sperre *f*; (*at factory gate etc*) Schranke *f*. **(b)** (*Naut*) Baum *m*. **(c)** (*Tech: also* **derrick ~**) Ladebaum *m*; (*jib of crane*) Ausleger *m*. **(d)** (*for microphone*) Galgen *m*.

boom[2] [1] *n* (*of sea, waves, wind*) Brausen *nt*; (*of thunder*) Hallen *nt*; (*of guns*) Donnern *nt*; (*of organ, voice*) Dröhnen *nt*.
[2] *vi* **(a)** (*sea, wind*) brausen; (*thunder*) hallen. **(b)** (*organ, person, voice: also* **~ out**) dröhnen; (*guns*) donnern.
[3] *interj* bum.

◆**boom out** [1] *vi see* **boom[2] 2 (b)**.
[2] *vt sep* (*person*) *order* brüllen ◆ **to ~ ~ a command to sb** jdm mit Donnerstimme einen Befehl zubrüllen; **the bass ~s ~ the chorus** der Baß singt den Refrain mit dröhnender Stimme.

boom[3] [1] *vi* (*trade, sales*) einen Aufschwung nehmen, boomen (*inf*); (*prices*) anziehen, in die Höhe schnellen ◆ **business/he is ~ing** das Geschäft blüht *or* floriert/er floriert.
[2] *n* (*of business, fig*) Boom, Aufschwung *m*; (*period of economic growth*) Hochkonjunktur *f*; (*of prices*) Preissteigerung *f* ◆ **to undergo** *or* **have a sudden ~** einen plötzlichen Aufschwung nehmen *or* erfahren.

boomerang ['bu:məræŋ] [1] *n* (*lit, fig*) Bumerang *m* ◆ **to have a ~ effect** einen Bumerangeffekt haben.
[2] *vi* (*fig inf: words, actions*) wie ein Bumerang zurückkommen (*on* zu).

booming ['bu:mɪŋ] *adj sound* dröhnend; *surf* brausend.

boom: ~ microphone *n* Mikrophon *nt* am Galgen; **~-slump cycle** *n* Konjunktur-Zyklus *m*; **~ town** *n* Goldgräberstadt *f*.

boon[1] [bu:n] *n* **(a)** (*blessing, advantage*) Segen *m* ◆ **it's such a ~** es ist ein wahrer Segen. **(b)** (*obs: favour, wish*) Gunst, Gnade *f*.

boon[2] *adj*: **~ companion** (*old, liter*) lustiger Gesell (*old*).

boondockers ['bu:ndɒkəz] *npl* (*US inf: heavy boots*) (schwere) Stiefel *pl*.

boondocks ['bu:ndɒks] *npl* (*US inf: backwoods*) Wildnis *f* ◆ **in the ~** irgendwo j.w.d. (*inf*).

boondoggle ['bu:ndɒgl] (*US inf*) [1] *vi* auf Staatskosten Zeit und Geld verplempern (*inf*).
[2] *n* Zeitverschwendung *f or* Kleinkrämerei *f* auf Staatskosten.

boondoggler ['bu:ndɒgləʳ] *n* (*US inf*) staatlich angestellte Niete, kleinkarierte Beamtenseele, beamteter Kleinkrämer.

boor [bʊəʳ] *n* Rüpel, Flegel *m*.

boorish *adj*, **~ly** *adv* ['bʊərɪʃ, -lɪ] rüpelhaft, flegelhaft.

boorishness ['bʊərɪʃnɪs] *n* Rüpelhaftigkeit, Flegelhaftigkeit *f*.

boost [bu:st] [1] *n* Auftrieb *m no pl*; (*Elec, Aut*) Verstärkung *f*; (*rocket*) Zusatzantrieb *m* ◆ **to give sb/sth a ~** jdm/einer Sache Auftrieb geben, jdn aufmöbeln (*inf*)/etw ankurbeln *or* in Schwung bringen; (*by advertising*) für jdn/etw die Werbetrommel rühren; **to give my bank account a ~** um meinem Bankkonto eine Finanzspritze zu verabreichen; **this device gives the heart/electric charge/motor a ~** dieser Apparat verstärkt den Herzschlag/die elektrische Ladung/die Motorleistung; **to give a ~ to sb's morale/confidence** jdm Auftrieb geben *or* Mut machen/jds Selbstvertrauen stärken.
[2] *vt production, output, sales, economy* ankurbeln; *electric charge, engine, heart beat etc* verstärken; *confidence, sb's ego* stärken; *morale* heben.

booster ['bu:stəʳ] *n* **(a)** (*Elec*) Puffersatz *m*; (*Rad*) Zusatzverstärker *m*; (*TV*) Zusatzgleichrichter *m*; (*Comput: on cable*) Zwischengenerator *m*; (*Aut*) (*supercharger*) Kompressor *m*; (*for heating*) Gebläse *nt*; (*~ rocket*) Booster *m*; (*for launching*) Booster *m*, Startrakete *f*; (*Aviat*) Hilfstriebwerk *nt*; (*Space*) Booster *m*, Zusatztriebwerk *nt* ◆ **to act as a ~** zur Verstärkung dienen. **(b)** (*Med: also* **~ shot**) Wiederholungsimpfung *f* ◆ **~ dose** zusätzliche Dosis.

boot[1] [bu:t] [1] *n* **(a)** Stiefel *m* ◆ **the ~ is on the other foot** (*fig*) es ist genau umgekehrt; (*the other side is responsible*) die Verantwortung/Schuld liegt, ganz im Gegenteil, bei den anderen; **to give sb the (order of the** *hum*) **~** (*inf*) jdn rausschmeißen (*inf*), jdn an die Luft setzen (*inf*); **to get the ~** (*inf*) rausgeschmissen werden (*inf*); **it's the ~ for him** (*inf*) der fliegt (*inf*); **to die with one's ~s on** (*inf*) über der Arbeit *or* in den Sielen sterben; **to put the ~ in** (*sl*) kräftig zutreten.
(b) (*Brit: of car etc*) Kofferraum *m*.
(c) (*inf: kick*) **to give sb/sth a ~** jdm/einer Sache einen Tritt geben *or* versetzen.
(d) (*Brit pej sl: woman*) Schreckschraube *f* (*inf*).
[2] *vt* **(a)** (*inf: kick*) einen (Fuß)tritt geben (+*dat*); *ball* kicken. **(b)** (*Comput*) laden, urladen.
[3] *vi* (*Comput*) laden.

◆**boot out** *vt sep* (*inf: lit, fig*) rausschmeißen (*inf*).

◆**boot up** *vti sep* (*Comput*) laden.

boot[2] *adv* (*hum, form*): **to ~** obendrein, noch dazu.

bootblack ['bu:tblæk] *n* Schuhputzer *m*.

boot camp *n* (*US Mil inf*) Armee-Ausbildungslager *nt*.

bootee [bu:'ti:] *n* (*baby's*) gestrickter Babyschuh.

booth [bu:ð] *n* **(a)** (*at fair*) (Markt)bude *f or* -stand *m*; (*at show*) (Messe)stand *m*. **(b)** (*telephone ~*) (offene) Zelle *f*; (*polling ~, in cinema, language laboratory*) Kabine *f*; (*in restaurant*) Nische *f*, Séparée *nt* (*geh*).

boot: ~jack *n* Stiefelknecht *m*; **~lace** *n* Schnürsenkel *m*; **to pull oneself up by one's own ~laces** (*inf*) sich am eigenen Haar herausziehen; **~leg** [1] *vt* **(a)** (*US*) (*make*) *liquor* schwarz brennen (*inf*); (*sell*) schwarz verkaufen; (*transport*) schmuggeln; **(b)** (*inf: produce illegally*) schwarz herstellen; *cassettes etc* schwarz mitschneiden; [2] *adj whisky etc* schwarz gebrannt; *goods* schwarz hergestellt; *cassettes etc* schwarz mitgeschnitten; **~legger** *n* (*US*) Bootlegger *m*; (*seller also*) Schwarzhändler *m*.

bootless ['bu:tlɪs] *adj* (*liter*) nutzlos, eitel (*liter*).

boot: ~licker *n* (*pej inf*) Speichellecker *m* (*pej inf*); **~maker** *n* Schuhmacher *m*; **~ polish** *n* Schuhcreme *f*.

boots [bu:ts] *n sing* (*Brit*) Hausbursche *or* -diener *m*.

bootstraps ['bu:tstræpz] *npl see* **bootlace**.

booty ['bu:tɪ] *n* (*lit, fig*) Beute *f*.

booze [bu:z] (*inf*) [1] *n* (*alcoholic drink*) Alkohol *m*; (*spirits also*) Schnaps *m*; (*drinking bout*) Sauftour *f* (*inf*) ◆ **keep off the ~** laß das Saufen sein (*inf*); **bring some ~** bring was zu schlucken mit (*inf*); **he's gone on the ~ again** er säuft wieder (*inf*).
[2] *vi* saufen (*inf*) ◆ **all this boozing** diese Sauferei (*inf*); **boozing party** Besäufnis *nt* (*inf*); **to go out boozing** saufen gehen (*inf*).

boozed(-up) ['bu:zd(ʌp)] *adj* (*inf*) blau (*inf*), alkoholisiert (*inf*).

boozer ['bu:zəʳ] *n* **(a)** (*pej inf: drinker*) Säufer(in *f*) (*pej inf*), Schluckspecht (*inf*) *m*. **(b)** (*Brit sl: pub*) Kneipe *f* (*inf*).

booze-up ['bu:zʌp] *n* (*inf*) Besäufnis *nt* (*inf*).

boozy ['bu:zɪ] *adj* (+*er*) (*inf*) *look, face* versoffen (*inf*) ◆ **a ~ person** ein Schluckspecht *m* (*inf*); (*stronger*) ein versoffenes Loch (*sl*); **to have ~ breath** eine Fahne haben (*inf*); **~ party** Sauferei *f* (*inf*); **~ lunch** Essen *nt* mit reichlich zu trinken.

bop [bɒp] [1] *n* **(a)** (*Mus*) Bebop *m*. **(b)** (*inf: dance*) Schwof *m* (*inf*). **(c)** (*inf: blow*) Knuff (*inf*), Puff (*inf*) *m* ◆ **to give sb a ~ on the nose** jdm eins auf die Nase geben.
[2] *vi* (*inf: dance*) schwofen (*inf*).
[3] *vt* (*inf*) **to ~ sb on the head** jdm eins auf den Kopf geben.

boracic [bə'ræsɪk] *adj* (*Chem*) Bor-, borhaltig.

borage ['bɒrɪdʒ] *n* Borretsch *m*.

borax ['bɔ:ræks] *n* Borax *m*.

border ['bɔ:dəʳ] [1] *n* **(a)** (*edge, side: woods, field*) Rand *m*.
(b) (*boundary, frontier*) Grenze *f* ◆ **on the French ~** an der französischen Grenze; **on the ~s of France** an der französischen Grenze; **on the ~s of France and Switzerland** an der Grenze zwischen Frankreich und der Schweiz, an der französisch-schweizerischen Grenze; **the B~s** (*Brit Geog*) *das Grenzgebiet zwischen England und Schottland*; **north/south of the ~** (*Brit*) in/nach Schottland/England; **~ dispute** Grenzstreitigkeit *f*; (*fighting*) Grenzzwischenfall *m*.
(c) (*in garden*) Rabatte *f*; *see* **herbaceous**.
(d) (*edging: on dress*) Bordüre *f*; (*of carpet*) Einfassung *f*; (*of picture*) Umrahmung *f* ◆ **black ~** (*on notepaper*) schwarzer Rand, Trauerrand *m*.
[2] *vt* **(a)** (*line edges of*) *road, path* säumen; *garden, estate etc* begrenzen; (*on all sides*) umschließen.
(b) (*land etc: lie on edge of*) grenzen an (+*acc*).

◆**border on** *or* **upon** *vi* +*prep obj* (*lit, fig*) grenzen an (+*acc*) ◆ **it was ~ing ~ being rude** das grenzte an Unhöflichkeit.

borderer ['bɔ:dərəʳ] *n* Grenzbewohner(in *f*) *m*; (*Brit*) *Bewohner m des Grenzgebiets zwischen England und Schottland*.

border: ~ guard *n* Grenzsoldat *m*; **~ incident** *n* Grenzzwischenfall *m*.

bordering ['bɔ:dərɪŋ] *adj country* angrenzend.

border: ~land *n* (*lit*) Grenzgebiet *nt*; (*fig*) Grenzbereich *m*; **~line** [1] *n* **(a)** (*between states, districts*) Grenzlinie, Grenze *f*; **(b)** (*fig: between categories, classes etc*) Grenze *f*; **to be on the ~line** an der Grenze liegen, ein Grenzfall sein; **his marks were on the ~line between a pass and a fail** er stand mit seinen Noten auf der Kippe; [2] *adj* (*fig*) **a ~line case** ein Grenzfall *m*; **it was a ~line pass/fail** er *etc* ist ganz knapp durchgekommen/durchgefallen; **he/it is ~line** er/es ist ein Grenzfall; **it's too ~line** das liegt zu sehr an der Grenze; **~ raid** *n* Grenzüberfall *m*; **~ state** *n* Grenzstaat *m*; **~ town** *n* Grenzstadt *f*.

bore[1] [bɔ:ʳ] [1] *vt hole, well, tunnel* bohren; *rock* durchbohren.
[2] *vi* bohren (*for* nach).
[3] *n* (*hole*) Bohrloch *nt*; (*of tube, pipe*) lichte Weite, Durchmesser *m*; (*of shotgun, cannon*) Kaliber *nt* ◆ **a 12 ~ shotgun** eine Flinte vom Kaliber 12.

bore[2] [1] *n* **(a)** (*person*) Langweiler *m* ◆ **what a ~ he is!** das ist ein Langweiler!, der kann einen langweilen *or* anöden (*inf*); **the club/office ~** der Langweiler vom Dienst.
(b) (*thing, profession, situation etc*) **to be a ~** langweilig sein.
(c) (*nuisance*) **don't be a ~** nun sei doch nicht so (schwierig)!; **he's a ~, he never wants ...** er ist eine Plage, er will nie ...; **this car is such a ~** das Auto ist wirklich eine Plage; **it's such a ~ having to go** es ist wirklich zu dumm *or* lästig, daß ich *etc* gehen muß; **oh what a ~!** das ist aber auch zu dumm *or* lästig!
[2] *vt* langweilen ◆ **to ~ sb stiff** *or* **to death** *or* **to tears, to ~ the pants off sb** (*inf*) jdn zu Tode langweilen; **to be/get ~d** sich langweilen; **I'm ~d** mir ist es langweilig, ich langweile mich; **he is/gets ~d with her/his job** sie/seine Arbeit langweilt ihn; **he was ~d with reading/life** er war des Lesens/Lebens überdrüssig (*geh*), er hatte das Lesen/Leben über.

bore[3] *pret of* **bear[1]**.

bore[4] *n* (*tidal wave*) Flutwelle *f*.

boredom ['bɔ:dəm] *n* Lang(e)weile *f*; (*boringness*) Stumpfsinn *m*, Langweiligkeit *f* ◆ **with a look of utter ~ on his face** mit einem völlig gelangweilten Gesichtsausdruck.

bore-hole ['bɔ:həʊl] *n* Bohrloch *nt*.

borer ['bɔ:rəʳ] *n* (*Tech*) Bohrer *m*; (*insect*) Bohrkäfer *m*.

boric [ˈbɔːrɪk] *adj (Chem)* Bor-.

boring[1] [ˈbɔːrɪŋ] [1] *n (Tech) (act)* Bohren *nt*; *(hole)* Bohrloch *nt*.
[2] *adj* **~ machine** Bohrmaschine *f*.

boring[2] *adj* langweilig.

born [bɔːn] [1] *ptp of* **bear[1] 1 (h)** ◆ **to be ~** geboren werden; *(fig)* entstehen; *(idea)* geboren werden; **I was ~ in 1948** ich bin *or* wurde 1948 geboren; **when were you ~?** wann sind Sie geboren?; **to be ~ again** wiedergeboren werden; **every baby ~ into the world** jedes Kind, das auf die Welt kommt; **he was ~ to a life of hardship/into a rich family** er wurde in ein schweres Leben/eine reiche Familie hineingeboren; **to be ~ lucky/deaf** unter einem glücklichen Stern/taub geboren sein; **he was just ~ to be Prime Minister** er war zum Premierminister geboren; **I wasn't ~ yesterday** *(inf)* ich bin nicht von gestern *(inf)*; **there's one ~ every minute!** *(fig inf)* die Dummen werden nicht alle!; **the characteristics which are ~ in us** die uns angeborenen Eigenschaften; **he was ~ of poor parents** er war das Kind armer Eltern; **with that confidence ~ of experience** mit dem aus Erfahrung hervorgegangenen Selbstvertrauen.
[2] *adj suf* **(a)** *(native of)* **he is Chicago-~** er ist ein gebürtiger *or* geborener Chicagoer; **his foreign-/French-~ wife** seine Frau, die Ausländerin/gebürtige Französin ist. **(b) high-/low-~** von vornehmer/niedriger Geburt.
[3] *adj* geboren ◆ **he is a ~ poet/teacher** er ist der geborene Dichter/Lehrer; **an Englishman ~ and bred** ein echter *or* waschechter *(inf)* Engländer; **in all my ~ days** *(inf)* mein Lebtag *(dated)*, in meinem ganzen Leben.

born-again [ˈbɔːnəˌgen] *adj Christian etc* wiedergeboren.

borne [bɔːn] *ptp of* **bear[1]**.

Borneo [ˈbɔːnɪəʊ] *n* Borneo *nt*.

borough [ˈbʌrə] *n* **(a)** *(also* **municipal ~***)* Bezirk *m*, Stadtgemeinde *f*. **(b)** *(Parl)* städtischer Wahlbezirk.

borrow [ˈbɒrəʊ] [1] *vt* **(a)** (sich *dat*) borgen, sich *(dat)* leihen *(from* von); *£5000 (from bank), car* sich *(dat)* leihen; *library book* ausleihen; *word* entlehnen; *(fig) idea, methodology* borgen *(inf)*, übernehmen *(from* von) ◆ **to ~ money from the bank/another country** Kredit bei der Bank/eine Anleihe bei einem anderen Land aufnehmen; **~ed word** Lehnwort *nt*; **he is living on ~ed time** seine Uhr ist abgelaufen.
(b) *(Math: in subtraction)* borgen *(inf)*.
[2] *vi* borgen; *(from bank)* Kredit aufnehmen ◆ **~ing country** kreditnehmendes Land.

borrower [ˈbɒrəʊəʳ] *n* Entleiher(in *f*) *m*; *(of capital, loan etc)* Kreditnehmer(in *f*) *m* ◆ **he's a terrible ~** er borgt ständig.

borrowing [ˈbɒrəʊɪŋ] *n see vt* Borgen, Leihen *nt*; Ausleihen *nt*; Entlehnung *f*; Übernahme *f* ◆ **~ of money from the bank** Kreditaufnahme *or (short-term)* Geldaufnahme *f* bei der Bank; **government ~** staatliche Kreditaufnahme; **consumer ~** Verbraucherkredit *m*; **~s** *(Fin)* aufgenommene Schulden *pl*; *(of country also)* Anleihen *pl*; **~ requirements** Kreditbedarf *m*.

borstal [ˈbɔːstl] *n (Brit)* Jugendheim *nt*, Besserungsanstalt *f*.

borzoi [ˈbɔːzɔɪ] *n* Barsoi *m*.

bosh [bɒʃ] *n (dated inf)* Quatsch *(inf)*, Quark *(dated inf) m*.

bo's'n [ˈbəʊsn] *n see* **boatswain**.

Bosnia [ˈbɒznɪə] *n* Bosnien *nt*.

Bosnia-Herzegovina [ˈbɒznɪəˌhɜːtsəgəˈviːnə] *n* Bosnien-Herzegowina *nt*.

Bosnian [ˈbɒznɪən] [1] *adj* bosnisch.
[2] *n* Bosnier(in) *m(f)*.

bosom [ˈbʊzəm] [1] *n* **(a)** *(lit, fig: of person)* Busen *m* ◆ **to lay bare one's ~ to sb** *(fig liter)* jdm sein Herz erschließen *(liter)*, jdm sein Innerstes offenbaren *(liter)*. **(b)** *(of dress)* Brustteil *m*. **(c)** *(fig)* **in the ~ of his family** im Schoß der Familie; **deep in the ~ of the earth/sea** *(liter)* tief im Schoße der Erde *(liter)*/in den Tiefen des Meeres *(liter)*.
[2] *adj attr friend etc* Busen-.

bosomy [ˈbʊzəmɪ] *adj (inf)* vollbusig.

Bosp(h)orus [ˈbɒsfərəs, bɒspərəs] *n*: **the ~** der Bosporus.

boss[1] [bɒs] *n* Chef, Boß *(inf) m* ◆ **industrial/union ~es** Industrie-/Gewerkschaftsbosse *pl (inf)*; **his wife is the ~** seine Frau hat das Sagen, bei ihm zu Hause bestimmt die Frau; **OK, you're the ~** in Ordnung, du hast zu bestimmen.

◆**boss about** *or* **around** *vt sep (inf)* rumkommandieren *(inf)*.

boss[2] *n (knob on shield)* Buckel *m*; *(Archit)* Schlußstein *m*.

bossa nova [ˌbɒsəˈnəʊvə] *n* Bossa Nova *m*.

boss-eyed [bɒsˈaɪd] *adj (inf)* schielend *attr* ◆ **to be ~** schielen, einen Knick in der Optik haben *(inf)*.

bossiness [ˈbɒsɪnɪs] *n* Herrschsucht *f*, herrische Art.

boss man *n (sl)* Boß *m (inf)*.

bossy [ˈbɒsɪ] *adj (+er)* herrisch ◆ **don't you get ~ with me!** kommandier mich nicht so rum *(inf)*; **she tends to be rather ~** sie kommandiert einen gern rum *(inf)*.

Boston (crab) [ˈbɒstən(kræb)] *n (Wrestling)* Beinschraube *f*.

bosun [ˈbəʊsn] *n see* **boatswain**.

BOT *(Brit) abbr of* **Board of Trade** *Regierungsausschuß m für Handel und Export*.

botanical [bəˈtænɪkəl] *adj* botanisch, Pflanzen- ◆ **~ gardens** botanischer Garten.

botanist [ˈbɒtənɪst] *n* Botaniker(in *f*) *m*.

botany [ˈbɒtənɪ] *n* Botanik, Pflanzenkunde *f*.

botch [bɒtʃ] *(inf)* [1] *vt (also* **~ up***)* verpfuschen, vermurksen *(inf)*; *plans etc* vermasseln *(inf)*.
[2] *n* Murks *(inf)*, Pfusch *(inf) m* ◆ **to make a ~ of sth** etw verpfuschen/vermasseln *(inf)*.

botcher [ˈbɒtʃəʳ] *n (inf)* Murkser *(inf)*, Pfuscher *(inf) m*.

botch-up [ˈbɒtʃʌp] *(inf) n see* **botch 2**.

botchy [ˈbɒtʃɪ] *adj (inf)* verpfuscht, vermurkst *(inf)*.

▼ **both** [bəʊθ] [1] *adj* beide ◆ **~ (the) boys** beide Jungen.
[2] *pron* beide; *(two different things)* beides ◆ **~ of them were there, they were ~ there** sie waren (alle) beide da; **two pencils/a pencil and a picture - he took ~** zwei Bleistifte/ein Bleistift und ein Bild - er hat beide/beides genommen; **~ of these answers/you are wrong** beide Antworten sind falsch/ihr habt (alle) beide unrecht; **come in ~ of you** kommt beide herein; **I meant ~ of you** ich habe euch beide gemeint.
▼ [3] *adv* **~ ... and ...** sowohl ..., als auch ...; **~ you and I** wir beide; **John and I ~ came** John und ich sind beide gekommen; **she was ~ laughing and crying** sie lachte und weinte zugleich *or* gleichzeitig; **I'm ~ pleased and not pleased** ich freue mich und auch wieder nicht; **is it black or white? — ~** ist es schwarz oder weiß? — beides; **you and me ~** *(esp US inf)* wir zwei beide *(inf)*.

▼ **bother** [ˈbɒðəʳ] [1] *vt* **(a)** *(annoy, trouble: person, noise)* belästigen; *(sb's behaviour, tight garment, hat, long hair)* ärgern, stören; *(cause disturbance to: light, noise, sb's presence, mistakes etc)* stören; *(give trouble: back, teeth etc)* zu schaffen machen *(+dat)*; *(worry)* Sorgen machen *(+dat)*; *(matter, problem, question)* beschäftigen, keine Ruhe lassen *(+dat)* ◆ **I'm sorry to ~ you but ...** es tut mir leid, daß ich Sie damit belästigen muß, aber ...; **well I'm sorry I ~ed you** entschuldigen Sie, daß ich (überhaupt) gefragt habe; **don't ~ your head about that** zerbrechen Sie sich *(dat)* darüber nicht den Kopf; **don't ~ yourself about that** machen Sie sich *(dat)* darüber mal keine Gedanken *or* Sorgen; **I wouldn't let it ~ me** darüber würde ich mir keine Sorgen *or* Gedanken machen; **I shouldn't let it ~ you** machen Sie sich mal keine Sorgen; **don't ~ me!** laß mich in Frieden!; **he was always ~ing me to lend him money** er hat mich dauernd um Geld angegangen; **could I ~ you for a light?** dürfte ich Sie vielleicht um Feuer bitten?; **one thing is still ~ing him** eins stört ihn noch; **what's ~ing you?** was haben Sie denn?; **is something ~ing you?** haben Sie etwas?; *see* **hot**.
▼ **(b) I/he can't be ~ed** ich habe/er hat keine Lust; **I can't be ~ed with people like him/opera** für solche Leute/für Opern habe ich nichts übrig; **I can't be ~ed with doing that** ich habe einfach keine Lust, das zu machen; **he can't be ~ed about** *or* **with small matters like that** mit solchen Kleinigkeiten gibt er sich nicht ab; **do you want to stay or go? — I'm not ~ed** willst du bleiben oder gehen? — das ist mir egal; **I'm not ~ed about him/the money** seinetwegen/wegen des Geldes mache ich mir keine Gedanken.
[2] *vti (take trouble to do)* **don't ~ to do it again/to ask** das brauchen Sie nicht nochmals zu tun/Sie brauchen nicht (zu) fragen; **don't ~!** nicht nötig!; **I won't ~ to ask you again!** dich werde ich bestimmt nicht mehr fragen!; **she didn't even ~ to ask/check** sie hat gar nicht erst gefragt/nachgesehen; **please don't ~ to get up** bitte, bleiben Sie doch sitzen; **you needn't ~ to come** Sie brauchen wirklich nicht (zu) kommen; **really you needn't have ~ed!** das wäre aber wirklich nicht nötig gewesen!
[3] *vi* sich kümmern *(about* um); *(get worried)* sich *(dat)* Sorgen machen *(about* um) ◆ **don't ~ about me!** machen Sie sich meinetwegen keine Sorgen; *(sarcastic)* ist ja egal, was ich will; **to ~ with sb** sich mit jdm abgeben; **he/it is not worth ~ing about** über ihn/darüber brauchen wir gar nicht zu reden, er/das ist nicht der Mühe wert; **I'm not going to ~ with that** das lasse ich; **I didn't ~ about lunch** ich habe das Mittagessen ausgelassen.
[4] *n* **(a)** *(nuisance)* Plage *f* ◆ **it's such a ~** das ist wirklich lästig *or* eine Plage; **I've forgotten it, what a ~** ich habe es vergessen, wie ärgerlich *or* so was Ärgerliches; **he/the car can be a bit of a ~** er/das Auto kann einem wirklich Schwierigkeiten machen; **I know it's an awful ~ for you but ...** ich weiß, daß Ihnen das fürchterliche Umstände macht, aber ...
(b) *(trouble, contretemps etc)* Ärger *m*; *(difficulties)* Schwierigkeiten *pl* ◆ **she's in a spot of ~** sie hat Schwierigkeiten; **we had a spot** *or* **bit of ~ with the car** wir hatten Ärger mit dem Auto; **I didn't have any ~ getting the visa** es war kein Problem, das Visum zu bekommen; **I'll do it tonight, no ~** *(inf)* kein Problem, das mache ich heute abend; **that's all right, it's no ~** bitte schön, das tue ich doch gern; **it wasn't any ~** *(don't mention it)* das ist gern geschehen; *(not difficult)* das war ganz einfach; **the children were no ~ at all** wir hatten mit den Kindern überhaupt keine Probleme; **to go to a lot of ~ to do sth** sich *(dat)* mit etw viel Mühe geben; **please don't put yourself to any ~ on my account** machen Sie meinetwegen keine Umstände.
[5] *interj* Mist *(inf)* ◆ **~ that man!** zum Kuckuck mit ihm! *(inf)*; **oh ~ this lock!** das ist ein doofes Schloß! *(inf)*.

botheration [ˌbɒðəˈreɪʃən] *interj* verflixt und zugenäht *(inf)*.

bothersome [ˈbɒðəsəm] *adj* lästig; *child* unleidlich ◆ **the cooker has been rather ~ lately** mit dem Herd hatte ich *etc* in letzter Zeit viel Ärger.

bothie [ˈbɒθɪ] *n see* **bothy**.

Bothnia [ˈbɒθnɪə] *n*: **Gulf of ~** Bottnischer Meerbusen.

bothy [ˈbɒθɪ] *n (Scot)* Schutzhütte *f*.

Botswana [ˌbɒtˈswaːnə] *n* Botsuana, Botswana *nt*.

bottle [ˈbɒtl] [1] *n* **(a)** Flasche *f* ◆ **a ~ of wine** eine Flasche Wein.
(b) *(Brit sl)* Mumm (in den Knochen) *m (inf)*.
(c) *(fig inf: drink)* Flasche *f (inf)* ◆ **to be on/off the ~** trinken/nicht mehr trinken; **to take to the ~** zur Flasche greifen; **he's too fond of the ~** er trinkt zu gern; *see* **hit**.
[2] *vt* in Flaschen abfüllen ◆ **~d in ...** abgefüllt in ...
[3] *vi (Brit sl: lose nerve)* die Nerven verlieren.

◆**bottle out** *vi see* **bottle 3**.

◆**bottle up** *vt sep emotion* in sich *(dat)* aufstauen, in sich *(acc)* hineinfressen *(inf)* ◆ **there's a lot of hate ~d ~ inside her** es ist viel aufgestauter Haß in ihr.

➤ LANGUAGE IN USE: **both: 3** → 26.2 **bother: 1b** → 7.5

bottle: ~ bank *n* Altglascontainer *m*; **~ blonde** *n* (*inf*) Wasserstoffblondine *f* (*inf*).
bottled ['bɒtld] *adj wine* in Flaschen (abgefüllt); *gas* in Flaschen; *beer* Flaschen-; *fruit* eingemacht.
bottle: ~-fed *adj* **he is ~-fed** er wird aus der Flasche ernährt; **a ~-fed baby** ein Flaschenkind *nt*; **~-feed** *vt* aus der Flasche ernähren; **~ green** *adj* flaschengrün; **~neck** *n* (*lit, fig*) Engpaß *m*; **~ opener** *n* Flaschenöffner *m*; **~ party** *n* Bottle-Party *f*; **~ rack** *n* Flaschengestell *nt*; **~-washer** *n* Flaschenreiniger *m*.
bottling ['bɒtlɪŋ] *n* Abfüllen *nt*; (*of fruit*) Einmachen *nt* ◆ **~ plant** Abfüllanlage *f*.
bottom ['bɒtəm] [1] *n* **(a)** (*lowest part*) (*of receptacle, box, glass*) Boden *m*; (*of mountain, pillar, spire, printed character*) Fuß *m*; (*of well, canyon*) Grund *m*; (*of page, screen, wall*) unteres Ende; (*of list, road*) Ende *nt*; (*of trousers*) unteres Beinteil; (*of dress*) Saum *m* ◆ **trousers with wide/narrow ~s** unten ausgestellte/enge Hosen; **the ~ of the league** das Tabellenende, der Tabellenschluß; **which end is the ~?** wo ist unten?; **the ~ of the tree/page/list/wall** *etc* **is ...** der Baum/die Seite/Liste/Wand *etc* ist unten ...; **at the ~ of the page/list/league/hill/wall/tree** *etc* unten auf der Seite/Liste/in der Tabelle/am Berg/an der Wand/am Baum *etc*; **at the ~ of the canyon** unten in der Schlucht; **at the ~ of the mountain/cliff** am Fuß des Berges/Felsens; **to be (at the) ~ of the class** der/die Letzte in der Klasse sein; **he's near the ~ in English** in Englisch gehört er zu den Schlechtesten; **at the ~ of the garden** hinten im Garten; **at the ~ of the table/road** am unteren Ende des Tisches/am Ende der Straße; **~(s) up!** hoch die Tassen (*inf*); **from the ~ of my heart** aus tiefstem Herzen; **he took a card from the ~ of the pack** er nahm eine Karte unten aus dem Stapel; **at ~** (*fig*) im Grunde; **to knock the ~ out of an argument** ein Argument gründlich widerlegen; **the ~ fell out of his world** (*inf*) für ihn brach alles zusammen; **the ~ dropped** *or* **fell out of the market** die Marktlage hat einen Tiefstand erreicht.
(b) (*underneath, underside*) Unterseite *f*, untere Seite ◆ **on the ~ of the tin/ashtray** unten an der Dose/am Aschenbecher.
(c) (*of sea, lake, river*) Grund, Boden *m* ◆ **on the ~ of the sea** auf dem Meeresboden *or* -grund (*geh*); **to send a ship to the ~** ein Schiff versenken; **the ship went to the ~** das Schiff sank auf den Grund.
(d) (*of chair*) Sitz *m*, Sitzfläche *f*.
(e) (*of person*) Hintern (*inf*), Po (*inf*) *m*; (*of trousers etc*) Hosenboden *m*.
(f) (*fig: causally*) **to be at the ~ of sth** (*person*) hinter etw (*dat*) stecken; (*thing*) einer Sache (*dat*) zugrunde liegen; **to get to the ~ of sth** einer Sache (*dat*) auf den Grund kommen, hinter etw (*acc*) kommen; **let's get to the ~ of the matter** wir wollen der Sache auf den Grund gehen.
(g) (*Naut: of ship*) Boden *m* ◆ **the ship floated ~ up** das Schiff trieb kieloben.
(h) (*Brit Aut: gear*) erster Gang ◆ **in ~** im ersten Gang.
(i) (*US: low land*) **~s** Ebene *f*.
[2] *adj attr* (*lower*) untere(r, s); (*lowest*) unterste(r,s); *price* niedrigste(r, s); (*Fin*) Tiefst-; *pupil* schlechteste(r, s) ◆ **~ half** (*of box*) untere Hälfte; (*of list, class*) zweite Hälfte.
◆**bottom out** *vi* (*reach lowest point*) die Talsohle erreichen (*at* bei); (*pass lowest point*) die Talsohle verlassen *or* überwinden.
bottom: ~ drawer *n* (*Brit*) **to put sth away in one's ~ drawer** etw für die Aussteuer beiseite legen; **~ gear** *n* (*Brit Aut*) erster Gang; **we're still in ~ gear** (*inf*) wir sind immer noch nicht richtig auf Touren gekommen (*inf*); **~less** *adj* (*lit*) bodenlos; (*fig*) *despair* tiefste(r, s); **a ~less pit** (*fig*) ein Faß ohne Boden; **~ line** *n* **(a)** (*of accounts etc*) Saldo *m*; **if the balance sheet shows a healthy ~ line** wenn die Bilanz einen gesunden Saldo aufweist; **(b)** (*fig*) **that's the ~ line (of it)** (*decisive factor*) das ist das Entscheidende (dabei); (*what it amounts to*) darauf läuft es im Endeffekt hinaus; **~-line** *adj attr management, publishing* gewinnorientiert; **~most** *adj* allerunterste(r, s); **~-up** *adj approach, view, analysis* von unten nach oben.
botulism ['bɒtjʊlɪzəm] *n* Nahrungsmittelvergiftung *f*, Botulismus *m*.
bouclé [buː'kleɪ] *n* Bouclé *nt*.
boudoir ['buːdwɑːʳ] *n* Boudoir *nt* (*old*).
bouffant ['buːfɔ̃ːŋ] *adj hairstyle* aufgetürmt.
bougainvillea [ˌbuːgən'vɪlɪə] *n* Bougainvillea *f*.
bough [baʊ] *n* Ast *m*.
bought [bɔːt] *pret, ptp of* **buy**.
bouillon ['buːjɔ̃ːŋ] *n* Bouillon *f*, klare Fleischbrühe ◆ **~ cube** (*US*) Brühwürfel *m*.
boulder ['bəʊldəʳ] *n* Felsblock, Felsbrocken *m*.
boulder clay *n* (*Geol*) Geschiebelehm *m*.
boulevard ['buːləvɑːʳ] *n* Boulevard *m*.
bounce [baʊns] [1] *vi* **(a)** (*ball etc*) springen; (*Sport: ball*) aufspringen; (*chins, breasts etc*) wackeln ◆ **rubber ~s** Gummi federt; **the child ~d up and down on the bed** das Kind hüpfte auf dem Bett herum; **the car ~d along the bumpy road** das Auto holperte die schlechte Straße entlang; **he came bouncing into the room** er kam munter ins Zimmer; **he ~d up out of his chair** er sprang von seinem Stuhl hoch.
(b) (*inf: cheque*) platzen (*inf*).
[2] *vt* **(a)** aufprallen lassen, prellen (*Sport*) ◆ **he ~d the ball against the wall** er warf den Ball gegen die Wand; **he ~d the baby on his knee** er ließ das Kind auf den Knien reiten.
(b) (*sl: throw out*) rausschmeißen (*inf*).
[3] *n* **(a)** (*of ball: rebound*) Aufprall *m* ◆ **to hit a ball on the ~** den Ball beim Aufprall nehmen; **count the number of ~s** zählen Sie, wie oft der Ball *etc* aufspringt. **(b)** *no pl* (*of ball*) Sprungkraft *f*; (*of hair also, rubber*) Elastizität *f*; (*inf: of person*) Schwung *m* (*inf*).
◆**bounce back** [1] *vt sep ball* zurückprallen lassen.
[2] *vi* abprallen, zurückprallen; (*fig inf: person*) sich nicht unterkriegen lassen (*inf*); (*to boyfriend*) zurückkommen.
◆**bounce off** [1] *vt always separate* **to ~ sth ~ sth** etw von etw abprallen lassen; *radio waves etc* etw an etw (*dat*) reflektieren; **to ~ an idea ~ sb** (*fig inf*) eine Idee an jdm testen (*inf*).
[2] *vi* abprallen; (*radio waves*) reflektieren.
bouncer ['baʊnsəʳ] *n* (*inf*) Rausschmeißer *m* (*inf*).
bouncing ['baʊnsɪŋ] *adj* **~ baby** strammer Säugling.
bouncy ['baʊnsɪ] *adj* (+*er*) **(a)** *ball* gut springend; *mattress, step* federnd; *springs, hair* elastisch; *ride* holpernd. **(b)** (*fig inf: exuberant*) vergnügt und munter, quietschvergnügt (*inf*).
bouncy castle ® *n* Hüpfburg *f*.
bound[1] [baʊnd] [1] *n usu pl* (*lit, fig*) Grenze *f* ◆ **to keep within ~s** innerhalb der Grenzen bleiben; **to keep within the ~s of propriety** den Anstand wahren, im Rahmen bleiben, **within the ~s of probability** im Bereich des Wahrscheinlichen; **there are no ~s to his ambition** sein Ehrgeiz kennt keine Grenzen; **the pub/this part of town is out of ~s** das Betreten des Lokals ist verboten/dieser Stadtteil ist Sperrzone.
[2] *vt usu pass country* begrenzen; *area also* abgrenzen.
bound[2] [1] *n* Sprung, Satz *m*; *see* **leap**.
[2] *vi* springen; (*rabbit*) hoppeln ◆ **to ~ in/away/back** herein-/weg-/zurückspringen; **the dog came ~ing up** der Hund kam angesprungen; **the ball ~ed back** der Ball prallte zurück.
bound[3] [1] *pret, ptp of* **bind**.
[2] *adj* **(a)** gebunden ◆ **~ hand and foot** an Händen und Füßen gebunden.
(b) *book* gebunden ◆ **paper-~, ~ in paper** broschiert; **~ in boards** kartoniert.
(c) **~ variable** (*Math*) abhängige Variable; **~ form** (*Ling*) gebundene Form.
(d) (*sure*) **to be ~ to do sth** etw bestimmt tun; **but then of course he's ~ to say that** das muß er ja sagen; **it's ~ to happen** das muß so kommen.
(e) (*obliged*) *person* verpflichtet; (*by contract, word, promise*) gebunden ◆ **but I'm ~ to say ...** (*inf*) aber ich muß schon sagen ...; **if you say X then you're ~ to say that ...** wenn Sie X behaupten, müssen Sie zwangsläufig sagen, daß ...; **I'm not ~ to agree** ich muß nicht zwangsläufig zustimmen; *see* **honour**.
bound[4] *adj pred* **to be ~ for London** (*heading for*) auf dem Weg nach London sein, nach London unterwegs sein; (*about to start*) (*ship, plane, lorry etc*) nach London gehen; (*person*) nach London reisen wollen; **the plane/all passengers ~ for London will ...** das Flugzeug/alle Passagiere nach London wird/werden ...; **where are you ~ for?** wohin geht die Reise?, wohin wollen Sie?; **we were northward-/California-~** wir waren nach Norden/Kalifornien unterwegs; *see* **homeward**.
boundary ['baʊndərɪ] *n* Grenze *f*; (*Cricket*) Spielfeldgrenze *f* ◆ **to hit/score a ~** den Ball über die Spielfeldgrenze schlagen/4 oder 6 Punkte für einen Schlag über die Spielfeldgrenze erzielen.
boundary: ~ line *n* Grenzlinie *f*; (*Sport*) Spielfeldgrenze *f*; **~ rider** *n* (*Austral*) *Arbeiter, der die Grenzen des Weidelandes abreitet*; **~ stone** *n* Grenzstein *m*.
bounden ['baʊndən] *adj*: **~ duty** (*old, liter*) Pflicht und Schuldigkeit *f* (*geh*).
bounder ['baʊndəʳ] *n* (*dated Brit inf*) Lump *m* (*dated inf*).
boundless ['baʊndlɪs] *adj* (*lit, fig*) grenzenlos.
bounteous ['baʊntɪəs], **bountiful** ['baʊntɪfʊl] *adj* großzügig; *sovereign, god* gütig; *harvest, gifts* (über)reich.
bounteousness ['baʊntɪəsnɪs], **bountifulness** ['baʊntɪfʊlnɪs] *n see adj* Großzügigkeit *f*; Güte *f*; reiche Fülle (*geh*).
bounty ['baʊntɪ] *n* **(a)** (*generosity*) Freigebigkeit *f*; (*of nature*) reiche Fülle (*geh*). **(b)** (*gift*) großzügige *or* reiche Gabe (*geh*). **(c)** (*reward money*) Kopfgeld *nt* ◆ **~ hunter** Kopfgeldjäger *m*.
bouquet ['bʊkeɪ] *n* **(a)** Strauß *m*, Bukett *nt* (*geh*) ◆ **~ garni** (*Cook*) Kräutermischung *f*. **(b)** (*of wine*) Bukett *nt*, Blume *f*.
Bourbon ['bʊəbən] *n* (*Hist*) Bourbone *m*, Bourbonin *f*.
bourbon ['bɜːbən] *n* (*also* **~ whisky**) Bourbon *m*.
bourgeois ['bʊəʒwɑː] [1] *n* Bürger(in *f*), Bourgeois (*esp Sociol*) *m*; (*pej*) Spießbürger(in *f*), Spießer *m*.
[2] *adj* bürgerlich; (*pej*) spießbürgerlich, spießig.
bourgeoisie [ˌbʊəʒwɑː'ziː] *n* Bürgertum *nt*, Bourgeoisie *f*.
bout [baʊt] *n* **(a)** (*of flu etc*) Anfall *m*; (*of negotiations*) Runde *f* ◆ **a ~ of fever/rheumatism** ein Fieber-/Rheumaanfall *m*; **a drinking ~** eine Zecherei; **I did another final ~ of revision before the exam** ich habe vor dem Examen noch einmal alles wiederholt. **(b)** (*Boxing, Wrestling, Fencing*) Kampf *m*. **to have a ~ with sb** einen Kampf mit jdm austragen.
boutique [buː'tiːk] *n* Boutique *f*.
bovine ['bəʊvaɪn] [1] *adj* (*lit*) Rinder-; *appearance* rinderartig; (*fig*) stupide, einfältig.
[2] *n* Rind *nt*.
bovver ['bɒvəʳ] *n* (*Brit sl*) Schlägerei *f* (*inf*) ◆ **~ boots** Rockerstiefel *pl*; **~ boys** (*dated*) Schlägertypen *pl*.
bow[1] [bəʊ] [1] *n* **(a)** (*for shooting arrows*) Bogen *m* ◆ **a ~ and arrow** Pfeil und Bogen *pl*. **(b)** (*Mus*) Bogen *m* ◆ **up ~/down ~ stroke** Auf-/Abstrich *m*. **(c)** (*knot: of ribbon etc*) Schleife *f*.
[2] *vi* (*Mus*) den Bogen führen.
[3] *vt* (*Mus*) streichen.
bow[2] [baʊ] [1] *n* (*with head, body*) Verbeugung *f*; (*by young boy*) Diener *m* ◆ **to make one's ~ to sb** sich vor jdm verbeugen *or* verneigen (*geh*), jdm seine Reverenz erweisen (*form*).

[2] *vi* **(a)** sich verbeugen, sich verneigen (*geh*) (*to sb* vor jdm); (*young boy*) einen Diener machen ◆ **to ~ and scrape** katzbuckeln (*pej*), liebedienern (*pej*).
(b) (*bend: branches etc*) sich biegen *or* beugen.
(c) (*fig: defer, submit*) sich beugen (*before* vor +*dat*, *under* unter +*dat*, *to dat*) ◆ **to ~ to the majority/inevitable** sich der Mehrheit beugen/sich in das Unvermeidliche fügen.
[3] *vt* **(a) to ~ one's head** den Kopf senken; (*in prayer*) sich verneigen. **(b)** (*bend*) *branches* beugen ◆ **old age had not ~ed his head/him** er war vom Alter ungebeugt (*geh*).
◆**bow down** [1] *vi* (*lit*) sich beugen *or* neigen ◆ **to ~ ~ to** *or* **before sb** (*fig*) sich jdm beugen.
[2] *vt sep* **~ed ~ with snow/cares** schneebeladen/mit Sorgen beladen.
◆**bow out** [1] *vi* (*fig*) sich verabschieden.
[2] *vt sep* unter Verbeugungen hinausgeleiten.
bow[3] [baʊ] *n often pl* Bug *m* ◆ **in the ~s** im Bug; **on the port/starboard ~** backbord(s)/steuerbord(s) voraus; **~ doors** Bugtor *nt*.
Bow Bells [ˌbəʊ'belz] *npl*: **he was born within the sound of ~** er ist ein waschechter Cockney (*Londoner*).
bowdlerize ['baʊdləraɪz] *vt book* von anstößigen Stellen säubern, reinigen ◆ **a ~d version** eine zensierte Ausgabe.
bowel ['baʊəl] *n usu pl* **(a)** (*Anat*) (*of person*) Eingeweide *nt usu pl*, Gedärm *nt usu pl*; (*of animal also*) Innereien *pl* ◆ **a ~ movement** Stuhl(gang) *m*; **to move/control one's ~s** Stuhl(gang) haben/seine Darmentleerung kontrollieren; **he had something wrong with his ~s** mit seiner Verdauung stimmte etwas nicht.
(b) (*fig*) **the ~s of the earth/ship** *etc* das Erdinnere/Schiffsinnere *etc*, das Innere der Erde/der Schiffsbauch.
bower ['baʊə^r] *n* Laube *f*.
bowing ['bəʊɪŋ] *n* (*Mus*) Bogenführung *f*.
bowl[1] [bəʊl] *n* **(a)** Schüssel *f*; (*smaller, shallow also, finger~*) Schale *f*; (*for sugar etc*) Schälchen *nt*; (*for animals, prisoners also*) Napf *m*; (*punch ~*) Bowle *f*; (*wash~ also*) Becken *nt* ◆ **a ~ of milk** eine Schale/ein Napf Milch.
(b) (*of pipe*) Kopf *m*; (*of spoon*) Schöpfteil *m*; (*of lavatory*) Becken *nt*; (*of lamp*) Schale *f*; (*of wineglass*) Kelch *m*; (*of retort*) Bauch *m*.
(c) (*Geog*) Becken *nt*.
(d) (*US: stadium*) Stadion *nt*.
bowl[2] [1] *n* (*Sport: ball*) Kugel *f*; *see also* **bowls**.
[2] *vi* **(a)** (*Bowls*) Bowling/Boccia/Boule spielen; (*tenpin*) bowlen, Bowling spielen; (*skittles*) kegeln.
(b) (*Cricket*) (*mit gestrecktem Arm*) werfen.
(c) (*travel: car, cycle etc*) brausen (*inf*) ◆ **he came ~ing down the street** er kam auf der Straße angerauscht (*inf*).
[3] *vt* **(a)** (*roll*) *ball* rollen; *hoop also* treiben.
(b) (*Cricket*) *ball* werfen; *batsman* ausschlagen.
◆**bowl along** *vi* dahergerauscht kommen/dahinrauschen (*prep obj* auf +*dat*) (*inf*).
◆**bowl out** *vt sep* (*Cricket*) ausschlagen.
◆**bowl over** *vt sep* **(a)** (*lit*) (*with ball etc*) umwerfen; (*in car etc*) umfahren, über den Haufen fahren (*inf*). **(b)** (*fig*) umwerfen, umhauen (*inf*) ◆ **to be ~ed ~** sprachlos *or* platt (*inf*) sein; **he was ~ed ~ by the news/her/the idea** die Nachricht/sie/die Idee hat ihn (einfach) überwältigt *or* umgehauen (*inf*).
bow [bəʊ]: **~-legged** *adj* O-beinig; **~legs** *npl* O-Beine *pl*.
bowler[1] ['bəʊlə^r] *n* (*Sport*) **(a)** Bowlingspieler(in *f*) *m*; (*of bowls also*) Boccia-/Boulespieler(in *f*) *m*. **(b)** (*Cricket*) Werfer *m*.
bowler[2] *n* (*Brit*) (*also* **~ hat**) Melone *f* ◆ **~ hat brigade** (*hum*) Bürohengste *pl* (*inf*).
bowline ['bəʊlɪn] *n* Palstek, Pfahlstek *m*; (*rope*) Bulin(e) *f*.
bowling ['bəʊlɪŋ] *n* **(a)** (*Cricket*) Werfen *nt* ◆ **renowned for his fast ~** für seine schnellen Bälle berühmt. **(b)** (*tenpin ~*) Bowling *nt*; (*skittles*) Kegeln *nt* ◆ **to go ~** bowlen/kegeln gehen.
bowling: ~ alley *n* Bowlingbahn *f*; **~ green** *n* Spiel- *or* Rasenfläche *f* für Bowling/Boccia/Boule.
bowls [bəʊlz] *n* Bowling *nt*; (*Italian, German*) Boccia *nt*; (*French*) Boule *nt*.
bowman ['bəʊmən] *n*, *pl* **-men** [-mən] Bogenschütze *m*.
bows [baʊz] *npl see* **bow**[3].
bowsprit ['bəʊsprɪt] *n* Bugspriet *nt or m*.
Bow Street runner [bəʊ-] *n* (*Brit Hist*) Büttel *m* (*der offiziellen Detektei in der Londoner Bow Street*).
bow [bəʊ]: **~string** *n* (*Mus*) (Bogen)bezug *m*; (*in archery*) (Bogen)sehne *f*; **~ tie** *n* Fliege *f*; **~ window** *n* Erkerfenster *nt*.
bow-wow ['baʊ'waʊ] (*baby-talk*) [1] *interj* wauwau (*baby-talk*).
[2] ['baʊwaʊ] *n* (*dog*) Wauwau *m* (*baby-talk*).
box[1] [bɒks] [1] *vti* (*Sport*) boxen.
[2] *vt* **to ~ sb's ears** *or* **sb on the ears** jdn ohrfeigen, jdm eine Ohrfeige geben.
[3] *n* **a ~ on the ear** *or* **round the ears** eine Ohrfeige, eine Backpfeife (*inf*).
box[2] *n* (*Bot*) Buchsbaum *m*.
box[3] [1] *n* **(a)** (*made of wood or strong cardboard*) Kiste *f*; (*cardboard ~*) Karton *m*; (*made of light cardboard*, *~ of matches*) Schachtel *f*; (*snuff~, cigarette ~ etc, biscuit tin*) Dose *f*; (*of crackers, chocolates etc*) Packung, Schachtel *f*; (*jewellery ~*) Schatulle *f*, Kasten *m*; (*tool ~*) (Werkzeug)kasten *m*; (*ballot ~*) Urne *f*; (*money ~*) (*with lid and lock*) Kassette *f*; (*for saving*) Sparbüchse *or* -dose *f*; (*collection ~*) (Sammel)büchse *f*; (*in church*) Opferbüchse *f*; (*fixed to wall etc*) Opferstock *m*; (*Brit old: trunk*) (Schrank)koffer *m*.
(b) (*two-dimensional*) (umrandetes) Feld; (*Baseball*) Box *f*; (*in road junction*) *gelb schraffierter Kreuzungsbereich* ◆ **draw a ~ round it** umranden Sie es.
(c) (*Theat*) Loge *f*; (*jury ~*) Geschworenenbank *f*; (*witness ~*) Zeugenstand *m*; (*press ~*) Pressekabine *f*; (*outside*) Pressetribüne *f*; (*in court*) Pressebank *f*.
(d) (*Tech: housing*) Gehäuse *nt* ◆ **gear ~** Getriebe *nt*.
(e) (*building*) (*sentry ~*) Schilderhaus *nt*; (*signal ~*) Häuschen *nt*; (*hunting ~*) (Jagd)hütte *f*.
(f) (*horse~*) Box *f*.
(g) (*Brit: pillar-~*) (Brief)kasten *m*.
(h) (*Brit: phone ~*) Zelle *f*.
(i) (*Brit inf: TV*) Glotze *f* (*inf*), Glotzkasten *m* (*inf*) ◆ **what's on the ~?** was gibt's im Fernsehen?; **I was watching the ~** ich habe in die Röhre geguckt (*inf*) *or* geglotzt (*sl*).
(j) (*Brit: gift of money*) Geldgeschenk *nt*.
(k) (*on stagecoach*) (Kutsch)bock *m*.
[2] *vt* **(a)** (in eine(r) Schachtel *etc*) verpacken. **(b) to ~ the compass** (*Naut*) alle Kompaßpunkte der Reihe nach aufzählen.
◆**box in** *vt sep* **(a)** *player* in die Zange nehmen; *parked car* einklemmen; (*fig*) einengen, keinen *or* zuwenig Spielraum lassen (+*dat*). **(b)** *bath etc* verkleiden; (*with wood also*) verschalen.
◆**box off** *vt sep* abteilen, abtrennen.
◆**box up** *vt sep* **(a)** (*confine*) einsperren. **(b)** (*put in boxes*) (in Kartons) einpacken.
box: ~ bed *n* Klappbett *nt*; **~ calf** *n* Boxkalf *nt*; **~ camera** *n* Box *f*; **~car** *n* (*US Rail*) (geschlossener) Güterwagen.
boxer ['bɒksə^r] *n* **(a)** (*Sport*) Boxer *m*. **(b)** (*dog*) Boxer *m*.
boxer shorts *npl* (*Brit*) Boxer-Shorts *pl*.
box: ~ file *n* Flachordner *m*; **~ girder** *n* Kastenträger *m*; **~ hedge** *n* streng geschnittene Hecke.
boxing ['bɒksɪŋ] *n* Boxen *nt*.
boxing *in cpds* Box-; **B~ Day** *n* (*Brit*) zweiter Weihnachts(feier)tag; **~ match** *n* Boxkampf *m*; **~ ring** *n* Boxring *m*.
box: ~ junction *n* (*Mot*) gelbschraffierte Kreuzung(, *in die bei Stau nicht eingefahren werden darf*); **~ kite** *n* Kastendrachen *m*; **~ number** *n* Chiffre *f*; (*at post office*) Postfach *nt*; **~ office** [1] *n* Kasse, Theater-/Kinokasse *f*; **to be good ~ office** ein Kassenschlager sein; [2] *attr* **~ office success/hit/attraction** Kassenschlager *m*; **~ pleat** *n* Kellerfalte *f*; **~room** *n* (*Brit*) Abstellraum *m*; **~ spanner** *n* Steckschlüssel *m*; **~ tree** *n* Buchsbaum *m*; **~wood** *n* Buchsbaum(holz *nt*) *m*.
boxy ['bɒksɪ] *adj* (*usu pej*) *building, car* kastenförmig.
boy [bɔɪ] *n* **(a)** (*male child*) Junge, Bub (*dial*) *m* ◆ **bad** *or* **naughty ~!** du frecher Bengel; (*to animal*) böser Hund! *etc*; **sit, ~!** (*to dog*) sitz!; **the Jones ~** der Junge von Jones; **~s will be ~s** Jungen sind nun mal so; **a school for ~s** eine Jungenschule; **good morning, ~s** guten Morgen(, Jungs)!; *see* **old ~**.
(b) (*inf: fellow*) Knabe *m* (*inf*) ◆ **the old ~** (*boss*) der Alte (*inf*); (*father*) mein *etc* alter Herr.
(c) (*friend*) **the ~s** meine/seine Kumpels; **our ~s** (*team*) unsere Jungs; **jobs for the ~s** Vetternwirtschaft *f*.
(d) (*native servant, lift~*) Boy *m*; (*messenger ~, ship ~*) Junge *m*; (*butcher's etc ~*) (Lauf)junge *m*; (*page~*) (Hotel)boy *m*; (*stable ~*) Stalljunge *or* (*older*) -bursche *m*.
(e) oh ~! (*inf*) Junge, Junge! (*inf*).
boycott ['bɔɪkɒt] [1] *n* Boykott *m* ◆ **to put a ~ on sth** den Boykott über etw (*acc*) verhängen.
[2] *vt* boykottieren.
boy: ~friend *n* Freund *m*; **~hood** *n* Kindheit *f*; (*as teenager*) Jugend(zeit) *f*.
boyish ['bɔɪɪʃ] *adj* jungenhaft; (*woman*) knabenhaft.
boyo ['bɔɪəʊ] *interj* (*Welsh*) Junge *m*.
Boys' Brigade *n Jugendorganisation*, ≃ Junge Pioniere *pl* (*DDR*).
boy: ~ scout *n* Pfadfinder *m*; **B~ Scouts** *n sing* Pfadfinder *pl*.
bozo ['bəʊzəʊ] *n* (*US*) (primitiver) Kerl (*inf*).
bpi (*Comput*) *abbr of* **bits per inch** Bits pro Zoll.
BR *abbr of* **British Rail** *die britischen Eisenbahnen*.
bra [brɑː] *n abbr of* **brassière** BH *m*.
brace[1] [breɪs] *n*, *pl* - (*pair: of pheasants etc*) Paar *nt*.
brace[2] [1] *n* **(a)** (*Build*) Strebe *f*. **(b)** (*tool*) (*wheel ~*) Radschlüssel *m*; (*to hold bit*) Bohrwinde *f* ◆ **~ and bit** Bohrer *m* (mit Einsatz). **(c)** (*on teeth*) Klammer, Spange *f*; (*Med*) Stützapparat *m*. **(d)** (*Typ*) geschweifte Klammer, Akkolade *f*.
[2] *vt* **(a)** (ab)stützen; (*horizontally*) verstreben; (*in vice etc*) verklammern. **(b)** (*climate etc: invigorate*) stärken, kräftigen.
[3] *vr* sich bereit halten; (*fig*) sich wappnen (*geh*), sich bereit machen ◆ **to ~ oneself for sth** sich auf etw (*acc*) gefaßt machen; **~ yourself, I've got bad news for you** mach dich auf eine schlechte Nachricht gefaßt.
bracelet ['breɪslɪt] *n* Armband *nt*; (*bangle*) Armreif(en) *m*; (*ankle ~*) Fußreif(en) *m* ◆ **~s** (*inf: handcuffs*) Handschellen *pl*.
bracer ['breɪsə^r] *n* **(a)** (*inf: drink*) kleine Stärkung, Schnäpschen *nt*. **(b)** (*Sport*) Armschutz *m*.
braces ['breɪsɪz] *npl* (*Brit*) Hosenträger *pl* ◆ **a pair of ~** (ein Paar) Hosenträger.
bracing ['breɪsɪŋ] *adj* belebend, anregend; *climate* Reiz-.
bracken ['brækən] *n* Adlerfarn *m*.
bracket ['brækɪt] [1] *n* **(a)** (*angle ~*) Winkelträger *m*; (*for shelf*) (Regal)träger *m*; (*Archit*) Konsole *f*; (*of stone*) Kragstein *m*.
(b) (*gas ~*) Anschluß *m*; (*for electric light*) (Wand)arm *m*.
(c) (*Typ, Mus*) Klammer *f* ◆ **in ~s** in Klammern.
(d) (*group*) Gruppe, Klasse *f* ◆ **the lower income ~** die untere Einkommens-

gruppe; **tax ~** Steuerklasse *f.*
[2] *vt* **(a)** *(put in ~s)* einklammern. **(b)** *(also* **~ together***)* *(join by ~s)* mit einer Klammer verbinden; *(Mus also)* mit einer Akkolade verbinden; *(fig: group together)* zusammenfassen.

brackish ['brækɪʃ] *adj water* brackig.

bract [brækt] *n* Tragblatt *nt.*

brad [bræd] *n* Stift *m.*

bradawl ['brædɔːl] *n* Ahle *f*, Pfriem *m.*

brae [breɪ] *n (Scot)* Berg *m.*

brag [bræg] [1] *vi* prahlen, angeben *(about, of* mit).
[2] *vt* prahlen ◆ **to ~ that** prahlen, daß, damit angeben, daß.
[3] *n* **(a)** *(boast)* Prahlerei, Angeberei *f.* **(b)** *(inf) see* **braggart.**

braggart ['brægət] *n* Prahler, Angeber *m.*

bragging ['brægɪŋ] *n* Prahlerei, Angeberei *f.*

braid [breɪd] [1] *n* **(a)** *(of hair)* Flechte *f (geh)*, Zopf *m.* **(b)** *(trimming)* Borte *f*; *(self-coloured)* Litze *f.* **(c)** *(Mil)* Tressen *pl* ◆ **gold ~** Goldtressen *pl.* **(d)** *(to tie hair)* (Haar)band *nt.*
[2] *vt* **(a)** *(plait) hair, straw etc* flechten. **(b)** *(trim)* mit einer Borte besetzen. **(c)** *(tie up with ~) hair* binden.

braille [breɪl] [1] *n* Blinden- *or* Brailleschrift *f.*
[2] *adj* Blindenschrift- ◆ **~ library** Blindenbücherei *f*; **~ books** Bücher in Blindenschrift.

brain [breɪn] [1] *n* **(a)** *(Anat, of machine)* Gehirn *nt* ◆ **he's got sex/cars on the ~** *(inf)* er hat nur Sex/Autos im Kopf; **I've got that tune on the ~** *(inf)* das Lied geht *or* will mir nicht aus dem Kopf.
(b) ~s *pl (Anat)* Gehirn *nt*; *(Cook)* Hirn *nt.*
(c) *(mind)* Verstand *m* ◆ **~s** *pl (intelligence)* Intelligenz *f*, Grips *m (inf)*, Köpfchen *nt (inf)*; **to have a good ~** einen klaren *or* guten Verstand haben; **he has ~s** er ist intelligent, er hat Grips *(inf) or* Köpfchen *(inf)*; **he's the ~s of the family** er ist das Familiengenie *(hum)*, er ist der Schlauste in der Familie; **you're the one with the ~s** du bist doch der Schlaue *or* Intelligente hier; **use your ~s** streng mal deinen Kopf *or* Grips *(inf)* an; **he didn't have the ~s to ...** er ist nicht einmal darauf gekommen, zu ...
[2] *vt* den Schädel einschlagen *(sb* jdm).

brain: ~box *n (hum inf)* Schlauberger *m (inf)*; **~child** *n* Erfindung *f*; *(idea)* Geistesprodukt *nt*; **~-damaged** *adj (lit)* hirngeschädigt; *(fig inf)* (ge)hirnamputiert *(hum inf)*; **~-dead** *adj* (ge)hirntot; **~ death** *n* (Ge)hirntod *m*; **~ drain** *n* Abwanderung *f* von Wissenschaftlern, Brain-Drain *m*; **~ fever** *n* Hirnhautentzündung *f*; **~less** *adj plan, idea* hirnlos, dumm; *person also* unbedarft; **~ scan** *n* Computertomographie *f* des Schädels; **~ scanner** *n* Computertomograph *m (zur Untersuchung des Gehirns)*; **~storm** *n* **(a)** *(Brit)* **to have a ~storm** geistig weggetreten sein *(inf)*; **(b)** *(US: ~wave)* Geistesblitz *m*; **~storming** *n* gemeinsame Problembewältigung, Brainstorming *nt*; **to have a ~storming session** ein Brainstorming veranstalten *or* abhalten.

brains trust *n (discussion)* Podiumsdiskussion *f*; *(panel)* Gruppe *f* von Sachverständigen *or* Experten.

brain: ~ teaser *n* Denksportaufgabe *f*; **~ trust** *n (US)* Brain Trust, Expertenausschuß *m*; **~ tumour** *n* Gehirntumor *m*; **~wash** *vt* einer Gehirnwäsche *(dat)* unterziehen; **to ~wash sb into believing/accepting** *etc* **that ...** jdm (ständig) einreden, daß ...; **~washing** *n* Gehirnwäsche *f*; **~wave** *n (Brit)* Geistesblitz *m*; **~-work** *n* Kopfarbeit *f.*

brainy ['breɪnɪ] *adj (+er) (inf)* gescheit, helle *pred (inf).*

braise [breɪz] *vt (Cook)* schmoren.

brake¹ [breɪk] *n (thicket)* Unterholz *nt.*

brake² *n (Bot)* (Adler)farn *m.*

brake³ *n (shooting ~)* Kombi(wagen) *m.*

brake⁴ [1] *n (Tech)* Bremse *f* ◆ **to put the ~s on** *(lit, fig)* bremsen; **to put the ~s on sth** *(fig)* etw bremsen; **to act as a ~** *(lit)* als Bremse wirken *(on* auf *+acc)*; *(fig)* dämpfend wirken *(on* auf *+acc)*, bremsen *(on acc).*
[2] *vi* bremsen.

brake *in cpds* Brems-; **~ block** *n* Bremsbacke *f*; **~ drum** *n* Bremstrommel *f*; **~ fluid** *n* Bremsflüssigkeit *f*; **~ horsepower** *n* Bremsleistung *f*; **~light** *n* Bremslicht *nt*; **~ lining** *n* Bremsbelag *m*; **~man** *n (US Rail)* Bremser *m*; **~ pad** *n* Bremsklotz *m*; **~ shoe** *n* Bremsbacke *f*; **~ van** *n* Bremswagen *m.*

braking ['breɪkɪŋ] *n* Bremsen *nt.*

braking: ~ distance *n* Bremsweg *m*; **~ power** *n* Bremskraft *f.*

bramble ['bræmbl] *n* **(a)** *(thorny shoot)* dorniger Zweig, Dornenzweig *m.* **(b)** *(blackberry)* Brombeere *f*; *(bush also)* Brombeerstrauch *m* ◆ **~ jam** Brombeermarmelade *f.*

bran [bræn] *n* Kleie *f.*

branch [brɑːntʃ] [1] *n* **(a)** *(Bot)* Zweig *m*; *(growing straight from trunk)* Ast *m.*
(b) *(of river, pipe, duct)* Arm *m*; *(of road)* Abzweigung *f*; *(of family, race, language)* Zweig *m*; *(of railway)* Abzweig *m*; *(of antler)* Sprosse *f*, Ende *nt.*
(c) *(in river, road, railway, pipe, duct)* Gabelung *f.*
(d) *(Comm)* Filiale, Zweigstelle *f*; *(of company, bank also)* Geschäftsstelle *f* ◆ **main ~** Haupt(geschäfts)stelle *f*; *(of store)* Hauptgeschäft *nt*; *(of bank)* Hauptgeschäftsstelle, Zentrale *f.*
(e) *(field: of subject etc)* Zweig *m.*
[2] *vi (divide: river, road etc)* sich gabeln; *(in more than two)* sich verzweigen.

◆**branch off** *vi (road)* abzweigen; *(driver)* abbiegen.

◆**branch out** *vi (fig: person, company)* sein Geschäft erweitern *or* ausdehnen *(into* auf *+acc)* ◆ **the firm is ~ing into cosmetics** die Firma erweitert ihren (Geschäfts)bereich jetzt auf Kosmetika; **to ~ ~ on one's own** sich selbständig machen.

branch: ~ line *n (Rail)* Zweiglinie, Nebenlinie *f*; **~ manager** *n* Filialleiter *m*; **~ office** *n* Filiale, Zweigstelle *f.*

brand [brænd] [1] *n* **(a)** *(make)* Marke *f.* **(b)** *(mark)* *(on cattle)* Brandzeichen *nt*; *(on criminal, prisoner, fig)* Brandmal *nt.* **(c)** *see* **branding iron.** **(d)** *(obs, poet: sword)* Klinge *f (liter).*
[2] *vt* **(a)** *goods* mit seinem Warenzeichen versehen ◆ **~ed goods** Markenartikel *pl.* **(b)** *cattle, property* mit einem Brandzeichen kennzeichnen. **(c)** *(stigmatize) person* brandmarken.

brand: ~ awareness *n* Markenbewußtsein *nt*; **~ image** *n* Marken-Image *nt.*

branding iron ['brændɪŋ,aɪən] *n* Brandeisen *nt.*

brandish ['brændɪʃ] *vt* schwingen, fuchteln mit *(inf).*

brand: ~ leader *n* führende Marke; **~ loyalty** *n* Markentreue *f*; **~ name** *n* Markenname *m*; **~-new** *adj* nagelneu, brandneu *(inf).*

brandy ['brændɪ] *n* Weinbrand, Brandy *m.*

brandy: ~ butter *n* Weinbrandbutter *f*; **~snap** *n Gebäckröllchen nt aus dünnem, mit Ingwer gewürztem Teig.*

brash [bræʃ] *adj (+er)* naßforsch, dreist; *(tasteless colour etc)* laut, aufdringlich.

brashness ['bræʃnɪs] *n see adj* naßforsche Art, Dreistigkeit *f*; Aufdringlichkeit *f.*

brasier *n see* **brazier.**

brass [brɑːs] [1] *n* **(a)** Messing *nt.*
(b) the ~ *(Mus)* die Blechbläser *pl*, das Blech *(inf).*
(c) *(thing made of ~)* *(plaque)* Messingtafel *or* -schild *nt*; *(in church: on tomb)* Grabplatte *f* aus Messing; *(no pl: ~ articles)* Messing *nt* ◆ **to do** *or* **clean the ~(es)** das Messing putzen.
(d) *(inf)* **the top ~** die hohen Tiere *(inf).*
(e) *(sl: impudence)* Frechheit *f.*
(f) *(sl: money)* Moos *nt (sl)*, Kies *m (sl).*
[2] *adj (made of ~)* Messing-, messingen *(rare)*; *(Mus)* Blech- ◆ **~ player** Blechbläser *m*; **~ section** Blech(bläser *pl*) *nt*; **I don't care** *or* **give a ~ farthing** *(inf)* es ist mir wurscht(egal) *(inf)*; **real ~ monkey weather, eh?** *(hum sl)* arschkalt, was? *(sl)*; **to get down to ~ tacks** *(inf)* zur Sache kommen; **to have a ~ neck** Nerven haben *(inf).*

brass: ~ band *n* Blaskapelle *f*; **~ foundry** *n* Messinggießerei *f*; **~ hat** *n (Brit Mil sl)* hohes Tier *(inf).*

brassière ['bræsɪə^r] *n (dated, form)* Büstenhalter *m.*

brass: ~ knuckles *npl (inf)* Schlagring *m*; **~ plaque** *or* **plate** *n* Messingschild *nt*; *(in church)* Messinggedenktafel *f*; **~ rubbing** *n (activity)* Durchpausen *or* -zeichnen *nt (des Bildes auf einer Messinggrabtafel)*; *(result)* Pauszeichnung *f (des Bildes auf einer Messinggrabtafel).*

brassy ['brɑːsɪ] *adj (+er)* **(a)** *metal* messingartig; *hair, blonde* messingfarben; *sound* blechern. **(b)** *(inf: impudent)* frech, dreist.

brat [bræt] *n (pej inf)* Balg *m or nt (inf)*, Gör *nt (inf)*; *(esp girl)* Göre *f (inf)* ◆ **all these ~s** *(boys and girls)* diese Gören.

bravado [brə'vɑːdəʊ] *n (showy bravery)* Draufgängertum *nt*, Wagemut *m*; *(hiding fear)* gespielte Tapferkeit ◆ **this is just literary ~** das ist nur ein literarisches Bravourstückchen.

brave [breɪv] [1] *adj (+er)* **(a)** *person, act* mutig, unerschrocken *(geh)*; *(showing courage, suffering pain)* tapfer; *attack* mutig; *smile* tapfer ◆ **be ~!** nur Mut!; *(more seriously)* sei tapfer!
(b) *(obs, liter: fine)* schmuck *(dated)*, ansehnlich ◆ **~ new world** schöne neue Welt.
[2] *n (Indian)* Krieger *m.*
[3] *vt* die Stirn bieten *(+dat)*; *weather, elements* trotzen *(+dat)*; *death* tapfer ins Auge sehen *(+dat).*

◆**brave out** *vt sep* **to ~ it ~** es *or* das durchstehen.

bravely ['breɪvlɪ] *adv see adj.*

braveness ['breɪvnɪs], **bravery** ['breɪvərɪ] *n see adj* Mut *m*; Tapferkeit *f.*

bravo [brɑː'vəʊ] [1] *interj* bravo!
[2] *n, pl* **-es** Bravoruf *m.*

bravura [brə'vʊərə] *n* Bravour *f*; *(Mus)* Bravourstück *nt.*

brawl [brɔːl] [1] *vi* sich schlagen.
[2] *n* Schlägerei *f.*

brawling ['brɔːlɪŋ] *n* Schlägereien *pl.*

brawn [brɔːn] *n* **(a)** *(Cook)* Preßkopf *m*, Sülze *f.* **(b)** Muskeln *pl*, Muskelkraft *f* ◆ **to have plenty of ~** starke Muskeln haben, ein Muskelpaket *or* Muskelprotz sein *(inf)*; **he's all ~ and no brains** (er hat) Muskeln, aber kein Gehirn.

brawny ['brɔːnɪ] *adj (+er)* muskulös, kräftig.

bray [breɪ] [1] *n (of ass)* (Esels)schrei *m*; *(inf: laugh)* Wiehern, Gewieher *nt.*
[2] *vi (ass)* schreien; *(inf: person)* wiehern.

brazen ['breɪzn] *adj* **(a)** *(impudent)* unverschämt, dreist; *lie* schamlos. **(b)** *(obs: of brass)* messingen *(rare).*

◆**brazen out** *vt sep* **to ~ it ~** durchhalten; *(by lying)* sich durchmogeln *(inf).*

brazen-faced ['breɪzn,feɪst] *adj* schamlos, unverschämt.

brazenly ['breɪznlɪ] *adv see adj* unverschämt, dreist; schamlos.

brazenness ['breɪznnɪs] *n see adj* Unverschämtheit, Dreistigkeit *f*; Schamlosigkeit *f.*

brazier ['breɪzɪə^r] *n* (Kohlen)feuer *nt* (im Freien); *(container)* Kohlenbecken *nt.*

brazil [brə'zɪl] *n (also* **~ nut***)* Paranuß *f.*

Brazil [brə'zɪl] *n* Brasilien *nt.*

Brazilian [brə'zɪlɪən] [1] *n* Brasilianer(in *f*) *m.*
[2] *adj* brasilianisch.

breach [bri:tʃ] 1 *n* **(a)** Verletzung *f* (*of gen*), Verstoß *m* (*of gegen*); (*of law*) Übertretung *f* (*of gen*), Verstoß *m* ◆ **a ~ of confidence/contract/faith** ein Vertrauens-/Vertrags-/Vertrauensbruch *m*; **~ of the peace** (*Jur*) öffentliche Ruhestörung; **~ of privilege** Privilegienmißbrauch *m*; **~ of promise** (*Jur*) Bruch *m* des Eheversprechens.
(b) (*estrangement: in friendship etc*) Bruch *m*.
(c) (*gap*) (*in wall etc*) Bresche, Lücke *f*; (*in security*) Lücke *f* ◆ **to make a ~ in the enemy's lines** (*Mil*) eine Bresche in die feindlichen Linien schlagen; **to step into/throw oneself into the the ~** (*fig*) in die Bresche springen.
2 *vt* **(a)** *wall* eine Bresche schlagen (in +*acc*); *defences, security* durchbrechen. **(b)** *contract, treaty* verletzen.

bread [bred] 1 *n* **(a)** Brot *nt* ◆ **a piece of ~ and butter** ein Butterbrot *nt*; **we just had ~ and butter** wir aßen nur Brot mit Butter; **he was put on (dry) ~ and water** er saß bei Wasser und (trocken) Brot; **he knows which side his ~ is buttered (on)** er weiß, wo was zu holen ist.
(b) (*food, livelihood*) **daily ~** tägliches Brot; **to earn one's daily ~** (sich *dat*) sein Brot verdienen; **writing is his ~ and butter** er verdient sich seinen Lebensunterhalt mit Schreiben; **to take the ~ out of sb's mouth** (*fig*) jdn seiner Existenzgrundlage (*gen*) berauben; **to break ~ with sb** (*old*) sein Brot mit jdm teilen, das Brot mit jdm brechen (*old*).
(c) (*sl: money*) Moos *nt* (*inf*), Kies *m* (*inf*), Flöhe *pl* (*sl*).
2 *vt* panieren.

bread: ~-and-butter letter *or* **note** *n* Bedankemichbrief *m*; **~-and-butter pudding** *n* Brotauflauf *m*; **~ basket** *n* **(a)** Brotkorb *m*; **(b)** (*sl*) Bauch *m*; **~bin** *n* Brotkasten *m*, **~board** *n* Brot(schneide)brett *nt*; **~crumb** *n* Brotkrume *f* or -krümel *m*; **~crumbs** *npl* (*Cook*) Paniermehl *nt*; **in ~crumbs** paniert; **~fruit** *n* Brotfrucht *f*; **~knife** *n* Brotmesser *nt*; **~line** *n Schlange f vor einer Nahrungsmittelausgabestelle*; **to be on the ~line** (*fig*) nur das Allernotwendigste zum Leben haben; **~ roll** *n* Brötchen *nt*; **~ sauce** *n* Brottunke *f*.

breadth [bretθ] *n see* **broad 1 (a, d)** Breite *f*; Großzügigkeit *f*; (*of ideas, of theory*) (Band)breite *f* ◆ **a hundred metres in ~** hundert Meter breit; **his ~ of outlook** (*open-mindedness*) seine große Aufgeschlossenheit; (*variety of interests*) seine große Vielseitigkeit; **the ~ of his comprehension/theory** sein umfassendes Verständnis/seine umfassende Theorie.

breadthways ['bretθweɪz], **breadthwise** ['bretθwaɪz] *adv* in der Breite, der Breite nach.

breadwinner ['bredwɪnəʳ] *n* Ernährer, Brotverdiener *m*.

break [breɪk] (*vb: pret* **broke,** *ptp* **broken**) 1 *n* **(a)** (*fracture*) (*in bone, pipe etc*) Bruch *m*; (*in pottery, vase etc*) Sprung *m*; (*Gram, Typ: word break*) (Silben)trennung *f* ◆ **... he said with a ~ in his voice ...** sagte er mit stockender Stimme; **~ in the circuit** (*Elec*) Stromkreisunterbrechung *f*.
(b) (*gap*) Lücke *f*; (*in rock*) Spalte *f*, Riß *m*; (*in drawn line*) Unterbrechung *f* ◆ **row upon row of houses without a ~** Häuserzeile auf Häuserzeile, ohne Lücke *or* lückenlos.
(c) (*pause, rest: in conversation, tea ~, Brit Sch etc*) Pause *f*; (*in journey also*) Unterbrechung *f* ◆ **without a ~** ohne Unterbrechung *or* Pause, ununterbrochen; **to take** *or* **have a ~** (eine) Pause machen; **at ~** (*Sch*) in der Pause.
(d) (*end of relations*) Bruch *m*.
(e) (*change*) (*in contest etc*) Wende *f*, Umschwung *m*; (*holiday, change of activity etc*) Abwechslung *f* ◆ **just to give you a ~** nur zur Abwechslung, damit du mal was anderes siehst/hörst/machst; **~ in the weather** Wetterumschwung *m*.
(f) at ~ of day bei Tagesanbruch.
(g) (*inf: escape*) Ausbruch *m* ◆ **they made a ~ for it** sie versuchten zu entkommen.
(h) (*inf: luck, opportunity*) **to have a good/bad ~** Glück *or* Schwein (*inf*) *nt*/Pech *nt* haben; **we had a few lucky ~s** wir haben ein paarmal Glück *or* Schwein (*inf*) gehabt; **give me a ~!** gib mir eine Chance!
(i) (*Billiards*) Ballfolge, Serie *f*.
2 *vt* **(a)** (*fracture, snap*) *bone* sich (*dat*) brechen; *stick* zerbrechen; *rope* zerreißen; (*smash*) kaputtschlagen, kaputtmachen; *glass, cup also* zerbrechen; *window also* einschlagen; *egg* aufbrechen ◆ **to ~ sth from sth** etw von etw abbrechen; **to ~ one's leg** sich (*dat*) das Bein brechen; *see* **heart**.
(b) (*put out of working order*) *toy, chair* kaputtmachen.
(c) (*violate*) *promise, treaty, vow* brechen; *traffic laws, rule, commandment* verletzen; *appointment* nicht einhalten ◆ **to ~ bail** die Haftverschonung brechen.
(d) (*interrupt*) *journey, current, silence, fast* unterbrechen; *spell* brechen; (*relieve*) *monotony, routine also* auflockern ◆ **to ~ a holiday short** seinen Urlaub abbrechen.
(e) (*penetrate*) *skin* ritzen; *surface, shell* durchbrechen.
(f) (*surpass*) *sound barrier* durchbrechen; *record* brechen ◆ **his skin is grazed but not broken** die Haut ist zwar abgeschürft, aber nicht aufgeplatzt; **to ~ surface** (*submarine*) auftauchen.
(g) (*open up*) *path* schlagen, sich (*dat*) bahnen; *see* **ground**.
(h) to ~ a habit mit einer Gewohnheit brechen, sich (*dat*) etw abgewöhnen; **he couldn't ~ the habit of smoking** er konnte sich das Rauchen nicht abgewöhnen; **to ~ sb of a habit** jdm etw abgewöhnen.
(i) (*tame, discipline*) *horse* zureiten; *spirit, person* brechen; *wilful child* fügsam machen.
(j) (*destroy*) *sb* kleinkriegen (*inf*), mürbe machen; *sb's health* ruinieren, kaputtmachen (*inf*); *resistance, strike* brechen; *alibi* entkräften; *code* entziffern; (*Sport*) *serve* durchbrechen ◆ **his spirit was broken by her death** ihr Tod hatte ihn seelisch gebrochen; **to ~ sb** (*financially*) jdn ruinieren, jdn bankrott machen; (*with grief*) jdn seelisch brechen; **to ~ the bank** (*Gambling*) die Bank sprengen; **37p, well that won't exactly ~ the bank** 37 Pence, na, davon gehe ich/gehen wir noch nicht bankrott; **his service was broken** (*Tennis*) er hat das Aufschlagspiel abgegeben.
(k) (*soften, weaken*) *fall* dämpfen, abfangen ◆ **the wall ~s the force of the wind** der Wind bricht sich an der Mauer.
(l) (*get out of, escape from*) *jail, one's bonds* ausbrechen aus ◆ **to ~ step** (*Mil*) aus dem Schritt fallen; *see* **camp, cover, rank.**
(m) (*disclose*) *news* mitteilen ◆ **how can I ~ it to her?** wie soll ich es ihr sagen?
(n) (*start spending*) *five-dollar bill* anbrechen; (*give change for*) kleinmachen.
3 *vi* **(a)** (*snap, be fractured*) (*twig, bone*) brechen; (*rope*) zerreißen; (*smash: window, cup*) kaputtgehen; (*cup, glass etc also*) zerbrechen ◆ **~ing strain** *or* **strength** Belastbarkeit *f*.
(b) (*stop working etc: toy, watch, chair*) kaputtgehen; (*toy, chair etc also*) zerbrechen.
(c) (*become detached*) **to ~ from sth** von etw abbrechen.
(d) (*pause*) (eine) Pause machen, unterbrechen.
(e) (*wave*) sich brechen.
(f) (*day, dawn*) anbrechen; (*suddenly: storm*) losbrechen.
(g) (*change: weather, luck*) umschlagen.
(h) (*disperse*) (*clouds*) aufreißen; (*crowd*) sich teilen.
(i) (*give way*) (*health*) leiden, Schaden nehmen; (*stamina*) gebrochen werden; (*under interrogation etc*) zusammenbrechen ◆ **his courage/spirit broke** sein Mut verließ ihn.
(j) (*voice*) (*with emotion*) brechen ◆ **his voice is beginning to ~** (*boy*) er kommt in den Stimmbruch.
(k) (*become known: story, news, scandal*) bekanntwerden, an den Tag *or* ans Licht kommen ◆ **the news broke on Wall Street yesterday** gestern platzte diese Nachricht in der Wall Street.
(l) (*end relations*) brechen.
(m) (*let go: Boxing etc*) sich trennen ◆ **~!** break!
(n) (**~ away, escape**) (*from jail*) ausbrechen (*from* aus) ◆ **to ~ even** seine (Un)kosten decken; *see* **loose**.
(o) (*ball*) **to ~ to the right/left** nach rechts/links wegspringen.
(p) (*Billiards*) anstoßen.

◆**break away** 1 *vi* **(a)** (*chair leg, handle etc*) abbrechen (*from* von); (*railway coaches, boats*) sich losreißen (*from* von).
(b) (*dash away*) weglaufen (*from* von); (*prisoner*) sich losreißen (*from* von); (*Ftbl*) sich absetzen ◆ **he broke ~ from the rest of the field** er hängte das ganze Feld ab.
(c) (*cut ties*) sich trennen *or* lossagen (*from* von); (*US Sport: start too soon*) fehlstarten, zu früh starten ◆ **to ~ ~ from a group** sich von einer Gruppe trennen; **to ~ ~ from the everyday routine** aus der täglichen Routine ausbrechen; **to ~ ~ from an idea** sich von einer Vorstellung lösen.
2 *vt sep* abbrechen (*from* von).

◆**break down** 1 *vi* **(a)** (*vehicle*) eine Panne haben; (*machine*) versagen; (*binding machine etc*) stehenbleiben.
(b) (*fail*) (*negotiations, plan, marriage*) scheitern; (*communications, law and order*) zusammenbrechen.
(c) (*give way*) (*argument, resistance, person: start crying, have a breakdown*) zusammenbrechen ◆ **his health has broken ~** ihm geht es gesundheitlich schlecht.
(d) (*be analysed*) (*expenditure*) sich aufschlüsseln or -gliedern; (*theory*) sich unter- or aufgliedern (lassen); (*Chem: substance*) sich zerlegen (lassen); (*change its composition: substance*) sich aufspalten (*into* in +*acc*).
2 *vt sep* **(a)** (*smash down*) *door* einrennen; *wall* niederreißen.
(b) (*overcome*) *opposition* brechen; *hostility, reserve, shyness, suspicion* überwinden.
(c) (*to constituent parts*) *expenditure* aufschlüsseln, aufgliedern; *argument* auf- or untergliedern; aufspalten; (*change composition of*) umsetzen.

◆**break forth** *vi* (*liter*) (*light, water*) hervorbrechen; (*smile*) sich ausbreiten; (*storm*) losbrechen.

◆**break in** 1 *vi* **(a)** (*interrupt*) unterbrechen (*on sb/sth* jdn/etw). **(b)** (*enter illegally*) einbrechen.
2 *vt sep* **(a)** *door* aufbrechen. **(b)** (*tame, train*) *horse* zureiten; *new employee* einarbeiten. **(c)** *shoes* einlaufen.

◆**break into** *vi +prep obj* **(a)** *house* einbrechen in (+*acc*); *safe, car* aufbrechen ◆ **his house/car has been broken ~** bei ihm ist eingebrochen worden/sein Auto ist aufgebrochen worden.
(b) (*use part of*) *savings, £5 note, rations* anbrechen.
(c) (*begin suddenly*) **to ~ ~ song/a run/a trot** zu singen/laufen/traben anfangen, in Laufschritt/Trab (ver)fallen; **to ~ ~ a laugh** in Lachen ausbrechen.

◆**break off** 1 *vi* **(a)** abbrechen (*from* von).
(b) (*stop*) abbrechen, aufhören; (*stop speaking*) abbrechen; (*temporarily*) unterbrechen ◆ **to ~ ~ from work** die Arbeit abbrechen; **we ~ ~ at 5 o'clock** wir hören um 5 Uhr auf.
2 *vt sep* **(a)** *twig, piece of chocolate etc* abbrechen. **(b)** *negotiations, relations* abbrechen; *engagement* lösen ◆ **she's broken it ~** sie hat die Verlobung gelöst.

◆**break open** 1 *vi* aufspringen.
2 *vt sep* aufbrechen.

◆**break out** *vi* **(a)** (*epidemic, fire, war*) ausbrechen.
(b) to ~ ~ in a rash/in(to) spots einen Ausschlag/Pickel bekommen; **he broke ~ in a sweat/a cold sweat** er kam ins Schwitzen, ihm brach der Schweiß/Angstschweiß aus.

(**c**) (*escape*) ausbrechen (*from, of* aus).
(**d**) (*speak suddenly*) herausplatzen, losplatzen.

◆**break through** [1] *vi* (*Mil, sun*) durchbrechen.
[2] *vi +prep obj defences, barrier, crowd* durchbrechen ◆ **to ~ ~ sb's reserve** jdn aus der Reserve locken.

◆**break up** [1] *vi* (**a**) (*road*) aufbrechen; (*ice also*) bersten; (*ship in storm*) zerbersten; (*on rocks*) zerschellen.
(**b**) (*clouds*) sich lichten; (*crowd, group*) auseinanderlaufen; (*meeting, partnership*) sich auflösen; (*marriage, relationship*) in die Brüche gehen; (*party*) zum Ende kommen; (*Pol: party*) sich auflösen, auseinandergehen; (*friends, partners*) sich trennen; (*sentence, theory*) sich aufspalten, zerfallen; (*empire*) auseinanderfallen; (*inf: with laughter*) sich totlachen (*inf*) ◆ **when did the party ~ ~ last night?** wie lange ging die Party gestern abend?
(**c**) (*Brit Sch*) (*school, pupils*) aufhören ◆ **when do you ~ ~?** wann hört bei euch die Schule auf, wann gibt es Ferien?
[2] *vt sep* (**a**) *ground, road* aufbrechen; *oil slick* auflösen; *ship* auseinanderbrechen lassen; (*in breaker's yard*) abwracken.
(**b**) *estate, country* aufteilen; *room also, paragraph, sentence* unterteilen; *empire* auflösen; *lines, expanse of colour* unterbrechen; (*make more interesting*) auflockern.
(**c**) (*bring to an end, disperse*) *marriage, home* zerstören; *meeting* (*police etc*) auflösen; (*trouble-makers*) sprengen; *crowd* (*police*) zerstreuen, auseinandertreiben ◆ **he broke ~ the fight** er trennte die Kämpfer; **~ it ~!** auseinander!

breakable ['breɪkəbl] [1] *adj* zerbrechlich.
[2] *n* **~s** *pl* zerbrechliche Ware.

breakage ['breɪkɪdʒ] *n* (**a**) (*in chain, link*) Bruch *m*. (**b**) (*of glass, china*) Bruch *m* ◆ **to pay for ~s** für zerbrochene Ware *or* Bruch bezahlen; **were there any ~s?** hat es Bruch gegeben?, ist irgend etwas kaputtgegangen *or* zu Bruch gegangen?

breakaway ['breɪkəˌweɪ] [1] *n* (**a**) (*Pol*) Abfall *m*; (*of state also*) Loslösung *f*. (**b**) (*Sport*) Aus- *or* Durchbruch *m*. (**c**) (*US Sport: false start*) Fehlstart *m*.
[2] *adj group* Splitter-.

break: ~ command *n* (*Comput*) Unterbrechungsbefehl *m*; **~ dance** *vi* Breakdance tanzen; **~ dancer** *n* Breakdance-Tänzer(in *f*) *m*; **~ dancing** *n* Breakdance *m*.

breakdown ['breɪkdaʊn] *n* (**a**) (*of machine*) Betriebsschaden *m*; (*of vehicle*) Panne *f*, Motorschaden *m*.
(**b**) (*of communications, system*) Zusammenbruch *m*.
(**c**) (*Med: physical, mental*) Zusammenbruch *m*.
(**d**) (*of figures, expenditure etc*) Aufschlüsselung *f*; (*of thesis, theory etc*) Auf- *or* Untergliederung *f*.
(**e**) (*Chem*) Aufspaltung *f*; (*change in composition*) Umsetzung *f*.

breakdown: ~ service *n* Pannendienst *m*; **~ truck** *or* **van** *n* Abschleppwagen *m*.

breaker ['breɪkə^r] *n* (**a**) (*wave*) Brecher *m*. (**b**) **~'s (yard): to send a ship to the ~'s (yard)** ein Schiff abwracken.

break-even point [breɪk'iːvənˌpɔɪnt] *n* Gewinnschwelle *f*, Break-even-Punkt *m* (*spec*).

breakfast ['brekfəst] [1] *n* (**a**) Frühstück *nt* ◆ **to have ~** frühstücken, Frühstück essen; **for ~** zum Frühstück. (**b**) **wedding ~** Hochzeitsessen *nt*.
[2] *vi* frühstücken ◆ **he ~ed on bacon and eggs** er frühstückte Eier mit Speck.

breakfast *in cpds* Frühstücks-; **~ cereal** *n* Cornflakes, Getreideflocken *pl*; **~ meeting** *n* Arbeitsfrühstück *nt*; **~ set** *n* Frühstücksservice *nt*; **~ television** *n* Frühstücksfernsehen *nt*; **~-time** *n* Frühstückszeit *f*.

break-in ['breɪkɪn] *n* Einbruch *m* ◆ **we've had a ~** bei uns ist eingebrochen worden.

breaking ['breɪkɪŋ] *n* **~ and entering** (*Jur*) Einbruch *m*.

breaking point *n* (**a**) (*Tech*) Festigkeitsgrenze *f*. (**b**) (*fig*) **she has reached** *or* **is at ~** sie ist nervlich völlig am Ende (ihrer Kräfte).

break: ~neck *adj* **at ~neck speed** mit halsbrecherischer Geschwindigkeit; **~-out** *n* Ausbruch *m*; **~ point** *n* (*Tennis*) Breakpunkt *m*; **~through** *n* (*Mil, fig*) Durchbruch *m*; **~-up** *n* (**a**) (*lit*) (*of ship*) Zerbersten *nt*; (*on rocks*) Zerschellen *nt*; (*of ice*) Bersten *nt*; (**b**) (*fig*) (*of friendship*) Bruch *m*; (*of marriage*) Zerrüttung *f*; (*of empire*) Zerfall *m*; (*of political party*) Zersplitterung *f*; (*of partnership, meeting*) Auflösung *f*; (*by trouble-makers*) Sprengung *f*; **~-up value** *n* (*Fin*) Liquidationswert *m*; **~water** *n* Wellenbrecher *m*.

bream [briːm] *n* Brasse *f*, Brachsen *m*.

breast [brest] [1] *n* (**a**) (*chest*) Brust *f*; (*Cook: of chicken, lamb*) Brust(stück *nt*) *f*. (**b**) (*of woman*) Brust *f* ◆ **a child/baby at the ~** ein Kind/Säugling an der Brust. (**c**) (*fig liter*) Brust *f*, Busen *m* (*liter*).
[2] *vt* (**a**) **to ~ the waves/the storm** gegen die Wellen/den Sturm ankämpfen. (**b**) **to ~ the tape** (*Sport*) durchs Ziel gehen.

breastbone ['brestbəʊn] *n* Brustbein *nt*; (*of bird*) Brustknochen *m*.

-breasted ['brestɪd] *adj suf woman* -brüstig ◆ **a double-/single-~ jacket** ein Einreiher *m*/Zweireiher *m*.

breast: ~fed *adj* **to be ~fed** gestillt werden; **~fed child** Brustkind *nt*; **~feed** *vti* stillen; **~feeding** *n* Stillen *nt*; **~ milk** *n* Muttermilch *f*; **~plate** *n* (*on armour*) Brustharnisch *m*; (*of high priest*) Brustplatte *f or* -gehänge *nt*; **~ pocket** *n* Brusttasche *f*; **~ stroke** *n* Brustschwimmen *nt*; **to swim** *or* **do the ~ stroke** brustschwimmen; **~work** *n* (*Mil*) Brustwehr *f*.

breath [breθ] *n* (**a**) Atem *m* ◆ **to take a deep ~** einmal tief Luft holen; (*before diving, singing etc*) einmal tief einatmen; **bad ~** Mundgeruch *m*; **to have bad ~** aus dem Mund riechen, Mundgeruch haben; **with one's dying ~** mit dem letzten Atemzug; **to draw one's last ~** (*liter*) seinen letzten Atemzug tun; **out of** *or* **short of ~** außer Atem, atemlos; **to stop for ~** sich verschnaufen, eine Pause zum Luftholen machen; **in the same ~** im selben Atemzug; **to say sth all in one ~** etw in einem Atemzug sagen; **to take sb's ~ away** jdm den Atem verschlagen; **to say sth under one's ~** etw vor sich (*acc*) hin murmeln; **save your ~** spar dir die Spucke (*inf*); **you're wasting your ~** du redest umsonst; **to go out for a ~ of (fresh) air** an die frische Luft gehen, frische Luft schnappen gehen; **she brought a ~ of fresh air to the ward** (*fig*) sie brachte etwas Schwung in die Station; **you're like a ~ of fresh air** du bist so erfrischend.
(**b**) (*slight stirring*) **~ of wind** Lüftchen *nt*; **there wasn't a ~ of air** es regte sich *or* wehte kein Lüftchen.
(**c**) (*fig: whisper*) Hauch *m*, Sterbenswörtchen *nt*.

breathalyze ['breθəlaɪz] *vt* (*Brit*) blasen lassen ◆ **he refused to be ~d** er weigerte sich, (ins Röhrchen) zu blasen.

Breathalyzer ® ['breθəlaɪzə^r] *n* (*Brit*) Promillemesser *m* ◆ **to give sb a ~** jdn (ins Röhrchen) blasen lassen; **to blow into the ~** ins Röhrchen blasen.

breathe [briːð] [1] *vi* atmen; (*inf: rest*) verschnaufen, Luft holen *or* schöpfen; (*liter: live*) leben ◆ **now we can ~ again** jetzt können wir wieder frei atmen; (*have more space*) jetzt haben wir wieder Luft; **I don't want him breathing down my neck** (*inf*) ich will ihn nicht auf dem Hals haben (*inf*).
[2] *vt* (**a**) *air* einatmen ◆ **to ~ one's last (breath)** seinen letzten Atemzug tun; **to ~ the air of one's own country again** wieder auf heimatlichem Boden sein *or* stehen.
(**b**) (*exhale*) atmen, (*into* in *+acc*) ◆ **he ~d alcohol/garlic all over me** er hatte eine solche Fahne, er verströmte einen solchen Alkohol-/Knoblauchgeruch; **to ~ fire** Feuer spucken; **he ~d new life into the firm** er brachte neues Leben in die Firma.
(**c**) (*utter*) *prayer* flüstern, hauchen ◆ **to ~ a sigh of relief** erleichtert aufatmen; **don't ~ a word of it!** sag kein Sterbenswörtchen darüber!

◆**breathe in** *vi, vt sep* einatmen.

◆**breathe out** *vi, vt sep* ausatmen.

breather ['briːðə^r] *n* (*short rest*) Atempause, Verschnaufpause *f* ◆ **to give sb a ~** jdn verschnaufen lassen; **to take** *or* **have a ~** sich verschnaufen.

breathing ['briːðɪŋ] *n* (*respiration*) Atmung *f* ◆ **the child's peaceful ~** die ruhigen Atemzüge des Kindes.

breathing: ~ apparatus *n* Sauerstoffgerät *nt*; **~ space** *n* (*fig*) Atempause, Ruhepause *f*.

breathless ['breθlɪs] *adj* atemlos; (*with exertion also*) außer Atem ◆ **he said in a ~ voice** sagte er, nach Luft ringend; **he is rather ~** (*through illness*) er leidet an Atemnot; **it left me ~** (*lit, fig*) es verschlug mir den Atem.

breathlessly ['breθlɪslɪ] *adv see adj* atemlos; außer Atem.

breathlessness ['breθlɪsnɪs] *n* (*due to exertion*) Atemlosigkeit *f*; (*due to illness*) Kurzatmigkeit *f*.

breath: ~taking *adj* atemberaubend; **~ test** *n* Atemalkoholtest *m*; **~ testing** *n* Atemalkoholkontrolle *f*.

breathy ['breθɪ] *adj* (*+er*) rauchig; (*through shyness*) hauchig.

bred [bred] *pret, ptp of* **breed**.

-bred *adj suf* -erzogen.

breech[1] [briːtʃ] *n* (*of gun*) Verschluß *m* ◆ **~-loader** (*Mil*) Hinterlader *m*.

breech[2] *adj attr* (*Med*) *birth, delivery* Steiß- ◆ **~ presentation** Steißlage *f*; **to be a ~ baby** eine Steißlage sein.

breeches ['brɪtʃɪz] *npl* Kniehose *f*; (*riding ~*) Reithose *f*; (*for hiking*) (Knie)bundhose *f*.

breeches buoy *n* Hosenboje *f*.

breed [briːd] (*vb: pret, ptp* **bred**) [1] *n* (*lit, fig*) (*species*) Art, Sorte *f* ◆ **they produced a new ~** sie haben eine neue Züchtung hervorgebracht; **a ~ apart** (*fig*) eine besondere *or* spezielle Sorte *or* Gattung.
[2] *vt* (**a**) (*raise, rear*) *animals, flowers* züchten; *see* **born**.
(**b**) (*fig: give rise to*) erzeugen ◆ **dirt ~s disease** Schmutz verursacht Krankheit, Schmutz zieht Krankheit nach sich.
[3] *vi* (*animals*) Junge haben; (*birds*) brüten; (*pej, hum: people*) sich vermehren ◆ **rabbits ~ quickly** Kaninchen vermehren sich schnell.

breeder ['briːdə^r] *n* (**a**) (*person*) Züchter *m*. (**b**) (*Phys: also* **~ reactor**) Brutreaktor, Brüter *m*.

breeding ['briːdɪŋ] *n* (**a**) (*reproduction*) Fortpflanzung und Aufzucht *f* der Jungen. (**b**) (*rearing*) Zucht *f*. (**c**) (*upbringing, good manners: also* **good ~**) gute Erziehung, Kinderstube *f*.

breeding: ~ place *n* (*lit, fig*) Brutstätte *f*; **~ season** *n* (*of birds*) Brutzeit *f*; (*of animal*) Zeit *f* der Fortpflanzung und Aufzucht der Jungen.

breeze [briːz] *n* Brise *f* ◆ **it's a ~** (*US inf*) das ist kinderleicht.

◆**breeze in** *vi* fröhlich angetrabt kommen *or* hereinschneien ◆ **he ~d ~to the room** er kam fröhlich ins Zimmer geschneit.

◆**breeze out** *vi* vergnügt abziehen (*of* aus).

◆**breeze through** *vi +prep obj* (*inf: do easily*) spielend *or* mit Leichtigkeit schaffen.

breezeblock ['briːzblɒk] *n* (*Build*) Ytong ® *m*.

breezily ['briːzɪlɪ] *adv* (*fig*) forsch-fröhlich.

breeziness ['briːzɪnɪs] *n* (*fig*) Forschheit *f*.

breezy ['briːzɪ] *adj* (*+er*) (**a**) *weather, day* windig; *corner, spot also* luftig. (**b**) *manner* forsch-fröhlich.

Bren gun ['brengʌn] *n* (*Mil*) leichtes Maschinengewehr ◆ **~ carrier, Bren carrier** kleines leichtes Panzerfahrzeug.

brer, br'er [brɛə^r] *n* (*old*) Gevatter *m* (*old*).

brethren ['breðrɪn] *npl* (*obs, Eccl*) Brüder *pl*.

Breton ['bretən] [1] *adj* bretonisch.
[2] *n* (**a**) Bretone *m*, Bretonin *f*. (**b**) (*language*) Bretonisch *nt*.

breve [bri:v] *n (Mus)* Brevis *f.*
breviary ['bri:vɪərɪ] *n* Brevier *nt.*
brevity ['brevɪtɪ] *n* **(a)** *(shortness)* Kürze *f.* **(b)** *(conciseness)* Kürze, Bündigkeit, Knappheit *f* ◆ **~ is the soul of wit** *(Prov)* in der Kürze liegt die Würze *(Prov).*
brew [bru:] 1 *n* **(a)** *(beer)* Bräu *nt.* **(b)** *(of tea)* Tee *m,* Gebräu *nt (iro); (of herbs)* Kräutermischung *f* ◆ **witch's ~** Zaubertrank *m.*
2 *vt* **(a)** *beer, ale* brauen; *tea* aufbrühen, aufgießen, kochen. **(b)** *(fig) scheme, mischief, plot* ausbrüten, aushecken ◆ **to ~ a plot** ein Komplott schmieden.
3 *vi* **(a)** *(beer)* gären; *(tea)* ziehen. **(b)** *(make beer)* brauen. **(c)** *(fig)* **there's trouble/mischief/a storm** *etc* **~ing (up)** da braut sich ein Konflikt/Unheil/ein Sturm zusammen; **there's something ~ing** da braut sich etwas zusammen.
◆**brew up** *vi* **(a)** *(inf: make tea)* sich *(dat)* einen Tee machen. **(b)** *(fig) see* **brew 3 (c).**
brewer ['bru:əʳ] *n* Brauer *m* ◆ **~'s yeast** Bierhefe *f.*
brewery ['bru:ərɪ] *n* Brauerei *f.*
brew-up ['bru:ʌp] *n (inf)* **to have a ~** Tee kochen.
briar ['braɪəʳ] *n* **(a)** *(also* **~wood)** Bruyère(holz) *nt; (also* **~ pipe)** Bruyère(pfeife) *f.* **(b)** *see* **brier (a).**
bribable ['braɪbəbl] *adj* bestechlich.
bribe [braɪb] 1 *n* Bestechung *f; (money also)* Bestechungsgeld *nt* ◆ **as a ~** als Bestechung; **to take a ~** sich bestechen lassen, Bestechungsgeld nehmen; **to offer sb a ~** jdn bestechen wollen, jdm Bestechungsgeld anbieten.
2 *vt* bestechen ◆ **to ~ sb to do sth** jdn bestechen, damit er etw tut.
bribery ['braɪbərɪ] *n* Bestechung *f* ◆ **open to ~** bestechlich.
bric-à-brac ['brɪkəbræk] *n* Nippes *m,* Nippsachen *pl.*
brick [brɪk] *n* **(a)** *(Build)* Ziegel- *or* Backstein *m* ◆ **you can't make ~s without straw** *(Prov)* wo nichts ist, kann auch nichts werden; **he came** *or* **was down on me like a ton of ~s** *(inf)* er hat mich unheimlich fertiggemacht *(inf);* **to drop a ~** *(fig inf)* ins Fettnäpfchen treten; **to drop sb/sth like a hot ~** *(inf)* jdn/etw wie eine heiße Kartoffel fallenlassen.
(b) *(toy)* (Bau)klotz *m* ◆ **box of (building) ~s** Baukasten *m.*
(c) *(of ice-cream)* Block *m.*
(d) *(dated inf)* feiner Kerl *(inf)* ◆ **be a ~!** sei ein Kumpel!
◆**brick in** *or* **up** *vt sep door, window* zumauern.
brick *in cpds* Backstein-; **~bat** *n (missile)* Backsteinbrocken *m; (fig)* Beschimpfung *f.*
brickie ['brɪkɪ] *n (Brit inf)* Maurer *m.*
brick: ~-kiln *n* Ziegelofen *m;* **~layer** *n* Maurer *m;* **~laying** *n* Maurerarbeit *f; (trade)* Maurerhandwerk *nt;* **~ red** *adj* ziegelrot; **~ wall** *n (fig inf)* **I might as well be talking to a ~ wall** ich könnte genausogut gegen eine Wand reden; **it's like beating** *or* **banging one's head against a ~ wall** es ist, wie wenn man mit dem Kopf gegen die Wand rennt; **to come up against a ~ wall** plötzlich vor einer Mauer stehen; **~work** *n* Backsteinmauerwerk *nt;* **~works** *npl,* **~yard** *n* Ziegelei *f.*
bridal ['braɪdl] *adj* Braut-; *procession also, feast* Hochzeits- ◆ **~ party** Angehörige und Freunde *pl* der Braut; **~ vow** Eheversprechen *nt* der Braut.
bride [braɪd] *n* Braut *f* ◆ **the ~ and (bride)groom** Braut und Bräutigam, das Hochzeitspaar; **~ of Christ** Braut Christi.
bridegroom ['braɪdgru:m] *n* Bräutigam *m.*
bridesmaid ['braɪdzmeɪd] *n* Brautjungfer *f.*
bridge[1] [brɪdʒ] 1 *n* **(a)** *(lit, fig)* Brücke *f.* **(b)** *(Naut)* (Kommando)brücke *f.* **(c)** *(of nose)* Sattel *m; (of spectacles, violin)* Steg *m.* **(d)** *(Dentistry)* Brücke *f.* **(e)** *(Billiards)* Steg *m.*
2 *vt river, railway* eine Brücke schlagen *or* bauen über (+*acc*); *(fig)* überbrücken ◆ **to ~ the gap** *(fig)* die Zeit überbrücken; *(between people)* die Kluft überbrücken.
bridge[2] *n (Cards)* Bridge *nt.*
bridge: ~-building *n* Brückenbau *m;* **~head** *n* Brückenkopf *m;* **to establish a ~head** einen Brückenkopf errichten; **~house** *n* Brückenhaus *nt;* **~ roll** *n* längliches Brötchen.
bridging ['brɪdʒɪŋ]: **~ finance** *n* Zwischenfinanzierung *f;* **~ loan** *n* Überbrückungskredit *m.*
bridle ['braɪdl] 1 *n (of horse)* Zaum *m.*
2 *vt* **(a)** *horse* aufzäumen. **(b)** *(fig) one's tongue, emotions* im Zaume halten.
3 *vi* sich entrüstet wehren *(at* gegen).
bridlepath ['braɪdl,pɑ:θ] *n* Reitweg *m.*
brief [bri:f] 1 *adj* (+*er*) kurz; *(curt also) manner* kurz angebunden ◆ **in ~** kurz; **to be ~** um es kurz zu machen; **could you give me a ~ idea ...** könnten Sie mir kurz erzählen ...
2 *n* **(a)** *(Jur)* Auftrag *m (an einen Anwalt); (document)* Unterlagen *pl* zu dem/einem Fall; *(instructions)* Instruktionen *pl* ◆ **to take a ~** *(Jur)* einen Fall annehmen; **to hold a ~ for sb** *(Jur)* jds Sache vor Gericht vertreten; **I hold no ~ for him** *(fig)* ich will nicht für ihn plädieren. **(b)** *(instructions)* Auftrag *m.*
3 *vt* **(a)** *(Jur) lawyer* instruieren; *(employ)* beauftragen.
(b) *(give instructions, information to)* instruieren *(on* über +*acc)* ◆ **the pilots were ~ed on what they had to do** die Piloten wurden instruiert, was sie tun sollten.
briefcase ['bri:fkeɪs] *n* (Akten)tasche, (Akten)mappe *f.*
briefing ['bri:fɪŋ] *n (instructions)* Instruktionen *pl,* Anweisungen *pl; (also* **~ session)** Einsatzbesprechung *f.*
briefly ['bri:flɪ] *adv* kurz.
briefness ['bri:fnɪs] *n* Kürze *f.*
briefs [bri:fs] *npl* Slip *m* ◆ **a pair of ~** ein Slip.
brier ['braɪəʳ] *n* **(a)** *(wild rose)* wilde Rose; *(bramble runner)* Ranke *f; (thorny bush)* Dornbusch *m.* **(b)** *see* **briar (a).**
Brig. *abbr of* **brigadier.**
brig [brɪg] *n* **(a)** *(ship)* Brigg *f.* **(b)** *(US: cell)* Arrestzelle *f (auf einem Schiff); (US Mil sl)* Bunker *m (sl).*
brigade [brɪ'geɪd] *n (Mil)* Brigade *f.*
brigadier [,brɪgə'dɪəʳ] *n (Brit)* Brigadegeneral *m.*
brigadier (general) *n (Brit Hist, US)* Brigadegeneral *m.*
brigand ['brɪgənd] *n (old)* Räuber, Bandit *m.*
bright [braɪt] *adj* (+*er*) **(a)** hell; *colour* leuchtend; *sunshine, star also, eyes, gem* strahlend; *day, weather* heiter; *reflection* stark; *metal* glänzend ◆ **~ red** knallrot; **it was really ~** *or* **a ~ day outside** es war wirklich sehr hell draußen; **~ with lights** hell erleuchtet; **~ intervals** *or* **periods** *(Met)* Aufheiterungen *pl;* **the outlook is ~er** *(Met)* die Aussichten sind etwas freundlicher; *(fig)* es sieht etwas besser aus; **the ~ lights** *(inf)* der Glanz der Großstadt.
(b) *(cheerful) person, smile* fröhlich, heiter ◆ **I wasn't feeling too ~** es ging mir nicht besonders gut; **~ and early** in aller Frühe; *see* **side.**
(c) *(intelligent) person* intelligent, schlau; *child* aufgeweckt; *idea* glänzend; *(iro)* intelligent ◆ **I'm not very ~ this morning** ich habe heute morgen Mattscheibe *(inf);* **I forgot to tell him — that's ~** *(inf)* ich habe vergessen, ihm das zu sagen — toll! *(inf).*
(d) *(favourable) future* glänzend; *prospects also* freundlich ◆ **things aren't looking too ~** es sieht nicht gerade rosig aus.
brighten (up) ['braɪtn(ʌp)] 1 *vt (sep)* **(a)** *(make cheerful) spirits, person* aufmuntern, aufheitern; *room, atmosphere* aufhellen, aufheitern; *conversation* beleben; *prospects, situation* verbessern.
(b) *(make bright) colour, hair* aufhellen; *metal* aufpolieren.
2 *vi* **(a)** *(weather, sky)* sich aufklären *or* aufheitern.
(b) *(person)* fröhlicher werden; *(face)* sich aufhellen *or* aufheitern; *(eyes)* aufleuchten; *(prospects)* sich verbessern, freundlicher werden; *(future)* freundlicher aussehen.
bright-eyed ['braɪtaɪd] *adj* mit strahlenden Augen.
brightly ['braɪtlɪ] *adv* **(a)** hell; *reflected* stark. **(b)** *see adj (b)* fröhlich, heiter. **(c)** *see adj (c)* intelligent, schlau ◆ **he very ~ left it at home** *(iro)* er hat es intelligenterweise zu Hause gelassen.
brightness ['braɪtnɪs] *n see adj* **(a)** Helligkeit *f;* Leuchten *nt;* Strahlen *nt;* Heiterkeit *f;* Stärke *f;* Glanz *m* ◆ **~ control** Helligkeitsregler *m.* **(b)** Fröhlichkeit, Heiterkeit *f.* **(c)** Intelligenz, Schlauheit *f;* Aufgewecktheit *f.* **(d)** Freundlichkeit *f* ◆ **the ~ of the future** die glänzende Zukunft.
Bright's disease ['braɪtsdɪ,zi:z] *n* Brightsche Krankheit.
brill[1] [brɪl] *n* Glattbutt *m.*
brill[2] *adj (Brit inf)* toll *(inf).*
brilliance ['brɪljəns] *n* **(a)** heller Glanz, Strahlen *nt; (of colour)* Strahlen *nt.* **(b)** *(fig) see adj (b)* Großartigkeit *f;* Brillanz *f* ◆ **a man of such ~** ein Mann von so hervorragender Intelligenz.
brilliant ['brɪljənt] *adj* **(a)** *sunshine, light, eyes, colour* strahlend. **(b)** *(fig)* großartig *(also iro); scientist, artist, wit, achievement also* glänzend, brillant; *student* hervorragend ◆ **she is a ~ woman** sie ist eine sehr intelligente Frau.
brilliantine [,brɪljən'ti:n] *n* Brillantine, Haarpomade *f.*
brilliantly ['brɪljəntlɪ] *adv* **(a)** *shine* hell; *sunny* strahlend.
(b) *(very well, superbly)* großartig; *talented* glänzend; *play, perform* brillant; *funny, witty, simple* herrlich ◆ **a ~ original idea** eine Idee von glänzender Originalität.
Brillo pad ® ['brɪləʊ,pæd] *n* Scheuertuch *nt aus Stahlwolle.*
brim [brɪm] 1 *n (of cup)* Rand *m; (of hat also)* Krempe *f* ◆ **full to the ~** randvoll.
2 *vi* strotzen *(with* von *or* vor +*dat)* ◆ **her eyes were ~ming with tears** ihre Augen schwammen in Tränen.
◆**brim over** *vi (lit, fig)* überfließen *(with* vor +*dat).*
brimful ['brɪm'fʊl] *adj (lit)* randvoll; *(fig)* voll *(of, with* von) ◆ **he is ~ of energy** er sprüht vor Energie.
-brimmed [brɪmd] *adj suf hat* -krempig.
brimstone ['brɪmstəʊn] *n (sulphur)* Schwefel *m.*
brindled ['brɪndld] *adj* gestreift.
brine [braɪn] *n* **(a)** *(salt water)* Sole *f; (for pickling)* Lake *f.* **(b)** *(sea water)* Salzwasser *nt; (liter: sea)* See *f.*
bring [brɪŋ] *pret, ptp* **brought** *vt* **(a)** bringen; *(also:* **~ with one)** mitbringen ◆ **did you ~ the car/your guitar** *etc*? haben Sie den Wagen/die Gitarre *etc* mitgebracht?; **to ~ sb across/inside** *etc* jdn herüber-/hereinbringen *etc.*
(b) *(result in, be accompanied by) snow, rain, luck* bringen ◆ **to ~ a blush/tears to sb's cheeks/eyes** jdm die Röte ins Gesicht/die Tränen in die Augen treiben.
(c) (+*infin: persuade)* **I cannot ~ myself to speak to him** ich kann es nicht über mich bringen, mit ihm zu sprechen; **to ~ sb to do sth** jdn dazu bringen *or* bewegen, etw zu tun.
(d) *(esp Jur: present for trial, discussion) case, matter* bringen *(before* vor +*acc)* ◆ **the trial will be brought next week** der Prozeß findet nächste Woche statt; *see* **action, charge.**
(e) *(sell for, earn) price, income* (ein)bringen.
(f) *in phrases see also relevant nouns* **to ~ sth to a close** *or* **end** etw zu Ende bringen; **to ~ sb low** jdn auf Null bringen *(inf);* **to ~ sth to sb's knowledge/attention** jdm etw zur Kenntnis bringen/jdn auf etw *(acc)* aufmerksam machen; **to ~ to perfection** perfektionieren, vervollkommnen.
◆**bring about** *vt sep* **(a)** *(cause)* herbeiführen, verursachen. **(b)** *(Naut)* wenden ◆ **he brought us ~** er wendete.
◆**bring along** *vt sep* **(a)** mitbringen. **(b)** *see* **bring on (b).**

◆**bring around** *vt sep see* **bring round (a, d).**
◆**bring away** *vt sep person* wegbringen; *memories, impression* mitnehmen.
◆**bring back** *vt sep* **(a)** *(lit) person, object* zurückbringen.
(b) *(restore) custom, hanging* wieder einführen; *government* wiederwählen ◆ **a rest will ~ him ~ to normal** ein wenig Ruhe wird ihn wiederherstellen; **to ~ sb ~ to life/health** jdn wieder lebendig/gesund machen; **to ~ a government ~ to power** eine Regierung wieder an die Macht bringen.
(c) *(recall) memories* zurückbringen, wecken; *events* erinnern an (+*acc*).
◆**bring down** *vt sep* **(a)** *(out of air) (shoot down) bird, plane* herunterholen; *(land) plane, kite* herunterbringen ◆ **to ~ sb's wrath ~ (up)on one** sich *(dat)* jds Zorn zuziehen; **you'll ~ the boss ~ on us** da werden wir es mit dem Chef zu tun bekommen.
(b) *opponent, footballer* zu Fall bringen; *(by shooting) animal* zur Strecke bringen; *person* niederschießen; *see* **house.**
(c) *government etc* zu Fall bringen.
(d) *(reduce) temperature, prices, cost of living* senken; *swelling* reduzieren, zurückgehen lassen.
◆**bring forth** *vt sep (old, liter)* **(a)** *fruit* hervorbringen *(geh)*; *child, young* zur Welt bringen *(geh)*. **(b)** *(fig) ideas* hervorbringen; *suggestions* vorbringen; *protests* auslösen.
◆**bring forward** *vt sep* **(a)** *(lit) person, chair* nach vorne bringen. **(b)** *(fig: present) witness* vorführen; *evidence, argument, proposal* vorbringen, unterbreiten. **(c)** *(advance time of) meeting* vorverlegen; *clock* vorstellen. **(d)** *(Comm) figure, amount* übertragen ◆ **amount brought ~** Übertrag *m.*
◆**bring in** *vt sep* **(a)** *(lit) person, object* hereinbringen *(prep obj, -to* in +*acc)*; *harvest* einbringen, bergen *(esp DDR)*; *sails* einziehen ◆ **to ~ ~ the New Year** das Neue Jahr begrüßen.
(b) *(fig: introduce) fashion, custom* einführen; *(Parl) bill* einbringen ◆ **to ~ sth ~(to) fashion** etw in Mode bringen.
(c) *(involve, call in) police, consultant etc* einschalten *(on* bei) ◆ **don't ~ him ~ to it** laß ihn aus der Sache raus; **she's bound to ~ Freud ~** sie wird bestimmt Freud mit hereinbringen; **why ~ Freud/that ~?** was hat Freud/das damit zu tun?
(d) *(Fin) income, money, interest* (ein)bringen *(-to sb* jdm); *(Comm) business* bringen.
(e) *(Jur: jury) verdict* fällen.
◆**bring into** *vt always separate* **to ~ ~ action/blossom/view** zum Einsatz bringen/blühen lassen/sichtbar werden lassen.
◆**bring off** *vt sep* **(a)** *people from wreck* retten, wegbringen *(prep obj* von). **(b)** *(succeed with) plan* zustande *or* zuwege bringen ◆ **to ~ ~ a coup** ein Ding drehen *(inf)*; **he brought it ~!** er hat es geschafft! *(inf)*. **(c)** *(sl: bring to orgasm)* befriedigen.
◆**bring on** *vt sep* **(a)** *(cause) illness, quarrel* herbeiführen, verursachen; *attack also* auslösen.
(b) *(help develop) pupil, young athlete* weiterbringen; *crops, flowers* herausbringen.
(c) *(Theat) person* auftreten lassen; *thing* auf die Bühne bringen; *(Sport) player* einsetzen ◆ **to ~ sb ~ the scene** *(fig)* jdn auf die Szene rufen.
(d) to ~ sth (up)~ oneself sich *(dat)* etw selbst aufladen; **you brought it (up)~ yourself** das hast du dir selbst zuzuschreiben.
◆**bring out** *vt sep* **(a)** *(lit)* (heraus)bringen *(of* aus); *(of pocket)* herausholen *(of* aus).
(b) *(draw out) person* die Hemmungen nehmen (+*dat*) ◆ **can't you ~ him ~ a bit?** können Sie nichts tun, damit er ein bißchen aus sich herausgeht?
(c) *(elicit) greed, bravery* zum Vorschein bringen; *best qualities also* herausbringen ◆ **to ~ ~ the best/worst in sb** das Beste/Schlimmste in jdm zum Vorschein bringen.
(d) *(also* **~ ~ on strike)** *workers* auf die Straße schicken.
(e) *(make blossom) flowers* herausbringen.
(f) *(to society) debutante* in die Gesellschaft einführen.
(g) *(bring on the market) new product, book* herausbringen.
(h) *(emphasize, show up)* herausbringen, hervorheben.
(i) *(utter) few words* herausbringen; *cry* ausstoßen.
(j) to ~ sb ~ in spots/a rash bei jdm Pickel/einen Ausschlag verursachen.
◆**bring over** *vt sep* **(a)** *(lit)* herüberbringen. **(b)** *(fig) (to ideas)* überzeugen *(to* von); *(to other side)* bringen *(to* auf +*acc*).
◆**bring round** *vt sep* **(a)** *(to one's house etc)* vorbeibringen. **(b)** *(steer) discussion, conversation* bringen *(to* auf +*acc*). **(c)** *unconscious person* wieder zu Bewußtsein bringen. **(d)** *(convert)* herumkriegen *(inf)*.
◆**bring through** *vt always separate patient, business* durchbringen ◆ **to ~ sb ~ a crisis/an illness** jdn durch eine Krise bringen/jdm helfen, eine Krankheit zu überstehen.
◆**bring to** *vt always separate* **(a)** *(Naut)* stoppen. **(b)** *unconscious person* wieder zu Bewußtsein bringen. **(c) to ~ sb ~ himself/herself** jdn wieder zu sich bringen.
◆**bring together** *vt sep* zusammenbringen.
◆**bring under** [1] *vt always separate (subdue)* unterwerfen.
[2] *vt +prep obj (categorize)* bringen unter (+*dat*) ◆ **this can be brought ~ four main headings** dies läßt sich in vier Kategorien gliedern; *see* **control.**
◆**bring up** *vt sep* **(a)** *(to a higher place)* heraufbringen; *(to the front)* her-/hinbringen.
(b) *(raise, increase) amount, reserves* erhöhen *(to* auf +*acc*); *level, standards* anheben ◆ **to ~ sb ~ to a certain standard** jdn auf ein gewisses Niveau bringen.
(c) *(rear) child, animal* groß- *or* aufziehen; *(educate)* erziehen ◆ **a well/badly brought ~ child** ein gut/schlecht erzogenes Kind; **to ~ sb ~ to do sth** jdn dazu erziehen, etw zu tun; **he was brought ~ to believe that ...** man hatte ihm beigebracht, daß ...
(d) *(vomit up)* brechen; *(esp baby, patient)* spucken *(inf)*.
(e) *(mention) fact, problem* zur Sprache bringen, erwähnen ◆ **do you have to ~ that ~?** müssen Sie davon anfangen?
(f) *(Jur)* **to ~ sb ~ (before a judge)** jdn (einem Richter) vorführen.
(g) *(Mil) battalion* heranbringen; *see* **rear.**
(h) to ~ sb ~ short jdn innehalten lassen.
(i) to ~ sb ~ against sth jdn mit etw konfrontieren.
◆**bring upon** *vt sep +prep obj see* **bring on (d).**
bring-and-buy (sale) ['brɪŋənd'baɪ(ˌseɪl)] *n (Brit)* Basar *m, wo mitgebrachte Sachen angeboten und verkauft werden.*
brink [brɪŋk] *n (lit, fig)* Rand *m* ◆ **on the ~ of sth/doing sth** *(lit, fig)* am Rande von etw/nahe daran, etw zu tun.
brinkmanship ['brɪŋkmənʃɪp] *n (inf)* Spiel *nt* mit dem Feuer.
briny ['braɪnɪ] [1] *adj* salzhaltig, salzig.
[2] *n (inf)* See *f.*
Bri-nylon ® [ˌbraɪ'naɪlən] *n (Brit) britische Kunstfaser.*
briquet(te) [brɪ'ket] *n* Brikett *nt.*
brisk [brɪsk] *adj* (+*er*) **(a)** *person, way of speaking* forsch; *sales assistant, service* flott, flink; *walk, pace* flott ◆ **to go for a ~ walk** einen ordentlichen Spaziergang machen.
(b) *(fig) trade, betting, bidding* lebhaft, rege ◆ **business** *etc* **was ~** das Geschäft *etc* ging lebhaft *or* war rege; **the market made a ~ start** der Markt begann lebhaft.
(c) *wind, weather* frisch.
brisket ['brɪskɪt] *n (Cook)* Bruststück *nt.*
briskly ['brɪsklɪ] *adv see adj* **(a)** forsch; flott, flink; flott. **(b)** lebhaft, rege.
briskness ['brɪsknɪs] *n see adj* **(a)** Forschheit *f*; Flottheit, Flinkheit *f.* **(b)** Lebhaftigkeit *f.* **(c)** Frische *f.*
brisling ['brɪzlɪŋ] *n* Brisling *m*, Sprotte *f.*
bristle ['brɪsl] [1] *n (of brush, boar etc)* Borste *f*; *(of beard)* Stoppel *f.*
[2] *vi* **(a)** *(animal's hair)* sich sträuben ◆ **the dog ~d** dem Hund sträubte sich das Fell.
(b) *(fig: person)* zornig werden ◆ **to ~ with anger** vor Wut schnauben.
(c) *(fig)* **to be bristling with people/mistakes** von *or* vor Leuten/Fehlern wimmeln; **bristling with difficulties** mit Schwierigkeiten gespickt; **the dress was bristling with pins** das Kleid steckte voller Nadeln; **the soldiers ~d with weapons** die Soldaten waren bis an die Zähne bewaffnet.
bristly ['brɪslɪ] *adj* (+*er*) *animal* borstig; *chin* Stoppel-, stoppelig; *hair, beard* borstig.
Bristol fashion ['brɪstəlˌfæʃn] *adj see* **shipshape.**
bristols ['brɪstəlz] *npl (Brit sl)* Titten *pl (sl)*.
Brit [brɪt] *n (inf)* Engländer, Tommy *(inf) m.*
Britain ['brɪtən] *n* Großbritannien *nt*; *(in ancient history)* Britannien *nt.*
Britannia [brɪ'tænɪə] *n (poet: country)* Britannien *nt*; *(personification)* Britannia *f.*
Britannic [brɪ'tænɪk] *adj*: **Her/His ~ Majesty** Ihre/Seine Britannische Majestät.
briticism ['brɪtɪsɪzəm] *n* Britizismus *m.*
briticize ['brɪtɪsaɪz] *vt* anglisieren, britifizieren.
British ['brɪtɪʃ] [1] *adj* britisch ◆ **I'm ~** ich bin Brite/Britin; **the ~ Isles** die Britischen Inseln; **~ Empire** Britisches Weltreich; **~ English** britisches Englisch; **and the best of ~ (luck)!** *(inf)* na, dann mal viel Glück!
[2] *n* **the ~** *pl* die Briten *pl.*
Britisher ['brɪtɪʃə^r] *n (US)* Brite *m*, Britin *f.*
British Honduras *n* Britisch-Honduras *nt.*
Briton ['brɪtən] *n* Brite *m*, Britin *f.*
Brittany ['brɪtənɪ] *n* die Bretagne.
brittle ['brɪtl] *adj* **(a)** spröde, zerbrechlich; *old paper* bröcklig; *biscuits* mürbe ◆ **~ bones** schwache Knochen. **(b)** *(fig) nerves* schwach; *person* empfindlich; *voice, laugh* schrill ◆ **to have a ~ temper** aufbrausend sein.
brittleness ['brɪtəlnɪs] *n see adj* **(a)** Sprödigkeit, Zerbrechlichkeit *f*; Bröckligkeit *f*; Mürbheit *f.* **(b)** Schwäche *f*; Empfindlichkeit *f*; Schrillheit *f.*
broach [brəʊtʃ] *vt* **(a)** *barrel* anstechen, anzapfen. **(b)** *subject, topic* anschneiden.
B-road ['biːrəʊd] *n (Brit)* ≃ Landstraße *f.*
broad [brɔːd] [1] *adj* (+*er*) **(a)** *(wide)* breit ◆ **to grow ~er** breiter werden; *(road, river also)* sich verbreitern; **to make ~er** verbreitern; **it's as ~ as it is long** *(fig)* es ist Jacke wie Hose *(inf)*.
(b) *(widely applicable) theory* umfassend; *(general)* allgemein.
(c) *(not detailed) distinction, idea, outline* grob; *instructions* vage; *sense* weit ◆ **as a very ~ rule** als Faustregel.
(d) *(liberal) mind, attitude, ideas* großzügig, tolerant ◆ **a man of ~ sympathies** ein aufgeschlossener Geist.
(e) *wink, hint* deutlich; *(indelicate) humour* derb.
(f) *(strongly marked) accent* stark; *(with long vowel sounds also)* breit ◆ **he speaks ~ Scots** er spricht breit(est)es Schottisch *or* starken schottischen Dialekt.
[2] *n* **(a)** *(widest part)* **the ~ of the back** die Schultergegend.
(b) the (Norfolk) B~s *pl* die Norfolk Broads.
(c) *(esp US sl: woman)* Frau *f*; *(younger)* Mieze *f (sl)*.
broad bean *n* dicke Bohne, Saubohne *f.*
broadcast ['brɔːdkɑːst] *(vb: pret, ptp ~)* [1] *n (Rad, TV)* Sendung *f*; *(of match*

etc) Übertragung *f* ◆ ~s Programm *nt*, Sendungen *pl*.
[2] *vt* **(a)** *(Rad, TV)* senden, ausstrahlen; *football match, event* übertragen. **(b)** *(fig) news, rumour etc* verbreiten. **(c)** *(Agr) seed* aussäen.
[3] *vi (Rad, TV: station)* senden; *(person)* im Rundfunk/Fernsehen sprechen ◆ **we're not ~ing tonight** heute abend strahlen wir kein Programm aus.

broadcaster ['brɔːdkɑːstəʳ] *n (Rad, TV) (announcer)* Rundfunk-/Fernsehsprecher(in *f*) *m*; *(personality)* Rundfunk-/Fernsehpersönlichkeit *f* ◆ **he's not a very good ~** er ist nicht besonders gut im Fernsehen/Rundfunk; **a famous ~** eine vom Rundfunk/Fernsehen bekannte Persönlichkeit.

broadcasting ['brɔːdkɑːstɪŋ] [1] *n (Rad, TV)* Sendung *f*; *(of event)* Übertragung *f* ◆ **end of ~** Ende des Programms; **to work in ~** beim Rundfunk/Fernsehen arbeiten; **the early days of ~** die Anfänge des Rundfunks/Fernsehens.
[2] *attr (Rad)* Rundfunk-; *(TV)* Fernseh- ◆ **~ station** *(Rad)* Rundfunkstation *f*; *(TV)* Fernsehstation *f*.

broadcloth ['brɔːdklɒθ] *n* merzerisierter Baumwollstoff.

broaden (out) ['brɔːdn(aʊt)] [1] *vt (sep) road etc* verbreitern; *(fig) person, attitudes* aufgeschlossener machen ◆ **to ~ one's mind/one's horizons** *(fig)* seinen Horizont erweitern.
[2] *vi* breiter werden, sich verbreitern; *(fig) (person, attitudes)* aufgeschlossener werden; *(horizon)* sich erweitern.

broad: ~ gauge *n* Breitspur *f*; **~ jump** *n (US Sport)* Weitsprung *m*; **~loom** *adj carpet* überbreit.

broadly ['brɔːdlɪ] *adv* **(a)** *(in general terms)* allgemein, in großen Zügen; *outline, describe* grob ◆ **~ speaking** ganz allgemein gesprochen. **(b)** *(greatly, widely) differ* beträchtlich; *applicable* allgemein. **(c)** *grin, smile, laugh* breit; *hint, wink* deutlich. **(d)** *see adj (f) speak a dialect* stark; breit.

broad: ~-minded *adj* großzügig, tolerant; **~-mindedness** *n* Großzügigkeit, Toleranz *f*; **~ness** *n see* **breadth**; **~sheet** *n* Flugblatt *nt*; **~-shouldered** *adj* breitschult(e)rig; **~side** *(Naut)* [1] *n* Breitseite *f*; *(fig also)* Attacke *f*; **to fire a ~side** eine Breitseite abgeben *or* abfeuern; **he let him have a ~side** *(fig)* er attackierte ihn heftig; [2] *adv* **~side on** mit der Breitseite *(to* nach); **~sword** *n* breites Schwert.

brocade [brəʊ'keɪd] [1] *n* Brokat *m*.
[2] *attr* Brokat-, brokaten.

brocaded [brəʊ'keɪdɪd] *adj* (wie Brokat) verziert *or* bestickt.

broccoli ['brɒkəlɪ] *n* Brokkoli *pl*, Spargelkohl *m*.

brochure ['brəʊʃjʊəʳ] *n* Broschüre *f*, Prospekt *m*.

brogue[1] [brəʊg] *n (shoe)* ≃ Haferlschuh *(Aus)*, Budapester *m*.

brogue[2] *n (Irish accent)* irischer Akzent.

broil [brɔɪl] *vti (Cook)* grillen.

broiler ['brɔɪləʳ] *n* **(a)** *(chicken)* Brathähnchen *nt*, (Gold)broiler *m (dial)*. **(b)** *(grill)* Grill *m*.

broke [brəʊk] [1] *pret of* **break**.
[2] *adj pred (inf)* abgebrannt *(inf)*, pleite *(inf)* ◆ **to go for ~** *(inf)* den Bankrott riskieren.

broken ['brəʊkən] [1] *ptp of* **break**.
[2] *adj* **(a)** kaputt *(inf)*; *twig* geknickt; *bone* gebrochen; *rope also* gerissen; *(smashed) cup, glass etc also* zerbrochen.
(b) *(fig) voice* brüchig; *chord* gebrochen; *heart, spirit, man* gebrochen; *health, marriage* zerrüttet ◆ **surely his voice has ~ by now** er muß den Stimmbruch schon hinter sich *(dat)* haben; **from a ~ home** aus zerrütteten Familienverhältnissen.
(c) *promise* gebrochen; *appointment* nicht (ein)gehalten.
(d) *road, surface, ground* uneben; *coastline* zerklüftet; *water, sea* aufgewühlt, bewegt; *set* unvollständig.
(e) *(interrupted) journey* unterbrochen; *line also* gestrichelt; *sleep also* gestört.
(f) *English, German etc* gebrochen.

broken: ~-down *adj machine, car* kaputt *(inf)*; *horse* ausgemergelt; **~-hearted** *adj* untröstlich; **~ white** *n* gebrochenes Weiß; **~-winded** *adj* kurzatmig, dämpfig *(spec)*.

broker ['brəʊkəʳ] *n (St Ex, Fin, real estate)* Makler *m* ◆ **yachting ~** Bootshändler *m*.

brokerage ['brəʊkərɪdʒ] *n* **(a)** *(commission)* Maklergebühr *f*; *(of insurance broker also)* Maklerlohn *m*. **(b)** *(trade)* Maklergeschäft *nt*.

broking ['brəʊkɪŋ] *n* Geschäft *nt* eines Maklers ◆ **there was some rather dubious ~ involved** es wurden dabei einige recht zweifelhafte Maklergeschäfte getätigt.

brolly ['brɒlɪ] *n (Brit inf)* (Regen)schirm *m*.

bromide ['brəʊmaɪd] *n* **(a)** *(Chem)* Bromid *nt*; *(Typ)* Bromsilberdruck *m*; *(Med inf)* Beruhigungsmittel *nt* ◆ **~ paper** *(Phot)* Bromsilberpapier *nt*. **(b)** *(fig: platitude)* Platitüde *f*, Allgemeinplatz *m*.

bronchia ['brɒŋkɪə] *npl* Bronchien *pl*.

bronchial ['brɒŋkɪəl] *adj* bronchial ◆ **~ tubes** Bronchien *pl*.

bronchitis [brɒŋ'kaɪtɪs] *n* Bronchitis *f*.

bronchus ['brɒŋkəs] *n, pl* **bronchi** ['brɒŋkiː] Bronchus *m*.

bronco ['brɒŋkəʊ] *n wildes oder halbwildes Pferd in den USA.*

broncobuster ['brɒŋkəʊ,bʌstəʳ] *n (inf) Zureiter m wilder oder halbwilder Pferde.*

brontosaurus [,brɒntə'sɔːrəs] *n* Brontosaurus *m*.

Bronx cheer [brɒŋks'tʃɪəʳ] *n (US inf)* **to get a ~** ausgelacht werden; **to give sb a ~** jdn auslachen.

bronze [brɒnz] [1] *n (all senses)* Bronze *f*.
[2] *vi (person)* braun werden, bräunen.
[3] *vt* **(a)** *metal* bronzieren. **(b)** *face, skin* bräunen.
[4] *adj* Bronze-.

Bronze: ~ Age *n* Bronzezeit *f*; **~ Age man** *n* der Mensch der Bronzezeit.

bronzed [brɒnzd] *adj face, person* braun, (sonnen)gebräunt.

bronzing ['brɒnzɪŋ] *adj attr* Bräunungs- ◆ **~ powder** Bräunungspuder *m*; **~ gel** Bräunungsgel *nt*.

brooch [brəʊtʃ] *n* Brosche *f*.

brood [bruːd] [1] *n (lit, fig)* Brut *f*.
[2] *vi* **(a)** *(bird)* brüten. **(b)** *(fig: person)* grübeln; *(despondently also)* brüten.

◆**brood over** *or* **(up)on** *vi + prep obj* nachgrübeln über *(+acc)*; *(despondently also)* brüten über *(+dat)*.

brood mare *n* Zuchtstute *f*.

broody ['bruːdɪ] *adj* **(a)** *hen* brütig ◆ **the hen is ~** die Henne gluckt; **to be feeling ~** *(hum inf)* den Wunsch nach einem Kind haben. **(b)** *person* grüblerisch; *(sad, moody)* schwerblütig.

brook[1] [brʊk] *n* Bach *m*.

brook[2] *vt (liter: tolerate)* dulden ◆ **to ~ no delay** keinen Aufschub dulden.

brooklet ['brʊklɪt] *n* Bächlein *nt*.

broom [bruːm] *n* **(a)** Besen *m* ◆ **a new ~ sweeps clean** *(Prov)* neue Besen kehren gut *(Prov)*. **(b)** *(Bot)* Ginster *m*.

broom: ~ cupboard *n* Besenschrank *m*; **~stick** *n* Besenstiel *m*; **a witch on her ~stick** eine Hexe auf ihrem Besen.

Bros *npl (Comm) abbr of* **Brothers** Gebr.

broth [brɒθ] *n* Fleischbrühe *f*; *(thickened soup)* Suppe *f*.

brothel ['brɒθl] *n* Bordell *nt*, Puff *m (inf)*.

brothel: ~-creepers *npl (hum)* Leisetreter *pl (hum)*; **~-keeper** *n* Bordellwirt(in *f*) *m*.

brother ['brʌðəʳ] *n, pl* **-s** *or (obs, Eccl)* **brethren** **(a)** *(also Eccl)* Bruder *m* ◆ **they are ~ and sister** sie sind Geschwister, sie sind Bruder und Schwester; **my/his ~s and sisters** meine/seine Geschwister; **the Clarke ~s** die Brüder Clarke; *(Comm)* die Gebrüder Clarke; **oh ~!** *(esp US inf)* Junge, Junge! *(inf)*.
(b) *(in trade unions)* Kollege *m*.
(c) *(fellow man, DDR Pol)* Bruder *m* ◆ **his ~ officers** seine Offizierskameraden; **our ~ men, our ~s** unsere Mitmenschen *or* Brüder *(geh, Eccl)*.

brother: ~hood *n* **(a)** brüderliches Einvernehmen, Brüderlichkeit *f*; **sense of ~hood** *(lit)* Brudersinn *m*; *(fig)* Gefühl *nt* der Brüderlichkeit; **(b)** *(organization)* Bruderschaft *f*; **~hood of man** Gemeinschaft *f* der Menschen; **~-in-arms** *n* Waffenbruder *m*; **~-in-law** *n, pl* **~s-in-law** Schwager *m*.

brotherliness ['brʌðəlɪnɪs] *n* Brüderlichkeit *f*.

brotherly ['brʌðəlɪ] *adj* brüderlich.

brougham ['bruːəm] *n* Brougham *m*.

brought [brɔːt] *pret, ptp of* **bring**.

brow [braʊ] *n* **(a)** *(eyebrow)* Braue *f*. **(b)** *(forehead)* Stirn *f*. **(c)** *(of hill)* (Berg)kuppe *f*.

browbeat ['braʊbiːt] *pret* **~**, *ptp* **~en** *vt* unter (moralischen) Druck setzen ◆ **to ~ sb into doing sth** jdn so unter Druck setzen, daß er etw tut; **I can't ~ you into accepting it** ich kann euch natürlich nicht (dazu) zwingen, es anzunehmen; **I won't be ~en** ich lasse mich nicht tyrannisieren *or* unter Druck setzen.

brown [braʊn] [1] *adj (+er)* braun; *(Cook) roast etc also* braun gebraten.
[2] *n* Braun *nt*.
[3] *vt (sun) skin, person* bräunen; *(Cook)* (an)bräunen; *meat also* anbraten.
[4] *vi* braun werden.

◆**brown off** *vt* **to be ~ed ~ with sb/sth** *(esp Brit inf)* jdn/etw satt haben *(inf)*; **I was pretty ~ed ~ at the time** ich hatte es damals ziemlich satt; **you're looking a bit ~ed ~** du siehst so aus, als hättest du alles ziemlich satt.

brown: ~ ale *n* Malzbier *nt*; **~ bear** *n* Braunbär *m*; **~ bread** *n* Grau- *or* Mischbrot *nt*; *(from wholemeal)* Vollkornbrot *nt*; *(darker)* Schwarzbrot *nt*.

brownie ['braʊnɪ] *n* **(a)** *(fairy)* Heinzelmännchen *nt*. **(b)** **B~** *(in Guide Movement)* Wichtel *m*; **B~ points** Pluspunkte *pl*; **let's give him B~ points for trying** daß er es versucht hat, können wir ihm ja anrechnen; **to get B~ points with sb** sich bei jdm beliebt machen.
(c) *(chocolate cake) kleiner Schokoladenkuchen.*

browning ['braʊnɪŋ] *n (Cook) (act)* Anbraten *nt*; *(substance)* Bratensoße(npulver *nt*) *f*.

brownish ['braʊnɪʃ] *adj* bräunlich.

brown: ~ owl *n* **(a)** *(Orn)* Waldkauz *m*; **(b)** **B~ Owl** *(in Brownies)* die Weise Eule; **~ paper** *n* Packpapier *nt*; **~ rice** *n* geschälter Reis; **B~shirt** *n* Braunhemd *nt*; **~stone** *n (US) (material)* rötlichbrauner Sandstein; *(house)* (rotes) Sandsteinhaus *nt*; **~ study** *n* **to be in a ~ study** *(liter)* geistesabwesend sein, in Gedanken verloren sein; **~ sugar** *n* brauner Zucker.

browse [braʊz] [1] *vi* **(a)** **to ~ among the books** in den Büchern schmökern; **to ~ through a book** in einem Buch schmökern; **to ~ (around)** sich umsehen. **(b)** *(cattle)* weiden; *(deer)* äsen.
[2] *n* **to have a ~ (around)** sich umsehen; **to have a ~ through the books** in den Büchern schmökern; **to have a ~ around the book-shops** sich in den Buchläden umsehen.

Bruges [bruːʒ] *n* Brügge *nt*.

bruin ['bruːɪn] *n* (Meister) Petz *m*.

bruise [bruːz] [1] *n (on person)* blauer Fleck, Bluterguß *(esp Med) m*; *(on fruit)* Druckstelle *f*.
[2] *vt person* einen blauen Fleck/blaue Flecke(n) schlagen *(+dat) or* beibringen *(+dat)*; *fruit* beschädigen; *(fig) person, spirit, feelings* verletzen ◆ **to ~ oneself/one's elbow** sich stoßen, sich *(dat)* einen blauen Fleck holen/sich *(dat)* einen blauen Fleck am Ellbogen holen; **the fruit is ~d** das Obst hat Druckstellen; **I feel ~d all over** mir tut's am ganzen Körper weh.

3 *vi* (*person, part of body*) einen blauen Fleck/blaue Flecke(n) bekommen; (*fruit*) eine Druckstelle/Druckstellen bekommen; (*fig: person, feelings*) verletzt werden ◆ **he ~s easily** er bekommt leicht blaue Flecken; (*fig*) er ist sehr empfindlich.

bruiser ['bru:zəʳ] *n* (*inf*) Rabauke, Räuber (*hum*) *m*.

brunch [brʌntʃ] *n* Brunch *m, Frühstück und Mittagessen nt in einem*.

brunette [bru:'net] 1 *n* Brünette *f*.
2 *adj* brünett.

brunt [brʌnt] *n*: **to bear the (main) ~ of the attack/work/costs** die volle Wucht des Angriffs/die Hauptlast der Arbeit/Kosten tragen; **to bear the ~** das meiste abkriegen.

brush [brʌʃ] 1 *n* **(a)** Bürste *f*; (*artist's ~, paint~, shaving ~, pastry ~*) Pinsel *m*; (*hearth ~*) Besen *m*; (*with dustpan*) Handbesen *or* -feger *m*; (*flue ~*) Stoßbesen *m*; (*flue ~ with weight*) Sonne *f* ◆ **to be as daft as a ~** (*inf*) total meschugge sein (*inf*).
(b) (*action*) **to give sth a ~** etw bürsten; *jacket, shoes* etw abbürsten; **your jacket/hair/teeth could do with a ~** du solltest deine Jacke/dein Haar/deine Zähne mal wieder bürsten.
(c) (*light touch*) leichte, flüchtige Berührung, Streifen *nt* ◆ **I felt the ~ of the cobwebs against my face** ich spürte, wie Spinnweben mein Gesicht streiften.
(d) (*of fox*) Lunte *f*.
(e) (*undergrowth*) Unterholz *nt*.
(f) (*Mil: skirmish*) Zusammenstoß *m*, Scharmützel *nt*; (*quarrel, incident*) Zusammenstoß *m* ◆ **to have a ~ with sb** mit jdm aneinandergeraten.
(g) (*Elec: of commutator*) Bürste *f*.
2 *vt* **(a)** bürsten; (*with hand*) wischen ◆ **to ~ one's teeth/hair** sich (*dat*) die Zähne putzen/sich (*dat*) das Haar bürsten. **(b)** (*sweep*) *dirt* fegen, kehren; (*with hand, cloth*) wischen. **(c)** (*touch lightly*) streifen. **(d)** *fabric* bürsten, aufrauhen.

◆**brush against** *vi +prep obj* streifen.

◆**brush aside** *vt sep obstacle, person* (einfach) zur Seite schieben; *objections* (einfach) abtun; *ideas* verwerfen.

◆**brush away** *vt sep* (*with brush*) abbürsten; (*with hand, cloth*) ab- *or* wegwischen; *insects* verscheuchen.

◆**brush down** *vt sep* abbürsten; *horse* striegeln.

◆**brush off** 1 *vt sep* **(a)** *mud, snow* abbürsten; *insect* verscheuchen. **(b)** (*inf: reject*) *person* abblitzen lassen (*inf*); *suggestion, criticism* zurückweisen.
2 *vi* (*mud etc*) sich abbürsten *or* (*with hand, cloth*) abwischen lassen.

◆**brush past** *vi* streifen (*prep obj acc*) ◆ **as he ~ed ~** als er mich/ihn *etc* streifte.

◆**brush up** *vt sep* **(a)** *crumbs, dirt* auffegen, aufkehren ◆ **to ~ sth ~ into a pile** etw zusammenfegen *or* -kehren.
(b) *wool, nap* aufrauhen, rauhen (*form*).
(c) (*fig: also ~ ~ on*) *subject, one's German* auffrischen.

brushed nylon [,brʌʃt'naɪlən] *n* Nylon-Velours *m*.

brush: ~-off *n* (*inf*) Abfuhr *f*; **to give sb the ~-off** jdn abblitzen lassen (*inf*), jdm einen Korb geben (*inf*); **to get the ~-off** abblitzen (*inf*), einen Korb kriegen (*inf*); **~stroke** *n* Pinselstrich *m*; (*way of painting*) Pinselführung *f*; **~-up** *n* (*inf*) **I must give my Italian a ~-up** ich muß meine Italienischkenntnisse auffrischen; **~wood** *n* **(a)** (*undergrowth*) Unterholz *nt*; **(b)** (*cut twigs*) Reisig *nt*; **~work** *n* (*Art*) Pinselführung *f*.

brusque [bru:sk] *adj* (*+er*) *person, tone, manner* brüsk, schroff.

brusquely ['bru:sklɪ] *adv behave* brüsk, schroff; *speak* brüsk, in schroffem Ton.

brusqueness ['bru:sknɪs] *n* Schroffheit *f*.

Brussels ['brʌslz] *n* Brüssel *nt*.

Brussels: ~ lace *n* Brüsseler Spitze(n *pl*) *f*; **~ sprouts** *npl* Rosenkohl *m*.

brutal ['bru:tl] *adj* brutal.

brutalism ['bru:təlɪzəm] *n* (*Archit*) Brutalismus *m*.

brutality [bru:'tælɪtɪ] *n* Brutalität *f*.

brutalize ['bru:təlaɪz] *vt* brutalisieren, verrohen lassen.

brutally ['bru:təlɪ] *adv* brutal ◆ **I'll be ~ frank** ich werde schonungslos offen sein.

brute [bru:t] 1 *n* **(a)** Tier, Vieh (*pej*) *nt*.
(b) (*person*) brutaler Kerl; (*savage*) Bestie *f* ◆ **drink brings out the ~ in him** Alkohol bringt das Tier in ihm zum Vorschein.
(c) (*inf: thing*) **it's a ~ of a problem** es ist ein höllisches Problem (*inf*); **this nail's a real ~ (to get out)** dieser Nagel geht höllisch schwer raus (*inf*).
2 *adj attr strength* roh; *passion* tierisch, viehisch (*pej*) ◆ **by ~ force** mit roher Gewalt.

brutish ['bru:tɪʃ] *adj person, behaviour* viehisch, brutal.

BS (*US sl*) *abbr of* **bullshit**.

BSc *abbr of* **Bachelor of Science**.

BSc Econ *abbr of* **Bachelor of Economic Science**.

BSE *abbr of* **bovine spongiform encephalopathy** BSE *f*, Rinderwahn *m*.

BSI *abbr of* **British Standards Institution** *britischer Normenausschuß*.

B-side *n* (*of record*) B-Seite *f*.

BST *abbr of* **British Summer Time; British Standard Time**.

BT *abbr of* **British Telecom** *britisches Telekommunikationsunternehmen*.

Bt. *abbr of* **baronet**.

bubble ['bʌbl] 1 *n* Blase *f*; (*on plane etc*) (Glas)kuppel *f* ◆ **to blow ~s** Blasen machen; **the ~ has burst** (*fig*) alles ist wie eine Seifenblase zerplatzt.
2 *vi* **(a)** (*liquid*) sprudeln; (*heated also*) strudeln; (*wine*) perlen; (*gas*) Blasen/Bläschen machen *or* bilden.
(b) (*make bubbling noise*) blubbern (*inf*); (*cooking liquid, geyser etc*) brodeln; (*stream*) plätschern.

◆**bubble out** *vi* (*liquid*) heraussprudeln.

◆**bubble over** *vi* (*lit*) überschäumen; (*fig*) übersprudeln (*with* vor *+dat*).

◆**bubble up** *vi* (*liquid*) aufsprudeln; (*gas*) in Blasen/Bläschen hochsteigen; (*excitement, emotions*) aufsteigen, hochkommen.

bubble: ~-and-squeak *n* (*Brit*) *zusammen gebratene Fleischreste und Gemüse*; **~ bath** *n* Schaumbad *nt*; **~ car** *n* (*Brit*) (*opening at the top*) Kabinenroller *m*; (*opening at the front*) Isetta ® *f*; **~ chamber** *n* Blasenkammer *f*; **~ gum** *n* Bubble-Gum *m*; **~-jet printer** *n* (*Comput*) Bubble-Jet-Drucker *m*; **~ memory** *n* (*Comput*) Blasenspeicher *m*; **~ pack** *n* (Klar)sichtpackung *f*.

bubbly ['bʌblɪ] 1 *adj* (*+er*) (*lit*) sprudelnd; (*fig inf*) *personality* temperamentvoll, lebendig; *mood* übersprudelnd.
2 *n* (*inf*) Schampus *m* (*inf*).

bubonic plague [bju:'bɒnɪk'pleɪg] *n* Beulenpest *f*.

buccaneer [,bʌkə'nɪəʳ] *n* Seeräuber *m*; (*ship*) Piratenschiff *nt*.

Bucharest [,bju:kə'rest] *n* Bukarest *nt*.

buck [bʌk] 1 *n* **(a)** (*male of deer*) Bock *m*; (*rabbit, hare*) Rammler *m* ◆ **~ rabbit** Rammler *m*.
(b) (*old, hum: dandy*) Stutzer, Geck (*old*) *m*.
(c) (*US inf: dollar*) Dollar *m* ◆ **20 ~s** 20 Dollar; **to make a fast ~** (*also Brit*) schnell Kohle machen (*inf*).
(d) **to pass the ~** (*difficulty, unpleasant task*) den Schwarzen Peter weitergeben; (*responsibility also*) die Verantwortung abschieben; **to pass the ~ to sb** jdm den Schwarzen Peter zuschieben; jdm die Verantwortung aufhalsen; **the ~ stops here** der Schwarze Peter bleibt bei mir/uns *etc* hängen.
(e) (*leap by horse*) Bocken *nt*.
(f) (*in gymnastics*) Bock *m*.
2 *vi* **(a)** (*horse*) bocken.
(b) (*resist, object*) sich sträuben (*at* gegen).
3 *vt* **(a)** **you can't ~ the market** gegen den Markt kommt man nicht an; *see* **system**. **(b)** (*horse*) *rider* abwerfen.

◆**buck for** *vi +prep obj* (*US inf*) **to ~ ~ promotion** mit aller Gewalt *or* auf Teufel komm raus (*inf*) befördert werden wollen.

◆**buck off** *vt sep rider* abwerfen.

◆**buck up** (*inf*) 1 *vi* **(a)** (*hurry up*) sich ranhalten (*inf*), rasch *or* fix machen (*inf*) ◆ **~ ~!** halt dich ran! (*inf*).
(b) (*cheer up*) aufleben. **~ ~!** Kopf hoch!
2 *vt sep* **(a)** (*make hurry*) Dampf machen (*+dat*) (*inf*).
(b) (*make cheerful*) aufmuntern.
(c) **to ~ one's ideas ~** sich zusammenreißen (*inf*).

buckaroo [,bʌkə'ru:] *n* (*US*) Cowboy *m*.

buckboard ['bʌkbɔ:d] *n* (*US*) (einfache, offene) Kutsche.

bucket ['bʌkɪt] 1 *n* (*also of dredger, grain elevator*) Eimer *m*; (*of excavator, water wheel*) Schaufel *f* ◆ **a ~ of water** ein Eimer *m* Wasser; **to weep** *or* **cry ~s (of tears)** (*inf*) wie ein Schloßhund heulen (*inf*); *see* **kick, drop**.
2 *vi* (*inf*) **it's ~ing!, the rain is ~ing (down)!** es gießt *or* schüttet wie aus *or* mit Kübeln (*inf*).

◆**bucket about** *vt sep usu pass* (*inf*) durchrütteln.

◆**bucket along** *vi* (*dated inf*) mit einem Affenzahn dahin-/entlangkutschen (*inf*) *or* -karriolen (*inf*).

◆**bucket down** *vi* (*inf*) *see* **bucket 2**.

bucketful ['bʌkɪtfʊl] *n* Eimer *m*.

bucket: ~ seat *n* Schalensitz *m*; **~ shop** *n* (*Fin*) unreelle Maklerfirma, Schwindelmakler *m*; (*travel agent*) Agentur *f* für Billigreisen.

buckeye ['bʌkaɪ] *n* (*US*) Roßkastanie *f*; (*seed*) Kastanie *f*.

buckle ['bʌkl] 1 *n* **(a)** (*on belt, shoe*) Schnalle, Spange *f*.
(b) (*in metal etc*) Beule *f*; (*concave also*) Delle *f* ◆ **there's a nasty ~ in this girder/wheel** dieser Träger ist übel eingebeult *or* (*twisted*) verbogen/dieses Rad ist übel verbogen.
2 *vt* **(a)** *belt, shoes* zuschnallen.
(b) *wheel, girder etc* verbiegen; (*dent*) verbeulen.
3 *vi* **(a)** (*belt, shoe*) mit einer Schnalle *or* Spange geschlossen werden. **(b)** (*wheel, metal*) sich verbiegen.

◆**buckle down** *vi* (*inf*) sich dahinterklemmen (*inf*), sich dranmachen (*inf*) ◆ **to ~ ~ to a task** sich hinter eine Aufgabe klemmen (*inf*), sich an eine Aufgabe machen.

◆**buckle on** *vt sep armour* anlegen; *sword, belt* umschnallen.

◆**buckle to** *vi* sich am Riemen reißen (*inf*).

buckram ['bʌkrəm] 1 *n* Buckram *m*.
2 *adj attr* Buckram-.

Bucks [bʌks] *abbr of* **Buckinghamshire**.

bucksaw ['bʌksɔ:] *n* Handsäge *f*.

buckshee [bʌk'ʃi:] *adj* (*Brit inf*) gratis, umsonst.

buck: ~shot *n* grober Schrot, Rehposten (*spec*) *m*; **~skin** *n* **(a)** Wildleder *nt*, Buckskin *m*; **(b)** **~skins** *pl* Lederhose(n *pl*) *f*; **~tooth** *n* vorstehender Zahn; **~toothed** *adj* mit vorstehenden Zähnen; **~wheat** *n* Buchweizen *m*.

bucolic [bju:'kɒlɪk] *adj* (*liter*) bukolisch (*liter*).

bud[1] [bʌd] 1 *n* **(a)** Knospe *f* ◆ **to be in ~** knospen, Knospen treiben. **(b)** (*Anat*) *see* **taste ~**.
2 *vi* (*plant, flower*) knospen, Knospen treiben; (*tree also*) ausschlagen; (*horns*) wachsen.

bud[2] *interj* (*US inf*) *see* **buddy**.

Budapest [,bju:də'pest] *n* Budapest *nt*.

Buddha ['bʊdə] *n* Buddha *m*.

Buddhism ['bʊdɪzəm] *n* Buddhismus *m*.
Buddhist ['bʊdɪst] 1 *n* Buddhist(in *f*) *m*.
2 *adj* buddhistisch.
budding ['bʌdɪŋ] *adj* knospend; *(fig) poet etc* angehend.
buddy ['bʌdɪ] *n* *(US inf)* Kumpel *m* ◆ **hey, ~!** he, Kumpel, hör mal!; *(threatening)* hör mal zu, Kumpel *or* Freundchen *(inf)*.
buddy-buddy ['bʌdɪbʌdɪ] *adj* *(US inf)* **to be ~ with sb** mit jdm dick befreundet sein *(inf)*; **to try to get ~ with sb** sich bei jdm anbiedern.
budge [bʌdʒ] 1 *vi* **(a)** *(move)* sich rühren, sich bewegen ◆ **~ up** *or* **over!** mach Platz!, rück mal ein Stückchen!
(b) *(fig: give way)* nachgeben, weichen ◆ **I will not ~ an inch** ich werde keinen Fingerbreit nachgeben *or* weichen; **he is not going to ~** er gibt nicht nach, der bleibt stur *(inf)*.
2 *vt* **(a)** *(move)* (von der Stelle) bewegen.
(b) *(force to give way)* zum Nachgeben bewegen ◆ **we can't ~ him** er läßt sich durch nichts erweichen.
budgerigar ['bʌdʒərɪgɑːʳ] *n* Wellensittich *m*.
budget ['bʌdʒɪt] 1 *n* Etat *m*, Budget *nt*; *(Parl also)* Haushalt(splan) *m* ◆ **~ day** ≃ Haushaltsdebatte *f*; **~ deficit** Haushaltsdefizit *nt*; **~ speech** Etatrede *f*.
2 *vi* haushalten, wirtschaften ◆ **responsible for ~ing** für das Budget *or* den Etat *or* *(Parl also)* den Haushalt verantwortlich.
3 *vt* **(a)** *money, time* verplanen. **(b)** *(also* **~ for***)* *item* kostenmäßig einplanen; *costs* einplanen ◆ **~ed costs/expense** Vorgabekosten, vorgesehene Kosten *pl*; **~ed revenue** Sollertrag *m*.
◆**budget for** *vi +prep obj* (im Etat) einplanen.
budget account *n* Kundenkonto *nt*.
budgetary ['bʌdʒɪtrɪ] *adj* Etat-, Budget-, Haushalts-.
budgeting ['bʌdʒɪtɪŋ] *n* Kalkulation, Budgetierung *f*.
budgie ['bʌdʒɪ] *n* *(inf) abbr of* **budgerigar** Wellensittich *m*.
Buenos Aires ['bweɪnɒs'aɪrɪz] *n* Buenos Aires *nt*.
buff[1] [bʌf] 1 *n* **(a)** *(leather)* (kräftiges, weiches) Leder. **(b) in the ~** nackt, im Adams-/Evaskostüm *(hum)*. **(c)** *(polishing disc)* Schwabbelscheibe *(spec)*, Polierscheibe *f*; *(cylinder)* Schwabbelwalze *f (spec)*. **(d)** *(colour)* Gelbbraun *nt*.
2 *adj* **(a)** ledern, Leder-. **(b)** gelbbraun.
3 *vt metal* polieren.
buff[2] *n* *(inf)* *(movie/theatre etc ~)* Fan *m* *(inf)*.
buffalo ['bʌfələʊ] *n*, *pl* **-es**, *collective pl* - Büffel *m*.
buffalo grass *n* *(US)* Büffelgras *nt*.
buffer[1] ['bʌfəʳ] *n* *(lit, fig, Comput)* Puffer *m*; *(Rail: at terminus)* Prellbock *m*.
buffer[2] *n* *(Brit inf)* Heini *m* *(inf)*.
buffering ['bʌfərɪŋ] *n* *(Comput)* Pufferung *f*.
buffer: ~ solution *n* *(Chem)* Puffer(lösung *f*) *m*; **~ state** *n* *(Pol)* Pufferstaat *m*.
buffet[1] ['bʌfɪt] 1 *n* *(blow)* Schlag *m*.
2 *vt* hin und her werfen ◆ **~ed by the wind** vom Wind gerüttelt; **~ing wind** böiger Wind.
buffet[2] ['bʊfeɪ] *n* Büffet *nt*; *(Brit Rail)* Speisewagen *m*; *(meal)* Stehimbiß *m*; *(cold ~)* kaltes Büffett.
buffet car ['bʊfeɪ-] *n* *(Brit Rail)* Speisewagen *m*.
buffeting ['bʌfɪtɪŋ] *n* heftiges Schaukeln; *(Aviat)* Rütteln *nt* ◆ **to get** *or* **take a ~** hin und her geworfen *or* *(Aviat)* gerüttelt werden.
buffet ['bʊfeɪ-]: **~ lunch/meal/supper** *n* Stehimbiß *m*.
buffoon [bə'fuːn] *n* Clown *m*; *(stupid)* Blödmann *m* *(pej inf)* ◆ **to act** *or* **play the ~** den Clown *or* Hanswurst spielen.
buffoonery [bə'fuːnərɪ] *n* Clownerie *f*.
bug [bʌg] 1 *n* **(a)** Wanze *f*; *(inf: any insect)* Käfer *m* ◆ **~s** *pl* Ungeziefer *nt*.
(b) *(bugging device)* Wanze *f*.
(c) *(inf: germ, virus)* Bazillus *f* ◆ **I might get your ~** du könntest mich anstecken; **he picked up a ~ while on holiday** er hat sich *(dat)* im Urlaub eine Krankheit geholt; **there must be a ~ about** das geht zur Zeit um.
(d) *(inf: obsession)* **now he's got the ~** jetzt hat's ihn gepackt *(inf)*; **she's got the travel ~** die Reiselust hat sie gepackt.
(e) *(inf: snag, defect)* Fehler *m* ◆ **~s** Mucken *pl* *(inf)*.
(f) *(Comput)* Programmfehler *m*, Wanze *f*.
2 *vt* **(a)** *room, building* verwanzen *(inf)*, Wanzen *pl* installieren in *(+dat)* *or* einbauen in *(+acc)* *(inf)*; *conversation, telephone lines* abhören ◆ **this room is ~ged** hier sind Wanzen *(inf)*, das Zimmer ist verwanzt *(inf)*.
(b) *(inf)* *(worry)* stören; *(annoy)* nerven *(sl)*, den Nerv töten *(+dat)* *(inf)* ◆ **don't let it ~ you** mach dir nichts draus *(inf)*.
bugaboo ['bʌgəbuː] *n* Schreckgespenst *nt*.
bug: ~bear *n* Schreckgespenst *nt*; **~-eyed** *adj* mit vorstehenden *or* vorquellenden Augen; **~-free** *adj* *(Comput)* fehlerfrei.
bugger ['bʌgəʳ] 1 *n* *(sl)* Scheißkerl *m* *(sl)*, Arschloch *nt* *(vulg)*; *(when not contemptible)* Kerl *m* *(inf)*; *(thing)* Scheißding *nt* *(sl)* ◆ **this nail's a ~, it won't come out** dieser Scheißnagel geht einfach nicht raus *(sl)*; **you lucky ~!** du hast vielleicht ein Schwein! *(inf)*; **to play silly ~s** *(inf)* Scheiß machen *(sl)*.
2 *interj* *(sl)* Scheiße *(sl)* ◆ **~ this car/pen!** dieses Scheißauto *(sl)*/dieser Scheißstift *(sl)*; **~ him** dieser Scheißkerl *(sl)*; *(he can get lost)* der kann mich mal *(sl)*; **~ me!** *(surprise)* (du) meine Fresse! *(sl)*; *(annoyance)* so'n Scheiß! *(sl)*.
3 *vt* **(a)** *(lit)* anal verkehren mit. **(b)** *(Brit sl)* versauen *(sl)* ◆ **I couldn't be ~ed** es ist/war mir scheißegal *(sl)*; **well, I'll be ~ed!** ich glaub', ich krieg' die Tür nicht zu! *(sl)*.
◆**bugger about** *or* **around** *(Brit sl)* 1 *vi* *(laze about etc)* rumgammeln *(sl)*; *(be ineffective)* blöd rummachen *(sl)* ◆ **stop ~ing ~ and get on with it** nun mach mal Nägel mit Köpfen *(inf)*; **he's not serious about her, he's just ~ing ~** ihm ist es nicht ernst mit ihr, er treibt nur sein Spielchen *(inf)*; **to ~ ~ with sth** an etw *(dat)* rumpfuschen *(inf)*.
2 *vt sep* verarschen *(sl)*.
◆**bugger off** *vi* *(Brit sl)* abhauen *(inf)*, Leine ziehen *(sl)*.
◆**bugger up** *vt sep* *(Brit sl)* versauen *(sl)* ◆ **I'm sorry if I've ~ed you ~** tut mir leid, daß ich dich in eine solche Scheißlage gebracht habe *(sl)*.
bugger all [,bʌgər'ɔːl] *n* *(Brit sl: nothing)* rein gar nichts.
buggery ['bʌgərɪ] *n* Analverkehr *m*; *(with animals)* Sodomie *f*.
bugging ['bʌgɪŋ] *n* Abhören *nt* ◆ **the use of ~** der Gebrauch von Abhörgeräten; **elaborate ~** raffiniertes Abhörsystem.
bugging device *n* Abhörgerät *nt*, Wanze *f* *(inf)*.
buggy ['bʌgɪ] *n* *(with horse)* Buggy *m*, leichter Einspänner ◆ **baby ~** *(Brit)* Sportwagen *m*; *(US)* Kinderwagen *m*; **beach ~** Buggy *m*; **moon ~** Mondauto *nt*.
bugle ['bjuːgl] *n* Bügelhorn *nt* ◆ **~ call** Hornsignal *nt*.
bugler ['bjuːgləʳ] *n* Hornist *m*.
bug: ~proof *adj room, telephone* abhörsicher; **~-ridden** *adj* **(a)** *hotel, mattress* von Wanzen befallen, verwanzt *(inf)*; **(b)** *(Comput) software etc* voller Fehler.
build [bɪld] *(vb: pret, ptp* **built***)* 1 *n* Körperbau *m*.
2 *vt* **(a)** *(generally)* bauen ◆ **the house is being built** das Haus ist im Bau *or* befindet sich im Bau. **(b)** *(fig) new nation, relationship, career, system etc* aufbauen; *a better future* schaffen.
3 *vi* bauen ◆ **to ~ on a piece of land** auf einem Grundstück bauen; *(cover with houses etc)* ein Grundstück bebauen.
◆**build in** *vt sep* *(lit, fig)* *wardrobe, proviso etc* einbauen; *(fig) extra time* einplanen; *see* **built-in**.
◆**build on** 1 *vt sep* anbauen ◆ **to ~ ~to sth** etw an etw *(acc)* anbauen.
2 *vi +prep obj* bauen auf *(+acc)*.
◆**build up** 1 *vi* **(a)** entstehen; *(anticyclone, atmosphere also)* sich aufbauen; *(increase)* zunehmen; *(Tech: pressure)* sich erhöhen ◆ **the music ~s ~ to a huge crescendo** die Musik steigert sich zu einem gewaltigen Crescendo.
(b) *(traffic)* sich verdichten; *(queue, line of cars)* sich bilden.
(c) the parts ~ ~ into a complete ... die Teile bilden zusammen ein vollständiges ...
2 *vt sep* **(a)** aufbauen *(into* zu*)*; *finances* aufbessern ◆ **to ~ ~ a reputation** sich *(dat)* einen Namen machen.
(b) *(increase)* *ego, muscles, forces* aufbauen; *production, pressure* steigern, erhöhen; *forces* *(mass)* zusammenziehen; *health* kräftigen; *sb's confidence* stärken ◆ **porridge ~s you ~** von Porridge wirst du groß und stark; **growing children need lots of vitamins to ~ them ~** Kinder im Wachstumsalter brauchen viele Vitamine als Aufbaustoffe; **to ~ ~ sb's hopes** jdm Hoffnung(en) machen.
(c) *(cover with houses) area, land* (ganz) bebauen.
(d) *(publicize) person* aufbauen ◆ **he wasn't as good as he had been built ~ to be** er war nicht so gut, wie die Werbung erwarten ließ.
builder ['bɪldəʳ] *n* *(worker)* Bauarbeiter(in *f*) *m*; *(of ships)* Schiffsbauer *m*; *(contractor)* Bauunternehmer *m*; *(future owner)* Bauherr *m*; *(fig: of state)* Baumeister *(geh)*, Erbauer *m* ◆ **John Higgins, B~s** Bauunternehmen John Higgins; **~'s labourer** Bauarbeiter *m*; **~'s merchant** Baustoffhändler *m*.
building ['bɪldɪŋ] *n* **(a)** Gebäude *nt*; *(usually big or in some way special also)* Bau *m* ◆ **it's the next ~ but one** das ist zwei Häuser weiter; **the ~s in the old town** die Häuser *or* Gebäude in der Altstadt. **(b)** *(act of constructing)* Bau *m*, Bauen *nt*; *(of new nation etc)* Aufbau *m*.
building: ~ block *n* *(in toy set)* Bauklotz *m*; *(fig)* Baustein *m*; **~ contractor** *n* Bauunternehmer *m*; **~ contractors** *npl* Bauunternehmen *nt*; **~ industry** *n* Bauindustrie *f*; **~ materials** *npl* Baumaterial *nt*, Baustoffe *pl*; **~ site** *n* Baustelle *f*; **~ society** *n* *(Brit)* Bausparkasse *f*; **~ trade** *n* Baugewerbe *nt*; **~ worker** *n* Bauarbeiter *m*.
build-up ['bɪldʌp] *n* **(a)** *(inf)* Werbung *f* ◆ **publicity ~** Werbekampagne *f*; **they gave the play a good ~** sie haben das Stück ganz groß herausgebracht *(inf)*; **the chairman gave the speaker a tremendous ~** der Vorsitzende hat den Redner ganz groß angekündigt. **(b)** *(of pressure)* Steigerung *f*; *(Tech also)* Verdichtung *f* ◆ **~ of troops** Truppenmassierungen *pl*; **a traffic ~, a ~ of traffic** eine Verkehrsverdichtung.
built [bɪlt] *pret, ptp of* **build**.
built: ~-in *adj cupboard etc* eingebaut, Einbau-; *(fig: instinctive)* instinktmäßig; **~-in obsolescence** geplanter Verschleiß; **~-up** *adj shoulders* gepolstert; **~-up area** bebautes Gebiet; *(Mot)* geschlossene Ortschaft; **~-up shoes** Schuhe *pl* mit überhoher Sohle; *(Med)* orthopädische Schuhe *pl*.
bulb [bʌlb] *n* **(a)** Zwiebel *f*; *(of garlic)* Knolle *f*. **(b)** *(Elec)* (Glüh)birne *f*. **(c)** *(of thermometer etc)* Kolben *m*.
bulbous ['bʌlbəs] *adj plant* knollig, Knollen-; *(bulb-shaped) growth etc* knotig, Knoten- ◆ **~ nose** Knollennase *f*.
Bulgaria [bʌl'geərɪə] *n* Bulgarien *nt*.
Bulgarian [bʌl'geərɪən] 1 *adj* bulgarisch.
2 *n* **(a)** Bulgare *m*, Bulgarin *f*. **(b)** *(language)* Bulgarisch *nt*.
bulge [bʌldʒ] 1 *n* **(a)** *(in surface)* Wölbung *f*; *(irregular)* Unebenheit *f*; *(in jug, glass etc also)* Bauch *m*; *(in plaster, metal: accidental)* Beule *f*; *(in line)* Bogen *m*; *(in tyre)* Wulst *m* ◆ **the Battle of the B~** die Ardennenoffensive; **what's that ~ in your pocket?** was steht denn in deiner Tasche so vor?
(b) *(in birth rate etc)* Zunahme *f*, Anschwellen *nt* *(in gen)* ◆ **the post-war ~** der Babyboom der Nachkriegsjahre.
2 *vi* **(a)** *(also* **~ out***)* *(swell)* (an)schwellen; *(metal, sides of box)* sich wölben; *(plaster)* uneben sein; *(stick out)* vorstehen ◆ **his eyes were bulging out of his head** *(lit)* die Augen traten ihm aus dem Kopf; *(fig)* er bekam Stielaugen

(*inf*).
(**b**) (*pocket, sack*) prall gefüllt sein; gestopft voll sein (*inf*) (*with mit*); (*cheek*) voll sein (*with mit*) ◆ **his notebooks were absolutely bulging with ideas** seine Notizbücher waren berstend *or* zum Bersten voll mit Ideen.
bulge baby *n Kind nt der starken Nachkriegsjahrgänge*.
bulging ['bʌldʒɪŋ] *adj stomach* prall, vorstehend; *pockets, suitcase* prall gefüllt, gestopft voll (*inf*) ◆ **~ eyes** Glotzaugen *pl*.
bulimia [bə'lɪmɪə] *n* Bulimie *f*.
bulimic [bə'lɪmɪk] [1] *adj* bulimisch.
[2] *n* Bulimiker(in) *m(f)*.
bulk [bʌlk] [1] *n* (**a**) (*size*) Größe *f*; (*of task*) Ausmaß *nt*; (*large shape*) (*of thing*) massige Form; (*of person, animal*) massige Gestalt ◆ **of great ~** massig.
(**b**) (*also* **great ~**) größter Teil; (*of debt, loan also*) Hauptteil *m*; (*of work, mineral deposits also*) Großteil *m*; (*of people, votes also*) Gros *nt*; (*of property, legacy etc also*) Masse *f*.
(**c**) (*Comm*) **in ~** im großen, en gros.
[2] *vi*: **to ~ large** eine wichtige Rolle spielen.
bulk buying [,bʌlk'baɪɪŋ] *n* Mengen- *or* Großeinkauf *m*.
bulkhead ['bʌlkhed] *n* Schott *nt*; (*in tunnel*) Spundwand *f*.
bulkiness ['bʌlkɪnɪs] *n see adj* (**a**) Sperrigkeit *f*; Dicke *f*; Unförmigkeit *f*. (**b**) Massigkeit, Wuchtigkeit *f*.
bulky ['bʌlkɪ] *adj* (*+er*) (**a**) *object* sperrig; *book* dick; *sweater, space-suit* unförmig ◆ **~ goods** Sperrgut *nt*. (**b**) *person* massig, wuchtig.
bull[1] [bʊl] [1] *n* (**a**) Stier *m*; (*for breeding*) Bulle *m* ◆ **to take** *or* **seize the ~ by the horns** (*fig*) den Stier bei den Hörnern packen; **like a ~ in a china shop** (*inf*) wie ein Elefant im Porzellanladen (*inf*); **with a neck like a ~** stiernackig.
(**b**) (*male of elephant, whale etc*) Bulle *m* ◆ **a ~ elephant** ein Elefantenbulle *m*; **~ calf** Bullenkalb *nt*.
(**c**) (*St Ex*) Haussier, Haussespekulant(in *f*) *m* ◆ **~ market** Hausse *f*.
(**d**) (*Brit Mil sl*) Drill *m* und Routine *f*.
(**e**) (*inf: nonsense*) Unsinn, Quatsch (*inf*) *m*.
[2] *vi* (*St Ex*) auf Hausse spekulieren.
[3] *vt* (*St Ex*) *stocks, shares* hochtreiben ◆ **to ~ the market** die Kurse hochtreiben.
bull[2] *n* (*Eccl*) Bulle *f*.
bulldog ['bʊldɒg] *n* (**a**) Bulldogge *f* ◆ **he has the tenacity of a ~** er hat eine zähe Ausdauer. (**b**) (*Brit Univ*) Helfer *m* des Proctors.
bulldog: ~ breed *n* **he is one of the ~ breed** er ist ein zäher Mensch; **~ clip** *n* Papierklammer *f*.
bulldoze ['bʊldəʊz] *vt* (**a**) (*fig: force*) **to ~ sb into doing sth** jdn zwingen, etw zu tun, jdn so unter Druck setzen, daß er *etc* etw tut; **to ~ a measure through parliament** eine Maßnahme im Parlament durchpeitschen; **she ~d her way through the crowd** sie boxte sich durch die Menge.
(**b**) **they ~d the rubble out of the way** sie räumten den Schutt mit Bulldozern weg.
bulldozer ['bʊldəʊzə[r]] [1] *n* Planierraupe *f*, Bulldozer *m*.
[2] *adj attr* (*fig*) *tactics etc* Holzhammer- (*inf*).
bull-dyke ['bʊldaɪk] *n* (*sl*) kesser Vater (*sl*).
bullet ['bʊlɪt] *n* Kugel *f* ◆ **to bite the ~** in den sauren Apfel beißen (*inf*).
bullet: ~-headed *adj* rundköpfig; **~ hole** *n* Einschuß(loch *nt*) *m*.
bulletin ['bʊlɪtɪn] *n* (**a**) Bulletin *nt*, amtliche Bekanntmachung ◆ **health ~** Krankenbericht *m*, Bulletin *nt*; **~ board** (*US: notice board, Comput*) Schwarzes Brett; **a ~ to the press** ein Pressekommuniqué *nt*. (**b**) (*of club, society*) Bulletin *nt*.
bullet: ~proof [1] *adj* kugelsicher; [2] *vt* kugelsicher machen; **~ train** *n* (*japanischer*) Superexpreß; **~ wound** *n* Schußwunde *or* -verletzung *f*.
bull: ~fight *n* Stierkampf *m*; **~fighter** *n* Stierkämpfer *m*; **~fighting** *n* Stierkampf *m*; **~fighting is ...** der Stierkampf ist ...; **~finch** *n* Dompfaff, Gimpel *m*; **~frog** *n* Ochsenfrosch *m*; **~horn** *n* (*US*) Megaphon *nt*.
bullion ['bʊljən] *n, no pl* Gold-/Silberbarren *pl*.
bullish ['bʊlɪʃ] *adj* (**a**) *personality* selbstsicher ◆ **to be ~ about sth** in bezug auf etw (*acc*) zuversichtlich sein. (**b**) (*St Ex*) **the market was ~** der Markt war in Haussestimmung.
bull-necked ['bʊlnekt] *adj* stiernackig.
bullock ['bʊlək] *n* Ochse *m*.
bull: ~ring *n* Stierkampfarena *f*; **~'s eye** *n* (**a**) (*of target*) Scheibenmittelpunkt *m or* -zentrum *nt*; (*hit*) Schuß *m* ins Schwarze *or* Zentrum; (*in darts*) Bull's eye *nt*; (*in archery*) Mouche *f*; **to get a** *or* **hit the ~'s eye** (*lit, fig*) ins Schwarze treffen; **~'s eye!** (*lit, fig*) genau getroffen!, ein Schuß ins Schwarze!; (**b**) (*sweet*) hartes Pfefferminzbonbon; **~shit** (*vulg*) [1] *n* (*lit*) Kuhscheiße *f* (*vulg*); (*fig*) Bockmist (*sl*), Scheiß (*sl*) *m*; [2] *interj* Quatsch mit Soße (*sl*); **~shit, of course you can** red keinen Scheiß, klar kannst du das (*sl*); [3] *vi* Scheiß erzählen (*sl*); [4] *vt* **he ~shitted his way out of trouble** er hat sich ganz großkotzig aus der Affäre gezogen (*sl*); **~-shitter** *n* (*vulg*) Quatschkopf *m* (*inf*); **~-terrier** *n* Bullterrier *m*.
bully[1] ['bʊlɪ] [1] *n* (**a**) Tyrann *m*; (*esp Sch*) Rabauke *m* ◆ **you great big ~** du Rüpel; **to be a bit of a ~** den starken Mann markieren (*inf*); **don't be a ~ with your little sister** schikaniere *or* tyrannisiere deine kleine Schwester nicht.
(**b**) (*Hockey*) Bully *nt*.
[2] *vt* tyrannisieren, schikanieren; (*using violence*) drangsalieren; (*into doing sth*) unter Druck setzen ◆ **to ~ sb into doing sth** jdn so unter Druck setzen, daß er *etc* etw tut.
◆**bully about** *or* **around** *vt sep* herumkommandieren, tyrannisieren.
◆**bully off** *vi* (*Hockey*) das Bully machen.
bully[2] *interj* (*dated*) prima (*inf*), hervorragend ◆ **~ for you!** (*dated, iro*) gratuliere!
bully: ~ beef *n* (*Mil inf*) Corned beef *nt*; **~ boy** *n* (*inf*) Schlägertyp *m* (*inf*).
bullying ['bʊlɪɪŋ] [1] *adj person, manner* tyrannisch; *boss, wife also* herrisch.
[2] *n see vt* Tyrannisieren, Schikanieren *nt*; Drangsalieren *nt*; Anwendung *f* von Druck (*of* auf *+acc*).
bully-off [bʊlɪ'ɒf] *n* (*Hockey*) Bully *nt*.
bulrush ['bʊlrʌʃ] *n* Rohrkolben *m* ◆ **in the ~es** im Schilfrohr.
bulwark ['bʊlwək] *n* (**a**) (*lit, fig*) Bollwerk *nt*. (**b**) (*Naut*) Schanzkleid *nt*.
bum[1] [bʌm] *n* (*esp Brit inf*) Hintern (*inf*), Popo (*inf*) *m*.
bum[2] (*sl*) [1] *n* (**a**) (*good-for-nothing*) Rumtreiber *m* (*inf*); (*young*) Gammler *m*; (*down-and-out*) Penner, Pennbruder *m* (*sl*). (**b**) (*despicable person*) Saukerl *m* (*sl*).
(**c**) **to be on the ~** schnorren (*inf*); **he's always on the ~ for cigarettes** er schnorrt immer Zigaretten (*inf*).
[2] *adj* (*bad*) beschissen (*sl*); *trick* hundsgemein (*inf*) ◆ **~ rap** (*US sl*) falsche Anklage; **to give sb a ~ steer** (*US sl*) jdn auf die falsche Fährte locken.
[3] *vt* (**a**) *money, food* schnorren (*inf*) (*off sb* bei jdm) ◆ **could I ~ a lift into town?** kannst du mich in die Stadt mitnehmen?; **could I ~ a fag?** kann ich 'ne Kippe abstauben (*sl*) *or* schnorren (*inf*)?
(**b**) **he ~med his way round Europe** er ist durch Europa gegammelt (*sl*) *or* gezogen (*inf*).
[4] *vi* (*scrounge*) schnorren (*inf*) (*off sb* bei jdm).
◆**bum about** *or* **around** *vi* (*sl*) rumgammeln (*sl*); (*+prep obj*) ziehen durch (*inf*).
bumbag ['bʌmbæg] *n* (*Ski*) Gürteltasche *f*.
bumbershoot ['bʌmbəʃu:t] *n* (*US inf*) Musspritze *f* (*hum inf*).
bumble-bee ['bʌmblbi:] *n* Hummel *f*.
bumbledom ['bʌmbldəm] *n* (*inf*) kleinlicher Bürokratismus.
◆**bumble through** ['bʌmbl'θru:] *vi* sich durchwursteln (*inf*) *or* -mogeln (*inf*) (*+prep obj* durch).
bumbling ['bʌmblɪŋ] *adj* (*clumsy*) schusselig (*inf*) ◆ **some ~ idiot** irgend so ein Vollidiot (*inf*).
bumboat ['bʌmbəʊt] *n* Proviantboot *nt*.
bumf [bʌmf] *n see* **bumph**.
bummer ['bʌmə[r]] *n* (*sl: person*) Niete *f* ◆ **it's a ~** (*nuisance etc*) so 'ne Scheiße (*sl*); **this one's a real ~** das kannst du vergessen.
bump [bʌmp] [1] *n* (**a**) (*blow, noise, jolt*) Bums *m* (*inf*); (*of sth falling also*) Plumps *m* (*inf*) ◆ **to get a ~ on the head** sich (*dat*) den Kopf anschlagen; **I accidentally gave her a ~ on the chin** ich habe sie aus Versehen ans Kinn geboxt *or* gestoßen; **the car has had a few ~s** mit dem Auto hat es ein paarmal gebumst (*inf*); **each ~ was agony as the ambulance ...** jede Erschütterung war eine Qual, als der Krankenwagen ...; **~ and grind** (*inf*) erotische Zuckungen *pl*; (*sex*) Bumserei *f* (*inf*).
(**b**) (*on any surface*) Unebenheit *f*, Hubbel *m* (*inf*); (*on head, knee etc*) Beule *f*; (*on car*) Delle *f*.
(**c**) (*Aviat: rising air current*) Bö *f*.
[2] *vt* (**a**) stoßen; *car wing etc, one's own car* eine Delle fahren in (*+acc*); *another car* auffahren auf (*+acc*) ◆ **to ~ one's head/knee** sich (*dat*) den Kopf/das Knie anstoßen *or* anschlagen (*on against* an *+dat*); **her father sat ~ing her up and down on his knee** ihr Vater ließ sie auf den Knien reiten.
(**b**) (*Sch sl*) hochwerfen.
[3] *vi* (*move joltingly*) holpern ◆ **he fell and went ~ing down the stairs** er stürzte und fiel polternd die Treppe hinunter.
[4] *adv* **to go ~** bumsen (*inf*); **things that go ~ in the night** Geräusche im Dunkeln *or* in der Nacht.
◆**bump about** *vi* herumpoltern.
◆**bump into** *vi +prep obj* (**a**) (*knock into*) stoßen *or* bumsen (*inf*) gegen; (*driver, car*) fahren gegen; *another car* fahren auf (*+acc*). (**b**) (*inf: meet*) begegnen (*+dat*), treffen.
◆**bump off** *vt sep* (*inf*) abmurksen (*inf*), kaltmachen (*inf*).
◆**bump up** *vt sep* (*inf*) (*to* auf *+acc*) *prices* raufgehen mit (*inf*); *total* erhöhen; *salary* aufbessern.
◆**bump up against** *vi +prep obj* treffen.
bumper ['bʌmpə[r]] [1] *n* (*of car*) Stoßstange *f* ◆ **~ sticker** Aufkleber *m*.
[2] *adj* **~ crop** Rekordernte *f*; **a special ~ edition** eine Riesen-Sonderausgabe; **~ offer** großes Sonderangebot.
bumper car *n* Boxauto *nt* (*dial*), Autoskooter *m*.
bumph [bʌmf] *n* (*Brit inf*) (**a**) (*forms*) Papierkram *m* (*inf*). (**b**) (*toilet paper*) Klopapier *nt* (*inf*).
bumpiness ['bʌmpɪnɪs] *n see adj* Unebenheit, Hubbeligkeit (*inf*) *f*; Holp(e)rigkeit *f*; Böigkeit *f*.
bumpkin ['bʌmpkɪn] *n* (*also* **country ~**) (*man*) (Bauern)tölpel *m*; (*woman*) Trampel *f* vom Land.
bumptious ['bʌmpʃəs] *adj* aufgeblasen, wichtigtuerisch.
bumptiousness ['bʌmpʃəsnɪs] *n* Aufgeblasenheit, Wichtigtuerei *f*.
bumpy ['bʌmpɪ] *adj* (*+er*) *surface* uneben, hubbelig (*inf*); *road, drive* holp(e)rig; *flight* böig, unruhig ◆ **we had a very ~ drive** auf der Fahrt wurden wir tüchtig durchgerüttelt.
bum's rush *n*: **to give sb the ~** (*sl*) jdn rausschmeißen (*sl*).
bun [bʌn] *n* (**a**) (*bread*) Brötchen *nt*; (*iced ~ etc*) süßes Stückchen *or* Teilchen; (*N Engl: small cake*) Biskuittörtchen *nt* ◆ **to have a ~ in the oven** (*sl*) ein Kind kriegen (*inf*). (**b**) (*hair*) Knoten *m* ◆ **she wears her hair in a ~** sie trägt einen Knoten.
bunch [bʌntʃ] [1] *n* (**a**) (*of flowers*) Strauß *m*; (*of bananas*) Büschel *nt*; (*of radishes, asparagus*) Bund *nt*; (*of hair*) (Ratten)schwanz *m*, Zöpfchen *nt* ◆ **a ~**

of **roses/flowers** ein Strauß *m* Rosen/ein Blumenstrauß *m*; **~ of grapes** Weintraube *f*; **~ of keys** Schlüsselbund *m*; **to wear one's hair in ~es** (Ratten)schwänze *pl or* Zöpfchen *pl* haben; **the pick** *or* **best of the ~** die Allerbesten; (*things*) das Beste vom Besten; **to take the pick of the ~** sich (*dat*) die Allerbesten/das Beste aussuchen.
(b) (*inf: of people*) Haufen *m* (*inf*) ♦ **a small ~ of tourists** ein Häufchen *nt or* eine kleine Gruppe Touristen; **a ~ of fives** (*sl: fist*) 'ne Faust ins Gesicht (*sl*).
(c) (*inf: a lot*) **thanks a ~** (*esp iro*) schönen Dank; **there's still a whole ~ of things to do** es sind noch jede Menge Sachen zu erledigen (*inf*).
[2] *vi* (*dress*) sich bauschen; *see* **~ together 2, ~ up 2.**

♦**bunch together** [1] *vt sep* zusammenfassen; (*at random*) zusammenwürfeln ♦ **the girls/prisoners were sitting all ~ed ~** die Mädchen/Gefangenen saßen alle auf einem Haufen.
[2] *vi* (*people*) Grüppchen *or* einen Haufen bilden; (*atoms*) Cluster bilden ♦ **they ~ed ~ for warmth** sie kauerten sich aneinander, um sich zu wärmen; **don't ~ ~, spread out!** bleibt nicht alle auf einem Haufen, verteilt euch!

♦**bunch up** [1] *vt sep* (a) *dress, skirt* bauschen. (b) (*put together*) *objects* auf einen Haufen legen.
[2] *vi* (a) Grüppchen *or* Haufen bilden ♦ **don't ~ ~ so much, space out!** nicht alle auf einem Haufen, verteilt euch! (b) (*material*) sich bauschen.

bundle ['bʌndl] [1] *n* (a) Bündel *nt* ♦ **to tie sth in a ~** etw bündeln.
(b) (*fig*) **he is a ~ of nerves** er ist ein Nervenbündel; **that child is a ~ of mischief** das Kind hat nichts als Unfug im Kopf; **her little ~ of joy** (*inf*) ihr kleiner Wonneproppen (*inf*); **a ~ of fun** (*inf*) das reinste Vergnügen.
[2] *vt* (a) bündeln ♦ **~d software** (*Comput*) Software-Paket *nt*; **it comes ~d with ...** (*Comput*) ... ist im Software-Paket enthalten; *see* **~ up.** (b) (*put, send hastily*) *things* stopfen; *people* verfrachten, schaffen; (*into vehicle*) packen (*inf*), schaffen.

♦**bundle off** *vt sep person* schaffen ♦ **he was ~d ~ to Australia** er wurde nach Australien verfrachtet.

♦**bundle up** *vt sep* (*tie into bundles*) bündeln; (*collect hastily*) zusammenraffen ♦ **~d ~ in his overcoat** in seinen Mantel eingehüllt *or* gemummelt (*inf*).

bun fight *n* (*dated inf*) Festivitäten *pl* (*dated*).

bung [bʌŋ] [1] *n* (*of cask*) Spund(zapfen) *m*.
[2] *vt* (a) *cask* spunden, verstopfen. (b) (*Brit inf: throw*) schmeißen (*inf*).

♦**bung in** *vt sep* (*Brit inf: include*) dazutun.

♦**bung out** *vt sep* (*Brit inf*) rauswerfen (*inf*).

♦**bung up** *vt sep* (*inf*) *pipe* verstopfen ♦ **I'm all ~ed ~** meine Nase ist verstopft.

bungalow ['bʌŋgələʊ] *n* Bungalow *m*.

bungee jumping, bungy jumping ['bʌndʒɪ,dʒʌmpɪŋ] *n* Bungee-Springen *nt*.

bung-ho [bʌŋ'həʊ] *interj* (*dated inf*) famos (*dated inf*).

bunghole ['bʌŋhəʊl] *n* Spundloch *nt*.

bungle ['bʌŋgl] [1] *vt* verpfuschen, vermasseln (*inf*) ♦ **it was a ~d job** die Sache war vermasselt (*inf*) *or* verpfuscht.
[2] *vi* **I see you've ~d again, Higgins** wie ich sehe, haben Sie wieder einmal alles verpfuscht *or* vermasselt (*inf*), Higgins.
[3] *n* verpfuschte Sache, Stümperei *f*.

bungler ['bʌŋglə^r] *n* Nichtskönner, Stümper *m*.

bungling ['bʌŋglɪŋ] [1] *adj person* unfähig, trottelhaft, dusselig (*inf*); *attempt* stümperhaft ♦ **some ~ idiot has ...** irgendein Trottel hat ... (*inf*).
[2] *n* Stümperei, Dusseligkeit (*inf*) *f*.

bungy jumping *n see* **bungee jumping.**

bunion ['bʌnjən] *n* Ballen *m*.

bunk[1] [bʌŋk] *n*: **to do a ~** (*inf*) türmen (*inf*).

bunk[2] *n* (*inf*) Quatsch *m* (*inf*).

bunk[3] *n* (*in ship*) Koje *f*; (*in train, dormitory*) Bett *nt*.

♦**bunk down** *vi* (*inf*) kampieren (*inf*).

bunk-beds [bʌŋk'bedz] *npl* Etagenbett *nt*.

bunker ['bʌŋkə^r] [1] *n* (*Naut, Golf, Mil*) Bunker *m*.
[2] *vt* **he was ~ed** (*Golf*) er hatte den Ball in den Bunker geschlagen.

bunkhouse ['bʌŋkhaʊs] *n* Schlafbaracke *f*.

bunkum ['bʌŋkəm] *n* (*inf*) Blödsinn, Quatsch (*inf*) *m*.

bunny ['bʌnɪ] *n* (*also* **~ rabbit**) Hase *m*, Häschen *nt*.

bunny girl *n* Häschen *nt*.

Bunsen (burner) ['bʌnsn('bɜːnə^r)] *n* Bunsenbrenner *m*.

bunting[1] ['bʌntɪŋ] *n* (*Orn*) Ammer *f*; *see* **corn ~, reed ~.**

bunting[2] *n* (*material*) Fahnentuch *nt*; (*flags*) bunte Fähnchen *pl*, Wimpel *pl*.

buoy [bɔɪ] *n* Boje *f* ♦ **to put down a ~** eine Boje verankern.

♦**buoy up** *vt sep* (a) (*lit*) über Wasser halten. (b) (*fig*) *person* Auftrieb geben (+*dat*); *sb's hopes* beleben ♦ **~ed ~ by new hope** von neuer Hoffnung beseelt. (c) (*Fin*) *market, prices* Auftrieb geben (+*dat*).

buoyancy ['bɔɪənsɪ] *n* (a) (*of ship, object*) Schwimmfähigkeit *f*; (*of liquid*) Auftrieb *m* ♦ **~ chamber** (*Naut*) Trimmtank *m*; **~ tank** Luftkammer *f*. (b) (*fig: cheerfulness*) Schwung, Elan *m*. (c) (*Fin: of market, prices*) Festigkeit *f*; (*resilience*) Erholungsfähigkeit *f*.

buoyant ['bɔɪənt] *adj* (a) *ship, object* schwimmend; *liquid* tragend ♦ **fresh water is not so ~ as salt water** Süßwasser trägt nicht so gut wie Salzwasser. (b) (*fig*) *person, mood* heiter; (*energetic*) *step* federnd, elastisch. (c) (*Fin*) *market, prices* fest; (*resilient*) erholungsfähig; *trading* rege.

buoyantly ['bɔɪəntlɪ] *adv see adj.*

BUPA ['buːpə] *abbr of* **British United Provident Association** *private Krankenversicherung*.

buppie, buppy ['bʌpɪ] *n* (*inf*) *abbr of* **black upwardly mobile professional** schwarzer Yuppie.

bur, burr [bɜː^r] *n* (*Bot, fig inf*) Klette *f* ♦ **chestnut ~** Kastanienschale *f*.

burble ['bɜːbl] [1] *vi* (a) (*stream*) plätschern, gurgeln. (b) (*fig: person*) plappern; (*baby*) gurgeln ♦ **what's he burbling (on) about?** (*inf*) worüber quasselt er eigentlich? (*inf*).
[2] *n* (*of stream*) Plätschern, Gurgeln *nt*; (*on tape etc*) Gemurmel *nt*.

burbot ['bɜːbət] *n* Quappe *f*.

burden[1] ['bɜːdn] [1] *n* (a) (*lit*) Last *f* ♦ **it puts too much of a ~ on him/the engine** das überlastet ihn/den Motor; **beast of ~** Lasttier *nt*.
(b) (*fig*) Belastung *f* (*on, to* für) ♦ **he has such a ~ of responsibility** er hat eine schwere Last an Verantwortung zu tragen; **the guilt was a constant ~ on his mind** das Gefühl der Schuld belastete ihn sehr; **~ of taxation** steuerliche Belastung, Steuerlast *f*; **the ~ of years/debts** die Last der Jahre/die Schuldenlast; **I don't want to be a ~ on you** ich möchte Ihnen nicht zur Last fallen; **the ~ of proof lies with him** er muß den Beweis dafür erbringen *or* liefern; (*Jur*) er trägt die Beweislast.
(c) (*Naut*) Tragfähigkeit, Tragkraft *f*.
[2] *vt* belasten.

burden[2] *n* (a) (*of song*) Refrain, Kehrreim *m*. (b) (*of speech, essay etc*) Grundgedanke *m*.

burdensome ['bɜːdnsəm] *adj load* schwer; *condition* lästig; *task* mühsam ♦ **she finds the children ~** sie empfindet die Kinder als eine Belastung; **to be ~** eine Belastung darstellen.

burdock ['bɜːdɒk] *n* Klette *f*.

bureau [bjʊə'rəʊ] *n* (a) (*Brit: desk*) Sekretär *m*. (b) (*US: chest of drawers*) Kommode *f*. (c) (*office*) Büro *nt*. (d) (*government department*) Amt *nt*, Behörde *f* ♦ **federal ~** Bundesamt *nt*.

bureaucracy [bjʊə'rɒkrəsɪ] *n* Bürokratie *f*.

bureaucrat ['bjʊərəʊkræt] *n* Bürokrat *m*.

bureaucratic *adj*, **~ally** *adv* [,bjʊərəʊ'krætɪk, -əlɪ] bürokratisch.

burgeon ['bɜːdʒən] *vi* (*liter: also* **~ forth**) (*flower*) knospen (*liter*); (*plant*) sprießen (*liter*); (*fig*) hervorsprießen (*geh*) ♦ **when young love first ~s** wenn die junge Liebe erblüht (*liter*).

burger ['bɜːgə^r] *n* (*inf*) Hamburger *m*.

burgess ['bɜːdʒɪs] *n* (a) (freier) Bürger, (freie) Bürgerin. (b) (*Hist*) Abgeordnete(r) *mf*. (c) (*US*) *Abgeordneter m der Volksvertretung der Kolonien Maryland oder Virginia*.

burgh ['bʌrə] *n* (*Scot*) freie Stadt.

burgher ['bɜːgə^r] *n* (*old*) Bürger(in *f*) *m*.

burglar ['bɜːglə^r] *n* Einbrecher(in *f*) *m* ♦ **~ alarm** Alarmanlage *f*.

burglarize ['bɜːgləraɪz] *vt* (*US*) einbrechen in (+*acc*) ♦ **the place/he was ~d** in dem Gebäude/bei ihm wurde eingebrochen.

burglarproof ['bɜːgləpruːf] *adj* einbruchsicher.

burglary ['bɜːglərɪ] *n* Einbruch *m*; (*offence*) (Einbruchs)diebstahl *m*.

burgle ['bɜːgl] *vt* einbrechen in (+*acc*) ♦ **the place/he was ~d** in dem Gebäude/bei ihm wurde eingebrochen.

Burgundy ['bɜːgəndɪ] *n* Burgund *nt*; (*wine*) Burgunder *m*.

burial ['berɪəl] *n* Beerdigung, Bestattung *f*; (*~ ceremony also*) Begräbnis *nt*; (*in cemetery also*) Beisetzung *f* (*form*) ♦ **Christian ~** christliches Begräbnis; **~ at sea** Seebestattung *f*.

burial: ~ chamber *n* Grabkammer *f*; **~ ground** *n* Begräbnisstätte *f*; **~ mound** *n* Grabhügel *m*; **~ place** *n* Grabstätte *f*; **~ service** *n* Trauerfeier *f*.

burin ['bjʊərɪn] *n* (*Art*) Stichel *m*.

burlap ['bɜːlæp] *n* Sackleinen *nt*.

burlesque [bɜː'lesk] [1] *n* (a) (*parody*) Parodie *f*; (*Theat*) Burleske *f*; (*Liter*) Persiflage *f*.
(b) (*US Theat*) Varieté *nt*; (*show*) Varietévorstellung *f*.
[2] *adj* (a) *see n* parodistisch; burlesk; persiflierend.
(b) (*US Theat*) Varieté- ♦ **~ show** Varietévorstellung *f*.
[3] *vt* parodieren; *book, author, style* persiflieren.

burly ['bɜːlɪ] *adj* (+*er*) kräftig, stramm.

Burma ['bɜːmə] *n* Birma, Burma *nt*.

Burmese [bɜː'miːz] [1] *adj* birmanisch, burmesisch.
[2] *n* (a) Birmane, Burmese *m*, Birmanin, Burmesin *f*. (b) (*language*) Birmanisch, Burmesisch *nt*.

burn[1] [bɜːn] *n* (*Scot*) Bach *m*.

burn[2] (*vb: pret, ptp* **~ed** *or* **~t**) [1] *n* (a) (*on skin*) Brandwunde *f*; (*on material*) verbrannte Stelle, Brandfleck *m* ♦ **severe ~s** schwere Verbrennungen *pl*; **second degree ~s** Verbrennungen zweiten Grades; **cigarette ~** Brandfleck *m or* (*hole*) Brandloch *nt or* (*on skin*) Brandwunde *f* von einer Zigarette.
(b) (*Space: of rocket*) Zündung *f*.
[2] *vt* (a) verbrennen; *incense* abbrennen; *village* niederbrennen ♦ **he ~t me with his cigarette** er hat mich mit der Zigarette gebrannt; **to ~ oneself** sich verbrennen; **to be ~t to death** verbrannt werden; (*in accident*) verbrennen; **to be ~t alive** bei lebendigem Leibe verbrannt werden *or* (*in accident*) verbrennen; **to ~ a hole in sth** ein Loch in etw (*acc*) brennen; **to ~ one's fingers** (*lit, fig*) sich (*dat*) die Finger verbrennen; **he's got money to ~** (*fig*) er hat Geld wie Heu; **to ~ one's boats** *or* **bridges** (*fig*) alle Brücken hinter sich (*dat*) abbrechen; **to ~ the midnight oil** (*fig*) bis tief in die Nacht arbeiten.
(b) *meat, sauce, toast, cakes* verbrennen lassen; (*slightly*) anbrennen lassen; (*sun*) *person, skin* verbrennen.
(c) (*acid*) ätzen ♦ **the curry ~t his throat/lips** das Currygericht brannte ihm im Hals/auf den Lippen.
(d) (*use as fuel: ship etc*) befeuert werden mit; (*use up*) *petrol, electricity* verbrauchen.

3 *vi* **(a)** (*wood, fire etc*) brennen ◆ **you will ~ in hell** du wirst in der Hölle schmoren; **to ~ to death** verbrennen; *see* **ear**[1].
(b) (*meat, pastry etc*) verbrennen; (*slightly*) anbrennen ◆ **she/her skin ~s easily** sie bekommt leicht einen Sonnenbrand.
(c) (*ointment, curry, sun*) brennen; (*acid*) ätzen ◆ **the acid ~ed into the metal** die Säure fraß sich ins Metall.
(d) (*feel hot: wound, eyes, skin*) brennen ◆ **his face was ~ing (with heat/shame)** sein Gesicht glühte *or* war rot (vor Hitze/Scham); **it's so hot, I'm ~ing** es ist so heiß, ich komm bald um vor Hitze.
(e) **to be ~ing to do sth** darauf brennen, etw zu tun; **he was ~ing to get his revenge** er brannte auf Rache; **he was ~ing with anger/passion** er war wutentbrannt/er glühte in Leidenschaft (*geh*); **to ~ (with love/desire) for sb** (*liter*) von glühender Liebe/glühendem Verlangen nach jdm verzehrt werden (*liter*).
(f) (*Space: rockets*) zünden.

◆**burn away** 1 *vi* **(a)** (*go on burning*) vor sich hin brennen. **(b)** (*wick, candle, oil*) herunterbrennen; (*part of roof etc*) abbrennen.
2 *vt sep* abbrennen; (*Med*) wegbrennen.

◆**burn down** 1 *vi* **(a)** (*house etc*) abbrennen. **(b)** (*fire, candle, wick*) herunterbrennen.
2 *vt sep* abbrennen.

◆**burn off** *vt sep paint etc* abbrennen.

◆**burn out** 1 *vi* (*fire, candle*) ausbrennen, ausgehen; (*fuse, dynamo etc*) durchbrennen; (*rocket*) den Treibstoff verbraucht haben.
2 *vr* **(a)** (*candle, lamp*) herunterbrennen; (*fire*) ab- *or* ausbrennen. **(b)** (*fig inf*) **to ~ oneself ~** sich kaputtmachen (*inf*), sich völlig verausgaben.
3 *vt sep* **(a)** *enemy troops etc* ausräuchern ◆ **they were ~t ~ of house and home** ihr Haus und Hof war abgebrannt.
(b) *usu pass* **~t ~ lorries/houses** ausgebrannte Lastwagen/Häuser; **he/his talent is ~t ~** (*inf*) mit ihm/seinem Talent ist's vorbei (*inf*), er hat sich völlig verausgabt; **he looked ~t ~** (*inf*) er sah völlig kaputt (*inf*) *or* verbraucht aus.

◆**burn up** 1 *vi* **(a)** (*fire etc*) auflodern. **(b)** (*rocket etc in atmosphere*) verglühen. **(c)** +*prep obj* (*Brit sl*) **to ~ ~ the road** die Straße entlangbrausen (*inf*).
2 *vt sep* **(a)** *rubbish* verbrennen; *fuel, energy* verbrauchen; *excess fat also* abbauen.
(b) **he was ~ed ~ with envy** er verzehrte sich vor Neid (*geh*).
(c) (*US inf: make angry*) zur Weißglut bringen (*inf*).

burner ['bɜːnəʳ] *n* (*of gas cooker, lamp*) Brenner *m*.

burning ['bɜːnɪŋ] 1 *adj* **(a)** *candle, town* brennend; *coals also, (fig) face* glühend ◆ **I still have this ~ sensation in my mouth/on my skin** mein Mund/meine Haut brennt immer noch; **the ~ bush** (*Bibl*) der brennende Dornbusch. **(b)** (*fig*) *thirst* brennend; *desire also, fever, hate, passion* glühend; *question, topic* brennend.
2 *n* **there is a smell of ~, I can smell ~** es riecht verbrannt *or* (*Cook also*) angebrannt.

burning glass *n* Brennglas *nt*.

burnish ['bɜːnɪʃ] *vt metal* polieren.

burnt [bɜːnt] *adj* verbrannt ◆ **~ offering** (*Rel*) Brandopfer *nt*; (*hum: food*) angebranntes Essen; **there's a ~ smell** es riecht verbrannt *or* brenzlig *or* (*Cook also*) angebrannt; **the coffee has a slightly ~ taste** der Kaffee schmeckt wie frisch geröstet.

burn-up ['bɜːnʌp] *n* (*Brit inf*) Rennfahrt *f* ◆ **to go for a ~** eine Rennfahrt machen; **to have a ~** volle Pulle fahren (*inf*), voll aufdrehen (*inf*).

burp [bɜːp] (*inf*) 1 *vi* rülpsen (*inf*); (*baby*) aufstoßen.
2 *vt baby* aufstoßen lassen.
3 *n* Rülpser *m* (*inf*).

burp gun *n* (*inf*) MG *nt* (*inf*).

burr[1] [bɜːʳ] *n see* **bur**.

burr[2] *n* (*Ling*) *breiige Aussprache* (*von R*) ◆ **to speak with a ~** breiig sprechen.

burrow ['bʌrəʊ] 1 *n* (*of rabbit etc*) Bau *m*.
2 *vi* (*rabbits, dogs etc*) graben, buddeln (*inf*); (*make a ~*) einen Bau graben ◆ **they had ~ed under the fence** sie hatten sich (*dat*) ein Loch *or* (*below ground*) einen Gang unterm Zaun gegraben *or* gebuddelt (*inf*).
3 *vt hole* graben, buddeln (*inf*) ◆ **to ~ one's way underground** sich (*dat*) einen unterirdischen Gang graben *or* buddeln (*inf*).

bursar ['bɜːsəʳ] *n* Schatzmeister, Finanzverwalter *m*.

bursary ['bɜːsərɪ] *n* **(a)** (*grant*) Stipendium *nt*. **(b)** (*office*) Schatzamt *nt*; (*Univ*) Quästur *f*.

burst [bɜːst] (*vb: pret, ptp ~*) 1 *n* **(a)** (*of shell etc*) Explosion *f*.
(b) (*in pipe etc*) Bruch *m*.
(c) (*of anger, enthusiasm, activity etc*) Ausbruch *m*; (*of flames*) (plötzliches) Auflodern ◆ **~ of laughter** Lachsalve *f*; **~ of eloquence** Wortschwall *m*; **~ of applause** Beifallssturm *m*; **~ of speed** Spurt *m*; (*of cars etc*) Riesenbeschleunigung *f* (*inf*); **a ~ of automatic gunfire** eine Maschinengewehrsalve; **give them another ~** verpaß ihnen noch eine Salve.
2 *vi* **(a)** platzen ◆ **to ~ open** (*box, door etc*) aufspringen; (*buds, wound*) aufbrechen; (*abscess, wound*) aufplatzen.
(b) (*be full to overflowing: sack etc*) platzen, bersten ◆ **to fill sth to ~ing point** etw bis zum Platzen *or* Bersten füllen; **to be full to ~ing** zum Platzen *or* Bersten voll sein; **to be ~ing with health** vor Gesundheit strotzen; **to be ~ing with a desire to do sth** vor Begierde brennen, etw zu tun; **to be ~ing with pride** vor Stolz platzen; **if I eat any more, I'll ~** (*inf*) wenn ich noch mehr esse, platze ich (*inf*); **he was ~ing to tell us** (*inf*) er brannte darauf, uns das zu sagen; *see* **seam**.
(c) (*start, go suddenly*) **to ~ into tears/flames** in Tränen ausbrechen/in Flammen aufgehen; **he ~ past me/into the room** er schoß an mir vorbei/er platzte ins Zimmer; **we ~ through the enemy lines** wir durchbrachen die feindlichen Linien; **the sun ~ through the clouds** die Sonne brach durch die Wolken; **sunlight ~ into the room** Sonnenlicht fiel plötzlich ins Zimmer; **the oil ~ from the well** das Öl brach aus dem Brunnen; **to ~ into view** plötzlich in Sicht kommen; **to ~ into a gallop/into song/into bloom** losgaloppieren/lossingen/plötzlich aufblühen.
3 *vt balloon, bubble, tyre* zum Platzen bringen, platzen lassen; (*person*) kaputt machen (*inf*); *boiler, pipe, dyke* sprengen ◆ **the river has ~ its banks** der Fluß ist über die Ufer getreten; **to ~ one's sides with laughter** vor Lachen platzen; *see* **blood vessel**.

◆**burst forth** *vi* (*liter*) (*blood, sun*) hervorbrechen; (*blossoms*) ausbrechen.

◆**burst in** *vi* hinein-/hereinstürzen; (*on conversation*) dazwischenplatzen (*on* bei) ◆ **he ~ ~ on us** er platzte bei uns herein.

◆**burst out** *vi* **(a)** (*emotions*) hervorbrechen, herausbrechen; (*lava*) ausbrechen ◆ **she's ~ing ~ of that dress** sie sprengt das Kleid fast. **(b)** **to ~ ~ of a room** aus einem Zimmer stürzen *or* stürmen. **(c)** (*in speech*) losplatzen ◆ **he ~ ~ in a violent speech** er zog plötzlich vom Leder. **(d)** **to ~ ~ laughing/crying** in Gelächter/Tränen ausbrechen, loslachen/losheulen.

burthen ['bɜːðən] *n, vt* (*old, liter*) *see* **burden**[1].

burton ['bɜːtn] *n* (*Brit sl*) **to have gone for a ~** im Eimer sein (*sl*).

bury ['berɪ] *vt* **(a)** *person, animal, possessions, differences* begraben; (*with ceremony also*) beerdigen, bestatten (*geh*); (*hide in earth*) *treasure, bones* vergraben; (*put in earth*) *end of post, roots* eingraben ◆ **where is he buried?** wo liegt *or* ist er begraben?; (*in cemetery also*) wo liegt er?; **to ~ sb at sea** jdn auf See bestatten (*geh*), jdm ein Seemannsgrab geben; **he is dead and buried** er ist schon lange tot; **that's all dead and buried** (*fig*) das ist schon lange passé (*inf*); **she has buried three husbands** (*fig*) sie hat schon drei Männer begraben (*inf*); **buried by an avalanche** von einer Lawine verschüttet *or* begraben; **to be buried in work** (*fig*) bis zum Hals in Arbeit stecken; **to ~ one's head in the sand** (*fig*) den Kopf in den Sand stecken.
(b) (*conceal*) *one's face* verbergen ◆ **to ~ one's face in one's hands** das Gesicht in den Händen vergraben; **to ~ oneself under the blankets/(away) in the country** sich unter den Decken/auf dem Land vergraben; **a village buried in the heart of the country** ein im Landesinnern versteckt gelegenes Dorf.
(c) (*put, plunge*) *hands, fingers* vergraben (*in* in +*dat*); *claws, teeth* schlagen (*in* in +*acc*); *dagger* stoßen (*in* in +*acc*).
(d) (*engross: usu in ptp*) **to ~ oneself in one's books** sich in seinen Büchern vergraben; **buried in thought/in one's work** gedankenversunken, in Gedanken/in seine Arbeit versunken.

bus[1] [bʌs] 1 *n, pl* **-es** *or* (*US*) **-ses** **(a)** Bus *m* ◆ **by ~** mit dem Bus; *see* **miss**[1].
(b) (*inf: car, plane*) Kiste *f* (*inf*).
2 *vi* (*inf*) mit dem Bus fahren.
3 *vt* (*esp US*) mit dem Bus befördern *or* fahren.

bus[2] *n* (*Elec: also* **~bar**) Sammelschiene, Stromschiene *f*; (*Comput*) (Daten)bus *m*.

busboy ['bʌsbɔɪ] *n* (*US*) Bedienungshilfe *f*.

busby ['bʌzbɪ] *n* hohe Pelzmütze.

bus: ~ conductor *n* (Omni)busschaffner *m*; **~ conductress** *n* (Omni)busschaffnerin *f*; **~ depot** *n* (Omni)busdepot *nt*; **~ driver** *n* (Omni)busfahrer(in *f*) *m*; **~ garage** *n* (Omni)bushalle *f*.

bush[1] [bʊʃ] *n* **(a)** (*shrub*) Busch, Strauch *m*; (*thicket: also* **~es**) Gebüsch *nt* ◆ **to beat about the ~** (*fig*) um den heißen Brei herumreden; (*not act, take decision etc*) wie die Katze um den heißen Brei herumschleichen. **(b)** (*in Africa, Australia*) Busch *m*; (*Austral: the country*) freies *or* offenes Land. **(c)** (*fig*) **~ of hair** Haarschopf *m*; **~ of a beard** buschiger Bart.

◆**bush out** *vi* (*hair, tail*) buschig sein.

bush[2] *n* (*Tech*) Buchse *f*.

bushbaby ['bʊʃ,beɪbɪ] *n* Buschbaby *nt*.

bushed [bʊʃt] *adj* (*sl: exhausted*) groggy (*sl*).

bushel ['bʊʃl] *n* Scheffel *m* ◆ **to hide one's light under a ~** (*prov*) sein Licht unter den Scheffel stellen (*prov*).

bush fire *n* Buschfeuer *nt*.

bushiness ['bʊʃɪnɪs] *n* Buschigkeit *f*.

bushing ['bʊʃɪŋ] *n* (*US*) *see* **bush**[2].

bush: ~ league *n* (*US*) Provinzliga *f*; **~ leaguer** *n* (*US*) Provinzspieler *m*; (*fig*) Dilettant *m*; **~man** *n* (*Austral*) *jd, der im Busch lebt und arbeitet*; **B~man** *n* (*in S Africa*) Buschmann *m*; **~ranger** *n* **(a)** (*Austral*) Bandit, Strauchdieb (*dated*) *m*; **(b)** (*US, Canada*) *jd, der in der Wildnis lebt*; **~ telegraph** *n* (*lit*) Urwaldtelefon *nt*; **I heard it on the ~ telegraph** (*fig inf*) ich habe da so was läuten gehört (*inf*), das ist mir zu Ohren gekommen; **~whack** 1 *vi* in den Wäldern hausen; 2 *vt* (*ambush*) (aus dem Hinterhalt) überfallen; **~whacker** *n* (*frontiersman*) *jd, der in den Wäldern haust*; (*bandit*) Bandit *m*; (*guerilla*) Guerilla(kämpfer) *m*.

bushy ['bʊʃɪ] *adj* (+*er*) buschig.

busily ['bɪzɪlɪ] *adv* (*actively, eagerly*) eifrig.

business ['bɪznɪs] *n* **(a)** *no pl* (*commerce*) Geschäft *nt*; (*line of ~*) Branche *f* ◆ **to be in ~** Geschäftsmann sein; **I am in ~ with him** ich habe geschäftlich mit ihm zu tun; **to go into ~** Geschäftsmann werden; **to go into ~ with sb** mit jdm ein Geschäft gründen; **to be in the plastics/insurance ~** mit Plastik/Versicherungen zu tun haben, in der Plastikbranche/im Versicherungsgewerbe sein; **to set up in ~** ein Geschäft gründen; **to set up in ~ as a butcher/lawyer** *etc* sich als Fleischer/Rechtsanwalt *etc* niederlassen; **to go out of ~** zumachen; **to do ~ with sb** Geschäfte *pl* mit jdm machen; **~ is ~** Geschäft ist Geschäft; **how's ~?** wie gehen die Geschäfte?; **to look for ~** sich

nach Aufträgen umsehen; **I must be about my ~** *(form)* ich muß (jetzt) meinen Geschäften nachgehen; **to go to Paris on ~** geschäftlich nach Paris fahren; **he is here/away on ~** er ist geschäftlich hier/unterwegs; **to know one's ~** seine Sache verstehen; **to get down to ~** zur Sache kommen; **to combine ~ with pleasure** das Angenehme mit dem Nützlichen verbinden; **you shouldn't mix ~ with pleasure** Dienst ist Dienst und Schnaps ist Schnaps *(prov)*; **looking for ~?** *(asked by prostitute)* na, Süßer, wie wär's?
(b) *(fig inf)* **now we're in ~** jetzt kann's losgehen *(inf)*; **to mean ~** es ernst meinen.
(c) *(commercial enterprise)* Geschäft *nt*, Betrieb *m*.
(d) *(concern)* Sache, Angelegenheit *f*; *(task, duty also)* Aufgabe *f* ◆ **that's my ~ and none of yours** das ist meine Sache *or* Angelegenheit, das geht dich gar nichts an *(inf)*; **that's no ~ of mine/yours, that's none of my/your ~** das geht mich/dich nichts an; **to make it one's ~ to do sth** es sich *(dat)* zur Aufgabe machen, etw zu tun; **you should make it your ~ to see that all the products ...** Sie sollten sich darum kümmern, daß alle Produkte ...; **you've no ~ doing that** du hast kein Recht, das zu tun; **to send sb about his ~** jdn in seine Schranken weisen; *see* **mind**.
(e) *(difficult job)* Problem *nt*.
(f) *(inf: affair)* Sache *f* ◆ **I am tired of this protest ~** ich hab' genug von dieser Protestiererei *(inf)*; *see* **funny**.
(g) *(Theat)* dargestellte Handlung.
(h) *(inf: defecation: of dog, child)* Geschäft *nt (inf)* ◆ **to do one's ~** sein Geschäft machen *or* verrichten *(inf)*.

business: ~ address *n* Geschäftsadresse *f*; **~ card** *n* (Visiten)karte *f*; **~ centre** *n* Geschäftszentrum *nt*; **~ class** *n* Business Class *f*, Business-Klasse *f*; **~ college** *n* Wirtschaftshochschule *f*; **~ development loan** *n* Investitionskredit *m*; **~ end** *n (inf) (of knife, chisel etc)* scharfes Ende; *(of rifle etc)* Lauf *m*; **~ expenses** *npl* Spesen *pl*; **~ hours** *npl* Geschäftsstunden *pl*, Geschäftszeit *f*.

businesslike ['bɪznɪslaɪk] *adj person, firm (good at doing business)* geschäftstüchtig; *person, manner* geschäftsmäßig; *manner, transaction* geschäftlich; *(efficient) person, prose* kühl und sachlich, nüchtern.

business: ~man *n* Geschäftsmann *m*; **~ management** *n* Betriebswirtschaft(slehre) *f*; **~ park** *n* Industriegelände *nt*; **~ plan** *n* Geschäftsplan *m*; **~ proposition** *n (proposal)* Geschäftsangebot *nt*; *(idea)* Geschäftsvorhaben *nt*; **~ school** *n* Wirtschaftsschule *f*; **~ sense** *n* Geschäftssinn *m*; **~ studies** *npl* Wirtschaftslehre *f*; **~ suit** *n* Straßenanzug *m*; **~ trip** *n* Geschäftsreise *f*; **~woman** *n* Geschäftsfrau *f*.

busing *n see* **bussing**.

busk [bʌsk] *vi als Straßenmusikant vor Kinos, Theatern etc spielen.*

busker ['bʌskəʳ] *n* Straßenmusikant *m*.

bus: ~ lane *n (Brit)* Busspur *f*; **~load** *n* **a ~load of children** eine Busladung Kinder; **by the ~load** *(inf)*, **in ~loads** *(inf)* busweise *(inf)*; **~man** *n*: **a ~man's holiday** *(fig)* praktisch eine Fortsetzung der Arbeit im Urlaub; **~ route** *n* Buslinie *f*; **we're not on a ~ route** wir haben keine Busverbindungen; **~ service** *n* Busverbindung *f*; *(network)* Busverbindungen *pl*; **~ shelter** *n* Wartehäuschen *nt*.

bussing ['bʌsɪŋ] *n (esp US) Busbeförderung f von Schulkindern in andere Bezirke, um Rassentrennung zu verhindern.*

bus: ~ station *n* Busbahnhof *m*; **~ stop** *n* Bushaltestelle *f*.

bust¹ [bʌst] *n* Büste *f*; *(Anat also)* Busen *m* ◆ **~ measurement** Brustumfang *m*, Oberweite *f*.

bust² *(vb: pret, ptp ~) (inf)* [1] *adj* **(a)** *(broken)* kaputt *(inf)*.
(b) *(bankrupt)* pleite *(inf)*.
[2] *adv (bankrupt)* **to go ~** pleite gehen *or* machen *(inf)*.
[3] *n (US: failure)* Pleite *f (inf)*.
[4] *vt* **(a)** *(break)* kaputtmachen *(inf)* ◆ **the case ~ its sides** der Koffer ist an den Seiten kaputtgegangen *(inf)*; **they ~ed their way in** sie haben die Tür/das Fenster eingeschlagen; *(to a meeting)* sie haben sich hineingedrängt; **to ~ sth open** etw aufbrechen; **to ~ a gut** *(sl) or* **one's arse** *(vulg)* sich kaputtmachen *(inf)*; **he just about ~ a gut** *(sl) or* **his arse** *(vulg)* **doing it** er hat sich *(dat)* dabei fast einen abgebrochen *(sl)*.
(b) *(US: catch, convict)* hinter Schloß und Riegel bringen; *drugs, ring, syndicate* auffliegen lassen *(inf)*.
(c) *(US Mil: demote)* degradieren *(to* zu).
[5] *vi (break)* kaputtgehen *(inf)*.

◆**bust out** *(inf)* [1] *vi* ausbrechen.
[2] *vt sep* herausholen *(inf)*.

◆**bust up** *vt sep (inf) box, marriage* kaputtmachen *(inf)*; *meeting* auffliegen lassen *(inf)*; *(by starting fights)* stören ◆ **I hate to ~ ~ the party** tut mir leid, daß ich die traute Runde stören muß.

bustard ['bʌstəd] *n* Trappe *f*.

buster ['bʌstəʳ] *n (esp US inf: as address)* Meister *m (inf)*; *(threatening)* Freundchen *nt (inf)*.

bus ticket *n* Busfahrschein *m*.

bustle¹ ['bʌsl] [1] *n* Betrieb *m (of* in *+dat)*; *(of fair, streets also)* geschäftiges *or* reges Treiben *(of* auf *or* in *+dat)*.
[2] *vi* **to ~ about** geschäftig hin und her eilen *or* sausen *(inf)*; **to ~ in/out** geschäftig hinein-/herein-/hinaus-/herauseilen *or* -sausen *(inf)*; **the marketplace was bustling with activity** auf dem Markt herrschte großer Betrieb *or* ein reges Treiben.

bustle² *n (Fashion)* Turnüre *f*.

bustling ['bʌslɪŋ] *adj person* geschäftig; *place, scene* belebt, voller Leben.

bust-up ['bʌstʌp] *n (inf)* Krach *m (inf)* ◆ **they had a ~** sie haben Krach gehabt *(inf)*; *(split up)* sie haben sich verkracht *(inf)*.

busty ['bʌstɪ] *adj (+er) (inf) woman* vollbusig.

busway ['bʌsweɪ] *n (US)* Busspur *f*.

▼ **busy** ['bɪzɪ] [1] *adj (+er)* **(a)** *(occupied) person* beschäftigt ◆ **a very ~ man** ein vielbeschäftigter Mann; **are you ~?** haben Sie gerade Zeit?; *(in business)* haben Sie viel zu tun?; **not now, I'm ~** jetzt nicht, ich bin gerade beschäftigt; **the boss is always ~** der Chef hat immer viel zu tun; *(never available)* der Chef hat nie Zeit; **I'll come back when you're less ~** ich komme wieder, wenn Sie mehr Zeit haben; **to keep sb/oneself ~** jdn/sich selbst beschäftigen; **I was ~ studying when you called/all evening** ich war gerade beim Lernen, als Sie kamen/ich war den ganzen Abend mit Lernen beschäftigt; **she's always too ~ thinking about herself** sie ist immer zu sehr mit sich selbst beschäftigt; **they were ~ plotting against him** sie haben eifrig Pläne gegen ihn geschmiedet; **let's get ~** an die Arbeit!
(b) *(active) life, time* bewegt; *place, street, town* belebt; *(with traffic)* verkehrsreich; *street (with traffic)* stark befahren ◆ **it's been a ~ day/week** heute/diese Woche war viel los; **have you had a ~ day, dear?** hast du heute viel zu tun gehabt?; **he leads a very ~ life** bei ihm ist immer etwas los; **the shop was ~ all day** im Geschäft war den ganzen Tag viel los.
▼ **(c)** *(esp US) telephone line* besetzt ◆ **~ signal** Besetztzeichen *nt*.
(d) *(officious) person, manner* (über)eifrig.
(e) *pattern, design, print* unruhig.
[2] *vr* **to ~ oneself doing sth** sich damit beschäftigen, etw zu tun; **to ~ oneself with sth** sich mit etw beschäftigen.

busybody ['bɪzɪ'bɒdɪ] *n* Wichtigtuer, Gschaftlhuber *(S Ger) m* ◆ **don't be such a ~** misch dich nicht überall ein.

but [bʌt] [1] *conj* **(a)** aber ◆ **~ you must know that ...** Sie müssen aber wissen, daß ..., aber Sie müssen wissen, daß ...; **~ he didn't know that** aber er hat das nicht gewußt, er hat das aber nicht gewußt; **~ *he* didn't know that** er aber hat das nicht gewußt; **they all went ~ I didn't** sie sind alle gegangen, nur ich nicht.
(b) **not X ~ Y** nicht X sondern Y.
(c) *(subordinating)* ohne daß ◆ **never a week passes ~ she is ill** keine Woche vergeht, ohne daß sie krank ist; **I would have helped ~ that I was ill** *(old, liter)* ich hätte geholfen, wäre ich nicht krank gewesen *(old)*.
(d) **~ then he couldn't have known that** aber er hat das ja gar nicht wissen können; **~ then you must be my brother!** dann müssen Sie ja mein Bruder sein!; **~ then do you mean to say ...** wollen Sie dann etwa sagen ...; **~ then it is well paid** aber dafür wird es gut bezahlt.
[2] *adv* **she's ~ a child** sie ist doch noch ein Kind; **I cannot (help) ~ think that ...** ich kann nicht umhin, zu denken, daß ...; **one cannot ~ admire him/suspect that ...** man kann ihn nur bewundern/nur annehmen, daß ...; **you can ~ try** du kannst es immerhin versuchen; **I had no alternative ~ to leave** mir blieb keine andere Wahl, als zu gehen; **she left ~ a few minutes ago** sie ist erst vor ein paar Minuten gegangen.
[3] *prep* **no one ~ me could do it** niemand außer mir *or* nur ich konnte es tun; **who ~ Fred would ...?** wer außer Fred würde ...?; **anything ~ that!** (alles,) nur das nicht!; **it was anything ~ simple** das war alles andere als einfach; **he/it was nothing ~ trouble** er/das hat nichts als *or* nur Schwierigkeiten gemacht; **the last house ~ one/two/three** das vorletzte/vorvorletzte/drittletzte Haus; **the first ~ one** der/die/das zweite; **the next street ~ one/two/three** die übernächste/überübernächste Straße/vier Straßen weiter; **~ for you I would be dead** ohne Sie wäre ich tot, wenn Sie nicht gewesen wären, wäre ich tot.
[4] *n* **no ~s about it** kein Aber *nt*.

but and ben *n (Scot) Hütte f bestehend aus Küche und kleiner Schlafkammer.*

butane ['bjuːteɪn] *n* Butan *nt*.

butch [bʊtʃ] *adj (inf) clothes, hairstyle, manner* maskulin.

butcher ['bʊtʃəʳ] [1] *n* **(a)** Fleischer, Metzger *(dial)*, Schlachter *(N Ger) m* ◆ **~'s (shop)** Fleischerei, Metzgerei *(dial)*, Schlachterei *(N Ger) f*; **at the ~'s** beim Fleischer *etc*; **~'s boy** Fleischerjunge *etc m*; **~'s wife** Fleischersfrau *etc f*.
(b) *(fig: murderer)* Schlächter *m*.
(c) **~s** *(Brit sl: look)* **give us a ~s** laß mal gucken *(inf)*; **take** *or* **have a ~s (at that)** guck mal (das an) *(inf)*; **do you want a ~s?** willste mal gucken? *(inf)*.
[2] *vt animals* schlachten; *people* abschlachten, niedermetzeln; *(fig) play, piece of music, language* vergewaltigen ◆ **his ~ed body** seine schrecklich zugerichtete Leiche.

butchery ['bʊtʃərɪ] *n (slaughter)* Gemetzel *nt*, Metzelei *f* ◆ **the ~ of millions** das Abschlachten *or* Niedermetzeln von Millionen; **stop the fight, this is ~!** brechen Sie den Kampf ab, das ist ja das reinste Gemetzel!

butler ['bʌtləʳ] *n* Butler *m*.

butt¹ [bʌt] *n (for wine)* großes Faß; *(for rainwater)* Tonne *f*.

butt² *n (also ~ end)* dickes Ende; *(of rifle)* (Gewehr)kolben *m*; *(of cigar, cigarette)* Stummel *m* ◆ **the ~ end of the conversation** der letzte Rest der Unterhaltung.

butt³ *n (US sl: cigarette)* Kippe *f (inf)*.

butt⁴ *n* **(a)** *(target)* Schießscheibe *f*.
(b) *usu pl (on shooting range) (behind targets)* Kugelfang *m*; *(in front of targets)* Schutzwall *m*; *(range itself)* Schießstand *m*.
(c) *(fig: person)* Zielscheibe *f* ◆ **she's always the ~ of his jokes** sie ist immer (die) Zielscheibe seines Spottes.

butt⁵ [1] *n* (Kopf)stoß *m* ◆ **to give sb a ~** *see vt*.
[2] *vt* mit dem Kopf stoßen; *(goat also)* mit den Hörnern stoßen.

◆**butt at** *vi +prep obj (goat)* stoßen gegen.

◆**butt in** *vi* sich einmischen *(on* in *+acc)*, dazwischenfunken *or* -platzen *(inf)*

➤ LANGUAGE IN USE: **busy: 1c → 27.3**

(*on* bei).

◆**butt into** *vi +prep obj* sich einmischen in (+*acc*), dazwischenfunken *or* dazwischenplatzen bei (*inf*).

butt[6] *n* (*US sl: backside*) Arsch *m* (*sl*) ◆ **get up off your ~** setz mal deinen Arsch in Bewegung (*sl*).

butter ['bʌtə^r] [1] *n* Butter *f* ◆ **she looks as if ~ wouldn't melt in her mouth** sie sieht aus, als ob sie kein Wässerchen trüben könnte.
[2] *vt bread etc* mit Butter bestreichen, buttern.

◆**butter up** *vt sep* (*inf*) schöntun (+*dat*), um den Bart gehen (+*dat*) (*inf*).

butter: ~ball *n* (*US inf: fat person*) Fettkloß *m* (*inf*); **~ bean** *n* Mondbohne *f*; **~cup** *n* Butterblume *f*, Hahnenfuß *m*; **~dish** *n* Butterdose *f*; **~-fingers** *n sing* (*inf*) Schussel *m* (*inf*); **~-fingers!** du Schussel! (*inf*).

butterfly ['bʌtəflaɪ] *n* **(a)** Schmetterling *m* ◆ **I've got/I get butterflies (in my stomach)** mir ist/wird ganz flau im Magen (*inf*), mir ist/wird ganz mulmig zumute (*inf*).
(b) (*Swimming*) Schmetterlingsstil, Butterfly *m* ◆ **can you do the ~?** können Sie Butterfly *or* den Schmetterlingsstil?

butterfly: ~ kiss *n* Schmetterlingskuß *m*; **~ net** *n* Schmetterlingsnetz *nt*; **~ nut** *n* Flügelmutter *f*; **~ stroke** *n* Schmetterlingsstil, Butterfly *m*.

butter: ~ icing *n* ≃ Buttercreme *f*; **~ knife** *n* Buttermesser *nt*; **~milk** *n* Buttermilch *f*; **~scotch** [1] *n* ≃ Karamelbonbon *m*; [2] *adj* Karamel-.

buttery ['bʌtərɪ] *n* Vorratskammer *f*; (*Univ*) Cafeteria *f*.

buttock ['bʌtək] *n* (Hinter)backe, Gesäßhälfte (*form*) *f* ◆ **~s** *pl* Gesäß *nt*, Hintern *m* (*inf*).

button ['bʌtn] [1] *n* **(a)** Knopf *m* ◆ **not worth a ~** (*inf*) keinen Pfifferling wert (*inf*); **his answer was/he arrived right on the ~** (*inf*) seine Antwort hat voll ins Schwarze getroffen (*inf*)/er kam auf den Glockenschlag (*inf*). **(b)** (*mushroom*) junger Champignon. **(c) ~s** *sing* (*inf: pageboy*) (Hotel)page *m*.
[2] *vt garment* zuknöpfen ◆ **~ your lip** (*inf*) halt den Mund (*inf*).
[3] *vi* (*garment*) geknöpft werden.

◆**button up** *vt sep* zuknöpfen ◆ **to have a deal all ~ed ~** ein Geschäft unter Dach und Fach haben.

button: ~-down *adj collar* mit angeknöpften Enden; **~hole** [1] *n* **(a)** (*in garment*) Knopfloch *nt*; **~hole stitch** Knopflochstich *m*; **(b)** (*flower*) Blume *f* im Knopfloch; **to sell ~holes** Blumen fürs Knopfloch verkaufen; [2] *vt* (*fig*) zu fassen bekommen, sich (*dat*) schnappen (*inf*); **~hook** *n* (*for boots*) Stiefelknöpfer *m*; **~ mushroom** *n* junger Champignon.

buttress ['bʌtrɪs] [1] *n* (*Archit*) Strebepfeiler *m*; (*fig*) Pfeiler *m*.
[2] *vt* (*Archit*) *wall* (durch Strebepfeiler) stützen; (*fig*) stützen.

butty ['bʊtɪ] *n* (*N Engl inf*) Stulle *f* (*dial*).

buxom ['bʌksəm] *adj* drall.

buy [baɪ] (*vb: pret, ptp* **bought**) [1] *vt* **(a)** kaufen; (*Rail*) *ticket also* lösen ◆ **there are some things that money can't ~** es gibt Dinge, die man nicht kaufen kann; **all that money can ~** alles, was man mit Geld kaufen kann; **to ~ and sell goods** Waren an- und verkaufen.
(b) (*fig*) *victory, fame* sich (*dat*) erkaufen; *time* gewinnen ◆ **the victory was dearly bought** der Sieg war teuer erkauft.
(c) to ~ sth (*inf*) (*accept*) etw akzeptieren; (*believe*) jdm etw abnehmen (*inf*) *or* abkaufen (*inf*) ◆ **I'll ~ that** das ist o.k. (*inf*); (*believe*) ja, das glaube ich.
(d) (*sl: be killed*) **he bought it** den hat's erwischt (*sl*).
[2] *vi* kaufen.
[3] *n* (*inf*) Kauf *m* ◆ **to be a good ~** ein guter Kauf sein; (*clothes also, food*) preiswert sein.

◆**buy back** *vt sep* zurückkaufen.

◆**buy forward** *vt* (*Fin*) auf Termin kaufen.

◆**buy in** [1] *vt sep* (*acquire supply of*) *goods* einkaufen.
[2] *vi +prep obj* **to ~ ~ to a business** sich in ein Geschäft einkaufen.

◆**buy off** *vt sep* (*inf: bribe*) kaufen (*inf*).

◆**buy out** *vt sep* **(a)** *shareholders etc* auszahlen; *firm* aufkaufen. **(b)** (*from army*) los- *or* freikaufen (*of* von).

◆**buy over** *vt sep* kaufen; (*get on one's side*) für sich gewinnen.

◆**buy up** *vt sep* aufkaufen.

buy-back ['baɪˌbæk]: **~ option** *n* Rückkaufoption *f*; **~ price** *n* Rückkaufpreis *m*.

buyer ['baɪə^r] *n* Käufer *m*; (*agent*) Einkäufer *m* ◆ **~'s market** Käufermarkt *m*.

buy-out ['baɪaʊt] *n* Aufkauf *m*.

buzz [bʌz] [1] *vi* **(a)** (*insect*) summen, brummen; (*smaller or agitated insects*) schwirren; (*device*) summen ◆ **did you ~, sir?** haben Sie nach mir verlangt?; **Miss Jones, I've been ~ing for 10 minutes** Fräulein Jones, ich versuche schon seit 10 Minuten, Sie zu erreichen.
(b) my ears are ~ing mir dröhnen die Ohren; **my head is ~ing** mir schwirrt der Kopf; (*from noise*) mir dröhnt der Kopf.
(c) the town is ~ing in der Stadt ist was los (*inf*) *or* herrscht reges Leben; **the city was ~ing with excitement** die Stadt war in heller Aufregung; **the news set the town ~ing** die Nachricht versetzte die Stadt in helle Aufregung.
[2] *vt* **(a)** (*call*) *secretary* (mit dem Summer) rufen. **(b)** (*US inf: telephone*) anrufen. **(c)** (*plane*) *plane, building* dicht vorbeifliegen an (+*dat*) ◆ **we were ~ed** Flugzeuge flogen dicht an uns heran.
[3] *n* **(a)** *see vi* (*a*) Summen, Brummen *nt*; Schwirren *nt*. **(b)** (*of conversation*) Stimmengewirr, Gemurmel *nt* ◆ **~ of approval** beifälliges Gemurmel. **(c)** (*inf: telephone call*) Anruf *m*. **to give sb a ~** jdn anrufen; (*signal*) *secretary etc* jdn (mit dem Summer) rufen.

◆**buzz about** *or* **around** *vi* (*inf*) herumschwirren.

◆**buzz off** *vi* (*Brit inf*) abzischen (*inf*).

buzzard ['bʌzəd] *n* Bussard *m*.

buzz bomb *n* Fernrakete *f*.

buzzer ['bʌzə^r] *n* Summer *m*.

buzz (*inf*): **~ phrase** *n* Modeausdruck *m*; **~ word** *n* Modewort *nt*.

by [baɪ] [1] *prep* **(a)** (*close to*) bei, an (+*dat*); (*with movement*) an (+*acc*); (*next to*) neben (+*dat*); (*with movement*) neben (+*acc*) ◆ **~ the window/fire/river/church** am *or* beim Fenster/Feuer/Fluß/an *or* bei der Kirche; **a holiday ~ the sea** Ferien *pl* an der See; **come and sit ~ me** komm, setz dich neben mich; **she sat ~ me** sie saß neben mir; **to keep sth ~ one** etw bei sich haben.
(b) (*via*) über (+*acc*).
(c) (*past*) **to go/rush** *etc* **~ sb/sth** an jdm/etw vorbeigehen/-eilen *etc*.
(d) (*time: during*) **~ day/night** bei Tag/Nacht.
(e) (*time: not later than*) bis ◆ **can you do it ~ tomorrow?** kannst du es bis morgen machen?; **~ tomorrow I'll be in France** morgen werde ich in Frankreich sein; **~ the time I got there, he had gone** bis ich dorthin kam, war er gegangen; **but ~ that time** *or* **~ then I had understood/it will be too late/he will have forgotten** aber inzwischen hatte ich gemerkt .../aber dann ist es schon zu spät/aber bis dann *or* dahin hat er es schon vergessen; **~ now** inzwischen.
(f) (*indicating amount*) **~ the metre/kilo/hour/month** meter-/kilo-/stunden-/monatsweise; **one ~ one** einer nach dem anderen; **they came in two ~ two** sie kamen paarweise herein; **letters came in ~ the hundred** Hunderte von Briefen kamen.
(g) (*indicating agent, cause*) von ◆ **killed ~ a bullet** durch eine *or* von einer Kugel getötet; **indicated ~ an asterisk** durch Sternchen gekennzeichnet; **a painting ~ Picasso** ein Bild von Picasso; **surrounded ~** umgeben von.
(h) (*indicating method, means, manner: see also nouns*) **~ bus/car/bicycle** mit dem *or* per Bus/Auto/Fahrrad; **~ land and (~) sea** zu Land und zu Wasser; **to pay ~ cheque** mit Scheck bezahlen; **made ~ hand/machine** handgearbeitet/maschinell hergestellt; **~ daylight/moonlight** bei Tag(eslicht)/im Mondschein; **to know sb ~ name/sight** jdn dem Namen nach/vom Sehen her kennen; **to be known ~ the name of ...** unter dem Namen ... bekannt sein; **to lead ~ the hand** an der Hand führen; **to grab sb ~ the collar** jdn am Kragen packen; **he had a daughter ~ his first wife** von seiner ersten Frau hatte er eine Tochter; **~ myself/himself** *etc* allein.
(i) ~ saving hard he managed to ... durch eisernes Sparen *or* dadurch, daß er eisern sparte, gelang es ihm ...; **~ turning this knob** durch Drehen dieses Knopfes, wenn Sie an diesem Knopf drehen; **~ saying that I didn't mean ...** ich habe damit nicht gemeint ...; **animals which move ~ wriggling** Tiere, die sich schlängelnd fortbewegen; **he could walk ~ supporting himself on ...** gestützt auf ... könnte er gehen.
(j) (*according to: see also nouns*) nach ◆ **to judge ~ appearances** nach dem Äußern urteilen; **~ my watch it is nine o'clock** nach meiner Uhr ist es neun; **if you go ~ the rule** wenn du dich an die Regel hältst; **~ the terms of Article I** gemäß *or* nach (den Bestimmungen von) Artikel I; **to call sb/sth ~ his/its proper name** jdn/etw beim richtigen Namen nennen; **if it's OK ~ you/him** *etc* wenn es Ihnen/ihm *etc* recht ist; **it's all right ~ me** von mir aus gern *or* schon.
(k) (*measuring difference*) um ◆ **broader ~ a meter** um einen Meter breiter; **it missed me ~ inches** es verfehlte mich um Zentimeter.
(l) (*Math, Measure*) **to divide/multiply ~** dividieren durch/multiplizieren mit; **a room 20 metres ~ 30** ein Zimmer 20 auf *or* mal 30 Meter.
(m) (*points of compass*) **South ~ South West** Südsüdwest.
(n) (*in oaths*) bei ◆ **I swear ~ Almighty God** ich schwöre beim allmächtigen Gott; **~ heaven, I'll get you for this** das sollst *or* wirst du mir, bei Gott, büßen!
(o) ~ the right! (*Mil*) rechts, links ...!
(p) ~ the way *or* **by(e)** übrigens.
[2] *adv* **(a)** (*near*) *see* **close**[1]. **(b)** (*past*) **to pass/wander/rush** *etc* **~** vorbei- *or* vorüberkommen/-wandern/-eilen *etc*. **(c)** (*in reserve*) **to put** *or* **lay ~** beiseite legen. **(d)** (*phrases*) **~ and ~** irgendwann; (*with past tense*) nach einiger Zeit; **~ and large** im großen und ganzen.

by(e) [baɪ] *n* **(a)** (*Cricket*) *Lauf bei Bällen, die nicht vom Schlagmann geschlagen worden sind*. **(b) bye** (*Sport*) **to get a bye into the second round** spielfrei in die zweite Runde kommen.

bye [baɪ] *interj* (*inf*) tschüs ◆ **~ for now!** bis bald!

bye-bye ['baɪ'baɪ] [1] *interj* (*inf*) Wiedersehen (*inf*) ◆ **that's ~ £200** (da sind) £ 200 futsch! (*inf*).
[2] *n* **to go (to) ~s** (*baby-talk*) in die Heia gehen (*baby-talk*).

by(e)-election [baɪɪ'lekʃən] *n* Nachwahl *f*.

Byelorussia [bjeləˈrʌʃə] *n* Weißrußland *nt*.

Byelorussian [bjeləˈrʌʃən] [1] *adj* weißrussisch.
[2] *n* **(a)** Weißrusse *m*, Weißrussin *f*. **(b)** (*Ling*) Weißrussisch *nt*.

bygone ['baɪgɒn] [1] *adj* längst vergangen.
[2] *n* **to let ~s be ~s** die Vergangenheit ruhen lassen.

by: ~law *n* (*also* **bye-law**) Verordnung *f*; **~-line** *n* **(a)** (*Press*) *Zeile f mit dem Namen des Autors*; **(b)** (*Ftbl*) Seitenlinie *f*, Tor(aus)linie *f*; **~name** *n* Inbegriff *m* (*for* von); **X is a ~name for tractors** X ist *der* Name für Traktoren.

bypass ['baɪpɑːs] [1] *n* (*road*) Umgehungsstraße *f*; (*Tech: pipe etc*) Bypass *m*.
[2] *vt town, village*, (*Med*) umgehen; (*Tech*) *fluid, gas* umleiten; (*fig*) *person* übergehen; *intermediate stage also* überspringen; *difficulties* umgehen.

bypass: ~ operation *n* Bypass-Operation *f*; **~ surgery** *n* Bypass-Chirurgie *f*; **to have ~ surgery** sich einer Bypass-Operation unterziehen.

by: ~play *n* (*Theat*) Nebenhandlung *f*; **~-product** *n* (*lit, fig*) Nebenprodukt *nt*.

byre ['baɪə^r] *n* (Kuh)stall *m*.

by: ~road *n* Neben- *or* Seitenstraße *f*; **~stander** *n* Umstehende(r) *mf*, Zuschauer *m*; **innocent ~stander** unbeteiligter Zuschauer.

byte [baɪt] *n* (*Comput*) Byte *nt*.

by: ~way *n* Seitenweg *m*; *see* **highway**; **~word** *n* **to become a ~word for sth** gleichbedeutend mit etw werden.

Byzantine [baɪ'zæntaɪn] 1 *adj* byzantinisch. 2 *n* Byzantiner(in *f*) *m*.

Byzantium [baɪ'zæntɪəm] *n* Byzanz *nt*.

C, c [siː] C, c *nt* ◆ **C sharp/flat** Cis, cis *nt*/Ces, ces *nt*; *see also* **major, minor, natural.**

C *abbr of* **centigrade** C.

c *abbr of* **(a) cent** c, ct. **(b) circa** ca.

c/a *abbr of* **current account.**

CA *abbr of* **(a) chartered accountant. (b) Central America.**

cab [kæb] *n* **(a)** (*horsedrawn*) Droschke *f*; (*taxi*) Taxi *nt*, Taxe (*inf*), Droschke (*form*) *f* ◆ **~ driver** Taxifahrer(in *f*) *m*; **~ rank, ~ stand** Taxistand, Droschkenplatz (*form*) *m*. **(b)** (*of railway engine, lorry, crane*) Führerhaus *nt*.

cabal [kəˈbæl] *n* **(a)** (*intrigue*) Intrige *f*, Komplott *nt*, Kabale *f* (*old liter*). **(b)** (*group*) Clique, Kamarilla (*geh*) *f*.

cabaret [ˈkæbəreɪ] *n* Varieté *nt*; (*satire*) Kabarett *nt*.

cabbage [ˈkæbɪdʒ] *n* **(a)** Kohl *m*, Kraut *nt* (*esp S Ger*) ◆ **a head of ~** ein Kohlkopf *m*. **(b)** (*inf: person*) geistiger Krüppel (*inf*) ◆ **to become a ~** verblöden (*inf*); (*sick person*) dahinvegetieren.

cabbage: ~ lettuce *n* Kopfsalat *m*; **~ rose** *n* Zentifolie *f*; **~ white (butterfly)** *n* Kohlweißling *m*.

cab(b)alistic [ˌkæbəˈlɪstɪk] *adj* kabbalistisch.

cabby [ˈkæbɪ] *n* (*inf: of taxi*) Taxifahrer *m*; (*of horsedrawn vehicle*) Kutscher *m*.

caber [ˈkeɪbəʳ] *n* (*Scot*) Pfahl, Stamm *m*; *see* **toss.**

cabin [ˈkæbɪn] *n* **(a)** (*hut*) Hütte *f*. **(b)** (*Naut*) Kabine, Kajüte *f*; (*stateroom*) Kabine *f*. **(c)** (*of lorries, buses etc*) Führerhaus *nt*. **(d)** (*Aviat*) (*for passengers*) Passagierraum *m*; (*for pilot*) Cockpit *nt*, (Flug)kanzel *f*.

cabin: ~ boy *n* Schiffsjunge *m*; (*steward*) Kabinensteward *m*; **~ class** *n* zweite Klasse; **~ crew** *n* (*Aviat*) Flugbegleitpersonal *nt*; **~ cruiser** *n* Kajütboot *nt*.

cabinet [ˈkæbɪnɪt] *n* **(a)** Schränkchen *nt*; (*for display*) Vitrine *f*; (*for TV, record-player*) Schrank *m*, Truhe *f*; (*loudspeaker ~*) Box *f*. **(b)** (*Parl*) Kabinett *nt*, Regierungsmannschaft *f* (*inf*).

cabinet: ~maker *n* (Möbel)tischler, (Möbel)schreiner *m*; **~ making** *n* Tischlern *nt*, Tischlerei *f*; **~ meeting** *n* Kabinettssitzung *f*; **~ minister** *n* ≃ Mitglied *nt* des Kabinetts, Minister(in *f*) *m*; **~ reshuffle** *n* Kabinettsumbildung *f*; **~-size** *adj* (*Phot*) im Kabinettformat.

cabin: ~ luggage *n* Kabinengepäck *nt*; **~ trunk** *n* Schrank- *or* Überseekoffer *m*.

cable [ˈkeɪbl] 1 *n* **(a)** Tau *nt*; (*of wire*) Kabel *nt*, Trosse *f* (*Naut*).
(b) (*Elec*) Kabel *nt*, Leitung *f*.
(c) (*~gram*) Telegramm *nt*; (*from abroad*) (Übersee)telegramm, Kabel *nt* ◆ **by ~** per Telegramm/Kabel.
(d) (*~ television*) Kabelfernsehen *nt*.
2 *vt information* telegrafisch durchgeben; (*overseas*) kabeln ◆ **to ~ sb** jdm telegrafieren/kabeln.
3 *vi* telegrafieren, ein Telegramm/Kabel schicken.

cable: ~-car *n* (*hanging*) Drahtseilbahn *f*; (*streetcar*) (gezogene) Straßenbahn; (*funicular*) Standseilbahn *f*; **~gram** *n see* **cable 1 (c)**; **~ laying** *n* Kabelverlegung *f*, Kabellegen *nt*; **~ length** *n* (*Naut*) Kabellänge *f*; **~ railway** *n* Bergbahn *f*; **~ stitch** *n* (*Knitting*) Zopfmuster *nt*; **~ television** *n* Kabelfernsehen *nt*.

cabling [ˈkeɪblɪŋ] *n* (*cables*) Kabel *pl*; (*process*) Verkabelung *f*.

caboodle [kəˈbuːdl] *n* (*inf*): **the whole (kit and) ~** das ganze Zeug(s) (*inf*), der ganze Kram (*inf*).

caboose [kəˈbuːs] *n* **(a)** (*Naut*) Kombüse *f*. **(b)** (*US Rail*) Dienstwagen *m*.

cabriole [ˈkæbrɪəʊl] *n* (*of table etc*) geschwungenes *or* geschweiftes Bein.

cabriolet [ˌkæbrɪəʊˈleɪ] *n* Kabriolett *nt*.

cacao [kəˈkɑːəʊ] *n* (*tree, bean*) Kakao *m*.

cache [kæʃ] 1 *n* **(a)** Versteck *nt*, geheimes (Waffen-/Proviant)lager. **(b)** (*Comput: also* **~ memory**) Zwischenspeicher, Cache-Speicher *m*.
2 *vt* verstecken.

cachet [ˈkæʃeɪ] *n* Gütesiegel, Gütezeichen *nt* ◆ **the name has a certain ~ on the French market** der Name gilt auf dem französischen Markt als Gütezeichen; **it had given me a certain ~ in her parents' eyes** dadurch hatte ich bei ihren Eltern ein gewisses Ansehen.

cachou [ˈkæʃuː] *n* Cachou(bonbon) *m or nt*.

cack-handed [ˈkækˈhændəd] *adj* (*Brit inf*) tolpatschig (*inf*).

cackle [ˈkækl] 1 *n* (*of hens*) Gackern *nt*; (*laughter*) (meckerndes) Lachen; (*inf*) (*chatter*) Geblödel *nt* (*inf*).
2 *vi* (*hens*) gackern; (*inf*) (*talk*) schwatzen; (*laugh*) meckernd lachen.

cacophonous [kæˈkɒfənəs] *adj* mißtönend, kakophon (*geh*).

cacophony [kæˈkɒfənɪ] *n* Kakophonie *f* (*geh*), Mißklang *m*.

cactus [ˈkæktəs] *n* Kaktus *m*.

CAD [kæd] *abbr of* **computer-aided design** CAD.

cad [kæd] *n* (*dated*) Schurke (*old*), Schuft *m*.

cadaver [kəˈdævəʳ] *n* Kadaver *m*; (*of humans*) Leiche *f*.

cadaverous [kəˈdævərəs] *adj* (*corpse-like*) Kadaver-, Leichen-; (*gaunt*) ausgezehrt, ausgemergelt; (*pale*) leichenblaß.

CAD/CAM [ˈkædˈkæm] *abbr of* **computer-aided design/computer-aided manufacture** CAD/CAM.

caddie [ˈkædɪ] 1 *n* (*Golf*) Caddie *m*.
2 *vi* Caddie sein *or* spielen (*inf*).

caddis fly [ˈkædɪsˈflaɪ] *n* Köcherfliege, Frühlingsfliege *f*.

caddish [ˈkædɪʃ] *adj* (*dated*) schurkisch (*old*), niederträchtig.

caddy [ˈkædɪ] *n* **(a)** (*tea ~*) Behälter *m*, Büchse *f*. **(b)** (*US: shopping trolley*) Einkaufswagen *m*. **(c)** *see* **caddie.**

cadence [ˈkeɪdəns] *n* (*Mus*) Kadenz *f*; (*of voice*) Tonfall *m*, Melodie *f*; (*rhythm*) Rhythmus *m*, Melodie *f* ◆ **the ~s of his speech** seine Sprachmelodie.

cadenza [kəˈdenzə] *n* (*Mus*) Kadenz *f*.

cadet [kəˈdet] *n* **(a)** (*Mil etc*) Kadett *m* ◆ **~ corps** Kadettenkorps *nt*; **~ school** Kadettenanstalt *f*. **(b)** (*old*) jüngerer Sohn/Bruder.

cadge [kædʒ] 1 *vt* (er)betteln, abstauben (*inf*), schnorren (*inf*) (*from sb* bei *or* von jdm) ◆ **could I ~ a lift with you?** könnten Sie mich vielleicht (ein Stück) mitnehmen?
2 *vi* schnorren (*inf*).

cadger [ˈkædʒəʳ] *n* Schnorrer (*inf*), Abstauber (*inf*) *m*.

cadmium [ˈkædmɪəm] *n* Kadmium, Cadmium *nt*.

cadre [ˈkædrɪ] *n* (*Mil, fig*) Kader *m*.

caecum, (*US*) **cecum** [ˈsiːkəm] *n* (*Anat*) Blinddarm *m*.

Caesar [ˈsiːzəʳ] *n* Cäsar, Caesar *m*.

Caesarean, Caesarian [siːˈzeərɪən] 1 *adj* cäsarisch, Cäsaren-; (*of Caesar*) Cäsarisch.
2 *n* (*also* **~ section**) (*Med*) Kaiserschnitt *m* ◆ **he was a ~** er wurde mit Kaiserschnitt entbunden; **she had a (baby by) ~** sie hatte einen Kaiserschnitt.

caesium, (*US*) **cesium** [ˈsiːzɪəm] (*Chem*) *n* Cäsium *nt*.

caesura [sɪˈzjʊərə] *n* Zäsur *f*.

café [ˈkæfeɪ] *n* Café *nt*.

cafeteria [ˌkæfɪˈtɪərɪə] *n* Cafeteria *f*.

caff [kæf] *n* (*Brit sl*) Café *nt*.

caffein(e) [ˈkæfiːn] *n* Koffein *nt*.

caftan [ˈkæftæn] *n* Kaftan *m*.

cage [keɪdʒ] 1 *n* **(a)** Käfig *m*; (*small bird~*) Bauer *nt or m* ◆ **~ bird** Käfigvogel *m*. **(b)** (*of lift*) Aufzug *m*; (*Min*) Förderkorb *m*.
2 *vt* (*also* **~ up**) in einen Käfig sperren, einsperren.

cagey [ˈkeɪdʒɪ] *adj* (*inf*) vorsichtig; *behaviour, answer also* zugeknöpft (*inf*); (*evasive*) ausweichend ◆ **what are you being so ~ about?** warum tust du so geheimnisvoll?; **she was very ~ about her age** sie hat aus ihrem Alter ein großes Geheimnis gemacht; **he was very ~ about his plans** er hat mit seinen Absichten hinterm Berg gehalten.

cagily [ˈkeɪdʒɪlɪ] *adv see* **cagey.**

caginess [ˈkeɪdʒɪnɪs] *n* (*inf*) Vorsicht, Zugeknöpftheit (*inf*) *f*; (*evasiveness*) ausweichende Art.

cagoule [kəˈguːl] *n* Windhemd *nt*.

cahoots [kəˈhuːts] *n* (*inf*): **to be in ~ with sb** mit jdm unter einer Decke stecken.

caiman [ˈkeɪmən] *n* Kaiman *m*.

Cain [keɪn] *n* Kain *m* ◆ **to raise ~** (*inf*) (*be noisy*) Radau machen (*inf*), lärmen; (*protest*) Krach schlagen (*inf*).

cairn [kɛən] *n* **(a)** Steinpyramide *f*, Steinhügel *m*. **(b)** (*also* **~ terrier**) Cairn-Terrier *m*.

Cairo [ˈkaɪərəʊ] *n* Kairo *nt*.

caisson [ˈkeɪsən] *n* **(a)** (*Mil*) Munitionskiste *f*; (*wagon*) Munitionswagen *m*. **(b)** (*Tech: underwater ~*) Senkkasten, Caisson *m*.

cajole [kəˈdʒəʊl] *vt* gut zureden (+*dat*), beschwatzen (*inf*) ◆ **to ~ sb into doing sth** jdn dazu bringen *or* jdn beschwatzen (*inf*), etw zu tun; **to ~ sb out of**

doing sth jdm etw ausreden; **he would not be ~d** er ließ sich nicht beschwatzen (*inf*).

cajolery [kəˈdʒəʊlərɪ] *n* Überredung *f*, Beschwatzen *nt* (*inf*).

cake [keɪk] [1] *n* **(a)** Kuchen *m*; (*gateau*) Torte *f*; (*bun, individual ~*) Gebäckstück, Teilchen (*dial*) *nt* ◆ **~s and pastries** Gebäck *nt*; **a piece of ~** (*fig inf*) ein Kinderspiel *nt*, ein Klacks *m* (*inf*); **he/that takes the ~** (*inf*) das ist das Schärfste (*sl*); (*negatively also*) das schlägt dem Faß den Boden aus; **to sell like hot ~s** weggehen wie warme Semmeln (*inf*); **you can't have your ~ and eat it** (*prov*) beides auf einmal geht nicht; **he wants to have his ~ and eat it** (*prov*) er will das eine, ohne das andere zu lassen.
(b) (*of soap*) Stück *nt*, Riegel *m*; (*of chocolate*) Tafel *f*.
[2] *vt* dick einschmieren ◆ **my shoes are ~d with mud** meine Schuhe sind völlig verdreckt *or* dreckverkrustet.
[3] *vi* festtrocknen, eine Kruste bilden.

cake: ~ mix *n* Teigmischung *f*; **~ mixture** *n* Kuchenteig *m*; **~ shop** *n* Konditorei *f*; **~ tin** *n* (*for baking*) Kuchenform *f*; (*for storage*) Kuchenbüchse *f*.

calabash [ˈkæləbæʃ] *n* Kalebasse *f* ◆ **~ tree** Kalebassenbaum *m*.

calamine [ˈkæləmaɪn] *n* Galmei *m* ◆ **~ lotion** Galmeilotion *f*.

calamitous [kəˈlæmɪtəs] *adj* katastrophal.

calamity [kəˈlæmɪtɪ] *n* Katastrophe *f* ◆ **C~ Jane** Pechmarie *f*.

calcification [ˌkælsɪfɪˈkeɪʃən] *n* Kalkablagerung *f*; (*Med*) Verkalkung *f*.

calcify [ˈkælsɪfaɪ] [1] *vt* Kalk *m* ablagern auf/in (*+dat*), verkalken lassen.
[2] *vi* verkalken.

calcium [ˈkælsɪəm] *n* Kalzium, Calcium *nt* ◆ **~ carbonate** Kalziumkarbonat *nt*, kohlensaurer Kalk.

calculable [ˈkælkjʊləbl] *adj* berechenbar, kalkulierbar.

calculate [ˈkælkjʊleɪt] [1] *vt* **(a)** (*mathematically, scientifically*) berechnen; *costs also* ermitteln.
(b) (*fig: estimate critically*) kalkulieren, schätzen.
(c) to be ~d to do sth (*be intended*) auf etw (*acc*) abzielen; (*have the effect*) zu etw angetan sein.
(d) (*US inf: suppose*) schätzen, annehmen, meinen.
[2] *vi* (*Math*) rechnen ◆ **calculating machine** Rechenmaschine *f*.

◆**calculate on** *vi +prep obj* rechnen mit ◆ **I had ~d ~ finishing by this week** ich hatte damit gerechnet, diese Woche fertig zu werden.

calculated [ˈkælkjʊleɪtɪd] *adj* (*deliberate*) berechnet ◆ **~ insult** ein bewußter Affront; **a ~ risk** ein kalkuliertes Risiko.

calculating *adj*, **~ly** *adv* [ˈkælkjʊleɪtɪŋ, -lɪ] berechnend.

calculation [ˌkælkjʊˈleɪʃən] *n* Berechnung, Kalkulation *f*; (*critical estimation*) Schätzung *f* ◆ **to do a quick ~** die Sache schnell überschlagen; **you're out in your ~s** du hast dich verrechnet; **by my ~s he will arrive on Sunday** nach meiner Schätzung müßte er Sonntag ankommen.

calculator [ˈkælkjʊleɪtəʳ] *n* **(a)** (*machine*) Rechner *m*. **(b)** (*person*) Kalkulator, Rechnungsbeamte(r) *m*. **(c)** (*table of figures*) Rechentabelle *f*.

calculus [ˈkælkjʊləs] *n* **(a)** (*Math*) Infinitesimalrechnung, Differential- und Integralrechnung *f*. **(b)** (*Med*) Stein *m*.

Calcutta [kælˈkʌtə] *n* Kalkutta *nt*.

Caledonia [ˌkæləˈdəʊnɪə] *n* Kaledonien *nt*.

Caledonian [ˌkæləˈdəʊnɪən] *adj* kaledonisch.

calefactory [kæləˈfæktərɪ] *adj* (*form*) Wärme-.

calendar [ˈkæləndəʳ] *n* **(a)** Kalender *m* ◆ **~ month** Kalendermonat *m*. **(b)** (*schedule*) Terminkalender *m*; (*Jur*) Prozeßregister *nt* ◆ **~ of events** Veranstaltungskalender *m*; **Church ~** Kirchenkalender *m*, Kalendarium *nt*.

calender [ˈkæləndəʳ] [1] *n* Kalander *m*.
[2] *vt* kalandern.

calf[1] [kɑːf] *n*, *pl* **calves** **(a)** Kalb *nt* ◆ **a cow in** *or* **with ~** eine trächtige Kuh. **(b)** (*young elephant, seal etc*) Junge(s), -junge(s) *nt*. **(c)** (*leather*) Kalb(s)leder *nt*.

calf[2] *n*, *pl* **calves** (*Anat*) Wade *f*.

calf: ~ love *n* (jugendliche) Schwärmerei; **~skin** *n* Kalb(s)leder *nt*.

caliber *n* (*US*) *see* **calibre**.

calibrate [ˈkælɪbreɪt] *vt gun* kalibrieren; *meter, instrument also* eichen.

calibration [ˌkælɪˈbreɪʃən] *n see vt* Kalibrieren *nt*; Eichen *nt*; (*mark*) Kalibrierung *f*, Eichung *f*.

calibre, (*US*) **caliber** [ˈkælɪbəʳ] *n* (*lit*) Kaliber *nt*; (*fig also*) Format *nt* ◆ **a man of his ~** ein Mann seines Kalibers, ein Mann von seinem Format.

calico [ˈkælɪkəʊ] *n* Kattun *m*.

California [kælɪˈfɔːnɪə] *n* (*abbr* **Cal(if)**) Kalifornien *nt*.

Californian [kælɪˈfɔːnɪən] [1] *adj* kalifornisch.
[2] *n* Kalifornier(in *f*) *m*.

calipers [ˈkælɪpəz] *npl* (*US*) *see* **callipers**.

caliph [ˈkeɪlɪf] *n* Kalif *m*.

calisthenics [ˌkælɪsˈθenɪks] *n* (*US*) *see* **callisthenics**.

calk[1] [kɔːk] [1] *vt* mit Stollen versehen; *shoe also* mit Nägeln beschlagen.
[2] *n* Stollen *m*; (*on shoe also*) Nagel *m*.

calk[2] *vt drawing, design* durchpausen.

calk[3] *vt see* **caulk**.

▼ **call** [kɔːl] [1] *n* **(a)** (*shout, cry*) (*of person, bird etc*) Ruf *m*; (*of bugle*) Signal *nt* ◆ **to give sb a ~** jdn (herbei)rufen; (*inform sb*) jdm Bescheid sagen; (*wake sb*) jdn wecken; **they came at my ~** sie kamen auf meinen Ruf hin, als ich rief, kamen sie; **within ~** in Rufweite *f*; **a ~ for help** (*lit, fig*) ein Hilferuf *m*.
▼ **(b)** (*telephone ~*) Gespräch *nt*, Anruf *m* ◆ **I'll give you a ~** ich rufe Sie an; **to take a ~** ein Gespräch entgegennehmen; **will you take the ~?** nehmen Sie das Gespräch an?
(c) (*fig: summons*) (*for flight, meal*) Aufruf *m*; (*of religion*) Berufung *f*; (*Theat: to actors*) Aufruf *m*; (*fig: lure*) Ruf *m*, Verlockung *f* ◆ **to be on ~** Bereitschaftsdienst haben; **the doctor had a ~ at midnight** der Arzt wurde um Mitternacht zu einem Patienten gerufen; **that's your ~!** (*Theat*) Ihr Auftritt!; **the ~ of conscience/nature** die Stimme des Gewissens/der Natur; **to attend to a ~ of nature** (*euph*) mal kurz verschwinden gehen (*inf*); **the C~** *or* **~ came when he was 17** mit 17 Jahren spürte er die Berufung; **the ~ of duty** der Ruf der Pflicht; **with him the ~ of duty was particularly strong** er hatte ein besonders stark ausgeprägtes Pflichtgefühl; **to make a ~ for unity** zur Einigkeit aufrufen.
(d) (*visit*) Besuch *m* ◆ **to make** *or* **pay a ~ on sb** jdn besuchen, jdm einen Besuch abstatten (*form*); **I have several ~s to make** ich muß noch einige Besuche machen; **port of ~** Anlaufhafen *m*; (*fig*) Station *f*; **to pay a ~** (*euph*) mal verschwinden (*inf*).
(e) (*demand, claim*) Inanspruchnahme, Beanspruchung *f*; (*Comm*) Nachfrage *f* (*for* nach) ◆ **to have many ~s on one's purse/time** finanziell/zeitlich sehr in Anspruch genommen sein; **the sudden rain made for heavy ~s on the emergency services** die plötzlichen Regenfälle bedeuteten eine starke Belastung der Notdienste.
(f) at *or* **on ~** (*Fin*) auf Abruf.
(g) (*need, occasion*) Anlaß, Grund *m*, Veranlassung *f* ◆ **there is no ~ for you to worry** es besteht kein Grund zur Sorge, Sie brauchen sich (*dat*) keine Sorgen zu machen.
(h) (*Cards*) Ansage *f* ◆ **to make a ~ of three diamonds** drei Karo ansagen; **whose ~ is it?** wer sagt an?
(i) (*Tennis*) Entscheidung *f*.
[2] *vt* **(a)** (*shout out*) rufen ◆ **the landlord ~ed time** der Wirt rief „Feierabend"; **to ~ spades** (*Cards*) Pik reizen; **the ball was ~ed out** der Ball wurde für „aus" erklärt; *see* **halt**.
(b) (*name, consider*) nennen ◆ **to be ~ed** heißen; **what's he ~ed?** wie heißt er?; **what do you ~ your cat?** wie nennst du deine Katze?, wie heißt deine Katze?; **what's this ~ed in German?** wie heißt das auf Deutsch?; **let's ~ it a day** machen wir Schluß *or* Feierabend für heute; **~ it £5** sagen wir £ 5.
(c) (*summon*) *person, doctor* rufen; *meeting* einberufen; *elections* ausschreiben; *strike* ausrufen; (*Jur*) *witness* aufrufen; (*subpoena*) vorladen; (*waken*) wecken ◆ **he was ~ed to his maker** (*liter*) er ist in die Ewigkeit abberufen worden; **to ~ sth into being** etw ins Leben rufen; *see* **mind, question, bluff**[2].
▼ **(d)** (*telephone*) anrufen; (*contact by radio*) rufen.
(e) (*Fin*) *bond* aufrufen; *loan* abrufen.
(f) (*US Sport: call off*) abbrechen.
[3] *vi* **(a)** (*shout: person, animal*) rufen ◆ **to ~ for help** um Hilfe rufen; **to ~ to sb** jdm zurufen.
(b) (*visit*) vorbeigehen/-kommen ◆ **she ~ed to see her mother** sie machte einen Besuch bei ihrer Mutter; **the gasman ~ed about the meter** der Gasmann war wegen des Zählers da.
(c) (*Telec*) anrufen; (*by radio*) rufen ◆ **who's ~ing, please?** wer spricht da bitte?; **London ~ing!** (*Rad*) hier ist London; **thanks for ~ing** vielen Dank für den Anruf.

◆**call aside** *vt sep person* beiseite rufen.

◆**call at** *vi +prep obj* (*person*) vorbeigehen bei; (*Rail*) halten in (*+dat*); (*Naut*) anlaufen ◆ **a train for Lisbon ~ing ~ ...** ein Zug nach Lissabon über ...

◆**call away** *vt sep* weg- *or* abrufen ◆ **I was ~ed ~ on business** ich wurde geschäftlich abgerufen; **he was ~ed ~ from the meeting** er wurde aus der Sitzung gerufen.

◆**call back** *vti sep* zurückrufen.

◆**call down** *vt sep* **(a)** (*invoke*) **to ~ ~ curses on sb's head** jdn verfluchen. **(b) to ~ sb ~** (*lit*) jdn herunterrufen; (*US: reprimand*) jdn ausschimpfen, jdn herunterputzen (*inf*).

◆**call for** *vi +prep obj* **(a)** (*send for*) *person* rufen; *food, drink* kommen lassen; (*ask for*) verlangen (nach), fordern.
(b) (*need*) *courage, endurance* verlangen, erfordern ◆ **that ~s ~ a drink/celebration!** darauf muß ich/müssen wir einen trinken!, das muß begossen/gefeiert werden!
(c) (*collect*) *person, goods* abholen; (*come to see*) fragen nach ◆ **"to be ~ed ~"** (*goods sent by rail*) „bahnlagernd"; (*by post*) „postlagernd"; (*in shop*) „wird abgeholt".

◆**call forth** *vt insep protests* hervorrufen; *abilities etc* wachrufen, wecken.

◆**call in** [1] *vt sep* **(a)** *doctor* zu Rate ziehen. **(b)** (*withdraw*) *faulty goods etc* aus dem Verkehr ziehen; *currency also* aufrufen (*form*); *hire-boats* zurück- *or* aufrufen; *books* an- *or* zurückfordern.
[2] *vi* vorbeigehen *or* -schauen (*at, on* bei).

◆**call off** [1] *vt sep* **(a)** (*cancel*) *appointment, holiday* absagen; *deal* rückgängig machen; *strike* absagen, abblasen (*inf*); (*end*) abbrechen; *engagement* lösen ◆ **let's ~ the whole thing ~** blasen wir die ganze Sache ab (*inf*). **(b)** *dog* zurückrufen.
[2] *vi* absagen.

◆**call on** *vi +prep obj* **(a)** (*visit*) besuchen. **(b)** *see* **call upon**.

◆**call out** [1] *vi* rufen, schreien.
[2] *vt sep* **(a)** *names* aufrufen; (*announce*) ansagen. **(b)** *doctor* rufen; *troops, fire brigade* alarmieren. **(c)** (*order to strike*) zum Streik aufrufen.

◆**call out for** *vi +prep obj food* verlangen; *help* rufen um.

◆**call round** *vi* (*inf*) vorbeikommen.

◆**call up** [1] *vt sep* **(a)** (*Mil*) *reservist* einberufen; *reinforcements* mobilisieren ◆ **~ed ~ to go to Vietnam** nach Vietnam einberufen. **(b)** (*Telec*) anrufen. **(c)** (*fig*) (herauf)beschwören; *images, thoughts also* erwecken; *memories also*

➤ LANGUAGE IN USE: **call: 1b** → 27.1, 27.2, 27.3, 27.5 **2d** → 27.3, 27.4, 27.5, 27.7 **call back** → 27.4, 27.6

wachrufen ◆ **to ~ ~ the Devil** den Teufel beschwören.
[2] *vi (Telec)* anrufen.
◆**call upon** *vi +prep obj* **(a)** *(ask)* **to ~ ~ sb to do sth** jdn bitten *or* auffordern, etw zu tun; **I now ~ ~ the vicar to say a few words** ich möchte nun den Herrn Pfarrer um ein paar Worte bitten. **(b)** *(invoke)* **to ~ ~ sb's generosity** an jds Großzügigkeit *(acc)* appellieren; **to ~ ~ God** Gott anrufen.
callable ['kɔːləbl] *adj (Fin) money* abrufbar; *security* kündbar.
call: ~back *n (Comm: action)* Rückrufaktion *f*; **there were 1,000 ~backs** 1.000 wurden zurückbeordert; **~box** *n* Telefonzelle *f*, öffentlicher Fernsprecher; **~boy** *n (Theat)* Inspizientengehilfe *m (der die Schauspieler zu ihrem Auftritt ruft)*.
▼ **caller** ['kɔːləʳ] *n* **(a)** *(visitor)* Besuch(er) *m*. **(b)** *(Telec)* Anrufer *m* ◆ **hold the line please ~!** bitte bleiben Sie am Apparat!
call forwarding *n (Telec)* Anrufweiterschaltung *f*.
callgirl ['kɔːlgɜːl] *n* Callgirl *nt*.
calligraphic [ˌkælɪ'græfɪk] *adj* kalligraphisch, Schönschreib-.
calligraphy [kə'lɪgrəfɪ] *n* Kalligraphie *f*.
calling ['kɔːlɪŋ] *n* Berufung *f* ◆ **~ card** Visitenkarte *f*; **to leave one's ~ card** *(euph: cats or dogs)* seine Visitenkarte hinterlassen *(hum)*.
calliper *or (US)* **caliper brake** ['kælɪpəˌbreɪk] *n* Felgenbremse *f*.
callipers, *(US)* **calipers** ['kælɪpəz] *npl* Tastzirkel *m*.
callisthenics, *(US)* **calisthenics** [ˌkælɪs'θenɪks] *n sing or pl* Gymnastik *f*, Fitneß-Übungen *pl*, Kallisthenie *f (dated)*.
call money *n (Fin)* Tagesgeld *nt*, tägliches Geld.
callous ['kæləs] *adj* **(a)** *(cruel)* gefühllos, herzlos. **(b)** *(Med)* schwielig, kallös.
callously ['kæləslɪ] *adv* herzlos.
callousness ['kæləsnɪs] *n* Gefühllosigkeit, Herzlosigkeit *f*.
callow ['kæləʊ] *adj* unreif; *(ideas etc)* unausgegoren ◆ **a ~ youth** ein grüner Junge *(inf)*.
call: ~ sign *n (Rad)* Sendezeichen *nt*; **~-up** *n* Einberufung *f*; **~-up papers** *npl* Einberufungsbescheid *m*.
callus ['kæləs] *n (Med)* Schwiele *f*; *(of bone)* Kallus *m*, Knochenschwiele *f*; *(Bot)* Wundholz *nt*, Kallus *m*.
calm [kɑːm] [1] *adj (+er)* ruhig; *weather also* windstill ◆ **keep ~!** bleib ruhig!; **the weather grew ~ again after the storm** nach dem Sturm beruhigte sich das Wetter wieder.
[2] *n* **(a)** Ruhe, Stille *f*; *(at sea)* Flaute *f*; *(of wind)* Windstille *f* ◆ **a dead ~** absolute Stille, Totenstille *f*; **there was ~ after the hurricane** nach dem Orkan trat Stille ein *or* herrschte Stille; **the ~ before the storm** *(lit, fig)* die Ruhe vor dem Sturm.
(b) *(composure)* Ruhe, Gelassenheit *f*.
[3] *vt* beruhigen.
◆**calm down** [1] *vt sep* beruhigen, beschwichtigen.
[2] *vi* sich beruhigen; *(wind)* abflauen ◆ **~ ~!** beruhigen Sie sich!
calming ['kɑːmɪŋ] *adj* beruhigend.
calmly ['kɑːmlɪ] *adv speak, act* ruhig, gelassen ◆ **he spoke ~** er redete mit ruhiger Stimme; **she ~ told me that she'd crashed the car** sie erzählte mir seelenruhig, daß sie das Auto kaputtgefahren hatte.
calmness ['kɑːmnɪs] *n (of person)* Ruhe, Gelassenheit *f*; *(of wind, sea)* Stille *f*.
Calor gas ® ['kæləgæs] *n* Butangas *nt*.
caloric ['kælərɪk] *adj* kalorisch, Wärme-.
calorie ['kælərɪ] *n* Kalorie *f* ◆ **low on ~s** kalorienarm.
calorie *in cpds* Kalorien-, kalorien-; **~-conscious** *adj* kalorienbewußt.
calorific [ˌkælə'rɪfɪk] *adj* wärmeerzeugend ◆ **~ value** Heizwert *m*.
calumniate [kə'lʌmnɪeɪt] *vt (liter)* schmähen *(geh)*, verunglimpfen.
calumny ['kæləmnɪ] *n (liter)* Schmähung *(geh)*, Verunglimpfung *f*.
Calvary ['kælvərɪ] *n* **(a)** Golgatha *nt*, Kalvarienberg *m*. **(b) c~** Bildstock *m*, Marterl *nt (S Ger, Aus)*.
calve [kɑːv] *vi* kalben.
calves [kɑːvz] *pl of* **calf¹**, **calf²**.
Calvin ['kælvɪn] *n* Calvin *m*.
Calvinism ['kælvɪnɪzəm] *n* Kalvinismus *m*.
Calvinist ['kælvɪnɪst] [1] *n* Kalvinist(in *f*) *m*.
[2] *adj* kalvinistisch.
Calvinistic [ˌkælvɪ'nɪstɪk] *adj* kalvinistisch.
calypso [kə'lɪpsəʊ] *n* Calypso *m*.
calyx ['keɪlɪks] *n, pl* **calyces** ['keɪlɪsiːz] *or* **-es** ['keɪlɪksəz] Blütenkelch *m*.
CAM [kæm] *abbr of* **computer-aided manufacture** CAM.
cam [kæm] *n* Nocken *m*.
camaraderie [ˌkæmə'rɑːdərɪ] *n* Kameradschaft *f*.
camber ['kæmbəʳ] [1] *n (of road, ship, aircraft wing)* Wölbung *f*; *(of road also)* Überhöhung *f*; *(of wheels)* Radsturz *m*.
[2] *vt road, deck* wölben ◆ **a ~ed wheel** ein Rad *nt* mit Sturz.
Cambodia [kæm'bəʊdɪə] *n* Kambodscha *nt*.
Cambodian [kæm'bəʊdɪən] [1] *adj* kambodschanisch.
[2] *n* **(a)** Kambodschaner(in *f*) *m*. **(b)** *(language)* Kambodschanisch *nt*.
cambric ['keɪmbrɪk] *n (Tex)* Kambrik, Cambrai *m*, Kammertuch *nt*.
Cambs [kæmz] *abbr of* **Cambridgeshire**.
camcorder ['kæmkɔːdəʳ] *n* Camcorder, Kamera-Recorder *m*.
came [keɪm] *pret of* **come**.
camel ['kæməl] *n* Kamel *nt*.
camel *in cpds (colour) coat* kamelhaarfarben; **~ driver** *n* Kameltreiber *m*; **~-hair**, *(US)* **~'s-hair** [1] *n* Kamelhaar *nt*; [2] *attr coat, paintbrush* Kamelhaar-.
camellia [kə'miːlɪə] *n* Kamelie *f*.
cameo ['kæmɪəʊ] *n* **(a)** *(jewellery)* Kamee *f*. **(b)** *(Liter)* Miniatur *f*. **(c)** *(also ~ part)* Miniaturrolle *f*.
camera¹ ['kæmərə] *n* Kamera *f*; *(for stills also)* Fotoapparat *m*.
camera² *n (Jur)*: **in ~** unter Ausschluß der Öffentlichkeit; *(fig)* hinter verschlossenen Türen, in geschlossener Gesellschaft.
camera: ~man *n* Kameramann *m*; **~ obscura** ['kæmərəəb'skjʊrə] *n (Opt)* Camera obscura, Lochkamera *f*; **~-ready copy** *n* Druckvorlage *f*; **~-shy** *adj* kamerascheu; **~work** *n* Kameraführung *f*.
Cameroons [ˌkæmə'ruːnz] *npl* **the ~** Kamerun *nt*.
cami-knickers ['kæmɪˌnɪkəz] *npl* Spitzenhemdhöschen *nt*.
camisole ['kæmɪsəʊl] *n* Mieder, Leibchen *nt*.
camomile ['kæməʊmaɪl] *n* Kamille *f* ◆ **~ tea** Kamillentee *m*.
camouflage ['kæməflɑːʒ] [1] *n (Mil, fig)* Tarnung *f*; *(fig also)* Camouflage *f (geh)* ◆ **for ~** zur Tarnung.
[2] *vt (Mil, fig)* tarnen ◆ **she smiled but it didn't ~ her despair** ihr Lächeln konnte nicht über ihre Verzweiflung hinwegtäuschen.
camouflage *in cpds* Tarn-; **~ nets** *npl* Tarnnetze *pl*.
camp¹ [kæmp] [1] *n* **(a)** Lager *nt*; *(Mil)* (Feld)lager *nt* ◆ **to be in ~** im Lager leben *or* sein; *(Mil)* im Felde leben; **to pitch ~** Zelte *or* ein Lager aufschlagen; **to strike** *or* **break ~** die Zelte abbauen, das Lager *or* die Zelte abbrechen.
(b) *(fig)* Lager *nt* ◆ **to have a foot in both ~s** mit beiden Seiten zu tun haben; **the socialist ~** das sozialistische Lager.
[2] *vi* zelten, kampieren; *(Mil)* lagern ◆ **to go ~ing** zelten (gehen).
◆**camp out** *vi* zelten.
camp² *adj (theatrical, stagey)* übertrieben, extrem *(inf)*; *performance* manieriert, geschmäcklerisch; *person's appearance* aufgedonnert, aufgemotzt *(inf)*; *(effeminate)* tuntenhaft *(inf)*; *(homosexual)* schwul *(inf)*.
◆**camp up** *vt sep* **to ~ sth ~** *(vamp up)* etw aufmöbeln *(inf)*, etw aufmotzen *(inf)*; *(overact)* etw überziehen, in *or* bei etw zu dick auftragen; **to ~ it ~** *(overact, exaggerate)* es zu weit treiben; *(Theat)* es überziehen, zu dick auftragen; *(act homosexually)* sich tuntenhaft *(inf)* *or* wie eine Schwuchtel *(sl)* benehmen.
campaign [kæm'peɪn] [1] *n* **(a)** *(Mil)* Feldzug *m*, Kampagne *f (old)* ◆ **Hitler's Russian ~** Hitlers Rußlandfeldzug *m*. **(b)** *(fig)* Kampagne, Aktion *f*; *(election ~)* Feldzug *m*, Kampagne *f*.
[2] *vi* **(a)** *(Mil)* kämpfen, Krieg führen ◆ **~ing in Ruritania** im Einsatz in Ruritanien.
(b) *(fig)* *(for* für, *against* gegen) sich einsetzen, sich stark machen *(inf)*, agitieren; *(outdoors also)* auf die Straße gehen; *(politician, candidate)* im Wahlkampf stehen, den Wahlkampf führen; *(supporters)* Wahlwerbung treiben ◆ **we were out on the streets ~ing** wir waren auf der Straße im Einsatz.
campaigner [kæm'peɪnəʳ] *n* **(a)** *(Mil)* Krieger *m* ◆ **old ~** alter Kämpe. **(b)** *(fig)* Befürworter(in *f*) *m (for gen)*; Gegner(in *f*) *m (against gen)*; *(for politician)* Wahlwerber(in *f*) *m*.
camp: ~bed *n* Campingliege *f*; **~ chair** *n* Campingstuhl *m*.
camper ['kæmpəʳ] *n* **(a)** Camper(in *f*) *m*. **(b)** *(US: vehicle)* Wohnmobil *nt*.
camp: ~ fire *n* Lagerfeuer *nt*; **~ follower** *n* **(a)** Marketender(in *f*) *m*; **(b)** *(fig)* Anhänger(in *f*), Mitläufer(in *f*) *(pej)* *m*; **~ground** *n (US)* Campingplatz, Zeltplatz *m*.
camphor ['kæmfəʳ] *n* Kampfer *m*.
camphorated ['kæmfəreɪtɪd] *adj* mit Kampfer präpariert ◆ **~ oil** Kampferöl *nt*.
camping ['kæmpɪŋ] *n* Zelten, Camping *nt* ◆ **no ~** Zelten verboten!
camping *in cpds* Camping-; **~ gas** *n (US)* Campinggas *nt*; **~ ground** *n* Zeltplatz *m*; **~ site** *n (also* **camp site***)* Campingplatz, Zeltplatz *m*; **~ van** *n* Caravan *m*.
camp stool *n* Campinghocker *m*.
campus ['kæmpəs] *n* Campus *m*, Universitätsgelände *nt*.
campy ['kæmpɪ] *adj (sl) see* **camp²**.
camshaft ['kæmʃɑːft] *n* Nockenwelle *f*.
▼ **can¹** [kæn] *pret* **could** *modal aux vb, defective parts supplied by to be able to* **(a)** *(be able to)* können ◆ **~ you come tomorrow?** kannst du morgen kommen?; **I ~'t** *or* **~not go to the theatre tomorrow** ich kann morgen nicht ins Theater (gehen); **I'll do it if I ~** wenn ich kann(, tue ich es); **he'll help you all he ~** er wird sein möglichstes tun, er wird tun, was in seinen Kräften steht; **as soon as it ~ be arranged** sobald es sich machen läßt; **could you tell me ...** können *or* könnten Sie mir sagen, ...; **~ you speak German?** können *or* sprechen Sie Deutsch?; **we ~ but hope that, we ~ only hope that ...** wir können nur hoffen, daß ...; **they could not (help) but condemn it** sie konnten nicht anders, als das zu verurteilen.
▼ **(b)** *(may)* dürfen, können ◆ **~ I come too?** kann ich mitkommen?; **~** *or* **could I take some more?** darf ich mir noch etwas *or* noch einmal nehmen?; **you ~ go now** Sie können jetzt gehen; **~ I help?** darf *or* kann ich Ihnen helfen?; **could I possibly go with you?** könnte *or* dürfte ich vielleicht mitkommen?; **I'd like to go, ~ I? — no, you ~'t** ich würde gerne gehen, darf ich? — nein, du darfst nicht; **~ I use your car? — no, you ~'t** kann *or* darf ich dein Auto nehmen? — nein.
▼ **(c)** *(expressing surprise etc)* können ◆ **how ~/could you say such a thing!** wie können/konnten Sie nur *or* bloß so etwas sagen!; **where ~ it be?** wo kann das bloß sein?; **where ~ they have gone?** wo können sie denn nur hingegangen sein?; **you ~'t be serious** das kann doch wohl nicht dein Ernst sein.
▼ **(d)** *(expressing possibility)* können ◆ **it could be that he's got lost** vielleicht hat er sich verlaufen, (es ist) möglich, daß er sich verlaufen hat; **could he have got lost?** ob er sich wohl *or* vielleicht verlaufen hat?; **he could be on the**

next train er könnte im nächsten Zug sein; **and it could have been such a good party!** und es hätte so eine gute Party sein können!; **to think he could have become a doctor** wenn man bedenkt, daß er hätte Arzt werden können.
(e) (*with verbs of perception*) können ◆ **~ you hear me?** hören Sie mich?, können Sie mich hören?
(f) (*be capable of occasionally*) können ◆ **she ~ be very nice when she wants to** wenn sie will, kann sie sehr nett sein.
(g) (*indicating suggestion*) können ◆ **you could try telephoning him** Sie könnten ihn ja mal anrufen; **you could have been a little more polite** Sie hätten etwas höflicher sein können; **you could have told me** das hätten Sie mir auch sagen können.
(h) (*feel inclined to*) können ◆ **I could have murdered her** ich hätte sie umbringen können.
(i) we could do with some new furniture wir könnten neue Möbel gebrauchen; **I could do with a drink now** ich könnte jetzt etwas zu trinken vertragen; **this room could do with a coat of paint** das Zimmer könnte mal wieder gestrichen werden; **he looks as though he could do with a wash/haircut** ich glaube, er müßte sich mal waschen/er müßte sich (*dat*) mal wieder die Haare schneiden lassen.

can[2] [1] *n* **(a)** (*container*) Kanister *m*; (*milk~*) Kanne *f*; (*esp US: garbage ~*) (Müll)eimer *m* ◆ **in the ~** (*Film*) im Kasten; **the contract's in the ~** (*inf*) wir haben den Vertrag in der Tasche (*inf*); **to carry the ~** (*fig inf*) die Sache ausbaden (*inf*).
(b) (*tin*) Dose *f*; (*of food also*) Büchse *f* ◆ **a ~ of beer** eine Dose Bier; **a beer ~** eine Bierdose; **a ~ of paint** eine Dose Farbe; (*with handle*) ein Eimer Farbe.
(c) (*US sl: prison*) Knast *m* (*sl*).
(d) (*US sl: lavatory*) Klo (*inf*), Scheißhaus (*sl*) *nt*.
[2] *vt* **(a)** *foodstuffs* einmachen, eindosen; *see* **canned**.
(b) (*inf*) **~ it!** Klappe! (*inf*).

can *in cpds* Büchsen-, Dosen-.

Canaan ['keɪnən] *n* Kanaan *nt*.

Canaanite ['keɪnənaɪt] *n* Kanaaniter(in *f*) *m*.

Canada ['kænədə] *n* Kanada *nt*.

Canadian [kə'neɪdɪən] [1] *adj* kanadisch.
[2] *n* Kanadier(in *f*) *m*.

canal [kə'næl] *n* **(a)** Kanal *m* ◆ **~ barge** Schleppkahn *m*. **(b)** (*Anat*) Gang, Kanal *m*.

canalization [ˌkænəlaɪ'zeɪʃən] *n* (*lit*) Kanalisation *f*; (*fig*) Kanalisierung *f*.

canalize ['kænəlaɪz] *vt* (*lit, fig*) kanalisieren.

canapé ['kænəpeɪ] *n* Cocktail- *or* Appetithappen *m*.

canard [kæ'nɑːd] *n* (Zeitungs)ente *f*.

Canaries [kə'nɛərɪz] *npl see* **Canary Isles**.

canary [kə'nɛərɪ] *n* **(a)** Kanarienvogel *m*. **(b)** (*old: wine*) Kanarienwein *m* (*old*). **(c)** (*US sl: female singer*) Sängerin *f*.

canary *in cpds* (*colour: also* **~ yellow**) kanariengelb.

Canary Isles [kə'nɛərɪ'aɪlz] *npl* Kanarische Inseln *pl*.

canasta [kə'næstə] *n* Canasta *nt*.

cancan ['kænkæn] *n* Cancan *m*.

▼ **cancel** ['kænsəl] [1] *vt* **(a)** (*call off*) absagen; (*officially*) stornieren; *plans* aufgeben, fallenlassen; *train, bus* streichen ◆ **the last train has been ~led** der letzte Zug fällt aus.
(b) (*revoke, annul*) rückgängig machen; *command, invitation also* zurücknehmen; *contract also* (auf)lösen; *debt* streichen; *order for goods* stornieren; *magazine subscription* kündigen; *decree* aufheben; (*Aut*) *indicator* ausschalten ◆ **no, ~ that** (*in dictation etc*) nein, streichen Sie das.
(c) *stamp, ticket, cheque* entwerten, ungültig machen.
(d) (*Math*) kürzen ◆ **this X ~s that one** dieses X hebt das X auf.
[2] *vi* (*revoke commercial order, contract*) stornieren; (*call off appointment, holiday*) absagen.

◆**cancel out** [1] *vt sep* (*Math*) aufheben; (*fig*) zunichte machen ◆ **to ~ each other ~** (*Math*) sich aufheben, sich kürzen lassen; (*fig*) einander aufheben, sich gegenseitig aufheben.
[2] *vi* (*Math*) sich aufheben, sich wegkürzen lassen (*inf*).

cancellation [ˌkænsə'leɪʃən] *n see vt* **(a)** Absage *f*; Stornierung *f*; Aufgabe *f*; Streichung *f*, Ausfall *m*. **(b)** Rückgängigmachung *f*; Zurücknahme *f*; Auflösung *f*; Streichung *f*; Stornierung *f*; Kündigung *f*; Aufhebung *f*. **(c)** Entwertung *f*. **(d)** (*Math*) Kürzung *f*.

cancer ['kænsəʳ] *n* (*Med*) Krebs *m*; (*fig*) Krebsgeschwür *nt* ◆ **~ of the throat** Kehlkopfkrebs *m*; **~ research** Krebsforschung *f*; **C~** (*Astrol*) Krebs *m*.

cancerous ['kænsərəs] *adj* krebsartig ◆ **~ growth** (*lit, fig*) krebsartige Wucherung.

cancer stick *n* (*sl: cigarette*) Sargnagel *m* (*sl*).

candelabra [ˌkændɪ'lɑːbrə] *n* Kandelaber, Leuchter *m*.

candid ['kændɪd] *adj* offen, ehrlich ◆ **he was quite ~ about it** er war ganz offen, er sprach ganz offen darüber; **in my ~ opinion he ...** ich bin offen gesagt der Meinung, daß er ...

candida ['kændɪdə] *n* (*Med*) Candidose *f*.

candidacy ['kændɪdəsɪ] *n* Kandidatur *f*.

candidate ['kændɪdeɪt] *n* (*Pol*) Kandidat(in *f*) *m*; (*exam ~ also*) Prüfling *m* ◆ **to stand as (a) ~** kandidieren.

candidature ['kændɪdətʃəʳ] *n* (*Brit*) *see* **candidacy**.

candidly ['kændɪdlɪ] *adv* offen, ehrlich ◆ **quite ~, ...** offen gestanden, ...; **to speak ~** offen *or* ehrlich sein.

candidness ['kændɪdnɪs] *n* Offenheit, Ehrlichkeit *f*.

candied ['kændɪd] *adj* (*Cook*) kandiert, gezuckert ◆ **~ peel** (*of lemon*) Zitronat *nt*; (*of orange*) Orangeat *nt*; **his ~ words** seine schmeichelhaften *or* süßen Worte.

candle ['kændl] *n* Kerze *f* ◆ **to burn the ~ at both ends** mit seinen Kräften Raubbau treiben; **he can't hold a ~ to his brother** er kann seinem Bruder nicht das Wasser reichen; **the game is not worth the ~** das ist nicht der Mühe wert.

candle *in cpds* Kerzen-; **~ grease** *n* Kerzenwachs *nt*; **~light** *n* Kerzenlicht *nt*, Kerzenschein *m*; **by ~light** im Kerzenschein, bei Kerzenlicht; **a ~light dinner** ein Essen *nt* bei Kerzenlicht.

Candlemas ['kændlməs] *n* Mariä Lichtmeß *nt*.

candle: ~ power *n* (*old Elec*) Lichtstärke *f*; **a 20-~ power lamp** eine Lampe von 20 Kerzen, eine 20kerzige Lampe; **~stick** *n* Kerzenhalter *m*; **~wick** [1] *n* **(a)** Kerzendocht *m*; **(b)** (*Tex*) Frottierplüschmuster *nt*; [2] *attr bedspread* im Frottierplüschmuster.

candour, (*US*) **candor** ['kændəʳ] *n* Offenheit, Ehrlichkeit *f*.

candy ['kændɪ] [1] *n* (*US*) (*sweet*) Bonbon *m or nt*; (*sweets*) Süßigkeiten, Bonbons *pl*; (*bar of chocolate*) (Tafel) Schokolade *f*; (*individual chocolate*) Praline *f*.
[2] *vt sugar* kristallisieren lassen; *fruit etc* kandieren.

candy: ~floss *n* (*Brit*) Zuckerwatte *f*; **~ store** *n* (*US*) Süßwarenhandlung *f*, Bonbonladen *m* (*inf*); **~-striped** *adj* bunt gestreift (*auf weißem Hintergrund*).

cane [keɪn] [1] *n* **(a)** (*stem of bamboo, sugar etc*) Rohr *nt*; (*of raspberry*) Zweig *m*; (*for supporting plants*) Stock *m* ◆ **a chair made of ~** ein Rohrstuhl *m*.
(b) (*walking stick*) (Spazier)stock *m*; (*instrument of punishment*) (Rohr)stock *m* ◆ **to use the ~** den Rohrstock benutzen; **to get the ~** Prügel bekommen; (*on hand*) eine auf die Finger bekommen, eine Tatze bekommen (*S Ger*).
[2] *vt schoolboy* mit dem Stock schlagen.

cane *in cpds* Rohr-; **~ brake** *n* (*US*) Röhricht, Rohrdickicht *nt*; **~ chair** *n* Rohrstuhl *m*; **~ sugar** *n* Rohrzucker *m*.

canine ['keɪnaɪn] [1] *n* **(a)** (*animal*) Hund *m*. **(b)** (*also* **~ tooth**) Eckzahn *m*.
[2] *adj* Hunde-.

caning ['keɪnɪŋ] *n* (*beating with cane*) Schläge *pl* mit dem Stock, Prügeln *nt* (*inf*) ◆ **to give sb a ~** jdm eine Tracht Prügel verabreichen; **to get a ~** (*Sport*) haushoch geschlagen werden; (*new play etc*) verrissen werden.

canister ['kænɪstəʳ] *n* Behälter *m*; (*for tea, coffee etc also*) Dose *f* ◆ **~ shot** (*Mil*) Kartätsche *f*.

canker ['kæŋkəʳ] *n* (*Med*) Mund- *or* Lippengeschwür *nt*; (*Vet*) Hufkrebs *m*, Strahlfäule *f*; (*Bot*) Brand *m*; (*fig*) (Krebs)geschwür *nt*.

cankerous ['kæŋkərəs] *adj* (*Med*) entzündet; (*Vet, Bot*) brandig; (*fig*) krebsartig.

cannabis ['kænəbɪs] *n* Cannabis *m* ◆ **~ resin** Cannabisharz *nt*.

canned [kænd] *adj* **(a)** (*US*) *food, beer* Dosen-. **(b)** (*inf*) **~ music** Musikberieselung *f* (*inf*); **~ heat** Brennspiritus *m*. **(c)** (*sl: drunk*) blau (*inf*), voll (*sl*).

cannery ['kænərɪ] *n* (*US*) Konservenfabrik *f*.

cannibal ['kænɪbəl] [1] *n* (*person*) Kannibale, Menschenfresser *m* ◆ **these fishes are ~s** diese Fische fressen sich gegenseitig.
[2] *adj* kannibalisch; *animals* sich gegenseitig auffressend.

cannibalism ['kænɪbəlɪzəm] *n* (*of people*) Kannibalismus *m*, Menschenfresserei *f*.

cannibalize ['kænɪbəlaɪz] *vt old car etc* ausschlachten.

canning ['kænɪŋ] *n* Konservenabfüllung *f*; (*preserving*) Konservierung *f* ◆ **the ~ of meat** die Herstellung von Fleischkonserven.

cannon ['kænən] [1] *n* **(a)** (*Mil*) Kanone *f*. **(b)** (*Brit: Billiards*) Karambolage *f*.
[2] *vi* (*Brit: Billiards*) karambolieren.

◆**cannon into** *vi +prep obj* zusammenprallen mit.

cannonade [ˌkænə'neɪd] *n* Kanonade *f*.

cannon: ~ball *n* Kanonenkugel *f*; **~ fodder** *n* Kanonenfutter *nt*.

▼ **cannot** ['kænɒt] = **can not**.

canny ['kænɪ] *adj* (*+er*) (*Scot*) (*cautious*) vorsichtig; (*shrewd also*) schlau; (*careful with money also*) sparsam.

canoe [kə'nuː] [1] *n* Kanu *nt* ◆ **to paddle one's own ~** (*fig*) auf eigenen Füßen *or* Beinen stehen.
[2] *vi* Kanu fahren, paddeln.

canoeing [kə'nuːɪŋ] *n* Kanusport *m*, Kanufahren *nt*.

canoeist [kə'nuːɪst] *n* Kanufahrer(in *f*) *m*, Kanute *m*, Kanutin *f*.

canon[1] ['kænən] *n* (*all senses*) Kanon *m* ◆ **~ law** (*Eccl*) Kanon *m*, kanonisches Recht.

canon[2] *n* (*priest*) Kanoniker, Kanonikus *m*.

cañon *n* (*US*) *see* **canyon**.

canonical [kə'nɒnɪkəl] *adj* **(a)** (*Eccl*) kanonisch ◆ **~ dress** Priestergewand *nt*. **(b)** (*fig: accepted*) anerkannt, rechtmäßig.

canonization [ˌkænənaɪ'zeɪʃən] *n* (*Eccl*) Heiligsprechung, Kanonisation, Kanonisierung *f*.

canonize ['kænənaɪz] *vt* (*Eccl*) heiligsprechen, kanonisieren.

canoodle [kə'nuːdl] *vi* (*inf*) rumschmusen (*inf*).

can opener *n* Dosen- *or* Büchsenöffner *m*.

canopy ['kænəpɪ] *n* **(a)** (*awning*) Markise, Überdachung *f*; (*over entrance*) Vordach *nt*, Pergola *f*; (*of bed, throne*) Baldachin *m*; (*of aircraft*) Kanzeldach *nt*; (*of parachute*) Fallschirmkappe *f*. **(b)** (*fig liter: of sky, foliage*) Baldachin *m* (*liter*) ◆ **the ~ of the heavens** das Himmelszelt (*liter*).

canst [kænst] (*obs*) *2nd pers sing of* **can[1]**.

cant[1] [kænt] *n* **(a)** (*hypocrisy*) Heuchelei *f*, scheinheiliges *or* leeres Gerede. **(b)** (*jargon*) Jargon *m*, Kauderwelsch *nt*; (*of thieves, gipsies*) Rotwelsch *nt*.

cant[2] [1] *n* (*tilt*) Schräge *f*.

➤ LANGUAGE IN USE: **cancel: 1a** → 20.5, 21.4 **cannot** → 5.3, 10.4, 12.3, 16.3

[2] *vt* schräg stellen, kanten ◆ **the wind ~ed the boat** der Wind brachte das Boot zum Kippen.
[3] *vi* schräg *or* schief sein, sich neigen; (*boat*) kippen.
can't [kɑːnt] *contr of* **can not.**
Cantab ['kæntæb] *abbr of* **Cantabrigiensis** von der Universität Cambridge.
cantaloup(e) ['kæntəluːp] *n* Honigmelone, Buttermelone *f.*
cantankerous [kæn'tæŋkərəs] *adj* mürrisch, knurrig.
cantata [kæn'tɑːtə] *n* Kantate *f.*
canteen [kæn'tiːn] *n* **(a)** (*restaurant*) Kantine *f*; (*in university*) Mensa *f.* **(b)** (*Mil*) (*flask*) Feldflasche *f*; (*mess tin*) Kochgeschirr *nt.* **(c)** (*of cutlery*) Besteckkasten *m.*
canter ['kæntəʳ] [1] *n* Handgalopp, Kanter *m* ◆ **to ride at a ~** langsamen Galopp reiten; **to go for a ~** einen Ausritt machen.
[2] *vi* langsam galoppieren.
canticle ['kæntɪkl] *n* (*Eccl*) Lobgesang *m*; (*song*) Volksweise *f* ◆ **C~s** Hohelied *nt*, Hohes Lied.
cantilever ['kæntɪliːvəʳ] *n* Ausleger *m.*
cantilever *in cpds* Ausleger-; **~ bridge** *n* Auslegerbrücke *f.*
canto ['kæntəʊ] *n* (*Liter*) Canto, Gesang *m.*
canton ['kæntɒn] *n* Kanton *m.*
Cantonese [ˌkæntə'niːz] [1] *adj* kantonesisch.
[2] *n* **(a)** Kantonese *m*, Kantonesin *f.* **(b)** (*language*) Kantonesisch *nt.*
cantonment [kən'tuːnmənt] *n* Truppenunterkunft *f*, Kantonnement *nt* (*old*).
cantor ['kæntɔːʳ] *n* Kantor *m.*
Canuck [kə'nʌk] *n* (*US pej inf*) (Franko)kanadier(in *f*) *m.*
Canute [kə'njuːt] *n* Knut *m.*
canvas ['kænvəs] *n* Leinwand *f*; (*for sails*) Segeltuch *nt*; (*set of sails*) Segel *pl*; (*for tent*) Zeltbahn *f*; (*Art*) (*material*) Leinwand *f*; (*painting*) Gemälde *nt* ◆ **under ~** (*in a tent*) im Zelt; (*Naut*) mit gehißtem Segel; **~ chair** Liegestuhl, Klappstuhl *m*; **~ shoes** Segeltuchschuhe *pl.*
canvass ['kænvəs] [1] *vt* **(a)** (*Pol*) *district* Wahlwerbung machen in (+*dat*); *person* für seine Partei zu gewinnen suchen ◆ **to ~ the local electorate** in seinem Wahlkreis Stimmen werben *or* auf Stimmenfang gehen (*inf*).
(b) *customers, citizens etc* ansprechen, werben; *issue* unter die Leute bringen; *district* bereisen; (*sound out*) *opinions* erforschen.
[2] *vi* **(a)** (*Pol*) um Stimmen werben (*for sb* für jdn).
(b) (*Comm*) werben, eine Werbekampagne durchführen, Klinken putzen (*inf*) ◆ **to ~ for an applicant** (*for job*) einen Bewerber anpreisen, für einen Bewerber Stimmung machen.
[3] *n* (*Pol, Comm*) Aktion, Kampagne *f.*
canvasser ['kænvəsəʳ] *n* **(a)** (*Pol*) Wahlhelfer *m.* **(b)** (*Comm*) Vertreter, Klinkenputzer (*inf*) *m.*
canvassing ['kænvəsɪŋ] *n* **(a)** (*Pol*) Durchführung *f* des Wahlkampfs, Wahlwerbung *f.* **(b)** (*Comm*) Von-Haus-zu-Haus-Gehen, Klinkenputzen (*inf*) *nt*; (*sounding-out: of opinions*) Meinungsforschung *f* ◆ **~ for applicants is not allowed** es ist nicht gestattet, einen Bewerber anzupreisen *or* für einen Bewerber Stimmung zu machen.
canyon, (*US*) **cañon** ['kænjən] *n* Cañon *m.*
CAP *abbr of* **Common Agricultural Policy** *gemeinsame Agrarpolitik der EG*, GAP *f.*
cap¹ [kæp] [1] *n* **(a)** (*hat*) Mütze *f*; (*soldier's ~ also*) Käppi *nt*; (*nurse's ~*) Haube *f*; (*Jur, Univ*) Barett *nt*; (*for swimming*) Bademütze *or* -kappe *f*; (*of jester*) Kappe *f*; (*of cardinal*) Hut *m*; (*skull-~*) Käppchen *nt* ◆ **~ in hand** kleinlaut; **if the ~ fits(, wear it)** (*prov*) wem die Jacke paßt(, der soll sie sich anziehen); **to set one's ~ at sb** (*dated*) es auf jdn abgesehen haben; **~ and bells** Schellenkappe *f*; **in ~ and gown** mit Doktorhut und Talar; **he's got his ~ for England, he's an English ~** (*Sport*) er ist/war in der englischen Nationalmannschaft.
(b) (*lid, cover: of bottle*) Verschluß, Deckel *m*; (*of fountain pen*) (Verschluß)kappe *f*; (*of valve*) Kappe *f*; (*Mil: of shell, fuse*) Kapsel *f*; (*Aut: petrol ~, radiator ~*) Verschluß *m.*
(c) (*contraceptive*) Pessar *nt.*
(d) (*of mushroom*) Hut *m.*
(e) (*explosive*) Platzpatrone *f*; (*for toy gun*) Zündplättchen *nt.*
(f) (*of shoe*) Kappe *f.*
[2] *vt* **(a)** (*put ~ on*) *bottle etc* verschließen, zumachen; (*fig: cover top of*) *peaks* bedecken.
(b) (*Sport*) **he was ~ped four times for England** er wurde viermal für die englische Nationalmannschaft aufgestellt.
(c) (*do or say better*) überbieten ◆ **and then to ~ it all** ... und, um dem Ganzen die Krone aufzusetzen, ...
(d) (*Scot Univ*) einen akademischen Grad verleihen (+*dat*).
(e) (*Brit: in spending etc*) **the council was ~ped** dem Stadtrat wurde von der Regierung ein Höchstsatz für die Kommunalsteuer *etc* auferlegt.
cap² *n* (*Typ, inf*) großer Buchstabe ◆ **in ~s** in Großbuchstaben; *see also* **capital 1 (b).**
capability [ˌkeɪpə'bɪlɪtɪ] *n* **(a)** (*potential ability*) Fähigkeit *f*; (*no pl: capableness also*) Kompetenz *f.* **(b)** (*Mil*) Potential *nt.*
capable ['keɪpəbl] *adj* **(a)** (*skilful, competent*) fähig, kompetent; *mother* gut.
(b) to be ~ of doing sth etw tun können; (*person: have physical, mental ability also*) fähig sein, etw zu tun; **to be ~ of sth** etw können; zu etw fähig sein; **it's ~ of exploding any minute** es kann jede Minute explodieren; **it's ~ of speeds of up to** ... es erreicht Geschwindigkeiten bis zu ...; **he's ~ of better** er ist zu Besserem fähig; **the poem is ~ of several interpretations** das Gedicht läßt mehrere Interpretationsmöglichkeiten zu; **~ of improvement** verbesserungsfähig; **he's quite ~ of changing his mind at the last minute** er ist imstande *or* er bringt es fertig und ändert seine Meinung in der letzten Minute; **thank you but I'm quite ~ of doing that myself** danke, ich kann das durchaus allein.
capably ['keɪpəblɪ] *adv* kompetent, geschickt.
capacious [kə'peɪʃəs] *adj* geräumig; *dress* weit.
capacitance [kə'pæsɪtəns] *n* (*Elec*) Speicherkapazität *f.*
capacitor [kə'pæsɪtəʳ] *n* Kondensator *m.*
▼ **capacity** [kə'pæsɪtɪ] *n* **(a)** (*cubic content etc*) Fassungsvermögen *nt*, (Raum)inhalt *m*; (*maximum output*) Kapazität *f*; (*maximum weight*) Höchstlast *f*; (*Aut: engine ~*) Hubraum *m* ◆ **filled to ~** randvoll; (*hall*) bis auf den letzten Platz besetzt; **seating ~ of 400** 400 Sitzplätze; **to work to ~** voll ausgelastet sein; **working at full ~** voll ausgelastet; **the Stones played to ~ audiences** die Stones spielten vor ausverkauften Sälen.
(b) (*ability*) Fähigkeit *f* ◆ **his ~ for learning** seine Lern- *or* Aufnahmefähigkeit; **he has a great ~ for work** er kann sehr gut arbeiten; **this work is within/beyond his ~** er ist zu dieser Arbeit fähig/nicht fähig.
▼ **(c)** (*role, position*) Eigenschaft, Funktion *f* ◆ **in my ~ as a doctor** (in meiner Eigenschaft) als Arzt; **speaking in his official ~ as mayor, he said** ... er sagte in seiner Eigenschaft als Bürgermeister ...; **they refused to employ him in any ~ whatsoever** sie lehnten es ab, ihn in irgendeiner Form zu beschäftigen.
(d) (*legal power*) Befugnis *f.*
caparison [kə'pærɪsn] (*liter*) [1] *n* Schabracke *f* (*old*).
[2] *vt* mit einer Schabracke bedecken (*old*).
cape¹ [keɪp] *n* Cape *nt*, Umhang *m*, Pelerine *f* (*old*).
cape² *n* (*Geog*) Kap *nt.*
Cape: ~ Canaveral *n* Kap Canaveral *nt*; **~ coloured** *adj* farbig, gemischtrassig; **~ Horn** *n* Kap *nt* Hoorn; **~ of Good Hope** *n* Kap *nt* der guten Hoffnung.
caper¹ ['keɪpəʳ] [1] *vi* herumtollen.
[2] *n* **(a)** (*skip*) Luft- *or* Freudensprung *m.* **(b)** (*prank*) Eskapade, Kapriole *f.* **(c)** (*sl: crime*) Ding *nt* (*sl*).
caper² *n* (*Bot, Cook*) Kaper *f*; (*shrub*) Kapernstrauch *m.*
capercaillie, capercailzie [ˌkæpə'keɪlɪ] *n* Auerhahn *m.*
Cape: ~ Town *n* Kapstadt *nt*; **~ Verde Islands** *npl* Kapverdische Inseln, Kapverden *pl.*
capful ['kæpfʊl] *n* **one ~ to one litre of water** eine Verschlußkappe auf einen Liter Wasser.
capillary [kə'pɪlərɪ] [1] *adj* kapillar, Kapillar- ◆ **~ attraction** *or* **action** Kapillarwirkung *f.*
[2] *n* Kapillare *f*, Kapillargefäß *nt.*
capital ['kæpɪtl] [1] *n* **(a)** (*also* **~ city**) Hauptstadt *f.*
(b) (*also* **~ letter**) Großbuchstabe *m* ◆ **large/small ~s** Großbuchstaben, Versalien (*spec*) *pl*/Kapitälchen *pl* (*spec*); **please write in ~s** bitte in Blockschrift schreiben!
(c) *no pl* (*Fin*) Kapital *nt* ◆ **to make ~ out of sth** (*fig*) aus etw Kapital schlagen; **~ and labour** Kapital und Arbeit.
(d) (*Archit*) Kapitell *nt.*
[2] *adj* **(a)** *letter* Groß- ◆ **love with a ~ L** die große Liebe; **a car with a ~ C** ein richtiges Auto; **unity with a ~ U** hundertprozentige Einheit. **(b)** (*dated inf*) prächtig (*dated*), famos (*dated*).
capital *in cpds* Kapital-; **~ allowance** *n* Abschreibung *f*; **~ assets** *npl* Kapitalvermögen *nt*; **~ employed** *n* Betriebskapital *nt*; **~ equipment** *n* (Betriebs)anlagen *pl*; **~ expenditure** *n* Kapitalaufwendungen *pl*; **~ gains** *npl* Kapitalgewinn *m*; **~ gains tax** *n* Kapitalertragssteuer *f*; **~ goods** *npl* Investitionsgüter *pl*; **~-intensive** *adj* kapitalintensiv; **~ investment** *n* Kapitalanlage *f.*
capitalism ['kæpɪtəlɪzəm] *n* Kapitalismus *m.*
capitalist ['kæpɪtəlɪst] [1] *n* Kapitalist(in *f*) *m.*
[2] *adj* kapitalistisch.
capitalistic [ˌkæpɪtə'lɪstɪk] *adj* kapitalistisch.
capitalization [ˌkæpɪtəlaɪ'zeɪʃən] *n* **(a)** (*Fin*) Kapitalisierung, Kapitalisation *f.* **(b)** (*Typ*) Großschreibung *f.*
capitalize ['kæpɪtəˌlaɪz] *vt* **(a)** (*Fin*) kapitalisieren. **(b)** (*Typ*) *word* groß schreiben.
◆**capitalize on** *vi+prep* (*fig*) Kapital schlagen aus.
capital: ~ offence *n* Kapitalverbrechen *nt*; **~ punishment** *n* die Todesstrafe; **~ sum** *n* Kapitalbetrag *m*, Kapital *nt*; **~ transfer tax** *n* Kapitalverkehrssteuer *f*; (*for inheritance*) Erbschaftssteuer *f.*
capitation [ˌkæpɪ'teɪʃən] *n* Kopfsteuer *f.*
Capitol ['kæpɪtl] *n* Kapitol *nt.*
capitulate [kə'pɪtjʊleɪt] *vi* kapitulieren (*also Mil*) (*to* vor +*dat*), aufgeben (*to* gegenüber).
capitulation [kəˌpɪtjʊ'leɪʃən] *n* Kapitulation *f.*
capo ['kæpəʊ] *n* Kapodaster *m.*
capon ['keɪpən] *n* Kapaun *m.*
cappuccino [ˌkæpʊ'tʃiːnəʊ] *n* Cappuccino *m.*
Capri [kə'priː] *n* Capri *nt.*
caprice [kə'priːs] *n* **(a)** Laune(nhaftigkeit), Kaprice (*geh*) *f.* **(b)** (*Mus*) Capriccio *nt.*
capricious [kə'prɪʃəs] *adj* launisch, kapriziös (*geh*).
capriciously [kə'prɪʃəslɪ] *adv act, behave* launenhaft; *decide, do sth* einer Laune gehorchend (*geh*).
capriciousness [kə'prɪʃəsnɪs] *n* Launenhaftigkeit *f.*
Capricorn ['kæprɪkɔːn] *n* Steinbock *m.*

➤ LANGUAGE IN USE: **capacity: c → 19**

capsicum ['kæpsɪkəm] *n (Bot: plant, fruit)* Pfefferschote *f*, Peperoni *pl.*

capsize [kæp'saɪz] [1] *vi* kentern.
[2] *vt* zum Kentern bringen.

capstan ['kæpstən] *n* Poller *m.*

capsular ['kæpsjʊlə^r] *adj* Kapsel-.

capsule ['kæpsjuːl] *n* Kapsel *f.*

captain ['kæptɪn] *(abbr* **Capt**) [1] *n (Mil)* Hauptmann *m*; *(Naut, Aviat, Sport)* Kapitän *m*; *(US: in restaurant)* Oberkellner *m* ◆ **yes, ~!** jawohl, Herr Hauptmann/Kapitän!; **~ of industry** Industriekapitän *m.*
[2] *vt (Sport) team* anführen; *(Naut) ship* befehligen ◆ **he ~ed the team for years** er war jahrelang Kapitän der Mannschaft.

captaincy ['kæptənsɪ] *n* Befehligung *f*, Befehl *m*; *(Sport)* Führung *f* ◆ **to get one's ~** sein Kapitänspatent *nt* erhalten; **under his ~** mit ihm als Kapitän.

caption ['kæpʃən] [1] *n* Überschrift *f*, Titel *m*; *(under cartoon)* Bildunterschrift *f*; *(Film: subtitle)* Untertitel *m.*
[2] *vt* betiteln, mit einer Überschrift *or* einem Titel *etc* versehen.

captious ['kæpʃəs] *adj person* überkritisch, pedantisch; *remark* spitzfindig.

captivate ['kæptɪveɪt] *vt* faszinieren, entzücken.

captivating ['kæptɪveɪtɪŋ] *adj* bezaubernd; *personality* einnehmend.

captive ['kæptɪv] [1] *n* Gefangene(r) *mf* ◆ **to take sb ~** jdn gefangennehmen; **to hold sb ~** jdn gefangenhalten; *(fig)* jdn fesseln, jdn gefangennehmen.
[2] *adj person* gefangen ◆ **a ~ audience** ein unfreiwilliges Publikum; **~ balloon** Fesselballon *m*; **in a ~ state** in Gefangenschaft *f.*

captivity [kæp'tɪvɪtɪ] *n* Gefangenschaft *f.*

captor ['kæptə^r] *n* derjenige, der jdn gefangennimmt ◆ **his ~s treated him kindly** er wurde nach seiner Gefangennahme gut behandelt; **his ~s were Ruritanian** er wurde von Ruritaniern gefangengenommen; **his ~s later freed him** man ließ ihn später wieder frei.

capture ['kæptʃə^r] [1] *vt* **(a)** *town* einnehmen, erobern; *treasure* erobern; *person* gefangennehmen; *animal* (ein)fangen; *ship* kapern, aufbringen *(spec)* ◆ **they ~d the town from the enemy** sie eroberten die vom Feind beherrschte Stadt.
(b) *(fig) votes* erringen, auf sich *(acc)* vereinigen; *prizes* erringen; *(painter etc) atmosphere* einfangen; *attention, sb's interest* erregen.
(c) *(Comput) data* erfassen.
[2] *n* Eroberung *f*; *(thing captured also)* Fang *m*; *(of escapee)* Gefangennahme *f*; *(of animal)* Einfangen *nt*; *(Comput: of data)* Erfassung *f.*

capuchin ['kæpjʊtʃɪn] *n* **(a)** *(hooded cloak)* Kapuzencape *nt.* **(b)** *(Zool)* Kapuziner(affe) *m.* **(c)** *(Eccl)* **C~** Kapuziner(mönch) *m.*

car [kɑː^r] *n* **(a)** Auto *nt*, Wagen *m* ◆ **by ~** mit dem Auto *or* Wagen. **(b)** *(esp US: Rail, tram~)* Wagen *m.* **(c)** *(of airship, balloon, cable~)* Gondel *f*; *(US: of elevator)* Fahrkorb *m.*

carafe [kə'ræf] *n* Karaffe *f.*

caramel ['kærəməl] *n (substance)* Karamel *m*; *(sweet)* Karamelle *f.*

caramel *in cpds* Karamel-; **~-coloured** *adj* hellbraun; **~-flavoured** *adj* mit Karamelgeschmack.

carapace ['kærəpeɪs] *n* Schale *f*; *(of tortoise etc)* (Rücken)panzer *m.*

carat ['kærət] *n* Karat *nt* ◆ **nine ~ gold** neunkarätiges Gold.

caravan ['kærəvæn] *n* **(a)** *(Brit: Aut)* Wohnwagen, Caravan *m.* **(b)** *(gipsy ~)* Zigeunerwagen *m.* **(c)** *(desert ~)* Karawane *f.*

caravan holiday *n* Ferien *pl* im Wohnwagen.

caravanning ['kærəvænɪŋ] *n* Caravaning *nt*, Urlaub *m* im Wohnwagen ◆ **to go ~** Urlaub im Wohnwagen machen.

caravanserai [,kærə'vænsə,raɪ] *n* Karawanserei *f.*

caravan site *n* Campingplatz *m* für Wohnwagen.

caravel [kærə'vel] *n* Karavelle *f.*

caraway ['kærəweɪ] *n* Kümmel *m* ◆ **~ seeds** Kümmel(körner *pl*) *m.*

carbide ['kɑːbaɪd] *n* Karbid *nt.*

carbine ['kɑːbaɪn] *n* Karabiner *m.*

carbohydrate ['kɑːbəʊ'haɪdreɪt] *n* Kohle(n)hydrat *nt.*

carbolic [kɑː'bɒlɪk] *adj* **(a)** Karbol- ◆ **~ acid** Karbolsäure *f.* **(b)** *(also* **~ soap**) Karbolseife *f.*

car bomb *n* Autobombe *f.*

carbon ['kɑːbən] *n (Chem)* Kohlenstoff *m*; *(Elec)* Kohle *f.*

carbonaceous [,kɑːbə'neɪʃəs] *adj* Kohlenstoff-, kohlenstoffhaltig.

carbonate ['kɑːbənɪt] *n* Karbonat *nt.*

carbonated ['kɑːbə,neɪtəd] *adj* mit Kohlensäure (versetzt).

carbon: ~ copy *n* Durchschlag *m*; **to be a ~ copy of sth** das genaue Ebenbild einer Sache *(gen)* sein; **she's a ~ copy of her sister** sie sieht ihrer Schwester zum Verwechseln ähnlich; **~ dating** *n* Radiokarbonmethode, Kohlenstoffdatierung *f*; **~ dioxide** *n* Kohlendioxyd *nt*; **~ fibre** *n* Kohlenstoffaser *f.*

carbonic [kɑː'bɒnɪk] *adj* Kohlen- ◆ **~ acid** Kohlensäure *f.*

carboniferous [,kɑːbə'nɪfərəs] *adj (Geol)* kohlehaltig.

carbonization [,kɑːbənaɪ'zeɪʃən] *n* Karbonisation, Verkohlung *f.*

carbonize ['kɑːbənaɪz] *vt* karbonisieren, verkohlen (lassen).

carbonless ['kɑːbənlɪs] *adj* **~ paper** selbstdurchschreibendes Papier.

carbon: ~ monoxide *n* Kohlenmonoxyd *nt*; **~ paper** *n* Kohlepapier *nt*; **~ ribbon** *n* Kohlefarbband *nt.*

car-boot sale ['kɑːbuːt'seɪl] *n auf einem Parkplatz durchgeführter Verkauf persönlicher Gegenstände mit dem Kofferraum als Auslage.*

carboy ['kɑːbɔɪ] *n* Korbflasche *f.*

carbuncle ['kɑː,bʌŋkl] *n* **(a)** *(Med)* Karbunkel *m.* **(b)** *(jewel)* Karfunkel(stein) *m.*

carburettor, *(US)* **carburetor** [,kɑːbə'retə^r] *n* Vergaser *m.*

carcass ['kɑːkəs] *n* **(a)** *(corpse)* Leiche *f*; *(of animal)* Kadaver *m*, (Tier)leiche *f*; *(at butcher's)* Rumpf *m* ◆ **move your fat ~** *(inf)* geh mal mit deinem fetten Kadaver hier weg! *(sl)*. **(b)** *(of ship, house)* Skelett *nt*; *(remains)* Überbleibsel, Trümmer *pl.*

carcinogen [kɑː'sɪnədʒen] *n* Krebserreger *m*, Karzinogen *nt.*

carcinogenic [,kɑːsɪnə'dʒenɪk] *adj* karzinogen, krebserregend.

carcinoma [,kɑːsɪ'nəʊmə] *n* Karzinom *nt.*

car *in cpds* Auto-; **~ coat** *n* Dreivierteljacke *f*; **~ crash** *n* (Auto)unfall *m.*

card[1] [kɑːd] *n* **(a)** *no pl* (**~board**) Pappe *f.*
(b) *(greetings, business ~ etc)* Karte *f.*
(c) **~s** *pl (employment ~s)* Papiere *pl* ◆ **he asked for his ~s** *(inf)* er wollte sich *(dat)* seine Papiere geben lassen *(inf)*.
(d) *(Sport: programme)* Programm *nt.*
(e) *(playing ~)* (Spiel)karte *f* ◆ **to play ~s** Karten spielen; **to lose money at ~s** Geld beim Kartenspiel verlieren; **pack of ~s** Karten *pl*, Kartenspiel *nt*; **game of ~s** Kartenspiel *nt*; **house of ~s** *(lit, fig)* Kartenhaus *nt.*
(f) *(fig uses)* **put one's ~s on the table** seine Karten aufdecken *or* (offen) auf den Tisch legen; **to play one's ~s right/badly** geschickt/ungeschickt taktieren, taktisch geschickt/unklug vorgehen; **to hold all the ~s** alle Trümpfe in der Hand haben; **to play one's last/best ~** seinen letzten/höchsten Trumpf ausspielen; **it's on the ~s** das ist zu erwarten.
(g) *(dated inf: person)* ulkiger Vogel *(inf)*.

card[2] *(Tex)* [1] *n* Wollkamm *m*, Krempel, Karde *f.*
[2] *vt wool, cotton* kämmen, krempeln, karden.

cardamom ['kɑːdəməm] *n* Kardamom *m or nt.*

card: ~board [1] *n* Karton *m*, Pappe *f*;
[2] *attr* Papp-; *(fig) character* stereotyp, klischeehaft, schablonenhaft; **~board box** *n* (Papp)karton *m*, Pappschachtel *f*; **~-carrying** *adj* **a ~-carrying member** ein eingetragenes Mitglied; **~-carrying communist** Mitglied *nt* der Kommunistischen Partei; **~ catalogue** *or* **file** *n* Zettelkatalog *m*; *(in library)* Katalog(karten *pl*) *m*; **~ game** *n* Kartenspiel *nt.*

cardiac ['kɑːdɪæk] *adj* Herz- ◆ **~ arrest** Herzstillstand *m.*

cardigan ['kɑːdɪgən] *n* Strickjacke *f.*

cardinal ['kɑːdɪnl] [1] *n* **(a)** *(Eccl)* Kardinal *m.* **(b)** *see* **~ number.**
[2] *adj (chief)* Haupt-; *(utmost)* äußerste(r, s) *attr.*

cardinal: ~ number *n* Kardinalzahl *f*; **~ points** *npl* Himmelsrichtungen *pl*; **~ red** *n* Purpurrot *nt*; **~ sin** *n* Todsünde *f*; **~ virtue** *n* Kardinaltugend *f.*

card index *n* Kartei *f*; *(in library)* Katalog *m.*

cardio ['kɑːdɪəʊ] *pref* Kardio- ◆ **~gram** Kardiogramm *nt.*

cardiologist [,kɑːdɪ'ɒlɪdʒɪst] *n* Kardiologe *m*, Kardiologin *f.*

cardiology [,kɑːdɪ'ɒlədʒɪ] *n* Kardiologie *f.*

cardiopulmonary [,kɑːdɪəʊ'pʊlmənərɪ] *adj* Herz-Lungen- ◆ **~ resuscitation** Herz-Lungen-Wiederbelebung *f.*

cardiovascular [,kɑːdɪəʊ'væskjʊlə^r] *adj* kardiovaskulär.

card: ~phone *n* Kartentelefon *nt*; **~ punch** *n* Lochkartenmaschine *f*; **~ reader** *n* Lesemaschine *f*; **~ sharp(er)** *n* Falschspieler, Zinker *(inf) m*; **~ table** *n* Spieltisch *m*; **~ trick** *n* Kartenkunststück *nt*; **~ vote** *n (Brit)* ≃ Abstimmung *f* durch Wahlmänner.

CARE [keə^r] *abbr of* **Cooperative for American Relief Everywhere** ◆ **~ packet** Carepaket *nt.*

▼ **care** [keə^r] [1] *n* **(a)** *(worry, anxiety)* Sorge *f (of* um) ◆ **free from ~(s)** ohne Sorgen, frei von Sorge; **he hasn't a ~ in the world** er hat keinerlei Sorgen; **the ~s of the world** die Sorgen des Alltags; **the ~s of state** die Staatsgeschäfte *pl.*
(b) *(carefulness, attentiveness)* Sorgfalt *f* ◆ **driving without due ~ and attention** fahrlässiges Verhalten im Straßenverkehr; **to drive with due ~ and attention** sich umsichtig im Straßenverkehr verhalten; **"fragile, with ~", "handle with ~"** „Vorsicht, zerbrechlich"; **to take ~** aufpassen, achtgeben, vorsichtig sein; **take ~ he doesn't cheat you** sehen Sie sich vor *or* nehmen Sie sich in acht, daß er Sie nicht betrügt; **bye-bye, take ~** tschüs, mach's gut; **it got broken despite all the ~ we took** es ist trotz aller Vorsicht kaputtgegangen; **to take ~ to do sth/not to do sth** sich bemühen *or* sich *(dat)* Mühe geben, etw zu tun/etw nicht zu tun; **I'll take ~ not to trust him again** ich werde mich hüten, ihm noch einmal zu trauen; **to take ~ over** *or* **with sth/in doing sth** etw sorgfältig tun; **you should take more ~ with** *or* **over the details** Sie sollten sich sorgfältiger mit den Einzelheiten befassen; **have a ~** *(old: be careful)* gib acht *or* Obacht! *(old)*; *(inf: be considerate)* nun mach mal einen Punkt! *(inf)*.
(c) *(of teeth, skin, car, furniture etc)* Pflege *f* ◆ **to take ~ of sth** auf etw *(acc)* aufpassen; *of one's appearance, hair, car, furniture* etw pflegen; *(not treat roughly) car, furniture, health* schonen; **to take ~ of oneself** sich um sich selbst kümmern; *(as regards health)* sich schonen, auf sich *(acc)* aufpassen; *(as regards appearance)* etwas für sich tun, sich pflegen.
(d) *(of old people, children)* Versorgung, Fürsorge *f* ◆ **medical ~** ärztliche Versorgung; **he needs medical ~** er muß ärztlich behandelt werden; **he is in the ~ of Dr Smith** er ist bei Dr. Smith in Behandlung; **to take ~ of sb** sich um jdn kümmern; *of patients* jdn versorgen; *of one's family* für jdn sorgen; **they took good ~ of her in hospital** sie wurde im Krankenhaus gut versorgt.
(e) *(protection, supervision)* Obhut *f* ◆ **~ of** *(abbr* **c/o**) bei; **in** *or* **under sb's ~** in jds *(dat)* Obhut; **to take a child into ~** ein Kind in Pflege nehmen; **to be taken into ~** in Pflege gegeben werden; **the children/valuables in my ~** die mir anvertrauten Kinder/Wertsachen; **to take ~ of sth** *of valuables etc* auf etw *(acc)* aufpassen; *of plants, animals etc* sich um etw kümmern; *(over longer period)* etw versorgen.
(f) **to take ~ of sb/sth** *(see to)* sich um jdn/etw kümmern; *of arrangements,*

affairs etc also etw erledigen; **that takes ~ of him/it** er/das wäre abgehakt (*inf*), das wäre erledigt; **let me take ~ of that** lassen Sie mich das mal machen, überlassen Sie das mir; **that can take ~ of itself** das wird sich schon irgendwie geben; **let the housework take ~ of itself for a moment** nun laß doch mal einen Augenblick die Hausarbeit (sein).

(g) (*caringness, concern*) (*of person*) Anteilnahme, Fürsorglichkeit *f*; (*of state, council*) Interesse *nt* am Mitmenschen ♦ **if the city planners showed more ~** wenn die Städteplaner etwas mehr Menschenfreundlichkeit zeigen würden; **if only she showed a little ~** wenn sie nur nicht so gleichgültig wäre; **the party has a genuine ~ for senior citizens** der Partei liegt das Wohl der älteren Mitbürger am Herzen.

▼ 2 *vi* (*be concerned*) sich kümmern (*about* um) ♦ **we ~ about our image** wir kümmern uns um unser Image, wir sorgen für unser Image; **a company that ~s about its staff** eine Firma, die sich um ihr Personal kümmert *or* für ihr Personal sorgt; **money is all he ~s about** er interessiert sich nur fürs Geld, ihm liegt nur etwas am Geld; **that's all he ~s about** alles andere ist ihm egal; **he ~s deeply about her/this** sie/das liegt ihm sehr am Herzen; **he doesn't ~ about her** sie ist ihm gleichgültig; **I know you don't ~ about me/such things** ich weiß, daß ich dir gleichgültig bin/daß dir so etwas gleichgültig *or* egal ist; **I didn't know you ~d** (*hum*) ich wußte gar nicht, daß ich dir was bedeute; **the party that ~s** die Partei, die sich um Ihr Wohl kümmert, die Partei mit Herz; **I wish you'd ~ a bit more** ich wünschte, das wäre dir nicht alles egal *or* gleichgültig; **I don't ~** das ist mir egal *or* gleichgültig; **as if I ~d** als ob mir das etwas ausmachen würde; **for all I ~** meinetwegen, von mir aus; **who ~s?** na und?, und wenn schon?; **he just doesn't ~** das ist ihm so egal.

3 *vt* **(a)** (*mind*) **I don't ~ what people say** es ist mir egal *or* es kümmert mich nicht, was die Leute sagen; **don't you ~ that half the world is starving?** berührt es Sie überhaupt nicht, daß die halbe Welt hungert?; **what do I ~?** was geht mich das an?; **I couldn't ~ less what people say** es ist mir doch völlig egal *or* gleich(gültig), was die Leute sagen; **you don't ~ what happens to me — but I do ~** dir ist es ja egal, was mir passiert — nein, das ist mir überhaupt nicht egal; **I didn't think you ~d what I do** ich habe nicht gedacht, daß dich das kümmert, was ich mache, ich habe gedacht, das ist dir egal, was ich mache.

(b) (*like*) **to ~ to do sth** etw gerne tun mögen *or* wollen; **would you ~ to take off your coat?** würden Sie gerne Ihren Mantel ablegen?, wollen *or* möchten Sie nicht (Ihren Mantel) ablegen?; **can I help you? — if you ~ to** kann ich Ihnen helfen? — wenn Sie so freundlich wären; **I wouldn't ~ to meet him/try** ich würde keinen gesteigerten Wert darauf legen, ihn kennenzulernen/das zu probieren; **I don't ~ to believe him** ich bin nicht gewillt, ihm zu glauben; **but I don't ~ to** ich will aber nicht.

♦**care for** *vi +prep obj* **(a)** (*look after*) sich kümmern um; *invalid also* versorgen; *hands, furniture etc* pflegen ♦ **well ~d-~** *person* gut versorgt; *hands, garden, hair, house* gepflegt; **the children are being ~d ~ by their grandmother** die Großmutter kümmert sich um die Kinder.

(b) (*like*) **I don't ~ ~ that suggestion/picture/him** dieser Vorschlag/das Bild/er sagt mir nicht zu; **I don't ~ ~ your tone of voice** wie reden Sie denn mit mir?; **would you ~ ~ a cup of tea?** hätten Sie gerne eine Tasse Tee?; **~ ~ a drink?** wie wär's mit einem Drink?, etwas zu trinken?; **~ ~ another?** noch einen?; **I never have much ~d ~ his films** ich habe mir noch nie viel aus seinen Filmen gemacht; **yes, sir, what would you ~ ~?** was hätte der Herr gern?; **what sort of hotel would madam ~ ~?** an welche Art von Hotel hatten gnädige Frau gedacht?; **but you know I do ~ ~ you** aber du weißt doch, daß du mir viel bedeutest *or* daß du mir nicht egal *or* gleichgültig bist.

career [kə'rɪə^r] 1 *n* Karriere *f*; (*profession, job*) Beruf *m*; (*working life*) Laufbahn *f*; (*life, development, progress*) Werdegang *m* ♦ **~s officer** Berufsberater(in *f*) *m*; **~s guidance** Berufsberatung *f*; **journalism is his new ~** er hat jetzt die Laufbahn des Journalisten eingeschlagen; **to make a ~ for oneself** Karriere machen; **~s adviser** Berufsberater(in *f*) *m*.

2 *attr* Karriere-; *soldier, diplomat* Berufs- ♦ **~ girl** *or* **woman** Karrierefrau *f*.

3 *vi* rasen ♦ **to ~ along** rasen; **the car ~ed out of control** das Auto geriet außer Kontrolle.

careerist [kə'rɪərɪst] *n* Karrierist(in *f*), Karrieremacher(in *f*) *m*.

carefree ['kɛəfriː] *adj* sorglos, unbekümmert; *song* heiter.

▼ **careful** ['kɛəfʊl] *adj* sorgfältig; (*cautious, circumspect*) sorgsam, vorsichtig; (*with money etc*) sparsam ♦ **~!** Vorsicht!, passen Sie auf!; **to be ~** aufpassen (*of* auf *+acc*); **be ~ with the glasses** sei mit den Gläsern vorsichtig; **be ~ what you do** sieh dich vor, nimm dich in acht; **be ~ (that) they don't hear you** gib acht *or* sei vorsichtig, damit *or* daß sie dich nicht hören; **be ~ not to drop it** paß auf, daß du das nicht fallen läßt; **he is very ~ with his money** er hält sein Geld gut zusammen.

carefully ['kɛəfəlɪ] *adv see adj*.

carefulness ['kɛəfʊlnɪs] *n see adj* Sorgfalt *f*; Sorgsamkeit, Vorsicht *f*; Sparsamkeit *f*.

care label *n* Pflegeetikett *nt*.

careless ['kɛəlɪs] *adj* **(a)** (*negligent, heedless*) *person, worker, work* nachlässig; *driver* unvorsichtig; *driving* leichtsinnig; *remark* gedankenlos ♦ **~ mistake** Flüchtigkeitsfehler *m*; **to be ~ of one's health** nicht auf seine Gesundheit achten; **to be ~ of sb's feelings** nicht an jds (*acc*) Gefühle denken.

(b) (*carefree*) sorglos, unbekümmert.

(c) *dress, elegance* lässig.

carelessly ['kɛəlɪslɪ] *adv see adj*.

carelessness ['kɛəlɪsnɪs] *n see adj* **(a)** Nachlässigkeit *f*; Unvorsicht(igkeit) *f*; Leichtsinn *m*; Gedankenlosigkeit *f*. **(b)** Sorglosigkeit, Unbekümmertheit *f*. **(c)** Lässigkeit *f*.

carer ['kɛərə^r] *n* im Sozialbereich Tätige(r) *mf* ♦ **the handicapped and their ~s** die Behinderten und ihre Fürsorgenden.

caress [kə'res] 1 *n* Liebkosung, Zärtlichkeit *f usu pl*, Streicheln *nt no pl*.

2 *vt* streicheln, liebkosen.

caressing [kə'resɪŋ] *adj* zärtlich, sanft, streichelnd.

caret ['kærət] *n* (*Typ*) Einschaltungszeichen *nt*.

care: ~taker *n* Hausmeister *m*; **~taker government** *n* geschäftsführende Regierung; **~worn** *adj* von Sorgen gezeichnet.

car: ~ fare *n* (*US*) Fahrpreis *m*; **~-ferry** *n* Autofähre *f*.

cargo ['kɑːgəʊ] *n* (Schiffs)fracht *or* -ladung *f*, Kargo *m* (*spec*) ♦ **~ boat** Frachter, Frachtdampfer *m*, Frachtschiff *nt*.

car hire *n* Autovermietung *f*.

carhop ['kɑːhɒp] *n* (*US*) Bedienung *f* in einem Drive-in-Restaurant.

Caribbean [ˌkærɪ'biːən, (*US*) kæ'rɪbiːən] 1 *adj* karibisch ♦ **~ Sea** Karibisches Meer.

2 *n* Karibik *f*.

caribou ['kærɪbuː] *n* Karibu *m*.

caricature ['kærɪkətjʊə^r] 1 *n* Karikatur *f*.

2 *vt* karikieren.

caricaturist [ˌkærɪkə'tjʊərɪst] *n* Karikaturist(in *f*) *m*.

caries ['kɛəriiːz] *n* Karies *f*.

carillon [kə'rɪljən] *n* Glockenspiel *nt*.

caring ['kɛərɪŋ] *adj person, attitude* warmherzig, mitfühlend, einfühlsam; *parent, husband* liebevoll; *teacher* engagiert; *government, society* sozial, mitmenschlich ♦ **a child needs a ~ environment** ein Kind braucht Zuwendung *or* braucht eine Umgebung, die sich um es kümmert ♦ **~ profession** Sozialberuf *m*.

car insurance *n* Kfz-Versicherung, Kraftfahrzeugversicherung *f*.

carjacker ['kɑːdʒækə^r] *n Räuber m der seine Opfer in ihren Autos überfällt und beraubt*, Carjacker *m*.

carjacking ['kɑːdʒækɪŋ] *n* Autoraub *m*, Carjacking *nt*.

Carmelite ['kɑːməlaɪt] *n* Karmelit(in *f*), Karmeliter(in *f*) *m*.

carmine ['kɑːmaɪn] 1 *adj* karm(es)inrot.

2 *n* Karmesin- *or* Karmin(rot) *nt*.

carnage ['kɑːnɪdʒ] *n* Blutbad, Gemetzel *nt* ♦ **a scene of ~** ein blutiges Schauspiel; **fields covered with the ~ of battle** mit Toten *or* Leichen übersäte Schlachtfelder *pl*.

carnal ['kɑːnl] *adj* fleischlich, körperlich ♦ **~ desires** sinnliche Begierden; **~ lusts** Fleischeslust *f* (*liter*); **to have ~ knowledge of sb** mit jdm (Geschlechts)verkehr haben.

carnation [kɑː'neɪʃən] *n* Nelke *f*.

carnival ['kɑːnɪvəl] 1 *n* Volksfest *nt*; (*village ~ etc*) Schützenfest *nt*; (*based on religion*) Karneval *m*.

2 *attr* Fest-; Karnevals- ♦ **~ procession** Fest-/Karnevalszug *m*.

carnivore ['kɑːnɪvɔː^r] *n, pl* **carnivora** [kɑː'nɪvərə] (*animal*) Fleischfresser *m*; (*plant*) fleischfressende Pflanze.

carnivorous [kɑː'nɪvərəs] *adj* fleischfressend, karnivor.

carob ['kærəb] *n* Johannisbrotbaum *m*; (*fruit*) Johannisbrot *nt*.

carol ['kærəl] 1 *n* Lied *nt* ♦ **Christmas ~** Weihnachtslied *nt*.

2 *vi* (*old, liter*) (fröhlich) singen, jubilieren (*old, liter*); (*bird*) tirilieren (*old, liter*).

carol: ~ singers *npl* ≃ Sternsinger *pl*; **~ singing** *n* Weihnachtssingen *nt*.

carom ['kærəm] (*US*) 1 *n* Karambolage *f*.

2 *vi* (*Billiards*) karambolieren; (*rebound*) abprallen.

carotene ['kærətiːn] *n* Karotin *nt*.

carotid (artery) [kə'rɒtɪd('ɑːtərɪ)] *n* Halsschlagader, Karotide (*spec*) *f*.

carousal [kə'raʊzəl] *n* (*old*) (Zech)gelage *nt*, Schmaus *m*.

carouse [kə'raʊz] *vi* (*old*) zechen, Gelage feiern.

carousel [ˌkæruː'sel] *n see* **car(r)ousel**.

carp[1] [kɑːp] *n* (*fish*) Karpfen *m*.

carp[2] *vi* etwas auszusetzen haben, nörgeln ♦ **to ~ at sb/sth** an jdm/etw etwas auszusetzen haben, an jdm herummeckern (*inf*)/über etw (*acc*) meckern (*inf*).

carpal bone ['kɑːpl'bəʊn] *n* Handwurzelknochen *m*.

car: ~ park *n* (*Brit*) (*open-air*) Parkplatz *m*; (*covered*) Parkhaus *nt*; **~ parking** *n* **~ parking facilities are available** Parkplatz *or* Parkmöglichkeit(en) vorhanden; **~ park ticket** *n* Parkschein *m*.

Carpathians [kɑː'peɪθɪənz] *npl* (*Geog*) Karpaten *pl*.

carpel ['kɑːpl] *n* Fruchtblatt *nt*.

carpenter ['kɑːpɪntə^r] *n* Zimmermann *m*; (*for furniture*) Tischler *m*.

carpentry ['kɑːpɪntrɪ] *n* Zimmerhandwerk *nt*, (Bau)tischlerei *f*; (*as hobby*) Tischlern *nt* ♦ **a piece of ~** eine Tischlerarbeit.

carpet ['kɑːpɪt] 1 *n* (*lit, fig*) Teppich *m*; (*fitted*) Teppichboden *m* ♦ **the subject on the ~** das Thema, das zur Zeit diskutiert wird; **to have sb on the ~** (*inf*) jdn zur Minna machen (*inf*).

2 *vt* **(a)** *floor* (mit Teppichen/Teppichboden) auslegen ♦ **the wood ~ed in** *or* **with moss** der moosbedeckte Waldboden.

(b) (*inf: reprimand*) zur Minna machen (*inf*).

carpet: ~ bag *n* Reisetasche *f*; **~bagger** *n* (*US*) (*inf*) politischer Abenteurer; (*Hist*) *politischer Ämterjäger, der mit nichts als einer Reisetasche nach dem Sezessionskrieg in die besetzten Südstaaten kam*; **~-beater** *n* Teppich- *or* Ausklopfer *m*.

carpeting ['kɑːpɪtɪŋ] *n* Teppiche *pl*.

➤ LANGUAGE IN USE: **care: 2** → 7.5 **careful** → 2.3

carpet: ~ slippers *npl* Pantoffeln, Hausschuhe *pl*; **~ sweeper** *n* Teppichkehrer *m*, Teppichkehrmaschine *f*; **~ tile** *n* Teppichfliese *f*.
car phone *n* Autotelefon *nt*.
carping ['kɑːpɪŋ] [1] *adj* **a ~ old woman** eine alte Meckerziege (*inf*); **she grew weary of his ~ criticism** sie wurde sein ständiges Nörgeln leid.
[2] *n* Nörgelei(en *pl*) *f*, Gemecker *nt* (*inf*).
carpool ['kɑː,puːl] [1] *n* **(a)** (*people*) Fahrgemeinschaft *f*. **(b)** (*vehicles*) Fuhrpark *m*.
[2] *vi* eine Fahrgemeinschaft bilden (*with* mit).
carport ['kɑːpɔːt] *n* Einstellplatz *m*.
car radio *n* Autoradio *nt*.
carrel ['kærəl] *n* Arbeitsnische *f*, Arbeitsplatz *m* (*in Bibliothek*).
carriage ['kærɪdʒ] *n* **(a)** (*horse-drawn vehicle*) Kutsche *f*; (*esp US: baby* ~) Kinderwagen *m* ◆ **~ and pair** Zweispänner *m*.
(b) (*Brit Rail*) Wagen *m*.
(c) (*Comm: conveyance*) Beförderung *f*; (*cost of* ~ *also*) Beförderungskosten *pl* ◆ **~ forward** Fracht zahlt Empfänger; **~ free** frachtfrei; **~ paid** frei Haus.
(d) (*Typ*) Wagen *m* ◆ **~ return** Wagenrücklauf *m*; (*Comput*) Return *nt*.
(e) (*Mil: gun-*~) Lafette *f*.
(f) (*of person: bearing*) Haltung *f*.
carriage clock *n* ≃ Stiluhr *f*.
carriageway ['kærɪdʒ'weɪ] *n* (*Brit*) Fahrbahn *f*.
car ride *n* Autofahrt *f*, Fahrt *f* mit dem Auto.
carrier ['kærɪəʳ] *n* **(a)** (*goods haulier*) Spediteur, Transportunternehmer *m*.
(b) (*of disease*) Überträger *m*.
(c) (*aircraft* ~) Flugzeugträger *m*; (*troop* ~) Transportflugzeug *nt*/-schiff *nt*.
(d) (*Chem*) Träger(substanz *f*) *m*; (*catalyst*) Katalysator *m*.
(e) (*luggage rack*) Gepäckträger *m*.
(f) (*Brit also* **~ bag**) Tragetasche, Tragetüte *f*.
(g) (*also* **~ pigeon**) Brieftaube *f* ◆ **by ~ pigeon** mit der Taubenpost.
carrion ['kærɪən] *n* Aas *nt* ◆ **~ crow** Rabenkrähe *f*.
carrot ['kærət] *n* Mohrrübe, Karotte, Möhre *f*; (*fig*) Köder *m* ◆ **to dangle a ~ before sb** *or* **in front of sb** jdm einen Köder unter die Nase halten; **the stick and the ~** Zuckerbrot und Peitsche.
carrot-and-stick [,kærətən'stɪk] *adj* **~ policy** Politik *f* von Zuckerbrot und Peitsche.
carroty ['kærətɪ] *adj hair* kupferrot.
car(r)ousel [,kæruː'sel] *n* **(a)** Karussell *nt*. **(b)** (*for slides*) Rundmagazin *nt*.
carry ['kærɪ] [1] *vt* **(a)** tragen; *message* (über)bringen.
(b) (*vehicle: convey*) befördern; *goods also* transportieren ◆ **this coach carries 30 people** dieser Bus kann 30 Personen befördern; **a boat ~ing missiles to Cuba** ein Schiff mit Raketen für Kuba; **the boat was carried along by the wind** der Wind trieb das Boot dahin; **the sea carried the boat westward** das Boot wurde nach Westen abgetrieben, die Strömung trieb das Boot westwärts; **the wind carried the sound to him** der Wind trug die Laute zu ihm hin *or* an sein Ohr.
(c) (*have on person*) *documents, money* bei sich haben *or* führen (*form*); *gun, sword* tragen ◆ **to ~ sth about** *or* **around with one** etw mit sich herumtragen; **to ~ money on one** Geld bei sich haben; **to ~ the facts in one's head** die Fakten im Kopf haben; (*remember*) die Fakten (im Kopf) behalten; **the ship was ~ing too much sail** das Schiff hatte zu viele Segel gesetzt.
(d) (*fig*) **his voice carries conviction** seine Stimme klingt überzeugend; **he carried his audience with him** er riß das Publikum mit, er begeisterte das Publikum; **to ~ interest** (*Fin*) Zinsen tragen *or* abwerfen; **the loan carries 5% interest** das Darlehen wird mit 5% verzinst; **this job carries extra pay/a lot of responsibility** dieser Posten bringt eine höhere Bezahlung/viel Verantwortung mit sich; **the offence carries a penalty of £50** auf dies Vergehen *or* darauf steht eine Geldstrafe von £ 50.
(e) (*bridge etc: support*) tragen, stützen ◆ **he carries his drink well** er kann viel vertragen; **he can't ~ the responsibility** er ist der Verantwortung nicht gewachsen.
(f) (*Comm*) *goods, stock* führen, (auf Lager) haben.
(g) (*Tech: pipe*) *water, oil, electricity* führen; (*wire*) *sound* (weiter)leiten, übertragen.
(h) (*extend*) führen, (ver)legen ◆ **they carried the pipes under the street** sie verlegten die Rohre unter der Straße; **to ~ sth too far** (*fig*) etw zu weit treiben; **they carried the war into the enemy's territory** sie trugen den Krieg in feindliches Gebiet; **this theme is carried through the whole book** dies Thema zieht sich durch das ganze Buch.
(i) (*win*) einnehmen, erobern ◆ **to ~ the day** siegreich sein, den Sieg davontragen; **to ~ all** *or* **everything before one** freie Bahn haben; (*hum: woman*) viel Holz vor der Tür haben (*inf*); **the motion was carried unanimously** der Antrag wurde einstimmig angenommen; **he carried his point** er ist mit diesem Punkt durchgekommen; **he carried all seven states** er hat die Wahl in allen sieben Staaten gewonnen.
(j) he carries himself well/like a soldier er hat eine gute/soldatische Haltung; **he carries himself with dignity** er tritt würdig auf; **she carries her head very erect** sie trägt den Kopf sehr aufrecht.
(k) (*Press*) *story* bringen.
(l) (*be pregnant with*) erwarten, schwanger gehen mit (*geh*) ◆ **to be ~ing a child** schwanger sein, ein Kind erwarten.
(m) (*Math*) ... **and ~ 2** ... übertrage *or* behalte 2, ... und 2 im Sinn (*inf*).
[2] *vi* **(a)** (*voice, sound*) tragen ◆ **the sound of the alphorn carried for miles** der Klang des Alphorns war meilenweit zu hören. **(b)** (*ball, arrow*) fliegen.
◆**carry away** *vt sep* **(a)** (*lit*) (hin)wegtragen; (*torrent, flood*) (hin)wegspülen; (*whirlwind, tornado*) hinwegfegen.
(b) (*fig*) **to get carried ~** sich nicht mehr bremsen können (*inf*); **don't get carried ~!** übertreib's nicht!, brems dich (*inf*); **to get carried ~ by sth** bei etw in Fahrt kommen; **to be carried ~ by one's feelings** sich (in seine Gefühle) hineinsteigern; **don't get carried ~ by your success** daß dir dein Erfolg nicht in den Kopf steigt!; **she got carried ~ by the atmosphere of excitement** sie wurde von der Aufregung mitgerissen.
◆**carry back** *vt sep* (*fig*) *person* zurückversetzen (*to* in +*acc*).
◆**carry forward** *vt sep* (*Fin*) vortragen.
◆**carry off** *vt sep* **(a)** (*seize, carry away*) wegtragen. **(b)** (*win*) *prizes, medals* gewinnen, mit nach Hause nehmen (*inf*). **(c) to ~ it ~** es hinkriegen (*inf*). **(d)** (*kill*) (hin)wegraffen (*geh*).
◆**carry on** [1] *vi* **(a)** (*continue*) weitermachen; (*life*) weitergehen ◆ **here's £5/some work to be ~ing ~ with** hier sind erst einmal 5 Pfund/hier ist etwas Arbeit fürs nächste.
(b) (*inf*) (*talk*) reden und reden; (*make a scene*) ein Theater machen (*inf*) ◆ **to ~ ~ about sth** sich über etw (*acc*) auslassen; **they just kept ~ing ~ about it until somebody did something** sie haben so lange weitergebohrt, bis jemand etwas gemacht hat; **she does tend to ~ ~** sie redet und redet.
(c) (*have an affair*) etwas haben (*inf*) (*with sb* mit jdm).
[2] *vt sep* **(a)** (*continue*) *tradition, family business* fortführen.
(b) (*conduct*) *conversation, correspondence, business* führen; *profession, trade* ausüben.
◆**carry out** *vt sep* **(a)** (*lit*) heraustragen. **(b)** (*fig*) *order, rules, job* ausführen; *promises, obligations* erfüllen; *plan, reform, search, experiment* durchführen; *threats* wahrmachen.
◆**carry over** *vt sep* **(a)** (*Fin*) vortragen. **(b)** (*to next meeting etc*) vertagen.
◆**carry through** *vt sep* **(a)** (*carry out*) zu Ende führen. **(b)** (*sustain*) überstehen lassen.
◆**carry up** *vt sep* hinauftragen, hochtragen.
carry: ~-all *n* (*US*) (Einkaufs-/Reise)tasche *f*; **~-cot** *n* Säuglingstragetasche *f*.
carryings-on ['kærɪɪŋz'ɒn] *npl* (*inf*) übles Treiben (*inf*) ◆ **all these ~ next door** was die da nebenan alles so treiben (*inf*), was sich da nebenan alles so abspielt.
carry: ~-on *n* (*inf*) Theater *nt* (*inf*); **~-out** (*US, Scot*) [1] *n* **(a)** (*restaurant*) Imbißstube *f*/Restaurant *nt* für Außer-Haus-Verkauf; (*bar*) Schalter *m* für Außer-Haus-Verkauf, Gassenschenke *f* (*S Ger*); **(b)** (*meal, drink*) Speisen *pl*/Getränke *pl* zum Mitnehmen; **let's get a ~-out** kaufen wir uns etwas zum Mitnehmen; **~-outs aren't allowed in the grounds** auf das Gelände dürfen keine Getränke mitgebracht werden;
[2] *adj attr* Außer-Haus-; **the ~-out menu is quite different** für Gerichte zum Mitnehmen gibt es eine ganz andere Speisekarte; **~-over** *n* Überbleibsel *nt*; (*Fin*) Saldovortrag, Übertrag *m*; (*Math*) Rest *m*.
car: ~sick *adj* **I used to get ~sick** früher wurde mir beim Autofahren immer übel *or* schlecht; **~sickness** *n* Übelkeit *f* beim Autofahren.
cart [kɑːt] [1] *n* Wagen, Karren *m* ◆ **to put the ~ before the horse** (*prov*) das Pferd beim Schwanz aufzäumen (*prov*).
[2] *vt* (*fig inf*) mit sich schleppen.
◆**cart away** *or* **off** *vt sep* abtransportieren, wegbringen.
cartage ['kɑːtɪdʒ] *n* (*act, cost*) Transport *m*.
carte blanche ['kɑːt'blɑ̃nʃ] *n*, *no pl* Blankovollmacht *f* ◆ **to give sb ~** jdm Carte Blanche (*geh*) *or* (eine) Blankovollmacht geben.
cartel [kɑː'tel] *n* Kartell *nt*.
carter ['kɑːtəʳ] *n* Fuhrmann *m*.
Cartesian [kɑː'tiːzɪən] [1] *adj* kartesianisch, kartesisch.
[2] *n* Kartesianer *m*.
Carthage ['kɑːθɪdʒ] *n* Karthago *nt*.
Carthaginian [,kɑːθə'dʒɪnɪən] [1] *adj* karthagisch.
[2] *n* Karthager(in *f*) *m*.
carthorse ['kɑːthɔːs] *n* Zugpferd *nt*.
cartilage ['kɑːtɪlɪdʒ] *n* Knorpel *m*.
cartload ['kɑːtləʊd] *n* Wagenladung *f*.
cartographer [kɑː'tɒgrəfəʳ] *n* Kartograph(in *f*) *m*.
cartographic(al) [,kɑːtəʊ'græfɪk(əl)] *adj* kartographisch.
cartography [kɑː'tɒgrəfɪ] *n* Kartographie *f*.
cartomancy ['kɑːtə,mænsɪ] *n* Kartenlegen *nt*, Kartomantie *f* (*spec*).
carton ['kɑːtən] *n* (Papp)karton *m*; (*of cigarettes*) Stange *f*; (*of milk*) Tüte *f*.
cartoon [kɑː'tuːn] *n* **(a)** Cartoon *m or nt*; (*single picture*) Karikatur *f*. **(b)** (*Film, TV*) (Zeichen)trickfilm *m* ◆ **Mickey Mouse ~** Mickymausfilm *m*. **(c)** (*Art: sketch*) Karton *m*.
cartoon character *n* Comicfigur *f*.
cartoonist [,kɑː'tuːnɪst] *n* **(a)** Karikaturist(in *f*) *m*. **(b)** (*Film, TV*) Trickzeichner(in *f*) *m*.
cartoon strip *n* Cartoon *m or nt*, Comic *m*, Zeichengeschichte *f*.
cartouche ['kɑːtuːʃ] *n* Kartusche *f*.
cartridge ['kɑːtrɪdʒ] *n* (*for rifle, pen*) Patrone *f*; (*Phot, for tape recorder*) Kassette *f*; (*for record player*) Tonabnehmer *m*.
cartridge *in cpds* Patronen-; **~ belt** *n* Patronengurt *or* -gürtel *m*; **~ case** *n* Patronenhülse *f*; **~ clip** *n* Magazin *nt*; **~ paper** *n* Zeichenpapier *nt*.
cart: ~-track *n* Feldweg *m*; **~wheel** *n* (*lit*) Wagenrad *nt*; (*Sport*) Rad *nt*; **to turn** *or* **do ~wheels** radschlagen.
carve [kɑːv] [1] *vt* **(a)** (*Art: cut*) *wood* schnitzen; *stone etc* (be)hauen ◆ **~d out of** *or* **in wood/marble** aus Holz geschnitzt/aus Marmor gehauen; **to ~ sth on a stone** etw in einen Stein einmeißeln; **to ~ one's initials on a tree** seine Initialen in einen Baum einritzen *or* schnitzen; **a frieze ~d with flowers** ein

geschnitzter *or* (*in stone*) gemeißelter Blumenfries; **the sculptor was still carving the face** der Bildhauer schnitzte *or* (*in stone*) meißelte noch das Gesicht.
(b) (*Cook*) aufschneiden, zerteilen, tranchieren.
(c) (*fig*) **to ~ one's way through the crowd/jungle** sich (*dat*) seinen Weg durch die Menge/den Dschungel bahnen.
[2] *vi* (*Cook*) tranchieren.
◆**carve out** *vt sep* **(a)** (*in wood*) schnitzen; (*in stone*) meißeln. **(b)** (*fig*) *piece of land* abtrennen, loslösen. **(c) to ~ ~ a career for oneself** sich (*dat*) eine Karriere aufbauen.
◆**carve up** *vt sep* **(a)** *meat*, (*inf: surgeon*) aufschneiden; *body* zerstückeln. **(b)** (*fig*) *country* aufteilen, zerstückeln; *area of town etc* zerreißen, auseinanderreißen. **(c)** (*inf: with knife*) *person* (mit dem Messer) böse zurichten (*inf*) ◆ **to ~ ~ sb's face** jdm das Gesicht zerfetzen. **(d)** (*sl: driver*) schneiden.
carver ['kɑːvəʳ] *n* (*knife*) Tranchiermesser *nt* ◆ **a set of ~s** ein Tranchierbesteck *nt*.
carve-up ['kɑːvʌp] *n* (*inf*) (*of inheritance*) Verteilung *f*; (*of estate, country*) Zerstückelung *f*.
carving ['kɑːvɪŋ] *n* • (*Art*) (*thing carved*) Skulptur *f*; (*in wood also*) (Holz)schnitzerei *f*; (*relief*) Relief *nt*; (*in wood*) Holzschnitt *m* ◆ **~ knife** Tranchiermesser *nt*.
carwash ['kɑːwɒʃ] *n* (*place*) Autowaschanlage, Waschstraße *f*; (*wash*) Autowäsche *f*.
caryatid [,kærɪ'ætɪd] *n* Karyatide *f*.
casanova [,kæsə'nəʊvə] *n* (*hum*) Casanova *m* (*inf*).
cascade [kæs'keɪd] [1] *n* Kaskade *f*; (*fig*) (*of lace etc*) (Spitzen)besatz *m*; (*of sparks*) Regen *m* ◆ **a ~ of green sparks** ein grüner Funkenregen.
[2] *vi* (*also* **~ down**) (*onto* auf *+acc*) (in Kaskaden) herabfallen; (*sparks*) herabsprühen, herabregnen; (*hair*) wallend herabfallen; (*boxes etc*) herunterpurzeln (*inf*).
▼ **case**[1] [keɪs] *n* **(a)** (*situation*) Fall *m* ◆ **if that's the ~** wenn das der Fall ist, wenn das zutrifft *or* stimmt; **is that the ~ with you?** ist das bei Ihnen der Fall?, trifft das auf Sie zu?; **if it is the ~ that you're right** ... sollten Sie wirklich *or* tatsächlich recht haben ...; im Fall(e), daß Sie tatsächlich recht haben ...; **such being the ~** da das der Fall ist, da dem so ist (*geh*); **if it is a ~ of his not having been informed** wenn er nicht benachrichtigt worden ist; **as the ~ may be** je nachdem.
(b) (*instance, police ~, Med etc*) Fall *m* ◆ **in most ~s** meist(ens), in den meisten Fällen; **a typical ~ (of)** ein typischer Fall (von); **it's a clear ~ of lying** das ist eindeutig gelogen; **in ~** falls; **(just) in ~** für alle Fälle; **in ~ of emergency** im Notfall *m*, bei Gefahr *f*; **in any ~** sowieso; **in this/that ~** in dem Fall; **in no ~** unter keinen Umständen, auf keinen Fall; **five ~s of smallpox/pneumonia** fünf Pockenfälle/Fälle von Lungenentzündung *f*.
(c) (*Jur*) Fall *m* ◆ **to win one's ~** seinen Prozeß gewinnen; **the ~ for the defence/prosecution** die Verteidigung/Anklage; **what's the ~ for the prosecution?** worauf stützt sich die Anklage?; **could we hear the ~ for the defence?** das Wort hat die Verteidigung; **the Keeler ~** der Fall Keeler; **in the ~ Higgins v Schwarz** in der Sache Higgins gegen Schwarz; **to make out a good ~ for sth** überzeugende Argumente für etw liefern; **the ~ for/against the abolition of capital punishment** die Argumente für/gegen die Abschaffung der Todesstrafe; **you haven't got a ~** das Belastungsmaterial reicht nicht für ein Verfahren; (*fig*) Sie haben keine Handhabe; **to have a good ~** (*Jur*) gute Chancen haben, durchzukommen; **you/they have a good ~** es ist durchaus gerechtfertigt, was Sie/sie sagen; **there's a very good ~ for adopting this method** es spricht sehr viel dafür, diese Methode zu übernehmen; **they do not have a very good ~** sie haben nicht viel Chancen, damit durchzukommen; **to put one's ~** seinen Fall darlegen; **to put the ~ for sth** etw vertreten; **there's a strong ~ for legalizing pot** es spricht viel für die Legalisierung von Hasch; **there's a good ~ for voting Labour** es gibt viele Gründe, Labour zu wählen; **the court decided that there was no ~ against him** das Gericht entschied, daß nichts gegen ihn vorlag; **that is my ~** das war es, was ich sagen wollte; **a ~ of conscience** eine Gewissensfrage *or* -entscheidung.
(d) (*Gram*) Fall, Kasus *m* ◆ **in the genitive ~** im Genitiv.
(e) (*inf: person*) Witzbold *m*, Type *f* (*inf*) ◆ **he's a ~** das ist vielleicht 'ne Type (*inf*); **a hard ~** ein schwieriger Fall.
case[2] [1] *n* **(a)** (*suit~*) Koffer *m*; (*crate, packing ~*) Kiste *f*; (*display ~*) Vitrine *f*, Schau- *or* Glaskasten *m* ◆ **~s of oranges** Apfelsinenkisten *pl*.
(b) (*box*) Schachtel *f*; (*for jewels*) Schatulle *f*, Kästchen *nt*; (*for spectacles*) Etui, Futteral *nt*; (*seed~*) Hülse, Hülle *f*; (*for umbrella*) Hülle *f*; (*pillow~*) Bezug *m*; (*for musical instrument*) Kasten *m*; (*of watch*) Gehäuse *nt*.
(c) (*Typ*) (Setz)kasten *m*; (*of book*) Schuber *m* ◆ **upper/lower ~** groß/klein geschrieben.
[2] *vt* (*sl*) *bank, house* inspizieren ◆ **to ~ the joint** sich (*dat*) den Laden ansehen (*sl*).
case: ~book *n* (*Med*) (Kranken)fälle *pl*; (*in social work, Jur*) Fallsammlung *f*; **~-bound** *adj* (*Typ*) mit Pappeinband; **~ ending** *n* (*Gram*) Endung *f*; **~ file** *n* **~ file on X** Akte *f* zum Fall X; **~-harden** *vt metal* verstählen, vereisenen; **~-hardened** *adj* (*fig*) abgebrüht (*inf*); **~ history** *n* (*Med*) Krankengeschichte *f*; (*Sociol, Psych*) Vorgeschichte *f*; **~ law** *n* (*Jur*) Fallrecht *nt*; **~-load** *n* **to have a heavy/light ~-load** viele/wenig Fälle haben.
casement ['keɪsmənt] *n* (*window*) Flügelfenster *nt*; (*frame*) Fensterflügel *m*.
case: ~ study *n* Fallstudie *f*; **~work** *n* (*Sociol*) ≃ Sozialarbeit *f*; **~worker** *n* (*Sociol*) ≃ Sozialarbeiter(in *f*) *m*.
cash [kæʃ] [1] *n* **(a)** Bargeld *nt*; (*change also*) Kleingeld *nt* ◆ **~ in hand** Barbestand, Kassenbestand *m*; **to pay (in) ~** bar bezahlen; **ready ~** verfügbares Geld; **how much do you have in ready ~?** wieviel Geld haben Sie verfügbar?
(b) (*immediate payment*) Barzahlung *f*; (*not credit*) Sofortzahlung *f* ◆ **~ down** Barzahlung *f*; Sofortzahlung *f*; **£250 ~ down and the rest over ...** £ 250 sofort (zu bezahlen), und der Rest über ...; **to pay ~ (down)** (in) bar/sofort bezahlen; **~ with order** zahlbar bei Bestellung; **~ on delivery** per Nachnahme.
(c) (*money*) Geld *nt* ◆ **to be short of ~** knapp bei Kasse sein (*inf*); **I'm out of ~** ich bin blank (*inf*), ich habe kein Geld.
[2] *vt cheque* einlösen.
◆**cash in** [1] *vt sep* einlösen.
[2] *vi* **to ~ ~ on sth** aus etw Kapital schlagen, sich (*dat*) etw zunutze machen; **we want to stop others ~ing ~ (on the act)** (*inf*) wir wollen verhindern, daß andere aus der Sache Kapital schlagen.
◆**cash up** *vi* (*Brit*) Kasse machen.
cash: ~ advance *n* Vorschuß *m*; **~-and-carry** [1] *adj* Cash-and-carry-; [2] *n* (*for retailers*) Cash and Carry, Abholmarkt *m*; (*for public*) Verbrauchermarkt *m*; **~ book** *n* Kassenbuch *nt*; **~ box** *n* (Geld)kassette *f*; **~ card** *n* (Geld)automatenkarte *f*; **~ crop** *n* zum Verkauf bestimmte Ernte; **~desk** *n* Kasse *f*, Kassentisch *m*; **~ discount** *n* Skonto *m or nt*, Rabatt *m* bei Barzahlung; **~ dispenser** *n* Geldautomat *m*.
cashew [kæ'ʃuː] *n* (*tree*) Nierenbaum *m*; (*nut*) Cashewnuß *f*.
cash-flow ['kæʃfləʊ] *n* Cash-flow *m* ◆ **~ analysis** Cash-flow-Analyse *f*; **~ forecast** Cash-flow-Prognose *f*; **~ position** Bruttoertragslage *f*; **~ problems** Liquiditätsprobleme *pl*; **I've got ~ problems** (*personal*) ich bin in Geldschwierigkeiten.
cashier[1] [kæ'ʃɪəʳ] *n* Kassierer(in *f*) *m*.
cashier[2] *vt* (*Mil*) (unehrenhaft) entlassen, kassieren (*old*).
cashless ['kæʃləs] *adj* bargeldlos.
cashmere [kæʃ'mɪəʳ] *n* Kaschmir *m* ◆ **~ wool** Kaschmirwolle *f*.
cash: ~ offer *n* Bar(zahlungs)angebot *nt*; **~ office** *n* Kasse *f*, Kassenbüro *nt*; **~ payment** *n* Barzahlung *f*; **~point** *n* Kasse *f*; **~ price** *n* Bar(zahlungs)preis *m*; **~ receipts** *npl* (*in shop*) Bareinnahmen *pl*; **~ reduction** *n see* **~ discount**; **~ register** *n* Registrierkasse *f*; **~ reserves** *npl* Bargeldreserven *pl*; **~ sale** *n* Barverkauf *m*; **~ transaction** *n* Bargeldtransfer *m*.
casing ['keɪsɪŋ] *n* (*Tech*) Gehäuse *nt*; (*of cylinder, tyre*) Mantel *m*; (*of sausage*) Haut *f*, Darm *m*.
casino [kə'siːnəʊ] *n* (Spiel)kasino *nt*, Spielbank *f*.
cask [kɑːsk] *n* Faß *nt*.
casket ['kɑːskɪt] *n* Schatulle *f*; (*for cremated ashes*) Urne *f*; (*US: coffin*) Sarg *m*, Totenschrein *m* (*geh*).
Caspian Sea ['kæspɪən'siː] *n* Kaspisches Meer.
Cassandra [kə'sændrə] *n* (*Myth*) Kassandra *f* ◆ **despite all the C~s** (*fig*) allen Kassandrarufen *or* Unkenrufen zum Trotz.
cassava [kə'sɑːvə] *n* Maniok *m*.
casserole ['kæsərəʊl] [1] *n* (*Cook*) Schmortopf *m*, Kasserolle *f* ◆ **a lamb ~, a ~ of lamb** eine Lammkasserolle.
[2] *vt* schmoren.
cassette [kæ'set] *n* Kassette *f* ◆ **~ deck** Kassettendeck *nt*; **~ player, ~ recorder** Kassettenrecorder *m*.
cassock ['kæsək] *n* Talar *m*, Soutane *f*.
cast [kɑːst] (*vb: pret, ptp* **~**) [1] *n* **(a)** (*of dice, net, line*) Wurf *m*.
(b) (*mould*) (Guß)form *f*; (*object moulded*) Abdruck *m*; (*in metal*) (Ab)guß *m*.
(c) (*plaster ~*) Gipsverband *m*.
(d) (*Theat*) Besetzung *f* ◆ **~ (in order of appearance)** Mitwirkende *pl* (in der Reihenfolge ihres Auftritts); **the ~ includes several famous actors** das Stück ist mit mehreren berühmten Schauspielern besetzt; **who's in the ~?** wer spielt mit?
(e) the ~ of sb's features jds Gesichtsschnitt *m*; **~ of mind** Gesinnung *f*; **he's a man of quite a different ~** er ist aus anderem Holz geschnitzt, er ist ein Mensch von ganz anderem Zuschnitt.
(f) (*tinge*) Schimmer *m*.
(g) (*of worm*) aufgeworfene Erde; (*of bird*) Gewölle *nt*.
(h) (*Med: squint*) schielender Blick ◆ **to have a ~ in one eye** auf einem Auge schielen.
[2] *vt* **(a)** (*lit liter, fig: throw*) werfen; *anchor, net, fishing lines* auswerfen; *horoscope* erstellen ◆ **to ~ one's vote** seine Stimme abgeben; **a picture of the bishop ~ing his vote** ein Bild des Bischofs bei der Stimmabgabe; **to ~ lots** (aus)losen; **to ~ in one's lot with sb** sich auf jds (*acc*) Seite stellen; **to ~ one's eyes over sth** einen Blick auf etw (*acc*) werfen; **to ~ the blame on sb** jdm die Schuld geben, die Schuld auf jdn abwälzen; **to ~ a shadow** (*lit, fig*) einen Schatten werfen (*on* auf *+acc*).
(b) (*shed*) **to ~ its skin** sich häuten; **to ~ a shoe** ein Hufeisen *nt* verlieren; **to ~ its feathers** (*form*) sich mausern; **to ~ its leaves** (*form*) die Blätter abwerfen; **to ~ its young** (*form*) (Junge) werfen.
(c) (*Tech, Art*) gießen; *see* **mould**[1].
(d) (*Theat*) *parts, play* besetzen; *parts also* verteilen ◆ **he was well/badly ~** die Rolle paßte gut/schlecht zu ihm; **he was ~ for the part of Hamlet** er sollte den Hamlet spielen; **I don't know why they ~ him as the villain** ich weiß nicht, warum sie ihm die Rolle des Schurken gegeben *or* zugeteilt haben.
[3] *vi* **(a)** (*Fishing*) die Angel auswerfen.
(b) (*Theat*) die Rollen verteilen, die Besetzung vornehmen.
◆**cast about** *or* **around for** *vi +prep obj* zu finden versuchen; *for new job etc also* sich umsehen nach ◆ **he was ~ing ~ (in his mind) ~ something to say** er

➤ LANGUAGE IN USE: **case**[1]: **a** → 26.1

suchte nach Worten; (*for answer/excuse*) er suchte nach einer Antwort/Ausrede.

◆**cast aside** *vt sep cares, prejudices, inhibitions, habits* ablegen; *old clothes etc* ausrangieren; *person* fallenlassen.

◆**cast away** *vt sep* wegwerfen ◆ **to be ~ ~** (*Naut*) gestrandet sein; **he was ~ ~ on a desert island** er wurde auf eine einsame Insel verschlagen.

◆**cast back** [1] *vi* (*fig*) **to ~ ~ (in one's mind)** im Geiste zurückdenken (*to* an *+acc*).
[2] *vt sep* **to ~ one's thoughts** *or* **mind ~** seine Gedanken zurückschweifen lassen (*to* in *+acc*).

◆**cast down** *vt sep eyes* niederschlagen; (*liter: throw down*) *weapons* hinwerfen ◆ **to be ~ ~** (*fig*) niedergeschlagen sein.

◆**cast off** [1] *vt sep* (a) (*get rid of*) abwerfen; *friends* fallenlassen ◆ **she ~ ~ three boyfriends in one week** in einer Woche hat sie drei Freunden den Laufpaß gegeben. (b) *stitches* abketten. (c) (*Naut*) losmachen.
[2] *vi* (a) (*Naut*) losmachen. (b) (*in knitting*) abketteln.

◆**cast on** *vti sep* (*Knitting*) anschlagen.

◆**cast out** *vt sep* (*liter*) vertreiben; *demons* austreiben.

◆**cast up** *vt sep* (a) **to ~ one's eyes ~ (to the heavens)** seine Augen (zum Himmel) emporrichten.
(b) (*wash up*) *flotsam, sailors* anspülen ◆ **they were ~ ~ on a desert island** sie wurden auf einer einsamen Insel an Land gespült; **~ ~ on the shores of life** im Leben gestrandet.
(c) (*refer to*) *sb's misdemeanours etc* aufbringen ◆ **to ~ sth ~ (at sb)** jdm etw vorhalten.

castanets [ˌkæstəˈnets] *npl* Kastagnetten *pl*.

castaway [ˈkɑːstəweɪ] *n* (*lit, fig*) Schiffbrüchige(r) *mf*.

caste [kɑːst] [1] *n* Kaste *f* ◆ **to lose ~** an Rang verlieren, absteigen; **he lost ~ with** *or* **among his friends** er verlor in den Augen seiner Freunde *or* bei seinen Freunden an Ansehen.
[2] *adj attr mark, system* Kasten- ◆ **a high/low ~ family** eine Familie, die einer hohen/niedrigen Kaste angehört.

castellan [ˈkæstələn] *n* Schloßvogt, Kastellan *m*.

castellated [ˈkæstəleɪtɪd] *adj* mit (Türmen und) Zinnen.

caster [ˈkɑːstəʳ] *n see* **castor.**

castigate [ˈkæstɪgeɪt] *vt person* (*old: physically*) züchtigen; (*verbally*) geißeln.

castigation [ˌkæstɪˈgeɪʃən] *n see vt* Züchtigung *f*; Geißelung *f*.

Castile [kæˈstiːl] *n* Kastilien *nt*.

Castilian [kæˈstɪljən] [1] *adj* kastilisch.
[2] *n* (a) (*language*) Kastilisch *nt*. (b) (*person*) Kastilier(in *f*) *m*.

casting [ˈkɑːstɪŋ] *n* (a) (*Fishing*) Auswerfen *nt*; (*Tech, Art: act, object*) (Ab)guß *m*; (*in plaster*) Abdruck, Abguß *m*. (b) (*Theat*) Rollenverteilung, Besetzung *f* ◆ **~ director** Besetzungsleiter(in *f*) *m*; **she got the part through the ~ couch** (*hum*) sie bekam die Rolle, weil sie mit dem Regisseur geschlafen hat.

casting vote *n* ausschlaggebende Stimme ◆ **he used his ~** seine Stimme gab den Ausschlag.

cast iron [1] *n* Gußeisen *nt*.
[2] *adj* **(~-iron)** (a) (*lit*) gußeisern; (b) (*fig*) *will, constitution* eisern; *case, alibi* hieb- und stichfest.

castle [ˈkɑːsl] [1] *n* (a) Schloß *nt*; (*medieval fortress*) Burg *f* ◆ **to build ~s in the air** *or* **in Spain** Luftschlösser bauen. (b) (*Chess*) Turm *m*.
[2] *vi* (*Chess*) rochieren.

castling [ˈkɑːslɪŋ] *n* (*Chess*) Rochade *f*.

cast: ~-off *adj clothes* abgelegt *attr*; **~-offs** *npl* (*inf*) abgelegte Kleider *pl*; **she's one of his ~-offs** (*fig inf*) sie ist eine seiner ausrangierten Freundinnen (*inf*).

castor [ˈkɑːstəʳ] *n* (a) (*Brit: for sugar, salt etc*) Streuer *m*. (b) (*wheel*) Rolle *f*, Rad *nt*.

castor: ~ oil *n* Rizinus(öl) *nt*; **~ sugar** *n* (*Brit*) Sandzucker *m*.

castrate [kæsˈtreɪt] *vt* kastrieren; (*fig*) *text* verstümmeln.

castrati [kæsˈtrɑːtiː] *pl of* **castrato.**

castration [kæsˈtreɪʃən] *n* Kastration *f*.

castrato [kæsˈtrɑːtəʊ] *n, pl* **castrati** Kastrat *m*.

casual [ˈkæʒjʊl] [1] *adj* (a) (*not planned*) zufällig; *acquaintance, glance* flüchtig ◆ **we were in the area, so we paid them a ~ visit** wir waren gerade in der Gegend und haben sie bei der Gelegenheit besucht; **~ sex** Gelegenheitssex *m*; freie Liebe.
(b) (*offhand, careless*) lässig; *attitude* gleichgültig; *remark* beiläufig; (*lacking emotion*) gleichgültig ◆ **it was just a ~ remark** das war nicht so ernst gemeint, das habe ich/hat er *etc* nur so gesagt; **he was very ~ about it** es war ihm offensichtlich gleichgültig; (*in reaction*) das hat ihn kaltgelassen *or* nicht tangiert (*inf*); **you shouldn't be so ~ about it** du solltest das nicht so leicht *or* auf die leichte Schulter nehmen; **he tried to sound ~** er tat so, als ob ihm das nichts ausmachen würde; **he had a rather ~ manner for a policeman** für einen Polizisten war er ziemlich salopp *or* lässig.
(c) (*informal*) zwanglos; *discussion, chat also* ungezwungen; *clothes* leger ◆ **a ~ shirt** ein Freizeithemd *nt*; **~ wear** Freizeitkleidung *f*; **he was wearing ~ clothes** er war leger gekleidet.
(d) (*irregular*) *work, worker, labourer* Gelegenheits-.
[2] *n* (a) **~s** *pl* (*shoes*) Slipper *pl*. (b) (**~ worker**) Gelegenheitsarbeiter(in *f*) *m* ◆ **~s** Aushilfen *pl*. (c) (*also* **football ~**) Fußballrowdy *m*.

casually [ˈkæʒjʊlɪ] *adv* (*without planning*) zufällig; (*without emotion*) ungerührt; (*incidentally, in an offhand manner*) beiläufig; (*without seriousness*) lässig; (*informally*) zwanglos; *dressed* leger.

casualness [ˈkæʒjʊlnɪs] *n* (*informality*) Zwanglosigkeit *f*; (*carelessness*) Lässigkeit *f*; (*lack of emotion*) Ungerührtheit, Schnodderigkeit (*inf*) *f*; (*offhand nature: of remark*) Beiläufigkeit *f* ◆ **the ~ of his dress** seine legere Kleidung.

casualty [ˈkæʒjʊltɪ] *n* (a) (*lit, fig*) Opfer *nt*; (*injured also*) Verletzte(r) *mf*; (*killed also*) Tote(r) *mf* ◆ **were there many casualties?** gab es viele Opfer?; (*Mil*) gab es hohe Verluste? (b) (*also* **~ unit** *or* **ward**) Unfallstation, Notaufnahme *f* ◆ **to/in ~** in die/in der Unfallstation *or* Notaufnahme.

casualty: ~ list *n* Verlustliste *f*; **~ ward** *n* Unfallstation *f*.

casuist [ˈkæzjʊɪst] *n* Kasuist *m*.

casuistry [ˈkæzjʊɪstrɪ] *n* Kasuistik *f*.

cat [kæt] *n* (a) Katze *f*; (*tiger etc*) (Raub)katze *f* ◆ **the (big) ~s** die großen Katzen; **to let the ~ out of the bag** die Katze aus dem Sack lassen; **to wait to see which way the ~ jumps** (abwarten, um zu) sehen, wie der Hase läuft; **they fight like ~ and dog** die sind *or* die vertragen sich wie Hund und Katze; **to play a ~-and-mouse game with sb** mit jdm Katz und Maus spielen; **there isn't room to swing a ~ (in)** (*inf*) man kann sich nicht rühren(, so eng ist es); **a ~ may look at a king** (*prov*) es wird doch noch erlaubt sein zu gucken!; **it's enough to make a ~ laugh** da lachen ja die Hühner! (*inf*); **to be like a ~ on hot bricks, to be like a ~ on a hot tin roof** wie auf glühenden Kohlen sitzen; **that's put the ~ among the pigeons!** da hast du *etc* aber was (Schönes) angerichtet!; **he thinks he's the ~'s whiskers** (*inf*) er hält sich für wer weiß was; **when the ~'s away the mice will play** (*Prov*) wenn die Katze aus dem Haus ist, tanzen die Mäuse (*Prov*); **has the ~ got your tongue?** (*inf*) du hast wohl die Sprache verloren?
(b) (*inf: woman*) Katze *f*.
(c) (*whip*) (neunschwänzige) Katze.
(d) (*dated US sl*) Typ *m* (*inf*).
(e) (*inf: caterpillar tractor*) Raupe *f*.

catabolism [kəˈtæbəlɪzm] *n* Abbaustoffwechsel, Katabolismus (*spec*) *m*.

cataclysm [ˈkætəklɪzəm] *n* Verheerung *f*; (*fig*) Umwälzung *f*.

cataclysmic [ˌkætəˈklɪzmɪk] *adj* verheerend; (*fig*) umwälzend.

catacombs [ˈkætəkuːmz] *npl* Katakomben *pl*.

catafalque [ˈkætəfælk] *n* Katafalk *m*.

catalepsy [ˈkætəlepsɪ] *n* Katalepsie, Starrsucht *f*.

cataleptic [ˌkætəˈleptɪk] *adj* kataleptisch.

catalogue, (*US*) **catalog** [ˈkætəlɒg] [1] *n* Katalog *m*.
[2] *vt* katalogisieren.

catalysis [kəˈtæləsɪs] *n* Katalyse *f*.

catalyst [ˈkætəlɪst] *n* (*lit, fig*) Katalysator *m*.

catalytic [ˌkætəˈlɪtɪk] *adj* (*lit, fig*) katalytisch ◆ **~ converter** (*Aut*) Katalysator *m*.

catamaran [ˌkætəməˈræn] *n* Katamaran *m*.

catapult [ˈkætəpʌlt] [1] *n* (*slingshot*) Schleuder *f*; (*Mil, Aviat*) Katapult *nt or m* ◆ **~ launching** (*Aviat*) Katapultstart *m*.
[2] *vt* schleudern, katapultieren; (*Aviat*) katapultieren.
[3] *vi* geschleudert *or* katapultiert werden.

cataract [ˈkætərækt] *n* (a) (*rapids*) Katarakt *m*. (b) (*Med*) grauer Star.

catarrh [kəˈtɑːʳ] *n* Katarrh *m*.

catarrhal [kəˈtɑːrəl] *adj* katarrhalisch.

catastrophe [kəˈtæstrəfɪ] *n* Katastrophe *f* ◆ **to end in ~** verhängnisvoll *or* in einer Katastrophe enden; **to be heading for ~** auf eine Katastrophe zusteuern; **to be the final ~ for sb** jdm schließlich zum Verhängnis werden.

catastrophic [ˌkætəˈstrɒfɪk] *adj* katastrophal; *event, decision, course also* verhängnisvoll.

catastrophically [ˌkætæˈstrɒfɪkəlɪ] *adv see adj*.

catatonia [ˌkætəˈtəʊnɪə] *n* Katatonie *f*.

catatonic [ˌkætəˈtɒnɪk] (*Med*) [1] *adj* katatonisch.
[2] *n* Katatoniker(in *f*) *m*.

cat: ~bird *n* (*US*) amerikanische Spottdrossel; **~ burglar** *n* Fassadenkletterer *m*; **~call** (*Theat*) [1] *n* **~calls** Pfiffe und Buhrufe *pl*; [2] *vi* pfeifen.

catch [kætʃ] (*vb: pret, ptp* **caught**) [1] *n* (a) (*of ball etc*) **to make a (good) ~** (gut) fangen; **good ~!** gut gefangen!; **it was a difficult ~** das war schwer zu fangen; **he missed an easy ~** er hat einen leichten Ball nicht gefangen.
(b) (*Fishing, Hunt*) Fang *m*; (*of trawler etc also*) Fischzug *m* ◆ **he didn't get a ~** er hat nichts gefangen; **he's a good ~** (*fig inf*) er ist ein guter Fang; (*for marriage also*) er ist eine gute Partie.
(c) (*children's game*) Fangen *nt*.
(d) (*trick, snag*) Haken *m* ◆ **where's the ~?** wo liegt *or* ist (da) der Haken?; **there's a ~ in it somewhere!** die Sache hat irgendwo einen Haken, da ist irgendwo ein Haken dabei; **~-22** ausweglose Falle, Sackgasse *f*; **a ~-22 situation** (*inf*) eine Zwickmühle; **~ question** Fangfrage *f*.
(e) (*device for fastening*) Verschluß(vorrichtung *f*) *m*; (*hook*) Haken *m*; (*latch*) Riegel *m*.
(f) (*break in voice*) Stocken *nt* ◆ **with a ~ in one's voice** mit stockender Stimme.
(g) (*Mus*) *Kanon m für Singstimmen mit heiter-komischem Text.*
(h) (*fragment*) Bruchstück *nt*.
[2] *vt* (a) *object* fangen; *batsman* durch Abfangen des Balls ausscheiden lassen.
(b) *fish, mice* fangen; *thief, offender* fassen, schnappen (*inf*), erwischen (*inf*); *escaped animal* (ein)fangen; (*inf: manage to see*) erwischen (*inf*) ◆ **to ~ sb by the arm** jdn am Arm fassen; **to ~ sight/a glimpse of sb/sth** jdn/etw erblicken *or* zu sehen kriegen (*inf*); **to ~ sb's attention/eye** jdn auf sich (*acc*) aufmerksam machen.
(c) (*take by surprise*) erwischen, ertappen ◆ **to ~ sb at sth** jdn bei etw erwischen; **I caught him flirting with my wife** ich habe ihn (dabei) erwischt, wie er mit meiner Frau flirtete; **you won't ~ me signing any contract** (*inf*) ich

unterschreibe doch keinen Vertrag; **you won't ~ me in that restaurant** (*inf*) in das Restaurant gehe ich garantiert *or* bestimmt nicht; **(you won't) ~ me doing that again!** (*inf*) das mache ich bestimmt nicht wieder!; **you won't ~ me falling for that trick again** (*inf*) auf den Trick falle ich nicht noch einmal herein; **aha, caught you** hab' ich dich doch erwischt (*inf*); (*with question*) ha ha, reingefallen (*inf*); **caught in the act** auf frischer Tat ertappt; (*sexually*) in flagranti erwischt; **we were caught in a storm** wir wurden von einem Unwetter überrascht; **to ~ sb on the wrong foot** *or* **off balance** (*fig*) jdn überrumpeln.
(d) (*take*) *bus, train etc* nehmen.
(e) (*be in time for*) *train, bus* erreichen, kriegen (*inf*) ◆ **can I still ~ the post?** kommt der Brief noch mit?; **if you want to ~ the 4 o'clock post ...** wenn das mit der Vieruhrleerung mitsoll ...
(f) (*become entangled*) hängenbleiben mit ◆ **a nail caught her dress** ihr Kleid blieb an einem Nagel hängen; **I caught my finger in the car door** ich habe mir den Finger in der Wagentür eingeklemmt; **he caught his foot in the grating** er ist mit dem Fuß im Gitter hängengeblieben.
(g) (*with stitches*) mit ein paar Stichen befestigen ◆ **to ~ a dress (in) at the waist** ein Kleid an der Taille fassen.
(h) (*understand, hear*) mitkriegen (*inf*).
(i) **to ~ an illness** sich (*dat*) eine Krankheit zuziehen *or* holen (*inf*); **he's always ~ing cold(s)** er erkältet sich leicht; **you'll ~ your death (of cold)!** du holst dir den Tod! (*inf*).
(j) (*portray*) *mood, atmosphere etc* einfangen.
(k) **to ~ one's breath** (*after exercise etc*) Luft holen, verschnaufen; **to ~ sb a blow** jdm einen Schlag versetzen; **the blow/ball caught him on the arm** der Schlag/Ball traf ihn am Arm; **she caught him one on the nose** (*inf*) sie haute ihm auf die Nase; **you'll ~ it!** (*inf*) es setzt was! (*inf*), du kannst (aber) was erleben! (*inf*); **he caught it all right!** (*inf*) (*physically*) der hat vielleicht eine Abreibung bekommen! (*inf*); (*verbally*) der hat aber was zu hören bekommen! (*inf*).
[3] *vi* **(a)** (*with ball*) fangen. **(b)** (*fire*) in Gang kommen, brennen; (*wood etc*) Feuer fangen, brennen; (*Cook*) anbrennen. **(c)** (*get stuck*) klemmen, sich verklemmen; (*get entangled*) hängenbleiben, sich verfangen ◆ **her dress caught in the door** sie blieb mit ihrem Kleid in der Tür hängen.

◆**catch at** *vi +prep obj* (*grab for*) greifen nach; *opportunity* ergreifen.

◆**catch on** *vi* (*inf*) **(a)** (*become popular*) ankommen; (*fashion also*) sich durchsetzen; (*book etc also*) einschlagen. **(b)** (*understand*) kapieren (*inf*).

◆**catch out** *vt sep* (*fig*) überführen; (*with trick question etc*) hereinlegen (*inf*); (*Sport*) abfangen ◆ **I caught you ~ there!** du bist durchschaut; (*with trick question*) jetzt bist du aber reingefallen (*inf*); **to ~ sb ~ in a lie** jdn beim Lügen ertappen.

◆**catch up** [1] *vi* aufholen ◆ **to ~ ~ on one's sleep** Schlaf nachholen; **to ~ ~ on** *or* **with one's work** Arbeit nachholen; **to ~ ~ with sb** (*running, in work etc*) jdn einholen; **hurry, they're ~ing ~!** beeil dich, sie holen auf!; **you've got a lot of ~ing ~ to do** du mußt noch eine Menge nachholen.
[2] *vt sep* **(a)** **to ~ sb ~** (*walking, working etc*) jdn einholen.
(b) (*snatch up*) (vom Boden) hochheben; *hair* hochstecken ◆ **she caught ~ her skirts** sie raffte *or* schürzte ihre Röcke.
(c) **to get caught ~ in sth** (*entangled*) sich in etw (*dat*) verheddern *or* verfangen; *in traffic* in etw (*acc*) kommen; *in discussion* in etw (*acc*) verwickelt werden.

catch: ~all *n* (*US*) (*drawer etc*) Schublade *f* für Krimskrams (*inf*); (*phrase, clause etc*) allgemeine Bezeichnung/Klausel/allgemeiner Rahmen *etc*; **~-as-catch-can** *n* (*Sport*) Catch-as-catch-can *nt*; **~crop** *n* Zwischenfrucht *f*.

catcher ['kætʃəʳ] *n* Fänger *m* ◆ **he's a good ~** er ist gut im Fangen, er fängt gut.

catching ['kætʃɪŋ] *adj* (*Med, fig*) ansteckend.

catchment ['kætʃmənt] *n*: **~ area** Einzugsgebiet *nt*, Einzugsbereich *m*; **~ basin** Einzugsgebiet *nt*.

catch: ~penny *adj* (*dated*) publikumswirksam, zugkräftig; **~phrase** *n* Schlagwort *nt*, Slogan *m*.

catchup ['kætʃəp] *n* (*US*) *see* **ketchup**.

catch: ~ weight *adj* (*Sport*) ohne Gewichtsklasse; **~ word** *n* Schlagwort *nt*.

catchy ['kætʃɪ] *adj* (*+er*) *tune* eingängig.

catechism ['kætɪkɪzəm] *n* (*instruction*) Katechese *f*; (*fig*) Verhör *nt*; (*book*) Katechismus *m*.

catechize ['kætɪkaɪz] *vt* katechisieren.

categorical [ˌkætɪ'gɒrɪkəl] *adj statement, denial* kategorisch ◆ **he was quite ~ about it** er hat das mit Bestimmtheit gesagt; **~ imperative** kategorischer Imperativ.

categorically [ˌkætɪ'gɒrɪkəlɪ] *adv* kategorisch; *say* mit Bestimmtheit.

categorization [ˌkætɪgəraɪ'zeɪʃən] *n* Kategorisierung *f*.

categorize ['kætɪgəraɪz] *vt* kategorisieren.

category ['kætɪgərɪ] *n* Kategorie, Klasse *f*.

cater ['keɪtəʳ] *vi* (*provide food*) die Speisen und Getränke liefern.

◆**cater for** *vi +prep obj* **(a)** (*serve*) mit Speisen und Getränken versorgen; *coach party etc* (mit Speisen und Getränken) bedienen ◆ **weddings and functions ~ed ~** wir richten Hochzeiten und andere Veranstaltungen aus; **that café ~s mainly ~ students** das Café ist hauptsächlich auf Studenten eingestellt.
(b) ausgerichtet *or* eingestellt sein auf (*+acc*); (*also* **cater to**) *needs, tastes* gerecht werden (*+dat*), etwas zu bieten haben (*+dat*) ◆ **to ~ ~ all tastes** jedem Geschmack gerecht werden, für jeden (Geschmack) etwas zu bieten haben; **a region which ~s more ~ old people** eine Gegend, die mehr für alte Menschen tut *or* die alten Menschen mehr zu bieten hat; **a town which ~s ~ children** eine kinderfreundliche Stadt; **a dictionary which ~s ~ the user** ein benutzerfreundliches Wörterbuch.
(c) (*expect, be prepared for*) **I hadn't ~ed ~ that** darauf bin/war ich nicht eingestellt.

cater-cornered ['keɪtə'kɔːnəd] *adj* (*US*) diagonal.

caterer ['keɪtərəʳ] *n* Lieferfirma *f* für Speisen und Getränke; (*for parties etc*) Lieferfirma, die Partys *etc* ausrichtet; (*owner, manager*) Gastronom(in *f*) *m*.

catering ['keɪtərɪŋ] *n* Versorgung *f* mit Speisen und Getränken (*for gen*); (*trade*) Gastronomie *f* ◆ **who's doing the ~?** wer liefert das Essen und die Getränke?; **~ trade** (Hotel- und) Gaststättengewerbe *nt*.

caterpillar ['kætəpɪləʳ] *n* (*Zool*) Raupe *f*; (*Tech*) Raupe(nkette), Gleiskette *f*; (*vehicle*) Raupenfahrzeug *nt*.

caterpillar: (*Tech*) **~-track** *n* Raupenkette, Gleiskette *f*; **~ tractor** *n* Raupenfahrzeug, Gleiskettenfahrzeug *nt*.

caterwaul ['kætəwɔːl] *vi* jaulen.

caterwauling ['kætəwɔːlɪŋ] *n* Gejaule *nt*.

catgut ['kætgʌt] *n* Katgut *nt*.

catharsis [kə'θɑːsɪs] *n* **(a)** (*Med*) Darmreinigung, Darmentleerung *f*. **(b)** (*Liter, Philos*) Katharsis, Läuterung *f*.

cathartic [kə'θɑːtɪk] [1] *adj* **(a)** (*Med*) abführend. **(b)** (*Liter, Philos*) kathartisch.
[2] *n* (*Med*) Abführmittel *nt*.

cathedral [kə'θiːdrəl] *n* Dom *m*; (*esp in England, France, Spain*) Kathedrale *f* ◆ **~ town/city** Domstadt *f*.

Catherine ['kæθərɪn] *n* Katharina *f* ◆ **c~ wheel** Feuerrad *nt*.

catheter ['kæθɪtəʳ] *n* Katheter *m*.

catheterize ['kæθɪtəraɪz] *vt* katheterisieren.

cathode ['kæθəʊd] *n* Kathode *f*.

cathode: ~ ray *n* Kathodenstrahl *m*; **~-ray tube** *n* Kathodenstrahlröhre *f*.

catholic ['kæθəlɪk] *adj* (*varied*) vielseitig ◆ **he's a man of very ~ tastes** er ist (ein) sehr vielseitig interessiert(er Mensch).

Catholic [1] *adj* (*Eccl*) katholisch ◆ **the ~ Church** die katholische Kirche.
[2] *n* Katholik(in *f*) *m*.

Catholicism [kə'θɒlɪsɪzəm] *n* Katholizismus *m*.

cat: ~kin *n* (*Bot*) Kätzchen *nt*; **~lick** *n* (*inf*) Katzenwäsche *f*; **~like** *adj* katzenhaft, katzengleich; **~ litter** *n* Katzenstreu *f*; **~mint** *n* Katzenminze *f*; **~nap** [1] *n* **to have a ~nap** ein Nickerchen *nt* machen (*inf*); [2] *vi* dösen; **~nip** *n* (*US*) *see* **~mint**; **~-o'-nine-tails** *n* neunschwänzige Katze.

CAT scan ['kætˌskæn] *n* Computertomographie *f*.

cat: ~'s cradle *n* Abnehmespiel, Fadenspiel *nt*; **~'s eye** *n* Katzenauge *nt*, Rückstrahler *m*; **~'s paw** *n* Handlanger *m*; **~suit** *n* einteiliger Hosenanzug.

catsup ['kætsəp] *n* (*US*) *see* **ketchup**.

cattail ['kætˌteɪl] *n* (*US*) Rohrkolben, Kanonenputzer (*inf*) *m*.

cattle ['kætl] *npl* Rind(vieh) *nt* ◆ **500 head of ~** 500 Rinder, 500 Stück Vieh; **"~ crossing"** „Vorsicht Viehtrieb!"; **they were treated like ~** sie wurden wie Vieh behandelt.

cattle: ~ breeding *n* Rinderzucht *f*; **~ grid** *n* Weidenrost *m*, Viehtor *nt*; **~man** *n* Rinderzüchter *m*; **~ market** *n* (*lit*) Viehmarkt *m*; (*fig inf: beauty contest etc*) Fleischbeschau *f* (*inf*); (*fig inf: for pick-ups*) Abschleppladen *m* (*inf*); **~ rustler** *n* Viehdieb *m*; **~ shed** *n* Viehstall *m*; **~ show** *n* Rinder(zucht)schau *f*; **~ truck** *n* (*Aut*) Viehanhänger *m*; (*Rail*) Viehwagen *m*.

catty ['kætɪ] *adj* (*+er*) gehässig, boshaft.

catwalk ['kætwɔːk] *n* Steg *m*, Brücke *f*; (*for models*) Laufsteg *m*.

Caucasian [kɔː'keɪzɪən] [1] *adj* kaukasisch.
[2] *n* Kaukasier(in *f*) *m*.

Caucasus ['kɔːkəsəs] *n* Kaukasus *m*.

caucus ['kɔːkəs] *n* (*committee*) Gremium *nt*, Ausschuß *m*; (*US: meeting*) Sitzung *f*.

caudal ['kɔːdl] *adj* Schwanz-, kaudal (*spec*) ◆ **the ~ vertebrae/fin** die Schwanzwirbel *pl*/die Schwanzflosse.

caught [kɔːt] *pret, ptp of* **catch**.

caul [kɔːl] *n* Glückshaube *f*.

cauldron ['kɔːldrən] *n* großer Kessel; (*witch's ~*) (Hexen)kessel *m*.

cauliflower ['kɒlɪflaʊəʳ] *n* Blumenkohl *m* ◆ **~ cheese** Blumenkohl mit Käsesoße; **~ ear** Boxerohr *nt*.

caulk [kɔːk] *vt seams, joints* abdichten; (*on ship*) kalfatern.

caulking ['kɔːkɪŋ] *n* Material *nt* zum Abdichten; (*Naut*) Teer *m*.

causal ['kɔːzəl] *adj* kausal, ursächlich ◆ **~ relationship** Kausalzusammenhang *m*.

causality [kɔː'zælɪtɪ] *n* Kausalität *f*.

causally ['kɔːzəlɪ] *adv* kausal, ursächlich ◆ **they are ~ connected** dazwischen besteht ein Kausalzusammenhang.

causation [kɔː'zeɪʃən] *n* Kausalität *f*; (*of particular event*) Ursache *f* ◆ **the law of ~** das Kausalgesetz *or* -prinzip.

causative ['kɔːzətɪv] [1] *adj factor* verursachend; (*Gram*) kausativ.
[2] *n* (*Gram*) Kausativ *nt*.

▼ **cause** [kɔːz] [1] *n* **(a)** Ursache *f* (*of* für) ◆ **~ and effect** Ursache und Wirkung; **what was the ~ of the fire?** wodurch ist das Feuer entstanden?
(b) (*reason*) Grund, Anlaß *m* ◆ **she has no ~ to be angry** sie hat keinen Grund, sich zu ärgern; **the ~ of his failure** der Grund für sein Versagen; **with/without (good) ~** mit (triftigem)/ohne (triftigen) Grund; **there's no ~ for alarm** es besteht kein Grund *or* Anlaß zur Aufregung; **you have every ~ to be worried** du hast allen Anlaß zur Sorge; **you have good ~ for complaint** Sie haben allen Grund zur Klage, Sie beklagen sich zu Recht.

(c) (*purpose, ideal*) Sache *f* ◆ **to make common ~ with sb** mit jdm gemeinsame Sache machen; **to work for** *or* **in a good ~** sich für eine gute Sache einsetzen; **he died for the ~ of peace** er starb für den Frieden *or* für die Sache des Friedens; **in the ~ of justice** für die (Sache der) Gerechtigkeit, im Namen der Gerechtigkeit; **it's all in a good ~** es ist für eine gute Sache.
(d) (*Jur: action*) Fall *m*, Sache *f* ◆ **~ célèbre** Cause célèbre *f*.
[2] *vt* verursachen ◆ **to ~ grief to sb** jdm Kummer machen; **to ~ sb to do sth** (*form*) jdn veranlassen, etw zu tun (*form*).

causeway ['kɔːzweɪ] *n* Damm *m*.

caustic ['kɔːstɪk] *adj* (*Chem*) ätzend, kaustisch; (*fig*) ätzend; *remark* bissig ◆ **he was very ~ about the project** er äußerte sich sehr bissig über das Projekt; **~ soda** Ätznatron *nt*.

caustically ['kɔːstɪklɪ] *adv* in ätzendem *or* bissigem Ton.

cauterization [ˌkɔːtəraɪ'zeɪʃən] *n* (*Med*) Kaustik, Kauterisation *f*.

cauterize ['kɔːtəraɪz] *vt* (*Med*) kauterisieren.

caution ['kɔːʃən] [1] *n* **(a)** (*circumspection*) Vorsicht, Umsicht *f*, Bedacht *m* ◆ **"~!"** „Vorsicht!"; **to act with ~** umsichtig *or* mit Bedacht vorgehen, Vorsicht walten lassen.
(b) (*warning*) Warnung *f*; (*official*) Verwarnung *f*.
(c) (*inf*) **to be a real ~** zum Piepen sein (*inf*).
[2] *vt* **to ~ sb** jdn warnen (*against* vor *+dat*); (*officially*) jdn verwarnen; **to ~ sb against doing sth** jdn davor warnen, etw zu tun.

cautionary ['kɔːʃənərɪ] *adj* belehrend; *sign* Warn- ◆ **a ~ tale** eine Geschichte mit Moral.

cautious ['kɔːʃəs] *adj* vorsichtig ◆ **to play a ~ game** Vorsicht walten lassen.

cautiously ['kɔːʃəslɪ] *adv see adj*.

cautiousness ['kɔːʃəsnɪs] *n* Vorsicht *f*.

cavalcade [ˌkævəl'keɪd] *n* Kavalkade *f*.

cavalier [ˌkævə'lɪəʳ] [1] *n* (*horseman, knight*) Kavalier *m* ◆ **C~** (*Hist*) Kavalier *m*.
[2] *adj* **(a)** (*Hist*) **C~: the C~ resistance** der Widerstand der Kavaliere. **(b)** (*offhand*) *person, nature* unbekümmert; *disregard, overruling also* ungeniert, kaltlächelnd ◆ **... he said in his ~ tone** ... sagte er leichthin; **treat it seriously, don't be so ~** nehmen Sie das ernst, und gehen Sie nicht so leichthin darüber hinweg.

cavalierly [ˌkævə'lɪəlɪ] *adv* unbekümmert, kaltlächelnd; *say* leichthin.

cavalry ['kævəlrɪ] *n* Kavallerie, Reiterei *f*.

cavalry: ~man *n* Kavallerist *m*; **~ officer** *n* Kavallerieoffizier *m*; **~ twill** *n* Reitertrikot *m*, *strapazierfähiger Hosenstoff*.

cave¹ ['keɪvɪ] *n*: **to keep ~** (*dated Brit Sch sl*) Schmiere stehen (*inf*).

cave² [keɪv] [1] *n* Höhle *f*.
[2] *vi* **to go caving** auf Höhlenexpedition(en) gehen; **he did a lot of caving in his youth** in seiner Jugend hat er viel Höhlenforschung betrieben.

◆**cave in** *vi* **(a)** einstürzen; (*fig: scheme etc*) zusammenbrechen. **(b)** (*inf: surrender, yield*) nachgeben, kapitulieren.

caveat ['kævɪæt] *n* Vorbehalt *m* ◆ **to enter** *or* **file a ~** (*Jur*) Einspruch einlegen.

cave: ~-dweller *n* Höhlenbewohner *m*; **~-in** *n* Einsturz *m*; (*place*) Einsturzstelle *f*; **~man** *n* Höhlenmensch *m*; (*fig*) Tier *nt* (*inf*), Urmensch *m*; **~man instincts** Urinstinkte *pl*; **~ painting** *n* Höhlenmalerei *f*.

cavern ['kævən] *n* Höhle *f*.

cavernous ['kævənəs] *adj* **(a)** *cellar, pit, darkness* tief; *hole* gähnend; *eyes* tiefliegend; *cheeks* eingefallen, hohl; *voice* hohl(tönend); *yawn* herzhaft, breit. **(b)** *mountain etc* höhlenreich, voller Höhlen.

caviar(e) ['kævɪɑːʳ] *n* Kaviar *m*.

cavil ['kævɪl] *vi* kritteln ◆ **to ~ at sth** an etw (*dat*) herumkritteln.

cavity ['kævɪtɪ] *n* Hohlraum *m*, Höhlung *f*; (*in tooth*) Loch *nt* ◆ **nasal/chest ~** (*Anat*) Nasen-/Brusthöhle *f*; **~ block** Hohlraumziegel *m*; **~ wall** Hohlwand *f*; **~ wall insulation** Schaumisolierung *f*.

cavort [kə'vɔːt] *vi* tollen, toben ◆ **to ~ about** herumtollen *or* -toben.

cavy ['keɪvɪ] *n* Meerschweinchen *nt*.

caw [kɔː] [1] *vi* krächzen.
[2] *n* (heiserer) Schrei.

cawing ['kɔːɪŋ] *n* Krächzen, Gekrächz(e) *nt*.

cay [keɪ] *n* (kleine) Insel, Koralleninsel *f*.

cayenne pepper ['keɪen'pepəʳ] *n* Cayennepfeffer *m*.

CB *abbr of* **Citizens' Band** CB ◆ **~ radio** CB-Funk *m*.

CBC *abbr of* **Canadian Broadcasting Company.**

CBE (*Brit*) *abbr of* **Commander of the Order of the British Empire.**

CBI (*Brit*) *abbr of* **Confederation of British Industry** ≃ BDI.

CBS *abbr of* **Columbia Broadcasting System** CBS.

cc¹ *abbr of* **cubic centimetre** cc, cm³.

cc² *abbr of* **carbon copy** [1] *n* Kopie *f*.
[2] *vt* eine Kopie senden an (*+acc*) ◆ **~:** ... Kopie (an): ...

CC (*Brit*) *abbr of* **(a) County Council. (b) Cricket Club.**

CD *abbr of* **(a) compact disc** CD *f* ◆ **~ player** CD-Spieler *m*. **(b) corps diplomatique. (c) civil defence. (d)** (*US*) **Congressional District.**

Cdr *abbr of* **Commander.**

CD-ROM ['siːdiː'rɒm] *abbr of* **compact disk - read only memory** CD-ROM.

CD-ROM drive *n* CD-ROM-Laufwerk *nt*.

CDT (*US*) *abbr of* **Central Daylight Time.**

cease [siːs] [1] *vi* enden, aufhören; (*noise, shouting etc*) verstummen ◆ **we shall not ~ from our endeavours** (*liter*) wir werden in unserem Streben nicht nachlassen (*geh*); **without ceasing** ohne Pause, unaufhörlich; **to ~ from doing sth** (*form*) von etw ablassen (*geh*).
[2] *vt* beenden; *fire, payments, production* einstellen ◆ **to ~ doing sth** aufhören, etw zu tun; **to ~ to exist** aufhören zu bestehen; **~ fire!** Feuer halt!
[3] *n* **without ~** (*liter*) unaufhörlich, ohne Unterlaß (*liter*).

ceasefire [siːs'faɪəʳ] *n* Feuerpause *or* -einstellung *f*; (*longer*) Waffenruhe *f*, Einstellung *f* der Kampfhandlungen ◆ **to give** *or* **sound the ~** den Befehl zur Feuereinstellung geben.

ceaseless ['siːslɪs] *adj* endlos, unaufhörlich; (*relentless*) *vigilance* unablässig.

ceaselessly ['siːslɪslɪ] *adv see adj*.

cecum ['siːkəm] *n see* **caecum.**

cedar ['siːdəʳ] *n* **(a)** (*tree*) Zeder *f*. **(b)** (*also* **~wood**) Zedernholz *nt* ◆ **~ of Lebanon** Libanonzeder *f*.

cede [siːd] *vt territory* abtreten (*to* an *+acc*) ◆ **to ~ a point in an argument** in einem Punkt *or* in einer Sache nachgeben.

cedilla [sɪ'dɪlə] *n* Cedille *f*.

Ceefax ® ['siːfæks] *n Videotext m der BBC*.

ceiling ['siːlɪŋ] *n* **(a)** (Zimmer)decke *f*; *see* **hit 2 (l)**. **(b)** (*Aviat*) (*cloud ~*) Wolkenhöhe *f*; (*aircraft's ~*) Gipfelhöhe *f*. **(c)** (*fig: upper limit*) ober(st)e Grenze, Höchstgrenze *f* ◆ **price ~** oberste Preisgrenze; **to put a ~ on sth** etw nach oben begrenzen.

celadon ['selədɒn] [1] *n* Seladon *nt*.
[2] *adj* seladongrün.

celandine ['seləndaɪn] *n* **(a)** (*greater ~*) Schöllkraut *nt*. **(b)** (*lesser ~*) Scharbockskraut *nt*.

celebrant ['selɪbrənt] *n* (*Eccl*) Zelebrant *m*.

celebrate ['selɪbreɪt] [1] *vt* **(a)** feiern; *event, birthday also* begehen. **(b)** (*extol*) *sb's name, deeds* feiern, preisen (*geh*). **(c)** *mass, ritual* zelebrieren; *communion* feiern.
[2] *vi* feiern.

celebrated ['selɪbreɪtɪd] *adj* gefeiert (*for* wegen), berühmt (*for* für).

celebration [ˌselɪ'breɪʃən] *n* **(a)** (*party, festival*) Feier *f*; (*commemoration, jubilee also*) Gedenkfeier *f*; (*act of celebrating*) Feiern *nt* ◆ **during the centenary ~s** während der Hundertjahrfeier(n); **in ~ of** zur Feier (*+gen*).
(b) (*praise*) Verherrlichung *f*.
(c) (*of mass, ritual*) Zelebration *f*; (*of communion*) Feier *f*.

celebrity [sɪ'lebrɪtɪ] *n* Berühmtheit *f*; (*person also*) berühmte Persönlichkeit.

celeriac [sə'lerɪæk] *n* (Knollen)sellerie *f*.

celerity [sɪ'lerɪtɪ] *n* (*form*) Geschwindigkeit *f*.

celery ['selərɪ] *n* Stangensellerie *m or f* ◆ **three stalks of ~** drei Stangen Sellerie; **~ hearts** Sellerieherzen *pl*.

celesta [sɪ'lestə], **celeste** [sɪ'lest] *n* (*Mus*) Celesta *f*.

celestial [sɪ'lestɪəl] *adj* himmlisch; (*Astron*) Himmels-.

celibacy ['selɪbəsɪ] *n* Zölibat *nt or m*; (*fig*) Enthaltsamkeit *f*.

celibate ['selɪbɪt] [1] *adj* (*Rel*) keusch, zölibatär (*spec*); (*fig*) enthaltsam.
[2] *n* **to be a ~** im Zölibat leben.

cell [sel] *n* (*all meanings*) Zelle *f* ◆ **~ wall** Zellwand *f*.

cellar ['seləʳ] *n* Keller *m* ◆ **he keeps an excellent ~** er hat einen ausgezeichneten Weinkeller.

cellarage ['selərɪdʒ] *n* (*cellar space*) Kellerfläche *f*; (*storage cost*) Lagerkosten *pl*.

cellist ['tʃelɪst] *n* Cellist(in *f*) *m*.

cello, 'cello ['tʃeləʊ] *n* Cello *nt*.

cellophane ® ['seləfeɪn] *n* Cellophan ® *nt*.

cellular ['seljʊləʳ] *adj* **(a)** zellenförmig, zellular, Zell- ◆ **~ phone** Funktelefon *nt*. **(b)** (*of textiles*) aus porösem Material.

cellulite ['seljʊlaɪt] *n* Unterhautfettgewebe *nt*.

celluloid ['seljʊlɔɪd] *n* Zelluloid *nt* ◆ **~ heroes** Zelluloidhelden *pl*; **on the ~** auf der Leinwand.

cellulose ['seljʊləʊs] [1] *n* Zellulose *f*, Zellstoff *m*.
[2] *adj* Zellulose-.

Celsius ['selsɪəs] *adj* Celsius- ◆ **30 degrees ~** 30 Grad Celsius.

Celt [kelt, selt] *n* Kelte *m*, Keltin *f*.

Celtic ['keltɪk, 'seltɪk] [1] *adj* keltisch.
[2] *n* (*language*) Keltisch *nt*.

cembalo ['tʃembələʊ] *n* (*Mus*) Cembalo *nt*.

cement [sə'ment] [1] *n* **(a)** (*Build*) Zement *m*; (*inf: concrete*) Beton *m* ◆ **~ mixer** Betonmischmaschine *f*.
(b) (*glue*) Leim, Klebstoff *m*; (*for holes etc, fig*) Kitt *m*.
(c) (*of tooth*) (Zahn)zement *m*.
[2] *vt* (*Build*) zementieren; (*glue*) leimen; kitten; (*fig*) festigen, zementieren.

cemetery ['semɪtrɪ] *n* Friedhof *m*.

cenotaph ['senətɑːf] *n* Mahnmal, Ehrenmal *nt*, Kenotaph *m*.

censer ['sensəʳ] *n* (*Eccl*) Rauchfaß, Räuchergefäß *nt*.

censor ['sensəʳ] [1] *n* Zensor *m*.
[2] *vt* zensieren; (*remove*) *chapter* herausnehmen.

censorious [sen'sɔːrɪəs] *adj remark, glance* strafend ◆ **he was very ~ of the new policy** er kritisierte die neue Politik scharf.

censorship ['sensəʃɪp] *n* Zensur *f* ◆ **~ of the press** Pressezensur *f*.

censure ['senʃəʳ] [1] *vt* tadeln.
[2] *n* Tadel *m* ◆ **vote of ~** Tadelsantrag *m*.

census ['sensəs] *n* Zensus *m*, Volkszählung *f*; (*Bibl*) Schätzung *f*; (*traffic ~*) Verkehrszählung *f* ◆ **to take a ~ (of the population)** eine Volkszählung durchführen.

cent [sent] *n* Cent *m* ◆ **I haven't a ~** (*US*) ich habe keinen Pfennig.

centaur ['sentɔːʳ] *n* Zentaur *m*.

centenarian [ˌsentɪ'neərɪən] [1] *adj* hundertjährig.
[2] *n* Hundertjährige(r) *mf*, Zentenar *m* (*geh*).

centenary [sen'tiːnərɪ] *n* (*anniversary*) hundertster Jahrestag; (*birthday*)

➤ LANGUAGE IN USE: **cause: 2** → 17.2, 26.3 **celebrate: 1a** → 25.1, 25.2

hundertster Geburtstag; *(100 years)* Jahrhundert *nt* ◆ **she has just passed her ~** sie ist gerade hundert Jahre alt geworden; **~ celebrations** Hundertjahrfeier *f.*

centennial [sen'tenɪəl] 1 *adj* hundertjährig, hundertjährlich.
2 *n (esp US)* Hundertjahr- *or* Zentenarfeier *(geh) f.*

center *n (US) see* **centre.**

centesimal [sen'tesɪməl] *adj* zentesimal, hundertteilig.

centigrade ['sentɪgreɪd] *adj* Celsius- ◆ **one degree ~** ein Grad Celsius.

centigramme, *(US)* **centigram** ['sentɪgræm] *n* Zentigramm *nt.*

centilitre, *(US)* **centiliter** ['sentɪ,li:tə^r] *n* Zentiliter *m or nt.*

centimetre, *(US)* **centimeter** ['sentɪ,mi:tə^r] *n* Zentimeter *m or nt.*

centipede ['sentɪpi:d] *n* Tausendfüßler *m.*

central ['sentrəl] 1 *adj* **(a)** zentral, Zentral-; *(main, chief)* Haupt- ◆ **the ~ area of the city** das Innenstadtgebiet; **our house is very ~** unser Haus liegt sehr zentral.
(b) *(fig)* wesentlich; *importance, figure* zentral ◆ **to be ~ to sth** das Wesentliche an etw *(dat)* sein; **he plays a ~ part in** ... er spielt eine zentrale *or* wesentliche Rolle bei ...
2 *n (US: exchange, operator)* (Telefon)zentrale *f,* Fernamt *nt.*

central: C~ America *n* Mittelamerika *nt;* **C~ American** 1 *adj* mittelamerikanisch; 2 *n* Mittelamerikaner(in *f*) *m;* **C~ Europe** *n* Mitteleuropa *nt;* **C~ European** 1 *adj* mitteleuropäisch; 2 *n* Mitteleuropäer(in *f*) *m;* **~ government** *n* Zentralregierung *f;* **~ heating** *n* Zentralheizung *f.*

centralism ['sentrəlɪzəm] *n (esp Pol)* Zentralismus *m.*

centralist ['sentrəlɪst] *adj (esp Pol)* zentralistisch.

centralization [,sentrəlaɪ'zeɪʃən] *n* Zentralisierung *f.*

centralize ['sentrəlaɪz] *vt* zentralisieren.

central locking *n* Zentralverriegelung *f.*

centrally ['sentrəlɪ] *adv* zentral ◆ **~ heated** zentralbeheizt.

central: ~ nervous system *n* Zentralnervensystem *nt;* **~ reservation** *n* Mittelstreifen *m;* Grünstreifen *m;* **~ station** *n* Hauptbahnhof *m.*

centre, *(US)* **center** ['sentə^r] 1 *n* **(a)** *(chief place)* Zentrum *nt* ◆ **business ~** Geschäftszentrum *nt.*
(b) *(middle, Pol)* Mitte *f;* *(of circle)* Mittelpunkt *m;* *(town ~)* Stadtmitte *f;* *(city ~)* Zentrum *nt,* City *f* ◆ **~ of gravity** Schwerpunkt *m;* **~ of attraction** Hauptanziehungspunkt *m,* Hauptattraktion *f;* *(person)* Mittelpunkt *m* der Aufmerksamkeit; **she always wants to be the ~ of attraction** sie will immer im Mittelpunkt stehen; **left of ~** *(Pol)* links der Mitte; **the ~ of the field** *(Sport)* das Mittelfeld; **a politician of the ~** ein Politiker der Mitte; **let's go into the ~** komm, wir gehen in die Stadt!
(c) *(community ~, sports ~, shopping ~)* Zentrum, Center *nt.*
(d) *(Rugby)* mittlerer Dreiviertelspieler; *(Basketball, Netball)* Center *m.*
2 *vt* **(a)** *(also Comput)* zentrieren. **(b)** *(concentrate)* konzentrieren. **(c)** *(Sport) ball* zur Mitte (ab)spielen.

◆**centre up** *vt sep* zentrieren.

◆**centre (up)on** *vi +prep obj (thoughts, problem, talk etc)* kreisen um, sich drehen um.

centre: ~-bit *n (Tech)* Zentrumbohrer *m;* **~-board** *n (Naut)* (Kiel)schwert *nt;* **~-fold** *n doppelseitiges Bild in der Mitte einer Zeitschrift;* **~-fold girl** *n weibliches Aktmodell, dessen Foto auf den Mittelseiten einer Zeitschrift abgedruckt ist;* **~-forward** *n (Sport)* Mittelstürmer *m;* **~-half** *n (Sport)* Stopper *m;* **~ party** *n* Partei *f* der Mitte; **~-piece** *n* Tafelaufsatz *m;* **~-three-quarter** *n (Rugby)* mittlerer Dreiviertelspieler.

centrifugal [,sentrɪ'fjʊgəl] *adj* zentrifugal ◆ **~ force** Zentrifugal- *or* Fliehkraft *f.*

centrifuge ['sentrɪfju:ʒ] *n (Tech)* Zentrifuge, Schleuder *f.*

centripetal [,sentrɪ'pɪtl] *adj* zentripetal ◆ **~ force** Zentripetalkraft *f.*

centrist ['sentrɪst] *n* Anhänger(in *f*) *m* der politischen Mitte; *(politician)* Politiker(in *f*) *m* der Mitte.

centuries-old ['sentjʊrɪz'əʊld] *adj* jahrhundertealt.

centurion [sen'tjʊərɪən] *n* Zenturio *m.*

century ['sentjʊrɪ] *n* **(a)** Jahrhundert *nt* ◆ **in the twentieth ~** im zwanzigsten *(written:* 20.) Jahrhundert. **(b)** *(Cricket)* Hundert *f.*

CEO *(US) abbr of* **chief executive officer.**

cephalic [sɪ'fælɪk] *adj (form)* Kopf-, Schädel-.

ceramic [sɪ'ræmɪk] 1 *adj* keramisch ◆ **~ hob** Glaskeramik-Kochfeld *nt.*
2 *n* Keramik *f.*

ceramics [sɪ'ræmɪks] *n* **(a)** *sing (art)* Keramik *f.* **(b)** *pl (articles)* Keramik(en *pl*) *f,* Keramikwaren *pl.*

cereal ['sɪərɪəl] *n* **(a)** *(crop)* Getreide *nt* ◆ **~ crop** Getreideernte *f;* **the growing of ~s** der Getreideanbau; **maize, rye and other ~s** Mais, Roggen und andere Getreidearten. **(b)** *(food)* Corn-flakes *pl*/Müsli *nt etc.*

cerebellum [,serɪ'beləm] *n* Kleinhirn, Zerebellum *(spec) nt.*

cerebral ['serɪbrəl] *adj (Physiol)* zerebral; *(intellectual)* geistig; *person* durchgeistigt, vergeistigt.

cerebration [,serɪ'breɪʃən] *n (usu hum)* Reflexion *f.*

cerebrum ['serəbrəm] *n* Großhirn, Zerebrum *(spec) nt.*

ceremonial [,serɪ'məʊnɪəl] 1 *adj* zeremoniell.
2 *n* Zeremoniell *nt.*

ceremonially [,serɪ'məʊnɪəlɪ] *adv* feierlich, zeremoniell.

ceremonious [,serɪ'məʊnɪəs] *adj* förmlich, zeremoniös *(geh).*

ceremoniously [,serɪ'məʊnɪəslɪ] *adv* mit großem Zeremoniell.

▼ **ceremony** ['serɪmənɪ] *n* **(a)** *(event etc)* Zeremonie, Feier(lichkeiten *pl*) *f.* **(b)** *(formality)* Förmlichkeit(en *pl*) *f* ◆ **to stand on ~** förmlich sein.

cerise [sə'ri:z] 1 *adj* kirschrot, cerise *pred.*
2 *n* Kirschrot *nt.*

cert¹ [sɜ:t] *abbr of* **certificate.**

cert² *n (sl)* **a (dead) ~** eine todsichere Sache *(inf);* **it's a dead ~ he'll be coming** er kommt todsicher *(inf).*

▼ **certain** ['sɜ:tən] *adj* **(a)** *(positive, convinced)* sicher; *(inevitable, guaranteed)* bestimmt, gewiß ◆ **are you ~ of** *or* **about that?** sind Sie sich *(dat)* dessen sicher?; **is he ~?** weiß er das genau?; **there's no ~ cure for this disease/for inflation** für *or* gegen diese Krankheit/gegen die Inflation gibt es kein sicheres Mittel; **for ~** ganz sicher, ganz genau; **I don't know for ~, but I think** ... ich bin mir nicht ganz sicher, aber ich glaube ...; **I can't say for ~** ich kann das nicht genau *or* mit Sicherheit sagen; **he is ~ to come** er wird ganz bestimmt *or* gewiß kommen; **we are ~ to succeed** wir werden ganz bestimmt Erfolg haben; **to make ~ of sth** *(check)* sich einer Sache *(gen)* vergewissern, etw nachprüfen; *(ensure)* für etw sorgen; **to make ~ of a seat** sich *(dat)* einen Platz sichern; **will you please make ~?** vergewissern Sie sich bitte noch einmal; **be ~ to tell him** vergessen Sie bitte nicht, ihm das zu sagen; **that was ~ to happen** das mußte ja so kommen.
(b) *(attr: not named or specified)* gewiß; *reason, conditions* bestimmt ◆ **a ~ gentleman** ein gewisser Herr; **to a ~ extent** in gewisser Hinsicht, zu einem bestimmten Grade.

▼ **certainly** ['sɜ:tənlɪ] *adv (admittedly)* sicher(lich); *(positively, without doubt)* bestimmt, gewiß *(geh)* ◆ **~ not!** ganz bestimmt nicht, auf keinen Fall!; **I ~ will not!** ich denke nicht daran!; **~!** sicher, gewiß! *(geh).*

certainty ['sɜ:təntɪ] *n* **(a)** *(sure fact)* Gewißheit *f* ◆ **to know for a ~ that** ... mit Sicherheit wissen, daß ...; **he was faced with the ~ of defeat** er sah seiner sicheren Niederlage entgegen; **his success is a ~** er wird mit Sicherheit Erfolg haben, sein Erfolg ist gewiß; **the ultimate ~ of death** die letztliche Gewißheit des Todes; **will it happen? — yes, it's a ~** wird das passieren? — ja, mit Sicherheit; **it's a ~ that** ... es ist absolut sicher, daß ...
(b) *no pl (conviction)* Gewißheit, Sicherheit *f.*

CertEd *(Brit) abbr of* **Certificate of Education.**

certifiable [,sɜ:tɪ'faɪəbl] *adj* **(a)** *fact, claim* nachweisbar. **(b)** *(Psych)* unzurechnungsfähig; *(inf: mad)* nicht zurechnungsfähig.

certificate [sə'tɪfɪkɪt] *n* Bescheinigung *f,* Nachweis *m;* *(of qualifications)* Zeugnis *nt,* Urkunde *f;* *(of health)* Zeugnis *nt;* *(marriage ~)* Trauschein *m;* *(of baptism)* Taufschein *m;* *(share ~)* Zertifikat *nt;* *(Film)* Freigabe *f.*

certification [,sɜ:tɪfɪ'keɪʃən] *n* **(a)** *(of film)* Klassifizierung *f.* **(b)** *(Jur: document)* Beglaubigung *f.*

certify ['sɜ:tɪfaɪ] 1 *vt* **(a)** bescheinigen, bestätigen; *(Jur)* beglaubigen ◆ **this is to ~ that** ... hiermit wird bescheinigt *or* bestätigt, daß ...; **certified as a true copy** beglaubigte Abschrift; **certified cheque** gedeckter Scheck; **certified mail** *(US)* Einschreiben *nt;* **certified milk** *(US)* Vorzugsmilch *f;* **certified public accountant** *(US)* geprüfter Buchhalter.
(b) *(Psych)* für unzurechnungsfähig erklären; *(put in asylum)* in eine Anstalt einweisen ◆ **he should be certified** *(inf)* der ist doch nicht ganz zurechnungsfähig *(inf).*
2 *vi* **to ~ to sb/sth** sich für jdn/etw verbürgen.

certitude ['sɜ:tɪtju:d] *n* Gewißheit, Sicherheit *f.*

cervical ['sɜ:vɪkəl, sə'vaɪkəl] *adj* zervikal *(spec)* ◆ **~ cancer** Gebärmutterhalskrebs *m;* **~ smear** Abstrich *m.*

cervix ['sɜ:vɪks] *n (of uterus)* Gebärmutterhals *m.*

cesium *n (US) see* **caesium.**

cessation [se'seɪʃən] *n* Ende *nt;* *(of hostilities)* Einstellung *f* ◆ **the ~ of the heartbeat** Herzstillstand *m.*

cession ['seʃən] *n* Abtretung *f* ◆ **~ of lands/territories** Gebietsabtretung(en *pl*) *f.*

cesspit ['sespɪt] *n see* **cesspool (a).**

cesspool ['sespu:l] *n* **(a)** Senk- *or* Jauchegrube, Latrine *f.* **(b)** *(fig)* Sumpf *m* ◆ **a ~ of vice** ein Sündenpfuhl *m.*

CET *abbr of* **Central European Time** MEZ.

cetacean [sɪ'teɪʃɪən] 1 *n* Wal *m,* Zetazee *f (spec).*
2 *adj* Wal(fisch)-, Zetazeen- *(spec).*

Ceylon [sɪ'lɒn] *n* Ceylon *nt.*

Ceylonese [sɪlɒ'ni:z] 1 *adj* ceylonesisch.
2 *n* Ceylonese *m,* Ceylonesin *f.*

CF *(US) abbr of* **cost and freight** cf.

cf *abbr of* **confer** vgl.

c/f *abbr of* **carry forward.**

CFC *abbr of* **chlorofluorocarbon** FCKW *m.*

CFI *(US) abbr of* **cost, freight and insurance** cif.

CFO *abbr of* **chief financial officer.**

CG *(US) abbr of* **coastguard.**

cg *abbr of* **centigram(s), centigramme(s)** cg.

CGA *(Comput) abbr of* **colour graphics adaptor** CGA.

ch *abbr of* **(a) chapter** Kap. **(b) central heating** ZH.

cha-cha ['tʃɑ:tʃɑ:] 1 *n* Cha-Cha-Cha *m.*
2 *vi* Cha-Cha-Cha tanzen.

Chad [tʃæd] *n* der Tschad.

chafe [tʃeɪf] 1 *vt* **(a)** *(rub, abrade)* (auf)scheuern, wundscheuern ◆ **his shirt ~d his neck** sein (Hemd)kragen scheuerte (ihn); **the rope was ~d** das Seil war durchgescheuert.
(b) *(fig)* aufregen, nervös machen.
2 *vi* **(a)** *(rub)* sich auf- *or* wundscheuern; *(cause soreness)* scheuern ◆ **her skin ~s easily** ihre Haut wird leicht wund; **the rope was chafing against the railings** das Seil scheuerte an der Reling. **(b)** *(fig)* sich ärgern *(at, against* über

➤ LANGUAGE IN USE: **ceremony: a** → 24.3 **certain: a** → 15.1, 16.1, 26.3 **certainly** → 26.1, 26.3

+acc).
[3] n wundgescheuerte Stelle.
chaff¹ [tʃɑːf] n (a) (husks of grain) Spreu f; see **wheat.** (b) (straw) Häcksel m or nt.
chaff² [1] n (banter: also **~ing**) Scherze pl, Flachserei f (inf).
[2] vt aufziehen (about mit).
chaffinch ['tʃæfɪntʃ] n Buchfink m.
chagrin ['ʃægrɪn] [1] n Ärger, Verdruß (geh) m.
[2] vt ärgern, verdrießen (geh) ◆ **he was much ~ed by the news** die Nachricht bekümmerte or verdroß (geh) ihn sehr.
chain [tʃeɪn] [1] n (a) Kette f ◆ **~s** (lit, fig: fetters) Ketten, Fesseln pl; (Aut) (Schnee)ketten pl; **~ of office** Amtskette f; **to keep a dog on a ~** einen Hund an der Kette halten; **in ~s** in Ketten.
(b) (of mountains) (Berg)kette, (Gebirgs)kette f; (of atoms etc) Kette f ◆ **~ of shops** Ladenkette f; **to make a ~** eine Kette bilden; **~ of ideas** Gedankenkette f; **~ of events** Kette von Ereignissen.
(c) (measure of length) Meßkette f.
[2] vt (lit, fig) anketten, festketten; dog an die Kette legen, anketten ◆ **to ~ sb/sth to sth** jdn/etw an etw (acc) ketten.
◆**chain up** vt sep prisoner in Ketten legen; dog an die Kette legen, anketten.
chain in cpds Ketten-; **~ drive** n Kettenantrieb m, Kettengetriebe f; **~ gang** n Truppe f aneinandergeketteter Sträflinge, Sträflingskolonne f; **~ letter** n Kettenbrief m; **~ lightning** n Linienblitz m; **~-link fence** n Maschendrahtzaun m; **~mail** n Kettenhemd nt; **~ reaction** n Kettenreaktion f; **~saw** n Kettensäge f; **~-smoke** vi eine (Zigarette) nach der anderen rauchen, kettenrauchen infin only; **~-smoker** n Kettenraucher(in f) m; **~ stitch** n (Sew) Kettenstich m; **~ store** n Kettenladen m.
chair [tʃɛəʳ] [1] n (a) (seat) Stuhl m; (arm~) Sessel m; (sedan ~) Sänfte f ◆ **please take a ~** bitte nehmen Sie Platz!
(b) (in committees etc) Vorsitz m ◆ **to be in/take the ~** den Vorsitz führen; **to address the ~** sich an den Vorsitzenden/die Vorsitzende wenden; **all questions through the ~, please** bitte alle Fragen (direkt) an den Vorsitzenden richten!
(c) (professorship) Lehrstuhl m (of für).
(d) (electric ~) (elektrischer) Stuhl.
[2] vt (a) meeting den Vorsitz führen bei.
(b) (Brit: carry in triumph) auf den Schultern (davon)tragen.
chair: ~bound adj an den Rollstuhl gefesselt; **~lift** n Sessellift m; **~man** n Vorsitzende(r) mf; **Mr/Madam C~man** Herr Vorsitzender/Frau Vorsitzende; **~manship** n Vorsitz m; **under the ~manship of** unter (dem) Vorsitz von; **~person** n Vorsitzende(r) mf; **~woman** n Vorsitzende f.
chaise [ʃeɪz] n (Hist) Einspänner m.
chaise longue [ˌʃeɪz'lɑ̃ːŋ] n Chaiselongue f.
chalet ['ʃæleɪ] n Chalet nt; (in motel etc) Apartment nt.
chalice ['tʃælɪs] n (poet, Eccl) Kelch m.
chalk [tʃɔːk] [1] n Kreide f; (limestone also) Kalkstein m ◆ **~ pit** Kalk(stein)bruch m; **not by a long ~** (Brit inf) bei weitem nicht, noch nicht einmal annähernd; **they're as different as ~ and cheese** sie sind (so verschieden) wie Tag und Nacht.
[2] vt message etc mit Kreide schreiben; luggage etc mit Kreide kennzeichnen; billiard cue mit Kreide einreiben.
◆**chalk up** vt sep (a) (lit) (mit Kreide) aufschreiben, notieren. (b) (fig: gain, win) success, victory verbuchen; medal einheimsen. (c) (fig: mark up as credit) anschreiben (inf).
chalkiness ['tʃɔːkɪnɪs] n Kalkigkeit f; (chalky content) Kalkhaltigkeit f.
chalky ['tʃɔːkɪ] adj (+er) (containing chalk) kalkhaltig, kalkig; (like chalk) kalkartig; (covered with chalk) voller Kalk.
challenge ['tʃælɪndʒ] [1] n (a) (to duel, match etc) Herausforderung f (to an +acc); (fig: demands) Anforderung(en pl) f ◆ **to issue a ~ to sb** jdn herausfordern; **this job is a ~** bei dieser Arbeit ist man gefordert; **I see this task as a ~** ich sehe diese Aufgabe als Herausforderung; **the ~ of modern life** die Anforderungen des heutigen Lebens; **those who rose to the ~** diejenigen, die sich der Herausforderung stellten; **the office job held no ~ for him** die Bürotätigkeit stellte keine Ansprüche an ihn; **the ~ of new ideas/the unknown** der Reiz neuer Ideen/des Unbekannten.
(b) (bid: for leadership etc) Griff m (for nach) ◆ **a direct ~ to his authority** eine direkte Infragestellung seiner Autorität.
(c) (Mil: of sentry) Anruf, Werdaruf m.
(d) (Jur: of witness) Ablehnung f.
[2] vt (a) person, champion (to duel, race etc) herausfordern; world record etc überbieten wollen ◆ **to ~ sb to a duel** jdn zum Duell fordern; **to ~ sb to a match** jdn zu einem Kampf or einer Begegnung etc herausfordern.
(b) (fig: make demands on) fordern.
(c) (fig) remarks, sb's authority in Frage stellen, anfechten.
(d) (sentry) anrufen.
(e) (Jur) witnesses ablehnen; evidence, verdict anfechten.
challenger ['tʃælɪndʒəʳ] n (to duel, match etc) Herausforderer m ◆ **a ~ of traditional beliefs** einer, der überkommene Glaubenssätze in Frage stellt.
challenging ['tʃælɪndʒɪŋ] adj (provocative) herausfordernd; (thought-provoking) reizvoll; (demanding) anspruchsvoll, fordernd ◆ **a ~ idea** eine reizvolle Vorstellung; **I don't find this work very ~** diese Arbeit fordert mich nicht.
chamber ['tʃeɪmbəʳ] n (a) (old) (room) Gemach nt (old), Raum m; (bedroom) Schlafgemach nt (old) ◆ **~ of horrors** Horrorkabinett nt. (b) (Brit) **~s** (of solicitor) Kanzlei f; (of judge) Dienst- or Amtszimmer nt. (c) **C~ of Commerce** Handelskammer f; **the Upper/Lower C~** (Parl) die Erste/Zweite Kammer. (d) (Anat) (Herz)kammer f. (e) (of revolver) Kammer f.
chamberlain ['tʃeɪmbəlɪn] n Kammerherr m.
chamber: ~maid n Zimmermädchen nt, Kammerzofe f (old); **~ music** n Kammermusik f; **~ orchestra** n Kammerorchester nt; **~ pot** n Nachttopf m.
chambray ['tʃæmbreɪ] n (US) see **cambric.**
chameleon [kə'miːlɪən] n (Zool, fig) Chamäleon nt.
chamfer ['tʃæmfəʳ] [1] n Fase, Schrägkante f.
[2] vt abfasen, abschrägen.
chamois ['ʃæmwɑː] n (a) (leather) Gamsleder nt ◆ **a ~ (leather)** ein Ledertuch nt, ein Fensterleder nt. (b) (Zool) Gemse f.
champ¹ [tʃæmp] vt (animals) geräuschvoll mahlen or kauen; (people) mampfen (inf) ◆ **to ~ at the bit** (lit) an der Gebißstange kauen; (fig) vor Ungeduld fiebern.
champ² n (inf) Meister, Champion m ◆ **listen, ~** hör zu, Meister.
champagne [ʃæm'peɪn] [1] n Sekt, Schaumwein m; (French ~) Champagner m ◆ **~ glass** Sekt-/Champagnerglas nt.
[2] adj (also **~-coloured**) champagner(farben).
champers ['ʃæmpəz] n (inf) Schampus m (inf).
champion ['tʃæmpjən] [1] n (a) (Sport) Meister(in f), Champion m ◆ **~s** (team) Meister m; **world ~** Weltmeister(in f) m; **boxing ~** Boxchampion m; **heavyweight ~ of the world** Weltmeister m im Schwergewicht. (b) (of a cause) Verfechter m.
[2] adj (a) (prize-winning) siegreich; dog, bull, show animal preisgekrönt ◆ **~ boxer** erfolgreicher Boxer; **~ horse** (racing) Turfsieger m; (show-jumping) siegreiches Turnierpferd.
(b) (N Engl inf) klasse inv (inf), prima inv (inf).
[3] vt person, action, cause eintreten für, sich engagieren für.
championship ['tʃæmpjənʃɪp] n (a) (Sport) Meisterschaft f ◆ **he defended his ~** er verteidigte den Titel. (b) **~s** pl (event) Meisterschaftskämpfe pl. (c) (support) Eintreten, Engagement nt (of für).
➤ **chance** [tʃɑːns] [1] n (a) (coincidence) Zufall m; (luck, fortune) Glück nt ◆ **by ~** durch Zufall, zufällig; **a game of ~** ein Glücksspiel nt; **would you by any ~ be able to help?** könnten Sie mir wohl or vielleicht behilflich sein?; **to leave things to ~** die Dinge dem Zufall überlassen; **to trust to ~** auf sein Glück vertrauen.
➤ (b) (possibility) Aussicht(en pl), Chance(n pl) f; (probability, likelihood) Möglichkeit f ◆ **the ~s are that ...** aller Wahrscheinlichkeit nach ..., wahrscheinlich ...; **the ~s are against that happening** vieles spricht dagegen or die Wahrscheinlichkeit ist gering, daß das eintritt; **what are the ~s of him agreeing?** wie sind die Aussichten or wie stehen die Chancen, daß er zustimmt?; **is there any ~ of us meeting again?** könnten wir uns vielleicht wiedersehen?; **what are the ~s of his coming?** wie groß ist die Wahrscheinlichkeit, daß er kommt?; **is there any ~ he might be lost?** besteht die Möglichkeit, daß er sich verirrt hat?; **on the ~ of your returning** für den Fall, daß du or falls du zurückkommst or zurückkommen solltest; **he has not much/a good ~ of winning** er hat wenig/gute Aussicht zu gewinnen, er hat nicht sehr gute/gute Siegeschancen; **to be in with a ~** eine Chance haben; **he doesn't stand** or **hasn't got a ~** er hat keine(rlei) Chance(n); **no ~!** (inf) nee! (inf), ist nicht drin (inf); **will you lend me £50 — sorry, no ~** leihst du mir £ 50? — bedaure, nichts zu machen or ist nicht drin (inf).
(c) (opportunity) Chance f ◆ **the ~ of a lifetime** eine einmalige Chance; **you won't get another ~ of going there** or **to go there** die Gelegenheit, dahin zu fahren, bietet sich (dir) nicht noch einmal; **you won't get another ~** das ist eine einmalige Gelegenheit; **I had the ~ to go** or **of going** ich hatte (die) Gelegenheit, dahin zu gehen; **now's your ~!** das ist deine Chance!; **this is my big ~** das ist die Chance für mich; **to take one's ~** die Gelegenheit nutzen; **to have an eye to the main ~** (pej) nur auf seinen Vorteil bedacht sein; **he never had a ~ in life** er hat im Leben nie eine Chance gehabt; **give me a ~!** nun mach aber mal langsam (inf); **to give sb a ~** jdm eine Chance geben; **you never gave me a ~ to explain** du hast mir ja nie die Chance gegeben, das zu erklären; **~ would be a fine thing!** (inf) schön wär's!
(d) (risk) Risiko nt ◆ **to take a ~** es darauf ankommen lassen; **aren't you taking a bit of a ~?** ist das nicht ein bißchen riskant?; **he's not taking any ~s** er geht kein Risiko ein.
[2] attr zufällig ◆ **~ meeting** zufällige Begegnung.
[3] vi **it ~d that ...** es traf or fügte (geh) sich, daß ...
[4] vt (a) **to ~ to do sth** zufällig etw tun.
(b) **I'll ~ it!** (inf) ich versuch's mal (inf); **to ~ one's arm** (inf) (et)was riskieren; **to ~ one's luck** (have a try) sein Glück versuchen; (risk) das Glück herausfordern; **I'll just have to ~ that happening** das muß ich eben riskieren.
◆**chance (up)on** vi +prep obj person zufällig begegnen (+dat), zufällig treffen; thing zufällig stoßen auf (+acc).
chancel ['tʃɑːnsəl] n Chor, Altarraum m.
chancellery ['tʃɑːnsələrɪ] n (offices) Kanzleramt nt; (position) Kanzlerschaft f.
chancellor ['tʃɑːnsələʳ] n (Jur, Pol, Univ) Kanzler m ◆ **C~ (of the Exchequer)** (Brit) Schatzkanzler, Finanzminister m.
chancellorship ['tʃɑːnsələʃɪp] n Kanzlerschaft f.
chancer ['tʃɑːnsəʳ] n (inf) Windhund m (inf).
chancery ['tʃɑːnsərɪ] n: **ward in ~** Mündel nt in Amtsvormundschaft.
chancre ['ʃæŋkəʳ] n Schanker m.
chancy ['tʃɑːnsɪ] adj (+er) (inf: risky) riskant.
chandelier [ˌʃændə'lɪəʳ] n Kronleuchter m.
chandler ['tʃɑːndləʳ] n (for candles) Kerzenmacher m; (shop) Kerzenladen m

➤ LANGUAGE IN USE: **chance: 1b** → 16.2, 16.3

◆ **ship's ~** Schiffsausrüster *m.*

▼ **change** [tʃeɪndʒ] [1] *n* **(a)** Veränderung *f*; (*modification also*) Änderung *f* (*to gen*) ◆ **a ~ for the better/worse** ein Fortschritt *m*, eine Verbesserung/ein Rückschritt *m*, eine Verschlechterung; **~ of address** Adressen- *or* Anschriftenänderung *f*; **a ~ in the weather** eine Wetterveränderung; **a ~ of air** eine Luftveränderung; **a ~ is as good as a rest** (*prov*) Abwechslung wirkt *or* tut Wunder; **no ~** unverändert; **I need a ~ of scene** ich brauche Tapetenwechsel; **to make ~s (to sth)** (an etw *dat*) (Ver)änderungen vornehmen; **to make a ~/a considerable ~ in sth** etw ändern/bedeutend verändern; **the ~ of life** die Wechseljahre; **he needs a ~ of clothes** er müßte sich mal wieder umziehen; **I didn't have a ~ of clothes with me** ich hatte nichts zum Wechseln mit; **a ~ of job** ein Stellenwechsel *m.*
(b) (*variety*) Abwechslung *f* ◆ **(just) for a ~** zur Abwechslung (mal); **that makes a ~** das ist mal was anderes; (*iro*) das ist ja was ganz Neues!; **it'll make a nice ~** das wäre eine nette Abwechslung; *see* **ring.**
(c) *no pl* (*changing*) Veränderung *f* ◆ **those who are against ~** diejenigen, die gegen jegliche Veränderung sind; **the constant ~ will only confuse people** der ständige Wechsel verwirrt die Leute nur.
(d) (*of one thing for another*) Wechsel *m* ◆ **a ~ of government** ein Regierungswechsel, ein Wechsel in der Regierung; **a wheel ~** ein Radwechsel.
(e) *no pl* (*money*) Wechselgeld *nt*; (*small ~*) Kleingeld *nt* ◆ **can you give me ~ for a pound?** können Sie mir ein Pfund wechseln?; **I haven't got any ~** ich habe kein Kleingeld; **I haven't got ~ for £5** ich kann auf £ 5 nicht rausgeben *or* £ 5 nicht wechseln; **you won't get much ~ out of £5** von £ 5 wird wohl nicht viel übrigbleiben; **keep the ~** der Rest ist für Sie; **you won't get much ~ out of him** (*fig*) aus ihm wirst du nicht viel rauskriegen.
(f) (*St Ex*) **C~** Börse *f.*
[2] *vt* **(a)** (*by substitution*) wechseln; *address, name* ändern ◆ **to ~ trains/buses** *etc* umsteigen; **to ~ one's clothes** sich umziehen; **to ~ a wheel/the oil** einen Rad-/Ölwechsel vornehmen, ein Rad/das Öl wechseln; **to ~ a baby's nappy** *or* **a baby** (bei einem Baby) die Windeln wechseln, ein Baby wickeln; **to ~ the sheets** *or* **the bed** die Bettwäsche wechseln, das Bett neu beziehen; **to ~ one's seat** den Platz wechseln, sich woanders hinsetzen; **to ~ hands** den Besitzer wechseln; **would you ~ the record?** kannst du (mal) ein andere Platte auflegen?; (*turn it over*) kannst du mal die andere Seite auflegen?; **to ~ places with sb** mit jdm den Platz tauschen; **she ~d places with him/Mrs Brown** er/Frau Brown und sie tauschten die Plätze; **I wouldn't ~ places with him for the world** ich möchte *or* würde um nichts in der Welt mit ihm tauschen; **to ~ horses in midstream** (*fig*) plötzlich einen anderen Kurs einschlagen.
(b) (*alter*) (ver)ändern; *person, ideas* ändern; (*transform*) verwandeln ◆ **to ~ sb/sth into sth** jdn/etw in etw (*acc*) verwandeln; **you won't be able to ~ her** du kannst sie nicht ändern; **a chameleon can ~ its colour** das Chamäleon kann seine Farbe wechseln.
(c) (*exchange: in shop etc*) umtauschen ◆ **she ~d the dress for one of a different colour** sie tauschte das Kleid gegen ein andersfarbiges um; **he ~d his Rolls Royce for a Mini** er vertauschte seinen Rolls Royce mit einem Mini; *see* **guard.**
(d) *money* (*into smaller money*) wechseln; (*into other currency*) (ein)wechseln, (um)tauschen.
(e) (*Aut*) **to ~ gear** schalten.
[3] *vi* **(a)** sich ändern; (*town, person also*) sich verändern ◆ **you've ~d!** du hast dich aber verändert!; **he will never ~** er wird sich nie ändern, der ändert sich nie!; **to ~ from sth into ...** sich aus etw in ... (*acc*) verwandeln.
(b) (*~ clothes*) sich umziehen ◆ **she ~d into an old skirt** sie zog sich einen alten Rock an; **I'll just ~ out of these old clothes** ich muß mir noch die alten Sachen ausziehen.
(c) (*~ trains etc*) umsteigen ◆ **you ~ at York** in York müssen Sie umsteigen; **all ~!** Endstation!, alle aussteigen!
(d) (*~ gear*) schalten; (*traffic lights*) umspringen (*to* auf +*acc*).
(e) (*from one thing to another*) (*seasons*) wechseln ◆ **to ~ to a different system** auf ein anderes System umstellen, zu einem anderen System übergehen; **I ~d to philosophy from maths** ich habe von Mathematik zu Philosophie gewechselt; **do you want to ~ with me?** (*places*) möchten Sie mit mir tauschen?

◆**change down** *vi* (*Aut*) einen niedrigeren Gang einlegen, in einen niedrigeren Gang schalten, (he)runterschalten.

◆**change over** [1] *vi* **(a)** (*change to sth different*) sich umstellen auf (+*acc*) ◆ **we have just ~d ~ from gas to electricity** hier *or* bei uns ist gerade von Gas auf Strom umgestellt worden.
(b) (*exchange places, activities etc*) wechseln; (*Sport also*) die Seiten wechseln ◆ **do you mind if I ~ ~?** (*TV*) hast du was dagegen, wenn ich umschalte?
[2] *vt sep* austauschen.

◆**change round** [1] *vi see* **change over 1 (b).**
[2] *vt sep room* umräumen; *furniture* umstellen; *tyres* austauschen, auswechseln.

◆**change up** *vi* (*Aut*) einen höheren Gang einlegen, in einen höheren Gang schalten, höherschalten (*inf*) ◆ **to ~ ~ into top** in den höchsten Gang schalten.

changeability [ˌtʃeɪndʒəˈbɪlɪtɪ] *n* Unbeständigkeit, Veränderlichkeit *f.*

changeable [ˈtʃeɪndʒəbl] *adj person, character* unbeständig; *weather* veränderlich, wechselhaft; *mood, winds* wechselnd.

changeless [ˈtʃeɪndʒlɪs] *adj* unveränderlich.

changeling [ˈtʃeɪndʒlɪŋ] *n* (*child*) Wechselbalg *m.*

➤ LANGUAGE IN USE: **change: 1a → 19.3**

change machine *n* Geldwechsler *m.*

changeover [ˈtʃeɪndʒəʊvər] *n* Umstellung *f* (*to* auf +*acc*); (*of governments*) Regierungswechsel *m*; (*in relay race*) (Stab)wechsel *m*; (*of teams changing ends*) Seitenwechsel *m.*

changing [ˈtʃeɪndʒɪŋ] [1] *adj* sich verändernd, wechselnd ◆ **the fast-~ face of Munich** das sich rapide wandelnde Gesicht *or* Stadtbild Münchens.
[2] *n* **the ~ of the Guard** die Wachablösung.

changing-room [ˈtʃeɪndʒɪŋˈruːm] *n* (*in store*) Ankleideraum *m*, Kabine *f*; (*Sport*) Umkleideraum *m*, Umkleidekabine *f.*

channel [ˈtʃænl] [1] *n* **(a)** (*watercourse*) (Fluß)bett *nt*; (*strait*) Kanal *m*; (*deepest part of river etc*) Fahrrinne *f* ◆ **the (English) C~** der Ärmelkanal; **C~ Islands** Kanalinseln *pl*; **C~ Tunnel** Kanaltunnel *m.*
(b) (*fig, usu pl*) (*of bureaucracy etc*) Dienstweg *m*; (*of information etc*) Kanal *m*; (*of thought, interest etc*) Bahn *f* ◆ **if you go through the right ~s** wenn Sie sich an die richtigen Stellen wenden; **to go through the official ~s** den Dienstweg gehen; **you'll have to go through ~s** (*US*) Sie werden den Dienstweg einhalten müssen; **through the usual ~s** auf dem üblichen Wege.
(c) (*groove*) Furche, Rinne *f.*
(d) (*TV, Rad*) Kanal *m*, Programm *nt.*
[2] *vt* **(a)** (*dig out, furrow*) *way, course* sich (*dat*) bahnen.
(b) (*direct*) *water, river* (hindurch)leiten (*through* durch).
(c) (*fig*) *efforts, interest* lenken (*into* auf +*acc*); *energy also* kanalisieren; *crowd also* dirigieren.

◆**channel off** *vt sep* (*lit*) ableiten; (*fig*) abzweigen.

channel-hop [ˈtʃænlˌhɒp] *vi* (*Brit TV inf*) ständig umschalten *or* den Kanal wechseln.

channel-hopping [ˈtʃænlˌhɒpɪŋ] *n* (*Brit TV inf*) ständiges Umschalten.

channel-surf [ˈtʃænlˌsɜːf] *vi* (*US TV inf*) *see* **channel-hop.**

channel-surfing [ˈtʃænlˌsɜːfɪŋ] *n* (*US TV inf*) *see* **channel-hopping.**

chant [tʃɑːnt] [1] *n* (*Eccl, Mus*) Gesang, Cantus *m*; (*monotonous song*) Sprechgesang, Singsang *m*; (*of football fans*) Sprechchor *m* ◆ **tribal ~s** Stammesgesänge *pl.*
[2] *vt* im (Sprech)chor rufen; (*Eccl*) singen.
[3] *vi* Sprechchöre anstimmen; (*Eccl*) singen.

chanterelle [ˈtʃæntərel] *n* Pfifferling *m.*

chanticleer [ˈtʃæntɪkliːər] *n* (*old*) Hahn *m.*

chaos [ˈkeɪɒs] *n* Chaos, Durcheinander *nt* ◆ **complete ~** ein totales Durcheinander.

chaotic *adj*, **~ally** *adv* [keɪˈɒtɪk, -əlɪ] chaotisch.

chap[1] [tʃæp] [1] *n* (*Med: of skin*) **he's got ~s on his hands** seine Hände sind aufgesprungen *or* rauh.
[2] *vi* (*skin*) aufspringen.
[3] *vt* spröde machen ◆ **~ped lips** aufgesprungene *or* rauhe Lippen.

chap[2] *n* (*Brit inf: man*) Kerl (*inf*), Typ (*inf*) *m* ◆ **old ~** alter Junge (*inf*) *or* Knabe (*inf*); **poor little ~** armer Kleiner!, armes Kerlchen!; **now look here you ~s** hört mal zu, Jungs (*inf*).

chap[3] *abbr of* **chapter** Kap.

chapel [ˈtʃæpəl] *n* **(a)** Kapelle *f*; (*Sch, Univ: service*) Andacht *f* ◆ **~ of rest** *Kapelle f in einem Bestattungsunternehmen, wo Tote aufgebahrt werden.* **(b)** (*nonconformist church*) Sektenkirche *f.* **(c)** (*Press: of union*) *Betriebsgruppe f innerhalb der Gewerkschaft der Drucker und Journalisten.*

chaperon(e) [ˈʃæpərəʊn] [1] *n* **(a)** (*for propriety*) Anstandsdame *f*, Anstandswauwau *m* (*hum inf*). **(b)** (*escort*) Begleiter(in *f*) *m.* **(c)** (*esp US: supervisor*) Aufsichts- *or* Begleitperson *f.*
[2] *vt* **(a)** (*for propriety*) begleiten, Anstandsdame spielen bei. **(b)** (*escort*) begleiten. **(c)** (*US*) beaufsichtigen.

chaplain [ˈtʃæplɪn] *n* Kaplan *m.*

chaplaincy [ˈtʃæplənsɪ] *n* Amt *nt or* Stelle *f* eines Kaplans; (*building*) Diensträume *pl* eines Kaplans.

chaplet [ˈtʃæplɪt] *n* (*of flowers etc*) Kranz *m.*

chappy [ˈtʃæpɪ] *n* (*inf*) Kerlchen *nt* (*inf*).

chaps [tʃæps] *npl* lederne Reithosen, Cowboyhosen *pl.*

chapter [ˈtʃæptər] *n* **(a)** (*of book*) Kapitel *nt* ◆ **to give ~ and verse (for sth)** (*fig*) etw genau belegen. **(b)** (*fig*) Kapitel *nt* ◆ **a ~ of accidents** eine Serie von Unfällen. **(c)** (*Eccl*) Kapitel *nt* ◆ **~ house** Kapitel(saal *m*) *nt.* **(d)** (*esp US: branch*) Ortsgruppe *f.*

char[1] [tʃɑːr] *vt* (*burn black*) verkohlen.

char[2] (*Brit inf*) [1] *n* (*charwoman*) Putzfrau *f.*
[2] *vi* putzen ◆ **to ~ for sb** bei jdm putzen.

char[3] *n* (*fish*) Saibling *m.*

char[4] *n* (*Brit inf: tea*) Tee *m.*

charabanc, char-à-banc [ˈʃærəbæŋ] *n* (*old*) *offener Omnibus für Ausflugsfahrten.*

character [ˈkærɪktər] *n* **(a)** (*nature*) Charakter *m*; (*of people*) Wesen *nt no pl*, Wesensart *f* ◆ **there's quite a difference in ~ between them** sie sind wesensmäßig sehr verschieden; **to be in ~ for sb** typisch für jdn sein; **it is out of ~ for him to behave like that** solches Benehmen ist untypisch für ihn; **it's out of ~ for him to do that** es ist eigentlich nicht seine Art, so etwas zu tun; **to be of good/bad ~** ein guter/schlechter Mensch sein.
(b) *no pl* (*strength of ~*) Charakter *m* ◆ **a man of ~** ein Mann von Charakter; **she's got no ~** sie hat keinen Charakter.
(c) *no pl* (*individuality*) (*of towns etc*) Charakter *m*; (*of person*) Persönlichkeit *f* ◆ **she has no ~** sie hat keine Persönlichkeit; **her face is full of ~** sie hat ein Charaktergesicht.

(d) (*in novel*) (Roman)figur, (Roman)gestalt *f*; (*Theat*) Gestalt *f*.
(e) (*person in public life*) Persönlichkeit, Gestalt *f*; (*original person*) Original *nt*; (*inf: person*) Typ *m* (*inf*), Type *f* (*inf*).
(f) (*reference*) Zeugnis *nt*.
(g) (*Typ, Comput*) Zeichen *nt*; (*Chinese etc also*) Schriftzeichen *nt* ◆ **to type 100 ~s per minute** 100 Anschläge pro Minute machen; **Gothic ~s** gotische Schrift.

character *in cpds* (*Theat*) Charakter-; ~ **actor** *n* Charakterdarsteller *m*; ~ **assassination** *n* Rufmord *m*.

characteristic [ˌkærɪktəˈrɪstɪk] [1] *adj* charakteristisch, typisch (*of* für).
[2] *n* (typisches) Merkmal, Charakteristikum *nt*; (*Math*) Charakteristik, Kennziffer *f* ◆ **one of the main ~s of his style is ...** besonders charakteristisch für seinen Stil ist ..., eines der Hauptmerkmale seines Stils ist ...; **he has all the ~s of the true aristocrat** er hat alle Züge des echten Aristokraten.

characteristically [ˌkærɪktəˈrɪstɪkəlɪ] *adv* typisch.

characterization [ˌkærɪktəraɪˈzeɪʃən] *n* (*in a novel etc*) Personenbeschreibung *f*; (*of one character*) Charakterisierung *f*.

characterize [ˈkærɪktəraɪz] *vt* **(a)** (*be characteristic of*) kennzeichnen, charakterisieren. **(b)** (*describe*) beschreiben.

characterless [ˈkærɪktəlɪs] *adj person* nichtssagend, farblos; *room* nichtssagend, nichts Besonderes *pred*; *wine* fade.

character: ~ **part** *n* Charakterrolle *f*; ~ **reference** *n* Referenz *f*; ~ **set** *n* (*Comput*) Zeichensatz *m*; ~ **sketch** *n* Charakterstudie *f*; ~ **space** *n* (*Comput*) Zeichenplatz *m*; ~ **string** *n* (*Comput*) Zeichenkette *f*.

charade [ʃəˈrɑːd] *n* Scharade *f*; (*fig*) Farce *f*, Affentheater *nt* (*inf*).

charcoal [ˈtʃɑːkəʊl] *n* Holzkohle *f*; (*drawing*) Kohlezeichnung *f*; (*pencil*) Kohle(stift *m*) *f*.

charcoal: ~ **burner** *n* (*person*) Köhler, Kohlenbrenner (*rare*) *m*; (*stove*) Holzkohlenofen *m*; ~ **drawing** *n* Kohlezeichnung *f*; **~-grey** *adj* schwarzgrau.

charge [tʃɑːdʒ] [1] *n* **(a)** (*Jur: accusation*) Anklage *f* (*of* wegen) ◆ **convicted on all three ~s** in allen drei Anklagepunkten für schuldig befunden; **to bring a ~ against sb** gegen jdn Anklage erheben, jdn unter Anklage stellen; **to press ~s (against sb)** (gegen jdn) Anzeige erstatten; **what is the ~?** wessen werde ich/wird er *etc* beschuldigt?; **to be on a murder ~** unter Mordanklage stehen; **he was arrested on a ~ of murder** er wurde wegen *or* unter Mordverdacht festgenommen; **to give sb in ~** (*form*) jdn in polizeilichen Gewahrsam bringen (*form*); **it was laid to his ~** (*form*) es wurde ihm angelastet *or* zur Last gelegt; **to be on a ~** (*soldier*) eine Disziplinarstrafe verbüßen; **to put a soldier on a ~** über einen Soldaten eine Disziplinarstrafe verhängen, einen Soldaten verknacken (*sl*); **you're on a ~, Smith!** das gibt eine Disziplinarstrafe, Smith!
(b) (*attack: of soldiers, bull etc*) Angriff *m*; (*trumpet-call*) Signal *nt* ◆ **to sound the ~** zum Angriff blasen.
(c) (*fee*) Gebühr *f* ◆ **what's the/your ~?** was kostet das?/was verlangen Sie?; **to make a ~ (of £5) for sth** (£ 5 für) etw berechnen *or* in Rechnung stellen; **he made no ~ for mending my watch** er hat mir für die Reparatur der Uhr nichts berechnet; **there's an extra ~ for delivery** die Lieferung wird zusätzlich berechnet; **his ~s are quite reasonable** seine Preise sind ganz vernünftig; **free of ~** kostenlos, gratis; **delivered free of ~** Lieferung frei Haus.
(d) (*explosive ~*) (Spreng)ladung *f*; (*in firearm, Elec, Phys*) Ladung *f* ◆ **to put a battery on ~** eine Batterie aufladen; **to be on ~** aufgeladen werden.
(e) (*position of responsibility*) Verantwortung *f* (*of* für) ◆ **to be in ~** verantwortlich sein, die Verantwortung haben; **who is in ~ here?** wer ist hier der Verantwortliche?; **look, I'm in ~ here** hören Sie mal zu, hier bestimme ich!; **to be in ~ of sth** für etw die Verantwortung haben; *of department* etw leiten; **to put sb in ~ of sth** jdm die Verantwortung für etw übertragen; *of department* jdm die Leitung von etw übertragen; **while in ~ of a car** (*form*) am Steuer eines Kraftfahrzeuges; **the man in ~** der Verantwortliche, die verantwortliche Person; **the children were placed in their aunt's ~** die Kinder wurden der Obhut der Tante anvertraut; **the patients in** *or* **under her ~** die ihr anvertrauten Patienten; **to take ~ of sth** etw übernehmen; **to take ~** das Kommando übernehmen; **he took ~ of the situation** er nahm die Sache in die Hand.
(f) (*ward*) (*child*) Schützling *m*; (*of authorities*) Mündel *nt*; (*patient*) Patient(in *f*) *m*.
(g) (*financial burden*) **to be a ~ on sb** jdm zur Last fallen.
[2] *vt* **(a)** (*with gen*) (*Jur*) anklagen; (*fig*) beschuldigen.
(b) (*attack*) stürmen; *troops* angreifen; (*bull etc*) losgehen auf (*+acc*); (*Sport*) *goalkeeper, player* angehen ◆ **the forwards ~d the defence** die Stürmer griffen die Deckung an; **to ~ sb off the ball** jdn vom Ball abdrängen.
(c) (*ask in payment*) berechnen ◆ **I won't ~ you for that** das kostet Sie nichts, ich berechne Ihnen nichts dafür.
(d) (*record as debt*) in Rechnung stellen ◆ **~ it to the company** stellen Sie das der Firma in Rechnung, das geht auf die Firma (*inf*); **please ~ all these purchases to my account** bitte setzen Sie diese Einkäufe auf meine Rechnung.
(e) *firearm* laden; (*Phys, Elec*), *battery* (auf)laden.
(f) (*form: command*) **to ~ sb to do sth** jdn beauftragen *or* anweisen (*form*), etw zu tun.
(g) (*form: give as responsibility*) **to ~ sb with sth** jdn mit etw beauftragen.
[3] *vi* **(a)** (*attack*) stürmen; (*at people*) angreifen (*at sb* jdn); (*bull*) losgehen (*at sb* auf jdn) ◆ **~!** vorwärts!
(b) (*inf: rush*) rennen ◆ **he ~d into a brick wall** er rannte gegen eine Mauer; **he ~d into the room/upstairs** er stürmte ins Zimmer/die Treppe hoch.

◆**charge up** *vt sep* **(a)** (*credit*) in Rechnung stellen (*to sb* jdm) ◆ **I'll ~ the expenses ~** das geht auf Geschäftskosten. **(b)** (*Elec*) aufladen.

chargeable [ˈtʃɑːdʒəbl] *adj* **(a)** (*Jur*) **to be ~ with sth** für etw angeklagt werden können. **(b) to be ~ to sb** auf jds Kosten (*acc*) gehen; **are these expenses ~?** geht das auf Geschäftskosten?

charge: ~ **account** *n* Kunden(kredit)konto *nt*; **~-cap** *vt* (*Brit*) **the council was ~capped** dem Stadtrat wurde ein Höchstsatz für die Kommunalsteuer auferlegt; ~ **capping** [ˈtʃɑːdʒˌkæpɪŋ] *n* (*Brit*) *Festlegung f eines Kommunalsteuer-Höchstsatzes durch die Zentralregierung*; ~ **card** *n* Kundenkreditkarte *f*.

charged [ˈtʃɑːdʒd] *adj* (*lit, fig*) geladen; (*Elec also*) aufgeladen ◆ **~ with emotion** emotionsgeladen.

chargé d'affaires [ˈʃɑːʒeɪdæˈfɛəʳ] *n* Chargé d'affaires *m*.

charge: **~hand** *n* Vorarbeiter(in *f*) *m*; ~ **nurse** *n* (*Brit*) Stationsleiter *m* (*im Pflegedienst*).

charger [ˈtʃɑːdʒəʳ] *n* **(a)** (*battery ~*) Ladegerät *nt*. **(b)** (*horse*) Roß *nt*. **(c)** (*old: dish*) Platte *f*.

charge sheet *n* Anklageprotokoll *nt*.

charily [ˈtʃɛərɪlɪ] *adv* vorsichtig.

chariness [ˈtseərɪnɪs] *n* Vorsicht *f*.

chariot [ˈtʃærɪət] *n* Wagen, Streitwagen (*liter*) *m*.

charioteer [ˌtʃærɪəˈtɪəʳ] *n* Wagenlenker *m*.

charisma [kæˈrɪzmə] *n* Charisma *nt*.

charismatic [ˌkærɪzˈmætɪk] *adj* charismatisch.

charitable [ˈtʃærɪtəbl] *adj* menschenfreundlich, gütig; (*dispensing charity*) *trust, organization* Wohltätigkeits-, karitativ; (*financially generous, tolerant*) großzügig; *thought, remark etc* freundlich ◆ **a ~ deed** eine gute Tat; **he wasn't very ~ about his boss** er äußerte sich nicht gerade schmeichelhaft über seinen Chef; **I'm feeling ~ today, here's £5** ich habe heute meinen sozialen Tag, hier hast du £ 5.

charitably [ˈtʃærɪtəblɪ] *adv* großzügig; *say etc* freundlich.

charity [ˈtʃærɪtɪ] *n* **(a)** (*Christian virtue*) tätige Nächstenliebe, Barmherzigkeit *f*.
(b) (*tolerance, kindness*) Menschenfreundlichkeit *f* ◆ **for ~'s sake, out of ~** aus reiner Menschenfreundlichkeit; **~ begins at home** (*Prov*) man muß zuerst an seine eigene Familie/sein eigenes Land *etc* denken.
(c) (*alms*) **to live on ~** von Almosen leben.
(d) (*charitable society*) Wohltätigkeitsverein *m*, karitative Organisation; (*charitable purposes*) Wohlfahrt *f* ◆ **to work for ~** für die Wohlfahrt arbeiten; **a collection for ~** eine Sammlung für wohltätige *or* karitative Zwecke.

charity *in cpds* Wohltätigkeits-.

charlady [ˈtʃɑːˌleɪdɪ] *n* (*Brit*) Putz- *or* Reinemachefrau *f*.

charlatan [ˈʃɑːlətən] *n* Scharlatan *m*.

Charlemagne [ˈʃɑːləmeɪn] *n* Karl der Große.

Charles [tʃɑːlz] *n* Karl *m*.

charleston [ˈtʃɑːlstən] *n* Charleston *m*.

charley horse [ˈtʃɑːlɪhɔːs] *n* (*US inf*) steifes Bein.

Charlie [ˈtʃɑːlɪ] *n* **(a)** *dim of* **Charles. (b) c~** (*inf: fool*) Heini (*inf*), Blödmann (*sl*) *m*; **I felt a real c~** ich kam mir richtig blöd vor (*inf*); **I must have looked a proper c~** ich muß ziemlich dumm aus der Wäsche geguckt haben (*inf*).

Charlotte [ˈʃɑːlət] *n* **(a)** Charlotte *f*. **(b)** (*Cook*) **c~** Charlotte *f*; **c~ russe** Charlotte Malakoff.

charm [tʃɑːm] [1] *n* **(a)** (*attractiveness*) Charme *m no pl*; (*of person also*) Anziehungskraft *f*; (*of cottage, village, countryside*) Reiz *m* ◆ **feminine ~s** (weibliche) Reize *pl*; **he fell victim to her ~s** er erlag ihrem Charme; **to turn on the ~** seinen (ganzen) Charme spielen lassen.
(b) (*spell*) Bann *m* ◆ **it worked like a ~** das hat hervorragend geklappt.
(c) (*amulet*) Talisman *m*; (*trinket*) Anhänger *m*.
[2] *vt* **(a)** (*attract, please*) bezaubern ◆ **he could ~ the birds out of the trees** (*prov*) er könnte mit seinem Charme alles erreichen. **(b)** (*cast spell on*) bannen; *snakes* beschwören ◆ **to lead a ~ed life** einen Schutzengel haben.

◆**charm away** *vt sep fears, worries etc* zerstreuen.

charm bracelet *n* Armband *nt* mit Anhängern.

charmer [ˈtʃɑːməʳ] *n* **to be/look a real ~** wirklich charmant sein/zum Verlieben aussehen.

charming [ˈtʃɑːmɪŋ] *adj* reizend, charmant ◆ **~!** (*iro*) wie reizend! (*iro*), na, das ist ja reizend! (*iro*).

charmingly [ˈtʃɑːmɪŋlɪ] *adv* reizend ◆ **she behaved/welcomed us quite ~** sie war/begrüßte uns äußerst charmant.

charnel-house [ˈtʃɑːnlhaʊs] *n* (*old*) Leichenhalle *f*; (*for bones*) Beinhaus *nt*.

chart [tʃɑːt] [1] *n* **(a)** Tabelle *f*; (*graph, diagram*) Schaubild, Diagramm *nt*; (*map, weather ~*) Karte *f* ◆ **on a ~** in einer Tabelle/einem Diagramm; **to keep a ~ of sth** etw in eine Tabelle eintragen/in einem Diagramm festhalten.
(b) ~s *pl* (*top twenty*) Hitliste *f*; **~ topper** (*hit record*) Spitzenreiter *m*.
[2] *vt* (*make a map of*) kartographisch erfassen; (*record progress of*) auswerten; (*keep a ~ of*) aufzeichnen, erfassen; (*plan*) festlegen ◆ **to ~ the progress of a project** die Entwicklung eines Projekts schriftlich festhalten.

charter [ˈtʃɑːtəʳ] [1] *n* **(a)** Charta *f*; (*town ~, Univ also*) Gründungsurkunde *f*; (*of a society*) Satzung *f*; (*permission to become established*) Charter *f or m*, Freibrief *m*. **(b)** (*Naut, Aviat: hire*) **on ~** gechartert; **the plane is available for ~** das Flugzeug kann gechartert werden.
[2] *vt plane, bus etc* chartern.

charter *in cpds* Charter-.

chartered accountant [ˌtʃɑːtədəˈkaʊntənt] *n* staatlich geprüfte(r) Bilanzbuchhalter.

charter: ~ **flight** *n* Charterflug *m*; ~ **party** *n* Chartergesellschaft *f*; ~

plane *n* Charterflugzeug *nt.*

charwoman ['tʃɑːˌwʊmən] *n (Brit) see* **charlady.**

chary ['tʃɛərɪ] *adj (+er) (cautious)* vorsichtig; *(sparing)* zurückhaltend *(of* mit) ◆ **I'd be ~ of taking lifts from strangers if I were you** an deiner Stelle würde ich nicht so ohne weiteres mit Fremden mitfahren; **he is ~ of giving praise** er ist mit Lob zurückhaltend.

Charybdis [kə'rɪbdɪs] *n* Charybdis *f.*

Chas *abbr of* **Charles.**

chase¹ [tʃeɪs] [1] *n* Verfolgungsjagd *f*; *(Hunt)* Jagd *f* ◆ **a car ~** eine Verfolgungsjagd im Auto; **to give ~** die Verfolgung aufnehmen; **to give ~ to sb** jds Verfolgung aufnehmen.

[2] *vt* jagen; *(follow)* verfolgen; *member of opposite sex* hinterherlaufen *(+dat)*, nachlaufen *(+dat)* ◆ **go and ~ yourself!** *(sl)* scher dich zum Teufel! *(inf)*; **he's been chasing that girl for months** er ist schon seit Monaten hinter der Frau her; **this letter has been chasing you all over London** dieser Brief ist dir schon durch ganz London gefolgt.

[3] *vi* **to ~ after sb** hinter jdm herrennen *(inf)*; *(in vehicle)* hinter jdm herrasen *(inf)*; **to ~ around** herumrasen *(inf)*.

◆**chase away** *or* **off** [1] *vi* losrasen *(inf)*; *(on foot also)* losrennen.

[2] *vt sep* wegjagen; *(fig) sorrow etc* vertreiben.

◆**chase up** *vt sep person* rankriegen *(inf)*; *information etc* ranschaffen *(inf)* ◆ **we'll have to ~ them ~ a bit (about ...)** wir werden ihnen ein bißchen Dampf machen müssen (wegen ...).

chase² *vt (Tech) silver, metal* ziselieren.

chaser ['tʃeɪsə^r] *n* **(a)** *(pursuer)* Verfolger *m.* **(b)** *(drink)* **have a whisky ~** trinken Sie einen Whisky dazu.

chasm ['kæzəm] *n (Geol)* Spalte, Kluft *(also fig) f* ◆ **a yawning ~** ein gähnender Abgrund; **the future lay before him, a great black ~** die Zukunft tat sich wie ein riesiger dunkler Abgrund vor ihm auf.

chassis ['ʃæsɪ] *n* Chassis *nt*; *(Aut also)* Fahrgestell *nt.*

chaste [tʃeɪst] *adj (+er) (pure, virtuous)* keusch; *(simple, unadvanced) style, elegance* schlicht.

chastely ['tʃeɪstlɪ] *adv see adj.*

chasten ['tʃeɪsn] *vt* nachdenklich stimmen, zur Einsicht bringen; *pride, stubborn nature* zügeln ◆ **~ed by ...** durch ... zur Einsicht gelangt.

chasteness ['tʃeɪstnɪs] *n see adj* Keuschheit *f*; Schlichtheit *f.*

chastening ['tʃeɪsnɪŋ] *adj thought, experience* ernüchternd.

chastise [tʃæs'taɪz] *vt* züchtigen *(geh)*; *(scold)* schelten.

chastisement ['tʃæstɪzmənt] *n see vt* Züchtigung *f (geh)*; Schelte *f.*

chastity ['tʃæstɪtɪ] *n (sexual purity)* Keuschheit *f*; *(virginity also)* Unberührtheit, Reinheit *f* ◆ **~ belt** Keuschheitsgürtel *m.*

chasuble ['tʃæzjʊbl] *n* Meßgewand *nt*, Kasel *f.*

chat [tʃæt] [1] *n* Unterhaltung *f*; *(about unimportant things also)* Plauderei *f*, Schwatz *m (inf)* ◆ **could we have a ~ about it?** können wir uns mal darüber unterhalten?; **she dropped in for a ~** sie kam zu einem Schwätzchen rein *(inf)*.

[2] *vi* plaudern; *(2 people also)* sich unterhalten.

◆**chat up** *vt sep (inf) person* einreden auf *(+acc)*; *prospective girl-/boyfriend* sich heranmachen an *(+acc)*, anquatschen *(inf)*.

chat-up line ['tʃætʌpˌlaɪn] *n* Anmacherspruch *m.*

chatelaine ['ʃætəleɪn] *n* **(a)** *(of castle) (housekeeper)* Schloßverwalterin *f*; *(owner)* Schloßherrin *f.* **(b)** *(old) Gürtel, an dem ein Schlüsselbund getragen wird.*

chat show *n (Brit)* Talkshow *f.*

chattels ['tʃætlz] *npl (Jur)* bewegliches Vermögen, bewegliche Habe ◆ **all his (goods and) ~** seine gesamte Habe.

chatter ['tʃætə^r] [1] *n (of person)* Geschwätz, Geplapper *nt*; *(of birds)* Schwatzen *nt*; *(of monkeys)* Geschnatter *nt*; *(of teeth)* Klappern *nt*; *(of guns)* Knattern, Geknatter *nt.*

[2] *vi see n* schwatzen, schwätzen *(esp S Ger)*, plappern; schnattern; knattern.

chatterbox ['tʃætəbɒks] *n* Quasselstrippe *f (inf)*.

chattering ['tʃætərɪŋ] [1] *n* Geschwätz *nt.*

[2] *adj attr* **the ~ classes** *(Brit pej inf)* das Bildungsbürgertum.

chatty ['tʃætɪ] *adj (+er) person* geschwätzig, schwatzhaft ◆ **written in a ~ style** im Plauderton geschrieben.

chauffeur ['ʃəʊfə^r] *n* Chauffeur, Fahrer *m* ◆ **~-driven** mit Fahrer *or* Chauffeur; **to be ~-driven** einen Fahrer haben.

chauffeuse [ʃəʊ'fɜːz] *n* Chauffeuse, Fahrerin *f.*

chauvinism ['ʃəʊvɪnɪzəm] *n* Chauvinismus *m.*

chauvinist ['ʃəʊvɪnɪst] [1] *n (jingoist)* Chauvinist(in *f*) *m*; *(male ~)* männlicher Chauvinist.

[2] *adj* chauvinistisch ◆ **(male) ~ pig** Chauvinistenschwein *nt (sl)*.

chauvinistic [ˌʃəʊvɪ'nɪstɪk] *adj* chauvinistisch.

cheap [tʃiːp] [1] *adj (+er)* **(a)** *also adv (inexpensive)* billig ◆ **to hold sth ~** etw geringachten; **it's ~ at the price** es ist spottbillig; **I got it ~** ich habe es billig gekriegt.

(b) *(poor quality)* billig, minderwertig ◆ **everything they sell is ~ and nasty** sie verkaufen nur Ramsch.

(c) *(fig) (mean, shallow, sexually ~) joke, flattery, thrill, girl* billig; *person, behaviour, appearance* ordinär ◆ **to feel ~** sich *(dat)* schäbig vorkommen; **how can you be so ~!** wie kannst du nur so gemein sein!; **to make oneself ~** sich entwürdigen; *(by loose living)* sich wegwerfen; **that was a ~ shot** *(US)* das ging unter die Gürtellinie *(inf)*.

[2] *n* **on the ~** auf die billige Tour *(inf)*; **to buy sth on the ~** *(inf)* etw für einen Pappenstiel *(inf) or* einen Apfel und ein Ei *(inf)* kaufen; **to make sth on the ~** *(inf)* etw ganz billig produzieren.

cheapen ['tʃiːpən] [1] *vt (lit)* verbilligen, herabsetzen; *(fig)* herabsetzen, schlechtmachen ◆ **to ~ oneself** sich entwürdigen.

[2] *vi* billiger werden, sich verbilligen.

cheapie ['tʃiːpɪ] *n, adj (inf) see* **cheapo.**

cheapjack ['tʃiːpdʒæk] *adj* Ramsch- *(pej)*.

cheaply ['tʃiːplɪ] *adv see adj.*

cheapness ['tʃiːpnɪs] *n see adj* **(a)** billiger Preis. **(b)** Billigkeit, Minderwertigkeit *f.* **(c)** Billigkeit *f*; ordinäre Art.

cheapo ['tʃiːpəʊ] *(inf)* [1] *n* Billigartikel *m*, billiges Ding *(inf)*.

[2] *adj* Billig-.

cheap shot *n* unfaire Bemerkung ◆ **that was a ~** das war unfair.

cheapskate ['tʃiːpskeɪt] *n (inf)* Knicker *(inf)*, Knauser *(inf) m.*

cheat [tʃiːt] [1] *vt* betrügen; *authorities also* täuschen ◆ **to ~ sb out of sth** jdn um etw betrügen.

[2] *vi* betrügen; *(in exam, game etc)* mogeln *(inf)*, schummeln *(Sch sl)*; *(in card games also)* falschspielen, mogeln *(inf)*.

[3] *n* **(a)** *(person)* Betrüger(in *f*) *m*; *(in exam, game etc)* Mogler(in *f*) *(inf)*, Schummler(in *f*) *(Sch sl) m*; *(in card games also)* Falschspieler(in *f*), Mogler(in *f*) *(inf) m.*

(b) *(dishonest trick)* Betrug *m*, Täuschung *f.*

◆**cheat on** *vi +prep obj* betrügen.

cheating ['tʃiːtɪŋ] [1] *n see* **cheat 2** Betrügen *nt*, Betrug *m*; Mogeln *(inf)*, Schummeln *(Sch sl) nt*; Falschspielen, Mogeln *(inf) nt.*

[2] *adj* betrügerisch.

Chechen ['tʃetʃən] [1] *n, pl* **Chechens** *or* **Chechen** Tschetschene *m*, Tschetschenin *f.*

[2] *adj* tschetschenisch ◆ **the ~ Republic** die Tschetschenische Republik.

Chechnya ['tʃetʃnjɑː] *n* Tschetschenien *nt.*

check [tʃek] [1] *n* **(a)** *(examination)* Überprüfung, Kontrolle *f* ◆ **to give sth a ~** etw überprüfen *or* nachsehen; **to make a ~ on sb/sth** jdn/etw überprüfen, bei jdm/etw eine Kontrolle durchführen; **a random ~** eine Stichprobe; **to keep a ~ on sb/sth** jdn/etw überwachen *or* kontrollieren.

(b) *(restraint)* Hemmnis *nt*, Erschwernis *f*; *(Mil: to army)* Hindernis *nt*, Sperre *f* ◆ **an efficient ~ on population growth** ein wirksames Mittel zur Eindämmung des Bevölkerungswachstums; **to hold** *or* **keep sb in ~** jdn in Schach halten; **to hold** *or* **keep one's temper in ~** sich beherrschen; **(a system of) ~s and balances** ein Sicherungssystem *nt*; **to act as a ~ (up)on sth** etw unter Kontrolle *(dat)* halten.

(c) *(pattern)* Karo(muster) *nt*; *(square)* Karo *nt.*

(d) *(Chess)* Schach *nt* ◆ **to be in ~** im Schach stehen; **to put sb in ~** jdm Schach bieten.

(e) *(US) (cheque)* Scheck *m*; *(bill)* Rechnung *f* ◆ **~ please** bitte (be)zahlen.

(f) *(US) (room) (Rail)* Gepäckaufbewahrung *f*; *(Theat)* Garderobe *f*; *(ticket)* (Gepäck)schein *m*; (Garderoben)marke *f.*

(g) *(US: tick)* Haken *m.*

[2] *vt* **(a)** *(examine)* überprüfen, checken *(inf)*; *(in book also)* nachschlagen; *tickets also* kontrollieren.

(b) *(act as control on)* kontrollieren; *(stop) enemy, advance* aufhalten; *anger* unterdrücken, beherrschen ◆ **I was going to say it, but I just managed to ~ myself in time** ich wollte es sagen, aber ich konnte mich gerade noch beherrschen.

(c) *(Chess)* Schach bieten *(+dat)*.

(d) *(US) coat etc* abgeben; *(Rail) luggage (register)* aufgeben; *(deposit)* abgeben, zur Aufbewahrung geben.

(e) *(US: tick)* abhaken.

[3] *vi* **(a)** *(make sure)* nachfragen *(with* bei); *(have a look)* nachsehen, nachgucken ◆ **I was just ~ing** ich wollte nur nachprüfen. **(b)** *(stop, pause)* stocken; *(horse)* scheuen.

◆**check back** *vi (look back in records)* zurückgehen *(in* zu), nachsehen *(in* in *+dat)*; *(re-contact)* rückfragen *(with* bei).

◆**check in** [1] *vi (at airport)* sich bei der Abfertigung melden, einchecken; *(at hotel)* sich anmelden ◆ **what time do you have to ~ ~?** wann mußt du am Flughafen sein?

[2] *vt sep (at airport) luggage* abfertigen lassen; *(at hotel) person* anmelden ◆ **he isn't ~ed ~ at this hotel** er wohnt nicht in diesem Hotel; **they ~ed me ~ at a first-class hotel** ich wurde in einem erstklassigen Hotel untergebracht.

◆**check off** *vt sep (esp US)* abhaken.

◆**check on** *vi +prep obj see* **check up on.**

◆**check out** [1] *vi* sich abmelden; *(leave hotel)* abreisen; *(sign out)* sich austragen; *(clock out)* stempeln, stechen.

[2] *vt sep* **(a)** *figures, facts, persons* überprüfen ◆ **~ it ~ with the boss** klären Sie das mit dem Chef ab; **~ ~ our new range** *(inf)* sehen Sie sich *(dat)* unser neues Sortiment an. **(b)** *(hotel, airline etc)* abfertigen.

◆**check over** *vt sep* überprüfen.

◆**check through** *vt sep* **(a)** *account, proofs* durchsehen, durchgehen. **(b) they ~ed my bags ~ to Berlin** mein Gepäck wurde nach Berlin durchgecheckt.

◆**check up** *vi* überprüfen.

◆**check up on** *vi +prep obj* überprüfen; *person also* Nachforschungen anstellen über *(+acc)*; *(keep a check on) sb* kontrollieren.

checkbook ['tʃekbʊk] *n (US)* Scheckbuch *nt.*

checked [tʃekt] *adj* kariert ◆ **~ pattern** Karomuster *nt.*

checker ['tʃekə^r] *n* **(a)** *(of documents etc)* Prüfer(in *f*) *m.* **(b)** *(US: in supermarket)* Kassierer(in *f*) *m.* **(c)** *(US: for coats etc)* Garderobenfrau *f*/-mann *m.*

checkerboard ['tʃekəbɔ:d] *n (US)* Damebrett *nt*; *(chessboard)* Schachbrett *nt*.
checkered *adj (US) see* **chequered**.
checkers ['tʃekəz] *n (US)* Damespiel *nt* ♦ **to play ~** Dame spielen.
check-in (desk) ['tʃekın('desk)] *n* Abfertigung *f*, Abfertigungsschalter *m*; *(Aviat)* Abflugschalter *m*; *(US: in hotel)* Rezeption, Anmeldung *f*.
checking ['tʃekıŋ] *n* Überprüfung, Kontrolle *f* ♦ **it needs more ~** es muß gründlicher überprüft werden; **~ account** *(US)* Girokonto *nt*.
check: ~ list *n* Prüf- *or* Checkliste *f*; **~mate** 1 *n* Schachmatt *nt*; **~mate!** *(Chess)* matt!; *(fig)* aus!; **he found himself in ~mate** *(lit, fig)* er war matt gesetzt; 2 *vt* matt setzen; **~-out** *n (in supermarket)* Kasse *f*; **~point** *n* Kontrollpunkt *m*; **C~point Charlie** *n* Checkpoint Charlie *m*, Ausländerübergang *m* Friedrichstraße; **~room** *n (US) (Theat)* Garderobe *f*; *(Rail)* Gepäckaufbewahrung *f*; **~-up** *n (Med)* Untersuchung *f*, Check-up *m*; **to have a ~-up/to go for a ~-up** einen Check-up machen lassen.
cheddar ['tʃedəʳ] *n* Cheddar(käse) *m*.
cheek [tʃi:k] 1 *n* **(a)** Backe, Wange *(liter) f* ♦ **to be ~ by jowl (with sb)** Tuchfühlung mit jdm haben, auf Tuchfühlung (mit jdm) sein; **to dance ~ to ~** Wange an Wange tanzen; **~ bone** Wangenknochen *m*, Jochbein *nt (spec)*; **~ pouch** Futtertasche *f*; **to turn the other ~** die andere Wange hinhalten.
(b) *(buttock)* Backe *f*.
(c) *(impudence)* Frechheit, Unverschämtheit, Dreistigkeit *f* ♦ **to have the ~ to do sth** die Frechheit *or* Stirn haben, etw zu tun, sich erfrechen, etw zu tun; **they gave him a lot of ~** sie waren sehr frech zu ihm; **enough of your ~!** jetzt reicht's aber!; **of all the ~!, the ~ of it!** so eine Frechheit *or* Unverschämtheit!
2 *vt* **to ~ sb** frech sein zu jdm *or* gegen jdn.
-cheeked ['tʃi:kd] *adj suf* -backig ♦ **rosy-~** rotbackig.
cheekily ['tʃi:kılı] *adv* frech, vorwitzig, dreist.
cheekiness ['tʃi:kınıs] *n* Frechheit, Dreistigkeit *f*, Vorwitz *m (geh)*; *(of person also)* freche Art.
cheeky ['tʃi:kı] *adj (+er)* frech, vorwitzig, dreist; *remark, person, smile also* schnippisch; *hat, dress* keß, flott; *driving* schneidig, schnittig, frech ♦ **it's a bit ~ asking for another pay rise so soon** es ist etwas unverschämt, schon wieder eine Gehaltserhöhung zu verlangen; **~ girl** freche Göre.
cheep [tʃi:p] 1 *n* Piep, Piepser *m*.
2 *vi* piepsen.
cheer [tʃıəʳ] 1 *n* **(a)** Hurra- *or* Beifallsruf *m*; *(cheering)* Hurrageschrei *nt*, Jubel *m* ♦ **to give three ~s for sb** jdn dreimal hochleben lassen, ein dreifaches Hoch auf jdn ausbringen; **three ~s for Mike!** ein dreifaches Hurra für Mike!; **~s!** *(Brit inf) (your health)* prost!; *(goodbye)* tschüs! *(inf)*; *(thank you)* danke schön!; **~leader** Anführer *m*.
(b) *(comfort)* Aufmunterung, Ermutigung *f* ♦ **the news gave us some ~** die Nachricht munterte uns auf; **words of ~** aufmunternde Worte, Zuspruch *m*.
(c) *(old)* **be of good ~** seid guten Mutes *or* wohlgemut *(old)*.
(d) *(old: food etc)* **good ~** Tafelfreude(n *pl*) *f (old)*.
2 *vt* **(a)** *person* zujubeln *(+dat)*; *thing, event* bejubeln.
(b) *(gladden)* aufmuntern, aufheitern, froh machen.
3 *vi* jubeln, hurra rufen.
♦**cheer on** *vt sep* anspornen, anfeuern.
♦**cheer up** 1 *vt sep* aufmuntern, aufheitern; *room, place* aufheitern ♦ **he needed a bit of ~ing ~** er brauchte etwas Aufmunterung *or* Aufheiterung; **tell him that, that'll ~ him ~** sag ihm das, dann freut er sich.
2 *vi (person)* vergnügter *or* fröhlicher werden, bessere Laune bekommen; *(things)* besser werden ♦ **~ ~!** laß den Kopf nicht hängen!, nun lach doch mal!; **~ ~, it's not that bad** Kopf hoch *or* nur Mut, so schlimm ist es auch wieder nicht.
cheerful ['tʃıəfʊl] *adj* fröhlich, vergnügt; *person also* gutgelaunt *attr*, heiter *(geh)*; *place, colour etc* heiter; *prospect, news* erfreulich; *(iro)* heiter; *tune* fröhlich; *fire* lustig ♦ **you're a ~ one, aren't you?** *(iro)* du bist (mir) vielleicht ein schöner Miesmacher *(inf)*; **that's ~!** *(iro)* das ist ja heiter!
cheerfully ['tʃıəfʊlı] *adv* fröhlich, vergnügt; *decorated* lustig, heiter ♦ **the fire was burning ~** das Feuer brannte lustig.
cheerfulness ['tʃıəfʊlnıs] *n see adj* Fröhlichkeit *f*; gute Laune, Vergnügtheit *f*, Frohsinn *m (geh)*; Heiterkeit *f*; Erfreulichkeit *f*; fröhlicher Charakter ♦ **I love the ~ of a log fire** ich mag es gern, wenn das offene Feuer so lustig brennt.
cheerily ['tʃıərılı] *adv* fröhlich, vergnügt.
cheering ['tʃıərıŋ] 1 *n* Jubel *m*, Jubeln, Hurrageschrei *nt*; *(~ on)* anfeuernde Zurufe *pl*.
2 *adj* **(a)** *news, prospect* beglückend. **(b)** *crowds* jubelnd.
cheerio ['tʃıərı'əʊ] *interj (esp Brit inf)* **(a)** *(goodbye)* Wiedersehen *(inf)*, Servus *(S Ger, Aus)*; *(to friends)* tschüs *(inf)*. **(b)** *(your health)* prost.
cheerless ['tʃıəlıs] *adj* freudlos, trüb; *person* trübselig, trübsinnig; *prospect* trübe, düster, traurig; *scenery* grau.
cheers [tʃıərz] *interj see* **cheer 1 (a)**.
cheery ['tʃıərı] *adj (+er)* fröhlich; *tune, colour also* lustig.
cheese [tʃi:z] *n* Käse *m* ♦ **hard ~!** *(dated inf)* Künstlerpech! *(inf)*; **say ~!** *(Phot)* bitte recht freundlich, sag „cheese".
cheese *in cpds* Käse-; **~board** *n* Käsebrett *nt*; *(course)* Käseplatte *f*; **~burger** *n* Cheeseburger *m*; **~cake** *n (Cook)* Käsekuchen *m*; *(sl)* (nacktes) Fleisch *(inf)*; **~cloth** *n* Käseleinen *nt*, indische Baumwolle *f*.
cheesed-off [tʃi:zd'ɒf] *adj (Brit sl)* angeödet *(sl)* ♦ **I'm ~ with this job/her** diese Arbeit/sie ödet mich an *(sl) or* stinkt mir *(sl)*.
cheese: ~paring 1 *n* Pfennigfuchserei *(inf)*, Knauserei *f*; 2 *adj* knauserig, knickerig *(inf)*; **~ straw** *n* kleine Käsestange.
cheesy ['tʃi:zı] *adj (+er)* **(a)** käsig ♦ **to taste ~** nach Käse schmecken; **a ~ taste** ein Käsegeschmack; **a ~ smile** ein Pepsodentlächeln *nt (inf)*. **(b)** *(US sl: shoddy)* mies *(inf)*.
cheetah ['tʃi:tə] *n* Gepard *m*.
chef [ʃef] *n* Küchenchef *m*; *(as profession)* Koch *m*; *(head ~)* Chefkoch *m*.
chemical ['kemıkəl] 1 *adj* chemisch ♦ **~ accident** Chemieunfall *m*; **~ engineering** Chemotechnik *f*; **~ warfare** chemische Krieg(s)führung.
2 *n* Chemikalie *f*.
chemically ['kemıkəlı] *adv* chemisch.
chemise [ʃə'mi:z] *n* Unterkleid *nt*.
chemist ['kemıst] *n* **(a)** *(expert in chemistry)* Chemiker(in *f*) *m*. **(b)** *(Brit: in shop)* Drogist(in *f*) *m*; *(dispensing)* Apotheker(in *f*) *m* ♦ **~'s shop** Drogerie *f*, Apotheke *f*.
chemistry ['kemıstrı] *n* **(a)** Chemie *f*; *(chemical make-up)* chemische Zusammensetzung *(fig)* ♦ **~ set** Chemiebaukasten *m*.
(b) *(fig)* Verträglichkeit *f* ♦ **the good/bad ~ between them** ihre gute Verträglichkeit/ihre Unverträglichkeit; **the ~ between us was perfect** wir haben uns sofort vertragen, es hat sofort zwischen uns gefunkt *(inf)*; **the ~'s all wrong (between us)** wir sind einfach zu verschieden; **the ~ of physical attraction/of love** das Kräftespiel der körperlichen Anziehung/in der Liebe.
chemotherapy [,keməʊ'θerəpı] *n* Chemotherapie *f*.
chenille [ʃə'ni:l] *n* Chenille *f*.
▼ **cheque,** *(US)* **check** [tʃek] *n* Scheck *m* ♦ **a ~ for £100** ein Scheck über £ 100; **to pay by ~** mit (einem) Scheck bezahlen; **~book** Scheckheft, Scheckbuch *nt*; **~book journalism** Scheckbuch-Journalismus *m*; **~ card** Scheckkarte *f*.
chequered, *(US)* **checkered** ['tʃekəd] *adj (lit)* kariert; *(dappled)* gefleckt, gesprenkelt; *(fig) career, history* bewegt.
cherish ['tʃerıʃ] *vt* **(a)** *person* liebevoll sorgen für ♦ **to love and to ~** zu lieben und zu ehren. **(b)** *feelings, hope* hegen; *idea, illusion* sich hingeben *(+dat)* ♦ **I shall always ~ that memory/present** die Erinnerung (daran)/das Geschenk wird mir immer lieb und teuer sein; **to ~ sb's memory** jds Andenken in Ehren halten.
Cherokee (Indian) ['tʃerəʊki:('ındıən)] *n* Tscherokese *m*, Tscherokesin *f*.
cheroot [ʃə'ru:t] *n* Stumpen *m*.
cherry ['tʃerı] 1 *n* Kirsche *f*; *(colour)* Kirschrot *nt* ♦ **wild ~** Vogelkirsche *f*.
2 *adj (colour)* kirschrot; *(Cook)* Kirsch-.
cherry *in cpds* Kirsch-; **~ brandy** *n* Cherry Brandy *m*; **~ orchard** *n* Kirschgarten *m*; **~ red** *adj* kirschrot.
cherub ['tʃerəb] *n* **(a)** *pl* **-im** ['tʃerəbım] *(Eccl)* Cherub *m*. **(b)** *pl* **-s** *(Art)* Putte *f*, Putto *m (form)*; *(baby)* Engelchen *nt*.
chervil ['tʃɜ:vıl] *n* Kerbel *m*.
chess [tʃes] *n* Schach(spiel) *nt* ♦ **~ board** Schachbrett *nt*; **~man, ~ piece** Schachfigur *f*.
chest[1] [tʃest] *n (for tea, tools etc)* Kiste *f*; *(piece of furniture, for clothes, money etc)* Truhe *f* ♦ **~ of drawers** Kommode *f*.
chest[2] *n (Anat)* Brust *f*, Brustkorb *m (esp Med)* ♦ **the boxer's broad ~** der breite Brustkasten des Boxers; **to measure sb's ~** jds Brustweite *or* Brustumfang messen; **to get sth off one's ~** *(fig inf)* sich *(dat)* etw von der Seele reden, etw loswerden; **to have a weak ~** schwach auf der Brust sein *(inf)*; **a cold on the ~** Bronchialkatarrh *m*; **~ infection** Lungeninfekt *m*; **~ pains** Schmerzen *pl* in der Brust; **~ specialist** Facharzt *m*/-ärztin *f* für Lungenkrankheiten, Lungenfacharzt *m*/-ärztin *f*.
-chested ['tʃestıd] *adj suf* -brüstig.
chesterfield ['tʃestəfi:ld] *n* Chesterfieldsofa *nt*.
chestnut ['tʃesnʌt] 1 *n* **(a)** *(nut, tree)* Kastanie *f*. **(b)** *(colour)* Kastanienbraun *nt*. **(c)** *(horse)* Fuchs *m*. **(d)** *(inf: old joke)* alte *or* olle Kamelle *(inf)*.
2 *adj (colour) hair* kastanienbraun, rötlichbraun ♦ **a ~ horse** ein Fuchs *m*.
chesty ['tʃestı] *adj (+er) (inf) person* erkältet, grippig *(inf)*; *cough* rauh, schnarrend ♦ **I'm a bit ~ this morning** ich hab's heute etwas auf der Brust *(inf)*.
cheval glass [ʃə'vælglɑ:s] *n* Standspiegel *m* (zum Kippen).
chevron ['ʃevrən] *n* Winkel *m*.
chew [tʃu:] 1 *n* Kauen *nt* ♦ **to have a good ~ on sth** auf *or* an etw *(dat)* gründlich herumkauen.
2 *vt* kauen ♦ **this meat takes a lot of ~ing** an *or* bei diesem Fleisch muß man viel (herum)kauen; **that dog's been ~ing the carpet again** der Hund hat schon wieder am Teppich gekaut; **don't ~ your fingernails** kaue nicht an deinen Nägeln; **she always ~s her nails** sie kaut Nägel; *see* **cud**.
♦**chew away** 1 *vi* lange herumkauen an *or* auf *(+dat)* ♦ **the rats have been ~ing ~ at the woodwork** die Ratten haben am Holz herumgenagt.
2 *vt sep* wegfressen.
♦**chew off** *or* **out** *vt sep (US inf)* zur Schnecke machen *(inf)*.
♦**chew on** *vi +prep obj* **(a)** *(lit)* (herum)kauen auf *(+dat)*. **(b)** *(also* **chew over***)* *(inf) facts, problem* sich *(dat)* durch den Kopf gehen lassen.
♦**chew up** *vt sep* **(a)** *(lit)* aufessen, fertigessen; *(animal)* auffressen; *pencil etc* zerkauen; *ground, road surface* zerstören; *paper* zerfressen, zermalmen. **(b)** *(sl: tell off)* fertigmachen *(inf)*, runterputzen *(inf)*.
chewing gum ['tʃu:ıŋgʌm] *n* Kaugummi *m or nt*.
chewy ['tʃu:ı] *adj meat* zäh; *pasta* kernig; *sweets* weich.
chiaroscuro [kı,ɑ:rəs'kʊərəʊ] *n* Chiaroscuro, Helldunkel *nt*.
chic [ʃi:k] 1 *adj (+er)* schick, elegant.
2 *n* Chic, Schick *m*.

➤ LANGUAGE IN USE: **cheque** → 20.7

chicane [ʃɪ'keɪn] *n* (*Sport*) Schikane *f*.
chicanery [ʃɪ'keɪnərɪ] *n* (*trickery*) Machenschaften *pl*; (*legal*) Winkelzüge *pl*.
chichi ['tʃiːtʃiː] *adj* (*inf*) todschick (*iro inf*), auf schön gemacht (*inf*); *dress etc* verspielt, niedlich.
chick [tʃɪk] *n* **(a)** (*of chicken*) Küken *nt*; (*young bird*) Junge(s) *nt*. **(b)** (*inf: child*) Kleine(s) *nt*. **(c)** (*sl: girl*) Mieze *f* (*sl*) ◆ **she's some ~** sie ist nicht ohne (*inf*).
chicken ['tʃɪkɪn] 1 *n* **(a)** Huhn *nt*; (*for roasting, frying*) Hähnchen *nt* ◆ **she's no ~** (*inf*) sie ist nicht mehr die Jüngste; **~ liver** Hühner- *or* Geflügelleber *f*; **don't count your ~s before they're hatched** (*Prov*) man soll den Tag nicht vor dem Abend loben (*Prov*); **it's a ~ and egg situation** (*inf*) das ist eine Zwickmühle.
(b) (*inf: coward*) feiges Huhn (*inf*), Feigling *m*.
2 *adj* (*inf*) feig ◆ **he's ~** er ist ein Feigling *or* ein feiges Huhn (*inf*); **he's too ~ to do it** er ist zu feig(e).
◆**chicken out** *vi* (*inf*) kneifen (*inf*).
chicken *in cpds* Hühner-; **~-farmer** *n* Hühnerzüchter *m*; **~feed** *n* **(a)** (*lit*) Hühnerfutter *nt*; **(b)** (*inf: insignificant sum*) ein paar Pfennige; **they expect us to work for ~feed** sie erwarten, daß wir für'n Appel und'n Ei arbeiten (*inf*); **~-hearted** *adj* feige, hasenherzig (*old, liter*); **~pox** *n* Windpocken *pl*; **~-run** *n* Hühnerhof, Auslauf *m*; **~ wire** *n* Hühnerdraht *m*.
chick: ~pea *n* Kichererbse *f*; **~weed** *n* Sternmiere *f*.
chicle ['tʃɪkl] *n* Chiclegummi *m*.
chicory ['tʃɪkərɪ] *n* Chicorée *f or m*; (*in coffee*) Zichorie *f*.
chide [tʃaɪd] *pret* **chid** [tʃɪd] (*old*) *or* **~d** ['tʃaɪdɪd], *ptp* **chidden** ['tʃɪdn] (*old*) *or* **~d** *vt* schelten, rügen.
chief [tʃiːf] 1 *n, pl* **-s** **(a)** (*of organization*) Leiter, Chef (*inf*) *m*; (*of clan*) Oberhaupt *nt*; (*of tribe*) Häuptling *m*; (*of gang*) Anführer *m*; (*inf: boss*) Boss (*inf*), Chef *m* ◆ **~ of police** Polizeipräsident *or* -chef *m*; **~ of staff** (*Mil*) Stabschef *m*; **~ of state** Staatschef *m*. **(b)** (*Her*) Schildhaupt *nt*. **(c) in ~** hauptsächlich.
2 *adj* **(a)** (*most important*) Haupt-, wichtigste(r, s), bedeutendste(r, s) ◆ **the ~ thing** das Wichtigste, die Hauptsache; **~ reason** Hauptgrund *m*.
(b) (*most senior*) Haupt-, Ober-, erste(r) ◆ **~ clerk** Bürochef *m*; **~ constable** (*Brit*) Polizeipräsident *or* -chef *m*; **~ executive officer** Generaldirektor *m*; **~ justice** (*Brit*) ≈ Oberrichter *m*; (*US*) Oberster Bundesrichter.
chiefly ['tʃiːflɪ] *adv* hauptsächlich, in erster Linie, vor allem.
chieftain ['tʃiːftən] *n* (*of tribe*) Häuptling *m*; (*of clan*) Oberhaupt *nt*, Älteste(r) *m*; (*of robber band*) Hauptmann *m* ◆ **the village ~** der Dorfälteste.
chiffon ['ʃɪfɒn] 1 *n* Chiffon *m*.
2 *adj* Chiffon-.
chignon ['ʃiːnjɔ̃ːŋ] *n* Nackenknoten, Chignon *m*.
chihuahua [tʃɪ'waʊwɑː] *n* Chihuahua *m*.
chilblain ['tʃɪlbleɪn] *n* Frostbeule *f*.
child [tʃaɪld] *n, pl* **children** (*lit, fig*) Kind *nt* ◆ **when I was a ~** in *or* zu meiner Kindheit; **she was with ~** (*old, liter*) sie trug ein Kind unter ihrem Herzen (*old, liter*); **the ~ of his imagination** das Produkt seiner Phantasie.
child *in cpds* Kinder-; **~ abuse** *n* Kindesmißhandlung *f*; (*sexually*) Notzucht *f* mit Kindern; **~ abuser** *n jd, der Kinder mißhandelt*; (*sexually*) Kinderschänder *m*; **~-bearing** 1 *n* Mutterschaft *f*, Kinderkriegen *nt* (*inf*); **ten years of ~-bearing exhausted her** zehn Jahre mit kleinen Kindern erschöpften sie; 2 *adj* **of ~-bearing age** im gebärfähigen Alter; **good ~-bearing hips** gebärfreudiges Becken; **~ benefit** *n* (*Brit*) Kindergeld *nt*; **~birth** *n* Geburt *f*, Gebären *nt*; **to die in ~birth** bei der Geburt sterben; **~ care** *n* Kinderpflege *f*; (*social work dept*) Jugendfürsorge *f*; **~-friendly** *adj* kinderfreundlich; **~ guidance** *n* Erziehungsberatung *f*; (*social work agency*) Erziehungsberatungsstelle *f*; **~hood** *n* Kindheit *f*; **to be in one's second ~hood** seine zweite Kindheit erleben.
childish *adj*, **~ly** *adv* ['tʃaɪldɪʃ, -lɪ] (*pej*) kindisch.
childishness ['tʃaɪldɪʃnɪs] *n* (*pej*) kindisches Gehabe.
child: ~ labour *n* Kinderarbeit *f*; **~less** *adj* kinderlos; **~like** *adj* kindlich; **~ lock** *n* Kindersicherung *f*; **~minder** *n* Tagesmutter *f*; **~minding** *n* Beaufsichtigung *f* von Kindern; **~ prodigy** *n* Wunderkind *nt*; **~proof** *adj* kindersicher.
children ['tʃɪldrən] *pl of* **child**.
child: ~-resistant *adj* bruchsicher; **~'s play** *n* ein Kinderspiel *nt*; **~('s) seat** *n* Kindersitz *m*; **~ welfare** *n* Jugendfürsorge *f*; **C~ Welfare Centre** Kinderabteilung *f* im Gesundheitsamt.
Chile ['tʃɪlɪ] *n* Chile *nt*.
Chilean ['tʃɪlɪən] 1 *adj* chilenisch.
2 *n* Chilene *m*, Chilenin *f*.
chill [tʃɪl] 1 *n* **(a)** Frische *f* ◆ **there's quite a ~ in the air** es ist ziemlich frisch; **the sun took the ~ off the water** die Sonne hat das Wasser ein bißchen erwärmt; **you should take the ~ off the wine** Sie sollten den Wein nicht so eiskalt servieren.
(b) (*Med*) fieberhafte Erkältung; (*shiver*) Schauder *m*, Frösteln *nt* ◆ **to catch a ~** sich verkühlen.
(c) (*fig*) **a distinct ~ in East/West relations** eine deutliche Abkühlung der Ost-West-Beziehungen; **his presence cast a ~ over the meeting** durch seine Anwesenheit wurde das Treffen sehr kühl *or* frostig.
2 *adj* (*lit*) kühl, frisch; (*fig liter*) *reception* kühl, frostig.
3 *vt* **(a)** (*lit*) *wine, meat* kühlen ◆ **I was ~ed to the bone** *or* **marrow** die Kälte ging mir bis auf die Knochen.
(b) (*fig*) *blood* gefrieren lassen; *enthusiasm etc* abkühlen.
chil(l)i ['tʃɪlɪ] *n* Peperoni *pl*; (*spice, meal*) Chili *m*.
chill(i)ness ['tʃɪl(ɪ)nɪs] *n* (*lit*) Kühle, Frische *f*; (*fig*) Kühle, Frostigkeit *f*.
chilling ['tʃɪlɪŋ] *adj look* frostig, eisig; *prospect, thought* äußerst unerquicklich, beunruhigend.
chilly ['tʃɪlɪ] *adj* (*+er*) *weather* kühl, frisch; *manner, look, smile etc* kühl, frostig ◆ **to feel ~** frösteln, frieren; **I feel ~** mich fröstelt's, mir ist kühl.
chime [tʃaɪm] 1 *n* Glockenspiel, Geläut *nt*; (*of door-bell*) Läuten *nt no pl*.
2 *vt* schlagen.
3 *vi* läuten.
◆**chime in** *vi* (*inf*) sich einschalten.
◆**chime in with** *vi +prep obj* (*plans*) in Einklang stehen mit.
chimera [kaɪ'mɪərə] *n* Chimäre *f*; (*fig*) Schimäre *f*.
chimerical [kaɪ'merɪkəl] *adj* schimärisch.
chimney ['tʃɪmnɪ] *n* Schornstein *m*; (*on factory also*) Schlot *m*; (*open fire-place*) Kamin *m*; (*of lamp*) Zylinder *m*; (*of stove*) Rauchfang *m*; (*Mountaineering*) Kamin *m*.
chimney: ~breast *n* Kaminvorsprung *m*; **~piece** *n* Kaminsims *m*; **~pot** *n* Schornsteinkopf *m*; **~stack** *n* Schornstein *m*; **~sweep** *n* Schornsteinfeger *m*.
chimp [tʃɪmp] (*inf*), **chimpanzee** [ˌtʃɪmpæn'ziː] *n* Schimpanse *m*.
chin [tʃɪn] 1 *n* Kinn *nt* ◆ **to have a weak/strong ~** wenig Kinn/ein ausgeprägtes Kinn haben; **to keep one's ~ up** die Ohren steifhalten (*inf*); **keep your ~ up!** Kopf hoch!, nur Mut!; **he took it on the ~** (*fig inf*) er hat's mit Fassung getragen.
2 *vt* (*Sport*) **to ~ the bar** einen Klimmzug machen.
China ['tʃaɪnə] *n* China *nt*.
china ['tʃaɪnə] 1 *n* Porzellan *nt*.
2 *adj* Porzellan-.
china: ~ cabinet *n* Porzellanvitrine *f*; **~ clay** *n* Kaolin *m*; **C~man** *n* Chinese *m*; (*US pej*) Schlitzauge *nt*; **C~ Sea** *n* **East/South C~ Sea** Ost-/Südchinesisches Meer; **C~town** *n* Chinesenviertel *nt*; **~ware** *n* Porzellanware(n *pl*) *f*.
chinchilla [tʃɪn'tʃɪlə] *n* Chinchilla *f*; (*fur*) Chinchilla(pelz) *m*.
Chinese [tʃaɪ'niːz] 1 *n* **(a)** (*person*) Chinese *m*, Chinesin *f*. **(b)** (*language, fig: gibberish*) Chinesisch *nt*. **(c)** (*inf*) (*restaurant*) Chinarestaurant *nt*; (*meal*) chinesisches Essen.
2 *adj* chinesisch ◆ **~ lantern** Lampion *m*; **~ leaves** Chinakohl *m*; **~ puzzle** *ein Gegenstand zum Zusammensetzen als Geduldsspiel*; **~ restaurant** Chinarestaurant *nt*; **~ white** Chinesischweiß *nt*.
chink[1] [tʃɪŋk] 1 *n* Riß *m*, Ritze *f*; (*in door*) Spalt *m* ◆ **a ~ of light** ein dünner Lichtstreifen *or* -strahl; **the ~ in sb's armour** (*fig*) jds schwacher Punkt.
2 *vt* (*US*) stopfen.
chink[2] 1 *n* (*sound*) Klirren *nt*; (*of coins*) Klimpern *nt*.
2 *vt* klirren mit; *coins* klimpern mit.
3 *vi* klirren; (*coins*) klimpern.
Chink [tʃɪŋk] *n* (*pej*) Schlitzauge *nt*, Chinese *m*, Chinesin *f*.
chinkie ['tʃɪŋkɪ] (*inf*) 1 *n* (*restaurant*) Chinarestaurant *nt*; (*meal*) chinesisches Essen.
2 *adj restaurant, meal*, (*esp pej*) *friends etc* chinesisch.
chin: ~less *adj* **to be ~less** (*lit*) ein fliehendes Kinn haben; (*fig*) willensschwach sein; **~less wonder** *n* (*hum*) leicht vertrottelter Vertreter der Oberschicht; **~ rest** *n* Kinnstütze *f*; **~ strap** *n* Kinnriemen *m*.
chintz [tʃɪnts] 1 *n* Chintz *m*.
2 *attr curtains* Chintz-.
chintzy ['tʃɪntsɪ] *adj* (*+er*) schmuck; (*pej*) kitschig.
chin-up ['tʃɪnʌp] *n* Klimmzug *m*.
chinwag ['tʃɪnwæg] *n* (*Brit inf*) Schwatz *m* (*inf*).
chip [tʃɪp] 1 *n* **(a)** Splitter *m*; (*of glass also*) Scherbe *f*; (*of wood*) Span *m* ◆ **he's a ~ off the old block** er ist ganz der Vater; **to have a ~ on one's shoulder** einen Komplex haben (*about* wegen); **sb with a ~ on his shoulder** jd, der sich ständig angegriffen fühlt.
(b) (*potato ~*) Pomme frite *m or nt usu pl*; (*US: crisp*) Chip *m usu pl* ◆ **~ basket** Frittiersieb *nt*; **~-pan** Friteuse *f*.
(c) (*in crockery, furniture etc*) abgeschlagene *or* abgestoßene Ecke *or* Stelle ◆ **this cup has a ~** diese Tasse ist angeschlagen.
(d) (*in poker etc*) Chip *m*, Spielmarke *f* ◆ **to cash in one's ~s** (*euph*) den Löffel abgeben (*sl euph*); **he's had his ~s** (*inf*) d(er hat ausgespielt (*inf*); **to be in the ~s** (*US inf*) Kleingeld haben (*inf*), flüssig sein (*inf*); **when the ~s are down** wenn es drauf ankommt.
(e) to give the ball a ~ (*Golf, Tennis*) den Ball chippen.
(f) (*Comput: micro~*) Chip *nt*.
2 *vt* **(a)** *cup, stone* anschlagen; *varnish, paint* abstoßen; *wood* beschädigen; (*~ off*) wegschlagen, abstoßen ◆ **to be badly ~ped** stark angeschlagen sein.
(b) (*Brit Cook*) **~ped potatoes** Pommes frites *pl*. **(c)** (*Sport*) *ball* chippen.
3 *vi* (*cup etc*) angeschlagen werden, Macken/eine Macke bekommen (*inf*); (*paint*) abspringen; (*stone*) splittern ◆ **this pottery ~s easily** diese Keramik ist schnell angeschlagen.
◆**chip away** 1 *vt sep* weghauen ◆ **the woodpecker ~ped ~ the bark** der Specht hackte die Rinde ab.
2 *vi* **the sculptor ~ped ~ until ...** der Bildhauer meißelte am Stein herum, bis ...
◆**chip in** *vi* (*inf*) **(a)** (*interrupt*) sich einschalten. **(b)** (*contribute*) **he ~ped ~ with £3** er steuerte £ 3 bei; **would you like to ~ ~?** würdest du gerne etwas beisteuern?
◆**chip off** 1 *vt sep paint etc* wegschlagen; *piece of china* abstoßen, abschlagen.
2 *vi* (*paint etc*) absplittern.
chipboard ['tʃɪpbɔːd] *n* Spanholz *nt* ◆ **piece of ~** Spanplatte *f*.

chipmunk ['tʃɪpmʌŋk] *n* Backenhörnchen *nt*.
chipolata [tʃɪpə'lɑːtə] *n* (*Brit*) Cocktailwürstchen *nt*.
chippie ['tʃɪpɪ] *n see* **chippy (b)**.
chippings ['tʃɪpɪŋz] *npl* Splitter *pl*; (*of wood*) Späne *pl*; (*road* ~) Schotter *m*.
chippy ['tʃɪpɪ] *n* (*inf*) **(a)** (*joiner*) Schreiner *m*. **(b)** (*chip shop*) Frittenbude (*inf*), Pommesbude (*inf*) *f*.
chip shot *n* (*Golf*) Chip(shot) *m*; (*Tennis*) Chip *m*.
chiromancer ['kaɪərəmænsəʳ] *n* Chiromant(in *f*) *m*.
chiromancy ['kaɪərəmænsɪ] *n* Chiromantie *f*.
chiropodist [kɪ'rɒpədɪst] *n* Fußpfleger(in *f*) *m*.
chiropody [kɪ'rɒpədɪ] *n* Fußpflege *f*.
chiropractic [ˌkaɪərə'præktɪk] *n* Chiropraktik *f*.
chiropractor ['kaɪərəʊˌpræktəʳ] *n* Chiropraktiker(in *f*) *m*.
chirp [tʃɜːp] **1** *vi* (*birds*) zwitschern; (*crickets*) zirpen.
2 *n* (*of birds*) Piepser *m*; (~*ing*) Piepsen, Zwitschern *nt no pl*; (*of crickets*) Zirpen *nt no pl* ♦ **I don't want to hear another ~ from you** ich möchte keinen Muckser mehr von dir hören (*inf*).
chirpy ['tʃɜːpɪ] *adj* (+*er*) (*inf*) munter.
chirrup ['tʃɪrəp] *see* **chirp**.
chisel ['tʃɪzl] **1** *n* Meißel *m*; (*for wood*) Beitel *m*.
2 *vt* meißeln; (*in wood*) stemmen ♦ **her finely ~led features** ihr fein geschnittenes Gesicht.
chit¹ [tʃɪt] *n* junges Ding ♦ **she's a mere ~ of a girl** sie ist ja noch ein halbes Kind.
chit² *n* (*also* **~ of paper**) Zettel *m*.
chitchat ['tʃɪttʃæt] *n* (*inf*) Geschwätz, Gerede *nt*.
chivalric ['ʃɪvəlrɪk] *adj* ritterlich.
chivalrous *adj*, **~ly** *adv* ['ʃɪvəlrəs, -lɪ] ritterlich.
chivalry ['ʃɪvəlrɪ] *n* Ritterlichkeit *f*; (*medieval concept*) Rittertum *nt* ♦ **~ is not dead** es gibt noch Kavaliere.
chives [tʃaɪvz] *n* Schnittlauch *m*.
chivvy ['tʃɪvɪ] *vt* (*Brit inf*) (*also* **~ along** *or* **up**) antreiben ♦ **to ~ sb into doing sth** jdn dazu antreiben, etw zu tun.
chlorate ['klɔːreɪt] *n* Chlorat *nt*.
chloric ['klɔːrɪk] *adj* chlorig, chlorhaltig ♦ **~ acid** Chlorsäure *f*.
chloride ['klɔːraɪd] *n* Chlorid *nt* ♦ **~ of lime** Chlorkalk *m*.
chlorinate ['klɒrɪneɪt] *vt water* chloren.
chlorination [klɒrɪ'neɪʃən] *n* (*of water*) Chloren *nt*.
chlorine ['klɔːriːn] *n* Chlor *nt*.
chlorofluorocarbon [ˌklɒrəʊflʊərə'kɑːbən] *n* Chlorfluorkohlenwasserstoff *m*.
chloroform ['klɒrəfɔːm] **1** *n* Chloroform *nt*.
2 *vt* mit Chloroform betäuben, eine Chloroformnarkose geben (+*dat*).
chlorophyll ['klɒrəfɪl] *n* Chlorophyll *nt*.
choc-ice ['tʃɒkaɪs] *n* Eismohrle *nt* (*Eiscreme mit Schokoladenüberzug*).
chock [tʃɒk] **1** *n* Bremskeil, Bremsklotz *m*; (*Naut: under boat*) Bock *m*; (*Naut: for cables*) Lippe, Lippklampe *f* ♦ **~s away** Bremsklötze weg.
2 *vt wheel* blockieren; *boat* aufbocken.
chock-a-block ['tʃɒkəblɒk], **chock-full** ['tʃɒkfʊl] *adj* (*inf*) knüppelvoll (*inf*), gerammelt voll (*inf*).
chocolate ['tʃɒklɪt] **1** *n* **(a)** Schokolade *f* ♦ (**hot** *or* **drinking**) **~** Schokolade *f*, Kakao *m*; **a ~** eine Praline. **(b)** (*colour*) Schokoladenbraun *nt*.
2 *adj* Schokoladen-; (~-*coloured*) schokoladenbraun.
chocolate: ~ bar *n* (*slab*) Tafel *f* Schokolade; (*Mars* ® *bar etc*) Schokoladenriegel *m*; **~ biscuit** *n* Schokoladenkeks *m*; **~-box** *adj look, picture* Postkarten-; **~ cake** *n* Schokoladenkuchen *m*; **~-coloured** *adj* schokoladenbraun; **~-flavoured** *adj* mit Schokoladengeschmack; **~ fudge cake** *n* Schokoladencremetorte *f*; **~ pudding** *n* Schokoladenkuchen *m*; (*whip*) Schokoladenpudding *m*; **~ sauce** *n* Schokoladensoße *f*.
▼ **choice** [tʃɔɪs] **1** *n* **(a)** (*act of, possibility of choosing*) Wahl *f* ♦ **it's your ~** du hast die Wahl; **to make a ~** eine Wahl treffen; **to take one's ~** sich (*dat*) etwas aussuchen; **I didn't do it from ~** ich habe es mir nicht ausgesucht; **he had no ~ but to obey** er hatte keine (andere) Wahl *or* es blieb ihm nichts anderes übrig, als zu gehorchen; **for ~ I would ...** wenn ich die Wahl hätte, würde ich ...; **the prize is a holiday of your own ~** zu gewinnen ist eine Urlaubsreise an einen Ort Ihrer Wahl.
(b) (*person, thing chosen*) Wahl *f* ♦ **it was your ~** du wolltest es ja so.
(c) (*variety to choose from*) Auswahl *f* (*of* an +*dat*, von).
2 *adj* **(a)** (*Comm*) *goods, fruit, wine* Qualitäts-, erstklassig ♦ **~ fruit** Obst erster Wahl; **~st** allerfeinste(r, s), auserlesen.
(b) *language* (*elegant*) gewählt; (*euph: strong*) sauber (*euph*).
choir ['kwaɪəʳ] *n* **(a)** Chor *m*. **(b)** (*Archit*) Chor(raum) *m*.
choir *in cpds* Chor-; **~boy** *n* Chor- *or* Sängerknabe *m*; **~ loft** *n* Chorempore *f*; **~ master** *n* Chorleiter *m*; **~ practice** *n* Chorprobe *f*; **~ school** *n* Konvikt *nt* für Sängerknaben; **~ stall** *n* Chorstuhl *m*; **~ stalls** *npl* Chorgestühl *nt*.
choke [tʃəʊk] **1** *vt* **(a)** *person* ersticken; (*throttle*) (er)würgen, erdrosseln ♦ **don't eat so fast, you'll ~ yourself** iß nicht so schnell, sonst erstickst du daran; **to ~ the life out of sb/sth** (*lit, fig*) jdm/einer Sache den Garaus machen; **in a voice ~d with sobs** mit tränenerstickter Stimme.
(b) (*fig*) *pipe, tube, street* verstopfen; *fire, plants* ersticken.
2 *vi* ersticken (*on* an +*dat*) ♦ **he was choking with laughter/anger** er erstickte fast *or* halb vor Lachen/Wut.
3 *n* (*Aut*) Choke, Starterzug *m* ♦ **give it a bit of ~** zieh den Choke etwas heraus.
♦**choke back** *vt sep feelings, tears, reply* unterdrücken.
♦**choke down** *vt sep* hinunterschlucken.
♦**choke off** *vt sep* **(a)** *supplies* drosseln. **(b)** (*sl*) *person* (*interrupt*) das Wort abschneiden (+*dat*); (*put off*) abwimmeln (*inf*). **(c)** (*sl: make fed up*) **I'm ~d ~** mir stinkt's! (*sl*).
♦**choke up** *vt sep* **(a)** (*block*) *pipe, drain etc* verstopfen. **(b)** (*usu pass*) *voice* ersticken ♦ **you sound a bit ~d ~** du klingst etwas verschnupft. **(c) to get/be ~d ~** (*sl*) ganz fuchtig (*inf*) werden/sein (*about* wegen).
choke chain *n* Stachelhalsband *nt*.
choked [tʃəʊkt] *adj* (*inf*) pikiert.
chokedamp ['tʃəʊkdæmp] *n* Ferch *m*, böse *or* giftige Wetter *pl*.
choker ['tʃəʊkəʳ] *n* (*collar*) Vatermörder *m*; (*necklace*) enger Halsreif; (*of velvet etc*) Kropfband *nt*.
choler ['kɒləʳ] *n* (*old*) (*bile*) (gelbe) Galle; (*bad temper*) Zorn *m*.
cholera ['kɒlərə] *n* Cholera *f*.
choleric ['kɒlərɪk] *adj* cholerisch, leicht aufbrausend.
cholesterol [kɒ'lestərəl] *n* Cholesterin *nt*.
chomp [tʃɒmp] *vt* laut mahlen; (*person*) mampfen (*inf*).
choo-choo ['tʃuːtʃuː] *n* (*Brit baby-talk: train*) Puff-Puff *f* (*baby-talk*).
choose [tʃuːz] *pret* **chose**, *ptp* **chosen** **1** *vt* **(a)** (*select*) (aus)wählen, sich (*dat*) aussuchen ♦ **to ~ a team** eine Mannschaft auswählen *or* zusammenstellen; **they chose him as their leader** *or* **to be their leader** sie wählten ihn zu ihrem Anführer; **in a few well-chosen words** in wenigen wohlgesetzten Worten.
(b) (*decide, elect*) **to ~ to do sth** es vorziehen, etw zu tun; **may I come earlier? — if you ~ to** darf ich früher kommen? — wenn Sie wollen.
2 *vi* **(a) to ~ (between** *or* **among/from)** wählen *or* eine Wahl treffen (zwischen +*dat*/aus *or* unter +*dat*); **there is nothing to ~ between them** sie sind gleich gut; **there aren't many to ~ from** die Auswahl ist nicht sehr groß.
(b) (*decide, elect*) **as/if you ~** wie/wenn Sie wollen.
choos(e)y ['tʃuːzɪ] *adj* (+*er*) wählerisch.
chop¹ [tʃɒp] **1** *n* **(a)** (*blow*) Schlag *m*.
(b) (*Cook*) Kotelett *nt*.
(c) (*Sport*) harter (Kurz)schlag; (*Karate*) Karateschlag *m*.
(d) (*of waves*) Klatschen, Schlagen *nt*.
(e) (*sl*) **to get the ~** (*be axed*) unter die Sense kommen (*sl*), dem Rotstift zum Opfer fallen; (*be fired*) rausgeschmissen werden (*inf*); **to give sb the ~** jdn rausschmeißen (*inf*).
2 *vt* **(a)** hacken; *meat, vegetables etc* kleinschneiden ♦ **to ~ one's way through the undergrowth** sich (*dat*) einen Weg durchs Dickicht schlagen.
(b) (*Sport*) *ball* (ab)stoppen; (*Wrestling etc*) *opponent* einen Schlag versetzen (+*dat*).
♦**chop at** *vi* +*prep obj* hacken *or* schlagen nach; (*with axe*) einhacken auf (+*acc*).
♦**chop back** *vt sep* zurück- *or* wegschneiden.
♦**chop down** *vt sep tree* fällen.
♦**chop off** *vt sep* abhacken, abschlagen, abhauen ♦ **to ~ ~ the ends of one's words** abgehackt sprechen.
♦**chop up** *vt sep* zerhacken, zerkleinern; (*fig*) *country* aufteilen; *company* aufspalten.
chop² *vi* **(a)** (*Naut: wind*) drehen, umspringen. **(b)** (*fig*) **to ~ and change** ständig seine Meinung ändern; **if you keep ~ping and changing with your jobs ...** wenn du weiterhin ständig die Stelle wechselst, ...
chop-chop ['tʃɒp'tʃɒp] (*inf*) *adv, interj* hopp, hopp (*inf*).
chophouse ['tʃɒphaʊs] *n* Steakhaus *nt*.
chopper ['tʃɒpəʳ] *n* **(a)** (*axe*) Hackbeil *nt*. **(b)** (*inf: helicopter*) Hubschrauber *m*. **(c)** (*bicycle*) BMX-Rad *nt*; (*sl: motorcycle*) Maschine *f* (*inf*).
choppers ['tʃɒpəz] *npl* (*sl: teeth*) Beißerchen *pl* (*inf*).
chopping ['tʃɒpɪŋ]: **~ block** *n* Hackklotz *m*; (*for wood, executions etc*) Block *m*; **~ board** *n* Hackbrett *nt*; **~ knife** *n* Hackmesser *nt*; (*with rounded blade*) Wiegemesser *nt*.
choppy ['tʃɒpɪ] *adj* (+*er*) *sea* kabbelig; *wind* böig, wechselhaft.
chops [tʃɒps] *npl* (*of dog*) Lefzen *pl*; (*inf: of person*) Visage *f* (*sl*).
chop: ~stick *n* Stäbchen *nt*; **~-suey** *n* Chop-Suey *nt*.
choral ['kɔːrəl] *adj* Chor- ♦ **~ society** Gesangverein, Chor *m*.
chorale [kɒ'rɑːl] *n* Choral *m*.
chord [kɔːd] *n* **(a)** (*Mus*) Akkord *m* ♦ **to strike the right/a sympathetic ~** (*fig*) den richtigen Ton treffen/auf Verständnis stoßen. **(b)** (*Geometry*) Sehne *f*. **(c)** (*Anat*) Band *nt*.
chordal ['kɔːdl] *adj* (*Mus*) Akkord-.
chore [tʃɔːʳ] *n* lästige Pflicht ♦ **~s** *pl* Hausarbeit *f*; **to do the ~s** den Haushalt machen, die Hausarbeit erledigen.
choreograph ['kɒrɪəʊgrɑːf] *vt* choreographieren.
choreographer [ˌkɒrɪ'ɒgrəfəʳ] *n* Choreograph(in *f*) *m*.
choreographic [ˌkɒrɪəʊ'græfɪk] *adj* choreographisch.
choreography [ˌkɒrɪ'ɒgrəfɪ] *n* Choreographie *f*.
chorister ['kɒrɪstəʳ] *n* (Kirchen)chormitglied *nt*; (*boy*) Chorknabe *m*.
chortle ['tʃɔːtl] **1** *vi* gluckern, glucksen ♦ **he was chortling over the newspaper/the article** er lachte in sich hinein *or* vor sich hin, als er die Zeitung/den Artikel las.
2 *n* Gluckser *m*.
chorus ['kɔːrəs] **1** *n* **(a)** (*refrain*) Refrain *m*.
(b) Chor *m*; (*of opera*) Opernchor *m*; (*dancers*) Tanzgruppe *f* ♦ **she's in the ~** sie singt im Chor/sie ist bei der Tanzgruppe; **in ~** im Chor; **he was greeted with a ~ of good morning, sir** als er hereinkam, riefen alle im Chor: guten

➤ LANGUAGE IN USE: **choice: 1a** → 1.1, 10.1, 18.3

Morgen!
2 *vi* im Chor singen/sprechen/rufen.
chorus: ~ girl *n* Revuetänzerin *f or* -girl *nt*; **~ line** *n* Revue *f*.
chose [tʃəuz] *pret of* **choose**.
chosen ['tʃəuzn] 1 *ptp of* **choose**.
2 *adj* **the ~ people** das auserwählte Volk; **the ~ few** die wenigen Auserwählten.
choux pastry ['ʃuː'peɪstrɪ] *n* Brandteig *m*.
chow [tʃau] *n* (*sl: food*) Futterage *f* (*inf*), Proviant *m*.
chow(chow) ['tʃau(tʃau)] *n* (*dog*) Chow-Chow *m*.
chowder ['tʃaudəʳ] *n* (*US*) sämige Fischsuppe.
Christ [kraɪst] 1 *n* Christus *m*.
2 *interj* (*sl*) Herrgott (*inf*).
christen ['krɪsn] *vt* **(a)** taufen ◆ **to ~ sb after sb** jdn nach jdm (be)nennen. **(b)** (*inf: use for first time*) einweihen.
Christendom ['krɪsndəm] *n* (*old*) die Christenheit.
christening ['krɪsnɪŋ] *n* Taufe *f* ◆ **~ robe** Taufkleid *nt*.
Christian ['krɪstɪən] 1 *n* Christ *m*.
2 *adj* (*lit, fig*) christlich.
Christianity [,krɪstɪ'ænɪtɪ] *n* **(a)** (*faith, religion*) Christentum *nt*, christlicher Glaube; (*body of Christians*) Christenheit *f*.
(b) (*being a Christian*) Christlichkeit, Frömmigkeit *f* ◆ **his ~ did not prevent him from doing it** sein christlicher Glaube hinderte ihn nicht daran(, das zu tun).
(c) (*Christian character*) christliche Haltung *or* Gesinnung.
Christianize ['krɪstɪənaɪz] *vt* christianisieren.
Christian: ~ name *n* Vor- *or* Rufname *m*; **~ Science** *n* Christian Science *f*; **~ Scientist** *n* Anhänger(in *f*) *m* der Christian Science.
Christlike ['kraɪstlaɪk] *adj* Christus-gleich.
➤ **Christmas** ['krɪsməs] *n* Weihnachten *nt* ◆ **are you going home for ~?** fährst du (über) Weihnachten nach Hause?; **what did you get for ~?** was hast du zu Weihnachten bekommen?; **merry** *or* **happy ~!** frohe *or* fröhliche Weihnachten!
Christmas: ~ box *n* (*Brit*) Trinkgeld *nt* zu Weihnachten, ≃ Neujahrsgeld *nt*; **~ cake** *n Früchtekuchen m mit Zuckerguß zu Weihnachten*; **~ card** *n* Weihnachtskarte *f*; **~ carol** *n* Weihnachtslied *nt*; **~ Day** *n* der erste Weihnachtstag; **on ~ Day** an Weihnachten, am ersten (Weihnachts)feiertag; **~ Eve** *n* Heiligabend *m*; **on ~ Eve** Heiligabend; **~ Island** *n* Weihnachtsinsel *f*; **~ present** *n* Weihnachtsgeschenk *nt*; **~ pudding** *n* Plumpudding *m*; **~ rose** *n* Christrose *f*; **~ stocking** *n Strumpf m, in den Weihnachtsgeschenke gelegt werden*; **~ time** *n* Weihnachtszeit *f*; **at ~ time** zur *or* in der Weihnachtszeit; **~ tree** *n* Weihnachtsbaum, Christbaum (*esp S Ger*) *m*.
chromatic [krə'mætɪk] *adj* (*Art, Mus*) chromatisch.
chrome [krəum] *n* Chrom *nt* ◆ **~ steel** Chromstahl *m*.
chromium ['krəumɪəm] *n* Chrom *nt*.
chromium: ~ plate *n* Chromschicht *f*; **~ plated** *adj* verchromt; **~ plating** *n* Verchromung *f*.
chromosome ['krəuməsəum] *n* Chromosom *nt*.
chronic ['krɒnɪk] *adj* **(a)** (*Med, fig*) *disease, invalid, liar etc* chronisch. **(b)** (*inf: terrible*) schlecht, miserabel (*inf*).
chronicle ['krɒnɪkl] 1 *n* Chronik *f* ◆ **C~s** (*Bibl*) Bücher *pl* der Chronik.
2 *vt* aufzeichnen; *historic events also* eine Chronik (*+gen*) verfassen.
chronicler ['krɒnɪkləʳ] *n* Chronist *m*.
chronological *adj*, **~ly** *adv* [,krɒnə'lɒdʒɪkəl, -ɪ] chronologisch ◆ **~ly arranged** in chronologischer Reihenfolge.
chronology [krə'nɒlədʒɪ] *n* zeitliche Abfolge, Chronologie (*form*) *f*; (*list of dates*) Zeittafel *f*.
chronometer [krə'nɒmɪtəʳ] *n* Chronometer *m*.
chrysalis ['krɪsəlɪs] *n*, *pl* **-es** (*Biol*) Puppe *f*; (*covering*) Kokon *m*.
chrysanthemum [krɪ'sænθəməm], **chrysanth** [krɪ'sænθ] (*inf*) *n* Chrysantheme *f*.
chub [tʃʌb] *n*, *pl* - Döbel, Aitel *m*.
chubby ['tʃʌbɪ] *adj* (*+er*) pummelig, rundlich ◆ **~ cheeks** Pausbacken *pl*; **~-cheeked** pausbäckig.
chuck[1] [tʃʌk] 1 *vt* (*inf*) **(a)** (*throw*) schmeißen (*inf*). **(b)** (*sl*) *girlfriend etc* Schluß machen mit (*inf*); *job* hinschmeißen (*inf*) ◆ **~ it!** (*stop it*) Schluß jetzt! **(c) to ~ sb under the chin** jdm einen Kinnstüber versetzen.
2 *n* **(a)** (*sl: dismissal*) Rausschmiß *m* (*inf*) ◆ **to give sb the ~** jdn rausschmeißen (*inf*), jdn an die Luft setzen (*inf*); **he got the ~** er ist rausgeflogen (*inf*), den haben sie an die Luft gesetzt (*inf*).
(b) to give sb a ~ under the chin *see vt (c)*.
◆**chuck about** *vt sep* (*inf*) rumschmeißen (mit) (*inf*).
◆**chuck away** *vt sep* (*inf*) (*throw out*) wegschmeißen (*inf*); (*waste*) *money* aus dem Fenster schmeißen (*inf*).
◆**chuck in** *vt sep* (*inf*) *job* hinschmeißen (*inf*), an den Nagel hängen (*inf*) ◆ **to ~ it (all)** ~ den Laden hinschmeißen (*inf*).
◆**chuck out** *vt sep* (*inf*) rausschmeißen (*inf*); *useless articles also* wegschmeißen (*inf*) ◆ **to be ~ed ~** rausfliegen (of aus) (*inf*).
◆**chuck up** *vt sep* (*inf*) *job* hinschmeißen (*inf*).
chuck[2] *n* (*Tech*) Spannfutter *nt*.
chuck[3] *n* (*US sl: food*) Essen *nt* ◆ **~ wagon** Proviantwagen *m* mit fahrbarer Küche.
chucker-out ['tʃʌkər'aut] *n* (*inf*) Rausschmeißer *m* (*inf*).
chuckle ['tʃʌkl] 1 *n* leises Lachen, Kichern *nt no pl* ◆ **to have a good ~ about sth** sich (*dat*) eins lachen über etw (*acc*) (*inf*).
2 *vi* leise in sich (*acc*) hineinlachen, sich (*dat*) eins lachen (*inf*) ◆ **to ~ away** vor sich hin lachen *or* kichern.
chuffed [tʃʌft] *adj* (*Brit sl*) vergnügt und zufrieden; (*flattered*) gebauchpinselt (*inf*) (*about* wegen) ◆ **I was dead ~ about it** ich freute mich darüber wie ein Schneekönig (*inf*); **to be/look ~ with oneself** auf sich (*acc*) selbst stolz sein/ sehr zufrieden aussehen.
chug [tʃʌg] 1 *n* Tuckern *nt*.
2 *vi* tuckern.
◆**chug along** *vi* entlangtuckern; (*fig inf*) gut vorankommen.
chukka, chukker ['tʃʌkəʳ] *n* (*Polo*) Chukka, Chukker *nt*.
chum [tʃʌm] *n* (*inf*) Kamerad, Kumpel (*inf*), Spezi (*S Ger*) *m*.
◆**chum up** *vi* sich anfreunden.
chummy ['tʃʌmɪ] *adj* (*+er*) (*inf*) kameradschaftlich ◆ **to be ~ with sb** mit jdm sehr dicke sein (*inf*); **to get ~ with sb** sich mit jdm anfreunden.
chump [tʃʌmp] *n* **(a)** (*inf*) Trottel *m*, dummes Stück, Hornochse *m* (*inf*). **(b) he's off his ~** (*Brit inf*) der hat 'ne Meise (*inf*).
chump chop *n* Kotelett *nt*.
chunk [tʃʌŋk] *n* großes Stück; (*of meat*) Batzen *m*; (*of stone*) Brocken *m*.
chunky ['tʃʌŋkɪ] *adj* (*+er*) (*inf*) *legs, arms* stämmig; *person also* untersetzt, gedrungen; *knitwear* dick, klobig; *book* kompakt; *glass* massiv.
Chunnel ['tʃʌnəl] *n* (*inf*) Kanaltunnel *m*.
church [tʃɜːtʃ] *n* Kirche *f*; (*service*) die Kirche ◆ **to go to ~** in die Kirche gehen; **the C~ Fathers** die Kirchenväter; **the C~ of England** die Anglikanische Kirche; **he has gone into** *or* **entered the C~** er ist Geistlicher geworden.
church *in cpds* Kirchen-; **~-goer** *n* Kirchgänger(in *f*) *m*; **~-going** *adj* **a ~-going family** eine Familie, die regelmäßig in die Kirche geht; **~ hall** *n* Gemeindehalle *f*; **~man** *n* (*clergyman*) Geistliche(r), Seelsorger *m*; (*~goer*) Kirchgänger *m*; **~ mouse** *n*: **as poor as a ~ mouse** arm wie eine Kirchenmaus; **~ service** *n* Gottesdienst *m*; **~warden** *n* Gemeindevorsteher *m*.
churchy ['tʃɜːtʃɪ] *adj* (*+er*) (*inf*) *person* kirchlich.
churchyard ['tʃɜːtʃjɑːd] *n* Friedhof, Kirchhof (*old, dial*) *m*.
churlish *adj*, **~ly** *adv* ['tʃɜːlɪʃ, -lɪ] ungehobelt.
churlishness ['tʃɜːlɪʃnɪs] *n* ungehobeltes Benehmen.
churn [tʃɜːn] 1 *n* (*for butter*) Butterfaß *nt*; (*Brit: milk-~*) Milchkanne *f*.
2 *vt* **(a) to ~ butter** buttern, Sahne buttern. **(b)** (*agitate*) *sea, mud etc* aufwühlen.
3 *vi* (*water, mud*) wirbeln, strudeln; (*wheels, rage etc*) wühlen; (*propeller*) wirbeln, sich wild drehen ◆ **the ~ing sea** die stampfende See.
◆**churn away** *vi* sich wild drehen; (*engine*) stampfen.
◆**churn out** *vt sep* am laufenden Band produzieren.
◆**churn up** *vt sep* aufwühlen.
chute [ʃuːt] *n* **(a)** Rutsche *f*; (*garbage ~*) Müllschlucker *m*. **(b)** (*rapid in river*) Stromschnelle *f*. **(c)** (*inf: parachute*) Fallschirm *m*. **(d)** (*in playground*) Rutschbahn, Rutsche *f*.
chutney ['tʃʌtnɪ] *n* Chutney *m*.
chutzpah ['tʃʌtspɑː] *n* Chuzpe *f*.
CI *abbr of* **Channel Islands.**
CIA *abbr of* **Central Intelligence Agency** CIA *m*.
ciborium [sɪ'bɔːrɪəm] *n* Ziborium *nt*.
cicada [sɪ'kɑːdə] *n* Zikade *f*.
cicatrix ['sɪkətrɪks] *n*, *pl* **cicatrices** [sɪkə'traɪsiːz] wildes Fleisch, Granulationsgewebe *nt* (*spec*); (*scar*) Narbe *f*.
cicerone [,tʃɪtʃə'rəunɪ] *n* Cicerone *m*.
CID (*Brit*) *abbr of* **Criminal Investigation Department** ≃ Kripo *f*.
cider ['saɪdəʳ] *n* Apfelwein, Cidre *m* ◆ **hard ~** (*US*) (*voll vergorener*) Apfelwein; **sweet ~** süßer (*teilweise vergorener*) Apfelwein, Rauscher *m* (*dial*); **rough ~** Apfelwein *m* (*mit größerem Alkoholgehalt*).
cider: ~ apple *n* Mostapfel *m*; **~ press** *n* Apfelpresse *f*.
cif *abbr of* **cost, insurance and freight** cif.
cigar [sɪ'gɑːʳ] *n* Zigarre *f*.
cigar: ~ box *n* Zigarrenkiste *f*; **~ cutter** *n* Zigarrenabschneider *m*.
cigarette [,sɪgə'ret] *n* Zigarette *f*.
cigarette: ~ box *n* Zigarettenschachtel *f*; **~ case** *n* Zigarettenetui *nt*; **~ end** *n* Zigarettenstummel *m*; **~ holder** *n* Zigarettenspitze *f*; **~ lighter** *n* Feuerzeug *nt*; **~ paper** *n* Zigarettenpapier *nt*.
cigarillo [sɪgə'rɪləu] *n* Zigarillo *m or nt*.
cigar: ~ lighter *n* (*in car*) Zigarettenanzünder *m*; **~-shaped** *adj* zigarrenförmig.
ciggy ['sɪgɪ] *n* (*inf*) Glimmstengel *m* (*inf*), Kippe *f* (*inf*).
C-in-C *abbr of* **Commander in Chief.**
cinch [sɪntʃ] 1 *n* **(a)** (*US: saddle girth*) Sattelgurt *m*. **(b)** (*sl*) **it's a ~** (*easy*) das ist ein Kinderspiel *or* ein Klacks (*inf*); (*esp US: certain*) es ist todsicher (*inf*).
2 *vt* (*US*) **(a) to ~ a horse** den Sattelgurt anziehen. **(b)** (*sl*) *deal* regeln (*sl*).
cinder ['sɪndəʳ] *n* **~s** *pl* Asche *f*; (*lumpy*) Schlacke *f*; (*still burning*) glühendes Kohlestück ◆ **burnt to a ~** (*fig*) verkohlt.
Cinderella [,sɪndə'relə] *n* (*lit, fig*) Aschenputtel *nt*.
cinder track *n* Aschenbahn *f*.
cineaste ['sɪnɪæst] *n* Cineast(in *f*), Kinoliebhaber(in *f*) *m*.
cine-camera [,sɪnɪ'kæmərə] *n* (*Brit*) (Schmal)filmkamera *f*.
cine-film ['sɪnɪfɪlm] *n* (*Brit*) Schmalfilm *m*.
cinema ['sɪnəmə] *n* (*esp Brit*) Kino *nt*; (*films collectively also*) Film *m* ◆ **at/to the ~** im/ins Kino.
cinema (*esp Brit*): **~ complex** *n* Kinocenter *nt*; **~goer** *n* Kinogänger(in *f*) *m*;

➤ LANGUAGE IN USE: **Christmas** → 23.2

~-going [1] *n* **the popularity of ~-going** die Beliebtheit des Kinos; [2] *adj* **the ~-going public** das Kinopublikum, die Kinogänger *pl*; **~-loving** *adj* kinofreudig.
Cinemascope ® ['sɪnəməskəʊp] *n* Cinemascope *nt*.
cinematic [sɪnə'mætɪk] *adj* filmisch ◆ **~ art** Filmkunst *f*.
cinematograph [,sɪnə'mætəgrɑːf] *n* (*dated*) Kinematograph *m* (*dated*).
cine-projector [,sɪnɪprə'dʒektəʳ] *n* (*Brit*) Filmprojektor *m*.
cinerama ® [,sɪnə'rɑːmə] *n* Cinerama ® *nt*.
cinerary ['sɪnərərɪ] *adj* Aschen-.
cinnabar ['sɪnəbɑːʳ] *n* Zinnober *m*.
cinnamon ['sɪnəmən] [1] *n* Zimt *m*.
[2] *adj attr* **(a)** *cake, biscuit* Zimt-. **(b)** (*colour*) zimtfarben.
CIO (*US*) *abbr of* **Congress of Industrial Organizations** *amerikanischer Gewerkschafts-Dachverband*.
cipher ['saɪfəʳ] [1] *n* **(a)** (*Arabic numeral*) Ziffer, Zahl *f*.
(b) (*zero*) Null *f*.
(c) (*nonentity*) Niemand *m no pl*.
(d) (*code*) Chiffre *f*, Code *m* ◆ **~ clerk** (De)chiffreur *m*; **~s officer** (*army*) Fernmeldeoffizier *m*; (*secret service etc*) (De)chiffreur *m*; **in ~** chiffriert.
(e) (*monogram*) Monogramm, Namenszeichen *nt*.
[2] *vt* (*encode*) verschlüsseln, chiffrieren.
circ *abbr of* **circa** ca.
circa ['sɜːkə] *prep* zirka, circa.
circle ['sɜːkl] [1] *n* **(a)** Kreis *m* ◆ **to stand in a ~** im Kreis stehen; **to go round in ever decreasing ~s** (*lit*) Spiralen drehen; (*fig*) sich unablässig im Kreis drehen; **to turn full ~** (*lit*) sich ganz herumdrehen, eine Volldrehung machen; **we're just going round in ~s** (*fig*) wir bewegen uns nur im Kreise; **to come full ~** (*fig*) zum Ausgangspunkt zurückkehren; **things have come full ~** der Kreis hat sich geschlossen; **when the seasons have come full ~** wenn sich der Kreis der Jahreszeiten schließt.
(b) (*of hills etc*) Ring *m*, Kette *f*; (*round the eyes*) Ring *m* (*round* unter +*dat*); (*in gymnastics*) Welle *f* ◆ **a Celtic stone ~** ein keltischer Steinkreis; **the ~ of the seasons** der Zyklus *or* Kreislauf der Jahreszeiten.
(c) (*Brit: Theat*) Rang *m*; *see* **dress, upper.**
(d) (*group of persons*) Kreis, Zirkel (*geh*) *m* ◆ **a close ~ of friends** ein enger Freundeskreis; **in political ~s** in politischen Kreisen; **the family ~** der engste Familienkreis; **the whole family ~** die ganze Familie; **he's moving in different ~s now** er verkehrt jetzt in anderen Kreisen.
[2] *vt* **(a)** (*surround*) umgeben. **(b)** (*move around*) kreisen um ◆ **the enemy ~d the town** der Feind kreiste die Stadt ein. **(c)** (*draw a ~ round*) einen Kreis *or* Kringel machen um ◆ **he ~d (off) several of the addresses** er machte einen Kreis um mehrere der Anschriften; **~d in red** rot umkringelt.
[3] *vi* (*fly in a ~*) kreisen.
◆**circle around** *vi* (*people*) umhergehen *or* -wandern; (*birds*) Kreise ziehen; (*vehicles*) kreisen, Runden drehen; (*ships*) kreisen ◆ **the wolves/Indians ~d ~, waiting** die Wölfe/Indianer kreisten lauernd um uns/sie/das Lager *etc*.
circlet ['sɜːklɪt] *n* Reif *m*.
circlip ['sɜːklɪp] *n* Sicherungsring *m*.
circuit ['sɜːkɪt] [1] *n* **(a)** (*journey around etc*) Rundgang *m*/-fahrt *f*/-reise *f* (*of* um) ◆ **to make a ~ of sth** um etw herumgehen/-fahren, einen Rundgang/eine Rundfahrt um etw machen; **three ~s of the racetrack** drei Runden auf der Rennbahn; **they made a wide ~ to avoid the enemy** sie machten einen großen Bogen um den Feind; **the diagram shows the ~ the oil takes** das Diagramm zeigt die Zirkulation des Öls.
(b) (*of judges etc*) Gerichtsbezirk *m* ◆ **to go on ~** den (Gerichts)bezirk bereisen; **he is on the eastern ~** er bereist *or* hat den östlichen (Gerichts)bezirk.
(c) (*Theat*) Theaterring *m or* -kette *f* ◆ **to travel the ~** die Theater (der Reihe nach) bereisen.
(d) (*Elec*) Stromkreis *m*; (*apparatus*) Schaltung *f*.
(e) (*Sport: track*) Rennbahn *f*.
(f) **the professional golf/tennis ~** die Golf-/Tennisturnierrunde (der Berufsspieler).
[2] *vt track, course* eine Runde drehen um.
circuit: ~ board *n* (*Tech*) Platine, Leiterplatte *f*; **~ breaker** *n* Stromkreisunterbrecher *m*; **~ court** *n* Bezirksgericht, *das an verschiedenen Orten eines Gerichtsbezirks Sitzungen abhält*; **~ diagram** *n* Schaltplan *m*; **~ judge** *n* Richter *m* an einem Bezirksgericht.
circuitous [sɜː'kjʊɪtəs] *adj* umständlich ◆ **~ path** Schlängelpfad *m*.
circuitously [sɜː'kjʊɪtəslɪ] *adv* umständlich ◆ **the road winds ~** die Straße schlängelt sich.
circuitousness [sɜː'kjʊɪtəsnɪs] *n* Umständlichkeit *f*; (*of route*) Gewundenheit *f*.
circuitry ['sɜːkətrɪ] *n* Schaltkreise *pl*.
circuit training *n* Circuittraining *nt*.
circuity [sɜː'kjʊətɪ] *n see* **circuitousness.**
circular ['sɜːkjʊləʳ] [1] *adj object* kreisförmig, rund ◆ **~ saw** Kreissäge *f*; **~ motion** Kreisbewegung *f*; **~ tour** Rundfahrt *f*/-reise *f*; **a ~ tour of the island** eine Inselrundfahrt; **~ argument** Zirkelschluß *m*; **~ letter** Rundschreiben *nt*, Rundbrief *m*.
[2] *n* (*in firm*) Rundschreiben *nt*, Rundbrief *m*; (*single copy*) Umlauf *m*; (*printed advertisement*) Wurfsendung *f*.
circularize ['sɜːkjʊləraɪz] *vt person* durch Rundschreiben informieren; *letter, memo* zirkulieren lassen.
circulate ['sɜːkjʊleɪt] [1] *vi* **(a)** (*water, blood, money*) fließen, zirkulieren; (*traffic*) fließen; (*news, rumour*) kursieren, in Umlauf sein; (*news*) sich verbreiten. **(b)** (*person: at party*) die Runde machen ◆ **to keep the guests circulating** dafür sorgen, daß die Gäste keine Grüppchen bilden.
[2] *vt news, rumour* verbreiten, in Umlauf bringen; *memo etc* zirkulieren lassen; *water* pumpen.
circulating ['sɜːkjʊleɪtɪŋ]: **~ capital** *n* flüssiges Kapital, Umlaufkapital *nt*; **~ library** *n* Fahrbücherei *f*; **~ medium** *n* (*Fin*) Zahlungs- *or* Umlaufsmittel *nt*.
circulation [,sɜːkjʊ'leɪʃən] *n* **(a)** (*Med*) (*act of circulating*) Kreislauf *m*, Zirkulation *f*; (*of traffic*) Ablauf, Fluß *m*; (*of money also*) Umlauf *m*; (*of news, rumour*) Kursieren *nt*, Verbreitung *f* ◆ **to have poor ~** Kreislaufstörungen haben; **to put notes into ~** Banknoten in Umlauf bringen; **this coin was withdrawn from** *or* **taken out of ~** diese Münze wurde aus dem Verkehr gezogen; **new words which come into ~** Wörter, die neu in Umlauf kommen; **he's back in ~ now** (*inf*) er mischt wieder mit (*inf*); **the ideas then in ~** die Ideen, die damals im Schwang(e) waren.
(b) (*of newspaper etc*) Auflage(nziffer) *f* ◆ **for private ~** zum privaten Gebrauch.
circulatory [,sɜːkjʊ'leɪtərɪ] *adj* Kreislauf- ◆ **~ system** Blutkreislauf *m*.
circum- ['sɜːkəm-] *pref* um-, um ... herum.
circumcise ['sɜːkəmsaɪz] *vt* beschneiden.
circumcision [,sɜːkəm'sɪʒən] *n* Beschneidung *f* ◆ **the C~** (*Eccl*) der Tag der Beschneidung des Herrn.
circumference [sə'kʌmfərəns] *n* Umfang *m* ◆ **the tree is 10 ft in ~** der Baum hat einen Umfang von 10 Fuß.
circumflex ['sɜːkəmfleks] *n* Zirkumflex *m*.
circumlocution [,sɜːkəmlə'kjuːʃən] *n* Weitschweifigkeit *f*; (*evasiveness*) Umschreibung *f*, Drumherumreden *nt* (*inf*).
circumlocutory [,sɜːkəmlə'kjuːtərɪ] *adj* weitschweifig; *expression* umschreibend.
circumnavigate [,sɜːkəm'nævɪgeɪt] *vt the globe* umfahren; (*in yacht also*) umsegeln; *cape, island also* umschiffen.
circumnavigation ['sɜːkəm,nævɪ'geɪʃən] *n* Fahrt *f* (*of* um); (*in yacht also*) Umseglung *f* ◆ **~ of the globe** Fahrt um die Welt; Weltumseglung *f*.
circumnavigator [,sɜːkəm'nævɪgeɪtəʳ] *n* **~ of the globe** Weltumsegler(in *f*) *m*.
circumscribe ['sɜːkəmskraɪb] *vt* **(a)** (*Math*) einen Kreis umbeschreiben (+*dat*). **(b)** (*restrict*) eingrenzen.
circumscription [,sɜːkəm'skrɪpʃən] *n* **(a)** (*restriction*) Eingrenzung *f*. **(b)** (*on coin*) Umschrift *f*.
circumspect *adj*, **~ly** *adv* ['sɜːkəmspekt, -lɪ] umsichtig.
circumspection [,sɜːkəm'spekʃən] *n* Umsicht *f*.
circumstance ['sɜːkəmstəns] *n* **(a)** Umstand *m* ◆ **in** *or* **under the ~s** unter diesen Umständen; **in** *or* **under no ~s** unter gar keinen Umständen, auf keinen Fall; **in certain ~s** unter Umständen, eventuell; **what were the ~s surrounding the case?** wie waren die näheren Umstände des Falls?
(b) **~s** *pl* (*financial condition*) finanzielle Verhältnisse, Umstände (*form*) *pl* ◆ **in poor ~s** in ärmlichen Verhältnissen.
(c) *see* **pomp.**
circumstantial [,sɜːkəm'stænʃəl] *adj* **(a)** (*detailed*) *report, statement* ausführlich, detailliert. **(b)** (*Jur*) **~ evidence** Indizienbeweis *m*. **(c)** (*secondary*) nebensächlich.
circumstantiate [,sɜːkəm'stænʃɪeɪt] *vt* (*form*) belegen.
circumvent [,sɜːkəm'vent] *vt* umgehen.
circumvention [,sɜːkəm'venʃən] *n* Umgehung *f*.
circus ['sɜːkəs] *n* Zirkus *m*; (*in place names*) Platz *m*.
cirrhosis [sɪ'rəʊsɪs] *n* Zirrhose *f*.
cirrus ['sɪrəs] *n*, *pl* **cirri** ['sɪraɪ] Zirruswolke *f*.
CIS *abbr of* **Commonwealth of Independent States** GUS.
cisalpine ['siːzælpaɪn] *adj* zisalpin.
cissy ['sɪsɪ] *n see* **sissy.**
Cistercian [sɪs'tɜːʃən] [1] *n* Zisterzienser *m*.
[2] *adj* Zisterzienser-.
cistern ['sɪstən] *n* Zisterne *f*; (*of WC*) Spülkasten *m*.
citadel ['sɪtədl] *n* Zitadelle *f*.
citation [saɪ'teɪʃən] *n* **(a)** (*quote*) Zitat *nt*; (*act of quoting*) Zitieren *nt*. **(b)** (*Mil*) Belobigung *f*, lobende Erwähnung. **(c)** (*Jur*) Vorladung *f* (vor Gericht).
cite [saɪt] *vt* **(a)** (*quote*) anführen, zitieren. **(b)** (*Mil*) belobigen, lobend erwähnen (*for* wegen). **(c)** (*Jur*) vorladen ◆ **he was ~d to appear** er wurde vorgeladen, er erhielt eine Vorladung; **he was ~d as the co-respondent** (*mentioned*) er wurde als der Dritte in der Scheidungssache genannt.
citizen ['sɪtɪzn] *n* **(a)** Bürger(in *f*) *m* ◆ **C~s' Band** CB-Funk *m*. **(b)** (*of a state*) (Staats)bürger(in *f*) *m* ◆ **French ~** französischer Staatsbürger, Franzose *m*, Französin *f*; **~ of the world** Weltbürger *m*.
citizenry ['sɪtɪznrɪ] *n* (*liter*) Bürgerschaft *f*.
Citizens' Advice Bureau *n* (*Brit*) ≃ Bürgerberatungsstelle *f*.
citizen's arrest *n Festnahme f durch eine Zivilperson*.
citizenship ['sɪtɪznʃɪp] *n* Staatsbürgerschaft *f*.
citrate ['sɪtreɪt] *n* Zitrat *nt*.
citric ['sɪtrɪk] *adj* Zitrus- ◆ **~ acid** Zitronensäure *f*.
citron ['sɪtrən] *n* (*fruit*) Zitrone *f*; (*tree*) Zitronenbaum *m*.
citrus ['sɪtrəs] *n* Zitrusgewächs *nt* ◆ **~ fruits** Zitrusfrüchte *pl*.
city ['sɪtɪ] *n* **(a)** Stadt, Großstadt *f* ◆ **towns and cities** Städte und Großstädte; **the ~ of Glasgow** die Stadt Glasgow. **(b)** (*in London*) **the C~** die City, das Banken- und Börsenviertel.
city: ~ boy *n* Großstadtkind *nt*, Großstadtjunge *m*; **~ bred** *adj* in der

(Groß)stadt aufgewachsen; ~ **centre** *n* Stadtmitte *f*, Stadtzentrum *nt*, Innenstadt *f*, City *f*; ~ **desk** *n* (*Brit*) Finanz- und Wirtschaftsabteilung *f* (*einer Redaktion*); (*US*) Abteilung *f* für Lokalnachrichten; ~ **dweller** *n* Stadtbewohner(in *f*) *m*; ~ **editor** *n* (*Brit*) Wirtschaftsredakteur(in *f*) *m*; (*US*) Lokalredakteur(in *f*) *m*; ~ **father** *n* Stadtverordnete(r) *m*; **the ~ fathers** die Stadtväter *pl*; ~ **hall** *n* Rathaus *nt*; (*US: municipal government*) Stadtverwaltung *f*; ~ **life** *n* (Groß)stadtleben *nt*; ~ **manager** *n* (*US*) Oberstadtdirektor *m*; ~ **page** *n* (*Brit*) Wirtschaftsseite *f*; **~scape** *n* (Groß)stadtlandschaft *f*; ~ **slicker** *n* (*pej inf*) feiner Pinkel aus der (Groß)stadt (*pej inf*); (*dishonest*) schlitzohriger Großstädter (*pej inf*); ~ **state** *n* Stadtstaat *m*; **C~ Technology College** *n* (*Brit*) ≃ Technische Fachschule; ~ **type** *n* (Groß)stadtmensch *m*.

civet ['sɪvɪt] *n* (*substance*) Zibet *m*; (*cat*) Zibetkatze *f*.

civic ['sɪvɪk] *adj rights, virtues* bürgerlich, Bürger-; *guard, authorities* Stadt-, städtisch ♦ **~ centre** (*Brit*) Verwaltungszentrum *nt* einer Stadt.

civics ['sɪvɪks] *n sing* Staatsbürgerkunde *f*.

civies ['sɪvɪz] *npl* (*sl*) *see* **civvies**.

civil ['sɪvl] *adj* (**a**) (*of society*) bürgerlich; *duties* staatsbürgerlich, Bürger-. (**b**) (*polite*) höflich; (*in behaviour also*) aufmerksam, zuvorkommend ♦ **cigar? — very ~ of you** Zigarre? — sehr zuvorkommend (von Ihnen). (**c**) (*Jur*) zivilrechtlich.

civil: C~ Aviation Authority *n* Behörde *f* für Zivilluftfahrt; ~ **defence** *n* Zivilschutz *m*; **~ defence worker** Beauftragte(r) *mf* des Zivilschutzes; ~ **disobedience** *n* ziviler Ungehorsam; **~ disobedience campaign** Kampagne *f* für zivilen Ungehorsam; ~ **engineer** *n* Bauingenieur *m*; ~ **engineering** *n* Hoch- und Tiefbau *m*.

civilian [sɪ'vɪlɪən] 1 *n* Zivilist *m*.
2 *adj* zivil, Zivil- ♦ **in ~ clothes** in Zivil; **~ casualties** Verluste unter der Zivilbevölkerung.

civility [sɪ'vɪlɪtɪ] *n* Höflichkeit *f*.

civilization [,sɪvɪlaɪ'zeɪʃən] *n* (**a**) (*civilized world*) Zivilisation *f* ♦ **all ~** die ganze zivilisierte Welt; **~!, the explorer exclaimed** Menschen!, rief der Forscher aus. (**b**) (*state: of Greeks etc*) Kultur *f*. (**c**) (*act*) Zivilisierung *f*.

civilize ['sɪvɪlaɪz] *vt* zivilisieren; *person also* Kultur beibringen (+*dat*).

civilized ['sɪvɪlaɪzd] *adj* (**a**) zivilisiert ♦ **all ~ nations** alle Kulturnationen. (**b**) *working hours, conditions, hour* zivil; (*cultured*) *lifestyle, age etc* kultiviert ♦ **a more ~ place to live in** ein etwas zivilerer Ort zum Leben; **brandy after dinner, very ~** Weinbrand nach dem Essen, sehr gepflegt.

civil: ~ law *n* Zivilrecht *nt*, Bürgerliches Recht; ~ **liberty** *n* Freiheitsrecht *nt*; ~ **list** *n* Zivilliste *f*.

civilly ['sɪvɪlɪ] *adv* (*politely*) höflich, zuvorkommend.

civil: ~ marriage *n* standesamtliche Trauung, Ziviltrauung *f*; ~ **rights** 1 *npl* (staats)bürgerliche Rechte *pl*; 2 *attr march, campaign, demonstration* Bürgerrechts-; ~ **servant** *n* ≃ Staatsbeamte(r) *m*, Staatsbeamtin *f*; ~ **service** *n* ≃ Staatsdienst *m* (*ohne Richter und Lehrer*); (~ *servants collectively*) Beamtenschaft *f*; ~ **war** *n* Bürgerkrieg *m*.

civvies ['sɪvɪz] *npl* (*sl*) Zivil *nt* ♦ **he put his ~ on** er schmiß sich in Zivil (*inf*).

civvy street ['sɪvɪ'stri:t] *n* (*Brit sl*) Zivilleben *nt* ♦ **on ~** im Zivilleben.

CJD *abbr of* **Creutzfeldt-Jakob disease** CJK.

cl *abbr of* **centilitre(s)** cl.

clack [klæk] 1 *n* Klappern, Geklapper *nt*.
2 *vi* klappern.

clad [klæd] 1 (*old*) *pret, ptp of* **clothe**.
2 *adj* (*liter*) gekleidet.
3 *adj suf* **fur-/silk-~** in Pelze/Seide gekleidet; **iron-/steel-~** mit Eisen/Stahl verkleidet; **ivy-~** efeubewachsen.

claim [kleɪm] 1 *vt* (**a**) (*demand as one's own or due*) Anspruch erheben auf (+*acc*); *social security, benefits, sum of money* (*apply for*) beantragen; (*draw*) beanspruchen; *lost property* abholen ♦ **he ~ed diplomatic immunity** er berief sich auf seine diplomatische Immunität; **to ~ sth as one's own** etw für sich beanspruchen, Anspruch auf etw (*acc*) erheben; **both armies ~ed the victory** beide Armeen nahmen den Sieg für sich in Anspruch; **territories ~ed by the Arabs** von den Arabern beanspruchte Gebiete; **does anyone ~ this wallet?** gehört diese Brieftasche jemandem?
(**b**) (*profess, assert*) behaupten ♦ **he ~s to have seen you** er behauptet, Sie gesehen zu haben, er will Sie gesehen haben; **the club can ~ a membership of ...** der Verein kann ... Mitglieder vorweisen; **the advantages ~ed for this technique** die Vorzüge, die man dieser Methode zuschreibt.
(**c**) *one's attention, interest* in Anspruch nehmen.
2 *vi* (**a**) (*Insur*) Ansprüche geltend machen; (*for damage done by people*) Schadenersatz verlangen.
(**b**) (*for expenses etc*) **to ~ for sth** sich (*dat*) etw zurückgeben *or* -zahlen lassen; **you can ~ for your travelling expenses** Sie können sich (*dat*) Ihre Reisekosten zurückerstatten lassen.
3 *n* (**a**) (*demand*) Anspruch *m*; (*pay ~, Ind*) Forderung *f* ♦ **his ~ to the throne/title/property** *etc* sein Anspruch auf den Thron/Titel/das Grundstück *etc*; **I have many ~s on my time** meine Zeit ist *or* ich bin sehr in Anspruch genommen; **you have no ~ on me** du hast keine Ansprüche an mich (zu stellen); **children have first ~ on their parents** die Kinder müssen an erster Stelle stehen, die Kinder müssen vorgehen; **to make ~s on sb's friendship** an jds Freundschaft (*acc*) appellieren; **to lay ~ to sth** Anspruch auf etw (*acc*) erheben; **to put in a ~ (for sth)** etw beantragen; (*Insur*) Ansprüche geltend machen; **they put in a ~ for extra pay** sie forderten einen Zuschlag; **we want the ~ back-dated** wir wollen das Geld rückwirkend; **he put in an expenses ~ for £100** er reichte Spesen in Höhe von £ 100 ein; **the ~s were all paid** (*Insur*) der Schaden wurde voll ersetzt.
(**b**) (*assertion*) Behauptung *f* ♦ **to make a ~** eine Behauptung aufstellen; **have you heard his ~?** haben Sie gehört, was er behauptet?; **the exaggerated ~s made for the new washing powder** die übertriebenen Eigenschaften, die man diesem neuen Waschpulver zuschreibt; **the book makes no ~ to be original** das Buch erhebt keinen Anspruch auf Originalität; **I make no ~ to be a genius** ich erhebe nicht den Anspruch, ein Genie zu sein.
(**c**) (*Min*) Claim *m* (*Anteil an einem Goldfeld etc*); *see* **stake**.

➤ LANGUAGE IN USE: **claim: 1b** → 17.1

♦**claim back** *vt sep* zurückfordern ♦ **to ~ sth ~ (as expenses)** sich (*dat*) etw zurückzahlen *or* -geben *or* -erstatten lassen.

claimant ['kleɪmənt] *n* (*for social security etc*) Antragsteller(in *f*) *m*; (*for inheritance etc*) Anspruchsteller(in *f*) *m* (*to* auf +*acc*); (*Jur*) Kläger(in *f*) *m* ♦ **a ~ to a title/throne** ein Titel-/Thronanwärter *m*, eine Titel-/Thronanwärterin.

claim form *n* Antragsformular *nt*.

clairvoyance [klɛə'vɔɪəns] *n* Hellsehen *nt*, Hellseherei *f* ♦ **thanks to the ~ of the management** dank der Hellsichtigkeit der Firmenleitung.

clairvoyant [klɛə'vɔɪənt] 1 *n* Hellseher(in *f*) *m*.
2 *adj* hellseherisch ♦ **I'm not ~** ich bin (doch) kein Hellseher!

clam [klæm] *n* Venusmuschel *f* ♦ **he shut up like a ~** aus ihm war kein Wort mehr herauszubekommen.

♦**clam up** *vi* (*inf*) keinen Piep (mehr) sagen (*inf*) ♦ **he ~med ~ on me** ich habe kein Wort mehr aus ihm herausgekriegt (*inf*).

clambake ['klæmbeɪk] *n* (*US*) Muschelessen *nt* am Strand; (*inf: party*) Fete *f* (*inf*).

clamber ['klæmbə^r] 1 *vi* klettern, kraxeln (*esp S Ger*) ♦ **to ~ up a hill** auf einen Berg klettern, einen Berg hinaufklettern; **the baby ~ed all over the sofa** das Baby krabbelte auf dem Sofa herum.
2 *n* Kletterei, Kraxelei (*esp S Ger*) *f*.

clamminess ['klæmɪnɪs] *n* Feuchtigkeit, Klammheit *f*.

clammy ['klæmɪ] *adj* (+*er*) feucht, klamm ♦ **a ~ handshake** ein feuchter Händedruck.

clamor *n* (*US*) *see* **clamour**.

clamorous ['klæmərəs] *adj* (*liter*) (**a**) *mob* lärmend. (**b**) *demands* lautstark.

clamour, (*US*) **clamor** ['klæmə^r] 1 *n* (**a**) (*noise*) Lärm *m*, Lärmen *nt* ♦ **the ~ of the battle** der Kampf- *or* Schlachtenlärm.
(**b**) (*demand*) lautstark erhobene Forderung (*for* nach) ♦ **a ~ against sth** ein Aufschrei *m* gegen etw; **continuous ~ against the EC** ständiges Geschrei gegen die EG.
2 *vi* **to ~ for/against sth** nach etw schreien/sich gegen etw empören; **the paper ~ed against the government** die Zeitung wetterte gegen die Regierung; **the men were ~ing to go home** die Männer forderten lautstark die Heimkehr.

clamp[1] [klæmp] 1 *n* Schraubzwinge *f*; (*Med, Elec*) Klemme *f*.
2 *vt* (ein)spannen.

♦**clamp down** 1 *vt sep* (*lit*) festmachen.
2 *vi* (*fig*) (*on expenses etc*) gewaltig bremsen (*inf*); (*police, government*) rigoros durchgreifen.

♦**clamp down on** *vi +prep obj person* an die Kandare nehmen; *expenditure, activities* einen Riegel vorschieben (+*dat*); *news broadcasts* unterdrücken ♦ **the government ~ed ~ ~ private radio stations** die Regierung holte zum Schlag gegen private Rundfunksender aus.

clamp[2] *n* (*Brit: of potatoes*) Miete *f*.

clamp-down ['klæmpdaʊn] *n* Schlag *m* (*on* gegen) ♦ **he ordered the ~ on the porn merchants** er hat dafür gesorgt, daß es den Pornohändlern an den Kragen ging (*inf*); **the ~ has made tax-evasion almost impossible** das harte Durchgreifen hat Steuerhinterziehung fast unmöglich gemacht.

clan [klæn] *n* (*lit, fig*) Clan *m*.

clandestine [klæn'destɪn] *adj* geheim; *meeting, society* Geheim-; *rendezvous* heimlich.

clang [klæŋ] 1 *n* Klappern *nt*; (*of hammer*) Hallen, Dröhnen *nt*; (*of swords*) Klirren *nt*.
2 *vi* klappern; (*hammer*) hallen, dröhnen; (*swords*) klirren.
3 *vt* mit etw klappern; *cymbal* schlagen; *bell* läuten.

clanger ['klæŋə^r] *n* (*Brit inf*) Fauxpas, Schnitzer (*inf*) *m* ♦ **to drop a ~** ins Fettnäpfchen treten (*inf*).

clangor ['klæŋgə^r] *n* (*US*) *see* **clangour**.

clangorous ['klæŋgərəs] *adj* (*liter*) hallend.

clangour ['klæŋgə^r] *n* Hallen *nt*; (*irritating*) Getöse *nt*.

clank ['klæŋk] 1 *n* Klirren *nt*.
2 *vt* klirren mit.
3 *vi* klirren.

clannish ['klænɪʃ] *adj group* klüngelhaft, verfilzt (*inf*); *person* cliquenbewußt ♦ **the office became unbearably ~** im Büro entwickelte sich eine unerträgliche Cliquenwirtschaft.

clansman ['klænzmən] *n, pl* **-men** [-mən] Clanmitglied *nt* ♦ **all the McTaggart clansmen** alle Mitglieder des Clans McTaggart.

clap[1] [klæp] *n* (*sl*) Tripper *m* ♦ **to pick up a dose of the ~** sich (*dat*) was *or* den Tripper (weg)holen (*sl*).

clap[2] 1 *n* Klatschen *nt no pl*; (*no pl: applause*) (Beifall)klatschen *nt* ♦ **a ~ of thunder** ein Donnerschlag *m*; **give him a ~!** klatscht ihm Beifall!, alle(s) klatschen!; **the audience gave him a big ~** das Publikum klatschte (ihm) begeistert Beifall; **a ~ on the back** ein Schlag *m* auf die Schulter.
2 *vt* (**a**) (*applaud*) Beifall klatschen (+*dat*).
(**b**) **to ~ one's hands** in die Hände klatschen; **to ~ sb on the back** jdm auf die Schulter klopfen.

(c) *(put quickly)* **he ~ped his hand over my mouth** er hielt mir den Mund zu; **to ~ sb into prison** jdn ins Gefängnis stecken; **to ~ eyes on sb/sth** *(inf)* jdn/ etw zu sehen kriegen *(inf)*.
[3] *vi* (Beifall) klatschen.

◆**clap on** *vt sep handcuffs* anlegen *(prep obj dat)* ◆ **to ~ ~ one's hat** sich *(dat)* den Hut aufstülpen; **to ~ ~ sail** *(Naut)* Beisegel setzen; **to ~ ~ the brakes** *(Aut)* auf die Bremse latschen *(inf)*.

◆**clap to** *vti always separate door* zuklappen.

clapboard ['klæpbɔːd] *n* Schindel *f*.

clapped-out ['klæptaʊt] *adj (inf)* klapprig ◆ **a ~ old car** ein klappriges Auto, eine alte Klapperkiste *(inf)*; **I feel really ~** ich bin total geschafft *(inf)*.

clapper ['klæpə^r] *n (of bell)* (Glocken)klöppel *m* ◆ **to go/drive/work like the ~s** *(Brit sl)* einen Affenzahn draufhaben *(sl)*.

clapping ['klæpɪŋ] *n* (Beifall)klatschen *nt*, Beifall *m*.

claptrap ['klæptræp] *n (inf)* Geschwafel *nt (inf)*.

claque [klæk] *n (Theat)* Claque *f*, Claqueure *pl*.

claret ['klærət] [1] *n* **(a)** *(wine)* roter Bordeauxwein. **(b)** *(colour)* Weinrot *nt*.
[2] *adj* weinrot.

clarification [ˌklærɪfɪ'keɪʃən] *n* **(a)** Klarstellung *f* ◆ **the whole issue needs a lot more ~** die Sache bedarf noch der Klärung; **I'd like a little ~ on this point** ich hätte diesen Punkt gerne näher erläutert; **in** *or* **as ~** zur Klarstellung. **(b)** *(of wine)* Klärungsprozeß *m*.

clarificatory [klærɪfɪ'keɪtərɪ] *adj* erklärend.

clarify ['klærɪfaɪ] [1] *vt* **(a)** klären, klarstellen; *text* erklären; *statement* näher erläutern ◆ **the matter has now clarified itself** die Sache hat sich jetzt geklärt. **(b)** *sugar, fat* raffinieren; *wine* klären.
[2] *vi (wine)* sich klären.

clarinet [ˌklærɪ'net] *n* Klarinette *f*.

clarinettist [ˌklærɪ'netɪst] *n* Klarinettist(in *f*) *m*.

clarion ['klærɪən] *n (liter)* Fanfare *f* ◆ **a ~ call for liberty/to duty** ein Ruf nach Freiheit/zur Pflicht.

clarity ['klærɪtɪ] *n* Klarheit *f*.

clash [klæʃ] [1] *vi* **(a)** *(armies, demonstrators)* zusammenstoßen ◆ **the chairman ~ed with the committee at the last meeting** der Vorsitzende hatte auf der letzten Sitzung eine Auseinandersetzung mit dem Komitee; **unions ~ with government** Konflikt zwischen Gewerkschaften und Regierung.
(b) *(colours)* nicht harmonieren, sich beißen; *(interests)* kollidieren, aufeinanderprallen; *(programmes, films)* sich überschneiden ◆ **our personalities** *or* **we ~ too much** wir passen einfach nicht zusammen.
(c) *(cymbals etc: also* **~ together**) aneinanderschlagen; *(swords)* klirrend aneinanderschlagen.
[2] *vt cymbals, swords* schlagen.
[3] *n* **(a)** *(of armies, demonstrators etc)* Zusammenstoß *m*; *(between people, parties)* Konflikt *m* ◆ **there's bound to be a ~ between the chairman and the vice-chairman** zwischen dem Vorsitzenden und seinem Stellvertreter muß es ja zu einem Zusammenstoß kommen.
(b) *(of personalities)* grundsätzliche Verschiedenheit, Unvereinbarkeit *f* ◆ **we want to avoid a ~ of personalities in the office** wir wollen keine Leute im Büro, die absolut nicht miteinander harmonieren; **it's such a ~ of personalities** sie sind charakterlich grundverschieden; **I don't like that ~ of red and turquoise** mir gefällt diese Zusammenstellung von Rot und Türkis nicht; **what a (horrible) ~!** was für eine (schreckliche) Zusammenstellung!; **a ~ of interests** eine Interessenkollision.
(c) *(of swords)* Aufeinanderprallen *nt*.

clasp [klɑːsp] [1] *n* **(a)** *(on brooch etc)* (Schnapp)verschluß *m*.
(b) *(with one's arms)* Umklammerung *f*; *(with hand)* Griff *m* ◆ **he had a firm ~ on the rope** er klammerte sich am Seil fest.
(c) *(Mil: of medals)* Ansteckabzeichen *nt*, Metallspange *f* auf dem Ordensband.
[2] *vt* **(a)** (er)greifen ◆ **to ~ sb's hand** jds Hand ergreifen; **to ~ one's hands (together)** die Hände falten; **with his hands ~ed in prayer** mit zum Gebet gefalteten Händen; **with his hands ~ed behind his back** mit auf dem Rücken verschränkten Händen; **to ~ sb in one's arms** jdn in die Arme nehmen *or* schließen; **they lay ~ed in each other's arms** sie lagen sich in den Armen; **to ~ sb to one's heart** jdn ans Herz drücken.
(b) *(to fasten with a ~)* befestigen, zuschnappen lassen ◆ **she ~ed the bracelet round her wrist** sie legte ihr Armband an.

clasp knife *n* Taschenmesser *nt*.

➤ **class** [klɑːs] [1] *n* **(a)** *(group, division)* Klasse *f* ◆ **what ~ are you travelling?** in welcher Klasse reisen Sie?; **he's not in the same ~ as his brother** sein Bruder ist eine Klasse besser; **they're just not in the same ~** man kann sie einfach nicht vergleichen; **in a ~ by himself/itself** weitaus der/das Beste.
(b) *(social rank)* gesellschaftliche Stellung, Stand *m (dated)*, Klasse *f (Sociol)* ◆ **the ruling ~** die herrschende Klasse, die Herrschenden *pl*; **considerations of ~** Standeserwägungen *(dated)*, Klassengesichtspunkte *pl*; **it was ~ not ability that determined who ...** (die gesellschaftliche) Herkunft und nicht die Fähigkeiten bestimmten, wer ...; **what ~ does he come from?** aus welcher Schicht *or* Klasse kommt er?; **are you ashamed of your ~?** schämst du dich deines Standes *(dated)* *or* deiner Herkunft?; **~ and educational background** Klassenzugehörigkeit und Erziehung; **a society riddled with prejudice and ~** eine von Vorurteilen und Standesdünkel beherrschte Gesellschaft; **we were talking about ~** wir sprachen über die gesellschaftlichen Klassen.
(c) *(Sch, Univ)* Klasse *f* ◆ **I don't like her ~es** ihr Unterricht gefällt mir nicht; **you should prepare each ~ in advance** du solltest dich auf jede (Unterrichts)stunde vorbereiten; **to give** *or* **take a Latin ~** Latein unterrichten *or* geben; *(Univ)* eine Lateinvorlesung halten; ein Lateinseminar *etc* abhalten; **the French ~** *(lesson)* die Französischstunde; *(people)* die Französischklasse; **an evening ~** ein Abendkurs *m*; **eating in ~** Essen während des Unterrichts; **the ~ of 1980** *(US)* der Jahrgang 1980, *die Schul-/Universitätsabgänger etc des Jahres 1980.*
(d) *(Bot, Zool)* Klasse *f*.
(e) *(Brit Univ: of degree)* Prädikat *nt* ◆ **a first-~ degree** ein Prädikatsexamen *nt*; **second-/third-~ degree** ≃ Prädikat Gut/Befriedigend.
(f) *(inf: quality, tone)* Stil *m* ◆ **to have ~** Stil haben, etwas hermachen *(inf)*; *(person)* Format haben; **that gives the place a bit of ~** das macht (doch) (et)was her *(inf)*; **I see we've got a bit of ~ in tonight, two guys in dinner jackets** heute abend haben wir ja vornehme *or* exklusive Gäste, zwei Typen im Smoking; **she's a real piece of ~** sie ist was Besseres *(inf)*.
[2] *adj (sl)* erstklassig, exklusiv.
[3] *vt* einordnen, klassifizieren ◆ **he was ~ed with the servants** er wurde genauso eingestuft wie die Diener.
[4] *vi* eingestuft werden, sich einordnen lassen.

class: ~ conscious *adj* standesbewußt, klassenbewußt; **~ consciousness** *n* Standesbewußtsein, Klassenbewußtsein *nt*; **~ distinction** *n* gesellschaftlicher Unterschied, Klassenunterschied *m*; **there is too much ~ distinction** die gesellschaftlichen Unterschiede/Klassenunterschiede sind zu groß; **~ feeling** *n (antagonism)* Klassenantagonismus *m (Sociol)*; *(solidarity)* Solidarität *f*, Klassenbewußtsein *nt*.

classic ['klæsɪk] [1] *adj (lit, fig)* klassisch ◆ **it was ~!** *(inf)* das war geradezu klassisch!
[2] *n* Klassiker *m*.

classical ['klæsɪkəl] *adj* klassisch; *(in the style of ~ architecture)* klassizistisch; *education* humanistisch; *method, solution also* altbewährt ◆ **the ~ world** die antike Welt; **a ~ scholar** ein Altphilologe *m*.

classicism ['klæsɪsɪzəm] *n* Klassik *f*; *(style of classic architecture)* Klassizismus *m*.

classicist ['klæsɪsɪst] *n* Altphilologe *m*/-philologin *f*.

classics ['klæsɪks] *n sing (Univ)* Altphilologie *f*.

classifiable ['klæsɪfaɪəbl] *adj* klassifizierbar.

classification [ˌklæsɪfɪ'keɪʃən] *n* Klassifizierung, Einteilung *f*.

classified ['klæsɪfaɪd] *adj* in Klassen *or* Gruppen eingeteilt ◆ **~ ad(vertisement)** Kleinanzeige *f*; **~ information** *(Mil)* Verschlußsache *f*; *(Pol)* Geheimsache *f*.

classify ['klæsɪfaɪ] *vt* **(a)** klassifizieren, (nach Klassen, Gruppen) ordnen. **(b)** *information* für geheim erklären.

classiness ['klɑːsɪnɪs] *n (inf)* Exklusivität *f*.

class: ~less *adj society* klassenlos; **~ list** *n (Brit Univ)* Benotungsliste *f*; **~mate** *n* Klassenkamerad(in *f*), Mitschüler(in *f*) *m*; **~ridden** *adj society* von Klassengegensätzen beherrscht; **~room** *n* Klassenzimmer *nt*; **~ society** *n* Klassengesellschaft *f*; **~ struggle** *n* Klassenkampf *m*; **~ war(fare)** *n* Klassenkrieg *m*.

classy ['klɑːsɪ] *adj (+er) (inf)* nobel *(inf)*, exklusiv ◆ **~ hotel** eine Nobelherberge *(inf)*; **a ~ woman** eine Klassefrau *(inf)*.

clatter ['klætə^r] [1] *n* Klappern, Geklapper *nt*; *(of hooves also)* Trappeln, Getrappel *nt* ◆ **her workbox fell with a ~ to the ground** mit lautem Klappern fiel der Nähkasten zu Boden.
[2] *vi* klappern; *(hooves also)* trappeln ◆ **the box of tools went ~ing down the stairs** der Werkzeugkasten polterte die Treppe hinunter; **the cart ~ed over the cobbles** der Wagen polterte *or* rumpelte über das Pflaster.
[3] *vt* klappern mit.

clause [klɔːz] *n* **(a)** *(Gram)* Satz *m*. **(b)** *(Jur etc)* Klausel *f*.

claustrophobia [ˌklɔːstrə'fəʊbɪə] *n* Klaustrophobie, Platzangst *(inf) f*.

claustrophobic [ˌklɔːstrə'fəʊbɪk] *adj* klaustrophob(isch) *(Psych)* ◆ **it's so ~ in here** hier kriegt man Platzangst *(inf)*; **I get this ~ feeling** ich kriege Platzangst *(inf)*; **a room of ~ proportions** ein Zimmer, in dem man Platzangst kriegt *(inf)*.

clave [kleɪv] *ptp of* **cleave**[2].

clavichord ['klævɪkɔːd] *n* Klavichord *nt*.

clavicle ['klævɪkl] *n* Schlüsselbein *nt*.

claw [klɔː] [1] *n* Kralle *f*; *(of lions, birds of prey also, of excavator)* Klaue *f*; *(of lobster etc)* Schere, Zange *f*; *(of hammer)* Nagelklaue *f* ◆ **to show one's ~s** die Krallen zeigen; **to get one's ~s into sb** *(inf)* (dauernd) auf jdm herumhacken; **once a woman like that has got her ~s into a man ...** wenn eine Frau wie die erst einmal einen Mann in den Klauen hat, ...
[2] *vt* kratzen ◆ **badly ~ed** schlimm zerkratzt; **the prisoners ~ed a tunnel through the earth** die Gefangenen gruben mit bloßen Händen einen Tunnel unter der Erde; **the mole ~s its way through the soil** der Maulwurf wühlt sich durch das Erdreich; **two women, like cats, ~ing each other** zwei Frauen, die wie Hyänen aufeinander losgingen; **he ~ed back the sheets** er riß die Laken weg.
[3] *vi* **to ~ at sth** sich an etw *(acc)* krallen; **he ~ed desperately for the handle** er krallte verzweifelt nach der Klinke.

◆**claw back** *vt sep (taxman etc)* sich *(dat)* zurückholen.

◆**claw out** *vt sep* auskratzen ◆ **to ~ ~ sth ~ of sth** etw mit der Tatze *or* *(excavator)* mit der Klaue aus etw herausholen.

claw: ~back *n (for individual)* Rückerstattung *f*; **from this sale the government got a £3m ~back** aus diesem Verkauf flossen 3 Millionen Pfund in die Staatskasse zurück; **~ hammer** *n* Tischlerhammer *m*; **~ mark** *n* Kratzer *m*.

clay [kleɪ] *n* Lehm *m* ◆ **potter's ~** Ton *m*.

clayey ['kleɪɪ] *adj* lehmig; *soil also* Lehm-.

➤ LANGUAGE IN USE: **class: 1a** → 5.2

claymore ['kleɪmɔːʳ] *n* zweischneidiges Langschwert.

clay: ~ pigeon *n* Tontaube *f*; **~ pigeon shooting** *n* Tontaubenschießen *nt*; **~ pipe** *n* Tonpfeife *f*.

clean [kliːn] [1] *adj* (+*er*) **(a)** (*not dirty, also bomb*) sauber ◆ **to wash/wipe/brush sth ~** etw abwaschen/-reiben/-bürsten; **to wipe a disk ~** (*Comput*) alle Daten von einer Diskette löschen; **she has very ~ habits, she's a very ~ person** sie ist sehr sauber.
(b) (*new, not used*) *sheets, paper* sauber, neu ◆ **I want to see a nice ~ plate** ich will einen schön leer gegessenen Teller sehen; **the vultures picked the carcass/bone ~** die Geier nagten den Kadaver bis aufs Skelett ab/nagten den Knochen ganz ab; **to make a ~ start** ganz von vorne anfangen; (*in life*) ein neues Leben anfangen.
(c) *joke* stubenrein; *film* anständig; (*Typ*) *proof* sauber ◆ **keep television ~** das Fernsehen muß sauber *or* anständig bleiben; **he's ~, no guns** (*inf*) alles in Ordnung, nicht bewaffnet.
(d) (*well-shaped*) *lines* klar.
(e) (*regular, even*) *cut, break* sauber, glatt.
(f) (*Sport*) *fight, match* sauber, fair; *boxer* fair.
(g) (*acceptable to religion*) rein.
(h) to make a ~ breast of sth etw gestehen, sich (*dat*) etw von der Seele reden; *see* **sweep**.
[2] *adv* glatt ◆ **I ~ forgot** das habe ich glatt(weg) vergessen (*inf*); **he got ~ away** er verschwand spurlos; **he got ~ away from the rest of the field** er ließ das übrige Feld weit hinter sich; **the ball/he went ~ through the window** der Ball flog glatt/er flog achtkantig durch das Fenster; **to cut ~ through sth** etw ganz durchschneiden/durchschlagen *etc*; **to come ~** (*inf*) auspacken (*inf*); **we're ~ out (of matches)** es sind keine (Streichhölzer) mehr da.
[3] *vt* saubermachen; (*with cloth also*) abwischen; *carpets also* reinigen; (*remove stains etc*) säubern; *clothes also* säubern (*form*); (*dry~*) reinigen; *nails, paint-brush, furniture also, dentures, old buildings* reinigen; *window, shoes* putzen, reinigen (*form*); *fish, wound* säubern; *chicken* ausnehmen; *vegetables* putzen; *apple, grapes etc* säubern (*form*); (*wash*) (ab)waschen; (*wipe*) abwischen; *cup, plate etc* säubern (*form*); (*wash*) spülen; (*wipe*) aus-/abwischen; *car* waschen, putzen ◆ **the cat is ~ing itself** die Katze putzt sich; **to ~ one's hands** (*wash*) sich (*dat*) die Hände waschen *or* (*wipe*) abwischen *or* (*scrape, with grease remover*) säubern; **to ~ one's teeth** sich (*dat*) die Zähne putzen *or* (*with toothpick*) säubern; **to ~ one's face** (*wash*) sich (*dat*) das Gesicht waschen *or* (*wipe*) abwischen; **~ the dirt off your face** wisch dir den Schmutz vom Gesicht!; **~ your shoes before you come inside** putz dir die Schuhe ab, bevor du reinkommst!; **to ~ a room** ein Zimmer saubermachen, in einem Zimmer putzen; **clothes which are easy to ~** pflegeleichte Kleider *pl*.
[4] *vi* reinigen ◆ **this paint ~s easily** diese Farbe läßt sich leicht reinigen; **brand X ~s better** die Marke X reinigt gründlicher.
[5] *n see vt* **to give sth a ~** etw saubermachen/reinigen/putzen *etc*; **your face/this house/the suit needs a good ~** du könntest dein Gesicht mal richtig waschen/das Haus/dieser Anzug müßte mal richtig gereinigt werden.

◆**clean down** *vt sep car, lorry* waschen; *walls* abwaschen.

◆**clean off** [1] *vt sep* (*wash*) abwaschen; (*rinse*) abspülen; (*wipe*) abwischen; (*scrape, rub*) abreiben; *dirt, barnacles, rust* entfernen, abmachen (*inf*).
[2] *vi* sich abwaschen *etc* lassen.

◆**clean out** *vt sep* **(a)** (*lit*) gründlich saubermachen; (*with water also*) ausspülen; *stables also* ausmisten; *carburettor* reinigen; *stomach* auspumpen *or* -räumen.
(b) (*inf: to leave penniless*) *person* ausnehmen (wie eine Weihnachtsgans) (*inf*); *bank* ausräumen (*inf*); (*gambling*) sprengen ◆ **to be ~ed ~** abgebrannt sein (*inf*).
(c) (*inf: take all stock*) **to ~ sb ~ of sth** jdm alles wegkaufen.

◆**clean up** [1] *vt sep* **(a)** saubermachen; *old building, old painting* reinigen; *mess* aufräumen ◆ **to ~ oneself ~** sich saubermachen.
(b) (*fig*) **the new mayor ~ed ~ the city** der neue Bürgermeister hat für Sauberkeit in der Stadt gesorgt; **to ~ ~ television** den Bildschirm (von Gewalt, Sex *etc*) säubern.
(c) (*sl: make money*) einstecken (*inf*), absahnen (*sl*).
[2] *vi* **(a)** (*lit*) aufräumen. **(b)** (*sl*) abkassieren (*inf*), absahnen (*sl*) ◆ **he certainly ~ed ~ on that sale** bei dem Verkauf hat er kräftig abgesahnt (*sl*).

clean-cut ['kliːnkʌt] *adj* klar, klar umrissen; *sort of person* gepflegt ◆ **the ~ lines of his new suit** der klare *or* einfache Schnitt seines neuen Anzuges; **~ features** klare Gesichtszüge *pl*.

cleaner ['kliːnəʳ] *n* **(a)** (*person*) Reinemachefrau *f*; Gebäudereiniger *m* (*form*) ◆ **a firm of office ~s** eine Büroreinigungsfirma; **the ~s come once a week** das Reinigungspersonal kommt einmal pro Woche.
(b) (*shop*) **~'s** Reinigung *f*; **to take sb to the ~'s** (*inf*) (*con, trick*) jdn übers Ohr hauen (*inf*), jdn reinlegen (*inf*); (*defeat easily*) jdn in die Pfanne hauen (*inf*).
(c) (*thing*) Reiniger *m*; *see* **vacuum ~**.
(d) (*substance*) Reiniger *m*, Reinigungsmittel *nt*.

cleaning ['kliːnɪŋ] *n* **the ladies who do the ~** die Frauen, die (hier) saubermachen; **~ fluid** Reinigungsflüssigkeit *f*; **~ lady** Reinemachefrau *f*.

clean-limbed ['kliːn'lɪmd] *adj* gutgebaut *attr*, gut gebaut *pred*.

cleanliness ['klenlɪnɪs] *n* Reinlichkeit *f* ◆ **~ is next to godliness** (*Prov*) Sauberkeit ist alles!

clean-living ['kliːn'lɪvɪŋ] *adj* anständig, sauber.

cleanly¹ ['kliːnlɪ] *adv* sauber ◆ **the bone broke ~** es war ein glatter Knochenbruch.

cleanly² ['klenlɪ] *adj* (+*er*) sauber; *person* reinlich.

cleanness ['kliːnnɪs] *n* **(a)** Sauberkeit *f*.
(b) (*of joke*) Anständigkeit, Stubenreinheit *f*; (*of film*) Anständigkeit *f*; (*Typ: of proof*) Sauberkeit *f*.
(c) (*of outline*) Klarheit *f*.
(d) (*of break etc*) Sauberkeit, Glätte *f* ◆ **thanks to the ~ of the break** weil es ein glatter Bruch war.

clean-out ['kliːnaʊt] *n* **to give sth a ~** etw saubermachen.

cleanse [klenz] *vt* reinigen; (*spiritually*) läutern (*of* von).

cleanser ['klenzəʳ] *n* (*detergent*) Reiniger *m*, Reinigungsmittel *nt*; (*for skin*) Reinigungscreme *f*; Reinigungsmilch *f*.

clean-shaven ['kliːn'ʃeɪvn] *adj* glattrasiert.

cleansing ['klenzɪŋ] *adj agent* Reinigungs- ◆ **~ cream** Reinigungscreme *f*; **~ department** Stadtreinigung *f*; **~ lotion** Reinigungslotion *f*.

clean-up ['kliːnʌp] *n* **(a)** (*of person*) **give yourself a good ~ before you come down to dinner** wasch dich erst einmal, bevor du zum Essen kommst; **to give sth a ~** etw saubermachen. **(b)** (*by police*) Säuberung *f*. **(c)** (*sl: profit*) Schnitt *m* (*sl*).

▼ **clear** [klɪəʳ] [1] *adj* (+*er*) **(a)** *water, soup, sky, head, weather etc* klar; *complexion* rein; *conscience* rein, gut *attr*; *photograph* scharf ◆ **on a ~ day** bei klarem Wetter.
(b) (*of sounds*) klar.
▼ **(c)** (*to one's understanding, distinct, obvious*) klar ◆ **to be ~ to sb** jdm klar sein; **it's still not ~ to me why** es ist mir immer noch nicht klar, warum, ich bin immer noch im unklaren (darüber), warum; **a ~ case of murder** ein klarer *or* eindeutiger Fall von Mord; **to have a ~ advantage** eindeutig *or* klar im Vorteil sein; **you weren't very ~** du hast dich nicht sehr klar ausgedrückt; **to make oneself** *or* **one's meaning ~** sich klar ausdrücken; **is that ~?** alles klar?; **do I make myself ~?** habe ich mich klar (genug) ausgedrückt?; **to make it ~ to sb that ...** es jdm (unmißverständlich) klarmachen, daß ...; **to make sth ~ to sb** (*explain*) jdm etw klarmachen; **I wish to make it ~ that ...** ich möchte einmal ganz klar sagen, daß ...; **let's get this ~, I'm the boss** eins wollen wir mal klarstellen — ich bin hier der Chef; **as ~ as day** sonnenklar; **as ~ as mud** (*inf*) klar wie Kloßbrühe (*inf*).
(d) to be ~ on sth über etw (*acc*) im klaren sein; **I'm not ~ on the implications** ich bin mir nicht sicher, was das impliziert.
(e) (*lit, fig: free of obstacles, danger etc*) *road, way* frei ◆ **I want to keep the weekend ~** ich möchte mir das Wochenende freihalten; **is it ~ now?** (*of road*) ist jetzt frei?; **there's not a single ~ space on his desk** auf seinem Schreibtisch ist überhaupt kein Platz; **there's a small patch of ~ ground between the houses** zwischen den Häusern ist ein kleines Stück Land frei; **all ~!** (alles) frei!; **is it all ~ now?** ist alles in Ordnung?, ist die Luft rein?; **to be ~ of sth** (*freed from*) von etw befreit sein; **at last we were/got ~ of the prison walls** endlich hatten wir die Gefängnismauern hinter uns; **I'll come when I get ~ of all this work** ich komme, wenn ich diese ganze Arbeit erledigt *or* hinter mir habe; **you're ~, said the customs officer** alles in Ordnung, sagte der Zollbeamte; **the plane climbed until it was ~ of the clouds** das Flugzeug stieg auf, bis es aus den Wolken heraus war; **the lion got ~ of the net** der Löwe konnte sich aus dem Netz befreien; **he's ~ of all suspicion** er ist frei von jedem Verdacht; **the car was ~ of the town** das Auto hatte die Stadt hinter sich gelassen; **~ of debts** schuldenfrei; **the screw should be 2 mm ~ of the wire** zwischen Schraube und Draht müssen 2 mm Zwischenraum sein; **the bottom of the door should be about 3 mm ~ of the floor** zwischen Tür und Fußboden müssen etwa 3 mm Luft sein; **hold the blow-lamp about 6 cm ~ of the paint** die Lötlampe in etwa 6 cm Abstand zum Lack halten; **park at least 20 cm ~ of the pavement** parken Sie wenigstens 20 cm vom Bürgersteig entfernt; **OK, keep going, you're ~ of the wall** in Ordnung, fahr, bis zur Mauer ist noch ein ganzes Stück Platz; **hold his head well ~ of the water** den Kopf gut über Wasser halten; **the mortars landed well ~ of us** die Mörser schlugen ein ganzes Stück neben uns ein.
(f) a ~ profit ein Reingewinn *m*; **three ~ days** drei volle Tage; **a ~ majority** eine klare Mehrheit; **to have a ~ lead** klar führen.
[2] *n* **(a)** (*of message*) **in ~** in/im Klartext.
(b) to be in the ~ nichts zu verbergen haben; **we're not in the ~ yet** (*not out of debt, difficulties*) wir sind noch nicht aus allem heraus; **this puts Harry in the ~** damit ist Harry entlastet.
[3] *adv* **(a)** *see* **loud**.
(b) he got ~ away er verschwand spurlos; **he kicked the ball ~ across the field** er schoß den Ball quer über das Spielfeld.
(c) to steer ~ of sth (*Naut*) um etw herumsteuern; **to steer** *or* **keep ~ of sb/sth/a place** jdm aus dem Wege gehen/etw meiden/um etw einen großen Bogen machen; **keep ~ of the whisky for a while** du solltest mal eine Zeitlang die Finger vom Whisky lassen; **you'd better keep ~ of that pub** um die Kneipe würde ich lieber einen großen Bogen machen; **keep ~ of Slobodia until the revolution's over** fahr nicht nach Slobodia, solange die Revolution nicht vorüber ist; **I prefer to keep ~ of town during the rush hour** während der Hauptverkehrszeit meide ich die Stadt nach Möglichkeit; **the public was asked to keep ~ of the area** die Öffentlichkeit wurde aufgefordert, dem Gebiet fernzubleiben; **exit, keep ~** Ausfahrt freihalten!; **dangerous chemicals, keep ~** Vorsicht, giftige Chemikalien!; **keep ~ of the testing area** Versuchsgebiet nicht betreten!; **personnel not wearing protective clothing must keep well ~ of the dump** Angestellte ohne Schutzkleidung dürfen sich nicht in unmittelbarer Nähe der Deponie aufhalten; **to stand ~** zurücktreten; zurückbleiben; **stand ~ of the doors!** bitte von den Türen zurücktreten!; **he kicked the ball ~** er klärte; **the helicopter lifted him ~** der Hubschrauber brachte ihn außer Gefahr; **he leapt ~ of the burning**

➤ LANGUAGE IN USE: **clear: 1c** → 26.1, 26.3

car er rettete sich durch einen Sprung aus dem brennenden Auto.

4 vt (a) *(remove obstacles etc from) pipe* reinigen; *blockage* beseitigen; *land, road, railway line, snow* räumen; *(Comput) screen* löschen; *one's conscience* erleichtern ♦ **to ~ the table** den Tisch abräumen; **to ~ the decks (for action)** *(lit)* das Schiff gefechtsklar machen; *(fig)* alles startklar machen; **to ~ a space for sth** für etw Platz schaffen; **to ~ sth of sth** etw von etw räumen; **he ~ed all the rubbish off his desk** er räumte den ganzen Kram von seinem Schreibtisch; **to ~ the way for sb/sth** den Weg für jdn/etw freimachen; **to ~ the streets of ice** das Eis auf den Straßen beseitigen; **~ the way!** Platz machen!, Platz da!; **to ~ a way through the crowd** sich *(dat)* einen Weg durch die Menge bahnen; **to ~ a room** *(of people)* ein Zimmer räumen; *(of things)* ein Zimmer ausräumen; **her singing ~ed the room in no time** ihr Gesang ließ die Leute fluchtartig den Raum verlassen; **to ~ the court** den Gerichtssaal räumen lassen; **to ~ the ground for further talks** den Boden für weitere Gespräche bereiten.

(b) *letterbox* leeren.

(c) *(free from guilt etc, Jur: find innocent) person* freisprechen; *one's/sb's name* reinwaschen ♦ **that ~s him** das beweist seine Unschuld; **he will easily ~ himself** er wird seine Unschuld leicht beweisen können.

(d) *(get past or over)* **he ~ed the bar easily** er übersprang die Latte mit Leichtigkeit; **the horse ~ed the gate by 10 cm/easily** das Pferd übersprang das Gatter mit 10 cm Zwischenraum /das Pferd nahm das Gatter mit Leichtigkeit; **the door should ~ the floor by 3 mm** zwischen Tür und Fußboden müssen 3 mm Luft sein; **raise the car till the wheel ~s the ground** das Auto anheben, bis das Rad den Boden nicht mehr berührt; **the ship's keel only just ~ed the reef** der Kiel des Schiffes kam an dem Riff nur um Haaresbreite vorbei.

(e) *(Med) blood* reinigen; *bowels* (ent)leeren ♦ **to ~ one's head** (wieder) einen klaren Kopf bekommen.

(f) *(Ftbl etc)* **to ~ the ball** klären.

(g) *(make profit of)* machen, rausholen *(inf)* ♦ **I didn't even ~ my expenses** ich habe nicht einmal meine Ausgaben wieder hereinbekommen.

(h) *debt* begleichen, zurückzahlen.

(i) *stock etc* räumen.

(j) *(pass, OK)* abfertigen; *ship* klarieren; *expenses, appointment* bestätigen; *goods* zollamtlich abfertigen ♦ **to ~ a cheque** bestätigen, daß ein Scheck gedeckt ist; *(enquire)* nachfragen, ob der Scheck gedeckt ist; **you'll have to ~ that with management** Sie müssen das mit der Firmenleitung regeln *or* abklären; **~ed by security** von den Sicherheitsbehörden für unbedenklich erklärt; **to ~ a plane for take-off** einem Flugzeug die Starterlaubnis erteilen, ein Flugzeug zum Start freigeben.

5 vi *(weather)* aufklaren, schön werden; *(mist, smoke)* sich legen, sich auflösen; *(crystal ball)* sich klären.

♦**clear away** 1 vt sep wegräumen; *dirty dishes also* abräumen.

2 vi (a) *(mist etc)* sich auflösen, sich legen. (b) *(to ~ ~ the table)* den Tisch abräumen.

♦**clear off** 1 vt sep *debts* begleichen, zurückzahlen; *(Comm) stock* räumen; *mortgage* abzahlen, abtragen; *arrears of work* aufarbeiten.

2 vi *(inf)* abhauen *(inf)*, verschwinden *(inf)*.

♦**clear out** 1 vt sep *cupboard, room* ausräumen; *unwanted objects also* entfernen ♦ **he ~ed everyone ~ of the room** er schickte alle aus dem Zimmer.

2 vi *(inf)* (a) verschwinden *(inf)*. (b) *(leave home etc)* sich absetzen *(inf)*.

♦**clear up** 1 vt sep (a) *point, matter* klären; *mystery, crime* aufklären, aufdecken; *doubts* beseitigen. (b) *(tidy)* aufräumen; *litter* wegräumen.

2 vi (a) *(weather)* (sich) aufklären; *(rain)* aufhören. (b) *(tidy up)* aufräumen.

clearance ['klɪərəns] n (a) *(act of clearing)* Entfernen *nt*, Beseitigung *f* ♦ **slum ~s** Slumsanierungen *or* -beseitigungen *pl*.

(b) *(free space)* Spielraum *m*; *(headroom)* lichte Höhe.

(c) *(Ftbl etc)* **a good ~ by the defender saved a nasty situation** der Verteidiger klärte gekonnt und rettete die Lage.

(d) *(of cheque)* Bestätigung *f* der Deckung.

(e) *(by customs)* Abfertigung *f*; *(by security)* Unbedenklichkeitserklärung *f*; *(document)* Unbedenklichkeitsbescheinigung *f* ♦ **get your security ~ first** Sie müssen erst noch von den Sicherheitsorganen für unbedenklich erklärt werden; **the despatch was sent to the Foreign Office for ~** der Bericht wurde zur Überprüfung ans Außenministerium geschickt; **~ to land** Landeerlaubnis *f*; **~ for take-off** Startfreigabe *f*.

(f) *(Naut)* Klarierung *f* ♦ **~ outwards** Ausklarierung *f*; **~ inwards** Einklarierung *f*.

clearance: ~ certificate n *(Naut)* Verzollungspapiere *pl*; **~ sale** n *(Comm)* Räumungsverkauf *m*.

clear-cut ['klɪə'kʌt] *adj decision* klar; *features* scharf.

clearing ['klɪərɪŋ] n *(in forest)* Lichtung *f*.

clearing: ~ bank n *(Brit)* Clearingbank *f*; **~ house** n Clearingstelle *f*.

▼ **clearly** ['klɪəlɪ] *adv* (a) *(distinctly)* klar ♦ **~ visible** klar *or* gut zu sehen; **to stand out ~ from the rest** sich deutlich vom übrigen hervorheben *or* abheben.

▼ (b) *(obviously)* eindeutig ♦ **is that so? — ~** ist das der Fall? — natürlich *or* selbstverständlich; **~ we cannot allow ...** wir können keinesfalls zulassen, ...; **this ~ can't be true** das muß eindeutig falsch sein, das kann auf keinen Fall stimmen.

clearness ['klɪənɪs] n (a) *see* **clear 1 (a)** Klarheit *f*; Reinheit *f*; Schärfe *f*. (b) *see* **clear 1 (b, c)** Klarheit *f*.

clear: ~-sighted *adj (fig)* klar- *or* scharfsichtig; **~-sightedness** n *(fig)* Klar- *or* Scharfsicht *f*; **~way** n *(Brit)* Straße *f* mit Halteverbot, Schnellstraße *f*.

cleat [kliːt] n *(on shoes)* Stoßplatte *f*; *(made of metal)* Absatzeisen *nt*; *(on gang-plank etc)* Querleiste *f*; *(for rope)* Klampe *f*.

cleavage ['kliːvɪdʒ] n (a) *(split)* Spalte, Kluft *(geh) f*; *(fig)* Spaltung, Kluft *f*. (b) *(of woman's breasts)* Dekolleté *nt*.

cleave[1] [kliːv] *pret* **clove** *or* **cleft** *or* **~d**, *ptp* **cleft** *or* **cloven** 1 vt spalten; **to ~ in two** in zwei Teile spalten; **to ~ a way through sth** sich *(dat)* einen Weg durch etw bahnen.

2 vi (a) **to ~ through the waves** die Wellen durchschneiden. (b) *(Biol)* sich spalten.

cleave[2] vi *pret* **~d** *or* **clave**, *ptp* **~d** *(adhere)* festhalten *(to* an *+dat)*, beharren *(to* auf *+dat)* ♦ **through all the difficulties they ~d fast to each other** *(liter)* durch alle Schwierigkeiten hindurch hielten sie fest zusammen.

cleaver ['kliːvəʳ] n Hackbeil *nt*.

clef [klef] n (Noten)schlüssel *m*.

cleft [kleft] 1 *pret, ptp of* **cleave[1]**.

2 *adj* gespalten ♦ **~ palate** Gaumenspalte *f*, Wolfsrachen *m*; **to be in a ~ stick** in der Klemme sitzen *(inf)*.

3 n Spalte, Kluft *(geh) f*; *(fig)* Spaltung, Kluft *f*.

clematis ['klemətɪs] n Waldrebe, Klematis *f*.

clemency ['klemənsɪ] n Milde *f (towards sb* jdm gegenüber*)* ♦ **the prisoner was shown ~** dem Gefangenen wurde eine milde Behandlung zuteil.

clement ['klemənt] *adj* mild *(towards sb* jdm gegenüber*)*.

clementine ['kleməntaɪn] n *(fruit)* Klementine *f*.

clench [klentʃ] vt (a) *fist* ballen; *teeth* zusammenbeißen; *(grasp firmly)* packen ♦ **to ~ sth between one's teeth** etw zwischen die Zähne klemmen; **to ~ sth in one's hands** etw mit den Händen umklammern; **~ed-fist salute** Arbeiterkampfgruß *m*. (b) *see* **clinch 1 (a)**.

Cleopatra [ˌkliːə'pætrə] n Kleopatra *f*.

clerestory ['klɪəstɔːrɪ] n *(Archit)* Lichtgaden *m*.

clergy ['klɜːdʒɪ] *npl* Klerus *m*, Geistlichkeit *f*, die Geistlichen *pl* ♦ **to join the ~** Geistlicher werden.

clergyman ['klɜːdʒɪmən] n, *pl* **-men** [-mən] Geistliche(r), Pfarrer *m*.

cleric ['klerɪk] n Geistliche(r) *m*.

clerical ['klerɪkəl] *adj* (a) *(Eccl)* geistlich ♦ **~ collar** Stehkragen *m (des Geistlichen)*, Priesterkragen *m*.

(b) **~ work/job** Schreib- *or* Büroarbeit *f*; **~ worker** Schreib- *or* Bürokraft *f*; **~ staff** Schreibkräfte *pl*, Büropersonal *nt*; **~ error** Versehen *nt*; *(in figures, wording etc)* Schreibfehler *m*; **~ duties** Büroarbeiten *pl*; **~ inaccuracies** Versehen *nt*, Nachlässigkeit *f*; **the ~ branch of the civil service** ≃ die mittlere Beamtenlaufbahn.

clericalism ['klerɪkəlɪzəm] n Klerikalismus *m*.

clerihew ['klerɪhjuː] n Clerihew *nt*, witziger Vierzeiler.

clerk [klɑːk, *(US)* klɜːrk] n (a) (Büro)angestellte(r) *mf*. (b) *(secretary)* Schriftführer(in *f*) *m* ♦ **C~ of the Court** *(Jur)* Protokollführer(in *f*) *m*; **~ of works** *(Brit)* Bauleiter(in *f*) *m*. (c) *(US: shop assistant)* Verkäufer(in *f*) *m*. (d) *(US: in hotel)* Hotelsekretär(in *f*) *m*.

clever ['klevəʳ] *adj* (a) *(mentally bright)* schlau; *animal also* klug ♦ **to be ~ at French** gut in Französisch sein; **how ~ of you to remember my birthday!** wie aufmerksam von dir, daß du an meinen Geburtstag gedacht hast!

(b) *(ingenious, skilful, witty)* klug; *person, move in chess also* geschickt; *idea also* schlau; *device, machine* raffiniert, geschickt ♦ **to be ~ at sth** Geschick zu etw haben, in etw *(dat)* geschickt sein; **to be ~ with one's hands** geschickte Hände haben; **~ Dick** *(inf)* Schlaumeier *(inf)*, Schlaukopf *(inf) m*.

(c) *(cunning, smart)* schlau, clever *(inf)*.

clever-clever ['klevə'klevəʳ] *adj (inf)* ausgeklügelt; *person* oberschlau *(inf)*.

cleverly ['klevəlɪ] *adv* geschickt; *(wittily)* schlau, klug ♦ **he very ~ remembered it** schlau wie er war, hat er es nicht vergessen.

cleverness ['klevənɪs] n *see adj* (a) Schlauheit *f*; Klugheit *f*. (b) Klugheit *f*; Geschicktheit *f*; Schlauheit *f*; Raffiniertheit *f*. (c) Schläue, Cleverness *f*.

clew [kluː] 1 n (a) *(thread)* Knäuel *nt*. (b) *(Naut: of sail)* Schothorn *nt*; *(of hammock)* Schlaufe *f*. (c) = **clue**.

2 vt (a) *thread* aufwickeln. (b) *(Naut)* **to ~ (up)** aufgeien.

cliché ['kliːʃeɪ] n Klischee *nt* ♦ **~-ridden** voller Klischees.

clichéd ['kliːʃeɪd] *adj* klischeehaft.

click [klɪk] 1 n Klicken *nt*; *(of joints)* Knacken *nt*; *(of light-switch)* Knipsen *nt*; *(of fingers)* Knipsen, Schnipsen *nt*; *(of latch, key in lock)* Schnappen *nt*; *(of tongue, Phon)* Schnalzen *nt* ♦ **he turned with a sharp ~ of his heels** er drehte sich um und klappte zackig die Hacken zusammen.

2 vi (a) *see n* klicken; knacken; knipsen; knipsen, schnipsen; schnappen; schnalzen; *(high heels)* klappern.

(b) *(inf: be understood)* funken *(inf)* ♦ **suddenly it all ~ed (into place)** plötzlich hatte es gefunkt *(inf)*.

(c) *(inf: get on well)* funken *(inf)* ♦ **they ~ed right from the moment they first met** zwischen ihnen hatte es vom ersten Augenblick an gefunkt *(inf)*; **some people you ~ with straight away** mit manchen Leuten versteht man sich auf Anhieb.

(d) *(inf: catch on)* ankommen *(inf) (with* bei*)*.

3 vt *heels* zusammenklappen; *fingers* schnippen mit; *tongue* schnalzen mit; *(Comput: mouse)* anklicken ♦ **to ~ a door shut** eine Tür zuklinken; **to ~ sth into place** etw einschnappen lassen.

♦**click on** vi (a) *(inf: understand)* es schnallen *(inf)* ♦ **he just didn't ~ ~** er hat es einfach nicht geschnallt *(inf)*. (b) *(Comput)* anklicken.

client ['klaɪənt] n (a) Kunde *m*, Kundin *f*; *(of solicitor)* Klient(in *f*) *m*; *(of barrister)* Mandant(in *f*) *m*. (b) *(US: receiving welfare)* Bezieher *m* ♦ **~ state** Schützling, Satellitenstaat *m*.

clientele [ˌkliːɑ̃ːn'tel] n Kundschaft, Klientel *f* ♦ **the regular ~** die

➤ LANGUAGE IN USE: **clearly: b → 15.1**

Stammkundschaft.

cliff [klɪf] *n* Klippe *f*; *(along coast also)* Kliff *nt*; *(inland also)* Felsen *m* ◆ **the ~s of Cornwall/Dover** die Kliffküste Cornwalls/die Felsen von Dover.

cliff: ~-dweller *n vorgeschichtlicher Höhlenbewohner im Colorado-Cañon*; **~hanger** *n* Superthriller *m* *(inf)*; **~-hanging** *adj conclusion* spannungsgeladen.

climacteric [klaɪ'mæktərɪk] *n (Med)* Klimakterium *nt*; *(fig)* (Lebens)wende *f*, Wendepunkt *m* (im Leben).

climactic [klaɪ'mæktɪk] *adj* **the conclusion was ~ in the extreme** der Schluß war ein absoluter Höhepunkt; **a ~ scene** ein Höhepunkt.

climate ['klaɪmɪt] *n (lit, fig)* Klima *nt* ◆ the **two countries have very different ~s** die beiden Länder haben (ein) sehr unterschiedliches Klima; **America has many different ~s** Amerika hat viele verschiedene Klimazonen; **to move to a warmer ~** in eine wärmere Gegend *or* in eine Gegend mit wärmerem Klima ziehen; **the ~ of popular opinion** die Stimmung in der Öffentlichkeit, das öffentliche Klima.

climatic [klaɪ'mætɪk] *adj* klimatisch, Klima-.

climatologist [,klaɪmə'tɒlədʒɪst] *n* Klimaforscher(in *f*) *m*.

climatology [,klaɪmə'tɒlədʒɪ] *n* Klimatologie, Klimakunde *f*.

climax ['klaɪmæks] *n (all senses)* Höhepunkt *m*; *(sexual also)* Orgasmus *m* ◆ **this brought matters to a ~** damit erreichte die Angelegenheit ihren Höhepunkt.

climb [klaɪm] [1] *vt* **(a)** *(also* **~ up)** klettern auf (*+acc*); *wall also, hill* steigen auf (*+acc*); *mountains also* besteigen; *ladder, steps* hoch- *or* hinaufsteigen; *pole, cliffs* hochklettern ◆ **my car can't ~ that hill** mein Auto schafft den Berg nicht *or* kommt den Berg nicht hoch; **to ~ a rope** an einem Seil hochklettern.
(b) *(also* **~ over)** *wall etc* steigen *or* klettern über (*+acc*).
[2] *vi* klettern; *(as mountaineer)* bergsteigen; *(into train, car etc)* steigen; *(road)* ansteigen; *(aircraft)* (auf)steigen; *(sun)* steigen; *(prices)* steigen, klettern *(inf)* ◆ **when the sun had ~ed to its highest point** als die Sonne am höchsten stand; **he ~ed to the top of his profession** er hat den Gipfel seiner beruflichen Laufbahn erklommen.
[3] *n* **(a)** *(climbing)* **we're going out for a ~** wir machen eine Kletter- *or* Bergtour; *(as mountaineers)* wir gehen bergsteigen; **that was some ~!** das war eine Kletterei!; **Ben Lomond is an easy ~** Ben Lomond ist leicht zu besteigen; **I've never done that ~** den habe ich noch nicht bestiegen.
(b) *(of aircraft)* Steigflug *m* ◆ **the plane went into a steep ~** das Flugzeug zog steil nach oben.

◆**climb down** [1] *vi* **(a)** *(lit)* *(person)* *(from tree, wall)* herunterklettern; *(from horse, mountain)* absteigen; *(from ladder)* heruntersteigen; *(road)* abfallen. **(b)** *(admit error)* nachgeben ◆ **it'll be a pleasure to make him ~ ~** es wird ein Vergnügen sein, ihn von seinem hohen Roß herunterzuholen.
[2] *vi +prep obj tree, wall* herunterklettern von; *ladder* heruntersteigen; *mountain etc* absteigen.

◆**climb in** *vi* einsteigen; *(with difficulty also)* hineinklettern.

◆**climb up** [1] *vi see* **climb 2**.
[2] *vi +prep obj ladder etc* hinaufsteigen; *tree, wall* hochklettern.

climbable ['klaɪməbl] *adj* besteigbar.

climb-down ['klaɪmdaʊn] *n (fig)* Abstieg *m* ◆ **it was quite a ~ for the boss to have to admit that he was wrong** der Chef mußte ziemlich zurückstecken und zugeben, daß er unrecht hatte.

climber ['klaɪmə^r] *n* **(a)** *(mountaineer)* Bergsteiger(in *f*) *m*; *(rock ~)* Kletterer(in *f*) *m*. **(b)** *(socially)* Aufsteiger *m*. **(c)** *(plant)* Kletterpflanze *f*.

climbing ['klaɪmɪŋ] [1] *adj* **(a)** *club* Berg(steiger)-; Kletter- ◆ **~ frame** Klettergerüst *nt*; **we are going on a ~ holiday** wir gehen im Urlaub zum Bergsteigen/Klettern; **~-irons** Steigeisen *pl*; **~ speed** *(Aviat)* Steiggeschwindigkeit *f*. **(b)** *plant* Kletter-.
[2] *n* Bergsteigen *nt*; *(rock ~)* Klettern *nt* ◆ **we did a lot of ~** wir sind viel geklettert.

clime [klaɪm] *n (old, liter)* Himmelsstrich *(old, liter)*, Landstrich *(geh)* *m* ◆ **in these ~s** in diesen Breiten; **he moved to warmer ~s** er zog in wärmere Breiten.

clinch [klɪntʃ] [1] *vt* **(a)** *(Tech: also* **clench)** *nail* krumm schlagen.
(b) *argument* zum Abschluß bringen ◆ **to ~ the deal** den Handel perfekt machen, den Handel besiegeln; **that ~es it** damit ist der Fall erledigt.
[2] *vi (Boxing)* in den Clinch gehen, clinchen.
[3] *n (Boxing, fig)* Clinch *m* ◆ **in a ~** im Clinch *(inf)*.

clincher ['klɪntʃə^r] *n (inf)* ausschlaggebendes Argument ◆ **that was the ~** das gab den Ausschlag.

cling¹ [klɪŋ] *pret, ptp* **clung** *vi (hold on tightly)* sich festklammern (*to* an *+dat*), sich klammern (*to* an *+acc*); *(to opinion also)* festhalten (*to* an *+dat*); *(remain close)* sich halten (*to* an *+acc*); *(clothes, fabric)* sich anschmiegen (*to dat*); *(smell)* haften (*to* an *+dat*), sich setzen (*to* in *+acc*) ◆ **~ on tight!** halt dich gut fest!; **the car clung to the road** das Auto lag sicher auf der Straße; **to ~ together** sich aneinanderklammern; *(lovers)* sich umschlingen, sich umschlungen halten; **in spite of all the difficulties they've clung together** trotz aller Schwierigkeiten haben sie zusammengehalten; **she clung around her father's neck** sie hing ihrem Vater am Hals; **the boat clung to the shoreline** das Schiff hielt sich dicht an die Küste; **women who ~** Frauen, die sich an einen klammern.

cling² [1] *n* Klingen *nt*; *(of cash register)* Klingeln *nt*.
[2] *vi* klingen; *(cash register)* klingeln.

clingfilm ['klɪŋfɪlm] *n* Frischhaltefolie *f*.

clinging ['klɪŋɪŋ] *adj garment* sich anschmiegend; *smell* lange haftend, hartnäckig ◆ **she's the ~ sort** sie ist wie eine Klette *(inf)*; **~ vine** *(inf)* Klette *f* *(inf)*.

cling(stone) peach ['klɪŋ(stəʊn)'piːtʃ] *n* Klingstone *m* *(nichtsteinlösende Pfirsichsorte)*.

clinic ['klɪnɪk] *n* **(a)** Klinik *f*. **(b)** *(medical course)* klinischer Unterricht, Klinik *f*.

clinical ['klɪnɪkəl] *adj* **(a)** *(Med)* klinisch ◆ **~ thermometer** Fieberthermometer *nt*. **(b)** *(fig)* *(sterile) room, atmosphere* steril, kalt; *(detached, dispassionate)* klinisch, nüchtern; *sb's appearance* streng.

clink¹ [klɪŋk] [1] *vt* klirren lassen; *(jingle)* klimpern mit ◆ **she ~ed a coin against the window** sie schlug mit einer Münze gegen die Scheibe, daß es klirrte; **to ~ glasses with sb** mit jdm anstoßen.
[2] *vi* klirren; *(jingle)* klimpern ◆ **the thermometer ~ed against the glass** das Thermometer stieß klirrend an das Glas.
[3] *n, no pl* Klirren *nt*; Klimpern *nt* ◆ **the ~ of glasses as they drank to his health** das Klingen der Gläser, als auf sein Wohl getrunken wurde.

clink² *n (sl: prison)* Knast *m (sl)* ◆ **in ~** im Knast.

clinker ['klɪŋkə^r] *n* **(a)** *(from fire)* Schlacke *f* ◆ **a ~** ein Stück Schlacke. **(b)** *(brick)* Klinker *m*.

clinker-built ['klɪŋkəbɪlt] *adj (Naut)* klinkergebaut.

clip¹ [klɪp] [1] *n* **(a)** *(for holding things)* Klammer *f*. **(b)** *(jewel)* Klips *m*. **(c)** *(of gun)* Ladestreifen *m*.
[2] *vt* **to ~ on** anklemmen; *(papers also)* anheften; **to ~ sth onto sth** etw an etw *(acc)* anklemmen/-heften; **to ~ two things together** zwei Dinge zusammenklemmen/-heften.
[3] *vi* **to ~ on**(**to sth** an etw *acc*) angeklemmt werden; **to ~ together** zusammengeklemmt werden.

clip² [1] *vt* **(a)** scheren; *dog also* trimmen; *hedge also, fingernails* schneiden; *wings* stutzen ◆ **to ~ sb's wings** *(fig)* jdm einen Dämpfer aufsetzen; **they'll find that the young baby will ~ their wings a bit** sie werden merken, daß das Kleinkind sie recht unbeweglich macht.
(b) *(also* **~ out)** *article from paper* ausschneiden; *(also* **~ off)** *hair* abschneiden ◆ **the bullet ~ped a few inches off the wall** die Kugel schlug ein paar Zentimeter aus der Mauer.
(c) *(Brit) ticket* lochen, knipsen, entwerten.
(d) to ~ (the ends of) one's words abgehackt sprechen.
(e) *(hit)* treffen; *(graze: car, bullet)* streifen ◆ **he ~ped him round the ear** er gab ihm eine Ohrfeige; **he ~ped his opponent on the jaw** er traf seinen Gegner am Unterkiefer; **the left jab just ~ped him on the chin** die linke Gerade streifte sein Kinn.
[2] *n* **(a)** *see vt (a)* Scheren *nt*; Trimmen *nt*; Schneiden *nt*; Stutzen *nt* ◆ **to give the sheep/hedge a ~** die Schafe scheren/die Hecke scheren *or* (be)schneiden; **to give one's fingernails a ~** sich *(dat)* die Fingernägel schneiden.
(b) *(sound)* Klappern *nt*.
(c) *(hit)* Schlag *m* ◆ **he gave him a ~ round the ears** er gab ihm eins hinter die Ohren *(inf)*.
(d) *(inf: high speed)* **at a fair ~** mit einem unheimlichen Zahn *(sl)*; **he made off at a fair ~** er legte ganz schön los *(inf)*.
(e) *(from film)* Ausschnitt, Clip *m*.

clip: ~board *n* Klemmbrett *nt*, Manuskripthalter *m*; **~ clop** *n* Klipp-Klapp *nt*; **~ joint** *n (sl)* Nepplokal *nt (inf)*; **~-on** *adj brooch* mit Klips; *tie* zum Anstecken; **~-on earrings** Clips *pl*.

clipped [klɪpt] *adj accent* abgehackt ◆ **~ form** Kurzform *f*.

clipper ['klɪpə^r] *n (Naut)* Klipper *m*; *(Aviat)* Clipper *m*.

clippers ['klɪpəz] *npl* *(also* **pair of ~)** Schere *f*; *(for hedge also)* Heckenschere *f*; *(for hair)* Haarschneidemaschine *f*; *(for fingernails)* Zwicker *m*, Nagelzange *f*.

clippie ['klɪpɪ] *n (Brit inf)* Schaffnerin *f*.

clipping ['klɪpɪŋ] *n* *(newspaper ~)* Ausschnitt *m* ◆ **nail ~s** abgeschnittene Nägel.

clique [kliːk] *n* Clique *f*, Klüngel *m (inf)*.

cliquish ['kliːkɪʃ] *adj* cliquenhaft, klüngelhaft *(inf)*.

cliquishness ['kliːkɪʃnɪs] *n* Cliquenwirtschaft *f*, Klüngel *m (inf)*.

clitoris ['klɪtərɪs] *n* Klitoris *f*, Kitzler *m*.

cloak [kləʊk] [1] *n (lit)* Umhang *m*; *(fig)* *(disguise)* Deckmantel *m*; *(veil: of secrecy etc)* Schleier *m* ◆ **under the ~ of darkness** im Schutz der Dunkelheit.
[2] *vt (fig)* verhüllen ◆ **fog ~ed the town** die Stadt war in Nebel gehüllt.

cloak: ~-and-dagger *adj* mysteriös, geheimnisumwittert; **~-and-dagger play** Kriminalstück *nt*; **a ~-and-dagger operation** eine Nacht-und-Nebel-Aktion; **~room** *n* **(a)** *(for coats)* Garderobe *f*; **(b)** *(Brit euph)* Waschraum *m* *(euph)*.

clobber ['klɒbə^r] *(sl)* [1] *n (Brit: clothes, belongings)* Klamotten *pl (sl)*.
[2] *vt* **(a)** *(hit, defeat)* **to get ~ed** eins übergebraten kriegen *(sl)*; **to ~ sb one** jdm ein paar vor den Latz knallen *(sl)*. **(b)** *(charge a lot)* schröpfen. **the taxman really ~ed me** das Finanzamt hat mir ganz schön was abgeknöpft *(inf)*.

clobbering ['klɒbərɪŋ] *n (sl)* *(beating, defeat)* Tracht *f* Prügel *(inf)*, Dresche *f* *(inf)* ◆ **to get a ~** Dresche *(inf)* *or* eine Tracht Prügel *(inf)* beziehen; *(from the taxman)* ganz schön geschröpft werden *or* was abgeknöpft kriegen *(inf)*.

cloche [klɒʃ] *n* **(a)** *(hat)* Topfhut *m*. **(b)** *(for plants)* Folien-/Glasschutz *m* ◆ **~ tunnel** Folientunnel *m*.

clock [klɒk] [1] *n* **(a)** Uhr *f* ◆ **round the ~** rund um die Uhr; **against the ~** *(Sport)* nach *or* auf Zeit; **to work against the ~** gegen die Uhr arbeiten; **to put the ~ back/forward** *or* **on** *(lit)* die Uhr zurückstellen/vorstellen; **to put** *or* **set** *or* **turn the ~ back** *(fig)* die Zeit zurückdrehen.
(b) *(inf)* *(speedometer, milometer)* Tacho *m (inf)*; *(of taxi)* Uhr *f* ◆ **it's got 100 on**

the ~ es hat einen Tachostand von 100.
[2] *vt* **(a)** *(Sport)* **he ~ed four minutes for the mile** er lief die Meile in vier Minuten; **he's ~ed the fastest time this year** er ist die schnellste Zeit dieses Jahres gelaufen/gefahren.
(b) *(Brit inf: hit)* **he ~ed him one** er hat ihm eine runtergehauen *(inf)*.
(c) *(Brit sl: see)* sehen.

◆**clock in** *vi (Sport)* **he ~ed ~ at 3 minutes 56 seconds** seine Zeit war 3 Minuten 56 Sekunden.

◆**clock in** *or* **on** [1] *vi* (den Arbeitsbeginn) stempeln *or* stechen.
[2] *vt sep* **to ~ sb ~** für jdn stempeln *or* stechen.

◆**clock off** *or* **out** [1] *vi* (das Arbeitsende) stempeln *or* stechen.
[2] *vt sep* **to ~ sb ~** für jdn stempeln *or* stechen.

◆**clock up** *vt sep* **(a)** *(athlete, competitor) time* laufen; fahren; schwimmen *etc*. **(b)** *speed, distance* fahren. **(c)** *(inf) success* verbuchen ◆ **that's another successful deal to ~ ~ to Jim** noch ein erfolgreiches Geschäft, das Jim für sich verbuchen kann; **to ~ ~ overtime** Überstunden machen.

clock *in cpds* Uhr(en)-; ~ **face** *n* Zifferblatt *nt*; ~ **golf** *n* Uhrengolf *nt*; ~ **maker** *n* Uhrmacher(in *f*) *m*; ~**-radio** *n* Radiouhr *f*; ~ **tower** *n* Uhrenturm *m*; ~**-watcher** *n* **she's a terrible ~-watcher** sie sieht *or* guckt dauernd auf die Uhr; ~**-watching** *n* Auf-die-Uhr-Schauen *nt*; ~**wise** *adj, adv* im Uhrzeigersinn; **in a ~wise direction** im Uhrzeigersinn; ~**work** [1] *n (of clock)* Uhrwerk *nt*; *(of toy)* Aufziehmechanismus *m*; **driven by ~work, ~work driven** zum Aufziehen; **like ~work** wie am Schnürchen; [2] *attr* **(a)** *train, car* aufziehbar, zum Aufziehen; **(b) with ~work precision/regularity** mit der Präzision/Regelmäßigkeit eines Uhrwerks; **he arrives every day at 9.30 with ~work regularity** er kommt jeden Tag pünktlich auf die Minute um 9^{30} Uhr.

clod [klɒd] *n* **(a)** *(of earth)* Klumpen *m*. **(b)** *(fig: person; also* **~pole***)* Trottel *m* ◆ **this silly great ~** dieser Obertrottel *(inf)*.

clodhopper ['klɒd,hɒpəʳ] *n (inf)* **(a)** *(person)* Trampel *nt (inf)*, Tolpatsch *m*. **(b)** *(shoe)* Quadratlatschen *m (inf)*.

clog [klɒg] [1] *n (shoe)* Holzschuh *m* ◆ **~s** *(modern)* Clogs *pl*; ~ **dance** Holzschuhtanz *m*.
[2] *vt (also* **~ up***) pipe, drain etc* verstopfen; *mechanism, wheels* blockieren ◆ **don't ~ your argument with inessential points** verlieren Sie sich nicht in Nebensächlichkeiten.
[3] *vi (also* **~ up***) (pipe etc)* verstopfen; *(mechanism etc)* blockiert werden.

cloggy ['klɒgɪ] *adj (inf)* klumpig.

cloister ['klɔɪstəʳ] [1] *n* **(a)** *(covered walk)* Kreuzgang *m*. **(b)** *(monastery)* Kloster *nt*.
[2] *vr* **to ~ oneself (away)** sich von der Welt abkapseln.

cloistered ['klɔɪstəd] *adj* **(a)** *(fig)* weltabgeschieden; *way of thinking* weltfremd *or* -fern *(liter)* ◆ **to lead a ~ life** *(isolated)* in klösterlicher Abgeschiedenheit leben; *(sheltered)* ein streng *or* klösterlich behütetes Leben führen.
(b) *(Archit)* **a ~ courtyard** ein Klosterhof *m* mit Kreuzgang.

clone [kləʊn] [1] *n* Klon *m*.
[2] *vt* klonen.

clonk [klɒŋk] *(inf)* [1] *vt* hauen.
[2] *n (blow)* Schlag *m*; *(sound)* Plumps *m*.

close¹ [kləʊs] [1] *adj (+er)* **(a)** *(near)* nahe *(to gen)*, in der Nähe *(to gen*, von) ◆ **is Glasgow ~ to Edinburgh?** liegt Glasgow in der Nähe von Edinburgh?; **the buildings which are ~ to the station** die Gebäude in der Nähe des Bahnhofs *or* in Bahnhofsnähe; **in ~ proximity** in unmittelbarer Nähe *(to gen)*; **in such ~ proximity (to one another)** so dicht zusammen; **you're very ~** *(in guessing etc)* du bist dicht dran; **~ combat** Nahkampf *m*; **at ~ quarters** aus unmittelbarer Nähe; **he chose the ~st cake** er nahm den Kuchen, der am nächsten lag; **we use this pub because it's ~/the ~st** wir gehen in dieses Lokal, weil es in der Nähe/am nächsten ist.
(b) *(in time)* nahe (bevorstehend) ◆ **nobody realized how ~ a nuclear war was** es war niemandem klar, wie nahe ein Atomkrieg bevorstand.
(c) *(fig) friend, co-operation, connection etc* eng; *relative* nahe; *resemblance* groß, stark ◆ **they were very ~ (to each other)** sie waren *or* standen sich *or* einander *(geh)* sehr nahe.
(d) *(not spread out) handwriting, print* eng; *texture, weave* dicht, fest; *grain* dicht, fein; *ranks* dicht, geschlossen; *(fig) argument* lückenlos, stichhaltig; *reasoning, (Sport) game* geschlossen ◆ **they played a very ~ game** sie spielten mit kurzen Pässen *or* geschlossen.
(e) *(exact, painstaking) examination, study* eingehend, genau; *translation* originalgetreu; *watch* streng, scharf; *arrest* scharf ◆ **now pay ~ attention to me** jetzt hör mir gut zu; **you have to pay very ~ attention to the traffic signs** du mußt genau auf die Verkehrszeichen achten; **to keep a ~ lookout for sb/sth** scharf nach jdm/etw Ausschau halten.
(f) *(stuffy)* schwül; *(inside)* stickig.
(g) *(almost equal) fight, result* knapp ◆ **a ~(-fought) match** ein (ganz) knappes Spiel; **a ~ finish** ein Kopf-an-Kopf-Rennen *nt*; **a ~ election** ein Kopf-an-Kopf-Rennen *nt*, eine Wahl mit knappem Ausgang; **it was a ~ thing** *or* **call** das war knapp!
(h) ~ on nahezu; **~ on sixty/midnight** an die sechzig/kurz vor Mitternacht.
[2] *adv (+er)* nahe; *(spatially also)* dicht ◆ **~ by** in der Nähe; **~ by us** in unserer Nähe; **stay ~ to me** bleib dicht bei mir; **~ to the water/ground** nahe *or* dicht am Wasser/Boden; **~ to** *or* **by the bridge** nahe (bei) der Brücke; **he followed ~ behind me** er ging dicht hinter mir; **don't stand too ~ to the fire** stell dich nicht zu nahe *or* dicht ans Feuer; **to be ~ to tears** den Tränen nahe sein; **~ together** dicht *or* nahe zusammen; **my exams were so ~ together** meine Prüfungen lagen so kurz hintereinander; **the ~r the exams came the more nervous he got** je näher die Prüfung rückte, desto nervöser wurde er; **that brought the two brothers ~r together** das brachte die beiden Brüder einander näher; **please stand ~r together** bitte rücken Sie näher *or* dichter zusammen; **this pattern comes ~/~st to the sort of thing we wanted** dieses Muster kommt dem, was wir uns vorgestellt haben, nahe/am nächsten; **what does it look like from ~ in/up?** wie sieht es von nahem aus?; **if you get too ~ up ...** wenn du zu nahe herangehst ...
[3] *n (in street names)* Hof *m*; *(of cathedral etc)* Domhof *m*; *(Scot: outside passage)* offener Hausflur.

close² [kləʊz] [1] *vt* **(a)** schließen; *eyes, door, shop, window, curtains also* zumachen; *(permanently) business, shop etc also* schließen; *factory* stillegen; *(block) opening etc* verschließen; *road* sperren ◆ **"~d"** „geschlossen"; **sorry, we're ~d** tut uns leid, wir haben geschlossen *or* zu; **don't ~ your mind to new ideas** du solltest dich neuen Ideen nicht verschließen; **to ~ one's eyes/ears to sth** sich einer Sache gegenüber blind/taub stellen; **to ~ ranks** *(Mil, fig)* die Reihen schließen.
(b) *(bring to an end) church service, meeting* schließen, beenden; *affair, discussion also* abschließen; *bank account etc* auflösen; *sale* abschließen ◆ **the matter is ~d** der Fall ist abgeschlossen.
(c) *(Elec) circuit* schließen.
[2] *vi* **(a)** *(shut, come together)* sich schließen; *(door, window, box, lid, eyes, wound also)* zugehen; *(can be shut)* schließen, zugehen; *(shop, factory)* schließen, zumachen; *(factory: permanently)* stillgelegt werden ◆ **his eyes ~d** die Augen fielen ihm zu; *(in death)* seine Augen schlossen sich.
(b) *(come to an end)* schließen; *(tourist season)* aufhören, enden, zu Ende gehen; *(Theat: play)* auslaufen.
(c) *(approach)* sich nähern, näherkommen; *(boxers etc)* aufeinander losgehen ◆ **the battleship ~d to 100 metres** das Kriegsschiff kam bis auf 100 Meter heran.
(d) *(Comm: accept offer)* abschließen, zu einem Abschluß kommen.
(e) *(St Ex)* schließen ◆ **the shares ~d at £5** die Aktien erreichten eine Schlußnotierung von £ 5.
[3] *n* Ende *nt*, Schluß *m* ◆ **to come to a ~** enden, aufhören, zu Ende gehen; **to draw to a ~** sich dem Ende nähern, dem Ende zugehen; **to draw** *or* **bring sth to a ~** etw beenden; **at/towards the ~ of (the) day** am/gegen Ende des Tages; **at the ~ (of business)** bei Geschäfts- *or (St Ex)* Börsenschluß.

◆**close about** *or* **around** *vi +prep obj* umschließen, sich schließen um ◆ **the waters ~d ~ the drowning man** die Wellen schlugen über dem Ertrinkenden zusammen.

◆**close down** [1] *vi* **(a)** *(business, shop etc)* schließen, zumachen *(inf)*; *(factory: permanently)* stillgelegt werden. **(b)** *(Rad, TV)* das Programm beenden ◆ **programmes ~ ~ at about 12** Sendeschluß (ist) gegen 24 Uhr; **we're now closing ~ for the night** (und) damit ist unser heutiges Programm beendet.
[2] *vt sep shop etc* schließen; *factory (permanently)* stillegen.

◆**close in** [1] *vi (evening, winter)* anbrechen; *(night, darkness)* hereinbrechen; *(days)* kürzer werden; *(enemy etc)* bedrohlich nahekommen ◆ **the troops ~d ~ around the enemy** die Truppen zogen sich um den Feind zusammen; **to ~ ~ on sb** *(gang, individual etc)* jdm auf den Leib rücken; **the walls were slowly closing ~ on him** die Wände kamen langsam auf ihn zu; **the police are closing ~ on him** die Polizei zieht das Netz um ihn zu; *(physically)* die Polizisten umzingeln ihn.
[2] *vt sep* umgeben, umfrieden *(geh)*.

◆**close off** *vt sep* abriegeln, (ab)sperren; *(separate off) area of office etc* abteilen, abtrennen.

◆**close on** *vi +prep obj* einholen.

◆**close round** *vi +prep obj see* **close about**.

◆**close up** [1] *vi* **(a)** *(line of people)* aufschließen, zusammenrücken; *(Mil)* aufschließen; *(wound)* (sich) schließen. **(b)** *(lock up)* ab- *or* zuschließen, ab- *or* zusperren.
[2] *vt sep* **(a)** *house, shop* zumachen; *house also* verschließen; *shop also* ab- *or* zuschließen, ab- *or* zusperren. **(b)** *(block up)* zumachen.

◆**close with** *vi +prep obj* **(a)** *enemy* zum Nahkampf übergehen mit; *boxer etc* ringen *or* kämpfen mit. **(b)** *(strike bargain with)* handelseinig sein *or* werden mit; *(accept) offer* eingehen auf.

close-cropped [,kləʊs'krɒpt] *adj hair* kurzgeschnitten.

closed [kləʊzd]: ~ **circuit** *n* geschlossener Stromkreis; **~-circuit television** *n* interne Fernsehanlage; *(for supervision)* Fernsehüberwachungsanlage *f*.

close-down ['kləʊzdaʊn] *n* **(a)** *(of shop, business etc)* (Geschäfts)schließung *f*; *(of factory)* Stillegung *f*. **(b)** *(Rad, TV)* Sendeschluß *m*.

closed [kləʊzd]: ~ **scholarship** *n* an eine bestimmte Schule gebundenes Stipendium; ~ **season** *n* Schonzeit *f*; ~ **session** *n (Jur)* Sitzung *f* unter Ausschluß der Öffentlichkeit; ~ **shop** *n* Closed Shop *m*; **we have a ~ shop** wir haben Gewerkschaftszwang.

close [kləʊs]: **~-fisted** *adj* geizig, knauserig *(inf)*; **~-fitting** *adj* enganliegend, eng sitzend; **~-grained** *adj* fein gemasert; **~-harmony singing** *n* Gesang *m* in geschlossener Harmonie; **~-harmony singers** *npl Vokalgruppe f, die im Barbershop-Stil singt*; **~-knit** *adj, comp* **~r-knit** *community* eng *or* fest zusammengewachsen.

closely ['kləʊslɪ] *adv* **(a)** eng, dicht; *work, connect* eng; *woven* fest; *related* nah(e), eng; *follow (in time)* dicht ◆ **he was ~ followed by a policeman** ein Polizist ging dicht hinter ihm; **she held the baby ~** sie drückte das Baby (fest) an sich; **~ reasoned** schlüssig dargestellt *or* -gelegt; **the match was ~ contested** der Spielausgang war hart umkämpft.
(b) *(attentively) watch, listen etc* genau; *study also* eingehend; *guard* scharf,

streng.

close-mouthed [ˌkləʊsˈmaʊðd] *adj* verschwiegen.

closeness [ˈkləʊsnɪs] *n* **(a)** *(nearness, in time)* Nähe *f* ◆ **she could feel his ~ to her** sie konnte seine Nähe fühlen.
(b) *(fig) (of friendship)* Innigkeit *f* ◆ **thanks to the ~ of their co-operation** ... dank ihrer engen Zusammenarbeit ...; **the ~ of their relationship/resemblance caused problems** ihre so enge Beziehung/ihre große Ähnlichkeit verursachte Probleme.
(c) *(fig: of reasoning)* Schlüssigkeit *f*; *(Sport: of game)* Geschlossenheit *f* ◆ **the ~ of the print/weave** die große Druck-/(Ge)webedichte; **the ~ of the grain** die feine Maserung.
(d) *(of examination, interrogation)* Genauigkeit *f*; *(of watch)* Strenge *f*; *(of translation)* Textnähe *or* -treue *f*.
(e) the ~ (of the air) die Schwüle; *(indoors)* die stickige Luft.
(f) *(of race etc)* knapper Ausgang ◆ **the ~ of the finish** der knappe Ausgang des Rennens.

close: ~-run *adj, comp* **~r-run** *race* mit knappem Ausgang; **it was a ~-run thing** es war eine knappe Sache; **~ season** *n* **(a)** *(Ftbl)* Saisonpause *f*; **(b)** *(Hunting, Fishing)* Schonzeit *f*; **~-set** *adj, comp* **~r-set** *eyes* eng zusammenstehend; *print* eng; **~-shaven** *adj* glattrasiert.

closet [ˈklɒzɪt] *(vb: pret, ptp* **~ed** [ˈklɒzɪtɪd]) 1 *n* **(a)** Wandschrank *m* ◆ **to come out of the ~** *(fig)* sich als Homosexueller bekennen; *(woman)* sich als Lesbierin bekennen. **(b)** *(dated: water-~)* Klosett *nt*. **(c)** *(old: small room)* Kabinett, Nebenzimmer *nt*.
2 *vt* **to be ~ed** hinter verschlossenen Türen sitzen *(with sb* mit jdm).
3 *adj attr (secret)* heimlich.

close-up [ˈkləʊsʌp] 1 *n* Nahaufnahme *f* ◆ **in ~** in Nahaufnahme; *(of face)* in Großaufnahme.
2 *attr shot, view* Nah- ◆ **lens** für Nahaufnahmen.

closing [ˈkləʊzɪŋ] 1 *n* Schließung *f*; *(of factory: permanently)* Stillegung *f*.
2 *adj* **(a)** *remarks, words etc* abschließend, Schluß-.
(b) ~ date *(for competition etc)* Einsendeschluß *m*; **~ time** Geschäfts- *or* Ladenschluß *m*; *(Brit) (in pub)* Polizei- *or* Sperrstunde *f*; **when is ~ time?** wann schließt die Bank/das Geschäft/der Laden/das Lokal *etc*?
(c) *(St Ex)* **~ prices** Schlußkurse, Schlußnotierungen *pl*.

closure [ˈkləʊʒəʳ] *n* **(a)** *(act of closing)* Schließung *f*; *(of road)* Sperrung *f*; *(of wound, incision)* Schließen *nt*; *(of factory, mine etc also)* Stillegung *f*.
(b) *(Parl)* Schluß *m* der Debatte ◆ **to move the ~** den Schluß der Debatte beantragen; **to apply the ~ to a debate** das Ende einer Debatte erklären.

clot [klɒt] 1 *n* **(a)** *(of blood)* (Blut)gerinnsel *nt*; *(of milk)* (Sahne)klumpen *m*.
(b) *(inf: person)* Trottel *m*.
2 *vt blood* zum Gerinnen bringen.
3 *vi (blood)* gerinnen; *(milk)* dick werden.

cloth [klɒθ] *n* **(a)** Tuch *nt*, Stoff *m*; *(as book-cover)* Leinen *nt* ◆ **a nice piece of ~** ein schöner Stoff, ein gutes Tuch; **~ of gold** goldenes Tuch.
(b) *(dish~, tea~ etc)* Tuch *nt*; *(for cleaning also)* Lappen *m*; *(table~)* Tischdecke *f*, Tischtuch *nt*.
(c) *no pl (Eccl)* **a gentleman of the ~** ein geistlicher Herr; **the ~** der geistliche Stand, die Geistlichkeit.

cloth: ~-bound *adj book* in Leinen (gebunden); **~ cap** *n* Schlägermütze *f*.

clothe [kləʊð] *pret, ptp* **clad** *(old) or* **~d** *vt* **(a)** *(usu pass: dress)* anziehen, kleiden ◆ **she appeared ~d in white** *(liter)* sie erschien (ganz) in Weiß. **(b)** *(provide clothes for)* anziehen. **(c)** *(fig liter)* kleiden *(liter)* ◆ **~d in glory** mit Ruhm bedeckt; **the hills ~d in mist** die nebelverhangenen Hügel.

cloth: ~-eared *adj (inf)* doof *(inf)*; **~-ears** *n sing (inf)* Doofmann *m (inf)*.

clothes [kləʊðz] *npl* **(a)** *(garments)* Kleider *pl*; *(clothing, outfit also)* Kleidung *f no pl* ◆ **his mother still washes his ~** seine Mutter macht ihm immer noch die Wäsche; **with one's ~ on/off** angezogen, (voll) bekleidet/ausgezogen; **you can't swim properly with your ~ on** mit *or* in Kleidern kann man nicht richtig schwimmen; **to put on/take off one's ~** sich an-/ausziehen.
(b) *(bed~)* Bettzeug *nt*.

clothes: ~ basket *n* Wäschekorb *m*; **~ brush** *n* Kleiderbürste *f*; **~ drier** *or* **dryer** *n* Wäschetrockner *m*; **~ hanger** *n* Kleiderbügel *m*; **~ horse** *n* Wäscheständer *m*; **she's a real ~ horse** *(US inf)* sie hat einen Kleiderfimmel *(inf)*; **~ line** *n* Wäscheleine *f*; **~ moth** *n* Kleidermotte *f*; **~ peg**, *(US)* **~ pin** *n* Wäscheklammer *f*; **~ pole** *or* **prop** *n* Wäschestütze *f*; **~ shop** *n* Bekleidungsgeschäft *nt*.

clothier [ˈkləʊðɪəʳ] *n (seller of clothes) (for men)* Herrenausstatter *m*; *(for women)* Modegeschäft *nt or* -salon *m*.

clothing [ˈkləʊðɪŋ] *n* Kleidung *f*.

clotted [ˈklɒtɪd] *adj* **hair ~ with mud** mit Schlamm verklebtes Haar; **~ cream** Sahne *f (aus erhitzter Milch)*.

clottish [ˈklɒtɪʃ] *adj (inf)* trottelig ◆ **a ~ thing to do** eine Eselei.

cloud [klaʊd] 1 *n* **(a)** Wolke *f* ◆ **low ~(s) delayed take-off** tiefhängende Wolken verzögerten den Start; **to have one's head in the ~s** in höheren Regionen schweben; *(momentarily)* geistesabwesend sein; **to be up in the ~s** *(inf)* überglücklich sein; **to be on ~ nine** *(inf)* im siebten Himmel sein *or* schweben *(inf)*; **every ~ has a silver lining** *(Prov)* kein Unglück ist so groß, es hat sein Glück im Schoß *(Prov)*.
(b) *(of smoke, dust etc)* Wolke *f*; *(of insects)* Schwarm, Haufen *m*; *(of gas, smoke from fire)* Schwaden *m* ◆ **~ of dust/smoke** Staub-/Rauchwolke *f*; **a ~ of controversy/confusion surrounded the whole matter** die ganze Angelegenheit wurde von Kontroversen überschattet/nebulöses Durcheinander herrschte in der ganzen Angelegenheit; **the ~ of suspicion hanging over him suddenly dispersed** der Verdacht, der über ihm schwebte, verflog plötzlich; **he's been under a ~ for weeks** *(under suspicion)* seit Wochen haftet ein Verdacht an ihm; *(in disgrace)* die Geschichte hängt ihm schon wochenlang nach; **the ~s are gathering** *(lit, fig)* es braut sich etwas zusammen.
(c) *(in liquid, marble)* Wolke *f* ◆ **her cold breath formed ~s/a ~ on the mirror** durch ihren kalten Atem beschlug der Spiegel.
2 *vt* **(a)** *(lit) sky, view* verhängen *(geh)*; *mirror* trüben ◆ **a ~ed sky** ein bewölkter Himmel.
(b) *(fig) (cast gloom on) prospect, sb's enjoyment* trüben; *face, expression* umwölken *(geh)*; *(mar, spoil) friendship, sb's future* überschatten; *(make less clear) mind, judgement, awareness* trüben; *nature of problem* verschleiern ◆ **to ~ the issue** *(complicate)* es unnötig kompliziert machen; *(hide deliberately)* die Angelegenheit verschleiern.
3 *vi see* **~ over**.

◆**cloud over** *vi (sky)* sich bewölken, sich bedecken; *(mirror etc)* (sich) beschlagen, anlaufen ◆ **his face ~ed ~** seine Stirn umwölkte sich *(geh)*.

◆**cloud up** 1 *vi (mirror etc)* beschlagen ◆ **it's ~ing ~** *(weather)* es bezieht sich.
2 *vt sep* **the steam ~ed ~ the windows** die Fenster beschlugen (vom Dampf).

cloud: ~ bank *n* Wolkenwand *f*; **~burst** *n* Wolkenbruch *m*; **~-capped** *adj (liter)* **the ~-capped mountains/peaks** die wolkenverhangenen Berge/Gipfel; **~ chamber** *n* Nebelkammer *f*; **~-cuckoo-land** *n* Wolkenkuckucksheim *nt*; **you're living in ~-cuckoo-land if you think** ... du lebst auf dem Mond, wenn du glaubst, ... *(inf)*.

cloudiness [ˈklaʊdɪnɪs] *n (of sky)* Bewölkung *f*; *(of liquid, diamond, glass, plastic etc)* Trübung *f*.

cloudless [ˈklaʊdlɪs] *adj sky* wolkenlos.

cloudy [ˈklaʊdɪ] *adj (+er)* **(a)** *sky* wolkig, bewölkt, bedeckt; *weather* grau ◆ **we had only three ~ days** wir hatten nur drei Tage, an denen es bewölkt war; **it's getting ~** es bewölkt sich; **the weather will be ~** es ist mit Bewölkung zu rechnen.
(b) *liquid, diamond, glass etc* trüb.

clout [klaʊt] 1 *n* **(a)** *(inf: blow)* Schlag *m* ◆ **to give sb/sth a ~** jdm eine runterhauen *(inf)*/auf etw *(acc)* schlagen *or* hauen *(inf)*; **to give sb a ~ round the ears/on the arm** jdm eine Ohrfeige geben/jdm eins *or* eine auf den Arm schlagen *or* hauen *(inf)*; **to give oneself a ~ on the knee, to give one's knee a ~** sich *(dat)* aufs Knie hauen *(inf)*; *(against door etc)* sich *(dat)* das Knie (an)stoßen *or* anschlagen.
(b) *(political, industrial)* Schlagkraft *f*.
2 *vt (inf)* schlagen, hauen *(inf)* ◆ **to ~ sb one** jdm eine runterhauen *(inf) or* eins verpassen *(inf)*.

clove[1] [kləʊv] *n* **(a)** Gewürznelke *f* ◆ **oil of ~s** Nelkenöl *nt*. **(b) ~ of garlic** Knoblauchzehe *f*.

clove[2] *pret of* **cleave**[1].

clove hitch *n* Webeleinstek *m*.

cloven [ˈkləʊvn] *ptp of* **cleave**[1].

cloven hoof *n* Huf *m* der Paarhufer *or* -zeher; *(of devil)* Pferdefuß *m* ◆ **pigs have ~ hooves** Schweine sind Paarzeher.

clover [ˈkləʊvəʳ] *n* Klee *m* ◆ **to be/live in ~** wie Gott in Frankreich leben; **~ leaf** *(Bot, Mot)* Kleeblatt *nt*.

clown [klaʊn] 1 *n (in circus etc)* Clown *m*; *(inf: foolish person also)* Kasper, Hanswurst *m*; *(pej)* Idiot, Trottel *m* ◆ **to act the ~** den Clown *or* Hanswurst spielen, herumkaspern *(inf)*.
2 *vi (also* **~ about** *or* **around)** herumblödeln *(inf) or* -kaspern *(inf)*.

cloy [klɔɪ] *vi (lit, fig)* zu süßlich sein/werden; *(pleasures)* an Reiz verlieren.

cloying [ˈklɔɪɪŋ] *adj (lit)* übermäßig süß ◆ **these ~ pleasures** diese Freuden, deren man so schnell überdrüssig wird.

cloze test [ˈkləʊzˌtest] *n* Worterganzungstest *m*.

club [klʌb] 1 *n* **(a)** *(weapon)* Knüppel, Prügel *m*, Keule *f*; *(golf ~)* Golfschläger *m*; *(Indian ~)* Keule *f*.
(b) *(Cards)* **~s** *pl* Kreuz *nt* ◆ **the ace/nine of ~s** (das) Kreuz-As/(die) Kreuz-Neun.
(c) *(society)* Klub, Verein *m*; *(tennis ~, golf ~, gentleman's ~, night~)* Klub, Club *m*; *(Ftbl)* Verein *m* ◆ **to be in the ~** *(inf)* in anderen Umständen sein *(inf)*, ein Kind kriegen *(inf)*; **to get** *or* **put sb in the ~** *(inf)* jdm ein Kind machen *(sl)*; **join the ~!** *(inf)* gratuliere! du auch!
2 *vt* einknüppeln auf (+*acc*), knüppeln.

◆**club together** *vi* zusammenlegen.

clubbable [ˈklʌbəbl] *adj* geeignet, in einen Klub aufgenommen zu werden; *(sociable)* gesellschaftsfähig.

club: ~ class *n (Aviat)* Club-Klasse, Businessklasse *f*; **~ foot** *n* Klumpfuß *m*; **~-footed** *adj* klumpfüßig; **~house** *n* Klubhaus *nt*; **~land** *n* Klubviertel *m*, *vornehmer Stadtteil, in dem sich besonders viele Klubs befinden*; **~man** *n* **he isn't much of a ~man** er interessiert sich nicht besonders für Klubs; **~ member** *n* Vereins- *or* Klubmitglied *nt*; **~ room** *n* Klubraum *nt*; **~ sandwich** *n* Club-Sandwich *nt*.

cluck [klʌk] 1 *vi* gackern; *(hen: to chicks)* glucken.
2 *n* Gackern *nt*; Glucken *nt*.

clue [kluː] *n* Anhaltspunkt, Hinweis *m*; *(in police search also: object)* Spur *f*; *(in crosswords)* Frage *f* ◆ **to find a/the ~ to sth** den Schlüssel zu etw finden; **I'll give you a ~** ich gebe dir einen Tip; **I haven't a ~!** (ich hab') keine Ahnung!

◆**clue up** *vt sep (inf) person* informieren ◆ **to get ~d ~ on** *or* **about sth** sich mit etw vertraut machen; **to be ~d ~ on** *or* **about sth** über etw *(acc)* im Bilde sein; *(about subject)* mit etw vertraut sein.

clueless [ˈkluːlɪs] *adj (inf)* ahnungslos, unbedarft *(inf)*; *expression, look* ratlos.

cluelessly [ˈkluːlɪslɪ] *adv (inf) see adj*.

clump [klʌmp] [1] *n* **(a)** (*of trees, flowers etc*) Gruppe *f*; (*of earth*) Klumpen *m* ◆ **a ~ of shrubs** ein Gebüsch *nt*. **(b)** (*inf: blow*) Schlag, Hieb *m*.
[2] *vt* (*inf: hit*) schlagen, hauen (*inf*).
[3] *vi* trampeln; (*with adv of place*) stapfen ◆ **to ~ about** herumtrampeln; (*in snow, mud etc*) herumstapfen.
clumsily ['klʌmzɪlɪ] *adv* **(a)** ungeschickt; (*in an ungainly way*) schwerfällig; *act* ungeschickt. **(b)** (*inelegantly*) *written, translated etc* schwerfällig, unbeholfen. **(c)** (*awkwardly, tactlessly*) ungeschickt, unbeholfen; *compliment also* plump.
clumsiness ['klʌmzɪnɪs] *n* **(a)** Ungeschicklichkeit, Schwerfälligkeit *f*. **(b)** (*of tool, shape*) Unförmigkeit *f*; (*of prose, translation etc*) Schwerfälligkeit, Unbeholfenheit *f*. **(c)** (*awkwardness of apology, excuse etc*) Unbeholfenheit *f*.
clumsy ['klʌmzɪ] *adj* (+*er*) **(a)** ungeschickt; (*all thumbs also*) tolpatschig; (*ungainly*) schwerfällig.
(b) (*unwieldy*) plump; *tool also* wuchtig, klobig; *shape also* unförmig, klobig; (*inelegant*) *prose, translation etc* schwerfällig, unbeholfen; (*careless*) *mistake* dumm.
(c) (*awkward, tactless*) plump, ungeschickt.
clung [klʌŋ] *pret, ptp of* **cling**[1].
clunk [klʌŋk] [1] *n* dumpfes Geräusch.
[2] *vi* **the door ~ed into place** die Tür schloß sich mit einem dumpfen Geräusch.
clunker ['klʌŋkəʳ] *n* (*US pej: car*) Kiste (*pej inf*), Mühle (*pej inf*) *f*.
cluster ['klʌstəʳ] [1] *n* (*of trees, flowers, houses*) Gruppe *f*, Haufen *m*; (*of curls, bananas*) Büschel *nt*; (*of bees, people, grapes*) Traube *f*; (*of islands*) Gruppe *f*; (*of diamonds*) Büschel *nt*; (*Phon*) Häufung *f* ◆ **the flowers grow in a ~ at the top of the stem** die Blumen sitzen *or* wachsen doldenförmig am Stengel; (*of roses etc*) mehrere Blüten wachsen am gleichen Stiel; **~ bomb** Splitterbombe *f*.
[2] *vi* (*people*) sich drängen *or* scharen ◆ **they all ~ed round to see what he was doing** alle drängten *or* scharten sich um ihn, um zu sehen, was er tat.
clutch[1] [klʌtʃ] [1] *n* **(a)** (*grip*) Griff *m* ◆ **he made a sudden ~ at the rope** er griff plötzlich nach dem Seil.
(b) (*Aut*) Kupplung *f* ◆ **to let in/out the ~** ein-/auskuppeln; **~ pedal** Kupplungspedal *nt*.
(c) (*fig*) **to fall into sb's ~es** jdm in die Hände fallen, jdm ins Netz gehen; **to be in sb's ~es** in jds Gewalt (*dat*) sein; **to have sb in one's ~es** jdn im Netz *or* in den Klauen haben; **he escaped her ~es** er entkam ihren Klauen.
[2] *vt* (*grab*) umklammern, packen; (*hold tightly*) umklammert halten ◆ **to ~ sth in one's hand** etw umklammern.
◆**clutch at** *vi +prep obj* (*lit*) schnappen nach (+*dat*), greifen; (*hold tightly*) umklammert halten; (*fig*) sich klammern an (+*acc*); *see* **straw**.
clutch[2] *n* (*of chickens*) Brut *f*; (*of eggs*) Gelege *nt*.
clutch bag *n* Unterarmtasche *f*.
clutter ['klʌtəʳ] [1] *n* (*confusion*) Durcheinander *nt*; (*disorderly articles*) Kram *m* (*inf*) ◆ **his desk was in a ~** auf seinem Schreibtisch war ein fürchterliches Durcheinander; **his essay was a ~ of unrelated details** sein Aufsatz war ein Sammelsurium *or* Wirrwarr von zusammenhangslosen Einzelheiten.
[2] *vt* (*also* **~ up**) zu voll machen (*inf*)/stellen; *painting, photograph* überladen; *mind* vollstopfen ◆ **to be ~ed with sth** (*mind, room, drawer etc*) mit etw vollgestopft sein; (*floor, desk etc*) mit etw übersät sein; (*painting etc*) mit etw überladen sein; **the floor/his desk was absolutely ~ed** auf dem Fußboden lag alles verstreut/sein Schreibtisch war ganz voll.
cm *abbr of* **centimetre** cm.
Cmdr *abbr of* **Commander.**
CNAA *abbr of* **Council for National Academic Awards.**
CND *abbr of* **Campaign for Nuclear Disarmament.**
Co *abbr of* **(a) company** KG *f*. **(b) county.**
CO *abbr of* **Commanding Officer.**
c/o *abbr of* **(a) care of** bei, c/o. **(b) carried over** Übertr.
co- [kəʊ-] *pref* Mit-, mit-.
coach [kəʊtʃ] [1] *n* **(a)** (*horsedrawn*) Kutsche *f*; (*state ~*) (Staats)karosse *f* ◆ **~ and four** Vierspänner *m*.
(b) (*Rail*) (Eisenbahn)wagen, Waggon *m*.
(c) (*Brit: motor ~*) (Reise)bus *m* ◆ **by ~** mit dem Bus; **~ travel/journeys** Busreisen *pl*; **~ driver** Busfahrer *m*.
(d) (*tutor*) Nachhilfelehrer(in *f*) *m*; (*Sport*) Trainer *m*.
[2] *vt* **(a)** (*Sport*) trainieren. **(b) to ~ sb for an exam** jdn aufs Examen vorbereiten; **he had been ~ed in what to say** man hatte mit ihm eingeübt, was er sagen sollte.
coach: ~ box *n* (Kutsch)bock *m*; **~builder** *n* (*Brit*) Karosseriebauer *m*; **~building** *n* (*Brit*) Karosseriebau *m*; **~-house** *n* (*old*) Remise *f*.
coaching ['kəʊtʃɪŋ] *n* (*Sport*) Trainerstunden *pl*; (*Tennis*) Training *nt*; (*tutoring*) Nachhilfe *f*.
coach: ~load *n* (*Brit*) *see* **busload**; **~man** *n* Kutscher *m*; **~ party** *n* (*Brit*) Busreisegruppe *f*; **~ station** *n* (*Brit*) Busbahnhof *m*; **~ trip** *n* (*Brit*) Busfahrt *f*; **~work** *n* (*Brit*) Karosserie *f*.
coagulate [kəʊ'ægjʊleɪt] [1] *vi* (*blood*) gerinnen, koagulieren (*spec*); (*milk*) dick werden; (*jelly*) fest werden; (*paint*) zähflüssig werden, eindicken.
[2] *vt blood* gerinnen lassen; *milk* dick werden lassen; *jelly* fest werden lassen.
coagulation [kəʊˌægjʊ'leɪʃən] *n see vb* Gerinnen *nt*, Gerinnung, Koagulation (*spec*) *f*; Dickwerden *nt*; Festwerden *nt*; Eindicken *nt*.
coal [kəʊl] *n* Kohle *f* ◆ **we still burn ~** wir heizen noch mit Kohle; **to carry ~s to Newcastle** (*Prov*) Eulen nach Athen tragen (*Prov*); **to haul sb over the ~s** jdm eine Standpauke halten, jdm die Leviten lesen; **to heap ~s of fire on sb's head** feurige Kohlen auf jds Haupt (*dat*) sammeln.
coal *in cpds* Kohlen-; **~-bin, ~-bunker** *n* Kohlenkasten *m*; **~ black** *adj* kohlrabenschwarz; **~-cellar** *n* Kohlenkeller *m*; **~-dust** *n* Kohlenstaub, (Kohlen)grus *m*.
coalesce [ˌkəʊə'les] *vi* (*Phys, Chem*) sich verbinden, eine Verbindung eingehen; (*fig*) sich vereinigen, zusammengehen; (*views, opinions etc*) sich verquicken (*geh*).
coalescence [ˌkəʊə'lesəns] *n see vi* Verbindung *f*; Vereinigung *f*; Verquickung *f* (*geh*).
coal: ~-face *n* Streb *m*; **men who work at** *or* **on the ~-face** Männer, die im Streb *or* vor Ort arbeiten; **~field** *n* Kohlenrevier *nt*; **~ fire** *n* Kamin *m*; **a ~ fire heats better** ein Kohlenfeuer wärmt besser; **~-fired** *adj* Kohle(n)-; **~-fired power station** Kohlekraftwerk *nt*; **~ hod** *n* Kohleneimer *m*; **~-hole** *n* Kohlenbunker *m*.
coalition [ˌkəʊə'lɪʃən] *n* Koalition *f* ◆ **~ government** Koalitionsregierung *f*.
coal: ~man *n* Kohlenmann *m*; **~-merchant** *n* Kohlenhändler *m*; **~-mine** *n* Grube, Zeche *f*, Kohlenbergwerk *nt*; **~-miner** *n* Bergmann, Kumpel (*inf*) *m*; **~-mining** *n* Kohle(n)bergbau *m*; **~-mining area** *n* Kohlenrevier *nt*; **the ~-mining industry** der Kohle(n)bergbau; **~-pit** *n see* **~-mine**; **~ scuttle** *n* Kohleneimer, Kohlenkasten *m*; **~shed** *n* Kohlenschuppen *m*; **~ strike** *n* Bergarbeiterstreik *m*; **~ tar** *n* Kohlenteer *m*; **~ tar soap** *n* Teerseife *f*; **~ tit** *n* (*Orn*) Tannenmeise *f*; **~ yard** *n* Kohlenhof *m*.
coarse [kɔːs] *adj* (+*er*) **(a)** (*in texture, not delicate*) grob; *sand, sugar also* grobkörnig; *features also* derb ◆ **~-grained** grobfaserig; **~-grained fibre** grobe Faser; **~-grained paper** ungeleimtes Papier, Zeitungspapier *nt*.
(b) (*uncouth*) gewöhnlich; *person, manners also* grob, ungehobelt, ungeschliffen; *laugh also* rauh, derb; *joke also* derb, unanständig.
(c) (*common*) *food* derb, einfach ◆ **~ red wine** einfacher (Land)rotwein; **~ fish** Süßwasserfisch *m* (*mit Ausnahme aller Lachs- und Forellenarten*); **~ fishing** Angeln *nt* von Süßwasserfischen.
coarsely ['kɔːslɪ] *adv see adj* (*a, b*).
coarsen ['kɔːsn] [1] *vt person* derber machen; *skin* gerben.
[2] *vi* (*person*) derber werden; (*skin*) gröber werden.
coarseness ['kɔːsnɪs] *n* **(a)** (*of texture*) Grobheit *f*.
(b) (*fig*) *see adj* (*b, c*) Gewöhnlichkeit *f*; Grobheit, Ungeschliffenheit *f*; Derbheit *f*; Unanständigkeit *f*; Einfachheit *f* ◆ **the ~ of his laugh** sein rauhes Lachen.
coast [kəʊst] [1] *n* Küste *f*, Gestade *nt* (*poet*) ◆ **at/on the ~** an der Küste/am Meer; **we're going to the ~** wir fahren an die Küste *or* ans Meer; **the ~ is clear** (*fig*) die Luft ist rein.
[2] *vi* **(a)** (*car, cyclist*) (*in neutral*) (im Leerlauf) fahren; (*cruise effortlessly*) dahinrollen; (*athlete*) locker laufen; (*US: on sled*) hinunterrodeln. **(b)** (*fig*) **to be ~ing along** mühelos *or* spielend vorankommen; **he was just ~ing up to the exam** er steuerte ohne große Mühe aufs Examen zu.
coastal ['kəʊstəl] *adj* Küsten- ◆ **~ traffic** Küstenschiffahrt *f*.
coaster ['kəʊstəʳ] *n* **(a)** (*Naut*) Küstenmotorschiff *nt*. **(b)** (*drip mat*) Untersetzer *m*. **(c)** (*US*) (*sled*) (Rodel)schlitten *m*; (*roller-~*) Achterbahn, Berg- und Talbahn *f*. **(d)** (*US*) **~ brake** Rücktrittbremse *f*.
coast: ~guard *n* Küstenwache *f*; **the ~guards** die Küstenwacht; **~guard boat/station** Küstenwachtboot *nt*/-posten *m*; **~line** *n* Küste *f*.
coat [kəʊt] [1] *n* **(a)** (*outdoor wear*) Mantel *m*; (*doctor's ~ etc also*) (Arzt)kittel *m*; (*jacket of suit etc*) Jacke *f*; (*for men also*) Jackett *nt* ◆ **~ and skirt** Kostüm *nt*.
(b) (*Her*) **~ of arms** Wappen *nt*.
(c) ~ of mail Panzerhemd *nt*; (*of chainmail*) Kettenhemd *nt*.
(d) (*of animal*) Fell *nt*.
(e) (*of paint, tar etc*) (*application*) Anstrich *m*; (*actual layer*) Schicht *f* ◆ **a thick ~ of fur on his tongue** ein dicker pelziger Belag auf seiner Zunge; **give it a second ~** streich es noch einmal.
[2] *vt* (*with paint etc*) streichen; (*with chocolate, icing etc*) überziehen ◆ **to be ~ed with rust/dust/mud** mit einer Rost-/Staub-/Schmutzschicht überzogen sein, eine Rost-/Staub-/Schmutzschicht haben; **my hands were ~ed with grease/flour** meine Hände waren voller Schmiere/Mehl; **his tongue was ~ed** seine Zunge war belegt; **~ed paper** gestrichenes Papier; **the chassis was ~ed with an anti-rust preparation** das Chassis war mit einem Rostschutzmittel beschichtet *or* (*sprayed*) gespritzt.
coat-hanger ['kəʊtˌhæŋəʳ] *n* Kleiderbügel *m*.
coating ['kəʊtɪŋ] *n* Überzug *m*, Schicht *f*; (*of paint*) Anstrich *m*.
coat: ~less *adj* ohne Mantel; **~stand** *n* Garderobenständer *m*; **~-tails** *npl* Rockschöße *pl*.
co-author ['kəʊˌɔːθəʳ] *n* Mitautor, Mitverfasser *m* ◆ **they were ~s of the book** sie haben das Buch gemeinsam geschrieben.
coax [kəʊks] *vt* überreden ◆ **to ~ sb into doing sth** jdn beschwatzen (*inf*) *or* dazu bringen, etw zu tun; **he ~ed the engine into life** er brachte den Motor mit List und Tücke in Gang; **you have to ~ the fire** du mußt dem Feuer ein bißchen nachhelfen; **to ~ sth out of sb** jdm etw entlocken.
coaxing ['kəʊksɪŋ] [1] *n* gutes Zureden, Zuspruch *m* ◆ **with a little ~ the engine/fire started** mit etwas List und Tücke kam der Motor/das Feuer in Gang.
[2] *adj* einschmeichelnd.
coaxingly ['kəʊksɪŋlɪ] *adv* **to speak/ask ~** mit einschmeichelnder Stimme reden/fragen; **however ~ she spoke to him** ... so sehr sie auch versuchte, ihn zu überreden ...
cob [kɒb] *n* **(a)** (*horse*) *kleines, gedrungenes Pferd*. **(b)** (*swan*) (männlicher) Schwan. **(c)** (*also* **~-nut**) (große) Haselnuß. **(d)** (*corn*) (Mais)kolben *m*; (*bread*) rundes Brot ◆ **corn on the ~** Maiskolben *m*; **a ~ of coal** ein Stück Eier- *or* Nußkohle.
cobalt ['kəʊbɒlt] *n* Kobalt *nt* ◆ **~ blue** kobaltblau.

cobber ['kɒbəʳ] *n (Austral inf)* Kumpel *m (inf)*.
cobble ['kɒbl] 1 *n (also* **~stone***)* Kopfstein *m*.
2 *vt* **(a)** *shoe* flicken. **(b) a ~d street** eine Straße mit Kopfsteinpflaster.
◆**cobble together** *vt sep (inf) essay etc* zusammenschustern.
cobbler ['kɒbləʳ] *n* **(a)** Schuster, Flickschuster *m*. **(b)** *(esp US: fruit pie) Obst mit Teig überbacken*; *(drink)* Cobbler *m*.
cobblers ['kɒbləz] *npl (Brit sl: rubbish)* Scheiße *f (sl)*, Mist *m (inf)* ◆ **(what a load of old) ~!** was für'n Haufen Mist! *(inf)*.
cobblestone ['kɒblstəʊn] *n see* **cobble 1**.
COBOL ['kəʊbɒl] *abbr of* **common business oriented language** COBOL.
cobra ['kəʊbrə] *n* Kobra *f*.
cobweb ['kɒbweb] *n (single thread, threads)* Spinn(en)webe *f*; *(network)* Spinnennetz *nt* ◆ **a brisk walk will blow away the ~s** *(fig)* ein ordentlicher Spaziergang, und man hat wieder einen klaren Kopf.
cocaine [kə'keɪn] *n* Kokain *nt*.
coccyx ['kɒksɪks] *n* Steißbein *nt*.
cochineal ['kɒtʃɪniːl] *n (insect, colouring)* Koschenille *f*.
cock [kɒk] 1 *n* **(a)** *(rooster)* Hahn *m*; *(weather~)* Wetterhahn *m* ◆ **(the) ~ of the walk** *or* **roost** der Größte *(inf)*.
(b) *(male bird)* Männchen *nt* ◆ **turkey ~** Truthahn, Puter *m*.
(c) *(tap)* (Wasser)hahn *m* ◆ **fuel ~** Treibstoffhahn *m*.
(d) *(of rifle)* Hahn *m*.
(e) *(of hat)* schiefer Sitz.
(f) *(Brit inf: mate)* Kumpel *m (inf)*.
(g) *(vulg: penis)* Schwanz *m (vulg)*.
2 *vt* **(a) to ~ the gun** den Hahn spannen.
(b) *ears* spitzen ◆ **the parrot ~ed its head on one side** der Papagei legte seinen Kopf schief *or* auf die Seite; **to ~ a snook at sb** *(lit)* jdm eine lange Nase machen; *(fig)* zeigen, daß man auf jdn pfeift; **he ~ed his hat at a jaunty angle** er setzte seinen Hut keck auf; **~ed hat** *(with two points)* Zweispitz *m*; *(with three points)* Dreispitz *m*; **to knock sb into a ~ed hat** *(inf) (lit beat up)* jdm Kleinholz machen; *(fig)* jdn total an die Wand spielen; **this painting knocks all the others into a ~ed hat** *(inf)* dieses Gemälde stellt alle anderen in den Schatten.
◆**cock up** *vt sep (Brit sl: mess up)* versauen *(sl)*.
cockade [kɒ'keɪd] *n* Kokarde *f*.
cock: ~-a-doodle-doo *n* Kikeriki *nt*; **~-a-hoop** *adj* ganz aus dem Häuschen, außer sich vor Freude; **~-a-leekie (soup)** *n* Lauchsuppe *f* mit Huhn.
cockamamie [ˌkɒkə'meɪmɪ] *adj (US inf: poor quality)* mies *(inf)*.
cock-and-bull story [ˌkɒkən'bʊlˌstɔːrɪ] *n* Lügengeschichte *f* ◆ **to give sb a ~** jdm eine Lügengeschichte erzählen.
cockatoo [ˌkɒkə'tuː] *n* Kakadu *m*.
cockatrice ['kɒkətrɪs] *n* Basilisk *m*.
cockchafer ['kɒkˌtʃeɪfəʳ] *n* Maikäfer *m*.
cockcrow ['kɒkkrəʊ] *n (old: dawn)* Hahnenschrei *m* ◆ **at ~** beim ersten Hahnenschrei.
cocker ['kɒkəʳ] *n (also* **~ spaniel***)* Cocker(spaniel) *m*.
cockerel ['kɒkərəl] *n* junger Hahn.
cock: ~-eyed *adj (inf)* **(a)** *(crooked)* schief; **(b)** *(absurd) idea* verrückt, widersinnig; **~fight** *n* Hahnenkampf *m*; **~horse** *n (old)* Steckenpferd *nt*.
cockiness ['kɒkɪnɪs] *n (inf)* Großspurigkeit *f*.
cockle ['kɒkl] *n* **(a)** *(shellfish: also* **~shell***)* Herzmuschel *f*. **(b)** *(boat)* kleines Boot, Nußschale *f*. **(c) it warmed the ~s of my heart** es wurde mir warm ums Herz.
cockney ['kɒknɪ] 1 *n* **(a)** *(dialect)* Cockney *nt*. **(b)** *(person)* Cockney *m*.
2 *adj* Cockney-.
cockpit ['kɒkpɪt] *n* **(a)** *(Aviat, of racing car)* Cockpit *nt*; *(Naut: on yacht)* Plicht *f*, Cockpit *nt*. **(b)** *(for cockfighting)* Hahnenkampfplatz *m*.
cockroach ['kɒkrəʊtʃ] *n* Küchenschabe *f*, Kakerlak *m*.
cockscomb ['kɒkskəʊm] *n* **(a)** *(Orn, Bot)* Hahnenkamm *m*. **(b)** *see* **coxcomb**.
cock: ~ sparrow *n* (männlicher) Spatz; **~sure** *adj* (ganz) sicher, fest überzeugt; **don't you be so ~sure** sei dir deiner Sache *(gen)* nicht zu sicher; **to be ~sure of oneself** von sich *(dat)* selber *or* selbst sehr überzeugt sein.
cocktail ['kɒkteɪl] *n* **(a)** Cocktail *m* ◆ **we're invited for ~s** wir sind zum Cocktail eingeladen. **(b) fruit ~** Obstsalat *m*.
cocktail *in cpds* Cocktail-; **~ bar** *n* Cocktail-Bar *f*; **~ cabinet** *n* Hausbar *f*; **~ lounge** *n* Cocktail-Bar *f*.
cock-up ['kɒkʌp] *n (Brit sl)* **to be a ~** in die Hose gehen *(sl)*; **to make a ~ of sth** bei *or* mit etw Scheiße bauen *(sl)*.
cocky ['kɒkɪ] *adj (+er) (inf)* anmaßend, großspurig ◆ **he was so ~ before the exams** er tat so großspurig vorm Examen.
cocoa ['kəʊkəʊ] *n* Kakao *m* ◆ **~ bean** Kakaobohne *f*.
coconut ['kəʊkənʌt] 1 *n* Kokosnuß *f*.
2 *attr* Kokos- ◆ **~ ice** Kokosnußriegel *m*; **~ matting** Kokosläufer *m*; **~ oil** Kokosöl *nt*; **~ palm, ~ tree** Kokospalme *f*; **~ shy** Wurfbude *f*.
cocoon [kə'kuːn] 1 *n* Kokon *m*; *(fig) (of scarves, blankets etc)* Hülle *f* ◆ **the old warships were put in ~s** die alten Kriegsschiffe wurden mit Planen abgedeckt.
2 *vt* einhüllen; *ship etc* abdecken ◆ **she looks well ~ed against the wind/winter** sie ist warm eingemummt.
COD *abbr of* **cash** *(Brit) or* **collect** *(US)* **on delivery**.
cod [kɒd] *n* Kabeljau *m*; *(in Baltic)* Dorsch *m*.
coda ['kəʊdə] *n* Koda *f*.
coddle ['kɒdl] *vt* **(a)** *child, invalid* umhegen, verhätscheln. **(b)** *(Cook) eggs* im Backofen pochieren.
code [kəʊd] 1 *n* **(a)** *(cipher)* Kode, Code *m*, Chiffre *f* ◆ **in ~** verschlüsselt, chiffriert; **to put into ~** verschlüsseln, chiffrieren.
(b) *(Jur)* Gesetzbuch *nt*, Kodex *m*.
(c) *(rules, principles)* Kodex *m* ◆ **~ of honour/behaviour** Ehren-/Sittenkodex *m*; **~ of practice** Verfahrensregeln *pl*.
(d) post *or* **zip** *(US)* **~** Postleitzahl *f*.
(e) *(Comput)* Code *m*.
(f) *(Ling, Sociol)* Code, Kode *m*.
2 *vt* verschlüsseln, chiffrieren; *(Comput)* kodieren.
code breaker *n* Kode-Knacker *m*.
codeine ['kəʊdiːn] *n* Kodein *nt*.
code: ~ letter *n* Kodebuchstabe *m*; **~ name** *n* Deckname *m*; **~ number** *n* Kennziffer *f*; **~ word** *n* Kodewort *nt*; *(Comput also)* Paßwort, Kennwort *nt*.
codex ['kəʊdeks] *n, pl* **codices** Kodex *m*.
codfish ['kɒdfɪʃ] *n see* **cod**.
codger ['kɒdʒəʳ] *n (inf)* komischer (alter) Kauz.
codices ['kɒdɪsiːz] *pl of* **codex**.
codicil ['kɒdɪsɪl] *n* Kodizill *nt*.
codify ['kəʊdɪfaɪ] *vt laws* kodifizieren.
coding ['kəʊdɪŋ] *n* **(a)** Chiffrieren *nt* ◆ **a new system of ~** ein neues Chiffriersystem; **I don't understand the ~** ich verstehe den Kode nicht. **(b)** *(Comput: codes)* Kodierung(en *pl*) *f*.
cod: ~-liver-oil *n* Lebertran *m*; **~piece** *n* Hosenbeutel *m*.
co-driver ['kəʊdraɪvəʳ] *n* Beifahrer *m*.
codswallop ['kɒdzwɒləp] *n (Brit inf)* Stuß *m (dated inf)*.
co-ed, coed ['kəʊ'ed] 1 *n (inf) (Brit: school)* gemischte Schule, Koedukationsschule *f*; *(US: girl student)* Schülerin *or* Studentin *f* einer gemischten Schule.
2 *adj school* gemischt, Koedukations-.
3 *adv* **to go ~** Koedukation einführen.
coedition [ˌkəʊɪ'dɪʃən] *n* gemeinsame Ausgabe.
co-editor ['kəʊ'edɪtəʳ] *n* Mitherausgeber *m*.
coeducation ['kəʊˌedjʊ'keɪʃən] *n* Koedukation *f*.
coeducational ['kəʊˌedjʊ'keɪʃənl] *adj teaching* koedukativ; *school* Koedukations-.
coefficient [ˌkəʊɪ'fɪʃənt] *n (Math, Phys)* Koeffizient *m*.
coerce [kəʊ'ɜːs] *vt* zwingen ◆ **to ~ sb into doing sth** jdn dazu zwingen *or* nötigen *(geh)*, etw zu tun.
coercion [kəʊ'ɜːʃən] *n* Zwang *m*; *(Jur)* Nötigung *f*.
coercive [kəʊ'ɜːsɪv] *adj* Zwangs-.
coeval [kəʊ'iːvəl] *(form)* 1 *adj* der gleichen Periode *or* Zeit *(with* wie); *manuscripts, authors etc also* zeitgenössisch *attr*.
2 *n* Zeitgenosse *m*.
coexist [ˌkəʊɪg'zɪst] *vi* koexistieren *(Pol, Sociol, geh)*, nebeneinander bestehen ◆ **to ~ with** *or* **alongside sb/sth** neben *or* mit jdm/etw bestehen *or* existieren.
coexistence [ˌkəʊɪg'zɪstəns] *n* Koexistenz *f*.
coexistent [ˌkəʊɪg'zɪstənt] *adj* koexistent *(geh)*, nebeneinander bestehend ◆ **the two states are now peacefully ~** die beiden Staaten leben jetzt friedlich nebeneinander *or* in friedlicher Koexistenz.
coextensive [ˌkəʊɪk'stensɪv] *adj (in time)* zur gleichen Zeit; *(in area)* flächengleich; *(in length)* längengleich; *(fig) (concepts)* bedeutungs- *or* inhaltsgleich ◆ **to be ~ with sth** mit etw zusammenfallen; *(spatially)* sich mit etw decken.
C of E *abbr of* **Church of England**.
coffee ['kɒfɪ] *n* Kaffee *m* ◆ **two ~s, please** zwei Kaffee, bitte.
coffee *in cpds* Kaffee-; **~ bar** *n* Café *nt*; **~ bean** *n* Kaffeebohne *f*; **~ break** *n* Kaffeepause *f*; **~ cake** *n* Mokkakuchen *m*; **~ cup** *n* Kaffeetasse *f*; **~ filter** *n* Kaffeefilter *m*; **~ grinder** *n* Kaffeemühle *f*; **~ house** *n (also Hist)* Kaffeehaus *nt*; **~ machine** *n (~ maker)* Kaffeemaschine *f*; *(vending machine)* Kaffee-Verkaufsautomat *m*; **~ maker** *n* Kaffeemaschine *f*; **~ percolator** *n* Kaffeemaschine *f*; **~ pot** *n* Kaffeekanne *f*; **~ table** *n* Couchtisch *m*; **~-table book** Bildband *m*; **~ whitener** *n* Kaffeeweißer *m*.
coffer ['kɒfəʳ] *n* **(a)** Truhe *f*. **(b)** *(fig)* **the ~s** die Schatulle, das Geldsäckel; *(of state)* das Staatssäckel. **(c)** *(Archit)* Kassette *f*.
cofferdam ['kɒfədæm] *n* Caisson *m*.
coffin ['kɒfɪn] *n* Sarg *m*.
cog [kɒg] *n (Tech)* Zahn *m*; *(~wheel)* Zahnrad *nt* ◆ **he's only a ~ in the machine** *(fig)* er ist nur ein Rädchen im Getriebe; **each employee is a vital ~ in the company** jeder einzelne Angestellte ist ein wichtiger Teil in der Firma.
cogency ['kəʊdʒənsɪ] *n* Stichhaltigkeit *f*.
cogent ['kəʊdʒənt] *adj* stichhaltig; *argument, reason also* zwingend; *reasoning also* überzeugend.
cogently ['kəʊdʒəntlɪ] *adv* stichhaltig.
cogitate ['kɒdʒɪteɪt] 1 *vi (about, (up)on* über *+acc)* nachdenken, grübeln.
2 *vt* nachdenken über *(+acc)*; *(devise)* ersinnen.
cogitation [ˌkɒdʒɪ'teɪʃən] *n* Nachdenken *nt* ◆ **my ~s on the subject** meine Überlegungen zu dem Thema.
cognac ['kɒnjæk] *n* Kognak *m*; *(French)* Cognac *m*.
cognate ['kɒgneɪt] 1 *adj* verwandt; *(Ling)* urverwandt.
2 *n (Ling)* urverwandtes Wort; urverwandte Sprache ◆ **"night" is a ~ of "Nacht"** „night" ist mit „Nacht" verwandt.
cognition [kɒg'nɪʃən] *n* Erkenntnis *f*; *(visual)* Wahrnehmung *f*.
cognitive ['kɒgnɪtɪv] *adj powers, faculties* kognitiv.
cognizance ['kɒgnɪzəns] *n (form)* **(a)** *(conscious knowledge, awareness)* Kenntnis *f*; *(range of perception)* Erkenntnisbereich *m* ◆ **to take ~ of sth** etw

zur Kenntnis nehmen.
(**b**) (*jurisdiction*) Zuständigkeit, Befugnis *f*; (*Jur*) Gerichtsbarkeit *f*.

cognizant ['kɒgnɪzənt] *adj* (*form*) (**a**) (*aware, conscious*) **to be ~ of sth** sich (*dat*) einer Sache (*gen*) bewußt sein. (**b**) (*having jurisdiction*) zuständig.

cognoscente [,kɒgnəʊ'ʃentɪ] *n, pl* **cognoscenti** [,kɒgnəʊ'ʃenti:] Kenner *m*.

cog: ~ railway *n* (*US*) Zahnradbahn *f*; **~wheel** *n* Zahnrad *nt*.

cohabit [kəʊ'hæbɪt] *vi* (*esp Jur*) in nichtehelicher Lebensgemeinschaft leben, zusammenleben.

cohabitation [,kəʊhæbɪ'teɪʃən] *n* eheähnliche Gemeinschaft.

cohabitee [,kəʊhæbɪ'ti:] *n Partner(in f) m in einer nichtehelichen Lebensgemeinschaft.*

coheir ['kəʊ'ɛə^r] *n* Miterbe *m* (*to gen*) ◆ **they were ~s to the fortune** sie waren gemeinsame Erben des Vermögens.

coheiress ['kəʊ'eərɪs] *n* Miterbin *f* (*to gen*).

cohere [kəʊ'hɪə^r] *vi* (**a**) (*lit*) zusammenhängen. (**b**) (*fig*) (*community*) ein Ganzes *or* eine Einheit bilden; (*essay, symphony etc*) in sich geschlossen sein; (*argument, reasoning, style*) kohärent *or* zusammenhängend sein.

coherence [kəʊ'hɪərəns] *n* (**a**) (*lit*) Kohärenz *f*.
(**b**) (*of community*) Zusammenhalt *m*; (*of essay, symphony etc*) Geschlossenheit *f*; (*of argument, reasoning, style*) Kohärenz *f* ◆ **his address lacked ~** seiner Rede (*dat*) fehlte der Zusammenhang.
(**c**) (*fig: comprehensibility*) **after five whiskies he lacked ~** nach fünf Whiskys gab er nur noch unzusammenhängendes Zeug von sich.

coherent [kəʊ'hɪərənt] *adj* (**a**) (*comprehensible*) zusammenhängend. (**b**) (*cohesive*) *logic, reasoning etc* kohärent, schlüssig; *case* schlüssig.

coherently [kəʊ'hɪərəntlɪ] *adv* (**a**) (*comprehensibly*) zusammenhängend. (**b**) (*cohesively*) kohärent, schlüssig.

cohesion [kəʊ'hi:ʒən] *n* (*Sci*) Kohäsion *f*; (*fig also*) Zusammenhang *m*; (*of group*) Zusammenhalt *m*, Geschlossenheit *f*.

cohesive [kəʊ'hi:sɪv] *adj* (*Sci*) Binde-, Kohäsiv-; (*fig*) geschlossen.

cohesively [kəʊ'hi:sɪvlɪ] *adv* (*Sci*) kohäsiv; (*fig*) *write, argue* im Zusammenhang.

cohort ['kəʊhɔ:t] *n* Kohorte *f*, Trupp *m*.

COHSE ['kəʊzɪ] (*Brit*) *abbr of* **Confederation of Health Service Employees** *Gewerkschaft f der Angestellten des Gesundheitsdienstes.*

coif [kɔɪf] *n* (*Hist, Eccl*) Haube *f*; (*skullcap*) Kappe *f*.

coiffure [kwɒ'fjʊə^r] *n* Haartracht, Coiffure (*geh*) *f*.

coil [kɔɪl] 1 *n* (**a**) (*of rope, wire etc*) Rolle *f*; (*in light-bulb*) Glühdraht *m*; (*on loop*) Windung *f*; (*of smoke*) Kringel *m*; (*of hair*) Kranz *m* ◆ **~ spring** Sprungfeder *f*; **she wore her hair in ~s** (*round head*) sie hatte eine Gretchenfrisur; (*round ears*) sie trug ihr Haar in Schnecken; **the sinewy ~s of the snake** die kraftvoll gespannte Spirale des Schlangenkörpers.
(**b**) (*Elec*) Spule *f*.
(**c**) (*contraceptive*) Spirale *f*.
2 *vt* aufwickeln, aufrollen; *wire* aufspulen, aufwickeln ◆ **to ~ sth round sth** etw um etw wickeln; **the python ~ed itself around the rabbit/(up) in the basket** die Pythonschlange umschlang das Kaninchen/rollte sich im Korb zusammen.
3 *vi* sich ringeln; (*smoke also*) sich kringeln; (*river*) sich schlängeln *or* winden.

coin [kɔɪn] 1 *n* (**a**) Münze *f* ◆ **~-box** (*telephone*) Münzfernsprecher *m*; (*box*) Geldkasten *m*; (*on telephone, meter*) Münzzähler *m*; **~-operated** Münz-.
(**b**) (*no pl*) Münzen *pl* ◆ **in the ~ of the realm** in der Landeswährung; **I'll pay you back in your own ~** (*fig*) das werde ich dir in gleicher Münze heimzahlen; **the other side of the ~** (*fig*) die Kehrseite der Medaille.
2 *vt* (*lit, fig*) *money, phrase* prägen ◆ **he's ~ing money** (*fig inf*) er scheffelt Geld (*inf*); ..., **to ~ a phrase** ..., um mich mal so auszudrücken.

coinage ['kɔɪnɪdʒ] *n* (**a**) (*act*) Prägen *nt*, Prägung *f*; (*coins*) Münzen *pl*, Hartgeld *nt no pl*; (*system*) Währung *f*. (**b**) (*fig*) Prägung, Neuschöpfung *f*.

coincide [,kəʊɪn'saɪd] *vi* (*in time, place*) zusammenfallen; (*in area*) sich decken; (*agree*) übereinstimmen ◆ **the two concerts ~** die beiden Konzerte finden zur gleichen Zeit statt.

coincidence [kəʊ'ɪnsɪdəns] *n* (**a**) Zufall *m*, Fügung *f* (*geh*) ◆ **what a ~!** welch ein Zufall!; **it is no ~ that** ... es ist kein Zufall, daß ..., es ist nicht von ungefähr, daß ... (**b**) (*occurring or coming together*) (*in time*) Zusammentreffen *nt*; (*in place*) Zusammenfall *m*; (*agreement*) Übereinstimmung *f*.

coincident [kəʊ'ɪnsɪdənt] *adj* (*in time*) zusammentreffend; (*in place*) zusammenfallend; (*agreeing*) übereinstimmend.

coincidental *adj*, **~ly** *adv* [kəʊ,ɪnsɪ'dentl, -təlɪ] zufällig.

coir [kɔɪə^r] *n* Kokosfaser *f*, Coir *nt or f*.

coition [kəʊ'ɪʃən], **coitus** ['kɔɪtəs] *n* (*form*) Koitus, Akt *m* ◆ **coitus interruptus** Coitus interruptus *m*.

coke[1] [kəʊk] *n* Koks *m*.

coke[2] *n* (*sl: cocaine*) Koks *m*.

Coke ® [kəʊk] *n* (*inf*) (Coca-®)Cola *f*, Coke ® *nt*.

col[1] [kɒl] *n* Sattel, Paß *m*.

col[2] *abbr of* **column** Sp.

Col *abbr of* **Colonel**.

colander ['kʌləndə^r] *n* Seiher *m*, Sieb *nt*.

▼ **cold** [kəʊld] 1 *adj* (*+er*) (**a**) kalt ◆ **~ meats** Aufschnitt *m*; **I am ~** mir ist kalt, ich friere; **my hands are ~/are getting ~** ich habe/kriege kalte Hände; **don't get ~** paß auf, daß du nicht frierst!; **if you get ~** wenn es dir zu kalt wird, wenn du frierst.
▼ (**b**) (*fig*) kalt; *answer, reception* betont kühl; *personality* kühl; (*dispassionate, not sensual*) kühl ◆ **to be ~ to sb** jdn kühl behandeln; **that leaves me ~** das läßt mich kalt.
(**c**) (*inf: unconscious*) bewußtlos; (*knocked out*) k.o ◆ **to be out ~** bewußtlos/k.o. sein.
(**d**) (*inf: in guessing*) kalt ◆ **you're still ~** immer noch kalt.
(**e**) (*Hunt*) *scent* kalt.
(**f**) (*phrases*) **in ~ blood** kaltblütig; **~ comfort** ein schwacher Trost; **to get/have ~ feet** (*fig inf*) kalte Füße kriegen (*inf*); **to give sb the ~ shoulder** (*inf*) jdm die kalte Schulter zeigen; **to be in a ~ sweat** vor Angst schwitzen; **that brought him out in a ~ sweat** dabei brach ihm der kalte Schweiß *or* der Angstschweiß aus; **to throw ~ water on sb's plans/hopes** (*inf*) jdm eine kalte Dusche geben/jds Hoffnungen (*dat*) einen Dämpfer aufsetzen.
2 *adv* **to come to sth ~** unvorbereitet an eine Sache herangehen; **to learn/know sth ~** (*US*) etw gut lernen/können; **he stopped ~ when ...** (*US*) er hielt unvermittelt an, als ...; **she quit her job ~** sie hat glatt *or* eiskalt gekündigt (*inf*); **he was turned down ~** er wurde glatt abgelehnt.
3 *n* (**a**) Kälte *f* ◆ **to feel the ~** kälteempfindlich sein; **don't go out in this ~!** geh nicht raus bei dieser Kälte!; **to be left out in the ~** (*fig*) ausgeschlossen werden, links liegengelassen werden; **to feel left out in the ~** sich ausgeschlossen fühlen.
(**b**) (*Med*) Erkältung *f*; (*runny nose*) Schnupfen *m* ◆ **a heavy** *or* **bad ~** eine schwere Erkältung; **to have a ~** erkältet sein; (einen) Schnupfen haben; **to get** *or* **catch a ~** sich erkälten, sich (*dat*) eine Erkältung holen; **to catch ~** sich erkälten; **~ in the head/on the chest** Schnupfen *m*/Bronchialkatarrh *m*.

cold: ~-blooded *adj* (*Zool, fig*) kaltblütig; **~-blooded animal** Kaltblüter *m*; **~-bloodedly** ['kəʊld'blʌdɪdlɪ] *adv* kaltblütig; **~ box** *n* Kühlbox *f*; **~ chisel** *n* Kaltmeißel *m*; **~ cream** *n* Cold Cream *f or nt*, halbfette Feuchtigkeitscreme; **~ cuts** *npl* Aufschnitt *m*; **~ frame** *n* (*Hort*) Frühbeet *nt*; **~-hearted** *adj* kaltherzig.

coldly ['kəʊldlɪ] *adv* (*lit, fig*) kalt; *answer, receive* betont kühl ◆ **they ~ planned the murder** der Mord wurde von ihnen kaltblütig geplant.

coldness ['kəʊldnɪs] *n* (*lit, fig*) Kälte *f*; (*of answer, reception, welcome*) betonte Kühle ◆ **the unexpected ~ of the weather** die unerwartete Kälte; **the ~ with which they planned the murder** die Kaltblütigkeit, mit der sie den Mord planten.

cold: ~ room *n* Kühlraum *m*; **~ selling** *n* Cold selling *nt*; **~-shoulder** *vt* (*inf*) links liegenlassen (*inf*); **~ sore** *n* (*Med*) Bläschenausschlag *m*; **~ start** *n* (*Aut, Comput*) Kaltstart *m*; **~ storage** *n* Kühllagerung *f*; **to put sth into ~ storage** (*lit*) *food* etw kühl lagern; (*fig*) *idea, plan* etw auf Eis legen; **~ store** *n* Kühlhaus *nt*; **~ turkey** (*sl*) 1 *adj* **a ~ turkey cure** sofortiger Totalentzug; 2 *adv* **to come off drugs ~ turkey** eine radikale Entziehung(skur) machen; **~ war** *n* kalter Krieg; **~ warrior** *n* kalter Krieger.

coleslaw ['kəʊlslɔ:] *n* Krautsalat *m*.

colic ['kɒlɪk] *n* Kolik *f*.

coliseum [,kɒlɪ'si:əm] *n* Kolosseum *nt*.

collaborate [kə'læbəreɪt] *vi* (**a**) zusammenarbeiten ◆ **they asked him to ~** sie baten ihn mitzuarbeiten, sie baten um seine Mitarbeit; **to ~ with sb on** *or* **in sth** mit jdm bei etw zusammenarbeiten. (**b**) (*with enemy*) kollaborieren ◆ **he was suspected of collaborating** er wurde der Kollaboration verdächtigt.

collaboration [kə,læbə'reɪʃən] *n* (**a**) Zusammenarbeit *f*; (*of one party*) Mitarbeit *f* ◆ **helpful ~** Mithilfe *f*. (**b**) (*with enemy*) Kollaboration *f*.

collaborator [kə'læbəreɪtə^r] *n* (**a**) Mitarbeiter(in *f*) *m*. (**b**) (*with enemy*) Kollaborateur(in *f*) *m*.

collage [kɒ'lɑ:ʒ] *n* Collage *f*.

collapse [kə'læps] 1 *vi* (**a**) (*person*) zusammenbrechen; (*mentally, have heart attack also*) einen Kollaps erleiden *or* haben ◆ **his health ~d** er hatte einen Kollaps; **they all ~d with laughter** sie konnten sich alle vor Lachen nicht mehr halten.
(**b**) (*fall down, cave in*) zusammenbrechen; (*building, wall, roof also*) einstürzen; (*lungs*) zusammenfallen, kollabieren.
(**c**) (*fig: fail*) zusammenbrechen; (*negotiations also*) scheitern; (*civilization*) zugrunde gehen; (*prices*) stürzen, purzeln (*inf*); (*government*) zu Fall kommen, stürzen; (*plans*) scheitern, zu Fall kommen; (*hopes*) sich zerschlagen ◆ **his whole world ~d about him** eine ganze Welt stürzte über ihm zusammen; **their whole society ~d** ihre ganze Gesellschaftsordnung brach zusammen.
(**d**) (*fold*) (*table, umbrella, bicycle etc*) sich zusammenklappen lassen; (*telescope, walking-stick*) sich zusammenschieben lassen; (*life raft*) sich zusammenlegen *or* -falten lassen ◆ **a collapsing bicycle/chair** ein Klappfahrrad *nt*/-stuhl *m*.
2 *vt table, umbrella, bicycle etc* zusammenklappen; *telescope, walking-stick* zusammenschieben; *life-raft* zusammenlegen *or* -falten.
3 *n* (**a**) (*of person*) Zusammenbruch *m*; (*nervous breakdown also, heart attack*) Kollaps *m*.
(**b**) *see vi (b)* Zusammenbruch *m*; Einsturz *m*; Kollaps *m*.
(**c**) (*failure*) *see vi (c)* Zusammenbruch *m*; Scheitern *nt*; Untergang *m*; Sturz *m*; Zerschlagung *f*.

collapsible [kə'læpsəbl] *adj see vi (d)* zusammenklappbar, Klapp-; zusammenschiebbar; zusammenlegbar, zusammenfaltbar, Falt-.

collar ['kɒlə^r] 1 *n* (**a**) Kragen *m* ◆ **he got hold of him by the ~** er packte ihn am Kragen; **~-bone** Schlüsselbein *nt*; **~ stud** Kragenknopf *m*. (**b**) (*for dogs*) Halsband *nt*; (*for horses*) Kum(me)t *nt*. (**c**) (*chain and insignia*) Hals- *or* Ordenskette *f*. (**d**) (*Mech: on pipe etc*) Bund *m*.
2 *vt* (*capture*) fassen; (*latch onto*) abfangen, schnappen (*inf*).

collate [kɒ'leɪt] *vt* (**a**) vergleichen, kollationieren. (**b**) (*Typ*) kollationieren, zusammentragen.

➤ LANGUAGE IN USE: **cold: 1b** → 7.5

collateral [kɒ'lætərəl] 1 *adj* **(a)** (*connected but secondary*) *evidence, questions etc* zusätzlich, Zusatz-; *events* Begleit-.
(b) (*parallel, side by side*) *states etc* nebeneinanderliegend; (*fig*) *aims etc* Hand in Hand gehend.
(c) *descent, branch of family* seitlich, kollateral (*spec*).
(d) (*Fin*) *security* zusätzlich.
2 *n* (*Fin*) (zusätzliche) Sicherheit.
collation [kɒ'leɪʃən] *n* **(a)** (*collating*) Vergleich *m*, Kollationieren *nt*; (*Typ*) Kollationieren, Zusammentragen *nt*. **(b)** (*form: meal*) Imbiß *m*.
colleague ['kɒli:g] *n* Kollege *m*, Kollegin *f* ◆ **my ~s at work** meine Arbeitskollegen.
collect[1] ['kɒlekt] *n* (*Eccl*) Kirchen- *or* Tagesgebet *nt*.
▼ **collect**[2] [kə'lekt] 1 *vt* **(a)** (*accumulate*) ansammeln; (*furniture*) *dust* anziehen; *empty glasses, exam papers, tickets etc* einsammeln; *litter* aufsammeln; *belongings* zusammenpacken *or* -sammeln; (*assemble*) sammeln; *one's thoughts also* ordnen; *information also* zusammentragen; *volunteers* zusammenbringen ◆ **she ~ed a lot of praise/five points for that** das hat ihr viel Lob/fünf Punkte eingebracht *or* eingetragen; **to ~ interest** Zinsen bringen; **the train ~s electricity from overhead cables** der Zug entnimmt den Strom der Oberleitung (*dat*).
(b) (*pick up, fetch*) *things, persons* abholen (*from* bei).
(c) *stamps, coins* sammeln.
(d) *taxes* einziehen; *money, jumble for charity* sammeln; *rent, fares* kassieren; *debts* eintreiben.
2 *vi* **(a)** (*gather*) sich ansammeln; (*dust*) sich absetzen.
(b) (*~ money*) kassieren; (*for charity*) sammeln.
(c) (*Comm: call for goods*) abholen.
3 *adj* **~ call** R-Gespräch; **~ cable** (*US*) vom Empfänger bezahltes Telegramm.
▼ 4 *adv* **to pay ~** (*US*) bei Empfang bezahlen; **to call ~** ein R-Gespräch führen; **to pay ~ on delivery** bei Lieferung bezahlen; (*through post*) per Nachnahme bezahlen.
◆**collect together** *vt sep* zusammensammeln; *information* zusammentragen; *team of people* auf- *or* zusammenstellen ◆ **the officer ~ed his men ~** der Offizier rief seine Leute zusammen.
◆**collect up** *vt sep* einsammeln; *litter* aufsammeln; *belongings* zusammenpacken *or* -sammeln.
collected [kə'lektɪd] *adj* **(a) the ~ works of Oscar Wilde** Oscar Wildes gesammelte Werke. **(b)** (*calm*) ruhig, gelassen.
collectedly [kə'lektɪdlɪ] *adv* ruhig, gelassen.
collection [kə'lekʃən] *n* **(a)** (*group of people, objects*) Ansammlung *f*; (*of stamps, coins etc*) Sammlung *f* ◆ **they're an odd ~ of people** das ist ein seltsamer Verein (*inf*).
(b) (*collecting*) (*of facts, information*) Zusammentragen *nt*; (*of goods, person*) Abholung *f*; (*of mail*) Abholung *f*; (*from letterbox*) Leerung *f*; (*of stamps, coins*) Sammeln *nt*; (*of money, jumble for charity*) Sammlung *f*; (*in church*) Kollekte *f*; (*of rent, fares*) Kassieren *nt*; (*of taxes*) Einziehen *nt*; (*of debts*) Eintreiben *nt* ◆ **the police organized the ~ of all firearms** die Polizei ließ alle Schußwaffen einsammeln; **to make** *or* **hold a ~ for sb/sth** für jdn/etw eine Sammlung durchführen; **bill for ~** Inkassowechsel *m*.
(c) (*Fashion*) Kollektion *f*.
collective [kə'lektɪv] 1 *adj* **(a)** kollektiv, Kollektiv-; *responsibility, agreement, action also* gemeinsam ◆ **~ bargaining** Tarifverhandlungen *pl*; **~ ticket** Sammelfahrschein *m*; **~ farm** landwirtschaftliche Produktionsgenossenschaft.
(b) (*accumulated*) *wisdom, discoveries, experience* gesamt *attr* ◆ **the ~ unconscious** das kollektive Unbewußte.
(c) (*Gram*) **~ noun** Kollektivum *nt*, Sammelbegriff *m*.
2 *n* Kollektiv *nt*; (*farm also*) Produktionsgenossenschaft *f*.
collectively [kə'lektɪvlɪ] *adv* gemeinsam, zusammen; (*in socialist context also*) kollektiv.
collectivism [kə'lektɪvɪzəm] *n* Kollektivismus *m*.
collectivist [kə'lektɪvɪst] 1 *n* Kollektivist *m*.
2 *adj* kollektivistisch.
collectivize [kə'lektɪvaɪz] *vt* kollektivieren.
collector [kə'lektə^r] *n* **(a)** (*of taxes*) Einnehmer(in *f*) *m*; (*of rent, cash*) Kassierer(in *f*) *m*; (*ticket ~*) *Bahnbediensteter, der die abgefahrenen Fahrkarten einsammelt.* **(b)** (*of stamps, coins etc*) Sammler(in *f*) *m* ◆ **~'s** *item, piece, price* Sammler-, Liebhaber-; **~'s car** Liebhaberauto *nt*. **(c) current ~** Stromabnehmer *m*.
colleen ['kɒli:n] *n* (*Ir*) junges Mädchen, Mädel *nt*.
college ['kɒlɪdʒ] *n* **(a)** (*part of university*) College *nt*; Institut *nt* ◆ **to go to ~** (*university*) studieren; **to start ~** sein Studium beginnen; **we met at ~** wir haben uns im Studium kennengelernt. **(b)** (*of music, agriculture, technology etc*) Fachhochschule *f* ◆ **~ of Art** Kunstakademie *f*. **(c)** (*body*) **~ of Cardinals** Kardinalskollegium *nt*; **~ of Physicians/Surgeons** Ärztebund *m*, Ärztekammer *f*.
collegiate [kə'li:dʒɪɪt] *adj* College- ◆ **~ life** das Collegeleben, das Leben auf dem College; **Oxford is a ~ university** Oxford ist eine auf dem College-System aufgebaute Universität.
collide [kə'laɪd] *vt* **(a)** (*lit*) zusammenstoßen *or* -prallen; (*Naut*) kollidieren ◆ **they ~d head-on** sie stießen frontal zusammen; **to ~ with sb/sth** mit jdm zusammenstoßen/gegen etw prallen. **(b)** (*fig*) (*person*) eine heftige Auseinandersetzung haben (*with* mit); (*interest, demands*) kollidieren.
collie ['kɒlɪ] *n* Collie *m*.

➤ LANGUAGE IN USE: **collect**[2]**: 4 → 27.2**

collier ['kɒlɪə^r] *n* **(a)** Bergmann, Kumpel (*inf*) *m*. **(b)** (*coal-ship*) Kohlenschiff *nt*.
colliery ['kɒlɪərɪ] *n* Grube, Zeche *f*.
collimate ['kɒlɪmeɪt] *vt* kollimieren.
collision [kə'lɪʒən] *n* (*lit*) Zusammenstoß, Zusammenprall *m*; (*fig*) Zusammenstoß, Konflikt *m*, Kollision *f*; (*Naut*) Kollision *f* ◆ **on a ~ course** (*lit, fig*) auf Kollisionskurs; **to be in ~ with sth** mit etw zusammenstoßen; **to come into ~ with sth** (*lit, fig*) mit etw zusammenstoßen; (*Naut*) mit etw kollidieren.
collocate ['kɒləkeɪt] *vt* (*Gram*) nebeneinanderstellen ◆ **to be ~d** nebeneinanderstehen.
collocation [kɒlə'keɪʃən] *n* (*Gram*) Kollokation *f*.
colloquial [kə'ləʊkwɪəl] *adj* umgangssprachlich.
colloquialism [kə'ləʊkwɪəlɪzəm] *n* umgangssprachlicher Ausdruck.
colloquially [kə'ləʊkwɪəlɪ] *adv* umgangssprachlich.
colloquium [kə'ləʊkwɪəm] *n* Kolloquium *nt*.
colloquy ['kɒləkwɪ] *n* (*form*) Gespräch *nt*; (*Liter*) Dialog *m* ◆ **in ~** im Gespräch.
collusion [kə'lu:ʒən] *n* (geheime) Absprache ◆ **they're acting in ~** sie haben sich abgesprochen; **there's been some ~ between those two pupils** diese beiden Schüler haben zusammengearbeitet.
collywobbles ['kɒlɪ,wɒblz] *npl* (*inf*) **the ~** (*upset stomach*) Bauchgrimmen *nt* (*inf*); (*nerves*) ein flaues Gefühl im Magen.
Cologne [kə'ləʊn] 1 *n* Köln *nt*.
2 *adj* Kölner, kölnisch.
cologne [kə'ləʊn] *n* Kölnischwasser, Eau de Cologne *nt*.
colon[1] ['kəʊlən] *n* (*Anat*) Dickdarm *m*.
colon[2] *n* (*Gram*) Doppelpunkt *m*; (*old, Typ*) Kolon *nt*.
colonel ['kɜ:nl] *n* Oberst *m*; (*as address*) Herr Oberst.
colonial [kə'ləʊnɪəl] 1 *adj* Kolonial-, kolonial ◆ **~ architecture** Kolonialstil *m*; **~ type** Typ *m* des Herrenmenschen (*iro*).
2 *n* Bewohner(in *f*) *m* einer Kolonie/der Kolonien.
colonialism [kə'ləʊnɪəlɪzəm] *n* Kolonialismus *m*.
colonialist [kə'ləʊnɪəlɪst] 1 *adj* kolonialistisch.
2 *n* Kolonialist(in *f*) *m*.
colonist ['kɒlənɪst] *n* Kolonist(in *f*), Siedler(in *f*) *m*.
colonization [,kɒlənaɪ'zeɪʃən] *n* Kolonisation *f*.
colonize ['kɒlənaɪz] *vt* kolonisieren.
colonnade [,kɒlə'neɪd] *n* Kolonnade *f*, Säulengang *m*.
colony ['kɒlənɪ] *n* Kolonie *f*.
colophon ['kɒləfən] *n* Kolophon *m*, Signet *nt*.
color *etc* (*US*) *see* **colour** *etc*.
colorant ['kʌlərənt] *n* (*US*) *see* **colourant**.
Colorado beetle [,kɒlə'rɑ:dəʊ'bi:tl] *n* Kartoffelkäfer *m*.
coloration [,kʌlə'reɪʃən] *n* Färbung *f*.
coloratura [kɒlərə'tʊ:rə] *n* Koloratur *f*.
color guard *n* (*US*) *see* **colour party**.
coloscopy [kə'lɒskəpɪ] *n* (*Med*) Koloskopie *f*.
colossal [kə'lɒsl] *adj* riesig, ungeheuer, gewaltig; *fool, cheek, mistake* ungeheuer; *car, man, park, lake, city* riesig; *prices, damage, building also* kolossal.
colosseum [kɒlɪ'si:əm] *n* Kolosseum *nt*.
colossi [kə'lɒsaɪ] *pl of* **colossus**.
Colossians [kə'lɒʃəns] *n* **(Epistle to the) ~** Kolosserbrief *m*.
colossus [kə'lɒsəs] *n, pl* **colossi** *or* **-es** (*statue*) Koloß *m*; (*person also*) Riese *m* ◆ **this ~ of the world of music** dieser Gigant *or* Titan der Musik.
colostomy [kə'lɒstəmɪ] *n* (*Med*) Kolostomie *f*.
colour, (*US*) **color** ['kʌlə^r] 1 *n* **(a)** (*lit, fig*) Farbe *f* ◆ **what ~ is it?** welche Farbe hat es?; **red/yellow in ~** rot/gelb; **a good sense of ~** ein guter Farbensinn; **let's see the ~ of your money first** (*inf*) zeig erst mal dein Geld her (*inf*); **the ~ of a note** (*Mus*) die Klangfarbe eines Tons; *see* **glowing**.
(b) (*complexion*) (Gesichts)farbe *f* ◆ **to change ~** die Farbe wechseln; **to get one's ~ back** wieder Farbe bekommen; **to bring the ~ back to sb's cheeks** jdm wieder Farbe geben; **to have a high ~** eine gesunde Gesichtsfarbe haben; (*look feverish*) rot im Gesicht sein.
(c) (*racial*) Hautfarbe *f* ◆ **I don't care what ~ he is** seine Hautfarbe interessiert mich nicht.
(d) ~s *pl* (*paints*) Farben *pl* ◆ **a box of ~s** ein Mal- *or* Tuschkasten *m*.
(e) (*fig: bias*) (*of newspaper, report*) Färbung *f*.
(f) (*of place, period etc*) Atmosphäre *f* ◆ **to add ~ to a story** einer Geschichte (*dat*) Farbe geben; **the pageantry and ~ of Elizabethan England** der Prunk und die Farbenpracht des Elisabethanischen England; **local ~** Lokalkolorit *nt*.
(g) (*appearance of truth*) **to give** *or* **lend ~ to a tale** eine Geschichte ausschmücken.
(h) ~s *pl* (*symbols of membership*) Farben *pl*.
(i) (*flag*) **~s** Fahne *f*; **the regimental ~s** die Regimentsfahne; **to serve with/join the ~s** (*old*) der Fahne dienen (*dated*)/den bunten Rock anziehen (*old*); **to nail one's ~s to the mast** (*fig*) Farbe bekennen; **to sail under false ~s** (*fig*) unter falscher Flagge segeln; **to show one's true ~s** (*fig*) sein wahres Gesicht zeigen.
(j) (*Sport*) **~s** (Sport)abzeichen *nt*.
2 *vt* **(a)** (*lit*) anmalen; (*Art*) kolorieren; (*dye*) färben.
(b) (*fig*) beeinflussen; (*bias deliberately*) färben.
3 *vi* **(a)** (*leaves*) sich (ver)färben.
(b) (*person: also ~ up*) rot werden, erröten.

◆**colour in** *vt sep* anmalen; (*Art*) kolorieren.
colour *in cpds* Farb-; (*racial*) Rassen-; (*Mil*) Fahnen-.
colourant, (*US*) **colorant** ['kʌlərənt] *n* Farbstoff *m*.
colour: ~-bar *n* Rassenschranke *f*; (*in country also*) Rassenschranken *pl*; **to operate a ~-bar** Rassentrennung praktizieren; **~-blind** *adj* farbenblind; **~-blindness** *n* Farbenblindheit *f*; **~-code** *vt* farbig kennzeichnen *or* kodieren.
coloured, (*US*) **colored** ['kʌləd] [1] *adj* **(a)** bunt; *fabric, walls also* farbig. **(b)** (*fig*) (*biased*) gefärbt; (*exaggerated*) ausgeschmückt. **(c)** *person, race* farbig; (*of mixed blood*) gemischtrassig.
[2] *n* Farbige(r) *mf*; (*of mixed blood*) Mischling *m*.
-coloured, (*US*) **-colored** *adj suf* **yellow-/red-~** gelb/rot; **straw-/dark-~** strohfarben/dunkel.
colourfast, (*US*) **colorfast** ['kʌləfɑːst] *adj* farbecht.
colourful, (*US*) **colorful** ['kʌləfʊl] *adj* **(a)** (*lit*) bunt; *spectacle* farbenfroh *or* -prächtig. **(b)** (*fig*) *style of writing, account etc* farbig, anschaulich; *life, historical period* (bunt)bewegt; *personality* (bunt)schillernd.
colourfully, (*US*) **colorfully** ['kʌləfəlɪ] *adv see adj*.
colourfulness, (*US*) **colorfulness** ['kʌləfʊlnɪs] *n see adj* **(a)** (*lit*) Buntheit *f*; Farbenpracht *f*. **(b)** (*fig*) Farbigkeit, Anschaulichkeit *f*; Bewegtheit *f* ◆ **the ~ of his character** sein schillernder Charakter.
colour illustration *n* farbige Illustration.
colouring, (*US*) **coloring** ['kʌlərɪŋ] *n* **(a)** (*complexion*) Gesichtsfarbe *f*, Teint *m*. **(b)** (*substance*) Farbstoff *m*. **(c)** (*painting*) Malen *nt* ◆ **~ book** Malbuch *nt*; **~ set** Mal- *or* Tuschkasten *m*; (*box of crayons*) Schachtel *f* Buntstifte. **(d)** (*coloration*) Farben *pl*. **(e)** (*fig: of news, facts etc*) Färbung *f*.
colourist, (*US*) **colorist** ['kʌlərɪst] *n* Farbkünstler(in *f*) *m*.
colourless, (*US*) **colorless** ['kʌləlɪs] *adj* (*lit, fig*) farblos; *existence also* grau.
colourlessly, (*US*) **colorlessly** ['kʌləlɪslɪ] *adv see adj*.
colourlessness, (*US*) **colorlessness** ['kʌləlɪsnɪs] *n* Farblosigkeit *f*.
colour: ~ party *n* Fahnenträgerkommando *nt*; **~ photograph** *n* Farbfoto *nt*; **~ postcard** *n* bunte Ansichtskarte; **~ scheme** *n* Farbzusammenstellung *f*; **~ sergeant** *n* (*Mil*) Fahnenträger *m*; **~ supplement** *n* Farbbeilage *f*, Magazin *nt*; **~ television** *n* Farbfernsehen *nt*; (*set*) Farbfernseher *m*; **~wash** *n* Farbtünche *f*.
colt [kəʊlt] *n* Hengstfohlen *nt*; (*dated fig: youth*) junger Dachs (*inf*).
Co Ltd *abbr of* **company limited** GmbH *f*.
columbine ['kɒləmbaɪn] *n* (*Bot*) Akelei *f*.
Columbus [kə'lʌmbəs] *n* Kolumbus *m*.
column ['kɒləm] *n* **(a)** (*Archit, of smoke, water etc*) Säule *f* ◆ **~ of mercury** Quecksilbersäule *f*. **(b)** (*of figures, names*) Kolonne *f*; (*division of page*) Spalte, Kolumne (*spec*) *f*; (*article in newspaper*) Kolumne *f*. **(c)** (*of vehicles, soldiers etc*) Kolonne *f*.
columnist ['kɒləmnɪst] *n* Kolumnist(in *f*) *m*.
coma ['kəʊmə] *n* Koma *nt* ◆ **to be in a/to go** *or* **fall into a ~** im Koma liegen/ins Koma fallen.
comatose ['kəʊmətəʊs] *adj* komatös.
comb [kəʊm] [1] *n* **(a)** (*also Tech, of fowl*) Kamm *m*. **(b)** (*act*) **to give one's hair a ~** sich kämmen; **your hair could do with a ~** du könntest dich (auch) mal wieder kämmen. **(c)** (*honey~*) Wabe *f*.
[2] *vt* **(a)** *hair, wool* kämmen; *horse* striegeln ◆ **to ~ one's hair** sich (*dat*) die Haare kämmen, sich kämmen. **(b)** (*search*) durchkämmen; *newspapers* durchforsten.
◆**comb out** *vt sep* **(a)** *hair* auskämmen. **(b)** *mistakes* ausmerzen; *useless stuff* aussortieren.
◆**comb through** *vi +prep obj hair* kämmen; *files, book etc* durchgehen; *shops* durchstöbern.
combat ['kɒmbæt] [1] *n* Kampf *m* ◆ **ready for ~** kampfbereit, einsatzbereit.
[2] *vt* (*lit, fig*) bekämpfen.
[3] *vi* kämpfen.
combatant ['kɒmbətənt] *n* (*lit, fig*) Kombattant *m*.
combat: ~ dress *n* Kampfanzug *m*; **~ fatigue** *n* Kriegsmüdigkeit *f*.
combative ['kɒmbətɪv] *adj* (*pugnacious*) kämpferisch; (*competitive*) aggressiv.
combat: ~ jacket *n* Feldjacke, Kampfjacke *f*; **~ mission** *n* Kampfeinsatz *m*; **~ troops** *npl* Kampftruppen *pl*; **~ zone** *n* Kampfgebiet *nt or* -zone *f*.
combination [ˌkɒmbɪ'neɪʃən] *n* **(a)** Kombination *f*; (*combining: of organizations, people etc*) Vereinigung *f*, Zusammenschluß *m*; (*of events*) Verkettung *f* ◆ **in ~** zusammen, gemeinsam; **an unusual colour ~** eine ungewöhnliche Farbzusammenstellung; **pink is a ~ of red and white** Rosa ist eine Mischung aus Rot und Weiß; **they're a strange ~, that couple** die beiden sind ein seltsames Paar; **those two boys together are a nasty ~** diese beiden Jungen zusammen sind ein übles Duo.
(b) ~s *pl* (*undergarment*) Kombination, Hemdhose *f*.
(c) (*motorcycle ~*) Motorrad *nt* mit Beiwagen.
(d) (*for lock*) Kombination *f* ◆ **~ lock** Kombinationsschloß *nt*.
combine [kəm'baɪn] [1] *vt* kombinieren, verbinden ◆ **couldn't we ~ the two suggestions?** lassen sich die beiden Vorschläge nicht kombinieren *or* miteinander verbinden?; **your plan ~s the merits of the other two** Ihr Plan vereinigt die Vorzüge der beiden anderen.
[2] *vi* sich zusammenschließen; (*Chem*) sich verbinden ◆ **everything ~d against him** alles hat sich gegen ihn verschworen.
[3] ['kɒmbaɪn] *n* **(a)** Firmengruppe *f*, Konzern *m*; (*in socialist countries*) Kombinat *nt*. **(b)** (*also* **~ harvester**) Mähdrescher *m*.
combined [kəm'baɪnd] *adj* gemeinsam; *talents, efforts* vereint; *forces* vereinigt ◆ **~ with** in Kombination mit; (*esp clothes, furniture*) kombiniert mit; **a ~ clock and wireless/radio and tape recorder** eine Radiouhr/Radio und Tonband in einem.
combining form [kəm'baɪnɪŋfɔːm] *n* Affix, Wortbildungselement *nt*.
combo ['kɒmbəʊ] *n* (*Mus*) Combo *f*.
combustibility [kəm'bʌstɪbɪlɪtɪ] *n* Brennbarkeit *f*.
combustible [kəm'bʌstɪbl] [1] *adj* brennbar.
[2] *n* brennbarer Stoff.
combustion [kəm'bʌstʃən] *n* Verbrennung *f* ◆ **~ chamber** Brennkammer *f*.
come [kʌm] *pret* **came,** *ptp* **~** [1] *vi* **(a)** kommen ◆ **~!** (*form: ~ in*) herein!; **~ and get it!** (das) Essen ist fertig!, Essen fassen! (*esp Mil*); **to ~ and go** kommen und gehen; (*vehicle*) hin- und herfahren; **the picture/sound ~s and goes** das Bild/der Ton geht immerzu weg; **~ and see me soon** besuchen Sie mich bald einmal; **he has ~ a long way** er hat einen weiten Weg hinter sich; (*fig*) er ist weit gekommen; **the project has ~ a long way** das Projekt ist schon ziemlich weit; **he came running/hurrying/laughing into the room** er kam ins Zimmer gerannt/er eilte ins Zimmer/er kam lachend ins Zimmer; **coming!** ich komme (gleich)!; ich komm' ja schon!; **~ ~!, ~ now!** (*fig*) komm, (komm), na, na!; **Christmas is coming** bald ist Weihnachten.
(b) (*arrive*) kommen; (*reach, extend*) reichen (*to* an/in/bis *etc +acc*) ◆ **they came to a town/castle** sie kamen in eine Stadt/zu einem Schloß; **it came into my head that ...** ich habe mir gedacht, daß ...; **to ~ before a judge** vor den Richter kommen.
(c) (*have its place*) kommen ◆ **May ~s before June** Mai kommt vor Juni; **the adjective must ~ before the noun** das Adjektiv muß vor dem Substantiv stehen; **where does your name ~ in the list?** an welcher Stelle auf der Liste steht Ihr Name?; **that must ~ first** das muß an erster Stelle kommen.
(d) (*happen*) geschehen ◆ **~ what may** ganz gleich, was geschieht, komme, was (da) mag (*geh*); **you could see it coming** das konnte man ja kommen sehen, das war ja zu erwarten; **she had had it coming to her** (*inf*) das mußte ja so kommen; **you've got it coming to you** (*inf*) mach dich auf was gefaßt!; **recovery came slowly** nur allmählich trat eine Besserung ein.
(e) how ~? (*inf*) wieso?, weshalb?; **how ~ you're so late?, how do you ~ to be so late?** wieso *etc* kommst du so spät?
(f) (*be, become*) werden ◆ **his dreams came true** seine Träume wurden wahr; **the handle has ~ loose** der Griff hat sich gelockert; **it ~s less expensive to shop in town** es ist *or* kommt billiger, wenn man in der Stadt einkauft; **everything came all right in the end** zuletzt *or* am Ende wurde doch noch alles gut.
(g) (*Comm: be available*) erhältlich sein ◆ **milk now ~s in plastic bottles** es gibt jetzt Milch in Plastikflaschen.
(h) (*+infin: be finally in a position to*) **I have ~ to believe him** inzwischen *or* mittlerweile glaube ich ihm; **I'm sure you will ~ to agree with me** ich bin sicher, daß du mir schließlich zustimmst; **(now I) ~ to think of it** wenn ich es mir recht überlege.
(i) the years/weeks *etc* **to ~** die kommenden *or* nächsten Jahre/Wochen; **in days/time to ~** in Zukunft/in künftigen Zeiten; **the life (of the world) to ~** das ewige Leben.
(j) (*inf uses*) **... ~ next week** nächste Woche ...; **I've known him for three years ~ January** im Januar kenne ich ihn drei Jahre; **how long have you been away? — a week ~ Monday** wie lange bist du schon weg? — (am) Montag acht Tage (*inf*) *or* eine Woche; **a week ~ Monday I'll be ...** Montag in acht Tagen (*inf*) *or* in einer Woche bin ich ...; **~ again?** wie bitte?; **she is as vain as they ~** sie ist so eingebildet wie nur was (*inf*).
(k) (*inf: have orgasm*) kommen (*inf*).
[2] *vt* (*sl: act as if one were*) spielen ◆ **don't ~ the innocent with me** spielen Sie hier bloß nicht den Unschuldigen!, kommen Sie mir bloß nicht auf die unschuldige Tour (*inf*)!; **he tried to ~ the innocent with me** er hat versucht, den Unschuldigen zu markieren (*inf*), er hat es auf die unschuldige Tour versucht (*inf*); **don't ~ that game** *or* **that (with me)!** kommen Sie mir bloß nicht mit *der* Tour! (*inf*), *die* Masche zieht bei mir nicht! (*inf*); **that's coming it a bit strong!** das ist reichlich übertrieben.
[3] *n* (*sl: semen*) Soße *f* (*sl*).
◆**come about** *vi* **(a)** *impers* (*happen*) passieren ◆ **how does it ~ ~ that you are here?** wie kommt es, daß du hier bist?; **this is why it came ~** das ist so gekommen; **this is how it came ~ ...** das kam so ... **(b)** (*Naut*) (*wind*) drehen; (*ship*) beidrehen.
◆**come across** [1] *vi* **(a)** (*cross*) herüberkommen. **(b)** (*be understood*) verstanden werden; (*message, speech*) ankommen. **(c)** (*make an impression*) wirken ◆ **he wants to ~ ~ like a tough guy** er mimt gerne den starken Mann (*inf*). **(d)** (*inf*) (*do what is wanted*) mitmachen (*inf*).
[2] *vi +prep obj* (*find or meet by chance*) treffen auf (*+acc*) ◆ **if you ~ ~ my watch ...** wenn du zufällig meine Uhr siehst.
◆**come across with** *vi +prep obj* (*inf*) *information* rausrücken mit (*inf*); *money* rausrücken (*inf*).
◆**come after** *vi +prep obj* **(a)** (*follow in sequence, be of less importance than*) kommen nach ◆ **the noun ~s ~ the verb** das Substantiv steht nach *or* hinter dem Verb. **(b)** (*pursue*) herkommen hinter (*+dat*). **(c)** *also vi* (*follow later*) nachkommen.
◆**come along** *vi* **(a)** (*hurry up, make an effort etc: also* **come on**) kommen.
(b) (*attend, accompany*) mitkommen ◆ **~ ~ with me** kommen Sie mal (bitte) mit.
(c) (*develop: also* **come on**) **to be coming ~** sich machen, vorangehen; (*person*) sich machen; **how is your broken arm? — it's coming ~ nicely** was macht dein gebrochener Arm? — dem geht's ganz gut *or* prima; **the bulbs are coming ~ nicely** die Blumenzwiebeln wachsen gut; **the new apprentice is**

coming ~ nicely der neue Lehrling macht sich gut; **my play isn't coming ~ at all well** mein Stück macht überhaupt keine Fortschritte.
(d) *(arrive, turn up)* kommen, auftauchen; *(chance etc)* sich ergeben.

◆**come apart** *vi (fall to pieces)* kaputtgehen, auseinanderfallen; *(be able to be taken apart)* zerlegbar sein.

◆**come at** *vi +prep obj (attack) sb* losgehen auf *(+acc)*; *(approach) runway* anfliegen; *problem* angehen.

◆**come away** *vi* **(a)** *(leave)* (weg)gehen ◆ **~ ~ with me for a few days** fahr doch ein paar Tage mit mir weg!; **~ ~ from there!** komm da weg!; **~ ~ in!** *(Scot)* kommen Sie doch rein! **(b)** *(become detached)* abgehen.

◆**come back** *vi* **(a)** *(return)* zurückkommen; *(drive back)* zurückfahren ◆ **to ~ ~ to what I was saying** um noch einmal auf das zurückzukommen, was ich vorhin gesagt habe; **we always ~ ~ to the same difficulty** wir stoßen immer wieder auf dieselbe Schwierigkeit; **can I ~ ~ to you on that one?** kann ich später darauf zurückkommen?; **the colour is coming ~ to her cheeks** langsam bekommt sie wieder Farbe; **will his memory ever ~ ~?** wird er je das Gedächtnis wiedererlangen?
(b) *(return to one's memory)* **his face is coming ~ to me** langsam erinnere ich mich wieder an sein Gesicht; **ah yes, it's all coming ~** ach ja, jetzt fällt mir alles wieder ein; **your German will very quickly ~ ~** du wirst ganz schnell wieder ins Deutsche reinkommen *(inf)*.
(c) *(become popular again)* wieder in Mode kommen.
(d) *(make a comeback)* **they thought Sinatra would never ~ ~** man glaubte, Sinatra würde niemals ein Comeback machen; **he came ~ strongly into the game** er spielte mächtig auf.
(e) *(reply)* reagieren ◆ **she came ~ at him with a fierce accusation** sie entgegnete ihm mit einer heftigen Anschuldigung.

◆**come between** *vi +prep obj people, lovers* treten zwischen *(+acc)* ◆ **I never let anything ~ ~ me and my evening pint** ich lasse mich durch nichts von meinem abendlichen Bier(chen) abhalten; **he tried to ~ ~ the two men fighting** er versuchte, die beiden Kampfhähne zu trennen.

◆**come by** [1] *vi +prep obj (obtain)* kriegen; *illness, bruise* sich *(dat)* holen; *idea* kommen auf *(+acc)*.
[2] *vi (visit)* vorbeikommen.

◆**come close to** *vi +prep obj see* **come near to.**

◆**come down** *vi* **(a)** *(from ladder, stairs)* herunterkommen; *(aircraft also)* landen; *(from mountain also)* absteigen; *(snow, rain)* fallen ◆ **~ ~ from there at once!** komm da sofort runter!; **we came ~ to 6,000 metres** wir gingen auf 6.000 m runter.
(b) *(be demolished: building etc)* abgerissen werden; *(fall down)* (he)runterfallen.
(c) *(drop: prices)* sinken, runtergehen *(inf)*; *(seller)* runtergehen *(to* auf *+acc)*.
(d) *(be a question of)* ankommen *(to* auf *+acc)* ◆ **it all ~s ~ to something very simple** das ist letzten Endes ganz einfach.
(e) *(lose social rank)* sinken, absteigen ◆ **you've ~ ~ in the world a bit** du bist aber ganz schön tief gesunken.
(f) *(reach)* reichen *(to* bis auf *+acc,* zu) ◆ **her hair ~s ~ to her shoulders** die Haare gehen *or* fallen ihr bis auf die Schultern; **the dress ~s ~ to her knees** das Kleid geht ihr bis zum Knie.
(g) *(be transmitted: tradition, story etc)* überliefert werden.
(h) *(from university)* **when did you ~ ~?** wann bist du von der Uni runter? *(inf)*, wann haben Sie die Universität verlassen?; *(for vac)* seit wann habt ihr Semesterferien?
(i) *(US inf: be about to happen)* **there's a bank robbery coming ~ next week** für nächste Woche ist ein Banküberfall geplant.

◆**come down on** *vi +prep obj* **(a)** *(punish, rebuke)* rannehmen *(inf)*, zusammenstauchen *(inf)*; *see* **brick. (b)** *(decide in favour of)* setzen auf *(+acc)* ◆ **he came ~ ~ the side of expansion** er setzte auf Expansion; **you've got to ~ ~ one side or the other** du mußt dich so oder so entscheiden.

◆**come down with** *vi +prep obj illness* kriegen.

◆**come for** *vi +prep obj* kommen wegen.

◆**come forward** *vi* **(a)** sich melden. **(b) to ~ ~ with help/money** Hilfe/Geld anbieten; **to ~ ~ with a good suggestion** mit einem guten Vorschlag kommen.

◆**come from** *vi +prep obj* kommen aus; *(suggestion)* kommen *or* stammen von ◆ **where does he/it ~ ~?** wo kommt er/das her?

◆**come in** *vi* **(a)** (he)reinkommen; *(person also)* eintreten ◆ **~ ~!** herein!; **to ~ ~ out of the cold** aus der Kälte kommen.
(b) *(arrive)* ankommen, eintreffen; *(train also)* einfahren; *(ship also)* einlaufen.
(c) *(tide)* kommen.
(d) *(report, information etc)* hereinkommen ◆ **a report has just ~ ~ of ...** uns ist gerade eine Meldung über ... zugegangen.
(e) *(become seasonable)* **when do strawberries ~ ~?** wann ist die Zeit für Erdbeeren?, wann gibt es (frische) Erdbeeren?
(f) *(fashions, vogue)* aufkommen, in Mode kommen.
(g) *(in a race)* **he came ~ fourth** er wurde vierter, er belegte den vierten Platz; **where did he ~ ~?** wievielter ist er denn geworden?, welchen Platz hat er belegt?
(h) *(Pol: be elected to power)* **when the socialists came ~** als die Sozialisten ans Ruder *or* an die Regierung kamen.
(i) *(be received as income)* **he has £15,000 coming ~ every year** er kriegt *(inf) or* hat £ 15.000 im Jahr.
(j) *(have a part to play)* **where do I ~ ~?** welche Rolle spiele ich dabei?; **... but where does your brother ~ ~?** ... aber was hat dein Bruder mit der ganzen Sache zu tun?; **that will ~ ~ handy** *(inf) or* **useful** das kann ich/man noch gut gebrauchen.
(k) *(Telec)* **~ ~, Panda 5** Panda 5, melden!

◆**come in for** *vi +prep obj attention, admiration* erregen; *criticism etc also* hinnehmen *or* einstecken müssen.

◆**come in on** *vi +prep obj venture, scheme etc* mitmachen bei, sich beteiligen an *(+dat)*.

◆**come into** *vi +prep obj* **(a)** *legacy etc (inherit)* erben ◆ **to ~ ~ one's own** zeigen, was in einem steckt.
(b) *(be involved)* **I don't see where I ~ ~ all this** ich verstehe nicht, was ich mit der ganzen Sache zu tun habe; **this is a donation, publicity doesn't ~ ~ it** es handelt sich hier um eine Spende, Publicity ist dabei nicht im Spiel.
(c) *(in fixed collocations)* **to ~ ~ being** *or* **existence** entstehen; **to ~ ~ blossom/bud** zu blühen/knospen beginnen; **to ~ ~ sb's possession** in jds Besitz *(acc)* gelangen.

◆**come near to** *vi +prep obj* **to ~ ~ ~ doing sth** nahe daran *or* drauf und dran sein, etw zu tun; **he came ~ ~ (committing) suicide** er war *or* stand kurz vor dem Selbstmord.

◆**come of** *vi +prep obj* **(a)** *(result from)* **nothing came ~ it** es ist nichts daraus geworden, es führte zu nichts; **that's what ~s ~ disobeying!** das kommt davon, wenn man nicht hören will!
(b) *(be descended from)* kommen *or* stammen aus.

◆**come off** [1] *vi* **(a)** *(person: off bicycle etc)* runterfallen.
(b) *(button, handle, paint etc)* abgehen; *(be removable also)* sich abnehmen lassen.
(c) *(stains, marks)* weg- *or* rausgehen.
(d) *(take place)* stattfinden ◆ **her wedding didn't ~ ~ after all** aus ihrer Hochzeit ist nun doch nichts geworden.
(e) *(plans etc)* klappen *(inf)*; *(attempts, experiments etc also)* glücken, gelingen.
(f) *(acquit oneself)* abschneiden ◆ **he came ~ well in comparison to his brother** im Vergleich zu seinem Bruder ist er gut weggekommen; **he always came ~ badly in fights** bei Schlägereien zog er immer den kürzeren; **several companies are likely to ~ ~ badly with the new tax laws** mehrere Firmen kommen in der neuen Steuergesetzgebung schlecht weg.
(g) *(sl: have orgasm)* kommen *(inf)* ◆ **eventually he came ~** endlich kam es ihm *(sl)*.
[2] *vi +prep obj* **(a)** *bicycle, horse etc* fallen von.
(b) *(button, paint, stain)* abgehen von.
(c) *case, assignment etc* abgeben ◆ **to ~ ~ the gold standard** *(Fin)* vom Goldstandard abgehen.
(d) *(be removed from price of)* runtergehen von *(inf)*.
(e) *(inf)* **~ ~ it!** nun mach mal halblang! *(inf)*.
(f) *(inf: have orgasm)* kommen *(inf)*.

◆**come on** [1] *vi* **(a)** *(follow)* nachkommen.
(b) *see* **come along (a) ~ ~!** komm!; **~ *on!*** komm schon!
(c) *(continue to advance)* zukommen *(towards* auf *+acc)*.
(d) *(progress, develop) see* **come along (c).**
(e) *(start) (night)* hereinbrechen; *(storm)* ausbrechen, einsetzen ◆ **it came ~ to rain, the rain came ~** es begann zu regnen, es fing an zu regnen; **I've a cold coming ~** ich kriege eine Erkältung; **winter *etc* is coming ~** es wird Winter *etc*.
(f) *(Jur: case)* verhandelt werden.
(g) *(Sport: player)* ins Spiel kommen; *(Theat) (actor)* auftreten, auf die Bühne kommen; *(play)* gegeben werden.
(h) *(inf)* **she's coming ~ seventeen** sie wird siebzehn.
(i) *(sl: make impression, behave)* **he tries to ~ ~ like a tough guy** er versucht, den starken Mann zu mimen *(inf)*; **he came ~ with this bit about knowing the director** er gab damit an, den Direktor zu kennen; **to ~ ~ strong** groß auftreten *(inf)*.
[2] *vi +prep obj* = **come (up)on.**

◆**come on to** *vi +prep obj (esp US inf: make advances to)* anmachen *(inf)*.

◆**come out** *vi* **(a)** (he)rauskommen ◆ **to ~ ~ of a room/meeting *etc*** aus einem Zimmer/einer Versammlung *etc* kommen; **can you ~ ~ tonight?** kannst du heute abend weg?; **do you want to ~ ~ with me?** gehst du mit mir weg?; **he asked her to ~ ~ for a meal/drive** er lud sie zum Essen/einer Spazierfahrt ein.
(b) *(be published, marketed) (book, magazine)* erscheinen, herauskommen; *(new product)* auf den Markt kommen; *(film)* (in den Kinos) anlaufen; *(become known) (exam results)* herauskommen, bekannt werden; *(news)* bekannt werden.
(c) *(Ind)* **to ~ ~ (on strike)** in den Streik treten, streiken.
(d) *(Phot: film, photograph)* **the photo of the hills hasn't ~ ~ very well** das Foto von den Bergen ist nicht sehr gut geworden; **let's hope the photos ~ ~** hoffentlich sind die Bilder was geworden *(inf) or* gut geworden; **you always ~ ~ well on *or* in photos** du bist sehr fotogen; **all the details have ~ ~ clearly** alle Einzelheiten kommen klar (he)raus.
(e) *(show itself)* sich zeigen ◆ **his kindness/arrogance ~s ~ in everything he says** bei allem, was er sagt, spürt man seine Freundlichkeit/bei allem, was er sagt, kommt seine Arroganz durch.
(f) *(splinter, stains, dye etc)* (he)rausgehen.
(g) *(Math: of problems, divisions etc)* aufgehen.
(h) *(total, average)* betragen ◆ **the total ~s ~ at £500** das Ganze beläuft sich auf *(acc) or* macht *(inf)* £ 500.
(i) *(in exams etc)* **he came ~ third in French** er wurde Drittbester in Französisch; **she came ~ of the interview well** sie hat bei dem Vor-

stellungsgespräch einen guten Eindruck gemacht.
(j) (*stars, sun, flowers*) (he)rauskommen.
(k) (*truth, meaning etc*) (he)rauskommen ◆ **no sooner had the words ~ ~ than** ... kaum waren die Worte heraus, als ....
(l) (*go into society: girl*) debütieren.
(m) (*be released: prisoner*) (he)rauskommen.
(n) (*homosexual*) sich als Homosexueller bekennen; (*woman*) sich als Lesbierin bekennen.
(o) **his face came ~ in pimples** er bekam lauter Pickel im Gesicht; **he came ~ in a rash** er bekam einen Ausschlag; **he came ~ in a sweat** ihm brach der Schweiß aus.
(p) **to ~ ~ against/in favour of** *or* **for sth** sich gegen/für etw aussprechen, etw ablehnen/befürworten.
(q) **to ~ ~ of sth badly/well** bei etw schlecht/nicht schlecht wegkommen; **to ~ ~ on top** sich durchsetzen, Sieger bleiben.

◆**come out with** *vi +prep obj truth, facts* rausrücken mit (*inf*); *remarks, nonsense* loslassen (*inf*).

◆**come over** [1] *vi* (a) (*lit*) herüberkommen ◆ **he came ~ to England** er kam nach England.
(b) (*change one's opinions, allegiance*) **he came ~ to our side** er trat auf unsere Seite über; **he came ~ to our way of thinking** er machte sich unsere Denkungsart zu eigen.
(c) (*inf: become suddenly*) werden ◆ **I came ~ (all) queer** *or* **funny** mir wurde ganz komisch (*inf*) *or* ganz merkwürdig; **it came ~ cloudy** es bewölkte sich.
(d) (*be understood*) *see* **come across 1 (b).**
(e) (*make an impression*) *see* **come across 1 (c).**
[2] *vi +prep obj* (*feelings*) überkommen ◆ **I don't know what came ~ her to speak like that!** ich weiß nicht, was über sie gekommen ist, so zu reden!; **what's ~ ~ you?** was ist denn (auf einmal) mit dir los?, was ist in dich gefahren?

◆**come round** *vi* (a) **the road was blocked and we had to ~ ~ by the farm** die Straße war blockiert, so daß wir einen Umweg über den Bauernhof machen mußten.
(b) (*call round*) vorbeikommen *or* -schauen.
(c) (*recur*) **your birthday will soon ~ ~ again** du hast ja bald wieder Geburtstag; **Christmas has ~ ~ again** nun ist wieder Weihnachten.
(d) (*change one's opinions*) es sich (*dat*) anders überlegen ◆ **eventually he came ~ to our way of thinking** schließlich machte er sich (*dat*) unsere Denkungsart zu eigen.
(e) (*regain consciousness*) wieder zu sich (*dat*) kommen.
(f) **to ~ ~ to doing sth** (*get round*) dazu kommen, etw zu tun.
(g) (*throw off bad mood*) wieder vernünftig werden (*inf*).
(h) (*Naut: boat*) wenden.

◆**come through** [1] *vi* (a) (*phone-call, order*) durchkommen ◆ **your expenses/papers haven't ~ ~ yet** (*be cleared*) wir haben Ihre Ausgaben noch nicht durchgekriegt/Ihre Papiere sind noch nicht fertig. (b) (*survive*) durchkommen.
[2] *vi +prep obj* (*survive*) *illness, danger* überstehen.

◆**come to** [1] *vi* (a) (*regain consciousness: also* **~ ~ oneself**) wieder zu sich kommen. (b) (*Naut*) beidrehen.
[2] *vi +prep obj* (a) **he/that will never ~ ~ much** aus ihm/ daraus wird nie etwas werden; **that won't ~ ~ much** daraus wird nicht viel werden; **that didn't ~ ~ anything** daraus ist nichts geworden.
(b) (*impers*) **when it ~s ~ mathematics ...** wenn es um Mathematik geht, ...; **when it ~s ~ choosing, he ...** wenn er die Wahl hat *or* vor die Wahl gestellt wird, ...; **if it ~s ~ that we're sunk** wenn es dazu kommt, sind wir verloren; **~ ~ that** *or* **if it ~s ~ that, he's just as good** was das betrifft *or* an(be)langt, ist er genauso gut; **let's hope it never ~s ~ a court case** wollen wir hoffen, daß es nie zum Prozeß kommt; **it ~s ~ the same thing** das kommt *or* läuft auf dasselbe hinaus.
(c) (*price, bill*) **how much does it ~ ~?** wieviel macht das?; **it ~s ~ much less/more than I thought** es kommt viel billiger/teurer, als ich dachte.
(d) (*touch on*) *point, subject etc* kommen auf (*+acc*); (*tackle*) *problem, job etc* herangehen an (*+acc*).
(e) (*in certain collocations*) **to ~ ~ a decision** zu einer Entscheidung kommen; **it's coming ~ something when ...** es will schon etwas heißen, wenn ...; **what are things** *or* **what is the world coming ~!** wohin soll das noch führen!; *see* **blow[1], light** *etc.*

◆**come together** *vi* zusammenkommen, sich treffen ◆ **he and his wife have ~ ~ again** er ist wieder mit seiner Frau zusammen; **it's all coming ~ for him** (*sl*) es regelt sich jetzt alles für ihn (*inf*).

◆**come under** *vi +prep obj* (a) (*be subject to*) **to ~ ~ sb's influence/domination** unter jds Einfluß/Herrschaft geraten; **this shop has ~ ~ new management** dieser Laden hat einen neuen Besitzer/Pächter; **this ~s ~ another department** das ist Sache einer anderen Abteilung.
(b) *category, heading* kommen unter (*+acc*).

◆**come up** *vi* (a) (*lit*) hochkommen; (*upstairs*) hoch- *or* raufkommen; (*diver, submarine*) nach oben kommen; (*sun, moon*) aufgehen ◆ **do you ~ ~ to town often?** kommen Sie oft in die Stadt?; **he came ~ (to Oxford) last year** (*Univ*) er studiert seit letztem Jahr (in Oxford); **you've ~ ~ in the world** du bist ja richtig vornehm geworden!; **he came ~ to me with a smile** er kam lächelnd auf mich zu.
(b) (*supplies, troops etc*) herangeschafft werden.
(c) (*Jur*) (*case*) verhandelt werden, drankommen (*inf*); (*accused*) vor Gericht kommen.
(d) (*plants*) herauskommen.
(e) (*matter for discussion*) aufkommen, angeschnitten werden; (*name*) erwähnt werden.
(f) (*number in lottery etc*) gewinnen ◆ **to ~ ~ for sale/auction** *etc* zum Verkauf/zur Auktion *etc* kommen.
(g) (*post, job*) frei werden.
(h) (*be vomited*) wieder hochkommen.
(i) (*shine, show colour*) herauskommen.

◆**come up against** *vi +prep obj* stoßen auf (*+acc*); *opposing team* treffen auf (*+acc*) ◆ **his plan was doing well until he came ~ ~ the directors** sein Vorhaben machte gute Fortschritte, bis er an die Geschäftsleitung geriet; **the new teacher keeps coming ~ ~ the headmaster** der neue Lehrer gerät ständig mit dem Direktor aneinander.

◆**come (up)on** *vi +prep obj* (a) (*lit*) (*attack by surprise*) überfallen; (*fig*) (*disaster*) hereinbrechen über (*+acc*) ◆ **and the fear of the Lord came upon them** (*Bibl*) und die Furcht des Herrn kam über sie (*Bibl*). (b) (*find*) stoßen auf (*+acc*).

◆**come up to** *vi +prep obj* (a) (*reach up to*) gehen *or* reichen bis zu *or* an (*+acc*) ◆ **the water came ~ ~ his knees** das Wasser ging *or* reichte ihm bis an die Knie *or* bis zu den Knien.
(b) (*equal*) *hopes* erfüllen; *expectations* entsprechen (*+dat*).
(c) (*inf: approach*) **she's coming ~ ~ twenty** sie wird bald zwanzig; **we're coming ~ ~ 150 km/h** wir haben gleich 150 km/h drauf (*inf*); **it's just coming ~ ~ 10** es ist gleich 10.

◆**come up with** *vi +prep obj answer* haben; *idea, solution also* kommen auf (*+acc*); *plan* sich (*dat*) ausdenken, entwickeln; *suggestion* machen, bringen ◆ **I can't ~ ~ ~ any answers either** ich habe auch keine Antwort; **let me know if you ~ ~ ~ anything** sagen Sie mir Bescheid, falls Ihnen etwas einfällt.

come-at-able [kʌm'ætəbl] *adj* (*inf*) leicht erreichbar.

comeback ['kʌmbæk] *n* (a) (*Theat etc, fig*) Comeback *nt* ◆ **to make** *or* **stage a ~** ein Comeback versuchen/machen. (b) (*inf: redress*) Anspruch *m* auf Schadenersatz; (*reaction*) Reaktion *f* ◆ **we've got no ~ in this situation** wir können da nichts machen.

Comecon ['kɒmɪkɒn] *abbr of* **Council for Mutual Economic Aid** Comecon *m or nt*.

comedian [kə'miːdɪən] *n* Komiker(in *f*) *m*; (*fig also*) Witzbold *m*.

comedienne [kə,miːdɪ'en] *n* Komikerin *f*; (*actress*) Komödiendarstellerin *f*.

comedown ['kʌmdaʊn] *n* (*inf*) Abstieg *m*.

comedy ['kɒmɪdɪ] *n* (a) (*Theat*) Komödie *f*, Lustspiel *nt* ◆ **~ programme** Unterhaltungsprogramm *nt*; **~ writer** Lustspielautor *or* (*classical*) -dichter *m*; **"C~ of Errors"** „Komödie der Irrungen"; **the entire deal was just one ~ of errors** (*fig*) bei dem Geschäft ging aber auch alles daneben; **low/high ~** Klamauk *m*/echte *or* gekonnte Komödie; **to act (in) ~** Komödiendarsteller(in *f*) *m* sein.
(b) (*fig*) Komödie *f*, Theater *nt* (*inf*).

come-hither [kʌm'hɪðə[r]] *adj* (*inf*) **she gave him a ~ look** sie warf ihm einladende *or* aufmunternde Blicke zu.

comeliness ['kʌmlɪnɪs] *n* (*liter*) Wohlgestalt *f* (*liter*).

comely ['kʌmlɪ] *adj* (*+er*) (*liter*) wohlgestaltet (*geh*).

come-on ['kʌmɒn] *n* (*sl: lure, enticement*) Köder *m* (*fig*) ◆ **to give sb the ~** (*woman*) jdn anmachen (*sl*).

comer ['kʌmə[r]] *n* **this competition is open to all ~s** an diesem Wettbewerb kann sich jeder beteiligen; **"open to all ~s"** „Teilnahme für jedermann".

comestible [kə'mestɪbl] [1] *n usu pl* Nahrungsmittel *pl*.
[2] *adj* eßbar ◆ **~ goods** Nahrungsmittel *pl*.

comet ['kɒmɪt] *n* Komet *m*.

come-to-bed *adj*: **she has ~ eyes** (*inf*) sie hat Schlafzimmeraugen (*inf*).

come-uppance [,kʌm'ʌpəns] *n* (*inf*): **to get one's ~** die Quittung kriegen (*inf*).

comfit ['kɒmfɪt] *n* (*old*) Konfekt, Zuckerwerk (*old*) *nt*.

comfort ['kʌmfət] [1] *n* (a) Komfort *m*, Bequemlichkeit *f* ◆ **relax in the ~ of a leather armchair** entspannen Sie sich in unseren behaglichen Ledersesseln; **he likes his ~s** er liebt seinen Komfort *or* seine Bequemlichkeit; **to live in ~** komfortabel leben; **a flat with every modern ~** eine Wohnung mit allem Komfort.
(b) (*consolation*) Beruhigung *f*, Trost *m* ◆ **to take ~ from the fact that ...** sich mit dem Gedanken *or* sich damit trösten, daß ...; **your presence is/you are a great ~ to me** es beruhigt mich sehr, daß Sie da sind; **it is a ~ to know that ...** es ist tröstlich *or* beruhigend zu wissen, daß ...; **it is no ~ to know that ...** es ist nicht sehr tröstlich zu wissen, daß ...; **some ~ you are!** (*iro*) das ist ja ein schöner Trost! (*iro*), du bist gut! (*iro*); **small ~** schwacher Trost; **a pipe is a great ~** Pfeiferauchen hat etwas sehr Beruhigendes; **your poems brought a little ~ to my life** Ihre Gedichte haben ein wenig Trost in mein Leben gebracht.
(c) (*US*) **~ station** Bedürfnisanstalt *f*, öffentliche Toilette.
[2] *vt* (*console*) trösten ◆ **the child needed a lot of ~ing** es dauerte eine ganze Weile, bis das Kind sich trösten ließ; **he stayed with the injured man to ~ him** er blieb bei dem Verletzten, um ihm Beistand zu leisten; **the hot soup ~ed him a little** nach dem Genuß der heißen Suppe fühlte er sich etwas wohler.

comfortable ['kʌmfətəbl] *adj* (a) *armchair, bed, shoes, life* bequem; *room, hotel etc* komfortabel; *temperature* angenehm ◆ **to make sb/oneself ~** es jdm/sich bequem machen; (*make at home*) es jdm/sich gemütlich machen; **the sick man had a ~ night** der Kranke hatte *or* verbrachte eine ruhige Nacht; **the patient/his condition is ~** der Patient/er ist wohlauf; **are you ~?, asked the**

nurse liegen/sitzen *etc* Sie bequem?, fragte die Schwester; **are you too hot? — no, I'm just ~** ist es Ihnen zu heiß? — nein, es ist angenehm so.
(b) *(fig) income, pension* ausreichend; *life* geruhsam, angenehm; *majority, lead* sicher; *figure* mollig ◆ **he's very ~ to be with** bei ihm fühlt man sich sehr wohl; **she had quite a ~ feeling about it** sie hatte ein gutes Gefühl dabei; **I'm not very ~ about it** mir ist nicht ganz wohl bei der Sache; **I'm not too ~ about giving her the job** mir ist nicht ganz wohl bei dem Gedanken, ihr die Stelle zu geben.

comfortably ['kʌmfətəblɪ] *adv* **(a)** *lie, sit, dress etc* bequem; *furnished, upholstered* komfortabel.
(b) *(fig) win, lead* sicher; *live* geruhsam, angenehm; *afford* gut und gern; *claim, say* ruhig ◆ **they are ~ off** es geht ihnen gut; **he was ~ certain of winning** er wiegte sich in der Gewißheit, daß er gewinnen würde.

comfort eating *n* Essen *nt* als Trost.

comforter ['kʌmfətə^r] *n* **(a)** *(person)* Tröster(in *f*) *m* ◆ **my wife was my ~ in times of stress** in schweren Zeiten war meine Frau mein Beistand. **(b)** *(dated: scarf)* Wollschal *m*. **(c)** *(dummy, teat)* Schnuller *m*. **(d)** *(US: quilt)* Deckbett *nt*.

comforting ['kʌmfətɪŋ] *adj* tröstlich, beruhigend ◆ **a ~ cup of tea** eine Tasse Tee zur Beruhigung.

comfortless ['kʌmfətlɪs] *adj* **(a)** *chair etc* unbequem; *room, hotel* ohne Komfort. **(b)** *(fig) person* ungemütlich; *life* unbequem; *thought, prospect* unerfreulich, unangenehm.

comfort zone *n Bereich m, in dem man sich sicher fühlt* ◆ **two goals in two minutes put Rangers in the ~** nach zwei Toren in zwei Minuten fühlten Rangers sich sicher.

comfy ['kʌmfɪ] *adj (+er) (inf) chair* bequem; *hotel, flat, room* gemütlich ◆ **are you ~?** sitzt/liegst du bequem?; **make yourself ~** machen Sie es sich *(dat)* bequem *or* gemütlich *(inf)*.

comic ['kɒmɪk] [1] *adj* komisch ◆ **~ actor** Komödiendarsteller, Komöde *(geh) m*; **~ book** Comicbuch *nt*; **~ opera** komische Oper; **~ relief** befreiende Komik; **~ strip** Comic strip *m*; **~ verse** humoristische Gedichte *pl*.
[2] *n* **(a)** *(person)* Komiker(in *f*) *m*. **(b)** *(magazine)* Comic-Heft(chen) *nt*. **(c)** *(US)* **~s** Comics *pl*.

comical *adj*, **~ly** *adv* ['kɒmɪkəl, -ɪ] komisch, ulkig.

coming ['kʌmɪŋ] [1] *n* Kommen *nt* ◆ **you can sense the ~ of spring** man fühlt *or* spürt das Herannahen des Frühlings; **the first/second ~ (of the Lord)** die Ankunft/Wiederkunft des Herrn; **the ~ of a new manager** die Ankunft eines neuen Geschäftsführers; **~ and going/~s and goings** Kommen und Gehen *nt*; **~-out** gesellschaftliches Debüt, (offizielle) Einführung in die Gesellschaft; **~-out party** Debütantinnenparty *f*; **~ of age** Erreichung *f* der Volljährigkeit.
[2] *adj (lit, fig)* kommend; *year, week also* nächst ◆ **a ~ politician** einer der kommenden Männer in der Politik; **it's the ~ thing** *(inf)* das ist zur Zeit groß im Kommen *(inf)*.

comma ['kɒmə] *n* Komma *nt*.

command [kə'mɑːnd] [1] *vt* **(a)** *(order)* befehlen, den Befehl geben *(sb* jdm) ◆ **he ~ed that the prisoners be released** er befahl, die Gefangenen freizulassen.
(b) *(be in control of) army, ship* befehligen, kommandieren.
(c) *(be in a position to use) money, resources, vocabulary* verfügen über *(+acc)*, gebieten über *(+acc) (geh)* ◆ **to ~ sb's services** jds Dienste *or* Hilfe in Anspruch nehmen.
(d) to ~ sb's admiration/respect jdm Bewunderung/Respekt abnötigen, jds Bewunderung/Respekt erheischen *(geh)*; **antiques ~ a high price** Antiquitäten stehen hoch im Preis.
(e) *(overlook) valley* überragen; *view* bieten *(of* über *+acc)*.
[2] *vi* **(a)** *(order)* befehlen.
(b) *(Mil, Naut: to be in ~)* das Kommando führen.
[3] *n* **(a)** *(order)* Befehl *m* ◆ **at/by the ~ of** auf Befehl *+gen*; **at the word of ~** auf Kommando; **on ~** auf Befehl *or* Kommando.
(b) *(Mil: power, authority)* Kommando *nt*, Befehlsgewalt *f* ◆ **to be in ~** das Kommando *or* den (Ober)befehl haben *(of* über *+acc)*; **to take ~** das Kommando übernehmen *(of gen)*; **the new colonel arrived to take ~ of his regiment** der neue Oberst kam, um sein Regiment zu übernehmen; **during/under his ~** unter seinem Kommando; **the battalion is under the ~ of ...** das Bataillon steht unter dem Kommando von ... *or* wird befehligt von ...; **to be second in ~** zweiter Befehlshaber sein.
(c) *(Mil) (troops)* Kommando *nt*; *(district)* Befehlsbereich *m*; *(~ post)* Posten *m*.
(d) *(Comput)* Befehl *m* ◆ **~ language** Befehlssprache *f*; **~ line** Befehlszeile *f*.
(e) *(fig: possession, mastery)* Beherrschung *f* ◆ **~ of the seas** Seeherrschaft *f*; **the gymnast's remarkable ~ over his body** die bemerkenswerte Körperbeherrschung des Turners; **his ~ of English is excellent** er beherrscht das Englische ausgezeichnet; **to have sb/sth at one's ~** über jdn/etw verfügen *or* gebieten *(geh)*; **I am at your ~** ich stehe zu Ihrer Verfügung.

commandant [ˌkɒmən'dænt] *n (Mil)* Kommandant *m*.

command economy *n* Kommandowirtschaft *f*.

commandeer [ˌkɒmən'dɪə^r] *vt (Mil) men* einziehen; *(from another battalion, fig)* abbeordern, abkommandieren; *stores, ship, car etc (lit, fig)* beschlagnahmen, requirieren.

commander [kə'mɑːndə^r] *n* **(a)** Führer *m*; *(Mil, Aviat)* Befehlshaber, Kommandant *m*; *(Naut)* Fregattenkapitän *m*; *(Brit Police) Distriktleiter m der Londoner Polizei* ◆ **~/~s-in-chief** Oberbefehlshaber *m/pl*. **(b)** *(of order of chivalry)* Komtur *m*.

commanding [kə'mɑːndɪŋ] *adj* **(a)** *position* Befehls- ◆ **~ officer** *(Mil)* befehlshabender Offizier. **(b)** *personality, voice, tone* gebieterisch; *voice, tone also* Kommando- *(pej)*. **(c)** *(of place)* beherrschend ◆ **~ heights** Kommandohöhen *pl*.

commandment [kə'mɑːndmənt] *n (esp Bibl)* Gebot *nt* ◆ **to break a ~** gegen ein Gebot verstoßen.

command module *n (Space)* Kommandokapsel *f*.

commando [kə'mɑːndəʊ] *n, pl* **-s** *(Mil) (soldier)* Angehörige(r) *m* eines Kommando(trupp)s; *(unit)* Kommando(trupp *m*) *nt*.

command: ~ performance *n (Theat)* königliche Galavorstellung; **~ post** *n (Mil)* Kommandoposten *m*.

commemorate [kə'meməreɪt] *vt* gedenken *(+gen)* ◆ **a festival to ~ the event** eine Feier zum Gedenken an das Ereignis.

commemoration [kəˌmemə'reɪʃən] *n* Gedenken *nt* ◆ **in ~ of** zum Gedenken an *(+acc)*.

commemorative [kə'memərətɪv] *adj* Gedenk- ◆ **~ plaque** Gedenktafel *f*.

commence [kə'mens] *vti (form)* beginnen.

commencement [kə'mensmənt] *n* **(a)** *(form)* Beginn *m*. **(b)** *(Univ: Cambridge, Dublin, US)* Abschlußfeier *f (zur Verleihung der Diplome etc)*.

commend [kə'mend] [1] *vt* **(a)** *(praise)* loben; *(recommend)* empfehlen. **(b)** *(entrust)*, *(Bibl) spirit, soul* befehlen *(to dat)* ◆ **~ me to Mr Smith** *(form)* empfehlen Sie mich Herrn Smith *(form)*.
[2] *vr* sich empfehlen *(to dat)*.

commendable [kə'mendəbl] *adj* lobenswert, löblich.

commendably [kə'mendəblɪ] *adv* lobenswerterweise.

commendation [ˌkɒmen'deɪʃən] *n (no pl: praise)* Lob *nt*; *(award)* Auszeichnung *f*; *(official recognition)* Belobigung *f*.

commendatory [kə'mendətrɪ] *adj* anerkennend.

commensurate [kə'menʃərɪt] *adj* entsprechend *(with dat)* ◆ **to be ~ with sth** einer Sache *(dat)* entsprechen; **they made salaries ~ with those in comparable professions** die Gehälter wurden denen in vergleichbaren Berufen angeglichen.

commensurately [kə'menʃərətlɪ] *adv* entsprechend, angemessen.

➤ **comment** ['kɒment] [1] *n (remark)* Bemerkung *f (on, about* über *+acc*, zu); *(official)* Kommentar *m (on* zu); *(no pl: talk, gossip)* Gerede *nt*; *(textual or margin note etc)* Anmerkung *f* ◆ **no ~** kein Kommentar!; **to make a ~** eine Bemerkung machen/einen Kommentar abgeben.
➤ [2] *vi* sich äußern *(on* über *+acc*, zu), einen Kommentar abgeben *(on* zu) ◆ **need I ~?** Kommentar überflüssig!
[3] *vt* bemerken, äußern.

commentary ['kɒməntərɪ] *n* Kommentar *m (on* zu) ◆ **he used to do the commentaries for football matches** früher war er Reporter bei Fußballspielen; **I don't need a constant ~ from you** ich brauche deine ständigen Kommentare nicht.

commentate ['kɒmenteɪt] *vi (Rad, TV)* Reporter(in) sein *(on* bei).

commentator ['kɒmenteɪtə^r] *n* **(a)** *(Rad, TV)* Reporter(in *f*) *m*. **(b)** *(on texts etc)* Interpret(in *f*) *m*; *(of Bible)* Exeget(in *f*) *m*.

commerce ['kɒmɜːs] *n* **(a)** Handel *m*; *(between countries also)* Handelsverkehr *m* ◆ **in the world of ~** im Geschäftsleben; **he is in ~** er ist Geschäftsmann. **(b)** *(form: dealings)* Verkehr *m*.

commercial [kə'mɜːʃəl] [1] *adj* Handels-; *custom also, ethics, training* kaufmännisch; *language, premises, vehicle* Geschäfts-; *production, radio, project, success, attitude etc* kommerziell ◆ **the ~ world** die Geschäftswelt; **of no ~ value** ohne Verkaufswert; **to think in ~ terms** kaufmännisch denken; **it makes good ~ sense** das läßt sich kaufmännisch durchaus vertreten.
[2] *n (Rad, TV)* Werbespot *m* ◆ **during the ~s** während der (Fernseh)werbung.

commercial: ~ art *n* Werbegraphik *f*; **~ artist** *n* Werbegraphiker(in *f*) *m*; **~ bank** *n* Handelsbank *f*; **~ college** *n* Fachschule *f* für kaufmännische Berufe.

commercialese [kəmɜːʃə'liːz] *n* Wirtschaftssprache *f*.

commercialism [kə'mɜːʃəlɪzəm] *n* Kommerzialisierung *f*; *(connected with art, literature also)* Kommerz *m*.

commercialization [kəˌmɜːʃəlaɪ'zeɪʃən] *n* Kommerzialisierung *f*.

commercialize [kə'mɜːʃəlaɪz] *vt* kommerzialisieren.

commercially [kə'mɜːʃəlɪ] *adv* geschäftlich; *manufacture, succeed* kommerziell ◆ **to be ~ minded** kaufmännisch veranlagt *or* kommerziell eingestellt *(usu pej)* sein.

commercial: ~ television *n* kommerzielles Fernsehen; **~ traveller** *n* Handelsvertreter(in *f*) *m*.

commie ['kɒmɪ] *(pej inf)* [1] *n* Rote(r) *mf (pej inf)*.
[2] *adj* rot *(pej inf)*.

commingle [kɒ'mɪŋgl] *vi (liter)* sich vermischen; *(colours)* ineinander verschwimmen.

commiserate [kə'mɪzəreɪt] *vi* mitfühlen *(with* mit) ◆ **we ~ with you in the loss of your husband** wir nehmen Anteil am Tode Ihres Gatten.

commiseration [kəˌmɪzə'reɪʃən] *n* Mitgefühl *nt no pl*, (An)teilnahme *f no pl* ◆ **my ~s** herzliches Beileid *(on* zu).

commissar ['kɒmɪsɑː^r] *n* Kommissar *m*.

commissariat [ˌkɒmɪ'sɛərɪət] *n* **(a)** *(Mil)* Intendantur *f*. **(b)** *(in USSR etc)* Kommissariat *nt*.

commissary ['kɒmɪsərɪ] *n* **(a)** *(Mil)* Intendant *m*. **(b)** *(delegate)* Beauftragte(r) *mf*. **(c)** *(US Comm)* Laden *m* in Lagern/auf Baustellen *etc*.

commission [kə'mɪʃən] [1] *n* **(a)** *(committing)* Begehen *nt (form)*.
(b) *(for building, painting etc)* Auftrag *m*.
(c) *(Comm)* Provision *f* ◆ **on ~, on a ~ basis** auf Provision(sbasis); **~ agent**

➤ LANGUAGE IN USE: **comment: 2 → 6.3**

Komissionär(in *f*) *m*.
(d) (*Mil*) Patent *nt*.
(e) (*special committee*) Kommission *f*, Ausschuß *m* ◆ **~ of enquiry** Untersuchungskommission *f or* -ausschuß *m*.
(f) (*Naut, fig: use*) **to put in(to) ~** in Dienst stellen; **to take out of ~** aus dem Verkehr ziehen; **in/out of ~** in/außer Betrieb.
(g) (*form: task, errand*) Erledigung *f* ◆ **I was given a ~ to recruit new members** ich wurde (damit) beauftragt, neue Mitglieder zu werben.
(h) the (EC) C~ die EG-Kommission.
2 *vt* **(a)** *person* beauftragen; *book, painting* in Auftrag geben ◆ **to ~ sb to do sth** jdn damit beauftragen, etw zu tun. **(b)** (*Mil*) *sb* zum Offizier ernennen; *officer* ernennen ◆ **~ed officer** Offizier *m*. **(c)** *ship* in Dienst stellen; *power station etc* in Betrieb nehmen ◆ **~ing ceremony** Eröffnungszeremonie *f*.
commissionaire [kəˌmɪʃəˈnɛəʳ] *n* Portier *m*.
commissioner [kəˈmɪʃənəʳ] *n* **(a)** (*member of commission*) Ausschußmitglied *nt*. **(b)** (*of police*) Polizeipräsident *m*. **(c)** (*Jur*) **~ of** *or* **for oaths** Notar(in *f*) *m*.
commit [kəˈmɪt] **1** *vt* **(a)** (*perpetrate*) begehen ◆ **the crimes they ~ted against humanity** ihre Verbrechen gegen die Menschlichkeit.
(b) to ~ sb (to prison/to a home) jdn ins Gefängnis/in ein Heim einweisen; **to have sb ~ted (to an asylum)** jdn in eine Anstalt einweisen lassen; **to ~ sb for trial** jdn einem Gericht überstellen; **to ~ sb/sth to sb's care** jdn/etw jds Obhut (*dat*) anvertrauen; **to ~ to writing** *or* **to paper** zu Papier bringen; **to ~ to the flames** den Flammen übergeben *or* überantworten.
(c) (*involve, obligate*) festlegen (*to* auf *+acc*) ◆ **to ~ troops to a battle** Truppen in ein Gefecht schicken; **to ~ resources/manpower to a project** Mittel/Arbeitskräfte für ein Projekt einsetzen; **that doesn't ~ you to buying the book** das verpflichtet Sie nicht zum Kauf des Buches; **I don't want to be ~ted** ich möchte mich nicht festlegen.
(d) (*Parl*) *bill* an den (zuständigen) Ausschuß überweisen.
2 *vr* sich festlegen (*to* auf *+acc*) ◆ **to ~ oneself on an issue** sich in einer Frage festlegen; **you have to ~ yourself totally to the cause** man muß sich voll und ganz für die Sache einsetzen *or* engagieren; **the government has ~ted itself to (undertake) far-reaching reforms** die Regierung hat sich zu weitreichenden Reformen bekannt *or* verpflichtet; **... without ~ting myself to the whole contract** ... ohne damit an den ganzen Vertrag gebunden zu sein.
commitment [kəˈmɪtmənt] *n* **(a)** (*act*) *see* **committal (a)**.
(b) (*obligation*) Verpflichtung *f*; (*dedication*) Engagement *nt* ◆ **his family/teaching ~s** seine familiären Verpflichtungen *pl*/seine Lehrverpflichtungen *pl*; **there's no ~ (to buy)** es besteht kein(erlei) Kaufzwang; **the trainer demands one hundred per cent ~ from his team** der Trainer verlangt von seiner Mannschaft hundertprozentigen Einsatz; **his ~ to his job is total** er geht völlig in seiner Arbeit auf; **political/military ~** politisches/militärisches Engagement.
(c) (*Parl: of bill*) Überweisung *f* an den (zuständigen) Ausschuß.
committal [kəˈmɪtl] *n* **(a)** (*to prison, asylum etc*) Einweisung *f* ◆ **his ~ for trial** seine Überstellung ans Gericht; **~ proceedings** gerichtliche Voruntersuchung. **(b)** (*of crime etc*) Begehen *nt* (*form*). **(c) ~ to memory** Auswendiglernen *nt*; (*of single fact*) Sich-Einprägen *nt*. **(d)** (*Parl*) *see* **commitment (c)**.
committed [kəˈmɪtɪd] *adj* (*dedicated*) engagiert ◆ **he is so ~ to his work that ...** er geht so in seiner Arbeit auf, daß ...; **all his life he has been ~ to this cause** er hat sich sein Leben lang für diese Sache eingesetzt.
committee [kəˈmɪtɪ] *n* Ausschuß *m* (*also Parl*), Komitee *nt* ◆ **to be** *or* **sit on a ~** in einem Ausschuß *or* Komitee sein *or* sitzen; **C~ of 100** (*Brit*) Komitee der Hundert; **~ meeting** Ausschußsitzung *f*; **~ member** Ausschußmitglied *nt*; **the bill didn't reach the ~ stage** der Gesetzentwurf ist gar nicht erst an den (zuständigen) Ausschuß gelangt; **the ~ stage lasted weeks** der Gesetzentwurf wurde mehrere Wochen im Ausschuß verhandelt.
commode [kəˈməʊd] *n* **(a)** (*chest of drawers*) Kommode *f*. **(b)** (*night-~*) (Nacht)stuhl *m*.
commodious [kəˈməʊdɪəs] *adj* geräumig.
commodity [kəˈmɒdɪtɪ] *n* Ware *f*; (*agricultural*) Erzeugnis *nt* ◆ **basic** *or* **staple commodities** (*natural*) Grundstoffe *pl*; (*St Ex*) Rohstoffe *pl*; (*manufactured*) Bedarfsgüter *pl*; (*foodstuffs*) Grundnahrungsmittel *pl*; **~ market** Rohstoffmarkt *m*; **electricity is a ~ which every country needs** Strom ist ein (Versorgungs)gut, das jedes Land braucht; **~ exchange** (*St Ex*) Warenbörse *f*.
commodore [ˈkɒmədɔːʳ] *n* (*Naut*) Flottillenadmiral *m* (*BRD*); (*senior captain*) Kommodore *m*; (*of yacht club*) Präsident *m*.
▼ **common** [ˈkɒmən] **1** *adj* (*+er*) **(a)** (*shared by many*) gemeinsam; *property also* Gemein-, gemeinschaftlich ◆ **~ land** Allmende *f*; **~ prostitute** Straßendirne *f*; **it is ~ knowledge that ...** es ist allgemein bekannt, daß ...; **it is to the ~ advantage that ...** es ist von allgemeinem Nutzen, daß ...; **very little/no ~ ground** kaum eine/keine gemeinsame Basis.
(b) (*frequently seen or heard etc*) häufig; *word also* weitverbreitet *attr*, weit verbreitet *pred*, geläufig; *experience also* allgemein; *animal, bird* häufig *pred*, häufig anzutreffend *attr*; *belief, custom*, (*over large area*) *animal, bird* (weit)verbreitet *attr*, weit verbreitet *pred*; (*customary, usual*) normal ◆ **it's quite a ~ sight** das sieht man ziemlich häufig; **it's ~ for visitors to feel ill here** Besucher fühlen sich hier häufig krank; **nowadays it's quite ~ for the man to do the housework** es ist heutzutage ganz normal, daß der Mann die Hausarbeit macht.
(c) (*ordinary*) gewöhnlich ◆ **the ~ man** der Normalbürger; **the ~ people** die einfachen Leute; **a ~ soldier** ein einfacher *or* gemeiner (*dated*) Soldat; **the ~ run of mankind** die (breite) Masse; **the ~ touch** das Volkstümliche; **the Book of C~ Prayer** (*Eccl*) die Agende; **it's only ~ decency to apologize** es ist nur recht und billig, daß man sich entschuldigt.
(d) (*vulgar, low-class*) gewöhnlich ◆ **to be as ~ as muck** (*inf*) schrecklich gewöhnlich *or* ordinär sein.
2 *n* **(a)** (*land*) Anger *m*, Gemeindewiese *f*.
(b) nothing out of the ~ nichts Besonderes.
▼ **(c) to have sth in ~** etw miteinander gemein haben; **to have a lot/nothing in ~** viel/nichts miteinander gemein haben, viele/keine Gemeinsamkeiten haben; **we do at least have that in ~** wenigstens das haben wir gemein; **in ~ with many other people/towns/countries** (ebenso *or* genauso) wie viele andere (Leute)/Städte/Länder ...; **I, in ~ with ...** ich, ebenso wie ...
commonalty [ˈkɒmənəltɪ] *n* (*form*) **the ~** die Bürgerlichen *pl*.
common: ~ cold *n* Schnupfen *m*; **~ core** *n* (*Sch*) Pflichtfächer *pl*; **~ denominator** *n* (*Math, fig*) gemeinsamer Nenner; **~ divisor** *n* gemeinsamer Teiler; **~ entrance (examination)** *n* Aufnahmeprüfung *f* (*für eine britische Public School*).
commoner [ˈkɒmənəʳ] *n* **(a)** Bürgerliche(r) *mf*. **(b)** (*Brit Univ*) *Student, der kein Universitätsstipendium erhält*.
common: ~ factor *n* gemeinsamer Teiler; **~ fraction** *n* gemeiner Bruch; **~ gender** *n* (*Gram*) doppeltes Geschlecht; **~ law 1** *n* Gewohnheitsrecht *nt*; **2** *adj* **she is his ~-law wife** sie lebt mit ihm in eheähnlicher Gemeinschaft; **the law regarded her as his ~-law wife** vor dem Gesetz galt ihre Verbindung als eheähnliche Gemeinschaft.
commonly [ˈkɒmənlɪ] *adv* **(a)** (*often*) häufig; (*widely*) gemeinhin, weithin ◆ **a ~ held belief** eine weitverbreitete Ansicht. **(b)** (*vulgarly*) gewöhnlich, ordinär.
common: C~ Market *n* Gemeinsamer Markt; **C~ Marketeer** *n* Befürworter(in *f*) *m* des Gemeinsamen Marktes; **~ multiple** *n* gemeinsame(s) Vielfache(s); **the lowest** *or* **least ~ multiple** das kleinste gemeinsame Vielfache.
commonness [ˈkɒmənnɪs] *n* **(a)** *see adj (b)* Häufigkeit *f*; weite Verbreitung, Geläufigkeit *f*; Allgemeinheit *f*. **(b)** (*vulgarity*) Gewöhnlichkeit *f*; (*of person also*) ordinäre Art.
common: ~ noun *n* Gattungsbegriff *m*; **~-or-garden** *adj* Feld-, Wald- und Wiesen- (*inf*); *topic, novel etc* ganz gewöhnlich; **~place 1** *adj* alltäglich; (*banal*) *remark* banal; **2** *n* Gemeinplatz *m*; **a ~place** (*frequent sight or event*) etwas Alltägliches; **~room** *n* Aufenthalts- *or* Tagesraum *m*; (*for teachers*) Lehrerzimmer *nt*; (*Univ*) Dozentenzimmer *nt*.
commons [ˈkɒmənz] *npl* **(a) the C~** (*Parl*) das Unterhaus; *see* **house**. **(b) on short ~** auf Kurzration gesetzt.
common: ~ sense *n* gesunder Menschenverstand; **~sense** *adj* vernünftig; *attitude also* gesund; **it's the ~sense thing to do** das ist das Vernünftigste; **~ time** *n* Viervierteltakt *m*; **~weal** *n* (*form*) Gemeinwohl *nt*; **~wealth** *n* **(a)** Staat *m*, Gemeinwesen *nt*; (*US*) *Bezeichnung für die US-Bundesstaaten Kentucky, Massachusetts, Pennsylvania und Virginia*; **the C~wealth of Australia** der Australische Bund; **the (British) C~wealth, the C~wealth of Nations** das Commonwealth; **(b)** (*Hist*) **the C~wealth** *die englische Republik unter Cromwell*.
commotion [kəˈməʊʃən] *n* Aufregung *f usu no indef art*; (*noise*) Lärm, Spektakel *m* ◆ **to cause a ~** Aufsehen erregen; **to make a ~** Theater machen (*inf*); (*noise*) Krach machen.
comms [kɒmz] *n see* **communications**.
communal [ˈkɒmjuːnl] *adj* **(a)** (*of a community*) Gemeinde- ◆ **~ life** Gemeinschaftsleben *nt*. **(b)** (*owned, used in common*) gemeinsam; *bathroom, kitchen also* Gemeinschafts-.
communally [ˈkɒmjuːnəlɪ] *adv* gemeinsam ◆ **to be ~ owned** Gemein- *or* Gemeinschaftseigentum sein.
communard [ˈkɒmjʊˌnɑːd] *n* Kommunarde *m*, Kommunardin *f*.
commune[1] [kəˈmjuːn] *vi* **(a)** Zwiesprache halten ◆ **to ~ with the spirits** mit den Geistern verkehren. **(b)** (*esp US Eccl*) (*Catholic*) kommunizieren, die Kommunion empfangen; (*Protestant*) das Abendmahl empfangen.
commune[2] [ˈkɒmjuːn] *n* Kommune *f*; (*administrative division also*) Gemeinde *f*.
communicable [kəˈmjuːnɪkəbl] *adj* **(a)** *disease* übertragbar. **(b)** *ideas, knowledge* kommunizierbar, vermittelbar.
communicant [kəˈmjuːnɪkənt] *n* (*Eccl*) Kommunikant(in *f*) *m*.
communicate [kəˈmjuːnɪkeɪt] **1** *vt news etc* übermitteln; *ideas, feelings* vermitteln; *illness* übertragen (*to* auf *+acc*).
2 *vi* **(a)** (*be in communication*) in Verbindung *or* Kontakt stehen ◆ **the ship was unable to ~ with the shore** das Schiff konnte keine Verbindung zum Festland herstellen.
(b) (*convey or exchange thoughts*) sich verständigen, kommunizieren ◆ **the inability of modern man to ~** die Unfähigkeit des heutigen Menschen zur Kommunikation.
(c) (*rooms*) verbunden sein ◆ **communicating rooms** Zimmer *pl* mit einer Verbindungstür.
(d) (*Eccl*) (*Catholic*) kommunizieren; (*Protestant*) das Abendmahl empfangen.
communication [kəˌmjuːnɪˈkeɪʃən] *n* **(a)** (*communicating*) Verständigung, Kommunikation *f*; (*of ideas, information*) Vermittlung *f*; (*of disease*) Übertragung *f*; (*contact*) Verbindung *f* ◆ **system/means of ~** Kommunikationssystem *nt*/-mittel *nt*; **to be in ~ with sb** mit jdm in Verbindung stehen (*about* wegen).
(b) (*exchanging of ideas*) Verständigung, Kommunikation *f*.
(c) (*letter, message*) Mitteilung *f*.
(d) ~s (*roads, railways, telegraph lines etc*) Kommunikationswege *pl*, Kommunikationsnetz *nt*; **all ~s with the mainland have been cut off**

➤ LANGUAGE IN USE: common: 2c → 5.5

sämtliche Verbindungen zum Festland sind unterbrochen; **they're trying to restore ~s** man versucht, die Verbindung wiederherzustellen.
(e) ~s (*Telec*) Telekommunikation *f*.
(f) (*between rooms etc*) Verbindung *f*.
communication: ~ breakdown *n* Zusammenbruch *m* der Kommunikation; **~ cord** *n* (*Brit Rail*) ≃ Notbremse *f*; **~ gap** *n* Kommunikationslücke *f*; **~ problem** *n* Kommunikationsproblem *nt*; **~ skills** *npl* Kommunikationsfähigkeit *f*.
communications: ~ package *n* Kommunikationssoftware *f*; **~ satellite** *n* Kommunikations- *or* Nachrichtensatellit *m*; **~ software** *n* Kommunikationssoftware *f*; **~ technology** *n* Nachrichtentechnik *f*.
communication: ~ studies *npl* Kommunikationswissenschaften *pl*; **~ trench** *n* Verbindungsgraben *m*.
communicative [kə'mju:nɪkətɪv] *adj* mitteilsam, gesprächig.
communion [kə'mju:nɪən] *n* **(a)** (*intercourse, exchange of feelings etc*) Zwiesprache *f*; (*with spirits*) Verkehr *m* ♦ **a sense of ~ with nature** ein Gefühl der Verbundenheit mit der Natur.
(b) (*religious group*) Gemeinde *f*; (*denomination*) Religionsgemeinschaft *f* ♦ **the ~ of saints/the faithful** die Gemeinschaft der Heiligen/Gläubigen.
(c) (*Eccl: also* **C~**) (*Protestant*) Abendmahl *nt*; (*Catholic*) Kommunion *f* ♦ **to receive** *or* **take ~** die Kommunion/das Abendmahl empfangen.
communion: ~ rail *n* Kommunionsbank *f*; **~ service** *n* Abendmahlsgottesdienst *m*; **~ table** *n* Abendmahlstisch *m*.
communiqué [kə'mju:nɪkeɪ] *n* Kommuniqué *nt*, (amtliche) Verlautbarung.
communism ['kɒmjʊnɪzəm] *n* Kommunismus *m*.
communist ['kɒmjʊnɪst] 1 *n* Kommunist(in *f*) *m*.
2 *adj* kommunistisch ♦ **C~ Manifesto** Kommunistisches Manifest; **C~ Party** Kommunistische Partei.
communistic [,kɒmjʊ'nɪstɪk] *adj* pro-kommunistisch; (*esp US: communist*) kommunistisch.
community [kə'mju:nɪtɪ] *n* **(a)** (*social, cultural etc group*) Gemeinschaft *f*; (*ethnic also*) Bevölkerungsgruppe *f* ♦ **the ~ at large** das ganze Volk; **the great ~ of nations** die große Völkergemeinschaft; **a sense of ~** (ein) Gemeinschaftsgefühl *nt*; **to work in the ~** im Sozialbereich tätig sein.
(b) (*the public*) Allgemeinheit *f*.
(c) (*Eccl: of monks, nuns*) (Ordens)gemeinschaft *f*.
(d) (*holding in common*) **the ~ of love/goods** die Liebes-/Gütergemeinschaft; **they have no ~ of interests** sie haben keine gemeinsamen Interessen.
community: ~ centre *n* Gemeindezentrum *nt*; **~ charge** *n Kopfsteuer f zur Finanzierung der Stadt- und Gemeindeverwaltungen*; **~ chest** *n* (*US*) Wohltätigkeits- *or* Hilfsfonds *m*; **~ college** *n* (*US*) Gemeinde-College *nt*; **~ relations** *npl* das Verhältnis zwischen den Bevölkerungsgruppen; **~ service** *n* (*Jur*) Sozialdienst *m*; **~ singing** *n* gemeinsames Singen; **~ worker** *n* Sozialberufler(in *f*) *m*.
communize ['kɒmjʊnaɪz] *vt* kommunistisch machen.
commutable [kə'mju:təbl] *adj* (*Jur*) umwandelbar.
commutation [,kɒmjʊ'teɪʃən] *n* **(a)** (*Jur*) Umwandlung *f*. **(b) ~ ticket** (*US*) Zeitnetzkarte *f*.
commutator ['kɒmjʊteɪtə^r] *n* (*Elec*) Kommutator *m*.
commute [kə'mju:t] 1 *vt* (*all senses*) umwandeln.
2 *vi* (*travel as commuter*) pendeln.
commuter [kə'mju:tə^r] *n* Pendler(in *f*) *m* ♦ **the ~ belt** das Einzugsgebiet, der Einzugsbereich; **a ~ belt** ein städtischer Einzugsbereich; **~ traffic** Pendlerverkehr *m*; **~ train** Pendlerzug *m*.
commuting [kə'mju:tɪŋ] *n* Pendeln *nt*; (*commuter traffic*) Pendelverkehr *m* ♦ **I hate ~** ich hasse es zu pendeln; **increased ~ levels** erhöhter Pendelverkehr.
comp [kɒmp] *n* (*Typ inf*) Setzer(in *f*) *m*.
compact[1] [kəm'pækt] 1 *adj* (*+er*) kompakt; *style of writing, prose also* gedrängt; *soil, snow* fest ♦ **the print is too ~** der Druck ist zu eng, es ist zu eng bedruckt; **~ camera** Kompaktkamera *f*.
2 *vt* **(a)** *snow, soil* festtreten/-walzen/-fahren *etc*. **(b)** (*fig liter*) **to be ~ed of ...** sich aus ... zusammensetzen.
compact[2] ['kɒmpækt] *n* **(a)** (*powder ~*) Puderdose *f*. **(b)** (*US: car*) Kompaktauto *nt or* -wagen *m*. **(c)** (*camera*) Kompaktkamera *f*.
compact[3] ['kɒmpækt] *n* (*form: agreement*) Vereinbarung, Übereinkunft *f*.
compact disc *n* Compact-disc *f* ♦ **~ player** CD-Spieler *m*.
compactly [kəm'pæktlɪ] *adv* kompakt; *expressed* gedrängt; *printed* eng.
compactness [kəm'pæktnɪs] *n* Kompaktheit *f*; (*of style also*) Gedrängtheit *f*; (*of print*) Dichte, Enge *f*.
companion [kəm'pænjən] 1 *n* **(a)** (*person with one*) Begleiter(in *f*) *m* ♦ **~s in arms** Kampfgefährten, Waffenbrüder (*geh*) *pl*; **my ~s on the journey** meine Reisegefährten *pl*; **travelling/holiday/drinking ~** Reisebegleiter(in *f*) *m*/Urlaubsgefährte *m*, -gefährtin *f*/Zechgenosse *m*, -genossin *f*.
(b) (*friend*) Freund(in *f*), Kamerad(in *f*) *m* ♦ **his elder brother is not much of a ~ for him** sein älterer Bruder ist ihm kein richtiger Freund; **a faithful ~ for fifty years** ein treuer Gefährte über fünfzig Jahre.
(c) (*one of pair of objects*) Pendant *nt*.
(d) (*lady ~*) Betreuerin *f*.
(e) (*handbook*) **"the Gardener's C~"** „der Ratgeber für den Gartenfreund".
(f) (*of order of knighthood*) Ritter *m*.
2 *attr* passend; *volume* Begleit- ♦ **they have just brought out a ~ set of Dickens** in derselben Reihe ist jetzt eine Dickens-Ausgabe erschienen.
companionable [kəm'pænjənəbl] *adj* freundlich.
companionably [kəm'pænjənəblɪ] *adv* vertraut; *smile also* freundlich.
companion: ~ship *n* Gesellschaft *f*; **~way** *n* (*Naut*) Niedergang *m*.
▼ **company** ['kʌmpənɪ] 1 *n* **(a)** Gesellschaft *f* ♦ **to keep sb ~** jdm Gesellschaft leisten; **I enjoy ~** ich bin gern in Gesellschaft, ich habe gern Gesellschaft; **female ~** Damengesellschaft *f*; **he arrived with female ~** er kam in Damenbegleitung; **he's good ~** seine Gesellschaft ist angenehm; **just for ~** nur, um Gesellschaft zu haben; **he came along just for ~** (*to provide ~*) er kam bloß, um mir/uns Gesellschaft zu leisten; **he doesn't know how to behave in ~** er weiß nicht, wie man sich in Gesellschaft benimmt; **I/he in ~ with ...** ich/er, genauso wie ...; **she is no** *or* **not fit ~ for your sister** sie ist nicht der richtige Umgang für deine Schwester; **a man is known by the ~ he keeps** (*prov*) sage mir, mit wem du umgehst, so sage ich dir, wer du bist (*prov*); **she keeps a cat, it's ~ for her** sie hält sich eine Katze, da hat sie (wenigstens) Gesellschaft; **you'll be in good ~ if ...** wenn du ..., bist du in guter Gesellschaft.
(b) (*guests*) Besuch *m*.
(c) (*Comm*) Firma, Gesellschaft *f* ♦ **Smith & C~, Smith & Co.** Smith & Co.; **shipping ~** Schiffahrtsgesellschaft, Reederei *f*; **publishing ~** Verlagshaus *nt*, Verlag *m*; **a printing/clothes ~** ein Druckerei-/Textilbetrieb *m*; **that's paid for by the ~** das bezahlt die Firma.
(d) (*Theat*) (Schauspiel)truppe *f*.
(e) (*Naut*) **ship's ~** Besatzung *f*.
(f) (*Mil*) Kompanie *f*.
2 *attr* Firmen- ♦ **he has a ~ BMW** er hat einen BMW als Firmenwagen.
company: ~ car *n* Firmenwagen *m*; **~ commander** *n* (*Mil*) Kompaniechef *m*; **~ director** *n* Direktor(in *f*), Firmenchef(in *f*) *m*; **~ law** *n* Gesellschaftsrecht *nt*; **~ lawyer** *n* (*for ~ law*) Gesellschaftsrechtler(in *f*) *m*; (*within ~*) Hausjurist(in *f*) *m*; **~ loyalty** *n* Firmentreue *f*; **~ man** *n* treues *or* loyales Firmenmitglied; **~ policy** *n* Geschäftspolitik *f*; **~ secretary** *n* (*Brit Comm*) ≃ Prokurist(in *f*) *m*; **~ sergeant-major** *n* (*Mil*) Kompaniefeldwebel *m*; **~ time** *n* Arbeitszeit *f*.
comparable ['kɒmpərəbl] *adj* vergleichbar (*with, to* mit).
comparably ['kɒmpərəblɪ] *adv* gleichermaßen.
comparative [kəm'pærətɪv] 1 *adj* **(a)** *religion, philology etc* vergleichend ♦ **~ literature** vergleichende Literaturwissenschaft, Komparatistik *f*. **(b) the ~ form** (*Gram*) der Komparativ, die erste Steigerungsstufe. **(c)** (*relative*) relativ ♦ **to live in ~ luxury** relativ luxuriös leben.
2 *n* (*Gram*) Komparativ *m*.
▼ **comparatively** [kəm'pærətɪvlɪ] *adv* **(a)** vergleichend. **(b)** (*relatively*) verhältnismäßig, relativ.
▼ **compare** [kəm'peə^r] 1 *vt* vergleichen (*with, to* mit) ♦ **~d with** im Vergleich zu, verglichen mit; **they cannot be ~d** man kann sie nicht vergleichen, sie lassen sich nicht vergleichen; **his car is not to be** *or* **can't be ~d with my new one** sein Wagen ist überhaupt kein Vergleich zu meinem neuen Auto; **to ~ notes** Eindrücke/Erfahrungen austauschen.
▼ 2 *vi* sich vergleichen lassen (*with* mit) ♦ **it ~s badly/well** es schneidet vergleichsweise schlecht/gut ab; **it doesn't ~ very well at all** es schneidet im Vergleich überhaupt nicht gut ab; **how do the two cars ~ for speed?** wie sieht ein Geschwindigkeitsvergleich der beiden Wagen aus?; **the old car can't ~ for speed with the new one** in puncto Geschwindigkeit läßt sich der alte Wagen nicht mit dem neuen vergleichen.
3 *n*: **beyond** *or* **without** *or* **past ~** unvergleichlich; **beautiful beyond ~** unvergleichlich schön.
▼ **comparison** [kəm'pærɪsn] *n* **(a)** Vergleich *m* (*to* mit) ♦ **in ~ with** im Vergleich zu; **to make** *or* **draw a ~** einen Vergleich anstellen; **to bear ~** einem Vergleich standhalten, einen Vergleich aushalten; **there's no ~** das ist gar kein Vergleich.
(b) (*Gram*) Steigerung *f* ♦ **degree of ~** Steigerungsstufe *f*.
compartment [kəm'pɑ:tmənt] *n* (*in fridge, desk etc*) Fach *nt*; (*Rail*) Abteil *nt*; (*Naut*) Schott(e *f*) *nt*; (*fig*) (Schub)fach *nt*.
compartmentalize [,kɒmpɑ:t'mentəlaɪz] *vt* aufsplittern ♦ **their excessively ~d view of life** ihre übertrieben genau gegliederte Lebensanschauung.
compass ['kʌmpəs] 1 *n* **(a)** Kompaß *m* ♦ **by the ~** nach dem Kompaß. **(b) ~es** *pl*, **pair of ~es** Zirkel *m*. **(c)** (*fig: extent*) Rahmen *m*; (*of human mind, experience*) Bereich *m*; (*Mus: of voice*) Umfang *m*.
2 *vt see* **encompass** ♦ **~ed about with enemies** (*form*) von Feinden umzingelt.
compass: ~ bearing *n* Kompaßpeilung *f*; **~ card** *n* Kompaßscheibe, Windrose *f*; **~ course** *n* Navigationskurs *m*.
compassion [kəm'pæʃən] *n* Mitgefühl, Mitleid *nt* (*for* mit); (*esp Bibl*) Erbarmen *nt* (*on, for* mit).
compassionate [kəm'pæʃənɪt] *adj* mitfühlend, voller Mitgefühl *or* Mitleid ♦ **on ~ grounds** aus familiären Gründen; **~ leave** Beurlaubung *f* wegen einer dringenden Familienangelegenheit.
compass rose *n* Windrose *f*.
compatibility [kəm,pætə'bɪlɪtɪ] *n* Vereinbarkeit, Kompatibilität (*geh*) *f*; (*Med*) Verträglichkeit, Kompatibilität (*spec*) *f*; (*Comput*) Kompatibilität *f* ♦ **their ~/lack of ~ was obvious** es war offensichtlich, daß die beiden gut/schlecht zueinander paßten.
compatible [kəm'pætɪbl] *adj* vereinbar, kompatibel (*geh*); (*Med*) verträglich, kompatibel (*spec*); *people* zueinander passend; *colours, furniture* passend; (*Comput*) kompatibel ♦ **to be ~** (*people*) zueinander passen; (*colours, furniture*) zusammenpassen; (*plan*) vereinbar sein; **a salary ~ with the dangers of the job** ein Gehalt, das den Gefahren des Berufs entspricht.
compatibly [kəm'pætɪblɪ] *adv* **to be ~ matched** gut zueinander passen; **to be ~ married** in der Ehe gut zueinander passen.

➤ LANGUAGE IN USE: **company: 1a** → 25.1 **comparatively: a** → 5.1 **compare: 1** → 5.1, 26.3 **2** → 5.3 **comparison: a** → 5.2, 5.5, 26.3

compatriot [kəm'pætrɪət] *n* Landsmann *m*, Landsmännin *f*.
compel [kəm'pel] *vt* **(a)** zwingen ◆ **I feel ~led to tell you** ... ich sehe mich (dazu) gezwungen *or* veranlaßt, Ihnen mitzuteilen, ... **(b)** *admiration, respect* abnötigen (*from sb* jdm); *obedience* erzwingen (*from sb* von jdm).
compelling [kəm'pelɪŋ] *adj* zwingend; *performance, personality, eyes* bezwingend.
compellingly [kəm'pelɪŋlɪ] *adv see adj* ◆ **he presented his case ~** er legte seinen Fall mit zwingender Logik dar.
compendious [kəm'pendɪəs] *adj notes etc* umfangreich.
compendium [kəm'pendɪəm] *n* Handbuch, Kompendium *nt* ◆ **~ of games** Spielemagazin *nt*.
compensate ['kɒmpənseɪt] **1** *vt* (*recompense*) entschädigen; (*Mech*) ausgleichen.
2 *vi* (*Psych*) kompensieren.
◆**compensate for** *vi +prep obj* (*in money, material goods etc*) ersetzen; (*make up for, offset*) wieder wettmachen *or* ausgleichen; (*Psych*) kompensieren ◆ **he was awarded £900 to ~ ~ the damage** er erhielt £ 900 Schadenersatz *or* -ausgleich.
compensation [ˌkɒmpən'seɪʃən] *n* (*damages*) Entschädigung *f*; (*fig*) Ausgleich *m*; (*Psych*) Kompensation *f* ◆ **he had the ~ of knowing that** ... er hatte die Genugtuung zu wissen, daß ...; **in ~** als Entschädigung/Ausgleich/ Kompensation.
compensatory [kəm'pensətərɪ] *adj* kompensierend, ausgleichend; *education*, (*Psych*) kompensatorisch.
compère ['kɒmpɛəʳ] (*Brit*) **1** *n* Conférencier *m*.
2 *vt* **to ~ a show** bei einer Show der Conférencier sein.
compete [kəm'piːt] *vi* **(a)** konkurrieren ◆ **to ~ with each other** sich (gegenseitig) Konkurrenz machen; **to ~ for sth** um etw kämpfen *or* (*esp Comm*) konkurrieren; **able to ~ industrially** industriell konkurrenzfähig; **his poetry can't ~ with Eliot's** seine Gedichte können sich nicht mit denen Eliots messen; **he can't ~ (any more)** er kann nicht mehr mithalten.
(b) (*Sport*) teilnehmen ◆ **to ~ for the championship** um die Meisterschaft kämpfen; **to ~ with/against sb** gegen jdn kämpfen *or* antreten.
competence ['kɒmpɪtəns], **competency** ['kɒmpɪtənsɪ] *n* **(a)** Fähigkeit *f*; (*of lawyer, scientist etc also, Ling*) Kompetenz *f* ◆ **to do sth with surprising ~** etw mit erstaunlichem Geschick tun; **his ~ in handling money/dealing with awkward clients** sein Geschick im Umgang mit Geld/schwierigen Kunden; **what level of ~ has the class reached in Spanish?** auf welchem Stand ist die Klasse in Spanisch?
(b) (*form: income*) Einkommen *nt*.
(c) (*Jur*) Zuständigkeit *f*.
competent ['kɒmpɪtənt] *adj* **(a)** fähig, befähigt (*in* zu); (*in a particular field*) kompetent; (*adequate*) *knowledge, understanding* angemessen, adäquat ◆ **his English is quite ~** sein Englisch ist recht gut. **(b)** (*Jur*) zuständig; *evidence, witness* zulässig. **(c)** (*form: relevant*) **to be ~/not ~** (*business, question*) von/ohne *or* nicht von Belang sein.
competently ['kɒmpɪtəntlɪ] *adv* geschickt, kompetent.
competition [ˌkɒmpɪ'tɪʃən] *n* **(a)** *no pl* Konkurrenz *f* (*for* um) ◆ **to keep an eye on the ~** die Konkurrenz beobachten; **unfair ~** unlauterer Wettbewerb; **a spirit of ~** Wettbewerbs- *or* Konkurrenzdenken *nt*; **to be in ~ with sb** mit jdm wetteifern *or* (*esp Comm*) konkurrieren; **to choose by ~** einem Auswahlverfahren unterziehen, durch Auswahl ermitteln.
(b) (*contest*) Wettbewerb *m*; (*in newspapers etc*) Preisausschreiben *nt* ◆ **beauty/swimming ~** Schönheitskonkurrenz *f or* -wettbewerb *m*/ Schwimmwettbewerb *m*.
competitive [kəm'petɪtɪv] *adj* **(a)** *person, attitude* vom Konkurrenzdenken geprägt; *sport* (Wett)kampf- ◆ **~ spirit** Wettbewerbs- *or* Konkurrenzgeist *m*; (*of team*) Kampfgeist *m*; **he's a very ~ sort of person** er genießt Wettbewerbssituationen; (*in job etc*) er ist ein sehr ehrgeiziger Mensch; **the exam system encourages children to be too ~** das Prüfungssystem regt die Kinder zu sehr zum Konkurrenzdenken an; **the recruitment procedure is not ~** die Stellenvergabe erfolgt nicht auf Grund eines Auswahlverfahrens; **~ advantage** Wettbewerbsvorteil *m*; **a ~ examination** eine Auswahlprüfung.
(b) (*Comm*) *business, prices, salaries* wettbewerbs- *or* konkurrenzfähig ◆ **a highly ~ market** ein Markt mit starker Konkurrenz; **retailing is highly ~** der Einzelhandel ist stark wettbewerbsbetont *or* -orientiert.
competitiveness [kəm'petɪtɪvnɪs] *n* (*competitive spirit*) Wettbewerbs- *or* Konkurrenzgeist *m*; (*of product, company, prices*) Wettbewerbsfähigkeit *f*.
competitor [kəm'petɪtəʳ] *n* **(a)** (*Sport, in contest*) Teilnehmer(in *f*) *m*; (*for job*) Mitbewerber(in *f*) *m* ◆ **to be a ~** teilnehmen; **to be sb's ~** jds Gegner sein. **(b)** (*Comm*) Konkurrent(in *f*) *m* ◆ **our ~s** unsere Konkurrenz *or* Konkurrenten.
compilation [ˌkɒmpɪ'leɪʃən] *n see vt* Zusammenstellung *f*, Sammlung *f*, Abfassung *f*.
compile [kəm'paɪl] *vt* zusammenstellen, erstellen (*form*); *material* sammeln, zusammentragen; *dictionary* verfassen; (*Comput*) kompilieren.
compiler [kəm'paɪləʳ] *n* (*of dictionary*) Verfasser(in *f*) *m*; (*Comput*) Compiler *m* ◆ **who's the ~ of this list?** wer hat diese Liste zusammengestellt?
complacence [kəm'pleɪsəns], **complacency** [kəmp'leɪsnsɪ] *n* Selbstzufriedenheit, Selbstgefälligkeit *f*.
complacent [kəm'pleɪsənt] *adj* selbstzufrieden *or* -gefällig ◆ **don't get ~ just because** ... jetzt werde bloß nicht selbstgefällig *or* überheblich, nur weil ...
complacently [kəm'pleɪsəntlɪ] *adv* selbstzufrieden *or* -gefällig ◆ **those who ~ accept their parents' beliefs** diejenigen, die die Ansichten ihrer Eltern unreflektiert übernehmen.
complain [kəm'pleɪn] *vi* sich beklagen, klagen (*about* über *+acc*); (*to make a formal complaint*) sich beschweren, Beschwerde einlegen (*form*) (*about* über *+acc, to* bei) ◆ **to ~ that** ... sich darüber beklagen/beschweren, daß ...; **(I) can't ~** (*inf*) ich kann nicht klagen (*inf*); **stop ~ing!** beklag dich nicht dauernd!; **to ~ of sth** über etw (*acc*) klagen; **she's always ~ing** sie muß sich immer beklagen, sie hat immer etwas zu klagen; **to ~ of not having enough time** über Zeitmangel klagen.
complainant [kəm'pleɪnənt] *n* Beschwerdeführer(in *f*) *m*; (*in court*) Kläger(in *f*) *m*.
complaint [kəm'pleɪnt] *n* **(a)** Klage *f*; (*formal ~*) Beschwerde *f* (*to* bei) ◆ **I have no cause for ~** ich kann mich nicht beklagen; **I wouldn't have any ~(s) if** ... ich würde mich nicht beklagen, wenn ...; **to lodge** *or* **lay a ~ against sb with the police** jdn bei der Polizei anzeigen, gegen jdn Anzeige erstatten.
(b) (*illness*) Beschwerden *pl* ◆ **a very rare ~** eine sehr seltene Krankheit, ein sehr seltenes Leiden.
complaisance [kəm'pleɪzəns] *n* (*liter*) Gefälligkeit *f*.
complaisant *adj*, **~ly** *adv* [kəm'pleɪzənt, -lɪ] gefällig, entgegenkommend; *smile* wohlwollend.
complement ['kɒmplɪmənt] **1** *n* **(a)** Ergänzung *f* (*to gen*); (*to perfect sth*) Vervollkommnung *f* (*to gen*); (*colour*) Komplementärfarbe *f* (*to* zu).
(b) (*full number*) volle Stärke; (*crew of ship*) Besatzung *f* ◆ **the battalion didn't have its full ~ of soldiers** das Bataillon hatte seine Sollstärke nicht; **we've got our full ~ in the office now** unser Büro ist jetzt komplett *or* voll besetzt.
(c) (*Gram*) Ergänzung *f*.
(d) (*Math: angle*) Ergänzungswinkel *m*.
2 ['kɒmplɪment] *vt* **(a)** ergänzen; (*make perfect*) vervollkommnen, abrunden; (*colour*) herausbringen ◆ **to ~ each other** sich ergänzen; (*colours*) aufeinander abgestimmt sein.
(b) (*Gram*) die Ergänzung bilden zu.
(c) (*Math*) zu 90° ergänzen.
complementary [ˌkɒmplɪ'mentərɪ] *adj colour* Komplementär-; *angle* Ergänzungs- ◆ **a ~ pair** ein zusammengehöriges Paar; **two ~ characters** zwei einander ergänzende Charaktere; **they are ~ to each other** sie ergänzen sich *or* einander; **they have ~ interests** ihre Interessen ergänzen sich.
complete [kəm'pliːt] **1** *adj* **(a)** (*entire, whole*) ganz *attr*; *set also, wardrobe, deck of cards* vollständig, komplett; (*having the required numbers*) vollzählig; *edition* Gesamt- ◆ **my happiness/disappointment was ~** mein Glück/meine Enttäuschung war perfekt *or* vollkommen; **my life is now ~** mein Leben ist erfüllt; **our victory was ~** unser Sieg war vollkommen; **the ~ works of Shakespeare** die gesammelten Werke Shakespeares; **a very ~ account** ein sehr umfassender *or* detaillierter Bericht; **are we ~?** sind wir vollzählig?
(b) *attr* (*total, absolute*) völlig; *failure, beginner, disaster, flop also, victory* total; *surprise, shambles also* komplett; *satisfaction also, approval* voll ◆ **we were ~ strangers** wir waren uns *or* einander völlig fremd.
(c) (*finished*) fertig ◆ **his novel is not yet ~** sein Roman ist noch nicht abgeschlossen; **my life's work is now ~** mein Lebenswerk ist nun vollbracht.
(d) **~ with** komplett mit; **he came ~ with rucksack and boots** er erschien komplett ausgerüstet mit Rucksack und Stiefeln.
(e) *sportsman, gardener etc* perfekt.
2 *vt* **(a)** (*make whole*) *collection, set* vervollständigen, komplettieren; *team* vollzählig machen; *education, meal* abrunden ◆ **to ~ our numbers** damit wir vollzählig sind; **that ~s my collection** damit ist meine Sammlung vollständig.
(b) (*fig*) *happiness* vollkommen machen ◆ **and to ~ their misery** ... und zu allem Unglück ...
(c) (*finish*) beenden, abschließen, zum Abschluß *or* zu Ende bringen; *building, work* fertigstellen; *prison sentence* verbüßen ◆ **~ this phrase** ergänzen Sie diesen Ausspruch; **it's not ~d yet** es ist noch nicht fertig; **when you've ~d your repayments** wenn Sie es ganz abbezahlt haben.
(d) *form, questionnaire* ausfüllen.
completely [kəm'pliːtlɪ] *adv* völlig, vollkommen ◆ **he's ~ wrong** er irrt sich gewaltig, er hat völlig unrecht; **he's not ~ normal** er ist nicht ganz normal.
completeness [kəm'pliːtnɪs] *n* Vollständigkeit *f* ◆ **the design has a sense of ~ about it** das Design erscheint vollendet *or* vollkommen; **a work which demonstrates the ~ of his talent** ein Werk, das sein vollendetes Talent beweist.
completion [kəm'pliːʃən] *n* **(a)** (*finishing*) Fertigstellung *f*; (*of work also*) Beendigung *f*; (*of project, course, education*) Abschluß *m*; (*of prison sentence*) Verbüßung *f* ◆ **near ~** kurz vor dem Abschluß; **to bring sth to ~** etw zum Abschluß bringen; **we need more people for the ~ of the work** wir brauchen noch mehr Leute, um die Arbeit zum Abschluß zu bringen; **on ~ of the course** am Ende *or* nach Abschluß des Kurses; **on ~ of the contract/sale** bei Vertrags-/Kaufabschluß; **~ date** Fertigstellungstermin *m*.
(b) (*making whole*) Vervollständigung *f*; (*of education, meal*) Abrundung *f*; (*of happiness etc*) Vervollkommnung *f*.
(c) (*filling in: of form etc*) Ausfüllen *nt*.
complex ['kɒmpleks] **1** *adj* **(a)** komplex; *person, mind, issue, question, problem, poem also* vielschichtig; *theory, task, system also, machine, pattern* differenziert, kompliziert; *situation also, paragraph* verwickelt, kompliziert.
(b) (*Gram*) **a ~ sentence** ein Satzgefüge *nt*.
2 *n* **(a)** Komplex *m* ◆ **industrial ~** Industriekomplex *m*. **(b)** (*Psych*) Komplex *m* ◆ **he has a ~ about his ears** er hat Komplexe *or* einen Komplex wegen seiner Ohren; **don't get a ~ about it** deswegen brauchst du keine Komplexe zu bekommen.
complexion [kəm'plekʃən] *n* **(a)** Teint *m*; (*skin colour*) Gesichtsfarbe *f*. **(b)**

(*fig: aspect*) Anstrich, Aspekt *m* ◆ **to put a new/different** *etc* **~ on sth** etw in einem neuen/anderen *etc* Licht erscheinen lassen; **of a different political/religious ~** mit anderen politischen/religiösen Anschauungen.

complexity [kəm'pleksɪtɪ] *n see adj (a)* Komplexität *f*; Vielschichtigkeit *f*; Differenziertheit, Kompliziertheit *f*.

compliance [kəm'plaɪəns] *n* Einverständnis *nt*; (*with rules etc*) Einhalten *nt* (*with* gen); (*submissiveness*) Willfährigkeit (*geh*), Fügsamkeit *f* ◆ **in ~ with the law/our wishes** *etc* dem Gesetz/unseren Wünschen *etc* gemäß.

compliant [kəm'plaɪənt] *adj* entgegenkommend, gefällig; (*submissive*) nachgiebig, willfährig (*geh*).

complicate ['kɒmplɪkeɪt] *vt* komplizieren.

complicated ['kɒmplɪkeɪtɪd] *adj* kompliziert.

complication [,kɒmplɪ'keɪʃən] *n* Komplikation *f*; (*condition*) Kompliziertheit *f* ◆ **his life had reached such a level of ~** sein Leben war so kompliziert *or* verwickelt geworden.

complicity [kəm'plɪsɪtɪ] *n* Mittäterschaft *f* (*in* bei).

compliment ['kɒmplɪmənt] [1] *n* **(a)** Kompliment *nt* (*on* zu, wegen) ◆ **to pay sb a ~** jdm ein Kompliment machen; **that's quite a ~, coming from you** wenn Sie das sagen, heißt das schon etwas *or* ist das wahrhaftig ein Kompliment; **(give) my ~s to the chef** mein Lob *or* Kompliment dem Koch/der Köchin.

(b) (*form*) **~s** *pl* Grüße *pl* ◆ **give him my ~s** empfehlen Sie mich ihm (*dated form*); **to pay one's ~s to sb** (*on arrival*) jdn begrüßen; (*on departure*) sich jdm empfehlen (*dated form*); (*visit*) jdm einen Höflichkeitsbesuch abstatten (*form*); **the ~s of the season** frohes Fest; **"with the ~s of Mr X/the management"** „mit den besten Empfehlungen von Herrn X/der Geschäftsleitung"; **"with the ~s of the publishers"** „zur gefälligen Kenntnisnahme, der Verlag"; **~s slip** (*Comm*) Empfehlungszettel *m*.

[2] ['kɒmplɪment] *vt* ein Kompliment/Komplimente machen (+*dat*) (*on* wegen, zu).

complimentary [,kɒmplɪ'mentərɪ] *adj* **(a)** (*praising*) schmeichelhaft ◆ **~ close** Schlußformel *f*. **(b)** (*gratis*) *seat, ticket* Frei- ◆ **~ copy** Freiexemplar *nt*; (*of magazine*) Werbenummer *f*.

compline ['kɒmplɪn] *n* (*Eccl*) Komplet *f*.

▼ **comply** [kəm'plaɪ] *vi* (*person*) einwilligen; (*object, system etc*) die Bedingungen erfüllen, den Bedingungen entsprechen ◆ **to ~ with sth** einer Sache (*dat*) entsprechen; (*system*) in Einklang mit etw stehen; **to ~ with a clause in a contract** eine Vertragsbedingung erfüllen; **to ~ with a request/a wish/instructions** einer Bitte/einem Wunsch/den Anordnungen nachkommen (*form*) *or* entsprechen (*form*); **to ~ with sb's wishes** sich jds Wünschen (*dat*) fügen; **to ~ with a time limit/the rules** eine Frist einhalten/sich an die Regeln halten.

component [kəm'pəʊnənt] [1] *n* Teil *nt*, Bestandteil *m*; (*Chem, Phys*) Komponente *f*.

[2] *adj* **a ~ part** ein (Bestand)teil *m*; **the ~ parts** die Bestand- *or* Einzelteile *pl*; **the ~ parts of a machine/sentence** die einzelnen Maschinen-/Satzteile *pl*.

comport [kəm'pɔːt] (*form*) [1] *vr* sich verhalten.

[2] *vi* **to ~ with** sich vereinbaren lassen mit.

comportment [kəm'pɔːtmənt] *n* Verhalten *nt* ◆ **to study ~** Anstandsunterricht nehmen.

compose [kəm'pəʊz] *vt* **(a)** *music* komponieren; *letter* abfassen, aufsetzen; *poem* verfassen.

(b) (*constitute, make up*) bilden ◆ **to be ~d of** sich zusammensetzen aus; **water is ~d of ...** Wasser besteht aus ...

(c) to ~ oneself sich sammeln; **to ~ one's features** sich wieder in die Gewalt bekommen; **to ~ one's thoughts** Ordnung in seine Gedanken bringen.

(d) (*Typ*) setzen.

composed *adj*, **~ly** *adv* [kəm'pəʊzd, -zədlɪ] beherrscht, gelassen.

composer [kəm'pəʊzəʳ] *n* **(a)** (*Mus*) Komponist(in *f*) *m*. **(b)** (*of letter, poem etc*) Verfasser(in *f*) *m*.

composite ['kɒmpəzɪt] [1] *adj* **(a)** zusammengesetzt ◆ **~ motion** Sammelantrag *m*; **~ photograph** Photomontage *f*; **~ structure** gegliederter Aufbau. **(b)** (*Bot*) Korbblütler-; *flower* zur Familie der Korbblütler gehörig. **(c)** (*Math*) *number* teilbar.

[2] *n* (*Bot*) Korbblütler *m*.

composition [,kɒmpə'zɪʃən] *n* **(a)** (*act of composing*) (*of music*) Komponieren *nt*; (*of letter*) Abfassen, Aufsetzen *nt*; (*of poem*) Verfassen *nt* ◆ **music/verse of his own ~** selbstkomponierte Musik/selbstverfaßte Verse.

(b) (*arrangement, Mus, Art*) Komposition *f*; (*Mus: theory of ~ also*) Kompositionslehre *f*.

(c) (*Sch: essay*) Aufsatz *m*.

(d) (*constitution, make-up*) Zusammensetzung *f*; (*of sentence*) Aufbau *m*, Konstruktion *f* ◆ **to change/decide on the ~ of sth** die Zusammenstellung einer Sache (*gen*) ändern/etw zusammenstellen; **this medicine/manure is a ~ of ...** dieses Medikament/dieser Dünger setzt sich aus ... zusammen; **there is a touch of madness in his ~** (*old, liter*) in ihm findet sich die Anlage zum Wahnsinn.

(e) (*artificial substance*) Kunststoff *m*.

(f) (*Typ*) Setzen *nt* ◆ **~ by hand** Handsatz *m*, manueller Satz.

(g) (*Jur*) Vergleich *m*.

composition *in cpds* Kunst-; **~ rubber** *n* synthetischer Kautschuk; **~ sole** *n* Kunststoffsohle *f*.

compositor [kəm'pɒzɪtəʳ] *n* (*Typ*) (Schrift)setzer(in *f*) *m*.

compos mentis ['kɒmpəs'mentɪs] *adj* **I'm never really ~ first thing in the morning** frühmorgens ist mein Verstand noch nicht so klar *or* bin ich noch nicht voll da (*inf*); **he's quite ~** er ist voll zurechnungsfähig; **he's not quite ~** er ist nicht voll zurechnungsfähig, er ist nicht ganz bei Trost (*inf*).

compost ['kɒmpɒst] *n* Kompost *m* ◆ **~ heap** Komposthaufen *m*.

composure [kəm'pəʊʒəʳ] *n* Beherrschung, Fassung *f* ◆ **to lose/regain one's ~** die Beherrschung verlieren/seine Selbstbeherrschung wiederfinden.

compote ['kɒmpəʊt] *n* Kompott *nt*.

compound[1] ['kɒmpaʊnd] [1] *n* (*Chem*) Verbindung *f*; (*Gram*) Kompositum *nt*, zusammengesetztes Wort.

[2] *adj* **(a)** (*Chem*) **~ substance** Verbindung *f*.

(b) (*Math*) **~ fraction** Doppelbruch *m*; **~ interest** Zinseszins *m*; **~ number** zusammengesetzte Zahl.

(c) (*Med*) **~ fracture** offener *or* komplizierter Bruch.

(d) (*Gram*) *tense, word* zusammengesetzt ◆ **~ sentence** Satzgefüge *nt*; (*of two or more main clauses*) Satzreihe, Parataxe *f*.

(e) (*Zool*) **~ eye** Facetten- *or* Netzauge *nt*.

[3] [kəm'paʊnd] *vt* **(a)** (*rare: combine*) verbinden; (*Chem*) mischen ◆ **to be ~ed of ...** (*liter*) sich zusammensetzen aus ...

(b) (*Jur*) *debt* begleichen, tilgen; *quarrel* beilegen ◆ **to ~ a crime** ein Verbrechen wegen erhaltener Entschädigung nicht verfolgen.

(c) (*make worse*) verschlimmern; *problem* verstärken, vergrößern ◆ **this only ~s our difficulties** das erschwert unsere Lage *or* Situation noch zusätzlich.

[4] [kəm'paʊnd] *vi* einen Vergleich schließen; (*with creditors*) sich vergleichen ◆ **to ~ with sb for sth** sich mit jdm auf etw (*acc*) einigen.

compound[2] ['kɒmpaʊnd] *n* (*enclosed area*) Lager *nt*; (*in prison*) Gefängnishof *m*; (*living quarters*) Siedlung *f*; (*in zoo*) Gehege *nt*.

compounding ['kɒmpaʊndɪŋ] *n* (*Ling*) Zusammensetzungen *pl*.

comprehend [,kɒmprɪ'hend] *vt* **(a)** (*understand*) begreifen, verstehen. **(b)** (*include*) enthalten, umfassen, einschließen.

comprehensibility [,kɒmprɪ,hensɪ'bɪlɪtɪ] *n* Verständlichkeit *f*.

comprehensible [,kɒmprɪ'hensəbl] *adj* verständlich ◆ **such behaviour is just not ~** ein solches Verhalten ist einfach unbegreiflich *or* unverständlich.

comprehension [,kɒmprɪ'henʃən] *n* **(a)** (*understanding*) Verständnis *nt*; (*ability to understand*) Begriffsvermögen *nt* ◆ **that is beyond my ~** das übersteigt mein Begriffsvermögen; (*behaviour*) das ist mir unbegreiflich.

(b) (*inclusion*) Aufnahme *f*.

(c) (*school exercise*) Fragen *pl* zum Textverständnis.

comprehensive [,kɒmprɪ'hensɪv] [1] *adj* umfassend ◆ **~ school** (*Brit*) Gesamtschule *f*; **to go ~** (*Sch*) (eine) Gesamtschule werden; **~ insurance** Vollkasko(versicherung *f*) *nt*; **are you ~?** (*Insur*) sind Sie vollkaskoversichert?, haben Sie Vollkasko? (*inf*).

[2] *n* (*Brit*) Gesamtschule *f*.

comprehensively [,kɒmprɪ'hensɪvlɪ] *adv* umfassend.

comprehensiveness [,kɒmprɪ'hensɪvnɪs] *n* Ausführlichkeit *f* ◆ **the ~ of his report** sein umfassender Bericht.

compress[1] [kəm'pres] [1] *vt* komprimieren (*into* auf +*acc*); *air etc also*, (*Comput*) *data* verdichten; *materials* zusammenpressen (*into* zu) ◆ **the storyline is too ~ed** die Geschichte ist zu komprimiert *or* gedrängt erzählt.

[2] *vi* sich verdichten, sich komprimieren lassen.

compress[2] ['kɒmpres] *n* Kompresse *f*, feuchter Umschlag.

compressed air [kəm'prest'eəʳ] *n* Druck- *or* Preßluft *f*.

compression [kəm'preʃən] *n* Verdichtung, Kompression *f*; (*of information etc*) Komprimieren *nt* ◆ **~ ratio** Verdichtungs- *or* Kompressionsverhältnis *nt*; **the gas is in a state of very high ~** das Gas ist stark verdichtet *or* komprimiert.

compressor [kəm'presəʳ] *n* Kompressor, Verdichter *m* ◆ **~ program** (*Comput*) Verdichtungsprogramm *nt*.

comprise [kəm'praɪz] *vt* bestehen aus, umfassen.

compromise ['kɒmprəmaɪz] [1] *n* Kompromiß *m* ◆ **to come to** *or* **reach** *or* **make a ~** zu einem Kompromiß kommen *or* gelangen, einen Kompromiß schließen; **one has to make ~s** man muß auch mal Kompromisse schließen.

[2] *adj attr* Kompromiß- ◆ **~ decision** Kompromiß(lösung *f*) *m*; **~ solution** Kompromißlösung *f*.

[3] *vi* Kompromisse schließen (*about* in +*dat*) ◆ **we agreed to ~** wir einigten uns auf einen Kompromiß.

[4] *vt* **(a)** kompromittieren ◆ **to ~ oneself** sich kompromittieren; **to ~ one's reputation** seinem guten Ruf schaden.

(b) (*imperil*) gefährden.

compromising ['kɒmprəmaɪzɪŋ] *adj* kompromittierend.

comptroller [kən'trəʊləʳ] *n* (*form*) Rechnungsprüfer, Bücherrevisor *m* ◆ **C~ of the Queen's Household** *Beamter des Rechnungshofes, der die königlichen Finanzen überprüft*.

compulsion [kəm'pʌlʃən] *n* Zwang, Druck *m*; (*Psych*) innerer Zwang ◆ **under ~** unter Druck *or* Zwang; **you are under no ~** Sie sind nicht gezwungen, niemand zwingt Sie.

compulsive [kəm'pʌlsɪv] *adj* zwanghaft, Zwangs-; *neurosis* Zwangs-; *behaviour* zwanghaft ◆ **the ~ buying of ...** der krankhafte Zwang, ... zu kaufen; **~ buying as a form of disease** Kaufzwang, eine Art Krankheit; **he has a ~ desire to ...** er steht unter dem Zwang, zu ...; **he is a ~ eater** er hat die Eßsucht, er leidet an einem Eßzwang; **he is a ~ liar** er hat einen krankhaften Trieb zu lügen; **he's a ~ smoker** das Rauchen ist bei ihm zur Sucht geworden; **she's a ~ talker** sie muß unbedingt reden; **it makes ~ reading/viewing** das muß man einfach lesen/sehen; **this ~ TV-watching**

➤ LANGUAGE IN USE: **comply** → 11.3

ruins every conversation diese ständige Fernseherei zerstört jede Unterhaltung!

compulsively [kəm'pʌlsɪvlɪ] *adv see adj* **to act ~** unter einem (inneren) Zwang handeln.

compulsorily [kəm'pʌlsərɪlɪ] *adv* zwangsweise.

▼ **compulsory** [kəm'pʌlsərɪ] *adj* obligatorisch; *liquidation, measures* Zwangs-; *subject, member* Pflicht- ◆ **that is ~** das ist Pflicht *or* obligatorisch; **education is ~** es besteht (allgemeine) Schulpflicht; **~ purchase** Enteignung *f*; **~ purchase order** Enteignungsbeschluß *m*; **to put a ~ purchase order on a place** die Enteignung eines Grundstückes verfügen; **~ retirement** Zwangspensionierung *f*; **~ service** (*US*) Wehrpflicht *f*.

compunction [kəm'pʌŋkʃən] *n* (*liter*) Schuldgefühle, Gewissensbisse *pl* ◆ **with no ~/without the slightest ~** ohne sich schuldig/im geringsten schuldig zu fühlen.

computation [ˌkɒmpjʊ'teɪʃən] *n* Berechnung, Kalkulation *f*.

computational [ˌkɒmpjʊ'teɪʃənəl] *adj* **~ linguistics** Computerlinguistik *f*.

compute [kəm'pjuːt] *vt* berechnen (*at* auf *+acc*), errechnen.

computer [kəm'pjuːtə^r] *n* Computer, Rechner *m*; (*data processing also*) Datenverarbeitungsanlage *f* ◆ **to put/have sth on ~** etw im Computer speichern/(gespeichert) haben; **it's all done by ~** das geht alles per Computer.

computer *in cpds* Computer-; **~ age** *n* Computerzeitalter *nt*; **~-aided** *adj* rechnergestützt; **~-aided design** *n* rechnergestützter Entwurf.

computerate [kəm'pjuːtərɪt] *adj* **to be ~** sich mit Computern auskennen.

computer: ~-based *adj* auf Computerbasis; **~-controlled** *adj* rechnergesteuert; **~ crime** *n* Computerkriminalität *f*; **~-dating** *n* Partnervermittlung *f* per Computer; **~-dating agency** *or* **bureau** *n* Partnervermittlungsbüro *nt* auf Computerbasis; **~-designed** *adj* durch Computer *or* mit Computerunterstützung entworfen.

computerese [kəmˌpjuːtə'riːz] *n* (*inf: jargon*) Computerjargon *m*.

computer: ~ freak *n* (*inf*) Computerfreak *m* (*inf*); **~ game** *n* Computerspiel *nt*; **~ games software** *n* Software *f* für Computerspiele; **~-generated** *adj image, graphics* computergeneriert; **~ graphics** *npl* Computergrafik *f*, grafische Datenverarbeitung.

computerization [kəm'pjuːtəraɪ'zeɪʃən] *n* (*of information etc*) Computerisierung *f* ◆ **the ~ of the factory** die Umstellung der Fabrik auf Computer.

computerize [kəm'pjuːtəraɪz] *vt information* computerisieren; *company, accounting methods* auf Computer *or* EDV umstellen.

computer: ~ language *n* Computersprache *f*; **~ literacy** *n* Computerkenntnisse *pl*; **~ literate** *adj* **to be ~ literate** sich mit Computern auskennen; **~ model** *n* Computermodell *nt*; **~ network** *n* Computer-Netzwerk *nt*; (*larger also*) Rechnerverbund *m*; **~-operated** *adj* computergesteuert; **~ operator** *n* Operator, Bildschirmarbeiter(in *f*) *m*; **~ peripheral** *n* Peripheriegerät *nt*; **~ printout** *n* (Computer-)Ausdruck *m*; **~ program** *n* (Computer)programm *nt*; **~ programmer** *n* Programmierer(in *f*) *m*; **~ science** *n* Informatik *f*; **~ scientist** *n* Informatiker(in *f*) *m*; **~ search** *n* Suche *f* per Computer; (*in criminal contexts*) Rasterfahndung *f*; **~ skills** *npl* Computerkenntnisse *pl*; **~ studies** *npl* Computerwissenschaft *f*; **~-typeset** *vt* in Computersatz herstellen; **~ typesetting** *n* Computersatz *m*; **~ virus** *n* Computer-Virus *m*.

computing [kəm'pjuːtɪŋ] [1] (**a**) (*subject*) Computerwissenschaft *f* ◆ **her husband's in ~** ihr Mann ist in der Computerbranche. (**b**) (*act*) Berechnung *f*.
[2] *attr problem, task* rechnerisch.

comrade ['kɒmrɪd] *n* Kamerad *m*; (*Pol*) Genosse *m*, Genossin *f* ◆ **~-in-arms** Waffenbruder (*old*), Kriegskamerad *m*.

comradely ['kɒmrɪdlɪ] *adj* kameradschaftlich.

comradeship ['kɒmrɪdʃɪp] *n* Kameradschaft(lichkeit) *f* ◆ **the spirit of ~** der Kameradschaftsgeist.

comsat ['kɒmsæt] *abbr of* **communications satellite**.

con[1] [kɒn] *vt* (*rare: learn*) sich (*dat*) einprägen.

con[2] *adv, n see* **pro[3]**.

con[3] *vt* (*Naut*) steuern, lenken.

con[4] (*inf*) [1] *n* Schwindel, Beschiß (*sl*) *m* ◆ **it's a ~!** das ist alles Schwindel *or* Beschiß (*sl*); **~ artist** Schwindler(in *f*) *m*.
[2] *vt* hereinlegen (*inf*), bescheißen (*sl*) ◆ **he ~ned her out of all her money** er hat sie um ihr ganzes Geld gebracht; **to ~ sb into doing sth** jdn durch einen faulen Trick dazu bringen, daß er etw tut (*inf*); **don't let him ~ you into believing it** laß dir das bloß nicht von ihm aufbinden (*inf*) *or* einreden; **he ~ned his way through the security check** er hat sich durch die Sicherheitskontrolle gemogelt (*inf*).

con[5] (*inf*) *abbr of* **convict** Knastbruder *m* (*inf*).

concatenation [kɒnˌkætɪ'neɪʃən] *n* Verkettung *f*.

concave ['kɒn'keɪv] *adj* konkav; *mirror* Konkav-, Hohl-.

concavity [kɒn'kævɪtɪ] *n* Konkavität *f*.

concavo-convex [kɒnˌkeɪvəʊkɒn'veks] *adj* konkav-konvex.

conceal [kən'siːl] *vt* (*hide*) *object, emotions, thoughts* verbergen; (*keep secret*) verheimlichen (*sth from sb* jdm etw) ◆ **why did they ~ this information from us?** warum hat man uns diese Informationen vorenthalten?; **to ~ the fact that ...** (die Tatsache) verheimlichen, daß ...; **the chameleon was completely ~ed against its background** das Chamäleon war nicht mehr von seiner Umgebung zu unterscheiden.

concealed [kən'siːld] *adj* verborgen; *lighting, wiring, turning, entrance* verdeckt; *camera* versteckt, Geheim-.

concealment [kən'siːlmənt] *n* (*of facts*) Verheimlichung *f*; (*of evidence*) Unterschlagung *f*; (*of criminal*) Gewährung *f* von Unterschlupf (*of* an *+acc*) ◆ **to come out of ~** aus dem Versteck auftauchen; **to stay in ~** sich versteckt halten.

concede [kən'siːd] [1] *vt* (**a**) (*yield, give up*) *privilege* aufgeben; *lands* abtreten (*to* an *+acc*) ◆ **to ~ a privilege/right to sb** jdm ein Privileg/Recht überlassen; **to ~ victory to sb** vor jdm kapitulieren; **to ~ a match** (*give up*) aufgeben, sich geschlagen geben; (*lose*) ein Match abgeben; **to ~ a penalty** einen Elfmeter verursachen; **to ~ a point to sb** jdm in einem Punkt recht geben; (*Sport*) einen Punkt an jdn abgeben.
(**b**) (*admit, grant*) zugeben, einräumen (*form*); *privilege* einräumen (*to sb* jdm); *right* zubilligen, zugestehen (*to sb* jdm) ◆ **it's generally ~d that ...** es ist allgemein anerkannt, daß ...; **to ~ defeat** sich geschlagen geben.
[2] *vi* nachgeben, kapitulieren.

conceit [kən'siːt] *n* (**a**) (*pride*) Einbildung *f* ◆ **he's full of ~** er ist schrecklich eingebildet; **of all the ~!** diese Einbildung! (**b**) **he is wise in his own ~** (*liter*) er dünkt sich weise (*liter*). (**c**) (*Liter*) Konzetto *nt*.

conceited [kən'siːtɪd] *adj* eingebildet.

conceitedly [kən'siːtɪdlɪ] *adv see adj* ◆ **he ~ claimed ...** eingebildet wie er ist, hat er behauptet ...

conceitedness [kən'siːtɪdnɪs] *n* Eingebildetheit, Einbildung *f*.

conceivable [kən'siːvəbl] *adj* denkbar, vorstellbar ◆ **it is hardly ~ that ...** es ist kaum denkbar, daß ..., man kann sich (*dat*) kaum vorstellen, daß ...; **it's not ~ that she would have gone without us** ich kann mir nicht vorstellen, daß sie ohne uns gegangen ist.

conceivably [kən'siːvəblɪ] *adv* **she may ~ be right** es ist durchaus denkbar, daß sie recht hat; **will it happen? — ~** wird das geschehen? — das ist durchaus denkbar.

conceive [kən'siːv] [1] *vt* (**a**) *child* empfangen.
(**b**) (*imagine*) sich (*dat*) denken *or* vorstellen; *idea, plan* haben; *novel* die Idee haben zu ◆ **it was originally ~d as quite a different sort of book** ursprünglich war das Buch ganz anders geplant *or* konzipiert (*geh*); **it was ~d in a Paris café** die Idee (dazu) wurde in einem Pariser Café geboren; **the way he ~s his role** seine Vorstellung *or* Auffassung von seiner Rolle; **she ~s it to be her duty** sie erachtet (*geh*) *or* betrachtet es als ihre Pflicht; **I can't ~ why** ich verstehe *or* begreife nicht, warum.
(**c**) **to ~ a dislike for sb/sth** eine Abneigung gegen jdn/etw entwickeln; **to ~ a liking for sb/sth** Zuneigung für jdn empfinden/seine Vorliebe für etw entdecken.
[2] *vi* (*woman*) empfangen.

◆**conceive of** *vi +prep obj* sich (*dat*) vorstellen ◆ **who first ~d ~ the idea?** wer hatte die Idee zuerst?, wem kam die Idee zuerst?; **he absolutely refuses to ~ ~ cheating** Betrug käme ihm überhaupt nicht in den Sinn.

concentrate ['kɒnsəntreɪt] [1] *vt* (**a**) konzentrieren (*on* auf *+acc*) ◆ **to ~ all one's energies on sth** sich (voll und) ganz auf etw (*acc*) konzentrieren; **to ~ one's mind on sth** seine Gedanken *or* sich auf etw (*acc*) konzentrieren; **it's amazing how he's ~d so much material into one novel** es ist erstaunlich, wieviel Material er in einem Roman zusammengedrängt hat. (**b**) (*Mil*) *troops* konzentrieren. (**c**) (*Chem*) konzentrieren.
[2] *vi* (**a**) (*give one's attention*) sich konzentrieren ◆ **to ~ on doing sth** sich darauf konzentrieren, etw zu tun.
(**b**) (*people*) sich sammeln; (*troops also*) sich konzentrieren.
[3] *adj* (*Chem*) konzentriert.
[4] *n* (*Chem*) Konzentrat *nt*.

concentration [ˌkɒnsən'treɪʃən] *n* (**a**) Konzentration *f* ◆ **powers of ~** Konzentrationsfähigkeit *f*. (**b**) (*gathering*) Ansammlung *f*. (**c**) (*Chem*) Konzentration *f*.

concentration camp *n* Konzentrationslager, KZ *nt*.

concentric [kən'sentrɪk] *adj circles* konzentrisch.

concept ['kɒnsept] *n* Begriff *m*; (*conception*) Vorstellung *f* ◆ **the ~ of evil** der Begriff des Bösen; **our ~ of the world** unser Weltbild *nt*; **his ~ of marriage** seine Vorstellungen von der Ehe; **the ~ of the play was good** das Stück war gut konzipiert (*geh*) *or* war in der Anlage *or* vom Konzept her gut.

concept album *n* (*Mus*) Konzeptalbum *nt*.

conception [kən'sepʃən] *n* (**a**) (*forming ideas*) Vorstellung *f* ◆ **the writer's powers of ~** die Vorstellungskraft *or* das Vorstellungsvermögen des Schriftstellers.
(**b**) (*idea*) Vorstellung *f*; (*way sth is conceived*) Konzeption *f* ◆ **what's your ~ of the ideal life?** was ist Ihrer Vorstellung nach ein ideales Leben?; **the Buddhist ~ of life/nature/morality** die buddhistische Auffassung vom Leben/Vorstellung von der Natur/Moralvorstellung; **the classical ~ of beauty** das klassische Schönheitsideal; **they have a totally different ~ of justice** sie haben eine völlig unterschiedliche Auffassung *or* Vorstellung von Gerechtigkeit; **in their ~ they are ...** sie sind von der Konzeption her ...; **he has no ~ of how difficult it is** er macht sich (*dat*) keinen Begriff davon *or* er hat keine Vorstellung, wie schwer das ist.
(**c**) (*of child*) die Empfängnis, die Konzeption (*form*).

conceptual [kən'septjʊəl] *adj thinking* begrifflich ◆ **is this a ~ possibility?** ist ein solcher Begriff überhaupt denkbar?

conceptualism [kən'septjʊəlɪzəm] *n* Konzeptualismus *m*.

conceptualization [kənˌseptjʊəlaɪ'zeɪʃən] *n* Begriffsbildung *f* ◆ **the ~ of experience** die begriffliche Erfassung der Erfahrung.

conceptualize [kən'septjʊəlaɪz] [1] *vt* in Begriffe fassen.
[2] *vi* begrifflich denken.

conceptually [kən'septjʊəlɪ] *adv* begrifflich ◆ **X is ~ impossible** X ist begrifflich undenkbar; **it only exists ~** das existiert nur in der Vorstellung.

▼ **concern** [kən'sɜːn] [1] *n* (**a**) (*relation, connection*) **do you have any ~ with bank-**

➤ LANGUAGE IN USE: **compulsory** → 10.3

ing? haben Sie etwas mit dem Bankwesen zu tun?; **to have no ~ with sth** mit etw nichts zu tun haben.
(b) (*business, affair*) Angelegenheit(en *pl*) *f*; (*matter of interest and importance to a person*) Anliegen *nt* ◆ **the day-to-day ~s of government** die täglichen Regierungsgeschäfte; **it's no ~ of his** das geht ihn nichts an; **what ~ is it of yours?** was geht Sie das an?; **my ~ is with his works, not his life** mir geht es um sein Werk, nicht um seine Biographie.
(c) (*Comm*) Konzern *m*; *see* **going.**
(d) (*share*) Beteiligung *f* ◆ **he has a ~ in the business** er ist an dem Geschäft beteiligt; **what is your ~ in it?** wie hoch sind Sie beteiligt?, wie hoch ist Ihre Beteiligung?
(e) (*anxiety*) Sorge, Besorgnis *f* ◆ **a look of ~** ein besorgter *or* sorgenvoller Blick; **the situation in the Middle East is causing ~** die Lage im Nahen Osten ist besorgniserregend; **there's some/no cause for ~** es besteht Grund/kein Grund zur Sorge; **he showed great ~ for your safety** er war *or* zeigte sich (*geh*) sehr um Ihre Sicherheit besorgt; **don't you feel any ~ for the starving millions?** berührt Sie die Tatsache, daß Millionen am Verhungern sind, überhaupt nicht?
(f) (*importance*) Bedeutung *f* ◆ **a matter of economic ~** eine Angelegenheit von wirtschaftlicher Bedeutung; **issues of national ~** Fragen von nationalem Interesse.
[2] *vt* **(a)** (*be about*) handeln von ◆ **it ~s the following issue** es geht um die folgende Frage; **the last chapter is ~ed with ...** das letzte Kapitel behandelt ...
▼**(b)** (*be the business of, involve*) angehen, betreffen; (*affect*) betreffen ◆ **that doesn't ~ you** das betrifft Sie nicht; (*as snub*) das geht Sie nichts an; **to whom it may ~** (*on certificate*) Bestätigung *f*; (*on reference*) Zeugnis *nt*; **the countries ~ed with oil-production** die Länder, die mit der Ölproduktion zu tun haben; **where money/honour is ~ed** wenn es um Geld/die Ehre geht; **as far as the money is ~ed** was das Geld betrifft *or* angeht; **is it important? — not as far as I'm ~ed** ist es denn wichtig? — was mich betrifft, nicht; **as far as he is ~ed it's just another job, but ...** für ihn ist es nur ein anderer Job, aber ...; **as far as I'm ~ed you can do what you like** von mir aus kannst du tun und lassen, was du willst; **where we are ~ed** wo es um uns geht; (*in so far as we are affected*) wo wir betroffen sind; **the department ~ed** (*relevant*) die zuständige Abteilung; (*involved*) die betreffende Abteilung; **who are the people ~ed in this report?** wer sind die Leute, um die es in diesem Bericht geht?; **the persons ~ed** die Betroffenen, die betroffenen Personen; **my brother is the most closely ~ed** mein Bruder ist am meisten davon betroffen; **the men ~ed in the robbery** die in den Überfall verwickelten Männer; **he's ~ed in some complicated court case** er ist in irgendeinen komplizierten Fall verwickelt.
(c) (*interest*) **he is only ~ed with facts** ihn interessieren nur die Fakten; (*is only dealing with*) ihm geht es nur um die Fakten; **to ~ oneself in** *or* **with** *or* **about sth** sich für etw interessieren; **I'm not ~ed now** *or* **I don't want to ~ myself now with the economic aspect of the problem** mir geht es jetzt nicht um den ökonomischen Aspekt des Problems.
(d) (*have at heart*) **we should be ~ed more with** *or* **about quality** Qualität sollte uns ein größeres Anliegen sein; **a mother is naturally ~ed about the well-being of her children** das Wohl ihrer Kinder ist einer Mutter natürlich ein Anliegen; **he's not at all ~ed with** *or* **about her well-being** ihr Wohl kümmert ihn überhaupt nicht; **there's no need for you to ~ yourself about that** darum brauchen Sie sich nicht zu kümmern.
(e) (*worry: usu pass*) **to be ~ed about sth** sich (*dat*) um etw Sorgen machen, um etw besorgt sein; **I was very ~ed to hear about your illness** ich habe mir Sorgen gemacht, als ich von Ihrer Krankheit hörte; **he was ~ed at the news** die Nachricht beunruhigte ihn; **don't ~ yourself** machen Sie sich keine Sorgen; **I was very ~ed about** *or* **for your safety** ich war sehr um Ihre Sicherheit besorgt; **I am ~ed to hear that ...** es beunruhigt mich, daß ...; **a ~ed look** ein besorgter Blick.

concerning [kən'sɜːnɪŋ] *prep* bezüglich, hinsichtlich, betreffs (*form*) (*all +gen*) ◆ **~ your request ...** apropos Ihrer Anfrage ..., was Ihre Anfrage betrifft ...; **~ what?** worüber?

concert¹ ['kɒnsət] *n* **(a)** (*Mus*) Konzert *nt* ◆ **were you at the ~?** waren Sie in dem Konzert?; **Madonna in ~** Madonna live. **(b)** (*of voices etc*) **in ~** im Chor, gemeinsam. **(c)** (*fig*) **in ~** gemeinsam; **to work in ~ with sb** mit jdm zusammenarbeiten.

concert² [kən'sɜːt] *vt efforts* vereinen.

concerted [kən'sɜːtɪd] *adj efforts, action, attack* gemeinsam, konzertiert (*esp Pol*) ◆ **with** *or* **through their ~ efforts ...** mit vereinten Kräften ...; **to take ~ action** gemeinsam vorgehen; **to make a ~ attack** gemeinsam *or* geballt angreifen.

concert: ~goer *n* Konzertbesucher(in *f*) *or* -gänger(in *f*) *m*; **~ grand** *n* Konzertflügel *m*; **~ hall** *n* Konzerthalle *f or* -saal *m*.

concertina [ˌkɒnsə'tiːnə] [1] *n* Konzertina *f*.
[2] *vi* sich wie eine Ziehharmonika zusammenschieben.

concertmaster ['kɒnsətmæstəʳ] *n* (*US*) Konzertmeister *m*.

concerto [kən'tʃɜːtəʊ] *n* Konzert, Concerto *nt*.

concert: ~ performer *n* Konzertkünstler(in *f*) *m*; **~ pianist** *n* Pianist(in *f*) *m*; **~ pitch** *n* Kammerton *m*; **~ tour** *n* Konzerttournee *f*.

concession [kən'seʃən] *n* Zugeständnis *nt*, Konzession *f* (*to* an *+acc*); (*Comm*) Konzession *f* ◆ **to make ~s to sb** jdm Konzessionen *or* Zugeständnisse machen.

concessionaire [kənˌseʃə'nɛəʳ] *n* (*Comm*) Konzessionär *m*.

concessionary [kən'seʃənərɪ] *adj* (*Comm*) Konzessions-; (*reduced*) *rates, fares* verbilligt.

concessive [kən'sesɪv] *adj* (*Gram*) konzessiv, Konzessiv-.

conch [kɒntʃ] *n große, spiralige Meeresschnecke*; (*used as trumpet*) Trompetenschnecke *f*, Tritonshorn *nt* (*also Myth*).

conchy ['kɒntʃɪ] *n* (*pej sl*) Kriegsdienstverweigerer, Drückeberger (*pej inf*) *m*.

concierge ['kɒnsɪɜːʒ] *n* Portier *m*, Portiersfrau *f*.

conciliate [kən'sɪlɪeɪt] *vt* **(a)** (*placate*) besänftigen; (*win the goodwill of*) *person* versöhnlich stimmen. **(b)** (*reconcile*) *opposing views* auf einen Nenner bringen, in Einklang bringen.

conciliation [kənˌsɪlɪ'eɪʃən] *n see vt (a)* Besänftigung *f*; Versöhnung *f* ◆ **~ board** (*in industry*) Schlichtungskommission *f*.

conciliator [kən'sɪlɪeɪtəʳ] *n* Vermittler(in *f*) *m*.

conciliatory [kən'sɪlɪətərɪ] *adj* versöhnlich; (*placatory*) beschwichtigend, besänftigend.

concise [kən'saɪs] *adj* präzis(e), exakt ◆ **~ dictionary** Handwörterbuch *nt*.

concisely [kən'saɪslɪ] *adv* präzis(e), exakt.

conciseness [kən'saɪsnɪs],

concision [kən'sɪʒən] *n* Präzision, Exaktheit *f*.

conclave ['kɒnkleɪv] *n* **(a)** Klausur *f* ◆ **in ~** in Klausur; **to meet in ~** eine Klausurtagung abhalten. **(b)** (*Eccl*) Konklave *nt*.

▼**conclude** [kən'kluːd] [1] *vt* **(a)** (*end*) *meeting, letter, speech* beenden, schließen; *meal* abschließen, beenden ◆ **this, gentlemen, ~s our business** damit, meine Herren, sind wir mit unserer Besprechung am Ende; **and now, to ~ tonight's programmes** zum Abschluß unseres heutigen Abendprogramms.
(b) (*arrange*) *treaty, transaction, deal* abschließen.
▼**(c)** (*infer*) schließen, folgern (*from* aus) ◆ **what did you ~?** was haben Sie daraus geschlossen *or* gefolgert?
▼**(d)** (*decide, come to conclusion*) zu dem Schluß kommen ◆ **what have you ~d about his suggestion?** zu welchem Schluß sind Sie in bezug auf seinen Vorschlag gekommen?
[2] *vi* (*meetings, events*) enden; (*letter, speech etc also*) schließen ◆ **to ~ I must say ...** abschließend wäre noch zu bemerken *or* bliebe noch zu sagen, ...

concluding [kən'kluːdɪŋ] *adj remarks, words* abschließend, Schluß- ◆ **~ bars/lines** Schlußtakte/-zeilen *pl*; **the ~ years of ...** die letzten Jahre von ...

▼**conclusion** [kən'kluːʒən] *n* **(a)** (*end*) Abschluß *m*; (*of essay, novel etc*) Schluß *m* ◆ **in ~** zum (Ab)schluß, abschließend.
(b) (*settling: of treaty etc*) Abschluß *m*, Zustandekommen *nt*.
▼**(c)** Schluß(folgerung *f*) *m* ◆ **what ~ do you draw** *or* **reach from all this?** welchen Schluß *or* welche Schlußfolgerung ziehen Sie daraus *or* aus alldem?; **let me know your ~s** lassen Sie mich wissen, zu welchem Schluß Sie gekommen sind; **a rash ~** ein voreiliger Schluß; **one is forced to the ~ that ...** man kommt unweigerlich zu dem Schluß, daß ...
(d) (*Logic*) Folgerung *f*.

conclusive [kən'kluːsɪv] *adj* (*convincing*) schlüssig, überzeugend; (*decisive, final*) endgültig; (*Jur*) *evidence* einschlägig; *proof* schlüssig, eindeutig.

conclusively [kən'kluːsɪvlɪ] *adv see adj* schlüssig, überzeugend; endgültig; *prove* eindeutig, unwiderleglich ◆ **this ~ settles this issue** damit ist die Sache endgültig beigelegt.

concoct [kən'kɒkt] *vt* **(a)** (*Cook etc*) zusammenstellen, (zu)bereiten; (*hum*) kreieren, zurechtzaubern. **(b)** (*fig*) sich (*dat*) zurechtlegen; *scheme, plan also* ausbrüten *or* -hecken; *excuse also* sich (*dat*) ausdenken; *new dress, hat* zaubern.

concoction [kən'kɒkʃən] *n* **(a)** (*food*) Kreation, Zusammenstellung *f*; (*drink*) Gebräu *nt* ◆ **one of her little ~s** eines ihrer Spezialrezepte. **(b)** (*story etc*) Erdichtung *f*; (*fashion*) Zauberei, Spielerei *f* ◆ **the plot is an amazing ~ of bizarre events** der Plot ist eine erstaunliche Verkettung der merkwürdigsten Ereignisse.

concomitant [kən'kɒmɪtənt] [1] *adj* Begleit-.
[2] *n* Begleiterscheinung *f*.

concord ['kɒŋkɔːd] *n* (*harmony*) Eintracht *f*; (*about decision etc*) Einvernehmen *nt*, Übereinstimmung *f*.

concordance [kən'kɔːdəns] *n* **(a)** (*agreement*) Übereinstimmung *f* ◆ **in ~ with your specifications** (*form*) Ihren Angaben *or* Anweisungen gemäß. **(b)** (*Bibl, Liter*) Konkordanz *f*.

concordant [kən'kɔːdənt] *adj* (*form*) übereinstimmend ◆ **to be ~ with** entsprechen (*+dat*).

concordat [kɒn'kɔːdæt] *n* Konkordat *nt*.

concourse ['kɒŋkɔːs] *n* **(a)** (*liter: of people*) Menschenmenge *f*, Menschenauflauf *m*; (*of two rivers*) Zusammenfluß *m* ◆ **a fortuitous ~ of atoms** eine willkürliche Verbindung von Atomen. **(b)** (*place*) Eingangshalle *f*; (*US: in park*) freier Platz ◆ **station ~** Bahnhofshalle *f*.

concrete¹ ['kɒŋkriːt] *adj object, evidence, example* konkret ◆ **a chair is a ~ object** ein Stuhl ist gegenständlich *or* etwas Gegenständliches; **~ noun** Konkretum *nt*; **~ music** konkrete Musik; **~ poetry** Bilderlyrik *f*; **could you put your argument in a more ~ form?** könnten Sie etwas konkreter werden?

concrete² [1] *n* (*Build*) Beton *m* ◆ **~ mixer** Betonmischmaschine *f*.
[2] *adj* Beton-.
[3] *vt wall, floor* betonieren.

concretely [kən'kriːtlɪ] *adv* konkret ◆ **to express sth ~/more ~** etw konkretisieren/etw konkreter ausdrücken.

concretion [kən'kriːʃən] *n* (*coalescence*) Verschmelzung *f*; (*Geol also*) Konkretion *f*; (*Med*) Konkrement *nt*.

concubine ['kɒŋkjʊbaɪn] *n* **(a)** (*old*) Konkubine, Mätresse *f*. **(b)** (*in polygamy*) Konkubine, Nebenfrau *f*.

➤ LANGUAGE IN USE: **concern: 2b** → 26.2 **conclude: 1c** → 26.1 **1d** → 26.1 **conclusion: c** → 26.1, 26.3

concupiscence [kən'kju:pɪsəns] *n* Lüsternheit *f.*

concupiscent [kən'kju:pɪsənt] *adj* lüstern.

concur [kən'kɜ:ʳ] *vi* **(a)** *(agree)* übereinstimmen; *(with a suggestion etc)* beipflichten *(with dat)*; *(Math)* zusammenlaufen ◆ **John and I ~red** John und ich waren einer Meinung; **I ~ with that** ich pflichte dem bei.
(b) *(happen together)* zusammentreffen, auf einmal eintreten ◆ **everything ~red to bring about a successful result** alles trug zu einem erfolgreichen Ergebnis bei.

concurrence [kən'kʌrəns] *n* **(a)** *(accordance)* Übereinstimmung *f*; *(agreement, permission)* Einverständnis *nt*, Zustimmung *f.* **(b)** *(of events)* Zusammentreffen *nt.* **(c)** *(Math)* Schnittpunkt *m* ◆ **at the ~ of the two lines** im Schnittpunkt der beiden Geraden.

concurrent [kən'kʌrənt] *adj* **(a)** *(occurring at the same time)* gleichzeitig ◆ **to be ~ with sth** mit etw zusammentreffen, zur gleichen Zeit wie etw stattfinden.
(b) *(acting together)* vereint, gemeinsam.
(c) *(in agreement)* übereinstimmend; *interpretation, statement also* gleichlautend ◆ **to be ~ with sth** mit etw übereinstimmen.
(d) *(Math)* zusammenlaufend; *(intersecting)* sich schneidend.

concurrently [kən'kʌrəntlɪ] *adv* gleichzeitig ◆ **the two sentences to run ~** *(Jur)* unter gleichzeitigem Vollzug beider Freiheitsstrafen.

concuss [kən'kʌs] *vt (usu pass)* **to be ~ed** eine Gehirnerschütterung haben.

concussion [kən'kʌʃən] *n* Gehirnerschütterung *f.*

▼ **condemn** [kən'dem] *vt* **(a)** *(censure)* verurteilen.
(b) *(Jur)* verurteilen ◆ **to ~ sb to death/10 years' imprisonment** jdn zum Tode/zu 10 Jahren Gefängnis verurteilen; **the ~ed man** der zum Tode Verurteilte; **the ~ed cell** die Todeszelle.
(c) *(fig)* verdammen, verurteilen *(to* zu).
(d) *(declare unfit) building, slums* für abbruchreif erklären; *ship* für nicht mehr seetüchtig erklären ◆ **these houses are/should be ~ed** diese Häuser stehen auf der Abrißliste/sollten abgerissen werden; **the fruit was ~ed as unfit for consumption** das Obst wurde für den Verzehr ungeeignet erklärt.
(e) *(US Jur)* beschlagnahmen; *land* enteignen.

▼ **condemnation** [ˌkɒndem'neɪʃən] *n* **(a)** Verurteilung *f*; *(fig also)* Verdammung *f* ◆ **the state of these houses is a ~ of society** der Zustand dieser Häuser stellt der Gesellschaft ein Armutszeugnis aus; **what a ~** was für ein Armutszeugnis.
(b) *(of slums, ship)* Kondemnation *f (spec)* ◆ **the new council was responsible for the immediate ~ of some of the old city slums** die neue Stadtverwaltung war dafür verantwortlich, daß einige der alten Slums sofort auf die Abrißliste kamen.
(c) *(US Jur)* Beschlagnahme *f*; *(of land)* Enteignung *f.*

condemnatory [kɒndem'neɪtərɪ] *adj* aburteilend; *frown* mißbilligend; *criticism* verdammend; *conclusion* vernichtend.

condensation [ˌkɒnden'seɪʃən] *n* **(a)** *(of vapour)* Kondensation *f*; *(liquid formed)* Kondensat *nt*; *(on window panes etc)* Kondenswasser *nt* ◆ **the windows/walls are covered with ~** die Fenster/Wände sind beschlagen.
(b) *(short form)* Kurzfassung *f*; *(act)* Kondensierung, Zusammenfassung *f.*

condense [kən'dens] [1] *vt* **(a)** kondensieren ◆ **~d milk** Kondensmilch, Büchsen- *or* Dosenmilch *f.* **(b)** *(Phys) gas* kondensieren; *(compress)* verdichten; *rays* bündeln. **(c)** *(shorten)* zusammenfassen. **in a very ~d form** in sehr gedrängter Form.
[2] *vi (gas)* kondensieren, sich niederschlagen.

condenser [kən'densəʳ] *n (Elec, Phys)* Kondensator *m*; *(Opt)* Kondensor *m*, Sammellinse *f.*

condescend [ˌkɒndɪ'send] *vi* **(a)** *(stoop)* sich herab- *or* herbeilassen ◆ **to ~ to do sth** sich herab- *or* herbeilassen, etw zu tun, geruhen *(geh, iro) or* so gnädig sein, etw zu tun.
(b) *(be ~ing towards)* herablassend behandeln *(to sb* jdn) ◆ **he doesn't like being ~ed to** er läßt sich nicht gerne von oben herab behandeln.

condescending *adj*, **~ly** *adv* [ˌkɒndɪ'sendɪŋ, -lɪ] *(pej)* herablassend, von oben herab.

condescension [ˌkɒndɪ'senʃən] *n (pej)* Herablassung *f*; *(attitude also)* herablassende Haltung.

condiment ['kɒndɪmənt] *n* Würze *f* ◆ **would you pass the ~s?** würden Sie mir bitte Pfeffer und Salz reichen?

condition [kən'dɪʃən] [1] *n* **(a)** *(determining factor)* Bedingung *f (also Jur, Comm)*; *(prerequisite)* Voraussetzung *f* ◆ **~s of sale** Verkaufsbedingungen *pl*; **on ~ that ...** unter der Bedingung *or* Voraussetzung, daß ...; **on this ~** unter folgender Bedingung *or* Voraussetzung; **on what ~?** zu welchen Bedingungen?, unter welchen Voraussetzungen?; **on no ~** auf keinen Fall; **to make ~s** Bedingungen stellen; **he made it a ~ that ...** er machte es zur Bedingung, daß ...
(b) **~s** *pl (circumstances)* Verhältnisse, Zustände *(pej) pl* ◆ **working ~s** Arbeitsbedingungen *pl*; **living ~s** Wohnverhältnisse *pl*; **weather ~s** die Wetterlage; **in** *or* **under (the) present ~s** bei den derzeitigen Verhältnissen.
(c) *no pl (state)* Zustand *m* ◆ **he is in good/bad ~** er ist in guter/schlechter Verfassung; **it is in good/bad ~** es ist in gutem/schlechtem Zustand; **not in your ~!** nicht in deinem Zustand!; **he/the car is in no ~ to make a journey** er ist nicht reisefähig/so wie das Auto ist, kann man damit keine Reise machen; **you're in no ~ to drive** du bist nicht mehr fahrtüchtig; **to be in/out of ~** eine gute/keine Kondition haben; **to keep in/get into ~** in Form bleiben/kommen; *(Sport also)* seine Kondition beibehalten/sich *(dat)* eine gute Kondition antrainieren; **in an interesting ~** *(dated hum inf)* in anderen Umständen; **to change one's ~** *(old)* sich verehelichen *(dated)*.
(d) *(Med)* Beschwerden *pl* ◆ **heart/thyroid ~** Herz-/Schilddrüsenleiden *nt*; **he has a heart ~** er ist herzkrank.
(e) *(old: rank)* Stand *m*, Schicht *f* ◆ **in every ~ of life** aus allen Ständen.
[2] *vt* **(a)** *(esp pass: determine)* bedingen, bestimmen ◆ **to be ~ed by** bedingt sein durch, abhängen von.
(b) *(bring into good ~) hair, athlete, animal* in Form bringen ◆ **~ing powder** Aufbaumittel *nt.*
(c) *(Psych etc: train)* konditionieren; *(accustom)* gewöhnen ◆ **they have become ~ed to believing it** sie sind so konditioniert, daß sie es glauben; **~ed reflex** bedingter Reflex.

conditional [kən'dɪʃənl] [1] *adj* **(a)** mit Vorbehalt, bedingt, vorbehaltlich; *(Comm, Jur) sale* mit Auflagen ◆ **a ~ yes** ein Ja mit Vorbehalt; **to be ~ (up)on sth** von etw abhängen.
(b) *(Gram)* konditional, Konditional-, Bedingungs- ◆ **the ~ mood/tense** der Konditional.
[2] *n (Gram)* Konditional *m.*

conditionally [kən'dɪʃnəlɪ] *adv* unter *or* mit Vorbehalt.

conditioner [kən'dɪʃənəʳ] *n (for hair)* Pflegespülung *f*; *(for washing)* Weichspüler *m.*

condo ['kɒndəʊ] *n (US inf) see* **condominium (b)**.

condole [kən'dəʊl] *vi* **to ~ with sb (on** *or* **upon sth)** jdm (zu etw) sein Mitgefühl aussprechen; *(on death also)* jdm (zu etw) kondolieren.

condolence [kən'dəʊləns] *n* Beileid *nt no pl*, Anteilnahme, Kondolenz *(form) f no pl* ◆ **letter of ~** Kondolenzbrief *m*; **please accept my ~s on the death of your mother** (meine) aufrichtige Anteilnahme zum Tode Ihrer Mutter.

condom ['kɒndɒm] *n* Kondom *nt or m*, Präservativ *nt.*

condominium ['kɒndə'mɪnɪəm] *n* **(a)** *(Pol)* Kondominium *nt*; *(rule also)* Kondominat *nt.* **(b)** *(US) (apartment house)* ≃ Haus *nt* mit Eigentumswohnungen, Eigentumsblock *m*; *(single apartment)* ≃ Eigentumswohnung *f.*

condone [kən'dəʊn] *vt (overlook)* (stillschweigend) hinwegsehen über *(+acc)*; *(approve)* (stillschweigend) dulden.

condor ['kɒndɔ:ʳ] *n* Kondor *m.*

conduce [kən'dju:s] *vi* **to ~ to** *(form)* förderlich sein *(+dat)*.

conducive [kən'dju:sɪv] *adj* förderlich, dienlich *(to dat)*.

conduct ['kɒndʌkt] [1] *n* **(a)** *(behaviour)* Verhalten, Benehmen *nt (towards* gegenüber); *(of children also)* Betragen *nt*; *(of prisoner)* Führung *f* ◆ **the rules of ~** die Verhaltensregeln; **~ sheet** *(Mil)* militärische Beurteilung.
(b) *(management)* Führung *f*; *(of conference, commission of inquiry)* Leitung *f*; *(of investigation)* Durchführung *f* ◆ **his ~ of the war/inquiry** seine Kriegsführung/die Art, wie er die Untersuchung durchführte.
[2] [kən'dʌkt] *vt* **(a)** *(guide)* führen; *(ceremoniously)* geleiten *(geh)* ◆ **~ed tour (of)** *(of country)* Gesellschaftsreise *f* (durch); *(of building)* Führung *f* (durch).
(b) *(direct, manage) war, campaign, correspondence, conversation* führen; *meeting, business also* leiten; *investigation* durchführen; *private affairs* handhaben ◆ **he ~ed his own defence** er übernahm seine eigene Verteidigung.
(c) *(Mus)* dirigieren.
(d) *(Phys, Physiol)* leiten; *lightning* ableiten, erden.
[3] [kən'dʌkt] *vi* **(a)** *(Mus)* dirigieren. **(b)** *(Phys)* leiten.
[4] [kən'dʌkt] *vr* sich verhalten, sich benehmen; *(prisoner)* sich führen ◆ **her husband ~ed himself abominably** ihr Mann führte sich unmöglich auf.

conduction [kən'dʌkʃən] *n (Phys, Physiol)* Leitung *f (along* durch *or (Physiol)* entlang).

conductive [ˌkɒn'dʌktɪv] *adj* leitfähig, leitend.

conductivity [ˌkɒndʌk'tɪvɪtɪ] *n (Phys, Physiol)* Leitfähigkeit *f.*

conductor [kən'dʌktəʳ] *n* **(a)** *(Mus)* Dirigent(in *f*) *m*; *(of choir also)* Leiter(in *f*) *m.* **(b)** *(bus, tram ~)* Schaffner *m*; *(US Rail: guard)* Zugführer *m.* **(c)** *(Phys)* Leiter *m*; *(lightning ~)* Blitzableiter *m* ◆ **~ rail** (Fahr)leitung(sschiene) *f.*

conductress [kən'dʌktrɪs] *n (on bus etc)* Schaffnerin *f.*

conduit ['kɒndɪt] *n* Leitungsrohr *nt*; *(Elec)* Rohrkabel *nt.*

cone [kəʊn] *n* **(a)** Kegel *m*; *(Geol: of volcano)* (Berg)kegel *m*; *(storm ~)* Windsack *m*; *(traffic ~)* Pylon(e *f*) *m (form)*, Leitkegel *m*; *(Space: nose ~)* Nase *f* ◆ **a ~ of light** ein Lichtkegel *m.* **(b)** *(Bot)* Zapfen *m.* **(c)** *(ice-cream ~)* (Eis)tüte *f.*

◆**cone off** *vt sep* mit Pylonen absperren.

cone-shaped ['kəʊnʃeɪpt] *adj* kegelförmig.

coney *n see* **cony**.

confab ['kɒnfæb] *n (inf)* kleine Besprechung ◆ **we'd better have a quick ~** wir bekakeln das am besten mal schnell *(inf)*.

confection [kən'fekʃən] *n* **(a)** *(sweets)* Konfekt *nt*, Zucker- *or* Naschwerk *nt (old)*. **(b)** *(Comm: item of ladies' clothing)* modischer Artikel ◆ **a charming little ~ from Dior** eine bezaubernde kleine Kreation von Dior.

confectioner [kən'fekʃənəʳ] *n (maker)* Konditor, Zuckerbäcker *(old) m*; *(seller also)* Süßwarenverkäufer *m* ◆ **~'s (shop)** Süßwarenladen *m*; **~'s custard** Puddingmasse *f*; **~'s sugar** *(US)* Puderzucker *m.*

confectionery [kən'fekʃənərɪ] *n* Konditorwaren, Süßwaren *pl*; *(chocolates)* Konfekt *nt.*

confederacy [kən'fedərəsɪ] *n (Pol) (confederation)* Bündnis *nt*; *(of nations)* Staatenbund *m*, Konföderation *f* ◆ **the C~** *(US Hist)* die Konföderierten Staaten von Amerika.

confederate [kən'fedərɪt] [1] *adj system* konföderiert; *nations also* verbündet ◆ **the C~ States** *(US Hist)* die Konföderierten Staaten von Amerika.
[2] *n (Pol: ally)* Verbündete(r), Bündnispartner, Bundesgenosse *m*; *(pej: accomplice)* Komplize *m (pej)* ◆ **the C~s** *(US Hist)* die Konföderierten *pl.*

➤ LANGUAGE IN USE: **condemn: a → 26.3** **condemnation: a → 14**

confederation [kən,fedə'reɪʃən] *n* **(a)** (*Pol*) (*alliance*) Bündnis *nt*, Bund *m*; (*system of government*) Staatenbund *m*, Konföderation *f* ◆ **the Swiss C~** die Schweizerische Eidgenossenschaft. **(b)** (*association*) Bund *m* ◆ **C~ of British Industry** Verband *m* der britischen Industrie.

confer [kən'fɜːʳ] [1] *vt* (*on, upon sb* jdm) *title, degree* verleihen; *power also* übertragen.

[2] *vi* sich beraten, konferieren (*geh*).

conference ['kɒnfərəns] *n* **(a)** Konferenz *f*; (*more informal*) Besprechung *f* ◆ **to be in a ~ (with)** eine Besprechung *or* Unterredung haben (mit); **to get round the ~ table** sich an den Konferenztisch setzen; **to get sb to the ~ table** jdn an den Konferenztisch bringen; **I'm sorry, he's in ~** tut mir leid, er ist in *or* bei einer Konferenz/Besprechung; **~ call** (*Telec*) Konferenzschaltung *f*; **~ room** Konferenzzimmer *nt*.

(b) (*convention*) Konferenz, Tagung *f*.

conferencing ['kɒnfərənsɪŋ] *n* (*Telec*) Konferenzschaltungen *pl*.

conferment [kən'fɜːmənt], **conferral** [kən'fɜːrəl] *n* (*of title, degree*) Verleihung *f*.

confess [kən'fes] [1] *vt* **(a)** (*acknowledge*) gestehen, zugeben; *ignorance, mistake also* bekennen, beichten (*hum inf*).

(b) (*Eccl*) *sins* bekennen; (*to priest*) beichten; (*priest*) *penitent* die Beichte abnehmen (+*dat*).

[2] *vi* **(a)** gestehen (*to acc*) ◆ **to ~ to sth** etw gestehen, sich zu etw bekennen; **if you did it, you might as well ~** wenn du es warst, warum gestehst du es (dann) nicht?

(b) (*Eccl*) beichten ◆ **to ~ to sb/to sth** jdm/etw (*acc*) beichten.

confessed [kən'fest] *adj* (*admitted*) *plan* zugegeben, erklärt, eingestanden; (*having confessed*) *criminal* geständig; (*self-~*) *revolutionary* erklärt; *alcoholic, criminal* eigenen Eingeständnisses, nach eigenen Angaben.

confessedly [kən'fesɪdlɪ] *adv* zugegebenermaßen.

confession [kən'feʃən] *n* **(a)** Eingeständnis *nt*; (*of guilt, crime etc*) Geständnis *nt* ◆ **on his own ~** laut eigener Aussage; **to make a full ~ of sth to sb** (*Jur also*) jdm ein volles Geständnis einer Sache (*gen*) ablegen; **I have a ~ to make** ich muß dir etwas beichten (*inf*) *or* gestehen; (*Jur*) ich möchte ein Geständnis ablegen; **"~s of a ..."** „Bekenntnisse eines/einer ..."; **~ magazine** Zeitschrift *f* mit Geschichten, die das Leben schrieb.

(b) (*Eccl*) (*of sins*) Beichte *f*, (Schuld- *or* Sünden)bekenntnis *nt* ◆ **general ~/~ of faith** allgemeines Sündenbekenntnis/Glaubensbekenntnis *nt*; **to make one's ~** seine Sünden bekennen; **to hear ~** (die) Beichte hören.

(c) (*faith*) (Glaubens)bekenntnis *nt*, Konfession *f* ◆ **what ~ are you?** welche Konfession *or* Glaubenszugehörigkeit haben Sie?

confessional [kən'feʃənl] *n* Beichtstuhl *m* ◆ **the secrecy of the ~** das Beichtgeheimnis.

confessor [kən'fesəʳ] *n* **(a)** (*Eccl*) Beichtvater *m*. **(b) Edward the C~** Edward der Bekenner.

confetti [kən'feti:] *n, no pl* Konfetti *nt*.

confidant [,kɒnfɪ'dænt] *n* Vertraute(r) *m*.

confidante [,kɒnfɪ'dænt] *n* Vertraute *f*.

confide [kən'faɪd] *vt* anvertrauen (*to sb* jdm).

◆**confide in** *vi +prep obj* **(a)** (*tell secrets to*) sich anvertrauen (+*dat*) ◆ **to ~ ~ sb about sth** jdm etw anvertrauen. **(b)** (*old: trust*) sein Vertrauen setzen in (+*acc*), bauen auf (+*acc*).

confidence ['kɒnfɪdəns] *n* **(a)** (*trust*) Vertrauen *nt*; (*in sb's abilities also*) Zutrauen *nt* (*in* zu); (*confident expectation*) Zuversicht *f* ◆ **to have (every/no) ~ in sb/sth** (volles/kein) Vertrauen zu jdm/etw haben *or* in jdn/etw setzen; **they have no ~ in his ability/the future** sie haben kein Vertrauen *or* Zutrauen zu seinen Fähigkeiten/kein Vertrauen in die Zukunft; **I have every ~ that ...** ich bin ganz zuversichtlich, daß ...; **to put one's ~ in sb/sth** auf jdn/etw bauen, sich auf jdn/etw verlassen; **I wish I had your ~** ich wünschte, ich hätte deine Zuversicht(lichkeit); **we look with ~ ...** wir schauen zuversichtlich ...; **can you leave your car here with ~?** kann man hier sein Auto beruhigt abstellen?; **he talked with ~ on the subject** er äußerte sich sehr kompetent zu dem Thema; **I can't talk with any ~ about ...** ich kann nichts Bestimmtes über (+*acc*) ... sagen; **in the full ~ that ...** im festen Vertrauen darauf, daß ...; **issue of ~** (*Parl*) Vertrauensfrage *f*; **to give/ask for a vote of ~** (*Parl*) das Vertrauen aussprechen/die Vertrauensfrage stellen; **motion/vote of no ~** Mißtrauensantrag *m*/-votum *nt*.

(b) (*self-~*) (Selbst)vertrauen *nt*, Selbstsicherheit *f*.

(c) (*confidential relationship*) Vertrauen *nt* ◆ **in (strict) ~** (streng) vertraulich; **to take sb into one's ~** jdn ins Vertrauen ziehen; **to be in** *or* **enjoy sb's ~** jds Vertrauen besitzen *or* genießen.

(d) (*information confided*) vertrauliche Mitteilung.

confidence: ~ trick, ~ trickster *n see* **con trick, con-man.**

confident ['kɒnfɪdənt] *adj* **(a)** (*sure*) überzeugt, zuversichtlich (*of gen*); *look etc* zuversichtlich ◆ **to be ~ of success** *or* **succeeding** vom Erfolg überzeugt sein, zuversichtlich *or* überzeugt sein, daß man gewinnt; **it will happen — are you ~?** es wird geschehen — sind Sie davon überzeugt *or* dessen sicher?; **to be ~ in sb/sth** Vertrauen zu jdm/etw haben, jdm/einer Sache vertrauen; **~ in her love** ihrer Liebe gewiß (*geh*).

(b) (*self-assured*) (selbst)sicher.

confidential [,kɒnfɪ'denʃəl] *adj* **(a)** *information, whisper* vertraulich. **(b)** (*enjoying sb's confidence*) **~ secretary** Privatsekretär(in *f*) *m*; **~ agent** Sonderbeauftragte(r) *mf* mit geheimer Mission. **(c)** (*inclined to confide*) vertrauensselig.

confidentiality [,kɒnfɪ,denʃɪ'ælɪtɪ] *n* Vertraulichkeit *f*.

confidentially [,kɒnfɪ'denʃəlɪ] *adv* vertraulich, im Vertrauen.

➤ LANGUAGE IN USE: **confidence: c → 19.4**

confidently ['kɒnfɪdəntlɪ] *adv* **(a)** zuversichtlich; *look forward also* vertrauensvoll. **(b)** (*self-~*) selbstsicher; (*with conviction*) mit Überzeugung.

confiding *adj*, **~ly** *adv* [kən'faɪdɪŋ, -lɪ] vertrauensvoll.

configuration [kən,fɪgjʊ'reɪʃən] *n* Konfiguration *f* (*form*); (*Geog*) Form, Gestalt *f*; (*Sci*) Struktur *f*, Aufbau *m*; (*Comput*) Konfiguration *f*; (*Astron*) Anordnung *f*, Aspekt *m* (*spec*).

configure [kən'fɪgəʳ] *vt* (*Comput*) konfigurieren.

confine [kən'faɪn] [1] *vt* **(a)** (*keep in*) *person, animal* (ein)sperren; *flood* eindämmen ◆ **~d to bed/the house** ans Bett/ans Haus gefesselt; **to be ~d to barracks/one's room/one's house** Kasernen-/Stubenarrest haben/unter Hausarrest stehen; **with her body ~d in a corset** in ein Korsett gezwängt.

(b) (*limit*) *remarks* beschränken (*to* auf +*acc*) ◆ **to ~ oneself to doing sth** sich darauf beschränken, etw zu tun; **the damage was ~d to ...** der Schaden beschränkte *or* erstreckte sich nur auf (+*acc*) ...; **he finds life here too confining** er findet das Leben hier zu beengend *or* eingeengt; **lions are ~d to Africa** Löwen gibt es nur in Afrika.

(c) (*dated pass: in childbirth*) **to be ~d** niederkommen (*old*).

[2] **~s** ['kɒnfaɪnz] *npl* (*of space, thing etc*) Grenzen *pl*.

confined [kən'faɪnd] *adj space* beschränkt, begrenzt; *atmosphere* beengend.

confinement [kən'faɪnmənt] *n* **(a)** (*imprisonment*) (*act*) Einsperren *nt*; (*in hospital*) Einweisung *f*; (*of animals*) Gefangenhalten *nt*; (*state*) Eingesperrtsein *nt*; (*in jail*) Haft *f*; (*of animals*) Gefangenschaft *f*; (*Mil*) Arrest *m* (*also hum*) ◆ **~ to barracks/one's room** Kasernen-/Stubenarrest *m*; **to put sb in ~** jdn einsperren; **to keep sb in close ~** jdn in strengem Gewahrsam halten.

(b) (*restriction*) Beschränkung *f* (*to* auf +*acc*).

(c) (*dated: childbirth*) Entbindung, Niederkunft (*old*) *f*.

confirm [kən'fɜːm] *vt* **(a)** (*verify*) bestätigen. **(b)** (*strengthen*) bestärken; *one's resolve also* bekräftigen. **(c)** (*Eccl*) konfirmieren; *Roman Catholic* firmen.

confirmation [,kɒnfə'meɪʃən] *n* **(a)** Bestätigung *f* ◆ **a letter in ~ (of)** ein Brief *m* zur *or* als Bestätigung (+*gen*). **(b)** (*Eccl*) Konfirmation *f*; (*of Roman Catholics*) Firmung *f* ◆ **~ classes** Konfirmandenstunde *f or* -unterricht *m*; Firmunterricht *m*.

confirmatory [,kɒnfɜː'meɪtərɪ] *adj* bestätigend.

confirmed [kən'fɜːmd] *adj* erklärt; *bachelor* eingefleischt.

confirming bank [kən'fɜːmɪŋ,bæŋk] *n* bestätigende Bank.

confiscate ['kɒnfɪskeɪt] *vt* beschlagnahmen, konfiszieren ◆ **to ~ sth from sb** jdm etw abnehmen.

confiscation [,kɒnfɪs'keɪʃən] *n* Beschlagnahme, Konfiszierung *f*.

confiscatory [,kɒnfɪs'keɪtərɪ] *adj* **they have ~ powers** sie sind zur Beschlagnahme befugt.

conflagration [,kɒnflə'greɪʃən] *n* (*of forest, towns*) Feuersbrunst *f* (*geh*); (*of building*) Großbrand *m*.

conflate [kən'fleɪt] *vt* zusammenfassen.

conflation [kən'fleɪʃən] *n* Zusammenfassung *f*.

conflict ['kɒnflɪkt] [1] *n* Konflikt *m*; (*of moral issues, ideas also*) Widerstreit, Zwiespalt *m*; (*between two accounts etc*) Widerspruch *m*; (*fighting*) Zusammenstoß *m* ◆ **to be in ~ with sb/sth** mit jdm/etw im Konflikt liegen; im Widerspruch zu jdm/etw stehen; **the ego is always in ~ with the id** das Ich ist immer im Widerstreit mit dem Es; **to come into ~ with sb/sth** mit jdm/etw in Konflikt geraten; **open/armed ~** offener Konflikt/ bewaffneter Zusammenstoß; **border ~** Grenzkonflikt *m*; **~ of interests/opinions** Interessen-/Meinungskonflikt *m*.

[2] [kən'flɪkt] *vi* im Widerspruch stehen (*with* zu), widersprechen (*with dat*) ◆ **their opinions on the subject ~** in diesem Punkt stehen ihre Ansichten im Widerspruch zueinander.

conflicting [kən'flɪktɪŋ] *adj* widersprüchlich.

confluence ['kɒnfluəns] *n* (*of rivers*) Zusammenfluß *m*.

conform [kən'fɔːm] *vi* **(a)** (*things: comply with*) entsprechen (*to dat*); (*people: socially*) sich anpassen (*to* an +*acc*); (*things, people: to rules etc*) sich richten (*to* nach); (*agree*) übereinstimmen, konform gehen (*with* mit). **(b)** (*Brit Eccl*) sich (der englischen Staatskirche *dat*) unterwerfen.

conformance [kən'fɔːməns] *n see* **conformity.**

conformist [kən'fɔːmɪst] [1] *n* Konformist *m* (*also Brit Eccl*).

[2] *adj* konformistisch.

conformity [kən'fɔːmɪtɪ] *n* **(a)** (*uniformity*) Konformismus *m*.

(b) (*compliance*) Übereinstimmung *f*; (*of manners*) Konformismus *m*; (*socially*) Anpassung *f* (*with* an +*acc*) ◆ **the outward ~ of his social manner and way of life** sein äußerer Konformismus in Benehmen und Lebensweise; **in ~ with sth** einer Sache (*dat*) entsprechend *or* gemäß; **to be in ~ with sth** einer Sache (*dat*) entsprechen; **to bring sth into ~ with sth** etw mit etw in Einklang *or* Übereinstimmung bringen.

confound [kən'faʊnd] *vt* **(a)** (*amaze*) verblüffen.

(b) (*throw into confusion*) verwirren, durcheinanderbringen.

(c) (*liter: mistake for sth else*) verwechseln.

(d) (*inf*) **~ it!** vermaledeit (*dated*) *or* verflixt (*inf*) noch mal!; **~ him!** der vermaledeite (*dated*) *or* verflixte (*inf*) Kerl!

confounded [kən'faʊndɪd] *adj* (*inf*) vermaledeit (*dated inf*), verflixt (*inf*); *cheek also* verflucht (*inf*); *noise also* Heiden- (*inf*); *nuisance* elend (*inf*).

confoundedly [kən'faʊndɪdlɪ] *adv* (*dated inf*) verflucht (*inf*).

confront [kən'frʌnt] *vt* **(a)** (*face*) *danger, enemy, the boss* gegenübertreten (+*dat*); (*fig*) *problems, issue also* begegnen (+*dat*); (*stand or be ~ing*) *wall of ice etc* gegenüberstehen (+*dat*); (*problems, decisions*) sich stellen (+*dat*) ◆ **he found a lion ~ing him** er fand sich einem Löwen gegenüber.

(b) (*bring face to face with*) konfrontieren ◆ **to ~ sb with sb/sth** jdn jdm gegenüberstellen, jdn mit jdm/etw konfrontieren; **to be ~ed with sth** mit etw konfrontiert sein, vor etw (*dat*) stehen; **(when) ~ed with** angesichts (*+gen*).

confrontation [ˌkɒnfrənˈteɪʃən] *n* Konfrontation *f* (*also Pol*); (*defiant also*) Auseinandersetzung *f*; (*with witnesses, evidence etc*) Gegenüberstellung *f*.

Confucian [kənˈfjuːʃən] **1** *adj* konfuzianisch.
2 *n* Konfuzianer(in *f*) *m*.

Confucianism [kənˈfjuːʃənɪzm] *n* Konfuzianismus *m*.

Confucius [kənˈfjuːʃəs] *n* Konfuzius, Konfutse *m*.

confuse [kənˈfjuːz] *vt* **(a)** (*bewilder, muddle*) *people* konfus machen, verwirren, durcheinanderbringen; (*make unclear*) *situation* verworren machen ◆ **am I confusing you?** bringe ich Sie durcheinander?, verwirrt Sie das?; **don't ~ the issue!** bring (jetzt) nicht alles durcheinander!
(b) (*mix up*) *people* verwechseln; *matters, issues also* durcheinanderbringen ◆ **to ~ two problems** zwei Probleme durcheinanderbringen *or* miteinander verwechseln.

confused [kənˈfjuːzd] *adj* **(a)** (*muddled*) wirr, konfus; *person also* verwirrt; (*through old age, after anaesthetic etc*) wirr im Kopf; *idea, report, situation also* verworren; *sound, jumble* wirr. **(b)** (*embarrassed*) verwirrt, verlegen, betreten.

confusedly [kənˈfjuːzɪdlɪ] *adv* verwirrt; (*in disorder also*) wirr; (*embarrassedly also*) verlegen, betreten.

confusing [kənˈfjuːzɪŋ] *adj* verwirrend.

confusion [kənˈfjuːʒən] *n* **(a)** (*disorder*) Durcheinander *nt*, Wirrwarr *m*, Unordnung *f*; (*jumble*) Wirrwarr *m* ◆ **to be in ~** in Unordnung sein, durcheinander sein; **scenes of ~** allgemeines *or* wildes Durcheinander; **to retire in ~** (*Mil*) einen ungeordneten Rückzug antreten; **to throw everything into ~** alles durcheinanderbringen; **in the ~ of the battle/robbery** im Durcheinander der Schlacht/während des Raubüberfalls; **to run about in ~** wild durcheinanderlaufen.
(b) (*perplexity*) Verwirrung, Unklarheit *f*; (*mental ~: after drugs, blow on head etc*) Verwirrtheit *f*; (*through old age etc*) Wirrheit *f* ◆ **in the ~ of the moment** im Eifer des Gefechts.
(c) (*embarrassment*) Verlegenheit *f*; (*at being found out*) Betroffenheit *f* ◆ **covered in ~** schamrot vor Verlegenheit; **to be covered in ~** vor Verlegenheit erröten.
(d) (*mixing up*) Verwechslung *f*.

confutation [kɒnfjuːˈteɪʃən] *n* Widerlegung *f*.

confute [kənˈfjuːt] *vt* widerlegen.

conga [ˈkɒŋgə] *n* Conga *f*.

congeal [kənˈdʒiːl] **1** *vi* erstarren, starr werden; (*glue, mud*) hart *or* fest werden; (*blood*) gerinnen; (*with fear*) erstarren.
2 *vt* erstarren lassen (*also fig*); *glue, mud* hart werden lassen; *blood* gerinnen lassen.

congelation [kɒndʒəˈleɪʃən] *n see vi* Erstarren *nt*; Festwerden *nt*; Gerinnen *nt*.

congenial [kənˈdʒiːnɪəl] *adj* **(a)** (*pleasant*) ansprechend; *person also* sympathisch; *place, job also, atmosphere* angenehm. **(b)** (*liter: of like nature*) kongenial (*liter*), geistesverwandt.

congenital [kənˈdʒenɪtl] *adj* angeboren, kongenital (*spec*) ◆ **~ defect** Geburtsfehler *m*; **~ idiot** (*inf*) Erzdepp *m* (*inf*).

conger [ˈkɒŋgəʳ] *n* (*also* **~ eel**) Seeaal *m*.

congeries [kənˈdʒɪriːz] *n sing* (*liter*) Konglomerat *nt*, Ansammlung, Anhäufung *f*.

congested [kənˈdʒestɪd] *adj* überfüllt; (*with traffic*) verstopft; (*with people also*) voll; *pavement* übervoll; (*highly populated*) über(be)völkert ◆ **his lungs are ~** in seiner Lunge hat sich Blut angestaut *or* ist es zu einem Blutstau gekommen.

congestion [kənˈdʒestʃən] *n* (*traffic, pedestrians*) Stau *m*, Stockung *f*; (*in corridors etc*) Gedränge *nt*; (*overpopulation*) Übervölkerung *f*; (*Med*) Blutstau, Blutandrang *m* ◆ **the ~ in the city centre is getting so bad ...** die Verstopfung in der Innenstadt nimmt derartige Ausmaße an ...

conglomerate [kənˈglɒmərɪt] **1** *adj nation* zusammengewürfelt; *language* Misch- ◆ **~ rock** (*Geol*) Konglomeratgestein *nt*.
2 *n* (*also Geol, Comm*) Konglomerat *nt*.
3 [kənˈglɒməreɪt] *vi* sich zusammenballen, sich vereinigen, verschmelzen.

conglomeration [kənˌglɒməˈreɪʃən] *n* Ansammlung *f*, Haufen *m*; (*of ideas*) Gemisch *nt*.

Congo [ˈkɒŋgəʊ] *n* Kongo *m*.

Congolese [ˌkɒŋgəʊˈliːz] **1** *adj* kongolesisch.
2 *n* Kongolese *m*, Kongolesin *f*.

congrats [kənˈgræts] *interj* (*dated inf*) gratuliere!

congratulate [kənˈgrætjʊleɪt] *vt* gratulieren (*+dat*) (*also on birthday, engagement etc*), beglückwünschen (*on* zu) ◆ **you are to be ~d on not having succumbed** man kann Ihnen nur gratulieren, daß Sie nicht nachgegeben haben.

congratulation [kənˌgrætjʊˈleɪʃən] *n* Gratulation *f*; Gratulieren *nt* ◆ **there was a tone of ~ in his voice** seine Stimme hatte einen anerkennenden Ton.

▼ **congratulations** [kənˌgrætjʊˈleɪʃənz] **1** *npl* Glückwunsch *m*, Glückwünsche *pl* ◆ **to offer/send one's ~** gratulieren, jdn beglückwünschen/jdm gratulieren, jdm seine Glückwünsche senden.
▼ **2** (*iro*) gratuliere! ◆ **~ (on ...)!** herzlichen Glückwunsch *or* herzliche Glückwünsche (zu ...)!

congratulatory [kənˈgrætjʊlətərɪ] *adj card, telegram* Glückwunsch-; *look, tone* anerkennend ◆ **I wrote him a ~ letter on ...** ich gratulierte ihm brieflich zu ...

congregate [ˈkɒŋgrɪgeɪt] *vi* sich sammeln; (*on a particular occasion*) sich versammeln ◆ **to be ~d in ...** sich sammeln in (*+dat*) ...; sich versammeln in (*+dat*) ...

congregation [ˌkɒŋgrɪˈgeɪʃən] *n* **(a)** Versammlung *f*; (*not planned*) Ansammlung *f*; (*people in cities etc*) Zusammenballung *f*. **(b)** (*Eccl*) Gemeinde *f*; (*of cardinals*) Kongregation *f*.

congregational [ˌkɒŋgrɪˈgeɪʃənl] *adj* **(a)** **C~** kongregationalistisch. **(b)** (*of a congregation*) Gemeinde-.

Congregationalism [ˌkɒŋgrɪˈgeɪʃənəlɪzəm] *n* Kongregationalismus *m*.

Congregationalist [ˌkɒŋgrɪˈgeɪʃənəlɪst] *n* Kongregationalist(in *f*) *m*.

congress [ˈkɒŋgres] *n* **(a)** (*meeting*) Kongreß *m*, Tagung *f*; (*of political party*) Parteitag *m*. **(b)** **C~** (*US etc Pol*) der Kongreß.

congressional [kɒŋˈgreʃənl] *adj delegate, meeting* Kongreß- ◆ **C~ District** Kongreßwahlbezirk *m*; **C~ Record** Veröffentlichung *f* der Kongreßdebatten.

Congressman [ˈkɒŋgresmən] *n, pl* **-men** [-mən] Kongreßabgeordnete(r) *m*.

Congresswoman [ˈkɒŋgresˌwʊmən] *n, pl* **-women** [-ˌwɪmɪn] Kongreßabgeordnete *f*.

congruence [ˈkɒŋgrʊəns] *n* Kongruenz, Übereinstimmung *f*; (*Geometry*) Deckungsgleichheit, Kongruenz *f*.

congruent [ˈkɒŋgrʊənt] *adj* **(a)** *see* **congruous**. **(b)** (*Math*) *number* kongruent; (*Geometry also*) deckungsgleich.

congruity [kəŋˈgruːɪtɪ] *n* Übereinstimmung, Kongruenz (*geh*) *f*.

congruous [ˈkɒŋgrʊəs] *adj* **(a)** (*corresponding*) sich deckend, übereinstimmend ◆ **to be ~ with sth** sich mit etw decken. **(b)** (*appropriate, proper*) vereinbar.

conic [ˈkɒnɪk] *adj* **(a)** (*Math*) Kegel-, konisch ◆ **~ section** Kegelschnitt *m*. **(b)** (*also* **~al**) kegelförmig, Kegel-, konisch ◆ **~ projection** (*Geog*) Kegelprojektion *or* -abbildung *f*.

conifer [ˈkɒnɪfəʳ] *n* Nadelbaum *m*, Konifere *f* (*spec*) ◆ **~s** Nadelhölzer *pl*.

coniferous [kəˈnɪfərəs] *adj tree, forest* Nadel-.

conjectural [kənˈdʒektʃərəl] *adj* auf Vermutungen *or* Mutmaßungen beruhend ◆ **a conclusion which must remain ~** ein Schluß, der Vermutung *or* Mutmaßung bleiben muß; **it is entirely ~** es ist reine Vermutung.

conjecture [kənˈdʒektʃəʳ] **1** *vt* vermuten, mutmaßen (*geh*).
2 *vi* Vermutungen *or* Mutmaßungen anstellen, mutmaßen (*geh*) ◆ **it was just as scientists had ~d** es verhielt sich geradeso, wie es die Wissenschaftler gemutmaßt *or* vermutet hatten.
3 *n* Vermutung, Mutmaßung (*geh*) *f* ◆ **what will come next is a matter of** *or* **for ~** was folgt, das kann man nur vermuten *or* das bleibt unserer Vermutung überlassen.

conjoin [kənˈdʒɔɪn] *vt* (*form*) verbinden.

conjoint *adj*, **~ly** *adv* [kənˈdʒɔɪnt, -lɪ] gemeinsam.

conjugal [ˈkɒndʒʊgəl] *adj rights, bliss, duties* ehelich; *state* Ehe- ◆ **~ affection** Gattenliebe *f*.

conjugate [ˈkɒndʒʊgeɪt] **1** *vt* (*Gram*) konjugieren, beugen.
2 *vi* (*Gram*) sich konjugieren lassen; (*Biol*) konjugieren.

conjugation [ˌkɒndʒʊˈgeɪʃən] *n* (*Gram, Biol*) Konjugation *f*.

conjunction [kənˈdʒʌŋkʃən] *n* **(a)** (*Gram*) Konjunktion *f*, Bindewort *nt*.
(b) (*association*) Verbindung *f*; (*co-occurrence: of events*) Zusammentreffen *nt* ◆ **in ~** zusammen; **in ~ with the new evidence** in Verbindung mit dem neuen Beweismaterial; **the programme was broadcast/produced in ~ with the NBC** die Sendung wurde von NBC übernommen/das Programm wurde in Zusammenarbeit mit NBC aufgezeichnet.
(c) (*Astron*) Konjunktion *f*.

conjunctive [kənˈdʒʌŋktɪv] *adj* (*Gram, Anat*) Binde-.

conjunctivitis [kənˌdʒʌŋktɪˈvaɪtɪs] *n* (*Med*) Bindehautentzündung, Konjunktivitis (*spec*) *f*.

conjuncture [kənˈdʒʌŋktʃəʳ] *n* Zusammentreffen *nt*.

conjure[1] [kənˈdʒʊəʳ] *vt* (*liter: appeal to*) beschwören.

conjure[2] [ˈkʌndʒəʳ] *vti* zaubern ◆ **a name to ~ with** ein Name, der Wunder wirkt *or* der eine Ausstrahlung hat.

◆**conjure away** *vt sep* (*lit, fig*) wegzaubern.

◆**conjure up** *vt sep ghosts, spirits* beschwören; (*fig*) *memories etc* heraufbeschwören; (*provide, produce*) hervorzaubern; *meal* zusammenzaubern.

conjurer [ˈkʌndʒərəʳ] *n* Zauberer, Zauberkünstler(in *f*) *m*.

conjuring [ˈkʌndʒərɪŋ] *n* Zaubern *nt*; (*performance*) Zauberei *f* ◆ **~ set** Zauberkasten *m*; **~ trick** Zaubertrick *m*, (Zauber)kunststück *nt*.

conjuror [ˈkʌndʒərəʳ] *n see* **conjurer**.

conk [kɒŋk] (*inf*) **1** *n* (*esp Brit: nose*) Zinken *m* (*inf*).
2 *vt* (*hit*) hauen (*inf*).

◆**conk out** *vi* (*inf*) es aufstecken (*inf*), den Geist aufgeben; (*person*) (*faint*) umkippen (*inf*); (*die*) ins Gras beißen (*sl*).

conker [ˈkɒŋkəʳ] *n* (*Brit inf*) (Roß)kastanie *f* ◆ **~s** (*game*) *Spiel nt, bei dem zwei Spieler mit an Fäden befestigten Kastanien wechselseitig versuchen, die Kastanie des Gegenspielers zu treffen und zu zerstören.*

con-man [ˈkɒnmæn] *n, pl* **-men** [-men] (*inf*) Schwindler, Bauernfänger (*inf*) *m*; (*pretending to have social status*) Hochstapler *m*; (*promising marriage*) Heiratsschwindler *m*.

▼ **connect** [kəˈnekt] **1** *vt* **(a)** (*join*) verbinden (*to, with* mit); (*Elec etc: also* **~ up**) *appliances, subscribers* anschließen (*to* an *+acc*) ◆ **I'll ~ you** (*Telec*) ich verbinde (Sie); **to be ~ed** (*two things*) miteinander verbunden sein; (*several things*) untereinander verbunden sein; **to ~ to earth** erden; **~ed by telephone** telefonisch verbunden; *see* **parallel**.
(b) (*fig: associate*) in Verbindung *or* Zusammenhang bringen ◆ **I always ~**

Paris with springtime ich verbinde Paris immer mit Frühling; **these things are ~ed in my mind** diese Dinge gehören für mich zusammen; **I'd never ~ed them** ich hatte sie nie zueinander in Beziehung gesetzt.

▼**(c)** (*esp pass: link*) *ideas, theories etc* verbinden ◆ **to be ~ed with** eine Beziehung haben zu, in einer Beziehung *or* in Verbindung stehen zu; (*be related to*) verwandt sein mit; **he's ~ed with the BBC/university** er hat mit der BBC/der Universität zu tun; **to be ~ed by marriage** verschwägert sein; **to be ~ed** (*ideas etc*) in Beziehung zueinander stehen; (*firms*) geschäftlich miteinander verbunden sein; **loosely ~ed ideas** lose verknüpfte Ideen.

2 *vi* **(a)** (*join*) (*two rooms*) eine Verbindung haben (*to, with* zu); (*two parts, wires etc*) Kontakt haben ◆ **~ing rooms** angrenzende Zimmer *pl* (*mit Verbindungstür*).

(b) (*Rail, Aviat etc*) Anschluß haben (*with* an *+acc*) ◆ **~ing flight** Anschlußflug *m*.

(c) (*inf: hit*) (*fist etc*) landen (*inf*) (*with* auf *+dat*); (*golf-club etc*) treffen (*with acc*) ◆ **he really ~ed** er hat voll getroffen.

◆**connect up** *vt sep* (*Elec etc*) anschließen (*to, with* an *+acc*).

connecting rod [kəˈnektɪŋˌrɒd] *n* Pleuel- *or* Kurbelstange *f*.

connection [kəˈnekʃən] *n* **(a)** Verbindung *f* (*to, with* zu, mit); (*telephone line also, wire*) Leitung *f*; (*to mains*) Anschluß *m* (*to* an *+acc*); (*connecting part*) Verbindung(sstück *nt*) *f* ◆ **parallel/series ~** Parallel-/Reihenschaltung *f*.

(b) (*fig: link*) Zusammenhang *m*, Beziehung *f* (*with* zu) ◆ **in this ~** in diesem Zusammenhang; **in ~ with** in Zusammenhang mit.

(c) (*relationship, business ~*) Beziehung, Verbindung *f* (*with* zu); (*family ~*) familiäre Beziehung; (*old, form: relative*) (entfernter) Verwandter, (entfernte) Verwandte ◆ **to have ~s** Beziehungen haben; **to break off a ~ (with sb)** die Beziehung *or* Verbindung (zu jdm) abbrechen; **there is some family ~** sie/wir *etc* sind weitläufig miteinander verwandt.

(d) (*Rail etc*) Anschluß *m* ◆ **the train makes a ~ with the bus** der Zug hat Anschluß an den Bus.

connective [kəˈnektɪv] 1 *n* (*Gram*) Bindewort *nt*.

2 *adj* verbindend ◆ **~ tissue** Bindegewebe *nt*.

connexion [kəˈnekʃən] *n see* **connection**.

conning tower [ˈkɒnɪŋtaʊəʳ] *n* Kommandoturm *m*.

connivance [kəˈnaɪvəns] *n* (*tacit consent*) stillschweigendes Einverständnis; (*dishonest dealing*) Schiebung *f* ◆ **his ~ at the wrong-doing** seine Mitwisserschaft bei dem Vergehen; **to do sth in ~ with sb** etw mit jds Wissen tun; **to be in ~ with sb** mit jdm gemeinsame Sache machen.

connive [kəˈnaɪv] *vi* **(a)** (*conspire*) sich verschwören, gemeinsame Sache machen ◆ **he's a conniving little wretch** (*inf*) er ist ein hinterhältiger Tropf (*inf*).

(b) (*deliberately overlook*) **to ~ at sth** etw stillschweigend dulden; **to ~ at a crime** einem Verbrechen Vorschub leisten.

connoisseur [ˌkɒnəˈsɜːʳ] *n* Kenner, Connaisseur (*geh*) *m* ◆ **~ of wines/women** Wein-/Frauenkenner *m*.

connotation [ˌkɒnəʊˈteɪʃən] *n* Assoziation, Konnotation (*spec*) *f* ◆ **the ~s of this word** die mit diesem Wort verbundenen Assoziationen, die Konnotationen dieses Wortes (*spec*).

connotative [ˈkɒnəteɪtɪv] *adj meaning* Neben-, assoziativ, konnotativ (*spec*).

connote [kɒˈnəʊt] *vt* suggerieren.

connubial [kəˈnjuːbɪəl] *adj* ehelich, Ehe-.

conquer [ˈkɒŋkəʳ] *vt* **(a)** (*lit*) *country* erobern; *enemy, nation* besiegen. **(b)** (*fig*) *difficulties, feelings, disease* bezwingen, besiegen; *sb's heart* erobern; *mountain* bezwingen.

conquering [ˈkɒŋkərɪŋ] *adj hero* siegreich.

conqueror [ˈkɒŋkərəʳ] *n* (*of country, heart*) Eroberer *m*; (*of enemy, difficulties, feelings, disease*) Sieger (*of* über *+acc*), Besieger *m*; (*of difficulties, feelings, mountains*) Bezwinger *m* ◆ **William the C~** Wilhelm der Eroberer.

conquest [ˈkɒŋkwest] *n* Eroberung *f*; (*of enemy etc, disease*) Sieg *m* (*of* über *+acc*), Bezwingung *f*; (*inf: person*) Eroberung *f*.

Cons *abbr of* **Conservative**.

consanguinity [ˌkɒnsæŋˈgwɪnɪtɪ] *n* Blutsverwandtschaft *f*.

conscience [ˈkɒnʃəns] *n* Gewissen *nt* ◆ **to have a clear/easy/bad/guilty ~** ein reines/gutes/schlechtes/böses Gewissen haben (*about* wegen); **doesn't it give you a guilty ~ telling lies?** haben Sie keine Gewissensbisse *or* kein schlechtes Gewissen, wenn Sie lügen?; **with an easy ~** mit ruhigem Gewissen, ruhigen Gewissens (*geh*); **he has no ~ about lying** er macht sich (*dat*) kein Gewissen daraus zu lügen; **it/he will be on your ~ all your life** Sie werden das/ihn ihr Leben lang auf dem Gewissen haben; **she/it is on my ~** ich habe ihretwegen/deswegen Gewissensbisse; **it's still on my ~** (*I still haven't done it*) es steht mir noch bevor; **my ~ won't let me do it** das kann ich mit meinem Gewissen nicht vereinbaren; **in (all) ~** allen Ernstes; **I can't in all ~ ...** ich kann unmöglich ...; **let your ~ be your guide!** hör auf dein Gewissen; **it's between you and your ~** das mußt du mit dir selbst *or* mit deinem Gewissen abmachen.

conscience: ~ clause *n* (*Jur*) ≃ Gewissensklausel *f*; **~ money** *n* **his donation looks like ~ money** mit der Spende will er wohl sein Gewissen beruhigen; **~-stricken** *adj* schuldbewußt.

conscientious [ˌkɒnʃɪˈenʃəs] *adj* (*diligent*) gewissenhaft; (*conscious of one's duty*) pflichtbewußt ◆ **~ objector** Wehrdienst- *or* Kriegsdienstverweigerer *m* (*aus Gewissensgründen*); **he had ~ objections** er war aus Gewissens gründen dagegen.

conscientiously [ˌkɒnʃɪˈenʃəslɪ] *adv see adj*.

conscientiousness [ˌkɒnʃɪˈenʃəsnɪs] *n* Gewissenhaftigkeit *f*; (*sense of duty*) Pflichtbewußtsein, Pflichtgefühl *nt*.

conscious [ˈkɒnʃəs] *adj* **(a)** (*Med*) bei Bewußtsein. **(b)** (*aware*) bewußt (*also Psych*) ◆ **the ~ mind** das Bewußtsein; **to be/become ~ of sth** sich (*dat*) einer Sache (*gen*) bewußt sein/werden; **I was/became ~ that** es war/wurde mir bewußt, daß. **(c)** (*deliberate*) *effort etc* bewußt; *humour also* absichtlich.

-conscious *adj suf* -bewußt ◆ **weight-~** gewichtsbewußt.

consciously [ˈkɒnʃəslɪ] *adv* bewußt; (*deliberately also*) absichtlich.

consciousness [ˈkɒnʃəsnɪs] *n* **(a)** (*Med*) Bewußtsein *nt* ◆ **to lose/regain ~** das Bewußtsein verlieren/wiedererlangen, bewußtlos werden/wieder zu sich kommen.

(b) (*awareness*) Bewußtsein, Wissen *nt* ◆ **her ~ of her abilities** das Wissen um ihre Fähigkeiten.

(c) (*conscious mind*) Bewußtsein *nt* ◆ **to be ~-raising** den Bewußtseinsgrad erhöhen, bewußtseinserweiternd sein.

-consciousness *n suf* -bewußtheit *f*.

conscript [kənˈskrɪpt] 1 *vt* einziehen, einberufen; *army* ausheben.

2 [ˈkɒnskrɪpt] *n* Wehrpflichtige(r) *m*.

conscription [kənˈskrɪpʃən] *n* Wehrpflicht *f*; (*act of conscripting*) Einberufung *f*; (*of army*) Aushebung *f*.

consecrate [ˈkɒnsɪkreɪt] *vt* (*lit, fig*) weihen.

consecration [ˌkɒnsɪˈkreɪʃən] *n* Weihe *f*; (*in Mass*) Wandlung *f*.

consecutive [kənˈsekjʊtɪv] *adj* **(a)** aufeinanderfolgend; *numbers* fortlaufend ◆ **on four ~ days** vier Tage hintereinander; **this is the third ~ morning he's been late** er ist jetzt dreimal hintereinander morgens zu spät gekommen.

(b) (*Gram*) *clause* Konsekutiv-, Folge-.

consecutively [kənˈsekjʊtɪvlɪ] *adv* nacheinander, hintereinander; *numbered* fortlaufend.

consensus [kənˈsensəs] *n* Übereinstimmung *f*; (*accord also*) Einigkeit *f* ◆ **what's the ~?** was ist die allgemeine Meinung?; **the ~ is that ...** man ist allgemein der Meinung, daß ...; **there's a ~ of opinion in favour of ...** die allgemeine Mehrheit ist für ...; **cabinet decisions are based on ~** Entscheidungen des Kabinetts beruhen auf einem Mehrheitsbeschluß; **there was no ~ (among them)** sie waren sich nicht einig, es gab keinen Konsens unter ihnen (*form*); **~ politics** Politik *f* des Konsensus *or* Miteinander.

▼**consent** [kənˈsent] 1 *vi* zustimmen (*to dat*), einwilligen (*to* in *+acc*) ◆ **to ~ to do sth** sich bereit erklären, etw zu tun; **to ~ to sb doing sth** einwilligen *or* damit einverstanden sein, daß jd etw tut; **homosexuality between ~ing adults** homosexuelle Beziehungen zwischen erwachsenen Männern.

▼2 *n* Zustimmung (*to* zu), Einwilligung (*to* in *+acc*) *f* ◆ **it/he is by common** *or* **general ~ ...** man hält es/ihn allgemein für ...; **to be chosen by general ~** einstimmig gewählt werden; **by mutual ~** in gegenseitigem Einverständnis; *see* **age 1 (c)**.

▼**consequence** [ˈkɒnsɪkwəns] *n* **(a)** (*result, effect*) Folge *f*; (*of actions also*) Konsequenz *f* ◆ **in ~** folglich; **in ~ of** infolge (*+gen*); **in ~ of which** infolgedessen; **and the ~ is that we have ...** und folglich haben wir ...; **as a ~ of ...** als Folge (*+gen*); **with the ~ that he ...** was zur Folge hatte *or* mit dem Erfolg, daß er ...; **to take the ~s** die Folgen *or* Konsequenzen tragen.

(b) (*importance*) Wichtigkeit, Bedeutung *f* ◆ **a person of ~** eine bedeutende *or* wichtige Persönlichkeit; **did he have anything of ~ to say?** hatte er irgend etwas Wichtiges zu sagen?; **he's (a man) of no ~** er hat nichts zu sagen; **it's of no ~/no ~ to me** das spielt keine Rolle/das ist mir einerlei; **of what ~ is that to you?** was tangiert Sie das? (*inf*).

(c) **~s** *sing* (*game*) *Schreibspiel nt, bei dem auf gefaltetem Papier ein nicht bekannter Vorsatz ergänzt wird.*

consequent [ˈkɒnsɪkwənt] *adj attr* daraus folgend, sich daraus ergebend; (*temporal*) darauffolgend ◆ **to be ~ upon sth** (*form, liter*) sich aus etw ergeben.

consequential [ˌkɒnsɪˈkwenʃəl] *adj* **(a)** *see* **consequent**. **(b)** (*self-important*) wichtigtuerisch; *smile, tone also* überheblich. **(c)** (*logically consistent*) folgerichtig.

consequentially [ˌkɒnsɪˈkwenʃəlɪ] *adv* (*as a result*) daraufhin.

▼**consequently** [ˈkɒnsɪkwəntlɪ] *adv* folglich.

conservancy [kənˈsɜːvənsɪ] *n* **(a)** (*Brit: board*) Schutzbehörde *f*; (*for ports, rivers etc*) Wasserschutzamt *nt*; (*for forests*) Forstamt *nt*. **(b)** (*official conservation*) Erhaltung *f*, Schutz *m*.

conservation [ˌkɒnsəˈveɪʃən] *n* **(a)** (*preservation*) Erhaltung *f*, Schutz *m* ◆ **~ area** Naturschutzgebiet *nt*; (*in town*) unter Denkmalschutz stehendes Gebiet; **~ technology** Umweltschutztechnik *f*. **(b)** (*Phys*) Erhaltung *f*.

conservationist [ˌkɒnsəˈveɪʃənɪst] *n* Umweltschützer(in *f*) *m*; (*as regards old buildings etc*) Denkmalpfleger *m*.

conservatism [kənˈsɜːvətɪzəm] *n* Konservatismus *m*.

conservative [kənˈsɜːvətɪv] 1 *adj* **(a)** *person, style* konservativ; (*cautious, moderate*) vorsichtig ◆ **at a ~ estimate** bei vorsichtiger Schätzung. **(b)** (*Pol*) konservativ. **the C~ Party** (*Brit*) die Konservative Partei.

2 *n* (*Pol: C~*) Konservative(r) *mf* ◆ **I'm a ~ in such matters** in solchen Dingen bin ich konservativ.

conservatively [kənˈsɜːvətɪvlɪ] *adv* konservativ; *estimate, invest* vorsichtig.

conservatoire [kənˈsɜːvətwɑːʳ] *n* Konservatorium *nt*.

conservatory [kənˈsɜːvətrɪ] *n* **(a)** (*Hort*) Wintergarten *m*. **(b)** (*esp US: Mus etc*) Konservatorium *nt*.

conserve [kənˈsɜːv] *vt* erhalten, bewahren, konservieren; *building* erhalten; *one's strength* schonen; *strength, energy* (auf)sparen.

conserves [kənˈsɜːvz] *npl* Eingemachte(s) *nt*.

▼**consider** [kənˈsɪdəʳ] *vt* **(a)** (*reflect upon*) *plan, idea, offer* sich (*dat*) überlegen, nachdenken über (*+acc*); *possibilities* sich (*dat*) überlegen ◆ **I'll ~ the matter** ich werde mir die Sache überlegen *or* durch den Kopf gehen lassen.

(b) (*have in mind*) in Erwägung ziehen ◆ **we're ~ing a few changes** wir ziehen ein paar Änderungen in Erwägung; **I'm ~ing going abroad** ich spiele

➤ LANGUAGE IN USE: **connect: 1c** → 17.2 **consent: 1** → 9.3 **2** → 11.2 **consequence: a** → 26.3 **consequently** → 26.3 **consider: a** → 26.1

mit dem Gedanken, ins Ausland zu gehen, ich erwäge einen Auslandsaufenthalt (*geh*); **he is being ~ed for the job** er wird für die Stelle in Erwägung *or* Betracht gezogen.

(c) (*entertain*) in Betracht ziehen ♦ **he refused even to ~ the possibility** er verwarf die Möglichkeit sofort, er weigerte sich, die Möglichkeit überhaupt in Betracht zu ziehen; **I won't even ~ the idea of ...** der Gedanke, zu ..., kommt für mich überhaupt nicht in Betracht; **I won't even ~ it!** ich denke nicht daran!; **would you ~ £500?** hielten Sie £ 500 für angemessen?; **I'm sure he would never ~ doing anything criminal** ich bin überzeugt, es käme ihm nie in den Sinn, etwas Kriminelles zu tun.

(d) (*think of*) denken an (+*acc*) ♦ **~ George** denken Sie an George; **~ my position** überlegen Sie sich meine Lage; **~ this case, for example** nehmen Sie zum Beispiel diesen Fall; **~ how he must have felt** überlegen Sie sich, wie ihm zumute gewesen sein muß; **~ how much you owe him** denken Sie daran *or* bedenken Sie, wieviel Sie ihm schulden; **have you ~ed going by train?** haben Sie daran gedacht, mit dem Zug zu fahren?

(e) (*take into account*) denken an (+*acc*); *cost, difficulties, dangers also, facts* bedenken, berücksichtigen; *person, feelings also* Rücksicht nehmen auf (+*acc*) ♦ **when one ~s that ...** wenn man bedenkt, daß ...; **all things ~ed** alles in allem.

(f) (*regard as, deem*) betrachten als; *person* halten für ♦ **to ~ sb to be** *or* **as ...** jdn als ... betrachten, jdn für ... halten; **to ~ oneself lucky/honoured** sich glücklich schätzen/geehrt fühlen; **~ it (as) done!** schon so gut wie geschehen!; **(you can) ~ yourself sacked** betrachten Sie sich als entlassen; **I ~ it an honour** ich betrachte es als besondere Ehre.

(g) (*look at*) (eingehend) betrachten.

considerable [kən'sɪdərəbl] *adj* beträchtlich, erheblich; *sum of money, achievement also* ansehnlich; *loss also, interest, income* groß; (*used admiringly*) *number, size, achievement, effort etc* beachtlich ♦ **to a ~ extent** *or* **degree** weitgehend.

considerably [kən'sɪdərəblɪ] *adv* (*in comparisons*) *changed, older, better, grown* beträchtlich, um einiges; (*very*) *upset, impressed* höchst.

considerate [kən'sɪdərɪt] *adj* rücksichtsvoll (*to(wards)* gegenüber); (*kind*) aufmerksam.

considerately [kən'sɪdərɪtlɪ] *adv see adj.*

consideration [kən,sɪdə'reɪʃən] *n* (a) *no pl* (*careful thought*) Überlegung *f* ♦ **I'll give it my ~** ich werde es mir überlegen.

(b) *no pl* (*regard, account*) **to take sth into ~** etw bedenken, etw berücksichtigen; *factors also* etw in Erwägung ziehen; **taking everything into ~** alles in allem; **to leave sth out of ~** etw außer acht lassen; **your request/the matter is under ~** Ihr Gesuch/die Sache wird zur Zeit geprüft (*form*), wir gehen der Sache zur Zeit nach; **in ~ of** (*in view of*) mit Rücksicht auf (+*acc*), in Anbetracht (+*gen*); (*in return for*) als Dank für.

(c) *no pl* (*thoughtfulness*) Rücksicht *f* (*for* auf +*acc*) ♦ **to show sb ~, to show** *or* **have ~ for sb's feelings** Rücksicht auf jdn *or* jds Gefühle nehmen; **his lack of ~ (for others)** seine Rücksichtslosigkeit (anderen gegenüber).

(d) (*sth taken into account*) Erwägung *f*, Gesichtspunkt, Faktor *m* ♦ **on no ~** auf keinen Fall; **money is no ~/a minor ~/his first ~** Geld spielt keine Rolle/eine unbedeutendere Rolle/bei ihm die größte Rolle; **it's a ~** das wäre zu überlegen.

(e) (*reward, payment*) Entgelt *nt*, Gegenleistung *f*, kleine Anerkennung (*hum*) ♦ **for a ~** gegen Entgelt, für eine Gegenleistung *or* kleine Anerkennung (*hum*).

considered [kən'sɪdɪd] *adj opinion* ernsthaft.

considering [kən'sɪdərɪŋ] [1] *prep* für (+*acc*), wenn man ... (*acc*) bedenkt.

[2] *conj* wenn man bedenkt ♦ **~ (that) he's been ill ...** wenn man bedenkt, daß er krank war ..., dafür, daß er krank war ...

[3] *adv* eigentlich ♦ **it's not too bad ~** es ist eigentlich gar nicht so schlecht; **yes it is, ~** ach ja, eigentlich schon.

consign [kən'saɪn] *vt* (a) (*Comm*) (*send*) versenden, verschicken; (*address*) adressieren (*to* an +*acc*) ♦ **the goods are ~ed to ...** die Waren sind für ... bestimmt. (b) (*commit*) übergeben (*to dat*); (*entrust also*) anvertrauen ♦ **it was ~ed to the rubbish heap** es landete auf dem Abfallhaufen; **to ~ a child to sb's care** ein Kind in jds Obhut (*acc*) geben.

consignee [,kɒnsaɪ'ni:] *n* Empfänger *m.*

consigner [kən'saɪnəʳ] *n see* **consignor.**

consignment [kən'saɪnmənt] *n* (*Comm*) (a) (*of goods*) Versendung, Verschickung *f* ♦ **goods for ~ abroad** ins Ausland gehende Ware; **on ~** in Kommission; (*overseas*) in Konsignation; **~ note** Frachtbrief *m.* (b) (*goods*) Sendung *f*; (*bigger*) Ladung *f.*

consignor [kən'saɪnəʳ] *n* (*Comm*) Versender *m.*

consist [kən'sɪst] *vi* (a) (*be composed*) **to ~ of** bestehen aus. (b) (*have as its essence*) **to ~ in sth** in etw (*dat*) bestehen; **his happiness ~s in helping others** sein Glück besteht darin, anderen zu helfen.

consistency [kən'sɪstənsɪ] *n* (a) *no pl see adj (a)* Konsequenz *f*; Übereinstimmung, Vereinbarkeit *f*; Logik, Folgerichtigkeit *f*; Stetigkeit *f* ♦ **his statements lack ~** seine Aussagen widersprechen sich *or* sind nicht miteinander vereinbar.

(b) *no pl see adj (b)* Beständigkeit *f*; Stetigkeit *f*; Einheitlichkeit *f.*

(c) (*of substance*) Konsistenz *f*; (*of liquids also*) Dicke *f*; (*of glue, dough, rubber etc also*) Festigkeit(sgrad *m*) *f* ♦ **beat it to a thick ~** zu einer festen Masse schlagen; **the steak had the ~ of leather** das Steak war zäh wie Leder.

consistent [kən'sɪstənt] *adj* (a) konsequent; *statements* übereinstimmend, miteinander vereinbar; (*logical*) *argument* logisch, folgerichtig; (*constant*) *failure* ständig, stetig.

(b) (*uniform*) *quality* beständig; *performance, results* gleichbleibend, stetig; *method, style* einheitlich.

(c) (*in agreement*) **to be ~ with sth** einer Sache (*dat*) entsprechen; **what you're saying now is not ~ with what you said before** was Sie jetzt sagen, widerspricht dem *or* läßt sich mit dem nicht vereinbaren, was Sie davor gesagt haben.

consistently [kən'sɪstəntlɪ] *adv* (a) *argue* konsequent; (*constantly*) *fail* ständig. (b) (*uniformly*) einheitlich, durchweg. (c) (*in agreement*) entsprechend (*with dat*).

consolation [,kɒnsə'leɪʃən] *n* Trost *m no pl*; (*act*) Tröstung *f* ♦ **it is some ~ to know that ...** es ist tröstlich *or* ein Trost zu wissen, daß ...; **that's a big ~!** (*iro*) das ist ein schwacher Trost!; **old age has its ~s** das Alter hat auch seine guten Seiten; **a few words of ~** ein paar tröstende Worte; **~ prize** Trostpreis *m.*

consolatory [kən'sɒlətərɪ] *adj* tröstlich, tröstend.

console¹ [kən'səʊl] *vt* trösten ♦ **to ~ sb for sth** jdn über etw (*acc*) hinwegtrösten.

console² ['kɒnsəʊl] *n* (a) (*control panel*) (Kontroll)pult *nt*; (*of organ*) Spieltisch *m.* (b) (*cabinet*) Schrank *m*, Truhe *f* ♦ **our TV is a ~ (model)** wir haben eine Fernsehtruhe. (c) (*ornamental bracket*) Konsole *f* ♦ **~ table** Konsoltischchen *nt.*

consolidate [kən'sɒlɪdeɪt] *vt* (a) (*confirm*) festigen. (b) (*combine*) zusammenlegen, vereinigen; *companies* zusammenschließen; *funds, debts* konsolidieren ♦ **C~d Fund** (*Brit*) konsolidierter Staatsfonds, unablösbare Anleihe; **~d balance sheet** konsolidierte Bilanz.

consolidation [kən,sɒlɪ'deɪʃən] *n see vt* (a) Festigung *f.* (b) Zusammenlegung, Vereinigung *f*; Zusammenschluß *m*; Konsolidierung *f.*

consoling [kən'səʊlɪŋ] *adj* tröstlich, tröstend.

consols ['kɒnsɒlz] *npl* (*Brit Fin*) Konsols, konsolidierte Staatsanleihen *pl.*

consommé [kɒn'sɒmeɪ] *n* Kraftbrühe, Konsommee (*old*) *f.*

consonance ['kɒnsənəns] *n* (*Mus*) Konsonanz *f*; (*Poet*) Konsonantengleichklang *m*; (*fig*) (*of agreement, ideas*) Einklang *m*, Harmonie *f*; (*consistency*) Übereinstimmung *f.*

consonant ['kɒnsənənt] [1] *n* (*Phon*) Konsonant, Mitlaut *m* ♦ **~ shift** Lautverschiebung *f.*

[2] *adj* (*Mus*) konsonant (*with* zu) ♦ **to be ~ with sth** (*fig*) mit etw in Einklang zu bringen sein.

consonantal [,kɒnsə'næntl] *adj* konsonantisch.

consort ['kɒnsɔ:t] [1] *n* (*form: spouse*) Gemahl(in *f*) *m* (*form*), Gatte *m* (*form*), Gattin *f* (*form*).

[2] [kən'sɔ:t] *vi* (*form*) (a) verkehren (*with* mit). (b) (*be consistent*) passen (*with* zu), sich vereinbaren lassen (*with* mit).

consortium [kən'sɔ:tɪəm] *n* Konsortium *nt.*

conspicuous [kən'spɪkjʊəs] *adj person, clothes, behaviour* auffällig, auffallend; (*easily visible*) *road signs* deutlich sichtbar, auffällig; (*obvious*) *lack of sympathy etc* deutlich, offensichtlich, auffallend; (*outstanding*) *bravery* bemerkenswert, hervorragend ♦ **to be/make oneself ~** auffallen; **why don't you put it in a more ~ position?** warum stellen Sie es nicht irgendwohin, wo es eher auffällt?; **to be/not to be ~ for sth** sich/sich nicht gerade durch etw auszeichnen; **he was ~ by his absence** er glänzte durch Abwesenheit; **he showed a ~ lack of tact** er fiel durch sein mangelndes Taktgefühl (unangenehm) auf; **~ consumption** Prestigekäufe *pl.*

conspicuously [kən'spɪkjʊəslɪ] *adv see adj* auffällig, auffallend; deutlich sichtbar; deutlich, offensichtlich; bemerkenswert ♦ **he's not ~ intelligent** (*iro*) er fällt nicht gerade durch Intelligenz auf.

conspicuousness [kən'spɪkjʊəsnɪs] *n see adj* Auffälligkeit *f*; deutliche Sichtbarkeit, Auffälligkeit *f*; Deutlichkeit *f.*

conspiracy [kən'spɪrəsɪ] *n* Verschwörung *f*, Komplott *nt*, Konspiration *f* (*form*); (*Jur*) (strafbare) Verabredung ♦ **~ to defraud/murder** Verabredung zum Betrug/Mordkomplott; **a ~ of silence** ein verabredetes Schweigen; **he thinks it's all a ~ against him** er meint, man hätte sich gegen ihn verschworen.

conspirator [kən'spɪrətəʳ] *n* Verschwörer *m.*

conspiratorial [kən,spɪrə'tɔ:rɪəl] *adj* verschwörerisch.

conspire [kən'spaɪəʳ] *vi* (a) (*people*) sich verschwören, sich zusammentun, konspirieren (*form*) (*against* gegen) ♦ **to ~ (together) to do sth** sich verabreden *or* heimlich planen, etw zu tun. (b) (*events*) zusammenkommen, sich verschwören (*geh*); (*fate etc*) sich verschwören (*against* gegen).

constable ['kʌnstəbl] *n* (*Brit: police ~*) Polizist, Gendarm (*dial*) *m*; (*in address*) Herr Wachtmeister.

constabulary [kən'stæbjʊlərɪ] *n* (*Brit*) Polizei *f no pl.*

constancy ['kɒnstənsɪ] *n* (a) (*of support, supporter*) Beständigkeit, Konstanz (*liter*) *f*; (*of feelings*) Unveränderlichkeit, Unwandelbarkeit *f*; (*of friend, lover*) Treue *f*; (*also* **~ of purpose**) Ausdauer *f.* (b) (*of temperature etc*) Beständigkeit *f.*

constant ['kɒnstənt] [1] *adj* (a) (*continuous*) *quarrels, interruptions, noise* dauernd, ständig, konstant (*geh*) ♦ **we have ~ hot water** wir haben ständig heißes Wasser.

(b) (*unchanging*) *temperature* gleichmäßig, gleichbleibend, konstant ♦ **x remains ~ while y ...** x bleibt konstant, während y ...; **the price is not ~** der Preis bleibt nicht gleich *or* konstant; **~ load** (*Tech*) Grundlast *f.*

(c) (*steadfast*) *affection, devotion* unwandelbar, beständig; *friend, supporter, lover* treu.

[2] *n* (*Math, Phys, fig*) Konstante *f*, konstante Größe.

constantly ['kɒnstəntlɪ] *adv* (an)dauernd, ständig.

➤ LANGUAGE IN USE: **consider:** f → 21.4, 26.3

constellation [ˌkɒnstəˈleɪʃən] *n* Sternbild *nt*, Konstellation *f* (*also fig*).

consternation [ˌkɒnstəˈneɪʃən] *n* (*dismay*) Bestürzung *f*; (*concern, worry*) Sorge *f*; (*fear and confusion*) Aufruhr *m* ◆ **to my great ~** zu meiner großen Bestürzung; **to cause ~** (*state of £, sb's behaviour*) Grund zur Sorge geben; (*news*) Bestürzung auslösen; **the mouse caused ~ among the ladies** die Maus versetzte die Damen in Aufruhr; **with a look of ~ on his face** mit bestürzter Miene; **the news filled me with ~** ich war bestürzt, als ich das hörte.

constipate [ˈkɒnstɪpeɪt] *vt* Verstopfung hervorrufen bei, verstopfen.

constipated [ˈkɒnstɪpeɪtɪd] *adj bowels* verstopft ◆ **he is ~** er hat Verstopfung, er ist verstopft (*inf*); **it'll make you ~** davon bekommst du Verstopfung, das stopft.

constipation [ˌkɒnstɪˈpeɪʃən] *n, no pl* Verstopfung *f*.

constituency [kənˈstɪtjʊənsɪ] *n* (*Pol*) Wahlkreis *m*.

constituent [kənˈstɪtjʊənt] [1] *adj* **(a)** (*Pol*) *assembly* konstituierend. **(b)** *attr part, element* einzeln ◆ **~ part** *or* **element** (*of machine, matter*) Bestandteil *m*.
[2] *n* **(a)** (*Pol*) Wähler(in *f*) *m*. **(b)** (*part, element*) Bestandteil *m*. **(c)** (*Ling*) Satzteil *m*.

constitute [ˈkɒnstɪtjuːt] *vt* **(a)** (*make up*) bilden, ausmachen ◆ **society is so ~d that ...** die Gesellschaft ist so aufgebaut, daß ... **(b)** (*amount to*) darstellen ◆ **that ~s a lie** das ist eine glatte Lüge. **(c)** (*set up, give legal authority to*) *committee, court* einrichten, konstituieren (*form*). **(d)** (*form: appoint*) ernennen *or* bestimmen zu ◆ **he ~d himself our judge** er warf sich zu unserem Richter auf.

constitution [ˌkɒnstɪˈtjuːʃən] *n* **(a)** (*Pol*) Verfassung *f*; (*of club etc*) Satzung *f*. **(b)** (*of person*) Konstitution, Gesundheit *f* ◆ **to have a strong/weak ~** eine starke/schwache Konstitution haben. **(c)** (*way sth is made*) Aufbau *m*; (*what sth is made of*) Zusammensetzung *f*. **(d)** (*setting up: of committee etc*) Einrichtung *f*.

constitutional [ˌkɒnstɪˈtjuːʃənl] [1] *adj* **(a)** (*Pol*) *reform, crisis, theory* Verfassungs-; *monarchy* konstitutionell; *government, action* verfassungsmäßig ◆ **~ law** Verfassungsrecht *nt*; **it's not ~** das ist verfassungswidrig. **(b)** (*Med*) konstitutionell (*spec*), körperlich bedingt; (*fig*) *dislike etc* naturgegeben *or* -bedingt.
[2] *n* (*hum inf*) Spaziergang *m*.

constitutionally [ˌkɒnstɪˈtjuːʃənəlɪ] *adv* (*Pol*) verfassungsmäßig; (*as the constitution says also*) nach der Verfassung; (*in accordance with the constitution*) verfassungsgemäß; (*Med*) körperlich; (*fig*) von Natur aus.

constrain [kənˈstreɪn] *vt* zwingen; *one's temper* zügeln ◆ **to find oneself/feel ~ed to ...** sich gezwungen sehen/fühlen, zu ...

constrained [kənˈstreɪnd] *adj* (*forced*) gezwungen.

constraint [kənˈstreɪnt] *n* **(a)** (*compulsion*) Zwang *m* ◆ **to act under ~** unter Zwang handeln. **(b)** (*restriction*) Beschränkung, Einschränkung *f* ◆ **to place ~s on sth** einer Sache (*dat*) Zwänge auferlegen. **(c)** (*in manner etc*) Gezwungenheit *f*; (*embarrassment*) Befangenheit *f*.

constrict [kənˈstrɪkt] *vt* **(a)** (*compress*) einzwängen, einengen; *muscle* zusammenziehen; *vein* verengen. **(b)** (*hamper, limit*) *movements* behindern, einschränken (*also fig*); (*rules, traditions etc*) einengen; *outlook, view etc* beschränken.

constriction [kənˈstrɪkʃən] *n* **(a)** (*of muscles*) Zusammenziehen *nt* ◆ **he felt a ~ in his chest** er hatte ein Gefühl der Enge in der Brust. **(b)** *see vt* (*b*) Behinderung *f*; (*limiting*) Einengung *f*; Beschränkung *f*.

constrictor [kənˈstrɪktər] *n* **(a)** (*muscle*) Schließmuskel, Konstriktor (*spec*) *m*. **(b)** (*snake*) Boa (constrictor) *f*.

construct [kənˈstrʌkt] [1] *vt* bauen; *bridge, machine also*, (*Geom*) konstruieren; *sentence* bilden, konstruieren; *novel, play etc* aufbauen; *theory* entwickeln, konstruieren.
[2] [ˈkɒnstrʌkt] *n* Gedankengebäude *nt*.

construction [kənˈstrʌkʃən] *n* **(a)** (*of building, road*) Bau *m*; (*of bridge, machine also, of geometrical figures*) Konstruktion *f*; (*of novel, play etc*) Aufbau *m*; (*of theory*) Entwicklung, Konstruktion *f* ◆ **in course of** *or* **under ~** in *or* im Bau.
(b) (*way sth is constructed*) Struktur *f*; (*of building*) Bauweise *f*; (*of machine, bridge*) Konstruktion *f*; (*of novel, play etc*) Aufbau *m*.
(c) (*sth constructed*) Bau *m*, Bauwerk *nt*; (*bridge, machine*) Konstruktion *f* ◆ **primitive ~s** primitive Bauten.
(d) (*interpretation*) Deutung *f* ◆ **to put a wrong/bad ~ on sth** etw falsch auffassen *or* auslegen/etw schlecht aufnehmen; **I don't know what ~ to put on it** ich weiß nicht, wie ich das auffassen soll.
(e) (*Gram*) Konstruktion *f* ◆ **sentence ~** Satzbau *m*.

construction *in cpds* Bau-.

constructional [kənˈstrʌkʃənl] *adj* baulich; *technique, tool* Bau-; *fault, toy* Konstruktions-.

construction industry *n* Bauindustrie *f*.

constructive [kənˈstrʌktɪv] *adj* konstruktiv.

constructively [kənˈstrʌktɪvlɪ] *adv* konstruktiv; *critical* auf konstruktive Art ◆ **he suggested, not very ~, that ...** er machte den nicht gerade konstruktiven Vorschlag, zu ...

construe [kənˈstruː] [1] *vt* **(a)** (*Gram*) *words* analysieren; *sentence also* zerlegen ◆ **in English it is ~d as an adjective** im Englischen wird das als Adjektiv betrachtet. **(b)** (*interpret*) auslegen, auffassen.
[2] *vi* (*Gram: sentence*) sich zerlegen *or* aufgliedern *or* analysieren lassen.

consubstantiation [ˌkɒnsəbˌstænʃɪˈeɪʃən] *n* (*Eccl*) Konsubstantiation *f*.

consuetude [ˌkɒnswɪˈtjuːd] *n* (*form*) normative Kraft des Faktischen (*form*).

consul [ˈkɒnsəl] *n* Konsul *m*.

consular [ˈkɒnsjʊlər] *adj* konsularisch.

consulate [ˈkɒnsjʊlɪt] *n* Konsulat *nt*.

➤ LANGUAGE IN USE: **contact: 1a → 21.1**

consul general *n, pl* **-s** - Generalkonsul *m*.

consulship [ˈkɒnsəlʃɪp] *n* Konsulat *nt*.

consult [kənˈsʌlt] [1] *vt* **(a)** sich besprechen mit, konsultieren; *lawyer, doctor etc* konsultieren, zu Rate ziehen; *dictionary* nachschlagen in (+*dat*), konsultieren (*geh*); *map* nachsehen auf (+*dat*); *oracle* befragen; *horoscope* nachlesen; *clock* sehen auf (+*acc*) ◆ **he might have ~ed me** das hätte er auch mit mir besprechen können, er hätte mich auch konsultieren können; **you don't have to ~ me about every little detail** Sie brauchen mich nicht wegen jeder Kleinigkeit zu fragen; **he did it without ~ing anyone** er hat das getan, ohne jemanden zu fragen.
(b) (*form: consider*) bedenken.
[2] *vi* (*confer*) sich beraten, beratschlagen ◆ **to ~ together (over sth)** (etw) gemeinsam beraten; **to ~ with sb** sich mit jdm beraten.

consultancy [kənˈsʌltənsɪ] *n* (*act*) Beratung *f*; (*business*) Beratungsbüro *nt*.

consultant [kənˈsʌltənt] [1] *n* (*Brit Med*) Facharzt *m am Krankenhaus*; (*other professions*) Berater *m*.
[2] *adj attr* beratend.

consultation [ˌkɒnsəlˈteɪʃən] *n* Beratung, Besprechung, Konsultation (*form*) *f*; (*of doctor, lawyer*) Konsultation *f* (*of gen*), Beratung *f* (*of* mit) ◆ **in ~ with** in gemeinsamer Beratung mit; **to have a ~ with one's doctor/lawyer** seinen Arzt/Rechtsanwalt konsultieren; **to hold a ~ (with sb)** sich (mit jdm) beraten, eine Besprechung (mit jdm) abhalten.

consultative [kənˈsʌltətɪv] *adj document* beratend, konsultativ (*form*) ◆ **in a ~ capacity** in beratender Funktion.

consulting [kənˈsʌltɪŋ] *adj engineer, architect, psychiatrist* beratend ◆ **~ hours/room** (*Brit*) Sprechstunde *f*/-zimmer *nt*.

consumable [kənˈsjuːməbl] *n* Konsumgut, Verbrauchsgut *nt* ◆ **~s** (*Comput*) Verbrauchsmaterial *nt*.

consume [kənˈsjuːm] *vt* **(a)** *food, drink* zu sich nehmen, konsumieren (*form*); *food also* verzehren (*geh*), aufessen, vertilgen (*hum inf*); (*Econ*) konsumieren.
(b) (*destroy*) (*fire*) vernichten; (*use up*) *fuel, money* verbrauchen; *money, energy* aufbrauchen, verzehren (*geh*); *time* in Anspruch nehmen ◆ **he was ~d with desire/jealousy/rage** er wurde von Begierde/Eifersucht verzehrt (*geh*)/die Wut fraß ihn nahezu auf.

consumer [kənˈsjuːmər] *n* Verbraucher, Konsument (*form*) *m*.

consumer *in cpds* Verbraucher-; **~ advice centre** *n* Verbraucherzentrale *f*; **~ credit** *n* Verbraucherkredit *m*; **~ demand** *n* (konsumptive *spec*) Nachfrage; **~ durables** *npl* (langlebige) Gebrauchsgüter *pl*; **~ goods** *npl* Konsumgüter *pl*.

consumerism [kənˈsjuːmərɪzəm] *n* Konsumismus *m*, Konsumdenken *nt* ◆ **the age of ~** das Konsumzeitalter.

consumer: ~ protection *n* Verbraucherschutz *m*; **~ research** *n* Verbraucherbefragung *f*; **~ resistance** *n* Kaufunlust *f*; **~ society** *n* Konsumgesellschaft *f*.

consuming [kənˈsjuːmɪŋ] *adj ambition, interest* glühend, brennend; *desire, passion also* verzehrend (*geh*).

consummate [kənˈsʌmɪt] [1] *adj skill, folly* vollendet, vollkommen; *politician* unübertrefflich ◆ **with ~ ease** mit spielender Leichtigkeit.
[2] [ˈkɒnsəmeɪt] *vt marriage* vollziehen.

consummation [ˌkɒnsəˈmeɪʃən] *n* **(a)** (*of marriage*) Vollzug *m*. **(b)** (*fig*) (*peak*) Höhepunkt *m*; (*fulfilment*) Erfüllung *f*.

consumption [kənˈsʌmpʃən] *n* **(a)** (*of food, fuel etc*) Konsum *m*; (*of non-edible products*) Verbrauch *m*; (*of food also*) Verzehr *m* (*geh*) ◆ **this letter is for private ~ only** (*inf*) der Brief ist nur für den privaten Gebrauch; **not fit for human ~** zum Verzehr ungeeignet; **world ~ of oil** Weltölverbrauch *m*; **his daily ~ of three litres of beer** sein täglicher Konsum von drei Litern Bier.
(b) (*Med old*) Auszehrung (*old*), Schwindsucht *f*.

consumptive [kənˈsʌmptɪv] (*old*) [1] *n* Schwindsüchtige(r) *mf*.
[2] *adj* schwindsüchtig.

▼ **contact** [ˈkɒntækt] [1] *n* **(a)** Kontakt *m*; (*touching also*) Berührung *f*; (*communication also*) Verbindung *f* ◆ **to be in ~ with sb/sth** (*be touching*) jdn/etw berühren; (*in communication*) mit jdm/etw in Verbindung *or* Kontakt stehen; **to come into ~ with sb/sth** (*lit, fig*) mit jdm/etw in Berührung kommen; *with disease carrier also* mit jdm in Kontakt kommen; **he has no ~ with his family** er hat keinen Kontakt zu seiner Familie; **his first ~ with death** seine erste Berührung mit dem Tod; **on ~ with air/water** wenn es mit Luft/Wasser in Berührung kommt; **I'll get in ~** ich werde mich melden (*inf*), ich werde von mir hören lassen; **I'll get in(to) ~ with you** ich werde mich mit Ihnen in Verbindung setzen; **how can we get in(to) ~ with him?** wie können wir ihn erreichen?; **to make ~** (*two things*) sich berühren; (*wires, wheels etc*) in Berührung *or* Kontakt (miteinander) kommen; (*two people*) (*get in touch*) sich miteinander in Verbindung setzen; (*by radio etc*) eine Verbindung herstellen; (*psychologically*) Kontakt bekommen; **he could make ~ by radio** er konnte sich durch Funk in Verbindung setzen; **as soon as the glue makes ~ (with the surface)** sobald der Klebstoff mit der Fläche in Berührung *or* Kontakt kommt; **to make ~ with sb/sth** (*touch*) jdn/etw berühren, mit jdm/etw in Berührung kommen; (*wire, wheels etc also*) mit jdm/etw in Kontakt kommen; (*get in touch with*) sich mit jdm/etw in Verbindung setzen; (*psychologically*) Kontakt zu jdm/etw bekommen; **I finally made ~ with him at his office** ich habe ihn schließich im Büro erreicht; **to lose ~ (with sb/sth)** den Kontakt *or* die Verbindung (zu jdm/etw) verlieren; **point of ~** (*Math, fig*) Berührungspunkt *m*.
(b) (*Elec*) (*act*) Kontakt *m*; (*equipment*) Kontakt- *or* Schaltstück *nt* ◆ **to make/break ~** den Kontakt herstellen/unterbrechen.
(c) (*person*) Kontaktperson *f* (*also Med*); (*in espionage*) Verbindungsmann,

V-Mann *m* ◆ **~s** *pl* Kontakte, Verbindungen *pl*; **to make ~s** Kontakte herstellen; **he's made a useful ~** er hat einen nützlichen Kontakt hergestellt.
[2] *vt person, agent, lawyer* sich in Verbindung setzen mit; (*for help*) *police* sich wenden an (*+acc*) ◆ **I've been trying to ~ you for hours** ich versuche schon seit Stunden, Sie zu erreichen; **he doesn't want to be ~ed unless it's urgent** er möchte, daß man sich nur in dringenden Fällen mit ihm in Verbindung setzt.

contact: ~-breaker *n* Unterbrecher *m*; **~ flight** *n* Sichtflug *m*; **~ lens** *n* Kontaktlinse *f*; **~ man** *n* Kontakt- *or* Mittelsmann *m*; **~ print** *n* (*Phot*) Kontaktabzug *m*.

contagion [kən'teɪdʒən] *n* (*contact*) Ansteckung *f*; (*disease*) Ansteckungskrankheit *f*; (*epidemic*) Seuche *f* (*also fig*); (*fig: spreading influence*) schädlicher Einfluß.

contagious [kən'teɪdʒəs] *adj* (*Med, fig*) ansteckend; *disease also* direkt übertragbar ◆ **he's not ~** (*Med*) seine Krankheit ist nicht ansteckend; (*hum*) er ist nicht giftig (*inf*).

contain [kən'teɪn] *vt* (**a**) (*hold within itself*) enthalten ◆ **the envelope ~ed money** im Umschlag befand sich Geld, der Umschlag enthielt Geld.
(**b**) (*have capacity for: box, bottle, room*) fassen.
(**c**) (*control*) *emotions, oneself* beherrschen; *tears* zurückhalten; *laughter* unterdrücken; *disease, inflation, sb's power* in Grenzen halten; *epidemic, flood* aufhalten, unter Kontrolle bringen; *enemy*, (*Sport*) in Schach halten; *attack* abwehren ◆ **he could hardly ~ himself** er konnte kaum an sich (*acc*) halten.
(**d**) (*Math*) *angle* einschließen.

container [kən'teɪnəʳ] [1] *n* (**a**) Behälter *m*; (*bottle, jar etc also*) Gefäß *nt*. (**b**) (*Comm: for transport*) Container *m*.
[2] *adj attr* Container- ◆ **by ~ transport** per Container.

containerization [kən,teɪnəraɪ'zeɪʃən] *n* (*of goods*) Verpackung *f* in Container; (*of ports*) Umstellung *f* auf Container.

containerize [kən'teɪnəraɪz] *vt freight* in Container verpacken; *port* auf Container umstellen.

containment [kən'teɪnmənt] *n* (*Mil*) In-Schach-Halten *nt*; (*of attack*) Abwehr *f* ◆ **their efforts at ~ (of the rebels)** ihre Bemühungen, die Rebellen in Schach zu halten.

contaminate [kən'tæmɪneɪt] *vt* verunreinigen, verschmutzen; (*poison*) vergiften; (*radioactivity*) verseuchen, kontaminieren (*spec*); (*fig*) *mind* verderben ◆ **the oranges were ~d by poison** in den Orangen befanden sich Giftstoffe.

contamination [kən,tæmɪ'neɪʃən] *n, no pl see vt* Verunreinigung, Verschmutzung *f*; Vergiftung *f*; Verseuchung, Kontaminierung (*spec*) *f*; (*substance*) Giftstoffe *pl*; (*fig*) schädlicher Einfluß (*of* auf *+acc*); (*fig: contaminated state*) Verdorbenheit *f*.

contango [kən'tæŋgəʊ] *n* (*Fin*) Report *m*.

contd *abbr of* **continued** Forts., Fortsetzung *f*.

contemplate ['kɒntempleɪt] *vt* (**a**) (*look at*) betrachten.
(**b**) (*think about, reflect upon*) nachdenken über (*+acc*); (*consider*) *changes, a purchase, action, accepting an offer* in Erwägung ziehen, erwägen (*geh*); *a holiday* denken an (*+acc*) ◆ **he ~d the future with some misgivings** er sah der Zukunft mit einem unguten Gefühl entgegen; **he would never ~ violence** der Gedanke an Gewalttätigkeit würde ihm nie kommen; **it's too awful to ~** schon der Gedanke (daran) ist zu entsetzlich.
(**c**) (*expect*) voraussehen.
(**d**) (*intend*) **to ~ doing sth** daran denken, etw zu tun.

contemplation [,kɒntem'pleɪʃən] *n, no pl* (**a**) (*act of looking*) Betrachtung *f*.
(**b**) (*act of thinking*) Nachdenken *nt* (*of* über *+acc*); (*deep thought*) Besinnung, Betrachtung, Kontemplation (*esp Rel*) *f* ◆ **a life of ~** ein beschauliches *or* kontemplatives (*esp Rel*) Leben; **a life of inner ~** ein Leben der inneren Einkehr; **deep in ~** in Gedanken versunken.
(**c**) (*expectation*) Erwartung *f* ◆ **in ~ of their visit** in Erwartung ihres Besuches.

contemplative [kən'templətɪv] *adj look* nachdenklich; *mood also* besinnlich; *life, religious order* beschaulich, kontemplativ.

contemplatively [kən'templətɪvlɪ] *adv* nachdenklich; *sit also* in Gedanken.

contemporaneous [kən,tempə'reɪnɪəs] *adj* gleichzeitig stattfindend *attr* ◆ **a manuscript ~ with ...** ein Manuskript aus derselben Zeit *or* Epoche wie ...; **events ~ with the rebellion** Ereignisse zur Zeit des Aufstandes.

contemporary [kən'tempərərɪ] [1] *adj* (**a**) (*of the same time*) *events* gleichzeitig; *records, literature, writer* zeitgenössisch; (*of the same age*) *manuscript* gleich alt ◆ **records ~ with the invasion** Aufzeichnungen aus der Zeit der Invasion.
(**b**) (*of the present time*) *life* heutig; *art, design* zeitgenössisch, modern.
[2] *n* Altersgenosse *m*/-genossin *f*; (*in history*) Zeitgenosse *m*/-genossin *f*; (*at university*) Kommilitone *m*, Kommilitonin *f*.

contempt [kən'tempt] *n* (**a**) Verachtung *f*; (*disregard also*) Geringachtung, Geringschätzung *f* (*for* von) ◆ **to have** *or* **hold in/bring into ~** verachten/in Verruf bringen; **to fall into ~** (an) Ansehen einbüßen *or* verlieren; (*lose popularity*) (an) Popularität einbüßen; **in ~ of public opinion** die öffentliche Meinung außer acht lassend, ohne Ansehen der öffentlichen Meinung; **beneath ~** unter aller Kritik.
(**b**) (*Jur: also* **~ of court**) Mißachtung *f* (der Würde) des Gerichts, Ungebühr *f* vor Gericht; (*through non-appearance*) Ungebühr *f* durch vorsätzliches Ausbleiben; (*by press*) Beeinflussung *f* der Rechtspflege ◆ **to be in ~ (of court)** das Gericht *or* die Würde des Gerichts mißachten.

contemptible [kən'temptəbl] *adj* verachtenswert, verächtlich.

contemptuous [kən'temptjʊəs] *adj manner, gesture, look* geringschätzig, verächtlich ◆ **to be ~ of sb/sth** jdn/etw verachten; **she was quite ~ of my offer** sie reagierte ziemlich verächtlich auf mein Angebot.

contemptuously [kən'temptjʊəslɪ] *adv see adj*.

contend [kən'tend] [1] *vi* (**a**) kämpfen ◆ **to ~ (with sb) for sth** (mit jdm) um etw kämpfen; **then you'll have me to ~ with** dann bekommst du es mit mir zu tun; **but I've got two directors to ~ with** aber ich habe es mit zwei Direktoren zu tun. (**b**) (*cope*) **to ~ with sb/sth** mit jdm/etw fertigwerden.
[2] *vt* behaupten.

contender [kən'tendəʳ] *n* Kandidat(in *f*), Anwärter(in *f*) *m* (*for* auf *+acc*); (*for job also*) Bewerber(in *f*) *m* (*for* um); (*Sport*) Wettkämpfer(in *f*) *m* (*for* um).

contending [kən'tendɪŋ] *adj emotions* widerstreitend ◆ **the ~ parties** (*Sport*) die Wettstreiter *pl*, die Wettkampfteilnehmer *pl*; (*in lawsuit*) die streitenden Parteien *pl*.

content[1] [kən'tent] [1] *adj pred* zufrieden (*with* mit) ◆ **to be/feel ~** zufrieden sein; **she's quite ~ to stay at home** sie bleibt ganz gern zu Hause.
[2] *n* Zufriedenheit *f* ◆ **a grunt of ~** ein zufriedenes Grunzen.
[3] *vt person* zufriedenstellen ◆ **there's no ~ing him** er ist mit nichts zufrieden; **to ~ oneself with** sich zufriedengeben *or* begnügen *or* abfinden mit; **to ~ oneself with doing sth** sich damit zufriedengeben *or* begnügen *or* abfinden, etw zu tun.

content[2] ['kɒntent] *n* (**a**) **~s** *pl* (*of room, one's pocket, book etc*) Inhalt *m*; **(table of) ~s** Inhaltsverzeichnis *nt*. (**b**) *no pl* (*substance, component*) Gehalt *m*; (*of speech, book etc also*) Inhalt *m* ◆ **gold/vitamin ~** Gold-/Vitamingehalt *m*.

contented *adj*, **~ly** *adv* [kən'tentɪd, -lɪ] zufrieden.

contentedness [kən'tentɪdnɪs] *n see* **contentment**.

contention [kən'tenʃən] *n* (**a**) (*dispute*) Streit *m* ◆ **~s** Streitigkeiten *pl*; **the matter in ~** die strittige Angelegenheit; **that is no longer in ~** das steht nicht mehr zur Debatte. (**b**) (*argument*) Behauptung *f* ◆ **it is my ~ that ...** ich behaupte, daß ...

contentious [kən'tenʃəs] *adj subject, issue* strittig, umstritten; *person* streitlustig, streitsüchtig.

contentment [kən'tentmənt] *n* Zufriedenheit *f*.

contest ['kɒntest] [1] *n* (*for* um) Kampf *m*; (*competition also*) Wettkampf, Wettstreit (*geh*) *m*; (*beauty ~ etc*) Wettbewerb *m* ◆ **boxing ~** Boxkampf *m*; **election ~** Wahlkampf *m*; **it's no ~** das ist ein ungleicher Kampf; **it was a real ~ of skill** es kam dabei wirklich aufs Können an.
[2] [kən'test] *vt* (**a**) (*fight over*) kämpfen um; (*fight against, oppose*) kämpfen gegen; (*Parl*) *election* teilnehmen an (*+dat*) ◆ **to ~ a seat** (*Parl*) um einen Wahlkreis kämpfen; **the seat was not ~ed** es gab keinen Kampf um den Wahlkreis.
(**b**) (*dispute*) *statement* bestreiten, angreifen; *measure* angreifen; (*Jur*) *will, right, legal action* anfechten ◆ **a ~ed measure** eine umstrittene Maßnahme; **to ~ sb's right to do sth** jdm das Recht streitig machen *or* jds Recht anfechten, etw zu tun.
[3] [kən'test] *vi* kämpfen (*for* um).

contestant [kən'testənt] *n* (Wettbewerbs)teilnehmer(in *f*) *m*; (*Parl, in quiz*) Kandidat(in *f*) *m*; (*Sport*) (Wettkampf)teilnehmer(in *f*) *m*; (*Mil*) Kämpfende(r) *m* ◆ **the ~s in the election** die Wahlkandidaten.

context ['kɒntekst] *n* Zusammenhang, Kontext (*geh*) *m* ◆ **(taken) out of ~** aus dem Zusammenhang *or* Kontext (*geh*) gerissen; **in the wider European ~** im weiteren europäischen Zusammenhang *or* Kontext (*geh*) *or* Rahmen; **in this ~** in diesem Zusammenhang; **in an office ~** im Rahmen eines Büros.

contextual [kən'tekstjʊəl] *adj* kontextuell (*form*); *meaning* aus dem Zusammenhang *or* Kontext (*geh*) ersichtlich.

contextualize [kən'tekstjʊəlaɪz] *vt* in einen Zusammenhang *or* Kontext (*geh*) setzen.

contiguity [,kɒntɪ'gjʊɪtɪ] *n* (unmittelbare) Nachbarschaft.

contiguous [kən'tɪgjʊəs] *adj* (*form*) aneinandergrenzend, sich berührend; (*in time*) (unmittelbar) aufeinanderfolgend ◆ **the estates are ~** die Grundstücke grenzen aneinander.

continence ['kɒntɪnəns] *n* (**a**) (*Med*) Kontinenz *f* (*spec*), Fähigkeit *f*, Stuhl und/oder Urin zurückzuhalten. (**b**) (*abstinence*) Enthaltsamkeit *f*.

continent[1] ['kɒntɪnənt] *adj* (*self-controlled*) mäßig, beherrscht, maßvoll; (*sexually*) (sexuell) enthaltsam ◆ **the old lady was not ~** (*Med*) die alte Dame konnte ihre Darmtätigkeit/Blasentätigkeit nicht mehr kontrollieren.

continent[2] *n* (*Geog*) Kontinent, Erdteil *m*; (*mainland*) Festland *nt* ◆ **the C~** (*Brit*) Kontinentaleuropa *nt*; **on the C~** in Europa, auf dem Kontinent.

continental [,kɒntɪ'nentl] [1] *adj* (**a**) (*Geog*) kontinental. (**b**) (*Brit: European*) europäisch; *holidays* in Europa.
[2] *n* (Festlands)europäer(in *f*) *m*.

continental: ~ breakfast *n* kleines Frühstück; **~ drift** *n* (*Geog*) Kontinentaldrift *f*; **~ quilt** *n* Steppdecke *f*; **~ shelf** *n* (*Geog*) Kontinentalschelf, Kontinentalsockel *m*.

contingency [kən'tɪndʒənsɪ] *n* (**a**) möglicher Fall, Eventualität *f* ◆ **in this ~, should this ~ arise** in diesem Fall, für diesen Fall, sollte dieser Fall eintreten; **~ fund** Eventualfonds *m*; **to provide for all contingencies** alle Möglichkeiten einplanen, alle Eventualitäten berücksichtigen; **a ~ plan** ein Ausweichplan *m*; **~ planning** Planung *f* für Eventualfälle.
(**b**) (*Philos*) Kontingenz *f*.

contingent [kən'tɪndʒənt] [1] *adj* (**a**) **~ upon** (*form*) abhängig von; **to be ~ upon** abhängen von. (**b**) (*Philos*) kontingent.
[2] *n* Kontingent *nt*; (*section*) Gruppe *f*; (*Mil*) Trupp *m*.

continual [kən'tɪnjʊəl] *adj* (*frequent*) dauernd, ständig; (*unceasing*) ununterbrochen, pausenlos.

continually [kən'tɪnjʊəlɪ] *adv see adj* (an)dauernd, ständig; ununterbrochen, pausenlos.

➤ LANGUAGE IN USE: **context** → 26.2

continuance [kən'tɪnjʊəns] *n* **(a)** (*duration*) Dauer *f.* **(b)** *see* **continuation (a)**.

continuation [kən,tɪnjʊ'eɪʃən] *n* **(a)** Fortsetzung, Fortführung *f* ◆ **the ~ of the human race** der Weiterbestand *or* Fortbestand der menschlichen Rasse; **the Government's ~ in office** das Verbleiben der Regierung im Amt.
(b) (*retention: of arrangement etc*) Beibehaltung *f.*
(c) (*resumption*) Fortsetzung, Wiederaufnahme *f.*
(d) (*sth continued*) Fortsetzung, Weiterführung *f.*

continue [kən'tɪnju:] [1] *vt* **(a)** (*carry on*) fortfahren mit; *policy, tradition, struggle* fortsetzen, fortführen, weiterführen; *activity, piece of work, meal* fortsetzen, weitermachen mit ◆ **to ~ doing** *or* **to do sth** etw weiter tun, fortfahren, etw zu tun; **to ~ to fight/sing/read/eat, to ~ fighting/singing/reading/eating** weiterkämpfen/-singen/-lesen/-essen; **the patient ~s to improve** das Befinden des Patienten bessert sich ständig.
(b) (*resume*) fortsetzen; *conversation, work, journey also* wiederaufnehmen ◆ **to be ~d** Fortsetzung folgt; **~d on p 10** weiter *or* Fortsetzung auf Seite 10.
(c) (*prolong*) *line* verlängern, weiterführen.
[2] *vi* (*go on*) (*person*) weitermachen; (*crisis, speech*) fortdauern, (an)dauern; (*influence*) fortdauern, andauern; (*weather*) anhalten; (*road, forest etc*) weitergehen, sich fortsetzen; (*concert etc*) weitergehen ◆ **to ~ on one's way** weiterfahren; (*on foot*) weitergehen; **he ~d after a short pause** er redete/schrieb/las *etc* nach einer kurzen Pause weiter; **to ~ with one's work** seine Arbeit fortsetzen, mit seiner Arbeit weitermachen; **please ~** bitte machen Sie weiter; (*in talking*) fahren Sie fort; **to ~ to be obstinate/cheerful** weiterhin starrköpfig/fröhlich bleiben; **he ~s (to be) optimistic** er ist nach wie vor optimistisch; **to ~ at university/with a company/as sb's secretary** auf der Universität/bei einer Firma/jds Sekretärin bleiben; **to ~ in office** im Amt verbleiben; **his influence ~d after his death** sein Einfluß überdauerte seinen Tod.

continuing [kən'tɪnju:ɪŋ] *adj* ständig, fortgesetzt; *process* stetig, kontinuierlich (*geh*).

continuity [,kɒntɪ'nju:ɪtɪ] *n* **(a)** Kontinuität *f* ◆ **the story lacks ~** der Geschichte fehlt der rote Faden. **(b)** (*Film*) Anschluß *m;* (*Rad*) (verbindende) Ansagen *pl* ◆ **~ girl** Scriptgirl *nt.*

continuo [kən'tɪnjʊəʊ] *n* Continuo *nt* ◆ **to play the ~** Continuo spielen.

continuous [kən'tɪnjʊəs] *adj* dauernd, ständig, kontinuierlich (*geh*); *line* durchgezogen, ununterbrochen; *rise, movement etc* stetig, stet *attr* (*geh*), gleichmäßig; (*Math*) *function* stetig ◆ **~ paper** (*Comput*) Endlospapier *nt;* (*pre-printed*) Endlosformular *nt;* **~ performance** (*Film*) durchgehende Vorstellung; **~ tense** (*Gram*) Verlaufsform *f;* **present/past ~** (*Gram*) Verlaufsform *f* Präsens/Imperfekt.

continuously [kən'tɪnjʊəslɪ] *adv see adj* dauernd, ständig, kontinuierlich (*geh*); ununterbrochen; stetig, gleichmäßig.

continuum [kən'tɪnjʊəm] *n* Kontinuum *nt.*

contort [kən'tɔ:t] *vt* **(a)** *one's features, metal* verziehen (*into* zu); *limbs* verrenken, verdrehen ◆ **a face ~ed by pain** ein schmerzverzerrtes Gesicht; **a ~ed smile** ein verkrampftes Lächeln. **(b)** (*fig*) *words* verdrehen; *report also* verzerren.

contortion [kən'tɔ:ʃən] *n* (*esp of acrobat*) Verrenkung *f;* (*of features*) Verzerrung *f* ◆ **mental ~s** geistige Verrenkungen *pl or* Klimmzüge *pl;* **he went through all sorts of ~s to avoid telling the truth** er hat sich gedreht und gewendet, um nicht die Wahrheit sagen zu müssen.

contortionist [kən'tɔ:ʃənɪst] *n* Schlangenmensch *m.*

contour ['kɒntʊə^r] [1] *n* **(a)** (*outline*) Kontur *f,* Umriß *m.* **(b)** (*shape*) **~s** *pl* Konturen *pl* ◆ **the ~s of her body** ihre Konturen. **(c)** (*Geog*) *see* **~ line**.
[2] *vt road* der Gegend anpassen; *land* hügelig anlegen; *map* mit Höhenlinien versehen ◆ **the road was ~ed around the hill** die Straße wurde/war der Landschaft angepaßt und um den Hügel herumgeführt; **~ed seat** Kontursitz *m.*

contour: ~ line *n* (*Geog*) Höhenlinie *f;* **~ map** *n* Höhenlinienkarte *f.*

contra- ['kɒntrə-] *pref* Gegen-, Kontra-; (*Mus: pitched lower*) Kontra-.

contraband ['kɒntrəbænd] [1] *n, no pl* (*goods*) Konterbande, Schmuggelware *f;* (*form: smuggling*) Schleichhandel *m,* Schmuggeln *nt* ◆ **~ of war** Kriegskonterbande *f.*
[2] *adj* Schmuggel- ◆ **~ goods** Konterbande, Schmuggelware *f.*

contraception [,kɒntrə'sepʃən] *n* Empfängnisverhütung *f.*

contraceptive [,kɒntrə'septɪv] [1] *n* empfängnisverhütendes Mittel; (*sheath*) Verhütungsmittel, Präventivmittel (*form*) *nt.*
[2] *adj* empfängnisverhütend; *pill* Antibaby-; *advice* über Empfängnisverhütung.

contract¹ ['kɒntrækt] [1] *n* **(a)** (*agreement*) Vertrag, Kontrakt (*old*) *m;* (*document also*) Vertragsdokument *nt;* (*Comm*) (*order*) Auftrag *m;* (*delivery ~*) Liefervertrag *m* ◆ **to enter into** *or* **make a ~ (with sb)** (mit jdm) einen Vertrag eingehen *or* (ab)schließen; **to be under ~** unter Vertrag stehen (*to* bei, mit); **to be bound by ~** vertraglich gebunden sein (*to* an *+acc*); **to put work out to ~** Arbeiten außer Haus machen lassen; **to put a ~ on sb** (*to kill*) einen Killer auf jdn ansetzen; **terms of ~** Vertragsbedingungen *or* -bestimmungen *pl.*
(b) (*Bridge*) Kontrakt *m* ◆ **~ bridge** Kontrakt-Bridge *nt.*
[2] *adj price, date* vertraglich festgelegt *or* vereinbart ◆ **~ work** Auftragsarbeit *f.*
[3] [kən'trækt] *vt* **(a)** (*acquire*) *debts* machen, ansammeln; *illness* erkranken an (*+dat*); *vices, habit* sich (*dat*) zulegen, entwickeln, annehmen; *passion* entwickeln.
(b) (*enter into*) *marriage, alliance* schließen, eingehen.
[4] [kən'trækt] *vi* **(a)** (*Comm*) **to ~ to do sth** sich vertraglich verpflichten, etw zu tun.
(b) (*form: make an arrangement*) sich verbünden.

◆**contract in** *vi* sich anschließen (*-to dat*); (*into insurance scheme*) beitreten (*-to dat*).

◆**contract out** [1] *vi* (*withdraw*) austreten, aussteigen (*inf*) (*of* aus); (*not join*) sich nicht anschließen (*of dat*); (*of insurance scheme*) nicht beitreten (*of dat*).
[2] *vt sep* (*Comm*) *work* außer Haus machen lassen (*to* von), vergeben (*to* an *+acc*).

contract² [kən'trækt] [1] *vt* **(a)** zusammenziehen; *brow* in Falten legen, hochziehen; *pupil* verengen. **(b)** (*Ling*) zusammenziehen, kontrahieren (*spec*) (*into* zu).
[2] *vi* (*muscle, metal etc*) sich zusammenziehen; (*pupil also*) sich verengen; (*fig: influence, business*) (zusammen)schrumpfen.

contraction [kən'trækʃən] *n* **(a)** (*of metal, muscles*) Zusammenziehen *nt,* Zusammenziehung *f;* (*of pupils*) Verengung *f;* (*fig*) Schrumpfung *f.* **(b)** (*Ling*) Kontraktion *f.* **(c)** (*in childbirth*) **~s** Wehen *pl.* **(d)** (*form: acquisition*) (*of debts*) Ansammlung *f;* (*of habit*) Entwicklung, Annahme *f* ◆ **his ~ of polio** seine Erkrankung an Kinderlähmung.

contractor [kən'træktə^r] *n* (*individual*) Auftragnehmer *m,* beauftragter Elektriker/Monteur *etc;* (*company also*) beauftragte Firma; (*building ~*) Bauunternehmer *m;* (*company*) Bauunternehmen *nt,* Bauunternehmer *m* ◆ **that is done by outside ~s** damit ist eine andere Firma beauftragt.

contractual [kən'træktʃʊəl] *adj* vertraglich.

▼ **contradict** [,kɒntrə'dɪkt] *vt* (*person*) widersprechen (*+dat*); (*event, action, statement also*) im Widerspruch stehen zu ◆ **to ~ oneself** sich (*dat*) widersprechen; **he ~ed every word I said** er widersprach mir bei jedem Wort; **he can't stand being ~ed** er duldet keinen Widerspruch.

contradiction [,kɒntrə'dɪkʃən] *n* Widerspruch *m* (*of* zu); (*contradictory*) Widersprechen *nt* ◆ **full of ~s** voller Widersprüchlichkeiten; **to give a flat ~** einfach *or* rundheraus widersprechen (*+dat*).

contradictory [,kɒntrə'dɪktərɪ] *adj person* widersprüchlich; *statements also* (sich) widersprechend ◆ **to be ~ to sth** einer Sache (*dat*) widersprechen, zu etw im Widerspruch stehen; **it is not ~ to say ...** es ist kein Widerspruch, zu behaupten ...; **he was in a ~ mood** er war voller Widerspruchsgeist.

contradistinction [,kɒntrədɪs'tɪŋkʃən] *n* (*form*): **in ~ to** im Gegensatz *or* Unterschied zu.

contra-flow ['kɒntrə'fləʊ] (*Mot*) [1] *n* Gegenverkehr *m.*
[2] *adj* Gegenverkehrs-.

contraindication [,kɒntrə,ɪndɪ'keɪʃən] *n* (*Med*) Kontraindikation, Gegenanzeige *f.*

contralto [kən'træltəʊ] [1] *n* (*voice*) Alt *m;* (*singer also*) Altist(in *f*) *m.*
[2] *adj voice* Alt- ◆ **the ~ part** die Altstimme, der Alt.

contraption [kən'træpʃən] *n* (*inf*) Apparat *m* (*inf*); (*vehicle also*) Vehikel *nt* (*inf*), Kiste *f* (*inf*).

contrapuntal [,kɒntrə'pʌntl] *adj* kontrapunktisch.

contrarily [kən'trɛərɪlɪ] *adv* (*perversely*) widerborstig; (*of horse etc*) widerspenstig.

contrariness [kən'trɛərɪnɪs] *n see* **contrary²** Widerborstigkeit *f;* Widerspruchsgeist *m;* Widerspenstigkeit *f.*

▼ **contrary¹** ['kɒntrərɪ] [1] *adj* (*opposite*) entgegengesetzt; *effect, answer also* gegenteilig; (*conflicting*) *views, statements also* gegensätzlich; (*adverse*) *winds, tides* widrig ◆ **in a ~ direction** in entgegengesetzter Richtung; **sth is ~ to sth** etw steht im Gegensatz zu etw; **it is ~ to our agreement** es entspricht nicht unseren Abmachungen; **~ to nature** wider die Natur; **~ to our hopes/intentions** wider all unsere Hoffnungen/Absichten, entgegen unseren Hoffnungen/Absichten; **~ to what I expected** entgegen meinen Erwartungen.
▼ [2] *n* Gegenteil *nt* ◆ **on the ~** im Gegenteil; **the ~ of what I expected** das Gegenteil von dem, was ich erwartet hatte; **unless you hear to the ~** sofern Sie nichts Gegenteiliges hören.

contrary² [kən'trɛərɪ] *adj* widerborstig, widerspenstig; *person also* voll Widerspruchsgeist; *horse* widerspenstig.

▼ **contrast** ['kɒntrɑ:st] [1] *n* **(a)** (*contrasting*) Gegenüberstellung *f.*
▼ **(b)** Gegensatz *m* (*with, to* zu); (*visual, striking difference of opposites*) Kontrast *m* (*with, to* zu) ◆ **by** *or* **in ~** im Gegensatz dazu; **to be in ~ with** *or* **to sth** im Gegensatz/in Kontrast zu etw stehen; **the red makes a good ~** das Rot stellt einen guten Kontrast dar; **she's quite a ~ to her sister** es besteht ein ziemlicher Gegensatz *or* Unterschied zwischen ihr und ihrer Schwester; **the ~ between the state of the £ now and last year** der Unterschied zwischen dem jetzigen Stand des Pfundes und seinem Wert im letzten Jahr; **and now, by way of ~** und nun etwas ganz anderes; **what a ~!** welch ein Gegensatz!
(c) (*Art, Phot, TV*) Kontrast *m.*
[2] [kən'trɑ:st] *vt* einen Vergleich anstellen (*with* zwischen *+dat*), gegenüberstellen (*with dat*).
[3] [kən'trɑ:st] *vi* im Gegensatz *or* in Kontrast stehen (*with* zu), kontrastieren (*with* mit); (*colours also*) sich abheben (*with* von), abstechen (*with* von) ◆ **to ~ unfavourably with sth** bei einem Vergleich mit *or* im Vergleich zu etw schlecht abschneiden; **his promises and his actions ~ sharply** seine Versprechungen und seine Handlungsweise stehen in scharfem Kontrast *or* Gegensatz zueinander; **blue and yellow ~ nicely** Blau und Gelb ergeben einen hübschen Kontrast.

contrasting [kən'trɑ:stɪŋ] *adj opinions, lifestyle etc* gegensätzlich, kontrastierend (*form*); *colours* kontrastierend, Kontrast-.

contrastive [kən'trɑ:stɪv] *adj* gegenüberstellend; (*Ling*) kontrastiv.

contravene [,kɒntrə'vi:n] *vt law, custom etc* (*action, behaviour*) verstoßen gegen, verletzen; (*person also*) zuwiderhandeln (*+dat*).

➤ LANGUAGE IN USE: **contradict** → 26.3 **contrary¹: 1** → 26.2 **2** → 22, 26.3 **contrast: 1b** → 5.1

contravention [ˌkɒntrəˈvenʃən] *n* Verstoß *m* (*of* gegen), Verletzung *f* (*of gen*); (*of law also*) Übertretung *f* (*of gen*) ◆ **to be in ~ of** ... gegen ... verstoßen; **to act in ~ of sth** einer Sache (*dat*) zuwiderhandeln.

contretemps [ˈkɒntrəˌtɒŋ] *n, no pl* Zwischenfall *m*; (*unexpected hitch also*) kleines Mißgeschick.

contribute [kənˈtrɪbjuːt] [1] *vt* beitragen (*to* zu); *food, money, supplies* beisteuern (*to* zu); (*to charity*) spenden (*to* für); *time, talent* zur Verfügung stellen (*to dat*); *press article also, information* liefern (*to* für), beisteuern (*to dat*) ◆ **to ~ one's share** sein(en) Teil dazu beitragen.

[2] *vi* beitragen (*to* zu); (*to pension fund etc*) einen Beitrag leisten (*to* zu); (*to present*) beisteuern (*to* zu); (*to charity*) spenden (*to* für); (*to newspaper, conference, society etc*) einen Beitrag leisten (*to* zu); (*regularly: to a magazine etc*) mitwirken (*to* an *+dat*) ◆ **do you want me to ~?** möchten Sie, daß ich etwas dazu beisteuere *or* (*to charity*) etwas spende?

contribution [ˌkɒntrɪˈbjuːʃən] *n* Beitrag *m* (*to* zu); (*donation also*) Spende *f* (*to* für) ◆ **to make a ~ to sth** einen Beitrag zu etw leisten; **the beer is my ~** das Bier stelle ich; **I appreciate the ~ of so much of your time/effort** ich weiß es zu schätzen, daß Sie Ihre Zeit so großzügig zur Verfügung gestellt/solche Anstrengungen unternommen haben.

contributor [kənˈtrɪbjʊtə^r] *n* (*to magazine etc*) Mitarbeiter(in *f*) *m* (*to* an *+dat*); (*of goods, money*) Spender(in *f*) *m* ◆ **to be a ~ to a newspaper/an appeal** für eine Zeitung schreiben/auf einen Appell hin etwas spenden.

contributory [kənˈtrɪbjʊtərɪ] *adj* **(a) it's certainly a ~ factor/cause** es ist sicherlich ein Faktor, der dazu beiträgt *or* der mit eine Rolle spielt; **to be a ~ cause of a disease** ein Faktor sein, der zu einer Krankheit beiträgt; **~ negligence** (*Jur*) Mitverschulden *nt*. **(b)** *pension scheme* beitragspflichtig.

con trick *n* (*inf*) Schwindel *m*.

contrite *adj*, **~ly** *adv* [ˈkɒntraɪt, -lɪ] reuig, zerknirscht.

contrition [kənˈtrɪʃən] *n* Reue *f* ◆ **act of ~** (*Eccl*) Buße *f*.

contrivance [kənˈtraɪvəns] *n* **(a)** (*device*) Vorrichtung *f*; (*mechanical*) Gerät *nt*, Apparat *m*. **(b)** (*devising, scheming*) Planung *f*; (*invention*) Erfindung *f*; (*inventiveness*) Findigkeit, Erfindungsgabe *f* ◆ **a plan/device of his ~** ein seinem Kopf entstammender Plan/ein von ihm erfundenes Gerät. **(c)** (*plan, scheme*) List *f*.

contrive [kənˈtraɪv] *vt* **(a)** (*devise*) *plan, scheme* entwickeln, entwerfen, ersinnen; (*make*) fabrizieren ◆ **to ~ a means of doing sth** einen Weg finden, etw zu tun.

(b) (*manage, arrange*) bewerkstelligen, zuwege bringen; *meeting also* arrangieren ◆ **to ~ to do sth** es fertigbringen (*also iro*) *or* zuwege bringen, etw zu tun; **can you ~ to be here at three o'clock?** können Sie es so einrichten, daß Sie um drei Uhr hier sind?; **he always ~s to get his own way** er versteht (es) immer, seinen Kopf durchzusetzen.

contrived [kənˈtraɪvd] *adj* gestellt; *style also* gekünstelt.

control [kənˈtrəʊl] [1] *n* **(a)** *no pl* (*management, supervision*) Aufsicht *f* (*of* über *+acc*); (*of money, fortune*) Verwaltung *f* (*of gen*); (*of situation, emotion, language*) Beherrschung *f* (*of gen*); (*self-~*) (Selbst)beherrschung *f*; (*physical ~*) (Körper)beherrschung *f* (*of gen*); (*authority, power*) Gewalt, Macht *f* (*over* über *+acc*); (*over territory*) Gewalt *f* (*over* über *+acc*); (*regulation*) (*of prices, disease, inflation*) Kontrolle *f* (*of gen*); (*of traffic*) Regelung *f* (*of gen*); (*of pollution*) Einschränkung *f* (*of gen*) ◆ **to be in ~ of sth, to have ~ of sb/sth** *business, office* etw leiten, etw unter sich (*dat*) haben; *children* jdn beaufsichtigen; *money* etw verwalten; **I'm in ~ here** ich habe hier die Leitung; **to be in ~ of sb/sth, to have sth under ~** etw in der Hand haben; *children, class also* jdn/etw unter Kontrolle haben; *situation also* Herr einer Sache (*gen*) sein, etw beherrschen; *car, inflation, disease, pollution* etw unter Kontrolle haben; **to be in ~ of oneself/one's emotions** sich in der Hand *or* in der Gewalt haben/Herr über seine Gefühle sein, Herr seiner Gefühle sein; **to have some/no ~ over sb** Einfluß/keinen Einfluß auf jdn haben; **she has no ~ over how the money is spent/what her children do** sie hat keinen Einfluß darauf, wie das Geld ausgegeben wird/was ihre Kinder machen; **to have some/no ~ over sth** etw in der Hand/nicht in der Hand haben; *over money* Kontrolle/keine Kontrolle über etw (*acc*) haben; *over environment* Einfluß/keinen Einfluß auf etw (*acc*) haben; **to lose ~ (of sth)** etw nicht mehr in der Hand haben, (über etw *acc*) die Gewalt *or* Herrschaft verlieren; *of business* die Kontrolle (über etw *acc*) verlieren; *of car* die Herrschaft (über etw *acc*) verlieren; **to lose ~ of oneself** die Beherrschung verlieren; **to lose ~ of the situation** nicht mehr Herr der Lage sein; **to be/get out of ~** (*child, class*) außer Rand und Band sein/geraten; (*situation*) außer Kontrolle sein/geraten; (*car*) nicht mehr zu halten sein; (*inflation, prices, disease, pollution*) sich jeglicher Kontrolle (*dat*) entziehen/nicht mehr zu halten *or* zu bremsen (*inf*) sein; (*fire*) nicht unter Kontrolle sein/außer Kontrolle geraten; **the car spun out of ~** der Wagen begann sich ganz unkontrollierbar zu drehen; **under state ~** unter staatlicher Kontrolle *or* Aufsicht; **to bring** *or* **get sth under ~** etw unter Kontrolle bringen; *situation* Herr einer Sache (*gen*) werden; *car* etw in seine Gewalt bringen; **to be under ~** unter Kontrolle sein; (*children, class*) sich benehmen; (*car*) (wieder) lenkbar sein; **everything** *or* **the situation is under ~** wir/sie *etc* haben die Sache im Griff (*inf*); **the situation was beyond their ~** die Sache war ihnen völlig aus der Hand geglitten, sie hatten die Sache nicht mehr in der Hand; **he was beyond his parents' ~** er war seinen Eltern über den Kopf gewachsen; **circumstances beyond our ~** nicht in unserer Hand liegende Umstände; **his ~ of the ball** seine Ballführung.

(b) (*check*) Kontrolle *f* (*on gen*, über *+acc*) ◆ **wages/price ~s** Lohn-/Preiskontrolle *f*.

(c) (*~ room*) die Zentrale; (*Aviat*) der Kontrollturm.

(d) (*knob, switch*) Regler *m*; (*of vehicle, machine*) Schalter *m* ◆ **to be at the ~s** (*of spaceship, airliner*) am Kontrollpult sitzen; (*of small plane, car*) die Steuerung haben; **to take over the ~s** die Steuerung übernehmen.

(e) (*Sci*) (*person*) Kontrollperson *f*; (*animal*) Kontrolltier *nt*; (*group*) Kontrollgruppe *f*.

(f) (*Spiritualism*) *Geist m einer Persönlichkeit, dessen Äußerungen das Medium wiedergibt.*

(g) (*Comput*) **~-F1** Control-F1.

[2] *vt* **(a)** (*direct, manage*) kontrollieren; *business* führen, leiten, unter sich (*dat*) haben; *sea* beherrschen; *organization* in der Hand haben; *animal, child, class* fertigwerden mit; *car* steuern, lenken; *traffic* regeln; *emotions, movements* beherrschen, unter Kontrolle halten; *hair* bändigen ◆ **to ~ oneself/one's temper** sich beherrschen; **~ yourself!** nimm dich zusammen!; **please try to ~ your children/dog** bitte sehen Sie zu, daß sich Ihre Kinder benehmen/sich Ihr Hund benimmt.

(b) (*regulate, check*) *prices, rents, growth etc* kontrollieren; *temperature, speed* regulieren; *disease* unter Kontrolle bringen; *population* eindämmen, im Rahmen halten.

control: ~ centre *n* Kontrollzentrum *nt*; **~ character** *n* (*Comput*) Steuerzeichen *nt*; **~ column** *n* Steuersäule *f* (*form*), Steuerknüppel *m*; **~ experiment** *n* Kontrollversuch *m*; **~ freak** *n* (*inf*) **most men are total ~ freaks** die meisten Männer müssen immer alles unter Kontrolle haben; **~ group** *n* (*Med, Psych*) Kontrollgruppe *f*; **~ key** *n* (*Comput*) Control-Taste *f*; **~ knob** *n* (*on TV etc*) Kontrollknopf *m*.

controllable [kənˈtrəʊləbl] *adj* kontrollierbar, zu kontrollieren *pred*; *child, animal* lenkbar.

controlled [kənˈtrəʊld] *adj emotion, movement, voice* beherrscht; *passion* gezügelt; *conditions, rent* kontrolliert; *prices* gebunden; *temperature* geregelt; ◆ **~ drugs** *or* **substances** verschreibungspflichtige Medikamente.

controller [kənˈtrəʊlə^r] *n* **(a)** (*director*) (*Rad*) Intendant *m*; (*Aviat*) (Flug)lotse *m*. **(b)** (*financial head*) Leiter *m* des Finanzwesens.

controlling [kənˈtrəʊlɪŋ] *adj attr factor* beherrschend; *body* Aufsichts- ◆ **~ interest** Mehrheitsanteil *m*.

control: ~ panel *n* Schalttafel, Schaltblende *f*; (*on aircraft, TV*) Bedienungsfeld *nt*; (*on machine*) Steuer- *or* Bedienungs- *or* Betriebspult *nt*; (*on car*) Armaturenbrett *nt*; **~ point** *n* Kontrollpunkt *m*, Kontrollstelle *f*; **~ rod** *n* Regelstab *m*; **~ room** *n* Kontrollraum *m*; (*Naut also*) Kommandoraum *m*; (*Mil*) (Operations)zentrale *f*; (*of police*) Zentrale *f*; **~ stick** *n see* **~ column**; **~ tower** *n* (*Aviat*) Kontrollturm *m*; **~ unit** *n* (*Comput*) Steuerwerk *nt*, Steuereinheit *f*.

controversial [ˌkɒntrəˈvɜːʃəl] *adj speech etc* kontrovers; (*debatable*) *matter, decision also* umstritten, strittig ◆ **it is still ~ whether** ... es ist immer noch umstritten, ob ...; **he is deliberately ~** er gibt sich bewußt kontrovers.

controversy [ˈkɒntrəvɜːsɪ, kənˈtrɒvəsɪ] *n* Kontroversen *pl*, Streit *m* ◆ **there was a lot of ~ about it** es gab deswegen große Kontroversen *or* Differenzen; **to give rise to ~** Anlaß zu Kontroversen geben; **statements/facts that are beyond ~** völlig unumstrittene Behauptungen/Tatsachen.

controvert [ˈkɒntrəvɜːt] *vt* (*form*) anfechten, bestreiten.

contumacious *adj*, **~ly** *adv* [ˌkɒntjʊˈmeɪʃəs, -lɪ] verstockt; (*insubordinate*) den Gehorsam verweigernd.

contumacy [ˈkɒntjʊməsɪ] *n see adj* Verstocktheit *f*; Gehorsamsverweigerung *f*.

contumely [ˈkɒntjʊmɪlɪ] *n* (*no pl: abuse*) Schmähen *nt* (*geh*); (*insult*) Schmähung *f* (*geh*).

contuse [kənˈtjuːz] *vt* (*form*) quetschen, prellen.

contusion [kənˈtjuːʒən] *n* Quetschung, Kontusion (*spec*) *f*.

conundrum [kəˈnʌndrəm] *n* (*lit, fig*) Rätsel *nt*.

conurbation [ˌkɒnɜːˈbeɪʃən] *n* Ballungsgebiet *nt or* -raum *m or* -zentrum *nt*, Conurbation *f* (*spec*).

convalesce [ˌkɒnvəˈles] *vi* genesen (*from, after* von) ◆ **while convalescing** während der Genesung(szeit).

convalescence [ˌkɒnvəˈlesəns] *n* Genesung *f*; (*period*) Genesungszeit *f*.

convalescent [ˌkɒnvəˈlesənt] [1] *n* Rekonvaleszent(in *f*) *m* (*form*), Genesende(r) *mf*.

[2] *adj* genesend ◆ **to be ~** auf dem Wege der Besserung sein; **~ home** Genesungsheim *nt*.

convection [kənˈvekʃən] *n* Konvektion *f*.

convector [kənˈvektə^r] *n* (*also* **~ heater**) Heizlüfter *m*.

convene [kənˈviːn] [1] *vt meeting* einberufen; *group of people* zusammenrufen, versammeln.

[2] *vi* zusammenkommen, sich versammeln; (*parliament, court*) zusammentreten.

convener [kənˈviːnə^r] *n Person, die Versammlungen einberuft.*

convenience [kənˈviːnɪəns] *n* **(a)** *no pl* (*usefulness, advantageousness*) Annehmlichkeit *f*; (*functionalness*) Zweckmäßigkeit *f* ◆ **for the sake of ~** aus praktischen Gründen; **~ foods** Fertiggerichte *pl*.

(b) *no pl* **to consider the ~ of the inhabitants/driver** *etc* daran denken, was für die Bewohner/den Fahrer *etc* praktisch und bequem ist, die Zweckmäßigkeit für die Bewohner/den Fahrer *etc* in Betracht ziehen; **for your ~** zum gefälligen Gebrauch; **these chairs are for the ~ of customers** diese Stühle sind für unsere Kunden gedacht; **I'm not changing it for** *or* **to suit his ~** ich werde es seinetwegen *or* nur um es ihm recht zu machen nicht ändern; **he did not find that date to his ~** der Termin paßte ihm nicht *or* kam ihm nicht gelegen; **at your own ~** zu einem Ihnen angenehmen Zeitpunkt, wann es Ihnen paßt (*inf*); **at your earliest ~** (*Comm*) möglichst bald, baldmöglichst (*form*).

(c) (*convenient thing, amenity*) Annehmlichkeit *f* ♦ **a house with every ~/with all modern ~s** ein Haus mit allem/allem modernen Komfort.
(d) (*Brit form: public ~*) (öffentliche) Toilette, Bedürfnisanstalt *f* (*dated form*).

convenient [kən'vi:nɪənt] *adj* (*useful, functional*) zweckmäßig, praktisch; *area, house* (*for shops etc*) günstig gelegen; *time* günstig, passend ♦ **at a more ~ time** zu einem passenderen *or* günstigeren Zeitpunkt; **if it is ~** wenn es Ihnen (so) paßt; **if it is ~ to** *or* **for you** wenn es Ihnen (so) paßt, wenn es Ihnen keine Umstände macht; **a place/time ~ for all of us** ein Ort, der/eine Zeit, die uns allen paßt *or* für uns alle günstig ist; **is tomorrow ~ (to** *or* **for you)?** paßt (es) Ihnen morgen?, geht es morgen?; **well, then, you'd better make it ~** nun, dann machen Sie es eben passend (*inf*); **he sat down on a ~ chair** er setzte sich auf einen Stuhl, der gerade dastand; **the trams are very ~** (*nearby*) die Straßenbahnhaltestellen liegen sehr günstig; (*useful*) die Straßenbahn ist sehr praktisch; **a ~ place to stop** eine geeignete *or* günstige Stelle zum Anhalten; **is there a ~ train?** gibt es einen geeigneten *or* passenden Zug?; **her resignation was most ~ (for him)** ihr Rücktritt kam ihm äußerst gelegen; **how ~!** sehr günstig!

conveniently [kən'vi:nɪəntlɪ] *adv* günstigerweise; *situated* günstig, vorteilhaft; (*usefully*) *designed* praktisch, zweckmäßig ♦ **he very ~ arrived home early** er kam früh nach Hause, was äußerst günstig war; **if you could ~ do it then** wenn es Ihnen paßte; **it ~ started to rain** wie bestellt, fing es an zu regnen; **the house is ~ close to the shops** das Haus liegt in praktischer Nähe der Läden.

convent ['kɒnvənt] *n* (Frauen)kloster *nt* ♦ **to enter a ~** ins Kloster gehen; **~ school** Klosterschule *f*.

convention [kən'venʃən] *n* **(a)** Brauch *m*, Sitte *f*; (*social rule*) Konvention *f* ♦ **~ requires** *or* **demands that ...** die Sitte *or* der Brauch will es so, daß ...; **it's a ~ that ...** es ist so üblich *or* Sitte *or* Brauch, daß ...; **it's a ~ of our society** es ist in unserer Gesellschaft so üblich; (*point of etiquette*) es ist eine gesellschaftliche Konvention; **to disregard ~(s)** sich nicht an die herkömmlichen Bräuche *or* Konventionen halten.
(b) (*agreement*) Abkommen *nt*.
(c) (*conference*) Tagung, Konferenz *f*; (*Pol*) Versammlung *f*.

conventional [kən'venʃənl] *adj dress, attitudes, warfare, weapons* konventionell; *person, behaviour also* konventionsgebunden; *philosophy, beliefs, theory, manner, technique* herkömmlich; *theatre, music, style* traditionell; *symbol, mealtimes* normalerweise üblich ♦ **it is ~ to do sth** es ist normalerweise üblich, etw zu tun.

conventionality [kən,venʃə'nælɪtɪ] *n see adj* Konventionalität *f*; Konventionsgebundenheit *f*; Herkömmlichkeit *f*; traditionelle Art.

conventionally [kən'venʃnəlɪ] *adv see adj* konventionell; konventionsgebunden; herkömmlicherweise; traditionell; normalerweise, üblicherweise ♦ **~ one would be expected to ...** herkömmlicherweise würde erwartet, daß man ...

converge [kən'vɜ:dʒ] *vi* (*road, lines*) zusammenlaufen (*at* in *or* an *+dat*); (*river also*) zusammenströmen (*at* in *or* an *+dat*); (*Math, Phys*) konvergieren (*at* in *+dat*); (*fig: views etc*) sich aneinander annähern, konvergieren (*geh*) ♦ **to ~ on sb/sth/New York** von überallher zu jdm/etw/nach New York strömen.

convergence [kən'vɜ:dʒəns] *n see vi* Zusammenlaufen *nt*; Zusammenströmen *nt*; Konvergenz *f*; Annäherung *f* ♦ **point of ~** Schnittpunkt *m*; (*of rays*) Brennpunkt *m*; (*of rivers*) Zusammenfluß *m*.

convergent [kən'vɜ:dʒənt], **converging** [kən'vɜ:dʒɪŋ] *adj see vi* zusammenlaufend; zusammenströmend; konvergent (*form*), konvergierend; sich (aneinander) annähernd.

conversant [kən'vɜ:sənt] *adj pred* vertraut.

conversation [,kɒnvə'seɪʃən] *n* Gespräch *nt*, Unterhaltung *f*; (*Sch*) Konversation *f* ♦ **to make ~** sich unterhalten; (*small talk*) Konversation machen; **to get into/be in ~ with sb** mit jdm ins Gespräch kommen/im Gespräch sein; **deep in ~** ins Gespräch vertieft; **to have a ~/several ~s with sb (about sth)** sich mit jdm/oft mit jdm (über etw *acc*) unterhalten; **he has no ~** mit ihm kann man sich nicht unterhalten; **his ~ is so amusing** er ist ein unterhaltsamer Gesprächspartner; **a subject of ~** ein Gesprächsthema *nt*; **words used only in ~** Wörter, die nur in der gesprochenen Sprache gebraucht werden; **we only mentioned it in ~** wir haben das nur gesprächsweise erwähnt; **the art of ~** die Kunst der gepflegten Konversation *or* Unterhaltung.

conversational [,kɒnvə'seɪʃənl] *adj tone, style* Unterhaltungs-, Plauder-, leger ♦ **~ German** gesprochenes Deutsch; **his tone was quiet and ~** er sagte es in ruhigem Gesprächston; **that gave him a ~ opening** das ermöglichte es ihm, sich in die Unterhaltung einzuschalten *or* (*to get talking*) eine Unterhaltung anzufangen.

conversationalist [,kɒnvə'seɪʃnəlɪst] *n* guter Unterhalter *or* Gesprächspartner, gute Unterhalterin *or* Gesprächspartnerin ♦ **not much of a ~** nicht gerade ein Konversationsgenie.

conversationally [,kɒnvə'seɪʃnəlɪ] *adv write* im Plauderton.

conversation: ~ mode *n* (*Comput*) Dialogbetrieb *m*; **~ piece** *n* Gesprächsgegenstand *m*; **~ stopper** *n* **that was a real ~ stopper** das brachte die Unterhaltung zum Erliegen.

converse[1] [kən'vɜ:s] *vi* (*form*) sich unterhalten, konversieren (*old*).

converse[2] ['kɒnvɜ:s] [1] *adj* umgekehrt; (*Logic also*) konvers (*spec*); *opinions etc* gegenteilig.
[2] *n* (*opposite*) Gegenteil *nt*; (*Logic: proposition*) Umkehrung, Konverse (*spec*) *f* ♦ **the ~ is true** das Gegenteil trifft zu; **quite the ~** ganz im Gegenteil.

conversely [kɒn'vɜ:slɪ] *adv* umgekehrt.

conversion [kən'vɜ:ʃən] *n* **(a)** Konversion *f* (*into* in *+acc*); (*Fin, Sci also*) Umwandlung *f* (*into* in *+acc*); (*Rugby*) Verwandlung *f*; (*of measures*) Umrechnung *f* (*into* in *+acc*); (*of van, caravan etc*) Umrüstung *f*, Umbau *m*; (*model*) Spezialausführung *f*; (*of building*) Umbau *m* (*into* zu); (*of appliances*) Umstellung *f* (*to* auf *+acc*) ♦ **the attic flat is a ~** die Wohnung ist ein ausgebauter Dachstock; **~ table** Umrechnungstabelle *f*.
(b) (*Rel, fig*) Bekehrung, Konversion *f* (*to* zu).

convert ['kɒnvɜ:t] [1] *n* (*lit, fig*) Bekehrte(r) *mf*; (*to another denomination*) Konvertit *m* ♦ **to become a ~ to sth** (*lit, fig*) sich zu etw bekehren.
[2] [kən'vɜ:t] *vt* **(a)** konvertieren (*into* in *+acc*); (*Fin, Sci also*) umwandeln (*into* in *+acc*); (*Rugby*) verwandeln; *measures* umrechnen (*into* in *+acc*); *van, caravan etc* umrüsten, umbauen (*into* zu); *attic* ausbauen (*into* zu); *building* umbauen (*into* zu); *appliance* umstellen (*to* auf *+acc*) ♦ **a sofa that can be ~ed into a bed** ein Sofa, das sich in ein Bett verwandeln läßt; **most of the town has now been ~ed to natural gas** der größte Teil der Stadt ist jetzt auf Erdgas umgestellt.
(b) (*Rel, fig*) bekehren (*to* zu); (*to another denomination*) konvertieren.
[3] [kən'vɜ:t] *vi* sich verwandeln lassen (*into* in *+acc*).

converter [kən'vɜ:tə^r] *n* (*Elec*) Konverter *m*; (*for AC/DC*) Stromgleichrichter *m*.

convertibility [kən,vɜ:tə'bɪlɪtɪ] *n* (*of currency*) Konvertierbarkeit, Konvertibilität *f*; (*of appliances*) Umstellbarkeit *f*.

convertible [kən'vɜ:təbl] [1] *adj* verwandelbar; *currency* konvertibel, konvertierbar; *car* mit aufklappbarem Verdeck; *appliances* umstellbar ♦ **a ~ sofa** ein Sofa, das sich in ein Bett verwandeln läßt.
[2] *n* (*car*) Kabriolett, Kabrio *nt*.

convex [kɒn'veks] *adj lens, mirror* konvex, Konvex-.

convexity [kɒn'veksɪtɪ] *n* Konvexität *f*.

convey [kən'veɪ] *vt* **(a)** befördern; *goods* spedieren; *water* leiten.
(b) (*make known or felt*) *opinion, idea* vermitteln; (*make understood*) *meaning* klarmachen; (*transmit*) *message, order, best wishes* übermitteln, überbringen ♦ **what does this poem/music ~ to you?** was sagt Ihnen dieses Gedicht/diese Musik?; **words cannot ~ what I feel** was ich empfinde, läßt sich nicht mit Worten ausdrücken; **try to ~ to him that he should ...** versuchen Sie doch, ihm klarzumachen, daß er ... sollte.
(c) (*Jur*) *property* übertragen (*to* auf *+acc*).

conveyance [kən'veɪəns] *n* **(a)** (*transport*) Beförderung *f*; (*of goods also*) Spedition *f* ♦ **~ of goods** Güterverkehr *m*; **means of ~** Beförderungsmittel *nt*. **(b)** (*old, form: vehicle*) Gefährt *nt*. **public ~** öffentliches Verkehrsmittel. **(c)** (Eigentums)übertragung *f* (*to* auf *+acc*); (*document*) Übertragungsurkunde *f*.

conveyancing [kən'veɪənsɪŋ] *n* (*Jur*) (Eigentums)übertragung *f*.

conveyor [kən'veɪə^r] *n* (*of message etc*) Überbringer(in *f*) *m*; (*Tech*) Förderer *m* ♦ **~ belt** Fließband *nt*; (*for transport, supply*) Förderband *nt*.

convict ['kɒnvɪkt] [1] *n* Sträfling *m*, Zuchthäusler(in *f*) *m*.
[2] [kən'vɪkt] *vt* **(a)** (*Jur*) *person* verurteilen (*of* wegen), für schuldig erklären (*of gen*) ♦ **a ~ed criminal** ein verurteilter Verbrecher; **to get sb ~ed** jds Verurteilung (*acc*) bewirken.
(b) (*actions etc: betray*) überführen ♦ **to stand ~ed by one's own actions** durch sein Handeln überführt werden.
[3] [kən'vɪkt] *vi* jdn verurteilen ♦ **the jury refused to ~** die Geschworenen lehnten es ab, einen Schuldspruch zu fällen.

conviction [kən'vɪkʃən] *n* **(a)** (*Jur*) Verurteilung *f* ♦ **five previous ~s** fünf Vorstrafen; **to get a ~** (*police, prosecution*) einen Schuldspruch erreichen.
(b) (*belief, act of convincing*) Überzeugung *f* ♦ **to be open to ~** sich gern eines Besseren belehren lassen; **to carry ~** überzeugend klingen; **his speech lacked ~** seine Rede klang wenig überzeugend; **he's a socialist by ~** er ist ein überzeugter Sozialist; **he did it in the ~ that ...** er tat es in der Überzeugung, daß ...; **a man of strong ~s** ein Mann, der feste Anschauungen vertritt; **his fundamental political/moral ~s** seine politische/moralische Gesinnung; *see* **courage**.

▼ **convince** [kən'vɪns] *vt* überzeugen ♦ **I'm trying to ~ him that ...** ich versuche, ihn davon zu überzeugen, daß ...

convinced [kən'vɪnst] *adj* überzeugt.

▼ **convincing** *adj*, **~ly** *adv* [kən'vɪnsɪŋ, -lɪ] überzeugend.

convivial [kən'vɪvɪəl] *adj* heiter und unbeschwert; *person also* fröhlich; (*sociable*) gesellig.

conviviality [kən,vɪvɪ'ælɪtɪ] *n see adj* unbeschwerte Heiterkeit; Fröhlichkeit *f*; Geselligkeit *f*.

convocation [,kɒnvə'keɪʃən] *n* (*form*) (*calling together*) Einberufung *f*; (*meeting, Eccl*) Versammlung *f*.

convoke [kən'vəʊk] *vt meeting* einberufen; (*Parl also*) zusammentreten lassen.

convolute ['kɒnvəlu:t] *adj shell* spiralig aufgewunden; *petal, leaf* eingerollt.

convoluted ['kɒnvəlu:tɪd] *adj* **(a)** (*involved*) verwickelt; *plot also* verschlungen; *style* gewunden. **(b)** (*coiled*) gewunden; *shell* spiralig aufgewunden.

convolution [,kɒnvə'lu:ʃən] *n usu pl* Windung *f*; (*of plot*) Verschlungenheit *f no pl*; (*of style*) Gewundenheit *f no pl*.

convolvulus [kən'vɒlvjʊləs] *n* Winde *f*.

convoy ['kɒnvɔɪ] [1] *n* **(a)** (*escort*) Konvoi *m*, Geleit *nt* ♦ **under ~** mit Geleitschutz, unter Konvoi; **one of our ~ was torpedoed** eines unserer Geleitboote *or* Begleitboote wurde torpediert; **to be on ~ duty** als Geleitschutz abgeordnet sein.
(b) (*vehicles under escort, fig*) Konvoi *m*; (*ships also*) Verband *m* ♦ **in ~** im Konvoi/Verband.
[2] *vt* Geleitschutz geben (*+dat*), begleiten ♦ **the ships were ~ed across** die

➤ LANGUAGE IN USE: **convince** → 6.2, 15.1, 26.2 **convincing** → 26.1, 26.3

Schiffe wurden unter Konvoi hinübergebracht.

convulse [kən'vʌls] *vt* (*earthquake, war etc*) *land* erschüttern; (*fig also*) schütteln; *sb's body, muscles* krampfhaft zusammenziehen ◆ **to be ~d with laughter/pain** sich vor Lachen schütteln/Schmerzen krümmen; **a face ~d with rage/agony** ein vor Wut/Qual verzerrtes Gesicht; **a joke which ~d the audience** ein Witz *m*, bei dem sich das Publikum vor Lachen bog.

convulsion [kən'vʌlʃən] *n* **(a)** (*Med*) Schüttelkrampf *m no pl*, Konvulsion *f* (*spec*); (*caused by crying*) Weinkrampf *m no pl*. **(b)** (*caused by social upheaval etc*) Erschütterung *f*. **(c)** (*inf: of laughter*) **to go into/be in ~s** sich biegen *or* schütteln vor Lachen; **he had the audience in ~s** er rief beim Publikum wahre Lachstürme hervor.

convulsive [kən'vʌlsɪv] *adj* konvulsiv(isch) (*spec*), Krampf-; *movement also* krampfhaft ◆ **~ laughter** Lachkrämpfe *pl*.

convulsively [kən'vʌlsɪvlɪ] *adv* krampfartig ◆ **she laughed ~** sie schüttelte sich vor Lachen.

cony, coney ['kəʊnɪ] *n* **(a)** (*US*) Kaninchen *nt*. **(b)** (*also* **~ skin**) Kaninchenfell *nt*.

coo [ku:] [1] *vi* (*pigeon, fig*) gurren.
[2] *vt* gurren, girren.
[3] *n* Gurren, Girren *nt*.
[4] *interj* (*Brit inf*) ui.

cooee ['ku:i:] [1] *interj* huhu.
[2] *vi* huhu rufen.

cook [kʊk] [1] *n* Koch *m*, Köchin *f* ◆ **she is a good ~/good plain ~** sie kocht gut/sie kocht gute Hausmannskost; **too many ~s spoil the broth** (*Prov*) viele Köche verderben den Brei (*Prov*); **to be chief ~ and bottlewasher** (*inf*) Küchendienst machen.
[2] *vt* **(a)** *food, meal* machen, zubereiten; (*in water, milk etc*) kochen; (*fry, roast*) braten; *pie, pancake also* backen ◆ **how are you going to ~ the duck?** wie willst du die Ente zubereiten?; **a ~ed meal/breakfast/supper** eine warme Mahlzeit/ein warmes Abendessen/ein Frühstück *nt* mit warmen Gerichten; **to ~ sb's goose** (*fig*) jdm die Suppe versalzen.
(b) (*inf: falsify*) *accounts* frisieren (*inf*).
[3] *vi* (*person, food*) kochen; (*fry, roast*) braten; (*pie*) backen ◆ **it will ~ quickly** das ist schnell gekocht; **the pie ~s in half an hour** die Pastete ist in einer halben Stunde fertig; **what's ~ing?** (*fig inf*) was ist los?

◆**cook up** *vt sep* (*fig inf*) *story, excuse* sich (*dat*) einfallen lassen, zurechtbasteln (*inf*) ◆ **~ed ~ story** Lügenmärchen *nt*.

cookbook ['kʊkbʊk] *n* Kochbuch *nt*.

cooker ['kʊkə^r] *n* **(a)** (*Brit: stove*) Herd *m*. **(b)** (*apple*) Kochapfel *m*.

cookery ['kʊkərɪ] *n* Kochen *nt* (*also Sch*), Kochkunst *f* ◆ **French/native ~** französische/einheimische Küche; **~ book** Kochbuch *nt*; **~ classes** Kochkurs *m*; Kochkurse *pl*.

cookhouse ['kʊkhaʊs] *n* (*Naut*) Kombüse *f*; (*Mil*) Feldküche *f*.

cookie, cooky ['kʊkɪ] *n* **(a)** (*US: biscuit*) Keks *m*, Plätzchen *nt* ◆ **that's the way the ~ crumbles** (*inf, also Brit*) so ist das nun mal (im Leben), das ist der Lauf der Welt *or* der Dinge.
(b) (*inf: smart person*) Typ *m* ◆ **he's a pretty sharp/tough ~** er ist ein richtiger Schlauberger/ziemlich zäher Typ.

cooking ['kʊkɪŋ] *n* Kochen *nt*; (*food*) Essen *nt* ◆ **plain ~** einfaches Essen, Hausmannskost *f*; **French ~** die französische Küche, französisches Essen; **her ~ is atrocious** sie kocht miserabel.

cooking *in cpds* Koch-; **~ apple** *n* Kochapfel *m*; **~ chocolate** *n* Blockschokolade *f*; **~ foil** *n* Backfolie *f*; **~ salt** *n* Kochsalz *nt*.

cookout ['kʊkaʊt] *n* (*US*) Kochen *nt* am Lagerfeuer; (*on charcoal brazier*) Grillparty *f*.

cooky *n see* **cookie**.

cool [ku:l] [1] *adj* (*+er*) **(a)** *water, weather, drink* kühl; *clothes* luftig, leicht ◆ **serve ~** kalt *or* (gut) gekühlt servieren; **it's nice to slip into something ~** es ist angenehm, in etwas Luftiges *or* Leichtes schlüpfen zu können; **"keep in a ~ place"** „kühl aufbewahren".
(b) (*calm, unperturbed*) *person, manner* besonnen; *voice* kühl ◆ **to keep ~, to keep a ~ head** einen kühlen Kopf behalten; **keep ~!** reg dich nicht auf!, (nur) ruhig Blut!; **as ~ as you please** mit kühler Gelassenheit, in aller Seelenruhe.
(c) (*audacious*) kaltblütig, unverfroren (*pej*), kaltschnäuzig (*inf*) ◆ **as ~ as you please** mit größter Unverfrorenheit (*pej*), seelenruhig; **that was very ~ of him** da hat er sich ein starkes Stück geleistet.
(d) (*unenthusiastic, unfriendly*) *greeting, reception, look* kühl ◆ **to be ~ to(wards) sb** sich jdm gegenüber kühl verhalten; **play it ~!** immer mit der Ruhe!; **she decided to play it ~** sie entschied sich, ganz auf kühl zu machen.
(e) (*inf: with numbers etc*) glatt (*inf*) ◆ **he earns a ~ thirty thousand a year** er verdient glatte dreißigtausend im Jahr (*inf*).
(f) (*sl: great, smart*) *idea, disco, pub, dress etc* stark (*sl*), cool (*sl*) ◆ **~ jazz** Cool Jazz *m*.
[2] *n* **(a)** (*lit, fig*) Kühle *f* ◆ **in the ~ of the evening** in der Abendkühle; **to keep sth in the ~** etw kühl aufbewahren; **go/stay in the ~** geh ins Kühle/bleib im Kühlen.
(b) (*inf*) **keep your ~!** reg dich nicht auf!, immer mit der Ruhe!; **to lose one's ~** durchdrehen (*inf*); **he doesn't have the ~ to be a TV announcer** er hat nicht die Nerven für einen Fernsehansager.
[3] *vt* **(a)** kühlen; (*~ down*) abkühlen; *wine also* kalt stellen.
(b) (*sl*) **~ it!** (*don't get excited*) reg dich ab! (*inf*), mach mal langsam (*inf*); (*don't cause trouble*) mach keinen Ärger! (*inf*); **tell those guys to ~ it** sag den Typen, sie sollen keinen Ärger machen (*inf*); **I think we should ~ it** ich glaube wir sollten etwas langsamer treten (*inf*).
[4] *vi* (*lit, fig*) abkühlen; (*anger*) verrauchen, sich legen; (*enthusiasm, interest*) nachlassen ◆ **he has ~ed towards her** er ist ihr gegenüber kühler geworden.

◆**cool down** [1] *vi* **(a)** (*lit*) abkühlen; (*weather also, person*) sich abkühlen. **(b)** (*feelings etc*) sich abkühlen; (*anger also*) verrauchen; (*critical situation, person: calm down*) sich beruhigen ◆ **look, just ~ ~ will you!** komm, reg dich (bloß wieder) ab! (*inf*); **to let things ~ ~** die Sache etwas ruhen lassen.
[2] *vt sep* **(a)** *food, drink* abkühlen; (*let ~ ~*) abkühlen lassen ◆ **to ~ oneself ~** sich abkühlen. **(b)** *situation* beruhigen ◆ **put him in a cell, that'll ~ him ~** steck ihn in eine Zelle, dann wird er sich schon wieder beruhigen.

◆**cool off** *vi* **(a)** (*liquid, food*) abkühlen; (*person*) sich abkühlen.
(b) (*fig*) (sich) abkühlen; (*enthusiasm, interest*) nachlassen; (*become less angry*) sich beruhigen; (*become less friendly*) kühler werden (*about or towards sb* jdm gegenüber).

coolant ['ku:lənt] *n* Kühlmittel *nt*.

cool: ~ bag *n* Kühltasche *f*; **~ box** *n* Kühlbox *f*.

cooler ['ku:lə^r] *n* **(a)** (*for milk etc*) Kühlapparat *m*; (*for wine*) Kühler *m*. **(b)** (*sl: solitary*) Bau *m* (*inf*).

cool-headed [ku:l'hedɪd] *adj* kühl (und besonnen).

coolie ['ku:lɪ] *n* Kuli *m*.

cooling ['ku:lɪŋ] *adj drink, shower* kühlend; *effect* (ab)kühlend; *affection* abnehmend; *enthusiasm, interest* nachlassend ◆ **~ fan** Lüfter *m*.

cooling-off ['ku:lɪŋ'ɒf] *n* (*in relationship etc*) Abkühlung *f* ◆ **there's been a distinct ~ (of interest) about this project** das Interesse an diesem Projekt hat merklich nachgelassen.
[2] *adj* **~ period** (*gesetzlich festgelegter*) *Zeitraum für Schlichtungsverhandlungen* (*bei Arbeitskämpfen*).

cooling tower *n* Kühlturm *m*.

coolly ['ku:lɪ] *adv* **(a)** (*calmly*) ruhig, gefaßt, besonnen. **(b)** (*unenthusiastically, in an unfriendly way*) kühl. **(c)** (*audaciously*) kaltblütig, unverfroren (*pej*), kaltschnäuzig (*inf*).

coolness ['ku:lnɪs] *n see adj* **(a)** Kühle *f*; Luftigkeit, Leichtigkeit *f*. **(b)** Besonnenheit *f*; Kühle *f*. **(c)** Kaltblütigkeit, Unverfrorenheit (*pej*), Kaltschnäuzigkeit (*inf*) *f*. **(d)** Kühle *f*.

coomb [ku:m] *n* Tal(mulde *f*) *nt*.

coon [ku:n] *n* **(a)** (*Zool*) Waschbär *m*. **(b)** (*pej*) Nigger *m* (*pej*).

coop [ku:p] *n* (*also* **hen ~**) Hühnerstall *m* ◆ **to fly the ~** (*fig inf*) sich aus dem Staub machen (*inf*).

◆**coop up** *vt sep person* einsperren; *several people* zusammenpferchen (*inf*).

co-op ['kəʊ'ɒp] *n* Genossenschaft *f*; (*shop*) Coop, Konsum *m*.

cooper ['ku:pə^r] *n* Böttcher, Küfer (*dial*) *m*.

cooperate [kəʊ'ɒpəreɪt] *vi* kooperieren, zusammenarbeiten; (*go along with, not be awkward*) mitmachen ◆ **to ~ towards a common end** auf ein gemeinsames Ziel hinarbeiten; **even the weather ~d in making it a day to remember** auch das Wetter trug dazu bei, es zu einem denkwürdigen Tag zu machen; **if the weather ~s** wenn das Wetter mitmacht.

cooperation [kəʊ,ɒpə'reɪʃən] *n* Kooperation, Zusammenarbeit *f*; (*help*) Mitarbeit, Kooperation *f* ◆ **we produced this model in ~ with ...** wir haben dieses Modell in Gemeinschaftsarbeit *or* Kooperation *or* gemeinsam mit ... produziert; **to further ~ between EC countries** um die Kooperation *or* Zusammenarbeit zwischen EG-Ländern zu fördern; **with the ~ of all members then ...** wenn alle Mitglieder mitmachen, dann ...

cooperative [kəʊ'ɒpərətɪv] [1] *adj* **(a)** (*prepared to comply*) kooperativ; (*prepared to help*) hilfsbereit ◆ **if any member does not have a ~ attitude** wenn ein Mitglied nicht bereit ist mitzumachen.
(b) *firm* auf Genossenschaftsbasis ◆ **~ society** Genossenschaft, Kooperative *f*; **~ farm** Bauernhof *m* auf Genossenschaftsbasis; **~ bank** (*US*) Genossenschaftsbank *f*.
[2] *n* Genossenschaft, Kooperative *f*; (*also* **~ farm**) Bauernhof *m* auf Genossenschaftsbasis.

cooperatively [kəʊ'ɒpərətɪvlɪ] *adv see adj (a)* kooperativ; hilfsbereit.

coopt [kəʊ'ɒpt] *vt* selbst (hinzu)wählen, kooptieren (*spec*) ◆ **he was ~ed onto the committee** er wurde vom Komitee selbst dazugewählt.

coordinate [kəʊ'ɔ:dnɪt] [1] *adj* gleichwertig; (*in rank*) gleichrangig; (*Gram*) nebengeordnet (*with* zu) ◆ **~ geometry** analytische Geometrie.
[2] *n* (*Math etc*) Koordinate *f*; (*equal*) etwas Gleichwertiges ◆ **~s** (*clothes*) Kleidung *f* zum Kombinieren.
[3] [kəʊ'ɔ:dɪneɪt] *vt* **(a)** *movements, muscles, pieces of work* koordinieren; (*two people, firms*) *operations etc also* aufeinander abstimmen; *thoughts also* ordnen ◆ **to ~ one thing with another** eine Sache auf eine andere abstimmen.
(b) (*Gram*) nebenordnen, koordinieren ◆ **co-ordinating conjunction** nebenordnende *or* koordinierende Konjunktion.

coordination [kəʊ,ɔ:dɪ'neɪʃən] *n* Koordination, Koordinierung *f*.

coordinator [kəʊ'ɔ:dɪneɪtə^r] *n* Koordinator *m*; (*Gram*) koordinierende *or* nebenordnende Konjunktion.

coot [ku:t] *n* Wasserhuhn *nt* ◆ **bald as a ~** völlig kahl; **to be as bald as a ~** eine Platte haben (*inf*); **daft as a ~** (*inf*) doof (*inf*); (*mad*) leicht übergeschnappt (*inf*).

cootie ['ku:tɪ] *n* (*US inf*) Laus *f*.

co-owner ['kəʊ'əʊnə^r] *n* Mitbesitzer(in *f*), Miteigentümer(in *f*) *m*.

co-ownership ['kəʊ'əʊnəʃɪp] *n* Mitbesitz *m*.

cop [kɒp] [1] *n* **(a)** (*inf: policeman*) Polizist(in *f*), Bulle (*pej inf*) *m* ◆ **to play ~s and robbers** Räuber und Gendarm spielen. **(b)** (*Brit sl: arrest*) **it's a fair ~** jetzt hat's mich erwischt (*inf*). **(c)** (*Brit sl*) **it's no great ~** das ist nichts Besonderes.
[2] *vt* (*sl: catch*) *sb* schnappen (*inf*), erwischen (*inf*); *clout, thump* fangen (*inf*)

♦ **he ~ped one right on the nose** er fing eine genau auf der Nase (*inf*); **when they found out he didn't have a licence he really ~ped it** als sie herausfanden, daß er keinen Führerschein hatte, war er dran (*inf*); **hey, ~ a load of this!** he, hör dir das mal an! (*inf*).

♦**cop out** *vi* (*sl*) aussteigen (*sl*) (*of* aus).

cop *in cpds* (*sl*) Polizei-, Bullen- (*pej inf*).

copartner ['kəʊ'pɑːtnəʳ] *n* Teilhaber(in *f*), Partner *m*.

copartnership ['kəʊ'pɑːtnəʃɪp] *n* Teilhaberschaft, Partnerschaft *f*.

cope¹ [kəʊp] *n* **(a)** (*Eccl*) Pluviale *nt*. **(b)** (*Archit*) *see* **coping.**

cope² *vi* zurechtkommen; (*with work*) es schaffen ♦ **to ~ with** *difficulties, children, difficult person* fertigwerden mit, zurechtkommen mit; **how do you ~ all by yourself?** wie werden Sie so allein fertig?, wie kommen Sie so allein zurecht?; **I can't ~ with all this work** ich bin mit all der Arbeit überfordert; **she can't ~ with the stairs any more** sie schafft die Treppe nicht mehr.

Copenhagen [ˌkəʊpn'heɪgən] *n* Kopenhagen *nt*.

Copernican [kə'pɜːnɪkən] *adj* kopernikanisch.

Copernicus [kə'pɜːnɪkəs] *n* Kopernikus *m*.

copestone ['kəʊpstəʊn] *n* **(a)** (*Archit*) Abdeckplatte *f*. **(b)** (*fig*) (*of career etc*) Krönung *f*; (*of theory*) Schlußstein *m*.

copier ['kɒpɪəʳ] *n* (*copyist*) Kopist(in *f*) *m*; (*imitator also*) Nachmacher *m*; (*of writer, painter etc*) Imitator(in *f*) *m*; (*machine*) Kopiergerät *nt*, Kopierer *m* (*inf*).

co-pilot ['kəʊ'paɪlət] *n* Kopilot *m*.

coping ['kəʊpɪŋ] *n* Mauerkrone *f*.

coping: ~ saw *n* Laubsäge *f*; **~ stone** *n see* **copestone.**

copious ['kəʊpɪəs] *adj supply* groß, reichlich; *information, details, illustrations* zahlreich; *writer* fruchtbar ♦ **amidst ~ tears** unter einer Flut von Tränen.

copiously ['kəʊpɪəslɪ] *adv* reichlich ♦ **she wept ~** sie vergoß Ströme von Tränen.

copiousness ['kəʊpɪəsnɪs] *n see adj* Größe, Reichlichkeit *f*; Fülle *f*, Reichtum *m*; Fruchtbarkeit *f*.

cop-out ['kɒpaʊt] *n* (*sl: going back on sth*) Rückzieher *m* (*inf*); (*deliberate evasion*) Ausweichmanöver *nt* ♦ **this solution/translation is just a ~** diese Lösung/Übersetzung weicht dem Problem nur aus.

copper ['kɒpəʳ] *n* **(a)** (*metal*) Kupfer *nt*. **(b)** (*colour*) Kupferrot *nt*. **(c)** (*esp Brit inf: coin*) Pfennig *m* ♦ **~s** Kleingeld *nt*. **(d)** (*inf: policeman*) Polizist(in *f*), Bulle (*pej inf*) *m*. **(e)** (*for boiling clothes etc*) Kupferkessel, Waschkessel *m*.

copper: ~ beech *n* Rotbuche *f*; **~-bottomed** *adj* mit Kupferboden; (*Fin, fig*) gesund; **~-coloured** *adj* kupferfarben; **~ mine** *n* Kupfermine *f*; **~nob** *n* (*inf*) Rotkopf *m* (*inf*); **~plate** [1] *vt* verkupfern; [2] *n* **(a)** (*plate for engraving*) Kupferplatte *f*; (*engraving*) Kupferstich *m*; **(b)** (*handwriting*) lateinische (Ausgangs)schrift; [3] *adj* **~plate engraving** Kupferstich *m*; (*process also*) Kupferstechen *nt*; **~plate (hand)writing** lateinische (Ausgangs)schrift; **in your best ~plate writing** in deiner besten Sonntagsschrift; **he does this real ~plate handwriting** er schreibt wie gestochen; **~-plating** *n* Verkupferung *f*; **~smith** *n* Kupferschmied *m*.

coppery ['kɒpərɪ] *adj* kupfern, kupferrot.

coppice ['kɒpɪs] *n see* **copse.**

copra ['kɒprə] *n* Kopra *f*.

coprocessor ['kəʊ'prəʊsesəʳ] *n* (*Comput*) Koprozessor *m* ♦ **maths ~** Arithmetikprozessor *m*.

coprophilia ['kɒprəfɪlɪə] *n* Koprophilie *f*.

copse [kɒps] *n* Wäldchen *nt*.

cop-shop ['kɒpʃɒp] *n* (*Brit sl*) Revier *nt*.

copter ['kɒptəʳ] *n* (*inf*) Hubschrauber *m*.

Coptic ['kɒptɪk] *adj* koptisch.

copula ['kɒpjʊlə] *n* Kopula *f*, Satzband *nt*.

copulate ['kɒpjʊleɪt] *vi* kopulieren.

copulation [ˌkɒpjʊ'leɪʃən] *n* Kopulation *f*.

copulative ['kɒpjʊlətɪv] (*Gram*) [1] *n* Kopula *f*.
[2] *adj* kopulativ.

copy ['kɒpɪ] [1] *n* **(a)** Kopie *f* (*also Comput*); (*of document*) (*separately written or typed also*) Abschrift *f*; (*typed carbon also*) Durchschlag *m*; (*handwritten carbon also*) Durchschrift *f*; (*Phot*) Abzug *m* ♦ **to take** *or* **make a ~ of sth** eine Kopie/Zweitschrift *etc* von etw machen; **to write out a fair ~** etw ins reine schreiben, eine Reinschrift herstellen.
(b) (*of book etc*) Exemplar *nt* ♦ **have you got a ~ of today's "Times"?** hast du die „Times" von heute?
(c) (*Press etc*) (*subject matter*) Stoff *m*; (*material to be printed*) Artikel *m*; (*Typ*) (Manu)skript *nt* ♦ **that's always good ~** das zieht immer; **this murder story will make good ~** aus diesem Mord kann man etwas machen.
(d) (*in advertising*) Werbetext *m* ♦ **who did the ~ for this campaign?** wer hat den Text/die Texte für diese Werbekampagne gemacht?; **he writes good ~** er schreibt gute Werbetexte.
[2] *vi* (*imitate*) nachahmen; (*Sch etc*) abschreiben.
[3] *vt* **(a)** (*make a ~ of*) *see n* kopieren (*also Comput*); eine Abschrift anfertigen von; einen Durchschlag/eine Durchschrift machen von; abziehen; (*write out again*) abschreiben ♦ **to ~ sth to a disk** etw auf eine Diskette kopieren.
(b) (*imitate*) nachmachen; *gestures, person also* nachahmen ♦ **they always ~ Ford** sie machen Ford immer alles nach.
(c) (*Sch etc*) *sb else's work* abschreiben; (*painting*) abmalen ♦ **to ~ Brecht** (von) Brecht abschreiben.
(d) (*send a ~ to*) einen Durchschlag/eine Durchschrift senden an (*+acc*).

copy: ~book [1] *n* Schönschreibheft *nt*; *see* **blot;** [2] *adj attr* mustergültig, wie es/er/sie im Lehrbuch steht; **a ~book landing** eine Bilderbuchlandung; **~ boy** *n* (*Press*) Laufjunge *m*; **~cat** [1] *n* (*inf*) Nachahmer(in *f*) *m*; (*with written work*) Abschreiber(in *f*) *m*; **she's a terrible ~cat** sie macht immer alles nach; sie schreibt immer ab; **~cat!** Nachmachen gilt nicht! (*inf*); [2] *adj attr* **his was a ~cat crime** er war ein Nachahmungstäter; **~ desk** *n* (*Press*) Redaktionstisch *m*; **~-edit** *vt see* **~ editor** redigieren; lektorieren; bearbeiten; **~ editor** *n* (*Press*) Redakteur(in *f*) *m*; (*publishing also*) Lektor(in *f*) *m*; Manuskriptbearbeiter(in *f*) *m*.

copyist ['kɒpɪɪst] *n* Kopist(in *f*) *m*.

copy (*Comput*)**: ~-protected** *adj disk* kopiergeschützt; **~ protection** *n* Kopierschutz *m*.

copyreader ['kɒpɪriːdəʳ] *n see* **copy editor.**

copyright ['kɒpɪraɪt] [1] *n* Copyright, Urheberrecht *nt* ♦ **out of ~** urheberrechtlich nicht mehr geschützt.
[2] *adj* urheberrechtlich geschützt.
[3] *vt book* urheberrechtlich schützen; (*author*) urheberrechtlich schützen lassen.

copy: ~ typist *n* Schreibkraft *f*; **~writer** *n* Werbetexter(in *f*) *m*.

coquetry ['kɒkɪtrɪ] *n* Koketterie *f*.

coquette [kə'ket] *n* kokettes Mädchen, kokette Frau.

coquettish [kə'ketɪʃ] *adj* kokett, keß.

cor [kɔːʳ] *interj* (*Brit sl*) Mensch (*inf*), Mann (*sl*).

coracle ['kɒrəkl] *n kleines ovales Ruderboot aus mit Leder bezogenem Flechtwerk.*

coral ['kɒrəl] *n* **(a)** Koralle *f*. **(b)** (*colour*) Korallenrot *nt*.

coral *in cpds* Korallen-; **~-coloured** *adj* korallenfarbig; **~ island** *n* Koralleninsel *f*; **~ necklace** *n* Korallenkette *f*; **~ reef** *n* Korallenriff *nt*; **C~ Sea** *n* Korallenmeer *nt*; **~ snake** *n* Korallennatter *f*.

cor anglais ['kɔːrɒŋgleɪ] *n* (*esp Brit*) Englischhorn *nt*.

corbel ['kɔːbəl] *n* Kragstein *m*, Konsole *f*.

cord [kɔːd] [1] *n* **(a)** Schnur *f*; (*for clothes*) Kordel *f*; (*US Elec*) Schnur *f*. **(b) ~s** *pl* (*also* **a pair of ~s**) Kordhosen *pl*. **(c)** (*Tex*) *see* **corduroy. (d)** (*Anat*) *see* **spinal, umbilical, vocal.**
[2] *attr* Kord- ♦ **~ jacket** Kordjacke *f*; **~ trousers** Kordhosen *pl*.

cordage ['kɔːdɪdʒ] *n, no pl* Tauwerk *nt*.

corded ['kɔːdɪd] *adj* (*ribbed*) gerippt.

cordial ['kɔːdɪəl] [1] *adj* freundlich, höflich; *dislike* heftig.
[2] *n* (*drink*) Fruchtsaftkonzentrat *nt*; (*alcoholic*) Fruchtlikör *m*.

cordiality [ˌkɔːdɪ'ælɪtɪ] *n* Freundlichkeit, Höflichkeit *f*.

cordially ['kɔːdɪəlɪ] *adv* freundlich, höflich ♦ **~ yours** mit freundlichen Grüßen.

cordite ['kɔːdaɪt] *n* Cordit *nt*.

cordless ['kɔːdlɪs] *adj telephone* schnurlos.

cordon ['kɔːdn] [1] *n* **(a)** Kordon *m*, Postenkette *f* ♦ **to put** *or* **fling a ~ round sth** einen Kordon um etw ziehen, etw (hermetisch) abriegeln. **(b)** (*ribbon of an Order*) Kordon *m*, (Ordens)band *nt*. **(c)** (*Hort*) Kordon, Schnurbaum *m*.
[2] *vt see* **~ off.**

♦**cordon off** *vt sep area, building* absperren, abriegeln.

cordon bleu [ˌkɔːdɒn'blɜː] [1] *n* (*Cook*) (*award*) Meisterkochdiplom *nt*; (*chef, cook*) Meisterkoch *m*, Meisterköchin *f*.
[2] *adj cook* vorzüglich ♦ **she's taking a ~ cookery course** sie macht einen Kochkurs für die feine Küche (mit).

corduroy ['kɔːdərɔɪ] *n* Kordsamt *m* ♦ **~s** Kord(samt)hosen *pl*.

corduroy *in cpds* Kord(samt)-; **~ road** *n* Knüppeldamm *m*.

CORE [kɔːʳ] (*US*) *abbr of* **Congress of Racial Equality** *Verband m zur Bekämpfung von Rassendiskriminierung.*

core [kɔːʳ] [1] *n* (*lit, fig*) Kern *m*; (*of apple, pear*) Kernhaus *nt*, Butzen *m* (*dial*); (*of rock*) Innere(s) *nt*; (*of nuclear reactor*) Kern *m* ♦ **rotten/English to the ~** (*fig*) durch und durch schlecht/englisch; **to get to the ~ of the matter** (*fig*) zum Kern der Sache kommen.
[2] *adj attr issue* Kern-; (*Sch*) *subject* Haupt-, Pflicht-; *curriculum* Haupt-.
[3] *vt fruit* entkernen; *apple, pear* das Kernhaus (*+gen*) entfernen *or* ausschneiden.

corelate *vti see* **correlate.**

co-religionist ['kəʊrɪ'lɪdʒənɪst] *n* Glaubensgenosse *m*/-genossin *f*.

corer ['kɔːrəʳ] *n* (*Cook*) Apfelstecher *m*.

co-respondent ['kəʊrɪs'pɒndənt] *n* (*Jur*) Mitbeklagte(r) *or* Dritte(r) *mf* (*im Scheidungsprozeß*), Scheidungsgrund *m* (*hum*).

core time *n* Kernzeit *f*.

Corfu [kɔː'fuː] *n* Korfu *nt*.

corgi ['kɔːgɪ] *n* Corgi *m*.

coriander [ˌkɒrɪ'ændəʳ] *n* Koriander *m*.

Corinth ['kɒrɪnθ] *n* Korinth *nt*.

Corinthian [kə'rɪnθɪən] [1] *adj* korinthisch.
[2] *n* Korinther(in *f*) *m* ♦ **~s** *+sing vb* (*Eccl*) Korinther *pl*.

Coriolanus ['kɒrɪə'leɪnəs] *n* Coriolan *m*.

cork [kɔːk] [1] *n* **(a)** *no pl* (*substance*) Kork *m*. **(b)** (*stopper*) Korken *m* ♦ **put a ~ in it!** (*inf*) halt die Klappe! (*inf*). **(c)** (*Fishing: also* **~ float**) Schwimmer *m*.
[2] *vt* (*also* **~ up**) *bottle, wine* zu- *or* verkorken.
[3] *adj* Kork-, korken (*rare*).

corkage ['kɔːkɪdʒ] *n* Korkengeld *nt*.

corked [kɔːkt] *adj* **the wine is ~** der Wein schmeckt nach Kork.

corker ['kɔːkəʳ] *n* (*dated sl*) **a ~** einsame Klasse (*inf*).

cork *in cpds* Kork-; **~ flooring** *n* Kork(fuß)boden *m*.

corking ['kɔːkɪŋ] *adj* (*dated Brit sl*) Klasse- (*inf*).

cork: ~screw *n* Korkenzieher *m*; **~screw curls** *npl* Korkenzieherlocken *pl*; **~ shoes** *npl* Schuhe *pl* mit Korksohlen; **~ tile** *n* Korkfliese *f*; **~-tipped** *adj* *cigarette* mit Korkfilter; ~ **tree** *n* Korkbaum *m.*

corky ['kɔːkɪ] *adj* Kork-, korkartig; *taste* Kork-, korkig.

corm [kɔːm] *n* Knolle *f.*

cormorant ['kɔːmərənt] *n* Kormoran *m.*

corn[1] [kɔːn] *n* **(a)** *no pl* (*cereal*) Getreide, Korn *nt.* **(b)** (*seed of* ~) Korn *nt.* **(c)** *no pl* **sweet~** (*esp US: maize*) Mais *m*; *see* **cob.**

corn[2] *n* Hühnerauge *nt* ♦ ~ **plaster** Hühneraugenpflaster *nt*; **to tread on sb's ~s** (*fig*) jdm auf die Hühneraugen treten.

corn[3] *n* (*inf*) (*sentiment etc*) Kitsch *m*, sentimentales Zeug; (*trite humour*) olle Kamellen *pl* (*inf*).

corn: C~ Belt *n* (*Geog*) Getreidegürtel *m*; ~ **bread** *n* (*US*) Maisbrot *nt*; **~bunting** *n* (*Orn*) Grauammer *f*; ~ **chandler** *n* Kornhändler *m*; **~cob** *n* Maiskolben *m*; **~-coloured** *adj* strohfarben, strohgelb; **~crake** *n* (*Orn*) Wachtelkönig *m*; **~crib** *n* (*US*) Maisspeicher *m*; ~ **dodger** *n* (*US*) Maisfladen *m.*

cornea ['kɔːnɪə] *n* Hornhaut, Cornea (*spec*) *f.*

corned beef ['kɔːnd'biːf] *n* Corned beef *nt.*

corner ['kɔːnəʳ] [1] *n* **(a)** (*generally, Boxing*) Ecke *f*; (*of sheet also*) Zipfel *m*; (*of mouth, eye*) Winkel *m*; (*sharp bend in road*) Kurve *f*; (*fig: awkward situation*) Klemme *f* (*inf*) ♦ **at** *or* **on the ~** an der Ecke; **the teacher made him stand in the ~** der Lehrer stellte ihn in die Ecke; **it's just round the ~** es ist gleich um die Ecke; **to turn the ~** (*lit*) um die Ecke biegen; **we've turned the ~ now** (*fig*) wir sind jetzt über den Berg; **the pages are curling up at the ~s** die Seiten haben Eselsohren; **out of the ~ of one's eye** aus dem Augenwinkel (heraus); **he always has a cigarette hanging out of the ~ of his mouth** er hat immer eine Zigarette im Mundwinkel (hängen); **to cut ~s** (*lit*) Kurven schneiden; (*fig*) das Verfahren abkürzen; **to drive sb into a ~** (*fig*) jdn in die Enge treiben; **all four ~s of the world** alle vier Winde; **he has travelled to all four ~s of the world** er hat die ganze Welt bereist; **in every ~ of Europe/the globe/the house** in allen (Ecken und) Winkeln Europas/der Erde/des Hauses; **an attractive ~ of Britain** eine reizvolle Gegend Großbritanniens.
(b) (*out-of-the-way place*) Winkel *m* ♦ **have you got an odd ~ somewhere where I could store my books?** hast du irgendwo ein Eckchen *or* Plätzchen, wo ich meine Bücher lagern könnte?
(c) (*Comm: monopoly*) Monopol *nt* ♦ **to make/have a ~ in sth** das Monopol für *or* auf etw (*acc*) erwerben/haben.
(d) (*Ftbl*) Ecke *f*, Eckball, Corner (*Aus*) *m* ♦ **to take a ~** eine Ecke ausführen.
[2] *vt* **(a)** (*lit, fig: trap*) in die Enge treiben.
(b) (*Comm*) *the market* monopolisieren.
[3] *vi* (*take a* ~) (*person*) Kurven/die Kurve nehmen ♦ **this car ~s well** dieses Auto hat eine gute Kurvenlage.

corner *in cpds* Eck-; ~ **cabinet** *n* Eckschrank *m*; ~ **chair** *n* Eckstuhl *m.*

-cornered ['kɔːnəd] *adj suf* -eckig ♦ **three-~** dreieckig.

corner flag *n* (*Sport*) Eckfahne *f.*

cornering ['kɔːnərɪŋ] *n* (*of car*) Kurvenlage *f*; (*of driver*) Kurventechnik *f.*

corner: ~ kick *n* (*Ftbl*) Eckstoß *m*; ~ **post** *n* (*Ftbl*) Eckfahne *f*; ~ **seat** *n* (*Rail*) Eckplatz *m*; ~ **shop** *n* Laden *m* an der Ecke; **~stone** *n* (*lit, fig*) Grundstein, Eckstein *m*; ~ **table** *n* Tisch *m* in der Ecke, Ecktisch *m*; **~ways, ~wise** *adv* über Eck, diagonal.

cornet ['kɔːnɪt] *n* **(a)** (*Mus*) Kornett *nt.* **(b)** (*ice-cream* ~) (Eis)tüte *f.*

corn: C~ Exchange *n* Getreidebörse *f*; **~-fed** *adj* mit Getreide gefüttert; **~field** *n* (*Brit*) Korn- *or* Weizenfeld *nt*; (*US*) Maisfeld *nt*; **~flakes** *npl* Cornflakes *pl*; **~flour** *n* (*Brit*) Stärkemehl *nt*; **~flower** [1] *n* **(a)** Kornblume *f*; **(b)** (*colour*) Kornblumenblau *nt*; [2] *adj* (*also* **~flower blue**) kornblumenblau.

cornice ['kɔːnɪs] *n* (*Archit: of wall, column*) (Ge)sims *nt*; (*fig: of snow*) Wächte *f.*

Cornish ['kɔːnɪʃ] [1] *adj* kornisch, aus Cornwall ♦ ~ **pasty** (*Brit*) *Gebäckstück nt aus Blätterteig mit Fleischfüllung.*
[2] *n* (*dialect*) Kornisch *nt.*

Cornishman ['kɔːnɪʃmən] *n, pl* **-men** [-mən] Bewohner *m* Cornwalls.

corn: ~meal *n* (*US*) Maismehl *nt*; ~ **oil** *n* (Mais)keimöl *nt*; ~ **pone** *n* (*US*) *see* ~ **bread**; ~ **poppy** *n* Klatschmohn *m*, Mohnblume *f*; ~ **shock** *n* (Getreide)garbe *f*; **~starch** *n* (*US*) Stärkemehl *nt*; ~ **syrup** *n* (*US*) (Mais)sirup *m.*

cornucopia [kɔːnjʊ'kəʊpɪə] *n* (*Myth, horn-shaped container*) Füllhorn *nt*; (*fig: abundance*) Fülle *f.*

corn whisky *n* (*US*) Maiswhisky *m.*

corny ['kɔːnɪ] *adj* (+*er*) (*inf*) *joke* blöd (*inf*); (*sentimental*) kitschig ♦ **what a ~ old joke!** der Witz hat (so) einen Bart (*inf*).

corolla [kə'rɒlə] *n* (*Bot*) Blumenkrone, Korolla (*spec*) *f.*

corollary [kə'rɒlərɪ] [1] *n* (logische) Folge, Korollar *nt* (*also Math*) ♦ **this would prove, as a ~, that ...** damit würde dann gleichzeitig auch bewiesen, daß ...
[2] *adj* Begleit-.

corona [kə'rəʊnə] *n* (*Astron*) (*of sun, moon etc*) Hof *m*; (*part of sun's atmosphere*) Korona *f*; (*of tooth*) Krone *f*; (*Bot*) Nebenkrone *f*; (*cigar*) Corona *f.*

coronary ['kɒrənərɪ] [1] *adj* (*Med*) Koronar- (*spec*) ♦ ~ **artery** Kranzarterie *f*; ~ **failure** Herzversagen *nt* (*inf*), Koronarinsuffizienz *f*; ~ **thrombosis** Herzinfarkt *m.*
[2] *n* Herzinfarkt *m.*

coronation [,kɒrə'neɪʃən] *n* Krönung *f.*

coronation *in cpds* Krönungs-; ~ **robes** *npl* Krönungsgewänder *pl.*

coroner ['kɒrənəʳ] *n Beamter, der Todesfälle untersucht, die nicht eindeutig eine natürliche Ursache haben* ♦ **~'s inquest** *Untersuchung f nicht eindeutig natürlicher Todesfälle*; **~'s jury** *Untersuchungskommission f bei nicht eindeutig natürlichen Todesfällen.*

coronet ['kɒrənɪt] *n* Krone *f*; (*jewellery*) Krönchen *nt.*

corp. *abbr of* **corporation.**

corporal[1] ['kɔːpərəl] *n* (*abbr* **corp**) (*Mil*) Stabsunteroffizier *m.*

corporal[2] *adj* körperlich; *pleasures, needs* leiblich ♦ ~ **punishment** Prügel- *or* Körperstrafe *f.*

corporate ['kɔːpərɪt] *adj* **(a)** (*of a group*) gemeinsam, korporativ ♦ ~ **action/decision** geschlossenes *or* gemeinsames Vorgehen/gemeinsame Entscheidung; **to work for the ~ good** für das Gemeinwohl arbeiten; **to take out ~ membership of another society** als geschlossene Gruppe Mitglied eines anderen Vereins werden.
(b) (*of a corporation*) korporativ; (*of a company*) Firmen-; (*Jur*) Korporations- ♦ **I'm not a ~ man** ich bin ein Mensch, der sich in großen Firmen nicht wohl fühlt; **the ~ life of an organization** das Leben in einer großen Vereinigung; **I was meaning "we" in the ~ sense** ich meinte „wir" als Firma; **our ~ liabilities** unsere Verbindlichkeiten als Firma; ~ **body** Körperschaft *f*; ~ **finance** Unternehmensfinanzen *pl*; ~ **financing** Unternehmensfinanzierung *f*; ~ **hospitality** *Unterhaltung und Bewirtung von Firmenkunden*; ~ **identity** Firmenimage *nt*; ~ **law** Gesellschaftsrecht *nt*; ~ **planning** Unternehmensplanung *f.*

corporately ['kɔːpərɪtlɪ] *adv see adj* **(a)** gemeinsam. **(b)** körperschaftlich.

corporation [,kɔːpə'reɪʃən] *n* **(a)** (*municipal* ~) Gemeinde, Stadt *f* ♦ **the Mayor and C~** der Bürgermeister und die Stadt.
(b) (*Brit Comm: incorporated company*) Handelsgesellschaft *f*; (*US Comm: limited liability company*) Gesellschaft *f* mit beschränkter Haftung ♦ **private/public ~** (*Comm*) Privatunternehmen *nt*/staatliches Unternehmen.
(c) (*Brit hum: large belly*) Schmerbauch *m.*

corporation: ~ bus *n* Stadtbus *m*, städtischer Omnibus; ~ **property** *n* gemeindeeigener Besitz; ~ **tax** *n* Körperschaftssteuer *f*; ~ **tram** *n* städtische Straßenbahn; ~ **transport** *n* städtisches Verkehrsmittel.

corporatism ['kɔːpərɪtɪzəm] *n* **the growth of ~** die steigende Zahl der Großunternehmen; **a sense of ~** ein Zusammengehörigkeitsgefühl *nt* innerhalb des/eines Unternehmens.

corporeal [kɔː'pɔːrɪəl] *adj* körperlich.

corps [kɔːʳ] *n, pl* - (*Mil*) Korps *nt* ♦ ~ **de ballet** Corps de ballet *nt*; ~ **diplomatique** diplomatisches Korps; *see* **diplomatic ~.**

corpse [kɔːps] [1] *n* Leiche *f*, Leichnam *m* (*geh*).
[2] *vi* (*Theat sl*) einen Lachanfall bekommen.

corpulence ['kɔːpjʊləns] *n* Korpulenz *f.*

corpulent ['kɔːpjʊlənt] *adj* korpulent.

corpus ['kɔːpəs] *n* **(a)** (*collection*) Korpus *m*; (*of opinions*) Paket *nt.* **(b)** (*main body*) Großteil *m* ♦ **the main ~ of his work** der Hauptteil seiner Arbeit. **(c)** (*Fin*) Stammkapital *nt.*

Corpus Christi ['kɔːpəs'krɪstɪ] *n* (*Eccl*) Fronleichnam *m.*

corpuscle ['kɔːpʌsl] *n* Korpuskel *nt* (*spec*) ♦ **blood ~** Blutkörperchen *nt.*

corpuscular [kɔː'pʌskjuːləʳ] *adj* Korpuskular- (*spec*).

corpus delicti ['kɔːpəsdə'lɪktaɪ] *n* (*Jur*) Corpus delicti *nt*; (*corpse*) Leiche *f.*

corral [kə'rɑːl] [1] *n* Korral *m.*
[2] *vt cattle* in den Korral treiben.

correct [kə'rekt] [1] *adj* **(a)** (*right*) richtig; *answer, pronunciation also* korrekt; *time also* genau ♦ **am I ~ in thinking that ...?** gehe ich recht in der Annahme, daß ...?
(b) (*proper, suitable, perfectly mannered*) korrekt ♦ **it's the ~ thing to do** das gehört sich so.
[2] *vt* **(a)** korrigieren; *person, pronunciation, error etc also* berichtigen, verbessern; *bad habit* sich/jdm abgewöhnen ♦ **to ~ proofs** Korrektur lesen; **~ me if I'm wrong** Sie können mich gern berichtigen; **I stand ~ed** ich nehme alles zurück.
(b) (*old*) (*by punishment, scolding*) maßregeln; (*by corporal punishment*) züchtigen.

correction [kə'rekʃən] *n see vt* **(a)** Korrektion, Korrektur *f*, Berichtigung, Verbesserung *f*, Abgewöhnung *f* ♦ ~ **of proofs** Korrekturlesen *nt*; **I am open to ~** ich lasse mich gerne berichtigen; **to do one's ~s** (*Sch*) die Verbesserung machen; ~ **key** Korrekturtaste *f*; ~ **tape** (*on typewriter*) Korrekturband *nt.*
(b) (*old*) Maßregelung *f*, Züchtigung *f* ♦ **house of ~** Besserungsanstalt *f.*

correctitude [kə'rektɪtjuːd] *n see* **correctness (b).**

corrective [kə'rektɪv] [1] *adj* korrigierend ♦ **to take ~ action** korrigierend eingreifen; **to have ~ surgery** sich einem korrigierenden Eingriff unterziehen.
[2] *n* (*Pharm*) Korrektiv *nt.*

correctly [kə'rektlɪ] *adv* **(a)** (*accurately*) richtig; *answer, pronounce also* korrekt ♦ **he had ~ assumed that ...** er hatte richtigerweise angenommen, daß ... **(b)** (*in proper way*) *behave, speak, dress* korrekt.

correctness [kə'rektnɪs] *n* **(a)** (*accuracy*) Richtigkeit *f.* **(b)** (*of behaviour etc*) Korrektheit *f.*

correlate ['kɒrɪleɪt] [1] *vt two things* zueinander in Beziehung setzen, korrelieren (*geh*) ♦ **to ~ sth with sth** etw mit etw in Beziehung setzen, etw mit etw korrelieren (*geh*).
[2] *vi* (*two things*) sich entsprechen ♦ **to ~ with sth** mit etw in Beziehung stehen.

correlation [,kɒrɪ'leɪʃən] *n* (*correspondence*) Beziehung *f*; (*close relationship*) enger *or* direkter Zusammenhang; (*Math, Statistics*) Korrelation *f.*

correlative [kɒ'relətɪv] [1] *n* Korrelat *nt.*
[2] *adj* (*directly related*) entsprechend; (*Gram*) korrelativ.

▼ **correspond** [,kɒrɪs'pɒnd] *vi* **(a)** (*be equivalent*) entsprechen (*to, with dat*); (*two or more: to one another*) sich entsprechen; (*be in accordance also*) sich decken (*with* mit) ♦ **your version doesn't ~** Ihre Version deckt sich nicht damit.
(b) (*exchange letters*) korrespondieren (*with* mit).

➤ LANGUAGE IN USE: **correspond: a → 5.4**

correspondence [ˌkɒrɪsˈpɒndəns] *n* **(a)** *(agreement, equivalence)* Übereinstimmung *f (between* zwischen, *with* mit).
(b) *(letter-writing)* Korrespondenz *f*; *(letters also)* Briefe *pl*; *(in newspaper)* Leserzuschriften *or* -briefe *pl* ◆ **to be in ~ with sb** mit jdm in Korrespondenz stehen *(form)*, mit jdm korrespondieren; *(private)* mit jdm in Briefwechsel stehen, mit jdm korrespondieren *(geh)*.
correspondence: ~ card *n* Briefkarte *f*; **~ column** *n (Press)* Leserbriefspalte *f*; **~ course** *n* Fernkurs *m*; **~ school** *n* Fernlehrinstitut *nt*.
correspondent [ˌkɒrɪsˈpɒndənt] 1 *n* **(a)** *(letter-writer)* Briefschreiber(in *f*) *m* ◆ **to be a good/bad ~** ein eifriger Briefschreiber sein/schreibfaul sein; **according to my ~** wie man mir geschrieben hat. **(b)** *(Press)* Korrespondent(in *f*) *m*. **(c)** *(Comm)* Entsprechung *f*, Gegenstück *nt*.
2 *adj see* **corresponding.**
corresponding [ˌkɒrɪsˈpɒndɪŋ] *adj* entsprechend.
correspondingly [ˌkɒrɪsˈpɒndɪŋlɪ] *adv* (dem)entsprechend.
corridor [ˈkɒrɪdɔːʳ] *n* Korridor *m*; *(in building also, in train, bus)* Gang *m* ◆ **in the ~s of power** an den Schalthebeln der Macht; **~ train** D-Zug *m*.
corrie [ˈkɒrɪ] *n (Geol)* Kar *m*.
corrigendum [kɒrɪˈdʒendəm] *n, pl* **corrigenda** [kɒrɪˈdʒendə] Corrigendum *nt (geh)*.
corroborate [kəˈrɒbəreɪt] *vt* bestätigen; *theory also* bekräftigen, erhärten, untermauern.
corroboration [kəˌrɒbəˈreɪʃən] *n see vt* Bestätigung *f*; Bekräftigung, Erhärtung, Untermauerung *f* ◆ **in ~ of** zur Untermauerung *or* Unterstützung *(+gen)*; **through lack of ~** *(Jur)* mangels unterstützenden Beweismaterials; *(from witnesses)* mangels bestätigender Zeugenaussagen.
corroborative [kəˈrɒbərətɪv] *adj see vt* bestätigend; bekräftigend, erhärtend, untermauernd *all attr* ◆ **to be ~ of sth** etw bestätigen/untermauern.
corrode [kəˈrəʊd] 1 *vt metal* zerfressen; *(fig)* zerstören.
2 *vi (metal)* korrodieren.
corrosion [kəˈrəʊʒən] *n* Korrosion *f*; *(fig)* Zerstörung *f*.
corrosive [kəˈrəʊzɪv] 1 *adj* korrosiv; *(fig)* zerstörend.
2 *n* Korrosion verursachendes Mittel.
corrugated [ˈkɒrəgeɪtɪd] *adj* gewellt ◆ **~ cardboard** dicke Wellpappe; **~ iron** Wellblech *nt*; **~ paper** Wellpappe *f*.
corrugation [ˌkɒrəˈgeɪʃən] *n* Welle *f*.
corrupt [kəˈrʌpt] 1 *adj* verdorben, verworfen, schlecht; *(open to bribery)* korrupt, bestechlich; *text, language* verderbt, korrumpiert; *(Comput) disk* korrupt.
2 *vt (morally)* verderben; *(ethically)* korrumpieren; *(form: bribe)* bestechen, korrumpieren; *(Comput) data* korrumpieren ◆ **to become ~ed** *(text, language)* korrumpiert werden.
corruptible [kəˈrʌptəbl] *adj* korrumpierbar; *(bribable also)* bestechlich.
corruption [kəˈrʌpʃən] *n* **(a)** *(act)* *(of person)* Korruption *f*; *(by bribery also)* Bestechung *f*; *(Comput: of data)* Korrumpierung *f*.
(b) *(corrupt nature)* Verdorbenheit, Verderbtheit *f*; *(by bribery)* Bestechlichkeit *f*; *(of morals)* Verfall *m*; *(of language, text)* Korrumpierung *f*.
(c) *(form: decay of bodies etc)* Zersetzung, Fäulnis *f*.
corsage [kɔːˈsɑːʒ] *n* **(a)** *(bodice)* Mieder *nt*. **(b)** *(flowers)* Ansteckblume *f*.
corsair [ˈkɔːsɛəʳ] *n (ship)* Piratenschiff *nt*, Korsar *m*; *(pirate)* Pirat, Korsar *m*.
corselet [kɔːsəˈlet] *n* **(a)** *(corset)* Korselett *nt*. **(b)** *see* **corslet.**
corset [ˈkɔːsɪt] *n (also* **~s***)* Korsett *nt*; *(to give wasp waist)* Schnürmieder *nt* ◆ **surgical ~** Stützkorsett *nt*.
corseted [ˈkɔːsɪtɪd] *adj* geschnürt.
corsetry [ˈkɔːsɪtrɪ] *n* Miederwarenherstellung *f*; *(corsets)* Miederwaren *pl* ◆ **~ department** Miederwarenabteilung *f*.
Corsica [ˈkɔːsɪkə] *n* Korsika *nt*.
Corsican [ˈkɔːsɪkən] 1 *adj* korsisch ◆ **~ holiday** Urlaub auf Korsika.
2 *n* **(a)** Korse *m*, Korsin *f*. **(b)** *(language)* Korsisch *nt*.
corslet [ˈkɔːslɪt], **corselet** *n* Brust- (und Rücken)panzer *m*.
cortège [kɔːˈteɪʒ] *n (retinue)* Gefolge *nt*; *(procession)* Prozession *f*; *(funeral ~)* Leichenzug *m*.
cortex [ˈkɔːteks] *n, pl* **cortices** *(Anat)* *(of brain)* Hirnrinde *f*; *(of kidney)* Nierenrinde *f*; *(Bot)* Kortex *m*.
cortical [ˈkɔːtɪkl] *adj (Anat, Bot)* kortikal.
cortices [ˈkɔːtɪsiːz] *pl of* **cortex.**
cortisone [ˈkɔːtɪzəʊn] *n* Kortison *nt*.
corundum [kəˈrʌndəm] *n (Geol)* Korund *m*.
coruscate [ˈkɒrəskeɪt] *vi* funkeln ◆ **coruscating wit/humour** *(fig)* sprühender Geist/Witz.
corvette [kɔːˈvet] *n (Naut)* Korvette *f*.
cos¹ [kɒs] *abbr of* **cosine** cos.
cos² *n (also* **~ lettuce***)* Romagna-Salat, römischer Salat *m*.
cos³ *conj (inf)* = **because.**
cosec [ˈkəʊsek] *abbr of* **cosecant** cosec.
cosecant [ˈkəʊsekænt] *n* Kosekans *m*.
cosh [kɒʃ] 1 *vt* auf den Schädel schlagen, eins über den Schädel ziehen *(+dat) (inf)*.
2 *n (instrument)* Totschläger *m*; *(blow)* Schlag *m* (auf den Kopf).
cosignatory [ˈkəʊˈsɪgnətərɪ] *n* Mitunterzeichner(in *f*) *m*.
cosine [ˈkəʊsaɪn] *n* Kosinus *m*.
cosiness, *(US)* **coziness** [ˈkəʊzɪnɪs] *n* Gemütlichkeit, Behaglichkeit *f*; *(warmth)* mollige Wärme; *(of chat)* Freundschaftlichkeit, Traulichkeit *(dated) f*.
cosmetic [kɒzˈmetɪk] 1 *adj (lit, fig)* kosmetisch ◆ **~ surgery** kosmetische Chirurgie; **she's had ~ surgery** sie hat eine Schönheitsoperation gehabt.
2 *n* Kosmetikum, Schönheitspflegemittel *nt*.
cosmetician [kɒzməˈtɪʃən] *n* Kosmetiker(in *f*) *m*.
cosmic [ˈkɒzmɪk] *adj* kosmisch ◆ **~ dust** Weltraumnebel *m*.
cosmogony [kɒzˈmɒgənɪ] *n* Kosmogonie *f*.
cosmography [kɒzˈmɒgrəfɪ] *n* Kosmographie *f*.
cosmologist [kɒzˈmɒlədʒɪst] *n* Kosmologe *m*, Kosmologin *f*.
cosmology [kɒzˈmɒlədʒɪ] *n* Kosmologie *f*.
cosmonaut [ˈkɒzmənɔːt] *n* Kosmonaut(in *f*) *m*.
cosmopolitan [ˌkɒzməˈpɒlɪtən] 1 *adj* kosmopolitisch, international.
2 *n* Kosmopolit, Weltbürger *m*.
cosmos [ˈkɒzmɒs] *n* **(a)** Kosmos *m*. **(b)** *(Bot)* Kosmee *f*.
cossack [ˈkɒsæk] 1 *n* Kosak(in *f*) *m*.
2 *adj* Kosaken- ◆ **~ hat** Kosakenmütze *f*.
cosset [ˈkɒsɪt] *vt* verwöhnen.
cost [kɒst] *(vb: pret, ptp ~)* 1 *vt* **(a)** *(lit, fig)* kosten ◆ **how much does it ~?** wieviel kostet es?; **how much will it ~ to have it repaired?** wieviel kostet die Reparatur?; **it ~ (him) a lot of money** das hat (ihn) viel Geld gekostet; **driving without a seat belt ~ him dear** Fahren ohne Sicherheitsgurt kam ihn teuer zu stehen; **it ~ him a great effort/a lot of time** es kostete ihn viel Mühe/viel Zeit; **that mistake could ~ you your life** der Fehler könnte dich das Leben kosten; **~ what it may** koste es, was es wolle; **politeness doesn't ~ (you) anything** es kostet (dich) nichts, höflich zu sein; **it'll ~ you** *(inf)* das kostet dich was *(inf)*.
(b) *pret, ptp* **~ed** *(work out ~ of) project etc* veranschlagen.
(c) *pret, ptp* **~ed** *(Comm: put a price on) articles for sale* auspreisen *(at* zu).
2 *n* **(a)** Kosten *pl (of* für) ◆ **to bear the ~ of sth** die Kosten für etw tragen, für die Kosten von etw aufkommen; **the ~ of electricity/petrol these days** die Strom-/Benzinpreise heutzutage; **to buy sth at great ~** etw zu einem hohen Preis kaufen; **at little ~ to oneself** ohne große eigene Kosten; **to buy sth at ~** etw zum Selbstkostenpreis kaufen; **~ of sales** Verkaufskosten *pl*.
(b) *(fig)* Preis *m* ◆ **at all ~s** um jeden Preis; **whatever the ~** kostet es, was es wolle; **at the ~ of one's health/job/marriage** *etc* auf Kosten seiner Gesundheit/Stelle/Ehe *etc*; **at great/little personal ~** unter großen/geringen eigenen Kosten; **he found out to his ~ that ...** er machte die bittere Erfahrung, daß ...
(c) *(Jur)* **~s** *pl* Kosten *pl* ◆ **to be ordered to pay ~s** zur Übernahme der Kosten verurteilt werden.
◆**cost out** *vt sep* (kostenmäßig) kalkulieren.
Costa Brava [ˈkɒstəˈbrɑːvə] *n* Costa Brava *f*.
cost: ~ accountant *n* Kostenbuchhalter(in *f*) *m*; **~ accounting** *n* Kalkulation *f*.
Costa del Sol [ˈkɒstədelˈsɒl] *n* Costa del Sol *f*.
co-star [ˈkəʊstɑːʳ] 1 *n (Film, Theat)* einer der Hauptdarsteller ◆ **Burton and Taylor were ~s** Burton und Taylor spielten die Hauptrollen.
2 *vt* **the film ~s R. Burton** der Film zeigt R. Burton in einer der Hauptrollen.
3 *vi* als Hauptdarsteller auftreten.
Costa Rica [ˈkɒstəˈriːkə] *n* Costa Rica *nt*.
Costa Rican [ˈkɒstəˈriːkən] 1 *adj* costaricanisch.
2 *n* Costaricaner(in *f*) *m*.
cost: ~-benefit analysis *n* Kosten-Nutzen-Analyse *f*; **~ centre** *n* Kostenstelle *f*; **~ clerk** *n* Angestellte(r) *mf* in der Kostenbuchhaltung; **~-conscious** *adj* kostenbewußt; **~-cutting** 1 *n* Kostenverringerung *f*; 2 *adj attr* **~-cutting exercise** kostendämpfende Maßnahmen *pl*; **~-effective** *adj* rentabel, kosteneffizient *(spec)*; **~-effectiveness** *n* Rentabilität, Kosteneffizienz *(spec) f*.
coster(monger) [ˈkɒstə(ˌmʌŋgəʳ)] *n (Brit)* Straßenhändler *m*.
costing [ˈkɒstɪŋ] *n* Kalkulation *f* ◆ **~ department** Kostenbuchhaltung *f*, betriebliches Rechnungswesen.
costive [ˈkɒstɪv] *adj (form) (constipated)* verstopft; *(constipating)* stopfend.
costliness [ˈkɒstlɪnɪs] *n* Kostspieligkeit *f*; *(in business, industry)* hoher Kostenaufwand ◆ **the ~ of buying a new car** die mit dem Kauf eines neuen Wagens verbundenen hohen Kosten.
costly [ˈkɒstlɪ] *adj* teuer, kostspielig; *tastes, habits* teuer ◆ **~ in terms of time/labour** zeitaufwendig/arbeitsintensiv.
cost: ~ of living *n* Lebenshaltungskosten *pl*; **~-of-living bonus** *n* Lebenshaltungskostenzuschlag *m*; **~-of-living index** *n* Lebenshaltungsindex *m*; **~-plus** *adj* **calculated on a ~-plus basis** unter Einbeziehung einer Gewinnspanne berechnet; **~ price** *n* Selbstkostenpreis *m*.
costume [ˈkɒstjuːm] *n* Kostüm *nt*; *(bathing ~)* Badeanzug *m* ◆ **national ~** Nationaltracht *f*.
costume: ~ ball *n* Kostümfest *nt*; **~ jewellery** *n* Modeschmuck *m*; **~ piece, ~ play** *n* Schauspiel *nt* in historischen Kostümen; **~ ring** *n* Modeschmuckring *m*.
costumier [kɒsˈtjuːmɪəʳ], *(US)* **costumer** [kɒsˈtjuːməʳ] *n* **(a)** *(theatrical ~)* Kostümverleih *m*. **(b)** *(form: dressmaker)* Schneider(in *f*) *m*.
cosy, *(US)* **cozy** [ˈkəʊzɪ] 1 *adj (+er) room, atmosphere* gemütlich, behaglich; *(warm)* mollig warm; *(fig) chat* gemütlich, traulich *(dated)* ◆ **to feel ~** *(person)* sich wohl und behaglich fühlen; *(room etc)* einen behaglichen *or* gemütlichen Eindruck machen; **I'm very ~ here** ich fühle mich hier sehr wohl, ich finde es hier sehr gemütlich; **a ~ little tête-à-tête** *(fig)* ein trautes Tête-à-tête; **warm and ~** mollig warm.
2 *n (tea ~, egg ~)* Wärmer *m*.

cot [kɒt] *n* (*esp Brit: child's bed*) Kinderbett *nt*; (*US: camp bed*) Feldbett *nt* ◆ **~ death** Krippentod *m*, plötzlicher Kindstod.

cote [kəʊt] *n* (*dove~*) Taubenschlag *m*; (*sheep~*) Schafstall *m*.

coterie ['kəʊtərɪ] *n* Clique *f*; (*literary ~*) Zirkel *m*.

cotill(i)on [kə'tɪljən] *n* Kotillon *m*.

cotta ['kɒtə] *n* (*Eccl*) Chorhemd *nt*.

cottage ['kɒtɪdʒ] *n* **(a)** Cottage, Häuschen *nt*; (*US: in institution*) Wohneinheit *f*. **(b)** (*for gays*) Schwulentreff *m* (*inf*).

cottage: ~ cheese *n* Hüttenkäse *m*; **~ hospital** *n* (*Brit*) *kleines Krankenhaus für leichtere Fälle*; **~ industry** *n* Manufaktur, Heimindustrie *f*; **~ loaf** *n* (*Brit*) *eine Art rundes, hohes Weißbrot*; **~ pie** *n Hackfleisch mit Kartoffelbrei überbacken*.

cottager ['kɒtɪdʒəʳ] *n* (*Brit*) Cottage-Bewohner(in *f*) *m*.

cotter (pin) ['kɒtə(,pɪn)] *n* Splint *m*.

cotton ['kɒtn] [1] *n* Baumwolle *f*; (*plant*) Baumwollstrauch *m*; (*fibre*) Baumwollfaser *f*; (*fabric*) Baumwollstoff *m*; (*sewing thread*) (Baumwoll)garn *nt* ◆ **absorbent ~** (*US*) Watte *f*.
[2] *adj* Baumwoll-, baumwollen; *clothes, fabric also* aus Baumwolle.

◆**cotton on** *vi* (*inf*) es kapieren (*inf*), es schnallen (*sl*) ◆ **has he ~ed ~ yet?** hat er es endlich kapiert (*inf*) *or* geschnallt? (*sl*).

◆**cotton to** *vi +prep obj* (*inf*) *plan, suggestion* gut finden.

cotton *in cpds* Baumwoll-; **~ batting** *n* (*US*) Gaze *f*; **~ cake** *n* Futtermittel *nt*; **~ candy** *n* (*US*) Zuckerwatte *f*; **~ gin** *n* Entkörnungsmaschine *f* (für Baumwolle); **~ grass** *n* Wollgras *nt*; **~ mill** *n* Baumwollspinnerei *f*; **~-picker** *n* Baumwollpflücker(in *f*) *m*; (*machine*) Baumwoll-Pflückmaschine *f*; **~-picking** *adj* (*US inf*) verflucht (*inf*); **~ plant** *n* Baumwollstaude *f or* -strauch *m*; **~ print** *n* (*fabric*) bedruckter Baumwollstoff; **~seed** *n* Baumwollsamen *m*; **~seed cake** *n see* **~ cake**; **~seed oil** *n* Baumwollsamenöl *nt*; **~tail** *n* (*US*) Kaninchen, Karnickel *nt*; **~wood** *n* Pyramidenpappel *f*; **~wool** *n* (*Brit*) Watte *f*; **to bring a child up in ~wool** (*fig*) ein Kind wohlbehütet aufwachsen lassen; **to wrap sb in ~wool** (*fig*) jdn in Watte packen; **my legs feel like ~wool** meine Beine sind wie Butter.

cotyledon [,kɒtɪ'li:dən] *n* Keimblatt *nt*.

couch [kaʊtʃ] [1] *n* Sofa *nt*; (*studio ~*) Schlafcouch *f*; (*doctor's ~*) Liege *f*; (*psychiatrist's ~*) Couch *f*; (*poet: bed*) Lager *nt*.
[2] *vt* **(a)** (*put in words*) *request* formulieren, abfassen ◆ **~ potato** (*US inf*) Dauerglotzer(in *f*) *m* (*inf*).
(b) (*lower*) *spear, lance* anlegen.
[3] *vi* (*liter: lion, cat etc*) lauern, auf der Lauer liegen.

couchant ['ku:ʃənt] *adj* (*Her*) liegend.

couchette [ku:'ʃet] *n* (*Rail*) Liegewagen(platz) *m*.

couchgrass ['kaʊtʃgrɑ:s] *n* Quecke *f*.

cougar ['ku:gəʳ] *n* Puma, Kuguar *m*.

cough [kɒf] [1] *n* Husten *m* ◆ **to give a warning ~** sich warnend räuspern; **to clear one's throat with a loud ~** sich laut *or* vernehmlich räuspern; **a smoker's ~** Raucherhusten *m*.
[2] *vi* husten.
[3] *vt blood* husten.

◆**cough out** *vt sep* aushusten, ausspucken.

◆**cough up** [1] *vt sep* (*lit*) aushusten.
[2] *vt insep* (*fig inf*) *money* rausrücken (*inf*), ausspucken (*sl*), rüberkommen mit (*sl*).
[3] *vi* (*fig inf*) blechen (*inf*), ausspucken (*sl*).

cough: ~ drop *n* Hustenpastille *f*; **~ mixture** *n* Hustensaft *m or* -mittel *nt*; **~ sweet** *n* Hustenbonbon *nt*.

▼ **could** [kʊd] *pret of* **can¹**.

couldn't ['kʊdnt] *contr of* **could not**.

council ['kaʊnsl] [1] *n* (*body of representatives*) Rat *m*; (*meeting*) Sitzung, Beratung *f* ◆ **city/town ~** Stadtrat *m*; **to be on the ~** im Rat sitzen, Ratsmitglied sein; **to hold ~** Beratungen abhalten, Rat halten (*old*); **~ of war** Kriegsrat *m*; **C~ of Europe** Europarat *m*.
[2] *attr estate* (*Brit*) des sozialen Wohnungsbaus ◆ **~ flat** Sozialwohnung *f*; **~ house/housing** (*Brit*) Sozialwohnung *f*/sozialer Wohnungsbau; **~ chamber** Sitzungssaal *m* des Rats; **~ meeting** Ratssitzung *f*.

councillor, (*US*) **councilor** ['kaʊnsələʳ] *n* Ratsmitglied *nt*; (*town ~*) Stadtrat *m*/-rätin *f* ◆ **~ Smith** Herr Stadtrat/Frau Stadträtin Smith.

counsel ['kaʊnsəl] [1] *n* **(a)** (*form: advice*) Rat(schlag) *m* ◆ **to hold ~ with sb over** *or* **about sth** mit jdm etw beraten *or* beratschlagen; **to keep one's own ~** seine Meinung für sich behalten, mit seiner Meinung zurückhalten; **~s of perfection** schlaue Ratschläge.
(b) *pl* - (*Jur*) Rechtsanwalt *m* ◆ **~ for the defence/prosecution** Verteidiger(in *f*) *m*/Vertreter(in *f*) *m* der Anklage, ≃ Staatsanwalt *m*/-anwältin *f*; **~ on both sides** Verteidigung und Anklage.
[2] *vt* **(a)** (*form*) *person* beraten; *course of action* empfehlen, raten zu ◆ **to ~ sb to do sth** jdm raten *or* empfehlen, etw zu tun.
(b) (*in social work etc*) beraten.

counselling, (*US*) **counseling** ['kaʊnsəlɪŋ] *n* soziale Beratung ◆ **to give sb ~ on social problems** jdn bei sozialen Problemen beraten.

counsellor, (*US*) **counselor** ['kaʊnsələʳ] *n* **(a)** (*adviser*) Berater(in *f*) *m*. **(b)** (*US, Ir: lawyer*) Rechtsanwalt *m*/-anwältin *f*.

count¹ [kaʊnt] [1] *n* **(a)** Zählung *f*; (*Sport*) Auszählen *nt*; (*of votes*) (Stimmen)zählung, (Stimmen)auszählung *f* ◆ **I'll have a ~** ich zähle es mal (ab); **she lost ~ when she was interrupted** sie kam mit dem Zählen durcheinander, als sie unterbrochen wurde; **I've lost all ~ of her boyfriends** ich habe die Übersicht über ihre Freunde vollkommen verloren; **to keep ~ (of sth)** (etw) mitzählen; (*keep track*) die Übersicht über etw (*acc*) behalten; **she couldn't keep ~ of them** sie verlor die Übersicht; **at the last ~ there were twenty members** bei der letzten Zählung waren es zwanzig Mitglieder; **all together now, on the ~ of three** und jetzt alle zusammen, bei drei geht's los; **he was out for the ~, he took the ~** (*Sport*) er wurde ausgezählt; (*fig*) er war k.o.; **he took a ~ of eight** (*Sport*) er ging bis acht zu Boden.
(b) (*Jur: charge*) Anklagepunkt *m* ◆ **on that ~** (*fig*) in dem Punkt; **on all ~s** in jeder Hinsicht.
(c) *no pl* (*notice*) **don't take any ~ of what he says** hören Sie nicht auf das, was er sagt; **she never takes much/any ~ of him** sie nimmt wenig/keine Notiz von ihm.
[2] *vt* **(a)** (ab)zählen; (*~ again*) nachzählen; *votes* (aus)zählen ◆ **to ~ ten** bis zehn zählen; **I only ~ed ten people** ich habe nur zehn Leute gezählt; **to ~ the cost** (*lit*) auf die Kosten achten, jeden Pfennig umdrehen; **she'll help anyone without ~ing the cost to herself** sie hilft jedem, ohne an sich selbst zu denken.
(b) (*consider*) ansehen, betrachten; (*include*) mitrechnen, mitzählen ◆ **to ~ sb (as) a friend/among one's friends** jdn als Freund ansehen/zu seinen Freunden zählen; **you should ~ yourself lucky to be alive** Sie sollten froh und glücklich sein *or* Sie können noch von Glück sagen, daß Sie noch leben; **ten people (not) ~ing the children** zehn Leute, die Kinder (nicht) mitgerechnet *or* eingerechnet; **to ~ sth against sb** etw gegen jdn anrechnen.
[3] *vi* **(a)** zählen ◆ **~ing from today** von heute an (gerechnet).
(b) (*be considered*) betrachtet *or* angesehen werden; (*be included*) mitgerechnet *or* mitgezählt werden; (*be important*) wichtig sein ◆ **the children don't ~** die Kinder zählen nicht; **he doesn't ~ amongst her friends** er zählt nicht zu ihren Freunden; **that doesn't ~** das zählt nicht; **every minute/it all ~s** jede Minute ist/das ist alles wichtig; **appearance ~s a lot** es kommt sehr auf die äußere Erscheinung an; **to ~ against sb** gegen jdn sprechen.

◆**count down** [1] *vi* den Countdown durchführen ◆ **they started ~ing ~ last night** sie haben gestern abend mit dem Countdown angefangen; **to ~ ~ to blast-off** bis zum Abschuß (der Rakete) rückwärts zählen.
[2] *vt sep* **to ~ a rocket ~** den Countdown (für eine Rakete) durchführen.

◆**count for** *vi +prep obj* **to ~ ~ a lot** sehr viel bedeuten; **to ~ ~ nothing** nichts gelten.

◆**count in** *vt sep* mitzählen; *person also* mitrechnen, berücksichtigen, einplanen ◆ **to ~ sb ~ on sth** davon ausgehen *or* damit rechnen, daß jd bei etw mitmacht; **you can ~ me ~!** Sie können mit mir rechnen, da mache ich mit.

◆**count off** *vt sep, vi* abzählen.

◆**count on** *vi +prep obj* (*depend on*) rechnen mit, sich verlassen auf (*+acc*) ◆ **to ~ ~ doing sth** die Absicht haben, etw zu tun; **to ~ ~ being able to do sth** damit rechnen, etw tun zu können; **you can ~ ~ him to help you** du kannst auf seine Hilfe zählen.

◆**count out** *vt sep* **(a)** (*Sport*) auszählen. **(b)** *money, books etc* abzählen. **(c)** (*Brit Parl*) **to ~ the House ~** *eine Sitzung des Unterhauses wegen zu geringer Abgeordnetenzahl vertagen*. **(d)** (*inf: exclude*) **(you can) ~ me ~ (of that)!** ohne mich!, da mache ich nicht mit!; **~ him ~ of it** plane ihn besser nicht ein.

◆**count up** *vt sep* zusammenzählen *or* -rechnen.

◆**count upon** *vi +prep obj see* **count on**.

count² *n* Graf *m*.

countable ['kaʊntəbl] *adj* zählbar (*also Gram*).

countdown ['kaʊntdaʊn] *n* Countdown *m* ◆ **to start the ~** mit dem Countdown beginnen.

countenance ['kaʊntɪnəns] [1] *n* **(a)** (*old, form: face*) Angesicht (*old, Eccl*), Antlitz (*old*) *nt*; (*expression*) Gesichtsausdruck *m* ◆ **to keep one's ~** (*fig*) die Fassung *or* Haltung bewahren; **to lose ~** (*fig*) das Gesicht verlieren; **to put sb out of ~** jdn aus der Fassung bringen. **(b)** (*support*) **to give/lend ~ to sth** etw ermutigen/unterstützen.
[2] *vt behaviour* gutheißen; *plan, suggestion also, person* unterstützen.

counter ['kaʊntəʳ] [1] *n* **(a)** (*in shop*) Ladentisch, Tresen (*N Ger*) *m*; (*in cafe*) Theke *f*; (*in bank, post office*) Schalter *m* ◆ **to sell/buy sth under/over the ~** etw unter dem/über den Ladentisch verkaufen/bekommen; **medicines which can be bought over the ~** Medikamente, die man rezeptfrei bekommt; **under-the-~ dealings** (*fig*) dunkle Geschäfte, Schiebereien *pl*.
(b) (*small disc for games*) Spielmarke *f*.
(c) (*Tech*) Zähler *m*.
(d) (*Sport*) (*Fencing*) Parade *f*; (*Boxing also*) Konter *m*.
(e) (*reply*) Entgegnung, Erwiderung, Replik (*geh*) *f*.
[2] *vt* (*retaliate against*) antworten auf (*+acc*), kontern (*also Sport*) ◆ **how dare you ~ my orders!** (*countermand*) wie können Sie es wagen, meine Anweisungen *or* (*Mil*) Befehle aufzuheben; **to ~ the loss** den Verlust wettmachen *or* ausgleichen.
[3] *vi* kontern (*also Sport*).
[4] *adv* **~ to** gegen (*+acc*); **to go** *or* **run ~ to sb's wishes** jds Wünschen (*dat*) zuwiderlaufen; **the results are ~ to expectations** die Ergebnisse widersprechen den Erwartungen.

counter: ~act *vt* (*make ineffective*) neutralisieren; (*act in opposition to*) entgegenwirken (*+dat*); *disease* bekämpfen; **~action** *n see vt* Neutralisierung *f*; Gegenwirkung *f*; Bekämpfung *f*; **~active** *adj* entgegenwirkend, Gegen-; **~active measures** Gegenmaßnahmen *pl*; **~attack** [1] *n* Gegenangriff *m*; [2] *vt* einen Gegenangriff starten gegen; (*argue against*) kontern, beantworten; [3] *vi* einen Gegenangriff starten, zurückschlagen; **~attraction** *n* Gegenattraktion *f* (*to* zu); (*on TV etc*) Konkurrenzprogramm *nt*; **~balance** [1] *n* Gegengewicht *nt*; [2] *vt* ausgleichen; **~charge** *n* **(a)** (*Jur*) Gegenklage *f*; **(b)**

➤ LANGUAGE IN USE: **could** → 1.1, 1.2, 2.2, 4, 9.1, 15.3, 26.3

(*Mil*) Gegenattacke *f*; **~check** *n* Gegenkontrolle *f*; **~claim** *n* (*Jur*) Gegenanspruch *m*; **~ clerk** *n* (*in bank, booking office etc*) Angestellte(r) *mf* im Schalterdienst; (*in post office etc*) Schalterbeamte(r) *m*/-beamtin *f*; **~clockwise** *adj, adv* (*US*) *see* **anti-clockwise**; **~espionage** *n* Gegenspionage, Spionageabwehr *f*; **~-example** *n* Gegenbeispiel *nt*.

counterfeit ['kaʊntəfi:t] 1 *adj* gefälscht; (*fig*) falsch ◆ **~ money/coins** Falschgeld *nt*.
2 *n* Fälschung *f*.
3 *vt* fälschen; (*fig*) vortäuschen.

counterfoil ['kaʊntəfɔɪl] *n* Kontrollabschnitt *m*.

counter: ~insurgency *n* Kampf *m* gegen Aufständische; **~insurgency measures** Maßnahmen *pl* gegen Aufständische; **~insurgent** *n* Anti-Guerilla-Kämpfer *m*; **~intelligence** *n see* **~espionage**; **~irritant** *n* (*Med*) Gegenreizmittel *nt*; **~-jumper** *n* (*US sl*) Ladenschwengel *m* (*hum*), Verkäuferin *f*.

countermand ['kaʊntəmɑ:nd] *vt order* aufheben, widerrufen; *attack, plan* rückgängig machen ◆ **unless ~ed** bis auf gegenteilige Anweisung *or* (*Mil*) Order.

counter: ~march (*Mil*) 1 *n* Rückmarsch *m*; 2 *vi* zurückmarschieren; **~measure** *n* Gegenmaßnahme *f*; **~offensive** *n* (*Mil*) Gegenoffensive *f*; **~offer** *n* Gegenangebot *nt*; **~pane** *n* Tagesdecke *f*; **~part** *n* (*equivalent*) Gegenüber *nt*; (*complement*) Gegenstück, Pendant *nt*; **~plot** 1 *n* Gegenanschlag *m*; 2 *vi* einen Gegenanschlag planen; **~point** *n* (*Mus*) Kontrapunkt *m*; **~poise** 1 *n* (**a**) (*weight*) Gegengewicht *nt*; (*force, fig*) Gegenkraft *f*; (**b**) *no pl* (*equilibrium, fig*) Gleichgewicht *nt*; **to be in ~poise** im Gleichgewicht sein; 2 *vt* (*lit, fig*) ausgleichen; **~-productive** *adj* unsinnig, widersinnig; *criticism, measures, policies* destruktiv; **that wouldn't help us at all, in fact it would be ~-productive** das würde uns nicht weiterbringen, sondern sogar das Gegenteil bewirken; **C~-Reformation** *n* (*Hist*) Gegenreformation *f*; **~-revolution** *n* Gegen- *or* Konterrevolution *f*; **~-revolutionary** *adj* konterrevolutionär; **~shaft** *n* (*Tech*) Vorgelegewelle *f*; **~sign** 1 *n* (*Mil*) Parole *f*, Kennwort *nt*; 2 *vt cheque etc* gegenzeichnen; **~-signature** *n* Gegenunterschrift *f*; **~sink** 1 *n* (*tool*) Versenker, Spitzsenker *m*; 2 *vt hole* senken; *screw* versenken; **~ staff** *npl* (*in shop*) Verkäufer *pl*; **~sunk** *adj screw* Senk-; **~tenor** *n* (*Mus*) Kontratenor *m*; **~-terrorism** *n* Terrorismusbekämpfung *f*; **~weight** *n* Gegengewicht *nt*.

countess ['kaʊntɪs] *n* Gräfin *f*.

counting house ['kaʊntɪŋhaʊs] *n* (*old*) Kontor *nt*.

countless ['kaʊntlɪs] *adj* unzählig *attr*, zahllos *attr*.

count palatine *n, pl* **-s** - Pfalzgraf *m*.

countrified ['kʌntrɪfaɪd] *adj* ländlich, bäuerlich.

country ['kʌntrɪ] *n* (**a**) (*state*) Land *nt*; (*people also*) Volk *nt* ◆ **his own ~** seine Heimat; **to die for one's ~** für sein Land sterben; **to go to the ~** Neuwahlen ausschreiben.
(**b**) *no pl* (*as opposed to town*) Land *nt*; (*scenery, countryside also*) Landschaft *f* ◆ **in/to the ~** auf dem/aufs Land; **the surrounding ~** das umliegende Land, die Umgebung; **this is good hunting/fishing ~** das ist eine gute Jagd-/Fischgegend; **this is mining ~** dies ist ein Bergbaugebiet; **we're back in familiar ~ again** (*fig*) wir befinden uns wieder auf vertrautem Boden; **this subject is new ~ to me** das ist Neuland für mich.

country *in cpds* Land-; **~-and-western** 1 *n* Country- und Westernmusik *f*; 2 *adj* Country- und Western-; **~-born** *adj* auf dem Land geboren; **~-bred** *adj* auf dem Land aufgewachsen; *animals* auf dem Land gezogen; **~ bumpkin** *n* (*pej*) Bauerntölpel (*inf*), Bauer (*pej inf*) *m*; (*girl*) Bauerntrampel *nt* (*inf*); **~ club** *n Klub m auf dem Lande*; **~ cousin** *n* Vetter *m*/Base *f* vom Lande; **~ dance** *n* Volkstanz *m*; **~ dancing** *n* Volkstanz *m*; **to go ~ dancing** zum Volkstanz gehen; **~ dweller** *n* Landbewohner(in *f*) *m*; **~ folk** *npl* Leute *pl* vom Lande; **~ gentleman** *n* Landbesitzer *m*; **~ gentry** *npl* Landadel *m*; **~ house** *n* Landhaus *nt*; **~ life** *n* das Landleben, das Leben auf dem Lande; **~man** *n* (**a**) (*landsman*) Landsmann *m*; **his fellow ~men** seine Landsleute; (**b**) (*country-dweller*) Landmann *m*; **~ music** *n* Country-Musik *f*; **~ people** *npl* Leute *pl* vom Land(e); **~ road** *n* Landstraße *f*; **~ seat** *n* Landsitz *m*; **~side** *n* (*scenery*) Landschaft, Gegend *f*; (*rural area*) Land *nt*; **it's beautiful ~side** das ist eine herrliche Landschaft *or* Gegend; **to live in the middle of the ~side** mitten auf dem Land leben; **~ town** *n* Kleinstadt *f*; **~-wide** *adj* landesweit, im ganzen Land; **~woman** *n* (**a**) (*landswoman*) Landsmännin *f*; (**b**) (*country-dweller*) Landfrau *f*.

county ['kaʊntɪ] 1 *n* (*Brit*) Grafschaft *f*; (*US*) (Verwaltungs)bezirk *m*.
2 *adj* (*Brit*) *family* zum Landadel gehörend; *accent, behaviour* vornehm; *occasion* für den Landadel ◆ **the ~ set** die feinen Pinkel (*inf*).

county: ~ borough *n* (*Brit*) *Stadt f mit grafschaftlichen Rechten*; **~ council** *n* (*Brit*) Grafschaftsrat *m*; **~ court** *n* (*Brit*) Grafschaftsgericht *nt*; **~ seat** *n* (*US*) *Hauptstadt f eines Verwaltungsbezirkes*; **~ town** *n* (*Brit*) *Hauptstadt f einer Grafschaft*.

coup [ku:] *n* (**a**) (*successful action*) Coup *m*. (**b**) (*~ d'état*) Staatsstreich, Coup d'Etat *m*.

coup: ~ de grâce [ˌku:də'grɑ:s] *n* (*lit, fig*) Gnadenstoß *m*; (*with gun*) Gnadenschuß *m*; **~ d'état** ['ku:deɪ'tɑ:] *n see* **coup (b)**.

coupé ['ku:peɪ] *n* (*car*) Coupé *nt*.

couple ['kʌpl] 1 *n* (**a**) (*pair*) Paar *nt*; (*married ~*) Ehepaar *nt* ◆ **courting ~s** Liebespaare *pl*; **the happy ~** das glückliche Paar; **in ~s** paarweise.
(**b**) (*inf*) **a ~** (*two*) zwei; (*several*) ein paar, einige; **a ~ of letters/friends** *etc* ein paar *or* einige Briefe/Freunde *etc*; **we had a ~ in the pub** wir haben in der Kneipe ein paar getrunken; **a ~ of times** ein paarmal; **it took a ~ of minutes/hours** es hat einige *or* ein paar Minuten/ungefähr zwei Stunden gedauert.
2 *vt* (**a**) (*link*) *names, circuit* verbinden; *carriages etc* koppeln.
(**b**) (*mate*) *animals* paaren.
3 *vi* (*mate*) sich paaren.

◆**couple on** *vt sep* anhängen.

◆**couple up** *vt sep* ankoppeln.

coupler ['kʌplə^r] *n* (*Comput*) Koppler *m*.

couplet ['kʌplɪt] *n* Verspaar *nt* ◆ **rhyming ~** Reimpaar *nt*.

coupling ['kʌplɪŋ] *n* (**a**) (*linking*) Verbindung *f*; (*of carriages etc*) Kopplung *f* ◆ **the continual ~ of his name with ...** daß sein Name ständig mit ... in Verbindung gebracht wird/wurde. (**b**) (*mating*) Paarung *f*. (**c**) (*linking device*) Kupplung *f*.

coupon ['ku:pɒn] *n* (**a**) (*voucher*) Gutschein *m*; (*ration ~*) (Zuteilungs)schein *m*. (**b**) (*Ftbl*) Totoschein, Wettschein *m*. (**c**) (*Fin*) Kupon *m*.

courage ['kʌrɪdʒ] *n* Mut *m*, Courage *f* (*inf*) ◆ **I haven't the ~ to refuse** ich habe einfach nicht den Mut, nein zu sagen; **take ~!** (*liter*) nur Mut!; **to take ~ from sth** sich durch etw ermutigt fühlen; **to lose one's ~** den Mut verlieren; **to have/lack the ~ of one's convictions** Zivilcourage/keine Zivilcourage haben; **to take one's ~ in both hands** sein Herz in beide Hände nehmen.

courageous [kə'reɪdʒəs] *adj* mutig; (*with courage of convictions*) couragiert (*inf*).

courageously [kə'reɪdʒəslɪ] *adv see adj*.

courgette [kʊə'ʒet] *n* (*Brit*) Zucchini *f*.

courier ['kʊrɪə^r] *n* (**a**) (*messenger*) Kurier *m* ◆ **by ~** per Kurier. (**b**) (*tourist guide*) Reiseleiter(in *f*) *m*.

▼ **course**[1] [kɔ:s] *n* (**a**) (*direction, path*) (*of plane, ship*) Kurs *m*; (*of river*) Lauf *m*; (*fig*) (*of illness, relationship*) Verlauf *m*; (*of history*) Lauf *m*; (*of action etc, way of proceeding*) Vorgehensweise *f* ◆ **to set (one's) ~ for** *or* **towards a place** Kurs auf einen Ort nehmen; **to change** *or* **alter ~** den Kurs wechseln *or* ändern; **to be on/off ~** auf Kurs sein/vom Kurs abgekommen sein; **to let sth take** *or* **run its ~** einer Sache (*dat*) ihren Lauf lassen, etw (*acc*) seinen Lauf nehmen lassen; **the affair has run its ~** die Angelegenheit ist zu einem Ende gekommen; **the ~ of true love ne'er did run smooth** (*prov*) Liebe geht oft seltsame Wege (*prov*); **which ~ of action did you take?** wie sind Sie vorgegangen?; **that was an unwise ~ of action** es war unklug, so vorzugehen; **the best ~ (of action) would be ...** das beste wäre ...; **we have no other ~ (of action) but to ...** es bleibt uns nichts anderes übrig als zu ...; **to take a middle ~** einen gemäßigten Kurs einschlagen.
(**b**) **in the ~ of his life/the next few weeks/the meeting** *etc* während seines Lebens/der nächsten paar Wochen/der Versammlung *etc*; **in the ~ of time/the conversation** im Laufe der Zeit/Unterhaltung; **it's in the ~ of being done** es wird gerade gemacht; **in the ~ of shaving** beim Rasieren; **in the ordinary ~ of things, you could expect ...** unter normalen Umständen könnte man erwarten ...; **to be in the ~ of nature** in der Natur der Sache liegen; *see* **due**.
▼ (**c**) **of ~** (*admittedly*) natürlich; (*naturally, obviously also*) selbstverständlich; **of ~!** natürlich!, selbstverständlich!, klar! (*inf*); **of ~ I will!** aber natürlich *or* selbstverständlich!; **of ~ I'm coming** natürlich *or* selbstverständlich komme ich, klar, ich komme (*inf*); **don't you like me? — of ~ I do** magst du mich nicht? — doch, natürlich; **he's rather young, of ~, but ...** er ist natürlich ziemlich jung, aber ...
(**d**) (*Sch, Univ*) Studium *nt*; (*shorter, summer ~ etc*) Kurs(us) *m*; (*at work*) Lehrgang *m*; (*Med: of treatment*) Kur *f* ◆ **to go to/on a French ~** einen Französischkurs(us) besuchen; **a ~ on/in first aid** ein Kurs über Erste Hilfe/ein Erste-Hilfe-Kurs; **a ~ of lectures, a lecture ~** eine Vorlesungsreihe; **a ~ of pills/treatment** eine Pillenkur/eine Behandlung.
(**e**) (*Sports*) (*race~*) Kurs *m*; (*golf ~*) Platz *m* ◆ **to stay** *or* **last the ~** (*lit*) das Rennen durchhalten; (*fig*) bis zum Ende durchhalten.
(**f**) (*Cook*) Gang *m* ◆ **first ~** erster Gang; **a three-~ meal** ein Essen *nt* mit drei Gängen.
(**g**) (*Build*) Schicht *f*.
(**h**) (*Naut: sail*) Untersegel *nt*.

course[2] 1 *vt* (*Hunt*) *hare, stag* hetzen, jagen.
2 *vi* (**a**) (*blood, tears*) strömen. (**b**) (*Hunt, fig*) hetzen, jagen ◆ **to go coursing** auf Hetzjagd gehen.

courser ['kɔ:sə^r] *n* (**a**) (*dog*) Hatz- *or* Hetzhund *m*. (**b**) (*poet: horse*) (schnelles) Roß (*liter*).

coursing ['kɔ:sɪŋ] *n* (*Sport*) Hetzjagd, Hatz, Hetze *f*.

court [kɔ:t] 1 *n* (**a**) (*Jur*) (*also* **~ of justice** *or* **law**) Gericht *nt*; (*body of judges also*) Gerichtshof *m*; (*room*) Gerichtssaal *m* ◆ **~ of Session** (*Scot*) *höchstes schottisches Zivilgericht*; **to appear in ~** vor Gericht erscheinen; **the evidence was ruled out of ~** das Beweismaterial wurde nicht zugelassen; **his suggestion was ruled out of ~** (*fig*) sein Vorschlag wurde verworfen; **to take sb to ~** jdn verklagen *or* vor Gericht bringen; **to go to ~ over a matter** eine Sache vor Gericht bringen, mit einer Sache vor Gericht gehen; **the case comes up in ~ next week** der Fall wird nächste Woche verhandelt; **Sir James is still in ~** Sir James ist noch beim Gericht; *see* **settle**.
(**b**) (*royal*) Hof *m* ◆ **to be presented at ~** bei Hofe vorgestellt werden; **the C~ of St James** der englische Königshof.
(**c**) (*Sport*) Platz *m*; (*for squash*) Halle *f*; (*marked-off area*) Spielfeld *nt*; (*service ~ etc*) Feld *nt* ◆ **grass/hard ~** Rasen-/Hartplatz *m*; **on ~** auf dem Platz/in der Halle; **out of the ~** außerhalb des Spielfeldes.
(**d**) (*~yard, Univ: quadrangle*) Hof *m* ◆ **inner ~** Innenhof *m*.
(**e**) (*old form: courtship*) Hof *m* ◆ **to pay ~ to a woman** einer Frau (*dat*) den Hof machen.

➤ LANGUAGE IN USE: **course**[1]: **c** → **9.2, 11.3**

[2] *vt* **(a)** *(dated) woman* umwerben, werben um, den Hof machen (+*dat*). **(b)** *(fig) person's favour* werben um, buhlen um *(pej)*; *danger, defeat* herausfordern.

[3] *vi (dated) (man)* auf Freiersfüßen gehen *(dated, hum)* ◆ **they were ~ing at the time** zu der Zeit gingen sie zusammen; **she's ~ing** sie hat einen Freund; **are you ~ing?** hast du jemanden?

court: ~ card *n (Brit)* Bildkarte *f*; **~ circular** *n* Hofnachrichten *pl*; **~ dress** *n* Hoftracht *f*.

courteous *adj*, **~ly** *adv* ['kɜːtiəs, -lɪ] höflich.

courtesan [ˌkɔːtɪ'zæn] *n* Kurtisane *f*.

courtesy ['kɜːtɪsɪ] *n* Höflichkeit *f* ◆ **(by) ~ of** freundlicherweise zur Verfügung gestellt von; **would you do me the ~ of shutting up!** würden Sie mir den Gefallen tun und den Mund halten!

courtesy: ~ bus *n* gebührenfreier Bus; Hotelbus *m*; **~ light** *n (Aut)* Innenleuchte *f*; **~ title** *n* Höflichkeitstitel *m*; **~ visit** *n* Höflichkeitsbesuch *m*.

court: ~ guide *n* Hofkalender *m*; **~house** *n (Jur)* Gerichtsgebäude *nt*.

courtier ['kɔːtɪəʳ] *n* Höfling *m*.

courtliness ['kɔːtlɪnɪs] *n see adj* Höflichkeit *f*; Vornehmheit *f*.

courtly ['kɔːtlɪ] *adj manners* höflich; *grace, elegance* vornehm ◆ **~ love** Minne *f*.

court: ~-martial [1] *n, pl* **~-martials** *or* **~s-martial** *(Mil)* Militärgericht *nt*; *(in wartime also)* Kriegsgericht *nt*; **to be tried by ~-martial** vor das/ein Militär-/Kriegsgericht gestellt werden *or* kommen; [2] *vt* vor das/ein Militär-/Kriegsgericht stellen *(for* wegen*)*; **~ order** *n* gerichtliche Verfügung; **I'll get a ~ order** ich werde eine gerichtliche Verfügung beantragen; **~room** *n (Jur)* Gerichtssaal *m*.

courtship ['kɔːtʃɪp] *n (dated)* (Braut)werbung *f (dated) (of* um*)* ◆ **during their ~** während er um sie warb *or* freite *(dated)*.

court: ~ shoe *n* Pumps *m*; **~ tennis** *n (US)* Tennis *nt*; **~yard** *n* Hof *m*.

cousin ['kʌzn] *n (male)* Cousin, Vetter *(dated) m*; *(female)* Cousine, Kusine, Base *(old) f* ◆ **Kevin and Susan are ~s** Kevin und Susan sind Cousin und Cousine.

cousinly ['kʌznlɪ] *adj* verwandtschaftlich.

couture [kuː'tjʊəʳ] *n* Couture *f*.

couturier [kuː'tjʊərɪəʳ] *n* Couturier *m*.

cove¹ [kəʊv] *n (Geog)* (kleine) Bucht.

cove² *n (dated Brit inf: fellow)* Kerl *m (inf)* ◆ **queer** *or* **odd ~** komischer Kauz.

coven ['kʌvn] *n* Hexenzirkel *m*; *(meeting)* Hexensabbat *m*.

covenant ['kʌvɪnənt] [1] *n* Schwur *m*; *(Bibl)* Bund *m*; *(Jur)* Verpflichtung *f* zu regelmäßigen Spenden ◆ **to swear a solemn ~ that ...** feierlich schwören, daß ...

[2] *vt* **to ~ to do sth** durch ein Abkommen versprechen, etw zu tun; *(Jur)* sich vertraglich verpflichten, etw zu tun.

[3] *vi* ein Abkommen/einen Bund schließen.

Coventry ['kɒvəntrɪ] *n*: **to send sb to ~** *(Brit inf)* jdn schneiden *(inf)*.

cover ['kʌvəʳ] [1] *n* **(a)** *(lid)* Deckel *m*; *(of lens)* (Schutz)kappe *f*; *(loose ~: on chair)* Bezug *m*; *(cloth: for typewriter, umbrella etc)* Hülle *f*; *(on lorries, tennis court)* Plane *f*; *(sheet: over merchandise, shop counter)* Decke *f*, Tuch *nt*; *(blanket, quilt)* (Bett)decke *f* ◆ **he put a ~ over her/it** er deckte sie/es zu.

(b) *(of book)* Einband *m*; *(of magazine)* Umschlag *m*; *(dust ~)* (Schutz)umschlag *m* ◆ **to read a book from ~ to ~** ein Buch von Anfang bis Ende *or* von der ersten bis zur letzten Seite lesen; **on the ~** auf dem Einband/Umschlag; *(of magazine)* auf der Titelseite, auf dem Titel(blatt).

(c) *(Comm: envelope)* Umschlag *m* ◆ **under separate ~** getrennt; **under plain ~** in neutralem Umschlag.

(d) *no pl (shelter, protection)* Schutz *m (from* vor +*dat*, gegen*)*; *(Mil)* Deckung *f (from* vor +*dat*, gegen*)* ◆ **to take ~** *(from rain)* sich unterstellen, Schutz suchen *(from* vor +*dat)*; *(Mil)* in Deckung gehen *(from* vor +*dat)*; **under the ~ of the rocks** im Schutz der Felsen; **these plants/the car should be kept under ~** diese Pflanzen sollten/das Auto sollte abgedeckt sein *or (under roof)* durch ein Dach geschützt sein; **to get oneself under ~** sich unterstellen; *(for longer period)* Unterschlupf finden; **under ~ of darkness** im Schutz(e) der Dunkelheit; **to give sb ~** *(Mil)* jdm Deckung geben.

(e) *(Hunt)* Deckung *f* ◆ **to break ~** aus der Deckung hervorbrechen.

(f) *(place at meal)* Gedeck *nt* ◆ **she laid ~s for six** sie deckte für sechs Personen, sie legte sechs Gedecke auf.

(g) *(Comm, Fin)* Deckung *f*; *(insurance ~)* Versicherung *f* ◆ **to operate without ~** ohne Deckung arbeiten; **to take out ~ for a car/against fire** ein Auto versichern/eine Feuerversicherung abschließen; **to get ~ for sth** etw versichern (lassen); **do you have adequate ~?** sind Sie ausreichend versichert?

(h) *(assumed identity)* Tarnung *f*; *(front organization also)* Deckung *f* ◆ **under ~ as** getarnt als; **to operate under ~** als Agent tätig sein; **to blow sb's ~** jdn enttarnen.

[2] *vt* **(a)** bedecken; *(cover over)* zudecken; *(with loose cover) chair etc* beziehen ◆ **a ~ed wagon/way** ein Planwagen *m*/überdachter Weg; **to ~ one's head** den Kopf bedecken; **the car ~ed us in mud** das Auto bespritzte uns von oben bis unten mit Schlamm; **the mountain was ~ed with** *or* **in snow** der Berg war schneebedeckt *or* mit Schnee bedeckt; **you're all ~ed with dog hairs** du bist voller Hundehaare; **to ~ oneself in** *or* **with glory** Ruhm ernten; **~ed in** *or* **with shame** zutiefst beschämt.

(b) *(hide) surprise* verbergen; *mistake, tracks also* verdecken ◆ **to ~ one's face in** *or* **with one's hands** sein Gesicht in den Händen verstecken *or* verbergen.

(c) *(Mil, Sport, Chess: protect)* decken ◆ **he only said that to ~ himself** er hat das nur gesagt, um sich abzudecken *or* zu decken; **I'll keep you ~ed** ich gebe dir Deckung.

(d) *(point a gun at etc) door etc* sichern; *sb* in Schach halten; *(be on guard near)* sichern ◆ **to keep sb ~ed** jdn in Schach halten; **I've got you ~ed!** *(with gun etc)* ich hab' auf dich angelegt; *(fig: Chess etc)* ich hab' dich.

(e) *(Fin) loan* decken; *expenses, costs also* abdecken; *(Insur)* versichern ◆ **will £30 ~ the petrol?** reichen £ 30 für das Benzin?; **he gave me £30 to ~ the petrol** er gab mir £ 30 für Benzin.

(f) *(take in, include)* behandeln; *(law also)* erfassen; *(allow for, anticipate) possibilities, eventualities* vorsehen.

(g) *(Press: report on)* berichten über (+*acc*).

(h) *(travel) miles, distance* zurücklegen.

(i) *(salesman etc) territory* zuständig sein für.

(j) *(play a higher card than)* überbieten.

(k) *(animals: copulate with)* decken.

◆**cover for** *vi +prep obj* vertreten, einspringen für.

◆**cover in** *vt sep* **(a)** *(fill in) grave etc* auffüllen, zuschütten. **(b)** *(roof in)* überdachen.

◆**cover over** *vt sep (put a cover over)* zudecken; *(for protection), tennis court* abdecken; *(roof over)* überdachen.

◆**cover up** [1] *vi* **(a)** *(wrap up)* sich einmummen. **(b)** *(conceal a fact)* alles vertuschen *or* verheimlichen ◆ **don't try to ~ ~** versuchen Sie nicht, Ihren Fehler zu vertuschen; **to ~ ~ for sb** jdn decken.

[2] *vt sep* **(a)** *child* zudecken; *object also, tennis court* abdecken. **(b)** *(hide) truth, facts* vertuschen, verheimlichen.

coverage ['kʌvərɪdʒ] *n, no pl* **(a)** *(in media)* Berichterstattung *f (of* über +*acc)* ◆ **to give full ~ to an event** ausführlich über ein Ereignis berichten; **the games got excellent TV ~** die Spiele wurden ausführlich im Fernsehen gebracht. **(b)** *(Insur)* Versicherung *f* ◆ **this policy gives you full ~ for ...** diese Versicherung bietet Ihnen volle Deckung bei ...

cover: ~all *n usu pl (US)* Overall *m*; **~ charge** *n* Kosten *pl* für ein Gedeck; **~ girl** *n* Titel(bild)mädchen, Covergirl *nt*.

covering ['kʌvərɪŋ] *n* Decke *f*; *(floor ~)* Belag *m* ◆ **a ~ of dust/snow** eine Staub-/Schneedecke; **what kind of ~ did you put over the hole?** womit haben Sie das Loch ab- *or* zugedeckt?

covering letter *n* Begleitbrief *m*.

coverlet ['kʌvəlɪt] *n* Tagesdecke *f*.

cover: ~ note *n* Deckungszusage *f*, vorläufiger Versicherungsschein; **~ organization** *n* Deckorganisation *f*; **~ price** *n* Einzel(exemplar)preis *m*; **~ story** *n (of paper)* Titelgeschichte *f*; *(of spy)* Geschichte *f*.

covert ['kʌvət] [1] *adj threat, attack* versteckt; *glance also* verstohlen.

[2] *n* Versteck *nt*; *see* **draw²**.

covertly ['kʌvətlɪ] *adv see adj* versteckt; verstohlen.

cover-up ['kʌvərʌp] *n* Vertuschung, Verschleierung *f* ◆ **the Watergate ~** die Vertuschung von Watergate.

covet ['kʌvɪt] [1] *vt* begehren.

[2] *vi* begehrlich *or* begierig sein.

covetous ['kʌvɪtəs] *adj* begehrlich ◆ **to be ~ of sth** *(liter)* etw begehren.

covetously ['kʌvɪtəslɪ] *adv* begehrlich.

covetousness ['kʌvɪtəsnɪs] *n* Begierde *f (of* auf +*acc)*, Begehren *nt (of* nach*)*.

covey ['kʌvɪ] *n (of partridges)* Kette *f*.

coving ['kəʊvɪŋ] *n* Wölbung *f*.

cow¹ [kaʊ] *n* **(a)** Kuh *f* ◆ **a ~ elephant** eine Elefantenkuh; **till the ~s come home** *(fig inf)* bis in alle Ewigkeit *(inf)*; **you'll be waiting till the ~s come home** *(fig inf)* da kannst du warten, bis du schwarz wirst *(inf)*. **(b)** *(pej inf: woman) (stupid)* Kuh *f (inf)*; *(nasty)* gemeine Ziege *(inf)*.

cow² *vt person, animal* einschüchtern, verschüchtern ◆ **she had a ~ed look about her** sie machte einen eingeschüchterten *or* verschüchterten Eindruck; **to ~ sb into obedience** jdn (durch Einschüchterung) gefügig machen.

coward ['kaʊəd] *n* Feigling *m*.

cowardice ['kaʊədɪs],

cowardliness ['kaʊədlɪnɪs] *n* Feigheit *f*.

cowardly ['kaʊədlɪ] *adj* feig(e).

cow: ~bell *n* Kuhglocke *f*; **~boy** *n* **(a)** Cowboy *m*; **to play ~boys and Indians** Indianer spielen; **(b)** *(fig inf) (incompetent)* Pfuscher *m*; *(dishonest)* Gauner *m (inf)*; **a ~boy outfit** ein windiges Unternehmen *(inf)*; **~boy hat** *n* Cowboyhut *m*; **~catcher** *n (Rail)* Schienenräumer *m*; **~ dung** *n* Kuhmist *m*.

cower ['kaʊəʳ] *vi* sich ducken; *(squatting)* kauern ◆ **to ~ before sb** vor jdm ducken; **he stood ~ing in a corner** er stand geduckt in einer Ecke; **the ~ing peasants** die geduckten Bauern.

◆**cower away** *vi* (furchtsam) ausweichen *(from* dat*)*.

◆**cower down** *vi* sich niederkauern.

cow: ~girl *n* Cowgirl *nt*; **~hand** *n* Hilfscowboy *m*; *(on farm)* Stallknecht *m*; **~herd** *n* Kuhhirte *m*; **~hide** *n* **(a)** *(untanned)* Kuhhaut *f*; *(no pl: leather)* Rindsleder *nt*; **(b)** *(US: whip)* Lederpeitsche *f*.

cowl [kaʊl] *n* **(a)** *(monk's hood)* Kapuze *f*. **(b)** *(chimney ~)* (Schornstein)kappe *f*.

cowlick ['kaʊlɪk] *n* Tolle *f*.

cowling ['kaʊlɪŋ] *n (Aviat)* Motorhaube *f*.

cowl neck *n* Schalrollkragen *m*.

cowman ['kaʊmən] *n, pl* **-men** [-mən] *(farm labourer)* Stallbursche *m*; *(US: cattle rancher)* Viehzüchter *m*.

co-worker ['kəʊ'wɜːkəʳ] *n* Kollege *m*, Kollegin *f*.

cow: ~-parsley *n* Wiesenkerbel *m*; **~-pat** *n* Kuhfladen *m*; **~poke** *n (US inf)*

Kuhheini (*pej inf*), Cowboy *m*; **~pox** *n* Kuhpocken *pl*; **~puncher** *n* (*US inf*) Cowboy *m*.
cowrie, cowry ['kaʊrɪ] *n* Kaurischnecke *f*.
cow: ~shed *n* Kuhstall *m*; **~slip** *n* (*Brit: primrose*) Schlüsselblume *f*; (*US: kingcup*) Sumpfdotterblume *f*.
cox [kɒks] 1 *n* Steuermann *m*.
2 *vt crew* Steuermann sein für.
3 *vi* steuern.
coxcomb ['kɒkskəʊm] *n* (*old*) Stutzer *m* (*old*).
coxless ['kɒkslɪs] *adj* ohne Steuermann.
coxswain ['kɒksn] *n* **(a)** (*in rowing*) *see* **cox 1**. **(b)** (*Naut*) Boot(s)führer *m*.
coy *adj* (*+er*), **~ly** *adv* [kɔɪ, -lɪ] (*affectedly shy*) verschämt; (*coquettish*) neckisch, kokett.
coyness ['kɔɪnɪs] *n see adj* Verschämtheit *f*; neckisches *or* kokettes Benehmen.
coyote [kɔɪ'əʊtɪ] *n* Kojote *m*.
coypu ['kɔɪpuː] *n* Sumpfbiber *m*.
cozy *adj* (*US*) *see* **cosy**.
CP *abbr of* **Communist Party** KP *f*.
cp *abbr of* **compare** vgl.
CPA (*US*) *abbr of* **certified public accountant**.
cpi *abbr of* **characters per inch** cpi.
CPI (*US*) *abbr of* **Consumer Price Index**.
Cpl *abbr of* **Corporal**.
CP/M *abbr of* **control program/monitor** CP/M.
CPO *abbr of* **(a)** (*Naut*) **chief petty officer**. **(b)** (*Police*) **crime prevention officer**.
CPR *abbr of* **cardiopulmonary resuscitation**.
cps *abbr of* **characters per second** cps, Zeichen *pl* pro Sekunde.
CPU *abbr of* **central processing unit** CPU, Zentraleinheit *f*.
crab¹ [kræb] *n* **(a)** Krabbe *f*; (*small also*) Krebs *m*; (*as food*) Krabbe *f* ♦ **to catch a ~** (*Rowing*) einen Krebs fangen. **(b)** (*~-louse*) Filzlaus *f*. **(c)** (*Gymnastics*) Brücke *f*.
crab² *vi* nörgeln.
crab apple *n* (*fruit*) Holzapfel *m*; (*tree*) Holzapfelbaum *m*.
crabbed ['kræbd] *adj* **(a)** (*person*) griesgrämig, mürrisch. **(b)** *handwriting* kritzelig, unleserlich.
crabby ['kræbɪ] *adj* (*+er*) *see* **crabbed (a)**.
crab: ~ grass *n* Fingerhirse *f*; **~louse** *n* Filzlaus *f*.
crack [kræk] 1 *n* **(a)** Riß *m*; (*between floorboards etc*) Ritze *f*; (*wider hole etc*) Spalte *f*; (*fine line: in pottery, glass etc*) Sprung *m* ♦ **leave the window open a ~** laß das Fenster einen Spalt offen; **at the ~ of dawn** in aller Frühe.
(b) (*sharp noise*) (*of wood etc breaking*) Knacks *m*; (*of gun, whip*) Knall(en *nt no pl*) *m*; (*of thunder*) Schlag *m* ♦ **at the ~ of doom** beim Jüngsten Gericht.
(c) (*sharp blow*) Schlag *m* ♦ **to give sb/oneself a ~ on the head** jdm eins auf den Kopf geben/sich (*dat*) den Kopf anschlagen.
(d) (*inf*) (*gibe*) Stichelei *f*; (*joke*) Witz *m* ♦ **to make a ~ about sb/sth** einen Witz über jdn/etw reißen.
(e) (*inf: attempt*) **to have a ~ at sth** etw mal probieren (*inf*).
(f) (*Drugs*) Crack *nt*.
2 *adj attr* erstklassig; (*Mil*) Elite- ♦ **~ shot** Meisterschütze *m*.
3 *vt* **(a)** (*make a ~ in*) *glass, china, pottery* einen Sprung machen in (*+acc*); *bone* anbrechen, anknacksen (*inf*); *skin, ground* rissig machen; *ground, ice* einen Riß/Risse machen in (*+acc*) ♦ **to ~ a rib** sich (*dat*) eine Rippe anbrechen.
(b) (*break*) *nuts, safe* (*inf*), (*fig*) *code* knacken; *case, problem* lösen ♦ **to ~ (open) a bottle** einer Flasche (*dat*) den Hals brechen; **I've ~ed it** (*solved it*) ich hab's!
(c) *joke* reißen.
(d) *whip* knallen mit; *finger, joint* knacken mit.
(e) (*hit sharply*) schlagen ♦ **he ~ed his head against the pavement** er krachte mit dem Kopf aufs Pflaster.
(f) (*distil*) *petroleum* kracken ♦ **~ing plant** Krackanlage *f*.
4 *vi* **(a)** (*get a ~*) (*pottery, glass*) einen Sprung/Sprünge bekommen, springen; (*ice, road*) einen Riß/Risse bekommen; (*lips, skin*) spröde *or* rissig werden; (*bones*) einen Knacks bekommen (*inf*); (*break*) brechen ♦ **at last his stern face ~ed and he laughed** schließlich verzog sich seine ernste Miene zu einem Lachen.
(b) (*make a ~ing sound*) (*twigs, joints*) knacken, krachen; (*whip, gun*) knallen.
(c) (*hit sharply*) schlagen, krachen.
(d) (*break: voice*) (*with emotion*) versagen ♦ **his voice is ~ing/beginning to ~** (*boy*) er ist im/kommt in den Stimmbruch.
(e) (*inf*) **to get ~ing** loslegen (*inf*), sich daran machen; **to get ~ing with** *or* **on sth** mit etw loslegen (*inf*), sich an etw (*acc*) machen; **get ~ing!** los jetzt!; (*speed up*) mach(t) mal ein bißchen Dampf! (*inf*).
(f) *see* **~ up 1 (b)**. **the spy ~ed under torture** der Agent ist unter der Folter zusammengebrochen.
♦**crack down** *vi* **(a)** (*whip*) niederknallen, niederkrachen. **(b)** (*clamp down*) hart durchgreifen (*on* bei).
♦**crack up** 1 *vi* **(a)** (*break into pieces*) zerbrechen; (*road surface, lips*) aufspringen, rissig werden; (*ice*) brechen; (*machine, plane*) auseinanderbrechen, auseinanderfallen; (*make-up*) rissig werden.
(b) (*fig inf*) (*person*) durchdrehen (*inf*); (*under strain*) zusammenbrechen; (*have a mental breakdown*) einen Nervenzusammenbruch haben; (*organization*) auseinanderfallen, zusammenbrechen; (*lose ability, strength: athlete etc*) abbauen ♦ **I/he must be ~ing ~** (*hum*) so fängt's an (*inf*); **she ~ed ~ in the witness box** sie brach auf der Zeugenbank zusammen.
2 *vt sep* (*inf*) **he's/it's not all he's/it's ~ed ~ to be** so toll ist er/es dann auch wieder nicht; **he's ~ed ~ to be some sort of genius** er wird als eine Art Genie gepriesen; **to ~ sb/sth ~ to be really good** jdn/etw über den grünen Klee loben (*inf*).
crackajack *n, adj* (*US*) *see* **crackerjack**.
crack: ~brained ['krækbreɪnd] *adj* (*inf*) verrückt, irre; **~-down** *n* (*inf*) scharfes Durchgreifen; **to order a ~-down on sth** anordnen, bei etw scharf durchzugreifen.
cracked [krækt] *adj* **(a)** *glass, plate, ice* gesprungen; *rib, bone* angebrochen, angeknackst (*inf*); (*broken*) gebrochen; *surface, walls, make-up* rissig. **(b)** (*inf: mad*) übergeschnappt (*inf*).
cracker ['krækəʳ] *n* **(a)** (*biscuit*) Kräcker *m*. **(b)** (*fire~*) Knallkörper *m*; (*Christmas ~*) Knallbonbon *nt*. **(c)** **~s** *pl* (*nut ~s*) Nußknacker *m*. **(d)** (*Brit inf*) tolle Frau (*inf*); toller Mann (*inf*); tolles Ding (*inf*).
crackerjack, (*US*) **crackajack** ['krækədʒæk] 1 *n* (*person*) Kanone *f* (*inf*); (*thing*) Knüller *m* (*inf*).
2 *adj* bombig (*inf*).
crackers ['krækəz] *add pred* (*Brit inf*) übergeschnappt (*inf*) ♦ **to go ~** überschnappen (*inf*).
cracking ['krækɪŋ] *adj* (*inf*) *pace* scharf; (*dated: good*) *novel* klasse *inv* (*inf*), phantastisch.
crack-jaw ['krækdʒɔː] (*inf*) 1 *adj attr word, name* zungenbrecherisch.
2 *n* Zungenbrecher *m*.
crackle ['krækl] 1 *vi* (*dry leaves*) rascheln; (*paper also*) knistern; (*fire*) knistern, prasseln; (*twigs, telephone line*) knacken; (*machine gun*) knattern; (*bacon*) brutzeln ♦ **the line was crackling so much** es knackte so stark in der Leitung.
2 *vt paper* rascheln *or* knistern mit.
3 *n* **(a)** (*crackling noise*) *see vi* Rascheln *nt*; Knistern *nt*; Knistern, Prasseln *nt*; Knacken *nt*; Knattern *nt*; Brutzeln *nt*.
(b) (*on china, porcelain*) Craquelé, Krakelee *m or nt*.
crackleware ['kræklwɛəʳ] *n* Craqueléporzellan *nt*.
crackling ['kræklɪŋ] *n, no pl* **(a)** *see* **crackle 3 (a)**. **(b)** (*Cook*) Kruste *f* (*des Schweinebratens*).
cracknel ['kræknl] *n* (harter) Keks.
crackpot ['krækpɒt] (*inf*) 1 *n* Spinner(in *f*) *m* (*inf*), Irre(r) *mf*.
2 *adj* verrückt, irre.
cracksman ['kræksmən] *n, pl* **-men** [-mən] (*sl*) Safeknacker *m* (*inf*).
crack-up ['krækʌp] *n* (*inf*) Zusammenbruch *m*.
cradle ['kreɪdl] 1 *n* (*cot, fig: birthplace*) Wiege *f*; (*support*) (*of phone*) Gabel *f*; (*for invalids*) Schutzgestell *nt* (*zum Abhalten des Bettzeugs von Verletzungen*); (*for ship*) (Ablauf)schlitten *m*; (*Build, for window-cleaners*) Hängegerüst *nt*; (*in sea rescues*) Hosenboje *f*; (*for mechanic under car*) Schlitten *m* ♦ **from the ~ to the grave** von der Wiege bis zur Bahre; **right from the ~** von klein auf, von Kindesbeinen an.
2 *vt* **(a)** (*hold closely*) an sich (*acc*) drücken ♦ **he was cradling his injured arm** er hielt sich (*dat*) seinen verletzten Arm; **to ~ sb/sth in one's arms/lap** jdn/etw fest in den Armen/auf dem Schoß halten; **the baby lay ~d in her lap** das Baby lag (geborgen) in ihrem Schoß; **he ~d the telephone under his chin** er klemmte sich (*dat*) den Hörer unters Kinn; **the way he ~s the guitar** wie er die Gitarre zärtlich hält.
(b) *receiver* auflegen.
cradle: ~ cap *n* Milchschorf *m*; **~-snatcher** *n* (*inf*) *see* **baby-snatcher**; **~-snatching** *n* (*inf*) *see* **baby-snatching**; **~-song** *n* Wiegenlied *nt*.
craft [krɑːft] *n* **(a)** (*handicraft*) Kunst *f*, Handwerk *nt*; (*trade*) Handwerk, Gewerbe *nt*; (*weaving, pottery etc*) Kunstgewerbe *nt* ♦ **it's a real ~** das ist eine echte Kunst; *see* **art¹**.
(b) (*guild*) (Handwerker)innung, (Handwerks)zunft (*Hist*) *f*.
(c) *no pl* (*skill*) Geschick(lichkeit *f*) *nt*, Kunstfertigkeit *f*.
(d) *no pl* (*cunning*) List *f* ♦ **to obtain sth by ~** sich (*dat*) etw erlisten, etw durch List bekommen.
(e) *pl* - (*boat*) Boot *nt*.
craft fair *n* Handwerksmarkt *m*.
craftily ['krɑːftɪlɪ] *adv* schlau, clever.
craftiness ['krɑːftɪnɪs] *n* Schlauheit, Cleverness *f*.
craftsman ['krɑːftsmən] *n, pl* **-men** [-mən] Handwerker *m* ♦ **he's a real ~** er ist ein echter Künstler.
craftsmanship ['krɑːftsmənʃɪp] *n* Handwerkskunst *f*; (*of person also*) handwerkliches Können, Kunstfertigkeit *f* ♦ **there's no ~ left these days** heutzutage gibt es einfach keine Handwerkskunst mehr.
craft union *n* Handwerkergewerkschaft *f*.
crafty ['krɑːftɪ] *adj* (*+er*) schlau, clever ♦ **he is a ~ one** (*inf*) er ist ein ganz Schlauer (*inf*); **he's as ~ as a fox** er ist ein schlauer Fuchs; **he took a ~ glance at ...** er riskierte einen verstohlenen Blick auf (*+acc*) ...
crag [kræg] *n* Fels *m*.
craggy ['krægɪ] *adj* (*+er*) (*rocky*) felsig; (*jagged*) zerklüftet; *face* kantig ♦ **he was good-looking in a ~ sort of way** er sah auf eine herbe, kantige Art gut aus.
crake [kreɪk] *n* Ralle *f*.
cram [kræm] 1 *vt* **(a)** (*fill*) vollstopfen, vollpacken; (*stuff in*) hineinstopfen (*in(to)* in *+acc*); *people* hineinzwängen (*in(to)* in *+acc*) ♦ **the room was ~med** der Raum war gestopft voll; **we were all ~med into one room** wir waren alle in einem Zimmer zusammengepfercht; **he ~med his hat (down) over his eyes** er zog sich (*dat*) den Hut tief ins Gesicht.
(b) (*for exam*) *Latin verbs etc* pauken (*inf*), büffeln (*inf*); (*teach for exam*) *pupil* pauken mit (*inf*) ♦ **to ~ sth into sb** jdm etw einpauken (*inf*).
2 *vi* (*swot*) pauken (*inf*), büffeln (*inf*).
♦**cram in** *vi* (*people*) sich hinein-/hereindrängen *or* -quetschen *or* -zwängen

(*-to* in *+acc*).

cram-full ['kræmfʊl] *adj (inf)* vollgestopft (*of* mit), gestopft voll (*inf*).

crammer ['kræməʳ] *n (tutor)* Einpauker *m*; *(student)* Büffler(in *f*) *m (inf)*; *(book)* Paukbuch *nt*; *(school)* Paukschule *f*.

cramp¹ [kræmp] 1 *n (Med)* Krampf *m* ◆ **to have ~ in one's leg** einen Krampf im Bein haben; **to have the ~s** *(US)* Krämpfe haben; **writer's ~** Schreibkrampf *m*.

2 *vt* **(a)** *(also* **~ up**) *persons* zusammenpferchen, einpferchen; *writing* eng zusammenkritzeln. **(b)** *(fig: hinder)* behindern ◆ **to ~ sb's style** jdm im Weg sein. **(c)** *(give ~ to)* Krämpfe *pl* verursachen in *(+dat)*.

cramp² 1 *n (also* **~ iron**) Bauklammer *f*.

2 *vt* klammern.

cramped [kræmpt] *adj* **(a)** *space* eng, beschränkt ◆ **we are very ~ (for space)** wir sind räumlich sehr beschränkt. **(b)** *position* verkrampft. **(c)** *handwriting* eng zusammengekritzelt.

crampon ['kræmpən] *n* Steigeisen *nt*.

cranberry ['krænbərɪ] *n* Preiselbeere, Kronsbeere *f* ◆ **~ sauce** Preiselbeersoße *f*.

crane [kreɪn] 1 *n* **(a)** Kran *m* ◆ **~ driver** Kranführer *m*. **(b)** *(Orn)* Kranich *m*.

2 *vt*: **to ~ one's neck** den Hals recken, sich *(dat)* fast den Hals verrenken *(inf)*.

3 *vi (also* **~ forward**) den Hals *or* den Kopf recken.

cranefly ['kreɪnflaɪ] *n* Schnake *f*.

cranesbill ['kreɪnzbɪl] *n (Bot)* Storchschnabel *m*.

crania ['kreɪnɪə] *pl of* **cranium**.

cranial ['kreɪnɪəl] *adj (Anat)* Schädel-, kranial *(spec)*.

cranium ['kreɪnɪəm] *n, pl* **crania** *(Anat)* Schädel *m*, Cranium *nt (spec)*.

crank¹ [kræŋk] *n (eccentric person)* Spinner(in *f*) *m (inf)*; *(US: cross person)* Griesgram *m*.

crank² 1 *n (Mech)* Kurbel *f*.

2 *vt (also:* **~ up**) ankurbeln.

crankcase ['kræŋkkeɪs] *n (Aut)* Kurbelgehäuse *nt*.

crankiness ['kræŋkɪnɪs] *n* **(a)** *(eccentricity)* Verrücktheit *f*. **(b)** *(US: bad temper)* Griesgrämigkeit *f*.

crankshaft ['kræŋkʃɑːft] *n (Aut)* Kurbelwelle *f*.

cranky ['kræŋkɪ] *adj (+er)* **(a)** *(eccentric)* verrückt. **(b)** *(US: bad-tempered)* griesgrämig.

cranny ['krænɪ] *n* Ritze, Spalte *f*; *see* **nook**.

crap [kræp] *(vulg)* 1 *n* **(a)** Scheiße *f (vulg)* ◆ **to go for/have a ~** scheißen gehen/scheißen *(vulg)*. **(b)** *(sl: rubbish)* Scheiße *f (sl)* ◆ **a load of ~** *(sl)* große Scheiße *(sl)*.

2 *vi* scheißen *(vulg)*.

3 *attr joke, job* Scheiß-.

◆**crap out** *vi (US sl)* kneifen *(of* vor *+dat)*.

crap game *n (US)* Würfelspiel *nt (mit zwei Würfeln)*.

crappy ['kræpɪ] *adj (+er) (sl)* beschissen *(sl)*, Scheiß- *(sl)*.

craps [kræps] *n (US)* Würfelspiel *nt* ◆ **to shoot ~** Würfel spielen.

crapshooter ['kræpʃuːtəʳ] *n* Würfelspieler *m*.

crash [kræʃ] 1 *n* **(a)** *(noise)* Krach(en *nt*) *m no pl*; *(of thunder, cymbals also, of drums)* Schlag *m* ◆ **there was a ~ upstairs** es hat oben gekracht; **the vase fell to the ground with a ~** die Vase fiel krachend zu Boden; **a ~ of thunder** ein Donnerschlag *m*; **the ~ of the waves against ...** das Krachen der Wellen gegen ...

(b) *(accident)* Unfall *m*, Unglück *nt*; *(collision also)* Zusammenstoß *m*; *(with several cars)* Karambolage *f*; *(plane ~)* (Flugzeug)unglück *nt* ◆ **to be in a (car) ~** in einen (Auto)unfall verwickelt sein; **to have a ~** (mit dem Auto) verunglücken, einen (Auto)unfall haben; *(cause it)* einen Unfall verursachen *or* bauen *(inf)*; **the impact of the ~** die Wucht des Aufpralls; *(into another car)* die Wucht des Zusammenstoßes.

(c) *(Fin)* Zusammenbruch *m*.

2 *adv* krach ◆ **he went ~ into a tree** er krachte gegen einen Baum; **~, bang, wallop!** *(inf)* bums! *(inf)*, krach! *(inf)*.

3 *vt* **(a)** *car, bicycle* einen Unfall haben mit; *plane* abstürzen mit ◆ **if you let him use your car he's bound to ~ it** wenn du ihm dein Auto gibst, fährt er es dir bestimmt kaputt *(inf)*; **to ~ one's car into sth** mit dem Auto gegen etw krachen *or* knallen *(inf)*; **the car was found ~ed** das Auto wurde demoliert aufgefunden.

(b) *(with particle: bang)* **he ~ed it to the ground** er knallte es auf den Boden *(inf)*; **stop ~ing the plates around** hör auf, mit den Tellern zu scheppern *(inf)*; **he ~ed the cymbals together** er schlug scheppernd die Becken zusammen; **he ~ed his head against the windscreen** er krachte mit dem Kopf gegen die Windschutzscheibe; **he ~ed the car through the barrier** er fuhr mit dem Auto voll durch die Absperrung *(inf)*.

(c) *(inf: gatecrash)* **to ~ a party** uneingeladen zu einer Party gehen, in eine Party hineinplatzen.

4 *vi* **(a)** *(have an accident)* verunglücken, einen Unfall haben; *(plane)* abstürzen ◆ **to ~ into sth** gegen etw *(acc)* krachen *or* knallen *(inf)*.

(b) *(with particle: move with a ~)* krachen ◆ **to ~ to the ground/through sth** zu Boden/durch etw krachen; **they went ~ing through the undergrowth** sie brachen krachend durchs Unterholz; **his fist ~ed into Tom's face** seine Faust landete krachend in Toms Gesicht; **the whole roof came ~ing down (on him)** das ganze Dach krachte auf ihn herunter; **his whole world ~ed about him** *or* **his ears** seine ganze Welt brach zusammen.

(c) *(Fin)* pleite machen *(inf)* ◆ **when Wall Street ~ed** als Wall Street zusammenbrach.

(d) *(inf: sleep: also* **~ out**) pofen *(sl)*; *(fall asleep)* einpofen *(sl)*; *(become unconscious)* wegtreten *(sl)*.

crash: ~ barrier *n* Leitplanke *f*; **~ course** *n* Schnell- *or* Intensivkurs *m*; **~ diet** *n* Radikalkur *f*; **~ dive** 1 *n* Schnelltauchmanöver *nt*; 2 *vti* schnelltauchen; **~ helmet** *n* Sturzhelm *m*.

crashing ['kræʃɪŋ] *adj (inf)* **he's/it's a ~ bore** er/es ist fürchterlich *or* zum Einschlafen langweilig *(inf)*.

crash: ~-land 1 *vi* eine Bruchlandung machen, bruchlanden; 2 *vt* eine Bruchlandung machen mit, bruchlanden mit; **~-landing** *n* Bruchlandung *f*; **~ programme** *n* Intensivprogramm *nt*.

crass [krɑːs] *adj (+er) (stupid, unsubtle)* kraß; *ignorance also* haarsträubend; *(coarse) behaviour* unfein, derb ◆ **must you be so ~ about it?** müssen Sie sich so kraß ausdrücken?

crassly ['krɑːslɪ] *adv* kraß; *behave* unfein.

crassness ['krɑːsnɪs] *n see adj* Kraßheit *f*; Derbheit *f*.

crate [kreɪt] 1 *n (also inf: car, plane)* Kiste *f*; *(beer ~, milk ~)* Kasten *m*.

2 *vt goods* (in Kisten/eine Kiste) (ver)packen.

crater ['kreɪtəʳ] *n* Krater *m*.

cravat(te) [krə'væt] *n* Halstuch *nt*.

crave [kreɪv] *vt (liter: beg)* erbitten; *mercy also* erflehen; *(desire) attention, drink etc* sich sehnen nach ◆ **to ~ sb's pardon** *(form)* jdn um Verzeihung anflehen; **ladies and gentlemen, may I ~ your indulgence?** *(form)* meine Damen und Herren, darf ich um Ihre werte Aufmerksamkeit bitten?; **may I ~ your indulgence a moment longer?** *(form)* darf ich Ihre Geduld noch etwas länger in Anspruch nehmen?

◆**crave for** *vi +prep obj* sich sehnen nach.

craven ['kreɪvən] 1 *adj* feig(e) ◆ **a ~ coward** ein elender Feigling, eine feige Memme *(geh)*.

2 *n (liter)* Memme *f (geh)*.

craving ['kreɪvɪŋ] *n* Verlangen *nt* ◆ **to have a ~ for sth** Verlangen nach etw haben; **pregnant women have strange ~s** schwangere Frauen haben eigenartige Gelüste.

crawfish ['krɔːfɪʃ] *n see* **crayfish (b)**.

crawl [krɔːl] 1 *n* **(a)** *(on hands and knees)* Kriechen *nt*; *(slow speed)* Schnecken- *or* Kriechtempo *nt*; *(Brit inf: pub-~)* Kneipenbummel *m* ◆ **it was a long ~** wir mußten lange kriechen; *(in car)* wir sind lange nur im Kriechtempo vorangekommen; **we could only go at a ~** wir kamen nur im Schnecken- *or* Kriechtempo voran; **to join the ~ to the coast** sich der (Auto)schlange zur Küste anschließen.

(b) *(swimming stroke)* Kraul(stil) *m*, Kraulen *nt* ◆ **to do the ~** kraulen; **she's very fast at the ~** sie ist sehr schnell im Kraulen.

2 *vi* **(a)** kriechen; *(baby, insects also)* krabbeln; *(time also)* schleichen ◆ **he tried to ~ away** er versuchte wegzukriechen.

(b) *(be infested)* wimmeln *(with* von) ◆ **the place is ~ing!** hier wimmelt es von Ungeziefer!; **the meat was ~ing with flies** das Fleisch wimmelte nur so von Fliegen; **the street was ~ing with policemen** auf der Straße wimmelte es von Polizisten.

(c) **spiders make my flesh** *or* **skin ~** wenn ich Spinnen sehe, kriege ich eine Gänsehaut.

(d) *(inf: suck up)* kriechen *(to* vor *+dat)* ◆ **he went ~ing to teacher** er ist gleich zum Lehrer gerannt.

crawler ['krɔːləʳ] *n* **(a)** *(inf: sycophant)* Kriecher(in *f*) *m*. **(b)** **~s** *pl (rompers)* Spielanzug *m*.

crawler lane *n (Brit Aut)* Kriechspur *f*.

crayfish ['kreɪfɪʃ] *n* **(a)** *(freshwater)* Flußkrebs *m*. **(b)** *(saltwater: also* **crawfish**) Languste *f*.

crayon ['kreɪən] 1 *n* **(a)** *(pencil)* Buntstift *m*; *(wax ~)* Wachs(mal)stift *m*; *(chalk ~)* Pastellstift *m*, Malkreide *f*. **(b)** *(picture)* Pastell *nt*, Kreide- *or* Pastellzeichnung *f*.

2 *vti* (mit Bunt-/Wachsmal-/Pastellstiften) zeichnen *or* malen.

◆**crayon in** *vt sep drawing* ausmalen.

craze [kreɪz] 1 *n* Fimmel *m (inf)* ◆ **it's all the ~** *(inf)* das ist große Mode; **there's a ~ for collecting old things just now** es ist zur Zeit große Mode, alte Sachen zu sammeln.

2 *vt* **(a)** *(make insane)* **to be half ~d with grief** vor Schmerz halb wahnsinnig sein; **he had a ~d look on his face** er hatte den Gesichtsausdruck eines Wahnsinnigen. **(b)** *pottery, glazing* rissig machen.

3 *vi (pottery)* rissig werden.

crazily ['kreɪzɪlɪ] *adv (madly)* verrückt; *lean, tilt* unwahrscheinlich.

crazy ['kreɪzɪ] *adj (+er)* **(a)** verrückt *(with* vor *+dat)* ◆ **to send** *or* **drive sb ~** jdn verrückt *or* wahnsinnig machen; **to go ~** verrückt *or* wahnsinnig werden; **that's ~** das ist doch verrückt!; **like ~** *(inf)* wie verrückt *(inf)*.

(b) *(inf: enthusiastic)* verrückt *(inf)* ◆ **to be ~ about sb/sth** ganz verrückt *or* wild auf jdn/etw sein *(inf)*; **football-~** Fußball-verrückt *(inf)*; **to be ~ for sb** verrückt nach jdm sein *(inf)*.

(c) *angle, tilt* unwahrscheinlich.

crazy: ~ bone *n (US)* Musikantenknochen *m*; **~ paving** *n* Mosaikpflaster *nt*; **~ quilt** *n (US)* Flickendecke *f*.

CRC ['siːɑː'siː] *n abbr of* **camera-ready copy**.

CRE *(Brit) abbr of* **Commission for Racial Equality**.

creak [kriːk] 1 *n* Knarren *nt no pl*; *(of hinges, bed springs)* Quietschen *nt no pl*; *(of knees etc)* Knacken *nt no pl* ◆ **to give a loud ~** laut knarren/quietschen/knacken; **a series of ~s** knarrende/quietschende/knackende Geräusche.

2 *vi* knarren; *(hinges, bed springs)* quietschen; *(knees etc)* knacken.

creaky ['kriːkɪ] *adj (+er) see vi* knarrend; quietschend; knackend.

cream [kriːm] [1] *n* **(a)** Sahne *f*, Rahm *m* (*S Ger*); (*~ pudding, artificial ~*) Creme, Krem *f* ◆ **~ of tomato/chicken soup** Tomaten-/Hühnercremesuppe *f*; **~ of tartar** Weinstein *m*.
(b) (*lotion*) Creme *f*.
(c) (*colour*) Creme(farbe *f*) *nt* ◆ **a skirt in a pale shade of ~** ein blaßcremefarbener Rock.
(d) (*fig: best*) die Besten; (*of society also*) Crème, Elite *f* ◆ **our rivals take the ~ of the applicants** unsere Konkurrenz sahnt die besten Bewerber ab; **the ~ of society** die Crème der Gesellschaft; **to take the ~** den Rahm abschöpfen.
[2] *adj* **(a)** (*colour*) creme *inv*, cremefarben *or* -farbig.
(b) (*made with ~*) Sahne-; Creme- ◆ **~ soups** Cremesuppen *pl*.
[3] *vt* **(a)** (*put ~ on*) *face etc* eincremen. **(b)** *butter, eggs etc* cremig rühren; *potatoes, fruit* pürieren ◆ **~ed potatoes** Kartoffelpüree *nt*. **(c)** (*skim*) *milk* entrahmen. **(d)** (*allow to form a ~*) *milk* aufrahmen lassen. **(e)** (*US inf: defeat easily*) in die Pfanne hauen (*inf*), putzen (*sl*).
[4] *vi* (*milk*) aufrahmen.
◆**cream off** *vt sep* (*lit*) abschöpfen; (*fig*) *profits also, the best* absahnen.
cream: ~ bun *n* Eclair *nt*; **~ cake** *n* Sahnetorte *f*; Cremetorte *f*; (*small*) Sahnetörtchen *nt*; Cremetörtchen *nt*; **~ cheese** *n* (Doppelrahm)frischkäse *m*.
creamer ['kriːməʳ] *n* **(a)** (*jug*) Sahnekännchen *nt*. **(b)** (*skimming machine*) Milchzentrifuge *or* -schleuder *f*. **(c)** (*dried milk*) Milchpulver *nt*.
creamery ['kriːmərɪ] *n* Molkerei *f*; (*shop*) Milchgeschäft *nt*.
cream: ~ puff *n* Windbeutel *m*; **~ soda** *n* Sodawasser *nt* mit Vanillegeschmack; **~ tea** *n* Nachmittagstee *m*.
creamy ['kriːmɪ] *adj* (*+er*) **(a)** (*tasting of cream*) sahnig; (*smooth*) cremig ◆ **a ~ complexion** ein zarter Teint. **(b)** (*cream-coloured*) creme(farben *or* -farbig).
crease [kriːs] [1] *n* **(a)** Falte *f*; (*deliberate fold*) (*in material also*) Kniff *m*; (*in paper also*) Falz, Kniff *m*; (*ironed: in trousers etc*) (Bügel)falte *f* ◆ **to be a mass of ~s** völlig zerknittert sein; **to put a ~ in a pair of trousers** eine Falte in ein Paar Hosen bügeln.
(b) (*Sport*) Linie *f*.
[2] *vt* (*deliberately*) *clothes* Falten/eine Falte machen in (*+acc*); *material, paper* Kniffe/einen Kniff machen in (*+acc*); *paper* falzen; (*unintentionally*) zerknittern ◆ **smartly ~d trousers** Hosen mit sauberen Bügelfalten.
[3] *vi* knittern ◆ **his face ~d with laughter** er fing an zu lachen.
◆**crease up** *vi* (*inf: with laughter*) sich kringeln (*inf*).
crease-proof ['kriːspruːf], **crease-resistant** ['kriːsrɪzɪstənt] *adj* knitterfrei.
create [kriː'eɪt] [1] *vt* **(a)** schaffen; *new style, fashion also* kreieren; *the world, man* erschaffen; *draught, noise, fuss* verursachen; *difficulties* machen; *problems* (*person*) schaffen; (*action, event*) verursachen, hervorbringen; *impression* machen; (*Comput*) *file* anlegen ◆ **to ~ a sensation** eine Sensation sein; **to ~ a fuss** Theater machen (*inf*).
(b) (*appoint*) *peer* ernennen ◆ **peers can only be ~d by the reigning monarch** nur der regierende Monarch kann jemanden in den Adelsstand erheben; **to ~ sb baron** jdn zum Baron erheben *or* ernennen.
[2] *vi* (*Brit inf*) Theater machen (*inf*).
creation [kriː'eɪʃən] *n* **(a)** *no pl see vt* Schaffung *f*; Kreation *f*; Erschaffung *f*; Verursachung *f*; Schaffen *nt*; Verursachung *f*; Erhebung, Ernennung *f*.
(b) *no pl* **the C~** die Schöpfung; **all ~, the whole of ~** die Schöpfung, alle Kreatur *f*, alle Geschöpfe *pl*.
(c) (*created object*) (*Art*) Werk *nt*; (*Fashion*) Kreation *f*.
creative [kriː'eɪtɪv] *adj power, skill etc* schöpferisch; *approach, attitude, person* kreativ ◆ **~ writing** dichterisches Schreiben; **~ toys** Spielzeug *nt* zum Gestalten und Werken.
creativeness [ˌkriː'eɪtɪvnɪs], **creativity** [ˌkriːeɪ'tɪvɪtɪ] *n* schöpferische Begabung *or* Kraft; (*of person also, of approach, attitude*) Kreativität *f*.
creator [kriː'eɪtəʳ] *n* Schöpfer(in *f*) *m*.
creature ['kriːtʃəʳ] *n* **(a)** Geschöpf, (Lebe)wesen *nt*, Kreatur *f* ◆ **what a superb ~!** welch ein herrliches Geschöpf!; **all dumb ~s** die stumme Kreatur; **she's a funny/beautiful ~** sie ist ein komisches/schönes Geschöpf; **there wasn't a ~ in sight** nirgends regte sich etwas, kein Lebewesen war zu sehen.
(b) (*subordinate person*) Geschöpf *nt*.
creature comforts *npl* leibliches Wohl.
crèche [kreɪʃ] *n* **(a)** (*esp Brit: day nursery*) (Kinder)krippe *f or* -hort *m*; (*esp US: children's home*) Kinderheim *nt*. **(b)** (*crib*) Krippe *f*.
cred [kred] *see* **street ~**.
credence ['kriːdəns] *n* **(a)** *no pl* (*belief*) Glaube *m* ◆ **to lend ~ to sth** etw glaubwürdig erscheinen lassen *or* machen; **worthy of ~** glaubwürdig; **to give** *or* **attach ~ to sth** einer Sache (*dat*) Glauben schenken; **letter of ~** Beglaubigungsschreiben *nt*.
(b) (*Eccl: also* **~ table**) Kredenz *f*.
credentials [krɪ'denʃəlz] *npl* (*references*) Referenzen, Zeugnisse *pl*; (*papers of identity*) (Ausweis)papiere *pl* ◆ **to present one's ~** seine Papiere vorlegen.
credibility [ˌkredə'bɪlɪtɪ] *n* Glaubwürdigkeit *f* ◆ **~ gap** Mangel *m* an Glaubwürdigkeit; **his ~ gap widened** er verlor immer mehr an Glaubwürdigkeit; **his ~ rating is pretty low** er wird als nicht sehr glaubwürdig eingestuft.
credible *adj*, **-bly** *adv* ['kredɪbl, -ɪ] glaubwürdig.
credit ['kredɪt] [1] *n* **(a)** *no pl* (*Fin*) Kredit *m*; (*in pub, hotel, shop etc*) Stundung *f* ◆ **the bank will let me have £5,000 ~** die Bank räumt mir einen Kredit von £ 5.000 ein; **to buy/sell on ~** auf Kredit kaufen/gegen Kredit verkaufen; **his ~ is good** er ist kreditwürdig; (*in small shop*) er ist vertrauenswürdig; **to give sb (unlimited) ~** jdm (unbegrenzt) Kredit geben; **we can't give you ~** (*bank*) wir können Ihnen keinen Kredit geben; (*corner shop etc*) wir können Ihnen nichts stunden; **pubs do not usually give ~** in Lokalen bekommt man normalerweise nichts gestundet; **letter of ~** Kreditbrief *m*, Akkreditiv *nt*.
(b) (*Fin: money possessed by person, firm*) (Gut)haben *nt*; (*Comm: sum of money*) Kreditposten *m* ◆ **to be in ~** Geld auf dem Konto haben; **to keep one's account in ~** sein Konto nicht überziehen; **to place a sum to one's ~** sich (*dat*) eine Summe gutschreiben lassen; **the ~s and debits** Soll und Haben *nt*; **how much have we got to our ~?** wieviel haben wir auf dem Konto?
(c) *no pl* (*standing*) Ansehen *nt* ◆ **a man of good ~** ein angesehener Mann.
(d) *no pl* (*honour*) Ehre *f*; (*recognition*) Anerkennung *f*; (*Sch, Univ: distinction*) Auszeichnung *f* ◆ **he's a ~ to his family** er macht seiner Familie Ehre; **that's to his ~** das ehrt ihn; **well, all ~ to you for not succumbing** alle Achtung, daß Sie nicht nachgegeben haben; **at least he has this to his ~** das spricht immerhin für ihn; **to reflect great ~ on sb** jdm große Ehre machen; **to come out of sth with ~** ehrenvoll aus etw hervorgehen; **to get all the ~** die ganze Anerkennung *or* Ehre einstecken; **I do all the work and he gets all the ~** ich mache die Arbeit, und ihm wird es als Verdienst angerechnet; **the ~ for that should go to him** das ist sein Verdienst; **to take the ~ for sth** das Verdienst für etw in Anspruch nehmen; **~ where ~ is due** (*prov*) Ehre, wem Ehre gebührt (*prov*).
(e) *no pl* (*belief*) Glaube *m* ◆ **to give ~ to sth** etw glauben, einer Sache (*dat*) Glauben schenken; **to lend ~ to sth** etw glaubwürdig erscheinen lassen *or* machen; **to gain ~** an Glaubwürdigkeit gewinnen; **I gave you ~ for more sense** ich habe Sie für vernünftiger gehalten; **worthy of ~** glaubwürdig.
(f) (*esp US Univ*) Schein *m* ◆ **to take** *or* **do ~s** Scheine machen.
(g) **~s** *pl* (*Film etc*) Vor-/Nachspann *m*; (*in book*) Herausgeber- und Mitarbeiterverzeichnis *nt*.
[2] *vt* **(a)** (*believe*) glauben ◆ **would you ~ it!** ist das denn zu glauben!, ist das denn die Möglichkeit!
(b) (*attribute*) zuschreiben (*+dat*) ◆ **I ~ed him with more sense** ich habe ihn für vernünftiger gehalten; **he was ~ed with having invented it/with having found that solution** die Erfindung wurde ihm zugeschrieben/es wurde als sein Verdienst angerechnet *or* es wurde ihm zugute gehalten, diese Lösung gefunden zu haben; **it's ~ed with (having) magic powers** ihm werden Zauberkräfte zugeschrieben; **one is hardly able to ~ him with having done such a silly thing** man kann kaum glauben, daß er so etwas Dummes getan hat.
(c) (*Fin*) gutschreiben ◆ **to ~ a sum to sb's account** jds Konto (*dat*) einen Betrag gutschreiben (lassen); **he had been ~ed with £100** ihm waren £ 100 gutgeschrieben worden.
creditable ['kredɪtəbl] *adj* **(a)** (*praiseworthy*) lobenswert, anerkennenswert.
(b) (*credible*) glaublich ◆ **I find it hardly ~** ich finde es höchst unglaublich.
creditably ['kredɪtəblɪ] *adv* löblich.
credit: ~ account *n* Kreditkonto *nt*; **~ agency** *n* (*giving credit*) Finanzierungsinstitut *nt*; (*for credit investigation*) Kreditschutzverein *m*; **~ arrangements** *npl* Kreditvereinbarungen *pl*; **~ balance** *n* Kontostand, Saldo *m*; **~ card** *n* Kreditkarte *f*; **~ check** *n* Überprüfung *f* der Kreditwürdigkeit; **to run a ~ check on sb** jds Kreditwürdigkeit überprüfen; **~ control** *n* Kreditüberwachung *f*; **~ facilities** *npl* Kreditmöglichkeiten *pl*; **~ limit** *n* Kreditgrenze *f*; **~ note** *n* Gutschrift *f*.
creditor ['kredɪtəʳ] *n* Gläubiger *m*.
credit: ~ page *n* Herausgeber- und Mitarbeiterverzeichnis *nt*; **~ rating** *n* Kreditwürdigkeit *f*; **to have a good/bad ~ rating** als kreditwürdig/als nicht kreditwürdig eingestuft werden; **~ rating agency** *n* Kreditschutzverein *m*, ≃ Schufa *f*; **~ sales** *npl* Kreditkäufe *pl*; **~ side** *n* (*lit, fig*) Habenseite *f*; **on the ~ side he's young** für ihn spricht, daß er jung ist; **~ squeeze** *n* Kreditbeschränkung *or* -knappheit *f*; **~ terms** *npl* Kreditbedingungen *pl*; **~ titles** *npl* (*Film*) *see* **credit 1 (g)**; **~-worthiness** *n* Kreditwürdigkeit *f*; **~-worthy** *adj* kreditwürdig.
credo ['kreɪdəʊ] *n* (*lit, fig*) Kredo, Glaubensbekenntnis *nt*.
credulity [krɪ'djuːlɪtɪ] *n, no pl* Leichtgläubigkeit *f*.
credulous *adj*, **~ly** *adv* ['kredjʊləs, -lɪ] leichtgläubig.
creed [kriːd] *n* (*Eccl*) (*prayer*) Glaubensbekenntnis *nt*; (*as part of service, fig also*) Kredo *nt*.
creek [kriːk] *n* (*esp Brit: inlet*) (kleine) Bucht; (*US: brook*) Bach *m* ◆ **to be up the ~** (*inf*) (*be in trouble*) in der Tinte sitzen (*inf*); (*be completely wrong*) auf dem falschen Dampfer sein (*inf*).
creel [kriːl] *n* Korb *m*.
creep [kriːp] (*vb: pret, ptp* **crept**) [1] *vi* **(a)** (*move quietly or slowly*) schleichen; (*with the body close to the ground, insects*) kriechen; (*plants*) (*horizontally*) kriechen; (*vertically*) klettern, sich ranken ◆ **ivy is a ~ing plant** Efeu ist eine Kletterpflanze; **time's ~ing on** die Zeit verrinnt; **~ing paralysis** schleichende Lähmung; **the water-level crept higher and higher** der Wasserspiegel kletterte immer höher.
(b) **the story made my flesh ~** bei der Geschichte überlief es mich kalt *or* bekam ich eine Gänsehaut.
[2] *n* **(a)** (*inf*) (*unpleasant person*) Widerling *m* (*inf*), widerlicher *or* fieser Typ (*inf*) ◆ **you little ~!** du fieser Typ (*inf*).
(b) (*inf*)**stop giving me the ~s** hör auf, da bekomme ich eine Gänsehaut; **her make-up gives me the ~s** wenn ich ihr Make-up sehe, kriege ich das kalte Grausen (*inf*); **he/this old house gives me the ~s** er ist mir nicht geheuer/in dem alten Haus ist es mir nicht geheuer.
◆**creep in** *vi* (sich) hinein-/hereinschleichen (*-to* in *+acc*); (*mistakes, doubts*) sich einschleichen (*-to* in *+acc*).
◆**creep over** *vi +prep obj* (*feeling, doubt etc*) beschleichen, überkommen; (*pleasant feeling*) überkommen.

◆**creep up** *vi* **(a)** *(person)* sich heranschleichen *(on* an *+acc)*; *(prices)* (in die Höhe) klettern. **(b) to ~ ~ on sb** *(time, exam)* langsam auf jdn zukommen; **old age is ~ing ~ on him** er wird langsam alt.

creeper ['kri:pəʳ] *n* **(a)** *(plant) (along ground)* Kriechpflanze *f*; *(upwards)* Kletterpflanze *f*. **(b)** *(bird)* Baumläufer *m*. **(c) ~s** *pl (US) Schuhe pl mit dicken Gummisohlen*, Leisetreter *pl (inf)*.

creepy ['kri:pɪ] *adj (+er) (frightening)* unheimlich; *story, place also* gruselig.

creepy-crawly ['kri:pɪ'krɔ:lɪ] *(inf)* [1] *adj insect* krabbelig *(inf)*, kribbelnd, krabbelnd; *feeling* unheimlich.
[2] *n* Krabbeltier *nt*.

cremate [krɪ'meɪt] *vt* einäschern, kremieren *(rare)*.

cremation [krɪ'meɪʃən] *n* Einäscherung, Kremation *f*.

crematorium [,kremə'tɔ:rɪəm], *(esp US)* **crematory** ['kremə,tɔ:rɪ] *n* Krematorium *nt*.

crème de la crème ['kremdəlæ'krem] *n* Crème de la crème *f*.

crème de menthe ['kremdə'mɒnt] *n* Pfefferminzlikör *m*.

crenellated ['krenɪleɪtɪd] *adj battlements* mit Zinnen versehen, kreneliert *(spec)*; *moulding, pattern* zinnenartig.

crenellation [,krenɪ'leɪʃən] *n usu pl (on castle)* Zinnen *pl*, Krenelierung *f (spec)*; *(on moulding)* Zinnenmuster *nt*.

Creole ['kri:əʊl] [1] *n* **(a)** *(language)* Kreolisch *nt*. **(b)** *(person)* Kreole *m*, Kreolin *f*.
[2] *adj* kreolisch.

creolized ['kreɪəlaɪzd] *adj* kreolisiert.

creosote ['krɪəsəʊt] [1] *n* Kreosot *nt*.
[2] *vt* mit Kreosot streichen.

crêpe [kreɪp] [1] *n* **(a)** *(Tex)* Krepp, Crêpe *m*. **(b)** *see* **~ rubber**. **(c)** *see* **~ paper**.
[2] *adj (made of ~)* Krepp-.

crêpe: ~ bandage *n* elastische Binde, elastischer Verband; **~ de Chine** [,krepdə'ʃi:n] *n* Crêpe de Chine, Chinakrepp *m*; **~ paper** *n* Kreppapier *nt*; **~ rubber** [1] *n* Kreppgummi *m*; [2] *adj* Kreppgummi-; **~-soled** ['kreɪp'səʊld] *adj* mit Kreppsohle(n), Krepp-; **~ suzette** [,kreɪpsu:'zet] *n* Crêpe Suzette *f*.

crepitate ['krepɪteɪt] *vi (liter)* prasseln.

crept [krept] *pret, ptp of* **creep**.

crepuscular [krɪ'pʌskjʊləʳ] *adj (liter)* dämmerig ◆ **~ animals** *(Zool)* Dämmerungstiere *pl*.

crescendo [krɪ'ʃendəʊ] [1] *n (Mus)* Crescendo *nt*; *(fig)* Zunahme *f* ◆ **~ of excitement** Anschwellen *nt* der Aufregung.
[2] *vi (Mus, fig)* anschwellen.

crescent ['kresnt] [1] *n* Halbmond *m*; *(in street names)* Weg *m (halbmondförmig verlaufende Straße)*.
[2] *adj* **~-shaped** *adj* halbmond- *or* sichelförmig; **the ~ moon** die Mondsichel.

cress [kres] *n* (Garten)kresse *f*; *(water~)* Brunnenkresse *f*.

crest [krest] [1] *n* **(a)** *(of bird)* Haube *f*; *(of cock)* Kamm *m*; *(on hat etc)* Federbusch *m*; *(plume on helmet)* Helmbusch *m*.
(b) *(Her)* Helmzierde *f*; *(coat of arms)* Wappen *nt*.
(c) *(of wave, hill, Anat: of horse etc)* Kamm *m*; *(fig: of excitement, popularity)* Höhepunkt, Gipfel *m*; *(Phys: of oscillation)* Scheitel(punkt) *m* ◆ **he's riding on the ~ of a wave** *(fig)* er schwimmt im Augenblick oben.
[2] *vt (reach the ~ of)* erklimmen.

crested ['krestɪd] *adj notepaper, seal* verziert; *(bird)* Hauben- ◆ **~ coot** Kammbleßralle *f*; **~ tit** Haubenmeise *f*.

crestfallen ['krest,fɔ:lən] *adj* geknickt, niedergeschlagen.

cretaceous [krɪ'teɪʃəs] *adj* Kreide-, kretazeisch *(spec)* ◆ **the ~ age** *(Geol)* die Kreide(zeit).

Cretan ['kri:tən] [1] *adj* kretisch.
[2] *n* Kreter(in *f*) *m*.

Crete [kri:t] *n* Kreta *nt*.

cretin ['kretɪn] *n (Med)* Kretin *m*; *(inf)* Schwachkopf *m (inf)*.

cretinism ['kretɪnɪzəm] *n (Med)* Kretinismus *m*; *(inf)* Schwachsinn *m*, Idiotie *f*.

cretinous ['kretɪnəs] *adj (Med)* kretinoid; *(inf)* schwachsinnig.

cretonne [kre'tɒn] *n* Cretonne *f or m*.

crevasse [krɪ'væs] *n* (Gletscher)spalte *f*.

crevice ['krevɪs] *n* Spalte *f*.

crew[1] [kru:] [1] *n* **(a)** Mannschaft *(also Sport)*, Crew *f*; *(including officers: of ship also, of plane, tank)* Besatzung, Crew *f* ◆ **50 passengers and 20 ~** 50 Passagiere und 20 Mann Besatzung; **the ground ~** *(Aviat)* das Bodenpersonal; **is Mary your ~** macht Mary Vorschotmann?
(b) *(inf: gang)* Bande *f* ◆ **they were a motley ~** sie waren ein bunt zusammengewürfelter Haufen *(inf)*.
[2] *vi* **to ~ for sb** bei jdm den Vorschotmann machen.
[3] *vt yacht* die Mannschaft *or* Crew sein von; *(one person in race)* den Vorschotmann machen auf *(+dat)*.

crew[2] *(old) pret of* **crow**.

crew: ~-cut *n* Bürstenschnitt *m*; **~-member** *n* Mitglied *nt* der Mannschaft, Besatzungsmitglied *nt*; **~-neck** *n* runder Halsausschnitt; *(also* **~-neck pullover** *or* **sweater***)* Pullover *m* mit rundem Halsausschnitt.

crib [krɪb] [1] *n* **(a)** *(cradle)* Krippe *f*; *(US: cot)* Kinderbett *nt* ◆ **~ death** *(US)* Krippentod *m*, plötzlicher Kindstod. **(b)** *(manger)* Krippe, Raufe *f*; *(fig: nativity scene)* Krippe *f*. **(c)** *(US: maize bin)* Trockengerüst *nt* für Maiskolben. **(d)** *(Sch: cheating aid)* Spickzettel *m (inf)*; *(inf: plagiary)* Anleihe *f (inf)*.
[2] *vti (esp Sch inf)* abschreiben *(inf)*, spicken *(inf)*.

cribbage ['krɪbɪdʒ] *n* Cribbage *nt*.

crick [krɪk] [1] *n* **a ~ in one's neck/back** ein steifes Genick/ein steifer Rücken.
[2] *vt* **to ~ one's neck/back** sich *(dat)* ein steifes Genick/einen steifen Rücken zuziehen.

cricket[1] ['krɪkɪt] *n (insect)* Grille *f*.

cricket[2] *n (Sport)* Kricket *nt* ◆ **that's not ~** *(fig inf)* das ist nicht fair.

cricket *in cpds* Kricket-; **~ bat** *n* (Kricket)schlagholz *nt*.

cricketer ['krɪkɪtəʳ] *n* Kricketspieler(in *f*) *m*.

cricket: ~ match *n* Kricketspiel *nt*; **~ pitch** *n* Kricketfeld *nt*.

cri de cœur [ˈkri:də'kɜ:ʳ] *n* verzweifelter Stoßseufzer.

crier ['kraɪəʳ] *n (town ~)* Ausrufer *m*; *(court ~)* Gerichtsdiener *m*.

crikey ['kraɪkɪ] *interj (dated Brit inf)* Mann *(inf)*.

crime [kraɪm] *n* **(a)** Straftat *f*; *(murder, robbery with violence etc also, fig)* Verbrechen *nt* ◆ **it's not a ~!** das ist nicht verboten; **it's a ~ to throw away all that good food** es ist eine Sünde *or* eine Schande, all das gute Essen wegzuwerfen.
(b) *no pl* Verbrechen *pl* ◆ **~ and punishment** Verbrechen und Verbrechensverfolgung; **to lead a life of ~** kriminell leben; **~ is on the increase** die Zahl der Verbrechen nimmt zu; **~ doesn't pay** Verbrechen lohnen sich nicht.

Crimea [kraɪ'mɪə] *n (Geog)* Krim *f*; *(inf: Crimean War)* der Krimkrieg.

Crimean [kraɪ'mɪən] [1] *n (person)* Krimbewohner(in *f*) *m*.
[2] *adj* Krim- ◆ **she's ~** sie kommt von der Krim.

crime: ~ prevention *n* Verbrechensverhütung *f*, präventive Verbrechensbekämpfung *(form)*; **~ prevention officer** *n Polizeibeamter, der sich aktiv um die Verhütung von Verbrechen bemüht*; **~ rate** *n* Verbrechensrate *f*; **~ story** *n* Kriminalgeschichte *f*, Krimi *m (inf)*; **~ wave** *n* Verbrechenswelle *f*.

criminal ['krɪmɪnl] [1] *n* Straftäter(in *f*) *m (form)*, Kriminelle(r) *mf*; *(guilty of capital crimes also, fig)* Verbrecher(in *f*) *m*.
[2] *adj* **(a)** kriminell, verbrecherisch; *action also* strafbar ◆ **~ assault** Körperverletzung *f*; **C~ Investigation Department** *(Brit)* Kriminalpolizei *f*; **~ code** Strafgesetzbuch *nt*; **~ damage** *(Jur)* Sachbeschädigung *f*; **~ law** Strafrecht *nt*; **~ lawyer** Anwalt *m* für Strafsachen; *(specializing in defence)* Strafverteidiger *m*; **~ offence** strafbare Handlung; **to take ~ proceedings against sb** strafrechtlich gegen jdn vorgehen; **to have a ~ record** vorbestraft sein; **C~ Records Office** Kriminaldienststelle *f* zur Führung der Verbrecherkartei.
(b) *(fig)* kriminell ◆ **it's ~ to stay in in this weather** es ist eine Schande, bei diesem Wetter drinnen zu bleiben.

criminality [,krɪmɪ'nælɪtɪ] *n* Kriminalität *f*.

criminalization [,krɪmɪnəlaɪ'zeɪʃən] *n* Kriminalisierung *f*.

criminalize ['krɪmɪnəlaɪz] *vt* kriminalisieren.

criminally ['krɪmɪnəlɪ] *adv* kriminell, verbrecherisch ◆ **he thought she behaved quite ~** *(fig)* seiner Meinung nach hat sie sich kriminell verhalten.

criminologist [,krɪmɪ'nɒlədʒɪst] *n* Kriminologe *m*, Kriminologin *f*.

criminology [,krɪmɪ'nɒlədʒɪ] *n* Kriminologie *f*.

crimp [krɪmp] *vt hair* (mit der Brennschere) wellen.

crimplene ® ['krɪmpli:n] *n* ≃ knitterfreier Trevira ®.

crimson ['krɪmzn] [1] *adj* purpurn, purpurrot; *sky* blutrot, purpurrot; *(through blushing)* knallrot *(inf)*, dunkelrot ◆ **to turn** *or* **go ~** *person, face* knallrot *(inf) or* dunkelrot werden *or* anlaufen; *(sky)* sich blutrot färben.
[2] *n* Purpur, Purpurrot *nt*.

cringe [krɪndʒ] *vi* **(a)** *(shrink back)* zurückschrecken *(at* vor *+dat)*; *(fig)* schaudern ◆ **to ~ before sb** vor jdm zurückweichen *or* -schrecken; **he ~d at the thought** er *or* ihn schauderte bei dem Gedanken; **he ~d when she mispronounced his name** er zuckte zusammen, als sie seinen Namen falsch aussprach.
(b) *(humble oneself, fawn)* katzbuckeln, kriechen *(to* vor *+dat)* ◆ **to go cringing to sb** zu jdm gekrochen kommen; **a cringing person** ein Kriecher *m*; **cringing behaviour** kriecherisches Benehmen.

crinkle ['krɪŋkl] [1] *n* (Knitter)falte *f*; *(in skin)* Fältchen *nt*.
[2] *vt paper, foil, dress etc* (zer)knittern; *cardboard, plastic etc* knicken; *edge of paper* wellen ◆ **the paper was all ~d** das Papier war ganz zerknittert.
[3] *vi (wrinkle) (paper, foil, dress etc)* knittern; *(face, skin)* (Lach)fältchen bekommen; *(edges of paper)* sich wellen, wellig werden; *(curl: hair)* sich krausen ◆ **the skin round his eyes ~d when he smiled** er bekam tausend Fältchen um die Augen, wenn er lächelte.

crinkly ['krɪŋklɪ] *adj (+er) (inf) (wrinkled) paper, foil etc* zerknittert; *edges* wellig; *hair* krauselig *(inf)*.

crinoline ['krɪnəli:n] *n* Krinoline *f*.

cripes [kraɪps] *interj (dated Brit inf)* Mann *(inf)*.

cripple ['krɪpl] [1] *n* Krüppel *m*.
[2] *vt person* zum Krüppel machen; *arm, legs etc* verkrüppeln; *ship, plane* aktionsunfähig machen; *(fig) industry, exports* lahmlegen, lähmen ◆ **the ship was ~d** das Schiff war nicht mehr aktionsfähig; **~d with rheumatism** von Rheuma praktisch gelähmt; **to be ~d for life** lebenslang ein Krüppel sein.

crippling ['krɪplɪŋ] *adj taxes, mortgage repayments* erdrückend; *strikes* alles lähmend *attr*; *pain* lähmend.

cripplingly ['krɪplɪŋlɪ] *adv expensive* unerschwinglich.

crisis ['kraɪsɪs] *n, pl* **crises** ['kraɪsi:z] Krise *f (also Med)* ◆ **to reach ~ point** den Höhepunkt erreichen; **that was a ~ in his life** *(decisive moment)* das war ein entscheidender Punkt in seinem Leben; *(emotional ~)* das war eine Krise in seinem Leben; **in this time of ~** in dieser krisenreichen *or* schweren Zeit; **in times of ~** in Krisenzeiten.

crisis: ~ centre *n* Einsatzzentrum *nt für Krisenfälle*; **rape ~ centre** Beratungsstelle *f für Frauen, die Opfer einer Vergewaltigung geworden sind*; **~ management** *n* Krisenmanagement *nt*.

crisp [krɪsp] [1] *adj (+er) apple, lettuce* knackig, fest; *bread, biscuits, bacon* knusprig; *snow* verharscht; *leaves* trocken; *appearance* adrett, frisch; *curls, clothes* steif; *manner, voice, style of writing, remark* knapp; *air, weather, colour* frisch; *sound* klar; (*Sport*) *shot* sauber; *pound note* brandneu.
[2] *n* (*Brit: potato ~*) Chip *m* ◆ **to burn sth to a ~** etw verbrutzeln lassen; *toast* etw verkohlen lassen.
[3] *vt* (*also* **~ up**) *bread* aufbacken.

crispbread ['krɪspbred] *n* Knäckebrot *nt*.

crispen (up) ['krɪspn('ʌp)] *vt* (*sep*) *bread* aufbacken; *blouse etc* auffrischen.

crisper ['krɪspəʳ] *n* (*in fridge*) Gemüsefach *nt*.

crisply ['krɪsplɪ] *adv* knackig; *baked, fried* knusprig; *starched* steif; *dressed* adrett, frisch; *write, speak* knapp ◆ **the snow crunched ~ under his feet** der Schnee knirschte unter seinen Füßen; **the notes rang out ~** die Töne kamen klar.

crispness ['krɪspnɪs] *n see adj* Knackigkeit, Festheit *f*; Knusprigkeit *f*; Verharschtheit *f*; Trockenheit *f*; Adrettheit, Frische *f*; Steifheit *f*; Knappheit *f*; Klarheit *f*; Sauberkeit *f*.

crispy ['krɪspɪ] *adj* (*+er*) (*inf*) knusprig.

criss-cross ['krɪskrɒs] [1] *n* Kreuzundquer *nt*.
[2] *adj pattern* Kreuz-.
[3] *adv* kreuz und quer.
[4] *vt* mit einem Kreuzmuster versehen.

crit [krɪt] *n* (*inf: of book etc*) Kritik *f*.

criterion [kraɪ'tɪərɪən] *n, pl* **criteria** [kraɪ'tɪərɪə] Kriterium *nt* ◆ **then, by the same ~, he is guilty too** dann ist er ebenso schuldig.

critic ['krɪtɪk] *n* Kritiker(in *f*) *m* ◆ **literary ~** Literaturkritiker(in *f*) *m*; **he's a terrible ~** (*very critical*) er ist schrecklich kritisch; **he's his own worst ~** er kritisiert sich selbst am meisten, er ist sein schlimmster Kritiker; **he is a constant ~ of the government** er kritisiert ständig die Regierung *or* an der Regierung.

critical ['krɪtɪkəl] *adj* **(a)** (*fault-finding, discriminating*) kritisch ◆ **the book was a ~ success** das Buch kam bei den Kritikern an; **~ reviews** Kritiken *pl*; **~ edition** kritische Ausgabe; **to cast a ~ eye over sth** sich (*dat*) etw kritisch ansehen; **to be ~ of sb/sth** jdn/etw kritisieren.
(b) (*dangerous, Sci*) kritisch; (*crucial also*) entscheidend.
(c) ~ path kritischer Pfad; **~ path analysis** kritische Pfadanalyse.

critically ['krɪtɪkəlɪ] *adv* **(a)** kritisch. **(b)** *ill* schwer ◆ **to be ~ important** von kritischer Bedeutung sein.

▼ **criticism** ['krɪtɪsɪzəm] *n* Kritik *f* ◆ **literary ~** Literaturkritik *f*; **to come in for a lot of ~** schwer kritisiert werden.

▼ **criticize** ['krɪtɪsaɪz] *vti* kritisieren.

critique [krɪ'tiːk] *n* Kritik *f*.

critter ['krɪtəʳ] *n* (*US dial*) *see* **creature**.

croak [krəʊk] [1] *n* (*of frog*) Quaken *nt no pl*; (*of raven, person*) Krächzen *nt no pl* ◆ **~, went the frog/raven** quak, machte der Frosch/krakra, machte der Rabe.
[2] *vti* **(a)** (*frog*) quaken; (*raven, person*) krächzen.
(b) (*sl: die*) **he ~ed (it)** er ist abgekratzt (*sl*).

croaky ['krəʊkɪ] *adj* (*+er*) (*inf*) *voice* krächzend ◆ **you sound a bit ~** du klingst etwas heiser.

Croat ['krəʊæt] *n* (*person*) Kroate *m*, Kroatin *f*; (*language*) Kroatisch *nt*.

Croatia [krəʊ'eɪʃɪə] *n* Kroatien *nt*.

Croatian [krəʊ'eɪʃɪən] [1] *n see* **Croat**.
[2] *adj* kroatisch.

crochet ['krəʊʃeɪ] [1] *n* (*also* **~ work**) Häkelei *f* ◆ **~ hook** Häkelnadel *f*; **to do a lot of ~** viel häkeln.
[2] *vti* häkeln.

crock¹ [krɒk] *n* (*jar*) Topf *m*; (*pottery chip*) Scherbe *f*.

crock² *n* (*inf*) (*vehicle*) Kiste *f* (*inf*); (*person*) Wrack *nt* (*inf*); (*horse*) Klepper *m* ◆ **an old ~s race** ein Oldtimer-Rennen *nt*.

crockery ['krɒkərɪ] *n* (*Brit*) Geschirr *nt*.

crocodile ['krɒkədaɪl] *n* **(a)** Krokodil *nt*. **(b)** (*Brit Sch*) **to walk in a ~** zwei und zwei hintereinandergehen; **the long ~ of little girls** der lange Zug kleiner Mädchen, die zwei und zwei hintereinander gingen/gehen.

crocodile: ~ clip *n* Krokodilklemme *f*; **~ tears** *npl* Krokodilstränen *pl*.

crocus ['krəʊkəs] *n* Krokus *m*.

Croesus ['kriːsəs] *n* Krösus *m* ◆ **to be as rich as ~** ein (richtiger) Krösus sein.

croft [krɒft] *n* (*esp Scot*) kleines Pachtgrundstück; (*house*) Kate *f*.

crofter ['krɒftəʳ] *n* (*esp Scot*) Kleinpächter(in *f*) *m*.

croissant ['krwɑːsɒŋ] *n* Hörnchen *nt*.

crone [krəʊn] *n* Tante *f* (*inf*).

crony ['krəʊnɪ] *n* Freund(in *f*), Spießgeselle (*hum*) *m*.

crook¹ [krʊk] [1] *n* **(a)** (*dishonest person*) Gauner *m* (*inf*).
(b) (*staff*) (*of shepherd*) Hirtenstab, Krummstab *m*; (*of bishop also*) Bischofsstab *m*; *see* **hook**.
(c) (*bend: in road, river*) Biegung *f*; (*in arm*) Beuge *f*.
[2] *vt finger* krümmen; *arm* beugen ◆ **she only has to ~ her (little) finger and he comes running** sie braucht nur mit dem kleinen Finger zu winken, und schon kommt er angerannt.

crook² *adj* (*Austral inf*) **(a)** (*sick*) krank ◆ **he's ~ with the flu/a cold** er hat die Grippe/eine Erkältung; **he feels/is ~** er fühlt sich mies (*inf*) *or* lausig (*inf*)/es geht ihm mies (*inf*). **(b)** (*not functioning*) kaputt (*inf*); (*not good*) mies (*inf*). **(c)** (*angry*) wild (*inf*) ◆ **to go ~ at** *or* **on sb** wegen jdm wild werden.

crooked ['krʊkɪd] *adj* (*lit*) (*bent*) krumm; (*tilted, sloping also*), *smile* schief; (*fig inf: dishonest*) *method* krumm; *person* unehrlich ◆ **your hat's ~** dein Hut sitzt schief.

croon [kruːn] [1] *vt* (*sing softly*) leise *or* sanft singen; (*usu pej: sentimentally*) gefühlvoll *or* schmalzig (*pej inf*) singen.
[2] *vi* (*sing softly*) leise *or* sanft singen; (*usu pej: sentimentally*) Schnulzen (*pej inf*) *or* sentimentale Lieder singen.

crooner ['kruːnəʳ] *n* Sänger *m* (sentimentaler Lieder), Schnulzensänger *m* (*pej inf*).

crop [krɒp] [1] *n* **(a)** (*produce*) Ernte *f*; (*species grown*) (Feld)frucht *f*; (*fig: large number*) Schwung *m* ◆ **cereal ~s** Getreidearten *pl*; **the cereal ~s were destroyed** die Getreideernte wurde zerstört; **the barley ~ is looking good** die Gerste steht gut; **a good ~ of fruit/potatoes** eine gute Obst-/Kartoffelernte; **the beef ~** die Rindfleischproduktion; **to be in** *or* **under/out of ~** bebaut/nicht bebaut sein; **he grows a different ~ every year** er baut jedes Jahr etwas anderes an; **to bring the ~s in** die Ernte einbringen; **a ~ of lies/questions** eine Masse Lügen/Fragen (*inf*).
(b) (*of bird*) Kropf *m*.
(c) (*of whip*) Stock *m*; (*hunting ~*) Reitpeitsche *f*.
(d) (*hairstyle*) Kurzhaarschnitt *m* ◆ **to give sb a close ~** jdm die Haare gehörig stutzen.
[2] *vt hair* stutzen; *horse's or dog's tail also* kupieren ◆ **it's best to keep the grass ~ped short** man sollte das Gras kurz halten; **the goat ~ped the grass** die Ziege fraß das Gras ab; **~ped hair, hair ~ped short** kurzgeschnittenes Haar.

◆**crop out** *vi* auftauchen; (*minerals*) zutage treten.

◆**crop up** *vi* aufkommen ◆ **something's ~ped ~** es ist etwas dazwischengekommen; **he was ready for anything that might ~ ~** er war auf alle Eventualitäten gefaßt.

crop dusting *n* Schädlingsbekämpfung *f* (*aus dem Flugzeug*).

cropper ['krɒpəʳ] *n* **(a)** (*person*) Anbauer *m* ◆ **these plants are poor ~s** diese Pflanzen bringen nicht viel Ertrag. **(b)** (*inf*) **to come a ~** (*lit: fall*) hinfliegen (*inf*); (*fig: fail*) auf die Nase fallen.

crop: ~ rotation *n* Fruchtwechsel *m*; **~ sprayer** *n* (*person*) Schädlingsbekämpfer *m*; (*plane*) Schädlingsbekämpfungsflugzeug *nt*; (*tractor*) Schädlingsbekämpfungsfahrzeug, Besprühungsfahrzeug *nt*; **~ spraying** *n* Schädlingsbekämpfung *f* (*durch Besprühen*).

croquet ['krəʊkeɪ] *n* Krocket(spiel) *nt* ◆ **~ lawn** Krocketrasen *m*.

croquette [krəʊ'ket] *n* Krokette *f*.

crosier, crozier ['krəʊʒɪəʳ] *n* Bischofsstab, Hirtenstab, Krummstab *m*.

▼ **cross**¹ [krɒs] [1] *n* **(a)** Kreuz *nt* ◆ **to make one's ~** sein Kreuz(chen) machen *or* setzen; **to make the sign of the C~** das Kreuzzeichen machen *or* schlagen; **the C~ and the Crescent** Kreuz und Halbmond; **to bear/take up one's ~** (*fig*) sein Kreuz tragen/auf sich (*acc*) nehmen; **we all have our ~ to bear/our little ~es** (*inf*) wir haben alle unser Kreuz zu tragen.
(b) (*bias*) **on the ~** schräg; **to be cut on the ~** schräg geschnitten sein.
(c) (*hybrid*) Kreuzung *f*; (*fig*) Mittelding *nt*.
[2] *attr* (*transverse*) *street, line etc* Quer-.
[3] *vt* **(a)** (*go across*) *road, river, mountains* überqueren; (*on foot*) *picket line etc* überschreiten; *country, desert, room* durchqueren ◆ **to ~ the road** über die Straße gehen, die Straße überqueren; **to ~ sb's path** (*fig*) jdm über den Weg laufen; **it ~ed my mind that ...** es fiel mir ein, daß ..., mir kam der Gedanke, daß ...; **don't ~ your bridges until you come to them** (*prov*) laß die Probleme auf dich zukommen; **we'll ~ that bridge when we come to it** lassen wir das Problem mal auf uns zukommen, das sind ungelegte Eier (*inf*).
▼ **(b)** (*put at right-angles, intersect*) kreuzen ◆ **to ~ one's legs/arms** die Beine übereinanderschlagen/die Arme verschränken; **the lines are ~ed** (*Telec*) die Leitungen überschneiden sich; **line AB ~es line CD at point E** AB schneidet CD in E; **to ~ sb's palm with silver** jdm ein Geldstück in die Hand drücken; **keep your fingers ~ed for me!** (*inf*) drück *or* halt mir die Daumen! (*inf*); **I'm keeping my fingers ~ed** (*inf*) ich drücke *or* halte die Daumen (*inf*).
(c) (*put a line across*) *letter, t* einen Querstrich machen durch; (*Brit*) *cheque* ≃ *zur Verrechnung ausstellen* ◆ **a ~ed cheque** ein Verrechnungsscheck *m*; **to ~ sth through** etw durchstreichen; *see* **dot**.
(d) (*make the sign of the C~*) **to ~ oneself** sich bekreuzigen; **~ my/your heart** (*inf*) Ehrenwort, Hand aufs Herz.
(e) (*mark with a ~*) ankreuzen.
(f) (*go against*) *plans* durchkreuzen ◆ **to ~ sb** jdn verärgern; **to be ~ed in love** in der Liebe enttäuscht werden.
(g) *animal, fruit* kreuzen.
[4] *vi* **(a)** (*across road*) hinübergehen, die Straße überqueren; (*across Channel etc*) hinüberfahren ◆ **"~ now"** „gehen"; **to ~ on the green light** bei Grün über die Straße gehen.
(b) (*intersect*) sich kreuzen; (*lines also*) sich schneiden ◆ **our paths have ~ed several times** (*fig*) unsere Wege haben sich öfters gekreuzt.
(c) (*pass: letters etc*) sich kreuzen.

◆**cross off** *vt sep* streichen (*prep obj* aus, von).

◆**cross out** *vt sep* ausstreichen.

◆**cross over** [1] *vi* **(a)** (*cross the road*) hinübergehen, die Straße überqueren.
(b) (*change sides*) übergehen, überwechseln (*to* zu).
[2] *vi +prep obj road, street* überqueren.

cross² *adj* (*+er*) böse, sauer (*inf*) ◆ **to be ~ with sb** mit jdm *or* auf jdn böse sein.

cross: ~-action *n* (*Jur*) Widerklage *f*; **~bar** *n* (*of bicycle*) Stange *f*; (*Sport*) Querlatte *f*; **~beam** *n* (*girder*) Querbalken *m*; (*Sport*) Schwebebalken *m*;

~bench *n usu pl (Parl) Bank, wo die weder zur Regierungs- noch zur Oppositionspartei gehörenden Abgeordneten sitzen;* **~bencher** ['krɒsbentʃəʳ] *n (Parl) Abgeordneter, der weder der Regierungs- noch der Oppositionspartei angehört;* **~bill** *n (Orn)* Kreuzschnabel *m;* **~bones** *npl* gekreuzte Knochen *pl (unter einem Totenkopf); see* **skull**; **~bow** *n* (Stand)armbrust *f;* **~bred** *adj (Zool, Biol)* gekreuzt; **~breed** *(Zool, Biol)* [1] *n* Kreuzung *f;* [2] *vt* kreuzen; **~-Channel** *attr ferries, swimmer* Kanal-; **a ~-Channel swim** ein Durchschwimmen des Kanals; **~-check** [1] *n* Gegenprobe *f;* [2] *vt facts, figures* überprüfen; *equation* die Gegenprobe machen bei; **~-compiler** *n (Comput)* Cross-Compiler *m;* **~-country** [1] *adj* Querfeldein-; **~-country ski** Langlaufski *m;* **~-country skier** Langläufer(in *f*) *m;* **~-country skiing** Langlauf *m;* **~-country ski track** (Langlauf)loipe *f;* [2] *adv* querfeldein; [3] *n (race)* Querfeldeinrennen *nt;* **~-current** *n* Gegenströmung *f;* **~-dresser** *n* Transvestit *m;* **~-dressing** *n* Transvestismus *m;* **~-examination** *n* Kreuzverhör *nt (of* über *+acc);* **~-examine** *vt* ins Kreuzverhör nehmen; **~-eyed** *adj* schielend; **to be ~-eyed** schielen; **~-fertilization** *n, no pl (Bot)* Kreuzbefruchtung, Fremdbestäubung *f; (fig)* gegenseitige Befruchtung; **~-fertilize** *vt (Bot)* kreuzbefruchten; **~fire** *n* Kreuzfeuer *nt;* **to be caught in the ~fire** *(lit, fig)* ins Kreuzfeuer geraten; **~-gartered** *adj (old)* mit kreuzweise geschnürten Waden; **~-grained** *adj wood* quergefasert; *(grumpy)* mürrisch; *(perverse)* querköpfig; **~hatch** *vt* mit Kreuzlagen schattieren; **~hatching** *n* Kreuzschattierung *f.*

crossing ['krɒsɪŋ] *n* **(a)** *(act)* Überquerung *f; (sea ~)* Überfahrt *f.* **(b)** *(~ place)* Übergang *m; (crossroads)* Kreuzung *f.*

cross: ~-keys *npl (Her)* gekreuzte Schlüssel *pl;* **~kick** *n (Ftbl)* Querpaß *m* (nach innen); **~-legged** *adj, adv* mit gekreuzten Beinen; *(on ground)* im Schneidersitz.

crossly ['krɒslɪ] *adv* böse, verärgert.

cross: ~-match *vt (Med)* kreuzen; **~-matching** *n (Med)* Kreuzprobe *f;* **~over** *n (Rail)* Gleiskreuzung *f;* **~patch** *n (inf)* Brummbär *m (inf);* **~piece** *n (bar)* Querstange *f;* **~-ply** [1] *adj* Diagonal-; [2] *n (inf)* Diagonalreifen *m;* **~-pollinate** *vt* fremdbestäuben; **~-pollination** *n* Fremdbestäubung *f;* **~-purposes** *npl* **to be** *or* **talk at ~-purposes** aneinander vorbeireden; **he was at ~-purposes with her** sie haben aneinander vorbeigeredet; **~-question** *vt see* **~-examine**; **~-refer** *vt* verweisen *(to* auf *+acc);* **~-reference** [1] *n* (Quer)verweis *m (to* auf *+acc);* [2] *vt see* **~-refer**; **~roads** *n sing or pl (lit)* Kreuzung *f; (fig)* Scheideweg *m;* **~ section** *n* Querschnitt *m;* **to draw sth in ~ section** etw im Querschnitt zeichnen; **a ~ section of the population** ein Querschnitt durch die Bevölkerung; **~-stitch** [1] *n (Sew)* Kreuzstich *m;* [2] *vt* im Kreuzstich arbeiten; **~talk** *n, no pl* **(a)** *(witty)* Wortgefecht *nt;* Wortgefechte *pl;* **(b)** *(Telec)* Nebensprechen *nt;* **~-town** *adj (US)* quer durch die Stadt; **~walk** *n (US)* Fußgängerüberweg *m;* **~ways** *adv see* **~wise**; **~wind** *n* Seitenwind *m;* **~wise** *adv* quer; **~word (puzzle)** *n* Kreuzworträtsel *nt;* **~wort** *n* gewöhnliches Kreuzlabkraut.

crotch [krɒtʃ] *n* **(a)** *(in tree etc)* Gabelung *f.* **(b)** *(of trousers)* Schritt *m; (Anat)* Unterleib *m* ◆ **a kick in the ~** ein Tritt zwischen die Beine; **she wears her skirts about an inch below the ~** ihre Röcke reichen nur ein Paar Zentimeter über den Po *(inf).*

crotchet ['krɒtʃɪt] *n* **(a)** *(Mus)* Viertelnote *f* ◆ **~ rest** Viertelpause *f.* **(b)** *(inf: cross person)* Miesepeter *m (inf).*

crotchety ['krɒtʃɪtɪ] *adj (inf: cross)* schlecht gelaunt, miesepetrig *(inf); child* quengelig *(inf).*

crouch [krautʃ] [1] *vi* sich zusammenkauern, kauern ◆ **to ~ down** sich niederkauern.
[2] *n* Hocke *f; (of animal)* Kauerstellung *f.*

croup¹ [kru:p] *n, no pl (Med)* Krupp *m,* Kehlkopfdiphtherie *f.*

croup² *n (of horse)* Kruppe *f.*

croupier ['kru:pɪeɪ] *n* Croupier *m.*

crouton ['kru:tɒn] *n* Crouton *m.*

crow¹ [krəʊ] *n* **(a)** *(Orn)* Krähe *f* ◆ **as the ~ flies** (in der) Luftlinie; **to eat ~** *(US inf)* zu Kreuze kriechen. **(b)** *(inf) see* **crowbar**.

crow² [1] *n (of cock, baby)* Krähen *nt no pl; (of person)* J(a)uchzer *m* ◆ **a ~ of delight** ein Freudenjauchzer *m.*
[2] *vi* **(a)** *pret* **~ed** *or (old)* **crew**, *ptp* **~ed** *(cock)* krähen.
(b) *pret, ptp* **~ed** *(baby)* krähen; *(person)* j(a)uchzen; *(fig) (boast)* sich brüsten, angeben *(about* mit); *(exalt)* hämisch frohlocken *(over* über *+acc).*

crow: ~bar *n* Brecheisen *nt;* **~berry** *n* Krähenbeere *f.*

crowd [kraud] [1] *n* **(a)** Menschenmenge *f; (Sport, Theat)* Zuschauermenge *f* ◆ **to be swept along by the ~** von der *or* in der Menge mitgerissen werden; **to get lost in the ~(s)** in der Menge verlorengehen; **~s of people** Menschenmassen, große Menschenmengen *pl;* **that would pass in a ~** *(fig)* das geht (durch), wenn man nicht zu genau hinsieht; **to get a good ~ at a match** bei einem Spiel eine Menge Zuschauer haben; **we were quite a ~** wir waren eine ganze Menge Leute; **a whole ~ of us** ein ganzer Haufen von uns *(inf);* **~ scene** *(Theat)* Massenszene *f.*
(b) *(set, of people, clique)* Clique *f,* Haufen *m (inf)* ◆ **the university ~** der Uni-Haufen *(inf),* die Uni-Clique; **I'm not in that ~** *or* **one of that ~** ich gehöre nicht zu diesem Haufen *(inf) or* zu denen; **they're a nice ~** sie sind ein netter Haufen *(inf).*
(c) *no pl (the masses)* **the ~** die (breite) Masse; **to go with** *or* **follow the ~** mit der Herde laufen; **she hates to be just one of the ~** sie geht nicht gern in der Masse unter.
[2] *vi* (sich) drängen ◆ **to ~ (a)round/together/in** sich herumdrängen/sich zusammendrängen/(sich) hereindrängen; **to ~ (a)round sb/sth** (sich) um jdn/etw herumdrängen.
[3] *vt* **(a) to ~ the streets** die Straßen bevölkern; **to ~ a room with furniture** eine Wohnung mit Möbeln vollstopfen; **to ~ furniture into a room** Möbel in eine Wohnung stopfen; **a room ~ed with children** ein Zimmer voller Kinder; **it will really ~ the office having three new people** mit drei neuen Leuten wird es im Büro sicherlich eng werden; **to ~ things together** Dinge eng zusammendrängen; **the holiday was ~ed with incidents** die Ferien waren sehr ereignisreich; **a mind ~ed with facts** eine Ansammlung von Faktenwissen (im Kopf).
(b) *(inf: harass)* **to ~ sb** jdn drängeln, jdm auf den Füßen stehen *(inf); (creditors)* jdn bedrängen.

◆**crowd out** *vt sep (not let in)* wegdrängen; *(make leave)* herausdrängen; *(Press) article etc* verdrängen ◆ **the pub was ~ed ~** das Lokal war gerammelt voll *(inf) or* proppenvoll *(inf).*

crowded ['kraudɪd] *adj train, shop etc* überfüllt ◆ **the streets/shops/trains are ~** es ist voll auf den Straßen/in den Geschäften/Zügen; **to play to a ~ house** *(Theat)* vor vollem Haus spielen.

crowd-pleaser ['kraudpli:zəʳ] *n (person)* Publikumsliebling *m; (event etc)* Publikumserfolg *m.*

crowd-puller ['kraudpʊləʳ] *n* Kassenmagnet *m.*

crowfoot ['krəʊfʊt] *n (Bot)* Hahnenfuß *m.*

crown [kraun] [1] *n* **(a)** Krone *f* ◆ **~ of thorns** Dornenkrone *f;* **the C~** die Krone; **to wear the ~** auf dem Thron sitzen; **to be heir to the ~** Thronfolger(in) sein; **to succeed to the ~** die Thronfolge antreten.
(b) *(coin)* Krone *f.*
(c) *(top) (of head)* Wirbel *m; (skull itself)* Schädel *m; (head measurement)* Kopf(umfang) *m; (of hat)* Kopf *m; (of road)* Wölbung *f; (of arch)* Scheitelpunkt *m; (of roof)* First *m; (of tooth, tree)* Krone *f; (of hill)* Kuppe *f.*
(d) *(size of paper) englisches Papierformat (ca. 45 × 38 cm²).*
(e) *(fig: climax, completion)* Krönung *f.*
[2] *vt* **(a)** krönen ◆ **he was ~ed king** er ist zum König gekrönt worden; **~ed head** gekröntes Haupt.
(b) *(usu pass: top)* **the hill is ~ed with trees** die Bergkuppe ist mit Bäumen bewachsen; **the cake was ~ed with marzipan decorations** der Kuchen war zur Krönung des Ganzen (noch) mit Marzipanfiguren geschmückt; **to be ~ed with success** *(fig)* von Erfolg gekrönt sein.
(c) *(fig: form climax to)* krönen ◆ **to ~ it all it began to snow** *(inf)* zur Krönung des Ganzen begann es zu schneien; **that ~s everything!** *(inf)* das ist doch der Gipfel *or* die Höhe! *(inf).*
(d) *(in draughts etc)* eine Dame bekommen mit.
(e) *tooth* eine Krone machen für ◆ **the tooth had already been ~ed before** der Zahn hatte schon vorher eine Krone gehabt.
(f) *(inf: hit)* eine runterhauen *(+dat) (inf).*

crown: ~ cap *n see* **cork**; **~ colony** *n* Kronkolonie *f;* **~ cork** *n* Kronenkorken *m;* **~ court** *n Bezirksgericht nt für Strafsachen.*

crowning ['kraunɪŋ] [1] *n* Krönung *f.*
[2] *adj success, achievement* krönend ◆ **her hair was her ~ glory** ihr Haar war ihre größte Zierde; **that symphony was his ~ glory** diese Symphonie war die Krönung seines Werkes.

crown: ~ jewels *npl* Kronjuwelen *pl;* **~ lands** *npl* königliche Ländereien *pl,* Ländereien *pl* der Krone; **~ prince** *n* Kronprinz *m;* **~ princess** *n* Kronprinzessin *f;* **~ wheel** *n* Kronenrad, Kammrad *nt;* **~ witness** *n* Zeuge *m*/Zeugin *f* der Anklage.

crow's: ~ feet *npl* Krähenfüße *pl;* **~ nest** *n (Naut)* Mastkorb *m; (on foremast)* Krähennest *nt.*

crozier *n see* **crosier**.

crucial ['kru:ʃəl] *adj* **(a)** *(decisive)* entscheidend *(to* für). **(b)** *(very important)* äußert wichtig. **(c)** *(Med) incision etc* kreuzförmig, Kreuz-.

crucially ['kru:ʃəlɪ] *adv* ausschlaggebend; *different* bedeutend ◆ **~ necessary** äußerst wichtig; **~ important** von entscheidender Bedeutung.

crucible ['kru:sɪbl] *n* (Schmelz)tiegel *m* ◆ **~ steel** Tiegelgußstahl *m.*

crucifix ['kru:sɪfɪks] *n* Kruzifix *nt.*

crucifixion [ˌkru:sɪ'fɪkʃən] *n* Kreuzigung *f.*

cruciform ['kru:sɪfɔ:m] *adj* kreuzförmig.

crucify ['kru:sɪfaɪ] *vt* **(a)** kreuzigen. **(b)** *(fig) play, author* verreißen; *person* in der Luft zerreißen *(inf).* **(c)** *(mortify) the flesh* abtöten.

cruddy ['krʌdɪ] *adj (+er) (inf)* blöd *(inf),* bescheuert *(inf).*

crude [kru:d] [1] *adj (+er)* **(a)** *(unprocessed)* Roh-, roh. **(b)** *(vulgar) expression, story etc* ordinär, derb. **(c)** *(unsophisticated) method, model, implement* primitiv; *sketch* grob; *manners* ungehobelt, grob; *attempt* unbeholfen.
[2] *n* Rohöl *nt.*

crudely ['kru:dlɪ] *adv* **(a)** *(vulgarly)* ordinär, derb. **(b)** *(unsophisticatedly)* primitiv; *draw* grob; *behave* ungehobelt ◆ **to put it ~** um es ganz grob auszudrücken.

crudeness ['kru:dnɪs], **crudity** ['kru:dɪtɪ] *n* **(a)** *(vulgarity)* Derbheit *f.* **(b)** *see adj (c)* Primitivität *f;* Grobheit *f;* Ungehobelte(s) *nt (of gen,* in *+dat);* Unbeholfenheit *f.*

cruel ['krʊəl] *adj* grausam *(to* zu); *remark, wit, critic, winter also* unbarmherzig ◆ **to be ~ to animals/one's dog** ein Tierquäler sein/seinen Hund quälen; **that is ~ to animals** das ist Tierquälerei; **don't be ~!** sei nicht so gemein!; **sometimes you have to be ~ to be kind** manchmal ist es letzten Endes besser, wenn man hart ist.

cruelly ['krʊəlɪ] *adv (+vb)* grausam; *(+adj)* auf grausame Art.

cruelty ['krʊəltɪ] *n see adj* Grausamkeit *f (to* gegenüber); Unbarmherzigkeit *f* ◆ **~ to children** Kindesmißhandlung *f;* **~ to animals** Tierquälerei *f;* **physical/mental ~** Grausamkeit *f*/seelische Grausamkeit.

cruet ['kru:ɪt] *n* **(a)** (*set*) Gewürzständer *m*, Menage *f*; (*for oil*) Krügchen *nt* ◆ **would you pass the ~?** könnten Sie mir bitte die Gewürze reichen? **(b)** (*Eccl*) Krügchen *nt*.

cruise [kru:z] 1 *vi* **(a)** eine Kreuzfahrt/Kreuzfahrten machen; (*ship also*) kreuzen.
(b) (*travel at cruising speed*) (*car*) Dauergeschwindigkeit fahren; (*aircraft*) (mit Reisegeschwindigkeit) fliegen; (*athlete*) locker laufen; (*drive around*) herumfahren ◆ **the car ~s happily at 90** 90 ist eine ideale Fahrgeschwindigkeit für das Auto; **we were cruising along the road** wir fuhren (gemächlich) die Straße entlang; **we are now cruising at a height/speed of ...** wir fliegen nun in einer Flughöhe/mit einer Reisegeschwindigkeit von ...; **the cyclist ~d down the hill** der Radfahrer rollte den Berg hinunter.
2 *vt* (*ship*) befahren; (*car*) *streets* fahren auf (+*dat*); *area* abfahren.
3 *n* Kreuzfahrt *f* ◆ **to go on** *or* **for a ~** eine Kreuzfahrt machen.

cruise missile *n* Cruise Missile *nt*, Marschflugkörper *m*.

cruiser ['kru:zə^r] *n* (*Naut*) Kreuzer *m*; (*pleasure ~*) Vergnügungsjacht *f*.

cruiserweight ['kru:zəweɪt] *n* (*Boxing*) Halbschwergewicht *nt*.

cruising ['kru:zɪŋ] *n* Kreuzfahrten *pl* ◆ **to go ~** eine Kreuzfahrt/Kreuzfahrten machen.

cruising: ~ altitude *n* Reiseflughöhe *f*; **~ speed** *n* Reisegeschwindigkeit *f*; **~ yacht** *n* Vergnügungsjacht *f*.

cruller ['krʌlə^r] *n* (*US Cook*) *Art f Berliner*.

crumb [krʌm] 1 *n* **(a)** (*of bread etc*) Krümel *m*, Krume *f*, Brösel *m*; (*inside of loaf*) Krume *f* ◆ **can you spare a ~?** haben Sie eine Scheibe Brot für einen hungrigen Menschen?; **~s from the rich man's/master's table** Brosamen, die von des Reichen/des Herren Tisch fallen; **~s of wisdom** ein bißchen Weisheit; **a few ~s of information** ein paar Informationsbrocken; **that's one ~ of comfort** das ist (wenigstens) ein winziger Trost.
(b) (*sl*) (*fool*) Depp *m* (*inf*); (*brute*) Lump *m* (*inf*).
2 *interj* **~s!** (*inf*) Mensch! (*inf*), Mensch Meier! (*inf*).
3 *vt* (*Cook*) *fish etc* panieren.

crumble ['krʌmbl] 1 *vt* zerkrümeln, zerbröckeln ◆ **to ~ sth into/onto sth** etw in/auf etw (*acc*) krümeln *or* bröckeln.
2 *vi* (*brick, earth*) bröckeln; (*bread, cake etc*) krümeln; (*also* **~ away**) (*earth, building*) zerbröckeln; (*fig*) (*resistance, opposition*) sich auflösen, schmelzen; (*hopes*) schwinden; (*plans*) ins Wanken geraten.
3 *n* (*Cook*) Obst *nt* mit Streusel; (*topping*) Streusel *pl* ◆ **apple/rhubarb ~** *mit Streuseln bestreutes, überbackenes Apfel/Rhabarberdessert*.

crumbly ['krʌmblɪ] *adj* (+*er*) *stone, earth* bröckelig; *cake, bread* krümelig, bröselig.

crummy ['krʌmɪ] *adj* (+*er*) (*inf*) mies (*inf*), Scheiß- (*sl*).

crumpet ['krʌmpɪt] *n* **(a)** (*Cook*) *kleiner dicker Pfannkuchen*. **(b)** (*esp Brit sl: women*) Miezen *pl* (*sl*) ◆ **he fancied a bit of ~** ihm war nach ein bißchen Sex; **she's a nice bit of ~** sie ist sehr sexy.

crumple ['krʌmpl] 1 *vt* (*also* **~ up**) *paper, dress, fabric* (*crease*) zer- *or* verknittern, zerknautschen; (*screw up*) zusammenknüllen; *metal* eindrücken ◆ **the force of the impact ~d the bonnet/car** die Wucht des Aufpralls drückte die Kühlerhaube ein/quetschte das Auto zusammen.
2 *vi* (*lit, fig: collapse*) zusammenbrechen; (*get creased: paper*) krumpeln, knittern; (*car, metal*) zusammengedrückt werden ◆ **her face ~d** ihr Gesicht verzog sich (zum Weinen).

crumple zone *n* Knautschzone *f*.

crunch [krʌntʃ] 1 *vt* **(a)** *biscuit etc* mampfen (*inf*). **(b) he ~ed the beetle/ice/gravel underfoot** der Käfer zerknackte/das Eis zersplitterte/der Kies knirschte unter seinen Füßen; **to ~ the gears** (*Aut*) den Gang/die Gänge reinwürgen (*inf*). **(c)** (*Comput*) *numbers* verarbeiten.
2 *vi* **(a)** (*gravel, snow etc*) knirschen; (*gears*) krachen ◆ **he ~ed across the gravel** er ging mit knirschenden Schritten über den Kies. **(b) he was ~ing on a carrot** er mampfte eine Möhre (*inf*); **he ~ed into the apple** er biß knackend in den Apfel.
3 *n* **(a)** (*sound*) Krachen *nt*; (*of footsteps, gravel etc*) Knirschen *nt* ◆ **the two cars collided with a ~** die zwei Autos krachten zusammen (*inf*); **~!** Krach!
(b) (*inf: car crash*) Zusammenstoß *m*.
(c) (*inf: moment of reckoning*) **the ~** der große Krach; **when it comes to the ~** wenn es darauf ankommt; **this is the ~** jetzt ist der spannende Moment; **it's/we've come to the ~** jetzt kommt es drauf an, jetzt geht es hart auf hart.

◆**crunch up** *vt sep* (*eat*) *carrot etc* zerbeißen; (*crush noisily*) *garbage etc* (krachend) zermahlen.

crunchy ['krʌntʃɪ] *adj* (+*er*) *apple* knackig; *biscuit* knusprig; *snow* verharscht.

crupper ['krʌpə^r] *n* **(a)** (*of harness*) Schweifriemen *m*. **(b)** (*hindquarters*) Kruppe *f*.

crusade [kru:'seɪd] 1 *n* (*Hist, fig*) Kreuzzug *m*; (*evangelical ~*) Missionsfeldzug, Glaubensfeldzug *m*.
2 *vi* (*Hist, fig*) einen Kreuzzug/Kreuzzüge führen; (*as evangelist*) missionieren.

crusader [kru:'seɪdə^r] *n* (*Hist*) Kreuzritter *m*; (*fig*) Apostel *m*; (*evangelical ~*) Glaubensjünger *m*.

crush [krʌʃ] 1 *n* **(a)** (*crowd*) Gedrängel *nt* ◆ **it'll be a bit of a ~** es wird ein bißchen eng werden; **~ barrier** Absperrung, Barrikade *f*.
(b) (*inf*) (*infatuation*) Schwärmerei *f*; (*object of infatuation*) Schwarm *m* ◆ **to have a ~ on sb** für jdn schwärmen, in jdn verschossen sein (*inf*); **schoolgirl ~** Schulmädchenschwärmerei *f*.
(c) (*drink*) Saftgetränk *nt*.
2 *vt* **(a)** (*squeeze, press tightly*) quetschen; (*damage*) *soft fruit etc* zerdrücken, zerquetschen; *finger, toes etc* quetschen; (*rock, car etc*) *sb* zerquetschen; (*kill*) zu Tode quetschen; (*grind, break up*) *spices, garlic* (zer)stoßen; *ice* stoßen; *ore, stone* zerkleinern, zerstampfen; *scrap metal, garbage* zusammenpressen; (*crease*) *clothes, paper* zerknittern, zerdrücken; (*screw up*) *paper* zerknüllen ◆ **~ed pineapple** *klein geschnetzelte Ananas*; **I was ~ed between two enormous men in the plane** ich war im Flugzeug zwischen zwei fetten Männern eingequetscht *or* eingeklemmt; **she ~ed the child to her breast** sie drückte das Kind fest an die Brust; **to ~ sb/sth into sth** jdn in etw (*acc*) quetschen/etw in etw (*acc*) stopfen.
(b) (*fig*) *enemy, hopes, self-confidence, sb* vernichten; *revolution, opposition* niederschlagen; (*oppress*) *people, peasants* unterdrücken ◆ **she ~ed him with one glance** sie vernichtete ihn mit einem Blick; **to ~ sb's spirit** jdn brechen.
3 *vi* **(a)** (*crowd*) (sich) drängen ◆ **to ~ past/round sb** sich an jdm vorbeidrängen/sich um jdn herumdrängen; **they ~ed into the car** sie quetschten *or* drängten sich in das Auto.
(b) (*clothes, fabric*) knittern, knautschen (*inf*).

◆**crush in** 1 *vt sep* hineinstopfen (*prep obj, -to* in +*acc*).
2 *vi* (sich) hinein-/hereindrängen.

◆**crush out** *vt sep juice etc* auspressen, ausquetschen (*inf*).

◆**crush up** *vt sep* **(a)** (*pulverize*) zerstoßen. **(b)** (*pack tightly together*) zusammendrücken *or* -quetschen ◆ **we were (sitting) all ~ed ~** wir saßen alle zusammengequetscht.

crushing ['krʌʃɪŋ] *adj defeat* zerschmetternd; *blow, look, reply* vernichtend; *experience* niederschmetternd.

crush-resistant ['krʌʃrɪzɪstənt] *adj* knitterfrei.

crust [krʌst] 1 *n* (*all senses*) Kruste *f* ◆ **the earth's ~** die Erdkruste.
2 *vi* verkrusten ◆ **~ed port** Portwein *m* mit Kruste.

crustacean [krʌs'teɪʃən] 1 *n* Schalentier *nt*, Krustazee *f* (*spec*).
2 *adj characteristics, class* der Schalentiere *or* Krustazeen (*spec*); *appearance* krebsähnlich.

crustily ['krʌstɪlɪ] *adv* (*fig*) barsch.

crusty ['krʌstɪ] *adj* (+*er*) knusprig; (*fig: irritable*) barsch.

crutch [krʌtʃ] *n* **(a)** (*for walking*) Krücke *f* ◆ **to use sb/sth as a ~** (*fig*) sich an jdn/etw klammern. **(b)** (*Naut*) Baumstütze, Baumschere *f*. **(c)** *see* **crotch (b)**.

crux [krʌks] *n* (*of matter, problem*) Kern *m* ◆ **this is the ~ (of the matter)** das ist der springende Punkt.

cry [kraɪ] 1 *n* **(a)** (*inarticulate shout*) Schrei *m*; (*call*) Ruf *m* ◆ **to give** *or* **utter a ~** (auf)schreien, einen Schrei ausstoßen; **a ~ of fear/pain** ein Angstschrei *m*/Schmerzensschrei *m*; **a ~ for help** ein Hilferuf *m*; **he gave a ~ for help** er rief um Hilfe; **within ~** in Rufweite; *see* **far**.
(b) (*of animal*) Schrei *m*; (*Hunt: of hounds*) Geheul, Gebell *nt* ◆ **the pack is in full ~** die Meute hetzt laut bellend *or* heulend hinter der Beute her; **to be in full ~ after sb** (*fig*) sich mit großem Geheul auf jdn stürzen.
(c) (*slogan*) Parole *f*; (*battle ~*) Schlachtruf *m*.
(d) (*outcry*) **a ~ for/against sth** ein Ruf *m* nach etw/ein Protest *m* gegen etw.
(e) (*weep*) **a ~ will do you good** weine ruhig, das wird dir guttun; **to have a good/little ~** sich einmal richtig ausweinen *or* ausheulen (*inf*)/ein bißchen weinen.
2 *vi* **(a)** (*weep*) weinen, heulen (*inf*); (*baby*) schreien ◆ **she was ~ing for her teddy bear** sie weinte nach ihrem Teddy; **... or I'll give you something to ~ for** *or* **about** ... und dann weißt du, warum du heulst (*inf*).
(b) (*call*) rufen; (*louder, animal, bird*) schreien; (*Hunt: hounds*) heulen ◆ **to ~ for help** um Hilfe rufen/schreien; **she cried for a nurse/for somebody to come** sie rief/schrie nach einer Krankenschwester/nach jemandem.
3 *vt* **(a)** (*shout out*) rufen; (*louder*) schreien ◆ **to ~ mercy** (*old, liter*) um Gnade flehen; **he cried to me to go away** er rief mir zu, daß ich verschwinden solle; *see* **shame, wolf**.
(b) (*announce*) ausrufen.
(c) (*weep*) *bitter tears etc* weinen ◆ **to ~ one's eyes/heart out** sich (*dat*) die Augen ausweinen/herzzerreißend weinen; **to ~ oneself to sleep** sich in den Schlaf weinen.

◆**cry down** *vt sep* (*decry*) herabsetzen.

◆**cry off** *vi* einen Rückzieher machen, aussteigen (*inf*) ◆ **to ~ ~ from sth** aus etw aussteigen (*inf*), etw (wieder) abblasen (*inf*).

◆**cry out** *vi* **(a)** aufschreien ◆ **to ~ ~ to sb** jdm etwas zuschreien; **he cried ~ to me to fetch help** er schrie mir zu, ich solle Hilfe holen; **well for ~ing ~ loud!** (*inf*) na, das darf doch wohl nicht wahr sein! (*inf*).
(b) (*fig*) **to be ~ing ~ for sth** nach etw schreien; (*be suitable for also*) sich (geradezu) zu etw anbieten; **that building is just ~ing ~ to be turned into a pub** dieses Gebäude schreit (geradezu) danach, daß man es in ein Lokal verwandelt.

◆**cry up** *vt sep* **it's/he's not all it's/he's cried ~ to be** so großartig ist es/er dann auch wieder nicht.

crybaby ['kraɪbeɪbɪ] *n* (*inf*) Heulsuse *f* (*inf*).

crying ['kraɪɪŋ] 1 *adj* (*fig: outrageous*) *injustice* schreiend; *need* dringend ◆ **it is a ~ shame** es ist jammerschade *or* ein Jammer.
2 *n* (*weeping*) Weinen *nt*; (*of baby*) Schreien *nt*.

crypt [krɪpt] *n* Krypta *f*; (*burial ~*) Gruft *f*.

cryptic ['krɪptɪk] *adj remark etc* hintergründig, rätselhaft, schleierhaft; *clue, riddle etc* verschlüsselt ◆ **you're being very ~** du drückst dich sehr rätselhaft *or* schleierhaft aus.

cryptically ['krɪptɪkəlɪ] *adv* hintergründig, rätselhaft, schleierhaft ◆ **~ worded** *letter, remark* hintergründig *etc* formuliert; *clue* verschlüsselt formuliert.

crypto- ['krɪptəʊ] *pref* Krypto-, krypto-.

cryptogram ['krɪptəʊgræm] *n* Kryptogramm *nt*.

cryptographer [krɪpˈtɒgrəfəʳ], **cryptographist** [krɪpˈtɒgrəfɪst] *n* Kryptograph *m.*

cryptographic [ˌkrɪptəʊˈgræfɪk] *adj* kryptographisch, in Geheimschrift verschlüsselt.

cryptography [krɪpˈtɒgrəfɪ] *n* Kryptographie *f.*

crystal [ˈkrɪstl] 1 *n* (*Chem, Rad*) Kristall *m*; (*on watch*) (Uhr)glas *nt*; (~ *glass*) Kristall *nt*; (*quartz*) (Quarz)kristall *m.*
2 *adj* **(a)** (*crystalline*) Kristall-, kristallin; (*like a* ~) kristallartig; (~*-glass*) Kristall-, kristallen; (*quartz*) Quarzkristall-. **(b)** (*fig*) *waters* kristallklar, glasklar.

crystal: ~ ball *n* Glaskugel *f*; **I don't have a ~ ball** (*inf*) ich bin (doch) kein Hellseher; **you didn't see that in your ~ ball, did you?** (*inf*) das hast du wohl nicht vorausgesehen?; **~-ball gazer** *n* Hellseher(in *f*) *m*; **~-ball gazing** *n* Hellseherei *f*; **~-clear** *adj* (*lit, fig*) glasklar, völlig klar, vollständig klar; **~-detector** *n* (*Rad*) Kristalldetektor *m*; **~-gazer** *n see* **~-ball gazer**; **~-gazing** 1 *n see* **~-ball gazing**; 2 *adj* **all these ~-gazing so-called experts** alle diese sogenannten Experten, die aus dem Kaffeesatz wahrsagen; **~ lattice** *n* Kristallgitter *nt.*

crystalline [ˈkrɪstəlaɪn] *adj* Kristall-, kristallin ♦ **~ lens** (Augen)linse *f.*

crystallization [ˈkrɪstəlaɪzeɪʃən] *n* **(a)** (*lit*) Kristallisierung *f*; (*out of another substance*) Auskristallisierung *f.*
(b) (*fig*) (Heraus)kristallisierung *f*; (*crystallized form*) kristallisierte Form ♦ **after the ~ of these ideas into a theory** nachdem sich aus diesen Gedanken eine Theorie herauskristallisiert hatte.

crystallize [ˈkrɪstəlaɪz] 1 *vt* (*lit*) zum Kristallisieren bringen; (*separating out*) auskristallisieren; *fruit* kandieren; (*fig*) (feste) Form geben (*+dat*).
2 *vi* (*lit*) kristallisieren; (*separate out*) (sich) auskristallisieren; (*fig*) feste Form annehmen ♦ **this theory ~d out of many years' research** diese Theorie hat sich nach jahrelanger Forschung herauskristallisiert.

crystallized [ˈkrɪstəlaɪzd] *adj* kristallisiert; *fruit* kandiert.

crystallography [ˌkrɪstəˈlɒgrəfɪ] *n* Kristallographie *f.*

crystal set *n* (*Rad*) Detektorempfänger *m.*

CSE (*Brit*) *abbr of* **Certificate of Secondary Education.**

CS gas *n* (*Brit*) ≃ Tränengas *nt.*

CST *abbr of* **Central Standard Time.**

ct *abbr of* **(a) cent. (b) carat.**

cub [kʌb] 1 *n* **(a)** (*of animal*) Junge(s) *nt.* **(b) C~** (*C~ Scout*) Wölfling *m.* **(c)** (~ *reporter*) junger Reporter, junge Reporterin. **(d)** (*inf: boy*) grüner Junge.
2 *vi* werfen.

Cuba [ˈkjuːbə] *n* Kuba *nt.*

Cuban [ˈkjuːbən] 1 *adj* kubanisch ♦ **~ heel** Blockabsatz *m.*
2 *n* Kubaner(in *f*) *m.*

cubby-hole [ˈkʌbɪhəʊl] *n* **(a)** (*compartment*) Fach *nt.* **(b)** (*room*) Kabäuschen, Kabuff *nt.*

cube [kjuːb] 1 *n* **(a)** (*shape, object*) Würfel *m* ♦ **~ sugar** Würfelzucker *m.*
(b) (*Math: power of three*) dritte Potenz ♦ **~ root** Kubikwurzel *f*; **the ~ of 3 is 27** die dritte Potenz von 3 ist 27, 3 hoch 3 ist 27.
2 *vt* **(a)** (*Math*) in die dritte Potenz erheben, hoch 3 nehmen ♦ **four ~d** vier hoch drei.
(b) (*Cook*) würfelig *or* in Würfel schneiden.

cubic [ˈkjuːbɪk] *adj* **(a)** (*of volume*) Kubik-, Raum- ♦ **~ capacity** Fassungsvermögen *nt*; (*of engine*) Hubraum *m*; **~ content** Raum- *or* Kubikinhalt *m*; **~ measure** Raum- *or* Kubikmaß *nt*; **~ metre/foot/feet** Kubikmeter *m or nt*/Kubikfuß *m.* **(b)** (*Math*) kubisch ♦ **~ equation** Gleichung *f* dritten Grades.

cubicle [ˈkjuːbɪkəl] *n* Kabine *f*; (*in dormitory etc also*) Alkoven *m*; (*in toilets*) (Einzel)toilette *f.*

cubiform [ˈkjuːbɪfɔːm] *adj* (*form*) kubisch, würfelförmig.

cubism [ˈkjuːbɪzəm] *n* Kubismus *m.*

cubist [ˈkjuːbɪst] 1 *n* Kubist(in *f*) *m.*
2 *adj* kubistisch.

cubit [ˈkjuːbɪt] *n* Elle *f.*

cub: C~ mistress *n* Wölflingsmutter *f*; **~ reporter** *n* junger Reporter, junge Reporterin; **C~ Scout** *n* Wölfling *m.*

cuckold [ˈkʌkəld] 1 *n* Hahnrei *m* (*old*), betrogener Ehemann.
2 *vt* zum Hahnrei machen (*old*), betrügen, Hörner aufsetzen (*+dat*).

cuckoo [ˈkʊkuː] 1 *n* Kuckuck *m.*
2 *adj pred* (*inf*) meschugge (*inf*) ♦ **to go ~** überschnappen (*inf*).

cuckoo: ~ clock *n* Kuckucksuhr *f*; **~-pint** *n* (*Bot*) Gefleckter Aronsstab; **~-spit** *n* (*secretion*) Kuckucksspeichel *m*; (*insect*) Schaumzikade *f.*

cucumber [ˈkjuːkʌmbəʳ] *n* (Salat)gurke *f* ♦ **as cool as a ~** seelenruhig.

cud [kʌd] *n* wiedergekäutes Futter ♦ **to chew the ~** (*lit*) wiederkäuen; (*fig*) vor sich hin grübeln, sinnieren.

cuddle [ˈkʌdl] 1 *n* Liebkosung *f* ♦ **to give sb a ~** jdn in den Arm nehmen; **to need a ~** Zärtlichkeit brauchen, geknuddelt (*inf*) *or* liebkost werden müssen; **to have a ~** schmusen.
2 *vt* in den Arm nehmen; (*amorously also*) schmusen mit.
3 *vi* schmusen.

♦**cuddle down** *vi* sich kuscheln.

♦**cuddle up** *vi* sich kuscheln (*to, against* an *+acc*) ♦ **to ~ ~ beside sb** sich neben jdm zusammenkuscheln; **to ~ ~ in bed** sich im Bett zusammenkuscheln, sich ins Bett kuscheln; **I'm cold — well, ~ ~ then** mir ist kalt — na, dann kuschel dich ran (*inf*); **we all had to ~ ~ in the tent to keep warm** wir mußten uns alle im Zelt aneinanderkuscheln, um es warm zu haben.

cuddlesome [ˈkʌdlsəm] *adj see* **cuddly.**

cuddly [ˈkʌdlɪ] *adj* (*+er*) (*wanting a cuddle*) verschmust (*inf*), anschmiegsam; (*good to cuddle*) *toy, doll* zum Liebhaben, knuddelig (*inf*); *person* knuddelig (*inf*) ♦ **to be in a ~ mood** in einer verschmusten Laune *or* in Schmuselaune sein; **~ toy** Schmusetier *nt* (*inf*).

cudgel [ˈkʌdʒəl] 1 *n* Knüppel *m* ♦ **to take up the ~s for** *or* **on behalf of sb/sth** (*fig*) für jdn/etw eintreten *or* eine Lanze brechen, für jdn/etw auf die Barrikaden gehen.
2 *vt* prügeln ♦ **to ~ one's brains** (*fig*) sich (*dat*) das (Ge)hirn zermartern.

cue [kjuː] 1 *n* **(a)** (*Theat, fig*) Stichwort *nt*; (*action*) (Einsatz)zeichen *nt*; (*Film, TV*) Zeichen *nt* zum Aufnahmebeginn; (*Mus*) Einsatz *m*; (*written: preceding bars*) Hilfsnoten *pl* ♦ **to give sb his ~** (*Theat*) jdm das *or* sein Stichwort geben; (*action*) jdm das (Einsatz)zeichen geben; (*Mus*) jdm den Einsatz geben; **that sounds like a ~ for a song** das hört sich ganz nach einem Lied an; **whenever he hears the word "strike" that's his ~ to launch into an attack on the unions** das Wort „Streik" ist für ihn jedesmal (das) Stichwort für einen Angriff auf die Gewerkschaften; **to take one's ~ from sb** sich nach jdm richten; **right on ~** (*Theat*) genau auf's Stichwort; (*fig*) wie gerufen.
(b) (*Billiards*) Queue *nt.*
2 *vt* (*Theat*) das Stichwort geben (*+dat*); (*with gesture etc*) das Einsatzzeichen geben (*+dat*); (*TV, Film*) *scene* abfahren lassen; (*Mus*) *player* den Einsatz geben (*+dat*); *trumpet flourish etc* den Einsatz geben für ♦ **~!** (*Film, TV*) ab!

♦**cue in** *vt sep* den Einsatz geben (*+dat*); (*TV, Film*) *scene* abfahren lassen; *tape etc* (zur rechten Zeit) einspielen.

cue: ~-ball *n* Spielball *m*; **~ card** *n* (*TV*) Neger *m*; **~ rest** *n* Stütze *f* für das Queue.

cuff[1] [kʌf] *n* **(a)** Manschette *f*; (*turned back also*) Stulpe *f* ♦ **off the ~** aus dem Handgelenk, aus dem Stegreif. **(b)** (*US: of trousers*) (Hosen)aufschlag *m.* **(c)** *usu pl* (*inf: handcuff*) Handschelle *f.* **(d)** (*US inf: credit*) **on the ~** auf Stottern (*inf*).

cuff[2] 1 *vt* (*strike*) einen Klaps geben (*+dat*), eins um die Ohren geben (*+dat*) (*inf*).
2 *n* (*blow*) Klaps *m.*

cuff-link [ˈkʌflɪŋk] *n* Manschettenknopf *m.*

cuirass [kwɪˈræs] *n* Küraß, Brustharnisch *m.*

cuirassier [ˌkwɪrəˈsɪəʳ] *n* Kürassier *m.*

cuisine [kwɪˈziːn] *n* Küche *f.*

cul-de-sac [ˈkʌldəsæk] *n* (*esp Brit*) Sackgasse *f.*

culinary [ˈkʌlɪnərɪ] *adj* kulinarisch; *skill, talents etc* Koch-; *implements* Küchen-.

cull [kʌl] 1 *n* **(a)** (*selection*) Auswahl *f.* **(b)** (*killing of surplus*) *Erlegen nt überschüssiger Tierbestände*, Reduktionsabschuß *m* ♦ **~ of seals** Robbenschlag *m.* **(c)** (*rejected item*) Ausschuß *m.*
2 *vt* **(a)** (*pick*) *flowers* pflücken.
(b) (*collect*) entnehmen (*from dat*); *legends* (zusammen)sammeln (*from* aus).
(c) (*kill as surplus*) (als überschüssig) erlegen ♦ **to ~ seals** Robbenschlag *m* betreiben.

cullender *n see* **colander.**

culminate [ˈkʌlmɪneɪt] 1 *vi* (*Astron*) kulminieren, den *or* seinen Höchst-/Tiefststand erreichen; (*fig*) (*reach a climax: career, music etc*) gipfeln, kulminieren (*geh*) (*in* in *+dat*); (*end*) herauslaufen (*in* auf *+acc*), enden (*in* mit).
2 *vt* (*US*) den Höhepunkt *or* Gipfel (*+gen*) darstellen.

culmination [ˌkʌlmɪˈneɪʃən] *n* (*Astron*) Kulminationspunkt, Höchst-/Tiefststand *m*; (*fig*) (*high point: of career etc*) Höhepunkt *m*; (*end*) Ende *nt*, Ausgang *m.*

culottes [kjuːˈlɒts] *npl* Hosenrock *m* ♦ **a pair of ~** ein Hosenrock.

culpability [ˌkʌlpəˈbɪlɪtɪ] *n* (*form*) Schuld *f.*

culpable [ˈkʌlpəbl] *adj* (*form*) schuldig ♦ **~ homicide** (*Jur*) fahrlässige Tötung; **~ negligence** grobe Fahrlässigkeit.

culprit [ˈkʌlprɪt] *n* Schuldige(r) *mf*; (*Jur*) Täter(in *f*) *m*; (*inf: thing, person causing trouble*) Übeltäter *m.*

cult [kʌlt] 1 *n* (*Rel, fig*) Kult *m* ♦ **to make a ~ of sth** (einen) Kult mit etw treiben.
2 *attr movie etc* Kult-.

cultivable [ˈkʌltɪvəbl] *adj* kultivierbar.

cultivate [ˈkʌltɪveɪt] *vt* **(a)** kultivieren; *soil also* bebauen; *crop, fruit etc also* anbauen; *beard* wachsen lassen.
(b) (*fig*) *friendship, links etc* pflegen, kultivieren; *art, skill, taste* entwickeln; *sb* sich (*dat*) warmhalten (*inf*), die Beziehung zu ... pflegen ♦ **a connection like that is definitely worth cultivating** es lohnt sich bestimmt, so eine Verbindung aufrechtzuerhalten; **to ~ one's mind** sich bilden.

cultivated [ˈkʌltɪveɪtɪd] *adj* (*Agr, fig*) kultiviert.

cultivation [ˌkʌltɪˈveɪʃən] *n see vt* **(a)** Kultivieren *nt*, Kultivierung *f*; Anbau *m* ♦ **to be under ~** bebaut werden.
(b) Pflege *f* (*of* von); Entwicklung *f*; Bemühung *f* (*of* um) ♦ **his constant ~ of influential friendships** seine ständigen Bemühungen um einflußreiche Freunde.
(c) (*cultivated state*) Kultiviertheit *f.*

cultivator [ˈkʌltɪveɪtəʳ] *n* **(a)** (*machine*) Kultivator, Grubber *m.* **(b)** (*person*) **a ~ of the soil/of new friendships** *etc* jemand, der den Boden bebaut/neue Freundschaften pflegt.

cultural [ˈkʌltʃərəl] *adj* **(a)** Kultur-; *differences, resemblances also, events* kulturell ♦ **what sort of ~ activities are there?** was wird kulturell geboten?; **we enjoyed a very ~ evening** wir hatten einen sehr gebildeten Abend; **could you not do something a little more ~ with your spare time?** könntest du

deine Freizeit nicht etwas kultivierter gestalten *or* verbringen?
(b) (*Agr*) Kultur-.

culturally ['kʌltʃərəlɪ] *adv* kulturell.

culture ['kʌltʃəʳ] [1] *n* (a) Kultur *f* ♦ **physical ~** (*dated*) Körperkultur *f* (*dated*); **a man of ~/of no ~** ein kultivierter/unkultivierter Mann, ein Mann mit/ohne Kultur; **to study German ~** die deutsche Kultur studieren.
(b) (*Agr, Biol, Med*) Kultur *f*; (*of animals*) Zucht *f*.
[2] *vt* (*Biol, Med*) eine Kultur anlegen von.

cultured ['kʌltʃəd] *adj* kultiviert; (*Agr*) Kultur-; (*Biol, Med*) gezüchtet ♦ **~ pearl** Zuchtperle *f*.

culture *in cpds* Kultur-; **~ dish** *n* (*Biol, Med*) Petrischale *f*; **~ fluid** *n* (*Biol, Med*) Nährlösung *f*; **~ gap** *n* Kulturlücke *f*; **~ medium** *n* (*Biol, Med*) Kulturmedium *nt*, (künstlicher) Nährboden; **~ shock** *n* Kulturschock *m*; **~ vulture** *n* (*hum*) Kulturfanatiker(in *f*) *m*.

culvert ['kʌlvət] *n* unterirdischer Kanal, (Abwasser)kanal *m*; (*for cables*) Kabeltunnel *m*.

cum [kʌm] *prep* in einem, gleichzeitig ♦ **a sort of sofa-~-bed** eine Art von Sofa und Bett in einem.

cumbersome ['kʌmbəsəm] *adj clothing, coat* (be)hinderlich; *spacesuit, movements, gesture, style, piece of music* schwerfällig; *vehicle* unhandlich (*inf*), schwer zu manövrieren; *suitcases, parcels* sperrig, unhandlich; *procedure, regulations* beschwerlich, mühselig ♦ **it's so ~ having to wear all this heavy clothing** es ist so lästig, daß man alle diese schweren Kleidungsstücke tragen muß.

cumbersomely ['kʌmbəsəmlɪ] *adv move, write* schwerfällig; *phrased also* umständlich; *dressed* hinderlich.

cumbrous ['kʌmbrəs] *adj see* **cumbersome**.

cumin ['kʌmɪn] *n* Kreuzkümmel *m*.

cummerbund ['kʌməbʌnd] *n* Kummerbund *m*.

cumulative ['kju:mjʊlətɪv] *adj* gesamt-, kumulativ (*geh*) ♦ **~ evidence** (*Jur*) Häufung *f* von Beweisen/Zeugenaussagen; **~ interest** (*Fin*) Zins und Zinseszins; **~ voting** Wählen *nt* durch Kumulieren *or* Stimmenhäufung *or* nach dem Kumulierungssystem; **the ~ debts of ten years** die Schulden, die sich im Lauf von zehn Jahren angehäuft haben/hatten.

cumulonimbus ['kju:mjələʊ'nɪmbəs] *n* Kumulonimbus *m*.

cumulus ['kju:mjələs] *n* Kumulus *m*.

cuneiform ['kju:nɪfɔ:m] [1] *adj* keilförmig; *characters, inscription* in Keilschrift, Keilschrift- ♦ **~ writing** Keilschrift *f*.
[2] *n* Keilschrift *f*.

cunnilingus [ˌkʌnɪ'lɪŋgəs] *n* Cunnilingus *m*.

cunning ['kʌnɪŋ] [1] *n* (*cleverness*) Schlauheit, Listigkeit, Gerissenheit *f*; (*liter: skill*) (Kunst)fertigkeit *f*, Geschick *nt*.
[2] *adj* (a) *plan* schlau; *person also* listig, gerissen; *smile, expression* verschmitzt, verschlagen (*pej*); (*ingenious*) *gadget* schlau *or* clever (*inf*) ausgedacht. (b) (*US inf*) drollig.

cunningly ['kʌnɪŋlɪ] *adv* schlau; (*with reference to people also*) listig, gerissen; *smile, look* verschmitzt, verschlagen (*pej*); (*ingeniously*) geschickt ♦ **a ~ designed little gadget** ein geschickt *or* clever ausgedachtes Ding.

cunt [kʌnt] *n* (*vulg*) (*vagina*) Fotze (*vulg*), Möse (*vulg*) *f*; (*intercourse*) Fick *m* (*vulg*); (*term of abuse*) Arsch *m* (*vulg*) ♦ **she's a nice bit of ~** das ist eine tolle Fotze (*vulg*).

cup [kʌp] [1] *n* (a) Tasse *f*; (*goblet*) Pokal, Kelch *m*; (*mug*) Becher *m*; (*Eccl*) Kelch *m* ♦ **in his ~s** (*dated inf*) angezecht.
(b) (*cupful*) Tasse *f*; (*Cook: standard measure: 8 fl oz = 0,22 l*) ♦ **a ~ of tea/water** eine Tasse Tee/Wasser; **that's just/that's not my ~ of tea** (*fig inf*) das ist genau/ist nicht mein Fall.
(c) (*prize, football ~ etc*) Pokal *m* ♦ **they're out of the C~** sie sind aus dem Pokal(wettbewerb) ausgeschieden.
(d) (*drink*) -mix, -becher *m*.
(e) (*Bot: of flower*) Kelch *m*; (*of bra*) Körbchen *nt*; (*Golf*) Metallbüchse *f* (*im Loch*); (*Med: ~ping glass*) Schröpfkopf *m*.
(f) (*fig liter: portion*) Kelch *m* ♦ **to drain the ~ of sorrow (to the dregs)** den Kelch des Leidens (bis zur Neige) leeren (*liter*); **my ~ is overflowing** (*liter*) *or* **runneth over** (*Bibl*) ich bin über alle Maßen glücklich, mein Glück ist vollkommen.
[2] *vt* (a) *hands* hohl machen ♦ **~ped hand** hohle Hand; **he ~ped his hands and blew into them** er blies sich (*dat*) in die Hände; **to ~ sth in one's hands** etw in der hohlen Hand halten; **he ~ped his chin in his hand** er stützte das Kinn in die Hand; **to ~ one's** *or* **a hand to one's ear** die Hand ans Ohr halten; **to ~ one's hands around sth** etw mit der hohlen Hand umfassen.
(b) (*Med*) schröpfen.
(c) (*Golf*) einlochen mit.

cup: ~-and-ball *n* Fangbecherspiel *nt*; **~bearer** *n* Mundschenk *m*.

cupboard ['kʌbəd] *n* Schrank *m* ♦ **~ love** fauler Schmus (*inf*), Zweckfreundlichkeit *f*; **what's all this ~ love, what are you after?** was soll der faule Schmus, worauf willst du hinaus? (*inf*).

cup: ~-cake *n kleiner, runder Kuchen*; **C~ Final** *n* Pokalendspiel *nt*; (*international also*) Cupfinale *nt*; **C~ Finalist** *n* Teilnehmer *m* am Pokalendspiel; **~ful** *n, pl* **~sful, ~fuls** Tasse *f*.

cupid ['kju:pɪd] *n* Amorette *f* ♦ **C~** Cupido, Amor *m*; **C~'s dart** (*liter*) Amors Pfeil (*liter*), Liebespfeil *m*.

cupidity [kju:'pɪdɪtɪ] *n* (*liter*) Begierde (*pej*), Gier (*pej*) *f*.

Cupid's bow ['kju:pɪdz'bəʊ] *adj* bogenförmig geschwungen ♦ **~ mouth** Kußmund, Herzmund *m*.

cup match *n* Pokalspiel *nt*.

cupola ['kju:pələ] *n* (*Archit*) Kuppel *f*; (*roof also*) Kuppeldach *nt*; (*furnace*) Kupolofen *m*.

cuppa ['kʌpə] *n* (*Brit inf*) Tasse Tee *f*, Täßchen Tee *nt* (*inf*).

cupping ['kʌpɪŋ] *n* (*Med*) Schröpfen *nt* ♦ **~-glass** Schröpfkopf *m*.

cupreous ['kju:prɪəs] *adj* Kupfer-, kupfern.

cuprite ['kju:praɪt] *n* Kupferoxyd, Rotkupfererz *nt*.

cupronickel ['kju:prəʊ'nɪkl] *n* Kupfernickel *nt*, Kupfer-Nickel-Legierung *f*.

cuprous ['kju:prəs] *adj* Kupfer-, kupfern.

cup: ~ size *n* (*of bra*) Körbchengröße *f*; **~ tie** *n* Pokalspiel *nt*.

cupule ['kju:pju:l] *n* (*Bot*) Becher *m*, Cupula *f* (*spec*).

Cup-winners ['kʌpwɪnəz] *npl* Pokalsieger *m* ♦ **~' Cup** (*Ftbl*) Europapokal *m* der Pokalsieger.

cur [kɜ:ʳ] *n* (*pej*) (*dog*) Köter *m* (*pej*); (*old: man*) Kanaille *f* (*dated pej*), Hundsfott *m* (*dated pej*).

curable ['kjʊərəbl] *adj* heilbar ♦ **is he ~?** ist er zu heilen?

curaçao [ˌkju:rə'səʊ] *n* Curaçao *m*.

curate ['kjʊərɪt] *n* (*Catholic*) Kurat *m*; (*Protestant*) Vikar *m* ♦ **it's like the ~'s egg** es ist streckenweise gar nicht so schlecht.

curative ['kjʊərətɪv] [1] *adj* Heil-, heilend.
[2] *n* Heilmittel *nt*.

curator [kjʊə'reɪtəʳ] *n* (a) (*of museum etc*) Kustos *m*. (b) (*Jur: guardian*) Kurator, Vormund *m*.

curb [kɜ:b] [1] *n* (a) (*of harness*) (*bit*) Kandare *f*; (*chain*) Kinnkette, Kandarenkette *f*.
(b) (*fig*) Behinderung *f*; (*deliberate also*) Beschränkung *f* ♦ **to put a ~ on sb/sth** jdn im Zaum *or* in Schranken halten/etw einschränken; **this acted as a ~ on his musical development** das (be)hinderte seine musikalische Entwicklung.
(c) (*esp US: curbstone*) *see* **kerb**.
[2] *vt* (a) *horse* zügeln. (b) (*fig*) zügeln; *immigration, investment etc* in Schranken halten, bremsen (*inf*).

curb: ~ bit *n* Kandare *f*; **~ rein** *n* Kandarenzügel *m*; **~ roof** *n* (*Archit*) Mansardendach *nt*; **~ service** *n* (*US*) Bedienung *f* am Fahrzeug; **~stone** *n* (*esp US*) *see* **kerbstone**.

curd [kɜ:d] [1] *n* (*often pl*) Quark *m* ♦ **~ cheese** Weißkäse *m*.
[2] *vt* gerinnen lassen.
[3] *vi* gerinnen.

curdle ['kɜ:dl] [1] *vt* (*lit, fig*) gerinnen lassen ♦ **to ~ sb's blood** jdm das Blut in den Adern gerinnen lassen.
[2] *vi* gerinnen ♦ **his blood ~d** das Blut gerann ihm in den Adern.

cure [kjʊəʳ] [1] *vt* (a) (*Med*) *illness, person* heilen, kurieren (*inf*) ♦ **to be/get ~d (of sth)** (von etw) geheilt *or* kuriert (*inf*) sein/werden; **he used to be an alcoholic but he's been ~d** er war früher Alkoholiker, aber jetzt ist er geheilt *or* kuriert (*inf*).
(b) (*fig*) *inflation, ill etc* abhelfen (*+dat*) ♦ **to ~ sb of sth/doing sth** jdm etw austreiben, jdn von etw kurieren; **I'll ~ him!** dem werde ich das schon austreiben!
(c) *food* haltbar machen; (*salt*) pökeln; (*smoke*) räuchern; (*dry*) trocknen; *skins, tobacco* trocknen.
[2] *vi* (a) (*be healed*) heilen.
(b) (*food, bacon, fish*) *see vt* (c) **it is left to ~** es wird zum Pökeln eingelegt/zum Räuchern aufgehängt/zum Trocknen aufgehängt *or* ausgebreitet.
[3] *n* (a) (*Med*) (*remedy*) (Heil)mittel *nt* (*for* gegen); (*treatment*) Heilverfahren *nt* (*for sb* für jdn, *for sth* gegen etw); (*recovery*) Heilung *f*; (*health ~*) Kur *f*; (*fig: remedy*) Mittel *nt* (*for* gegen) ♦ **to take** *or* **follow a ~** zur *or* in Kur gehen, eine Kur machen, sich einer Kur unterziehen (*geh*); **beyond** *or* **past ~** (*patient*) unheilbar krank; (*illness*) unheilbar; (*fig: state of affairs, laziness etc*) hoffnungslos; **there's no ~ for that** (*lit*) das ist unheilbar; (*fig*) dagegen kann man nichts machen.
(b) (*Eccl: spiritual care*) **the ~ of souls** die Seelsorge; **to have the ~ of souls** (der) Seelsorger sein.

cure-all ['kjʊərɔ:l] *n* (*lit, fig*) Allheilmittel *nt*.

curettage ['kjʊərətɪdʒ] *n* (*Med*) Ausschabung, Kürettage *f*.

curet(te) [kjʊə'ret] *n* (*Med*) Kürette *f*.

curfew ['kɜ:fju:] *n* Ausgangssperre *f*, Ausgehverbot *nt*; (*old: evening bell*) Abendglocke *f* ♦ **to impose a/lift the ~** das Ausgehverbot verhängen/aufheben; **is the ~ still on?** ist noch Ausgangssperre?

curie ['kjʊərɪ] *n* (*Phys*) Curie *nt*.

curio ['kjʊərɪəʊ] *n* Kuriosität *f*.

curiosity [ˌkjʊərɪ'ɒsɪtɪ] *n* (a) *no pl* (*inquisitiveness*) Neugier *f*; (*for knowledge also*) Wißbegier(de) *f* ♦ **out of** *or* **from ~** aus Neugier; **~ killed the cat** (*Prov*) sei nicht so neugierig. (b) (*object, person*) Kuriosität *f* ♦ **~ shop** Kuriositätenladen *m*.

curious ['kjʊərɪəs] *adj* (a) (*inquisitive*) neugierig ♦ **I'm ~ to know what he'll do/how he did it** ich bin mal gespannt, was er macht/ich bin neugierig zu erfahren, wie er das gemacht hat; **I'd be ~ to know how you got on** ich wüßte (ganz) gern, wie du zurechtgekommen bist; **the neighbours were ~ to know** ... die Nachbarn wollten zu gerne wissen ...
(b) (*odd*) sonderbar, seltsam, eigenartig ♦ **how ~!** wie seltsam!; **it's ~ the way he already knew that** sonderbar *etc*, daß er das schon gewußt hat.

curiously ['kjʊərɪəslɪ] *adv* (a) (*inquisitively*) neugierig.
(b) (*oddly*) *behave, speak etc* seltsam, eigenartig, merkwürdig, sonderbar; *disappeared* auf sonderbare *or* seltsame Weise; *unconcerned* seltsam, merkwürdig ♦ **they are ~ similar** sie ähneln sich merkwürdig *or* auf seltsame Weise; **it was ~ quiet** es war merkwürdig ruhig; **any sense of humour is ~**

absent seltsamerweise *or* eigenartigerweise fehlt jeglicher Sinn für Humor; **~ enough** merkwürdigerweise.

curiousness ['kjʊərɪəsnɪs] *n* **(a)** *see* **curiosity (a)**. **(b)** *(oddness)* Merkwürdigkeit, Sonderbarkeit *f*.

curl [kɜːl] **1** *n (of hair)* Locke *f* ♦ **in ~(s)** in Locken, gelockt; *(tight)* gekräuselt, kraus; **a ~ of smoke/of wood** ein Rauchkringel *m*/(geringelter) Hobelspan; **with a ~ of his lips** mit gekräuselten Lippen; **its tail was just a little ~** es hatte nur ein kleines Kringelschwänzchen.
2 *vt hair* locken; *(with curlers)* in Locken legen; *(in tight curls)* kräuseln; *lips (person)* kräuseln; *(animal)* hochziehen; *edges* umbiegen ♦ **he ~ed the ball into the back of the net** er zirkelte den Ball mit einem Bogenschuß ins Netz.
3 *vi* **(a)** *(hair)* sich locken; *(tightly)* sich kräuseln; *(naturally)* lockig sein; *(paper)* sich wellen; *(wood)* sich verziehen; *(road)* sich schlängeln, sich winden ♦ **his lips ~ed** er kräuselte die Lippen; **it's enough to make your hair ~** *(fig inf)* da stehen einem ja die Haare zu Berge *(inf)*.
(b) *(Sport)* Curling spielen.

♦**curl up** **1** *vi* **(a)** *(animal)* sich zusammenkugeln; *(person also)* sich zusammenkuscheln; *(hedgehog)* sich einigeln; *(paper)* sich wellen; *(metal)* sich rollen; *(leaf)* sich hochbiegen ♦ **his moustache ~s ~ at the ends** sein Schnurrbart ist nach oben gezwirbelt; **to ~ ~ in bed/in an armchair** sich ins Bett/in einen Sessel kuscheln; **to ~ ~ with a good book** es sich *(dat)* mit einem guten Buch gemütlich machen; **he just ~ed ~ and died** er legte sich einfach hin und starb.
(b) the smoke ~ed ~ der Rauch ringelte sich hoch.
(c) *(inf)* **the way he behaves just makes me want to ~ ~** es macht mich krank, wie er sich benimmt *(inf)*; **I just wanted to ~ ~ and die** ich wäre am liebsten im Boden versunken.
2 *vt sep ends of moustache, piece of paper etc* wellen; *metal* rollen; *edges* hochbiegen ♦ **to ~ oneself/itself ~** sich zusammenkugeln/zusammenringeln.

curler ['kɜːləʳ] *n* **(a)** *(hair ~)* Lockenwickel, Lockenwickler *m* ♦ **to put one's ~s in** sich *(dat)* die Haare eindrehen *or* auf (Locken)wickler drehen; **have you never seen her in ~s?** hast du sie noch nie mit Lockenwickeln gesehen?; **I was in ~s, I had my ~s in** ich hatte Lockenwickel *or* Lockenwickler im Haar.
(b) *(Sport)* Curlingspieler(in *f*) *m*.

curlew ['kɜːljuː] *n* Brachvogel *m*.

curlicue ['kɜːlɪkjuː] *n* Schnörkel *m*.

curling ['kɜːlɪŋ] *n (Sport)* Curling, Eisschießen *nt* ♦ **~ stone** Curlingstein, Eisstock *m*.

curling-irons ['kɜːlɪŋ,aɪənz] *or* **curling-tongs** ['kɜːlɪŋ,tɒŋz] *npl* Lockenschere, Brennschere *f*; *(electric)* Lockenstab *m*.

curl paper *n* (Papier)lockenwickel *m*.

curly ['kɜːlɪ] **1** *adj (+er) hair* lockig; *(tighter)* kraus; *tail* Ringel-, geringelt; *lettuce* kraus; *leaf* gewellt; *pattern, writing* verschnörkelt, Schnörkel- ♦ **she was much curlier** ihr Haar war viel lockiger.
2 *n (inf: person)* Krauskopf *m*.

curly: ~-haired *adj* lockig, lockenköpfig; *(tighter)* krausköpfig; **~-head** *n (inf)* Lockenkopf *m*; *(tighter)* Krauskopf *m*; **~-headed** *adj see* **~-haired**.

currant ['kʌrənt] *n* **(a)** *(dried fruit)* Korinthe *f* ♦ **~ bun** Rosinenbrötchen *nt*.
(b) *(Bot)* Johannisbeere *f* ♦ **~ bush** Johannisbeerstrauch *m*.

currency ['kʌrənsɪ] *n* **(a)** *(Fin)* Währung *f* ♦ **foreign ~** Devisen *pl*.
(b) Verbreitung *f*; *(of word, expression)* Gebräuchlichkeit *f* ♦ **to be in ~** in Umlauf sein, verbreitet sein; **to gain ~** sich verbreiten, um sich greifen; **to give ~ to a rumour/theory** ein Gerücht/eine Theorie verbreiten *or* in Umlauf setzen.

currency: ~ appreciation *n* Geldaufwertung *f*; **~ depreciation** *n* Geldabwertung *f*; **~ market** *n* Devisenmarkt *m*; **~ snake** *n* Währungsschlange *f*; **~ speculator** *n* Währungsspekulant(in *f*) *m*.

current ['kʌrənt] **1** *adj (present)* augenblicklich, gegenwärtig; *policy, price* aktuell, gegenwärtig, Tages-; *research, month, week* laufend; *edition* letzte(r, s); *(prevalent) opinion* verbreitet; *spelling, word* gebräuchlich ♦ **to be no longer ~** nicht mehr aktuell sein; *(coins)* nicht mehr in Umlauf sein; **a ~ rumour** ein Gerücht, das zur Zeit in Umlauf ist; **~ affairs** Tagespolitik *f*, aktuelle Fragen *pl*, Aktuelle(s) *nt*; **in ~ use** allgemein gebräuchlich.
2 *n* **(a)** *(of water)* Strömung *f*, Strom *m*; *(of air)* Luftströmung *f*, Luftstrom *m* ♦ **with/against the ~** mit dem/gegen den Strom; **air/ocean ~** Luft-/Meeresströmung *f or* -strom *m*; **upward/downward ~** Aufwind *m*/Abwind *m*.
(b) *(Elec)* Strom *m*.
(c) *(fig: of events, opinions etc)* Tendenz *f*, Trend *m* ♦ **to go against/with the ~ of popular opinion** gegen den Strom *or* die Strömung der öffentlichen Meinung anschwimmen/mit dem Strom *or* der Strömung der öffentlichen Meinung schwimmen; **if you try to go against the ~ of events** wenn Sie versuchen, gegen den Strom der Ereignisse anzuschwimmen; **the ~ of public feeling is now in favour of/against ...** die öffentliche Meinung tendiert zur Befürwortung/Ablehnung von ...; **a politician who ignores the ~ of popular opinion** ein Politiker, der die Tendenz(en) der öffentlichen Meinung *or* den Trend (in) der öffentlichen Meinung unbeachtet läßt.

current: ~ account *n* Girokonto *nt*; **~ assets** *npl* Umlaufvermögen *nt*; **~ collector** *n (Rail etc)* Stromabnehmer *m*; **~ expenses** *npl* laufende Ausgaben *pl*; **~ liabilities** *npl* kurzfristige Verbindlichkeiten *pl*.

currently ['kʌrəntlɪ] *adv* momentan, zur Zeit, gegenwärtig ♦ **it is ~ thought that ...** die aktuelle Meinung ist, daß ...

curricle ['kʌrɪkl] *n* offener Zweispänner.

curricula [kə'rɪkjʊlə] *pl of* **curriculum**.

curricular [kə'rɪkjʊləʳ] *adj activities* lehrplanmäßig.

curriculum [kə'rɪkjʊləm] *n, pl* **curricula** Lehrplan *m* ♦ **to be on the ~** auf dem Lehrplan stehen; **~ vitae** Lebenslauf *m*.

currish ['kɜːrɪʃ] *adj (dated) behaviour* hundsföttisch *(dated)*.

curry[1] ['kʌrɪ] *(Cook)* **1** *n* Curry *m or nt* ♦ **~-powder** Currypulver *nt*; **~ sauce** Currysauce *f*.
2 *vt* mit Curry zubereiten.

curry[2] *vt horse* striegeln; *leather* zurichten ♦ **to ~ favour (with sb)** sich (bei jdm) einschmeicheln *or* lieb Kind machen.

curry-comb ['kʌrɪkəʊm] **1** *n* Striegel *m*.
2 *vt* striegeln.

curse [kɜːs] **1** *n* **(a)** *(malediction)* Fluch *m* ♦ **to be under a ~** unter einem Fluch stehen; **to put sb under a ~** jdn mit einem Fluch belegen, einen Fluch über jdn aussprechen; **to call down ~s on sb** jdn verfluchen; **a ~** *or* **a thousand ~s on him/this pen!** *(old, hum)* den/den Füller soll doch der Kuckuck holen! *(inf)*, dieser vermaledeite Mensch/Füller *(old)*; **~s!** *(inf)* verflucht! *(inf)*.
(b) *(swear-word)* Fluch *m*.
(c) *(fig: affliction)* Fluch *m*; *(inf: nuisance)* Plage *f (inf)* ♦ **it's the ~ of my life** das ist der Fluch meines Lebens; **the ~ of drunkenness** der Fluch des Alkohols; **the ~** *(inf: menstruation)* die Tage *pl (inf)*; **she has the ~** sie hat ihre Tage *(inf)*.
2 *vt* **(a)** *(to put a curse on)* verfluchen ♦ **~ you/it!** *(inf)* verflucht! *(inf)*, verdammt! *(sl)*, Mist! *(inf)*; **I could ~ you for forgetting it** ich könnte dich verwünschen, daß du das vergessen hast; **where is he now, ~ the man** *or* **~ him!** *(inf)* wo steckt er jetzt, der verfluchte Kerl *(inf)*; **~ these trains!** *(inf)* diese verfluchten Züge! *(inf)*.
(b) *(swear at or about)* fluchen über *(+acc)*.
(c) *(fig: to afflict)* **to be ~d with sb/sth** mit jdm/etw geschlagen *or* gestraft sein.
3 *vi* fluchen ♦ **he started cursing and swearing** er fing an, wüst zu schimpfen und zu fluchen.

cursed ['kɜːsɪd] *adj (inf)* verflucht *(inf)*.

cursive ['kɜːsɪv] **1** *adj* kursiv, Kursiv-.
2 *n* Kursivschrift *f*.

cursively ['kɜːsɪvlɪ] *adv* kursiv.

cursor ['kɜːsəʳ] *n (Comput)* Cursor *m* ♦ **~ control** Cursorsteuerung *f*; **~ movements** Cursorbewegungen *pl*.

cursorily ['kɜːsərɪlɪ] *adv see adj* flüchtig; oberflächlich.

cursoriness ['kɜːsərɪnɪs] *n see adj* Flüchtigkeit *f*; Oberflächlichkeit *f*.

cursory ['kɜːsərɪ] *adj glance* flüchtig; *inspection, investigation also* oberflächlich.

curst [kɜːst] *adj see* **cursed**.

curt [kɜːt] *adj (+er) person* kurz angebunden; *verbal reply also* knapp; *letter, nod, refusal* kurz, knapp ♦ **to be ~ with sb** zu jdm kurz angebunden sein.

curtail [kɜː'teɪl] *vt* kürzen.

curtailment [kɜː'teɪlmənt] *n* Kürzung *f*.

curtain ['kɜːtn] **1** *n* **(a)** Vorhang *m*; *(on windows also)* Gardine *f* ♦ **to draw** *or* **pull the ~s** *(open)* den Vorhang/die Vorhänge aufziehen; *(close)* den Vorhang/die Vorhänge zuziehen.
(b) *(Theat)* Vorhang *m* ♦ **the ~ rises/falls** der Vorhang hebt sich/fällt; **the ~ rises on a scene of domestic harmony** der Vorhang hebt sich und gibt den Blick auf eine Szene häuslichen Glücks frei; **to take a ~** *(inf)* vor den Vorhang treten.
(c) *(fig) (of mystery)* Schleier *m* ♦ **a ~ of smoke/flames/rain** eine Rauch-/Flammen-/Regenwand; **if you get caught it'll be ~s for you** *(inf)* wenn sie dich erwischen, ist für dich der Ofen aus *(inf) or* bist du weg vom Fenster *(inf)*.
2 *vt* mit Vorhängen/einem Vorhang ausstatten ♦ **a ~ed bed** ein Himmelbett *nt*.

♦**curtain off** *vt sep* durch einen Vorhang/Vorhänge abtrennen.

curtain: ~-call *n (Theat)* Vorhang *m*; **to get/take a ~-call** einen Vorhang bekommen/vor den Vorhang treten; **~ hook** *n* Gardinengleithaken *m*; **~ pole** *n* Vorhangstange *f*; **~ rail** *n* Vorhangschiene *f*; **~-raiser** *n (Theat)* kurzes Vorspiel; **~ ring** *n* Gardinenring *m*; **~ rod** *n* Gardinenstange *f*; **~ runner** *n* Vorhangschiene *f*; *(for ~ rings)* Gardinenstange *f*.

curtly ['kɜːtlɪ] *adv reply, nod* kurz, knapp; *refuse* kurzerhand.

curtness ['kɜːtnɪs] *n see adj* Kurzangebundenheit *f*; Kürze, Knappheit *f*.

curts(e)y ['kɜːtsɪ] **1** *n* Knicks *m*; *(to royalty)* Hofknicks *m* ♦ **to drop a ~** einen Knicks/Hofknicks machen.
2 *vi* knicksen *(to* vor *+dat)*.

curvaceous [kɜː'veɪʃəs] *adj* üppig; *figure also* kurvenreich.

curvaceously [kɜː'veɪʃəslɪ] *adv* üppig, prall ♦ **she stretched ~** sie räkelte ihre üppigen Formen.

curvature ['kɜːvətʃəʳ] *n* Krümmung *f*; *(misshapen)* Verkrümmung *f* ♦ **~ of the spine** *(normal)* Rückgratkrümmung *f*; *(abnormal)* Rückgratverkrümmung *f*; **the ~ of space** die Raumkrümmung.

curve [kɜːv] **1** *n* Kurve *f*; *(of body, vase etc)* Rundung, Wölbung *f*; *(of river)* Biegung *f*; *(of archway)* Bogen *m* ♦ **there's a ~ in the road** die Straße macht einen Bogen; **the price ~** die Preiskurve; **her ~s** *(inf)* ihre Kurven *or* Rundungen *pl (inf)*.
2 *vt* biegen; *(build with a ~) arch, roof, side of ship* wölben ♦ **gravity ~s the path of light** die Gravitation krümmt den Lichtweg; **he ~d the ball around the wall** er zirkelte den Ball um die Mauer herum.
3 *vi* **(a)** *(line, road)* einen Bogen machen; *(river)* eine Biegung machen ♦ **her lips ~d into a smile** ihre Lippen verzogen sich zu einem Lächeln; **the road/river ~d in and out among the hills** die Straße/der Fluß wand *or* schlängelte

sich durch die Berge; **the road ~s around the city** die Straße macht einen Bogen um die Stadt; **to make a ball ~ (through the air)** einen Ball anschneiden, einem Ball einen Drall geben.
(b) *(be curved)* *(space, horizon)* gekrümmt sein; *(side of ship, surface, arch)* sich wölben; *(hips, breasts)* sich runden; *(metal strip etc)* sich biegen; *(arch)* sich wölben.

curved [kɜːvd] *adj line* gebogen; *table-legs etc also* geschwungen; *horizon* gekrümmt; *surface, arch, sides of ship* gewölbt; *hips* rund ◆ **space is ~** der Raum ist gekrümmt.

curvet [kɜː'vet] 1 *n* Kruppade *f*.
2 *vi* eine Kruppade springen.

curvilinear ['kɜːvɪ'lɪnɪəʳ] *adj (full of curves) tracery etc* mit vielen Rundungen *or* Kurven; *(curved) motion, course* gewunden; *(Geometry) figure* krummlinig begrenzt.

curvy ['kɜːvɪ] *adj (+er) (inf) road, figure* kurvenreich.

cushion ['kʊʃən] 1 *n* Kissen *nt*; *(pad, fig: buffer)* Polster *nt*; *(Billiards)* Bande *f* ◆ **a stroke off the ~** ein Stoß gegen die Bande; **a ~ of air/moss** ein Luftkissen *nt*/Moospolster *nt*; **~ cover** Kissenüberzug, Kissenbezug *m*.
2 *vt* **(a)** *(absorb, soften) fall, blow* auffangen, dämpfen; *(fig) disappointment* dämpfen.
(b) *(fig: protect)* **to ~ sb against sth** jdn gegen etw abschirmen, jdn vor etw *(dat)* behüten; **he ~ed the vase against his chest** er barg die Vase an seiner Brust.
(c) *(Billiards) ball* gegen die Bande spielen.

cushioning ['kʊʃənɪŋ] *adj* **to have a ~ effect** (stoß)dämpfend wirken; *(fig)* mildernd wirken.

cushy ['kʊʃɪ] *adj (+er) (inf)* bequem ◆ **to have a ~ time of it/be onto a ~ number** eine ruhige Kugel schieben *(inf)*; **a ~ job** ein gemütlicher *or* ruhiger Job; **that job is a ~ number** in dem Job reißt man sich *(dat)* kein Bein aus *(inf)*.

cusp [kʌsp] *n (of tooth)* Höcker *m*; *(of moon)* Spitze *f* (der Mondsichel); *(Astrol)* Eintritt *m* in ein neues Zeichen.

cuspid ['kʌspɪd] *n* Eckzahn *m*.

cuspidor ['kʌspɪdɔːʳ] *n (US)* Spucknapf *m*.

cuss [kʌs] *(inf)* 1 *n* **(a)** *(person)* Kauz *m (inf)*. **(b) he's not worth a (tinker's) ~** der ist keinen roten Heller wert *(inf)*; **he doesn't care a ~ (about it)** das ist ihm völlig Wurst *(inf) or* schnuppe *(inf)*. **(c)** *(oath)* Fluch *m*.
2 *vi* fluchen ◆ **to ~ and swear** schimpfen und fluchen.

cussed ['kʌsɪd] *adj (inf)* stur.

cussedness ['kʌsɪdnɪs] *n (inf)* Sturheit *f* ◆ **out of sheer ~** aus lauter *or* reiner Sturheit.

custard ['kʌstəd] *n (pouring ~)* ≃ Vanillesoße *f*; *(set)* ≃ Vanillepudding *m*.

custard: ~ apple *n (Bot)* Zimt- *or* Rahmapfel *m*; **~ cream (biscuit)** *n* Doppelkeks *m* (mit Vanillecremefüllung); **~ pie** *n (in slapstick)* Sahnetorte *f*; **~ powder** *n* ≃ Vanillepuddingpulver, Vanillesoßenpulver *nt*; **~-tart** *n* ≃ Puddingtörtchen *nt*.

custodial [kʌs'təʊdɪəl] *adj (form)* **(a)** *duties etc* als Aufseher. **(b) ~ sentence** Gefängnisstrafe *f*.

custodian [kʌs'təʊdɪən] *n (of building, park, museum)* Aufseher, Wächter *m*; *(of treasure)* Hüter *m*; *(of tradition, cultural heritage, world peace, of public morality etc)* Hüter, Gralshüter *(pej) m*.

custody ['kʌstədɪ] *n* **(a)** *(keeping, guardianship)* Obhut *f*; *(of person also)* Aufsicht *f (of* über *+acc)*; *(of object also)* Aufbewahrung *f (of gen, with* bei); *(Jur: of children)* Vormundschaft *f (of* für, über *+acc)* ◆ **to put** *or* **place sth in sb's ~** etw jdm zur Aufbewahrung anvertrauen, etw in jds Obhut *(acc) or* Gewahrsam *(acc)* geben; **the child/money is in safe ~** das Kind/Geld ist gut aufgehoben; **he is in the ~ of his aunt** seine Tante hat die Vormundschaft für *or* über ihn; **the mother was awarded ~ of the children after the divorce** die Kinder wurden (bei der Scheidung) der Mutter zugesprochen; **the country's future is placed in the ~ of its teachers** die Zukunft des Landes liegt in den Händen der Lehrer; **whilst these goods are in the ~ of the police** während sich die Gegenstände in Polizeiaufbewahrung befinden.
(b) *(police detention)* (polizeilicher) Gewahrsam, Haft *f* ◆ **to take sb into ~** jdn verhaften; **he will be kept in ~ until ...** er wird inhaftiert bleiben, bis ...

custom ['kʌstəm] 1 *n* **(a)** *(established behaviour, convention)* Sitte *f*, Brauch *m* ◆ **~ demands ...** es ist Sitte *or* Brauch ...; **as ~ has it** wie es Sitte *or* (der) Brauch ist; **our ~s** unsere Bräuche *pl*, unsere Sitten und Gebräuche.*pl*.
(b) *(habit)* (An)gewohnheit *f* ◆ **it was his ~ to rest each afternoon** er pflegte am Nachmittag zu ruhen *(geh)*; **as was his ~** wie er es gewohnt war, wie er es zu tun pflegte *(geh)*.
(c) *no pl (Comm: patronage)* Kundschaft *f* ◆ **to get sb's ~** jdn als Kunden gewinnen; **to take one's ~ elsewhere** (als Kunde) anderswo hingehen, woanders Kunde werden; **we get a lot of ~ from tourists** wir machen viel Geschäft mit Touristen.
(d) ~s *pl (duty, organization)* Zoll *m*; **(the) C~s** der Zoll; **the C~s and Excise Department** die Britische Zollbehörde; **to go through ~s** durch den Zoll gehen; **to get sth through the ~s** etw durch den Zoll bekommen.
(e) *(Jur)* Gewohnheitsrecht *nt* ◆ **that is ~ and practice** das ist allgemein üblich.
2 *adj (US) tailor* Maß-; *suit, shoes also* maßgefertigt; *carpenter* auf Bestellung arbeitend; *car (also Brit)* spezialgefertigt, Spezial-.

customarily ['kʌstəmərəlɪ] *adv* normaler- *or* üblicherweise.

customary ['kʌstəmərɪ] *adj (conventional)* üblich; *(habitual)* gewohnt ◆ **it's ~ to apologize/to wear a tie** man entschuldigt sich normalerweise *or* gewöhnlich/man trägt normalerweise *or* gewöhnlich eine Krawatte; **~ laws** Gewohnheitsrecht *nt*.

custom-built ['kʌstəmbɪlt] *adj* spezialangefertigt.

customer ['kʌstəməʳ] *n* **(a)** *(Comm: patron)* Kunde *m*, Kundin *f* ◆ **our ~s** unsere Kundschaft; **~ base** Kundenstamm *m*; **~ service** Kundendienst *m*; **~ service department** Kundendienstabteilung *f*. **(b)** *(inf: person)* Kunde *m (inf)*.

customize ['kʌstəmaɪz] *vt car etc* individuell aufmachen.

custom-made ['kʌstəmmeɪd] *adj clothes, shoes* maßgefertigt, nach Maß; *furniture, car* spezialangefertigt.

customs: ~ clearance *n* Zollabfertigung *f*; **to get ~ clearance for sth** etw zollamtlich abfertigen lassen; **~ declaration** *n* Zollerklärung *f*; **~ duty** *n* Zoll(abgabe *f*) *m*; **~ house** *n* Zollamt *nt*; **~ inspection** *n* Zollkontrolle *f*; **~ officer** *n* Zollbeamte(r) *m*; **~ union** *n* Zollunion *f*.

cut [kʌt] *(vb: pret, ptp ~)* 1 *n* **(a)** *(result of cutting)* Schnitt *m*; *(wound also)* Schnittwunde *f* ◆ **to make a ~ in sth** in etw *(acc)* einen Einschnitt machen.
(b) *(act of cutting, slash)* Schnitt *m*; *(with sword, whip)* Hieb, Schlag *m* ◆ **his hair could do with a ~** seine Haare könnten mal wieder geschnitten werden; **the ~ and thrust of politics/publishing** das Spannungsfeld der Politik/der Trubel des Verlagswesens; **the ~ and thrust of the debate** die Hitze der Debatte; **a ~ from his sword** ein Schlag mit seinem Schwert.
(c) *(reduction) (in gen) (in prices)* Senkung, Ermäßigung, Herabsetzung *f*; *(in quality)* Verminderung *f*; *(in quantity, length etc)* Verringerung *f*; *(in expenses, salaries)* Kürzung *f*; *(in working hours, holidays)* (Ver)kürzung *f*; *(in programme, text, film)* Streichung *f (in* in *+dat)*; *(in production, output)* Einschränkung *f*; *(in expenditure, budget etc)* Kürzung, Einsparung *f* ◆ **the censor had made so many ~s** die Zensur hatte so viel gestrichen; **he had to take a ~ in (his) salary** er mußte eine Gehaltskürzung hinnehmen.
(d) *(of clothes, hair)* Schnitt *m*; *(of jewel also)* Schliff *m*.
(e) *(of meat)* Stück *nt* ◆ **~s of meat are different here** das Fleisch wird hier anders geschnitten.
(f) *(inf: share)* Anteil *m*, Teil *m or nt* ◆ **to get one's ~** sein(en) Teil abbekommen.
(g) *(gibe)* Spitze *f*, spitze Bemerkung; *(action)* Beleidigung *f* ◆ **the unkindest ~ of all** *(prov)* der schlimmste Schlag.
(h) *(short route)* Abkürzung *f*; *(connecting alley-way etc)* Verbindungsweg *m*.
(i) *(Sport)* **to give a ~ to the ball** den Ball anschneiden.
(j) *(Elec)* Unterbrechung *f (in gen)*; *(planned)* Sperre *f* ◆ **power/electricity ~** Stromausfall *m*; *(planned)* Stromsperre *f*.
(k) *(Cards)* Abheben *nt* ◆ **it's your ~** du hebst ab.
(l) *(also* **wood~***)* Holzschnitt *m*.
(m) he's a ~ above the rest of them er ist den anderen um einiges überlegen.
2 *adj* **(a)** *usu attr flowers, tobacco* Schnitt-; *bread* (auf)geschnitten; *grass* gemäht; *prices* ermäßigt, herabgesetzt, Billig- ◆ **finely ~ features** feingeschnittene Züge *pl*; **a well-~ dress** ein gutgeschnittenes Kleid; **~-and-dried** *(fig) (fixed beforehand)* abgesprochen, (eine) abgemachte Sache; *(fixed and unchangeable)* festgelegt; **~-and-dried opinions** festgefahrene Meinungen *pl*; **as far as he's concerned the whole issue is now ~-and-dried** für ihn ist die ganze Angelegenheit erledigt; **it's not all that ~-and-dried** so eindeutig ist das nicht.
(b) *pred (inf: drunken)* voll *(inf)* ◆ **to be half ~** einen in der Krone haben *(inf)*.
3 *vt* **(a)** *(with knife, scissors)* schneiden; *grass* mähen; *cake* anschneiden; *rope* durchschneiden; *(Naut)* kappen; *(~ out) fabric, suit* zuschneiden; *(~ off)* abschneiden; *(with sword, axe)* abschlagen, abhacken ◆ **to ~ one's finger/lip/leg** sich *(dat)* am Finger/an der Lippe/am Bein schneiden; *(with knife, razor etc also)* sich *(dat)* in den Finger/in die Lippe/ins Bein schneiden; **to ~ one's nails** sich *(dat)* die Nägel schneiden; **to ~ sth in half/three** etw halbieren/dritteln, etw in zwei/drei Teile schneiden; **the road ~s the village in two** die Straße schneidet das Dorf in zwei Teile; **to ~ to pieces** zerstückeln; *sb's reputation* zerstören; *(gunfire) enemy line* auseinanderreißen; **to ~ open** aufschneiden; **he ~ his head open** *(on stone etc)* er hat sich *(dat)* den Kopf aufgeschlagen; *(on nail etc)* er hat sich *(dat)* den Kopf aufgerissen; *(on blade etc)* er hat sich *(dat)* den Kopf aufgeschnitten; **to have** *or* **get one's hair ~** sich *(dat)* die Haare schneiden lassen; **to ~ sb free/loose** jdn losschneiden.
(b) *(shape) steps* schlagen, hauen; *channel, trench* graben, ausheben; *figure (in wood)* schnitzen *(in* aus); *(in stone)* hauen *(in* aus); *glass, crystal, diamond* schleifen; *key* anfertigen; *record* pressen; *(singer)* machen ◆ **to ~ one's coat according to one's cloth** *(Prov)* sich nach der Decke strecken; **to ~ a fine/sorry figure** eine gute/schlechte Figur machen *or* abgeben.
(c) *(fig: break off) electricity* abstellen; *(interrupt, accidentally)* unterbrechen; *gas also* (ab)sperren; *ties, links* abbrechen ◆ **to ~ all one's ties** *(fig)* alle Verbindungen abbrechen *(with* zu); **to ~ sb short** *(fig)* jdm das Wort abschneiden; **to ~ sth short** etw vorzeitig abbrechen; **to ~ a long story short** kurz und gut, der langen Rede kurzer Sinn.
(d) *(ignore, avoid) person* schneiden ◆ **to ~ sb dead** jdn wie Luft behandeln.
(e) *(skip, not attend) lecture, class* schwänzen *(inf)*.
(f) *(intersect) (line)* schneiden; *(path, road)* kreuzen.
(g) *(reduce) prices* senken, ermäßigen, herabsetzen; *quality* vermindern; *quantity* reduzieren; *working hours, holidays* (ver)kürzen; *expenses, salary, text, programme, film* kürzen; *production, output* verringern, einschränken.
(h) *(eliminate) part of programme or text or film* streichen; *(censor) film* Teile streichen aus ◆ **the ~ version of a film** die zensierte *or* gekürzte Fassung eines Films.
(i) *(cause pain or suffering to)* **it ~ me to the quick** es schnitt mir ins Herz *or* in die Seele; **the wind ~ his face** der Wind schnitt ihm ins Gesicht.
(j) to ~ a tooth zahnen, einen Zahn bekommen; **to ~ one's teeth on sth**

(*fig*) sich (*dat*) die (ersten) Sporen an *or* mit etw (*dat*) verdienen.
(k) (*Cards*) **to ~ the cards/the pack** abheben.
(l) (*Sport*) *ball* (an)schneiden.
(m) (*edit*) *film* schneiden, cutten.
(n) (*stop*) *engine* abstellen; (*inf*) *noise* aufhören mit.
(o) (*divide*) **if we ~ the profits three ways** wenn wir den Gewinn dritteln *or* unter drei verteilen *or* aufteilen.
(p) **don't ~ it too fine with your revision** laß es mit deiner Wiederholung nicht auf die letzte Minute ankommen; **£10 would be ~ting it rather fine** £ 10 wären etwas knapp (bemessen); **2.20 would be ~ting it a bit fine** 2[20] wäre ein bißchen knapp; **aren't you ~ting it a bit fine?** ist das nicht ein bißchen knapp?; **to ~ one's losses** eine Sache abschließen, ehe der Schaden (noch) größer wird.
[4] *vi* (a) (*knife, scissors*) schneiden; (*lawnmower also*) mähen ◆ **to ~ both ways** (*fig*) auch umgekehrt zutreffen; (*have disadvantages too*) ein zweischneidiges Schwert sein.
(b) (*material*) **paper ~s easily** Papier läßt sich leicht schneiden.
(c) (*intersect: lines, roads*) sich schneiden.
(d) (*Film*) (*change scenes*) überblenden (*to* zu); (*stop filming*) aufhören, abbrechen ◆ **~!** Schnitt!, aus!
(e) (*Cards*) abheben ◆ **to ~ for dealer** (*durch Ziehen einer Karte*) den Geber auslosen.
(f) (*Sport*) den Ball/die Bälle (an)schneiden ◆ **to ~ at a ball** einen Ball anschneiden.
(g) **to ~ and run** abhauen (*inf*), die Beine in die Hand nehmen (*inf*); **to ~ loose** (*Naut*) losmachen; (*fig*) sich losmachen; (*US inf*) loslegen (*inf*).

◆**cut across** *vi +prep obj* (a) hinüber-/herübergehen *etc* (*prep obj* über *+acc*) ◆ **you can ~ ~ here** Sie können hier hinüber/herüber; **if you ~ ~ the fields** wenn Sie über die Felder gehen; **to ~ ~ country** querfeldein gehen/fahren *etc.* (b) (*fig*) *theory etc* widersprechen (*prep obj dat*).

◆**cut along** *vi* (*dated inf*) sich auf die Socken machen (*inf*).

◆**cut away** *vt sep* wegschneiden ◆ **the dress was ~ ~ at the back** das Kleid war hinten *or* im Rücken (tief) ausgeschnitten.

◆**cut back** [1] *vi* (a) (*go back*) zurückgehen/-fahren; (*Film also*) zurückblenden.
(b) (*reduce expenditure etc*) sich einschränken ◆ **to ~ ~ on expenses** *etc*/**production** die Ausgaben *etc* einschränken/die Produktion zurückschrauben; **to ~ ~ on smoking/sweets** weniger rauchen/weniger Süßigkeiten essen.
[2] *vt sep* (a) *plants* zurückschneiden. (b) *production* zurückschrauben; *outgoings* einschränken; *programme* kürzen.

◆**cut down** [1] *vt sep* (a) *tree* fällen; *corn* schneiden; *person* (*with sword*) (mit dem Schwert) niederstrecken.
(b) (*make smaller*) *number, expenses* einschränken; *text* zusammenstreichen (*to* auf *+acc*) ◆ **to ~ sb ~ to size** jdn auf seinen Platz verweisen.
(c) *usu pass* (*kill*) dahinraffen (*geh*) ◆ **a young man ~ ~ in his prime** ein junger Mann, der im Frühling seiner Jahre dahingerafft wurde (*liter*).
[2] *vi* (*reduce intake, expenditure etc*) sich einschränken ◆ **to ~ ~ on sth** etw einschränken.

◆**cut in** [1] *vi* (a) (*interrupt*) sich einschalten ◆ **to ~ ~ on sb/sth** jdn unterbrechen/sich in etw (*acc*) einschalten.
(b) (*cut towards the centre*) (*blade*) einschneiden ◆ **to ~ ~ on sb's market** sich in jds Revier (*acc*) drängen (*inf*); **he ~ ~ to the centre of the pitch** er zog ins Mittelfeld herüber.
(c) (*Aut: swerve in front*) sich direkt vor ein anderes/das andere Auto setzen ◆ **to ~ ~ in front of sb** jdn schneiden; **he ~ ~ so sharply that the car behind had to swerve** er zog so schnell herüber, daß das nachfolgende Auto ausweichen mußte.
[2] *vt sep* **to ~ sb ~ on sth** jdn an etw (*dat*) beteiligen.

◆**cut into** *vi +prep obj* (a) (*make a cut in*) *cake, meat* anschneiden. (b) (*interrupt*) *conversation* fallen in (*+acc*). (c) (*swerve into*) *line of traffic* sich drängeln in (*+acc*); *woods, alley-way* schnell einbiegen in (*+acc*). (d) (*fig: make inroads in*) *savings* ein Loch reißen in (*+acc*); *holidays* verkürzen.

◆**cut off** *vt sep* (a) (*with knife etc*) abschneiden; (*with sword etc*) abschlagen ◆ **to ~ ~ sb's head** jdm den Kopf abschlagen.
(b) *town, supply* abschneiden; *allowance* sperren ◆ **to ~ ~ the enemy's retreat/supplies** dem Feind den Rückzug/die Zufuhr abschneiden; **his deafness ~ him ~ from others** seine Taubheit schnitt ihn von der Umwelt ab; **we're very ~ ~ out here** wir leben hier draußen sehr abgeschieden.
(c) (*disinherit*) enterben ◆ **to ~ sb ~ without a penny** jdn enterben.
(d) (*disconnect*) *gas, telephone etc* abstellen ◆ **operator, I've been ~ ~** wir sind unterbrochen worden.
(e) (*break off*) *discussion, relations* abbrechen.

◆**cut out** [1] *vi* (*engine, radio transmission*) aussetzen.
[2] *vt sep* (a) (*remove by cutting*) ausschneiden; *malignant growth etc* herausschneiden.
(b) (*form by cutting*) *coat, dress* zuschneiden ◆ **they had ~ ~ a path through the jungle** sie hatten (sich *dat*) einen Weg durch den Dschungel geschlagen *or* gebahnt.
(c) (*delete*) (heraus)streichen; (*not bother with*) verzichten auf (*+acc*), sich (*dat*) schenken; *smoking, swearing etc* aufhören mit, sein lassen (*inf*); *rival* ausstechen ◆ **~ it ~!** (*inf*) hör auf damit!, laß das (sein)! (*inf*); **~ ~ the nonsense** laß den Unsinn; **~ ~ the talking!** (*inf*) halt den Mund! (*inf*); **and you can ~ ~ the self-pity for a start!** und mit Selbstmitleid brauchst du gar nicht erst zu kommen *or* anzufangen!
(d) (*fig*) **to be ~ ~ for sth** zu etw geeignet *or* gemacht sein; **to be ~ ~ to be sth** dazu geeignet sein, etw zu sein *or* zu werden; **he's not ~ ~ to be** *or* **for a doctor** er ist nicht zum Arzt geeignet, er hat nicht das Zeug zum Arzt.
(e) **to have one's work ~ ~** alle Hände voll zu tun haben.

◆**cut through** *vt sep* **he couldn't ~ his way ~** es gelang ihm nicht, durchzukommen; **we ~ ~ the housing estate** wir gingen/fuhren durch die Siedlung.

◆**cut up** [1] *vi* **to ~ ~ rough** Krach schlagen (*inf*).
[2] *vt sep* (a) *meat* aufschneiden; *wood* spalten; (*fig*) *enemy, army* vernichten. (b) *pass* (*inf: upset*) **he was very ~ ~ about it** das hat ihn schwer getroffen *or* ziemlich mitgenommen.

cutaneous [kjuːˈteɪnɪəs] *adj* Haut-, kutan (*spec*).

cutaway [ˈkʌtəweɪ] [1] *n* Cut(away) *m*.
[2] *adj* **~ coat** Cut(away) *m*; **~ diagram** Schnittdiagramm *nt*.

cut-back [ˈkʌtbæk] *n* (a) Kürzung *f*. (b) (*Film*) Rückblende *f*.

cute [kjuːt] *adj* (*+er*) (a) (*inf: sweet*) süß, niedlich. (b) (*esp US inf: clever*) *idea, gadget* dufte (*inf*), prima (*inf*); (*shrewd*) *person, move* schlau, gerissen, clever (*inf*) ◆ **that was pretty ~ of him** das hat er ganz schön schlau hingekriegt (*inf*).

cut glass [1] *n* geschliffenes Glas.
[2] *adj* (a) (*lit*) aus geschliffenem Glas. (b) *accent* vornehm.

cuticle [ˈkjuːtɪkl] *n* (*of nail*) Nagelhaut *f*; (*Anat*) Epidermis *f*; (*Bot*) Kutikula *f* ◆ **~ remover** Nagelhautentferner *m*.

cutie [ˈkjuːtɪ] *n* (*esp US inf*) (*attractive*) flotter Käfer (*inf*), dufte Biene (*inf*); (*child*) süßer Fratz (*inf*); (*shrewd*) gewitzter Kerl, Schlitzohr (*pej*) *m*.

cutie-pie [ˈkjuːtɪpaɪ] *n* (*esp US inf*) süßer Fratz (*inf*).

cutlass [ˈkʌtləs] *n* Entermesser *nt*.

cutler [ˈkʌtlə^r] *n* Messerschmied *m*.

cutlery [ˈkʌtlərɪ] *n, no pl* (*esp Brit*) Besteck *nt*.

cutlet [ˈkʌtlɪt] *n* (*boneless chop*) Schnitzel *nt*; (*fish fillet*) (Fisch)schnitzel *nt*; (*of chopped meat*) (paniertes) Hacksteak.

cut: ~ loaf *n* aufgeschnittenes Brot; **~-off** *n* (a) (*Tech: device*) Ausschaltmechanismus *m*; (b) (*also* **~-off point**) Trennlinie *f*; **~-out** [1] *n* (a) (*model*) Ausschneidemodell *nt*; (*figure, doll*) Ausschneidepuppe *f*; **~-out book** Ausschneidebogen *m*; (b) (*of engine*) Aussetzen *nt*; **it has an automatic ~-out** es setzt automatisch aus; (c) (*Elec*) Sperre *f*; [2] *adj* (a) *model etc* Ausschneide-; (b) (*Elec*) Abschalt-, Ausschalt-; **~-price** *adj* zu Schleuderpreisen; *offer* Billig-; **~-rate** *adj* zu verbilligtem Tarif; **~-sheet feed** *n* Einzelblatteinzug *m*.

cutter [ˈkʌtə^r] *n* (a) (*tool*) Messer *nt* ◆ **a pair of (wire-)~s** eine Drahtschere; (*Elec*) ein Seitenschneider *m*. (b) (*of clothes*) Zuschneider(in *f*) *m*; (*of jewel*) Schleifer(in *f*) *m*; (*of glass*) Glasschneider *m*; (*Film*) Cutter(in *f*) *m*. (c) (*boat*) Kutter *m*; (*US: coastguard's boat*) Boot *nt* der Küstenwache. (d) (*US: sleigh*) leichter Pferdeschlitten.

cut-throat [ˈkʌtθrəʊt] [1] *n* (*murderous type*) Strolch, Verbrechertyp (*inf*) *m*.
[2] *adj* (a) *competition, business* unbarmherzig, mörderisch. (b) **~ razor** (offenes) Rasiermesser.

cutting [ˈkʌtɪŋ] [1] *n* (a) Schneiden *nt*; (*of grass*) Mähen *nt*; (*of cake*) Anschneiden *nt*; (*of rope*) Durchschneiden, Kappen *nt*; (*of garment*) Zuschneiden *nt*, Zuschnitt *m*; (*~ off*) Abschneiden *nt*; (*with sword*) Abschlagen *nt*; (*of electricity*) Sperrung *f*; (*interruption, accidental*) Unterbrechung *f*; (*of steps*) Schlagen *nt*; (*of channel, trench*) Graben *nt*; (*of figure*) (*in wood*) Schnitzen *nt* (*in* aus); (*in stone*) Hauen *nt* (*in* aus); (*of glass, crystal, jewel*) Schliff *m*; (*of key*) Anfertigung *f*; (*of record*) Pressen *nt*, Herstellung *f*; (*snubbing: of person*) Schneiden *nt*; (*of lecture, class*) Schwänzen *nt* (*inf*); (*of prices*) Senkung, Herabsetzung *f*; (*of quality*) Verminderung *f*; (*of quantity*) Reduzierung *f*; (*of working hours*) Verkürzung *f*; (*of expenses, salary*) Kürzung *f*; (*Film*) Schnitt *m*; (*of production*) Drosselung *f*; (*of part of text*) Streichung *f*; (*of ties*) Lösen *nt*, Abbruch *m* ◆ **~ room** (*Film*) Schneideraum *m*.
(b) (*Brit: road ~, railway ~*) Durchstich *m*.
(c) (*Brit: clipping*) (*from newspaper*) Ausschnitt *m*; (*of cloth*) Schnipsel *m*, Stückchen (Stoff) *nt*.
(d) (*Hort*) Ableger *m* ◆ **to take a ~** einen Ableger nehmen.
[2] *adj* (a) *blade, edge* scharf. (b) (*fig*) *wind, cold* schneidend; *remark also, tongue* scharf, spitz ◆ **to be ~ to sb** jdm gegenüber spitze Bemerkungen machen.

cuttle-bone [ˈkʌtlbəʊn] *n* Schulp *m*.

cuttlefish [ˈkʌtlfɪʃ] *n* Tintenfisch *m*, Sepie *f*, Kuttelfisch *m*.

CV *abbr of* **curriculum vitae**.

cwm [kuːm] *n* Kar *nt*.

cwo *abbr of* **cash with order**.

cwt *abbr of* **hundredweight**.

cyanide [ˈsaɪənaɪd] *n* Zyanid, Blausäuresalz *nt* ◆ **~ poisoning** Blausäurevergiftung *f*.

cybernetics [ˌsaɪbəˈnetɪks] *n sing* Kybernetik *f*.

cyberpunk [ˈsaɪbəpʌŋk] *n* (*Liter*) Cyberpunk *m*.

cyberspace [ˈsaɪbəspeɪs] *n* Cyberspace *m*.

cyclamen [ˈsɪkləmən] *n* Alpenveilchen, Zyklamen (*spec*) *nt*.

cycle [ˈsaɪkl] [1] *n* (a) Zyklus, Kreislauf *m*; (*of events*) Gang *m*; (*of poems, songs*) Zyklus *m*; (*Elec*) Periode *f* ◆ **life ~** Lebenszyklus *or* -kreislauf *m*; **menstrual ~** Monatszyklus, Menstruationszyklus *m*; **the moon's ~** der Mondwechsel.
(b) (*bicycle*) (Fahr)rad *nt*; (*sl: motorbike*) Maschine *f* (*sl*).
[2] *vi* mit dem (Fahr)rad fahren ◆ **can you ~?** kannst du radfahren?

cycle: ~ clip *n* Fahrradklammer *f*; **~ path** *n* (Fahr)radweg *m*.

cycler [ˈsaɪklə^r] *n* (*US*) *see* **cyclist**.

cycle: ~ race *n* Radrennen *nt;* **~ rack** *n* Fahrradständer *m;* **~ shed** *n* Fahrradstand *m;* **~-track** *n* (*path*) (Fahr)radweg *m;* (*for racing*) Radrennbahn *f.*
cycleway ['saɪklweɪ] *n* Radweg *m.*
cyclic(al) ['saɪklɪk(əl)] *adj* zyklisch; (*Elec*) periodisch.
cycling ['saɪklɪŋ] *n* Radfahren *nt* ◆ **I enjoy ~** ich fahre gern Rad.
cycling: ~ cape *n* Radmantel *m,* Radcape *nt;* **~ holiday** *n* Urlaub *m* mit dem Fahrrad; **~ tour** *n* Radtour *f.*
cyclist ['saɪklɪst] *n* (Fahr)radfahrer(in *f*) *m;* (*motor* ~) Motorradfahrer(in *f*) *m.*
cyclometer [saɪ'klɒmɪtə^{r}] *n* Kilometerzähler *m.*
cyclone ['saɪkləʊn] *n* Zyklon *m* ◆ **~ cellar** (*US*) *tiefer Keller zum Schutz vor Zyklonen.*
cyclonic [saɪ'klɒnɪk] *adj* zyklonartig.
cyclopaedia [ˌsaɪkləʊ'piːdɪə] *n* Enzyklopädie *f.*
Cyclops ['saɪklɒps] *n* Zyklop *m.*
cyclorama [ˌsaɪklə'rɑːmə] *n* Rundhorizont *m.*
cygnet ['sɪgnɪt] *n* Schwanjunge(s) *nt.*
cylinder ['sɪlɪndə^{r}] *n* (*Math, Aut*) Zylinder *m;* (*of revolver, typewriter*) Walze *f* ◆ **a four-~ car** ein Vierzylinder *m,* ein vierzylindriges Auto; **to be firing on all four ~s** (*lit*) auf allen vier Zylindern laufen; (*fig*) in Fahrt sein/kommen.
cylinder: ~ block *n* (*Aut*) Zylinderblock *m;* **~ capacity** *n* (*Aut*) Hubraum *m;* **~ head** *n* (*Aut*) Zylinderkopf *m;* **~ head gasket** *n* Zylinderkopfdichtung *f.*
cylindrical *adj,* **~ly** *adv* [sɪ'lɪndrɪkəl, -ɪ] zylindrisch.
cymbal ['sɪmbəl] *n* Beckenteller *m* ◆ **~s** Becken *nt;* **to play the ~s** das Becken schlagen.
cynic ['sɪnɪk] *n* **(a)** Zyniker(in *f*) *m* ◆ **don't be such a ~** sei nicht so zynisch. **(b) C~** (*Philos*) Kyniker, Zyniker *m.*
cynical ['sɪnɪkəl] *adj* **(a)** zynisch ◆ **he was very ~ about it** er äußerte sich sehr zynisch dazu. **(b) C~** (*Philos*) kynisch, zynisch.
cynically ['sɪnɪklɪ] *adv* zynisch.
cynicism ['sɪnɪsɪzəm] *n* **(a)** *no pl* Zynismus *m.* **(b)** (*cynical remark*) zynische Bemerkung. **(c) C~** (*Philos*) Kynismus, Zynismus *m.*
cynosure ['saɪnəʃʊə^{r}] *n* **to be the ~ of every eye** (*liter*) alle Blicke auf sich ziehen *or* vereinigen.
cypher *see* **cipher.**
cypress ['saɪprɪs] *n* Zypresse *f.*
Cyprian ['sɪprɪən] *n* (*old*) *see* **Cypriot.**
Cypriot ['sɪprɪət] 1 *adj* zypriotisch, zyprisch.
2 *n* Zypriot(in *f*), Zyprer(in *f*) *m.*
Cyprus ['saɪprəs] *n* Zypern *nt.*
Cyrillic ['sɪrɪlɪk] *adj* kyrillisch.
cyst [sɪst] *n* Zyste *f.*
cystitis [sɪs'taɪtɪs] *n* Blasenentzündung, Zystitis (*spec*) *f.*
cytology [saɪ'tɒlədʒɪ] *n* Zytologie, Zellenlehre *f.*
cytoplasm ['saɪtəʊplæzm] *n* Zytoplasma, Zellplasma *nt.*
CZ (*US*) *abbr of* **Canal Zone** Kanalzone *f, Gebiet nt um den Panamakanal.*
czar [zɑː^{r}] *n* Zar *m.*
czarevitch ['zɑːrəvɪtʃ] *n* Zarewitsch *m.*
czarina [zɑː'riːnə] *n* Zarin *f.*
czarism ['zɑːrɪzəm] *n* Zarismus *m.*
czarist ['zɑːrɪst] 1 *adj* zaristisch.
2 *n* Zarist(in *f*) *m.*
Czech [tʃek] 1 *adj* tschechisch.
2 *n* **(a)** Tscheche *m,* Tschechin *f.* **(b)** (*language*) Tschechisch *nt.*
Czechoslovak ['tʃekəʊ'sləʊvæk] 1 *adj* tschechoslowakisch.
2 *n* Tschechoslowake *m,* Tschechoslowakin *f.*
Czechoslovakia ['tʃekəʊslə'vækɪə] *n* die Tschechoslowakei.
Czechoslovakian ['tʃekəʊslə'vækɪən] *adj, n see* **Czechoslovak.**
Czech Republic *n* Tschechische Republik, Tschechien *nt.*

D

D, d [di:] *n* D, d *nt*; (*Sch: as a mark*) ausreichend ◆ **D sharp/flat** Dis, dis *nt*/Des, des *nt*; *see also* **major, minor, natural.**
D (*US Pol*) *abbr of* **Democratic** dem.
d *abbr of* **(a)** (*Brit old*) **pence. (b) died** gest.
'd = had, would.
DA (*US*) *abbr of* **District Attorney.**
D/A *abbr of* **deposit account.**
dab¹ [dæb] 1 *n* **(a)** (*small amount*) Klecks *m*; (*applied with puff, of cream etc*) Tupfer *m*; (*of liquid, perfume, glue etc*) Tropfen *m*; (*of butter*) Klacks *m* ◆ **a ~ of powder/ointment** *etc* etwas *or* ein bißchen Puder/Salbe *etc*; **to give sth a ~ of paint** etw überstreichen. **(b) ~s** *pl* (*sl: fingerprints*) Fingerabdrücke *pl*.
2 *vt* (*with powder etc*) betupfen; (*with towel etc*) tupfen ◆ **to ~ one's eyes** sich (*dat*) die Augen tupfen; **she ~bed ointment/powder over her face/the wound** sie betupfte sich (*dat*) das Gesicht/die Wunde mit Salbe/Puder.
◆**dab at** *vi +prep obj* betupfen.
◆**dab off** *vt sep* abtupfen.
◆**dab on** *vt sep* auftragen (*prep obj* auf *+acc*).
dab² *n* (*fish*) Kliesche, Scharbe *f*.
dab³ *adj* (*inf*) **to be a ~ hand at sth/doing sth** gut in etw (*dat*) sein/sich darauf verstehen, etw zu tun.
dabble ['dæbl] 1 *vt* **to ~ one's hands/feet in the water** mit den Händen/Füßen im Wasser plan(t)schen.
2 *vi* **(a)** plan(t)schen. **(b)** (*fig*) **to ~ in/at sth** sich (nebenbei) mit etw beschäftigen; **are you a serious photographer? — no, I only ~ (in it)** beschäftigen Sie sich ernsthaft mit der Fotografie? — nein, nur so nebenbei; **he ~s in stocks and shares/antiques** er versucht sich an der Börse/in Antiquitäten.
dabbler ['dæbləʳ] *n* Amateur *m*.
dabchick ['dæbtʃɪk] *n* Steißfuß *m*.
dace [deɪs] *n, pl* - Weißfisch *m*.
dacha ['dætʃə] *n* Datscha, Datsche *f*.
dachshund ['dækshʊnd] *n* Dackel, Dachshund (*rare*) *m*.
dacron ® ['dækrɒn] *n* Dacron ® *nt*.
dactyl ['dæktɪl] *n* (*Zool*) Zehe *f*; Finger *m*; (*Liter*) Daktylus *m*.
dactylic [dæk'tɪlɪk] *adj* daktylisch.
dad [dæd] *n* (*inf*) Vater *m*; (*affectionately also*) Vati, Papa *m*.
Dada ['dɑ:dɑ:] *n* (*Art*) Dada *m*.
Dadaism ['dɑ:dɑ:ɪzm] *n* Dadaismus *m*.
daddy ['dædɪ] *n* (*inf*) Papa, Vati *m* (*inf*) ◆ **the ~ of them all** (*inf*) der Größte.
daddy-long-legs [,dædɪ'lɒŋlegz] *n, pl* - (*Brit*) Schnake *f*; (*US*) Weberknecht *m*.
dado ['deɪdəʊ] *n* (*of pedestal*) Basis *f*; (*of wall*) Paneel *nt*.
daemon ['di:mən] *n* (*liter*) *see* **demon.**
daffodil ['dæfədɪl], **daff** [dæf] (*inf*) *n* Osterglocke, Narzisse *f*.
daffy ['dæfɪ] *adj* (*+er*) (*inf*) *see* **daft.**
daft [dɑ:ft] *adj* (*+er*) doof, blöd, bekloppt (*all inf*) ◆ **~ in the head** (*inf*) blöd (*inf*), bekloppt (*inf*); **what a ~ thing to do** so was Doofes *or* Blödes *or* Bekopptes (*all inf*); **he's ~ about her/football** (*inf*) er ist verrückt nach ihr/nach Fußball (*inf*).
daftie ['dɑ:ftɪ], **daft ha'porth** ['dɑ:fteɪpəθ] *n* (*Brit inf*) Dussel *m* (*inf*).
dagger ['dægəʳ] *n* **(a)** Dolch *m* ◆ **to be at ~s drawn with sb** (*fig*) mit jdm auf (dem) Kriegsfuß stehen; **to look ~s at sb** jdn mit Blicken durchbohren. **(b)** (*Typ*) Kreuz *nt*.
dago ['deɪgəʊ] *n* (*pej*) Südländer, Kanake (*pej sl*) *m* (*verächtlich für Spanier, Portugiese oder Südamerikaner*).
daguerreotype [də'gerəʊtaɪp] 1 *n* Daguerreotypie *f*.
2 *vt* nach dem Daguerreotypieverfahren fotografieren.
dahlia ['deɪlɪə] *n* Dahlie *f*.
Dáil Eireann [daɪl'ɛərən] *n Unterhaus nt der Republik Irland.*
daily ['deɪlɪ] 1 *adj* täglich; *wage, newspaper* Tages- ◆ **~ dozen** (*inf*) Morgengymnastik *f*; **~ grind** täglicher Trott; **he is employed on a ~ basis** er ist tageweise angestellt; (*labourer*) er ist als Tagelöhner beschäftigt, er steht im Tagelohn.
2 *adv* täglich.
3 *n* **(a)** (*newspaper*) Tageszeitung *f*.
(b) (*also* **~ help, ~ woman**) Putzfrau *f*.
daintily ['deɪntɪlɪ] *adv* zierlich; *hold, walk, move* anmutig.
daintiness ['deɪntɪnɪs] *n* Zierlichkeit *f*; (*of movement, manners etc*) Anmutigkeit, Geziertheit (*pej*) *f*.
dainty ['deɪntɪ] 1 *adj* (*+er*) **(a)** zierlich; *lace, handkerchief* fein; *movement, music* anmutig ◆ **she has ~ little ways** bei ihr ist alles fein und zierlich. **(b)** *food* appetitlich ◆ **~ morsel** Appetithappen *m*. **(c)** (*refined*) geziert, etepetete (*inf*).
2 *n* Leckerei *f*.
daiquiri ['daɪkərɪ] *n Cocktail m aus Rum, Limonensaft und Zucker.*
dairy ['dɛərɪ] *n* Molkerei *f*; (*on farm*) Milchkammer *f*; (*shop*) Milchgeschäft *nt*.
dairy: ~ butter *n* Markenbutter *f*; **~ cattle** *npl* Milchvieh *nt*; **~ cow** *n* Milchkuh *f*; **~ farm** *n* auf Milchviehhaltung spezialisierter Bauernhof; **~ farming** *n* Milchviehhaltung *f*; **~ herd** *n* Herde *f* Milchkühe; **~ ice cream** *n* Milchspeiseeis *nt*.
dairying ['dɛərɪɪŋ] *n* Milchwirtschaft *f*.
dairy: ~maid *n* Melkerin *f*; (*worker*) Molkereiangestellte *f*; **~man** *n* Melker *m*; Molkereiangestellte(r) *m*; (*milkman*) Milchmann *m*; **~ produce** *n* Milch- *or* Molkereiprodukte *pl*.
dais ['deɪɪs] *n* Podium *nt*.
daisy ['deɪzɪ] *n* Gänseblümchen *nt* ◆ **~ chain** Kette *f* aus Gänseblümchen; **to be as fresh as a ~** taufrisch sein; **to be pushing up the daisies** (*sl*) sich (*dat*) die Radieschen von unten besehen (*sl*).
daisy-wheel ['deɪzɪwi:l] *n* (*Typ, Comput*) Typenrad *m* ◆ **~ (printer)** Typenraddrucker *m*; **~ typewriter** Typenradschreibmaschine *f*.
dale [deɪl] *n* (*N Engl, liter*) Tal *nt*.
dalesman ['deɪlzmən] *n, pl* **-men** [-mən] Bewohner *m* des Gebiets der Dales in Yorkshire.
dalliance ['dælɪəns] *n* (*liter*) Tändelei *f* (*liter*).
dally ['dælɪ] *vi* **(a)** (*waste time*) (herum)trödeln, bummeln ◆ **without ~ing** ohne zu trödeln *or* bummeln. **(b)** (*flirt*) **to ~ with sb/an idea** mit jdm schäkern/mit einem Gedanken liebäugeln.
Dalmatia [dæl'meɪʃə] *n* Dalmatien *nt*.
Dalmatian [dæl'meɪʃən] 1 *adj* dalmatinisch, dalmatisch.
2 *n* **(a)** (*person*) Dalmatiner(in *f*) *m*. **(b)** (*dog*) Dalmatiner *m*.
daltonism ['dɔ:ltənɪzəm] *n* Farbenblindheit *f*, Daltonismus *m* (*dated spec*); Rotgrünblindheit *f*.
dam¹ [dæm] 1 *n* (*lit, fig*) Damm *m*; (*reservoir*) Stausee *m*.
2 *vt* (*also* **~ up**) **(a)** *river, lake* (auf)stauen; *valley* eindämmen. **(b)** (*fig*) *flow of words* eindämmen; *feelings* aufstauen.
dam² *n* (*mother*) Muttertier *nt*.
damage ['dæmɪdʒ] 1 *n* **(a)** Schaden *m* (*to* an *+dat*) ◆ **to do a lot of ~** großen Schaden anrichten; **to do sb/sth a lot of ~** jdm/einer Sache (*dat*) großen Schaden zufügen; **the ~ to his pride/ego/reputation** die Verletzung seines Stolzes/Erschütterung seines Selbstbewußtseins/Schädigung seines Rufs; **it did no ~ to his reputation** das hat seinem Ruf nicht geschadet.
(b) (*Jur*) **~s** Schaden(s)ersatz *m*.
(c) (*inf: cost*) **what's the ~?** was kostet der Spaß? (*inf*).
2 *vt* schaden (*+dat*); *machine, car, furniture, fruit, tree* beschädigen; *health, reputation, relations also* schädigen ◆ **to ~ one's eyesight** sich (*dat*) die Augen verderben; **smoking can ~ your health** Rauchen ist gesundheitsschädlich, Rauchen schadet Ihrer Gesundheit; **to ~ one's chances** sich (*dat*) die Chancen verderben.
damaging ['dæmɪdʒɪŋ] *adj* schädlich; *remarks* abträglich ◆ **to be ~ to sth** sich auf etw (*acc*) schädigend *or* schädlich auswirken, schädlich für etw sein; **that was a ~ blow to his opponent's chin/his pride** der Schlag ans Kinn seines Gegners saß/das hat seinem Stolz einen empfindlichen Schlag versetzt.
damascene ['dæməsi:n] *vt* damaszieren ◆ **~d blades** Damaszenerklingen *pl*.
Damascus [də'mɑ:skəs] *n* Damaskus *nt* ◆ **~ steel** Damaszener Stahl *m*.
damask ['dæməsk] 1 *n* **(a)** Damast *m*. **(b) ~ (steel)** Damaszener Stahl *m*. **(c) ~ rose** Damaszenerrose *f*.
2 *adj* **(a)** Damast-, aus Damast. **(b)** (*liter*) *colour* rosig.
dam-buster ['dæmbʌstəʳ] *n jd, der Staudämme in die Luft sprengt.*
dame [deɪm] *n* **(a) D~** (*Brit*) *Titel der weiblichen Träger des „Order of the British Empire".* **(b)** (*old: lady*) Dame *f* ◆ **D~ Fortune** Frau Fortuna *f*. **(c)** (*Theat: in pantomime*) (komische) Alte. **(d)** (*US inf*) Weib *nt* (*inf*).
damfool ['dæm'fu:l] *adj attr* (*inf*) idiotisch (*inf*).

dammit ['dæmɪt] *interj (inf)* verdammt *(inf)*, Teufel noch mal *(inf)* ◆ **it weighs 2 kilos as near as ~** es wiegt so gut wie 2 Kilo.

damn [dæm] 1 *interj (inf)* verdammt *(inf)*.
2 *n (inf)* **he doesn't care** *or* **give a ~** er schert sich den Teufel *or* einen Dreck (darum) *(inf)*; **I don't give a ~** das ist mir piepegal *(inf) or* scheißegal *(sl)*; **it's not worth a ~** das ist keinen Pfifferling wert.
3 *adj attr (inf)* verdammt ◆ **it's one ~ thing after another** verdammt noch mal, da kommt aber auch eins nach dem andern; **it's a ~ nuisance** das ist ein verdammter Mist *(inf)*, das ist wirklich zu blöd *(inf)*; **I can't/couldn't see a ~ thing** verdammt (noch mal) *(inf)*, ich kann überhaupt nichts sehen/das war vielleicht ein Mist *(inf)*, ich konnte überhaupt nichts sehen.
4 *adv (inf)* verdammt ◆ **I should ~ well hope/think so** das will ich aber auch stark hoffen/ich doch stark annehmen; **a ~ sight better/worse** verdammt viel besser/schlechter *(inf)*; **~-all** nicht die Bohne *(inf)*; **I've done ~-all today** ich hab heute überhaupt nichts gemacht.
5 *vt* **(a)** *(Rel)* verdammen.
(b) *(bring condemnation, ruin on)* das Genick brechen (+*dat*); *(evidence)* überführen.
(c) *(judge and condemn)* verurteilen; *book etc also* verreißen ◆ **to ~ sb/sth with faint praise** jdn/etw auf eine Weise loben, die ihn bloßstellt; **to ~ sb to sth** jdn zu etw verdammen.
(d) *(inf)* **~ him/you!** *(annoyed)* verdammt! *(inf)*; *(I don't care about him/you)* der kann/du kannst mich mal! *(inf)*; **~ him for forgetting** so ein (verdammter) Mist, er hat's vergessen *(inf)*; **~ Richard, he's pinched my book** der verdammte Richard hat mein Buch geklaut *(inf)*; **~ it!** verdammt (noch mal)! *(inf)*; **~ it all!** zum Donnerwetter! *(inf)*; *(in surprise)* Donnerwetter! *(inf)*, Teufel auch! *(inf)*; **well, I'll be ~ed!** Donnerwetter! *(inf)*; **I'll be ~ed if I'll go there** ich denk nicht (im Schlaf) dran *(inf)*, da hinzugehen; **I'll be ~ed if I know** weiß der Teufel *(inf)*.

damnable *adj*, **-bly** *adv* ['dæmnəbl, -ɪ] gräßlich.

damnation [dæm'neɪʃən] 1 *n (Eccl) (act)* Verdammung *f*; *(state of ~)* Verdammnis *f*.
2 *interj (inf)* verdammt *(inf)*.

damned [dæmd] 1 *adj* **(a)** *soul* verdammt. **(b)** *(inf) see* **damn 3**.
2 *adv see* **damn 4**.
3 *n (Eccl, liter)* **the ~** *pl* die Verdammten *pl*.

damnedest ['dæmdɪst] *n* **to do** *or* **try one's ~** *(inf)* (verdammt noch mal *inf*) sein möglichstes tun.

damning ['dæmɪŋ] *adj* vernichtend; *evidence* belastend ◆ **he was pretty ~ about it** er hat sich ziemlich vernichtend darüber geäußert.

Damocles ['dæməkli:z] *n*: **sword of ~** Damoklesschwert *nt*.

damp [dæmp] 1 *adj* (+*er*) feucht ◆ **a ~ squib** *(fig)* ein Reinfall *m*.
2 *n* **(a)** Feuchtigkeit *f*. **(b)** *(Min) (choke-~)* Schlagwetter *nt*; *(fire-~)* Grubengas *nt*.
3 *vt* **(a)** befeuchten, anfeuchten; *ironing also* einsprengen *or* -spritzen. **(b)** *(fig) enthusiasm etc* dämpfen ◆ **to ~ sb's spirits** jdm einen Dämpfer aufsetzen. **(c)** *sounds, vibrations* dämpfen; *(also* **~ down**) *fire* ersticken.

damp course *n* Dämmschicht *f*.

dampen ['dæmpən] *vt see* **damp 3 (a, b)**.

damper ['dæmpə^r] *n* **(a)** *(of chimney)* (Luft)klappe *f*; *(of piano)* Dämpfer *m*. **(b) to put a ~ on sth** einer Sache *(dat)* einen Dämpfer aufsetzen. **(c)** *(Austral: bread)* Fladenbrot *nt*.

dampish ['dæmpɪʃ] *adj* etwas feucht.

dampness ['dæmpnɪs] *n* Feuchtigkeit *f*.

damp-proof ['dæmppru:f] *adj* feuchtigkeitsbeständig.

damsel ['dæmzəl] *n (obs, liter)* Maid *f (obs, liter)*.

damsel fly *n* Seejungfer, Schlankjungfer *f*.

damson ['dæmzən] *n (fruit)* Damaszenerpflaume *f*; *(tree)* Damaszenerpflaumenbaum *m*.

Dan [dæn] *n (Sport)* Dan *m*.

dance [dɑ:ns] 1 *n* **(a)** Tanz *m* ◆ **the D~ of Death** der Totentanz; **may I have the next ~?** darf ich um den nächsten Tanz bitten?; **she's led him a fine** *or* **pretty ~** sie hat ihn ja ganz schön an der Nase herumgeführt; *(caused a lot of trouble)* ihretwegen hat er sich *(dat)* die Hacken abgelaufen.
(b) *(ball)* Tanz *m*; Tanzabend *m* ◆ **public ~** öffentliche Tanzveranstaltung; **end-of-term ~** Semesterball *m*; **to give** *or* **hold a ~** einen Tanz(abend) veranstalten; *(privately)* eine Tanzparty geben; **to go to a ~** tanzen gehen, zum Tanzen gehen.
2 *vt* tanzen ◆ **to ~ attendance on sb** jdn von hinten und vorn bedienen *(inf)*.
3 *vi* **(a)** tanzen ◆ **would you like to ~?** möchten Sie tanzen?
(b) *(move here and there)* **to ~ about/up and down** (herum)tänzeln/auf- und abhüpfen; **to ~ for joy** einen Freudentanz aufführen.
(c) *(fig)* tanzen; *(boat on waves also)* schaukeln.

dance *in cpds* Tanz-; **~ band** *n* Tanzkapelle *f*; **~ floor** *n* Tanzboden *m*; *(in restaurant)* Tanzfläche *f*; **~ hall** *n* Tanzsaal *m*; **~ music** *n* Tanzmusik *f*.

dancer ['dɑ:nsə^r] *n* Tänzer(in *f*) *m*.

dancing ['dɑ:nsɪŋ] 1 *n* Tanzen *nt*.
2 *attr* Tanz- ◆ **~ dervish** tanzender Derwisch; **~ girl** Tänzerin *f*; **~ shoe** Tanzschuh *m*; **put on your ~ shoes!** *(fig)* mach dich hübsch *or* zurecht!

D and C *abbr of* **dilation and curettage**.

dandelion ['dændɪlaɪən] *n* Löwenzahn *m*.

dander ['dændə^r] *n (inf)*: **to get sb's/one's ~ up** jdn auf die Palme bringen *(inf)*/seine *or* die Borsten aufstellen *(fig)*.

dandified ['dændɪfaɪd] *adj* stutzerhaft.

dandle ['dændl] *vt* schaukeln (*on* auf +*dat*).

dandruff ['dændrəf] *n* Schuppen *pl*.

dandy ['dændɪ] 1 *n* Dandy, Stutzer *(dated)*, Geck *(dated) m*.
2 *adj (esp US inf)* prima *(inf)*.

Dane [deɪn] *n* Däne *m*, Dänin *f*.

dang [dæŋ] *(dated inf) adj, adv, vt see* **damn 3, 4, 5 (d)**.

danger ['deɪndʒə^r] *n* **(a)** Gefahr *f* ◆ **he likes ~** er liebt die Gefahr; **to put sb/sth in ~** jdn/etw in Gefahr bringen, jdn/etw gefährden; **to run into ~** in Gefahr geraten; **to be in ~ of doing sth** Gefahr laufen, etw zu tun; **the country is in ~ of invasion** dem Land droht eine Invasion; **out of ~** außer Gefahr; **there is a ~ of fire** es besteht Feuergefahr; **there is a ~ of his getting lost** es besteht die Gefahr, daß er sich verirrt; **he ran the ~ of being recognized** er lief Gefahr, erkannt zu werden; **there is no ~ of that** die Gefahr besteht nicht; **to be a ~ to sb/sth** für jdn/etw eine Gefahr bedeuten.
(b) "**~**" „Achtung, Lebensgefahr!"; *(Mot)* „Gefahrenstelle"; "**~, high-tension cables/road up**" „Achtung, Hochspannung!/Straßenarbeiten"; "**~, ice**" „Glatteisgefahr"; "**~, keep out**" „Zutritt verboten, Lebensgefahr!"; **the signal was at ~** *(Rail)* das Signal stand auf Rot.

danger: ~ area *n* Gefahrenzone *f or* -bereich *m*; **~ list** *n*: **on/off the ~ list** in/außer Lebensgefahr; **~ money** *n* Gefahrenzulage *f*; **to get ~ money** eine Gefahrenzulage kriegen.

dangerous ['deɪndʒrəs] *adj* gefährlich.

dangerously ['deɪndʒrəslɪ] *adv* gefährlich ◆ **the deadline is getting ~ close** der Termin rückt bedenklich nahe.

danger: ~ point *n* Gefahrengrenze *f*; **to reach ~ point** die Gefahrengrenze erreichen; **~ signal** *n (lit, fig)* Warnsignal *nt*; *(Rail)* Deckungssignal *nt* vor Gefahr *(spec)*; **~ zone** *n* Gefahrenzone *f*.

dangle ['dæŋgl] 1 *vt* baumeln lassen ◆ **to ~ sth in front of** *or* **before sb** *(fig)* jdm etw verlockend in Aussicht stellen.
2 *vi* **(a)** baumeln. **(b) to ~ after sb** jdm nachlaufen; **to ~ around an important person** um eine bedeutende Persönlichkeit herumscharwenzeln.

Danish ['deɪnɪʃ] 1 *adj* dänisch ◆ **~ blue (cheese)** (Blau)schimmelkäse *m*; **~ pastry** Plundergebäck *nt*.
2 *n (language)* Dänisch *nt* ◆ **the ~** *pl (people)* die Dänen.

dank [dæŋk] *adj* (unangenehm) feucht.

Dante ['dæntɪ] *n* Dante *m*.

Dantean ['dæntɪən] *adj* dantisch; *works* Dantisch.

Dantesque ['dæntesk] *adj* dantesk.

Danube ['dænju:b] *n* Donau *f*.

dapper ['dæpə^r] *adj* gepflegt, gediegen.

dapple ['dæpl] *vt* sprenkeln.

dappled ['dæpld] *adj* gefleckt; *(with small flecks)* gesprenkelt; *sky* wolkig; *horse* scheckig.

dapple grey (horse) *n* Apfelschimmel *m*.

DAR *abbr of* **Daughters of the American Revolution** Töchter *pl* der amerikanischen Revolution.

Darby and Joan ['dɑ:bɪən'dʒəʊn] *npl glückliches, älteres Ehepaar* ◆ **~ club** Altenclub *m*.

Dardanelles [,dɑ:də'nelz] *npl* Dardanellen *pl*.

➤ **dare** [deə^r] 1 *vi (be bold enough)* es wagen; *(have the confidence)* sich trauen ◆ **you/he wouldn't ~!** du wirst dich/er wird sich schwer hüten; **you ~!** untersteh dich!; **how ~ you!** was fällt dir ein!
2 *vt* **(a) to ~ (to) do sth** (es) wagen, etw zu tun; sich trauen, etw zu tun; **I didn't ~ (to) go upstairs** ich habe mich nicht getraut, die Treppe hinaufzugehen, ich habe mich nicht die Treppe hinauf getraut; **he wouldn't ~ say anything bad about his boss** er wird sich hüten *or* unterstehen, etwas Schlechtes über seinen Chef zu sagen; **he ~ not** *or* **~n't do it** das wagt er nicht!; **how ~ you say such things?** wie kannst du es wagen *or* was unterstehst du dich, so etwas zu sagen?; **don't you ~ say that to me** untersteh dich, das zu mir zu sagen; **~ you do it?** trauen Sie sich?; **she ~d a smile** sie riskierte ein Lächeln.
(b) I ~ say it gets quite cold here ich könnte mir denken, daß es hier ziemlich kalt wird; **I ~ say he'll be there** es kann (gut) sein, daß er dort sein wird; **he's bound to be there — I ~ say** er ist sicher dort — das kann gut sein; **he was very sorry — I ~ say** es tat ihm sehr leid — das glaube ich gerne.
(c) *(face the risk of)* riskieren; *danger also* trotzen (+*dat*) ◆ **to ~ death/one's life** sein Leben riskieren *or* aufs Spiel setzen.
(d) *(challenge)* **go on, I ~ you!** Feigling!; **are you daring me?** wetten, daß? *(inf)*; **(I) ~ you to jump off** spring doch, du Feigling!
3 *n* Mutprobe *f* ◆ **to do sth for a ~** etw als Mutprobe tun.

daredevil ['deə,devl] 1 *n* Waghals *m*.
2 *adj* waghalsig.

daring ['deərɪŋ] 1 *adj* kühn *(geh)*; *(in physical matters)* waghalsig; *remark, attempt* gewagt, kühn *(geh)*; *opinion, dress* gewagt.
2 *n* Schneid *m*, Kühnheit *f (geh)*; *(in physical matters)* Waghalsigkeit *f*, Schneid *m (geh)*.

daringly ['deərɪŋlɪ] *adv* kühn; *(in physical matters)* waghalsig; *dress* gewagt ◆ **he spoke very ~ to the boss** er hat in sehr kühnem Ton mit dem Chef gesprochen.

➤ **dark** [dɑ:k] 1 *adj* (+*er*) **(a)** dunkel; *room, night also* finster ◆ **it's getting** *or* **growing ~** es wird dunkel; *(in evening also)* es wird Nacht; **the sky is getting ~** der Himmel wird dunkel; *(before storm)* der Himmel verfinstert sich; **~ blue** dunkelblau; **a ~ blue** ein dunkles Blau; **in ~est Africa** im tiefsten Afrika.
(b) *(fig: sinister)* dunkel; *thoughts, threats also* finster ◆ **to keep sth ~** etw geheimhalten; **~ deeds** dunkle Geschäfte.

➤ LANGUAGE IN USE: **dare: 1 → 14**

(c) (*gloomy, sad*) düster ◆ **to look on the ~ side of things** schwarzsehen, schwarzseherisch sein.
[2] *n* (a) Dunkelheit *f* ◆ **after ~** nach Einbruch der Dunkelheit; **until ~** bis zum Einbruch der Dunkelheit.
▼ (b) (*fig: ignorance*) Dunkel *nt* ◆ **to be in the ~** keine Ahnung haben (*about* von); **he has kept me in the ~ as to what they were planning** er hat mich über das, was sie vorhatten, im dunkeln gelassen; **to work in the ~** im dunkeln *or* finstern tappen; **it was a shot in the ~** das war nur so auf gut Glück *or* aufs Geratewohl gesagt/getan/geraten.
dark: D~ Ages *npl* finsteres Mittelalter; **~-complexioned** ['dɑːkkəm,plekʃənd] *adj* mit dunklem Teint; **D~ Continent** *n* **the D~ Continent** der Schwarze Erdteil.
darken ['dɑːkən] [1] *vt* (a) dunkel machen; *sky also* verdunkeln; (*before storm*) verfinstern; *brilliance also* trüben ◆ **the sun ~ed her skin** die Sonne hat ihre Haut gebräunt.
(b) (*fig*) trüben; *mind also* umnachten; *future also* verdüstern ◆ **an angry frown ~ed his brow** ein ärgerliches Runzeln verfinsterte seine Stirn; **never ~ my door again!** lassen Sie sich hier nicht mehr blicken!
[2] *vi see vt* (a) dunkel werden; sich verdunkeln; sich verfinstern; sich trüben. (b) sich trüben; sich umnachten; sich verdüstern; (*brow*) sich verfinstern.
dark: ~-eyed ['dɑːkaɪd] *adj* dunkeläugig; **~ glasses** *npl* Sonnenbrille *f*; **~ horse** *n* (*fig*) stilles Wasser (*fig*); (*unexpected winner*) unbekannte Größe.
darkie, darky ['dɑːkɪ] *n* (*pej inf*) Schwarze(r) *mf*.
darkish ['dɑːkɪʃ] *adj* ziemlich dunkel.
darkly ['dɑːklɪ] *adv* (*lit, fig*) dunkel; *think, threaten also* finster.
darkness ['dɑːknɪs] *n* (a) Dunkelheit *f*; (*of room, night also*) Finsternis *f* ◆ **in total ~** in totaler *or* völliger Dunkelheit, in tiefem Dunkel (*geh*); **the house was in ~** das Haus lag im Dunkeln. (b) (*fig: sinisterness*) Finsterkeit *f*. (c) (*fig: gloominess, sadness*) Düsterkeit *f*.
dark: ~room *n* (*Phot*) Dunkelkammer *f*; **~-skinned** ['dɑːkskɪnd] *adj* dunkelhäutig.
darky *n* (*pej inf*) *see* **darkie**.
darling ['dɑːlɪŋ] [1] *n* (a) Schatz *m*; (*child also*) Schätzchen *nt* ◆ **he is mother's ~/the ~ of the public** er ist Mamas Liebling/der Liebling aller; **she's a little ~** sie ist ein süßer kleiner Schatz; **that cat is a little ~** diese Katze ist ein liebes kleines Tierchen; **be a ~ and ...** sei so lieb *or* nett *or* sei ein Schatz und ...
(b) (*form of address*) Liebling, Schatz *m*, Schätzchen *nt*; (*to child also*) Goldschatz *m*.
[2] *adj cat, dress etc* süß, goldig; *wife etc* lieb.
darn[1] [dɑːn] (*Sew*) [1] *n* gestopfte Stelle.
[2] *vt* stopfen.
darn[2] (*inf*) [1] *interj* verflixt (*inf*).
[2] *adj attr* verflixt (*inf*) ◆ **I can't/couldn't see a ~ thing** verflixt (noch mal) (*inf*), ich kann überhaupt nichts sehen/das war vielleicht ein Mist (*inf*), ich konnte überhaupt nichts sehen.
[3] *adv* verflixt (*inf*) ◆ **a ~ sight better/worse** ein ganzes Ende besser/schlechter (*inf*).
[4] *n* **I don't give a ~** (*inf*) das ist mir völlig schnurz (*inf*).
[5] *vt* **~ him!** zum Kuckuck mit ihm! (*inf*); **~ him for coming late** zum Kuckuck mit ihm, warum kommt er auch zu spät!; **~ it!** verflixt (noch mal) (*inf*); **well I'll be ~ed!** Donnerwetter! (*inf*); **I'll be ~ed if I ...** das wäre ja noch schöner, wenn ich ... (*inf*); **I'll be ~ed if I know** und wenn du dich auf den Kopf stellst, ich weiß es einfach nicht (*inf*).
darned [dɑːnd] *adj, adv* (*inf*) *see* **darn**[2] **2, 3**.
darning ['dɑːnɪŋ] *n* Stopfen *nt*; (*things to be darned*) Flick- *or* Stopfsachen *pl*, Flickarbeit *f* ◆ **I've a lot of ~ to do** ich habe viel zu stopfen; **~ needle** Stopfnadel *f*; **~ mushroom** Stopfpilz *m*.
dart [dɑːt] [1] *n* (a) (*movement*) Satz *m* ◆ **to make a sudden ~ at sb/sth** einen plötzlichen Satz auf jdn/etw zu machen; **the fish made a ~ for the shelter of the weeds** der Fisch schnellte ins schützende Seegras; **with a ~ of its tongue the chameleon caught its prey** die Zunge schnellte heraus, und das Chamäleon hatte seine Beute gefangen.
(b) (*weapon*) Pfeil *m*; (*fig: of sarcasm etc*) Spitze *f*; (*Sport*) (Wurf)pfeil *m*.
(c) (*liter*) (*of serpent*) (Gift)zahn *m*; (*of bee*) Stachel *m*.
(d) (*Sew*) Abnäher *m*.
[2] *vi* flitzen; (*fish*) schnellen ◆ **to ~ out** (*person*) heraus-/hinausflitzen; (*fish, tongue*) herausschnellen; **to ~ in** (*person*) hinein-/hereinstürzen; (*into water: otter etc*) sich hineinstürzen; **he ~ed behind a bush** er hechtete hinter einen Busch; **he ~ed off** er flitzte davon; **her eyes ~ed round the room** ihre Blicke schossen blitzschnell im Zimmer hin und her; **her thoughts were ~ing here and there** tausend Gedanken schossen ihr durch den Kopf.
[3] *vt look* werfen ◆ **to ~ a glance at sb** jdm einen Blick zuwerfen; **the snake ~ed its tongue out** die Schlange ließ ihre Zunge hervorschnellen.
dart board *n* Dartscheibe *f*.
darts [dɑːts] *n sing* Darts, Pfeilwurfspiel *nt* ◆ **a game of ~** ein Dartspiel *nt*.
Darwinian [dɑː'wɪnɪən] [1] *n* Darwinist(in *f*) *m*.
[2] *adj* darwinistisch.
Darwinism ['dɑːwɪnɪzəm] *n* Darwinismus *m*.
dash [dæʃ] [1] *n* (a) (*sudden rush*) Jagd *f* ◆ **to make a ~** losstürzen; **he made a ~ for the door/across the road** er stürzte auf die Tür zu/über die Straße; **to make a ~ for freedom** versuchen, in die Freiheit zu entkommen; **his ~ for freedom was unsuccessful** sein Versuch, in die Freiheit zu entkommen, war vergeblich; **she made a ~ for it** sie rannte, so schnell sie konnte.
(b) (*hurry*) Hetze *f*.
(c) (*style, vigour*) Schwung, Elan *m* ◆ **to cut a ~** eine schneidige Figur machen.
(d) (*small amount*) etwas, ein bißchen; (*of wine, vinegar, spirits also*) Schuß *m*; (*of seasoning etc also*) Prise *f*; (*of lemon also*) Spritzer *m*.
(e) (*Typ*) Gedankenstrich *m*.
(f) (*in morse*) Strich *m*.
(g) *see* **dashboard**.
[2] *vt* (a) (*throw violently*) schleudern ◆ **to ~ sth to pieces** etw in tausend Stücke zerschlagen; **to ~ one's head against sth** mit dem Kopf gegen etw schlagen *or* prallen; **the ship was ~ed against a rock** das Schiff wurde gegen eine Klippe geschleudert.
(b) (*discourage*) *sb's hopes* zunichte machen ◆ **that ~ed his spirits** das hat ihn völlig geknickt.
(c) (*inf*) *see* **darn**[2] **5**.
[3] *vi* (a) (*rush*) sausen (*inf*) ◆ **to ~ into/across a room** in/quer durch ein Zimmer stürzen *or* stürmen; **to ~ away/back/up** fort-/zurück-/hinaufstürzen.
(b) (*knock, be hurled*) schlagen; (*waves also*) peitschen.
[4] *interj* **~ (it)!** (*inf*) verflixt! (*inf*), (verflixter) Mist! (*inf*).
◆**dash off** [1] *vi* losstürzen ◆ **sorry to have to ~ ~ like this** es tut mir leid, daß ich so forthetzen muß.
[2] *vt sep letter, essay* hinwerfen; *drawing also* mit ein paar Strichen hinwerfen.
dashboard ['dæʃbɔːd] *n* Armaturenbrett *nt*.
dashed [dæʃt] *adj, adv see* **darn**[2] **2, 3**.
dashing ['dæʃɪŋ] *adj person, appearance* flott, schneidig; *behaviour* schneidig.
dashpot ['dæʃpɒt] *n* (*Tech*) Pralltopf *m*.
dastardly ['dæstədlɪ] *adj* niederträchtig, gemein.
DAT *n abbr of* **digital audio tape** DAT *nt* ◆ **~ cassette** DAT-Kassette *f*.
data ['deɪtə] *pl of* **datum** *usu with sing vb* Daten *pl* ◆ **the actual ~ is quite surprising** die eigentlichen Daten sind recht erstaunlich; **a piece of ~** eine Angabe; (*Math*) ein (Zahlen)wert *m*; **what's the ~ on Kowalski?** (*inf*) welche Angaben haben wir über Kowalski?; **we have a significant amount of ~ on ...** wir haben einen beträchtlichen Datenbestand über (+*acc*).
data: ~ bank *n* Datenbank *f*; **~base** *n* Datenbank *f*; **we have a large ~base of ...** wir haben große Datenbestände an ... (*dat*); **~ block** *n* Datenblock *m*; **~ buffer** *n* Datenpuffer *m*; **~ capture** *n* Datenerfassung *f*; **~ carrier** *n* Datenträger *m*; **~ file** *n* Datei *f*; **~-handling system** *n* Datenerfassungssystem *nt*; **~ input** *n* Dateneingabe *f*; **~ pen** *n* (*Comput*) Lichtgriffel *m*; **~ processing** *n* Datenverarbeitung *f*; **~ protection** *n* Datenschutz *m*; **~ protection act** *n* Datenschutzgesetz *m*; **~ retrieval** *n* Datenabruf *m*; **~ switch** *n* Datenschalter *m*; **~ transfer** *n* Datentransfer *m*; **~ transmission** *n* Datenübertragung *f*.
date[1] [deɪt] *n* (*fruit*) Dattel *f*; (*tree*) Dattelpalme *f*.
date[2] [1] *n* (a) Datum *nt*; (*historical ~*) Geschichts- *or* Jahreszahl *f*; (*for appointment*) Termin *m* ◆ **~ of birth** Geburtsdatum *nt*; **what's the ~ today?** der Wievielte ist heute?, welches Datum haben wir heute?; **what ~ is he coming on?** wann *or* an welchem Tag kommt er?; **what is the ~ of that letter?** von wann ist der Brief datiert?; **to ~** bis heute, bis dato (*form, dated*); **of early/recent ~** älteren/neueren *or* jüngeren Datums.
(b) (*on coins, medals etc*) Jahreszahl *f*.
(c) (*appointment*) Verabredung *f*; (*with girlfriend etc also*) Rendezvous *nt* ◆ **who's his ~?** mit wem trifft er sich?; **my ~ didn't show up** derjenige, mit dem/diejenige, mit der ich ausgehen wollte, hat mich versetzt (*inf*); **to make a ~ with sb** sich mit jdm verabreden; **she's out on a ~** sie hat eine Verabredung *or* ein Rendezvous.
[2] *vt* (a) mit dem Datum versehen; *letter etc also* datieren ◆ **letter ~d the seventh of August** ein vom siebten August datierter Brief; **a coin ~d 1390** eine Münze von 1390.
(b) (*establish age of*) *work of art etc* datieren ◆ **that really ~s you** daran merkt man, wie alt Sie sind.
(c) (*take out*) *girlfriend etc* ausgehen mit; (*regularly also*) gehen mit (*inf*).
[3] *vi* (a) **to ~ back to** zurückdatieren auf (+*acc*); **to ~ from** zurückgehen auf (+*acc*); (*antique etc*) stammen aus. (b) (*become old-fashioned*) veralten. (c) (*have boyfriend etc*) einen Freund/eine Freundin haben; (*couple*) miteinander gehen.
dated ['deɪtɪd] *adj* altmodisch; *clothes, manners also* überholt.
date: ~less *adj* (a) *manuscript* undatiert, ohne Jahreszahl; (b) (*never old-fashioned*) zeitlos; **~ line** *n* (*Geog*) Datumsgrenze *f*; (*Typ*) Datumszeile *f*; **~ palm** *n* Dattelpalme *f*; **~rape** *n Vergewaltigung f nach einem Rendezvous*; **~-stamp** [1] *n* Datumsstempel *m*; [2] *vt* mit Datumsstempel versehen.
dative ['deɪtɪv] [1] *n* Dativ *m* ◆ **in the ~** im Dativ.
[2] *adj* Dativ-, dativisch ◆ **the ~ case** der Dativ.
datum ['deɪtəm] *n, pl* **data** (*rare*) Faktum, Datum *nt*.
daub [dɔːb] [1] *vt walls, canvas, face* beschmieren; *paint, slogans, make-up* schmieren; (*coat with grease etc*) *axle* einschmieren; (*coat with mud, clay*) *walls* bewerfen; (*spread on*) *grease, mud, clay* streichen ◆ **she ~ed cream all over her face** sie hat sich (*dat*) das ganze Gesicht mit Creme zu- *or* vollgeschmiert.
[2] *n* (a) (*Build*) Bewurf *m*.
(b) (*pej: bad picture*) Kleckserei *f*.
dauber ['dɔːbəʳ] *n* (*pej*) Kleckser *m*.
daughter ['dɔːtəʳ] *n* (*lit, fig*) Tochter *f* ◆ **~-in-law** Schwiegertochter *f*.
daughterboard ['dɔːtə,bɔːd] *n* (*Comput*) Zusatzplatine *f*.
daunt [dɔːnt] *vt* entmutigen ◆ **he is never ~ed** er ist nie verzagt; **nothing ~ed** unverzagt.

➤ LANGUAGE IN USE: **dark: 2b → 16.1**

daunting ['dɔːntɪŋ] *adj* entmutigend.
dauntless ['dɔːntlɪs] *adj* unerschrocken, beherzt; *courage* unbezähmbar.
davenport ['dævnpɔːt] *n* **(a)** (*esp US: sofa*) Sofa *nt*, Couch *f*. **(b)** (*Brit: desk*) Sekretär *m*.
David ['deɪvɪd] *n* David *m*.
davit ['dævɪt] *n* (*Naut*) Davit *m or nt*.
Davy ['deɪvɪ] *n dim of* **David** ◆ **to go to ~ Jones' locker** den Seemannstod sterben; **treasures from ~ Jones' locker** Schätze vom Grunde des Meeres; **~ lamp** (Gruben-)Sicherheitslampe *f*.
dawdle ['dɔːdl] *vi* (*be too slow*) trödeln; (*stroll*) bummeln ◆ **to ~ on the way** unterwegs trödeln; **to ~ over one's work** bei der Arbeit bummeln *or* trödeln.
◆**dawdle along** *vi* dahinbummeln; (*+prep obj*) entlangbummeln.
◆**dawdle away** *vt sep time* vertrödeln.
dawdler ['dɔːdlə^r] *n* Trödler(in *f*) *m*; (*as regards work also*) Bummelant(in *f*), Bummler(in *f*) (*inf*) *m*.
dawdling ['dɔːdlɪŋ] *adj* **at a ~ pace** im Bummeltempo.
dawn [dɔːn] **1** *n* (*lit, fig*) (Morgen)dämmerung, Morgenröte (*liter*) *f*; (*no art: time of day*) Tagesanbruch *m*, Morgengrauen *nt* ◆ **at ~** bei Tagesanbruch, im Morgengrauen; **it's almost ~** es ist fast Morgen, es dämmert schon bald; **when is ~?** wann wird es hell?; **from ~ to dusk** von morgens bis abends.
2 *vi* **(a) day was already ~ing** es dämmerte schon; **the day ~ed rainy** der Tag fing mit Regen an; **the day will ~ when ...** (*fig*) der Tag wird kommen, wo ...
(b) (*fig*) (*new age etc*) dämmern, anbrechen; (*hope*) erwachen.
(c) (*inf*) **to ~ (up)on sb** jdm dämmern *or* zum Bewußtsein kommen; **the idea ~ed on him that ...** es wurde ihm langsam klar, daß ..., es dämmerte ihm, daß ...
dawn: ~ chorus *n* Morgenkonzert *nt* der Vögel; **~ patrol** *n* (*Aviat*) Morgenpatrouille *f*; **~ raid** *n* **(a)** (*by police*) Razzia *f* (*in den frühen Morgenstunden*). **(b)** (*Fin*) *plötzlicher Aufkauf von Aktien*, Überraschungsangriff *m*.
day [deɪ] *n* **(a)** Tag *m* ◆ **he's coming in three ~s' time** *or* **in three ~s** er kommt in drei Tagen; **it will arrive any ~ now** es muß jeden Tag kommen; **what ~ is it today?** welcher Tag ist heute?, was haben wir heute?; **what ~ of the month is it?** der wievielte ist heute?; **twice a ~** zweimal täglich *or* am Tag; **the ~ before yesterday** vorgestern; **(on) the ~ after/before, (on) the following/previous ~** am Tag danach/zuvor, am (darauf)folgenden/vorhergehenden Tag; **the ~ after tomorrow** übermorgen; **this ~ week** (*inf*) heute in acht Tagen (*inf*); **from that ~ on(wards)** von dem Tag an; **from this ~ forth** (*old*) von diesem Tage an; **two years ago to the ~** heute/morgen *etc* auf den Tag genau vor zwei Jahren; **one ~** eines Tages; **one ~ we went swimming, and the next ...** einen Tag gingen wir schwimmen, und den nächsten ...; **one of these ~s** irgendwann(einmal), eines Tages; **~ in, ~ out** tagein, tagaus; **they went to London for the ~** sie machten einen Tagesausflug nach London; **for ~s on end** tagelang; **~ after ~** Tag für Tag, tagtäglich; **~ by ~** jeden Tag, täglich; **the other ~** neulich; **at the end of the ~** (*fig*) letzten Endes; **to live from ~ to ~** von einem Tag auf den andern leben; **today of all ~s** ausgerechnet heute; **some ~ soon** demnächst; **I remember it to this ~** daran erinnere ich mich noch heute; **he's fifty if he's a ~** er ist mindestens *or* wenigstens fünfzig; **all ~** den ganzen Tag; **to travel during the** *or* **by ~** tagsüber *or* während des Tages reisen; **at that time of ~** zu der Tageszeit; **to work ~ and night** Tag und Nacht arbeiten; **good ~!** guten Tag!; (*good-bye*) auf Wiedersehen; **(the) ~ is done** (*liter*) der Tag ist vorüber; **to be paid by the ~** tageweise bezahlt werden; **let's call it a ~** machen wir Schluß; **some time during the ~** irgendwann im Laufe des Tages; **to have a nice/lazy ~** einen schönen Tag verbringen/einen Tag faulenzen; **have a nice ~!** viel Spaß!; (*esp US: said by storekeeper etc*) schönen Tag noch!; **did you have a nice ~?** war's schön?; **did you have a good ~ at the office?** wie war's im Büro?; **to have a good/bad ~** einen guten/schlechten Tag haben; **what a ~!** (*terrible*) so ein fürchterlicher Tag!; (*lovely*) so ein herrlicher Tag!; **it's all in the** *or* **a ~'s work!** das ist (doch) selbstverständlich; **to work an eight hour ~** einen Achtstundentag haben, acht Stunden am Tag arbeiten; **on a wet ~** an einem regnerischen Tag; **that'll be the ~** das möcht' ich sehen *or* erleben; *see* **make**.
(b) (*period of time: often pl*) **these ~s** heute, heutzutage; **what are you doing these ~s?** was machst *or* treibst du denn so?; **in this ~ and age** heutzutage; **the talking-point of the ~** das Tagesgespräch; **in ~s to come** künftig, in künftigen Zeiten *or* Tagen (*geh*); **from his young ~s** von Kindesbeinen *or* frühester Jugend an; **in his younger ~s** als er noch jünger war; **in Queen Victoria's ~, in the ~s of Queen Victoria** zu Königin Viktorias Zeiten; **the happiest ~s of my life** die glücklichste Zeit meines Lebens; **those were the ~s** das waren noch Zeiten; **in the old ~s** früher; **in the good old ~s** in der guten alten Zeit; **it's early ~s yet** es ist noch zu früh; **during the early ~s of the war** in den ersten Kriegstagen; **he/this material has seen better ~s** er/dieser Stoff hat (auch) schon bessere Zeiten *or* Tage gesehen; **to end one's ~s in misery** im Elend sterben.
(c) (*with poss adj: lifetime, best time*) **famous in her ~** in ihrer Zeit berühmt; **it has had its ~** das hat seine Glanzzeit überschritten; **his ~ will come** sein Tag wird kommen; **everything has its ~** für alles kommt einmal die richtige Zeit.
(d) *no pl* (*contest, battle*) **to win** *or* **carry the ~** den Sieg bringen; **to lose/save the ~** (den Kampf) verlieren/retten.
day: ~ bed *n* Ruhebett *nt*; **~ boarder** *n* (*Brit Sch*) Externe(r) *mf*; **~book** *n* (*Comm*) Journal, Tagebuch *nt*; **~ boy** *n* (*Sch*) Externe(r) *m*; **~break** *n* Tagesanbruch *m*; **at ~break** bei Tagesanbruch; **~ care** *n* **to be in ~ care** (*child*) in einer Tagesstätte untergebracht sein; (*old person*) in einer Altentagesstätte untergebracht sein; **~ (care) centre** *n* (*for children*) Tagesstätte *f*; (*for old people*) Altentagesstätte *f*; **~ coach** *n* (*US*) (Eisenbahn)personenwagen *m*; **~dream** **1** *n* Tagtraum *m*, Träumerei *f*; **2** *vi* (mit offenen Augen) träumen; **~ girl** *n* (*Sch*) Externe *f*; **~ labourer** *n* Tagelöhner *m*.
daylight ['deɪlaɪt] *n* **(a)** (*daybreak*) Tagesanbruch *m*.
(b) Tageslicht *nt* ◆ **it is still ~** es ist noch hell; **it was broad ~** es war heller *or* hellichter Tag; **in broad ~** am hellen *or* hellichten Tage: **I'd like to get there in ~** ich möchte gern bei Tag ankommen; **I began to see ~** (*fig*) (*to understand*) mir ging ein Licht auf; (*to see the end appear*) so langsam habe ich Land gesehen (*inf*); **to beat the living ~s out of sb** (*inf*) jdn windelweich schlagen (*inf*); **to scare the living ~s out of sb** (*inf*) jdm einen fürchterlichen Schreck einjagen (*inf*).
daylight: ~ robbery *n* (*inf*) Halsabschneiderei *f* (*inf*), offener Diebstahl; **~ saving time** *n* (*esp US*) Sommerzeit *f*.
day: ~ long *adj* 24 Stunden-, den ganzen Tag dauernd; **~ nurse** *n* Tagesschwester *f*; **~ nursery** *n* Kindertagesstätte *f*; (*in private house*) Kinderzimmer *nt*; **~-old** *adj* Eintags-, einen Tag alt; **two-/three-~ old** zwei/drei Tage alt; **~ pupil** *n* (*Sch*) Externe(r) *mf*; **~ release** *n* tageweise Freistellung von Angestellten zur Weiterbildung; **~ release course** *n* Tageskurs *m* für Berufstätige; **~ return (ticket)** *n* (*Brit Rail*) Tagesrückfahrkarte *f*; **~ school** *n* Tagesschule *f*; **~ shift** *n* Tagschicht *f*; **to be on** *or* **work ~ shift** Tagschicht arbeiten.
daytime ['deɪtaɪm] **1** *n* Tag *m* ◆ **in the ~** bei Tage, tagsüber, während des Tages.
2 *attr* am Tage; *course, programme* Tages-; *raid* am hellen *or* hellichten Tage.
day: ~-to-day *adj occurrence* alltäglich; *way of life* Alltags-, täglich; **on a ~-to-day basis** tageweise; **~ trip** *n* Tagesausflug *m*; **~ tripper** *n* Tagesausflügler(in *f*) *m*.
daze [deɪz] **1** *n* Benommenheit *f* ◆ **in a ~** ganz benommen.
2 *vt* benommen machen.
dazed [deɪzd] *adj* benommen.
dazzle ['dæzl] *vt* (*lit, fig*) blenden.
dazzling ['dæzlɪŋ] *adj* (*lit*) blendend.
dazzlingly ['dæzlɪŋlɪ] *adv* (*lit, fig*) blendend ◆ **~ beautiful** strahlend schön.
dB *abbr of* **decibel** dB.
DC *abbr of* **(a) direct current. (b) District of Columbia.**
DCC ® *abbr of* **digital compact cassette** DCC *f*.
DD *abbr of* **Doctor of Divinity** Dr. Theol.
D/D *abbr of* **direct debit.**
D-day ['diːdeɪ] *n* (*Hist, fig*) der Tag X.
DDT *abbr of* **dichloro-diphenyl-trichloroethane** DDT *nt*.
deacon ['diːkən] *n* Diakon *m*.
deaconess ['diːkənes] *n* Diakonissin *f*.
deaconry ['diːkənrɪ] *n* Diakonat *nt*.
deactivate [diː'æktɪveɪt] *vt* entschärfen.
dead [ded] **1** *adj* **(a)** tot; *plant also* abgestorben, eingegangen ◆ **he has been ~ for two years** er ist seit zwei Jahren tot; **to drop (down)** *or* **fall down ~** tot umfallen; **to shoot sb ~** jdn erschießen *or* totschießen (*inf*); **to strike sb ~** jdn erschlagen; **over my ~ body** (*inf*) nur über meine Leiche (*inf*).
(b) (*not sensitive*) *limbs* abgestorben, taub ◆ **my fingers are ~** meine Finger sind wie abgestorben; **he is ~ to reason** er ist gegen alle vernünftigen Argumente taub; **he is ~ to pity** er kennt kein Mitleid; **to be ~ from the neck up** (*inf*) nur Stroh im Kopf haben (*inf*), gehirnamputiert sein (*sl*); **to be ~ to the world** vollkommen weggetreten sein (*inf*).
(c) (*without activity etc*) *town, season* tot; *business also* flau.
(d) (*Elec*) *cable* stromlos; (*Telec*) tot ◆ **to go ~** ausfallen.
(e) (*burnt out*) *fire* aus *pred*; *match* abgebrannt.
(f) (*inf: finished with*) *glass* ausgetrunken; (*Typ*) *copy* abgesetzt ◆ **are these glasses ~?** können diese Gläser weg?
(g) (*Sport*) *ball* tot.
(h) (*obsolete*) *language etc* tot; *custom* ausgestorben.
(i) (*absolute, exact*) total, völlig ◆ **~ silence** Totenstille *f*; **~ calm** (*Naut*) absolute *or* totale Windstille; **she was in a ~ faint** sie war völlig bewußtlos; **to come to a ~ stop** völlig zum Stillstand kommen; **he's the ~ spit of his father** (*sl*) er ist seinem Vater wie aus dem Gesicht geschnitten; **to be on a ~ level with sb** mit jdm genau gleichauf sein; *see* **cert, set.**
(j) *colour* tot, stumpf, matt; *sound* dumpf.
(k) (*Typ*) *key* Tot-.
(l) (*inf: exhausted*) tot (*inf*), völlig kaputt (*inf*).
2 *adv* **(a)** (*exactly*) genau ◆ **~ straight** schnurgerade; **to be ~ on time** auf die Minute pünktlich kommen; (*clock*) auf die Minute genau gehen; **~ on course** voll *or* genau auf Kurs; **the parachutists landed ~ on target** die Fallschirmspringer sind genau im Ziel gelandet.
(b) (*inf: very*) total (*inf*), völlig ◆ **~ drunk/tired** total betrunken, stockvoll (*inf*)/todmüde; **you're ~ right** Sie haben völlig recht; **he was ~ lucky** er hat Schwein gehabt (*inf*), er hat irrsinnig Glück gehabt; **~ slow** ganz langsam; **"~ slow"** „Schritt fahren"; **to be ~ certain about sth** (*inf*) bei etw todsicher sein; **he's ~ against it** er ist total dagegen.
(c) to stop ~ abrupt stehenbleiben *or* (*talking*) innehalten.
3 *n* **(a) the ~** *pl* die Toten *pl*. **(b) at ~ of night** mitten in der Nacht; **in the ~ of winter** mitten im Winter.
dead: ~-and-alive *adj* (*inf*) *party, place* tot, langweilig; **~-ball line** *n* (*Rugby*) Feldauslinie *f*; **~-beat** *adj* (*inf*) völlig kaputt (*inf*), total fertig (*inf*); **~-beat** *n* (*down-and-out*) Gammler *m*; (*failure*) Versager *m*; **~ duck** *n* **to be a ~ duck** passé sein; **politically he's/it's a ~ duck** politisch ist er/es gestorben (*inf*).

deaden ['dedn] *vt shock* auffangen; *pain* mildern; *force, blow* abschwächen; *nerve, passions* abtöten; *sound, noise* dämpfen; *mind, feeling* abstumpfen.

dead: ~ end *n* Sackgasse *f*; **to come to a ~ end** (*lit*) (*road*) in einer Sackgasse enden; (*driver*) an eine Sackgasse kommen; (*fig*) in eine Sackgasse geraten; **~-end** *adj attr* **~-end street** (*esp US*) Sackgasse *f*; **to be in ~-end street** (*fig*) keine Chancen haben; **~-end kids** Gassenkinder *pl*; **a ~-end job** ein Job *m* ohne Aufstiegsmöglichkeiten; **~ heat** *n* totes Rennen; **~ letter** *n* (*lit*) unzustellbarer Brief; (*Jur*) toter Buchstabe; **~line** *n* (letzter) Termin; **to fix** *or* **set a ~line** eine Frist setzen; **to work to a ~line** auf einen Termin hinarbeiten; **he was working to a six o'clock ~line** um 6 Uhr mußte er die Arbeit fertig haben; **can you meet the ~line?** können Sie den Termin *or* die Frist einhalten?; **copy ~line** (*Press*) Redaktionsschluß *m*.

deadliness ['dedlɪnɪs] *n* (*of poison, weapon*) tödliche Wirkung; (*of wit, sarcasm*) vernichtende Wirkung; (*inf*) (*boringness*) tödliche Langeweile; (*awfulness*) Entsetzlichkeit *f*.

deadlock ['dedlɒk] *n* **to reach (a) ~** sich festfahren, in eine Sackgasse geraten; **to break the ~** aus der Sackgasse herauskommen; **"union talks: it's ~"** „Verhandlungen mit der Gewerkschaft festgefahren".

deadly ['dedlɪ] 1 *adj* (*+er*) **(a)** *poison, hatred, weapon, accuracy* tödlich; *sin, enemy* Tod-; *wit, sarcasm* vernichtend ◆ **his aim was ~** er traf mit tödlicher Sicherheit; **he's in ~ earnest** er meint es todernst, es ist sein voller Ernst.
(b) (*inf*) (*boring*) todlangweilig; (*awful*) *taste* entsetzlich.
2 *adv boring* tod- ◆ **~ pale** totenbleich.

deadly nightshade *n* Tollkirsche *f*.

dead: ~ man's handle *n* SIFA-Schalttaste, Totmannkurbel *f*; **~ march** *n* Totenmarsch *m*; **~ men's shoes** *n*: **to wait for ~ men's shoes** warten, bis eine Stelle frei wird.

deadness ['dednɪs] *n* (*of limbs*) Taubheit *f*; (*of colour*) Langweiligkeit *f* ◆ **there is nothing to compare with the ~ of Hull** keine Stadt ist so tot wie Hull.

dead: ~pan 1 *adj face* unbewegt; *style, humour* trocken; **with a ~pan expression** mit unbeweglicher Miene; 2 *n* (*face, expression*) unbewegliche Miene; **~ reckoning** *n* (*Naut*) Koppelung *f*; **D~ Sea** *n* Totes Meer; **D~ Sea scrolls** *npl* Schriftrollen *pl* vom Toten Meer; **~ weight** *n* (*Tech*) Eigen- *or* Totgewicht *nt*; **that box/she was a ~ weight** die Kiste/sie war furchtbar schwer; **~wood** *n* (*lit*) morsches Holz; (*Naut*) Totholz *nt*; (*fig*) Ballast *m*; **to cut out the ~wood from the manuscript** allen Ballast im Manuskript abwerfen; **to cut out the ~wood from the staff** die Nieten unter den Mitarbeitern entlassen.

deaf [def] 1 *adj* (*+er*) (*lit, fig*) taub ◆ **as ~ as a (door)post** stocktaub; **he was ~ to her pleas** er blieb gegen alle ihre Bitten taub, er verschloß sich ihren Bitten; **to turn a ~ ear to sb/sth** sich jdm/einer Sache (*dat*) gegenüber taub stellen; **our pleas fell on ~ ears** unsere Bitten fanden kein Gehör.
2 *n* **the ~** *pl* die Tauben *pl*.

deaf: ~-aid *n* Hörgerät *nt*; **~-and-dumb** *adj* taubstumm; *language* Taubstummen-.

deafen ['defn] *vt* (*lit*) taub machen; (*fig*) betäuben.

deafening ['defnɪŋ] *adj noise* ohrenbetäubend; *row* lautstark ◆ **a ~ silence** ein eisiges Schweigen.

deaf-mute ['def'mju:t] *n* Taubstumme(r) *mf*.

deafness ['defnɪs] *n* (*lit, fig*) Taubheit *f* (*to* gegenüber).

▼ **deal¹** [di:l] 1 *n* (*amount*) Menge *f* ◆ **a good** *or* **great ~** eine Menge, (ziemlich) viel; **not a great ~** nicht (besonders) viel; **there's still a (good** *or* **great) ~ of work left** es ist noch ein schönes Stück *or* eine Menge Arbeit; **there's a great** *or* **good ~ of truth in what he says** es ist schon ziemlich viel Wahres an dem, was er sagt; **it says a good ~ for him** das spricht sehr für ihn; **and that's saying a good ~** und damit ist schon viel gesagt; **to mean a great ~ to sb** jdm viel bedeuten.
2 *adv* **a good** *or* **great ~**, **a ~** (*inf*) (*+vb*) (ziemlich) viel; (*+adj*) viel; **not a great ~** nicht viel; **did you swim much? — not a great ~** seid ihr viel geschwommen? — nicht besonders viel.

deal² (*vb: pret, ptp* **dealt**) 1 *n* **(a)** (*also* **business ~**) Geschäft *nt*, Handel *m*; (*arrangement*) Handel *m*, Abkommen *nt*, Deal *m* (*inf*) ◆ **to do** *or* **make a ~ with sb** mit jdm ein Geschäft *or* einen Deal (*inf*) machen, mit jdm ein Geschäft abschließen; **it's a ~** abgemacht!; **I'll make** *or* **do a ~ with you** ich schlage Ihnen ein Geschäft vor; **can I suggest a ~?** kann ich einen Vorschlag machen?; **I never make ~s** ich lasse mich nie auf Geschäfte ein; **are you forgetting our ~?** hast du unsere Abmachung vergessen?; **a ~ on the Stock Exchange** ein Börsengeschäft; *see* **big**.
(b) (*inf*) **to give sb a fair ~** jdn anständig behandeln; **a better ~ for the lower paid** bessere Bedingungen für die schlechter bezahlten Arbeiter; **the Tories/management offered us a new ~** die Tories haben uns ein neues Programm vorgelegt/die Firmenleitung hat uns ein neues Angebot gemacht.
(c) (*Cards*) **it's your ~** Sie geben.
2 *vt* **(a)** (*also* **~ out**) *cards* geben, austeilen. **(b)** *see* **blow¹**.
3 *vi* **(a) to ~ well/badly by sb** jdn gut/schlecht behandeln.
(b) (*Cards*) geben, austeilen.

◆**deal in** 1 *vi +prep obj* (*Comm*) handeln mit.
2 *vt sep* (*Cards*) *player* Karten geben (*+dat*).

◆**deal out** *vt sep gifts, money* verteilen (*to* an *+acc*); *cards* (aus)geben (*to* dat) ◆ **to ~ ~ justice** Recht sprechen; **a judge who was not afraid to ~ ~ justice to powerful men** ein Richter, der keine Angst davor hatte, auch mächtige Männer zur Rechenschaft zu ziehen.

◆**deal with** *vi +prep obj* **(a)** (*do business with*) verhandeln mit ◆ **he's not easy to**
▼ **~ ~** es ist nicht leicht, mit ihm zu verhandeln.
(b) (*manage, handle*) sich kümmern um; (*with job*) sich befassen mit; (*successfully*) fertigwerden mit; (*Comm*) *orders* erledigen; (*be responsible for also*) zuständig sein für ◆ **let's ~ ~ the adjectives first** behandeln wir zuerst die Adjektive; **to know how to ~ ~ sb** wissen, wie man mit jdm fertig wird *or* umgeht; **you bad boy, I'll ~ ~ you later** (*inf*) dich knöpf' *or* nehm' ich mir später vor, du Lausebengel! (*inf*); **the problem has been successfully ~t ~** man ist gut mit dem Problem fertiggeworden; **if the government doesn't know how to ~ ~ the problem/doesn't ~ ~ the problem soon** wenn die Regierung mit dem Problem nicht fertigwerden kann/sich nicht bald mit dem Problem befaßt; **to ~ ~ a case** (*judge*) einen Fall verhandeln; (*lawyer*) sich mit einem Fall befassen.
▼ **(c)** (*be concerned with*) (*book, film etc*) handeln von; (*author*) sich beschäftigen *or* befassen mit.

deal³ 1 *n* (*wood*) Kiefern- *or* Tannenholz *nt*.
2 *adj attr* aus Kiefern- *or* Tannenholz, Kiefern-, Tannen-.

dealer ['di:ləʳ] *n* **(a)** (*Comm*) Händler *m*; (*wholesaler*) Großhändler *m* ◆ **a ~ in furs** ein Pelzhändler. **(b)** (*with drugs*) Dealer *m*. **(c)** (*Cards*) Kartengeber *m*.

dealing ['di:lɪŋ] *n* **(a)** (*trading*) Handel *m*; (*on stock exchange also*) Transaktionen *pl* ◆ **now that all the ~ is over** jetzt, wo alle Verhandlungen vorüber sind; **there's some crooked ~ involved here** da ist irgend etwas gedreht *or* gemauschelt (*inf*) worden.
(b) (*of cards*) Geben, Aus- *or* Verteilen *nt*.
(c) ~s *pl* (*Comm*) Geschäfte *pl*; (*generally*) Umgang *m* ◆ **to have ~s with sb** mit jdm zu tun haben; (*Comm also*) Geschäftsbeziehungen zu jdm haben; **he had secret ~s with the enemy** er stand heimlich mit dem Feind in Verbindung.

dealt [delt] *pret, ptp of* **deal²**.

dean [di:n] *n* (*Eccl, Univ*) Dekan *m*.

deanery ['di:nərɪ] *n* **(a)** Dekanat *nt*. **(b)** (*Eccl: house*) Dekanei *f*.

deanship ['di:nʃɪp] *n* (*Eccl, Univ*) Dekanat *nt*.

dear [dɪəʳ] 1 *adj* (*+er*) **(a)** (*loved*) lieb, teuer (*liter*) ◆ **that/she was ~est of all to him** das/sie war ihm das Liebste *or* Teuerste; **I hold him/it ~** er/es ist mir lieb und teuer; **that is my ~est wish** das ist mein sehnlichster *or* innigster Wunsch; **my ~ chap** mein lieber Freund; **you are very ~ to me** du bist mir lieb und teuer; **these memories are very ~ to him** diese Erinnerungen sind ihm teuer.
(b) (*lovable, sweet*) *child* lieb, süß, reizend; *thing* süß, entzückend, reizend ◆ **what a ~ little dress/baby/kitten** was für ein süßes *or* entzückendes Kleidchen/Kind/Kätzchen!
(c) (*in letter-writing etc*) **~ Daddy/John** lieber Vati/John!; **~ Sir/Madam** sehr geehrter Herr X/sehr geehrte Frau X!, sehr verehrte gnädige Frau! (*geh*); (*no name known*) sehr geehrte Damen und Herren!; **~ Mr Kemp** sehr geehrter Herr Kemp!; (*less formal*) lieber Herr Kemp!; **D~ John letter** (*US inf*) Abschiedsbrief *m*.
(d) (*expensive*) *goods, shop* teuer; *prices also* hoch ◆ **to get ~er** (*goods*) teuer werden; (*prices*) steigen.
2 *interj* **~ ~!**, **~ me!** (ach) du liebe Zeit!, (du) meine Güte!; **oh ~!** oje!, ach du meine Güte *or* du liebe Zeit!
3 *n* **hello/thank you ~** hallo/vielen Dank; **Veronika/Robert ~** Veronika/Robert; **yes, ~** (*husband to wife etc*) ja, Schätzchen *or* Liebling; **Edward, my ~** (*elderly lady to nephew/brother etc*) mein lieber Edward, Edward, mein Lieber; **my ~est** meine Teuerste (*geh*), mein Teuerster (*geh*), (meine) Liebste, (mein) Liebster; **are you being served, ~?** (*inf*) werden Sie schon bedient?; **looking for company, ~?** (*inf*) suchst du Gesellschaft, Süßer?; **give it to me, there's a ~** (*inf*) gib es mir, sei (doch) so lieb *or* gut; **be a ~** (*inf*) sei so lieb *or* gut; **poor ~** die Arme, der Arme; **your mother is a ~** (*inf*) deine Mutter ist ein Engel (*inf*) *or* richtig lieb; **her little boy is such a little ~** ihr kleiner Junge ist ein süßer Knopf (*inf*); **this old ~ came up to me** dieses Muttchen kam zu mir her (*inf*).
4 *adv* (*lit, fig*) *buy, pay, sell* teuer.

dearie, deary ['dɪərɪ] *n* (*inf*) *usu not translated*; (*woman to child*) Kleine(r, s) ◆ **thanks for your help, ~** (*old woman*) vielen Dank für deine Hilfe, mein Kind/Sohn; **coming inside, ~?** (*tart*) kommst du rein, Süßer?

dearly ['dɪəlɪ] *adv* **(a)** (*very much*) *love* von ganzem Herzen ◆ **I should ~ like** *or* **love to live here** ich würde für mein Leben gern hier wohnen. **(b)** (*lit, fig*) *pay etc* teuer.

dearness ['dɪənɪs] *n* **(a)** (*expensiveness*) hoher Preis. **(b)** (*being loved*) **her ~ to him** daß sie ihm lieb und teuer war.

dearth [dɜ:θ] *n* Mangel *m* (*of* an *+dat*); (*of ideas*) Armut *f* (*of* an *+dat*) ◆ **~ of water/ideas** Wassermangel *m*/Gedankenarmut *f*; **there is no ~ of young men** an jungen Männern ist *or* herrscht kein Mangel.

deary *n see* **dearie**.

▼ **death** [deθ] *n* Tod *m*; (*of planet, city also, of plans, hopes etc*) Ende *nt* ◆ **~ to all traitors!** Tod allen Verrätern!; **D~ is portrayed as ...** der Tod wird als ... dargestellt; **to be afraid of ~** sich vor dem Tod fürchten; **to be burnt to ~** verbrennen; (*at stake*) verbrannt werden; **how many ~s were there?** wieviele Tote *or* Todesfälle gab es?; **to die a hero's ~** den Heldentod sterben; **a fight to the ~** ein Kampf auf Leben und Tod; **to put sb to ~** jdn hinrichten; **to do sb to ~** (*old*) jdn umbringen; **to drink oneself to ~** sich zu Tode trinken; **to work oneself to ~** sich totarbeiten; **he works his men to ~** er schindet seine Leute zu Tode; **to be at ~'s door** an der Schwelle des Todes stehen; **it will be the ~ of you** (*inf*) das wird dein Tod sein; **he will be the ~ of me** (*inf*) (*he's so funny*) ich lach' mich noch einmal tot über ihn (*inf*); (*he's annoying*) er bringt mich noch ins Grab; **to catch one's ~ (of cold)** (*inf*) sich (*dat*) den Tod holen; **I am sick to ~ of all this** (*inf*) das alles hängt mir gründlich zum Halse raus, ich bin das alles gründlich satt *or* leid; **he looked like ~ warmed**

➤ LANGUAGE IN USE: **deal¹: 1** → 26.1 **deal with: c** → 26.3 **death** → 24.4

up (*inf*) er sah wie der Tod auf Urlaub aus (*inf*).

death: ~bed *n* Sterbebett *nt*; **~bed scene** *n* Szene *f* am Sterbebett; **~ benefit** *n* (*Insur*) Versicherungsprämie *f* im Todesfall; **~-blow** *n* (*lit, fig*) Todesstoß *m*; **~ camp** *n* Vernichtungslager *nt*; **~ cell** *n* Todeszelle *f*; **~ certificate** *n* Sterbeurkunde *f*, Totenschein *m*; **~-dealing** *adj blow, missile* tödlich; **~ duties** *npl* (*Brit*) Erbschaftssteuern *pl*; **~ instinct** *n* (*Psych*) Todestrieb *m*; **~ knell** *n* (*fig*) Todesstoß *m*; **~less** *adj* unsterblich; **~like** *adj* totenähnlich.

deathly ['deθlɪ] [1] *adj* (*+er*) **(a)** **~ hush** *or* **stillness** Totenstille *f*; **~ silence** eisiges Schweigen; **~ pallor** Totenblässe *f*. **(b)** *blow etc* tödlich.
[2] *adv* **~ pale** totenbleich, leichenblaß.

death: ~-mask *n* Totenmaske *f*; **~ penalty** *n* Todesstrafe *f*; **~ rate** *n* Sterbeziffer *f*; **~-rattle** *n* Todesröcheln *nt*; **~ ray** *n* Todesstrahl *m*; **~-roll** *n* Verlust- *or* Gefallenenliste *f*; **~ row** *n* Todestrakt *m*; **~ sentence** *n* Todesurteil *nt*; **~'s head** *n* (*on flag etc*) Totenkopf *m*; **~'s head moth** *n* Totenkopf(schwärmer) *m*; **~ squad** *n* Todeskommando *nt*; **~ throes** *npl* (*lit, fig*) Todeskampf *m*; **in his ~ throes** im Todeskampf; **~ toll** *n* Zahl *f* der (Todes)opfer *or* Toten; **~-trap** *n* Todesfalle *f*; **~-warrant** *n* Hinrichtungsbefehl *m*; (*fig*) Todesurteil *nt*; **~-watch** *n* Totenwache *f*; **~-watch beetle** *n* Totenuhr *f*, Klopfkäfer *m*; **~-wish** *n* Todestrieb *m*.

deb [deb] *n* (*inf*) Debütantin *f*.

débâcle [de'bɑ:kl] *n* Debakel *nt* (*over* bei).

debag [ˌdi:'bæg] *vt* (*Brit inf*) die Hosen runterziehen (*+dat*).

debar [dɪ'bɑ:ʳ] *vt* (*from club, competition*) ausschließen (*from* von) ◆ **to ~ sb from doing sth** jdn davon ausschließen, etw zu tun.

debark [dɪ'bɑ:k] [1] *vi* sich ausschiffen, an Land gehen.
[2] *vt* ausschiffen; *troops* landen.

debarkation [ˌdi:bɑ:'keɪʃən] *n* Ausschiffung, Landung *f*; (*of troops*) Landen *nt*.

debarment [dɪ'bɑ:mənt] *n* Ausschluß *m* ◆ **his ~ from the club** sein Ausschluß aus dem Klub.

debase [dɪ'beɪs] *vt* **(a)** *person* erniedrigen, entwürdigen ◆ **to ~ oneself by doing sth** sich selbst so weit erniedrigen, daß man etw tut. **(b)** *virtues, qualities* mindern, herabsetzen. **(c)** *metal* verschlechtern; *coinage also* den Wert mindern von.

debasement [dɪ'beɪsmənt] *n see vt* **(a)** Erniedrigung, Entwürdigung *f*. **(b)** Minderung, Herabsetzung *f*. **(c)** Verschlechterung *f*; Wertminderung *f* ◆ **~ of the coinage** Münzverschlechterung *f*.

debatable [dɪ'beɪtəbl] *adj* fraglich; *frontier* umstritten ◆ **it's a ~ point whether ...** es ist fraglich, ob ...

debate [dɪ'beɪt] [1] *vt question* debattieren, diskutieren.
[2] *vi* debattieren, diskutieren (*with* mit, *about* über *+acc*) ◆ **he was debating with himself/his conscience whether to go or not** er überlegte hin und her, ob er gehen sollte.
[3] *n* Debatte *f* ◆ **after much ~** nach langer Debatte; **the ~ was on** *or* **about ...** die Debatte ging über ... (*+acc*); **the death penalty was under ~** zur Debatte stand die Todesstrafe.

debater [dɪ'beɪtəʳ] *n* Debattierer(in *f*), Debatter (*Press sl*) *m*.

debating [dɪ'beɪtɪŋ] [1] *n* Debattieren, Diskutieren *nt*.
[2] *adj attr* Debattier- ◆ **~ society** Debattierklub *m*.

debauch [dɪ'bɔ:tʃ] [1] *vt* verderben.
[2] *n* Orgie *f*.

debauched [dɪ'bɔ:tʃt] *adj person, look* verderbt; *life* zügellos, ausschweifend.

debauchee [ˌdebɔ:'tʃi:] *n* Wüstling, Lüstling *m*.

debauchery [dɪ'bɔ:tʃərɪ] *n* Ausschweifung, Debauche (*old*) *f* ◆ **a life of ~** ein zügelloses *or* ausschweifendes Leben.

debenture [dɪ'bentʃəʳ] *n* (*Fin*) Schuldschein *m*; (*Customs*) Rückzollschein *m*.

debenture: ~ bond *n* Schuldverschreibung, Obligation *f*; **~ stock** *n* Schuldverschreibungen, Obligationen *pl*.

debilitate [dɪ'bɪlɪteɪt] *vt* schwächen.

debilitating [dɪ'bɪlɪteɪtɪŋ] *adj* schwächend; *lack of funds etc also* lähmend; *shyness, self-doubt* hinderlich, hemmend.

debility [dɪ'bɪlɪtɪ] *n* Schwäche *f*.

debit ['debɪt] [1] *n* Schuldposten *m*, Debet *nt* ◆ **~ account/balance** Debetkonto *nt*/Soll- *or* Debetsaldo *m*; **to enter sth to the ~ side of an account** etw auf der Sollseite verbuchen; **on the ~ side** (*fig*) auf der Minusseite.
[2] *vt* **to ~ sb/sb's account with a sum, to ~ a sum to sb/sb's account** jdn/jds Konto mit einer Summe belasten *or* debitieren (*form*).

debit: ~ card *n* Kundenkarte *f*; **~ entry** *n* Abbuchung *f*.

debonair [ˌdebə'neəʳ] *adj* flott.

debouch [dɪ'baʊtʃ] *vi* (*troops*) hervorbrechen, debouchieren (*old*); (*river*) münden, sich ergießen.

Debrett [də'bret] *n* ≃ Gotha *m*.

debrief [ˌdi:'bri:f] *vt* befragen ◆ **to be ~ed** Bericht erstatten.

debriefing [ˌdi:'bri:fɪŋ] *n* (*also* **~ session**) Einsatzbesprechung *f* (nach dem Flug *etc*).

debris ['debri:] *n* Trümmer *pl*, Schutt *m*; (*Geol*) Geröll *nt*.

debt [det] *n* (*money owed, obligation*) Schuld *f* ◆ **~ of honour** Ehrenschuld *f*; **National D~** Staatsschulden *pl*, Verschuldung *f* der öffentlichen Hand; **to be in ~** verschuldet sein (*to* gegenüber); **to be £5 in ~** £ 5 Schulden haben (*to* bei); **he is in my ~** (*for money*) er hat Schulden bei mir; (*for help etc*) er steht in meiner Schuld; **to run** *or* **get into ~** Schulden machen, sich verschulden; **to get out of ~** aus den Schulden herauskommen; **to be out of ~** schuldenfrei sein; **to repay a ~** (*lit, fig*) eine Schuld begleichen; **I shall always be in your ~** ich werde ewig in Ihrer Schuld stehen; **to pay one's ~ to nature** das Zeitliche segnen.

debt: ~ collection agency *n* Inkassobüro *nt*; **~-collector** *n* Inkassobeauftragte(r) *mf*, Schuldeneintreiber *m* (*inf*).

debtor ['detəʳ] *n* Schuldner(in *f*) *m*.

debt rescheduling ['detrɪ'ʃedʒʊəlɪŋ] *n* Umschuldung *f*.

debug [ˌdi:'bʌg] *vt* **(a)** *mattress* entwanzen. **(b)** (*remove technical faults from*) die Fehler beseitigen bei. **(c)** (*remove bugging equipment from*) entwanzen (*sl*). **(d)** (*Comput*) entwanzen ◆ **~ging program** Fehlerkorrekturprogramm *nt*, Debugger *m*.

debugger [ˌdi:'bʌgəʳ] *n* (*Comput*) Debugger *m*.

debunk [ˌdi:'bʌŋk] *vt claim* entlarven; *politician* vom Sockel stoßen.

début ['deɪbju:] *n* (*lit, fig*) Debüt *nt* ◆ **to make one's ~** (*in society*) in die Gesellschaft eingeführt werden; (*Theat*) debütieren, sein Debüt geben; (*fig*) sein Debüt geben.

débutante ['debju:tɑ̃:nt] *n* Debütantin *f*.

dec *abbr of* **deceased** gest.

Dec *abbr of* **December** Dez.

decade ['dekeɪd] *n* **(a)** (*ten years*) Jahrzehnt *nt*, Dekade *f*. **(b)** (*Eccl: of rosary*) Gesätz *nt*.

decadence ['dekədəns] *n* Dekadenz *f*.

decadent ['dekədənt] [1] *adj* dekadent.
[2] *n* (*Liter*) Vertreter *m* der Dekadenz, Décadent *m* (*geh*).

de-caff ['di:kæf] *n abbr of* **decaffeinated** (*inf*) Koffeinfreie(r) *m* (*inf*).

decaffeinated [ˌdi:'kæfɪneɪtɪd] *adj* koffeinfrei, entkoffeiniert.

decagramme, (*US*) decagram ['dekəgræm] *n* Dekagramm *nt*.

decal [dɪ'kæl] *n* (*US*) Abziehbild *nt*; (*process*) Abziehen *nt*.

decalitre, (*US*) decaliter ['dekəˌli:təʳ] *n* Dekaliter *m or nt*.

decalogue ['dekəlɒg] *n* Dekalog *m*.

decametre, (*US*) decameter ['dekəˌmi:təʳ] *n* Dekameter *nt*.

decamp [dɪ'kæmp] *vi* **(a)** (*Mil*) das Lager abbrechen. **(b)** (*inf*) verschwinden, sich aus dem Staube machen (*inf*).

decant [dɪ'kænt] *vt* umfüllen, dekantieren (*form*).

decanter [dɪ'kæntəʳ] *n* Karaffe *f*.

decapitate [dɪ'kæpɪteɪt] *vt* enthaupten (*geh*), köpfen, dekapitieren (*form*) ◆ **she was ~d in the accident** bei dem Unfall wurde ihr der Kopf abgetrennt.

decapitation [dɪˌkæpɪ'teɪʃən] *n* Enthauptung *f* (*geh*).

decarbonization ['di:ˌkɑ:bənaɪ'zeɪʃən] *n* (*Aut*) Entkohlung, Dekarbonisierung *f*.

decarbonize [ˌdi:'kɑ:bənaɪz] *vt pistons etc* dekarbonisieren, entkohlen.

decasyllable ['dekəsɪləbl] *n* Zehnsilber *m*.

decathlete [dɪ'kæθli:t] *n* Zehnkämpfer *m*.

decathlon [dɪ'kæθlən] *n* Zehnkampf *m*.

decay [dɪ'keɪ] [1] *vi* **(a)** verfallen; (*building also, Phys*) zerfallen; (*rot*) (*dead body, flesh also, vegetable matter*) verwesen; (*food*) schlecht werden, verderben; (*tooth also*) schlecht werden, faulen; (*bones, wood also*) morsch werden.
(b) (*fig*) verfallen; (*health also*) sich verschlechtern; (*beauty also*) verblühen, vergehen; (*civilization, race*) untergehen; (*friendship*) auseinandergehen, zerfallen; (*one's faculties*) verkümmern; (*business, family*) herunterkommen ◆ **a ~ing old actress** eine verblühende alte Schauspielerin.
[2] *vt food* schlecht werden lassen, verderben; *tooth* faulen lassen, schlecht werden lassen; *wood* morsch werden lassen.
[3] *n* **(a)** *see vi (a)* Verfall *m*; Zerfall *m*; Verwesung *f*; Schlechtwerden *nt*; Morschwerden *nt* ◆ **it prevents (tooth) ~** es verhindert Zahnverfall; **to fall into ~** in Verfall geraten, verfallen.
(b) (*~ed part or area*) Fäule, Fäulnis *f*.
(c) (*fig*) Verfall *m*; (*of friendship, civilization*) Zerfall *m*; (*of race, family, business*) Untergang *m*; (*of faculties*) Verkümmern *nt*.

decayed [dɪ'keɪd] *adj wood etc* morsch; *tooth* faul; *food* schlecht; *body, vegetable matter* verwest.

decease [dɪ'si:s] (*Jur, form*) [1] *n* Ableben *nt* (*form*).
[2] *vi* sterben, verscheiden (*geh*).

deceased [dɪ'si:st] (*Jur, form*) [1] *adj* ge- *or* verstorben ◆ **John Brown, ~** der verstorbene John Brown.
[2] *n*: **the ~** der/die Tote *or* Verstorbene; die Toten *or* Verstorbenen *pl*.

deceit [dɪ'si:t] *n* Betrug *m no pl*, Täuschung *f* ◆ **these unending ~s** diese endlosen Täuschungsmanöver; **a character full of evil and ~** ein durch und durch übler und falscher Charakter.

deceitful [dɪ'si:tfʊl] *adj* falsch, betrügerisch.

deceitfully [dɪ'si:tfəlɪ] *adv* betrügerischerweise; *behave* falsch, betrügerisch.

deceitfulness [dɪ'si:tfʊlnɪs] *n* Falschheit *f*; (*deceitful acts*) Betrügereien *pl*.

deceive [dɪ'si:v] [1] *vt* täuschen, trügen (*geh*); *one's wife, husband* betrügen ◆ **to ~ sb into doing sth** jdn durch Täuschung dazu bringen, etw zu tun; **are my eyes deceiving me, — is it really you?** täuschen mich meine Augen, oder bist du es wirklich?; **to ~ oneself** sich (*dat*) selbst etwas vormachen; **his hopes were ~d** er sah sich in seinen Hoffnungen betrogen (*geh*).
[2] *vi* trügen (*geh*), täuschen.

deceiver [dɪ'si:vəʳ] *n* Betrüger(in *f*) *m*.

decelerate [di:'seləreɪt] [1] *vi* (*car, train*) langsamer werden; (*driver*) die Geschwindigkeit herabsetzen; (*production*) sich verlangsamen.
[2] *vt* verlangsamen.

deceleration ['di:ˌselə'reɪʃən] *n see vi* Langsamerwerden *nt*; Herabsetzung *f* der Geschwindigkeit; Verlangsamung *f*.

December [dɪ'sembəʳ] *n* Dezember *m*; *see also* **September**.

decency ['di:sənsɪ] *n* (*good manners etc*) Anstand *m*; (*of dress etc*) Anständigkeit *f*; (*of behaviour*) Schicklichkeit *f* ◆ **~ demands that ...** der Anstand fordert, daß ...; **it's only common ~ to ...** es gehört sich einfach, zu ...; **have you no sense of ~?** haben Sie denn kein Anstandsgefühl!; **to observe the decencies** den Anstand wahren; **for ~'s sake** anstandshalber; **he could have had/I hope you'll have the ~ to tell me** er hätte es mir anständigerweise auch sagen können/ich hoffe, du wirst die Anständigkeit besitzen, es mir zu sagen.

decent ['di:sənt] *adj (all senses)* anständig ◆ **are you ~?** *(inf)* bist du schon salonfähig? *(inf)*; **another gin? — very ~ of you** noch ein Gin? — sehr liebenswürdig!

decently ['di:səntlı] *adv* anständig ◆ **you can't ~ ask him ...** Sie können ihn jetzt kaum bitten ...; **he very ~ offered to help out** es war sehr anständig von ihm, seine Hilfe anzubieten.

decentralization ['di:,sentrəlaı'zeıʃən] *n* Dezentralisierung *f*.

decentralize [di:'sentrəlaız] *vti* dezentralisieren.

decentralized [di:'sentrəlaızd] *adj* dezentral.

deception [dı'sepʃən] *n* **(a)** *(act of deceiving)* Täuschung *f*, Betrug *m no pl (of* an *+dat)*; *(of wife etc)* Betrug *m* ◆ **all the little ~s we practise** all die kleinen Betrügereien, die wir verüben. **(b)** *(state of being deceived)* Täuschung *f*. **(c)** *(that which deceives)* Täuschung *f*.

deceptive [dı'septıv] *adj* irreführend; *similarity, side-step* täuschend; *simplicity* trügerisch ◆ **to be ~** täuschen, trügen *(geh)*; **appearances are** *or* **can be ~** der Schein trügt.

deceptively [dı'septıvlı] *adv* täuschend ◆ **the village looks ~ near** das Dorf scheint täuschend nahe; **he seemed ~ calm** seine Ruhe war täuschend echt.

deceptiveness [dı'septıvnıs] *n* Täuschende(s) *nt* ◆ **the ~ of the effects of perspective** die trügerischen Effekte der Perspektive; **beware of the ~ of statistics** Vorsicht, Statistiken sind irreführend.

decibel ['desıbel] *n* Dezibel *nt*.

▼ **decide** [dı'saıd] [1] *vt* **(a)** *(come to a decision)* (sich) entscheiden; *(take it into one's head)* beschließen, sich entschließen ◆ **what did you ~?** *(yes or no)* wie habt ihr euch entschieden?; *(what measures)* was habt ihr beschlossen?; **did you ~ anything?** habt ihr irgendwelche Entscheidungen getroffen?; **you must ~ what to do** du mußt (dich) entscheiden, was du tun willst; **you can't suddenly ~ you're going to leave home just like that** du kannst nicht plötzlich beschließen, daß du einfach von zu Hause weggehst; **I have ~d we are making a big mistake** ich bin zu der Ansicht gekommen, daß wir einen großen Fehler machen; **I'll ~ what we do!** ich bestimme, was wir tun!; **she always wants to ~ everything** sie will immer alles bestimmen; **the car seems to have ~d it's not going to start** das Auto scheint beschlossen zu haben, nicht anzuspringen; **the weather hasn't ~d what it's going to do yet** das Wetter hat (sich) noch nicht entschlossen, was es will.
(b) *(settle) question, war etc* entscheiden ◆ **to ~ sb's fate** jds Schicksal bestimmen, (über) jds Schicksal entscheiden.
(c) to ~ sb to do sth jdn veranlassen, etw zu tun; **that eventually ~d me** das hat schließlich für mich den Ausschlag gegeben.
[2] *vi* (sich) entscheiden ◆ **I don't know,** *you* **~** ich weiß nicht, entscheiden *or* bestimmen *Sie!*; **I don't know, I can't ~** ich kann mich nicht entscheiden; **to ~ for/ against sth** (sich) für/gegen etw entscheiden; **to ~ for** *or* **in favour of/against sb/sth** *(Jur)* zu jds Gunsten/Ungunsten *or* für/gegen jdn/etw entscheiden.

◆**decide on** *vi +prep obj* sich entscheiden für ◆ **the date which has been ~d ~** der Termin, für den man sich entschieden hat.

decided [dı'saıdıd] *adj* **(a)** *(clear, definite) improvement* entschieden; *difference* deutlich ◆ **there was a ~ smell of burning** es roch entschieden verbrannt. **(b)** *(determined) manner* entschlossen, bestimmt; *opinion* entschieden ◆ **it's my ~ opinion that ...** ich bin entschieden der Meinung, daß ....

decidedly [dı'saıdıdlı] *adv* **(a)** *(definitely)* entschieden ◆ **she is ~ lazy** sie ist (ganz) entschieden faul. **(b)** *act* entschlossen.

decider [dı'saıdə^r] *n* **(a) the ~ was that ...** was den Ausschlag gab, war, daß ..., ausschlaggebend war, daß ... **(b)** *(game)* Entscheidungsspiel *nt*; *(goal)* Entscheidungstreffer *m*.

deciding [dı'saıdıŋ] *adj* entscheidend; *factor also* ausschlaggebend; *game, goal also* Entscheidungs-.

deciduous [dı'sıdjʊəs] *adj tree* Laub-; *leaves* die jedes Jahr abfallen; *antler* das abgeworfen wird.

decimal ['desıməl] [1] *adj* Dezimal- ◆ **to three ~ places** auf drei Dezimalstellen; **to go ~** sich auf das Dezimalsystem umstellen; **~ point** Komma *nt*.
[2] *n* Dezimalzahl *f* ◆ **~s** Dezimalzahlen *pl*.

decimalization [,desıməlaı'zeıʃən] *n* Umstellung *f* auf das Dezimalsystem, Dezimalisierung *f (form)*.

decimalize ['desıməlaız] *vt system, currency* auf das Dezimalsystem umstellen, dezimalisieren *(form)*.

decimate ['desımeıt] *vt* dezimieren.

decipher [dı'saıfə^r] *vt (lit, fig)* entziffern.

decipherable [dı'saıfərəbl] *adj (lit, fig)* entzifferbar.

decision [dı'sıʒən] *n* **(a)** Entscheidung *f (on* über *+acc)*, Entschluß *m*; *(esp of committee etc)* Beschluß *m*; *(of judge)* Entscheidung *f* ◆ **to make a ~** eine Entscheidung treffen *or* fällen, einen Entschluß/Beschluß fassen; **she always wants to make all the ~s** sie will immer über alles bestimmen; **I can't make your ~s for you** ich kann nicht für dich entscheiden; **it's your ~** das mußt du entscheiden; **I can't give you a ~ now** ich kann das jetzt nicht entscheiden; **to come to a ~** zu einer Entscheidung kommen; **I've come to the ~ it's a waste of time** ich bin zu dem Schluß gekommen, daß Zeitverschwendung ist; **~s ~s!** immer diese Entscheidungen!
(b) *no pl (of character)* Entschlußkraft, Entschlossenheit *f* ◆ **a man of ~** ein Mann von Entschlußkraft.

decision: ~-maker *n* Entscheidungsträger *m*; **~-making** [1] *n* Entscheidungsfindung *f*; **to show an aptitude for ~-making** Entschlußkraft zeigen; **he's hopeless at ~-making** er kann einfach keine Entscheidungen treffen; [2] *adj attr* **~-making skills/abilities** Entschlußkraft *f*; **the ~-making function of management** die Aufgabe des Managements, Entschlüsse zu fassen *or* Entscheidungen zu treffen.

decisive [dı'saısıv] *adj* **(a)** entscheidend; *factor also* ausschlaggebend; *battle also* Entscheidungs-. **(b)** *manner, answer* bestimmt, entschlossen; *person* entschlußfreudig.

decisively [dı'saısıvlı] *adv see adj* **(a)** entscheidend. **(b)** bestimmt, entschlossen.

decisiveness [dı'saısıvnıs] *n see adj* **(a)** entscheidende Bedeutung ◆ **a victory of such ~** ein so entscheidender Sieg. **(b)** Bestimmtheit, Entschlossenheit *f*.

deck [dek] [1] *n* **(a)** *(Naut)* Deck *nt* ◆ **on ~** auf Deck; **to go up on ~** an Deck gehen; **to go (down) below ~(s)** unter Deck gehen.
(b) *(of bus, plane)* Deck *nt* ◆ **top** *or* **upper ~** Oberdeck *nt*.
(c) *(of cards)* Spiel *nt*.
(d) *(of record-player)* Laufwerk *nt*; *(part of hi-fi unit)* Plattenspieler *m* ◆ **tape ~** Tape-deck *nt*.
[2] *vt (also* **~ out)** schmücken ◆ **to ~ oneself out in one's Sunday best** sich in seinen Sonntagsstaat werfen *(inf)*, sich herausputzen; **all ~ed out in his Sunday best** ganz fesch in seinem Sonntagsstaat.

deck: ~ cabin *n* Deckkabine *f*; **~ cargo** *n* Deckladung *f*; **~chair** *n* Liegestuhl *m*.

-decker ['dekə^r] *n suf* -decker *m* ◆ *(Naut)* **a three-~** ein Dreidecker *m*; *see* **single-decker, double-decker.**

deck: ~-hand *n* Deckshelfer *m*; **~-house** *n* Deckshaus *nt*.

deckle-edge ['dekledʒ] *n* Büttenrand *m*.

deckle-edged ['dekledʒd] *adj* mit Büttenrand; *paper* Bütten-.

deck tennis *n* Decktennis *nt*.

declaim [dı'kleım] [1] *vi* deklamieren ◆ **to ~ against sth** gegen etw wettern.
[2] *vt* deklamieren, vortragen.

declamation [,deklə'meıʃən] *n* Deklamation *f*; *(against sth)* Tirade *f*.

declamatory [dı'klæmətərı] *adj* deklamatorisch, pathetisch.

declarable [dı'kleərəbl] *adj goods* verzollbar.

declaration [,deklə'reıʃən] *n (of love, war, income etc)* Erklärung *f*; *(Cards)* Ansage *f*; *(customs also)* Deklaration *f (form)* ◆ **~ of intent** Absichtserklärung *f*; **~ of love/bankruptcy** Liebeserklärung *f*/Konkursanmeldung *f*; **to make a ~** eine Erklärung abgeben; **~ of the results** *(Pol)* Bekanntgabe des Ergebnisses/der Ergebnisse.

▼ **declare** [dı'kleə^r] [1] *vt* **(a)** *intentions* erklären, kundtun *(geh)*; *results* bekanntgeben, veröffentlichen; *goods* angeben, deklarieren *(form)* ◆ **have you anything to ~?** haben Sie etwas zu verzollen?; **to ~ one's income** sein Einkommen angeben; **to ~ oneself** *or* **one's feelings** *(to a woman)* sich erklären; **to ~ war (on sb)** (jdm) den Krieg erklären; **to ~ sb bankrupt** jdn für bankrott erklären; **I ~ this meeting/motorway officially open** ich erkläre diese Sitzung/diese Autobahn für offiziell eröffnet; **I ~ this meeting closed** ich erkläre die Sitzung für geschlossen; **to ~ sb the winner** jdn zum Sieger erklären.
▼ **(b)** *(assert)* erklären, beteuern, versichern.
[2] *vi* **(a) to ~ for/against sb/sth** sich für/gegen jdn/etw erklären; **well I (do) ~!** *(dated)* ist es denn die Möglichkeit!
(b) *(Sport)* die Runde für beendet erklären.

declared [dı'kleəd] *adj* erklärt.

declaredly [dı'kleərıdlı] *adv* erklärtermaßen.

declassification [dı,klæsıfı'keıʃən] *n (of information)* Freigabe *f*.

declassify [di:'klæsıfaı] *vt information* freigeben.

declension [dı'klenʃən] *n (Gram)* Deklination *f*.

declinable [dı'klaınəbl] *adj (Gram)* deklinierbar.

▼ **decline** [dı'klaın] [1] *n* **(a)** *(in standards, birthrate, business, sales, prices)* Rückgang *m*; *(of empire, a party's supremacy)* Untergang, Niedergang *m* ◆ **to be on the ~** *see vi*; **at the ~ of his life/the day** *(liter)* als sein Leben/der Tag zur Neige ging *(liter)*.
(b) *(Med)* Verfall *m* ◆ **she went into a ~** es ging bergab mit ihr.
▼ [2] *vt* **(a)** *invitation, honour* ablehnen ◆ **he ~d to come** er hat es abgelehnt, zu kommen. **(b)** *(Gram)* deklinieren.
[3] *vi* **(a)** *(empire)* verfallen; *(fame)* verblassen; *(health)* sich verschlechtern; *(prices, business)* zurückgehen; *(importance, significance, value)* geringer werden; *(custom)* aussterben; *(popularity, enthusiasm, interest)* abnehmen; *(population, influence)* abnehmen, zurückgehen ◆ **cases of real poverty are declining** Fälle von echter Armut gibt es immer weniger.
(b) *(refuse, say no)* ablehnen.
(c) *(slope: ground)* abfallen.
(d) *(sun)* untergehen; *(liter: life, day)* zur Neige gehen *(liter)* ◆ **in his declining years** gegen Ende seiner Tage *(liter)*; **in declining health** bei schlechter werdender Gesundheit.
(e) *(Gram)* dekliniert werden.

declivity [dı'klıvıtı] *n* Abschüssigkeit *f*.

declutch [,di:'klʌtʃ] *vi* auskuppeln.

decoction [dı'kɒkʃən] *n* Abkochung *f*, Absud *m*; *(Pharm)* Dekokt *nt (spec)*.

decode [,di:'kəʊd] *vt* dekodieren, dechiffrieren, entschlüsseln; *(Comput, TV)* dekodieren.

decoder [,di:'kəʊdə^r] *n (Comput, TV)* Dekoder, Decoder, Dekodierer *m*.

➤ LANGUAGE IN USE: **decide: 1a** → 8.2 **declare: 1b** → 26.2 **decline: 2a** → 12.3

decoke [diː'kəʊk] *vt* entrußen.
decollate ['diːkɒleɪt] *vt* (*Comput*) trennen.
decollator ['diːkɒleɪtə^r] *n* (*Comput*) Formulartrenner *m*, Trennmaschine *f*.
décolletage [deɪ'kɒltɑːʒ], **décolleté** *n* Dekolleté *nt*, (tiefer) Ausschnitt.
décolleté [deɪ'kɒlteɪ] *adj* dekolletiert, (tief) ausgeschnitten.
decolonize [diː'kɒlənaɪz] *vt* entkolonisieren.
decommission [ˌdiːkə'mɪʃən] *vt power plant* stillegen; *warship* außer Dienst nehmen.
decompose [ˌdiːkəm'pəʊz] 1 *vt* (*Chem, Phys*) zerlegen; (*rot*) zersetzen.
2 *vi* zerlegt werden; (*rot*) sich zersetzen.
decomposition [ˌdiːkɒmpə'zɪʃən] *n* (*Phys: of light*) Zerlegung *f*; (*Chem also*) Abbau *m*; (*rotting*) Zersetzung *f*, Verfaulen *nt*.
decompress [ˌdiːkəm'pres] 1 *vt diver* einer Dekompression (*dat*) unterziehen.
2 *vi* sich einer Dekompression (*dat*) unterziehen.
decompression [ˌdiːkəm'preʃən] *n* Dekompression, Druckverminderung *f*.
decompression: ~ chamber *n* Dekompressionskammer *f*; **~ sickness** *n* Dekompressions- *or* Taucherkrankheit *f*.
decongestant [ˌdiːkən'dʒestənt] 1 *adj* abschwellend.
2 *n* abschwellendes Mittel; (*drops etc*) Nasentropfen *pl*/-spray *nt*.
deconstruct [ˌdiːkən'strʌkt] *vt* (*esp Liter*) dekonstruieren.
decontaminate [ˌdiːkən'tæmɪneɪt] *vt* entgiften, dekontaminieren (*form*); (*from radioactivity*) entseuchen.
decontamination ['diːkənˌtæmɪ'neɪʃən] *n* Entgiftung, Dekontamination (*form*) *f*; (*from radioactivity*) Entseuchung *f*, Dekontaminieren *nt*.
decontrol [ˌdiːkən'trəʊl] *vt* (*Comm*) *trade, prices* freigeben.
décor ['deɪkɔː^r] *n* (*in room*) Ausstattung *f*; (*Theat*) Dekor *m or nt* ◆ **he did his front room with a 1930s ~** er richtete sein vorderes Zimmer im Stil der dreißiger Jahre ein.
decorate ['dekəreɪt] *vt* **(a)** *cake, hat* verzieren; *street, building, Christmas tree* schmücken; *room* tapezieren; (*paint*) (an)streichen; (*for special occasion*) dekorieren. **(b)** *soldier* dekorieren, auszeichnen.
decorating ['dekəreɪtɪŋ] *n* Tapezieren *nt*; (*painting*) Streichen *nt*.
decoration [ˌdekə'reɪʃən] *n* **(a)** (*action*) *see vt (a)* Verzierung *f*; Schmücken *nt*; Tapezieren *nt*; (An)streichen *nt*; Dekoration *f*.
(b) (*ornament*) (*on cake, hat etc*) Verzierung *f*; (*on Christmas tree, building, in street*) Schmuck *m no pl* ◆ **Christmas ~s** Weihnachtsdekorationen *pl or* -schmuck *m*; **interior ~** Innenausstattung *f*; **his secretary is just for ~** seine Sekretärin ist nur zur Dekoration da.
(c) (*Mil*) Dekoration, Auszeichnung *f*.
decorative ['dekərətɪv] *adj* dekorativ.
decorator ['dekəreɪtə^r] *n* (*Brit*) Maler *m*.
decorous ['dekərəs] *adj action, behaviour* geziemend, schicklich; *dress* schicklich.
decorously ['dekərəslɪ] *adv see adj*.
decorum [dɪ'kɔːrəm] *n* Anstand *m*, Dekorum *nt* (*old, form*) ◆ **to have a sense of ~** Gefühl für Anstand haben; **to behave with ~** sich mit gebührendem Anstand benehmen.
decoy ['diːkɔɪ] 1 *n* (*lit, fig*) Köder *m*; (*person*) Lockvogel *m* ◆ **to act as a ~** als Köder fungieren; Lockvogel spielen; **police ~** Lockvogel *m* der Polizei; **~ manoeuvre** Falle *f*.
2 *vt* **(a)** *bird* anlocken. **(b)** *person* locken ◆ **to ~ sb into doing sth** jdn durch Lockmittel dazu bringen, etw zu tun.
decrease [diː'kriːs] 1 *vi* abnehmen; (*figures, output, life expectancy also, birthrate, production*) zurückgehen; (*strength, enthusiasm, intensity*) nachlassen; (*in knitting*) abnehmen ◆ **in decreasing order of importance** in der Reihenfolge ihrer Bedeutung; **it ~s in value** es verliert an Wert.
2 *vt* verringern, reduzieren.
3 ['diːkriːs] *n see vi* Abnahme *f*; Rückgang *m*; Nachlassen *nt*; Abnehmen *nt* ◆ **~ in speed** Verminderung *or* Abnahme *f* der Geschwindigkeit; **to be on the ~** *see vi*.
decreasingly [diː'kriːsɪŋlɪ] *adv* immer weniger ◆ **~ popular** immer unbeliebter.
decree [dɪ'kriː] 1 *n* Anordnung, Verordnung, Verfügung *f*; (*Pol, of king etc*) Erlaß *m*; (*Eccl*) Dekret *nt*; (*Jur*) Verfügung *f*; (*of tribunal, court*) Entscheid *m*, Urteil *nt* ◆ **by royal/government ~** auf königlichen Erlaß/auf Erlaß der Regierung; **to issue a ~** einen Erlaß herausgeben; **~ nisi/absolute** vorläufiges/ endgültiges Scheidungsurteil.
2 *vt* verordnen, verfügen ◆ **he ~d an annual holiday on 1st April** er erklärte den 1. April zum (ständigen) Feiertag.
decrepit [dɪ'krepɪt] *adj staircase etc* altersschwach; *building also* baufällig, heruntergekommen; *person also* klapprig (*inf*).
decrepitude [dɪ'krepɪtjuːd] *n see adj* Altersschwäche *f*; Baufälligkeit *f*; Klapprigkeit *f* (*inf*).
decriminalization [ˌdiːkrɪmɪnəlaɪ'zeɪʃən] *n* Entkriminalisierung *f*.
decriminalize [diː'krɪmɪnəlaɪz] *vt* entkriminalisieren.
decry [dɪ'kraɪ] *vt* schlechtmachen.
dedicate ['dedɪkeɪt] *vt* **(a)** *church* weihen. **(b)** *book, music* widmen (*to sb* jdm) ◆ **to ~ oneself** *or* **one's life to sb/sth** sich *or* sein Leben jdm/einer Sache widmen, sich einer Sache hingeben.
dedicated ['dedɪkeɪtɪd] *adj* **(a)** *attitude* hingebungsvoll; *service also* treu; (*in one's work*) engagiert ◆ **a ~ nurse/teacher** *etc* eine Krankenschwester/eine Lehrerin *etc*, die mit Leib und Seele bei der Sache ist; **to become a top-class dancer you have to be really ~** um ein erstklassiger Tänzer zu werden, muß man wirklich mit Leib und Seele dabei sein; **he is completely ~, he thinks of nothing but his work** er hat sich völlig seiner Arbeit verschrieben, er denkt an nichts anderes; **it's very ~ of you to stay on this late, Robinson** das ist sehr aufopfernd von Ihnen, so lange zu bleiben, Robinson.
(b) ~ word processor dediziertes Textverarbeitungssystem.
dedication [ˌdedɪ'keɪʃən] *n* **(a)** (*quality*) Hingabe *f* (*to* an *+acc*). **(b)** (*act*) (*of church*) Einweihung, Weihe *f* ◆ **his ~ of his life to helping the poor** daß er sein Leben in den Dienst der Armen gestellt hat. **(c)** (*in book*) Widmung *f*.
deduce [dɪ'djuːs] *vt* folgern, schließen (*from* aus); (*Logic*) deduzieren (*from* von).
deducible [dɪ'djuːsɪbl] *adj* zu schließen, ableitbar (*from* aus); (*Logic*) deduzierbar (*from* von).
deduct [dɪ'dʌkt] *vt* abziehen (*from* von); (*from wages also*) einbehalten ◆ **to ~ sth from the price** etw vom Preis ablassen; **to ~ sth for expenses** etwas für Spesen zurückbehalten; **to ~ income tax at source** Einkommenssteuer einbehalten; **after ~ing 5%** nach Abzug von 5%.
deductible [dɪ'dʌktəbl] *adj* abziehbar; (*tax ~*) absetzbar.
deduction [dɪ'dʌkʃən] *n* **(a)** (*act of deducting*) Abziehen *nt*, Abzug *m*; (*sth deducted*) (*from price*) Nachlaß *m* (*from* für, auf *+acc*); (*from wage*) Abzug *m*.
(b) (*act of deducing*) Folgern *nt*, Folgerung *f*; (*sth deduced*) (Schluß)folgerung *f*; (*Logic*) Deduktion *f* ◆ **by a process of ~** durch Folgern.
deductive [dɪ'dʌktɪv] *adj* deduktiv.
deed [diːd] 1 *n* **(a)** Tat, Handlung *f*; (*feat*) Tat, Leistung *f* ◆ **good ~** gute Tat; **in word and ~** in Wort und Tat; **to do a black** *or* **a foul ~** eine Gemeinheit begehen, etwas Böses *or* Gemeines tun.
(b) in ~ tatsächlich, in der Tat; **he is master in ~ if not in name** er ist der eigentliche *or* tatsächliche Herr, wenn auch nicht offiziell *or* nach außen hin.
(c) (*Jur*) Übertragungsurkunde *f* ◆ **the ~s of a house** die Übertragungsurkunde eines Hauses; **~ of covenant** Vertragsurkunde *f*.
2 *vt* (*US*) überschreiben (*to* auf *+acc*).
deed poll *n* (einseitige) Absichtserklärung.
deejay ['diːdʒeɪ] *n* (*inf*) Diskjockey *m*.
deem [diːm] *vt* **to ~ sb/sth (to be) sth** jdn/etw für etw erachten (*geh*) *or* halten; **he was ~ed worthy of the honour** (*geh*) er wurde der Ehre (*gen*) für würdig erachtet (*geh*) *or* gehalten.
deep [diːp] 1 *adj* (*+er*) **(a)** *water, hole, wound* tief ◆ **the pond/snow was 4 metres ~** der Teich war/der Schnee lag 4 Meter tief; **a two-metre ~ trench** ein zwei Meter tiefer Graben; **two metres ~ in snow/water** mit zwei Meter Schnee bedeckt/zwei Meter tief unter Wasser; **the ~ end** (*of swimming pool*) das Tiefe; **to go off (at) the ~ end** (*fig inf*) auf die Palme gehen (*inf*); **to go** *or* **plunge in at the ~ end** (*fig*) sich kopfüber in die Sache stürzen; **to be thrown in at the ~ end** (*fig*) gleich zu Anfang richtig ranmüssen (*inf*).
(b) *shelf, cupboard* tief; (*wide*) *border, edge* breit ◆ **a plot of ground 15 metres ~** ein 15 Meter tiefes Stück Land; **the spectators stood ten ~** die Zuschauer standen zu zehnt hintereinander.
(c) *voice, sound, note, colour* tief.
(d) *breathing, sigh* tief.
(e) (*fig*) *mystery, sleep, secret, mourning* tief; (*profound*) *thinker, book also, remark, writer* tiefsinnig; (*heartfelt*) *concern, relief, interest* groß; *sorrow* tief (empfunden); (*devious*) *person* verschlagen, hintergründig; *dealings* undurchsichtig ◆ **~ in thought/a book** in Gedanken/in ein Buch vertieft *or* versunken; **~ in debt** hoch verschuldet; **to be in ~ trouble** in großen Schwierigkeiten sein; **he's a ~ one** (*inf*) er ist ein ganz stilles Wasser, er ist ein ganz verschlagener Kerl.
2 *adv* (*+er*) ◆ **~ into the night** bis tief in die Nacht hinein; **to drink ~** (*liter*) (*one draught*) einen tiefen Zug tun; (*all evening*) viel trinken; **to breathe ~** tief atmen; **he's in it pretty ~** (*inf*) er steckt *or* hängt ganz schön tief da drin (*inf*).
3 *n* **(a)** (*liter*) **the ~** das Meer, die See.
(b) in the ~ of winter mitten im tiefsten Winter.
deepen ['diːpən] 1 *vt* (*lit, fig*) vertiefen; *concern, sorrow also* vergrößern; *love, friendship also* verstärken; *colour also* dunkler machen; *mystery* vergrößern; *sound* tiefer machen.
2 *vi* (*lit, fig*) sich vergrößern, tiefer werden; (*sorrow, concern, interest*) zunehmen, größer werden; (*colour, sound, voice*) tiefer werden; (*mystery*) größer werden.
deepening ['diːpənɪŋ] 1 *adj sorrow, concern etc* zunehmend, wachsend; *friendship, love also* sich vertiefend; *colour, mystery* sich vertiefend, tiefer werdend.
2 *n* (*of hole, mystery*) Vergrößerung *f*; (*of sorrow, interest, concern*) Zunahme *f*; (*of friendship, love*) Vertiefung *f*.
deep: ~-freeze 1 *n* Tiefkühltruhe *f*; (*upright*) Gefrierschrank *m*; 2 *vt* einfrieren; **~-freezing** *n* Einfrieren, Tiefgefrieren *nt*; **~-frozen** *adj* tiefgefroren; **~-frozen foods** Tiefkühlkost *f*; **~-fry** *vt* fritieren, im schwimmenden Fett backen; **~ grammar** *n* Tiefengrammatik *f*; **~ kiss** *n* Zungenkuß *m*; **~-laid** *adj*, *comp* **~er-laid** *plot* (sorgfältig) ausgetüftelt (*inf*) *or* ausgearbeitet.
deeply ['diːplɪ] *adv* **(a)** *cut, breathe* tief; *think also* gründlich; *drink* schwer ◆ **to go ~ into sth** sich gründlich mit etw befassen. **(b)** *grateful, concerned* zutiefst; *offended also, indebted* tief; *love* innig(lich); *interested* höchst; *aware* voll(kommen).
deepness ['diːpnɪs] *n* (*lit, fig*) Tiefe *f*; (*of border, edge*) Breite *f*; (*profundity: of thinker, remark etc*) Tiefsinnigkeit *f*; (*of concern, relief, interest*) Größe *f*.
deep: ~-ray therapy *n* Tiefenbestrahlung *f*; **~-rooted** *adj*, *comp* **~er-rooted** (*fig*) tiefverwurzelt; **~-sea** *adj plant, current* Meeres-; *animal also*

Tiefsee-; **~-sea diver** *n* Tiefseetaucher *m*; **~-sea fishery** *or* **fishing** *n* Hochseefischerei *f*; **~-seated** *adj, comp* **~er-seated** tiefsitzend; **~-set** *adj, comp* **~er-set** tiefliegend; **D~ South** *n* Tiefer Süden; **~ space** *n* der äußere Weltraum; **~ structure** *n (Ling)* Tiefenstruktur *f*; **~-throated** [ˈdiːpˌθrəʊtɪd] *adj* kehlig.

deer [dɪəʳ] *n, pl* - Hirsch *m*; *(roe ~)* Reh *nt* ◆ **the (red/fallow) ~ in the forest** das (Rot-/Dam)wild im Wald.

deer: ~-hound *n* Deerhound *m*; **~-park** *n* Wildpark *m*; **~skin** *n* Hirsch-/Rehleder *nt*; **~stalker** *n* **(a)** *(person) jd, der auf die Pirsch geht*; **(b)** *(hat)* ≃ Sherlock-Holmes-Mütze *f*; **~stalking** *n* Pirschen *nt*, Pirsch *f*; **to go ~stalking** auf die Pirsch gehen.

de-escalate [ˌdiːˈeskəleɪt] *vt* deeskalieren.

de-escalation [ˌdiːeskəˈleɪʃən] *n* Deeskalation *f*.

deface [dɪˈfeɪs] *vt* verunstalten.

de facto [deɪˈfæktəʊ] *adj, adv* de facto.

defamation [ˌdefəˈmeɪʃən] *n* Diffamierung, Verleumdung *f* ◆ **~ of character** Rufmord *m*.

defamatory [dɪˈfæmətərɪ] *adj* diffamierend, verleumderisch.

defame [dɪˈfeɪm] *vt* diffamieren, verleumden.

default [dɪˈfɔːlt] [1] *n* **(a)** *(failure to appear) (Jur)* Nichterscheinen *nt* vor Gericht; *(Sport)* Nichtantreten *nt*; *(failure to perform duty)* Versäumnis *f*; *(failure to pay)* Nichtzahlung *f* ◆ **judgement by ~** *(Jur)* Versäumnisurteil *nt*; **to win by ~** *(Sport)* kampflos gewinnen.
(b) *(lack, absence)* Mangel *m* ◆ **in ~ of, due to ~ of** in Ermangelung *+gen*.
(c) [ˈdiːfɔːlt] *(Comput)* Default *m*, Voreinstellung *f*.
[2] *vi (not appear) (Jur)* nicht erscheinen; *(Sport)* nicht antreten; *(not perform duty, not pay)* säumig sein ◆ **to ~ in one's payments** seinen Zahlungsverpflichtungen nicht nachkommen; **it always ~s to drive C** *(Comput)* es wird immer das Laufwerk C angesprochen.
[3] *attr (Comput)* Default-*drive* Standard-; *parameter* voreingestellt.

defaulter [dɪˈfɔːltəʳ] *n see* **default 1 (a)** nichterscheinende Partei; nichtantretender Spieler, nichtantretende Spielerin; Säumige(r) *mf*; säumiger Zahler; *(Mil, Naut)* Straffällige(r) *mf*.

defeat [dɪˈfiːt] [1] *n (defeating)* Besiegung *f*, Sieg *m (of* über *+acc)*; *(of motion, bill)* Ablehnung *f*; *(of hopes, plans)* Vereitelung *f*; *(being defeated)* Niederlage *f* ◆ **their ~ of/by the enemy** ihr Sieg über den Feind/ihre Besiegung *or* Niederlage durch den Feind; **to admit ~** sich geschlagen geben; **to suffer a ~** eine Niederlage erleiden.
[2] *vt army, team* besiegen, schlagen; *government also* eine (Abstimmungs)Niederlage beibringen *(+dat)*; *motion, bill* ablehnen; *hopes, plans* vereiteln ◆ **to ~ one's own ends** *or* **object** sich *(dat or acc)* ins eigene Fleisch schneiden; **that would be ~ing the purpose of the exercise** dann verliert die Übung ihren Sinn; **it ~s me why ...** *(inf)* es will mir einfach nicht in den Kopf, warum ... *(inf)*.

defeatism [dɪˈfiːtɪzəm] *n* Defätismus *m*.

defeatist [dɪˈfiːtɪst] [1] *n* Defätist *m*.
[2] *adj* defätistisch.

defecate [ˈdefəkeɪt] *vi* den Darm entleeren, defäkieren *(form)*.

defecation [ˌdefəˈkeɪʃən] *n* Entleerung *f* des Darms, Defäkation *f (form)*.

defect[1] [ˈdiːfekt] *n* Fehler, Schaden *m*; *(in mechanism also)* Defekt *m* ◆ **physical ~** körperlicher Schaden *or* Defekt; **a character ~** ein Charakterfehler *m*.

defect[2] [dɪˈfekt] *vi (Pol)* sich absetzen; *(fig)* abtrünnig werden, abfallen ◆ **to ~ to the enemy** zum Feind überlaufen.

defection [dɪˈfekʃən] *n (Pol)* Überlaufen *nt*; *(fig)* Abtrünnigkeit *f*, Abfall *m*.

defective [dɪˈfektɪv] [1] *adj* **(a)** *material etc* fehlerhaft; *machine also* defekt; *(fig) reasoning etc* fehlerhaft; *hearing, sight* mangelhaft, gestört ◆ **his heart/liver is ~** bei ihm ist die Herz-/Lebertätigkeit gestört. **(b)** *(Gram)* unvollständig, defektiv. **(c)** *(mentally ~)* geistesgestört.
[2] *n* **(a)** *(Gram)* Defektivum *nt*.
(b) *(retarded person)* Geistesgestörte(r) *mf*.

defence, (US) defense [dɪˈfens] *n* **(a)** *no pl* Verteidigung *f no pl* ◆ **in his ~** zu seiner Verteidigung; **to come to sb's ~** jdn verteidigen; **to put up a stubborn ~** sich hartnäckig verteidigen; **his only ~ was ...** seine einzige Rechtfertigung war ....
(b) *(form of protection)* Abwehr- *or* Schutzmaßnahme *f*; *(Mil: fortification etc)* Befestigung, Verteidigungsanlage *f* ◆ **as a ~ against** als Schutz gegen; **his ~s were down** er war wehrlos; **she caught me when my ~s were down** sie erwischte mich in einem schwachen Augenblick *(inf)*.
(c) *(Jur, Sport)* Verteidigung *f*.

defence: ~ counsel *n* Verteidiger(in *f*) *m*; **~ expenditure** *n* Verteidigungsausgaben *pl*; **~less** *adj* schutzlos; **~ mechanism** *n (Physiol, Psych)* Abwehrmechanismus *m*; **~ minister** *n* Verteidigungsminister *m*; **~ witness** *n* Zeuge *m*/Zeugin *f* der Verteidigung.

defend [dɪˈfend] *vt* verteidigen *(also Jur) (against* gegen) ◆ **to ~ oneself** sich verteidigen.

defendant [dɪˈfendənt] [1] *n* Angeklagte(r) *mf*; *(in civil cases)* Beklagte(r) *mf*.
[2] *adj* angeklagt; beklagt.

defender [dɪˈfendəʳ] *n* Verteidiger *m* ◆ **D~ of the Faith** Fidei Defensor *m*.

defending [dɪˈfendɪŋ] *adj*: **~ counsel** Verteidiger(in *f*) *m*.

defense *etc* [dɪˈfens] *(US) see* **defence** *etc*.

defensible [dɪˈfensɪbl] *adj* **(a)** *(lit)* wehrhaft ◆ **because of its position the town wasn't ~** die Stadt war wegen ihrer Lage nicht zu verteidigen. **(b)** *(justifiable) behaviour, argument* vertretbar, zu verteidigen *pred*.

defensive [dɪˈfensɪv] [1] *adj* defensiv *(also fig)*, Verteidigungs- ◆ **a good ~ player** ein guter Verteidiger.
[2] *n (Mil)* Verteidigungs- *or* Abwehraktion *f* ◆ **to be on the ~** *(Mil, fig)* in der Defensive sein; **to go onto the ~** *(fig)* sich in die Defensive begeben.

defer[1] [dɪˈfɜːʳ] *vt (delay)* verschieben; *event also* verlegen ◆ **to ~ doing sth** es verschieben, etw zu tun.

defer[2] *vi (submit)* **to ~ to sb/sb's wishes** sich jdm beugen *or* fügen/sich jds Wünschen *(dat)* fügen.

deference [ˈdefərəns] *n* Achtung *f*, Respekt *m* ◆ **out of** *or* **in ~ to** aus Achtung *(dat) or* Respekt *(dat)* vor; **with all due ~ to you** bei aller schuldigen Achtung *or* allem schuldigen Respekt Ihnen gegenüber.

deferential [ˌdefəˈrenʃəl] *adj* ehrerbietig, respektvoll ◆ **to be ~ to sb** jdm mit Respekt *or* Achtung begegnen.

deferentially [ˌdefəˈrenʃəlɪ] *adv see adj*.

deferment [dɪˈfɜːmənt] *n see* **defer[1]** Verschiebung *f*, Verlegung *f*.

deferred [dɪˈfɜːd] *adj* **~ shares** Nachzugsaktien *pl*; **~ annuity** nach bestimmter Zeit fällige Rente; **~ pay** *(Mil)* einbehaltener Sold; *(Naut)* einbehaltene Heuer; **sale on the ~ payment system** Verkauf *m* auf Ratenzahlungsbasis, Ratenzahlungs- *or* Abzahlungsgeschäft *nt*; **~ taxation** Steuerrückstellung *f*; **~ terms** Teilzahlung *f*.

defiance [dɪˈfaɪəns] *n* Trotz *m (of sb* jdm gegenüber); *(of order, law also, of death, danger)* Mißachtung *f (of gen)* ◆ **an act of ~** eine Trotzhandlung; **in ~ of sb/sb's orders** jdm/jds Anordnungen zum Trotz, jds Anordnungen mißachtend; **that is in ~ of the laws of nature** das widerspricht den Gesetzen der Natur.

defiant [dɪˈfaɪənt] *adj (rebellious)* aufsässig; *esp child also, answer* trotzig; *(challenging) attitude* herausfordernd.

defiantly [dɪˈfaɪəntlɪ] *adv see adj*.

deficiency [dɪˈfɪʃənsɪ] *n (shortage)* Mangel *m*; *(Fin)* Defizit *nt*, Fehlbetrag *m*; *(defect: in character, system)* Schwäche *f* ◆ **vitamin/iron ~** Vitamin-/Eisenmangel *m*; **~ disease** *(Med)* Mangelkrankheit *f*.

deficient [dɪˈfɪʃənt] *adj* unzulänglich ◆ **sb/sth is ~ in sth** jdm/einer Sache fehlt es an etw *(dat)*; *see* **mentally**.

deficit [ˈdefɪsɪt] *n* Defizit *nt*.

defile[1] [ˈdiːfaɪl] [1] *n* Hohlweg *m*
[2] *vi* hintereinander marschieren.

defile[2] [dɪˈfaɪl] *vt (pollute, sully)* verschmutzen, verunreinigen; *(desecrate)* schänden, entweihen.

defilement [dɪˈfaɪlmənt] *n* Verschmutzung, Verunreinigung *f*; *(desecration)* Schändung, Entweihung *f*.

definable [dɪˈfaɪnəbl] *adj see vt* definierbar; bestimmbar; erklärbar.

define [dɪˈfaɪn] *vt* **(a)** *word* definieren; *conditions, boundaries, powers, duties also* bestimmen, festlegen; *feeling, attitude also* erklären. **(b)** *(show in outline)* betonen ◆ **clearly/not well ~d** scharf/nicht scharf; **to be clearly ~d against the sky** sich klar *or* scharf gegen den Himmel abzeichnen.

definite [ˈdefɪnɪt] *adj* **(a)** *(fixed, concrete, explicit)* definitiv; *answer, decision, possibility also* klar, eindeutig; *agreement, date, plan, decision, intention, wish also* fest; *command, request* bestimmt ◆ **is that ~?** ist das sicher?; *(agreed by contract etc also)* steht das fest?; **we've arranged to meet at 5, that's ~** wir haben fest abgemacht, uns um 5 Uhr zu treffen.
(b) *(distinct, pronounced) mark, stain, lisp* deutlich; *advantage, improvement also* klar, eindeutig; *problem* echt.
(c) *(positive, decided) tone, manner* bestimmt ◆ **she was very ~ about it** sie war sich *(dat)* sehr sicher.
(d) *(Gram)* definitiv.

▼ **definitely** [ˈdefɪnɪtlɪ] *adv* **(a)** *decide, agree, arrange* fest, definitiv. **(b)** *(without doubt)* bestimmt ◆ **he ~ wanted to come** er wollte bestimmt kommen; **that's ~ an improvement/advantage** das ist zweifelsohne *or* ganz sicherlich eine Verbesserung/ein Vorteil. **(c)** *(positively, decidedly) speak* bestimmt.

definiteness [ˈdefɪnɪtnɪs] *n* **(a)** *see adj (a)* Definitive *nt*; Klarheit, Eindeutigkeit *f*. **(b)** *see adj (c)* Bestimmtheit *f*.

definition [ˌdefɪˈnɪʃən] *n* **(a)** *(of word, concept)* Definition *f* ◆ **by ~** per definitionem, definitionsgemäß. **(b)** *(of powers, duties, boundaries)* Festlegung, Bestimmung *f*. **(c)** *(Phot, TV)* Bildschärfe *f*; *(Rad)* Tonschärfe *f*; *(Opt: of lens)* Schärfe *f*.

definitive [dɪˈfɪnɪtɪv] [1] *adj (decisive) victory, answer* entschieden; *(authoritative) book* maßgeblich *(on* für); *(defining) laws* Rahmen-; *term* beschreibend.
[2] *n (stamp)* Briefmarke *f* einer Dauerserie.

definitively [dɪˈfɪnɪtɪvlɪ] *adv see adj*.

deflate [ˌdiːˈfleɪt] [1] *vt tyre, balloon* etwas/die Luft ablassen aus ◆ **to ~ the currency** *(Fin)* eine Deflation herbeiführen; **he was a bit ~d when ...** es war ein ziemlicher Dämpfer für ihn, daß ...
[2] *vi (Fin)* eine Deflation herbeiführen.

deflation [ˌdiːˈfleɪʃən] *n (of tyre, ball)* Luftablassen *nt (of* aus); *(Fin)* Deflation *f*.

deflationary [ˌdiːˈfleɪʃənərɪ] *adj (Fin)* Deflations-, deflationistisch.

deflect [dɪˈflekt] [1] *vt* ablenken; *ball, bullet also* abfälschen; *steam, air current also* ableiten; *(Phys) light* beugen.
[2] *vi (compass needle)* ausschlagen; *(projectile)* abweichen.

deflection [dɪˈflekʃən] *n see vb* Ablenkung *f*, Abfälschung *f*, Ableitung *f*, Beugung *f*; Ausschlag *m*; Abweichung *f*.

deflective [dɪˈflektɪv] *adj* ablenkend; *(Phys)* beugend.

deflector [dɪˈflektəʳ] *n* Deflektor *m*, Ablenkvorrichtung *f*.

defloration [ˌdiːflɔːˈreɪʃən] *n (liter: of girl)* Entjungferung, Defloration *f*.

deflower [ˌdiːˈflaʊəʳ] *vt (liter) girl* entjungfern, deflorieren.

➤ LANGUAGE IN USE: **definitely: b → 8.2**

defoliant [ˌdiːˈfəʊlɪənt] *n* Entlaubungsmittel *nt.*
defoliate [ˌdiːˈfəʊlɪeɪt] *vt* entlauben, entblättern.
defoliation [ˌdiːfəʊlɪˈeɪʃən] *n* Entlaubung *f.*
deforest [ˌdiːˈfɒrɪst] *vt* entwalden.
deforestation [diːˌfɒrɪˈsteɪʃən] *n* Entwaldung *f.*
deform [dɪˈfɔːm] *vt* deformieren, verunstalten; (*Tech*) verformen; *mind, tastes* verderben.
deformation [ˌdiːfɔːˈmeɪʃən] *n see vt* Deformierung, Deformation, Verunstaltung *f*; Verformung *f*; Verderben *nt.*
deformed [dɪˈfɔːmd] *adj* deformiert, verunstaltet; (*Tech*) verformt; *person, limb also* mißgestaltet; *mind* krankhaft.
deformity [dɪˈfɔːmɪtɪ] *n see adj* Deformität, Verunstaltung *f*, Verformung *f*; Mißgestalt *f*; Krankhaftigkeit *f.*
defraud [dɪˈfrɔːd] *vt* betrügen, hintergehen ◆ **to ~ sb of sth** jdn um etw betrügen *or* bringen.
defrauder [dɪˈfrɔːdə^r] *n* Betrüger(in *f*) *m.*
defray [dɪˈfreɪ] *vt* tragen, übernehmen.
defrayal [dɪˈfreɪəl], **defrayment** [dɪˈfreɪmənt] *n* Übernahme *f.*
defrock [ˌdiːˈfrɒk] *vt* aus dem Priesteramt verstoßen.
defrost [ˌdiːˈfrɒst] *vti fridge, windscreen* entfrosten, abtauen; *food* auftauen.
defroster [ˌdiːˈfrɒstə^r] *n* Defroster, Entfroster *m.*
deft *adj* (*+er*), **~ly** *adv* [deft, -lɪ] flink, geschickt.
deftness [ˈdeftnɪs] *n* Flinkheit, Geschicktheit *f.*
defunct [dɪˈfʌŋkt] *adj person* verstorben; (*fig*) *institution etc* eingegangen; *idea* untergegangen; *law* außer Kraft.
defuse [ˌdiːˈfjuːz] *vt* (*lit, fig*) entschärfen.
defy [dɪˈfaɪ] *vt* **(a)** (*refuse to submit to, disobey*) *person* sich widersetzen (*+dat*); (*esp child also*) trotzen (*+dat*); *orders, law, death, danger* verachten, trotzen (*+dat*).
(b) (*fig: make impossible*) widerstehen (*+dat*) ◆ **the suitcase defied our efforts to close it** der Koffer widerstand unseren Bemühungen, ihn zu schließen; **to ~ definition** nicht definiert werden können; **to ~ description** jeder Beschreibung spotten.
(c) (*challenge*) **I ~ you to do it/to buy one more cheaply** machen Sie es doch/kaufen Sie doch einen billigeren(, wenn Sie können).
degeneracy [dɪˈdʒenərəsɪ], **degenerateness** *n* Degeneration *f.*
degenerate [dɪˈdʒenərɪt] **1** *adj* degeneriert; *race, morals also* entartet.
2 *n* degenerierter Mensch.
3 [dɪˈdʒenəreɪt] *vi* degenerieren; (*people, morals also*) entarten.
degenerateness [dɪˈdʒenərɪtnɪs] *n see* **degeneracy.**
degeneration [dɪˌdʒenəˈreɪʃən] *n see vi* Degeneration *f*; Entartung *f.*
degenerative [dɪˈdʒenərətɪv] *adj* (*Med*) Abbau-.
degradation [ˌdegrəˈdeɪʃən] *n see vt* Erniedrigung *f*; Degradierung *f*; Erosion *f*; Abbau *m.*
degrade [dɪˈgreɪd] *vt* erniedrigen; (*esp Mil: lower in rank*) degradieren; (*Geol*) erodieren; (*Chem*) abbauen ◆ **to ~ oneself** sich erniedrigen; **I wouldn't ~ myself by doing that** ich würde mich nicht dazu erniedrigen, das zu tun.
degrading [dɪˈgreɪdɪŋ] *adj* erniedrigend.
degree [dɪˈgriː] *n* **(a)** (*unit of measurement*) Grad *m no pl* ◆ **an angle of 90 ~s** ein Winkel *m* von 90 Grad; **it was 35 ~s in the shade** es waren 35 Grad im Schatten.
(b) (*extent*) (*of risk, uncertainty etc*) Maß *nt* ◆ **to some ~, to a (certain) ~** einigermaßen, zu einem gewissen Grad, in gewissem Maße; **to a high ~** in hohem Maße; **to such a ~ that ...** so sehr *or* in solchem Maße, daß ...; **to what ~ was he involved?** wieweit *or* in welchem Maße war er verwickelt?
(c) (*step in scale*) Grad *m* ◆ **~ of kinship/consanguinity** Verwandschaftsgrad *m*; **by ~s** nach und nach; **first/second ~ murder** (*Jur*) Mord *m* /Totschlag *m.*
(d) (*Univ*) akademischer Grad ◆ **first/higher (academic) ~** erster/höherer akademischer Grad; **to do a ~** studieren; **when did you do your ~?** wann haben Sie das Examen gemacht?; **I'm taking** *or* **doing a science ~** *or* **a ~ in science** ich studiere Naturwissenschaften; **to get one's ~** seinen akademischen Grad erhalten.
(e) (*position in society*) Rang, Stand *m.*
degree: ~ course *n* Universitätskurs, der mit dem ersten akademischen Grad abschließt; **~ day** *n* Tag *m* der Gradverleihung.
dehumanize [ˌdiːˈhjuːmənaɪz] *vt* entmenschlichen.
dehydrate [ˌdiːhaɪˈdreɪt] *vt* Wasser entziehen (*+dat*), dehydrieren (*spec*).
dehydrated [ˌdiːhaɪˈdreɪtɪd] *adj* dehydriert (*spec*); *vegetables, milk also* Trocken-; *milk, eggs also* pulverisiert; *person, skin also* ausgetrocknet.
dehydration [ˌdiːhaɪˈdreɪʃən] *n* Austrocknung, Dehydration (*spec*) *f*; (*of vegetables, milk etc*) Trocknung, Dehydration (*spec*) *f.*
de-ice [ˌdiːˈaɪs] *vt* enteisen.
de-icer [ˌdiːˈaɪsə^r] *n* Enteiser *m*; (*spray for cars*) Defroster *m.*
deictic [ˈdaɪktɪk] *adj* (*Ling*) deiktisch.
deification [ˌdiːɪfɪˈkeɪʃən] *n* Vergötterung *f.*
deify [ˈdiːɪfaɪ] *vt* vergöttern.
deign [deɪn] *vt* **to ~ to do sth** geruhen *or* sich herablassen, etw zu tun; **he didn't ~ to** er ließ sich nicht dazu herab.
deism [ˈdiːɪzəm] *n* Deismus *m.*
deist [ˈdiːɪst] *n* Deist(in *f*) *m.*
deity [ˈdiːɪtɪ] *n* Gottheit *f* ◆ **the D~** Gott *m.*
deixis [ˈdaɪksɪs] *n* (*Ling*) Deixis *f.*
déjà vu [ˈdeɪʒɑːˈvjuː] *n* Déjà-vu-Erlebnis *nt* ◆ **a feeling** *or* **sense of ~** das Gefühl, das schon einmal gesehen zu haben.
deject [dɪˈdʒekt] *vt* deprimieren.

dejected *adj*, **~ly** *adv* [dɪˈdʒektɪd, -lɪ] niedergeschlagen, deprimiert.
dejection [dɪˈdʒekʃən] *n* Niedergeschlagenheit, Depression *f.*
de jure [ˌdiːˈdʒʊərɪ] *adj, adv* de jure.
dekko [ˈdekəʊ] *n* (*Brit inf*) kurzer Blick (*at* auf *+acc*) ◆ **let's have a ~ (at it)** (*show me*) laß (das) mal sehen; (*let's go and see it*) gucken wir uns das mal an.
delay [dɪˈleɪ] **1** *vt* **(a)** (*postpone*) verschieben, aufschieben ◆ **to ~ doing sth** es verschieben *or* aufschieben, etw zu tun; **he ~ed paying until ...** er wartete solange mit dem Zahlen, bis ...; **he ~ed writing the letter** er schob den Brief auf; **rain ~ed play** der Beginn des Spiels verzögerte sich wegen Regens.
(b) (*hold up*) *person, train, traffic* aufhalten.
2 *vi* **to ~ in doing sth** es verschieben *or* aufschieben, etw zu tun; **if you ~ too long in booking** wenn Sie zu lange mit der Buchung warten; **he ~ed in paying the bill** er schob die Zahlung der Rechnung hinaus; **don't ~!** verlieren Sie keine Zeit!, tun Sie es unverzüglich!; **don't ~ in sending it in** senden Sie es unverzüglich ein.
3 *n* (*hold-up*) Aufenthalt *m*; (*to traffic*) Stockung *f*; (*to train, plane*) Verspätung *f*; (*time lapse*) Verzögerung *f* ◆ **to have a ~** aufgehalten werden; **roadworks are causing ~s to traffic of up to 1 hour** Straßenbauarbeiten verursachen Verkehrsstockungen bis zu 1 Stunde; **there are ~s to all trains** alle Züge haben Verspätung; **a split second's ~** eine Verzögerung von einem Bruchteil einer Sekunde; **without ~** unverzüglich; **without further ~** ohne weitere Verzögerung.
delayed-action [dɪˈleɪdˌækʃən] *adj attr bomb, mine* mit Zeitzünder ◆ **~ shutter release** (*Phot*) Selbstauslöser *m.*
delaying [dɪˈleɪɪŋ] *adj action* verzögernd, hinhaltend, Verzögerungs- ◆ **~ tactics** Verzögerungs- *or* Hinhaltetaktik *f.*
delectable [dɪˈlektəbl] *adj* köstlich; (*fig*) reizend.
delectation [ˌdiːlekˈteɪʃən] *n* **for sb's ~** als besonderen Genuß für jdn.
delegate [ˈdelɪgeɪt] **1** *vt person* delegieren; *authority, power, job also* übertragen (*to sb* jdm) ◆ **to ~ sb to do sth** jdn dazu abordnen *or* damit beauftragen, etw zu tun.
2 *vi* delegieren ◆ **you must ~ more** Sie sollten nicht alles selber machen.
3 [ˈdelɪgət] *n* Delegierte(r) *mf.*
delegation [ˌdelɪˈgeɪʃən] *n* **(a)** (*of responsibility etc*) Delegation *f* ◆ **he's no good at ~** er gibt die Verantwortung nicht gern aus der Hand. **(b)** (*group of delegates*) Delegation, Abordnung *f.*
delete [dɪˈliːt] *vt* streichen (*from* von); (*Comput*) löschen ◆ **"~ where not applicable"** „Nichtzutreffendes (bitte) streichen".
deleterious [ˌdelɪˈtɪərɪəs] *adj* (*form*) schädlich (*to* für).
deletion [dɪˈliːʃən] *n* Streichung *f*; (*Comput*) Löschung *f* ◆ **who made those ~s?** wer hat das gestrichen?
delft [delft] *n* Delfter Fayencen *pl.*
deli [ˈdelɪ] *n* (*inf*) *see* **delicatessen.**
deliberate [dɪˈlɪbərɪt] **1** *adj* **(a)** (*intentional*) absichtlich; *action, insult, lie also* bewußt. **(b)** (*cautious, thoughtful*) besonnen; *action, judgement* (wohl)überlegt; (*slow*) *movement, step, voice* bedächtig.
2 [dɪˈlɪbəreɪt] *vi* (*ponder*) nachdenken (*on, upon* über *+acc*); (*discuss*) sich beraten (*on, upon* über *+acc*, wegen).
3 [dɪˈlɪbəreɪt] *vt* (*ponder*) bedenken, überlegen; (*discuss*) beraten.
deliberately [dɪˈlɪbərɪtlɪ] *adv* **(a)** (*intentionally*) absichtlich, mit Absicht, bewußt. **(b)** (*purposefully, slowly*) bedächtig.
deliberateness [dɪˈlɪbərɪtnɪs] *n see adj* Absichtlichkeit *f*; Besonnenheit *f*; Überlegtheit *f*; Bedächtigkeit *f.*
deliberation [dɪˌlɪbəˈreɪʃən] *n* **(a)** (*consideration*) Überlegung *f* (*on* zu) ◆ **after due/careful ~** nach reiflicher/sorgfältiger Überlegung. **(b)** (*discussion*) Beratungen *pl* (*of, on* in *+dat*, über *+acc*). **(c)** (*purposefulness, slowness*) Bedächtigkeit *f.*
deliberative [dɪˈlɪbərətɪv] *adj speech* abwägend ◆ **~ assembly** beratende Versammlung.
delicacy [ˈdelɪkəsɪ] *n* **(a)** *see* **delicateness. (b)** (*food*) Delikatesse *f*, Leckerbissen *m.*
delicate [ˈdelɪkɪt] **1** *adj* **(a)** (*fine, exquisite, dainty*) fein; *fabric also, bones, colour* zart; (*fragile*) *person, bones, china also* zerbrechlich; *fabric, flower* empfindlich.
(b) (*Med*) *health, person* zart; *liver* empfindlich ◆ **in a ~ condition** (*dated euph*) in anderen Umständen.
(c) (*sensitive*) *person* feinfühlig; *manner also* delikat; *instrument* empfindlich; *task* fein; *playing* gefühlvoll; *painting* zart ◆ **he has a ~ touch** (*pianist, artist*) er hat sehr viel Gefühl; (*doctor*) er ist sehr behutsam.
(d) (*requiring skilful handling*) *operation, subject, situation* heikel, delikat.
(e) *food* delikat; *flavour* fein.
2 *n* **~s** *pl* (*fabrics*) Feinwäsche *f.*
delicately [ˈdelɪkɪtlɪ] *adv see adj (a, c, e).*
delicateness [ˈdelɪkɪtnɪs] *n see adj* **(a)** Feinheit *f*; Zartheit *f*; Zerbrechlichkeit *f*; Empfindlichkeit *f.*
(b) Zartheit *f*; Empfindlichkeit *f.*
(c) Feinfühligkeit *f*; Empfindlichkeit *f*; Feinheit *f*; Gefühl(volle) *nt*; Zartheit *f.*
(d) Heikle *nt*, Delikatheit *f.*
(e) Delikatheit *f*; Feinheit *f.*
delicatessen [ˌdelɪkəˈtesn] *n* Feinkostgeschäft *nt.*
delicious [dɪˈlɪʃəs] *adj* **(a)** *food etc* köstlich, lecker (*inf*). **(b)** (*delightful*) herrlich.
delight [dɪˈlaɪt] **1** *n* Freude *f* ◆ **to my ~** zu meiner Freude; **he takes great ~ in doing that** es bereitet ihm große Freude, das zu tun; **to give sb ~** jdn erfreuen; **sensual ~s** Sinnesfreuden *pl*; **he's a ~ to watch, it's a ~ to watch him**

➤ LANGUAGE IN USE: **deliberately: a → 18.4**

es ist eine Freude, ihm zuzusehen.

[2] *vt person, ear, eye etc* erfreuen; *see* **delighted.**

[3] *vi* sich erfreuen (*in* an *+dat*) ♦ **she ~s in doing that** es bereitet ihr große Freude, das zu tun.

▼ **delighted** [dɪ'laɪtɪd] *adj* (*with* über *+acc*) erfreut, entzückt ♦ **to be ~** sich sehr freuen (*at* über *+acc, that* daß); **absolutely ~** hocherfreut, ganz entzückt; **~ to meet you!** sehr angenehm!; **we shall be ~ to accept (your invitation)** wir nehmen Ihre Einladung gern an; **I'd be ~ to help you** ich würde Ihnen sehr gern helfen.

delightful [dɪ'laɪtfʊl] *adj* reizend; *weather, party, meal* wunderbar.

delightfully [dɪ'laɪtfəlɪ] *adv* wunderbar.

delimit [di:'lɪmɪt] *vt* abgrenzen.

delimitation [ˌdi:lɪmɪ'teɪʃən] *n* Abgrenzung *f.*

delimiter [di:'lɪmɪtəʳ] *n* (*Comput*) Trennzeichen *nt,* Delimiter *m.*

delineate [dɪ'lɪnɪeɪt] *vt* (*draw*) skizzieren; (*describe*) beschreiben, darstellen ♦ **the mountains were clearly ~d against the sky** die Berge zeichneten sich klar gegen den Himmel ab.

delineation [dɪˌlɪnɪ'eɪʃən] *n see vt* Skizzierung *f;* Beschreibung, Darstellung *f.*

delinquency [dɪ'lɪŋkwənsɪ] *n* Kriminalität, Delinquenz (*spec*) *f* ♦ **an act of ~** eine Straftat; (*fig*) ein Verbrechen *nt.*

delinquent [dɪ'lɪŋkwənt] [1] *adj* **(a)** straffällig. **(b)** *bill* überfällig; *account* rückständig.

[2] *n* Delinquent *m.*

delirious [dɪ'lɪrɪəs] *adj* (*Med*) im Delirium; (*fig*) im Taumel ♦ **to be ~ with joy** im Freudentaumel sein.

deliriously [dɪ'lɪrɪəslɪ] *adv see adj* **~ happy** überglücklich.

delirium [dɪ'lɪrɪəm] *n* (*Med*) Delirium *nt;* (*fig*) Taumel *m* ♦ **~ tremens** Delirium tremens, Säuferwahn(sinn) *m.*

deliver [dɪ'lɪvəʳ] [1] *vt* **(a)** *goods* liefern; *note* zustellen, überbringen; (*on regular basis*) *papers etc* zustellen; (*on foot*) austragen; (*by car*) ausfahren ♦ **to ~ sth to sb** jdm etw liefern/zustellen; **~ed free** frei Haus; **to ~ sb/sth into sb's care** jdn/etw in jds Obhut (*acc*) geben; **he ~ed me right to the door** er brachte mich bis zur Tür; **to ~ the goods** (*fig inf*) es bringen (*inf*), es schaffen.

(b) (*liter: rescue*) befreien ♦ **~ us from evil** (*Bibl*) erlöse uns von dem Übel *or* Bösen.

(c) (*pronounce*) *speech, sermon* halten; *ultimatum* stellen; *verdict* sprechen, verkünden.

(d) (*Med*) *baby* zur Welt bringen; (*old*) *woman* entbinden ♦ **to be ~ed of a son** (*old*) eines Jungen genesen (*old*).

(e) (*hand over: also* **~ up**) aushändigen, übergeben ♦ **to ~ a town (up) into the hands of the enemy** eine Stadt dem Feind ausliefern; *see* **stand.**

(f) (*aim, throw*) *blow* versetzen, landen (*inf*); *ball* werfen ♦ **Ali ~ed a punch to Bugner's jaw** Ali landete einen Schlag an Bugners Kinn (*inf*); **to ~ a broadside** eine Breitseite abfeuern.

[2] *vi* **(a)** liefern. **(b)** (*fig sl: be good enough*) es bringen (*sl*) ♦ **they didn't ~** sie brachten's nicht (*sl*).

deliverance [dɪ'lɪvərəns] *n* (*liter*) Befreiung, Erlösung *f* (*from* von).

deliverer [dɪ'lɪvərəʳ] *n* **(a)** (*Comm*) Lieferant *m.* **(b)** (*liter: rescuer*) Erlöser, Retter *m.*

▼ **delivery** [dɪ'lɪvərɪ] *n* **(a)** (*of goods*) (Aus)lieferung *f;* (*of parcels, letters*) Zustellung *f* ♦ **to take ~ of a parcel** ein Paket in Empfang nehmen; **to pay on ~** bei Empfang zahlen.

(b) (*Med*) Entbindung *f.*

(c) (*of speaker*) Vortrag *m,* Vortragsweise *f.*

(d) (*liter: rescue*) Rettung, Befreiung *f.*

(e) (*of punch, blow*) Landung *f* (*inf*); (*Cricket*) Wurf *m.*

delivery: ~ boy *n* Bote *m;* (*for newspapers*) Träger *m;* **~ man** *n* Lieferant *m;* **~ note** *n* Lieferschein *m;* **~ room** *n* Kreißsaal, Entbindungssaal *m;* **~ service** *n* Zustelldienst *m;* **~ time** *n* Lieferzeit *f;* **~ van** *n* (*Brit*) Lieferwagen *m.*

dell [del] *n* kleines bewaldetes Tal.

delouse [ˌdi:'laʊs] *vt* entlausen.

Delphic ['delfɪk] *adj* (*lit, fig*) delphisch ♦ **the ~ oracle** das Delphische Orakel, das Orakel von Delphi.

delphinium [del'fɪnɪəm] *n* Rittersporn *m.*

delta ['deltə] *n* Delta *nt.*

delta: ~ ray *n* (*Phys*) Deltastrahl *m;* **~ rhythm** *or* **wave** *n* (*Physiol*) Deltawelle *f;* **~ wing** *n* (*Aviat*) Deltaflügel *m.*

delude [dɪ'lu:d] *vt* täuschen, irreführen (*with* mit) ♦ **to ~ sb into thinking sth** (*incident*) jdn dazu verleiten, etw zu glauben; (*person also*) jdm etw weismachen; **to ~ oneself** sich (*dat*) Illusionen machen, sich (*dat*) etwas vormachen; **stop deluding yourself/don't ~ yourself that ...** hör auf, dir vorzumachen, daß .../mach dir doch nicht vor, daß ...; **~d** voller Illusionen; **poor ~d creature** armer Irrer, arme Irre.

deluge ['delju:dʒ] [1] *n* (*lit*) Überschwemmung *f;* (*of rain*) Guß *m;* (*fig: of complaints, letters etc*) Flut *f* ♦ **the D~** (*Bibl*) die Sintflut.

[2] *vt* (*lit, fig*) überschwemmen, überfluten.

delusion [dɪ'lu:ʒən] *n* Illusion *f,* Irrglaube *m no pl;* (*Psych*) Wahnvorstellung *f* ♦ **to be** *or* **labour under a ~** in einem Wahn leben; **to have ~s of grandeur** den Größenwahn haben.

delusive [dɪ'lu:sɪv], **delusory** [dɪ'lu:sərɪ] *adj* irreführend, täuschend, trügerisch.

de luxe [dɪ'lʌks] *adj* Luxus-, De-luxe-.

delve [delv] *vi* (*into subject*) sich eingehend befassen (*into* mit); (*into book*) sich vertiefen (*into* in *+acc*) ♦ **to ~ in(to) one's pocket/a drawer** tief in die Tasche/eine Schublade greifen.

Dem (*US Pol*) *abbr of* **Democratic** dem.

demagnetize [ˌdi:'mægnɪtaɪz] *vt* entmagnetisieren.

demagogic [ˌdemə'gɒgɪk] *adj* demagogisch.

demagogue, (*US*) **demagog** ['deməgɒg] *n* Demagoge *m,* Demagogin *f.*

demagoguery [ˌdemə'gɒgərɪ], **demagogy** ['deməgɒgɪ] *n* Demagogie *f.*

▼ **demand** [dɪ'mɑ:nd] [1] *vt* verlangen, fordern (*of, from* von); (*situation, task etc*) erfordern, verlangen; *time* beanspruchen ♦ **he ~ed my name/to see my passport** er wollte meinen Namen wissen/meinen Paß sehen; **he ~ed to know what had happened** er verlangte zu wissen, was passiert war.

[2] *n* **(a)** Forderung *f,* Verlangen *nt* (*for* nach); (*claim for better pay, of kidnapper etc*) Forderung *f* (*for* nach) ♦ **by popular ~** auf allgemeinen Wunsch; **payable on ~** zahlbar bei Vorlage; **to make ~s on sb** Forderungen *or* Ansprüche an jdn stellen; **he makes too many ~s on my patience/time/pocket** er (über)strapaziert meine Geduld/er belegt mich *or* meine Zeit zu sehr mit Beschlag/er liegt mir zu sehr auf der Tasche; **I have many ~s on my time** meine Zeit ist sehr mit Beschlag belegt.

(b) *no pl* (*Comm*) Nachfrage *f* ♦ **to create a ~ for a product** Nachfrage für ein Produkt schaffen; **there's no ~ for it** es ist nicht gefragt, es besteht keine Nachfrage danach; **to be in great ~** (*article, person*) sehr gefragt sein.

demanding [dɪ'mɑ:ndɪŋ] *adj child* anstrengend; *task also, teacher, boss* anspruchsvoll ♦ **physically ~** körperlich anstrengend.

demand: ~ management *n* Steuerung *f* der Nachfrage; **~ note** *n* Zahlungsaufforderung *f.*

de-manning [ˌdi:'mænɪŋ] *n* (*Brit: of industry*) Personal- *or* Stellenabbau *m.*

demarcate ['di:mɑ:keɪt] *vt* abgrenzen, demarkieren.

demarcation [ˌdi:mɑ:'keɪʃən] *n* Abgrenzung, Demarkation *f* ♦ **~-line** Demarkationslinie *f;* **~ dispute** Streit *m* um den Zuständigkeitsbereich.

démarche ['deɪmɑ:ʃ] *n* Demarche *f.*

dematerialize [ˌdi:mə'tɪərɪəlaɪz] [1] *vt* entmaterialisieren.

[2] *vi* sich entmaterialisieren.

demean [dɪ'mi:n] *vr* **(a)** (*lower*) sich erniedrigen ♦ **I will not ~ myself (so far as) to do that** ich werde mich nicht (dazu) erniedrigen, das zu tun; **~ing** erniedrigend. **(b)** (*behave*) sich benehmen *or* verhalten.

demeanour, (*US*) **demeanor** [dɪ'mi:nəʳ] *n* (*behaviour*) Benehmen, Auftreten *nt;* (*bearing*) Haltung *f.*

demented [dɪ'mentɪd] *adj* verrückt, wahnsinnig ♦ **~ with worry** verrückt vor Angst.

dementia [dɪ'menʃɪə] *n* Schwachsinn *m,* Demenz *f* (*spec*) ♦ **~ praecox** Jugendirresein *nt,* Dementia praecox *f* (*spec*).

demerara (sugar) [ˌdemə'rɛərə('ʃʊgəʳ)] *n* brauner Rohrzucker.

demerge [ˌdi:'mɜ:dʒ] *vt company* entflechten.

demerit [di:'merɪt] *n* Schwäche *f,* Fehler *m;* (*US: black mark*) Minuspunkt *m.*

demesne [dɪ'meɪn] *n* Grundbesitz *m* ♦ **to hold sth in ~** etw in Besitz haben.

demi ['demɪ-] *pref* Halb-, halb- ♦ **~god** Halbgott *m;* **~john** Demijohn *m;* (*in wickerwork also*) bauchige Korbflasche; **~-monde** [ˌdemɪ'mɔ̃d] Halbwelt *f.*

demilitarization ['di:ˌmɪlɪtəraɪ'zeɪʃən] *n* Entmilitarisierung *f.*

demilitarize [ˌdi:'mɪlɪtəraɪz] *vt* entmilitarisieren ♦ **~d zone** *n* entmilitarisierte Zone.

demise [dɪ'maɪz] *n* (*death*) Tod *m;* (*of person also*) Ableben *nt* (*geh*); (*fig: of institution, newspaper etc*) Ende *nt.*

demisemiquaver [ˌdemɪsemɪ'kweɪvəʳ] *n* Zweiunddreißigstelnote *f.*

demist [ˌdi:'mɪst] *vt windscreen* freimachen.

demister [ˌdi:'mɪstəʳ] *n* Gebläse *nt.*

demitasse ['demɪtæs] *n* (*US*) (*cup*) Mokkatasse *f;* (*coffee*) Kaffee *m.*

demo ['deməʊ] [1] *n abbr of* **demonstration** Demo(nstration) *f.*

[2] *adj attr* **~ disk** Demodiskette *f;* **~ tape** Demoband *nt.*

demob [ˌdi:'mɒb] (*Brit*) [1] *n abbr of* **demobilization** Entlassung *f* aus dem Kriegsdienst.

[2] *vt abbr of* **demobilize** aus dem Kriegsdienst entlassen, demobilisieren.

demobilization ['di:ˌməʊbɪlaɪ'zeɪʃən] *n* (*of army*) Demobilmachung, Demobilisierung *f;* (*of soldier*) Entlassung *f* aus dem Kriegsdienst, Demobilisierung *f.*

demobilize [di:'məʊbɪlaɪz] *vt* aus dem Kriegsdienst entlassen, demobilisieren.

democracy [dɪ'mɒkrəsɪ] *n* Demokratie *f.*

democrat ['deməkræt] *n* Demokrat(in *f*) *m.*

democratic *adj,* **~ally** *adv* [ˌdemə'krætɪk, -əlɪ] demokratisch.

democratize [dɪ'mɒkrətaɪz] *vt* demokratisieren.

demographer [dɪ'mɒgrəfəʳ] *n* Demograph(in *f*) *m.*

demographic [ˌdemə'græfɪk] *adj* demographisch.

demography [dɪ'mɒgrəfɪ] *n* Demographie *f.*

demolish [dɪ'mɒlɪʃ] *vt building* ab- *or* einreißen, abbrechen; *fortifications* niederreißen; (*fig*) *opponent, theory* zunichte machen, vernichten; (*hum*) *cake etc* vertilgen.

demolition [ˌdemə'lɪʃən] *n* Abbruch *m.*

demolition: ~ area *n see* **~ zone; ~ squad** *n* Abbruchkolonne *f;* **~ zone** *n* Abbruchgebiet *nt.*

demon ['di:mən] *n* Dämon *m;* (*inf: child*) Teufel *m* ♦ **to be a ~ for work** ein Arbeitstier sein; **the D~ Drink** König Alkohol *m.*

demoniac [dɪ'məʊnɪæk] [1] *adj* dämonisch.

[2] *n* Besessene(r) *mf.*

demoniacal [ˌdi:məʊ'naɪəkəl] *adj* dämonisch.

demonic [dɪ'mɒnɪk] *adj* dämonisch.

demonstrable ['demənstrəbl] *adj* beweisbar, offensichtlich.

demonstrably ['demənstrəblɪ] *adv see adj* ◆ **~ false** nachweislich falsch.

demonstrate ['demənstreɪt] 1 *vt* **(a)** *truth, emotions, needs, good will* zeigen, beweisen; *(by experiment, example also)* demonstrieren. **(b)** *appliance etc* vorführen; *operation also* demonstrieren.
2 *vi (Pol etc)* demonstrieren.

demonstration [ˌdemən'streɪʃən] 1 *n* **(a)** *see vt* Zeigen *nt*, Beweis *m*; Demonstration *f*; Vorführung *f*; Demonstration *f* ◆ **to give a ~ (of sth)** etw demonstrieren; *(of gadgets)* eine Vorführung machen, etw vorführen. **(b)** *(Pol etc)* Demonstration *f*. **to hold a ~** eine Demonstration veranstalten *or* durchführen.
2 *attr car, lesson* Vorführ-, Demonstrations-.

demonstrative [dɪ'mɒnstrətɪv] *adj* demonstrativ; *(Gram) adjective also* hinweisend.

demonstrator ['demənstreɪtə^r] *n* **(a)** *(Comm)* Vorführer(in *f*) *m* (von technischen Geräten), Propagandist(in *f*) *m*; *(Sch, Univ)* Demonstrator *m*. **(b)** *(Pol)* Demonstrant(in *f*) *m*.

demoralization [dɪˌmɒrəlaɪ'zeɪʃən] *n see vt* Entmutigung *f*; Demoralisierung *f*.

demoralize [dɪ'mɒrəlaɪz] *vt* entmutigen; *troops etc* demoralisieren.

demoralizing [dɪ'mɒrəlaɪzɪŋ] *adj see vt* entmutigend; demoralisierend.

demote [dɪ'məʊt] *vt (Mil)* degradieren *(to* zu); *(in business etc)* zurückstufen ◆ **~d to captain** zum Hauptmann degradiert.

demotic [dɪ'mɒtɪk] *adj* **(a)** *Greek* demotisch. **(b)** *(of the people)* volkstümlich.

demotion [dɪ'məʊʃən] *n (Mil)* Degradierung *f*; *(in business etc)* Zurückstufung *f*.

demur [dɪ'mɜː^r] 1 *vi* Einwände erheben, Bedenken haben *(to, at* gegen); *(Jur)* Einspruch erheben *or* einlegen.
2 *n (form)* Einwand *m*, Bedenken *pl*; *(Jur)* Einspruch *m* ◆ **without ~** widerspruchslos.

demure [dɪ'mjʊə^r] *adj (+er) (coy) look, girl, smile* spröde; *(sedate)* ernst, gesetzt; *(sober)* nüchtern, gelassen ◆ **a ~ little hat** ein schlichter kleiner Hut.

demurely [dɪ'mjʊəlɪ] *adv see adj*.

demureness [dɪ'mjʊənɪs] *n see adj* Sprödigkeit *f*; Ernst *m*, Gesetztheit *f*; Nüchternheit, Gelassenheit *f*; Schlichtheit *f*.

demurrage [dɪ'mʌrɪdʒ] *n (Comm) (charge)* (Über)liegegeld *nt*; *(time)* Überliegezeit *f*.

demystification [ˌdiːmɪstɪfɪ'keɪʃən] *n* Entmystifizierung *f*.

demystify [diː'mɪstɪfaɪ] *vt* entmystifizieren.

demythologize ['diːmɪ'θɒlədʒaɪz] *vt* entmythologisieren.

den [den] *n* **(a)** *(of lion, tiger etc)* Höhle *f*, Versteck *nt*; *(of fox)* Bau *m*. **(b) ~ of iniquity** *or* **vice** Lasterhöhle *f*; **~ of thieves** Spelunke, Räuberhöhle *(hum) f*; *see* **gambling, opium ~**. **(c)** *(study)* Arbeitszimmer *nt*; *(private room)* gemütliches Zimmer, Bude *f (inf)* ◆ **hobby ~** Hobbyraum *m*.

denationalization ['diːˌnæʃnəlaɪ'zeɪʃən] *n* Entstaatlichung *f*.

denationalize [ˌdiː'næʃnəlaɪz] *vt* entstaatlichen.

denature [ˌdiː'neɪtʃə^r] *vt* denaturieren; *(make unfit for eating, drinking also)* ungenießbar machen.

denazification ['diːˌnætsɪfɪ'keɪʃən] *n* Entnazifizierung *f*.

denazify [ˌdiː'nætsɪfaɪ] *vt* entnazifizieren.

dendrite ['dendraɪt] *n* Dendrit *m*.

denial [dɪ'naɪəl] *n* **(a)** *(of accusation, guilt)* Leugnen *nt* ◆ **~ of (the existence of) God** Gottesleugnung *f*; **the government issued an official ~** die Regierung gab ein offizielles Dementi heraus.
(b) *(refusal: of request etc)* Ablehnung *f*, abschlägige Antwort; *(official)* abschlägiger Bescheid; *(of rights)* Verweigerung *f* ◆ **he regarded this as a ~ of his sons** er war der Ansicht, daß seine Söhne übergangen worden waren.
(c) *(disowning)* Verleugnung *f* ◆ **Peter's ~ of Christ** die Verleugnung des Petrus.
(d) *(self-~)* Selbstverleugnung *f*.

denier ['denɪə^r] *n (of stockings)* Denier *nt*.

denigrate ['denɪgreɪt] *vt* verunglimpfen.

denigration [ˌdenɪ'greɪʃən] *n* Verunglimpfung *f*.

denim ['denɪm] 1 *n* **(a)** Jeansstoff, Köper *m*. **(b) ~s** *pl* Blue Jeans, Jeans *pl*.
2 *adj attr* Jeans-, Köper- ◆ **~ jacket** Jeansjacke *f*; **~ suit** Jeansanzug *m*.

denitrification [ˌdiːnaɪtrɪfɪ'keɪʃən] *n* Entstickung *f*.

denizen ['denɪzn] *n* Bewohner(in *f*) *m*; *(person)* Einwohner(in *f*) *m* ◆ **~s of the forest/deep** Waldbewohner *pl*/Bewohner *pl* der Tiefe.

Denmark ['denmɑːk] *n* Dänemark *nt*.

denominate [dɪ'nɒmɪneɪt] *vt* benennen, bezeichnen.

denomination [dɪˌnɒmɪ'neɪʃən] *n* **(a)** *(Eccl)* Konfession *f*. **(b)** *(name, naming)* Benennung, Bezeichnung *f*. **(c)** *(of money)* Nennbetrag *m*; *(of weight, measures)* Einheit *f*. **(d)** *(class, kind)* Klasse, Gruppe *f*.

denominational [dɪˌnɒmɪ'neɪʃənl] *adj (Eccl)* konfessionell, Konfessions-.

denominator [dɪ'nɒmɪneɪtə^r] *n (Math)* Nenner *m*.

denotation [ˌdiːnəʊ'teɪʃən] *n* **(a)** *(Philos: of term, concept)* Denotation *f*, Begriffsumfang *m*; *(of word)* Bedeutung *f*. **(b)** *(name: of object)* Bezeichnung *f*; *(symbol)* Symbol *nt*.

denotative [dɪ'nəʊtətɪv] *adj (Ling)* denotativ.

denote [dɪ'nəʊt] *vt* bedeuten; *symbol, word* bezeichnen; *(Philos)* den Begriffsumfang angeben von.

dénouement [deɪ'nuːmɒŋ] *n (Theat, Liter)* (Auf)lösung *f*; *(fig)* Ausgang *m*.

denounce [dɪ'naʊns] *vt* **(a)** *(accuse publicly)* anprangern, brandmarken; *(inform against)* anzeigen, denunzieren *(sb to sb* jdn bei jdm). **(b)** *(condemn as evil) alcohol, habit etc* verurteilen, denunzieren *(geh)*. **(c)** *treaty* (auf)kündigen.

denouncement [dɪ'naʊnsmənt] *n see* **denunciation**.

dense [dens] *adj (+er)* **(a)** *fog, forest, crowd, population* dicht. **(b)** *(Phot) negative* überbelichtet. **(c)** *(inf: stupid) person* beschränkt, blöd *(inf)* ◆ **are you being ~?** stellst du dich dumm?

densely ['denslɪ] *adv* **(a)** dicht ◆ **~ wooded/populated** dicht bewaldet *pred*, dichtbewaldet *attr*/dicht bevölkert *pred*, dichtbevölkert *attr*. **(b)** *(inf: stupidly)* blöd *(inf)*.

denseness ['densnɪs] *n* **(a)** *see* **density**. **(b)** *(inf)* Beschränktheit, Blödheit *(inf) f*.

density ['densɪtɪ] *n* Dichte *f* ◆ **population ~** Bevölkerungsdichte *f*.

dent [dent] 1 *n (in metal)* Beule, Delle *(inf) f*; *(in wood)* Kerbe, Delle *(inf) f* ◆ **that made a ~ in his savings** *(inf)* das hat ein Loch in seine Ersparnisse gerissen; **that made a bit of a ~ in his pride** das hat seinen Stolz ganz schön angeknackst *(inf)*.
2 *vt hat, car, wing* einbeulen, verbeulen; *wood, table* eine Delle machen in (+*acc*); *(inf) pride* anknacksen *(inf)*.
3 *vi (metal etc)* sich einbeulen; *(wood, table)* eindellen.

dental ['dentl] 1 *adj* **(a)** Zahn-; *treatment* zahnärztlich; *training* zahnmedizinisch *(form)* ◆ **~ floss** Zahnseide *f*; **~ surgeon** Zahnarzt *m*/-ärztin *f*; **~ technician** Zahntechniker(in *f*) *m*. **(b)** *(Ling)* Dental-, dental.
2 *n (Ling)* Dental, Zahnlaut *m*.

dentifrice ['dentɪfrɪs] *n* Zahnpasta *f*.

dentist ['dentɪst] *n* Zahnarzt *m*, Zahnärztin *f* ◆ **at the ~('s)** beim Zahnarzt.

dentistry ['dentɪstrɪ] *n* Zahnmedizin, Zahnheilkunde *f* ◆ **a nice bit of ~** eine gute (Zahnarzt)arbeit.

dentition [den'tɪʃən] *n (process of teething)* Zahnen *nt*, Dentition *f (spec)*; *(arrangement of teeth)* Gebißform *f*.

dentures ['dentʃəz] *npl* Zahnprothese *f*; *(full)* Gebiß *nt*.

denude [dɪ'njuːd] *vt (of trees etc)* entblößen *(of gen)*; *(fig also)* berauben *(of gen)*.

denunciation [dɪˌnʌnsɪ'eɪʃən] *n see* **denounce** Anprangerung, Brandmarkung *f*; Denunziation *f*; Verurteilung *f*; (Auf)kündigung *f* ◆ **the book is a sustained ~ of ...** das Buch ist eine einzige Anklage gegen ...

Denver boot [ˌdenvə'buːt] *n (inf: car clamp)* Parkkralle, Kralle *(inf) f*.

▼ **deny** [dɪ'naɪ] *vt* **(a)** *charge, accusation etc* bestreiten, abstreiten, (ab)leugnen; *existence of God* leugnen; *(officially)* dementieren ◆ **do you ~ having said that?** leugnen *or* bestreiten Sie, das gesagt zu haben?; **there's no ~ing it** das läßt sich nicht bestreiten *or* leugnen; **I ~ that there is a real need for it** ich bestreite, daß ein echtes Bedürfnis danach besteht.
(b) *(refuse)* **to ~ sb a request/his rights/aid/a privilege/admittance/credit** jdm eine Bitte abschlagen/jdm seine Rechte vorenthalten/jdm Hilfe/ein Privileg versagen/jdm den Zugang verwehren/jdm Kredit verweigern; **I can't ~ her anything** ich kann ihr nichts abschlagen; **I had to ~ myself the pleasure of his company** ich mußte mir das Vergnügen seiner Gesellschaft versagen; **why should I ~ myself these little comforts?** warum sollte ich mir das bißchen Komfort nicht gönnen?
(c) *(disown) leader, religion, principles* verleugnen.
(d) to ~ oneself sich selbst verleugnen; **to ~ the flesh** der Sinneslust entsagen *(liter)*, sich kasteien.

deodorant [diː'əʊdərənt] 1 *adj* desodor(is)ierend.
2 *n* Deodorant *m*.

deodorize [diː'əʊdəraɪz] *vt* desodor(is)ieren.

deontology [ˌdiːɒn'tɒlədʒɪ] *n* Pflichtethik, Deontologie *f*.

deoxidize [diː'ɒksɪdaɪz] *vt* desoxydieren.

deoxyribonucleic acid [dɪ'ɒksɪˌraɪbəʊnjuː'kleɪɪkˌæsɪd] *n* Desoxyribonukleinsäure *f*.

dep *abbr of* **departure** Abf.

depart [dɪ'pɑːt] 1 *vi* **(a)** *(go away)* weggehen; *(on journey)* abreisen; *(by bus, car etc)* wegfahren; *(train, bus etc)* abfahren ◆ **the train at platform 6 ~ing for ...** der Zug auf Bahnsteig 6 nach ...; **guests are asked to sign the register before they ~** Gäste werden gebeten, vor der Abreise einen Meldezettel auszufüllen; **to be ready to ~** *(person)* start- *or* abfahrbereit sein; **the train was/visitors were about to ~** der Zug war im Begriff abzufahren/die Gäste waren im Begriff aufzubrechen; **to ~ on one's way** *(liter, old)* sich aufmachen, aufbrechen; **this is the point from which we ~ed** *(fig)* das war unser Ausgangspunkt.
(b) *(deviate: from opinion etc)* abweichen, abgehen.
2 *vt (liter)* **to ~ this world** *or* **life** aus dieser Welt *or* diesem Leben scheiden *(liter)*.

departed [dɪ'pɑːtɪd] 1 *adj* **(a)** *(liter: dead)* verstorben, verschieden *(geh)*. **(b)** *(bygone) friends* verloren; *glory, happiness also* vergangen.
2 *n* **the (dear) ~** der/die (liebe) Verstorbene; die (lieben) Verstorbenen *pl*.

department [dɪ'pɑːtmənt] *n* **(a)** *(generally)* Abteilung *f*; *(Geog: in France)* Departement *nt*; *(in civil service)* Ressort *nt* ◆ **D~ of Employment** *(Brit)* Arbeitsministerium *nt*; **D~ of State** *(US)* Außenministerium *nt*; **that's not my ~** *(fig)* dafür bin ich nicht zuständig. **(b)** *(Sch, Univ)* Fachbereich *m*.

departmental [ˌdiːpɑː't'mentl] *adj* **(a)** Abteilungs- ◆ **~ store** *(dated)* Warenhaus *nt*. **(b)** *(Sch, Univ)* Fachbereichs-.

departmentalism [ˌdiːpɑːt'mentəlɪzəm] *n* Gliederung *f* in Abteilungen.

departmentalize [ˌdiːpɑːt'mentəlaɪz] *vt* in Abteilungen einteilen *or* (auf)gliedern.

departmentally [ˌdiːpɑːt'mentəlɪ] *adv* abteilungsweise.

department store *n* Kaufhaus, Warenhaus *nt*.

departure [dɪ'pɑːtʃə^r] *n* **(a)** *(of person)* Weggang *m*; *(on journey)* Abreise *f*

➤ LANGUAGE IN USE: **deny: a → 15.1, 26.3**

(*from* aus); (*of vehicle*) Abfahrt *f*; (*of plane*) Abflug *m* ♦ **to be on the point of ~** im Aufbruch (begriffen) sein; **there are three ~s daily for Stockholm** es gibt täglich drei Flüge nach Stockholm; **"~s"** „Abfahrt"; (*at airport*) „Abflug"; **at the hour of our ~ from this life** (*liter*) in der Stunde unseres Dahinscheidens (*liter*).
(b) (*fig: from custom, principle*) Abweichen, Abgehen *nt* (*from* von); (*from truth*) Abweichen *nt*.
(c) (*fig*) (*change in policy etc*) Richtung *f*; (*in science, philosophy also*) Ansatz *m* ♦ **this is a new ~ for us** das ist eine neue Richtung für uns.
departure: ~ board *n* (*Rail*) Abfahrtstafel *f*; (*Aviat*) Abfluganzeige *f*; **~ gate** *n* Flugsteig, Ausgang *m*; **~ language** *n* (*Ling*) Ausgangssprache *f*; **~ lounge** *n* Abflughalle *f*; (*for single flight*) Warteraum *m*; **~ signal** *n* Abfahrtssignal *nt*; **~ time** *n* (*Aviat*) Abflugzeit *f*; (*Rail, bus*) Abfahrtzeit *f*.
▼ **depend** [dɪˈpend] *vi* **(a)** abhängen (*on sb/sth* von jdm/etw) ♦ **it ~s on what you mean by reasonable** es kommt darauf an, was Sie unter vernünftig verstehen; **it all ~s (on whether ...)** das kommt ganz darauf an(, ob ...); **that ~s** das kommt darauf an, je nachdem; **~ing on his mood/the sum needed/how late we arrive** je nach seiner Laune/Höhe des erforderlichen Betrags/je nachdem, wie spät wir ankommen.
(b) (*rely*) sich verlassen (*on, upon* auf +*acc*) ♦ **you may ~ (up)on his coming** Sie können sich darauf verlassen, daß er kommt; **you can ~ (up)on it!** darauf können Sie sich verlassen!
(c) (*person: be dependent on*) **to ~ on** abhängig sein von, angewiesen sein auf (+*acc*).
dependability [dɪˌpendəˈbɪlɪtɪ] *n* Zuverlässigkeit, Verläßlichkeit *f*.
dependable [dɪˈpendəbl] *adj* zuverlässig, verläßlich.
dependant, dependent [dɪˈpendənt] *n* Abhängige(r) *mf* ♦ **do you have ~s?** haben Sie (abhängige) Angehörige?
dependence [dɪˈpendəns] *n* **(a)** (*state of depending*) Abhängigkeit *f* (*on, upon* von). **(b)** (*reliance*) **I could never put much ~ on him** ich habe nie sehr viel von seiner Zuverlässigkeit gehalten.
dependency [dɪˈpendənsɪ] *n* **(a)** (*country*) Schutzgebiet *nt*, Kolonie *f*. **(b)** *see* **dependence (a)**.
dependent [dɪˈpendənt] **1** *adj* abhängig (*on, upon* von) ♦ **to be ~ on charity/sb's good will** auf Almosen/jds Wohlwollen (*acc*) angewiesen sein.
2 *n see* **dependant**.
depersonalize [diːˈpɜːsənəlaɪz] *vt* entpersönlichen, depersonalisieren (*Psych*).
depict [dɪˈpɪkt] *vt* darstellen; (*in words also*) beschreiben.
depiction [dɪˈpɪkʃən] *n see vt* Darstellung *f*; Beschreibung *f*.
depilatory [dɪˈpɪlətərɪ] **1** *adj* enthaarend, Enthaarungs-.
2 *n* Enthaarungsmittel *nt*.
deplenish [dɪˈplenɪʃ] *vt supplies etc* verringern.
deplete [dɪˈpliːt] *vt* **(a)** (*exhaust*) erschöpfen; (*reduce*) vermindern, verringern; *funds* verringern ♦ **our supplies are/the larder is somewhat ~d** unsere Vorräte sind ziemlich erschöpft/die Speisekammer ist ziemlich leer; **the audience had become somewhat ~d** die Zuschauerreihen hatten sich ziemlich gelichtet.
(b) (*Med*) entleeren.
depletion [dɪˈpliːʃən] *n see vt* Erschöpfung *f*; Verminderung, Verringerung *f*; Entleerung *f*; (*of stock also, of membership*) Abnahme *f*.
deplorable [dɪˈplɔːrəbl] *adj* beklagenswert, bedauerlich.
deplorably [dɪˈplɔːrəblɪ] *adv see adj* **to be in ~ bad taste** von bedauernswert schlechtem Geschmack zeugen.
deplore [dɪˈplɔːʳ] *vt* (*regret*) bedauern, beklagen; (*disapprove of*) mißbilligen ♦ **his attitude is to be ~d** seine Haltung ist bedauerlich.
deploy [dɪˈplɔɪ] **1** *vt* **(a)** (*Mil*) (*use, employ*) einsetzen; (*position*) aufstellen ♦ **the number of troops/missiles ~ed in Germany** die Zahl der in Deutschland stationierten Streitkräfte/Raketen. **(b)** (*fig*) *resources, staff, arguments* einsetzen.
2 *vi* (*Mil*) sich aufstellen; aufmarschieren.
deployment [dɪˈplɔɪmənt] *n see vb* Einsatz *m*; Aufstellung *f*; Stationierung *f*.
depoliticize [ˈdiːpɒˈlɪtɪsaɪz] *vt* entpolitisieren.
deponent [dɪˈpəʊnənt] **1** *n* (*Ling*) Deponens *nt*; (*Jur*) vereidigter Zeuge.
2 *adj* **~ verb** Deponens *nt*.
depopulate [ˌdiːˈpɒpjʊleɪt] *vt* entvölkern.
depopulation [ˈdiːˌpɒpjʊˈleɪʃən] *n* Entvölkerung *f*.
deport [dɪˈpɔːt] **1** *vt prisoner* deportieren; *alien* abschieben.
2 *vr* (*behave*) sich benehmen *or* verhalten.
deportation [ˌdiːpɔːˈteɪʃən] *n see vt* Deportation *f*; Abschiebung *f*.
deportation order *n* Abschiebungsanordnung *f*.
deportee [diːpɔːˈtiː] *n* Deportierte(r) *mf*; (*alien awaiting deportation*) Abzuschiebende(r) *mf*.
deportment [dɪˈpɔːtmənt] *n* Haltung *f*; (*behaviour*) Verhalten, Benehmen *nt* ♦ **lessons in ~** Haltungsschulung *f*; Anstandsunterricht *m*.
depose [dɪˈpəʊz] **1** *vt sovereign* entthronen, absetzen; *official* absetzen.
2 *vi* (*Jur*) unter Eid aussagen.
deposit [dɪˈpɒzɪt] **1** *vt* **(a)** (*put down*) hinlegen; (*upright*) hinstellen ♦ **the turtle ~s her eggs in the sand** die Schildkröte legt ihre Eier im Sand ab. **(b)** *money, valuables* deponieren (*with* bei). **(c)** (*Geol*) ablagern.
2 *n* **(a)** (*Fin: in bank*) Einlage *f*, Guthaben *nt* ♦ **to have £500 on ~** ein Guthaben *or* eine Einlage von £ 500 haben.
(b) (*Comm*) (*part payment*) Anzahlung *f*; (*returnable security*) Sicherheit, Kaution *f*; (*for bottle*) Pfand *nt* ♦ **to put down a ~ on a car** eine Anzahlung für ein Auto leisten, (auf) ein Auto anzahlen; **to leave a ~** eine Sicherheit *or* Kaution hinterlegen; **to lose one's ~** (*Pol*) seine Kaution verlieren.
(c) (*Chem: in wine, Geol*) Ablagerung *f*; (*accumulation of ore, coal, oil*) (Lager)stätte *f* ♦ **to form a ~** sich ablagern.
deposit account *n* Sparkonto *nt*.
depositary [dɪˈpɒzɪtərɪ] *n* Treuhänder(in *f*) *m*.
deposition [ˌdiːpəˈzɪʃən] *n* **(a)** (*of sovereign*) Entthronung, Absetzung *f*; (*of official*) Absetzung *f*. **(b)** (*Jur*) Aussage *f* unter Eid. **(c)** (*Art, Rel*) **~ from the cross** Kreuzabnahme *f*.
depositor [dɪˈpɒzɪtəʳ] *n* Deponent(in *f*), Einzahler(in *f*) *m*.
depository [dɪˈpɒzɪtərɪ] *n* Verwahrungsort *m*; (*warehouse*) Lagerhaus *nt*.
deposit slip *n* Einzahlungsbeleg *m*.
depot [ˈdepəʊ] *n* **(a)** (*bus garage etc*) Depot *nt*; (*store also*) (Lager)haus *nt*. **(b)** (*US Rail*) Bahnhof *m*.
depot ship *n* Versorgungsschiff *nt*.
depravation [ˌdeprəˈveɪʃən] *n* **(a)** (*depraving*) Verderbung *f*. **(b)** (*depravity*) Verderbtheit, Verworfenheit *f*.
deprave [dɪˈpreɪv] *vt* verderben.
depraved [dɪˈpreɪvd] *adj* verderbt, verkommen, verworfen.
depravity [dɪˈprævɪtɪ] *n* Verderbtheit, Verworfenheit *f*.
deprecate [ˈdeprɪkeɪt] *vt* (*form*) mißbilligen.
deprecating [ˈdeprɪkeɪtɪŋ] *adj* **(a)** (*disapproving*) mißbilligend. **(b)** (*apologetic*) abwehrend.
deprecatingly [ˈdeprɪkeɪtɪŋlɪ] *adv see adj*.
deprecation [deprɪˈkeɪʃən] *n* (*form*) Mißbilligung *f*.
deprecatory [ˈdeprɪkətərɪ] *n see* **deprecating**.
depreciate [dɪˈpriːʃɪeɪt] **1** *vt* **(a)** *value* mindern ♦ **to ~ a currency** die Kaufkraft einer Währung mindern. **(b)** (*belittle*) herabsetzen *or* -mindern *or* -würdigen.
2 *vi* an Wert verlieren; (*currency*) an Kaufkraft verlieren.
depreciation [dɪˌpriːʃɪˈeɪʃən] *n* **(a)** (*of property, value*) Wertminderung *f*; (*in accounting*) Abschreibung *f*; (*of currency*) Kaufkraftverlust *m*. **(b)** (*belittlement*) Herabsetzung *or* -minderung *or* -würdigung *f*.
depreciatory [dɪˈpriːʃɪətərɪ] *adj* abschätzig, herabsetzend.
depredation [ˌdeprɪˈdeɪʃən] *n usu pl* Verwüstung *f*.
depress [dɪˈpres] *vt* **(a)** *person* deprimieren; (*discourage*) entmutigen. **(b)** (*press down*) *lever* niederdrücken, herunterdrücken; *push button* drücken, betätigen.
depressant [dɪˈpresnt] **1** *n* Beruhigungsmittel, Sedativ(um) (*spec*) *nt*.
2 *adj* beruhigend, dämpfend, sedativ (*spec*).
depressed [dɪˈprest] *adj* **(a)** *person* deprimiert, niedergeschlagen; (*sad*) bedrückt; (*discouraged*) entmutigt. **(b)** *industry* notleidend; *area* Notstands-; *market, trade, business* schleppend, flau.
depressing [dɪˈpresɪŋ] *adj* deprimierend, bedrückend ♦ **don't be so ~** hör auf, ständig schwarzzusehen.
depressingly [dɪˈpresɪŋlɪ] *adv* deprimierend, bedrückend.
depression [dɪˈpreʃən] *n* **(a)** Depression *f*; (*Med*) Depressionen *pl*.
(b) (*of lever*) Herunter- *or* Niederdrücken *nt*; (*of key, push button*) Drücken, Betätigen *nt*, Betätigung *f*.
(c) (*in ground*) Vertiefung, Senke, Mulde *f*.
(d) (*Met*) Tief(druckgebiet) *nt* ♦ **a deep/shallow ~** ein ausgedehntes/schwaches Tief(druckgebiet).
(e) (*Econ*) Flaute *f*; (*St Ex*) Baisse *f* ♦ **the D~** die Weltwirtschaftskrise.
depressive [dɪˈpresɪv] **1** *adj* depressiv.
2 *n* an Depressionen Leidende(r) *mf* ♦ **to be a ~** depressiv sein.
depressurize [diːˈpreʃəraɪz] *vt* den Druck herabsetzen in (+*dat*) ♦ **should the cabin become ~d** bei Druckverlust in der Kabine.
deprivation [ˌdeprɪˈveɪʃən] *n* **(a)** (*depriving*) Entzug *m*; (*loss*) Verlust *m*; (*Psych*) Deprivation *f*; (*of rights*) Beraubung *f*.
(b) (*state*) Entbehrung *f*; (*lack of necessities*) Mangel *m* ♦ **the ~s of the war** die Entbehrungen des Krieges.
deprive [dɪˈpraɪv] *vt* **to ~ sb of sth** jdm etw entziehen; **they had been ~d of a decent education/the benefit of ...** ihnen wurde eine anständige Erziehung/der Vorteil von ... vorenthalten; **I wouldn't want to ~ you of the pleasure of ...** ich möchte dir das Vergnügen ... nicht vorenthalten; **I don't want to ~ you** ich will dir das/die *etc* nicht vorenthalten; **those who are ~d of any sense of national identity** die, denen jedes Gefühl für nationale Identität fehlt; **to ~ oneself of sth** sich (*dat*) etw nicht gönnen.
deprived [dɪˈpraɪvd] *adj* **~ child** benachteiligtes Kind; **~ families** benachteiligte *or* deprivierte (*Sociol*) Familien; **are you feeling ~?** (*inf*) fühlst du dich benachteiligt?
dept *abbr of* **department** Abt.
depth [depθ] *n* **(a)** Tiefe *f* ♦ **the ~s of the ocean** die Tiefen des Ozeans; **at a ~ of 3 metres** in einer Tiefe von 3 Metern, in 3 Meter Tiefe; **don't go out of your ~** geh nicht zu tief rein!; **to get out of one's ~** (*lit*) den Boden unter den Füßen verlieren; (*fig also*) ins Schwimmen geraten; **I'm out of my ~ there** davon habe ich keine Ahnung, da muß ich passen.
(b) (*of knowledge, feeling, colour*) Tiefe *f* ♦ **to sing/act with great ~ of feeling** sehr gefühlvoll singen/sehr einfühlsam spielen; **in ~** eingehend, intensiv; *see* **in-depth**.
(c) (*fig*) **~(s)** Tiefen *pl* ♦ **in the ~s of despair** in tiefster Verzweiflung; **in the ~s of winter/the forest** im tiefsten Winter/Wald; **from the ~s of the earth** aus den Tiefen der Erde (*geh*).
depth: ~ charge *n* Wasserbombe *f*; **~ of field** *n* (*Phot*) Tiefenschärfe *f*; **~ psychology** *n* Tiefenpsychologie *f*.
deputation [ˌdepjʊˈteɪʃən] *n* (*act*) Abordnung *f*; (*people also*) Delegation *f*.

➤ LANGUAGE IN USE: **depend: a → 6.3**

depute [dɪ'pjuːt] *vt person* abordnen, delegieren; *power, authority* delegieren, übertragen (*to sb* jdm).

deputize ['depjʊtaɪz] [1] *vi* vertreten (*for sb* jdn), als Vertreter fungieren (*for sb* für jdn).
[2] *vt* ernennen, abordnen.

deputy ['depjʊtɪ] [1] *n* **(a)** Stellvertreter(in *f*) *m*. **(b)** (*in deputation*) Delegierte(r) *mf*. **(c)** (*also* ~ **sheriff**) Hilfssheriff *m*. **(d)** (*in France*) Deputierte(r) *mf*; (*US: in foreign parliaments*) Abgeordnete(r) *mf*.
[2] *adj attr* stellvertretend.

derail [dɪ'reɪl] [1] *vt* zum Entgleisen bringen, entgleisen lassen ◆ **to be ~ed** entgleisen.
[2] *vi* entgleisen.

derailleur gears [dɪ'reɪljə'gɪəz], **derailleurs** [dɪ'reɪljəz] (*inf*) *npl* Kettenschaltung *f*.

derailment [dɪ'reɪlmənt] *n* Entgleisung *f*.

derange [dɪ'reɪndʒ] *vt* **(a)** (*make insane*) verrückt *or* wahnsinnig machen. **(b)** *plan* durcheinanderbringen, umwerfen.

deranged [dɪ'reɪndʒd] *adj mind* gestört, verwirrt, verstört ◆ **to be (mentally) ~** (*person*) geistesgestört sein.

derangement [dɪ'reɪndʒmənt] *n* **(a)** Geistesgestörtheit *f*. **(b)** (*of order*) Unordnung *f*, Durcheinander *nt*.

Derby ['dɑːbɪ, (*US*) 'dɜːbɪ] *n* **(a)** (*US: also* ~ **hat**) Melone *f*. **(b)** (*local* ~) (Lokal)derby *nt*. **(c)** (*Racing*) Derby *nt*.

deregulate [diː'regjʊleɪt] *vt* deregulieren; *buses etc* dem freien Wettbewerb überlassen.

deregulation [ˌdiːregjʊ'leɪʃən] *n see vt* Deregulierung *f*; Wettbewerbsfreiheit *f* (*of* für).

derelict ['derɪlɪkt] [1] *adj* (*abandoned*) verlassen, aufgegeben; (*ruined*) verfallen, heruntergekommen.
[2] *n* **(a)** (*Naut*) (treibendes) Wrack. **(b)** (*person*) Obdachlose(r) *mf*.

dereliction [ˌderɪ'lɪkʃən] *n* **(a)** (*state: of property*) Verfall *m*, Heruntergekommenheit *f*. **(b)** ~ **of duty** Pflichtversäumnis *nt*.

derestricted [ˌdiːrɪ'strɪktɪd] *adj road, area* ohne Geschwindigkeitsbegrenzung *or* -beschränkung.

deride [dɪ'raɪd] *vt* sich lustig machen über (+*acc*), verspotten.

derision [dɪ'rɪʒən] *n* Hohn, Spott *m* ◆ **object of ~** Zielscheibe *f* des Spotts; **to be greeted with ~** mit Spott *or* spöttisch aufgenommen werden.

derisive *adj*, **~ly** *adv* [dɪ'raɪsɪv, -lɪ] spöttisch, höhnisch; (*malicious*) hämisch, verächtlich.

derisory [dɪ'raɪsərɪ] *adj* **(a)** *amount, offer* lächerlich. **(b)** *see* **derisive.**

derivable [dɪ'raɪvəbl] *adj* (*Ling, Philos, Chem*) ableitbar,

derivation [ˌderɪ'veɪʃən] *n* (*Ling, Philos*) Ableitung *f*; (*Chem*) Derivation *f*.

derivative [dɪ'rɪvətɪv] [1] *adj* abgeleitet; (*Ling, Chem also*) derivativ; (*fig*) *style, composition, literary work etc* nachgeahmt, imitiert.
[2] *n* Ableitung *f*; (*Ling also, Chem*) Derivat *nt*.

derive [dɪ'raɪv] [1] *vt ideas, names, origins* her- *or* ableiten (*from* von); *profit* ziehen (*from* aus); *satisfaction, comfort, pleasure* gewinnen (*from* aus) ◆ **this word is ~d from the Greek** dieses Wort stammt aus dem Griechischen.
[2] *vi* **to ~ from** sich her- *or* ableiten von; (*power, fortune*) beruhen auf (+*dat*), herkommen *or* -rühren von; (*ideas*) kommen *or* stammen von; **it all ~s from the fact that ...** das beruht alles auf der Tatsache, daß ...

dermatitis [ˌdɜːmə'taɪtɪs] *n* Hautentzündung, Dermatitis *f*.

dermatologist [ˌdɜːmə'tɒlədʒɪst] *n* Hautarzt *m*, Hautärztin *f*, Dermatologe *m*, Dermatologin *f*.

dermatology [ˌdɜːmə'tɒlədʒɪ] *n* Dermatologie *f* ◆ **~ clinic** Hautklinik *f*.

derogate ['derəgeɪt] *vi* **to ~ from sth** (*form*) einer Sache (*dat*) Abbruch tun; **without derogating from his authority/merits** ohne seine Autorität/Verdienste schmälern zu wollen.

derogation [ˌderə'geɪʃən] *n* (*form: of power, dignity etc*) Beeinträchtigung, Schmälerung *f*, Abbruch *m* (*of, from gen*).

derogatory [dɪ'rɒgətərɪ] *adj* abfällig, abschätzig.

derrick ['derɪk] *n* Derrickkran, Montagekran *m*; (*above oilwell*) Bohrturm *m*.

derring-do ['derɪŋ'duː] *n* (*old*) Verwegenheit, Tollkühnheit *f* ◆ **deeds of ~** verwegene *or* tollkühne Taten.

derringer ['derɪndʒə^{r}] *n* Derringer *m or f*.

derv [dɜːv] *n* (*Brit*) Diesel(kraftstoff) *m*, Dieselöl *nt*.

dervish ['dɜːvɪʃ] *n* Derwisch *m*.

DES *abbr of* **Department of Education and Science** Bildungs- und Wissenschaftsministerium *nt*.

desalinate [diː'sælɪneɪt] *vt* entsalzen.

desalination [diːˌsælɪ'neɪʃən], **desalinization** [diːˌsælɪnaɪ'zeɪʃən] *n* Entsalzung *f* ◆ **~ plant** Meerwasserentsalzungsanlage *f*.

desalinize [diː'sælɪnaɪz] *vt* entsalzen.

desalt [diː'sɔːlt] *vt* (*esp US*) entsalzen ◆ **~ing plant** Meerwasserentsalzungsanlage *f*.

descale [diː'skeɪl] *vt* entkalken.

descant ['deskænt] [1] *n* (*Mus*) Diskant *m* ◆ **~ recorder** Sopranflöte *f*.
[2] [des'kænt] *vi* sich auslassen *or* verbreiten (*upon* über +*acc*), ausgiebig kommentieren.

descend [dɪ'send] [1] *vi* **(a)** (*go down: person*) herunter-/hinuntergehen, hinabschreiten (*geh*); (*lift, vehicle*) herunter-/hinunterfahren; (*road*) herunter-/hinunterführen, herunter-/hinuntergehen; (*hill*) abfallen; (*from horse*) absteigen; (*Astron*) untergehen ◆ **in ~ing order of importance** nach Wichtigkeit geordnet.
(b) (*have as ancestor*) abstammen (*from* von).
(c) (*pass by inheritance*) (*property*) übergehen (*from* von, *to* auf +*acc*); (*customs*) überliefert werden (*from* von, *to* auf +*acc*); (*rights*) vererbt werden (*from* von, *to* auf +*acc*).
(d) (*attack suddenly*) herfallen (*on, upon* über +*acc*), überfallen (*on, upon sb* jdn); (*plague*) hereinbrechen (*on, upon* über +*acc*); (*come over: sadness etc*) befallen (*on, upon sb* jdn).
(e) (*inf: visit*) **to ~ (up)on sb** jdn überfallen (*inf*).
(f) (*lower oneself*) **to ~ to sth** sich zu etw herablassen *or* erniedrigen; **I wouldn't ~ to lying** ich würde mich nie dazu herablassen *or* erniedrigen zu lügen; **he even ~ed to bribery** er scheute selbst vor Bestechung nicht zurück.
[2] *vt* **(a)** *stairs* hinunter-/heruntergehen *or* -steigen, hinabschreiten (*geh*). **(b) to be ~ed from** abstammen von.

descendant [dɪ'sendənt] *n* **(a)** Nachkomme *m*. **(b)** (*Astron, Astrol*) **in the ~** im Deszendenten.

descender [dɪ'sendə^{r}] *n* (*Typ*) Unterlänge *f*.

descent [dɪ'sent] *n* **(a)** (*going down*) (*of person*) Hinunter-/Heruntergehen, Absteigen *nt*; (*from mountain, of plane, into underworld*) Abstieg *m*; (*of gymnast*) Abgang *m*; (*slope, of road*) Abfall *m* ◆ **the ~ of the mountain** der Abstieg vom Berg; **the road made a sharp ~** die Straße fiel steil ab; **~ by parachute** Fallschirmabsprung *m*; **the ~ from the cross** (*Art, Rel*) die Kreuzabnahme.
(b) (*ancestry*) Abstammung, Herkunft *f* ◆ **of noble ~** von adliger Abstammung *or* Herkunft; **he is the thirteenth in ~ from ...** er ist der dreizehnte Nachkomme von ...
(c) (*of property*) Vererbung, Übertragung *f* (*to* auf +*acc*); (*of customs*) Überlieferung *f* (*to* auf +*acc*).
(d) (*Mil, fig: attack*) Überfall *m* (*on* auf +*acc*).
(e) (*inf: visit*) Überfall *m* (*inf*) ◆ **sorry about our unannounced ~ on you last night** entschuldige, daß wir dich gestern abend so unangemeldet überfallen haben.
(f) (*fig: into crime etc*) Absinken *nt* (*into* in +*acc*).

describe [dɪ'skraɪb] *vt* **(a)** beschreiben, schildern ◆ **~ him for us** beschreiben Sie ihn uns (*dat*); **which cannot be ~d** was unbeschreiblich ist. **(b)** (+*as*) bezeichnen ◆ **he ~s himself as a doctor** er bezeichnet sich (als) Arzt. **(c)** (*Math*) beschreiben.

description [dɪ'skrɪpʃən] *n* **(a)** Beschreibung *f*; (*of event, situation also*) Schilderung *f* ◆ **of a beauty beyond ~** von unbeschreiblicher Schönheit. **(b)** (+*as*) Bezeichnung *f*; *see* **answer 2 (b)**. **(c)** (*sort*) Art *f* ◆ **vehicles of every ~** Fahrzeuge aller Art. **(d)** (*Math*) Beschreibung *f*.

descriptive [dɪ'skrɪptɪv] *adj* **(a)** beschreibend; *account, adjective, passage* anschaulich ◆ **~ writing** Beschreibung *f*; **to be ~ of sth** etw beschreiben. **(b)** *linguistics, science etc* deskriptiv.

descriptivism [dɪ'skrɪptɪvɪzəm] *n* (*Ling, Philos*) Deskriptivismus *m*.

descriptivist [dɪ'skrɪptɪvɪst] (*Ling, Philos*) [1] *n* Deskriptivist(in *f*) *m*.
[2] *adj* deskriptivistisch.

descry [dɪ'skraɪ] *vt* (*form, liter*) gewahren (*geh*), erblicken.

desecrate ['desɪkreɪt] *vt* entweihen, schänden.

desecration [ˌdesɪ'kreɪʃən] *n* Entweihung, Schändung *f*.

desegregate [ˌdiː'segrɪgeɪt] *vt schools* desegregieren ◆ **~d schools** gemischtrassige Schulen *pl*.

desegregation ['diːˌsegrɪ'geɪʃən] *n* Aufhebung *f* der Rassentrennung (*of* in +*dat*), Desegregation *f*.

deselect [ˌdiːsɪ'lekt] *vt MP etc* nicht wieder (als Kandidat) aufstellen.

desensitize [ˌdiː'sensɪtaɪz] *vt* (*Phot*) lichtunempfindlich machen; (*Med*) desensibilisieren.

desert^{1} ['dezət] [1] *n* (*lit, fig*) Wüste *f*.
[2] *adj attr region, climate* Wüsten- ◆ **~ island** einsame *or* verlassene Insel; **~ boots** Boots *pl*; **~ rat** (*Brit fig inf*) Wüstensoldat *m*.

desert^{2} [dɪ'zɜːt] [1] *vt* (*leave*) verlassen; *cause, party* im Stich lassen ◆ **by the time the police arrived the place was ~ed** als die Polizei eintraf, war niemand mehr da; **in winter the place is ~ed** im Winter ist der Ort verlassen.
[2] *vi* (*Mil*) desertieren, Fahnenflucht begehen; (*fig also*) fahnenflüchtig werden ◆ **to ~ to the rebels** zu den Rebellen überlaufen.

deserter [dɪ'zɜːtə^{r}] *n* (*Mil, fig*) Deserteur *m*.

desertion [dɪ'zɜːʃən] *n* **(a)** (*act*) Verlassen *nt*; (*Jur: of wife, family*) böswilliges Verlassen; (*Mil*) Desertion, Fahnenflucht *f*; (*fig*) Fahnenflucht *f* ◆ **~ to the enemy** Überlaufen *nt* zum Feind. **(b)** (*state*) Verlassenheit *f*.

deserts [dɪ'zɜːts] *npl* Verdienste *pl*; (*reward, also iro*) verdiente Belohnung; (*punishment*) verdiente Strafe ◆ **according to one's ~** nach seinen Verdiensten; **to get one's just ~** bekommen, was man verdient, seine gerechte Belohnung bekommen.

deserve [dɪ'zɜːv] [1] *vt* verdienen ◆ **he ~s to win** er verdient den Sieg; **he ~s to be punished** er verdient es, bestraft zu werden.
[2] *vi* **he ~s well of his country** (*form*) sein Land ist ihm zu Dank verpflichtet.

deservedly [dɪ'zɜːvɪdlɪ] *adv* verdientermaßen ◆ **and ~ so** und das verdientermaßen.

deserving [dɪ'zɜːvɪŋ] *adj person, action, cause* verdienstvoll ◆ **the ~ poor** die Bedürftigen; **to be ~ of sth** etw verdienen.

deshabille [ˌdezə'biːl] *n see* **dishabille.**

desiccate ['desɪkeɪt] *vt* trocknen.

desiccated ['desɪkeɪtɪd] *adj* getrocknet; (*fig*) vertrocknet.

desiccation [ˌdesɪ'keɪʃən] *n* Trocknung *f*, Trocknen *nt*.

desideratum [dɪˌzɪdə'rɑːtəm] *n, pl* **desiderata** [dɪˌzɪdə'rɑːtə] Desiderat(um) (*liter*), Erfordernis *nt*.

design [dɪ'zaɪn] 1 *n* (a) *(planning, shaping etc)* *(of building, book, picture etc)* Entwurf *m*; *(of dress also)* Design *nt*; *(of car, machine, plane etc)* Konstruktion *f* ◆ **it's still at the ~ stage** es befindet sich noch in der Konstruktion *or* im Konstruktionsstadium; **a machine with a good/faulty ~** eine gut/schlecht konstruierte Maschine; **a new ~** *(Aut)* ein neues Modell.
(b) *no pl* *(as subject, art of designing)* Design *nt* ◆ **industrial ~** Konstruktionslehre *f*.
(c) *(pattern: on pottery, material)* Muster *nt*.
(d) *(intention)* Plan *m*, Absicht *f* ◆ **by ~** absichtlich; **to have ~s on sb/sth** mit jdm/etw etwas im Sinn haben, es auf jdn/etw abgesehen haben; **he has ~s on her** er hat etwas mit ihr vor.
2 *vt* (a) entwerfen; *machine* konstruieren ◆ **a well ~ed machine** eine gut durchkonstruierte Maschine. (b) *(intend)* **to be ~ed for sb/sth** für jdn/etw vorgesehen *or* bestimmt sein.
3 *vi* planen, Pläne *or* Entwürfe machen.
4 *adj attr engineer, team* Design-.

designate ['dezɪgneɪt] 1 *vt* (a) *(name)* kennzeichnen, benennen; *(appoint)* bestimmen, ernennen, designieren *(form)* ◆ **to ~ sb as sth** jdn zu etw ernennen. (b) *(indicate, specify, mark)* festlegen, bestimmen.
2 ['dezɪgnɪt] *adj* **the Prime Minister ~** der designierte Premierminister.

designation [,dezɪg'neɪʃən] *n see vt* Kennzeichnung, Benennung *f*; Bestimmung, Ernennung *f*; Festlegung *f*.

designedly [dɪ'zaɪnɪdlɪ] *adv* absichtlich, vorsätzlich.

designer [dɪ'zaɪnə^r] 1 *n* Designer, Gestalter *m*; *(fashion ~)* Modeschöpfer(in *f*) *m*; *(of machines etc)* Konstrukteur *m*; *(Theat)* Bühnenbildner(in *f*) *m*.
2 *adj attr* Designer- ◆ **~ drug** Modedroge *f*; **~ stubble** *(hum)* Dreitagebart *m* *(inf)*.

designing [dɪ'zaɪnɪŋ] *adj* intrigant, hinterhältig.

desirability [dɪ,zaɪərə'bɪlɪtɪ] *n* Wünschbarkeit *f* ◆ **they discussed the ~ of the plan** sie erörterten, ob das Vorhaben wünschenswert sei; **in his eyes this only increased her ~** das machte sie in seinen Augen um so begehrenswerter; **to increase the ~ of these houses** um die Attraktivität dieser Häuser zu erhöhen.

desirable [dɪ'zaɪərəbl] *adj* (a) *action, progress* wünschenswert, erwünscht. (b) *position, offer, house, area* reizvoll, attraktiv. (c) *woman* begehrenswert.

▼ **desire** [dɪ'zaɪə^r] 1 *n* *(for* nach*)* Wunsch *m*; *(longing)* Sehnsucht *f*; *(sexual)* Verlangen, Begehren *nt* ◆ **her sexual ~s** ihre sexuellen Wünsche; **a ~ for peace** ein Verlangen nach Frieden; **heart's ~** Herzenswunsch *m*; **I have no ~ to see him** ich habe kein Verlangen, ihn zu sehen; **I have no ~ to cause you any trouble** ich möchte Ihnen keine Unannehmlichkeiten bereiten.
2 *vt* wünschen; *object* sich *(dat)* wünschen; *woman* begehren; *peace* haben wollen, verlangen nach ◆ **it leaves much to be ~d** das läßt viel zu wünschen übrig ◆ **to ~ sb to do sth** *(form: request)* jdn bitten *or* ersuchen, etw zu tun.

desirous [dɪ'zaɪərəs] *adj see vt* **to be ~ of sth** *(form)* etw wünschen/wollen/begehren.

desist [dɪ'zɪst] *vi (form)* Abstand nehmen, absehen *(from doing sth* davon, etw zu tun, *from sth* von etw*)* ◆ **would you kindly ~!** unterlassen Sie das gefälligst!

desk [desk] *n* Schreibtisch *m*; *(for pupils, master)* Pult *nt*; *(in shop, restaurant)* Kasse *f*; *(in hotel)* Empfang *m*; *(Press)* Ressort *nt* ◆ **information ~** Information(sschalter *m*) *f*.

desk: ~bound *adj* an den Schreibtisch gebunden; **~ clerk** *n (US)* Empfangschef *m*; **~ diary** *n* Tischkalender *m*; **~ editor** *n* Lektor(in *f*), Manuskriptbearbeiter(in *f*) *m*; *(Press)* Ressortchef(in *f*) *m*; **~ job** *n* Bürojob *m*; **~ pad** *n* Schreibunterlage *f*.

desktop ['desktɒp] *n* Arbeitsfläche *f*.

desktop: ~ computer *n* Desktop-Computer, Tischrechner *m*; **~ publishing** *n* Desktop-Publishing *nt*.

desk work *n* Schreibarbeit *f*.

desolate ['desəlɪt] 1 *adj* (a) *place (devastated)* verwüstet; *(barren)* trostlos; *(fig) outlook* trostlos. (b) *(grief-stricken)* tieftraurig, zu Tode betrübt; *(friendless)* verlassen; *cry* verzweifelt, der Verzweiflung.
2 ['desəleɪt] *vt* (a) *country* verwüsten. (b) *person* zu Tode betrüben, untröstlich machen.

desolately ['desəlɪtlɪ] *adv see adj*.

desolation [,desə'leɪʃən] *n* (a) *(of country by war)* Verwüstung *f*. (b) *(of landscape)* Trostlosigkeit *f*. (c) *(grief)* Trostlosigkeit *f*; *(friendlessness)* Verlassenheit *f*.

despair [dɪ'speə^r] 1 *n* Verzweiflung *f (about, at* über *+acc)* ◆ **to be in ~** verzweifelt sein; **he was filled with ~** Verzweiflung überkam *or* ergriff ihn; **in ~, she gave up** in ihrer Verzweiflung gab sie auf; **his ~ of ever being able to return home** seine Verzweiflung darüber, vielleicht nie mehr nach Hause zurückkehren zu können; **to be the ~ of sb** jdn zur Verzweiflung bringen.
2 *vi* verzweifeln, alle Hoffnung aufgeben ◆ **to ~ of doing sth** alle Hoffnung aufgeben, etw zu tun; **to ~ of sth** alle Hoffnung auf etw *(acc)* aufgeben; **his life was ~ed of** man gab ihm keine Überlebenschancen; **to make sb ~** jdn zur Verzweiflung bringen *or* treiben.

despairing *adj*, **~ly** *adv* [dɪs'peərɪŋ, -lɪ] verzweifelt.

despatch [dɪ'spætʃ] *vt, n see* **dispatch**.

desperado [,despə'rɑːdəʊ] *n, pl* **-(e)s** Desperado *m*.

desperate ['despərɪt] *adj* (a) verzweifelt; *criminal* zum Äußersten entschlossen; *(urgent) need etc* dringend ◆ **to feel ~** verzweifelt sein; **to get ~** verzweifeln, in Verzweiflung geraten; **I haven't had a cigarette for hours, I'm getting ~** *(inf)* ich habe schon seit Stunden keine mehr geraucht, jetzt brauche ich (aber) dringend eine; **to be ~ for sth** etw dringend brauchen *or* benötigen; **I'm/it's not that ~!** so dringend ist es nicht!; **I was ~ to get the job** ich wollte die Stelle unbedingt haben; **don't do anything ~!** lassen Sie sich nicht zu einer Verzweiflungstat hinreißen; **to do something ~** sich zu einer Verzweiflungstat hinreißen lassen; **that was a rather ~ solution** das war (doch) eine recht extreme Lösung.
(b) *situation etc* verzweifelt, hoffnungslos ◆ **things are getting ~** die Lage wird allmählich verzweifelt *etc*.
(c) *(inf: very bad) colour etc* schrecklich ◆ **what a ~ idiot he is** er ist (doch) wirklich der letzte Idiot *(inf)*.

desperately ['despərɪtlɪ] *adv* (a) verzweifelt, voller Verzweiflung; *(urgently) need* dringend ◆ **~ in love** verliebt bis über beide Ohren; **~ ill** schwerkrank *attr*, schwer krank *pred*; **do you want ...? — not ~** möchten Sie ...? — nicht unbedingt; **was it good/are you busy? — not ~** war's schön/hast du zu tun? — nicht gerade übermäßig, es hielt/hält sich in Grenzen.
(b) *(inf) cold, frightened, funny* fürchterlich *attr*.

desperation [,despə'reɪʃən] *n* Verzweiflung *f* ◆ **an act of ~** eine Verzweiflungstat; **in (sheer) ~** aus (reiner) Verzweiflung; **in ~ of ever seeing him** weil sie *etc* alle Hoffnung aufgegeben hatte, ihn je zu sehen *or* zu Gesicht zu bekommen; **to drive sb to ~** jdn zur Verzweiflung bringen *or* treiben; **to be in ~** verzweifelt sein; **to fight with ~** verzweifelt kämpfen.

despicable [dɪ'spɪkəbl] *adj* verabscheuungswürdig; *person* verachtenswert, widerwärtig, ekelhaft ◆ **don't be so ~** sei (doch) nicht ekelhaft.

despicably [dɪ'spɪkəblɪ] *adv* verabscheuungswürdig, widerwärtig, ekelhaft ◆ **he was ~ rude** er war so ekelhaft *or* widerwärtig grob.

despise [dɪ'spaɪz] *vt* verachten; *presents, food also* verschmähen.

despising *adj*, **~ly** *adv* [dɪ'spaɪzɪŋ, -lɪ] verächtlich, voller Verachtung, verachtungsvoll.

despite [dɪ'spaɪt] *prep* trotz *(+gen)* ◆ **in ~ of** *(old, liter)* trotz, ungeachtet *(+gen)*; **~ his warnings** seinen Warnungen zum Trotz; **~ what she says** trotz allem, was sie sagt.

despoil [dɪ'spɔɪl] *vt person* berauben *(of gen)*; *country* plündern ◆ **~ed of all its treasures** all seiner Schätze beraubt.

despondence [dɪ'spɒndəns], **despondency** [dɪ'spɒndənsɪ] *n* Niedergeschlagenheit, Mutlosigkeit *f*.

despondent [dɪ'spɒndənt] *adj* niedergeschlagen, mutlos ◆ **to be ~ about sth** über etw *(acc)* bedrückt sein; **to grow** *or* **get ~** den Mut verlieren.

despondently [dɪ'spɒndəntlɪ] *adv* niedergeschlagen, mutlos.

despot ['despɒt] *n (lit, fig)* Despot *m*.

despotic *adj*, **~ally** *adv* [des'pɒtɪk, -əlɪ] *(lit, fig)* despotisch, herrisch.

despotism ['despətɪzəm] *n* Despotie *f*; *(as ideology)* Despotismus *m*.

des res ['dez'rez] *n (hum inf)* attraktiver Wohnsitz.

dessert [dɪ'zɜːt] *n* Nachtisch *m*, Dessert *nt* ◆ **for ~** als *or* zum Nachtisch.

dessert: ~ apple *n* Dessertapfel *m*; **~ plate** *n* Dessertteller *m*; **~spoon** *n* Dessertlöffel *m*; **~ wine** *n* Dessertwein *m*.

destabilization [,diːsteɪbɪlaɪ'zeɪʃən] *n* Destabilisierung *f*.

destabilize [diː'steɪbɪlaɪz] *vt* destabilisieren.

destination [,destɪ'neɪʃən] *n* *(of person)* Reiseziel *nt*; *(of goods)* Bestimmungsort *m*; *(fig: of person)* Bestimmung *f*; *(of money)* Zweck *m* ◆ **port of ~** Bestimmungshafen *m*; **to know one's ~ in life** seine Bestimmung kennen.

destine ['destɪn] *vt* (a) *(set apart, predestine) person* bestimmen, ausersehen; *object* bestimmen ◆ **to be ~d to do sth** dazu bestimmt *or* ausersehen sein, etw zu tun; **the qualities which ~d him for leadership** die Eigenschaften, die ihn für Führungsaufgaben prädestinierten.
(b) *usu pass (be fated)* **we were ~d to meet** das Schicksal hat es so gewollt, daß wir uns begegnen; **I was ~d never to see them again** ich sollte sie nie (mehr) wiedersehen; **at the ~d hour** zu der vom Schicksal (vor)bestimmten Stunde.

destined ['destɪnd] *adj*: **~ for** *(ship)* unterwegs nach; *(goods)* für; **where is the cargo ~ for?** wo geht diese Fracht hin?

destiny ['destɪnɪ] *n* (a) *no art (determining power)* Schicksal *nt*, Vorsehung *f* ◆ **D~** das Schicksal, die Vorsehung.
(b) *(individual fate, fated event)* Schicksal, Geschick, Los *nt* ◆ **the destinies of Germany during this period** die Geschicke Deutschlands während dieser Zeit; **to control one's own ~** sein Schicksal selbst in die Hand nehmen; **it was his ~** es war sein Schicksal *or* Los; **will it be our ~ to meet again?** wird uns das Schicksal (je) wieder zusammenführen?

destitute ['destɪtjuːt] 1 *adj* (a) *(poverty-stricken)* mittellos ◆ **to be utterly ~** bettelarm sein. (b) *(lacking)* bar *(of gen)*.
2 *npl* **the ~** die Mittellosen, die, die im Elend leben.

destitution [,destɪ'tjuːʃən] *n* (bittere) Not, Elend *nt*; *(esp financially)* Mittellosigkeit *f*.

destroy [dɪ'strɔɪ] *vt* (a) zerstören; *box, toy, watch etc* kaputtmachen; *documents etc also* vernichten; *trace also* tilgen; *(fire also)* verwüsten ◆ **to ~ oneself** sich zugrunde richten; **to be ~ed by fire** durch Brand vernichtet werden.
(b) *(kill)* vernichten; *animal* einschläfern.
(c) *(put an end to)* zerstören; *influence, hopes, chances* zunichte machen, vernichten; *reputation, mood, beauty* ruinieren; *morals* zersetzen ◆ **you'll ~ your appetite** du verdirbst dir den Appetit; **they are trying to ~ him as party leader** sie versuchen, seine Stellung als Parteiführer zu ruinieren.

destroyer [dɪ'strɔɪə^r] *n (Naut)* Zerstörer *m*.

destruct [dɪ'strʌkt] 1 *vi (esp Space)* sich selbst zerstören.
2 *attr mechanism etc* Selbstzerstörungs-.

destructible [dɪ'strʌktəbl] *adj* vernichtbar.

destruction [dɪ'strʌkʃən] *n* (a) *(destroying: of town, building, hope)* Zerstörung *f*; *(of enemy, people, insects, documents)* Vernichtung *f*; *(of reputation also)*

➤ LANGUAGE IN USE: **desire: 1 → 8.3**

Ruinierung *f*; (*of character, soul*) Zerstörung, Zersetzung *f*. **(b)** (*damage: caused by war, fire*) Verwüstung, Zerstörung *f*.

destructive [dɪ'strʌktɪv] *adj* **(a)** *wind, fire, war* zerstörerisch; *tendencies also* destruktiv; *urge* Zerstörungs- ◆ **a ~ child** ein Kind, das zum Zerstören neigt, ein destruktives Kind (*Psych*); **to be ~ of sth** etw zerstören. **(b)** (*fig*) *criticism etc* destruktiv.

destructively [dɪ'strʌktɪvlɪ] *adv* destruktiv.

destructiveness [dɪ'strʌktɪvnɪs] *n* **(a)** (*of fire, war*) zerstörende Wirkung; (*of person, child etc*) Destruktivität (*esp Psych*), Zerstörungswut *f*. **(b)** (*of criticism*) Destruktivität *f*, zersetzende Wirkung.

destructor [dɪ'strʌktəʳ] *n* (*Tech: also* **refuse ~**) Müllverbrennungsanlage *f*.

desuetude [dɪ'sjuːtjuːd] *n* (*form*) **to fall into ~** außer Gebrauch kommen.

desulphurization [ˌdiːsʌlfəraɪ'zeɪʃən] *n* Entschwefelung *f* ◆ **~ plant** Entschwefelungsanlage *f*.

desultoriness ['desəltərɪnɪs] *n see adj* Flüchtigkeit *f*; Halbherzigkeit *f*; Zwanglosigkeit *f*.

desultory ['desəltərɪ] *adj reading* flüchtig; *manner, approach, attempt* halbherzig; *firing* vereinzelt, sporadisch ◆ **to have a ~ conversation** eine zwanglose Unterhaltung führen.

detach [dɪ'tætʃ] *vt* **(a)** (*separate, unfasten*) *rope, cart* loslösen (*from* von); *section of form, document* abtrennen (*from* von); *part of machine, wooden leg, collar, hood* abnehmen (*from* von); *lining* herausnehmen (*from* aus); *coach from train* abhängen (*from* von) ◆ **to ~ oneself from a group** sich von einer Gruppe lösen *or* trennen; **a section became ~ed from ...** ein Teil löste sich von ...; **these buildings are ~ed from the main block** diese Gebäude stehen gesondert vom Hauptkomplex.
(b) (*Mil, Naut*) abkommandieren.

detachable [dɪ'tætʃəbl] *adj part of machine, collar* abnehmbar; *section of document* abtrennbar (*from* von); *lining* ausknöpfbar; (*with zip*) ausreißbar; *lens* auswechselbar.

detached [dɪ'tætʃt] *adj* **(a)** (*unbiased*) *opinion* distanziert, unvoreingenommen; (*unemotional*) *manner* kühl, distanziert. **(b) ~ house** alleinstehendes Haus, Einzelhaus *nt*.

detachment [dɪ'tætʃmənt] *n* **(a)** (*act of separating*) *see vt* (*a*) Loslösen *nt*; Abtrennen *nt*; Abnehmen *nt*; Herausnehmen *nt*; Abhängen *nt*. **(b)** (*emotionlessness*) Distanz *f*; (*objectivity*) Abstand *m*. **(c)** (*Mil*) Sonderkommando *nt*, Abordnung *f*.

▼ **detail** ['diːteɪl] [1] *n* **(a)** Detail *nt*; (*particular*) Einzelheit *f*; (*part of painting, photo etc*) Ausschnitt *m*; (*insignificant circumstance*) unwichtige Einzelheit ◆ **in ~** im Detail, in Einzelheiten; **in great ~** in allen Einzelheiten, ausführlich; **in every ~** mit *or* in allen Einzelheiten; **every ~ was taken care of** jede Kleinigkeit wurde beachtet; **there's one little ~ you've forgotten** eine Kleinigkeit haben Sie (noch) vergessen; **please send me further ~s** bitte schicken Sie mir nähere *or* weitere Einzelheiten; **I didn't want to hear the ~s** ich wollte die Einzelheiten (gar) nicht hören; **to go into ~s** auf Einzelheiten eingehen, ins Detail gehen; **his attention to ~** seine Aufmerksamkeit für das Detail; **but that's a ~!** das ist doch (wirklich) nur eine (unwichtige) Einzelheit, das ist doch unwichtig!
(b) (*Mil*) Sondertrupp *m*.
[2] *vt* **(a)** *facts, story* ausführlich *or* genau erzählen *or* berichten ◆ **the specifications are fully ~ed on page 3** die genaue Ausführung wird auf Seite 3 aufgeführt.
(b) (*Mil*) *troops* abkommandieren (*for* zu, *to do* um zu tun).

detail drawing *n* Detailzeichnung *f*.

detailed ['diːteɪld] *adj* ausführlich, genau, detailliert.

detain [dɪ'teɪn] *vt* (*keep back*) aufhalten; (*police*) in Haft nehmen ◆ **to be ~ed** (*be arrested*) verhaftet werden; (*be in detention*) sich in Haft *or* polizeilichem Gewahrsam befinden; **to ~ sb for questioning** jdn zur Vernehmung festhalten.

detainee [diteɪ'niː] *n* Häftling *m*.

detect [dɪ'tekt] *vt* entdecken, herausfinden; (*see, make out*) ausfindig machen; *culprit* entlarven; *crime* aufdecken; *a tone of sadness, movement, noise* wahrnehmen; *mine, gas* aufspüren ◆ **do I ~ a note of irony?** höre ich da nicht eine gewisse Ironie (heraus)?

detectable [dɪ'tektəbl] *adj* (*able to be found*) *trace* feststellbar ◆ **sb/sth is ~** (*discernible*) jd läßt sich ausfindig machen/etw läßt sich wahrnehmen; **no ~ difference** kein erkennbarer Unterschied.

detection [dɪ'tekʃən] *n* **(a)** (*of criminal*) Entlarvung *f*; (*of crime*) Entdeckung, Aufdeckung *f*; (*of fault*) Entdeckung, Feststellung *f*; (*detective work*) Ermittlungsarbeit *f* ◆ **to escape ~** (*criminal*) nicht gefaßt *or* dingfest gemacht werden; (*mistake*) der Aufmerksamkeit (*dat*) entgehen; **he tried to escape ~ by ...** er versuchte, unentdeckt zu bleiben, indem ...; **a brilliant piece of ~** ein glänzendes Stück Detektivarbeit.
(b) (*of gases, mines*) Aufspürung *f*.

detective [dɪ'tektɪv] *n* (*police ~*) Kriminalbeamte(r) *mf*; (*private ~*) Detektiv *m*; (*fig*) Detektiv *m*.

detective: ~ agency *n* Detektivbüro *nt*, Detektei *f*; **~ chief inspector** *n* (*Brit*) Kriminaloberinspektor *m*; **~ chief superintendent** *n* (*Brit*) Kriminalhauptkommissar *m*; **~ constable** *n* (*Brit*) Kriminalbeamte(r) *m*; **~ inspector** *n* Kriminalinspektor *m*; **~ sergeant** *n* Kriminalmeister *m*; **~ story** *n* Kriminalgeschichte *f*, Kriminalroman, Krimi (*inf*) *m*; **~ superintendent** *n* (*Brit*) Kriminalkommissar *m*; **~ work** *n* kriminalistische Arbeit.

detector [dɪ'tektəʳ] *n* (*Rad, Tech*) Detektor *m* ◆ **~ van** Funkmeßwagen *m*.

détente [deɪ'tɑːnt] *n* Entspannung, Détente *f*.

detention [dɪ'tenʃən] *n* **(a)** (*captivity*) Haft *f*, Gewahrsam *m*; (*act*) Festnahme *f*; (*Mil*) Arrest *m*; (*Sch*) Nachsitzen *nt* ◆ **to give a pupil two hours' ~** einen Schüler zwei Stunden nachsitzen lassen; **he's in ~** (*Sch*) er sitzt nach.
(b) (*being held up, delayed*) Verzögerung *f*, Aufenthalt *m*.

detention centre *n* Jugendstrafanstalt *f*.

deter [dɪ'tɜːʳ] *vt* (*prevent*) abhalten, hindern; (*discourage*) abschrecken ◆ **to ~ sb from sth** jdn von etw abhalten *or* an etw (*dat*) hindern; **he won't be ~red** er läßt sich nicht abhalten/abschrecken; **don't let him ~ you** lassen Sie sich nicht von ihm abhalten *or* abbringen.

detergent [dɪ'tɜːdʒənt] [1] *n* Reinigungs- *or* Säuberungsmittel *nt*; (*soap powder etc*) Waschmittel *nt*.
[2] *adj* reinigend.

deteriorate [dɪ'tɪərɪəreɪt] *vi* sich verschlechtern; (*materials*) verderben; (*species*) entarten; (*morals, brickwork*) verfallen.

deterioration [dɪˌtɪərɪə'reɪʃən] *n see vi* Verschlechterung *f*; Verderben *nt*; Entartung *f*; Verfall *m*.

determinable [dɪ'tɜːmɪnəbl] *adj* **(a)** *quantity* bestimmbar. **(b)** (*Jur*) befristet.

determinant [dɪ'tɜːmɪnənt] [1] *adj* determinierend *attr*, entscheidend.
[2] *n* ausschlaggebender Faktor; (*Math, Biol etc*) Determinante *f*.

determinate [dɪ'tɜːmɪnɪt] *adj number, period etc* bestimmt, begrenzt; *concept also* fest(gelegt).

determination [dɪˌtɜːmɪ'neɪʃən] *n* **(a)** (*firmness of purpose*) Entschlossenheit *f* ◆ **he has great ~** er ist ein Mensch von großer Entschlußkraft; **an air of ~** eine entschlossene Miene; **there is an air of ~ about him** er hat etwas Entschlossenes an sich.
(b) (*determining*) Determinierung *f*; (*of character, future also*) Bestimmung *f*; (*of cause, nature, position*) Ermittlung, Bestimmung *f*; (*of frontiers*) Festlegung, Festsetzung *f*.

determinative [dɪ'tɜːmɪnətɪv] (*Gram*) [1] *n* Determinativ(um) *nt*.
[2] *adj* determinativ.

determine [dɪ'tɜːmɪn] *vt* **(a)** (*be a decisive factor in*) *sb's character, future etc* bestimmen, determinieren.
(b) (*settle, fix*) *conditions, price* festlegen, festsetzen.
(c) (*ascertain*) *cause, nature, position* ermitteln, bestimmen.
(d) (*resolve*) beschließen.
(e) (*cause to decide*) *person* veranlassen ◆ **to ~ sb to do sth** jdn dazu veranlassen *or* bewegen, etw zu tun.
(f) (*Jur*) *contract* beenden.

◆**determine on** *vi +prep obj course of action, alternative* sich entschließen zu ◆ **to ~ ~ doing sth** beschließen *or* sich entschließen, etw zu tun.

▼ **determined** [dɪ'tɜːmɪnd] *adj person, appearance* entschlossen ◆ **he is ~ that ...** er hat fest beschlossen, daß ...; **they are ~ to succeed** sie sind (fest) entschlossen, erfolgreich zu sein; **he's ~ to make me lose my temper** (*inf*) er legt es darauf an, daß ich wütend werde; **you seem ~ to exhaust yourself** du scheinst dich mit aller Gewalt kaputtmachen zu wollen.

determinedly [dɪ'tɜːmɪndlɪ] *adv* voller Entschlossenheit, entschlossen.

determiner [dɪ'tɜːmɪnəʳ] *n* (*Gram*) Bestimmungswort *nt*.

determining [dɪ'tɜːmɪnɪŋ] *adj* entscheidend, bestimmend.

determinism [dɪ'tɜːmɪnɪzəm] *n* Determinismus *m*.

determinist [dɪ'tɜːmɪnɪst] [1] *adj* deterministisch.
[2] *n* Determinist(in *f*) *m*.

deterministic [dɪˌtɜːmɪ'nɪstɪk] *adj* deterministisch.

deterrence [dɪ'terəns] *n* Abschreckung *f*.

deterrent [dɪ'terənt] [1] *n* (*also Mil*) Abschreckungsmittel *nt* ◆ **to act as a ~** als Abschreckung(smittel) dienen (*to* für); **to be a ~** abschrecken.
[2] *adj* abschreckend, Abschreckungs-.

detest [dɪ'test] *vt* verabscheuen, hassen ◆ **I ~ having to get up early** ich hasse es, früh aufstehen zu müssen; **~ed by all** von allen gehaßt.

detestable [dɪ'testəbl] *adj* widerwärtig, abscheulich; *character also* verabscheuungswürdig.

detestably [dɪ'testəblɪ] *adv* widerwärtig, abscheulich.

detestation [ˌdiːtes'teɪʃən] *n* **(a)** Abscheu *m* (of vor *+dat*). **(b)** (*object of hatred*) **to be the ~ of sb** jds Abscheu erregen.

dethrone [diː'θrəʊn] *vt* entthronen.

dethronement [diː'θrəʊnmənt] *n* Entthronung *f*.

detonate ['detəneɪt] [1] *vi* (*fuse*) zünden; (*bomb also*) detonieren.
[2] *vt* zur Explosion bringen ◆ **detonating device** Detonator *m*.

detonation [ˌdetə'neɪʃən] *n* Zündung *f*.

detonator ['detəneɪtəʳ] *n* Zünd- *or* Sprengkapsel *f*; (*Rail*) Nebelsignal *nt*.

detour ['diːˌtʊəʳ] [1] *n* **(a)** (*in road, fig*) Umweg *m*; (*in river*) Schleife *f*, Bogen *m*; (*from a subject*) Abschweifung *f* ◆ **to make a ~** einen Umweg machen. **(b)** (*for traffic*) Umleitung *f*.
[2] *vt traffic* umleiten.

detoxification [ˌdiːtɒksɪfɪ'keɪʃən] *n* Entgiftung *f*.

detoxify [diː'tɒksɪfaɪ] *vt* entgiften.

detract [dɪ'trækt] *vi* **to ~ from sth** etw beeinträchtigen, einer Sache (*dat*) Abbruch tun; *pleasure, merit also* etw schmälern.

detraction [dɪ'trækʃən] *n* Beeinträchtigung, Schmälerung *f* (*from* gen).

detractor [dɪ'træktəʳ] *n* Kritiker(in *f*) *m*.

detrain [diː'treɪn] [1] *vt* ausladen.
[2] *vi* (*troops, esp US: passengers*) aussteigen.

detribalize [diː'traɪbəlaɪz] *vt* die Stammesstruktur auflösen in (*+dat*) ◆ **as Africa becomes increasingly ~d** mit dem zunehmenden Verfall der Stammesstruktur in Afrika.

detriment ['detrɪmənt] *n* Schaden, Nachteil *m* ◆ **to the ~ of** zum Schaden

➤ LANGUAGE IN USE: **detail: 1a** → 19.1, 20.1, 21.3, 26.3 **determined** → 8.2

(*+gen*) *or* von; **without ~ to** ohne Schaden für; **I don't know anything to his ~** ich weiß nichts Nachteiliges über ihn.

detrimental [ˌdetrɪ'mentl] *adj* (*to health, reputation*) schädlich (*to dat*); *effect also* nachteilig (*to* für); (*to case, cause, one's interest*) abträglich (*to dat*).

detritus [dɪ'traɪtəs] *n* (*Geol*) Geröll *nt*; (*fig*) Müll *m*.

de trop [də'trəʊ] *adj* fehl am Platz, überflüssig.

deuce[1] [dju:s] *n* **(a)** (*Cards*) Zwei *f*. **(b)** (*Tennis*) Einstand *m* ◆ **after ten ~s** nachdem es zehnmal Einstand gegeben hatte; **to be at ~** den Einstand erreicht haben.

deuce[2] *n* (*dated inf*) Teufel *m*; *for phrases see* **devil 1 (c)**.

deuced ['djʊsɪd] (*dated inf*) [1] *adj* verteufelt (*dated inf*), verdammt (*inf*) ◆ **that ~ dog** dieser verdammte Hund (*inf*).
[2] *adv* **what ~ bad weather** verteufelt schlechtes Wetter! (*dated inf*).

deucedly ['dju:sɪdlɪ] *adv* (*dated inf*) verteufelt (*dated inf*).

deus ex machina ['deɪəseks'mækɪnə] *n* Deus ex machina *m*.

deuterium [dju:'tɪərɪəm] *n* Deuterium *nt*.

Deuteronomy [ˌdju:tə'rɒnəmɪ] *n* das fünfte Buch Mose(s), Deuteronomium *nt* (*spec*).

devaluate [di:'væljʊeɪt] *vt see* **devalue**.

devaluation [ˌdɪvæljʊ'eɪʃən] *n* Abwertung *f*.

devalue [di:'vælju:] *vt* abwerten.

devastate ['devəsteɪt] *vt* **(a)** (*lit*) *town, land* verwüsten; (*fig*) *opposition* vernichten. **(b)** (*inf: overwhelm*) umhauen (*inf*) ◆ **I was ~d** das hat mich umgehauen (*inf*).

devastating ['devəsteɪtɪŋ] *adj* **(a)** (*destructive*) *wind, storm* verheerend, vernichtend.
(b) (*fig: overwhelming*) *power* verheerend; *passion* zerstörerisch; *news* niederschmetternd; *grief* überwältigend.
(c) (*inf*) *argument, attack, reply* vernichtend; *effect, consequences* verheerend; *wit, humour, charm, woman* umwerfend, überwältigend.

devastatingly ['devəsteɪtɪŋlɪ] *adv beautiful, funny* umwerfend.

devastation [ˌdevə'steɪʃən] *n* Verwüstung *f*.

develop [dɪ'veləp] [1] *vt* **(a)** *mind, body* entwickeln.
(b) *argument, thesis, outlines* (weiter)entwickeln, weiter ausführen; *original idea* (weiter)entwickeln; *plot of novel* (*unfold*) entfalten; (*fill out*) weiterentwickeln, ausbauen; (*Mus*) *theme* durchführen.
(c) *natural resources, region, ground* erschließen; *old part of a town* sanieren; *new estate* erschließen; *new series, new model* entwickeln; *business* (*expand*) erweitern, ausbauen; (*from scratch*) aufziehen ◆ **they plan to ~ this area into a ...** es ist geplant, dieses Gebiet als ... zu erschließen.
(d) *liking, taste, talent* entwickeln; *cold* sich (*dat*) zuziehen.
(e) (*Phot, Math*) entwickeln.
[2] *vi* **(a)** (*person, region, country*) sich entwickeln ◆ **to ~ into sth** sich zu etw entwickeln, etw werden. **(b)** (*illness, tendency, feeling*) sich entwickeln; (*talent, plot etc*) sich entfalten. **(c)** (*Phot*) entwickelt werden. **(d)** (*event, situation*) sich entwickeln ◆ **it later ~ed that he had never seen her** später stellte sich heraus *or* zeigte es sich, daß er sie nie gesehen hatte.

developer [dɪ'veləpə^r] *n* **(a)** *see* **property ~**. **(b)** (*Phot*) Entwickler *m*. **(c) late ~** Spätentwickler *m*.

developing [dɪ'veləpɪŋ] [1] *adj crisis, storm* aufkommend; *industry* neu entstehend; *interest* wachsend.
[2] *n* **(a)** *see* **development (a, d)**. **(b)** (*Phot*) Entwickeln *nt*.

developing: ~ bath *n* Entwicklerbad *nt*; **~ country** *n* Entwicklungsland *nt*; **~ tank** *n* Entwicklerschale *f*.

development [dɪ'veləpmənt] *n* **(a)** (*of person, mind, body*) Entwicklung *f*.
(b) (*way subject, plot etc is developed*) Ausführung *f*; (*of interests also*) Entfaltung *f*; (*of argument etc*) (Weiter)entwicklung *f*; (*Mus*) Durchführung *f*.
(c) (*change in situation*) Entwicklung *f* ◆ **new ~s in ...** neue Entwicklungen in ...; **to await ~s** die Entwicklung abwarten.
(d) (*of area, site, new town*) Erschließung *f*; (*of old part of town*) Sanierung *f*; (*of industry*) (*from scratch*) Entwicklung *f*; (*expansion*) Ausbau *m* ◆ **we live in a new ~** wir leben in einer neuen Siedlung; **unauthorized ~** illegale Baumaßnahmen *pl*.
(e) (*Phot, Math*) Entwicklung *f*.

developmental [dɪveləp'mentl] *adj stage* Entwicklungs-.

development: ~ area *n* Entwicklungsgebiet *nt*; (*in town*) Erschließungsgebiet *nt*; (*in old town*) Sanierungsgebiet *nt*; **~ company** *n* (Wohnungs)baugesellschaft *f*; **~ costs** *npl* Erschließungskosten *pl*; **~ grant** *n* Entwicklungsförderung *f*.

deviancy ['di:vɪənsɪ] *n* abweichendes Verhalten, Devianz *f*.

deviant ['di:vɪənt] [1] *adj behaviour* abweichend, deviant (*spec*).
[2] *n* jd, der von der Norm abweicht, Deviant *m* (*spec*).

deviate ['di:vɪeɪt] *vi* **(a)** (*person: from truth, former statement, routine*) abweichen. **(b)** (*ship, plane, projectile*) vom Kurs abweichen *or* abkommen; (*deliberately*) vom Kurs abgehen.

deviation [ˌdi:vɪ'eɪʃən] *n* Abweichen *nt*, Abweichung *f*.

deviationism [ˌdi:vɪ'eɪʃənɪzəm] *n* Abweichlertum *nt*.

deviationist [ˌdi:vɪ'eɪʃənɪst] [1] *adj* abweichend.
[2] *n* Abweichler(in *f*) *m*.

device [dɪ'vaɪs] *n* **(a)** (*gadget etc*) Gerät *nt*; (*extra fitment*) Vorrichtung *f* ◆ **nuclear ~** atomarer Sprengkörper; **a rhetorical ~** ein rhetorischer Kunstgriff. **(b) to leave sb to his own ~s** jdn sich (*dat*) selbst überlassen.
(c) (*emblem*) Emblem *nt*; (*motto*) Motto *nt*, Devise *f*.

devil ['devl] [1] *n* **(a)** (*evil spirit*) Teufel *m*.
(b) (*inf*) (*person, child*) Teufel *m* (*inf*); (*object, screw etc*) Plage *f*; (*daring person*) Teufelskerl *m* ◆ **you poor ~** (du) armer Teufel!; **he's a ~ with the ladies** er ist ein Weiberheld; **you little ~!** du kleiner Satansbraten!; **shall I have another? — go on, be a ~** soll ich noch einen trinken? *etc* — los, nur zu, riskier's! (*inf*); **be a ~ and say yes** riskier mal was und sag ja.
(c) (*inf: as intensifier*) **a ~ of a job** eine Heidenarbeit; **I had the ~ of a job getting here** es war verdammt schwierig, hierher zu kommen; **the ~ of a wind** ein scheußlicher Wind; **a ~ of a fellow** ein Teufelskerl *m*; **to live a ~ of a long way away** verdammt weit weg wohnen; **how/what/why/who the ~ ...?** wie/was/warum/wer zum Teufel *or* in drei Teufels Namen ...?; **to work like the ~** wie ein Pferd schuften (*inf*); **to run like the ~** wie ein geölter Blitz sausen (*inf*); **to shout like the ~** wie am Spieß brüllen (*inf*); **they were making the ~ of a noise** sie machten einen Höllenlärm; **to be in a ~ of a mess** ganz schön in der Patsche *or* Klemme sitzen (*inf*) *or* sein (*inf*); **there will be the ~ to pay** das dicke Ende kommt nach.
(d) (*in expressions*) **(to be) between the D~ and the deep blue sea** (sich) in einer Zwickmühle (befinden); **to play the ~ with sth** (*inf*) etw ruinieren; **go to the ~!** (*inf*) scher dich zum Teufel! (*inf*); **the ~ take him/it** (*old inf*) der Teufel soll ihn/es holen (*old, inf*), hol's der Teufel (*inf*); **the ~ finds work for idle hands** (*Prov*) Müßiggang ist aller Laster Anfang (*Prov*); **he has the ~ in him today** ihn reitet heute der Teufel; **speak** *or* **talk of the ~!** wenn man vom Teufel spricht!; **give the ~ his due** das muß der Neid ihm lassen; **to have the ~'s own luck** (*inf*) *or* **the luck of the ~** (*inf*) ein Schweineglück (*inf*) *or* unverschämtes Glück haben; **better the ~ you know (than the ~ you don't)** (*prov*) von zwei Übeln wählt man besser das, was man schon kennt; **(the) ~ take the hindmost** den Letzten beißen die Hunde (*Prov*).
(e) printer's ~ Setzerjunge *m*.
[2] *vi* (*Jur, Typ, Liter etc*) Handlangerdienste tun.
[3] *vt* (*Cook*) *kidneys* scharf gewürzt grillen.

devil fish *n* (*ray*) Rochen *m*; (*octopus*) Tintenfisch *m*.

devilish ['devlɪʃ] [1] *adj* **(a)** *invention* teuflisch. **(b)** (*inf: terrible*) schrecklich.
[2] *adv* (*dated inf: very*) verteufelt (*dated inf*); *funny, amusing* furchtbar.

devilishly ['devlɪʃlɪ] *adv* **(a)** *behave* abscheulich. **(b)** (*dated inf*) *see* **devilish 2**.

devilishness ['devlɪʃnɪs] *n* Teuflische(s) *nt* (*of an +dat*); (*of behaviour*) Abscheulichkeit *f*.

devil-may-care [ˌdevlmeɪ'kɛə^r] *adj* leichtsinnig, vollständig unbekümmert; (*in a selfish way*) Nach-mir-die-Sintflut-.

devilment ['devlmənt] *n* (grober) Unfug ◆ **out of sheer ~** aus lauter Übermut; **a piece of ~** (*old*) (grober) Unfug; **full of ~** voller Übermut.

devilry ['devlrɪ] *n* **(a)** (*mischief*) (grober) Unfug ◆ **a piece of childish ~** ein Dummejungenstreich *m*. **(b)** (*black magic*) Teufelskunst *f*. **(c)** (*extreme wickedness, cruelty*) Teufelei *f*.

devil's advocate *n* des Teufels Advokat, Advocatus Diaboli *m*; **to play ~** den Advocatus Diaboli spielen.

devious ['di:vɪəs] *adj* **(a)** *path, argumentation* gewunden ◆ **by a ~ route** auf einem Umweg; **he has a very ~ mind** er hat sehr verschlungene Gedankengänge, er denkt immer um viele Ecken (*inf*). **(b)** (*dishonest*) *method, manoeuvre, route* krumm (*inf*), fragwürdig; *person* verschlagen, hinterhältig ◆ **he has a very ~ mind** er ist durch und durch verschlagen.

deviously ['di:vɪəslɪ] *adv* verschlagen, hinterhältig ◆ **~ worded** verklausuliert.

deviousness ['di:vɪəsnɪs] *n see adj* **(a)** Gewundenheit *f*. **(b)** Fragwürdigkeit *f*; Verschlagenheit, Hinterhältigkeit *f*.

devise [dɪ'vaɪz] [1] *vt* **(a)** *scheme, style* sich (*dat*) ausdenken. **(b)** (*Jur*) hinterlassen, vermachen.
[2] *n* (*Jur*) Vermächtnis *nt*, Hinterlassenschaft *f*.

devitalization [di:ˌvaɪtəlaɪ'zeɪʃən] *n* Schwächung *f*.

devitalize [di:'vaɪtəlaɪz] *vt* schwächen.

devoid [dɪ'vɔɪd] *adj*: **~ of** bar (*+gen*), ohne.

devolution [ˌdi:və'lu:ʃən] *n* **(a)** (*of power*) Übertragung *f* (*from ... to* von ... auf *+acc*); (*Pol*) Dezentralisierung *f*. **(b)** (*Jur: of property*) (*active devolving*) Übertragung *f*; (*being devolved*) Übergang *m*. **(c)** (*Biol*) Rückentwicklung, Degeneration *f*.

devolve [dɪ'vɒlv] (*on, upon* auf *+acc*) [1] *vi* (*duty, property etc*) übergehen.
[2] *vt duty* übertragen.

devote [dɪ'vəʊt] *vt time, life, oneself, book, chapter, attention* widmen (*to dat*); *thought* verwenden (*to* auf *+acc*); *building* verwenden (*to* für); *resources* bestimmen (*to* für).

devoted [dɪ'vəʊtɪd] *adj* ergeben; *followers, service, friendship* treu; *admirer* eifrig ◆ **he/his time is ~ to his work/children** er geht in seiner Arbeit/seinen Kindern auf/seine Zeit ist seiner Arbeit/seinen Kindern gewidmet; **your ~ servant/son** (*old*) Ihr ergebener Diener/Sohn (*old*).

devotedly [dɪ'vəʊtɪdlɪ] *adv* hingebungsvoll; *serve, follow* treu; *support* eifrig.

devotee [ˌdevəʊ'ti:] *n* Anhänger(in *f*) *m*; (*of a writer*) Verehrer(in *f*) *m*; (*of music also, poetry*) Liebhaber(in *f*) *m*.

devotion [dɪ'vəʊʃən] *n* **(a)** (*to friend, wife etc*) Ergebenheit *f* (*to* gegenüber); (*to work*) Hingabe *f* (*to* an *+acc*) ◆ **~ to duty** Pflichteifer *m*. **(b)** (*of part of building, time etc*) (*to* für) Verwendung *f*; (*of resources*) Bestimmung *f*. **(c)** (*Rel*) **~s** *pl* Andacht *f*; **to be at one's ~s** in Andacht versunken sein.

devotional [dɪ'vəʊʃənl] *adj book, literature* religiös ◆ **~ objects** Devotionalien *pl*.

devour [dɪ'vaʊə^r] *vt* (*lit, fig*) verschlingen ◆ **I could ~ you** ich habe dich zum Fressen gern, du bist wirklich zum Fressen; **to be ~ed by jealousy/an all-consuming passion** von Eifersucht/einer unersättlichen Leidenschaft verzehrt werden.

devouring [dɪ'vaʊərɪŋ] *adj hunger, passion* verzehrend.

devout [dɪ'vaʊt] *adj person* fromm; *hope* sehnlich(st).
devoutly [dɪ'vaʊtlɪ] *adv pray* fromm; *hope* sehnlich(st).
dew [dju:] *n* Tau *m*.
dew: ~claw *n* Afterkralle *or* -klaue *f*; **~drop** *n* Tautropfen *m*; **~lap** *n* (*on cow*) Wamme *f*; (*hum: on person*) Doppelkinn *nt*; **~pond** *n flacher Teich, der sich aus Regenwasser bildet*.
dewy ['dju:ɪ] *adj* (*+er*) *grass* taufeucht; *skin* taufrisch ◆ **her eyes were ~** ihre Augen hatten einen feuchten Schimmer.
dewy-eyed ['dju:ɪaɪd] *adj* (*innocent, naive*) naiv; (*trusting*) vertrauensselig ◆ **to go all ~** feuchte Augen bekommen; **to look all ~** mit großen Augen in die Welt schauen.
dexterity [deks'terɪtɪ] *n* **(a)** Geschick *nt*. **(b)** (*right-handedness*) Rechtshändigkeit *f*.
dexterous, dextrous ['dekstrəs] *adj* **(a)** (*skilful*) geschickt. **(b)** (*rare: right-handed*) rechtshändig.
dextrose ['dekstrəʊz] *n* Dextrose *f*, Traubenzucker *m*.
dg *abbr of* **decigram(s), decigramme(s)** dg.
DHSS (*Brit*) *abbr of* **Department of Health and Social Security** Ministerium *nt* für Gesundheit und Soziales.
diabetes [ˌdaɪə'bi:ti:z] *n* Zuckerkrankheit *f*, Diabetes *m*, Zucker *no art* (*inf*).
diabetic [ˌdaɪə'betɪk] **1** *adj* **(a)** zuckerkrank, diabetisch (*spec*). **(b)** *beer, chocolate* Diabetiker-.
2 *n* Zuckerkranke(r) *mf*, Diabetiker(in *f*) *m*.
diabolic(al) [ˌdaɪə'bɒlɪk(əl)] *adj* **(a)** *power, invention, action* diabolisch, teuflisch. **(b)** (*sl*) *weather, child, heat* saumäßig (*sl*) ◆ **it's diabolical!** das ist ja saumäßig! (*sl*).
diabolically [ˌdaɪə'bɒlɪkəlɪ] *adv see adj*.
diachronic [ˌdaɪə'krɒnɪk] *adj* diachron.
diacritic [ˌdaɪə'krɪtɪk] **1** *adj* diakritisch.
2 *n* diakritisches Zeichen.
diacritical [ˌdaɪə'krɪtɪkəl] *adj* diakritisch.
diadem ['daɪədem] *n* Diadem *nt*.
diaeresis, (*US*) **dieresis** [daɪ'erɪsɪs] *n* Diärese *f*; (*sign*) Trema *nt*.
diagnose ['daɪəgnəʊz] *vt* (*Med, fig*) diagnostizieren.
diagnosis [ˌdaɪəg'nəʊsɪs] *n, pl* **diagnoses** [ˌdaɪəg'nəʊsi:z] Diagnose *f* ◆ **to make a ~** eine Diagnose stellen.
diagnostic [ˌdaɪəg'nɒstɪk] *adj* diagnostisch ◆ **~ test bay** Diagnosestand *m*.
diagnostician [ˌdaɪəgnɒs'tɪʃən] *n* Diagnostiker(in *f*) *m*.
diagnostics [ˌdaɪəg'nɒstɪks] *n sing or pl* Diagnose *f* ◆ **~ program** (*Comput*) Diagnoseprogramm *nt*.
diagonal [daɪ'ægənl] **1** *adj* diagonal.
2 *n* Diagonale *f*.
diagonally [daɪ'ægənəlɪ] *adv cut, fold* diagonal; (*loosely: crossways*) schräg ◆ **~ across sth** *walk* schräg über etw (*acc*); *be placed* schräg über etw (*dat*); **to be ~ opposite sth** einer Sache (*dat*) schräg gegenüber sein; **the car was struck ~ by a lorry** das Auto wurde schräg von hinten/vorn von einem Lastwagen gerammt.
diagram ['daɪəgræm] *n* (*Math*) Diagramm *nt*; (*of machine etc also*) Schaubild *nt*; (*chart: of figures etc*) graphische Darstellung ◆ **as shown in the ~** wie das Schaubild *or* Diagramm/die graphische Darstellung zeigt; **you don't have to draw me a ~** (*fig inf*) Sie brauchen es mir nicht aufzuzeichnen (*inf*).
diagrammatic [ˌdaɪəgrə'mætɪk] *adj* diagrammatisch ◆ **in ~ form** in einem Schaubild *or* Diagramm/graphisch dargestellt.
▼ **dial** ['daɪəl] **1** *n* **(a)** (*of clock*) Zifferblatt *nt*; (*of speedometer, pressure gauge*) Skala *f*; (*Telec*) Wähl- *or* Nummernscheibe *f*; (*on radio etc*) (Frequenzbereich-) Einstellskala *f*.
(b) (*sl: face*) Visage *f* (*sl*).
▼ **2** *vt* (*Telec*) wählen ◆ **to ~ direct** durchwählen; **you can ~ London direct** man kann nach London durchwählen; **to ~ 999** den Notruf wählen; **to ~ a wrong number** eine falsche Nummer wählen, sich verwählen.
3 *vi* (*Telec*) wählen.
dialect ['daɪəlekt] **1** *n* Dialekt *m*; (*local, rural also*) Mundart *f* ◆ **the country people spoke in ~** die Landbevölkerung sprach Dialekt; **the play is in ~** das Stück ist in Dialekt *or* Mundart geschrieben.
2 *attr word* Dialekt-.
dialectal [ˌdaɪə'lektl] *adj see n* dialektal, Dialekt-; mundartlich, Mundart-.
dialectical [ˌdaɪə'lektɪkəl] *adj* dialektisch ◆ **~ materialism** dialektischer Materialismus.
dialectician [ˌdaɪəlek'tɪʃən] *n* Dialektiker(in *f*) *m*.
dialectic(s) [ˌdaɪə'lektɪk(s)] *n* (*with sing vb*) Dialektik *f*.
dialling ['daɪəlɪŋ]: **~ code** *n* Vorwahl(nummer), Ortsnetzkennzahl (*form*) *f*; **~ tone** *n* (*Brit Telec*) Amtszeichen *nt*.
dialogue, (*US*) **dialog** ['daɪəlɒg] *n* (*all senses*) Dialog *m* ◆ **~ coach** Dialogregisseur *m*.
dial tone *n* (*US Telec*) Amtszeichen *nt*.
dial-up ['daɪəl'ʌp] *adj attr service* Wähl- ◆ **~ modem** (Wähl)modem *nt*.
dialysis [daɪ'æləsɪs] *n* Dialyse *f*.
diamanté [ˌdaɪə'mæntɪ] *n* Straß *m*; (*rare: fabric*) mit Pailletten besetzter Stoff.
diameter [daɪ'æmɪtə^r] *n* Durchmesser *m* ◆ **to be one metre in ~** einen Durchmesser von einem Meter haben; **what's its ~?** welchen Durchmesser hat es?, wie groß ist es im Durchmesser?
diametrical [ˌdaɪə'metrɪkəl] *adj* (*Math, fig*) diametral.
diametrically [ˌdaɪə'metrɪkəlɪ] *adv* diametral ◆ **~ opposed (to)** diametral entgegengesetzt (*+dat*).

➤ LANGUAGE IN USE: **dial: 2** → 27.1, 27.2, 27.7

diamond ['daɪəmənd] *n* **(a)** Diamant *m* ◆ **it was a case of ~ cut ~** (*Prov*) da sind die Richtigen aneinandergeraten; *see* **rough ~**. **(b) ~s** (*Cards*) Karo *nt*; **the King of ~s** der Karo-König. **(c)** (*Baseball*) Innenfeld *nt*. **(d)** (*Math: rhombus*) Raute *f*.
diamond *in cpds ring etc* Diamant-; **~ cutter** *n* Diamantschneider(in *f*) *m*; (*Ind*) Diamantschleifer(in *f*) *m*; **~ cutting** *n* Diamantschleifen *nt*; **~ drill** *n* Diamantbohrer *m*; **~ merchant** *n* Diamantenhändler(in *f*) *m*; **~-shaped** *adj* rautenförmig; **~ wedding** *n* diamantene Hochzeit.
Diana [daɪ'ænə] *n* Diana *f*.
diapason [ˌdaɪə'peɪzən] *n* (*also Mus*) Diapason *m or nt* ◆ **open/stopped ~** Prinzipal *nt*/gedacktes Prinzipal.
diaper ['daɪəpə^r] *n* (*US*) Windel *f*.
diaphanous [daɪ'æfənəs] *adj* durchscheinend.
diaphragm ['daɪəfræm] *n* (*Anat, Phys, Chem*) Diaphragma *nt*; (*abdominal also*) Zwerchfell *nt*; (*Phot also*) Blende *f*; (*in telephone*) Membran *f*; (*contraceptive*) Pessar *nt*.
diarist ['daɪərɪst] *n* (*of personal events*) Tagebuchschreiber(in *f*) *m*; (*of contemporary events*) Chronist *m*.
diarrhoea, (*US*) **diarrhea** [ˌdaɪə'ri:ə] *n* Durchfall *m*, Diarrhöe *f* ◆ **verbal ~** Laberei *f* (*inf*); **the speaker was suffering from verbal ~** der Redner hatte geistigen Dünnschiß (*sl*).
diary ['daɪərɪ] *n* (*of personal experience*) Tagebuch *nt*; (*for noting dates*) (Termin)kalender *m* ◆ **to keep a ~** Tagebuch führen; **desk/pocket ~** Schreibtisch-/Taschenkalender *m*; **I've got it in my ~** es steht in meinem (Termin)kalender.
Diaspora [daɪ'æspərə] *n* Diaspora *f*.
diastole [daɪ'æstəlɪ] *n* Diastole *f*.
diatonic [ˌdaɪə'tɒnɪk] *adj* diatonisch.
diatribe ['daɪətraɪb] *n* Schmährede *f*.
dibble ['dɪbl] **1** *n* Pflanz- *or* Setzholz *nt*.
2 *vt plant* setzen, pflanzen; *hole* machen, graben.
dice [daɪs] **1** *n, pl* - Würfel *m* ◆ **to play ~** Würfel spielen, würfeln; **~ cup** *or* **box** Würfelbecher *m*; **no ~** (*sl*) (das) ist nicht drin (*inf*).
2 *vi* würfeln ◆ **to ~ with death** mit dem Tode spielen.
3 *vt* (*Cook*) würfelig *or* in Würfel schneiden.
dicey ['daɪsɪ] *adj* (*Brit inf*) riskant.
dichotomy [dɪ'kɒtəmɪ] *n* Trennung, Dichotomie *f*.
dick [dɪk] *n* **(a)** (*sl: detective*) Schnüffler *m* (*inf*) ◆ **private ~** Privatdetektiv *m*; *see* **clever**. **(b)** (*vulg: penis*) Schwanz *m* (*sl*).
dickens ['dɪkɪnz] *n* (*euph inf: devil*) Teufel *m*; *for phrases see* **devil 1 (c)**.
Dickensian [dɪ'kenzɪən] *adj character, novel* Dickenssch *attr*; (*old-fashioned*) antiquiert ◆ **it's all very ~** das ist alles wie aus einem Roman von Dickens.
dicker ['dɪkə^r] *vi* (*US*) feilschen.
dickey, dicky ['dɪkɪ] *n* **(a)** (*inf*) (*on shirt*) Hemdbrust *f*; (*bow-tie*) Fliege *f*. **(b)** (*also* **~ seat**) Notsitz *m in einem Zweisitzer*.
dicky ['dɪkɪ] *adj* (*inf*) *heart* angeknackst (*inf*) ◆ **I feel a bit ~** (*dated*) ich bin ziemlich ab (*inf*) *or* erschossen (*inf*).
dickybird ['dɪkɪbɜ:d] *n* (*baby-talk*) Piepmatz *m* (*baby-talk*) ◆ **I didn't see a ~** (*inf*) ich habe überhaupt nichts gesehen.
dicta ['dɪktə] *pl of* **dictum**.
dictaphone ® ['dɪktəfəʊn] *n* Diktaphon *nt*.
dictate [dɪk'teɪt] **1** *vti* (*all senses*) diktieren.
2 ['dɪkteɪt] *n usu pl* Diktat *nt*; (*of reason*) Gebote *pl*.
◆**dictate to** *vi +prep obj person* diktieren (*+dat*), Vorschriften machen (*+dat*) ◆ **I won't be ~d ~** ich lasse mir nicht diktieren, ich lasse mir keine Vorschriften machen.
dictation [dɪk'teɪʃən] *n* (*also Sch*) Diktat *nt* ◆ **to take a ~** ein Diktat aufnehmen; **to read at ~ speed** in Diktiertempo lesen.
dictator [dɪk'teɪtə^r] *n* **(a)** (*Pol, fig*) Diktator *m*. **(b)** (*of letter, passage*) Diktierende(r) *mf*.
dictatorial *adj*, **~ly** *adv* [ˌdɪktə'tɔ:rɪəl, -ɪ] (*Pol, fig*) diktatorisch.
dictatorship [dɪk'teɪtəʃɪp] *n* (*Pol, fig*) Diktatur *f*.
diction ['dɪkʃən] *n* **(a)** (*Liter*) Diktion *f* ◆ **poetic ~** poetische Sprache. **(b)** (*way of speaking*) Diktion *f*.
dictionary ['dɪkʃənrɪ] *n* Wörterbuch *nt*.
dictum ['dɪktəm] *n, pl* **dicta** Diktum *nt*.
did [dɪd] *pret of* **do²**.
didactic *adj*, **~ally** *adv* [dɪ'dæktɪk, -əlɪ] didaktisch.
diddle ['dɪdl] *vt* (*inf*) übers Ohr hauen (*inf*), beschummeln ◆ **you have been ~d** man hat Sie übers Ohr gehauen; **to ~ sb out of sth** jdm etw abgaunern (*inf*).
diddler ['dɪdlə^r] *n* (*inf*) Spitzbube, Gauner *m*.
diddums ['dɪdəmz] *interj* (*inf*) du Armer/Arme.
didn't ['dɪdənt] = **did not**; *see* **do²**.
didst [dɪdst] (*obs*) = **didst thou**; *see* **do²**.
die¹ [daɪ] **1** *vi* **(a)** sterben; *soldier also* fallen; (*motor, engine*) absterben; (*planet*) vergehen ◆ **to ~ of hunger/pneumonia/grief** Hungers (*geh*) *or* vor Hunger/an Lungenentzündung/vor *or* aus Kummer sterben; **to ~ by one's own hand** von eigener Hand sterben, Hand an sich legen; **he ~d a hero** er starb als Held; **to be dying** im Sterben liegen; **never say ~!** nur nicht aufgeben!; **to ~ laughing** (*inf*) sich totlachen (*inf*).
(b) to be dying to do sth (*fig*) darauf brennen, etw zu tun, brennend gern etw tun wollen; **I'm dying for a cigarette** ich brauche jetzt unbedingt eine Zigarette; **I'm dying to know what happened** ich bin schrecklich gespannt zu hören, was passiert ist; **he's dying to meet you/to get home** er möchte Sie

brennend gern kennenlernen/er brennt darauf, heimzukommen.
(c) *(love)* vergehen, ersterben *(geh)*, erlöschen *(geh)*; *(memory)* (ver)schwinden; *(custom)* aussterben; *(empire)* untergehen ◆ **the secret ~d with him** er nahm das Geheimnis mit ins Grab; **rumours ~ hard** Gerüchte sind nicht totzukriegen.
[2] *vt* **to ~ a hero's/a violent death** den Heldentod/eines gewaltsamen Todes sterben; **to ~ the death** *(plan etc)* sterben *(inf)*.

◆**die away** *vi (sound, voice)* schwächer *or* leiser werden; *(wind)* nachlassen, sich legen; *(anger)* sich legen, vergehen.

◆**die back** *vi* absterben.

◆**die down** *vi* nachlassen; *(fire)* herunterbrennen; *(flames)* kleiner werden; *(storm, wind also)* sich legen, schwächer werden; *(noise also)* leiser werden, schwächer werden; *(emotion also)* sich legen; *(quarrel, protest also)* schwächer werden.

◆**die off** *vi* (hin)wegsterben; *(animals, people also)* (der Reihe nach) sterben.

◆**die out** *vi* aussterben.

die[2] *n* **(a)** *(form) pl* **dice** Würfel *m* ◆ **the ~ is cast** *(prov)* die Würfel sind gefallen; *see also* **dice**. **(b)** *pl* **-s** *(Tech)* Gesenk *nt*, Gußform *f*; *(in minting)* Prägestempel *m*.

die casting *n (article)* Spritzguß(stück *nt*) *m*; *(process)* Spritzgußverfahren *nt*.

die-hard ['daɪhɑːd] [1] *n* zäher Kämpfer; *(resistant to change)* Ewiggestrige(r) *mf*.
[2] *adj* zäh; *(pej)* reaktionär.

dielectric [ˌdaɪɪ'lektrɪk] *adj* dielektrisch.

dieresis *n (US) see* **diaeresis**.

diesel ['diːzəl] *n (train)* Dieseltriebwagen *m*; *(car)* Diesel *m*; *(fuel)* Dieselöl *nt*, Diesel *no art*.

diesel: ~-electric *adj* dieselelektrisch; **~ engine** *n* Dieselmotor *m*; **~ oil** *n* Dieselöl *nt*; **~ train** *n* Dieseltriebwagen *m*.

die: ~ sinker *n* Werkzeugmacher(in *f*) *m*; **~ stamp** *n* Prägestempel *m*.

diet[1] ['daɪət] [1] *n* Nahrung *f*; *(special ~)* Diät *f*; *(slimming ~)* Schlankheitskur *f* ◆ **he lives on a ~ of hamburgers and chips** er ernährt sich von Hamburgern und Pommes frites; **there's nothing wrong with my ~** meine Ernährung ist völlig in Ordnung; **to put sb on a ~/special ~** jdm eine Schlankheitskur/Diät verordnen; **to be/go on a ~** eine Schlankheitskur machen; **high protein ~** proteinreiche Diät; **~ sheet** Diät-/Schlankheits(fahr)plan *m*.
[2] *vi* eine Schlankheitskur machen.

diet[2] *n (assembly)* Abgeordnetenversammlung *f* ◆ **the German/Japanese ~** der deutsche/japanische Reichstag; **the D~ of Worms** der Reichstag zu Worms.

dietary ['daɪətərɪ] *adj* Diät-, diätetisch, Ernährungs- ◆ **~ fibre** Ballaststoff *m*.

dietetic [ˌdaɪə'tetɪk] *adj* Diät-, diätetisch, Ernährungs-.

dietetics [ˌdaɪə'tetɪks] *n sing* Diätlehre, Diätetik *f*.

dietician [ˌdaɪə'tɪʃən] *n* Diätist(in *f*), Ernährungswissenschaftler(in *f*) *m*.

differ ['dɪfəʳ] *vi* **(a)** *(be different)* sich unterscheiden *(from* von*)* ◆ **tastes ~** die Geschmäcker sind verschieden; **I ~ from you in that ...** ich unterscheide mich von Ihnen darin, daß ... **(b)** *(disagree)* **to ~ with sb over sth** über etw *(acc)* anderer Meinung sein als jd; **we ~ed sharply over that** darin waren wir völlig verschiedener Meinung; *see* **agree, beg**.

▼ **difference** ['dɪfrəns] *n* **(a)** Unterschied *m*; *(in age)* (Alters)unterschied *m (in, between* zwischen *+dat)* ◆ **that makes a big ~ to me** das ist für mich ein großer Unterschied; **to make a ~ to** *or* **in sth** einen Unterschied bei etw machen; **that makes a big ~, that makes all the ~** das ändert die Sache völlig, das gibt der Sache *(dat)* ein ganz anderes Gesicht; **a bottle of wine would make all the ~** es fehlt nur noch eine Flasche Wein dazu; **it makes all the ~ in the world** da liegt der entscheidende Unterschied; **what ~ does it make if ...?** was macht es schon, wenn ...?; **what ~ is that to you?** was macht dir das aus?; **it makes no ~** es ist egal *(inf)*; **it makes no ~ to me** das ist mir egal *or* einerlei; **it makes a lot of ~** das ist ein erheblicher *or* gewaltiger Unterschied; **cooperation makes all the ~** Zusammenarbeit macht viel aus; **for all the ~ it makes** obwohl es ja eigentlich egal ist; **a car/dress with a ~** *(inf)* ein Auto/Kleid, das mal was anderes ist.
(b) *(between numbers, amounts)* Differenz *f* ◆ **to pay the ~** die Differenz *or* den Rest(betrag) bezahlen.
(c) *(quarrel)* Differenz, Auseinandersetzung *f* ◆ **a ~ of opinion** eine Meinungsverschiedenheit; **to settle one's ~s** die Differenzen *or* Meinungsverschiedenheiten beilegen.

different ['dɪfrənt] *adj* **(a)** andere(r, s), anders *pred (from, to* als*)*; *two people, things* verschieden, unterschiedlich ◆ **completely ~** völlig verschieden; *(changed)* völlig verändert; **that's ~!** das ist was anderes!; **in what way are they ~?** wie unterscheiden sie sich?; **to feel a ~ person** ein ganz anderer Mensch sein; **to do something ~** etwas anderes tun; **that's quite a ~ matter** das ist etwas völlig anderes; **she's quite ~ from what you think** sie ist ganz anders, als Sie denken; **he wants to be ~** er will unbedingt anders *or* etwas Besonderes sein.
(b) *(various)* verschieden.

differential [ˌdɪfə'renʃəl] [1] *adj (different) rates of pay, treatment* unterschiedlich, verschieden; *(distinguishing) feature* unterscheidend ◆ **~ calculus** Differentialrechnung *f*; **~ coefficient** *(Math)* Ableitung *f*; **~ gear** Differential(getriebe) *nt*.
[2] *n* **(a)** *(difference)* Unterschied *m*; *(Math)* Differential *nt* ◆ **wage/salary ~** Lohn-/Gehaltsunterschiede *or* -differenzen *pl*.
(b) *(Aut)* Differential(getriebe) *nt*.

differentially [ˌdɪfə'renʃəlɪ] *adv (Tech)* differential.

▼ **differentiate** [ˌdɪfə'renʃɪeɪt] [1] *vt* unterscheiden; *(Math)* differenzieren ◆ **to ~ x and y/x from y** x und y voneinander/x von y unterscheiden.
[2] *vi (see difference)* unterscheiden, einen Unterschied machen, differenzieren; *(two things: become different)* sich unterschiedlich *or* anders entwickeln ◆ **to ~ between people** einen Unterschied zwischen Menschen machen.

differentiation [ˌdɪfərenʃɪ'eɪʃən] *n* Unterscheidung, Differenzierung *f*.

differently ['dɪfrəntlɪ] *adv* anders *(from* als*)*; *(from one another)* verschieden, unterschiedlich ◆ **he thinks ~ (from you)** er denkt anders (als Sie).

▼ **difficult** ['dɪfɪkəlt] *adj* **(a)** schwierig, schwer; *(hard to understand)* schwer, diffizil *(geh)*; *writer* kompliziert, schwierig ◆ **sth is ~ to do** es ist schwierig *or* schwer, etw zu tun; **it is ~ for me** *or* **I find it ~ to believe that** es fällt mir *or* ist für mich schwer, das zu glauben; **we'll make things ~ for him** wir werden es ihm schwer *or* nicht leicht machen; **it's ~ to know whether ...** es ist schwer zu sagen, ob ...; **there's nothing ~ about it** das ist nicht schwierig *or* schwer; **the ~ thing is ...** die Schwierigkeit liegt darin ...; **it's ~ to deny that ...** es läßt sich kaum leugnen, daß ...; **he's just trying to be ~** er will nur Schwierigkeiten machen.
(b) *neighbour, character, child* schwierig ◆ **she is ~ to get on with** es ist schwer, mit ihr auszukommen.

difficulty ['dɪfɪkəltɪ] *n* Schwierigkeit *f* ◆ **with/without ~** mit/ohne Schwierigkeiten *pl*; **he had ~ in doing that** es fiel ihm schwer *or* nicht leicht, das zu tun, er hatte Schwierigkeiten dabei; **a slight ~ in breathing** leichte Atembeschwerden *pl*; **there was some ~ in finding him** es war schwierig *or* nicht leicht, ihn zu finden; **the ~ is in choosing** *or* **to choose** die Wahl ist nicht leicht; **they hadn't appreciated the ~ of finding somewhere to live** sie hatten nicht bedacht, wie schwierig es sein würde, eine Wohnung zu finden; **in ~** *or* **difficulties** in Schwierigkeiten *pl*; **to get into difficulties** in Schwierigkeiten geraten; **to get out of difficulties** Schwierigkeiten überwinden; **he was working under great difficulties** er arbeitete unter äußerst schwierigen Bedingungen.

diffidence ['dɪfɪdəns] *n* Bescheidenheit, Zurückhaltung *f*; *(of smile)* Zaghaftigkeit *f*.

diffident ['dɪfɪdənt] *adj* zurückhaltend, bescheiden; *smile* zaghaft ◆ **he was very ~ about offering his help** er hat zaghaft seine Hilfe angeboten.

diffidently ['dɪfɪdəntlɪ] *adv see adj*.

diffract [dɪ'frækt] *vt* beugen.

diffraction [dɪ'frækʃən] *n* Diffraktion, Beugung *f*.

diffuse [dɪ'fjuːz] [1] *vt light, heat, gas, rays* ausstrahlen, verbreiten; *fluid* ausgießen, ausschütten; *(Chem)* diffundieren, verwischen; *perfume* verbreiten, verströmen; *knowledge, custom, news* verbreiten.
[2] *vi* ausstrahlen, sich ver- *or* ausbreiten; *(fluid)* sich ausbreiten; *(Chem)* diffundieren, sich verwischen; *(perfume, odour)* ausströmen; *(custom, news)* sich verbreiten.
[3] [dɪ'fjuːs] *adj* **(a)** *gas, rays, light* diffus.
(b) *(verbose) style, writer* langatmig, weitschweifig.

diffused [dɪ'fjuːzd] *adj* verbreitet; *lighting* indirekt.

diffuseness [dɪ'fjuːsnɪs] *n (of style)* Weitschweifigkeit *f*.

diffuser [dɪ'fjuːzəʳ] *n (for light)* (Licht)diffusor *m*.

diffusion [dɪ'fjuːʒən] *n (of light, heat, rays, fluid etc)* Ausbreitung *f*; *(Chem)* Diffusion *f*; *(of perfume, odour)* Ausströmung *f*; *(of knowledge, custom, news)* Verbreitung *f*.

dig [dɪg] *(vb: pret, ptp* **dug***)* [1] *vt* **(a)** *ground* graben; *trench, hole, tunnel etc also* ausheben ◆ **to ~ potatoes** Kartoffeln roden; **they dug their way out of prison** sie gruben sich *(dat)* einen (Flucht)tunnel aus dem Gefängnis.
(b) *(poke, thrust)* bohren *(sth into sth* etw in etw *acc)* ◆ **to ~ sb in the ribs** jdm *or* jdn in die Rippen stoßen.
(c) *(sl) (enjoy)* stehen auf *(+dat) (inf)*; *(take notice of)* sich *(dat)* angucken; *(understand)* kapieren *(inf)*.
[2] *vi* **(a)** *(person)* graben; *(dog, pig also)* wühlen; *(Tech)* schürfen; *(Archeol)* (aus)graben, Ausgrabungen machen ◆ **to ~ for minerals** Erz schürfen; **to ~ in one's pockets for sth** in seinen Taschen nach etw suchen *or* wühlen.
(b) *(inf: taunt)* **to ~ at sb** jdn anschießen *or* anmotzen *(inf)*.
[3] *n* **(a)** *(with hand, elbow)* Puff, Stoß *m* ◆ **to give sb a ~ in the ribs** jdm einen Rippenstoß geben.
(b) *(sarcastic remark)* Seitenhieb *m*, Spitze *f* ◆ **to have a ~ at sb/sth** eine Spitze gegen jdn loslassen *(inf)*, eine spitze Bemerkung über jdn machen.
(c) *(Archeol)* (Aus)grabung *f*; *(site)* Ausgrabungsstätte *f*.

◆**dig around** *vi (inf)* herumsuchen.

◆**dig in** [1] *vi* **(a)** *(also ~ oneself ~)* *(Mil, fig)* sich eingraben. **(b)** *(inf: eat)* reinhauen *(inf)*.
[2] *vt sep* **(a)** *compost* unter- *or* eingraben. **(b)** *(Mil) troops, tanks* eingraben. **(c) to ~ one's spurs ~** (dem Pferd) die Sporen geben; **to ~ one's heels ~** *(lit)* die Hacken in den Boden stemmen; *(fig)* sich auf die Hinterbeine stellen *(inf)*.

◆**dig into** *vi +prep obj* **(a)** *(inf) cake, pie* herfallen über *(+acc) (inf)*. **(b)** *sb's past* wühlen in *(+dat)*.

◆**dig out** *vt sep (lit, fig)* ausgraben *(of* aus*)*.

◆**dig over** *vt sep soil, garden* umgraben.

◆**dig up** *vt sep* **(a)** *earth* aufwühlen; *lawn, garden* umgraben. **(b)** *plants, treasure, body, idea* ausgraben; *weeds* (aus)jäten; *(fig) fact, information also* auftun; *solution* finden ◆ **where did you ~ her ~?** *(inf)* wo hast du die denn aufgegabelt? *(inf)*.

digest [daɪ'dʒest] [1] *vt (lit, fig)* verdauen.
[2] *vi* verdauen.
[3] ['daɪdʒest] *n* **(a)** *(of book, facts)* Digest *m or nt*, Auswahl *f*. **(b)** *(Jur)* Gesetzessammlung *f*.

digestible [dɪ'dʒestəbl] *adj* verdaulich.

➤ LANGUAGE IN USE: **difference: a** → 5.4 **differentiate: 1** → 5.1 **difficult: a** → 5.1, 26.3

digestion [dɪ'dʒestʃən] *n* Verdauung *f*.
digestive [dɪ'dʒestɪv] *adj* Verdauungs- ◆ ~ **(biscuit)** (*Brit*) *Keks m aus Roggenmehl*.
digger ['dɪgəʳ] *n* **(a)** (*person*) (*miner*) Bergmann *m*; Goldgräber *m*; (*navvy*) Straßenarbeiter *m*; (*Tech: excavator*) Bagger *m*. **(b)** (*sl*) australischer/ neuseeländischer Soldat; (*Austral inf: pal*) Kumpel *m*.
diggings ['dɪgɪŋz] *npl* **(a)** (*Min*) Bergwerk *nt*; (*minerals*) Funde *pl*; (*Archeol*) Grabungsort *m*. **(b)** (*US*) *see* **digs**.
digit ['dɪdʒɪt] *n* **(a)** (*finger*) Finger *m*; (*toe*) Zehe *f*. **(b)** (*Math*) Ziffer *f* ◆ **a four-~ number** eine vierstellige Zahl.
digital ['dɪdʒɪtəl] 1 *adj* **(a)** *clock, computer* Digital- ◆ ~ **recording** Digitalaufnahme *f*. **(b)** (*Anat*) Finger-.
2 *n* (*of piano, organ*) Taste *f*.
digitalin [ˌdɪdʒɪ'teɪlɪn] *n* Digitalis *nt*.
digitalis [ˌdɪdʒɪ'teɪlɪs] *n* Digitalis *f*.
digitalization [ˌdɪdʒɪtəlaɪ'zeɪʃən] *n* Digitalisierung *f*.
digitally ['dɪdʒɪtəlɪ] *adv* digital ◆ ~ **recorded** im Digitalverfahren aufgenommen; ~ **remastered** digital aufbereitet.
digitize ['dɪdʒɪtaɪz] *vt* (*Comput*) digitalisieren.
digitizer ['dɪdʒɪtaɪzəʳ] *n* (*Comput*) Digitalisierer *m*.
dignified ['dɪgnɪfaɪd] *adj person* (ehr)würdig; *behaviour, manner* fein ◆ **he maintained a ~ silence** er schwieg würdevoll.
dignify ['dɪgnɪfaɪ] *vt* ehren, auszeichnen ◆ **to ~ sth with the name of ...** etw mit dem anspruchsvollen Namen ... belegen.
dignitary ['dɪgnɪtərɪ] *n* Würdenträger(in *f*) *m* ◆ **the local dignitaries** die Honoratioren am Ort.
dignity ['dɪgnɪtɪ] *n* **(a)** (*of person, occasion, work*) Würde *f* ◆ **to stand on one's ~** förmlich sein; **to lose one's ~** sich blamieren; **that would be beneath my ~** das wäre unter meiner Würde. **(b)** (*high rank, post*) Rang *m*, (hohe) Stellung; (*title*) Würde *f*.
digraph ['daɪgræf] *n* Digraph *m*.
digress [daɪ'gres] *vi* abschweifen ◆ **but I ~** doch ich schweife ab.
digression [daɪ'greʃən] *n* Abschweifung *f*, Exkurs *m* ◆ **this by way of ~** aber das nur nebenbei.
digressive [daɪ'gresɪv] *adj* abschweifend, abweichend.
digs [dɪgz] *npl* (*Brit*) Bude *f* (*inf*) ◆ **to be in ~** ein möbliertes Zimmer *or* eine Bude (*inf*) haben.
dihedral [daɪ'hiːdrəl] 1 *adj* zweiflächig.
2 *n* V-Winkel *m*; (*Aviat*) V-Stellung *f*.
dike [daɪk] *n, vt see* **dyke**.
dilapidated [dɪ'læpɪdeɪtɪd] *adj house* verfallen, heruntergekommen, baufällig; *book, clothes* schäbig.
dilapidation [dɪˌlæpɪ'deɪʃən] *n* **(a)** (*of building*) Baufälligkeit *f*, Verfall *m*; (*of book, clothes*) Schäbigkeit *f* ◆ **in a state of ~** in schlechtem Zustand. **(b)** (*Geol*) Verwitterung *f*.
dilatation [ˌdaɪlə'teɪʃən], **dilation** [daɪ'leɪʃən] *n* Ausdehnung, Erweiterung *f*; (*of pupils*) Erweiterung *f* ◆ ~ **and curettage** Dilation und Kürettage (*spec*), Ausschabung *f*.
dilate [daɪ'leɪt] 1 *vt* weiten, dehnen.
2 *vi* sich weiten, sich dehnen; (*pupils*) sich erweitern ◆ **~d pupils** erweiterte Pupillen *pl*; **to ~ (up)on** (*talk at length*) sich verbreiten über (+*acc*).
dilatoriness ['dɪlətərɪnɪs] *n* Langsamkeit *f*, Zögern *nt* (*in doing sth* etw zu tun).
dilatory ['dɪlətərɪ] *adj* **(a)** *person* langsam; *reply* verspätet ◆ **to be ~** sich (*dat*) Zeit lassen; **he was rather ~ in answering** er ließ sich mit der Antwort Zeit. **(b)** (*delaying*) *action, policy* Verzögerungs-, Hinhalte-.
dildo ['dɪldəʊ] *n* Godemiché *m*.
dilemma [daɪ'lemə] *n* Dilemma *nt* ◆ **to be in a ~** sich in einem Dilemma befinden, in der Klemme sitzen (*inf*); **to place sb in a ~** jdn in eine Klemme (*inf*) *or* ein Dilemma bringen.
dilettante [ˌdɪlɪ'tæntɪ] 1 *n, pl* **dilettanti** [ˌdɪlɪ'tæntɪ] Amateur(in *f*), Dilettant(in *f*) *m*; (*Art*) Kunstliebhaber(in *f*) *m*.
2 *adj* amateurhaft, stümperhaft.
dilettantism [ˌdɪlɪ'tæntɪzəm] *n* Dilettantismus *m*; Kunstliebhaberei *f*.
diligence ['dɪlɪdʒəns] *n* Eifer *m*; (*in work etc also*) Fleiß *m*.
diligent ['dɪlɪdʒənt] *adj person* eifrig; (*in work etc also*) fleißig; *search, work* sorgfältig, genau ◆ **to be ~ in doing sth** etw eifrig *or* mit großem Eifer tun.
diligently ['dɪlɪdʒəntlɪ] *adv see adj*.
dill [dɪl] *n* Dill *m*.
dilly-dally ['dɪlɪdælɪ] *vi* (*over work etc*) trödeln; (*when walking also*) bummeln ◆ **without ~ing** ohne zu trödeln/bummeln; **no ~ing!** ein bißchen dalli!
dilute [daɪ'luːt] 1 *vt orange juice, milk etc* verdünnen; *colour* dämpfen, abschwächen; (*fig*) mildern, (ab)schwächen ◆ ~ **to taste** nach Geschmack verdünnen.
2 *adj* verdünnt.
dilution [daɪ'luːʃən] *n see vt* Verdünnung *f*; Dämpfung, Abschwächung *f*; Milderung *f*.
dim [dɪm] 1 *adj* (+*er*) **(a)** *light* schwach, trüb, schummerig (*inf*); *lamp* schwach, dunkel, trüb; *room, forest etc* halbdunkel, dämmerig, schummerig (*inf*) ◆ **to grow ~** schwach *or* dunkel werden; **the room grew ~** im Zimmer wurde es dunkel; **it's a ~ look-out for him** es sieht sehr trübe *or* schlecht für ihn aus.
(b) *eyesight* schwach; *colour* gedeckt, glanzlos; *eyes* trüb; *metal* matt, glanzlos.
(c) *sound, memory* schwach, verschwommen; *outline, shape* undeutlich, verschwommen, unscharf.
(d) (*mentally*) begriffsstutzig, beschränkt; (*inf: stupid*) schwer von Begriff *or* Kapee (*inf*).
(e) (*inf*) **to take a ~ view of sb/sth** wenig *or* nicht viel von jdm/etw halten; **she took a ~ view of his selling the car** sie hielt nichts davon, daß er das Auto verkaufte.
2 *vt* **(a)** *light* dämpfen; *lamp* verdunkeln ◆ **to ~ the lights** (*Theat*) das Licht langsam ausgehen lassen; **to ~ one's headlights** (*esp US*) abblenden.
(b) *sight, mind, senses* trüben; *colour* dämpfen, decken; *metal* mattieren; *beauty* beeinträchtigen; *glory* beeinträchtigen, verblassen lassen.
(c) *sound* dämpfen; *outline* unscharf *or* undeutlich machen; *memory* trüben.
3 *vi* **(a)** (*light*) schwach *or* trübe werden; (*lamps*) verlöschen, dunkler werden.
(b) (*sight*) nachlassen, getrübt werden; (*colour*) gedämpft *or* matter werden; (*metal*) mattiert werden; (*beauty*) getrübt werden, verblassen; (*glory*) verblassen, vergehen.
(c) (*sound*) leiser werden; (*outline*) undeutlich *or* unscharf werden, verschwimmen; (*memory*) nachlassen.
◆**dim out** *vt sep* (*US*) *city* verdunkeln.
dime [daɪm] *n* (*US*) Zehncentstück *nt* ◆ **it's not worth a ~** (*inf*) das ist keinen (roten) Heller *or* keine fünf Pfennig *or* keinen Sechser (*dial*) wert; **they're a ~ a dozen** das ist Dutzendware; ~ **novel** Groschen- *or* Schundroman *m*.
dimension [daɪ'menʃən] *n* Dimension *f*; (*measurement*) Abmessung(en *pl*) *f*, Maß *nt* ◆ **a project of vast ~(s)** ein Projekt von gewaltigen Ausmaßen *or* von gewaltiger Größenordnung; **it adds a new ~ to ...** das gibt ... (*dat*) eine neue Dimension.
-dimensional [-daɪ'menʃənl] *adj suf* -dimensional.
diminish [dɪ'mɪnɪʃ] 1 *vt* **(a)** verringern; *price, speed, authority also* herabsetzen; *value, strength also* (ver)mindern; *number also* verkleinern; *enthusiasm* dämpfen; *reputation* schmälern ◆ **a ~ed staff** eine reduzierte Belegschaft; **~ed responsibility** (*Jur*) verminderte Zurechnungsfähigkeit.
(b) (*Mus*) (um einen Halbton) vermindern ◆ **~ed** vermindert.
2 *vi* sich verringern; (*speed, authority, strength also*) abnehmen, sich vermindern; (*price also*) fallen, sinken; (*value also*) sich vermindern; (*number also*) sich verkleinern; (*enthusiasm*) nachlassen; (*reputation*) schlechter werden ◆ **law of ~ing returns** (*Econ*) Gesetz *nt* von der fallenden Profitrate; **to ~ in numbers** weniger werden, zahlenmäßig abnehmen; **to ~ in value** im Wert sinken, an Wert verlieren.
diminuendo [dɪˌmɪnjʊ'endəʊ] 1 *adv* diminuendo.
2 *n* Diminuendo *nt*.
diminution [ˌdɪmɪ'njuːʃən] *n* (*in gen*) Verringerung *f*; (*of reputation*) Schmälerung *f*; (*in enthusiasm*) Nachlassen *nt*.
diminutive [dɪ'mɪnjʊtɪv] 1 *adj* winzig, klein; (*Gram*) diminutiv.
2 *n* (*Gram*) Verkleinerungsform *f*, Diminutiv(um) *nt*.
dimity ['dɪmɪtɪ] *n* Dimitz *m*.
dimly ['dɪmlɪ] *adv* **(a)** *shine* schwach; *hear also* gedämpft, undeutlich; *remember also* undeutlich; *see* verschwommen; *lit* schwach. **(b)** (*inf: stupidly*) einfältig, begriffsstutzig.
dimmer ['dɪməʳ] *n* (*Elec*) Dimmer *m*; (*US Aut*) Abblendschalter *or* -hebel *m* ◆ ~ **switch** Dimmer *m*; (*US Aut*) Abblendschalter *m*; **~s** (*US Aut*) Abblendlicht *nt*; (*sidelights*) Begrenzungsleuchten *pl*.
dimness ['dɪmnɪs] *n see adj* **(a)** (*of light, sight*) Schwäche, Trübheit *f*; Halbdunkel, Dämmerlicht *nt*.
(b) Schwäche *f*; Glanzlosigkeit *f*; Trübheit *f*; Mattheit *f*.
(c) Schwäche, Verschwommenheit *f*; Undeutlichkeit, Unschärfe *f*.
(d) Begriffsstutzigkeit, Beschränktheit *f*.
dim-out ['dɪmaʊt] *n* (*US*) Verdunkelung *f*.
dimple ['dɪmpl] 1 *n* (*on cheek, chin*) Grübchen *nt*; (*depression*) Delle, Vertiefung *f*; (*on water*) Kräuselung *f*.
2 *vi* (*cheeks*) Grübchen bekommen; (*person*) Grübchen zeigen; (*surface*) sich einbeulen; (*water*) sich kräuseln.
3 *vt* **a smile ~d her cheeks** sie lächelte und zeigte dabei ihre Grübchen.
dimpled ['dɪmpld] *adj cheek, chin, arm* mit Grübchen.
dim: ~wit *n* (*inf*) Blödmann *m* (*inf*); **~-witted** *adj* (*inf*) blöd (*inf*), dämlich (*inf*).
din [dɪn] 1 *n* Lärm *m*, Getöse *nt* ◆ **an infernal ~** ein Höllenlärm *or* -spektakel *m*.
2 *vt* **to ~ sth into sb** jdm etw einbleuen.
3 *vi* **the noise was still ~ning in his ears** der Lärm dröhnte ihm immer noch in den Ohren.
dine [daɪn] 1 *vi* speisen, dinieren (*old, geh*) (*on* etw) ◆ **to ~ out** außer Haus *or* auswärts speisen; **he ~d out on that story for months** diese Geschichte hat ihm monatelang Einladungen zum Essen verschafft.
2 *vt* bewirten, beköstigen.
diner ['daɪnəʳ] *n* **(a)** (*person*) Speisende(r) *mf*; (*in restaurant*) Gast *m*. **(b)** (*café etc*) Eßlokal *nt*. **(c)** (*Rail*) Speisewagen *m*.
dinette [daɪ'net] *n* Eßecke *f*.
ding-a-ling ['dɪŋə'lɪŋ] *n* **(a)** Klingeling *nt*; (*fire-engine*) Tatütata *nt*. **(b)** (*US inf: fool*) Depp *m* (*inf*).
ding-dong ['dɪŋ'dɒŋ] 1 *n* Bimbam *nt*.
2 *adj* (*fig*) *battle* hin- und herwogend.
ding(e)y, dinghy ['dɪŋgɪ] *n* Ding(h)i *nt*; (*collapsible*) Schlauchboot *nt*.
dinginess ['dɪndʒɪnɪs] *n* Unansehnlichkeit *f*.
dingle ['dɪŋgl] *n* baumbestandene Mulde.
dingo ['dɪŋgəʊ] *n* Dingo *m*, australischer Wildhund.

dingy[1] ['dɪndʒɪ] *adj place, furniture* schmuddelig.
dingy[2] ['dɪŋgɪ] *n see* **ding(e)y.**
dining ['daɪnɪŋ]: **~ car** *n* Speisewagen *m*; **~ chair** *n* Eßzimmerstuhl *m*; **~ hall** *n* Speisesaal *m*; **~ room** *n* Eßzimmer *nt*; *(in hotel)* Speiseraum *m*; **~-table** *n* Eßtisch *m*.
dink [dɪŋk] *n* **(a)** *(inf) abbr of* **double income, no kids** ♦ **~s** Doppelverdiener *pl* ohne Kinder. **(b)** *(US pej: Vietnamese)* Vietnamese *m*, Vietnamesin *f*.
dinkum ['dɪŋkəm] *(Austral inf)* 1 *adj* ehrlich; *person also* anständig, redlich. 2 *adv* ehrlich.
dinky[1] ['dɪŋkɪ] *adj* **(a)** *(Brit inf)* schnuckelig *(inf)*. **(b)** ® *(also* **D~**) *car* Modell-.
dinky[2] *n (inf) abbr of* **double income, no kids yet** ♦ **~s** noch kinderlose Doppelverdiener *pl*.
▼ **dinner** ['dɪnəʳ] *n (evening meal)* (Haupt)mahlzeit *f*, Abendessen *nt*; *(formal)* (Abend)essen *nt*; *(lunch)* Mittagessen *nt*; *(for cat, dog)* Fressen *nt* ♦ **to be at ~** beim Essen sein, (gerade) essen; **to be eating** *or* **having one's ~** zu Abend/ Mittag essen; *(dog, cat)* (gerade) fressen; **we're having people to ~** wir haben Gäste zum Essen; **~'s ready** das Essen ist fertig; **to finish one's ~** zu Ende essen; **what time do you finish ~?** wann bist du mit dem Essen fertig?; **to go out to ~** *(in restaurant)* auswärts *or* außer Haus essen (gehen); *(at friends')* zum Essen eingeladen sein; **to give a ~ in sb's honour** ein Essen zu jds Ehren geben; **a formal ~** ein offizielles Essen.
dinner: ~ bell *n* (Essens)glocke *f*; **the ~ bell has gone** es hat (zum Essen) geläutet; **~-dance** *n Abendessen nt mit Tanz*; **~ duty** *n* **to do ~ duty** Tischaufsicht haben; **~ jacket** *n* Smokingjacke *f*; **~ knife** *n* Tafelmesser *nt*; **~ party** *n* Abendgesellschaft *f* (mit Essen); **to have a small ~ party** ein kleines Essen geben; **~ plate** *n* Tafelteller *m*; **~ service** *n* Tafelservice *nt*; **~ suit** *n* Smoking *m*; **~ table** *n* Tafel *f*; **we were already sitting at the ~ table** wir hatten schon zum Essen Platz genommen; **~time** *n* Essenszeit *f*; **~ trolley** *or* **wagon** *n* Servierwagen *m*.
dinosaur ['daɪnəsɔːʳ] *n* Dinosaurier *m*.
dinosaurian [daɪnə'sɔːriːən] *adj* Dinosaurier-.
dint [dɪnt] 1 *n* **(a) by ~ of** durch, kraft *(+gen)*; **we succeeded by ~ of working 24 hours a day** wir schafften es, indem wir 24 Stunden pro Tag arbeiteten. **(b)** *see* **dent.**
2 *vt see* **dent.**
diocesan [daɪ'ɒsɪsən] *adj* Diözesan-, Bistums-.
diocese ['daɪəsɪs] *n* Diözese *f*, Bistum *nt*.
diode ['daɪəʊd] *n* Diode *f* ♦ **light-emitting ~** Leuchtdiode *f*.
Dionysian [,daɪə'nɪzɪən] *adj* dionysisch.
Dionysus [,daɪə'naɪsɪs] *n* Dionysos, Dionys *m*.
dioptre, *(US)* **diopter** [daɪ'ɒptəʳ] *n* Dioptrie *f*.
diorama [daɪə'rɑːmə] *n* Diorama *nt*.
dioxide [daɪ'ɒksaɪd] *n* Dioxyd *nt*.
dioxin [daɪ'ɒksɪn] *n* Dioxin *nt*.
Dip *abbr of* **diploma.**
dip [dɪp] 1 *vt* **(a)** *(in(to)* in *+acc)* *(into liquid)* tauchen; *pen, hand* eintauchen; *bread* (ein)tunken, stippen *(inf)*; *candles* ziehen; *sheep* in Desinfektionslösung baden, dippen.
(b) *(into bag, basket) hand* stecken.
(c) *(Brit Aut) headlights* abblenden ♦ **to drive on ~ped headlights** mit Abblendlicht fahren.
(d) to ~ one's flag *(Naut)* die Flagge dippen.
2 *vi (ground)* sich senken; *(temperature, pointer on scale, prices)* fallen, sinken; *(boat)* tauchen ♦ **the sun ~ped behind the mountains** die Sonne verschwand hinter den Bergen.
3 *n* **(a)** *(swim)* **to go for a** *or* **to have a ~** kurz *or* schnell mal schwimmen gehen, kurz reinspringen; **after a/her ~ she lay and sunbathed** nach einem kurzen Bad sonnte sie sich.
(b) *(liquid) (for cleaning animals)* Desinfektionslösung *f*; *(Tech)* Lösung *f*.
(c) *(in ground) (hollow)* Bodensenke *f*; *(slope)* Abfall *m* ♦ **the road took a ~** die Straße fiel ab.
(d) *(Phys: also* **angle of ~**) Inklination *f*, Neigungswinkel *m*.
(e) *(Naut: of flag)* Dippen *nt*.
(f) *(Cook)* Dip *m*; *see* **lucky.**
(g) *(candle)* gezogene Kerze.
(h) *(Sport)* Beugestütz *m*.
(i) *(sl: pickpocket)* Taschendieb, Langfinger *(inf) m*.
♦**dip into** *vi +prep obj* **(a)** *(lit)* **she ~ped ~ her bag for money** sie griff in ihre Tasche, um Geld zu holen. **(b)** *(fig)* **to ~ ~ one's pocket** tief in die Tasche greifen; **to ~ ~ one's savings** seine Ersparnisse angreifen, an seine Ersparnisse gehen. **(c)** *book* einen kurzen Blick werfen in *(+acc)*.
diphtheria [dɪf'θɪərɪə] *n* Diphtherie *f*.
diphthong ['dɪfθɒŋ] *n* Diphthong *m*.
diphthongize ['dɪfθɒŋgaɪz] *vti* diphthongieren.
diploma [dɪ'pləʊmə] *n* Diplom *nt* ♦ **teacher's ~** Lehrerdiplom *nt*; **to hold a ~ in** ein Diplom haben in *(+dat)*.
diplomacy [dɪ'pləʊməsɪ] *n (Pol, fig)* Diplomatie *f* ♦ **to use ~** diplomatisch vorgehen.
diplomat ['dɪpləmæt] *n (Pol, fig)* Diplomat(in *f*) *m*.
diplomatic *adj*, **~ally** *adv* [,dɪplə'mætɪk, -əlɪ] *(lit, fig)* diplomatisch.
diplomatic: ~ bag *n* Diplomatenpost *f*; **~ corps** *n* diplomatisches Korps; **~ immunity** *n* Immunität *f*; **~ pouch** *n (US) see* **~ bag**; **~ service** *n* diplomatischer Dienst.
diplomatist [dɪ'pləʊmətɪst] *n see* **diplomat.**
dip needle *n* Inklinationsnadel *f*.
dipole ['daɪpəʊl] *n* Dipol *m*.
dipper ['dɪpəʳ] *n* **(a)** *(ladle)* Schöpflöffel *m*, Kelle *f*.
(b) *(Tech: person)* Eintaucher(in *f*) *m*.
(c) *(Orn)* Taucher *m*, Tauchente *f*.
(d) *(Tech) (bulldozer)* Bagger *m*; *(scoop)* Schaufel *f*.
(e) *(at fair: also* **Big D~**) Achterbahn *f*.
(f) *(Brit Aut: for headlamps)* Abblendschalter *m*.
(g) *(US Astron)* **the Big** *or* **Great/Little D~** der Große/Kleine Wagen *or* Bär.
dippy ['dɪpɪ] *adj (inf)* plemplem *(inf)*, meschugge *(inf)*.
dip rod *n (US) see* **dipstick.**
dipso ['dɪpsəʊ] *n abbr of* **dipsomaniac.**
dipsomania [,dɪpsəʊ'meɪnɪə] *n* Trunksucht *f*.
dipsomaniac [,dɪpsəʊ'meɪnɪæk] *n* Trunksüchtige(r) *mf*.
dip: ~stick *n* Ölmeßstab *m*; **~switch** *n (Aut)* Abblendschalter *m*.
DIP switch ['dɪpswɪtʃ] *n (Comput)* DIP-Schalter *m*.
diptera ['dɪptərə] *npl* Dipteren *(spec)*, Zweiflügler *pl*.
dipterous ['dɪptərəs] *adj* zweiflüg(e)lig.
diptych ['dɪptɪk] *n* Diptychon *nt*.
▼ **dire** [daɪəʳ] *adj* schrecklich, furchtbar, gräßlich; *poverty* äußerste(r, s) ♦ **~ necessity** dringende Notwendigkeit; **to be in ~ need** in großer Verlegenheit sein (of nach); *see* **strait.**
▼ **direct** [daɪ'rekt] 1 *adj* **(a)** direkt; *(following straight on, uninterrupted) link, result, heir, contact also* unmittelbar; *responsibility, cause, danger* unmittelbar; *train* durchgehend; *opposite* genau ♦ **~ access** *(Comput)* Direktzugriff *m*; **~ action** direkte Aktion; **to pay by ~ debit** per Einzugsauftrag bezahlen; **to be a ~ descendant of sb** von jdm in direkter Linie abstammen, ein direkter Nachkomme von jdm sein; **~ dialling** Selbstwahl *f*; **~ grant (school)** *(Brit) Privatschule f mit staatlicher Unterstützung*; **"keep away from ~ heat"** „vor unmittelbarer Wärmeeinstrahlung schützen"; **~ heating** Zimmerheizung *f*; **~ hit** Volltreffer *m*; **~-mail advertising** Postwurfsendungen *pl*; **~ marketing** Direktmarketing *nt*; **~ method** direkte Methode.
(b) *(blunt) person, remark* direkt, offen; *refusal, denial* glatt.
(c) *(Gram)* **~ object** direktes Objekt, Akkusativobjekt *nt*; **~ speech** *or* **discourse** *(US)* direkte Rede.
(d) *(Elec)* **~ current** Gleichstrom *m*.
2 *vt* **(a)** *(address, aim) remark, letter* richten *(to* an *+acc)*; *efforts* richten *(towards* auf *+acc)* ♦ **to ~ one's steps to(wards) sb/sth** auf jdn/etw zugehen; **to ~ sb's attention to sb/sth** jds Aufmerksamkeit auf jdn/etw lenken; **can you ~ me to the town hall?** können Sie mir den Weg zum Rathaus sagen?
(b) *(supervise, control) person's work, business* leiten, lenken; *traffic* regeln.
(c) *(order)* anweisen *(sb to do sth* jdn, etw zu tun); *(Jur) jury* Rechtsbelehrung erteilen *(+dat)* ♦ **the judge ~ed the jury to ...** der Richter belehrte die Schöffen darüber, daß ...; **as ~ed** *(Med)* wie verordnet.
(d) *film* Regie führen bei; *play also* Spielleitung haben von; *group of actors* dirigieren; *radio/TV programme* leiten.
▼ 3 *adv* direkt.
direction [dɪ'rekʃən] *n* **(a)** *(lit, fig: way)* Richtung *f* ♦ **in every ~** in jede Richtung; **in the wrong/right ~** *(lit, fig)* in die falsche/richtige Richtung; **in the ~ of Hamburg/the star** in Richtung Hamburg/des Sterns; **what ~ did he go in?** in welche Richtung ist er gegangen/gefahren?; **a sense of ~** *(lit)* Orientierungssinn *m*; *(fig)* ein Ziel *nt* im Leben; **new ~s in modern philosophy** neue Wege in der modernen Philosophie.
(b) *(management: of company etc)* Leitung, Führung *f*.
(c) *(of film, actors)* Regie *f*; *(of play also)* Spielleitung *f*; *(of radio/TV programme)* Leitung *f* ♦ **under the ~ of** unter der Regie von.
(d) ~s *pl (instructions)* Anweisungen *pl*; *(to a place)* Angaben *pl*; *(for use)* (Gebrauchs)anweisung *or* -anleitung *f*; *(in recipe etc)* Hinweise *pl*.
directional [dɪ'rekʃənl] *adj* Richtungs-, gerichtet ♦ **~ antenna** Richtantenne *f*.
direction: ~ finder *n* Peilantenne *f*; **~ indicator** *n (Aut)* Winker *m*; *(flashing)* Blinker *m*.
directive [dɪ'rektɪv] *n* Direktive, Weisung *f*.
directly [dɪ'rektlɪ] 1 *adv* **(a)** *(following straight on)* direkt, unmittelbar; *(in a short time)* sofort, gleich ♦ **to come ~ to the point** direkt zur Sache kommen; **to be ~ descended from sb** in direkter Linie *or* direkt von jdm abstammen.
(b) *(frankly) speak* direkt, ohne Umschweife.
(c) *(completely) opposite* genau, unmittelbar; *opposed* völlig.
2 *conj* sobald, sowie ♦ **he'll come ~ he's ready** er kommt, sobald *or* sowie er fertig ist.
directness [daɪ'rektnɪs] *n* Direktheit *f*.
director [dɪ'rektəʳ] *n* **(a)** *(of company, institution)* Direktor(in *f*), Leiter(in *f*) *m*; *(Univ)* Rektor(in *f*) *m* ♦ **~ of studies** Studienberater(in *f*) *m*; **~ of music** Musikdirektor(in *f*) *m*; **~ of Public Prosecutions** ≃ Oberstaatsanwalt *m*; **~ general** Generaldirektor(in *f*) *m*. **(b)** *(Rad, TV)* Direktor(in *f*) *m*; *(Film, Theat)* Regisseur(in *f*) *m* ♦ **~'s chair** Regiestuhl *m*. **(c)** *(Mil)* Richtgerät *nt*.
directorate [daɪ'rektərɪt] *n (period of office)* Dienstzeit *f* als Direktor; *(board of directors)* Aufsichtsrat *m*.
directorship [dɪ'rektəʃɪp] *n* Direktorstelle *f or* -posten *m* ♦ **under his ~** unter seiner Leitung.
▼ **directory** [dɪ'rektərɪ] *n* **(a)** Adreßbuch *nt*; *(telephone ~)* Telefonbuch *nt*; *(trade ~)* Branchenverzeichnis *nt* ♦ **~ enquiries** *or (US)* **assistance** *(Telec)* (Fernsprech)auskunft *f*. **(b)** *(Comput)* Inhaltsverzeichnis, Directory *nt* ♦ **to change directories** das Directory wechseln. **(c)** *(Hist)* **the D~** das Direktorium.
dirge [dɜːdʒ] *n* Grab- *or* Trauer- *or* Klagegesang *m*.

➤ LANGUAGE IN USE: **dinner** → 25.1, 25.2 **dire** → 17.2, 20.7 **direct: 3** → 27.1, 27.3 **directory: a** → 27.1

dirigible ['dɪrɪdʒəbl] [1] *n* (lenkbares) Luftschiff.
[2] *adj* lenkbar.

dirk [dɜːk] *n (Scot)* Dolch *m*.

dirt [dɜːt] *n* **(a)** Schmutz *m*; *(soil)* Erde *f*; *(excrement)* Dreck *m*; *(rubbish also)* Unrat, Kehricht *m* ◆ **to be covered in ~** völlig verschmutzt sein; **to eat ~** *(fig)* sich widerspruchslos demütigen *or* beleidigen lassen; **to treat sb like ~** jdn wie (den letzten) Dreck behandeln *(inf)*; **he looked at me as though I was a bit of ~** er sah mich an, als wäre ich ein Stück Dreck *(inf)*.
(b) *(fig: obscenity)* Schmutz *m*; *(scandal also)* schmutzige Wäsche ◆ **go and wash the ~ out of your mouth!** schäm dich, solche Worte in den Mund zu nehmen!

dirt: ~-cheap *adj, adv (inf)* spottbillig; **~ farmer** *n (US)* Kleinbauer *m*.

dirtily ['dɜːtɪlɪ] *adv* **(a)** schmutzig; *eat, live* wie ein Ferkel. **(b)** *(fig) (meanly)* gemein, schäbig; *(obscenely)* schmutzig.

dirtiness ['dɜːtɪnɪs] *n* Schmutzigkeit *f*; *(of story also)* Unanständigkeit *f*.

dirt: ~ road *n* unbefestigte Straße; **~ track** *n* Feldweg *m*; *(Sport)* Aschenbahn *f*; **~-track racing** *n* Aschenbahnrennen *nt*.

dirty ['dɜːtɪ] [1] *adj (+er)* **(a)** schmutzig; *hands, clothes, shoes etc also, wound* verschmutzt ◆ **~ weather** Dreckwetter, Sauwetter *(inf) nt*; *(Naut)* stürmisches Wetter; **a ~ colour** eine Schmutzfarbe; **to get ~** schmutzig *or* dreckig werden; **to get sth ~** etw schmutzig machen; **to give sb a ~ look** *(fig)* jdm einen bösen *or* giftigen Blick zuwerfen.
(b) *(fig: obscene)* schmutzig, unanständig ◆ **to have a ~ mind** eine schmutzige Phantasie haben; **~ old man** fieser alter Kerl, alte Drecksau *(sl)*; **you ~ old man!** Sie Schmutzfink!; **the ~ raincoat brigade** *(hum)* ≃ die Spanner *pl*; **they're having a ~ weekend** *(inf)* sie sind zusammen übers Wochenende weggefahren.
(c) *(fig) (despicable)* gemein, niederträchtig; *(Sport) player, match* unfair ◆ **a ~ bastard** *(sl)* ein richtiges Schwein *(sl)*; **~ work** Dreck(s)arbeit *f (inf)*.
[2] *vt* beschmutzen; *machine* verschmutzen.
[3] *n* **to do the ~ on sb** *(Brit inf)* jdn reinlegen *(inf)*.

disability [ˌdɪsə'bɪlɪtɪ] *n* **(a)** *(handicap, injury etc)* Behinderung *f* ◆ **~ for work** Arbeitsunfähigkeit *f*; **sb's ~ to do sth** jds Unfähigkeit *f or* Unvermögen *nt*, etw zu tun; **~ allowance** Behindertenfreibetrag *m*; **~ pension** Invalidenrente *f*. **(b)** *(Jur)* Rechtsunfähigkeit *f*.

disable [dɪs'eɪbl] *vt* **(a) to ~ sb for work** jdn arbeitsunfähig machen. **(b)** *tank, gun* unbrauchbar machen; *ship* kampfunfähig machen. **(c)** *(Jur) (make incapable)* rechtsunfähig machen; *(disqualify)* für unfähig erklären *(from doing sth* etw zu tun).

disabled [dɪs'eɪbld] [1] *adj* **(a)** behindert ◆ **~ ex-serviceman** Kriegsversehrte(r) *m*. **(b)** *tank, gun* unbrauchbar; *ship* nicht seetüchtig. **(c)** *(Jur)* nicht rechtsfähig.
[2] *npl* **the ~** die Behinderten *pl*; **the war ~** die Kriegsversehrten *pl*.

disablement [dɪs'eɪblmənt] *n* **(a)** Behinderung *f*. **(b)** *(of tank, gun, ship)* Unbrauchbarmachen *nt*.

disabuse [ˌdɪsə'bjuːz] *vt* **to ~ sb of sth** jdn von etw befreien.

disadvantage [ˌdɪsəd'vɑːntɪdʒ] *n (obstacle, unfavourable factor)* Nachteil *m*; *(detriment also)* Schaden *m* ◆ **to be at a ~** sich im Nachteil befinden, benachteiligt *or* im Nachteil sein; **to put sb at a ~** jdn benachteiligen; **to show oneself at a ~** sich von einer ungünstigen *or* unvorteilhaften Seite zeigen; **he felt his ~** er empfand seine Benachteiligung; **it would be to your ~** es wäre zu Ihrem Nachteil.

disadvantaged [ˌdɪsəd'vɑːntɪdʒd] *adj* benachteiligt.

disadvantageous *adj*, **~ly** *adv* [ˌdɪsædvɑːn'teɪdʒəs, -lɪ] nachteilig.

disaffected [ˌdɪsə'fektɪd] *adj* entfremdet ◆ **to become ~** sich entfremden.

disaffection [ˌdɪsə'fekʃən] *n* Entfremdung *f (from* von).

disagree [ˌdɪsə'griː] *vi* **(a)** *(with person, views)* nicht übereinstimmen; *(with plan, suggestion etc)* nicht einverstanden sein; *(two people)* sich nicht einig sein.
(b) *(quarrel)* eine Meinungsverschiedenheit haben.
(c) *(be different: figures, reports)* nicht übereinstimmen.
(d) *(climate, food)* **to ~ with sb** jdm nicht bekommen; **mutton ~s with me** ich vertrage Hammelfleisch nicht, Hammelfleisch bekommt mir nicht.

disagreeable [ˌdɪsə'griːəbl] *adj smell, work, experience* unangenehm; *(bad-tempered) person* unsympathisch.

disagreeableness [ˌdɪsə'griːəblnɪs] *n see adj* Unangenehme(s) *nt*; unangenehme Art, unsympathische Art.

disagreeably [ˌdɪsə'griːəblɪ] *adv see adj*.

disagreement [ˌdɪsə'griːmənt] *n* **(a)** *(with opinion, between opinions)* Uneinigkeit *f* ◆ **my ~ with that view is based on ...** ich bin mit dieser Ansicht nicht einverstanden, weil ...; **there is still ~** es herrscht noch Uneinigkeit. **(b)** *(quarrel)* Meinungsverschiedenheit *f*. **(c)** *(between figures, reports)* Diskrepanz *f*.

disallow [ˌdɪsə'laʊ] *vt evidence* nicht anerkennen; *claim also* zurückweisen; *plan etc* ablehnen; *(Sport) goal* nicht anerkennen, nicht geben.

disambiguate [ˌdɪsæm'bɪgjʊeɪt] *vt term etc* eindeutig machen, disambiguieren *(spec)*.

disappear [ˌdɪsə'pɪəʳ] [1] *vi* verschwinden; *(worries, fears, difficulties also)* sich in Nichts auflösen; *(rage also)* verrauchen; *(memory)* schwinden; *(objections)* sich zerstreuen ◆ **he ~ed from (our) sight** er verschwand; **to make sth ~** etw verschwinden lassen; **to do one's ~ing trick** *(inf)* sich verdünnisieren *(inf)*, sich verdrücken *(inf)*.
[2] *vt (esp Pol inf)* verschwinden lassen ◆ **the ~ed** die Verschwundenen *pl*.

disappearance [ˌdɪsə'pɪərəns] *n see vi* Verschwinden *nt*; Verrauchen *nt*; Schwinden *nt*; Zerstreuung *f*.

➤ LANGUAGE IN USE: **disagree: a** → 12.1 **disappointed** → 14

disappoint [ˌdɪsə'pɔɪnt] *vt* enttäuschen.

disappointed [ˌdɪsə'pɔɪntɪd] *adj* enttäuscht ◆ **to be ~ in sb/sth** von jdm/etw enttäuscht sein; **to be ~ in love** eine Enttäuschung in der Liebe erleben.

disappointing [ˌdɪsə'pɔɪntɪŋ] *adj* enttäuschend ◆ **how ~!** so eine Enttäuschung!

disappointingly [ˌdɪsə'pɔɪntɪŋlɪ] *adv* enttäuschend ◆ **rather ~ he didn't have the opportunity** es war ziemlich enttäuschend, daß er keine Gelegenheit hatte; **he did ~ in the exams** er hat in den Prüfungen enttäuschend abgeschnitten *or* enttäuscht.

disappointment [ˌdɪsə'pɔɪntmənt] *n* Enttäuschung *f*; *(of hopes also, ambition)* Nichterfüllung *f*.

disapprobation [ˌdɪsæprə'beɪʃən] *n* Mißbilligung *f*.

disapproval [ˌdɪsə'pruːvl] *n* Mißbilligung *f* ◆ **murmur of ~** mißbilligendes Gemurmel.

disapprove [ˌdɪsə'pruːv] [1] *vt* mißbilligen.
[2] *vi* dagegen sein ◆ **if you don't ~, I'd like to ...** wenn Sie nichts dagegen haben, würde ich gerne ...; **to ~ of sth** etw mißbilligen; **he ~s of children smoking** er mißbilligt es, wenn Kinder rauchen.

disapproving *adj*, **~ly** *adv* [ˌdɪsə'pruːvɪŋ, -lɪ] mißbilligend.

disarm [dɪs'ɑːm] [1] *vt (lit, fig)* entwaffnen.
[2] *vi (Mil)* abrüsten.

disarmament [dɪs'ɑːməmənt] *n* Abrüstung *f*.

disarming *adj*, **~ly** *adv* [dɪs'ɑːmɪŋ, -lɪ] entwaffnend.

disarrange ['dɪsə'reɪndʒ] *vt* durcheinanderbringen.

disarranged ['dɪsə'reɪndʒd] *adj* unordentlich.

disarray [ˌdɪsə'reɪ] [1] *n* Unordnung *f* ◆ **to be in ~** *(troops)* in Auflösung (begriffen) sein; *(thoughts, organization, political party)* durcheinander *or* in Unordnung sein; *(person)* aufgelöst sein; *(clothes)* in unordentlichem Zustand sein.
[2] *vt* in Unordnung bringen; *enemy* verwirren.

disassemble ['dɪsə'sembl] *vt* auseinandernehmen; *prefabricated building* abbauen.

disassociate ['dɪsə'səʊʃɪeɪt] *vt see* **dissociate**.

disaster [dɪ'zɑːstəʳ] *n* Katastrophe *f*; *(Aviat, Min, Rail also)* Unglück *nt*; *(fiasco)* Fiasko, Desaster *nt* ◆ **doomed to ~** zum Untergang verdammt *or* verurteilt.

disaster: ~ area *n* Katastrophengebiet *nt*; *(fig inf: person)* Katastrophe *f*; **~ fund** *n* Katastrophenfonds *m*; **~ movie** *n* Katastrophenfilm *m*.

disastrous *adj*, **~ly** *adv* [dɪ'zɑːstrəs, -lɪ] katastrophal, verheerend.

disavow ['dɪsə'vaʊ] *vt* verleugnen; *one's words* ableugnen.

disavowal [ˌdɪsə'vaʊəl] *n see vt* Verleugnung *f*; Ableugnung *f*.

disband [dɪs'bænd] [1] *vt* auflösen.
[2] *vi (army, club)* sich auflösen; *(soldiers, club members)* auseinandergehen.

disbar [dɪs'bɑːʳ] *vt (Jur)* die Lizenz entziehen (+*dat*).

disbelief ['dɪsbə'liːf] *n* Ungläubigkeit *f*; *(Rel)* Unglaube *m* ◆ **in ~** ungläubig.

disbelieve ['dɪsbə'liːv] *vt* nicht glauben.

disbeliever ['dɪsbə'liːvəʳ] *n* Ungläubige(r) *mf*.

disburden [dɪs'bɜːdn] *vt (lit, fig)* entlasten.

disburse [dɪs'bɜːs] *vt* aus(be)zahlen.

disbursement [dɪs'bɜːsmənt] *n* Auszahlung *f*.

disc, *(esp US)* **disk** [dɪsk] *n* **(a)** *(flat, circular object)* (runde) Scheibe; *(Anat)* Bandscheibe *f*; *(Mil: identity ~)* (Erkennungs)marke *f*; *see* **slip**. **(b)** *(record, Comput)* Platte *f*; *see also* **disk**.

discard [dɪ'skɑːd] [1] *vt* **(a)** *unwanted article, person* ausrangieren; *idea, plan* verwerfen; *(take off) coat* ausziehen; *antlers, leaves* abwerfen. **(b)** *also vi (Cards)* abwerfen.
[2] *n* **(a)** *(Cards)* Abwerfen *nt*.
(b) *(Ind, Comm)* Ausschuß(ware *f*) *m*.

disc: ~ brake *n* Scheibenbremse *f*; **~ camera** *n* Disc-Kamera *f*.

discern [dɪ'sɜːn] *vt (with senses)* wahrnehmen; *(mentally also)* erkennen ◆ **he was too young to ~ right from wrong** er war zu jung, um Recht von Unrecht unterscheiden zu können.

discernible [dɪ'sɜːnəbl] *adj (with senses)* wahrnehmbar; *(mentally)* erkennbar.

discernibly [dɪ'sɜːnəblɪ] *adv see adj*.

discerning [dɪ'sɜːnɪŋ] *adj clientele, reader* anspruchsvoll, kritisch; *eye, ear* fein.

discernment [dɪ'sɜːnmənt] *n* **(a)** *(ability to discern) (observation)* feines Gespür; *(discriminating taste)* kritisches Urteilsvermögen. **(b)** *(act of discerning) see vt* Wahrnehmung *f*; Erkennen *nt*.

discharge [dɪs'tʃɑːdʒ] [1] *vt* **(a)** *employee, prisoner, patient etc* entlassen; *accused* freisprechen; *bankrupt* entlasten ◆ **he ~d himself (from hospital)** er hat das Krankenhaus auf eigene Verantwortung verlassen.
(b) *(emit) (Elec)* entladen; *liquid, gas (pipe etc)* ausstoßen; *(workers)* ausströmen lassen; *(Med)* ausscheiden, absondern ◆ **the tanker was discharging its oil into the Channel** das Öl lief aus dem Tanker in den (Ärmel)kanal; **how much oil has been ~d?** wieviel Öl ist ausgelaufen?; *(deliberately)* wieviel Öl hat man abgelassen?
(c) *(unload) ship, cargo* löschen ◆ **the bus ~d its load of ...** aus dem Bus strömten die ...
(d) *(gun)* abfeuern.
(e) *debt* begleichen; *duty* nachkommen (+*dat*); *function* erfüllen ◆ **~d bankrupt** entlasteter Konkursschuldner.
[2] *vi (wound, sore)* eitern.
[3] ['dɪstʃɑːdʒ] *n* **(a)** *(dismissal) see vt (a)* Entlassung *f*; Freispruch *m*; Entlastung *f*; *(of soldier)* Abschied *m*.
(b) *(Elec)* Entladung *f*; *(of gas)* Ausströmen *nt*; *(of liquid, Med: vaginal ~)* Aus-

fluß *m*; (*of pus*) Absonderung *f*.
(c) (*of cargo*) Löschen *nt*.
(d) (*of debt*) Begleichung *f*; (*of duty, function*) Erfüllung *f*.
disc harrow *n* Scheibenegge *f*.
disciple [dɪ'saɪpl] *n* (*lit, fig*) Jünger *m*; (*fig: non-emotional*) Schüler(in *f*) *m*.
disciplinarian [ˌdɪsɪplɪ'neərɪən] *n* Zuchtmeister(in *f*) *m* ◆ **to be a strict ~** eiserne Disziplin halten.
disciplinary ['dɪsɪplɪnərɪ] *adj* Disziplinar-, disziplinarisch.
discipline ['dɪsɪplɪn] 1 *n* (*all senses*) Disziplin *f*; (*punishment*) disziplinarische Maßnahmen *pl* ◆ **to maintain ~** die Disziplin aufrechterhalten.
2 *vt* **(a)** (*train, make obedient*) disziplinieren; *reactions, emotions* in Zucht *or* unter Kontrolle halten ◆ **to ~ sb/oneself to do sth** jdn/sich dazu anhalten *or* zwingen, etw zu tun.
(b) (*punish*) bestrafen; (*physically*) züchtigen.
disciplined ['dɪsɪplɪnd] *adj* diszipliniert; *behaviour, reactions, emotions also* beherrscht ◆ **well/badly ~** diszipliniert/disziplinlos, undiszipliniert.
disc jockey *n* Diskjockey *m*.
disclaim [dɪs'kleɪm] *vt* **(a)** abstreiten, (weit) von sich (*dat*) weisen ◆ **to ~ all responsibility** jede Verantwortung von sich weisen. **(b)** (*Jur*) *a right* verzichten auf (+*acc*).
disclaimer [dɪs'kleɪməʳ] *n* **(a)** Dementi *nt* ◆ **to issue a ~** eine Gegenerklärung abgeben. **(b) to put in a ~ of sth** (*Jur*) eine Verzichterklärung auf etw (*acc*) abgeben.
disclose [dɪs'kləʊz] *vt secret* enthüllen; *intentions, news* bekanntgeben *or* -machen.
disclosure [dɪs'kləʊʒəʳ] *n* **(a)** *see vt* Enthüllung *f*; Bekanntgabe *f*. **(b)** (*fact etc revealed*) Mitteilung *f*.
disco ['dɪskəʊ] *n* Disko, Disco *f* ◆ **~ dancing** Diskotanzen *nt*.
discography [dɪs'kɒgrəfɪ] *n* Diskographie *f*.
discolor *vti* (*US*) *see* **discolour**.
discoloration [dɪsˌkʌlə'reɪʃən] *n* Verfärben *nt*; (*mark*) Verfärbung *f*.
discolour [dɪs'kʌləʳ] 1 *vt* verfärben.
2 *vi* sich verfärben.
discomfit [dɪs'kʌmfɪt] *vt* Unbehagen verursachen (+*dat*).
discomfiture [dɪs'kʌmfɪtʃəʳ] *n* Unbehagen *nt*.
discomfort [dɪs'kʌmfət] *n* (*lit*) Beschwerden *pl*; (*fig: uneasiness, embarrassment*) Unbehagen *nt* ◆ **the injury gives me a little ~ now and again** die Verletzung verursacht mir ab und zu leichte Beschwerden.
disconcert [ˌdɪskən'sɜːt] *vt* beunruhigen.
disconcerting *adj*, **~ly** *adv* [ˌdɪskən'sɜːtɪŋ, -lɪ] beunruhigend.
disconnect ['dɪskə'nekt] *vt pipe etc* trennen; *TV, iron* ausschalten; (*cut off supply of*) *gas, electricity* abstellen ◆ **to ~ a call** (*Telec*) ein Gespräch unterbrechen; **I've been ~ed** (*for non-payment*) man hat mir das Telefon/den Strom/das Gas *etc* abgestellt; (*in mid-conversation*) das Gespräch ist unterbrochen worden.
disconsolate [dɪs'kɒnsəlɪt] *adj* niedergeschlagen ◆ **to grow ~** verzweifeln, verzagen.
discontent ['dɪskən'tent] *n* Unzufriedenheit *f*.
discontented ['dɪskən'tentɪd] *adj* unzufrieden (*with, about* mit).
discontentment ['dɪskən'tentmənt] *n* Unzufriedenheit *f*.
discontinuation [dɪskənˌtɪnju'eɪʃən] *n see vt* Aufgabe *f*; Abbruch *m*; (Produktions)einstellung *f*; Einstellung *f*.
discontinue ['dɪskən'tɪnjuː] *vt* aufgeben; *class, project also, conversation* abbrechen; (*Comm*) *line* auslaufen lassen, die Produktion einstellen von; *production*, (*Jur*) *case* einstellen ◆ **to ~ one's subscription to a newspaper** seine Zeitung abbestellen; **a ~d line** (*Comm*) eine ausgelaufene Serie.
discontinuity [ˌdɪskɒntɪ'njuːɪtɪ] *n* mangelnde Kontinuität, Diskontinuität (*geh*) *f* ◆ **a certain amount of ~** ein gewisser Mangel an Kontinuität; **to reduce any ~ to a minimum** die Kontinuität möglichst wenig unterbrechen.
discontinuous *adj*, **~ly** *adv* ['dɪskən'tɪnjʊəs, -lɪ] nicht kontinuierlich.
discord ['dɪskɔːd] *n* **(a)** Uneinigkeit *f*. **(b)** (*Mus*) Disharmonie *f*.
discordance [dɪs'kɔːdəns] *n* **(a)** Uneinigkeit *f*. **(b)** (*of colours, sounds, music*) Disharmonie *f*.
discordant [dɪs'kɔːdənt] *adj opinions, colours* nicht miteinander harmonierend; *meeting, atmosphere* unharmonisch; (*Mus*) disharmonisch.
discotheque ['dɪskəʊtek] *n* Diskothek *f*.
▼ **discount** ['dɪskaʊnt] 1 *n* **(a)** (*on article*) Rabatt *m*; (*for cash*) Skonto *nt or m* ◆ **to give a ~ on sth** Rabatt *or* Prozente (*inf*) auf etw (*acc*) geben; **to give sb a 5% ~** jdm 5% Rabatt/Skonto geben; **at a ~** auf Rabatt/Skonto; **~ for cash** Skonto *or* Rabatt bei Barzahlung.
(b) to be at a ~ (*Fin*) unter pari sein; (*fig*) nicht *or* wenig gefragt sein.
2 *vt* **(a)** (*Comm*) *sum of money* nachlassen; *bill, note* diskontieren ◆ **~ed bill** Diskontwechsel *m*. **(b)** [dɪs'kaʊnt] *person's opinion* unberücksichtigt lassen ◆ **to ~ sth as exaggeration/untrue** etw als Übertreibung/unwahr abtun.
discount: ~ broker *n* Wechselmakler *m*; **~ house** *n* **(a)** (*Fin*) Diskontbank *f*. **(b)** (*store*) Discountgeschäft *nt or* -laden *m*.
discourage [dɪs'kʌrɪdʒ] *vt* **(a)** (*dishearten*) entmutigen ◆ **to become ~d** entmutigt werden; (*generally disheartened*) mutlos werden.
(b) (*dissuade*) **to ~ sb from sth/from doing sth** jdm von etw abraten/jdm abraten, etw zu tun; (*successfully*) jdn von etw abbringen/jdn davon abbringen, etw zu tun.
(c) (*deter, hinder*) abhalten; *friendship, advances, plan* zu verhindern suchen; *praise, evil* abwehren; *pride* nicht ermutigen ◆ **the weather ~d people from going away** das Wetter hielt die Leute davon ab wegzufahren.
discouragement [dɪs'kʌrɪdʒmənt] *n* **(a)** (*depression*) Mutlosigkeit *f*. **(b)** (*dissuasion*) Abraten *nt*; (*with success*) Abbringen *nt*. **(c)** (*deterrence, hindrance*) Abhaltung *f*; (*of friendship*) Verhinderung *f*; (*of praise*) Abwehr *f*. **(d)** (*discouraging thing*) **to be a ~** entmutigend sein.
discouraging [dɪs'kʌrɪdʒɪŋ] *adj* entmutigend ◆ **he was rather ~ about her chances** er äußerte sich ziemlich entmutigend über ihre Chancen.
discouragingly [dɪs'kʌrɪdʒɪŋlɪ] *adv see adj*.
discourse ['dɪskɔːs] 1 *n* Diskurs *m* (*geh*) ◆ **~ analysis** (*Ling*) Diskursanalyse *f*.
2 *vi* einen Diskurs geben (*geh*); (*converse*) einen Diskurs führen (*geh*).
discourteous *adj*, **~ly** *adv* [dɪs'kɜːtɪəs, -lɪ] unhöflich.
discourteousness [dɪs'kɜːtɪəsnɪs], **discourtesy** [dɪs'kɜːtɪsɪ] *n* Unhöflichkeit *f*.
discover [dɪs'kʌvəʳ] *vt* entdecken; *culprit* finden; *secret also* herausfinden; (*after search*) *house, book also* ausfindig machen; (*notice*) *mistake, loss also* feststellen, bemerken ◆ **did you ever ~ who ...?** haben Sie jemals herausgefunden, wer ...?
discoverer [dɪs'kʌvərəʳ] *n* Entdecker(in *f*) *m*.
discovery [dɪs'kʌvərɪ] *n* Entdeckung *f*.
discredit [dɪs'kredɪt] 1 *vt* **(a)** (*cast slur/doubt on*) *report, theory* in Mißkredit bringen; *family, company also* diskreditieren.
(b) (*disbelieve*) keinen Glauben schenken (+*dat*).
2 *n* **(a)** *no pl* (*dishonour, disbelief*) Mißkredit *m* ◆ **to bring ~ (up)on sb/sth** jdn/etw in Mißkredit bringen; **without any ~ to you** ohne daß Sie dadurch diskreditiert *or* in Mißkredit gebracht werden.
(b) to be a ~ to sb eine Schande für jdn sein.
discreditable [dɪs'kredɪtəbl] *adj* diskreditierend ◆ **to be ~ to sb** jdn diskreditieren, jdn in Mißkredit bringen.
discreditably [dɪs'kredɪtəblɪ] *adv see adj*.
discreet [dɪ'skriːt] *adj* diskret; (*in quiet taste also*) dezent.
discreetly [dɪ'skriːtlɪ] *adv* diskret; *dressed also, decorated* dezent.
discreetness [dɪ'skriːtnɪs] *n see adj* Diskretheit *f*; dezente Art.
discrepancy [dɪ'skrepənsɪ] *n* Diskrepanz *f* (*between* zwischen +*dat*).
discrete [dɪ'skriːt] *adj* diskret.
discretion [dɪ'skreʃən] *n* **(a)** Diskretion *f* ◆ **~ is the better part of valour** (*Prov*) Vorsicht ist die Mutter der Porzellankiste (*inf*).
(b) (*freedom of decision*) Ermessen *nt* ◆ **to leave sth to sb's ~** etw in jds Ermessen (*acc*) stellen; **use your own ~** Sie müssen nach eigenem Ermessen handeln; **to be at sb's ~** in jds Ermessen (*dat*) stehen.
discretionary [dɪ'skreʃənərɪ] *adj* Ermessens- ◆ **~ powers** Ermessensspielraum *m*.
discriminate [dɪ'skrɪmɪneɪt] 1 *vi* **(a)** (*be discriminating*) kritisch sein; (*distinguish*) unterscheiden (*between* zwischen +*dat*). **(b)** (*make unfair distinction*) Unterschiede machen (*between* zwischen +*dat*) ◆ **to ~ in favour of sb** jdn bevorzugen.
2 *vt* unterscheiden, einen Unterschied machen zwischen (+*dat*) ◆ **to ~ good and/from bad** Gut und Böse/Gut von Böse unterscheiden können.
◆**discriminate against** *vi + prep obj* diskriminieren ◆ **they were ~d** sie wurden diskriminiert.
discriminating [dɪ'skrɪmɪneɪtɪŋ] *adj* **(a)** *person, judgement, mind* kritisch; *clientele* verwöhnt; *taste* fein. **(b)** *tariff, duty* Differential-.
discrimination [dɪˌskrɪmɪ'neɪʃən] *n* **(a)** (*differential treatment*) Diskriminierung *f* ◆ **racial ~** Rassendiskriminierung *f*; **sexual ~** Diskriminierung auf Grund des Geschlechts. **(b)** (*differentiation*) Unterscheidung *f* (*between* zwischen +*dat*). **(c)** (*discernment*) kritisches Urteilsvermögen.
discriminatory [dɪ'skrɪmɪnətərɪ] *adj* diskriminierend.
discursive [dɪ'skɜːsɪv], **discursory** [dɪ'skɜːsərɪ] *adj* **(a)** *style* weitschweifig. **(b)** (*Philos*) diskursiv.
discus ['dɪskəs] *n* Diskus *m* ◆ **~ thrower** Diskuswerfer(in *f*) *m*; **in the ~** im Diskuswerfen.
discuss [dɪ'skʌs] *vt* besprechen; *politics, theory* diskutieren; *in essay, speech etc* erörtern, diskutieren ◆ **I don't want to ~ it any further** ich möchte darüber nicht weiter reden, ich möchte das nicht weiter diskutieren; **I am not willing to ~ it** ich bin nicht gewillt, darüber zu diskutieren.
discussant [dɪ'skʌsənt] *n* (*US*) Diskussionsteilnehmer(in *f*) *m*.
discussion [dɪ'skʌʃən] *n* Diskussion *f*; (*meeting*) Besprechung *f* ◆ **after a lot of ~** nach langen Diskussionen; **to be under ~** zur Diskussion stehen; **that is still under ~** das ist noch in der Diskussion; **a subject for ~** ein Diskussionsthema *nt*.
disdain [dɪs'deɪn] 1 *vt sb* verachten; *sth also* verschmähen ◆ **he ~ed to notice them** er hielt es für unter seiner Würde, ihnen Beachtung zu schenken.
2 *n* Verachtung *f*.
disdainful *adj*, **~ly** *adv* [dɪs'deɪnfʊl, -fəlɪ] verächtlich.
disease [dɪ'ziːz] *n* (*lit, fig*) Krankheit *f*.
diseased [dɪ'ziːzd] *adj* (*lit, fig*) krank; *tissue, plant* befallen.
disembark [ˌdɪsɪm'bɑːk] 1 *vt* ausschiffen.
2 *vi* von Bord gehen.
disembarkation [ˌdɪsembɑː'keɪʃən] *n* Landung *f*.
disembodied ['dɪsɪm'bɒdɪd] *adj* körperlos; *voice* geisterhaft.
disembowel [ˌdɪsɪm'baʊəl] *vt* die Eingeweide herausnehmen (+*dat*); (*murder*) den Bauch aufschlitzen (+*dat*).
disenchant ['dɪsɪn'tʃɑːnt] *vt* ernüchtern ◆ **he became ~ed with her/it** sie/es ernüchterte ihn.
disenfranchise ['dɪsɪn'fræntʃaɪz] *vt* **(a)** *person* die bürgerlichen Ehrenrechte aberkennen (+*dat*); *town* das Recht nehmen, einen Abgeordneten ins Parlament zu senden (+*dat*). **(b)** (*Comm*) die Konzession entziehen (+*dat*).

➤ LANGUAGE IN USE: **discount: 1a → 20.3**

disenfranchisement ['dɪsɪn'fræntʃaɪzmənt] *n* (*of person*) Aberkennung *f* der bürgerlichen Ehrenrechte; (*of town*) Entzug *m* des Rechts, einen Abgeordneten ins Parlament zu senden.

disengage [ˌdɪsɪn'geɪdʒ] [1] *vt* **(a)** (*extricate*) losmachen, lösen (*from* aus). **(b)** (*Tech*) ausrücken (*form*) ◆ **to ~ the clutch** (*Aut*) auskuppeln. **(c)** (*Mil*) (*from country*) abziehen; (*from battle also*) abrücken lassen.
[2] *vi* **(a)** (*Tech*) ausrücken (*form*). **(b)** (*Mil*) auseinanderrücken; (*opponents*) sich trennen. **(c)** (*Fencing*) sich (aus seiner Bindung) lösen.

disengagement [ˌdɪsɪn'geɪdʒmənt] *n see vt* **(a)** Lösung *f*. **(b)** Ausrücken *nt* (*form*) ◆ **~ of the clutch** das Auskuppeln. **(c)** Abzug *m*.

disentail ['dɪsɪn'teɪl] *vt* (*Jur*) das Fideikommiß (*+gen*) auflösen.

disentangle ['dɪsɪn'tæŋgl] *vt* (*lit, fig*) entwirren; *problem, mystery also* enträtseln ◆ **to ~ oneself from sth** (*lit*) sich aus etw lösen; (*fig*) sich von etw lösen.

disestablish ['dɪsɪs'tæblɪʃ] *vt the Church* vom Staat trennen.

disestablishment [ˌdɪsɪs'tæblɪʃmənt] *n* Trennung *f* (vom Staat).

disfavour, (*US*) **disfavor** [dɪs'feɪvəʳ] *n* **(a)** (*displeasure*) Ungnade *f*; (*dislike*) Mißfallen *nt* ◆ **to fall into/be in ~** in Ungnade fallen/sein (*with* bei); **to look with ~ upon sb/sth** jdn/etw mit Mißfallen betrachten.
(b) (*disadvantage*) **in/to his ~** zu seinen Ungunsten.

disfigure [dɪs'fɪgəʳ] *vt* verunstalten; *person also* entstellen.

disfigurement [dɪs'fɪgəmənt] *n see vt* Verunstaltung *f*; Entstellung *f*.

disfranchise ['dɪs'fræntʃaɪz] *vt see* **disenfranchise.**

disfranchisement [dɪs'fræntʃaɪzmənt] *n see* **disenfranchisement.**

disgorge [dɪs'gɔːdʒ] [1] *vt food* ausspucken, ausspeien; (*stomach*) ausstoßen; (*fig*) (*spew forth*) ausspeien; (*river*) *waters* ergießen; (*give up*) (widerwillig) her(aus)geben *or* herausrücken.
[2] *vi* (*river*) aus einer Schlucht austreten.

disgrace [dɪs'greɪs] [1] *n* **(a)** *no pl* (*dishonour, shame*) Schande *f* ◆ **to bring ~ on sb** jdm Schande machen *or* bringen; **to be in/fall into ~** in Ungnade (gefallen) sein/fallen (*with* bei).
(b) (*cause of shame*) (*thing*) Schande, Blamage *f* (*to* für); (*person*) Schandfleck *m* (*to gen*).
[2] *vt* Schande machen (*+dat*); *country, family also* Schande bringen über (*+acc*) ◆ **don't ~ us!** mach uns keine Schande!, blamier uns nicht; **to ~ oneself** sich blamieren; (*child, dog*) sich schlecht benehmen; **to be ~d** blamiert sein; (*politician, officer etc*) in Unehre gefallen sein.

disgraceful [dɪs'greɪsfʊl] *adj* erbärmlich (schlecht); *behaviour, performance, exam results also* skandalös ◆ **it's quite ~ how/that ...** es ist wirklich eine Schande, wie/daß ....

disgracefully [dɪs'greɪsfəlɪ] *adv* (*+adj*) erbärmlich; (*+vb*) erbärmlich schlecht.

disgruntle [dɪs'grʌntl] *vt* verstimmen ◆ **~d** verstimmt.

disgruntlement [dɪs'grʌntlmənt] *n* Verstimmung *f*.

disguise [dɪs'gaɪz] [1] *vt* unkenntlich machen; *sb, oneself also* verkleiden; *voice* verstellen; *vehicle, aircraft, building also* tarnen; *facts, mistakes, interest, feelings* verschleiern.
[2] *n* (*lit*) Verkleidung *f*; (*of vehicle, aircraft, building*) Tarnung *f*; (*fig*) Deckmantel *m* ◆ **in ~** verkleidet; getarnt; **in the ~ of** in der Verkleidung als, verkleidet als/getarnt als/unter dem Deckmantel von *or* der Maske (*+gen*).

disgust [dɪs'gʌst] [1] *n* Ekel *m*; (*at sb's behaviour*) Entrüstung, Empörung *f* ◆ **to go away in ~** sich voller Ekel/Empörung abwenden; **much to his ~ he was given raw fish to eat/they left** Ekel überkam ihn, als ihm roher Fisch vorgesetzt wurde/sehr zu seiner Empörung gingen sie.
[2] *vt* (*person, sight*) anekeln, anwidern; (*actions*) empören.

disgusted [dɪs'gʌstɪd] *adj* angeekelt; (*at sb's behaviour*) empört ◆ **I am ~ with you** ich bin empört über dich.

disgustedly [dɪs'gʌstɪdlɪ] *adv* voller Ekel; (*at sb's behaviour*) empört.

disgusting [dɪs'gʌstɪŋ] *adj* widerlich; (*physically nauseating also*) ekelhaft; (*euph: obscene*) *mind* schmutzig; *behaviour, language* anstößig; (*inf: terrible also*) ekelhaft ◆ **don't be ~** sei nicht so ordinär; **that's ~** das ist eine Schweinerei (*inf*).

disgustingly [dɪs'gʌstɪŋlɪ] *adv* widerlich, ekelhaft; *rich* stink-.

dish [dɪʃ] [1] *n* **(a)** Schale *f*; (*for serving also*) Schüssel *f*. **(b) ~es** *pl* (*crockery*) Geschirr *nt*; **to do the ~es** Geschirr spülen, abwaschen. **(c)** (*food*) Gericht *nt*. **(d)** (*Elec*) Parabolreflektor *m*; (*also* **~ aerial** (*Brit*) *or* **antenna** *US*) Parabolantenne, Schüssel (*inf*) *f*. **(e)** (*sl*) (*girl*) duftes Mädchen (*inf*); (*man*) toller Typ (*inf*).
[2] *vt* **(a)** (*serve*) anrichten. **(b)** (*inf*) *chances* zunichte machen.

◆**dish out** *vt sep* (*inf*) austeilen ◆ **he can really ~ it ~** er kann ganz schön austeilen (*inf*).

◆**dish up** [1] *vt sep* **(a)** (*lit*) auf dem Teller anrichten; (*in bowls*) auftragen. **(b)** (*fig inf*) *facts* auftischen (*inf*).
[2] *vi* anrichten.

dishabille [ˌdɪsə'biːl] *n* **in a state of ~** (*woman*) im Negligé; (*man*) halb angezogen.

disharmony ['dɪs'hɑːmənɪ] *n* (*lit, fig*) Disharmonie *f*.

dishcloth ['dɪʃklɒθ] *n* (*for drying*) Geschirrtuch *nt*; (*for washing*) Spüllappen *m* *or* -tuch *nt*.

dishearten [dɪs'hɑːtn] *vt* entmutigen ◆ **don't be ~ed!** nun verlieren Sie nicht gleich den Mut!, nur Mut!

disheartening *adj*, **~ly** *adv* [dɪs'hɑːtnɪŋ, -lɪ] entmutigend.

dished [dɪʃt] *adj* (*Tech*) konkav (gewölbt); *wheels* gestürzt.

dishevelled, (*US*) **disheveled** [dɪ'ʃevəld] *adj* ramponiert (*inf*), unordentlich; *hair* zerzaust.

dish mop *m* Spülbürste *f*.

dishonest [dɪs'ɒnɪst] *adj* unehrlich; (*cheating also*) *businessman* unredlich; (*lying also*) verlogen; *plan, scheme* unlauter.

dishonestly [dɪs'ɒnɪstlɪ] *adv see adj*.

dishonesty [dɪs'ɒnɪstɪ] *n see adj* Unehrlichkeit *f*; Unredlichkeit *f*; Verlogenheit *f*; Unlauterkeit *f*.

dishonour, (*US*) **dishonor** [dɪs'ɒnəʳ] [1] *n* Schande, Unehre *f* ◆ **to bring ~ upon sb** Schande über jdn bringen.
[2] *vt* **(a)** schänden, entehren; *family* Schande machen (*+dat*).
(b) (*Comm, Fin*) *cheque* nicht honorieren; *bill* nicht bezahlen.
(c) *agreement* nicht einhalten; *promise also* nicht einlösen.

dishonourable, (*US*) **dishonorable** [dɪs'ɒnərəbl] *adj* unehrenhaft.

dishonourableness, (*US*) **dishonorableness** [dɪs'ɒnərəblnɪs] *n* Unehrenhaftigkeit *f*.

dishonourably, (*US*) **dishonorably** [dɪs'ɒnərəblɪ] *adv see adj* ◆ **to behave ~ to sb** sich jdm gegenüber unehrenhaft *or* unanständig verhalten; **to be ~ discharged** (*Mil*) unehrenhaft entlassen werden.

dish: ~pan hands *npl* rauhe und rissige Hände; **~ rack** *n* Geschirrständer *m*; (*in ~washer*) (Einsatz)korb *m*; **~ towel** *n* (*US, Scot*) Geschirrtuch *nt*; **~washer** *n* (*person*) Tellerwäscher(in *f*), Spüler(in *f*) *m*; (*machine*) (Geschirr)spülmaschine *f*; **~washer-proof** *adj* spülmaschinenfest; **~water** *n* Abwasch- *or* Spülwasser *nt*; **this coffee is like ~water** der Kaffee schmeckt wie Abwasch- *or* Spülwasser.

dishy ['dɪʃɪ] *adj* (*+er*) (*Brit sl*) *woman, man* dufte (*inf*).

disillusion [ˌdɪsɪ'luːʒən] [1] *vt* desillusionieren ◆ **I hate to ~ you, but ...** es tut mir leid, Ihnen Ihre Illusionen rauben *or* Sie desillusionieren zu müssen, aber ...
[2] *n* Desillusion *f*.

disillusionment [ˌdɪsɪ'luːʒənmənt] *n* Desillusionierung *f*.

disincentive [ˌdɪsɪn'sentɪv] *n* Entmutigung *f* ◆ **to be a ~ to sth** keinen Anreiz für etw bieten; **it acts as a ~** es hält die Leute ab.

disinclination [ˌdɪsɪnklɪ'neɪʃən] *n* Abneigung, Unlust *f*.

disinclined ['dɪsɪn'klaɪnd] *adj* abgeneigt.

disinfect [ˌdɪsɪn'fekt] *vt* desinfizieren.

disinfectant [ˌdɪsɪn'fektənt] [1] *n* Desinfektionsmittel *nt*.
[2] *adj* desinfizierend, Desinfektions-.

disinfection [ˌdɪsɪn'fekʃən] *n* Desinfektion *f*.

disinformation [ˌdɪsɪnfɔː'meɪʃən] *n* Desinformation *f*.

disingenuous [ˌdɪsɪn'dʒenjʊəs] *adj* unaufrichtig.

disingenuousness [ˌdɪsɪn'dʒenjʊəsnɪs] *n* Unaufrichtigkeit *f*.

disinherit ['dɪsɪn'herɪt] *vt* enterben.

disinheritance ['dɪsɪn'herɪtəns] *n* Enterbung *f*.

disintegrate [dɪs'ɪntɪgreɪt] [1] *vi* zerfallen; (*rock, cement*) auseinanderbröckeln; (*road surface*) rissig werden; (*car*) sich in seine Bestandteile auflösen; (*group also, institution*) sich auflösen; (*theory*) zusammenbrechen.
[2] *vt* zerfallen lassen; *rock, cement* auseinanderbröckeln lassen; *road surface* brüchig werden lassen; *group, institution* auflösen; *theory* zusammenbrechen lassen.

disintegration [dɪsˌɪntɪ'greɪʃən] *n see vi* Zerfall *m*; Auseinanderbröckeln *nt*; Rissigkeit *f*; Auflösung *f* in seine Bestandteile; Auflösung *f*; Zusammenbruch *m*.

disinter ['dɪsɪn'tɜːʳ] *vt* ausgraben.

disinterest [dɪs'ɪntrəst] *n* Desinteresse *nt* (*in* an *+dat*) ◆ **it's a matter of complete ~ to me** die Sache interessiert mich in keiner Weise, ich bin an der Sache völlig desinteressiert.

disinterested [dɪs'ɪntrɪstɪd] *adj* **(a)** (*unbiased*) unvoreingenommen, unparteiisch. **(b)** (*bored*) desinteressiert.

disinterestedly [dɪs'ɪntrɪstɪdlɪ] *adv see adj*.

disinterestedness [dɪs'ɪntrɪstɪdnɪs] *n see adj* **(a)** Unvoreingenommenheit *f*. **(b)** Desinteresse *nt*.

disinterment [ˌdɪsɪn'tɜːmənt] *n* Ausgrabung *f*.

disjointed *adj*, **~ly** *adv* [dɪs'dʒɔɪntɪd, -lɪ] unzusammenhängend, zusammenhanglos.

disjointedness [dɪs'dʒɔɪntɪdnɪs] *n* Zusammenhanglosigkeit *f*.

disjunctive [dɪs'dʒʌŋktɪv] (*Gram*) [1] *adj* disjunktiv.
[2] *n* Disjunktion *f*.

disk *n* (*Comput*) Platte *f*; (*floppy ~*) Diskette *f* ◆ **on ~** auf Platte/Diskette.

disk (*Comput*): **~ controller** *n* Plattencontroller *m*; **~ drive** *n* Diskettenlaufwerk *nt*; (*hard ~ drive*) Festplattenlaufwerk *nt*.

diskette [dɪs'ket] *n* (*Comput*) Diskette *f*.

diskless ['dɪsklɪs] *adj* (*Comput*) plattenlos.

disk operating system *n* (*Comput*) (Platten-)Betriebssystem *nt*.

dislike [dɪs'laɪk] [1] *vt* nicht mögen, nicht gern haben ◆ **to ~ doing sth** etw ungern *or* nicht gern tun; **to ~ sb doing sth** es nicht gern haben *or* sehen, wenn jd etw tut; **I ~ him/it intensely** ich mag ihn/es überhaupt nicht; **I don't ~ it** ich habe nichts dagegen.
[2] *n* Abneigung *f* (*of* gegen) ◆ **to take a ~ to sb/sth** eine Abneigung gegen jdn/etw entwickeln.

dislocate ['dɪsləʊkeɪt] *vt* (*Med*) ver- *or* ausrenken; (*fig*) *plans* durcheinanderbringen ◆ **to ~ one's shoulder** sich (*dat*) den Arm auskugeln.

dislocation [ˌdɪsləʊ'keɪʃən] *n* (*Med*) *see vt* Verrenkung *f*; (*fig*) Durcheinanderbringen *nt*; Auskugeln *nt*.

dislodge [dɪs'lɒdʒ] *vt obstruction, stone* lösen; (*prise, poke out*) herausstochern; (*knock out*) herausschlagen *or* -klopfen; *enemy* verdrängen ◆ **a few bricks/stones have been ~d** einige Ziegelsteine/Steine sind verschoben worden.

disloyal [dɪs'lɔɪəl] *adj* illoyal ◆ **to be ~ to sb/the cause** sich jdm/der Sache gegenüber illoyal verhalten.
disloyalty [dɪs'lɔɪəltɪ] *n* Illoyalität *f* (*to* gegenüber).
dismal ['dɪzməl] *adj* düster, trist; *person* trübselig, trübsinnig; *failure, result* kläglich.
dismally ['dɪzməlɪ] *adv* trostlos; *fail* kläglich; *think, say* trübselig ◆ **the sky remained ~ overcast** der Himmel blieb trüb.
dismantle [dɪs'mæntl] *vt* (*take to pieces*) auseinandernehmen; *scaffolding* abbauen; (*permanently*) *arms factory, machinery* demontieren; *ship* abwracken.
dismast [dɪs'mɑːst] *vt* entmasten.
dismay [dɪs'meɪ] 1 *n* Bestürzung *f* ◆ **in ~** bestürzt.
2 *vt* bestürzen.
dismember [dɪs'membəʳ] *vt* (*lit*) *animal, body* zerstückeln; (*Med*) zergliedern; (*fig*) *empire* zersplittern.
dismemberment [dɪs'membəmənt] *n* (*lit*) Zergliederung *f*; (*fig*) Zersplitterung *f*.
dismiss [dɪs'mɪs] *vt* **(a)** (*from job*) entlassen; *official, officer also* den Abschied geben (*+dat*). **(b)** (*allow to go*) entlassen; *assembly* auflösen, aufheben ◆ **~!** wegtreten! **(c)** (*brush aside*) *point, objection* abtun. **(d)** (*Jur*) *accused* entlassen; *appeal* abweisen ◆ **to ~ a case** die Klage abweisen. **(e)** (*Sport*) *batsman, team* ausschlagen. **he was ~ed for 52 runs** er wurde nach 52 Läufen ausgeschlagen.
dismissal [dɪs'mɪsəl] *n see vt* **(a)** Entlassung *f*; Abschied *m*. **(b)** Entlassung *f*; Auflösung *f*. **(c)** Abtun *nt*. **(d)** Entlassung *f*; Abweisung *f*; Einstellung *f*. **(e)** Ausschlagen *nt*.
dismissive [dɪs'mɪsɪv] *adj remark* wegwerfend ◆ **to be ~ about sth** etw abtun; **... he said with a ~ wave of his hand ...** sagte er mit einer abweisenden Handbewegung.
dismount [dɪs'maʊnt] 1 *vi* absteigen.
2 *vt* **(a)** *rider* abwerfen. **(b)** (*Tech*) *machine, gun* abmontieren.
disobedience [ˌdɪsə'biːdɪəns] *n* Ungehorsam *m* (*to* gegenüber) ◆ **an act of ~** ungehorsames Verhalten.
disobedient [ˌdɪsə'biːdɪənt] *adj* ungehorsam.
disobey ['dɪsə'beɪ] *vt parents, teacher* nicht gehorchen (*+dat*); *officer* den Gehorsam verweigern (*+dat*); *rule, law* übertreten.
disoblige [ˌdɪsə'blaɪdʒ] *vt* keinen Gefallen tun (*+dat*).
disobliging *adj*, **~ly** *adv* [ˌdɪsə'blaɪdʒɪŋ, -lɪ] ungefällig.
disorder [dɪs'ɔːdəʳ] 1 *n* **(a)** Durcheinander *nt*; (*in room etc also*) Unordnung *f* ◆ **in ~** durcheinander; in Unordnung; **to throw sth into ~** etw durcheinanderbringen/in Unordnung bringen; **to retreat in ~** (*Mil*) einen ungeordneten Rückzug antreten.
(b) (*Pol: rioting*) Unruhen *pl*.
(c) (*Med*) Funktionsstörung *f* ◆ **kidney/mental ~** Nieren-/Geistesstörung; **stomach ~** Magenbeschwerden *pl*.
2 *vt* **(a)** durcheinanderbringen; *room* in Unordnung bringen.
(b) (*Med*) angreifen.
disordered [dɪs'ɔːdəd] *adj* **(a)** *room, thoughts* unordentlich, durcheinander *pred*; *plans, papers also* wirr; *existence* ungeordnet. **(b)** (*Med*) *stomach, liver* angegriffen; *mind* gestört, verwirrt; *imagination* wirr.
disorderliness [dɪs'ɔːdəlɪnɪs] *n see adj* Unordentlichkeit *f*, Durcheinander *nt*; Wirrheit *f*; Ungeordnetheit *f*.
disorderly [dɪs'ɔːdəlɪ] *adj* (*untidy*) *desk, room* unordentlich; *life* unsolide; *mind* wirr; (*unruly*) *crowd* aufrührerisch; *pupils also* ungebärdig, außer Rand und Band; *behaviour* ungehörig ◆ **~ conduct** (*Jur*) ungebührliches Benehmen; **~ house** (*brothel*) Bordell, Freudenhaus *nt*; (*gambling den*) Spielhölle *f*.
disorganization [dɪsˌɔːgənaɪ'zeɪʃən] *n* Desorganisation *f*; (*state of confusion*) Durcheinander *nt*.
disorganize [dɪs'ɔːgənaɪz] *vt* durcheinanderbringen.
disorganized [dɪs'ɔːgənaɪzd] *adj* systemlos; *life also, person* chaotisch; *filing system etc* durcheinander *pred*, ungeordnet ◆ **he/the office is completely ~** bei ihm/im Büro geht alles drunter und drüber; **he was completely ~ about it** er ist dabei völlig unsystematisch vorgegangen.
disorient [dɪs'ɔːrɪənt], **disorientate** [dɪs'ɔːrɪənteɪt] *vt* (*lit, fig*) verwirren, desorientieren.
disorientation [dɪsˌɔːrɪən'teɪʃən] *n* Verwirrung, Desorientierung *f*.
disown [dɪs'əʊn] *vt* verleugnen; *child also* verstoßen; *signature* nicht (als seine eigene) anerkennen; *suggestion* nicht wahrhaben wollen ◆ **I'll ~ you if you go out in that hat** wenn du mit dem Hut ausgehst, tue ich so, als ob ich nicht zu dir gehöre.
disparage [dɪ'spærɪdʒ] *vt* herabsetzen; *work, achievements also* schmälern.
disparagement [dɪ'spærɪdʒmənt] *n see vt* Herabsetzung *f*; Schmälerung *f*.
disparaging *adj*, **~ly** *adv* [dɪ'spærɪdʒɪŋ, -lɪ] abschätzig, geringschätzig.
disparate ['dɪspərɪt] *adj* ungleich, disparat (*geh*).
disparity [dɪ'spærɪtɪ] *n* Ungleichheit, Disparität (*geh*) *f*.
dispassion [dɪs'pæʃən] *n* Objektivität *f*.
dispassionate *adj*, **~ly** *adv* [dɪs'pæʃənɪt, -lɪ] objektiv.
dispatch [dɪ'spætʃ] 1 *vt* **(a)** senden, schicken; *letter, telegram also* aufgeben; *person, troops etc also* entsenden.
(b) (*deal with*) *job etc* (prompt) erledigen.
(c) (*kill*) töten; (*shoot also*) den Todesschuß geben (*+dat*).
(d) (*inf*) *food* fertig werden mit (*inf*).
2 *n also* ['dɪspætʃ] **(a)** *see vt* (*a — c*) Senden, Schicken *nt*; Aufgabe *f*; Entsendung *f*; prompte Erledigung; Tötung *f* ◆ **date of ~** Absendedatum *nt*. **(b)** (*message, report*) Depesche *f*; (*Press*) Bericht *m* ◆ **to be mentioned in ~es** (*Mil*) in den Kriegsberichten erwähnt werden. **(c)** (*promptness*) Promptheit *f*. **with ~** prompt.
dispatch: ~ box *n* (*Brit Parl*) Depeschenkassette *f*; **~ documents** *npl* (*Comm*) Versandpapiere *pl*; **~ note** *n* (*in advance*) Versandanzeige *f*; (*with goods*) Begleitschein *m*; **~ rider** *n* (*motorcyclist*) Melder, Meldefahrer *m*.
dispel [dɪ'spel] *vt clouds, fog* auflösen, vertreiben; *doubts, fears* zerstreuen; *sorrows* vertreiben.
dispensability [dɪˌspensɪ'bɪlɪtɪ] *n* Entbehrlichkeit *f*.
dispensable [dɪ'spensəbl] *adj* entbehrlich.
dispensary [dɪ'spensərɪ] *n* (*in hospital*) (Krankenhaus)apotheke *f*; (*in chemist's*) Apothekenabteilung *f*; (*clinic*) Dispensarium *nt*.
dispensation [ˌdɪspen'seɪʃən] *n* **(a)** (*handing out*) Verteilung *f*; (*of charity*) Austeilung *f* ◆ **~ of justice** Rechtsprechung *f*.
(b) (*exemption, Eccl*) Dispens *m*, Dispensation *f*.
(c) (*system, regime*) System *nt*; (*Rel*) Glaubenssystem *nt* ◆ **~ of Providence** Fügung *f* der Vorsehung *or* des Schicksals.
dispense [dɪ'spens] 1 *vt* **(a)** verteilen, austeilen (*to* an *+acc*); *advice also* erteilen ◆ **to ~ one's favours** seine Gunst verschenken; **to ~ justice** Recht sprechen.
(b) (*Pharm*) *medicine* abgeben; *prescription* zubereiten.
(c) (*form: exempt*) dispensieren, befreien ◆ **to ~ sb from doing sth** jdn davon befreien *or* dispensieren, etw zu tun.
2 *vi* (*Pharm*) Medizin abgeben, dispensieren (*form*) ◆ **dispensing chemist's** Apotheke *f*.
◆**dispense with** *vi +prep obj* verzichten auf (*+acc*) ◆ **I could/couldn't ~ ~ that** ich könnte darauf gut/nicht verzichten, ich könnte ohne das auskommen/nicht auskommen; **that can be ~d ~** das ist entbehrlich.
dispenser [dɪ'spensəʳ] *n* **(a)** (*Pharm*) Apotheker(in *f*) *m*. **(b)** (*container*) Spender *m*; (*slot-machine*) Automat *m*.
dispersal [dɪ'spɜːsəl] *n see vt* Verstreuen *nt*; Verteilung *f*; Zerstreuung, Auflösung *f*; Streuung *f*; Dispersion *f*; Verbreitung *f*; (*of efforts*) Verzettelung, Zersplitterung *f*.
dispersant [dɪ'spɜːsənt] *n* Lösungsmittel *nt*.
disperse [dɪ'spɜːs] 1 *vt* (*scatter widely*) verstreuen; (*Bot*) *seed* verteilen; (*dispel*) *crowd, mist* zerstreuen, auflösen; *oil slick* auflösen; (*Opt*) *light* streuen; (*Chem*) *particles* dispergieren; (*fig*) *knowledge etc* verbreiten.
2 *vi* sich zerstreuen *or* auflösen; (*oil slick*) sich auflösen.
dispersion [dɪ'spɜːʃən] *n see* **dispersal**.
dispirit [dɪ'spɪrɪt] *vt* entmutigen.
dispirited *adj*, **~ly** *adv* [dɪ'spɪrɪtɪd, -lɪ] entmutigt.
dispiriting *adj*, **~ly** *adv* [dɪ'spɪrɪtɪŋ, -lɪ] entmutigend.
displace [dɪs'pleɪs] *vt* **(a)** (*move*) verschieben. **(b)** (*replace*) ablösen, ersetzen. **(c)** (*Naut, Phys*) *water, air etc* verdrängen. **(d)** (*in office*) verdrängen, ausbooten (*inf*).
displaced: ~ emotion *n* verlagertes Gefühl; **~ person** *n* Verschleppte(r) *mf*, Zwangsvertriebene(r) *mf*.
displacement [dɪs'pleɪsmənt] *n* **(a)** (*act of displacing*) *see vt* Verschiebung *f*; Ablösung *f*, Ersatz *m*; Verdrängung *f*; Ausbootung *f* (*inf*). **(b)** (*distance sth is moved*) Verschiebung *f*; (*Geol: of rocks*) Dislokation *f*. **(c)** (*volume displaced*) (*Phys*) verdrängte Menge; (*Naut*) Verdrängung *f*.
displacement: ~ activity *n* (*Psych*) Ersatzbefriedigung *f*; **~ ton** *n* (*Naut*) Verdrängungstonne *f*.
display [dɪ'spleɪ] 1 *vt* **(a)** zeigen; *interest, courage also* beweisen; *interest, ignorance* an den Tag legen, beweisen; (*ostentatiously*) *new clothes etc also* vorführen; *luxury, sth sensational* zur Schau stellen; *power* demonstrieren; *exam results, notice* aushängen. **(b)** (*Comm*) *goods* ausstellen. **(c)** (*Typ, Press*) hervorheben.
2 *vi* Imponiergehabe zeigen; (*birds also*) balzen.
3 *n* **(a)** *see vt (a)* Zeigen *nt*; Beweis *m*; Vorführung *f*; Zurschaustellung *f*; Demonstration *f*; Aushängen *nt* ◆ **to make a great ~ of sth/one's feelings** etw groß zur Schau stellen/seine Gefühle deutlich zeigen; **to be on ~** ausgestellt sein; **these are only for ~** die sind nur zur Ansicht; **I hope we don't have another ~ (of temper) like that** ich hoffe, wir kriegen nicht noch einmal denselben Tanz *or* dieselbe Schau (*inf*).
(b) (*exhibition of paintings etc*) Ausstellung *f*; (*dancing ~ etc*) Vorführung *f*; (*military, air ~*) Schau *f*.
(c) (*Comm*) Auslage *f*, Display *nt*.
(d) (*Typ, Press*) **to give top ~ to sth** etw groß herausbringen.
(e) (*Zool*) Imponiergehabe *nt*; (*of bird also*) Balz *f*.
(f) (*visual ~*) Anzeige *f*.
display *in cpds* (*Comm*) Ausstellungs-; **~ advertisement** *n* Display-Anzeige *f*; **~ advertising** *n* Displaywerbung *f*; **~ cabinet** *n* Schaukasten *m*; **~ case** *n* Vitrine *f*; **~ pack** *n* Display-Packung *f*; **~ unit** *n* (*Comput*) (Daten)sichtgerät, Bildschirmgerät *nt*; **~ window** *n* Schaufenster *nt*.
displease [dɪs'pliːz] *vt* mißfallen (*+dat*), nicht gefallen (*+dat*); (*annoy*) verstimmen, verärgern ◆ **he was rather ~d to hear that ...** er hörte nur sehr ungern, daß ...; **he is easily ~d** er ist leicht verstimmt.
displeasing [dɪs'pliːzɪŋ] *adj* unangenehm ◆ **to be ~ to sb** jdm mißfallen *or* nicht gefallen; (*annoy*) jdn verstimmen *or* verärgern; **the idea was not ~ to her** der Gedanke war ihr gar nicht so unangenehm.
displeasure [dɪs'pleʒəʳ] *n* Mißfallen *nt* (*at* über *+acc*).
disport [dɪ'spɔːt] *vr* (*old*) sich ergötzen (*old*).
disposable [dɪ'spəʊzəbl] *adj* **(a)** (*to be thrown away*) Wegwerf-, wegwerfbar; *nappy also* Papier-; *cup, plate* Papp-/Plastik-; *bottle, syringe* Einweg- ◆ **easily ~** leicht zu vernichten.
(b) (*available*) *capital, money* verfügbar, disponibel (*spec*). (*Fin*) **~ assets**

disponibles (*spec*) *or* frei verfügbares Vermögen; ~ **income** verfügbares Einkommen.

disposal [dɪ'spəʊzəl] *n* **(a)** *see* **dispose of (a)** Loswerden *nt*; Veräußerung *f*; Beseitigung *f*; Erledigung, Regelung *f* ◆ **(waste) ~ unit** Müllschlucker *m*.
(b) (*control: over resources, funds, personnel*) Verfügungsgewalt *f* ◆ **the means at one's ~** die jdm zur Verfügung stehenden Mittel; **to put sth at sb's ~** jdm etw zur Verfügung stellen; **we had the entire staff/afternoon at our ~** die ganze Belegschaft/der ganze Nachmittag stand uns zur Verfügung.
(c) (*form: arrangement*) (*of ornaments, furniture*) Anordnung *f*, Arrangement *nt*; (*Mil: of troops*) Aufstellung *f*.

dispose [dɪ'spəʊz] [1] *vt* **(a)** (*form: arrange*) *shrubs, ornaments* anordnen; *people, troops* aufstellen; *papers* ordnen.
(b) (*make willing*) **to ~ sb towards sb/sth** jdn für jdn/etw gewinnen; **to ~ sb to do sth** jdn geneigt machen, etw zu tun.
[2] *vi see* **propose.**

◆**dispose of** *vi +prep obj* **(a)** (*get rid of*) *furniture* loswerden; (*by selling also*) veräußern; *unwanted person or goods also, litter* beseitigen; *opponent, difficulties* aus dem Weg schaffen; *question, matter, difficulties* erledigen, regeln.
(b) (*have at disposal*) *fortune, time* verfügen über (*+acc*).

disposed [dɪ'spəʊzd] *adj* bereit ◆ **to be well/ill ~ towards sb** jdm wohlwollen/übelwollen.

disposition [ˌdɪspə'zɪʃən] *n* **(a)** (*form: arrangement*) (*of buildings, ornaments*) Anordnung *f*; (*of forces*) Aufstellung *f*. **(b)** (*temperament*) Veranlagung *f* ◆ **her cheerful/friendly ~** ihre fröhliche/freundliche Art.

dispossess ['dɪspə'zes] *vt* enteignen.

dispossession [ˌdɪspə'zeʃən] *n* Enteignung *f*.

disproportion [ˌdɪsprə'pɔːʃən] *n* Mißverhältnis *nt*.

disproportionate [ˌdɪsprə'pɔːʃnɪt] *adj* **to be ~ (to sth)** in keinem Verhältnis (zu etw) stehen; **a ~ amount of money/time** ein unverhältnismäßig hoher/niedriger Geldbetrag/eine unverhältnismäßig lange/kurze Zeit.

disproportionately [ˌdɪsprə'pɔːʃnɪtlɪ] *adv* unverhältnismäßig.

disprovable [dɪs'pruːvəbl] *adj* widerlegbar.

▼ **disprove** [dɪs'pruːv] *vt* widerlegen.

disputable [dɪ'spjuːtəbl] *adj* sehr zweifelhaft, disputabel.

disputant [dɪ'spjuːtənt] *n* Disputant(in *f*) *m*.

disputation [ˌdɪspjuː'teɪʃən] *n* Disput *m*, Kontroverse *f*.

disputatious [ˌdɪspjuː'teɪʃəs] *adj* streitbar, streitlustig.

dispute [dɪ'spjuːt] [1] *vt* **(a)** (*argue against*) *statement* bestreiten, anfechten; *claim to sth, will* anfechten ◆ **I would ~ that** das möchte ich bestreiten.
(b) (*debate*) *question, subject* sich streiten über (*+acc*); (*scholars etc also*) disputieren über (*+acc*) ◆ **the issue was hotly ~d** das Thema wurde hitzig diskutiert.
(c) (*contest*) *championship, possession* jdm streitig machen; *territory* beanspruchen.
[2] *vi* (*argue*) streiten; (*debate: scholars etc also*) disputieren.
[3] *n also* ['dɪspjuːt] **(a)** *no pl* (*arguing, controversy*) Disput *m*, Kontroverse *f* ◆ **a lot of ~** ein größerer Disput, eine größere Kontroverse; **to be beyond ~** außer Frage stehen; **without ~** zweifellos; **beyond** *or* **without ~ he would be ...** er wäre zweifelsohne *or* unbestritten ...; **there is some ~ about which horse won** es ist umstritten, welches Pferd gewonnen hat; **a territory in** *or* **under ~** ein umstrittenes Gebiet; **to be open to ~** anfechtbar *or* umstritten sein; **the case is in** *or* **under ~** (*Jur*) der Fall wird verhandelt.
(b) (*quarrel, argument*) Streit *m*; (*debate: between scholars etc also*) Kontroverse *f*.
(c) (*Ind*) Auseinandersetzung *f* ◆ **the union is in ~ (with the management)** zwischen Gewerkschaft und Betriebsleitung bestehen Unstimmigkeiten; **wages ~** Tarifauseinandersetzungen *pl*; **to be in ~** (*on strike*) im Ausstand sein.

disqualification [dɪsˌkwɒlɪfɪ'keɪʃən] *n* **(a)** Ausschluß *m*; (*Sport also*) Disqualifizierung, Disqualifikation *f* ◆ **~ (from driving)** Führerscheinentzug *m*. **(b)** (*disqualifying factor*) Grund *m* zur Disqualifikation.

disqualify [dɪs'kwɒlɪfaɪ] *vt* (*make ineligible*) untauglich *or* ungeeignet machen (*from* für); (*Sport etc*) disqualifizieren, ausschließen ◆ **to ~ sb from driving** jdm den Führerschein entziehen; **that disqualifies you from criticizing him** das nimmt Ihnen jedes Recht, ihn zu kritisieren.

disquiet [dɪs'kwaɪət] [1] *vt* beunruhigen.
[2] *n* (*also* **disquietude**) Unruhe *f*.

disquisition [ˌdɪskwɪ'zɪʃən] *n* (lange, ausführliche) Abhandlung *or* (*speech*) Rede (*on* über *+acc*).

disregard ['dɪsrɪ'gɑːd] [1] *vt* ignorieren; *remark, feelings also* nicht beachten, nicht achten auf (*+acc*); *danger, advice, authority also* mißachten.
[2] *n* Nichtbeachtung, Mißachtung *f* (*for gen*); (*for danger also, money*) Geringschätzung *f* (*for gen*) ◆ **to show complete ~ for sth** etw völlig außer acht lassen.

disrepair ['dɪsrɪ'peəʳ] *n* Baufälligkeit *f* ◆ **in a state of ~** baufällig; **to fall into ~** verfallen.

disreputable [dɪs'repjʊtəbl] *adj* (*dishonest, dishonourable*) übel; (*not respectable*) unfein; *clothes* unansehnlich; *area* anrüchig, verrufen, übel.

disreputably [dɪs'repjʊtəblɪ] *adv behave* (*dishonourably*) übel, gemein; (*not respectably*) unfein; *dress* schlecht.

disrepute ['dɪsrɪ'pjuːt] *n* schlechter Ruf ◆ **to bring sth into ~** etw in Verruf bringen; **to fall into ~** in Verruf kommen *or* geraten.

disrespect ['dɪsrɪs'pekt] *n* Respektlosigkeit *f* (*for* gegenüber) ◆ **I don't mean any ~, but ...** ich will nicht respektlos sein, aber ...

disrespectful *adj*, **~ly** *adv* [ˌdɪsrɪs'pektfʊl, -fəlɪ] respektlos (*to* gegenüber).

disrobe [dɪs'rəʊb] [1] *vi* (*judge*) seine Gewänder ablegen; (*form, hum: undress*) sich entkleiden, sich entblättern (*hum inf*).
[2] *vt* (*form, hum: undress*) entkleiden.

disrupt [dɪs'rʌpt] *vt* stören; *lesson, meeting, conversation, train service, communications also* unterbrechen.

disruption [dɪs'rʌpʃən] *n see vt* Störung *f*; Unterbrechung *f*.

disruptive [dɪs'rʌptɪv] *adj* störend ◆ **~ element** störendes Element, Störenfried *m*.

dissatisfaction ['dɪsˌsætɪs'fækʃən] *n* Unzufriedenheit *f*.

dissatisfied [dɪs'sætɪsfaɪd] *adj* unzufrieden (*with* mit).

dissect [dɪ'sekt] *vt plant* präparieren; *animal also* sezieren; (*fig*) *report, theory* sezieren, zergliedern.

dissection [dɪ'sekʃən] *n* **(a)** (*act*) *see vt* Präparation *f*; Sektion *f*; Zergliederung *f*. **(b)** (*plant, animal*) Präparat *nt*.

dissemble [dɪ'sembl] [1] *vt* (*cover up*) verbergen; (*feign*) vortäuschen, heucheln.
[2] *vi* (*liter*) sich verstellen; (*feign illness*) simulieren.

dissembler [dɪ'səmbləʳ] *n* Heuchler(in *f*) *m*.

disseminate [dɪ'semɪneɪt] *vt* verbreiten.

dissemination [dɪˌsemɪ'neɪʃən] *n* Verbreitung *f*.

dissension [dɪ'senʃən] *n* Meinungsverschiedenheit, Differenz *f* ◆ **a great deal of ~** große Differenzen *or* Meinungsverschiedenheiten *pl*; **to cause ~** zu Meinungsverschiedenheiten *or* Differenzen führen; (*person*) Meinungsverschiedenheiten *or* Differenzen verursachen.

dissent [dɪ'sent] [1] *vi* **(a)** anderer Meinung sein, differieren (*geh*) ◆ **I strongly ~ from what he says** ich muß dem, was er sagt, entschieden widersprechen.
(b) (*Eccl*) sich weigern, die Staatskirche anzuerkennen.
[2] *n* **(a)** Dissens *m* (*geh*), Nichtübereinstimmung *f* ◆ **to voice/express one's ~ (with sth)** erklären, daß man (mit etw) nicht übereinstimmt; **in the absence of any ~** da keine Gegenstimme laut wurde; **the motion was carried with almost no ~** der Antrag wurde fast ohne Gegenstimmen angenommen.
(b) (*Eccl*) Weigerung *f*, die (englische) Staatskirche anzuerkennen.

dissenter [dɪ'sentəʳ] *n* Abweichler(in *f*) *m*; (*Eccl also*) Dissenter *m*.

dissentient [dɪ'senʃɪənt] *adj* (*form*) *see* **dissenting.**

dissenting [dɪ'sentɪŋ] *adj attr opinion* abweichend ◆ **there was not a single ~ voice** es wurde keine Gegenstimme laut.

dissertation [ˌdɪsə'teɪʃən] *n* wissenschaftliche Arbeit; (*for PhD*) Dissertation *f*; (*fig*) Vortrag *m*.

disservice [dɪs'sɜːvɪs] *n* **to do sb a ~** jdm einen schlechten Dienst erweisen; **to be a ~/of ~ to sb** sich nachteilig für jdn auswirken, jdm schaden.

dissidence ['dɪsɪdəns] *n* Opposition *f*; (*Pol*) Dissidententum *nt*.

dissident ['dɪsɪdənt] [1] *n* Dissident(in *f*), Regimekritiker(in *f*) *m*.
[2] *adj* dissident, regimekritisch.

dissimilar ['dɪ'sɪmɪləʳ] *adj* unterschiedlich, verschieden (*to* von); *two things* verschieden ◆ **not ~ (to sb/sth)** (jdm/einer Sache) nicht ungleich *or* (*in appearance*) nicht unähnlich.

dissimilarity [ˌdɪsɪmɪ'lærɪtɪ] *n* Unterschiedlichkeit, Verschiedenheit *f*; (*in appearance also*) Unähnlichkeit *f*.

dissimulate [dɪ'sɪmjʊleɪt] [1] *vt* verbergen.
[2] *vi* sich verstellen.

dissimulation [dɪˌsɪmjʊ'leɪʃən] *n* Verstellung, Heuchelei *f* ◆ **by this ~ of his real feelings** dadurch, daß er so seine wahren Gefühle verbarg *or* nicht zeigte.

dissipate ['dɪsɪpeɪt] [1] *vt* **(a)** (*dispel*) *fog* auflösen; *doubts, fears* zerstreuen. **(b)** *energy, efforts* verschwenden, vergeuden; *fortune* verschwenden.
[2] *vi* (*clouds, fog*) sich auflösen; (*crowd, doubts, fear also*) sich zerstreuen.

dissipated ['dɪsɪpeɪtɪd] *adj behaviour, society* zügellos; *person also* leichtlebig; (*in appearance*) verlebt; *life* ausschweifend.

dissipation [ˌdɪsɪ'peɪʃən] *n see vt* **(a)** Auflösung *f*; Zerstreuung *f*. **(b)** Verschwendung, Vergeudung *f*. **(c)** (*debauchery*) Ausschweifung *f* ◆ **a life of ~** ein ausschweifendes Leben.

▼ **dissociate** [dɪ'səʊʃɪeɪt] *vt* trennen, dissoziieren (*geh, Chem*) ◆ **to ~ oneself from sb/sth** sich von jdm/etw distanzieren; **two aspects which have become largely ~d** zwei Aspekte, die sich weitgehend voneinander gelöst haben.

dissociation [dɪˌsəʊsɪ'eɪʃən] *n* Trennung, Dissoziation (*geh, Chem, Psych*) *f* ◆ **in ~ from** getrennt *or* losgelöst von.

dissoluble [dɪ'sɒljʊbl] *adj* (*Chem*) löslich, dissolubel (*spec*).

dissolute ['dɪsəluːt] *adj person* zügellos, freizügig; *way of life also* ausschweifend; *appearance* verlebt.

dissoluteness ['dɪsəluːtnɪs] *n see adj* Zügellosigkeit, Freizügigkeit *f*; Verlebtheit *f*.

dissolution [ˌdɪsə'luːʃən] *n* **(a)** (*Chem, Jur, Pol*) Auflösung *f*. **(b)** (*of relationship*) Auflösung *f*; (*of faith*) Abbröckeln *nt*.

dissolve [dɪ'zɒlv] [1] *vt* **(a)** (*lit, Jur, Pol, fig*) auflösen; *marriage also* scheiden. **(b)** (*Film*) überblenden (*into* in *or* auf *+acc*).
[2] *vi* **(a)** (*lit, Jur, Pol, fig*) sich (auf)lösen; (*fig*) sich in nichts auflösen ◆ **it ~s in water** es ist wasserlöslich, es löst sich in Wasser; **to ~ into tears** in Tränen zerfließen. **(b)** (*Film*) überblenden (*into* in *or* auf *+acc*).
[3] *n* (*Film*) Überblendung *f*.

dissolvent [dɪ'zɒlvənt] [1] *adj* lösend.
[2] *n* Lösungsmittel *nt*.

dissonance ['dɪsənəns] *n* (*Mus, fig*) Dissonanz *f*.

dissonant ['dɪsənənt] *adj* (*Mus*) dissonant; (*fig*) *opinions, temperaments* unvereinbar; *colours* disharmonisch.

➤ LANGUAGE IN USE: **disprove** → 26.3 **dissociate** → 26.2

dissuade [dɪ'sweɪd] *vt* **to ~ sb (from sth)/from doing sth** jdn von etw abbringen, jdm etw ausreden/jdn davon abbringen *or* jdm ausreden, etw zu tun; **to try to ~ sb from sth** versuchen, jdn von etw abzubringen; **he wouldn't be ~d** er ließ sich nicht davon abbringen, er ließ sich das nicht ausreden.

dissuasion [dɪ'sweɪʒən] *n* Abraten *nt* ◆ **no amount of ~ would make him change his mind** so sehr man ihm auch abriet, er änderte seinen Entschluß nicht.

dissuasive [dɪ'sweɪsɪv] *adj* abratend ◆ **he was most ~** er riet sehr davon ab; **I found his argument ~ rather than persuasive** statt mich dazu zu überreden, brachten mich seine Argumente eher davon ab.

dissuasively [dɪ'sweɪsɪvlɪ] *adv see adj.*

dissuasiveness [dɪ'sweɪsɪvnɪs] *n* (*of person*) Abraten *nt* ◆ **the ~ of his tone/voice/ arguments** sein abratender Ton/seine abratende Stimme/seine abratenden Argumente.

distaff ['dɪstɑːf] *n* **(a)** (*in spinning*) Spinnrocken *m*, Kunkel *f*. **(b) on the ~ side** mütterlicherseits.

distance ['dɪstəns] **1** *n* **(a)** (*in space*) Entfernung *f*; (*gap, interval*) Abstand *m*, Distanz *f* (*geh*); (*distance covered*) Strecke *f*, Weg *m* ◆ **we now measure ~ in metres** wir geben Entfernungen jetzt in Metern an; **at a ~ of two metres** in zwei Meter(n) Entfernung; **stopping ~** Bremsweg *m*; **the ~ between the eyes/railway lines** der Abstand der Augen *or* zwischen den Augen/der Abstand zwischen den Eisenbahnschienen; **at an equal ~ from each other** gleich weit voneinander entfernt *or* weg; **the ~ between London and Glasgow is ...** die Entfernung zwischen London und Glasgow beträgt ...; **what's the ~ from London to Glasgow?** wie weit ist es von London nach Glasgow?; **I don't know the exact ~** ich weiß nicht genau, wie weit es ist; **we covered the ~ between London and Glasgow in five hours** wir haben für die Strecke London-Glasgow fünf Stunden gebraucht; **he went with me (for) part of the ~** er ging einen Teil der Strecke *or* des Weges mit mir; **in the (far) ~** (ganz) in der Ferne, (ganz) weit weg; **he admired her at** *or* **from a ~** (*fig*) er bewunderte sie aus der Ferne; **it's within walking ~** es ist zu Fuß erreichbar; **it's no ~** es ist überhaupt nicht weit, es ist nur ein Katzensprung; **quite a/a short ~ (away)** ziemlich weit/nicht weit (entfernt *or* weg); **we drove 600 miles — that's quite a ~** wir sind 600 Meilen gefahren — das ist eine ganz schöne Strecke; **the race is over a ~ of 3 miles** das Rennen geht über eine Distanz von 3 Meilen; **the fight went the ~** der Kampf ging über alle Runden; **to go the ~** durchhalten, es durchstehen; **to keep one's ~** Abstand halten.

(b) (*in time*) **at a ~ of 400 years** aus einem Abstand von 400 Jahren; **at this ~ in time** nach einem so langen Zeitraum.

(c) (*fig: in social rank*) Unterschied *m* ◆ **to keep sb at a ~** jdn auf Distanz halten; **to keep one's ~** (*be aloof*) auf Distanz bleiben, Abstand *or* Distanz wahren (*geh*); **he keeps his ~** er bleibt immer auf Distanz, er ist immer sehr distanziert.

2 *vt* **(a)** (*Sport etc*) *see* **outdistance.**

(b) to ~ oneself from sb/sth sich von jdm/etw distanzieren.

distance: ~ event *n* Langstreckenlauf *m*; **~ runner** *n* Langstreckenläufer(in *f*) *m*.

distant ['dɪstənt] **1** *adj* **(a)** (*far away*) *country* weit entfernt, fern ◆ **we had a ~ view of the church** wir sahen in der Ferne die Kirche; **that's not so far ~ from the truth** das ist gar nicht so weit von der Wahrheit entfernt.

(b) (*in past*) *age* fern, weit zurückliegend; *recollection* entfernt ◆ **that was in the ~ past** das liegt weit zurück.

(c) (*in future*) **that's a ~ prospect** das liegt noch in weiter Ferne; **in the ~ future** in ferner Zukunft; **in the not too ~ future** in nicht allzu ferner Zukunft; **the exams are still very ~** bis zu den Prüfungen ist noch viel Zeit.

(d) *relationship, likeness, cousin* entfernt.

(e) (*fig: aloof*) *person, manner* distanziert, kühl, reserviert.

2 *adv* entfernt ◆ **two miles ~** zwei Meilen entfernt.

distantly ['dɪstəntlɪ] *adv* **(a)** (*lit*) entfernt, fern ◆ **the lights shone ~ on the horizon** die Lichter leuchteten weit weg am Horizont. **(b)** (*fig*) *resemble* entfernt; *be related also* weitläufig. **(c)** (*fig: aloofly*) *speak, behave* kühl, distanziert, reserviert.

distaste [dɪs'teɪst] *n* Widerwille *m* (*for* gegen).

distasteful [dɪs'teɪstfʊl] *adj task* unangenehm; *photo, magazine* geschmacklos ◆ **to be ~ to sb** jdm zuwider *or* unangenehm sein; **he's finding his duties more and more ~** seine Pflichten werden ihm immer mehr zuwider.

distemper¹ [dɪs'tempəʳ] **1** *n* (*paint*) Temperafarbe *f*.

2 *vt* mit Temperafarbe streichen.

distemper² *n* **(a)** (*Vet*) Staupe *f*. **(b)** (*old: ill temper*) Verstimmung *f*.

distend [dɪ'stend] **1** *vt balloon* (auf)blasen; *sails, stomach* (auf)blähen.

2 *vi* sich blähen.

distension [dɪ'stenʃən] *n* Blähen *nt*; (*of stomach also*) (Auf)blähung *f*.

distil, (*US*) **distill** [dɪ'stɪl] **1** *vt* **(a)** (*Chem*) destillieren; *whisky etc also* brennen; (*fig*) herausarbeiten, (heraus)destillieren.

(b) (*drip slowly*) tropfenweise ausscheiden *or* absondern.

2 *vi* **(a)** (*Chem*) sich herausdestillieren; (*whisky also*) gebrannt werden; (*fig also*) sich herauskristallisieren.

(b) (*drip slowly*) langsam heraustropfen, heraustöpfeln.

distillation [ˌdɪstɪ'leɪʃən] *n* (*Chem etc*) (*act*) Destillation *f*; (*of whisky etc also*) Brennen *nt*; (*product*) Destillat *nt*; (*fig*) (*act*) Verarbeitung *f*; (*product*) Destillat *nt*.

distiller [dɪ'stɪləʳ] *n* Destillateur, (Branntwein)brenner *m* ◆ **~s of whisky/gin** Whisky-/Ginbrenner *or* -destillateure *pl*.

distillery [dɪ'stɪlərɪ] *n* Destillerie, (Branntwein)brennerei *f*.

distinct [dɪ'stɪŋkt] *adj* **(a)** deutlich, klar, distinkt (*geh*); *landmark, shape also* deutlich *or* klar erkennbar; *preference also* ausgesprochen; *likeness also* ausgeprägt, ausgesprochen; *increase, progress also* merklich, entschieden ◆ **I have a ~ memory of him putting it there** ich erinnere mich deutlich daran, daß er es dahin gelegt hat; **a ~ lack of respect** ein deutlicher Mangel an Respekt; **I had the ~ feeling that something bad was going to happen** ich hatte das bestimmte Gefühl, daß etwas Schlimmes passieren würde; **he has a ~ Scottish accent** er hat einen unverkennbar schottischen Akzent; **he has a ~ advantage over her** er ist ihr gegenüber klar *or* deutlich im Vorteil, er hat ihr gegenüber einen deutlichen Vorteil.

(b) (*different*) verschieden; (*separate*) getrennt ◆ **as ~ from** im Unterschied zu; **to keep sth ~ from sth** etw und etw auseinanderhalten.

(c) (*distinctive*) eigen, individuell ◆ **in his own ~ style** in seinem eigenen unverwechselbaren *or* unverkennbaren Stil.

distinction [dɪ'stɪŋkʃən] *n* **(a)** (*difference*) Unterschied *m*; (*act of distinguishing*) Unterscheidung *f* ◆ **to make a ~ (between two things)** (zwischen zwei Dingen) unterscheiden *or* einen Unterschied machen; **is there any ~ in meaning here?** liegt hier ein Bedeutungsunterschied vor?

(b) *no pl* (*preeminence*) (hoher) Rang *m*, Distinktion *f* (*dated geh*); (*refinement*) Vornehmheit *f* ◆ **she has an air of ~** sie hat etwas Vornehmes *or* Distinguiertes (*geh*); **to win ~** sich hervortun *or* auszeichnen; **a pianist of ~** ein Pianist von Rang.

(c) (*Sch, Univ: grade*) Auszeichnung *f* ◆ **he got a ~ in French** er hat das Französischexamen mit Auszeichnung bestanden; **he was awarded several academic ~s** ihm sind mehrere akademische Auszeichnungen verliehen worden.

distinctive [dɪ'stɪŋktɪv] *adj colour, plumage* auffällig; (*unmistakable*) unverwechselbar; *gestures, walk, voice, bird call etc* unverwechselbar, unverkennbar; *characteristic, feature* kennzeichnend ◆ **with his ~ irony** mit der ihm eigenen *or* für ihn charakteristischen Ironie; **it wasn't a very ~ car** es war nichts Besonderes an dem Auto.

distinctively [dɪ'stɪŋktɪvlɪ] *adv see adj.*

distinctly [dɪ'stɪŋktlɪ] *adv* **(a)** deutlich, klar; *prefer also, alike, rude* ausgesprochen; *better, increased* entschieden ◆ **his accent was ~ Bavarian** sein Akzent war eindeutig bayrisch. **(b)** (*differently*) verschieden; (*separately*) getrennt.

distinguish [dɪ'stɪŋgwɪʃ] **1** *vt* **(a)** (*make different*) unterscheiden ◆ **only the length of their hair ~es the twins** die Zwillinge unterscheiden sich nur durch ihre Haarlänge.

(b) (*tell apart*) unterscheiden, auseinanderhalten ◆ **he can't ~ green from/and red** er kann Rot nicht von Grün unterscheiden, er kann Rot und Grün nicht auseinanderhalten.

(c) (*make out*) *landmark, shape* erkennen, ausmachen.

2 *vi* **to ~ between** unterscheiden zwischen (+*dat*), einen Unterschied machen zwischen (+*dat*).

3 *vr* sich auszeichnen, sich hervortun.

distinguishable [dɪ'stɪŋgwɪʃəbl] *adj* **(a)** (*which can be differentiated*) *two things, people* unterscheidbar ◆ **to be (easily/scarcely) ~ from sb/sth** (gut/kaum) von jdm/etw zu unterscheiden sein; **the twins are hardly ~** die Zwillinge sind kaum auseinanderzuhalten *or* voneinander zu unterscheiden.

(b) (*discernible*) *landmark, shape* erkennbar, zu erkennen; *change, improvement* merklich, deutlich.

distinguished [dɪ'stɪŋgwɪʃt] *adj* **(a)** (*eminent*) *pianist, scholar* von hohem Rang; *career* hervorragend. **(b)** (*refined, elegant*) *person, manner* distinguiert (*geh*), vornehm; *voice* gepflegt.

distinguishing [dɪ'stɪŋgwɪʃɪŋ] *adj* kennzeichnend, charakteristisch ◆ **the ~ feature of his work is ...** was seine Arbeit auszeichnet *or* kennzeichnet, ist ...

distort [dɪ'stɔːt] **1** *vt* verzerren (*also Phys*); *truth, words* verdrehen; *facts* verzerrt darstellen, verdrehen; *judgement* trüben, beeinträchtigen ◆ **a ~ed report/view of life** ein verzerrter Bericht/ein verzerrtes Bild von der Wirklichkeit; **she has a ~ed impression of what is happening** sie sieht die Ereignisse völlig verzerrt.

2 *vi* verzerrt werden.

distortion [dɪ'stɔːʃən] *n see vt* Verzerrung *f*; Verdrehung *f*; verzerrte Darstellung; Trübung, Beeinträchtigung *f*.

distract [dɪ'strækt] *vt* **(a)** (*divert attention of*) ablenken. **(b)** (*old: amuse*) zerstreuen, die Zeit vertreiben (+*dat*).

distracted [dɪ'stræktɪd] *adj* (*worried, anxious*) besorgt, beunruhigt; (*grief-stricken, distraught*) außer sich (*with* vor +*dat*) ◆ **she screamed like one ~** sie schrie wie eine Irre.

distractedly [dɪ'stræktɪdlɪ] *adv see adj.*

distraction [dɪ'strækʃən] *n* **(a)** *no pl* (*lack of attention*) Unaufmerksamkeit *f* ◆ **in a state of ~** zerstreut.

(b) (*interruption: from work etc*) Ablenkung *f*.

(c) (*entertainment*) Zerstreuung *f*.

(d) (*anxiety*) Ruhelosigkeit, Unruhe *f*; (*distraughtness*) Verstörung *f* ◆ **to love sb to ~** jdn wahnsinnig lieben; **to drive sb to ~** jdn zum Wahnsinn *or* zur Verzweiflung treiben.

distrain [dɪ'streɪn] *vi* (*Jur*) **to ~ upon sb's goods** jds Eigentum beschlagnahmen.

distraint [dɪ'streɪnt] *n* (*Jur*) Beschlagnahmung, Beschlagnahme *f* ◆ **~ order** Beschlagnahmungsverfügung *f*.

distraught [dɪ'strɔːt] *adj* verzweifelt, außer sich (*dat*) *pred*; *look, voice* verzweifelt.

distress [dɪ'stres] [1] *n* **(a)** Verzweiflung *f*; (*physical*) Leiden *nt*; (*mental, cause of* ~) Kummer *m*, Sorge *f* ♦ **to be in great** ~ sehr leiden; (*physical also*) starke Schmerzen haben; **to cause** ~ **to sb** jdm Kummer *or* Sorge/starke Schmerzen bereiten.
(b) (*great poverty*) Not *f*, Elend *nt*.
(c) (*danger*) Not *f* ♦ **a ship/plane in** ~ ein Schiff in Seenot/ein Flugzeug in Not; ~ **call** Notsignal *nt*.
[2] *vt* (*worry*) Kummer machen (*+dat*), Sorge bereiten (*+dat*) ♦ **don't** ~ **yourself** machen Sie sich (*dat*) keine Sorgen!
distressed [dɪ'strest] *adj* **(a)** (*upset*) bekümmert; (*grief-stricken*) erschüttert (*about* von). **(b)** (*poverty-stricken*) **in** ~ **circumstances** in erbärmlichen *or* armseligen Umständen *or* Verhältnissen; ~ **area** Notstandsgebiet *nt*; ~ **gentlewoman** verarmte Dame von Stand.
distressing [dɪ'stresɪŋ] *adj* (*upsetting*) besorgniserregend; (*stronger*) erschreckend; (*regrettable*) betrüblich.
distressingly [dɪ'stresɪŋlɪ] *adv see adj*.
distress: ~ **rocket** *n* Notrakete *f*; ~**-signal** *n* Notsignal *nt*.
distributary [dɪ'strɪbjʊtərɪ] [1] *n* (*Geog*) Nebenarm *m*, Flußarm *m* eines Deltas.
[2] *adj network* Verteiler-.
distribute [dɪ'strɪbju:t] *vt* verteilen; (*Comm*) *goods* vertreiben; *films* verleihen; *dividends* ausschütten ♦ **to** ~ **to/amongst** verteilen auf (*+acc*)/unter (*+acc*); vertreiben/ausschütten an (*+acc*); **this disease is evenly** ~**d throughout the classes** diese Krankheit tritt in allen Schichten gleich häufig auf.
distribution [ˌdɪstrɪ'bju:ʃən] *n see vt* Verteilung *f*; Vertrieb *m*; Verleih *m*; Ausschüttung *f* ♦ ~ **network** Vertriebsnetz *nt*; ~ **rights** Vertriebsrechte *pl*.
distributive [dɪ'strɪbjʊtɪv] [1] *adj* (*Gram*) distributiv.
[2] *n* (*Gram*) Distributivum *nt*.
distributor [dɪ'strɪbjʊtə^r^] *n* Verteiler *m* (*also Aut*); (*Comm*) (*wholesaler*) Großhändler *m*; (*retailer*) Händler *m*; (*of films*) Verleih(er) *m* ♦ ~ **discount** Händlerrabatt *m*.
distributorship [dɪ'strɪbjʊtəʃɪp] *n* Konzession *f*.
district ['dɪstrɪkt] *n* (*of country*) Gebiet *nt*; (*of town*) Stadtteil *m*, Viertel *nt*; (*administrative area*) (Verwaltungs)bezirk *m* ♦ **all the girls in the** ~ alle Mädchen in der Gegend.
district: ~ **attorney** *n* (*US*) Bezirksstaatsanwalt *m*; **D**~ **Commissioner** *n hoher Regierungsbeamter in einer Kolonie*; ~ **council** *n* (*Brit*) ≃ Bezirksregierung *f*; ~ **court** *n* (*US Jur*) Bezirksgericht *nt*; ~ **manager** *n* (*Comm*) Bezirksdirektor *m*; ~ **nurse** *n* Gemeindeschwester *f*; ~ **surveyor** *n* Bauinspektor *m*, Beamte(r) *m* des regionalen Bauaufsichtsamtes.
distrust [dɪs'trʌst] [1] *vt* mißtrauen (*+dat*).
[2] *n* Mißtrauen *nt* (*of* gegenüber).
distrustful [dɪs'trʌstfʊl] *adj* mißtrauisch (*of* gegenüber).
disturb [dɪ'stɜ:b] [1] *vt* **(a)** *person, sleep, silence, balance* stören ♦ **you** ~**ed my sleep** du hast mich im Schlaf gestört; **I hope I'm not** ~**ing you** ich hoffe, ich störe (Sie) nicht.
(b) (*alarm*) *person* beunruhigen.
(c) *waters* bewegen; *sediment* aufwirbeln; *papers* durcheinanderbringen; (*fig*) *peace of mind* stören.
[2] *vi* stören ♦ **"please do not** ~**"** „bitte nicht stören".
disturbance [dɪ'stɜ:bəns] *n* **(a)** (*political, social*) Unruhe *f*; (*in house, street*) (Ruhe)störung *f* ♦ **to cause** *or* **create a** ~ Unruhe *or* eine Ruhestörung verursachen.
(b) (*interruption: in work, routine*) Störung *f*.
(c) *no pl* (*disarranging*) *see vt (c)* Bewegung *f*; Aufwirbeln *nt*; Durcheinanderbringen *nt*; Störung *f*.
(d) *no pl* (*alarm, uneasiness*) Unruhe *f* ♦ **I don't want to cause any** ~ **but** ... ich will Sie ja nicht beunruhigen, aber...
disturbed [dɪ'stɜ:bd] *adj* **(a)** (*unbalanced*) (*mentally*) geistig gestört; (*socially*) verhaltensgestört ♦ **his mind is** ~ er ist geistig gestört.
(b) (*worried, unquiet*) beunruhigt (*at, by* über *+acc*, von) ♦ **your father was rather** ~ **to hear of your trouble with the police** dein Vater hat sich sehr beunruhigt, als er von deinen Schwierigkeiten mit der Polizei hörte.
(c) to have a ~ **night** eine unruhige Nacht verbringen.
(d) *waters* unruhig; *surface* bewegt.
disturbing [dɪ'stɜ:bɪŋ] *adj* (*alarming*) beunruhigend; (*distracting*) störend ♦ **some viewers may find these scenes** ~ einige Zuschauer könnten an diesen Szenen Anstoß nehmen.
disturbingly [dɪ'stɜ:bɪŋlɪ] *adv see adj*.
disulphide, (*US*) **disulfide** [daɪ'sʌlfaɪd] *n* Disulfid *nt*.
disunite ['dɪsju:'naɪt] *vt* spalten, entzweien.
disunity [ˌdɪs'ju:nɪtɪ] *n* Uneinigkeit *f*.
disuse ['dɪs'ju:s] *n* **to fall into** ~ nicht mehr benutzt werden; (*custom*) außer Gebrauch kommen; **rusty from** ~ wegen mangelnder Benutzung verrostet.
disused ['dɪs'ju:zd] *adj building* leerstehend; *mine, railway line* stillgelegt; *vehicle, machine* nicht mehr benutzt.
ditch [dɪtʃ] [1] *n* **(a)** Graben *m*. **(b)** (*Aviat sl*) Bach *m* (*sl*) ♦ **the plane came down in the** ~ die Maschine fiel in den Bach (*sl*).
[2] *vt* (*sl: get rid of*) *person* abhängen (*inf*); *employee, boyfriend* abservieren (*inf*); *plan, project* badengehen lassen (*sl*); *car* stehenlassen; *old manuscript, unwanted object* wegschmeißen (*inf*) ♦ **to** ~ **a plane** eine Maschine im Bach landen (*sl*).
[3] *vi* (*Aviat sl*) in den Bach gehen.
dither ['dɪðə^r^] [1] *n* **to be all of a** ~**, to be in a** ~ ganz aufgeregt *or* am Rotieren (*inf*) sein.
[2] *vi* zaudern, schwanken ♦ **to** ~ **over a decision** mit einer Entscheidung zaudern *or* nicht zu Potte kommen (*inf*); **stop** ~**ing (about) and get on with it!** jetzt laß doch dieses ewige Hin und Her und fang endlich mal an.
dithyrambs ['dɪθɪræmz] *npl* Dithyramben *pl*.
ditto ['dɪtəʊ] *n* **I'd like coffee — ~ (for me)** (*inf*) ich möchte Kaffee — ich auch, dito (*inf*); ~ **marks,** ~ **sign** Wiederholungszeichen *nt*.
ditty ['dɪtɪ] *n* Liedchen *nt*, Weise *f*.
diuretic [ˌdaɪjʊə'retɪk] [1] *adj* harntreibend, diuretisch (*spec*).
[2] *n* harntreibendes Mittel, Diuretikum *nt* (*spec*).
diurnal [daɪ'ɜ:nl] [1] *adj* (*liter: of the daytime*) Tages-; (*Bot, Zool*) Tag- ♦ **the sun's** ~ **course** der Tageslauf der Sonne, der tägliche Lauf der Sonne; **this pallid** ~ **moon** dieser blasse Mond am Tageshimmel.
[2] *n* (*Eccl*) Diurnal(e) *nt*.
div *abbr of* **dividend**.
divan [dɪ'væn] *n* Diwan *m* ♦ ~ **bed** Liege *f*.
dive [daɪv] (*vb: pret* ~**d** *or* (*US*) **dove**, *ptp* ~**d**) [1] *n* **(a)** (*by swimmer*) Sprung *m*; (*by plane*) Sturzflug *m*; (*Ftbl*) Hechtsprung, Hechter (*inf*) *m* ♦ **divers are only allowed to make two** ~**s a day** Taucher dürfen nur zweimal am Tag unter Wasser; **the deepest** ~ **yet made** die bisher größte Tauchtiefe; **to make a** ~ **for sth** (*fig inf*) sich auf etw (*acc*) stürzen; **to take a** ~ (*sl: boxer*) ein K.O. vortäuschen; (*inf: pound, dollar etc: plunge*) absacken (*inf*); (*inf: confidence, hopes*) sich in nichts auflösen.
(b) (*pej inf: club etc*) Spelunke *f* (*inf*).
[2] *vi* **(a)** (*person*) (*from diving-board*) springen; (*from side of lake, pool etc*) (mit dem Kopf voraus) springen, hechten; (*under water*) tauchen; (*submarine*) untertauchen; (*plane*) einen Sturzflug machen ♦ **to** ~ **for pearls** nach Perlen tauchen; **the goalie** ~**d for the ball** der Torwart hechtete nach dem Ball; ~**!** (*Naut*) auf Tauchstation!
(b) (*inf*) **he** ~**d into the crowd/under the table** er tauchte in der Menge unter/verschwand blitzschnell unter dem Tisch; **to** ~ **for cover** eilig in Deckung gehen; **he** ~**d into his car and raced off** er stürzte (sich) ins Auto und raste davon; **he** ~**d into his pocket** er fischte eilig in seiner Tasche.
♦**dive in** *vi* **(a)** (*swimmer*) (mit dem Kopf voraus) hineinspringen. **(b)** (*inf: start to eat*) ~**!** hau(t) rein! (*inf*).
dive: ~**-bomb** *vt* im Sturzflug bombardieren; ~**-bomber** *n* Sturzkampfbomber, Stuka *m*; ~**-bombing** *n* Sturzkampfbombardierung *f*.
diver ['daɪvə^r^] *n* (*also bird*) Taucher *m*; (*off high board*) Turmspringer(in *f*) *m*; (*off springboard*) Kunstspringer(in *f*) *m*.
diverge [daɪ'vɜ:dʒ] *vi* abweichen (*from* von), divergieren (*geh, Math*); (*two things*) voneinander abweichen.
divergence [daɪ'vɜ:dʒəns] *n* Divergenz *f* (*geh, Math*), Auseinandergehen *nt*; (*from a standard etc*) Abweichung *f*.
divergent [daɪ'vɜ:dʒənt] *adj opinions etc* auseinandergehend, divergent (*geh, Math*), divergierend (*geh, Math*).
divers ['daɪvɜ:z] *adj attr* mehrere, diverse.
diverse [daɪ'vɜ:s] *adj* verschieden(artig), unterschiedlich.
diversification [daɪˌvɜ:sɪfɪ'keɪʃən] *n* (*change, variety*) Abwechslung *f*; (*of business etc*) Diversifikation *f*.
diversify [daɪ'vɜ:sɪfaɪ] [1] *vt* abwechslungsreich(er) gestalten; *interests* breit(er) fächern; *business etc* diversifizieren.
[2] *vi* (*Comm*) diversifizieren ♦ **to** ~ **into new markets** sich in neue Märkte ausdehnen.
diversion [daɪ'vɜ:ʃən] *n* **(a)** (*of traffic, stream*) Umleitung *f*.
(b) (*relaxation*) Unterhaltung *f* ♦ **for** ~ zur Unterhaltung *or* Zerstreuung; **it's a** ~ **from work** es ist eine angenehme Abwechslung von der Arbeit.
(c) (*Mil, fig: that which distracts attention*) Ablenkung *f* ♦ **to create a** ~ ablenken; **as a** ~ um abzulenken.
diversionary [daɪ'vɜ:ʃnərɪ] *adj* ablenkend, Ablenkungs- ♦ ~ **tactics** (*Mil, fig*) eine Ablenkungstaktik/Ablenkungstaktiken *pl*; **a** ~ **manoeuvre** (*Mil, fig*) ein Ablenkungsmanöver *nt*; ~ **behaviour** Ablenkungsgebaren *nt*.
diversity [daɪ'vɜ:sɪtɪ] *n* Vielfalt *f* ♦ ~ **of opinion** Meinungsvielfalt *f*.
divert [daɪ'vɜ:t] *vt* **(a)** *traffic, stream* umleiten; *attention* ablenken; *conversation* in eine andere Richtung lenken; *blow* abwenden. **(b)** (*amuse*) unterhalten.
diverting [daɪ'vɜ:tɪŋ] *adj* unterhaltsam, kurzweilig.
divest [daɪ'vest] *vt* **(a)** (*of clothes, leaves*) berauben (*sb of sth* jdn einer Sache *gen*) ♦ **he tried to** ~ **the book of technical expressions** er versuchte, das Buch von Fachausdrücken zu reinigen; ~**ed of its rhetoric the speech says very little** ihrer Rhetorik entkleidet, ist die Rede recht nichtssagend; **he** ~**ed himself of his heavy overcoat** (*hum, form*) er entledigte sich seines schweren Mantels; **the country has** ~**ed itself of the last traces of imperialism** das Land hat sich der letzten Reste des Imperialismus entledigt.
(b) to ~ **sb of office/his authority** jdn des *or* seines Amtes entkleiden (*geh*)/seiner Macht entheben; **to** ~ **sb of (his) rank** jdn seiner Würden entkleiden (*geh*).
divide [dɪ'vaɪd] [1] *vt* **(a)** (*separate*) trennen ♦ **the wall which** ~**s the two offices** die Wand, die die beiden Büros trennt.
(b) (*split into parts: also* ~ *up*) *money, work, property, kingdom, room* teilen (*into* in *+acc*); (*in order to distribute*) aufteilen ♦ **the river** ~**s the city into two** der Fluß teilt die Stadt; ~ **the piece of paper into three parts** teilen Sie das Blatt in drei Teile (ein); **she** ~**d the cake into five parts** sie teilte den Kuchen in fünf Stücke (auf); **the book can be** ~**d into three main parts** das Buch kann in drei Hauptteile gegliedert werden.
(c) (*share out*) *money, time, food* verteilen ♦ **she** ~**d the food evenly among the children** sie verteilte das Essen gleichmäßig an die Kinder.
(d) (*Math*) dividieren, teilen ♦ **to** ~ **6 into 36, to** ~ **36 by 6** 36 durch 6 teilen

or dividieren; **what is 12 ~d by 3?** was ist 12 (geteilt *or* dividiert) durch 3?
(e) *(cause disagreement among) friends* entzweien.
(f) *(Brit Parl)* **to ~ the House** durch Hammelsprung abstimmen lassen.
[2] *vi* **(a)** *(river, road, room, cells)* sich teilen; *(book etc)* sich gliedern *(into* in *+acc)* ◆ **to ~ into groups** sich in Gruppen aufteilen; *(be classified)* sich gliedern lassen; **the policy of ~ and rule** die Politik des „divide et impera".
(b) *(Math: number)* sich teilen *or* dividieren lassen *(by* durch) ◆ **we're learning to ~** wir lernen Teilen *or* Dividieren; **he can't ~** er kann nicht teilen *or* dividieren.
(c) *(Brit Parl)* **the House ~d** das Parlament stimmte durch Hammelsprung ab; **~, ~!** abstimmen!
[3] *n (Geog)* Wasserscheide *f* ◆ **the Great D~** *(Geog)* die (nord)amerikanische Wasserscheide; *(fig)* die Kluft; *(death)* der Tod; **to cross the Great D~** *(fig)* den Schritt über die Schwelle tun; *(die)* die Schwelle des Todes überschreiten.
◆**divide off** [1] *vi* sich (ab)trennen; *(be separable)* sich (ab)trennen lassen.
[2] *vt sep* (ab)trennen.
◆**divide out** *vt sep* aufteilen *(among* unter *+acc or dat)*.
◆**divide up** [1] *vi see* **divide 2 (a)**.
[2] *vt sep see* **divide 1 (b)**.
divided [dɪˈvaɪdɪd] *adj* **(a)** *(lit)* geteilt ◆ **~ highway** *(US)* Schnellstraße *f*; **~ skirt** Hosenrock *m*. **(b)** *(in disagreement) opinion, country, self* geteilt; *couple* getrennt ◆ **a people ~ against itself** ein unter sich *(dat)* uneiniges Volk.
dividend [ˈdɪvɪdend] *n* **(a)** *(Fin)* Dividende *f* ◆ **to pay ~s** *(fig)* sich bezahlt machen. **(b)** *(Math)* Dividend *m*.
dividers [dɪˈvaɪdəz] *npl* Stechzirkel *m*.
dividing [dɪˈvaɪdɪŋ] *adj* (ab)trennend ◆ **~ wall** Trennwand *f*; **~ line** *(lit, fig)* Trennungslinie *f*.
divination [ˌdɪvɪˈneɪʃən] *n* Prophezeiung, Weissagung *f*.
divine [dɪˈvaɪn] [1] *adj (Rel, fig inf)* göttlich ◆ **~ worship** Anbetung *f* Gottes.
[2] *n* Theologe *m*; *(priest also)* Geistliche(r) *m*.
[3] *vt* **(a)** *(foretell) the future* weissagen, prophezeien. **(b)** *(liter: make out) sb's intentions* erahnen, erspüren *(liter)*. **(c)** *(find) water, metal* aufspüren.
divinely [dɪˈvaɪnlɪ] *adv see adj*.
diviner [dɪˈvaɪnəʳ] *n* **(a)** *(of future)* Wahrsager(in *f*) *m*. **(b)** *see* **water ~**.
diving [ˈdaɪvɪŋ] *n (under water)* Tauchen *nt*; *(into water)* Springen *nt*; *(Sport)* Wasserspringen *nt*.
diving: ~-bell *n* Taucherglocke *f*; **~-board** *n* (Sprung)brett *nt*; **~-suit** *n* Taucheranzug *m*.
divining-rod [dɪˈvaɪnɪŋˈrɒd] *n* Wünschelrute *f*.
divinity [dɪˈvɪnɪtɪ] *n* **(a)** *(divine being)* göttliches Wesen, Gottheit *f*. **(b)** *(divine quality)* Göttlichkeit *f*. **(c)** *(theology)* Theologie *f*; *(Sch)* Religion *f* ◆ **doctor of ~** Doktor der Theologie.
divisible [dɪˈvɪzəbl] *adj* teilbar *(by* durch).
division [dɪˈvɪʒən] *n* **(a)** *(act of dividing, state of being divided)* Teilung *f*; *(Math)* Teilen *nt*, Division *f* ◆ **we're learning ~** wir sind beim Teilen; **the ~ of labour** die Arbeitsteilung.
(b) *(Mil)* Division *f*.
(c) *(result of dividing) (in administration)* Abteilung *f*; *(in box, case)* Fach *nt*; *(part)* Teil *m*; *(category)* Kategorie *f*.
(d) *(that which divides) (in room)* Trennwand *f*; *(fig: between social classes etc)* Schranke *f*; *(dividing line: lit, fig)* Trennungslinie *f* ◆ **where does the syllable ~ come?** wie ist die Silbentrennung hier?
(e) *(fig: discord)* Uneinigkeit *f*.
(f) *(Brit Parl)* **to call for a ~** eine Abstimmung durch Hammelsprung verlangen.
(g) *(Sport)* Liga *f*.
division-bell [dɪˈvɪʒənˌbel] *n (Parl) Klingel, mit der die Abgeordneten zur Abstimmung gerufen werden.*
division sign *n (Math)* Teilungszeichen *nt*.
divisive [dɪˈvaɪsɪv] *adj* **to be ~** Uneinigkeit schaffen.
divisor [dɪˈvaɪzəʳ] *n (Math)* Divisor *m*.
divorce [dɪˈvɔːs] [1] *n (Jur)* Scheidung *f (from* von); *(fig)* Trennung *f* ◆ **he wants a ~** er will sich scheiden lassen; **to get a ~ (from sb)** sich (von jdm) scheiden lassen; **~ court** Scheidungsgericht *m*; **~ proceedings** Scheidungsprozeß *m*.
[2] *vt* **(a)** *husband, wife* sich scheiden lassen von ◆ **to get ~d** sich scheiden lassen. **(b)** *(fig)* trennen.
[3] *vi* sich scheiden lassen ◆ **they ~d last year** sie haben sich letztes Jahr scheiden lassen.
divorced [dɪˈvɔːst] *adj (Jur)* geschieden *(from* von) ◆ **to be ~ from sth** *(fig)* keine(rlei) Beziehung zu etw haben.
divorcee [dɪˌvɔːˈsiː] *n* Geschiedene(r) *mf*, geschiedener Mann, geschiedene Frau ◆ **he is a ~** er ist geschieden.
divot [ˈdɪvɪt] *n vom Golfschläger etc ausgehacktes Rasenstück.*
divulge [daɪˈvʌldʒ] *vt* preisgeben *(sth to sb* jdm etw).
divvy [ˈdɪvɪ] *(Brit inf) dim of* **dividend** Dividende *f*.
◆**divvy up** *(inf)* [1] *vt sep (divide up)* aufteilen.
[2] *vi* aufteilen.
dixie [ˈdɪksɪ] *n (Brit Mil sl)* Gulaschkanone *f (inf)*; *(for eating)* Eßgeschirr *nt*.
Dixie *n (also* **~land**) Dixie(land) *m*.
DIY *abbr of* **do it yourself**.
dizzily [ˈdɪzɪlɪ] *adv* **(a)** *(giddily) stagger* taumelnd, schwankend ◆ **the pound rose ~ to DM 3.20** das Pfund stieg auf schwindelerregende DM 3,20. **(b)** *(inf: foolishly) behave* verrückt.
dizziness [ˈdɪzɪnɪs] *n* Schwindel *m* ◆ **attack of ~** Schwindelanfall *m*.
dizzy [ˈdɪzɪ] *adj (+er)* **(a)** *(lit, fig) person* schwind(e)lig; *height, speed* schwindelerregend ◆ **~ spell** Schwindelanfall *m*; **I feel ~** mir ist *or* ich bin schwindlig; **it makes me ~ to think of it** mir wird ganz schwindelig bei dem Gedanken.
(b) *(inf: foolish)* verrückt.
DJ *abbr of* **(a) dinner jacket. (b) disc jockey.**
dl *abbr of* **decilitre(s)** dl.
D Lit *abbr of* **Doctor of Letters** Dr. phil.
DM *abbr of* **Deutschmark** DM; **Doctor of medicine** Dr. med.
dm *abbr of* **decimetre(s)** dm.
D-mark [ˈdiːmɑːk] *n abbr of* **Deutschmark** D-Mark *f*.
D Mus *abbr of* **Doctor of Music.**
DNA *abbr of* **de(s)oxyribonucleic acid** DNS *f*.
DNA fingerprinting, DNA profiling *n see* **genetic fingerprinting.**
do¹ [dəʊ] *n (Mus)* Do *nt*.
do² [duː] *(vb: pret* **did,** *ptp* **done)** [1] *v aux* **(a)** *(used to form interrog and neg in present and pret vbs)* **~ you understand?** verstehen Sie?; **I ~ not** *or* **don't understand** ich verstehe nicht; **didn't you** *or* **did you not know?** haben Sie das nicht gewußt?; **never did I see so many** ich habe noch nie so viele gesehen.
(b) *(for emphasis: with stress on do)* **~ come!** kommen Sie doch (bitte)!; **~ shut up!** (nun) sei doch (endlich) ruhig!; **~ tell him that ...** sagen Sie ihm doch (bitte), daß ...; **~ I remember him!** und ob ich mich an ihn erinnere!; **but I ~ like it** aber es gefällt mir wirklich; **it's very dear, but I ~ like it** es ist zwar sehr teuer, aber es gefällt mir nun mal; **so you ~ know them!** Sie kennen sie also wirklich *or* tatsächlich!; *(and were lying etc)* Sie kennen sie also doch!; **you don't do meals, do you? — yes, we ~ do meals** Essen gibt's bei Ihnen nicht? — doch.
(c) *(used to avoid repeating vb)* **you speak better than I ~** Sie sprechen besser als ich; **he likes cheese and so ~ I** er ißt gern Käse und ich auch; **he doesn't like cheese and neither ~ I** er mag keinen Käse und ich auch nicht; **they said he would go and he did** sie sagten, er würde gehen, und das tat er (dann) auch.
(d) *(in question tags)* oder ◆ **you know him, don't you?** Sie kennen ihn doch?, Sie kennen ihn (doch), oder *or* nicht wahr?; **so you know/don't know him, ~ you?** Sie kennen ihn also/also nicht, oder?; **you do understand, don't you?** das verstehen Sie doch (sicherlich)(, nicht wahr *or* oder)?; **he didn't go, did he?** er ist (doch) nicht gegangen, oder?
(e) *(in answers: replacing vb)* **do you see them often? — yes, I ~/no, I don't** sehen Sie sie oft? — ja/nein; **they speak French — oh, ~ they?** sie sprechen Französisch — ja?, ach, wirklich *or* tatsächlich?; **they speak French — ~ they really?** sie sprechen Französisch — wirklich?; **may I come in? — ~!** darf ich hereinkommen? — ja, bitte; **shall I open the window? — no, don't!** soll ich das Fenster öffnen? — nein, bitte nicht!; **who broke the window? — I did** wer hat das Fenster eingeschlagen? — ich.
[2] *vt* **(a)** *(be busy with, be involved in, carry out)* tun, machen ◆ **what are you ~ing (with yourself) on Saturday?** was machen *or* tun Sie am Sonnabend?; **I've got nothing to ~** ich habe nichts zu tun; **are you ~ing anything this evening?** haben Sie heute abend schon etwas vor?; **I shall ~ nothing of the sort** ich werde nichts dergleichen tun; **he does nothing but complain** er nörgelt immer nur, er tut nichts als nörgeln *(inf)*; **what must I ~ to get better?** was soll ich tun, um wieder gesund zu werden?; **what shall we ~ for money?** wie machen wir es mit Geld?
(b) *(perform, accomplish)* tun; *homework* machen ◆ **I've done a stupid thing** ich habe da was Dummes gemacht *or* getan; **to ~ a play** ein Stück aufführen; **to ~ a film** einen Film machen *or* drehen; **to ~ one's military service** seinen Wehrdienst ableisten *or* machen *(inf)*; **to ~ the housework** die Hausarbeit machen; **we'll have to ~ something about this/him** wir müssen da etwas tun *or* unternehmen/müssen mit ihm etwas tun *or* unternehmen; **how do you ~ it?** wie macht man das?; *(in amazement)* wie machen Sie das bloß?; **what's to be done?** was ist da zu tun?; **what can you ~?** was kann man da machen?; **sorry, it's impossible, it can't be done** tut mir leid, (ist) ausgeschlossen, es läßt sich nicht machen; **well, ~ what you can** mach *or* tu (eben), was du kannst; **what can I ~ for you?** was kann ich für Sie tun?; *(by shop assistant also)* was darf's sein?; **can you ~ it by yourself?** schaffst du das allein, kannst du das allein machen?; **what do you want me to ~ (about it)?** und was soll ich da tun *or* machen?; **he knows it's a mistake but he can't ~ anything about it** er weiß, daß es ein Fehler ist, aber er kann nichts dagegen machen *or* daran ändern; **to ~ sth again** etw noch (ein)mal tun *or* machen; **~ something for me, will you ... shut up** tu mir bloß den (einen) Gefallen und halt den Mund; **you ~ something to me** du hast es mir angetan; **does that ~ anything for you?** macht dich das an? *(inf)*; **Brecht doesn't ~ anything for me** Brecht läßt mich kalt *(inf) or* sagt mir nichts; **what have you done to him?** was haben Sie mit ihm gemacht?; **that's done it** *(inf)* so, da haben wir's, da haben wir die Bescherung; **that does it!** jetzt reicht's mir!; **oh God, now what have you done!** ach du Schreck, was hast du jetzt bloß wieder angestellt *or* gemacht?
(c) *(make, produce)* **~ this letter and six copies** tippen Sie den Brief mit sechs Durchschlägen; **I'll ~ a translation for you** ich werde eine Übersetzung für Sie machen; *see* **wonder** *etc*.
(d) *(Sch etc: study)* durchnehmen, haben ◆ **we've done Milton** wir haben Milton gelesen *or* durchgenommen; **I've never done any German** ich habe nie Deutsch gelernt *or* gehabt.
(e) *(solve)* lösen; *sum, crossword, puzzle etc also* machen.
(f) *(arrange)* **to ~ the flowers** die Blumen arrangieren; **to ~ one's hair** sich

frisieren, sich (*dat*) die Haare (zurecht)machen (*inf*); **who does your hair?** zu welchem Friseur gehen Sie?; **who did your hair last time, madam?** wer hat Sie letztes Mal bedient?; **I can't ~ my tie** ich kann meine Krawatte nicht binden.
(g) (*clean, tidy*) **to ~ one's nails** sich (*dat*) die Nägel schneiden *or* (*varnish*) lackieren; **to ~ one's teeth** sich (*dat*) die Zähne putzen; **to ~ the shoes** Schuhe putzen; **this room needs ~ing today** dieses Zimmer muß heute gemacht werden (*inf*); **to ~ the dishes** spülen, den Abwasch machen.
(h) (*deal with*) **the barber said he'd ~ me next** der Friseur sagte, er würde mich als Nächsten drannehmen; **who did the choreography/the jacket design?** wer hat die Choreographie/ den Umschlagentwurf gemacht?; **you ~ the painting and I'll ~ the papering** du streichst an und ich tapeziere; **we'll have to get someone to ~ the roof** wir müssen jemanden bestellen, der das Dach macht (*inf*); **he does the film crits for the magazine** er schreibt die Filmkritiken für die Zeitschrift; **we only ~ one make of gloves** wir haben *or* führen nur eine Sorte Handschuhe; (*produce*) wir stellen nur eine Sorte Handschuhe her; **I'll ~ the talking** ich übernehme das Reden; **who's ~ing the flowers?** wer besorgt die Blumen?; **who did the food for your reception?** wer hat bei Ihrem Empfang für das Essen gesorgt?; **I'll ~ you** (*sl*) dir besorg' ich's noch! (*inf*).
(i) (*in pret, ptp only: complete, accomplish*) **the work's done now** die Arbeit ist gemacht *or* getan *or* fertig; **what's done cannot be undone** was geschehen ist, kann man nicht ungeschehen machen; **I haven't done telling you what I think of you** mit dir bin ich noch lange nicht fertig; **done!** abgemacht!; **it's all over and done with** (*is finished*) das ist alles erledigt; (*has happened*) das ist alles vorbei *or* überstanden; **to get done with sth** etw fertigmachen.
(j) (*visit, see sights of*) *city, country, museum* besuchen, abhaken (*inf*); (*take in also*) mitnehmen (*inf*).
(k) (*Aut etc*) fahren, machen (*inf*) ◆ **this car does** *or* **can ~** *or* **will ~ 100** das Auto fährt *or* macht (*inf*) 100; **we did London to Edinburgh in 8 hours** wir haben es in 8 Stunden von London bis Edinburgh geschafft.
(l) (*inf*) (*be suitable*) passen (*sb* jdm); (*be sufficient for*) reichen (*sb* jdm) ◆ **that will ~ me nicely** das reicht dicke (*inf*) *or* allemal.
(m) (*Theat*) *part* spielen ◆ **to ~ Hamlet** den Hamlet spielen.
(n) (*take off, mimic*) nachmachen.
(o) (*inf: cheat*) übers Ohr hauen (*inf*), reinlegen (*inf*) ◆ **you've been done!** du bist reingelegt *or* übers Ohr gehauen worden (*inf*); **I was done for £80 for that table** mit £ 80 für den Tisch hat man mich ganz schön übers Ohr gehauen (*inf*).
(p) (*sl: burgle*) einbrechen in (+*acc*) ◆ **the office was done last night** im Büro ist gestern nacht ein Bruch gemacht worden (*sl*).
(q) (*provide service of*) **sorry, we don't ~ lunches** wir haben leider keinen Mittagstisch; **we don't ~ telegrams** wir können keine Telegramme annehmen.
(r) (*inf: provide food, lodgings for*) **they ~ you very well at that hotel/restaurant** in dem Hotel ist man gut untergebracht *or* aufgehoben/in dem Restaurant ißt man sehr gut.
(s) (*Cook*) machen (*inf*); *vegetables etc also* kochen ◆ **to ~ the cooking/food** Essen machen; **how do you like your steak done?** wie möchten Sie Ihr Steak?; **well done** durch(gebraten).
(t) (*inf: tire out*) **I'm absolutely done!** ich bin völlig geschafft *or* erledigt *or* fertig (*all inf*).
(u) (*inf: in prison*) *6 years* sitzen, abreißen (*inf*).
(v) (*old, liter: translate*) **done into the English by** ... ins Englische übertragen von ...
[3] *vi* **(a)** (*act*) **~ as I ~** mach es wie ich; **he did well to take advice** er tat gut daran, sich beraten zu lassen; **he did right** er hat richtig gehandelt, es war richtig von ihm; **he did right/well to go** es war richtig/gut, daß er gegangen ist.
(b) (*get on, fare*) **how are you ~ing?** wie geht's (Ihnen)?; **I'm not ~ing so badly** es geht mir gar nicht so schlecht; **the patient is ~ing very well** dem Patienten geht es recht ordentlich; **he's ~ing well at school** er ist gut in der Schule; **his business is ~ing well** sein Geschäft geht gut; **the roses are ~ing well this year** die Rosen stehen dieses Jahr gut; **I married and did quite well out of it** ich habe geheiratet und bin dabei ganz gut gefahren; **what's ~ing?** was ist los?
(c) (*finish*) **the meat, is it done?** ist das Fleisch fertig (gebraten) *or* durch?; **have you done?** sind Sie endlich *or* schon (*iro*) fertig?
(d) (*suit, be convenient*) gehen ◆ **that will never ~!** das geht nicht!; **this room will ~** das Zimmer geht (*inf*) *or* ist in Ordnung; **will it ~ if I come back at 8?** geht es, wenn ich um 8 Uhr zurück bin?; **it doesn't ~ to keep a lady waiting** es gehört sich *or* geht nicht, daß man eine Dame warten läßt; **will she/it ~?** geht sie/das?; **this coat will ~ for** *or* **as a cover** dieser Mantel geht als Decke; **you'll have to make ~ with £10** £ 10 müssen Ihnen reichen, Sie werden mit £ 10 auskommen müssen.
(e) (*be sufficient*) reichen ◆ **can you lend me some money? — will £10 ~?** können Sie mir etwas Geld leihen? — reichen £ 10?; **yes, that'll ~** ja, das reicht; **that'll ~!** jetzt reicht's aber!
(f) (*inf: char*) putzen.
[4] *vr* **to ~ oneself well** es sich (*dat*) gutgehen lassen.
[5] *n* (*inf*) **(a)** Veranstaltung, Sache (*inf*) *f*; (*party*) Fete *f* (*inf*). **(b)** (*Brit: swindle*) Schwindel *m*. **(c)** (*in phrases*) **it's a poor ~!** das ist ja schwach (*inf*) *or* ein schwaches Bild! (*inf*); **the ~s and don'ts** was man tun und nicht tun sollte (*for* als); (*highway code*) die Ge- und Verbote; **fair ~s all round** gleiches Recht für alle.
◆**do away with** *vi +prep obj* **(a)** *custom, law* abschaffen; *document* vernichten; *building* abreißen. **(b)** (*kill*) umbringen.
◆**do by** *vi +prep obj* **to ~ well/badly ~ sb** jdn gut/schlecht behandeln; **do as you would be done ~** (*Prov*) was du nicht willst, daß man dir tu, das füg auch keinem andern zu (*Prov*); *see* **hard**.
◆**do down** *vt sep* (*Brit*) heruntermachen, schlechtmachen.
◆**do for** *vi +prep obj* **(a)** (*inf: finish off*) *person* fertigmachen (*inf*); *project* zunichte machen ◆ **to be done ~** (*person*) erledigt *or* fertig (*inf*) sein; (*project*) gestorben sein (*inf*). **(b)** (*inf: charlady*) putzen für *or* bei.
◆**do in** *vt sep* (*inf*) **(a)** (*kill*) um die Ecke bringen (*inf*). **(b)** (*usu pass: exhaust*) **to be** *or* **feel done ~** fertig *or* geschafft sein (*inf*).
◆**do out** *vt sep* **(a)** *room* auskehren *or* -fegen. **(b) to ~ sb ~ of a job/his rights** jdn um eine Stelle/seine Rechte bringen; **to ~ sb ~ of £100** jdn um £ 100 bringen *or* erleichtern (*inf*).
◆**do over** *vt sep* **(a)** (*redecorate*) (neu) herrichten. **(b)** (*sl: beat up*) zusammenschlagen. **(c)** (*US: do again*) noch einmal machen.
◆**do up** [1] *vi* (*dress etc*) zugemacht werden.
[2] *vt sep* **(a)** (*fasten*) zumachen ◆ **~ yourself ~, sir!** machen Sie Ihre Hose zu!
(b) (*parcel together*) *goods* zusammenpacken ◆ **books done ~ in brown paper** in Packpapier eingewickelte Bücher; **to ~ sth ~ in a parcel** etw einpacken.
(c) *house, room* (neu) herrichten ◆ **to ~ ~ one's face** sich schminken; **to ~ oneself ~** sich zurechtmachen.
◆**do with** *vi +prep obj* **(a)** (*with can or could: need*) brauchen ◆ **do you know what I could ~ ~?** weißt du, was ich jetzt brauchen könnte?; **it could ~ ~ a clean** es müßte mal saubergemacht werden.
(b) (*dial: in neg, with can or could: tolerate*) ausstehen, vertragen ◆ **I can't be ~ing ~ this noise** ich kann den Lärm nicht vertragen *or* ausstehen.
(c) he has to ~ ~ the steel industry er hat mit der Stahlindustrie zu tun; **what has that got to ~ ~ it?** was hat das damit zu tun?; **I won't have anything to ~ ~ it!** ich möchte nichts damit zu tun haben!; **that has** *or* **is nothing to ~ ~ you!** das geht Sie gar nichts an!; **this debate has to ~ ~** ... in dieser Debatte geht es um ...; **well, it's to ~ ~ this letter you sent** es geht um den Brief, den Sie geschickt haben; **money has a lot to ~ ~ it** Geld spielt eine große Rolle dabei.
(d) what have you done ~ my gloves/your face? was haben Sie mit meinen Handschuhen/Ihrem Gesicht gemacht?
(e) he doesn't know what to ~ ~ himself er weiß nicht, was er mit sich anfangen soll; **the children can always find something to ~ ~ themselves** die Kinder finden immer etwas, womit sie sich beschäftigen können.
(f) to be done ~ sb/sth (*finished*) mit jdm/etw fertig sein.
◆**do without** *vi +prep obj* auskommen ohne ◆ **I can ~ ~ your advice** Sie können sich Ihren Rat sparen; **I could have done ~ that!** das hätte mir (wirklich) erspart bleiben können; **you'll have to ~ ~** Sie müssen ohne auskommen.
do[3] *written abbr of* **ditto**.
DOA *abbr of* **dead on arrival**.
d.o.b. *abbr of* **date of birth**.
Doberman (pinscher) ['dəubəmən('pɪnʃəʳ)] *n* Dobermann(pinscher) *m*.
doc [dɒk] *n* (*inf*) *abbr of* **doctor** Herr Doktor *m*.
docile ['dəusaɪl] *adj* sanftmütig; *horse* fromm; *engine* schwach.
docility [dəʊ'sɪlɪtɪ] *n* Sanftmut *f*.
dock[1] [dɒk] [1] *n* Dock *nt*; (*for berthing*) Pier, Kai *m* ◆ **~s** *pl* Hafen *m*; **my car is in ~** (*inf*) mein Wagen ist in der Werkstatt.
[2] *vt* docken; (*Space also*) ankoppeln.
[3] *vi* **(a)** (*Naut*) anlegen. **(b)** (*Space: two spacecraft*) docken (*spec*), ankoppeln.
dock[2] *n* (*Jur*) Anklagebank *f* ◆ **to stand in the ~** auf der Anklagebank sitzen; **"prisoner in the ~"** „Angeklagte(r)".
dock[3] [1] *vt* **(a)** *dog's tail* kupieren; *horse's tail* stutzen. **(b)** *wages* kürzen. **to ~ £5 off sb's wages** jds Lohn um 5 Pfund kürzen.
[2] *n* kupierter Schwanz; (*of horse*) gestutzer Schweif.
dock[4] *n* (*Bot*) Ampfer *m*.
docker ['dɒkəʳ] *n* (*Brit*) Hafenarbeiter, Docker *m*.
docket ['dɒkɪt] [1] *n* **(a)** (*on document, parcel etc*) Warenbegleitschein, Laufzettel *m*. **(b)** (*Jur: judgements register*) Urteilsregister *nt*; (*list of cases*) *Liste f der Gerichtstermine*. **(c)** (*customs certificate*) Zollinhaltserklärung *f*.
[2] *vt* **(a)** *contents*, (*Jur*) *judgement, information etc* zusammenfassen, eine Kurzfassung geben *or* herstellen von. **(b)** *contents* angeben; (*put ~ on*) *crate* mit einem Warenbegleitschein *or* Laufzettel versehen.
dock gates *npl* Hafeneingang *m*; (*in water*) Docktor *nt*.
docking ['dɒkɪŋ] *n* (*Space*) Docking *nt* (*spec*), Ankoppelung *f*.
docking: ~ manoeuvre *n* (*Space*) (An)koppelungsmanöver *nt*; **~ techniques** *npl* (*Space*) (An)koppelungstechnik *f*; **~ time** *n* Liegezeit *f*.
dock: ~ labourer *n* Hafenarbeiter *m*; **~land** *n* Hafenviertel *nt*; **~ strike** *n* Hafenarbeiterstreik *m*; **~ worker** *n* Hafenarbeiter *m*; **~yard** *n* Werft *f*.
Doc Martens ® [dɒk'mɑ:tənz] *npl* Springerstiefel *pl*.
doctor ['dɒktəʳ] [1] *n* **(a)** (*Med*) Arzt *m*, Ärztin *f*, Doktor(in *f*) *m* (*inf*) ◆ **D~ Smith** Doktor Smith; **yes, ~** ja, Herr Doktor; **to send for the ~** den Arzt holen; **he is a ~** er ist Arzt; **a woman ~** eine Ärztin; **he's under the ~** (*inf*) er ist in Behandlung; **it's just what the ~ ordered** (*fig inf*) das ist genau das richtige.
(b) (*Univ etc*) Doktor *m* ◆ **to take one's ~'s degree** promovieren, seinen Doktor machen; **~ of Law/of Science** *etc* Doktor der Rechte/der Naturwissenschaften *etc*; **Dear Dr Smith** Sehr geehrter Herr Dr./Sehr geehrte Frau Dr. Smith.
[2] *vt* **(a)** *cold* behandeln ◆ **she's always ~ing herself** sie doktort dauernd an sich (*dat*) herum. **(b)** (*inf: castrate*) kastrieren. **(c)** (*tamper with*) *accounts*

frisieren; *text* verfälschen ◆ **the food's/wine's been ~ed** dem Essen/Wein ist etwas beigemischt worden.

doctoral ['dɒktərəl] *adj* **~ thesis** Doktorarbeit *f*.

doctorate ['dɒktərɪt] *n* Doktorwürde *f* ◆ **~ in science/philosophy** Doktor(titel) *m* in Naturwissenschaften/Philosophie; **to get one's ~** die Doktorwürde verliehen bekommen; **to do one's ~** seinen Doktor machen; **he's still doing his ~** er sitzt immer noch an seiner Doktorarbeit.

doctrinaire [,dɒktrɪ'neəʳ] *adj* doktrinär.

doctrinal [dɒk'traɪn!] *adj* doktrinell ◆ **on ~ matters** in Sachen der Doktrin.

doctrine ['dɒktrɪn] *n* Doktrin, Lehre *f*.

docudrama ['dɒkjʊ,drɑːmə] *n* Dokumentarspiel *nt*.

document ['dɒkjʊmənt] [1] *n* Dokument *nt*, Urkunde *f*.
[2] *vt* (a) *case* beurkunden, (urkundlich) belegen ◆ **his argument/theory is well ~ed** sein Argument/seine Theorie ist gut belegt. **(b)** *ship* mit Papieren versehen.

documentary [,dɒkjʊ'mentərɪ] [1] *adj* (a) dokumentarisch, urkundlich ◆ **~ credit** *(Fin)* Dokumentenakkreditiv *nt*; **~ evidence** *(Jur)* urkundliche Beweise *pl*. **(b)** *(Film, TV)* **a ~ film** ein Dokumentarfilm *m*; **in ~ form** in Form einer Dokumentation.
[2] *n (Film, TV)* Dokumentarfilm *m*.

documentation [,dɒkjʊmen'teɪʃən] *n* Dokumentation *f*.

DOD *(US) abbr of* **Department of Defense** Verteidigungsministerium *nt*.

dodder ['dɒdəʳ] *vi* tapern.

dodderer ['dɒdərəʳ] *n (inf)* Tattergreis *m (inf)*.

doddering ['dɒdərɪŋ], **doddery** ['dɒdərɪ] *adj walk* unsicher; *person* taperig ◆ **the ~ old fool** *(inf)* der vertrottelte alte Opa *(inf)*.

dodge [dɒdʒ] [1] *n* (a) *(lit)* Sprung *m* zur Seite, rasches Ausweichen; *(Ftbl, Boxing)* Ausweichen *nt*.
(b) *(trick)* Trick, Kniff *m*; *(ingenious plan)* Glanzidee *f (inf)* ◆ **to be up to all the ~s** mit allen Wassern gewaschen sein.
[2] *vt blow, ball, question, difficulty* ausweichen (+*dat*); *tax* umgehen; *(shirk) work, military service* sich drücken vor (+*dat*) ◆ **to ~ the issue** der (eigentlichen) Frage *or* dem Problem ausweichen *or* aus dem Weg gehen.
[3] *vi* ausweichen ◆ **to ~ out of sight** blitzschnell verschwinden, sich blitzschnell verdrücken *(inf)*; **to ~ out of the way** zur Seite springen; *(to escape notice)* blitzschnell verschwinden; **to ~ behind a tree** hinter einen Baum springen *or* schlüpfen; **to ~ through the traffic** sich durch den Verkehr schlängeln.

dodgem ['dɒdʒəm] *n* (Auto)skooter *m* ◆ **did you go on the ~s?** bist du (Auto)skooter gefahren?

dodger ['dɒdʒəʳ] *n* (a) *(trickster)* Schlawiner *m (inf)*; *see* **artful**. **(b)** *(Naut)* Wetterschutz *m*.

dodgy ['dɒdʒɪ] *adj* (+*er*) *(Brit inf: tricky) situation* vertrackt *(inf)*, verzwickt *(inf)*; *(dubious)* zweifelhaft; *engine* nicht einwandfrei, launisch *(inf)* ◆ **this translation/his spelling/the carburettor is a bit ~** diese Übersetzung/seine Rechtschreibung/der Vergaser ist nicht einwandfrei.

dodo ['dəʊdəʊ] *n* (a) Dodo *m*, Dronte *f* ◆ **as dead as the/a ~** mausetot. **(b)** *(US inf: silly person)* Trottel *m (inf)*.

DOE *abbr of* **(a)** *(Brit)* **Department of the Environment** Umweltministerium *nt*. **(b)** *(US)* **Department of Energy** Energieministerium *nt*.

doe [dəʊ] *n (roe deer)* Reh(geiß *f*) *nt*, Ricke *f*; *(red deer)* Hirschkuh *f*; *(rabbit)* (Kaninchen)weibchen *nt*; *(hare)* Häsin *f*.

doer ['duːəʳ] *n* (a) *(author of deed)* Täter(in *f*) *m* ◆ **he's a great ~ of crosswords** *(inf)* er macht sehr gerne Kreuzworträtsel.
(b) *(active person)* Mann *m* der Tat, Macher *m (inf)* ◆ **more of a ~ than a thinker** eher ein Mann der Tat als der Theorie.

does [dʌz] *3rd pers sing of* **do²**.

doeskin ['dəʊskɪn] *n* Rehfell *nt*; *(treated)* Rehleder *nt*.

doesn't ['dʌznt] *contr of* **does not**.

doff [dɒf] *vt hat* ziehen, lüften; *(old) garment* ablegen.

dog [dɒg] [1] *n* (a) Hund *m* ◆ **the ~s** *(Brit Sport)* das Hunderennen.
(b) *(fig phrases)* **to lead a ~'s life** ein Hundeleben führen, wie ein Hund leben; **it's a ~'s life** es ist ein Hundeleben; **to go to the ~s** *(person, business, district, institution)* vor die Hunde gehen *(inf)*; **give a ~ a bad name (and hang him)** wer einmal ins Gerede *or* in Verruf kommt(, dem hängt das sein Leben lang an); **~ in the manger** Spielverderber(in *f*) *m*; **~-in-the-manger attitude** mißgünstige Einstellung; **every ~ has his day** jeder hat einmal Glück im Leben; **it's (a case of) ~ eat ~** es ist ein Kampf aller gegen alle; **~-eat-~ society** Ellenbogengesellschaft *f*; **you can't teach an old ~ new tricks** der Mensch ist ein Gewohnheitstier; **to put on the ~** *(US inf)* auf fein machen *(inf)*; **~'s dinner** *or* **breakfast** *(fig inf)* Schlamassel *m (inf)*; **he made a complete ~'s breakfast of it** *(inf)* er hat dabei totalen Mist gebaut *(inf)*; **she was done up like a ~'s dinner** *(inf)* sie war aufgetakelt wie eine Fregatte *(inf)*.
(c) *(male fox, wolf)* Rüde *m*.
(d) *(inf: man)* **lucky ~** Glückspilz *m*; **gay ~** lockerer Vogel *(inf)*; **dirty ~** gemeiner Hund; **sly ~** gerissener Hund *(inf)*; **there's life in the old ~ yet** noch kann man ihn nicht zum alten Eisen werfen; **Tom Jones, you old ~!** Tom Jones, du alter Schwerenöter!; *see* **top ~**.
(e) *(Tech: clamp)* Klammer *f*.
(f) **~s** *pl (sl: feet)* Quanten *pl (sl)*.
(g) *(US inf: failure)* Pleite *f (inf)*.
(h) *(US inf: unattractive woman)* Schreckschraube *f (inf)*.
[2] *vt* (a) *(follow closely)* **to ~ sb** *or* **sb's footsteps** jdm hart auf den Fersen sein/bleiben. **(b)** *(harass)* verfolgen. **~ged by misfortune** vom Pech verfolgt.

dog: ~ basket *n* Hundekorb *m*; **~ biscuit** *n* Hundekuchen *m*; **~ breeder** *n* Hundezüchter(in *f*) *m*; **~ breeding** *n* Hundezucht *f*; **~cart** *n* Dogcart *m*; **~-collar** *n (lit)* Hundehalsband *nt*; *(vicar's) steifer, hoher Kragen*; **~ days** *npl* Hundstage *pl*; **~-eared** ['dɒgɪəd] *adj* mit Eselsohren; **~-fancier** *n* Hundefreund(in *f*) *m*; *(breeder, seller)* Hundezüchter(in *f*) *m*; **~fight** *n (Aviat)* Luftkampf *m*; **~fish** *n* Hundshai *m*; **~ food** *n* Hundefutter *nt*; **~ fox** *n* Fuchsrüde *m*.

dogged *adj*, **~ly** *adv* ['dɒgɪd, -lɪ] beharrlich, zäh.

doggedness ['dɒgɪdnɪs] *n* Beharrlichkeit, Zähigkeit *f*.

doggerel ['dɒgərəl] *n (also* **~ verse***)* Knittelvers *m*.

doggie, doggy ['dɒgɪ] [1] *n (inf)* kleiner Hund, Hündchen *nt*.
[2] *adj smell* Hunde-; *(dog loving)* hundenärrisch.

doggie bag *n Beutel m für Essensreste, die nach Hause mitgenommen werden.*

doggo ['dɒgəʊ] *adv (inf)*: **to lie ~** sich nicht mucksen *(inf)*; *(go underground)* von der Bildfläche verschwinden *(inf)*.

doggone [,dɒg'gɒn] *interj (US sl)* **~ (it)!** verdammt noch mal!

doggoned [,dɒg'gɒn(d)] *adj (US sl)* verdammt.

dog: ~ handler *n* Hundeführer *m*; **~house** *n* Hundehütte *f*; **he's in the ~house** *(inf)* er ist in Ungnade; *(with wife)* bei ihm hängt der Haussegen schief; **~ iron** *n* Kaminbock *m*; **~ Latin** *n* Küchenlatein *nt*; **~leg** *n* Knick *m*; *(in road also)* scharfe Kurve; *(in pipe also)* starke Krümmung; **~ licence** *n* Hundemarke *f*; **a ~ licence costs ...** die Hundesteuer beträgt ...; **~like** *adj* Hunde-, hundeähnlich; **~like devotion** hündische Ergebenheit.

dogma ['dɒgmə] *n* Dogma *nt*.

dogmatic [dɒg'mætɪk] *adj* dogmatisch ◆ **D~ theology** Dogmatik *f*; **to be very ~ about sth** in etw (*dat*) sehr dogmatisch sein.

dogmatically [dɒg'mætɪkəlɪ] *adv see adj*.

dogmatism ['dɒgmətɪzəm] *n* Dogmatismus *m*.

dogmatize ['dɒgmətaɪz] [1] *vi (Rel, fig)* dogmatisch sein/dogmatische Behauptungen aufstellen.
[2] *vt (Rel, fig)* dogmatisieren, zum Dogma erheben.

do-gooder ['duː'gʊdəʳ] *n (pej)* Weltverbesserer *m*.

dog: ~ paddle *n* **to do (the) ~ paddle** paddeln, Hundepaddeln machen; **~rose** *n* Hundsrose *f*.

dogsbody ['dɒgzbɒdɪ] *n* **she's/he's the general ~** sie/er ist (das) Mädchen für alles.

dog: ~ show *n* Hundeausstellung *f*; **~ sled** *n* Hundeschlitten *m*; **~ star** *n* Hundsstern, Sirius *m*; **~ tag** *n (US Mil inf)* Erkennungsmarke, Hundemarke *(inf) f*; **~-tired** *adj* hundemüde; **~tooth** *n (Archit)* Hundszahn *m*; **~ track** *n* Hunderennbahn *f*; **~trot** *n* gemächlicher *or* leichter Trott; **~watch** *n (Naut)* Hundewache *f*; **~wood** *n* Hartriegel, Hornstrauch *m*.

doily ['dɔɪlɪ] *n* (Spitzen- *or* Zier)deckchen *nt*.

doing ['duːɪŋ] *n* (a) Tun *nt* ◆ **this is your ~** das ist dein Werk; **it was none of my ~** ich hatte nichts damit zu tun; **that takes some ~** da gehört (schon) etwas dazu; **there is a difference between ~ and saying** zwischen Taten und Worten besteht ein Unterschied. **(b)** *(inf)* **~s** *pl* Handlungen, Taten *pl*.

doings ['duːɪŋz] *n sing (Brit inf)* Dingsbums *nt (inf)*.

do-it-yourself ['duːɪtjə'self] [1] *adj shop* Bastler-, Hobby- ◆ **~ fan** Heimwerker(in *f*), Bastler(in *f*) *m*; **the ~ craze** die Do-it-yourself-Bewegung; **~ kit** *(for household jobs)* Heimwerkerausrüstung *f*; *(for radio etc)* Bausatz *m*.
[2] *n* Heimwerken, Do-it-yourself *nt*.

dol *abbr of* **dollar**.

Dolby ® ['dɒlbɪ] *n* Dolby ® *nt*.

doldrums ['dɒldrəmz] *npl* (a) *(Geog) (area)* Kalmengürtel *m or* -zone *f*; *(weather)* Windstille, Kalme *f*. **(b)** **to be in the ~** *(people)* Trübsal blasen; *(business etc)* in einer Flaute stecken.

dole [dəʊl] *n (Brit inf)* Arbeitslosenunterstützung, Alu *(inf) f* ◆ *(inf)* **to go/be on the ~** stempeln (gehen).

◆**dole out** *vt sep* austeilen, verteilen.

doleful ['dəʊlfʊl] *adj* traurig; *face, expression, prospect also* trübselig; *tune, song also* klagend.

dolefully ['dəʊlfəlɪ] *adv see adj*.

dolichocephalic ['dɒlɪkəʊse'fælɪk] *adj* dolichozephal.

doll [dɒl] *n* (a) Puppe *f* ◆ **~'s house** Puppenhaus *nt*; **~'s pram** Puppenwagen *m*. **(b)** *(esp US inf: girl)* Mädchen *nt*; *(pretty girl)* Puppe *f (inf)* ◆ **thanks Betty, you're a ~** danke Betty, du bist klasse *(inf)*.

◆**doll up** *vt sep (inf)* herausputzen ◆ **to ~ oneself ~, to get ~ed ~** sich herausputzen *or* aufdonnern *(inf)*.

dollar ['dɒləʳ] *n* Dollar *m*.

dollar: ~ area *n* Dollarraum, Dollarblock *m*; **~ bill** *n* Dollarnote *f*; **~ diplomacy** *n* Finanzdiplomatie *f*; **~ gap** *n* Dollar-Lücke *f*; **~ rate** *n* Dollarkurs *m*; **~ sign** *n* Dollarzeichen *nt*.

dollop ['dɒləp] *n (inf)* Schlag *m (inf)*.

dolly ['dɒlɪ] [1] *n* (a) *(inf: doll)* Püppchen *nt*.
(b) *(wheeled frame)* (Transport)wagen *m*; *(Film, TV)* Dolly, Kamerawagen *m*; *(Rail)* Schmalspurrangierlokomotive *f*.
(c) *(for washing clothes)* Wäschestampfer *m*.
(d) *(Tech: for rivet)* Gegenhalter *m*.
(e) *(inf: girl: also* **~-bird***)* Puppe *f*.
(f) *(Sport inf)* lahmer Ball *(inf)*.
[2] *adj (Sport inf) shot* lahm; *catch* leicht.

◆**dolly in** *vti sep (Film, TV)* vorfahren.

◆**dolly out** *vti sep (Film, TV)* zurückfahren.

dolly-bird ['dɒlɪbɜːd] [1] *n (inf)* Puppe *f*.
[2] *adj attr* puppig.

dolman ['dɒlmən] *n* Dolman *m* ◆ **~ sleeve** angeschnittener Ärmel.

dolomite [ˈdɒləmaɪt] *n* Dolomit *m* ◆ **the D~s** die Dolomiten *pl*.
dolphin [ˈdɒlfɪn] *n* Delphin *m*.
dolphinarium [ˌdɒlfɪˈnɛərɪəm] *n* Delphinarium *nt*.
dolt [dəʊlt] *n* Tölpel *m*.
domain [dəʊˈmeɪn] *n* **(a)** (*lit: estate*) Gut *nt*; (*belonging to state, Crown*) Domäne *f* ◆ **the Crown ~s** die Ländereien der Krone. **(b)** (*fig*) Domäne *f*; *see* **public**. **(c)** (*Math*) Funktionsbereich *m*.
dome [dəʊm] *n* **(a)** (*Archit: on building*) Kuppel *f*. **(b)** (*of heaven, skull*) Gewölbe *nt*; (*of hill*) Kuppe *f*; (*of branches*) Kuppel *f*. **(c)** (*lid, cover etc*) Haube *f*.
domed [dəʊmd] *adj forehead* gewölbt; *roof* kuppelförmig ◆ **~ building** Kuppelbau *m*.
domestic [dəˈmestɪk] [1] *adj* **(a)** *duty, bliss, life* häuslich ◆ **~ servants** Hausangestellte *pl*, Hauspersonal *nt*; **she was in ~ service** sie arbeitete als Hausmädchen, sie war Hausgehilfin; **everything of a ~ nature** alles, was den Haushalt angeht; **~ rubbish** (*Brit*) *or* **garbage** (*US*) Hausmüll *m*.
(b) (*Pol, Econ*) *policy, politician* Innen-; *news* Inland-, aus dem Inland; *produce* einheimisch; *trade* Binnen-; *flight* Inland- ◆ **~ quarrels** innenpolitische Auseinandersetzungen *pl*; **~ affairs** Inneres *nt*, innere Angelegenheiten *pl*.
(c) *animal* Haus-.
[2] *n* Domestik *m* (*old*), Hausangestellte(r) *mf*.
domesticate [dəˈmestɪkeɪt] *vt wild animal*, (*hum*) *person* domestizieren; (*house-train*) *dog, cat* stubenrein machen.
domesticated [dəˈmestɪkeɪtɪd] *adj* domestiziert; *cat, dog* stubenrein ◆ **she's very ~** sie ist sehr häuslich.
domestication [dəmestɪˈkeɪʃən] *n see vt* Domestikation, Domestizierung *f*; Gewöhnung *f* ans Haus.
domesticity [ˌdəʊmesˈtɪsɪtɪ] *n* häusliches Leben ◆ **a life of simple ~** ein (gut)bürgerliches Leben.
domestic science *n* Hauswirtschaftslehre *f* ◆ **~ college** Frauenfachschule *f*.
domicile [ˈdɒmɪsaɪl] [1] *n* (*Admin*) Wohnsitz *m*; (*Fin*) Zahlungs- *or* Erfüllungsort *m*.
[2] *vt* (*Admin*) unterbringen (*with* bei, in *+dat*); (*Fin*) domizilieren (*at* bei) ◆ **~d bill** Domizilwechsel *m*.
domiciliary [ˌdɒmɪˈsɪlɪərɪ] *adj* (*Admin*) *expenses* Haushalts-; *care of invalids* Haus- ◆ **~ visit of a doctor** Hausbesuch *m*.
dominance [ˈdɒmɪnəns] *n* Vorherrschaft, Dominanz *f* (*also Biol*) (*over* über *+acc*).
dominant [ˈdɒmɪnənt] [1] *adj* **(a)** (*controlling, masterful*) dominierend; *nation also* vorherrschend, mächtig; *gene* dominant, überdeckend; (*more prominent*) *colour, building, industry, mountain* beherrschend, dominierend; *feature also* hervorstechend, herausragend ◆ **~ male** (*animal*) männliches Leittier; (*fig inf*) Platzhirsch *m* (*inf*).
(b) (*Mus*) dominant ◆ **~ seventh** Dominantseptakkord *m*.
[2] *n* (*Mus*) Dominante *f*.
dominate [ˈdɒmɪneɪt] [1] *vi* dominieren.
[2] *vt* beherrschen; (*colour, feature also, species, gene*) dominieren.
domination [ˌdɒmɪˈneɪʃən] *n* (Vor)herrschaft *f* ◆ **under the ~ of the Romans** unter römischer Herrschaft; **his ~ of his younger brothers** sein dominierendes Verhalten seinen jüngeren Brüdern gegenüber; **her ~ of the conversation** die Tatsache, daß sie die Unterhaltung beherrschte.
domineer [ˌdɒmɪˈnɪər] *vi* tyrannisieren (*over sb* jdn).
domineering [ˌdɒmɪˈnɪərɪŋ] *adj* herrisch; *mother-in-law, husband etc also* herrschsüchtig.
Dominican[1] [dəˈmɪnɪkən] (*Geog*) [1] *adj* dominikanisch ◆ **~ Republic** Dominikanische Republik.
[2] *n* Dominikaner(in *f*) *m*.
Dominican[2] (*Eccl*) [1] *n* Dominikaner *m*.
[2] *adj* Dominikaner-, dominikanisch.
dominion [dəˈmɪnɪən] *n* **(a)** *no pl* Herrschaft *f* (*over* über *+acc*) ◆ **to have ~ over sb** Macht über jdn haben.
(b) (*territory*) Herrschaftsgebiet *nt* ◆ **overseas ~s** überseeische Gebiete *pl*; **the D~ of Canada** das Dominion Kanada; **D~ Day** *gesetzlicher Feiertag in Kanada zur Erinnerung an die Übertragung der vollen politischen Autonomie*.
domino [ˈdɒmɪnəʊ] *n, pl* **-es (a)** Domino(stein) *m* ◆ **a game of ~es** ein Dominospiel *nt*; **to play ~es** Domino spielen; **~ effect** Dominowirkung *f or* -effekt *m*; **~ theory** Dominoeffekt *m*. **(b)** (*costume, mask*) Domino *m*.
don[1] [dɒn] *n* (*Brit Univ*) *Universitätsdozent m, besonders in Oxford und Cambridge*.
don[2] *vt garment* anziehen, anlegen (*dated*); *hat* aufsetzen.
donate [dəʊˈneɪt] *vt blood, kidney* spenden; *money, gifts to a charity also* stiften.
donation [dəʊˈneɪʃən] *n* (*act of giving*) (*of money, gifts*) Spenden *nt*; (*on large scale*) Stiften *nt*; (*of blood*) Spenden *nt*; (*gift*) Spende *f*; (*large scale*) Stiftung *f* ◆ **to make a ~ of 50p/£10,000** 50 Pence spenden /£ 10.000 stiften.
done [dʌn] [1] *ptp of* **do[2]**.
[2] *adj* **(a)** (*finished*) *work* erledigt; (*cooked*) *vegetables* gar; *meat* durch ◆ **to get sth ~** (*finished*) etw fertigkriegen; **is that ~ yet?** ist das schon erledigt?
(b) (*inf: tired out*) **I'm ~** ich bin geschafft (*inf*) *or* fertig.
(c) it's not the ~ thing, that's not ~ das tut man nicht.
(d) (*inf: used up*) **the butter is ~** die Butter ist alle.
doner kebab [ˈdɒnəkəˈbæb] *n* Döner-Kebab *m*.
dong [dɒŋ] *n* (*US sl: penis*) Apparat *m* (*inf*).
Don Juan [ˌdɒnˈdʒuːən] *n* (*lit, fig*) Don Juan *m*.
donkey [ˈdɒŋkɪ] *n* Esel *m* ◆ **~'s years** (*inf*) eine Ewigkeit, ewig und drei Tage (*inf*); **she's been here for ~'s years** (*inf*) sie ist schon ewig und drei Tage (*inf*) *or* eine Ewigkeit hier.
donkey: ~ engine *n* (*Rail*) (kleines) Hilfsaggregat; **~ jacket** *n dicke* (*gefütterte*) *Jacke*; **~ ride** *n* Ritt *m* auf dem/einem Esel, Eselsritt *m*; **~work** *n* Routinearbeit, Dreckarbeit (*inf*) *f*.
donnish [ˈdɒnɪʃ] *adj* gebildet; *tone* belehrend.
donor [ˈdəʊnər] *n* (*Med: of blood, organ for transplant*) Spender(in *f*) *m*; (*to charity etc also*) Stifter(in *f*) *m*.
don't [dəʊnt] *contr of* **do not**.
don't-know [ˌdəʊntˈnəʊ] *n* (*in opinion poll*) **30% were ~s** 30% hatten keine Meinung.
donut [ˈdəʊnʌt] *n* (*esp US*) *see* **doughnut**.
doodah [ˈduːdɑː] *n* (*inf*) Dingsbums (*inf*), Dingsda (*inf*) *nt*.
doodle [ˈduːdl] [1] *vi* Männchen malen.
[2] *vt* kritzeln.
[3] *n* Gekritzel *nt*.
doodlebug [ˈduːdlbʌg] *n* **(a)** (*Brit: bomb*) V1-Rakete *f*. **(b)** (*US: larva*) Ameisenlarve *f*.
doohickey [ˈduːhɪkɪ] *n* (*US inf: thingummy*) Dings(bums) *nt*.
doolally [duːˈlælɪ] *adj* (*inf*) plemplem *pred* (*sl*).
doom [duːm] [1] *n* (*fate*) Schicksal *nt*; (*ruin*) Verhängnis *nt* ◆ **to go to one's ~** seinem Verhängnis entgegengehen; **to send sb to his ~** jdn ins Verhängnis stürzen; **he met his ~** das Schicksal ereilte ihn.
[2] *vt* verurteilen, verdammen ◆ **to be ~ed** verloren sein; **the project was ~ed from the start** das Vorhaben war von Anfang an zum Scheitern verurteilt; **the ~ed ship** das dem Untergang geweihte Schiff; **~ed to die** dem Tode geweiht; **~ed to failure/to perish** zum Scheitern/Untergang verurteilt; **this country was ~ed to become a second-rate nation** dieses Land war dazu verdammt, zur Zweitrangigkeit abzusinken.
doomsday [ˈduːmzdeɪ] *n* der Jüngste Tag ◆ **... otherwise we'll be here till ~** (*inf*) ... sonst sind wir in zwanzig Jahren noch hier.
door [dɔːr] *n* **(a)** Tür *f*; (*entrance: to cinema etc*) Eingang *m* ◆ **there's someone at the ~** da ist jemand an der Tür; **was that the ~?** hat es geklingelt/geklopft?; **to stand in the ~** in der Tür stehen; **to be on the ~** (*bouncer etc*) Türsteher sein; (*collecting ticket money etc*) Türdienst haben; **to pay at the ~** (*Theat etc*) an der (Abend)kasse zahlen; **"~s open 2.20"** „Einlaß $14.^{20}$ Uhr"; **to go from ~ to ~** (*salesman etc*) von Tür zu Tür gehen, Klinken putzen (*inf*); **he lives three ~s away** er wohnt drei Häuser weiter.
(b) (*phrases*) **the ~ to success** der Schlüssel zum Erfolg; **to lay sth at sb's ~** jdm etw vorwerfen *or* anlasten; **to leave the ~ open to** *or* **for further negotiations** die Tür zu weiteren *or* für weitere Verhandlungen offen lassen; **to open the ~ to sth** einer Sache (*dat*) Tür und Tor öffnen; **to show sb the ~** jdm die Tür weisen; **to shut** *or* **close the ~ on sth** etw ausschließen; **we don't want to shut any ~s** wir möchten uns (*dat*) keine Möglichkeiten verbauen; **when one ~ shuts, another ~ opens** (*prov*) irgendwie geht es immer weiter; **out of ~s** im Freien.
door *in cpds* Tür-; **~bell** *n* Türglocke *or* -klingel *f*; **there's the ~bell** es hat geklingelt.
do-or-die [ˈduːɔːˈdaɪ] *adj* verbissen.
door: ~frame *n* Türrahmen *m*; **~ handle** *n* Türklinke *f*; (*knob*) Türknauf *m*; **~keeper** *n* (*of hotel, block of flats*) Portier *m*; **~ knob** *n* Türknauf *m*; **~knocker** *n* Türklopfer *m*; **~man** *n* Portier *m*; **~mat** *n* Fußmatte *f*, Abtreter *m*; (*fig*) Fußabtreter *m*; **~nail** *n*: **as dead as a ~nail** mausetot; **~plate** *n* Türschild *nt*; **~post** *n* Türpfosten *m*; **deaf as a ~post** stocktaub; **~step** *n* Eingangsstufe *f*; (*hum: hunk of bread*) dicke Scheibe Brot; **the bus stop is just on my ~step** (*fig*) die Bushaltestelle ist direkt vor meiner Tür; **~stop(per)** *n* Türanschlag *m*; **~-to-~** *adj* **(a) ~-to-~ salesman** Vertreter *m*; **(b)** *delivery* von Haus zu Haus; **how's that for ~-to-~ service?** na, ist das nicht ein Service?; **~way** *n* (*of room*) Tür *f*; (*of building, shop*) Eingang *m*; (*fig: to success etc*) Weg *m*.
dope [dəʊp] [1] *n* **(a)** *no pl* (*inf: drugs*) Rauschgift *nt*, Stoff *m* (*inf*), Drogen *pl*; (*Sport*) Anregungs- *or* Aufputschmittel *nt* ◆ **to test for ~** eine Dopingkontrolle machen.
(b) *no pl* (*inf: information*) Information(en *pl*) *f* ◆ **to give sb the ~** jdn informieren, jdm etw stecken (*sl*) (*on* über *+acc*); **what's the ~ on ...?** was wissen wir über (*+acc*) ...?
(c) (*inf: stupid person*) Esel (*inf*), Trottel (*inf*) *m*.
(d) (*varnish*) Lack *m*.
(e) (*for explosives*) Benzinzusatz(mittel *nt*) *m*.
[2] *vt horse, person* dopen; *food, drink* präparieren, ein Betäubungsmittel untermischen (*+dat*).
dope: ~ fiend (*inf*), **~head** (*sl*) *n* Junkie *m* (*inf*); **~ peddler** *or* **pusher** *n* Drogenhändler, Dealer (*sl*), Pusher (*sl*) *m*.
dopey, dopy [ˈdəʊpɪ] *adj* (*+er*) (*inf*) (*stupid*) bekloppt (*inf*), blöd (*inf*); (*sleepy, half-drugged*) benommen, benebelt (*inf*).
doping [ˈdəʊpɪŋ] *n* (*Sport*) Doping *nt*.
Doppler effect [ˈdɒplərɪˌfekt] *n* Dopplereffekt *m*.
Doric [ˈdɒrɪk] *adj* (*Archit*) dorisch.
dorm [dɔːm] (*inf*) *abbr of* **dormitory**.
dormant [ˈdɔːmənt] *adj* (*Zool, Bot*) ruhend; *volcano* untätig; *energy* verborgen, latent; *passion* schlummernd; (*Her*) liegend ◆ **to let a matter lie ~** eine Sache ruhen *or* liegen lassen; **to lie ~** (*evil etc*) schlummern.
dormer (window) [ˈdɔːmə(ˈwɪndəʊ)] *n* Mansardenfenster *nt*.
dormice [ˈdɔːmaɪs] *pl of* **dormouse**.
dormitory [ˈdɔːmɪtrɪ] *n* Schlafsaal *m*; (*US: building*) Wohnheim *nt* ◆ **~ suburb** *or* **town** Schlafstadt *f*.
dormobile ® [ˈdɔːməbiːl] *n* Wohnmobil *nt*, Campingbus *m*.

dormouse ['dɔːmaʊs] *n, pl* **dormice** Haselmaus *f*.
dorsal ['dɔːsl] [1] *adj* Rücken-, dorsal (*spec*).
[2] *n* (*Phon*) Dorsal(laut) *m*.
dory ['dɔːrɪ] *n* (*US*) *Ruderboot mit spitzem Bug und schmalem Heck*.
DOS [dɒs] (*Comput*) *abbr of* **disk operating system** DOS *nt*.
dosage ['dəʊsɪdʒ] *n* Dosis *f*; (*giving of medicine*) Dosierung *f* ◆ **~ meter** Dosimeter *nt*.
dose [dəʊs] [1] *n* **(a)** (*Med*) Dosis *f*; (*fig: of punishment etc*) Ration *f* ◆ **give him a ~ of medicine** gib ihm Medizin; **in small/large ~s** (*fig*) in kleinen/großen Mengen; **she's all right in small ~s** sie ist nur (für) kurze Zeit zu ertragen; **I can stand this weather in small ~s** ich kann dies Wetter nur für kurze Zeit vertragen.
(b) (*inf: venereal disease*) Tripper *m* ◆ **to catch a ~** sich (*dat*) etwas holen (*inf*), sich (*dat*) den Tripper holen.
(c) (*inf: bout of illness*) Anfall *m* ◆ **she's just had a ~ of the flu** sie hat gerade Grippe gehabt.
[2] *vt person* Arznei geben (*+dat*) ◆ **she's always dosing herself** sie nimmt *or* schluckt ständig Medikamente; **I've tried dosing myself with cough mixture** ich habe versucht, mich mit Hustensaft zu kurieren.
dosh [dɒʃ] *n* (*sl: money*) Moos *nt* (*sl*), Knete *f* (*sl*).
doss [dɒs] (*Brit sl*) [1] *n* Schlafplatz *m*, Bleibe *f* (*inf*).
[2] *vi* (*also* **~ down**) pennen (*inf*), sich hinhauen (*inf*) ◆ **to ~ down for the night** sich für die Nacht einquartieren (*inf*).
dosser ['dɒsəʳ] *n* (*Brit sl*) Penner(in *f*), Stadtstreicher(in *f*) *m*.
dosshouse ['dɒshaʊs] *n* (*Brit sl*) Penne *f* (*sl*), Obdachlosenheim *nt*.
dossier ['dɒsɪeɪ] *n* Dossier *m or nt* ◆ **they are keeping a ~ on him** sie haben ein Dossier über ihn angelegt.
dost [dʌst] (*obs*) *2nd pers sing of* **do²**.
DOT (*US*) *abbr of* **Department of Transportation** Verkehrsministerium *nt*.
dot [dɒt] [1] *n* **(a)** Punkt *m*; (*over i also*) Pünktchen, Tüpfelchen *nt*; (*on material*) Tupfen, Punkt *m* ◆ **morse code is made up of ~s and dashes** das Morsealphabet besteht aus kurzen und langen Signalen; **~, dash, ~** (*morse*) kurz, lang, kurz; **~, ~, ~** (*in punctuation*) drei Punkte.
(b) (*phrases*) **to arrive on the ~** auf die Minute pünktlich (an)kommen; **at 3 o'clock on the ~** haargenau *or* auf die Minute genau um 3 Uhr; **in the year ~** (*inf*) Anno dazumal (*inf*) *or* Tobak (*inf*); **she has lived here since the year ~** sie lebt schon ewig hier *or* schon seit ewigen Zeiten hier.
[2] *vt* **(a) to ~ an i** einen i-Punkt setzen; **to ~ one's i's and cross one's t's** peinlich genau *or* penibel sein; **~ted line** punktierte Linie; **to tear along the ~ted line** an der *or* entlang der punktierten Linie abtrennen; **to sign on the ~ted line** (*fig*) seine formelle Zustimmung geben, formell zustimmen.
(b) (*sprinkle*) verstreuen ◆ **a field ~ted with flowers** ein mit Blumen übersätes Feld; **cars were ~ted along the side of the road** an der Straße entlang stand hier und da ein Auto; **he has friends ~ted about all over Germany** seine Freunde leben über ganz Deutschland verteilt.
(c) to ~ sb one (*inf*) jdm eine langen (*inf*).
dotage ['dəʊtɪdʒ] *n* Senilität, Altersschwäche *f* ◆ **to be in one's ~** in seiner zweiten Kindheit sein, senil sein.
dot command *n* (*Comput*) Punktbefehl *m*.
dote on ['dəʊtɒn] *vi +prep obj* abgöttisch lieben.
doth [dʌθ] (*obs*) *3rd pers sing of* **do²**.
doting ['dəʊtɪŋ] *adj* **her ~ parents** ihre sie vergötternden *or* abgöttisch liebenden Eltern.
dot matrix (printer) *n* Matrixdrucker, Nadeldrucker *m*.
dottle ['dɒtl] *n* Tabakrest *m*.
dotty ['dɒtɪ] *adj* (*+er*) (*Brit inf*) kauzig, schrullig ◆ **to be ~ about sb/sth** (*like*) nach jdm/etw verrückt sein.
double ['dʌbl] [1] *adj* **(a)** (*twice as much, twofold*) doppelt; (*having two similar parts, in pairs*) Doppel- ◆ **he got a ~ amount of work** er mußte die doppelte Arbeit tun, er erhielt doppelt soviel Arbeit; **a ~ whisky** ein doppelter Whisky; **her salary is ~ what it was ten years ago** sie bekommt doppelt soviel Gehalt wie vor zehn Jahren; **~ bottom** doppelter Boden; **~ consonant** Doppelkonsonant *m*; **~ knot** doppelter Knoten; **~ track** (*Rail*) zweigleisige Strecke; **an egg with a ~ yolk** ein Ei mit zwei Dottern; **it is spelt with a ~ "p"** es wird mit Doppel-p *or* mit zwei „p" geschrieben; **~ six** (*in ludo etc*) Doppelsechs *f*; (*in dominoes, dice*) Sechserpasch *m*; **~ seven five four/~ seven five** (*Telec*) siebenundsiebzig vierundfünfzig/sieben sieben fünf.
(b) (*made for two*) Doppel- ◆ **~ room** Doppelzimmer *nt*.
(c) (*dual, serving two purposes*) doppelt ◆ **it has a ~ meaning/ interpretation** es ist zwei- *or* doppeldeutig/läßt zwei Auslegungen zu; **~ standards** Doppelmoral *f*; **society applies ~ standards** die Gesellschaft mißt mit zweierlei Maß *or* legt zwei (verschiedene) Maßstäbe an.
(d) (*underhand, deceptive*) **to lead a ~ life** ein Doppelleben führen; **to play a ~ game** ein Doppelspiel treiben.
(e) (*Bot*) gefüllt.
(f) ~ time (*Mil*) Laufschritt *m*.
[2] *adv* **(a)** (*twice*) doppelt ◆ **that costs ~ what it did last year** das kostet doppelt soviel wie letztes Jahr; **I have ~ what you have** ich habe doppelt soviel wie du; **he did it in ~ the time it took me** er brauchte doppelt so lange wie ich; **he's ~ your age** er ist doppelt so alt wie du; **~ six is twelve** zweimal sechs ist zwölf; **to see ~** doppelt sehen.
(b) to be bent ~ with pain sich vor Schmerzen krümmen, vor Schmerz gekrümmt sein; **fold it ~** falte es (einmal).
[3] *n* **(a)** (*twice a quantity, number, size etc*) das Doppelte, das Zweifache ◆ **~ or quits** doppelt oder nichts; **he earns the ~ of what I do** er verdient doppelt soviel wie ich.
(b) (*person*) Ebenbild *nt*, Doppelgänger(in *f*) *m*; (*Film, Theat: stand-in*) Double *nt*; (*actor taking two parts*) Schauspieler, der eine Doppelrolle spielt ◆ **I've got the ~ of that clock** ich habe genau die gleiche Uhr.
(c) at the ~ (*also Mil*) im Laufschritt; (*fig*) auf der Stelle.
(d) (*Cards*) (*increase*) Verdoppelung *f*; (*hand*) *Blatt, das die Verdoppelung rechtfertigt*; (*in racing*) Doppelwette *f*; (*in dice*) Pasch *m*; (*in dominoes*) Doppelstein, Pasch *m*.
[4] *vt* **(a)** (*increase twofold*) verdoppeln.
(b) (*fold in two*) *piece of paper* (einmal) falten.
(c) (*Film, Theat*) **he ~s the parts of courtier and hangman** er hat die Doppelrolle des Höflings und Henkers; **the producer decided to ~ the parts of pimp and judge** der Produzent beschloß, die Rollen des Zuhälters und des Richters mit demselben Schauspieler zu besetzen; **who is doubling for him?** wer doubelt ihn?, wer ist sein Double?
(d) (*Naut: sail round*) umsegeln.
(e) (*Cards*) *one's opponent, his call* verdoppeln; (*Bridge*) kontrieren.
[5] *vi* **(a)** (*increase twofold*) sich verdoppeln; (*price also*) um das Doppelte steigen.
(b) (*Mus*) zwei Instrumente spielen ◆ **he ~s on flute and clarinet** er spielt Flöte und Klarinette.
(c) (*Film, Theat*) **to ~ for sb** jds Double sein, jdn doubeln; **he ~s as the butler and the duke** er hat die Doppelrolle des Butlers und Herzogs.
(d) (*Cards*) verdoppeln; (*Bridge*) kontrieren.
◆**double back** [1] *vi* (*person*) kehrtmachen, zurückgehen/-fahren; (*animal*) kehrtmachen, zurücklaufen; (*road, river*) sich zurückwinden *or* -schlängeln.
[2] *vt sep blanket* umschlagen; *page* umknicken.
◆**double over** [1] *vi see* **double up 1 (a)**.
[2] *vt sep see* **double back 2**.
◆**double up** [1] *vi* **(a)** (*bend over*) sich krümmen; (*with laughter*) sich biegen, sich kringeln (*inf*) ◆ **he ~d when the bullet hit him** er klappte (*inf*) *or* brach zusammen, als die Kugel ihn traf.
(b) (*share room*) das Zimmer/Büro *etc* gemeinsam benutzen; (*share bed*) in einem Bett schlafen ◆ **you'll have to ~ ~ with Mary** du mußt dir ein Zimmer mit Mary teilen.
(c) (*Brit Betting*) *den Einsatz bis zum ersten Gewinn verdoppeln*.
[2] *vt sep* **(a)** *paper* falten, knicken; *blanket* zusammenlegen.
(b) the bullet/blow ~d him ~ von der Kugel/dem Schlag getroffen, brach er zusammen.
double: ~-acting *adj engine* doppelwirkend; **~ agent** *n* Doppelagent *m*; **~ bar** *n* (*Mus*) Doppelstrich *m*; **~-barrelled,** (*US*) **~-barreled** [ˌdʌbl'bærəld] *adj surname* Doppel-; **~-barrel(l)ed shotgun** *n* doppelläufiges Gewehr, Zwilling *m*; **~ bass** *n* Kontrabaß *m*; **~ bassoon** *n* Kontrafagott *nt*; **~ bed** *n* Doppelbett *nt*; **~ bend** *n* S-Kurve *f*; **~ bill** *n* Vorstellung *f* mit zwei Filmen/ Stücken; **~-blind** *adj* (*Sci*) *experiment* Doppelblind-; **~ boiler** *n* (*US*) Turmtopf *m*; **~-book** *vt room, seat* zweimal reservieren; *flight* zweimal buchen; **very sorry, I've ~-booked you** tut mir sehr leid, ich habe ein Zimmer/ einen Platz für Sie reserviert, das/der schon vergeben war; **~-breasted** *adj* zweireihig; **~-breasted jacket/suit** Zweireiher *m*; **~-check** *vti* noch einmal (über)prüfen; **~ chin** *n* Doppelkinn *nt*; **~-click** *vti* (*Comput*) doppelklicken; **~ cream** *n* Schlagsahne *f*; **~-cross** (*inf*) [1] *vt* ein Doppelspiel *or* falsches Spiel treiben mit; **the ~-crossing swines!** diese falschen Hunde! (*inf*); [2] *n* Doppelspiel *nt*; **~-crosser** *n* (*inf*) falscher Freund *or* Hund (*inf*); **~-date** *vt* **he's ~-dating me** er trifft sich außer mit mir noch mit einer anderen; **~-dealer** *n* Betrüger *m*; **~-dealing** [1] *n* Betrügerei(en *pl*) *f*; [2] *adj* betrügerisch; **~-decker** *n* (*all senses*) Doppeldecker *m*; **~-declutch** *vi* (*Aut*) mit Zwischengas schalten; **~-density** *adj* (*Comput*) *disk* mit doppelter Dichte; **~ dutch** *n* (*Brit*) Kauderwelsch *nt*; **to talk ~ dutch** Unsinn *or* Kauderwelsch reden; **it was ~ dutch to me** das waren für mich böhmische Dörfer; **~ eagle** *n* (*US*) *alte amerikanische Goldmünze mit einem Wert von $ 20*; **~-edged** *adj* (*lit, fig*) zweischneidig; **~ entendre** ['duːblɑ̃ːn'tɑ̃ːndr] *n* Zweideutigkeit *f*; **~-entry bookkeeping** *n* doppelte Buchführung; **~ exposure** *n* doppelt belichtetes Foto; **~ fault** *n* (*Tennis*) Doppelfehler *m*; **~ feature** *n* Programm *nt* mit zwei Hauptfilmen; **~ first** *n* (*Brit Univ*) **he got a ~ first** er bestand beide Fächer mit „sehr gut" (*in einem honours degree course*); **~ flat** *n* (*Mus*) Doppel-b *nt*; **~-glaze** *vt* mit Doppelverglasung versehen; **~ glazing** *n* Doppelfenster *pl*; **~ Gloucester** *n englische Käsesorte*; **~-header** *n* (*US Sport*) Doppelspieltag *m*; **~ honours (course)** *n* (*Brit Univ*) ≃ Doppelstudium *nt*; **~-jointed** *adj* äußerst elastisch, sehr gelenkig; **~-knitting (wool)** *n* ≃ Sportwolle *f*; **~ knot** *n* Doppelknoten *m*; **~ lock** *n* Doppelschloß *nt*; **~-lock** *vt* zweimal abschließen; **~ negative** *n* doppelte Verneinung; **~-page spread** *n* Doppelseite *f*; **~ park** *vi* in der zweiten Reihe parken; **~ parking** *n* Parken *nt* in der zweiten Reihe; **~ pneumonia** *n* doppelseitige Lungenentzündung; **~-quick** (*inf*) [1] *adv* sehr schnell; [2] *adj* **in ~-quick time** im Nu, in Null Komma nichts (*inf*).
doubles ['dʌblz] *n sing or pl* (*Sport*) Doppel *nt*.
double: ~ saucepan *n* Turmtopf *m*; **~-sharp** *n* (*Mus*) Doppelkreuz *nt*; **~-sided** *adj* (*Comput*) *disk* zweiseitig; **~-sided (adhesive) tape** Doppelklebeband *nt*; **~-space** *vt* (*Typ*) mit doppeltem Zeilenabstand drucken; **~ spacing** *n* doppelter Zeilenabstand; **~ star** *n* Doppelstern *m*; **~ stop** [1] *n* (*Mus*) Doppelgriff *m*; [2] *vi* mit Doppelgriff spielen; **~ stopping** *n* (*Mus*) Doppelgriffe *pl*; **~ strike** *n* (*Comput: printing*) Doppeldruck *m*.
doublet ['dʌblɪt] *n* **(a)** Wams *nt*. **(b)** (*Ling*) Dublette *f*.
double: ~ take *n* **he did a ~ take** er mußte zweimal hingucken; **~talk** *n* (*ambiguous*) zwei- *or* doppeldeutiges Gerede; (*deceitful*) doppelzüngiges

Gerede; **~think** *n* widersprüchliches Denken; **~ time** *n* (*in wages*) doppelter Lohn; **~-tongue** *vi* (*Mus*) mit Doppelzunge blasen; **~-tonguing** *n* Doppelzunge *f*; **~ vision** *n* **to suffer from ~ vision** doppelt sehen; **~ windows** *npl* Doppelfenster *pl*.

doubloon [dʌ'blu:n] *n* Dublone *f*.

doubly ['dʌblɪ] *adv* doppelt ◆ **this road is dangerous, ~ so when it's icy** diese Straße ist gefährlich, vor allem bei Glatteis.

▼ **doubt** [daʊt] [1] *n* Zweifel *m* ◆ **his honesty is in ~** seine Ehrlichkeit wird angezweifelt; **I am in (some) ~ about his honesty** ich habe Zweifel an seiner Ehrlichkeit; **to be in great ~ as to sth** schwere Bedenken hinsichtlich einer Sache (*gen*) haben; **it is still in ~** es ist noch zweifelhaft; **I am in no ~ as to what** *or* **about what he means** ich bin mir völlig im klaren darüber, was er meint; **to have one's ~s as to** *or* **about sth** (so) seine Bedenken hinsichtlich einer Sache (*gen*) haben; **I have my ~s whether he will come** ich bezweifle, daß er kommt; **to cast ~ on sth** etw in Zweifel ziehen; **there is room for ~** es ist durchaus nicht sicher; **there's no ~ about it** daran gibt es keinen Zweifel; **I have no ~ about it** ich bezweifle das nicht; **I have no ~s about taking the job** ich habe keine Bedenken, die Stelle anzunehmen; **no ~ he will come tomorrow** höchstwahrscheinlich kommt er morgen; **without (a) ~** ohne Zweifel; **yes, no ~, but ...** ja, zweifelsohne, aber ...; **it's beyond ~ that ...** es steht außer Zweifel, daß ...; **when in ~** im Zweifelsfall.

▼[2] *vt* bezweifeln; *sb's honesty, truth of statement* anzweifeln, Zweifel haben an (*+dat*) ◆ **I'm sorry I ~ed you** (*what you said*) es tut mir leid, daß ich dir nicht geglaubt habe; (*your loyalty etc*) es tut mir leid, daß ich an dir gezweifelt habe; **I ~ it (very much)** das möchte ich (doch stark) bezweifeln, das bezweifle ich (sehr); **I don't ~ it** das bezweifle ich (auch gar) nicht; **I ~ whether he will come** ich bezweifle, daß er kommen wird.

[3] *vi* Zweifel haben *or* hegen ◆ **~ing Thomas** ungläubiger Thomas.

doubter ['daʊtə^r] *n* Skeptiker, Zweifler *m*.

▼ **doubtful** ['daʊtfʊl] *adj* **(a)** (*uncertain*) unsicher, zweifelhaft; *outcome, result, future* ungewiß ◆ **to be ~ about sb/sth** jdm/einer Sache gegenüber Zweifel hegen *or* voller Zweifel sein; **to be ~ about doing sth** zweifeln *or* Bedenken haben, ob man etw tun soll; **he might do it, but I'm a bit ~** es kann sein, daß er es macht, aber ganz sicher bin ich nicht; **to look ~** (*person*) skeptisch aussehen; **the weather was** *or* **looked a bit ~** es sah nach schlechtem Wetter aus; **it is ~ whether/that ...** es ist unsicher *or* zweifelhaft, ob ...; **he's a ~ starter** (*in race*) es ist zweifelhaft, ob er starten wird *or* (*for job etc*) ob er anfangen wird.

(b) (*of questionable character*) zweifelhaft; *person, affair also* zwielichtig; *reputation also* fragwürdig; *joke* zweideutig.

doubtfully ['daʊtfəlɪ] *adv* skeptisch, voller Zweifel.

doubtfulness ['daʊtfʊlnɪs] *n see adj* **(a)** Unsicherheit *f*; Ungewißheit *f* ◆ **because of the ~ of the weather** weil es nach schlechtem Wetter aussah. **(b)** Zweifelhaftigkeit *f*; Zwielichtigkeit *f*; Fragwürdigkeit *f*; Zweideutigkeit *f*.

▼ **doubtless** ['daʊtlɪs] *adv* ohne Zweifel, zweifelsohne.

douche [du:ʃ] [1] *n* Spülung, Irrigation (*spec*) *f*; (*instrument*) Irrigator *m* ◆ **like a cold ~** (*inf*) wie eine kalte Dusche.

[2] *vi* eine Spülung machen.

[3] *vt* spülen.

dough [dəʊ] *n* **(a)** Teig *m*. **(b)** (*sl: money*) Kohle *f*, Kies, Zaster *m* (*all inf*).

dough: ~ball *n* Kloß *m*; **~boy** *n* (*US Mil sl*) Landser *m* (*inf*); **~nut** *n* Berliner (Pfannkuchen), Krapfen (*S Ger*) *m*.

doughty ['daʊtɪ] *adj* (*liter*) kühn, tapfer.

doughy ['dəʊɪ] *adj* **(a)** *consistency* zäh, teigig; (*pej*) *bread* klitschig, nicht durchgebacken. **(b)** (*pej*) *complexion* käsig.

Douglas fir [ˌdʌgləs'fɜ:^r] *or* **pine** [-'paɪn] *n* Douglastanne *f*.

dour ['dʊə^r] *adj* (*silent, unfriendly*) mürrisch, verdrießlich; *struggle* hart, hartnäckig ◆ **to be ~-faced** mürrisch *or* verdrießlich aussehen.

douse [daʊs] *vt* **(a)** (*pour water over*) Wasser schütten über (*+acc*); (*put into water*) ins Wasser tauchen; *plants* reichlich wässern. **(b)** *light* ausmachen, löschen ◆ **~ that light!** Licht aus!

dove¹ [dʌv] *n* (*lit, fig*) Taube *f*.

dove² [dəʊv] (*US*) *pret of* **dive**.

dove [dʌv-]: **~-coloured** *adj* taubenblau; **~cot(e)** *n* ['dʌvkɒt] Taubenschlag *m*; **~ grey** *adj* taubengrau.

dovetail ['dʌvteɪl] [1] *n* Schwalbenschwanz *m* ◆ **~ joint** Schwalbenschwanzverbindung *f*.

[2] *vt* (schwalbenschwanzförmig) überblatten; (*fig*) *plans* koordinieren.

[3] *vi* (*plans*) übereinstimmen.

dowager ['daʊədʒə^r] *n* (adlige) Witwe ◆ **~ duchess** Herzoginwitwe *f*.

dowdiness ['daʊdɪnɪs] *n* absoluter Mangel an Schick.

dowdy ['daʊdɪ] *adj* (*+er*) ohne jeden Schick.

dowel ['daʊəl] *n* Dübel *m*.

dower house ['daʊəhaʊs] *n Haus nt für eine Witwe*.

Dow-Jones average [ˌdaʊ'dʒəʊnz'ævərɪdʒ] *n* Dow-Jones-Index *m*.

down¹ [daʊn] [1] *adv* **(a)** (*indicating movement*) (*towards speaker*) herunter; (*away from speaker*) hinunter; (*downstairs also*) nach unten ◆ **~!** (*to dog*) Platz!; **~ it goes!** (*taking medicine, child eating*) nun schluck mal schön runter; (*of stone, tree etc*) da fällt er; **and ~ he fell** und da fiel er hinunter/herunter; **to jump ~** hinunter-/herunterspringen; **~ with school/traitors!** nieder mit der Schule/den Verrätern!; **on his way ~ from the hilltop** auf seinem Weg vom Gipfel herab/hinab; **all the way ~ to the bottom** bis ganz nach unten.

(b) (*indicating static position*) unten ◆ **~ there** da unten; **I shall stay ~ here** ich bleibe hier unten; **~ in the valley** unten im Tal; **it needs a bit of paint ~ at the bottom** es muß unten herum neu gestrichen werden; **don't hit a man when he's ~** man soll jemanden nicht fertigmachen, wenn er schon angeschlagen ist *or* wenn's ihm dreckig geht (*inf*); **head ~** mit dem Kopf nach unten; **the sun is ~** die Sonne ist untergegangen; **the sun was well ~ in the sky** die Sonne stand schon ziemlich tief; **the blinds were ~** die Jalousien waren unten *or* heruntergelassen; **John isn't ~ yet** (*hasn't got up*) John ist noch nicht unten; **I'll be ~ in a minute** ich komme sofort runter; **to be ~ for the count** (*Boxing*) ausgezählt werden; **I've been ~ with flu** ich habe mit Grippe (im Bett) gelegen; **he was (feeling) a bit ~** er fühlte sich ein wenig niedergeschlagen *or* down (*sl*).

(c) (*to or at another place*) *usu not translated* **he came ~ from London yesterday** er kam gestern aus London; (*to south also*) er ist gestern von London runtergekommen (*inf*); **on the way ~ from London** auf dem Weg von London hierher *or* runter (*inf*); **he's ~ in London** er ist in London; **~ South** im Süden/in den Süden; **~ here in Italy** hier unten in Italien; **we're going ~ to the sea/to Dover** wir fahren an die See/nach Dover; **~ in Australia** in Australien; **he's ~ at his brother's** er ist bei seinem Bruder.

(d) (*in volume, degree, status*) **his shoes were worn ~** seine Schuhe waren abgetragen; **the tyres are ~** die Reifen sind platt; **his temperature is ~** sein Fieber ist zurückgegangen; **the price of meat is ~ on last week** der Fleischpreis ist gegenüber der letzten Woche gefallen; **I'm £20 ~ on what I expected** ich habe £ 20 weniger, als ich dachte; **their team is three points ~ (on their opponents)** ihre Mannschaft liegt (verglichen mit ihren Gegnern) um drei Punkte zurück; **they're still three goals ~** sie liegen immer noch mit drei Toren zurück.

(e) (*in writing, planning*) **to write sth ~** etw aufschreiben; **I've got it ~ in my diary** ich habe es in meinem Kalender notiert; **let's get it ~ on paper** schreiben wir es auf, halten wir es schriftlich fest; **when you see it ~ on paper** wenn man es schwarz auf weiß sieht; **to be ~ for the next race** für das nächste Rennen gemeldet sein; **it's ~ for next month** es steht für nächsten Monat auf dem Programm/Stundenplan *etc*.

(f) (*indicating succession of things, events, in hierarchy*) *usu not translated* **from 1700 ~ to the present** seit 1700 bis zur Gegenwart; **(all or right) ~ through the ages** von jeher; **right ~ to the present day** bis zum heutigen Tag; **from the biggest ~** vom Größten angefangen; **from the biggest ~ to the smallest** vom Größten bis zum Kleinsten; **from the chairman (all the way) ~ to the doorman** vom Vorsitzenden bis (herunter) zum Pförtner.

(g) to pay £20 ~ £ 20 anzahlen; **how much do they want ~?** was verlangen sie als Anzahlung?; **to be ~ on sb** jdn schikanieren *or* triezen (*inf*).

(h) (*not working*) **to be ~** außer Betrieb sein.

(i) to be ~ to sb/sth (*be caused by*) an jdm/etw liegen; **it's ~ to you to decide** die Entscheidung liegt bei Ihnen.

[2] *prep* **(a)** (*indicating movement to*) **to go/come ~ the hill/street** *etc* den Berg/die Straße *etc* hinuntergehen/herunterkommen; **she let her hair fall ~ her back** sie ließ ihr Haar über die Schultern fallen; **he ran his finger ~ the list** er ging (mit dem Finger) die Liste durch.

(b) (*at a lower part of*) **he's already ~ the hill** er ist schon unten; **the other skiers were further ~ the slope** die anderen Skifahrer waren weiter unten; **she lives ~ the street (from us)** sie wohnt ein Stückchen weiter die Straße entlang.

(c) ~ the ages/centuries durch die Jahrhunderte (hindurch).

(d) (*along*) **he was walking/coming ~ the street** er ging/kam die Straße entlang; **looking ~ this road, you can see ...** wenn Sie die Straße hinunterblicken, können Sie ... sehen.

(e) (*Brit inf: to, in, at*) **he's gone ~ the pub** er ist in die Kneipe gegangen; **she's ~ the shops** sie ist einkaufen gegangen; **he works ~ the garage** er arbeitet in der Autowerkstatt; **let's go ~ Jimmy's place** gehen wir doch zu Jimmy.

[3] *n* **to have a ~ on sb** (*inf*) jdn auf dem Kieker haben (*inf*); *see* **up**.

[4] *vt opponent* niederschlagen, zu Fall bringen; *enemy planes* abschießen, (he)runterholen (*inf*); *beer etc* runterkippen *or* -schütten (*inf*) ◆ **to ~ tools** die Arbeit niederlegen.

down² *n* (*feathers*) Daunen, Flaumfedern *pl*; (*youth's beard*) Flaum *m*.

down³ *n usu pl* (*Geog*) Hügelland *nt no pl* ◆ **on the ~(s)** im Hügelland.

down: ~-and-out [1] *n* (*tramp*) Penner *m* (*inf*); [2] *adj* heruntergekommen; *appearance also* abgerissen; **~-beat** [1] *n Taktstockführung f, die den ersten betonten Taktteil anzeigt*, erster Taktteil; [2] *adj* (*fig*) *ending* undramatisch; **~-bow** *n* (*Mus*) Abstrich *m*; **~cast** [1] *adj* **(a)** (*depressed*) *person, expression* niedergedrückt, entmutigt; **(b)** *eyes* niedergeschlagen; *look* gesenkt; [2] *n* (*Min*) Wetterschacht *m*; **~ draught,** (*US*) **~ draft** *n* (*Met*) Fallwind *m*; (*Tech*) Fallstrom *m*.

downer ['daʊnə^r] *n* (*sl*) Downer *m* (*sl*), Beruhigungsmittel *nt*.

down: ~fall *n* **(a)** Sturz, Fall *m*; (*of empire also*) Untergang *m*; (*cause of ruin: drink etc*) Ruin *m*; **(b)** (*of rain*) heftiger Niederschlag, Platzregen *m*; **~grade** [1] *n* (*Rail*) Gefälle *nt*; **to be on the ~grade** (*fig*) auf dem absteigenden Ast sein; (*health, quality*) sich verschlechtern; [2] *vt hotel, job, work* herunterstufen; *person also* degradieren; **~-hearted** *adj* niedergeschlagen, entmutigt; **~hill** [1] *adv* **to go ~hill** (*road*) bergab führen *or* gehen; (*car*) hinunter *or* herunterfahren; (*person*) hinunter- *or* heruntergehen; (*fig*) (*person*) auf dem absteigenden Ast sein; (*work, health*) sich verschlechtern; [2] *adj* (*lit*) abfallend *attr*, bergab führend *attr*; **the path is ~hill for 2 miles** der Weg führt zwei Meilen bergab; **the ~hill path to drug addiction** der abschüssige Weg in die Drogensucht; **~ line** *n* (*Rail*) *Eisenbahnlinie f von der Stadt aufs Land oder aus der Hauptstadt heraus*; **~load** (*Comput*) [1] *vt* laden; [2] *vi* **it won't ~load** Runterladen ist nicht möglich; [3] *attr font, character* ladbar; **~loadable** *adj* (*Comput*) ladbar; **~market** [1] *adj product* für den

Massenmarkt; *area* weniger anspruchsvoll; *person, language* ordinär; **we used to have a ~market range** unser Sortiment war früher auf den Massenmarkt ausgerichtet; [2] *adv* **we decided to go ~market** (*shop*) wir beschlossen, uns mehr auf den Massenmarkt zu konzentrieren; **~ payment** *n* (*Fin*) Anzahlung *f*; **~pipe** *n* Abflußrohr, Fallrohr *nt*; **~pour** *n* Platzregen, Wolkenbruch *m*; **~right** [1] *adj refusal, lie* glatt; *rudeness, scoundrel, liar* ausgesprochen; [2] *adv rude, angry* ausgesprochen; **~river** *adv* flußabwärts (*from* von); **~river from Bonn** unterhalb von Bonn; **~size** [ˌdaʊn'saɪz] [1] *vt business, workforce* verkleinern; **~sized economy** *durch Rationalisierung und Stellenabbau gekennzeichnete wirtschaftliche Lage*; [2] *vi* (*company*) sich verkleinern ◆ **downsizing** (*Comput*) Downsizing *nt*; **~spout** *n* Abflußrohr, Fallrohr *nt*.

Down's syndrome ['daʊnz'sɪndrəʊm] (*Med*) [1] *n* Down-Syndrom *nt*.
[2] *attr* **a ~ baby** ein an Down-Syndrom leidendes Kind.

down: ~stage *adv* (*at the front*) im vorderen Teil der Bühne; (*towards the front*) zum vorderen Teil der Bühne; **he was standing ~stage from her** er stand von ihr aus gesehen weiter vorne auf der Bühne; **~stairs** [1] *adv go, come* nach unten; *be* unten; **the people ~stairs** die Leute unter uns *or* von unten; [2] *adj flat* Parterre-; **the ~stairs rooms** die unteren Zimmer, die Zimmer unten; **our ~stairs neighbours** die Nachbarn unter uns; [3] *n* Parterre *nt*; **~stream** *adv* fluß- *or* stromabwärts (*from* von); **~stroke** *n* (*in writing*) Abstrich *m*; (*Mech: of piston*) Ansaugtakt *m*; **~swept** *adj wings* abwärtsgerichtet; **~ swing** *n* Abwärtsschwingen *nt*; **~time** *n* Ausfallzeit *f*; **~-to-earth** *adj attitude, approach* nüchtern; **he's a ~-to-earth sort of person** (*practical*) er steht mit beiden Füßen auf der Erde; (*rather boring*) er ist eher nüchtern; **~town** [1] *adj* **~town district** Zentrum *nt*, Innenstadt *f*; (*US*) Geschäftsviertel *nt*; **~town Chicago** das Zentrum *or* die City *or* Innenstadt von Chicago; [2] *adv* **to go ~town** in die (Innen)stadt *or* ins Zentrum gehen; **to live ~town** im (Stadt)zentrum *or* in der Innenstadt wohnen; **~ train** *n Zug, der von der Stadt aufs Land fährt oder von der Hauptstadt abgeht*; **~-trodden** *adj people* unterdrückt, geknechtet; **~trend** *n* (*Econ*) Abwärtstrend *m*; **to be in** *or* **on a ~trend** sich im Abwärtstrend befinden; **~turn** *n* (*in prices, business*) Rückgang *m*, Abflauen *nt*; **to take a ~turn** zurückgehen, abflauen; **his fortunes took a ~turn** sein Glücksstern sank; **~ under** (*Brit inf*) [1] *n* Australien *nt*; Neuseeland *nt*; [2] *adv* in/nach Australien/Neuseeland.

downward ['daʊnwəd] [1] *adj movement, pull* nach unten; *slope* abfallend ◆ **he's on the ~ path** (*fig*) mit ihm geht's bergab.
[2] *adv* (*also* **downwards**) **(a)** *go, look* nach unten ◆ **to slope gently ~** sanft abfallen. **(b)** (*fig*) **from the 10th century ~** seit dem 10. Jahrhundert; **from the king ~** beim König angefangen.

downwind ['daʊnwɪnd] *adv* in Windrichtung (*of or from sth* einer Sache *gen*).

downy ['daʊnɪ] *adj* (*+er*) *skin, leaf, peach* flaumig, mit (feinen) Härchen bedeckt; *cushion* Daunen-; *softness* flaumweich, daunenweich.

dowry ['daʊrɪ] *n* Mitgift *f*.

dowse[1] [daʊz] *vt see* **douse**.

dowse[2] *vi* (*divine*) mit einer Wünschelrute suchen ◆ **dowsing rod** Wünschelrute *f*.

dowser ['daʊzəʳ] *n* Wünschelrutengänger(in *f*) *m*.

doxology [dɒk'sɒlədʒɪ] *n* Lobpreisung *f*, Verherrlichung *f* Gottes.

doyen ['dɔɪən] *n* (*senior and expert member of group*) Nestor *m*; (*of diplomatic corps*) Doyen *m*.

doyenne ['dɔɪen] *n see* **doyen** Nestorin *f*; Doyenne *f*.

doz *abbr of* **dozen**.

doze [dəʊz] [1] *n* Nickerchen *nt* ◆ **to have a ~** dösen, ein Nickerchen machen.
[2] *vi* (vor sich hin) dösen.

◆**doze off** *vi* einschlafen, einnicken.

dozen ['dʌzn] *n* Dutzend *nt* ◆ **80p a ~** 80 Pence das Dutzend; **half a ~** sechs, ein halbes Dutzend; **~s** jede Menge; (*fig inf*) eine ganze Menge; **~s of times** (*inf*) x-mal (*inf*), tausendmal; **there are ~s like that** (*inf*) das gibt's wie Sand am Meer; **~s of people came** (*inf*) Dutzende von Leute kamen.

dozily ['dəʊzɪlɪ] *adv* verschlafen, schläfrig.

dozy ['dəʊzɪ] *adj* (*+er*) **(a)** (*sleepy*) schläfrig, verschlafen. **(b)** (*sl: stupid*) dösig (*inf*).

DP *abbr of* **data processing** DV *f*.

D Phil *abbr of* **Doctor of Philosophy** Dr. phil.

DPP *abbr of* **Director of Public Prosecutions.**

dpt *abbr of* **department** Abt.

Dr *abbr of* **doctor** Dr.

drab [dræb] [1] *adj* (*+er*) trist; *colour also* düster; *town also* grau.
[2] *n, no pl* (*Tex*) grober, graubrauner Wollstoff.

drably ['dræblɪ] *adv see adj*.

drabness ['dræbnɪs] *n see adj* Tristheit *f*, Düsterkeit *f*, Grauheit *f*.

drachma ['drækmə] *n*, *pl* **-e** ['drækmiː] *or* **-s** Drachme *f*.

draconian [drə'kəʊnɪən] *adj* drakonisch.

draft [drɑːft] [1] *n* **(a)** (*rough outline*) Entwurf *m*.
(b) (*Fin, Comm*) Wechsel *m*, Tratte *f*.
(c) (*Mil: group of men*) Sonderkommando *nt*.
(d) (*US Mil*) (*group of conscripts*) Rekruten *pl*; (*conscription*) Einberufung (zum Wehrdienst).
(e) (*US*) *see* **draught.**
(f) (*Comput*) Draft(druck) *m*, Schnellschrift *f*.
[2] *vt* **(a)** *letter, speech, bill, contract* entwerfen.
(b) (*US Mil*) *conscript* einziehen, einberufen (*into* zu) ◆ **he was ~ed into the Cabinet** (*fig*) er wurde ins Kabinett berufen; **to ~ sb to do sth** (*Mil*) jdn dazu abkommandieren, etw zu tun; (*fig*) jdn beauftragen, etw zu tun.
[3] *attr* (*Comput*) *mode, quality* Draft-.

draft: ~ board *n* (*US Mil*) Einberufungsbehörde *f*; (*panel*) Einberufungsausschuß *m*; **~ card** *n* (*US Mil*) Wehrpaß *m*; **~ dodger** *n* (*US Mil*) *Wehrpflichtiger, der sich vor dem Wehrdienst drückt*, Drückeberger *m* (*pej inf*).

draftee ['drɑːftiː] *n* (*US Mil*) Wehrpflichtige(r) *m*.

draftiness *etc* (*US*) *see* **draughtiness** *etc*.

draft: ~ letter *n* Entwurf *m* eines/des Briefes; **~ version** *n* Entwurf *m*.

drag [dræg] [1] *n* **(a)** (*object pulled along*) (*for dredging etc*) Suchanker *m*; (*Naut: cluster of hooks*) Dregganker, Draggen *m*; (*~-net*) Schleppnetz *nt*; (*heavy sledge*) Lastschlitten *m*; (*Agr: harrow*) schwere Egge.
(b) (*resistance*) (*Aviat*) Luft- *or* Strömungswiderstand *m*; (*Naut*) Wasserwiderstand *m*.
(c) (*brake*) Hemmklotz, Hemmschuh *m*.
(d) (*slow laborious progress*) **it was a long ~ up to the top of the hill** es war ein langer, mühseliger Aufstieg zum Gipfel, der Aufstieg auf den Gipfel war ein furchtbarer Schlauch (*inf*).
(e) (*inf: hindrance*) **to be a ~ on sb** für jdn ein Klotz am Bein *or* ein Hemmschuh sein.
(f) (*inf*) **what a ~!** (*boring*) Mann, ist der/die/das langweilig! (*inf*); (*nuisance*) so'n Mist (*inf*); **what a ~ having to go back!** so'n Mist, daß wir zurückmüssen (*inf*); **the film was a ~** der Film war stinklangweilig (*inf*); **he suddenly decided that his girlfriend was a real ~** es wurde ihm plötzlich klar, daß seine Freundin ihn anödete (*inf*).
(g) (*inf: pull on cigarette*) Zug *m* (*on, at* an *+dat*) ◆ **give me a ~** laß mich mal ziehen, gib mir mal'n Zug (*inf*).
(h) (*inf: women's clothing worn by men*) (*von Männern getragene*) Frauenkleidung *f* ◆ **in** *or* **wearing ~** in Frauenkleidung, im Fummel (*sl*), als Tunte (*sl*).
(i) (*US inf: influence*) Einfluß *m* ◆ **to use one's ~** seinen Einfluß ausüben.
(j) (*US inf: street*) **the main ~** die Hauptstraße.
[2] *vt* **(a)** *person, object* schleppen, schleifen, ziehen ◆ **the dog was ~ging its broken leg** der Hund schleifte sein gebrochenes Bein hinter sich her; **to ~ one's feet** (*lit*) (mit den Füßen) schlurfen; (*fig*) alles/die Sache schleifen lassen; **to ~ anchor** (*Naut*) vor Anker treiben; **to ~ the truth out of sb** aus jdm die Wahrheit mühsam herausholen; **he ~ged the words out of him** er mußte ihm jedes Wort einzeln aus der Nase ziehen (*inf*).
(b) *river* absuchen.
[3] *vi* **(a)** schleifen; (*feet*) schlurfen; (*Naut: anchor*) treiben.
(b) (*lag behind: person*) hinterherhinken.
(c) (*fig*) (*time, work*) sich hinziehen; (*play, book*) sich in die Länge ziehen; (*conversation*) sich (mühsam) hinschleppen.

◆**drag along** *vt sep person* mitschleppen ◆ **to ~ oneself ~** sich mühsam dahinschleppen; **to ~ sth ~ behind one** etw hinter sich (*dat*) her schleppen *or* schleifen.

◆**drag apart** *vt sep* auseinanderzerren, trennen.

◆**drag away** *vt sep* (*lit, fig*) wegschleppen *or* -ziehen ◆ **you'll have to ~ him ~ from the television** den muß man mit Gewalt vom Fernsehen wegziehen; **if you can ~ yourself ~ from the television for a second ...** wenn du dich vielleicht mal für eine Sekunde vom Fernsehen losreißen könntest ...

◆**drag behind** [1] *vt +prep obj* **to ~ sb/sth ~ one** jdn/etw hinter sich (*dat*) herschleppen *or* herschleifen.
[2] *vi* (*in class*) zurück sein, hinterherhinken; (*in race*) hinterherlaufen *or* -fahren; (*on a walk*) zurückbleiben, hinterhertrödeln.

◆**drag down** *vt sep* (*lit*) herunterziehen; (*fig*) mit sich ziehen ◆ **to ~ sb ~ to one's own level** (*fig*) jdn auf sein eigenes Niveau herabziehen; **his illness is ~ging him ~** seine Krankheit macht ihn fertig (*inf*); **you shouldn't let these things ~ you ~ so** du solltest dich dadurch nicht so entmutigen lassen.

◆**drag in** *vt sep* **(a)** (*lit*) hineinziehen. **(b)** (*fig*) *subject* aufs Tapet bringen; *remark* anbringen.

◆**drag off** *vt sep* (*lit*) wegzerren *or* -ziehen; (*fig*) wegschleppen ◆ **to ~ sb ~ to a concert** jdn in ein Konzert schleppen.

◆**drag on** *vi* sich in die Länge ziehen; (*meeting, lecture also*) sich hinziehen; (*conversation*) sich hinschleppen ◆ **it ~ged ~ for 3 hours** es zog sich über 3 Stunden hin.

◆**drag out** *vt sep meeting, discussion etc* in die Länge ziehen.

◆**drag up** *vt sep* **(a)** *scandal, story* ausgraben; *person* aufgabeln (*inf*), auftun (*inf*). **(b)** (*inf*) *child* mehr schlecht als recht aufziehen ◆ **~ged ~ rather than brought up** mehr schlecht als recht aufgezogen.

drag: ~ and drop *n* (*Comput*) Drag-and-Drop *nt*; **~ artist** *n* (*inf*) *Künstler, der in Frauenkleidung auftritt*; **~ coefficient** *n* Luftwiderstandsbeiwert *m*.

dragée ['dræʒeɪ] *n* (*Med*) Dragee *nt*.

drag factor *n* Widerstandsbeiwert *m*.

draggy ['drægɪ] *adj* (*sl*) anödend (*inf*).

drag lift *n* (*Ski*) Schlepplift *m*.

dragnet ['drægnet] *n* (*for fish*) Schleppnetz *nt*; (*police hunt*) großangelegte Polizeiaktion ◆ **to slip through the ~** (der Polizei) durch die Maschen schlüpfen.

dragoman ['drægəʊmən] *n* Dragoman *m*.

dragon ['drægən] *n* (*lit, fig inf*) Drache *m*.

dragonfly ['drægənˌflaɪ] *n* Libelle *f*.

dragoon [drə'guːn] [1] *n* (*Mil*) Dragoner *m*.
[2] *vt* **to ~ sb into doing sth** jdn zwingen *or* mit Gewalt dazu bringen, etw zu tun.

drag: ~ queen *n* (*sl*) Fummeltrine (*sl*), Tunte (*sl*) *f*; **~race** *n* Beschleunigungsrennen *nt;* ~**rope** *n* Schlepptau *nt;* ~ **show** *n* Transvestitenshow *f.*

dragster ['drægstəʳ] *n* Dragster *m (sl).*

drain [dreɪn] [1] *n* **(a)** *(pipe)* Rohr *nt; (under sink etc)* Abfluß(rohr *nt*) *m; (under the ground)* Kanalisationsrohr *nt;* (~ *cover)* Rost *m* ◆ **open** ~ (Abfluß)rinne *f;* **to throw one's money down the** ~ *(fig inf)* das Geld zum Fenster hinauswerfen; **all his hopes have gone down the** ~ **now** *(inf)* er hat alle seine Hoffnungen begraben (müssen); **this country's going down the** ~ *(inf)* dieses Land geht vor die Hunde *(inf);* **I had to watch all our efforts go down the** ~ ich mußte zusehen, wie alle unsere Bemühungen zunichte (gemacht) wurden; **to laugh like a** ~ *(inf)* sich vor Lachen ausschütten wollen.
(b) *(on resources etc)* Belastung *f (on gen)* ◆ **looking after her father has been a great** ~ **on her strength** die Pflege ihres Vaters hat sehr an ihren Kräften gezehrt; *see* **brain** ~.
[2] *vt* **(a)** drainieren; *land, marshes also* entwässern; *vegetables* abgießen; *(let* ~) abtropfen lassen; *mine* auspumpen; *reservoir* trockenlegen; *boiler, radiator* das Wasser ablassen aus; *engine oil* ablassen.
(b) *(fig)* **to** ~ **sb of strength** an jds Kräften *(acc)* zehren; **to feel** ~**ed (of energy)** sich ausgelaugt fühlen; **to** ~ **a country of resources** ein Land auslaugen *or* auspowern *(sl);* **to** ~ **sb dry** jdn ausnehmen *(inf).*
(c) *glass* austrinken, leeren.
[3] *vi (vegetables, dishes)* abtropfen; *(land into river)* entwässert werden.

◆**drain away** [1] *vi (liquid)* ablaufen; *(strength)* dahinschwinden.
[2] *vt sep liquid* ableiten.

◆**drain off** *vt sep* abgießen; *(let drain)* abtropfen lassen.

drainage ['dreɪnɪdʒ] *n* **(a)** *(draining)* Dränage *f; (of land also)* Entwässerung *f.* **(b)** *(system)* Entwässerungssystem *nt; (in house, town)* Kanalisation *f.* **(c)** *(sewage)* Abwasser *nt.* **(d)** *(Geol)* Drän(ier)ung *(spec),* Entwässerung *f.*

drainage: ~ **area,** ~ **basin** *n (Geol)* Einzugsgebiet *f;* ~ **channel** *n (Build)* Entwässerungsgraben, Abzugsgraben *m;* ~ **tube** *n (Med)* Drain, Drän *m.*

drain: ~**ing board,** *(US)* ~ **board** *n* Ablauf *m;* ~ **pipe** *n* Kanalisations-/Abflußrohr *nt;* ~**pipes,** ~**pipe trousers** *npl* Röhrenhosen *pl.*

drake [dreɪk] *n* Erpel, Enterich *m; see* **duck[1]**.

dram [dræm] *n* **(a)** *(measure, Pharm)* ≃ Drachme *f (old).* **(b)** *(small drink)* Schluck *m* (Whisky).

drama ['drɑːmə] *n (art, play, incident)* Drama *nt; (no pl: quality of being dramatic)* Dramatik *f* ◆ **18th-century German** ~ das deutsche Drama des 18. Jahrhunderts; **family** ~ *(TV series)* Familienserie *f.*

drama: ~ **critic** *n* Theaterkritiker(in *f*) *m;* ~ **school** *n* Schauspielschule *f;* ~ **student** *n* Schauspielschüler(in *f*) *m.*

dramatic [drə'mætɪk] *adj* dramatisch; *criticism* Theater-; *ability of actor* schauspielerisch.

dramatically [drə'mætɪkəlɪ] *adv* dramatisch; *(in a theatrical manner)* theatralisch ◆ **he flung his book** ~ **to the ground** mit theatralischer Geste schleuderte er sein Buch auf den Boden; **it's not** ~ **different** so dramatisch ist der Unterschied nicht.

dramatics [drə'mætɪks] *npl* **(a)** *(Theat)* Dramaturgie *f; see* **amateur. (b)** *(fig)* theatralisches Getue.

dramatis personae ['dræmətɪspɜː'səʊnaɪ] *npl* Personen der Handlung, dramatis personae *(old) pl.*

dramatist ['dræmətɪst] *n* Dramatiker *m.*

dramatization [,dræmətaɪ'zeɪʃən] *n see vt* Bühnen-/Fernsehbearbeitung *f;* Dramatisierung *f.*

dramatize ['dræmətaɪz] [1] *vt* **(a)** *novel* für die Bühne/das Fernsehen bearbeiten, dramatisieren. **(b)** *(make vivid) event* dramatisieren.
[2] *vi* **(a)** *(novel etc)* sich für die Bühne/das Fernsehen bearbeiten lassen. **(b)** *(exaggerate)* übertreiben.

drank [dræŋk] *pret of* **drink.**

drape [dreɪp] [1] *vt* **(a)** drapieren; *window* mit Vorhängen versehen; *person* hüllen; *altar also* behängen.
(b) *curtain, length of cloth* drapieren ◆ **to** ~ **sth over sth** etw über etw *(acc)* drapieren; **she** ~**d herself over the sofa** *(inf)* sie drapierte sich malerisch auf das Sofa.
[2] *n* **(a)** ~**s** *pl (US)* Gardinen *pl.* **(b)** *(way sth hangs)* Fall *m.*

draper ['dreɪpəʳ] *n (Brit)* Textilkaufmann *m* ◆ ~**'s (shop)** Textilgeschäft *nt.*

drapery ['dreɪpərɪ] *n* **(a)** *(Brit) (cloth etc)* Stoff *m; (business: also* ~ **shop)** Stoffladen *m.* **(b)** *(hangings)* Draperie *f (old); (on wall also)* Behang *m; (around bed etc)* Vorhänge *pl; (clothing, fig liter)* Gewand *nt.*

drastic ['dræstɪk] *adj* **(a)** drastisch ◆ **you'll have to do something** ~ Sie werden da drastische Maßnahmen ergreifen müssen; **there's no need to be so** ~ man braucht nicht so radikal *or* drastisch vorzugehen; **he's had a very** ~ **haircut** er hat sich die Haare radikal abschneiden lassen.
(b) *(urgent, serious)* bedrohlich ◆ **things are getting** ~ die Sache wird bedrohlich; **there's a** ~ **need for medical supplies** es besteht dringender Bedarf an Medikamenten.

drastically ['dræstɪkəlɪ] *adv see adj* **(a)** drastisch. **(b)** bedrohlich ◆ **they're** ~ **short of supplies** ihre Vorräte sind bedrohlich knapp.

drat [dræt] *interj (inf)* ~ **(it)!** verflixt! *(inf);* ~ **the child!** dieses verflixte Kind! *(inf).*

dratted ['drætɪd] *adj (inf)* verflixt *(inf).*

draught, *(US)* **draft** [drɑːft] *n* **(a)** (Luft)zug *m; (through* ~) Durchzug *m; (for fire)* Zug *m* ◆ **there's a terrible** ~ **in here** hier zieht es fürchterlich; **what a** ~! das zieht ja fürchterlich!; **I'm sitting in a** ~ ich sitze im Zug; **are you in a** ~? zieht's Ihnen?; **I've got a** ~ **blowing round the back of my neck** mir zieht's im Genick; **open the window so we'll get a nice cool** ~ **in here** mach mal das Fenster auf, damit wir etwas frische Luft bekommen; **open the flues to increase the** ~ mach die Klappen auf, damit der Ofen mehr Zug bekommt; **he's beginning to feel the** ~ *(fig inf)* ihm wird allmählich das Geld knapp.
(b) *(swallow, drink)* Zug *m* ◆ **a** ~ **of mead** ein Schluck *m* Met.
(c) (~ *beer)* Faß- *or* Schankbier *nt* ◆ **on** ~ vom Faß.
(d) *(Naut)* Tiefgang *m.*
(e) *(of fish)* Fischzug *m.*
(f) *(Brit: game)* ~**s** *(+sing vb)* Damespiel *nt; (+pl vb: pieces)* Damesteine *pl.*
(g) *(rough sketch) see* **draft 1 (a).**

draught: ~ **animal** *n* Zugtier *nt;* ~ **beer** *n* Faßbier *nt,* Bier *nt* vom Faß; ~**board** *n* Damebrett *nt;* ~ **excluder** *n* Dichtungsmaterial *nt.*

draughtiness, *(US)* **draftiness** ['drɑːftɪnɪs] *n* Zugigkeit *f.*

draughtproof, *(US)* **draftproof** ['drɑːftpruːf] *adj windows, doors* dicht; *room* gegen Zugluft geschützt.

draughtproofing, *(US)* **draftproofing** ['drɑːft,pruːfɪŋ] *n* Zugluftisolierung *f; (material)* Isoliermaterial *nt* gegen Zugluft.

draughtsman ['drɑːftsmən] *n, pl* **-men** [-mən] **(a)** *(US:* **draftsman)** *(of plans)* Zeichner *m; (of documents, treaty etc)* Verfasser *m.* **(b)** *(Brit: in game)* Damestein *m.*

draughtsmanship, *(US)* **draftsmanship** ['drɑːftsmənʃɪp] *n* **you can tell by the** ~ **that** ... an der Qualität der Zeichnung/des Entwurfs kann man sehen, daß ...; **the skills of** ~ das zeichnerische Können; **an excellent piece of** ~ ein hervorragendes Beispiel zeichnerischen Könnens.

draughty, *(US)* **drafty** ['drɑːftɪ] *adj (er)* zugig ◆ **it's** ~ **in here** hier zieht es.

draw[1] [drɔː] *pret* **drew,** *ptp* **drawn** [1] *vt (lit, fig)* zeichnen; *line* ziehen ◆ **we must** ~ **the line somewhere** *(fig)* irgendwo muß Schluß sein; **I** ~ **the line there** da ist bei mir Schluß, da hört's bei mir auf; **I** ~ **the line at scrubbing floors** beim Schrubben von Fußböden ist bei mir Schluß *or* hört's bei mir auf; **some people just don't know where to** ~ **the line** manche Leute wissen einfach nicht, wie weit sie gehen können.
[2] *vi* zeichnen.

draw[2] *(vb: pret* **drew,** *ptp* **drawn)** [1] *vt* **(a)** *(move by pulling)* ziehen; *bolt* zurückschieben; *bow* spannen; *curtains (open)* aufziehen; *(shut)* zuziehen; *(Med) abscess* schneiden ◆ **he drew the book towards him** er zog das Buch näher (zu sich heran); **he drew his finger along the edge of the table** er fuhr mit dem Finger die Tischkante entlang; **he drew his hat over his eyes** er zog sich *(dat)* den Hut ins Gesicht; **he drew the smoke down into his lungs** er machte einen (tiefen) Lungenzug.
(b) *(move by pulling behind) coach, cart* ziehen.
(c) *(extract, remove) teeth, sword* ziehen; *cork* herausziehen ◆ **with** ~**n sword** mit gezogenem *or* gezücktem Schwert.
(d) *(obtain from source)* holen; *wine also (from barrel)* zapfen ◆ **to** ~ **a bath** das Badewasser einlassen; **to** ~ **money from the bank** Geld (vom Konto) abheben; **he's bitten her — has he** ~**n blood?** er hat sie gebissen — blutet sie?; **to** ~ **a cheque on a bank** einen Scheck auf eine Bank ausstellen; **to** ~ **first prize** den ersten Preis gewinnen; **to** ~ **inspiration from sb/sth/somewhere** sich von jdm/von etw/von irgendwas inspirieren lassen; **to** ~ **comfort from sth** sich mit etw trösten; **her singing drew tears from the audience** ihr Singen rührte die Zuhörer zu Tränen; **her singing drew tremendous applause from the audience** ihr Singen rief brausenden Beifall hervor; **to** ~ **a big salary/the dole** ein großes Gehalt/Arbeitslosenunterstützung beziehen; **to** ~ **a smile/a laugh from sb** jdm ein Lächeln/ein Lachen entlocken.
(e) *(attract) interest* erregen; *customer, crowd* anlocken ◆ **the play has** ~**n a lot of criticism** das Theaterstück hat viel Kritik auf sich *(acc)* gezogen; **to feel** ~**n towards sb** sich zu jdm hingezogen fühlen; **to** ~ **sb into sth** jdn in etw *(acc)* hineinziehen *or* verwickeln; **to** ~ **sb away from sb/sth** jdn von jdm/etw weglocken; **I was irresistibly** ~**n to the conclusion that** ... ich kam unweigerlich zu dem Schluß, daß ...; **her shouts drew me to the scene** ihr Rufen brachte mich an den Ort des Geschehens.
(f) to ~ **a (deep) breath** (tief) Luft holen; **to** ~ **a long breath** einmal tief Luft holen.
(g) *(cause to speak, to disclose feelings)* **I could** ~ **no reply from him** ich konnte keine Antwort aus ihm herausbringen; **he refuses to be** ~**n** *(will not speak)* aus ihm ist nichts herauszubringen; *(will not be provoked)* er läßt sich auf nichts ein; **I won't be** ~**n on that one** dazu möchte ich mich nicht äußern.
(h) *(establish, formulate) conclusion, comparison* ziehen; *distinction* treffen ◆ **well,** ~ **your own conclusions!** zieh deine eigenen Schlüsse!; **you can** ~ **whatever conclusion you like** du kannst daraus schließen, was du willst.
(i) *(Naut)* **the boat** ~**s 4 metres** das Boot hat 4 m Tiefgang.
(j) *(Sport)* **to** ~ **a match** sich unentschieden trennen, unentschieden spielen.
(k) we've been ~**n (to play) away/at home** wir sind für ein Auswärtsspiel/Heimspiel gezogen worden; **France has been** ~**n against Scotland** Frankreich ist für ein Spiel gegen Schottland gezogen worden.
(l) *(Cards)* **to** ~ **a card from the pack** eine Karte vom Haufen abheben *or* nehmen; **to** ~ **trumps** Trümpfe herauszwingen.
(m) *(Cook) fowl* ausnehmen; *see* **hang.**
(n) *(Hunt) fox* aufstöbern ◆ **to** ~ **a covert** ein Tier aus seinem Versteck aufstöbern *or* aufjagen.
(o) to ~ **sth to a close** etw zu Ende bringen, etw beenden.
[2] *vi* **(a)** *(move, come: of person, time, event)* kommen ◆ **he drew towards the door** er bewegte sich auf die Tür zu; **he drew to one side** er ging/fuhr zur Seite; **to** ~ **round the table** sich um den Tisch versammeln; **to** ~ **to an end** zu Ende gehen; **he drew ahead of the other runners** er zog den anderen

Läufern davon; **the two horses drew level** die beiden Pferde zogen gleich; **to ~ near** herankommen (*to* an *+acc*); **to ~ nearer** (immer) näher (heran)kommen (*to* an *+acc*); *see* **near**.
(b) (*allow airflow: of chimney, pipe*) ziehen.
(c) (*Sport: of teams in matches*) unentschieden spielen ◆ **they drew 2-2** sie trennten sich *or* spielten 2:2 unentschieden; **the teams drew for second place** im Kampf um den 2. Platz trennten sich die Mannschaften unentschieden.
(d) (*Cards*) **to ~ for partners** die Partner durch Kartenziehen bestimmen.
(e) (*infuse: tea*) ziehen.
3 *n* **(a)** (*lottery*) Ziehung, Ausspielung *f*; (*for sports competitions*) Auslosung, Ziehung *f*; *see* **luck**.
(b) (*Sport*) Unentschieden *nt* ◆ **the match ended in a ~** das Spiel endete unentschieden *or* mit einem Unentschieden; **the team had five wins and two ~s** die Mannschaft hat fünfmal gewonnen und zweimal unentschieden gespielt.
(c) (*attraction: play, film etc*) (Kassen)schlager, Knüller (*inf*) *m*; (*person*) Attraktion *f*.
(d) to be quick on the ~ (*lit*) schnell mit der Pistole sein, schnell (den Revolver) ziehen; (*fig*) schlagfertig sein; **to beat sb to the ~** schneller sein als jd; (*lit: cowboy etc also*) schneller ziehen als jd.

◆**draw alongside** *vi* heranfahren/-kommen (*+prep obj* an *+acc*).

◆**draw apart** 1 *vi* (*move away*) sich lösen; (*couple*) sich auseinanderleben; (*from political party etc*) abrücken.
2 *vt sep person* beiseite nehmen.

◆**draw aside** *vt sep person* beiseite nehmen; *curtains* zur Seite ziehen.

◆**draw away** 1 *vi* **(a)** (*move off: car etc*) losfahren; (*procession*) sich entfernen. **(b)** (*move ahead: runner etc*) davonziehen (*from sb* jdm). **(c)** (*move away: person*) sich entfernen ◆ **she drew ~ from him when he put his arm around her** sie rückte von ihm ab, als er den Arm um sie legte.
2 *vt sep person* weglocken; *object* wegnehmen.

◆**draw back** 1 *vi* zurückweichen.
2 *vt sep* zurückziehen; *curtains also* aufziehen.

◆**draw down** *vt sep blinds* herunterlassen ◆ **to ~ sth ~ on oneself** (*fig*) etw auf sich (*acc*) ziehen.

◆**draw in** 1 *vi* **(a)** (*train*) einfahren; (*car*) anhalten.
(b) (*get shorter: days*) kürzer werden.
2 *vt sep* **(a)** *breath, air* einziehen.
(b) (*attract, gain*) *crowds* anziehen ◆ **to ~ sb ~ on a project** jdn für ein Projekt gewinnen; **I don't want to be ~n ~to your problems** ich möchte nicht in Ihre Probleme verwickelt *or* hineingezogen werden.
(c) to ~ ~ one's claws (*lit, fig*) die Krallen einziehen; *see* **horn**.
(d) (*pull on*) *reins* anziehen ◆ **to ~ ~ one's belt** den Gürtel enger schnallen.

◆**draw off** 1 *vi* (*car*) losfahren.
2 *vt sep* **(a)** *gloves, garment* ausziehen. **(b)** *excess liquid* abgießen; *blood* abnehmen.

◆**draw on** 1 *vi* **as the night drew ~** mit fortschreitender Nacht; **winter ~s ~** der Winter naht; **time is ~ing ~** es wird spät.
2 *vi +prep obj* (*use as source: also* **~ upon**) sich stützen auf (*+acc*) ◆ **you'll have to ~ ~ your powers of imagination** Sie müssen Ihre Phantasie zu Hilfe nehmen; **the author ~s ~ his experiences in the desert** der Autor schöpft aus seinen Erfahrungen in der Wüste.
3 *vt sep* (*put on*) *stockings, gloves* anziehen.

◆**draw out** 1 *vi* **(a)** (*train*) ausfahren; (*car*) herausfahren (*of* aus). **(b)** (*become longer: days*) länger werden.
2 *vt sep* **(a)** (*take out*) herausziehen.
(b) (*make longer*) ziehen ◆ **he drew the elastic ~ as far as it would go** er zog das Gummi so lang, wie es ging.
(c) (*prolong*) in die Länge ziehen, hinausziehen ◆ **a long-~n-~ meeting** eine sehr in die Länge gezogene Konferenz.
(d) (*cause to speak*) **to ~ sb ~/sb ~ of his shell** jdn aus der Reserve locken.

◆**draw over** *vi* **the policeman told the motorist to ~ ~ (to the side of the road)** der Polizist sagte dem Autofahrer, er solle an den Straßenrand fahren.

◆**draw together** *vt sep threads* miteinander verknüpfen; *bits of argument also* in einen Zusammenhang bringen.

◆**draw up** 1 *vi* (*stop: car*) (an)halten.
2 *vt sep* **(a)** (*formulate*) entwerfen; *contract, agreement also, will* aufsetzen; *list* aufstellen.
(b) *chair* heranziehen; *boat* aufschleppen (*spec*), an Land ziehen ◆ **to ~ oneself ~ (to one's full height)** sich (zu seiner vollen Größe) aufrichten.
(c) (*set in line*) *troops* aufstellen.
(d) (*make stop*) **this thought drew him ~ sharp** dieser Gedanke ließ ihn mit einem Ruck innehalten.

◆**draw upon** *vi +prep obj see* **draw on 2**.

draw: ~back *n* Nachteil *m*; **~bridge** *n* Zugbrücke *f*.

drawee [drɔːˈiː] *n* (*Fin*) Bezogene(r) *mf*; Trassat *m* (*spec*).

drawer *n* **(a)** [drɔːʳ] (*in desk etc*) Schublade *f*; *see* **chest**[1]. **(b)** [ˈdrɔːəʳ] (*person: of pictures*) Zeichner *m*. **(c)** [ˈdrɔːəʳ] (*of cheque etc*) Aussteller, Trassant (*spec*) *m*. **(d) ~s** [drɔːz] *pl* (*dated, hum*) (*for men*) Unterhose(n *pl*) *f*; (*for women also*) Schlüpfer *m*.

drawing [ˈdrɔːɪŋ] *n* Zeichnung *f* ◆ **I'm no good at ~** ich bin nicht gut im Zeichnen, ich kann nicht gut zeichnen.

drawing: ~-board *n* Reißbrett *nt*; **the scheme is still on the ~-board** (*fig*) das Projekt ist noch in der Planung; **well, it's back to the ~-board** (*fig*) das muß noch einmal ganz neu überdacht werden; **~ paper** *n* Zeichenpapier *nt*; **~ pen** *n* Zeichenfeder *f*; **~-pin** *n* (*Brit*) Reißzwecke *f*; **~ room** *n* Wohnzimmer *nt*; (*in mansion*) Salon *m*.

drawl [drɔːl] 1 *vi* schleppend sprechen.
2 *vt* schleppend aussprechen.
3 *n* schleppende Sprache ◆ **a Texan/Southern ~** schleppendes Texanisch/ein schleppender südlicher Dialekt.

drawn [drɔːn] 1 *ptp of* **draw**[1] *and* **draw**[2].
2 *adj* **(a)** (*haggard*) (*from tiredness*) abgespannt; (*from worry*) abgehärmt, verhärmt ◆ **his face ~ with pain** sein vor Schmerzen verzerrtes Gesicht. **(b)** (*equal*) *game, match* unentschieden.

drawstring [ˈdrɔːstrɪŋ] *n* Kordel *f* zum Zuziehen.

dray [dreɪ] *n* Rollwagen *f*.

dray: ~-horse *n* Zugpferd *nt*; (*in brewery*) Brauereipferd *nt*; **~man** *n* Rollkutscher *m*.

dread [dred] 1 *vt* sich fürchten vor (*+dat*), große Angst haben vor (*+dat*) ◆ **his violent temper was ~ed by the whole school** seine Wutausbrüche waren von der ganzen Schule gefürchtet; **the ~ed monster from outer space** das gefürchtete Ungeheuer aus dem All; **and now the ~ed moment, here are the exam results** der mit Schrecken erwartete Augenblick ist da, hier sind die Examensergebnisse; **I ~ to think what may happen** ich wage nicht daran zu denken, was passieren könnte; **I ~** *or* **I'm ~ing seeing her again** ich denke mit Schrecken an ein Wiedersehen mit ihr; **he ~s going to the dentist** er hat schreckliche Angst davor, zum Zahnarzt zu gehen; **I ~ to think of it** (*inf*) das wage ich nicht, mir vorzustellen.
2 *n* **an object of ~ to the whole world** etwas, was der ganzen Welt Furcht und Schrecken einjagt; **to go** *or* **live in ~ of the secret police/being found out** in ständiger Angst vor der Geheimpolizei leben/in ständiger Angst davor leben, entdeckt zu werden.
3 *adj* (*liter*) gefürchtet.

▼ **dreadful** [ˈdredfʊl] *adj* schrecklich, furchtbar ◆ **what a ~ thing to happen** wie entsetzlich *or* furchtbar, daß das passieren mußte; **I feel ~** (*ill*) ich fühle mich schrecklich *or* scheußlich; (*mortified*) es ist mir schrecklich peinlich.

dreadfully [ˈdredfəlɪ] *adv* schrecklich ◆ **are you keen to come? — not ~** (*inf*) möchten Sie gern kommen? — nicht übermäßig.

dreadlocks [ˈdredlɒks] *npl* Dreadlocks *pl*.

dreadnought [ˈdrednɔːt] *n* (*Naut*) Dreadnought *m*.

▼ **dream** [driːm] (*vb: pret, ptp* **dreamt** *or* **~ed**) 1 *n* **(a)** Traum *m* ◆ **to have a bad ~** schlecht träumen; **the whole business was like a bad ~** die ganze Angelegenheit war wie ein böser Traum; **sweet ~s!** träum was Schönes!, träume süß!; **to have a ~ about sb/sth** von jdm/etw träumen; **to see sb/sth in a ~** jdn/etw im Traum sehen; **life is but a ~** das Leben ist nur ein Traum; **it worked like a ~** (*inf*) das ging wie im Traum.
(b) (*when awake*) **lost in ~s** traumverloren; **she goes round in a ~** sie lebt wie im Traum; **to be in a ~** (mit offenen Augen) träumen; **to go into a ~** zu träumen anfangen; **sorry, I didn't hear you, I was in a ~** Entschuldigung, ich habe Sie nicht gehört, ich habe geträumt.
(c) (*fantasy, vision*) Traum *m* ◆ **the house of his ~s** das Haus seiner Träume, sein Traumhaus; **she was happy beyond her wildest ~s** sie war so glücklich, wie sie es in ihren kühnsten Träumen nicht für möglich gehalten hätte; **to have ~s of becoming rich** davon träumen, reich zu werden; **all his ~s came true** all seine Träume gingen in Erfüllung; **I have a ~ of a better world** ich träume von einer besseren Welt; **it's just idle ~s** das sind nichts als Wunschträume.
(d) (*inf*) Schatz *m* ◆ **darling, you're a ~!** Liebling, du bist ein Schatz; **a ~ of a hat** ein traumhaft schöner Hut; **a ~ of a girl** ein Schatz von einem Mädchen; **a ~ of a father** ein toller Vater.
2 *vi* (*lit, fig*) träumen (*about, of* von) ◆ **I'm sorry, I was ~ing** es tut mir leid, ich habe geträumt.
▼ 3 *vt* (*lit, fig*) träumen; *dream* haben ◆ **he ~s of being free one day** er träumt davon, eines Tages frei zu sein; **I should never have ~t of doing such a thing** ich hätte nicht im Traum daran gedacht, so etwas zu tun; **I wouldn't ~ of it/of telling her** das würde mir nicht im Traum einfallen/es fiele mir nicht im Traum ein, es ihr zu erzählen; **I little ~t it would be so complicated** ich habe mir nicht träumen lassen, daß es so kompliziert sein würde; **I never ~t (that) he would come** ich hätte mir nie *or* nicht träumen lassen, daß er kommen würde.
4 *adj attr car, holiday* Traum- ◆ **~boat** (*dated sl*) Traumfrau *f*/-mann *m*; **~land** Traumland *nt*; **~ world** Traumwelt *f*.

◆**dream away** *vt sep time* verträumen; *one's life* mit Träumen verbringen.

◆**dream up** *vt sep* (*inf*) *idea* sich (*dat*) einfallen lassen *or* ausdenken ◆ **where did you ~ that ~?** wie bist du denn bloß darauf gekommen?

dreamer [ˈdriːməʳ] *n* Träumer(in *f*) *m*.

dreamily [ˈdriːmɪlɪ] *adv* verträumt.

dreamless [ˈdriːmlɪs] *adj sleep* traumlos.

dreamlike [ˈdriːmlaɪk] *adj* traumähnlich; *music* traumhaft.

dreamt [dremt] *pret, ptp of* **dream**.

dream ticket *n* (*Pol etc, inf*) (*individual*) ideale Besetzung; (*pair*) Traumpaar *nt*; (*group*) ideales Team.

dreamy [ˈdriːmɪ] *adj* (*+er*) **(a)** *person* verträumt; *expression also* versonnen. **(b)** *music* zum Träumen ◆ **soft ~ colours** weiche, verträumte Farben; **the ~ quality of the music** die Verträumtheit der Musik. **(c)** (*inf: lovely*) traumhaft.

drear [drɪəʳ] *adj* (*poet*) *see* **dreary**.

drearily [ˈdrɪərɪlɪ] *adv* eintönig, langweilig; *say, stare* trüb ◆ **the music droned on ~ for another hour** die Musik plärrte noch eine Stunde weiter; **it rained ~ all day** den ganzen Tag über war es trüb und regnerisch.

➤ LANGUAGE IN USE: **dreadful** → 7.3 **dream: 3** → 12.3

dreariness ['drɪərɪnɪs] *n see adj* Eintönigkeit *f*; Trübheit *f*; Langweiligkeit, Farblosigkeit *f*.

dreary ['drɪərɪ] *adj* (+*er*) eintönig; *weather* trüb; *person, speech* langweilig, farblos ◆ **how ~ for you!** wie langweilig für Sie.

dredge[1] [dredʒ] [1] *n* Bagger *m*; (*net*) Schleppnetz *nt*; (*vessel*) *see* **dredger**[1].
[2] *vt river, canal* ausbaggern, schlämmen.

◆**dredge up** *vt sep* (*lit*) ausbaggern; (*fig*) *unpleasant facts* ans Licht zerren.

dredge[2] *vt* (*Cook*) bestäuben, bestreuen.

dredger[1] ['dredʒəʳ] *n* (*ship*) Schwimmbagger *m*; (*machine*) Bagger *m*.

dredger[2] *n* (*Cook*) Streuer *m*; (*also* **sugar ~**) Zuckerstreuer *m*.

dredging[1] ['dredʒɪŋ] *n* Ausbaggern *nt*.

dredging[2] *n* (*Cook*) Bestreuen *nt*.

dregs [dregz] *npl* **(a)** (Boden)satz *m* ◆ **to drink sth to the ~** etw bis auf den letzten Tropfen austrinken. **(b)** (*fig*) Abschaum *m* ◆ **the ~ of society** der Abschaum der Gesellschaft.

drench [drentʃ] *vt* **(a)** durchnässen ◆ **I'm absolutely ~ed** ich bin durch und durch naß; **to get ~ed to the skin** bis auf die Haut naß werden; **sprinkle some water on it, don't ~ it** besprengen Sie es mit Wasser, aber ersäufen Sie es nicht (*inf*).
(b) (*Vet*) Arznei einflößen (+*dat*).

drenching ['drentʃɪŋ] [1] *n* **to get a ~** bis auf die Haut naß werden.
[2] *adj*: **~ rain** Regen, der bis auf die Haut durchgeht; **he's been working out in the ~ rain all day** er hat den ganzen Tag draußen im strömenden Regen gearbeitet.

Dresden ['drezdən] *n* (*also* **~ china**) ≃ Meißner Porzellan *nt*.

dress [dres] [1] *n* **(a)** (*for woman*) Kleid *nt*.
(b) *no pl* (*clothing*) Kleidung *f* ◆ **articles of ~** Kleidungsstücke *pl*; **to be in eastern ~** orientalisch gekleidet sein.
(c) *no pl* (*way of dressing*) Kleidung *f*, Kleider *pl* ◆ **to be modest/careless in one's ~** sich einfach/nachlässig kleiden.
[2] *vt* **(a)** (*clothe*) *child* anziehen; *family* kleiden; *recruits etc* einkleiden ◆ **to get ~ed** sich anziehen; **are you ~ed?** bist du schon angezogen?; **he's old enough to ~ himself** er ist alt genug, um sich allein anzuziehen; **to ~ sb in sth** jdm etw anziehen; **she ~es herself with great fastidiousness** sie kleidet sich sehr sorgfältig; **~ed in black** in Schwarz, schwarz gekleidet; **~ed in a sailor's uniform** im Matrosenanzug; **to be ~ed for the country/town/tennis** fürs Land/für die Stadt/zum Tennisspielen angezogen sein.
(b) (*Theat*) *play* Kostüme entwerfen für.
(c) (*arrange, decorate*) (*Naut*) *ship* beflaggen; (*Comm*) *shop-window* dekorieren ◆ **to ~ sb's hair** jdm das Haar frisieren.
(d) (*Cook*) *salad* anmachen; *food for table* anrichten; *chicken* brat- *or* kochfertig machen ◆ **~ed crab** farcierter Krebs.
(e) *skins* gerben; *material* appretieren; *timber* hobeln; *stone* schleifen.
(f) *wound* verbinden.
(g) *troops* ausrichten.
(h) (*Agr*) *fields* vorbereiten.
[3] *vi* **(a)** sich anziehen *or* kleiden ◆ **to ~ in black** sich schwarz kleiden; **she ~es very well** sie zieht sich sehr gut an *or* kleidet sich sehr gut; **to ~ for dinner** sich zum Essen umziehen.
(b) (*soldiers*) sich ausrichten ◆ **right, ~!** rechts, richt't euch!

◆**dress down** *vt sep* **(a)** *horse* striegeln. **(b)** *see* **dressing down**.

◆**dress up** [1] *vi* **(a)** (*in smart clothes*) sich feinmachen, sich schön anziehen.
(b) (*in fancy dress*) sich verkleiden ◆ **he came ~ed ~ as Father Christmas** er kam als Weihnachtsmann (verkleidet); **to ~ ~ as a pirate** sich als Pirat verkleiden.
[2] *vt sep* **(a)** (*disguise*) verkleiden ◆ **it's just his old plan ~ed ~ in a new way** das ist bloß sein alter Plan in einem neuen Gewand. **(b)** (*smarten*) *sb* herausputzen ◆ **~ yourself ~ a bit!** mach dich ein bißchen schön!

dressage ['dresɑːʒ] *n* Dressur *f*.

dress: ~ circle *n* erster Rang; **~ coat** *n* Frack *m*; **~ designer** *n* Modezeichner(in *f*) *m*.

dresser[1] ['dresəʳ] *n* **(a)** (*Theat*) Garderobier *m*, Garderobiere *f*. **(b)** (*Med*) **his ~** sein Assistent bei der Operation. **(c)** (*tool: for wood*) Hobel *m*; (*for stone*) Schleifstein *m*. **(d)** (*Comm: also* **window-~**) Dekorateur(in *f*) *m*. **(e) she's a stylish ~** sie kleidet sich stilvoll.

dresser[2] *n* **(a)** Anrichte *f*. **(b)** (*US: dressing-table*) Frisierkommode *f*.

dressing ['dresɪŋ] *n* **(a)** (*act*) Anziehen, Ankleiden *nt*.
(b) (*Med: bandage, ointment*) Verband *m*.
(c) (*Cook*) Soße *f*.
(d) (*Agr*) Dünger *m* ◆ **a ~ of phosphate** Phosphatdünger *m*.
(e) (*of material*) Appretieren *nt*; (*of stone*) Schleifen *nt*; (*of leather*) Gerben *nt*; (*of wood*) Hobeln *nt*; (*for material*) Appreturmittel *nt*; (*for leather*) Gerbmittel *nt*.

dressing: ~ down *n* (*inf*) Standpauke *f* (*inf*); **to give sb a ~ down** jdn herunterputzen (*inf*), jdm eine Standpauke halten; **to get a ~ down** eins auf den Deckel *or* das Dach kriegen (*inf*); **~-gown** *n* (*in towelling: for bather, boxer, etc*) Bademantel *m*; (*for women: négligé*) Morgenrock *m*; **~-room** *n* (*in house*) Ankleidezimmer *nt*; (*Theat*) (Künstler)garderobe *f*; (*Sport*) Umkleidekabine *f*; **~-station** *n* Verbandsplatz *m*; **~-table** *n* Frisiertoilette *or* -kommode *f*; **~-table set** Toilettengarnitur *f*.

dress: ~maker *n* (Damen)schneider(in *f*) *m*; **~making** *n* Schneidern *nt*; **~ rehearsal** *n* (*lit, fig*) Generalprobe *f*; **~ shield** *n* Arm- *or* Schweißblatt *nt*; **~ shirt** *n* Frackhemd *nt*; **~ suit** *n* Abendanzug *m*; **~ uniform** *n* Galauniform *f*.

dressy ['dresɪ] *adj* (+*er*) (*inf*) *person* fein angezogen, aufgedonnert (*pej*) ◆ **she's a very ~ person** sie ist immer sehr fein angezogen; **do you think I look a bit too ~?** meinst du, daß ich zu fein angezogen bin?; **a long skirt would be a bit too ~** ein langer Rock wäre etwas übertrieben; **you need something a bit more ~** es müßte etwas Eleganteres sein.

drew [druː] *pret of* **draw**[1] *and* **draw**[2].

dribble ['drɪbl] [1] *vi* **(a)** (*liquids*) tropfen. **(b)** (*baby, person*) sabbern; (*animal*) geifern. **(c)** (*Sport*) dribbeln. **(d)** (*people*) **to ~ back/in** *etc* kleckerweise (*inf*) zurückkommen/hereinkommen *etc*.
[2] *vt* **(a)** (*Sport*) **to ~ the ball** mit dem Ball dribbeln.
(b) (*baby etc*) kleckern ◆ **to ~ saliva** sabbern; **he ~d his milk all down his chin** er kleckerte sich (*dat*) Milch übers Kinn.
[3] *n* **(a)** (*of water*) ein paar Tropfen ◆ **a slow ~ of water was still coming out of the pipe** es tröpfelte immer noch etwas aus der Leitung. **(b)** (*of saliva*) Tropfen *m* ◆ **don't expect me to clean up all your dog's ~** erwarten Sie nicht, daß ich dauernd aufwische, wo Ihr Hund gesabbert hat. **(c)** (*Sport*) Dribbling *nt*.

dribbler ['drɪbləʳ] *n* **(a)** (*Sport*) Dribbelkünstler, Dribbler *m*. **(b) he's a terrible ~** (*when drinking etc*) er kleckert ständig (*inf*).

driblet ['drɪblɪt] *n* (*drop*) Tropfen *m* ◆ **in ~s** (*money*) in kleinen Raten, kleckerweise (*inf*); **~s of intelligence began to come through** Informationen fingen an durchzusickern.

dribs and drabs ['drɪbzən'dræbz] *npl*: **in ~** kleckerweise (*inf*).

dried [draɪd] *adj* getrocknet; *fruit also* Dörr- ◆ **~ eggs/milk** Trockenei *nt*/-milch *f*, Ei-/Milchpulver *nt*.

drier *n see* **dryer**.

drift [drɪft] [1] *vi* **(a)** (*Naut, Aviat, snow*) treiben; (*sand*) wehen; (*Rad*) verschwimmen ◆ **to ~ off course** abtreiben; **rally drivers have a technique of ~ing round corners** Rallye-Fahrer haben eine Technik, sich durch Kurven tragen zu lassen.
(b) (*fig: person*) sich treiben lassen ◆ **to let things ~** die Dinge treiben lassen; **he ~ed into marriage** er ist in die Ehe hineingeschlittert (*inf*); **he ~ed from job to job** er ließ sich planlos von Job zu Job treiben; **he was ~ing aimlessly along** er wanderte ziellos umher; (*in life etc*) er lebte planlos in den Tag hinein, er ließ sich plan- und ziellos treiben; **the nation was ~ing towards a crisis** das Land trieb auf eine Krise zu; **young people are ~ing away from the villages** junge Leute wandern aus den Dörfern ab; **to ~ apart** (*people*) sich auseinanderleben; **we're ~ing apart** wir leben uns immer mehr auseinander; **as the smoke ~ed away** als sich der Rauch verzog; **the audience started ~ing away** das Publikum begann wegzugehen.
[2] *vt* treiben; (*wind*) *clouds, snow also* vor sich her treiben.
[3] *n* **(a)** (*of air, water current*) Strömung *f* ◆ **the ~ of the current** (*speed*) die (Stärke der) Strömung; (*direction*) die Strömung(srichtung).
(b) (*mass caused by ~ing*) (*of sand, fallen snow*) Verwehung *f*; (*of leaves*) Haufen *m*.
(c) (*of ship, aircraft*) (Ab)drift, Abweichung *f* ◆ **to allow for ~** Abdriften *or* Abweichungen (mit) einkalkulieren.
(d) (*Geol: deposits*) Geschiebe *nt* ◆ **glacial ~** Moräne *f*; **continental ~** Kontinentalverschiebung *or* -drift *f*.
(e) (*tendency*) **the ~ to the city** der Drang in die Stadt; **moving with the general ~ of events** dem allgemeinen Zug der Ereignisse folgend; **the ~ of opinion away from this view** das (allmähliche) Abrücken von dieser Ansicht.
(f) (*general meaning: of questions*) Richtung, Tendenz *f* ◆ **I caught the ~ of what he said** ich verstand, worauf er hinauswollte; **if I get your ~** wenn ich Sie recht verstehe.
(g) (*Ling*) Tendenz *f*.

drift anchor *n* (*Naut*) Treibanker *m*.

drifter ['drɪftəʳ] *n* **(a)** (*person*) Gammler *m* ◆ **he's a bit of a ~** ihn hält's nirgends lange; **there's no place for ~s in this business** ziellose und unentschlossene Leute haben in diesem Geschäft keinen Platz. **(b)** (*boat*) Drifter *m*.

drift: ~-ice *n* Treibeis *nt*; **~ing mine** *n* Treibmine *f*; **~-net** *n* Treibnetz *nt*; **~sand** *n* Treibsand *m*; **~wood** *n* Treibholz *nt*.

drill[1] [drɪl] [1] *n* (*for metal, wood, oil, dentist's*) Bohrer *m*.
[2] *vti* bohren ◆ **to ~ for oil** nach Öl bohren; **have they started ~ing yet?** haben sie schon mit den Bohrungen angefangen?

◆**drill down** *vi* (in die Tiefe) bohren ◆ **we kept ~ing ~ until we hit oil** wir bohrten bis wir auf Öl stießen; **we ~ed ~ 500 feet** wir bohrten in eine Tiefe von 500 Fuß.

drill[2] [1] *n* **(a)** *no pl* (*esp Mil, fig*) Drill *m*; (*marching etc*) Exerzieren *nt* ◆ **we get ~ every morning** jeden Morgen müssen wir exerzieren.
(b) (*in grammar etc*) Drillübung *f* ◆ **pattern ~** Patterndrill *m*.
(c) (*inf: procedure*) **what's the ~?** wie geht das?, wie macht man das?; **he doesn't know the ~** er weiß nicht, wie der Laden läuft (*inf*) *or* wie die Sache angefaßt werden muß.
[2] *vt* **(a)** *soldiers* drillen; (*in marching etc*) exerzieren. **(b) to ~ pupils in grammar** mit den Schülern Grammatik pauken. **(c) to ~ good manners into a child** einem Kind gute Manieren eindrillen (*inf*); **I ~ed it into him that he must not ...** ich habe es ihm eingebläut (*inf*), daß er nicht ... darf.
[3] *vi* (*Mil*) gedrillt werden; (*marching etc*) exerzieren.

drill[3] (*Agr*) [1] *n* **(a)** (*furrow*) Furche *f*. **(b)** (*machine*) Drillmaschine *f*.
[2] *vt* drillen.

drill[4] *n* (*Tex*) Drillich *m*.

drill ground *n* Exerzierplatz *m*.

drilling ['drɪlɪŋ] *n* (*for oil*) Bohrung *f*; (*by dentist*) Bohren *nt* ◆ **when does ~**

start? wann fangen die Bohrungen an?; **~ operations begin next week** die Bohrungen fangen nächste Woche an; **~ rig** Bohrturm *m*; *(at sea)* Bohrinsel *f*.

drill sergeant *n* Ausbilder *m*.

drily ['draɪlɪ] *adv see* **dryly**.

drink [drɪŋk] *(vb: pret* **drank**, *ptp* **drunk**) [1] *n* **(a)** *(liquid to ~)* Getränk *nt* ◆ **food and ~** Essen und Getränke; **may I have a ~?** kann ich etwas zu trinken haben?; **would you like a ~ of water?** möchten Sie etwas Wasser?; **to give sb a ~** jdm etwas zu trinken geben; **~s can** Getränkedose *f*.
(b) *(glass of alcoholic ~)* Glas *nt*, Drink *m* ◆ **have a ~!** trink doch was *or* einen!; **let's have a ~** trinken wir was; **I need a ~!** ich brauche was zu trinken!; **he likes a ~** er trinkt gern (einen); **to ask friends in for ~s** Freunde auf ein Glas *or* einen Drink einladen; **afterwards there will be ~s** anschließend Getränke; **he's got a few ~s in him** *(inf)* er hat einige intus *(inf)*.
(c) *no pl (alcoholic liquor)* Alkohol *m* ◆ **the ~ problem** der Alkoholismus; **he has a ~ problem** er trinkt; **~ was his ruin** der Alkohol hat ihn ruiniert; **to be the worse for ~** betrunken sein; **to take to ~** zu trinken anfangen; **his worries/she drove him to ~** vor lauter Sorgen fing er an zu trinken/sie war der Grund, warum er zu trinken anfing; **it's enough to drive you to ~!** da könnte man wirklich zum Trinker werden.
(d) *(esp Naut, Aviat sl: sea)* Bach *m (sl)* ◆ **three planes went down into the ~** drei Flugzeuge gingen in den Bach *(sl)*.
[2] *vt* trinken ◆ **would you like something to ~?** möchten Sie etwas zu trinken (haben)?; **is the water fit to ~?** ist das Trinkwasser?, kann man das Wasser trinken?; **he ~s all his wages** er vertrinkt seinen ganzen Lohn; **to ~ oneself into debt** Haus und Hof versaufen *(inf)*; **to ~ oneself silly** sich dumm und dämlich trinken *(inf) or* saufen *(inf)*; **this car ~s petrol** dieses Auto säuft das Benzin nur so *(inf)*; **they drank the pub dry** sie tranken die Kneipe leer.
[3] *vi* trinken ◆ **he doesn't ~** er trinkt nicht, er trinkt keinen Alkohol; **his father drank** sein Vater hat getrunken *or* war Trinker; **to go out ~ing** einen trinken gehen; **one shouldn't ~ and drive** nach dem Trinken soll man nicht fahren; **~ing and driving** Alkohol am Steuer; **to ~ to sb** auf jdn trinken; *(to one's neighbour at table etc)* jdm zuprosten *or* zutrinken; **to ~ to sth** auf etw *(acc)* trinken; **I'll ~ to that** darauf trinke ich.

◆**drink away** *vt sep fortune* vertrinken; *sorrows* im Alkohol ersäufen.

◆**drink down** *vt sep* hinuntertrinken, hinunterschlucken.

◆**drink in** *vt sep* **(a)** *(plants etc) water* aufsaugen; *(person) air* einsaugen, einatmen; *sunshine* in sich *(acc)* aufsaugen. **(b)** *(fig) a sight, his words etc* (begierig) in sich aufnehmen.

◆**drink off** *vt sep* austrinken, leeren ◆ **he drank ~ the wine in one long gulp** er trank den Wein in einem Zug aus.

◆**drink up** [1] *vi* austrinken ◆ **~ ~!** trink aus!
[2] *vt sep* austrinken.

drinkable ['drɪŋkəbl] *adj* **(a)** *(not poisonous) water* trinkbar, Trink-. **(b)** *(palatable)* genießbar, trinkbar ◆ **a very ~ little wine** ein sehr süffiges Weinchen.

drink-driving ['drɪŋk'draɪvɪŋ] [1] *n* Trunkenheit *f* am Steuer.
[2] *attr conviction* wegen Trunkenheit am Steuer ◆ **the number of ~ offences** die Zahl der Fälle von Trunkenheit am Steuer.

drinker ['drɪŋkəʳ] *n* Trinker(in *f*) *m*.

drinking ['drɪŋkɪŋ] *n (act)* Trinken *nt*; *(drunkenness)* das Trinken, das Saufen *(inf)* ◆ **there was a lot of heavy ~** es wurde viel getrunken; **his ~ caused his marriage to break up** an seiner Trunksucht ging seine Ehe in die Brüche; **under-age ~** der Alkoholkonsum von Minderjährigen.

drinking: ~ bout *n* Sauftour *f (inf)*; **to go on a ~ bout** auf Sauftour gehen *(inf)*; **when his wife died he went on a ~ bout for three months** als seine Frau starb, hat er drei Monate lang nur getrunken; **~ chocolate** *n* Trinkschokolade *f*; **~ companion** *n* Saufbruder *(inf)*, Zechkumpan *m*; **~ fountain** *n* Trinkwasserbrunnen *m*; **~-song** *n* Trinklied *nt*; **~ trough** *n* Tränke *f*; **~-up time** *n (Brit) die letzten zehn Minuten vor der Polizeistunde*; **~-water** *n* Trinkwasser *nt*.

drip [drɪp] [1] *vi (water, tap)* tropfen ◆ **careful with that beer, you're ~ping!** paß auf mit dem Bier, es tropft!; **to be ~ping with sweat/blood** schweißüberströmt *or* schweißgebadet sein/vor Blut triefen; **sweat was ~ping off his forehead** der Schweiß triefte ihm von der Stirn; **the walls were ~ping (with water)** die Wände waren triefnaß; **the film positively ~s with sentimentality** der Film trieft förmlich vor Schmalz.
[2] *vt liquid* träufeln, tropfen ◆ **he was ~ping water/blood all over the carpet** Wasser/sein Blut tropfte überall auf den Teppich; **his clothes were ~ping water all over the carpet** von seinen Kleidern tropfte Wasser überall auf den Teppich; **careful, you're ~ping paint over my coat** paß auf, die Farbe tropft mir auf den Mantel!
[3] *n* **(a)** *(sound: of water, rain, tap)* Tropfen *nt*.
(b) *(drop)* Tropfen *m*.
(c) *(Med)* Infusionsapparat, Tropf *(inf) m* ◆ **to be on a ~** eine Infusion bekommen, am Tropf hängen *(inf)*.
(d) *(inf: silly person)* Flasche *f (inf)*.

drip: ~-dry [1] *adj shirt* bügelfrei; [2] *vt* tropfnaß aufhängen; [3] *vi* bügelfrei sein; **~-dry** *(on label)* bügelfrei; **let it ~-dry** hängen Sie es tropfnaß auf; **~-feed** *(Med)* [1] *n* künstliche Ernährung; [2] *vt* künstlich ernähren.

dripping ['drɪpɪŋ] [1] *n* **(a)** *(Cook)* Bratenfett *nt*.
(b) *(action: of water etc)* Tropfen *nt*.
[2] *adj* **(a)** *tap, trees* tropfend; *washing* tropfnaß.
(b) *(inf: very wet) coat, clothes* triefend, klatschnaß ◆ **I'm absolutely ~!** ich bin klatschnaß!; **~ wet** triefnaß, klatschnaß.
(c) **~ pan** *(Cook)* Fettpfanne *f*.

drippy ['drɪpɪ] *adj (+er) (inf) person* müde *(inf)*; *(sentimental) singer, film, novel* schmalzig; *(US) day* regnerisch.

drivability [draɪvə'bɪlɪtɪ] *n (Aut) (performance)* Fahreigenschaften *pl*; *(ease of handling)* Fahrkomfort *m*.

drive [draɪv] *(vb: pret* **drove**, *ptp* **driven**) [1] *n* **(a)** *(Aut: journey)* (Auto)fahrt *f* ◆ **to go for a ~** ein bißchen (raus)fahren; **to go for a ~ to the coast** ans Meer fahren; **he took her for a ~ in his new car** er machte mit ihr eine Spazierfahrt in seinem neuen Auto; **it's about one hour's ~ from London** es ist etwa eine Stunde Fahrt von London (entfernt).
(b) *(into house: also* **~way**) Einfahrt *f*; *(longer)* Auffahrt, Zufahrt *f*.
(c) *(Golf, Tennis)* Treibschlag *m*.
(d) *(Psych etc)* Trieb *m* ◆ **the sex ~** der Geschlechtstrieb, der Sexualtrieb.
(e) *(energy)* Schwung, Elan, Tatendrang *m* ◆ **you're losing your ~** Ihr Elan *or* Schwung läßt nach; **he has no ~ to improve his job** ihm fehlt es an Elan *or* Schwung, sich beruflich zu verbessern.
(f) *(Comm, Pol etc)* Aktion *f* ◆ **this is part of a ~ for new members** das ist Teil einer Mitgliederwerbeaktion; **fund-raising ~** Sammelaktion *f*; **sales ~** Verkaufskampagne *f*; *see* **export**.
(g) *(Mil: offensive)* kraftvolle Offensive.
(h) *(Mech: power transmission)* Antrieb *m* ◆ **front-wheel/rear-wheel ~** Vorderrad-/Hinterradantrieb *m*.
(i) *(Aut)* Steuerung *f* ◆ **left-hand ~** Linkssteuerung *f*.
(j) *(Cards) see* **whist**.
(k) *(Comput)* Laufwerk *nt*.
[2] *vt* **(a)** *(cause to move) people, animals, dust, clouds etc* treiben ◆ **to ~ sb out of the country** jdn aus dem Land (ver)- treiben; **Christ drove them out of the temple** Jesus vertrieb *or* jagte sie aus dem Tempel; **to ~ a nail/stake into sth** einen Nagel/Pfahl in etw *(acc)* treiben; **to ~ sth into sb's head** *(fig)* jdm etw einhämmern *or* einbläuen; **the gale drove the ship off course** der Sturm trieb das Schiff vom Kurs ab.
(b) *cart, car, train* fahren ◆ **he ~s a taxi (for a living)** er ist Taxifahrer, er fährt Taxi *(inf)*.
(c) *(convey in vehicle) person* fahren ◆ **I'll ~ you home** ich fahre Sie nach Hause; **could you ~ us there?** können Sie uns dahin fahren?
(d) *(provide power for, operate) motor (belt, shaft)* antreiben; *(electricity, fuel)* betreiben; *(Comput)* ansteuern ◆ **steam-~n train** Zug *m* mit Dampflokomotive; **machine ~n by electricity** elektrisch betriebene Maschine, Maschine mit Elektroantrieb.
(e) *(Tennis, Golf) ball* driven *(spec)* ◆ **to ~ the ball** einen Treibball spielen.
(f) *(cause to be in a state or to become)* treiben ◆ **to ~ sb/oneself mad** *or* **round the bend** *(inf)* jdn/sich selbst verrückt machen; **to ~ sb to rebellion** jdn in die Rebellion treiben; **I was ~n to it** ich wurde dazu getrieben; **who/what drove you to do that?** wer/was trieb *or* brachte Sie dazu(, das zu tun)?
(g) *(force to work hard) person* hart herannehmen, schinden *(pej)* ◆ **you're driving him too hard** Sie nehmen ihn zu hart ran, Sie schinden ihn zu sehr; **you don't ~ them hard enough** Sie nehmen sie nicht hart genug ran; **he ~s himself very hard** er fordert sich selbst sehr stark.
(h) *tunnel* treiben; *well* ausheben; *nail* schlagen.
[3] *vi* **(a)** *(travel in vehicle)* fahren ◆ **he's learning to ~** er lernt Auto fahren; **to ~ at 50 km an hour** mit (einer Geschwindigkeit von) 50 km in der Stunde fahren; **to ~ on the right** rechts fahren; **did you come by train? — no, we drove** sind Sie mit der Bahn gekommen? — nein, wir sind mit dem Auto gefahren; **it's cheaper to ~** mit dem Auto ist es billiger.
(b) *(move violently)* schlagen, peitschen ◆ **the rain was driving in our faces** der Regen peitschte uns *(dat)* ins Gesicht.

◆**drive along** [1] *vi (vehicle, person)* dahinfahren.
[2] *vt sep (wind, current) person, boat* (voran)treiben ◆ **he was ~n ~ by the wind** der Wind trieb ihn voran.

◆**drive at** *vi +prep obj (fig: intend, mean)* hinauswollen auf *(+acc)* ◆ **what are you driving ~?** worauf wollen Sie hinaus?; **I don't see what he's driving ~ in this article of his** ich weiß nicht, worauf er in seinem Artikel hinauswill.

◆**drive away** [1] *vi (car, person)* wegfahren.
[2] *vt sep (lit, fig) person, cares* vertreiben; *suspicions* zerstreuen.

◆**drive back** [1] *vi (car, person)* zurückfahren.
[2] *vt sep* **(a)** *(cause to retreat) person* zurückdrängen; *enemy also* zurücktreiben. **(b)** *(convey back in vehicle) person* zurückfahren.

◆**drive home** *vt sep nail* einschlagen, einhämmern; *argument* einhämmern ◆ **she drove ~ her point that ...** sie legte eindringlich und überzeugend dar, daß ...; **how can I ~ it ~ to him that it's urgent?** wie kann ich (es) ihm nur klarmachen, daß es dringend ist?

◆**drive in** [1] *vi (car, person)* (hinein)fahren ◆ **he drove ~to the garage** er fuhr in die Garage.
[2] *vt sep nail* (hin)einschlagen, (hin)einhämmern; *screw* (r)eindrehen.

◆**drive off** [1] *vi* **(a)** *(person, car)* weg- *or* abfahren. **(b)** *(Golf)* abschlagen.
[2] *vt sep* **(a)** *person, enemy* vertreiben. **(b)** **she was ~n ~ in a big Mercedes/an ambulance** sie fuhr in einem großen Mercedes weg/sie wurde in einem Krankenwagen weggebracht *or* abtransportiert.

◆**drive on** [1] *vi (person, car)* weiterfahren.
[2] *vt sep (incite, encourage) person* antreiben; *(to do sth bad)* anstiften.

◆**drive out** [1] *vi* heraus-/hinausfahren ◆ **he drove ~ onto the street** er fuhr auf die Straße (hinaus).
[2] *vt sep person* hinaustreiben *or* jagen; *evil thoughts* austreiben.

◆**drive over** [1] *vi* hinüberfahren.
[2] *vt always separate (in car) person* hinüberfahren ◆ **he drove his family ~ to**

see us er hat seine Familie (mit dem Auto) zu uns gebracht.
3 *vi +prep obj dog* überfahren.

◆**drive up** *vi (car, person)* vorfahren ◆ **a car drove ~ outside the house** ein Auto fuhr vor dem Haus vor.

drive: ~ belt *n* Treibriemen *m*; **~-in** *adj* **~-in cinema** Autokino *nt*; **~-in bank** Autoschalter *m*; **to watch a ~-in movie** sich (*dat*) einen Film in Autokino ansehen.

drivel ['drɪvl] 1 *n (pej)* Blödsinn, Kokolores (*inf*) *m* ◆ **what utter ~!** das ist ja kompletter Blödsinn!; **meaningless ~** leeres Gefasel.
2 *vi (pej)* Unsinn reden ◆ **what's he ~ling (on) about?** was faselt er da?, worüber labert er da? (*inf*).

driven ['drɪvn] *ptp of* **drive.**

-driven ['drɪvn] *suf* -betrieben.

driver ['draɪvəʳ] *n* **(a)** (*of car, taxi, lorry, bus*) Fahrer(in *f*) *m*; (*Brit: of locomotive*) Führer *m*; (*of coach*) Kutscher *m* ◆ **~'s seat** (*lit*) Fahrersitz *m*; **to be in the ~'s seat** (*fig*) das Steuer führen, die Zügel in der Hand haben. **(b)** (*of animals*) Treiber *m*. **(c)** (*golf-club*) Driver *m*. **(d)** (*Comput*) Treiber *m*.

driver's license *n (US)* Führerschein *m*.

drive: ~ shaft *n* Antriebswelle *f*; (*Aut*) Kardanwelle *f*; **~way** *n* Auffahrt *f*; (*longer*) Zufahrtsstraße *f or* -weg *m*; **~ wheel** *n* Antriebsrad, Treibrad *nt*.

driving ['draɪvɪŋ] 1 *n* Fahren *nt* ◆ **his ~ is awful** er fährt schrecklich (schlecht); **that was a very bad piece of ~** da sind Sie/ist er *etc* aber wirklich schlecht gefahren; **I do a lot of ~ in my job** in meinem Beruf muß ich sehr viel fahren; **~ is his hobby** Autofahren ist sein Hobby; **I don't like ~** ich fahre nicht gern (Auto); **dangerous ~** (*Jur*) rücksichtsloses Fahren.
2 *adj* **(a) he was the ~ force behind it all** bei der ganzen Angelegenheit war er die treibende Kraft.
(b) ~ rain peitschender Regen.

driving: ~ instructor *n* Fahrlehrer(in *f*) *m*; **~ iron** *n (Golf)* Driving-Iron *m*; **~ lesson** *n* Fahrstunde *f*; **~ licence** *n (Brit)* Führerschein *m*; **~ mirror** *n* Rückspiegel *m*; **~ range** *n (Golf)* Drivingrange *nt*; **~ school** *n* Fahrschule *f*; **~ test** *n* Fahrprüfung *f*; **to take/fail/pass one's ~ test** die Fahrprüfung machen/nicht bestehen/bestehen; **~ wheel** *n* Antriebsrad *nt*.

drizzle ['drɪzl] 1 *n* Nieselregen, Sprühregen *m*.
2 *vi* nieseln.

drizzly ['drɪzlɪ] *adj weather* Niesel- ◆ **it was such a ~ afternoon** es hat den ganzen Nachmittag so genieselt.

dromedary ['drɒmɪdərɪ] *n* Dromedar *nt*.

drone [drəʊn] 1 *n* **(a)** (*bee, fig*) Drohne *f*.
(b) (*sound*) (*of bees*) Summen *nt*; (*of engine, aircraft*) Brummen *nt*.
(c) (*monotonous way of speaking*) monotone Stimme.
(d) (*Mus*) (*bass voice part*) Baß *m*; (*of bagpipes*) Brummer *m*; (*sound*) Bordun(ton) *m*.
(e) (*Aviat: robot plane*) ferngesteuertes Flugzeug.
2 *vi* **(a)** (*bee*) summen; (*engine, aircraft*) brummen.
(b) (*speak monotonously: also* **~ away** *or* **on**) eintönig sprechen; (*in reciting*) leiern ◆ **he ~d on and on for hours** er redete stundenlang in seinem monotonen Tonfall; **we had to listen to him droning on** wir mußten seinem monotonen Geschwafel zuhören (*inf*).

◆**drone out** *vt sep speech* monoton vortragen; (*reciting*) leiern.

drool [druːl] *vi* sabbern.

◆**drool over** *vi +prep obj* richtig verliebt sein in (*+acc*) ◆ **the young mother ~s ~ her little boy** die junge Mutter ist ganz vernarrt in ihren kleinen Jungen; **he sat there ~ing ~ a copy of Playboy** er geilte sich an einem Playboyheft auf (*sl*).

droop [druːp] 1 *vi* **(a)** (*lit*) (*person*) vornüber gebeugt stehen, krumm stehen, sich schlecht halten; (*shoulders*) hängen; (*head*) herunterfallen; (*eyelids*) herunterhängen; (*with sleepiness*) zufallen; (*flowers*) die Köpfe hängen lassen; (*feathers, one's hand, breasts*) schlaff herunterhängen; (*rope, roof etc*) durchhängen ◆ **stand up straight, don't ~** halte dich aufrecht, steh nicht so krumm.
(b) (*fig: one's interest, energy*) erlahmen; (*audience etc*) erschlaffen, schlaff werden ◆ **his spirits were beginning to ~** sein Mut begann zu schwinden *or* sinken; **don't let your spirits ~** laß den Mut nicht sinken; **the heat made him ~** die Hitze machte ihn schlaff *or* matt.
2 *vt head* hängen lassen.
3 *n (lit)* (*of body*) Gebeugtsein *nt*; (*of eyelids*) Schwere *f* ◆ **I recognized her by the familiar ~ of her shoulders** ich habe sie an ihren hängenden Schultern erkannt.

drooping ['druːpɪŋ] *adj* **(a)** *head, shoulders, breasts, feathers, leaves, tail* hängend: *flowers* welk; *hand* herunterhängend; *eyelids* herunterhängend; (*with sleep*) schwer; *roof* durchhängend. **(b) a drink to revive his ~ spirits** ein Schluck, um seine (geschwundenen) Lebensgeister wieder zu wecken.

droopy ['druːpɪ] *adj* **(a)** schlaff; *tail* herabhängend; *moustache* nach unten hängend. **(b)** (*inf: tired, weak*) schlaff, schlapp (*inf*).

drop [drɒp] 1 *n* **(a)** (*of liquid, also fig*) Tropfen *m* ◆ **~ by ~** tropfenweise; **a ~ of blood** ein Blutstropfen *m*, ein Tropfen Blut; **it's a ~ in the ocean** *or* **bucket** (*fig*) das ist ein Tropfen auf den heißen Stein.
(b) (*alcohol*) Tropfen *m* ◆ **just a ~ for me** für mich nur einen Tropfen; **this is a nice little ~** das ist ein guter Tropfen; **a ~ of wine?** ein Schlückchen Wein?; **he's had a ~ too much** er hat einen über den Durst getrunken; **he likes a ~** er trinkt ganz gern mal einen.
(c) (*sweet*) Drops *m*.
(d) (*fall: in temperature, prices*) Rückgang *m*; (*sudden*) Sturz *m* ◆ **a ~ in prices** ein Preissturz *m*/-rückgang *m*; **20% is quite a ~** 20%, das ist stark gefallen; **he took a large ~ in salary when he changed jobs** als er die Stelle wechselte, nahm er eine beträchtliche Gehaltsverschlechterung in Kauf; **a sudden/noticeable ~ in the temperature** ein plötzlicher/merklicher Temperaturabfall; **~ in the voltage** Spannungsabfall *m*.
(e) (*difference in level*) Höhenunterschied *m*; (*fall*) Sturz, Fall *m*; (*parachute jump*) (Ab)sprung *m* ◆ **a ~ of ten metres** ein Höhenunterschied von zehn Metern; **there's a ~ of ten metres down to the ledge** bis zu dem Felsvorsprung geht es zehn Meter hinunter; **it was only a short ~ off the wall** es war nur ein kleiner Sprung von der Mauer; **it's a long ~** es geht tief hinunter; **it was a sheer ~ from the top of the cliff into the sea** die Klippen fielen schroff zum Meer ab; **careful, it's a nasty ~** paß auf, da geht es tief hinunter.
(f) (*of supplies, arms*) Abwurf *m* ◆ **the Red Cross made a ~ of medical supplies into the flood zone** das Rote Kreuz warf Medikamente über dem Überschwemmungsgebiet ab.
(g) (*of gallows*) Falltür *f*.
(h) (*Theat: also* **~-curtain**) Vorhang *m*.
(i) (*for secret mail*) toter Briefkasten.
(j) to have the ~ on sb (*lit: in shooting*) schneller schießen als jd; **to have/get the ~ on sb** jdn ausstechen können/sich (*dat*) einen Vorteil gegenüber jdm verschaffen.
2 *vt* **(a)** (*cause to fall in ~s*) *liquid* tropfen.
(b) (*allow to fall*) fallen lassen; *bomb, supplies, pamphlets, burden* abwerfen; *parachutist* absetzen; *lampshade* (*from ceiling*) aufhängen; *curtsy* machen; *voice* senken; (*Knitting*) *stitch* fallen lassen; (*lower*) *hemline* herunterlassen; (*Theat*) *curtain* herunterlassen ◆ **I ~ped my watch** meine Uhr ist runtergefallen; **don't ~ it!** laß es nicht fallen!; **he ~ped his heavy cases on the floor** er setzte *or* stellte seine schweren Koffer auf dem Boden ab; **~ that gun!** laß die Pistole fallen!; **to ~ a letter in the postbox** einen Brief einwerfen *or* in den Briefkasten werfen; **he ~ped the ball into the back of the court** (*Tennis*) er schlug einen hohen Ball in die hintere Hälfte des Feldes.
(c) (*kill*) *bird* abschießen; (*sl*) *person* abknallen (*sl*); (*send sprawling*) zu Fall bringen, zu Boden strecken.
(d) (*set down*) (*from car*) *person* absetzen; *thing* abliefern; (*from boat*) *cargo* löschen.
(e) (*utter casually*) *remark, name* fallenlassen; *clue* geben; *hint* machen ◆ **to ~ a word in sb's ear** mal mit jdm reden, es jdm stecken (*inf*); **he let ~ that he was going to be married** (*by mistake*) es rutschte ihm raus (*inf*), daß er heiraten wollte; (*deliberately*) er erwähnte so nebenbei, daß er heiraten wollte.
(f) (*send, write casually*) *postcard, note, line* schreiben ◆ **to ~ sb a note** *or* **a line** jdm ein paar Zeilen schreiben.
(g) (*omit*) *word, reference* auslassen; (*deliberately also*) weglassen (*from* in *+dat*); *programme* absetzen ◆ **this word ~s the "e" in the plural** bei diesem Wort fällt das „e" im Plural weg; **the newspaper editor refused to ~ the story** der Herausgeber der Zeitung weigerte sich, den Artikel herauszunehmen; **he ~s his h's** er verschluckt immer das „h"; **to ~ sb from a team** jdn aus einer Mannschaft nehmen.
(h) (*cease to associate with, dismiss*) *candidate, minister, friend* fallenlassen; *girlfriend* Schluß machen mit.
(i) (*give up*) *work, habit, life-style* aufgeben; *idea, plan also* fallenlassen; *discussion, conversation also* abbrechen; (*Jur*) *case* niederschlagen ◆ **you'll find it hard to ~ the habit** es wird Ihnen schwerfallen, sich (*dat*) das abzugewöhnen; **let's ~ the subject** lassen wir das Thema; **you'd better ~ the idea** schlagen Sie sich (*dat*) das aus dem Kopf; **~ it!** (*inf*) hör auf (damit)!; **~ everything!** (*inf*) laß alles stehen und liegen!
(j) (*lose*) *money* verlieren, loswerden (*inf*) ◆ **she ~ped the first three games** (*Tennis*) sie gab die ersten drei Spiele ab.
(k) (*give birth to: animal*) werfen.
3 *vi* **(a)** (*drip: liquid*) (herunter)tropfen.
(b) (*fall: object*) (herunter)fallen; (*Theat: curtain*) fallen ◆ **don't let it ~** laß es nicht fallen; *see* **penny, pin.**
(c) (*fall: rate, temperature etc*) sinken; (*wind*) sich legen; (*voice*) sich senken ◆ **to ~ astern** (*Naut*) zurückfallen.
(d) (*to the ground: person*) fallen; (*collapse*) umfallen, umkippen (*inf*) ◆ **to ~ to the ground** sich zu Boden fallen lassen; **to ~ to one's knees** auf die Knie fallen *or* sinken; **I'm ready to ~ (with fatigue)** ich bin zum Umfallen müde; **she ~ped into an armchair** sie sank in einen Sessel, sie ließ sich in einen Sessel fallen; **... till you ~/she ~s** *etc* (*inf*) ... bis zum Gehtnichtmehr (*inf*); **to ~ (down) dead** tot umfallen; **~ dead!** (*sl: expressing contempt*) geh zum Teufel! (*inf*); (*in games*) du bist tot!
(e) (*end: conversation etc*) aufhören ◆ **you can't just let the matter ~** Sie können die Sache nicht einfach auf sich beruhen lassen; **shall we let it ~?** sollen wir es darauf beruhen lassen?; **there the matter ~ped** dabei ist es dann geblieben.

◆**drop across** *or* **around** *vi (inf)* vorbeikommen/-gehen ◆ **we ~ped ~ to see him** wir sind bei ihm vorbeigegangen; **~ ~ and see us some time** kommen Sie doch mal (bei uns) vorbei.

◆**drop away** *vi* **(a)** (*become fewer: numbers*) **people have been ~ping ~ at recent meetings** in letzter Zeit sind immer weniger Leute zu den Versammlungen gekommen. **(b)** (*cliffs*) jäh *or* steil *or* schroff abfallen.

◆**drop back** *vi* zurückfallen.

◆**drop behind** 1 *vi* zurückfallen.
2 *vi +prep obj* **to ~ ~ sb** hinter jdn zurückfallen.

◆**drop by** *vi (inf)* vorbeikommen, hereinschauen.

◆**drop down** 1 *vi (fruit, monkeys)* herunterfallen ◆ **he ~ped ~ behind the hedge** er duckte sich hinter die Hecke; **we ~ped ~ to the coast for a few**

days wir sind für ein paar Tage an die Küste gefahren; **he ~ped ~ onto his knees** er sank in *or* fiel auf die Knie; **the hawk ~ped ~ out of the sky and caught the rabbit** der Habicht stürzte sich aus der Luft (herunter) auf das Kaninchen; **the cliffs ~ ~ to the sea** die Klippen fallen jäh *or* steil zum Meer (hin) ab.
2 *vt sep* fallen lassen.

◆**drop in** *vi* (*inf: visit casually*) vorbeikommen, hereinschauen ◆ **~ ~ on the Smiths** schauen Sie doch mal bei den Smiths herein; **to ~ ~ at the grocer's** beim Lebensmittelgeschäft vorbeigehen; **I've just ~ped ~ for a minute** ich wollte nur mal kurz hereinschauen.

◆**drop off** 1 *vi* **(a)** (*fall off*) abfallen; (*come off*) abgehen. **(b)** (*fall asleep*) einschlafen; (*for brief while*) einnicken. **(c)** (*sales*) zurückgehen; (*speed, interest, popularity also*) nachlassen; (*friends*) abfallen.
2 *vt sep* (*set down from car etc*) *person* absetzen; *parcel* abliefern.

◆**drop out** *vi* **(a)** (*of box etc*) herausfallen (*of* aus).
(b) (*from competition etc*) ausscheiden (*of* aus) ◆ **to ~ ~ of a race** (*before it*) an einem Rennen nicht teilnehmen; (*during it*) aus dem Rennen ausscheiden; **he ~ped ~ of the philosophy course** er gab den Kurs in Philosophie auf, er hängte den Philosophiekurs an den Nagel (*inf*); **to ~ ~ of society/university** aus der Gesellschaft aussteigen/sein Studium abbrechen; **he decided to ~ ~** er beschloß, auszusteigen (*inf*).
(c) **the "t" ~s ~** das „t" fällt weg.

◆**drop over** *vi* (*inf*) *see* **drop across.**

drop: ~ ceiling *n* Hängedecke *f*; **~ curtain** *n* (*Theat*) (Fall)vorhang *m*; **~-forge** *vt* (*Metal*) gesenkschmieden; **~ goal** *n* (*Rugby*) Tor *nt* durch Dropkick; **~ hammer** *n* Fallhammer *m*; **~ handlebars** *npl* Rennlenker *m*; **~ kick** *n* (*Rugby*) Dropkick *m*; **~-leaf table** *n* Tisch *m* mit herunterklappbaren Seitenteilen.

droplet ['drɒplɪt] *n* Tröpfchen *nt*.

dropout ['drɒpaʊt] *n* (*from society*) Aussteiger (*inf*), Drop-out (*sl*) *m*; (*pej*) Asoziale(r) *mf*; (*university ~*) Studienabbrecher(in *f*) *m* ◆ **at 25 he became a ~** mit 25 ist er ausgeflippt (*sl*); **the ~ rate at universities** die Zahl der Studienabbrecher.

dropper ['drɒpə^r] *n* (*Med*) Pipette *f*; (*on bottle*) Tropfer *m*.

droppings ['drɒpɪŋz] *npl* Kot *m*; (*of horse*) Äpfel *pl* (*inf*); (*of sheep*) Bohnen, Köttel (*inf*) *pl*.

drop: ~ scene *n* (*Theat*) (Zwischen)vorhang *m*; **~ shot** *n* (*Tennis*) Stopball *m*.

dropsical ['drɒpsɪkəl] *adj* wassersüchtig.

dropsy ['drɒpsɪ] *n* Wassersucht *f*.

drop zone *n* (*for supplies*) Abwurfgebiet *nt*; (*for parachutists*) Absprunggebiet *nt*.

drosophila [drəʊ'sɒfɪlə] *n* Drosophila, Taufliege *f*.

dross [drɒs] *n, no pl* (*Metal*) Schlacke *f*; (*fig*) Schund *m* ◆ **wealth and fame are but ~** Reichtum und Ruhm sind eitel und nichtig.

drought [draʊt] *n* Dürre *f* ◆ **three ~s in three years** drei Dürrekatastrophen in drei Jahren.

drove[1] [drəʊv] *n* (*of animals*) Herde *f*; (*of people*) Schar *f* ◆ **they came in ~s** sie kamen in hellen Scharen.

drove[2] *pret of* **drive.**

drover ['drəʊvə^r] *n* Viehtreiber *m*.

drown [draʊn] 1 *vi* ertrinken.
2 *vt* **(a)** *person, animal* ertränken ◆ **to be ~ed** ertrinken; **he looks like a ~ed rat** (*inf*) er sieht wie eine gebadete Maus aus (*inf*); **to ~ one's sorrows (in drink)** seine Sorgen (im Alkohol) ertränken; **to ~ one's whisky** seinen Whisky verwässern.
(b) (*submerge, flood*) *land* überschwemmen, überfluten ◆ **with her face ~ed in tears** mit tränenüberströmtem Gesicht.
(c) (*render inaudible: also* **~ out**) *noise, voice* übertönen; *speaker* niederschreien.

drowning ['draʊnɪŋ] 1 *adj person* ertrinkend ◆ **a ~ man will clutch at a straw** (*Prov*) dem Verzweifelten ist jedes Mittel recht.
2 *n* Ertrinken *nt* ◆ **there were three ~s here last year** im letzten Jahr sind hier drei Leute ertrunken.

drowse [draʊz] 1 *vi* (vor sich (*acc*) hin) dösen *or* dämmern.
2 *n* Halbschlaf, Dämmerschlaf *m*.

◆**drowse off** *vi* eindämmern, eindösen (*inf*).

drowsily ['draʊzɪlɪ] *adv* schläfrig, dösig (*inf*); (*after sleeping*) verschlafen.

drowsiness ['draʊzɪnɪs] *n* Schläfrigkeit *f* ◆ **to cause ~** schläfrig machen.

drowsy ['draʊzɪ] *adj* (+*er*) **(a)** *person* schläfrig, dösig (*inf*); (*after sleep*) verschlafen ◆ **to grow/get ~** schläfrig werden; **to feel ~** schläfrig sein. **(b)** *afternoon* träge; *atmosphere* schläfrig ◆ **I had a ~ afternoon** ich habe den Nachmittag verdöst.

drub [drʌb] *vt* (*thrash*) *person* (ver)prügeln, schlagen.

drubbing ['drʌbɪŋ] *n* **(a)** (*thrashing*) Prügel *pl* ◆ **to give sb a sound ~** jdm eine Tracht Prügel verpassen. **(b)** (*defeat*) Niederlage *f* ◆ **to take a good ~** ganz schön Prügel kriegen (*inf*).

drudge [drʌdʒ] 1 *n* (*person*) Arbeitstier *nt* (*inf*); (*job*) stumpfsinnige Plackerei *or* Schufterei (*inf*) ◆ **is the lexicographer a harmless ~?** ist der Lexikograph ein Mensch, der nur brav vor sich hin schuftet?
2 *vi* sich placken, schuften (*inf*).

drudgery ['drʌdʒərɪ] *n* stumpfsinnige Plackerei *or* Schufterei (*inf*) ◆ **it's sheer ~** es ist eine einzige Plackerei.

drug [drʌg] 1 *n* **(a)** (*Med, Pharm*) Medikament, Arzneimittel *nt*; (*Sport*) Dopingmittel *nt* ◆ **~s test** Dopingtest *m*; **he's on ~s** er muß Medikamente nehmen; **to put sb on ~s** jdm Medikamente verordnen.
(b) (*addictive substance*) Droge *f*, Rauschgift *nt* ◆ **to be on ~s/to take ~s** drogen- *or* rauschgiftsüchtig sein/Drogen *or* Rauschgift nehmen; *see* **hard ~, soft.**
(c) (*inducing unconsciousness*) Betäubungsmittel *nt*.
(d) (*Comm: unsaleable goods*) **a ~ on the market** unverkäufliche Ware; (*in shop*) ein Ladenhüter *m*.
2 *vt* **(a)** (*render unconscious by ~s*) *person* betäuben ◆ **to be in a ~ged sleep** in tiefer Betäubung liegen; **to be ~ged with sleep** (*fig*) schlaftrunken sein; **to be ~ged from lack of sleep** vor Müdigkeit ganz benommen sein.
(b) (*food, drink*) **to ~ sth** ein Betäubungsmittel in etw (*acc*) mischen ◆ **her whisky was ~ged** in ihrem Whisky war ein Betäubungsmittel.
(c) (*Med*) *patient* Medikamente geben (+*dat*) ◆ **to be/get ~ged up to the eyeballs on tranquillizers** (*inf*) mit Beruhigungsmittel vollgepumpt sein (*inf*)/sich mit Beruhigungsmitteln vollpumpen (*inf*).

drug: ~ abuse *n* Drogenmißbrauch *m*; **~ abuser** *n jd, der Drogenmißbrauch betreibt*; **~ addict** *n* Drogen- *or* Rauschgiftsüchtige(r), Drogen- *or* Rauschgiftabhängige(r) *mf*; **~ addiction** *n* Rauschgiftsucht, Drogenabhängigkeit *or* -sucht *f*; **~ baron** *n* Drogenbaron *m*; **~ culture** *n* Drogenkultur *f*; **~ dealer** *n* Drogenhändler(in) *m(f)*, Dealer(in) *m(f)*; **~ dependency** *n* Drogenabhängigkeit *f*.

druggist ['drʌgɪst] *n* (*US*) Drogist(in *f*) *m*.

drug: ~ pusher *n* Dealer (*sl*), Pusher (*sl*) *m*; **~ runner** *n* Drogenschmuggler *m*; **~ squad** *n* Rauschgiftdezernat *nt*, Drogenfahndung *f*; **~ squad officer** Drogenfahnder(in *f*) *m*; **~store** *n* (*US*) Drugstore *m*; **~ taker** *n* jd, der Drogen *or* Rauschgift nimmt; **~ taking** *n* Einnehmen *nt* von Drogen *or* Rauschgift; **~ traffic** *n* Drogenhandel *m*; **~ trafficker** *n* (Drogen)dealer(in) *m(f)*; **~ trafficking** *n see* **~ traffic**; **~ user** *n* Drogenbenutzer(in *f*) *m*.

druid ['dru:ɪd] *n* Druide *m*.

drum [drʌm] 1 *n* **(a)** (*Mus*) Trommel *f* ◆ **Joe Jones on ~s** am Schlagzeug: Joe Jones; **the ~s** die Trommeln *pl*; (*pop, jazz*) das Schlagzeug; **to beat the ~ for sb/sth** (*fig*) die Trommel für jdn/etw rühren.
(b) (*for oil, petrol*) Tonne *f*; (*cylinder for wire*) Trommel, Rolle *f*; (*Tech: machine part*) Trommel, Walze *f*; (*Phot*) Entwicklertrommel *f*; (*Archit*) (*wall*) Tambour *m*, Trommel *f*; (*shaft*) Säulentrommel *f*.
(c) (*Anat: also* **ear~**) Trommelfell *nt*.
2 *vi* (*Mus, fig: rain etc*) trommeln ◆ **the noise is still ~ming in my ears** das Geräusch dröhnt mir noch in den Ohren.
3 *vt* **to ~ one's fingers on the table** mit den Fingern auf den Tisch trommeln.

◆**drum into** *vt always separate* **to ~ sth ~ sb** *or* **sb's head** jdm etw eintrichtern (*inf*) *or* einpauken (*inf*).

◆**drum out** *vt sep* (*out of army, club*) ausstoßen.

◆**drum up** *vt sep enthusiasm* erwecken; *support* auftreiben ◆ **to ~ ~ business** Aufträge anbahnen.

drum: ~beat *n* Trommelschlag *m*; **~ brake** *n* Trommelbremse *f*; **~fire** *n* (*Mil*) Trommelfeuer *nt*; **~head** *n* Trommelfell *nt*; **~head court martial** *n* Standgericht *nt*; **~ kit** *n* Schlagzeug *nt*; **~-major** *n* Tambourmajor *m*; **~-majorette** *n* (*US*) Tambourmajorin *f*.

drummer ['drʌmə^r] *n* **(a)** (*in orchestra*) Trommelschläger *m*; (*in band, pop-group*) Schlagzeuger *m*; (*Mil, in parade etc also*) Trommler *m*. **(b)** (*US inf*) Vertreter *m*.

drummer boy *n* Trommler *m*.

drumstick ['drʌmstɪk] *n* **(a)** (*Mus*) Trommelschlegel *or* -stock *m*. **(b)** (*on chicken etc*) Keule *f*.

drunk [drʌŋk] 1 *ptp of* **drink.**
2 *adj* **(a)** betrunken ◆ **I'm going out to get ~** ich gehe mich jetzt betrinken *or* besaufen (*inf*); **to get ~ (on)** betrunken werden (von); (*on purpose*) sich betrinken (mit); **he gets ~ on two pints of beer** er ist schon nach zwei Halben betrunken; **to get sb ~** jdn betrunken *or* blau (*inf*) machen; **~ and disorderly** (*Jur*) durch Trunkenheit öffentliches Ärgernis erregend; **as ~ as a lord** blau wie ein Veilchen (*inf*), voll wie ein Amtmann (*inf*).
(b) (*fig*) trunken, berauscht ◆ **~ with blood** *killers etc* im Blutrausch; **~ with joy** freudetrunken; **~ with success** erfolgsselig, vom Erfolg berauscht.
3 *n* Betrunkene(r) *mf*; (*habitually*) Trinker(in *f*), Säufer(in *f*) (*inf*) *m*.

drunkard ['drʌŋkəd] *n* Trinker(in *f*), Säufer(in *f*) (*inf*) *m*.

drunk driving *n* (*esp US*) Trunkenheit *f* am Steuer.

drunken ['drʌŋkən] *adj* **(a)** *person* betrunken, blau (*inf*) ◆ **a ~ old fool** ein alter Saufkopp (*inf*); **~ driving** (*Jur*) Trunkenheit *f* am Steuer. **(b)** *orgy* feucht-fröhlich, Sauf-; *brawl* mit/von Betrunkenen; *fury* betrunken; *voice* betrunken, besoffen (*inf*) ◆ **I can't read this ~ scrawl** ich kann nicht lesen, was er in seinem betrunkenen Zustand da geschmiert hat.

drunkenly ['drʌŋkənlɪ] *adv* betrunken; *stagger* blau, wie er *etc* war (*inf*); *behave* wie ein Betrunkener *or* eine Betrunkene.

drunkenness ['drʌŋkənnɪs] *n* (*state*) Betrunkenheit *f*; (*habit, problem*) Trunksucht *f*.

drunkometer [drʌŋ'kɒmɪtə^r] *n* (*US*) *see* **breathalyzer.**

dry [draɪ] 1 *n* **come into the ~** komm ins Trockene; **to give sth a ~** etw trocknen.
2 *adj* (+*er*) (*all senses*) trocken ◆ **to wipe sth ~** etw trockenwischen; **the river ran ~** der Fluß trocknete aus; **as ~ as a bone** *land, clothes* knochentrocken (*inf*); *mouth, ditches* völlig ausgetrocknet; **~ bread** trocken(es) Brot; **to feel/to be ~** (*thirsty*) durstig sein, eine trockene Kehle haben (*inf*); **the cow has gone ~** die Kuh steht trocken.

3 *vt* trocknen; (~ *out*) *skin* austrocknen; *fruit also* dörren; (*with cloth*) *dishes, one's hands* (ab)trocknen ◆ **to ~ one's eyes** sich (*dat*) die Tränen abwischen; **the dishes will ~ themselves** das Geschirr trocknet von selbst; **to ~ oneself** sich abtrocknen.
4 *vi* trocknen, trocken werden.
◆dry off *vi* (*clothes etc*) trocknen, trocken werden.
◆dry out 1 *vi* **(a)** (*clothes*) trocknen; (*ground, skin etc*) austrocknen. **(b)** (*inf: alcoholic*) eine Entziehungskur machen.
2 *vt sep clothes* trocknen; *ground, skin* austrocknen.
◆dry up 1 *vi* **(a)** (*stream, well*) austrocknen, versiegen; (*moisture*) trocknen; (*inspiration, source of income*) versiegen; (*author*) keine Ideen mehr haben ◆ **then business started ~ing ~** dann wurden die Aufträge immer spärlicher.
(b) (*dishes*) abtrocknen.
(c) (*actor*) steckenbleiben (*inf*); (*speaker also*) den Faden verlieren.
(d) (*inf: be quiet*) **~ ~!** halt den Mund! (*inf*); **to make sb ~ ~** jdn zum Schweigen bringen.
2 *vt sep mess* aufwischen; *dishes* abtrocknen; (*sun*) *well* austrocknen.
dryad ['draɪæd] *n* Dryade *f*.
dry: ~-as-dust *adj* fürchterlich trocken, staubtrocken; **~ battery** *n* (*Elec*) Trockenbatterie *f*; **~ cell** *n* (*Elec*) Trockenelement *nt*; **~ cell battery** *n* Trockenbatterie *f*; **~-clean** 1 *vt* chemisch reinigen; **to have a dress ~-cleaned** ein Kleid chemisch reinigen lassen; **~-clean only** (*on label*) chemisch reinigen!; 2 *vi* **will it ~-clean?** läßt es sich chemisch reinigen?; **~-cleaner's** *n* chemische Reinigung; **~-cleaning** *n* chemische Reinigung; **~ dock** *n* (*Naut*) Trockendock *nt*.
dryer, drier ['draɪəʳ] *n* (*for clothes*) Wäschetrockner *m*; (*spin ~*) Wäscheschleuder *f*; (*for hair*) Fön, Haartrockner *m*; (*over head*) Trockenhaube *f*; (*in paint*) Trockenstoff *m*.
dry: ~ farming *n* Trockenfarmsystem *nt*; **~-fly fishing** *n* Trockenfliegenfischen *nt*; **~ goods** *npl* (*Comm*) Kurzwaren *pl*; **~ ice** *n* Trockeneis *nt*.
drying ['draɪɪŋ]: **~ cupboard** *n* (Wäsche)trockenschrank *m*; **~ room** *n* Trockenboden *m*; Trockenkeller *m*; **~-up** *n* Abtrocknen *nt*; **to do the ~-up** abtrocknen.
dry land *n* fester Boden ◆ **I'll be glad to be on ~ again** ich bin froh, wenn ich wieder festen Boden unter den Füßen habe.
dryly ['draɪlɪ] *adv* trocken.
dry measure *n* Trockenmaß *nt*.
dryness ['draɪnɪs] *n* (*all senses*) Trockenheit *f*.
dry: ~ nurse *n* Säuglingsschwester *f*; **~ rot** *n* (Haus- *or* Holz)schwamm *m*; **~ run** *n* Probe *f*; (*Mil*) Trockentraining *nt*; **~ shampoo** *n* Trockenshampoo *nt*; **~ ski slope** *n* Trockenskipiste *f*; **~ spell** *n* (*Met*) Trockenperiode *f*; **~-stone wall** *n* Bruchsteinmauer *f*; **~ valley** *n* Trockental *nt*.
DSC *abbr of* **Distinguished Service Cross** *Auszeichnung f für besondere Verdienste.*
DSc *abbr of* **Doctor of Science** Dr. rer. nat.
DSM *abbr of* **Distinguished Service Medal** *Auszeichnung f für besondere Verdienste.*
DSO *abbr of* **Distinguished Service Order** *Auszeichnung f für besondere Verdienste.*
DST (*US*) *abbr of* **daylight saving time.**
DTI (*Brit*) *abbr of* **Department of Trade and Industry** ≃ Wirtschaftsministerium *nt*.
DTP *abbr of* **desktop publishing** DTP *nt*.
DTs ['di:'ti:z] *abbr of* **delirium tremens** ◆ **to have the ~** vom Saufen den Tatterich haben (*inf*).
dual ['djʊəl] *adj* (*double*) doppelt, Doppel-; (*two kinds of*) zweierlei ◆ **in his ~ rôles of ...** in seiner Doppelrolle als ...; **it has a ~ function** es hat doppelte *or* zweierlei Funktion; **the ~ criteria of quality and price** die zwei Kriterien Qualität und Preis; **~ carriageway** (*Brit*) *Straße f mit Mittelstreifen und Fahrbahnen in beiden Richtungen*, ≃ Schnellstraße *f*; **~ control** (*Aut*) Doppelsteuerung *f*; **~ nationality** doppelte Staatsangehörigkeit; **the company is under ~ ownership** die Firma hat zwei Eigentümer; **~ personality** gespaltene Persönlichkeit.
dualism ['djʊəlɪzəm] *n* Dualismus *m*.
dualist ['djʊəlɪst] *n* Dualist *m*.
dualistic [ˌdjʊə'lɪstɪk] *adj* dualistisch.
duality [djʊ'ælɪtɪ] *n* Dualität *f*.
dual-purpose ['djʊəl'pɜ:pəs] *adj* zweifach verwendbar.
dub¹ [dʌb] *vt* **(a) to ~ sb (a) knight** jdn zum Ritter schlagen. **(b)** (*nickname*) taufen. **(c)** *film* synchronisieren.
◆dub in *vt sep* (*Film*) synchron (zum Bild) aufnehmen.
dub² *n* (*US inf*) Tolpatsch *m*.
Dubai [du:'baɪ] *n* Dubai *nt*.
dubbin ['dʌbɪn] *n* Lederfett *nt*.
dubbing ['dʌbɪŋ] *n* (*Film*) Synchronisation *f*.
dubiety [dju:'baɪətɪ] *n* (*form*) Zweifel *pl*.
dubious ['dju:bɪəs] *adj* **(a)** (*uncertain*) *matter etc* zweifelhaft, ungewiß; *look* zweifelnd ◆ **he's ~ whether ...** er weiß nicht *or* ist im Zweifel, ob ...; **I'm very ~ about it** ich habe da (doch) starke Zweifel; **he gave me a ~ look** er sah mich zweifelnd an.
(b) *people, company, reputation* zweifelhaft, fragwürdig.
(c) (*questionable*) *honour, advantage* zweifelhaft, fragwürdig.
dubiously ['dju:bɪəslɪ] *adv look* zweifelnd, ungewiß; *behave* zweifelhaft, fragwürdig.
dubiousness ['dju:bɪəsnɪs] *n* **(a)** *see adj (a)* Zweifelhaftigkeit, Ungewißheit *f* ◆ **there was a certain ~ in his voice** es lag ein gewisser Zweifel in seiner Stimme.
(b) *see adj (b, c)* Zweifelhaftigkeit, Fragwürdigkeit *f*.
ducal ['dju:kəl] *adj* herzoglich; *palace also* Herzogs-.
ducat ['dʌkɪt] *n* (*Hist*) Dukaten *m*.
duchess ['dʌtʃɪs] *n* Herzogin *f*.
duchy ['dʌtʃɪ] *n* Herzogtum *nt*.
duck¹ [dʌk] 1 *n* **(a)** (*bird*) Ente *f* ◆ **wild ~** Wildente *f*; **roast ~** gebratene Ente, Entenbraten *m*; **to play ~s and drakes** Steine (über das Wasser) springen lassen; **to play ~s and drakes with sth** (*squander*) mit etw furchtbar aasen (*inf*); **to take to sth like a ~ to water** bei etw gleich in seinem Element sein; **it's like water off a ~'s back** das prallt alles an ihm/ihr *etc* ab.
(b) (*Brit sl*) *see* **duckie.**
(c) a funny old ~ (*sl*) eine komische alte Tante.
(d) (*Mil inf*) Amphibienfahrzeug *nt*.
(e) (*Cricket*) **he made** *or* **scored a ~** er hat keinen Punkt gemacht; **to be out for a ~** ohne Punktgewinn aus sein.
2 *vi* **(a)** (*also* **~ down**) sich ducken ◆ **he ~ed down out of sight** er duckte sich, so daß man ihn nicht mehr sehen konnte; **he ~ed under the water** er tauchte (im Wasser) unter.
(b) he ~ed out of the room er verschwand aus dem Zimmer.
3 *vt* **(a)** (*push under water*) untertauchen.
(b) to ~ one's head den Kopf einziehen.
(c) (*avoid*) *difficult question etc* ausweichen (+*dat*).
duck² *n* (*Tex*) Segeltuch *nt* ◆ **~s** Segeltuchhosen *pl*.
duck: ~-bill, ~-billed platypus *n* Schnabeltier *nt*; **~board** *n* Lattenrost *m*; **~-egg blue** *n* zartes Blau.
duckie ['dʌkɪ] *n* (*Brit sl: also* **duck, ducks**) *often not translated* (*bus conductress to passenger*) junger Mann/junge Frau; (*actors, homosexuals, prostitute client*) Süße(r) *mf* ◆ **he is a ~** er ist süß *or* ein süßer Knopf (*inf*).
ducking ['dʌkɪŋ] *n* Untertauchen, Tauchen *nt* ◆ **to give sb a ~** jdn untertauchen *or* tunken.
ducking-and-diving [ˌdʌkɪŋən'daɪvɪŋ] *n* (*inf*) Ausweichmanöver *pl*; (*verbal also*) Ausflüchte *pl* ◆ **~ is all part of political life** Ausweichmanöver gehören zur Politik.
ducking-stool ['dʌkɪŋˌstu:l] *n Sitz m auf einem Balken, mit dem Übeltäter zur Strafe ins Wasser getaucht wurden.*
duckling ['dʌklɪŋ] *n* Entenküken, Entlein *nt* ◆ **roast ~** gebratene junge Ente; *see* **ugly.**
duck pond *n* Ententeich *m*.
ducks [dʌks] *n* (*Brit sl*) *see* **duckie.**
duck: ~ shooting *n* Entenjagd *f*; **~weed** *n* Entenflott *nt*, Entengrütze, Wasserlinse *f*.
ducky *n* (*Brit sl*) *see* **duckie.**
duct [dʌkt] *n* **(a)** (*Anat*) Röhre *f* ◆ **tear ~** Tränenkanal *m*.
(b) (*for liquid, gas*) (Rohr)leitung *f*, Rohr *nt*; (*Elec*) Rohr *nt*, Röhre *f*.
ductile ['dʌktaɪl] *adj* **(a)** *metal* hämmerbar; (*stretchable*) dehnbar, streckbar. **(b)** (*fig liter*) *person* leicht lenkbar.
ductless gland ['dʌktlɪs'glænd] *n* endokrine *or* innersekretorische Drüse.
dud [dʌd] (*inf*) 1 *adj* **(a) ~ shell/bomb** Blindgänger *m*.
(b) *tool* nutzlos; *saw* stumpf; *actor, teacher* mies (*inf*), schlecht; *coin* falsch; *cheque* ungedeckt; (*forged*) gefälscht ◆ **~ note** Blüte *f* (*inf*); **we had pretty ~ holidays** unsere Ferien waren ein ziemlicher Reinfall *or* waren ziemlich mies (*inf*).
2 *n* **(a)** (*shell, bomb*) Blindgänger *m*. **(b)** (*cheque*) ungedeckter *or* (*forged*) gefälschter Scheck; (*note*) Blüte *f* (*inf*). **(c)** (*person*) Blindgänger (*inf*), Versager *m*.
dude [dju:d] *n* (*US*) **(a)** (*dandy*) Dandy *m*. **(b)** (*city type*) Städter *m*, feiner Stadtpinkel (*pej inf*). **(c)** (*inf: man*) Kerl *m* (*inf*).
dude ranch *n* (*US*) Touristenranch, Ferienranch *f*.
dudgeon ['dʌdʒən] *n*: **in high ~** sehr empört, sehr aufgebracht.
duds [dʌdz] *npl* (*sl: clothes*) Klamotten *pl* (*inf*).
due [dju:] 1 *adj* **(a)** (*to be paid, owing*) fällig ◆ **the sum/respect which is ~ to him** die Summe, die ihm zusteht/der Respekt, der ihm gebührt; **the amount ~ as compensation** der Betrag, der als Schadenersatz gezahlt werden soll; **to fall ~** fällig werden *or* sein; **I am ~ six days off/(for) a rise** mir stehen sechs Tage Urlaub zu/mir steht eine Gehaltserhöhung zu; **I was ~ a bit of luck** es wurde auch Zeit, daß ich ein bißchen Glück hatte.
(b) (*expected, scheduled*) **to be ~ to do sth** etw tun sollen; **the train is ~** *or* **~ to arrive at midday** der Zug soll laut Fahrplan um zwölf Uhr ankommen; **when are we ~ in?** wann kommen wir an?, wann sollen wir dasein?; **I'm ~ in London tomorrow** ich soll morgen in London sein; **he's ~ back tomorrow** er müßte morgen zurück sein; **this building is ~ to be demolished** dies Gebäude soll demnächst abgerissen werden; **when is the baby/she ~?** wann wird das Baby kommen/bekommt sie ihr Baby?; **his next novel is about ~** sein nächster Roman ist demnächst fällig.
(c) (*proper, suitable*) *respect, regard* gebührend, geziemend (*geh*), nötig ◆ **with all ~ respect** bei allem Respekt; **buried with all honour ~ to his rank** mit allen Ehren begraben, die ihm rangmäßig zustehen; **with the respect ~ from a son to his father** mit allem Respekt, den ein Sohn seinem Vater schuldet; **in ~ form** in geziemender (*geh*) *or* gebührender Form; **we'll let you know in ~ course** *or* **time** wir werden Sie zu gegebener Zeit benachrichtigen; **the man who was, in ~ course, to become ...** derjenige, der dann im Laufe der Zeit ... wurde; **after ~ consideration** nach reiflicher Überlegung; **after ~ process of law** nach einem ordentlichen (Gerichts)verfahren.

(d) ~ **to** aufgrund (*+gen*), wegen (*+gen or dat*); **what's it ~ to?** worauf ist dies zurückzuführen?; **his failure was entirely ~ to himself/his carelessness** an seinem Versagen war nur er selbst/seine Sorglosigkeit schuld; **it is ~ to you that we lost/are alive today** wir haben es euch zu verdanken, daß wir verloren haben/heute am Leben sind.
[2] *adv* ~ **west** direkt nach Westen; ~ **east of the village** genau im Osten *or* östlich des Dorfes.
[3] *n* **(a)** ~**s** *pl (fees)* Gebühr *f*, Gebühren *pl*.
(b) *no pl* **(to) give the man his ~, it was an extremely difficult task** man muß gerechterweise zugeben, daß es äußerst schwierig war; **give him his ~, he did have some success** das muß der Neid ihm lassen, er hatte doch einigen Erfolg; **(to) give him his ~, he did try hard** das muß man ihm lassen, er hat sich wirklich angestrengt; *see* **devil**.

duel ['djʊəl] [1] *n (lit, fig)* Duell *nt* ◆ ~**ling pistols** Duellierpistolen *pl*; **students' ~** Mensur *f*; ~ **of wits** geistiger Wettstreit.
[2] *vi* sich duellieren; *(German students)* eine Mensur schlagen.

duellist ['djʊəlɪst] *n* Duellant *m*.

duet [dju:'et] *n* Duo *nt*; *(for voices)* Duett *nt* ◆ **violin ~** Geigenduo.

duff[1] [dʌf] *n (Cook)* Mehlpudding *m*; *see* **plum ~**.

duff[2] *adj (Brit sl)* Scheiß- *(sl)*; *suggestion, idea* doof *(inf)*.

◆**duff up** *vt sep (Brit sl)* zusammenschlagen *(inf)*.

duffel ['dʌfl]: ~ **bag** *n* Matchbeutel *or* -sack *m*; ~**-coat** *n* Dufflecoat *m*.

duffer ['dʌfə^r] *n (Brit sl)* **(a)** *(esp Sch)* Blödmann *m (inf)* ◆ **to be a ~ at football/French** eine Flasche im Fußball sein *(inf)*/eine Niete in Französisch sein *(inf)*. **(b)** *(silly old man)* (alter) Trottel *(inf)*.

dug[1] [dʌg] *n (of animal)* Zitze *f*.

dug[2] *pret, ptp of* **dig**.

dugout ['dʌgaʊt] *n (Mil)* Schützengraben, Unterstand *m*; *(also ~* **canoe**) Einbaum *m*.

duke [dju:k] *n* Herzog *m*.

dukedom ['dju:kdəm] *n (territory)* Herzogtum *nt*; *(title)* Herzogswürde *f*.

dukes [dju:ks] *npl (dated sl: fists)* Fäuste *pl* ◆ **put up your ~** zeig mal deine Fäuste *(inf)*.

dulcet ['dʌlsɪt] *adj (liter, hum, iro)* wohlklingend, melodisch ◆ **so nice to hear your ~ tones again** *(hum, iro)* wie nett, deine liebliche *or (to man)* sonore Stimme wieder zu hören *(hum, iro)*.

dulcimer ['dʌlsɪmə^r] *n* Cymbal, Hackbrett *nt*.

dull [dʌl] [1] *adj (+er)* **(a)** *(slow-witted) person* langsam, schwerfällig ◆ **the ~ ones** *(Sch)* die schwächeren *or* langsameren Schüler *pl*; **his senses/intellectual powers are growing ~** seine Sinne/geistigen Kräfte lassen langsam nach.
(b) *(boring)* langweilig; *person, book, evening etc also* lahm *(inf)* ◆ **as ~ as ditchwater** stinklangweilig *(inf)*.
(c) *(lacking spirit) person, mood, humour* lustlos ◆ **he felt very ~ all day** er hatte den ganzen Tag zu nichts so richtig Lust.
(d) *colour, light* trüb; *eyes also* glanzlos, matt; *mirror* blind; *(matt) colour* matt; *(tarnished) metal* angelaufen, stumpf.
(e) *(overcast) weather* trüb, grau; *sky also* verhangen, bedeckt ◆ **it's ~ today** es ist trüb(es Wetter) heute.
(f) *(muffled) sound* dumpf ◆ **he fell to the ground with a ~ thud** er schlug dumpf auf den Boden auf.
(g) *(blunted) blade* stumpf; *(fig) pain* dumpf.
(h) *(St Ex) market* flau; *(Comm) trade* träge, schleppend.
[2] *vt* **(a)** *senses, memory* trüben, schwächen; *mind* abstumpfen ◆ **emotionally ~ed** (emotional) abgestumpft.
(b) *(lessen) pain* betäuben; *pleasure* dämpfen.
(c) *(muffle) sound* dämpfen.
(d) *(blunt) edge, blade* stumpf machen.
(e) *(make less bright) colour* dämpfen; *mirror* blind *or* matt machen; *metal* stumpf werden lassen, anlaufen lassen.

dullard ['dʌləd] *n* Dummkopf *m*.

dullness ['dʌlnɪs] *n see adj* **(a)** Langsamkeit, Schwerfälligkeit *f*.
(b) Langweiligkeit *f*; Lahmheit *f (inf)*.
(c) Lustlosigkeit *f*.
(d) Trübheit *f*; Glanzlosigkeit, Mattheit *f*; Blindheit *f*; Stumpfheit *f*.
(e) Trübheit, Grauheit *f*; Bedecktheit *f*.
(f) Dumpfheit *f*.
(g) Stumpfheit *f*; Dumpfheit *f*.
(h) Flauheit *f*.

dully ['dʌllɪ] *adv* **(a)** *(in a listless way) look* lustlos. **(b)** *(boringly) talk, write* langweilig, einfallslos. **(c)** *(dimly) shine* matt, schwach; *sense, perceive* dumpf.

duly ['dju:lɪ] *adv* entsprechend; *(properly)* gebührend, wie es sich gehört; *(according to regulations etc)* ordnungsgemäß, vorschriftsmäßig ◆ **he was ~ surprised** er war entsprechend überrascht; **when all the details have been ~ considered** wenn alle Einzelheiten gebührend bedacht sind; **and the parcel ~ arrived the next morning** und das Paket kam dann auch am nächsten Morgen.

dumb [dʌm] *adj (+er)* **(a)** stumm ◆ **a ~ person** ein Stummer, eine Stumme; **the ~** die Stummen *pl*; ~ **animals** die Tiere *pl*; **our ~ friends** unsere stummen Freunde *(geh)*; **that's cruelty to ~ animals** *(fig)* das ist ja Tierquälerei!; **to strike sb ~** *(lit)* jdm die Sprache nehmen; **he was (struck) ~ with fear/horror** es hatte ihm vor Furcht/Schreck die Sprache verschlagen.
(b) *(esp US inf: stupid)* doof *(inf)*, dumm ◆ **that's a pretty ~ thing to do** wie kann man nur so was Doofes machen!; **a ~ blonde** eine doofe Blondine; **to act ~** sich dumm stellen.

dumb: ~**-bell** *n (Sport)* Hantel *f*; ~ **cluck** *n (inf: fool)* Doofi *m (inf)*.

dumbfound ['dʌmfaʊnd] *vt* verblüffen ◆ **I'm ~ed!** ich bin sprachlos!

dumbness ['dʌmnɪs] *n* **(a)** Stummheit *f*. **(b)** *(esp US inf. stupidity)* Doofheit *(inf)*, Dummheit *f*.

dumbo ['dʌmbəʊ] *n (inf: stupid person)* Doofkopp *m (inf)*.

dumb: ~ **show** *n (Theat) pantomimische Einlage in einem Stück*; **in ~ show** in Mimik; ~ **terminal** *n (Comput)* Einfachterminal *nt*, dummes Terminal; ~ **waiter** *n* Speiseaufzug *m*; *(trolley)* Serviertisch *m*, stummer Diener.

dum-dum ['dʌmdʌm] *n (inf)* Doofie *m (inf)*.

dumdum (bullet) *n* Dumdum(geschoß) *nt*.

dummy ['dʌmɪ] [1] *n* **(a)** *(sham object)* Attrappe *f*; *(Comm also)* Schaupackung *f*; *(for clothes)* (Schaufenster- *or* Kleider)puppe *f*; *(of book)* Blindband *m* ◆ **the manager is only a ~** der Direktor ist nur ein Strohmann; *see* **tailor**.
(b) *(Brit: baby's teat)* Schnuller *m*.
(c) *(Cards) (person)* Strohmann *m*; *(cards)* Tisch *m*.
(d) *(inf: fool)* Dummkopf, Idiot *(inf)*, Doofie *(inf) m*.
(e) *(Ftbl etc)* Finte *f* ◆ **to sell sb a ~** jdn antäuschen.
[2] *adj attr (not real)* unecht ◆ **it's just a ~ ...** das ist nur die Attrappe eines/einer ...; **a ~ rifle** eine Gewehrattrappe; ~ **run** Probe *f*; *(of air attack)* Übung *f*.

dump [dʌmp] [1] *n* **(a)** *(pile of rubbish)* Schutthaufen, Abfallhaufen *m*; *(place)* Müllplatz *m*, Müllkippe *f*. **(b)** *(Mil)* Depot *nt*. **(c)** *(pej inf: town)* Kaff *nt (inf)*; *(house, building)* Dreckloch *nt (pej inf)*; *(school etc)* Sauladen *m (pej sl)*. **(d)** *(inf)* **to be (down) in the ~s** deprimiert *or* down *(sl)* sein. **(e)** *(Comput)* Dump, Abzug *m*.
[2] *vt* **(a)** *(get rid of) rubbish* abladen ◆ **they ~ed the cargo/bodies overboard** sie warfen die Ladung/Leichen über Bord.
(b) *(put down, let fall) load, rubbish* abladen; *sand, bricks also* kippen; *bags etc (drop)* fallen lassen; *(leave)* lassen ◆ **where can I ~ these books?** wo kann ich diese Bücher lassen?
(c) *(inf: abandon, get rid of) person, girlfriend* abschieben; *car* abstellen, loswerden; *sth unwanted* abladen.
(d) *(Comm) goods* zu Dumpingpreisen verkaufen.
(e) *(Comput)* ausgeben, abziehen, dumpen.

◆**dump down** *vt sep* fallenlassen.

◆**dump off** *vt sep (inf)* **will you ~ me ~ on the way home?** kannst du mich auf der Rückfahrt absetzen?

dumper ['dʌmpə^r] *n (also* **dump truck**) Kipper *m*.

dumping ['dʌmpɪŋ] *n* **(a)** *(of load, rubbish)* Abladen *nt* ◆ **"no ~"** „Schuttabladen verboten!" **(b)** *(Comm)* Dumping *nt*.

dumping ground *n* Müllkippe *f*, Schuttabladeplatz *m*; *(fig)* Abladeplatz *m*.

dumpling ['dʌmplɪŋ] *n* **(a)** *(Cook)* Kloß, Knödel *m* ◆ **apple ~** Apfel *m* im Schlafrock. **(b)** *(inf: person)* Dickerchen *(inf) nt*.

Dumpster ['dʌmpstə^r] ® *n (US)* (Müll)container *m*.

dump truck *n* Kipper *m*.

dumpy ['dʌmpɪ] *adj* pummelig; *glasses* klein und massiv.

dun[1] [dʌn] [1] *adj* graubraun.
[2] *n* Graubraun *nt*.

dun[2] *vt* mahnen ◆ **to ~ sb for the money he owes** bei jdm seine Schulden anmahnen.

dunce [dʌns] *n (Sch)* langsamer Lerner *or* Schüler; *(stupid person)* Dummkopf *m* ◆ **to be a ~ at maths** eine Niete *or* schlecht in Mathe sein *(inf)*; **the ~ of the class** das Schlußlicht der Klasse; ~**'s cap** *spitzer Papierhut, der früher zur Strafe dem schlechtesten Schüler aufgesetzt wurde*.

dunderhead ['dʌndəhed] *n* Dummkopf, Dummerjan *(inf) m*.

dune [dju:n] *n* Düne *f*.

dung [dʌŋ] [1] *n* Dung *m*; *(of birds)* Dreck *m*; *(Agr: manure also)* Mist, Dünger *m*.
[2] *vt field* düngen, misten.

dungarees [ˌdʌŋgə'ri:z] *npl (workman's, child's)* Latzhose *f* ◆ **a pair of ~** eine Latzhose.

dung: ~ **beetle** *n* Mistkäfer *m*; ~ **cart** *n* Mistkarren *m*.

dungeon ['dʌndʒən] *n* Verlies *nt*, Kerker *m*.

dunghill ['dʌŋhɪl] *n* Mist- *or* Dunghaufen *m*.

dunk [dʌŋk] *vt* (ein)tunken.

dunning letter ['dʌnɪŋˌletə^r] *n* Mahnbrief *m*.

dunno ['dʌnəʊ] = **(I) don't know.**

duo ['dju:əʊ] *n* Duo *nt*.

duodenal [ˌdju:əʊ'di:nl] *adj* Duodenal- *(form)* ◆ ~ **ulcer** Zwölffingerdarmgeschwür *nt*.

duodenum [ˌdju:əʊ'di:nəm] *n* Zwölffingerdarm *m*, Duodenum *nt (spec)*.

dupe [dju:p] [1] *vt* betrügen, überlisten, übertölpeln ◆ **he was ~d into believing it** er fiel darauf rein.
[2] *n* Betrogene(r) *mf*.

duple ['dju:pl] *adj (Mus)* ~ **time** Zweiertakt *m*.

duplex ['dju:pleks] [1] *adj* **(a)** *(Elec, Tech)* doppelt, Doppel-, Duplex-. **(b)** ~ **apartment** *(esp US)* zweistöckige Wohnung; ~ **house** *(US)* Zweifamilienhaus *nt*.
[2] *n (esp US) see adj (b)*.

duplicate ['dju:plɪkeɪt] [1] *vt* **(a)** *(make a copy of) document* ein Duplikat *nt or* eine Zweitschrift anfertigen von.
(b) *(make copies of: on machine)* kopieren, vervielfältigen.
(c) *(repeat) action etc* wiederholen, noch einmal machen; *(wastefully)* doppelt *or* zweimal machen ◆ **that is merely duplicating work already done** da wird doch nur schon Erledigtes noch einmal gemacht.
[2] ['dju:plɪkɪt] *n (of document)* Duplikat *nt*, Kopie *f*; *(of work of art)* Kopie *f*; *(of*

key etc) Zweitschlüssel *m* ◆ **I have a watch which is the exact ~ of yours** ich habe genau die gleiche Uhr wie Sie; **in ~** in doppelter Ausfertigung.
[3] ['dju:plɪkɪt] *adj* doppelt, zweifach ◆ **a ~ copy of the text** ein Duplikat *nt or* eine Kopie des Textes; **a ~ receipt** eine Empfangsbescheinigung in doppelter Ausfertigung; **a ~ cheque** ein Scheckduplikat *nt*; **a ~ key** ein Zweitschlüssel *m*.

duplicating machine ['dju:plɪkeɪtɪŋmə∫i:n], **duplicator** *n* Vervielfältigungsapparat *m*.

duplication [ˌdju:plɪ'keɪ∫ən] *n (of documents) (act)* Vervielfältigung *f*; *(thing also)* Kopie *f*; *(double)* Doppel *nt*; *(of efforts, work)* Wiederholung *f* ◆ **save expenses by avoiding ~ of efforts** tun Sie nichts zweimal, sparen Sie Kosten.

duplicator ['dju:plɪkeɪtə^r] *n see* **duplicating machine.**

duplicity [dju:'plɪsɪtɪ] *n* Doppelspiel *nt*.

durability [ˌdjʊərə'bɪlɪtɪ] *n see adj* Dauer *f*; Haltbarkeit *f*; Widerstandsfähigkeit *f*.

durable ['djʊərəbl] *adj friendship* dauerhaft; *material* haltbar; *metal* widerstandsfähig.

duration [djʊə'reɪ∫ən] *n (of play, war etc)* Länge, Dauer *f* ◆ **of long/short ~** von langer/kurzer Dauer; **after a struggle of six years' ~** nach sechsjährigem Kampf; **~ of life** Lebensdauer *f*; **he joined up for the ~** er hat sich bis zum Ende verpflichtet; **it looks as though we are here for the ~** *(inf)* es sieht so aus, als ob wir bis zum Ende hier sind.

duress [djʊə'res] *n* Zwang *m* ◆ **he signed the form under ~** er hat die Unterschrift unter Zwang geleistet.

durex ® ['djʊəreks] *n* Gummi *m (inf)*.

during ['djʊərɪŋ] *prep* während *(+gen)*.

durst [dɜ:st] *(obs) pret of* **dare.**

dusk [dʌsk] *n (twilight)* (Abend)dämmerung *f*; *(gloom)* Finsternis *f* ◆ **at ~** bei Einbruch der Dunkelheit.

duskiness ['dʌskɪnɪs] *n* Dunkelheit *f*.

dusky ['dʌskɪ] *adj (+er)* dunkel ◆ **~ maidens** dunkelhäutige Mädchen *pl*; **~ pink** altrosa.

dust [dʌst] [1] *n, no pl* **(a)** Staub *m* ◆ **covered in ~** staubbedeckt; *furniture etc also* ganz verstaubt; **to make** *or* **raise a lot of ~** *(lit, fig)* eine Menge Staub aufwirbeln; **a bit of ~** ein Staubkorn, ein Körnchen Staub *nt*; **clouds of interstellar ~** staubförmige interstellare Materie; **when the ~ had settled** *(fig)* als sich die Wogen wieder etwas geglättet hatten; *see* **bite.**
(b) to give sth a ~ etw abstauben.
[2] *vt* **(a)** *furniture* abstauben; *room* Staub wischen in *(+dat)*. **(b)** *(Cook)* bestäuben.
[3] *vi (housewife etc)* Staub wischen ◆ **she spent the morning ~ing** sie verbrachte den Morgen mit Staubwischen.

◆**dust down** *vt sep person, sb's clothes (with brush)* abbürsten; *(with hand)* abklopfen ◆ **to ~ oneself ~** sich abbürsten; sich *(dat)* den Staub abklopfen.

◆**dust off** *vt sep dirt* abwischen, wegwischen; *table, surface* abstauben.

◆**dust out** *vt sep box, cupboard* auswischen.

dust: ~ bag *n* Staubbeutel *m*; **~bath** *n* Staubbad *nt*; **~bin** *n (Brit)* Mülltonne *f*; **~bin man** *n (Brit)* Müllmann *m*: **~ bowl** *n* Trockengebiet *nt*; **~cart** *n (Brit)* Müllwagen *m*; **~ cloud** *n* Staubwolke *f*; **~coat** *n* Kittel *m*; **~cover** *n (on book)* (Schutz)umschlag *m*; *(on furniture)* Schonbezug *m*.

duster ['dʌstə^r] *n* **(a)** Staubtuch *nt*; *(Sch)* (Tafel)schwamm *m*. **(b)** *(Naut)* Schiffsflagge; *see* **red ~.** **(c)** *(US: ~coat)* Kittel *m*.

dustfree ['dʌstfri:] *adj* staubfrei.

dusting ['dʌstɪŋ] *n* **(a)** Staubwischen *nt* ◆ **to give sth a ~** etw abstauben, von etw den Staub abwischen; **to do the ~** Staub wischen; **when I've finished the ~** wenn ich mit Staubwischen fertig bin.
(b) *(Cook etc: sprinkling)* (Be)stäuben *nt*.
(c) *(dated inf)* **the colonel gave his officers a good ~ down** der Oberst putzte seine Offiziere gründlich herunter *(inf)*.

dusting powder *n* Talkpuder *m*.

dust: ~ jacket *n* (Schutz)umschlag *m*; **~man** *n (Brit)* Müllmann *m*; **the ~men come on Fridays** freitags ist Müllabfuhr; **~pan** *n* Kehr- *or* Müllschaufel *f*; **~proof** *adj* staubdicht; **~sheet** *n* Tuch *nt (zum Abdecken unbenutzter Möbel)*; **~ storm** *n* Staubsturm *m*; **~-trap** *n* Staubfänger *m*; **~-up** *n (dated inf)* Streit *m*, (handgreifliche) Auseinandersetzung.

dusty ['dʌstɪ] *adj (+er) table, path* staubig ◆ **to get ~** staubig werden; **the furniture gets very ~ in this room** die Möbel verstauben in diesem Zimmer sehr; **to get a ~ answer** *(dated inf)* eine unklare Antwort bekommen; **not so ~** *(dated inf)* gar nicht so übel *or* unflott *(dated inf)*.

Dutch [dʌt∫] [1] *adj* holländisch, niederländisch *(esp form)* ◆ **the ~ School** *(Art)* die Niederländische Schule; **~ auction** *Versteigerung f mit stufenweise erniedrigtem Ausbietungspreis*; **~ cap** *(contraceptive)* Pessar *nt*; **~ cheese** Holländer Käse *m*; **~ barn** *(Brit)* (offene) Scheune; **that's just ~ courage** *(inf)* er hat sich *(dat)* Mut angetrunken; **I need a little ~ courage** *(inf)* ich muß mir ein bißchen Mut antrinken; **~ door** quergeteilte Tür; **~ elm disease** Ulmensterben *nt*; **to talk to sb like a ~ uncle** *(inf)* jdm eine Standpauke halten.
[2] *adv* **to go ~** *(inf)* getrennte Kasse machen.
[3] *n* **(a) the ~** die Holländer *or* Niederländer *pl*.
(b) *(language)* Holländisch, Niederländisch *(esp form) nt*.
(c) my old ~ *(Brit sl)* meine gute Alte *(inf)*.

Dutchman ['dʌt∫mən] *n, pl* **-men** [-mən] Holländer, Niederländer *(esp form) m* ◆ **he did say that or I'm a ~** *(inf)* ich fresse einen Besen, wenn er das nicht gesagt hat *(inf)*.

Dutchwoman ['dʌt∫ˌwʊmən] *n, pl* **-women** [-ˌwɪmɪn] Holländerin, Niederländerin *(esp form) f*.

dutiable ['dju:tɪəbl] *adj* zollpflichtig.

dutiful ['dju:tɪfʊl] *adj child* gehorsam; *husband, employee* pflichtbewußt ◆ **your ~ son** *(old, form: in letters)* Dein treuer Sohn *(old, form)*.

dutifully ['dju:tɪfəlɪ] *adv obey* gehorsam; *act* pflichtbewußt.

▼ **duty** ['dju:tɪ] *n* **(a)** Pflicht *f* ◆ **to do one's ~** seine Pflicht tun; **to do one's ~ by sb** seine Pflicht gegenüber jdm tun *or* erfüllen; **it is my ~ to say** *or* **I am (in) ~ bound to say that ...** es ist meine Pflicht zu sagen, daß ...; **one's ~ to one's parents** seine Pflicht (und Schuldigkeit) seinen Eltern gegenüber; **it is my painful ~ to admit ...** ich habe die schwere *or* traurige Pflicht, Ihnen zu gestehen ...; **you don't know? but it's your ~ to know!** du weißt das nicht? aber es ist deine verdammte Pflicht und Schuldigkeit, es zu wissen! *(inf)*; **to make it one's ~ to do sth** es sich *(dat)* zur Pflicht machen, etw zu tun.
▼ **(b)** *(often pl: responsibility)* Aufgabe, Pflicht *f* ◆ **to take up one's duties** seine Pflichten aufnehmen; **to be on ~** *(doctor etc)* im Dienst sein; *(Sch etc)* Aufsicht haben; **who's on ~ tomorrow?** wer hat morgen Dienst/Aufsicht?; **to be off ~** nicht im Dienst sein; **he comes off ~ at 9** sein Dienst endet um 9; **Tuesday I'm off ~** Dienstag habe ich dienstfrei; **he was called for overseas ~** er wurde nach Übersee eingezogen; **to return to ~** den Dienst wieder aufnehmen; **night ~** Nachtdienst *m*; **he's been neglecting his duties as a husband** er hat seine ehelichen Pflichten vernachlässigt; **the box does ~ for a table** die Kiste dient als Tisch.
(c) *(Fin: tax)* Zoll *m* ◆ **to pay ~ on sth** Zoll auf etw *(acc)* zahlen; *see* **estate ~** *etc.*

duty: ~ call *n*: **a ~ call** ein Höflichkeitsbesuch *m*; **~-free** [1] *adj* zollfrei; **~-free shop** Duty-free-Shop *m*; [2] *n* zollfreie Ware; **~ NCO** *n* UvD *m*; **~ officer** *n* Offizier *m* vom Dienst; **~ roster** *n* Dienstplan *m*.

DV *abbr of* **deo volente** so Gott will.

DVLA *(Brit) abbr of* **Driver and Vehicle Licensing Agency.**

dwarf [dwɔ:f] [1] *n, pl* **dwarves** [dwɔ:vz] Zwerg *m*; *(tree)* Zwergbaum *m*; *(star also)* Zwergstern *m*.
[2] *adj person* zwergenhaft; *tree, star* Zwerg-.
[3] *vt* **(a)** klein erscheinen lassen, überragen; *(through achievements, ability etc)* in den Schatten stellen.
(b) *(Hort) tree* klein züchten.

dweeb [dwi:b] *n (esp US sl)* mickeriger Typ *(inf)*.

dwell [dwel] *pret, ptp* **dwelt** *vi* **(a)** *(liter: live)* weilen *(geh)*, leben, wohnen. **(b)** *(fig)* **the thought dwelt in his mind** der Gedanke haftete in seinem Gedächtnis.

◆**dwell (up)on** *vi +prep obj* **(a)** verweilen bei, sich länger aufhalten bei; *(in thought)* verweilen bei, länger nachdenken über *(+acc)* ◆ **to ~ ~ the past** sich ständig mit der Vergangenheit befassen; **don't let's ~ ~ it** wir wollen uns nicht (länger) damit aufhalten. **(b)** *(Mus) note* halten.

dweller ['dwelə^r] *n* Bewohner(in *f*) *m*.

dwelling ['dwelɪŋ] *n (form: also* **~ place)** Wohnsitz *m (form)*, Wohnung *f* ◆ **~ house** Wohnhaus *nt*.

dwelt [dwelt] *pret, ptp of* **dwell.**

dwindle ['dwɪndl] *vi (strength, interest, relevance)* schwinden, abnehmen; *(numbers, audiences)* zurückgehen, abnehmen; *(supplies)* schrumpfen, zur Neige gehen.

◆**dwindle away** *vi (strength, person)* dahinschwinden; *(supplies)* zusammenschrumpfen.

dwindling ['dwɪndlɪŋ] [1] *n (of strength)* Schwinden *nt*, Abnahme *f*; *(of supplies)* Schwinden *nt*; *(of interest)* Nachlassen *nt*, Abnahme *f*.
[2] *adj* schwindend; *resources* versiegend.

dye [daɪ] [1] *n* Farbstoff *m* ◆ **hair ~** Haarfärbmittel *nt*; **the ~ will come out in the wash** die Farbe geht bei der Wäsche heraus; **a crime of so deep a ~** *(liter)* ein derart abscheuliches *or* verwerfliches Verbrechen; **a villain of the deepest ~** *(liter)* ein Schurke übelster *or* schlimmster Sorte.
[2] *vt* färben.
[3] *vi (cloth etc)* sich färben lassen.

dyed-in-the-wool ['daɪdɪnðəˌwʊl] *adj* Erz-, durch und durch *pred*; *attitude* eingefleischt, in der Wolle gefärbt *attr (geh)*.

dyer ['daɪə^r] *n* Färber(in *f*) *m* ◆ **~'s and cleaner's** Färberei und Reinigung *f*.

dye: ~stuffs *npl* Farbstoffe *pl*; **~works** *n sing or pl* Färberei *f*.

dying ['daɪɪŋ] [1] *adj person* sterbend; *tradition, art, race, civilization* aussterbend; *embers* verglühend; *civilization* untergehend; *year* ausklingend ◆ **he's a ~ man** er liegt im Sterben; **to my ~ day** bis an mein Lebensende, bis zu meinem Tode; **~ wish** letzter Wunsch; **~ words** letzte Worte.
[2] *n* **the ~** die Sterbenden.

dyke, dike [daɪk] [1] *n* **(a)** *(channel)* (Entwässerungs)graben, Kanal *m*. **(b)** *(barrier)* Deich, Damm *m*; *(causeway)* Fahrdamm *m*. **(c)** *(sl: lesbian)* Lesbe *f (sl)*.
[2] *vt land* eindeichen; *river* eindämmen.

dynamic [daɪ'næmɪk] [1] *adj* dynamisch.
[2] *n* Dynamik *f*.

dynamically [daɪ'næmɪkəlɪ] *adv* dynamisch.

dynamics [daɪ'næmɪks] *n sing or pl* Dynamik *f*.

dynamism ['daɪnəmɪzəm] *n* Dynamismus *m*; *(of person)* Dynamik *f*.

dynamite ['daɪnəmaɪt] [1] *n (lit)* Dynamit *nt*; *(fig)* Zünd- *or* Sprengstoff *m* ◆ **this new actress is ~** diese neue Schauspielerin ist eine Wucht *(inf)*; **this new piece of evidence is ~** dieses neue Beweisstück wird wie eine Bombe einschlagen; **that story is ~** diese Geschichte ist der reinste Zündstoff.
[2] *vt rocks, bridge* sprengen.

dynamo ['daɪnəməʊ] *n* Dynamo *m*; *(Aut)* Lichtmaschine *f* ◆ **she's a human ~**

➤ LANGUAGE IN USE: **duty: a** → 10.1 **b** → 19.2, 19.5

sie steckt voller Dynamik.
dynastic [daɪ'næstɪk] *adj* dynastisch.
dynasty ['dɪnəstɪ] *n* Dynastie *f.*
dysentery ['dɪsɪntrɪ] *n* Dysenterie, Ruhr *f.*
dysfunction [dɪs'fʌnkʃən] *n* Funktionsstörung, Fehlfunktion *f.*
dyslexia [dɪs'leksɪə] *n* Legasthenie *f.*
dyslexic [dɪs'leksɪk] [1] *adj* legasthenisch.
[2] *n* Legastheniker(in *f*) *m.*
dysmenorrhoea [ˌdɪsmenə'rɪə] *n* Dysmenorrhöe *f.*
dyspepsia [dɪs'pepsɪə] *n* Dyspepsie, Verdauungsstörung *f* ◆ **nervous ~** nervöse Magenbeschwerden *pl.*
dyspeptic [dɪs'peptɪk] [1] *adj* dyspeptisch.
[2] *n* jd, der an Dyspepsie leidet.
dysphasia [dɪs'feɪzɪə] *n* Dysphasie *f.*
dystrophy ['dɪstrəfɪ] *n* Dystrophie, Ernährungsstörung *f* ◆ **muscular ~** Muskelschwund *m.*

E, e [iː] *n* E, e *nt*; (*Mus*) E, e *nt* ◆ **E flat/sharp** Es, es *nt*/Eis, eis *nt*; *see also* **major, minor, natural.**

E *abbr of* **east** O.

each [iːtʃ] [1] *adj* jede(r, s) ◆ **~ one of us/ ~ and every one of us** jeder einzelne von uns; **~ and every boy** jeder einzelne Junge (ohne Ausnahme); **to back a horse ~ way** auf alle drei Gewinnplätze setzen.
[2] *pron* **(a)** jede(r, s) ◆ **~ of them gave their** (*inf*) *or* **his opinion** sie sagten alle ihre Meinung, jeder (von ihnen) sagte seine Meinung; **a little of ~ please** ein bißchen von jedem, bitte; **we ~ had our own ideas about it** jeder von uns hatte seine eigene Vorstellung davon.
(b) ~ other sich, einander (*geh*); **they haven't seen ~ other for a long time** sie haben sich *or* einander lange nicht gesehen; **they wrote (to) ~ other** sie haben sich (*dat*) *or* einander geschrieben; **we visit ~ other** wir besuchen uns (gegenseitig), wir besuchen einander; **they were sorry for ~ other** sie bedauerten sich gegenseitig, sie bedauerten einander; **the respect/love they have for ~ other** die Achtung, die sie voreinander haben/die Liebe, die sie füreinander empfinden; **you must help ~ other** ihr müßt einander helfen *or* euch gegenseitig helfen; **on top of ~ other/next to ~ other** aufeinander/nebeneinander.
[3] *adv* je ◆ **we gave them one apple ~** wir haben ihnen je einen Apfel gegeben; **two classes of 20 pupils ~** zwei Klassen mit je 20 Schülern; **the books are £10 ~** die Bücher kosten je £ 10; **carnations at one mark ~** Nelken zu einer Mark das Stück.

eager [ˈiːgə^{r}] *adj person, discussion, pursuit* eifrig ◆ **the ~ looks on their faces** der erwartungsvolle Ausdruck in ihren Gesichtern; **to be ~ to do sth** darauf erpicht sein, etw zu tun, etw unbedingt tun wollen; **he was ~ to please her/to help** er war eifrig bedacht, sie zufriedenzustellen/äußerst willig zu helfen; **children who are ~ to learn** Kinder, die lerneifrig *or* lernbegierig *or* lernwillig sind; **to be ~ for sth** auf etw (*acc*) erpicht *or* aus sein; **~ for knowledge** wißbegierig; **he was ~ for happiness/affection** es verlangte ihn nach Glück/Liebe; **~ beaver** (*inf*) Arbeitstier *nt* (*inf*).

eagerly [ˈiːgəlɪ] *adv* eifrig; *look, wait* voll gespannter Ungeduld ◆ **we look forward ~ to the day when ...** wir warten ungeduldig auf den Tag, an dem ...; **they agreed so ~ it was suspicious** sie stimmten so bereitwillig zu, daß es schon verdächtig war.

eagerness [ˈiːgənɪs] *n* Eifer *m* ◆ **~ for knowledge/profit/power/vengeance/independence** Wißbegierde *f*/Profit-/Machtgier *f*/Rachgier *f*/Unabhängigkeitsstreben *nt*; **such was his ~ to please/help** er war so darauf bedacht zu gefallen/seine Bereitwilligkeit zu helfen war so groß, ...

eagle [ˈiːgl] *n* Adler *m*; (*Golf*) Eagle *nt*.

eagle-eyed [ˈiːglaɪd] *adj* **the ~ detective** der Detektiv mit seinen Adleraugen.

eaglet [ˈiːglɪt] *n* Adlerjunge(s) *nt*.

E & OE *abbr of* **errors and omissions excepted** ausgenommen evtl. Fehler und Auslassungen.

ear[1] [ɪə^{r}] *n* **(a)** (*Anat, fig*) Ohr *nt* ◆ **to keep one's ~s open** die Ohren offenhalten; **to keep an ~ to the ground** die Ohren aufsperren *or* offenhalten; **to be all ~s** ganz Ohr sein; **your ~s must have been burning** Ihnen müssen die Ohren geklungen haben; **to lend an ~ to sb** jdm sein Ohr leihen; **if that came to** *or* **reached his ~s** wenn ihm das zu Ohren kommt; **he has the ~ of the king** der König hört auf ihn; **it goes in one ~ and out the other** das geht zum einen Ohr hinein und zum anderen wieder hinaus; **to be up to the ~s in debt** bis über die *or* über beide Ohren in Schulden stecken; **to set two people by the ~s** zwei Leute gegeneinander aufbringen; **he'll be out on his ~** (*inf*) dann fliegt er raus (*inf*); **to bend sb's ~** (*inf*) jdn vollquatschen (*inf*) *or* vollsülzen (*sl*).
(b) (*sense of hearing*) Gehör, Ohr *nt* ◆ **to have a good ~ for music** ein feines Gehör für Musik haben; **to play by ~** (*lit*) nach (dem) Gehör spielen; **to play it by ~** (*fig*) improvisieren; **these sounds are pleasing to the ~** diese Klänge schmeicheln dem Ohr *or* sind ein Ohrenschmaus *m*.

ear[2] *n* (*of grain, plant*) Ähre *f*; (*of maize*) Kolben *m*.

ear: ~ache *n* Ohrenschmerzen *pl*; **~ drops** *npl* (*Med*) Ohrentropfen *pl*; **~drum** *n* Trommelfell *nt*.

-eared [-ɪəd] *adj suf* **long-/short-~** lang-/kurzohrig.

ear: ~ flap *n* Ohrenschützer *m*; **~ful** *n* (*inf*) **to get an ~ful** mit einer Flut von Beschimpfungen überschüttet werden.

earl [ɜːl] *n* Graf *m*.

earldom [ˈɜːldəm] *n* (*land*) Grafschaft *f*; (*title*) Grafentitel *m*; (*rank*) Grafenstand *m*.

earlobe [ˈɪələʊb] *n* Ohrläppchen *nt*.

early [ˈɜːlɪ] [1] *adj* (*+er*) **(a) it was ~ in the morning** es war früh am Morgen; **to be an ~ riser** ein Frühaufsteher sein; **the ~ bird catches the worm** (*Prov*) Morgenstund hat Gold im Mund (*Prov*); (*first come first served*) wer zuerst kommt, mahlt zuerst (*Prov*); **~ to bed, ~ to rise (makes Jack healthy, wealthy and wise)** (*Prov*) früh ins Bett und früh heraus, frommt dem Leib, dem Geist, dem Haus (*Prov*); **in the ~ hours** in den frühen Morgenstunden; *see* **day.**
(b) (*near to beginning of period of time*) **in the ~ morning/afternoon** am frühen Morgen/Nachmittag; **in ~ spring** zu Anfang des Frühjahrs; **in his ~ youth** in seiner frühen Jugend; **in his earlier years he had ...** in jüngeren Jahren hatte er ...; **from an ~ age** von frühester Jugend *or* Kindheit an; **she's in her ~ forties** sie ist Anfang Vierzig; **in the ~ part of the century** Anfang des Jahrhunderts; **an ~ Baroque church** eine frühbarocke Kirche, eine Kirche aus dem Frühbarock.
(c) (*first, primitive*) vor- *or* frühgeschichtlich ◆ **E~ Church** Urkirche *f*; **the ~ masters** (*Art*) die frühen Meister; **this is an ~ form of writing** das ist eine frühe Schriftform; **the mystery plays as an ~ form of moral education** die Mysterienspiele als Frühform der Moralerziehung.
(d) (*sooner than expected*) zu früh; *fruit, vegetable* Früh-.
(e) (*in the future*) **at an ~ date** bald; **at an earlier date** früher, eher; **at the earliest possible moment** so bald wie (irgend) möglich; **to promise ~ delivery** baldige Lieferung versprechen.
[2] *adv* früh(zeitig) ◆ **good morning, you're ~ today** guten Morgen, Sie sind heute ja früh dran; **post ~** geben Sie Ihre Post früh(zeitig) auf; **I get up earlier in summer** im Sommer stehe ich früher *or* zeitiger auf; **I cannot come earlier than Thursday** ich kann nicht vor Donnerstag *or* eher als Donnerstag kommen; **he told me earlier on this evening** er hat es mir früher am Abend gesagt; **I saw him earlier on this week** ich habe ihn Anfang der Woche gesehen; **earlier on that year Jim had ...** Jim hatte früher in dem Jahr ...; **the earliest he can come is ...** er kann frühestens ... kommen; **earlier on in the novel** an einer früheren Stelle in dem Roman; **~ in the morning** früh am Morgen; **~ in the year/in winter** Anfang des Jahres/Winters; **~ in May** Anfang Mai; **I learned that ~ in life** ich habe das früh im Leben gelernt; **too ~** zu früh; **as ~ as possible** so früh wie möglich, möglichst früh; **she left ten minutes ~** sie ist zehn Minuten früher gegangen; **he was half an hour ~ for the meeting** er kam eine halbe Stunde zu früh zur Versammlung.

early: ~ bird *n* (*in morning*) Frühaufsteher (in *f*) *m*; (*arriving etc*) Frühankömmling *m*; **~ closing** *n* **it's ~ closing today** die Geschäfte haben *or* sind heute nachmittag geschlossen *or* zu (*inf*); **~ retirement** *n* vorgezogener *or* vorzeitiger Ruhestand; **to take ~ retirement** vorzeitig in den Ruhestand gehen; **to have taken ~ retirement** Frührentner(in *f*) *m* sein; **~-warning system** *n* Frühwarnsystem *nt*.

ear: ~mark [1] *n* (*on animal*) Ohrmarke *f*; [2] *vt* (*fig*) vorsehen, bestimmen; **~-muffs** *npl* Ohrenschützer *pl*.

earn [ɜːn] *vt money, praise, rest* verdienen; (*Fin*) *interest* bringen ◆ **this ~ed him a lot of money/respect** das trug ihm viel Geld/große Achtung ein, damit verdiente er sich (*dat*) viel Geld/große Achtung; **he's ~ed it** das hat er sich (*dat*) verdient; **~ed income** Arbeitseinkommen *nt*; **~ing capacity** Verdienstmöglichkeiten *pl*.

earner [ˈɜːnə^{r}] *n* **(a)** (*person*) Verdiener(in *f*) *m* ◆ **big ~s** Großverdiener *pl*. **(b)** (*Brit sl*) Einnahmequelle *f* ◆ **that video shop is a nice little ~** der Videoladen wirft ganz schön was ab (*inf*).

earnest [ˈɜːnɪst] [1] *adj* **(a)** (*serious, determined*) ernsthaft.
(b) *hope etc* aufrichtig; *prayer, desire also* ernstgemeint.
(c) ~ money Angeld *nt*.
[2] *n* **in ~** (*with determination*) ernsthaft; (*without joking*) im Ernst; **this time I'm in ~** diesmal meine ich es ernst, das ist mein Ernst; **it is snowing in ~ now** jetzt schneit es richtig.

earnestly [ˈɜːnɪstlɪ] *adv speak* ernsthaft; *beseech* ernstlich; *hope* aufrichtig.

earnestness [ˈɜːnɪstnɪs] *n* Ernsthaftigkeit *f*; (*of voice*) Ernst *m*.

earnings [ˈɜːnɪŋz] *npl* (*of person*) Verdienst *m*; (*of a business also*) Ertrag *m*.

ear: ~, nose and throat *adj attr* Hals-Nasen-Ohren-; **~phones** *npl*

Kopfhörer *pl*; **~-piece** *n* Hörer *m*; **~-piercing** *adj scream* ohrenbetäubend; **~-plug** *n* Ohrwatte *f*, Ohropax ® *nt*; **~-ring** *n* Ohrring *m*; **~shot** *n*: **out of/within ~shot** außer/in Hörweite; **~-splitting** *adj sound, scream* ohrenbetäubend; *din* Höllen- (*inf*).

earth [ɜ:θ] 1 *n* (a) (*world*) Erde *f* ◆ **the ~, E~** die Erde; **on ~** auf der Erde, auf Erden (*liter*); **to the ends of the ~** bis ans Ende der Welt; **where/who etc on ~?** (*inf*) wo/wer etc ... bloß?; **what on ~?** (*inf*) was in aller Welt (*inf*), was bloß (*inf*); **nothing on ~ will stop me now** keine Macht der Welt hält mich jetzt noch auf; **heaven on ~** der Himmel auf Erden; **it cost the ~** (*inf*) das hat eine schöne Stange Geld gekostet (*inf*); **it won't cost the ~** (*inf*) es wird schon nicht die Welt kosten (*inf*).
(b) (*ground*) Erde *f* ◆ **to fall to ~** zur Erde fallen; **to come back** *or* **down to ~ (again)** (*fig*) wieder auf den Boden der Tatsachen (zurück)kommen; **to bring sb down to ~ (with a bump)** (*fig*) jdn (unsanft) wieder auf den Boden der Tatsachen zurückholen.
(c) (*soil*) Erde *f*.
(d) (*Brit Elec*) Erde *f*.
(e) (*of fox, badger etc*) Bau *m* ◆ **to go to ~** (*fox*) im Bau verschwinden; (*criminal etc*) untertauchen; **to run sb/sth to ~** (*fig*) jdn/etw ausfindig machen *or* aufstöbern.
2 *vt* (*Brit Elec*) erden.

◆**earth up** *vt sep plant* ausgraben.

earth: ~-bound *adj* (a) erdgebunden; (b) **the spacecraft is on its ~-bound journey** das Raumschiff ist auf dem Rückflug zur Erde; **~ closet** *n* Trockenabort *m*.

earthen ['ɜ:θən] *adj* irden.

earthenware ['ɜ:θənweəʳ] 1 *n* (*material*) Ton *m*; (*dishes etc*) Tongeschirr *nt*.
2 *adj* aus Ton, Ton-.

earthiness ['ɜ:θɪnɪs] *n* Derbheit *f*.

earthling ['ɜ:θlɪŋ] *n* (*pej*) Erdenwurm *m*.

earthly ['ɜ:θlɪ] 1 *adj* (a) (*of this world*) irdisch.
(b) (*inf: possible*) **there is no ~ reason to think ...** es besteht nicht der geringste Grund für die Annahme ...; **for no ~ reason** ohne den geringsten Grund; **this thing is of no ~ use** das Ding hat nicht den geringsten Nutzen.
2 *n* (*inf*) **she hasn't got an ~** sie hat nicht die geringste Chance.

earth: ~man *n* (*Sci-Fi*) Erdenmensch, Terraner(in *f*) *m*; **~mother** *n* (*Myth*) Erdmutter *f*; (*fig*) Urmutter *f*; **~-moving equipment** *n* Maschinen *pl* für Erdbewegungen; **~quake** *n* Erdbeben *nt*; **~ sciences** *npl* Geowissenschaften *pl*; **~-shattering** *adj* (*fig*) welterschütternd; **~ tremor** *n* Erdstoß *m*; **~ward(s)** *adv* auf die Erde zu, in Richtung Erde, erdwärts (*geh*); **~work** *n* (*Build*) Erdarbeiten *pl*; (*Mil*) Schanzwerk *nt*, Schanze *f*; **~worm** *n* Regenwurm *m*.

earthy ['ɜ:θɪ] *adj* (+*er*) (a) *taste, smell* erdig. (b) *person, humour* derb.

ear: ~-trumpet *n* Hörrohr *nt*; **~-wax** *n* Ohrenschmalz *nt*; **~wig** *n* Ohrwurm *m*.

ease [i:z] 1 *n* (a) (*freedom from discomfort*) Behagen *nt* ◆ **I am never at ~ in this dress** ich fühle mich in diesem Kleid nie ganz wohl; **I am never at ~ in his company** in seiner Gesellschaft fühle ich mich immer befangen *or* fühle ich mich nie frei und ungezwungen; **to put** *or* **set sb at his ~** jdm die Befangenheit nehmen; **to put** *or* **set sb's mind at ~** jdn beruhigen; **my mind is at ~ now** jetzt bin ich beruhigt; **to take one's ~** es sich (*dat*) bequem machen; (*Mil*) **(stand) at ~!** rührt euch!
(b) (*absence of difficulty*) Leichtigkeit *f* ◆ **with ~** mit Leichtigkeit; **the ~ of his manners** seine Ungezwungenheit.
(c) (*absence of work*) Muße *f* ◆ **he lives a life of ~** er führt ein Leben der Muße.
2 *vt* (a) (*relieve*) *pain* lindern; *mind* erleichtern ◆ **to ~ sb of a burden/a few pounds** (*hum inf*) jdm eine Last von der Seele nehmen/jdn um ein paar Pfund erleichtern (*hum inf*).
(b) (*make less, loosen*) *rope, strap* lockern, nachlassen; *dress etc* weiter machen; *pressure, tension* verringern.
(c) **to ~ a key into a lock** einen Schlüssel behutsam in ein Schloß stecken *or* einführen; **to ~ in the clutch** (*Aut*) die Kupplung behutsam kommen lassen; **he ~d the car into gear** er legte behutsam einen Gang ein; **he ~d out the screw** er drehte die Schraube behutsam heraus; **he ~d the lid off** er löste den Deckel behutsam ab; **he ~d his broken leg up onto the stretcher** er hob sein gebrochenes Bein behutsam auf die Trage.
3 *vi* nachlassen; (*situation*) sich entspannen; (*prices also*) nachgeben ◆ **he ~d down into second gear** er schaltete behutsam in den zweiten Gang zurück.

◆**ease off** *or* **up** *vi* (a) (*slow down, relax*) langsamer werden; (*driver*) verlangsamen; (*situation*) sich entspannen ◆ **~ ~ a bit!** (etwas) langsamer!, sachte, sachte!; **the doctor told him to ~ ~ a bit at work** der Arzt riet ihm, bei der Arbeit etwas kürzer zu treten; **things usually ~ ~ a little just after Christmas** nach Weihnachten wird es normalerweise etwas ruhiger *or* geruhsamer; **there'll be no easing ~ until we've finished!** es wird keine Ruhepause geben, bis wir fertig sind.
(b) (*pain, rain*) nachlassen.

easel ['i:zl] *n* Staffelei *f*.

easily ['i:zɪlɪ] *adv* (a) (*without difficulty*) leicht ◆ **he learnt to swim ~** er lernte mühelos schwimmen; **he can run 3 miles ~** er läuft leicht *or* mit Leichtigkeit drei Meilen.
(b) (*without doubt*) gut und gerne ◆ **he is ~ the best/winner** er ist mit Abstand der beste/der Sieger; **it's ~ 25 miles** es sind gut und gerne 25 Meilen.
(c) (*possibly*) leicht ◆ **he may ~ change his mind** er kann es sich (*dat*) leicht noch anders überlegen.
(d) (*calmly*) gelassen.

easiness ['i:zɪnɪs] *n* Leichtigkeit *f*.

east [i:st] 1 *n* (a) Osten *m* ◆ **in/to the ~** im Osten/nach *or* gen (*old, poet*) Osten; **from the ~** von Osten; **to the ~ of** östlich von; **the wind is blowing from the ~** der Wind kommt von Ost(en) *or* aus (dem) Osten. (b) (*Geog, Pol*) **the E~** der Osten; **from the E~** aus dem Osten; *see* **Far E~, Middle E~, Near E~.**
2 *adv* nach Osten, ostwärts ◆ **~ of** östlich von.
3 *adj* östlich, Ost- ◆ **~ wind** Ostwind *m*.

east: E~ Africa *n* Ostafrika *nt*; **E~ Berlin** *n* Ostberlin *nt*; **~bound** *adj traffic, carriageway* (in) Richtung Osten; **E~ End** *n*: **the E~ End** der (Londoner) Osten.

Easter ['i:stəʳ] 1 *n* Ostern *nt* ◆ **at ~** an *or* zu Ostern.
2 *adj attr week, egg* Oster- ◆ **~ Island** Osterinsel *f*; **~ Monday** Ostermontag *m*; **~ Sunday, ~ Day** Ostersonntag *m*.

easterly ['i:stəlɪ] *adj* östlich, Ost- ◆ **in an ~ direction** in östlicher Richtung.

eastern ['i:stən] *adj* Ost-, östlich; *attitude* orientalisch ◆ **the ~ bloc** der Ostblock.

easterner ['i:stənəʳ] *n* (*esp US*) Oststaatler(in *f*) *m* ◆ **he's an ~** er kommt aus dem Osten.

easternmost ['i:stənməʊst] *adj* östlichste(r, s).

east: E~ German *adj* ostdeutsch, DDR-; **E~ Germany** *n* Ostdeutschland *nt*, die DDR; **E~ Indies** *npl* Ostindien *nt* (*old*), der Malaiische Archipel; **~ward, ~wardly** 1 *adj* östlich; **in an ~wardly direction** nach Osten, (in) Richtung Osten; 2 *adv* (*also* **~wards**) ostwärts, nach Osten.

easy ['i:zɪ] 1 *adj* (+*er*) (a) (*not difficult*) leicht ◆ **it is as ~ as anything** das ist kinderleicht; **it is ~ to see that ...** es ist leicht zu sehen, daß ...; **it is ~ for him to do that** das ist leicht für ihn; **it's ~ for you to say that** du hast leicht reden; **he was an ~ winner, he came in an ~ first** es war ihm ein leichtes zu gewinnen (*geh*), er hat mühelos gewonnen; **he is ~ to work with** man kann gut mit ihm arbeiten; **he is ~ to get on with** mit ihm kann man gut auskommen; **~ money** leicht verdientes Geld.
(b) (*free from discomfort etc*) bequem, leicht; *manners, movement* ungezwungen; *style* flüssig ◆ **in ~ stages** in bequemen Etappen; (*pay, persuade sb*) nach und nach; **on ~ terms** (*Comm*) zu günstigen Bedingungen; **I'm ~** (*inf*) mir ist alles recht; **at an ~ pace** in gemütlichem Tempo; **a colour which is ~ on the eyes** eine Farbe, die angenehm für die Augen ist.
(c) (*St Ex*) *market* ruhig.
2 *adv* **~!, ~ now!, ~ does it!** immer sachte!; **to take things** *or* **it ~** (*healthwise*) sich schonen; **take it ~ !** (*don't worry*) nimm's nicht so schwer; (*don't get carried away, don't rush*) immer mit der Ruhe!; **to go ~ on** *or* **with sth** sparsam mit etw umgehen; **to go ~ on the brakes/one's liver** die Bremsen/seine Leber schonen; **to go ~ on sb** nicht zu hart *or* streng mit jdm sein; **look, go ~, that's got to last us all night** sachte, sachte (*inf*), das muß die ganze Nacht reichen; **stand ~!** (*Mil*) rührt euch!

easy: ~ chair *n* Sessel *m*; **~ come ~ go** *interj* wie gewonnen, so zerronnen (*Prov*); **~-come ~-go** *adj* unbekümmert; **~-going** *adj* (*not anxious*) gelassen; (*lax*) lax, lässig.

eat [i:t] (*vb: pret* **ate**, *ptp* **eaten**) 1 *vt* (*person*) essen, fressen (*pej inf*); (*animal*) fressen ◆ **to ~ one's breakfast** frühstücken; **" ~ before July 2"** „zu verzehren bis: 2. Juli"; **he ate his way through ...** er aß sich durch ...; **he's ~ing us out of house and home** (*inf*) der (fr)ißt uns noch arm *or* die Haare vom Kopf (*inf*); **to ~ one's words** (alles,) was man gesagt hat, zurücknehmen; **I'll make him ~ his words** ich bringe ihn dazu, daß er das zurücknimmt; **he won't ~ you** (*inf*) er wird dich schon nicht fressen (*inf*); **what's ~ing you?** (*inf*) was hast du denn?
2 *vi* essen, fressen (*pej inf*); (*animal*) fressen ◆ **I haven't ~en for ages** ich habe schon ewig nichts mehr gegessen.
3 *n* (*inf*) **~s** *pl* Fressalien *pl* (*inf*); ◆ **time for ~s!** Fütterung der Raubtiere! (*inf*).

◆**eat away** *vt sep* (*sea*) auswaschen; (*acid*) zerfressen.

◆**eat into** *vi* +*prep obj metal* anfressen; *capital* angreifen.

◆**eat out** 1 *vi* zum Essen ausgehen.
2 *vt sep* **to ~ one's heart ~** Trübsal blasen, sich vor Gram verzehren (*geh*); **Michael Parkinson, ~ your heart ~** Michael Parkinson, da kannst du vor Neid erblassen.

◆**eat up** 1 *vt sep* (a) aufessen; (*animal*) auffressen. (b) (*fig: use up, consume*) verbrauchen, fressen (*inf*) ◆ **this car ~s ~ the miles** der Wagen gibt ganz schön was her (*inf*). (c) **he was ~en ~ with envy** der Neid nagte *or* zehrte an ihm.
2 *vi* aufessen.

eatable ['i:təbl] *adj* eßbar, genießbar ◆ **it's very ~** das ist durchaus genießbar.

eat-by date ['i:tbaɪdeɪt] *n* Haltbarkeitsdatum *nt*.

eaten ['i:tn] *ptp of* **eat**.

eater ['i:təʳ] *n* (a) Esser(in *f*) *m*. (b) (*apple*) Eßapfel *m*.

eatery ['i:tərɪ] *n* (*hum inf: restaurant etc*) Eßlokal (*inf*), Freßlokal (*hum inf*) *nt*.

eating ['i:tɪŋ] *n* Essen *nt* ◆ **to make good ~** gut zum Essen sein.

eating: ~ apple *n* Eßapfel *m*; **~-house** *n* Gasthaus *nt*; **~ place** *n* Eßlokal *nt*.

eau de Cologne ['əʊdəkə'ləʊn] *n* Kölnisch Wasser, Eau de Cologne *nt*.

eaves [i:vz] *npl* Dachvorsprung *m*.

eavesdrop ['i:vzdrɒp] *vi* (heimlich) lauschen ◆ **to ~ on a conversation** ein Gespräch belauschen.

eavesdropper ['i:vzdrɒpəʳ] *n* Lauscher *m*.

ebb [eb] 1 *n* Ebbe *f* ◆ **~ and flow** Ebbe und Flut *f*; (*fig*) Auf und Ab *nt*; **~ tide**

Ebbe; **at a low ~** (*fig*) auf einem Tiefstand.
[2] *vi* (a) (*tide*) zurückgehen ◆ **to ~ and flow** (*lit, fig*) kommen und gehen. (b) (*fig: also* **~ away**) (*enthusiasm etc*) ab- *or* verebben.
ebonite ['ebənaɪt] *n* Ebonit *nt.*
ebony ['ebənɪ] [1] *n* Ebenholz *nt.*
[2] *adj colour* schwarz wie Ebenholz; *material* aus Ebenholz.
ebullience [ɪ'bʌlɪəns] *n* Überschwenglichkeit *f* ◆ **the ~ of youth** jugendlicher Überschwang.
ebullient [ɪ'bʌlɪənt] *adj person* überschwenglich; *spirits, mood* übersprudelnd.
EC *abbr of* **European Community** EG *f.*
eccentric [ɪk'sentrɪk] [1] *adj* (a) *person* exzentrisch. (b) *load* schief, ungleich; *orbit, curve, circles* exzentrisch.
[2] *n* (a) (*person*) Exzentriker(in *f*) *m.* (b) (*Tech*) Exzenter *m.*
eccentrically [ɪk'sentrɪkəlɪ] *adv* exzentrisch.
eccentricity [,eksən'trɪsɪtɪ] *n* (*all senses*) Exzentrizität *f.*
Ecclesiastes [ɪ,kli:zɪ'æsti:z] *n* (der Prediger) Salomo *m.*
ecclesiastic [ɪ,kli:zɪ'æstɪk] *n* Kleriker *m.*
ecclesiastical [ɪ,kli:zɪ'æstɪkəl] *adj* kirchlich.
ECG *abbr of* **electrocardiogram** EKG *nt.*
echelon ['eʃəlɒn] *n* (*Mil*) (*formation*) Staffelung *f*, Echelon *m* (*old*) ◆ **the higher ~s** die höheren Ränge *pl.*
echo ['ekəʊ] [1] *n* Echo *nt*, Widerhall *m*; (*fig*) Anklang *m* (*of an +acc*); (*Comput*) Rückmeldung *f* ◆ **he was cheered to the ~** er bekam brausenden *or* rauschenden Beifall.
[2] *vt sound* zurückwerfen; (*fig*) wiedergeben.
[3] *vi* (*sounds*) widerhallen; (*room*) hallen ◆ **to ~ with sth** von etw widerhallen; **it ~es in here** hier ist ein Echo.
echo: ~ chamber *n* Hallraum *m*; (*for electric guitar*) Nachhall- Erzeuger *m*; **~-sounder** *n* Echolot *nt.*
ECLA *abbr of* **Economic Commission for Latin America**..
éclair [eɪ'kleəʳ] *n* Eclair *nt*, Liebesknochen *m.*
eclampsia [ɪ'klæmpsɪə] *n* (*Med*) Eklampsie *f.*
eclectic [ɪ'klektɪk] *adj* eklektisch.
eclecticism [ɪ'klektɪsɪzəm] *n* Eklektizismus *m.*
eclipse [ɪ'klɪps] [1] *n* (*Astron*) Eklipse (*spec*), Finsternis *f*; (*fig*) (*of fame, theory*) Verblassen *nt*; (*of person*) Niedergang *m* ◆ **~ of the sun/moon** Sonnen-/Mondfinsternis *f*; **to be in ~** (*sun, moon*) verfinstert sein; (*fig*) in der Versenkung verschwunden sein.
[2] *vt* (*Astron*) verfinstern; (*fig*) in den Schatten stellen.
eco- ['i:kəʊ-] *pref* Öko-, öko- ◆ **~-friendly** umweltfreundlich.
ecological [,i:kəʊ'lɒdʒɪkəl] *adj* ökologisch ◆ **~ damage** Umweltbelastung *f.*
ecologically [,i:kəʊ'lɒdʒɪkəlɪ] *adv* ökologisch ◆ **~ conscious** umweltbewußt; **~ harmful** umweltschädigend.
ecologist [ɪ'kɒlədʒɪst] *n* Ökologe *m*, Ökologin *f.*
ecology [ɪ'kɒlədʒɪ] *n* Ökologie *f.*
economic [,i:kə'nɒmɪk] *adj* wirtschaftlich, ökonomisch; *development, growth, system also, geography, miracle* Wirtschafts- ◆ **~ migrant** *or* **refugee** Wirtschaftsflüchtling *m*; **~ war** Wirtschaftskrieg *m.*
economical [,i:kə'nɒmɪkəl] *adj* wirtschaftlich, ökonomisch; *person also* sparsam ◆ **to be ~ with sth** mit etw haushalten *or* sparsam umgehen; **he's a very ~ runner** er geht beim Laufen sehr sparsam mit seinen Kräften um; **to be ~ (to run)** (*car*) (in der Haltung) wirtschaftlich sein.
economically [,i:kə'nɒmɪkəlɪ] *adv* wirtschaftlich; (*thriftily*) sparsam ◆ **to use sth ~** mit etw wirtschaftlich *or* sparsam umgehen; etw sparsam verwenden; **one has to be ~ minded** man muß wirtschaftlich *or* ökonomisch denken.
economics [,i:kə'nɒmɪks] *n* (a) *with sing or pl vb* Volkswirtschaft *f*, Wirtschaftswissenschaften *pl*; (*social ~*) Volkswirtschaft *f*; (*in management studies*) Betriebswirtschaft *f.*
(b) *pl* (*economic aspect*) Wirtschaftlichkeit, Ökonomie *f* ◆ **the ~ of the situation** die wirtschaftliche Seite der Situation.
economist [ɪ'kɒnəmɪst] *n see* **economics** Wirtschaftswissenschaftler(in *f*) *m*; Volkswirt(in *f*), Volkswirtschaftler(in *f*) *m*; Betriebswirt(in *f*), Betriebswirtschaftler(in *f*) *m.*
economize [ɪ'kɒnəmaɪz] *vi* sparen.
◆**economize on** *vi +prep obj* sparen.
economy [ɪ'kɒnəmɪ] *n* (a) (*system*) Wirtschaft *f no pl*; (*from a monetary aspect*) Konjunktur *f* ◆ **what is the state of the ~?** wie ist die Wirtschaftslage/Konjunktur?; **to improve our economies** um die Wirtschaft (unserer Länder) zu verbessern/Konjunktur (in unseren Ländern) anzukurbeln.
(b) (*in time, money*) Sparmaßnahme, Einsparung *f* ◆ **an ~ in time** eine Zeitersparnis; **a false ~** falsche Sparsamkeit; **economies of scale** Einsparungen *pl* durch erhöhte Produktion.
(c) (*thrift*) Sparsamkeit *f* ◆ **to practise ~** Sparsamkeit walten lassen; **his ~ of style** sein knapper Stil; **he has run the race with great ~** er hat seine Kräfte gut eingeteilt; **with ~ of effort** mit sparsamem Kräfteaufwand.
economy: ~ class *n* Touristenklasse *f*; **~ drive** *n* Sparmaßnahmen *pl*; **we'll have to have an ~ drive** wir werden Sparmaßnahmen ergreifen müssen; **~ size** *n* Sparpackung *f.*
eco: ~sphere *n* Ökosphäre *f*; **~ system** *n* Ökosystem *nt*; **~-tourism** *n* Ökotourismus *m.*
ecru [e'kru:] *adj* (*US*) naturfarben, ekrü.
ecstasy ['ekstəsɪ] *n* Ekstase, Verzückung *f* ◆ **to go into/to be in ecstasies over sth** über etw (*acc*) in Ekstase *or* Verzückung geraten; **~! she sighed** welche Wonne! seufzte sie.
ecstatic *adj*, **~ally** *adv* [eks'tætɪk, -əlɪ] ekstatisch, verzückt.
ECT *abbr of* **electro-convulsive therapy** Elektroschock *m*, Elektrokrampftherapie *f.*
ectomorph ['ektəʊmɔ:f] *n* ektomorpher Konstitutionstyp.
ectopic [ek'tɒpɪk] *adj* **~ pregnancy** ektopische *or* ektope Schwangerschaft.
ectoplasm ['ektəʊplæzəm] *n* Ektoplasma *nt.*
ECU ['eɪkju:, i:si:'ju:] *n abbr of* **European Currency Unit** ECU *m*, Ecu *m.*
ecu ['eɪkju:] *n* Ecu *m.*
Ecuador ['ekwədɔ:ʳ] *n* Ecuador, Ekuador *nt.*
Ecuador(i)an [,ekwə'dɔ:r(ɪ)ən] [1] *adj* ecuadorianisch, ekuadorianisch.
[2] *n* Ecuadorianer(in *f*), Ekuadorianer(in *f*) *m.*
ecumenical [,i:kjʊ'menɪkəl] *adj* ökumenisch ◆ **E~ Council** Ökumenischer Rat.
ecumenicism [,i:kjʊ'menɪsɪzm] *n* Ökumenismus *m.*
eczema ['eksɪmə] *n* Ekzem *nt*, (Haut)ausschlag *m.*
ed *abbr of* **editor** Verf., Verfasser *m*; **edition** Ausg., Ausgabe *f*; **edited** hg., herausgegeben.
Edam ['i:dæm] *n* Edamer (Käse) *m.*
eddy ['edɪ] [1] *n* Wirbel *m*; (*of water also*) Strudel *m* ◆ **the wind swept the leaves in eddies down the avenue** der Wind wirbelte die Blätter durch die Allee.
[2] *vi* wirbeln; (*water also*) strudeln.
edelweiss ['eɪdlvaɪs] *n* Edelweiß *nt.*
edema [ɪ'di:mə] *n* (*esp US*) Ödem *nt.*
Eden ['i:dn] *n* (*also fig*): **Garden of ~** Garten *m* Eden.
edge [edʒ] [1] *n* (a) (*of knife, razor*) Schneide *f* ◆ **to put an ~ on a knife** ein Messer schleifen; **to take the ~ off a blade** eine Klinge stumpf machen; **to take the ~ off sth** (*fig*) *sensation* etw der Wirkung (*gen*) berauben; *pain* etw lindern; **that took the ~ off my appetite** das nahm mir erst einmal den Hunger; **the noise/taste sets my teeth on ~** das Geräusch geht mir durch und durch/der Geschmack ist mir unangenehm an den Zähnen; **to be on ~** nervös sein; **my nerves are all on ~** ich bin schrecklich nervös; **to have the ~ on sb/sth** jdm/etw überlegen sein; **but the professional had just that little extra ~** aber der Profi war eben doch noch etwas besser; **it gives her/it that extra ~** darin besteht eben der kleine Unterschied.
(b) (*outer limit*) Rand *m*; (*of cloth, table also, of brick, cube*) Kante *f*; (*of lake, river also, of sea*) Ufer *nt*; (*of estates etc*) Grenze *f* ◆ **a book with gilt ~s** ein Buch mit Goldschnitt; **the trees at the ~ of the road** die Bäume am Straßenrand; **to be on the ~ of disaster** am Rande des Untergangs stehen.
[2] *vt* (a) (*put a border on*) besetzen, einfassen ◆ **to ~ a coat with fur** einen Mantel mit Pelz verbrämen.
(b) (*sharpen*) *tool, blade* schärfen, schleifen, scharf machen.
(c) **to ~ one's way towards sth** (*slowly*) sich allmählich auf etw (*acc*) zubewegen; (*carefully*) sich vorsichtig auf etw (*acc*) zubewegen; **she ~d her way through the crowd** sie schlängelte sich durch die Menge; **the prisoner ~d his way along the wall** der Gefangene schob sich langsam an der Wand entlang; **he ~d his chair nearer the door** er rückte mit seinem Stuhl allmählich auf die Tür zu.
[3] *vi* sich schieben ◆ **to ~ out of a room** sich aus einem Zimmer stehlen; **to ~ away** sich davonstehlen; **to ~ away from sb/sth** sich allmählich immer weiter von jdm/etw entfernen; **to ~ up to sb** sich an jdn heranmachen; **he ~d past me** er drückte *or* schob sich an mir vorbei.
◆**edge out** [1] *vt sep* (*of job, position etc*) beiseite drängen ◆ **to ~ sb ~ of his job** jdn aus seiner Stelle drängen.
[2] *vi* **she ~d ~ onto the balcony** sie tastete sich auf den Balkon vor; **the driver ~d ~ onto the main road** der Fahrer fuhr vorsichtig auf die Hauptstraße.
◆**edge up** [1] *vt sep prices etc* hochdrücken.
[2] *vi* (*prices etc*) hochgehen.
edgeways ['edʒweɪz] *adv* mit der Schmalseite voran ◆ **to stand a brick ~** einen Ziegel hochkant stellen; **I couldn't get a word in ~** ich bin überhaupt nicht zu Wort gekommen.
edginess ['edʒɪnɪs] *n* Nervosität *f.*
edging ['edʒɪŋ] *n* Borte, Einfassung *f*; (*of ribbon, silk also*) Paspel *f* ◆ **~-shears** Rasenschere *f.*
edgy ['edʒɪ] *adj* (*+er*) *person* nervös.
edibility [,edɪ'bɪlɪtɪ] *n* Eßbarkeit, Genießbarkeit *f.*
edible ['edɪbl] *adj* eßbar, genießbar ◆ **very ~!** durchaus genießbar!
edict ['i:dɪkt] *n* Erlaß *m*; (*Hist*) Edikt *nt.*
edification [,edɪfɪ'keɪʃən] *n* Erbauung *f* ◆ **for the ~ of ...** zur Erbauung der ...
edifice ['edɪfɪs] *n* (*lit, fig*) Gebäude *nt*; (*fig also*) Gefüge *nt.*
edify ['edɪfaɪ] *vt* erbauen.
edifying ['edɪfaɪɪŋ] *adj* erbaulich.
edit ['edɪt] [1] *vt series, author, newspaper, magazine* herausgeben, edieren; *newspaper story, book, text* redigieren, bearbeiten; *film, tape* schneiden, cutten, montieren; (*Comput*) editieren ◆ **~ed by: ...** (*Film*) Schnitt: ...
[2] *vi* redigieren, redaktionell arbeiten.
◆**edit out** *vt sep* herausnehmen; (*from film, tape*) herausschneiden; *character from story* herausstreichen.
editable ['edɪtəbl] *adj* (*Comput*) *file* editierbar.
editing ['edɪtɪŋ] *n see vt* Herausgabe *f*; Redaktion, Bearbeitung *f*; Schnitt *m*, Montage *f*; Editieren *nt.*
edition [ɪ'dɪʃən] *n* Ausgabe, Edition *f*; (*impression*) Auflage *f.*
editor ['edɪtəʳ] *n* (*of text, newspaper, magazine, series, author*) Herausgeber(in *f*) *m*; (*publisher's*) (Verlags)lektor(in *f*) *m*; (*Film*) Cutter(in *f*) *m*; (*Comput*) Editor *m* ◆ **political/sports ~** politischer Redakteur/Sportredakteur *m*; **~-in-chief**

Herausgeber *m*; (*of newspaper*) Chefredakteur *m*; **the ~s in our educational department** die Redaktion unserer Schulbuchabteilung; **the ~ of this passage obviously misunderstood** der, der diese Stelle redigierte, hat offensichtlich nicht richtig verstanden.

editorial [ˌedɪ'tɔːrɪəl] 1 *adj* redaktionell, Redaktions- ◆ **~ assistant** Redaktionsassistent(in *f*) *m*; **~ office** Redaktion *f*; (*Publishing also*) (Verlags)lektorat *nt*; **~ staff** Redaktion(sangestellte *pl*) *f*; **he is ~ staff** er arbeitet in der Redaktion; **there's an ~ job going in the Bible Department** in der Bibelabteilung ist eine Lektorenstelle zu besetzen; **some ~ problems in the text** einige redaktionelle Textprobleme.
2 *n* Leitartikel *m*.

editorially [ˌedɪ'tɔːrɪəlɪ] *adv* redaktionell.

editorship ['edɪtəʃɪp] *n* (*of newspaper, magazine*) Chefredaktion, Schriftleitung *f* ◆ **under the general ~ of** ... unter ... als Herausgeber.

EDP *abbr of* **electronic data processing** EDV *f*.

EDT (*US*) *abbr of* **Eastern Daylight Time** *östliche Sommerzeit in den USA und Kanada*.

educable ['edjʊkəbl] *adj* erziehbar; (*academically*) ausbildbar.

educate ['edjʊkeɪt] *vt* **(a)** erziehen; *public* informieren ◆ **he was ~d at Eton** er ist in Eton zur Schule gegangen.
(b) *the mind* schulen; *one's tastes* (aus)bilden.

educated ['edjʊkeɪtɪd] *adj* gebildet ◆ **to make an ~ guess** eine fundierte *or* wohlbegründete Vermutung anstellen.

education [ˌedjʊ'keɪʃən] *n* Erziehung *f*; (*studies, training*) Ausbildung *f*; (*knowledge, culture*) Bildung *f* ◆ **Ministry of E~** Ministerium *nt* für Erziehung und Unterricht, Kultusministerium *nt*; **lecturer in ~** Dozent(in *f*) *m* für Pädagogik; **College of E~** Pädagogische Hochschule; (*for graduates*) Studienseminar *nt*; **(local) ~ authority** Schulbehörde *f*; **to study ~** Pädagogik *or* Erziehungswissenschaften studieren; **if the Government neglects ~** wenn die Regierung das Erziehungs- und Ausbildungswesen vernachlässigt; **the ~ budget** der Etat für das Erziehungs- und Ausbildungswesen; **~ is free** die Schulausbildung ist kostenlos; **his ~ was interrupted** seine Ausbildung wurde unterbrochen; **the ~ which he received at school** seine Schulbildung; **haven't you got any ~?** hast du denn überhaupt keine Bildung?; **a good literary/scientific ~** eine gute literarische/ naturwissenschaftliche Bildung; **the ~ of one's taste buds to appreciate** ... (Aus)bildung seines Geschmacks für ...

educational [ˌedjʊ'keɪʃənl] *adj* pädagogisch; *methods, work also* Erziehungs-; *films, games also* Lehr-; *role, function also* erzieherisch; *publisher also* Schulbuch-, Lehrbuch- ◆ **a very ~ experience** eine sehr lehrreiche Erfahrung; **~ technology** Unterrichtstechnologie *f*.

education(al)ist [ˌedjʊ'keɪʃn(əl)ɪst] *n* Pädagoge *m*, Pädagogin *f*, Erziehungswissenschaftler(in *f*) *m*.

educationally [ˌedjʊ'keɪʃnəlɪ] *adj* pädagogisch ◆ **~ subnormal** lernbehindert.

educative ['edjʊkətɪv] *adj* erzieherisch.

educator ['edjʊkeɪtə^r] *n* Pädagoge, Erzieher *m* ◆ **an ~ of the people** ein Erzieher des Volkes.

educe [ɪ'djuːs] *vt* (*form*) ableiten (*from sth* von etw); entlocken (*from sb* jdm).

edutainment [edjʊ'teɪnmənt] *n* (*esp US*) Edutainment *nt*.

Edward ['edwəd] *n* Eduard *m*.

Edwardian [ed'wɔːdɪən] 1 *adj* aus der Zeit Eduards VII ◆ **in ~ days** unter Eduard VII, im ersten Jahrzehnt des 20. Jahrhunderts.
2 *n* Zeitgenosse *m* Eduards VII.

EEC *abbr of* **European Economic Community** EG, EWG (*dated*) *f*.

EEG *abbr of* **electroencephalogram** EEG *nt*.

eel [iːl] *n* Aal *m*; *see* **slippery**.

e'en [iːn] *adv* (*poet*) *contr of* **even**[1].

EENT (*US Med*) *abbr of* **eye, ear, nose and throat. ~ specialist** Augen- und HNO-Arzt *m*/-Ärztin *f*.

e'er [eə^r] *adv* (*poet*) *contr of* **ever**.

eerie, eery *adj* (+*er*), **eerily** *adv* ['ɪərɪ, -lɪ] unheimlich.

EET *abbr of* **Eastern European Time** OEZ *f*.

efface [ɪ'feɪs] *vt* auslöschen ◆ **to ~ oneself** sich zurückhalten.

effect [ɪ'fekt] 1 *n* **(a)** (*result*) Wirkung *f*, Effekt *m*; (*repercussion*) Auswirkung *f* ◆ **the ~ of an acid on metal** die Wirkung einer Säure auf Metall; **alcohol has the ~ of dulling your senses** Alkohol bewirkt eine Abstumpfung der Sinne; **the ~ of this rule will be to prevent** ... diese Regelung wird die Verhinderung von ... bewirken *or* zur Folge haben; **the ~ of this is that** ... das hat zur Folge, daß ...; **the ~s of radioactivity on the human body** die Auswirkungen radioaktiver Strahlen auf den menschlichen Körper; **to feel the ~s of an accident/of drink** die Folgen eines Unfalls/des Trinkens spüren; **to no ~** erfolglos, ergebnislos; **our warning was to no ~** unsere Warnung hatte keine Wirkung; **to such good ~ that** ... so wirkungsvoll, daß ...; **to put one's knowledge into ~** seine Kenntnisse anwenden; **to have an ~ on sb/sth** eine Wirkung auf jdn/etw haben; **to have no ~** keine Wirkung haben; **to take ~** (*drug*) wirken.
(b) (*impression*) Wirkung *f*, Effekt *m* ◆ **to create an ~** eine Wirkung *or* einen Effekt erzielen; **to give a good ~** einen guten Effekt ergeben; **literary ~** literarischer Effekt; **~s of light** (*Art*) Lichteffekte *pl*; **the sword was only for ~** der Degen war nur zum Effekt da; **it's all done solely for ~** es wird alles bloß des Effekts wegen *or* aus Effekthascherei (*pej*) getan.
(c) (*meaning*) **his letter is to the ~ that** ... sein Brief hat zum Inhalt, daß ...; **we received his letter to the ~ that** ... wir erhielten sein Schreiben des Inhalts, daß ...; **an announcement to the ~ that** ... eine Erklärung des Inhalts, daß ...; **he used words to that ~** sinngemäß drückte er sich so aus; ... **or words to that ~** ... oder etwas in diesem Sinne *or* etwas ähnliches.
(d) ~s *pl* (*property*) Effekten *pl*.
(e) (*reality*) **in ~** in Wirklichkeit, im Effekt.
(f) (*of laws*) **to be in ~** gültig *or* in Kraft sein; **to come into ~** in Kraft treten; **to put sth into ~** etw in Kraft setzen; **to take ~** in Kraft treten.
2 *vt* **(a)** bewirken, herbeiführen ◆ **to ~ one's purpose** seine Absicht verwirklichen; **to ~ an entry** (*form*) sich (*dat*) Zutritt verschaffen. **(b)** (*form*) *sale, purchase* tätigen; *payment* leisten; *insurance* abschließen; *settlement* erzielen.

effective [ɪ'fektɪv] *adj* **(a)** (*achieving a result*) wirksam, effektiv ◆ **to become ~** (*law*) in Kraft treten, wirksam werden; (*drug*) wirken; **the ~ date of an insurance policy** der Vertragsbeginn einer Versicherungspolice.
(b) (*creating a striking impression*) wirkungsvoll, effektvoll ◆ **a very ~ use of colours** eine sehr wirkungsvolle Farbgebung.
(c) (*real*) *aid, contribution* tatsächlich; *profit, performance also* effektiv ◆ **~ troops** einsatzbereite Truppen.

effectively [ɪ'fektɪvlɪ] *adv see adj* **(a)** wirksam, effektiv. **(b)** wirkungsvoll, effektvoll. **(c)** effektiv ◆ **but they are ~ the same** aber effektiv sind sie gleich.

effectiveness [ɪ'fektɪvnɪs] *n see adj* **(a)** Wirksamkeit, Effektivität *f*. **(b)** Wirkung *f*, Effekt *m*.

effectual *adj*, **~ly** *adv* [ɪ'fektjʊəl, -ɪ] wirksam.

effectuate [ɪ'fektjʊeɪt] *vt* bewirken.

effeminacy [ɪ'femɪnəsɪ] *n* feminines Wesen, Effemination *f* (*geh*).

effeminate [ɪ'femɪnɪt] *adj* feminin, effeminiert (*geh*).

effervesce [ˌefə'ves] *vi* sprudeln; (*fig: person*) überschäumen.

effervescence [ˌefə'vesns] *n* (*lit*) Sprudeln *nt*; (*fig*) Überschäumen *nt*; überschäumendes Temperament.

effervescent [ˌefə'vesnt] *adj* sprudelnd; (*fig*) überschäumend.

effete [ɪ'fiːt] *adj* schwach; *person* saft- und kraftlos.

efficacious [ˌefɪ'keɪʃəs] *adj* wirksam.

efficacy ['efɪkəsɪ] *n* Wirksamkeit *f*.

efficiency [ɪ'fɪʃənsɪ] *n* (*of person*) Fähigkeit, Tüchtigkeit *f*; (*of machine, engine, factory*) Leistungsfähigkeit *f*; (*of method, organization*) Rationalität, Effizienz (*geh*) *f* ◆ **~-minded** leistungsorientiert; **when jobs are lost for the sake of ~** wenn Stellen wegrationalisiert werden; **software that improves the ~ of translators** Software, die die Leistungsfähigkeit von Übersetzern erhöht.

efficient [ɪ'fɪʃənt] *adj person* fähig, effizient (*geh*); *worker, secretary etc also* tüchtig; *machine, engine, factory, company, department* leistungsfähig; *method, organization* rationell, effizient (*geh*) ◆ **to be ~ at sth/at doing sth** etw gut verstehen/es gut verstehen, etw zu tun, in etw (*dat*) tüchtig sein; **the ~ working of a mechanism** das gute Funktionieren eines Mechanismus.

efficiently [ɪ'fɪʃəntlɪ] *adv* gut, effizient (*geh*) ◆ **the new machines were installed smoothly and ~** die neuen Maschinen wurden glatt und reibungslos eingebaut.

effigy ['efɪdʒɪ] *n* Bildnis *nt* ◆ **to burn sb in ~** jds Puppe verbrennen.

effing ['efɪŋ] (*euph vulg*) 1 *adj* Scheiß- (*sl*).
2 *n*: **~ and blinding** Fluchen, Geschimpfe *nt*.
3 *vi* (*only in -ing form*) **he was ~ and blinding** er erging sich in wüsten Schimpfereien.

efflorescent [ˌeflɔː'resnt] *adj* (*Chem*) ausblühend, effloreszierend (*spec*); (*Bot*) aufblühend.

effluence ['eflʊəns] *n* Abwasser *nt*.

effluent ['eflʊənt] 1 *adj* ausfließend; *gas* ausströmend.
2 *n* (*from a lake*) Ausfluß *m*; (*sewage*) Abwasser *nt*.

effluvium [e'fluːvɪəm] *n* Ausdünstung *f*.

eff off ['efɒf] *vi* (*euph vulg*) sich verpissen (*sl*).

effort ['efət] *n* **(a)** (*attempt*) Versuch *m*; (*strain, hard work*) Anstrengung, Mühe *f*; (*Mech*) Leistung *f* ◆ **to make an ~ to do sth** den Versuch unternehmen, etw zu tun, sich bemühen, etw zu tun; **to make every ~** *or* **a great ~ to do sth** sich sehr bemühen *or* anstrengen, etw zu tun; **to make every possible ~ to do sth** jede nur mögliche Anstrengung *or* große Anstrengungen unternehmen *or* machen, etw zu tun; **he made no ~ to be polite** er machte sich (*dat*) nicht die Mühe, höflich zu sein; **it's an ~ (to get up in the morning)** es kostet einige Mühe *or* Anstrengung(, morgens aufzustehen); **it's an awful ~ to start working again** es kostet große Mühe, wieder mit der Arbeit anzufangen; **I'll try to persuade him but it'll be an ~** ich will versuchen, ihn zu überreden, aber es wird einige Mühe kosten; **with an ~** mühsam; **he had to double his ~s** er mußte seine Anstrengungen verdoppeln; **if it's not too much of an ~ for you** (*iro*) wenn es dir nicht zu viel Mühe macht; **come on, make an ~** komm, streng dich an.
(b) (*inf*) Unternehmen *nt* ◆ **it was a pretty poor ~** das war eine ziemlich schwache Leistung; **he made a pretty poor ~ of the repair** er hat bei der Reparatur ziemlich gepfuscht *or* ziemliche Pfuscharbeit geleistet; **it's not bad for a first ~** das ist nicht schlecht für den Anfang; **what did you think of his latest ~?** was halten Sie von seinem jüngsten Unternehmen?; **do you understand those rationalization ~s?** verstehen Sie diese Rationalisierungsbestrebungen?; **his first ~ at making a film** sein erster Versuch, einen Film zu drehen; **what's this peculiar cylinder ~?** was ist denn das Zylinder-Ding da? (*inf*).

effortless ['efətlɪs] *adj* mühelos, leicht; *style* leicht, flüssig.

effortlessly ['efətlɪslɪ] *adv* mühelos, leicht.

effrontery [ɪ'frʌntərɪ] *n* Unverschämtheit *f* ◆ **how can you have the ~ to deny the charge?** daß Sie die Frechheit besitzen, den Vorwurf abzustreiten!

effusion [ɪ'fjuːʒən] *n* (*lit, fig*) Erguß *m*.

effusive [ɪ'fju:sɪv] *adj* überschwenglich; *person, character, style also* exaltiert.
effusively [ɪ'fju:sɪvlɪ] *adv* überschwenglich.
effusiveness [ɪ'fju:sɪvnɪs] *n* Überschwenglichkeit *f*.
EFL *abbr of* **English as a Foreign Language** Englisch als Fremdsprache ♦ **~ teacher** Lehrer(in *f*) *m* für Englisch als Fremdsprache.
EFTA ['eftə] *abbr of* **European Free Trade Association** EFTA *f*.
EFTPOS ['eftpɒs] *abbr of* **electronic funds transfer at point of sale.**
eg *abbr of* **for example** z.B.
EGA (*Comput*) *abbr of* **enhanced graphics adapter** EGA.
egad [ɪ'gæd] *interj* (*old, hum*) fürwahr (*old, hum*).
egalitarian [ɪ,gælɪ'teərɪən] 1 *n* Verfechter(in *f*) *m* des Egalitarismus.
2 *adj person* egalitär (*geh*); *principle also* Gleichheits-.
egalitarianism [ɪ,gælɪ'teərɪənɪzəm] *n* Egalitarismus *m*.
egg [eg] *n* Ei *nt* ♦ **to put all one's ~s in one basket** (*prov*) alles auf eine Karte setzen; **as sure as ~s is ~s** (*inf*) so sicher wie das Amen in der Kirche (*inf*); **to have ~ all over one's face** (*fig inf*) dumm dastehen (*inf*); **he's a good/bad ~** (*dated inf*) er ist ein famoser Kerl (*dated*)/ein übler Kunde (*inf*); **the plan is still in the ~** der Plan ist noch im Entstehen.
♦**egg on** *vt sep* anstacheln ♦ **don't ~ him ~!** jetzt stachel ihn doch nicht auch noch an!
egg: ~ and dart *n* Eierstab *m* (*spec*); **~ and spoon race** *n* Eierlauf *m*; **~-beater** *n* Schneebesen *m*; **~-cup** *n* Eierbecher *m*; **~ custard** *n* Eiercreme *f*; **~-flip** *n* Ei-Flip *m*; **~head** *n* (*pej inf*) Intellektuelle(r) *mf*, Eierkopf *m* (*inf*); **~-plant** *n* Aubergine *f*; **~ roll** *n* Eibrötchen *nt*; **~ sandwich** *n* Sandwich *nt* mit Ei; **~shell** 1 *n* Eierschale *f*; 2 *adj* Eierschalen-; **~ spoon** *n* Eierlöffel *m*; **~-timer** *n* Eieruhr *f*; **~-whisk** *n* Schneebesen *m*; **~-white** *n* Eiweiß *nt*; **~ yolk** *n* Eidotter *m*, Eigelb *nt*.
eglantine ['egləntaɪn] *n* Weinrose *f*.
ego ['i:gəʊ] *n* (*Psych*) Ego, Ich *nt*; (*inf*) Selbstbewußtsein *nt*; (*conceit*) Einbildung *f* ♦ **this will boost his ~** das wird sein Selbstbewußtsein stärken, das wird ihm Auftrieb geben; **his ~ won't allow him to admit that he is wrong** sein Stolz läßt ihn nie zugeben, daß er unrecht hat.
egocentric(al) [,egəʊ'sentrɪk(əl)] *adj* egozentrisch, ichbezogen.
egoism ['egəʊɪzəm] *n* Egoismus *m*, Selbstsucht *f*.
egoist ['egəʊɪst] *n* Egoist *m*, selbstsüchtiger Mensch.
egoistical [,egəʊ'ɪstɪkəl] *adj* egoistisch, selbstsüchtig, eigennützig.
egomania [,i:gəʊ'meɪnɪə] *n* Egomanie *f*, übersteigerte Ichbezogenheit.
egomaniac [,i:gəʊ'meɪnɪæk] *n* Egomane *m*, Egomanin *f*.
egotism ['egəʊtɪzəm] *n* Ichbezogenheit *f*, Egotismus *m*.
egotist ['egəʊtɪst] *n* Egotist *m*, ichbezogener Mensch.
egotistic(al) [,egəʊ'tɪstɪk(əl)] *adj* von sich eingenommen, ichbezogen, egotistisch.
ego-trip ['i:gəʊtrɪp] *n* (*inf*) Ego-Trip *m* (*inf*).
egregious [ɪ'gri:dʒəs] *adj* ausgemacht, ungeheuerlich.
egret ['i:grɪt] *n* (*Orn*) Reiher *m*; (*ornament*) Reiherfeder *f*.
Egypt ['i:dʒɪpt] *n* Ägypten *nt*.
Egyptian [ɪ'dʒɪpʃən] 1 *adj* ägyptisch.
2 *n* (**a**) Ägypter(in *f*) *m*. (**b**) (*language*) Ägyptisch *nt*.
Egyptology [,i:dʒɪp'tɒlədʒɪ] *n* Ägyptologie *f*.
eh [eɪ] *interj* (**a**) (*inviting repetition*) **I've found a gold mine — ~?** ich habe eine Goldmine entdeckt — was? *or* hä? (*inf*). (**b**) (*inviting agreement*) **it's good, ~?** gut, nicht?
eider ['aɪdəʳ] *n* Eiderente *f*.
eiderdown ['aɪdədaʊn] *n* (*quilt*) Federbett *nt*, Daunendecke *f*; (*feathers*) Daunen, Flaumfedern *pl*.
eidetic [aɪ'detɪk] *adj* eidetisch.
eight [eɪt] 1 *adj* acht; *see* **six.**
2 *n* (**a**) Acht *f*; *see* **six.** (**b**) (*Rowing*) Achter *m*. (**c**) **to have had one over the ~** (*inf*) einen über den Durst *or* einen zuviel getrunken haben (*inf*).
eighteen ['eɪ'ti:n] 1 *adj* achtzehn.
2 *n* Achtzehn *f*.
eighteenth ['eɪ'ti:nθ] 1 *adj* achtzehnte(r, s).
2 *n* (*fraction*) Achtzehntel *nt*; (*of series*) Achtzehnte(r, s); *see* **sixteenth.**
eighth [eɪtθ] 1 *adj* achte(r, s).
2 *n* (*fraction*) Achtel *nt*; (*of series*) Achte(r, s); *see* **sixth.**
eighth-note ['eɪtθnəʊt] *n* (*US Mus*) Achtelnote *f*, Achtel *nt*.
eightieth ['eɪtɪəθ] 1 *adj* achtzigste(r, s).
2 *n* (*fraction*) Achtzigstel *nt*; (*of series*) Achtzigste(r, s); *see* **sixtieth.**
eightsome (reel) ['eɪtsəm('ri:l)] *n schottischer Volkstanz für 8 Tänzer.*
eighty ['eɪtɪ] 1 *adj* achtzig.
2 *n* Achtzig *f*; *see* **sixty.**
Eire ['ɛərə] *n* Irland, Eire *nt*.
▼ **either** ['aɪðəʳ, 'i:ðəʳ] 1 *adj, pron* (**a**) (*one or other*) eine(r, s) (von beiden) ♦ **there are two boxes on the table, take ~** auf dem Tisch liegen zwei Schachteln, nimm eine davon; **if on ~ side of the road there is a line of trees** wenn eine Straßenseite mit Bäumen bestanden ist.
(**b**) (*each, both*) jede(r, s), beide *pl* ♦ **~ day would suit me** beide Tage passen mir; **which bus will you take? — ~ (will do)** welchen Bus wollen Sie nehmen? — das ist egal; **I don't admire ~** ich bewundere keinen von beiden, ich bewundere beide nicht; **on ~ side of the street** auf beiden Seiten der Straße; **it wasn't in ~ (box)** es war in keiner der beiden (Kisten).
2 *adv, conj* (**a**) (*after neg statement*) auch nicht ♦ **he sings badly and he can't act ~** er ist ein schlechter Sänger, und spielen kann er auch nicht; **I have never heard of him — no, I haven't ~** ich habe noch nie von ihm gehört — ich auch nicht.

➤ LANGUAGE IN USE: **either: 2b → 26.2**

▼ (**b**) **~ ... or** entweder ... oder; (*after a negative*) weder ... noch; **he must be ~ lazy or stupid** er muß entweder faul oder dumm sein; **~ be quiet or go out!** entweder bist du ruhig oder du gehst raus!; **I have never been to ~ Paris or Rome** ich bin weder in Paris noch in Rom gewesen.
(**c**) (*moreover*) **she inherited a sum of money and not such a small one ~** sie hat Geld geerbt, und (zwar) gar nicht so wenig.
ejaculate [ɪ'dʒækjʊleɪt] 1 *vi* (*cry out*) aufschreien; (*Physiol*) ejakulieren.
2 *vt* (*utter*) ausstoßen, ausrufen; (*Physiol*) ejakulieren, ausspritzen.
3 [ɪ'dʒækjʊlɪt] *n* Ejakulat *m*.
ejaculation [ɪ,dʒækjʊ'leɪʃən] *n* (**a**) (*cry*) Ausruf *m*. (**b**) (*Physiol*) Ejakulation *f*, Samenerguß *m*.
ejaculatory [ɪ'dʒækjʊlətərɪ] *adj style, language* stoßhaft; (*Physiol*) Ejakulations-.
eject [ɪ'dʒekt] 1 *vt* (**a**) (*throw out*) *heckler, tenant* hinauswerfen. (**b**) *cartridge* auswerfen; (*Tech*) ausstoßen, auswerfen; *pilot* herausschleudern.
2 *vi* (*pilot*) den Schleudersitz betätigen.
ejection [ɪ'dʒekʃən] *n* Hinauswurf *m*; (*of cartridge*) Auswerfen *nt*; (*Tech*) Ausstoß *m* ♦ **~ is the pilot's last resort** Betätigung des Schleudersitzes ist die letzte Rettung für den Piloten.
ejector [ɪ'dʒektəʳ] *n* (*on gun*) Auswerfer, Ejektor *m* ♦ **~ seat** (*Aviat*) Schleudersitz *m*.
eke out ['i:kaʊt] *vt sep food, supplies* strecken, verlängern; *money, income* aufbessern ♦ **to ~ ~ a living** sich (recht und schlecht) durchschlagen.
el [el] *n* (*US*) *abbr of* **elevated railroad** Hochbahn *f*.
elaborate [ɪ'læbərɪt] 1 *adj design, hairstyle, pattern, drawing* kunstvoll, kompliziert; *style* (*of writing*) *also, document* ausführlich, detailliert; *plan* ausgefeilt, ausgeklügelt; *sculpture, style* kunstvoll; *preparations also* umfangreich; *clothes, meal* üppig; *joke* ausgeklügelt ♦ **I could cook something a little more ~** ich könnte etwas Anspruchsvolleres kochen; **an ~ meal** ein großes Menü.
2 [ɪ'læbəreɪt] *vt* (*work out in detail*) ausarbeiten; (*describe in detail*) ausführen.
3 [ɪ'læbəreɪt] *vi* **could you ~?** könnten Sie das etwas näher ausführen?; **there's no need to ~** Sie brauchen nichts weiter zu sagen.
♦**elaborate on** *vi +prep obj* näher ausführen.
elaborately [ɪ'læbərɪtlɪ] *adv designed, drawn, structured* kunstvoll, kompliziert; *detailed* ausführlich; *worked out* detailliert; *prepared* umfangreich.
elaborateness [ɪ'læbərɪtnɪs] *n see adj* Kompliziertheit *f*; Ausführlichkeit, Detailliertheit *f*; Umfang *m*; Üppigkeit *f*.
elaboration [ɪ,læbə'reɪʃən] *n* (*working out in detail*) (*of plan*) Ausfeilung *f*; (*description: of details etc*) nähere Ausführung; (*that which elaborates: details etc*) Ausschmückung *f* ♦ **an author who goes in for a great deal of tedious ~** ein Schriftsteller, der eine Menge langatmiger Beschreibungen bringt.
élan [eɪ'læn] *n* Elan *m*.
elapse [ɪ'læps] *vi* vergehen, verstreichen.
elastic [ɪ'læstɪk] 1 *adj* (*lit, fig*) elastisch ♦ **~ band** (*Brit*) Gummiband *nt*; **~ stockings** Gummistrümpfe *pl*.
2 *n* Gummi(band *nt*) *m*; (*US: rubber band*) Gummi *m*.
elasticity [,i:læs'tɪsɪtɪ] *n* Elastizität *f*.
Elastoplast ® [ɪ'læstəʊplɑ:st] *n* (*Brit*) Hansaplast ® *nt*.
elate [ɪ'leɪt] *vt* begeistern, in Hochstimmung versetzen.
elated [ɪ'leɪtɪd] *adj* begeistert ♦ **~ mood** Hochstimmung *f*.
elation [ɪ'leɪʃən] *n* Begeisterung (*at* über *+acc*), Hochstimmung *f*; (*of crowd also*) Jubel *m* ♦ **a mood of such ~** eine solche Hochstimmung.
elbow ['elbəʊ] 1 *n* (**a**) Ellbogen *m* ♦ **out at the ~s** an den Ellbogen durchgewetzt; **since he's been rubbing ~s with senators** (*esp US*) seit er sich in Senatorenkreisen bewegt. (**b**) (*of pipe, river, road*) Knie *nt*.
2 *vt* **to ~ one's way forward** sich durchdrängen; **he ~ed his way through the crowd** er boxte sich durch die Menge; **to ~ sb aside** jdn beiseite stoßen; **he ~ed me in the stomach** er stieß mir *or* mich mit dem Ellbogen in den Magen.
♦**elbow out** *vt sep* (*fig*) hinausdrängeln.
elbow: ~-grease *n* (*inf*) Muskelkraft *f*; **~-rest** *n* Armstütze *f*; **~-room** *n* (*inf: lit, fig*) Ellbogenfreiheit *f* (*inf*).
elder[1] ['eldəʳ] 1 *adj attr comp of* **old** (**a**) (*older*) *brother etc* ältere(r, s). (**b**) (*senior*) **Pliny the ~** Plinius der Ältere, der ältere Plinius. (**c**) **~ statesman** (alt)erfahrener Staatsmann.
2 *n* (**a**) **respect your ~s and betters** du mußt Respekt vor Älteren haben. (**b**) (*of tribe, Church*) Älteste(r) *m*. (**c**) (*Presbyterian*) Gemeindeälteste(r), Presbyter *m*.
elder[2] ['eldəʳ] *n* (*Bot*) Holunder *m*.
elderberry ['eldə,berɪ] *n* Holunderbeere *f* ♦ **~ wine** Holunderwein *m*.
elderly ['eldəlɪ] *adj* ältlich, ältere(r, s) *attr*.
eldest ['eldɪst] *adj attr superl of* **old** älteste(r, s) ♦ **their ~** ihr Ältester/ihre Älteste.
elec *abbr of* (**a**) **electricity.** (**b**) **electric** elektr.
elect [ɪ'lekt] 1 *vt* (**a**) wählen ♦ **he was ~ed chairman/MP** er wurde zum Vorsitzenden/Abgeordneten gewählt; **to ~ sb to the Senate** jdn in den Senat wählen.
(**b**) (*choose*) (er)wählen, sich entscheiden für ♦ **to ~ to do sth** sich dafür entscheiden, etw zu tun; **to ~ French nationality** sich für die französische Staatsangehörigkeit entscheiden.
2 *adj* **the president ~** der designierte *or* künftige Präsident.
3 *npl* (*esp Rel*) **the ~** die Auserwählten *pl*.
election [ɪ'lekʃən] *n* Wahl *f*.
election *in cpds* Wahl-; **~ campaign** *n* Wahlkampf *m*.
electioneer [ɪ,lekʃə'nɪəʳ] *vi* als Wahlhelfer arbeiten, Wahlhilfe leisten ♦ **he's**

just ~ing for X er macht nur Wahlpropaganda für X.
electioneering [ɪˌlekʃə'nɪərɪŋ] [1] *n (campaign)* Wahlkampf *m*; *(propaganda)* Wahlpropaganda *f*.
[2] *adj campaign* Wahl-; *speech* Wahlkampf-.
elective [ɪ'lektɪv] [1] *adj* **(a)** Wahl- ◆ ~ **assembly** Wahlversammlung *f*. **(b)** *(Chem)* **~-attraction** Wahlverwandtschaft *f*; *(fig)* **~-affinity** Wahlverwandtschaft *f*. **(c)** *(US) class, course* wahlfrei.
[2] *n (US)* Wahlfach *nt*.
elector [ɪ'lektə^r] *n* **(a)** Wähler(in *f*) *m*. **(b)** *(Hist)* **E~** Kurfürst *m*. **(c)** *(US)* Wahlmann *m*.
electoral [ɪ'lektərəl] *adj* Wahl- ◆ ~ **college** *(US)* Wahlmänner-gremium *nt*; ~ **district** *or* **division** Wahlbezirk *m*; ~ **roll** Wählerverzeichnis *nt*.
electorate [ɪ'lektərɪt] *n* Wähler *pl*, Wählerschaft *f*.
electric [ɪ'lektrɪk] *adj appliance, current, wire* elektrisch; *generator* Strom- ◆ **the atmosphere was** ~ es herrschte große Spannung; **the effect was** ~ *(inf)* das hatte eine tolle Wirkung.
electrical [ɪ'lektrɪkəl] *adj* Elektro-, elektrisch ◆ ~ **engineer** Elektrotechniker *m*; *(with Univ etc degree)* Elektroingenieur *m*; ~ **engineering** Elektrotechnik *f*.
electric: ~ **blanket** *n* Heizdecke *f*; ~ **blue** [1] *n* Stahlblau *nt*; [2] *adj* stahlblau; ~ **chair** *n* elektrischer Stuhl; ~ **charge** *n* elektrische Ladung; ~ **cooker** *n* Elektroherd *m*; ~ **current** *n* elektrischer Strom; ~ **eel** *n* Zitteraal *m*; ~ **eye** *n* Photozelle *f*; ~ **fence** *n* Elektrozaun *m*; ~ **field** *n* elektrisches Feld; ~ **fire,** ~ **heater** *n* elektrisches Heizgerät; ~ **guitar** *n* elektrische Gitarre, E-Gitarre *f*.
electrician [ɪlek'trɪʃən] *n* Elektriker *m*.
electricity [ɪlek'trɪsɪtɪ] *n* Elektrizität *f*; *(electric power for use)* (elektrischer) Strom ◆ **to have** ~ **installed** Stromanschluß *or* elektrischen Strom bekommen; **to turn on/off the** ~ den Strom an-/abschalten.
electricity: ~ **(generating) board** *(Brit) n* Elektrizitätswerk *nt*; ~ **meter** *n* Stromzähler *m*; ~ **strike** *n* Streik *m* in den Elektrizitätswerken.
electric: ~ **light** *n* elektrisches Licht; ~ **motor** *n* Elektromotor *m*; ~ **organ** *n* elektrische Orgel; ~ **ray** *n (Zool)* Zitterrochen *m*; ~ **shock** [1] *n* elektrischer Schlag, Stromschlag *m*; *(Med)* Elektroschock *m*; [2] *adj attr* ~ **shock treatment** Elektroschocktherapie *f*; **to give sb** ~ **shock treatment** jdn mit Elektroschock behandeln; ~ **storm** *n* Gewitter *nt*.
electrification [ɪˌlektrɪfɪ'keɪʃən] *n* Elektrifizierung *f*.
electrify [ɪ'lektrɪfaɪ] *vt* **(a)** *(Rail)* elektrifizieren. **(b)** *(charge with electricity)* unter Strom setzen. **(c)** *(fig)* elektrisieren.
electrifying [ɪ'lektrɪfaɪɪŋ] *adj (fig)* elektrisierend.
electro- [ɪ'lektrəʊ-] *pref* Elektro- ◆ **~cardiogram** Elektrokardiogramm *nt*; **~cardiograph** Elektrokardiograph *m*; **~chemical** elektrochemisch; **~convulsive therapy** Elektroschocktherapie *f*.
electrocute [ɪ'lektrəkju:t] *vt* durch einen (Strom)schlag töten; *(execute)* durch den *or* auf dem elektrischen Stuhl hinrichten.
electrocution [ɪˌlektrə'kju:ʃən] *n see vt* Tötung *f* durch Stromschlag; Hinrichtung *f* durch den elektrischen Stuhl.
electrode [ɪ'lektrəʊd] *n* Elektrode *f*.
electro: **~dynamics** *n* Elektrodynamik *f*; **~encephalogram** *n* Elektroenzephalogramm *nt*; **~encephalograph** *n* Elektroenzephalograph *m*.
electrolysis [ɪlek'trɒlɪsɪs] *n* Elektrolyse *f*.
electrolyte [ɪ'lektrəʊlaɪt] *n* Elektrolyt *m*.
electro: **~magnet** *n* Elektromagnet *m*; **~magnetic** *adj* elektromagnetisch; **~magnetism** *n* Elektromagnetismus *m*.
electron [ɪ'lektrɒn] *n* Elektron *nt* ◆ ~ **beam** Elektronenstrahl *m*; ~ **camera** Elektronenkamera *f*; ~ **gun** Elektronenkanone *f*; ~ **microscope** Elektronenmikroskop *nt*.
electronic [ɪlek'trɒnɪk] *adj* elektronisch.
electronic: ~ **banking** *n* elektronischer Geldverkehr; ~ **brain** *n* Elektronen(ge)hirn *nt*; ~ **mail** *n* elektronische Post; ~ **mailbox** *n* elektronischer Briefkasten.
electronics [ɪlek'trɒnɪks] *n* **(a)** *sing (subject)* Elektronik *f*. **(b)** *pl (of machine etc)* Elektronik *f*.
electro [ɪ'lektrəʊ]: **~plate** [1] *vt* galvanisieren; [2] *n, no pl* Galvanisierung *f*; **is it silver? — no, ~plate** ist das Silber? — nein, nur versilbert; **~plated** *adj* (galvanisch) versilbert/verchromt *etc*; **~shock therapy** *n* Elektroschocktherapie *or* -behandlung *f*; **~static** *adj* elektrostatisch.
elegance ['elɪgəns] *n* Eleganz *f*.
elegant *adj*, **~ly** *adv* ['elɪgənt, -lɪ] elegant.
elegiac [ˌelɪ'dʒaɪək] [1] *adj* elegisch.
[2] *n* **~s** *pl* elegische Verse *pl*, Verse *pl* im elegischen Versmaß.
elegize ['elɪdʒaɪz] *vi* (in Elegien) klagen *(upon* über *+acc)*.
elegy ['elɪdʒɪ] *n* Elegie *f*.
element ['elɪmənt] *n (all senses)* Element *nt*; *(Chem also)* Grundstoff *m*; *(usu pl: of a subject also)* Grundbegriff *m* ◆ **the ~s of mathematics** die Grundbegriffe *or* Anfangsgründe *(geh) pl* der Mathematik; **an ~ of danger** ein Gefahrenelement *nt*; **the ~ of chance** das Zufallselement; **an ~ of truth** eine Spur *or* ein Element *nt* von Wahrheit; **the personal ~** das persönliche Element; **undesirable ~s** unerwünschte Elemente *pl*; **the (four) ~s** die (vier) Elemente; **to be in one's ~** in seinem Element sein; **to be out of one's ~** *(with group of people)* sich fehl am Platze fühlen; *(with subject)* sich nicht auskennen.
elemental [ˌelɪ'mentl] *adj* **(a)** *(concerning the four elements) force, power, gods* elementar. **(b)** *(simple)* einfach, elementar ◆ ~ **truth** einfache Wahrheit. **(c)** *(Chem, Phys)* Grundstoff-.
elementary [ˌelɪ'mentərɪ] *adj* **(a)** *(simple)* einfach, simpel, elementar.
(b) *(first, basic)* elementar, Grund- ◆ ~ **education** Elementarunterricht *m*; ~ **geometry course** Geometrie-Grundkursus *m*; ~ **particle** *(Phys)* Elementarteilchen *nt*; ~ **politeness requires that** ... es ist ein einfaches Gebot der Höflichkeit, daß ...; **still in the ~ stages** noch in den Anfängen; ~ **school** Grundschule *f*; ~ **science** elementare Naturwissenschaften *pl*; *(Sch)* Grundkurs *m* in Naturwissenschaften.
elephant ['elɪfənt] *n* Elefant *m*; *see* **pink, white ~**.
elephantiasis [ˌelɪfən'taɪəsɪs] *n* Elephantiasis *f*.
elephantine [ˌelɪ'fæntaɪn] *adj (heavy, clumsy)* schwerfällig, wie ein Elefant; *(large)* mammuthaft, Mammut-.
elevate ['elɪveɪt] *vt* **(a)** heben ◆ **by elevating the house a full 3 metres above** ... indem man das Haus ganze 3 Meter über *(+acc)* ... setzt.
(b) *(fig) mind* erbauen; *soul* erheben ◆ **elevating reading** erbauliche Lektüre.
(c) to ~ sb to the peerage jdn in den Adelsstand erheben; **since he's been ~d to top management** *(hum)* seit er ins Spitzenmanagement berufen worden ist.
elevated ['elɪveɪtɪd] *adj* **(a)** *position* hoch(liegend), höher; *platform* erhöht ◆ ~ **railway** Hochbahn *f*; ~ **motorway** *(Brit)* Hochstraße *f*. **(b)** *(fig) position, style, language* gehoben; *thoughts* erhaben.
elevation [ˌelɪ'veɪʃən] *n* **(a)** *(lit)* Hebung *f*; *(to higher rank)* Erhebung *f (to* in *+acc)*; *(Eccl)* Elevation *f*.
(b) *(of thought)* Erhabenheit *f*; *(of position, style)* Gehobenheit *f*.
(c) *(above sea level)* Höhe *f* über dem Meeresspiegel *or* über N.N.; *(hill etc)* (Boden)erhebung, Anhöhe *f*.
(d) angle of ~ Höhen- *or* Elevationswinkel *m*.
(e) *(of gun)* Elevation, Erhöhung *f*.
(f) *(Archit: drawing)* Aufriß *m* ◆ **front ~** Frontansicht *f*, Fassadenaufriß *m*.
elevator ['elɪveɪtə^r] *n* **(a)** *(US)* Fahrstuhl, Lift, Aufzug *m*. **(b)** *(storehouse)* Silo *m*. **(c)** *(Aviat)* Höhenruder *nt*. **(d)** *(with buckets etc)* Aufzug *m*; *(hoist)* Winde *f*.
elevator shoe *n* Schuh *m* mit Plateausohle.
eleven [ɪ'levn] [1] *n* **(a)** *(number)* Elf *f* ◆ **the ~ plus** *(old Brit Sch)* *Aufnahmeprüfung f in eine weiterführende Schule*. **(b)** *(Sport)* Elf *f*. **the German ~** die deutsche (National)elf; **the second ~** die zweite Mannschaft.
[2] *adj* elf; *see also* **six**.
elevenses [ɪ'levnzɪz] *n sing or pl (Brit)* zweites Frühstück.
eleventh [ɪ'levnθ] [1] *adj* elfte(r, s) ◆ **at the ~ hour** *(fig)* in letzter Minute, fünf Minuten vor zwölf.
[2] *n (fraction)* Elftel *nt*; Elfte(r, s); *(of series)* Elfte(r, s); *see also* **sixth**.
elf [elf] *n, pl* **elves** Elf *m*, Elfe *f*; *(mischievous)* Kobold *m*.
elfin ['elfɪn] *adj light, music* Elfen-, elfisch.
elfish ['elfɪʃ] *adj* elfisch; *(mischievous)* koboldhaft.
elicit [ɪ'lɪsɪt] *vt* entlocken *(from sb* jdm*)*.
elide [ɪ'laɪd] [1] *vt* elidieren, auslassen.
[2] *vi* elidiert werden, weg- *or* ausfallen.
eligibility [ˌelɪdʒə'bɪlɪtɪ] *n* **(a)** Berechtigung *f* ◆ **because of his undoubted ~ for the post** da er für die Stelle zweifelsohne in Frage kommt/kam. **(b)** Wählbarkeit *f*.
eligible ['elɪdʒəbl] *adj* **(a)** in Frage kommend; *(for competition etc also)* teilnahmeberechtigt; *(for student flights, grants etc also)* berechtigt; *(for membership)* aufnahmeberechtigt ◆ **to be ~ for a job/an office/a pension** für einen Posten/ein Amt in Frage kommen/pensionsberechtigt sein; **an ~ bachelor** ein begehrter Junggeselle. **(b)** *(able to be elected)* wählbar.
eliminate [ɪ'lɪmɪneɪt] *vt* **(a)** ausschließen; *alternative also* ausscheiden; *possibility of error also, competitor* ausschalten; *(Physiol)* ausscheiden, eliminieren; *(Math)* eliminieren ◆ **our team/candidate was ~d in the second round** unsere Mannschaft/unser Kandidat *m* schied in der zweiten Runde aus. **(b)** *(kill) enemy* ausschalten, eliminieren.
elimination [ɪˌlɪmɪ'neɪʃən] *n see vt* **(a)** Ausschluß *m*; Ausscheidung *f*; Ausschaltung *f*; Elimination *f* ◆ **by (a) process of ~** durch negative Auslese; **our ~ at the hands of the German team** die Ausschaltung unserer Mannschaft durch die deutsche. **(b)** Ausschaltung, Eliminierung *f*.
elision [ɪ'lɪʒən] *n* Elision *f*.
élite [eɪ'li:t] *n* Elite *f*.
élitism [eɪ'li:tɪzəm] *n* Elitedenken *nt*.
élitist [eɪ'li:tɪst] *adj* elitär.
elixir [ɪ'lɪksə^r] *n* Elixier *nt*, Auszug *m* ◆ ~ **of life** Lebenselixier *nt*.
Elizabeth [ɪ'lɪzəbəθ] *n* Elisabeth *f*.
Elizabethan [ɪˌlɪzə'bi:θən] [1] *adj* elisabethanisch.
[2] *n* Elisabethaner(in *f*) *m*.
elk [elk] *n* Elch *m* ◆ **Canadian ~** Wapiti(-Hirsch) *m*.
ellipse [ɪ'lɪps] *n* Ellipse *f*.
ellipsis [ɪ'lɪpsɪs] *n, pl* **ellipses** [ɪ'lɪpsi:z] *(Gram)* Ellipse *f*.
elliptic(al) [ɪ'lɪptɪk(əl)] *adj (Math, Gram)* elliptisch.
elm [elm] *n* Ulme *f*.
elocution [ˌelə'kju:ʃən] *n* Sprechtechnik *f* ◆ **teacher of ~** Sprecherzieher(in *f*) *m*; ~ **classes** Sprecherziehung *f*.
elocutionist [ˌelə'kju:ʃənɪst] *n* Sprecherzieher(in *f*) *m*.
elongate ['i:lɒŋgeɪt] [1] *vt* verlängern; *(stretch out)* langziehen, strecken.
[2] *vi* länger werden.
elongated ['i:lɒŋgeɪtɪd] *adj (extra length added)* verlängert; *(stretched) neck* ausgestreckt; *shape* länglich.
elongation [ˌi:lɒŋ'geɪʃən] *n* Verlängerung *f*; *(stretching)* Ausstrecken *nt*.
elope [ɪ'ləʊp] *vi* durchbrennen *(inf)*, ausreißen *(inf)* ◆ **they've ~d** sie sind von zu Hause durchgebrannt *or* ausgerissen, um zu heiraten *(inf)*.
elopement [ɪ'ləʊpmənt] *n* Durchbrennen, Ausreißen *(inf) nt*.

eloquence ['eləkwəns] *n see adj* Beredsamkeit, Eloquenz (*geh*), Wortgewandtheit *f*; Gewandtheit *f*; Wohlgesetztheit *f*; Beredtheit *f* ◆ **phrased with such ~** mit einer solchen Eloquenz ausgedrückt.

eloquent ['eləkwənt] *adj person* beredt, beredsam, wortgewandt; *words* gewandt; *speech* wohlgesetzt; (*fig*) *look, gesture* beredt, vielsagend ◆ **this is ~ proof of ...** das spricht wohl deutlich dafür, daß ...

eloquently ['eləkwəntlı] *adv* wortgewandt, mit beredten Worten ◆ **very ~ put** *or* **phrased** sehr gewandt ausgedrückt.

else [els] *adv* **(a)** (*after pron*) andere(r, s) ◆ **anybody ~ would have done it** jeder andere hätte es gemacht; **is there anybody ~ there?** (*in addition*) ist sonst (noch) jemand da?; **since John doesn't want it, does anybody ~ want it?** da John es nicht will, will jemand anders es haben?; **may I speak to somebody ~?** kann ich mit jemand anders *or* sonst jemand sprechen?; **I'd prefer something ~** ich möchte lieber etwas anderes; **I'd prefer anything ~** alles andere wäre mir lieber; **have you anything ~ to say?** haben Sie sonst noch etwas zu sagen?; **do you find this species anywhere ~?** findet man die Gattung sonstwo *or* auch anderswo?; **but they haven't got anywhere ~ to go** aber sie können sonst nirgends anders hingehen; **somebody ~** sonst jemand, jemand anders; **is there somebody ~?, she asked** ist da jemand anders?, fragte sie; **this is somebody ~'s umbrella** dieser Schirm gehört jemand anders; **something ~** etwas anderes, sonst etwas; **if all ~ fails** wenn alle Stricke reißen; **will there be anything ~, sir?** (*in shop*) darf es sonst noch etwas sein?; (*butler*) haben Sie sonst noch Wünsche?
(b) somewhere ~, someplace ~ (*esp US*) woanders, anderswo; (*with motion*) woandershin, anderswohin; **from somewhere ~** anderswoher, woandersher, von woanders.
(c) (*after pron, neg*) **nobody ~, no one ~** sonst niemand, niemand anders; **nobody ~ understood** sonst hat es niemand verstanden, niemand anders hat es verstanden; **nothing ~** sonst nichts, nichts anderes; **nothing ~ would be good enough** alles andere wäre nicht gut genug; **what do you want? — nothing ~, thank you** was möchten Sie? — danke, nichts weiter; **that this is a result of the cold and nothing ~** daß dies allein auf die Kälte zurückzuführen ist; **nowhere ~** sonst nirgends *or* nirgendwo, nirgendwo anders; (*with motion*) sonst nirgendwohin, nirgendwo andershin; **there's nothing ~ for it but to ...** da gibt es keinen anderen Ausweg, als zu ...
(d) (*after interrog*) **where ~?** wo sonst?, wo anders?; **who ~?** wer sonst?; **who ~ but John could have done a thing like that?** wer anders als John hätte so etwas tun können?; **what ~?** was sonst?; **how ~ can I do it?** wie kann ich es denn sonst *or* anders machen?; **what ~ could I have done?** was hätte ich sonst tun können?
(e) (*adv of quantity*) **they sell books and toys and much ~** sie führen Bücher, Spielzeug und vieles andere; **there is little ~ to be done** da bleibt nicht viel zu tun übrig.
(f) (*otherwise, if not*) sonst, andernfalls ◆ **do it now (or) ~ you'll be punished** tu es jetzt, sonst setzt es Strafe *or* oder es setzt Strafe; **do it or ~ ...!** mach das, sonst *or* oder ...!; **you better had, or ~ ...!** mach das bloß, sonst *or* oder ...!

elsewhere [,els'weəʳ] *adv* woanders, anderswo; (*to another place*) woandershin, anderswohin ◆ **from ~** von woanders (her), woandersher; **... which is found in Wales and ~** das unter anderem in Wales gefunden wird; **my mind was ~** ich war mit meinen Gedanken woanders.

ELT *abbr of* **English Language Teaching.**

elucidate [ı'lu:sıdeıt] *vt text* erklären; *mystery* aufklären, aufhellen.

elucidation [ı,lu:sı'deıʃən] *n see vt* Erklärung *f*; Aufklärung, Aufhellung *f*.

elucidatory [ı'lu:sıdeıtərı] *adj* erklärend.

elude [ı'lu:d] *vt observation, justice* sich entziehen (*+dat*); *sb's gaze* ausweichen (*+dat*); *police, enemy* entkommen (*+dat*), entwischen (*+dat*) ◆ **to ~ sb's grasp** sich nicht fassen lassen; **the name ~s me** der Name ist mir entfallen.

elusive [ı'lu:sıv] *adj* schwer faßbar; *concept, meaning also* schwer definierbar; *thoughts, memory* flüchtig; *happiness* unerreichbar; *answer* ausweichend; *fox etc* schwer zu fangen ◆ **he tried hard but success was** *or* **remained ~** er gab sich (*dat*) alle Mühe, aber der Erfolg wollte sich nicht einstellen.

elusively [ı'lu:sıvlı] *adv answer* ausweichend ◆ **the fox slipped ~ past the traps** der Fuchs schlüpfte an den Fallen vorbei; **this prospect of happiness which hovered ~ before him** diese Aussicht auf ein Glück, das so nah und doch nicht faßbar war.

elusiveness [ı'lu:sıvnıs] *n* (*of thoughts*) Flüchtigkeit *f*; (*of happiness*) Unerreichbarkeit *f*; (*of answer*) Ausweichen *nt* ◆ **the ~ of this concept** die Schwierigkeit, diesen Begriff zu definieren.

elves [elvz] *pl of* **elf.**

'em [əm] *pron* (*inf*) = **them.**

emaciated [ı'meısıeıtıd] *adj* ab- *or* ausgezehrt, stark abgemagert ◆ **to become ~** stark abmagern.

emaciation [ı,meısı'eıʃən] *n* Auszehrung *f*, starke Abmagerung.

E-mail, e-mail ['i:meıl] *n see* **electronic mail.**

emanate ['eməneıt] *vi* ausgehen (*from* von); (*light also*) ausstrahlen (*from* von); (*odour also*) ausströmen (*from* von); (*documents, instructions etc*) stammen (*from* aus) ◆ **according to instructions emanating from regional headquarters** (*form*) nach Anweisungen der Bezirksstelle.

emanation [,emə'neıʃən] *n see vi* Ausgehen *nt*; Ausstrahlung *f*; Ausströmen *nt*, (*Rel*) Emanation *f*.

emancipate [ı'mænsıpeıt] *vt women* emanzipieren; *slaves* freilassen; (*fig*) emanzipieren, befreien, frei machen.

emancipated [ı'mænsıpeıtıd] *adj woman, outlook* emanzipiert; *slave* freigelassen.

emancipation [ı,mænsı'peıʃən] *n* (*lit, fig*) Emanzipation *f*; (*of slave*) Freilassung *f*.

emasculate [ı'mæskjʊleıt] *vt* **(a)** (*weaken*) entkräften. **(b)** (*lit*) *man* entmannen.

emasculated [ı'mæskjʊleıtıd] *adj style etc* (saft- und) kraftlos.

embalm [ım'bɑ:m] *vt corpse* einbalsamieren ◆ **~ing fluid/oil** Balsamierflüssigkeit *f*/-öl *nt*.

embankment [ım'bæŋkmənt] *n* (Ufer)böschung *f*; (*along path, road*) Böschung *f*; (*for railway*) Bahndamm *m*; (*holding back water*) (Ufer)damm, Deich *m*; (*roadway beside a river*) Ufer(straße *f*) *nt*.

embargo [ım'bɑ:gəʊ] *n, pl* **-es (a)** Embargo *nt* ◆ **to lay** *or* **place** *or* **put an ~ on sth** etw mit einem Embargo belegen, ein Embargo über etw (*acc*) verhängen; **there's still an ~ on petrol, petrol is still under an ~** es besteht immer noch ein Embargo für Benzin. **(b)** (*fig*) Sperre *f*. **to put an ~ on further spending** alle weiteren Ausgaben sperren.

embark [ım'bɑ:k] **1** *vt* einschiffen; *goods also* verladen.
2 *vi* **(a)** (*Naut*) sich einschiffen; (*troops*) eingeschifft werden. **(b)** (*fig*) **to ~ up(on) sth** etw anfangen, etw beginnen.

embarkation [,embɑ:'keıʃən] *n* **(a)** Einschiffung *f* ◆ **~ officer** Verladeoffizier *m*; **~ papers** Bordpapiere *pl*. **(b)** (*of cargo*) Verladung, Übernahme *f*.

embarrass [ım'bærəs] *vt* **(a)** in Verlegenheit bringen, verlegen machen; (*generosity etc*) beschämen ◆ **to look ~ed** verlegen aussehen; **I feel so ~ed about it** das ist mir so peinlich; **she was ~ed by the question** die Frage war ihr peinlich; **there's no need to feel ~ed, here, take the money** das braucht Ihnen gar nicht peinlich zu sein, hier, nehmen Sie das Geld.
(b) to be ~ed by lack of money in einer finanziellen Verlegenheit sein; **I am ~ed as to which one to choose** die Wahl bringt mich in Verlegenheit.
(c) ~ed by his cumbersome greatcoat durch seinen unförmigen Übermantel behindert.

embarrassed [ım'bærəst] *adj* verlegen.

embarrassing [ım'bærəsıŋ] *adj* peinlich; *generosity etc* beschämend.

embarrassingly [ım'bærəsıŋlı] *adv see adj* **he said a few rather ~ candid things** er machte ein paar Bemerkungen, deren Offenheit schon peinlich war.

embarrassment [ım'bærəsmənt] *n* Verlegenheit *f*; (*through generosity also*) Beschämung *f* ◆ **to cause ~ to sb** jdn in Verlegenheit bringen, jdn verlegen machen; **to be a source of ~ to sb** jdn ständig in Verlegenheit bringen; (*thing also*) jdm peinlich sein; **much to my ~ she ...** sie ..., was mir sehr peinlich war; **she's an ~ to her family** sie blamiert die ganze Familie (*inf*); **financial ~** finanzielle Verlegenheit.

embassy ['embəsı] *n* Botschaft *f*.

embattled [ım'bætld] *adj army* kampfbereit; *building* (mit Zinnen) bewehrt, befestigt.

embed [ım'bed] *vt* **(a)** einlassen ◆ **the screws/tyres were so firmly ~ded that ...** die Schrauben/Reifen steckten so fest, daß ...; **the bullet ~ded itself in the wall** die Kugel bohrte sich in die Wand; **to be ~ded in sth** (*fig*) fest in etw (*dat*) verwurzelt sein; **the belief is now firmly ~ded in their minds** der Glaube ist jetzt fest in ihrem Denken verankert.
(b) (*Comput*) **~ded commands** eingebettete Befehle.
(c) (*Ling*) einschieben ◆ **~ded clauses** eingeschobene Gliedsätze.

embellish [ım'belıʃ] *vt* (*adorn*) schmücken, verschönern; (*fig*) *tale, account* ausschmücken; *truth* beschönigen.

embellishment [ım'belıʃmənt] *n* Schmuck *m*; (*act also*) Verschönerung *f*; (*of story*) Ausschmückung *f*; (*of truth*) Beschönigung *f*; (*of handwriting*) Verzierung *f*; Schnörkel *m*; (*Mus*) Verzierung *f*.

embers ['embəz] *npl* Glut *f*; *see* **fan¹.**

embezzle [ım'bezl] *vt* unterschlagen, veruntreuen.

embezzlement [ım'bezlmənt] *n* Unterschlagung *f*.

embezzler [ım'bezləʳ] *n* jd, der eine Unterschlagung begangen hat ◆ **he was accused of being an ~** er wurde beschuldigt, Geld unterschlagen *or* veruntreut zu haben.

embitter [ım'bıtəʳ] *vt person* verbittern; *relations* trüben, vergiften.

emblazon [ım'bleızən] *vt* **(a)** (*Her*) schmücken, (ver)zieren. **(b)** (*display boldly*) *name* stolz hervorheben ◆ **the name "Jones" was ~ed on the cover** der Name „Jones" prangte auf dem Umschlag. **(c)** (*extol*) überschwenglich preisen.

emblem ['embləm] *n* Emblem *nt*; (*of political party, trade also*) Wahrzeichen *nt*.

emblematic [,emblə'mætık] *adj* emblematisch (*of* für).

embodiment [ım'bɒdımənt] *n* **(a)** Verkörperung *f* ◆ **to be the ~ of virtue** die Tugend in Person sein. **(b)** (*inclusion*) Aufnahme, Eingliederung *f*.

embody [ım'bɒdı] *vt* **(a)** (*give form to*) *one's thoughts* ausdrücken, Ausdruck geben (*+dat*), in Worte kleiden. **(b)** *one's ideal* verkörpern. **(c)** (*include*) enthalten ◆ **to become embodied in sth** in etw (*acc*) aufgenommen werden.

embolden [ım'bəʊldən] *vt* ermutigen, Mut machen (*+dat*) ◆ **to ~ sb to do sth** jdn dazu ermutigen *or* jdm Mut machen, etw zu tun.

embolism ['embəlızəm] *n* (*Med*) Embolie *f*.

embonpoint [,ɒmbɒm'pwɑ:ŋ] *n* (*hum, euph*) Embonpoint *m or nt* (*dated*), Leibesfülle *f*.

emboss [ım'bɒs] *vt metal, leather* prägen; *silk, velvet* gaufrieren ◆ **~ed wallpaper** Prägetapete *f*; **~ed writing paper** Briefpapier mit geprägtem Kopf; **a silver vase ~ed with a design** eine silberne Vase mit erhaben herausgearbeitetem Muster; **an ~ed silver tray** ein Silbertablett mit Relief.

embouchure ['ɒmbʊ,ʃʊəʳ] *n* (*Mus*) Mundstück *nt*; (*of player*) Mundstellung *f*.

▼ **embrace** [ɪm'breɪs] [1] *vt* (a) (*hug*) umarmen, in die Arme schließen.
▼ (b) (*seize eagerly*) *religion* annehmen; *opportunity* wahrnehmen, ergreifen; *cause* sich annehmen (*+gen*); *offer* annehmen, ergreifen ◆ **he ~d the cause of socialism** er machte die Sache des Sozialismus zu seiner eigenen.
(c) (*include*) umfassen, erfassen ◆ **an all-embracing review** eine allumfassende Besprechung.
[2] *vi* sich umarmen.
[3] *n* (*hug*) Umarmung *f* ◆ **a couple in a tender ~** ein Paar in zärtlicher Umarmung; **he held her in his ~** er hielt sie umschlungen; **death's ~** (*liter*) die Arme des Todes.

embrasure [ɪm'breɪʒəʳ] *n* (*in parapet*) Schießscharte *f*; (*of door, window*) Laibung *f*.

embrocation [,embrəʊ'keɪʃən] *n* Einreibemittel *nt*.

embroider [ɪm'brɔɪdəʳ] [1] *vt cloth* besticken; *pattern* sticken; (*fig*) *facts, truth* ausschmücken.
[2] *vi* sticken.

embroidery [ɪm'brɔɪdərɪ] *n* (a) Stickerei *f*. (b) (*fig*) Ausschmückungen *pl*.

embroidery: ~ frame *n* Stickrahmen *m*; **~ thread** *n* Stickgarn *nt*.

embroil [ɪm'brɔɪl] *vt* **to ~ sb in sth** jdn in etw (*acc*) hineinziehen; **to become ~ed in a dispute** in einen Streit verwickelt *or* hineingezogen werden.

embroilment [ɪm'brɔɪlmənt] *n* Verwicklung *f* (*in* in *+acc*).

embryo ['embrɪəʊ] *n* (*lit, fig*) Embryo *m*; (*fig also*) Keim *m* ◆ **in ~** (*lit*) im Keim; (*animal*) als Embryo; (*fig*) im Keim.

embryologist [,embrɪ'ɒlədʒɪst] *n* Embryologe *m*, Embryologin *f*.

embryology [,embrɪ'ɒlədʒɪ] *n* Embryologie *f*.

embryonic [,embrɪ'ɒnɪk] *adj* (*lit, fig*) embryonisch; (*fig also*) keimhaft.

emcee ['em'siː] [1] *n* Conférencier *m*; (*on TV also*) Showmaster *m*; (*at private functions*) Zeremonienmeister, Maître de plaisir (*old, hum*) *m*.
[2] *vt show* als Conférencier *etc* leiten.

emend [ɪ'mend] *vt text* verbessern, korrigieren.

emendation [,iːmen'deɪʃən] *n* Verbesserung, Korrektur *f*.

emerald ['emərəld] [1] *n* (a) (*stone*) Smaragd *m*. (b) (*colour*) Smaragdgrün *nt*.
[2] *adj* smaragden, Smaragd-; *colour also* smaragdgrün ◆ **the E~ Isle** die Grüne Insel.

▼ **emerge** [ɪ'mɜːdʒ] *vi* (a) auftauchen ◆ **he ~d victorious/the winner** er ging als Sieger/siegreich hervor; **we ~d into the bright daylight** wir kamen heraus in das helle Tageslicht; **he ~d from behind the shed** er tauchte hinter dem Schuppen auf; **one arm ~d from beneath the blanket** ein Arm tauchte unter der Decke hervor.
(b) (*come into being: life, new nation*) entstehen ◆ **life ~d from the sea** das Leben entstammt dem *or* kommt aus dem Meer.
▼ (c) (*truth, nature of problem etc*) sich herausstellen, herauskommen (*from* bei); (*facts*) sich herausstellen, an den Tag kommen ◆ **it ~s that ...** es stellt sich heraus, daß ...; **but what ~s from all this?** aber was ergibt sich aus all dem?

emergence [ɪ'mɜːdʒəns] *n* Auftauchen *nt*; (*of new nation etc*) Entstehung *f*; (*of theory, school of thought*) Aufkommen *nt*.

emergency [ɪ'mɜːdʒənsɪ] [1] *n* Notfall *m*; (*state of ~*) Notlage *f* ◆ **in case of ~, in an ~** im Notfall; **to be prepared for any ~** für den Notfall vorbereitet sein; **to declare a state of ~** den Notstand erklären *or* ausrufen; **to declare a state of ~ in an area** eine Gegend zum Notstandsgebiet erklären; **there's always an ~ just before publication** kurz vor der Veröffentlichung kommt es immer zur Panik; **the doctor's been called out on an ~** der Arzt ist zu einem Notfall gerufen worden.
[2] *adj attr case, fund* Not- ◆ **for ~ use only** nur für den Notfall.

emergency *in cpds* Not-; **~ brake** *n* Notbremse *f*; **~ call** *n* Notruf *m*; **~ centre** *n* Rettungszentrum *nt* des Noteinsatzes; **~ doctor** *n* Notarzt *m*; **~ exit** *n* Notausgang *m*; **~ landing** *n* Notlandung *f*; **~ powers** *npl* Notstandsvollmachten *pl*; **~ rations** *npl* Notverpflegung *f*, eiserne Ration; **~ room** *n* (*US*) Unfallstation *f*; **~ service** *n* Not- *or* Hilfsdienst *m*; **~ services** *npl* Notdienst *m*; **~ stop** *n* (*Aut*) Vollbremsung *f*; **~ telephone** *n* Notrufelefon *nt*; **~ ward** *n* Unfallstation *f*.

emergent [ɪ'mɜːdʒənt] *adj nations* jung, aufstrebend.

emeritus [ɪ'merɪtəs] *adj* emeritiert.

emery ['emərɪ] *n* Schmirgel *m*.

emery: ~ board *n* Papiernagelfeile *f*; **~ cloth** *n* Schmirgelleinwand *f*; **~ paper** *n* Schmirgelpapier *nt*.

emetic [ɪ'metɪk] *n* Brechmittel, Emetikum (*spec*) *nt*.

emigrant ['emɪgrənt] [1] *n* Auswanderer *m*; (*esp for political reasons*) Emigrant(in *f*) *m*.
[2] *adj attr* Auswanderer-; Emigranten- ◆ **~ labourers** Arbeitsemigranten *pl*.

emigrate ['emɪgreɪt] *vi* auswandern; (*esp for political reasons*) emigrieren.

emigration [,emɪ'greɪʃən] *n* Auswanderung *f*; (*esp for political reasons*) Emigration *f*.

émigré ['emɪgreɪ] *n* Emigrant(in *f*) *m*.

eminence ['emɪnəns] *n* (a) (*distinction*) hohes Ansehen ◆ **doctors of ~** (hoch) angesehene Ärzte *pl*. (b) (*of ground*) Erhebung, Anhöhe *f*. (c) (*Eccl*) **His/Your E~** Seine/Eure Eminenz.

éminence grise ['emɪnəns'griːz] *n* graue Eminenz.

eminent ['emɪnənt] *adj person* (hoch)angesehen, berühmt; *suitability, fairness* ausgesprochen, eminent.

eminently ['emɪnəntlɪ] *adv* ausgesprochen, außerordentlich.

emir [e'mɪəʳ] *n* Emir m.

emirate ['emɪrɪt] *n* Emirat *nt*.

emissary ['emɪsərɪ] *n* Emissär *m*, Abgesandte(r) *mf*.

emission [ɪ'mɪʃən] *n* Ausstrahlung, Abstrahlung *f*; (*of light also, of fumes, X-rays*) Emission *f* (*spec*); (*of heat also, of sound*) Abgabe *f*; (*of gas also, of smell*) Verströmen, Ausströmen *nt*; (*of liquid*) Ausströmen *nt*; (*gradual*) Absonderung, Abscheidung *f*; (*of vapour, smoke*) (*continuous*) Abgabe *f*; (*of lava*) Ausstoßen *nt*; (*of sparks*) Versprühen *nt* ◆ **~ of semen** Samenerguß *m*.

emit [ɪ'mɪt] *vt* (a) *light* ausstrahlen, abstrahlen; *radiation also* aussenden, emittieren; *heat also, sound* abgeben; *gas also, smell* verströmen, ausströmen; *vapour, smoke* (*continuous*) abgeben; *lava, cry* ausstoßen; *liquid* (*gradually*) absondern, abscheiden; *sparks* versprühen. (b) *banknotes* ausgeben.

Emmy ['emɪ] *n* (*award*) Emmy *f*.

emollient [ɪ'mɒlɪənt] (*Med*) [1] *n* Linderungsmittel *nt*.
[2] *adj* lindernd.

emolument [ɪ'mɒljʊmənt] *n* (*usu pl: form*) Vergütung *f*; (*fee*) Honorar *nt*; (*salary*) Bezüge *pl*.

emote [ɪ'məʊt] *vi* seine Gefühle ausdrücken; (*actor*) Gefühle mimen ◆ **she's just emoting** (*inf*) sie spielt nur Theater (*inf*).

emotion [ɪ'məʊʃən] *n* (a) Gefühl *nt*, Gefühlsregung, Emotion *f* ◆ **one should not allow ~ to interfere with reason** der Verstand sollte nicht durch das Gefühl beeinflußt werden.
(b) *no pl* (*state of being moved*) (Gemüts)bewegung, Bewegtheit *f* ◆ **to show no ~** unbewegt bleiben; **in a voice full of ~** mit bewegter Stimme; **there was absolutely no ~ in his voice** seine Stimme war völlig emotionslos.

emotional [ɪ'məʊʃənl] *adj* (a) emotional, emotionell; *shock also* seelisch, Gefühls-; *story, film, speech also* gefühlsbetont; *moment, writing also* gefühlvoll; *decision also* gefühlsmäßig; *day, experience* erregend; *letter* erregt ◆ **~ state** Zustand *m* der Erregung; **~ disturbance** Störung *f* des Gefühlslebens; **it has an ~ appeal** es appelliert an das Gefühl; **sex without ~ involvement** Sex ohne echtes Gefühl.
(b) *person, character, disposition* (leicht) erregbar, emotional ◆ **don't get so ~ about it** reg dich nicht so darüber auf.

emotionalism [ɪ'məʊʃnəlɪzəm] *n* Gefühlsbetontheit, Rührseligkeit *f* ◆ **the article was sheer ~** der Artikel war reine Gefühlsduselei.

emotionally [ɪ'məʊʃnəlɪ] *adv behave, react* gefühlsmäßig, emotional; (*with feeling*) *speak* gefühlvoll; (*showing one is upset*) *respond etc* erregt ◆ **an ~ deprived child** ein Kind ohne Nestwärme; **to be ~ disturbed** seelisch gestört sein; **you're ~ deprived!** du bist ja total gefühlsarm!; **I don't want to get ~ involved (with her)** ich will mich (bei ihr) nicht ernsthaft engagieren.

emotionless [ɪ'məʊʃənlɪs] *adj face etc* ausdruckslos; *person* gefühllos, emotionslos.

emotive [ɪ'məʊtɪv] *adj* gefühlsbetont; *word also* emotional gefärbt; *force of a word* emotional.

empanel *vt see* **impanel**.

empathize ['empəθaɪz] *vi* sich hineinversetzen *or* einfühlen (*with* in *+acc*).

empathy ['empəθɪ] *n* Einfühlungsvermögen *nt*, Empathie *f*.

emperor ['empərəʳ] *n* Kaiser *m*; (*in Rome also*) Imperator *m*.

emperor penguin *n* Kaiserpinguin *m*.

emphasis ['emfəsɪs] *n* (a) (*vocal stress*) Betonung *f* ◆ **the ~ is on the first syllable** die Betonung *or* der Ton liegt auf der ersten Silbe; **to lay** *or* **put ~ on a word** ein Wort betonen; **to say sth with ~** etw mit Nachdruck *or* nachdrücklich betonen.
(b) (*importance*) Betonung *f*, (Schwer)gewicht *nt* ◆ **to lay ~** *or* **put the ~ on sth** etw betonen; **this year the ~ is on masculinity** dieses Jahr liegt der Akzent *or* die Betonung auf Männlichkeit; **there is too much ~ on ....** ... wird zu sehr betont; **a change of ~** eine Akzentverschiebung.

▼ **emphasize** ['emfəsaɪz] *vt word, syllable, hips* betonen; *point, importance, need also* hervorheben ◆ **this point cannot be too strongly ~d** das kann man gar nicht genug betonen.

emphatic [ɪm'fætɪk] *adj tone, manner* nachdrücklich, entschieden, emphatisch (*geh*); *denial also* energisch; *person* bestimmt, entschieden ◆ **I am ~ about this point** ich bestehe auf diesem Punkt.

emphatically [ɪm'fætɪkəlɪ] *adv state* mit Nachdruck, ausdrücklich, emphatisch (*geh*); *deny, refuse* strikt, energisch ◆ **most ~ not** auf gar keinen Fall.

empire ['empaɪəʳ] [1] *n* (a) Reich *nt*; (*ruled by Kaiser, emperor also*) Kaiserreich *nt*; (*world-wide*) Weltreich, Imperium *nt* ◆ **the responsibilities of ~** die Verantwortung einer Weltmacht; **the Holy Roman E~** das Heilige Römische Reich (deutscher Nation); **the British E~** das Britische Weltreich, das Empire.
(b) (*fig: esp Comm*) Imperium *nt*.
[2] *adj attr* **E~** *costume, furniture, style* Empire-.

empire: ~-builder *n* (*fig*) jd, der sich ein kleines Imperium aufbaut; **~-building** *n* (*fig*) Schaffung *f* eines eigenen kleinen Imperiums.

empiric [em'pɪrɪk] [1] *adj see* **empirical**.
[2] *n* Empiriker *m*.

empirical [em'pɪrɪkəl] *adj* empirisch, Erfahrungs-.

empirically [em'pɪrɪkəlɪ] *adv tested, testable* empirisch; *based* auf Erfahrung.

empiricism [em'pɪrɪsɪzəm] *n* Empirismus *m*; (*method*) Empirie *f*.

empiricist [em'pɪrɪsɪst] *n* Empiriker *m*.

emplacement [ɪm'pleɪsmənt] *n* (*Mil*) Stellung *f*.

employ [ɪm'plɔɪ] [1] *vt* (a) *person* beschäftigen; (*take on*) anstellen; *private detective* beauftragen ◆ **he has been ~ed with us for 15 years** er ist schon seit 15 Jahren bei uns.
(b) (*use*) *means, method, force, cunning* anwenden, einsetzen; *skill also, word, concept* verwenden; *time* verbringen ◆ **you can surely find a better way of ~ing your time** Sie können doch bestimmt Besseres mit Ihrer Zeit anfangen.

➤ LANGUAGE IN USE: **embrace: 1b** → 26.3 **emerge: c** → 17.2 **emphasize** → 26.3

(c) **to be ~ed in doing sth** damit beschäftigt sein, etw zu tun.
[2] *n* **to be in the ~ of sb** (*form*) bei jdm beschäftigt sein, in jds Diensten stehen (*geh*).

employable [ɪm'plɔɪəbl] *adj person* anstellbar, zu beschäftigen *pred*; (*useable*) *method etc* anwendbar; *word* verwendbar.

employee [,ɪmplɔɪ'iː] *n* Angestellte(r) *mf* ◆ **~s and employers** Arbeitnehmer und Arbeitgeber; **the ~s** (*of one firm*) die Belegschaft, die Beschäftigten *pl*.

employer [ɪm'plɔɪəʳ] *n* Arbeitgeber(in *f*), Brötchengeber (*hum inf*) *m*; (*Comm, industry also*) Unternehmer(in *f*) *m*; (*of domestics, servants, civil servants also*) Dienstherr *m* ◆ **~s' federation** Arbeitgeberverband *m*; **~'s contribution** Arbeitgeberanteil *m*; **~'s liability insurance** Arbeitgeberhaftpflichtversicherung *f*.

employment [ɪm'plɔɪmənt] *n* (a) (An)stellung, Arbeit *f* ◆ **to take up ~ with sb** eine Stelle bei jdm annehmen; **to be without ~** stellungslos *or* ohne Arbeit sein; **to seek ~** Arbeit *or* eine Stelle suchen; **to seek ~ with sb** sich bei jdm bewerben; **out of ~** stellungslos, arbeitslos; **to throw workers out of ~** Arbeiter um ihren Arbeitsplatz bringen; **how long is it since you were last in ~?** wann hatten Sie Ihre letzte Stellung?; **conditions/contract/place of ~** Arbeitsbedingungen *pl*/-vertrag *m*/-platz *m*; **to find ~ for sb** Arbeit *or* eine Anstellung für jdn finden; **what sort of ~ are you looking for?** welche Art von Tätigkeit suchen Sie?; **what's your ~?** als was sind Sie tätig?
(b) (*act of employing*) Beschäftigung *f*; (*taking on*) Anstellung *f*, Einstellen *nt*.
(c) (*use*) (*of means, method, force, cunning*) Anwendung *f*, Einsatz *m*; (*of skill also, word, concept*) Verwendung *f*.

employment: ~ agency *n* Stellenvermittlung *f*; **~ exchange** *n* (*dated*), **~ office** *n* Arbeitsamt *nt*.

emporium [em'pɔːrɪəm] *n* Warenhaus *nt*.

empower [ɪm'paʊəʳ] *vt* **to ~ sb to do sth** jdn ermächtigen *or* (*Jur*) jdm (die) Vollmacht erteilen, etw zu tun; **to be ~ed to do sth** ermächtigt *or* befugt sein/die Vollmacht haben, etw zu tun.

empress ['emprɪs] *n* Kaiserin *f*.

emptiness ['emptɪnɪs] *n* Leere, Leerheit *f*; (*of life etc*) Leere *f*.

empty ['emptɪ] [1] *adj* (*+er*) (*all senses*) leer; (*not occupied*) *house* leerstehend *attr*; *head* hohl ◆ **~ of** ohne, bar (*+gen*) (*liter*); **to be taken on an ~ stomach** auf nüchternen Magen zu nehmen; **I just feel ~** ich fühle mich innerlich völlig leer; **~ vessels make most noise** (*Prov*) die am wenigsten zu sagen haben, reden am meisten; **to look into ~ space** ins Leere blicken.
[2] *n usu pl* Leergut *nt no pl*.
[3] *vt* (a) leeren, leer machen; *container* (ent)leeren; *box, room also* ausräumen; *house* räumen; *glass, bottle also* (*by drinking*) austrinken; *pond, tank also* ablassen; *lorry* abladen ◆ **her singing emptied the hall in ten minutes flat** mit ihrem Singen schaffte sie es, daß der Saal innerhalb von zehn Minuten leer war; **the burglars emptied the shop** die Einbrecher haben den Laden ausgeräumt; **as though he had now emptied himself of all emotion** als ob er nun jegliches Gefühl verloren hätte.
(b) *liquid, contents* ausgießen, leeren ◆ **he emptied it into another container** er goß es in ein anderes Gefäß um.
[4] *vi* (*water*) auslaufen, abfließen; (*rivers*) münden, sich ergießen (*liter*) (*into* in *+acc*); (*theatre, streets*) sich leeren ◆ **the sink is not ~ing properly** der Ausguß läuft nicht richtig ab.

◆**empty out** *vt sep* ausleeren; *pockets also* ausräumen.

empty: ~-handed *adj* **to return ~-handed** mit leeren Händen zurückkehren, unverrichteterdinge zurückkehren; **~-headed** *adj* strohdumm; **she's an ~-headed girl** sie hat Stroh im Kopf.

EMS *abbr of* **European Monetary System** EWS *nt*.

emu ['iːmjuː] *n* Emu *m*.

emulate ['emjʊleɪt] *vt* (a) nacheifern (*+dat*), nachstreben (*+dat*) ◆ **I tried to ~ his success** ich versuchte, es ihm gleichzutun. (b) (*Comput*) emulieren.

emulation [,emjʊ'leɪʃən] *n* (a) Nacheiferung *f* ◆ **in ~ of sb** in dem Bestreben, es jdm gleichzutun. (b) (*Comput*) Emulation *f*.

emulsifier [ɪ'mʌlsɪfaɪəʳ] *n* Emulgator *m*.

emulsify [ɪ'mʌlsɪfaɪ] [1] *vt* emulgieren, zu einer Emulsion verbinden.
[2] *vi* emulgieren.

emulsion [ɪ'mʌlʃən] *n* (a) Emulsion *f*. (b) (*also* **~ paint**) Emulsionsfarbe *f*.

enable [ɪ'neɪbl] *vt* (a) (*make able*) **to ~ sb to do sth** es jdm ermöglichen *or* möglich machen, etw zu tun, jdn in den Stand setzen, etw zu tun (*geh*); **what ~s the seal to stay under water so long?** wodurch ist der Seehund fähig, so lange unter Wasser zu bleiben?; **the good weather ~d us to go out** das schöne Wetter machte es uns möglich auszugehen.
(b) (*Jur: authorize*) **to ~ sb to do sth** jdn (dazu) ermächtigen, etw zu tun.

enabling act [ɪ'neɪblɪŋ,ækt] *n* (*Parl*) Ermächtigungsgesetz *nt*.

enact [ɪ'nækt] *vt* (a) (*Pol*) *law* erlassen ◆ **it is hereby ~ed that** ... es wird hiermit verfügt, daß ... (b) (*perform*) *play* aufführen; *rôle* darstellen, spielen ◆ **the drama which was ~ed yesterday** (*fig*) das Drama, das sich gestern abgespielt hat.

enactment [ɪ'næktmənt] *n* (*of law*) Erlaß *m*; (*law also*) Verordnung, Verfügung *f*.

enamel [ɪ'næməl] [1] *n* Email *nt*, Emaille *f* (*inf*); (*paint*) Email(le)lack *m*; (*of tiles etc*) Glasur *f*; (*of teeth*) Zahnschmelz *m*; (*nail ~*) Nagellack *m*.
[2] *vt* emaillieren.
[3] *adj pot, pan* Email(le)- ◆ **~ paint** Email(le)lack *m*; **~ painting** Email(le)malerei *f*.

enamelled [ɪ'næməld] *adj* emailliert; *tile* glasiert.

enamelware [ɪ'næməl,weəʳ] *n* Email(le)waren *pl*.

enamour, (*US*) **enamor** [ɪ'næməʳ] *vt* **to be ~ed of sb/sth** (*in love with*) in jdn/etw verliebt sein; (*taken by*) von jdm/etw angetan *or* entzückt sein; **she was not exactly ~ed of the idea** sie war von der Idee nicht gerade begeistert.

enc. *see* **enc(l)**.

encamp [ɪn'kæmp] [1] *vi* das Lager aufschlagen.
[2] *vt* **where the troops were ~ed** wo die Truppen ihr Lager bezogen hatten.

encampment [ɪn'kæmpmənt] *n* Lager *nt*.

encapsulate [ɪn'kæpsjʊleɪt] *vt* (*Pharm*) in Kapseln abfüllen; (*express in condensed form*) zusammenfassen.

encase [ɪn'keɪs] *vt* verkleiden (*in* mit); *wires* umgeben (*in* mit); *cake* überziehen (*in* mit).

encash [ɪn'kæʃ] *vt cheque etc* einlösen.

encashment [ɪn'kæʃmənt] *n* (*of cheque etc*) Einlösung *f*.

encephalitis [,ensefə'laɪtɪs] *n* Gehirnentzündung *f*.

enchain [ɪn'tʃeɪn] *vt* (*lit*) in Ketten legen ◆ **to be ~ed** in Ketten liegen; (*fig*) gefangen sein.

enchant [ɪn'tʃɑːnt] *vt* (a) (*delight*) bezaubern, entzücken ◆ **to be ~ed with sth** von etw *or* über etw (*acc*) entzückt sein. (b) (*put under spell*) verzaubern. **the ~ed wood** der Zauberwald.

enchanting *adj*, **~ly** *adv* [ɪn'tʃɑːntɪŋ, -lɪ] bezaubernd, entzückend.

enchantment [ɪn'tʃɑːntmənt] *n* (a) (*delight*) Entzücken *nt*. (b) (*charm*) Zauber *m*.

enchantress [ɪn'tʃɑːntrɪs] *n* Zauberin *f*; (*enchanting woman*) bezaubernde Frau.

encipher [ɪn'saɪfəʳ] *vt* chiffrieren.

encircle [ɪn'sɜːkl] *vt* (*surround*) umgeben, umfassen; (*wall, belt also*) umschließen; (*troops*) einkreisen, umfassen; *building* umstellen ◆ **his arm ~d her waist** er hielt ihre Taille umfaßt; **the house is ~d by trees** das Haus ist von Bäumen umstanden.

encirclement [ɪn'sɜːklmənt] *n* (*Mil*) Einkreisung, Umfassung *f*; (*in a valley also*) Einkesselung *f*; (*of building*) Umstellung *f*.

encircling [ɪn'sɜːklɪŋ] [1] *n* (*Mil*) Umfassung *f*, Einkreisen *nt*; (*in valley*) Einkesseln *nt*; (*of building*) Umstellung *f*.
[2] *adj walls etc* umgebend; (*liter*) *night* alles umgebend *or* umfassend ◆ **~ movement** (*Mil*) Einkreisungs- *or* Umfassungsmanöver *nt*.

enc(l) *abbr of* **enclosure(s)** Anl.

enclave ['enkleɪv] *n* Enklave *f*.

enclitic [ɪn'klɪtɪk] *n* Enklitikon *nt*.

➤ **enclose** [ɪn'kləʊz] *vt* (a) (*shut in*) einschließen; (*surround*) umgeben; (*with fence etc*) *ground* einzäunen, einfrieden (*geh*) ◆ **the garden is completely ~d** der Garten ist völlig abgeschlossen.
➤ (b) (*in a parcel, envelope*) beilegen, beifügen ◆ **please find ~d a cheque for £200** als Anlage *or* anbei übersenden wir Ihnen einen Scheck über £ 200; **a banknote was ~d in the letter** dem Brief lag ein Geldschein bei; **to ~ sth in a letter** einem Brief etw beilegen; **the ~d cheque** der beiliegende Scheck; **I ~d your letter with mine** ich habe Ihren Brief mitgeschickt.

enclosure [ɪn'kləʊʒəʳ] *n* (a) (*ground enclosed*) eingezäuntes Grundstück *or* Feld, Einfriedung *f*; (*for animals*) Gehege *nt* ◆ (*on racecourse*) **the ~** der Zuschauerbereich; **royal ~** *abgeteilter Zuschauerbereich für die königliche Familie*.
(b) (*act*) Einzäunung, Einfried(ig)ung (*geh*) *f*.
(c) (*fence etc*) Umzäunung *f* ◆ **~ wall** Umfassungsmauer *f*.
(d) (*document etc enclosed*) Anlage *f*.

encode [ɪn'kəʊd] *vt* (*also Comput*) kodieren.

encoder [ɪn'kəʊdəʳ] *n* (*also Comput*) Kodierer *m*, Kodiergerät *nt*.

encomium [ɪn'kəʊmɪəm] *n* (*form*) Lobrede, Laudatio (*geh*) *f*.

encompass [ɪn'kʌmpəs] *vt* (a) (*liter: surround*) umfassen (*with* mit). (b) (*include*) umfassen. (c) (*liter: bring about*) *downfall* herbeiführen.

encore ['ɒŋkɔːʳ] [1] *interj* da capo, Zugabe.
[2] *n* Zugabe *f*, Dacapo *nt* ◆ **to call for/give an ~** eine Zugabe verlangen/ machen (*inf*) *or* singen/spielen *etc*.
[3] *vt artiste* um eine Zugabe bitten.

encounter [ɪn'kaʊntəʳ] [1] *vt enemy, opposition* treffen *or* stoßen auf (*+acc*); *difficulties* stoßen auf (*+acc*); *danger* geraten in (*+acc*); (*liter*) *person* begegnen (*+dat*), treffen ◆ **to ~ enemy fire** unter feindlichen Beschuß geraten.
[2] *n* Begegnung *f*, Treffen *nt*; (*in battle*) Zusammenstoß *m* ◆ **~ group** (*Psych*) Encountergruppe *f*.

encourage [ɪn'kʌrɪdʒ] *vt person* ermutigen, ermuntern (*to* zu); (*motivate*) anregen; (*give confidence also*) Mut machen (*+dat*); *arts, industry, projects* fördern; (*Sport*) *team, competitor also* anfeuern, anspornen; *sb's bad habits* unterstützen ◆ **he's lazy enough as it is, please don't ~ him** er ist schon faul genug, bitte ermuntern *or* unterstützen Sie ihn nicht noch; **that will ~ bad habits** das wird zu schlechten Gewohnheiten führen; **to ~ sb in a belief** jdn in einem Glauben bestärken; **you'll only ~ him to think** ... er wird dann nur noch eher glauben, daß ...; **this ~s me to think that maybe** ... das läßt mich vermuten, daß vielleicht ...

encouragement [ɪn'kʌrɪdʒmənt] *n* Ermutigung, Ermunterung *f*; (*motivation*) Anregung *f*; (*support*) Unterstützung, Förderung *f* ◆ **to give sb ~** jdn ermuntern; **it's an ~ to know** ... es ist ein Ansporn, zu wissen ...; **he doesn't need much ~** ihn braucht man nicht groß zu ermuntern.

encouraging [ɪn'kʌrɪdʒɪŋ] *adj* ermutigend ◆ **you are not very ~** du machst mir/uns *etc* nicht gerade Mut.

encouragingly [ɪn'kʌrɪdʒɪŋlɪ] *adv see adj*.

encroach [ɪn'krəʊtʃ] *vi* **to ~ (up)on** *land* vordringen in (*+acc*); *sphere, rights* eingreifen in (*+acc*); *privileges* übergreifen auf (*+acc*); *time* in Anspruch nehmen.

➤ LANGUAGE IN USE: **enclose: b** → 20.2, 20.3, 20.7, 21

encroachment [ɪn'krəʊtʃmənt] *n see vi* Vordringen *nt*; Eingriff *m*; Übergriff *m*; Beanspruchung *f*.

encrust [ɪn'krʌst] *vi (with earth, cement)* überkrusten; *(with pearls, ice etc)* überziehen.

encrustation [ɪn,krʌs'teɪʃən] *n* Kruste *f* ◆ **with ~s of diamonds** diamant(en)besetzt.

encumber [ɪn'kʌmbəʳ] *vt* beladen; *(with responsibility, debts also)* belasten ◆ **~ed by heavy clothes** durch schwere Kleidung behindert; **~ed property** *(Fin)* belasteter Grundbesitz.

encumbrance [ɪn'kʌmbrəns] *n (also Jur)* Belastung *f*; *(person also)* Last *f* ◆ **to be an ~ to sb** *(luggage)* jdn behindern; *(person)* eine Last für jdn sein; *(dependent, responsibility)* eine Belastung für jdn sein.

encyclical [ɪn'sɪklɪkəl] *n* Enzyklika *f*.

encyclop(a)edia [ɪn,saɪkləʊ'piːdɪə] *n* Lexikon *nt*, Enzyklopädie *f*.

encyclop(a)edic [ɪn,saɪkləʊ'piːdɪk] *adj* enzyklopädisch.

end [end] [1] *n* **(a)** Ende *nt*; *(of finger)* Spitze *f* ◆ **at the ~ of the procession** am Schluß *or* Ende der Prozession; **the fourth from the ~** der/die/das vierte von hinten; **to the ~s of the earth** bis ans Ende der Welt; **from ~ to ~** von einem Ende zum anderen; **to keep one's ~ up** *(inf) (stay cheerful)* sich nicht unterkriegen lassen *(inf)*; *(do one's share)* das Seine tun; **to stand on ~** *(barrel, box etc)* hochkant stehen; *(hair)* zu Berge stehen; **two hours on ~** zwei Stunden ununterbrochen; **for hours on ~** stundenlang ununterbrochen; **the ships collided ~-on** die Schiffe fuhren aufeinander auf; **~ to ~** mit den Enden aneinander; **to change ~s** *(Sport)* die Seiten wechseln; **to make (both) ~s meet** *(fig)* zurechtkommen *(inf)*, sich über Wasser halten; **to see no further than the ~ of one's nose** nicht weiter sehen als seine Nase (reicht); **how do things look at your ~?** wie sieht es bei Ihnen aus?; **we've got some problems at this ~** wir haben hier *or* bei uns einige Probleme; **to have one's ~ away** *(vulg)* einen wegstecken *(sl)*.

(b) *(remnant) (of rope)* Ende *nt*, Rest *m*; *(of candle, cigarette)* Stummel *m* ◆ **just a few odd ~s left** nur noch ein paar Reste.

(c) *(conclusion)* Ende *nt* ◆ **the ~ of the month** das Monatsende; **at/towards the ~ of December** Ende/gegen Ende Dezember; **at the ~ of (the) winter/the war/the opera/the book** am Ende des Winters/des Krieges/am Schluß der Oper/des Buches; **at the ~ of three weeks** nach drei Wochen; **is there no ~ to this?** hört das denn nie auf?; **as far as I'm concerned, that's the ~!** für mich ist die Sache erledigt; **we shall never hear the ~ of it** das werden wir noch lange zu hören kriegen; **to be at an ~** zu Ende sein; **to be at the ~ of one's patience/strength** mit seiner Geduld/seinen Kräften am Ende sein; **to see a film/read a book to the ~** einen Film/ein Buch bis zu Ende sehen/lesen; **that's the ~ of him** er ist erledigt *or* fertig *(inf)*; **that's the ~ of that** das ist damit erledigt; **to bring to an ~** zu Ende bringen, beenden; *relations* ein Ende setzen (+*dat*), beenden; **to come to an ~** zu Ende gehen; **to get to the ~ of the road/book/job/money** ans Ende der Straße/zum Schluß des Buches kommen/mit der Arbeit fertig werden/das Geld ausgegeben haben; **in the ~** schließlich, zum Schluß; **to put an ~ to sth** einer Sache *(dat)* ein Ende setzen; **to come to a bad ~** ein böses Ende nehmen; **to meet one's ~** den Tod finden; **were you with him at the ~?** warst du zum Schluß *or* am Ende bei ihm?

(d) *(inf phrases)* **we met no ~ of famous people** wir trafen viele berühmte Leute; **he's no ~ of a nice chap** er ist ein irrsinnig netter Kerl *(inf)*; **to think no ~ of sb** große Stücke auf jdn halten; **it pleased her no ~** das hat ihr maßlos *or* irrsinnig *(inf)* gefallen; **you're the ~** *(annoying)* du bist der letzte Mensch *(inf)*; *(funny)* du bist zum Schreien *(inf)*.

(e) *(purpose)* Ziel *nt*, Zweck *m* ◆ **with this ~ in view** mit diesem Ziel vor Augen; **to what ~?** *(form)* zu welchem Zweck?; **an ~ in itself** Selbstzweck *no art*; **the ~ justifies the means** *(prov)* der Zweck heiligt die Mittel *(prov)*.

[2] *adj attr* letzte(r, s); *house also* End-.

[3] *vt* beenden; *speech, one's days also* beschließen ◆ **the novel to ~ all novels** der größte Roman aller Zeiten; **the howler to ~ all howlers** der schlimmste Schnitzer aller Zeiten; **to ~ it all** *(commit suicide)* Schluß machen.

[4] *vi* enden ◆ **we'll have to ~ soon** wir müssen bald Schluß machen; **we ~ed with a song** zum Schluß sangen wir ein Lied; **to be ~ing** zu Ende gehen; **where's it all going to ~?** wo soll das nur enden?; **to ~ in an "s"** auf „s" enden; **a post which ~s in a point** ein zugespitzter Pfahl; **an argument which ~ed in a fight** ein Streit, der mit einer Schlägerei endete.

◆**end off** *vt sep* abschließen, beschließen.

◆**end up** *vi* enden, landen *(inf)* ◆ **to ~ ~ doing sth** schließlich etw tun; **to ~ ~ as a lawyer/an alcoholic** schließlich Rechtsanwalt werden/als Alkoholiker enden; **we ~ed ~ at Joe's** wir waren *or* landeten *(inf)* schließlich bei Joe; **you'll ~ ~ in trouble** Sie werden noch Ärger bekommen.

endanger [ɪn'deɪndʒəʳ] *vt* gefährden.

endear [ɪn'dɪəʳ] *vt* beliebt machen *(to* bei).

endearing [ɪn'dɪərɪŋ] *adj smile* lieb, gewinnend; *personality, characteristic also* liebenswert.

endearingly [ɪn'dɪərɪŋlɪ] *adv* lieb.

endearment [ɪn'dɪəmənt] *n* **term of ~** Kosename *m*, Kosewort *nt*; **words of ~** liebe Worte *pl*.

endeavour [ɪn'devəʳ] [1] *n (attempt)* Anstrengung, Bemühung *f*; *(liter: striving)* (Be)streben *nt no pl (geh)* ◆ **to make an ~ to do sth** sich anstrengen *or* bemühen, etw zu tun; **to make every ~ to do sth** sich nach Kräften bemühen, etw zu tun; **in an ~ to please her** um ihr eine Freude zu machen.

[2] *vt* sich anstrengen, sich bemühen, bestrebt sein *(geh)*

endemic [en'demɪk] *adj (lit, fig)* endemisch ◆ **petty embezzling seems to be ~ here** kleine Unterschlagungen scheinen hier eine Krankheit zu sein.

end game *n* Endspiel *nt*.

ending ['endɪŋ] *n (of story, book, events)* Ausgang *m*; *(of day)* Abschluß *m*; *(last part)* Ende *nt*, Schluß *m*; *(of word)* Endung *f* ◆ **a story with a happy ~** eine Geschichte mit einem Happy End; **the events had a happy ~** alles ging gut aus.

endive ['endaɪv] *n* (Winter)endivie *f*, Endiviensalat *m*.

endless ['endlɪs] *adj* endlos; *attempts also, times* unzählig; *possibilities* unendlich ◆ **this job is ~** diese Arbeit nimmt kein Ende; **~ belt** endloses Transportband, Endlosband *nt*.

endlessly ['endlɪslɪ] *adv* endlos; *patient, generous* unendlich.

endocrine ['endəʊkraɪn] *adj* endokrin ◆ **~ gland** endokrine Drüse.

endocrinologist [,endəʊkraɪ'nɒlədʒɪst] *n* Endokrinologe *m*, Endokrinologin *f*.

endocrinology [,endəʊkraɪ'nɒlədʒɪ] *n* Endokrinologie *f*.

endomorph ['endəʊmɔːf] *n* Pykniker *m*.

endomorphic ['endəʊmɔːfɪk] *adj* pyknisch.

endorphin [,en'dɔːfɪn] *n* Endorphin *nt*.

▼ **endorse** [ɪn'dɔːs] *vt* **(a)** *document, cheque* auf der Rückseite unterzeichnen, indossieren. **(b)** *(Brit Jur) driving licence* eine Strafe vermerken auf (+*dat*) ◆ **I had my licence ~d** ich bekam einen Strafvermerk auf meinem Führer-
▼ schein. **(c)** *(approve)* billigen, unterschreiben *(inf)* ◆ **I ~ that** dem stimme ich zu, dem pflichte ich bei.

endorsee [ɪn,dɔː'siː] *n (Fin)* Indossatar *m*.

endorsement [ɪn'dɔːsmənt] *n* **(a)** *(on cheque, bill of exchange)* Indossament *nt*; *(on policy)* Zusatz, Nachtrag *m*. **(b)** *(Brit Jur: on driving licence)* Strafvermerk *m* auf dem Führerschein. **(c)** *(of opinion)* Billigung *f* ◆ **management's ~ of our suggestion** die Billigung unseres Vorschlags durch die Betriebsleitung.

endorser [ɪn'dɔːsəʳ] *n (Fin)* Indossar *m*.

endoscope ['endəʊ,skəʊp] *n* Endoskop *nt*.

endoscopy [,en'dɒskəpɪ] *n* Endoskopie *f*.

endow [ɪn'daʊ] *vt* **(a)** *institution, church* eine Stiftung machen an *(acc)*; *(Univ, Sch) prize, chair* stiften ◆ **he ~ed the church with a large sum of money** er stiftete der Kirche eine große Summe; **an ~ed school** *eine mit Stiftungsgeldern gebaute und finanzierte Schule*.

(b) *(fig) usu pass* **to ~ sb with sth** jdm etw geben *or* schenken; **to be ~ed with a natural talent for singing** ein sängerisches Naturtalent sein; **the poor lad is not very well ~ed** *(inf)* mit dem armen Bengel ist nicht viel los; **she's well ~ed** *(hum)* sie ist von der Natur reichlich ausgestattet (worden).

endowment [ɪn'daʊmənt] *n* **(a)** Stiftung *f* ◆ **~s** Stiftungsgelder *pl*. **(b)** *(natural talent etc)* Begabung *f* ◆ **his/her physical ~s** *(hum)* womit ihn/sie die Natur ausgestattet hat.

endowment: ~ assurance *n* Versicherung *f* auf den Erlebensfall, Erlebensversicherung *f*; **~ mortgage** *n* Hypothek *f* mit Lebensversicherung; **~ policy** *n* Lebensversicherungspolice *f*.

end: ~papers *npl* Vorsatzblätter *pl*; **~ product** *n* Endprodukt *nt*; *(fig)* Produkt *nt*; **~ result** *n* Endergebnis *nt*.

endue [ɪn'djuː] *vt* versehen, begaben *(liter)* ◆ **to be ~d with sth** über etw *(acc)* verfügen, mit etw begabt sein.

endurable [ɪn'djʊərəbl] *adj* erträglich.

endurance [ɪn'djʊərəns] *n* Durchhaltevermögen *nt* ◆ **to have great powers of ~** großes Durchhaltevermögen haben; **to have great powers of ~ against the cold** sehr widerstandsfähig gegen Kälte sein; **what a feat of ~** welche Ausdauer!; **he was tried beyond ~** er wurde über die Maßen gereizt; **this is beyond ~** das ist ja nicht auszuhalten.

endurance: ~ race *n (Sport) Rennen nt, bei dem es vor allem auf die Ausdauer ankommt*; **~ test** *n* Belastungsprobe *f*; *(fig also)* Durchhaltetest *m*.

endure [ɪn'djʊəʳ] [1] *vt* **(a)** *(undergo) pain, insults, tribulations, hardship* (er)leiden. **(b)** *(put up with)* ertragen; *pains also* aushalten ◆ **she can't ~ being laughed at** sie kann es nicht vertragen *or* haben *(inf)*, wenn man über sie lacht.

[2] *vi* bestehen; *(work, memories also)* Bestand haben.

enduring [ɪn'djʊərɪŋ] *adj value, fame* bleibend, dauernd; *friendship, peace also* dauerhaft; *hardship* anhaltend.

end user *n (esp Comput)* Endbenutzer *m*.

endways ['endweɪz], **endwise** ['endwaɪz] *adv* mit dem Ende nach vorne *or* zuerst; *(end to end)* mit den Enden aneinander ◆ **put it ~ on** legen Sie es mit dem Ende *or* der Spitze an.

ENE *abbr of* **east-north-east** ONO.

enema ['enɪmə] *n* Klistier *nt*, Einlauf *m*; *(syringe)* Klistierspritze *f*.

enemy ['enəmɪ] [1] *n (lit, fig)* Feind *m* ◆ **to make enemies** sich *(dat)* Feinde machen *or* schaffen; **to make an ~ of sb** sich *(dat)* jdn zum Feind(e) machen; **he is his own worst ~** er schadet sich *(dat)* selbst am meisten; **~-occupied** vom Feind besetzt.

[2] *adj attr* feindlich; *position, advance, morale* des Feindes ◆ **destroyed by ~ action** vom Feind *or* durch Feindeinwirkung *(form)* zerstört.

energetic [,enə'dʒetɪk] *adj* **(a)** voller Energie, energiegeladen; *(active)* aktiv; *manager, government* tatkräftig, aktiv; *dancer, dancing, music, prose* schwungvoll ◆ **she is a very ~ person** sie ist immer sehr aktiv, sie steckt voller Energie; **if I'm feeling ~** wenn ich die Energie habe; **I've had a very ~ day** ich hatte einen anstrengenden Tag.

(b) *denial, refusal, protest* energisch, entschlossen.

energetically [,enə'dʒetɪkəlɪ] *adv* voller Energie; *dance* schwungvoll; *express oneself* energisch, entschieden ◆ **he has worked competently and ~** er hat mit sehr viel Kompetenz und Schwung gearbeitet.

energize ['enədʒaɪz] *vt rocket motor, particle* Antrieb geben (+*dat*); *(Elec)* unter

➤ LANGUAGE IN USE: **endorse: c → 11.1**

Strom setzen.

energy ['enədʒɪ] *n* Energie *f* ◆ **he put his speech over with a lot of ~** er hielt seine Rede mit viel Schwung; **chocolate gives you ~** Schokolade gibt neue Energie; **to apply all one's energies to sth** seine ganze Energie *or* Kraft für etw einsetzen; **I haven't the ~** mir fehlt die Energie dazu; **to conserve one's energies** mit seinen Kräften haushalten *or* sparsam umgehen.

energy: ~ conservation *n* Energieeinsparung *f*; **~ crisis** *n* Energiekrise *f*; **~-giving** *adj food* energiespendend; **~-intensive** *adj* energieintensiv; **~-saving** *adj* energiesparend; *measures also* Energiespar-; **~ supplies** *npl* Energievorräte *pl*.

enervate ['enɜːveɪt] *vt* (*physically*) entkräften, schwächen; (*mentally*) entnerven, enervieren (*geh*).

enervating ['enɜːveɪtɪŋ] *adj* strapazierend.

enfant terrible [ˌɒnfɒnte'riːblə] *n, pl* **-s -s** Enfant terrible *nt*.

enfeeble [ɪn'fiːbl] *vt* schwächen.

enfeeblement [ɪn'fiːblmənt] *n* Schwächung *f*.

enfold [ɪn'fəʊld] *vt* einhüllen (*in* in *+acc*) ◆ **to ~ sb in one's arms** jdn in die Arme schließen.

enforce [ɪn'fɔːs] *vt* **(a)** durchführen, Geltung verschaffen (*+dat*); *one's claims, rights* geltend machen; *silence, discipline* sorgen für, schaffen; *obedience* sich (*dat*) verschaffen ◆ **the police ~ the law** die Polizei sorgt für die Einhaltung der Gesetze; **to ~ silence/obedience** Ruhe/Gehorsam erzwingen; **to ~ sth (up)on sb** jdm etw aufzwingen.
(b) (*rare: give force to*) *demand* Nachdruck verschaffen (*+dat*); *argument* stützen, untermauern.

enforceable [ɪn'fɔːsəbl] *adj* durchsetzbar.

enforcement [ɪn'fɔːsmənt] *n* (*of law, policy, ruling*) Durchführung *f*; (*of obedience*) Erzwingung *f*.

enfranchise [ɪn'fræntʃaɪz] *vt* **(a)** (*give vote to*) das Wahlrecht geben *or* erteilen (*+dat*) ◆ **to be ~d** wahlberechtigt sein. **(b)** (*set free*) *slaves* freilassen.

enfranchisement [ɪn'fræntʃɪzmənt] *n* **(a)** (*Pol*) Erteilung *f* des Wahlrechts ◆ **after the ~ of women** nachdem die Frauen das Wahlrecht erhalten hatten. **(b)** (*of slave*) Freilassung *f*.

engage [ɪn'geɪdʒ] **1** *vt* **(a)** *servant, workers* an- *or* einstellen; *singer, performer* engagieren; *lawyer* sich (*dat*) nehmen.
(b) *room* mieten, sich (*dat*) nehmen.
(c) *the attention* in Anspruch nehmen; *interest also* fesseln ◆ **to ~ sb in conversation** jdn in ein Gespräch verwickeln.
(d) to ~ oneself to do sth (*form*) sich verpflichten, etw zu tun.
(e) *the enemy* angreifen, den Kampf eröffnen gegen.
(f) (*Tech*) *gear wheels* ineinandergreifen lassen ◆ **to ~ a gear** (*Aut*) einen Gang einlegen; **to ~ the clutch** (ein)kuppeln.
2 *vi* **(a)** (*form: promise*) sich verpflichten (*to do* zu tun).
(b) (*gear wheels*) ineinandergreifen; (*clutch*) fassen.
(c) to ~ in sth sich an etw (*dat*) beteiligen; **to ~ in politics** sich politisch betätigen; **to ~ in competition with sb** in Wettbewerb mit jdm treten.
(d) (*Mil*) angreifen.

▼ **engaged** [ɪn'geɪdʒd] *adj* **(a)** verlobt ◆ **~ to be married** verlobt; **to become ~** sich verloben (*to* mit); **the ~ couple** die Verlobten *pl*. **(b)** (*occupied*) beschäftigt. **(c) the parties ~ in this dispute** die streitenden *or* am Streit ▼ beteiligten Parteien; **~ in bitter conflict** in erbittertem Streit. **(d)** *seat, taxi, toilet,* (*Brit Telec*) besetzt ◆ **~ tone** (*Brit Telec*) Besetztzeichen *nt*.

▼ **engagement** [ɪn'geɪdʒmənt] *n* **(a)** (*appointment*) Verabredung *f*; (*of actor etc*) Engagement *nt* ◆ **public/social ~s** öffentliche/gesellschaftliche Ver- ▼ pflichtungen *pl*; **a dinner ~** eine Verabredung zum Essen. **(b)** (*betrothal*) Verlobung *f*. **(c)** (*form: undertaking*) Verpflichtung *f*. **(d)** (*Mil*) Gefecht *nt*, Kampf *m*. **(e)** (*of parts of machine*) Ineinandergreifen *nt*.

engagement: ~ diary *n* Terminkalender *m*; **~ ring** *n* Verlobungsring *m*.

engaging [ɪn'geɪdʒɪŋ] *adj personality* einnehmend; *smile, look, tone* gewinnend.

en garde [ɒŋ'gɑːd] *interj* en garde.

engender [ɪn'dʒendəʳ] *vt* (*fig*) erzeugen.

engenderment [ɪn'dʒendəmənt] *n* Erzeugung *f*.

engine ['endʒɪn] *n* **(a)** Maschine *f*; (*of car, plane etc*) Motor *m*; (*of ship*) Maschine *f*. **(b)** (*Rail*) Lokomotive, Lok *f*.

engine block *n* Motorblock *m*.

-engined [-'endʒɪnd] *adj suf* -motorig.

engine driver *n* (*Brit*) Lok(omotiv)führer(in *f*) *m*.

engineer [ˌendʒɪ'nɪəʳ] **1** *n* **(a)** Techniker(in *f*) *m*; (*with university degree etc*) Ingenieur(in *f*) *m* ◆ **the E~s** (*Mil*) die Pioniere *pl*. **(b)** (*Naut: on merchant ships*) Maschinist *m*; (*in Navy*) (Schiffs)ingenieur *m* ◆ **~ officer** Technischer Offizier. **(c)** (*US Rail*) Lokführer *m*. **(d)** (*fig: of scheme*) Arrangeur *m*.
2 *vt* **(a)** konstruieren. **(b)** (*fig*) *election, campaign* organisieren; *downfall, plot* arrangieren, einfädeln; *success, victory* in die Wege leiten; (*Sport*) *goal* einfädeln ◆ **to ~ a scheme** einen Plan aushecken.

engineering [ˌendʒɪ'nɪərɪŋ] *n* **(a)** Technik *f*; (*mechanical ~*) Maschinenbau *m*; (*engineering profession*) Ingenieurwesen *nt* ◆ **the ~ of the Tay Bridge** die Konstruktion der Tay-Brücke; **he's in some sort of ~** er ist irgend etwas Technisches (*inf*); **a brilliant piece of ~** eine Meisterkonstruktion; **a triumph of ~** ein Triumph *m* der Technik.
(b) (*fig*) *see vt* (*b*) Organisation *f*, Arrangement *nt*; (*manoeuvring*) Arrangements *pl*.

engineering: ~ department *n* technische Abteilung; (*mechanical*) Abteilung *f* für Maschinenbau; **~ faculty** *n* (*Univ*) Fakultät *f* für Maschinenbau; **~ industries** *npl* Maschinenindustrie *f*; **~ worker** *n* Techniker(in *f*) *m*; **~ works** *n sing or pl* Maschinenfabrik *f*.

engine: ~ oil *n* Motoröl *nt*; **~ room** *n* (*Naut*) Maschinenraum *m*; **~ shed** *n* (*Brit*) Lokomotivschuppen *m*.

England ['ɪŋglənd] **1** *n* England *nt*.
2 *adj attr* **the ~ team** die englische Mannschaft.

English ['ɪŋglɪʃ] **1** *adj* englisch ◆ **he is ~** er ist Engländer; **our ~ teacher** (*teaching ~*) unser Englischlehrer; (*~ by nationality*) unser englischer Lehrer; **~ translator** englischer Übersetzer; (*foreign*) Übersetzer *m* für Englisch; **~ breakfast** englisches Frühstück.
2 *n* **(a) the ~** *pl* die Engländer *pl*.
(b) Englisch *nt*; (*the ~ language in general, ~ grammar also*) das Englische; (*as university subject*) Anglistik *f* ◆ **can you speak ~?** können Sie Englisch?; **he doesn't speak ~** er spricht kein Englisch; **"~ spoken"** „hier wird Englisch gesprochen"; **they were speaking ~** sie sprachen englisch; **they were talking (in) ~ to each other** sie unterhielten sich auf englisch; **he speaks (a) very clear ~** er spricht (ein) sehr klares Englisch; **in ~** auf *or* in (*inf*) Englisch *or* englisch; **in good/modern-day ~** in gutem/modernem Englisch; **to translate sth into/from (the) ~** etw ins Englische/aus dem Englischen übersetzen; **verbal structures in ~** die Verbstruktur im Englischen; **is that ~?** (*correct*) ist das richtig?; **that's not ~** das ist verkehrt, das ist falsches Englisch; **~/teaching ~ as a foreign language** (*abbr* **EFL/TEFL**) Englisch als Fremdsprache; **King's/Queen's ~** die englische Hochsprache; *see* **old ~, plain.**

English: ~ Channel *n* Ärmelkanal *m*; **~ Heritage** *n* (*Brit*) *Organisation f für die Pflege von Denkmälern und historischen Bauwerken in England*; **~man** *n* Engländer *m*; **an ~man's home is his castle** (*Prov*) für den Engländer ist sein Haus seine Burg; **~-speaker** *n* Englischsprachige(r) *mf*; **~-speaking** *adj* englischsprachig; **~woman** *n* Engländerin *f*.

engorge [ɪn'gɔːdʒ] *vi* (an)schwellen.

engrave [ɪn'greɪv] *vt* eingravieren; (*on rock, stone*) einmeißeln; (*on wood*) einschnitzen, einkerben; (*fig*) einprägen ◆ **this picture is ~d on my memory** dieses Bild hat sich mir (unauslöschlich) eingeprägt.

engraver [ɪn'greɪvəʳ] *n* Graveur(in *f*) *m*; (*on stone*) Steinhauer(in *f*) *m*; (*on wood*) Holzschneider(in *f*) *m*, Hersteller *m* von Druckstöcken.

engraving [ɪn'greɪvɪŋ] *n* **(a)** (*process*) *see vt* Gravieren *nt*; Einmeißeln *nt*; Einschnitzen, Einkerben *nt* ◆ **~ needle** Graviernadel *f*. **(b)** (*copy*) (Kupfer-/Stahl)stich *m*; (*from wood*) Holzschnitt *m*; (*design*) Gravierung *f*; (*on wood, stone*) eingemeißelte Verzierung/Schrift *etc*.

engross [ɪn'grəʊs] *vt person, attention* gefangennehmen ◆ **to become ~ed in one's book** sich in sein Buch vertiefen; **to be ~ed in one's own thoughts** in Gedanken vertieft sein.

engrossing [ɪn'grəʊsɪŋ] *adj* fesselnd.

engulf [ɪn'gʌlf] *vt* verschlingen ◆ **to be ~ed by the sea** von den Wellen verschlungen werden (*liter*); **he was ~ed by a pile of work** er war mit Arbeit überhäuft; **his coat ~s him completely** er verschwindet völlig in seinem Mantel.

enhance [ɪn'hɑːns] *vt* verbessern; *chances also, price, value, attraction* erhöhen.

enigma [ɪ'nɪgmə] *n* Rätsel *nt*.

enigmatic *adj*, **~ally** *adv* [ˌenɪg'mætɪk, -əlɪ] rätselhaft.

enjambement [ɪn'dʒæmmənt] *n* (*Poet*) Enjambement *nt*.

enjoin [ɪn'dʒɔɪn] *vt* (*form*) **to ~ sb to silence/caution, to ~ silence/caution on sb** jdn eindringlich zur Ruhe/zur Vorsicht mahnen; **to ~ on sb the need for sth** jdm die Notwendigkeit einer Sache eindringlich vor Augen stellen; **to ~ sb to do sth** jdn eindringlich mahnen, etw zu tun.

▼ **enjoy** [ɪn'dʒɔɪ] **1** *vt* **(a)** (*take pleasure in*) genießen ◆ **he ~s swimming/reading** er schwimmt/liest gern, Lesen/Schwimmen macht ihm Spaß; **he ~s being rude to people** es macht ihm Spaß *or* ihm macht es Spaß, zu Leuten unhöflich zu sein; **he ~ed reading the book** er hat das Buch gern gelesen; **I ~ed the book/concert/film** das Buch/Konzert/der Film hat mir gefallen; **he ~ed the meal** das Essen hat ihm gut geschmeckt; **I've ~ed talking to you** es war mir eine Freude, mich mit Ihnen zu unterhalten, es war nett, sich mit Ihnen zu unterhalten; **I didn't ~ it at all** es hat mir überhaupt keinen Spaß gemacht; **the author didn't mean his book to be ~ed** dem Verfasser ging es nicht darum, daß man an seinem Buch Spaß *or* Vergnügen haben sollte; **to ~ life** das Leben genießen; **I ~ed a very pleasant weekend in the country** ich habe ein sehr angenehmes Wochenende auf dem Land verbracht; **did you ~ your holidays?** hat es Ihnen im Urlaub gefallen?; **I really ~ed my holidays** ich habe meinen Urlaub richtig genossen.
(b) *good health* sich erfreuen (*+gen*) (*geh*); *rights, advantages, respect, confidence also* genießen; *income also* haben.
2 *vr* **to ~ oneself** sich amüsieren; **~ yourself!** viel Spaß!, amüsieren Sie sich gut!

enjoyable [ɪn'dʒɔɪəbl] *adj* nett; *film, book also* unterhaltsam, amüsant; *evening also, meal* angenehm.

enjoyably [ɪn'dʒɔɪəblɪ] *adv* angenehm.

enjoyment [ɪn'dʒɔɪmənt] *n* **(a)** Vergnügen *nt*, Spaß *m* (*of an +dat*) ◆ **he got a lot of ~ from this book/from bird-watching** das Buch machte ihm großen Spaß/es machte ihm großen Spaß *or* er fand großen Spaß daran, Vögel zu beobachten.
(b) (*of rights, income, fortune*) Genuß *m*.

enlarge [ɪn'lɑːdʒ] **1** *vt* vergrößern; *hole, field of knowledge,* (*Med*) *organ, pore also* erweitern; *membership, majority also* erhöhen ◆ **~d edition** erweiterte Ausgabe.
2 *vi* **(a)** *see vt* sich vergrößern; sich erweitern; sich erhöhen. **(b) to ~ (up)on sth** sich über etw (*acc*) genauer äußern.

enlargement [ɪn'lɑːdʒmənt] *n* **(a)** (*Phot*) Vergrößerung *f*. **(b)** *see vt* Ver-

➤ LANGUAGE IN USE: **engaged: a** → 24.2 **d** → 27.3 **engagement: a** → 25.2 **b** → 24.2 **enjoy: 1a** → 7.2

größerung *f*; Erweiterung *f*; Erhöhung *f*.
enlarger [ɪn'lɑːdʒəʳ] *n (Phot)* Vergrößerungsapparat *m*.
enlighten [ɪn'laɪtn] *vt* aufklären *(on, as to, about* über *+acc)*; *(spiritually)* erleuchten ◆ **let me ~ you** darf ich es Ihnen erklären?
enlightened [ɪn'laɪtnd] *adj* aufgeklärt; *(spiritually)* erleuchtet.
enlightening [ɪn'laɪtnɪŋ] *adj* aufschlußreich.
enlightenment [ɪn'laɪtnmənt] *n* Aufklärung *f*; *(spiritual)* Erleuchtung *f* ◆ **the E~** die Aufklärung; **the age of E~** das Zeitalter der Aufklärung.
enlist [ɪn'lɪst] [1] *vi (Mil etc)* sich melden *(in* zu).
[2] *vt soldiers* einziehen; *recruits also* einstellen; *supporters, collaborators* anwerben, gewinnen; *assistance, sympathy, support* gewinnen ◆ **could I ~ your aid?** darf ich Sie um Hilfe bitten?; **~ed man** *(US)* gemeiner Soldat.
enlistment [ɪn'lɪstmənt] *n see vb* **(a)** Meldung *f*. **(b)** Einziehung *f*; Einstellung *f*; Anwerbung *f*; Gewinnung *f*.
enliven [ɪn'laɪvn] *vt* beleben.
enmesh [ɪn'meʃ] *vt (lit)* in einem Netz fangen; *(fig)* verstricken ◆ **to get ~ed in sth** *(fig)* in etw *(acc)* verstrickt werden.
enmity ['enmɪtɪ] *n* Feindschaft *f*.
ennoble [ɪ'nəʊbl] *vt (lit)* adeln, in den Adelsstand erheben; *(fig) mind, person* erheben *(geh)*.
enormity [ɪ'nɔːmɪtɪ] *n* **(a)** *no pl (of action, offence)* ungeheures Ausmaß. **(b)** *(crime)* Ungeheuerlichkeit *f*.
enormous [ɪ'nɔːməs] *adj* gewaltig, enorm; *person* enorm groß; *patience* enorm ◆ **an ~ number of people** ungeheuer viele Menschen; **an ~ amount of money/time** eine Unsumme *(inf)*, eine Unmenge Geld/Zeit.
enormously [ɪ'nɔːməslɪ] *adv* enorm, ungeheuer.
enough [ɪ'nʌf] [1] *adj* genug, genügend *attr* ◆ **to be ~** genügen, reichen; **is there ~ milk?, is there milk ~?** ist genug *or* genügend Milch da?, reicht die Milch?; **have you ~ to pay with?** haben Sie genug, um zu bezahlen?; **we have ~ to live on** wir haben genug zum Leben, es reicht uns zum Leben; **more than ~** mehr als genug; **I've had ~, I'm going home** mir reicht's *or* jetzt reicht's mir aber, ich gehe nach Hause; **I've had ~ of this novel** jetzt habe ich genug von diesem Roman; **I've had ~ of your impudence** jetzt habe ich aber genug von deiner Frechheit, jetzt reicht es mir aber mit deiner Frechheit; **one can never have ~ of this music** von dieser Musik kann man nie genug kriegen; **that's ~, thanks** danke, das ist genug *or* das reicht; **now children, that's ~!** Kinder, jetzt ist es aber genug *or* jetzt reicht es aber!; **~ of this!** genug davon!; **this noise is ~ to drive me mad** dieser Lärm macht mich noch ganz verrückt; **one song was ~ to show he couldn't sing** ein Lied genügte, um zu zeigen, daß er nicht singen konnte; **it is ~ for us to know that** ... es genügt uns zu wissen, daß ...; **~ is as good as a feast** *(prov)* allzuviel ist ungesund *(prov)*; **~ is ~** was zuviel ist, ist zuviel.
[2] *adv* **(a)** *(sufficiently) (+adj)* genug; *(+vb also)* genügend ◆ **not big ~** nicht groß genug; **this meat is not cooked ~** das Fleisch ist nicht richtig durch; **that's a good ~ excuse** die Entschuldigung kann man gelten lassen; **he knows well ~ what I said** er weiß ganz genau, was ich gesagt habe.
(b) *(tolerably)* **she is clever/pleasant ~** sie ist so weit ganz intelligent/nett; **he writes/sings well ~** er schreibt/singt ganz ordentlich; **it's good ~ in its way** es ist in seiner Art ganz ordentlich; **I like it well ~** mir gefällt es ganz gut.
(c) *(as intensifier)* **oddly/funnily ~, I saw him too** sonderbarerweise/komischerweise habe ich ihn auch gesehen; **and sure ~, he didn't come** und er kam auch prompt nicht.
enquire, inquire [ɪn'kwaɪəʳ] [1] *vt the time, a name, the way* sich erkundigen nach, fragen nach ◆ **to ~ sth of sb** sich bei jdm nach etw erkundigen; **he ~d what/whether/when** *etc* ... er erkundigte sich *or* fragte, was/ob/wann *etc* ...
[2] *vi* sich erkundigen *(about* nach), fragen *(about* nach, wegen) ◆ **"~ within"** „Näheres im Geschäft".
◆**enquire after** *vi +prep obj person, sb's health* sich erkundigen nach.
◆**enquire for** *vi +prep obj person* fragen nach.
◆**enquire into** *vi +prep obj* untersuchen.
enquirer [ɪn'kwaɪərəʳ] *n* Fragende(r) *mf*.
enquiring [ɪn'kwaɪərɪŋ] *adj* fragend; *mind* forschend.
▼ **enquiry, inquiry** [ɪn'kwaɪərɪ, *(US)* 'ɪnkwɪrɪ] *n* **(a)** *(question)* Anfrage *f (about* über *+acc)*; *(for tourist information, direction etc)* Erkundigung *f (about* über *+acc,* nach) ◆ **to make enquiries** Erkundigungen einziehen; *(police etc)* Nachforschungen anstellen *(about sb* über jdn, *about sth* nach etw); **all enquiries to** ... alle Anfragen an *(+acc)* ...; **Enquiries** *(office)* Auskunft *f*.
(b) *(investigation)* Untersuchung *f* ◆ **to hold an ~ into the cause of the accident** eine Untersuchung der Unfallursache durchführen; **court of ~** Untersuchungskommission *f*.
enrage [ɪn'reɪdʒ] *vt* wütend machen ◆ **it ~s me to think that** ... es macht mich wütend, wenn ich daran denke, daß ...
enrapture [ɪn'ræptʃəʳ] *vt* entzücken, bezaubern.
enrich [ɪn'rɪtʃ] *vt* bereichern; *soil, food* anreichern.
enrichment [ɪn'rɪtʃmənt] *n* Bereicherung *f*; *(of soil)* Anreicherung *f*.
enrol, *(US)* **enroll** [ɪn'rəʊl] [1] *vt* einschreiben; *members also* aufnehmen; *schoolchild (school, headmaster)* aufnehmen; *(parents)* anmelden; *(Univ)* immatrikulieren.
[2] *vi* sich einschreiben; *(in the army)* sich melden *(in* zu); *(as member also)* sich einschreiben lassen; *(for course also, at school)* sich anmelden; *(Univ also)* sich immatrikulieren.
enrolment [ɪn'rəʊlmənt] *n* **(a)** *(enrolling) see vt* Einschreibung *f*; Aufnahme *f*; Anmeldung *f*; Immatrikulation *f*.
(b) *(being enrolled) see vi* Einschreibung *f*; Meldung *f*; Einschreibung *f*; Anmeldung *f*; Immatrikulation *f*.
(c) an evening class/a university/school with a total ~ of ... ein Abendkurs mit einer (Gesamt)teilnehmerzahl von .../eine Universität mit ... immatrikulierten Studenten/eine Schule mit einer (Gesamt)schülerzahl von ...
en route [ɒŋ'ruːt] *adv* unterwegs, en route *(geh)* ◆ **we can see it ~ to Paris** wir können es auf dem Weg nach Paris sehen.
ensconce [ɪn'skɒns] *vr* sich niederlassen, sich häuslich niederlassen *(in* in *+dat)* ◆ **he was ~d in the front room** er hatte sich in dem vorderen Zimmer (häuslich) niedergelassen.
ensemble [ɑ̃ːn'sɑ̃ːmbl] *n (Mus, Fashion)* Ensemble *nt*.
enshrine [ɪn'ʃraɪn] *vt (fig)* bewahren.
ensign ['ensaɪn] *n* **(a)** *(flag)* Nationalflagge *f*. **(b)** *(Mil Hist)* Fähnrich *m*. **(c)** *(US Naut)* Fähnrich *m* zur See.
enslave [ɪn'sleɪv] *vt* zum Sklaven machen ◆ **he is ~d by tradition** er ist der Tradition sklavisch verhaftet; **he was ~d by her beauty** ihre Schönheit hat ihn zu ihrem Sklaven gemacht.
enslavement [ɪn'sleɪvmənt] *n (lit)* Versklavung *f*; *(fig)* sklavische Abhängigkeit.
ensnare [ɪn'sneəʳ] *vt (lit)* fangen; *(fig) (woman)* umgarnen; *(charms)* berücken, bestricken ◆ **his leg became ~d in the ropes** sein Bein verfing sich in den Seilen.
ensue [ɪn'sjuː] *vi* folgen *(from, on* aus) ◆ **it ~s that ...** daraus folgt, daß ...; **what ~d?** was folgte darauf(hin)?
ensuing [ɪn'sjuːɪŋ] *adj year, day* folgend; *events* nachfolgend.
en suite ['ɒn'swiːt] *adj* **room with ~ bathroom** Zimmer *nt* mit eigenem Bad.
ensure [ɪn'ʃʊəʳ] *vt* sicherstellen; *(secure)* sichern ◆ **can I ~ that I will have a seat?** kann ich sicher sein *or* sichergehen, daß ich einen Platz bekomme?
ENT *abbr of* **ear, nose and throat. ~ department** HNO-Abteilung *f*.
entablature [ɪn'tæblətjʊəʳ] *n* Gebälk *nt*.
entail [ɪn'teɪl] *vt* **(a)** *expense, inconvenience* mit sich bringen; *risk, difficulty also* verbunden sein mit; *(involve) work stages also* erforderlich machen ◆ **what is ~ed in buying a house?** was ist zum Hauskauf alles erforderlich?; **this will ~ (my) buying a new car** das bringt mit sich *or* macht es erforderlich, daß ich mir ein neues Auto kaufen muß.
(b) *(Logic)* **if a = b, not a ~s not b** wenn a = b ist, so folgt daraus, daß nicht a = nicht b ist.
(c) *(Jur)* **to ~ an estate** ein Gut als Fideikommiß vererben; **~ed estate** unveräußerliches Erbgut, Fideikommiß *nt*.
entangle [ɪn'tæŋgl] *vt* **(a)** *(catch up)* verfangen ◆ **to become ~d in sth** sich in etw *(dat)* verfangen; **their feet were ~d in the ropes** sie hatten sich mit den Füßen in den Seilen verfangen.
(b) *(get into a tangle) hair* verwirren; *wool, thread, ropes also* verwickeln ◆ **to become ~d** sich verwirren; sich verwickeln *or* verheddern *(inf)*; *(branches)* ineinanderwachsen.
(c) *(fig: in affair etc)* verwickeln, verstricken *(in* in *+acc)* ◆ **he became ~d in his lies/explanations** er hat sich in Lügen verstrickt/sich bei seinen Erklärungen verheddert *(inf)*.
entanglement [ɪn'tæŋglmənt] *n* **(a)** *(lit) (no pl: enmeshing)* Verfangen *nt*; *(tangle) (of ropes etc)* Durcheinander *nt*; *(esp Mil: of barbed wire)* Verhau *m*.
(b) *(fig) (in affair etc)* Verwicklung *f* ◆ **legal ~** Rechtskonflikt *m*; **he wanted to avoid any ~ with the police** er wollte auf keinen Fall etwas mit der Polizei zu tun kriegen; **emotional ~** gefühlsmäßiges Engagement; **she didn't want any emotional ~** sie wollte sich gefühlsmäßig nicht engagieren.
enter ['entəʳ] [1] *vt* **(a)** *(towards speaker)* hereinkommen in *(+acc)*; *(away from speaker)* hineingehen in *(+acc)*; *(walk into) building etc also* betreten, eintreten in *(+acc)*; *(drive into) car park, motorway* einfahren in *(+acc)*; *(turn into) road etc* einbiegen in *(+acc)*; *(flow into: river, sewage etc)* münden in *(+acc)*; *(penetrate: bullet etc)* eindringen in *(+acc)*; *(climb into) bus* einsteigen in *(+acc)*; *(cross border of) country* einreisen in *(+acc)* ◆ **to ~ harbour** (in den Hafen) einlaufen; **he is ~ing his 60th year** er tritt ins sechzigste Lebensjahr ein; **the thought never ~ed my head** *or* **mind** so etwas wäre mir nie eingefallen; **that idea *had* ~ed my mind** *(iro)* auf diesen Gedanken bin ich tatsächlich gekommen.
(b) *(join, become a member of)* eintreten in *(+acc)* ◆ **to ~ the Army/Navy** zum Heer/zur Marine gehen; **to ~ the Church** Geistlicher werden; **to ~ a school/the university** in eine Schule eintreten/die Universität beziehen; **to ~ a profession** einen Beruf ergreifen.
(c) *(record)* eintragen *(in* in *+acc)*; *(Comput) data* eingeben ◆ **to ~ a/one's name** einen Namen/sich eintragen; **~ these purchases to me** *(Comm)* tragen Sie diese Käufe auf meinen Namen ein; **~ key** *(Comput)* Enter-Taste *f*.
(d) *(enrol) (for school, exam etc, pupil)* anmelden; *(athlete, competitor also, horse, for race, contest etc)* melden.
(e) *(go in for) race, contest* sich beteiligen an *(+dat)* ◆ **only amateurs could ~ the race** es konnten nur Amateure an dem Rennen teilnehmen.
(f) *(submit) appeal, plea* einlegen ◆ **to ~ an action against sb** *(Jur)* gegen jdn einen Prozeß anstrengen *or* einleiten.
[2] *vi* **(a)** *(towards speaker)* hereinkommen; *(away from speaker)* hineingehen; *(walk in)* eintreten; *(into bus etc)* einsteigen; *(drive in)* einfahren; *(penetrate: bullet etc)* eindringen; *(cross into country)* einreisen. **(b)** *(Theat)* auftreten. **(c)** *(for race, exam etc)* sich melden *(for* zu).
[3] *n (Comput)* **hit ~** Enter drücken.
◆**enter into** *vi +prep obj* **(a)** *relations, negotiations, discussions* aufnehmen; *contract, alliance* schließen, eingehen ◆ **to ~ ~ conversation/a correspondence with sb** ein Gespräch mit jdm anknüpfen/mit jdm in Briefwechsel treten; *see* **spirit**.
(b) *(figure in)* eine Rolle spielen bei ◆ **that possibility did not ~ ~ our calcula-**

➤ LANGUAGE IN USE: **enquiry: a → 20.2**

tions diese Möglichkeit war in unseren Berechnungen nicht einkalkuliert *or* eingeplant.

◆**enter up** *vt sep* eintragen.

◆**enter (up)on** *vi +prep obj career, duties* antreten; *new era* eintreten in (+*acc*); *subject* eingehen auf (+*acc*).

enteric [en'terɪk] *adj* Darm- ◆ ~ **fever** (Unterleibs)typhus *m*.

enteritis [ˌentə'raɪtɪs] *n* Dünndarmentzündung *f*.

enterprise ['entəpraɪz] *n* **(a)** *no pl* (*initiative, ingenuity*) Initiative *f*; (*adventurousness*) Unternehmungsgeist *m*.
(b) (*project, undertaking, Comm: firm*) Unternehmen *nt* ◆ **free/public/private ~ (system)** freies/öffentliches Unternehmertum/Privatunternehmertum *nt*; ~ **zone** wirtschaftliches Fördergebiet.

enterprising ['entəpraɪzɪŋ] *adj person* (*with initiative, ingenious*) einfallsreich, erfindungsreich; (*adventurous*) unternehmungslustig; *idea, venture* kühn.

enterprisingly ['entəpraɪzɪŋlɪ] *adv see adj* einfallsreich, erfindungsreich; unternehmungslustig; kühn ◆ **he very ~ started his own business** unternehmungslustig, wie er war, machte er sein eigenes Geschäft auf.

entertain [ˌentə'teɪn] 1 *vt* **(a)** (*offer hospitality to*) einladen; (*to meal*) bewirten ◆ **to ~ sb to dinner** jdn zum Essen einladen. **(b)** (*amuse*) unterhalten; (*humorously: joke*) belustigen. **(c)** *thought, intention* sich tragen mit; *suspicion, doubt* hegen; *hope* nähren; *suggestion, proposal, offer* erwägen, in Erwägung ziehen.
2 *vi* **(a)** (*have visitors*) Gäste haben. **(b)** (*comedian, conjurer etc*) unterhalten.

entertainer [ˌentə'teɪnə[r]] *n* Unterhalter(in *f*), Entertainer(in *f*) *m*.

entertaining [ˌentə'teɪnɪŋ] 1 *adj* amüsant, unterhaltsam.
2 *n* **she does a lot of ~** sie hat sehr oft Gäste.

entertainingly [ˌentə'teɪnɪŋlɪ] *adv* amüsant, unterhaltsam.

entertainment [ˌentə'teɪnmənt] *n* **(a)** (*amusement*) Unterhaltung *f*; (*professional also*) Entertainment *nt* ◆ **much to the ~ of the onlookers** sehr zur Belustigung der Zuschauer; **for my own ~** nur so zum Vergnügen, zu meinem Privatvergnügen; **the cinema is my favourite ~** zur Unterhaltung gehe ich am liebsten ins Kino; **he/the film is good ~** er/der Film ist sehr unterhaltend; **the world of ~** die Unterhaltungsbranche.
(b) (*performance*) Darbietung *f* ◆ **a musical ~** eine musikalische Darbietung *or* Unterhaltung.

entertainment: ~ allowance *n* ≃ Aufwandspauschale *f*; **~ tax** *n* Vergnügungssteuer *f*; **~ value** *n* **to be good ~ value** großen Unterhaltungswert haben; (*person*) sehr unterhaltend sein.

enthral(l) [ɪn'θrɔːl] *vt* begeistern, berücken (*geh*); (*exciting story etc also*) packen, fesseln ◆ **(held) ~led by her beauty** von ihrer Schönheit gefesselt *or* bezaubert *or* berückt (*geh*).

enthralling [ɪn'θrɔːlɪŋ] *adj* spannend; *story also* packend.

enthrone [ɪn'θrəʊn] *vt* inthronisieren; *king also* auf den Thron erheben; *bishop also* feierlich einsetzen ◆ **to sit ~d** thronen.

enthuse [ɪn'θjuːz] *vi* schwärmen (*over* von).

enthusiasm [ɪn'θjuːzɪæzəm] *n* Begeisterung *f*, Enthusiasmus *m* (*for* für) ◆ **I can't rouse** *or* **find any ~ for going out** ich kann mich gar nicht dafür begeistern, auszugehen; **I can't rouse any ~ for the idea** ich kann mich für die Idee nicht begeistern.

enthusiast [ɪn'θjuːzɪæst] *n* Enthusiast *m* ◆ **sports/football/rock-and-roll ~** begeisterter Sportler/Fußballfreund *m*/Rock-'n'-Roll- Anhänger *m*.

enthusiastic [ɪnˌθjuːzɪ'æstɪk] *adj* begeistert, enthusiastisch ◆ **to be/get ~ about sth** von etw begeistert sein/sich für etw begeistern; **to become** *or* **get ~** in Begeisterung geraten.

enthusiastically [ɪnˌθjuːzɪ'æstɪkəlɪ] *adv* begeistert, enthusiastisch, mit Begeisterung.

entice [ɪn'taɪs] *vt* locken; (*lead astray*) verführen, verleiten ◆ **to ~ sb to do sth** *or* **into doing sth** jdn dazu verführen *or* verleiten, etw zu tun; **to ~ sb away** jdn weglocken.

enticement [ɪn'taɪsmənt] *n* (*act*) Lockung *f*; (*leading astray*) Verführung *f*; (*lure*) Lockmittel *nt*; (*fig*) Verlockung *f*.

enticing [ɪn'taɪsɪŋ] *adj* verlockend; *look* verführerisch.

entire [ɪn'taɪə[r]] *adj* **(a)** ganz; *set, waste of time* vollständig ◆ **the ~ week/edition** die ganze Woche/Auflage; **he has my ~ confidence** er hat mein ganzes *or* vollstes Vertrauen. **(b)** (*unbroken*) ganz, heil.

entirely [ɪn'taɪəlɪ] *adv* ganz ◆ **the money was given ~ to charity** das gesamte Geld wurde für wohltätige Zwecke ausgegeben; **I'm not ~ surprised** das kommt für mich nicht ganz überraschend; **it's ~ different** es ist völlig *or* ganz anders; **I don't ~ agree** ich bin nicht ganz der (gleichen) Meinung.

entirety [ɪn'taɪərətɪ] *n* Gesamtheit *f* ◆ **in its ~** in seiner Gesamtheit.

entitle [ɪn'taɪtl] *vt* **(a)** *book* betiteln ◆ **it is ~d ...** es hat den Titel ...
(b) (*give the right*) **to ~ sb to sth/to do sth** jdn zu etw berechtigen/jdn dazu berechtigen, etw zu tun; (*to compensation, legal aid, taking holiday*) jdm den Anspruch auf etw (*acc*) geben/jdm den Anspruch darauf *or* das Anrecht dazu geben, etw zu tun; **to be ~d to sth/to do sth** das Recht auf etw (*acc*) haben/das Recht haben, etw zu tun; (*to compensation, legal aid, holiday*) Anspruch auf etw (*acc*) haben/Anspruch darauf haben, etw zu tun; **he is ~d to two weeks' holiday** ihm stehen zwei Wochen Urlaub zu, er hat Anspruch auf zwei Wochen Urlaub.

entitlement [ɪn'taɪtlmənt] *n* Berechtigung *f* (*to* zu); (*to compensation, legal aid, holiday etc*) Anspruch *m* (*to* auf +*acc*) ◆ **what is your holiday ~?** wieviel Urlaub steht Ihnen zu?

entity ['entɪtɪ] *n* Wesen *nt* ◆ **legal ~** juristische Person.

entomb [ɪn'tuːm] *vt* beisetzen, bestatten ◆ **the mausoleum which ~s his body** das Mausoleum, in dem er beigesetzt ist.

entomologist [ˌentə'mɒlədʒɪst] *n* Entomologe *m*, Entomologin *f*.

entomology [ˌentə'mɒlədʒɪ] *n* Entomologie, Insektenkunde *f*.

entourage [ˌɒntʊ'rɑːʒ] *n* Gefolge *nt*, Entourage *f* (*geh*).

entr'acte ['ɒntrækt] *n* Zwischenspiel *nt*.

entrails ['entreɪlz] *npl* (*lit*) Eingeweide *pl*; (*fig: of watch etc*) Innereien *pl* (*hum*).

entrain [ɪn'treɪn] 1 *vt troops* (in Eisenbahnwaggons) verladen.
2 *vi* (in den Zug) einsteigen.

entrance[1] [ɪn'trɑːns] *vt* in Entzücken *or* Verzückung versetzen ◆ **to be ~d** verzückt sein; **to be ~d by/at sth** von etw entzückt sein.

entrance[2] ['entrəns] *n* **(a)** (*way in*) Eingang *m*; (*for vehicles*) Einfahrt *f*; (*hall*) Eingangshalle *f*, Entree *nt* (*geh*).
(b) (*entering*) Eintritt *m*; (*Theat*) Auftritt *m* ◆ **on his ~** bei seinem Eintritt/Auftritt; **to make an ~** in Erscheinung treten; **to make one's ~** (*Theat*) auftreten; (*fig also*) erscheinen.
(c) (*admission*) Eintritt *m* (*to* in +*acc*); (*to club etc*) Zutritt *m* (*to* zu); (*to school*) Aufnahme *f* (*to* in +*acc*) ◆ **to gain ~ to a university** die Zulassung zu einer Universität erhalten.

entrance: ~ card *n* Eintrittskarte *f*; **~ examination** *n* Aufnahmeprüfung *f*; **~ fee** *n* (*for museum etc*) Eintrittsgeld *nt*; (*for competition*) Teilnahmegebühr *f*; (*for club membership*) Aufnahmegebühr *f*; **~ qualifications** *npl* Zulassungsanforderungen *pl*; **~ ticket** *n* Eintrittskarte *f*; **~ visa** *n* Einreisevisum *nt*.

entrancing *adj*, **~ly** *adv* [ɪn'trɑːnsɪŋ, -lɪ] bezaubernd.

entrant ['entrənt] *n* (*to profession*) Berufsanfänger(in *f*) *m* (*to* in +*dat*); (*in contest*) Teilnehmer(in *f*) *m*; (*in exam*) Prüfling *m*.

entreat [ɪn'triːt] *vt* inständig *or* dringend bitten, anflehen (*for* um) ◆ **listen to him, I ~ you** ich bitte Sie inständig *or* ich flehe Sie an, ihn anzuhören.

entreatingly [ɪn'triːtɪŋlɪ] *adv* flehentlich.

entreaty [ɪn'triːtɪ] *n* dringende *or* flehentliche Bitte ◆ **they remained deaf to my entreaties** sie blieben gegen alle meine Bitten taub; **a look of ~** ein flehender Blick.

entrecôte (steak) ['ɒntrəkəʊt(ˌsteɪk)] *n* Entrecote *nt*.

entrée ['ɒntreɪ] *n* **(a)** Hauptgericht *nt*. **(b)** (*to club etc*) Zutritt *m*.

entrench [ɪn'trentʃ] *vt* **(a)** (*Mil*) eingraben, verschanzen.
(b) (*fig*) **to be/become ~ed in sth** (*word, custom*) sich in etw (*dat*) eingebürgert haben/einbürgern; (*idea, prejudice*) sich in etw (*dat*) festgesetzt haben/festsetzen; (*belief*) in etw (*dat*) verwurzelt sein/sich in etw (*dat*) verwurzeln.

entrenchment [ɪn'trentʃmənt] *n* (*Mil*) Verschanzung *f*.

entrepôt ['ɒntrəpəʊ] *n* (*warehouse*) Lagerhalle *f*; (*port*) Umschlaghafen *m*.

entrepreneur [ˌɒntrəprə'nɜː[r]] *n* Unternehmer *m*.

entrepreneurial [ˌɒntrəprə'nɜːrɪəl] *adj* unternehmerisch.

entropy ['entrəpɪ] *n* Entropie *f*.

entrust [ɪn'trʌst] *vt* anvertrauen (*to sb* jdm) ◆ **to ~ a child to sb's care** ein Kind jds Obhut anvertrauen; **to ~ sb with a task/a secret/one's valuables** *etc* jdn mit einer Aufgabe betrauen/jdm ein Geheimnis/seine Wertgegenstände anvertrauen.

entry ['entrɪ] *n* **(a)** (*into* in +*acc*) (*coming or going in*) Eintritt *m*; (*by car etc*) Einfahrt *f*; (*into country*) Einreise *f*; (*into club, school etc*) Aufnahme *f*; (*Theat*) Auftritt *m* ◆ **point of ~** (*of bullet etc*) Einschußstelle *f*; (*of inlet pipe etc*) Anschlußstelle *f*; **port of ~** Einreisehafen *m*; (*airport*) Landeflughafen *m*; **to make an/one's ~** auftreten; **"no ~"** (*on door etc*) „Zutritt verboten"; (*on one-way street*) „keine Einfahrt"; **on ~ into the earth's atmosphere** beim Eintritt in die Erdatmosphäre.
(b) (*way in*) Eingang *m*; (*for vehicles*) Einfahrt *f*.
(c) (*in diary, account book, dictionary etc*) Eintrag *m* ◆ **the dictionary has 30,000 entries** das Wörterbuch enthält 30.000 Stichwörter; **to make an ~ against sb** einen Betrag von jds Konto abbuchen.
(d) (*for race etc: competitor*) Meldung *f* ◆ **there is a large ~ for the 200m** für die 200 m sind viele Meldungen eingegangen.

entry: ~ form *n* Anmeldeformular *nt*; **~-level** *adj prices etc* Einführungs-; (*Comput*) *model* für Einsteiger; **~ permit** *n* Passierschein *m*; (*into country*) Einreiseerlaubnis *f*; **~ phone** *n* Türsprechanlage *f*; **~ qualifications** *npl* Zulassungsanforderungen *pl*; **~way** *n* (*US*) Eingang *m*; (*for vehicles*) Einfahrt *f*.

entwine [ɪn'twaɪn] 1 *vt* (*twist together*) *stems, ribbons* ineinanderschlingen ◆ **they ~d their hands** sie schlangen ihre Hände ineinander.
2 *vi* sich ineinanderschlingen *or* -winden.

E number *n* E-Nummer *f*.

enumerate [ɪ'njuːməreɪt] *vt* aufzählen.

enumeration [ɪˌnjuːmə'reɪʃən] *n* Aufzählung *f*.

enunciate [ɪ'nʌnsɪeɪt] *vti* artikulieren.

enunciation [ɪˌnʌnsɪ'eɪʃən] *n* Artikulation *f*.

enuresis [ˌenjə'riːsɪs] *n* (*Med spec*) Enurese *f*.

envelop [ɪn'veləp] *vt* einhüllen ◆ **flames ~ed the house** das Haus war von Flammen eingehüllt; **he came ~ed in a big coat** er kam in einen großen Mantel gehüllt.

envelope ['envələʊp] *n* **(a)** (Brief)umschlag *m*; (*large, for packets etc*) Umschlag *m*. **(b)** (*of balloon, Biol*) Hülle *f*; (*of airship*) Außenhaut *f*; (*of insect*) Hautpanzer *m*.

enveloping [ɪn'veləpɪŋ] *adj* alles umhüllend ◆ **the all-~ fog/ silence** die dichte Nebelhülle/die Hülle des Schweigens.

envelopment [ɪn'veləpmənt] *n* Einhüllung *f*.

envenom [ɪn'venəm] *vt* (*lit, fig*) vergiften.

enviable *adj*, **-bly** *adv* ['envɪəbl, -ɪ] beneidenswert.

➤ LANGUAGE IN USE: **enthusiastic** → 7.3, 14

envious ['envɪəs] *adj* neidisch (*of* auf +*acc*).
enviously ['envɪəslɪ] *adv* neidisch; *speak, think also* voll Neid.
environment [ɪn'vaɪərənmənt] *n* Umwelt *f*; (*of town etc, physical surroundings*) Umgebung *f*; (*social, cultural surroundings also*) Milieu *nt* ◆ **working-class ~** Arbeitermilieu *nt*; **cultural/hostile ~** kulturelle/feindliche Umwelt; **Department of the E~** (*Brit*) Umweltministerium *nt*; **Secretary** (*US*) *or* **Minister** (*Brit*) **of the E~** Umweltminister(in *f*) *m*.
environmental [ɪn,vaɪərən'mentl] *adj* Umwelt-; (*relating to social, cultural environment also*) Milieu- ◆ **~ protection** Umweltschutz *m*; **~ studies** (*Sch*) Umweltkunde *f*.
environmentalism [ɪn,vaɪərən'mentəlɪzəm] *n* Umweltbewußtsein *nt*.
environmentalist [ɪn,vaɪərən'mentəlɪst] [1] *n* Umweltschützer(in *f*) *m*.
[2] *adj issues, politics* Umwelt-.
environmentally [ɪn,vaɪərən'mentəlɪ] *adv* im Hinblick auf die Umwelt ◆ **~ beneficial/damaging** umweltfreundlich/-feindlich.
environment-friendly *adj* umweltfreundlich.
environs [ɪn'vaɪərənz] *npl* Umgebung *f* ◆ **Rome and its ~** Rom und Umgebung.
▼ **envisage** [ɪn'vɪzɪdʒ] *vt* sich (*dat*) vorstellen ◆ **do you ~ any price rises in the near future?** halten Sie Preisanstiege in nächster Zukunft für wahrscheinlich?
envoy ['envɔɪ] *n* Bote *m*; (*diplomat*) Gesandte(r) *mf*.
envy ['envɪ] [1] *n* Neid *m* ◆ **his house was the ~ of his friends** seine Freunde beneideten ihn um sein Haus; **a laboratory which would be the ~ of every scientist** ein Labor, das der Neid eines jeden Wissenschaftlers wäre.
[2] *vt person* beneiden ◆ **to ~ sb sth** jdn um *or* wegen etw beneiden; **that's a job I don't ~** das ist eine Arbeit, um die ich niemanden beneide.
enzyme ['enzaɪm] *n* Enzym, Ferment *nt*.
Eolithic [,iːəʊ'lɪθɪk] *adj* eolithisch.
eon ['iːɒn] *n see* **aeon**.
EP *abbr of* **extended play** EP *f*.
EPA (*US*) *abbr of* **Environmental Protection Agency** *US-Umweltbehörde f*.
epaulette ['epɔːlet] *n* Epaulette *f*, Schulterstück *nt*.
épée [eɪ'peɪ] *n* (Fecht)degen *m*.
ephebe [ɪ'fiːb] *n* Ephebe *m*.
ephemeral [ɪ'femərəl] *adj* ephemer (*geh, Zool*), kurzlebig; *happiness also* flüchtig.
epic ['epɪk] [1] *adj poetry* episch; *film, novel* monumental, Monumental-; *performance, match* gewaltig; *journey* lang und abenteuerlich.
[2] *n* (*poem*) Epos, Heldengedicht *nt*; (*film, novel*) Epos *nt*, monumentaler Film/Roman; (*match*) gewaltiges Spiel ◆ **an ~ of the screen** (*Film*) ein Filmepos *nt*.
epicentre, (*US*) **epicenter** ['epɪsentəʳ] *n* Epizentrum *nt*.
epicure ['epɪkjʊəʳ] *n* Feinschmecker(in *f*) *m*.
epicurean [,epɪkjʊə'riːən] [1] *adj* epikureisch (*geh*).
[2] *n* Epikureer (*geh*), Genußmensch *m*.
epicycle ['epɪsaɪkl] *n* Epizykel *m*.
epicyclic [,epɪ'saɪklɪk] *adj* epizykel-, epizyklisch.
epidemic [,epɪ'demɪk] [1] *n* Epidemie (*also fig*), Seuche *f*.
[2] *adj* epidemisch.
epidemiological [,epɪdiːmɪə'lɒdʒɪkəl] *adj* epidemiologisch.
epidemiologist [,epɪdiːmɪ'ɒlədʒɪst] *n* Epidemiologe *m*, Epidemiologin *f*.
epidemiology [,epɪdiːmɪ'ɒlədʒɪ] *n* Epidemiologie *f*.
epidermis [,epɪ'dɜːmɪs] *n* Epidermis, Oberhaut *f*.
epidural [,epɪ'djʊərəl] [1] *adj* epidural.
[2] *n* Epiduralanästhesie *f*.
epiglottis [,epɪ'glɒtɪs] *n* Kehldeckel *m*, Epiglottis *f* (*spec*).
epigram ['epɪgræm] *n* (*saying*) Epigramm, Sinngedicht *nt*.
epigrammatic(al) [,epɪgrə'mætɪk(əl)] *adj* epigrammatisch.
epigraph ['epɪgrɑːf] *n* Epigraph *nt*, Inschrift *f*; (*at beginning of book, chapter*) Motto *nt*, Sinnspruch *m*.
epilepsy ['epɪlepsɪ] *n* Epilepsie *f*.
epileptic [,epɪ'leptɪk] [1] *adj* epileptisch ◆ **~ fit** epileptischer Anfall.
[2] *n* Epileptiker(in *f*) *m*.
epilogue ['epɪlɒg] *n* Epilog *m*, Nachwort *nt*; (*Rad, TV*) Wort *nt* zum Tagesausklang.
Epiphany [ɪ'pɪfənɪ] *n* das Dreikönigs- *or* Erscheinungsfest.
episcopal [ɪ'pɪskəpəl] *adj* bischöflich, Bischofs-, episkopal (*spec*) ◆ **the E~ church** die Episkopalkirche.
episcopalian [ɪ,pɪskə'peɪlɪən] [1] *adj* zur Episkopalkirche gehörig.
[2] *n* **E~** Mitglied *nt* der Episkopalkirche, Episkopale(r) *mf* (*form*); **the E~s** die Episkopalkirche.
episiotomy [ə,piːzɪ'ɒtəmɪ] *n* Dammschnitt *m*, Episiotomie *f*.
episode ['epɪsəʊd] *n* Episode *f*; (*of story, TV, Rad*) Fortsetzung *f*; (*incident also*) Begebenheit *f*, Vorfall *m*.
episodic [,epɪ'sɒdɪk] *adj* episodenhaft, episodisch; *novel* in Episoden.
epistemic [,epɪ'stiːmɪk] *adj* (*Philos*) epistemisch (*spec*).
epistemological [ɪ,pɪstɪmə'lɒdʒɪkəl] *adj* erkenntnistheoretisch, epistemologisch (*spec*).
epistemology [ɪ,pɪstə'mɒlədʒɪ] *n* Erkenntnistheorie, Epistemologie (*spec*) *f*.
epistle [ɪ'pɪsl] *n* (*old, iro*) Epistel *f*; (*Bibl*) Brief *m* (*to* an +*acc*).
epistolary [ɪ'pɪstələrɪ] *adj* Brief-.
epitaph ['epɪtɑːf] *n* Epitaph *nt*; (*on grave also*) Grabinschrift *f*.
epithet ['epɪθet] *n* Beiname *m*, Epitheton *nt* (*geh*); (*insulting name*) Schimpfname *m*.
epitome [ɪ'pɪtəmɪ] *n* **(a)** (*of virtue, wisdom etc*) Inbegriff *m* (*of gen*, an +*dat*). **(b)** (*rare: of book*) Epitome *f* (*spec*).
epitomize [ɪ'pɪtəmaɪz] *vt* verkörpern.
epoch ['iːpɒk] *n* Zeitalter *nt* (*also Geol*), Epoche *f*.
epoch-making ['iːpɒk'meɪkɪŋ] *adj* epochemachend, epochal.
EPOS ['iːpɒs] *abbr of* **electronic point of sale** elektronisches Kassenterminal.
epoxy resin [ɪ'pɒksɪ'rezɪn] *n* Epoxydharz *nt*.
Epsom salts ['epsəm'sɔːlts] *npl* (Epsomer) Bittersalz *nt*.
equable ['ekwəbl] *adj* gleichmäßig, ausgeglichen; *person* ausgeglichen.
equably ['ekwəblɪ] *adv* gleichmäßig.
equal ['iːkwəl] [1] *adj* **(a)** gleich (*to* +*dat*) ◆ **the two groups were ~ in number** die beiden Gruppen waren zahlenmäßig gleich groß; **they are about ~ in value** sie haben ungefähr den gleichen Wert; **an ~ sum of money** eine gleich große *or* gleiche Summe Geld; **two halves are ~ to one whole** zwei Halbe sind gleich ein Ganzes; **she received blame and praise with ~ indifference** sie nahm Lob und Tadel mit derselben Gleichgültigkeit entgegen; **to be on an ~ footing** *or* **on ~ terms** auf der gleichen Stufe stehen (*with* mit); **~ pay for ~ work** gleicher Lohn für gleiche Arbeit; **~ opportunities** Chancengleichheit *f*; **~ opportunities employer** Arbeitgeber, der Chancengleichheit praktiziert; **(all) other things being ~** wenn nichts dazwischenkommt; **now we're ~** jetzt sind wir quitt; **all men are ~, but some are more ~ than others** (*hum*) alle Menschen sind gleich, nur einige sind gleicher.
(b) to be ~ to the situation/task der Situation/Aufgabe gewachsen sein; **to feel ~ to sth** sich zu etw imstande *or* in der Lage fühlen.
[2] *n* (*in rank*) Gleichgestellte(r) *mf*; (*in birth also*) Artgenosse *m*/-genossin *f* ◆ **she is his ~** sie ist ihm ebenbürtig; **he has no ~** er hat nicht seinesgleichen; **our ~s** unseresgleichen; **to treat sb as an ~** jdn als ebenbürtig behandeln.
[3] *vt* (*be same as, Math*) gleichen; (*match, measure up to*) gleichkommen (+*dat*) ◆ **three times three ~s nine** drei mal drei (ist) gleich neun; **let x ~ 3** wenn x gleich 3 ist; **he ~led his brother in generosity** er kam seinem Bruder an Großzügigkeit gleich; **not to be ~led** unvergleichlich; **this show is not to be ~led by any other** diese Show hat nicht ihresgleichen; **there is nothing to ~ it** nichts kommt dem gleich.
equality [ɪ'kwɒlɪtɪ] *n* Gleichheit *f*.
equalize ['iːkwəlaɪz] [1] *vt chances, opportunities* ausgleichen; *incomes* angleichen.
[2] *vi* (*Sport*) ausgleichen ◆ **the equalizing goal** das Ausgleichstor.
equalizer ['iːkwəlaɪzəʳ] *n* **(a)** (*Sport*) Ausgleich *m*; (*Ftbl etc also*) Ausgleichstor *nt or* -treffer *m* ◆ **to score** *or* **get the ~** den Ausgleich erzielen. **(b)** (*US sl: gun*) Kanone (*inf*), Bleispritze (*sl*) *f*.
▼ **equally** ['iːkwəlɪ] *adv* **(a) ~ gifted** gleich begabt *pred*, gleichbegabt *attr*, gleichermaßen begabt; **~ paid** gleich bezahlt *pred*, gleichbezahlt *attr*; **~ guilty** gleich schuldig *pred*, gleichermaßen schuldig. **(b)** *divide, distribute*
▼ gleichmäßig. **(c)** (*just as*) genauso ◆ **he is ~ unsuited** er ist genauso ungeeig-
▼ net. **(d) but then, ~, one must concede ...** aber dann muß man ebenso zugestehen, daß ...
equals sign ['iːkwəlz'saɪn] *n* Gleichheitszeichen *nt*.
equanimity [,ekwə'nɪmɪtɪ] *n* Gleichmut *m*, Gelassenheit *f* ◆ **to recover one's ~** seine Gelassenheit wiedergewinnen, das seelische Gleichgewicht wiederfinden.
equate [ɪ'kweɪt] *vt* **(a)** (*identify*) gleichsetzen, identifizieren (*with* mit); (*compare, treat as the same*) auf die gleiche Stufe stellen, als gleichwertig hinstellen *or* betrachten ◆ **do not ~ physical beauty with moral goodness** du mußt *or* darfst Schönheit nicht mit gutem Charakter gleichsetzen; **to ~ Eliot and Shakespeare** Eliot und Shakespeare auf eine Stufe stellen.
(b) (*Math*) gleichsetzen (*to* mit).
equation [ɪ'kweɪʒən] *n* (*Math, fig*) Gleichung *f* ◆ **~ of supply and demand** Ausgleich *m* von Angebot und Nachfrage; **work and leisure, how to get the ~ right** wie man Arbeit und Freizeit ins rechte Gleichgewicht bringt.
equator [ɪ'kweɪtəʳ] *n* Äquator *m* ◆ **at the ~** am Äquator.
equatorial [,ekwə'tɔːrɪəl] *adj* äquatorial, Äquatorial-.
equerry [ɪ'kwerɪ] *n* (*personal attendant*) persönlicher Diener (*eines Mitgliedes der königlichen Familie*); (*in charge of horses*) königlicher Stallmeister.
equestrian [ɪ'kwestrɪən] *adj* Reit-, Reiter- ◆ **~ act** (Kunst)reit- *or* Pferdenummer *f*; **~ events** Reitveranstaltung *f*; (*tournament*) Reitturnier *nt*; **~ prowess** Reitkunst *f*; **~ statue** Reiterstandbild *nt*.
equestrianism [ɪ'kwestrɪənɪzəm] *n* Pferdesport *m*, Reiten *nt*.
equidistant ['iːkwɪ'dɪstənt] *adj* gleichweit entfernt (*from* von).
equilateral ['iːkwɪ'lætərəl] *adj* gleichseitig.
equilibrium [,iːkwɪ'lɪbrɪəm] *n* Gleichgewicht *nt* ◆ **the political ~ of East Asia** das politische Gleichgewicht in Ostasien; **to keep/ lose one's ~** das Gleichgewicht halten/verlieren; **in ~** im Gleichgewicht.
equine ['ekwaɪn] *adj* Pferde-.
equinoctial [,iːkwɪ'nɒkʃəl] *adj gales, tides* äquinoktial.
equinox ['iːkwɪnɒks] *n* Tagundnachtgleiche *f*, Äquinoktium *nt*.
equip [ɪ'kwɪp] *vt ship, soldier, astronaut, army, worker* ausrüsten; *household, kitchen* ausstatten ◆ **to ~ a room as a laboratory** ein Zimmer als Labor einrichten; **to ~ a boy for life** (*fig*) einem Jungen das (nötige) Rüstzeug fürs Leben mitgeben; **he is well ~ped for the job** (*fig*) er hat die nötigen Kenntnisse *or* das nötige Rüstzeug für die Stelle; **you are better ~ped than I to tackle chemistry translations** du bringst für Chemieübersetzungen das bessere Rüstzeug mit.
equipage ['ekwɪpɪdʒ] *n* Equipage *f*.
equipment [ɪ'kwɪpmənt] *n, no pl* **(a)** (*objects*) (*of person*) Ausrüstung *f* ◆ la-

➤ LANGUAGE IN USE: **envisage** → 8.1 **equally: c** → 26.1, 26.2 **d** → 26.2

boratory ~ Laborausstattung *f*; **office ~** Büroeinrichtung *f*; **electrical ~** Elektrogeräte *pl*; **kitchen/domestic ~** Küchen-/Haushaltsgeräte *pl*.
(b) (*action*) *see vt* Ausrüstung *f*; Ausstattung *f*.
(c) (*mental, intellectual*) (geistiges) Rüstzeug.

equipoise ['ekwɪpɔɪz] *n* (*state*) Gleichgewicht *nt*; (*thing*) Gegengewicht *nt*.

equitable ['ekwɪtəbl] *adj* fair, gerecht, recht und billig.

equitableness ['ekwɪtəblnɪs] *n* Fairneß, Billigkeit *f*.

equitably ['ekwɪtəblɪ] *adv* fair, gerecht.

equity ['ekwɪtɪ] *n* (a) Fairneß, Billigkeit *f*. (b) (*Fin*) **equities** *pl* Stammaktien *pl*, Dividendenpapiere *pl*; **~ capital** Eigenkapital *nt*, Nettoanteil *m*; **~ stake** Kapitalbeteiligung *f*; **equities market** Aktienmarkt *m*. (c) (*Jur*) Billigkeitsrecht *nt*, billiges Recht. (d) (*Brit Theat*) **E~** Gewerkschaft *f* der Schauspieler.

equivalence [ɪ'kwɪvələns] *n* Äquivalenz, Entsprechung *f*.

equivalent [ɪ'kwɪvələnt] [1] *adj* (a) (*equal*) gleich, gleichwertig, äquivalent ◆ **three more or less ~ translations** drei mehr oder weniger gleichwertige Übersetzungen; **that's ~ to saying ...** das ist gleichbedeutend damit, zu sagen ...; **to be ~ in meaning** die gleiche Bedeutung haben.
(b) (*corresponding*) entsprechend, äquivalent ◆ **the ~ institution in America** die entsprechende Einrichtung in Amerika, das amerikanische Äquivalent dazu; **an ~ salary in 1935 would have been ...** ein entsprechendes Gehalt wäre im Jahre 1935 ... gewesen; **it is ~ to £30** das entspricht £ 30; **an ace is ~ to ...** ein As entspricht ...; **... or the ~ value in francs** ... oder der Gegenwert in Francs.
(c) (*Chem*) gleichwertig; (*Geometry*) äquivalent.
(d) **that's ~ to lying** das ist soviel wie gelogen; **as au pair girl she is ~ to nanny, maid and tutor all in one** als Au-pair-Mädchen ist sie soviel wie Kindermädchen, Dienstmädchen und Hauslehrerin in einer Person.
[2] *n* Äquivalent *nt*; (*counterpart*) (*thing also*) Gegenstück, Pendant *nt*; (*person also*) Pendant *nt* ◆ **what is the ~ in German marks?** was ist der Gegenwert in DM?; **the American ~ of the British public school** das amerikanische Gegenstück *or* Pendant zur britischen Public School; **the German ~ of the English word** die deutsche Entsprechung des englischen Wortes; **... or the ~ in cash** ...oder der/den Gegenwert in bar; **the ~ from another company** das gleiche von einer anderen Firma.

equivocal [ɪ'kwɪvəkəl] *adj behaviour* zweideutig; *words* doppeldeutig; *outcome* nicht eindeutig; (*vague*) unklar, unbestimmt.

equivocally [ɪ'kwɪvəkəlɪ] *adv see adj*.

equivocate [ɪ'kwɪvəkeɪt] *vi* ausweichen, ausweichend antworten.

equivocation [ɪ,kwɪvə'keɪʃən] *n* Ausflucht *f*, doppelsinnige *or* ausweichende Formulierung/Antwort ◆ **without so much ~** ohne so viele Ausflüchte.

ER *abbr of* **Elizabeth Regina**.

ERA (*US*) *abbr of* **Equal Rights Amendment** *Verfassungsartikel m zur Gleichberechtigung*.

era ['ɪərə] *n* Ära, Epoche *f*; (*Geol*) Erdzeitalter *nt* ◆ **the Christian ~** (die) christliche Zeitrechnung; **the end of an ~** das Ende einer Ära.

eradicate [ɪ'rædɪkeɪt] *vt* ausrotten.

eradication [ɪ,rædɪ'keɪʃən] *n* Ausrottung *f*.

erase [ɪ'reɪz] *vt* ausradieren; (*from tape, Comput*) löschen; (*from the mind*) streichen (*from* aus); (*sl: kill*) erledigen (*sl*) ◆ **~ head** (*on tape recorder*) Löschkopf *m*.

eraser [ɪ'reɪzə^r] *n* Radiergummi *nt or m*; (*for blackboard*) Schwamm *m*.

erasure [ɪ'reɪʒə^r] *n* (*act*) Auslöschen, Ausradieren *nt*; (*from tape*) Löschen *nt*; (*sth erased*) ausradierte Stelle, Radierstelle *f*; (*on tape*) gelöschte Stelle.

ere [ɛə^r] (*old, poet*) [1] *prep* ehe, bevor ◆ **~ now** bisher; **~ long** binnen kurzem.
[2] *conj* ehe, bevor.

erect [ɪ'rekt] [1] *adj* aufrecht, gerade; *penis* erigiert, steif ◆ **to hold oneself ~** sich gerade halten; **he went forward, his head ~** er ging mit hocherhobenem Kopf nach vorn; **with tail ~** mit hocherhobenem Schwanz.
[2] *vt wall, flats, factory* bauen; *statue, altar* errichten (*to sb* jdm); *machinery, traffic signs, collapsible furniture* aufstellen; *scaffolding* aufstellen, aufbauen; *tent* aufschlagen; *mast, flagpole* aufrichten; (*fig*) *barrier* errichten, aufbauen; *theoretical system* aufstellen.

erectile [ɪ'rektaɪl] *adj* Schwell-, erektil.

erection [ɪ'rekʃən] *n* (a) *see vt* (Er)bauen, Errichten *nt*; Bauen *nt*; Aufstellen *nt*; Aufbauen *nt*; Aufschlagen *nt*; Aufrichten *nt*. (b) (*the building, structure*) Gebäude *nt*, Bau *m*. (c) (*Physiol*) Erektion *f*.

erectly [ɪ'rektlɪ] *adv sit etc* gerade, aufrecht.

erg [ɜ:g] *n* Erg *nt*.

ergonomic [,ɜ:gəʊ'nɒmɪk] *adj* ergonomisch.

ergonomics [,ɜ:gəʊ'nɒmɪks] *n sing* Arbeitswissenschaft, Ergonomik, Ergonomie *f*.

ergot ['ɜ:gət] *n* Mutterkorn, Hungerkorn *nt*.

ergotism ['ɜ:gətɪzəm] *n* (*Med*) Mutterkornvergiftung *f*, Ergotismus *m*.

Erin ['ɪərɪn] *n* (*poet*) Irland *nt*.

ERM *n abbr of* **exchange rate mechanism**.

ermine ['ɜ:mɪn] *n* (*animal*) Hermelin *nt*; (*fur*) Hermelin *m*.

ERNIE *abbr of* **Electronic Random Number Indicator Equipment**.

erode [ɪ'rəʊd] *vt* (*glacier, water, sea*) auswaschen, erodieren (*spec*); (*acid*) ätzen; (*rust*) wegfressen, anfressen; (*fig*) *confidence, sb's beliefs* untergraben; *differentials* aushöhlen.

erogenous [ɪ'rɒdʒənəs] *adj* erogen ◆ **~ zone** erogene Zone.

erosion [ɪ'rəʊʒən] *n* (*by water, glaciers, rivers*) Erosion, Abtragung *f*; (*by acid*) Ätzung *f*; (*fig: of love etc*) Schwinden *nt*; (*of differentials*) Aushöhlen *nt* ◆ **an ~ of confidence in the pound** ein Vertrauensverlust *or* -schwund des Pfundes.

erosive [ɪ'rəʊzɪv] *adj effect of sea etc* abtragend; *effect of acid* ätzend.

erotic [ɪ'rɒtɪk] *adj* aufreizend; *literature, film* erotisch ◆ **he's a very ~ dancer** er ist ein sehr erotisch wirkender Tänzer; **I'm a very ~ person** für mich spielt Erotik eine große Rolle.

erotica [ɪ'rɒtɪkə] *npl* Erotika *pl*.

erotically [ɪ'rɒtɪkəlɪ] *adv* aufreizend; *written, photographed* erotisch.

eroticism [ɪ'rɒtɪsɪzəm] *n* Erotik *f*.

err [ɜ:^r] *vi* (a) (*be mistaken*) sich irren ◆ **to ~ in one's judgement** in seinem Urteil fehlgehen, sich in seinem Urteil irren; **to ~ is human(, to forgive divine)** (*Prov*) Irren ist menschlich(, Vergeben göttlich) (*Prov*); **it is better to ~ on the side of caution** man sollte im Zweifelsfall lieber zu vorsichtig sein.
(b) (*sin*) sündigen, Verfehlungen begehen.
(c) (*Rel: stray*) abgehen, in die Irre gehen ◆ **to ~ from the path of righteousness** vom Pfad der Tugend abweichen *or* abgehen.

errand ['erənd] *n* (*shopping etc*) Besorgung *f*; (*to give a message etc*) Botengang *m*; (*task*) Auftrag *m* ◆ **to send sb on an ~** jdn auf Besorgungen/einen Botengang schicken; **to go on** *or* **run ~s (for sb)** (für jdn) Besorgungen/Botengänge machen; **to give sb an ~ to do** jdm etw auftragen; **you can't trust him with any ~s** man kann ihm nichts auftragen; **to be on an ~** Besorgungen/einen Botengang machen, etwas erledigen; **~ of mercy** Rettungsaktion *f*; **~ boy** Laufbursche, Laufjunge *m*.

errant ['erənt] *adj* (a) **knight ~** fahrender Ritter. (b) (*erring*) *ways* sündig, verfehlt; *husband* abtrünnig; (*hum*) *Marxist, Freudian* fehlgeleitet, auf Irrwegen.

errata [e'rɑ:tə] *pl of* **erratum**.

erratic [ɪ'rætɪk] *adj* (a) unberechenbar; *person also* sprunghaft; *moods also* schwankend; *results also* stark schwankend; *work, performance* ungleichmäßig, unregelmäßig; *working of machine, freezer, weather also* launisch. (b) (*Geol*) erratisch.

erratically [ɪ'rætɪkəlɪ] *adv act* unberechenbar, launenhaft; *work* (*machine*) unregelmäßig; (*person*) ungleichmäßig; *drive* ungleichmäßig.

erratum [e'rɑ:təm] *n*, *pl* **errata** Erratum *nt*.

erring ['ɜ:rɪŋ] *adj see* **errant (b)**.

erroneous [ɪ'rəʊnɪəs] *adj* falsch; *assumption, belief* irrig.

erroneously [ɪ'rəʊnɪəslɪ] *adv* fälschlicherweise; *accuse* fälschlich ◆ **~ known as ...** fälschlich als ... bekannt; **~ labelled** falsch etikettiert.

error ['erə^r] *n* (a) (*mistake*) Fehler *m* ◆ **the elimination of ~** das Ausmerzen von Fehlern, die Ausmerzung von Fehlern; **~ in calculation** Rechenfehler *m*; **compass ~** (magnetische) Abweichung; **~s and omissions excepted** (*Comm*) Irrtum vorbehalten; **a pilot ~** ein Fehler *m* des Piloten; **the ~ rate** die Fehlerquote, die Fehlerrate; **~ message/correction** (*Comput*) Fehlermeldung/-korrektur *f*; *see* **margin**.
(b) (*wrongness*) Irrtum *m* ◆ **to be in ~** im Irrtum sein, sich im Irrtum befinden; **in ~** (*wrongly, accidentally*) irrtümlicherweise; **to see the ~ of one's ways** seine Fehler einsehen.

ersatz ['ɛəzæts] [1] *adj* Ersatz- ◆ **~ religion** Ersatzreligion *f*; **~ coffee** Kaffee-Ersatz *m*.
[2] *n* Ersatz *m*.

erstwhile ['ɜ:stwaɪl] [1] *adj* (*old, liter*) vormalig, einstig, ehemalig.
[2] *adv* (*old, liter*) vormals, ehedem, einst.

eructate [ɪ'rʌkteɪt] *vi* (*hum, form*) aufstoßen.

eructation [,ɪrʌk'teɪʃən] *n* (*hum, form*) Aufstoßen *nt* ◆ **an ~** ein Rülpser *m* (*inf*).

erudite ['erʊdaɪt] *adj* gelehrt; *person also* gebildet, belesen.

eruditely ['erʊdaɪtlɪ] *adv* gelehrt.

erudition [,erʊ'dɪʃən] *n* Gelehrsamkeit *f* ◆ **a book of great ~** ein sehr gelehrtes Buch.

erupt [ɪ'rʌpt] *vi* (*volcano, war, quarrel*) ausbrechen; (*spots*) zum Vorschein kommen; (*fig: person*) explodieren ◆ **he ~ed into a fit of rage** er bekam einen Wutanfall; **she/her face ~s in spots** sie bekommt im ganzen Gesicht Pickel.

eruption [ɪ'rʌpʃən] *n* (*of volcano, anger, violence*) Ausbruch *m*; (*Med*) (*of spots, rash*) Eruption *f* (*spec*), Ausbruch *m*, Auftreten *nt*; (*rash etc*) Hautausschlag *m*, Eruption *f* (*spec*).

erysipelas [,erɪ'sɪpɪləs] *n* (Wund)rose *f*.

escalate ['eskəleɪt] [1] *vt war* ausweiten, eskalieren; *costs* sprunghaft erhöhen.
[2] *vi* sich ausweiten, um sich greifen, eskalieren; (*costs*) eskalieren, in die Höhe schnellen.

escalation [,eskə'leɪʃən] *n* Eskalation *f*.

escalator ['eskəleɪtə^r] *n* Rolltreppe *f*.

escalator clause *n* Gleitklausel *f*.

escalope [ɪ'skæləp] *n* Schnitzel *nt*.

escapade [,eskə'peɪd] *n* Eskapade *f*.

escape [ɪ'skeɪp] [1] *vi* (a) flüchten (*from* aus), entfliehen (*geh*) (*from dat*); (*from pursuers*) entkommen (*from dat*); (*from prison, camp, cage, stall etc*) ausbrechen (*from* aus); (*bird*) entfliegen (*from dat*); (*water*) auslaufen (*from* aus); (*gas*) ausströmen (*from* aus) ◆ **to stop the prisoners escaping** um Gefängnisausbrüche zu verhindern; **he was shot while trying to ~** er wurde bei einem Fluchtversuch erschossen; **he's trying to ~ from his life in the suburbs** er versucht, seinem Leben in der Vorstadt zu entfliehen *or* zu entkommen; **in order to let the queen ~** (*Chess*) um die Königin davonkommen zu lassen; **an ~d prisoner/tiger** ein entsprungener Häftling/Tiger; **he ~d from the fire** er ist dem Feuer entkommen; **I've got you now, she said, and I won't let you ~** jetzt habe ich dich, sagte sie, und du entkommst mir so schnell nicht; **you cannot ~ from the passage of time** man kann dem Lauf der Zeit nicht

➤ LANGUAGE IN USE: error: a → 18.3, 20.6, 20.7

entrinnen; **I just feel I have to ~ from this job/place** ich habe einfach das Gefühl, daß ich hier weg muß; **she has to be able to ~ from her family sometimes** sie muß ab und zu die Möglichkeit haben, ihrer Familie zu entfliehen; **a room which I can ~ to** ein Zimmer, in das ich mich zurückziehen kann; **to ~ from oneself** vor sich (*dat*) selber fliehen; **it's no good trying to ~ from the world** es hat keinen Zweck, vor der Welt fliehen zu wollen.
(b) (*get off, be spared*) davonkommen ◆ **these cuts will affect everyone, nobody will ~** diese Kürzungen betreffen alle, keiner wird ungeschoren davonkommen; **the others were killed, but he ~d** die anderen wurden getötet, aber er kam mit dem Leben davon.
2 *vt* **(a)** *pursuers* entkommen (*+dat*).
(b) (*avoid*) *consequences, punishment, disaster* entgehen (*+dat*) ◆ **no department will ~ these cuts** keine Abteilung wird von diesen Kürzungen verschont bleiben; **he narrowly ~d danger/death** er ist der Gefahr/dem Tod mit knapper Not entronnen; **he narrowly ~d being run over** er wäre um ein Haar *or* um Haaresbreite überfahren worden; **but you can't ~ the fact that ...** aber du kannst nicht leugnen *or* abstreiten, daß ...; **there's no escaping this remorseless logic** man kann sich dieser unbarmherzigen Logik nicht entziehen.
(c) (*be unnoticed, forgotten by*) **his name/the word ~s me** sein Name/das Wort ist mir entfallen; **nothing ~s him** ihm entgeht nichts; **to ~ observation *or* notice** unbemerkt bleiben; **it had not ~d her notice** es war ihr nicht entgangen.
(d) the thoughtless words which ~d me die unbedachten Worte, die mir herausgerutscht *or* entfahren sind.
3 *n* **(a)** (*from prison etc*) Ausbruch *m*, Flucht *f*; (*attempted ~*) Ausbruchsversuch, Fluchtversuch *m*; (*from a country*) Flucht *f*; (*fig: from reality, one's family etc*) Flucht *f* ◆ **to make an ~** ausbrechen, entfliehen; **the ~ was successful** der Ausbruchs- *or* Fluchtversuch glückte *or* war erfolgreich; **there's been an ~** jemand ist ausgebrochen; **there were two ~s from this prison last month** im letzten Monat sind aus diesem Gefängnis zweimal Leute ausgebrochen; **the increasing number of ~s** die zunehmende Zahl von Ausbruchsfällen; **with this security system ~ is impossible** dieses Sicherheitssystem macht Ausbrechen unmöglich; **what are their chances of ~?** wie sind ihre Fluchtmöglichkeiten?, wie sind ihre Chancen zu entkommen?; **have you had any ~s at this zoo?** sind Ihnen aus dem Zoo schon Tiere ausgebrochen?; **there's been an ~ at London Zoo** aus dem Londoner Zoo ist ein Löwe/Tiger *etc* ausgebrochen; **to have a miraculous ~** (*from accident, illness*) auf wunderbare Weise davonkommen; **an ~ from reality** eine Flucht vor der Realität; **fishing/music is his ~** Angeln/Musik ist seine Zuflucht; **otherwise I don't get any ~ from my routine life/the demands of my family** sonst habe ich überhaupt keine Abwechslung von meiner Routine/ von den Ansprüchen meiner Familie; **there's no ~** (*fig*) es gibt keinen Ausweg *or* kein Entrinnen (*geh*); *see* **lucky**.
(b) (*of water*) Ausfließen *nt*; (*of gas*) Ausströmen *nt*; (*of steam, gas, in a machine*) Entweichen *nt* ◆ **due to an ~ of gas** auf Grund ausströmenden Gases.
(c) (*Comput*) **hit ~** Escape drücken.

escape: ~ artist *n* Entfesselungskünstler(in *f*) *m*; **~ attempt, ~ bid** *n* Fluchtversuch *m*; **~ chute** *n* (*on plane*) Notrutsche *f*; **~ clause** *n* (*Jur*) Befreiungsklausel *f*.

escapee [ɪskeɪ'piː] *n* entwichener Häftling *or* Gefangener.

escape: ~ hatch *n* (*Naut*) Notluke *f*; **~ key** *n* (*Comput*) Escape-Taste *f*; **~ mechanism** *n* Abwehrmechanismus *m*.

escapement [ɪ'skeɪpmənt] *n* (*of clock*) Hemmung *f*.

escape: ~ pipe *n* Überlaufrohr *nt*; (*for gas, steam*) Abzugsrohr *nt*; **~ plan** *n* Fluchtplan *m*; **~-proof** *adj* ausbruchsicher; **~ road** *n* Ausweichstraße *f*; **~ route** *n* Fluchtweg *m*; **~ valve** *n* Sicherheitsventil *nt*; **~ velocity** *n* (*Space*) Fluchtgeschwindigkeit *f*.

escapism [ɪ'skeɪpɪzəm] *n* Wirklichkeitsflucht *f*, Eskapismus *m* (*spec*).

escapist [ɪ'skeɪpɪst] **1** *n* jd, der vor der Wirklichkeit flieht, Eskapist *m* (*spec*).
2 *adj* eskapistisch (*spec*) ◆ **~ visions** unrealistische Träume *pl*; **~ literature** unrealistische, eine Phantasiewelt vorgaukelnde Literatur; **~ phantasies** Phantasiegebilde *pl*.

escapologist [ˌeskə'pɒlədʒɪst] *n* Entfesselungskünstler(in *f*) *m*.

escarpment [ɪ'skɑːpmənt] *n* Steilhang *m*; (*Geol*) Schichtstufe *f*; (*as fortification*) Böschung *f*.

eschatological [ˌeskətə'lɒdʒɪkəl] *adj* eschatologisch.

eschatology [ˌeskə'tɒlədʒɪ] *n* Eschatologie *f*.

eschew [ɪs'tʃuː] *vt* (*old, liter*) scheuen, (ver)meiden; *wine etc* sich enthalten (*+gen*); *temptation* aus dem Wege gehen (*+dat*).

escort ['eskɔːt] **1** *n* **(a)** Geleitschutz *m*; (*escorting vehicles, ships etc*) Eskorte *f*; Geleitschiff *nt*/-schiffe *pl*; (*police ~*) Begleitmannschaft, Eskorte *f*; (*guard of honour*) Eskorte *f* ◆ **under ~** unter Bewachung; **motor-cycle ~** Motorradeskorte *f*.
(b) (*male companion*) Begleiter *m*; (*hired female*) Hostess *f*.
2 [ɪ'skɔːt] *vt* begleiten; (*Mil, Naut*) *general* eskortieren, Geleit(schutz) geben (*+dat*).

escort: ~ agency *n* Hostessenagentur *f*; **~ duty** *n* Geleitdienst *m*; **to be on ~ duty** Geleitschutz geben; **~ fighter** *n* (*Aviat*) Begleitjäger *m*; **~ party** *n* Eskorte *f*; **~ vessel** *n* (*Naut*) Geleitschiff *nt*.

escrow ['eskrəʊ] *n* **~ account** Anderkonto *nt*; **to put money in ~** Geld auf ein Anderkonto legen.

escutcheon [ɪ'skʌtʃən] *n* Wappen *nt* ◆ **it is a blot on his ~** das ist ein Fleck auf seiner weißen Weste.

ESE *abbr of* **east-south-east** OSO.

Eskimo ['eskɪməʊ] **1** *adj* Eskimo-, eskimoisch.
2 *n* **(a)** Eskimo *m*, Eskimofrau *f*. **(b)** (*language*) Eskimosprache *f*.

ESL *abbr of* **English as a Second Language**.

ESN *abbr of* **educationally subnormal**.

esophagus *n* (*esp US*) *see* **oesophagus**.

esoteric [ˌesəʊ'terɪk] *adj* esoterisch.

ESP *abbr of* **extra-sensory perception** ASW *f*.

espalier [ɪ'spæljəʳ] *n* (*trellis*) Spalier *nt*; (*tree*) Spalierbaum *m*; (*method*) Anbau *m* von Spalierobst.

especial [ɪ'speʃəl] *adj* besondere(r, s).

▼ **especially** [ɪ'speʃəlɪ] *adv* besonders ◆ **everyone should come, ~ you** alle sollten kommen, vor allen Dingen du *or* du besonders; **you ~ ought to know** gerade du solltest wissen; **more ~ as** besonders da, zumal; **why me ~?** warum unbedingt *or* gerade ich/mich?; **I came ~ to see you** ich bin speziell *or* extra gekommen, um dich zu besuchen; **~ in the summer** besonders *or* zumal im Sommer.

Esperanto [ˌespə'ræntəʊ] *n* Esperanto *nt*.

espionage [ˌespɪə'nɑːʒ] *n* Spionage *f*.

esplanade [ˌesplə'neɪd] *n* (Strand)promenade *f*.

espousal [ɪ'spaʊzəl] *n* **(a)** (*old*) (*marriage*) Vermählung *f*; (*betrothal*) Verlobung *f*. **(b)** (*of cause etc*) Parteinahme *f* (of für).

espouse [ɪ'spaʊz] *vt* **(a)** (*old, form*) *woman* sich vermählen mit, zur Frau nehmen; (*get betrothed to*) sich anverloben (*+dat*) (*old*) ◆ **to become ~d to sb** jdm angetraut/anverlobt werden. **(b)** (*fig*) *cause* Partei ergreifen für, eintreten für.

espresso [e'spresəʊ] *n* Espresso *m* ◆ **~ bar** Espresso(bar *f*) *nt*.

esprit de corps [e'spriːdə'kɔː] *n* Korpsgeist *m*.

espy [ɪ'spaɪ] *vt* (*old, liter*) erspähen, erblicken.

esquire [ɪ'skwaɪəʳ] *n* (*Brit: on envelope, abbr* **Esq**) *als Titel nach dem Namen, wenn kein anderer Titel angegeben wird* ◆ **James Jones, Esq** Herrn James Jones.

essay¹ [e'seɪ] (*form*) **1** *vt* (*try*) (aus)probieren.
2 *n* Versuch *m*.

essay² ['eseɪ] *n* Essay *m or nt*; (*esp Sch*) Aufsatz *m*.

essayist ['eseɪɪst] *n* Essayist *m*.

essence ['esəns] *n* **(a)** (*Philos*) Wesen *nt*, Essenz *f*; (*substratum*) Substanz *f*.
(b) (*most important quality*) Wesen, Wesentliche(s) *nt*, Kern *m* ◆ **in ~ the theories are very similar** die Theorien sind im Wesentlichen *or* in ihrem Kern *or* essentiell (*geh*) sehr ähnlich; **how would you describe the situation, in ~?** wie würden Sie die Situation im wesentlichen beschreiben?; **well that's it, in ~** nun, das wäre es im wesentlichen; **good management is of the ~** gutes Management ist von entscheidender *or* ausschlaggebender Bedeutung; **the ~ of his thought** der Kern *or* die Essenz seines Denkens; **the note contained the ~ of what he had said** die Notiz enthielt den Kern dessen, was er gesagt hatte; **the ~ of stupidity/tact** der Inbegriff der Dummheit/des Taktes; **the ~ of Liberalism** die Essenz des Liberalismus.
(c) (*extract: Chem, Cook*) Essenz *f* ◆ **meat ~** Fleischextrakt *m*.

▼ **essential** [ɪ'senʃəl] **1** *adj* **(a)** (*necessary, vital*) (unbedingt *or* absolut) erforderlich *or* notwendig ◆ **it is ~ to act quickly** schnelles Handeln ist unbedingt *or* absolut erforderlich; **it is ~ that he come(s)** es ist absolut *or* unbedingt erforderlich, daß er kommt, er muß unbedingt kommen; **it is ~ that you understand this** du mußt das unbedingt verstehen; **do it now — is it really ~?** mach es jetzt — ist das wirklich unbedingt nötig?; **this is of ~ importance** dies ist von entscheidender Bedeutung; **it's ~ for a happy life** es ist eine notwendige Voraussetzung für ein glückliches Leben; **sleep is ~ for a healthy life** Schlaf ist die wesentliche Voraussetzung für ein gesundes Leben; **she's become ~ to me** sie ist mir unentbehrlich geworden; **the ~ thing is to ...** wichtig ist vor allem, zu ...
(b) (*of the essence, basic*) wesentlich, essentiell (*geh*); (*Philos*) essentiell, wesenhaft; *question* entscheidend ◆ **~ features** wesentliche Eigenschaften *pl*; **I don't doubt his ~ goodness** ich zweifle nicht an, daß er im Grunde ein guter Mensch ist; **he has an ~ honesty** er ist im Grunde (genommen) ehrlich; **the ~ feature of his personality** der Grundzug *or* der grundlegende Zug seiner Persönlichkeit.
(c) (*Chem*) **~ oils** ätherische Öle *pl*.
2 *n* **(a)** (*necessary thing*) **an ice-axe is an ~ for mountain climbing** ein Eispickel ist unbedingt notwendig zum Bergsteigen; **accuracy is an ~ *or* one of the ~s in this type of work** Genauigkeit ist für diese Art (von) Arbeit unabdingbar; **just bring the ~s** bring nur das Allernotwendigste mit; **with only the bare ~s** nur mit dem Allernotwendigsten ausgestattet.
(b) ~s *pl* (*most important points*) wichtige Punkte *pl*, Essentials *pl* ◆ **the ~s of German grammar** die Grundlagen *or* Grundzüge der deutschen Grammatik.

essentially [ɪ'senʃəlɪ] *adv* (*basically*) im Grunde genommen, im Prinzip; (*in essence*) dem Wesen nach, im wesentlichen ◆ **he's ~ a nervous person** im Grunde seines Wesens ist er ein nervöser Mensch; **our points of view are ~ similar** unsere Ansichten gleichen einander im Wesentlichen; **an ~ optimistic view** eine im wesentlichen optimistische Einstellung.

EST (*US*) *abbr of* **Eastern Standard Time** Ostküstenzeit *f*.

est *abbr of* **established** gegr.; **estimated** gesch.

▼ **establish** [ɪ'stæblɪʃ] **1** *vt* **(a)** (*found, set up*) gründen; *government* bilden; *religion also* stiften; *laws* geben, schaffen; *custom, new procedure* einführen; *relations* herstellen, aufnehmen; *links* anknüpfen; *post* einrichten, schaffen; *power, authority* sich (*dat*) verschaffen; *peace* stiften; *order* (wieder)herstellen; *list* (*in publishing*) aufstellen, zusammenstellen; *reputation* sich (*dat*) verschaffen; *precedent* setzen; *committee* einsetzen ◆ **once he had ~ed his power**

➤ LANGUAGE IN USE: **especially** → 26.3 **essential: 1a** → 10.1

as Emperor als er seine Macht als Kaiser begründet hatte; **his father ~ed him in business** sein Vater ermöglichte ihm den Start ins Geschäftsleben; **to ~ one's reputation as a scholar/writer** sich (*dat*) einen Namen als Wissenschaftler/Schriftsteller machen.
▼**(b)** (*prove*) *fact, innocence* beweisen, nachweisen; *claim* unter Beweis stellen ◆ **we have ~ed that ...** wir haben bewiesen *or* gezeigt, daß ...; **having ~ed his indispensability** nachdem er seine Unentbehrlichkeit unter Beweis gestellt hatte.
(c) (*determine*) *identity, facts* ermitteln, feststellen.
(d) (*gain acceptance for*) *product, theory, ideas* Anklang *or* Anerkennung finden für; *one's rights* Anerkennung finden für ◆ **if we can ~ our product on the market** wenn wir unser Produkt auf dem Markt etablieren können; **we have tried to ~ our product as the number-one model** wir haben versucht, unser Produkt als das Spitzenmodell einzuführen.
[2] *vr* (*in business, profession*) sich etablieren, sich niederlassen ◆ **he has now firmly ~ed himself within the company** er ist jetzt in der Firma fest etabliert; **he seems to have ~ed himself as an expert** er scheint sich (*dat*) einen Ruf als Experte verschafft zu haben.

established [ɪ'stæblɪʃt] *adj* **(a)** (*on firm basis*) *reputation* gesichert, gefestigt ◆ **well-~ business** gut eingeführte *or* alteingesessene Firma.
(b) (*accepted*) *fact* feststehend, akzeptiert; *truth* akzeptiert, anerkannt; *custom* althergebracht; *procedure* anerkannt; *belief* überkommen, herrschend; *government* herrschend; *laws* bestehend, geltend; *order* bestehend, etabliert ◆ **an ~ scientific fact** eine wissenschaftlich erwiesene Tatsache; **he deviated somewhat from the ~ procedure** er wich ein wenig vom üblichen *or* sonst allgemeinüblichen Verfahren ab.
(c) (*Eccl*) **the ~ Church** die Staatskirche.

establishment [ɪ'stæblɪʃmənt] *n* **(a)** *see vt (a)* Gründung *f*; Bildung *f*; Stiftung *f*; Schaffung *f*, Erlassen *nt*; Einführung *f*; Herstellung, Aufnahme *f*; Einrichtung *f*; (*of power, authority*) Festigung *f*; (Wieder)herstellung *f*; Aufstellung *f*, Zusammenstellen *nt*; (*of reputation*) Begründung *f*; Setzen *nt*; Einsetzen *nt*.
(b) (*proving*) Beweis *m* ◆ **the lawyer devoted a lot of time to the ~ of a few basic facts** der Rechtsanwalt verwandte viel Zeit darauf, ein paar Tatsachen unter Beweis zu stellen.
(c) (*determining*) Ermittlung *f* ◆ **~ of truth** Wahrheitsfindung *f*.
(d) (*institution etc*) Institution *f*; (*hospital, school etc also*) Anstalt *f* ◆ **that big house on the corner is a very dubious ~** das große Haus an der Ecke ist ein sehr zweifelhaftes Etablissement; **commercial ~** kommerzielles Unternehmen.
(e) (*household*) Haus *nt*, Haushalt *m* ◆ **to keep up a large ~** ein großes Haus führen.
(f) (*Mil, Naut etc: personnel*) Truppenstärke *f* ◆ **war/peace ~** Kriegs-/Friedensstärke *f*.
(g) (*Brit*) **the E~** das Establishment; **~ person** (Erz)konservative(r) *mf*; **~ figure** Mitglied *nt or* Angehörige(r) *mf* des Establishments.

estate [ɪ'steɪt] *n* **(a)** (*land*) Gut *nt* ◆ **country ~** Landgut *nt*; **family ~** Familienbesitz *m*.
(b) (*Jur: possessions*) Besitz(tümer *pl*) *m*, Eigentum *nt*; (*of deceased*) Nachlaß *m*, Erbmasse *f* ◆ **to leave one's ~ to sb** jdm seinen ganzen Besitz vermachen *or* hinterlassen; **personal ~** persönliches Eigentum; *see* **real**.
(c) (*esp Brit*) (*housing ~*) Siedlung *f*; (*trading ~*) Industriegelände *nt*.
(d) (*order, rank*) Stand *m* ◆ **the three ~s** die drei Stände; **person of high ~** (*old*) Standesperson *f* (*old*); **the holy ~ of matrimony** (*Rel*) der heilige Stand der Ehe; **to reach man's ~** (*liter*) in den Mannesstand treten (*old*).

estate: ~ agent *n* (*Brit*) Grundstücks- *or* Immobilienmakler(in *f*) *m*; **~ car** *n* (*Brit*) Kombi(wagen) *m*; **~ duty** *n* Erbschaftssteuer *f*.

esteem [ɪ'stiːm] [1] *vt* **(a)** (*consider*) ansehen, betrachten ◆ **I ~ it an honour** ich sehe es als eine Ehre an.
(b) (*think highly of*) *person* hochschätzen; *qualities* schätzen ◆ **my ~ed colleague** (*form*) mein verehrter Herr Kollege (*form*).
[2] *n* Wertschätzung *f* ◆ **to hold sb/sth in (high) ~** jdn/etw (hoch)schätzen, von jdm/etw eine hohe Meinung haben; **to be held in low/great ~** wenig/sehr geschätzt werden; **he went down in my ~** er ist in meiner Achtung gesunken.

esthete *etc* (*esp US*) *see* **aesthete** *etc*.

Est(h)onia [e'stəʊnɪə] *n* Estland *nt*.

Est(h)onian [e'stəʊnɪən] [1] *adj* estnisch.
[2] *n* **(a)** Este *m*, Estin *f*. **(b)** (*language*) Estnisch *nt*.

estimable ['estɪməbl] *adj* **(a)** (*deserving respect*) schätzenswert. **(b)** (*that can be estimated*) (ab)schätzbar.

estimate ['estɪmɪt] [1] *n* **(a)** (*approximate calculation*) Schätzung *f*; (*valuation: by antique dealer etc*) Taxierung *f* ◆ **what's your ~ of our chances of success?** wie schätzen Sie unsere Erfolgschancen ein?; **to form an ~ of sb's capabilities** sich (*dat*) ein Bild von jds Fähigkeiten machen, jds Fähigkeiten einschätzen; **£100/it is just an ~** £ 100/das ist nur geschätzt; **at a rough ~** grob geschätzt, über den Daumen gepeilt (*inf*); **at the lowest ~** mindestens, wenigstens.
(b) (*Comm: of cost*) (Kosten)voranschlag *m* ◆ **to get an ~** einen (Kosten)voranschlag einholen.
(c) (*government costs*) **~s** *pl* Haushalt *m*, Budget *nt*.
[2] ['estɪmeɪt] *vt cost, price* (ein)schätzen; *distance, speed* schätzen ◆ **his wealth is ~d at ...** sein Vermögen wird auf ... geschätzt; **it's hard to ~** es läßt sich schwer (ab)schätzen; **I ~ she must be 40** ich schätze sie auf 40, ich schätze, daß sie 40 ist; **I would ~ we'd need 30 people/£300** ich schätze, wir brauchen 30 Leute/£ 300.
[3] ['estɪmeɪt] *vi* schätzen ◆ **I'm just estimating** das schätze ich nur.

estimation [ˌestɪ'meɪʃən] *n* **(a)** Einschätzung *f* ◆ **in my ~** meiner Einschätzung nach. **(b)** (*esteem*) Achtung *f*. **to hold sb in high ~** jdn hochachten, viel von jdm halten; **he went up/down in my ~** er ist in meiner Achtung gestiegen/gesunken.

estimator ['estɪmeɪtə^r] *n* (*Insur etc*) Schätzer *m*.

estivate *etc* (*US*) *see* **aestivate** *etc*.

Estonia *etc see* **Est(h)onia** *etc*.

estrange [ɪ'streɪndʒ] *vt person* entfremden (*from +dat*) ◆ **to be/become ~d from sb** sich jdm entfremdet haben/entfremden; **they are ~d** (*married couple*) sie haben sich auseinandergelebt; **his ~d wife** seine von ihm getrennt lebende Frau.

estrangement [ɪ'streɪndʒmənt] *n* Entfremdung *f* (*from* von).

estrogen ['iːstrəʊdʒən] *n* (*US*) Östrogen *nt*.

estuary ['estjʊərɪ] *n* Mündung *f*.

Estuary English *n* (*Brit*) (*von Jugendlichen*) *in Südengland gesprochene Variante des Cockney*.

ET (*US*) *abbr of* **Eastern Time** Ostküstenzeit *f*.

ETA *abbr of* **estimated time of arrival** voraussichtliche Ankunft.

et al [et'æl] *adv* et al.

etcetera [ɪt'setərə] *adv* (*abbr* **etc**) und so weiter, et cetera.

etch [etʃ] *vti* ätzen; (*in copper*) kupferstechen; (*in other metals*) radieren ◆ **the event was ~ed** *or* **had ~ed itself on her mind** das Ereignis hatte sich ihr ins Gedächtnis eingegraben.

etching ['etʃɪŋ] *n see vb* **(a)** Ätzen *nt*; Kupferstechen *nt*; Radieren *nt*. **(b)** (*picture*) Ätzung *f*; Kupferstich *m*; Radierung *f* ◆ **come up and see my ~s** (*hum*) wollen Sie noch mit heraufkommen und sich (*dat*) meine Briefmarkensammlung ansehen? (*hum*).

eternal [ɪ'tɜːnl] [1] *adj* **(a)** ewig ◆ **the E~ City** die Ewige Stadt; **the ~ triangle** (*fig*) das Dreiecksverhältnis. **(b)** *complaints, gossiping* ewig.
[2] *n* **the E~** das Ewige; (*God*) der Ewige.

eternally [ɪ'tɜːnəlɪ] *adv* ewig, immer; (*unceasingly*) ewig.

eternity [ɪ'tɜːnɪtɪ] *n* (*lit, fig inf*) Ewigkeit *f*; (*Rel: the future life*) das ewige Leben ◆ **from here to ~** bis in alle Ewigkeit; **will we meet again in ~?** werden wir uns im Jenseits wiedersehen?; **it seemed an ~** es kam mir wie eine Ewigkeit vor; **~ ring** Memoire-Ring *m*.

ethane ['iːθeɪn] *n* Äthan *nt*.

ethanol ['eθənɒl] *n* Äthanol *nt*.

ether ['iːθə^r] *n* (*Chem, poet*) Äther *m*.

ethereal [ɪ'θɪərɪəl] *adj* **(a)** (*light, delicate, spiritual*) ätherisch. **(b)** (*of the upper air*) *regions* himmlisch.

ethic ['eθɪk] *n* Ethik *f*, Ethos *nt*.

ethical ['eθɪkəl] *adj* **(a)** (*morally right*) ethisch *attr*; (*of ethics*) *judgement, philosophy etc* Moral- ◆ **~ values** moralische Werte *pl*; **it is not ~ to ...** es ist unethisch *or* unmoralisch, zu ... **(b)** *medicine etc* verschreibungspflichtig.

ethically ['eθɪkəlɪ] *adv* ethisch, moralisch.

ethics ['eθɪks] *n* **(a)** *sing* (*study, system*) Ethik *f*. **(b)** *pl* (*morality*) Moral *f* ◆ **the ~ of abortion** die moralischen *or* ethischen Aspekte der Abtreibung.

Ethiopia [ˌiːθɪ'əʊpɪə] *n* Äthiopien *nt*.

Ethiopian [ˌiːθɪ'əʊpɪən] [1] *adj* äthiopisch.
[2] *n* **(a)** Äthiopier(in *f*) *m*. **(b)** (*language*) Äthiopisch(e) *nt*.

ethnic ['eθnɪk] *adj* **(a)** ethnisch, Volks- ◆ **~ groups/minority** ethnische Gruppen *pl*/Minderheit *f*; **~ Germans** Volksdeutsche *pl*; **~ violence** Rassenkrawalle *pl*; **they import their own ~ food** sie importieren ihre eigenen einheimischen Nahrungsmittel. **(b)** (*traditional, folksy etc*) *atmosphere, pub etc* urtümlich, urwüchsig; *clothes* folkloristisch; *food* einheimisch, landesüblich.

ethnic cleansing *n* ethnische Säuberung.

ethnographer [eθ'nɒgrəfə^r] *n* Völkerkundler(in *f*) *m*.

ethnography [eθ'nɒgrəfɪ] *n* (beschreibende) Völkerkunde, Ethnographie *f*.

ethnologist [eθ'nɒlədʒɪst] *n* Ethnologe *m*, Ethnologin *f*.

ethnology [eθ'nɒlədʒɪ] *n* (vergleichende) Völkerkunde, Ethnologie *f*.

ethologist [ɪ'θɒlədʒɪst] *n* Verhaltensforscher(in *f*) *m*.

ethology [ɪ'θɒlədʒɪ] *n* Verhaltensforschung, Ethologie *f*.

ethos ['iːθɒs] *n* Gesinnung *f*, Ethos *nt*.

ethyl ['iːθaɪl] *n* Äthyl *nt*.

ethylene ['eθɪliːn] *n* Äthylen *nt*.

etiolate ['iːtɪəʊleɪt] *vt* (*Bot*) etiolieren (*spec*); (*enfeeble*) auszehren.

etiology *etc* (*esp US*) *see* **aetiology** *etc*.

etiquette ['etɪket] *n* Etikette *f* ◆ **court ~** Hofetikette *f*; **that's not in accordance with medical ~** das entspricht nicht dem Berufsethos eines Arztes.

Eton ['iːtən]: **~ collar** *n breiter, steifer, weißer Umlegekragen*; **~ crop** *n* Bubikopf *m*, Herrenschnitt *m*.

Etruscan [ɪ'trʌskən] [1] *adj* etruskisch.
[2] *n* **(a)** Etrusker(in *f*) *m*. **(b)** (*language*) Etruskisch *nt*.

ETV (*US*) *abbr of* **Educational Television** ≃ Schulfernsehen *nt*.

etymological *adj*, **~ly** *adv* [ˌetɪmə'lɒdʒɪkəl, -ɪ] etymologisch.

etymology [ˌetɪ'mɒlədʒɪ] *n* Etymologie *f*.

EU *n abbr of* **European Union** EU *f*.

eucalyptus [ˌjuːkə'lɪptəs] *n* Eukalyptus *m* ◆ **~ (oil)** Eukalyptusöl *nt*.

Eucharist ['juːkərɪst] *n* (*Eccl*) (*service*) Abendmahlsgottesdienst *m* ◆ **the ~** das (heilige) Abendmahl, die Eucharistie.

➤ LANGUAGE IN USE: **establish: 1b** → 15.1

Euclid ['ju:klɪd] *n* Euklid *m.*
Euclidean [ju:'klɪdɪən] *adj* euklidisch.
eugenics [ju:'dʒenɪks] *n sing* Eugenik *f.*
eulogize ['ju:lədʒaɪz] *vt* eine Lobesrede halten auf (*+acc*).
eulogy ['ju:lədʒɪ] *n* Lobesrede, Eloge (*liter*) *f.*
eunuch ['ju:nək] *n* Eunuch *m.*
euphemism ['ju:fəmɪzəm] *n* Euphemismus *m,* Hüllwort *nt.*
euphemistic *adj,* **~ally** *adv* [ˌju:fə'mɪstɪk, -əlɪ] euphemistisch, verhüllend.
euphonic [ju:'fɒnɪk], **euphonious** [ju:'fəʊnɪəs] *adj* euphonisch, wohlklingend.
euphonium [ju:'fəʊnɪəm] *n* Euphonium *nt.*
euphony ['ju:fənɪ] *n* (*Mus, Ling*) Euphonie *f,* Wohlklang *m.*
euphoria [ju:'fɔ:rɪə] *n* Euphorie *f.*
euphoric [ju:'fɒrɪk] *adj* euphorisch.
Euphrates [ju:'freɪti:z] *n* Euphrat *m.*
Eurasia [jʊə'reɪʃə] *n* Eurasien *nt.*
Eurasian [jʊə'reɪʃn] **1** *adj* eurasisch.
2 *n* Eurasier(in *f*) *m.*
Euratom [jʊə'rætəm] *abbr of* **European Atomic Energy Community** Euratom *f.*
eureka [jʊə'ri:kə] *interj* heureka.
eurhythmics [ju:'rɪðmɪks] *n sing* Eurhythmie *f.*
Euro- ['jʊərəʊ] *pref* Euro-.
Eurobond ['jʊərəʊbɒnd] *n* Eurobond *m.*
Eurocrat ['jʊərəʊkræt] *n* Eurokrat(in *f*) *m.*
Eurodollar ['jʊərəʊdɒlə^r] *n* Eurodollar *m.*
Europe ['jʊərəp] *n* Europa *nt.*
European [ˌjʊərə'pi:ən] **1** *adj* europäisch ◆ **~ Court of Justice** Europäischer Gerichtshof; **~ Economic Community** Europäische Wirtschaftsgemeinschaft; **~ Currency Unit** Europäische Wahrungseinheit; **~ Parliament** Europäisches Parlament, Europaparlament *nt.*
2 *n* Europäer(in *f*) *m* ◆ **~ Union** Europäischer Union.
Euro-sceptic, Eurosceptic ['jʊərəʊˌskeptɪk] *n* Euroskeptiker(in) *m(f).*
Eurotunnel ['jʊərəʊˌtʌnl] *n* Kanaltunnel *m,* Eurotunnel *m.*
Eurovision ['jʊərəʊvɪʒn] *n* Eurovision *f* ◆ **~ Song Contest** Eurovisions-Schlagerwettbewerb *m.*
Eustachian tube [ju:'steɪʃən'tju:b] *n* Eustachische Röhre.
euthanasia [ˌju:θə'neɪzɪə] *n* Euthanasie *f.*
evacuate [ɪ'vækjʊeɪt] *vt* **(a)** (*leave*) *fort, house* räumen. **(b)** (*clear*) *danger area* räumen; *civilians, women, children* evakuieren. **(c)** *bowels* entleeren.
evacuation [ɪˌvækjʊ'eɪʃən] *n see vt* Räumung *f;* Evakuierung *f.*
evacuee [ɪˌvækjʊ'i:] *n* Evakuierte(r) *mf.*
evade [ɪ'veɪd] *vt* **(a)** *blow* ausweichen (*+dat*); *pursuit, pursuers* sich entziehen (*+dat*), entkommen (*+dat*).
(b) *obligation, justice* sich entziehen (*+dat*); *military service also* umgehen; *question, issue* ausweichen (*+dat*); *difficulty, person, sb's glance* ausweichen (*+dat*), (ver)meiden; *sb's vigilance* entgehen (*+dat*) ◆ **to ~ taxes** Steuern hinterziehen; **he successfully ~d the tax authorities for several years** mehrere Jahre kam das Finanzamt ihm nicht auf die Spur; **if you try to ~ paying import duty** wenn Sie versuchen, den Einfuhrzoll zu umgehen; **a concept which somehow ~s precise definition** ein Begriff, der sich einer genauen Definition entzieht.
evaluate [ɪ'væljʊeɪt] *vt house, painting, worth etc* schätzen (*at* auf *+acc*); *damages* festsetzen (*at* auf *+acc*); *chances, effectiveness, usefulness* einschätzen, beurteilen; *evidence, results* auswerten; *pros and cons* (gegeneinander) abwägen; *contribution, achievement* bewerten, beurteilen ◆ **to ~ sth at £100** etw auf £ 100 taxieren *or* schätzen.
evaluation [ɪˌvæljʊ'eɪʃən] *n see vt* (Ein)schätzung *f;* Festsetzung *f;* Einschätzung, Beurteilung *f;* Auswertung *f;* Abwägung *f;* Bewertung *f* ◆ **in my ~** nach meiner Schätzung; **on ~ of the evidence it became clear that** ... die Auswertung *or* Sichtung des Beweismaterials machte klar, daß ...
evanescence [ˌi:və'nesəns] *n* (*Liter*) Vergänglichkeit *f.*
evanescent [ˌi:və'nesənt] *adj* (*Liter*) vergänglich.
evangelic(al) [ˌi:væn'dʒelɪk(əl)] *adj* evangelisch.
evangelist [ɪ'vændʒəlɪst] *n* (*Bibl*) Evangelist(in *f*) *m;* (*preacher*) Prediger(in *f*) *m;* (*itinerant*) Wanderprediger(in *f*) *m.*
evangelize [ɪ'vændʒəlaɪz] **1** *vt* evangelisieren, bekehren.
2 *vi* das Evangelium predigen.
evaporate [ɪ'væpəreɪt] **1** *vi* **(a)** (*liquid*) verdampfen, verdunsten. **(b)** (*fig*) (*disappear*) sich in nichts *or* in Luft auflösen; (*hopes*) sich zerschlagen, schwinden.
2 *vt liquid* verdampfen *or* verdunsten (lassen) ◆ **~d milk** Kondens- *or* Büchsenmilch *f;* **evaporating dish** Abdampfschale *f.*
evaporation [ɪˌvæpə'reɪʃən] *n* Verdampfung *f,* Verdampfen *nt;* (*fig*) Schwinden *nt.*
evasion [ɪ'veɪʒən] *n* **(a)** (*of question etc*) Ausweichen *nt* (*of* vor *+dat*). **(b)** (*evasive answer etc*) Ausflucht *f.*
evasive [ɪ'veɪzɪv] *adj answer* ausweichend; *meaning, truth* schwer zu fassen, schwer zu greifen; *prey* schwer zu fangen ◆ **don't be so ~** weich nicht aus; **he was very ~ about it** er wollte (dazu) nicht mit der Sprache herausrücken, er wich dauernd aus; **to take ~ action** (*Mil, fig*) ein Ausweichmanöver machen.
evasively [ɪ'veɪzɪvlɪ] *adv say, answer* ausweichend.
Eve [i:v] *n* Eva *f.*
eve¹ [i:v] *n* Vorabend *m* ◆ **on the ~ of** am Tage vor (*+dat*); am Vorabend (*+gen,* von); **these weeks were the ~ of a revolution which** ... diese Wochen bildeten den Vorabend einer Revolution, die ...
eve² *n* (*obs, poet*) Abend *m.*
▼ **even¹** ['i:vən] **1** *adj* **(a)** *surface, ground* eben ◆ **to make sth ~** *ground, earth* etw ebnen; **they made the top of the cupboard ~ with the top of the oven** sie machten den Schrank genau so hoch wie den Herd; **the concrete has to be ~ with the ground** der Beton muß eben mit dem Boden abschließen.
(b) (*regular*) *layer etc* gleichmäßig; *progress* stetig; *breathing, pulse also* regelmäßig; *temper* ausgeglichen ◆ **his work is not ~** seine Leistung ist schwankend *or* ungleichmäßig.
(c) *quantities, distances, values* gleich ◆ **the score is ~** es steht unentschieden; **they are an ~ match** sie sind einander ebenbürtig; **I will get ~ with you for that** das werde ich dir heimzahlen; **that makes us ~** (*in game*) damit steht es unentschieden; (*fig*) damit sind wir quitt; **the odds** *or* **chances are about ~** die Chancen stehen etwa fifty-fifty; **to break ~** sein Geld wieder herausbekommen.
(d) *number* gerade ◆ **~ money** *Wette, bei der die doppelte Einsatzsumme als Gewinn ausgezahlt wird;* **I'll give you ~ money he's late** (*inf*) ich gehe jede Wette mit dir ein, daß er zu spät kommt; **~ parity** (*Comput*) gerade Parität.
(e) (*exact*) genau ◆ **let's make it an ~ hundred** nehmen wir eine runde Zahl und sagen 100.
▼ **2** *adv* **(a)** sogar, selbst ◆ **~ for a fast car that's good going** sogar *or* selbst für ein schnelles Auto ist das allerhand; **they ~ denied its existence** sie leugneten sogar seine Existenz; **it'll be difficult, impossible ~** das wird schwierig sein, oder sogar *or* wenn nicht (so)gar unmöglich.
▼ **(b)** (*with comp adj*) sogar noch ◆ **that's ~ better/more beautiful** das ist sogar (noch) besser/schöner.
(c) (*with neg*) **not ~** nicht einmal; **with not ~ a smile** ohne auch nur zu lächeln; **he didn't ~ answer the letter** er hat den Brief (noch) nicht einmal beantwortet.
▼ **(d) ~ if/though** sogar *or* selbst wenn; **~ if you were a millionaire** sogar *or* selbst wenn du ein Millionär wärst; **but ~ then** aber sogar *or* selbst dann; **~ as I spoke someone knocked at the door** noch während ich redete, klopfte es an der Tür; **~ as he had wished** genau, wie er es sich gewünscht hatte; **~ as ... so** (*old*) genau wie ... so; **~ so** (aber) trotzdem.
3 *vt surface* glatt *or* eben machen, glätten.
◆**even out** **1** *vi* **(a)** (*prices*) sich einpendeln. **(b)** (*ground*) eben werden, sich ebnen.
2 *vt sep* **(a)** *prices* ausgleichen. **(b)** *ground, cement* ebnen, glätten; (*mechanically also*) planieren. **(c)** *tax burden, wealth* gleichmäßig verteilen ◆ **that should ~ things ~ a bit** dadurch müßte ein gewisser Ausgleich erzielt werden; **that will ~ things ~ between us** damit sind wir wohl wieder quitt.
◆**even up** **1** *vt sep sum* aufrunden (*to* auf *+acc*) ◆ **that will ~ things ~** das wird die Sache etwas ausgleichen.
2 *vi* (*pay off debt*) Schulden begleichen (*with* bei) ◆ **can we ~ ~ later?** können wir später abrechnen?
even² *n* (*obs, poet*) Abend *m.*
evening ['i:vnɪŋ] *n* Abend *m* ◆ **in the ~** abends, am Abend; **this/ tomorrow/ yesterday ~** heute/morgen/gestern abend; **that ~** an jenem Abend; **that ~ was** ... jener Abend war ...; **on the ~ of the twenty-ninth** am Abend des 29., am 29. abends; **one ~ as I** ... eines Abends, als ich ...; **every Monday ~** jeden Montagabend; **all ~** den ganzen Abend (lang *or* über); **the ~ of his life** (*liter*) sein Lebensabend.
evening *in cpds* Abend-; **~ class** *n* Abendkurs *m;* **to do ~ classes** *or* **an ~ class in French** einen Abendkurs in Französisch besuchen; **~ dress** *n* (*men's*) Abendanzug, Gesellschaftsanzug *m;* (*women's*) Abendkleid *nt;* **~ gown** *n* Abendkleid *nt.*
evenly ['i:vənlɪ] *adv spread, breathe, space, distribute, divide* gleichmäßig; *say* gelassen ◆ **the two contestants were ~ matched** die beiden Gegner waren einander ebenbürtig.
evenness ['i:vənnɪs] *n* **(a)** (*of ground*) Ebenheit *f.* **(b)** (*regularity*) Gleichmäßigkeit *f;* (*of progress*) Stetigkeit *f;* (*of breathing, pulse also*) Regelmäßigkeit *f;* (*of temper*) Ausgeglichenheit *f.*
evensong ['i:vənsɒŋ] *n* Abendgottesdienst *m.*
event [ɪ'vent] *n* **(a)** (*happening*) Ereignis *nt* ◆ **~s are taking place in Belfast which** ... in Belfast ereignen sich *or* geschehen Dinge, die ...; **in the normal course of ~s** normalerweise; **to be overtaken by ~s** von den Ereignissen überholt werden; **~s have proved us right** die Ereignisse haben uns recht gegeben; **it's quite an ~** das ist wirklich ein Ereignis; **it's easy to be wise after the ~** hinterher ist man immer klüger; *see* **happy**.
(b) (*organized function*) Veranstaltung *f;* (*Sport*) Wettkampf *m* ◆ **what is your best ~?** in welcher Disziplin sind Sie am besten?
(c) (*case*) Fall *m* ◆ **in the ~ of her death** im Falle ihres Todes; **in the ~ of war/fire** im Falle eines Krieges/Brandes, im Kriegs-/Brandfall; **he said he wouldn't come, but in the ~ he did** er sagte, er würde nicht kommen, aber er kam dann schließlich *or* im Endeffekt doch; **in the unlikely ~ that** ... falls, was sehr unwahrscheinlich ist, ...; **but in any ~ I can't give you my permission** aber ich kann dir jedenfalls nicht meine Erlaubnis geben; **but in any ~ you have my permission** aber Sie haben auf alle Fälle meine Erlaubnis; **in either ~** in jedem Fall; **at all ~s** auf jeden Fall.
even-tempered ['i:vən'tempəd] *adj* ausgeglichen.
eventer [ɪ'ventə^r] *n* (*Sport*) Militaryreiter(in *f*) *m.*
eventful [ɪ'ventfʊl] *adj* ereignisreich; *life, period also* bewegt.
eventide ['i:vəntaɪd] *n* **(a)** (*obs, poet*) Abendzeit *f.* **(b) ~ home** Altenheim *nt.*
eventing [ɪ'ventɪŋ] *n* (*Sport*) Military *f.*
eventual [ɪ'ventʃʊəl] *adj* **the decline and ~ collapse of the Roman Empire** der

Niedergang und schließlich vollkommene Zerfall des Römischen Reiches; **he predicted the ~ fall of the government** er hat vorausgesagt, daß die Regierung am Ende *or* schließlich zu Fall kommen würde; **the ~ success of the project is not in doubt** es besteht kein Zweifel, daß das Vorhaben letzten Endes Erfolg haben wird.

eventuality [ɪˌventʃʊ'ælɪtɪ] *n* (möglicher) Fall, Eventualität *f* ◆ **in the ~ of fire** im Brandfall; **be ready for any ~** sei auf alle Eventualitäten gefaßt.

eventually [ɪ'ventʃʊəlɪ] *adv* schließlich, endlich ◆ **it ~ turned out that ...** es hat sich schließlich *or* zum Schluß herausgestellt, daß ...; **he will get used to it ~** er wird sich schließlich daran gewöhnen; **of course ~ he always changed his mind** natürlich hat er es sich (dann) zum Schluß immer noch einmal anders überlegt.

ever ['evəʳ] *adv* **(a)** je(mals) ◆ **not ~** nie; **nothing ~ happens** es passiert nie etwas; **it hardly ~ snows here** hier schneit es kaum (jemals); **if I ~ catch you doing that again** wenn ich dich noch einmal dabei erwische; **if you ~ see her** wenn Sie sie je sehen sollten; **seldom, if ~** selten, wenn überhaupt; **he's a rascal if ~ there was one** er ist ein richtiggehender kleiner Halunke; **as if I ~ would** als ob ich das jemals täte; **don't you ~ say that again!** sag das ja nie mehr!; **have you ~ ridden a horse?** bist du schon einmal (auf einem Pferd) geritten?; **have you ~ been to Glasgow?** bist du schon einmal in Glasgow gewesen?; **have you ~ known him tell a lie?** haben Sie ihn (schon) jemals lügen hören?; **more beautiful than ~** schöner denn je; **the best soup I have ~ eaten** die beste Suppe, die ich je(mals) gegessen habe; **the first ~** der *etc* allererste; **the first man ~ to step on the moon** der erste Mensch, der je(mals) den Mond betrat; **the coldest night ~** die kälteste Nacht seit Menschengedenken.
(b) (*at all times*) **~ since I was a boy** seit ich ein Junge war; **~ since I have lived here ...** seitdem ich hier lebe ...; **~ since then** seit der Zeit, seitdem; **for ~** für immer, für alle Zeit(en); **it seemed to go on for ~ (and ~)** es schien ewig zu dauern; **for ~ and a day** für alle Zeiten, ewig und drei Tage (*inf*); **~ increasing powers** ständig wachsende Macht; **an ~ present feeling** ein ständiges Gefühl; *see* **forever**.
(c) (*intensive*) **be he ~ so charming** wenn er auch noch so liebenswürdig ist, sei er auch noch so liebenswürdig; **come as quickly as ~ you can** komm so schnell du nur kannst; **she's the best grandmother ~** sie ist die beste Großmutter, die es gibt; **did you ~!** (*inf*) also so was!
(d) **what ~ shall we do?** was sollen wir bloß machen?; **when ~ will they come?** wann kommen sie denn bloß *or* endlich?; **why ~ not?** warum denn bloß nicht?; *see* **whatever, wherever** *etc.*
(e) (*inf*) **~ so/such** unheimlich; **~ so slightly drunk** ein ganz klein wenig betrunken; **he's ~ such a nice man** er ist ein ungemein netter Mensch; **I am ~ so sorry** es tut mir schrecklich leid; **thank you ~ so much** ganz herzlichen Dank.
(f) (*old: always*) allzeit (*old, liter*).
(g) (*in letters*) **yours ~, Wendy** viele Grüße, Ihre Wendy.

Everest ['evərest] *n*: **(Mount) ~** der Mount Everest.

everglade ['evəgleɪd] *n* (*US*) *sumpfiges Flußgebiet*.

evergreen ['evəgriːn] **[1]** *adj trees, shrubs* immergrün; (*fig*) *topic* immer aktuell ◆ **~ facility** (*Fin*) Revolving-Kredit *m*; **~ song** Evergreen *m*.
[2] *n* Nadelbaum *m*; immergrüner Busch.

everlasting [ˌevə'lɑːstɪŋ] **[1]** *adj* **(a)** *God* ewig; *gratitude* immerwährend; *glory* unvergänglich ◆ **~ flower** Strohblume, Immortelle *f*. **(b)** (*inf: constant*) ewig (*inf*).
[2] *n*: **from ~ to ~ thou art God** Du bist Gott von Ewigkeit zu Ewigkeit.

everlastingly [ˌevə'lɑːstɪŋlɪ] *adv* ewig.

evermore [ˌevə'mɔːʳ] *adv* immer, stets ◆ **for ~** auf alle Zeiten, in (alle) Ewigkeit (*esp Rel*), auf immer; **their name liveth for ~** ihr Name wird ewig fortleben.

every ['evrɪ] *adj* **(a)** jede(r, s) ◆ **you must examine ~ one** Sie müssen jeden (einzelnen) untersuchen; **~ man for himself** jeder für sich; **in ~ way** (*in all respects*) in jeder Hinsicht; (*by ~ means*) mit allen Mitteln; **he is ~ bit as clever as his brother** er ist ganz genauso schlau wie sein Bruder; **~ bit as much** ganz genauso viel; **~ single time** jedes einzelne Mal; **~ single time I ...** immer wenn ich ...
(b) (*all possible*) **I have ~ confidence in him** ich habe unbedingtes *or* uneingeschränktes Vertrauen zu ihm; **I have/there is ~ hope that ...** ich habe allen Grund/es besteht aller Grund zu der Hoffnung, daß ...; **we wish you ~ success/happiness** wir wünschen Ihnen alles (nur erdenklich) Gute/viel Glück und Zufriedenheit; **there was ~ prospect of success** es bestand alle Aussicht auf Erfolg.
(c) (*indicating recurrence*) **~ fifth day, ~ five days** jeden fünften Tag, alle fünf Tage; **~ other day** jeden zweiten Tag, alle zwei Tage; **write on ~ other line** bitte eine Zeile Zwischenraum lassen; **once ~ week** einmal jede *or* pro Woche; **~ so often, ~ once in a while, ~ now and then** *or* **again** hin und wieder, ab und zu, gelegentlich.
(d) (*after poss adj*) **his ~ action** jede seiner Handlungen; **his ~ word** jedes seiner Worte, jedes Wort, das er sagte.

everybody ['evrɪbɒdɪ], **everyone** *pron* jeder(mann), alle *pl* ◆ **~ has finished** alle sind fertig; **it's not ~ who can afford a deep-freeze** nicht jeder kann sich (*dat*) eine Tiefkühltruhe leisten; **~ knows ~ else here** hier kennt jeder jeden; **~ knows that** das weiß (doch) jeder.

everyday ['evrɪdeɪ] *adj* alltäglich; *language* Alltags-, Umgangs- ◆ **words in ~ use** Wörter der Alltags- *or* Umgangssprache.

➤ **everyone** ['evrɪwʌn] *pron see* **everybody**.

everything ['evrɪθɪŋ] *n* alles ◆ **~ possible/old** alles Mögliche/Alte; **~ you have** alles, was du hast; **time is ~** Zeit ist kostbar; **money isn't ~** Geld ist nicht alles; **money is ~ to him** Geld bedeutet ihm alles.

➤ LANGUAGE IN USE: **everyone** → 26.2

everywhere ['evrɪweəʳ] *adv* überall; (*with direction*) überallhin ◆ **from ~** überallher *or* von überall; **~ you look there's a mistake** wo man auch hinsieht, findet man Fehler.

evict [ɪ'vɪkt] *vt tenants* zur Räumung zwingen (*from gen*) ◆ **they were ~ed** sie wurden zum Verlassen ihrer Wohnung gezwungen.

eviction [ɪ'vɪkʃən] *n* Ausweisung *f* ◆ **~ order** Räumungsbefehl *m*.

evidence ['evɪdəns] **[1]** *n* **(a)** Beweis(e *pl*) *m* ◆ **what ~ is there for this belief?** welche Anhaltspunkte gibt es für diese Annahme?; **show me your ~** welche Beweise haben Sie?; **according to the ~ of our senses** nach dem, was wir mit unseren Sinnen erkennen können; **these marks are ~ of life on Mars** diese Spuren sind Beweis *or* ein Zeichen *nt* dafür, daß es auf dem Mars Leben gibt; **the car bore ~ of having been in an accident** das Auto trug deutliche Spuren eines Unfalls.
(b) (*Jur*) Beweismaterial *nt*; (*object, dagger etc also*) Beweisstück *nt*; (*testimony*) Aussage *f* ◆ **the lawyers are still collecting ~** die Anwälte holen immer noch Beweise ein; **we haven't got any ~** wir haben keinerlei Beweise; **there wasn't enough ~** die Beweise *or* Indizien reichten nicht aus; **for lack of ~** aus Mangel an Beweisen, mangels Beweisen (*form*); **on the ~ available ...** auf Grund des vorhandenen Beweismaterials ...; **not admissible as ~** als Beweismittel nicht zulässig; **all the ~ was against his claim** alles sprach *or* die Tatsachen sprachen gegen seine Behauptung; **to give ~ (for/against sb)** (für/gegen jdn) aussagen; **the ~ for the defence/prosecution** die Beweisführung für die Verteidigung/für die Anklage; **piece of ~** (*statement*) Zeugenaussage *f*; (*object*) Beweisstück *or* -mittel *nt*; **a fingerprint was the only ~** ein Fingerabdruck war der einzige Beweis; *see* **Queen's ~, State's ~**.
(c) **to be in ~** sichtbar sein; **political ideas which have been very much in ~ recently** politische Ideen, die in letzter Zeit deutlich in Erscheinung getreten sind; **his father was nowhere in ~** sein Vater war nirgends zu sehen; **she likes to be very much in ~** sie hat es gern, gesehen und beachtet zu werden; **a statesman very much in ~ at the moment** ein Staatsmann, der zur Zeit stark beachtet wird.
[2] *vt* zeugen von.

evident *adj*, **~ly** *adv* ['evɪdənt, -lɪ] offensichtlich.

evil ['iːvl] **[1]** *adj* böse; *person also, reputation, influence* schlecht; *consequence also*, (*inf*) *smell* übel ◆ **the E~ One** der Böse; **to fall on ~ days** in eine unglückliche Lage geraten; **he had his ~ way with her** (*hum inf*) er hat mit ihr gesündigt (*hum inf*).
[2] *n* Böse(s) *nt*; (*evil thing, circumstance etc*) Übel *nt* ◆ **the struggle of good against ~** der Kampf des Guten gegen das Böse *or* zwischen Gut und Böse; **the ~s of war and disease** die Übel von Krieg und Krankheit; **to choose the lesser of two ~s** von zwei Übeln das kleinere wählen; **social ~s** soziale Mißstände; **he fell victim to the ~s of drink** er fiel dem Laster des Trinkens zum Opfer; **we must combat the ~s of alcoholism** wir müssen das Übel der Trunksucht bekämpfen.

evil: ~-doer *n* Übeltäter(in *f*) *m*, Bösewicht *m* (*dated*); **~ eye** *n*: **the ~ eye** der böse Blick; **~-minded** *adj* bösartig; **~-smelling** *adj* übelriechend.

evince [ɪ'vɪns] *vt* an den Tag legen; *surprise, desire also* bekunden.

eviscerate [ɪ'vɪsəreɪt] *vt* ausnehmen; (*person*) entleiben.

evocation [ˌevə'keɪʃən] *n* Heraufbeschwören, Wachrufen *nt*.

evocative [ɪ'vɒkətɪv] *adj* evokativ (*geh*) ◆ **an ~ style/scent** ein Stil/Geruch, der Erinnerungen/Gedanken *etc* wachruft *or* heraufbeschwört; **to be ~ of sth** etw heraufbeschwören.

evoke [ɪ'vəʊk] *vt* evozieren (*geh*), heraufbeschwören; *memory also* wachrufen; *admiration* hervorrufen.

evolution [ˌiːvə'luːʃən] *n* **(a)** (*development, Biol*) Evolution, Entwicklung *f* ◆ **the ~ of events in Vietnam** die Entwicklung in Vietnam; **political ~ rather than revolution** eher politische Evolution als Revolution; **theory of ~** Evolutionstheorie *f*.
(b) *often pl* (*of troops*) Bewegung *f*; (*of dancers, skaters*) Figur, Bewegung *f*.

evolutionary [ˌiːvə'luːʃnərɪ] *adj* evolutionär; *theory* Evolutions-.

evolve [ɪ'vɒlv] **[1]** *vt system, theory, plan* entwickeln.
[2] *vi* sich entwickeln, sich herausbilden.

ewe [juː] *n* Mutterschaf *nt*.

ewer ['juːəʳ] *n* Wasserkrug *m*.

ex[1] [eks] *n* (*inf*) Verflossene(r) *mf* (*inf*).

ex[2] *abbr of* **example** Bsp., Beispiel *nt*.

ex- [eks-] *pref* **(a)** ehemalig, Ex- (*inf*) ◆ **~-president** früherer Präsident, Expräsident *m* (*inf*); **~-wife** frühere Frau, Exfrau *f* (*inf*). **(b)** **~-dividend** ohne Anrecht auf Dividende; **~-factory, ~-works** ab Werk; *see* **ex-officio**.

exacerbate [ek'sæsəbeɪt] *vt person* verärgern; *pain, disease* verschlimmern; *hate* vergrößern; *resentment, discontent* vertiefen; *situation* verschärfen.

exacerbation [ekˌsæsə'beɪʃən] *n* (*of pain, disease*) Verschlimmerung *f*; (*of situation*) Verschärfung *f*.

exact [ɪg'zækt] **[1]** *adj* genau; *figures, analysis etc also, science* exakt ◆ **that's the ~ word I was looking for** das ist genau das Wort, nach dem ich gesucht habe; **at that ~ moment** genau in dem Augenblick; **sorry I can't be more ~** leider kann ich es nicht genauer sagen; **47 to be ~** 47, um genau zu sein; **or, to be (more) ~ ...** oder, genauer gesagt ...; **to be very ~ in one's work** peinlich genau arbeiten.
[2] *vt money, obedience* fordern (*from* von); *payment* eintreiben (*from* von); *care* erfordern; *promise* abverlangen (*from sb* jdm).

exacting [ɪg'zæktɪŋ] *adj person, work* anspruchsvoll ◆ **to be too/very ~ with sb** zu viel/sehr viel von jdm verlangen; **he's very ~ about cleanliness** er ist peinlich genau, was Sauberkeit angeht, er nimmt es mit der Sauberkeit sehr genau.

exactingness [ɪɡ'zæktɪŋnɪs] *n* **because of his ~ as a teacher** da er ein so anspruchsvoller Lehrer ist/war.

exaction [ɪɡ'zækʃən] *n* **(a)** (*act*) (*of money*) Eintreiben *nt*; (*of promises*) Abverlangen *nt*; (*of obedience*) Fordern *nt*. **(b)** (*money exacted*) Forderung *f*; (*excessive demand*) übertriebene/überzogene Forderung.

exactitude [ɪɡ'zæktɪtjuːd] *n* Genauigkeit, Exaktheit *f*.

▼ **exactly** [ɪɡ'zæktlɪ] *adv* **(a)** (*with exactitude*) genau.
▼ **(b)** (*quite, precisely*) (ganz) genau ◆ **we don't ~ know** wir wissen es nicht genau; **I'm not ~ sure who he is** ich bin mir nicht ganz sicher, wer er ist; **that's ~ what I thought** genau das habe ich gedacht; **it is three o'clock ~** es ist genau *or* Punkt drei Uhr; **~!** genau!; **~ so!** ganz recht!, genau!; **not ~** nicht ganz; (*hardly*) nicht direkt *or* gerade; **it's not ~ a detective story** es ist eigentlich keine Kriminalgeschichte; **he wasn't ~ pleased** er war nicht gerade erfreut.

exactness [ɪɡ'zæktnɪs] *n* Genauigkeit *f*.

exaggerate [ɪɡ'zædʒəreɪt] **1** *vt* **(a)** (*overstate*) übertreiben ◆ **he ~d what really happened** er hat das, was wirklich geschehen war, übertrieben dargestellt. **(b)** (*intensify*) *effect* verstärken; *similarity* hervorheben.
2 *vi* übertreiben.

exaggerated [ɪɡ'zædʒəreɪtɪd] *adj* übertrieben ◆ **to have an ~ opinion of oneself** eine übertrieben hohe Meinung von sich selbst haben.

▼ **exaggeration** [ɪɡ,zædʒə'reɪʃən] *n* Übertreibung *f* ◆ **a bit of an ~** eine leichte Übertreibung, leicht übertrieben.

exalt [ɪɡ'zɔːlt] *vt* **(a)** (*in rank or power*) erheben. **(b)** (*praise*) preisen.

exaltation [,eɡzɔːl'teɪʃən] *n* (*feeling*) Begeisterung, Exaltation (*liter*) *f*.

exalted [ɪɡ'zɔːltɪd] *adj* **(a)** *position, style* hoch ◆ **the ~ ranks of ...** die erhabenen Ränge der ... **(b)** *mood, person* exaltiert, überschwenglich.

exam [ɪɡ'zæm] *n* Prüfung *f*.

examination [ɪɡ,zæmɪ'neɪʃən] *n* **(a)** (*Sch etc*) Prüfung *f*; (*Univ also*) Examen *nt* ◆ **geography ~** Geographieprüfung *f*.
(b) (*study, inspection*) Prüfung, Untersuchung *f*; (*of machine, premises, passports*) Kontrolle *f*; (*of question*) Untersuchung *f*; (*of accounts*) Prüfung *f* ◆ **on closer ~** bei genauer(er) Prüfung *or* Untersuchung; **it was found on ~ that ...** die Untersuchung ergab, daß ...; **the matter is still under ~** die Angelegenheit wird noch geprüft *or* untersucht; *see* **medical**.
(c) (*Jur: of suspect, accused, witness*) Verhör *nt*; (*of case, documents*) Untersuchung *f* ◆ **legal ~** Verhör *nt*.

▼ **examine** [ɪɡ'zæmɪn] *vt* **(a)** (*for* auf +*acc*) untersuchen; *documents, accounts* prüfen; *machine, passports, luggage* kontrollieren ◆ **you want to have your head ~d** (*inf*) du solltest dich mal auf deinen Geisteszustand untersuchen lassen.
(b) *pupil, candidate* prüfen (*in* in +*dat*, *on* über +*acc*).
(c) (*Jur*) *suspect, accused, witness* verhören.

examinee [ɪɡ,zæmɪ'niː] *n* (*Sch*) Prüfling *m*; (*Univ*) (Examens)kandidat(in *f*) *m*.

examiner [ɪɡ'zæmɪnəʳ] *n* (*Sch, Univ*) Prüfer *m* ◆ **board of ~s** Prüfungsausschuß *m*.

▼ **example** [ɪɡ'zɑːmpl] *n* Beispiel *nt* ◆ **for ~** zum Beispiel; **to set a good/bad ~** ein gutes/schlechtes Beispiel geben, mit gutem/schlechtem Beispiel vorangehen; **his conduct should be an ~ to us** sein Verhalten sollte uns ein Beispiel sein; **a leader who is an ~ to his men** ein Führer, der seinen Männern als Beispiel dient *or* mit leuchtendem Beispiel vorangeht; **to take sb as an ~** sich (*dat*) an jdm ein Beispiel nehmen; **to make an ~ of sb** an jdm ein Exempel statuieren; **to punish sb as an ~ to others** jdn exemplarisch bestrafen.

exasperate [ɪɡ'zɑːspəreɪt] *vt* zur Verzweiflung bringen, auf die Palme bringen (*inf*) ◆ **to become** *or* **get ~d** verzweifeln (*with* an +*dat*), sich aufregen (*with* über +*acc*); **~d at** *or* **by his lack of attention** verärgert über seine mangelnde Aufmerksamkeit.

exasperating [ɪɡ'zɑːspəreɪtɪŋ] *adj* ärgerlich; *delay, difficulty, job* leidig *attr* ◆ **it's so ~ not to be able to buy any petrol** es ist wirklich zum Verzweifeln, daß man kein Benzin bekommen kann; **you can be ~!** du kannst einen wirklich zur Verzweiflung *or* auf die Palme (*inf*) bringen!

exasperatingly [ɪɡ'zɑːspəreɪtɪŋlɪ] *adv* **this train/student is ~ slow** es ist zum Verzweifeln, wie langsam dieser Zug fährt/dieser Student ist.

exasperation [ɪɡ,zɑːspə'reɪʃən] *n* Verzweiflung *f* (*with* über +*acc*) ◆ **he cried out in ~** er schrie verzweifelt auf; **the negotiations ended with everyone in a state of ~** am Ende der Verhandlungen waren alle völlig frustriert.

excavate ['ekskəveɪt] **1** *vt ground* ausschachten; (*machine*) ausbaggern; (*Archeol*) *remains* ausgraben; *trench* ausheben.
2 *vi* (*Archeol*) Ausgrabungen machen.

excavation [,ekskə'veɪʃən] *n* **(a)** (*Archeol*) (Aus)grabung *f* ◆ **~s** (*site*) Ausgrabungsstätte *f*; **to carry out ~s** Ausgrabungen machen. **(b)** (*of tunnel etc*) Graben *nt*.

excavator ['ekskəveɪtəʳ] *n* (*machine*) Bagger *m*; (*Archeol: person*) Ausgräber(in *f*).

exceed [ɪk'siːd] *vt* **(a)** (*in value, amount, length of time*) übersteigen, überschreiten (*by* um) ◆ **to ~ 40 in number** die Zahl 40 übersteigen *or* überschreiten; **the guests ~ed 40 in number** die Zahl der Gäste überstieg 40; **to ~ 5 kilos in weight** das Gewicht von 5 kg übersteigen *or* überschreiten; **a fine not ~ing £500** eine Geldstrafe bis zu £ 500.
(b) (*go beyond*) hinausgehen über (+*acc*); *expectations, desires also* übertreffen, übersteigen; *limits, powers also, speed limit* überschreiten.

exceedingly [ɪk'siːdɪŋlɪ], **exceeding** (*old*) [ɪk'siːdɪŋ] *adv* äußerst.

excel [ɪk'sel] **1** *vi* sich auszeichnen, sich hervortun.
2 *vt* übertreffen (*in* in +*dat*, an +*dat*) ◆ **to ~ oneself** (*often iro*) sich selbst übertreffen.

excellence ['eksələns] *n* **(a)** (*high quality*) hervorragende Qualität, Vorzüglichkeit *f* ◆ **the ~ of the essay/weather** der ausgezeichnete *or* hervorragende Aufsatz/das ausgezeichnete *or* hervorragende Wetter; **we aim at ~** wir streben hervorragende Qualität an. **(b)** (*excellent feature*) Vorzug *m*, hervorragende Eigenschaft.

Excellency ['eksələnsɪ] *n* Exzellenz *f* ◆ **Your/His ~** Eure/Seine Exzellenz.

▼ **excellent** ['eksələnt] *adj* ausgezeichnet, hervorragend.

excellently ['eksələntlɪ] *adv* ausgezeichnet, hervorragend ◆ **you did ~** das hast du ausgezeichnet gemacht.

excelsior [ek'selsɪɔːʳ] *n* (*US: shavings*) Holzwolle *f*.

except [ɪk'sept] **1** *prep* **(a)** außer (+*dat*); (*after questions also*) (anders ...) als ◆ **what can they do ~ wait?** was können sie anders tun als warten?; **who would have done it ~ him?** wer hätte es außer ihm denn getan?
(b) **~ for** abgesehen von, bis auf (+*acc*); **~ that ...** außer *or* nur daß ...; **~ for the fact that** abgesehen davon, daß ...; **~ if** es sei denn(, daß), außer wenn; **~ when** außer wenn.
2 *conj* **(a)** (*only*) doch ◆ **I'd refuse ~ I need the money** ich würde ablehnen, doch ich brauche das Geld.
(b) (*old, form: unless*) es sei denn(, daß) ◆ **~ he be a traitor** es sei denn, er wäre ein Verräter.
3 *vt* ausnehmen ◆ **to ~ sb from sth** jdn bei etw ausnehmen; **none ~ed** ohne Ausnahme.

excepting [ɪk'septɪŋ] *prep* außer ◆ **not** *or* **without ~ X** ohne X auszunehmen *or* auszuschließen, X nicht ausgenommen; **always ~ ...** natürlich mit Ausnahme (+*gen*).

exception [ɪk'sepʃən] *n* **(a)** Ausnahme *f* ◆ **to make an ~** eine Ausnahme machen; **to make an ~ of/for sb** eine Ausnahme bei jdm/für jdn machen; **without ~** ohne Ausnahme; **with the ~ of** mit Ausnahme von; **this case is an ~ to the rule** dieser Fall ist eine Ausnahme, das ist ein Ausnahmefall; **the ~ proves the rule** (*prov*) Ausnahmen bestätigen die Regel (*prov*); **these strokes of luck are the ~** diese Glückstreffer sind die Ausnahme; **with this ~** mit der einen Ausnahme.
(b) **to take ~ to sth** Anstoß *m* an etw (*dat*) nehmen.

exceptional [ɪk'sepʃənl] *adj* außergewöhnlich ◆ **apart from ~ cases** abgesehen von Ausnahmefällen.

exceptionally [ɪk'sepʃənəlɪ] *adv* (*as an exception*) ausnahmsweise; (*outstandingly*) außergewöhnlich.

excerpt ['eksɜːpt] *n* Auszug *m*, Exzerpt *nt*.

excess [ɪk'ses] *n* **(a)** Übermaß *nt* (*of* an +*dat*) ◆ **an ~ of caution/details** allzuviel Vorsicht/allzu viele Einzelheiten; **to eat/drink to ~** übermäßig essen/trinken; **to carry sth to ~** etw übertreiben; **don't do anything to ~** man soll nichts übertreiben; **he does everything to ~** er übertreibt bei allem.
(b) **~es** *pl* Exzesse *pl*; (*drinking, sex etc also*) Ausschweifungen *pl*; (*brutalities also*) Ausschreitungen *pl*.
(c) (*amount left over*) Überschuß *m*.
(d) **to be in ~ of** hinausgehen über (+*acc*), überschreiten; **a figure in ~ of ...** eine Zahl über (+*dat*).
(e) (*Insur*) Selbstbeteiligung *f*.

excess *in cpds weight, production* Über-; *profit* Mehr-; **~ baggage** *n* Übergewicht *nt*; **~ charge** *n* zusätzliche Gebühr; (*for letter etc*) Nachgebühr *f*; **~ fare** *n* Nachlösegebühr *f*; **I had to pay ~ fare** ich mußte nachlösen; **~ fat** *n* Fettpolster *nt*, überschüssiges Fett.

excessive [ɪk'sesɪv] *adj* übermäßig; *demands, price, praise also* übertrieben ◆ **~ use of the clutch** zu häufiger Gebrauch der Kupplung; **isn't that rather ~?** ist das nicht etwas übertrieben?; **I think you're being ~** ich finde, Sie übertreiben.

excessively [ɪk'sesɪvlɪ] *adv* **(a)** (*to excess*) (+*vb*) *eat, drink, spend* übermäßig, allzuviel; (+*adj*) *optimistic, worried, severe* allzu. **(b)** (*extremely*) *ugly, boring* äußerst, ungemein.

excess postage *n* Nachgebühr *f*, Strafporto *nt* (*inf*).

exchange [ɪks'tʃeɪndʒ] **1** *vt books, glances, seats* tauschen; *foreign currency* wechseln, umtauschen (*for* in +*acc*); *courtesies, ideas, experiences etc* austauschen ◆ **to ~ words/letters/blows** einen Wortwechsel haben/einen Briefwechsel führen/sich schlagen; **to ~ one thing for another** eine Sache gegen eine andere austauschen *or* (*in shop*) umtauschen.
2 *n* **(a)** (*of goods, stamps*) Tausch *m*; (*of prisoners, views, secrets, diplomatic notes*) Austausch *m*; (*of one bought item for another*) Umtausch *m* ◆ **in ~** dafür; **in ~ for money** gegen Geld *or* Bezahlung; **in ~ for a table/for lending me your car** für einen Tisch/dafür, daß Sie mir Ihr Auto geliehen haben; **that's not a fair ~ for my bike** das ist kein fairer Tausch für mein Rad; **to lose by the ~** einen schlechten Tausch machen; **fair ~ is no robbery** (*Prov*) Tausch ist kein Raub (*Prov*).
(b) (*Fin*) (*act*) Wechseln *nt*; (*place*) Wechselstube *f* ◆ **~ control** Devisenkontrolle *f*; **~ market** (*Fin*) Devisenmarkt *m*; **~ rate** Wechselkurs *m*; **~ rate mechanism** Wechselkursmechanismus *m*.
(c) (*St Ex*) Börse *f*.
(d) **(telephone) ~** Fernvermittlungsstelle *f* (*form*), Fernamt *nt*; (*in office etc*) (Telefon)zentrale *f*.
(e) (*altercation*) Wortwechsel *m*.
3 *adj attr student, teacher* Austausch- ◆ **~ value** Tauschwert *m*.

➤ LANGUAGE IN USE: **exactly: b** → 17.2 **exaggeration** → 26.1 **examine: a** → 26.1 **example** → 26.1, 26.2 **excellent** → 19.2

exchangeable [ɪks'tʃeɪndʒəbl] *adj* austauschbar (*for* gegen); *goods bought* umtauschbar (*for* gegen) ◆ **goods bought in the sale are not ~** Ausverkaufsware ist vom Umtausch ausgeschlossen.
exchequer [ɪks'tʃekəʳ] *n* Finanzministerium *nt*; (*esp in GB*) Schatzamt *nt*; (*inf: personal*) Finanzen *pl* (*inf*); *see* **chancellor.**
excisable [ek'saɪzəbl] *adj* steuerpflichtig.
excise[1] ['eksaɪz] *n* **(a)** Verbrauchssteuer *f* (*on* auf +*acc*, für) ◆ **~ on beer/tobacco** Bier-/Tabaksteuer *f*. **(b)** (*Brit: department*) *Verwaltungsabteilung f für indirekte Steuern.*
excise[2] [ek'saɪz] *vt* (*Med*) herausschneiden, entfernen (*also fig*).
excise ['eksaɪz]: **~ duties** *npl* Verbrauchssteuern *pl*; **~man** *n* Steuereinnehmer *m*.
excision [ek'sɪʒən] *n* (*Med, fig*) Entfernung *f*.
excitability [ɪk,saɪtə'bɪlɪtɪ] *n see adj* Erregbarkeit *f*; Reizbarkeit *f*.
excitable [ɪk'saɪtəbl] *adj* (leicht) erregbar; (*Physiol also*) reizbar.
excite [ɪk'saɪt] *vt* **(a)** aufregen, aufgeregt machen; (*rouse enthusiasm in*) begeistern ◆ **the news had clearly ~d him** er war wegen der Nachricht sichtlich aufgeregt; **the whole village was ~d by the news** das ganze Dorf war über die Nachricht in Aufregung; **the prospect doesn't exactly ~ me** ich finde die Aussicht nicht gerade begeisternd.
(b) (*Physiol*) *nerve* reizen; (*sexually*) erregen.
(c) *sentiments, passion, admiration* erregen; *interest, curiosity also* wecken; *imagination, appetite* anregen.
excited [ɪk'saɪtɪd] *adj* aufgeregt; (*worked up, not calm also*) erregt; (*sexually*) erregt; (*enthusiastic*) begeistert ◆ **don't get ~!** (*angry etc*) reg dich nicht auf!; **don't get ~, I only said "perhaps"** sei nicht gleich so aufgeregt, ich habe nur „vielleicht" gesagt; **aren't you ~ about these developments?** finden Sie diese Entwicklungen nicht aufregend?; **aren't you ~ about what might happen?** sind Sie nicht gespannt, was passieren wird?; **he's very ~ about your idea** er ist sehr von deiner Idee begeistert.
excitedly [ɪk'saɪtɪdlɪ] *adv see adj* aufgeregt; erregt ◆ **we're waiting ~ to see what will happen** wir warten gespannt darauf, was passiert.
excitement [ɪk'saɪtmənt] *n* **(a)** Aufregung *f*; (*not being calm etc also*) Erregung *f* ◆ **the ~ of the elections** die Aufregung der Wahlen; **a mood of ~** eine Spannung; **a shriek of ~** ein aufgeregter Schrei; **in the ~ of the match** in der Aufregung des Spiels, im Eifer des Gefechts; **the ~ of a day in the office** der aufregende Tagesablauf im Büro; **she only did it for ~** sie hat es nur getan, um ein bißchen Aufregung zu haben; **what's all the ~ about?** wozu die ganze Aufregung?; **to be in a state of great ~** in heller Aufregung sein; **his novel has caused great ~** sein Roman hat große Begeisterung ausgelöst.
(b) (*Physiol*) Reizung *f*; (*sexual*) Erregung *f*.
exciting [ɪk'saɪtɪŋ] *adj moment, week, life, prospects, idea* aufregend; *story, film, event, adventure also* spannend; *author* sensationell; (*sexually*) erregend ◆ **a letter for me? how ~!** ein Brief für mich? prima!; **how ~ for you** prima!, wie aufregend (*also iro*).
excl *abbr of* **(a) excluding. (b) exclusive** exkl.
exclaim [ɪk'skleɪm] [1] *vi* **he ~ed in surprise when he saw it** er schrie überrascht auf, als er es sah.
[2] *vt* ausrufen ◆ **at last! she ~ed** endlich! rief sie (aus).
exclamation [,eksklə'meɪʃən] *n* Ausruf *m* (*also Gram*) ◆ **~ mark** *or* **point** (*US*) Ausrufezeichen *nt*; **an ~ of horror** ein Schreckensschrei *m*.
exclamatory [ɪk'sklæmətərɪ] *adj* Ausrufe-; *style* exklamatorisch ◆ **~ remarks** Ausrufe *pl*.
exclude [ɪk'sklu:d] *vt* ausschließen ◆ **to ~ sb from the team/an occupation** jdn aus der Mannschaft/von einer Beschäftigung ausschließen; **if we ~ all cases in which ...** wenn wir alle Fälle ausnehmen, in denen ...; **everything excluding petrol** alles außer *or* ausgenommen Benzin.
exclusion [ɪk'sklu:ʒən] *n* Ausschluß *m* (*from* von) ◆ **you can't just think about your job to the ~ of everything else** du kannst nicht ausschließlich an deine Arbeit denken; **~ clause** (*Insur*) Haftungsausschlußklausel *f*.
exclusive [ɪk'sklu:sɪv] [1] *adj* **(a)** *group, club etc* exklusiv; *right, interview also* Exklusiv- ◆ **this garage has ~ rights for VW** das ist eine VW-Vertragswerkstatt; **the two possibilities are mutually ~** die beiden Möglichkeiten schließen einander aus.
(b) (*fashionable, sophisticated*) vornehm, elegant.
(c) (*sole*) ausschließlich, einzig.
(d) (*not including*) **from 15th to 20th June ~** vom 15. bis zum 20. Juni ausschließlich; **~ of** ausschließlich (+*gen*), exklusive (+*gen*); **£30 ~ of postage** £ 30 exklusive Porto.
[2] *n* (*Press, TV*) (*interview*) Exklusivinterview *nt*; (*report*) Exklusivbericht *m*.
exclusively [ɪk'sklu:sɪvlɪ] *adv* ausschließlich.
exclusivity [,ɪksklu:'sɪvɪtɪ] *n* (*of dealership*) Alleinvertretung *f* ◆ **to build ~ into a contract** die Exklusivrechte in einen Vertrag aufnehmen.
excommunicate [,ekskə'mju:nɪkeɪt] *vt* exkommunizieren.
excommunication ['ekskə,mju:nɪ'keɪʃən] *n* Exkommunikation *f*.
ex-convict [,eks'kɒnvɪkt] *n* ehemaliger Häftling.
excrement ['ekskrɪmənt] *n* Kot *m*, Exkremente *pl*.
excrescence [ɪks'kresns] *n* Gewächs *nt*, Auswuchs *m* (*also fig*).
excreta [ɪk'skri:tə] *npl* Exkremente *pl*.
excrete [ɪk'skri:t] *vt* ausscheiden, absondern.
excretion [ɪk'skri:ʃən] *n* (*act*) Ausscheidung, Exkretion *f*; (*substance*) Exkret *nt*.
excruciating [ɪk'skru:ʃɪeɪtɪŋ] *adj pain, noise* gräßlich, fürchterlich, entsetzlich ◆ **it was ~** (*inf*) (*embarrassing, boring*) es war gräßlich *or* fürchterlich; (*hilarious*) es war zum Schreien (*inf*); (*painful*) es hat scheußlich weh getan (*inf*).
excruciatingly [ɪk'skru:ʃɪeɪtɪŋlɪ] *adv see adj* **it was ~ painful** es hat scheußlich weh getan (*inf*); **~ funny** urkomisch.
exculpate ['ekskʌlpeɪt] *vt* (*form*) *person* freisprechen, exkulpieren (*liter*) (*from* von) ◆ **to ~ oneself** sich rechtfertigen.
excursion [ɪk'skɜ:ʃən] *n* Ausflug *m*; (*fig: into a subject also*) Exkurs *m* ◆ **to go on an ~** einen Ausflug machen.
excursionist [ɪk'skɜ:ʃənɪst] *n* Ausflügler(in *f*) *m*.
excursion: ~ ticket *n* verbilligte Fahrkarte (zu einem Ausflugsort); **we are going on an ~ ticket** wir fahren zum Ausflugstarif; **~ train** *n* Sonderzug *m*.
excusable [ɪk'skju:zəbl] *adj* verzeihlich, entschuldbar.
excuse [ɪk'skju:z] [1] *vt* **(a)** (*seek to justify*) *action, person* entschuldigen ◆ **such rudeness cannot be ~d** so ein schlechtes Benehmen ist nicht zu entschuldigen; **to ~ oneself** sich entschuldigen (*for sth* für *or* wegen etw); **he ~d himself for being late** er entschuldigte sich, daß er zu spät kam.
(b) (*pardon*) **to ~ sb** jdm verzeihen; **to ~ sb's insolence** jds Frechheit entschuldigen, jdm seine Frechheit verzeihen; **to ~ sb for having done sth** jdm verzeihen, daß er etwas getan hat; **well, I think I can be ~d for believing him** nun, man kann es mir wohl nicht übelnehmen, daß ich ihm geglaubt habe; **if you will ~ the expression** wenn Sie mir den Ausdruck gestatten; **~ me for laughing** entschuldigen *or* verzeihen Sie, daß *or* wenn ich lache; **~ me!** (*to get attention, sorry*) Entschuldigung!, entschuldigen Sie!; (*indignant*) erlauben Sie mal!; **well, ~ me for asking!** entschuldige, daß ich gefragt habe!
(c) (*set free from obligation*) **to ~ sb from (doing) sth** jdn von einer Sache befreien, jdm etw erlassen; **he is ~d boots** er ist davon befreit worden, Stiefel zu tragen; **you are ~d** (*to children*) ihr könnt gehen; **can I be ~d?** darf ich mal verschwinden (*inf*)?; **and now if you will ~ me I have work to do** und nun entschuldigen Sie mich bitte, ich habe zu arbeiten.
[2] [ɪks'kju:s] *n* **(a)** (*justification*) Entschuldigung *f* ◆ **there's no ~ for it** dafür gibt es keine Entschuldigung; **to give sth as an ~** etw zu seiner Entschuldigung anführen *or* vorbringen; **the reasons he gave in ~ of his action** die Gründe, die er zu seiner Entschuldigung *or* als Entschuldigung für seine Tat anführte.
(b) (*pretext*) Ausrede, Entschuldigung *f* ◆ **to make up ~s for sb** jdn herausreden; **to make ~s for sb** jdn entschuldigen; **I have a good ~ for not going** ich habe eine gute Ausrede *or* Entschuldigung, warum ich nicht hingehen kann; **it was raining — well, that's your ~** es hat geregnet — das ist wohl deine Ausrede *or* Entschuldigung; **~s, ~s!** nichts als Ausreden!; **you're full of ~s** du hast immer eine Ausrede; **he's only making ~s** er sucht nur nach einer Ausrede; **a good ~ for a party** ein guter Grund, eine Party zu feiern.
(c) ~s *pl* (*apology*) Entschuldigung *f* ◆ **to offer one's ~s** sich entschuldigen.
(d) an ~ for steak/a heating system ein jämmerliches *or* armseliges Steak/eine jämmerliche Heizung.
excuse-me [ɪk'skju:zmi:] *n* (*dance*) Tanz *m* mit Abklatschen.
ex-directory [,eksdaɪ'rektərɪ] *adj* (*Brit*) **to be ~** nicht im Telefonbuch stehen.
execrable *adj*, **-bly** *adv* ['eksɪkrəbl, -ɪ] scheußlich, abscheulich.
execrate ['eksɪkreɪt] *vt* **(a)** (*hate*) verabscheuen. **(b)** (*curse*) verfluchen, verwünschen.
execration [,eksɪ'kreɪʃən] *n* **(a)** (*hatred*) Abscheu *m* ◆ **to hold in ~** verabscheuen. **(b)** (*curse*) Fluch *m*, Verwünschung *f*.
executable ['eksɪkju:təbl] *adj* ausführbar ◆ **~ file** (*Comput*) ausführbare Datei, Programmdatei *f*.
executant [ɪg'zekjʊtənt] *n* Ausführende(r) *mf*.
execute ['eksɪkju:t] *vt* **(a)** *plan, order, task etc* durchführen, ausführen; *movement, dance* ausführen; *duties* erfüllen, wahrnehmen; *purpose* erfüllen; (*Comput*) *command* abarbeiten, ausführen. **(b)** (*Mus*) (*perform*) vortragen; *cadenza etc* ausführen. **(c)** *criminal* hinrichten. **(d)** (*Jur*) *will* vollstrecken, ausführen; *contract* ausfertigen; (*sign*) *document* unterzeichnen.
execution [,eksɪ'kju:ʃən] *n* **(a)** *see vt (a)* Durchführung, Ausführung *f*; Erfüllung, Wahrnehmung *f* ◆ **to put sth into ~** etw ausführen; **in the ~ of his duties** bei der Ausübung seines Amtes. **(b)** (*Mus*) Vortrag *m*; (*musician's skill*) Ausführung *f*. **(c)** (*as punishment*) Hinrichtung, Exekution *f*. **(d)** (*Jur*) (*of will, judgement*) Vollstreckung *f*; (*of contract*) Ausfertigung *f*; (*signing*) Unterschreiben *nt*.
executioner [,eksɪ'kju:ʃnəʳ] *n* Henker, Scharfrichter *m*.
executive [ɪg'zekjʊtɪv] [1] *adj* **(a)** *powers, committee etc* exekutiv, Exekutiv-; (*Comm*) geschäftsführend ◆ **~ position** leitende Stellung *or* Position; **~ ability** Führungsqualität *f*; **I think he's ~ material** ich glaube, er hat das Zeug zum Manager. **(b) ~ model** (*of car*) Modell *nt* für Anspruchsvolle; **~ sauna facilities** Saunaräume *pl* für höchste Ansprüche.
[2] *n* **(a)** (*of government*) Exekutive *f*; (*of association, trades union*) Vorstand *m*. **(b)** (*person in business*) leitender Angestellter, leitende Angestellte, Manager *m*.
executive: ~ (brief)case *n* Diplomatenaktentasche *f*; **~ committee** *n* Vorstand *m*; **~ director** *n* Vorstandsmitglied *nt*; **~ jet** *n* Privatjet *m* (für Manager); **~ officer** *n* Erster Offizier; **~ suite** *n* (*in office*) Vorstandsetage *f*.
executor [ɪg'zekjʊtəʳ] *n* (*of will*) Testamentsvollstrecker *m*.
executrix [ɪg'zekjʊtrɪks] *n* Testamentsvollstreckerin *f*.
exegesis [,eksɪ'dʒi:sɪs] *n* Exegese, Auslegung *f*.
exegetical [,eksɪ'dʒetɪkəl] *adj* exegetisch.
exemplary [ɪg'zemplərɪ] *adj conduct, virtue, pupil* vorbildlich, beispielhaft ◆ **~ punishment** exemplarische Strafe; **~ damages** *über den verursachten Schaden hinausgehende Entschädigung*, Bußgeld *nt*.
exemplification [ɪg,zemplɪfɪ'keɪʃən] *n* Erläuterung, Veranschaulichung,

Exemplifizierung *(geh) f.*
exemplify [ɪg'zemplɪfaɪ] *vt* erläutern, veranschaulichen.
exempt [ɪg'zempt] [1] *adj* befreit *(from* von) ◆ **diplomats are ~** Diplomaten sind ausgenommen; **could I be made ~ (from that)?** könnte ich davon befreit werden?
[2] *vt person* befreien ◆ **to ~ sb from doing sth** jdn davon befreien, etw zu tun.
exemption [ɪg'zempʃən] *n* Befreiung *f* ◆ **~ from taxes** Steuerfreiheit *f.*
exercise ['eksəsaɪz] [1] *n* **(a)** *no pl (of right)* Wahrnehmung *f; (of physical, mental power)* Ausübung *f; (of patience, mental faculties)* Übung *f; (of imagination)* Anwendung *f* ◆ **in the ~ of his duties** bei der Ausübung seiner Pflichten.
(b) *(bodily or mental, drill, Mus etc)* Übung *f* ◆ **to do one's ~s in the morning** Morgengymnastik machen.
(c) *no pl (physical)* Bewegung *f* ◆ **physical ~** (körperliche) Bewegung; **a dog needs a lot of ~** ein Hund braucht viel Bewegung; **people who don't take** *or* **get enough ~** Leute, die sich nicht genug bewegen *or* die nicht genug Bewegung bekommen; **shall we go out and get some ~?** wollen wir rausgehen und uns ein wenig Bewegung verschaffen?; **what do you do for ~?** wie halten Sie sich fit?
(d) *(Mil: usu pl)* Übung *f* ◆ **to go on ~s** eine Übung machen.
(e) ~s *pl (US: ceremonies)* Feierlichkeiten *pl.*
[2] *vt* **(a)** *body, mind* üben, trainieren; *(Mil) troops* exerzieren; *horse* bewegen; *dog* spazierenführen ◆ **I'm not saying this just to ~ my voice** ich sage das nicht zum Spaß.
(b) *(use) one's authority, control, power* ausüben; *a right also* geltend machen; *patience, tact, discretion* üben; *influence* ausüben *(on* auf *+acc); talents* Gebrauch machen von ◆ **to ~ care in doing sth** Vorsicht walten lassen, wenn man etw tut.
[3] *vi* **if you ~ regularly ...** wenn Sie sich viel bewegen ...; **you don't ~ enough** du hast zuwenig Bewegung; **he was exercising on the parallel bars** er turnte (gerade) am Barren.
exercise: ~ bike *n* Heimtrainer *m;* **~ book** *n* Heft *nt.*
exerciser ['eksəsaɪzə^r] *n* Trainingsgerät *nt; (bigger)* Fitneß-Center *nt.*
exercise yard *n* Hof *m.*
exert [ɪg'zɜːt] [1] *vt pressure* ausüben *(on* auf *+acc); influence also* aufbieten; *authority* aufbieten, einsetzen *(on* bei); *force* gebrauchen, anwenden ◆ **to ~ a force on sth** eine Kraft auf etw *(acc)* ausüben.
[2] *vr* sich anstrengen.
exertion [ɪg'zɜːʃən] *n* **(a)** *(effort)* Anstrengung *f* ◆ **by one's own ~s** durch eigene Anstrengungen.
(b) *(of force, strength)* Anwendung *f,* Einsatz *m; (of authority)* Aufgebot *nt,* Einsatz *m; (of influence)* Aufgebot *nt* ◆ **the ~ of force/pressure on sth** die Ausübung von Kraft/Druck auf etw *(acc);* **the ~ of an influence on sb** die Ausübung eines Einflusses auf jdn; **by the ~ of a little pressure** durch Ausübung *or* Anwendung von etwas Druck; **rugby requires a lot of ~** Rugby fordert viel Einsatz; **after the day's ~s** nach des Tages Mühen.
exeunt ['eksɪʌnt] *(in stage directions)* ab ◆ **~ Brutus and Cassius** Brutus und Cassius ab.
ex gratia [eks'greɪʃə] *adj payment* Sonder-.
exhale [eks'heɪl] [1] *vt* **(a)** *(breathe out)* ausatmen. **(b)** *(give off) smoke* abgeben; *gas, vapour also* ablassen.
[2] *vi* ausatmen.
exhaust [ɪg'zɔːst] [1] *vt* **(a)** *(use up completely)* erschöpfen ◆ **my patience is ~ed** meine Geduld ist erschöpft *or* zu Ende.
(b) *(tire)* erschöpfen ◆ **the children are/this job is ~ing me** die Kinder sind/diese Arbeit ist eine Strapaze für mich.
[2] *n* **(a)** *(Aut etc)* Auspuff *m.* **(b)** *no pl (gases)* Auspuffgase *pl.*
exhausted [ɪg'zɔːstɪd] *adj* erschöpft.
exhaust fumes *npl* Auspuffgase, Abgase *pl.*
exhausting [ɪg'zɔːstɪŋ] *adj activity, work, person* anstrengend, strapaziös ◆ **the climate is ~** das Klima erschöpft einen.
exhaustion [ɪg'zɔːstʃən] *n* Erschöpfung *f.*
exhaustive *adj,* **~ly** *adv* [ɪg'zɔːstɪv, -lɪ] erschöpfend.
exhaust: ~ pipe *n* Auspuffrohr *nt;* **~ system** *n* Auspuff *m.*
exhibit [ɪg'zɪbɪt] [1] *vt* **(a)** *paintings etc* ausstellen; *goods also* auslegen; *membership card* vorzeigen, vorweisen. **(b)** *skill, ingenuity* zeigen, beweisen, an den Tag legen.
[2] *vi* ausstellen.
[3] *n* **(a)** *(in an exhibition)* Ausstellungsstück *nt.* **(b)** *(Jur)* Beweisstück *nt.*
exhibition [,eksɪ'bɪʃən] *n* **(a)** *(of paintings, furniture etc)* Ausstellung *f; (of articles for sale)* Auslage *f.*
(b) *(act of showing: of a technique, film etc)* Vorführung *f.*
(c) what an ~ of bad manners! was für schlechte Manieren!; **did you see her at the party last night? — what an ~!** hast du sie auf der Party gestern abend gesehen? — die hat sich vielleicht aufgeführt!; **to make an ~ of oneself** ein Theater machen *(inf);* **am I making an ~ of myself?** benehm ich mich daneben?
(d) *(Brit Univ: grant)* Stipendium *nt.*
exhibitioner [,eksɪ'bɪʃənə^r] *n (Brit Univ)* Stipendiat(in *f) m.*
exhibitionism [,eksɪ'bɪʃənɪzəm] *n* Exhibitionismus *m.*
exhibitionist [,eksɪ'bɪʃənɪst] [1] *n* Exhibitionist(in *f) m.*
[2] *adj* exhibitionistisch.
exhibitor [ɪg'zɪbɪtə^r] *n* Aussteller *m.*
exhilarate [ɪg'zɪləreɪt] *vt* in Hochstimmung versetzen; *(news also)* (freudig) erregen; *(sea air etc)* beleben, erfrischen.
exhilarated [ɪg'zɪləreɪtɪd] *adj laugh* erregt, aufgeregt ◆ **to feel ~** in Hochstimmung sein.
exhilarating [ɪg'zɪləreɪtɪŋ] *adj sensation, speed* erregend, berauschend; *conversation, music, work* anregend; *air, wind etc* belebend, erfrischend.
exhilaration [ɪg,zɪlə'reɪʃən] *n* Hochgefühl *nt* ◆ **the ~ of flying** das Hochgefühl beim Fliegen; **to fill sb with a feeling of ~** jdn in Hochstimmung versetzen.
exhort [ɪg'zɔːt] *vt* ermahnen.
exhortation [,egzɔː'teɪʃən] *n* Ermahnung *f.*
exhumation [,eksh*j*uː'meɪʃən] *n* Exhumierung, Exhumation *f.*
exhume [eks'hjuːm] *vt* exhumieren.
exigence ['eksɪdʒəns], **exigency** [ɪg'zɪdʒənsɪ] *n* **(a)** *usu pl (requirement)* (An)forderung *f; (of situation also)* Erfordernis *nt.* **(b)** *(emergency)* Notlage *f.* **(c)** *(urgency)* Dringlichkeit *f.*
exigent ['eksɪdʒənt] *adj (urgent)* zwingend, dringend; *(exacting) master* streng, gestreng *(old).*
exiguity [,egzɪ'gjuːɪtɪ] *n (form)* Winzigkeit *f; (meagreness)* Knappheit *f.*
exiguous [ɪg'zɪgjʊəs] *adj (form) space* klein, winzig; *income* gering, dürftig.
exile ['eksaɪl] [1] *n* **(a)** *(person)* Verbannte(r) *mf.* **(b)** *(banishment)* Exil *nt,* Verbannung *f* ◆ **to go into ~** ins Exil gehen; **in ~** im Exil.
[2] *vt* verbannen *(from* aus), ins Exil schicken ◆ **the ~d former president** der im Exil lebende frühere Präsident.
exist [ɪg'zɪst] *vi* **(a)** *(to be)* existieren, bestehen ◆ **everything that ~s** alles, was ist *or* existiert; **it only ~s in her imagination** das gibt es *or* das existiert nur in ihrer Phantasie; **I want to live, not just ~** ich möchte leben, nicht einfach nur existieren; **it doesn't ~** das gibt es nicht; **to cease to ~** zu bestehen aufhören; **to continue to ~** fort- *or* weiterbestehen; **doubts still ~** noch bestehen Zweifel; **the understanding which ~s between the two countries** das Einvernehmen zwischen den beiden Ländern; **there ~s a tradition that ...** es gibt den Brauch, daß ...
(b) *(live)* existieren, leben ◆ **we cannot ~ without water** wir können ohne Wasser nicht leben *or* existieren; **can life ~ on Mars?** kann auf dem Mars Leben existieren?; **she ~s on very little** sie kommt mit sehr wenig aus; **we manage to ~** wir kommen gerade aus; **is it possible to ~ on such a small salary?** kann man denn von so einem kleinen Gehalt leben?
(c) *(be found)* vorkommen ◆ **the penguins/natural resources which ~ in the Antarctic** die Pinguine/Bodenschätze, die in der Antarktis vorkommen.
existence [ɪg'zɪstəns] *n* **(a)** Existenz *f; (of custom, tradition, institution also)* Bestehen *nt* ◆ **to be in ~** existieren, bestehen; **to come into ~** entstehen; *(person)* auf die Welt kommen; **to go out of ~** zu bestehen *or* existieren aufhören; **do you believe in the ~ of angels?** glauben Sie daran, daß es Engel gibt?, glauben Sie an die Existenz von Engeln?; **the continued ~ of such a procedure** das Weiterbestehen *or* der Fortbestand eines solchen Verfahrens; **the only one in ~** der einzige, den es gibt.
(b) *(life)* Leben, Dasein *nt,* Existenz *f* ◆ **a miserable ~** ein elendes Leben, ein trostloses Dasein; **what are your means of ~?** wie verdienen Sie Ihren Lebensunterhalt?
existent [ɪg'zɪstənt] *adj* existent; *conditions, laws* bestehend ◆ **to be ~** existieren; **dinosaurs are no longer ~** Dinosaurier gibt es nicht mehr.
existential [,egzɪs'tenʃəl] *adj* existentiell.
existentialism [,egzɪs'tenʃəlɪzəm] *n* Existentialismus *m.*
existentialist [,egzɪs'tenʃəlɪst] [1] *n* Existentialist(in *f) m.*
[2] *adj* existentialistisch.
existing [ɪg'zɪstɪŋ] *adj law* bestehend; *director* gegenwärtig.
exit ['eksɪt] [1] *n* **(a)** *(from stage, life)* Abgang *m; (from room also)* Hinausgehen *nt (from* aus); *(from sb's life)* Scheiden *nt (geh)* ◆ **to make one's ~** *(from stage)* abgehen; *(from room)* hinausgehen; **he made a very dramatic ~** sein Abgang war sehr dramatisch.
(b) *(way out)* Ausgang *m; (for vehicles)* Ausfahrt *f.*
[2] *vi* hinausgehen; *(from stage)* abgehen; *(Comput)* das Programm/die Datei *etc* verlassen, aussteigen *(inf)* ◆ **~ the king** *(stage direction)* der König (tritt) ab.
[3] *vt (US) bus etc* verlassen, aussteigen aus; *(Comput) program, file* verlassen, aussteigen aus *(inf).*
exit: ~ permit *n* Ausreisegenehmigung *f;* **~ poll** *bei Wahlen unmittelbar nach Verlassen der Wahllokale durchgeführte Umfrage;* **~ visa** *n* Ausreisevisum *nt.*
exodus ['eksədəs] *n* **(a)** Auszug *m; (Bibl: of Hebrews, fig)* Exodus *m* ◆ **general ~** allgemeiner Aufbruch; **the ~ of city dwellers to the sea in summer** die sommerliche Völkerwanderung der Städter an die See. **(b) ~ of capital** Kapitalabwanderung *f.* **(c)** *(Bibl)* **E~** 2. Buch Mosis *or* Mose, Exodus *m.*
ex-officio [,eksə'fɪʃɪəʊ] [1] *adj* **to be ~ commander/an ~ member** von Amts wegen Kommandant/Mitglied sein.
[2] *adv* ex officio ◆ **to act ~** kraft seines Amtes handeln.
exonerate [ɪg'zɒnəreɪt] *vt* entlasten *(from* von).
exoneration [ɪg,zɒnə'reɪʃən] *n* Entlastung *f (from* von).
exorbitance [ɪg'zɔːbɪtəns] *n (of price)* Unverschämtheit *f; (of demands also)* Maßlosigkeit, Übertriebenheit *f.*
exorbitant [ɪg'zɔːbɪtənt] *adj price* astronomisch, unverschämt, exorbitant *(geh); demands* maßlos, übertrieben ◆ **£50 for that is ~!** £ 50 dafür ist Wucher.
exorbitantly [ɪg'zɔːbɪtəntlɪ] *adv expensive* maßlos, exorbitant *(geh).*
exorcism ['eksɔːsɪzəm] *n* Geisterbeschwörung *f,* Exorzismus *m,* Austreibung *f* böser Geister.

exorcist ['eksɔːsɪst] *n* Exorzist *m*.
exorcize ['eksɔːsaɪz] *vt* exorzieren; *evil spirit also* austreiben.
exoskeleton [ˌeksəʊ'skelɪtən] *n* Außenskelett *nt*.
exoteric [ˌeksəʊ'terɪk] *adj* exoterisch.
exotic [ɪg'zɒtɪk] [1] *adj* exotisch.
[2] *n* (*Bot*) exotische Pflanze.
exotica [ɪg'zɒtɪkə] *npl* Exotika *pl* ◆ **a museum of ~** (*fig*) ein Raritätenkabinett *nt*.
exotically [ɪg'zɒtɪkəlɪ] *adv see adj*.
exoticism [ɪg'zɒtɪsɪzəm] *n* Exotik *f*, Exotische *nt*.
expand [ɪk'spænd] [1] *vt metal, gas, liquid, empire, chest* ausdehnen, expandieren; *business, trade, production also* erweitern, ausweiten; *knowledge, mind, algebraic formula* erweitern; *influence also, experience* vergrößern; *summary, notes* weiter ausführen; *ideas* entwickeln ◆ **~ed polystyrene** Styropor ® *nt*.
[2] *vi* (*solids, gases, liquids, universe*) sich ausdehnen, expandieren; (*business, trade, empire*) expandieren, sich ausweiten, wachsen; (*volume of trade, exports, production*) zunehmen, expandieren; (*knowledge, experience, influence*) zunehmen, wachsen; (*fields of knowledge, study, mind*) breiter werden; (*horizons*) sich erweitern ◆ **we want to ~** wir wollen expandieren *or* (uns) vergrößern; **the market is ~ing** der Markt wächst; **could you ~ on that?** könnten Sie das weiter ausführen?; **~ing watch-strap** Gliederarmband *nt*.
expandable [ɪk'spændəbl] *adj* erweiterbar.
expander [ɪk'spændə^r] *n* Expander *m*.
expanse [ɪk'spæns] *n* Fläche *f*; (*of ocean etc*) Weite *f no pl* ◆ **an ~ of grass/woodland** eine Grasfläche/ein Waldgebiet *nt*.
expansion [ɪk'spænʃən] *n* (*of liquid, gas, metal, universe, property*) Ausdehnung, Expansion *f*; (*of business, trade, production*) Erweiterung, Ausweitung *f*; (*territorial, economic, colonial*) Expansion *f*; (*of subject, idea*) Entwicklung *f*; (*Math, of knowledge*) Erweiterung *f*; (*of experience, influence*) Vergrößerung *f*; (*of summary, notes*) Ausweitung *f*.
expansion (*Comput*): **~ board** *n* Erweiterungsplatine *f*; **~ card** *n* Erweiterungskarte *f*.
expansionism [ɪk'spænʃənɪzəm] *n* Expansionspolitik *f*.
expansionist [ɪk'spænʃənɪst] [1] *adj* expansionistisch, Expansions-.
[2] *n* Expansionspolitiker(in *f*) *m*.
expansion slot *n* (*Comput*) Erweiterungssteckplatz *m*.
expansive [ɪk'spænsɪv] *adj* **(a)** *person* mitteilsam ◆ **to be in an ~ mood** mitteilsam sein. **(b)** (*Phys*) expansiv.
expat ['eksˌpæt] *see* **expatriate 2, 3**.
expatiate [ɪk'speɪʃɪeɪt] *vi* sich verbreiten (*on* über *+acc*).
expatiation [ɪkˌspeɪʃɪ'eɪʃən] *n* weitläufige Erörterung.
expatriate [eks'pætrɪeɪt] [1] *vt* ausbürgern, expatriieren.
[2] [eks'pætrɪət] *adj person* im Ausland lebend ◆ **~ community** Auslandsgemeinde, Kolonie *f*; **there are a lot of ~ Englishmen/workers here** hier leben viele Engländer/ausländische Arbeitskräfte; **~ German** Auslandsdeutsche(r) *mf*.
[3] [eks'pætrɪət] *n* im Ausland Lebende(r) *mf* ◆ **the ~s in Abu Dhabi** die Ausländer in Abu Dhabi; **Hemingway would go drinking with other ~s** Hemingway pflegte mit anderen Exilamerikanern trinken zu gehen; **I'm an ~ too** ich bin hier auch im Exil (*hum*).
▼ **expect** [ɪk'spekt] [1] *vt* **(a)** (*anticipate*) erwarten; *esp sth bad also* rechnen mit ◆ **that was to be ~ed** das war zu erwarten, damit war zu rechnen; **I know what to ~** ich weiß, was mich erwartet; **we were ~ing war in 1939** 1939 haben wir mit Krieg gerechnet; **to ~ the worst** mit dem Schlimmsten rechnen; **I ~ed as much** das habe ich erwartet, damit habe ich gerechnet; **he failed as (we had) ~ed** er fiel, wie erwartet, durch; **he got first prize as was to be ~ed** wie erwartet, bekam er den ersten Preis; **to ~ to do sth** erwarten *or* damit rechnen, etw zu tun; **I didn't ~ to gain his sympathy** ich habe kein Mitleid von ihm erwartet; **he ~s to be elected** er rechnet damit, gewählt zu werden; **it is ~ed that ...** es wird erwartet, daß ..., man rechnet damit, daß ...; **it is hardly to be ~ed that** es ist kaum zu erwarten *or* damit zu rechnen, daß; **I was ~ing him to come** ich habe eigentlich erwartet, daß er kommt; **you can't ~ me to agree to that!** Sie erwarten doch wohl nicht, daß ich dem zustimme!; **I'll ~ to see you tomorrow then** dann sehen wir uns also morgen.
▼ **(b)** (*suppose*) denken, glauben ◆ **will they be on time? — yes, I ~ so** kommen sie pünktlich? — ja, ich glaube schon *or* denke doch; **this work is very tiring — yes, I ~ it is** diese Arbeit ist sehr anstrengend — (ja,) das glaube ich; **I ~ it will rain** höchstwahrscheinlich wird es regnen, es wird wohl regnen; **I ~ you'd like a drink** Sie möchten sicher etwas trinken, ich nehme an, Sie möchten etwas trinken; **I ~ you're tired** Sie werden sicher müde sein; **I ~ he turned it down** er hat wohl abgelehnt, ich nehme an, er hat abgelehnt; **well, I ~ he's right** er wird schon recht haben; **well, I ~ it's all for the best** das ist wohl nur gut so; **I ~ it was your father who telephoned** ich nehme an, es war dein Vater, der angerufen hat.
▼ **(c)** (*demand*) **to ~ sth of *or* from sb** etw von jdm erwarten; **to ~ sb to do sth** erwarten, daß jd etw tut; **I ~ you to be obedient** ich erwarte von dir Gehorsam; **what do you ~ me to do about it?** was soll ich da tun?; **don't ~ me to feel sorry** erwarte von mir kein Mitleid; **are we ~ed to tip the waiter?** müssen wir dem Kellner Trinkgeld geben?
(d) (*await*) *person, thing, action* erwarten; *baby also* bekommen ◆ **I will be ~ing you tomorrow** ich erwarte dich morgen; **I am ~ing them for supper** ich erwarte sie zum Abendessen; **we'll ~ you when we see you** (*inf*) wenn ihr kommt, dann kommt ihr (*inf*); **you'll have to ~ me when you see me** (*inf*) wenn ich da bin, bin ich da! (*inf*).
[2] *vi* **she's ~ing** sie ist in anderen Umständen, sie bekommt *or* erwartet ein Kind.
expectancy [ɪk'spektənsɪ] *n* Erwartung *f*.
expectant [ɪk'spektənt] *adj* erwartungsvoll; *mother* werdend.
expectantly [ɪk'spektəntlɪ] *adv* erwartungsvoll ◆ **to wait ~** gespannt *or* ungeduldig warten.
expectation [ˌekspek'teɪʃən] *n* **(a)** (*act of expecting*) Erwartung *f* ◆ **in ~ of** in Erwartung (*+gen*); **in the confident ~ of an easy victory** fest mit einem leichten Sieg rechnend.
(b) (*that expected*) Erwartung *f* ◆ **contrary to all ~(s)** wider Erwarten; **beyond all ~(s)** über Erwarten, über alle Erwartung; **to come up to sb's ~s** jds Erwartungen (*dat*) entsprechen.
(c) (*prospect*) Aussicht *f*.
(d) ~ of life Lebenserwartung *f*.
expectorant [ɪk'spektərənt] *n* Expektorans *nt* (*spec*).
expectorate [ɪk'spektəreɪt] *vti* (*form*) ausspeien.
expedience [ɪk'spiːdɪəns], **expediency** [ɪk'spiːdɪənsɪ] *n* **(a)** (*self-interest*) Zweckdenken *nt*, Berechnung *f*. **(b)** (*of measure etc*) (*politic nature*) Zweckdienlichkeit *f*; (*advisability*) Ratsamkeit *f*.
expedient [ɪk'spiːdɪənt] [1] *adj* (*politic*) zweckdienlich; (*advisable*) angebracht, ratsam.
[2] *n* Notbehelf *m*, Hilfsmittel *nt*.
expedite ['ekspɪdaɪt] *vt* **(a)** (*hasten*) beschleunigen, vorantreiben ◆ **see what you can do to ~ matters** sehen Sie zu, daß Sie die Sache beschleunigen. **(b)** (*rare*) *letters* expedieren (*spec*).
expedition [ˌekspɪ'dɪʃən] *n* **(a)** Expedition *f*; (*scientific also*) Forschungsreise *f*; (*Mil*) Feldzug *m* ◆ **shopping ~** Einkaufstour *f*; **to go on an ~/a shopping ~** auf (eine) Expedition *or* Forschungsreise gehen/eine Einkaufstour machen. **(b)** *no pl* (*old, form: speed*) Eile *f* ◆ **with all possible ~** eilends (*old, form*).
expeditionary [ˌekspɪ'dɪʃənrɪ] *adj* Expeditions- ◆ **~ force** (*Mil*) Expeditionskorps *nt*.
expeditious *adj*, **~ly** *adv* [ˌekspɪ'dɪʃəs, -lɪ] schnell, prompt.
expel [ɪk'spel] *vt* **(a)** vertreiben; (*officially: from country*) ausweisen (*from* aus); (*from school*) verweisen (*from* von, *gen*); (*from society*) ausstoßen, ausschließen. **(b)** *gas, liquid* ausstoßen.
expend [ɪk'spend] *vt* **(a)** (*spend, employ*) *money* ausgeben, verwenden; *time, energy, care* aufwenden (*on* für, *on doing sth* um etw zu tun), verwenden (*on* auf *+acc*, *on doing sth* darauf, etwas zu tun). **(b)** (*use up*) *resources* verbrauchen.
expendability [ɪkˌspendə'bɪlɪtɪ] *n see adj* Entbehrlichkeit *f*; Überflüssigkeit *f*.
expendable [ɪk'spendəbl] *adj* entbehrlich; *people also* überflüssig.
expenditure [ɪk'spendɪtʃə^r] *n* **(a)** (*money spent*) Ausgaben *pl*. **(b)** (*spending*) (*of money*) Ausgabe *f*; (*of time, energy*) Aufwand *m* (*on* an *+dat*) ◆ **the ~ of money on ...** Geld auszugeben für ...; **~ of time/energy** Zeit-/Energieaufwand *m*.
expense [ɪk'spens] *n* **(a)** Kosten *pl* ◆ **at my ~** auf meine Kosten; **at the public ~** auf Staatskosten; **at little/great ~** mit geringen/hohen Kosten; **it's a big ~** es ist eine große Ausgabe; **to go to the ~ of buying a car** (viel) Geld für ein Auto anlegen; **to go to great ~ to repair the house** es sich (*dat*) etwas kosten lassen, das Haus instand zu setzen; **don't go to any ~ over our visit** stürz dich nicht in Unkosten wegen unseres Besuchs.
(b) (*Comm: usu pl*) Spesen *pl* ◆ **to incur ~s** Unkosten haben; **your ~s will be entirely covered** alle Unkosten werden Ihnen vergütet; **put it on ~s** schreiben Sie es auf die Spesenrechnung; **it's all on ~s** das geht alles auf Spesen.
(c) (*fig*) **at sb's ~/at the ~ of sth** auf jds Kosten (*acc*)/auf Kosten einer Sache (*gen*); **to get rich at somebody else's ~/at the ~ of others** sich auf Kosten eines anderen/anderer bereichern; **at the ~ of a decrease in quality** auf Kosten der Qualität; **at the ~ of great personal suffering** unter großen persönlichen Verlusten.
expense: ~ account [1] *n* Spesenkonto *nt*; **this will go on his ~ account** das geht auf Spesen; [2] *adj attr* **~-account lunch** Mittagessen *nt* auf Spesen; **~-account living** Leben *nt* auf Spesen; **it's only ~-account types who stay in this hotel** (*inf*) in diesem Hotel wohnen nur Spesenreiter (*inf*); **~s form** *n* Spesenrechnung *f*; **~s-paid** *adj* auf Geschäftskosten.
expensive [ɪk'spensɪv] *adj* teuer; *goods, undertaking also* kostspielig.
expensively [ɪk'spensɪvlɪ] *adv* teuer ◆ **~ priced** teuer.
expensiveness [ɪk'spensɪvnɪs] *n* (*of goods, travel, services etc*) hoher Preis, Kostspieligkeit *f*; (*of living here etc*) Kostspieligkeit *f* ◆ **the ~ of her tastes** ihr teurer Geschmack; **the increasing ~ of basic commodities** die ständige Verteuerung von Grundbedarfsmitteln.
▼ **experience** [ɪk'spɪərɪəns] [1] *n* **(a)** (*knowledge, wisdom acquired*) Erfahrung *f* ◆ **~ of life** Lebenserfahrung *f*; **~ shows *or* proves that ...** die Erfahrung lehrt, daß ...; **to know sth by *or* from ~** etw aus Erfahrung wissen; **from my own personal ~** aus eigener Erfahrung; **a fact established by ~** eine Erfahrungstatsache; **he has no ~ of real grief** er hat nie wirklichen Kummer erfahren *or* erlebt; **he has no ~ of living in the country** er kennt das Landleben nicht; **I gained a lot of useful ~** ich habe viele nützliche Erfahrungen gemacht; **to have an ~** eine Erfahrung machen.
▼ **(b)** (*practice, skill*) Erfahrung *f* ◆ **he has had no practical ~** ihm fehlt die Praxis, er hat keine praktischen Kenntnisse, er hat keine Erfahrung; **to have ~ of a technique** Erfahrung in einer Methode haben; **have you had some ~ of driving a bus?** haben Sie Erfahrung im Busfahren?; **~ in a trade/in**

➤ LANGUAGE IN USE: **expect: 1a** → 8.2, 16.2 **1b** → 6.2, 26.3 **1c** → 10.2 **experience: 1b** → 19.2

business Berufs-/Geschäftserfahrung *f*; **to have a lot of teaching ~** große Erfahrung als Lehrer haben; **he lacks ~** ihm fehlt die Praxis *or* praktische Erfahrung; **he is working in a factory to gain ~** er arbeitet in einer Fabrik, um praktische Erfahrungen zu sammeln.
(c) *(event experienced)* Erlebnis *nt* ◆ **I had a nasty ~** mir ist etwas Unangenehmes passiert; **the trial was a very nasty ~** der Prozeß war eine sehr unangenehme Sache; **to go through** *or* **have a painful ~** Schreckliches erleben; **to go through some terrible ~s** viel durchmachen; **what an ~!** das war vielleicht was!; **it was a new ~ for me** es war völlig neu für mich.
2 *vt* **(a)** erleben; *(suffer, undergo) pain, grief, hunger also* erfahren; *difficult times also* durchmachen ◆ **to ~ difficulties** auf Schwierigkeiten stoßen, Schwierigkeiten haben.
(b) *(feel)* fühlen, spüren, empfinden.

experienced [ɪk'spɪərɪənst] *adj* erfahren; *eye, ear* geschult ◆ **to be ~ in sth** erfahren in etw *(dat)* sein.

experiential [ɪk,spɪərɪ'enʃəl] *adj* auf Erfahrung beruhend, Erfahrungs-.

experiment [ɪk'sperɪmənt] 1 *n (Chem, Phys, fig)* Versuch *m*, Experiment *nt* ◆ **to do an ~** einen Versuch *or* ein Experiment machen; **as an ~** versuchsweise, als Versuch.
2 *vi (Chem, Phys, fig)* experimentieren *(on* mit).

experimental [ɪk,sperɪ'mentl] *adj* **(a)** *(based on experiments) research, method, science, evidence* experimentell, Experimental-. **(b)** *laboratory, farm, engine, prototype, period* Versuchs-, Test-; *novel* experimentell; *theatre, cinema* Experimentier-, experimentell ◆ **at the ~ stage** im Versuchsstadium; **on an ~ basis** auf Versuchsbasis.

experimentally [ɪk,sperɪ'mentəlɪ] *adv* **(a)** *(by experiment) test, discover* durch Versuche, experimentell. **(b)** *(as an experiment)* versuchsweise, als Versuch.

experimentation [ɪk,sperɪmen'teɪʃən] *n* Experimentieren *nt*.

expert ['ekspɜːt] 1 *n* Fachmann, Experte *m*, Expertin *f*; *(Jur)* Sachverständige(r) *mf* ◆ **he is an ~ on the subject/at that sort of negotiation** er ist Fachmann *or* Experte auf diesem Gebiet/für solche Verhandlungen; **~ in geology** Fachmann *m* für Geologie, Geologieexperte *m*; **an ~ at chess** ein Schachexperte *m*; **he's an ~ at saying the wrong thing** er versteht es meisterhaft, genau das Falsche zu sagen; **with the eye of an ~** mit fachmännischem Blick; **to get the advice of ~s** Experten *or* Fachleute/Sachverständige zu Rate ziehen; **OK, you do it, you're the ~** gut, machen Sie's, Sie sind der Fachmann.
2 *adj work* ausgezeichnet, geschickt; *driver etc* erfahren, geschickt; *approach, advice* fachmännisch; *opinion* eines Fachmanns/Sachverständigen ◆ **to be ~ in an art/a science** sich in einer Kunst/Wissenschaft sehr gut auskennen; **~ witness** sachverständiger Zeuge; **what's your ~ opinion?** *(also iro)* was meinen Sie als Fachmann *or* Experte dazu?; **the ~ touch** die Meisterhand; **he is ~ in handling a boat/in repairing cars** er kann meisterhaft mit einem Boot umgehen/er ist ein Experte für Autoreparaturen; **to cast an ~ eye over sth** etw fachmännisch begutachten.

expertise [,ekspə'tiːz] *n* Sachverstand *m*, Sachkenntnis *f (in* in *+dat*, auf dem Gebiet *+gen)*; *(manual skills)* Geschick *nt (in* bei).

expertly ['ekspɜːtlɪ] *adv* meisterhaft; *drive, dribble* geschickt, gekonnt; *judge, examine* sachverständig, mit Sachverstand.

expert system *n (Comput)* Expertensystem *nt*.

expiate ['ekspɪeɪt] *vt* sühnen.

expiation [,ekspɪ'eɪʃən] *n* **in ~ of** als Sühne für.

expiatory ['ekspɪətərɪ] *adj offering, sacrifice* Sühne-, sühnend.

expiration [,ekspaɪə'reɪʃən] *n* **(a)** *see* **expiry**. **(b)** *(of breath)* Ausatmen *nt*, Ausatmung *f*.

expire [ɪk'spaɪə^r^] *vi* **(a)** *(lease, passport)* ablaufen, ungültig werden; *(time limit)* ablaufen, zu Ende gehen. **(b)** *(liter: die)* seinen Geist aufgeben *(liter)*. **(c)** *(breathe out)* ausatmen.

expiry [ɪk'spaɪərɪ] *n* Ablauf *m* ◆ **on the ~ of** nach Ablauf *(+gen)*; **date of ~, ~ date** Ablauftermin *m*; *(of voucher, special offer)* Verfallsdatum *nt*.

▼ **explain** [ɪk'spleɪn] 1 *vt* erklären *(to sb* jdm); *motives, situation, thoughts also* erläutern; *mystery* aufklären ◆ **it's all right, I can ~ everything** schon gut, ich kann das alles erklären; **that is easy to ~, that is easily ~ed** das läßt sich leicht erklären; **he wanted to see me but wouldn't ~ why** er wollte mich sehen, sagte aber nicht, warum *or* aus welchem Grunde; **the bad weather ~s why he is absent** das schlechte Wetter erklärt seine Abwesenheit; **so that ~s why he didn't react** ach, das erklärt, warum er nicht reagiert hat.
2 *vr (justify)* sich rechtfertigen ◆ **he'd better ~ himself** ich hoffe, er kann das erklären; **listen, my boy, I think you'd better start ~ing yourself** was hast du zu deiner Entschuldigung zu sagen, mein Junge?; **what do you mean "stupid"! ~ yourself!** was meinst du mit „dumm"! erkläre mir/uns das!; **~ yourself!** was soll das?, kannst du es/das erklären?
3 *vi* es/alles erklären ◆ **please ~** bitte erklären Sie das; **I think you've got a little ~ing to do** ich glaube, Sie müssen da einiges erklären.

◆**explain away** *vt sep* eine Erklärung finden für.

explainable [ɪk'spleɪnəbl] *adj* erklärlich ◆ **this is easily ~** das läßt sich leicht erklären; **that is ~ by ...** das läßt sich durch ... erklären.

▼ **explanation** [,eksplə'neɪʃən] *n* **(a)** *see vt* Erklärung *f*; Erläuterung *f*; Aufklärung *f* ◆ **it needs some/a little ~** es bedarf einer/einer kurzen Erklärung, man muß das etwas/ein wenig erklären; **he gave a long ~ of what he meant** er erklärte lange, was er meinte; **what is the ~ of this?** wie ist das zu erklären?
(b) *(justification)* Erklärung, Rechtfertigung *f* ◆ **has he anything to say in ~ of his conduct?** kann er irgend etwas zur Erklärung seines Verhaltens vorbringen?; **what is the ~ of this?** was soll das heißen?

explanatory [ɪk'splænətərɪ] *adj* erklärend; *remarks etc also* erläuternd ◆ **a few ~ remarks** ein paar Worte zur Erklärung.

expletive [ɪk'spliːtɪv] 1 *n (exclamation)* Ausruf *m*; *(oath)* Kraftausdruck, Fluch *m*; *(Gram: filler word)* Füllwort *nt*.
2 *adj* **~ word** *(Gram)* Füllwort *nt*.

explicable [ɪk'splɪkəbl] *adj* erklärbar.

explicate ['eksplɪkeɪt] *vt (form)* erläutern, ausführen.

explication [,eksplɪ'keɪʃən] *n (form)* Erläuterung, Ausführung *f*.

explicit [ɪk'splɪsɪt] *adj* deutlich, explizit *(geh)*; *text, meaning also* klar; *sex scene* deutlich, unverhüllt ◆ **in ~ terms** klar und deutlich; **there's no need to be quite so ~** Sie brauchen nicht so deutlich zu werden; **he was ~ on this point** er wurde an diesem Punkt ziemlich deutlich; **~ denial** deutliches Abstreiten.

explicitly [ɪk'splɪsɪtlɪ] *adv* deutlich, explizite *(geh)*; *(clearly also)* klar.

explode [ɪk'spləʊd] 1 *vi* **(a)** explodieren; *(powder, booby-trap, mine also)* in die Luft fliegen *(inf)*.
(b) *(fig: with anger)* explodieren, vor Wut platzen *(inf)*, in die Luft gehen *(inf)* ◆ **to ~ with laughter** in schallendes Gelächter ausbrechen, losplatzen *(inf)*.
2 *vt* **(a)** *bomb, plane* sprengen; *dynamite, gas* zur Explosion bringen. **(b)** *(fig) theory* zu Fall bringen ◆ **to ~ a popular fallacy** einen weitverbreiteten Irrtum aufdecken.

exploded [ɪk'spləʊdɪd] *adj* **~ diagram** Explosionszeichnung *f*.

exploit ['eksplɔɪt] 1 *n (heroic)* Heldentat *f* ◆ **~s** *(adventures)* Abenteuer *pl*.
2 [ɪks'plɔɪt] *vt* **(a)** *(use unfairly) workers* ausbeuten; *friend, sb's credulity, good nature* ausnutzen. **(b)** *(make use of) talent, the situation* ausnutzen, ausnützen *(dial)*; *coal seam* ausbeuten; *land, natural resources* nutzen.

exploitation [,eksplɔɪ'teɪʃən] *n see vt* Ausbeutung *f*; Ausnutzung *f*; Nutzung *f*.

exploration [,eksplɔː'reɪʃən] *n (of country, area)* Erforschung, Exploration *(geh) f*; *(of small area, town)* Erkundung *f*; *(of topic, possibilities)* Erforschung, Untersuchung, Sondierung *f*; *(Med)* Untersuchung, Exploration *f* ◆ **a voyage of ~** *(lit, fig)* eine Entdeckungsreise; **on his ~s** auf seinen Forschungsreisen/Erkundungen.

exploratory [ɪk'splɒrətərɪ] *adj drilling* Probe-; *excursion* Forschungs- ◆ **~ operation** *(Med)* Explorationsoperation *f*; **~ talks** Sondierungsgespräche *pl*.

explore [ɪk'splɔː^r^] 1 *vt* **(a)** *country, forest, unknown territory* erforschen, erkunden, explorieren *(geh)*; *(Med)* untersuchen.
(b) *(fig) question, possibilities* erforschen, untersuchen, sondieren ◆ **talks to ~ the ground** Sondierungsgespräche *pl*.
2 *vi* **to go exploring** auf Entdeckungsreise gehen; **he went off into the village to ~** er ging auf Entdeckungsreise ins Dorf.

explorer [ɪk'splɔːrə^r^] *n* Forscher(in *f*) *m*, Forschungsreisende(r) *mf*.

explosion [ɪk'spləʊʒən] *n* **(a)** Explosion *f*; *(noise also)* Knall *m*. **(b)** *(fig: of anger)* Wutausbruch *m*. **(c)** *(fig: in prices, figures etc)* Explosion *f*.

explosive [ɪk'spləʊzɪv] 1 *adj* **(a)** *gas, matter, mixture, weapons, force* explosiv, Explosiv-, Spreng- ◆ **~ device** Sprengkörper *m*. **(b)** *(fig) situation, combination* explosiv; *temper also* leicht aufbrausend.
2 *n* Sprengstoff *m*.

expo ['ekspəʊ] *n abbr of* **exposition** Ausstellung *f*.

exponent [ɪk'spəʊnənt] *n* **(a)** *(of theory)* Vertreter(in *f*), Exponent(in *f*) *m*. **(b)** *(Math)* Exponent *m*, Hochzahl *f*.

exponential [,ekspəʊ'nenʃəl] *adj* Exponential-.

export 1 [ɪk'spɔːt] *vti* exportieren *(also Comput)*, ausführen ◆ **countries which ~ oil** ölexportierende *or* Ölexport-Länder *pl*; **~ or die** wer nicht exportiert, geht unter.
2 ['ekspɔːt] *n* Export *m*, Ausfuhr *f* ◆ **ban on ~s** Exportverbot, Ausfuhrverbot *nt*.
3 ['ekspɔːt] *adj attr* Export-, Ausfuhr- ◆ **~ director** Exportdirektor *m*; **~ duty** Export- *or* Ausfuhrzoll *m*; **~ drive** Exportkampagne *f*; **~ licence** Ausfuhrgenehmigung *or* -lizenz, Exportgenehmigung *f*; **~ manager** Exportleiter(in *f*) *m*; **~ permit** Ausfuhrerlaubnis, Exporterlaubnis *f*; **~ trade** Exporthandel *m*.

exportable [ɪk'spɔːtəbl] *adj* exportfähig.

exportation [,ekspɔː'teɪʃən] *n* Export *m*, Ausfuhr *f*.

exporter [ɪk'spɔːtə^r^] *n (person)* Exporteur *m (of* von); *(country also)* Exportland *nt (of* für).

expose [ɪk'spəʊz] *vt* **(a)** *(uncover) rocks, remains* freilegen; *electric wire, nerve also* bloßlegen ◆ **a dress which leaves the back ~d** ein Kleid, bei dem der Rücken frei bleibt; **to be ~d to view** sichtbar sein; **~d position** *(Mil)* exponierte Stellung.
(b) *(to danger, rain, sunlight, radiation)* aussetzen *(to dat)*; *baby* aussetzen ◆ **not to be ~d to heat** vor Hitze (zu) schützen; **to ~ oneself to criticism** sich der Kritik aussetzen.
(c) *(display) one's ignorance* offenbaren; *one's wounds* (vor)zeigen; *(indecently) oneself* entblößen ◆ **darling, you're exposing yourself** du zeigst etwas viel, Liebling.
(d) *abuse, treachery* aufdecken; *scandal, plot also* enthüllen; *person, imposter, murderer, thief* entlarven ◆ **to ~ sb/sth to the press** jdn/etw der Presse ausliefern.
(e) *(Phot)* belichten.

exposé [ek'spəʊzeɪ] *n* Exposé *nt*; *(of scandal etc)* Aufdeckung *f*.

exposed [ɪk'spəʊzd] *adj* **(a)** *(to weather) place* ungeschützt ◆ **~ to the wind** dem Wind ausgesetzt; **it's quite ~ where you live** Sie wohnen ziemlich ungeschützt; **this house is very ~** dieses Haus steht sehr frei *or* ungeschützt.

➤ LANGUAGE IN USE: **explain: 1 → 26.3** **explanation: a → 26.1**

(b) (*insecure*) **to feel ~** sich allen Blicken ausgesetzt fühlen.
(c) (*to view*) sichtbar ◆ **the ~ parts of a motor** die frei liegenden Teile eines Motors.

exposition [ˌekspəˈzɪʃən] *n* **(a)** (*of facts, theory*) Darlegung, Exposition (*geh*) *f*; (*explanatory*) Erklärung, Erläuterung *f*; (*of literature, text*) Kommentar *m* (*of* zu), Erläuterung *f*; (*Mus*) Exposition *f*. **(b)** (*exhibition*) Ausstellung *f*.

expository [ɪkˈspɒzɪtərɪ] *adj* darlegend.

expostulate [ɪkˈspɒstjʊleɪt] *vi* protestieren ◆ **to ~ with sb** mit jdm disputieren.

expostulation [ɪkˌspɒstjʊˈleɪʃən] *n* Protest *m*.

exposure [ɪkˈspəʊʒəʳ] *n* **(a)** (*to sunlight, air, danger*) Aussetzung *f* (*to dat*) ◆ **~ of the body to strong sunlight** wenn man den Körper starkem Sonnenlicht aussetzt; **to be suffering from ~** an Unterkühlung leiden; **to die of ~** erfrieren.
(b) (*displaying*) Entblößung *f* ◆ **indecent ~** Erregung *f* öffentlichen Ärgernisses.
(c) (*unmasking: of person, thief, murderer*) Entlarvung *f*; (*of abuses, plots, vices, scandals, crime*) Aufdeckung *f* ◆ **to threaten sb with ~** drohen, jdn zu entlarven.
(d) (*position of building*) Lage *f* ◆ **southern ~** Südlage *f*.
(e) (*Phot*) Belichtung(szeit) *f* ◆ **~ meter** Belichtungsmesser *m*.
(f) (*Media*) Publicity *f* ◆ **his new film has been given a lot of ~** sein neuer Film hat viel Publicity bekommen.

expound [ɪkˈspaʊnd] *vt theory, one's views* darlegen, erläutern.

▼ **express** [ɪkˈspres] 1 *vt* **(a)** ausdrücken, zum Ausdruck bringen; (*in words*) *wish, one's sympathy, appreciation also* aussprechen ◆ **to ~ oneself** sich ausdrücken; **this ~es exactly the meaning of the word** das gibt genau die Bedeutung des Wortes wieder; **I haven't the words to ~ my thoughts** mir fehlen die Worte, um meine Gedanken auszudrücken; **the thought/feeling which is ~ed here** der Gedanke, der/das Gefühl, das hier zum Ausdruck kommt.
(b) (*be expressive of*) ausdrücken ◆ **a face which ~es candour/pride** ein Gesicht, das Aufrichtigkeit/Stolz ausdrückt.
(c) (*form*) *juice, milk* auspressen, ausdrücken.
(d) *letter etc* per Expreß *or* als Eilsendung schicken.
2 *adj* (*clear*) *instructions* ausdrücklich; *intention* bestimmt ◆ **with the ~ purpose of seeing him** mit der bestimmten Absicht, ihn zu sprechen.
3 *adv* **to send sth ~** etw per Expreß *or* als Eilgut schicken.
4 *n* **(a)** (*train*) Schnellzug *m*.
(b) **to send goods by ~** Waren per Expreß schicken.

express: ~ company *n* (*US*) Spedition *f* (für Expreßgut); **~ delivery** *n* (*Brit*) Eilzustellung *f*.

expression [ɪkˈspreʃən] *n* **(a)** (*expressing: of opinions, friendship, affection, joy*) Äußerung *f*, Ausdruck *m* ◆ **as an ~ of our gratitude** zum Ausdruck unserer Dankbarkeit; **to give ~ to sth** etw zum Ausdruck bringen; **feelings which found ~ in tears** Gefühle, die sich in Tränen äußerten *or* die in Tränen zum Ausdruck kamen.
(b) (*feeling: in music, art etc*) Ausdruck *m* ◆ **you need to put more ~ into it/your voice** Sie müssen das ausdrucksvoller spielen/vortragen; **to play with ~** ausdrucksvoll spielen.
(c) (*phrase etc*) Ausdruck *m*.
(d) (*of face*) (Gesichts)ausdruck *m* ◆ **you could tell by his ~ that ...** man konnte an seinem Gesichtsausdruck erkennen, daß ...
(e) (*Math*) Ausdruck *m*.

expressionism [ɪkˈspreʃənɪzəm] *n* Expressionismus *m*.

expressionist [ɪkˈspreʃənɪst] 1 *n* Expressionist(in *f*) *m*.
2 *adj* expressionistisch.

expressionistic [ɪkˌspreʃəˈnɪstɪk] *adj* expressionistisch.

expressionless [ɪkˈspreʃənlɪs] *adj* ausdruckslos.

expressive [ɪkˈspresɪv] *adj* ausdrucksvoll, expressiv (*geh*); *face also* ausdrucksfähig ◆ **a poem ~ of despair** (*liter*) ein Verzweiflung ausdrückendes Gedicht.

expressively [ɪkˈspresɪvlɪ] *adv* ausdrucksvoll.

expressiveness [ɪkˈspresɪvnɪs] *n* Ausdruckskraft *f*; (*of face also*) Ausdrucksfähigkeit *f*.

express letter *n* Eil- *or* Expreßbrief *m*.

expressly [ɪkˈspreslɪ] *adv* **(a)** (*explicitly*) *deny, prohibit* ausdrücklich. **(b)** (*on purpose*) **he did it ~ to annoy me** er hat es absichtlich getan, um mich zu ärgern.

express: ~ train *n* Schnellzug *m*; **~way** *n* Schnellstraße *f*.

expropriate [eksˈprəʊprɪeɪt] *vt* enteignen.

expropriation [eksˌprəʊprɪˈeɪʃən] *n* Enteignung, Expropriation (*dated*) *f*.

expulsion [ɪkˈspʌlʃən] *n* (*from a country*) Ausweisung *f* (*from* aus); (*driving out*) Vertreibung *f* (*from* aus); (*from school*) Verweisung *f* (von der Schule) ◆ **~ order** Ausweisungsbefehl *m*.

expunge [ɪkˈspʌndʒ] *vt* (*form*) ausstreichen (*from* aus); (*from record also*) auslöschen (*from* aus).

expurgate [ˈekspɜːgeɪt] *vt* zensieren, die anstößigen Stellen entfernen aus ◆ **~d edition** gereinigte Fassung.

exquisite [ɪkˈskwɪzɪt] *adj* **(a)** (*excellent*) *workmanship, sewing* ausgezeichnet, vorzüglich; *woman, dress, painting* exquisit; *food, wine* exquisit, köstlich; *taste, wine* gepflegt; *view* einmalig, herrlich; *sensibility, politeness* fein, außerordentlich; *sense of humour* köstlich.
(b) (*keenly felt*) *thrill, satisfaction, pleasure, pain* köstlich.

exquisitely [ɪkˈskwɪzɪtlɪ] *adv* **(a)** *paint, embroider, decorate, express* ausgezeichnet, vorzüglich; *dress, dine* exquisit, gepflegt ◆ **she has the most ~ delicate hands** sie hat wunderbar zarte Hände. **(b)** (*extremely*) äußerst.

ex-serviceman [eksˈsɜːvɪsmən] *n, pl* **-men** [-mən] altgedienter Soldat, Veteran *m*.

ext *abbr of* **extension** App., Apparat *m*.

extant [ekˈstænt] *adj* (noch) vorhanden *or* existent.

extemporaneous [ɪkˌstempəˈreɪnɪəs], **extemporary** [ɪkˈstempərɪ] *adj* unvorbereitet, aus dem Stegreif.

extempore [ɪksˈtempərɪ] 1 *adv speak* aus dem Stegreif, unvorbereitet.
2 *adj* **to give an ~ speech** eine Rede aus dem Stegreif halten, extemporieren (*geh*).

extemporize [ɪkˈstempəraɪz] *vti* aus dem Stegreif sprechen, extemporieren (*geh*); (*Mus, with makeshift*) improvisieren.

▼ **extend** [ɪkˈstend] 1 *vt* **(a)** (*stretch out*) *arms* ausstrecken ◆ **to ~ one's hand to sb** jdm die Hand reichen; **to ~ a wire between two posts** einen Draht zwischen zwei Pfosten spannen.
(b) (*prolong*) *street, line, visit, passport, holidays* verlängern ◆ **~ed credit** verlängerter Kredit.
(c) (*enlarge*) *research, powers, franchise* ausdehnen, erweitern; *knowledge* erweitern, vergrößern; *house* anbauen an (+*acc*); *property also* vergrößern; *limits* erweitern; *frontiers of a country* ausdehnen ◆ **~ed play record** Schallplatte *f* mit verlängerter Spielzeit; **~ed family** Großfamilie *f*; **in an ~ed sense of the word** im weiteren Sinne des Wortes.
▼ **(d)** (*offer*) (*to sb* jdm) *help* gewähren; *hospitality, friendship* erweisen; *invitation, thanks, condolences, congratulations* aussprechen ◆ **to ~ a welcome to sb** jdn willkommen heißen.
(e) (*usu pass: make demands on*) *person, pupil, athlete* fordern ◆ **in this job he is fully ~ed** in diesem Beruf wird sein ganzes Können gefordert.
2 *vi* **(a)** (*wall, estate, garden*) sich erstrecken, sich ausdehnen (*to, as far as* bis); (*ladder*) sich ausziehen lassen; (*meetings etc: over period of time*) sich ausdehnen *or* hinziehen.
(b) (*reach to*) **enthusiasm which ~s even to the children** Begeisterung, die sich sogar auf die Kinder überträgt; **does that ~ to me?** betrifft das auch mich?

extendable [ɪkˈstendɪbl], **extensible** [ɪkˈstensɪbl] *adj telescope* ausziehbar; *time-limit* ausdehnbar.

▼ **extension** [ɪkˈstenʃən] *n* **(a)** (*of property*) Vergrößerung *f*; (*of business, knowledge also*) Erweiterung *f*; (*of powers, franchise, research, frontiers*) Ausdehnung *f*; (*of road, line, period of time*) Verlängerung *f*; (*of house*) Anbau *m*; (*of time limit*) Verlängerung *f*, Aufschub *m*.
(b) (*addition to length of sth: of road, line*) Verlängerung *f*; (*of table, holidays, leave etc*) Verlängerung *f*; (*of house*) Anbau *m*.
▼ **(c)** (*telephone in offices, in private houses*) (Neben)anschluß *m* ◆ **~ 3714** Apparat 3714.
(d) (*Logic: of word, concept*) Extension *f*.

extension: ~ cable *n* Verlängerungskabel *nt*; **~ course** *n* (*Univ*) weiterführender Kurs; **~ ladder** *n* Ausziehleiter *f*; **~ lead** *n* Verlängerungsschnur *f*.

extensive [ɪkˈstensɪv] *adj land, forest* ausgedehnt, weit; *view* weit; *knowledge, press coverage* umfassend, umfangreich; *study, research, enquiries* umfangreich, ausgedehnt; *investments, operations, alterations* umfangreich; *damage* beträchtlich; *use* häufig; *plans, reforms, business, influence* weitreichend ◆ **~ use is made of the cottage** die Hütte wird häufig *or* viel benutzt.

extensively [ɪkˈstensɪvlɪ] *adv* weit; *study, investigate, cover* ausführlich; *altered, reformed, damaged* beträchtlich; *used* häufig, viel ◆ **he has travelled ~ in the South of France** er ist viel in Südfrankreich herumgefahren.

extensor [ɪkˈstensəʳ] *n* Streckmuskel *m*.

extent [ɪkˈstent] *n* **(a)** (*length*) Länge *f*; (*size*) Ausdehnung *f* ◆ **we could see the full ~ of the park** wir konnten den Park in seiner ganzen Ausdehnung sehen.
(b) (*range, scope*) (*of knowledge, alterations, power, activities*) Umfang *m*; (*of damage, commitments, losses also*) Ausmaß *nt* ◆ **debts to the ~ of £5,000** Schulden in Höhe von £ 5.000.
(c) (*degree*) Grad *m*, Maß *nt* ◆ **to some ~** bis zu einem gewissen Grade; **to what ~** inwieweit; **to a certain ~** in gewissem Maße; **to a large/slight ~** in hohem/geringem Maße; **to such an ~ that ...** dermaßen *or* derart, daß ...; **such was the ~ of the damage** so groß war der Schaden.

extenuate [ɪkˈstenjʊeɪt] *vt guilt* verringern, mindern; *offence, conduct* beschönigen ◆ **extenuating circumstances** mildernde Umstände.

extenuation [ɪkˌstenjʊˈeɪʃən] *n* (*act*) Verringerung, Minderung *f*; Beschönigung *f*; (*extenuating factor*) mildernde Umstände *pl* ◆ **he pleaded ... in ~ of his crime** (*form*) er führte ... als mildernden Umstand an.

exterior [ɪkˈstɪərɪəʳ] 1 *adj surface* äußere(r, s), Außen-; *decorating, angle* Außen-.
2 *n* **(a)** (*of house, box etc*) Außenseite *f*, Äußere(s) *nt*; (*of person*) Äußere(s) *nt* ◆ **on the ~** außen, an der Außenseite. **(b)** (*Film*) Außenaufnahme *f*.

exterminate [ɪkˈstɜːmɪneɪt] *vt* ausrotten, vernichten; *pests also* vertilgen; *disease, beliefs, ideas* ausrotten.

extermination [ɪkˌstɜːmɪˈneɪʃən] *n see vt* Ausrottung, Vernichtung *f*; Vertilgung *f*.

exterminator [ɪkˈstɜːmɪneɪtəʳ] *n* (*person*) (*of rats etc*) Entweser *m* (*form*); (*of pests*) Kammerjäger *m*; (*poison etc*) Vernichtungsmittel *nt*.

external [ekˈstɜːnl] 1 *adj wall* äußere(r, s), Außen-; *factors, help* extern ◆ **for ~ use only** (*Med*) nur äußerlich (anzuwenden); **~ examiner** (*Brit Univ*) externer Prüfer; **~ degree** Fernstudium *nt*; **he has an ~ degree in Maths** er

➤ LANGUAGE IN USE: **express: 1a** → 6.3, 24.2, 26.3 **extend: 1d** → 22 **extension: c** → 27.4, 27.5, 27.7

hat ein Fernstudium in Mathematik abgeschlossen; **the ~ world** (*Philos*) die Außenwelt *or* äußere Welt; **~ device** (*Comput*) Fremdgerät *nt*; **~ financing** Fremdfinanzierung *f*; **~ trade** Außenhandel *m*; **this is ~ to our present enquiry** das liegt außerhalb des Bereichs unserer momentanen Untersuchung.
[2] *n* (*fig*) **~s** *pl* Äußerlichkeiten *pl*.

externalize [ek'stɜːnəlaɪz] *vt* externalisieren.

externally [ek'stɜːnəlɪ] *adv* äußerlich ◆ **he remained ~ calm** er blieb äußerlich ruhig; **some of the work is done ~** ein Teil der Arbeit wird außer Haus erledigt.

extinct [ɪk'stɪŋkt] *adj volcano, love* erloschen; *species* ausgestorben ◆ **to become ~** aussterben; *volcano* erlöschen.

extinction [ɪk'stɪŋkʃən] *n* (*of fire*) Löschen *nt*; (*of race, family*) Aussterben *nt*; (*annihilation*) Auslöschung, Vernichtung *f*.

extinguish [ɪk'stɪŋgwɪʃ] *vt fire, candle* (aus)löschen; *light* löschen; *hopes, passion* zerstören; *debt* tilgen.

extinguisher [ɪk'stɪŋgwɪʃəʳ] *n* Feuerlöscher *m*, Löschgerät *nt*.

extirpate ['ekstɜːpeɪt] *vt* (*lit, fig*) (mit der Wurzel) ausrotten, (gänzlich) beseitigen.

extirpation [,ekstə'peɪʃən] *n* (*lit, fig*) Ausrottung *f*.

extol [ɪk'stəʊl] *vt* preisen, rühmen.

extort [ɪk'stɔːt] *vt money* erpressen (*from* von); *confession also* erzwingen (*from* von); *secret* abpressen (*from dat*).

extortion [ɪk'stɔːʃən] *n* (*of money*) Erpressung *f*; (*of signature*) Erzwingung *f* ◆ **this is sheer ~!** (*inf*) das ist ja Wucher!

extortionate [ɪk'stɔːʃənɪt] *adj prices* Wucher-; *tax, demand* ungeheuer.

extortioner [ɪk'stɔːʃənəʳ] *n* Erpresser(in *f*) *m*; (*charging high prices*) Wucherer(in *f*) *m*.

extra ['ekstrə] [1] *adj* **(a)** (*additional*) zusätzlich; *bus* Einsatz-, zusätzlich ◆ **we need an ~ chair** wir brauchen noch einen Stuhl; **to work ~ hours** Überstunden machen; **to make an ~ effort** sich besonders anstrengen; **I have had ~ work this week** ich habe in dieser Woche zusätzliche Arbeit gehabt; **to order an ~ helping** eine zusätzliche Portion *or* eine Portion extra bestellen; **~ charge** Zuschlag *m*; **to make an ~ charge** Zuschlag berechnen; **there is an ~ charge for wine** der Wein wird extra berechnet; **there will be no ~ charge** das wird nicht extra berechnet; **for ~ whiteness** für ein strahlendes Weiß; **~ time** (*Brit Ftbl*) Verlängerung *f*; **we had to play ~ time** es gab eine Verlängerung, es wurde nachgespielt; **~ pay** eine Zulage; **for ~ safety** zur größeren Sicherheit; **we need an ~ 10 minutes** wir brauchen 10 Minuten mehr *or* extra; **could you give me an ~ £3?** könnten Sie mir £ 3 mehr *or* extra geben?; **I have set an ~ place at the table** ich habe ein Gedeck mehr *or* extra aufgelegt.
(b) (*spare*) Reserve-, übrig ◆ **I bought a few ~ tins** ich habe ein paar Dosen mehr *or* extra gekauft; **I have brought an ~ pair of shoes** ich habe ein Paar Schuhe extra mitgebracht; **these copies are ~** diese Exemplare sind übrig; **are there any ~ helpings?** gibt es Nachschlag? (*inf*), kann man noch eine Portion haben?; **go and get some ~ potatoes from the kitchen** hol noch ein paar Kartoffeln aus der Küche.
[2] *adv* **(a)** (*especially*) extra, besonders ◆ **she was ~ kind that day** sie war besonders freundlich an diesem Tag.
(b) (*in addition*) extra ◆ **postage and packing ~** zuzüglich Porto- und Versandkosten; **the wine is ~** der Wein wird extra berechnet.
(c) (*inf: more*) **to work ~** länger arbeiten.
[3] *n* **(a)** (*perk*) Zusatzleistung *f*; (*for car*) Extra *nt* ◆ **they regard it as an ~** sie betrachten es als Luxus; **singing and piano are (optional) ~s** Gesang- und Klavierunterricht sind Wahl- *or* Zusatzfächer *pl*.
(b) **~s** *pl* (*~ expenses*) zusätzliche Kosten *pl*, Nebenkosten *pl*; (*in restaurant*) Zusätzliches *nt*; (*food*) Beilagen *pl*.
(c) (*Film, Theat*) Statist(in *f*), Komparse *m*, Komparsin *f*.
(d) (*remainder*) **what shall we do with the ~?** was sollen wir mit dem Rest machen?

extra- *pref* **(a)** (*outside*) außer-; (*esp with foreign words*) extra-.
(b) (*especially*) besonders, extra ◆ **~dry** *wine* herb; *champagne* extra dry; **~fine** besonders fein, extrafein; **~smart** besonders schick, todschick (*inf*); *see also* **extra 2 (a)**.

extract [ɪk'strækt] [1] *vt* **(a)** herausnehmen; *cork etc* (heraus)ziehen (*from* aus); *juice, minerals, oil* gewinnen (*from* aus); *tooth also* ziehen, extrahieren (*spec*); *bullet, foreign body also* entfernen ◆ **she ~ed herself from his arms** sie befreite sich aus seinen Armen.
(b) (*fig*) *information, secrets, confession, money* herausholen (*from* aus); *permission also, promise* abringen, abnehmen, entlocken (*from dat*); *the meaning, moral of a book also* herausarbeiten (*from* aus) ◆ **to ~ sounds from an instrument** einem Instrument Töne entlocken.
(c) (*Math*) *square root* ziehen.
(d) *quotation, passage* herausziehen, exzerpieren (*geh*).
[2] ['ekstrækt] *n* **(a)** (*from book etc*) Auszug *m*, Exzerpt *nt*. **(b)** (*Med, Cook*) Extrakt *m* ◆ **beef ~** Fleischextrakt *m*.

extraction [ɪk'strækʃən] *n* **(a)** *see vt* Herausnehmen *nt*; (Heraus)ziehen *nt*; Gewinnung *f*, (Zahn)ziehen *nt*, Extraktion *f* (*spec*); Entfernung *f*, Herausholen *nt*; Abnahme, Entlockung *f*, Herausarbeiten *nt*; Wurzelziehen *nt* ◆ **he had to have three ~s** ihm mußten drei Zähne gezogen werden.
(b) (*descent*) Herkunft, Abstammung *f* ◆ **of Spanish ~** spanischer Herkunft *or* Abstammung.

extractor [ɪk'stræktəʳ] *n* (*for juice*) Presse *f*, Entsafter *m*; (*for dust*) Sauganlage *f*; (*of gun*) Auszieher *m* ◆ **~ fan** Sauglüfter *m*.

extracurricular ['ekstrəkə'rɪkjʊləʳ] *adj* außerhalb des Stundenplans.

extraditable ['ekstrədaɪtəbl] *adj offence* auslieferungsfähig; *person* auszuliefern *pred*, auszuliefernd *attr*.

extradite ['ekstrədaɪt] *vt* ausliefern.

extradition [,ekstrə'dɪʃən] *n* Auslieferung *f* ◆ **~ order** (*request*) Auslieferungsantrag *m*; **~ treaty** Auslieferungsvertrag *m*.

extramarital ['ekstrə'mærɪtl] *adj* außerehelich.

extramural ['ekstrə'mjʊərəl] *adj courses* Volkshochschul-.

extraneous [ɪk'streɪnɪəs] *adj* **(a)** (*from outside*) *influence* von außen (her), extern. **(b)** (*unrelated*) **~ to** irrelevant für, ohne Beziehung zu. **(c)** (*not essential*) *detail* unwesentlich.

extraordinarily [ɪk'strɔːdnrɪlɪ] *adv* außerordentlich; *rude also* höchst ◆ **how ~ odd!** wie überaus seltsam!

extraordinary [ɪk'strɔːdnrɪ] *adj* **(a)** (*beyond what is common*) außerordentlich; (*not usual*) ungewöhnlich ◆ **there's nothing ~ about that** daran ist gar nichts Ungewöhnliches.
(b) (*odd, peculiar*) sonderbar, seltsam ◆ **it's ~ to think that ...** es ist (schon) seltsam *or* sonderbar, wenn man denkt, daß ...; **you are a most ~ person!** du bist wirklich sonderbar *or* seltsam!; **the ~ fact is that he succeeded** das Merkwürdige an der Sache ist, daß er Erfolg hatte; **it's ~ how much he resembles his brother** es ist erstaunlich, wie sehr er seinem Bruder ähnelt; **how ~!** ist das nicht seltsam!
(c) (*specially employed or arranged*) Sonder- ◆ **envoy ~** Sonderbeauftragter *m*; **an ~ meeting** eine Sondersitzung; **~ general meeting** außerordentliche Hauptversammlung.

extrapolate [ek'stræpəleɪt] *vti* extrapolieren (*from* aus).

extrapolation [ek,stræpə'leɪʃən] *n* Extrapolation *f*.

extrasensory ['ekstrə'sensərɪ] *adj* außersinnlich ◆ **~ perception** außersinnliche Wahrnehmung.

extra-special ['ekstrə'speʃəl] *adj* ganz besondere(r, s) ◆ **to take ~ care over sth** sich (*dat*) besonders viel Mühe mit etw geben; **~ occasion** ganz besondere Gelegenheit; **to make something ~ to eat** etwas ganz Besonderes zu essen machen.

extraterrestrial ['ekstrətɪ'restrɪəl] [1] *adj* außerirdisch, extraterrestrisch.
[2] *n* außerirdisches Lebewesen.

extraterritorial ['ekstrə,terɪ'tɔːrɪəl] *adj* exterritorial.

extravagance [ɪk'strævəgəns] *n* **(a)** Luxus *m no pl* ◆ **her ~** ihre Verschwendungssucht; **if you can't forgive her occasional ~s** wenn Sie es ihr nicht verzeihen können, daß sie sich ab und zu einen Luxus leistet; **the ~ of her tastes** ihr kostspieliger *or* teurer Geschmack; **a life of such ~** ein derart luxuriöser Lebensstil; **the ~ of this big wedding** der Aufwand einer solch großen Hochzeitsfeier.
(b) (*wastefulness*) Verschwendung *f*.
(c) (*of ideas, theories*) Extravaganz, Ausgefallenheit *f*; (*of claim, demand*) Übertriebenheit *f*.
(d) (*extravagant action or notion*) Extravaganz *f* ◆ **the ~s of a Nero** die Extravaganzen eines Nero.

extravagant [ɪk'strævəgənt] *adj* **(a)** (*with money*) *taste, habit* teuer, kostspielig; *wedding, lifestyle* aufwendig, luxuriös; *price* überhöht ◆ **she is ~** sie gibt das Geld mit vollen Händen aus; **it was very ~ of him to buy me this bracelet** es war gar zu großzügig, daß er mir dieses Armband gekauft hat; **isn't it rather ~ to have two cars?** ist das nicht ein Luxus, zwei Autos zu haben?; **I'll be ~ and treat myself to a new coat** ich leiste mir den Luxus und kaufe mir einen neuen Mantel; **go on, be ~** gönn dir doch den Luxus.
(b) (*wasteful: in consumption etc*) verschwenderisch.
(c) *behaviour* extravagant; *ideas, theories, tie, pattern also* ausgefallen; *claim, demand* übertrieben ◆ **he was given to indulging in rather ~ talk** er neigte dazu, lose Reden zu führen; **it would be ~ of me to claim that ...** es wäre eine Anmaßung, wenn ich behauptete, daß ...

extravagantly [ɪk'strævəgəntlɪ] *adv* **(a)** (*lavishly, with much expense*) *furnished* luxuriös; *spend* mit vollen Händen; *live* auf großem Fuß, luxuriös ◆ **I rather ~ bought myself a gold watch** ich habe mir den Luxus einer goldenen Uhr geleistet.
(b) (*wastefully*) *use, consume etc* verschwenderisch.
(c) (*excessively, flamboyantly*) *furnish, dress* extravagant; *praise, act* überschwenglich; *demand, claim* übertrieben ◆ **to talk ~** lose Reden führen.

extravaganza [ɪk,strævə'gænzə] *n* phantastische Dichtung *or* (*Mus*) Komposition; (*show*) Ausstattungsstück *nt*.

extravehicular [,ekstrəviː'hɪkjʊləʳ] *adj* (*Space*) außerhalb des Raumfahrzeugs.

extreme [ɪk'striːm] [1] *adj* **(a)** (*furthest off*) *limit* äußerste(r, s) ◆ **to the ~ right** ganz rechts; **at the ~ left of the photograph** ganz links im Bild; **at the ~ end of the path** ganz am Ende des Weges; **the ~ opposite** genau das Gegenteil; **they are ~ opposites** sie sind Extreme, sie sind völlig gegensätzliche Charaktere.
(b) (*of the highest degree*) *courage, pleasure, kindness, simplicity* äußerste(r, s); *rudeness also* maßlos, extrem; *urgency also* extrem; *penalty* höchste(r, s) ◆ **with ~ pleasure** mit größtem Vergnügen; **~ old age** ein äußerst hohes Alter; **in ~ danger** in größter *or* höchster Gefahr; **the most ~ poverty** die bitterste *or* größte Armut; **an ~ case** ein Extremfall *m*.
(c) (*exaggerated, drastic, Pol*) extrem; *praise, flattery* übertrieben; *exaggeration, demands* maßlos ◆ **to be ~ in one's opinions** extreme Ansichten haben; **he was rather ~ in his praise** er hat bei seinem Lob ziemlich übertrieben; **the ~ right/left** (*Pol*) die äußerste *or* extreme Rechte/Linke; *see* **unction**.
[2] *n* Extrem *nt* ◆ **the ~s of happiness and despair** höchstes Glück und tiefste

Verzweiflung; **between these two ~s** zwischen diesen beiden Extremen; **~s of temperature** extreme Temperaturen *pl*; **in the ~** im höchsten Grade; **it is bewildering in the ~** es ist höchst *or* im höchsten Grade verwirrend; **to go from one ~ to the other** von einem Extrem ins andere fallen; **to go to ~s** es übertreiben; **I wouldn't go to that ~** so weit würde ich nicht gehen; **to drive sb to ~s** jdn zum Äußersten treiben.

extremely [ɪk'stri:mlɪ] *adv* äußerst, höchst, extrem ◆ **was it difficult? — ~** war es schwierig? — sehr!

extremism [ɪk'stri:mɪzəm] *n* Extremismus *m*.

extremist [ɪk'stri:mɪst] [1] *adj view, opinion* extremistisch.
[2] *n* Extremist(in *f*) *m*.

extremity [ɪk'stremɪtɪ] *n* **(a)** (*furthest point*) äußerstes Ende ◆ **at the northernmost ~ of the continent** am nördlichsten Zipfel des Kontinents.
(b) (*extreme degree*) **in the ~ of his despair** in tiefster *or* äußerster Verzweiflung; **the ~ to which he had taken the theory** die Entwicklung der Theorie bis zu ihrem Extrem.
(c) (*state of need, distress*) Not *f* ◆ **to help sb in his ~** jdm in seiner Not helfen; **to be reduced to a sad ~** sich in einer Notlage befinden; **I haven't yet been reduced to that ~** es ist noch nicht so weit mit mir gekommen; **he was reduced to the ~ of having to sell his business** er mußte zum äußersten Mittel schreiten und sein Geschäft verkaufen.
(d) (*extreme actions*) **to resort to extremities** zu äußersten *or* extremen Mitteln greifen; **to drive sb to extremities** jdn zum Äußersten treiben.
(e) extremities *pl* (*hands and feet*) Extremitäten *pl*.

extricate ['ekstrɪkeɪt] *vt object* befreien ◆ **to ~ oneself from sth** sich aus etw befreien.

extrinsic [ek'strɪnsɪk] *adj value, qualities* äußerlich; *considerations* nicht hereinspielend ◆ **considerations ~ to the argument** Überlegungen, die in keinem direkten Zusammenhang mit der Frage stehen.

extroversion [ˌekstrəʊ'vɜ:ʃən] *n* Extravertiertheit *f*.

extrovert ['ekstrəʊvɜ:t] [1] *adj* extravertiert.
[2] *n* extravertierter Mensch, Extravertierte(r) *mf*.

extrude [ɪk'stru:d] [1] *vt sb, sth* ausstoßen; *metal* herauspressen; *plastic* extrudieren.
[2] *vi* herausstehen (*from* aus) ◆ **this bit of land ~s into our territory** dieses Stückchen Land ragt in unser Gebiet.

extrusion [ɪk'stru:ʒən] *n* (*Tech*) (*of metal*) Fließpressen *nt*; (*of plastic*) Extrudieren *nt*.

exuberance [ɪg'zu:bərəns] *n* **(a)** (*of person*) Überschwenglichkeit *f*; (*of joy, youth, feelings*) Überschwang *m*; (*joy*) überschwengliche Freude (*at* über +*acc*) ◆ **in his ~** (*rejoicing*) in seiner überschwenglichen Freude, im Überschwang der Gefühle; **in their youthful ~** (*high spirits*) in ihrem jugendlichen Überschwang.
(b) (*vitality: of prose, style*) Vitalität *f*.
(c) (*abundance*) Fülle *f*, Reichtum *m*.

exuberant [ɪg'zu:bərənt] *adj* überschwenglich; *imagination* übersprudelnd; *style* übersprudelnd, vital; *painting, colour* lebendig; *music, melody* mitreißend ◆ **they were ~ after their victory** nach ihrem Sieg waren sie in Jubelstimmung.

exude [ɪg'zju:d] [1] *vi* (*liquid*) austreten (*from* aus); (*blood, pus etc*) abgesondert werden (*from* von).
[2] *vt* **(a)** (*liquid*) ausscheiden; *dampness, sap also* ausschwitzen. **(b)** (*fig: radiate*) *confidence* ausstrahlen; (*pej*) *charm* triefen vor.

exult [ɪg'zʌlt] *vi* frohlocken ◆ **~ing at his own success** über seinen eigenen Erfolg jubelnd.

exultant [ɪg'zʌltənt] *adj* jubelnd; *shout also* Jubel- ◆ **to be ~, to be in an ~ mood** jubeln, in Jubelstimmung sein; **I had never seen her so ~** ich hatte sie noch nie in solcher Jubelstimmung gesehen; **exhausted but ~** erschöpft, aber triumphierend.

exultation [ˌegzʌl'teɪʃən] *n* Jubel *m* ◆ **sing in ~** (*Rel*) jauchzet und frohlocket; **their ~ at finding it** ihr Jubel, als sie es fanden.

eye [aɪ] [1] *n* **(a)** (*of human, animal, electronic*) Auge *nt* ◆ **with tears in her ~s** mit Tränen in den Augen; **with one's ~s closed/open** mit geschlossenen/offenen Augen; (*fig*) blind/mit offenen Augen; **an ~ for an ~** Auge um Auge; **~s right!** (*Mil*) (die) Augen rechts!; **~s front!** (*Mil*) Augen geradeaus!; **to be all ~s** große Augen machen; **they were all ~s watching the magician** sie beobachteten den Zauberer mit großen Augen; **that's one in the ~ for him** (*inf*) da hat er eins aufs Dach gekriegt (*inf*); **to do sb in the ~** (*inf*) jdn übers Ohr hauen (*inf*); **to cast** *or* **run one's ~s over sth** etw überfliegen; **to cast one's ~s round a room** seine Blicke durch ein Zimmer wandern *or* schweifen lassen; **his ~ fell on a small door** sein Blick fiel auf eine kleine Tür; **to let one's ~ rest on sth** seine Augen *or* den Blick auf etw (*dat*) ruhen lassen; **to look sb (straight) in the ~** jdm in die Augen sehen; **to set** *or* **clap** (*inf*) **~s on sb/sth** jdn/etw zu Gesicht bekommen; **to have a keen ~** ein scharfes Auge haben, einen scharfen Blick haben; **a strange sight met our ~s** ein seltsamer Anblick bot sich uns; **(why don't you) use your ~s!** hast du keine Augen im Kopf?; **with one's own ~s** mit eigenen Augen; **before my very ~s** (direkt) vor meinen Augen; **it was there all the time right in front of my ~s** es lag schon die ganze Zeit da, direkt vor meiner Nase; **under the watchful ~ of the guard/their mother** unter der Aufsicht des Wächters/ihrer Mutter; **your ~s are bigger than your stomach** deine Augen sind größer als dein Magen; **you need ~s in the back of your head** da muß man hinten und vorne Augen haben; **I don't have ~s in the back of my head** ich hab doch hinten keine Augen; **to keep an ~ on sb/sth** (*look after*) auf jdn/etw aufpassen; **the police are keeping an ~ on him** (*have him under surveillance*) die Polizei beobachtet ihn; **to keep one's ~ on the ball/main objective** sich auf den Ball/die Hauptsache konzentrieren; **to have one's ~s fixed on sth** etw nicht aus den Augen lassen; **never to take one's ~s off sb/sth** kein Auge von jdm/etw wenden; **to keep one's ~s open** *or* **peeled** (*inf*) *or* **skinned** (*inf*) die Augen offenhalten; **to keep an ~ open** *or* **out for a hotel** nach einem Hotel Ausschau halten; **to keep a watchful ~ on the situation** die Sache im Auge behalten; **to keep an ~ on expenditure** auf seine Ausgaben achten *or* aufpassen; **to open sb's ~s to sb/sth** jdm die Augen über jdn/etw öffnen; **to close one's ~s to sth** die Augen vor etw (*dat*) verschließen; **to see ~ to ~ with sb** mit jdm einer Meinung sein; **to make ~s at sb** jdm schöne Augen machen; **to catch sb's ~** jds Aufmerksamkeit erregen; **that colour caught my ~** die Farbe fiel *or* stach mir ins Auge; **she would buy anything that caught her ~** sie kaufte alles, was ihr ins Auge fiel; **he was a monster in their ~s** in ihren Augen war er ein Scheusal; **through somebody else's ~s** mit den Augen eines anderen; **to look at a question through the ~s of an economist** eine Frage mit den Augen *or* aus der Sicht eines Volkswirts betrachten; **in the ~s of the law** in den Augen des Gesetzes; **with a critical/an uneasy ~** mit kritischem/besorgtem Blick; **with an ~ to the future** im Hinblick auf die Zukunft; **with an ~ to buying sth** in der Absicht, etw zu kaufen; **to have an ~ to** *or* **for the main chance** jede Gelegenheit ausnutzen; **to take one's ~s off sb/sth** die Augen *or* den Blick von jdm/etw abwenden; **take your ~s off that woman!** starr die Frau nicht so an!; **he couldn't take his ~s off her/the cake** er konnte einfach den Blick nicht von ihr/dem Kuchen lassen; **don't take your ~ off the ball** konzentrier dich auf den Ball; **have you got your ~ on the ball all the time you're playing?** konzentrierst du dich auch während des ganzen Spiels auf den Ball?; **don't take your ~s off the magician's left hand** lassen Sie die linke Hand des Zauberkünstlers nicht aus den Augen; **just watch it, my boy, I've got my ~ on you** paß bloß auf, mein Freund, ich beobachte dich genau; **to have one's ~ on sth** (*want*) auf etw (*acc*) ein Auge geworfen haben; **to have an ~ on sb for a job** jdn für eine Stelle im Auge haben; **I only have ~s for you** ich habe nur Augen für dich; **she has an ~ for a bargain** sie hat einen Blick *or* ein Auge für günstige Käufe; **he has no ~ for beauty** ihm fehlt der Blick für Schönheit; **he has a good ~ for colour/form** er hat ein Auge für Farbe/Form; **you need an ~ for detail** man muß einen Blick fürs Detail haben; **to get one's ~ in** (*shooting*) sich einschießen; (*playing tennis etc*) sich einspielen; **to be up to the ~s in work** (*inf*) in Arbeit ersticken (*inf*); **he's in it up to the ~s** (*inf*) er steckt bis zum Hals drin (*inf*); **my ~!** (*inf*) Unsinn!; **that's all my ~** (*inf*) das ist doch alles Gewäsch (*inf*).
(b) (*of needle*) Öhr *nt*; (*of potato, on peacock's tail*) Auge *nt*; (*of hurricane*) Auge *nt* ◆ **in the ~ of the wind** (*Naut*) in *or* gegen den Wind; *see* **hook and eye**.
[2] *vt* anstarren ◆ **to ~ sb up and down** jdn von oben bis unten mustern.

◆**eye up** *vt sep girls, boys* mustern, begutachten.

eye *in cpds* Augen-; **~ball** *n* Augapfel *m*; **to be/meet ~ball to ~ball** sich direkt gegenüberstehen; **drugged up to the ~balls** (*inf*) total high (*inf*); **~bath** *n* Augenbad *nt*; (*container*) Augenbadewanne *f*; **~brow** *n* Augenbraue *f*; **to raise one's ~brows** die Augenbrauen hochziehen; **he never raised an ~brow** er hat sich nicht einmal gewundert; **that will raise a few ~brows, there will be a few raised ~brows (at that)** da werden sich einige wundern; **~brow pencil** *n* Augenbrauenstift *m*; **~catcher** *n* (*thing*) Blickfang *m*; **she's quite an ~catcher** sie zieht alle Blicke auf sich; **~catching** *adj* auffallend; *publicity, poster also* auffällig, ins Auge springend *or* stechend; **that's rather ~catching** das fällt *or* springt ins Auge; **~ contact** *n* Blickkontakt *m*; **I wasn't getting any ~ contact from her** es kam zu keinem Blickkontakt zwischen ihr und mir; **~-cup** *n* (*US*) Augenbadewanne *f*.

-eyed [-aɪd] *adj suf* -äugig ◆ **green-~** grünäugig; **sad-~** mit traurigen Augen.

eye drops ['aɪdrɒps] *npl* Augentropfen *pl*.

eyeful ['aɪfʊl] *n* **he got an ~ of soda water** er bekam Selterswasser ins Auge; **she's quite an ~** (*inf*) sie hat allerhand zu bieten (*inf*); **I opened the bathroom door and got quite an ~** ich öffnete die Badezimmertür und sah allerhand (*inf*).

eye: ~glass *n* (*old*) Augenglas *nt* (*old*); **~ glasses** *npl* (*US: spectacles*) Brille *f*; **~lash** *n* Augenwimper *f*; **~let** ['aɪlɪt] *n* Öse *f*; **~-level** *adj attr grill* in Augenhöhe; **~lid** *n* Augenlid *nt*; **~ liner** *n* Eyeliner *m*; **~-opener** *n* **(a) that was a real ~-opener to me** das hat mir die Augen geöffnet; **(b)** (*US inf: drink*) (alkoholischer) Muntermacher; **~ patch** *n* Augenklappe *f*; **~piece** *n* Okular *nt*; **~shade** *n* Augenblende *f*, Schild *m*; **~shadow** *n* Lidschatten *m*; **~sight** *n* Sehkraft *f*, Sehvermögen *nt*; **to have good ~sight** gute Augen haben; **to lose one's ~sight** das Augenlicht verlieren (*geh*), erblinden; **his ~sight is failing** seine Augen lassen nach, sein Sehvermögen läßt nach; **~sore** *n* Schandfleck *m*; **this carpet is a real ~sore** dieser Teppich sieht fürchterlich aus; **~strain** *n* Überanstrengung *or* Ermüdung *f* der Augen; **~ test** *n* Augentest *m or* -untersuchung *f*.

Eyetie ['aɪtaɪ] *n* (*sl*) Spaghettifresser (*pej inf*), Itaker (*pej sl*) *m*.

eye: ~ tooth *n* Eckzahn, Augenzahn *m*; **I'd give my ~ teeth for that** darum würde ich alles geben; **~wash** *n* (*Med*) Augenwasser *or* -bad *nt*; (*fig inf*) Gewäsch *nt* (*inf*); (*deception*) Augenwischerei *f*; **~witness** *n* Augenzeuge *m*.

eyrie ['ɪərɪ] *n* Horst *m*.

Ezekiel [ɪ'zi:kɪəl] *n* (*Bibl*) Hesekiel, Ezechiel *m*.

F, f [ef] *n* F, f *nt* ◆ **~ sharp/flat** Fis, fis *nt*/Fes, fes *nt*; *see also* **major, minor, natural.**

F *abbr of* **Fahrenheit** F.

f *abbr of* **(a) foot, feet. (b) feminine** f.

FA *abbr of* **Football Association.**

fa [fɑː] *n* (*Mus*) Fa *nt*.

fab [fæb] *adj* (*dated sl*) *abbr of* **fabulous** toll (*inf*), dufte (*inf*).

fable ['feɪbl] *n* Fabel *f*; (*legend, body of legend*) Sage *f*; (*fig: lie*) Märchen *nt* ◆ **to sort out fact from ~** Dichtung und Wahrheit unterscheiden.

fabled ['feɪbld] *adj* sagenhaft ◆ **Cleopatra, ~ for her beauty** Kleopatra, berühmt für ihre Schönheit.

fabric ['fæbrɪk] *n* **(a)** (*Tex*) Stoff *m*. **(b)** (*basic structure*) **the ~ of the building/church was quite sound** das Gebäude/Kirchengebäude als solches war ganz gut. **(c)** (*fig: of society etc*) Gefüge *nt*, Struktur *f*.

fabricate ['fæbrɪkeɪt] *vt* **(a)** (*invent*) *story* erfinden, ersinnen (*geh*). **(b)** (*manufacture*) herstellen, fabrizieren.

fabrication [,fæbrɪ'keɪʃən] *n* **(a)** (*act of inventing*) Erfindung *f*; (*story invented also*) Lügengeschichte *f*, Lügenmärchen *nt* ◆ **it's (a) pure ~** das ist ein reines Märchen *or* (eine) reine Erfindung. **(b)** (*manufacture*) Herstellung, Fabrikation *f*.

Fabrikoid ® ['fæbrɪkɔɪd] *n* (*US*) Kunstleder, Skai ® *nt*.

fabulous ['fæbjʊləs] *adj* sagenhaft; (*inf: wonderful also*) toll (*inf*), fabelhaft.

fabulously ['fæbjʊləslɪ] *adv* sagenhaft.

façade [fə'sɑːd] *n* (*lit, fig*) Fassade *f*.

face [feɪs] **1** *n* **(a)** Gesicht *nt* ◆ **I don't want to see your ~ here again** ich möchte Sie hier nie wieder sehen; **we were standing ~ to ~** wir standen einander Auge in Auge *or* von Angesicht zu Angesicht (*geh*) gegenüber; **next time I see him ~ to ~** das nächste Mal, wenn ich ihm begegne; **to bring two people ~ to ~** zwei Leute einander gegenüberstellen *or* miteinander konfrontieren; **to come ~ to ~ with sb/one's Maker/death** jdn treffen/Gott von Angesicht zu Angesicht sehen/dem Tod ins Auge sehen; **he told him so to his ~** er sagte ihm das (offen) ins Gesicht; **he shut the door in my ~** er schlug mir die Tür vor der Nase zu; **he laughed in my ~** er lachte mir ins Gesicht; **to look/be able to look sb in the ~** jdn ansehen/jdm in die Augen sehen können; **to fling** *or* **throw a remark back in sb's ~** jdm seine eigene Bemerkung wieder auftischen; **in the ~ of great difficulties/much opposition** *etc* angesichts *or* (*despite*) trotz größter Schwierigkeiten/starker Opposition *etc*; **courage in the ~ of the enemy** Tapferkeit vor dem Feind; *see* **flat[1]**.
(b) (*expression*) Gesicht(sausdruck *m*) *nt* ◆ **to make** *or* **pull a ~** das Gesicht verziehen; **to make** *or* **pull ~s/a funny ~** Gesichter *or* Grimassen/eine Grimasse machen *or* schneiden (*at sb* jdm); **to put a good ~ on it** gute Miene zum bösen Spiel machen; **to put a brave ~ on it** sich (*dat*) nichts anmerken lassen; (*do sth one dislikes*) (wohl oder übel) in den sauren Apfel beißen; **he has set his ~ against that** er stemmt sich dagegen.
(c) (*prestige*) **loss of ~** Gesichtsverlust *m*; **to save (one's)/lose ~** das Gesicht wahren/verlieren.
(d) (*of clock*) Zifferblatt *nt*; (*rock ~*) (Steil)wand *f*; (*coal~*) Streb *m*; (*type~*) Schriftart *f*; (*of playing card*) Bildseite *f*; (*of coin*) Vorderseite *f*; (*of house*) Fassade *f* ◆ **to put sth ~ up(wards)/down(wards)** etw mit der Vorderseite nach oben/unten legen; **to be ~ up(wards)/down(wards)** (*person*) mit dem Gesicht nach oben/unten liegen; (*thing*) mit der Vorderseite nach oben/unten liegen; (*book*) mit der aufgeschlagenen Seite nach oben/unten liegen; **to work at the (coal)~** vor Ort arbeiten; **to change the ~ of a town** das Gesicht *or* Aussehen einer Stadt verändern; **he/it vanished off the ~ of the earth** (*inf*) er/es war wie vom Erdboden verschwunden; **on the ~ of it** so, wie es aussieht.
(e) (*inf: effrontery*) **to have the ~ to do sth** die Stirn haben, etw zu tun.
2 *vt* **(a)** (*be opposite, have one's face towards*) gegenübersein/-stehen/-liegen *etc* (*+dat*); (*window, door*) *north, south* gehen nach; *street, garden etc* liegen zu; (*building, room*) *north, south* liegen nach; *park, street* liegen zu ◆ **to ~ the wall/light** zur Wand gekehrt/dem Licht zugekehrt sein; (*person*) mit dem Gesicht zur Wand/zum Licht stehen/sitzen *etc*; **sit down and ~ the front!** setz dich und sieh nach vorn!; **~ this way!** bitte sehen Sie hierher!; **he was facing me at dinner** er saß mir beim Essen gegenüber; **the picture/wall facing you** das Bild/die Wand Ihnen gegenüber; **facing one another** einander gegenüber; **the picture facing page 16** die Abbildung gegenüber Seite 16; **to sit facing the engine/front of the bus** in Fahrtrichtung sitzen.
(b) (*fig*) *possibility, prospect* rechnen müssen mit ◆ **to be ~d with sth** sich einer Sache (*dat*) gegenübersehen; **the problem facing us** das Problem, dem wir gegenüberstehen *or* mit dem wir konfrontiert sind; **you'll ~ a lot of criticism if you do that** Sie setzen sich großer Kritik aus, wenn Sie das tun; **to be ~d with a bill for £100** eine Rechnung über £ 100 präsentiert bekommen; **he is facing/will ~ a charge of murder** er steht unter Mordanklage, er ist/wird wegen Mordes angeklagt.
(c) (*meet confidently*) *situation, danger, criticism* sich stellen (*+dat*); *person, enemy* gegenübertreten (*+dat*) ◆ **he ~d defeat bravely** er hat sich tapfer mit der Niederlage abgefunden; **to ~ (the) facts** den Tatsachen ins Auge blicken *or* sehen; **let's ~ it** machen wir uns doch nichts vor; **you'd better ~ it, you're not going to get it** du mußt dich wohl damit abfinden, daß du das nicht bekommst; **why don't you ~ it, ...** mach dir doch nichts vor, ...
(d) (*inf: put up with, bear*) verkraften (*inf*); *another drink, cake etc* runterkriegen (*inf*) ◆ **to ~ doing sth** es fertigbringen (*inf*) *or* es über sich (*acc*) bringen, etw zu tun; **I can't ~ it** (*inf*) ich bringe es einfach nicht über mich.
(e) *building, wall* verblenden, verkleiden; (*Sew*) *garment* (mit Besatz) verstürzen.
(f) (*Cards*) aufdecken.
(g) *stone* glätten, (plan) schleifen.
3 *vi* (*house, room*) liegen (*towards park* dem Park zu, *onto road* zur Straße, *away from road* nicht zur Straße); (*window*) gehen (*onto, towards* auf *+acc*, zu, *away from* nicht auf *+acc*) ◆ **he was sitting facing away from me** er saß mit dem Rücken zu mir; **they were all facing towards the window** sie saßen alle mit dem Gesicht zum Fenster (hin); **the house ~s away from the sea** das Haus liegt nicht aufs Meer zu; **in which direction was he facing?** in welche Richtung stand er?; **you've parked facing in the wrong direction** Sie haben in der falschen Richtung geparkt; **the side of the house that ~s onto the road** die der Straße zugekehrte Seite des Hauses; **why was the house built facing away from the park?** warum wurde das Haus nicht mit Blick auf den Park gebaut?; **right ~!** (*Mil*) rechts um!

◆**face about** *vi* (*US Mil*) kehrtmachen.

◆**face out** *vt sep* durchstehen.

◆**face up to** *vi +prep obj fact, truth* ins Gesicht sehen (*+dat*); *danger* ins Auge sehen *or* blicken (*+dat*); *possibility* sich abfinden mit; *responsibility* auf sich (*acc*) nehmen ◆ **he won't ~ ~ ~ the fact that ...** er will es nicht wahrhaben, daß ...

face *in cpds* Gesichts-; **~ card** *n* Bild(er)karte *f*; **~cloth** *n* Waschlappen *m*; **~ cream** *n* Gesichtscreme *f*; **~ guard** *n* Schutzmaske *f*; **~less** *adj drawing* gesichtslos; (*fig*) anonym; **~lift** *n* (*lit*) Gesichts(haut)straffung *f*, Facelift(ing) *nt*; (*fig: for car, building etc*) Verschönerung *f*; **to have a ~lift** sich (*dat*) das Gesicht liften *or* straffen lassen; (*fig*) ein neues Aussehen bekommen; **to give the house a ~lift** das Haus renovieren, das Haus einer Verschönerungsaktion unterziehen; **~-off** *n* **(a)** (*US: confrontation*) Konfrontation *f*; **(b)** (*Ice-hockey*) Bully *nt*; **~ pack** *n* Gesichtspackung *f*; **~ powder** *n* Gesichtspuder *m*.

facer ['feɪsə^r] *n* (*Brit inf: difficulty*) harte Nuß (*inf*).

face: ~-saver *n* Ausrede *f*, um das Gesicht zu wahren; **~-saving** *adj* **a ~-saving excuse/remark/tactic** eine Entschuldigung/Bemerkung/Taktik, um das Gesicht zu wahren.

facet ['fæsɪt] *n* (*lit*) Facette *f*; (*fig*) Seite *f*, Aspekt *m*.

faceted ['fæsɪtɪd] *adj* (*Zool*) Facetten-; (*Miner also*) facettiert.

faceting ['fæsɪtɪŋ] *n* (*Miner*) Facettenschliff *m*.

facetious [fə'siːʃəs] *adj remark, speech, tone* witzelnd, spöttisch, mokant ◆ **to be ~ (about sth)** (über etw *acc*) Witze machen, sich (über etw *acc*) mokieren; **~ humour** Blödeleien *pl*; **if satire is merely ~** wenn Satire zur Blödelei wird; **I was just being ~** das war doch nur ein Witz *or* so eine Blödelei (*inf*).

facetiously [fə'siːʃəslɪ] *adv* albernd, witzelnd.

face: ~-to-~ *adj* persönlich, von Angesicht zu Angesicht (*geh*); *confrontation* direkt; **~ value** *n* (*Fin*) Nennwert, Nominalwert *m*; **to take sth at (its) ~ value** (*fig*) etw für bare Münze nehmen; **to take sb at ~ value** jdm unbesehen glauben; **~-worker** *n* (*Min*) Hauer *m*.

facial ['feɪʃəl] **1** *adj* Gesichts-.
2 *n* (*inf*) kosmetische Gesichtsbehandlung.

facile ['fæsaɪl] *adj* **(a)** (*glib, superficial*) oberflächlich; *emotions, mind also* ohne Tiefgang; *piece of writing also* seicht, ohne Tiefgang ◆ **he made a few ~ remarks** er hat einige nichtssagende Bemerkungen gemacht. **(b)** (*flowing*) *style* flüssig, gewandt. **(c)** (*easy*) *task, victory* leicht.

facilitate [fə'sɪlɪteɪt] *vt* erleichtern; (*make possible*) ermöglichen ◆ **it would ~ matters** es würde die Sache erleichtern.

facilitator [fə'sɪlɪteɪtə^r] *n* Vermittler(in) *m(f)* ◆ **the role of teachers as ~s** die Vermittlerrolle von Lehrern.

facility [fə'sɪlɪtɪ] *n* **(a)** Einrichtung *f* ◆ **to offer facilities** Möglichkeiten bieten; **to give sb every ~** jdm jede Möglichkeit bieten; **you will have every ~** *or* **all facilities for study** es wird Ihnen alles zur Verfügung stehen, was Sie zum Studium brauchen; **facilities for the disabled** Einrichtungen für Behinderte; **cooking facilities** Kochgelegenheit *f*.
(b) *no pl* (*ease*) Leichtigkeit *f*; (*dexterity*) Gewandtheit *f* ◆ **~ in learning** (leichte) Auffassungsgabe.

facing ['feɪsɪŋ] *n* **(a)** (*on wall*) Verblendung, Verkleidung *f*. **(b)** (*Sew*) Besatz *m*.

facsimile [fæk'sɪmɪlɪ] *n* Faksimile *nt*; (*Telec*) Faksimileübertragung *f*.

▼ **fact** [fækt] *n* **(a)** Tatsache *f*, Faktum *nt* (*geh*); (*historical, geographical etc*) Faktum *nt* ◆ **hard ~s** nackte Tatsachen *pl*; **the true ~s** der wahre Sachverhalt; **to know for a ~ that** (es) ganz genau *or* sicher wissen, daß; **the ~ is that** ... die Sache ist die, daß ...; **to stick to the ~s** bei den Tatsachen bleiben, sich an die Tatsachen *or* Fakten halten; (*not speculate also*) auf dem Boden der Tatsachen bleiben; **to look (the) ~s in the face** der Wirklichkeit *or* den Tatsachen (*dat*) ins Auge sehen; **the ~s of the case** (*Jur*) der Tatbestand, der Sachverhalt; **... and that's a ~** darüber besteht kein Zweifel!, Tatsache! (*inf*); **is that a ~?** tatsächlich?, Tatsache? (*inf*); *see* **face 2 (c)**.
(b) *no pl* (*reality*) Wirklichkeit, Realität *f* ◆ **~ and fiction** Dichtung und Wahrheit; **founded on ~** auf Tatsachen beruhend.
(c) in (point of *or* **actual) ~** eigentlich; (*in reality*) tatsächlich, in Wirklichkeit; (*after all*) (dann) doch; (*to make previous statement more precise*) nämlich; **in ~, as a matter of ~** eigentlich; (*to intensify previous statement*) sogar; **I don't suppose you know him/you want it? — in (point of** *or* **actual) ~** *or* **as a matter of ~ I do** Sie kennen ihn/möchten das nicht zufällig? — doch, eigentlich schon; **do you know him/want it? — in (point of** *or* **actual) ~** *or* **as a matter of ~ I do** kennen Sie ihn/möchten Sie das? — jawohl; **but in (point of** *or* **actual) ~ he didn't do it/there were a lot more** aber in Wirklichkeit hat er es gar nicht getan/waren viel mehr da; **I'd meant to do some work but in ~ I was too tired** ich wollte eigentlich etwas arbeiten, war aber dann zu müde; **I thought I could give you a lift, but in (point of** *or* **actual) ~ I won't be going/won't have a car** ich dachte, ich könnte dich mitnehmen, aber ich gehe doch nicht/habe doch kein Auto; **I'm going soon, in (point of** *or* **actual) ~ tomorrow** ich gehe bald, nämlich morgen; **it won't be easy, in ~** *or* **as a matter of ~ it'll be very difficult** es wird nicht einfach sein, es wird sogar sehr schwierig sein; **does it hurt? — as a matter of ~ it's very painful** tut's weh? — ja, und sogar ganz schön; **I bet you haven't done that! — as a matter of ~ I have!** du hast das bestimmt nicht gemacht! — und ob, aber ja doch!; **as a matter of ~ we were just talking about you** wir haben (nämlich) eben von Ihnen geredet; **do you know Sir Charles? — as a matter of ~ he's my uncle/yes, in ~ he's my uncle** kennen Sie Sir Charles? — ja, und er ist sogar/ja, er ist nämlich mein Onkel.
(d) (*Jur*) **to be an accessory before/after the ~** sich der Beihilfe/Begünstigung schuldig machen.

fact-finding ['fæktfaɪndɪŋ] *adj commission* Untersuchungs-; *mission* Erkundungs- ◆ **~ tour** Informationsreise *f*.

faction ['fækʃən] *n* **(a)** (*group*) (Partei)gruppe *f*; (*Pol*) Fraktion *f*; (*splinter group*) Splittergruppe *f*. **(b)** *no pl* (*strife*) interne Unstimmigkeiten *pl*; (*Pol also*) Parteihader *m*.

factious ['fækʃəs] *adj* (*liter*) streitsüchtig, händelsüchtig; *quarrelling* kleinlich, engherzig.

factitious [fæk'tɪʃəs] *adj* künstlich, unecht; *demand for goods* hochgespielt.

fact of life *n* **(a)** (*reality*) harte Tatsache ◆ **that's just a ~** so ist es nun mal im Leben. **(b) ~s ~ ~** *pl* (*sexual*) Aufklärung *f*; **to tell/teach sb the ~s ~ ~** jdn aufklären; **to know the ~s ~ ~** aufgeklärt sein.

▼ **factor** ['fæktə^r] 1 *n* **(a)** Faktor *m*. **(b)** (*Biol*) Erbfaktor *m*. **(c)** (*agent*) Makler *m*. **(d)** (*Comm: for debts*) Kommissionär *m*.
2 *vi* (*Comm*) Schulden aufkaufen.

factorize ['fæktəraɪz] *vt* in Faktoren zerlegen, faktorisieren.

factory ['fæktərɪ] *n* Fabrik *f*; (*plant also*) Werk *nt*.

factory: F~ Act *n* Arbeitsschutzgesetz *nt*; **~ farm** *n* industrieller Viehzuchtbetrieb, Großmästerei *f*; **~ farming** *n* industriell betriebene Viehzucht; **~ hand** *n* Fabrikarbeiter(in *f*) *m*; **~ inspector** *n* Gewerbeaufsichtsbeamte(r) *m*; **~ ship** *n* Fabrikschiff *nt*; **~ worker** *n* Fabrikarbeiter(in *f*) *m*.

factotum [fæk'təʊtəm] *n* Faktotum *nt*.

factsheet ['fæktʃiːt] *n* Informationsblatt *nt*.

factual ['fæktjʊəl] *adj* sachlich, Tatsachen-; (*real*) tatsächlich ◆ **~ error** Sachfehler *m*.

factually ['fæktjʊəlɪ] *adv* sachlich.

faculty ['fækəltɪ] *n* **(a)** (*power of mind*) Vermögen *nt*, Fähigkeit, Kraft *f*; (*ability, aptitude*) Begabung *f*, Talent *nt* ◆ **~ of reason** Vernunft *f*; **~ of speech/thought/sight** Sprech-/Denk-/Sehvermögen *nt*; **the mental faculties** die Geisteskräfte *pl*; **to be in (full) possession of (all) one's faculties** im Vollbesitz seiner Kräfte sein; **to have a ~ for doing sth** ein Talent dafür haben, etw zu tun.
(b) (*Univ*) Fakultät *f* ◆ **the medical ~, the ~ of medicine** die medizinische Fakultät; **the F~** (*staff*) der Lehrkörper.
(c) (*Eccl*) Vollmacht *f*.

fad [fæd] *n* Fimmel (*inf*), Tick (*inf*) *m*; (*fashion*) Masche *f* (*inf*) ◆ **it's just a ~** das ist nur ein momentaner Fimmel (*inf*) *or* Tick (*inf*); **that's the latest fashion ~** das ist die neuste Modemasche (*inf*); **his ~ for caviar/wearing one earring** sein Kaviarfimmel (*inf*)/sein Tick *or* Fimmel, nur einen Ohrring zu tragen (*inf*).

faddish ['fædɪʃ], **faddy** ['fædɪ] (*inf*) *adj* wählerisch.

fade [feɪd] 1 *vi* **(a)** verblassen; (*material, colour also*) verbleichen; (*on exposure to light*) verschießen; (*flower*) verblühen; (*lose shine*) seinen Glanz verlieren ◆ **guaranteed non-~** *or* **not to ~** garantiert farbecht.
(b) (*fig*) (*memory*) verblassen; (*sight, strength, inspiration, feeling*) nachlassen, schwinden (*geh*); (*hopes*) zerrinnen; (*smile*) vergehen, verschwinden; (*beauty*) verblühen; (*sound*) verklingen, verhallen; (*radio signal*) schwächer werden.
(c) (*Rad, TV, Film*) (*scene*) ausgeblendet werden; (*cameraman*) ausblenden ◆ **to ~ to another scene** (allmählich) zu einer anderen Szene überblenden.
(d) (*Tech: brakes*) nachlassen.
2 *vt* **(a)** (*cause to lose colour*) ausbleichen. **(b)** (*Rad, TV, Film*) ausblenden ◆ **to ~ one scene (in)to another** von einer Szene (allmählich) in eine andere überblenden.
3 *n* (*Rad, TV, Film*) Abblende *f*.

◆**fade away** *vi* (*sight*) schwinden (*geh*); (*memory also*) verblassen; (*hopes also*) zerrinnen; (*interest, strength, inspiration also*) nachlassen; (*sound*) verklingen, verhallen; (*person*) immer weniger *or* schwächer werden; (*from memory of the public*) aus dem Gedächtnis schwinden.

◆**fade in** (*Rad, TV, Film*) 1 *vi* allmählich eingeblendet werden.
2 *vt sep* allmählich einblenden.

◆**fade out** 1 *vi* **(a)** (*Rad, TV, Film*) abblenden. **(b) to ~ ~ of sb's life** aus jds Leben verschwinden.
2 *vt sep* (*Rad, TV, Film*) abblenden.

◆**fade up** *vt sep* (*Rad, TV, Film*) aufblenden; *sound* lauter werden lassen, anschwellen lassen.

faded ['feɪdɪd] *adj* verblaßt, verblichen; *material* (*after exposure to light*) verschossen; *flowers, beauty* verblüht.

fade: ~-in *n* (*Rad, TV, Film*) Aufblendung *f*; **~-out** *n* (*Rad, TV, Film*) Abblende *f*.

faeces, (*US*) **feces** ['fiːsiːz] *pl* Kot *m*.

faerie, faery ['fɛərɪ] (*old*) 1 *n* Fee *f*.
2 *adj* Feen-, Elfen- ◆ **~ king/queen** Elfenkönig *m*/-königin *f*.

faff about ['fæfə,baʊt] *vi* (*Brit inf*) herumbosseln (*inf*).

fag [fæg] (*inf*) 1 *n* **(a)** *no pl* (*drudgery*) Schinderei, Plackerei *f*.
(b) (*Brit: cigarette*) Kippe *f* (*inf*), Glimmstengel *m* (*inf*).
(c) (*Brit Sch*) *junger Internatsschüler, der einem älteren bestimmte Dienste zu leisten hat.*
(d) (*sl: homosexual*) Schwule(r) *m* (*inf*).
2 *vt* (*also* **~ out**) (*inf*) erschöpfen, schlauchen (*inf*) ◆ **to ~ oneself (out)** sich abschinden, sich abrackern (*inf*); **to be ~ged (out)** kaputt *or* geschafft sein (*inf*).
3 *vi* **(a)** (*also* **~ away**) sich abrackern (*inf*), sich abplagen. **(b)** (*Brit Sch*) *einem älteren Schüler Dienste leisten.*

fag end *n* **(a)** (*Brit inf: cigarette end*) Kippe *f* (*inf*), Stummel *m*. **(b)** (*inf: last part*) letztes Ende ◆ **the ~ of a conversation** die letzten Fetzen einer Unterhaltung.

faggot, (*US*) **fagot** ['fægət] *n* **(a)** Reisigbündel *nt*. **(b)** (*Cook*) Frikadelle *f*. **(c)** (*inf: person*) Blödmann *m* (*inf*) ◆ **you lazy ~** du Faulpelz (*inf*). **(d)** (*esp US sl: homosexual*) Schwule(r) *m* (*inf*).

Fahrenheit ['færənhaɪt] *n* Fahrenheit *nt*.

fail [feɪl] 1 *vi* **(a)** (*be unsuccessful*) keinen Erfolg haben; (*in mission, life etc*) versagen, scheitern; (*campaign, efforts, negotiations also, plan, experiment, marriage*) fehlschlagen, scheitern; (*undertaking, attempt*) fehlschlagen, mißlingen, mißglücken; (*applicant, application*) nicht angenommen werden; (*election candidate, Theat: play*) durchfallen; (*business*) eingehen; (*charm, attempts at persuasion etc also*) vergeblich *or* umsonst sein ◆ **I/he/they** *etc* **~ed (in doing sth)** es gelang mir/ihm/ihnen *etc* nicht(, etw zu tun); **I don't like ~ing** ich habe nicht gern Mißerfolge; **he ~ed in his attempt** sein Versuch schlug fehl *or* blieb erfolglos *or* mißglückte; **he ~ed in his application for the post** seine Bewerbung wurde nicht angenommen; **to ~ in one's duty** seine Pflicht nicht tun; **to ~ by 5 votes** (*motion*) mit 5 Stimmen Mehrheit abgelehnt werden; (*person*) um 5 Stimmen geschlagen werden; **if all else ~s** wenn alle Stricke reißen.
(b) (*not pass exam*) durchfallen.
(c) (*fall short*) **where he/the essay ~s is in not being detailed enough** sein Fehler/der Fehler des Aufsatzes ist, daß er nicht ausführlich genug ist; **this report ~s in that it comes up with no clear proposals** dieser Bericht läßt es an klaren Vorschlägen fehlen; **where you ~ is that you lack experience** Ihnen fehlt es an der notwendigen Erfahrung.
(d) (*grow feeble*) (*health*) sich verschlechtern; (*hearing, eyesight also*) nachlassen; (*invalid*) schwächer werden ◆ **he is ~ing fast** sein Zustand verschlechtert sich zusehends.
(e) (*stop working, be cut off etc*) (*generator, battery, radio, electricity*) ausfallen; (*pump, engine also, brakes*) versagen; (*supply, wind*) ausbleiben; (*heart*) versagen, aussetzen ◆ **the crops ~ed** es gab ein Mißernte; (*completely*) die Ernte fiel aus.
2 *vt* **(a)** *candidate* durchfallen lassen ◆ **to ~ an exam** eine Prüfung nicht be-

➤ LANGUAGE IN USE: **fact: a** → 15.1, 26.1, 26.2, 26.3 **factor: 1a** → 26.1

stehen, durch eine Prüfung fallen.
(b) (*let down: person, memory*) im Stich lassen; (*not live up to sb's expectations*) enttäuschen ◆ **his heart ~ed him** sein Herz setzte aus; **words ~ me** mir fehlen die Worte.
(c) to ~ to do sth etw nicht tun; (*neglect*) (es) versäumen, etw zu tun; **I ~ to see why** es ist mir völlig unklar, warum; (*indignantly*) ich sehe gar nicht ein, warum.
3 *n* **(a) without ~** ganz bestimmt, auf jeden Fall; (*inevitably*) garantiert, grundsätzlich.
(b) (*failed candidate, exam*) **there were ten ~s** zehn sind durchgefallen *or* durchgerasselt (*inf*); **she got a ~ in history** in Geschichte ist sie durchgefallen *or* hängengeblieben (*inf*).

failing ['feɪlɪŋ] **1** *n* Schwäche *f*, Fehler *m*.
2 *prep* **~ an answer** mangels (einer) Antwort (*geh*); **ask John if he knows, ~ him try Harry** fragen Sie John (danach), und wenn er es nicht weiß, versuchen Sie es bei Harry; **~ this/that** (oder) sonst, und wenn das nicht möglich ist; **~ which** ansonsten, widrigenfalls (*form*).

fail-safe ['feɪlseɪf] *adj* (ab)gesichert; *method* hundertprozentig sicher.

failure ['feɪljə^r] *n* **(a)** (*lack of success*) Mißerfolg *m*; (*of campaign, efforts, negotiations also, of plan, experiment, marriage*) Fehlschlag *m*, Scheitern *nt*; (*of undertaking, attempt*) Fehlschlag *m*; (*of application*) Ablehnung *f*; (*in exam, Theat: of play also*) Durchfall *m*; (*of business*) Eingehen *nt* ◆ **~ to do sth** vergeblicher Versuch, etw zu tun; **~ rate** (*in exams*) Mißerfolgsquote *f*; (*of machine*) Fehlerquote *f*.
(b) (*unsuccessful person*) Versager *m*, Niete *f* (*inf*) (*at* in +*dat*); (*unsuccessful thing*) Mißerfolg, Reinfall (*inf*) *m*, Pleite *f* (*inf*) ◆ **sb is a ~ at doing sth** jd ist in etw (*dat*) eine Niete (*inf*), es gelingt jdm nicht, etw zu tun; **I'm a bit of a ~ at making my own clothes** ich bin eine ziemliche Niete, wenn es darum geht, meine eigenen Kleider zu nähen (*inf*).
(c) (*omission, neglect*) **because of his ~ to reply/act** weil er nicht geantwortet/gehandelt hat, weil er es versäumt *or* unterlassen hat zu antworten/zu handeln; **his ~ to notice anything** weil er nichts bemerkt hat; **~ to pay will result in prosecution** im Nichteinbringungsfall erfolgt Anzeige (*form*); **~ to perform one's duty** Nichterfüllung *f* seiner Pflicht; **~ to appear** Nichterscheinen *nt* (*form*); **~ to observe a law** Nichtbeachtung *f* eines Gesetzes.
(d) (*of health*) Verschlechterung *f*; (*of hearing, eyesight also*) Nachlassen *nt*; (*of invalid*) Nachlassen *nt* der Kräfte.
(e) (*breakdown*) (*of generator, engine, electricity*) Ausfall *m*; (*of pump, engine also, of brakes*) Versagen *nt*; (*of supply, wind*) Ausbleiben *nt*; (*of heart*) Versagen, Aussetzen *nt* ◆ **~ of crops** Mißernte *f*; (*complete*) Ernteausfall *m*.

fain [feɪn] *adv* (*obs*) gern.

faint [feɪnt] **1** *adj* (+*er*) **(a)** schwach; *colour, recollection also* blaß; *suspicion, hope, sound also, wish* leise *attr*; *smell, tracks, line, smile also, amusement* leicht *attr*; *resemblance also* entfernt; *voice* (*feeble*) matt, schwach; (*distant, not loud*) leise ◆ **a ~ idea** eine leise Ahnung; **I haven't the ~est (idea)** ich habe keinen blassen (Schimmer) (*inf*); **I haven't the ~est idea about it** davon habe ich nicht die leiseste Ahnung.
(b) (*pred: physically*) **I feel a bit ~** mir ist ganz schwach; **she felt ~** ihr wurde schwach; **she looked ~** sie schien einer Ohnmacht nahe; **I feel ~ with hunger** mir ist (ganz) schwach vor Hunger.
(c) (*timid*) **~ heart never won fair lady** (*Prov*) wer nicht wagt, der nicht gewinnt (*Prov*).
2 *n* Ohnmacht *f* ◆ **to fall in a ~** in Ohnmacht fallen, ohnmächtig werden.
3 *vi* ohnmächtig werden, in Ohnmacht fallen (*with, from* vor +*dat*).

faint-hearted [feɪnt'hɑːtɪd] *adj* zaghaft.

faint-heartedness [feɪnt'hɑːtɪdnɪs] *n* Zaghaftigkeit *f*.

fainting fit ['feɪntɪŋfɪt] *n* Ohnmachtsanfall *m*.

faintly ['feɪntlɪ] *adv* schwach; *visible also* kaum; *suspect, hope, attempt, sound* leise; *smell, smile* leicht; *similar, resemble* entfernt; (*slightly*) *interested, disappointed* leicht.

faintness ['feɪntnɪs] *n* **(a)** *see adj* (*a*) **such was the ~ of his voice/the colour/the smell/the resemblance** *etc* ... seine Stimme war so schwach/die Farbe war so blaß/der Geruch war so schwach/die Ähnlichkeit war so schwach *or* entfernt *etc* ...
(b) (*dizziness*) flaues Gefühl, Schwächegefühl *nt*.
(c) ~ of heart (*liter*) Verzagtheit *f*.

fair¹ [fɛə^r] **1** *adj* (+*er*) **(a)** (*just*) gerecht, fair (*to/on sb* jdm gegenüber, gegen jdn) ◆ **to be ~ to/on sb** (*not unjust*) jdm gegenüber fair *or* gerecht sein *or* (*not mean*) anständig handeln; **he tried to be ~ to everybody** er versuchte, gegen alle gerecht zu sein *or* (*give everybody his due*) allen gerecht zu werden; **that's a ~ comment** das stimmt, das läßt sich nicht abstreiten; **it's only ~ for him to earn more than us** es ist doch nur gerecht *or* fair, daß er mehr verdient als wir; **it's only ~ to ask him/to give him a hand** *etc* man sollte ihn fairerweise fragen/ihm fairerweise helfen *etc*; **it's only ~ to expect ...** man kann doch wohl zu Recht erwarten ...; **~ enough!** na schön, na gut; **that's ~ enough** das ist nur recht und billig; **as is (only) ~** was nur recht und billig ist; **~'s ~!** wir wollen doch fair bleiben; **by ~ means or foul** ohne Rücksicht auf Verluste (*inf*); **~ and square** offen und ehrlich, redlich; **that's a ~ sample of ...** das ist ziemlich typisch für ...
(b) (*reasonable*) ganz ordentlich ◆ **only ~** nur mäßig *or* mittelprächtig (*inf*), so lala (*inf*); **~ to middling** gut bis mittelmäßig; **he's a ~ judge of character** er hat eine gute Menschenkenntnis; **to have a ~ idea of sth** eine ungefähre Vorstellung von etw haben; **to have a ~ idea (of) what/how** *etc* ... sich (*dat*) ziemlich gut vorstellen können, was/wie *etc* ...; **to have a ~ idea that ...** den leisen Verdacht haben, daß ...; **a ~ chance of success** recht gute Erfolgsaussichten *pl*.
(c) (*reasonably large, fast, strong*) *sum, number, speed* ziemlich, ansehnlich; *wind* frisch ◆ **a ~ amount** ziemlich viel; **to go at a ~ pace** ziemlich schnell gehen/fahren *etc*, ein ganz schönes Tempo drauf haben (*inf*).
(d) (*fine*) *weather* heiter, schön ◆ **set ~** beständig; **the barometer/weather is set ~** das Barometer steht auf Schönwetter/das Wetter ist beständig.
(e) *person* (*light-haired*) blond; (*light-skinned*) hell.
(f) (*old: beautiful*) hold (*old*), liebreizend (*liter*) ◆ **the ~ sex** (*not old*) das schöne Geschlecht, die holde Weiblichkeit (*hum*); **her ~ name** (*liter*) ihr unbescholtener Name (*geh*).
(g) to be in a ~ way to doing sth (*inf*) auf dem besten Wege sein, etw zu tun.
2 *adv* **(a) to play ~** (*Sport*) fair spielen; (*fig also*) fair sein.
(b) ~ and square (*honestly*) offen und ehrlich; (*accurately, directly*) genau, direkt; **he struck him ~ and square in the face** er schlug ihm mitten ins Gesicht.
(c) (*dial: pretty well*) ganz schön (*inf*), vielleicht (*inf*) ◆ **it ~ took my breath away** das hat mir glatt den Atem verschlagen.

fair² *n* (Jahr)markt *m*; (*fun~*) Volksfest *nt*; (*Comm*) Messe *f*.

fair: ~ copy *n* Reinschrift *f*; **to write out a ~ copy of sth** etw ins reine schreiben; **~ game** *n* (*lit*) jagdbares Wild; (*fig*) Freiwild *nt*; **the grouse is ~ game between the months of ...** das Moorhuhn darf in den Monaten ... bejagt (*spec*) *or* gejagt werden; **~ground** *n see* **fair²** Markt(platz) *m*; Festplatz *m*; **~-haired** *adj, comp* **~er-haired** blond; **~-haired boy** *n* (*US*) Lieblingskind *nt*, Liebling *m*.

fairing ['fɛərɪŋ] *n* (*Aviat, Aut*) Stromlinien-Verkleidung *f*.

fairly ['fɛəlɪ] *adv* **(a)** (*justly*) gerecht ◆ **~ and squarely beaten** nach allen Regeln der Kunst geschlagen. **(b)** (*rather*) ziemlich, recht. **(c)** (*pretty well*) *see* **fair¹ 2 (c)**.

fair-minded ['fɛəmaɪndɪd] *adj* gerecht.

fairness ['fɛənɪs] *n* **(a)** (*justice*) Gerechtigkeit, Fairneß *f* ◆ **in all ~** gerechterweise, fairerweise; **in (all) ~ to him we should wait** wir sollten fairerweise warten. **(b)** (*lightness*) (*of hair*) Blondheit *f*; (*of skin*) Hellhäutigkeit *f*. **(c)** (*of weather*) Schönheit *f*. **(d)** (*old: beauty*) Liebreiz *m* (*old*).

fair: ~ play *n* (*Sport, fig*) faires Verhalten, Fair play *nt*; **that's not ~ play** (*fig*) das ist nicht fair *or* gerecht; **~-sized** *adj* recht groß; **~way** *n* **(a)** (*Naut*) Fahrwasser *nt or* -rinne *f*; **(b)** (*Golf*) Fairway *nt*; **~-weather** *adj friends* nur in guten Zeiten.

fairy ['fɛərɪ] *n* **(a)** Fee *f* ◆ **he's away with the fairies** (*sl*) der hat einen Haschmich (*sl*) *or* Stich (*inf*). **(b)** (*pej inf: homosexual*) Homo (*inf*), Schwule(r) (*inf*) *m*.

fairy: ~ cycle *n* Kinderfahrrad *nt*; **~ footsteps** *npl* (*iro inf*) Stapfen *nt*; **~ godmother** *n* (*lit, fig*) gute Fee; **~land** *n* Märchenland *nt*; **~ lights** *npl* bunte Lichter *pl*; **~-like** *adj* feenhaft; **~ queen** *n* Elfenkönigin *f*; **~ ring** *n* Hexentanzplatz *m*; (*of mushrooms*) Hexenring *m*; **~ story, ~-tale** *n* (*lit, fig*) Märchen *nt*.

fait accompli [ˌfetə'kɒmpliː] *n* vollendete Tatsache, Fait accompli *nt* (*geh*) ◆ **to present sb with a ~** jdn vor vollendete Tatsachen stellen.

faith [feɪθ] *n* **(a)** (*trust*) Vertrauen *nt* (*in* zu); (*in human nature, medicine, science etc, religious ~*) Glaube *m* (*in* an +*acc*) ◆ **~ in God** Gottvertrauen *nt*; **to have ~ in sb** jdm (ver)trauen; **to have ~ in sth** Vertrauen in etw (*acc*) haben; **have ~** haben Sie Vertrauen!; **act of ~** Vertrauensbeweis *m*; **it was more an act of ~ than a rational decision** das war mehr auf gut Glück gemacht als eine rationale Entscheidung.
(b) (*religion*) Glaube *m no pl*, Bekenntnis *nt*.
(c) (*promise*) **to keep/break ~ with sb** jdm treu bleiben/untreu werden, jdm die Treue halten/brechen (*geh*).
(d) (*sincerity, loyalty*) Treue *f* ◆ **to act in good/bad ~** in gutem Glauben/böser Absicht handeln.

faith cure *n* Heilung *f* durch Gesundbeten.

faithful ['feɪθfʊl] **1** *adj* **(a)** treu ◆ **~ to one's promise** seinem Versprechen getreu. **(b)** (*accurate*) *account, translation* genau, getreu.
2 *npl* **the ~** (*Rel*) die Gläubigen *pl*.

faithfully ['feɪθfəlɪ] *adv* **(a)** treu; *promise* fest, hoch und heilig (*inf*) ◆ **yours ~** mit freundlichen Grüßen; (*more formally*) hochachtungsvoll. **(b)** *report etc* genau, getreu; *translate* wortgetreu, genau.

faithfulness ['feɪθfʊlnɪs] *n* (*loyalty*) Treue *f* (*to* zu); (*of servant, dog etc also*) Ergebenheit *f* (*to* gegenüber); (*of translation*) Genauigkeit *f*; (*of reproduction*) Originaltreue *f*.

faith: ~ healer *n* Gesundbeter(in *f*) *m*; **~ healing** *n* Gesundbeten *nt*; **~less** *adj* treulos; **~lessness** *n* Treulosigkeit *f*.

fake [feɪk] **1** *n* (*object*) Fälschung *f*; (*jewellery*) Imitation *f*; (*person*) (*trickster*) Schwindler *m*; (*feigning illness*) Simulant *m* ◆ **he's just a big ~!** (*inf*) das ist doch alles nur Schau! (*inf*).
2 *vt* vortäuschen; *picture, document, results etc* fälschen; *bill, burglary, crash* fingieren; *jewellery* imitieren, nachmachen; *elections* manipulieren ◆ **to ~ an illness** (eine Krankheit) simulieren *or* vortäuschen.

◆**fake up** *vt sep story* erfinden; *picture, passport* fälschen; *jewellery* imitieren.

fakir ['fɑːkɪə^r] *n* Fakir *m*.

falcon ['fɔːlkən] *n* Falke *m*.

falconer ['fɔːlkənə^r] *n* Falkner *m*.

falconry ['fɔːlkənrɪ] *n* Falknerei *f*; (*sport*) Falkenjagd *or* -beize *f*.

Falkland Islands ['fɔːklənd,aɪləndz], **Falklands** ['fɔːkləndz] *npl* Falkland-Inseln *pl*.

fall [fɔːl] (*vb: pret* **fell**, *ptp* **fallen**) **1** *n* **(a)** Fall *no pl*, Sturz *m*; (*decline: of empire*

etc) Untergang *m* ◆ **the F~ (of Man)** (*Eccl*) der Sündenfall; **to break sb's ~** jds Fall auffangen; **to have a ~** (hin)fallen, stürzen; **he had several ~s** er ist mehrmals hingefallen *or* gestürzt; **it's a long ~ from up here** von hier oben geht es tief hinunter; **to head** *or* **ride for a ~** in sein Verderben rennen.
(b) (*defeat*) (*of town, fortress etc*) Einnahme, Eroberung *f*; (*of Troy*) Fall *m*; (*of country*) Zusammenbruch *m*; (*of government*) Sturz *m*.
(c) **~ of rain/snow** Regen-/Schneefall *m*; **~ of rock** Steinschlag *m*; **there was another heavy ~ last night** es hat heute nacht wieder viel geschneit.
(d) (*of night*) Einbruch *m*.
(e) (*in gen*) (*lowering*) Sinken *nt*; (*in temperature also*) Abfall *m*; (*sudden*) Sturz *m*; (*of barometer*) Fallen *nt*; (*sudden*) Sturz *m*; (*in wind*) Nachlassen *nt*; (*in revs, population, membership*) Abnahme *f*; (*in graph*) Abfall *m*; (*in morals*) Verfall *m*; (*of prices, currency*) (*gradual*) Sinken *nt*; (*sudden*) Sturz *m* ◆ **~ in altitude** Höhenverlust *m*.
(f) (*slope*) (*of roof, ground*) Gefälle *nt*; (*steeper*) Abfall *m*.
(g) (*water~: also* **~s**) Wasserfall *m* ◆ **the Niagara F~s** der Niagarafall.
(h) (*Wrestling*) Schultersieg *m*.
(i) (*hang: of curtains etc*) Fall *m*.
(j) (*US: autumn*) Herbst *m* ◆ **in the ~** im Herbst.
[2] *vi* **(a)** fallen; (*Sport, from a height, badly*) stürzen; (*object: to the ground*) herunter-/hinunterfallen ◆ **to ~ to one's death** tödlich abstürzen; **to ~ into a trap** in die Falle gehen.
(b) (*hang down: hair, clothes etc*) fallen ◆ **his tie kept ~ing into the soup** seine Krawatte hing ihm dauernd in die Suppe.
(c) (*drop*) (*temperature, price*) fallen, sinken; (*population, membership etc*) abnehmen; (*voice*) sich senken; (*wind*) sich legen, nachlassen; (*land*) abfallen; (*graph, curve, rate*) abnehmen; (*steeply*) abfallen ◆ **her eyes fell** sie schlug die Augen nieder (*geh*); **his face fell** er machte ein langes Gesicht; **to ~ in sb's estimation** *or* **eyes** in jds Achtung (*dat*) sinken.
(d) (*be defeated*) (*country*) eingenommen werden; (*city, fortress also*) fallen, erobert werden; (*government, ruler*) gestürzt werden ◆ **to ~ to the enemy** vom Feind eingenommen werden; (*fortress, town also*) vom Feind erobert werden.
(e) (*be killed*) fallen ◆ **to ~ in battle** fallen.
(f) (*night*) hereinbrechen; (*silence*) eintreten.
(g) (*Bibl*) den Sündenfall tun; (*old: girl*) die Unschuld *or* Ehre verlieren (*dated*) ◆ **when Adam fell** nach Adams Sündenfall.
(h) (*occur*) (*birthday, Easter etc*) fallen (*on* auf *+acc*); (*accent*) liegen (*on* auf *+dat*); (*be classified*) gehören (*under* in *+acc*), fallen (*under* unter *+acc*) ◆ **it ~s under another category** das gehört in *or* fällt in eine andere Kategorie; **that ~s outside/within the scope ...** das fällt nicht in/in den Bereich ..., das liegt außerhalb/innerhalb des Bereichs ...
(i) (*be naturally divisible*) zerfallen, sich gliedern (*into* in *+acc*) ◆ **to ~ into three sections** sich in drei Teile gliedern; **to ~ into categories** sich in Kategorien gliedern lassen.
(j) (*fig*) **not a word fell from his lips** kein Wort kam über seine Lippen; **her eyes fell on a strange object** ihr Blick fiel auf einen merkwürdigen Gegenstand; **the responsibility ~s on you** Sie tragen *or* haben die Verantwortung; **the blame for that ~s on him** ihn trifft die Schuld daran; **where do you think the responsibility/blame for that will ~?** wem wird Ihrer Meinung nach die Verantwortung dafür/die Schuld daran gegeben?
(k) (*become*) werden ◆ **to ~ asleep** einschlafen; **to ~ ill** krank werden, erkranken (*geh*); **to ~ in/out of love with sb** sich in jdn verlieben/aufhören, jdn zu lieben; **she's forever ~ing in and out of love** sie verliebt sich dauernd neu.
(l) (*pass into a certain state*) **to ~ into despair** verzweifeln; **to ~ into a deep sleep** in tiefen Schlaf fallen *or* sinken; **to ~ into a state of unconsciousness/into a coma** das Bewußtsein verlieren, in Ohnmacht/in ein Koma fallen; **to ~ into bad ways** auf die schiefe Bahn geraten; **to ~ apart** *or* **to pieces** (*chairs, cars, book etc*) aus dem Leim gehen (*inf*); (*clothes, curtains*) sich in Wohlgefallen auflösen (*inf*); (*house*) verfallen; (*system, company, sb's life*) aus den Fugen geraten *or* gehen.
(m) **to ~ to doing sth** (*start*) anfangen, etw zu tun.
(n) (*in set constructions see also n, adj etc*) **to ~ into the hands of sb** jdm in die Hände fallen; **to ~ among thieves** unter die Räuber fallen *or* geraten.
[3] *vt* **to ~ prey/a victim to sb/sth** jdm/einer Sache zum Opfer fallen.
◆**fall about** (*also* **~ ~ laughing**) *vi* sich krank lachen (*inf*).
◆**fall away** *vi* **(a)** (*ground*) abfallen. **(b)** (*come away, crumble: plaster, bricks, river bank*) abbröckeln (*from* von). **(c)** *see* **fall off (b)**. **(d)** (*anxiety, fears*) weichen (*geh*) (*from* von). **(e)** (*from party, church*) abfallen.
◆**fall back** *vi* zurückweichen (*also Mil*).
◆**fall back (up)on** *vi +prep obj* zurückgreifen auf (*+acc*).
◆**fall behind** *vi* **(a)** (*race, school etc*) zurückbleiben (*prep obj* hinter *+dat*), zurückfallen (*prep obj* hinter *+acc*). **(b)** (*with rent, work etc*) in Rückstand *or* Verzug geraten.
◆**fall down** *vi* **(a)** (*person*) hinfallen; (*statue, vase*) herunter-/hinunterfallen; (*collapse: house, scaffolding etc*) einstürzen.
(b) (*down stairs, cliff face*) hinunterfallen (*prep obj acc*) ◆ **he fell right ~ to the bottom** er ist bis ganz nach unten gefallen.
(c) (*fig: be inadequate: person, theory, plan*) versagen ◆ **where he/the plan ~s ~ is ...** woran es ihm/dem Plan fehlt, ist ..., woran es bei ihm/dem Plan hapert, ist ... (*inf*); **he fell ~ badly that time** er hat damals übel versagt; **that was where we fell ~** daran sind wir gescheitert.
◆**fall for** *vi +prep obj* **(a)** **I really fell ~ him/that** er/das hatte es mir angetan. **(b)** (*be taken in by*) *sales talk, propaganda* hereinfallen auf (*+acc*).
◆**fall in** *vi* **(a)** (*into water etc*) hineinfallen ◆ **to ~ ~(to) sth** in etw (*acc*) fallen. **(b)** (*collapse*) einstürzen; (*building also*) zusammenbrechen. **(c)** (*Mil*) (*troops*) (in Reih und Glied) antreten; (*one soldier*) ins Glied treten ◆ **~ ~!** antreten!; **to ~ ~ beside** *or* **alongside sb** sich jdm anschließen.
◆**fall in with** *vi +prep obj* **(a)** (*meet, join up with*) sich anschließen (*+dat*); *bad company* geraten in (*+acc*). **(b)** (*agree to*) mitmachen bei; *request* unterstützen.
◆**fall off** *vi* **(a)** (*lit*) (*person, cup etc*) herunter-/hinunterfallen (*prep obj* von). **(b)** (*decrease*) zurückgehen, abnehmen; (*supporters*) abfallen; (*speed also*) sich verringern; (*support, enthusiasm*) nachlassen.
◆**fall on** *vi +prep obj* **(a)** (*trip on*) *stone* fallen über (*+acc*). **(b)** (*be the responsibility of, be borne by*) (*duty, decision, task*) zufallen (*+dat*); (*blame*) treffen (*+acc*). **(c)** (*attack*) herfallen über (*+acc*). **(d)** (*find*) stoßen auf (*+acc*).
◆**fall out** *vi* **(a)** (*of bed, boat, window*) heraus-/hinausfallen ◆ **to ~ ~ of sth** aus etw fallen. **(b)** (*quarrel*) sich (zer)streiten. **(c)** (*Mil*) wegtreten. **(d)** (*happen*) sich ergeben ◆ **just wait and see how things ~ ~** wart erst mal ab, wie alles wird; **if everything ~s ~ all right** wenn alles wunschgemäß verläuft *or* nach Wunsch geht; **it fell ~ that ...** (*liter*) es erwies sich, daß ... (*geh*).
◆**fall over** *vi* **(a)** (*person*) hinfallen; (*collapse*) umfallen; (*statue, vase also*) umkippen.
(b) *+prep obj* (*trip over*) *stone, sb's legs* fallen über (*+acc*) ◆ **he was always ~ing ~ himself** er stolperte ständig über seine eigenen Füße; **they were ~ing ~ each other to get the book** sie drängelten sich, um das Buch zu bekommen.
(c) **to ~ ~ oneself to do sth** sich (fast) umbringen (*inf*) *or* sich (*dat*) die größte Mühe geben, etw zu tun; **to ~ ~ backwards to do sth** sich (förmlich) überschlagen, etw zu tun (*inf*).
◆**fall through** *vi* (*plan*) ins Wasser fallen, fehlschlagen.
◆**fall to** *vi* **(a)** (*inf*) (*start eating*) sich dranmachen (*inf*), reinhauen (*inf*); (*start fighting, working*) loslegen (*inf*). **(b)** (*be the responsibility of*) zufallen (*+dat*), obliegen (*+dat*) (*geh*).
◆**fall upon** *vi +prep obj see* **fall on (b-d)**.
fallacious [fəˈleɪʃəs] *adj* irrig; *argument* trugschlüssig.
fallacy [ˈfæləsɪ] *n* Irrtum *m*; (*in logic*) Fehlschluß, Trugschluß *m* ◆ **a popular ~** ein weitverbreiteter Irrtum; **it's a ~ to think that ...** es ist ein Irrtum zu meinen, daß ...
fallen [ˈfɔːlən] [1] *ptp of* **fall**.
[2] *adj women, soldier, angel* gefallen; *leaf* abgefallen.
[3] *npl* **the F~** (*Mil*) die Gefallenen *pl*.
fall guy *n* (*esp US inf*) (*victim*) armes Opfer, Angeschmierte(r) (*inf*) *mf*; (*scapegoat*) Sündenbock *m*.
fallibility [ˌfælɪˈbɪlɪtɪ] *n* Fehlbarkeit *f*.
fallible [ˈfæləbl] *adj* fehlbar, nicht unfehlbar.
falling [ˈfɔːlɪŋ]: **~ sickness** *n* (*old*) Fallsucht *f* (*old*); **~ star** *n* Sternschnuppe *f*.
fall: **~ line** *n* (*Sci*) Fall-Linie *f*; **~-off** *n* (*in gen*) Rückgang *m*, Abnahme *f*; (*in numbers, attendances*) Abfall *m*; (*in speed*) Verringerung *f*; (*in enthusiasm, support*) Nachlassen *nt*.
Fallopian tube [fəˈləʊpɪənˈtjuːb] *n* Eileiter *m*.
fall-out [ˈfɔːlaʊt] *n* radioaktiver Niederschlag, Fall-out *m* (*spec*) ◆ **~ shelter** Atombunker *m*.
fallow¹ [ˈfæləʊ] *adj land* brach ◆ **to lie ~** brachliegen.
fallow² *adj* falb, gelbbraun ◆ **~ deer** Damwild *nt*.
false [fɔːls] [1] *adj* falsch; *friend also, lover* treulos; *ceiling, floor* Einschub-, Zwischen- ◆ **to put a ~ interpretation on sth** etw falsch auslegen *or* deuten; **~ labour** Vorwehen *pl*; **to put sb in a ~ position** jdn in eine Position drängen, die er sonst nicht vertritt; **to sail under ~ colours** unter falscher Flagge segeln; **to bear ~ witness** (*Bibl*) falsch(es) Zeugnis reden (*Bibl*); **under ~ pretences** unter Vorspiegelung falscher Tatsachen; **to be ~ to one's wife/word** seine Frau hintergehen/sein Wort brechen; **a box with a ~ bottom** eine Kiste mit doppeltem Boden.
[2] *adv*: **to play sb ~** mit jdm ein falsches Spiel treiben.
false: **~ alarm** *n* falscher *or* blinder Alarm; **~ dawn** *n* Zodiakal- *or* Tierkreislicht *nt*; **~ friend** *n* (*Ling*) falscher Freund; **~-hearted** *adj* falsch, treulos.
falsehood [ˈfɔːlshʊd] *n* **(a)** (*lie*) Unwahrheit *f*. **(b)** *no pl* (*of statement etc*) Unwahrheit *f*.
falsely [ˈfɔːlslɪ] *adv interpret, understand* falsch; *believe, claim, declare* fälschlicherweise; *accuse* zu Unrecht; *smile* unaufrichtig; *deceive, act* treulos ◆ **to promise ~ to do sth** sein Versprechen, etw zu tun, nicht ernst meinen.
false negative *n* (*Med*) **~ (result)** falsch negative Diagnose.
falseness [ˈfɔːlsnɪs] *n* (*of statement etc*) Unrichtigkeit, Falschheit *f*; (*of promise*) Unaufrichtigkeit, Falschheit *f*; (*artificiality: of pearls, eyelashes etc*) Unechtheit *f*; (*unfaithfulness: of lover etc*) Untreue, Treulosigkeit *f*.
false: **~ positive** *n* (*Med*) **~ positive (result)** falsch positive Diagnose; **~ rib** *n* falsche Rippe; **~ start** *n* Fehlstart *m*; **~ teeth** *npl* (künstliches) Gebiß, falsche Zähne *pl*.
falsetto [fɔːlˈsetəʊ] [1] *n* (*voice*) Fistelstimme *f*; (*Mus*) Falsett *nt*; (*person*) Falsettist *m*.
[2] *adj* Fistel-; (*Mus*) Falsett-.
[3] *adv sing* im Falsett.
falsies [ˈfɔːlsɪz] *npl* (*inf*) Gummibusen *m* (*inf*).
falsifiable [ˈfɒlsɪfaɪəbl] *adj* (*disprovable*) widerlegbar, falsifizierbar (*spec*).
falsification [ˌfɔːlsɪfɪˈkeɪʃən] *n* **(a)** (Ver)fälschung *f*. **(b)** (*disproving*) Widerlegung, Falsifikation (*spec*) *f*.
falsify [ˈfɔːlsɪfaɪ] *vt* **(a)** *records, evidence* fälschen; *report* entstellen. **(b)** (*dis-*

prove) widerlegen, falsifizieren (*spec*).

falsity ['fɔːlsɪtɪ] *n* (*incorrectness*) Unrichtigkeit *f*; (*artificiality: of smile*) Falschheit *f*; (*unfaithfulness*) Treulosigkeit *f*.

falter ['fɔːltəʳ] *vi* (*speaking*) stocken; (*steps, horse*) zögern.

faltering ['fɔːltərɪŋ] *adj voice* stockend, stammelnd; (*hesitating, wavering*) zögernd; (*unsteady*) taumelnd.

falteringly ['fɔːltərɪŋlɪ] *adv see adj.*

fame [feɪm] *n* Ruhm *m* ◆ **of ill ~** von üblem Ruf, berüchtigt; **to come to ~** Ruhm erlangen, zu Ruhm kommen; **to win ~ for oneself** sich (*dat*) einen Namen machen; **is that the Joseph Heller of "Catch-22" ~?** ist das der berühmte Joseph Heller, der „Catch-22" geschrieben hat?; **Borg of Wimbledon 1979 ~** Borg, der sich 1979 in Wimbledon einen Namen gemacht hat.

famed [feɪmd] *adj* berühmt.

familiar [fə'mɪljəʳ] 1 *adj* (a) (*usual, well-known*) *surroundings, sight, scene* gewohnt, vertraut; *street, person, feeling* bekannt; *phrase, title, song* geläufig, bekannt; *complaint, event, protest* häufig ◆ **his face is ~** das Gesicht ist mir bekannt; **among ~ faces** unter vertrauten Gesichtern; **to be/seem ~ to sb** jdm bekannt sein/vorkommen; **it looks very ~** es kommt mir sehr bekannt vor; **to sound ~** sich bekannt anhören (*to sb* jdm); **that sounds ~** das habe ich doch schon mal gehört; **to be on ~ ground** Bescheid wissen; **to be on ~ ground with sth** in etw (*dat*) zu Hause sein.

(b) (*conversant*) **I am ~ with the word/the town/him** das Wort/die Stadt/er ist mir bekannt *or* (*more closely*) vertraut; **I am not ~ with Ancient Greek/computer language** ich kann kein Altgriechisch/ich bin mit der Computersprache nicht vertraut; **are you ~ with these modern techniques?** wissen Sie über diese modernen Techniken Bescheid?; **is he ~ with our customs?** ist er mit unseren Bräuchen vertraut?; **to make oneself ~ with sth** sich mit etw vertraut machen.

(c) (*friendly*) *language* familiär; *greeting* freundschaftlich; *gesture* familiär, vertraulich; (*overfriendly*) familiär, plump-vertraulich ◆ **the ~ term of address** die Anrede für Familie und Freunde, die vertraute Anrede; **to be on ~ terms with sb** mit jdm auf vertrautem Fuß stehen; **we're all on pretty ~ terms** wir haben ein ziemlich ungezwungenes Verhältnis zueinander; **~ language/expressions** Umgangssprache *f*/umgangssprachliche Ausdrücke *pl*; **there's no need to get ~** kein Grund, gleich (plump-)vertraulich *or* familiär zu werden; **they're not the kind of people one wishes to become too ~ with** mit solchen Leuten möchte man sich nicht unbedingt näher einlassen.

2 *n* (a) (*liter: friend*) Vertraute(r) *mf* (*liter*). (b) (*of witch etc*) Hausgeist *m*.

familiarity [fə,mɪlɪ'ærɪtɪ] *n* (a) *no pl* Vertrautheit *f*.

(b) (*between people*) vertrautes Verhältnis; (*between colleagues etc*) ungezwungenes *or* familiäres Verhältnis; (*of language etc*) Familiarität *f*; (*of greeting*) Freundschaftlichkeit *f*; (*of gesture*) Vertraulichkeit, Familiarität *f*; (*pej*) plumpe Vertraulichkeit, Familiarität *f* ◆ **~ breeds contempt** (*Prov*) allzu große Vertrautheit erzeugt Verachtung.

(c) *usu pl* (*overfriendly action*) (plumpe) Vertraulichkeit.

familiarization [fə,mɪlɪəraɪ'zeɪʃən] *n* **process of ~** Gewöhnungsprozeß *m*; **he is responsible for the ~ of all new employees with ...** er ist dafür verantwortlich, daß alle neuen Angestellten mit ... vertraut gemacht werden.

familiarize [fə'mɪlɪəraɪz] *vt* **to ~ sb/oneself with sth** jdn/sich mit etw vertraut machen; **once you've ~d yourself with the job** wenn Sie sich eingearbeitet haben.

familiarly [fə'mɪljəlɪ] *adv speak, behave* familiär, vertraulich; (*pej*) familiär, plump- vertraulich ◆ **~ known as** besser allgemein bekannt als; **more ~ known as** besser bekannt als.

family ['fæmɪlɪ] 1 *n* (a) Familie *f*; (*including cousins, aunts etc*) Verwandtschaft *f*; (*lineage*) Familie *f*, Haus, Geschlecht (*geh*) *nt* ◆ **to start a ~** eine Familie gründen; **they plan to add to their ~** sie planen Familienzuwachs; **has he any ~?** hat er Familie?; **it runs in the ~** das liegt in der Familie; **of good ~** aus guter Familie *or* gutem Hause; **he's one of the ~** er gehört zur Familie; **with just the immediate ~** im engsten Familienkreis.

(b) (*of plants, animals, languages etc*) Familie *f* ◆ **the ~ of man** die Menschheit.

2 *attr* Familien- ◆ **a ~ friend** ein Freund des Hauses *or* der Familie; **she's in the ~ way** (*inf*) sie ist in anderen Umständen.

family: ~ allowance *n* Kindergeld *nt*; **~ butcher** *n* **D. Crosby, F~ Butcher** D. Crosby, Fleischermeister; **our/their/the ~ butcher** unsere/ihre/die Stammfleischerei; **~ credit** *n* (*Brit*) *Sozialleistung f für Geringverdiener, um das Familieneinkommen auf einen Mindestbetrag anzuheben*; **~ conference** *n* Familienrat *m*; **~ doctor** *n* Hausarzt *m*/-ärztin *f*; **~ hotel** *n* Familienpension *f*; **~ income supplement** *n* Beihilfe *f* (zum Lebensunterhalt) (*für Familien*); **~ man** *n* (*home-loving*) häuslich veranlagter Mann; (*with a ~*) Familienvater *m*; **~ planning** *n* Familienplanung *f*; **~ planning clinic** *n* Familienberatungsstelle *f*; **~ resemblance** *n* Familienähnlichkeit *f*; **~-size** *adj* in Haushaltsgröße; *car, packets* Familien-; *house* Einfamilien-; *refrigerator* Haushalts-; **~ tree** *n* Stammbaum *m*.

famine ['fæmɪn] *n* (*lit*) Hungersnot *f*; (*fig*) Knappheit *f* ◆ **to die of ~** verhungern.

famish ['fæmɪʃ] *vi* (*inf*) verhungern.

famished ['fæmɪʃt] *adj* (*inf*) verhungert, ausgehungert ◆ **I'm absolutely ~** ich sterbe vor Hunger (*inf*).

famous ['feɪməs] *adj* (a) berühmt (*for* durch, für) ◆ **~ last words!** (*inf*) man soll es nicht beschreien. (b) (*dated inf*) famos (*dated*).

famously ['feɪməslɪ] *adv* (*dated inf*) famos (*dated*), prächtig.

famulus ['fæmjʊləs] *n* Famulus *m*.

fan¹ [fæn] 1 *n* (a) (*hand-held*) Fächer *m*; (*mechanical, extractor ~, Aut: to cool engine*) Ventilator *m*; (*on scooter*) Lüfterrad *nt*; (*Aut: booster*) Gebläse *nt* ◆ **when the shit hits the ~** (*sl*) wenn die Kacke am Dampfen ist (*sl*) ◆ **then the shit will really hit the ~** (*sl*) dann ist die Kacke echt am Dampfen (*sl*); (b) (*of peacock, fig*) Fächer *m* ◆ **to spread sth out in a ~** etw fächerförmig ausbreiten.

2 *vt* (a) (*wind*) umwehen; (*person*) fächeln (*+dat*) ◆ **to ~ sb/oneself** jdm/sich (Luft) zufächeln; **to ~ the embers** die Glut anfachen; (*fig also*) das Feuer entfachen; **to ~ the flames** (*fig*) Öl ins Feuer gießen; **to ~ the flames of passion** das Feuer der Leidenschaft (noch) schüren. (b) *cards* fächerförmig ausbreiten ◆ **the peacock ~ned its tail** der Pfau schlug ein Rad.

◆**fan out** 1 *vi* (*searchers etc*) ausschwärmen.

2 *vt sep feathers* fächerförmig aufstellen; *cards* fächerförmig ausbreiten.

fan² *n* (*supporter*) Fan, Anhänger(in *f*) *m* ◆ **I'm quite a ~ of yours** ich bin ein richtiger Verehrer von Ihnen.

fan-assisted ['fænə,sɪstɪd] *adj* mit Gebläse ◆ **~ oven** Heißluftherd *m*.

fanatic [fə'nætɪk] *n* Fanatiker(in *f*) *m*.

fanatic(al) *adj*, **fanatically** *adv* [fə'nætɪk(əl), fə'nætɪkəlɪ] fanatisch.

fanaticism [fə'nætɪsɪzəm] *n* Fanatismus *m*.

fan belt *n* Keilriemen *m*.

fanciable ['fænsɪəbl] *adj* (*Brit: attractive*) attraktiv, anziehend.

fancied ['fænsɪd] *adj* (*imaginary*) eingebildet.

fancier ['fænsɪəʳ] *n* Liebhaber(in *f*) *m*.

fanciful ['fænsɪfʊl] *adj story, idea* phantastisch, abstrus; (*fancy*) *costume* reich verziert; *pattern* phantasievoll; (*unrealistic*) *plan etc* unrealistisch ◆ **I think you're being somewhat ~** ich glaube, das ist etwas weit hergeholt; **and I don't think it's ~ to claim that ...** und ich glaube nicht, daß es verstiegen ist zu behaupten, daß ...

fancifulness ['fænsɪfʊlnɪs] *n* (*of story etc*) Seltsamkeit *f*; (*of person*) blühende Phantasie; (*of costume*) reiche Verzierung; (*of pattern*) Phantasiereichtum *m*.

fan club *n* Fanclub *m*.

fancy ['fænsɪ] 1 *n* (a) (*liking*) **to have a ~ for sth** Lust zu etw *or* (*to eat or drink*) auf etw (*acc*) haben; **he had a ~ for sports cars** er hatte eine Vorliebe für Sportwagen; **a passing ~** nur so eine Laune; **he's taken a ~ to her/this car/the idea** sie/das Auto/die Idee hat es ihm angetan; **they took a ~ to each other** sie fanden sich sympathisch; **to take** *or* **catch sb's ~** jdn ansprechen, jdm gefallen; **he took a ~ to go swimming** er hatte Lust, schwimmen zu gehen; **to tickle sb's ~** jdn reizen; **just as the ~ takes me/you** ganz nach Lust und Laune; **he only works when the ~ takes him** er arbeitet nur, wenn ihm gerade danach ist.

(b) (*no pl: imagination*) Phantasie *f*; (*thing imagined also*) Phantasievorstellung *f* ◆ **that was just his ~** das hat er sich (*dat*) nur eingebildet.

(c) (*notion, whim*) **I have a ~ that ...** ich habe so ein Gefühl, daß ...; **he had a sudden ~ to go to Spain** ihn überkam eine plötzliche Laune, nach Spanien zu fahren.

2 *vt* (a) (*in exclamations*) **~ doing that!** so was(, das) zu tun!; **~ him doing that** nicht zu fassen, daß er das tut/getan hat!; **~ that!** (*inf*), **(just) ~!** (*inf*) (nein) so was!, denk mal an! (*inf*); **just ~, he ...** stell dir vor, er ...; **~ seeing you here!** so was, Sie hier zu sehen!; **~ him winning!** wer hätte gedacht, daß er gewinnt!

(b) (*imagine*) meinen, sich (*dat*) einbilden; (*think*) glauben ◆ **he fancied he heard footsteps** er meinte, Schritte zu hören; **I rather ~ he has gone out** ich glaube, er ist weggegangen.

(c) (*like, be attracted by*) **he fancies that car/the idea/her** (*likes*) das Auto/die Idee/sie gefällt ihm *or* hat es ihm angetan; **he fancies a house on Crete/her as a wife/her as his MP** (*would like to have*) er hätte gern ein Haus auf Kreta/er hätte sie gern zur Frau/als seine Abgeordnete; **he fancies a walk/steak/beer** (*feels like*) er hat Lust zu einem Spaziergang/auf ein Steak/Bier; **he fancies (the idea of) doing that** er würde *or* möchte das gern tun; (*feels like it*) er hätte Lust, das zu tun; **(do you) ~ a walk?** hast du Lust zu einem Spaziergang?; **count me out, I don't ~ the idea** ohne mich, das ist nichts für mich; **I don't ~ the idea, but I'll have to do it** ich habe gar keine Lust dazu, aber ich muß es ja wohl tun; **I don't ~** *that* **(idea)!** nur das nicht, nein, das finde ich nicht gut; **I didn't ~ that job/that party** die Stelle/die Party hat mich nicht gereizt; **I don't ~ a house in Glasgow** ich möchte kein Haus in Glasgow haben; **he fancies his chances** er meint, er hätte Chancen; **I don't ~ my chances of getting that job** ich rechne mir keine großen Chancen aus, die Stelle zu bekommen; **a bit of what you ~ does you good** man muß sich auch mal was Gutes gönnen.

3 *vr* von sich eingenommen sein, sich für wunder was halten (*inf*) ◆ **he fancies himself as an actor/expert on that** er hält sich für einen (guten) Schauspieler/einen Experten auf dem Gebiet; **do you ~ yourself as a teacher?** kannst du dir dich als Lehrer vorstellen?

4 *adj* (a) (*+er*) (*elaborate*) *hairdo, dancing steps, footwork* kunstvoll; (*unusual*) *food, pattern, decorations, cigarettes, furnishings* ausgefallen; *baking, cakes, bread* fein; (*inf*) *gadget, car, girlfriend etc* toll, schick (*inf*) ◆ **nothing ~** etwas ganz Einfaches; (*dress, furniture etc also*) etwas ganz Schlichtes; **a big ~ car** ein toller Schlitten (*inf*); **he always uses these big ~ words** er drückt sich immer so geschwollen aus; **that was a ~ bit of driving** das war ein tolles Manöver; **do you like my new stereo/dress? — very ~** gefällt dir meine neue Stereoanlage/mein neues Kleid? — toll, toll; **that's too ~ for me** das ist mir etwas zu übertrieben; **you won't get me eating any of these ~ German sausages** du kriegst mich nicht dazu, diese komischen deutschen Würste zu essen.

(b) (*fig pej*) *idea* überspannt, verstiegen; *cure* seltsam; *price* gepfeffert, stolz *attr*.

(c) (*US: extra good*) *goods, foodstuffs* Delikateß-.

fancy: ~ dress *n* (Masken)kostüm *nt*; **is it ~ dress?** geht man da verkleidet hin?; **they came in ~ dress** sie kamen verkleidet *or* kostümiert; **~-dress ball/party** *n* Maskenball *m*/Kostümfest *nt*; **~-free** *adj* frei und ungebunden; **~ goods** *npl* Geschenkartikel *pl*; **~ man** *n* (*pimp*) Zuhälter *m*; (*lover*) Liebhaber *m*; **~ woman** *n* Freundin *f*, Weibchen *nt* (*inf*); **~work** *n* feine Handarbeit.

fandango [fæn'dæŋgəʊ] *n* Fandango *m*.

fanfare ['fænfɛə^r] *n* Fanfare *f* ◆ **bugle ~** Fanfarenstoß *m*.

fanfold paper ['fænfəʊld'peɪpə^r] *n* (*Comput*) Endlospapier *nt*.

fang [fæŋ] *n* (*of snake*) Giftzahn *m*; (*of wolf, dog*) Fang *m*; (*of vampire*) Vampirzahn *m*; (*hum: of person*) Hauer *m* (*hum*).

fan: ~ heater *n* Heizlüfter *m*; **~light** *n* Oberlicht *nt*; **~ mail** *n* Verehrerpost *f*.

fanny ['fænɪ] *n* (a) (*esp US inf*) Po *m* (*inf*). (b) (*Brit vulg*) Möse *f* (*vulg*).

fan: ~-shaped *adj* fächerförmig; **~tail** *n* (*pigeon*) Pfautaube *f*.

fantasia [fæn'teɪzjə] *n* Fantasie *f*.

fantasize ['fæntəsaɪz] *vi* phantasieren; (*dream*) Phantasievorstellungen haben (*about* von).

fantastic [fæn'tæstɪk] *adj* (a) (*also* **~al**) phantastisch, skurril; *garment also* extravagant. (b) (*incredible*) phantastisch, unwahrscheinlich. (c) (*inf: wonderful*) toll (*inf*), phantastisch.

fantastically [fæn'tæstɪkəlɪ] *adv see adj*.

fantasy ['fæntəzɪ] *n* (a) (*imagination*) Phantasie *f*. (b) (*illusion*) Phantasie *f*, Hirngespinst *nt* (*pej*) ◆ **that's pure ~** *or* **a ~** das ist reine Phantasie *or* bloß ein Hirngespinst. (c) (*Mus, Liter*) Fantasie *f*.

fan: ~ tracery *n* fächerförmiges Maßwerk; **~ vaulting** *n* Fächergewölbe *nt*.

fanzine ['fænziːn] *n* Fan-Magazin *nt*.

▼ **far** [fɑː^r] *comp* **further, farther**, *superl* **furthest, farthest** [1] *adv* (a) (*in place*) weit ◆ **we don't live ~** *or* **we live not ~ from here** wir wohnen nicht weit von hier; **I'll go with you as ~ as the gate** ich komme/gehe bis zum Tor mit; **~ and wide** weit und breit; **from ~ and near** *or* **wide** von nah und fern; **~ above** hoch *or* weit über (*+dat*); **~ away** weit entfernt *or* weg; **~ away in the distance** weit in der Ferne; **~ into the jungle** weit in den Dschungel hinein; **I won't be ~ off** *or* **away** ich bin ganz in der Nähe; **~ out** weit draußen; **have you come ~?** kommen Sie von weit her?

(b) (*in time*) **as ~ back as I can remember** so weit ich (zurück)denken *or* mich erinnern kann; **as ~ back as 1945** schon (im Jahr) 1945; **~ into the night** bis spät in die Nacht; **~ into the future** bis weit in die Zukunft.

(c) (*in degree, extent*) weit ◆ **how ~ have you got with your plans?** wie weit sind Sie mit Ihren Plänen (gekommen)?; **~ longer/better** weit länger/besser; **it's ~ beyond what I can afford** das übersteigt meine Mittel bei weitem.

▼ (d) (*in set phrases*) **as** *or* **so ~ as I'm concerned** was mich betrifft; **it's all right as ~ as it goes** das ist soweit ganz gut; **in so ~ as** insofern als; **~ and away the best, by ~ the best, the best by ~** bei weitem *or* mit Abstand der/die/das Beste; **better by ~** weit besser; **~ from satisfactory** alles andere als befriedigend; **~ from liking him I find him quite unpleasant** nicht nur, daß ich ihn nicht leiden kann, ich finde ihn sogar ausgesprochen unsympathisch; **~ from it!** ganz und gar nicht, (ganz) im Gegenteil; **~ be it from me to ...** es sei mir ferne, zu ...; **so ~** (*up to now*) bisher, bis jetzt; (*up to this point*) soweit; **so ~ this week I've seen him once/three times/I haven't seen him at all** diese Woche habe ich ihn erst einmal/schon dreimal/noch nicht gesehen; **so ~ so good** so weit, so gut; **so ~ and no further** bis hierher und nicht weiter; **to go ~** (*money, supplies etc*) weit *or* (*last a long time also*) lange reichen; (*person: succeed*) es weit bringen; (*measures*) weit reichen; **these measures won't go very ~ towards stemming rising costs** diese Maßnahmen werden nicht viel dazu beitragen, die steigenden Kosten aufzuhalten; **I would go so ~ as to say ...** ich würde so weit gehen zu sagen ...; **that's going too ~** das geht zu weit; **to carry a joke too ~** einen Spaß zu weit treiben; **that's carrying a joke too ~** da hört der Spaß auf; **not ~ out** (*in guess*) nicht schlecht; **~ out** (*sl: fantastic*) einsame Klasse (*sl*); **not ~ off** (*in guess, aim*) fast (getroffen); (*almost*) nicht viel weniger; **~ gone** (*inf*) schon ziemlich hinüber (*inf*).

[2] *adj* (a) (*more distant of two*) weiter entfernt, hintere(r, s) ◆ **the ~ end of the room** das andere Ende des Zimmers; **the ~ window/door/wall** das Fenster/die Tür/Wand am anderen Ende des Zimmers; **on the ~ side of** auf der anderen Seite von; **when he reached the ~ bank** als er am anderen Ufer ankam; **which of these cars is yours? — the ~ one** welches ist dein Auto? — das, das weiter weg ist; **which bed will you have? — the ~ one** welches Bett möchtest du? — das da drüben.

(b) (*~-off*) *country, land* weitentfernt *attr* ◆ **in the ~ distance** in weiter Ferne; **it's a ~ cry from ...** (*fig*) das ist etwas ganz anderes als ...

faraway ['fɑːrəweɪ] *adj attr place* abgelegen; (*fig: dreamy*) verträumt, versonnen ◆ **a ~ voice** (*distant*) eine Stimme in *or* aus der Ferne; (*dreamy*) eine verträumte Stimme.

farce [fɑːs] *n* (*Theat, fig*) Farce *f*.

farcemeat ['fɑːsmiːt] *n see* **forcemeat**.

farcical ['fɑːsɪkəl] *adj* (*Theat*) possenhaft; (*fig: absurd*) absurd, grotesk.

fare [fɛə^r] [1] *n* (a) (*charge*) Fahrpreis *m*; (*on plane*) Flugpreis *m*; (*on boat*) Preis *m* für die Überfahrt; (*money*) Fahrgeld *nt* ◆ **what is the ~?** was kostet die Fahrt/der Flug/die Überfahrt?; **~s please!** noch jemand ohne (*inf*), noch jemand zugestiegen?; **have you got the right ~?** haben Sie das Fahrgeld passend?; **he gave me (the cost of/money for) the ~** er gab mir das Fahrgeld.

(b) (*passenger*) Fahrgast *m*.

(c) (*old, form: food*) Kost *f*.

[2] *vi* **he ~d well** es ging *or* erging (*geh*) ihm gut; **we all ~d the same** es ging uns allen gleich; **~ thee well** (*old*) leb(e) wohl (*old*).

Far East *n* **the ~** der Ferne Osten.

Far Eastern *adj* fernöstlich ◆ **~ politics** Fernostpolitik *f*; **~ travel** Fernostreisen *pl*.

fare stage *n* Fahrzone, Teilstrecke, Zahlgrenze *f*.

farewell [fɛə'wel] [1] *n* Abschied *m* ◆ **to make one's ~s** sich verabschieden; (*before a longer absence*) Abschied nehmen; **to bid sb ~** jdm auf Wiedersehen *or* Lebewohl (*old*) sagen.

[2] *interj* (*old*) lebt wohl (*old*); (*to friend, sweetheart*) leb(e) wohl (*old*).

farewell *in cpds* Abschieds-.

fare zone *n* Tarifzone *f*.

far: ~-fetched *adj* weithergeholt *attr*, weit hergeholt *pred*, an den Haaren herbeigezogen; **~-flung** *adj* (a) (*distant*) abgelegen; (b) (*widely spread*) weit auseinandergezogen.

farinaceous [ˌfærɪ'neɪʃəs] *adj* mehlhaltig.

farm [fɑːm] [1] *n* Bauernhof *m*; (*bigger*) Gut(shof *m*) *nt*; (*in US, Australia, health ~*) Farm *f*; (*fish ~*) Fischzucht, Teichwirtschaft (*form*) *f*; (*mink ~ etc*) (Pelztier)zuchtfarm *f*.

[2] *attr house* Bauern-; *produce, buildings* Landwirtschafts-; *labourer* Land- ◆ **~ animals** Tiere auf dem Bauernhof.

[3] *vt land* bebauen; *livestock* halten; *trout, mink etc* züchten.

[4] *vi* Landwirtschaft betreiben ◆ **man has been ~ing for thousands of years** der Mensch (be)treibt schon seit Jahrtausenden Ackerbau und Viehzucht.

◆**farm out** *vt sep work* vergeben (*on, to* an *+acc*); *children* in Pflege geben (*to dat*, bei).

farmer ['fɑːmə^r] *n* Bauer, Landwirt *m*; (*in US, Australia*) Farmer *m*; (*mink ~*) Züchter *m*; (*fish ~*) Teichwirt *m* (*form*); (*gentleman ~*) Gutsherr *m*; (*tenant ~*) Pächter *m* ◆ **~'s wife** Bäuerin *f*; **~'s co-operative** landwirtschaftliche Genossenschaft.

farm: ~hand *n* Landarbeiter *m*; (*living on small farm*) Knecht *m*; **~house** *n* Bauernhaus *nt*.

farming ['fɑːmɪŋ] *n* Landwirtschaft *f*; (*of crops also*) Ackerbau *m*; (*animals also*) Viehzucht *f*.

farm: ~ land *n* Ackerland *nt*; **~stead** *n* Bauernhof *m*, Gehöft *nt*; **~yard** *n* Hof *m*.

Far North *n* **the ~** der Hohe Norden.

faro ['fɛərəʊ] *n* Phar(a)o *nt*.

Faroes ['fɛərəʊz], **Faroe Islands** ['fɛərəʊˌaɪləndz] *npl* Färöer *pl*.

far-off ['fɑːrɒf] *adj* (weit)entfernt.

farrago [fə'rɑːgəʊ] *n* Gemisch, Allerlei *nt*.

far-reaching ['fɑːˌriːtʃɪŋ] *adj* weitreichend.

farrier ['færɪə^r] *n* Hufschmied *m*.

farrow ['færəʊ] [1] *vt piglets* werfen.

[2] *vi* ferkeln.

[3] *n* Wurf *m*.

far: ~-seeing *adj* weitblickend; **~-sighted** *adj* (a) (*lit*) weitsichtig; (b) (*fig*) *person* weitblickend; (*taking precautionary measures*) umsichtig; *measures* auf weite Sicht geplant; **~-sightedness** *n see adj* (a) Weitsichtigkeit *f*; (b) Weitblick *m*; Umsicht *f*; **the ~-sightedness of these measures** diese Maßnahmen, die Weitblick verraten.

fart [fɑːt] (*inf*) [1] *n* Furz *m* (*inf*).

[2] *vi* furzen (*inf*).

◆**fart about** *or* **around** *vi* (*inf*) (a) (*rush around*) hin und her sausen (*inf*). (b) (*loaf around*) herumbummeln (*inf*). (c) (*mess around*) herumalbern (*inf*) ◆ **stop ~ing ~ and make a decision** reiß dich am Riemen und komm zu einer Entscheidung (*inf*); **to ~ ~ with sth** an etw (*dat*) herumfummeln (*inf*).

farther ['fɑːðə^r] *comp of* **far** [1] *adv see* **further 1 (a)**.

[2] *adj* weiter entfernt, hintere(r, s) ◆ **at the ~ end** am anderen Ende.

farthermost ['fɑːðəməʊst] *adj see* **furthermost**.

farthest ['fɑːðɪst] *adj, adv superl of* **far** *see* **furthest 1, 2**.

farthing ['fɑːðɪŋ] *n* Farthing *m* (*ein Viertelpenny*) ◆ **I haven't a ~** ich habe keinen roten Heller (*dated*).

farthingale ['fɑːðɪŋgeɪl] *n* Reifrock *m*, Krinoline *f*.

fas *abbr of* **free alongside ship** frei Kai.

fascia ['feɪʃə] *n* (*Brit Aut*) Armaturentafel *f*.

fascicle ['fæsɪkl], **fascicule** ['fæsɪkjuːl] *n* (a) (*Bot*) Büschel *nt*; (*Anat*) Bündel *nt*. (b) (*of book*) Lieferung *f*, Faszikel (*old*) *m*.

fascinate ['fæsɪneɪt] *vt* faszinieren (*geh*); (*enchant: skill, beauty, singer etc also*) begeistern, bezaubern; (*hold spellbound: book, film, magician also*) fesseln; (*snake etc*) hypnotisieren ◆ **old houses ~/this subject ~s me** ich finde alte Häuser/dieses Gebiet hochinteressant *or* faszinierend (*geh*); **the audience watched/listened ~d** das Publikum sah/hörte gebannt zu; **it ~s me how skilfully he does these things** ich finde es erstaunlich, wie geschickt er das macht.

fascinating ['fæsɪneɪtɪŋ] *adj* faszinierend (*geh*); *subject, book, speaker, facts also* hochinteressant; *beauty, display, rhythm also* bezaubernd; *idea, person* außerordentlich, interessant; *selection* erstaunlich ◆ **I find it ~ how quickly he does it** ich finde es erstaunlich, wie schnell er das macht; **~!** (*iro*) umwerfend (*iro inf*), faszinierend (*iro geh*).

fascinatingly ['fæsɪneɪtɪŋlɪ] *adv* faszinierend (*geh*); *talk, describe* hochinteressant, fesselnd; *beautiful* bezaubernd.

fascination [ˌfæsɪ'neɪʃən] *n* Faszination *f* (*geh*); (*fascinating quality also*) Reiz *m* ◆ **to listen/watch in ~** gebannt zuhören/zusehen; **to have** *or* **hold a ~ for sb** auf jdn einen besonderen Reiz ausüben; **his ~ with the cinema** der Reiz, den

➤ LANGUAGE IN USE: **far: 1d** → 26.2

das Kino für ihn hat, die Faszination, die das Kino auf ihn ausübt (*geh*).

fascism ['fæʃɪzəm] *n* Faschismus *m*.

fascist ['fæʃɪst] [1] *n* Faschist(in *f*) *m*.
[2] *adj* faschistisch.

fash [fæʃ] *vt (Scot) (trouble)* ärgern; *(worry)* aufregen.

fashion ['fæʃən] [1] *n* **(a)** *no pl (manner)* Art (und Weise) *f* ◆ **(in the) Indian ~** auf Indianerart, nach Art der Indianer; **in the usual ~** wie üblich; **to behave in a peculiar ~** sich merkwürdig verhalten; **after** *or* **in a ~** in gewisser Weise; **were you successful/have you translated it? — after a ~** hast du Erfolg gehabt/es übersetzt? — so einigermaßen; **to do sth after** *or* **in a ~** etw recht und schlecht machen; **a novel after** *or* **in the ~ of D.H. Lawrence** ein Roman im Stil von D.H. Lawrence; **after** *or* **in this ~** auf diese Weise, so.
(b) *(in clothing, latest style)* Mode *f* ◆ **in ~** modern; **it's the/all the ~** es ist Mode/große Mode; **to come into/go out of ~** in Mode/aus der Mode kommen; **a man of ~** ein modischer Herr; **the Paris ~s** die Pariser Mode; **~s in women's clothes** die Damenmode; **to set a ~** eine Mode aufbringen.
(c) *(custom) (of society)* Sitte *f*, Brauch *m*; *(of individual)* Gewohnheit *f* ◆ **it was the ~ in those days** das war damals Sitte *or* Brauch; **as was his ~** *(old)* wie er zu tun pflegte (*geh*).
[2] *vt* formen, gestalten ◆ **to ~ sth after sth** etw einer Sache (*dat*) nachbilden.

fashionable ['fæʃnəbl] *adj (stylish) clothes, person* modisch; *custom* modern; *illness, colour* Mode-; *(patronized by ~ people) area, address* vornehm; *pub, artist, author* in Mode ◆ **all the ~ people go there** die Schickeria geht dahin; **a very ~ expression/artist** ein Modeausdruck/Mode- *or* Erfolgsautor; **it's (very) ~** es ist (große) Mode.

fashionably ['fæʃnəblɪ] *adv* modisch; *behave* modern.

fashion *in cpds* Mode-; **~-conscious** *adj* modebewußt; **~ designer** *n* Modezeichner(in *f*) *m*; **~ magazine** *n* Mode(n)heft *nt or* -zeitschrift *f*; **~ model** *n* Mannequin *nt*; *(man)* Dressman *m*; **~ parade** *n* Mode(n)schau *f*; **~ plate** *n* Modezeichnung *f*; **she looked like a ~ plate** sie sah aus wie aus der Modezeitung; **~ show** *n* Mode(n)schau *f*.

fast[1] [fɑːst] [1] *adj (+er)* **(a)** *(quick)* schnell ◆ **he's a ~ worker** *(lit)* er arbeitet schnell; *(fig)* er geht mächtig ran (*inf*); **to pull a ~ one (on sb)** (*inf*) jdn übers Ohr hauen (*inf*).
(b) to be ~/five minutes ~ *(clock, watch)* vorgehen/fünf Minuten vorgehen.
(c) *tennis court, squash ball etc* schnell.
(d) *(Phot) film* hochempfindlich; *lens* lichtstark.
(e) *(fig: immoral) behaviour, person* locker, flott, ausschweifend (*pej*).
[2] *adv* **(a)** schnell. **(b)** *(fig)* **to live ~** flott *or* locker leben. **(c)** *(old)* **~ by sth** *(close by)* dicht bei etw; **to follow ~ on sth** dicht auf etw (*acc*) folgen.

fast[2] [1] *adj* **(a)** *(film, secure)* fest ◆ **is the rope ~?** ist das Tau fest(gemacht)?; **to make a boat ~** ein Boot festmachen. **(b)** *colour, dye* farbecht; *(against light also)* lichtecht; *(against washing also)* waschecht. **(c)** *(staunch) friend* gut.
[2] *adv* **(a)** *(firmly, securely)* fest ◆ **to stick ~** festsitzen; *(with glue)* festkleben; **to stand ~** standhaft *or* fest bleiben; **to stand ~ by sb/sth** (treu) zu jdm stehen/an etw (*dat*) festhalten; **to hold ~ to sth** an etw (*dat*) festhalten; **to play ~ and loose with sb** mit jdm ein falsches *or* doppeltes Spiel treiben.
(b) *(soundly)* **to be ~ asleep** tief *or* fest schlafen.

fast[3] [1] *vi (not eat)* fasten.
[2] *n* Fasten *nt*; *(period of fasting)* Fastenzeit *f* ◆ **~ day** Fasttag *m*; **to break one's ~** das Fasten brechen.

fast: ~back *n* (Wagen *m* mit) Fließheck *nt*; **~ breeder reactor** *n* schneller Brüter.

fasten ['fɑːsn] [1] *vt* **(a)** *(attach)* festmachen, befestigen (*to, onto* an *+dat*); *(do up) parcel etc* zuschnüren; *buttons, buckle, dress etc* zumachen; *(tighten) screw etc* anziehen; *(lock) door* (ab)schließen ◆ **to ~ two things together** zwei Dinge zusammenmachen (*inf*) *or* aneinander befestigen.
(b) *(fig) thoughts, attention* zuwenden (*on sb* jdm) ◆ **to ~ the blame on sb** die Schuld auf jdn schieben, jdm die Schuld in die Schuhe schieben (*inf*); **to ~ one's eyes on sth** die Augen *or* den Blick auf etw (*acc*) heften.
[2] *vi* sich schließen lassen ◆ **the dress ~s at the back** das Kleid wird hinten zugemacht; **the door won't ~** die Tür läßt sich nicht schließen; **these two pieces ~ together** diese zwei Teile werden miteinander verbunden; **this piece ~s in here** dieses Teil wird hier befestigt *or* gehört hier hinein.

◆**fasten down** *vt sep* festmachen.

◆**fasten in** *vt sep* festschnallen (*+prep obj* in *+dat*).

◆**fasten on** [1] *vt sep* befestigen, festmachen (*+prep obj, -to* an *+dat*); *flower, badge* anheften (*+prep obj, -to* an *+dat*).
[2] *vi +prep obj (fig)* **the teacher always ~s ~ Smith** der Lehrer hackt immer auf Smith herum (*inf*).

◆**fasten onto** *vi +prep obj (fig)* **to ~ ~ sb** sich an jdn hängen.

◆**fasten up** *vt sep dress etc* zumachen ◆ **would you ~ me ~?** (*inf*) kannst du mir zumachen? (*inf*).

fastener ['fɑːsnər], **fastening** ['fɑːsnɪŋ] *n* Verschluß *m*.

fast food *n* Fast-Food *nt* ◆ **he lives mainly on ~** er ernährt sich hauptsächlich von Schnellgerichten.

fast food: ~ chain *n* Schnellimbißkette, Fast-Food-Kette *f*; **~ outlet** *n* Schnellimbiß *m*; **~ restaurant** *n* Schnell(imbiß)restaurant *nt*.

fast: ~ forward *n (on tape deck)* Vorspultaste *f*; **~-forward** *vti* vorspulen.

fastidious [fæs'tɪdɪəs] *adj* genau (*about* in bezug auf *+acc*); *(pej)* pingelig (*inf*) (*about* in bezug auf *+acc*).

fastidiousness [fæs'tɪdɪəsnɪs] *n* Genauigkeit *f*; Pingeligkeit *f* (*inf*).

fast lane *n* Überholspur *f* ◆ **life in the ~** *(fig)* Leben *nt* mit Tempo; **those in the ~ of life** diese dynamischen Erfolgstypen (*inf*).

fastness ['fɑːstnɪs] *n* **(a)** *(stronghold)* Feste *f* ◆ **mountain ~** Bergfeste *f*. **(b)** *(of colours)* Farbechtheit *f*; *(against light also)* Lichtechtheit *f*. **(c)** *(immorality)* Liederlichkeit *f*.

fast: ~ train *n* D-Zug *m*; **~ woman** *n* leichtlebige Frau.

fat [fæt] [1] *n (Anat, Cook, Chem)* Fett *nt* ◆ **now the ~'s in the fire** jetzt ist der Teufel los (*inf*); **to live off the ~ of the land** *(fig)* wie Gott in Frankreich *or* wie die Made im Speck (*inf*) leben; **to put on ~** Speck ansetzen; **to run to ~** in die Breite gehen (*inf*).
[2] *adj (+er)* **(a)** *(plump)* dick, fett (*pej*) ◆ **to get ~** dick werden; **she has got a lot ~ter** sie hat ziemlich zugenommen.
(b) *(containing fat) meat* fett.
(c) *(fig) volume* dick, umfangreich; *wallet, cigar* dick; *salary, cheque, profit* üppig, fett (*inf*); *part in play* umfangreich.
(d) *(iro inf)* **a ~ lot of good you are!** Sie sind ja 'ne schöne Hilfe! (*iro inf*); **a ~ lot he knows!** was der alles *or* nicht weiß (*iro inf*); **a ~ chance he's got** da hat er ja Mordschancen (*inf*).
(e) *land* fett.

fatal ['feɪtl] *adj (lit)* tödlich (*to* für); *(fig)* verheerend, fatal, verhängnisvoll; *(fateful) day, decision* schicksalsschwer ◆ **that would be ~** das wäre das Ende (*to gen*), das wäre tödlich (*inf*); **to be a ~ blow to sb/sth** ein schwerer Schlag für jdn/etw sein; **an incident that proved ~ to their diplomatic relations** ein Vorfall, der verheerende Auswirkungen auf ihre diplomatischen Beziehungen hatte; **it's ~ to say that** das ist fatal, so was zu sagen; **~ error** *(Comput)* schwerer Fehler.

fatalism ['feɪtəlɪzəm] *n* Fatalismus *m*.

fatalist ['feɪtəlɪst] *n* Fatalist(in *f*) *m*.

fatalistic *adj*, **~ally** *adv* [,feɪtə'lɪstɪk, -əlɪ] fatalistisch.

fatality [fə'tælɪtɪ] *n* **(a)** Todesfall *m*; *(in accident, war etc)* (Todes)opfer *nt*. **(b)** *(liter: inevitability)* Unabwendbarkeit *f*.

fatally ['feɪtəlɪ] *adv wounded* tödlich ◆ **to be ~ attracted to sb** jdm hoffnungslos verfallen sein.

fata morgana ['fɑːtəmɔː'gɑːnə] *n* Fata Morgana *f*.

fate [feɪt] *n* Schicksal *nt* ◆ **the F~s** *(Myth)* die Parzen *pl*; **~ decided otherwise** das Schicksal wollte es anders; **the examiners meet to decide our ~ next week** die Prüfer kommen nächste Woche zusammen, um über unser Schicksal zu entscheiden; **to leave sb to his ~** jdn seinem Schicksal überlassen; **to go to meet one's ~** seinem Schicksal entgegentreten; **to meet one's ~** vom Schicksal heimgesucht *or* ereilt (*geh*) werden; **as sure as ~ it will go wrong/it went wrong** das geht garantiert schief/das ist natürlich prompt schiefgegangen.

fated ['feɪtɪd] *adj* unglückselig; *project, plan* zum Scheitern verurteilt ◆ **to be ~** unter einem ungünstigen Stern stehen; **to be ~ to fail** *or* **be unsuccessful** zum Scheitern verurteilt sein; **they were ~ never to meet again** es war ihnen bestimmt, sich nie wiederzusehen; **their plans were ~ to be forgotten** ihre Pläne waren dazu verurteilt, vergessen zu werden.

fateful ['feɪtfʊl] *adj (disastrous)* verhängnisvoll; *(momentous)* schicksalsschwer.

fat: ~head *n (inf)* Dummkopf, Blödian (*inf*) *m*; **~headed** *adj (inf)* dumm, blöd (*inf*).

father ['fɑːðər] [1] *n* **(a)** *(lit, fig)* Vater *m* (*to sb* jdm) ◆ **from ~ to son** vom Vater auf den Sohn; **like ~ like son** der Apfel fällt nicht weit vom Stamm; **F~'s Day** Vatertag *m*; **(Old) F~ Time** die Zeit (*als Allegorie*).
(b) ~s *pl (ancestors)* Väter *pl*.
(c) *(founder)* Vater *m*; *(leader)* Führer, Vater (*liter*) *m* ◆ **the F~s of the Church** die Kirchenväter *pl*.
(d) *(God)* **F~** Vater *m*.
(e) *(priest)* Pfarrer *m*; *(monk)* Pater *m* ◆ **good morning, ~** guten Morgen, Herr Pfarrer/Pater X; **the Holy F~** der Heilige Vater; **~ confessor** Beichtvater *m*.
[2] *vt* **(a)** *child* zeugen; *(admit paternity)* die Vaterschaft anerkennen für; *(fig) idea, plan* Urheber (*+gen*) sein.
(b) *(saddle with responsibility)* **to ~ sth on sb** jdm die Verantwortung für etw aufhalsen (*inf*) *or* aufbürden; **to ~ the blame on sb** jdm die Schuld in die Schuhe schieben (*inf*).

father: F~ Christmas *n* der Weihnachtsmann; **~-figure** *n* Vaterfigur *f*; **~hood** *n* Vaterschaft *f*; **~-in-law** *n, pl* **~s-in-law** Schwiegervater *m*; **~land** *n* Vaterland *nt*; **~less** *adj* vaterlos.

fatherly ['fɑːðəlɪ] *adj* väterlich, wie ein Vater.

fathom ['fæðəm] [1] *n* Faden *m*.
[2] *vt* **(a)** *(lit)* ausloten. **(b)** *(understand)* ermessen (*geh*); *(inf: also ~ out)* verstehen ◆ **I just can't ~ him (out)** er ist mir ein Rätsel; **I couldn't ~ it (out)** ich kam der Sache nicht auf den Grund, ich kam nicht dahinter (*inf*).

fathomable ['fæðəməbl] *adj (fig)* faßbar ◆ **not ~** unerforschlich.

fathomless ['fæðəmlɪs] *adj (lit)* abgrundtief; *(fig) (boundless)* unermeßlich; *(incomprehensible)* unergründlich.

fatigue [fə'tiːg] [1] *n* **(a)** Abspannung, Erschöpfung, Ermüdung *f*. **(b)** *(Tech: metal ~)* Ermüdung *f*. **(c)** *(Mil: ~ duty)* Arbeitsdienst *m* ◆ **to be on ~** *(Mil)* Arbeitsdienst haben. **(d) ~s** *pl (Mil) see* **~ dress**.
[2] *vt* **(a)** *(tire)* ermüden; *(exhaust)* erschöpfen. **(b)** *(Tech) metal* ermüden.
[3] *vi* ermüden.

fatigue: ~ dress *n* Arbeitsanzug *m*; **in ~ dress** im Arbeitsanzug; **~ duty** *n* Arbeitseinsatz, Arbeitsdienst *m*; **~ party** *n* Arbeitskommando *nt*.

fatiguing [fə'tiːgɪŋ] *adj (tiring)* ermüdend; *(exhausting)* erschöpfend.

fatness ['fætnɪs] *n see adj (a-c)* **(a)** Dicke, Fettheit (*pej*) *f*. **(b)** Fettigkeit *f*. **(c)** Umfang *m*; Dicke *f*; Üppigkeit, Fettheit (*inf*) *f*. **(d)** *(fig: of land)* Fruchtbarkeit *f*.

fatso ['fætsəʊ] *n (inf)* Dicke(r) *(inf)*, Fettsack *(pej inf) m.*
fat stock *n* Mastvieh *nt.*
fatted ['fætɪd] *adj*: **to kill the ~ calf** einen Willkommensschmaus veranstalten.
fatten ['fætn] 1 *vt (also* **~ up***) animals* mästen; *people* herausfüttern *(inf)* ◆ **are you trying to ~ me up?** *(inf)* du willst mich wohl mästen? *(inf)*.
2 *vi (also* **~ up** *or* **out***) (animal)* fett werden; *(person)* dick werden; *(through overeating)* sich mästen *(inf)*.
fattening ['fætnɪŋ] *adj food* dick machend ◆ **chocolate is ~** Schokolade macht dick.
fatty ['fætɪ] 1 *adj* fett; *food also* fetthaltig; *(greasy)* fettig; *acid, tissue* Fett- ◆ **~ degeneration** *(Med)* Verfettung *f*; **~ tumour** Fettgeschwulst *f.*
2 *n (inf)* Dickerchen *nt (inf)*.
fatuity [fə'tjuːɪtɪ] *n* Albernheit *f*; *(remark, action also)* törichte Bemerkung/Tat *(geh)*.
fatuous ['fætjʊəs] *adj* töricht *(geh)*, albern.
faucet ['fɔːsɪt] *n (US)* Hahn *m.*
faugh [fɔː] *interj (old)* pfui.
▼ **fault** [fɔːlt] 1 *n* **(a)** *(mistake, defect)* Fehler *m*; *(Tech also)* Defekt *m*; *(in sth bought also)* Mangel *m* ◆ **generous to a ~** übermäßig großzügig; **to find ~ with sb/sth** etwas an jdm/etw auszusetzen haben; **he/my memory was at ~** er war im Unrecht/mein Gedächtnis hat mich getrogen; **you were at ~ in not telling me** es war nicht recht von Ihnen, daß Sie mir das nicht gesagt haben.
▼ **(b)** *no pl* **it won't be my/his ~ if ...** es ist nicht meine/seine Schuld, wenn ..., ich bin/er ist nicht schuld, wenn ...; **whose ~ is it?** wer ist schuld (daran)?; **it's all your own ~** das ist Ihre eigene Schuld, Sie sind selbst schuld.
(c) *(Geol)* Verwerfung *f.*
(d) *(Tennis, Horseriding)* Fehler *m.*
2 *vt* **(a)** Fehler finden an *(+dat)*, etwas auszusetzen haben an *(+dat)* ◆ **I can't ~ it** ich habe nichts daran auszusetzen; *(can't disprove it)* ich kann es nicht widerlegen. **(b)** *(Geol)* eine Verwerfung verursachen in *(+dat)*.
3 *vi (Geol)* sich verwerfen.
fault: ~-finder *n* Krittler(in *f*) *m*; **~-finding** 1 *adj* krittelig; 2 *n* Krittelei *f.*
faultily ['fɔːltɪlɪ] *adv* falsch.
faultless ['fɔːltlɪs] *adj appearance* tadellos, einwandfrei; *(without mistakes)* fehlerlos; *English* fehlerfrei, fehlerlos.
fault-tolerant *adj (Tech, Comput)* fehlertolerant.
faulty ['fɔːltɪ] *adj (+er) (Tech)* defekt; *(Comm)* fehlerhaft; *reasoning, logic* falsch, fehlerhaft.
faun [fɔːn] *n (Myth)* Faun *m.*
fauna ['fɔːnə] *n* Fauna *f.*
faux pas [fəʊ'pɑː] *n* Fauxpas *m.*
▼ **favour,** *(US)* **favor** ['feɪvəʳ] 1 *n* **(a)** *no pl (goodwill)* Gunst *f*, Wohlwollen *nt* ◆ **to win/lose sb's ~** jds Gunst *(acc)* erlangen *(geh)*/verscherzen; **to find ~ with sb** bei jdm Anklang finden; **to get back in(to) sb's ~** von jdm wieder in Gnaden aufgenommen werden; **to be in ~ with sb** bei jdm gut angeschrieben sein; *(fashion, pop star, writer etc)* bei jdm beliebt sein, bei jdm gut ankommen; **to be/fall out of ~** in Ungnade (gefallen) sein/fallen; *(fashion, pop star, writer etc)* nicht mehr beliebt sein *(with* bei)/nicht mehr ankommen *(with* bei).
▼ **(b) to be in ~ of sth** für etw sein; **a point in his ~** ein Punkt zu seinen Gunsten, ein Punkt, der für ihn spricht; **all those in ~ raise their hands** alle, die dafür sind, Hand hoch; *see* **balance.**
(c) *(partiality)* Vergünstigung *f* ◆ **to show ~ to sb** jdn bevorzugen.
(d) *(act of kindness)* Gefallen *m*, Gefälligkeit *f* ◆ **to ask a ~ of sb** jdn um einen Gefallen bitten; **to do sb a ~** jdm einen Gefallen tun; **do me a ~!** *(inf)* sei so gut!; **would you do me the ~ of returning my library books?** wären Sie bitte so freundlich und würden meine Bücher in die Bücherei zurückbringen?; **do me the ~ of shutting up!** *(inf)* tu mir einen Gefallen und halt den Mund!; **as a ~** aus Gefälligkeit; **as a ~ to him** ihm zuliebe.
(e) *(old: ribbon etc)* Schleife *f.*
(f) to enjoy sb's ~s *(old, euph)* jds (Liebes)gunst genießen *(dated geh)*.
(g) *(on wedding cake)* Verzierung, (Kuchen)dekoration *f.*
2 *vt* **(a)** *idea (be in ~ of)* für gut halten; *(prefer)* bevorzugen ◆ **I don't ~ the idea** ich halte nichts von der Idee; **I ~ the second suggestion** ich bin für den zweiten Vorschlag.
(b) *(show preference)* bevorzugen; *(king etc)* begünstigen.
(c) *(oblige, honour)* beehren *(form)* ◆ **to ~ sb with one's attention/a smile/an interview** jdm gütigerweise seine Aufmerksamkeit/ein Lächeln/ein Interview gewähren *(geh)*.
(d) *(be favourable for)* begünstigen.
(e) *(US: resemble)* ähneln *(+dat)*.
▼ **favourable,** *(US)* **favorable** ['feɪvərəbl] *adj* günstig, vorteilhaft *(for, to* für); *(expressing approval)* positiv.
favourableness, *(US)* **favorableness** ['feɪvərəblnɪs] *n* Günstigkeit *f* ◆ **the ~ of his reply/report** seine positive Antwort/sein positiver Bericht.
favourably, *(US)* **favorably** ['feɪvərəblɪ] *adv see adj* vorteilhaft, positiv ◆ **to be ~ inclined to sb/sth** sich positiv zu jdm/etw stellen, jdm/einer Sache gewogen sein *(geh)*.
favoured, *(US)* **favored** ['feɪvəd] *adj* **the/a ~ few** die wenigen Auserwählten/einige (wenige) Auserwählte; **a ~ friend** ein besonderer Freund.
▼ **favourite,** *(US)* **favorite** ['feɪvərɪt] 1 *n* **(a)** *(person)* Liebling *m*; *(Hist, pej)* Günstling *m* ◆ **he is a universal ~** er ist allgemein beliebt; **which of her children is her ~?** welches Kind mag sie am liebsten *or* ist ihr Liebling?
▼ **(b)** *(thing)* **this one is my ~** das habe ich am liebsten; **this film/dress is my ~** das ist mein Lieblingsfilm/-kleid; **we sang all the old ~s** wir haben all die alten Lieder gesungen.
(c) *(Sport)* Favorit(in *f*) *m* ◆ **Chelsea are the ~s** Chelsea ist (der) Favorit.
▼ 2 *adj attr* Lieblings- ◆ **~ son** *(US Pol)* regionaler Spitzenkandidat.
favouritism, *(US)* **favoritism** ['feɪvərɪtɪzəm] *n* Vetternwirtschaft *(inf)*, Günstlingswirtschaft *f*; *(in school)* Schätzchenwirtschaft *(inf)*, Lieblingswirtschaft *f.*
fawn[1] [fɔːn] 1 *n* **(a)** Hirschkalb *nt*; *(of roe deer)* Rehkitz *nt.* **(b)** *(colour)* Beige *nt.*
2 *adj colour* beige.
fawn[2] *vi (dog)* (mit dem Schwanz) wedeln; *(fig: person)* katzbuckeln *(on, upon* vor *+dat)*, herumscharwenzeln *(on, upon* um).
fawning ['fɔːnɪŋ] *adj person, manner* kriecherisch, liebedienernd; *dog* schwanzwedelnd.
fax [fæks] 1 *n* **(a)** *(also* **~ machine***)* Fax, Telefax *nt*, Fernkopierer *m* ◆ **to send sth by ~** etw per Fax *or* Telefax senden, etw faxen. **(b)** *(message)* Fax, Telefax *nt.*
2 *vt* faxen, telefaxen, fernkopieren ◆ **can you ~ us?** können Sie uns *(dat)* faxen?
◆**fax back** *vt sep document* zurückfaxen ◆ **can you ~ me ~?** können Sie mir per Fax antworten?
fax: ~ board *n* Faxkarte *f*; **~ bureau** *n* Faxbüro *nt*; **~ card** *n see* **~ board**; **~ machine** *n see* **fax 1 (a)**; **~ message** *n* Fax, Telefax *nt*; **~ number** *n* (Tele)faxnummer *f*; **~shot** 1 *n* Direktwerbung *f* per Fax; **to send out a ~shot** Werbemitteilungen per Fax senden; 2 *vt* Werbemitteilungen per Fax senden an *(+acc)*.
fay [feɪ] *n (liter: fairy)* Fee *f.*
faze [feɪz] *vt (inf)* **(a)** *(take aback)* verdattern *(inf)* ◆ **the question didn't ~ me** die Frage brachte mich nicht aus der Fassung. **(b)** *(daunt)* entmutigen.
FBI *(US) abbr of* **Federal Bureau of Investigation** FBI *nt.*
FC *abbr of* **football club** FC *m.*
Feb *abbr of* **February** Febr.
fealty ['fiːəltɪ] *n (Hist)* Lehnstreue *f.*
fear [fɪəʳ] 1 *n* **(a)** Angst, Furcht *f (for* vor *+dat)* ◆ **he has ~s for his sister's life** er fürchtet für *or* um das Leben seiner Schwester; **have no ~** *(old, hum)* fürchte dich nicht *(old, hum)*; **in ~ and trembling** mit schlotternden Knien; **to be/go in ~ of sb/sth** Angst vor jdm/etw haben/in (ständiger) Angst vor jdm/etw leben; **to be/go in ~ of one's life** um sein/ständig um sein Leben bangen; **for ~ that ...** aus Angst, daß ...; **she asked us to be quiet/she talked quietly for ~ of waking the child** sie bat uns, leise zu sein, damit wir das Kind nicht weckten/sie sprach leise, um das Kind nicht aufzuwecken; **without ~ or favour** ganz gerecht.
(b) *no pl (risk, likelihood)* **no ~!** *(inf)* nie im Leben! *(inf)*; **there's no ~ of that happening again** keine Angst, das passiert so leicht nicht wieder; **there's not much ~ of his coming** wir brauchen kaum Angst zu haben, daß er kommt.
(c) *(awe: of God)* Scheu, Ehrfurcht *f* ◆ **to put the ~ of God into sb** *(inf)* jdm gewaltig Angst einjagen *(inf)*.
2 *vt* **(a)** (be)fürchten ◆ **I ~ the worst** ich befürchte das Schlimmste; **he's a man to be ~ed** er ist ein Mann, vor dem man Angst haben muß; **they did not ~ to die** *(liter)* sie fürchteten den Tod nicht.
(b) *(feel awe for) God* Ehrfurcht haben vor *(+dat)*.
3 *vi* **to ~ for** fürchten für *or* um; **never ~!** keine Angst!
fearful ['fɪəfʊl] *adj* **(a)** *(frightening, inf: terrible)* furchtbar, schrecklich. **(b)** *(apprehensive)* ängstlich, bang ◆ **he was ~ lest he fail/be discovered** *(old)* ihm bangte davor zu versagen/entdeckt zu werden; **to be ~ for one's/sb's life** um sein/jds Leben fürchten; **I was ~ of waking her** ich befürchtete, daß ich sie aufwecken würde.
fearfully ['fɪəfəlɪ] *adv see adj.*
fearfulness ['fɪəfʊlnɪs] *n see adj* Furchtbarkeit, Schrecklichkeit *f*; Ängstlichkeit *f.*
fearless ['fɪəlɪs] *adj* furchtlos ◆ **~ of sth** ohne Angst *or* Furcht vor etw *(dat)*; **to be ~ of heights/the consequences** keine Angst vor Höhen/vor den Folgen haben, Höhen/die Folgen nicht fürchten.
fearlessly ['fɪəlɪslɪ] *adv see adj.*
fearlessness ['fɪəlɪsnɪs] *n* Furchtlosigkeit *f.*
fearsome *adj*, **~ly** *adv* ['fɪəsəm, -lɪ] furchterregend.
feasibility [ˌfiːzə'bɪlɪtɪ] *n* **(a)** *(of plan etc)* Durchführbarkeit, Machbarkeit *f* ◆ **~ study** Machbarkeitsstudie *f*; **the ~ of doing sth** die Möglichkeit, etw zu tun; **I doubt the ~ of doing that** ich glaube nicht, daß das möglich *or* machbar ist.
(b) *(plausibility: of story etc)* Wahrscheinlichkeit *f.*
feasible ['fiːzəbl] *adj* **(a)** möglich, machbar; *plan also* durchführbar, realisierbar; *route* gangbar, möglich. **(b)** *(likely, probable) excuse, story, theory* plausibel, wahrscheinlich.
feasibly ['fiːzəblɪ] *adv* **(a) if it can ~ be done** wenn es machbar ist *or* praktisch möglich ist; **it can't ~ be done** es ist praktisch nicht möglich, es ist nicht machbar. **(b)** plausibel ◆ **that could ~ be true** das könnte durchaus stimmen.
feast [fiːst] 1 *n* **(a)** *(banquet)* Festmahl, Festessen *nt*; *(Hist)* Festgelage *nt* ◆ **a ~ for the eyes** eine Augenweide.
(b) *(Eccl, Rel)* Fest *nt* ◆ **~ day** Festtag, Feiertag *m*; **movable/immovable ~** beweglicher/unbeweglicher Feiertag.

➤ LANGUAGE IN USE: **fault: 1b** → 18.3 **favour: 1b** → 11.2 **favourable** → 13 **favourite: 1b** → 7.3 **2** → 7.1, 7.2, 7.4

[2] *vi* (*lit*) Festgelage *pl*/ein Festgelage halten ◆ **to ~ on sth** sich an etw (*dat*) gütlich tun; (*person also*) in etw (*dat*) schwelgen; (*fig*) sich an etw (*dat*) weiden.
[3] *vt* (a) *guest* festlich bewirten ◆ **to ~ oneself** sich gütlich tun (*on* an +*dat*); (*person also*) schwelgen (*on* in +*dat*).
(b) **to ~ one's eyes on sb/sth** seine Augen an jdm/etw weiden.

feat [fi:t] *n* Leistung *f*; (*heroic, courageous etc*) Heldentat *f*; (*skilful*) Kunststück *nt*, Meisterleistung *f* ◆ **a ~ of courage/daring** eine mutige/wagemutige Tat; **a ~ of strength** eine Kraftleistung.

feather ['feðə^r] [1] *n* Feder *f* ◆ **~s** (*plumage*) Gefieder *nt*; (*on dart, arrow also*) Fiederung *f* ◆ **as light as a ~** federleicht; **in fine ~** (*inf*) (*in a good mood*) (in) bester Laune; (*in top form*) in Hochform; **that's a ~ in his cap** das ist ein Ruhmesblatt *nt* für ihn; **you could have knocked me down with a ~** (*inf*) ich war wie vom Donner gerührt; **that'll make the ~s fly** das wird die Gemüter bewegen; **they are birds of a ~** sie sind vom gleichen Schlag; **birds of a ~ flock together** (*Prov*) gleich und gleich gesellt sich gern (*Prov*); *see* **white ~**.
[2] *vt* (a) *arrow etc* mit Federn versehen ◆ **to ~ one's nest** (*fig*) sein Schäfchen ins trockene bringen. (b) (*Aviat*) *propeller* auf Segelstellung bringen. (c) (*Rowing*) *oar* flachdrehen.
[3] *vi* (*Rowing*) das Ruderblatt flachdrehen.

feather: ~-bed [1] *n* mit Federn gefüllte Matratze; [2] *vt* (*fig*) *person* verhätscheln; (*Ind*) (*with grants*) verhätscheln; (*by overmanning*) unnötige Arbeitskräfte zugestehen (+*dat*); **~-bedding** *n* (*fig*) Hätschelung *f*; (*with subsidies also*) unnötige Subventionierung; **~brain** *n* Spatzenhirn *nt*; **~brained** *adj* dümmlich; **~ duster** *n* Staubwedel *m*.

feathered ['feðəd] *adj* gefiedert.

feather: ~ headdress *n* Kopfschmuck *m* aus Federn; **~weight** (*Boxing*) [1] *n* Federgewicht *nt*; (*fig*) Leichtgewicht *nt*; [2] *adj* Federgewicht-.

feathery ['feðərɪ] *adj* (+*er*) fed(e)rig; *feel* zart.

feature ['fi:tʃə^r] [1] *n* (a) (*facial*) (Gesichts)zug *m*.
(b) (*characteristic*) Merkmal, Kennzeichen, Charakteristikum *nt*; (*of sb's character*) Grundzug *m* ◆ **a ~ of his style is ...** sein Stil ist durch ... gekennzeichnet; **a ~ of this book is ...** das Buch zeichnet sich durch ... aus; **special ~** Besonderheit *f*; **new ~** Neuheit *f*; **this model has all the latest ~s** dieses Modell ist mit allen (technischen) Neuheiten *or* Raffinessen ausgestattet.
(c) (*focal point: of room, building etc*) besonderes *or* herausragendes Merkmal ◆ **to make a ~ of sth** etw besonders betonen, etw zur Geltung bringen; **the main ~ of the new shopping centre** die Hauptattraktion des neuen Einkaufszentrums; **the main ~ of the exhibition** (*central area of interest*) der Schwerpunkt der Ausstellung; **the old volcano, the dominant ~ of the island,** ... der die Insel dominierende alte Vulkan ...
(d) (*Press*) (Sonder)beitrag *m*, Feature *nt*; (*Rad, TV*) (Dokumentar)bericht *m*, Feature *nt*.
(e) (*film*) Spielfilm *m*.
[2] *vt* (a) (*Press*) *story, picture* bringen.
(b) **this film ~s an English actress** in diesem Film spielt eine englische Schauspielerin mit; **the room ~s a large fireplace** eine Besonderheit des Zimmers ist der große Kamin.
[3] *vi* (a) (*occur*) vorkommen. (b) (*Film*) (mit)spielen.

feature: ~ article *n* Sonderbeitrag *m*, Feature *nt*; **~ film** *n* Spielfilm *m*; **~ fireplace** *n* offener Kamin; **~-length** *adj film* mit Spielfilmlänge; **~less** *adj* ohne besondere Merkmale; **~ story** *n* Sonderbericht *m*, Feature *nt*; **~ writer** *n* Feuilletonist(in *f*) *m*.

febrile ['fi:braɪl] *adj* fiebrig, fieberhaft.

February ['februərɪ] *n* Februar *m*; *see* **September**.

feces ['fi:si:z] *npl* (*US*) *see* **faeces**.

feckless ['feklɪs] *adj* nutzlos.

fecund ['fi:kənd] *adj* (*lit, fig*) fruchtbar.

fecundate ['fi:kəndeɪt] *vt* befruchten.

fecundity [fɪ'kʌndɪtɪ] *n* (*lit, fig*) Fruchtbarkeit *f*.

fed[1] [fed] *pret, ptp of* **feed**.

fed[2] *n* (*US inf*) FBI-Agent *m*.

Fedayeen [fedɑ:'ji:n] *npl* Freischärler *pl*.

federal ['fedərəl] [1] *adj* Bundes-; *system etc* föderalistisch; (*US Hist*) föderalistisch ◆ **~ state** (*in US*) (Einzel)staat *m*; **the F~ Republic of Germany** die Bundesrepublik Deutschland.
[2] *n* (*US Hist*) Föderalist *m*; (*US inf*) FBI-Mann *m*.

federalism ['fedərəlɪzəm] *n* Föderalismus *m*.

federalist ['fedərəlɪst] [1] *adj* föderalistisch.
[2] *n* Föderalist *m*.

federate ['fedəreɪt] [1] *vt* zu einem Bund vereinigen *or* zusammenschließen, föderieren (*rare*).
[2] *vi* sich zu einem Bund zusammenschließen.
[3] ['fedərɪt] *adj* verbündet, föderiert.

federation [,fedə'reɪʃən] *n* (a) (*act*) Zusammenschluß *m*, Föderation *f* (*rare*). (b) (*league*) Föderation *f*, Bund *m*.

▼**fed up** *adj* (*inf*) **I'm ~** ich habe die Nase voll (*inf*); **I'm ~ with him/it** er/es hängt mir zum Hals heraus (*inf*), ich habe ihn/es satt; **you're looking pretty ~** du siehst so aus, als hättest du die Nase voll (*inf*); **I'm ~ waiting for him** ich habe es satt *or* ich bin es leid, auf ihn zu warten.

fee [fi:] *n* (a) Gebühr *f*; (*of doctor, lawyer, artist, tutor*) Honorar *nt*; (*of stage performer*) Gage *f*; (*of director, administrator etc*) Bezüge *pl*; (*membership ~*) Beitrag *m* ◆ **(school) ~s** Schulgeld *nt*; **on payment of a small ~** gegen geringe Gebühr. (b) **land held in ~ simple** (*Jur*) unbeschränkt vererbbares Land.

feeble ['fi:bl] *adj* (+*er*) schwach; *voice, smile also* matt; *attempt* kläglich, schwach.

feeble: ~-minded *adj* dümmlich; **~ness** *n see adj* Schwäche *f*, Mattheit *f*, Kläglichkeit *f*.

feebly ['fi:blɪ] *adv see adj* schwach; matt; kläglich.

feed [fi:d] (*vb: pret, ptp* **fed**) [1] *n* (a) (*meal*) (*of animals*) Fütterung *f*; (*of baby, inf: of person*) Mahlzeit *f*; (*food*) (*of animals*) Futter *nt*; (*inf: of person*) Essen *nt* ◆ **when is the baby's next ~?** wann wird das Baby wieder gefüttert?; **to have a good ~** (*inf*) tüchtig futtern (*inf*); **he's off his ~** (*hum*) er hat keinen Appetit.
(b) (*Theat*) Stichwort *nt*.
(c) (*Tech*) (*to machine*) Versorgung *f* (*to gen*); (*to furnace*) Beschickung *f* (*to gen*); (*to computer*) Eingabe *f* (*into* in +*acc*).
[2] *vt* (a) (*provide food for*) *person, army* verpflegen; *family also* ernähren ◆ **to ~ oneself** sich selbst verpflegen; **he ~s himself well** er ißt gut.
(b) (*give food to*) *baby, invalid, animal* füttern ◆ **to ~ oneself** (*child*) allein *or* ohne Hilfe essen (können); **to ~ sth to sb/an animal** jdm/einem Tier etw zu essen/fressen geben; **they were fed to the lions** sie wurden den Löwen zum Fraß vorgeworfen.
(c) (*supply*) *machine* versorgen; *furnace* beschicken; *computer* füttern; *meter* Geld einwerfen in (+*acc*), füttern (*hum*); (*fire*) unterhalten, etwas legen auf (+*acc*); (*fig*) *hope, imagination, rumour* nähren, Nahrung geben (+*dat*) ◆ **two rivers ~ this reservoir** dieses Reservoir wird von zwei Flüssen gespeist; **to ~ sth into a machine** etw in eine Maschine geben; **to ~ coolant into a machine** einer Maschine (*dat*) Kühlmittel zuführen; **to ~ information to sb, to ~ sb with information** jdm Informationen zustecken, jdn mit Informationen versorgen.
(d) (*Tech: insert*) führen ◆ **to ~ sth along/through a tube** etw an einem Röhrchen entlang/durch ein Röhrchen führen.
(e) (*Theat, fig*) **to ~ sb (with) the right lines** jdm die richtigen Stichworte geben.
[3] *vi* (*animal*) fressen; (*baby*) gefüttert werden; (*hum: person*) futtern (*inf*).

◆**feed back** *vt sep facts, information* zurückleiten (*to* an +*acc*); (*Elec*) rückkoppeln ◆ **by the time the information had been fed ~ to him** als die Informationen schließlich zu ihm zurückkamen; **to ~ sth ~ into the computer** dem Computer etw wieder eingeben.

◆**feed in** *vt sep tape, wire etc* einführen (*prep obj* in +*acc*); *facts, information* eingeben (*prep obj* in +*acc*).

◆**feed on** [1] *vi* +*prep obj* sich (er)nähren von; (*fig*) sich nähren von.
[2] *vt sep* +*prep obj animal, baby* füttern mit; *person* ernähren mit.

◆**feed up** *vt sep animal* mästen ◆ **to ~ sb ~** jdn aufpäppeln; *see also* **fed up**.

feed: ~back *n* (*Psych, Comput*) Feedback *nt*, Rückmeldung *f*; (*Elec*) Rückkoppelung *f*; (*fig*) Reaktion *f*, Feedback *nt*; **~back of information** Rückinformation *f*; **in our discussion group each participant should try to get as much ~back as possible from the others** in unserer Diskussionsgruppe sollte jeder Teilnehmer von den anderen möglichst viel zurückbekommen; **to provide more ~back about sth** ausführlicher über etw (*acc*) berichten; **~bag** *n* (*US*) Futtersack *m*; **to put on the ~bag** (*inf*) eine Mahlzeit einlegen.

feeder ['fi:də^r] [1] *n* (a) (*person*) Versorger *m*; (*bottle*) Flasche *f* ◆ **automatic ~** Futterautomat *m*.
(b) (*eater*) Esser(in *f*) *m* ◆ **the cow is a good ~** die Kuh frißt gut.
(c) (*device supplying machine*) Zubringer *m*.
(d) (*contributory source*) (*river*) Zu(bringer)fluß *m*; (*road*) Zubringer(straße *f*) *m*; (*air, bus, rail service*) Zubringerlinie *f*; (*Elec*) Speiseleitung *f*, Feeder *m* ◆ **~ pipe** Zuleitungsrohr *nt*.
[2] *attr plane etc* Zubringer-.

feeding ['fi:dɪŋ]: **~ bottle** *n* Flasche *f*; **~ time** *n* (*for animal*) Fütterungszeit *f*; (*for baby*) Zeit *f* für die Mahlzeit.

▼**feel** [fi:l] (*vb: pret, ptp* **felt**) [1] *vt* (a) (*touch*) fühlen; (*examining*) befühlen ◆ **to ~ one's way** sich vortasten; **I'm still ~ing my way around** ich versuche noch, mich zu orientieren; **to ~ one's way into sth** sich in etw (*acc*) einfühlen.
(b) (*be aware of by touching, feeling*) *prick, sun etc* fühlen, spüren ◆ **I can't ~ anything in my left leg** ich habe kein Gefühl im linken Bein; **I felt it move** ich spürte, wie es sich bewegte.
(c) (*be conscious of in oneself*) *regret, joy, fear etc* fühlen, empfinden; *effects* spüren ◆ **I could ~ him getting angry** ich merkte *or* spürte, daß er wütend wurde; **he felt a sense of regret** er empfand Bedauern; **can't you ~ the sadness in this music?** können Sie nicht empfinden, wie traurig diese Musik ist?
(d) (*be affected by*) *heat, cold, insult* leiden unter (+*dat*); *loss also* empfinden ◆ **I don't ~ the cold as much as he does** die Kälte macht mir nicht so viel aus wie ihm; **a right hook which he really felt** ein rechter Haken, der saß; **she's fallen, I bet she felt that!** sie ist hingefallen, das hat bestimmt weh getan.
▼(e) (*think*) glauben ◆ **what do you ~ about him/it?** was halten Sie von ihm/davon?; **it was felt that ...** man war der Meinung, daß ...; **he felt it necessary** er hielt es für notwendig; **don't ~ you have to ...** glauben Sie nicht, Sie müßten ...
▼[2] *vi* (a) (*indicating physical or mental state: person*) sich fühlen ◆ **to ~ well/ill/secure/apprehensive/relaxed/depressed** sich wohl/elend/sicher/unsicher/entspannt/deprimiert fühlen; **how do you ~ today?** wie fühlen Sie sich heute?; **to ~ convinced/certain** überzeugt/sicher sein; **to ~ hungry/thirsty/sleepy** hungrig/durstig/müde sein; **I ~ hot/cold** mir ist heiß/kalt; **I felt very touched at** *or* **by his remarks** ich war sehr gerührt von seinen Bemerkungen; **I ~ much better** ich fühle mich viel besser, es geht mir viel besser; **you'll ~ all the better for a holiday** ein Urlaub wird Ihnen guttun; **he doesn't ~ quite**

himself today er ist heute nicht ganz auf der Höhe; **I felt sad/strange** mir war traurig/komisch zumute; **I felt as though I'd never been away/I'd seen him before** mir war, als ob ich nie weggewesen wäre/als ob ich ihn schon mal gesehen hätte; **I felt as if I was going to be sick/to explode** ich dachte, mir würde schlecht werden/ich würde gleich explodieren; **how do you ~ about him?** (*emotionally*) was empfinden Sie für ihn?; **you can imagine what I felt like** *or* **how I felt** Sie können sich (*dat*) vorstellen, wie mir zumute war.
(b) (*~ to the touch: material, ground, bricks etc*) sich anfühlen ◆ **to ~ hard/soft/rough** *etc* sich hart/weich/rauh *etc* anfühlen; **the room/air ~s warm** das Zimmer/die Luft kommt einem warm vor; **my skin ~s tight** mir spannt die Haut.
(c) (*think, have opinions*) meinen ◆ **how do you ~ about him/the idea/going for a walk?** was halten Sie von ihm/der Idee/von einem Spaziergang *or* davon spazierenzugehen?; **how do you ~ about these developments?** was meinen Sie zu dieser Entwicklung?; **that's just how I ~** das meine ich auch, ich bin genau derselben Meinung.
(d) to ~ like (*have desire for*) Lust haben auf (*+acc*); (*for food also*) Appetit haben auf (*+acc*); **I ~ like eating something/going for a walk** ich könnte jetzt etwas essen/ich habe Lust spazierenzugehen; **I felt like screaming/crying/giving up** ich hätte am liebsten geschrien/geheult/aufgegeben, ich hätte schreien/heulen/aufgeben können; **if you ~ like it** wenn Sie Lust haben, wenn Sie wollen *or* gern möchten.
(e) *impers* **what does it ~ like** *or* **how does it ~ to be all alone?** wie fühlt man sich *or* wie ist das so ganz allein?; **what does it ~ like** *or* **how does it ~ to be the boss?** wie fühlt man sich als Chef?, was ist das für ein Gefühl, Chef zu sein?; **it ~s like flying** es ist wie Fliegen.
3 *n, no pl* **(a) let me have a ~ (of it)!** laß (mich) mal fühlen!
(b) (*quality when touched*) **it has a velvety/scaly ~** es fühlt sich samten/schuppig an; **he recognizes things by their ~** er erkennt Dinge daran, wie sie sich anfühlen; **I don't like the ~ of wool against my skin** ich mag Wolle nicht auf der Haut.
(c) (*fig*) **to get/have a ~ for sth** ein Gefühl für etw bekommen/haben; **to get the ~ for sth** ein Gefühl für etw bekommen; **you must get the ~ of the poem** Sie müssen sich in das Gedicht einfühlen.

◆**feel about** *or* **around** *vi* umhertasten; (*in drawer, bag etc*) herumsuchen, herumtasten.

◆**feel for** *vi +prep obj* **(a)** (*sympathize with*) (mit)fühlen mit, Mitgefühl haben mit ◆ **I ~ ~ you** Sie tun mir leid. **(b)** (*search or grope for*) tasten nach; (*in pocket, bag etc*) kramen nach.

◆**feel up** *vt sep* (*inf: sexually*) befummeln (*inf*).

◆**feel up to** *vi +prep obj* sich gewachsen fühlen (*+dat*).

feeler ['fiːləʳ] *n* **(a)** (*Zool*) Fühler *m*; (*of sea animal*) Tentakel *m or nt.* **(b)** (*fig*) Fühler *m* ◆ **to throw** *or* **put out ~s/a ~** seine Fühler ausstrecken. **(c) ~s** *pl* (*also* **~ gauge**) Fühl(er)lehre *f.*

feeling ['fiːlɪŋ] *n* **(a)** (*sense of touch*) Gefühl *nt*, Empfindung *f* ◆ **I've lost all ~ in my right arm** ich habe kein Gefühl mehr im rechten Arm.
(b) (*physical, mental sensation, emotion*) Gefühl *nt* ◆ **a ~ of pain/warmth** ein Gefühl des Schmerzes/der Wärme; **I had a ~ of isolation** ich kam mir ganz isoliert vor; **he doesn't have much ~ for his sister** er hat nicht viel für seine Schwester übrig.
(c) (*presentiment*) (Vor)gefühl *nt* ◆ **I've a funny ~ she won't come** ich hab so das Gefühl, daß sie nicht kommt.
(d) (*opinion: also* **~s**) Meinung, Ansicht *f* (*on* zu) ◆ **there was a general ~ that ...** man war allgemein der Ansicht, daß ...; **ill** *or* **bad/good ~** Verstimmung *f*/Wohlwollen *nt*; **there's been a lot of bad ~ about this decision** wegen dieser Entscheidung hat es viel böses Blut gegeben.
(e) ~s Gefühle *pl* ◆ **you've hurt his ~s** Sie haben ihn verletzt; **no hard ~s!** ich nehme es dir nicht übel; **no hard ~s?** nimm es mir nicht übel.

feet [fiːt] *pl of* **foot.**

feign [feɪn] *vt* vortäuschen; *friendship, interest, sympathy, feelings also* heucheln ◆ **to ~ illness/madness/death** simulieren, sich krank/verrückt/tot stellen; **to ~ urgent business** dringende Geschäfte vorgeben *or* vorschützen.

feigned [feɪnd] *adj* vorgeblich *attr*; *illness also* simuliert; *interest, sympathy etc also* vorgetäuscht, geheuchelt.

feint [feɪnt] **1** *n* (*Sport*) Finte *f* ◆ **he made a ~ to the left and shot to the right** er hat links angetäuscht und nach rechts geschossen; **to make a ~** eine Finte anwenden (*at* gegenüber).
2 *vi* (*Sport*) fintieren, eine Finte anwenden (*also fig*) ◆ **he ~ed with the left and hit with the right** er hat links angetäuscht und rechts zugeschlagen.

feint(-ruled) ['feɪnt(ruːld)] *adj* fein liniert.

feisty ['faɪstɪ] (*adj*) (*US inf: lively*) lebendig.

felicitate [fɪ'lɪsɪteɪt] *vt* (*form*) beglückwünschen (*sb on sth* jdn zu etw), gratulieren (*sb on sth* jdm zu etw).

felicitation [fɪˌlɪsɪ'teɪʃən] *n usu pl* (*form*) Glückwunsch *m* ◆ **my ~s** herzliche Glückwünsche, ich gratuliere.

felicitous *adj*, **~ly** *adv* [fɪ'lɪsɪtəs, -lɪ] (*form*) glücklich.

felicity [fɪ'lɪsɪtɪ] *n* (*form*) **(a)** (*happiness*) Glück *nt*, Glückseligkeit *f* (*geh*). **(b)** (*aptness*) **he expresses himself with ~** er drückt sich sehr glücklich aus; **the ~ of the expression** die glückliche Wahl des Ausdrucks.

feline ['fiːlaɪn] **1** *adj* (*lit*) Katzen-; *species* der Katzen; (*fig*) *grace, suppleness* katzenartig, katzenhaft ◆ **she gave a ~ purr** sie schnurrte wie eine Katze.
2 *n* Katze *f.*

fell[1] [fel] *pret of* **fall.**

fell[2] *n* (*skin*) Fell *nt*, Balg *m.*

fell[3] *adj* (*liter*) fürchterlich ◆ **with one ~ blow** (*not liter*) mit einem einzigen gewaltigen *or* mächtigen Hieb; *see* **swoop.**

fell[4] *vt tree* fällen, schlagen; *person* niederstrecken, zu Boden strecken; *animal* zur Strecke bringen.

fell[5] *n* (*N Engl*) (*mountain*) Berg *m*; (*moor*) Moorland *nt.*

fellah ['felɑː] *n* **(a)** Fellache *m*, Fellachin *f.* **(b)** *see* **fellow.**

fellatio [fɪ'leɪʃɪəʊ] *n* Fellatio *f.*

fellow[1] ['feləʊ] *n* **(a)** Mann, Kerl (*usu pej*), Typ (*sl*) *m*; (*inf: boyfriend*) Freund, Typ (*sl*) *m* ◆ **a poor/nice/rude/an intelligent/a clever ~** ein armer/netter/unverschämter Kerl/ein kluger Kopf *or* Bursche/ein gescheiter Bursche, ein cleverer Typ (*sl*); **poor little ~** das arme Kerlchen; **listen to me, ~** (*US inf*) hör mal her, Mann (*inf*); **an old ~** ein alter Mann *or* Knabe (*inf*); **look here, old ~** hör mal her, alter Junge (*inf*); **young ~** junger Bursche; **this journalist ~** dieser komische Journalist; **my dear ~** mein lieber Freund *or* Mann (*inf*); **who is this ~?** wer ist denn der Typ (*sl*) *or* Kerl da?; **this ~ here** dieser Herr/junge Mann, dieser Typ (*sl*); (*rude*) dieser Kerl hier; **I'm not the sort of ~ who ...** ich bin nicht der Typ, der ...; **a ~ needs a bit of rest sometimes** (*inf*) man braucht doch auch mal 'ne Pause (*inf*).
(b) (*comrade*) Kamerad, Kumpel (*inf*) *m*; (*colleague*) Kollege *m*, Kollegin *f* ◆ **~s in misfortune** Leidensgenossen *pl*; **to get together with one's ~s** mit seinesgleichen zusammenkommen; **the company of his/their ~s** die Gesellschaft mit seines-/ihresgleichen.
(c) (*Univ*) Fellow *m*; *see* **research ~.**
(d) (*of a society*) Mitglied *nt.*
(e) (*of things: one of a pair*) Gegenstück *nt.*

fellow[2] *pref* **our ~ bankers/doctors** unsere Kollegen (im Bankwesen/in der Ärzteschaft), unsere Berufskollegen *pl*; **~ writers** Schriftstellerkollegen; **he is a ~ lexicographer** er ist auch Lexikograph; **our ~ communists/royalists** unsere kommunistischen/royalistischen Gesinnungsgenossen.

fellow: ~ being *n* Mitmensch *m*; **~ citizen** *n* Mitbürger(in *f*) *m*; **~ countryman** *n* Landsmann *m*/-männin *f*; **~ countrymen** *npl* Landsleute *pl*; **~ creature** *n* Mitmensch *m*; **~ feeling** *n* Mitgefühl *nt*; (*togetherness*) Zusammengehörigkeitsgefühl *nt*; **~ member** *n* (*in club*) Klubkamerad(in *f*) *m*; (*in party*) Parteigenosse *m*/-genossin *f*; **~ men** *npl* Mitmenschen *pl*; **~ passenger** *n* Mitreisende(r) *mf.*

fellowship ['feləʊʃɪp] *n* **(a)** *no pl* Kameradschaft *f*; (*company*) Gesellschaft *f*; (*Eccl*) Gemeinschaft *f* ◆ **... who lived without the ~ of other men ...**, der keinen Umgang mit anderen Menschen hatte; **there's no sense of ~ here** hier herrscht kein kameradschaftlicher Geist. **(b)** (*Univ: scholarship*) Forschungsstipendium *nt*; (*job*) *Position f eines Fellow.*

fellow: ~ student *n* Kommilitone *m*, Kommilitonin *f*; **~ sufferer** *n* Leidensgenosse *m*/-genossin *f*; **~ traveller** *n* **(a)** (*lit*) Mitreisende(r) *mf*; **(b)** (*Pol*) Sympathisant *m*; **~ worker** *n* Kollege *m*, Kollegin *f*, Mitarbeiter(in *f*) *m.*

fell-runner ['felrʌnəʳ] *n* Geländeläufer(in *f*) *m* (*über bergiges Gebiet*).

felon ['felən] *n* (Schwer)verbrecher *m.*

felonious [fɪ'ləʊnɪəs] *adj* verbrecherisch.

felony ['felənɪ] *n* (schweres) Verbrechen.

felspar ['felspɑːʳ] *n* Feldspat *m.*

felt[1] [felt] *pret, ptp of* **feel.**

felt[2] **1** *n* Filz *m*; *see* **roofing.**
2 *adj attr hat etc* Filz-.
3 *vi* (*wool etc*) (ver)filzen.

felt-tip (pen) ['felttɪp('pen)] *n* Filzstift, Filzschreiber *m.*

felucca [fe'lʌkə] *n* Feluke *f.*

female ['fiːmeɪl] **1** *adj* **(a)** weiblich; *labour, rights* Frauen- ◆ **a ~ doctor/student/slave/dog** eine Ärztin/Studentin/Sklavin/Hündin; **~ bear/fish/ant** Bären-/Fisch-/Ameisenweibchen *nt*; **~ bee** Biene *f*; **a ~ companion** eine Gesellschafterin; **a ~ football team** eine Damenfußballmannschaft; **~ impersonator** Damen-Imitator *m*; **a typical ~ attitude** typisch Frau.
(b) (*Tech*) *connector, plug* weiblich, Innen- ◆ **~ screw** (Schrauben)mutter, Mutterschraube *f*; **~ thread** Mutter- *or* Innengewinde *nt.*
2 *n* **(a)** (*animal*) Weibchen *nt.* **(b)** (*inf: woman*) Frau *f*; (*pej*) Weib (*pej*), Weibsbild (*pej inf*) *nt* ◆ **a typical ~** eine typische Frau; **to eye up all the ~s** die Frauen *or* Miezen (*inf*) beäugen.

feminine ['femɪnɪn] **1** *adj* (*also Gram*) feminin, weiblich; *rhyme* weiblich, klingend; (*effeminate*) feminin.
2 *n* (*Gram*) Femininum *nt* ◆ **in the ~** in der femininen *or* weiblichen Form.

femininity [ˌfemɪ'nɪnɪtɪ] *n* Weiblichkeit *f.*

feminism ['femɪnɪzəm] *n* Feminismus *m*, Frauenrechtlertum *nt.*

feminist ['femɪnɪst] **1** *n* Feminist(in *f*) *m.*
2 *adj* feministisch.

femur ['fiːməʳ] *n* Oberschenkelknochen *m.*

fen [fen] *n* Moor- *or* Sumpfland *nt* ◆ **the F~s** *die Niederungen pl in East Anglia.*

fence [fens] **1** *n* **(a)** Zaun *m*; (*Sport*) Hindernis *nt* ◆ **to sit on the ~** (*fig*) (*neutral*) neutral bleiben, nicht Partei ergreifen; (*irresolute*) unschlüssig sein, zaudern; **on the right side of the ~** (*fig*) auf der richtigen Seite. **(b)** (*inf: receiver of stolen goods*) Hehler *m.* **(c)** (*Tech*) Anschlag *m.*
2 *vt* **(a)** (*also* **~ in**) *land* ein- *or* umzäunen. **(b)** (*Sport*) fechten gegen. **(c)** (*inf*) hehlen ◆ **until we find somebody to ~ these jewels ...** bis wir einen Hehler für diese Juwelen finden ...
3 *vi* **(a)** (*Sport*) fechten. **(b)** (*fig*) ausweichen ◆ **to ~ with a question** einer Frage (*dat*) ausweichen. **(c)** (*inf: receive stolen goods*) hehlen, mit Diebesgut handeln.

◆**fence in** *vt sep* **(a)** ein- *or* umzäunen, mit einem Zaun umgeben. **(b)** (*fig*) **to ~ sb ~** jdn in seiner Freiheit ein- *or* beschränken, jds Freiheit beschneiden

➤ LANGUAGE IN USE: **feel: 2d** → 7.1, 8.4

or einengen; **don't ~ me ~** laß mir meine Freiheit; **to feel ~d ~ by restrictions** sich von Beschränkungen eingeengt fühlen.

◆**fence off** *vt sep piece of land* abzäunen.

fencer ['fensəʳ] *n* Fechter(in *f*) *m*.

fencing ['fensıŋ] *n* **(a)** (*Sport*) Fechten *nt* ◆ **~ instructor** Fechtlehrer(in *f*) *or* -meister *m*; **~ school** Fechtschule *f*. **(b)** (*fences, material*) Zaun *m*, Einzäunung *f*.

fend [fend] *vi* **to ~ for oneself** (*provide*) für sich (selbst) sorgen, sich allein durchbringen; (*defend*) sich (selbst) verteidigen; **could she ~ for herself in the big city?** konnte sie sich in der großen Stadt allein durchschlagen?

◆**fend off** *vt sep* abwehren; *attacker also* vertreiben.

fender ['fendəʳ] *n* **(a)** (*in front of fire*) Kamingitter *nt*. **(b)** (*US Aut*) Kotflügel *m*; (*of bicycle etc*) Schutzblech *nt*. **(c)** (*Naut*) Fender *m*. **(d)** (*US: on train, streetcar*) Puffer *m*.

fender-bender ['fendə,bendəʳ] *n* (*US inf*) kleiner Blechschaden.

fenestration [,fenıs'treıʃən] *n* **(a)** (*Archit*) Fensteranordnung *f*. **(b)** (*Med*) Fensterungsoperation *f*.

fennel ['fenl] *n* (*Bot*) Fenchel *m*.

feoff [fi:f] *n* (*old, form: land*) Lehen *nt*.

feral ['ferəl] *adj* (*form*) (*wild*) wild; *animals also* ungezähmt.

ferment ['fɜ:ment] **[1]** *n* **(a)** (*fermentation*) Gärung *f*; (*substance*) Ferment *nt*, Gärstoff *m*.
(b) (*fig*) Unruhe, Erregung *f* ◆ **the city/he was in a state of ~** es brodelte *or* gärte in der Stadt/in ihm.
[2] [fə'ment] *vi* (*lit, fig*) gären; (*plan also*) (aus)reifen.
[3] [fə'ment] *vt* (*lit*) fermentieren, zur Gärung bringen; (*fig*) anwachsen lassen.

fermentation [,fɜ:men'teıʃən] *n* **(a)** Gärung *f*; (*fig: of plan etc*) Ausreifen *nt* ◆ **~ lock** Gärventil *nt*. **(b)** (*fig: excitement*) Aufregung, Unruhe *f*.

fern [fɜ:n] *n* Farn(kraut *nt*) *m*.

ferocious [fə'rəʊʃəs] *adj appearance* wild, grimmig; *glance, look* böse, grimmig; *dog, animal* wild; *criticism, competition* scharf; *fight, resistance, temper* heftig; *attack* heftig, scharf; *virus* bösartig.

ferociously [fə'rəʊʃəslı] *adv* grimmig; *growl, bare teeth* wild; *fight, attack, resist* heftig; *criticize* scharf.

ferocity [fə'rɒsıtı] *n see adj* Wildheit, Grimmigkeit *f*; Bissigkeit *f*; Schärfe *f*; Heftigkeit *f*; Bösartigkeit *f*.

ferret ['ferıt] **[1]** *n* Frettchen *nt*.
[2] *vi* **(a)** (*Sport: also* **go ~ing**) mit dem Frettchen jagen.
(b) (*also* **~ about** *or* **around**) herumstöbern *or* -schnüffeln (*pej*) ◆ **she was ~ing (about** *or* **around) among my books** sie schnüffelte in meinen Büchern (herum); **he was ~ing for information** er schnüffelte nach Informationen.

◆**ferret out** *vt sep* aufstöbern, aufspüren.

ferric ['ferık] *adj* Eisen-, Eisen(III)- (*spec*).

Ferris wheel ['ferıs,wi:l] *n* Riesenrad *nt*.

ferrite ['feraıt] *n* Ferrit *m* ◆ **~ rod** Ferritstab *m*; **~ rod aerial** Ferritantenne *f*.

ferroconcrete ['ferəʊ'kɒŋkri:t] *n* Eisen- *or* Stahlbeton *m*.

ferrous ['ferəs] *adj* Eisen-, Eisen(II)- (*spec*) ◆ **~ chloride** Eisenchlorid *nt*.

fer(r)ule ['feru:l] *n* (*of umbrella, cane*) Zwinge *f*, Ring *m*.

ferry ['ferı] **[1]** *n* Fähre *f*.
[2] *vt* **(a)** (*by boat: also* **~ across** *or* **over**) übersetzen; (*by plane, car etc*) transportieren, bringen ◆ **to ~ sb across** *or* **over a river** jdn über einen Fluß setzen; **to ~ sb/sth back and forth** jdn/etw hin- und herbringen; **he ferried voters to and from the polls** er fuhr Wähler zum Wahllokal und wieder nach Hause.
(b) (*deliver*) *plane* überführen.

ferry: ~boat *n* Fährboot *nt*; **~man** *n* Fährmann *m*.

fertile ['fɜ:taıl] *adj* (*lit, fig*) fruchtbar; *land, soil also* ertragreich ◆ **the idea fell on ~ ground** der Gedanke fiel auf fruchtbaren Boden.

fertility [fə'tılıtı] **[1]** *n* (*lit, fig*) Fruchtbarkeit *f*; (*of soil, seed also*) Ergiebigkeit *f*.
[2] *attr cult, symbol* Fruchtbarkeits- ◆ **~ drug** Fruchtbarkeitspille *f*.

fertilization [,fɜ:tılaı'zeıʃən] *n* Befruchtung *f*; (*of soil*) Düngung *f*.

fertilize ['fɜ:tılaız] *vt animal, egg, flower* befruchten; *land, soil* düngen.

fertilizer ['fɜ:tılaızəʳ] *n* Dünger *m*, Düngemittel *nt* ◆ **artificial ~** Kunstdünger *m*.

ferule ['feru:l] *n* **(a)** Stock *m*. **(b)** *see* **fer(r)ule**.

fervency ['fɜ:vənsı] *n see* **fervour**.

fervent ['fɜ:vənt], **fervid** ['fɜ:vıd] *adj* leidenschaftlich; *desire, wish, hope also* inbrünstig, glühend; *tone of voice, expression, prayer also* inbrünstig.

fervently ['fɜ:vəntlı], **fervidly** ['fɜ:vıdlı] *adv* inbrünstig, leidenschaftlich.

fervour, (*US*) **fervor** ['fɜ:vəʳ] *n* Inbrunst *f*; (*of public speaker also*) Leidenschaft *f*; (*of lover*) Leidenschaftlichkeit *f*.

fester ['festəʳ] *vi* eitern, schwären (*old*); (*fig: insult, resentment etc*) nagen, fressen ◆ **~ing sore** (*fig*) Eiterbeule *f*.

festival ['festıvəl] *n* **(a)** (*Eccl etc*) Fest *nt* ◆ **Church ~s** kirchliche Feste, kirchliche Feiertage *pl*; **F~ of Lights** Lichterfest *nt*. **(b)** (*cultural*) Festspiele *pl*, Festival *nt*; (*lasting several days also*) Festwoche *f* ◆ **the Edinburgh/Salzburg F~** das Edinburgh-Festival/die Salzburger Festspiele *pl*.

festive ['festıv] *adj* festlich ◆ **the ~ season** die Festzeit; **he was in (a) ~ mood** er war in festlicher Stimmung *or* in Festtagslaune.

festivity [fe'stıvıtı] *n* **(a)** (*gaiety*) Feststimmung, Feiertagsstimmung *f* ◆ **there was an air of ~ in the office** im Büro herrschte Feststimmung *f*. **(b)** (*celebration*) Feier *f* ◆ **festivities** *pl* (*festive proceedings*) Feierlichkeiten, Festivitäten (*hum*) *pl*.

festoon [fe'stu:n] **[1]** *n* Girlande *f*; (*in curtain etc, Archit*) Feston *m*.
[2] *vt* **to ~ sb/sth with sth** jdn mit etw behängen/etw mit etw schmücken *or* verzieren; **to be ~ed with sth** mit etw behängt sein; **garlands ~ed the room** Girlanden schmückten den Raum.

fetal *adj* (*esp US*) *see* **foetal**.

fetch [fetʃ] **[1]** *vt* **(a)** (*bring*) holen; (*collect*) *person, thing* abholen ◆ **would you ~ a handkerchief for me** *or* **~ me a handkerchief?** kannst du mir ein Taschentuch holen (gehen)?; **I'll ~ her from the station** ich hole sie vom Bahnhof ab; **she ~ed in the washing** sie holte die Wäsche herein; **he's upstairs, I'll ~ him down** er ist oben, ich hole ihn herunter.
(b) *sigh, groan* ausstoßen.
(c) (*bring in*) *money* (ein)bringen.
(d) (*inf*) **to ~ sb a blow/one** jdm eine langen (*inf*); (*accidentally: with rucksack etc*) jdn erwischen (*inf*).
[2] *vi* **(a) to ~ and carry for sb** bei jdm Mädchen für alles sein.
(b) (*Naut*) Kurs halten; (*change course*) Kurs nehmen.

◆**fetch up** **[1]** *vi* (*inf*) landen (*inf*).
[2] *vt sep* (*Brit: vomit*) wieder von sich geben, erbrechen.

fetching ['fetʃıŋ] *adj* bezaubernd, reizend; *hat, dress also* entzückend; *smile also* gewinnend, einnehmend.

fête [feıt] **[1]** *n* Fest *nt* ◆ **village ~** Dorffest *nt*.
[2] *vt* (*make much of*) *sb, sb's success* feiern ◆ **to ~ sb** (*entertain*) zu jds Ehren ein Fest geben; **a much ~d actress** eine gefeierte Schauspielerin.

fetid ['fetıd] *adj* übelriechend.

fetish ['fetıʃ] *n* (*all senses*) Fetisch *m* ◆ **to have a ~ about leather/cleanliness** einen Leder-/Sauberkeitstick haben (*inf*), ein Leder-/Sauberkeitsfetischist sein; **to make a ~ of sth** einen Kult mit etw treiben, etw zum Fetisch machen *or* erheben.

fetishism ['fetıʃızəm] *n* Fetischismus *m*.

fetishist ['fetıʃıst] *n* Fetischist *m*.

fetishistic [,fetı'ʃıstık] *adj* fetischistisch ◆ **to get ~ about sth** etw zu einem Fetisch machen.

fetlock ['fetlɒk] *n* Fessel *f*; (*joint*) Fesselgelenk *nt*.

fetter ['fetəʳ] **[1]** *vt prisoner* fesseln; *goat* anpflocken; (*fig*) in Fesseln legen.
[2] *n* **~s** *pl* (Fuß)fesseln *pl*; (*fig*) Fesseln *pl* ◆ **to put a prisoner in ~s** einen Gefangenen in Fesseln legen.

fettle ['fetl] *n* **to be in fine** *or* **good ~** in bester Form sein; (*as regards health also*) in bester Verfassung *or* topfit sein (*inf*).

fetus *n* (*US*) *see* **foetus**.

feu [fju:] *n* (*Scot*) Lehen *nt* ◆ **~ duty** Lehnsabgabe *f*.

feud [fju:d] **[1]** *n* (*lit, fig*) Fehde *f* ◆ **to have a ~ with sb** mit jdm in Fehde liegen.
[2] *vi* (*lit, fig*) sich befehden, in Fehde liegen.

feudal ['fju:dl] *adj* Feudal-, feudal, Lehns-.

feudalism ['fju:dəlızəm] *n* Feudalismus *m*, Lehnswesen *nt*.

fever ['fi:vəʳ] *n* **(a)** Fieber *nt no pl* ◆ **tropical ~s** tropische Fieberkrankheiten *pl*; **to have a ~** eine Fieberkrankheit haben; (*high temperature*) Fieber haben.
(b) (*fig*) Aufregung, Erregung *f*, Fieber *nt* ◆ **election ~** Wahlfieber *nt*, Wahlrausch *m*; **in a ~ of excitement** in fieberhafter Erregung; **to go into a ~ of excitement** von fieberhafter Erregung ergriffen *or* befallen werden; **~ pitch** Siedepunkt *m*; **to reach ~ pitch** am Siedepunkt angelangt sein, den Siedepunkt erreichen; **to be working at ~ pitch** auf Hochtouren arbeiten.

feverish ['fi:vərıʃ] *adj* (*Med*) fiebernd *attr*; (*fig*) *activity* fieberhaft; *atmosphere* fiebrig ◆ **he's still ~** er fiebert noch, er hat noch Fieber.

feverishly ['fi:vərıʃlı] *adv* fieberhaft.

feverishness ['fi:vərıʃnıs] *n* Fiebrigkeit *f*.

few [fju:] **[1]** *adj* (*+er*) **(a)** (*not many*) wenige ◆ **~ people come to see him** nur wenige Leute besuchen ihn; **with ~ exceptions** mit wenigen Ausnahmen; **we are very ~** wir sind nur sehr wenige *or* nur ein kleines Häufchen; **~ and far between** dünn gesät; **as ~ books as you** genauso wenig(e) Bücher wie du; **as ~ as six objections** bloß sechs Einwände, nicht mehr als sechs Einwände; **how ~ they are!** wie wenige das sind!; **so ~ books** so wenige Bücher; **too ~ cakes** zu wenige Kuchen; **there were 3 too ~** es waren 3 zuwenig da; **10 would not be too ~** 10 wären nicht zuwenig; **he is one of the ~ people who ...** er ist einer der wenigen, die ...; **the exceptions are ~** es gibt nur wenige Ausnahmen; **such occasions are ~** solche Gelegenheiten sind selten *or* rar; **its days are ~** es hat nur ein kurzes Leben.
(b) a ~ ein paar; **a ~ more days** noch ein paar Tage; **a ~ times** ein paar Male; **there were quite a ~ waiting** ziemlich viele warteten; **he has quite a ~ girl-friends** er hat eine ganze Menge *or* ziemlich viele Freundinnen; **he's had a good ~ drinks** er hat ziemlich viel getrunken; **quite a ~ books** ziemlich viele Bücher, eine ganze Menge Bücher; **I saw a good ~** *or* **quite a ~ people** ich habe ziemlich viele Leute *or* eine ganze Menge Leute gesehen; **we'll go in a ~ minutes** wir gehen in ein paar Minuten; **in the next/past ~ days** in den nächsten/letzten paar Tagen; **every ~ days** alle paar Tage.
[2] *pron* **(a)** (*not many*) wenige ◆ **~ of them came** wenige von ihnen kamen; **some ~** gar nicht so wenige; **the F~** *Kampfflieger, die an der Luftschlacht um England im zweiten Weltkrieg teilnahmen*; **the lucky ~** die wenigen Glücklichen; **as ~ as you** genauso wenig wie du; **how ~ there are!** wie wenige das sind!; **however ~ there may be** wie wenig auch immer da ist; **I've got so/too ~ as it is** ich habe sowieso schon so/zu wenig(e); **so ~ have been sold** so wenige sind bis jetzt verkauft worden; **there are too ~ of you** ihr seid zu wenige.
(b) a ~ ein paar; **I'll take just a ~** ich nehme nur ein paar; **a ~ more** ein paar mehr; **quite a ~ did not believe him** eine ganze Menge Leute *or* ziemlich viele Leute glaubten ihm nicht; **quite a ~** eine ganze Menge; **some ~** ei-

nige; **there are always the ~ who ...** es gibt immer einige wenige Leute *or* ein paar Leute, die ...; **the ~ who knew him** die wenigen, die ihn kannten.
fewer ['fju:ə^r] *adj, pron comp of* **few** weniger ◆ **no ~ than** nicht weniger als.
fewest ['fju:ɪst] *superl of* **few** [1] *adj* die wenigsten ◆ **the ~ occasions possible** so wenig wie möglich, so selten wie möglich.
[2] *pron* die wenigsten, am wenigsten.
fey [feɪ] *adj* (*Scot*) todgeweiht; (*clairvoyant*) hellseherisch.
fez [fez] *n* Fes *m*.
ff *abbr of* **following** ff.
fiancé [fɪ'ɑ̃:ŋseɪ] *n* Verlobte(r) *m*.
fiancée [fɪ'ɑ̃:ŋseɪ] *n* Verlobte *f*.
fiasco [fɪ'æskəʊ] *n, pl* **-s,** (*US also*) **-es** Fiasko *nt* ◆ **what a ~ of a reception** was für ein Fiasko dieser Empfang ist/war.
fiat ['faɪæt] *n* **(a)** (*decree*) Befehl, Erlaß *m*, Anordnung *f* ◆ **you can't just get it done by ~** das erledigt sich nicht so einfach auf Befehl. **(b)** (*authorization*) Billigung *f*, Plazet *nt*.
fib [fɪb] (*inf*) [1] *n* Flunkerei (*inf*), Schwindelei (*inf*) *f* ◆ **(that's a) ~!** das ist geflunkert! (*inf*); **don't tell ~s** flunker *or* schwindel nicht! (*inf*); **it's all a big ~** das ist alles (ein) großer Schwindel!
[2] *vi* flunkern (*inf*), schwindeln *inf*).
fibber ['fɪbə^r] *n* (*inf*) Flunkerer (*inf*), Schwindler (*inf*) *m*.
fibbing ['fɪbɪŋ] *n* (*inf*) Flunkerei *f* (*inf*).
fibre, (*US*) **fiber** ['faɪbə^r] *n* **(a)** Faser *f*. **(b)** (*fig*) **moral ~** Charakterstärke *f*; **he has no moral ~** er hat keinen inneren Halt, er hat kein Rückgrat.
fibre: ~board *n* Faserplatte *f*; **~glass** [1] *n* Fiberglas *nt*; [2] *adj* Fiberglas-, aus Fiberglas; **~-optic cable** *n* faseroptisches Kabel; **~ optics** *n sing* Faseroptik *f*; **~-tip pen** *n* (*Brit*) Faserschreiber *m*.
fibroid ['faɪbrɔɪd] *adj* fibrös.
fibrositis [ˌfaɪbrə'saɪtɪs] *n* Bindegewebsentzündung *f*.
fibrous ['faɪbrəs] *adj* faserig.
fibula ['fɪbjʊlə] *n* Wadenbein *nt*.
fickle ['fɪkl] *adj* unbeständig, launenhaft; *person also* wankelmütig; *weather also* wechselhaft.
fickleness ['fɪklnɪs] *n* Wechselhaftigkeit, Unbeständigkeit *f*; (*of person also*) Wankelmütigkeit *f*.
fiction ['fɪkʃən] *n* **(a)** *no pl* (*Liter*) Erzähl- *or* Prosaliteratur *f* ◆ **you'll find that under ~** das finden Sie unter Belletristik; **work of ~** Erzählung *f*; (*longer*) Roman *m*; **light ~** (leichte) Unterhaltungsliteratur; **romantic ~** Liebesromane *pl*.
(b) (*invention*) (freie) Erfindung, Fiktion *f* ◆ **that's pure ~** das ist frei erfunden; **the unicorn is a ~** das Einhorn ist eine Fiktion.
(c) legal ~ juristische Fiktion.
fictional ['fɪkʃənl] *adj* erdichtet, erfunden ◆ **all these events are purely ~** alle diese Ereignisse sind frei erfunden; **his ~ writing** seine erzählenden Schriften; **a ~ representation of historical events** eine dichterische Darstellung historischer Ereignisse; **a ~ character** eine Gestalt aus der Literatur.
fictitious [fɪk'tɪʃəs] *adj* **(a)** (*imaginary*) fiktiv, frei erfunden ◆ **all characters in this film are ~** alle Gestalten in diesem Film sind frei erfunden. **(b)** (*false*) falsch. **(c) ~ person** (*Jur*) juristische Person.
fiddle ['fɪdl] [1] *n* **(a)** (*Mus inf*) Fiedel (*inf*), Geige *f* ◆ **first ~** erste Geige; **to play second ~ (to sb)** (*fig*) in jds Schatten (*dat*) stehen; **he refuses to play second ~** (*fig*) er will immer die erste Geige spielen; **as fit as a ~** kerngesund; **he had a face as long as a ~** er machte ein Gesicht wie drei Tage Regenwetter.
(b) (*Brit inf: cheat, swindle*) Manipulation, Schiebung *f*; (*with money*) faule Geschäfte *pl* (*inf*) ◆ **it's a ~** das ist Schiebung!; **he only got that job through some ~** er hat die Stelle nur durch Trickserei gekriegt (*inf*); **there are so many ~s going on** es wird so viel getrickst (*inf*) *or* manipuliert; **the accountants were well aware there had been some sort of ~** die Buchprüfer wußten ganz genau, daß da irgend etwas manipuliert *or* frisiert (*inf*) worden war; **tax ~** Steuermanipulation *f*; **to be on the ~** faule Geschäfte *or* krumme Dinger machen (*inf*).
[2] *vi* **(a)** (*Mus inf*) fiedeln (*inf*), geigen.
(b) (*fidget, play around*) herumspielen ◆ **don't ~ with the engine if you don't know what you're doing** spiel nicht am Motor herum, wenn du dich damit nicht auskennst; **he sat there nervously fiddling with his tie/cigarette lighter** er saß da und spielte nervös an seinem Schlips herum/spielte mit seinem Feuerzeug herum; **put that thing down and stop fiddling!** leg das Ding weg und hör endlich mit dem Herumspielen auf!
(c) (*split hairs, be over-precise etc*) Haare spalten, pingelig sein (*inf*) ◆ **that would just be fiddling** das wäre reine Haarspalterei *or* bloße Pingeligkeit (*inf*).
[3] *vt* (*inf*) **(a)** *accounts, results* frisieren (*inf*); *election* manipulieren ◆ **he ~d some money out of the firm** er hat der Firma ein bißchen Geld abgegaunert (*inf*); **he ~d it so that ...** er hat es so hingebogen *or* getrickst (*inf*), daß ...
(b) *tune* fiedeln (*inf*), geigen.
[4] *interj* ach du liebe Zeit, ach du liebes Lottchen (*hum inf*).
◆**fiddle about** *or* **around** *vi* **to ~ ~ with sth** an etw (*dat*) herumspielen *or* herumfummeln (*inf*); (*fidget with*) mit etw herumspielen; **he dived under the bonnet and ~d ~ for a while** er verschwand unter der Kühlerhaube und fummelte eine Weile herum (*inf*); **I'm not spending all day just fiddling ~ with this one little job!** ich werde doch nicht den ganzen Tag damit zubringen, an dieser einen Kleinigkeit rumzufummeln! (*inf*); **he wasn't really playing a tune, just fiddling ~** er spielte keine richtige Melodie, er spielte nur so rum (*inf*).
fiddle-faddle ['fɪdlfædl] *interj* (*dated: nonsense*) Quatsch (*inf*).
fiddler ['fɪdlə^r] *n* **(a)** (*Mus inf*) Geiger *m*. **(b) you little ~, now you've broken it** du mit deiner ewigen Herumspielerei, jetzt ist es kaputt. **(c)** (*inf: cheat*) Schwindler, Betrüger *m*.
fiddler crab *n* Winkerkrabbe *f*.
fiddlesticks ['fɪdlstɪks] *interj* (*nonsense*) Unsinn, Quatsch (*inf*); (*bother*) du liebe Zeit, du liebes Lottchen (*hum inf*).
fiddliness ['fɪdlɪnɪs] *n* (*inf: intricacy*) Kniffligkeit *f* (*inf*).
fiddling ['fɪdlɪŋ] *adj* (*trivial*) läppisch.
fiddly ['fɪdlɪ] *adj* (+*er*) (*inf: intricate*) knifflig (*inf*).
fidelity [fɪ'delɪtɪ] *n* **(a)** Treue *f* (*to* zu). **(b)** (*of translation etc*) Genauigkeit *f*; (*Rad etc*) Klangtreue *f*.
fidget ['fɪdʒɪt] [1] *vi* (*be restless*) zappeln ◆ **to ~ with sth** mit etw herumspielen *or* herumfummeln (*inf*); **don't ~** zappel nicht so rum; **he sat there ~ing on his chair** er rutschte auf seinem Stuhl hin und her.
[2] *n* **(a)** (*person*) Zappelphilipp *m* (*inf*).
(b) (*inf*) **to give sb the ~s** jdn zappelig *or* kribbelig machen; **have you got the ~s?** was bist du für ein Zappelphilipp! (*inf*); **to get the ~s** zappelig werden.
fidgety ['fɪdʒɪtɪ] *adj* zappelig; *audience etc* unruhig.
fiduciary [fɪ'dju:ʃɪərɪ] [1] *adj* treuhänderisch; *currency* ungedeckt.
[2] *n* Treuhänder *m*.
fie [faɪ] *interj* (*old*) pfui ◆ **~ upon you** pfui!
fief [fi:f] *n* (*Hist*) Lehen *nt*.
field [fi:ld] [1] *n* **(a)** (*Agr*) Feld *nt*, Acker *m*; (*area of grass*) Wiese *f*; (*for cows, horses etc*) Weide *f* ◆ **corn/wheat ~** Getreide-/Weizenfeld *nt*; **potato ~** Kartoffelacker *m*; **we had a picnic in a ~** wir machten auf einer Wiese Picknick; **he's working in the ~s** er arbeitet auf dem Feld *or* Acker; **the farm has 20 ~s** der Hof hat 20 Felder; **beasts of the ~** Feldtiere *pl*; **to cut across the ~s** quer über die Felder gehen.
(b) (*coal~, ice~, oil~ etc*) Feld *nt*.
(c) (*for football etc: ground*) Platz *m* ◆ **sports** *or* **games ~** Sportplatz *m*; **to take the ~** auf den Platz kommen, einlaufen.
(d) (*Mil*) **~ of battle** Schlachtfeld *nt*; **noted for his bravery in the ~** für seine Tapferkeit im Feld bekannt; **to take the ~** zur Schlacht antreten; **to hold the ~** das Feld behaupten; **the ~ was ours** der Sieg war unser (*geh*); **he died on the ~ of honour** er ließ sein Leben auf dem Feld der Ehre.
(e) (*of study, work etc*) Gebiet, Feld *nt* ◆ **to be first in the ~ with sth** (*Comm*) als erster etw auf den Markt bringen; **in all the ~s of human endeavour** (*liter*) im gesamten menschlichen Trachten (*liter*); **studies in the ~ of medicine** Studien auf dem Gebiet der Medizin; **this is, of course, a very broad ~** das ist natürlich ein weites Feld; **what ~ are you in?** auf welchem Gebiet *or* in welchem Feld arbeiten Sie?; **his ~ is Renaissance painting** sein Spezialgebiet ist die Malerei der Renaissance.
(f) (*area of practical observation or operation*) Praxis *f* ◆ **when a salesman goes out into the ~** wenn ein Verkäufer in den Außeneinsatz geht; **work in the ~** Feldforschung *f*; (*of sales rep*) Außendienst *m*; **to test sth in the ~** etw in der Praxis *or* vor Ort ausprobieren.
(g) (*Phys, Opt*) Feld *nt* ◆ **~ of vision** Blick- *or* Gesichtsfeld *nt*; **gravitational ~** Gravitationsfeld, Schwerefeld *nt*; **~ of force** Kraftfeld *nt*; **magnetic ~** Magnetfeld *nt*, magnetisches Feld.
(h) (*Sport: competitors*) Feld *nt*; (*Hunt also*) rotes Feld; (*Cricket, Baseball*) Fängerpartei *f* ◆ **the rest of the ~** (*in race*) der Rest des Feldes, die übrigen Läufer; **there's quite a strong ~ for this year's chess contest** das Teilnehmerfeld für den diesjährigen Schachwettbewerb ist ziemlich stark.
(i) (*Comput*) Datenfeld *nt*; (*on punch card*) Feld *nt*.
(j) (*on flag, Her*) Feld *nt*, Grund *m*.
[2] *vt* **(a)** (*Cricket, Baseball etc*) *ball* auffangen und zurückwerfen; (*fig*) *question etc* abblocken, abwehren.
(b) *team, side* aufs Feld *or* auf den Platz schicken.
[3] *vi* (*Cricket, Baseball etc*) als Fänger spielen ◆ **when we go out to ~** wenn wir die Fänger(partei) stellen.
field: ~ ambulance *n* (*Mil*) Sanka, Sanitätskraftwagen *m*; **~ artillery** *n* Feldartillerie *f*; **~ day** *n* **(a)** Manöver *nt*; **(b)** (*fig*) **I had a ~ day** ich hatte meinen großen Tag; **to have a ~ day** einen inneren Reichsparteitag haben (*inf*); **with the score at 6-0 the Scots are having a ~ day against the English** beim Stand von 6:0 machen die Schotten jetzt die Engländer nach allen Regeln der Kunst fertig (*inf*).
fielder ['fi:ldə^r] *n* (*Cricket, Baseball etc*) Fänger *m*.
field: ~ event *n* (*Athletics*) *Disziplin, die nicht auf der Aschenbahn ausgetragen wird*; **~ games** *npl* Feldspiele *pl*; **~ glasses** *npl* Feldstecher *m*; **~ goal** *n* (*US*) (*Basketball*) Korbwurf *m* aus dem Spielgeschehen; (*Ftbl*) Feldtor *nt*; **~ gun** *n* (*Mil*) Feldgeschütz *nt*; **~ hockey** *n* (*US*) Hockey *nt*; **~ hospital** *n* (*Mil*) (Feld)lazarett *nt*; **~ kitchen** *n* (*Mil*) Feldküche *f*; **~ marshal** *n* (*Mil*) Feldmarschall *m*; **~mouse** *n* Feldmaus *f*; **~ notes** *npl* Arbeitsnotizen *pl*; **~piece** *n* (*Mil*) Feldgeschütz *nt*.
fieldsman ['fi:ldzmən] *n, pl* **-men** [-mən] (*Cricket*) Fänger *m*.
field: ~ sports *npl* **(a)** Sport *m* im Freien (*Jagen und Fischen*); **(b)** *see* **~ games**; **~ study** *n* Feldforschung *f*; **a ~ study** eine Feldstudie; **~ test** *n* Feldversuch *m*; **~-test** *vt* in einem Feldversuch/in Feldversuchen testen; **~work** *n* **(a)** (*of geologist, surveyor etc*) Arbeit *f* im Gelände; (*of sociologist etc*) Feldarbeit, Feldforschung *f*; **(b)** (*Mil*) Feldbefestigung, Schanze *f*; **~worker** *n* Praktiker *m*.
fiend [fi:nd] *n* **(a)** (*evil spirit*) Teufel, Dämon *m*; (*person*) Teufel *m* ◆ **the F~** der böse Feind; **"sex ~ strikes again"** „Sexbestie schlägt wieder zu".
(b) (*inf: addict*) Fanatiker(in *f*) *m* ◆ **he's a real ~ for Verdi** er ist ein richtiger Verdinarr *or* -fanatiker; **tennis ~** Tennisnarr *m*; **a fresh-air ~** ein Frisch-

luftfanatiker *m.*

fiendish ['fi:ndɪʃ] *adj* teuflisch; *cruelty also* unmenschlich; (*inf*) *pace, heat* höllisch (*inf*), Höllen- (*inf*); (*inf*) *problem* verteufelt (*inf*), verzwickt ◆ **to take a ~ delight in doing sth** seine höllische Freude daran haben, etw zu tun (*inf*).

fiendishly ['fi:ndɪʃlɪ] *adv grin, chuckle* teuflisch; (*dated inf*) *difficult, complicated* verteufelt (*inf*).

fierce [fɪəs] *adj* (*+er*) *appearance* wild, grimmig; *glance, look* böse, grimmig; *dog* bissig; *lion, warrior* wild; *criticism, competition* scharf; *fight, resistance, temper* heftig; *attack* (*lit, fig*) heftig, scharf; *heat* glühend; *sun* grell, glühend.

fiercely ['fɪəslɪ] *adv see adj.*

fierceness ['fɪəsnɪs] *n see adj* Wildheit, Grimmigkeit *f*; Bissigkeit *f*; Schärfe *f*; Heftigkeit *f*; Glut *f*; Grellheit *f*.

fiery ['faɪərɪ] *adj* (*+er*) feurig, glühend; *sunset* rotglühend; (*fig*) *person, temper* feurig, hitzig; *curry* feurig ◆ **to have a ~ temper/to be ~** ein Hitzkopf *m* sein; **~ liquor** feuriger Schnaps.

fiesta [fɪ'estə] *n* Fiesta *f.*

FIFA ['fi:fə] *abbr of* **Federation of International Football Associations** FIFA *f.*

fife [faɪf] *n* (*Mus*) Querpfeife *f.*

fifteen ['fɪf'ti:n] [1] *adj* fünfzehn.
[2] *n* **(a)** Fünfzehn *f.* **(b) a rugby ~** eine Rugbymannschaft; **the Welsh ~** die Rugbynationalmannschaft von Wales.

fifteenth ['fɪf'ti:nθ] [1] *adj* fünfzehnte(r, s).
[2] *n* Fünfzehnte(r, s); (*part, fraction*) Fünfzehntel *nt*; *see also* **sixteenth.**

fifth [fɪfθ] [1] *adj* fünfte(r, s) ◆ **~ column** fünfte Kolonne; **~ columnist** Angehörige(r) *mf* der fünften Kolonne; **~ rate** fünftrangig.
[2] *n* Fünfte(r, s); (*part, fraction*) Fünftel *nt*; (*Mus*) Quinte *f* ◆ **to take the ~** (*US inf*) die Aussage verweigern; *see also* **sixth.**

fiftieth ['fɪftɪɪθ] [1] *adj* fünfzigste(r, s).
[2] *n* Fünfzigste(r, s); (*part, fraction*) Fünfzigstel *nt*.

fifty ['fɪftɪ] [1] *adj* fünfzig.
[2] *n* Fünfzig *f*; *see also* **sixty.**

fifty-fifty ['fɪftɪ,fɪftɪ] [1] *adj* halbe-halbe *pred inv*, fifty-fifty *pred inv* ◆ **we have a ~ chance of success** unsere Chancen stehen fifty-fifty.
[2] *adv* **to go ~ (with sb)** (mit jdm) halbe-halbe *or* fifty-fifty machen.

fig *abbr of* **figure(s)** Abb.

fig [fɪg] *n* Feige *f* ◆ **I don't care a ~** (*inf*) ich kümmere mich einen Dreck darum (*inf*); **I don't give a ~ for what he thinks!** seine Meinung kümmert mich einen (feuchten) Dreck (*inf*); **not worth a ~** keinen Deut wert.

fight [faɪt] (*vb: pret, ptp* **fought**) [1] *n* **(a)** (*lit, fig*) Kampf *m*; (*fist ~, scrap*) Rauferei, Prügelei, Schlägerei *f*; (*Mil*) Gefecht *nt*; (*argument, row*) Streit *m* ◆ **to have a ~ with sb** sich mit jdm schlagen; (*argue*) sich mit jdm streiten; **to give sb a ~** (*lit, fig*) jdm einen Kampf liefern; **to put up a ~** (*lit, fig*) sich zur Wehr setzen; **to put up a good ~** (*lit, fig*) sich tapfer zur Wehr setzen, sich tapfer schlagen; **do you want a ~?** willst du was?, du willst dich wohl mit mir anlegen?; **if he wants a ~, then ...** (*lit, fig*) wenn er Streit sucht, dann ...; **a politician who enjoys a good ~** ein streitlustiger Politiker; **he won't give in without a ~** er ergibt sich nicht kampflos; **in the ~ against disease** im Kampf gegen die Krankheit; **the big ~** (*Boxing*) der große Kampf.
(b) (*~ing spirit*) Kampfgeist *m* ◆ **there was no ~ left in him** sein Kampfgeist war erloschen; **to show ~** Kampfgeist zeigen.
[2] *vi* kämpfen; (*have punch-up etc*) raufen, sich prügeln, sich schlagen; (*argue, with wife etc*) sich streiten *or* zanken ◆ **the dogs were ~ing over a bone** die Hunde rauften um einen Knochen; **to ~ against disease** Krankheiten bekämpfen; **to ~ for sb/sth** um jdn/etw kämpfen; **to ~ for what one believes in** für seine Überzeugungen eintreten *or* streiten; **to ~ for one's life** um sein Leben kämpfen; **to go down ~ing** sich nicht kampflos ergeben; **to ~ shy of sth** einer Sache (*dat*) aus dem Weg gehen; **I've always fought shy of claiming that ...** ich habe immer bewußt vermieden, zu behaupten ...
[3] *vt* **(a)** *person* kämpfen mit *or* gegen; (*have punch-up with*) sich schlagen mit, sich prügeln mit; (*in battle*) kämpfen mit, sich (*dat*) ein Gefecht *nt* liefern mit ◆ **I'm prepared to ~ him/the government** (*argue with, take on*) ich bin bereit, das mit ihm/der Regierung durchzukämpfen; **I'll ~ him on that one** dazu nehme ich es mit ihm auf; **you can't ~ the whole company** du kannst es nicht mit der ganzen Firma aufnehmen.
(b) *fire, disease, cuts, policy* bekämpfen; *decision* ankämpfen gegen ◆ **there's no point in ~ing it, this thing is bigger than both of us** es hat keinen Zweck, dagegen anzukämpfen, dieses Gefühl ist stärker als wir beide.
(c) to ~ a duel ein Duell *nt* austragen, sich duellieren; **to ~ an action at law** einen Prozeß vor Gericht durchkämpfen *or* durchfechten; **to ~ one's way out of the crowd** sich aus der Menge freikämpfen; *see* **battle.**
(d) (*Mil, Naut: control in battle*) *army, ships* kommandieren.

◆**fight back** [1] *vi* (*in fight*) zurückschlagen; (*Mil*) sich verteidigen, Widerstand leisten; (*in argument*) sich wehren, sich zur Wehr setzen; (*after illness*) zu Kräften kommen; (*Sport*) zurückkämpfen.
[2] *vt sep tears etc* unterdrücken; *doubts also* zu besiegen versuchen ◆ **he fought his way ~ into the match/to the top** er hat sich ins Spiel/wieder an die Spitze zurückgekämpft.

◆**fight down** *vt sep anxiety* unterdrücken, bezwingen.

◆**fight off** *vt sep* (*Mil, fig*) *attack, disease* abwehren; *sleep* ankämpfen gegen; *a cold* erfolgreich bekämpfen ◆ **I'm still trying to ~ ~ this cold** ich kämpfe immer noch mit dieser Erkältung; **she has to keep ~ing men ~** sie muß dauernd Männer abwimmeln.

◆**fight on** *vi* weiterkämpfen.

◆**fight out** *vt sep* **to ~ it ~** es untereinander ausfechten.

fightback ['faɪtbæk] *n* Comeback *nt.*

fighter ['faɪtə^r] *n* **(a)** Kämpfer, Streiter *m*; (*Boxing*) Fighter *m* ◆ **he's a ~** (*fig*) er ist eine Kämpfernatur. **(b)** (*Aviat: plane*) Jagdflugzeug *nt*, Jäger *m.*

fighter: ~-bomber *n* Jagdbomber *m*; **~-interceptor** *n* Abfangjäger *m*; **~-pilot** *n* Jagdflieger *m.*

fighting ['faɪtɪŋ] [1] *n* (*Mil*) Kampf *m*, Gefecht *nt*; (*punch-ups, scrapping etc*) Prügeleien, Raufereien *pl*; (*arguments between husband and wife etc*) Streit, Zank *m* ◆ **~ broke out** Kämpfe brachen aus; *see* **street ~.**
[2] *adj attr person* kämpferisch, streitlustig; (*Mil*) *troops* Kampf-.

fighting: ~ chance *n* faire Chancen *pl*; **he's in with** *or* **he has a ~ chance** er hat eine Chance, wenn er sich anstrengt; **at least that gives you a ~ chance** damit hast du wenigstens eine Chance; **~ cock** *n* (*lit, fig*) Kampfhahn *m*; **~ forces** *npl* Kampftruppen *pl*; **~ line** *n* Front *f*; **~ man** *n* Krieger, Kämpfer *m*; **~ spirit** *n* Kampfgeist *m*; **to have a lot of ~ spirit** großen Kampfgeist haben; **~ strength** *n* (*Mil*) Kampf- *or* Einsatzstärke *f.*

figleaf ['fɪgli:f] *n* (*lit, fig*) Feigenblatt *nt.*

figment ['fɪgmənt] *n* **a ~ of the imagination** pure Einbildung, ein Hirngespinst *nt*; **it's all a ~ of his imagination** das ist alles eine Ausgeburt seiner Phantasie.

fig tree *n* Feigenbaum *m.*

figurative ['fɪgjʊrətɪv] *adj* **(a)** *language* bildlich; *use, sense* übertragen, figürlich. **(b)** (*Art*) gegenständlich.

figuratively ['fɪgjʊərətɪvlɪ] *adv* im übertragenen Sinne ◆ **~ speaking, of course** natürlich nicht im wörtlichen Sinn.

figure ['fɪgə^r] [1] *n* **(a)** (*number*) Zahl; (*digit also*) Ziffer *f*; (*sum*) Summe *f* ◆ **could you put some sort of ~ on the salary?** können Sie mir ungefähr die Höhe meines Gehaltes angeben?; **name your ~** nennen Sie Ihren Preis; **he's good at ~s** er ist ein guter Rechner; **a mistake in the ~s** eine Unstimmigkeit in den Zahlen; **have you seen last year's ~s?** haben Sie die Zahlen vom Vorjahr gesehen?; **Miss Jones, could you bring in the ~s for the Fotheringham contract?** Fräulein Jones, könnten Sie das Zahlenmaterial zum Fotheringham-Vertrag bringen?; **to get into double ~s** sich auf zweistellige Beträge belaufen, in die zweistelligen Zahlen gehen; **three-~ number** dreistellige Zahl; **to sell for a high ~** für eine hohe Summe verkauft werden; **he earns well into four ~s** er hat gut und gern ein vierstelliges Einkommen; **the ~s work** (*inf*) es rechnet sich (*inf*).
(b) (*in geometry, dancing, skating*) Figur *f* ◆ **~ of eight** Acht *f.*
(c) (*human form*) Gestalt *f.*
(d) (*shapeliness*) Figur *f* ◆ **she has a good ~** sie hat eine gute Figur; **I'm dieting to keep my ~** ich lebe Diät, um meine Figur zu behalten; **what a ~!** (was für) eine tolle Figur!; **she's a fine ~ of a woman** sie ist eine stattliche Frau; **he's a fine ~ of a man** er ist ein Bild von einem Mann; *see* **cut.**
(e) (*personality*) Persönlichkeit *f*; (*character in novel etc*) Gestalt *f* ◆ **the great ~s of history** die Großen der Geschichte; **a great public ~** eine bedeutende Persönlichkeit des öffentlichen Lebens; **~ of fun** Witzfigur *f*, lächerliche Erscheinung.
(f) (*statuette, model etc*) Figur *f.*
(g) (*Liter*) **~ of speech** Redensart, Redewendung *f*; **it's just a ~ of speech** das ist doch nur eine (leere) Redensart, das sagt man doch nur so.
(h) (*Mus*) Figur, Phrase *f*; (*notation*) Ziffer *f.*
(i) (*illustration*) Abbildung *f.*
[2] *vt* **(a)** (*decorate*) *silk etc* bemalen, mustern ◆ **~d velvet** bedruckter Samt. **(b)** (*Mus*) *bass* beziffern; *melody* verzieren. **(c)** (*imagine*) sich (*dat*) vorstellen, sich (*dat*) denken. **(d)** (*US inf: think, reckon*) glauben, schätzen (*inf*). **(e)** (*US inf: ~ out*) schlau werden aus, begreifen.
[3] *vi* **(a)** (*appear*) erscheinen, auftauchen ◆ **where does pity ~ in your scheme of things?** wo rangiert Mitleid in deiner Weltordnung?; **he ~d in a play** er trat in einem Stück auf; **he ~d prominently in the talks** er spielte eine bedeutende Rolle bei den Gesprächen.
(b) (*inf: make sense*) hinkommen (*inf*), hinhauen (*inf*) ◆ **that ~s** das hätte ich mir denken können; **it doesn't ~** das paßt *or* stimmt nicht zusammen; **it ~s that he would do that** typisch, daß er das getan hat.

◆**figure on** *vi +prep obj* (*esp US*) rechnen mit.

◆**figure out** *vt sep* **(a)** (*understand, make sense of*) begreifen, schlau werden aus ◆ **I can't ~ him ~ at all** ich werde überhaupt nicht schlau aus ihm; **I can't ~ it ~** ich werde daraus nicht schlau.
(b) (*work out*) ausrechnen; *answer, how to do sth* herausbekommen; *solution* finden ◆ **~ it ~ for yourself** das kannst du dir (leicht) selbst ausrechnen.

figure: ~-conscious *adj* figurbewußt; **~head** *n* (*Naut, fig*) Galionsfigur *f*; **~-hugging** *adj* figurbetont; **~-skate** *vi* eiskunstlaufen; **~-skater** *n* Eiskunstläufer(in *f*) *m*; **~-skating** *n* Eiskunstlaufen *nt.*

figurine [fɪgə'ri:n] *n* Figurine *f.*

Fiji ['fi:dʒi:] *n* Fidschiinseln *pl.*

Fijian [fɪ'dʒi:ən] [1] *adj* fidschianisch.
[2] *n* **(a)** Fidschiinsulaner(in *f*) *m.* **(b)** (*language*) Fidschianisch *nt.*

filament ['fɪləmənt] *n* (*Elec*) (Glüh- *or* Heiz)faden *m*; (*Bot*) Staubfaden *m.*

filch [fɪltʃ] *vt* filzen, mopsen, mausen (*all inf*).

file[1] [faɪl] [1] *n* (*tool*) Feile *f.*
[2] *vt* feilen ◆ **to ~ one's fingernails** sich (*dat*) die Fingernägel feilen.

◆**file away** *vt sep* abfeilen.

◆**file down** *vt sep* abfeilen.

file[2] [1] *n* **(a)** (*holder*) (Akten)hefter, Aktenordner *m*; (*for card index*) Karteikasten *m* ◆ **would you go to the ~s and get ...** könnten Sie bitte ... aus der Kartei holen; **it's in the ~s somewhere** das muß irgendwo bei den Akten sein.
(b) (*documents, information*) Akte *f* (*on sb* über jdn, *on sth* zu etw) ◆ **on ~**

aktenkundig, bei den Akten; **have we got that on ~?** haben wir das bei den Akten?; **to open** *or* **start a ~ on sb/sth** eine Akte über jdn/zu etw anlegen; **to keep a ~ on sb/sth** eine Akte über jdn/zu etw führen; **to close the ~ on sb/sth** jds Akte schließen/die Akte zu einer Sache schließen; **the Kowalski ~** die Akte Kowalski.
(c) *(Comput)* Datei *f*, File *m* ◆ **data on ~** gespeicherte Daten; **to have sth on ~** etw im *or* auf Computer haben.
[2] *vt* **(a)** *(put in ~) letters* ablegen, abheften ◆ **it's ~d under "B"** das ist unter „B" abgelegt. **(b)** *(Jur)* einreichen, erheben. **to ~ a petition at court** *(Jur)* ein Gesuch *nt* bei Gericht einreichen.
◆**file away** *vt sep papers* zu den Akten legen.
◆**file for** *vi +prep obj (Jur)* **to ~ ~ divorce** die Scheidung einreichen; **to ~ ~ bankruptcy** Konkurs anmelden; **to ~ ~ custody (of the children)** das Sorgerecht (für die Kinder) beantragen.
file³ [1] *n (row)* Reihe *f* ◆ **in Indian** *or* **single ~** im Gänsemarsch; *(Mil)* in Reihe; *see* **rank¹**.
[2] *vi* **to ~ in** hereinmarschieren *or* -kommen; **they ~d out of the classroom** sie gingen/kamen hintereinander *or* nacheinander aus dem Klassenzimmer; **the procession ~d under the archway** die Prozession zog unter dem Torbogen hindurch; **they ~d through the turnstile** sie kamen nacheinander durch das Drehkreuz; **the troops ~d past the general** die Truppen marschierten *or* defilierten am General vorbei; **the children ~d past the headmaster** die Kinder gingen in einer Reihe am Direktor vorbei; **a long line of refugees ~d over the bridge** eine lange Reihe von Flüchtlingen zog über die Brücke.
file: ~ cabinet *n (US)* Aktenschrank *m*; **~ clerk** *n (US)* Angestellte(r) *mf* in der Registratur; **~ management** *n (Comput)* Dateiverwaltung *f*; **~ name** *n (Comput)* Dateiname *m*; **~ server** *n (Comput)* File-server *m*; **~ size** *n (Comput)* Dateigröße *f or* -umfang *m*.
filial ['fɪlɪəl] *adj* Kindes- ◆ **with due ~ respect** mit dem Respekt, den eine Tochter/ein Sohn schuldig ist.
filibuster ['fɪlɪbʌstəʳ] *(esp US)* [1] *n (speech)* Obstruktion, Dauerrede *f*; *(person)* Filibuster, Dauerredner, Obstruktionist *m*.
[2] *vi* filibustern, Obstruktion betreiben.
filibusterer ['fɪlɪbʌstərəʳ] *n (esp US)* Filibuster, Dauerredner, Obstruktionist *m*.
filibustering ['fɪlɪbʌstərɪŋ] *n* Verschleppungstaktik *f*, Obstruktionismus *m*.
filigree ['fɪlɪgriː] [1] *n* Filigran(arbeit *f*) *nt*.
[2] *adj* Filigran-.
filing ['faɪlɪŋ] *n* **(a)** *(of documents)* Ablegen, Abheften *nt* ◆ **who does your ~?** wer ist bei Ihnen für die Ablage zuständig?; **have you done the ~?** haben Sie die Akten schon abgelegt? **(b)** *(Jur)* Einreichung *f*.
filing: ~ cabinet *n* Aktenschrank *m or* -regal *nt*; **~ clerk** *n (Brit)* Angestellte(r) *mf* in der Registratur.
filings ['faɪlɪŋz] *npl* Späne *pl*.
filing tray *n* Ablagekorb *m*.
Filipino [fɪlɪ'piːnəʊ] [1] *n* Filipino *m*.
[2] *adj* philippinisch.
fill [fɪl] [1] *vt* **(a)** *bottle, bucket, hole* füllen; *pipe* stopfen; *teeth also* plombieren; *(wind) sails* blähen; *(fig)* (aus)füllen ◆ **I had three teeth ~ed** ich bekam drei Zähne plombiert *or* gefüllt.
(b) *(permeate)* erfüllen ◆ **~ed with anger/admiration/longing** voller Zorn/Bewunderung/Verlangen, von Zorn/Bewunderung/Verlangen erfüllt *(geh)*; **the thought ~ed him with horror** der Gedanke erfüllte ihn mit Entsetzen.
(c) *post, position (employer)* besetzen; *(employee) (take up)* einnehmen; *(be in)* innehaben; *need* entsprechen *(+dat)* ◆ **we are looking for a young man to ~ the post of ...** wir suchen einen jungen Mann, der den Posten eines ... einnehmen soll; **I think he will ~ the job very nicely** ich denke, er wird die Stelle sehr gut ausfüllen *or* er ist der richtige Mann für den Job; **the position is already ~ed** die Stelle ist schon besetzt *or* vergeben.
[2] *vi* sich füllen.
[3] *n* **to drink one's ~** seinen Durst löschen; **to eat one's ~** sich satt essen; **to have had one's ~** gut satt sein; **I've had my ~ of him/it** *(inf)* ich habe von ihm/davon die Nase voll *(inf)*, ich habe ihn/das satt; **a ~ of tobacco** eine Pfeife Tabak.
◆**fill in** [1] *vi* **to ~ ~ for sb** für jdn einspringen.
[2] *vt sep* **(a)** *hole* auffüllen; *door, fireplace* zumauern ◆ **to ~ ~ the gaps in one's knowledge** seine Wissenslücken stopfen; **he's just ~ing ~ time until he gets another job** er überbrückt nur die Zeit, bis er eine andere Stelle bekommt.
(b) *form* ausfüllen; *name, address, missing word* eintragen.
(c) to ~ sb ~ (on sth) jdn (über etw *acc*) aufklären *or* ins Bild setzen; **could you ~ ~ the details for me?** könnten Sie mir die Einzelheiten nennen?
◆**fill out** [1] *vi* **(a)** *(sails etc)* sich blähen. **(b)** *(person: become fatter)* fülliger werden; *(cheeks, face)* runder *or* voller werden.
[2] *vt sep form* ausfüllen; *essay, article etc* strecken.
◆**fill up** [1] *vi* **(a)** *(Aut)* (auf)tanken.
(b) *(hall, barrel etc)* sich füllen.
[2] *vt sep* **(a)** *tank, cup* vollfüllen; *(driver)* volltanken; *hole* füllen, stopfen ◆ **to ~ sth right ~** etw bis zum Rand (an)füllen; **he ~ed the glass ~ to the brim** er füllte das Glas randvoll; **~ her ~!** *(Aut inf)* volltanken bitte!; **that pie has really ~ed me ~** ich fühle mich wirklich voll nach dieser Pastete; **you need something to ~ you ~** du brauchst was Sättigendes.
(b) *form* ausfüllen.
filler ['fɪləʳ] *n* **(a)** *(funnel)* Trichter *m*. **(b)** *(Build: paste for cracks)* Spachtelmasse *f*. **(c)** *(Press, TV)* Füllsel *nt*, (Lücken)füller *m*. **(d)** *(Chem: for plastics)* Füllstoff *m*. **(e)** *(Ling)* **~ (word)** Füllwort *nt*.
filler cap *n* Tankdeckel *m*.
fillet ['fɪlɪt] [1] *n* **(a)** *(Cook: of beef, fish)* Filet *nt* ◆ **~ steak** Filetsteak *nt*. **(b)** *(for the hair)* (Haar)band *nt*.
[2] *vt (Cook)* filetieren; *meat also* in Filets schneiden ◆ **~ed sole** Seezungenfilet *nt*.
filling ['fɪlɪŋ] [1] *n* **(a)** *(in tooth)* Füllung, Plombe *f* ◆ **my ~'s come out** ich hab eine Füllung *or* Plombe verloren; **I had to have three ~s** ich mußte mir drei Zähne plombieren *or* füllen lassen. **(b)** *(Cook: in pie, tart)* Füllung *f*.
[2] *adj food* sättigend.
filling station *n* Tankstelle *f*.
fillip ['fɪlɪp] *n (fig)* Ansporn *m*, Aufmunterung *f* ◆ **to give sb/sth a ~** jdn aufmuntern *or* anspornen/einer Sache *(dat)* (neuen) Schwung geben; **this gave a ~ to our business** dadurch hat unser Geschäft einen Aufschwung genommen.
fill-up ['fɪlʌp] *n (inf)* **to give sb a ~** jdm nachschenken; **do you want a ~?** soll ich nachschenken?
filly ['fɪlɪ] *n* Stutfohlen *nt*; *(dated inf)* Mädel *nt (dated)*.
film [fɪlm] [1] *n* **(a)** Film *m*; *(of dust)* Schicht *f*; *(of ice on water)* Schicht *f*; *(of mist, on the eye)* Schleier *m*; *(thin membrane)* Häutchen *nt*; *(on teeth)* Belag *m*; *(fine web)* feines Gewebe.
(b) *(Phot)* Film *m* ◆ **get your holiday on ~** bannen Sie Ihre Ferien auf den Film; **I wish I'd got that on ~** ich wünschte, ich hätte das aufnehmen können; **to take a ~ of sth** einen Film über etw *(acc)* drehen *or* machen.
(c) *(motion picture)* Film *m* ◆ **to make** *or* **shoot a ~** einen Film drehen *or* machen; **to make a ~** *(actor)* einen Film machen; **to go to the ~s** ins Kino gehen; **he's in ~s** er ist beim Film; **to go into ~s** zum Film gehen.
[2] *vt play* verfilmen; *scene* filmen; *people* einen Film machen von ◆ **he didn't know he was being ~ed** er wußte nicht, daß er gefilmt wurde.
[3] *vi* **she ~s well** sie ist sehr fotogen; **the story ~ed very well** die Geschichte ließ sich gut verfilmen; **~ing starts tomorrow** die Dreharbeiten fangen morgen an.
◆**film over** *or* **up** *vi (mirror, glass)* anlaufen.
film: ~ archives *npl* Filmarchiv(e *pl*) *nt*; **~ camera** *n* Filmkamera *f*; **~ clip** *n* Filmausschnitt *m*; **~ fan** *n* Filmliebhaber(in *f*) *m*, Filmfan *m*; **~ festival** *n* Filmfestival *nt*, Filmfestspiele *pl*; **~ library** *n* Cinemathek *f*; **~ maker** *n* Filmemacher(in *f*) *m*; **~ rights** *npl* Filmrechte *pl*; **~ script** *n* Drehbuch *nt*; **~ sequence** *n* Filmsequenz *f*; **~ set** *n* Filmset *nt*, Filmdekoration *f*; **~-set** *vt (Brit Typ)* lichtsetzen, fotosetzen; **~-setting** *n (Brit Typ)* Lichtsatz, Fotosatz *m*; **~star** *n* Filmstar *m*; **~strip** *n* Filmstreifen *m*; **~ studio** *n* Filmstudio *nt*; **~ test** *n* Probeaufnahmen *pl*; **to give sb a ~ test** Probeaufnahmen von jdm machen; **~ version** *n* Verfilmung *f*.
filmy ['fɪlmɪ] *adj (+er) material* dünn, zart.
Filofax ® ['faɪləʊfæks] *n* Filofax ® *m*.
filter ['fɪltəʳ] [1] *n* **(a)** Filter *m*; *(Phot, Rad, Mech)* Filter *nt or m*. **(b)** *(Brit: for traffic)* grüner Pfeil *(für Abbieger)*.
[2] *vt liquids, air* filtern.
[3] *vi* **(a)** *(light)* durchscheinen, durchschimmern; *(liquid, sound)* durchsickern. **(b)** *(Brit Aut)* sich einordnen ◆ **to ~ to the left** sich links einordnen.
◆**filter back** *vi (refugees etc)* allmählich zurückkommen.
◆**filter in** *vi (people)* langsam *or* allmählich eindringen; *(news)* durchsickern.
◆**filter out** [1] *vi (people)* einer nach dem anderen herausgehen/ -kommen.
[2] *vt sep (lit)* herausfiltern; *(fig)* heraussieben.
◆**filter through** *vi (liquid, sound, news)* durchsickern; *(light)* durchschimmern, durchscheinen.
filter: ~ bed *n* Klärbecken *nt*; **~ lane** *n (Brit)* Spur *f* zum Einordnen, Abbiegespur *f*; **~ paper** *n* Filterpapier *nt*; **~ tip** *n* Filter *m*; **~-tipped** *adj cigarette* Filter-.
filth [fɪlθ] *n (lit)* Schmutz, Dreck *m*; *(fig)* Schweinerei, Sauerei *(sl) f*; *(people)* Dreckspack, (Lumpen)gesindel *nt* ◆ **the ~** *(pej sl: police)* die Bullen *pl (sl)*; **all the ~ they wrote about him in the papers** all der Unflat, der über ihn in der Zeitung geschrieben wurde; **none of your ~!** keine Schweinereien, bitte!; **to talk ~** unflätig reden.
filthy ['fɪlθɪ] *adj (+er)* schmutzig, dreckig; *(inf) weather* Drecks- *(inf)*, Sau- *(sl)*; *day* Mist-; *temper* übel; *(obscene)* unanständig, schweinisch *(inf)* ◆ **your hands are ~!** deine Hände sind ja ganz dreckig *(inf) or* völlig verdreckt; **he's got a ~ mind** er hat eine schmutzige *or* schweinische *(inf)* Phantasie; **don't be ~** *(to child)* du Ferkel!; *(to grown-up)* Sie Schmutzfink!; **you ~ little boy!** du bist vielleicht ein Ferkel!; **you ~ swine!** du dreckiges Schwein! *(inf)*, du Drecksau! *(sl)*; **a ~ habit** eine widerliche Angewohnheit; **~ rich** *(inf)* stinkreich *(inf)*.
fin [fɪn] *n* **(a)** *(of fish)* Flosse *f*. **(b)** *(Aviat)* Seitenleitwerk *nt*, Seitenflosse *f*; *(of bomb, rocket, ship)* Stabilisierungsfläche *f*. **(c)** *(Aut: of radiator)* Kühlrippe *f*. **(d)** *(for swimming)* Schwimmflosse *f*.
final ['faɪnl] [1] *adj* **(a)** *(last)* letzte(r, s); *instalment, chapter, act also, examination, chord* Schluß-.
(b) *(ultimate) aim, result* letztendlich, End-; *version* endgültig, letzte(r, s); *offer* (aller)letzte(r, s) ◆ **~ score** Schlußstand *m*, Endergebnis *nt*.
(c) *(definite)* endgültig ◆ **~ word** letztes Wort; **we'll probably leave at 10, but that's not ~ yet** wir gehen wahrscheinlich um 10, aber das steht noch nicht endgültig fest; **you're not going and that's ~** du gehst nicht, und damit basta *(inf)*.
(d) ~ cause *(Philos)* Urgrund *m*; **~ clause** *(Gram)* Finalsatz *m*.
[2] *n* **(a) ~s** *pl (Univ)* Abschlußprüfung *f*. **(b)** *(Sport)* Finale, Endspiel *nt*; *(in quiz)* Finale *nt*, Endrunde *f* ◆ **the ~s** das Finale. **(c)** *(Press)* Spätausgabe *f*.

late-night ~ letzte Nachtausgabe.

finale [fɪ'nɑːlɪ] *n* (*Mus, in opera*) Finale *nt*; (*Theat*) Schlußszene *f*; (*fig*) Finale *nt* (*geh*), (Ab)schluß *m*.

finalist ['faɪnəlɪst] *n* (*Sport*) Endrundenteilnehmer(in *f*), Finalist(in *f*) *m*; (*Univ*) Examenskandidat(in *f*) *m*.

finality [faɪ'nælɪtɪ] *n* (*of decision etc*) Endgültigkeit *f*; (*of tone of voice*) Entschiedenheit, Bestimmtheit *f*.

finalization [ˌfaɪnəlaɪ'zeɪʃən] *n see vt* Beendigung *f*; endgültige Festlegung; endgültiger Abschluß; endgültige Formgebung.

finalize ['faɪnəlaɪz] *vt* fertigmachen, beenden; (*determine*) *plans, arrangements* endgültig festlegen; *deal* zum Abschluß bringen; *draft* die endgültige Form geben (+*dat*) ♦ **to ~ a decision** eine endgültige Entscheidung treffen.

▼ **finally** ['faɪnəlɪ] *adv* **(a)** (*at last, eventually*) schließlich; (*expressing relief etc*) endlich ♦ **at last he's ~ understood!** nun hat er es endlich verstanden!
▼ **(b)** (*at the end, lastly*) schließlich, zum Schluß.
(c) (*in a definite manner*) endgültig ♦ **he said it very ~** er hat es in sehr bestimmtem *or* entschiedenem Ton gesagt.
(d) we are, ~, all human beings wir sind doch letztlich *or* schließlich alle Menschen.

finance [faɪ'næns] **1** *n* **(a)** Finanzen *pl*, Finanz- *or* Geldwesen *nt* ♦ **high ~** Hochfinanz *f*; **to study ~** (*academically*) Finanzwissenschaft studieren; (*as training*) eine Finanzfachschule besuchen.
(b) (*money*) Geld *nt*, (Geld)mittel *pl* ♦ **it's a question of ~** das ist eine Geldfrage *or* Frage der Finanzen; **~s** Finanzen *pl*, Finanz- *or* Einkommenslage *f* ♦ **his ~s aren't sound** seine Finanzlage ist nicht gesund, seine Finanzen stehen nicht gut.
2 *vt* finanzieren.

finance: ~ company *n* Finanz(ierungs)gesellschaft *f*; **~ director** *n* Leiter *m* der Finanzabteilung.

financial [faɪ'nænʃəl] *adj* finanziell; *crisis* Finanz-; *news, page* Wirtschafts- ♦ **it makes good ~ sense** es ist finanziell sinnvoll; **~ paper** Börsenblatt *nt*; **~ planning** Finanzplanung *f*; **~ director** Leiter *m* der Finanzabteilung; **the ~ year** das Geschäftsjahr.

financially [faɪ'nænʃəlɪ] *adv* finanziell ♦ **the company is ~ sound** die Finanzlage der Firma ist gesund; **the planning was ~ disastrous** die Planung war ein finanzielles Fiasko.

financier [faɪ'nænsɪə^r] *n* Finanzier *m*.

finch [fɪntʃ] *n* Fink *m*.

find [faɪnd] (*vb: pret, ptp* **found**) **1** *vt* **(a)** finden ♦ **it's not to be found** es läßt sich nicht finden *or* auftreiben (*inf*); **to ~ sb out** *or* **away** jdn nicht (zu Hause) antreffen; **hoping this letter ~s you in good health** in der Hoffnung, daß Sie gesund sind; **we left everything as we found it** wir haben alles so gelassen, wie wir es vorgefunden haben; **he was found dead in bed** er wurde tot im Bett aufgefunden; **I can never ~ anything to say to him** ich weiß nie, was ich zu ihm sagen soll; **where am I going to ~ the money/time?** wo nehme ich nur das Geld/die Zeit her?; **you must take us as you ~ us** Sie müssen uns so nehmen, wie wir sind; **if you can ~ it in you to ...** wenn Sie es irgend fertigbringen, zu ...
(b) (*supply*) besorgen (*sb sth* jdm etw) ♦ **go and ~ me a needle** hol mir doch mal eine Nadel; **did you ~ him what he wanted?** haben Sie bekommen, was er wollte?; **we'll have to ~ him a car/secretary** wir müssen ihm ein Auto besorgen/eine Sekretärin für ihn finden.
(c) (*discover, ascertain*) feststellen; *cause also* (heraus)finden ♦ **we found the car wouldn't start** es stellte sich heraus, daß das Auto nicht ansprang; **I ~ I'm unable to ...** ich stelle fest, daß ich ... nicht kann; **you will ~ that I am right** Sie werden sehen, daß ich recht habe; **it has been found that this is so** es hat sich herausgestellt, daß es so ist.
(d) (*consider to be*) finden ♦ **I ~ Spain too hot** ich finde Spanien zu heiß; **I don't ~ it easy to tell you this** es fällt mir nicht leicht, Ihnen das zu sagen; **he always found languages easy/hard** ihm fielen Sprachen immer leicht/schwer; **I found all the questions easy** ich fand, daß die Fragen alle leicht waren; **did you ~ her a good worker?** fanden Sie, daß sie gut arbeitet?; **I ~ it impossible to understand him** ich kann ihn einfach nicht verstehen.
(e) I ~ myself in an impossible situation/in financial difficulties ich befinde mich in einer unmöglichen Situation/in finanziellen Schwierigkeiten; **one day he suddenly found himself a rich man/out of a job** eines Tages war er plötzlich ein reicher Mann/arbeitslos; **he awoke to ~ himself in prison/hospital** er erwachte und fand sich im Gefängnis/Krankenhaus wieder; **I found myself quite competent to deal with it** ich stellte fest, daß ich durchaus fähig war, damit zurechtzukommen; **I found myself unable/forced to .../surrounded** ich sah mich außerstande/gezwungen, zu .../umringt; **at the end of the tunnel I found myself in ...** am Ende des Tunnels befand ich mich in ...; **how do you ~ yourself this morning?** wie geht es Ihnen *or* wie befinden Sie sich (*geh*) heute morgen?
(f) this flower is found all over England diese Blume findet man in ganz England, diese Blume ist in ganz England vorzufinden; **you don't ~ bears here any more** man findet hier keine Bären mehr; **do you know where there is a chemist's to be found?** wissen Sie, wo hier eine Apotheke ist?; **there wasn't one to be found** es war keine(r) *etc* zu finden.
(g) £100 per week all found £ 100 pro Woche, (und freie) Kost und Logis *or* (*in institution*) bei freier Station.
(h) (*Jur*) **to ~ sb guilty** jdn für schuldig befinden, jdn schuldig sprechen; **how do you ~ the accused?** wie lautet Ihr Urteil?; **the court has found that ...** das Gericht hat befunden, daß ...
(i) (*Comput*) suchen ♦ **~ and replace** suchen und ersetzen.
2 *vi* (*Jur*) **to ~ for/against the accused** den Angeklagten freisprechen/verurteilen, für/gegen den Angeklagten entscheiden.
3 *n* Fund *m*.

♦**find out 1** *vt sep* **(a)** *answer, sb's secret* herausfinden ♦ **to help children ~ ~ about geometry** um Kindern dabei zu helfen, etwas über Geometrie (*acc*) herauszufinden; **to ~ ~ about sb/sth** (*discover existence of*) jdn/etw entdecken.
(b) (*discover the misdeeds etc of*) *person* erwischen; (*come to know about*) auf die Schliche kommen (+*dat*) (*inf*) ♦ **his wife has found him ~** seine Frau ist dahintergekommen; **don't get found ~** laß dich nicht erwischen; **you've been found ~** du bist entdeckt *or* ertappt (*inf*); **to ~ ~ about sb** jdm auf die Schliche kommen (*inf*); **your sins will ~ you ~** (*liter*) die Sonne bringt es an den Tag (*prov*).
2 *vi* es herausfinden; (*discover misdeeds, dishonesty etc also*) dahinterkommen ♦ **where is it? — ~ ~ for yourself!** wo ist es? — sieh doch selbst nach!; **where have you hidden it? — ~ ~!** wo hast du es versteckt? — such's doch!

finder ['faɪndə^r] *n* **(a)** (*of lost object*) Finder(in *f*) *m* ♦ **~s keepers** (*inf*) wer's findet, dem gehört's. **(b)** (*of telescope*) Sucher *m*.

finding ['faɪndɪŋ] *n* **(a) ~s** *pl* Ergebnis(se *pl*) *nt*; (*medical*) Befund *m* ♦ **the ~s of the commission of enquiry were as follows** die Untersuchungskommission kam zu folgendem Ergebnis. **(b)** (*Jur: verdict*) Urteil(sspruch *m*) *nt*.

fine[1] [faɪn] *adv*: **in ~** (*liter*) kurz und gut, kurzum.

fine[2] **1** *n* (*Jur*) Geldstrafe *f*; (*for less serious offences also*) Geldbuße *f*; (*driving also*) Bußgeld *nt*; (*for minor traffic offences*) (gebührenpflichtige) Verwarnung.
2 *vt see n* zu einer Geldstrafe verurteilen, mit einer Geldstrafe/-buße belegen; Bußgeld verhängen gegen; eine (gebührenpflichtige) Verwarnung erteilen (+*dat*) ♦ **he was ~d £100** er mußte £ 100 Strafe bezahlen; **he was ~d for speeding** er hat einen Strafzettel für zu schnelles Fahren bekommen.

fine[3] **1** *adj* (+*er*) **(a)** *weather* schön ♦ **it's going to be ~ this afternoon** heute nachmittag wird es schön; **one ~ day** eines schönen Tages; **I hope it keeps ~ for you!** ich hoffe, Sie haben schönes Wetter!; (*dated inf*) alles Gute!
(b) (*good*) gut; *example, selection, workmanship also, person, character* fein; *specimen, chap, woman* prächtig; *mind* fein, scharf; *pianist, novel, painting, shot* großartig; *complexion, holiday* schön; *holiday, meal, view* herrlich; (*elegant*) *clothes, manners etc* fein, vornehm ♦ **our ~st hour** unsere größte Stunde; **he did a ~ job there** da hat er gute Arbeit geleistet; **that's a ~ excuse** (*iro*) das ist ja eine schöne Ausrede; **a ~ time to ...** (*iro*) ein feiner Augenblick, zu ...; **a ~ friend you are** (*iro*) du bist mir ja ein schöner Freund!; **that's a ~ thing to say** (*iro*) das ist ja wirklich nett, so was zu sagen! (*iro*); **that's all very ~ but ...** das ist ja alles schön und gut, aber ...; **this is a ~ state of affairs** (*iro*) das sind ja schöne Zustände; **she likes to play at being the ~ lady** sie spielt sich gern als feine Dame auf.
(c) (*OK, in order*) gut, in Ordnung ♦ **more soup? — no thanks, I'm ~** noch etwas Suppe? — nein danke, ich habe genug; **everything was ~ until he came along** alles ging gut, bis er kam; **that's ~ by me** ich habe nichts dagegen; **(that's) ~** gut *or* in Ordnung; **~, fantastic!** gut, ausgezeichnet!; **~, let's do that then** ja *or* gut, machen wir das; **I got the tickets — oh that's ~, then** ich habe die Karten bekommen — fein *or* schön.
(d) (*healthwise, mentally*) **sb is** *or* **feels ~** jdm geht es gut; **I'm/he is ~ now** es geht mir/ihm wieder gut; **how are you? — ~** wie geht's? — gut.
(e) (*delicate*) *workmanship* fein; *material, china also* zart ♦ **~ feelings** Feingefühl *nt*; **to appeal to sb's ~r feelings** an jds besseres Ich appellieren; **it's no good trying to appeal to his ~r feelings** es hat keinen Wert, an seine Gefühle zu appellieren.
(f) *dust, sand* fein; *rain also* Niesel-.
(g) (*thin*) fein, dünn; (*sharp*) scharf; *handwriting* fein, zierlich ♦ **~ nib** spitze Feder; *see* **point**.
(h) (*Metal*) Fein-.
(i) (*discriminating*) *distinction, ear* fein ♦ **there's a very ~ line between ...** es besteht ein feiner Unterschied zwischen ...
2 *adv* **(a)** (*well*) gut, prima (*inf*) ♦ **these ~-sounding adjectives** diese wohlklingenden Adjektive.
(b) (+*er*) **to chop sth up ~** etw fein (zer)hacken; *see* **cut**.

♦**fine down** *vt sep wood etc* abhobeln/-feilen; *text, novel etc* straffen (*to* zu); *theory* reduzieren (*to* auf +*acc*).

fine: ~ art *n* **(a)** *usu pl* schöne Künste *pl*; **(b)** (*skill*) Kunststück *nt*, echte Kunst; **he's got it down to a ~ art** er hat den Bogen heraus (*inf*); **~-drawn** *adj* **(a)** *thread* fein gesponnen *or* (*synthetic*) gezogen; *wire* fein gezogen; **(b)** *features* fein (geschnitten); **~-grained** *adj wood* fein gemasert; *photographic paper* feinkörnig.

finely ['faɪnlɪ] *adv* fein; *worked, made* schön; *detailed* genau; *sliced also* dünn.

fineness ['faɪnnɪs] *n* **(a)** Schönheit *f*.
(b) (*of quality*) Güte *f*; (*of mind, novel*) Großartigkeit *f*; (*elegance*) Feinheit *f*.
(c) (*of piece of work*) Feinheit *f*; (*of material, feelings*) Zartheit *f*.
(d) (*of dust, sand*) Feinheit, Feinkörnigkeit *f*.
(e) (*thinness*) Feinheit, Dünnheit, Dünne *f*; (*sharpness*) Schärfe *f*; (*of handwriting*) Feinheit *f*; (*of nib*) Spitze *f*.
(f) (*of metal*) Feingehalt *m*.
(g) (*of distinction*) Feinheit *f*.

finery ['faɪnərɪ] *n* **(a)** (*of dress*) Staat *m*; (*liter: of nature etc also*) Pracht *f* ♦ **she had never seen so much ~** sie hatte noch nie so viel Eleganz gesehen. **(b)** (*Metal: furnace*) Frischofen *m*.

finesse [fɪ'nes] **1** *n* **(a)** (*skill, diplomacy*) Gewandtheit *f*, Geschick *nt*. **(b)** (*cunning*) Schlauheit, Finesse *f*. **(c)** (*Cards*) Schneiden *nt*.

➤ LANGUAGE IN USE: **finally: b → 26.1, 26.2**

[2] *vti* (*Cards*) schneiden.

fine-tooth comb ['faɪn'tu:θkəʊm] *n*: **to go through sth with a ~** etw genau unter die Lupe nehmen.

fine: ~-tune *vt* (*engine, fig: projection etc*) feinabstimmen; **~-tuning** *n* (*lit, fig*) Feinabstimmung *f*; (*fig also*) Detailarbeit *f*.

finger ['fɪŋgəʳ] [1] *n* Finger *m* ◆ **she can twist him round her little ~** sie kann ihn um den (kleinen) Finger wickeln; **to have a ~ in every pie** überall die Finger drin *or* im Spiel haben (*inf*), überall mitmischen (*inf*); **I forbid you to lay a ~ on him** ich verbiete Ihnen, ihm auch nur ein Härchen zu krümmen; **I didn't lay a ~ on her** ich habe sie nicht angerührt; **he wouldn't lift a ~ to help me** er würde keinen Finger rühren, um mir zu helfen; **he didn't lift a ~** er hat keinen Finger krumm gemacht (*inf*); **to point one's ~ at sb** mit dem Finger auf jdn zeigen; **to point the ~ at sb** (*fig*) mit Fingern auf jdn zeigen; **I can't put my ~ on it, but ...** ich kann es nicht genau ausmachen, aber ...; **you've put your ~ on it there** da haben Sie den kritischen Punkt berührt; **to put the ~ on sb** (*sl*) jdn verpfeifen (*inf*); **to get** *or* **pull one's ~ out** (*sl*) Nägel mit Köpfen machen (*sl*); **pull your ~ out!** (*sl*) es wird Zeit, daß du Nägel mit Köpfen machst! (*sl*); **to give sb the ~** (*esp US inf*) ≃ jdm den Vogel zeigen; *see* **cross.**

[2] *vt* **(a)** anfassen; (*toy, meddle with*) befingern, herumfingern an (+*dat*).
(b) (*Mus: mark for ~ing*) mit einem Fingersatz versehen ◆ **to ~ the keys/strings** in die Tasten/Saiten greifen.

finger: ~ alphabet *n* Fingeralphabet *nt*; **~ board** *n* Griffbrett *nt*; **~bowl** *n* Fingerschale *f*; **~ exercise** *n* Fingerübung *f*.

fingering ['fɪŋgərɪŋ] *n* **(a)** (*Mus*) (*in the notation*) Fingersatz *m*; (*of keys, strings*) (Finger)technik *f* ◆ **the ~ is very difficult** die Griffe sind sehr schwierig. **(b)** (*of goods in shop etc*) Anfassen, Berühren *nt*; (*toying, meddling*) Befingern *nt* (*of, with gen*), Herumfingern *nt* (*of, with* an +*dat*). **(c)** (*Tex*) Strumpfwolle *f*.

finger: ~mark *n* Fingerabdruck *m*; **~nail** *n* Fingernagel *m*; **~print** [1] *n* Fingerabdruck *m*; [2] *vt* **to ~print sb/sth** jdm die Fingerabdrücke *pl* abnehmen/von etw Fingerabdrücke *pl* abnehmen; **~print expert** *n* Sachverständige(r) *mf* für Fingerabdrücke; **~stall** *n* Fingerling *m*; **~tip** *n* Fingerspitze *f*; **to have sth at one's ~tips** (*fig*) (*know very well*) etw aus dem Effeff kennen (*inf*); (*have at one's immediate disposal*) etw im kleinen Finger (*inf*) *or* parat haben; **to one's ~tips** (*fig*) durch und durch; **~tip control** *n* (*of steering wheel etc*) mühelose Steuerung; **to have ~tip control** sich mühelos bedienen lassen.

finickiness ['fɪnɪkɪnɪs] *n* (*of person*) Pingeligkeit *f* (*inf*); (*about language also*) Wortklauberei, Haarspalterei *f*; (*of task*) Kniff(e)ligkeit *f* (*inf*) ◆ **because of his ~ about what he eats** weil er so wählerisch *or* heikel (*dial inf*) im Essen ist.

finicky ['fɪnɪkɪ] *adj person* schwer zufriedenzustellen, pingelig (*inf*); (*about language also*) wortklauberisch, haarspalterisch; (*about food, clothes etc also*) wählerisch, heikel (*dial inf*); *work, job* kniff(e)lig (*inf*); *detail* winzig.

finish ['fɪnɪʃ] [1] *n* **(a)** (*end*) Schluß *m*, Ende *nt*; (*of race*) Finish *nt*; (*~ing line*) Ziel *nt* ◆ **they never gave up, right to the ~** sie haben bis zum Schluß nicht aufgegeben; **he's got a good ~** (*Sport*) er hat einen starken Endspurt; **to be in at the ~** (*fig*) beim Ende dabeisein; **to fight to the ~** bis zum letzten Augenblick kämpfen.
(b) (*perfection: of manners*) Schliff *m*; (*of things*) Verarbeitung, Ausfertigung *f* ◆ **they lack the ~ of handmade ones** sie sind nicht so sorgfältig *or* sauber verarbeitet wie handgemachte; **it has a poor ~** die Verarbeitung *or* Ausfertigung ist nicht gut; **the style lacks ~** dem Stil fehlt der Schliff.
(c) (*of industrial products*) Finish *nt*; (*final coat of paint*) Deckanstrich *m*; (*of material*) Appretur *f*; (*of paper*) Oberflächenfinish *nt*; (*of pottery*) Oberfläche *f*; (*ornamental work*) Verzierung *f* ◆ **paper with a gloss/matt ~** Hochglanz-/Mattglanzpapier *nt*; **paint with a gloss/matt ~** Farbe mit Hochglanzeffekt/mattem Glanz; **highly polished to give it a good ~** hoch poliert, um Glanz zu erzielen.

[2] *vt* **(a)** beenden; *education, course also* abschließen; *work, business also* erledigen, abschließen ◆ **he's ~ed the painting/novel/job** er hat das Bild/den Roman/die Arbeit fertig(gemalt/-geschrieben/-gemacht); **to ~/have ~ed doing sth** mit etw fertig werden/sein; **to ~ writing/reading sth** etw zu Ende schreiben/lesen, etw fertigschreiben/-lesen; **let me ~ eating** laß mich zu Ende essen, laß mich fertigessen; **to have ~ed sth** etw fertig haben; *task, course* mit etw fertig sein, etw beendet haben; **when do you ~ work?** wann machen Sie Feierabend *or* Schluß?; **I'm in a hurry to get this job ~ed** ich möchte diese Sache so schnell wie möglich zu Ende bringen; **she never lets him ~ what he's saying** sie läßt ihn nie ausreden; **daddy, will you ~ (telling) that story?** Papa, erzählst du die Geschichte zu Ende *or* fertig?; **can I have that book when you've ~ed it?** kann ich das Buch haben, wenn du es ausgelesen hast?; **give me time to ~ my drink** laß mich austrinken; **~ what you're doing and we'll go** mach fertig, was du angefangen hast, und dann gehen wir; **that last kilometre nearly ~ed me** (*inf*) dieser letzte Kilometer hat mich beinahe geschafft (*inf*).
(b) (*give ~ to*) den letzten Schliff geben (+*dat*); *piece of handiwork* verarbeiten; *surface* eine schöne Oberfläche geben (+*dat*); *industrial product* ein schönes Finish geben (+*dat*) ◆ **the paintwork isn't very well ~ed** der Lack hat keine besonders schöne Oberfläche; **to ~ sth with a coat of varnish** etw zum Schluß lackieren; **the metal is ~ed with a high-speed disc** das Metall wird zum Schluß mit einer schnell rotierenden Scheibe poliert; **the paper is ~ed on the glazing rollers** das Papier wird zum Schluß mit dem Kalander bearbeitet.

[3] *vi* **(a)** zu Ende *or* aus sein; (*person: with task etc*) fertig sein; (*come to an end, ~ work*) aufhören; (*piece of music, story etc*) enden ◆ **when does the film ~?** wann ist der Film aus?; **my holiday ~es this week** mein Urlaub geht diese Woche zu Ende; **we'll ~ by singing a song** wir wollen mit einem Lied schließen, zum Schluß singen wir ein Lied; **I've ~ed** ich bin fertig.
(b) (*Sport*) das Ziel erreichen ◆ **to ~ first/second** als erster/zweiter durchs Ziel gehen.

◆**finish off** [1] *vi* **(a)** aufhören, Schluß machen.
(b) to ~ ~ with a glass of brandy zum (Ab)schluß ein Glas Weinbrand trinken; **we ~ed ~ by singing ...** wir schlossen mit dem Lied ..., wir sangen zum (Ab)schluß ...
[2] *vt sep* **(a)** *piece of work* fertigmachen; *job also* erledigen ◆ **to ~ ~ a painting/letter/story** ein Bild zu Ende malen/einen Brief zu Ende schreiben/eine Geschichte zu Ende erzählen.
(b) *food, meal* aufessen; *drink* austrinken.
(c) (*kill*) *wounded animal, person* den Gnadenstoß geben (+*dat*); (*by shooting*) den Gnadenschuß geben (+*dat*).
(d) (*do for*) *person* den Rest geben (+*dat*), erledigen (*inf*) ◆ **the last mile just about ~ed me ~** (*inf*) die letzte Meile hat mich ziemlich fertiggemacht (*inf*) *or* geschafft (*inf*).

◆**finish up** [1] *vi* **(a)** *see* **finish off 1 (a, b).**
(b) (*end up in a place*) landen (*inf*) ◆ **he ~ed ~ a nervous wreck** er war zum Schluß ein Nervenbündel; **he ~ed ~ in third place** er landete auf dem dritten Platz (*inf*); **you'll ~ ~ wishing you'd never started** du wünschst dir bestimmt noch, du hättest gar nicht erst angefangen; **I'll just ~ ~ by doing it all again** zum Schluß muß ich doch alles noch mal machen.
[2] *vt sep see* **finish off 2 (b).**

◆**finish with** *vi* +*prep obj* **(a)** (*no longer need*) nicht mehr brauchen ◆ **I've ~ed ~ the paper/book** ich habe die Zeitung/das Buch fertiggelesen; **I won't be ~ed ~ him/it for some time yet** ich werde noch eine Weile mit ihm/damit zu tun haben.
(b) (*want no more to do with*) **I've ~ed ~ him** ich will nichts mehr mit ihm zu tun haben, ich bin fertig mit ihm (*inf*); (*with boyfriend*) ich habe mit ihm Schluß gemacht.
(c) you wait till I've ~ed ~ you! (*inf*) wart nur, dich knöpfe ich mir noch vor (*inf*).

finished ['fɪnɪʃt] *adj* **(a)** *item, product* fertig; *woodwork, metal* fertig bearbeitet; (*polished also*) poliert; (*varnished, lacquered also*) lackiert; *performance* ausgereift, makellos; *appearance* vollendet ◆ **~ goods** Fertigprodukte *pl*; **beautifully ~ dolls** wunderschön gearbeitete Puppen.
(b) to be ~ (*person, task etc*) fertig sein; (*exhausted, done for etc*) erledigt sein; **the wine is/the chops are ~** es ist kein Wein/es sind keine Koteletts mehr da, der Wein ist/die Koteletts sind aus *or* alle (*inf*); **those days are ~** die Zeiten sind vorbei; **he's ~ as a politician** als Politiker ist er erledigt; **if you tell him that, you're ~** wenn Sie ihm das sagen, sind Sie erledigt; **I'm ~ with him/this company** er/diese Firma ist für mich erledigt *or* gestorben; **I'm ~ with politics/the theatre** mit der Politik/dem Theater ist es für mich vorbei; **it's all ~ (between us)** es ist alles aus (zwischen uns).

finishing ['fɪnɪʃɪŋ]: **~ line** *n* Ziellinie *f*; **~ school** *n* (Mädchen)pensionat *nt*.

finite ['faɪnaɪt] *adj* **(a)** begrenzt ◆ **a ~ number** eine endliche Zahl. **(b) ~ verb** (*Gram*) finites Verb, Verbum finitum *nt* (*spec*).

fink [fɪŋk] (*US sl*) [1] *n* **(a)** (*strikebreaker*) Streikbrecher *m*. **(b)** (*contemptible person*) Saftsack *m* (*sl*).
[2] *vi* **to ~ on sb** jdn verpfeifen (*inf*).

Finland ['fɪnlənd] *n* Finnland *nt*.

Finn [fɪn] *n* Finne *m*, Finnin *f*.

Finnish ['fɪnɪʃ] [1] *adj* finnisch.
[2] *n* Finnisch *nt*.

Finno-Ugric ['fɪnəʊ'ju:grɪk], **Finno-Ugrian** ['fɪnəʊ'ju:grɪən] *adj* (*Ling*) finnisch-ugrisch, finnougrisch.

fiord [fjɔ:d] *n* Fjord *m*.

fir [fɜ:ʳ] *n* Tanne *f*; (*~ wood*) Tanne(nholz *nt*) *f* ◆ **~ cone** Tannenzapfen *m*.

fire [faɪəʳ] [1] *n* **(a)** Feuer *nt* ◆ **the house was on ~** das Haus brannte; **to set ~ to sth, to set sth on ~** etw anzünden; (*so as to destroy*) etw in Brand stecken; **to catch ~** Feuer fangen; (*building, forest etc also*) in Brand geraten; **when man discovered ~** als der Mensch das Feuer entdeckte; **you're playing with ~** (*fig*) du spielst mit dem Feuer; **to fight ~ with ~** (*fig*) mit den gleichen Waffen kämpfen; **to go through ~ and water for sb** (*fig*) für jdn durchs Feuer gehen; *see* **house.**
(b) (*house ~, forest ~ etc*) Brand *m* ◆ **there was a ~ next door** nebenan hat es gebrannt; **~!** Feuer!, feurio (*old*); **Glasgow has more ~s than any other city** in Glasgow brennt es häufiger als in anderen Städten; **to insure oneself against ~** eine Feuerversicherung abschließen.
(c) (*in grate*) (Kamin)feuer *nt*; (*electric ~, gas ~*) Ofen *m* ◆ **they have an open ~** sie haben einen offenen Kamin.
(d) (*Mil*) Feuer *nt* ◆ **~!** Feuer!; **to come between two ~s** (*lit, fig*) zwischen zwei Feuer geraten; **to come under ~** (*lit, fig*) unter Beschuß geraten; **he came under ~ from the critics** er wurde von den Kritikern unter Beschuß genommen; **to be in the line of ~** (*lit, fig*) in der Schußlinie stehen.
(e) (*passion*) Feuer *nt* ◆ **he spoke with ~** er sprach mit Leidenschaft.
[2] *vt* **(a)** (*burn to destroy*) in Brand stecken.
(b) *pottery* brennen.
(c) *furnace* befeuern; *see* **oil-fired, gas-fired.**
(d) (*fig*) *imagination* beflügeln; *passions* entzünden, entfachen (*geh*); *enthusiasm* befeuern ◆ **to ~ sb with enthusiasm** jdn begeistern, jdn in Begeisterung versetzen.
(e) *gun* abschießen; *shot* abfeuern, abgeben; *rocket* zünden, abfeuern ◆ **to ~ a gun at sb** auf jdn schießen; **to ~ a salute** Salut schießen; **to ~ questions at**

sb Fragen auf jdn abfeuern.
(f) (*inf: dismiss*) feuern (*inf*).
[3] *vi* **(a)** (*shoot*) feuern, schießen (*at* auf *+acc*) ◆ **~!** (gebt) Feuer! **(b)** (*engine*) zünden ◆ **the engine is only firing on three cylinders** der Motor läuft nur auf drei Zylindern.
◆**fire away** *vi* (*inf: begin*) losschießen (*inf*).
◆**fire off** *vt sep gun, round, shell, questions* abfeuern.
fire: ~ **alarm** *n* Feueralarm *m*; (*apparatus*) Feuermelder *m*; **~arm** *n* Feuer- *or* Schußwaffe *f*; **~ball** *n* **(a)** (*of nuclear explosion*) Feuerball *m*; (*lightning*) Kugelblitz *m*; **(b)** (*meteor*) Feuerkugel *f*; **(c)** (*fig inf: person*) Energiebündel *nt* (*inf*); **~brand** *n* **(a)** Feuerbrand *m* (*old*); **(b)** (*mischief-maker*) Unruhestifter, Aufwiegler *m*; **~break** *n* (*strip of land*) Feuerschneise *f*; (*wall*) Brandmauer *f*; (*sandbags etc*) *(Schutz)wall m gegen die Ausbreitung eines Feuers*; **~brick** *n* Schamottestein *m*; ~ **brigade** *n* Feuerwehr *f*; **~bug** *n* (*inf*) Feuerteufel *m* (*inf*); **~clay** *n* Schamotte *f*; **~cracker** *n* Knallkörper *m*; **~damp** *n* (*Min*) Grubengas *nt*, schlagende Wetter *pl*; ~ **department** *n* (*US*) Feuerwehr *f*; **~dog** *n* Kaminbock *m*; ~ **door** *n* Feuertür *f*; ~ **drill** *n* Probealarm *m*; (*for firemen*) Feuerwehrübung *f*; **~-eater** *n* Feuerfresser *or* -schlucker *m*; **~-engine** *n* Feuerwehrauto *nt*; ~ **escape** *n* (*staircase*) Feuertreppe *f*; (*ladder*) Feuerleiter *f*; ~ **exit** *n* Notausgang *m*; (*external stairs*) Feuertreppe *f*; ~ **extinguisher** *n* Feuerlöscher *m*; **~-fighter** *n* (*fireman*) Feuerwehrmann *m*; (*voluntary help*) freiwilliger Helfer (bei der Feuerbekämpfung); **~-fighting** *adj attr techniques* Feuerbekämpfungs-; *equipment* (Feuer)lösch-; **~fly** *n* Leuchtkäfer *m*; **~guard** *n* (Schutz)gitter *nt* (*vor dem Kamin*); ~ **hazard** *n* **to be a ~ hazard** feuergefährlich sein; **these old houses are a ~ hazard** bei diesen alten Häusern besteht Brandgefahr; ~ **hose** *n* Feuerwehrschlauch *m*; ~ **house** *n* (*US*) Feuerwache, Feuerwehrzentrale *f*; ~ **hydrant** *n* Hydrant *m*; ~ **insurance** *n* Feuer- *or* Brandversicherung *f*; ~ **irons** *npl* Kaminbesteck *nt*; **~light** *n* Schein *m* des Feuers *or* der Flammen; **~lighter** *n* Feueranzünder *m*; **~man** *n* **(a)** Feuerwehrmann *m*; **(b)** (*Rail*) Heizer *m*; **~place** *n* Kamin *m*; **~plug** *n* (*US*) Hydrant *m*; **~power** *n* (*of guns, aircraft, army*) Feuerkraft *f*; ~ **prevention** *n* Brandschutz *m*; **~proof** [1] *adj* feuerfest; [2] *vt materials* feuerfest machen; **~-raiser** *n* Brandstifter *m*; **~-raising** *n* Brandstiftung *f*; ~ **regulations** *npl* Brandschutzbestimmungen *pl*; **~screen** *n* Ofenschirm *m*; **F~ Service** *n* Feuerwehr *f*; **~side** *n* **to sit by the ~side** am Kamin sitzen; **~side chair** *n* Lehnsessel *m*; ~ **station** *n* Feuerwache, Feuerwehrzentrale *f*; **~storm** *n* Feuersturm *m*; **~trap** *n* Feuerfalle *f*; **~wall** *n* Brandmauer *f*; **~warden** *n* Feuerwache *f*; **~water** *n* (*hum inf*) Feuerwasser *nt* (*inf*); **~wood** *n* Brennholz *nt*; **~works** *npl* Feuerwerkskörper *pl*; (*display*) Feuerwerk *nt*; **there's going to be ~works at the meeting** (*fig inf*) bei dem Treffen werden die Funken fliegen.
firing ['faɪrɪŋ] *n* **(a)** (*of pottery*) Brennen *nt*. **(b)** (*Mil*) Feuer *nt*; (*of gun, shot, rocket*) Abfeuern *nt* ◆ **the ~ of a salute** Salutschüsse *pl*. **(c)** (*inf: dismissal*) Rausschmiß *m* (*inf*). **(d)** (*Aut: of engine*) Zündung *f*.
firing: ~ **line** *n* (*Mil*) Feuer- *or* Schußlinie *f*; (*fig*) Schußlinie *f*; ~ **pin** *n* Schlagbolzen *m*; ~ **squad** *n* Exekutionskommando *nt*.
firm¹ [fɜːm] *n* Firma *f* ◆ ~ **of solicitors** Rechtsanwaltsbüro *nt*.
firm² [1] *adj* (*+er*) **(a)** fest; *base also* stabil; *look also* entschlossen; *friendship also* beständig; *hold, basis also* sicher ◆ **to be ~ with sb** jdm gegenüber bestimmt auftreten. **(b)** (*Comm*) fest; *market* stabil.
[2] *adv* **to stand ~ on sth** (*fig*) fest *or* unerschütterlich bei etw bleiben.
◆**firm up** *vt sep wall etc* (ab)stützen; *deal etc* unter Dach und Fach bringen.
firmament ['fɜːməmənt] *n* Firmament *nt*.
firmly ['fɜːmlɪ] *adv* fest ◆ **no, she said ~** nein, sagte sie in bestimmtem *or* entschiedenem Ton.
firmness ['fɜːmnɪs] *n see adj* **(a)** Festigkeit *f*; Stabilität *f*; Entschlossenheit *f*; Beständigkeit *f*; Sicherheit *f* ◆ ~ **of character** Charakterstärke *f*. **(b)** Festigkeit *f*; Stabilität *f*.
firmware ['fɜːmweəʳ] *n* (*Comput*) Firmware *f*.
▼ **first** [fɜːst] [1] *adj* erste(r, s) ◆ **he was ~ in the queue/in Latin/to do that** er war der erste in der Schlange/er war der Beste in Latein/er war der erste, der das gemacht hat; **who's ~?** wer ist der erste?; **I'm ~, I've been waiting longer than you** ich bin zuerst an der Reihe, ich warte schon länger als Sie; **(let's put) ~ things ~** eins nach dem anderen, immer (hübsch) der Reihe nach; **you have to put ~ things ~** du mußt wissen, was dir am wichtigsten ist; **he doesn't know the ~ thing about it/cars** davon/von Autos hat er keinen blassen Schimmer (*inf*); **we did it the very ~ time** wir haben es auf Anhieb geschafft; **in the ~ place** zunächst *or* erstens einmal; **why didn't you say so in the ~ place?** warum hast du denn das nicht gleich gesagt?
[2] *adv* **(a)** zuerst; (*before all the others*) *arrive, leave* als erste(r, s) ◆ **~, take three eggs** zuerst *or* als erstes nehme man drei Eier; **~ come ~ served** (*prov*) wer zuerst kommt, mahlt zuerst (*Prov*); **on a ~ come ~ served basis** nach dem Prinzip „wer zuerst kommt, mahlt zuerst"; **women and children ~** Frauen und Kinder zuerst; **ladies ~** Ladies first!, den Damen der Vortritt; **he says ~ one thing then another** er sagt mal so, mal so, er sagt mal hü, mal hott; **before he says anything I want to get in ~ with a few comments** bevor er irgend etwas sagt, möchte ich einige Bemerkungen anbringen; **that's not what you said ~** zuerst hast du etwas anderes gesagt; **you ~** du zuerst; **which things come ~ in your order of priorities?** was steht bei Ihnen an erster Stelle?, was ist Ihnen am wichtigsten?; **but darling, you know you always come ~** aber, mein Schatz, du weißt doch, daß du bei mir immer an erster Stelle stehst; **he always puts his job ~** seine Arbeit kommt bei ihm immer vor allem anderen.
▼ **(b)** (*before all else*) als erstes, zunächst; (*in listing*) erstens ◆ **~ of all** (*before all else, mainly*) vor allem; **~ of all I am going for a swim** als erstes *or* zu(aller)erst gehe ich schwimmen; **why can't I? — well, ~ of all it's not yours and ...** warum denn nicht? — nun, zunächst *or* erstens einmal gehört es nicht dir und ...; **~ and foremost** zunächst, vor allem; **~ and last** in erster Linie.
(c) (*for the ~ time*) zum ersten Mal, das erste Mal ◆ **when did you ~ meet him?** wann haben Sie ihn das erste Mal getroffen?; **when this model was ~ introduced** zu Anfang *or* zuerst, als das Modell herauskam; **when it ~ became known that ...** als zuerst bekannt wurde, daß ...
(d) (*before: in time*) (zu)erst ◆ **I must finish this ~** ich muß das erst fertigmachen; **think ~ before you sign anything** überlegen Sie es sich, bevor Sie etwas unterschreiben.
(e) (*in preference*) eher, lieber ◆ **I'd die ~!** eher *or* lieber würde ich sterben!
[3] *n* **(a) the ~** der/die/das Erste; **he was among the very ~ to arrive** er war unter den ersten, die ankamen; **they were the ~ to come** sie kamen als erste; **he was the ~ home/finished** er war als erster zu Hause/fertig.
(b) this is the ~ I've heard of it das ist mir ja ganz neu.
(c) at ~ zuerst, zunächst; **from the ~** von Anfang an; **from ~ to last** von Anfang bis Ende.
(d) (*Brit Univ*) Eins *f*, die Note „Eins" ◆ **he got a ~** er bestand (sein Examen) mit „Eins" *or* „sehr gut"; **he was supposed to get a ~** er war ein Einserkandidat.
(e) (*Aut*) **~ (gear)** der erste (Gang); **in ~** im ersten (Gang).
(f) (*US: Baseball*) erstes Base *or* Mal; *see also* **sixth.**
first: ~ **aid** *n* Erste Hilfe; **to give ~ aid** Erste Hilfe leisten; ~ **aid box** *n* Verbandskasten *m*; ~ **aid kit** *n* Erste-Hilfe-Ausrüstung *f*; ~ **aid post** *or* **station** *n* Sanitätswache *f*; **~-born** [1] *adj* erstgeboren; [2] *n* Erstgeborene(r) *mf*; **~-class** [1] *adj* **(a)** erstklassig; **~-class compartment** Erste(r)-Klasse-Abteil *nt*, Abteil *nt* erster Klasse; **~-class carriage** Erste(r)-Klasse-Wagen *m*; **~-class mail** *bevorzugt beförderte Post*; **~-class ticket** Erster-Klasse-Fahrkarte *f*, Fahrkarte *f* für die erste Klasse; **(b)** (*excellent*) erstklassig; **he's ~-class at tennis/cooking** er ist ein erstklassiger Tennisspieler/Koch; **that's absolutely ~-class** das ist einfach Spitze (*inf*); **oh ~-class!** (*dated*) oh pfundig! (*dated inf*); **(c)** (*Brit Univ*) **~-class degree** sehr gutes Examen; [2] *adv travel* erster Klasse; ~ **cousin** *n* Vetter *m* ersten Grades; **~-day cover** *n* Ersttagsbrief *m*; ~ **edition** *n* Erstausgabe *f*; **~-foot** *vt* (*Scot*) einen Neujahrsbesuch abstatten (*+dat*); ~ **form** *n* (*Brit Sch*) erste Klasse; **~-former** *n* (*Brit Sch*) Erstkläßler(in *f*) *m*; **~-generation** *adj citizen, computer* der ersten Generation; **~-hand** *adj, adv* aus erster Hand; **F~ Lady** *n* First Lady *f*; ~ **lieutenant** *n* Oberleutnant *m*.
▼ **firstly** ['fɜːstlɪ] *adv* erstens, zunächst (einmal).
first: ~ **mate** *n* (*Naut*) Erster Offizier; (*on small boats*) Bestmann *m*; ~ **name** *n* Vorname *m*; **they're on ~ name terms** sie reden sich mit Vornamen an; ~ **night** *n* (*Theat*) Premiere *f*; **~ night nerves** Premierenfieber *nt*; **~-nighter** *n* Premierenbesucher(in *f*) *m*; ~ **offender** *n* Ersttäter(in *f*) *m*; **he is a ~ offender** er ist nicht vorbestraft; ~ **officer** *n* (*Naut*) Erster Offizier; **~-past-the-post system** *n* (*Pol*) Mehrheitswahlrecht *nt*; ~ **performance** *n* (*Theat*) Uraufführung *f*; (*Mus also*) Erstaufführung *f*; ~ **person** *n* erste Person; **~-person** *adj narrative* Ich-; ~ **principles** *npl* Grundprinzipien *pl*; **to get down to ~ principles** den Dingen auf den Grund gehen; **~-rate** *adj see* **~-class 1 (b)**; **~-strike weapon** *n* Erstschlagwaffe *f*; **~-time buyer** *n jd, der zum ersten Mal ein Haus/eine Wohnung kauft*; ~ **violin** *n* erste Geige; **he is a ~ violin** er spielt in der ersten Geige.
firth [fɜːθ] *n* (*Scot*) Förde *f*, Meeresarm *m*.
fir tree *n* Tannenbaum *m*.
fiscal ['fɪskəl] [1] *adj* Finanz-; *measures* finanzpolitisch ◆ ~ **year** Steuerjahr *nt*.
[2] *n* (*Scot Jur*) Staatsanwalt *m*.
fish [fɪʃ] [1] *n, pl* - *or* (*esp for different types*) **-es** Fisch *m* ◆ ~ **and chips** Fisch und Pommes frites; **to drink like a ~** (*inf*) wie ein Loch saufen (*inf*); **to have other ~ to fry** (*fig inf*) Wichtigeres zu tun haben; **like a ~ out of water** wie ein Fisch auf dem Trockenen; **neither ~ nor fowl** (*fig*) weder Fisch noch Fleisch; **he's a queer ~!** (*inf*) er ist ein komischer Kauz; **there are plenty more ~ in the sea** (*fig inf*) es gibt noch mehr (davon) auf der Welt; **a big ~ in a little pond** der Hahn im Korb; **a little ~ in a big pond** nur einer von vielen; **The F~es** (*Astron*) die Fische *pl*.
[2] *vi* fischen; (*with rod also*) angeln ◆ **to go ~ing** fischen/angeln gehen; **to go salmon ~ing** auf Lachsfang gehen.
[3] *vt* fischen; (*with rod also*) angeln ◆ **to ~ a river** in einem Fluß fischen/angeln; **to ~ a river dry** einen Fluß abfischen.
◆**fish for** *vi +prep obj* **(a)** fischen/angeln, fischen/angeln auf (*+acc*) (*spec*). **(b)** (*fig*) *compliments* fischen nach ◆ **they were ~ing ~ information** sie waren auf Informationen aus.
◆**fish out** *vt sep* herausfischen *or* -angeln (*of or from sth* aus etw) ◆ **he ~ed it ~ from behind the cupboard** er angelte es hinter dem Schrank hervor.
◆**fish up** *vt sep* auffischen, herausziehen; (*fig: from memory etc*) hervorkramen *or* -holen.
fish: **~bone** *n* (Fisch)gräte *f*; ~ **bowl** *n* Fischglas *nt*; **~cake** *n* Fischfrikadelle *f*.
fisher ['fɪʃəʳ] *n* **(a)** (*old: ~man*) Fischer *m* ◆ **~s of men** (*Bibl*) Menschenfischer *pl* (*Bibl*). **(b)** (*animal*) Fischfänger *m*.
fisherman ['fɪʃəmən] *n, pl* **-men** [-mən] Fischer *m*; (*amateur*) Angler *m*; (*boat*) Fischereiboot *nt*.
fishery ['fɪʃərɪ] *n* (*area*) Fischereizone *f or* -gewässer *nt*; (*industry*) Fischerei *f*.
fish: **~-eye lens** *n* (*Phot*) Fischauge *nt*; ~ **farm** *n* Fischzucht(anlage) *f*; ~ **farmer** *n* Fischzüchter(in *f*) *m*; ~ **farming** *n* Fischzucht *f*; ~ **finger** *n* Fischstäbchen *nt*; ~ **glue** *n* Fischleim *m*; **~hook** *n* Angelhaken *m*.
fishing ['fɪʃɪŋ] *n* Fischen *nt*; (*with rod*) Angeln *nt*; (*as industry*) Fischerei *f*

➤ LANGUAGE IN USE: **first:** 1 → 19.2, 26.1 **2b** → 26.1, 26.2 **firstly** → 26.1, 26.2

◆ ~ **(is) prohibited** Angeln verboten!

fishing: ~ boat *n* Fischerboot *nt*; **~ fleet** *n* Fischereiflotte *f*; **~ grounds** *npl* Fischgründe *pl*; **~ industry** *n* Fischindustrie *f*; **~-line** *n* Angelschnur *f*; **~-net** *n* Fischnetz *nt*; **~ port** *n* Fischereihafen *m*; **~-rod** *n* Angelrute *f*; **~ tackle** *n* (*for sport*) Angelgeräte *pl*; (*for industry*) Fischereigeräte *pl*; **~ village** *n* Fischerdorf *nt*.

fish: ~ ladder *n* Fischleiter *f*; **~ market** *n* Fischmarkt *m*; **~monger** *n* (*Brit*) Fischhändler(in *f*) *m*; **~monger's** *n* (*Brit*) Fischgeschäft *nt*; **~-net stockings** *npl* Netzstrümpfe *pl*; **~ paste** *n* Fischpaste *f*; **~plate** *n* (*Rail*) Lasche *f*; **~pond** *n* Fischteich *m*; **~ slice** *n* (*for serving*) Fischvorlegemesser *nt*; **~ stick** *n* (*US*) *see* **~ finger**; **~ story** *n* (*US inf*) Seemannsgarn *nt*; **~ tank** *n* (*in house*) Aquarium *nt*; (*on fish farm*) Fischteich *m*; **~wife** *n* Fischfrau *f*; (*fig pej*) Marktweib *nt*.

fishy ['fɪʃɪ] *adj* (+*er*) **(a)** *smell* Fisch- ◆ **it smells rather ~** es riecht ziemlich nach Fisch. **(b)** (*inf*) verdächtig; *excuse, story* faul (*inf*) ◆ **there's something ~ about his story** an der Geschichte ist was faul (*inf*).

fissile ['fɪsaɪl] *adj* spaltbar.

fission ['fɪʃən] *n* (*Phys*) Spaltung *f*; (*Biol*) (Zell)teilung *f* ◆ **~ bomb** (konventionelle) Atombombe.

fissionable ['fɪʃnəbl] *adj* spaltbar.

fissure ['fɪʃəʳ] *n* Riß *m*; (*deep*) Kluft *f*; (*narrow*) Spalt(e *f*) *m*.

fissured ['fɪʃəd] *adj* rissig; (*with deep fissures*) zerklüftet.

fist [fɪst] *n* Faust *f* ◆ **to put up one's ~s** die Fäuste hochnehmen, in (Box)kampfstellung gehen.

fistful ['fɪstfʊl] *n* Handvoll *f* ◆ **a ~ of pound coins** eine Handvoll Pfundmünzen.

fisticuffs ['fɪstɪkʌfs] *npl* (*dated inf*) (*fighting*) Handgreiflichkeiten *pl*; (*boxing*) Boxen *nt* ◆ **I'm not much good at ~** ich tauge nicht viel mit den Fäusten; **resorting to ~ is no solution** handgreiflich (zu) werden ist keine Lösung.

fit[1] [fɪt] [1] *adj* (+*er*) **(a)** (*suitable, suited for sth*) geeignet; *time, occasion also* günstig ◆ **~ to eat** eßbar; **is this meat still ~ to eat?** kann man dieses Fleisch noch essen?; **~ for habitation** bewohnbar; **to be ~ to be seen** sich sehen lassen können; **the coat is ~ for nothing but the dustbin** der Mantel taugt nur noch für den Mülleimer.

(b) (*deserving*) **a man like that is not ~ to have such a good wife** ein Mann wie er verdient so eine gute Frau nicht *or* ist eine so gute Frau nicht wert; **you're not ~ to be spoken to** du bist es nicht wert *or* verdienst es nicht, daß man sich mit dir unterhält.

(c) (*right and proper*) richtig, angebracht ◆ **I'll do as I think ~** ich handle, wie ich es für richtig halte; **to see ~ to do sth** es für richtig *or* angebracht halten, etw zu tun; **as is only ~** wie es sich gebührt; **it is only ~** es ist nur recht und billig; **he did not see ~ to apologize** er hat es nicht für nötig gehalten, sich zu entschuldigen.

(d) (*in health*) gesund; *sportsman etc* fit, in Form ◆ **she is not yet ~ to travel** sie ist noch nicht reisefähig; **only the ~test survive** nur die Geeignetsten überleben; (*people*) nur die Gesunden überleben; (*in business etc*) nur die Starken können sich halten.

(e) to laugh ~ to burst vor Lachen beinahe platzen; **to be ~ to drop (with tiredness)** zum Umfallen müde sein.

[2] *n* (*of clothes*) Paßform *f* ◆ **it is a very good/bad ~** es sitzt *or* paßt wie angegossen/nicht gut; **it's a bit of a tight ~** (*clothes*) es ist etwas eng; (*suitcase, timing, parking*) es geht gerade (noch).

[3] *vt* **(a)** (*cover, sheet, nut etc*) passen auf (+*acc*); (*key etc*) passen in (+*acc*); (*clothes etc*) passen (+*dat*) ◆ **this coat ~s you better** dieser Mantel paßt Ihnen besser *or* sitzt besser; **that part won't ~ this machine** das Teil paßt nicht für diese Maschine; **to make a ring ~ sb** jdm einen Ring anpassen.

(b) (*be suitable for*) *sb's plans, a theory etc* passen in (+*acc*).

(c) to ~ a dress on sb jdm ein Kleid anprobieren.

(d) (*put on, attach*) anbringen (*to an* +*dat*); *tyre, lock also* montieren; *double-glazing also* einsetzen; (*put in*) einbauen (*in* in +*acc*); (*furnish, provide with*) ausstatten ◆ **to ~ a key in the lock/a bulb in its socket** einen Schlüssel ins Schloß stecken/eine Glühbirne in die Fassung drehen *or* schrauben; **to ~ a knob on a door** eine Tür mit einem Knauf versehen.

(e) (*match*) *description, facts* entsprechen (+*dat*); (*person also*) passen auf (+*acc*) ◆ **to make the punishment ~ the crime** eine dem Vergehen angemessene Strafe verhängen.

(f) to ~ oneself for a job/a hard winter sich für eine Stelle/einen strengen Winter rüsten.

[4] *vi* **(a)** passen.

(b) (*correspond*) zusammenstimmen *or* -passen ◆ **the facts don't ~** die Fakten sind widersprüchlich; **it all ~s** es paßt alles zusammen; **there's still one piece of evidence that doesn't ~** da ist immer noch ein Indiz, das nicht dazupaßt.

◆**fit in** [1] *vt sep* **(a)** (*find space for*) unterbringen.

(b) (*find time for*) *person* einen Termin geben (+*dat*); *meeting* unterbringen; (*squeeze in also*) einschieben; (*for treatment also*) drannehmen (*inf*) ◆ **Sir Charles could ~ you ~ at 3** um 3 Uhr hätte Sir Charles Zeit für Sie; **can you ~ this meeting ~(to) your schedule?** können Sie diese Konferenz noch in Ihrem Terminkalender unterbringen?

(c) (*make harmonize*) **to ~ sth ~ with sth** etw mit etw in Einklang bringen.

(d) (*fit, put in*) einsetzen, einbauen.

[2] *vi* **(a)** (*go into place*) hineinpassen.

(b) (*plans, ideas, word*) passen; (*facts etc*) übereinstimmen; (*match*) dazupassen ◆ **there is one fact that doesn't ~ ~** da ist ein Punkt, der nicht ins Ganze paßt; **how does this ~ ~?** wie paßt das ins Ganze?; **I see, it all ~s ~ now** jetzt paßt alles zusammen; **to ~ ~ with sth** (*plans, ideas*) in etw (*acc*) passen; (*facts*) mit etw übereinstimmen; (*match*) zu etw passen; **does that ~ ~ with your plans?** läßt sich das mit Ihren Plänen vereinbaren?; **he wants everybody to ~ ~ with him/his plans/his wishes** er will, daß sich jedermann nach ihm/seinen Plänen/Wünschen richtet.

(c) (*people: harmonize*) **he doesn't ~ ~ here/with the others/with such a firm** er paßt hier nicht her/nicht zu den anderen/nicht in eine solche Firma; **she's the sort who ~s ~ easily in any group** sie ist der Typ, der sich in jede Gruppe leicht einfügt; **the new director didn't ~ ~** der neue Direktor hat nicht in die Firma gepaßt *or* nicht reingepaßt (*inf*); **try to ~ ~ (with the others)** versuche, dich den anderen anzupassen.

◆**fit on** [1] *vi* **(a)** passen ◆ **will it ~ ~?** paßt es (darauf)? **(b)** (*be fixed*) befestigt *or* angebracht sein ◆ **where does this part ~ ~?** wo gehört dieses Teil drauf?, wo wird dieses Teil befestigt?

[2] *vt sep* **(a)** *dress* anprobieren; (*tailor*) anpassen (*prep obj dat*). **(b)** (*put in place, fix on*) anbringen.

◆**fit out** *vt sep expedition, person* (*for an expedition*) ausrüsten; *person, ship* ausstatten.

◆**fit up** *vt sep* **(a)** (*fix up*) anbringen; (*assemble*) zusammensetzen *or* -bauen. **(b)** (*supply with*) ausstatten, mit allem Nötigen versehen; (*with clothes also*) ausstaffieren; (*with implements, weapons etc also*) ausrüsten ◆ **to ~ sb/sth ~ with sth** jdn/etw mit etw versehen *or* ausstatten.

fit[2] *n* (*Med, fig*) Anfall *m* ◆ **~ of coughing/anger** Husten-/Wutanfall *m*; **in a ~ of anger** in einem Anfall von Wut; **~ of energy/generosity** Anwandlung *f or* Anfall von Aktivität/Großzügigkeit; **in** *or* **by ~s and starts** stoßweise; **he wrote this novel in ~s and starts** er hat diesen Roman in mehreren Anläufen geschrieben; **to be in ~s of laughter** sich vor Lachen biegen *or* kugeln (*inf*); **he'd have a ~** (*fig inf*) er würde (ja) einen Anfall kriegen (*inf*); **he'd do anything when the ~ was on him** wenn es ihn gepackt hat, war er zu allem fähig (*inf*).

fitful ['fɪtfʊl] *adj* unbeständig; *working, progress* stoßweise; *sleep* unruhig; *sun* launenhaft (*geh*); *enthusiasm* sporadisch.

fitfully ['fɪtfəlɪ] *adv progress* stoßweise; *work also, blow* sporadisch; *sleep* unruhig ◆ **the sun shone ~** die Sonne kam vereinzelt durch.

fitment ['fɪtmənt] *n* (*furniture*) Einrichtungsgegenstand *m*; (*of machine, car*) Zubehörteil *nt*.

fitness ['fɪtnɪs] *n* **(a)** (*health*) Gesundheit *f*; (*condition*) Fitness, Fitneß, Kondition *f* ◆ **~ training** Fitneß- *or* Konditionstraining *nt*. **(b)** (*suitability*) Geeignetheit *f*; (*for job also*) Eignung *f*; (*of remark etc*) Angemessenheit *f*.

fitted ['fɪtɪd] *adj* **(a)** *garment* tailliert ◆ **~ carpet** Teppichboden *m*; **~ kitchen/cupboards** Einbauküche *f*/Einbauschränke *pl*; **~ sheet** Spannbettuch *nt*. **(b)** *person* geeignet (*for* für).

fitter ['fɪtəʳ] *n* **(a)** (*for clothes*) Schneider(in *f*) *m*. **(b)** (*Tech*) (*of engines*) Monteur *m*; (*for machines*) (Maschinen)schlosser *m*; (*not specially qualified*) Montagearbeiter(in *f*) *m*; (*of pipes etc*) Installateur *m*.

fitting ['fɪtɪŋ] [1] *adj* (*suitable*) passend; *expression also* angebracht; *time also* geeignet; (*seemly, becoming*) schicklich (*dated*) ◆ **it is not ~ for a young lady ...** es schickt sich nicht *or* ist nicht schicklich (*dated*) für eine junge Dame ...

[2] *n* **(a)** Anprobe *f* ◆ **~ room** Anproberaum *m*; (*cubicle*) Anprobekabine *f*; **to go in for a ~** zur Anprobe gehen.

(b) (*part*) Zubehörteil *nt* ◆ **~s** Ausstattung *f*; (*furniture also*) Einrichtung *f*; (*pipes*) Installation *f*; **bathroom/office ~s** Badezimmer-/Büroeinrichtung *f*; **electrical ~s** Elektroinstallationen.

fittingly ['fɪtɪŋlɪ] *adv see adj.*

five [faɪv] [1] *adj* fünf.

[2] *n* Fünf *f*; *see also* **six**.

five: ~-and-ten *n* (*US*) billiges Kaufhaus; **~-a-side** *adj football* mit fünf Spielern pro Mannschaft; *team* Fünfer-; **~fold** *adj, adv* fünffach; **~-o'clock shadow** *n nachmittäglicher Anflug von Bartstoppeln.*

fiver ['faɪvəʳ] *n* (*inf*) Fünfpfund-/Fünfdollarschein *m*.

five: ~spot *n* (*US inf*) Fünfdollarschein *m*; **~-star hotel** *n* Fünf-Sterne-Hotel *nt*; **~-year plan** *n* Fünfjahresplan *m*.

fix [fɪks] [1] *vt* **(a)** (*make firm*) befestigen, festmachen (*sth to sth* etw an/auf etw +*dat*); (*put on, install*) *new aerial, new dynamo* anbringen; (*fig*) *ideas, images* verankern, festsetzen ◆ **to ~ a stake in the ground** einen Pfahl im Boden verankern; **to ~ the blame on sb** die Schuld auf jdn schieben, jdm die Schuld geben; **this image was firmly ~ed in his memory** diese Vorstellung war fest in seinem Gedächtnis verankert; **to ~ sth in one's mind** sich (*dat*) etw fest einprägen; **to ~ bayonets** die Bajonette aufpflanzen.

(b) *eyes, attention* richten (*on, upon* auf +*acc*) ◆ **she kept all eyes/everybody's attention ~ed on her** alle sahen sie wie gebannt an; **to ~ sb with an angry stare** (*liter*) jdn mit ärgerlichen Blicken durchbohren.

(c) *date, price, limit* festsetzen, festlegen; (*agree on*) ausmachen, beschließen ◆ **nothing has been ~ed yet** es liegt noch nichts fest; es ist noch nichts fest (ausgemacht *or* beschlossen worden).

(d) (*arrange*) arrangieren; *tickets, taxi etc* besorgen, organisieren (*inf*) ◆ **have you got anything ~ed for tonight?** haben Sie (für) heute abend schon etwas vor?

(e) (*straighten out, sort out*) in Ordnung bringen, regeln ◆ **don't worry I'll ~ things with him** mach dir keine Gedanken, ich regle das mit ihm *or* ich bringe das in Ordnung.

(f) (*inf: get even with, sort out*) **I'll ~ him** dem werd' ich's besorgen (*inf*); **the Mafia will ~ him** den wird sich (*dat*) die Mafia vornehmen (*inf*) *or* vorknöpfen (*inf*).

(g) (*repair*) in Ordnung bringen, (ganz) machen (*inf*); (*put in good order,*

adjust) machen (*inf*).
(h) *drink, meal* machen ◆ **to ~ one's hair** sich frisieren.
(i) (*inf*) *race, fight* manipulieren; *jury also* bestechen ◆ **the whole discussion/ interview was ~ed** die Diskussion/das Interview war gestellt; **the whole thing was ~ed** das war eine abgekartete Sache (*inf*).
(j) (*US inf: intend*) vorhaben ◆ **I'm ~ing on getting married soon** ich habe vor, bald zu heiraten.
(k) (*Chem, Phot*) fixieren.
(l) (*Naut, Aviat*) *position* bestimmen; *submarine etc* orten.
[2] *n* **(a)** (*inf: tricky situation*) Patsche (*inf*), Klemme (*inf*) *f* ◆ **to be in a ~** in der Patsche *or* Klemme sitzen (*inf*); **to get oneself into a ~** sich (*dat*) eine schöne Suppe einbrocken (*inf*).
(b) (*Naut*) Position *f*, Standort *m* ◆ **to take a ~ on sth** etw orten; **to get a ~ on sth** (*fig: get clear about*) sich (*dat*) Klarheit über etw (*acc*) verschaffen.
(c) (*sl: of drugs*) Fix *m* (*sl*) ◆ **to give oneself a ~** fixen (*sl*).
(d) (*inf*) **the fight/competition was a ~** der Kampf/Wettbewerb war eine abgekartete Sache (*inf*).
◆**fix down** *vt sep* befestigen.
◆**fix on** [1] *vt sep* festmachen (*prep obj* auf +*dat*); *badge etc also* anheften, anstecken; (*fit on*) anbringen; (*by sewing*) annähen.
[2] *vi* +*prep obj* (*decide on*) sich entscheiden für.
◆**fix together** *vt sep* zusammenmachen (*inf*).
◆**fix up** *vt sep* **(a)** *shelves* anbringen; *tent* aufstellen.
(b) (*arrange*) arrangieren; *holidays etc* festmachen; (*book*) *organized tour, hotel etc* buchen ◆ **it's all ~ed ~** es ist (schon) alles arrangiert/fest (*inf*) *or* festgemacht/fest gebucht; **have you got anything ~ed ~ for this evening?** haben Sie (für) heute abend schon etwas vor?
(c) to ~ sb ~ with sth jdm etw besorgen *or* verschaffen; **we ~ed them ~ for the night** wir haben sie für die Nacht untergebracht; **I stayed with him until I got myself ~ed ~ (with a room)** ich habe bei ihm gewohnt, bis ich ein Zimmer hatte.
(d) (*straighten out, sort out*) in Ordnung bringen, regeln.
fixated [fɪk'seɪtɪd] *adj* fixiert (*on* auf +*acc*).
fixation [fɪk'seɪʃən] *n* **(a)** (*Psych*) Fixierung *f* ◆ **she has this ~ about cleanliness** sie hat einen Sauberkeitsfimmel (*inf*). **(b)** (*Chem*) Fixierung *f*.
fixative ['fɪksətɪv] *n* Fixativ *nt*.
fixed [fɪkst] *adj* **(a)** fest; *idea* fix; *smile* starr ◆ **~ assets** feste Anlagen *pl*; **~ capital** Anlagevermögen, Anlagekapital *nt*; **~ costs** Fixkosten *pl*; **~ disk** (*Comput*) Festplatte *f*; **~ menu** Tagesmenü *nt*; **~ price** Festpreis *m*; (*Econ also*) gebundener Preis; **~ star** Fixstern *m*; **~ wing aircraft** Starrflügler *m*.
(b) (*inf*) **how are you ~ for time/food/money** *etc*? wie sieht's bei dir mit der Zeit/dem Essen/dem Geld *etc* aus? (*inf*), wie steht's (denn) bei dir mit Zeit/ Essen/Geld *etc*? (*inf*); **how are you ~ for tonight?** was hast du (für) heute abend vor?
fixedly ['fɪksɪdlɪ] *adv stare, look* starr, unbeweglich.
fixed-rate ['fɪkstreɪt] *adj mortgage* Festzins-
fixer ['fɪksəʳ] *n* (*Phot*) Fixiermittel *nt*; (*sl*) Schieber *m*.
fixing bath ['fɪksɪŋ,bɑːθ] *n* Fixierbad *nt*.
fixings ['fɪksɪŋz] *npl* (*US Cook*) Beilagen *pl*.
fixity ['fɪksɪtɪ] *n* (*liter*) **his ~ of purpose** seine Zielstrebigkeit.
fixture ['fɪkstʃəʳ] *n* **(a)** (*of a building etc*) **~s** Ausstattung *f*, unbewegliches Inventar (*form*); **~s and fittings** Anschlüsse und unbewegliches Inventar (*form*); **lighting ~s** elektrische Anschlüsse; **to be a ~** (*fig hum: person*) zum Inventar gehören.
(b) (*Brit Sport*) Spiel *nt* ◆ **~ list** Spielplan *m*.
fizz [fɪz] [1] *vi* (*champagne etc*) perlen, sprudeln, moussieren.
[2] *n* **(a)** (*of champagne etc*) Perlen, Moussieren *nt*. **(b)** (*drink*) Sprudel *m*; (*flavoured also*) (Brause)limonade, Brause *f*. **(c)** (*dated Brit inf: champagne*) Schampus *m* (*dated inf*).
◆**fizz up** *vi* (auf)sprudeln.
fizzle ['fɪzl] *vi* zischen, spucken (*inf*).
◆**fizzle out** *vi* (*firework, enthusiasm*) verpuffen; (*rocket*) vorzeitig verglühen; (*plan*) im Sande verlaufen.
fizzy ['fɪzɪ] *adj* (+*er*) sprudelnd ◆ **to be ~** sprudeln; **it's too ~** da ist zu viel Kohlensäure drin; **the soda water makes it ~** durch das Sodawasser sprudelt es; **a ~ drink** eine Brause.
fjord [fjɔːd] *n* Fjord *m*.
flab [flæb] *n* (*inf*) Speck *m* ◆ **to fight the ~** (*hum*) etwas für die schlanke Linie tun, sich trimmen.
flabbergast ['flæbəgɑːst] *vt* (*inf*) verblüffen, umhauen (*inf*) ◆ **I was ~ed to see him/at the price** ich war platt (*inf*) *or* von den Socken (*sl*), als ich ihn sah/als ich den Preis erfuhr.
flabbergasting ['flæbəgɑːstɪŋ] *adj pred* (*inf*) unglaublich.
flabbily ['flæbɪlɪ] *adv* schlaff; *written* schwammig.
flabbiness ['flæbɪnɪs] *n see adj* Schlaffheit *f*; Schwammigkeit *f*; Farblosigkeit *f*; Wabbeligkeit *f* (*inf*).
flabby ['flæbɪ] *adj* (+*er*) schlaff; *prose, argument, thesis* schwammig; *person, character* ohne Saft und Kraft, farblos; (*fat*) *stomach* schwammig, wabbelig (*inf*) ◆ **he's getting ~ round the middle** er setzt um die Taille Speck an.
flaccid ['flæksɪd] *adj* (*liter*) schlaff; *prose* saft- und kraftlos.
flag[1] [flæg] [1] *n* **(a)** Fahne *f*; (*small, on map, chart etc*) Fähnchen *nt*; (*national also, Naut*) Flagge *f*; (*for semaphore*) Signalflagge *or* -fahne *f* ◆ **to go down with all ~s flying** (*lit*) bis zum letzten kämpfen; (*fig*) mit Glanz und Gloria untergehen; **to keep the ~ flying** (*lit, fig*) die Stellung halten; **to show the ~** seine Präsenz *or* (*fig also*) seine Anwesenheit dokumentieren; **~ of convenience** (*Naut*) Billigflagge *f*.
(b) (*for charity*) Fähnchen *nt*.
(c) (*of taxi*) **the ~ was down** das Taxi war besetzt; **he put the ~ down** er stellte auf „besetzt".
(d) (*paper marker*) Kennzeichen *nt*.
[2] *vt* beflaggen.
◆**flag down** *vt sep taxi etc* anhalten.
◆**flag up** *vt sep* (*inf: mark, indicate*) markieren.
flag[2] *vi* erlahmen; (*interest, enthusiasm, strength etc also*) nachlassen; (*person also*) ermüden; (*plant*) den Kopf/die Blätter hängen lassen.
flag[3] *n* (*Bot*) Schwertlilie *f*; (*sweet ~*) Kalmus *m*.
flag[4] [1] *n* (*also* **~stone**) Steinplatte *f*; (*for floor also*) Fliese *f*.
[2] *vt* mit Steinplatten/Fliesen belegen; *floor also* fliesen.
flag day *n* **(a)** (*Brit*) *Tag m, an dem eine Straßensammlung für einen wohltätigen Zweck durchgeführt wird.* **(b) F~ D~** (*US*) *14. Juni, Gedenktag der Einführung der amerikanischen Nationalflagge.*
flagellate ['flædʒəleɪt] *vt* geißeln.
flagellation [,flædʒə'leɪʃən] *n* Geißelung *f*.
flag officer *n* (*Naut*) Flaggoffizier *m*.
flagon ['flægən] *n* (*bottle*) Flasche *f*; (*jug*) Krug *m*.
flagpole ['flægpəʊl] *n* Fahnenstange *f*.
flagrance ['fleɪgrəns], **flagrancy** ['fleɪgrənsɪ] *n* eklatante *or* krasse Offensichtlichkeit; (*of affair, defiance, disregard*) Unverhohlenheit *f* ◆ **such was the ~ of this injustice ...** das war eine derart eklatante *or* krasse *or* himmelschreiende Ungerechtigkeit ...; **the unabashed ~ of his abuse of privilege** die unverhohlene Art, mit der er seine Privilegien mißbraucht.
flagrant ['fleɪgrənt] *adj* eklatant, kraß; *injustice, crime also* himmelschreiend; *breach, violation also* flagrant (*geh*); *disregard, defiance also, affair* unverhohlen, offenkundig.
flagrantly ['fleɪgrəntlɪ] *adv* ganz eindeutig *or* offensichtlich; *abuse, flirt, disregard* unverhohlen, ganz offenkundig ◆ **he ~ parked right outside the police station** er hat ganz ungeniert *or* unverfroren direkt vor der Polizeiwache geparkt; **a ~ modernistic style** ein kraß modernistischer Stil.
flag: ~ship *n* (*lit, fig*) Flaggschiff *nt*; **~staff** *n* Fahnen- *or* Flaggenmast *m*; **~stone** *n* (Stein)platte *f*; (*on floor also*) Fliese *f*; **~waver** *n* Hurrapatriot(in *f*) *m*, Chauvinist *m*; **~waving** [1] *n* Hurrapatriotismus, Chauvinismus *m*; [2] *adj speech* chauvinistisch.
flail [fleɪl] [1] *n* (Dresch)flegel *m*.
[2] *vt* dreschen ◆ **he wildly ~ed his arms about** er schlug (mit den Armen) wild um sich.
[3] *vi* **to ~ about** herumfuchteln; **the dying deer with its legs ~ing in all directions** das verendende Reh, das mit seinen Läufen nach allen Richtungen ausschlug.
flail tank *n* Minenräumpanzer *m*.
flair [flɛəʳ] *n* (*for selecting the best etc*) Gespür *nt*, (feine) Nase (*inf*), Riecher *m* (*inf*); (*talent*) Talent *nt*; (*stylishness*) Flair *nt* ◆ **his great ~ for business** sein großes Geschäftstalent.
flak [flæk] *n* **(a)** Flakfeuer *nt* ◆ **~ jacket** kugelsichere Weste. **(b)** (*fig*) **he's been getting a lot of ~** er ist mächtig unter Beschuß geraten (*inf*); **I'm not taking the ~ for this** ich laß mich deswegen nicht zur Sau machen (*inf*).
flake [fleɪk] [1] *n* (*of snow, soap*) Flocke *f*; (*of paint, rust*) Splitter *m*; (*of plaster*) abgebröckeltes Stückchen; (*of metal, wood*) Span *m*; (*of skin*) Schuppe *f* ◆ **~s of paint/plaster were falling off the ceiling** die Farbe an der Decke blätterte ab/der Gips bröckelte von der Decke ab.
[2] *vi* (*stone, plaster etc*) abbröckeln; (*paint*) abblättern.
[3] *vt* (*Cook*) *chocolate, almonds* raspeln.
◆**flake off** *vi* (*plaster*) abbröckeln; (*paint, rust etc*) abblättern, absplittern; (*skin*) sich schälen, sich abschuppen.
◆**flake out** *vi* (*inf*) (*become exhausted*) abschlaffen (*inf*); (*pass out*) aus den Latschen kippen (*sl*); (*fall asleep*) einschlafen, einpennen (*sl*).
flaky ['fleɪkɪ] *adj* (+*er*) *potatoes* flockig; *paint, plaster etc* brüchig; *crust* blättrig; *skin* schuppig ◆ **~ pastry** Blätterteig *m*.
flamboyance [flæm'bɔɪəns] *n* Extravaganz *f*; (*of life style also*) Üppigkeit *f*; (*of colour*) Pracht *f*; (*of gesture*) Großartigkeit *f*.
flamboyant [flæm'bɔɪənt] *adj* extravagant; *life style also* üppig, aufwendig; *plumage* farbenprächtig; *colours* prächtig; *gesture* großartig ◆ **~ style** (*Archit*) Flamboyantstil *m*; **in the ~ court of Louis XIV** am prunkvollen Hof Ludwigs XIV.
flamboyantly [flæm'bɔɪəntlɪ] *adv* extravagant ◆ **in Hollywood, where nothing that is done is not done ~** in Hollywood, wo alles in großem Stil *or* Rahmen gemacht wird.
flame [fleɪm] [1] *n* **(a)** Flamme *f* ◆ **the house was in ~s** das Haus stand in Flammen. **(b)** (*of passion*) Flamme *f* (*geh*), Feuer *nt no pl* ◆ **the ~ of anger in his eyes** (*liter*) die Zornesglut in seinen Augen (*liter*). **(c)** (*inf: sweetheart*) Flamme *f* (*inf*).
[2] *vi* (*fire*) lodern, flammen (*geh*); (*liter: colour*) leuchten; (*gem*) funkeln, gleißen (*liter*).
◆**flame up** *vi* **(a)** (*fire*) auflodern. **(b)** (*fig*) (*person*) in Wut *or* Rage geraten; (*anger etc*) aufflammen, auflodern.
flame-coloured ['fleɪmkʌləd] *adj* feuerfarben.
flamenco [flə'meŋkəʊ] [1] *n* Flamenco *m*.
[2] *adj* Flamenco-.
flame: ~ red [1] *n* Feuerrot *nt*; [2] *adj* feuerrot; **~thrower** *n* Flammenwerfer *m*.
flaming ['fleɪmɪŋ] *adj* **(a)** brennend, lodernd; (*fig*) *colour* leuchtend; *rage*

hell; *passion* glühend ◆ **she was absolutely ~** (*Brit inf: angry*) sie kochte (vor Wut) (*inf*).
(b) (*Brit sl: bloody*) verdammt (*inf*), Scheiß- (*sl*) ◆ **it's a ~ nuisance/waste of time** Mensch, das ist vielleicht ein Mist/das ist die reinste Zeitverschwendung (*inf*); **it was there all the ~ time** Mensch (*inf*) *or* Scheiße (*sl*), das war die ganze Zeit da; **who does he ~ well think he is?** Mensch *or* verdammt noch mal, für wen hält der sich eigentlich? (*sl*).

flamingo [flə'mɪŋgəʊ] *n, pl* **-(e)s** Flamingo *m.*

flammable ['flæməbl] *adj* leicht entzündbar, feuergefährlich.

flan [flæn] *n* Kuchen *m* ◆ **fruit ~** Obstkuchen *m*; **~ case** Tortenboden *m.*

Flanders ['flɑːndəz] *n* Flandern *nt.*

flange [flændʒ] *n* (*on wheel etc*) Spurkranz *m*; (*Tech: ring, collar*) Flansch *m.*

flanged [flændʒd] *adj* gebördelt; *tube etc also* geflanscht.

flank [flæŋk] [1] *n* (*of animal, Mil*) Flanke *f*; (*of mountain, building*) Seite, Flanke (*old*) *f.*
[2] *vt* (a) flankieren. (b) (*Mil*) *the enemy* seitlich umgehen ◆ **~ing movement** Flankenbewegung *f.*

flannel ['flænl] [1] *n* (a) Flanell *m* ◆ **~s** *pl* (*trousers*) Flanellhose *f.* (b) (*Brit: face-~*) Waschlappen *m.* (c) (*Brit inf: waffle*) Geschwafel (*inf*), Gelaber (*inf*) *nt.*
[2] *adj trousers etc* Flanell-.
[3] *vi* (*Brit inf: waffle*) schwafeln (*inf*), labern (*inf*).

flannelette [ˌflænə'let] *n* Baumwollflanell *m* ◆ **~ sheet** Biberbettuch *nt.*

flap [flæp] [1] *n* (a) (*of pocket*) Klappe *f*; (*of table*) ausziehbarer Teil; (*Aviat*) (Lande)klappe *f* ◆ **a ~ of skin** ein Hautfetzen *m*; (*Med*) ein Hautlappen *m.*
(b) (*sound*) (*of sails, sheeting etc*) Flattern, Knattern *nt*; (*of wings*) Schlagen *nt.*
(c) (*motion*) **to give sth a ~** leicht auf etw (*acc*) klatschen.
(d) (*inf*) helle Aufregung, Panik *f* ◆ **to get in(to) a ~** in helle Aufregung geraten, ins Flattern geraten (*inf*); **there's a big ~ on** es herrscht große Panik, alles ist in heller Aufregung.
(e) (*Phon*) geschlagener Laut.
[2] *vi* (a) (*wings*) schlagen; (*door, shutters also*) klappern; (*sails, tarpaulin etc*) flattern ◆ **his coat ~ped about his legs** der Mantel schlackerte ihm um die Beine (*inf*); **his ears were ~ping** (*inf*) er spitzte die Ohren.
(b) (*inf*) in heller Aufregung sein ◆ **to start to ~** in helle Aufregung geraten; **don't ~** reg dich nicht auf; **there's no need to ~** (das ist) kein Grund zur Aufregung; **she's been ~ping around all morning** sie rennt schon den ganzen Morgen wie ein aufgescheuchtes Huhn durch die Gegend (*inf*).
[3] *vt* **to ~ its wings** mit den Flügeln schlagen; **he ~ped the newspaper at the fly** er schlug *or* klatschte mit der Zeitung nach der Fliege.

◆**flap away** *vi* (*bird*) davonfliegen.

flapjack ['flæpdʒæk] *n* Pfannkuchen *m.*

flapper ['flæpəʳ] *n modisches Mädchen in den 20er Jahren.*

flare [flɛəʳ] [1] *n* (a) Auflodern *nt*; (*fig: of anger*) Aufbrausen *nt.*
(b) (*signal*) Leuchtsignal *nt*; (*from pistol etc*) Leuchtrakete, Leuchtkugel *f*; (*fire, landing ~*) Leuchtfeuer *nt.*
(c) (*Fashion*) ausgestellter Schnitt ◆ **a skirt with a slight ~** ein leicht ausgestellter Rock; **trousers with ~s** ausgestellte Hose/Hosen, Hose *f*/Hosen *pl* mit Schlag.
(d) (*solar ~*) Sonneneruption, Fackel *f.*
(e) (*Phot*) Reflexlicht *nt.*
[2] *vi* (a) (*match, torch*) aufleuchten; (*sunspot also*) aufblitzen.
(b) (*trousers, skirts*) ausgestellt sein.
(c) (*nostrils*) sich blähen.

◆**flare up** *vi* (*lit, fig: situation, affair*) aufflackern, auflodern; (*fig*) (*person*) aufbrausen, auffahren; (*fighting, epidemic*) ausbrechen; (*anger*) zum Ausbruch kommen ◆ **she ~d ~ at me** sie fuhr mich an.

flared [flɛəd] *adj trousers, skirt* ausgestellt.

flare: ~ path *n* (*Aviat*) Leuchtpfad *m*; **~ pistol** *n* Leuchtpistole *f*; **~-up** *n see* **~ up** Aufflackern, Auflodern *nt*; Aufbrausen *nt*; Ausbruch *m*; (*sudden dispute*) (plötzlicher) Krach.

flash [flæʃ] [1] *n* (a) Aufblinken *nt no pl*; (*very bright*) Aufblitzen *nt no pl*; (*of metal, jewels etc*) Blitzen, Blinken *nt no pl*; (*Mot*) Lichthupe *f no pl* ◆ **to give sb a ~** (*Mot*) jdn (mit der Lichthupe) anblinken; **~ of lightning** Blitz *m*; **he gave two quick ~es with his torch** er blinkte zweimal kurz mit der Taschenlampe; **the ~es come at regular intervals** es blinkt in regelmäßigen Abständen; **three short ~es are the Morse sign for S** dreimal kurz blinken ist *or* drei kurze Blinkzeichen sind das Morsezeichen für S.
(b) (*fig*) (*news~*) Kurzmeldung *f*; (*interrupting programme also*) Zwischenmeldung *f* ◆ **~ of wit/inspiration** Geistesblitz *m*; **in a ~** blitzartig, wie der Blitz; **as quick as a ~** blitzschnell; **a ~ in the pan** (*inf*) ein Strohfeuer *nt.*
(c) (*Mil: on uniform*) Abzeichen *nt.*
(d) (*Phot*) Blitz(licht *nt*) *m* ◆ **to use a ~** Blitzlicht benutzen.
(e) (*US inf: torch*) Taschenlampe *f.*
[2] *vi* (a) aufblinken; (*very brightly*) aufblitzen; (*repeatedly: indicators etc*) blinken; (*metal, jewels, eyes*) blitzen, blinken; (*Mot*) die Lichthupe benutzen.
(b) (*move quickly*) (*vehicle*) sausen, schießen, flitzen (*all inf*); (*person also*) huschen ◆ **to ~ in and out** rein und raus sausen *etc*; **a smile ~ed across his face** ein Lächeln huschte über sein Gesicht; **to ~ past** *or* **by** vorbeisausen *etc*; (*holidays etc*) vorbeifliegen; **the time ~ed past** die Zeit verflog im Nu; **the thought ~ed through my mind that** ... mir kam plötzlich der Gedanke, daß ..., es schoß mir durch den Kopf, daß ...
[3] *vt* (a) *light* aufblitzen *or* aufleuchten lassen; *SOS, message* blinken ◆ **to ~ a torch on sb/sth** jdn/etw mit der Taschenlampe anleuchten; **to ~ one's headlights** die Lichthupe betätigen; **to ~ one's headlights at sb, to ~ sb** jdn mit der Lichthupe anblinken; **she ~ed him a look of contempt/gratitude** sie blitzte ihn verächtlich/dankbar an.
(b) (*inf: show, wave: also* **~ around**) schwenken (*inf*), protzen mit; *diamond ring* blitzen lassen ◆ **don't ~ all that money around** wedel nicht so mit dem vielen Geld herum (*inf*).
[4] *adj* (*inf*) (*showy*) protzig (*pej*); (*smart*) schick.

◆**flash back** *vi* (*Film*) zurückblenden (*to* auf *+acc*).

flash: ~back *n* (*Film*) Rückblende *f*; **~bulb** *n* (*Phot*) Blitzbirne *f*; **~ burn** *n* Verbrennung *f* (*durch kurzzeitige Strahlungshitze*); **~ card** *n* (*Sch*) Leselernkarte *f*; **~cube** *n* (*Phot*) Blitzwürfel *m.*

flasher ['flæʃəʳ] *n* (a) (*Mot*) Lichthupe *f.* (b) (*Brit inf: person exposing himself*) Exhibitionist *m.*

flash: ~ flood *n* flutartige Überschwemmung; **~ gun** *n* Elektronenblitzgerät *nt*; **~ Harry** *n* (*inf*) Lackaffe *m* (*pej inf*).

flashing ['flæʃɪŋ] *n* (*Build*) Verwahrung *f*, Kehlblech *nt.*

flash: ~light *n* (a) (*Phot*) Blitzlicht *nt*; (b) (*esp US: torch*) Taschenlampe *f*; (c) (*signal lamp*) Leuchtfeuer *nt*; **~ photography** *n* Blitz(licht)fotografie *f*; **~ point** *n* (*Chem*) Flammpunkt *m*; (*fig*) Siedepunkt *m.*

flashy ['flæʃɪ] *adj* (*+er*) auffallend, auffällig.

flask [flɑːsk] *n* Flakon *m*; (*Chem*) Glaskolben *m*; (*for spirits, carried in pocket*) Flachmann *m* (*inf*), Reiseflasche *f*; (*vacuum ~*) Thermosflasche *f.*

flat[1] [flæt] [1] *adj* (*+er*) (a) flach; *countryside also, tyre, nose, feet* platt; *surface* eben ◆ **he stood ~ against the wall** er stand platt gegen die Wand gedrückt; **as ~ as a pancake** (*inf*) (*tyre*) total platt; (*countryside*) total flach; (*girl*) flach wie ein (Plätt)brett, platt wie eine Flunder; **~ roof** Flachdach *nt*; **to fall ~ on one's face** auf die Nase fallen; **to lie ~** flach *or* platt liegen; **the earthquake laid the whole city ~** das Erdbeben machte die ganze Stadt dem Erdboden gleich.
(b) (*fig*) fad(e); *painting, photo also* flach, kontrastarm; *colour* matt, stumpf, glanzlos; *joke, remark* abgedroschen, öde, müde; *trade, market* lau, lahm, lustlos; (*stale*) *beer, wine* schal, abgestanden ◆ **she felt a bit ~** sie fühlte sich ein bißchen daneben (*inf*), sie hatte zu nichts Lust; **to fall ~** (*joke*) nicht ankommen; (*play etc*) durchfallen.
(c) *refusal, denial* glatt, deutlich ◆ **and that's ~** und damit basta.
(d) (*Mus*) *instrument* zu tief (gestimmt); *voice* zu tief.
(e) (*Comm*) Pauschal- ◆ **~ rate of pay** Pauschallohn *m*; **~ rate** Pauschale *f*; **to pay a ~ rate of income tax** eine Einkommenssteuerpauschale bezahlen; **to get a ~ rate of pay** pauschal bezahlt werden; **~ fare** Einheitstarif *m.*
(f) (*US inf: broke*) pleite (*inf*).
[2] *adv* (*+er*) (a) *turn down, refuse* rundweg, kategorisch ◆ **he told me ~ that ...** er sagte mir klipp und klar, daß ...
(b) (*Mus*) **to sing/play ~** zu tief singen/spielen.
(c) **in ten seconds ~** in sage und schreibe (nur) zehn Sekunden.
(d) **~ broke** (*Brit inf*) total pleite (*inf*).
(e) **~ out** (*inf*) (*exhausted*) total erledigt (*inf*); (*asleep, drunk*) hinüber (*inf*); **to go ~ out** voll aufdrehen (*inf*); (*in car also*) Spitze fahren (*inf*); **to work** *or* **go ~ out** auf Hochtouren arbeiten; **to be lying ~ out** platt am Boden liegen.
[3] *n* (a) (*of hand*) Fläche *f*; (*of blade*) flache Seite.
(b) (*Geog*) Ebene *f.*
(c) (*Mus*) Erniedrigungszeichen, b *nt* ◆ **you played E natural instead of a ~** du hast e statt es gespielt.
(d) (*Aut*) Platte(r) *m* (*inf*), (Reifen)panne *f.*
(e) (*Theat*) Kulisse *f.*
(f) (*Sport*) **the ~** das Flachrennen; (*season*) die Flachrennsaison.

flat[2] *n* (*Brit*) Wohnung *f.*

flat: ~-bed lorry *n* Tieflader *m*; **~-bottomed** ['flætˌbɒtəmd] *adj boat* flach; **~-chested** *adj* flachbrüstig; **~-dweller** *n* (*Brit*) Wohnungsbewohner(in *f*) *m*; **~ feet** *npl* Plattfüße *pl*; **~fish** *n* Plattfisch *m*; **~foot** *n* (*inf: policeman*) Polyp *m* (*inf*); **~-footed** *adj* plattfüßig; **~-hunting** *n* (*Brit*) Wohnungssuche *f*; **to go/be ~-hunting** auf Wohnungssuche gehen/sein; **~-iron** *n* (*old*) Plätteisen *nt*; **~let** *n* (*Brit*) kleine Wohnung.

flatly ['flætlɪ] *adv deny, refuse* rundweg, kategorisch; *say* klipp und klar, schlankweg.

flatmate ['flætmeɪt] *n* (*Brit*) Mitbewohner(in *f*) *m.*

flatness ['flætnɪs] *n see adj* (*a-c*) (a) Flachheit *f*; Plattheit *f*; Ebenheit *f.* (b) Fadheit *f*; Flachheit, Kontrastarmut *f*; Stumpfheit *f*; Abgedroschenheit *f*; Lustlosigkeit *f*; Schalheit *f.* (c) Deutlichkeit, Direktheit *f.*

flat: ~ pack *n* (*Brit: furniture*) flaches Paket ◆ **it arrives as a ~ pack** es kommt flach verpackt an; **~ pack furniture** Möbel *pl* zum Selberbauen; **~ race** *n* Flachrennen *nt*; **~ racing** *n* Flachrennen *nt*; **~ screen** *n* (*Comput*) Flachbildschirm *m*; **~ season** *n* Flachrennsaison *f.*

flatten ['flætn] [1] *vt* (a) *path, road, field* ebnen, planieren; *metal* flach *or* platt hämmern *or* schlagen; (*storm etc*) *crops* zu Boden drücken, niederdrücken; *trees* umwerfen; *town* dem Erdboden gleichmachen. (b) (*inf: demoralize, snub*) zu nichts reduzieren ◆ **that'll ~ him** das wird bei ihm die Luft rauslassen (*inf*).
[2] *vr* **to ~ oneself against sth** sich platt gegen *or* an etw drücken.

◆**flatten out** [1] *vi* (*countryside*) flach(er) *or* eben(er) werden; (*road*) eben(er) werden; (*Aviat*) ausschweben.
[2] *vt sep path* ebnen; *metal* glatt hämmern; *map, paper, fabric* glätten.

flatter ['flætəʳ] *vt* schmeicheln (*+dat*) ◆ **it ~s your figure** das ist sehr vorteilhaft; **I was very ~ed by his speech** ich fühlte mich von seiner Rede sehr geschmeichelt; **you can ~ yourself on being ...** Sie können sich (*dat*) etwas darauf einbilden, daß Sie ...; **he ~s himself he's a good musician** er schmeichelt sich (*dat*) *or* er bildet sich (*dat*) ein, ein guter Musiker zu sein.

flatterer ['flætərəʳ] *n* Schmeichler(in *f*) *m.*

flattering ['flætərɪŋ] *adj* schmeichelhaft; *clothes* vorteilhaft.

flatteringly ['flætərɪŋlɪ] *adv say* schmeichlerisch; *posed, dressed* vorteilhaft.

flattery ['flætərɪ] *n* (*compliments*) Schmeicheleien *pl* ◆ **~ will get you nowhere** mit Schmeicheln kommst du nicht weiter.

flat top *n* (*US inf: aircraft carrier*) Flugzeugträger *m*.

flatulence ['flætjʊləns] *n* Blähung(en *pl*), Flatulenz (*spec*) *f* ◆ **to cause ~** Blähungen verursachen, blähen.

flatulent ['flætjʊlənt] *adj* aufgebläht; *food* blähend.

flat: ~ware *n* (*US*) (*cutlery*) Besteck *nt*; (*plates etc*) Geschirr *nt*; **~work** *n* (*US*) Mangelwäsche *f*; **~worm** *n* Plattwurm *m*.

flaunt [flɔːnt] *vt wealth, knowledge* zur Schau stellen, protzen mit ◆ **she ~ed her femininity/independence at him** sie ließ ihre Reize vor ihm spielen/sie rieb ihm ihre Unabhängigkeit unter die Nase; **to ~ oneself** sich groß in Szene setzen.

flautist ['flɔːtɪst] *n* Flötist(in *f*) *m*.

flavour, (*US*) **flavor** ['fleɪvəʳ] [1] *n* (*taste*) Geschmack *m*; (*flavouring*) Aroma *nt*; (*fig*) Beigeschmack *m* ◆ **with a rum ~** mit Rumgeschmack; **20 different ~s** 20 verschiedene Geschmackssorten; **the film gives the ~ of Paris in the twenties** der Film vermittelt die Atmosphäre des Paris der zwanziger Jahre.
[2] *vt* Geschmack verleihen (*+dat*) *or* geben (*+dat*) ◆ **pineapple-~ed** mit Ananasgeschmack.

flavouring, (*US*) **flavoring** ['fleɪvərɪŋ] *n* (*Cook*) Aroma(stoff *m*) *nt* ◆ **vanilla/rum ~** Vanille-/Rumaroma *nt*.

flavourless, (*US*) **flavorless** ['fleɪvəlɪs] *adj* fad(e), geschmacklos.

flaw [flɔː] [1] *n* (*lit*) Fehler *m*; (*fig also*) Mangel *m*; (*in sb's character also*) Mangel, Defekt *m*; (*Jur: in contract etc*) (Form)fehler *m*.
[2] *vt argument, plan* einen Fehler aufzeigen *or* finden in (*+dat*) ◆ **his logic couldn't be ~ed** man konnte in seiner Logik keinen Fehler aufzeigen *or* finden.

flawed [flɔːd] *adj* fehlerhaft.

flawless ['flɔːlɪs] *adj performance* fehlerlos; *behaviour* untadelig, tadellos; *complexion* makellos; *diamond* lupenrein ◆ **~ English** fehlerloses *or* einwandfreies *or* tadelloses Englisch.

flax [flæks] *n* (*Bot*) Flachs *m*.

flaxen ['flæksən] *adj hair* flachsfarben, Flachs-; (*Tex*) flächse(r)n ◆ **~-haired** flachsblond.

flay [fleɪ] *vt* **(a)** (*skin*) *animal* abziehen, häuten; (*beat*) verdreschen; (*whip*) auspeitschen ◆ **to ~ sb alive** jdn gründlich verdreschen. **(b)** (*fig: criticize*) kein gutes Haar lassen an (*+dat*), heruntermachen (*inf*).

flea [fliː] *n* Floh *m* ◆ **to send sb off with a ~ in his/her ear** (*inf*) jdn wie einen begossenen Pudel abziehen lassen.

flea: ~bag *n* **(a)** (*US inf: hotel*) Flohbude (*inf*), Absteige *f*; **(b)** (*Brit inf: person*) Schrulle *f* (*inf*); **~ bite** *n* Flohbiß *m*; **it's a mere ~ bite** (*fig*) es ist eine Kleinigkeit; **~-bitten** *adj* voller Flohbisse; (*inf*) vergammelt (*inf*); **~ circus** *n* Flohzirkus *m*; **~ collar** *n* Flohhalsband *nt*; **~ market** *n* Flohmarkt *m*; **~pit** *n* (*Brit inf*) Flohkino *nt* (*inf*).

fleck [flek] [1] *n* (*of red etc*) Tupfen *m*; (*of mud, paint*) (*blotch*) Fleck(en) *m*; (*speckle*) Spritzer *m*; (*of fluff, dust*) Teilchen, Flöckchen *nt* ◆ **a ~ of dandruff** eine Schuppe.
[2] *vt* sprenkeln; (*with mud etc*) bespritzen ◆ **~ed wool** melierte Wolle; **blue ~ed with white** blau mit weißen Tupfen *or* Punkten, blau und weiß gesprenkelt; **the sky was ~ed with little clouds** der Himmel war mit Schäfchenwolken übersät.

fled [fled] *pret, ptp of* **flee**.

fledged [fledʒd] *adj bird* flügge; *see* **fully-~**.

fledg(e)ling ['fledʒlɪŋ] *n* **(a)** (*bird*) Jungvogel *m*. **(b)** (*fig: inexperienced person*) Grünschnabel *m*.

flee [fliː] *pret, ptp* **fled** [1] *vi* fliehen, flüchten (*from* vor *+dat*) ◆ **she fled to answer the door** sie eilte zur Tür, um aufzumachen; **to ~ from temptation** der Versuchung entfliehen.
[2] *vt town, country* fliehen *or* flüchten aus; *temptation, danger* entfliehen (*+dat*).

fleece [fliːs] [1] *n* Vlies, Schaffell *nt*; (*fabric*) (*natural*) Schaffell *nt*; (*artificial*) Webpelz, Flausch *m*.
[2] *vt* **(a)** *sheep* scheren. **(b)** (*fig inf*) **to ~ sb (of his money)** jdn schröpfen.

fleecy ['fliːsɪ] *adj* (*+er*) *blanket* flauschig; *snow* flockig ◆ **~ clouds** Schäfchenwolken *pl*; **~ lining** Wattierung *f*.

fleet[1] [fliːt] *n* **(a)** (*Naut*) Geschwader *nt*; (*entire naval force*) Flotte *f* ◆ **F~ Air Arm** Marineluftwaffe *f*; **merchant ~** Handelsflotte *f*. **(b)** (*of cars, coaches, buses etc*) (Fuhr)park *m* ◆ **he owns a ~ of lorries** er hat einen Lastwagenpark; **~ business** Firmenwagengeschäft *nt*.

fleet[2] *adj* (*+er*) schnell, flink ◆ **~ of foot, ~-footed** schnell- *or* leichtfüßig.

fleet admiral *n* (*US*) Großadmiral *m*.

fleeting ['fliːtɪŋ] *adj* flüchtig; *beauty* vergänglich ◆ **a ~ visit** eine Stippvisite; **the ~ years** die entfliehenden Jahre.

fleetingly ['fliːtɪŋlɪ] *adv* flüchtig.

Fleet Street *n* (*Brit*) Fleet Street *f* ◆ **he had a job on ~** er war Journalist in Fleet Street.

Fleming ['flemɪŋ] *n* Flame *m*, Flamin, Flämin *f*.

Flemish ['flemɪʃ] [1] *adj* flämisch.
[2] *n* **(a) the ~** *pl* die Flamen *pl*. **(b)** (*language*) Flämisch *nt*.

flesh [fleʃ] *n* **(a)** Fleisch *nt*; (*of fruit*) (Frucht)fleisch *nt*; (*of vegetable*) Mark *nt* ◆ **to put on ~** (*animals*) zunehmen; (*person also*) Fleisch auf die Rippen bekommen (*inf*); **all that bare ~ on the beach** diese Fleischbeschau am Strand.
(b) (*fig*) **one's own ~ and blood** sein eigen(es) Fleisch und Blut; **it was more than ~ and blood could bear** das war einfach nicht zu ertragen; **I'm only ~ and blood** ich bin auch nur aus Fleisch und Blut; **in the ~** in Person, in natura; **he's gone the way of all ~** er ist den Weg allen Fleisches gegangen; **to press the ~** (*inf*) Hände drücken.
(c) (*Rel*) Fleisch *nt* ◆ **sins of the ~** Sünden *pl* des Fleisches.

◆**flesh out** *vt sep idea, thesis etc* veranschaulichen, ausgestalten.

flesh: ~ colour *n* Fleischfarbe *f*; **~-coloured** *adj* fleischfarben; **~-eating** *adj* fleischfressend.

fleshings ['fleʃɪŋz] *npl* (*tights*) Trikotstrumpfhose(n *pl*) *f*.

flesh: ~pots *npl* Fleischtöpfe *pl*; **~ tints** *pl* Fleischtöne *pl*; **~ wound** *n* Fleischwunde *f*.

fleshy ['fleʃɪ] *adj* (*+er*) fleischig; *vegetable* Mark-.

fletch [fletʃ] *vt arrow* befiedern.

fletcher ['fletʃəʳ] *n* Pfeilmacher *m*.

fleur de lys [ˌflɜːdə'liː] *n, pl* **-s - -** [ˌflɜːdə'liːz] bourbonische Lilie.

flew [fluː] *pret of* **fly**[2], **fly**[3].

flex [fleks] [1] *n* (*Brit*) Schnur *f*; (*heavy duty*) Kabel *nt*.
[2] *vt body, knees* beugen ◆ **to ~ one's muscles** (*lit, fig*) seine Muskeln spielen lassen.

flexibility [ˌfleksɪ'bɪlɪtɪ] *n see adj* **(a)** Biegsamkeit *f*; Elastizität *f*. **(b)** Flexibilität *f*.

flexible ['fleksəbl] *adj* **(a)** *wire* biegsam; *material, plastic, branch also* elastisch. **(b)** (*fig*) flexibel ◆ **~ working hours** gleitende Arbeitszeit, Gleitzeit *f*.

flexion ['flekʃən] *n* (*Gram*) Flexion, Beugung *f*.

flexional ['flekʃənəl] *adj ending* Flexions-.

flex(i)time ['fleks(ɪ)taɪm] *n* Gleitzeit *f*.

flexor (muscle) ['fleksə(mʌsl)] *n* Beuger *m*.

flibbertigibbet ['flɪbətɪ'dʒɪbɪt] *n* (junges) Gänschen.

flick [flɪk] [1] *n* (*with finger*) Schnipsen *nt no pl*; (*of tail*) kurzer Schlag; (*with whip*) Schnalzen *nt no pl* ◆ **with a ~ of his fingers/whip** mit einem Fingerschnalzen/Peitschenschnalzen; **a ~ of the wrist** eine schnelle Drehung des Handgelenks; **she gave the room a quick ~ with the duster** sie ging kurz mit dem Staublappen durch das Zimmer.
[2] *vt whip* schnalzen *or* knallen mit; *fingers* schnalzen mit; (*with whip*) *horse etc* leicht schlagen; (*with fingers*) *switch* anknipsen; *dust, ash* wegschnipsen; (*with cloth*) wegwedeln ◆ **she ~ed her hair out of her eyes** sie strich sich (*dat*) die Haare aus den Augen; **I'll just ~ a duster round the sitting-room** (*inf*) ich wedel' *or* geh' eben mal mit dem Staubtuch durchs Wohnzimmer (*inf*); **he ~ed the pages of the book over** er blätterte flüchtig durch das Buch.
[3] *vi* **the snake's tongue ~ed in and out** die Schlange züngelte.

◆**flick off** *vt sep* wegschnippen; (*with duster*) wegwedeln.

◆**flick through** *vi +prep obj* (schnell) durchblättern.

flicker ['flɪkəʳ] [1] *vi* (*flame, candle*) flackern; (*light, TV also*) flimmern; (*needle on dial*) zittern; (*smile*) zucken; (*eyelid*) flattern, zucken ◆ **the snake's tongue ~ed in and out** die Schlange züngelte.
[2] *n see vi* Flackern *nt*; Flimmern *nt*; Zittern *nt*; Zucken *nt*; Flattern *nt* ◆ **a ~ of hope** ein Hoffnungsschimmer *nt*; **without a ~** ohne mit der Wimper zu zucken; **with not so much as the ~ of a smile** ohne (auch nur) das geringste Anzeichen eines Lächelns; **~-free** *screen etc* flimmerfrei.

flick knife *n* Klappmesser, Schnappmesser *nt*.

flicks [flɪks] *npl* (*Brit inf*) Kintopp *m or nt* (*inf*) ◆ **to/at the ~** in den *or* ins Kintopp (*inf*)/im Kintopp (*inf*).

flier ['flaɪəʳ] *n* **(a)** (*Aviat: pilot*) Flieger(in *f*) *m* ◆ **to be a good/bad ~** (*person*) Fliegen gut/nicht vertragen; (*bird*) ein guter/schlechter Flieger sein.
(b) (*US*) (*train*) Schnellzug *m*; (*fast coach*) Expreßbus *m*.
(c) to take a ~ (*leap*) einen Riesensprung *or* -satz machen; (*fall*) der Länge nach hinfallen.
(d) (*flying start*) fliegender Start ◆ **he got a ~** er hat einen fliegenden Start gemacht.
(e) (*leaflet*) Flugblatt *nt*.

flight[1] [flaɪt] *n* **(a)** Flug *m* ◆ **in ~** (*birds*) im Flug; (*Aviat*) in der Luft; **to take ~** (*bird*) davonfliegen, auffliegen; **the principles of ~** die Prinzipien des Fliegens.
(b) (*group*) (*of birds*) Schwarm *m*, Schar *f*; (*of aeroplanes*) Geschwader *nt*, Formation *f* ◆ **to be in the first** *or* **top ~** (*fig*) zur Spitze gehören; **the first** *or* **top ~ of scientists/novelists** die Spitzenwissenschaftler *pl*/-schriftsteller *pl*.
(c) (*of fancy, imagination*) Höhenflug *m* ◆ **~s of fancy** geistige Höhenflüge *pl*; **~s of oratory** rednerische Höhenflüge *pl*.
(d) ~ (of stairs) Treppe *f*; **he lives six ~s up** er wohnt sechs Treppen hoch; **a ~ of hurdles** eine Gruppe von Hürden; **he fell at the second ~** er fiel bei der zweiten Hürde; **a ~ of terraces** (eine Gruppe von) Terrassen *pl*.
(e) (*on dart, arrow*) Steuerfeder *f*.

flight[2] *n* Flucht *f* ◆ **to put the enemy to ~** den Feind in die Flucht schlagen; **to take (to) ~** die Flucht ergreifen; **the ~ of capital abroad** die Kapitalflucht ins Ausland.

flight: ~ attendant *n* Flugbegleiter(in *f*) *m*; **~ bag** *n* Schultertasche *f*; **~ crew** *n* Flugbesatzung *f*; **~ deck** *n* **(a)** (*Naut*) Flugdeck *nt*; **(b)** (*Aviat*) Cockpit *nt*; **~ engineer** *n* Bordingenieur *m*; **~ feather** *n* Schwungfeder *f*; **~less** *adj* nicht flugfähig; **~ lieutenant** *n* (*Brit Aviat*) Oberleutnant *m* der Luftwaffe; **~ log** *n* Bordbuch *nt*; **~ mechanic** *n* Bordmechaniker *m*; **~ number** *n* Flugnummer *f*; **~ path** *n* Flugbahn *f*; (*route*) Flugroute *f*; **incoming/outgoing ~ path** Einflug-/Ausflugschneise *f*; **~ plan** *n* Flugablaufplan *m*; **~ recorder** *n* Flugschreiber *m*; **~ sergeant** *n* Haupt- *or* Oberfeldwebel *m* (der Luftwaffe); **~ simulator** *n* Simulator *m*; **~-test** [1] *n*

Flugtest *m*; [2] *vt* im Flug testen, flugtesten.

flighty ['flaɪtɪ] *adj* (+*er*) (*fickle*) unbeständig, flatterhaft; (*empty-headed*) gedankenlos.

flim-flam ['flɪmflæm] *n* (*inf*) (*rubbish*) Blödsinn *m*; (*lies*) Schwindel *m*.

flimsily ['flɪmzɪlɪ] *adv dressed* leicht; *built, constructed also* nicht solide ◆ **a ~ bound book** ein schlecht gebundenes Buch.

flimsiness ['flɪmzɪnɪs] *n* (a) *see adj* (a) Dünne *f*; Leichtigkeit, Dürftigkeit *f*; leichte *or* wenig solide Bauweise; (*of book*) schlechte *or* billige Aufmachung; schlechte Qualität ◆ **in spite of the ~ of the wings** trotz der leichten Bauweise der Tragflächen. (b) (*of excuse*) Fadenscheinigkeit *f*; (*of reasoning*) mangelnde Stichhaltigkeit, Dürftigkeit *f*.

flimsy ['flɪmzɪ] [1] *adj* (+*er*) (a) *material* dünn; *clothing* leicht, dürftig; *house, aircraft* leicht gebaut, nicht stabil gebaut; *book* schlecht gebunden; *binding* schlecht ◆ **a ~ dress** ein Fähnchen *nt*; **these ~ houses** diese Billighäuser *pl* (*pej*).
(b) *excuse* fadenscheinig, schwach; *reasoning also* nicht stichhaltig, dürftig.
[2] *n* (*paper*) Durchschlagpapier *nt*.

flinch [flɪntʃ] *vi* (a) (*wince*) zurückzucken ◆ **without ~ing** ohne mit der Wimper zu zucken. (b) (*fig*) **to ~ from a task** vor einer Aufgabe zurückschrecken; **he ~ed from telling her the truth** er scheute sich, ihr die Wahrheit zu sagen.

fling [flɪŋ] (*vb: pret, ptp* **flung**) [1] *n* (a) (*act of ~ing*) Wurf *m*, Schleudern *nt no pl*.
(b) (*fig inf*) Anlauf *m* ◆ **to have a ~ at sth, to give sth a ~** sich an etw (*dat*) versuchen, etw (aus)probieren; **to have a ~ at doing sth** einen Anlauf machen, etw zu tun (*inf*); **youth must have its ~** die Jugend muß sich austoben; **to have a** *or* **one's ~** sich austoben; **he'll drop her when he's had his ~** wenn er erst mal seinen Spaß gehabt hat, läßt er sie fallen; **to go on a ~** einen draufmachen (*inf*); (*in shops*) sehr viel Geld ausgeben.
(c) *see* **Highland ~**.
[2] *vt* (*lit, fig*) schleudern ◆ **to ~ the window open/shut** das Fenster aufstoßen/zuwerfen; **the door was flung open** die Tür flog auf; **to ~ one's arms round sb's neck** jdm die Arme um den Hals werfen; **he flung himself at the intruder** er stürzte sich *or* warf sich auf den Eindringling; **to ~ a coat round one's shoulders** sich (*dat*) einen Mantel über die Schulter(n) werfen; **to ~ on one's coat** (sich *dat*) den Mantel überwerfen; **to ~ oneself into a job** sich auf eine Aufgabe stürzen; **to ~ oneself out of the window/into a chair** sich aus dem Fenster stürzen/sich in einen Sessel werfen; **you shouldn't just ~ yourself at him** (*fig inf*) du solltest dich ihm nicht so an den Hals werfen.

◆**fling away** *vt sep* wegwerfen, wegschmeißen (*inf*); (*fig*) *money, time* vergeuden, verschwenden.

◆**fling back** *vt sep one's head* zurückwerfen.

◆**fling down** *vt sep* (*lit*) runterschmeißen (*inf*) ◆ **to ~ ~ a challenge** den Fehdehandschuh hinwerfen *or* hinschleudern.

◆**fling off** *vt sep* (*lit*) *coat* abwerfen; *opponent* abschütteln; (*fig*) *remark* hinwerfen; *essay* hinhauen (*inf*); *restraints* von sich werfen.

◆**fling out** *vt sep unwanted object* wegwerfen, wegschmeißen (*inf*); *person* hinauswerfen, rausschmeißen (*inf*).

◆**fling up** *vt sep* (a) hochwerfen ◆ **to ~ one's arms ~ in horror** entsetzt die Hände über dem Kopf zusammenschlagen. (b) (*fig inf*) **to ~ sth ~ at sb** jdm etw unter die Nase reiben.

flint [flɪnt] *n* (a) (*for cigarette-lighter*) Feuerstein *m*. (b) (*stone*) Feuerstein, Flint(stein) *m*.

flint: ~ axe *n* (Feuer)steinbeil *nt*; **~ glass** *n* Flintglas *nt*; **~lock** *n* Steinschloßgewehr *nt*.

flinty ['flɪntɪ] *adj soil, rocks* aus Feuerstein; (*like flint*) wie Feuerstein; (*fig*) *heart* steinern.

flip [flɪp] [1] *n* (a) Schnipser *m* ◆ **to give sth a ~** etw in die Luft schnellen. (b) (*somersault*) Salto *m* ◆ **backwards ~** Salto rückwärts. (c) (*Aviat inf*) Rundflug *m*. (d) (*drink*) Flip *m*.
[2] *adj* (*inf: flippant*) schnodderig (*inf*).
[3] *vt* schnippen, schnipsen; (*inf*) *record* rumdrehen (*inf*) ◆ **to ~ a book open** ein Buch aufklappen *or* aufschlagen; **to ~ one's lid** (*inf*) durchdrehen (*inf*), aus dem Häuschen geraten (*inf*).
[4] *vi* (*sl*) durchdrehen (*inf*).
[5] *interj* (*Brit inf*) verflixt (*inf*).

◆**flip off** *vt sep* wegschnipsen; *ash from cigarette* abtippen; *top* aufklappen.

◆**flip over** [1] *vt sep* umdrehen; *pages of book* wenden.
[2] *vi* sich (um)drehen; (*plane*) sich in der Luft (um)drehen.

◆**flip through** *vi* +*prep obj book* durchblättern.

flipchart ['flɪptʃɑːt] *n* Flip-Chart *f*.

flip-flop ['flɪpflɒp] *n* (a) (*Sport*) Flickflack *m*. (b) (*Elec*) Flipflop *m*. (c) (*sandal*) Gummilatsche *f* (*inf*).

flip pack *n* Klappschachtel *f*.

flippancy ['flɪpənsɪ] *n* Frivolität, Leichtfertigkeit *f*.

flippant ['flɪpənt] *adj* leichtfertig, schnodderig (*inf*); *remarks* unernst, schnodderig (*inf*) ◆ **you shouldn't be so ~ (about it)** du solltest das etwas ernster nehmen.

flippantly ['flɪpəntlɪ] *adv see adj*.

flipper ['flɪpəʳ] *n* Flosse *f*; (*of diver*) (Schwimm)flosse *f*.

flipping ['flɪpɪŋ] *adj, adv* (*Brit inf*) verflixt.

flip: ~side *n* (*of record*) B-Seite *f*; **~ top** *n* Klappdeckel *m*.

flirt [flɜːt] [1] *vi* flirten ◆ **to ~ with an idea** mit einem Gedanken liebäugeln *or* spielen; **to ~ with death/disaster** den Tod/das Unglück herausfordern.
[2] *n* **he/she is just a ~** er/sie will nur flirten; **I'm a bit of a ~** ich flirte (für mein Leben) gern; **he's a great ~** er ist ein großer Charmeur.

flirtation [flɜː'teɪʃən] *n* Flirt *m*; (*flirting*) Flirten *nt* ◆ **his ~ with death/danger** sein Spiel mit dem Tod/der Gefahr.

flirtatious [flɜː'teɪʃəs] *adj woman* kokett ◆ **he/she is very ~** er/sie flirtet gern.

flit [flɪt] [1] *vi* (a) (*bats, butterflies etc*) flattern, huschen; (*ghost, person, image*) huschen ◆ **to ~ in and out** (*person*) rein- und rausflitzen; **an idea ~ted through my mind** ein Gedanke schoß mir *or* huschte mir durch den Kopf.
(b) (*Brit: move house secretly*) bei Nacht und Nebel ausziehen, sich bei Nacht und Nebel davonmachen.
(c) (*Scot, N Engl: move house*) umziehen.
[2] *n* (*Brit*) **to do a (moonlight) ~** bei Nacht und Nebel umziehen.

flitch [flɪtʃ] *n* Speckseite *f*; (*of halibut*) Heilbuttschnitte *f*.

float [fləʊt] [1] *n* (a) (*on fishing-line, in cistern, carburettor, on aeroplane*) Schwimmer *m*; (*anchored raft*) (verankertes) Floß, Schwimmplattform *f*; (*as swimming aid*) Schwimmkork *m*; (*of fish*) Schwimmblase *f*; (*on trawl net*) Korken *m*.
(b) (*vehicle*) (*in procession*) Festwagen *m*; (*for deliveries*) kleiner Elektrolieferwagen.
(c) (*ready cash: in till*) Wechselgeld *nt no indef art* (*zu Geschäftsbeginn*); (*loan to start business*) Startkapital *nt*; (*advance on expenses*) Vorschuß *m*.
[2] *vi* (a) (*on water*) schwimmen; (*move gently*) treiben; (*in air*) schweben ◆ **the corpse ~ed up to the surface** die Leiche trieb an die Wasseroberfläche; **it ~ed downriver** es trieb flußabwärts.
(b) (*Comm: currency*) floaten.
[3] *vt* (a) *boat* zu Wasser bringen ◆ **they ~ed the logs downstream** sie flößten die Baumstämme flußabwärts.
(b) (*Comm, Fin*) *company* gründen; *loan* lancieren; *shares* auf den Markt bringen; *bond issue* ausgeben; *currency* freigeben, floaten lassen; (*fig*) *ideas, suggestion* in den Raum stellen, zur Debatte stellen ◆ **the ~ing of the pound** die Freigabe *or* das Floaten *or* das Floating des Pfundes.

◆**float (a)round** *vi* (*rumour, news*) im Umlauf sein; (*person*) herumschweben (*inf*); (*things*) herumfliegen (*inf*).

◆**float away** *or* **off** *vi* (*on water*) abtreiben, wegtreiben; (*in air*) davonschweben; (*fig: person*) hinwegschweben.

floating ['fləʊtɪŋ] *adj* (a) *raft, logs* treibend ◆ **~ bridge** Schiffsbrücke *f*; **~ dock** Schwimmdock *nt*.
(b) (*fig*) *population* wandernd ◆ **~ voter** Wechselwähler *m*.
(c) (*Fin*) *currency* freigegeben ◆ **~ capital** Umlauf- *or* Betriebskapital *nt*; **~ debt** schwebende Schuld.
(d) (*Math*) *decimal point* Gleit- ◆ **~ accent** (*Comput*) fliegender Akzent; **~ point** (*Comput*) Gleitpunkt *m*, Gleitkomma *nt*.
(e) (*Med*) *kidney* Wander-; *rib* frei.

flock[1] [flɒk] [1] *n* (a) (*of sheep, geese, Eccl*) Herde *f*; (*of birds*) Schwarm *m*, Schar *f*.
(b) (*of people*) Schar *f*, Haufen *m* (*inf*) ◆ **they came in ~s** sie kamen haufenweise (*inf*) *or* in hellen Scharen.
[2] *vi* in Scharen kommen ◆ **to ~ in** hinein-/hereinströmen *or* -drängen; **to ~ out** hinaus-/herausströmen *or* -drängen; **to ~ together** zusammenströmen, sich versammeln; **to ~ around sb** sich um jdn scharen *or* drängen.

flock[2] *n* (*Tex*) Flocke *f* ◆ **~ wallpaper** Velourstapete *f*.

floe [fləʊ] *n* Treibeis *nt*, Eisscholle *f*.

flog [flɒg] *vt* (a) prügeln, schlagen; *thief, mutineer* auspeitschen ◆ **you're ~ging a dead horse** (*inf*) Sie verschwenden Ihre Zeit; **to ~ sth to death** (*fig*) etw zu Tode reiten. (b) (*Brit inf: sell*) verkloppen, verscherbeln, losschlagen (*all inf*).

◆**flog off** *vt sep* (*Brit inf*) verscheuern (*inf*), verkloppen (*inf*).

flogging ['flɒgɪŋ] *n* Tracht *f* Prügel; (*Jur*) Prügelstrafe *f*; (*of thief, mutineer*) Auspeitschen *nt* ◆ **he was given a ~** er bekam eine Tracht Prügel; (*Jur*) er wurde zu (einer) Prügelstrafe verurteilt; er wurde ausgepeitscht; **to bring back ~** die Prügelstrafe wiedereinführen; **a public ~** eine öffentliche Auspeitschung.

flood [flʌd] [1] *n* (a) (*of water*) Flut *f* ◆ **~s** Überschwemmung *f*, Hochwasser *nt*; (*in several places*) Überschwemmungen *pl*, Hochwasser *nt*; **the F~** die Sintflut; **the river is in ~** der Fluß führt Hochwasser; **she had a ~ in the kitchen** ihre Küche stand unter Wasser.
(b) (*fig*) Flut *f*, Schwall *m* ◆ **~s of tears** ein Strom von Tränen; **she was in ~s of tears** sie war in Tränen gebadet; **the scene was bathed in a ~ of light** die Szene war lichtüberflutet.
(c) (*also* **~-tide**) Flut *f*.
[2] *vt* (a) *fields, town* überschwemmen, unter Wasser setzen ◆ **the village/cellar was ~ed** das Dorf/der Keller war überschwemmt *or* stand unter Wasser; **to ~ the carburettor** den Motor absaufen lassen (*inf*).
(b) (*storm, rain*) *river, stream* über die Ufer treten lassen.
(c) (*fig*) überschwemmen, überfluten ◆ **~ed with light** lichtdurchflutet, von Licht durchflutet.
(d) (*Comm*) **to ~ the market** den Markt überschwemmen.
[3] *vi* (a) (*river*) über die Ufer treten; (*bath etc*) überfließen, überlaufen; (*cellar*) unter Wasser stehen; (*garden, land*) überschwemmt werden.
(b) (*people*) strömen, sich ergießen (*geh*) ◆ **the crowd ~ed into the streets** die Menge strömte auf die Straßen.

◆**flood in** *vi* (*people, sunshine*) hinein-/hereinströmen; (*water also*) hinein-/hereinfließen ◆ **the letters just ~ed ~** wir/sie hatten eine Flut von Briefen.

◆**flood out** *vt sep house* überfluten, unter Wasser setzen ◆ **the villagers were ~ed ~** die Dorfbewohner wurden durch das Hochwasser obdachlos.

flood: ~ control *n* Hochwasserschutz *m*; **~ disaster** *n* Flutkatastrophe *f*;

~gate *n* Schleusentor *nt;* **to open the ~gates** *(fig)* Tür und Tor öffnen *(to dat).*
flooding ['flʌdɪŋ] *n* Überschwemmung *f.*
flood: ~light *(vb: pret, ptp* **~lit)** [1] *vt buildings* anstrahlen; *football pitch* mit Flutlicht beleuchten; *(fig: light brightly)* beleuchten; [2] *n (device)* Scheinwerfer *m; (light)* Flutlicht *nt;* **under ~lights, by ~light** unter *or* bei Flutlicht; **~lighting** *n* **(a)** Flutlicht(anlage *f) nt;* **(b)** *(of building etc)* Beleuchtung *f;* **~lit** [1] *pret, ptp of* **~light;** [2] *adj* **~lit football** Fußball bei *or* unter Flutlicht; **~ plain** *n* Schwemmebene *f;* **~-tide** *n* Flut *f.*
floor [flɔːʳ] [1] *n* **(a)** Boden *m; (of room)* (Fuß)boden *m; (dance-~)* Tanzboden *m,* Tanzfläche *f* ◆ **stone/tiled ~** Stein-/Fliesenboden *m;* **to take the ~** *(dance)* aufs Parkett *or* auf den Tanzboden gehen; *(speak)* das Wort ergreifen; **to hold** *or* **have the ~** *(speaker)* das Wort haben.
(b) *(storey: in apartment block etc)* Stock(werk *nt) m* ◆ **first ~** *(Brit)* erster Stock; *(US)* Erdgeschoß *nt;* **on the second ~** *(Brit)* im zweiten Stock; *(US)* im ersten Stock.
(c) *(of prices etc)* Minimum *nt.*
(d) *(main part of chamber)* Plenar- *or* Sitzungssaal *m (also Parl); (of stock exchange)* Parkett *nt; (people present)* Zuhörerschaft *f; (Parl)* Abgeordnete *pl,* Haus *nt* ◆ **a question from the ~ (of the House)** eine Frage aus der Zuhörerschaft; *(Parl)* eine Frage aus dem Haus; **~ of the House** Plenarsaal *m* des Unterhauses; **to cross the ~** *(Parl)* die Partei wechseln.
[2] *vt* **(a)** *room etc* mit einem (Fuß)boden versehen.
(b) *(knock down) opponent* zu Boden schlagen.
(c) *(silence)* die Sprache verschlagen *(+dat); (bewilder)* verblüffen; *(defeat: question, problem etc)* schaffen *(inf)* ◆ **to be ~ed by a problem** mit einem Problem überhaupt nicht zu Rande kommen *(inf);* **he looked completely ~ed** er sah völlig perplex aus.
floor: ~ area *n* Bodenfläche *f;* **~board** *n* Diele, Bohle *f;* **~cloth** *n* Scheuer- *or* Putzlappen *m;* **~ exercise** *n* Bodenübung *f;* **~ lamp** *n* Stehlampe *f;* **~ manager** *n (in store)* Abteilungsleiter(in *f) m (im Kaufhaus); (TV)* Aufnahmeleiter(in *f) m;* **~ plan** *n* Grundriß *m* (eines Stockwerkes); **~ polish** *n* Bohnerwachs *nt;* **~ polisher** *n (tool)* Bohnerbesen *m;* **~ show** *n* Show, Vorstellung *f (im Nachtklub oder Kabarett);* **~ space** *n* Stellraum *m;* **if you've got a sleeping bag we have plenty of ~ space** wenn du einen Schlafsack hast, wir haben viel Platz auf dem Fußboden; **~-walker** *n (Comm)* Ladenaufsicht *f;* **~ wax** *n* Bohnerwachs *nt.*
floozie, floozy ['fluːzɪ] *n (inf)* Flittchen *nt (inf),* Schickse *f (inf).*
flop [flɒp] [1] *vi* **(a)** (lose) fallen; *(hard object)* knallen, plumpsen; *(inf: person)* sich fallenlassen, sich hinplumpsen lassen ◆ **the fish ~ped feebly in the basket** der Fisch zappelte matt im Korb; **he ~ped down on the bed** er ließ sich aufs Bett plumpsen *or* fallen; **I'm ready to ~** *(inf)* ich falle gleich um.
(b) *(inf: fail) (play, book)* durchfallen; *(actor, artiste)* nicht ankommen; *(party, picnic, scheme)* ein Reinfall sein.
[2] *n* **(a)** *(inf: failure)* Reinfall, Flop *(inf) m; (person)* Versager *m,* Niete *f.* **(b)** *(movement, sound)* Plumps *m.*
[3] *adv* **the whole business went ~** *(inf)* das ganze Geschäft ging hops *(inf).*
◆**flop around** *vi* herumzappeln; *(person: in slippers etc)* herumschlappen.
flophouse ['flɒphaʊs] *n* billige Absteige, Penne *f.*
floppy ['flɒpɪ] [1] *adj (+er)* schlaff, schlapp; *hat, ears* Schlapp-; *movement* schlaksig; *clothes* weit ◆ **~ disk** Floppy-disk, Diskette *f.*
[2] *n (disk)* Floppy-disk, Diskette *f.*
flora ['flɔːrə] *n* Flora *f.*
floral ['flɔːrəl] *adj arrangement, perfume* Blüten-; *fabric, dress* geblümt, mit Blumenmuster.
Florence ['flɒrəns] *n* Florenz *nt.*
Florentine ['flɒrəntaɪn] *adj* florentinisch.
florescence [flə'resəns] *n* Blüte *f.*
floret ['flɒrət] *n (of flower)* (Einzel)blütchen *nt; (of cauliflower)* Röschen *nt.*
florid ['flɒrɪd] *adj* **(a)** *complexion* kräftig ◆ **his ~ face** seine kräftigen (Gesichts)farben. **(b)** *(overelaborate)* überladen; *style, writing* blumig, schwülstig; *architecture, music also* zu reich verziert.
florin ['flɒrɪn] *n* Florin *m; (Dutch)* Gulden *m; (dated Brit)* Zweishillingstück *nt.*
florist ['flɒrɪst] *n* Blumenhändler(in *f),* Florist(in *f) m* ◆ **~'s shop** Blumengeschäft *nt.*
floss [flɒs] *n* Flockseide, Schappe *f; (thread)* Florettgarn *nt,* ungezwirntes Seidengarn; *(dental ~)* Zahnseide *f* ◆ **~ silk** Schappeseide, Florettseide *f.*
flotation [fləʊ'teɪʃən] *n (of ship)* Flottmachen *nt; (of log)* Flößen *nt; (Comm: of firm)* Gründung *f; (Metal)* Flotation, Schwimmaufbereitung *f* ◆ **~ collar** *(Space)* Schwimmkragen *m.*
flotilla [fləʊ'tɪlə] *n* Flotille *f.*
flotsam ['flɒtsəm] *n* Treibgut *nt* ◆ **~ and jetsam** *(floating)* Treibgut *nt; (washed ashore)* Strandgut *nt;* **the ~ and jetsam of our society** das Strandgut unserer Gesellschaft.
flounce¹ [flaʊns] [1] *vi* stolzieren ◆ **to ~ in/out/around** herein-/heraus-/herumstolzieren.
[2] *n* **she turned on her heel/left the room with a ~** sie drehte sich pikiert auf dem Absatz um/sie stolzierte aus dem Zimmer.
flounce² [1] *n (frill)* Volant *m,* Rüsche *f.*
[2] *vt* mit einem Volant/Volants *or* Rüschen besetzen.
flounced [flaʊnst] *adj skirt, dress* mit einem Volant/Volants *or* Rüschen besetzt.
flounder¹ ['flaʊndəʳ] *n (fish)* Flunder *f.*
flounder² *vi* **(a)** sich abstrampeln, sich abzappeln ◆ **a stranded whale ~ing on the beach** ein gestrandeter Wal, der sich am Strand abquält; **we ~ed along in the mud** wir quälten uns mühselig durch den Schlamm.
(b) *(fig)* sich abzappeln *(inf),* sich abstrampeln *(inf)* ◆ **to start to ~** ins Schwimmen kommen; **to ~ through sth** sich durch etw wursteln *(inf) or* mogeln *(inf);* **he ~ed on** er wurstelte weiter.
flour ['flaʊəʳ] [1] *n* Mehl *nt.*
[2] *vt (Cook) dough, rolling-pin etc* mit Mehl bestäuben; *one's hands also* (ein)mehlen.
flour: ~bin *n* Mehlbüchse *f;* **~ dredger** *n* Mehlstreuer *m.*
flourish ['flʌrɪʃ] [1] *vi (plants etc, person)* (prächtig) gedeihen; *(business)* blühen, florieren; *(type of literature, painting etc)* seine Blütezeit haben; *(writer, artist etc)* großen Erfolg haben, erfolgreich sein.
[2] *vt (wave about) stick, book etc* herumwedeln *or* -fuchteln mit, schwenken.
[3] *n* **(a)** *(curve, decoration etc)* Schnörkel *m.*
(b) *(movement)* schwungvolle Bewegung, eleganter Schwung ◆ **with a ~ of his stick** seinen Stock schwenkend.
(c) *(Mus) (fanfare)* Fanfare *f; (decorative passage)* Verzierung *f* ◆ **with a ~ of trumpets** mit einem Fanfarenstoß.
flourishing ['flʌrɪʃɪŋ] *adj plant, person* blühend *attr; business* gutgehend *attr,* florierend *attr.*
flour: ~ mill *n* (Korn)mühle *f;* **~ shaker** *n* Mehlstreuer *m.*
floury ['flaʊərɪ] *adj face, hands, potatoes* mehlig; *dish* bemehlt.
flout [flaʊt] *vt* sich hinwegsetzen über *(+acc),* mißachten; *convention, society* pfeifen auf *(+acc).*
flow [fləʊ] [1] *vi* **(a)** *(lit, fig)* fließen; *(tears also)* strömen; *(prose)* flüssig sein ◆ **where the river ~s into the sea** wo der Fluß ins Meer mündet; **tears were ~ing down her cheeks** Tränen liefen *or* flossen *or* strömten ihr übers Gesicht; **to keep the conversation ~ing** das Gespräch in Gang halten; **to keep the traffic ~ing** den Verkehr nicht ins Stocken kommen lassen; **try and keep the work ~ing smoothly** versuchen Sie, die Arbeit stetig voranzugehen zu lassen; **to ~ in** *(water, people, money etc)* hinein-/hereinströmen; **to ~ out of** herausströmen aus.
(b) *(dress, hair etc)* fließen, wallen.
(c) *(tide)* steigen, hereinkommen.
[2] *n* **(a)** Fluß *m* ◆ **the ~ of blood/traffic/information** der Blut-/Verkehrs-/Informationsfluß; **against the ~ of the river** gegen den Strom. **(b) the tide is on the ~** die Flut kommt. **(c)** *(of words etc)* Redefluß *m* ◆ **the ~ of his style** sein flüssiger Stil; **the powerful ~ of his prose** seine wortgewaltige Prosa.
flow chart *n* Flußdiagramm *nt.*
flower ['flaʊəʳ] [1] *n* **(a)** Blume *f; (blossom)* Blüte *f* ◆ **in ~** in Blüte; **to say sth with ~s** etw mit Blumen sagen; **"say it with ~s"** „laßt Blumen sprechen"; **no ~s by request** wir bitten von Blumenspenden abzusehen.
(b) *no pl (fig)* Blüte *f* ◆ **to be in the ~ of youth** in der Blüte seiner Jugend stehen; **the ~ of the army** die Blüte des Heeres; **~s of rhetoric** blumenreiche Ausdrücke *pl.*
(c) *(Chem)* **~s of sulphur** Schwefelblume *or* -blüte *f.*
[2] *vi (lit, fig)* blühen.
flower: ~ arrangement *n* Blumengesteck *nt;* **~-arranging** *n* Blumenstecken *nt;* **~bed** *n* Blumenbeet *nt;* **~ child** *n* Blumenkind *nt.*
flowered ['flaʊəd] *adj shirt, wallpaper* geblümt.
flower: ~ garden *n* Blumengarten *m;* **~ girl** *n* **(a)** *(seller)* Blumenmädchen *nt;* **(b)** *(at wedding etc)* Streukind *nt;* **~head** *n* Blütenkopf *m.*
flowering ['flaʊərɪŋ] *adj plant* Blüten-; *cherry, shrub* Zier-.
flower: ~ people *npl* Blumenkinder *pl;* **~pot** *n* Blumentopf *m;* **~ power** *n* Flower-power *f;* **~-seller** *n* Blumenverkäufer(in *f) m;* **~ shop** *n* Blumenladen *m,* Blumengeschäft *nt;* **~ show** *n* Blumenschau *f.*
flowery ['flaʊərɪ] *adj* **(a)** *meadow* Blumen-, mit Blumen übersät; *perfume* blumig; *dress, material* geblümt. **(b)** *(fig) language etc* blumig.
flowing ['fləʊɪŋ] *adj* fließend; *dress, hair also* wallend; *style of writing, painting* flüssig; *tide* auflaufend, hereinkommend.
flown [fləʊn] *ptp of* **fly², fly³.**
flu, 'flu [fluː] *n* Grippe *f* ◆ **to have (the) ~** (die *or* eine) Grippe haben.
fluctuate ['flʌktjʊeɪt] *vi* schwanken; *(in number also)* fluktuieren.
fluctuation [ˌflʌktjʊ'eɪʃən] *n* Schwankung *f,* Schwanken *nt no pl; (in number also)* Fluktuation *f; (fig: of opinions)* Schwanken *nt no pl.*
flue [fluː] *n* Rauchfang, Rauchabzug *m; (Mus: of organ) (pipe)* Labialpfeife *f; (opening)* Kernspalt *m* ◆ **~ brush** Stoßbesen *m.*
fluency ['fluːənsɪ] *n* Flüssigkeit *f; (of speaker)* Gewandtheit *f* ◆ **his ~ in English** ... daß er fließend Englisch spricht/sprach.
fluent ['fluːənt] *adj style* flüssig; *speaker, writer* gewandt ◆ **to be ~ in Italian, to speak ~ Italian** fließend Italienisch sprechen; **his ~ Italian** sein gutes Italienisch; **do you speak Greek? — yes, but I'm not ~** sprichst du Griechisch? — ja, aber nicht fließend.
fluently ['fluːəntlɪ] *adv speak a language* fließend; *write* flüssig, gewandt; *express oneself* gewandt.
fluff [flʌf] [1] *n, no pl (on birds, young animals)* Flaum *m; (from material)* Fusseln *pl; (dust)* Staubflocken *pl* ◆ **a bit of ~** eine Staubflocke/eine *or* ein Fussel; *(hum inf)* eine Mieze *(inf).*
[2] *vt* **(a)** *(also ~ out) feathers* aufplustern; *pillows* aufschütteln. **(b)** *opportunity, lines in play, entrance* vermasseln *(inf).*
◆**fluff up** *vt sep pillow etc* aufschütteln.
fluffy ['flʌfɪ] *adj (+er) bird* flaumig; *material, toy also* kuschelig, weich; *hair* locker, duftig.
fluid ['fluːɪd] [1] *adj substance* flüssig; *drawing, outline* fließend; *style* flüssig; *(fig) situation* ungewiß ◆ **the situation is still ~** die Dinge sind noch im Fluß;

~ ounce flüssige Unze.
[2] *n* Flüssigkeit *f.*
fluidity [flu:'ɪdɪtɪ] *n see adj* Flüssigkeit *f;* Fließende(s) *nt;* Ungewißheit *f.*
fluke[1] [flu:k] *n (inf)* Dusel *m (inf),* Schwein *nt (inf)* ♦ **by a ~** durch Dusel *(inf);* **it was a (pure) ~** das war (einfach) Dusel *(inf).*
fluke[2] *n (Naut)* Flunke *m; (of a whale's tail)* Fluke *f; (Fishing: flounder)* Flunder *f; (Zool: flatworm)* Plattwurm *m.*
fluky ['flu:kɪ] *adj (inf) wind* wechselnd ♦ **that was a ~ shot** das war ein Zufallstreffer.
flummox ['flʌməks] *vt (inf) person* durcheinanderbringen, aus dem Konzept bringen *(inf)* ♦ **to be ~ed** durcheinander sein.
flung [flʌŋ] *pret, ptp of* **fling.**
flunk [flʌŋk] *(inf)* [1] *vi* durchfallen *(inf),* durchrasseln *(sl),* durch die Prüfung fliegen *(inf).*
[2] *vt exam* verhauen *(inf); candidate* durchfallen *(inf) or* durchrasseln *(sl)* lassen ♦ **to ~ German/an exam** in Deutsch/bei einer Prüfung durchfallen.
flunk(e)y ['flʌŋkɪ] *n* Lakai *m; (flatterer)* Radfahrer *m (inf).*
fluorescence [flʊə'resəns] *n* Fluoreszenz *f.*
fluorescent [flʊə'resənt] *adj* Leucht-, fluoreszierend *(spec); lighting, tube* Leuchtstoff-.
fluoridate ['flu:rɪdeɪt] *vt* mit Fluor versetzen, fluorieren.
fluoridation [ˌflʊərɪ'deɪʃən] *n* Fluorzusatz *m (of* zu).
fluoride ['flʊəraɪd] *n* Fluorid *nt* ♦ **~ toothpaste** Fluorzahnpasta *f.*
fluorine ['flʊəri:n] *n* Fluor *nt.*
fluorocarbon [ˌflʊərəʊ'kɑ:bən] *n* Fluorkohlenwasserstoff *m.*
flurried ['flʌrɪd] *adj* **to get ~** sich aufregen, nervös werden.
flurry ['flʌrɪ] [1] *n* **(a)** *(of snow)* Gestöber *nt; (of rain)* Guß *m; (of wind)* Stoß *m* ♦ **a ~ of blows** ein Hagel *m* von Schlägen.
(b) *(fig)* Aufregung, Nervosität *f* ♦ **all in a ~** ganz aufgescheucht, in großer Aufregung; **a ~ of activity** eine Hektik; **in a ~ of excitement** in hektischer Aufregung.
[2] *vt* nervös machen, aufregen; *see* **flurried.**
flush[1] [flʌʃ] [1] *n* **(a)** *(lavatory ~)* (Wasser)spülung *f; (water)* Schwall *m.*
(b) *(blush)* Röte *f* ♦ **hot ~es** *(Med)* fliegende Hitze; **the ~ of blood to her cheeks** wie ihr das Blut in die Wangen schießt/schoß.
(c) *(of beauty, youth)* Blüte *f; (of joy)* Anfall *m; (of excitement)* Welle *f* ♦ **in the (first) ~ of victory** im (ersten) Siegestaumel; **in the first ~ of youth** in der ersten Jugendblüte; **she was in the full ~ of health** sie sah blühend aus.
[2] *vi* **(a)** *(person, face)* rot werden, rot anlaufen *(with* vor *+dat)* ♦ **to ~ crimson** dunkelrot anlaufen *or* werden. **(b)** *(lavatory)* spülen.
[3] *vt* **(a)** spülen; *(also* **~ out)** *drain* durch- *or* ausspülen ♦ **to ~ the lavatory** spülen, die Wasserspülung betätigen; **to ~ a wall down** eine Wand abspritzen; **to ~ sth down the lavatory** etw die Toilette hinunterspülen. **(b)** *face* röten.
♦**flush away** *vt sep waste matter etc* wegspülen.
♦**flush out** *vt sep* **(a)** *(with water) sink, bottle* ausspülen, auswaschen; *dirt* wegspülen, wegschwemmen. **(b)** *thieves, spies* aufstöbern, aufspüren.
flush[2] *adj pred* **(a)** bündig; *(horizontally also)* in gleicher Ebene ♦ **cupboards ~ with the wall** Schränke, die mit der Wand abschließen; **~ against the wall** direkt an die/der Wand; **~ left/right** *text* links-/rechtsbündig.
(b) *(inf)* **to be ~** gut bei Kasse sein *(inf).*
flush[3] *vt game, birds* aufstöbern, aufscheuchen.
flush[4] *n (Cards)* Flöte, Sequenz *f; (Poker)* Flush *m.*
flushed ['flʌʃt] *adj person* rot *(with* vor); *face also, (with fever)* gerötet ♦ **he came out of the meeting rather ~** er kam mit rotem Kopf aus der Besprechung; **they were ~ with happiness/success** sie strahlten förmlich vor Glück/über ihren Erfolg.
fluster ['flʌstəʳ] [1] *vt* nervös machen; *(confuse)* durcheinanderbringen ♦ **don't ~ me!** machen Sie mich nicht nervös!; **she got ~ed** sie wurde nervös; das brachte sie durcheinander; **to be ~ed** nervös *or* aufgeregt sein; durcheinander sein.
[2] *n* **in a (real) ~** (ganz) nervös *or* aufgeregt; *(confused)* (völlig) durcheinander.
flute [flu:t] [1] *n (Mus)* Querflöte *f; (organ stop)* Flötenregister *nt.*
[2] *vt column, pillar* kannelieren.
fluted ['flu:tɪd] *adj column, pillar* kanneliert; *border, edge* Bogen-, bogenförmig.
fluting ['flu:tɪŋ] *n (Archit)* Kannelierung *f,* Kanneluren *pl; (of border, edge)* Bogenform *f.*
flutist ['flu:tɪst] *n (US) see* **flautist.**
flutter ['flʌtəʳ] [1] *vi* **(a)** flattern *(also Med)* ♦ **her heart ~ed as he entered the room** sie bekam Herzklopfen, als er das Zimmer betrat; **to ~ away** *or* **off** davonflattern.
(b) *(person)* tänzeln; *(nervously)* flatterig sein ♦ **to ~ around** herumtänzeln; nervös herumfuhrwerken *(inf);* **she ~ed into/out of the room** sie tänzelte ins Zimmer/aus dem Zimmer.
[2] *vt fan, piece of paper* wedeln mit; *(birds) wings* flattern mit; *one's eyelashes* klimpern mit *(hum inf)* ♦ **to ~ one's eyelashes at sb** mit den Wimpern klimpern, jdn mit einem tollen Augenaufschlag bezirzen.
[3] *n* **(a)** Flattern *nt (also Med)* ♦ **this caused a ~ among the audience** dies verursachte leichte Unruhe im Publikum.
(b) *(nervousness)* **(all) in** *or* **of a ~** in heller Aufregung.
(c) *(Brit inf: gamble)* **to have a ~** sein Glück (beim Wetten) versuchen; **he likes his little ~ on a Friday night** er versucht Freitag abends gern sein Glück beim Wetten.
(d) *(Aviat)* Flattern *nt.*
flutter kick *n* Wechselschlag *m (beim Kraulen).*
fluty ['flu:tɪ] *adj (+er) voice* flötend.
fluvial ['flu:vɪəl] *adj* in Flüssen, fluvial *(spec)* ♦ **~ water** Flußwasser *nt.*
flux [flʌks] *n* **(a)** *(state of change)* Fluß *m* ♦ **things are in a state of ~** die Dinge sind im Fluß. **(b)** *(Med: no pl)* Ausfluß *m; (Phys)* Fluß *m.* **(c)** *(Metal)* Flußmittel *nt.*
fly[1] [flaɪ] *n* Fliege *f* ♦ **the epidemic killed them off like flies** sie starben während der Epidemie wie die Fliegen; **he wouldn't hurt a ~** er könnte keiner Fliege etwas zuleide tun; **there's a ~ in the ointment** *(inf)* da ist ein Haar in der Suppe; **he's the ~ in the ointment** er ist Sand im Getriebe; **there are no flies on him** *(inf)* ihn legt man nicht so leicht rein *(inf).*
fly[2] *(vb: pret* **flew,** *ptp* **flown)** [1] *vi* **(a)** fliegen.
(b) *(move quickly) (time)* (ver)fliegen; *(people)* sausen *(inf),* fliegen; *(sparks)* stieben, fliegen ♦ **time flies!** wie die Zeit vergeht!; **to ~ past** *(car, person)* vorbeisausen *(inf) or* -flitzen; **I am already late, I must ~** ich bin schon spät dran, ich muß jetzt wirklich sausen *(inf);* **the door flew open** die Tür flog auf; **to ~ to sb's assistance** jdm zu Hilfe eilen; **to ~ into a rage** einen Wutanfall bekommen; **to ~ at sb** *(inf)* auf jdn losgehen; **to ~ at sb's throat** jdm an die Kehle fahren; **to let ~ at sb** auf jdn losgehen; **he really let ~** er legte kräftig los; *(verbally also)* er zog kräftig vom Leder; **to let ~ a stone** einen Stein schleudern; **to knock** *or* **send sb/sth ~ing** jdn/etw umschmeißen *(inf) or* umwerfen; **he sent the ball ~ing over the wall** er schleuderte *or* schmiß *(inf)* den Ball über die Mauer; **to send a plate ~ing** einen Teller herunterschmeißen *(inf).*
(c) to ~ in the face of authority sich über jede Autorität hinwegsetzen; **to ~ in the face of reason** *(person, organization)* sich über jede Vernunft hinwegsetzen; *(idea, theory etc)* jeder Vernunft entbehren; **to ~ in the face of the evidence** in krassem Widerspruch zu den Tatsachen stehen.
(d) *(flag)* wehen.
[2] *vt* **(a)** *aircraft* fliegen; *kite* steigen lassen.
(b) *passengers, route, plane* fliegen; *Atlantic* überfliegen.
(c) *flag* führen, wehen lassen; *see* **flag**[1].
[3] *n* **to go for a ~** fliegen.
♦**fly away** *vi (person, plane, bird)* weg- *or* fortfliegen; *(plane, person also)* abfliegen; *(fig: hopes, cares)* schwinden.
♦**fly in** [1] *vi (troops, president, rescue plane etc)* einfliegen ♦ **we flew ~ to Heathrow at night** wir sind abends in Heathrow angekommen; **she flew ~ from New York this morning** sie ist heute morgen mit dem Flugzeug aus New York angekommen.
[2] *vt sep supplies, troops* einfliegen.
♦**fly off** *vi* **(a)** *(plane, person)* abfliegen, wegfliegen; *(bird)* wegfliegen, fortfliegen ♦ **to ~ ~ to the south** nach Süden fliegen; **a search plane flew ~ to look for them** ein Suchflugzeug flog los, um nach ihnen Ausschau zu halten; **as the plane flew ~ into the sunset** während das Flugzeug der untergehenden Sonne entgegenflog.
(b) *(come off: hat, lid etc)* wegfliegen; *(button)* abspringen.
♦**fly out** [1] *vi (troops, president, troop-plane)* ausfliegen ♦ **as we flew ~ of Heathrow** als wir von Heathrow abflogen; **I'll ~ ~ and come back by ship** ich werde hin fliegen und mit dem Schiff zurückkommen.
[2] *vt sep troops (to an area)* hinfliegen; *(out of an area)* ausfliegen ♦ **troops were flown ~ to the trouble area** Truppen wurden in das Krisengebiet geflogen; **the company will ~ you ~** die Firma wird Sie hinfliegen.
♦**fly past** *vi* **(a)** *+prep obj* **to ~ ~ sth** an etw *(dat)* vorbeifliegen. **(b)** *(ceremonially)* vorbeifliegen. **(c)** *(time)* verfliegen.
fly[3] *pret* **flew,** *ptp* **flown** [1] *vi (flee)* fliehen, flüchten ♦ **to ~ for one's life** um sein Leben laufen/fahren *etc.*
[2] *vt* **to ~ the country** aus dem Land flüchten.
fly[4] *n* **(a)** *(on trousers: also* **flies)** (Hosen)schlitz *m.* **(b)** *see* **flysheet. (c)** *(Theat)* **flies** *pl* Obermaschinerie *f.* **(d)** *see* **flywheel.**
fly[5] *adj (inf)* clever, gerissen.
fly-away ['flaɪəweɪ] *adj hair* fliegend, schwer zu bändigen.
fly-by-night ['flaɪbaɪnaɪt] [1] *n* **(a)** *(irresponsible man)* Windhund *m (inf); (woman)* leichtsinniges Ding *(inf).* **(b)** *(decamping debtor)* flüchtiger Schuldner.
[2] *adj* **(a)** *person* unzuverlässig, unbeständig. **(b)** *(Fin, Comm) firm, operation* zweifelhaft, windig *(inf).*
fly: ~catcher *n* **(a)** Fliegenschnäpper *m;* **(b)** *(trap for flies)* Fliegenfänger *m;* **~fishing** *n* Fliegenfischen *nt;* **~-half** *n (Rugby)* Halbspieler *m.*
flying ['flaɪɪŋ] *n* Fliegen *nt* ♦ **he likes ~** er fliegt gerne.
flying: ~ ambulance *n (helicopter)* Rettungshubschrauber *m; (plane)* Rettungsflugzeug *nt;* **~ boat** *n* Flugboot *nt;* **~-bomb** *n* V-Rakete *f;* **~ buttress** *n (Archit)* Strebebogen *m;* **~ colours** *npl* **to come through/pass** *etc* **with ~ colours** glänzend abschneiden; **~ doctor** *n* fliegender Arzt *(esp in Australien);* **F~ Dutchman** *n:* **The F~ Dutchman** der Fliegende Holländer; **~ fish** *n* fliegender Fisch; **~ fox** *n* Flughund *m;* **~ insect** *n* Fluginsekt *nt;* **~ jump** *n* (großer) Satz; **to take a ~ jump** einen großen Satz machen; **~ machine** *n (old, hum)* Flugmaschine *f;* **~ officer** *n (Brit)* Oberleutnant *m;* **~ picket** *n* mobiler Streikposten; **~ saucer** *n* fliegende Untertasse; **~ squad** *n* Bereitschaftsdienst *m;* **~ start** *n (Sport)* fliegender Start; **to get off to a ~ start** *(Sport)* hervorragend wegkommen *(inf); (fig)* einen glänzenden Start haben; **~ suit** *n* Pilotenanzug *m;* **~-time** *n* Flugzeit *f;* **~ trapeze** *n* Trapez, Schwebereck *nt;* **~ visit** *n* Blitzbesuch *m,* Stippvisite *f.*
fly: ~leaf *n* Vorsatzblatt *nt;* **~over** *n* Überführung *f;* **~paper** *n* Fliegenfänger *m;* **~-past** *n* Luftparade *f;* **~-posting** *n* illegales Plakate-

kleben; **~sheet** *n* (*entrance*) Überdach *nt*; (*outer tent*) Überzelt *nt*; **~-spray** *n* Fliegenspray *m*; **~-swat(ter)** *n* Fliegenklatsche *f*; **~-tipping** *n* illegales Müllabladen; **~weight** *n* (*Boxing*) Fliegengewicht *nt*; **~wheel** *n* Schwungrad *nt*.

FM *abbr of* **(a) frequency modulation** FM. **(b) field marshal.**

FO *abbr of* **Foreign Office.**

foal [fəʊl] 1 *n* Fohlen, Füllen *nt* ◆ **in ~** trächtig.
2 *vi* fohlen.

foam [fəʊm] 1 *n* Schaum *m*; (*of sea also*) Gischt *f*.
2 *vi* schäumen ◆ **to ~ at the mouth** (*lit*) Schaum vorm Mund/Maul haben; (*fig: person*) schäumen.

◆**foam up** *vi* (*liquid in container*) schäumen.

foam: ~ rubber *n* Schaumgummi *m*; **~ sprayer** *n* Schaumlöscher *m*.

foamy ['fəʊmɪ] *adj* (*+er*) schäumend.

fob[1] ['efəʊbiː] *abbr of* **free on board.**

fob[2] [fɒb] 1 *vt* **to ~ sb off (with promises)** jdn (mit leeren Versprechungen) abspeisen; **to ~ sth off on sb, to ~ sb off with sth** jdm etw andrehen.
2 *n* (*old: also* **~ pocket**) Uhrtasche *f* ◆ **~ watch** Taschenuhr *f*.

focal ['fəʊkəl] *adj* (*fig*) im Brennpunkt (stehend), fokal (*geh*).

focal: ~ length *n* Brennweite *f*; **~ plane** *n* Brennebene *f*; **~ point** *n* (*lit, fig*) Brennpunkt *m*; **his family is the ~ point of his life** seine Familie ist der Mittelpunkt seines Lebens, sein ganzes Leben dreht sich um seine Familie.

fo'c'sle ['fəʊksl] *n see* **forecastle.**

focus ['fəʊkəs] 1 *n, pl* **foci** ['fəʊkɪ] (*Phys, Math, fig*) Brennpunkt *m*; (*of storm*) Zentrum *nt*; (*of earthquake, Med*) Herd *m* ◆ **in ~** *camera* (scharf) eingestellt; *photo* scharf; **to bring into ~** (*lit*) klar *or* scharf einstellen; (*fig*) *topic* in den Brennpunkt rücken; **out of ~** (*lit*) *camera* unscharf eingestellt; *photo* unscharf; (*fig*) *ideas* vage; **to come into ~** ins Blickfeld rücken; **he was the ~ of attention** er stand im Mittelpunkt.
2 *vt instrument* einstellen (*on* auf *+acc*); *light, heat rays* bündeln; (*fig*) *one's efforts* konzentrieren (*on* auf *+acc*) ◆ **to ~ one's eyes on sth** den Blick auf etw (*acc*) richten; **all eyes were ~ed on him** alle Blicke waren auf ihn gerichtet; **to ~ one's attention** sich konzentrieren; **I should like to ~ your attention (up)on a new problem** ich möchte Ihre Aufmerksamkeit auf ein neues Problem lenken.
3 *vi* (*light, heat rays*) sich bündeln ◆ **to ~ on sth** sich auf etw (*acc*) konzentrieren; **his eyes ~ed on the book** sein Blick richtete sich auf das Buch; **I can't ~ properly** ich kann nicht mehr klar sehen.

fodder ['fɒdə^r] *n* (*lit, fig*) Futter *nt*.

foe [fəʊ] *n* (*liter*) Feind, Widersacher (*geh*) *m*.

foetal, (*esp US*) **fetal** ['fiːtl] *adj* fötal.

foetid ['fiːtɪd] *adj see* **fetid.**

foetus, (*esp US*) **fetus** ['fiːtəs] *n* Fötus, Fetus *m*.

fog [fɒg] 1 *n* **(a)** Nebel *m* ◆ **I am still in a ~ about it** (*dated inf*) das ist mir immer noch nicht klar. **(b)** (*Phot*) (Grau)schleier *m*.
2 *vt* **(a)** (*also* **~ up** *or* **over**) *mirror, glasses* beschlagen. **(b)** (*Phot*) verschleiern. **(c)** (*fig*) **to ~ the issue** die Sache vernebeln.
3 *vi* **(a)** (*also* **~ up** *or* **over**) (*mirror, glasses*) beschlagen.
(b) (*Phot: negative*) einen Grauschleier bekommen.

fog: ~ bank *n* Nebelbank *f*; **~bound** *adj ship, plane* durch Nebel festgehalten; *airport* wegen Nebel(s) geschlossen; **the motorway is ~bound** auf der Autobahn herrscht dichter Nebel.

fogey ['fəʊgɪ] *n* (*inf*) **old ~** alter Kauz (*inf*); (*woman*) Schrulle *f* (*inf*); **young ~** *junger Mensch, der sich bewußt konventionell benimmt und kleidet*, Junggreis *m* (*inf*).

foggy ['fɒgɪ] *adj* (*+er*) **(a)** *landscape, weather* neb(e)lig. **(b)** (*fig*) *ideas, reasoning* unklar, vage. **I haven't the foggiest (idea)** (*inf*) ich habe keinen blassen Schimmer (*inf*).

fog: ~horn *n* (*Naut*) Nebelhorn *nt*; **a voice like a ~horn** (*inf*) eine dröhnende Stimme; **~ lamp, ~ light** *n* Nebellampe *f*; (*Aut*) Nebelscheinwerfer *m*; **rear ~ light** (*Aut*) Nebelschlußleuchte *f*; **~ signal** *n* (*Naut, Rail*) Nebelsignal *nt*.

foible ['fɔɪbl] *n* Eigenheit *f*.

foil[1] [fɔɪl] *n* **(a)** (*metal sheet*) Folie *f*; (*of a mirror*) Spiegelfolie *f*; *see* **cooking ~, kitchen ~. (b)** (*fig*) Hintergrund *m*, Folie *f* ◆ **to act as a ~ to sb** jdm als Hintergrund *or* Folie dienen.

foil[2] *n* (*Fencing*) Florett *nt*.

foil[3] *vt plans* durchkreuzen; *attempts* vereiteln; *person* einen Strich durch die Rechnung machen (*+dat*) ◆ **~ed again!** (*hum*) wieder nichts!; **he was ~ed in his plans/attempts** ihm wurde ein Strich durch die Rechnung gemacht.

foist [fɔɪst] *vt* **(a) to ~ sth (off) on sb** *goods* jdm etw andrehen; *task* etw an jdn abschieben. **(b) to ~ oneself on(to) sb** sich jdm aufdrängen.

fold[1] [fəʊld] 1 *n* Falte *f*; (*Geol: of the earth*) (Boden)falte *f*.
2 *vt* **(a)** (*bend into ~s*) *paper* (zusammen)falten; *blanket also* zusammenlegen ◆ **to ~ a newspaper in two/four** eine Zeitung falten/zweimal falten.
(b) to ~ one's arms die Arme verschränken.
(c) (*wrap up*) einwickeln, einschlagen (*in* in *+acc*) ◆ **he ~ed the book in some paper** er schlug das Buch in Papier ein.
(d) to ~ sb in one's arms jdn in die Arme schließen; **to ~ sb to one's heart** (*liter*) jdn ans Herz drücken.
3 *vi* **(a)** (*chair, table*) sich zusammenklappen lassen; (*accidentally*) zusammenklappen ◆ **how does this map ~?** wie wird die Karte gefaltet?
(b) (*close down: business*) *see* **fold up.**

◆**fold away** 1 *vi* (*table, bed*) zusammenklappbar sein, sich zusammenlegen lassen.
2 *vt sep table, bed* zusammenklappen; *clothes* zusammenlegen; *newspaper* zusammenfalten.

◆**fold back** 1 *vt sep shutters, door* zurückfalten; *sheet, bedclothes* auf- *or* zurückschlagen.
2 *vi* (*door, shutters*) zurückfalten, sich zurückfalten lassen.

◆**fold down** *vt sep chair* zusammenklappen; *corner* kniffen.

◆**fold in** *vt sep* (*Cook*) *flour, sugar* unterziehen, unterheben.

◆**fold over** *vt sep paper* umknicken; *blanket* umschlagen.

◆**fold up** 1 *vi* **(a)** (*newspaper, business venture*) eingehen (*inf*); (*Theat: play*) abgesetzt werden. **(b) to ~ ~ with laughter** sich vor Lachen biegen.
2 *vt sep paper, blanket etc* zusammenfalten; *blanket also* zusammenlegen.

fold[2] *n* (*pen*) Pferch *m*; (*Eccl*) Herde, Gemeinde *f* ◆ **to return to the ~** (*fig*) in den Schoß der Gemeinde zurückkehren.

foldaway ['fəʊldəweɪ] *adj attr* zusammenklappbar.

folder ['fəʊldə^r] *n* **(a)** (*for papers*) Aktendeckel *m*, Aktenmappe *f*. **(b)** (*brochure*) Informationsblatt *nt*.

folding ['fəʊldɪŋ] *adj attr* **~ boat** Faltboot *nt*; **~ bed** Klappbett *nt*; **~ chair** Klappstuhl *m*; **~ doors** Falttür *f*; (*concertina doors also*) Harmonikatür *f*; (*grille on lift*) Scherengittertür *f*; **~ table** Klapptisch *m*.

foldout ['fəʊldaʊt] *adj section of book etc* ausklappbar.

foliage ['fəʊlɪɪdʒ] *n* Blätter *pl*; (*of tree also*) Laub(werk) *nt*.

foliation [ˌfəʊlɪ'eɪʃən] *n* **(a)** (*Bot*) Blattanordnung *f*; (*development*) Blattbildung *f*. **(b)** (*of book*) Foliierung, Blattzählung *f*. **(c)** (*Geol*) Schichtung *f*. **(d)** (*Archit*) Laubwerk *nt*.

folio ['fəʊlɪəʊ] *n* **(a)** (*sheet*) Folio *nt*. **(b)** (*volume*) Foliant *m*.

folk [fəʊk] *npl* **(a)** (*also* **~s** *inf*) (*people*) Leute *pl*; (*people in general*) die Leute, man ◆ **a lot of ~(s) believe ...** viele (Leute) glauben ...; **there were a lot of ~ at the concert** es waren eine Menge Leute bei dem Konzert; **come on ~s** (*inf*) na los, Leute!; **the young/old ~** die Jungen/Alten; **old ~ can't ...** alte Menschen können nicht ...
(b) (*inf: relatives: also* **~s**) **my ~s** meine Leute (*inf*); **the old ~(s) stayed at home** die alten Herrschaften blieben zu Haus.

folk: ~-dance *n* Volkstanz *m*; **~lore** *n* Folklore, Volkskunde *f*; **~-music** *n* Volksmusik *f*; **~-singer** *n* Sänger(in *f*) *m* von Volksliedern/Folksongs; **~-song** *n* Volkslied *nt*; (*modern*) Folksong *m*.

folksy ['fəʊksɪ] *adj* volkstümlich.

folk-tale ['fəʊkteɪl] *n* Volksmärchen *nt*.

follicle ['fɒlɪkl] *n* Follikel *nt*.

▼ **follow** ['fɒləʊ] 1 *vt* **(a)** folgen (*+dat*), nachgehen/-fahren *etc* (*+dat*); (*pursue also*) verfolgen; (*succeed*) folgen (*+dat*), kommen nach ◆ **he ~ed me about** er folgte mir überallhin; **he ~ed me out** er folgte mir nach draußen; **~ me** folgen Sie mir; (*by car also*) fahren Sie mir nach; **we're being ~ed** wir werden verfolgt; **to have sb ~ed** jdn verfolgen lassen; **he arrived first, ~ed by the ambassador** er kam als erster, gefolgt vom Botschafter; **he ~ed his father into the business** er folgte seinem Vater im Geschäft; **the earthquake was ~ed by an epidemic** auf das Erdbeben folgte eine Epidemie; **the dinner will be ~ed by a concert** im Anschluß an das Essen findet ein Konzert statt; **the toast was ~ed by a vote of thanks** auf den Trinkspruch folgten Worte des Dankes; **the years ~ one another** ein Jahr folgt auf das andere; **the years ~ one another in rapid succession** die Jahre vergehen in rascher Folge; **to ~ the hounds** (mit den Hunden) auf die Jagd gehen; **~ that (if you can)!** (*said after a good performance etc*) das soll mir/ihm *etc* erst mal einer nachmachen!; **how do you ~ that?** das ist kaum zu überbieten.
(b) (*keep to*) *road, path* folgen (*+dat*), entlanggehen/-fahren *etc* ◆ **the boat ~ed the coast** das Boot fuhr die Küste entlang; **the road ~s the valley** die Straße folgt dem Tal.
(c) (*understand*) folgen (*+dat*) ◆ **do you ~ me?** können Sie mir folgen?
(d) *profession* ausüben, nachgehen (*+dat*); *course of study, career* verfolgen ◆ **to ~ the sea/plough** (*liter*) zur See fahren/Bauersmann sein.
▼ **(e)** (*conform to*) *fashion* mitmachen; *advice, instructions* befolgen, folgen (*+dat*); *party line* folgen (*+dat*) ◆ **to ~ (the dictates of) one's heart/conscience** auf die Stimme seines Herzens/Gewissens hören.
(f) (*read, watch regularly*) *serial* verfolgen; *strip cartoon* regelmäßig lesen; (*take an interest in*) *progress, development, news* verfolgen; *athletics, swimming etc* sich interessieren für; (*listen to attentively*) *speech* (genau) verfolgen ◆ **to ~ the horses** sich für Pferderennen interessieren; **which team do you ~?** für welchen Verein sind Sie?
2 *vi* **(a)** (*come after*) folgen (*on sth* auf etw *acc*) ◆ **as ~s** wie folgt; **his argument was as ~s** er argumentierte folgendermaßen; **to ~ in sb's footsteps** (*fig*) in jds Fußstapfen (*acc*) treten; **what is there to ~?** (*at meals*) was gibt es noch *or* (*planning the meal*) hinterher *or* anschließend?; **what ~s** das Folgende.
(b) (*results, deduction*) folgen (*from* aus) ◆ **it ~s from this that ...** hieraus folgt, daß ...; **it doesn't ~ that ...** daraus folgt nicht, daß ...; **that doesn't ~** nicht unbedingt!; **your conclusion doesn't ~** Ihr Schluß ist nicht folgerichtig.
(c) (*understand*) folgen ◆ **I don't ~** das verstehe ich nicht, da komme ich nicht mit.

◆**follow on** *vi* **(a)** (*come after*) später folgen *or* kommen; (*person also*) nachkommen.
(b) (*results*) folgen, sich ergeben (*from* aus).
(c) (*continue*) **the story ~s ~ from his death** die Geschichte geht nach seinem Tod weiter; **she will ~ ~ from where he left off** sie wird da weitermachen, wo er aufgehört hat.
(d) (*Cricket*) zwei Innenrunden hintereinander spielen.

◆**follow out** *vt sep idea, plan* zu Ende verfolgen, durchziehen.

◆**follow through** 1 *vt sep argument* durchdenken, (zu Ende) verfolgen; *idea, plan, undertaking* (zu Ende) verfolgen, durchziehen.

➤ LANGUAGE IN USE: **follow: 1e → 11.3**

[2] *vi* (*Sport*) durchschwingen.

◆**follow up** [1] *vt sep* (**a**) (*pursue, take further action on*) *request* nachgehen (+*dat*); *offer, suggestion also* aufgreifen.
(**b**) (*investigate further*) sich näher beschäftigen *or* befassen mit; *suspect also* Erkundigungen einziehen über (+*acc*); *candidate also* in die engere Wahl nehmen; *matter also* weiterverfolgen; *rumour* nachgehen (+*dat*); *patient* nachuntersuchen; (*not lose track of*) *matter* im Auge behalten.
(**c**) (*reinforce*) *success, victory* fortsetzen, ausbauen ◆ **to ~ ~ insults with threats** auf Beleidigungen Drohungen folgen lassen; **he ~ed ~ his remark by punching him/by handing her a bouquet** er versetzte ihm zur Bekräftigung einen Schlag/er überreichte ihr zur Bekräftigung einen Blumenstrauß.
(**d**) (*get further benefit from*) *advantage* ausnutzen.
[2] *vi* (**a**) **to ~ ~ with sth** etw folgen lassen.
(**b**) (*Sport*) nachziehen.

follower ['fɒləʊəʳ] *n* (*disciple*) Anhänger(in *f*) *m*, Schüler(in *f*) *m*; (*old: servant*) Gefolgsmann *m* ◆ **to be a ~ of fashion** sehr modebewußt sein; **a ~ of Rangers** ein Rangers-Anhänger *m*.

▼ **following** ['fɒləʊɪŋ] [1] *adj* (**a**) folgend ◆ **the ~ day** der nächste *or* (darauf)folgende Tag; **he made the ~ remarks** er bemerkte folgendes. (**b**) **a ~ wind** Rückenwind *m*.
[2] *n* (**a**) (*followers*) Anhängerschaft, Gefolgschaft *f*.
(**b**) **he said the ~** er sagte folgendes; **see the ~ for an explanation** (*in documents etc*) Erläuterungen hierzu finden Sie im folgenden, Erklärungen im folgenden; **the ~ is/are of note** folgendes ist/folgende (Tatsachen *etc*) sind wichtig.

follow-through [ˌfɒləʊ'θruː] *n* (*Sport*) Durchziehen *nt*.

follow-up ['fɒləʊˌʌp] *n* (**a**) Weiterverfolgen, Weiterführen *nt*; (*event, programme etc coming after*) Fortsetzung *f* (*to gen*).
(**b**) (*letter*) Nachfaßschreiben *nt*; (*Press*) Fortsetzung *f*.
(**c**) (*Med*) Nachuntersuchung *f*.

follow-up: ~ advertising *n* Nachfaßwerbung *f*; **~ care** *n* (*Med*) Nachbehandlung *f*; **~ interview** *n* zweites Vorstellungsgespräch; **~ phonecall** *n* Anruf *m* zur Nachfrage *or* um nachzufragen.

folly ['fɒlɪ] *n* (*foolishness, foolish thing*) Torheit, Verrücktheit *f*; (*building*) *exzentrischer, meist völlig nutzloser Prachtbau* ◆ **it is sheer ~ (to do that)** es ist der reinste Wahnsinn(, das zu tun).

foment [fəʊ'ment] *vt trouble, discord* schüren; (*Med*) mit feuchten Umschlägen behandeln.

fomentation [ˌfəʊmen'teɪʃən] *n see vt* Schüren *nt*; feuchte Umschläge *pl*.

fond [fɒnd] *adj* (+*er*) (**a**) **to be ~ of sb** jdn gern haben *or* mögen; **to be ~ of sth** etw mögen; **to be ~ of doing sth** etw gern tun.
(**b**) (*loving*) *husband, parent, look* liebevoll, zärtlich; *hope* sehnsüchtig, leise; *ambition* leise ◆ **his ~est wish** sein Herzenswunsch *m*; **~est regards** mit lieben Grüßen, liebe Grüße.
(**c**) (*indulgent*) *parent, husband* allzu nachsichtig.
(**d**) (*unlikely to be realized*) *hope, ambition* (allzu) kühn.

fondant ['fɒndənt] *n* Fondant *m*.

fondle ['fɒndl] *vt* (zärtlich) spielen mit; (*stroke*) streicheln; *person* schmusen mit.

fondly ['fɒndlɪ] *adv see adj (b-d)*.

fondness ['fɒndnɪs] *n* Begeisterung *f*; (*for people*) Zuneigung, Liebe *f* (*for* zu); (*for food, place, writer etc*) Vorliebe *f* (*for* für) ◆ **his ~ for** *or* **of swimming** daß er gern schwimmen ging/geht.

fondue ['fɒnduː] *n* Fondue *nt* ◆ **~ set** Fondueset *nt*.

font [fɒnt] *n* (**a**) (*Eccl*) Taufstein *m*. (**b**) (*Typ*) Schrift *f*.

fontanel(le) [ˌfɒntə'nel] *n* (*Physiol*) Fontanelle *f*.

food [fuːd] *n* (**a**) Essen *nt*; (*for animals*) Futter *nt*; (*nourishment*) Nahrung *f*; (*~stuff*) Nahrungsmittel *nt*; (*groceries*) Lebensmittel *pl* ◆ **the ~ is awful here** das Essen hier ist scheußlich; **dog and cat ~** Hunde- und Katzenfutter; **~ and drink** Essen und Trinken; **milk is a ~ rather than a drink** Milch ist eher ein Nahrungsmittel als ein Getränk; **canned ~s** Konserven *pl*; **I haven't any ~ in the house** ich habe nichts zu essen im Haus; **to be off one's ~** keinen Appetit haben; **at last, ~!** endlich etwas zu essen; **the very thought of ~ made her ill** wenn sie nur ans Essen dachte, wurde ihr schon schlecht.
(**b**) (*fig*) Nahrung *f* ◆ **~ for thought** Stoff *m* zum Nachdenken.

foodchain ['fuːdtʃeɪn] *n* Nahrungskette *f* ◆ **to get into the ~** in die Nahrungskette gelangen.

foodie ['fuːdɪ] *n* (*inf: food fanatic*) Kochkünstler(in *f*), Kochfreak (*inf*) *m*.

food: ~ parcel *n* Lebensmittelpaket *nt*; **~ poisoning** *n* Lebensmittelvergiftung *f*; **~ processor** *n* Küchenmaschine *f*; **~ rationing** *n* Lebensmittelrationierung *f*; **~ stamp** *n* (*US*) Lebensmittelmarke *f*; **~stuff** *n* Nahrungsmittel *nt*; **~ value** *n* Nährwert *m*.

fool[1] [fuːl] [1] *n* (**a**) Dummkopf, Narr *m* ◆ **don't be a ~!** sei nicht (so) dumm!; **some ~ of a civil servant** irgend so ein blöder *or* doofer (*inf*) Beamter; **I was a ~ not to realize** wie konnte ich nur so dumm sein und das nicht merken; **have I been a ~!** war ich vielleicht dumm *or* blöd!, ich Idiot!; **he was a ~ not to accept** es war dumm von ihm, nicht anzunehmen; **to be ~ enough to ...** so dumm *or* blöd sein, zu ...; **to play** *or* **act the ~** Unsinn machen, herumalbern; **he made himself look a ~ in front of everyone** er machte sich vor allen lächerlich; **to make a ~ of sb** (*with ridicule*) jdn lächerlich machen; (*with a trick*) jdn zum besten *or* zum Narren haben; **he made a ~ of himself in the discussion** er hat sich in der Diskussion blamiert; **to go on a ~'s errand** einen nutzlosen Gang tun; **to live in a ~'s paradise** in einem Traumland leben; **there's no ~ like an old ~** (*Prov*) Alter schützt vor Torheit nicht (*Prov*); **~'s gold** Katzengold *nt*; **~s rush in (where angels fear to tread)** (*Prov*) blinder Eifer schadet nur (*Prov*); *see* **more, nobody**.
(**b**) (*jester*) Narr *m*.
[2] *adj* (*esp US inf*) doof (*inf*), schwachsinnig (*inf*).
[3] *vi* herumalbern, Blödsinn machen ◆ **stop ~ing (about)!** laß den Blödsinn!; **I was only ~ing** das war doch nur Spaß.
[4] *vt* zum Narren haben *or* halten; (*trick*) hereinlegen (*inf*); (*disguise, phoney accent etc*) täuschen ◆ **you won't ~ me so easily** so leicht können Sie mich nicht hereinlegen (*inf*); **I was completely ~ed** ich bin vollkommen darauf hereingefallen; **you had me ~ed** ich habe das tatsächlich geglaubt; **who are you trying to ~?** wem willst du das weismachen?; **they ~ed him into believing that ...** sie haben ihm weisgemacht, daß ...; **they ~ed him into believing it** er hat es ihnen tatsächlich abgenommen.

◆**fool about** *or* **around** *vi* (**a**) (*waste time*) herumtrödeln ◆ **he spends his time ~ing ~ with the boys** er verschwendet seine ganze Zeit mit den Jungs. (**b**) (*play the fool*) herumalbern. (**c**) **to ~ ~ with sth** mit etw Blödsinn machen. (**d**) (*sexually*) **he's just ~ing ~ with her** er treibt nur seine Spielchen mit ihr; **she was ~ing ~** sie hat sich mit anderen eingelassen.

fool[2] *n* (*Brit Cook*) *Sahnespeise f aus Obstpüree*.

foolery ['fuːlərɪ] *n* Albernheit *f*.

foolhardiness ['fuːlˌhɑːdɪnɪs] *n* Tollkühnheit *f*.

foolhardy ['fuːlˌhɑːdɪ] *adj* tollkühn.

foolish ['fuːlɪʃ] *adj* dumm, töricht ◆ **it is ~ to believe him** es ist dumm, ihm zu glauben; **to look ~** dumm aussehen *or* dreinsehen; **he's afraid of looking ~** er will sich nicht blamieren; **it made him look ~** dann stand er dumm da; **I felt very ~** ich kam mir sehr dumm vor.

foolishly ['fuːlɪʃlɪ] *adv* dumm, töricht ◆ **~, I assumed ...** törichterweise habe ich angenommen ...

foolishness ['fuːlɪʃnɪs] *n* Dummheit, Torheit *f* ◆ **enough of this ~** lassen wir diese Dummheiten *pl*.

foolproof ['fuːlpruːf] *adj* narrensicher, idiotensicher (*inf*).

foolscap ['fuːlskæp] *n* (*also* **~ paper**) ≃ Kanzleipapier *nt*, *britisches Papierformat* $13\frac{1}{2} \times 16\frac{1}{2}$ *Zoll* ◆ **a ~ sheet** ein Blatt *nt* Kanzleipapier.

foot [fʊt] [1] *n, pl* **feet** (**a**) Fuß *m* ◆ **to be on one's feet** (*lit, fig*) auf den Beinen sein; **to put sb (back) on his feet (again)** jdm (wieder) auf die Beine helfen; **on ~** zu Fuß; **to set ~ on dry land** den Fuß auf festen Boden setzen, an Land gehen; **I'll never set ~ here again!** hier kriegen mich keine zehn Pferde mehr her! (*inf*); **the first time he set ~ in the office** als er das erste Mal das Büro betrat; **to rise/jump to one's feet** aufstehen/aufspringen; **to put one's feet up** (*lit*) die Füße hochlegen; (*fig*) es sich (*dat*) bequem machen; **he never puts a ~ wrong** (*gymnast, dancer*) bei ihm stimmt jeder Schritt; (*fig*) er macht nie einen Fehler; **to catch sb on the wrong ~** (*Sport*) jdn auf dem falschen Fuß erwischen; (*fig*) jdn überrumpeln.
(**b**) (*fig uses*) **to put one's ~ down** (*act with decision or authority*) ein Machtwort sprechen; (*forbid, refuse*) es strikt verbieten; (*Aut*) Gas geben; **to put one's ~ in it** ins Fettnäpfchen treten; **to put one's best ~ forward** (*hurry*) die Beine unter den Arm nehmen; (*do one's best*) sich anstrengen; **to find one's feet** sich eingewöhnen, sich zurechtfinden; **to fall on one's feet** auf die Beine fallen; **to have one's** *or* **both feet (firmly) on the ground** mit beiden Beinen (fest) auf der Erde stehen; **to have one ~ in the grave** mit einem Bein im Grabe stehen; **to get/be under sb's feet** jdm im Wege stehen *or* sein; (*children also*) jdm vor den Füßen herumlaufen; **to get off on the right/wrong ~** einen guten/schlechten Start haben; **to have a/get one's** *or* **a ~ in the door** mit einem Fuß *or* Bein drin sein/mit einem Fuß *or* Bein hineinkommen; **to stand on one's own feet** auf eigenen Füßen *or* Beinen stehen; **to sit at sb's feet** jds Jünger sein.
(**c**) (*of stocking, list, page, stairs, hill etc*) Fuß *m*; (*of bed also*) Fußende *nt*; (*of sewing machine also*) Füßchen *nt*.
(**d**) (*measure*) Fuß *m* ◆ **3 ~** *or* **feet wide/long** 3 Fuß breit/lang.
(**e**) (*Poet*) (Vers)fuß *m*.
(**f**) *no pl* (*Mil*) Infanterie *f* ◆ **the 15th ~** das 15. Infanterieregiment; **ten thousand ~** zehntausend Fußsoldaten *pl*.
[2] *vt* (**a**) **to ~ it** (*inf*) (*walk*) marschieren (*inf*); (*dance*) tanzen.
(**b**) *bill* bezahlen, begleichen.

foot-and-mouth (disease) ['fʊtən'maʊθ(dɪˌziːz)] *n* Maul- und Klauenseuche *f*.

football ['fʊtbɔːl] *n* (**a**) Fußball(spiel *nt*) *m*; (*American* ~) Football *m*, amerikanischer Fußball. (**b**) (*ball*) Fußball *m*, Leder (*inf*) *nt*.

football: ~ boot *n* Fußballschuh, Fußballstiefel *m*; **~ casual** *n* Fußballprolo *m* (*inf*); **~ coupon** *n* (*Brit*) Tippzettel, Totoschein *m*.

footballer ['fʊtbɔːləʳ] *n* Fußball(spiel)er *m*; (*in American football*) Football-Spieler *m*.

football: ~ hooligan *n* Fußballrowdy *or* -hooligan *m*; **~ hooliganism** *n* Fußballkrawalle *pl*; **~ pools** *npl* Fußballtoto *m*; *see* **pool[2] (c)**.

foot: ~bath *n* Fußbad *nt*; **~board** *n* (*Rail, on coach*) Trittbrett *nt*; **~ brake** *n* Fußbremse *f*; **~bridge** *n* Fußgängerbrücke *f*.

-footed [-fʊtɪd] *adj suf* -füßig ◆ **four-~** vierfüßig.

footer ['fʊtər] *n* (*Comput*) Fußzeile *f*.

foot: ~fall *n* Schritt *m*; **~ fault** *n* (*Tennis*) Fußfehler *m*; **~gear** *n* Fußbekleidung *f*; **~hills** *npl* (Gebirgs)ausläufer *pl*; **~hold** *n* Stand, Halt *m*; (*fig*) sichere (Ausgangs)position; **he got a ~hold on the rock** er fand mit den Füßen Halt am Felsen; **to lose one's ~hold** (*lit, fig*) den Halt verlieren.

footing ['fʊtɪŋ] *n* (**a**) (*lit*) Stand, Halt *m* ◆ **to lose one's ~** den Halt verlieren; **to miss one's ~** danebentreten.
(**b**) (*fig: foundation, basis*) Basis *f*; (*relationship*) Beziehung *f*, Verhältnis *nt* ◆ **the business was on a secure ~** das Geschäft stand auf einer sicheren Basis;

➤ LANGUAGE IN USE: **following: 1a** → 20.2, 20.3, 26.2

to be on a friendly ~ with sb mit jdm auf freundschaftlichem Fuße stehen; **on an equal ~ (with each other)** auf gleicher Basis; **to be on a war ~** sich im Kriegszustand befinden; **to get a ~ in society** von der Gesellschaft akzeptiert werden.
(c) *(Archit)* Sockel *m.*

footle ['fu:tl] *vi* **to ~ about** *(inf)* herumpusseln.

footlights ['fʊtlaɪts] *npl (Theat)* Rampenlicht *nt* ◆ **the lure of the ~** *(fig)* die Anziehungskraft der Bühne *or* der Bretter.

footling ['fu:tlɪŋ] *adj* albern, dumm, läppisch.

foot: ~loose *adj* ungebunden, unbeschwert; **~loose and fancy-free** frei und ungebunden; **~man** *n* Lakai *m;* **~mark** *n* Fußabdruck *m;* **~note** *n* Fußnote *f;* *(fig)* Anmerkung *f;* **~path** *n* **(a)** *(path)* Fußweg *m;* **(b)** *(Brit: pavement)* Bürgersteig *m;* **~plate** *n* Führerstand *m;* **~platemen, ~plate workers** *npl* Lokomotivführer *pl;* **~-pound** *n britische Maßeinheit für Drehmoment und Energie;* **~print** *n* Fußabdruck *m;* *(fig: of machine)* Stellfläche, Grundfläche *f;* **~prints** *npl* Fußspuren *pl;* **~ pump** *n* Fußpumpe *f,* Blasebalg *m;* **~rest** *n* Fußstütze *f;* **~rot** *n (Vet)* Fußfäule *f.*

footsie ['fʊtsɪ] *n (inf)* **to play ~ with sb** mit jdm füßeln.

foot: ~-slog *vi (inf)* latschen *(inf),* marschieren; **~-slogger** *n (Mil sl)* Fußsoldat, Infanterist *m;* **~-sloggers** *(Mil sl)* Fußvolk *nt;* *(inf: walkers)* Spaziergänger, Tippler *(inf) pl;* **~ soldier** *n* Fußsoldat, Infanterist *m;* **~sore** *adj* **to be ~sore** wunde Füße haben; **~step** *n* Schritt *m; see* **follow;** **~stool** *n* Schemel *m,* Fußbank *f;* **~wear** *n* Schuhe *pl,* Schuhwerk *nt;* **~work** *n, no pl (Sport)* Beinarbeit *f.*

fop [fɒp] *n (dated)* Geck, Stutzer *(dated) m.*

foppish ['fɒpɪʃ] *adj* geckenhaft, stutzerhaft *(dated).*

for¹ [fɔ:ʳ] [1] *prep* **(a)** *(intention)* für; *(purpose also)* zu; *(destination)* nach ◆ **a letter ~ me** ein Brief für mich; **clothes ~ children** Kleidung für Kinder, Kinderkleidung *f;* **destined ~ greatness** zu Höherem bestimmt; **he is eager ~ praise** er ist lobeshungrig; **what ~?** wofür?, wozu?; **what is this knife ~?** wozu dient dieses Messer?; **he does it ~ pleasure** er macht es zum *or* aus Vergnügen; **what did you do that ~?** warum *or* wozu haben Sie das getan?; **a room ~ working in/sewing** ein Zimmer zum Arbeiten/Nähen; **a bag ~ carrying books (in)** eine Tasche, um Bücher zu tragen; **fit ~ nothing** zu nichts nutze *or* zu gebrauchen; **to get ready ~ a journey** sich für eine Reise fertigmachen; **ready ~ anything** zu allem bereit; **this will do ~ a hammer** das kann man als Hammer nehmen; **to go to Yugoslavia ~ one's holidays** nach Jugoslawien in Urlaub fahren; **train ~ Stuttgart** Zug nach Stuttgart; **to leave ~ the USA** in die USA *or* nach Amerika abreisen; **he swam ~ the shore** er schwamm auf die Küste zu, er schwamm in Richtung Küste; **to make ~ home** sich auf den Heimweg machen.
(b) *(indicating suitability)* **it's not ~ you to blame him** Sie haben kein Recht, ihm die Schuld zu geben; **it's not ~ me to say** es steht mir nicht zu, mich dazu zu äußern; **she's the woman** *or* **the one ~ me** sie ist die (richtige) Frau für mich.
(c) *(representing, instead of)* **I'll see her ~ you if you like** wenn Sie wollen, gehe ich an Ihrer Stelle *or* für Sie zu ihr; **to act ~ sb** für jdn handeln; **D ~ Daniel** D wie Daniel; **agent ~ Renault** Vertreter für Renault.
(d) *(in defence, in favour of)* für ◆ **are you ~ or against it?** sind Sie dafür oder dagegen?; **I'm all ~ it** ich bin ganz *or* sehr dafür; **I'm all ~ helping him** ich bin sehr dafür, ihm zu helfen.
(e) *(with regard to)* **anxious ~ sb** um jdn besorgt; **~ my part** was mich betrifft; **as ~ him/that** was ihn/das betrifft; **warm/cold ~ the time of year** warm/kalt für die Jahreszeit; **young ~ (a) president** jung für einen Präsidenten; **it's all right** *or* **all very well ~ you (to talk)** Sie haben gut reden.
(f) *(because of)* aus ◆ **~ this reason** aus diesem Grund; **he did it ~ fear of being left** er tat es aus Angst, zurückgelassen zu werden; **he is noted ~ his jokes/famous ~ his big nose** er ist für seine Witze bekannt/er ist wegen seiner großen Nase berühmt; **to shout ~ joy** aus *or* vor Freude jauchzen; **to go to prison ~ theft** wegen Diebstahls ins Gefängnis wandern; **to choose sb ~ his ability** jdn wegen seiner Fähigkeiten wählen; **if it were not ~ him** wenn er nicht wäre; **do it ~ me** tu es für mich.
(g) *(in spite of)* trotz *(+gen or (inf) +dat)* ◆ **~ all his wealth** trotz all seines Reichtums; **~ all that, you should have warned me** Sie hätten mich trotz allem warnen sollen.
(h) *(in exchange)* für ◆ **to pay four marks ~ a ticket** vier Mark für eine Fahrkarte zahlen; **he'll do it ~ ten pounds** er macht es für zehn Pfund.
(i) *(in contrast)* **~ one man who would do it there are ten who wouldn't** auf einen, der es tun würde, kommen zehn, die es nicht tun würden.
(j) *(in time)* seit; *(with future tense)* für ◆ **I have not seen her ~ two years** ich habe sie seit zwei Jahren nicht gesehen; **he's been here ~ ten days** er ist seit zehn Tagen hier; **I had/have known her ~ years** ich kannte/kenne sie schon seit Jahren; **then I did not see her ~ two years** dann habe ich sie zwei Jahre lang nicht gesehen; **he walked ~ two hours** er ist zwei Stunden lang marschiert; **I am going away ~ a few days** ich werde (für *or* auf) ein paar Tage wegfahren; **I shall be away ~ a month** ich werde einen Monat (lang) weg sein; **he won't be back ~ a week** er wird erst in einer Woche zurück sein; **can you get it done ~ Monday/this time next week?** können Sie es bis *or* für Montag/bis in einer Woche fertig haben?; **I've got a job for you ~ next week** ich habe für nächste Woche Arbeit für dich; **~ a while/time** (für) eine Weile/einige Zeit.
(k) *(distance)* **the road is lined with trees ~ two miles** die Straße ist auf *or* über zwei Meilen mit Bäumen gesäumt; **we walked ~ two miles** wir sind zwei Meilen weit gelaufen; **~ miles (ahead/around)** meilenweit (vor/um uns *etc*); **~ mile upon mile** Meile um Meile.
(l) *(with verbs)* **to pray ~ peace** für den *or* um Frieden beten; **to hope ~ news** auf Nachricht hoffen; **to look ~ sth** (nach) etw suchen; *see vbs.*
(m) *(after n indicating liking, aptitude etc)* für ◆ **a weakness ~ sweet things** eine Schwäche für Süßigkeiten; **his genius ~ saying the wrong thing** sein Talent, das Falsche zu sagen.
(n) *(with infin clauses)* **~ this to be possible** damit dies möglich wird/wurde; **it's easy ~ him to do it** für ihn ist es leicht, das zu tun, er kann das leicht tun; **I brought it ~ you to see** ich habe es mitgebracht, damit Sie es sich *(dat)* ansehen können; **the best would be ~ you to go** das beste wäre, wenn Sie weggingen; **there's still time ~ him to come** er kann immer noch kommen; **their one hope is ~ him to return** ihre einzige Hoffnung ist, daß er zurückkommt.
(o) *(phrases)* **to do sth ~ oneself** etw alleine tun; **~ example** zum Beispiel; **you're ~ it!** *(inf)* jetzt bist du dran! *(inf);* **oh ~ a cup a tea!** jetzt eine Tasse Tee — das wäre schön!
[2] *conj* denn ◆ **~ it was too late** denn es war zu spät.
[3] *adj pred (in favour)* dafür ◆ **17 were ~, 13 against** 17 waren dafür, 13 dagegen; **how many ~?** wieviele sind/waren dafür?

for² *abbr of* **free on rail** frei Bahn.

forage ['fɒrɪdʒ] [1] *n* **(a)** *(fodder)* Futter *nt.* **(b)** *(search for fodder)* Futtersuche *f;* *(Mil)* Überfall *m.*
[2] *vi* nach Futter suchen; *(Mil)* einen Überfall/Überfälle machen; *(fig: rummage)* herumstöbern *(for* nach) ◆ **~-cap** Schiffchen *nt.*

foray ['fɒreɪ] [1] *n* (Raub)überfall *m;* *(fig)* Exkurs *m (into* in *+acc)* ◆ **to make** *or* **go on a ~** auf Raubzug gehen.
[2] *vi* einen Raubüberfall/Raubüberfälle machen.

forbad(e) [fɔ:'bæd] *pret of* **forbid.**

forbear¹ [fɔ:'beəʳ] *pret* **forbore,** *ptp* **forborne** *vti (form)* **I forbore from expressing my opinion** ich verzichtete darauf *or* nahm Abstand davon, meine Meinung zu äußern; **he forbore to make any comment** er enthielt sich jeden Kommentars; **we begged him to ~** wir baten ihn, darauf zu verzichten.

forbear² ['fɔ:beəʳ] *n (form)* Vorfahr(in *f*), Ahn(e *f*) *m.*

forbearance [fɔ:'beərəns] *n* Nachsicht *f.*

▼ **forbid** [fə'bɪd] *pret* **forbad(e),** *ptp* **forbidden** *vt* **(a)** *(not allow)* verbieten ◆ **to ~ sb to do sth** jdm verbieten, etw zu tun; **to ~ sb alcohol** jdm Alkohol verbieten; **smoking ~den** Rauchen verboten; **it is ~den to ...** es ist verboten, zu ...
(b) *(prevent)* verhindern, nicht erlauben ◆ **my health ~s my attending the meeting** meine Gesundheit erlaubt es nicht, daß ich an dem Treffen teilnehme; **God ~!** Gott behüte *or* bewahre!

forbidden [fə'bɪdn] *adj* **~ fruit** verbotene Früchte *pl.*

forbidding [fə'bɪdɪŋ] *adj rocks, cliffs* bedrohlich, furchterregend; *sky* düster; *landscape* unfreundlich; *prospect* grauenhaft; *look, person* streng.

forbore [fɔ:'bɔ:ʳ] *pret of* **forbear¹.**

forborne [fɔ:'bɔ:n] *ptp of* **forbear¹.**

▼ **force** [fɔ:s] [1] *n* **(a)** *no pl (physical strength, power)* Kraft *f;* *(of blow also, of impact, collision)* Wucht *f;* *(physical coercion)* Gewalt *f;* *(Phys)* Kraft *f* ◆ **to resort to ~** Gewalt anwenden; **to settle sth by ~** etw gewaltsam *or* durch Gewalt beilegen; **by sheer ~** durch reine Gewalt; **by sheer ~ of numbers** aufgrund zahlenmäßiger Überlegenheit; **there is a ~ 5 wind blowing** es herrscht Windstärke 5; **the ~ of the wind was so great he could hardly stand** der Wind war so stark, daß er kaum stehen konnte; **they were there/came in ~** sie waren in großer Zahl *or* Stärke da/sie kamen in großer Zahl *or* Stärke.
(b) *no pl (fig) (of argument)* Überzeugungskraft *f;* *(of music, phrase)* Eindringlichkeit *f;* *(of character)* Stärke *f;* *(of words, habit)* Macht *f* ◆ **by ~ of will-power** durch Willensanstrengung *or* Willenskraft; **(the) ~ of circumstances** (der) Druck der Verhältnisse; **I see the ~ of that/of what he is saying** ich sehe ein, das ist zwingend/was er sagt, ist zwingend.
(c) *(powerful thing, person)* Macht *f* ◆ **F~s of Nature** Naturgewalten *pl;* **there are various ~s at work here** hier sind verschiedene Kräfte am Werk; **he is a powerful ~ in the trade union movement** er ist ein einflußreicher Mann in der Gewerkschaftsbewegung; *see* **life ~.**
(d) *(body of men)* **the ~s** *(Mil)* die Streitkräfte *pl;* **work ~** Arbeitskräfte *pl;* **sales ~** Verkaufspersonal *nt;* **the (police) ~** die Polizei; **to join** *or* **combine ~s** sich zusammentun.
(e) to come into/be in ~ in Kraft treten/sein.
▼[2] *vt* **(a)** *(compel)* zwingen ◆ **to ~ sb/oneself to do sth** jdn/sich zwingen, etw zu tun; **he was ~d to resign** er wurde gezwungen zurückzutreten; *(felt obliged to)* er sah sich gezwungen zurückzutreten; **he was ~d to conclude that ...** er sah sich zu der Folgerung gezwungen *or* gedrängt, daß ...
(b) *(extort, obtain by ~)* erzwingen ◆ **he ~d a confession out of** *or* **from me** er erzwang ein Geständnis von mir; **to ~ an error** *(Sport)* den Gegner/jdn ausspielen.
(c) to ~ sth (up)on sb *present, one's company* jdm etw aufdrängen; *conditions, obedience* jdm etw auferlegen; *conditions, decision, war* jdm etw aufzwingen; **I don't want to ~ myself on you** ich möchte mich Ihnen nicht aufdrängen.
(d) *(break open)* aufbrechen ◆ **to ~ an entry** sich *(dat)* gewaltsam Zugang *or* Zutritt verschaffen.
(e) *(push, squeeze)* **to ~ books into a box** Bücher in eine Kiste zwängen; **to ~ a splinter out** einen Splitter herausdrücken; **the liquid is ~d up the tube by a pump** die Flüssigkeit wird von einer Pumpe durch das Rohr nach oben gepreßt; **if it won't open/go in, don't ~ it** wenn es nicht aufgeht/paßt, wende keine Gewalt an; **to ~ one's way into sth** sich *(dat)* gewaltsam Zugang zu etw *or* in etw *(acc)* verschaffen; **to ~ one's way through** sich gewaltsam ei-

➤ LANGUAGE IN USE: **forbid: a** → 9.3, 9.5, 10.4 **force: 2a** → 10.3, 26.1

nen Weg bahnen; **to ~ a car off the road** ein Auto von der Fahrbahn drängen; **to ~ a bill through parliament** eine Gesetzesvorlage durch das Parlament peitschen.

(f) *plants* treiben.

(g) (*produce with effort*) **to ~ a smile** gezwungen lächeln; **to ~ the pace** das Tempo forcieren; **she can't sing top C without forcing her voice** sie kann das hohe C nur singen, wenn sie ihrer Stimme Gewalt antut; **it's just about possible to use the word like that, but it's forcing it a bit** man kann das Wort unter Umständen so verwenden, tut ihm aber damit ein bißchen Gewalt an; **don't ~ it** erzwingen Sie es nicht.

◆**force back** *vt sep* zurückdrängen; *tears* unterdrücken.

◆**force down** *vt sep food* sich (*dat*) hinunterquälen; *aeroplane* zur Landung zwingen; *price* drücken; *laugh* unterdrücken; *lid of suitcase etc* mit Gewalt zumachen.

◆**force off** *vt sep lid* mit Gewalt abmachen.

◆**force up** *vt sep prices* hochtreiben.

forced [fɔ:st] *adj smile* gezwungen, gequält; *plant* getrieben; *wording, translation* gezwungen, unnatürlich ◆ **~ landing** Notlandung *f*; **~ march** Gewaltmarsch *m*.

force-feed ['fɔ:sfi:d] (*vb: pret, ptp* **force-fed**) [1] *vt* zwangsernähren.

[2] *n* (*Tech*) Druckschmierung *f*.

forceful ['fɔ:sfʊl] *adj person* energisch, kraftvoll; *manner* überzeugend; *character* stark; *language, style* eindringlich, eindrucksvoll; *argument* wirkungsvoll, stark; *reasoning* eindringlich.

forcefully ['fɔ:sfəlɪ] *adv speak, write, argue, reason* eindringlich, eindrucksvoll; *behave* überzeugend.

forcefulness ['fɔ:sfʊlnɪs] *n see adj* Durchsetzungsvermögen *nt*, energische *or* kraftvolle Art; überzeugende Art; Stärke *f*; Eindringlichkeit *f*.

force majeure [,fɔ:smæ'ʒɜ:ʳ] *n* höhere Gewalt ◆ **to bow to ~** sich höherer Gewalt (*dat*) beugen.

forcemeat ['fɔ:smi:t] *n* (*Cook*) Fleischfüllung, Farce *f*.

forceps ['fɔ:seps] *npl* (*also* **pair of ~**) Zange *f* ◆ **~ delivery** Zangengeburt *f*.

forcible ['fɔ:səbl] *adj* **(a)** *entry* gewaltsam ◆ **~ feeding** Zwangsernährung. **(b)** *language, style* eindringlich, eindrucksvoll; *argument, reason* zwingend, überzeugend; *warning* eindringlich, nachdrücklich.

forcibly ['fɔ:səblɪ] *adv* **(a)** (*by force*) mit Gewalt ◆ **he was ~ fed** er wurde zwangsernährt. **(b)** (*vigorously*) *warn, object* eindringlich, nachdrücklich; *argue, speak* überzeugend.

forcing house ['fɔ:sɪŋhaʊs] *n* **(a)** (*Agr etc*) Gewächshaus *nt*. **(b)** (*fig: school*) Lernfabrik *f*.

ford [fɔ:d] [1] *n* Furt *f*.

[2] *vt* durchqueren; (*on foot also*) durchwaten.

fore [fɔ:ʳ] [1] *adj* (*esp Naut*) vordere(r, s), Vorder- ◆ **~ and aft sail** Schratsegel *nt*.

[2] *n* **(a)** (*Naut*) Vorderteil *nt*, Bug *m* ◆ **at the ~** am Bug.

(b) (*fig*) **to the ~** im Vordergrund, an der Spitze; **to come to the ~** ins Blickfeld geraten.

[3] *adv* (*Naut*) vorn ◆ **~ and aft** längsschiffs.

[4] *interj* (*Golf*) Achtung.

forearm[1] ['fɔ:rɑ:m] *n* Unterarm *m*.

forearm[2] [fɔ:r'ɑ:m] *vt* vorbereiten ◆ **to ~ oneself** sich wappnen; **he came ~ed** er kam vorbereitet; *see* **forewarn**.

forebear[1] ['fɔ:beəʳ] *n* Vorfahr(in *f*), Ahn(e *f*) *m*.

forebear[2] [fɔ:'beəʳ] *vti see* **forbear**[1].

forebode [fɔ:'bəʊd] *vt* (*be portent of*) ein Zeichen *or* Omen sein für, ahnen lassen, deuten auf (+*acc*).

foreboding [fɔ:'bəʊdɪŋ] *n* (*presentiment*) (Vor)ahnung *f*, Vorgefühl *nt*; (*feeling of disquiet*) ungutes Gefühl.

forebrain ['fɔ:breɪn] *n* Vorderhirn *nt*.

forecast ['fɔ:kɑ:st] [1] *vt* vorhersehen, voraussagen; (*Met*) voraussagen, vorhersagen.

[2] *n* Voraussage, Vorhersage, Prognose *f*; (*Met*) Voraus- *or* Vorhersage *f* ◆ **the ~ is good** der Wetterbericht *or* die Wettervorhersage ist günstig.

forecaster ['fɔ:kɑ:stəʳ] *n* (*Met*) Meteorologe *m*, Meteorologin *f* ◆ **economic ~** Wirtschaftsprognostiker *m*.

forecastle ['fəʊksl] *n* (*Naut*) Vorschiff, Vorderdeck *nt*; (*in Merchant Navy*) Logis *nt*.

foreclose [fɔ:'kləʊz] [1] *vt loan, mortgage* kündigen ◆ **to ~ sb** jds Kredit/Hypothek kündigen.

[2] *vi* (*on loan, mortgage*) ein Darlehen/eine Hypothek kündigen ◆ **to ~ on sth** etw kündigen.

foreclosure [fɔ:'kləʊʒəʳ] *n* Zwangsvollstreckung *f* (*on* bei).

forecourt ['fɔ:kɔ:t] *n* Vorhof *m*.

foredeck ['fɔ:dek] *n* Vor(der)deck *nt*.

forefather ['fɔ:,fɑ:ðəʳ] *n* Ahn, Vorfahr *m*.

forefinger ['fɔ:,fɪŋgəʳ] *n* Zeigefinger *m*.

forefoot ['fɔ:fʊt] *n* Vorderfuß *m*.

forefront ['fɔ:frʌnt] *n* **in the ~ of** an der Spitze (+*gen*).

foregather [fɔ:'gæðəʳ] *vi* zusammentreffen, sich versammeln.

forego [fɔ:'gəʊ] *pret* **forewent**, *ptp* **foregone** *vt* verzichten auf (+*acc*).

foregoing ['fɔ:gəʊɪŋ] *adj* vorhergehend, vorangehend ◆ **it can be seen from the ~ that ...** aus dem bisher Gesagten kann entnommen werden, daß ...

foregone [fɔ:'gɒn] [1] *ptp of* **forego**.

[2] ['fɔ:gɒn] *adj*: **it was a ~ conclusion** es stand von vornherein fest.

foreground ['fɔ:graʊnd] *n* (*Art, Phot*) Vordergrund *m* ◆ **in the ~** im Vordergrund.

forehand ['fɔ:hænd] (*Sport*) [1] *n* Vorhand *f*.

[2] *attr* Vorhand-.

forehead ['fɔ:hed, 'fɒrɪd] *n* Stirn *f*.

foreign ['fɒrən] *adj* **(a)** ausländisch; *customs, appearance* fremdartig, fremdländisch; *policy, trade* Außen- ◆ **is he ~?** ist er Ausländer?; **~ person** Ausländer(in *f*) *m*; **~ countries** das Ausland; **he came from a ~ country** er kam aus dem Ausland.

(b) (*not natural*) fremd ◆ **lying is quite ~ to him/his nature** Lügen ist seiner Natur fremd.

foreign: ~ affairs *npl* Außenpolitik *f*; **spokesman on ~ affairs** außenpolitischer Sprecher; **~ agent** *n* (*in espionage*) ausländischer Agent; (*Comm etc*) Auslandsvertreter(in *f*) *m*; **~-born** *adj* im Ausland geboren; **~ correspondent** *n* Auslandskorrespondent(in *f*) *m*; **~ currency** *n* Devisen *pl*.

foreigner ['fɒrənəʳ] *n* Ausländer(in *f*) *m*.

foreign: ~ exchange *n* Devisen *pl*; **~ exchange market** *n* Devisenmarkt *m*; **~ investment** *n* Auslandsinvestition *f*; **~ language** [1] *n* Fremdsprache *f*; **it was a ~ language to me** (*fig*) es war eine Sprache, die ich nicht verstand; [2] *attr* Fremdsprachen-; **~ legion** *n* Fremdenlegion *f*; **F~ Minister** *n* Außenminister *m*; **~ national** *n* ausländische(r) Staatsangehörige(r) *mf*; **F~ Office** *n* (*Brit*) Auswärtiges Amt; **F~ Secretary** *n* (*Brit*) Außenminister *m*.

foreknowledge [,fɔ:'nɒlɪdʒ] *n* vorherige Kenntnis.

foreland ['fɔ:lənd] *n* Vorland *nt*; (*promontory*) Landspitze *f*.

foreleg ['fɔ:leg] *n* Vorderbein *nt*.

forelimb ['fɔ:lɪm] *n* Vorderglied *nt*.

forelock ['fɔ:lɒk] *n* Stirnlocke *f*, Stirnhaar *nt* ◆ **to touch** *or* **tug one's ~ (to sb)** jdm Reverenz erweisen; **to take time by the ~** die Zeit (voll) nutzen.

foreman ['fɔ:mən] *n, pl* **-men** [-mən] (*in factory*) Vorarbeiter *m*; (*on building site*) Polier *m*; (*Jur: of jury*) Obmann *m*.

foremast ['fɔ:mɑ:st] *n* (*Naut*) Fockmast *m*.

foremost ['fɔ:məʊst] [1] *adj* (*lit*) erste(r, s), vorderste(r, s); (*fig*) *writer, politician etc* führend ◆ **the problem/thought which was ~ in his mind** das Problem, das/der Gedanke, der ihn hauptsächlich beschäftigte.

[2] *adv see* **first**.

forename ['fɔ:neɪm] *n* Vorname *m*.

forenoon ['fɔ:nu:n] *n* (*form*) Vormittag *m*.

forensic [fə'rensɪk] *adj* forensisch; (*Med also*) gerichtsmedizinisch ◆ **~ science** Kriminaltechnik *f*; **~ medicine** Gerichtsmedizin *f*, forensische Medizin; **~ expert** Spurensicherungsexperte *m*; **~ laboratory** Polizeilabor *nt*.

foreordain [,fɔ:,rɔ:'deɪn] *vt see* **preordain**.

foreplay ['fɔ:pleɪ] *n* Vorspiel *nt*.

forequarters ['fɔ:,kwɔ:təz] *npl* Vorderstücke *pl*.

forerunner ['fɔ:,rʌnəʳ] *n* Vorläufer *m* ◆ **a ~ of disaster** ein Vorbote *m* des Unglücks.

foresaid ['fɔ:sed] *adj see* **aforesaid**.

foresail ['fɔ:seɪl] *n* (*Naut*) Focksegel *nt*.

foresee [fɔ:'si:] *pret* **foresaw** [fɔ:'sɔ:], *ptp* **foreseen** [fɔ:'si:n] *vt* vorhersehen, voraussehen.

foreseeable [fɔ:'si:əbl] *adj* voraussehbar, absehbar ◆ **in the ~ future** in absehbarer Zeit.

foreshadow [fɔ:'ʃædəʊ] *vt* ahnen lassen, andeuten.

foresheet ['fɔ:ʃi:t] *n* (*Naut*) Fockschot *f*.

foreshore ['fɔ:ʃɔ:ʳ] *n* Küstenvorland *nt*; (*beach*) Strand *m*.

foreshorten [fɔ:'ʃɔ:tn] *vt* (*Art, Phot*) perspektivisch zeichnen/fotografieren ◆ **this has a ~ing effect** das läßt es kürzer erscheinen.

foreshortening [fɔ:'ʃɔ:tnɪŋ] *n* (*Art, Phot*) zeichnerische/fotografische Verkürzung.

foresight ['fɔ:saɪt] *n* Weitblick *m*.

foreskin ['fɔ:skɪn] *n* Vorhaut *f*.

forest ['fɒrɪst] *n* Wald *m*; (*for lumber etc*) Forst *m*; (*fig*) (*of TV aerials etc*) Wald *m*; (*of ideas, suggestions etc*) Wust *m*, Menge *f* ◆ **~ ranger** (*US*) Förster *m*.

forestall [fɔ:'stɔ:l] *vt sb, rival* zuvorkommen (+*dat*); *accident, eventuality* vorbeugen (+*dat*); *wish, desire* im Keim ersticken; *objection* vorwegnehmen.

forestage ['fɔ:steɪdʒ] *n* Vorbühne *f*.

forestation [fɒrɪ'steɪʃən] *n see* **afforestation**.

forestay ['fɔ:steɪ] *n* (*Naut*) Fockstag *nt*.

forested ['fɒrɪstɪd] *adj* bewaldet.

forester ['fɒrɪstəʳ] *n* Förster *m*.

forestry ['fɒrɪstrɪ] *n* Forstwirtschaft *f* ◆ **F~ Commission** (*Brit*) Forstverwaltung *f*.

foretaste ['fɔ:teɪst] *n* Vorgeschmack *m* ◆ **to give sb a ~ of sth** jdm einen Vorgeschmack von etw geben.

foretell [fɔ:'tel] *pret, ptp* **foretold** [fɔ:'təʊld] *vt* vorhersagen.

forethought ['fɔ:θɔ:t] *n* Vorbedacht *m*.

forever [fər'evəʳ] *adv* **(a)** (*constantly*) immer, ständig, ewig (*inf*) ◆ **he was ~ falling over** er fiel immer *or* ständig *or* ewig (*inf*) hin. **(b)** (*esp US: eternally*) = **for ever**; *see* **ever**.

forevermore [fər,evə'mɔ:ʳ] *adv* (*esp US*) = **for evermore**; *see* **evermore**.

forewarn [fɔ:'wɔ:n] *vt* vorher warnen ◆ **that should have ~ed him** das hätte ihm eine Vorwarnung sein sollen; **~ed is forearmed** (*Prov*) Gefahr erkannt, Gefahr gebannt (*Prov*).

forewent [fɔ:'went] *pret of* **forego**.

forewing ['fɔ:wɪŋ] *n* Vorderflügel *m*.

forewoman ['fɔːwʊmən] *n, pl* **-women** [-wɪmɪn] Vorarbeiterin *f.*

foreword ['fɔːwɜːd] *n* Vorwort *nt.*

forfeit ['fɔːfɪt] [1] *vt* **(a)** (*esp Jur*) verwirken; *one's rights also* verlustig gehen (+*gen*). **(b)** (*fig*) *one's life, health, honour, sb's respect* einbüßen ◆ **to ~ the right to criticize sb** sich (*dat*) das Recht verscherzen, jdn zu kritisieren.
[2] *n* (*esp Jur*) Strafe, Buße *f;* (*fig*) Einbuße *f;* (*in game*) Pfand *nt* ◆ **~s** *sing* (*game*) Pfänderspiel *nt;* **to pay a ~** (*in game*) ein Pfand (ab)geben; **his health was the ~ he paid** er zahlte mit seiner Gesundheit dafür.
[3] *adj* **to be ~** (*Jur*) verfallen sein; (*fig*) verwirkt sein.

forfeiture ['fɔːfɪtʃəʳ] *n* (*Jur, fig*) Verlust *m,* Einbuße *f;* (*of claim*) Verwirkung *f.*

forgather [fɔː'gæðəʳ] *vi see* **foregather.**

forgave [fə'geɪv] *pret of* **forgive.**

forge [fɔːdʒ] [1] *n* (*workshop*) Schmiede *f;* (*furnace*) Esse *f.*
[2] *vt* **(a)** *metal, (fig) friendship, plan* schmieden.
(b) (*counterfeit*) *signature, banknote* fälschen.
[3] *vi* **to ~ ahead** Fortschritte machen, vorwärtskommen; (*in career*) seinen Weg machen; (*Sport*) vorstoßen; **he ~d ahead of the rest of the field** er setzte sich weit vor die anderen.

forger ['fɔːdʒəʳ] *n* Fälscher(in *f*) *m.*

forgery ['fɔːdʒərɪ] *n* **(a)** (*act*) Fälschen *nt* ◆ **to be prosecuted for ~** wegen Fälschung angeklagt sein. **(b)** (*thing*) Fälschung *f.*

▼ **forget** [fə'get] *pret* **forgot,** *ptp* **forgotten** [1] *vt* vergessen; *ability, language also* verlernen ◆ **never to be forgotten** unvergeßlich, unvergessen; **and don't you ~ it!** und daß du das ja nicht vergißt!; **he never lets you ~ it either** er sorgt dafür, daß du auch immer daran denkst; **don't ~ the guide** vergessen Sie nicht, dem Führer ein Trinkgeld zu geben; **I was ~ting you knew him** ich habe ganz vergessen, daß Sie ihn kennen; **I ~ his name** sein Name ist mir entfallen; **I ~ what I wanted to say** es ist mir entfallen, was ich sagen wollte; **to ~ past quarrels** vergangene Streitigkeiten ruhen lassen; **~ it!** schon gut!; **you might as well ~ it** (*inf*) das kannst du vergessen (*inf*).
[2] *vi* es vergessen ◆ **don't ~!** vergiß (es) nicht!; **I never ~** ich vergesse nie etwas; **where is he? — I ~** wo ist er? — ich habe es vergessen *or* es ist mir entfallen.
[3] *vr* (*behave improperly*) sich vergessen, aus der Rolle fallen; (*act unselfishly*) sich selbst vergessen.

◆**forget about** *vi +prep obj* vergessen ◆ **I've forgotten all ~ what he did** ich habe völlig vergessen, was er getan hat.

forgetful [fə'getfʊl] *adj* (*absent-minded*) vergeßlich; (*of one's duties etc*) achtlos, nachlässig (*of* gegenüber).

forgetfulness [fə'getfʊlnɪs] *n see adj* Vergeßlichkeit *f;* Achtlosigkeit, Nachlässigkeit *f* (*of* gegenüber) ◆ **in a moment of ~** in einem Augenblick geistiger Abwesenheit.

forget-me-not [fə'getmɪnɒt] *n* (*Bot*) Vergißmeinnicht *nt.*

forgettable [fə'getəbl] *adj* **an eminently ~ second novel** ein zweiter Roman, den man getrost vergessen kann.

forgivable [fə'gɪvəbl] *adj* verzeihlich, verzeihbar.

▼ **forgive** [fə'gɪv] *pret* **forgave,** *ptp* **forgiven** [fə'gɪvn] *vti mistake, clumsiness* verzeihen, vergeben; *person* verzeihen (+*dat*), vergeben (+*dat*); (*esp Eccl*) *sin* vergeben, erlassen ◆ **to ~ sb sth** jdm etw verzeihen *or* vergeben; (*Eccl*) jdm etw vergeben *or* erlassen; **to ~ sb for sth** jdm etw verzeihen *or* vergeben; **to ~ sb for doing sth** jdm verzeihen *or* vergeben, daß er etw getan hat; **~ me, but ...** Entschuldigung, aber ...; **to ~ and forget** vergeben und vergessen.

forgiveness [fə'gɪvnɪs] *n, no pl* (*quality, willingness to forgive*) Versöhnlichkeit *f* ◆ **to ask/beg (sb's) ~** (jdn) um Verzeihung *or* Vergebung (*esp Eccl*) bitten; **her willing ~ of his rudeness surprised him** es überraschte ihn, daß sie ihm seine Grobheit so bereitwillig verzieh; **the ~ of sins** (*Eccl*) die Vergebung der Sünden; **full of ~** versöhnlich.

forgiving [fə'gɪvɪŋ] *adj* versöhnlich, nicht nachtragend.

forgo *pret* **forwent,** *ptp* **forgone** *vt see* **forego.**

forgot [fə'gɒt] *pret of* **forget.**

forgotten [fə'gɒtn] *ptp of* **forget.**

fork [fɔːk] [1] *n* **(a)** (*implement*) Gabel *f.* **(b)** (*in tree*) Astgabel *f;* (*in road, railway*) Gabelung *f* ◆ **take the left ~** nehmen Sie die linke Abzweigung.
[2] *vt* **(a)** *ground* mit einer Gabel umgraben; *hay* (*turn over*) wenden ◆ **to ~ hay onto a cart** Heu mit einer Gabel auf einen Wagen werfen. **(b)** *food* gabeln (*inf*).
[3] *vi* (*roads, branches*) sich gabeln ◆ **to ~ (to the) right** (*road*) nach rechts abzweigen; (*driver*) nach rechts abbiegen.

◆**fork out** *vti sep* (*inf*) blechen (*inf*).

◆**fork over** *vt sep ground* lockern; *hay* wenden.

◆**fork up** *vt sep soil* mit einer Gabel umgraben; *hay* hochheben; *food* gabeln (*inf*).

forked [fɔːkt] *adj branch, road* gegabelt; (*with lots of forks*) verästelt; *lightning* zickzackförmig; *tongue* gespalten ◆ **to speak with ~ tongue** mit gespaltener Zunge reden.

fork: ~-lift truck, ~-lift (*inf*) *n* Gabelstapler *m;* **~-luncheon** *n* (*Brit*) Gabelfrühstück *nt.*

forlorn [fə'lɔːn] *adj* (*deserted*) verlassen; *person* einsam und verlassen; (*desperate*) *attempt* verzweifelt; (*hope*) schwach ◆ **~ appearance** (*of house etc*) desolates *or* trostloses Aussehen.

form [fɔːm] [1] *n* **(a)** Form *f* ◆ **~ of government** Regierungsform *f;* **~ of life** Lebensform *f;* **the various ~s of energy** die verschiedenen Energieformen; **~ of address** Anrede *f;* **to choose another ~ of words** es anders formulieren; **~s of worship** Formen der Gottesverehrung; **a ~ of apology/punishment** eine Art der Entschuldigung/eine Form *or* Art der Bestrafung.
(b) (*condition, style, guise*) Form, Gestalt *f* ◆ **in the ~ of** in Form von *or* +*gen;* (*with reference to people*) in Gestalt von *or* +*gen;* **medicine in tablet ~** Arznei in Tablettenform; **water in the ~ of ice** Wasser in Form von Eis; **the same thing in a new ~** das gleiche in neuer Form *or* Gestalt; **the first prize will take the ~ of a trip to Rome** der erste Preis ist eine Reise nach Rom; **their discontent took various ~s** ihre Unzufriedenheit äußerte sich in verschiedenen Formen.
(c) (*shape*) Form *f* ◆ **to take ~** (*lit, fig*) Form *or* Gestalt annehmen; **a ~ approached in the fog** eine Gestalt näherte sich im Nebel.
(d) (*Art, Mus, Liter: structure*) Form *f* ◆ **~ and content** Form und Inhalt.
(e) (*Philos*) Form *f* ◆ **the world of ~s** die Ideenwelt.
(f) (*Gram*) Form *f* ◆ **the plural ~** die Pluralform, der Plural.
(g) *no pl* (*etiquette*) (Umgangs)form *f* ◆ **he did it for ~'s sake** er tat es der Form halber; **it's bad ~** so etwas tut man einfach nicht; **he pays attention to the ~s** er legt großen Wert auf Form; **what's the ~?** (*inf*) was ist üblich?
(h) (*document*) Formular *nt,* Vordruck *m* ◆ **printed ~** vorgedrucktes Formular; **application ~** Bewerbungsbogen *m.*
(i) (*physical condition*) Form, Verfassung *f* ◆ **to be in fine/good ~** gut in Form sein, in guter Form *or* Verfassung sein; **to be on/off ~** in/nicht in *or* außer Form sein; **he was in great ~ that evening** er war an dem Abend in Hochform; **to study (the) ~** (*Horse-racing*) die Form prüfen; **past ~** Papierform *f;* **on past ~** auf dem Papier.
(j) (*esp Brit: bench*) Bank *f.*
(k) (*Brit Sch*) Klasse *f.*
(l) *no pl* (*sl: criminal record*) **to have ~** vorbestraft sein.
(m) (*Tech: mould*) Form *f.*
(n) (*US Typ*) *see* **forme.**
(o) (*of hare*) Nest *nt,* Sasse *f* (*spec*).
[2] *vt* **(a)** (*shape*) formen, gestalten (*into* zu); (*Gram*) *plural, negative* bilden ◆ **he ~s his sentences well** er bildet wohlgeformte Sätze *pl.*
(b) (*train, mould*) *child, sb's character* formen.
(c) (*develop*) *liking, desire, idea* entwickeln; *habit also* annehmen; *friendship* schließen, anknüpfen; *opinion* sich (*dat*) bilden; *impression* gewinnen; *plan* ausdenken, entwerfen.
(d) (*set up, organize*) *government, committee* bilden; *company, society* gründen, ins Leben rufen.
(e) (*constitute, make up*) *part, basis* bilden ◆ **the committee is ~ed of ...** der Ausschuß wird von ... gebildet.
(f) (*take the shape or order of*) *queue, circle, pattern* bilden.
[3] *vi* **(a)** (*take shape*) Gestalt annehmen ◆ **the idea ~ed in my mind** die Idee nahm Gestalt an.
(b) (*esp Mil: also* **~ up**) sich aufstellen *or* formieren, antreten ◆ **to ~ into a queue/into two lines** eine Schlange/zwei Reihen bilden; **to ~ into a square** sich im Karree aufstellen; **to ~ into battle order** sich zur Schlachtordnung formieren.

formal ['fɔːməl] *adj* **(a)** formell; *person, manner, language etc also* förmlich; *reception, welcome (for head of state etc)* feierlich; *education, training* offiziell ◆ **~ dance/dress** Gesellschaftstanz *m*/-kleidung *f.*
(b) (*in form*) *distinction etc* formal (*also Philos*) ◆ **~ grammar** formalisierte Grammatik; **~ logic** formale Logik.

formaldehyde [fɔː'mældɪhaɪd] *n* Formaldehyd *m.*

formalin(e) ['fɔːməlɪn] *n* Formalin *nt.*

formalism ['fɔːməlɪzəm] *n* Formalismus *m.*

formality [fɔː'mælɪtɪ] *n* **(a)** *no pl* (*of person, dress, greeting, language, ceremony etc*) Förmlichkeit *f.*
(b) (*matter of form*) Formalität *f* ◆ **it's a mere ~** es ist (eine) reine Formsache *or* Formalität; **let's dispense with the formalities** lassen wir die Formalitäten beiseite.

formalize ['fɔːməlaɪz] *vt rules, grammar* formalisieren; *agreement, relationship* formell machen.

formally ['fɔːməlɪ] *adv* **(a)** formell; *behave, talk, agree, permit, invite etc also* förmlich; *welcome officially also* feierlich; *educated, trained* offiziell ◆ **to be ~ dressed** Gesellschaftskleidung tragen. **(b)** (*in form*) *alike, different, analyzed* formal.

format ['fɔːmæt] [1] *n* (*as regards size*) Format *nt;* (*as regards content*) Aufmachung *f;* (*Rad, TV: of programme*) Struktur *f* ◆ **page ~** Seitenformat *nt.*
[2] *vt* (*Comput*) *disk, page, paragraph* formatieren.

formation [fɔː'meɪʃən] *n* **(a)** (*act of forming*) Formung, Gestaltung *f;* (*Gram: of plural etc*) Bildung *f;* (*of character*) Formung *f;* (*of government, committee*) Bildung *f;* (*of company, society*) Gründung *f;* (*of desire, idea, impression, habit etc*) Entwicklung *f;* (*of friendship*) Schließen *nt,* Anknüpfung *f;* (*of opinion*) Bildung *f;* (*of plan*) Entwurf *m.*
(b) (*of aircraft, dancers*) Formation *f;* (*of troops also*) Aufstellung *f* ◆ **battle ~** Gefechtsaufstellung *f;* **in close ~** (*Aviat*) im geschlossenen Verband; **~ flying** Formationsflug *m;* **to dance in ~** in Formation tanzen; **~ dancing** Formationstanzen *nt.*
(c) (*Geol*) Formation *f.*

formative ['fɔːmətɪv] [1] *adj* formend, bildend; (*Gram*) Bildungs-; (*Biol*) morphogenetisch ◆ **~ years** entscheidende Jahre *pl.*
[2] *n* (*Gram*) Wortbildungselement, Formativ *nt.*

forme [fɔːm] *n* (*Brit Typ*) (Satz)form *f.*

▼ **former** ['fɔːməʳ] [1] *adj* **(a)** (*of an earlier period*) früher, ehemalig ◆ **the ~ mayor** der ehemalige Bürgermeister; **in a ~ life** in einem früheren Leben; **in ~ times/days** früher.
(b) (*first-mentioned*) erstere(r, s), erstgenannte(r, s).

➤ LANGUAGE IN USE: **forget: 1** → 26.3 **forgive** → 18.1, 18.2

▼[2] *n* **the ~** der/die/das erstere; **of these two theories I prefer the ~** von diesen beiden Theorien ziehe ich (die) erstere vor.
-former *n suf* (*Brit Sch*) -kläßler(in *f*) *m.*
formerly ['fɔːməlɪ] *adv* früher ◆ **we had ~ agreed that ...** wir hatten uns seinerzeit darauf geeinigt, daß ...; **~ known as ...** früher *or* ehemals als ... bekannt; **Mrs X, ~ Mrs Y** Frau X, die ehemalige *or* frühere Frau Y.
form: ~ feed *n* (*Comput*) Papiervorschub *m*; **~-fitting** *adj* enganliegend.
formica ® [fɔː'maɪkə] *n* Resopal ® *nt.*
formic acid ['fɔːmɪk'æsɪd] *n* Ameisensäure *f.*
formidable ['fɔːmɪdəbl] *adj* **(a)** *person, rock-face* furchterregend; *enemy, opponent also* bedrohlich, gefährlich; *height also* gewaltig; *opposition* übermächtig; *obstacles, debts, problems, task* gewaltig, enorm; *piece of work, theory* beeindruckend, beachtlich. **(b)** *achievement* gewaltig, ungeheuer.
form: ~less *adj* formlos; **~lessness** *n* Formlosigkeit *f*; **~ letter** *n* (*Comput*) Formbrief *m.*
formula ['fɔːmjʊlə] *n, pl* **-s** *or* **-e** ['fɔːmjʊliː] Formel *f* (*also Sci*); (*for lotion, medicine, soap powder*) Rezeptur *f* ◆ **there's no sure ~ for success** es gibt kein Patentrezept *nt* für Erfolg; **they changed the ~ of the programme** sie änderten die Aufmachung des Programms; **all his books use the same ~** alle seine Bücher sind nach demselben Rezept geschrieben; **~ 1/2** (*Motor-racing*) Formel 1/2.
formulate ['fɔːmjʊleɪt] *vt* formulieren.
formulation [,fɔːmjʊ'leɪʃən] *n* Formulierung *f.*
fornicate ['fɔːnɪkeɪt] *vi* Unzucht treiben.
fornication [,fɔːnɪ'keɪʃən] *n* Unzucht *f.*
fornicator ['fɔːnɪkeɪtə^r] *n* Hurer (*inf*), Hurenbock (*inf*) *m*; (*woman*) Hure *f* (*inf*).
forsake [fə'seɪk] *pret* **forsook** [fə'sʊk], *ptp* **forsaken** [fə'seɪkn] *vt* verlassen; *bad habits* aufgeben, entsagen (*+dat*) (*geh*) ◆ **my willpower ~s me on these occasions** meine Willenskraft läßt mich bei diesen Gelegenheiten im Stich.
forswear [fɔː'swɛə^r] *pret* **forswore** [fɔː'swɔː^r], *ptp* **forsworn** [fɔː'swɔːn] *vt* **(a)** (*renounce*) abschwören (*+dat*) ◆ **he has forsworn smoking** er hat hoch und heilig versprochen, nicht mehr zu rauchen. **(b)** (*deny*) unter Eid verneinen *or* leugnen.
forsythia [fɔː'saɪθɪə] *n* Forsythie *f.*
fort [fɔːt] *n* (*Mil*) Fort *nt* ◆ **to hold the ~** (*fig*) die Stellung halten.
forte ['fɔːtɪ] *n* (*strong point*) Stärke *f*, starke Seite.
forth [fɔːθ] *adv* **(a) to set ~** (*liter*) ausziehen (*liter*); **to stretch ~ one's hand** (*liter*) die Hand ausstrecken; *see vbs.* **(b)** (*in time*) **from this/that day ~** (*liter*) von diesem/jenem Tag an. **(c) and so ~** und so weiter.
forthcoming [fɔːθ'kʌmɪŋ] *adj* **(a)** *event* bevorstehend; *book* in Kürze erscheinend; *film, play* in Kürze anlaufend ◆ **~ events/attractions** Programmvorschau *f*; **~ books** *or* **titles** geplante Neuerscheinungen *pl*; **our ~ titles for next year** Titel, die nächstes Jahr erscheinen. **(b) to be ~** (*money*) kommen; (*help, information*) erfolgen. **(c)** (*esp Brit: frank, informative*) mitteilsam.
forthright ['fɔːθraɪt] *adj* offen; *answer also* unverblümt; *manner also* direkt.
forthwith [,fɔːθ'wɪθ] *adv* (*form*) umgehend, unverzüglich.
fortieth ['fɔːtɪɪθ] [1] *adj* vierzigste(r, s).
[2] *n* (*fraction*) Vierzigstel *nt*; (*in series*) Vierzigste(r, s).
fortification [,fɔːtɪfɪ'keɪʃən] *n* **(a)** *see vt* (*act of fortifying*) Befestigung *f*; Vergärung *f*; Anreicherung *f*; Bestärkung *f.* **(b)** (*often pl: Mil*) Befestigungen *pl*, Festungsanlagen *pl.*
fortify ['fɔːtɪfaɪ] *vt* (*Mil*) *town* befestigen; *wine* mit zuckerreichem Most vergären; *food* anreichern; *person* bestärken; (*food, drink*) stärken ◆ **fortified place** befestigte Stellung; **fortified wine** weinhaltiges Getränk, Südwein *m*; **have a drink to ~ you** nehmen Sie einen Schluck zur Stärkung.
fortitude ['fɔːtɪtjuːd] *n* (innere) Kraft *or* Stärke.
fortnight ['fɔːtnaɪt] *n* (*esp Brit*) vierzehn Tage, zwei Wochen ◆ **a ~'s holiday** zwei Wochen *or* vierzehn Tage Urlaub.
fortnightly ['fɔːtnaɪtlɪ] (*esp Brit*) [1] *adj* vierzehntägig, zweiwöchentlich.
[2] *adv* alle vierzehn Tage, alle zwei Wochen, vierzehntägig, zweiwöchentlich.
FORTRAN ['fɔːtræn] *abbr of* **formula translator** FORTRAN *nt.*
fortress ['fɔːtrɪs] *n* Festung *f* ◆ **~ mentality** Festungsmentalität *f.*
fortuitous *adj*, **~ly** *adv* [fɔː'tjuːɪtəs, -lɪ] zufällig.
fortuitousness [fɔː'tjuːɪtəsnɪs], **fortuity** [fɔː'tjuːɪtɪ] *n* Zufall *m.*
fortunate ['fɔːtʃənɪt] *adj circumstances, coincidence etc* glücklich ◆ **to be ~** (*person*) Glück haben; **you are very ~** *or* **you're a ~ man to be alive still** du kannst von Glück reden *or* dich glücklich schätzen, daß du noch lebst; **it was ~ that ...** es war (ein) Glück, daß ...; **we were ~ enough to meet him** wir hatten das Glück, ihn zu treffen; **how ~!** welch ein Glück!
fortunately ['fɔːtʃənɪtlɪ] *adv* glücklicherweise, zum Glück ◆ **he was more ~ situated** ihm ging es besser.
fortune ['fɔːtʃuːn] *n* **(a)** (*fate*) Schicksal, Geschick *nt*; (*chance*) Zufall *m* ◆ **she followed his ~s with interest** sie verfolgte sein Geschick mit Interesse; **the ~s of war** das Auf und Ab des Krieges; **he had the good ~ to have rich parents** er hatte das Glück, reiche Eltern zu haben; **by good ~** glücklicherweise, zum Glück; **by sheer good ~** rein zufällig; **~ has favoured him** das Glück war ihm hold; **~ favours the brave** *or* **bold** (*Prov*) das Glück ist nur dem Tüchtigen hold.
(b) (*money*) Reichtum *m*, Vermögen *nt* ◆ **to come into/make a ~** ein Vermögen erben/machen; **to seek/make one's ~** sein Glück versuchen/machen; **to marry a ~** reich heiraten; **it costs a ~** es kostet ein Vermögen; **she spends a (small) ~ on clothes** sie gibt ein (kleines) Vermögen für Kleidung aus.
fortune: ~ hunter *n* Mitgiftjäger *m*; **~-teller** *n* Wahrsager(in *f*) *m.*
forty ['fɔːtɪ] [1] *adj* vierzig ◆ **to have ~ winks** (*inf*) ein Nickerchen machen (*inf*).
[2] *n* Vierzig *f*; *see also* **sixty.**
forty-niner [,fɔːtɪ'naɪnə^r] *n Goldgräber, der im Zuge des Goldrausches von 1849 nach Kalifornien ging.*
forum ['fɔːrəm] *n* Forum *nt.*
forward ['fɔːwəd] [1] *adv* **(a)** (*also* **~s**) (*onwards, ahead*) vorwärts; (*to the front, to particular point, out of line*) nach vorn ◆ **please step ~** bitte vortreten; **to take two steps ~** zwei Schritte vortreten; **to rush ~** sich vorstürzen; **to go straight ~** geradeaus gehen; **~!** vorwärts!; **he went backward(s) and ~(s) between the station and the house** er ging/fuhr *etc* zwischen Haus und Bahnhof hin und her.
(b) (*in time*) **from this time ~** (*from then*) seitdem; (*from now*) von jetzt an; **if we think ~ to the next stage** wenn wir an die vor uns liegende nächste Stufe denken.
(c) (*into prominence*) **to come ~** sich melden; **to bring ~ new proof** neue Beweise *pl* vorlegen.
[2] *adj* **(a)** (*in place*) vordere(r, s); (*in direction*) Vorwärts- ◆ **~ march** Vormarsch *m*; **~ gears** (*Aut*) Vorwärtsgänge *pl*; **~ pass** (*Sport*) Vorwärtspaß *m*; **~ post** (*Mil*) Vorposten *m*; **this seat is too far ~** dieser Sitz ist zu weit vorn.
(b) (*in time*) *planning* Voraus-; (*Comm*) *buying, price* Termin-; (*well-advanced*) *season* (weit) fortgeschritten; *plants* Früh-, früh *pred*; *children* frühreif ◆ **I'd like to be further ~ with my work** ich wollte, ich wäre mit meiner Arbeit schon weiter; **good ~ thinking, Jones** gute Voraussicht, Jones.
(c) (*presumptuous, pert*) dreist.
[3] *n* (*Sport*) Stürmer *m.*
[4] *vt* **(a)** (*advance*) *plans etc* vorantreiben ◆ **we'll ~ your suggestions to the committee** wir werden Ihre Vorschläge an den Ausschuß weiterleiten.
(b) (*dispatch*) *goods* beförden, senden; (*send on*) *letter, parcel* nachsenden ◆ **please ~** bitte nachsenden.
forwarding ['fɔːwədɪŋ]: **~ address** *n* Nachsendeadresse *f*; **~ agent** *n* Spediteur *m*; **~ instructions** *npl* (*for goods*) Lieferanweisungen *pl*; (*for sending on mail*) Nachsendeanweisungen *pl.*
forward: ~-line *n* (*Sport*) Sturm *m*, Stürmerreihe *f*; **~-looking** *adj person* fortschrittlich, progressiv; *plan* vorausblickend.
forwardness ['fɔːwədnɪs] *n* (*presumption*) Dreistigkeit *f.*
forwards ['fɔːwədz] *adv see* **forward 1 (a).**
forwent [fɔː'went] *pret of* **forgo.**
Fosbury flop ['fɒzbrɪ'flɒp] *n* Fosbury-Flop *m.*
fossil ['fɒsl] [1] *n* (*lit*) Fossil *nt* ◆ **he's an old ~!** (*inf*) er ist so verknöchert.
[2] *adj* versteinert ◆ **~ fuels** fossile Brennstoffe *pl.*
fossilized ['fɒsɪlaɪzd] *adj* versteinert; (*fig*) *person* verknöchert; *customs* verkrustet, starr.
foster ['fɒstə^r] *vt* **(a)** *child* (*parents*) in Pflege nehmen; (*authorities:* **~ out**) in Pflege geben (*with* bei). **(b)** (*encourage, promote*) fördern. **(c)** (*have in one's mind*) *idea, thought* hegen.
◆**foster out** *vt sep* in Pflege geben (*with* bei).
foster: ~-brother *n* **(a)** Pflegebruder *m*; **(b)** (*fed by same mother*) Milchbruder *m*; **~-child** *n* Pflegekind *nt*; **~-father** *n* Pflegevater *m*; **~ home** *n* Pflegeheim *nt*; **~-mother** *n* **(a)** (*Jur*) Pflegemutter *f*; **(b)** (*wet-nurse*) Amme *f*; **(c)** (*apparatus*) Brutkasten *m*; **~-sister** *n* Pflegeschwester *f.*
fought [fɔːt] *pret, ptp of* **fight.**
foul [faʊl] [1] *adj* (*+er*) **(a)** (*putrid, stinking*) *smell* übel, schlecht; *water* faulig; *air* schlecht, stinkig (*inf*); *food* übelriechend, verdorben ◆ **~ deed** böse *or* schlechte Tat.
(b) (*horrible*) *day, weather, mood* ekelhaft, mies (*inf*); *person, behaviour* gemein, fies (*inf*) ◆ **he was really ~ to her** er war wirklich gemein *or* fies (*inf*) zu ihr; **he has a ~ temper** er ist ein ganz übellauniger Mensch.
(c) *language* unflätig.
(d) (*Sport*) *serve, throw-in* ungültig; *punch* unerlaubt, verboten ◆ **he was sent off for ~ play** er wurde wegen eines Fouls *or* wegen Regelverstößen vom Platz gestellt; **there was a lot of ~ play** es gab eine Menge Fouls *or* Regelverstöße.
(e) the police suspect ~ play es besteht Verdacht auf einen unnatürlichen *or* gewaltsamen Tod; **is there any possibility of ~ play?** könnte der Verdacht auf einen unnatürlichen *or* gewaltsamen Tod vorliegen?
(f) (*entangled*) verwickelt ◆ **to fall** *or* **run ~ of sb/the law** mit jdm/dem Gesetz in Konflikt geraten.
[2] *n* (*Sport*) Foul *nt*, Regelverstoß *m*; (*Boxing*) unerlaubter or verbotener Schlag.
[3] *vt* **(a)** (*pollute*) *air* verpesten; (*clog*) *pipe, chimney, gun-barrel* verstopfen; (*dog*) *pavement* verunreinigen.
(b) (*entangle*) *fishing line* verheddern; *propeller* (*seaweed etc*) sich verheddern in (*+dat*); (*collide with*) *ship* rammen ◆ **be careful not to ~ the propeller** paß auf, daß sich die Schraube nicht verheddert.
(c) (*Sport*) foulen.
[4] *vi* **(a)** (*Sport*) foulen, regelwidrig spielen.
(b) (*rope, line*) sich verwickeln, sich verheddern.
◆**foul up** *vt sep* (*inf*) versauen (*inf*).
fouler ['faʊlə^r] *n* (*Sport*) Foulspieler(in *f*) *m.*
foully ['faʊlɪ] *adv* (*horribly*) übel, schlimm.
foul-mouthed ['faʊlmaʊðd] *adj* unflätig, vulgär.
foulness ['faʊlnɪs] *n* **(a)** (*putridness, stink*) (*of water*) Fauligkeit *f*; (*of food*) Ver-

➤ LANGUAGE IN USE: **former: 2→26.2**

dorbenheit *f* ◆ **the ~ of the smell/air** der üble *or* schlechte Geruch/die schlechte Luft.
(b) *(horribleness)* **the ~ of the weather/wine** *etc* das schlechte Wetter/der schlechte Wein *etc*; **his ~ to her** sein gemeines Verhalten *or* seine Gemeinheit ihr gegenüber.
(c) *(of language)* Unflätigkeit *f*.
foul-smelling ['faʊlsmelɪŋ] *adj* übelriechend *attr*.
foul-tempered ['faʊl,tempəd] *adj* sehr übellaunig.
found¹ [faʊnd] *pret, ptp of* **find**.
found² *vt* **(a)** *(set up)* gründen; *town, school, hospital also* errichten. **(b) to ~ sth (up)on sth** *opinion, belief* etw auf etw *(dat)* gründen *or* stützen; **our society is ~ed on this** darauf beruht *or* basiert unsere Gesellschaft, das ist die Grundlage unserer Gesellschaft; **the novel is ~ed on fact** der Roman beruht *or* basiert auf Tatsachen.
found³ *vt* *(Metal) metal, glass* schmelzen und in eine Form gießen; *object* gießen.
foundation [faʊn'deɪʃən] *n* **(a)** *(act of founding)* *(of business, colony)* Gründung *f*; *(of town, school also)* Errichtung *f*. **(b)** *(institution)* Stiftung *f*. **(c) ~s** *pl* *(Build)* *(of house etc)* Fundament *nt*; *(of road)* Unterbau *m*. **(d)** *(fig: basis)* Grundlage *f*. **(e)** *(make-up)* Grundierungscreme *f*.
foundation: ~ cream *n* Grundierungscreme *f*; **F~ Day** *n* *(Austral)* *australischer gesetzlicher Feiertag zur Erinnerung an die Landung der Briten am 26. Januar 1788*; **~ garment** *n* Mieder *nt*; **~ stone** *n* Grundstein *m*.
founder¹ ['faʊndəʳ] *n* *(of school, colony, organization etc)* Gründer(in *f*) *m*; *(of charity, museum)* Stifter(in *f*) *m*.
founder² *vi* **(a)** *(ship: sink)* sinken, untergehen. **(b)** *(horse etc: stumble)* straucheln, stolpern. **(c)** *(fig: fail)* *(plan, project)* scheitern, fehlschlagen; *(hopes)* auf den Nullpunkt sinken.
founder³ *n* *(Metal)* Gießer *m*.
Founding Fathers ['faʊndɪŋ,fɑːðəz] *npl* *(US)* Väter *pl*.
foundling ['faʊndlɪŋ] *n* Findling *m*, Findelkind *nt* ◆ **~ hospital** Findelhaus, Findelheim *nt*.
foundry ['faʊndrɪ] *n* Gießerei *f*.
fount [faʊnt] *n* **(a)** *(liter)* *(fountain)* Born *m* *(poet)*, Quelle *f*; *(fig: source)* Quelle *f*. **(b)** *(Typ)* Schrift *f*.
fountain ['faʊntɪn] *n* Brunnen *m*; *(with upward jets also)* Springbrunnen *m*; *(jet, spurt: of water, lava etc)* Fontäne *f*; *(drinking ~)* (Trinkwasser)brunnen *m*; *(fig: source)* Quelle *f* ◆ **~ of youth** Jungbrunnen *m*.
fountain: ~-head *n* *(of river)* Quelle *f*; *(fig)* Quelle *f*, Ursprung *m*; **~-pen** *n* Füllfederhalter, Füller *m*.
four [fɔːʳ] **1** *adj* vier ◆ **open to the ~ winds** Wind und Wetter ausgesetzt; **the F~ Hundred** *(US)* ≃ die oberen Zehntausend.
2 *n* Vier *f* ◆ **on all ~s** auf allen vieren; **will you make up a ~ for bridge?** haben Sie Lust, beim Bridge den vierten Mann zu machen?; *see also* **six**.
four: ~-ball *n* *(Golf)* Vierer *m*; **~-colour** *adj* *(Typ)* Vierfarb-; **~-colour printing** *n* Vierfarbdruck *m*; **~-cycle** *adj* *(US)* *see* **~-stroke**; **~-dimensional** *adj* vierdimensional; **~-door** *attr* viertürig; **~-eyes** *n sing* *(hum inf)* Bebrillte(r) *mf* *(hum inf)*; *(woman also)* Brillenschlange *f* *(hum inf)*; **~-figure** *attr* vierstellig; **~fold** **1** *adj* vierfach; **2** *adv* um das Vierfache; **~-footed** *adj* vierfüßig; **~-four time** *n* *(Mus)* Viervierteltakt *m*; **~-handed** *adj* *(Mus)* vierhändig, für vier Hände, zu vier Händen; **~-in-hand** *n* Vierspänner *m*; **~-leaf clover, ~-leaved clover** *n* vierblättriges Kleeblatt; **~-letter word** *n* Vulgärausdruck *m*; **~-minute mile** *n* Vierminutenmeile *f*; **~-part** *attr serial, programme* vierteilig; *(Mus)* für vier Stimmen; **~-poster (bed)** *n* Himmelbett *nt*; **~ score** *adj* *(obs)* achtzig; **~-seater** **1** *adj* viersitzig; **2** *n* Viersitzer *m*; **~some** *n* Quartett *nt*; *(Sport)* Viererspiel *nt*; **to go out in a ~some** zu viert ausgehen; **~ square** *adj* **(a)** *(square)* viereckig, quadratisch; **(b)** *(firm, unyielding) attitude, decision* entschlossen, fest; **(c)** *(forthright) account* offen und ehrlich, direkt; **~-star** *adj hotel etc, (US) general* Vier-Sterne-; *(Brit) petrol* Super-; **~-stroke** *adj engine* Viertakt-.
fourteen ['fɔː'tiːn] **1** *adj* vierzehn.
2 *n* Vierzehn *f*.
fourteenth ['fɔː'tiːnθ] **1** *adj* vierzehnte(r, s).
2 *n* *(fraction)* Vierzehntel *nt*; *(of series)* Vierzehnte(r, s); *see also* **sixteenth**.
fourth [fɔːθ] **1** *adj* vierte(r, s) ◆ **the ~ dimension** die vierte Dimension; **the ~ estate** die Presse.
2 *n* *(fraction)* Viertel *nt*; *(in series)* Vierte(r, s) ◆ **to drive in ~** im vierten Gang fahren; **we need a ~ for our game of bridge** wir brauchen noch einen vierten zum Bridge; *see also* **sixth**.
fourthly ['fɔːθlɪ] *adv* viertens.
four: ~-way *adj* zu viert; *valve* Vierwege-; **~-wheel drive** *n* Vierradantrieb *m*.
fowl [faʊl] **1** *n* **(a)** *(poultry)* Geflügel *nt*; *(one bird)* Huhn *nt*; Gans *f*; Truthahn *m etc* ◆ **to keep ~** Hühner *etc* halten; **roast ~** *(Cook)* Brathuhn *nt*. **(b) the ~s of the air** *(liter)* die Vögel des Himmels.
2 *vi* *(also* **to go ~ing***)* auf Vogeljagd gehen.
fowling piece ['faʊlɪŋpiːs] *n* Schrotflinte *f*.
fowl pest *n* Hühnerpest *f*.
fox [fɒks] **1** *n* **(a)** *(lit, fig)* Fuchs *m* ◆ **he's a sly ~** *(fig)* er ist ein schlauer Fuchs. **(b)** *(~ fur)* Fuchs(pelz) *m*. **(c)** *(US inf: sexy woman)* scharfes Weib *(inf)*.
2 *vt* *(deceive)* täuschen, reinlegen *(inf)*; *(bewilder)* verblüffen ◆ **that's ~ed you, hasn't it?** da bist du baff, was? *(inf)*.
fox: ~ cub *n* Fuchsjunge(s) *nt*, Fuchswelpe *m*; **~glove** *n* *(Bot)* Fingerhut *m*; **~hole** *n* **(a)** Fuchsbau *m*; **(b)** *(Mil)* Schützengraben *m*, Schützenloch *nt*; **~hound** *n* Fuchshund *m*; **~-hunt** **1** *n* Fuchsjagd *f*; **2** *vi* auf (die) Fuchsjagd gehen; **~-hunting** *n* Fuchsjagd *f*; **to go ~-hunting** auf die *or* zur Fuchsjagd gehen; **~ terrier** *n* Foxterrier *m*; **~trot** *n* Foxtrott *m*.
foxy ['fɒksɪ] *adj* (+*er*) *(wily)* listig, pfiffig, verschlagen ◆ **~ lady** *(US inf)* scharfes Weib *(inf)*.
foyer ['fɔɪeɪ] *n* *(in theatre)* Foyer *nt*; *(in hotel also)* Empfangshalle *f*; *(esp US: in apartment house)* Diele *f*.
Fr *abbr of* **(a)** Father. **(b)** Friar.
fracas ['frækɑː] *n* Aufruhr, Tumult *m*.
fraction ['frækʃən] *n* **(a)** *(Math)* Bruch *m*. **(b)** *(fig)* Bruchteil *m*. **a ~ better/shorter** (um) eine Spur besser/kürzer; **move it just a ~ (of an inch)** verrücke es (um) eine Spur; **for a ~ of a second** einen Augenblick lang; **it missed me by a ~ of an inch** es verfehlte mich um Haaresbreite. **(c)** *(Eccl)* Brechen *nt* des Brotes.
fractional ['frækʃənl] *adj* **(a)** *(Math)* Bruch-; *(fig)* geringfügig ◆ **~ part** Bruchteil *m*. **(b)** *(Chem) distillation* fraktioniert.
fractionally ['frækʃənəlɪ] *adv* geringfügig; *ahead* um eine Nasenlänge.
fractious ['frækʃəs] *adj* verdrießlich; *child* aufsässig.
fractiousness ['frækʃəsnɪs] *n see adj* Verdrießlichkeit *f*; Aufsässigkeit *f*.
fracture ['fræktʃəʳ] **1** *n* Bruch *m*; *(Med also)* Fraktur *f* *(spec)*.
2 *vti* brechen ◆ **he ~d his shoulder** er hat sich *(dat)* die Schulter gebrochen; **~d skull** Schädelbruch *m*.
fragile ['frædʒaɪl] *adj china, glass* zerbrechlich; *butterfly's wing also, material, plant, leaf, complexion* zart; *(through age)* brüchig; *(fig) person (in health)* gebrechlich; *health* anfällig; *self-confidence, ego* labil, wackelig *(inf)* ◆ **"~, handle with care"** „Vorsicht, zerbrechlich"; **he's feeling a bit ~ this morning** *(inf)* er fühlt sich heute morgen etwas angeschlagen.
fragility [frə'dʒɪlɪtɪ] *n see adj* Zerbrechlichkeit *f*; Zartheit *f*; Brüchigkeit *f*; Gebrechlichkeit *f*; Anfälligkeit *f*; Labilität, Wackeligkeit *(inf) f*.
fragment ['frægmənt] **1** *n* **(a)** Bruchstück *nt*; *(of china, glass)* Scherbe *f*; *(of shell)* Stückchen *nt*; *(of paper, letter)* Schnipsel *m*; *(of programme, opera etc)* Bruchteil *m* ◆ **he smashed it to ~s** er schlug es in Stücke; **~s of conversation** Gesprächsfetzen *pl*.
(b) *(esp Liter, Mus: unfinished work)* Fragment *nt*.
2 [fræg'ment] *vi* *(rock, glass)* (zer)brechen, in Stücke brechen; *(fig)* *(hopes)* sich zerschlagen; *(society)* zerfallen.
3 [fræg'ment] *vt rock, glass* in Stücke brechen; *(with hammer etc)* in Stücke schlagen; *(fig) society, hopes* zerschlagen.
fragmentary ['frægməntərɪ] *adj* *(lit, fig)* fragmentarisch, bruchstückhaft.
fragmentation [,frægmen'teɪʃən] *n see vb* Zerbrechen *nt*; Zerschlagung *f* ◆ **~ bomb** Splitterbombe *f*.
fragmented [fræg'mentɪd] *adj* bruchstückhaft; *(broken up)* unzusammenhängend, ohne Zusammenhang.
fragrance ['freɪgrəns] *n* Duft, Wohlgeruch *m*.
fragrant ['freɪgrənt] *adj* duftend, wohlriechend; *(fig liter) memories* köstlich ◆ **~ smell** Duft *m*.
frail [freɪl] *adj* (+*er*) zart; *dried flowers, butterfly's wing, appearance also, old lady* zerbrechlich; *health also* anfällig; *old lace, old book* brüchig; *(fig) flesh, hope* schwach.
frailty ['freɪltɪ] *n see adj* Zartheit *f*; Zerbrechlichkeit *f*; Anfälligkeit *f*; Brüchigkeit *f*; Schwäche *f* ◆ **~, thy name is woman** Schwachheit, dein Name ist Weib.
frame [freɪm] **1** *n* **(a)** *(basic structure, border of picture)* Rahmen *m*; *(of building)* (Grund)gerippe *nt*; *(of ship)* Gerippe *nt*; *(Typ)* Setzregal *nt*; *(Hort)* Mistbeet, Frühbeet *nt*; *(of spectacles: also ~s)* Gestell *nt*; *(Billiards)* *(single game)* Spiel *nt*; *(triangle)* Rahmen *m*.
(b) *(of human, animal)* Gestalt *f* ◆ **her ~ was shaken by sobs** ihr Körper wurde von Schluchzen geschüttelt.
(c) ~ of mind *(mental state)* Verfassung *f*; *(mood)* Stimmung, Laune *f*; **in a cheerful ~ of mind** in fröhlicher Stimmung *or* Laune; **I am not in the right ~ of mind for singing** ich bin nicht in der (richtigen) Laune *or* Stimmung zum Singen.
(d) *(fig: framework, system)* grundlegende Struktur ◆ **~ of reference** *(lit, fig)* Bezugssystem *nt*; **within the ~ of ...** im Rahmen (+*gen*) ...
(e) *(Film, Phot)* (Einzel)bild *nt*; *(in comic strip)* Bild(chen) *nt*.
(f) *(TV)* Abtastbild, Rasterbild *nt*.
(g) *(Telec, Comput)* Datenübertragungsblock *m*.
2 *vt* **(a)** *picture* rahmen; *(fig) face etc* ein- *or* umrahmen ◆ **he appeared ~d in the door** er erschien im Türrahmen.
(b) *(draw up, construct) constitution, law, plan* entwerfen; *idea* entwickeln; *(express) answer, excuse* formulieren; *sentence* bilden; *words* bilden, formen.
(c) *(sl: incriminate falsely)* **he said he had been ~d** er sagte, man habe ihm die Sache angehängt *(inf)*.
3 *vi* *(develop)* sich entwickeln ◆ **his plans are framing well/badly** seine Pläne machen gute/keine Fortschritte *pl*.
frame-house ['freɪmhaʊs] *n* Holzhaus, Haus *nt* mit Holzrahmen.
framer ['freɪməʳ] *n* (Bilder)rahmer(in *f*) *m*.
frame: ~ rucksack *n* Rucksack *m* mit Traggestell; **~-saw** *n* Bügelsäge *f*; **~-up** *n* *(inf)* Komplott *nt*; **~work** *n* *(lit)* Grundgerüst *nt*; *(fig)* *(of essay, novel etc also)* Gerippe *nt*; *(of society, government etc)* grundlegende Struktur; **within the ~work of ...** im Rahmen (+*gen*) ...; **outside the ~work of ...** außerhalb des Rahmens (+*gen*) ...
franc [fræŋk] *n* Franc *m*.
France [frɑːns] *n* Frankreich *nt*.
franchise ['fræntʃaɪz] *n* **(a)** *(Pol)* Wahlrecht *nt*. **(b)** *(Comm)* Lizenz, Franchise *f*.

franchisee [ˌfræntʃaɪˈziː] *n (Comm)* Lizenz- *or* Franchisenehmer *m*.
franchisor [ˈfræntʃaɪzəʳ] *n (Comm)* Lizenz- *or* Franchisegeber *m*.
Francis [ˈfrɑːnsɪs] *n* Franz *m* ◆ **St ~ of Assisi** der heilige Franziskus von Assisi.
Franciscan [frænˈsɪskən] 1 *n* Franziskaner *m*.
2 *adj* Franziskaner-.
Franco- [ˈfræŋkəʊ-] *in cpds* Französisch-; **~-German** *adj* deutsch-französisch.
Franconia [fræŋˈkəʊnɪə] *n* Franken *nt*.
Franconian [fræŋˈkəʊnɪən] 1 *n (person)* Franke *m*, Fränkin *f*; *(dialect)* Fränkisch *nt*.
2 *adj* fränkisch.
franco: ~phile *n* **he is a ~phile** er ist frankophil; **~philia** *n* Frankophilie *f*; **~phobe** *n* Franzosenfeind *m*; **~phobia** *n* Frankophobie *f*; **~phone** *adj* französischsprechend; **F~-Prussian** *adj* **the F~-Prussian War** der Deutsch-Französische Krieg.
frangipane [ˈfrændʒɪpeɪn], **frangipani** [ˌfrændʒɪˈpænɪ] *n (shrub)* Roter Jasmin(baum); *(perfume)* Jasminparfüm *nt*.
Franglais [ˈfrɑ̃ːŋgleɪ] *n* Französisch *nt* mit vielen englischen Ausdrücken.
Frank [fræŋk] *n (Hist)* Franke *m*.
frank¹ [fræŋk] *adj (+er)* offen; *opinion also* ehrlich; *desire, distaste, dislike* unverhohlen ◆ **to be ~ with sb** mit jdm offen sein, zu jdm ehrlich sein; **he wasn't very ~ about it** er äußerte sich nicht sehr offen dazu; **to be (perfectly) ~** ehrlich gesagt.
frank² *vt letter* frankieren; *(postmark) letter* stempeln.
frankfurter [ˈfræŋkˌfɜːtəʳ] *n (sausage)* (Frankfurter) Würstchen *nt*.
frankincense [ˈfræŋkɪnsens] *n* Weihrauch *m*.
franking-machine [ˈfræŋkɪŋməˈʃiːn] *n* Frankiermaschine *f*.
Frankish [ˈfræŋkɪʃ] 1 *adj* fränkisch.
2 *n (Ling)* Fränkisch *nt*.
franklin [ˈfræŋklɪn] *n (Hist)* Freisasse *m*.
frankly [ˈfræŋklɪ] *adv* offen; *(to tell the truth)* ehrlich gesagt.
frankness [ˈfræŋknɪs] *n see adj* Offenheit *f*; Ehrlichkeit *f*; Unverhohlenheit *f*.
frantic [ˈfræntɪk] *adj effort, cry, scream* verzweifelt; *activity* fiebrig, rasend; *agitation* hell, höchste(r, s); *desire* übersteigert; *person* außer Fassung, außer sich ◆ **~ with pain/worry** außer sich *or* rasend vor Schmerzen/außer sich vor Sorge(n); **to go ~** außer sich geraten; *(with worry)* am Rande der Verzweiflung sein; **to drive sb ~** jdn zur Verzweiflung treiben; **he was driven ~ by anxiety** er war außer sich vor Sorge.
frantically [ˈfræntɪkəlɪ] *adv try, scream* verzweifelt; *gesticulate, rush around* wild, wie wildgeworden *(inf)*; *busy, worried* rasend; *(inf: terribly)* rasend, furchtbar.
frappé [ˈfræpeɪ] *n* Frappé *nt*.
frat [fræt] *n (US Univ inf) abbr of* **fraternity**.
fraternal [frəˈtɜːnl] *adj* brüderlich ◆ **~ twins** zweieiige Zwillinge *pl*.
fraternity [frəˈtɜːnɪtɪ] *n* **(a)** *no pl* Brüderlichkeit *f*. **(b)** *(community)* Vereinigung, Zunft *f*; *(Eccl)* Bruderschaft *f*; *(US Univ)* Verbindung *f* ◆ **the legal/medical/teaching ~** die Juristen *pl*/Mediziner *pl*/Lehrer *pl*; **~ pin** *(US Univ)* Mitgliedsabzeichen *nt (einer Verbindung)*.
fraternization [ˌfrætənaɪˈzeɪʃən] *n* (freundschaftlicher) Umgang, Verbrüderung *f (pej)*; *(Mil also)* Fraternisieren *nt*.
fraternize [ˈfrætənaɪz] *vi* (freundschaftlichen) Umgang haben, sich verbrüdern *(pej)*; *(Mil also)* fraternisieren.
fratricide [ˈfrætrɪsaɪd] *n* Brudermord *m*; *(person)* Brudermörder(in *f*) *m*.
fraud [frɔːd] *n* **(a)** *(no pl: trickery)* Betrug *m*; *(trick also)* Schwindel *m* ◆ **~s** Betrügereien *pl*; **~ squad** Betrugsdezernat *nt*.
(b) *(fraudulent person)* Betrüger(in *f*), Schwindler(in *f*) *m*; *(feigning illness)* Simulant(in *f*) *m*; *(fraudulent thing)* (reiner) Schwindel, fauler Zauber *(inf)* ◆ **you're not really angry, you big ~** du bist ja gar nicht wütend, du tust ja nur so; **the whole thing was a ~** das ganze war (ein einziger) Schwindel *or* reiner Schwindel; **to obtain sth by ~** sich *(dat)* etw erschwindeln.
fraudulence [ˈfrɔːdjʊləns], **fraudulency** [ˈfrɔːdjʊlənsɪ] *n* Betrügerei *f*; *(of action)* betrügerische Art.
fraudulent [ˈfrɔːdjʊlənt] *adj* betrügerisch.
fraught [frɔːt] *adj* geladen *(with* mit) ◆ **~ with danger** gefahrvoll; **~ with hatred** haßerfüllt; **~ with meaning** bedeutungsvoll *or* -schwer; **~ with tension** spannungsgeladen; **the situation/atmosphere was a bit ~** *(inf)* die Situation/Atmosphäre war ein bißchen gespannt.
fray¹ [freɪ] *n* Schlägerei *f*; *(Mil)* Kampf *m* ◆ **ready for the ~** *(lit, fig)* kampfbereit, zum Kampf bereit; **to be eager for the ~** *(lit, fig)* kampflustig sein; **to enter the ~** *(lit)* sich in den Kampf stürzen; *(fig)* sich in den Kampf *or* Streit einschalten.
fray² 1 *vt cloth* ausfransen; *cuff, rope* durchscheuern.
2 *vi (cloth)* (aus)fransen; *(cuff, trouser turn-up, rope)* sich durchscheuern ◆ **tempers began to ~** die Gemüter begannen sich zu erhitzen *or* zu erregen.
frayed [freɪd] *adj (fig)* gereizt, angespannt ◆ **my nerves are quite ~** ich bin mit den Nerven runter *(inf) or* am Ende *(inf)*; **tempers were ~** die Gemüter waren angespannt *or* erhitzt.
frazzle [ˈfræzl] 1 *n (inf)* **worn to a ~** *(exhausted)* am Boden zerstört *(inf)*; **burnt to a ~** *(toast, meat)* völlig verkohlt; *(sunburnt)* von der Sonne total verbrannt.
2 *vt (US inf)* **(a)** *(fray)* ausfransen. **(b)** *(fig: tire)* völlig erschöpfen *or* ermüden.
freak [friːk] 1 *n* **(a)** *(abnormal plant)* Mißbildung *f*; *(person, animal also)* Mißgeburt *f* ◆ **~ of nature** Laune *f* der Natur.
(b) *(abnormal event)* außergewöhnlicher Zufall; *(snowstorm etc)* Anomalie *f* ◆ **~ of fortune** Laune *f* des Zufalls.
(c) *(sl: hippy)* ausgeflippter Typ *(sl)* ◆ **he's an acid ~** er ist ein Säurekopf *m (inf)*, er nimmt LSD.
(d) *(sl)* **jazz ~** Jazzfan *m*; **movie ~** Kinofan *m*; **health ~** Gesundheitsapostel *m (inf)*.
(e) *(inf: weird person)* Irre(r) *mf* ◆ **he looked at me as though I was some sort of ~** er sah mich an, als ob ich vom Mond wäre.
2 *adj weather, conditions* anormal, abnorm; *error* verrückt; *(Statistics) values* extrem; *victory* Überraschungs-.
◆**freak out** *(sl)* 1 *vi* ausflippen *(sl)*; *(of society also)* aussteigen.
2 *vt sep* **it ~ed me ~** dabei bin ich ausgeflippt *(sl)*; **your prices ~ me ~!** bei euren Preisen flippt man aus! *(sl)*.
freakish [ˈfriːkɪʃ] *adj* **(a)** *see* **freak 2**. **(b)** *(changeable) weather* verrückt *(inf)*, launisch, unberechenbar; *person* ausgeflippt *(sl)*; *hairstyle, idea* verrückt *(inf)*, irre *(inf)*.
freak: ~-out *n (sl) (party)* Haschparty *f (inf)*; *(drug trip)* (Wahnsinns)trip *m (sl)*; **~ show** *n* Monstrositätenschau *f*.
freaky [ˈfriːkɪ] *adj (+er) (sl)* irre *(sl)*.
freckle [ˈfrekl] *n* Sommersprosse *f*.
freckled [ˈfrekld], **freckly** [ˈfreklɪ] *adj* sommersprossig.
Frederick [ˈfredrɪk] *n* Friedrich *m*.
free [friː] 1 *adj (+er)* **(a)** *(at liberty, unrestricted) person, animal, state, activity, translation, choice* frei ◆ **to set a prisoner ~** einen Gefangenen freilassen *or* auf freien Fuß setzen; **to go ~** *(not be imprisoned)* frei ausgehen; *(be set free)* freigelassen werden; **he is ~ to go** es steht ihm frei zu gehen; **the fishing is ~ here** diese Stelle hier ist zum Fischen freigegeben; **you're ~ to choose** die Wahl steht Ihnen frei; **you're ~ to come too/to ask him** Sie können ruhig auch kommen/Sie können ihn ruhig fragen; **you're ~ to refuse** Sie können auch ablehnen; **you're ~ to go now/decide** Sie können jetzt gehen(, wenn Sie wollen)/Sie können das selbst entscheiden; **I'm not ~ to do it** es steht mir nicht frei, es zu tun; **do feel ~ to help yourself** nehmen Sie sich ruhig; **feel ~!** *(inf)* bitte, gerne!; **to give sb a ~ hand** jdm freie Hand lassen; **he left one end of the string ~** er ließ ein Ende des Bindfadens lose; **his arms were left ~** *(not tied)* seine Arme waren frei(gelassen); **~ and easy** ungezwungen.
(b) *(+prep)* **~ from pain/worry** schmerzfrei/sorgenfrei *or* -los; **~ from blame/responsibility** frei von Schuld/Verantwortung; **~ of sth** frei von etw; **we chose a spot ~ of tourists/flies** wir suchten uns *(dat)* einen Platz ohne Touristen/Fliegen; **in two hours we were ~ of the city** nach zwei Stunden hatten wir die Stadt hinter uns.
(c) *(costing nothing)* kostenlos, Gratis-; *ticket also* frei, Frei-; *(Comm)* gratis ◆ **it's ~** das kostet nichts; **admission ~** Eintritt frei; **to get sth ~** etw umsonst bekommen; **we got in ~** *or* **for ~** *(inf)* wir kamen umsonst rein; **~, gratis and for nothing** gratis und umsonst; **I can tell you that for ~** *(inf)* das kann ich dir gratis sagen; **~ delivery** (porto)freier Versand; **~ gift** (Gratis)geschenk *nt*; **~ list** *(Theat)* Liste *f* der Empfänger von Freikarten; **~ alongside ship** *(Comm)* frei Kai; **~ on board** *(Comm)* frei Schiff.
(d) *(not occupied) room, seat, hour, person* frei ◆ **there are two ~ rooms left** es sind noch zwei Zimmer frei; **I wasn't able to get ~ earlier** ich konnte mich nicht eher freimachen; **to have one's hands ~** *(lit)* die Hände frei haben; *(fig: have no work to do)* nichts zu tun haben; **if you've got a ~ hand could you carry this?** wenn du eine Hand frei hast, kannst du mir das tragen?
(e) *(lavish, profuse)* großzügig, freigebig; *(licentious, improper) language, behaviour* frei, lose; *(over-familiar)* plump-vertraulich ◆ **to be ~ with one's money** großzügig mit seinem Geld umgehen; **to make ~ with other people's property** sich großzügig anderer Leute Sachen *(gen)* bedienen.
2 *vt prisoner (release)* freilassen; *(help escape)* befreien; *caged animal* freilassen; *nation* befreien; *(untie) person* losbinden; *tangle* (auf)lösen; *pipe* freimachen; *rusty screw, caught fabric* lösen ◆ **to ~ sb from anxiety** jdn von seiner Angst befreien; **to ~ oneself from sth** sich von etw frei machen.
◆**free up** *vt funds, resources* verfügbar machen.
-free *adj suf* -frei.
free association *n* freie Assoziation.
freebie, freebee [ˈfriːbiː] *n (inf: promotional gift)* Werbegeschenk *nt* ◆ **I got it as a ~** ich habe es gratis bekommen; **this one's a ~** das ist gratis *or* umsonst.
free: ~board *n* Freibord *nt*; **~booter** *n* Freibeuter *m*; **~-born** *adj* frei geboren; **F~ Church** *n* Freikirche *f*; **~ collective bargaining** *n* Tarifautonomie *f*.
freedman [ˈfriːdmæn] *n, pl* **-men** [-mən] befreiter *or* freigelassener Sklave.
freedom [ˈfriːdəm] *n* **(a)** Freiheit *f* ◆ **~ of action/speech/worship** Handlungs-/Rede-/Religionsfreiheit *f*; **~ of association** Vereinsfreiheit *f*; **~ of the press** Pressefreiheit *f*; **~ of the seas** Freiheit *f* der Meere; **to give sb ~ to do as he wishes** jdm (völlige) Freiheit lassen, zu tun, was er will; **~ from sth** Freiheit von etw.
(b) *(frankness)* Offenheit *f*; *(over-familiarity)* plumpe *(inf) or* zu große Vertraulichkeit ◆ **to speak with ~** offen reden.
(c) *(permission to use freely)* **the ~ of the city** die (Ehren)bürgerrechte *pl*; **to give sb the ~ of one's house** jdm sein Haus zur freien Verfügung stellen.
freedom fighter *n* Freiheitskämpfer(in *f*) *m*.
free: ~ elections *npl* freie Wahlen *pl*; **~ enterprise** *n* freies Unternehmertum; **~-fall** 1 *n* freier Fall; **in ~-fall** *(Space)* in freiem Fall; 2 *vi* frei fallen; **~ fight** *n* allgemeine Schlägerei.
freefone [ˈfriːfəʊn] *n* **call ~ 0800** rufen Sie gebührenfrei *or* zum Nulltarif 0800 an.
free: ~-for-all *n* Gerangel *nt (inf)*; *(fight)* Schlägerei *f*; **wages ~-for-all**

Tarifgerangel *nt*; **to stop the situation becoming a ~-for-all** es unterbinden, daß jeder mitmischen kann; **~-hand** [1] *adj drawing* Freihand-; [2] *adv* freihand, aus der Hand; **~-handed** *adj (generous)* großzügig, freigebig; **~hold** *n* **to own sth ~hold** etw besitzen; **he bought the ~hold on the house** er hat das Haus gekauft; **~hold property** *n* (freier) Grundbesitz; **~ house** *n (Brit) Wirtshaus, das nicht an eine bestimmte Brauerei gebunden ist*; **~ kick** *n (Sport)* Freistoß *m*; **~ labour** *n (non-unionized)* nicht organisierte Arbeiter(schaft *f*) *pl*; **~lance** [1] *n* Freiberufler(in *f*) *m*, freischaffender *or* freier Journalist/Schriftsteller *etc*, freischaffende *or* freie Journalistin/Schriftstellerin *etc*; *(with particular firm)* freier Mitarbeiter, freie Mitarbeiterin; [2] *adj journalist, designer etc* frei(schaffend), freiberuflich tätig; [3] *adv* freiberuflich; **to work ~lance** *see vi*; [4] *vi* freiberuflich tätig sein, frei arbeiten; *(with particular firm)* als freier Mitarbeiter/als freie Mitarbeiterin tätig sein; **~load** *vi (inf)* schmarotzen (*on* bei); **~loader** *n (inf)* Schmarotzer(in *f*) *m*; **~ love** *n* freie Liebe.

freely ['fri:lɪ] *adv* **(a)** *(lavishly) give* reichlich, großzügig ◆ **he spends his money ~** er gibt sein Geld mit vollen Händen aus. **(b)** *(unrestrictedly) speak* frei; *move also* ungehindert.

free: ~man *n* **(a)** *(not a slave)* Freie(r) *m*; **(b) ~man of a city** Ehrenbürger *m* einer Stadt; **~mason** *n* Freimaurer *m*; **~masonry** *n* Freimaurerei *f*; **~ port** *n* Freihafen *m*; **~-range** *adj (Brit) chicken* Farmhof-; *eggs* von freilaufenden Hühnern; **~ sample** *n* Gratisprobe *f*.

freesia ['fri:zɪə] *n (Bot)* Freesie *f*.

free: ~ speech *n* Redefreiheit *f*; **~-spoken** *adj* freimütig; **~-standing** *adj* frei stehend; **~style** [1] *n* Kür *f*; *(Swimming)* Freistil *m*; **the 200 metres ~style** die 200 Meter Freistil; [2] *attr* Kür-; *swimming, wrestling* Freistil-; **~thinker** *n* Freidenker, Freigeist *m*; **~thinking** *adj person* freidenkerisch, freigeistig; **~-trade** *n* Freihandel *m*; **~-trader** *n* Freihändler *m*; **~ verse** *n* freie Rhythmen *pl*; **~way** *n (US)* Autobahn *f*; **~wheel** [1] *vi* im Freilauf fahren; **a ~wheeling discussion** eine offene Diskussion; [2] *n* Freilauf *m*; **~ will** *n (Philos)* freier Wille; **he did it of his own ~ will** er hat es aus freien Stücken getan; **F~ World** *n* **the F~ World** die freie Welt.

freeze [fri:z] *(vb: pret* **froze**, *ptp* **frozen**) [1] *vi* **(a)** *(Met)* frieren; *(water, liquids)* gefrieren; *(lakes, rivers)* zufrieren; *(pipes)* einfrieren ◆ **it's freezing hard** es herrscht starker Frost, es friert stark *(inf)*; **it'll ~ hard tonight** es wird heute nacht starken Frost geben; **frozen solid** völlig gefroren/zugefroren/eingefroren; **I am/my hands are freezing** mir ist/meine Hände sind eiskalt; **to ~ to death** *(lit)* erfrieren; *(fig)* sich zu Tode frieren; *see* **frozen**.

(b) *(fig) (blood)* erstarren, gerinnen; *(heart)* aussetzen; *(smile)* erstarren, gefrieren ◆ **it made my blood ~** es ließ mir das Blut in den Adern gerinnen.

(c) *(keep still)* in der Bewegung verharren *or* erstarren ◆ **he froze in his tracks** er blieb wie angewurzelt stehen; **~!** keine Bewegung!

(d) *(Cook)* **meat ~s well** Fleisch läßt sich gut einfrieren.

[2] *vt* **(a)** *water* gefrieren; *(Med, Cook)* einfrieren. **(b)** *(Econ) assets* festlegen; *credit, wages, bank account* einfrieren; *(stop) film* anhalten. **(c)** *(Med) wound* vereisen. **(d)** *(fig)* **to ~ sb with a look** jdm einen eisigen Blick zuwerfen.

[3] *n* **(a)** *(Met)* Frost *m* ◆ **the big ~** der harte Frost. **(b)** *(Econ)* Stopp *m* ◆ **a wages ~, a ~ on wages** ein Lohnstopp *m*.

◆**freeze off** *vt sep* die kalte Schulter zeigen (+*dat*).

◆**freeze onto** *vi +prep obj (US inf)* **to ~ ~ sb** sich wie eine Klette an jdn hängen *or* heften.

◆**freeze out** *vt sep (US inf) person* herausekeln *(inf)*.

◆**freeze over** *vi (lake, river)* überfrieren; *(windscreen, windows)* vereisen.

◆**freeze up** [1] *vi* zufrieren; *(lock, car door etc also, pipes)* einfrieren; *(windscreen, windows)* vereisen.

[2] *vt sep* **we were frozen ~ last winter** letztes Jahr waren alle unsere Leitungen eingefroren.

freeze: ~-dry *vt* gefriertrocknen; **~ frame** *n (Phot)* Standbild *nt*.

freezer ['fri:zəʳ] *n* Tiefkühltruhe *f*; *(upright)* Gefrierschrank *m*; *(ice compartment of fridge)* Eisfach, (Tief)kühlfach, Gefrierfach *nt*.

freeze-up ['fri:zʌp] *n* **(a)** *(Met)* Dauerfrost *m*. **(b)** *(esp US: of lakes, rivers etc)* **during the ~ a lot of birds perish** während Seen und Flüsse zugefroren sind, kommen viele Vögel ums Leben.

freezing ['fri:zɪŋ] [1] *adj weather* eiskalt.

[2] *n* **(a)** *(Cook)* Einfrieren *nt*. **(b)** *(~ point)* **below ~** unter Null, unter dem Gefrierpunkt.

freezing point *n* Gefrierpunkt *m* ◆ **below ~** unter Null, unter dem Gefrierpunkt.

freight [freɪt] [1] *n (goods transported)* Fracht(gut *nt*) *f*; *(charge)* Frachtkosten *pl*, Fracht(gebühr) *f* ◆ **to send sth ~** etw als Frachtgut verschicken; **~ charges** Frachtkosten *pl*; **~ forward** Fracht gegen Nachnahme.

[2] *vt* **(a)** *(transport) goods* verfrachten.

(b) *(load) boat* beladen.

freightage ['freɪtɪdʒ] *n (charge)* Fracht(gebühr) *f*.

freight car *n (US Rail)* Güterwagen *m*.

freighter ['freɪtəʳ] *n (Naut)* Frachter *m*, Frachtschiff *nt*; *(Aviat)* Frachtflugzeug *nt*.

freight: ~ plane *n* Frachtflugzeug *nt*; **~ terminal** *n* Fracht- *or* Güterterminal *nt*; **~ train** *n* Güterzug *m*.

French [frentʃ] [1] *adj* französisch ◆ **the ~ people** die Franzosen *pl*, das französische Volk.

[2] *n* **(a) the ~** *pl* die Franzosen *pl*. **(b)** *(language)* Französisch *nt*; *see also* **English**.

French: ~ bean *n* grüne Bohne; **~-Canadian** [1] *adj* frankokanadisch, kanadisch-französisch; [2] *n* **(a)** Frankokanadier(in *f*) *m*; **(b)** *(language)* kanadisches Französisch; **~ chalk** *n* Schneiderkreide *f*; **~ doors** *npl (US) see* **~ window(s)**; **~ dressing** *n* Salatsoße, Vinaigrette *f*; **~ fried potatoes, ~ fries** *npl* Pommes frites *pl*; **~ Guiana** *n* Französisch-Guayana *nt*; **~ Guianan** [-gaɪ'ænən] [1] *n* Französisch-Guayaner(in *f*) *m*; [2] *adj* französisch-guayanisch; **~ horn** *n (Mus)* (Wald)horn *nt*.

frenchify ['frentʃɪfaɪ] *vt* französisieren; *clothes, restaurant also* auf französisch machen *(inf)* ◆ **frenchified ways** französisierte *or* welsche *(pej)* Manieren.

French: ~ kiss *n* Zungenkuß *m*; **~ knickers** *npl* French Knickers *pl*; **~ leave** *n* **to take ~ leave** sich (auf) französisch empfehlen; **~ letter** *n (Brit inf)* Pariser *m (inf)*; **~ loaf** *n* Baguette *f*; **~man** *n* Franzose *m*; **~ pleat** *or* **roll** *n Damenfrisur, bei der das Haar seitlich zurückgekämmt und in einer länglichen Rolle aufgesteckt wird*; **~ polish** [1] *n* Möbelpolitur *f* mit Schellack; [2] *vt* lackieren; **~ seam** *n (Sew)* französische Naht; **~ stick** *n* Baguette *f*, Stangenbrot *nt*; **~ toast** *n nur auf einer Seite gerösteter Toast*; *(with egg) in Ei getunktes gebratenes Brot*; **~ window(s** *pl*) *n* Verandatür *f*; **~woman** *n* Französin *f*.

frenetic [frə'netɪk] *adj* frenetisch, rasend.

frenzied ['frenzɪd] *adj* wahnsinnig; *applause, activity* rasend.

frenzy ['frenzɪ] *n* Raserei *f*, Rasen *nt* ◆ **in a ~** in heller *or* wilder Aufregung; **he worked himself/the audience up into a ~** er steigerte sich in eine Raserei (hinein)/er brachte die Menge zur Raserei *or* zum Rasen; **~ of delight** Freudentaumel *m*.

frequency ['fri:kwənsɪ] *n* Häufigkeit *f*; *(Statistics also, Phys)* Frequenz *f* ◆ **high/low ~** Hoch-/Niederfrequenz *f*.

frequency: ~ band *n* Frequenzband *nt*; **~ distribution** *n* Häufigkeitsverteilung *f*; **~ modulation** *n* Frequenzmodulation *f*.

frequent ['fri:kwənt] [1] *adj* häufig; *objection, criticism* häufig geäußert; *practice* landläufig ◆ **it's quite a ~ occurrence/state of affairs** es kommt recht häufig vor; **he is a ~ visitor to our house** er kommt uns oft *or* häufig besuchen.

[2] [frɪ'kwent] *vt* oft *or* häufig besuchen, frequentieren *(geh)*.

frequenter [frɪ'kwentəʳ] *n (of a house)* häufig gesehener Gast; *(of a pub)* Stammgast *m* ◆ **he's not a ~ of pubs** er geht nicht oft *or* regelmäßig ins Wirtshaus.

frequently ['fri:kwəntlɪ] *adv* oft, häufig ◆ **I have ~ said ...** ich habe schon oft gesagt ...; **I don't go to the cinema very ~** ich gehe nicht oft ins Kino.

fresco ['freskəʊ] *n (technique)* Freskomalerei *f*; *(painting)* Fresko(gemälde) *nt*.

fresh [freʃ] [1] *adj (+er)* **(a)** *(newly made, not stale or dirty or tinned or tired etc)* frisch ◆ **to keep one's clothes (looking) ~** seine Kleidung sauber und ordentlich halten; **it's still ~ in my memory/mind** es ist mir noch frisch in Erinnerung *or* im Gedächtnis; **~ water** *(not salt)* Süßwasser *nt*; **in the ~ air** an der frischen Luft; **let's have some ~ air in here** können wir hier mal lüften?; *see* **daisy**.

(b) *(new, different, original) supplies, sheet of paper, arrival, ideas, approach, courage* neu ◆ **it needs a ~ coat of paint** das muß frisch gestrichen werden, das hat einen neuen Anstrich nötig; **to make a ~ start** einen neuen Anfang machen, neu anfangen; **to start a ~ job/life** eine neue Stelle antreten/ein neues Leben anfangen; **a ~ arrival** ein Neuankömmling *m*.

(c) *(esp US: cheeky)* frech, mopsig *(inf)*, pampig *(inf)* ◆ **don't get ~ with me!** werd nicht frech!, komm mir bloß nicht frech!

(d) *(cool)* frisch ◆ **light breeze, becoming ~ towards the evening** leichte, gegen Abend auffrischende Winde *pl*; **~ breeze** *(Met, Naut)* frische Brise.

[2] *adv (+er) baked, picked etc* frisch ◆ **~ from the oven** ofenfrisch, frisch aus dem Ofen; **~ out of college** frisch von der Schule; **~ off the presses** druckfrisch, frisch von der Presse; **to come ~ to sth** neu zu etw kommen; **we're ~ out of eggs** *(sl)* uns sind die Eier ausgegangen; **sorry, we're ~ out** *(sl)* tut mir leid, davon ist leider nichts mehr da.

◆**fresh up** *vtir (US) see* **freshen up**.

freshen ['freʃn] [1] *vi (wind)* auffrischen; *(weather, air)* frisch werden.

[2] *vt shirt etc* aufbügeln; *bread* aufbacken.

◆**freshen up** [1] *vir* **to ~ ~ (oneself) ~** *(person)* sich frisch machen.

[2] *vt sep* **(a)** *child, invalid etc* frisch machen ◆ **that will ~ you ~** das wird Sie erfrischen. **(b)** *see* **freshen 2**.

fresher ['freʃəʳ] *n (Brit Univ inf)* Erstsemester *nt (inf)*.

freshly ['freʃlɪ] *adv* frisch.

freshman ['freʃmən] *n, pl* **-men** [-mən] *(US) see* **fresher**.

freshness ['freʃnɪs] *n* **(a)** *(of food, fruit, wind, dress etc)* Frische *f*; *(of approach also, of outlook)* Neuheit *f*. **(b)** *(esp US: cheekiness)* Frechheit, Mopsigkeit *(inf) f*.

freshwater ['freʃwɔ:təʳ] *adj attr* Süßwasser-.

fret[1] [fret] [1] *vi* **(a)** *(become anxious)* sich *(dat)* Sorgen machen; *(baby)* unruhig sein ◆ **don't ~** beruhige dich; **the child is ~ting for his mother** das Kind jammert nach seiner Mutter.

(b) *(horse)* **to ~ (at the bit)** sich (am Biß) reiben *or* scheuern.

[2] *vt* nagen an (+*dat*).

[3] *vr* sich *(dat)* Sorgen machen, sich aufregen.

[4] *n* **to be in a ~** sich *(dat)* Sorgen machen, in Sorge sein.

fret[2] *vt wood etc* laubsägen.

fret[3] *n (on guitar etc)* Bund *m*.

fretful ['fretfʊl] *adj (worried)* besorgt, in Sorge; *(peevish) child* quengelig; *baby* unruhig.

fretfulness ['fretfʊlnɪs] *n see adj* Besorgtheit *f*; Quengeligkeit *f*; Unruhe *f*.

fret: ~ saw *n* Laubsäge *f*; **~work** *n (in wood)* Laubsägearbeit *f*; *(Archit)* Mäander *m*.

Freudian ['frɔɪdɪən] [1] *adj (Psych, fig)* Freudsch *attr*, freudianisch ◆ **~ slip**

Freudsche Fehlleistung; (*spoken also*) Freudscher Versprecher; **very ~!** was Freud wohl dazu sagen würde!
[2] *n* Freudianer(in *f*) *m*.
FRG *abbr of* **Federal Republic of Germany** BRD *f*.
Fri *abbr of* **Friday** Fr.
friable ['fraɪəbl] *adj* bröckelig, krümelig.
friableness ['fraɪəblnɪs] *n* Bröckeligkeit, Krümeligkeit *f*.
friar ['fraɪəʳ] *n* Mönch *m* ◆ **F~ John** Bruder John; **Black/Grey/White F~s** Dominikaner/Franziskaner/Karmeliter *pl*.
friary ['fraɪərɪ] *n* Mönchskloster *nt*.
fricassee ['frɪkəsiː] [1] *n* Frikassee *nt*.
[2] *vt* frikassieren.
fricative ['frɪkətɪv] [1] *adj* Reibe- ◆ **~ consonant** Reibelaut *m*.
[2] *n* Reibelaut *m*.
friction ['frɪkʃən] *n* **(a)** Reibung *f*; (*Phys also*) Friktion *f* ◆ **~ clutch** Friktionskupplung, Reibungskupplung *f*; **~ feed** (*Comput*) Friktionsvorschub *m*; **~ tape** (*US*) Isolierband *nt*. **(b)** (*fig*) Reibung *f*, Reibereien *pl* ◆ **there is a lot of ~ between them** sie reiben sich ständig aneinander.
Friday ['fraɪdɪ] *n* Freitag *m*; *see also* **Tuesday**.
fridge [frɪdʒ] *n* (*Brit*) Eisschrank, Kühlschrank *m*.
fridge-freezer ['frɪdʒ'friːzəʳ] *n* Kühl- und Gefrierkombination *f*.
fried [fraɪd] *adj* Brat-; *egg* Spiegel-.
friend [frend] *n* **(a)** Freund(in *f*) *m*; (*less intimate*) Bekannte(r) *mf* ◆ **to make ~s with sb** sich mit jdm anfreunden, mit jdm Freundschaft schließen; **to make a ~ of sb** sich (*dat*) jdn zum Freund machen; **he makes ~s easily** er findet leicht Freunde; **a ~ of mine** ein Freund/eine Freundin von mir; ein Bekannter/eine Bekannte; **he's no ~ of mine** er ist nicht mein Freund; **to be ~s with sb** mit jdm befreundet sein, jds Freund(in) sein; **be a ~** sei so lieb; **I'm not ~s with you any more** (*inf*) du bist nicht mehr mein Freund/meine Freundin; **we're just (good) ~s** da ist nichts, wir sind nur gut befreundet; **my honourable** (*Parl*)/**learned** (*Jur*) **~** mein verehrter (Herr) Kollege; **a ~ at court** (*fig*) ein einflußreicher Freund; **a ~ in need is a ~ indeed** (*Prov*) Freunde in der Not gehen tausend auf ein Lot (*Prov*).
(b) (*helper, supporter*) Freund *m* ◆ **~ of the poor** Helfer *or* Freund der Armen; **~ of the arts** Förderer der schönen Künste.
(c) (*Rel*) **F~** Quäker(in *f*) *m*; **Society of F~s** Quäker *pl*.
friendless ['frendlɪs] *adj* ohne Freunde.
friendliness ['frendlɪnɪs] *n see adj* Freundlichkeit *f*; Freundschaftlichkeit *f*.
friendly ['frendlɪ] [1] *adj* **(a)** (*+er*) *person, smile, welcome* freundlich; *attitude also, advice, feelings* freundschaftlich; *breeze* angenehm ◆ **to be ~ to sb** zu jdm freundlich sein; **to be ~ with sb** mit jdm befreundet sein; **that wasn't a very ~ thing to do** das war nicht gerade sehr freundlich; **F~ Society** (*Brit*) Versicherungsverein *m* auf Gegenseitigkeit, Hilfskasse *f*.
(b) (*Sport*) *match* Freundschafts-.
[2] *n* (*Sport*) Freundschaftsspiel *nt*.
Friendly Islands *npl* Freundschafts-Inseln *pl*.
friendship ['frendʃɪp] *n* Freundschaft *f*.
Friesian ['friːʒən] [1] *adj* **(a)** friesisch ◆ **~ Islands** Friesische Inseln *pl*. **(b)** *cattle* holstein-friesisch.
[2] *n* **(a)** Friese *m*, Friesin *f*. **(b)** (*language*) Friesisch *nt*. **(c)** (*cow*) Holstein-Friese *m*/-Friesin *f*.
Friesland ['friːslənd] *n* Friesland *nt*.
frieze[1] [friːz] *n* (*Archit*) (*picture*) Fries *m*; (*thin band*) Zierstreifen *m*.
frieze[2] *n* (*Tex*) Fries *m*.
frigate ['frɪgɪt] *n* (*Naut*) Fregatte *f*.
frigging ['frɪgɪŋ] *adj, adv* (*sl*) *see* **fucking**.
fright [fraɪt] *n* **(a)** Schreck(en) *m* ◆ **to get** *or* **have a ~** sich erschrecken, einen Schreck bekommen; **to give sb a ~** jdm einen Schreck(en) einjagen, jdn erschrecken; **to take ~** es mit der Angst zu tun bekommen.
(b) (*inf: person*) Vogelscheuche *f* (*inf*) ◆ **she looks a ~ in that hat** mit dem Hut sieht sie verboten *or* zum Fürchten aus (*inf*).
frighten ['fraɪtn] [1] *vt* (*give a sudden fright*) erschrecken, Angst einjagen (*+dat*); (*make scared*) Angst machen (*+dat*), Angst einjagen (*+dat*); (*idea, thought*) ängstigen, Angst *or* Furcht einflößen (*+dat*) ◆ **I'm not easily ~ed** ich fürchte mich nicht so schnell, ich habe nicht so schnell Angst; (*with threats etc*) so schnell kann man mir keine Angst machen; **... he said in a ~ed voice ...** sagte er mit angsterfüllter Stimme; **to be ~ed by sth** vor etw (*dat*) erschrecken; **to be ~ed of sth** vor etw (*dat*) Angst haben; **don't be ~ed** (hab) keine Angst; **to be ~ed of doing sth** Angst davor haben *or* sich davor fürchten, etw zu tun; **I was ~ed out of my wits/to death** ich war zu Tode erschrocken.
[2] *vi* **she doesn't ~ easily** so leicht fürchtet sie sich nicht; (*with threats etc*) so leicht kann man ihr keine Angst machen.
◆**frighten away** *or* **off** *vt sep* abschrecken; (*deliberately*) verscheuchen.
frightening ['fraɪtnɪŋ] *adj* furchterregend, schreckerregend.
frighteningly ['fraɪtnɪŋlɪ] *adv* schrecklich, fürchterlich.
frightful *adj*, **~ly** *adv* ['fraɪtfʊl, -fəlɪ] schrecklich, furchtbar.
frightfulness ['fraɪtfʊlnɪs] *n* Schrecklichkeit, Furchtbarkeit *f*.
frigid ['frɪdʒɪd] *adj manner, welcome* kühl, frostig; (*Physiol, Psych*) frigid(e); (*Geog*) arktisch.
frigidity [frɪ'dʒɪdɪtɪ] *n* Kühle *f*; (*Physiol, Psych*) Frigidität *f*.
frill [frɪl] *n* **(a)** (*on dress, shirt etc*) Rüsche *f*; (*on animal, bird*) Kragen *m*; (*round meat, on plant pot etc*) Manschette *f*.
(b) **~s** *pl* (*fig: ornaments*) Kinkerlitzchen (*inf*), Verzierungen *pl* ◆ **with all the ~s** mit allem Drum und Dran (*inf*); **a simple meal without any ~s** ein schlichtes Essen.
frilly ['frɪlɪ] *adj* (*+er*) mit Rüschen, Rüschen-; (*fig*) *style* blumig.
fringe [frɪndʒ] [1] *n* **(a)** (*on shawl*) Fransenkante *f*, Fransen *pl*.
(b) (*Brit: hair*) Pony(fransen *pl*) *m*.
(c) (*fig: periphery*) Rand *m* ◆ **on the ~ of the forest** am Waldrand; **there is a ~ of the Labour Party which ...** es gibt eine Randgruppe der Labour-Party, die ...; **to live on the ~(s) of society** am Rande der Gesellschaft leben; **the outer ~s of a town** die Randbezirke einer Stadt; *see* **lunatic**.
[2] *vt* mit Fransen versehen ◆ **~d with silk** mit Seidenfransen; **a lawn ~d with trees** ein von Bäumen umsäumtes Rasenstück.
fringe: ~ benefits *npl* zusätzliche Leistungen *pl*; **~ group** *n* Randgruppe *f*; **~ theatre** *n* avantgardistisches Theater.
frippery ['frɪpərɪ] *n* (*pej*) (*cheap ornament*) Flitter *m*, Kinkerlitzchen *pl* (*inf*); (*on dress*) Tand, Flitterkram (*inf*) *m*.
frisbee ® ['frɪzbɪ] *n* Frisbee ® *nt*.
Frisian ['frɪsɪən] *adj, n see* **Friesian 1 (a), 2 (a, b).**
frisk [frɪsk] [1] *vi* (*leap about*) umhertollen.
[2] *vt suspect etc* durchsuchen, filzen (*inf*).
friskiness ['frɪskɪnɪs] *n* Verspieltheit *f*.
frisky ['frɪskɪ] *adj* (*+er*) verspielt.
fritillary [frɪ'tɪlərɪ] *n* (*butterfly*) Perlmutterfalter *m*.
fritter[1] ['frɪtəʳ] *vt* (*also* **~ away**) *money, time* vertun (*inf*), vergeuden, verplempern (*inf*).
fritter[2] *n* (*Cook*) Beignet *m*, Schmalzgebackenes *nt no pl* mit Füllung ◆ **apple ~** Apfel-Beignet *m*.
frivolity [frɪ'vɒlɪtɪ] *n* Frivolität *f*.
frivolous ['frɪvələs] *adj* frivol; *person, life, remark also* leichtsinnig, leichtfertig.
frivolously ['frɪvələslɪ] *adv* frivol; *remark also* leichtfertig.
frizz [frɪz] [1] *vt hair* kräuseln.
[2] *vi* sich kräuseln, kraus werden.
frizzle ['frɪzl] [1] *vi* (*sizzle*) brutzeln.
[2] *vt bacon etc* knusprig braten ◆ **the meat was all ~d up** das Fleisch war ganz verbraten.
frizz(l)y ['frɪz(l)ɪ] *adj* (*+er*) *hair* kraus.
fro [frəʊ] *adv see* **to, to-ing and fro-ing.**
frock [frɒk] *n* Kleid *nt*; (*of monk*) Kutte *f*.
frock coat *n* Gehrock *m*.
frog[1] [frɒg] *n* **(a)** Frosch *m* ◆ **to have a ~ in one's throat** einen Frosch im Hals haben. **(b)** **F~** (*Brit pej sl: French person*) Franzmann (*inf*), Franzose *m*, Französin *f*.
frog[2] *n* (*fastening*) Paspelverschluß *m*.
frog: ~ kick *n* Beinschlag *m* beim Brustschwimmen; **~man** *n* Froschmann *m*; **~march** *vt* (*Brit*) (ab)schleppen (*inf*), (weg)schleifen; (*carry*) zu viert wegtragen; **they ~marched him in** sie schleppten ihn herein (*inf*); **~spawn** *n* Froschlaich *m*.
frolic ['frɒlɪk] (*vb: pret, ptp* **~ked**) [1] *vi* (*also* **~ about** *or* **around**) umhertollen, umhertoben.
[2] *n* (*romp*) Herumtoben, Herumtollen *nt*; (*gaiety*) Ausgelassenheit *f*; (*prank*) Jux, Scherz, Spaß *m* ◆ **the children had a ~ on the lawn** die Kinder tobten *or* tollten auf dem Rasen herum.
frolicsome ['frɒlɪksəm] *adj* übermütig, ausgelassen.
from [frɒm] *prep* **(a)** (*indicating starting place*) von (*+dat*); (*indicating place of origin*) aus (*+dat*) ◆ **he/the train has come ~ London** er/der Zug ist von London gekommen; **he/this wine comes** *or* **is ~ Germany** er/dieser Wein kommt *or* ist aus Deutschland; **where has he come ~ today?** von wo ist er heute gekommen?; **where does he come ~?, where is he ~?** woher kommt *or* stammt er?; **the train ~ Manchester** der Zug aus Manchester; **the train ~ Manchester to London** der Zug von Manchester nach London; **~ London to Edinburgh** von London nach Edinburgh; **~ house to house** von Haus zu Haus.
(b) (*indicating time*) (*in past*) seit (*+dat*); (*in future*) ab (*+dat*), von (*+dat*) ... an ◆ **~ last week until** *or* **to yesterday** von letzter Woche bis gestern; **~ ... on** ab ...; **~ now on** von jetzt an, ab jetzt; **~ then on** von da an; (*in past also*) seither; **~ his childhood** von Kindheit an, von klein auf; **he comes ~ time to time** er kommt von Zeit zu Zeit; **commencing as ~ the 6th May** vom 6. Mai an, ab (dem) 6. Mai.
(c) (*indicating distance*) von (*+dat*) (... weg); (*from town etc also*) von (*+dat*) ... entfernt ◆ **the house is 10 km ~ the coast** das Haus ist 10 km von der Küste entfernt; **to go away ~ home** von zu Haus weg- *or* fortgehen.
(d) (*indicating sender, giver*) von (*+dat*) ◆ **tell him ~ me** richten Sie ihm von mir aus; **an invitation ~ the Smiths** eine Einladung von den Smiths; **"~ ..."** (*on envelope, parcel*) „Absender ...", „Abs. ...".
(e) (*indicating removal*) von (*+dat*); (*out of: from pocket, cupboard etc*) aus (*+dat*) ◆ **to take/grab** *etc* **sth ~ sb** jdm etw wegnehmen/wegreißen *etc*; **to steal sth ~ sb** jdm etw stehlen; **he took it ~ the top/middle/bottom of the pile** er nahm es oben vom Stapel/aus der Mitte des Stapels/unten vom Stapel weg.
(f) (*indicating source*) von (*+dat*); (*out of*) aus (*+dat*) ◆ **where did you get that ~?** wo hast du das her?, woher hast du das?; **I got that ~ the corner shop/the library/Kathy** ich habe das aus dem Laden an der Ecke/aus der Bücherei/von Kathy; **to drink ~ a stream/glass** aus einem Bach/Glas trinken; **quotation ~ Hamlet/the Bible/Shakespeare** Zitat *nt* aus Hamlet/aus der Bibel/nach Shakespeare; **translated ~ the English** aus dem Englischen übersetzt.

(g) *(modelled on)* nach *(+dat)* ◆ **painted ~ life** nach dem Leben gemalt.
(h) *(indicating lowest amount)* ab *(+dat)* ◆ **~ £2/the age of 16 (upwards)** ab £ 2/ab 16 Jahren (aufwärts); **dresses (ranging) ~ £60 to £80** Kleider *pl* zwischen £ 60 und £ 80; **there were ~ 10 to 15 people there** es waren zwischen 10 und 15 Leute da.
(i) *(indicating escape)* **he fled ~ the enemy** er floh vor dem Feind; **he got away ~ his pursuers** er entkam seinen Verfolgern; **he ran away ~ home** er rannte von zu Hause weg; **he escaped ~ prison** er entkam aus dem Gefängnis.
(j) *(indicating change)* **things went ~ bad to worse** es wurde immer schlimmer; **he went ~ office boy to director** er stieg vom Laufjungen zum Direktor auf; **a price increase ~ 1 mark to 1.50 marks** eine Preiserhöhung von 1 DM auf 1,50 DM; **~ log cabin to White House** aus der Blockhütte ins Weiße Haus.
(k) *(indicating difference)* **he is quite different ~ the others** er ist ganz anders als die andern; **to tell black ~ white** Schwarz und Weiß auseinanderhalten.
(l) *(because of, due to)* **to act ~ conviction** aus Überzeugung handeln; **to die ~ fatigue** an Erschöpfung sterben; **weak ~ hunger/tiredness** schwach vor Hunger/Müdigkeit.
(m) *(on the basis of)* **~ experience** aus Erfahrung; **to judge ~ appearances** nach dem Äußeren urteilen; **~ your point of view** von Ihrem Standpunkt aus (gesehen); **to conclude ~ the information** aus den Informationen einen Schluß ziehen, von den Informationen schließen; **~ what I heard** nach dem, was ich gehört habe; **~ what I can see ...** nach dem, was ich sehen kann, ...; **~ the look of things ...** (so) wie die Sache aussieht, ...
(n) *(in set phrases) see also other element* **to prevent/stop sb ~ doing sth** jdn daran hindern/davor zurückhalten, etw zu tun; **he prevented me ~ coming** er hielt mich davon ab, zu kommen; **to shelter ~ the rain** sich vor dem Regen unterstellen, vor dem Regen Zuflucht suchen.
(o) *(+adv)* von ◆ **~ inside/underneath** von innen/unten.
(p) *(+prep)* **~ above** *or* **over/across sth** über etw *(acc)* hinweg; **~ beneath** *or* **underneath sth** unter etw *(dat)* hervor; **~ out of sth** aus etw heraus; **~ before his mother's death** aus der Zeit vor dem Tod seiner Mutter; **~ among the trees** zwischen den Bäumen hervor; **~ inside/outside the house** von drinnen/draußen; **~ beyond the grave** aus dem Jenseits.

frond [frɒnd] *n (of fern)* Farnwedel *m*; *(of palm)* Palmwedel *m*.

front [frʌnt] [1] *n* **(a)** *(forward side, exterior)* Vorderseite *f*; *(forward part, including interior)* Vorderteil *nt*; *(of house etc: façade)* Vorderfront, Stirnseite *f*; *(of shirt, dress)* Vorderteil *nt*; *(dickey)* Hemdbrust *f*; *(Theat: auditorium)* Zuschauerraum *m* ◆ **in ~** vorne; *(in line, race etc also)* an der Spitze; **in ~ of sb/sth** vor jdm/etw; **at the ~ of** *(inside)* vorne in *(+dat)*; *(outside)* vor *(+dat)*; *(at the head of)* an der Spitze *(+gen)*; **to be in ~** vorne sein; *(Sport)* vorn(e) *or* an der Spitze liegen; **look in ~ of you** blicken Sie nach vorne; **in ~ of you you see ...** vor sich *(dat)* sehen Sie ...; **in** *or* **at the ~ of the train/class** vorne im Zug/Klassenzimmer; **he reached the ~ of the queue** er erreichte die Spitze der Schlange; **she spilt tea down the ~ of her dress** sie verschüttete Tee vorn über ihr Kleid.
(b) *(Mil, Pol, Met)* Front *f* ◆ **he fell at the ~** er ist an der Front gefallen; **they were attacked on all ~s** *(Mil)* sie wurden an allen Fronten angegriffen; *(fig)* sie wurden von allen Seiten angegriffen; **cold ~** *(Met)* Kalt(luft)front *f*; **we must present a common/united ~** wir müssen eine gemeinsame/geschlossene Front bieten; **on the wages ~** was die Löhne betrifft.
(c) *(Brit) (of sea)* Strandpromenade *f*; *(of lake)* Uferpromenade *f*.
(d) *(outward appearance)* Fassade *f* ◆ **to put on a bold ~** eine tapfere Miene zur Schau stellen; **to preserve a calm ~** nach außen hin ruhig bleiben; **it's just a ~** das ist nur Fassade.
(e) *(cover for illicit activity)* Tarnung, Fassade *f*.
(f) *(US: figurehead of organization)* Strohmann *m*, Aushängeschild *nt*.
(g) *no pl (effrontery)* Stirn *f* ◆ **to have the ~ to do sth** die Frechheit besitzen *or* die Stirn haben, etw zu tun.
(h) *(poet: brow, face)* Antlitz *nt (poet)*.
[2] *adv* **up ~** vorne; **to move up ~** nach vorne rücken; **50% up ~** 50% Vorschuß; **to attack ~ and rear** von vorn und hinten angreifen; **eyes ~!** *(Mil)* Augen geradeaus!; *see also* **up-front**.
[3] *vi* **the houses/windows ~ onto the street** die Häuser liegen/die Fenster gehen auf die Straße hinaus.
[4] *adj* vorderste(r, s); *row, page also* erste(r, s); *tooth, wheel, room, plan, elevation, view* Vorder-; *(Phon) vowel* Vorderzungen- ◆ **~ seat** Platz *m* in der ersten Reihe; *(Aut)* Vordersitz *m*; *(fig)* Logenplatz *m*; **~ garden** Vorgarten *m*; **the ~ end of the train** die Spitze des Zuges; **~ view** Vorderansicht *f*; *(Tech)* Aufriß *m*.

frontage [ˈfrʌntɪdʒ] *n (of building)* Front, Vorderseite *f*; *(ground in front of house)* Grundstück *or* Gelände *nt* vor dem Haus ◆ **the shop has a ~ on two streets** der Laden hat Schaufenster auf *or* zu zwei Straßen hinaus; **because of its ~ onto the sea** weil es zur See hinaus liegt.

frontal [ˈfrʌntl] *adj (Mil)* Frontal-; *(Anat)* Stirn-; *see* **full ~**.

front: ~ bench *n (Parl)* vorderste *or* erste Reihe *(wo die führenden Politiker sitzen)*; **~ door** *n* Haustür *f*; **~ end** *n (Comput)* Frontende *nt*.

frontier [ˈfrʌntɪəʳ] *n* Grenze, Landesgrenze *f*; *(boundary area)* Grenzgebiet *nt*; *(fig: of knowledge)* Grenze *f* ◆ **to push back the ~s of science** auf wissenschaftliches Neuland vorstoßen.

frontier *in cpds post, town, zone* Grenz-; **~ dispute** *n* Grenzstreitigkeiten *pl*.

frontiersman [ˈfrʌntɪəzmən] *n, pl* **-men** [-mən] Grenzbewohner, Grenzer *m*.

frontier station *n* Grenzposten *m*.

frontispiece [ˈfrʌntɪspiːs] *n* zweite Titelseite, Frontispiz *nt (obs)*.

front: ~ line *n* Front(linie) *f*; **~-line** *adj troops* Front-; *(fig) management etc* in vorderster Front; **~ loader** *n* Frontlader *m*; **~ man** *n* Mann *m* an der Spitze; *(pej)* Strohmann *m*; **~ matter** *n* Titelei *f*; **~ money** *n (US: paid up-front)* Vorschuß *m*; **~ organization** *n* Tarn- *or* Deckorganisation *f*; **~-page** [1] *adj news* auf der ersten Seite; **it's not exactly ~-page news** das wird nicht gerade Schlagzeilen machen; [2] *n* **~ page** erste Seite, Titelseite *f*; **to hit the ~ page** Schlagzeilen machen; **~ rank** *n* **to be in the ~ rank** *(fig)* zur Spitze zählen; **~-runner** *n* **(a)** Läufer(in *f*) *m* an der Spitze; **he's by nature a ~-runner** er läuft am liebsten an der Spitze; **(b)** *(fig)* Spitzenreiter *m*; **~-wheel drive** *n* Vorderradantrieb *m*.

frost [frɒst] [1] *n* **(a)** Frost *m*; *(on leaves etc)* Rauhreif *m* ◆ **late ~s** späte Frostperioden *pl*; **ten degrees of ~** zehn Grad Kälte. **(b)** *(fig: cold manner)* Kühle, Kälte, Frostigkeit *f*. **(c)** *(dated sl: failure)* Pleite *f (inf)*, Reinfall *m*.
[2] *vt* **(a)** *glass* mattieren. **(b)** *(esp US) cake* mit Zuckerguß überziehen, glasieren. **(c)** *(quick-freeze)* einfrieren, tiefkühlen.

frost: ~bite *n* Frostbeulen *pl*; *(more serious)* Erfrierungen *pl*; **to get ~bite on one's hands** Frostbeulen an den Händen bekommen; sich *(dat)* die Hände erfrieren; **~bitten** *adj hands, feet* erfroren; **~bound** *adj ground* hartgefroren.

frosted [ˈfrɒstɪd] *adj* **(a)** **~ glass** mattiertes Glas; *(textured)* geriffeltes Glas. **(b)** *(esp US Cook) cake* mit Zuckerguß überzogen, glasiert ◆ **~ icing** Zuckerguß *m*. **(c)** *(quick-frozen) food* tiefgekühlt, Tiefkühl-. **(d)** *(spoilt by frost) plants, vegetables* erfroren.

frostiness [ˈfrɒstɪnɪs] *n (of weather, welcome)* Frostigkeit *f*.

frosting [ˈfrɒstɪŋ] *n (esp US: icing)* Zuckerguß *m*.

frosty [ˈfrɒstɪ] *adj (+er) weather* frostig; *window* bereift, mit Eisblumen bedeckt; *(fig) welcome* frostig; *look* eisig.

froth [frɒθ] [1] *n* **(a)** *(on liquids, Med)* Schaum *m*.
(b) *(light conversation, frivolities)* Firlefanz *m*.
[2] *vi* schäumen ◆ **the beer ~ed over the edge of the glass** der Schaum floß über den Rand des Bierglases; **the dog was ~ing at the mouth** der Hund hatte Schaum vor dem Maul; **he was ~ing at the mouth (with rage)** er schäumte vor Wut.

frothy [ˈfrɒθɪ] *adj (+er) beer, liquid, sea* schäumend *attr*; *cream* schaumig, locker; *clouds* duftig; *talk etc* hohl, leer, seicht.

frown [fraʊn] [1] *n* Stirnrunzeln *nt no pl* ◆ **to give a ~** die Stirn(e) runzeln; ... **he said with a ~** ... sagte er mit einem Stirnrunzeln; **angry ~** finsterer Blick; **worried/puzzled ~** sorgenvoller/verdutzter Gesichtsausdruck, sorgenvolles/verdutztes Gesicht; **his worried ~** seine sorgenvoll gerunzelte Stirn.
[2] *vi (lit, fig)* die Stirn(e) runzeln *(at* über *+acc)*.

◆**frown (up)on** *vi +prep obj (fig) suggestion, idea* mißbilligen, mit Stirnrunzeln betrachten ◆ **not wearing a tie is ~ed ~** es wird beanstandet, wenn man keinen Schlips trägt.

frowning [ˈfraʊnɪŋ] *adj face, looks* finster; *(disapproving)* mißbilligend; *(fig) cliff* drohend, düster.

frowsy, frowzy [ˈfraʊzɪ] *adj (+er) (unkempt)* schlampig, schlud(e)rig.

froze [frəʊz] *pret of* **freeze**.

frozen [ˈfrəʊzn] [1] *ptp of* **freeze**.
[2] *adj* **(a)** *river* zugefroren, vereist; *North* eisig; *wastes* Eis-; *person* eiskalt; *body* erfroren; *pipes* eingefroren ◆ **I am ~** mir ist eiskalt; **I'm absolutely ~ stiff** ich bin total steifgefroren; **my hands are ~** meine Hände sind eiskalt *or* steifgefroren; **your tiny hand is ~** wie eiskalt ist dies Händchen.
(b) **~ foods** Tiefkühlkost *f*; **~ peas** tiefgekühlte *or* gefrorene Erbsen *pl*; **~ fish/meat** Gefrierfisch *m*/-fleisch *nt*.
(c) *(pegged) prices, wages* eingefroren ◆ **~ assets** *(Fin)* festliegendes Kapital, eingefrorene Guthaben *pl*.

FRS *abbr of* **Fellow of the Royal Society**.

fructification [ˌfrʌktɪfɪˈkeɪʃən] *n (lit, fig: making fruitful)* Befruchtung *f*; *(forming fruit)* Fruchtbildung *f*.

fructify [ˈfrʌktɪfaɪ] [1] *vt (lit, fig) seed, imagination* befruchten.
[2] *vi* Früchte tragen.

frugal [ˈfruːgəl] *adj person* sparsam, genügsam; *meal* einfach, schlicht, frugal *(geh)*.

frugality [fruːˈgælɪtɪ] *n (thrift)* Sparsamkeit *f*; *(of meal)* Schlichtheit, Frugalität *(geh) f*.

fruit [fruːt] [1] *n* **(a)** *(as collective)* Obst *nt*; *(fig)* Frucht *f*; *(Bot)* Frucht *f* ◆ **is it a ~ or a vegetable?** ist es Obst oder Gemüse?; **what is your favourite ~?** welches Obst magst du am liebsten?; **southern ~s** Südfrüchte *pl*; **the ~s of the earth** die Früchte *pl* des Feldes; **to bear ~** *(lit, fig)* Früchte tragen; **the ~(s) of my labour** die Früchte *pl* meiner Arbeit.
(b) *(dated Brit inf)* **old ~** alter Knabe *(inf)*.
(c) *(inf: homosexual)* Süße(r) *m (inf)*, warmer Bruder *(inf)*.
[2] *vi* Früchte tragen.

fruit: ~ bat *n* Flughund *m*; **~ cake** *n* englischer Kuchen; *(sl: eccentric)* Spinner *m (inf)*; **as nutty as a ~ cake** *(inf)* total verrückt; **~ cup** *n* **(a)** *(drink)* Cocktail *m* mit Früchten; **(b)** *(US)* Frucht- *or* Früchtebecher *m*; **~ dish** *n* Obstteller *m*; **~ drop** *n* Drops *m*, Früchtebonbon *m or nt*.

fruiterer [ˈfruːtərəʳ] *n (esp Brit)* Obsthändler *m*.

fruit: ~ farmer *n* Obstbauer *m*; **~ farming** *n* Obstanbau *m*; **~ fly** *n* Fruchtfliege, Taufliege *f*.

fruitful [ˈfruːtfʊl] *adj* **(a)** *plant, soil* fruchtbar, ertragreich. **(b)** *(fig) life, time at university, discussion* fruchtbar; *attempt* erfolgreich ◆ **were your enquiries ~?** waren Ihre Erkundigungen erfolgreich *or* von Erfolg gekrönt *(geh)*?

fruitfully ['fru:tfəlɪ] *adv see adj (b).*

fruitfulness ['fru:tfʊlnɪs] *n (lit, fig)* Fruchtbarkeit *f.*

fruition [fru:'ɪʃən] *n (of aims, plans, ideas)* Erfüllung, Verwirklichung *f* ◆ **to come to ~** sich verwirklichen; **to bring sth to ~** etw verwirklichen.

fruit knife *n* Obstmesser *nt.*

fruitless ['fru:tlɪs] *adj* **(a)** *plant* unfruchtbar. **(b)** *(fig) attempt, discussion, investigation* fruchtlos, ergebnislos ◆ **it would be ~ to try** ein Versuch wäre zwecklos.

fruit: ~ **machine** *n (Brit)* Spielautomat *m;* ~ **salad** *n* Obstsalat *m; (fig inf)* Lametta *nt;* ~ **tree** *n* Obstbaum *m.*

fruity ['fru:tɪ] *adj (+er)* **(a)** *(like fruit)* fruchtartig, obstartig; *taste, smell* Frucht-, Obst-; *wine* fruchtig ◆ **it has a ~ taste** es schmeckt nach Obst. **(b)** *(esp Brit inf) story* gesalzen, gepfeffert *(inf)* ◆ **to get ~** keck werden. **(c)** *voice* rauchig. **(d)** *(US inf: homosexual)* schwul *(sl).*

frump [frʌmp] *n (pej)* Vogelscheuche *f (inf)* ◆ **old ~** alte Schachtel *(inf).*

frumpish ['frʌmpɪʃ] *adj (pej)* tuntig *(inf),* tantenhaft.

frustrate [frʌ'streɪt] *vt hopes* zunichte machen; *plans, plot* durchkreuzen, zerstören; *person* frustrieren ◆ **he was ~d in his efforts** seine Anstrengungen waren umsonst *or* vergebens.

frustrated [frʌ'streɪtɪd] *adj person* frustriert.

frustrating [frʌ'streɪtɪŋ] *adj* frustrierend ◆ **it's so ~** das ist alles so frustrierend, so ein Frust *(sl).*

frustratingly [frʌ'streɪtɪŋlɪ] *adv slow, complex* frustrierend.

frustration [frʌ'streɪʃən] *n* Frustration *f no pl; (of hopes, plans, plot)* Zerschlagung *f* ◆ **the ~s of life in a city** die Frustration *or* der Frust *(sl)* eines Lebens in der Stadt; **he has had a number of ~s during the course of this project** er hat im Verlauf dieses Projektes eine Reihe von Rückschlägen gehabt.

fry¹ [fraɪ] *npl (fish)* kleine Fische *pl* ◆ **small ~** *(unimportant people)* kleine Fische *(inf); (children)* Kroppzeug *nt (inf).*

fry² [1] *vt* **(a)** *meat* (in der Pfanne) braten ◆ **to ~ an egg** ein Spiegelei machen, ein Ei in die Pfanne schlagen; **fried eggs** Spiegeleier *pl;* **fried potatoes** Bratkartoffeln *pl.* **(b)** *(US sl: electrocute)* auf dem elektrischen Stuhl hinrichten.

[2] *vi* **(a)** braten ◆ **we're absolutely ~ing in this heat** *(inf)* wir schmoren (in dieser Hitze) *(inf).* **(b)** *(US sl)* auf dem elektrischen Stuhl hingerichtet werden.

[3] *n (US)* Barbecue *nt.*

◆**fry up** *vt sep* (auf)braten, in die Pfanne hauen *(inf).*

frying pan ['fraɪɪŋ,pæn] *n* Bratpfanne *f* ◆ **to jump out of the ~ into the fire** *(Prov)* vom Regen in die Traufe kommen *(Prov).*

fry-up ['fraɪʌp] *n* Pfannengericht *nt* ◆ **to have a ~** sich *(dat)* etwas zusammenbrutzeln *(inf).*

ft *abbr of* **foot** ft; **feet** ft.

FT *abbr of* **Financial Times.**

FTC *(US) abbr of* **Federal Trade Commission.**

FTP, ftp *(Comput) abbr of* **file transfer protocol** FTP.

fuchsia ['fju:ʃə] *n* Fuchsie *f.*

fuck [fʌk] *(vulg)* [1] *vt* **(a)** *(lit)* ficken *(vulg).* **(b) you can get ~ed/~ you!** leck mich am Arsch *(vulg);* **~ him!** der kann mich doch am Arsch lecken *(vulg);* **~ what he thinks!** ich scheiß was auf seine Meinung *(sl);* **~ this car!** dieses Scheißauto! *(sl);* **~ me, he didn't say that, did he?** leck mich am Arsch, das hat der wirklich gesagt? *(sl).*

[2] *vi* ficken *(vulg).*

[3] *n* **(a)** Fick *m (vulg)* ◆ **to have a ~** ficken *(vulg);* **she's a good ~** sie fickt gut *(vulg).* **(b) I don't give** *or* **care a ~** ich kümmere mich einen Scheiß darum *(sl);* **who/what/where the ~ is that?** wer/was/wo ist denn das, verdammt noch mal? *(sl);* **like ~ he will!** das werden wir erst noch sehen, verdammt noch mal! *(inf).*

[4] *interj* (verdammte) Scheiße *(sl),* verdammt und zugenäht *(sl),* Herrgottsack *(S Ger vulg).*

◆**fuck about** *or* **around** *(vulg)* [1] *vi* rumgammeln *(inf)* ◆ **to ~ ~ with sb** jdn verarschen *(sl);* **someone's been ~ing ~ with the engine** verdammt, da hat irgend so ein Arsch am Motor rumgefummelt *(sl).*

[2] *vt sep* verarschen *(sl).*

◆**fuck off** *vi (vulg)* sich verpissen *(sl)* ◆ **~ ~!** verpiß dich! *(sl),* hau ab, du Arsch! *(sl).*

◆**fuck up** *(vulg)* [1] *vt sep* versauen *(sl); engine, piece of work also* Scheiße bauen mit *(sl)* ◆ **you've really ~ed me ~** *(let down, spoilt plans etc)* du hast mir die Sache echt versaut *(sl);* **she is really ~ed ~** *(psychologically)* sie ist total verkorkst *(inf).*

[2] *vi* Scheiß machen *(sl).*

fuck-all ['fʌkɔ:l] *(vulg)* [1] *n* einen Scheiß *(sl)* ◆ **he knows ~ about it** der hat keinen Schiß Ahnung davon *(sl);* **it's got ~ to do with him** einen Scheiß hat das mit ihm zu tun *(sl);* **there was ~ to drink** in dem ganzen Puff gab's nichts zu trinken *(sl);* **I've done ~ all day** ich hab den ganzen Tag nichts geschafft gekriegt *(inf);* **~ you care!** einen Scheiß kümmert es dich! *(sl).*

[2] *adj attr* **that's ~ use** das ist ja vielleicht ein Scheiß *(sl) or* total bekackt *(vulg) or* für'n Arsch *(vulg);* **he was ~ help** was der gemacht hat, war für'n Arsch *(vulg);* **he's got ~ idea how to do it** er hat keinen Schiß Ahnung, wie er das machen soll *(sl).*

fucker ['fʌkəʳ] *n (vulg)* Arsch(loch *nt*) *(vulg),* Saftsack *(vulg) m.*

fucking ['fʌkɪŋ] *(vulg)* [1] *adj* verdammt *(sl),* Scheiß- *(sl)* ◆ **all the ~ time** die ganze verdammte Zeit (über) *(sl);* **he doesn't have a ~ chance** für den ist nichts drin *(sl);* **~ hell!** verdammte Scheiße! *(sl),* verdammt noch mal! *(sl);* **it's a ~ nuisance** es ist eine verdammte Landplage *(sl);* **he's a ~ idiot/genius/millionaire** der ist ein verdammter Idiot/er ist ein Genie/Millionär, verdammt noch mal! *(all sl).*

[2] *adv* **it's ~ raining again** verdammte Scheiße, das regnet schon wieder *(sl).*

fuck-up ['fʌkʌp] *n (vulg)* **what a ~!** was für eine (totale) Scheiße! *(sl);* **there's been a ~** da hat einer Scheiße gebaut *(sl).*

fuddled ['fʌdld] *adj (muddled)* verwirrt, verdattert *(inf); (tipsy)* bedüdelt *(inf),* beschwipst, angesäuselt.

fuddy-duddy ['fʌdɪ,dʌdɪ] *(inf)* [1] *adj* verknöchert, verkalkt.

[2] *n* komischer Kauz *(inf)* ◆ **an old ~** ein alter Kauz.

fudge [fʌdʒ] [1] *n* **(a)** *(Cook)* Fondant *m.* **(b)** *(Press) (space for stop press)* Spalte *f* für letzte Meldungen; *(stop press news)* letzte Meldungen *pl.* **(c) her answer was a ~** ihre Antwort war ein Ausweichmanöver.

[2] *vt* **(a)** *(fake up) story, excuse* sich *(dat)* aus den Fingern saugen, (frei) erfinden. **(b)** *(dodge) question, issue* ausweichen *(+dat),* aus dem Wege gehen *(+dat).*

fuel [fjʊəl] [1] *n* Brennstoff *m,* Brennmaterial *nt; (for vehicle)* Kraftstoff *m; (petrol)* Benzin *nt; (Aviat, Space)* Treibstoff *m; (fig)* Nahrung *f* ◆ **lighter ~** Feuerzeugbenzin *nt;* **to add ~ to the flames** *or* **fire** *(fig)* Öl in die Flammen *or* ins Feuer gießen; **what kind of ~ do you use in your central heating?** womit betreiben Sie Ihre Zentralheizung?; *see* **solid ~.**

[2] *vt stove, furnace etc (fill)* mit Brennstoff versorgen; *(use for ~)* betreiben; *ships etc (fill)* auftanken, betanken; *(drive, propel)* antreiben; *(fig) debate* anfachen ◆ **they are now ~led atomically** sie sind jetzt atomgetrieben.

[3] *vi (ship, engine, aircraft)* Brennstoff/Treibstoff *m etc* aufnehmen, (auf)tanken ◆ **~ling station** *(US)* Tankstelle *f;* **~ling stop** Landung *f* zum Auftanken.

fuel: ~ **cell** *n* Brennstoffzelle *f;* ~ **gauge** *n* Benzinuhr, Tankuhr *f;* **~-injected** *adj* Einspritz-; ~ **injection** *n* (Benzin)einspritzung *f;* **engine with ~ injection** Einspritzmotor *m;* ~ **oil** *n* Gasöl *nt;* ~ **pump** *n* Benzinpumpe *f;* ~ **rod** *n* Brennstab *m;* ~ **shortage** *n* Brennstoffknappheit *f;* ~ **tank** *n* Öltank *m.*

fug [fʌg] *n (esp Brit inf)* Mief *m (inf).*

fuggy ['fʌgɪ] *adj (+er) (esp Brit inf)* muffig, miefig *(inf).*

fugitive ['fju:dʒɪtɪv] [1] *n* Flüchtling *m* ◆ **he is a ~ from the law** er ist auf der Flucht vor dem Gesetz.

[2] *adj* **(a)** *(runaway)* flüchtig, auf der Flucht. **(b)** *(liter) thought, happiness, hour* flüchtig.

fugue [fju:g] *n (Mus)* Fuge *f.*

fulcrum ['fʌlkrəm] *n* Dreh- *or* Stützpunkt *m; (fig: of argument, plan, organization)* Angelpunkt *m.*

fulfil, *(US)* **fulfill** [fʊl'fɪl] *vt condition, desire, one's duties, hopes* erfüllen; *task, order* ausführen ◆ **the prophecy was ~led** die Prophezeiung erfüllte sich; **being a mother didn't ~ her** sie fand im Muttersein keine Erfüllung; **to be** *or* **feel ~led** Erfüllung finden; **to ~ oneself** sich selbst verwirklichen.

fulfilling [fʊl'fɪlɪŋ] *adj* **a ~ job** ein Beruf, in dem man Erfüllung findet.

fulfilment, *(US)* **fulfillment** [fʊl'fɪlmənt] *n* Erfüllung *f* ◆ **to bring sth to ~** etw zur Erfüllung bringen; **to come to ~** in Erfüllung gehen; *(life's work)* seine Erfüllung finden.

full [fʊl] [1] *adj (+er)* **(a)** *(filled) room, theatre, train* voll ◆ **to be ~ of ...** voller *(+gen) or* voll von ... sein, voll sein mit ...; **he's ~ of good ideas** er steckt voll(er) guter Ideen; **a look ~ of hate** ein haßerfüllter Blick, ein Blick voller Haß; **his heart was ~** *(liter)* das Herz lief ihm über; **~ house** *(Theat)* (Vorstellung) ausverkauft; *(Cards)* Full house *nt;* **each night they played to ~ houses** sie spielten jeden Abend vor vollem Haus; **I am ~ (up)** *(inf),* ich bin (papp)satt, ich bin voll (bis obenhin) *(inf);* **we are ~ up for July** wir sind für Juli völlig ausgebucht.

(b) *(maximum, complete)* voll; *description, report* vollständig; *understanding, sympathy* vollste(r, s) ◆ **at ~ speed** in voller Fahrt; **to fall ~ length** der Länge nach hinfallen; **roses in ~ bloom** Rosen in voller Blüte; **that's a ~ day's work** damit habe ich *etc* den ganzen Tag zu tun; **I need a ~ night's sleep** ich muß mich (ein)mal gründlich ausschlafen; **to be in ~ flight** kopflos fliehen; **battalion at ~ strength** Bataillon in Sollstärke; **I waited two ~ hours** ich habe geschlagene zwei *or* zwei ganze Stunden gewartet; **the ~ particulars** die genauen *or* alle Einzelheiten; **a ~ colonel** ein Oberst *m;* **~ employment** Vollbeschäftigung *f;* **~ member** Vollmitglied *nt;* **~ name** Vor- und Zuname *m;* **to run ~ tilt into sth** mit voller Wucht *or* in voller Fahrt in etw *(acc) or* auf etw *(acc)* rennen; **to go at ~ tilt** rasen, Volldampf *(inf) or* volle Pulle *(inf)* fahren; **a very ~ colour** eine (sehr) satte Farbe; **it's in ~ colour** das ist in Farbe; **shots of the Rocky Mountains in ~ colour** schöne Farbaufnahmen von den Rocky Mountains.

(c) *(preoccupied)* **to be ~ of oneself** von sich (selbst) eingenommen sein, nur sich selbst im Kopf haben; **she was ~ of the news** sie platzte vor Neuigkeiten; **she was ~ of it** sie hat gar nicht mehr aufgehört, davon zu reden; **the papers were ~ of it for weeks** die Zeitungen waren wochenlang voll davon; **he's always so ~ of what he's going to do** er ist dauernd von seinen Plänen dran *(inf).*

(d) *(rounded) lips, face* voll; *figure, skirt etc* füllig; *(Naut) sails* voll, gebläht.

[2] *adv* **(a)** *(at least)* **it is a ~ five miles from here** es sind volle *or* gute fünf Meilen von hier.

(b) *(very, perfectly)* **I know it ~ well** ich weiß es sehr wohl.

(c) *(directly)* **to hit sb ~ in the face** jdn voll ins Gesicht schlagen; **to look sb ~ in the face** jdm voll in die Augen sehen.

(d) ~ out *work* auf Hochtouren; *drive* mit Vollgas.

[3] *n* **(a) in ~** ganz, vollständig; **to write one's name in ~** seinen Namen ausschreiben; **to pay in ~** den vollen Betrag bezahlen. **(b) to the ~** vollständig,

total.

full: ~-back *n* (*Sport*) Verteidiger *m*; **~-blooded** ['fʊlblʌdɪd] *adj* (*vigorous*) kräftig; *person also* Vollblut-; **~-blown** *adj* **(a)** *flower* voll aufgeblüht; **~-blown Aids** Vollbild-Aids *nt*; **(b)** (*fig*) *doctor, theory* richtiggehend, ausgewachsen (*inf*); **~-bodied** ['fʊl'bɒdɪd] *adj wine* schwer, vollmundig; **~-cream milk** *n* Vollmilch *f*.

full-dress ['fʊldres] *adj* **(a)** *clothes* Gala-. **(b)** (*fig: important, ceremonious*) **~ debate** wichtige Debatte.

fuller's earth ['fʊləz,ɜːθ] *n* Fullererde, Bleicherde *f*.

full: ~ face *adj portrait* mit zugewandtem Gesicht; **~ face helmet** Integralhelm *m*; **~-faced** ['fʊlfeɪst] *adj* rundgesichtig; **~-fledged** *adj* (*US*) *see* **fully-fledged**; **~ frontal** [1] *n* Nacktdarstellung *f*; [2] *adj* oben und unten ohne (*inf*); **the ~ frontal nudity in this play** die völlig nackten Schauspieler in diesem Stück; **~-grown** *adj* ausgewachsen; **~-length** *adj portrait* lebensgroß; *film* abendfüllend; **~-lipped** *adj* vollippig; **~ moon** *n* Vollmond *m*.

ful(l)ness ['fʊlnɪs] *n* (*of detail*) Vollständigkeit *f*; (*of voice*) Klangfülle *f*; (*of colour*) Sattheit *f*; (*of sound*) Fülle *f*; (*of skirt*) Fülle, Weite *f* ◆ **out of the ~ of his heart** (*liter*) aus der Fülle seines Herzens (*liter*); **out of the ~ of his sorrow** (*liter*) aus der Tiefe seines Leides *or* Schmerzes (*liter*); **in the ~ of time** (*eventually*) zu gegebener Zeit; (*at predestined time*) da *or* als die Zeit gekommen war, da *or* als die Zeit erfüllt war.

full: ~-page *adj advertisement etc* ganzseitig; **~-scale** *adj* **(a)** *drawing, replica* in Originalgröße; **(b)** *operation, search* groß angelegt; *revision, reorganization* umfassend, total; *retreat* auf der ganzen Linie; *war* richtiggehend, ausgewachsen (*inf*); **the factory starts ~-scale operation next month** die Fabrik nimmt den vollen Arbeitsbetrieb nächsten Monat auf; **~ size(d)** *adj bicycle, violin etc* richtig (groß); **~-sized** *adj model, drawing* lebensgroß; **~ stop** *n* Punkt *m*; **to come to a ~ stop** zum völligen Stillstand kommen; **I'm not going, ~ stop!** (*inf*) ich gehe nicht und damit basta (*inf*); **~-time** [1] *adv work* ganztags; [2] *adj employment* Ganztags-, ganztägig; **it's a ~-time job** (*fig*) das kann einen den ganzen Tag *or* rund um die Uhr auf Trab halten (*inf*); [3] *n* (*Sport*) **to blow for ~-time** das Spiel abpfeifen.

fully ['fʊlɪ] *adv* **(a)** (*entirely*) völlig, voll und ganz. **(b)** (*at least*) **it is ~ two hours since he went out** es ist volle *or* gute zwei Stunden her, daß er weggegangen ist; **it's ~ a year ago** es ist gut ein Jahr her.

fully: ~-fashioned ['fʊlɪ'fæʃnd] *adj stocking, jumper* mit Paßform; **~-fledged** *adj* **(a)** *bird* flügge; **(b)** (*fig: qualified*) *doctor, architect etc* richtiggehend, ausgewachsen (*inf*); **~ paid-up** *adj member* (*lit*) ohne Beitragsrückstände; (*fig*) eingeschrieben; **~-qualified** *adj* vollqualifiziert *attr*.

fulmar ['fʊlmər] *n* Eissturmvogel *m*.

fulminate ['fʌlmɪneɪt] *vi* (*fig*) wettern, donnern.

fulsome ['fʊlsəm] *adj praise* übertrieben; (*very full*) uneingeschränkt; *manner* übertrieben.

fumble ['fʌmbl] [1] *vi* (*also* **~ about** *or* **around**) umhertasten *or* -tappen ◆ **to ~ in the dark** im Dunkeln herumtasten *or* -tappen; **to ~ in one's pockets** in seinen Taschen wühlen; **to ~ (about) for sth** nach etw suchen *or* tasten; (*in case, pocket, drawer*) nach etw wühlen; **to ~ with sth** an etw (*dat*) herumfummeln; **to ~ for words** nach Worten suchen *or* ringen.

[2] *vt* vermasseln (*inf*), verpfuschen (*inf*) ◆ **to ~ the ball** den Ball nicht sicher fangen.

fumbler ['fʌmblər] *n* Stümper *m*.

fume [fjuːm] *vi* **(a)** (*liquids*) dampfen, rauchen; (*gases*) aufsteigen. **(b)** (*fig inf: person*) wütend sein, kochen (*inf*).

fumes [fjuːmz] *npl* Dämpfe *pl*; (*of car*) Abgase *pl* ◆ **petrol ~** Benzindämpfe *pl*.

fumigate ['fjuːmɪgeɪt] *vt* ausräuchern.

fun [fʌn] [1] *n* (*amusement*) Spaß *m* ◆ **to have great ~ doing sth** viel Spaß daran haben, etw zu tun, viel Spaß an etw (*dat*) haben; **for** *or* **in ~** (*as a joke*) im *or* als Scherz; **this is ~!** das macht Spaß *or* Freude!; **it's ~** es macht Spaß *or* Freude; **I'm not doing it for the ~ of it** ich mache das nicht zu meinem Vergnügen; **we just did it for ~** wir haben das nur aus *or* zum Spaß gemacht; **to spoil the ~** den Spaß verderben; **it's ~ doing this/being with him** es macht Spaß, das zu tun/mit ihm zusammen zu sein; **it's not much ~ for the others though** es ist allerdings für die anderen nicht gerade ein Vergnügen; **it takes all the ~ out of life/work** das nimmt einem den Spaß *or* die Freude am Leben/an der Arbeit; **life's not much ~ sometimes** das Leben ist manchmal nicht gerade das reinste Vergnügen; **it's no ~ living on your own/being broke** es macht nicht gerade Spaß, allein zu leben/pleite (*inf*) zu sein; **he is great ~** man kriegt mit ihm viel Spaß (*inf*) *or* viel zu lachen (*inf*); **but the children thought him great ~** aber die Kinder fanden ihn sehr lustig; **the visit was good ~** der Besuch hat viel Spaß gemacht; **what ~!** was für ein Spaß!; **you're no ~ to be with any more** es macht keinen Spaß mehr, mit dir zusammen zu sein; **that sounds like ~** das klingt gut; **I wasn't serious, I was just having a bit of ~** das hab ich nicht ernst gemeint, ich hab doch nur Spaß gemacht; **the children had ~ and games at the picnic** die Kinder haben beim Picknick viel Spaß gehabt; **there'll be ~ and games over this decision** (*inf*) mit dieser Entscheidung wird es noch Spaß geben; **that should be ~ and games** das kann ja (noch) heiter werden (*inf*); **he's having ~ and games with the au-pair girl** (*inf*) er amüsiert sich mit dem Au-pair-Mädchen; **to make ~ of** *or* **poke ~ at sb/sth** sich über jdn/etw lustig machen; **we had a bit of ~ getting the car started** (*inf*) wir hatten ein bißchen Theater, ehe das Auto ansprang (*inf*); **like ~** (*US inf*) (ja,) Pustekuchen! (*inf*).

[2] *adj attr* (*sl*) **squash is a ~ game** Squash macht Spaß; **he's a real ~ person** er ist wirklich ein lustiger Kerl; **that sounds like a ~ idea** das hört sich prima an (*inf*); **~ run** Volkslauf *m* (*oft für wohltätige Zwecke durchgeführt*).

function ['fʌŋkʃən] [1] *n* **(a)** (*of heart, tool, word etc*) Funktion *f*. **(b)** (*of person*) Aufgaben, Pflichten *pl* ◆ **in his ~ as judge** in seiner Eigenschaft als Richter; **his ~ in life** seine Lebensaufgabe. **(c)** (*meeting*) Veranstaltung *f*; (*reception*) Empfang *m*; (*official ceremony*) Feier *f*. **(d)** (*Math*) Funktion *f*.

[2] *vi* funktionieren; (*heart, kidney, brain also*) arbeiten ◆ **this line in the poem ~s in two separate ways** diese Zeile im Gedicht wirkt auf zweierlei Weise; **he can't ~ without his morning coffee** ohne seinen Kaffee am Morgen ist er nicht funktionsfähig; **to ~ as** fungieren als; (*person also*) die Rolle des/der ... spielen *or* ausfüllen; (*thing also*) dienen als.

functional ['fʌŋkʃənəl] *adj* **(a)** (*able to operate*) funktionsfähig. **(b)** (*utilitarian*) zweckmäßig, funktionell. **(c)** (*Med*) Funktions- ◆ **~ disease/disorder** Funktionsstörung *f*.

functionalism ['fʌŋkʃənəlɪzəm] *n* Funktionalismus *m*.

functionary ['fʌŋkʃənərɪ] *n* Funktionär *m*.

function key *n* (*Comput*) Funktionstaste *f*.

fund [fʌnd] [1] *n* **(a)** (*Fin*) Fonds *m* ◆ **to start a ~** einen Fonds einrichten *or* gründen.

(b) **~s** *pl* Mittel, Gelder *pl* ◆ **the public ~s** die öffentlichen Mittel, die Staatsgelder *pl*; **no ~s** (*Banking*) keine Deckung; **to be in ~s** zahlungsfähig *or* bei Kasse (*inf*) sein; **to be pressed for** *or* **short of ~s** knapp bei Kasse sein (*inf*); **at the moment I haven't the ~s** mir fehlen zur Zeit die Mittel *or* Gelder *pl*; **how are we off for ~s at the moment?** wie steht die Kasse zur Zeit?

(c) (*supply: of wisdom, humour etc*) Schatz (*of* von, *gen*), Vorrat (*of* an +*dat*) *m*.

(d) **~s** *pl* (*Brit: government securities*) Staatspapiere *pl*.

[2] *vt* **(a)** *debt* ausgleichen, bezahlen; (*put up money for*) *scheme, project* finanzieren.

(b) (*invest*) *money* anlegen, investieren.

➤ **fundamental** [,fʌndə'mentl] [1] *adj* (*basic*) grundlegend; *presupposition, importance, error also, indifference, problem* grundsätzlich, fundamental; *role, characteristics also* wesentlich; (*elementary*) Grund-; *beliefs also, likes* elementar; *nature* eigentlich ◆ **to be ~ to sth** für etw von grundlegender Bedeutung *or* Wichtigkeit sein; **his ~ ignorance of this subject** seine fundamentale Unkenntnis auf diesem Gebiet; **our ~ needs/beliefs** unsere Grundbedürfnisse *pl* *or* elementaren Bedürfnisse *pl*/unsere Grundüberzeugungen *pl*; **~ tone** (*Mus*) Grundton *m*; **~ research** Grundlagenforschung *f*.

[2] *n usu pl* Grundlage *f*.

fundamentalism [,fʌndə'mentəlɪzəm] *n* Fundamentalismus *m*.

fundamentalist [,fʌndə'mentəlɪst] [1] *adj* fundamentalistisch.

[2] *n* Fundamentalist(in *f*) *m*.

fundamentally [,fʌndə'mentəlɪ] *adv* grundlegend; (*in essence*) im Grunde (genommen), im wesentlichen ◆ **there is something ~ wrong with his argument** sein Argument enthält einen grundlegenden Fehler; **is man ~ good?** ist der Mensch im Grunde *or* im wesentlichen gut?; **this is quite ~ important for us** dies ist von grundlegender Bedeutung für uns; **we differ quite ~ on this** wir sind uns hierzu von Grund auf uneinig.

fund: ~-raiser *n* Spendenbeschaffer(in *f*) *or* -sammler(in *f*) *m*; **~-raising** *n* Geldbeschaffung *f*; **~-raising campaign** Aktion *f* zur Geldbeschaffung; (*for donations*) Spendenaktion *f*.

funeral ['fjuːnərəl] *n* Begräbnis *nt*, Beerdigung, Beisetzung (*form*) *f* ◆ **were you at his ~?** waren Sie auf seiner Beerdigung?; **that's his ~ if he wants to do it** (*inf*) wenn er das machen will, ist das sein Problem (*inf*); **well that's your ~** (*inf*) na ja, das ist dein persönliches Pech (*inf*), das ist dein Problem (*inf*).

funeral: ~ director *n* Beerdigungsunternehmer *m*; **~ home** *n* (*US*) Leichenhalle *f*; **~ march** *n* Trauermarsch *m*; **~ parlour** *n* Leichenhalle *f*; **~ procession** *n* Leichenzug *m*; **~ pyre** *n* Scheiterhaufen *m*; **~ service** *n* Trauergottesdienst *m*.

funereal [fjuː'nɪərɪəl] *adj* traurig, trübselig; *voice* Trauer-.

funfair ['fʌnfɛər] *n* Kirmes *f*.

fungal ['fʌŋgl] *adj infection, disease* Pilz-.

fungi ['fʌŋgaɪ] *pl of* **fungus**.

fungicide ['fʌŋgɪsaɪd] *n* Fungizid *nt*, pilztötendes Mittel.

fungoid ['fʌŋgɔɪd], **fungous** ['fʌŋgəs] *adj* schwammartig.

fungus ['fʌŋgəs] *n*, *pl* **fungi** (*Bot, Med*) Pilz *m*; (*hum sl: whiskers etc*) Sauerkohl *m* (*inf*).

funicular (railway) [fjuː'nɪkjʊlə('reɪlweɪ)] *n* Seilbahn *f*.

funk [fʌŋk] [1] *n* **(a)** (*esp Brit inf: fear*) Schiß (*inf*), Bammel (*inf*) *m* ◆ **to be in a (blue) ~** (vor Angst) die Hosen voll haben (*inf*), mächtig *or* ganz schön Schiß *or* Bammel haben (*inf*); **to go into a (blue) ~** mächtig Schiß *or* Bammel kriegen (*inf*); **to put sb in a blue ~** jdm mächtig Bammel einjagen (*inf*).

(b) (*Mus*) Funk *m*.

[2] *vt* kneifen vor (+*dat*) (*inf*) ◆ **he ~ed it** er hat (davor) gekniffen (*inf*).

funky ['fʌŋkɪ] *adj* (+*er*) **(a)** (*esp Brit inf: cowardly*) feige, ängstlich. **(b)** (*sl*) *music* irre (*sl*). **(c)** (*US sl: terrified*) **to be ~** (fürchterlich) Schiß haben (*sl*).

fun-loving ['fʌnlʌvɪŋ] *adj* lebenslustig ◆ **a ~ girl** (*euph*) ein lebenshungriges Mädchen.

funnel ['fʌnl] [1] *n* **(a)** (*for pouring*) Trichter *m*. **(b)** (*Naut, Rail*) Schornstein *m*. **two-~led steamer** Dampfer *m* mit zwei Schornsteinen. **(c)** (*US: ventilation shaft etc*) Luftschacht *m*.

[2] *vt liquid, grain* leiten; *attention, energies also* schleusen, kanalisieren; *information, traffic also* schleusen.

funnies ['fʌnɪz] *npl* (*US: comic strips*) Witze *pl*, Witzseite *f*.

funnily ['fʌnɪlɪ] *adv see adj* ◆ **~ enough** komischerweise.

funny ['fʌnɪ] *adj* (+*er*) **(a)** (*comic*) komisch, lustig ◆ **are you trying to be ~?, are you being ~?** das soll wohl ein Witz sein?; **don't you get ~ with me!** komm

➤ LANGUAGE IN USE: **fundamental: 1 → 26.1**

du mir bloß nicht komisch (*inf*); **it's not ~** das ist *or* das finde ich überhaupt nicht komisch.
(b) (*strange*) seltsam, komisch ◆ **he is ~ that way** (*inf*) in der Beziehung ist er komisch; **don't get any ~ ideas** komm bloß nicht auf komische Gedanken; **it's a ~ thing, only last week** ... (das ist doch) komisch, erst letzte Woche ...; **~, it was here just now** komisch, gerade war es noch da.
(c) (*inf: suspicious*) **~ business** faule Sache (*inf*); **none of your ~ tricks!** keine faulen Tricks! (*inf*); **there's something ~ going on here** hier ist doch was faul (*inf*).
(d) (*inf: unwell*) **I felt all ~** mir war ganz komisch *or* mulmig.

funny: ~ bone *n* Musikantenknochen *m*; **~ farm** *n* (*inf*) Klapsmühle *f* (*inf*); **~ money** *n* ein Wahnsinnsgeld *nt* (*inf*); **house prices in the realms of ~ money** Haus-/Wohnungspreise, die Irrsinnssummen erreichen (*inf*); **~ paper** *n* (*US*) Witzseiten *pl*.

fur [fɜːʳ] [1] *n* **(a)** (*on animal*) Fell *nt*, Pelz *m*; (*for clothing*) Pelz *m* ◆ **that will really make the ~ fly** (*inf*) da werden die Fetzen fliegen (*inf*); **a ~-lined coat** ein pelzgefütterter Mantel. **(b) ~s** *pl* Pelze *pl*. **(c)** (*in kettle etc*) Kesselstein *m*; (*Med: on tongue*) Belag *m*.
[2] *attr coat, stole* Pelz; *rug* Fell-.

◆**fur up** *vi* (*kettle, boiler*) verkalken, Kesselstein ansetzen; (*tongue*) pelzig werden ◆ **to be ~red ~** belegt *or* pelzig sein.

furbelow [ˈfɜːbɪləʊ] *n* **(a)** (*old*) Falbel *f*, Faltenbesatz *m*. **(b)** *usu pl* **~s** (*pej*) Firlefanz *m*.

furbish [ˈfɜːbɪʃ] *vt* **(a)** (*polish*) blank reiben, (auf)polieren. **(b)** (*smarten up*) aufpolieren.

furious [ˈfjʊərɪəs] *adj person* wütend; *storm, sea* stürmisch, wild; *struggle* wild; *speed* rasend, rasant ◆ **fast and ~** rasant; **things at the party were going fast and ~** die Party war richtig in Schwung *or* Fahrt gekommen; **the jokes/punches came fast and ~** die Witze kamen Schlag auf Schlag/es hagelte Schläge.

furiously [ˈfjʊərɪəslɪ] *adv see adj.*

furl [fɜːl] *vt sail, flag* einrollen; *umbrella* zusammenrollen.

furlong [ˈfɜːlɒŋ] *n* Achtelmeile *f*.

furlough [ˈfɜːləʊ] *n* (*Mil, Admin*) Urlaub *m* ◆ **to go on ~** in Urlaub gehen.

furn *abbr of* **furnished** möbl.

furnace [ˈfɜːnɪs] *n* Hochofen *m*; (*Metal*) Schmelzofen *m* ◆ **this room is like a ~** dieses Zimmer ist ja das reinste Treibhaus.

furnish [ˈfɜːnɪʃ] *vt* **(a)** *house* einrichten ◆ **~ed room** möbliertes Zimmer; **to live in ~ed accommodation** zur Untermiete wohnen; **~ing fabrics** Dekorationsstoffe *pl*. **(b)** *information, reason, excuse* liefern, geben ◆ **to ~ sb with sth** jdn mit etw versorgen, jdm etw liefern; *with reason, excuse* jdm etw liefern.

furnishings [ˈfɜːnɪʃɪŋz] *npl* Mobiliar *nt*; (*with carpets etc*) Einrichtung *f* ◆ **with ~ and fittings** voll eingerichtet.

furniture [ˈfɜːnɪtʃəʳ] *n* Möbel *pl* ◆ **a piece of ~** ein Möbelstück *nt*; **I must buy some ~** ich muß Möbel kaufen; **one settee and three chairs were all the ~** die Einrichtung bestand nur aus einem Sofa und drei Stühlen; **he treats her as part of the ~** er behandelt sie, als gehöre sie zur Einrichtung; **if I stay here much longer, I'll become a part of the ~** wenn ich noch viel länger hier bleibe, gehöre ich bald zum Inventar.

furniture: ~ depository, ~ depot (*US*) *n* Möbellager *nt*; **~ remover** *n* Möbelspediteur *m*; **~ van** *n* (*Brit*) Möbelwagen *m*.

furore [fjʊəˈrɔːrɪ], (*US*) **furor** [ˈfjʊrɔːʳ] *n* Protest(e *pl*) *m* ◆ **to cause a ~** einen Skandal verursachen.

furred [fɜːd] *adj* (*tongue*) belegt, pelzig.

furrier [ˈfʌrɪəʳ] *n* Kürschner *m*.

furrow [ˈfʌrəʊ] [1] *n* (*Agr*) Furche *f*; (*Hort: for flowers etc*) Rinne *f*; (*on brow*) Runzel *f*; (*on sea*) Furche *f*.
[2] *vt earth* pflügen, Furchen ziehen in (+*dat*); *brow* runzeln; (*worries etc*) furchen; (*boats*) *sea* Furchen ziehen in (+*dat*) ◆ **the old man's ~ed brow** die zerfurchte Stirn des alten Mannes.

furry [ˈfɜːrɪ] *adj* (+*er*) *animal* Pelz-; *toy* Plüsch-; *tongue* pelzig, belegt ◆ **the little kitten is so soft and ~** das Kätzchen ist so weich und kuschelig; **the soft ~ skin of the seal** das weiche Fell des Seehundes; **it has a ~ feel** es fühlt sich wie Pelz *or* Fell an.

▼ **further** [ˈfɜːðəʳ] [1] *adv, comp of* **far** **(a)** (*in place, time, fig*) weiter ◆ **~ on** weiter, weiter entfernt; **~ back** (*in place, time*) weiter zurück; (*in time*) früher; **he is ~ on than his brother** (*fig*) er ist weiter als sein Bruder; **nothing could be ~ from the truth** nichts könnte weiter von der Wahrheit entfernt sein; **to get ~ and ~ away** sich immer weiter entfernen; **we're no ~ advanced now** viel weiter sind wir jetzt (auch) nicht; **if we take this line of reasoning ~** wenn wir diese Argumente weiterverfolgen; **nothing is ~ from my thoughts** nichts liegt mir ferner; **to make the soup go ~** die Suppe strecken.
(b) (*more*) **he didn't question me ~** er hat mich nicht weiter *or* mehr gefragt; **until you hear ~** bis auf weiteres; **and ~** ... und darüberhinaus ...; **~ I want to say that** ... darüberhinaus möchte ich sagen, daß ...; **~ to your letter of** ... (*Comm*) bezugnehmend auf *or* in bezug auf Ihren Brief vom ... (*form*).
▼ [2] *adj* **(a)** *see* **farther**.
(b) (*additional*) weiter ◆ **to remand a case for ~ enquiry** (*Jur*) einen Fall zurückstellen, bis weitere Nachforschungen angestellt sind; **will there be anything ~?** kann ich sonst noch etwas für Sie tun?; **~ particulars** nähere *or* weitere Einzelheiten *pl*; **~ education** Weiterbildung, Fortbildung *f*.
[3] *vt one's interests, a cause* fördern.

furtherance [ˈfɜːðərəns] *n* Förderung *f* ◆ **in ~ of sth** zur Förderung einer Sache (*gen*).

▼ **furthermore** [ˈfɜːðəmɔːʳ] *adv* überdies, außerdem.

furthermost [ˈfɜːðəməʊst] *adj* äußerste(r, s).

furthest [ˈfɜːðɪst] [1] *adv* **the ~ north you can go** soweit nach Norden wie möglich; **he went the ~** er ging am weitesten; **of all the candidates he went ~ into this question** von allen Kandidaten drang er am tiefsten in diese Frage ein.
[2] *adj* **in the ~ depths of the forest** in den tiefsten Tiefen des Waldes; **5 km at the ~** höchstens 5 km; **the ~ way round** den längsten Weg; **at the ~ point from the centre** an dem vom Zentrum am weitesten entfernten Punkt.

furtive [ˈfɜːtɪv] *adj action* heimlich; *behaviour, person* heimlichtuerisch; (*suspicious*) verdächtig; *look* verstohlen.

furtively [ˈfɜːtɪvlɪ] *adv peer, creep, slink* verstohlen; (*suspiciously*) *behave* verdächtig.

furtiveness [ˈfɜːtɪvnɪs] *n see adj* Heimlichkeit *f*; Heimlichtuerei *f*; Verdachterregende(s) *nt*; Verstohlenheit *f*.

fury [ˈfjʊərɪ] *n* **(a)** (*of person*) Wut *f*; (*of storm also*) Ungestüm *nt*; (*of struggle, wind, passion*) Heftigkeit *f* ◆ **she flew into a ~** sie kam in Rage; **like ~** (*inf*) wie verrückt (*inf*). **(b)** (*Myth*) **the Furies** die Furien *pl*; **she's a little ~** sie ist ein kleiner Hitzkopf.

furze [fɜːz] *n* Stechginster *m*.

fuse, (*US*) **fuze** [fjuːz] [1] *vt* **(a)** *metals* verschmelzen. **(b)** (*Brit Elec*) **to ~ the lights** die Sicherung durchbrennen lassen; **I've ~d the lights** die Sicherung ist durchgebrannt. **(c)** (*fig*) vereinigen, verbinden; (*Comm*) fusionieren.
[2] *vi* **(a)** (*metals*) sich verbinden; (*atoms*) verschmelzen. **(b)** (*Brit Elec*) durchbrennen ◆ **the lights/the toaster ~d** die Sicherung war durchgebrannt/am Toaster war die Sicherung durchgebrannt. **(c)** (*fig: also* **~ together**) sich vereinigen.
[3] *n* **(a)** (*Elec*) Sicherung *f* ◆ **to blow the ~s** die Sicherung durchbrennen lassen; **he'll blow a ~** (*fig inf*) bei dem brennen die Sicherungen durch (*inf*); **she's got a short ~** (*fig inf*) bei ihr brennen leicht die Sicherungen durch (*inf*). **(b)** (*Brit Elec: act of fusing*) **there's been a ~ somewhere** irgendwo hat es einen Kurzschluß gegeben, da ist irgendwo ein Kurzschluß *or* Kurzer (*inf*). **(c)** (*in bombs etc, Min*) Zündschnur *f*.

fuse box *n* Sicherungskasten *m*.

fused [fjuːzd] *adj plug etc* gesichert.

fuselage [ˈfjuːzəlɑːʒ] *n* (Flugzeug)rumpf *m*.

fuse wire *n* Schmelzdraht *m*.

fusilier [ˌfjuːzɪˈlɪəʳ] *n* (*Brit*) Füsilier *m*.

fusillade [ˌfjuːzɪˈleɪd] *n* Salve *f*.

fusion [ˈfjuːʒən] *n* (*of metal, fig*) Verschmelzung, Fusion *f*; (*Phys: also* **nuclear ~**) (Kern)fusion, Kernverschmelzung *f* ◆ **~ reactor** Fusionsreaktor *m*.

fuss [fʌs] [1] *n* Theater *nt* (*inf*); (*bother also*) Umstände *pl* (*inf*), Aufheben(s) *nt*; (*lavish attention also*) Wirbel (*inf*), Wind (*inf*) *m*, Getue (*inf*) *nt* (*of* um) ◆ **don't go to a lot of ~** mach dir keine Umstände, mach nicht viel Theater (*inf*) *or* Aufhebens; **we had a bit of a ~ getting our money back** wir hatten ein bißchen Theater, ehe wir unser Geld zurückbekamen (*inf*); **to make a ~, to kick up a ~** Krach schlagen (*inf*); **to make a ~ about** *or* **over sth** viel Aufhebens *or* Wind (*inf*) *or* Wirbel (*inf*) um etw machen; **to avoid a ~** Streit *or* Krach (*inf*) vermeiden; **to make a ~ of sb** um jdn viel Wirbel (*inf*) *or* Wind (*inf*) *or* Getue (*inf*) machen; **to be in/get into a ~** Zustände haben/kriegen (*inf*); **a lot of ~ about nothing** viel Wind *or* Lärm um nichts.
[2] *vi* sich (unnötig) aufregen; (*get into a ~*) Umstände *pl* machen ◆ **there's no need to ~ if your son doesn't wear a vest** Sie brauchen nicht gleich Zustände zu kriegen, nur weil Ihr Sohn kein Unterhemd anhat (*inf*); **don't ~, mother!** ist ja gut, Mutter!; **a mother who ~es unnecessarily** eine übertrieben besorgte Mutter; **the mother bird starts to ~ when she senses the fox** die Vogelmutter wird ganz aufgeregt, wenn sie den Fuchs spürt; **with a crowd of attendants ~ing busily around her** mit einer Menge Bediensteter, die eifrig um sie herumhuschten *or* herumfuhrwerkten (*inf*).
[3] *vt person* nervös machen; (*pester*) keine Ruhe lassen (+*dat*) ◆ **don't ~ me** laß mich in Ruhe, laß mir meine Ruhe.

◆**fuss about** *or* **around** *vi* herumfuhrwerken (*inf*).

◆**fuss over** *vi* +*prep obj person* bemuttern; *guests* sich (*dat*) große Umstände machen mit.

fussbudget [ˈfʌsbʌdʒɪt] *n* (*US inf*) *see* **fusspot**.

fussily [ˈfʌsɪlɪ] *adv see adj.*

fussiness [ˈfʌsɪnɪs] *n see adj* **(a)** Kleinlichkeit, Pingeligkeit (*inf*) *f* ◆ **because of his incredible ~ about what he eats** weil er so eigen ist, was das Essen angeht. **(b)** Verspieltheit *f*; Ausgeklügeltheit *f*; Übergenauigkeit *f*.

fusspot [ˈfʌspɒt] *n* (*Brit inf*) Umstandskrämer *m* (*inf*); (*nag*) Nörgler(in *f*) *m*.

fussy [ˈfʌsɪ] *adj* (+*er*) **(a)** (*finicky*) kleinlich, pingelig (*inf*) ◆ **she is very ~ about what she eats/wears** sie ist sehr eigen, was das Essen/ihre Kleidung angeht; **don't be so ~** seien Sie nicht so pingelig (*inf*) *or* kleinlich, stellen Sie sich nicht so an (*inf*); **what do you want to do? — I'm not ~** was willst du machen? — ist mir egal; **you should be more ~** Sie sollten etwas wählerischer sein.
(b) (*elaborate*) *dress, pattern, architecture etc* verspielt; *style of writing* ausgeklügelt; *distinction* übergenau.

fustian [ˈfʌstɪən] [1] *n* (*Tex*) Barchent *m*.
[2] *adj* **(a)** (*Tex*) Barchent-. **(b)** (*fig: pompous*) schwülstig.

fusty [ˈfʌstɪ] *adj* (+*er*) (*lit, fig*) muffig.

futile [ˈfjuːtaɪl] *adj* sinnlos; *plan, idea* nutzlos; *effort, attempt* (*usu attr: in vain*) vergeblich; (*usu pred: pointless*) nutzlos.

futility [fjuːˈtɪlɪtɪ] *n see adj* Sinnlosigkeit *f*; Nutzlosigkeit *f*; Vergeblichkeit *f*.

futon [ˈfuːtɒn] *n* Futon *m*.

future [ˈfjuːtʃəʳ] [1] *n* **(a)** Zukunft *f* ◆ **in ~** in Zukunft, künftig; **in the near ~**

➤ LANGUAGE IN USE: **further: 1a** → 26.1 **2a** → 20.7 **furthermore** → 26.2, 26.3

bald, in der nahen Zukunft; **that is still very much in the ~** das liegt noch in weiter Ferne; **there's no ~ in this type of work** diese Art (von) Arbeit hat keine Zukunft; **he definitely has a ~ as an actor** er hat eine Zukunft als Schauspieler.
(b) (*Gram*) Zukunft *f*, Futur *nt* ◆ **in the ~** in der Zukunft, im Futur; **~ perfect** vollendete Zukunft.
(c) (*St Ex*) **~s** Termingeschäfte *pl* ◆ **~s market** Terminmarkt *m*, Terminbörse *f*.
2 *adj* **(a)** zukünftig ◆ **at some ~ date** zu *or* an einem zukünftigen *or* späteren Zeitpunkt.
(b) the ~ tense (*Gram*) das Futur(um), die Zukunft.
futurism ['fju:tʃərɪzəm] *n* Futurismus *m*.
futurist ['fju:tʃərɪst] *n* Futurist(in *f*) *m*.
futuristic [,fju:tʃə'rɪstɪk] *adj* futuristisch.
futurology [,fju:tʃər'ɒlədʒɪ] *n* Futurologie *f*.
fuze *n* (*US*) *see* **fuse**.
fuzz [fʌz] *n* **(a)** (*on peach, youth's chin etc*) Flaum *m*; (*inf*) (*bushy beard etc*) Gemüse *nt* (*inf*); (*frizzy hair*) Wuschelkopf *m*.
(b) (*inf: blur, blurred sound*) Unschärfen *pl*.
(c) (*sl: policeman*) Bulle (*pej sl*), Polyp (*sl*) *m* ◆ **the ~** (*collective*) die Bullen (*sl*), die Polypen (*sl*) *pl*.
fuzzy ['fʌzɪ] *adj* (*+er*) **(a)** *hair* kraus. **(b)** (*blurred*) *picture, sound, memory etc* verschwommen.
fuzzy-headed ['fʌzɪ,hedɪd] *adj* (*inf*) **(a)** (*not clear-thinking*) nicht (ganz) klar im Kopf; (*from headache, drugs, drink also*) benebelt. **(b)** (*curly-haired*) wuschelköpfig.
fuzzy-wuzzy ['fʌzɪ,wʌzɪ] *n* (*pej sl*) Krauskopf *m* (*inf*).
fwd *abbr of* **forward**.

G, g [dʒiː] *n* **(a)** G, g *nt.* **(b)** **g's** *pl* (*gravitational force*) g *nt.* **(c)** **G** (*US sl: one thousand dollars*) tausend Dollar *pl.* **(d)** (*Mus*) G, g *nt* ◆ **~ sharp/flat** Gis, gis *nt*/Ges, ges *nt*; *see also* **major, minor, natural.**

G (*US*) *abbr of* **general;** (*Film*) jugendfrei.

g *abbr of* **gram(s), gramme(s)** g.

gab [gæb] (*inf*) [1] *n* Gequassel (*inf*), Geschwätz *nt* ◆ **he's all ~** er ist ein Schwätzer (*inf*); **to have the gift of the ~** (*talk a lot*) wie ein Wasserfall reden (*inf*); (*be persuasive*) reden können, nicht auf den Mund gefallen sein.
[2] *vi* quatschen (*inf*), quasseln (*inf*).

gabardine, gaberdine [ˌgæbəˈdiːn] *n* Gabardine *m.*

gabble [ˈgæbl] [1] *vi* (*person*) brabbeln (*inf*); (*geese*) schnattern ◆ **he ~d through grace in two seconds flat** er rasselte das Tischgebet in zwei Sekunden herunter (*inf*).
[2] *vt poem, prayer* herunterrasseln (*inf*); *excuse, explanation* brabbeln (*inf*).
[3] *n* Gebrabbel *nt* (*inf*); (*of geese*) Geschnatter *nt* ◆ **the speaker ended in a ~** der Redner rasselte das Ende herunter (*inf*).

◆**gabble away** *vi* (*geese, people*) drauflosschnattern (*inf*).

◆**gabble on** *vi* reden und reden, quasseln und quasseln (*inf*).

gabby [ˈgæbɪ] *adj* (*inf*) geschwätzig, schwatzhaft.

gable [ˈgeɪbl] *n* Giebel *m* ◆ **~ end** Giebelwand *or* -seite *f*; **~ window** Giebelfenster *nt.*

gabled [ˈgeɪbld] *adj* Giebel-.

gad [gæd] *interj* **(by) ~!** (*old*) bei Gott! (*old*).

◆**gad about** *or* **around** *vi* herumziehen ◆ **he's always ~ding ~** er ist ständig auf Achse (*inf*); **to ~ ~ the country** im Land herumziehen *or* -reisen.

gadabout [ˈgædəbaʊt] *n* rastloser Geist; (*who likes travelling*) Reiseonkel *m*/ -tante *f* ◆ **she's a real ~, out somewhere every evening** sie ist sehr unternehmungslustig, jeden Abend ist sie irgendwo anders.

gadfly [ˈgædflaɪ] *n* (Vieh)bremse *f.*

gadget [ˈgædʒɪt] *n* Gerät *nt*, Vorrichtung *f*, Apparat *m* ◆ **with a lot of ~s** mit allen Schikanen (*inf*).

gadgetry [ˈgædʒɪtrɪ] *n* Vorrichtungen, Geräte *pl*; (*superfluous equipment*) technische Spielereien, Kinkerlitzchen (*inf*) *pl.*

gadzooks [gædˈzuːks] *interj* (*old*) Kruzitürken (*old*).

Gael [geɪl] *n* Gäle *m*, Gälin *f.*

Gaelic [ˈgeɪlɪk] [1] *adj* gälisch ◆ **~ coffee** Irish Coffee *m.*
[2] *n* (*language*) Gälisch *nt.*

gaff¹ [gæf] [1] *n* **(a)** (*Fishing*) Landungshaken *m*, Gaff *nt.* **(b)** (*Naut*) Gaffel *f.*
[2] *vt* (*Fishing*) mit dem (Landungs)haken *or* Gaff an Land ziehen.

gaff² *n*: **to blow the ~** (*sl*) nicht dichthalten (*inf*); **he blew the ~ (on it) to Joe** er hat es Joe auf die Nase gebunden (*inf*); **to blow the ~ on sth** etw ausquatschen (*sl*).

gaffe [gæf] *n* Fauxpas *m*; (*verbal*) taktlose Bemerkung ◆ **to make a ~** einen Fauxpas begehen; (*by saying sth*) ins Fettnäpfchen treten (*inf*).

gaffer [ˈgæfəʳ] *n* (*inf*) **(a)** (*Brit*) (*foreman*) Vorarbeiter, Vormann *m*; (*boss*) Chef, Boß (*inf*), Alte(r) (*inf*) *m.* **(b)** (*old man*) Alte(r), Opa (*inf*) *m.*

gag [gæg] [1] *n* **(a)** Knebel *m*; (*Med*) Mundsperre *f.*
(b) (*joke*) Gag *m.*
[2] *vt* knebeln; (*Med*) die Mundsperre einlegen (+*dat*); (*fig*) *person* zum Schweigen bringen; *press etc* mundtot machen, knebeln.
[3] *vi* **(a)** (*joke*) Witze machen; (*comedian*) Gags machen ◆ **..., he ~ged ...,** witzelte er. **(b)** (*esp US: retch*) würgen (*on* an +*dat*).

gaga [ˈgɑːˈgɑː] *adj* (*inf*) plemplem (*inf*), meschugge (*inf*); *old person* verkalkt (*inf*).

gage *n, vt* (*US*) *see* **gauge.**

gaggle [ˈgægl] [1] *n* (*of geese*) Herde *f*; (*hum: of girls, women*) Schar, Horde *f.*
[2] *vi* schnattern.

gaiety [ˈgeɪɪtɪ] *n* (*cheerfulness*) Fröhlichkeit, Heiterkeit *f*; (*usu pl: merrymaking*) Vergnügung *f.*

gaily [ˈgeɪlɪ] *adv* fröhlich; (*fig*) unbekümmert; (*colourfully*) farbenfroh ◆ **~ coloured** farbenfroh *or* -prächtig, lustig bunt.

gain [geɪn] [1] *n* **(a)** *no pl* (*advantage*) Vorteil *m*; (*profit*) Gewinn, Profit *m* ◆ **it will be to your ~** es wird zu Ihrem Vorteil sein; **the love of ~** Profitgier *f* (*pej*); **to do sth for ~** etw aus Berechnung (*dat*) *or* zum eigenen Vorteil tun; (*for money*) etw des Geldes wegen tun; **his loss is our ~** sein Verlust ist unser Gewinn, wir profitieren von seinem Verlust.
(b) **~s** *pl* (*winnings*) Gewinn *m*; (*profits also*) Gewinne *pl.*
(c) (*increase*) (*in gen*) Zunahme *f*; (*in speed also*) Erhöhung *f*; (*in wealth also*) Steigerung *f*; (*in health*) Besserung *f*; (*in knowledge*) Erweiterung, Vergrößerung *f* ◆ **~ in numbers** zahlenmäßiger Zuwachs; **a ~ in weight/productivity/height** eine Gewichtszunahme/eine Produktionssteigerung/ein Höhengewinn *m.*
[2] *vt* **(a)** (*obtain, win*) gewinnen; *knowledge, wealth* erwerben; *advantage, respect, entry* sich (*dat*) verschaffen; *the lead* übernehmen; *marks, points* erzielen; *sum of money* (*in deal*) verdienen; *liberty* erlangen; (*achieve*) *nothing, a little etc* erreichen ◆ **that ~ed something for us** damit haben wir etwas erreicht; **what does he hope to ~ by it?** was verspricht *or* erhofft er sich (*dat*) davon?; **to ~ sb's goodwill** jdn wohlwollend stimmen; **to ~ experience** Erfahrungen sammeln; **he ~ed a better view by climbing onto a wall** dadurch, daß er auf eine Mauer kletterte, hatte er einen besseren Ausblick; **they didn't ~ entry** sie wurden nicht eingelassen; **we ~ed an advantage over him** wir waren ihm gegenüber im Vorteil; **we stood to ~ over the others** wir waren den anderen gegenüber im Vorteil; **to ~ ground** (an) Boden gewinnen; (*disease*) um sich greifen, sich verbreiten; (*rumours*) sich verbreiten; **to ~ ground on sb** (*get further ahead*) den Vorsprung zu jdm vergrößern; (*catch up*) jdm gegenüber aufholen; **how did he ~ such a reputation?** wie ist er zu diesem Ruf gekommen?; **he ~ed a reputation for himself as ...** er hat sich (*dat*) einen Namen als ... gemacht.
(b) (*reach*) *other side, shore, summit* erreichen.
(c) (*increase*) **to ~ height** (an) Höhe gewinnen, höher steigen; **to ~ speed** schneller werden, beschleunigen; **she has ~ed weight/3 kilos** sie hat zugenommen/3 Kilo zugenommen; **as he ~ed confidence** als er sicherer wurde, als seine Selbstsicherheit wuchs *or* zunahm; **my watch ~s five minutes each day** meine Uhr geht fünf Minuten pro Tag vor.
[3] *vi* **(a)** (*watch*) vorgehen.
(b) (*get further ahead*) den Vorsprung vergrößern; (*close gap*) aufholen.
(c) (*profit: person*) profitieren (*by* von) ◆ **you can only ~ by it** das kann nur Ihr Vorteil sein, Sie können dabei nur profitieren; **his reputation ~ed greatly by that** dadurch wuchs sein Ansehen enorm; **society/the university would ~ from that** das wäre für die Gesellschaft/die Universität von Vorteil.
(d) **to ~ in knowledge/wealth** mehr Wissen/Reichtum erwerben, sein Wissen/seinen Reichtum vergrößern; **to ~ in confidence** mehr Selbstvertrauen bekommen; **to ~ in speed** schneller werden; **to ~ in height** (an) Höhe gewinnen; **to ~ in weight** zunehmen; **to ~ in prestige** an Ansehen gewinnen, sich (*dat*) größeres Ansehen verschaffen.

◆**gain (up)on** *vi* +*prep obj* (*get further ahead*) den Vorsprung zu ... vergrößern; (*close gap*) einholen; (*catch up with*) *work, rust etc* fertigwerden mit ◆ **it is ~ing/constantly ~ing ~ me** ich komme dagegen nicht (mehr)/immer weniger an; **the cold was ~ing ~ them, they could hardly move/they couldn't get the building finished** die Kälte übermannte sie, und sie konnten sich kaum bewegen/die Kälte brach herein, und sie konnten den Bau nicht fertigstellen.

gainer [ˈgeɪnəʳ] *n* **I/she** *etc* **was the ~** ich habe/sie hat *etc* dabei profitiert; **to be the ~ by doing sth** davon profitieren *or* einen Vorteil davon haben, daß man etw tut.

gainful [ˈgeɪnfʊl] *adj occupation etc* einträglich ◆ **to be in ~ employment** erwerbstätig sein.

gainsay [ˌgeɪnˈseɪ] *vt pret, ptp* **gainsaid** [ˈgeɪnˈsed] widersprechen (+*dat*); *fact* (ab)leugnen, bestreiten; *evidence, argument* widerlegen ◆ **it cannot be gainsaid** es läßt sich nicht leugnen; **there is no ~ing his honesty** seine Ehrlichkeit läßt sich nicht leugnen.

'gainst [geɪnst] *prep see* **against.**

gait [geɪt] *n* Gang *m*; (*of horse*) Gangart *f* ◆ **with unsteady ~** mit unsicheren Schritten.

gaiter [ˈgeɪtəʳ] *n* Gamasche *f.*

gal¹ [gæl] *n* (*dated inf*) Mädel *nt* (*dated*).

gal² *abbr of* **gallon(s).**

gala [ˈgɑːlə] *n* (*festive occasion*) großes Fest; (*Theat, Film, ball*) Galaveranstaltung *f* ◆ **swimming/sports ~** großes Schwimm-/Sportfest; **~ day** Festtag *m*; (*for person*) großer Tag; **~ dress** Gala *f*; (*uniform also*) Galauniform *f or* -anzug *m*; **~ night** Galaabend *m*; **~ occasion** festliche Veranstaltung; **~ performance** Galavorstellung, Festvorstellung *f.*

galactic [gəˈlæktɪk] *adj* galaktisch.
Galahad [ˈgæləhæd] *n* Galahad *m*; *(fig)* Kavalier, Ritter *m*.
galantine [ˈgælənti:n] *n kalt servierte, glasierte Fleisch- oder Geflügelroulade.*
galaxy [ˈgæləksɪ] *n* **(a)** *(Astron)* Milchstraße *f*, Sternsystem *nt*, Galaxis *f (spec)* ♦ **the G~** die Milchstraße *or* Galaxis *(spec)*. **(b)** *(fig)* Schar *f*, Heer *nt*.
gale [geɪl] *n* **(a)** Sturm *m* ♦ **it was blowing a ~** es stürmte, ein Sturm tobte *or* wütete; **~ force 8** Sturmstärke 8; **~-force winds** orkanartige Winde; **~ warning** Sturmwarnung *f*. **(b)** *(fig)* **~s of laughter** Lachsalven *pl*, stürmisches Gelächter.
Galicia [gəˈlɪsɪə] *n* **(a)** *(in Eastern Europe)* Galizien *nt*. **(b)** *(in Spain)* Galicien *nt*.
Galician [gəˈlɪsɪən] *see* **Galicia** 1 *adj* **(a)** galizisch. **(b)** galicisch.
2 *n* **(a)** Galizier(in *f*) *m*. **(b)** Galicier(in *f*) *m*.
Galilean [ˌgæləˈli:ən] 1 *adj* galiläisch.
2 *n* Galiläer(in *f*) *m*.
Galilee [ˈgælɪli:] *n* Galiläa *nt* ♦ **the Sea of ~** der See Genezareth, das Galiläische Meer.
gall [gɔ:l] 1 *n* **(a)** *(Physiol)* Galle(nsaft *m*) *f* ♦ **to dip one's pen in ~** *(fig)* seine Feder spitzen, seine Feder in Galle tauchen *(liter)*. **(b)** *(sore)* Wundstelle *f*; *(Bot)* Galle *f*; *(nut-shaped)* Gallapfel *m*. **(c)** *(fig liter)* Bitternis *f (geh)*. **(d)** *(inf)* Frechheit *f* ♦ **of all the ~!** so eine Frechheit *or* Unverschämtheit!
2 *vt (chafe)* wund reiben *or* scheuern; *(fig)* maßlos ärgern.
gallant [ˈgælənt] 1 *adj (brave)* tapfer; *(chivalrous, noble)* edel, ritterlich; *boat, appearance* stattlich; *sight, display* prächtig; *(attentive to women) person* galant, ritterlich; *poetry* galant.
2 *n (dashing man)* schneidiger Kavalier; *(ladies' man also)* Charmeur *m*; *(obs: suitor)* Galan *m (old, hum)*.
gallantly [ˈgæləntlɪ] *adv (bravely)* tapfer; *(nobly)* edelmütig; *(chivalrously, courteously)* galant.
gallantry [ˈgæləntrɪ] *n* **(a)** *(bravery)* Tapferkeit *f*; *(chivalry)* Edelmut *m*. **(b)** *(attentiveness to women)* Ritterlichkeit, Galanterie *f*. **(c)** *(compliment)* Galanterie, Artigkeit *(dated) f*.
gall bladder *n* Gallenblase *f*.
galleon [ˈgælɪən] *n* Galeone *f*.
gallery [ˈgælərɪ] *n* **(a)** *(balcony, corridor)* Galerie *f*; *(in church)* Empore *f*; *(Theat)* oberster Rang, Balkon *m*, Galerie *f* ♦ **to play to the ~** *(fig)* sich in Szene setzen. **(b)** *(Art)* (Kunst)galerie *f*. **(c)** *(underground)* Stollen *m*.
galley [ˈgælɪ] *n* **(a)** *(Naut) (ship)* Galeere *f*; *(kitchen)* Kombüse *f* ♦ **~ slave** Galeerensklave *m*. **(b)** *(Typ) (tray)* (Setz)schiff *nt*; *(also* **~ proof***)* Fahne(nabzug *m*) *f*.
Gallic [ˈgælɪk] *adj* gallisch.
gallicism [ˈgælɪsɪzəm] *n* Gallizismus *m*.
gallicize [ˈgælɪsaɪz] *vt* französisieren.
galling [ˈgɔ:lɪŋ] *adj* äußerst ärgerlich; *person* unausstehlich.
gallivant [ˌgælɪˈvænt] *vi* sich amüsieren ♦ **to ~ about** *or* **around** sich herumtreiben, herumzigeunern; **to ~ off** losziehen *(inf)*; **I was out ~ing last night** ich war gestern abend bummeln *or* auf Achse *(inf)*.
gallon [ˈgælən] *n* Gallone *f*.
gallop [ˈgæləp] 1 *n* Galopp *m* ♦ **at a ~** im Galopp; **at full ~** im gestreckten Galopp; **to go for a ~** ausreiten.
2 *vi* galoppieren, im Galopp reiten ♦ **to ~ away** davongaloppieren; **we ~ed through our work/the agenda** wir haben die Arbeit im Galopp erledigt *(inf)*/die Tagesordnung im Galopp abgehandelt *(inf)*; **to ~ through a book/meal** ein Buch in rasendem Tempo lesen *(inf)*/eine Mahlzeit hinunterschlingen.
3 *vt horse* galoppieren lassen.
galloping [ˈgæləpɪŋ] *adj (lit, fig)* galoppierend.
gallows [ˈgæləʊz] *n* Galgen *m* ♦ **to send/bring sb to the ~** jdn an den Galgen bringen; **he was sentenced to the ~** er wurde zum Tod am Galgen *or* durch den Strang verurteilt; **~ bird** *(inf)* Galgenvogel *m (inf)*; **~ humour** Galgenhumor *m*.
gallstone [ˈgɔ:lstəʊn] *n* Gallenstein *m*.
Gallup poll [ˈgæləpˌpəʊl] *n* Meinungsumfrage *f*.
galore [gəˈlɔ:ʳ] *adv* in Hülle und Fülle.
galoshes [gəˈlɒʃəz] *npl* Gummischuhe, Galoschen *pl*.
galumph [gəˈlʌmf] *vi (inf)* trapsen *(inf)*.
galvanic [gælˈvænɪk] *adj* **(a)** *(Elec)* galvanisch. **(b)** *(fig) movement* zuckend; *(stimulating)* mitreißend, elektrisierend.
galvanism [ˈgælvənɪzəm] *n* Galvanismus *m*.
galvanization [ˌgælvənaɪˈzeɪʃən] *n* Galvanisierung, Galvanisation *f*.
galvanize [ˈgælvənaɪz] *vt* **(a)** *(Elec)* galvanisieren. **(b)** *(fig)* elektrisieren ♦ **to ~ sb into action** jdn plötzlich aktiv werden lassen; **to ~ sb into doing sth** jdm einen Stoß geben, etw sofort zu tun; **he was ~d into life by the news** die Nachricht hat ihm enormen Auftrieb gegeben.
galvanized [ˈgælvənaɪzd] *adj iron, steel* galvanisiert.
galvanometer [ˌgælvəˈnɒmɪtəʳ] *n* Galvanometer *nt*.
Gambia [ˈgæmbɪə] *n* **(the) ~** Gambia *nt*.
Gambian [ˈgæmbɪən] 1 *adj* gambisch.
2 *n* Gambier(in *f*) *m*.
gambit [ˈgæmbɪt] *n* **(a)** *(Chess)* Gambit *nt*. **(b)** *(fig)* (Schach)zug *m* ♦ **his favourite ~ was to ...** was er am liebsten machte, war ...; **his favourite conversational ~ is ...** er fängt gern eine Unterhaltung mit ... an.
gamble [ˈgæmbl] 1 *n* **(a)** *(lit)* **I like the occasional ~** ich versuche gern mal mein Glück (im Spiel/bei Pferdewetten/bei Hundewetten *etc*); **to have a ~ on the horses/dogs/stock exchange** auf Pferde/Hunde wetten/an der Börse spekulieren.
(b) *(fig)* Risiko *nt* ♦ **it's a ~** es ist riskant *or* eine riskante Sache; **I'll take a ~ on it** ich riskiere es; **he took a ~ in buying this house** bei dem Hauskauf ist er ein Risiko eingegangen.
2 *vi* **(a)** *(lit)* (um Geld) spielen (*with* mit), sich an Glücksspielen beteiligen; *(on horses etc)* wetten ♦ **to ~ on the horses/stock exchange** bei Pferderennen wetten/an der Börse spekulieren; **he made a lot of money gambling at cards** er hat beim Kartenspiel viel Geld gewonnen.
(b) *(fig)* **to ~ on sth** sich auf etw *(acc)* verlassen; **she was gambling on his** *or* **him being late** sie hat sich darauf verlassen, daß er sich verspäten würde; **to ~ with sth** mit etw spielen, etw aufs Spiel setzen.
3 *vt* **(a)** *fortune* einsetzen ♦ **to ~ sth on sth** etw auf etw *(acc)* setzen. **(b)** *(fig)* aufs Spiel setzen.
♦**gamble away** *vt sep* verspielen.
gambler [ˈgæmbləʳ] *n (lit, fig)* Spieler(in *f*) *m* ♦ **he's a born ~** er ist eine Spielernatur.
gambling [ˈgæmblɪŋ] *n* Spielen *nt* (um Geld); *(on horses etc)* Wetten *nt* ♦ **to disapprove of ~** gegen das Glückspiel/Wetten sein; **~ debts** Spielschulden *pl*; **~ den** *or* **joint** Spielhölle *f*.
gambol [ˈgæmbəl] 1 *n* Tollen *nt*, Tollerei *f*; *(of lambs)* Herumspringen *nt* ♦ **to have a ~** herumtollen; herumspringen.
2 *vi* herumtollen; herumspringen.
game[1] [geɪm] 1 *n* **(a)** Spiel *nt*; *(sport)* Sport(art *f*) *m*; *(single ~)* *(of team sports, tennis)* Spiel *nt*; *(of table tennis)* Satz *m*; *(of billiards, board-games etc, informal tennis match)* Partie *f* ♦ **to have** *or* **play a ~ of football/tennis/chess** *etc* Fußball/Tennis/Schach *etc* spielen; **do you fancy a quick ~ of football/cards/tennis/chess** *etc*? hättest du Lust, ein bißchen Fußball/Karten/Tennis/Schach *etc* zu spielen?, hättest du Lust auf eine Partie Tennis/Schach?; **he plays a good ~** er spielt gut; **shall we play a ~ now?** wollen wir jetzt ein Spiel machen?; **to have a ~ with sb, to give sb a ~** mit jdm spielen; **winning the second set put him back in the ~ again** nachdem er den zweiten Satz gewonnen hatte, hatte er wieder Chancen; **to be off one's ~** nicht in Form sein; **~ of chance/skill** Glücksspiel *nt*/Geschicklichkeitsspiel *nt*; **~ set and match to X** Satz und Spiel (geht an) X; **~ to X** Spiel X; **that's ~** Spiel; **one ~ all** eins beide.
(b) *(fig)* Spiel *nt*; *(scheme, plan)* Absicht *f*, Vorhaben *nt* ♦ **to play the ~** sich an die Spielregeln halten; **to play ~s with sb** mit jdm spielen; **the ~ is up** das Spiel ist aus; **to play sb's ~** jdm in die Hände spielen; **two can play at that ~, that's a ~ (that) two can play** wie du mir, so ich dir *(inf)*; **to beat sb at his own ~** jdn mit den eigenen Waffen schlagen; **to give the ~ away** alles verderben; **to see through sb's ~** jds Spiel durchschauen, jdm auf die Schliche kommen; **to spoil sb's little ~** jdm das Spiel verderben, jdm die Suppe versalzen *(inf)*; **I wonder what the PM's ~ is?** ich frage mich, was der Premier vorhat *or* im Schilde führt; **so that's your ~, is it?** darauf willst du also hinaus!; **what's your little ~?** was führst du im Schilde?; **to be out of the ~** *(inf: be finished etc)* weg vom Fenster sein *(sl)*.
(c) **~s** *pl (Sports event)* Spiele *pl*.
(d) **~s** *sing (Sch)* Sport *m*; **to be good at ~s** gut in Sport sein; **gym on Tuesdays, ~s on Wednesdays** Turnen am Dienstag, Ballspiele/Leichtathletik *etc* am Mittwoch.
(e) *(inf: business, profession)* Branche *f* ♦ **how long have you been in this ~?** wie lange machen Sie das schon?; **the publishing ~** das Verlagswesen; **he's in the second-hand car ~** er macht in Gebrauchtwagen *(inf)*; **to be/go on the ~** auf den Strich gehen *(inf)*.
(f) *(inf: difficult time)* Theater *nt (inf)* ♦ **I had quite a ~ getting the tickets** das war (vielleicht) ein Theater, bis ich die Karten bekam! *(inf)*.
(g) *(Hunt)* Wild *nt*; *(Cook also)* Wildbret *nt*.
2 *vi* (um Geld) spielen.
3 *vt (also* **~ away***)* verspielen.
game[2] *adj (brave)* mutig ♦ **to be ~** *(willing)* mitmachen, dabeisein; **to be ~ for sth** (bei) etw mitmachen; **to be ~ to do sth** bereit sein, etw zu tun; **to be ~ for anything** für alles zu haben sein, zu allen Schandtaten bereit sein *(hum inf)*.
game[3] *adj (crippled)* lahm.
game: ~bag *n* Jagdtasche *f*; **~ bird** *n* Federwild *nt no pl*; **the pheasant is a ~ bird** der Fasan gehört zum Federwild.
Gameboy [ˈgeɪmbɔɪ] ® *n* Gameboy ® *m*.
game: ~cock *n* Kampfhahn *m*; **~ fish** *n* Sportfisch *m*; **~keeper** *n* Wildhüter *m*; **~ laws** *npl* Jagdgesetz *nt*; **~ licence** *n* Jagdschein *m*; **~ park** *n* Wildpark *m*; **~ plan** *n (Sport)* Spielplan *m*; *(fig)* Strategie *f*; **~ pie** *n* Wildpastete *f*; **~ point** *n* Spielpunkt *m*; **~ preserve** *n* Wildhegegebiet *nt*; **~ reserve** *n* Wildschutzgebiet *or* -reservat *nt*; **~ show** *n (TV)* Spielshow *f*.
games [geɪmz]: **~manship** *n* Ablenkungsmanöver *pl*; **~ master** *n* Sportlehrer *m*; **~ mistress** *n* Sportlehrerin *f*; **~ port** *n (Comput)* Spieleport *nt or m*; **~ software** *n* Software *f* für Computerspiele.
gamester [ˈgeɪmstəʳ] *n* Spieler(in *f*) *m*.
game: ~ theory *n (in business studies)* Spieltheorie *f*; **~warden** *n* Jagdaufseher *m*.
gamin [ˈgæmɛ̃] 1 *n* Straßenjunge *m*.
2 *attr* jungenhaft, knabenhaft.
gaming [ˈgeɪmɪŋ] *n see* **gambling** ♦ **~ machine** Spielautomat *m*.
gamma ray [ˈgæməˈreɪ] *n* Gammastrahl *m*.
gammon [ˈgæmən] *n (bacon)* leicht geräucherter Vorderschinken; *(ham)* (gekochter) Schinken ♦ **~ steak** *dicke Scheibe Vorderschinken zum Braten oder Grillen.*
gammy [ˈgæmɪ] *adj see* **game**[3].

gamp [gæmp] *n (dated hum)* Regenschirm *m*, Musspritze *f (dated hum)*.
gamut ['gæmət] *n (Mus)* Noten- *or* Tonskala *f*; *(fig)* Skala *f* ◆ **to run the (whole) ~ of emotion(s)** die ganze Skala der Gefühle durchlaufen.
gamy ['geɪmɪ] *adj* nach Wild schmeckend; *(high)* angegangen ◆ **~ taste** Wildgeschmack *m*; *(high)* Hautgout *m (geh)*, angegangener Geschmack.
gander ['gændəʳ] *n* **(a)** Gänserich, Ganter *(dial) m*. **(b)** *(inf)* **to have** *or* **take a ~ at sth** auf etw *(acc)* einen Blick werfen; **let's have a ~!** gucken wir mal! *(inf)*; *(let me/us look)* laß mal sehen.
gang [gæŋ] *n* Haufen *m*, Schar *f*; *(of workers, prisoners)* Kolonne *f*, Trupp *m*; *(of criminals, youths, terrorists)* Bande, Gang *f*; *(of friends etc, clique)* Clique *f*, Haufen *m (inf)* ◆ **there was a whole ~ of them** es war ein ganzer Haufen; **the G~ of Four** die Viererbande; **~ land** *(inf)* die Unterwelt.
◆**gang up** *vi* sich zusammentun ◆ **to ~ ~ against** *or* **on sb** sich gegen jdn verbünden *or* verschwören; *(to fight)* geschlossen auf jdn *or* gegen jdn losgehen.
gangbang ['gæŋbæŋ] *(inf)* [1] *n* **(a)** *(rape)* Gruppenvergewaltigung *f*. **(b)** *(voluntary)* **she had six men round for a ~** sie wurde von sechs Männern durchgebumst *(inf)*.
[2] *vt* **she was ~ed** *(raped)* sie wurde Opfer einer Gruppenvergewaltigung; *(voluntarily)* sie wurde von mehreren Männern hintereinander gebumst *(inf)*.
ganger ['gæŋəʳ] *n* Vorarbeiter, Vormann *m*.
Ganges ['gændʒiːz] *n* Ganges *m*.
ganglia ['gæŋglɪə] *pl of* **ganglion**.
gangling ['gæŋglɪŋ] *adj* schlaksig, hochaufgeschossen.
ganglion ['gæŋglɪən] *n, pl* **ganglia (a)** *(Anat)* Ganglion *nt*; *(Med also)* Überbein *nt*. **(b)** *(fig: of activity)* Zentrum *nt*.
gangplank ['gæŋplæŋk] *n* Laufplanke *f*, Landungssteg *m*.
gang rape *n* Gruppenvergewaltigung *f*.
gangrene ['gæŋgriːn] *n* Brand *m*, Gangrän *f or nt (spec)*.
gangrenous ['gæŋgrɪnəs] *adj* brandig, gangränös *(spec)*.
gangsta rap ['gæŋstə'ræp] *n (Mus)* Gangsta Rap *m*.
gangster ['gæŋstəʳ] *n* Gangster, Verbrecher *m*.
gangsterism ['gæŋstərɪzəm] *n* Gangstertum, Verbrechertum *nt*.
gangway ['gæŋweɪ] [1] *n* **(a)** *(Naut)* *(gangplank)* Landungsbrücke, Gangway *f*; *(ladder)* Fallreep *nt*. **(b)** *(passage)* Gang *m*.
[2] *interj* Platz da.
gannet ['gænɪt] *n (Zool)* Tölpel *m*.
gantry ['gæntrɪ] *n (for crane)* Portal *nt*; *(on motorway)* Schilderbrücke *f*; *(Rail)* Signalbrücke *f*; *(for rocket)* Abschußrampe *f*.
gaol [dʒeɪl] *n, vt see* **jail**.
gaoler ['dʒeɪləʳ] *n see* **jailer**.
gap [gæp] *n (lit, fig)* Lücke *f*; *(chink)* Spalt *m*; *(in surface)* Spalte *f*, Riß *m*; *(Geog)* Spalte *f*; *(Tech: spark ~)* Abstand *m*; *(fig) (in conversation, narrative)* Pause *f*; *(gulf)* Kluft *f* ◆ **a ~ in sb's education/memory** eine Bildungs-/Gedächtnislücke.
gape [geɪp] *vi* **(a)** *(open mouth wide) (person)* den Mund aufreißen *or* -sperren; *(bird)* den Schnabel aufsperren; *(chasm etc)* gähnen, klaffen; *(seam, wound)* klaffen.
(b) *(stare: person)* starren, gaffen ◆ **to ~ at sb/sth** jdn/etw (mit offenem Mund) anstarren; **to ~ up/down at sb/sth** zu jdm/etw hinaufstarren/auf jdn/etw hinunterstarren; **the people stood and ~d** die Leute sperrten Mund und Nase auf *(inf)*.
gaping ['geɪpɪŋ] *adj* **(a)** klaffend; *chasm also* gähnend; *wound* weit geöffnet; *beaks* weit aufgesperrt. **(b)** *(staring)* gaffend; *(astonished)* staunend.
gap: ~less *adj* lückenlos; **~-toothed** *adj* mit weiter Zahnstellung; *(with teeth missing)* mit Zahnlücken.
garage ['gærɑːʒ, *(US)* gə'rɑːʒ] [1] *n (for parking)* Garage *f*; *(for petrol)* Tankstelle *f*; *(for repairs etc)* (Reparatur)werkstatt *f* ◆ **~ mechanic** Kraftfahrzeug- *or* Kfz-Mechaniker *m*; **~ sale** *meist in einer Garage durchgeführter Verkauf von Haushaltsgegenständen und Trödel*.
[2] *vt* (in einer Garage) ab- *or* unterstellen; *(drive into ~)* in die Garage fahren ◆ **the car is kept ~d** das Auto wird in einer Garage aufbewahrt.
garaging ['gærɑːʒɪŋ, (US) gə'rɑːʒɪŋ] *n* Garagenplätze *pl*.
garb [gɑːb] [1] *n* Gewand *nt*; *(inf)* Kluft *f (inf)*.
[2] *vt* kleiden.
garbage ['gɑːbɪdʒ] *n (lit: esp US)* Abfall, Müll *m*; *(fig) (useless things)* Schund, Mist *(inf) m*; *(nonsense)* Blödsinn, Quatsch *m (inf)*; *(Comput)* Garbage *m* ◆ **~ in, ~ out** *(Comput)* garbage in, garbage out, Müll rein, Müll raus.
garbage: ~ can *n (US)* Müll- *or* Abfalleimer *m*; *(outside)* Mülltonne *f*; **~ collector** *n (US)* Müllarbeiter *m*; **~ collectors** *npl* Müllabfuhr *f*; **~ disposal unit** *n* Müllschlucker *m*; **~ man** *n (US) see* **~ collector**.
garble ['gɑːbl] *vt (deliberately) message* unverständlich machen ◆ **to ~ one's words** sich beim Sprechen überschlagen.
garbled ['gɑːbld] *adj* wirr ◆ **the message got ~ on its way** die Nachricht kam völlig entstellt an; **the facts got a little ~** die Tatsachen sind etwas durcheinandergebracht worden *or* durcheinandergeraten.
garda ['gɑːrdə] *n, pl* **gardaí** ['gɑːrdiː] *(Ir) (police)* Polizei *f*; *(policeman)* Polizist *m*.
garden ['gɑːdn] [1] *n* **(a)** Garten *m* ◆ **the G~ of Eden** der Garten Eden. **(b)** *(often pl: park)* Park *m*, Gartenanlagen *pl*.
[2] *vi* im Garten arbeiten, Gartenarbeit machen, gärtnern.
garden centre *n* Gartencenter *nt*, Gärtnereimarkt *m*.
gardener ['gɑːdnəʳ] *n* Gärtner(in *f*) *m*.
garden flat *n (Brit)* Souterrainwohnung *f*.
gardenia [gɑː'diːnɪə] *n* Gardenie *f*.
gardening ['gɑːdnɪŋ] *n* Gartenarbeit *f* ◆ **she loves ~** sie arbeitet gerne im Garten, sie gärtnert gerne; **~ tools** Gartengeräte *pl*.
garden *in cpds* Garten-; **~ party** *n* Gartenparty *f or* -fest *nt*; **~-party hat** *n* breitrandiger Sommerhut; **~ produce** *n (vegetables)* Gartengemüse *nt*; *(fruit)* Gartenobst *nt*; **~ shears** *npl* Heckenschere *f*.
gargantuan [gɑː'gæntjʊən] *adj* gewaltig, enorm.
gargle ['gɑːgl] [1] *vi* gurgeln.
[2] *n (liquid)* Gurgelwasser *nt* ◆ **to have a ~** gurgeln.
gargoyle ['gɑːgɔɪl] *n* Wasserspeier *m*.
garish ['gɛərɪʃ] *adj lights, illuminations etc* grell; *colour, decorations etc also* knallig *(inf)*; *colour also* schreiend; *clothes* knallbunt, auffallend.
garishly ['gɛərɪʃlɪ] *adv* in grellen *or* schreienden Farben; *colourful* auffallend, knallig *(inf)*; *illuminated* grell.
garishness ['gɛərɪʃnɪs] *n* grelle *or* schreiende Farben; *(of colours, illuminations)* Grellheit *f*.
garland ['gɑːlənd] [1] *n* Kranz *m*; *(festoon)* Girlande *f*.
[2] *vt* bekränzen.
garlic ['gɑːlɪk] *n* Knoblauch *m* ◆ **~ bread** Knoblauchbrot *nt*; **~ press** Knoblauchpresse *f*.
garlicky ['gɑːlɪkɪ] *adj taste* Knoblauch-; *food* knoblauchhaltig ◆ **she's got ~ breath** ihr Atem riecht nach Knoblauch.
garment ['gɑːmənt] *n* Kleidungsstück *nt*; *(robe)* Gewand *nt (liter)* ◆ **all her ~s** ihre ganzen Kleider; **~ industry** *(US)* Bekleidungsindustrie *f*.
garner ['gɑːnəʳ] *vt (lit, fig) (gather)* sammeln; *knowledge* erwerben; *(store)* speichern.
garnet ['gɑːnɪt] *n* Granat *m*.
garnish ['gɑːnɪʃ] [1] *vt* garnieren, verzieren; *(fig) story also, style* ausschmücken.
[2] *n* Garnierung *f*.
garnishing ['gɑːnɪʃɪŋ] *n (Cook)* Garnierung *f*; *(act also)* Garnieren *nt*; *(fig: of style, story etc)* Ausschmückung *f*.
garret ['gærət] *n (attic room)* Mansarde, Dachkammer *f*; *(attic)* Dachboden *m*.
garrison ['gærɪsən] [1] *n* Garnison *f* ◆ **~ duty/town** Garnisonsdienst *m*/Garnisonsstadt *f*.
[2] *vt troops* in Garnison legen; *town* mit einer Garnison belegen ◆ **to be ~ed** in Garnison liegen.
garrotte [gə'rɒt] [1] *vt (execute)* garrottieren, mit der Garrotte hinrichten; *(strangle)* erdrosseln ◆ **death by garrotting** Tod durch die Garrotte.
[2] *n* Garrotte *f*.
garrulity [gə'ruːlɪtɪ] *n* Geschwätzigkeit, Schwatzhaftigkeit *f*.
garrulous ['gærʊləs] *adj* geschwätzig, schwatzhaft.
garrulously ['gærʊləslɪ] *adv* **to talk/chat** *etc* **~** schwatzen, plappern.
garryowen [ˌgærɪ'əʊɪn] *n (Rugby)* hohe Selbstvorlage.
garter ['gɑːtəʳ] *n* Strumpfband *nt*; *(US: suspender)* Strumpfhalter *m* ◆ **the (Order of the) G~** der Hosenbandorden.
garter: ~ belt *n (US)* Strumpf- *or* Hüftgürtel *m*; **~ snake** *n (US)* Ringelnatter *f*; **~ stitch** *n* gerippt *or* rechts-rechts gestricktes Muster; **5 rows ~ stitch** 5 Reihen rechts-rechts gestrickt.
gas [gæs] [1] *n* **(a)** Gas *nt* ◆ **to cook by** *or* **with** *or* **on ~** mit Gas kochen; **to cook on a slow ~** auf niedriger Flamme kochen.
(b) *(US: petrol)* Benzin *nt*.
(c) *(anaesthetic)* Lachgas *nt* ◆ **to have ~** Lachgas bekommen; **to have a tooth out with ~** sich *(dat)* einen Zahn unter Lachgasnarkose ziehen lassen.
(d) *(Mil)* (Gift)gas *nt*.
(e) *(inf: talk)* leeres Gefasel *(inf)*; *(boastful)* großspuriges Gerede, Angeberei *f* ◆ **to have a good ~** einen Schwatz halten.
(f) *(sl)* **it's/he's a ~** *(fantastic)* es/er ist Klasse *or* dufte *or (all sl)*; *(hilarious)* es/er ist zum Schreien *(inf)*.
[2] *vt* vergasen ◆ **they were ~sed accidentally during their sleep** sie starben im Schlaf an Gasvergiftung; **to ~ oneself** den Gashahn aufdrehen, sich mit Gas vergiften.
[3] *vi (inf: talk)* schwafeln *(inf)*, faseln *(inf)*.
gas *in cpds* Gas-; **~bag** *n (inf)* Quasselstrippe *f (inf)*; **~ bracket** *n* Gasanschluß(stelle *f*) *m*, Gaszuleitungsrohr *nt*; *(for light)* Wandarm *m*; **~ chamber** *n* Gaskammer *f*; **~ cooker** *n* Gasherd *m*; **~ engine** *n* Gasmaschine *f or* -motor *m*.
gaseous ['gæsɪəs] *adj* gasförmig.
gas: ~ field *n* Erdgasfeld *nt*; **~ fire** *n* Gasofen *m*; **~-fired** *adj* Gas-, gasbefeuert *(form)*; **~ fitter** *n* Gasinstallateur *m*; **~ fittings** *npl* Gasgeräte *pl*; **~ fixture** *n* festinstalliertes Gasgerät; **~ guzzler** *n (US inf)* Säufer, Benzinschlucker *(inf) m*.
gash [gæʃ] [1] *n (wound)* klaffende Wunde; *(in earth, tree)* (klaffende) Spalte; *(slash)* tiefe Kerbe; *(in upholstery)* tiefer Schlitz.
[2] *vt* aufschlitzen; *furniture, wood* tief einkerben ◆ **he fell and ~ed his head/knee** er ist gestürzt und hat sich *(dat)* dabei den Kopf/das Knie aufgeschlagen; **I ~ed my foot open** ich habe mir den Fuß aufgeschlitzt.
gas: ~ heater *n* Gasofen *m*; **~-holder** *n* Gasometer *m*, (Groß)gasbehälter *m*; **~ jet** *n* Gasdüse *f*.
gasket ['gæskɪt] *n (Tech)* Dichtung *f*.
gas: ~ lamp *n* Gaslampe *f*; *(in streets)* Gaslaterne *f*; **~light** *n* **(a)** *see* **~ lamp**; **(b)** *no pl* Gaslicht *nt or* -beleuchtung *f*; **~ lighter** *n* **(a)** Gasanzünder *m*; **(b)** *(for cigarettes etc)* Gasfeuerzeug *nt*; **~ lighting** *n* Gasbeleuchtung *f*; **~-lit** *adj* mit Gasbeleuchtung; **~ main** *n* Gasleitung *f*; **~man** *n* Gasmann *m (inf)*; **~ mantle** *n* (Gas)glühstrumpf *m*; **~ mask** *n* Gasmaske *f*; **~ meter** *n* Gas-

zähler *m or* -uhr *f*.
gasoline ['gæsəʊliːn] *n (US)* Benzin *nt*.
gasometer [gæ'sɒmɪtəʳ] *n* Gasometer, (Groß)gasbehälter *m*.
gas oven *n* Gasherd *m*; *(gas chamber)* Gaskammer *f* ◆ **to put one's head in the ~** *(kill oneself)* den Gashahn aufdrehen.
gasp [gɑːsp] [1] *n (for breath)* tiefer Atemzug ◆ **the ~s of the runner** das Keuchen des Läufers; **to give a ~ (of surprise/fear etc)** (vor Überraschung/Angst *etc*) die Luft anhalten *or* nach Luft schnappen *(inf)*; **a ~ went up at his audacity** seine Verwegenheit verschlug den Leuten den Atem; **to be at one's last ~** in den letzten Zügen liegen; *(exhausted etc)* auf dem letzten Loch pfeifen *(inf)*.
[2] *vi (continually)* keuchen; *(once)* tief einatmen; *(with surprise etc)* nach Luft schnappen *(inf)* ◆ **to make sb ~** *(lit, fig)* jdm den Atem nehmen; **to ~ for breath** nach Atem ringen, nach Luft schnappen *(inf)*; **he ~ed with astonishment** er war so erstaunt, daß es ihm den Atem verschlug; **heavens, no!, she ~ed** um Himmels willen, nein!, stieß sie hervor.
◆**gasp out** *vt sep* hervorstoßen.
gasper ['gɑːspəʳ] *n (Brit sl)* Glimmstengel *m (inf)*.
gas: ~-permeable *adj lenses* gasdurchlässig; **~ pipe** *n* Gasrohr *nt or* -leitung *f*; **~ plasma** [1] *n* Gasplasma *nt*; [2] *adj screen* Gasplasma-; **~ pump** *n (US)* Zapfsäule *f*; **~ ring** *n* Gasbrenner *m*; *(portable)* Gaskocher *m*; **~ station** *n (US)* Tankstelle *f*; **~ stove** *n* Gasherd *m*; *(portable)* Gaskocher *m*.
gassy ['gæsɪ] *adj (+er)* **(a)** *(Sci)* gasförmig ◆ **it smells ~** es riecht nach Gas. **(b)** *drink* kohlensäurehaltig. **(c)** *(inf) person* geschwätzig.
gas: ~ tank *n (US)* Benzintank *m*; **~ tap** *n* Gashahn *m*; **~tight** *adj* gasdicht.
gastric ['gæstrɪk] *adj* Magen-, gastrisch *(spec)*.
gastric: ~ flu *or* **influenza** *n* Darmgrippe *f*; **~ juices** *npl* Magensäfte *pl*; **~ ulcer** *n* Magengeschwür *nt*.
gastritis [gæs'traɪtɪs] *n* Magenschleimhautentzündung, Gastritis *f*.
gastro- ['gæstrəʊ-] *pref* Magen-, Gastro- *(spec)* ◆ **~enteritis** Magen-Darm-Entzündung, Gastroenteritis *(spec) f*.
gastronome ['gæstrənəʊm] *n* Feinschmecker *m*.
gastronomic [,gæstrə'nɒmɪk] *adj* gastronomisch, kulinarisch.
gastronomy [gæs'trɒnəmɪ] *n* Gastronomie *f*.
gastropod ['gæstrəpɒd] *n* Bauchfüß(l)er, Gastropode *(spec) m*.
gasworks ['gæswɜːks] *n sing or pl* Gaswerk *nt*.
gat [gæt] *n (US sl)* Kanone, Knarre *(sl) f*.
gate [geɪt] [1] *n* **(a)** Tor *nt*; *(small, garden ~)* Pforte *f*; *(five-barred ~)* Gatter *nt*; *(in station)* Sperre *f*; *(in airport)* Flugsteig *m*; *(of level-crossing)* Schranke *f*; *(Sport: starting ~)* Startmaschine *f*; *(sports ground entrance)* Einlaß, Eingang *m* ◆ **to open/shut the ~s** das Tor *etc* öffnen/schließen; **the ~s of heaven** das Himmelstor, die Himmelstür *or* -pforte.
(b) *(Sport) (attendance)* Zuschauerzahl *f*; *(entrance money)* Einnahmen *pl*.
[2] *vt pupil, student* Ausgangssperre erteilen *(+dat)* ◆ **to be ~d** Ausgangssperre haben.
-gate [geɪt] *suf* -skandal *m*, -affäre *f* ◆ **Iran~** der Iran(gate)-Skandal, die Iran(gate)-Affäre..
gateau ['gætəʊ] *n* Torte *f*.
gate: ~crash *(inf)* [1] *vt* **to ~crash a party/meeting** in eine Party/Versammlung reinplatzen *(inf)*; *(crowd: to disrupt it)* eine Party/Versammlung stürmen; [2] *vi* einfach so hingehen *(inf)*; **~crasher** *n* ungeladener Gast; *(at meeting)* Eindringling *m*; **~house** *n* Pförtnerhaus *or* -häuschen *nt*; **~keeper** *n* Pförtner *m*; *(Rail)* Schrankenwärter *m*; **~-leg(ged) table** *n* Klapptisch *m*; **~ money** *n (Sport)* Einnahmen *pl*; **~post** *n* Torpfosten *m*; **between you, me and the ~post** *(inf)* unter uns gesagt; **~way** *n (lit, fig)* Tor *nt (to zu)*; *(archway, ~ frame)* Torbogen *m*.
gather ['gæðəʳ] [1] *vt* **(a)** *(collect, bring together)* sammeln; *crowd, people* versammeln; *flowers, cultivated fruit* pflücken; *potatoes, corn etc* ernten; *harvest* einbringen; *taxes* einziehen; *(collect up) broken glass, pins etc* zusammenlegen, aufsammeln; *one's belongings, books, clothes* (zusammen)packen; *an impression* gewinnen ◆ **to ~ one's strength/thoughts** Kräfte sammeln/seine Gedanken ordnen, sich sammeln; **velvet curtains ~ dust/dirt** Samtvorhänge sind Staub-/Schmutzfänger; **it just sat there ~ing dust** es stand nur da und verstaubte; **to be ~ed to one's fathers** *(liter)* heimgehen *(liter)*.
(b) *(increase)* **to ~ speed** schneller werden, an Geschwindigkeit gewinnen; **to ~ strength** stärker werden.
(c) *(infer)* schließen *(from* aus) ◆ **I ~ed that** das dachte ich mir; **I ~ from the papers that he has ...** wie ich aus den Zeitungen ersehe, hat er ...; **as far as I can ~** (so) wie ich es sehe; **I ~ she won't be coming** ich nehme an, daß sie nicht kommt; **as you will have/might have ~ed ...** wie Sie bestimmt/vielleicht bemerkt haben ...; **as will be ~ed from my report** wie aus meinem Bericht hervorgeht *or* zu ersehen ist.
(d) to ~ sb into one's arms jdn in die Arme nehmen *or* schließen; **she ~ed her mink around her** sie hüllte sich in ihren Nerz.
(e) *(Sew)* kräuseln, raffen; *(at seam)* fassen.
(f) *(Typ)* zusammentragen, kollationieren *(spec)*.
[2] *vi* **(a)** *(collect) (people)* sich versammeln; *(crowds also)* sich ansammeln; *(objects, dust etc)* sich (an)sammeln; *(clouds)* sich zusammenziehen; *(storm)* sich zusammenbrauen ◆ **tears ~ed in her eyes** ihre Augen füllten sich mit Tränen.
(b) *(increase: darkness, force etc)* zunehmen *(in* an *+dat)*.
(c) *(abscess etc)* sich mit Eiter füllen; *(pus)* sich sammeln.
[3] *n (Sew)* Fältchen *nt* ◆ **there were ~s at the waist (of the skirt)** der Rock war in der Taille gekräuselt *or* gerafft *or* gefaßt.
◆**gather in** *vt sep* **(a)** einsammeln; *crops* einbringen; *taxes* einziehen; *animals* zusammentreiben. **(b)** *cloth* fassen.
◆**gather round** *vi* zusammenkommen ◆ **come on, children, ~ ~!** kommt alle her, Kinder!; **they ~ed ~ the fire** sie versammelten *or* scharten sich um das Feuer.
◆**gather together** [1] *vi* zusammenkommen, sich versammeln.
[2] *vt sep* einsammeln; *one's belongings, books* zusammenpacken; *people* versammeln; *team* zusammenstellen; *animals* zusammentreiben ◆ **to ~ oneself ~** zu sich kommen; *(for jump etc)* sich bereit machen *(for* zu).
◆**gather up** *vt sep* aufsammeln; *one's belongings* zusammenpacken; *hair* hochstecken; *skirts* (hoch)raffen; *(fig) pieces* auflesen ◆ **he ~ed himself ~ to his full height** er reckte sich zu voller Größe auf.
gathering ['gæðərɪŋ] *n* **(a)** *(people at meeting etc)* Versammlung *f*; *(meeting)* Treffen *nt*; *(small group)* Gruppe *f*, Häufchen *nt*; *(of curious onlookers)* Ansammlung *f*. **(b)** *(Sew: gathers)* Krause *f*.
GATT [gæt] *abbr of* **General Agreement on Tariffs and Trade** GATT.
gauche *adj*, **~ly** *adv* [gəʊʃ, -lɪ] *(socially)* unbeholfen, tölpelhaft; *remark* ungeschickt; *(clumsy)* linkisch, ungeschickt.
gaucheness ['gəʊʃnɪs] *n* Unbeholfenheit, Tölpelhaftigkeit *f*; Ungeschicktheit *f*.
gaucherie ['gəʊʃəriː] *n* **(a)** *see* **gaucheness. (b)** *(act)* Tölpelei *f*; *(remark)* ungeschickte Bemerkung.
gaucho ['gaʊtʃəʊ] *n* Gaucho *m*.
gaudily ['gɔːdɪlɪ] *adv see adj*.
gaudiness ['gɔːdɪnɪs] *n* Knalligkeit *(inf)*, Buntheit *f*, Auffälligkeit *f*.
gaudy ['gɔːdɪ] *adj (+er)* knallig *(inf)*, auffällig bunt; *colours* auffällig, knallig *(inf)*.
gauge [geɪdʒ] [1] *n* **(a)** *(instrument)* Meßgerät *or* -instrument *nt*; *(to measure diameter, width etc)* (Meß)lehre *f*; *(for rings)* Ringmaß *nt*; *(to measure water level)* Pegel *m* ◆ **pressure/wind ~** Druck-/Windmesser *m*; **temperature ~** Temperaturanzeiger *m*; **petrol ~** Benzinuhr *f*; **oil ~** Ölstandsanzeiger *or* -messer *m*.
(b) *(thickness, width) (of wire, sheet metal etc)* Stärke *f*; *(of bullet)* Durchmesser *m*, Kaliber *nt*; *(Rail)* Spurweite *f* ◆ **standard/narrow ~** Normal- *or* Regel-/Schmalspur *f*.
(c) *(fig)* Maßstab *m (of* für).
[2] *vt* **(a)** *(Tech: measure)* messen. **(b)** *(fig: appraise) person's capacities, character* beurteilen; *reaction, course of events* abschätzen; *situation* abwägen; *(guess)* schätzen.
Gaul [gɔːl] *n (country)* Gallien *nt*; *(person)* Gallier(in *f*) *m*.
gaunt [gɔːnt] *adj (+er)* hager; *(from suffering)* abgezehrt, ausgemergelt; *trees* dürr und kahl; *landscape* öde, karg.
gauntlet[1] ['gɔːntlɪt] *n* **(a)** *(of armour)* Panzerhandschuh *m* ◆ **to throw down/pick up** *or* **take up the ~** *(fig)* den Fehdehandschuh hinwerfen/aufnehmen. **(b)** *(glove)* (Stulpen)handschuh *m*; *(part of glove)* Stulpe *f*.
gauntlet[2] *n*: **to run the ~** *(fig)* Spießruten laufen; **to (have to) run the ~ of sth** einer Sache *(dat)* ausgesetzt sein; **the child had to run the ~ of his tormentors** das Kind mußte einen Spießrutenlauf durch die Reihen seiner Peiniger veranstalten.
gauntness ['gɔːntnɪs] *n see adj* Hagerkeit *f*, Abgezehrtheit, Ausgemergeltheit *f*; Kahlheit *f*; Öde, Kargheit *f*.
gauze [gɔːz] *n* Gaze *f*; *(Med also)* (Verbands)mull *m* ◆ **wire ~** Drahtgaze *f or* -netz *nt*.
gauzy ['gɔːzɪ] *adj (+er)* hauchfein *or* -zart.
gave [geɪv] *pret of* **give**.
gavel ['gævl] *n* Hammer *m*.
gavotte [gə'vɒt] *n* Gavotte *f*.
gawk [gɔːk] *(inf)* [1] *n* Schlaks *m (inf)*.
[2] *vi see* **gawp**.
gawkily ['gɔːkɪlɪ] *adv see adj*.
gawkiness ['gɔːkɪnɪs] *n see adj* Schlaksigkeit, Staksigkeit *(inf) f*; Unbeholfenheit *f*.
gawky ['gɔːkɪ] *adj (+er) person, movement* schlaksig, staksig *(inf)*, linkisch; *animal* unbeholfen, staksig *(inf)*; *appearance* unbeholfen.
gawp [gɔːp] *vi (inf)* glotzen *(inf)*, gaffen ◆ **to ~ at sb/sth** jdn/etw anglotzen *(inf) or* angaffen; **what are you ~ing at?** was glotzt du da? *(inf)*.
gay [geɪ] [1] *adj (+er)* **(a)** *(happy)* fröhlich; *colours also* bunt; *one colour also* lebhaft; *company, occasion* lustig ◆ **with ~ abandon** hingebungsvoll. **(b)** *(pleasure-loving)* lebenslustig; *life* flott ◆ **~ dog** *(inf)* lockerer Vogel *(inf)*. **(c)** *(homosexual)* schwul *(inf)*.
[2] *n* Schwule(r) *mf* ◆ **G~ Lib** Schwulenbewegung *f*.
Gaza Strip ['gɑːzə'strɪp] *n* Gaza-Streifen *m*.
gaze [geɪz] [1] *n* Blick *m*.
[2] *vi* starren ◆ **to ~ at sb/sth** jdn/etw anstarren.
◆**gaze about** *or* **around** *vi* um sich blicken ◆ **he ~d ~ (him) at the strange scene** er sah sich *(dat)* erstaunt die seltsame Szene an.
gazebo [gə'ziːbəʊ] *n* Gartenlaube *f*.
gazelle [gə'zel] *n* Gazelle *f*.
gazette [gə'zet] [1] *n (magazine)* Zeitung, Gazette *(dated) f*; *(government publication)* Staatsanzeiger *m*, Amtsblatt *nt*.
[2] *vt* im Staatsanzeiger bekanntgeben.
gazetteer [,gæzɪ'tɪəʳ] *n* alphabetisches Ortsverzeichnis *(mit Ortsbeschreibung)*.
gazump [gə'zʌmp] *vt (Brit) entgegen mündlicher Zusage ein Haus an einen Höherbietenden verkaufen*.

GB *abbr of* **Great Britain** GB, Großbritannien *nt.*

gbh *abbr of* **grievous bodily harm.**

GC (*Brit*) *abbr of* **George Cross** *Tapferkeitsmedaille.*

GCE (*Brit*) *abbr of* **General Certificate of Education.**

GCHQ (*Brit*) *abbr of* **Government Communications Headquarters** *Zentralstelle f des britischen Nachrichtendienstes.*

GCSE (*Brit*) *abbr of* **General Certificate of Secondary Education.**

Gdns *abbr of* **Gardens.**

GDR *abbr of* **German Democratic Republic** DDR *f.*

gear [gɪəʳ] 1 *n* **(a)** (*Aut etc*) Gang *m* ◆ **~s** *pl* (*mechanism*) Getriebe *nt*; (*on bicycle*) Gangschaltung *f*; **a bicycle with three-speed ~s** ein Fahrrad mit Dreigangschaltung; **to put the car into ~** einen Gang einlegen; **the car is/you're in/out of ~** der Gang ist eingelegt *or* drin (*inf*)/das Auto ist im Leerlauf, es ist kein Gang drin (*inf*); **to leave the car in/out of ~** den Gang eingelegt lassen/das Auto im Leerlauf lassen; **to change ~** schalten; **to change into third ~** in den dritten Gang schalten, den dritten Gang einlegen; **the car jumps out of** *or* **won't stay in ~** der Gang springt heraus; **I am usually in bottom ~ in the mornings** morgens dauert bei mir alles länger.
(b) (*inf*) (*equipment*) Ausrüstung *f*, Zeug *nt* (*inf*), Sachen *pl* (*inf*); (*tools*) Gerät, Zeug (*inf*) *nt*; (*belongings*) Sachen *pl* (*inf*), Zeug(s) *nt* (*inf*); (*clothing*) Sachen *pl* (*inf*).
(c) (*Tech*) Vorrichtung *f*; *see* **landing ~, steering ~.**
2 *vt* (*fig*) abstellen, ausrichten (*to* auf +*acc*) ◆ **to be ~ed to sth** auf etw (*acc*) abgestellt sein; (*person, ambition*) auf etw (*acc*) ausgerichtet sein; (*have facilities for*) auf etw (*acc*) eingerichtet sein.
3 *vi* (*Tech*) eingreifen, im Eingriff sein.

◆**gear down** 1 *vi* (*driver*) herunterschalten, in einen niedrigeren Gang schalten.
2 *vt sep engine* niedertouriger auslegen *or* machen; (*fig*) drosseln.

◆**gear up** 1 *vi* heraufschalten, in einen höheren Gang schalten.
2 *vt sep engine* höhertourig auslegen *or* machen ◆ **to ~ oneself ~** (*fig*) sich bereit machen; **to ~ oneself ~ for sth** (*fig*) sich auf etw (*acc*) einstellen.

gear: ~box *n* Getriebe *nt*; **~ change** *n* Schalten *nt.*

-geared [-gɪəd] *adj suf* -tourig.

gearing ['gɪərɪŋ] *n* **(a)** (*Aut*) Auslegung *f* (der Gänge). **(b)** (*Fin: of company*) Verhältnis *nt* zwischen Eigen- und Fremdkapital.

gear: ~lever *n* Schaltknüppel *m*; (*column-mounted*) Schalthebel *m*; **~ ratio** *n* Übersetzung(sverhältnis *nt*) *f*; **~ shift** (*US*), **~ stick** *n see* **~ lever**; **~ wheel** *n* Zahnrad *nt.*

geddit? ['gedɪt] *inter* (*sl*) kapiert? (*inf*).

gee [dʒiː] *interj* **(a)** (*esp US inf*) Mensch (*inf*), Mann (*inf*) ◆ **~ whiz!** Mensch Meier! (*inf*). **(b)** (*to horse*) **~ up!** hü!

gee-gee ['dʒiːdʒiː] *n* (*baby-talk*) Hottehü *nt* (*inf*).

geek [giːk] *n* (*esp US inf*) Waschlappen *m* (*inf*).

geeky ['giːkɪ] *adj* (*esp US inf*) dämlich (*inf*).

geese [giːs] *pl of* **goose.**

geezer ['giːzəʳ] *n* (*sl*) Typ (*sl*), Kerl (*inf*) *m* ◆ **old ~** Opa *m* (*inf*).

Geiger counter ['gaɪgəˌkaʊntəʳ] *n* Geigerzähler *m.*

geisha (girl) ['geɪʃə(gɜːl)] *n* Geisha *f.*

gel [dʒel] 1 *n* Gel *nt.*
2 *vi* gelieren; (*jelly etc also*) fest werden; (*fig: plan, idea*) Gestalt annehmen.

gelatin(e) ['dʒelətiːn] *n* Gelatine *f.*

gelatinous [dʒɪ'lætɪnəs] *adj* gelatine- *or* gallertartig.

geld [geld] *vt* kastrieren, verschneiden.

gelding ['geldɪŋ] *n* kastriertes Tier, Kastrat *m* (*spec*); (*horse*) Wallach *m.*

gelignite ['dʒelɪgnaɪt] *n* Plastiksprengstoff *m.*

gem [dʒem] *n* Edelstein *m*; (*cut also*) Juwel *nt* (*geh*); (*fig*) (*person*) Juwel *nt*; (*of collection etc*) Prachtstück *or* -exemplar *nt* ◆ **be a ~ and** ... sei ein Schatz und ...; **that joke/story/this recording is a real ~** der Witz/die Geschichte/die Aufnahme ist Spitzenklasse (*inf*) *or* einmalig gut; **every one a ~** (*inf*) einer besser als der andere; **a ~ of a book/painting/watch** (*splendid*) ein meisterhaftes Buch/Gemälde/eine prachtvolle Uhr; (*sweet, amusing*) ein entzückendes Büchlein/Bildchen/Ührchen.

Gemini ['dʒemɪniː] *n* Zwillinge *pl* ◆ **he's a ~** er ist Zwilling.

gemstone ['dʒemstəʊn] *n* Edelstein *m.*

Gen *abbr of* **General** Gen.

gen [dʒen] *n* (*Brit inf*) Informationen *pl* ◆ **to give sb the ~ on** *or* **about sth** jdn über etw (*acc*) informieren; **what's the ~ on this?** worum geht es hier?

◆**gen up** (*Brit inf*) 1 *vi* **to ~ ~ on sth** sich über etw (*acc*) informieren.
2 *vt sep* **to ~ sb ~/get ~ned ~ on sth** jdn/sich über etw (*acc*) informieren; **to be (all) ~ned ~ on** *or* **about sth** sich (sehr gut) auskennen in etw (*dat*).

gender ['dʒendəʳ] *n* Geschlecht *nt* ◆ **what ~ is this word?** welches Geschlecht hat dieses Wort?; **the feminine/masculine ~** das Femininum/Maskulinum.

gender: ~-bender *n* (*inf*) **(a)** (*Comput*) *see* **~ changer**; **(b)** (*person*) **to be a ~-bender** (*man*) feminin wirken; (*woman*) maskulin wirken; **~ changer** *n* (*Comput*) Stecker-Stecker-Adapter *m*; Buchse-Buchse-Adapter *m*; **~ issues** *npl* geschlechtsspezifische Fragen *pl.*

gene [dʒiːn] *n* Gen *nt*, Erbfaktor *m* ◆ **~ bank** Gen-Bank *f*; **~ pool** Erbmasse *f.*

genealogical [ˌdʒiːnɪə'lɒdʒɪkəl] *adj* genealogisch ◆ **~ tree** Stammbaum *m.*

genealogist [ˌdʒiːnɪ'ælədʒɪst] *n* Genealoge *m*, Genealogin *f*, Stammbaumforscher(in *f*) *m.*

genealogy [ˌdʒiːnɪ'ælədʒɪ] *n* Genealogie, Stammbaumforschung *f*; (*ancestry*) Stammbaum *m.*

genera ['dʒenərə] *pl of* **genus.**

general ['dʒenərəl] 1 *adj* **(a)** allgemein; *view, enquiry, discussion also* generell; *manager, director, agent, agency* General-; *meeting* Voll-; (*of shareholders*) Haupt-; *user, reader* Durchschnitts-; *trader, dealer, store* Gemischtwaren- ◆ **as a ~ rule, in the ~ way (of things)** im allgemeinen; **it is ~ practice** *or* **a ~ custom** es ist allgemein üblich; **in ~ use** allgemein in Gebrauch; **for ~ use** für den allgemeinen *or* normalen Gebrauch; (*for use by everybody*) für die Allgemeinheit; **to be a ~ favourite** allgemein beliebt sein; **we just had a ~ chat** wir haben uns ganz allgemein unterhalten; **~ headquarters** Hauptquartier *nt*; (*Mil*) Generalhauptquartier *nt*; **~ editor** Allgemeinredakteur *m*; (*of particular book*) Herausgeber *m*; **to grant a ~ pardon** eine Generalamnestie erlassen (*to* für); **to explain sth in ~ terms** etw allgemein erklären; **the ~ plan** *or* **idea is that** ... wir/sie *etc* hatten uns/sich (*dat*) das so gedacht, daß ...; **the ~ idea of that is to** ... damit soll bezweckt werden *or* es geht dabei darum, daß ...; **that was the ~ idea** so war das (auch) gedacht; **the ~ idea is to wait and see** wir/sie *etc* wollen einfach mal abwarten; **I've got the ~ idea of it** ich habe eine Vorstellung *or* ich weiß so ungefähr, worum es geht; **to give sb a ~ idea/outline of a subject** jdm eine ungefähre Vorstellung von einem Thema geben/ein Thema in groben Zügen umreißen; **to be ~** (*not detailed or specific: wording, proposals*) allgemein gehalten sein; (*vague*) unbestimmt *or* vage sein; (*promises, clause*) unverbindlich sein; (*widespread: custom, weather etc*) weit verbreitet sein; (*customary*) allgemein üblich sein; **to make the wording/clause** *etc* **more ~** die Formulierung/Klausel *etc* allgemeiner fassen.
(b) (*after official title*) Ober- ◆ **Consul ~** Generalkonsul *m.*
2 *n* **(a) in ~** im allgemeinen; **to go from the ~ to the particular** vom Allgemeinen ins Besondere gehen.
(b) (*Mil*) General *m*; (*Caesar, Napoleon etc*) Feldherr *m.*

general: ~ anaesthetic *n* Vollnarkose *f*; **G~ Assembly** *n* (*of United Nations*) Voll- *or* Generalversammlung *f*; (*Eccl*) Generalsynode *f*; **G~ Certificate of Education** *n* (*Brit*) (*O-level*) ≃ Mittlere Reife; (*A-level*) ≃ Reifezeugnis, Abitur *nt*; **~ degree** *n nicht spezialisierter Studienabschluß*; **~ election** *n* Parlamentswahlen *pl.*

generalissimo [ˌdʒenərə'lɪsɪməʊ] *n* Generalissimus *m.*

generalist ['dʒenərəlɪst] *n* Generalist(in *f*) *m.*

generality [ˌdʒenə'rælɪtɪ] *n* **(a) to talk in/of generalities** ganz allgemein sprechen/sich über Allgemeines *or* Allgemeinheiten unterhalten. **(b)** (*general quality*) Allgemeinheit *f*; (*general applicability*) Allgemeingültigkeit *f* ◆ **a rule of great ~** eine fast überall anwendbare Regel.

generalization [ˌdʒenərəlaɪ'zeɪʃən] *n* Verallgemeinerung *f.*

generalize ['dʒenərəlaɪz] *vti* verallgemeinern ◆ **to ~ (a conclusion) from sth** allgemeine Schlüsse aus etw ziehen; **to ~ about sth** etw verallgemeinern.

general knowledge 1 *n* Allgemeinwissen *nt or* -bildung *f.*
2 *attr* zur Allgemeinbildung.

generally ['dʒenərəlɪ] *adv* (*usually*) im allgemeinen; (*for the most part also*) im großen und ganzen; (*widely, not in detail*) allgemein ◆ **~ speaking** im allgemeinen, im großen und ganzen.

general: ~ manager *n* Hauptgeschäftsführer(in *f*) *m*; **G~ Post Office** *n* (*Brit*) (*building*) Hauptpost(amt *nt*) *f*; (*dated: organization*) Post *f*; **~ practice** *n* (*Med*) Allgemeinmedizin *f*; **~ practitioner** *n* Arzt *m*/Ärztin *f* für Allgemeinmedizin, praktischer Arzt, praktische Ärztin; **~ public** *n* Öffentlichkeit, Allgemeinheit *f*; **~-purpose** *adj* Mehrzweck-, Universal-.

generalship ['dʒenərəlʃɪp] *n* (*Mil*) **(a)** (*office*) Generalsrang *m*; (*period of office*) Dienstzeit *f* als General ◆ **under his ~** als er General war. **(b)** (*skill*) Feldherrnkunst *f.*

general: ~ staff *n* (*Mil*) Generalstab *m*; **~ store** *n* Gemischtwarenhandlung *f*; **~ strike** *n* Generalstreik *m.*

generate ['dʒenəreɪt] *vt* (*lit, fig*) erzeugen; *heat, fumes also* entwickeln; (*Ling*) generieren ◆ **generating station** Kraftwerk, Elektrizitätswerk *nt.*

generation [ˌdʒenə'reɪʃən] *n* **(a)** (*lit, fig*) Generation *f*; (*period of time also*) Menschenalter *nt* ◆ **~ gap** Generationsproblem *nt or* -konflikt *m*. **(b)** (*act of generating*) Erzeugung *f.*

generative ['dʒenərətɪv] *adj* (*Ling*) generativ; (*Biol*) Zeugungs-, generativ (*spec*); (*Elec*) Erzeugungs-.

generator ['dʒenəreɪtəʳ] *n* Generator *m.*

generic [dʒɪ'nerɪk] *adj* artmäßig; (*Biol*) Gattungs- ◆ **~ name** *or* **term** Oberbegriff *m*; (*Biol*) Gattungsbegriff *or* -name *m*; **~ group** Gattung *f.*

generically [dʒɪ'nerɪkəlɪ] *adv* (*Biol*) gattungsmäßig ◆ **they could be ~ described as** ... sie könnten unter dem Oberbegriff ... zusammengefaßt werden.

generosity [ˌdʒenə'rɒsɪtɪ] *n* Großzügigkeit f; (*nobleness*) Großmut *m.*

generous ['dʒenərəs] *adj* **(a)** *person, action, gift* großzügig; (*noble-minded*) großmütig ◆ **he has a ~ mind** er ist großmütig. **(b)** (*large, plentiful*) reichlich; *figure* üppig ◆ **a ~ size 14** eine groß ausgefallene Größe 14.

generously ['dʒenərəslɪ] *adv see adj* ◆ **a ~ cut dress** ein groß ausgefallenes Kleid.

generousness ['dʒenərəsnɪs] *n* **(a)** *see* **generosity. (b)** *see adj (b)* Reichlichkeit *f*, Üppigkeit *f.*

genesis ['dʒenɪsɪs] *n, pl* **geneses** ['dʒenɪsiːz] Entstehung, Genese (*spec*) *f* ◆ **(the Book of) G~** (die) Genesis, die Schöpfungsgeschichte.

genetic [dʒɪ'netɪk] *adj* genetisch ◆ **does crime have a ~ cause?** ist Kriminalität erblich bedingt?; **~ information** Erbinformation *f.*

genetically [dʒɪ'netɪkəlɪ] *adv* genetisch ◆ **~ harmful** erbgutschädigend.

genetic: ~ counselling *n* genetische Beratung; **~ engineer** *n* Gentechniker(in *f*) *m*; **~ engineering** *n* Gentechnologie *f*; **~ fingerprint** *n* genetischer Fingerabdruck: **~ fingerprinting** *n* genetische Fingerab-

drücke *pl.*
geneticist [dʒɪˈnetɪsɪst] *n* Vererbungsforscher(in *f*), Genetiker(in *f*) *m.*
genetics [dʒɪˈnetɪks] *n sing* Vererbungslehre, Genetik *f.*
Geneva [dʒɪˈniːvə] *n* Genf *nt* ♦ **Lake ~** der Genfer See; **~ Convention** Genfer Konvention *f.*
genial [ˈdʒiːnɪəl] *adj* (*lit, fig*) freundlich; *person also* leutselig; *smile also* liebenswert; *atmosphere, climate also, company* angenehm; *warmth, influence* wohltuend.
geniality [ˌdʒiːnɪˈælɪtɪ] *n* (*lit, fig*) Freundlichkeit *f*; (*of person also*) Leutseligkeit *f*; (*of company*) Angenehmheit *f.*
genially [ˈdʒiːnɪəlɪ] *adv see adj.*
genie [ˈdʒiːnɪ] *n* dienstbarer Geist.
genii [ˈdʒiːnɪaɪ] *pl of* **genius.**
genital [ˈdʒenɪtl] *adj* Geschlechts-, Genital-, genital ♦ **~ herpes** Herpes genitalis *m*; **~ warts** Feigwarzen *pl.*
genitalia [ˌdʒenɪˈteɪlɪə] *npl* (*form*) Genitalien *pl.*
genitals [ˈdʒenɪtlz] *npl* Geschlechtsteile, Genitalien *pl.*
genitive [ˈdʒenɪtɪv] [1] *n* (*Gram*) Genitiv *m* ♦ **in the ~** im Genitiv.
[2] *adj* Genitiv- ♦ **~ case** Genitiv *m.*
genius [ˈdʒiːnɪəs] *n, pl* **-es** *or* **genii** **(a)** Genie *nt*; (*mental or creative capacity also*) Genius *m*, Schöpferkraft *f* ♦ **a man of ~** ein genialer Mensch, ein Genie *nt*; **to have a ~ for sth** eine besondere Gabe für etw haben; **his ~ for organization/languages** sein Organisationstalent *nt*/seine hohe Sprachbegabung; **he has a ~ for saying the wrong thing** er hat ein Talent *or* die Gabe, immer das Falsche zu sagen.
(b) (*spirit: of period, country etc*) (Zeit)geist *m.*
(c) (*bad influence*) **evil ~** böser Geist.
Genoa [ˈdʒenəʊə] *n* Genua *nt* ♦ **~ cake** *mandelverzierter Früchtekuchen.*
genocidal [ˈdʒenəʊsaɪdl] *adj war, campaign* völkermordähnlich ♦ **~ crime** Völkermord- *or* Genozidverbrechen *nt.*
genocide [ˈdʒenəʊsaɪd] *n* Völkermord *m*, Genozid *nt* (*geh*).
Genoese [ˌdʒenəʊˈiːz] [1] *adj* genuesisch.
[2] *n* Genuese *m*, Genuesin *f.*
genome [ˈdʒiːnəʊm] *n* Genom *nt.*
genotype [ˈdʒenəʊtaɪp] *n* Genotyp(us) *m*, Erbgut *nt.*
genre [ˈʒɑ̃ːŋrə] *n* Genre *nt* (*geh*), Gattung *f*; (*Art: also* **~ painting**) Genremalerei *f.*
gent [dʒent] *n* (*inf*) *abbr of* **gentleman** ♦ **~s' shoes/outfitter** (*Comm*) Herrenschuhe *pl*/-ausstatter *m*; **"G~s"** (*Brit: lavatory*) „Herren"; **where is the ~s?** wo ist die Herrentoilette?
genteel [dʒenˈtiːl] *adj* vornehm, fein; (*affected*) *manners* geziert ♦ **to live in ~ poverty** arm, aber vornehm leben.
genteelly [dʒenˈtiːlɪ] *adv* vornehm; (*affectedly*) geziert ♦ **she coughed ~** sie hüstelte.
gentian [ˈdʒenʃɪən] *n* Enzian *m.*
Gentile [ˈdʒentaɪl] [1] *n* Nichtjude *m.*
[2] *adj* nichtjüdisch.
gentility [dʒenˈtɪlɪtɪ] *n* Vornehmheit *f.*
gentle [ˈdʒentl] *adj* (*+er*) **(a)** sanft; (*not hard, vigorous*) *smack, breeze also, exercise* leicht; (*not loud*) *knock, sound* leise, zart; (*delicate*) *kiss, caress also, hint, reminder* zart; (*not harsh*) *words, humour* liebenswürdig, freundlich; *rebuke also, heat* mild; *person, disposition also* sanftmütig; *animal also* zahm; *heart* weich ♦ **~ reader** (*old*) geneigter Leser (*old*); **the ~ sex** das zarte Geschlecht; **to be ~ with sb** sanft *or* nett zu jdm sein; (*physically*) mit jdm sanft *or* behutsam umgehen; **to be ~ with sth** mit etw behutsam *or* vorsichtig umgehen; **to be ~ with one's hands** (*nurse, doctor*) behutsam sein; (*horseman*) eine leichte Hand haben; **~ as a lamb** sanft wie ein Lamm.
(b) (*old: well-born*) *knight, maiden* edel (*old*) ♦ **of ~ birth** von edler *or* vornehmer Geburt (*dated*).
gentlefolk [ˈdʒentlfəʊk] *npl* (*dated*) vornehme *or* feine Leute *pl.*
gentleman [ˈdʒentlmən] *n, pl* **-men** [-mən] **(a)** (*well-mannered, well-born*) Gentleman, Herr *m*; (*trustworthy also*) Ehrenmann *m* ♦ **he's a real ~** er ist ein richtiger Gentleman; **gentlemen's agreement** Gentlemen's Agreement *nt*; (*esp in business*) Vereinbarung *f* auf Treu und Glauben.
(b) (*man*) Herr *m* ♦ **gentlemen!** meine Herren!; (*in business letter*) sehr geehrte Herren!; **gentlemen of the jury/press!** meine Herren Geschworenen/von der Presse!
(c) (*dated: with private income*) Privatier *m*; (*Hist: rank*) Mann *m* von Stand; (*at court*) Höfling *m* ♦ **~ farmer** Gutsbesitzer *m*; **~-in-waiting** Kammerherr *m.*
gentlemanly [ˈdʒentlmənlɪ] *adj person, manners* zuvorkommend, gentlemanlike *pred*; *appearance* eines Gentleman, gentlemanlike *pred.*
gentleness [ˈdʒentlnɪs] *n see adj* Sanftheit *f*; Leichtheit *f*; Zartheit *f*; Liebenswürdigkeit, Freundlichkeit *f*; Milde *f*; Sanftmut *f*; Zahmheit *f*; Weichheit *f.*
gentlewoman [ˈdʒentlwʊmən] *n, pl* **-women** [-wɪmɪn] (*dated*) Dame *f* (von Stand); (*at court*) Hofdame *f*; (*Hist: attendant*) Zofe *f.*
gently [ˈdʒentlɪ] *adv see adj* ♦ **to handle sb/sth ~** mit jdm/etw behutsam umgehen; **~ does it!** sachte, sachte!
gentry [ˈdʒentrɪ] *npl* **(a)** Gentry *f*, niederer Adel ♦ **all the ~ were there** alles, was Rang und Namen hatte, war da. **(b)** (*dated pej: people*) Leute *pl.*
genuflect [ˈdʒenjʊflekt] *vi* (*Rel*) eine Kniebeuge machen.
genuflection, genuflexion [ˌdʒenjʊˈflekʃən] *n* (*Rel*) Kniebeuge *f.*
genuine [ˈdʒenjʊɪn] *adj* echt; *manuscript* authentisch, Original-; *offer* ernstgemeint, ernsthaft; (*sincere*) *sorrow, joy, willingness, disbelief also, belief* aufrichtig; *laughter, person* natürlich, ungekünstelt ♦ **the ~ article** (*not a copy*) das Original; **that's the ~ article!** das ist das Wahre!; (*not imitation*) das ist echt!; **she has a ~ belief in the supernatural** sie glaubt ernsthaft an das Übernatürliche.
genuinely [ˈdʒenjʊɪnlɪ] *adv* wirklich; (*sincerely also*) aufrichtig; (*authentically*) *old, antique* echt.
genuineness [ˈdʒenjʊɪnnɪs] *n see adj* Echtheit *f*; Ernsthaftigkeit *f*; Aufrichtigkeit *f*; Natürlichkeit, Ungekünsteltheit *f.*
genus [ˈdʒenəs] *n, pl* **genera** (*Biol*) Gattung *f.*
geocentric [ˌdʒiːəʊˈsentrɪk] *adj* geozentrisch.
geochemistry [ˌdʒiːəʊˈkemɪstrɪ] *n* Geochemie *f.*
geodesic [ˌdʒiːəʊˈdesɪk] *adj* geodätisch ♦ **~ dome** Traglufthalle *f.*
geodesy [dʒiːˈɒdɪsɪ] *n* Geodäsie *f.*
geographer [dʒɪˈɒɡrəfəʳ] *n* Geograph(in *f*) *m.*
geographic(al) [dʒɪəˈɡræfɪk(əl)] *adj*, **geographically** [dʒɪəˈɡræfɪkəlɪ] *adv* geographisch.
geography [dʒɪˈɒɡrəfɪ] *n* Geographie *f*; (*Sch also*) Erdkunde *f.*
geological *adj*, **~ly** *adv* [dʒɪəʊˈlɒdʒɪkəl, -ɪ] geologisch.
geologist [dʒɪˈɒlədʒɪst] *n* Geologe *m*, Geologin *f.*
geology [dʒɪˈɒlədʒɪ] *n* Geologie *f.*
geomancy [ˈdʒiːəʊmænsɪ] *n* Geomantie *f.*
geometric(al) [dʒɪəʊˈmetrɪk(əl)] *adj*, **geometrically** [dʒɪəʊˈmetrɪkəlɪ] *adv* geometrisch.
geometrician [ˌdʒɪəməˈtrɪʃən] *n* Fachmann *m* für Geometrie, Geometer *m* (*old*).
geometry [dʒɪˈɒmɪtrɪ] *n* (*Math*) Geometrie *f* ♦ **~ set** (Reißzeug *nt or* Zirkelkasten *m* mit) Zeichengarnitur *f.*
geophysics [ˌdʒiːəʊˈfɪzɪks] *n sing* Geophysik *f.*
geopolitics [ˌdʒiːəʊˈpɒlɪtɪks] *n sing* Geopolitik *f.*
Geordie [ˈdʒɔːdɪ] *n* (*inf*) *Bewohner(in f) m/Dialekt m der Bewohner von Newcastle upon Tyne und Umgebung.*
George [dʒɔːdʒ] *n* Georg *m* ♦ **by ~!** (*Brit dated*) potz Blitz! (*dated inf*); (*indicating determination*) bei Gott! (*dated*).
georgette [dʒɔːˈdʒet] *n* Georgette *f or m.*
Georgia [ˈdʒɔːdʒɪə] *n* (*US*) Georgia *nt*; (*USSR*) Georgien *nt.*
Georgian [ˈdʒɔːdʒɪən] *adj* (*Brit Hist*) georgianisch; (*US*) in/aus/von Georgia; (*USSR*) georgisch.
geostationary [ˌdʒiːəʊˈsteɪʃənərɪ] *adj* geostationär.
geothermal [ˌdʒiːəʊˈθɜːməl] *adj* geothermal.
geranium [dʒɪˈreɪnɪəm] *n* Geranie *f.*
gerbil [ˈdʒɜːbɪl] *n* Wüstenspringmaus *f.*
geriatric [ˌdʒerɪˈætrɪk] [1] *adj* geriatrisch, Greisen- (*often hum*); *nurse, nursing* Alten-; *home* Alters-; *patient* alt ♦ **~ medicine** Altersheilkunde *f*; **~ ward** geriatrische Abteilung, Pflegestation *f.*
[2] *n* alter Mensch, Greis *m* (*often hum*).
geriatrician [ˌdʒerɪəˈtrɪʃən] *n* Facharzt *m*/-ärztin *f* für Geriatrie, Geriater *m.*
geriatrics [ˌdʒerɪˈætrɪks] *n sing* Geriatrie, Altersheilkunde *f.*
germ [dʒɜːm] *n* (*lit, fig*) Keim *m*; (*of particular illness also*) Krankheitserreger *m*; (*esp of cold*) Bazillus *m* ♦ **don't spread your ~s around** behalte deine Bazillen für dich; **that contained the ~(s) of later conflict** darin lag der Keim für spätere Konflikte.
German [ˈdʒɜːmən] [1] *adj* deutsch.
[2] *n* **(a)** Deutsche(r) *mf.* **(b)** (*language*) Deutsch *nt*; *see* **English.**
German Democratic Republic *n* Deutsche Demokratische Republik.
germane [dʒɜːˈmeɪn] *adj* (*form*) von Belang (*geh*) (*to* für).
Germanic [dʒɜːˈmænɪk] *adj* germanisch.
germanium [dʒɜːˈmeɪnɪəm] *n* (*Chem*) Germanium *nt.*
germanize [ˈdʒɜːmənaɪz] *vt* germanisieren; *word* eindeutschen.
German: ~ measles *n sing* Röteln *pl*; **~ shepherd (dog)** *n* (*esp US*) deutscher Schäferhund; **~-speaking** *adj* deutschsprachig; **~-speaking Switzerland** die deutschsprachige Schweiz, die Deutschschweiz.
Germany [ˈdʒɜːmənɪ] *n* Deutschland *nt*; (*Hist*) Germanien *nt.*
germ: ~ carrier *n* Bazillenträger *m*; **~ cell** *n* (*Biol*) Keimzelle *f*; **~-free** *adj* keimfrei.
germicidal [ˌdʒɜːmɪˈsaɪdl] *adj* keimtötend.
germicide [ˈdʒɜːmɪsaɪd] *n* keimtötendes Mittel.
germinal [ˈdʒɜːmɪnəl] *adj* (*fig*) aufkeimend (*geh*).
germinate [ˈdʒɜːmɪneɪt] [1] *vi* keimen; (*fig*) aufkeimen (*geh*) ♦ **he let the idea ~ in his mind** er ließ die Idee in sich (*dat*) keimen.
[2] *vt* (*lit, fig*) keimen lassen.
germination [ˌdʒɜːmɪˈneɪʃən] *n* (*lit*) Keimung *f*; (*fig*) Aufkeimen *nt* (*geh*).
germ: ~-killer *n* keimtötendes Mittel; **~ warfare** *n* bakteriologische Kriegsführung, Bakterienkrieg *m.*
gerontocracy [ˌdʒerɒnˈtɒkrəsɪ] *n* Gerontokratie *f.*
gerontologist [ˌdʒerɒnˈtɒlədʒɪst] *n* Gerontologe *m*, Gerontologin *f.*
gerontology [ˌdʒerɒnˈtɒlədʒɪ] *n* Gerontologie *f.*
gerrymander [ˈdʒerɪmændəʳ] (*US Pol*) [1] *vt* **to ~ election districts** Wahlkreisschiebungen vornehmen.
[2] *n* Wahlkreisschiebung *f.*
gerrymandering [ˈdʒerɪmændərɪŋ] *n* (*US Pol*) Wahlkreisschiebungen *pl.*
gerund [ˈdʒerənd] *n* Gerundium *nt.*
gerundive [dʒɪˈrʌndɪv] *n* Gerundivum *nt.*
gestalt psychology [ɡəˈʃtæltsaɪˈkɒlədʒɪ] *n* Gestaltpsychologie *f.*
Gestapo [ɡeˈstɑːpəʊ] *n* Gestapo *f.*
gestate [dʒeˈsteɪt] [1] *vi* (*lit form*) (*animal*) trächtig sein, tragen (*form*); (*human*) schwanger sein; (*fig*) reifen.

2 *vt* tragen; *(fig)* in sich *(dat)* reifen lassen; *plan, idea* sich tragen mit *(geh)*.

gestation [dʒe'steɪʃən] *n (lit) (of animals)* Trächtigkeit *f*; *(of humans)* Schwangerschaft *f*; *(fig)* Reifwerden *nt* ◆ **his book was 10 years in ~** der Reifungsprozeß seines Buches dauerte 10 Jahre.

gesticulate [dʒe'stɪkjʊleɪt] *vi* gestikulieren.

gesticulation [dʒe,stɪkjʊ'leɪʃən] *n (act)* Gestikulieren *nt*; *(instance)* Gebärde *(geh)*, Geste *f* ◆ **all his ~s** all sein Gestikulieren.

gesture ['dʒestʃə^r] **1** *n (lit, fig)* Geste *f* ◆ **a ~ of denial/approval** eine verneinende/zustimmende Geste; **as a ~ of support** als Zeichen der Unterstützung; **his use of ~** seine Gestik.

2 *vi* gestikulieren.

3 *vt* **to ~ sb to do sth** jdm bedeuten, etw zu tun.

get [get] *pret, ptp* **got,** *(US) ptp* **gotten** **1** *vt* **(a)** *(receive)* bekommen, kriegen *(inf)*; *sun, light, full force of blow or anger* abbekommen, abkriegen *(inf)*; *wound also* sich *(dat)* zuziehen; *wealth, glory* kommen zu; *time, personal characteristics* haben *(from* von) ◆ **where did you ~ it (from)?** woher hast du das?; **this country ~s very little rain** in diesem Land regnet es sehr wenig; **the car got it on one wing** *(inf)* das Auto hat am Kotflügel etwas abbekommen *or* abgekriegt *(inf)*; **he wanted to ~ all the glory** er wollte all den Ruhm (haben); **he got the idea for his book while he was abroad/from some old document** die Idee zu dem Buch kam ihm, als er im Ausland war/er hatte die Idee zu seinem Buch von einem alten Dokument; **where do you ~ that idea (from)?** wie kommst du denn auf die Idee?; **I got quite a surprise/shock** ich war ziemlich überrascht/ich habe einen ziemlichen Schock bekommen *or* gekriegt *(inf)*; **you'll ~ it!** *(inf: be in trouble)* du wirst was erleben! *(inf)*.

(b) *(obtain by one's own efforts) object* sich *(dat)* besorgen; *visa, money also* sich *(dat)* beschaffen; *(find) staff, finances, partner, job* finden; *(buy)* kaufen; *(buy and keep) large item, car, cat* sich *(dat)* anschaffen ◆ **not to be able to ~ sth** etw nicht bekommen *or* kriegen *(inf)*; **to ~ sb/oneself sth, to ~ sth for sb/oneself** jdm/sich etw besorgen; *job* jdm/sich etw verschaffen; **she tried to ~ a partner for her friend** sie hat versucht, einen Partner für ihre Freundin zu finden; **to need to ~ sth** etw brauchen; **I've still three to ~** ich brauche noch drei; **you'll have to ~ a job/flat/more staff** Sie müssen zusehen, daß Sie eine Stelle/eine Wohnung/mehr Personal bekommen *or* finden; **he's been trying to ~ a house/job/partner** er hat versucht, ein Haus/eine Stelle/einen Partner zu bekommen; **why don't you ~ a flat of your own?** warum schaffen Sie sich *(dat)* nicht eine eigene Wohnung an?; *(rent)* warum nehmen Sie sich *(dat)* nicht eine eigene Wohnung?; **he got himself a wife/a fancy car/job** er hat sich *(dat)* eine Frau zugelegt *(inf)*/ein tolles Auto angeschafft *or* zugelegt/einen tollen Job verschafft; **what are you ~ting her for Christmas?** was schenkst du ihr zu Weihnachten?; **I got her a doll for Christmas** ich habe für sie eine Puppe zu Weihnachten besorgt; **we could ~ a taxi** wir könnten (uns *dat*) ein Taxi nehmen; **could you ~ me a taxi?** könnten Sie mir ein Taxi rufen *or* besorgen?

(c) *(fetch) person, doctor, object* holen ◆ **to ~ sb from the station** jdn vom Bahnhof abholen; **I got him/myself a drink** ich habe ihm/mir etwas zu trinken geholt; **can I ~ you a drink?** möchten Sie etwas zu trinken?; **why don't you ~ a dictionary/the contract and look it up?** warum sehen Sie nicht in einem Wörterbuch/im Vertrag nach?

(d) *(catch)* bekommen, kriegen *(inf)*; *cold, illness also* sich *(dat)* holen; *(in children's game)* fangen ◆ **to ~ sb by the arm/leg** jdn am Arm/Bein packen; **it** *or* **the pain ~s me here/when I move** *(inf)* es tut hier weh/es tut weh, wenn ich mich bewege; **he's got it bad** *(inf)* den hat's übel erwischt *(inf)*; **~ him/it!** *(to dog)* faß!; **(I've) got him/it!** *(inf)* (ich) hab' ihn/ich hab's *(inf)*; **got you!** *(inf)* hab' dich (erwischt)! *(inf)*; **ha, ha, can't ~ me!** ha, ha, mich kriegst du nicht! *(inf)*; **my big brother will ~ you!** mein großer Bruder, der zeigt's dir *or* macht dich fertig! *(inf)*; **he's out to ~ you** *(inf)* er hat's auf dich abgesehen *(inf)*; **we'll ~ them yet!** *(inf)* die werden wir schon noch kriegen! *(inf)*; **I'll ~ you for that!** *(inf)* das wirst du mir büßen!; **you've got me there!** *(inf)* da bin ich auch überfragt *(inf)*; **that'll/that question will ~ him** da/bei der Frage weiß er bestimmt auch nicht weiter.

(e) *(hit)* treffen, erwischen *(inf)* ◆ **the car got the lamppost with the front wing** das Auto hat den Laternenpfahl mit dem vorderen Kotflügel erwischt *(inf)*.

(f) *(Rad, TV)* bekommen, kriegen *(inf)*.

(g) *(Telec) (contact)* erreichen; *number* bekommen; *(put through to, get for sb)* geben ◆ **I'll ~ the number (for you)** ich wähle die Nummer (für Sie); *(switchboard)* ich verbinde Sie mit der Nummer; **~ me 339/Mr Johnston please** *(to secretary)* geben Sie mir bitte 339/Herrn Johnston; *(to switchboard)* verbinden Sie mich bitte mit 339/Herrn Johnston; **I must have got the wrong number** ich bin/war wohl falsch verbunden.

(h) *(prepare) meal* machen ◆ **I'll ~ you/myself some breakfast** ich mache dir/mir etwas zum Frühstück.

(i) *(eat)* essen ◆ **to ~ breakfast/lunch** *etc* frühstücken/zu Mittag essen *etc*; **to ~ a snack** eine Kleinigkeit essen.

(j) *(send, take)* bringen ◆ **to ~ sb to hospital** jdn ins Krankenhaus bringen; **to ~ sth to sb** jdm etw zukommen lassen; *(take it oneself)* jdm etw bringen; **where does that ~ us?** *(inf)* was bringt uns *(dat)* das? *(inf)*; **this discussion isn't ~ting us anywhere** diese Diskussion führt zu nichts; **tell him to ~ it there as quickly as possible** er soll zusehen, daß das so schnell wie möglich dort ist; *(take it himself also)* er soll das möglichst schnell dort hinbringen; **we'll ~ you there somehow** irgendwie kriegen wir dich schon dahin *(inf)*.

(k) *(manage to move)* kriegen *(inf)* ◆ **he couldn't ~ her/himself up the stairs** er kriegte sie nicht die Treppe rauf *(inf)*/er kam nicht die Treppe rauf.

(l) *(understand)* kapieren *(inf)*, mitbekommen; *(hear)* mitbekommen, mitkriegen *(inf)*; *(make a note of)* notieren ◆ **I don't ~ it/you** *or* **your meaning** *(inf)* da komme ich nicht mit *(inf)*/ich verstehe nicht, was du meinst; **~ it?** kapiert? *(inf)*.

(m) *(profit, benefit)* **what do you ~ from that?** was hast du davon?, was bringt dir das? *(inf)*; **I don't ~ much from his lectures** seine Vorlesungen geben mir nicht viel; **he's only in it for what he can ~** er will nur dabei profitieren.

(n) *(iro inf)* **~ (a load of) that!** was sagst du dazu! *(inf)*, hat man Töne! *(inf)*; **~ you!** *(regarding looks)* sag bloß! *(inf)*, Junge, Junge! *(inf)*; *(regarding ideas)* was du nicht sagst! *(inf)*; **~ her!** *(regarding looks)* was sagst du zu der da? *(inf)*; *(iro)* sieh dir bloß die mal an! *(inf)*; *(regarding ideas)* die ist ja ganz schön clever! *(inf)*; *(iro)* hör dir bloß das mal an! *(inf)*.

(o) *(inf) (annoy)* ärgern, aufregen; *(upset)* an die Nieren gehen (+*dat*) *(inf)*; *(thrill)* packen *(inf)*; *(amuse)* amüsieren ◆ **it ~s you there!** das packt einen so richtig! *(inf)*.

(p) **to ~ sb to do sth** *(have sth done by sb)* etw von jdm machen lassen; *(persuade sb)* jdn dazu bringen, etw zu tun; **I'll ~ him to phone you back** ich sage ihm, er soll zurückrufen; *(make him)* ich werde zusehen, daß er zurückruft; **you'll never ~ him to understand** du wirst es nie schaffen, daß er das versteht.

(q) (+*ptp*) *(cause to be done)* lassen; *(manage to ~ done)* kriegen *(inf)* ◆ **to ~ sth made for sb/oneself** jdm/sich etw machen lassen; **to ~ one's hair cut** sich *(dat)* die Haare schneiden lassen; **I'll ~ the grass cut/house painted soon** der Rasen wird bald gemäht/das Haus wird bald gestrichen; *(by sb else)* ich lasse bald den Rasen mähen/das Haus streichen; **to ~ sth done** etw gemacht kriegen *(inf)*; **to ~ the washing/dishes/some work done** die Wäsche waschen/abwaschen/Arbeit erledigen; **I'm not going to ~ much done** ich werde nicht viel geschafft bekommen *or* kriegen *(inf)*; **we ought to ~ it done soon** das müßte bald gemacht werden; **to ~ things done** was fertigkriegen *(inf)*; **can you ~ these things done for me?** können Sie das für mich erledigen?; **~ your fare paid by them** lassen Sie sich *(dat)* Ihre Fahrtkosten von ihnen bezahlen; **did you ~ the fare paid/question answered?** haben Sie die Fahrtkosten bezahlt/eine Antwort auf die Frage bekommen *or* gekriegt? *(inf)*; **you'll ~ me/yourself thrown out** du bringst es so weit, daß ich hinausgeworfen werde/du hinausgeworfen wirst; **that'll ~ him thrown out** da fliegt er hinaus.

(r) (+*infin or prp: cause to be*) kriegen *(inf)* ◆ **he can't ~ the sum to work out/lid to stay open** er kriegt es nicht hin, daß die Rechnung aufgeht/daß der Deckel aufbleibt *(inf)*; **I can't ~ the car to start/door to open** ich kriege das Auto nicht an *(inf)*/die Tür nicht auf *(inf)*; **can you ~ these two pieces to fit together/the wound to stop bleeding?** kriegen Sie die beiden Teile zusammen/können Sie etwas machen, daß die Wunde nicht mehr blutet?; **how do I ~ these two parts to stick together?** wie kriege ich die beiden Teile zusammengeklebt? *(inf)*; **once I've got this machine to work** wenn ich die Maschine erst einmal zum Laufen gebracht habe; **to ~ the fire to burn** das Feuer zum Brennen bringen; **to ~ sb talking** jdn zum Sprechen bringen.

(s) *(cause to be)* (+*adj*) machen; *(manage to make)* kriegen *(inf)*; (+*adv phrase*) tun ◆ **to ~ sb/sth/oneself ready** jdn/etw/sich fertigmachen; **to ~ sth clean/open/shut** *(person)* etw sauber-/auf-/zukriegen *(inf)*; **that'll ~ it clean/open/shut** damit wird es sauber/geht es auf/zu; **to ~ sb drunk** jdn betrunken machen/kriegen *(inf)*; **has she got the baby dressed yet?** hat sie das Baby schon angezogen?; **to ~ one's arm broken** sich *(dat)* den Arm brechen; **to ~ one's hands dirty** sich *(dat)* die Hände schmutzig machen; **to ~ one's things packed** seine Sachen packen; **~ the cat back in its box/out of the room** tu die Katze ins Körbchen zurück/aus dem Zimmer *(inf)*; **~ the children to bed** bring die Kinder ins Bett.

(t) *(inf: to form passive)* werden ◆ **when did it last ~ painted?** wann ist es zuletzt gestrichen worden?; **I got paid** ich wurde bezahlt.

(u) **to have got sth** *(Brit: have)* etw haben.

(v) *in set phrases see n, adj etc.*

2 *vi* **(a)** *(go, arrive)* kommen; gehen ◆ **to ~ home/here** nach Hause kommen/hier ankommen; **I've got as far as page 16** ich bin auf Seite 16; **to ~ far** *(lit)* weit kommen; *(fig)* es weit bringen; **~ (lost)!** verschwinde!

(b) *(fig inf)* **to ~ there** *(succeed)* es schaffen *(inf)*; *(understand)* dahinterkommen *(inf)*; **now we're ~ting there** *(to the truth)* jetzt kommt's raus! *(inf)*; **how's the work going? — we're slowly ~ting there** wie geht die Arbeit voran? — langsam wird's was *(inf)*; **to ~ somewhere/nowhere** *(in job, career etc)* es zu etwas/nichts bringen; *(with work, in discussion etc)* weiterkommen/nicht weiterkommen; **to ~ somewhere/nowhere (with sb)** (bei jdm) etwas/nichts erreichen; **we're not ~ting anywhere by arguing like this** wir erreichen doch gar nichts, wenn wir uns streiten; **now we're ~ting somewhere** jetzt wird die Sache *(inf)*; *(in interrogation, discussion etc)* jetzt kommen wir der Sache schon näher; **to ~ nowhere fast** *(inf)* absolut nichts erreichen.

(c) *(become, be, to form passive)* werden ◆ **to ~ old/tired/paid** *etc* alt/müde/bezahlt *etc* werden; **I'm/the weather is ~ting cold/warm** mir wird es/es wird kalt/warm; **to ~ dressed/shaved/washed** *etc* sich anziehen/rasieren/waschen *etc*; **to ~ married** heiraten; **how do people ~ like that** *or* **that way?** *(inf)* wie wird man nur so? *(inf)*.

(d) (+*infin*) **to ~ to know sb** jdn kennenlernen; **how did you ~ to know that?** wie hast du das erfahren?; **to ~ to like sb/sth** jdn sympathisch finden/an etw *(dat)* Gefallen finden; **after a time you ~ to realize ...** nach einiger Zeit merkt man ...; **to ~ to do sth** (~ *around to*) dazu kommen, etw zu tun; (~ *chance to*) die Möglichkeit haben, etw zu tun; **to ~ to be ...** (mit der Zeit) ... werden; **to ~ to see sb/sth** jdn/etw zu sehen bekommen; **to ~ to work** sich an die Arbeit machen.

(e) *(+prp or ptp)* **to ~ working/scrubbing** *etc* anfangen zu arbeiten/schrubben *etc*; **you lot, ~ cleaning/working!** ihr da, putzt/arbeitet!; **I got talking to him** ich kam mit ihm ins Gespräch; **to ~ going** *(person) (leave)* aufbrechen; *(start working)* sich daran machen; *(start talking)* loslegen *(inf)*; *(party etc)* in Schwung kommen; *(machine, fire etc)* in Gang kommen; **~ going!** fang an!; *(leave)* geh schon!; **let's ~ started** fangen wir an!
(f) *(inf: start)* **we got to talking about that** wir kamen darauf zu sprechen; **I got to thinking ...** ich habe mir überlegt, ...
(g) **to have got to do sth** *(be obliged to)* etw tun müssen; **I've got to** ich muß.
3 *vr see also vt (b, c, h, k)* **(a)** *(convey oneself)* gehen; kommen ◆ **I had to ~ myself to the hospital** ich mußte selbst ins Krankenhaus (gehen); **how did you ~ yourself home?** wie bist du nach Hause gekommen?; **~ yourself over here/out of here** komm hier rüber *(inf)*/mach, daß du hier rauskommst *(inf)*.
(b) *(+adj)* sich machen ◆ **to ~ oneself dirty/clean** sich schmutzig machen/sich saubermachen; **to ~ oneself pregnant/fit** schwanger/fit werden.
(c) *(+ptp)* **to ~ oneself washed/dressed** sich waschen/anziehen; **to ~ oneself married** heiraten; **he managed to ~ himself promoted** er hat es geschafft, daß er befördert wurde; **he got himself hit in the leg** er wurde am Bein getroffen.

◆**get about** *vi (prep obj* in *+dat)* **(a)** sich bewegen können; *(to different places)* herumkommen. **(b)** *(news)* sich herumsprechen; *(rumour)* sich verbreiten.

◆**get across** **1** *vi* **(a)** *(cross)* hinüber-/herüberkommen; *(+prep obj) road, river* kommen über *(+acc)* ◆ **to ~ ~ to the other side** auf die andere Seite kommen *or* gelangen.
(b) *(communicate) (play, joke, comedian etc)* ankommen *(to* bei); *(teacher etc)* sich verständlich machen *(to dat)*; *(idea, meaning)* klarwerden, verständlich werden *(to dat)*.
2 *vt always separate* **(a)** *(transport)* hinüber-/herüberbringen; *(manage to ~ ~)* hinüber-/herüberbekommen; *(+prep obj)* (hinüber-/herüber)bringen über *(+acc)*; (hinüber-/herüber)bekommen über *(+acc)*.
(b) *(communicate) play, joke* ankommen mit *(to* bei); *one's ideas, concepts* verständlich machen, klarmachen *(to sb* jdm).

◆**get ahead** *vi (make progress)* vorankommen *(in* in *+dat)*; *(in race)* sich *(dat)* einen Vorsprung verschaffen; *(from behind)* nach vorn kommen ◆ **to ~ ~ of sb** jdn überflügeln; *(in race)* einen Vorsprung zu jdm gewinnen; *(overtake)* jdn überholen; **if he ~s too far ~ in his reading** wenn er im Lesen den anderen zu weit voraus ist; **to ~ ~ of schedule** schneller als geplant vorankommen.

◆**get along** **1** *vi* **(a)** gehen ◆ **I must be ~ting ~** ich muß jetzt gehen, ich muß mich auf den Weg machen; **~ ~ now!** nun geh/geht schon!; **~ ~ with you!** *(inf)* jetzt hör aber auf! *(inf)*.
(b) *(manage)* zurechtkommen ◆ **to ~ ~ without sb/sth** ohne jdn/etw auskommen *or* zurechtkommen.
(c) *(progress)* vorankommen; *(work, patient, wound etc)* sich machen.
(d) *(be on good terms)* auskommen *(with* mit) ◆ **they ~ ~ quite well** sie kommen ganz gut miteinander aus.
2 *vt always separate* **to ~ sb ~ to sb/sth** *(send)* jdn zu jdm/etw schicken; *(take)* jdn zu jdm/etw mitnehmen/mitbringen; **to ~ sth ~ to sb** jdm etw zukommen lassen; *(take)* jdm etw bringen.

◆**get around** **1** *vi see* **get about**.
2 *vti +prep obj see* **get round 1 (b, d), 2 (c, d)**.

◆**get around to** *vi +prep obj see* **get round to**.

◆**get at** *vi +prep obj* **(a)** *(gain access to, reach)* herankommen an *(+acc)*; *town, house* erreichen, (hin)kommen zu; *(take, eat etc) food, money* gehen an *(+acc)* ◆ **put it where the dog/child won't ~ ~ it** stellen Sie es irgendwohin, wo der Hund/das Kind nicht drankommt *(inf)*; **don't let him ~ ~ the whisky** laß ihn nicht an den Whisky (ran); **let me ~ ~ him!** *(inf)* na, wenn ich den erwische! *(inf)*; **the mice have been ~ting ~ the cheese again** die Mäuse waren wieder am Käse *(inf)*; **woodworm/the damp had got ~ the furniture** der Holzwurm/die Feuchtigkeit war an die Möbel gekommen.
(b) *(discover, ascertain) sb's wishes, ideas, truth* herausbekommen *or* -finden; *facts* kommen an *(+acc)*.
(c) *(inf: mean)* hinauswollen auf *(+acc)* ◆ **what are you ~ting ~?** worauf willst du hinaus?
(d) **to ~ ~ sb** *(inf) (criticize)* an jdm etwas auszusetzen haben *(inf)*; *(nag)* an jdm herumnörgeln *(inf)*; **he had the feeling that he was being got ~** er hatte den Eindruck, daß ihm das galt *or* daß man ihm was am Zeug flicken wollte *(inf)*; **are you trying to ~ ~ me?** hast du was an mir auszusetzen? *(inf)*.
(e) *(inf: corrupt)* beeinflussen; *(by threats also)* unter Druck setzen *(inf)*; *(by bribes also)* schmieren *(inf)*.
(f) *(inf: start work on)* sich machen an *(+acc)*.

◆**get away** **1** *vi (leave)* wegkommen; *(for holiday also)* fortkommen; *(prisoner, thief)* entkommen, entwischen *(from sb* jdm, *from prison* aus dem Gefängnis); *(sportsman: from start)* loskommen *(inf)* ◆ **I must ~ ~ from here** ich muß hier weg *(inf)*; **could I ~ ~ early today?** könnte ich heute früher gehen *or* weg *(inf)*?; **I just can't ~ ~ from him/my work** ich kann ihm/der Arbeit einfach nicht entrinnen; **you can't ~ ~** *or* **there's no ~ting ~ from the fact that ...** man kommt nicht um die Tatsache herum, daß ...; **to ~ ~ from it all** sich von allem frei- *or* losmachen; **~ ~ (with you)!** *(inf)* ach, hör auf! *(inf)*.
2 *vt always separate* **(a)** *(remove)* wegbekommen; *(move physically) person* weg- *or* fortbringen; *objects* wegschaffen ◆ **~ her ~ from here/his influence** sehen Sie zu, daß sie hier/aus seinem Einflußbereich wegkommt; **~ them ~ from danger** bringen Sie sie außer Gefahr; **~ him ~ from the wall/propeller** sehen Sie zu, daß er von der Wand/dem Propeller weggeht; **~ him/that dog ~ from me** schaff ihn mir/mir den Hund vom Leib; **to ~ sth ~ from sb** *(take away)* jdm etw weg- *or* abnehmen.
(b) *(post) letter* weg- *or* fortschicken.

◆**get away with** *vi +prep obj* **(a)** *(abscond with)* entkommen mit.
(b) *(inf: escape punishment for)* **you'll/he'll** *etc* **never ~ ~ ~ that** das wird nicht gutgehen; **he** *etc* **got ~ ~ it** er ist ungestraft *or* ungeschoren *(inf)* davongekommen, es ist gutgegangen; **the things he ~s ~ ~!** was er sich *(dat)* alles erlauben kann!; **to let sb ~ ~ ~ sth** jdm etw durchgehen lassen.
(c) *(be let off with)* davonkommen mit.

◆**get back** **1** *vi* **(a)** *(return)* zurückkommen; zurückgehen ◆ **to ~ ~ (home)/to bed/to work** nach Hause kommen/wieder ins Bett gehen/wieder arbeiten; **I ought to be ~ting ~ (to the office/home)** ich sollte (ins Büro/nach Hause) zurück(gehen); **I must be ~ting ~ (home)** ich muß nach Hause.
(b) *(move backwards)* zurückgehen ◆ **~ ~!** zurück(treten)!
2 *vt sep* **(a)** *(recover) possessions, person* zurückbekommen; *good opinion, strength* zurückgewinnen ◆ **now that I've got you/it ~** jetzt, wo ich dich/es wiederhabe.
(b) *(bring back)* zurückbringen; *(put back in place)* zurücktun ◆ **he took it out and can't ~ it ~** er hat es herausgenommen und kriegt es nicht wieder hinein.

◆**get back at** *vi +prep obj (inf)* sich rächen an *(+dat)* ◆ **to ~ ~ ~ sb for sth** jdm etw heimzahlen *(inf)*.

◆**get back to** *vi +prep obj (esp Comm: recontact)* sich wieder in Verbindung setzen mit ◆ **I'll ~ ~ ~ you on that** ich werde darauf zurückkommen.

◆**get behind** *vi* **(a)** *(+prep obj) tree, person* sich stellen hinter *(+acc)*.
(b) *(fig)* zurückbleiben; *(person)* ins Hintertreffen geraten; *(+prep obj)* zurückbleiben hinter *(+dat)*; *(with schedule)* in Rückstand kommen ◆ **to ~ ~ with one's work/payments** mit seiner Arbeit/den Zahlungen in Rückstand kommen.

◆**get by** *vi* **(a)** *(move past)* vorbeikommen *(prep obj* an *+dat)* ◆ **to let sb/a vehicle ~ ~** jdn/ein Fahrzeug vorbeilassen.
(b) *(fig: pass unnoticed)* durchrutschen *(inf)* ◆ **how did that film ~ ~ the censors?** wie ist der Film nur durch die Zensur gekommen?; **how did that mistake ~ ~ the proofreader?** wie ist dieser Fehler dem Korrektor nur entgangen?
(c) *(inf: pass muster) (work, worker)* gerade noch annehmbar *or* passabel *(inf)* sein; *(knowledge)* gerade ausreichen ◆ **she would just about ~ ~ with her German in the exam** mit ihren Deutschkenntnissen müßte sie die Prüfung gerade so schaffen *(inf)*; **I haven't got a tie, do you think I'll ~ ~ without one?** ich habe keine Krawatte, meinst du, es geht auch ohne?
(d) *(inf: manage)* durchkommen *(inf)* ◆ **she ~s ~ on very little money** sie kommt mit sehr wenig Geld aus.

◆**get down** **1** *vi* **(a)** *(descend)* hinunter-/heruntersteigen *(prep obj, from* von); *(manage to ~ ~, in commands)* herunter-/hinunterkommen *(prep obj, from acc)*; *(from horse, bicycle)* absteigen *(from* von); *(from bus)* aussteigen *(from* aus) ◆ **to ~ ~ the stairs** die Treppe hinuntergehen/herunterkommen; **~ ~!** runter! *(inf)*.
(b) *(leave table)* aufstehen.
(c) *(bend down)* sich bücken; *(to hide)* sich ducken ◆ **to ~ ~ on one's knees** auf die Knie fallen; **to ~ ~ on all fours** sich auf alle viere begeben.
2 *vt sep* **(a)** *(take down)* herunternehmen; *trousers etc* herunterziehen; *(lift down)* herunterholen; *(carry down)* herunter-/hinunterbringen; *(manage to ~ ~)* herunterbringen *or* -kriegen *(inf)*.
(b) *(reduce) (to* auf *+acc)* beschränken; *(as regards length)* verkürzen; *temperature* herunterbekommen; *seller, price* herunterhandeln.
(c) *(swallow) food* hinunterbringen ◆ **~ this ~ (you)!** *(inf)* trink/iß das!
(d) *(make a note of)* aufschreiben, notieren.
(e) *(inf: depress)* fertigmachen *(inf)* ◆ **don't let it ~ you ~** laß dich davon nicht unterkriegen *(inf)*.

◆**get down to** *vi +prep obj* sich machen an *(+acc)*, in Angriff nehmen; *(find time to do)* kommen zu ◆ **to ~ ~ ~ business** zur Sache kommen.

◆**get in** **1** *vi* **(a)** *(enter)* hinein-/hereinkommen *(prep obj, -to* in *+acc)*; *(into car, train etc)* einsteigen *(prep obj, -to* in *+acc)*; *(into bath)* hinein-/hereinsteigen; *(into bed)* sich hineinlegen ◆ **to ~ ~(to) the bath** in die Badewanne steigen; **to ~ ~to bed** sich ins Bett legen; **the water/smoke got ~(to) my eyes** ich habe Wasser/Rauch in die Augen bekommen *or* gekriegt *(inf)*; **he can't ~ ~** er kann *(inf) or* kommt nicht herein/hinein; **he got ~ between them** *(in car, bed etc)* er hat sich zwischen sie gesetzt/gelegt/gestellt.
(b) *(arrive: train, bus)* ankommen *(-to* in *+dat, -to station* am Bahnhof).
(c) *(be admitted)* hinein-/hereinkommen *(-to* in *+acc)*; *(into school, profession)* ankommen, angenommen werden *(-to* in *+dat)*.
(d) *(Pol: be elected)* gewählt werden *(-to* in *+acc)*, es schaffen *(inf)*.
(e) *(get home)* nach Hause kommen.
(f) *(inf)* **to ~ ~ with a request** ein Gesuch anbringen; **he got ~ first/before me/him** *etc* er ist mir/ihm *etc* zuvorgekommen.
2 *vt* **(a)** *sep (bring in)* hinein-/hereinbringen *(prep obj, -to* in *+acc)*; *crops, harvest* einbringen; *taxes, debts* eintreiben; *(fetch)* herein-/hineinholen *(-to* in *+acc)*; *(help enter)* hinein-/hereinhelfen *(+dat) (prep obj, -to* in *+acc)* ◆ **I got the kids ~(to) bed** ich habe die Kinder ins Bett gebracht.
(b) *sep (receive) forms etc* bekommen; *(submit) forms* einreichen; *homework* abgeben.
(c) *sep (plant) (prep obj, -to* in *+acc) bulbs etc* einpflanzen; *seeds also* säen.
(d) *always separate (get admitted to) (into club etc) (prep obj, to* in *+acc) (as*

member) zur Aufnahme verhelfen (*+dat*); (*as guest*) mitnehmen ◆ **those exam results should ~ him ~to any university** mit den Zeugnissen müßte er auf jeder Universität angenommen werden *or* ankommen; **his parents wanted to ~ him ~to a good school** seine Eltern wollten ihn auf eine gute Schule schicken; **how did his parents ~ him ~(to this school)?** wie haben es seine Eltern geschafft, daß er (in der Schule) angenommen wurde?
(e) *always separate* (*get elected*) *candidate* zu einem Sitz verhelfen (*+dat*) (*-to* in *+dat*); *party* zu einem Wahlsieg verhelfen (*+dat*) ◆ **that got the Liberals ~to Parliament** dadurch kamen die Liberalen ins Parlament.
(f) *sep* (*fit, insert into, find room for*) hineinbringen *or* -bekommen *or* -kriegen (*inf*) (*-to* in *+acc*); (*fig*) *blow, punch, request, words* anbringen ◆ **he always tries to ~ it ~to the conversation that ...** er versucht immer, es in die Unterhaltung einfließen zu lassen, daß ...
(g) *sep* (*get a supply*) *groceries, coal* holen, ins Haus bringen ◆ **to ~ ~ supplies** sich (*dat*) Vorräte zulegen.
(h) *sep* (*send for*) *doctor, tradesman* holen, kommen lassen; *specialist, consultant etc* zuziehen.
(i) *always separate* **to ~ one's eye/hand ~** in Übung kommen.

◆**get in on** [1] *vi +prep obj* (*inf*) mitmachen bei (*inf*), sich beteiligen an (*+dat*) ◆ **to ~ ~ ~ the act** mitmachen, mitmischen (*inf*).
[2] *vt sep +prep obj* beteiligen an (*+dat*); (*let take part in*) mitmachen lassen bei; *specialist, consultant* zuziehen bei.

◆**get into** [1] *vi +prep obj see also* **get in 1 (a-d)** **(a)** *rage, panic, debt, situation, company etc* geraten in (*+acc*); *trouble, difficulties also* kommen in (*+acc*); (*inf: devil, something*) fahren in (*+acc*) (*inf*) ◆ **what's got ~ him?** (*inf*) was ist bloß in ihn gefahren? (*inf*).
(b) *bad habits* sich (*dat*) angewöhnen ◆ **to ~ ~ the way of (doing) sth** sich an etw (*acc*) gewöhnen; **to ~ ~ the habit of doing sth** sich (*dat*) angewöhnen, etw zu tun; **it's easy once you've got ~ the swing** *or* **way of it** es ist leicht, wenn Sie erst mal ein bißchen Übung darin haben.
(c) (*get involved in*) *book* sich einlesen bei; *work* sich einarbeiten in (*+acc*) ◆ **once I've got ~ this job** *or* **it** wenn ich mich erst einmal eingearbeitet habe.
(d) (*put on*) anziehen, schlüpfen in (*+acc*); (*fit into*) hineinkommen *or* -passen in (*+acc*).
[2] *vt +prep obj always separate see also* **get in 2 (a, c-f)** **(a)** *rage, debt, situation etc* bringen in (*+acc*) ◆ **to ~ sb/oneself ~ trouble** jdn/sich in Schwierigkeiten (*acc*) bringen (*also euph*); **who got you ~ that?** wer hat dir das eingebrockt? (*inf*).
(b) to ~ sb ~ bad habits jdm schlechte Angewohnheiten *pl* beibringen; **who/what got you ~ the habit of smoking?** wer/was ist daran schuld, daß Sie rauchen?; **who/what got you ~ the habit of getting up early?** wer hat Ihnen das angewöhnt/wieso haben Sie es sich angewöhnt, früh aufzustehen?
(c) to ~ sb ~ a dress jdm ein Kleid anziehen; (*manage to put on*) jdn in ein Kleid hineinbekommen *or* -kriegen (*inf*).

◆**get in with** *vi +prep obj* (*associate with*) Anschluß finden an (*+acc*); *bad company* geraten in (*+acc*); (*ingratiate oneself with*) sich gut stellen mit.

◆**get off** [1] *vi* **(a)** (*descend*) (*from bus, train etc*) aussteigen (*prep obj* aus); (*from bicycle, horse*) absteigen (*prep obj* von) ◆ **to tell sb where to ~ ~** (*inf*) *or* **where he ~s ~** (*inf*) jdm gründlich die Meinung sagen (*inf*); **he knows where he can ~ ~!** (*inf*) der kann mich mal! (*inf*).
(b) (*remove oneself*) (*prep obj* von) (*from premises*) weggehen, verschwinden; (*from lawn, ladder, sb's toes, furniture*) heruntergehen; (*stand up: from chair*) aufstehen ◆ **~ ~!** (*let me go*) laß (mich) los!; **let's ~ ~ this subject** lassen wir das Thema! (*inf*).
(c) (*leave*) weg- *or* loskommen; (*be sent away: letter etc*) wegkommen, abgeschickt werden ◆ **it's time you got ~ to school** es ist Zeit, daß ihr in die Schule geht; **to ~ ~ to an early start** früh wegkommen; **to ~ ~ to a good/bad start** (*Sport*) einen guten/schlechten Start haben; (*fig*) (*person*) einen guten/schlechten Anfang machen; (*campaign etc*) sich gut/schlecht anlassen.
(d) (*be excused*) *homework, task etc* nicht machen müssen ◆ **to ~ ~ work/school** nicht zur Arbeit/Schule gehen müssen; **he got ~ tidying up his room** er kam darum herum, sein Zimmer aufräumen zu müssen (*inf*).
(e) (*fig: escape, be let off*) davonkommen (*inf*) ◆ **to ~ ~ lightly/with a fine** billig/mit einer Geldstrafe davonkommen.
(f) (*fall asleep*) **to ~ ~ (to sleep)** einschlafen.
(g) (*from work etc*) gehen können (*prep obj* in *+dat*) ◆ **I'll see if I can ~ ~ (work) early** ich werde mal sehen, ob ich früher (im Büro/von der Arbeit) wegkann (*inf*); **what time do you ~ ~ work?** wann hören Sie mit der Arbeit auf?
[2] *vt* **(a)** *sep* (*remove*) wegbekommen *or* -bringen *or* -kriegen (*inf*) (*prep obj* von); *clothes, shoes* ausziehen; (*manage to ~ ~*) herunterbekommen *or* -kriegen (*inf*) (*prep obj* von); *cover, lid* heruntertun (*prep obj* von); (*manage to ~ ~*) abbekommen (*prep obj* von); *stains* herausmachen (*prep obj* aus); (*manage to ~ ~*) herausbekommen *or* -bringen *or* -kriegen (*inf*) (*prep obj* aus); (*take away from*) abnehmen (*prep obj dat*); *shipwrecked boat, stuck car etc* freibekommen *or* - kriegen (*inf*) ◆ **I want to ~ this ~ my desk** ich möchte das vom Tisch kriegen (*inf*); **~ your dirty hands ~ that** nimm deine schmutzigen Hände davon *or* da weg!; **~ your hat ~!** nimm den Hut ab!; **~ him ~ me!** schaff ihn mir vom Leib! (*inf*); **~ him ~ my property/chair/lawn!** *etc* vertreiben Sie ihn von meinem Grundstück/Stuhl/Rasen! *etc*; **can't you ~ him ~ that subject/topic?** können Sie ihn nicht von dem Thema abbringen?
(b) *always separate* (*from bus etc*) aussteigen lassen (*prep obj* aus); (*manage to ~ ~*) herausbekommen *or* -bringen (*prep obj* aus); (*from boat, roof, ladder etc*) herunterholen (*prep obj* von); (*manage to ~ ~*) herunterbringen *or* -bekommen *or* -kriegen (*inf*) (*prep obj* von).
(c) *+prep obj always separate* (*inf: obtain*) bekommen, kriegen (*inf*) (*prep obj* von) ◆ **I got that idea/pencil ~ John** ich habe die Idee/den Bleistift von John.
(d) *sep* (*send away*) *mail, children* losschicken ◆ **to ~ sb/sth ~ to a good start** jdm/einer Sache zu einem guten Start verhelfen; **to ~ sb/sth ~ to a bad start** jdn/etw schon schlecht anfangen lassen; **to ~ sb ~ to school** jdn für die Schule fertigmachen.
(e) *always separate* (*let off*) **that got him ~ school for the afternoon/doing that** dadurch mußte er am Nachmittag nicht in die Schule/dadurch ist er darum herumgekommen, es machen zu müssen.
(f) *sep* (*save from punishment*) *accused* (*lawyer*) freibekommen *or* -kriegen (*inf*); (*evidence etc*) entlasten ◆ **it was his good manners that got him ~** er ist nur wegen seines guten Benehmens davongekommen.
(g) *always separate* **to ~ sb ~ (to sleep)** jdn zum Schlafen bringen.
(h) *sep* (*from work etc*) *day, afternoon* freibekommen.

◆**get off on** *vi +prep obj* (*sl: become excited by*) sich aufgeilen an (*+dat*) (*sl*).

◆**get off with** *vi +prep obj* (*inf*) **(a)** (*start a relationship with*) aufreißen (*sl*); (*have sex with*) bumsen mit (*inf*). **(b)** *see* **get away with (c)**.

◆**get on** [1] *vi* **(a)** (*climb on*) hinauf-/heraufsteigen; (*+prep obj*) (hinauf-/herauf)steigen auf (*+acc*); (*on bus, train etc*) einsteigen (*prep obj, -to* in *+acc*); (*on bicycle, horse etc*) aufsteigen (*prep obj, -to* auf *+acc*) ◆ **to ~ ~ sth** auf etw (*acc*) aufsteigen *etc*; **~ ~ the back and I'll give you a lift** steigen Sie hinten auf, dann nehme ich Sie mit.
(b) (*continue: with work etc*) weitermachen; (*manage to ~ ~*) weiterkommen.
(c) (*get late, old*) **time is ~ting ~** es wird langsam spät; **he is ~ting ~ (in years)** er wird langsam alt.
(d) *see* **get along 1 (a)**.
(e) (*progress*) vorankommen; (*work also, patient, pupil*) Fortschritte machen; (*succeed*) Erfolg haben ◆ **to ~ ~ in the world** es zu etwas bringen.
(f) (*fare, cope: in exam etc*) zurechtkommen ◆ **how did you ~ ~ in the exam?** wie ging's (dir) in der Prüfung?; **how are you ~ting ~?** wie geht's?; **to ~ ~ without sb/sth** ohne jdn/etw zurechtkommen.
(g) (*have a good relationship*) sich verstehen, auskommen (*with* mit) ◆ **they don't ~ ~ (with each other)** sie kommen nicht miteinander aus, sie verstehen sich nicht.
[2] *vt* **(a)** *sep* (*prep obj* auf *+acc*) *clothes, shoes* anziehen; *hat, kettle* aufsetzen; *lid, cover* drauftun; *load* (*onto cart etc*) hinauftun; (*manage to ~ ~*) draufbekommen *or* -kriegen (*inf*).
(b) *always separate* (*on train, bus etc*) hineinsetzen; (*+prep obj, -to*) setzen in (*+acc*); (*manage to ~ ~*) hineinbekommen *or* -kriegen (*inf*) (*prep obj, -to* in *+acc*); (*on bicycle, horse*) hinaufsetzen; (*prep obj, -to*) setzen auf (*acc*).

◆**get on for** *vi +prep obj* (*time, person in age*) zugehen auf (*+acc*) ◆ **he's ~ting ~ ~ 40** er geht auf die 40 zu; **there were/he had ~ting ~ ~ 60** es waren/er hatte fast 60.

◆**get on to** *vi +prep obj* (*inf*) **(a)** (*trace, get on track of*) *person* auf die Spur *or* Schliche kommen (*+dat*) (*inf*); *dubious activity, double-dealing* aufdecken, herausfinden; *whereabouts* herausfinden ◆ **they got ~ ~ his trail/scent** sie kamen ihm auf die Spur/sie haben seine Fährte aufgenommen.
(b) (*move on to*) *next item, new subject* übergehen zu.
(c) (*contact*) sich in Verbindung setzen mit ◆ **I'll ~ ~ ~ him about it** ich werde ihn daraufhin ansprechen.
(d) (*nag*) herumhacken auf (*+dat*) (*inf*), herumnörgeln an (*+dat*) (*inf*).

◆**get onto** *vti +prep obj see* **get on 1 (a), 2 (a, b)**.

◆**get on with** *vi +prep obj* (*continue*) weitermachen mit; (*manage to ~ ~ ~*) weiterkommen mit ◆ **~ ~ ~ it!** nun mach schon! (*inf*); **~ ~ ~ what you're doing** mach weiter; **~ ~ ~ your meal, will you?** nun iß schon!; **to let sb ~ ~ ~ sth** jdn etw machen lassen; **to leave sb to ~ ~ ~ sth** jdn einfach machen lassen; **this will do to be ~ting ~ ~** das tut's wohl für den Anfang (*inf*).

◆**get out** [1] *vi* **(a)** heraus-/hinauskommen (*of* aus); (*walk out*) hinaus-/herausgehen (*of* aus); (*drive out*) hinaus-/herausfahren (*of* aus); (*climb out*) hinaus-/herausklettern *or* -steigen (*of* aus); (*of bus, train, car*) aussteigen (*of* aus); (*leave*) weggehen (*of* aus); (*fig*) (*of business, scheme, contract*) aussteigen (*inf*) (*of* aus); (*of job*) wegkommen (*of* von) ◆ **he has to ~ ~ of the country/town** er muß das Land/die Stadt verlassen; **let's ~ ~ (of here)!** bloß weg hier! (*inf*); **~ ~!** raus! (*inf*); **~ ~ of my house/room!** verlassen Sie mein Haus/Zimmer!, raus aus meinem Haus/Zimmer! (*inf*); **~ ~ of my life!** ich will nichts mehr mit dir zu tun haben, verschwinde und laß dich nicht mehr blicken!; **he couldn't ~ ~ (of the hole)** er kam (aus dem Loch) nicht mehr heraus; **I might need to ~ ~ in a hurry** es kann sein, daß ich schnell raus- (*inf*) *or* hinausmuß; **to ~ ~ of bed** aufstehen; **to ~ ~ while the going's good** gehen *or* (*of contract, affair etc*) aussteigen (*inf*), solange man das noch kann.
(b) (*go walking, shopping etc*) weggehen ◆ **you ought to ~ ~ (of the house) more** Sie müßten mehr rauskommen (*inf*); **I'd like to ~ ~ into the countryside** ich würde gern irgendwo ins Grüne kommen; **to ~ ~ and about** herumkommen.
(c) (*lit, fig: escape, leak out*) (*of* aus) herauskommen; (*animal, prisoner also*) entkommen; (*poisonous liquid, gas also*) entweichen; (*news*) an die Öffentlichkeit dringen.
[2] *vt sep* **(a)** (*remove*) (*of* aus) *cork, tooth, splinter, stain etc* herausmachen; *people* heraus-/hinausbringen; (*send out*) hinausschicken; (*manage to ~ ~*) heraus-/hinausbekommen *or* -kriegen (*inf*) ◆ **I couldn't ~ him/it ~** ich habe ihn/es nicht hinaus-/herausbekommen *etc*; **~ him ~ of my house/sight** schaff mir ihn aus dem Haus/aus den Augen!; **cold water will ~ the stain ~**

mit kaltem Wasser bekommen Sie *etc* den Fleck heraus.
(b) (*bring, take out*) herausholen *or* -nehmen (*of* aus); *car, boat, horse* herausholen (*of* aus).
(c) (*withdraw*) *money* abheben (*of* von).
(d) (*produce*) *words, apology* herausbekommen *or* -bringen *or* -kriegen (*inf*).
(e) (*publish, present*) *book, plans, list etc* herausbringen.
(f) (*borrow from library*) ausleihen (*of* aus).
(g) (*Sport*) *batsman* ausschlagen.
(h) (*derive*) **you only ~ ~ what you put in** Sie bekommen nur das zurück, was Sie hineinstecken.

◆**get out of** [1] *vi +prep obj see also* **get out 1 (a, c). (a)** (*avoid, escape*) *obligation, punishment* herumkommen um; *difficulty* herauskommen aus ◆ **you can't ~ ~ ~ it now** jetzt kannst du nicht mehr anders; **there's no ~ting ~ ~ it** man kommt nicht darum herum; **I have signed the contract and now I can't ~ ~ ~ it** ich habe den Vertrag unterschrieben, jetzt gibt es kein Zurück.
(b) (*become unaccustomed to*) **I've got ~ ~ the way of playing tennis** ich habe das Tennisspielen verlernt; **I'll ~ ~ ~ practice** ich verlerne es; **to ~ ~ ~ the habit of doing one's exercises** seine Übungen nicht mehr regelmäßig machen; **it's hard to ~ ~ ~ the habit of waking up early** es ist schwer, es sich abzugewöhnen, früh aufzuwachen.
[2] *vt +prep obj always separate see also* **get out 2 (a-c). (a)** (*extract*) *words, confession, truth* herausbekommen *or* -bringen *or* -kriegen (*inf*) aus ◆ **nothing could be got ~ ~ him** aus ihm war nichts herauszubekommen *etc.*
(b) (*gain from*) *profit* machen bei; *money* herausholen aus; *people* profitieren von; *benefit, knowledge, wisdom, much, little, nothing* haben von; *pleasure* haben an (*+dat*); *happiness etc* finden in (*+dat*) ◆ **there's nothing to be got ~ ~ his lectures** von seinen Vorlesungen hat man nichts; **to ~ the best/most ~ ~ sth** das Beste aus etw machen; **what can we ~ ~ ~ them/that?** wie können wir von ihnen/davon profitieren?; **what are you trying to ~ ~ ~ me?** was willst du von mir (haben)?
(c) to ~ sb ~ ~ a habit/(the habit of) doing sth jdm eine Unsitte abgewöhnen/es jdm abgewöhnen, etw zu tun.

◆**get over** [1] *vi* **(a)** (*cross*) hinüber-/herübergehen (*prep obj* über *+acc*); (*climb over*) hinüber-/herübersteigen *or* -klettern; (*+prep obj*) steigen *or* klettern über (*+acc*); (*manage to ~ ~*) hinüber-/herüberkommen; (*+prep obj*) kommen über (*+acc*) ◆ **they got ~ to the other side** sie kamen *or* gelangten auf die andere Seite.
(b) *+prep obj* (*lit, fig: recover from*) *disappointment, loss, sb's cheek, fact, experience* (hin)wegkommen über (*+acc*); *shock, surprise, illness* sich erholen von ◆ **I can't ~ ~ the fact that ...** ich komme gar nicht darüber hinweg, daß ...; **I can't ~ ~ it** (*inf*) da komm ich nicht drüber weg (*inf*).
(c) *+prep obj* (*overcome*) *problem, nervousness, handicap, obstacle* überwinden.
(d) (*communicate*) (*play, actor*) ankommen (*to* bei); (*speaker*) sich verständlich machen (*to dat*).
[2] *vt* **(a)** *always separate* (*transport across*) *person, animal, vehicle* hinüber-/herüberbringen (*prep obj* über *+acc*); (*manage to ~ ~*) hinüber-/herüberbekommen (*prep obj* über *+acc*); (*send*) hinüber-/herüberschicken; (*fetch*) holen; (*help sb to cross, climb*) hinüber-/herüberhelfen (*sb* jdm) (*prep obj* über *+acc*).
(b) *sep* (*make comprehensible*) *information, ideas etc* verständlich machen (*to dat*); (*impress upon*) klarmachen (*to dat*) ◆ **the actors got the scene ~ to the audience** die Schauspieler erreichten das Publikum mit dieser Szene; **she ~s her songs ~ well** sie kommt mit ihren Liedern gut an.
(c) *see* **get over with.**

◆**get over with** *vt always separate* hinter sich (*acc*) bringen ◆ **let's ~ it ~ (~)** bringen wir's hinter uns; **to ~ sth ~ and done ~** etw ein für allemal erledigen *or* hinter sich bringen.

◆**get past** [1] *vi see* **get by (a, b).**
[2] *vt sep* vorbeibringen (*prep obj* an *+dat*).

◆**get round** [1] *vi* **(a)** (*drive, walk etc round*) herumkommen (*prep obj* um, *the shops* in den Geschäften).
(b) *+prep obj* (*evade, circumvent*) herumkommen um; *difficulty also, law, regulations* umgehen.
(c) *+prep obj* (*persuade*) herumkriegen (*inf*).
(d) *+prep obj* **to ~ ~ the conference table** sich an einen Tisch setzen.
[2] *vt always separate* **(a)** (*restore to consciousness*) zu Bewußtsein *or* zu sich bringen.
(b) (*make agree*) herumbringen *or* -kriegen (*inf*) ◆ **I'm sure I can ~ her ~ to my way of thinking** ich bin sicher, daß ich sie überzeugen kann.
(c) *+prep obj* **to ~ one's tongue ~ a word** ein Wort aussprechen können.
(d) *+prep obj* **to ~ people (together) ~ the conference table** Leute an einem Tisch zusammenbringen.

◆**get round to** *vi +prep obj* (*inf*) **to ~ ~ ~ sth/doing sth** zu etw kommen/dazu kommen, etw zu tun.

◆**get through** [1] *vi* **(a)** (*through gap, snow etc*) durchkommen (*prep obj* durch) ◆ **why don't you ~ ~ there?** warum gehst/fährst/schlüpfst *etc* du nicht da durch?; **the news got ~ (to us)** die Nachricht kam (zu uns) durch.
(b) (*be accepted, pass*) durchkommen (*prep obj* bei) ◆ **to ~ ~ to the final** in die Endrunde kommen.
(c) (*Telec*) durchkommen (*inf*) (*to sb* zu jdm, *to London/Germany* nach London/Deutschland).
(d) (*communicate, be understood*) (*person*) durchdringen zu; (*idea etc*) klarwerden (*to dat*).
(e) *+prep obj* (*finish*) *work* fertigmachen, erledigen; (*manage to ~ ~*) schaffen (*inf*); *book* fertig- *or* auslesen ◆ **to ~ ~ doing sth** etw fertigmachen; **to ~ ~ writing/reading/cleaning sth** etw fertigschreiben/-lesen/-putzen; **when I've got ~ this** wenn ich damit fertig bin.
(f) *+prep obj* (*survive*) *days, time* herumbekommen *or* -kriegen (*inf*).
(g) *+prep obj* (*consume, use up*) verbrauchen; *clothes, shoes* abnutzen; *food* aufessen, verputzen (*inf*); *fortune* durchbringen (*inf*).
[2] *vt always separate* **(a)** *person, vehicle, object* durchbekommen *or* -bringen *or* -kriegen (*inf*) (*prep obj* durch) ◆ **to ~ a comb ~ one's hair** mit dem Kamm durchkommen.
(b) (*cause to succeed*) *candidate, proposal, bill* durchbekommen *or* -bringen (*prep obj* durch) ◆ **to ~ sb ~ an exam** (*teacher*) jdn durchs Examen bringen; **it was his English that got him ~** er hat das nur aufgrund seines Englisch geschafft (*inf*); **he got the team ~ to the finals** er hat die Mannschaft in die Endrunde gebracht.
(c) (*send*) *message* durchgeben (*to dat*); *supplies* durchbringen ◆ **they couldn't ~ the ammunition to the men** es ist ihnen nicht gelungen, Munition zu den Leuten zu bringen; **we eventually got supplies/a message ~ to them** wir konnten ihnen schließlich Vorräte/eine Nachricht zukommen lassen.
(d) (*make understand*) **to ~ sth ~ (to sb)** jdm etw klarmachen.

◆**get through with** *vi +prep obj* (*inf: finish*) hinter sich bringen; *job also, formalities, subject* erledigen; *book* auslesen (*inf*), durchbekommen (*inf*); *person* fertig werden mit ◆ **once I've got ~ ~ him** wenn ich mit ihm fertig bin; **I'll never ~ ~ ~ that** ich werde das nie schaffen.

◆**get to** *vi +prep obj* **(a)** (*lit, fig: arrive at*) kommen zu; *hotel, town etc also* ankommen in (*+dat*) ◆ **where have you got ~ in French/with that book?** wie weit seid ihr in Französisch/mit dem Buch?; **to ~ ~ a high position** auf einen hohen Posten kommen *or* gelangen.
(b) I got ~ thinking/wondering ich hab mir überlegt/mich gefragt.
(c) (*inf: annoy, upset*) aufregen ◆ **don't let them ~ ~ you with their sarcasm** laß dich von ihrem Sarkasmus nicht rausbringen (*inf*).

◆**get together** [1] *vi* zusammenkommen; (*estranged couple*) sich versöhnen; (*combine forces*) sich zusammenschließen ◆ **to ~ ~ about sth** zusammenkommen *or* sich zusammensetzen und etw beraten; **let's ~ ~ and decide ...** wir sollten uns zusammensetzen und entscheiden, ...; **why don't we ~ ~ later and have a drink?** warum treffen wir uns nicht später und trinken einen?
[2] *vt sep people, collection* zusammenbringen; *documents, papers* zusammentun *or* -suchen; *thoughts, ideas* sammeln ◆ **to ~ one's things ~** seine Sachen zusammenpacken; **once I've got my thoughts ~** wenn ich meine Gedanken beisammen habe (*inf*); **to ~ it ~** (*sl*) es bringen (*sl*); **that's no good, come on, ~ it ~** (*sl*) das taugt doch nichts, nun reiß dich mal am Riemen (*sl*).

◆**get under** [1] *vi* darunterkriechen; (*under umbrella etc*) daruntergehen/-kommen; (*+prep obj*) kriechen unter (*+acc*); kommen unter (*+acc*); (*manage to ~ ~*) darunterkommen; (*+prep obj*) kommen unter (*+acc*).
[2] *vt +prep obj always separate* bringen unter (*+acc*).

◆**get up** [1] *vi* **(a)** (*stand up, get out of bed*) aufstehen.
(b) (*climb up*) hinauf-/heraufsteigen *or* -klettern (*prep obj* auf *+acc*); (*on horse*) aufsteigen (*prep obj, on* auf *+acc*); (*manage to ~ ~*) hinauf-/heraufkommen (*prep obj, on* auf *+acc*); (*vehicle*) hinauf-/heraufkommen (*prep obj acc*) ◆ **to ~ ~ behind sb** hinter jdm aufsitzen; **~ting ~ is all right, coming down is much harder** hinauf *or* rauf (*inf*) kommt man leicht, nur hinunterzukommen ist schwieriger.
(c) (*get stronger*) (*wind*) aufkommen; (*sea*) stürmisch werden.
[2] *vt* **(a)** *always separate* (*get out of bed*) aus dem Bett holen; (*help to stand up*) aufhelfen (*+dat*); (*manage to ~ ~*) hochbringen ◆ **he couldn't ~ it ~** (*inf*) er hat ihn nicht hochgekriegt (*inf*); **I'll ~ myself ~ in the morning** ich stehe morgen früh allein auf.
(b) *always separate* (*carry up*) hinauf-/heraufbringen (*prep obj acc*); (*manage to ~ ~ also*) hinauf-/heraufbekommen *or* -kriegen (*inf*) (*prep obj acc*); (*help climb up*) hinauf-/heraufhelfen (*dat*) (*prep obj* auf *+acc*); (*fetch*) hinauf-/heraufholen ◆ **to ~ sb/sth ~ to the front** jdn/etw nach vorn *or* (*Mil*) an die Front bringen.
(c) *sep* (*gather*) *steam* aufbauen ◆ **to ~ ~ speed** sich beschleunigen; **to ~ one's strength ~, to ~ ~ one's strength** sich erholen, wieder neue Kräfte sammeln; **to ~ ~ an appetite/a thirst** (*inf*) Hunger/Durst bekommen *or* kriegen (*inf*).
(d) *sep* (*organize*) organisieren; *play also* auf die Beine stellen (*inf*).
(e) *always separate* (*dress up, make attractive*) *person, oneself* zurechtmachen; *article for sale* aufmachen, herrichten ◆ **to ~ oneself ~ as sb/sth** sich als jd/etw verkleiden; **to ~ sth ~ as sth** *or* **to look like sth** etw als etw aufmachen.

◆**get up against** *vi +prep obj* (*inf: come in conflict with*) sich anlegen mit (*inf*).

◆**get up to** [1] *vi +prep obj* **(a)** (*lit, fig: reach*) erreichen; *standard* herankommen an (*+acc*), kommen auf (*+acc*); *page* kommen bis ◆ **as soon as he got ~ ~ me** sobald er neben mir stand.
(b) (*be involved in*) anstellen (*inf*) ◆ **to ~ ~ ~ mischief** etwas anstellen; **what have you been ~ting ~ ~?** was hast du getrieben? (*inf*).
[2] *vt +prep obj always separate* (*bring up to*) *top of mountain* hinauf-/heraufbringen auf (*+acc*); *standard* bringen auf (*+acc*).

get: ~-at-able [ˌget'ætəbl] *adj* (*inf*) leicht erreichbar *or* zu erreichen *pred; house, person also* zugänglich; **it's not very ~-at-able** es ist schwer zu erreichen; **~away** [1] *n* Flucht *f*; **to make one's/a quick ~away** sich davonmachen (*inf*)/schnell abhauen (*inf*); [2] *adj attr car, plans* Flucht-.

Gethsemane [geθ'semənɪ] *n* Gethsemane, Gethsemani *no art.*

get: ~-together *n* (*inf*) Treffen *nt*; **we have a ~-together once a year** wir treffen uns einmal im Jahr; **~-up** *n (inf)* Aufzug *m (inf)*, Aufmachung *f (inf)*; **I want a new ~-up** ich möchte etwas Neues zum Anziehen; **~-up-and-go** *n (inf)* Elan *m*; **~-well card** *n* Karte *f* mit Genesungswünschen.

geyser ['gi:zəʳ] *n* **(a)** *(Geol)* Geiser, Geysir *m*. **(b)** *(domestic ~)* Durchlauferhitzer *m*.

G-force ['dʒi:fɔ:s] *n* g-Druck, Andruck *m*.

Ghana ['gɑ:nə] *n* Ghana *nt*.

Ghanaian [gɑ:'neɪən] **1** *adj* ghanaisch.
2 *n (person)* Ghanaer(in *f*) *m*.

ghastly ['gɑ:stlɪ] *adj* **(a)** *crime, injuries, accident* entsetzlich, grauenerregend; *mistake, tale* schrecklich. **(b)** *(inf: awful)* gräßlich *(inf)*, schauderhaft *(inf)*, scheußlich *(inf)* ◆ **to look ~** gräßlich aussehen *(inf)*; **I feel ~** mir geht's scheußlich *(inf)*. **(c)** *(pale, chalk-like) pallor* gespenstisch.

Ghent [gent] *n* Gent *nt*.

gherkin ['gɜ:kɪn] *n* Gewürz- *or* Essiggurke *f*.

ghetto ['getəʊ] *n (lit, fig)* G(h)etto *nt*.

ghetto-blaster ['getəʊblɑ:stəʳ] *n (inf)* Ghettoblaster *m (inf)*, großes Kofferradio.

ghettoization [,getəʊaɪ'zeɪʃən] *n* **the ~ of this district** die Ghettobildung in diesem Viertel.

ghettoize ['getəʊaɪz] *vt* zum Ghetto machen.

ghost [gəʊst] **1** *n* **(a)** *(apparition)* Geist *m*, Gespenst *nt*; *(of sb)* Geist *m*.
(b) *(fig)* **the ~ of a smile** der Anflug eines Lächelns; **she gave him the ~ of a smile** sie lächelte ihn zaghaft an; **to be a ~ of one's former self** nur noch ein Schatten seiner selbst sein; **I haven't the ~ of a chance** ich habe nicht die geringste Chance.
(c) to give up the ~ *(old, inf)* seinen *or* den Geist aufgeben.
(d) *(TV: also* **~ image***)* Geisterbild *nt*.
(e) *(writer)* Ghostwriter *m*.
2 *vi* Ghostwriter sein *(for sb* jds*)*.
3 *vt* **to be ~ed** von einem Ghostwriter geschrieben sein; **to get sth ~ed** sich *(dat)* etw von einem Ghostwriter schreiben lassen; **to ~ sb's books/speeches** für jdn Bücher/Reden (als Ghostwriter) schreiben.

ghost driver *n (US inf)* Geisterfahrer(in *f*) *m (inf)*.

ghosting ['gəʊstɪŋ] *n (TV)* Geisterbilder *pl*.

ghostly ['gəʊstlɪ] *adj (+er)* geisterhaft, gespenstisch ◆ **a ~ presence** die Gegenwart eines Geistes.

ghost *in cpds* Geister-; **~ story** *n* Geister- *or* Gespenstergeschichte *f*; **~ town** *n* Geisterstadt *f*; **~writer** *n* Ghostwriter *m*.

ghoul [gu:l] *n (evil spirit)* Ghul *m*; *(fig)* Mensch *m* mit schaurigen Gelüsten.

ghoulish ['gu:lɪʃ] *adj* makaber; *laughter, interest* schaurig.

ghoulishly ['gu:lɪʃlɪ] *adv see adj*.

GHQ *abbr of* **General Headquarters**.

G.I. *(US) abbr of* **government issue** **1** *n* GI, US-Soldat *m*.
2 *adj attr uniform, bride* GI-; *haircut, kitbag, shoes* (US-)Armee-.

giant ['dʒaɪənt] **1** *n* Riese *m*; *(star also)* Riesenstern *m*; *(fig)* (führende) Größe; *(company)* Gigant *m* ◆ **a ~ of a man** ein Riese (von einem Mann); **football ~** Fußballas *nt*, (führende) Größe im Fußball; **one of the ~s in that field** eine(r) der Großen auf dem Gebiet.
2 *adj (huge)* riesig, riesenhaft, Riesen-; *hill* enorm; *(in animal names)* Riesen-; *publisher etc* Groß-, Riesen- *(inf)* ◆ **~(-size) packet** Riesenpackung *f*; **~ strength** Riesenkräfte *pl*.

giantess ['dʒaɪəntes] *n* Riesin *f*.

giant: ~-killer *n (fig)* Goliathbezwinger *m*; **~ panda** *n* Großer Panda, Bambusbär *m*.

Gib [dʒɪb] *n abbr of* **Gibraltar**.

gibber ['dʒɪbəʳ] *vi (ape)* schnattern; *(foreigner also, idiot)* brabbeln ◆ **he ~ed at me** er schnatterte drauflos *(inf)*; **to ~ with rage/fear** vor Wut/Angst stammeln.

gibberish ['dʒɪbərɪʃ] *n* Quatsch *m (inf)*; *(foreign language, baby's ~)* Kauderwelsch *nt*.

gibbet ['dʒɪbɪt] *n* Galgen *m*.

gibbon ['gɪbən] *n* Gibbon *m*.

gibbous ['gɪbəs] *adj moon* Dreiviertel-.

gibe [dʒaɪb] **1** *n* Spöttelei, Stichelei *f*.
2 *vi* spotten, sticheln ◆ **to ~ at sb/sth** sich über jdn/etw lustig machen, spöttische Bemerkungen über jdn/etw machen.

giblets ['dʒɪblɪts] *npl* Geflügelinnereien *pl*.

Gibraltar [dʒɪ'brɔ:ltəʳ] *n* Gibraltar *nt*.

giddily ['gɪdɪlɪ] *adv* **(a)** benommen. **(b)** *climb etc* schwindelerregend; *spin* in schwindelerregendem Tempo. **(c)** *(fig)* leichtfertig, unbesonnen.

giddiness ['gɪdɪnɪs] *n* **(a)** *(dizziness)* Schwindelgefühl *nt*. **(b)** *(fig)* Leichtfertigkeit, Unbesonnenheit *f* ◆ **the ~ of the life they lead** der hektische Trubel ihres Lebens.

giddy ['gɪdɪ] *adj (+er)* **(a)** *(lit: dizzy)* schwind(e)lig; *feeling* Schwindel- ◆ **I feel ~** mir ist schwind(e)lig; **it makes me feel ~** mir wird (davon) schwind(e)lig; **heights always make me ~** ich bin nicht schwindelfrei.
(b) *(causing dizziness) climb, speed* schwindelerregend; *heights also* schwindelnd *(also fig)*; *spin* rasend schnell.
(c) *(fig: heedless, not serious)* leichtfertig, flatterhaft ◆ **their life was one ~ round of pleasure** ihr Leben bestand nur aus Jubel, Trubel, Heiterkeit; **that's the ~ limit!** *(dated inf)* das ist wirklich der Gipfel *or* die Höhe!

▼**gift** [gɪft] **1** *n* **(a)** *(thing given)* Geschenk *nt (inf)*, Gabe *f (liter)*; *(donation to charity)* Spende *f*; *(Jur)* Schenkung *f* ◆ **to make sb a ~** jdm ein Geschenk machen; **to make a ~ of sth to sb** jdm etw zum Geschenk machen *(form)*; **there is a free ~ with every purchase of ...** bei jedem Kauf von ... erhalten Sie ein Geschenk; **a free ~ of a tin of soup** eine Dose Suppe umsonst; **I wouldn't have it as a ~** ich möchte es nicht geschenkt haben; **that exam/question/goal was a ~** *(inf)* die Prüfung/die Frage/das Tor war ja geschenkt *(inf)*.
(b) *(form: right to give)* **sth is in the ~ of sb** jd kann etw vergeben.
▼**(c)** *(talent)* Gabe *f* ◆ **to have a ~ for sth** ein Talent für etw haben; **he has a ~ for languages/music** *etc* er ist sprachbegabt/musikalisch *etc* begabt; *see* **gab**.
2 *vt* als Schenkung überlassen.

gifted ['gɪftɪd] *adj* begabt *(in* für*)* ◆ **he is very ~ in languages/music** er ist sehr sprachbegabt/musikalisch sehr begabt.

gift: ~ horse *n*: **don't look a ~ horse in the mouth** *(Prov)* einem geschenkten Gaul schaut man nicht ins Maul *(Prov)*; **~ tax** *n* Schenkungssteuer *f*; **~ token** *or* **voucher** *n* Geschenkgutschein *m*; **~-wrap** *vt* in *or* mit Geschenkpapier einwickeln; **~-wrapping** *n* Geschenkpapier *nt*.

gig [gɪg] *n* **(a)** *(carriage, boat)* Gig *nt*. **(b)** *(inf: concert)* Konzert *nt*, Gig *m (inf)* ◆ **to do a ~** ein Konzert geben, auftreten. **(c)** *(US: temporary job)* Job *m*.

giga- ['gɪgə-] *pref* Giga-.

gigabyte ['gɪgəbaɪt] *n (Comput)* Gigabyte *nt*.

gigahertz ['gɪgəhɜ:ts] *n* Gigahertz *nt*.

gigantic [dʒaɪ'gæntɪk] *adj* riesig, riesengroß; *building, man, task also* gigantisch; *appetite, mistake also* gewaltig; *amount* riesenhaft, enorm, Riesen-; *yawn* kräftig, herzhaft; **it grew to ~ size** es wurde riesengroß.

giggle ['gɪgl] **1** *n* Gekicher, Kichern *nt no pl* ◆ **she has such a silly ~** sie kichert so dumm; **..., he said with a ~** ..., sagte er kichernd; **we had a good ~ about it** *(inf)* wir haben uns darüber gekringelt *(inf)*; **it was a bit of a ~** *(inf)* es war ganz lustig; **to get the ~s** anfangen herumzukichern.
2 *vi* kichern, gickeln *(inf)*.

giggly ['gɪglɪ] *adj (+er)* albern, gickelig *(inf)*.

GIGO ['gaɪgəʊ] *(Comput) abbr of* **garbage in, garbage out**.

gigolo ['ʒɪgələʊ] *n* Gigolo *m*.

gigot ['dʒɪgət] *n (old)* Hammelkeule *f* ◆ **~ chop** *(Scot)* Hammelkotelett *nt mit Mark im Knochen*.

gild [gɪld] *pret* **~ed**, *ptp* **~ed** *or* **gilt** *vt* vergolden ◆ **to ~ the lily** des Guten zuviel tun.

gilder ['gɪldəʳ] *n* Vergolder *m*.

gilding ['gɪldɪŋ] *n* Vergoldung *f*.

gill[1] [gɪl] *n (of fish)* Kieme *f* ◆ **green about the ~s** *(inf)* blaß um die Nase *(inf)*.

gill[2] [dʒɪl] *n (measure)* Gill *nt (0,148 l)*.

gillie ['gɪlɪ] *n (Scot)* Jagdaufseher *m*.

gilt [gɪlt] **1** *ptp of* **gild**.
2 *n (material)* Vergoldung *f* ◆ **a design in ~** ein vergoldetes Muster; **to take the ~ off the gingerbread** *(fig)* jdm die Freude verderben.
3 *adj* vergoldet.

gilt-edged [,gɪlt'edʒd] *adj* mit Goldrand, goldumrandet; *(Fin) securities, stocks* mündelsicher; *(fig)* solide.

gimcrack ['dʒɪmkræk] *adj* billig; *furniture, toys also* minderwertig.

gimlet ['gɪmlɪt] *n* Hand- *or* Vorbohrer *m* ◆ **to have eyes like ~s** Augen wie ein Luchs haben; **her eyes bored into him like ~s** ihre Augen durchbohrten ihn; **~-eyed** luchsäugig.

gimme ['gɪmɪ] *(sl)* = **give me**.

gimmick ['gɪmɪk] *n* Gag *m (inf)*; *(in film etc)* effekthaschender Gag, Spielerei *f*; *(gadget)* Spielerei *f* ◆ **changing the name and not the product is just a (sales) ~** den Namen, aber nicht das Produkt zu ändern, ist nur ein (Verkaufs)trick.

gimmickry ['gɪmɪkrɪ] *n* Effekthascherei *f*; *(in advertising, sales)* Gags *pl*; *(gadgetry)* Spielereien *pl*.

gimmicky ['gɪmɪkɪ] *adj* effekthascherisch.

gin[1] [dʒɪn] *n (drink)* Gin, Wacholder(schnaps) *m* ◆ **~ and tonic** Gin Tonic *m*; **~ and it** *Gin m und (italienischer) Wermut*.

gin[2] *n* **(a)** *(Hunt)* Falle *f*; *(snare)* Schlinge *f*. **(b)** *(Tex: cotton ~)* (Baumwoll)entkernungsmaschine *f*.

ginger ['dʒɪndʒəʳ] **1** *n* **(a)** Ingwer *m*. **(b)** *(pej inf: address for person)* Rotkopf *or* -schopf *m*.
2 *adj* **(a)** *(Cook) biscuit etc* Ingwer-. **(b)** *hair* kupferrot; *cat* rötlichgelb.

◆**ginger up** *vt sep (inf)* in Schwung *or* auf Vordermann *(inf)* bringen; *person also* aufmöbeln *(inf)*; *book* würzen.

ginger: ~-ale *n* Ginger Ale *nt*; **~ beer** *n* Ingwerlimonade *f*; **~bread** **1** *n* Leb- *or* Pfefferkuchen *m mit Ingwergeschmack*; **2** *adj attr* Lebkuchen-; **~ group** *n (Parl)* Aktionsgruppe *f*.

gingerly ['dʒɪndʒəlɪ] *adv* vorsichtig, behutsam; *(because sth is dirty)* mit spitzen Fingern; *(because sth is cold, hot etc)* zaghaft.

ginger: ~-nut *n* Ingwerplätzchen *nt*; **~-snap** *n* Ingwerwaffel *f*.

gingery ['dʒɪndʒərɪ] *adj taste* Ingwer-; *hair* rötlich.

gingham ['gɪŋəm] *n* Gingan, Gingham *m*.

gingivitis [,dʒɪndʒɪ'vaɪtɪs] *n* Zahnfleischentzündung *f*.

ginormous [dʒaɪ'nɔ:məs] *adj (sl: enormous)* riesig *(inf)*; *sum etc also* Wahnsinns- *(inf)*.

gin rummy *n* Rommé mit Zehn *nt*.

gippy tummy ['dʒɪpɪ'tʌmɪ] *n (inf)* Durchfall *m*.

gipsy, *(esp US)* **gypsy** ['dʒɪpsɪ] **1** *n* Zigeuner(in *f*) *m*.
2 *adj attr* Zigeuner- ◆ **~ moth** Schwammspinner *m*.

giraffe [dʒɪ'rɑ:f] *n* Giraffe *f*.

gird [gɜ:d] *pret, ptp* **~ed** *or (rare)* **girt** *vt (old)* gürten *(old)*; *(fig)* umgeben ◆ **to ~ oneself** sich gürten *(with* mit*)*; *(fig: prepare)* sich wappnen.

◆**gird up** *vt sep (old) robe* gürten ◆ **to ~ ~ one's loins** *(esp Bibl)* seine Lenden gürten *(Bibl)*; **to ~ oneself ~** *(fig)* sich wappnen; **he ~ed himself ~ for action**

➤ LANGUAGE IN USE: **gift: 1a** → 24.3 **1c** → 16.4

er machte sich bereit (zum Handeln).

girder ['gɜːdəʳ] *n* Träger *m*.

girdle[1] ['gɜːdl] 1 *n* **(a)** (*belt, fig*) Gürtel *m*. **(b)** (*corset*) Hüftgürtel *or* -halter *m*.
2 *vt* (*lit*) gürten; (*fig*) umgeben.

girdle[2] *n* (*Scot*) *see* **griddle**.

girl [gɜːl] *n* **(a)** Mädchen *nt*; (*daughter also*) Tochter *f* ◆ **an English ~** eine Engländerin; **they are hoping for a little ~** sie wünschen sich (*dat*) ein Töchterchen; **the Smith ~s** die Smith-Mädchen, die Mädchen von den Smiths; **my eldest ~** meine älteste Tochter, meine Älteste; **the ~s** (*colleagues*) die Damen; (*friends*) die/meine/ihre *etc* Freundinnen; **thank you, ~s** vielen Dank; **the old ~** die Alte (*inf*) *or* alte Frau; (*inf: wife, mother*) meine/seine *etc* Alte (*inf*).
(b) (*employee*) Mädchen *nt*; (*in shop also*) Verkäuferin *f*; (*in factory*) Arbeiterin *f*.

girl: ~ Friday *n* Allround-Sekretärin *f*; **~friend** *n* Freundin *f*; **~ guide** *n* (*Brit*) Pfadfinderin *f*; **~hood** *n* Mädchenzeit, Jugend *f*; **during her ~hood** in ihrer Jugend.

girlie ['gɜːlɪ] 1 *n* (*inf*) Mädchen *nt*.
2 *adj attr magazine* mit nackten Mädchen; *photos* von nackten Mädchen.

girlish ['gɜːlɪʃ] *adj behaviour, appearance* mädchenhaft; *laugh, confidences also* Mädchen- ◆ **she still looked ~** sie sah immer noch wie ein Mädchen aus.

girlishly ['gɜːlɪʃlɪ] *adv* mädchenhaft; *dress also* jugendlich.

girlishness ['gɜːlɪʃnɪs] *n* Mädchenhaftigkeit *f*.

girl scout *n* (*US*) Pfadfinderin *f*.

giro ['dʒaɪrəʊ] *n* (*Brit*) (*bank ~*) Giro(verkehr *m*) *nt*; (*post-office ~*) Postscheckverkehr *or* -dienst *m* ◆ **~ cheque** Postscheck *m*; (*social security*) Sozialhilfeüberweisung *f*; **to pay a bill by ~ (cheque)** eine Rechnung durch Giro/mit Postscheck bezahlen.

Girobank ['dʒaɪrəʊbæŋk] *n* Postsparkasse *f* ◆ **~ transfer** Postüberweisung *f*.

girt [gɜːt] (*rare*) *pret, ptp of* **gird**.

girth [gɜːθ] *n* **(a)** (*circumference*) Umfang *m* ◆ **in ~** im Umfang; **a man of ample ~** ein Mann mit beträchtlichem Umfang. **(b)** (*harness*) (Sattel)gurt *m*.

gismo *n* (*inf*) *see* **gizmo**.

gist [dʒɪst] *n, no pl* (*of report, conversation, argument*) Wesentliche(s) *nt* ◆ **that was the ~ of what he said** das war im wesentlichen, was er gesagt hat; **to give sb the ~ of sth** jdm sagen, worum es bei etw geht; **to get the ~ of sth/the conversation** im wesentlichen verstehen, worum es sich bei etw handelt/wovon geredet wird; **I got the ~ of it** das Wesentliche habe ich verstanden.

git [gɪt] *n* (*inf: stupid person*) Schwachkopf, Depp (*dial*) *m*.

give [gɪv] (*vb: pret* **gave**, *ptp* **given**) 1 *vt* **(a)** geben (*sb sth, sth to sb* jdm etw); (*as present*) schenken (*sb sth, sth to sb* jdm etw); (*donate also*) spenden ◆ **it was ~n to me by my uncle, I was ~n it by my uncle** ich habe es von meinem Onkel bekommen *or* (*as present also*) geschenkt bekommen; **she was ~n a sedative** sie hat ein Beruhigungsmittel bekommen, man hat ihr *or* ihr wurde ein Beruhigungs mittel gegeben; **the teacher gave us three exercises** der Lehrer hat uns drei Übungen gegeben *or* (*as homework*) aufgegeben; **we were ~n three exercises** wir haben drei Übungen bekommen *or* (*as homework*) aufbekommen; **he gave me a present of a book** *or* **a book as a present** er schenkte mir ein Buch, er machte mir ein Buch zum Geschenk; **they gave us food and drink** sie gaben uns zu essen und zu trinken; **they gave us roast beef for lunch** sie servierten uns Roastbeef zum (Mittag)essen; **to ~ sth for sth** (*sacrifice*) etw für etw (her)geben; (*exchange*) etw gegen etw tauschen; **what will you ~ me for it?** was gibst du mir dafür?; **what did you ~ for it?** was hast du dafür bezahlt?; **11 o'clock, ~ or take a few minutes** so gegen 11 Uhr; **six foot, ~ or take a few inches** ungefähr sechs Fuß; **to ~ as good as one gets** sich kräftig wehren; **he gave everything he'd got** (*fig*) er holte das Letzte aus sich heraus; **to ~ sb one's cold** (*inf*) jdn mit seiner Erkältung anstecken; **I'd ~ a lot/the world/anything to know** ... ich würde viel darum geben, wenn ich wüßte, ...
(b) (*fig*) geben; *pleasure, joy* machen, bereiten; *pain* bereiten; *trouble* machen; *one's love, attention* schenken; *hospitality* erweisen; *punishment* erteilen; *favour* gewähren ◆ **this incident gave him the basic plot of** *or* **idea for the story** durch dieses Ereignis bekam er die Grundidee zu seiner Geschichte; **who/what gave you that idea** *or* **notion?** wer hat dich denn auf die Idee gebracht/wie kommst du denn auf die Idee?; **to be ~n a choice** die Wahl haben; **I wasn't ~n the choice** ich hatte keine (andere) Wahl; **to ~ sb pain** jdm weh tun (*also fig*), jdm Schmerzen bereiten; **it ~s me great pleasure to** ... es ist mir eine große Freude ...; **he gave the impression/appearance of being disturbed** er machte einen verstörten Eindruck; **to ~ sb help** jdm helfen *or* Hilfe leisten; **to ~ sb support** jdn unterstützen; **(God) ~ me strength to do it** Gott gebe mir die Kraft, es zu tun!; **~ me strength/patience!** großer Gott! (*inf*); **he gave the child a spanking/100 lines** er gab *or* verabreichte dem Kind eine Tracht Prügel/er gab dem Kind 100 Zeilen als Strafarbeit auf; **to ~ sb five years** jdn zu fünf Jahren verurteilen, jdm fünf Jahre aufbrummen (*inf*); **he was ~n a spanking/five years** er hat eine Tracht Prügel/fünf Jahre bekommen; **to ~ sb to understand that** ... jdm zu verstehen geben, daß ...; **I was ~n to understand that** ... mir wurde zu verstehen gegeben, daß ...; **to ~ sb what for** (*inf*), **to ~ it to sb** (*inf*) jdm Saures geben (*inf*), es jdm geben (*inf*); **that will ~ you something to cry/think about** da hast du Grund zum Weinen/etwas, worüber du nachdenken kannst; **I'll ~ you something to cry about** ich werde schon zusehen, daß du weißt, warum du weinst; **~ me Shakespeare/Spain (every time)!** (*inf*) es geht doch nichts über Shakespeare/Spanien; **~ me Renoir and Rembrandt, not these surrealist artists** mir sind Renoir und Rembrandt viel lieber als diese Surrealisten; *see* **thrill, idea**.
(c) (*allow*) *time* geben ◆ **they gave me a week to do it** sie gaben *or* ließen mir eine Woche Zeit, um es zu machen; **~ yourself more time/half an hour** lassen Sie sich mehr Zeit/rechnen Sie mit einer halben Stunde; **I always ~ myself an extra hour in bed** ich genehmige mir eine Extrastunde im Bett; **how long do you ~ that marriage?** (*inf*) wie lange gibst du dieser Ehe? (*inf*); **I'll ~ you that** zugegeben; **he's a good worker, I'll ~ him that** eines muß man ihm lassen, er arbeitet gut.
(d) (*report, tell, pass on*) *information, details, description, answer, advice* geben; *one's name, particulars* angeben; *suggestion* machen; (*let sb know by letter, phone etc*) *decision, opinion, results* mitteilen ◆ **the court hasn't ~n a decision yet** das Gericht hat noch kein Urteil gefällt; **he wouldn't ~ me his decision/opinion** er wollte mir seine Meinung/Entscheidung nicht sagen; **they interrupted the programme to ~ the football results** sie unterbrachen das Programm, um die Fußballergebnisse zu bringen; **~ him my compliments** *or* **regards/thanks** bestellen Sie ihm (schöne) Grüße/bestellen Sie ihm, daß ich ihm danke, richten Sie ihm (schöne) Grüße von mir/meinen Dank aus; **to ~ the right/no answer** richtig/nicht antworten; **to ~ sb a warning** jdn warnen; **his letter gave us the latest news** in seinem Brief stand das Neueste; **she was ~n the news by John** John hat ihr das mitgeteilt; **he forgot to ~ us the date** er hat vergessen, uns das Datum anzugeben *or* (*verbally also*) zu sagen *or* (*by letter, phone etc also*) mitzuteilen; **who gave you that information?** wer hat Ihnen das gesagt *or* die Auskunft gegeben *or* erteilt?; *see* **message**.
(e) (*yield, produce*) *milk, warmth, light etc* geben; *results* (er)bringen; *answer* liefern ◆ **this TV ~s a very good picture** dieser Fernseher hat ein sehr gutes Bild; **this tree doesn't ~ much fruit** dieser Baum trägt nicht gut.
(f) (*hold, perform*) *party, dinner, play* geben; *speech* halten; *song* singen; *toast* ausbringen (*to sb* auf jdn) ◆ **~ us a song** sing uns was vor; **I ~ you Mary** (*as toast*) auf Mary!, auf Marys Wohl!; (*as speaker*) ich gebe Mary das Wort.
(g) (*devote*) widmen (*to dat*) ◆ **he has ~n himself entirely to medicine** er hat sich ganz der Medizin verschrieben; **he gave himself/his life to God** er weihte sich/sein Leben Gott.
(h) to ~ a cry/groan/laugh/sigh (auf)schreien/(auf)stöhnen/(auf)lachen/(auf)seufzen; **the child gave a little jump of excitement** das Kind machte vor Aufregung einen Luftsprung; **he gave a shrug of his shoulders** er zuckte mit den Schultern; **to ~ sb a look/smile** jdn ansehen/anlächeln; **to ~ sb a blow** jdn schlagen, jdm einen Schlag versetzen; **to ~ sb a push/kick** jdm einen Stoß/Tritt geben, jdn stoßen/treten; **to ~ sb's hand a squeeze** jdm die Hand drücken; **to ~ one's hair a brush/wash** sich (*dat*) die Haare bürsten/waschen.
(i) *in set phrases see under n* **to ~ chase** die Verfolgung aufnehmen; **to ~ evidence** (*Jur*) aussagen.
2 *vi* **(a)** (*also ~ way*) (*lit, fig: collapse, yield*) nachgeben; (*strength, health, nerve, voice*) versagen; (*break: rope, cable*) reißen; (*cold weather*) nachlassen ◆ **when you're under as much strain as that, something is bound to ~** (*inf*) wenn man unter so viel Druck steht, muß es ja irgendwo aushaken (*inf*).
(b) (*lit, fig: bend, be flexible*) nachgeben; (*bed*) federn; (*dress*) sich dehnen *or* weiten.
(c) (*~ money etc*) geben, spenden ◆ **it is more blessed to ~ than to receive** Geben ist seliger denn Nehmen; **you have to be prepared to ~ and take in this world/in marriage** (*fig*) man muß im Leben zu Kompromissen bereit sein *or* auch mal zurückstecken können/man muß in der Ehe geben und nehmen.
(d) (*sl*) **what ~s?** was gibt's? (*inf*), was ist los? (*inf*); **what ~s with him?** was ist los mit ihm? (*inf*); **what ~s in this town?** was ist hier (in der Stadt) los?
(e) (*US sl*) **OK, now ~!** also, raus mit der Sprache! (*inf*).
3 *n* Nachgiebigkeit, Elastizität *f*; (*of floor, bed, chair*) Federung *f* ◆ **this elastic hasn't got much ~ left** dieses Gummiband ist nicht mehr sehr elastisch; **it has a lot of ~** es gibt sehr stark nach; **he hasn't got enough ~** (*fig*) er ist nicht flexibel genug.

◆**give away** *vt sep* **(a)** (*give without charge*) weggeben; (*as present*) verschenken ◆ **at £5 I'm practically giving it ~** ich will £ 5 dafür, das ist fast geschenkt.
(b) *bride* (*als Brautvater etc*) zum Altar führen.
(c) (*hand out*) *prizes etc* vergeben, verteilen.
(d) (*fig: betray*) verraten (*to sb* an jdn) ◆ **to ~ the game** *or* **show ~** (*inf*) alles verraten.

◆**give back** *vt sep* zurück- *or* wiedergeben; *echo* widerhallen lassen, zurückgeben; (*mirror*) *image* reflektieren.

◆**give in** 1 *vi* (*surrender*) sich ergeben (*to sb* jdm); (*in guessing game etc*) aufgeben; (*accede, back down*) nachgeben (*to dat*) ◆ **to ~ ~ to sb's views/the majority/blackmail** sich jds Meinung/der Mehrheit beugen/auf Erpressung eingehen; **to ~ ~ to temptation** der Versuchung erliegen *or* nicht widerstehen.
2 *vt sep document, essay* einreichen; *parcel* abgeben ◆ **to ~ ~ sb's/one's name** jdn/sich anmelden.

◆**give off** *vt insep heat, gas* abgeben; *smell* verbreiten, ausströmen; *rays* ausstrahlen.

◆**give on to** *vi +prep obj* (*window*) hinausgehen auf (*+acc*); (*door*) hinausführen auf (*+acc*); *garden* hinausführen in (*+acc*).

◆**give out** 1 *vi* (*supplies, patience, strength, road*) zu Ende gehen *or* (*in past tense*) sein; (*engine, feet*) versagen; (*inspiration*) versiegen ◆ **my memory gave ~** mein Gedächtnis ließ mich im Stich.
2 *vt sep* **(a)** (*distribute*) aus- *or* verteilen. **(b)** (*announce*) bekanntgeben ◆ **to ~**

oneself ~ as sth *or* to be sth sich als etw ausgeben.
[3] *vt insep see* give off.
◆**give over** [1] *vt sep* **(a)** (*hand over*) übergeben (*to dat*).
(b) (*set aside, use for*) **to be ~n ~ to sth** für etw beansprucht werden.
(c) **to ~ oneself ~ to pleasure/despair** *etc* sich ganz dem Vergnügen/der Verzweiflung *etc* hingeben; **to be ~n ~ to pleasure** (*life*) ganz dem Vergnügen gewidmet sein.
[2] *vti* (*dial inf: stop*) aufhören ◆ **~ ~!** hör auf!; **~ ~ tickling me!** hör auf, mich zu kitzeln!.
◆**give up** [1] *vi* aufgeben ◆ **I ~ ~** ich gebe auf, ich geb's auf (*inf*).
[2] *vt sep* **(a)** aufgeben; *claim also* verzichten auf (+*acc*) ◆ **to ~ ~ doing sth** aufhören *or* es aufgeben, etw zu tun; **I'm trying to ~ ~ smoking** ich versuche, das Rauchen aufzugeben; **I gave it/him ~ as a bad job** das/ihn habe ich abgeschrieben; **to ~ sb/sth ~ as lost** jdn/etw verloren geben; **to ~ sb ~ as dead** jdn für tot halten.
(b) (*surrender*) *land, territory* abgeben, abtreten (*to dat*); *authority* abgeben, abtreten (*to* an +*acc*); *keys of city etc* übergeben (*to dat*); *seat, place* freimachen (*to* für), abtreten (*to dat*); *ticket* abgeben (*to* bei).
(c) (*hand over to authorities*) übergeben (*to dat*) ◆ **to ~ oneself ~** sich stellen; (*after siege etc*) sich ergeben.
(d) (*devote*) widmen ◆ **to ~ ~ one's life to music** sein Leben der Musik widmen *or* verschreiben; **he's ~n himself ~ to vice** er ist dem Laster verfallen.
(e) (*disclose, yield up*) *secret, treasure* enthüllen (*geh*).
◆**give way** *vi* **(a)** (*lit*) *see* **give 2 (a)**.
(b) (*fig: yield*) nachgeben (*to dat*) ◆ **to ~ ~ to intimidation** sich einschüchtern lassen; **don't ~ ~ to despair** überlaß dich nicht der Verzweiflung; **she gave ~ to tears** sie ließ den Tränen freien Lauf.
(c) (*be superseded*) **to ~ ~ to sth** von etw abgelöst werden; **tears gave ~ to smiles** die Tränen machten einem Lächeln Platz; **radio has almost ~n ~ to television** das Radio ist vom Fernsehen fast verdrängt worden.
(d) (*Brit Mot*) **~ ~ to oncoming traffic** der Gegenverkehr hat Vorfahrt; **who has to ~ ~ here?** wer hat hier Vorfahrt?; **I was expecting him to ~ ~** ich nahm an, er würde mir die Vorfahrt lassen; **"~ ~"** „Vorfahrt (beachten)".
give: ~ and take *n* Entgegenkommen *nt*; (*in personal relationships*) (gegenseitiges) Geben und Nehmen; **~-away** *n* **(a)** **the expression on her face was a ~-away** ihr Gesichtsausdruck verriet alles; **it was a real ~-away when he said ...** er verriet sich, als er sagte ...; **(b)** (*inf*) **that exam question was a ~-away** diese Prüfungsfrage war geschenkt (*inf*); **(c)** (*US Comm: gift*) Geschenk *nt*; **(d)** (*US Rad, TV*) Preisraten *nt*; **~-away price** *n* Schleuderpreis *m*.
given ['gɪvn] [1] *ptp of* **give**.
[2] *adj* **(a)** (*with indef art*) bestimmt; (*with def art*) angegeben ◆ **of a ~ size** von einer bestimmten Größe; **500 bottles of the ~ size** 500 Flaschen der angegebenen Größe.
(b) **~ name** (*esp US*) Vorname *m*.
(c) (*having inclination*) **to be ~ to sth** zu etw neigen; **I'm ~/not ~ to doing that** ich tue das gern/es ist nicht meine Art, das zu tun; **I'm not ~ to drinking on my own** ich habe nicht die Angewohnheit, allein zu trinken.
[3] *conj* **~ sth** (*with*) vorausgesetzt, man/er *etc* hat etw, wenn man/er *etc* etw hat; (*in view of*) angesichts einer Sache (*gen*); **~ that he ...** (*in view of the fact*) angesichts der Tatsache, daß er ...; (*assuming*) vorausgesetzt *or* angenommen, (daß) er ...; **~ time, we can/could do it** vorausgesetzt, wir haben/hätten genug Zeit *or* wenn wir genug Zeit haben/hätten, können/könnten wir es schaffen; **~ these circumstances/conditions** unter diesen Umständen/Voraussetzungen; **~ these premises you can work out the answer** anhand dieser Voraussetzungen kannst du die Lösung finden; **~ the triangle ABC** (*Math*) gegeben ist *or* sei das Dreieck ABC.
giver ['gɪvəʳ] *n* Spender(in *f*) *m* ◆ **he was a generous ~ to church funds** er hat großzügig für die Kirche gespendet.
give-way sign [gɪv'weɪ,saɪn] *n* (*Brit*) Vorfahrtsschild *nt*.
gizmo ['gɪzməʊ] *n* (*inf*) Ding *nt* (*inf*).
gizzard ['gɪzəd] *n* Muskelmagen *m*.
Gk *abbr of* **Greek** Griech.
glabrous ['glæbrəs] *adj* (*Zool*) unbehaart; (*liter*) *youth* bartlos.
glacé ['glæseɪ] *adj bun* mit Zuckerguß, glasiert; *fruit* kandiert; *leather* Glacé- ◆ **~ icing** Zuckerguß *m*.
glacial ['gleɪsɪəl] *adj* **(a)** (*Geol*) Gletscher-, glazial (*spec*) ◆ **~ epoch** *or* **era** Eiszeit *f*, Glazial *nt* (*form*). **(b)** (*cold*) *look, wind, temperature* eisig.
glaciated ['gleɪsɪeɪtɪd] *adj* (*covered with glaciers*) gletscherbedeckt, vergletschert; (*eroded by glaciers*) durch Gletschertätigkeit entstanden.
glacier ['glæsɪəʳ] *n* Gletscher *m*.
glaciology [,gleɪsɪ'ɒlədʒɪ] *n* Gletscherkunde, Glaziologie (*form*) *f*.
▼ **glad** [glæd] *adj* (+*er*) **(a)** (*pleased*) froh ◆ **to be ~ at** *or* **about sth** sich über etw (*acc*) freuen; **to be ~ of sth** über etw (*acc*) froh sein; **to be ~ that ...** sich freuen, daß ...; (*relieved*) froh sein, daß ...; **I'm ~ to see you** ich freue mich, Sie zu sehen; (*relieved*) ich bin froh, Sie zu sehen; **I'm so ~!** das freut mich, da bin ich aber froh!; **you'll be ~ to hear that ...** es wird Sie freuen zu hören, daß ...; **..., you'll be ~ to hear ...**, das wird Sie freuen; **to feel/look ~** sich freuen/erfreut *or* froh aussehen; (*relieved*) froh sein/froh *or* erleichtert aussehen; **we would be ~ of your help** wir wären froh, wenn Sie helfen könnten; **I'd be ~ of your opinion on this** ich würde gerne Ihre Meinung dazu hören; **you'll be ~ of it later** du wirst später (noch) froh darüber sein; **I'd be ~ to** aber gern!
(b) (*giving pleasure*) froh; *occasion, news also* freudig; *day also* Freuden- ◆ **the ~ tidings** die frohe Botschaft (*old, hum*).

➤ LANGUAGE IN USE: **glad: a** → 3.1, 25.2

gladden ['glædn] *vt person, heart* erfreuen.
glade [gleɪd] *n* Lichtung *f*.
glad: ~ eye *n* **to give sb the ~ eye** jdm schöne Augen machen (*inf*); **~ hand** *n* (*US*) **to give sb the ~ hand** jdn überschwenglich begrüßen.
gladiator ['glædɪeɪtəʳ] *n* Gladiator *m*.
gladiatorial [,glædɪə'tɔːrɪəl] *adj* Gladiatoren-.
gladiolus [,glædɪ'əʊləs] *n, pl* **gladioli** [,glædɪ'əʊlaɪ] Gladiole *f*.
gladly ['glædlɪ] *adv* **(a)** (*willingly*) gern. **(b)** (*joyfully*) fröhlich.
gladness ['glædnɪs] *n* **(a)** (*of person*) Freude *f*; (*relief*) Erleichterung *f*; (*of smile etc*) Fröhlichkeit *f*. **(b)** (*of occasion, news*) Freudigkeit *f*.
gladrags ['glæd,rægz] *npl* (*inf*) Sonntagsstaat *m* (*inf*) ◆ **to put/have one's ~ on** (*inf*) sich in Schale werfen/in Schale sein (*inf*).
gladsome ['glædsəm] *adj* (*old*) freudenreich (*liter*).
glam [glæm] *adj* (*inf*) schick.
glamor *n* (*US*) *see* **glamour**.
glamorize ['glæməraɪz] *vt* idealisieren, einen glamourösen Anstrich geben (+*dat*); *job, life-style also* einen besonderen Glanz *or* Reiz *or* eine besondere Faszination verleihen (+*dat*); *author, war* glorifizieren ◆ **to ~ one's image** sein Image aufpolieren; **to ~ oneself** sich (*dat*) einen raffinierten *or* glamourösen Anstrich geben.
glamorous ['glæmərəs] *adj* bezaubernd, betörend; *film star, life* glamourös; *job* Traum-, glamourös; *clothes* flott; *state occasion* glanzvoll.
glamorously ['glæmərəslɪ] *adv* glamourös ◆ **a ~ exciting life** ein fabelhaft aufregendes Leben.
glamour ['glæməʳ] *n* Glamour *m*; (*of occasion, situation*) Glanz *m* ◆ **she/the job doesn't have much ~** sie/dieser Beruf hat keinen besonderen Reiz; **she has ~ as well as prettiness** sie ist nicht nur hübsch, sondern besitzt auch noch einen besonderen Reiz.
glamour: ~ boy *n* (*inf*) Schönling *m* (*inf*); **~ girl** *n* (*inf*) Glamourgirl *nt*.
glance [glɑːns] [1] *n* Blick *m* ◆ **at a ~** auf einen Blick; **at first ~** auf den ersten Blick; **she gave him an angry/amorous ~** sie warf ihm einen wütenden/verliebten Blick zu; **to take a quick ~ at sth** einen kurzen Blick auf etw (*acc*) werfen; **he cast** *or* **had a quick ~ round the room** er sah sich kurz im Zimmer um.
[2] *vi* sehen, blicken, schauen (*esp S Ger*) ◆ **to ~ at sb/sth** jdn/etw kurz ansehen, einen kurzen Blick auf etw (*acc*) werfen; **to ~ at/through the newspaper/a report** einen kurzen Blick in die Zeitung/in einen Bericht werfen, die Zeitung/einen Bericht überfliegen *or* kurz durchsehen; **to ~ over sth** etw überfliegen; **to ~ across to sb** jdm einen Blick zuwerfen; **to ~ down/in** einen Blick hinunter-/hineinwerfen, kurz hinunter-/hineinsehen; **to ~ up/aside** aufsehen *or* -blicken (*from* von)/zur Seite sehen; **to ~ round** sich umblicken; **he ~d round the room** er sah sich im Zimmer um; **the book merely ~s at the problem** das Buch streift das Problem nur.
◆**glance off** *vi* (*prep obj* von) (*bullet etc*) abprallen; (*sword*) abgleiten; (*light*) reflektiert werden.
glancing ['glɑːnsɪŋ] *adj* **to strike sth a ~ blow** etw streifen; **she struck him a ~ blow** ihr Schlag streifte ihn; **it was only a ~ blow** ich/er *etc* wurde nur gestreift.
gland [glænd] *n* Drüse *f*; (*lymph ~*) Lymphdrüse *f or* -knoten *m*.
glandular ['glændjʊləʳ] *adj* Drüsen- ◆ **~ fever** Drüsenfieber *nt*.
glans penis ['glænz'piːnɪs] *n* Glans, Eichel *f*.
glare [glɛəʳ] [1] *n* **(a)** greller Schein; (*from sun, bulb, lamp also*) grelles Licht ◆ **the ~ of the sun** das grelle Sonnenlicht; **to avoid the ~ of publicity** das grelle Licht der Öffentlichkeit scheuen.
(b) (*stare*) wütender *or* stechender Blick ◆ **a ~ of hatred/anger** ein haßerfüllter/zorniger Blick; **there was a ~ of anger in her eyes** ihre Augen funkelten vor Zorn.
[2] *vi* **(a)** (*light, sun*) grell scheinen; (*headlights*) grell leuchten; (*bulb*) grell brennen. **(b)** (*stare*) (zornig) starren ◆ **to ~ at sb/sth** jdn/etw zornig anstarren. **(c)** (*fig*) **that mistake really ~s at you** dieser Fehler springt einem förmlich ins Gesicht.
[3] *vt* **(a)** **to ~ defiance/hatred at sb** jdn trotzig *or* voller Trotz/haßerfüllt *or* voll von Haß anstarren. **(b)** (*fig*) **to ~ sb in the face** jdm förmlich ins Gesicht springen.
glaring ['glɛərɪŋ] *adj* **(a)** *sun, colour* grell. **(b)** **her ~ eyes** ihr stechender Blick. **(c)** (*fig*) *omission* eklatant; *mistake also* grob; *contrast* kraß; *injustice* (himmel)schreiend.
glaringly ['glɛərɪŋlɪ] *adv* **(a)** *shine* grell ◆ **~ bright** grell. **(b)** (*fig*) **their words contrasted ~ with their deeds** ihre Worte standen in krassem Gegensatz zu ihren Taten; **it's ~ unjust/wrong** es ist eine himmelschreiende Ungerechtigkeit/das ist ein eklatanter Fehler; **it is ~ obvious that ...** es liegt klar auf der Hand, daß ...
glasnost ['glæznɒst] *n* Glasnost *f*.
glass [glɑːs] [1] *n* **(a)** (*substance*) Glas *nt* ◆ **a pane of ~** eine Glasscheibe; **to be grown under ~** (*Hort*) unter Glas gezogen werden.
(b) (*object, vessel, contents, ~ware*) Glas *nt*; (*dated: mirror*) Spiegel *m* ◆ **a ~ of wine** ein Glas Wein; **he gets quite cheerful when he's had a ~** (*inf*) er wird richtig fröhlich, wenn er ein Gläschen getrunken hat (*inf*).
(c) (*spectacles*) **~es** *pl*, **pair of ~es** Brille *f*; **he wears thick ~es** er trägt eine starke Brille *or* starke Gläser.
(d) (*instrument*) (*magnifying ~*) (Vergrößerungs)glas *nt*, Lupe *f*; (*telescope*) Teleskop, Fernrohr *nt*; (*barometer*) Barometer *nt* ◆ **~es** *pl* (*binoculars*) (Fern)glas *nt*.
[2] *vt* verglasen.
[3] *attr* Glas- ◆ **people who live in ~ houses shouldn't throw stones** (*Prov*) wer

im Glashaus sitzt, soll nicht mit Steinen werfen (Prov).

glass in cpds Glas-; **~-blower** n Glasbläser(in f) m; **~-blowing** n Glasbläserei f; **~ ceiling** n (fig) gläserne or unsichtbare Wand f (in Form von Vorurteilen und Traditionen, die Frauen am berufliche Fortkommen hindern) ◆ women who she hit the ~ ceiling Frauen, die beruflich nich mehr weiterkommen; **~-cloth** n Gläsertuch nt; **~-cutter** n (tool) Glasschneider m; (person) Glasschleifer m; **~ eye** n Glasauge nt; **~ fibre** n Glasfaser f; **~ful** n see glass 1 (b); **~house** n (a) (Brit Hort) Gewächshaus nt; (b) (Mil sl) Bau, Bunker m (sl); **~-paper** n Glaspapier nt; **~ware** n Glaswaren pl; **~ wool** n Glaswolle f; **~works** npl Glashütte f.

glassy ['glɑːsɪ] adj (+er) surface, sea etc spiegelglatt; eye, look glasig ◆ ~-eyed look glasig; to be ~-eyed einen glasigen Blick haben; to look at sb ~-eyed jdn mit glasigem Blick ansehen.

Glaswegian [glæs'wiːdʒən] [1] n (a) Glasgower(in f) m.
(b) (dialect) Glasgower Dialekt m.
[2] adj Glasgower, von Glasgow.

glaucoma [glɔː'kəʊmə] n grüner Star, Glaukom nt (form).

glaucous ['glɔːkəs] adj plums, grapes etc mit einer weißlichen Schicht überzogen ◆ ~ blue/green gräulich-blau/gräulich-grün.

glaze [gleɪz] [1] n (on pottery, tiles, Cook) Glasur f; (on paper, fabric) Appretur f; (on painting) Lasur f.
[2] vt (a) door, window verglasen. (b) pottery, tiles glasieren; fabric, paper appretieren; painting lasieren ◆ ~d tile Kachel f. (c) (Cook) cake glasieren; meat also mit Gelee überziehen; fruit kandieren ◆ a ~d ham Schinken in Aspik.
[3] vi (eyes: also ~ over) glasig werden.

glazier ['gleɪzɪəʳ] n Glaser m.

glazing ['gleɪzɪŋ] n (a) (act) Verglasen nt; (glass) Verglasung f; (trade) Glaserei f. (b) see glaze 1.

GLC abbr of Greater London Council.

gleam [gliːm] [1] n (a) Schein, Schimmer m; (of metal, water) Schimmern nt ◆ a ~ of light/red ein Lichtschimmer m/ein roter Schimmer; the ~ from his torch der Schein seiner Taschenlampe; a few ~s of moonlight came through the curtains das Mondlicht schimmerte durch die Vorhänge.
(b) (fig) a ~ of hope ein Hoffnungsschimmer m; a ~ of humour/intelligence/sense ein Anflug m von Humor/Intelligenz/ein Hauch m von Vernunft; not a ~ of hope/humour/intelligence/sense kein Funke m Hoffnung/Humor/Intelligenz/ Vernunft; he had a ~/a dangerous ~ in his eye seine Augen funkelten/funkelten gefährlich.
[2] vi schimmern; (hair also) glänzen; (eyes) funkeln.

gleaming ['gliːmɪŋ] adj schimmernd; hair, silver, water also glänzend; eyes funkelnd.

glean [gliːn] vt (lit) corn, field nachlesen; (fig) facts, news herausbekommen, ausfindig machen, erkunden (geh) ◆ to ~ sth from sb/sth etw von jdm erfahren/etw einer Sache (dat) entnehmen.

gleaner ['gliːnəʳ] n Ährenleser(in f) m.

gleanings ['gliːnɪŋz] npl (lit) Nachlese f, aufgelesene Ähren pl ◆ the ~ of twenty years of study die Ausbeute eines zwanzigjährigen Studiums; a few ~ from the press conference ein paar Informationen von der Pressekonferenz.

glebe [gliːb] n (Eccl) Pfarrland nt ◆ ~ house pfarreieigenes Haus; (vicarage) Pfarrhaus nt.

glee [gliː] n (a) Freude f; (malicious) Schadenfreude f ◆ he/they shouted in or with ~ er stieß einen Freudenschrei aus/sie brachen in (ein) Freudengeheul aus; he told the story with great ~ er erzählte die Geschichte mit großem Vergnügen; they were full of ~/malicious ~ sie waren (hell) begeistert/sie freuten sich hämisch or diebisch; his defeat caused great ~ among his enemies seine Feinde freuten sich diebisch or hämisch über seine Niederlage.
(b) (Mus) mehrstimmiges Lied ◆ ~ club (esp US) Chor m.

gleeful ['gliːfʊl] adj fröhlich, vergnügt; (maliciously) hämisch, schadenfroh ◆ they were all very ~ about his failure sie freuten sich alle diebisch über sein Versagen.

gleefully ['gliːfəlɪ] adv see adj.

glen [glen] n Tal nt.

glib [glɪb] adj (pej) gewandt; talker also zungenfertig; person glatt, zungenfertig, aalglatt (inf); reply, remark leichthin gemacht; speech, style glatt ◆ I don't want to sound ~ ich möchte nicht den Eindruck erwecken, das so leichthin zu sagen; to have a ~ tongue zungenfertig sein, eine glatte Zunge haben; he gave a ~ reply er war mit einer Antwort schnell bei der Hand; he was always ready with a ~ explanation er war immer schnell mit einer Erklärung bei der Hand.

glibly ['glɪblɪ] adv (pej) speak gewandt; say, remark, reply leichthin; lie geschickt ◆ he ~ produced a couple of excuses er war schnell mit ein paar Ausreden bei der Hand.

glibness ['glɪbnɪs] n (pej) (of speech, excuses, lies) Gewandtheit f; (of person) Zungenfertigkeit f ◆ the ~ of his explanation/reply seine leichthin gegebene Erklärung/Antwort; the ~ of such a remark eine so leichthin gemachte Bemerkung.

glide [glaɪd] [1] vi (a) gleiten; (through the air also) schweben ◆ to ~ into a room/in in ein Zimmer schweben/hereinschweben; to ~ off or away davongleiten; (person, ghost) davonschweben.
(b) (Aviat, bird) gleiten; (plane) im Gleitflug fliegen; (glider) gleiten, schweben; (fly in a glider) segelfliegen ◆ I would like to learn to ~ ich möchte Segelfliegen lernen; to ~ down to land zur Landung ansetzen.
[2] vt gleiten lassen; plane im Gleitflug fliegen (lassen).
[3] n (a) (dancing) Gleit- or Schleifschritt m. (b) (Mus) Portamento nt; (Phon) Gleitlaut m. (c) (Aviat) Gleitflug m.

glider ['glaɪdəʳ] n (Aviat) Segelflugzeug nt ◆ ~ pilot Segelflieger(in f) m.

gliding ['glaɪdɪŋ] n (Aviat) Segelfliegen nt ◆ ~ club Segelfliegerklub m.

glimmer ['glɪməʳ] [1] n (a) (of light, candle etc) Schimmer m; (of fire) Glimmen nt ◆ the ~ of the distant river das Schimmern des Flusses in der Ferne; a few ~s from the dying fire ein Aufglimmen nt des verlöschenden Feuers.
(b) (fig: also ~ing) see gleam 1 (b).
[2] vi (light, water) schimmern; (flame, fire) glimmen.

glimpse [glɪmps] [1] n Blick m ◆ it was our last ~ of home das war der letzte Blick auf unser Zuhause; a ~ of life in 18th century London ein (Ein)blick m in das Leben im London des 18. Jahrhunderts; to catch a ~ of sb/sth einen flüchtigen Blick auf jdn/etw werfen können or von jdm/etw erhaschen; (fig) eine Ahnung von etw bekommen; I hope I'll catch a ~ of him before he goes abroad ich hoffe, daß ich ihn noch einmal zu Gesicht bekomme, bevor er ins Ausland geht.
[2] vt kurz sehen, einen Blick erhaschen von.
[3] vi to ~ at sth einen Blick auf etw (acc) werfen; to ~ through a book ein Buch überfliegen.

glint [glɪnt] [1] n (of light, metal) Glitzern, Blinken nt no pl; (of cat's eyes) Funkeln nt no pl ◆ a ~ of light ein glitzernder Lichtstrahl; brown hair with golden ~s in it braunes Haar mit einem goldenen Schimmer; he has a wicked/merry ~ in his eyes seine Augen funkeln böse/lustig.
[2] vi glitzern, blinken; (eyes) funkeln.

glissade [glɪ'seɪd] n (in dancing) Glissade f.

glisten ['glɪsn] [1] vi glänzen; (dewdrops, eyes also, tears) glitzern.
[2] n Glänzen nt; Glitzern nt.

glister ['glɪstəʳ] n, vi (old) see glitter.

glitch [glɪtʃ] n (Comput) Funktionsstörung f.

glitter ['glɪtəʳ] [1] n Glitzern nt; (of eyes, diamonds) Funkeln nt; (for decoration) Glitzerstaub m; (fig) Glanz, Prunk m ◆ the ~ of life in London das glanzvolle Leben in London.
[2] vi glitzern; (eyes, diamonds) funkeln ◆ all that ~s is not gold (Prov) es ist nicht alles Gold, was glänzt (Prov).

glitterati [,glɪtə'rɑːtɪ] npl (inf) Hautevolee f.

glittering ['glɪtərɪŋ] adj glitzernd; eyes, diamonds funkelnd; occasion glanzvoll; career glänzend; prizes verlockend.

glittery ['glɪtərɪ] adj (inf) glitzernd.

glitzy ['glɪtsɪ] adj (inf) occasion glanzvoll, schillernd; dress schick.

gloaming ['gləʊmɪŋ] n (liter) Dämmer- or Zwielicht nt (geh).

gloat [gləʊt] vi (with pride at oneself) sich großtun (over, upon mit); (verbally also) sich brüsten (over, upon mit); (over sb's misfortune or failure) sich hämisch freuen (over, upon über +acc) ◆ to ~ over one's possessions/sb's misfortune sich an seinen Reichtümern/jds Unglück weiden; to ~ over one's successes sich in seinen Erfolgen sonnen; there's no need to ~! das ist kein Grund zur Schadenfreude!

gloating ['gləʊtɪŋ] [1] n Selbstgefälligkeit f; (over sb's misfortune or failure) Schadenfreude f ◆ his ~ over his possessions wie er sich genüßlich an seinem Besitz weidet; a look of ~ in his eyes ein selbstgefälliger/schadenfroher/ genüßlicher Blick; it wasn't pleasant to listen to their ~ es war kein Vergnügen, ihren selbstgefälligen Reden/schadenfrohen Bemerkungen zuzuhören; their ~ over their own success ihre selbstgefällige Freude über ihren Erfolg; their premature ~(s) ihre voreilige Freude.
[2] adj (self-satisfied) selbstgefällig; (malicious) hämisch, schadenfroh ◆ the ~ miser der Geizhals, der sich genüßlich an seinen Schätzen weidet; he cast a ~ look at the money er weidete sich genüßlich am Anblick des Geldes.

gloatingly ['gləʊtɪŋlɪ] adv see adj.

glob [glɒb] n (inf) Klacks m (inf); (of mud) Klümpchen nt.

global ['gləʊbl] adj global; peace, war Welt- ◆ taking a ~ view of the matter ... global gesehen ...; a ~ figure of £2 million eine Gesamtsumme von £ 2 Millionen; the world is considered as a ~ village die Welt wird als Dorf angesehen; ~ warming Erwärmung f der Erdatmosphäre.

globe [gləʊb] n (sphere) Kugel f; (map) Globus m; (fish-bowl) Glaskugel f ◆ terrestrial/celestial ~ Erd-/Himmelskugel f; the ~ (the world) der Globus, der Erdball; all over the ~ auf der ganzen Erde or Welt.

globe: ~ artichoke n Artischocke f; **~-fish** n Kugelfisch m; **~-trotter** n Globetrotter, Welt(en)bummler m; **~-trotting** [1] n Globetrotten nt; [2] attr Globetrotter-.

globular ['glɒbjʊləʳ] adj kugelförmig.

globule ['glɒbjuːl] n Klümpchen, Kügelchen nt; (of oil, water) Tröpfchen nt ◆ ~s of grease floating on the soup Fettaugen pl auf der Suppe.

glockenspiel ['glɒkənʃpiːl] n Glockenspiel nt.

gloom [gluːm] n (a) (darkness) Düsterkeit f.
(b) (sadness) düstere or gedrückte Stimmung ◆ an atmosphere of ~ eine düstere or gedrückte Atmosphäre; a look of ~ on his face seine düstere Miene; to cast a ~ over sth einen Schatten auf etw (acc) werfen; his future seemed to be filled with ~ seine Zukunft schien düster auszusehen; his speech was filled with ~ seine Rede war von düsteren Vorhersagen erfüllt.

gloomily ['gluːmɪlɪ] adv (fig) düster.

gloominess ['gluːmɪnɪs] n see adj Düsterkeit f; Finsterkeit f; Gedrücktheit f; Trübsinn m; Bedrückende(s) nt; Pessimismus m.

gloomster ['gluːmstəʳ] n (inf) Pessimist(in f), Schwarzmaler(in f) (inf) m.

gloomy ['gluːmɪ] adj (+er) düster; streets, forest also finster; atmosphere also gedrückt; thoughts also, character trübsinnig; news also bedrückend; outlook on life pessimistisch ◆ to take a ~ view of things schwarzsehen; to feel ~

niedergeschlagen *or* bedrückt sein; **just thinking about the situation makes me feel ~** es bedrückt mich, wenn ich nur über die Lage nachdenke; **he is very ~ about his chances of success** er beurteilt seine Erfolgschancen sehr pessimistisch; **to look ~ about sth** wegen etw ein trübsinniges Gesicht machen.

glorification [ˌglɔːrɪfɪˈkeɪʃən] *n* Verherrlichung *f*; (*of God also*) Lobpreis *m*; (*beautification*) Verschönerung *f*.

glorified [ˈglɔːrɪfaɪd] *adj* **this restaurant is just a ~ snack-bar** dieses Restaurant ist nur eine bessere Imbißstube.

glorify [ˈglɔːrɪfaɪ] *vt* verherrlichen; (*praise*) *God* lobpreisen.

glorious [ˈglɔːrɪəs] *adj* **(a)** (*lit*) *saint, martyr etc* glorreich; *deed, victory also* ruhmreich. **(b)** (*marvellous*) *weather, sky* herrlich, phantastisch ◆ **it was ~ fun** das war herrlich; **a ~ mess** (*iro*) ein schönes *or* herrliches Durcheinander.

gloriously [ˈglɔːrɪəslɪ] *adv see adj* ◆ **he was ~ drunk** (*inf*) er war herrlich betrunken (*inf*).

glory [ˈglɔːrɪ] [1] *n* **(a)** (*honour, fame*) Ruhm *m* ◆ **covered in ~** ruhmbedeckt. **(b)** (*praise*) Ehre *f* ◆ **~ to God in the highest** Ehre sei Gott in der Höhe; **~ be!** (*dated inf*) du lieber Himmel! (*inf*).
(c) (*beauty, magnificence*) Herrlichkeit *f* ◆ **the rose in all its ~** die Rose in ihrer ganzen Pracht *or* Herrlichkeit; **the glories of Nature** die Schönheiten *pl* der Natur; **Rome at the height of its ~** Rom in seiner Blütezeit.
(d) (*source of pride*) Stolz *m*.
(e) (*celestial bliss*) **the saints in ~** die Heiligen in der himmlischen Herrlichkeit; **Christ in ~** Christus in seiner Herrlichkeit; **to go to ~** (*euph liter*) ins ewige Leben *or* in die Ewigkeit eingehen (*euph liter*).
[2] *vi* **to ~ in one's skill/strength/ability** sich (*dat*) viel auf sein Geschick/ seine Kraft/Fähigkeit zugute tun; **to ~ in one's/sb's success** sich in seinem/ jds Erfolg sonnen; **to ~ in the knowledge/fact that .../one's independence** das Wissen/die Tatsache, daß .../seine Unabhängigkeit voll auskosten; **they gloried in showing me my mistakes** sie genossen es *or* kosteten es voll aus, mir meine Fehler zu zeigen; **to ~ in the name/title of ...** den stolzen Namen/Titel ... führen.

glory-hole [ˈglɔːrɪˌhəʊl] *n* **(a)** (*inf*) Rumpel- or Kramecke *f*; (*box*) Rumpelkiste *f*; (*drawer*) Kramschublade *f*. **(b)** (*Naut*) Logis *nt*.

gloss¹ [glɒs] *n* (*shine, lip ~*) Glanz *m*; (*fig: of respectability etc*) Schein *m* ◆ **paint with a high ~** Farbe mit Hochglanz; **to take the ~ off sth** (*lit*) etw stumpf werden lassen; (*fig*) einer Sache (*dat*) den Glanz nehmen; **to lose its ~** (*lit, fig*) seinen Glanz verlieren; **~ finish** (*Phot, on paper*) Glanz(beschichtung *f*) *m*; (*of paint*) Lackanstrich *m*; **the photos had a ~ finish** es waren Glanzabzüge.

◆**gloss over** *vt sep* (*try to conceal*) vertuschen; (*make light of*) beschönigen ◆ **he ~ed ~ the various points raised by the critics** er hat die verschiedenen Punkte der Kritiker einfach vom Tisch gewischt.

gloss² [1] *n* (*explanation*) Erläuterung *f*; (*note also*) Anmerkung, Glosse (*geh*) *f*.
[2] *vt* erläutern.

glossary [ˈglɒsərɪ] *n* Glossar *nt*.

glossily [ˈglɒsɪlɪ] *adj* glänzend ◆ **~ polished** blankpoliert.

glossiness [ˈglɒsɪnɪs] *n* Glanz *m*.

gloss (paint) *n* Glanzlack(farbe *f*) *m*.

glossy [ˈglɒsɪ] [1] *adj* (*+er*) glänzend; *paper, paint* Glanz-; (*Phot*) *print* (Hoch)glanz- ◆ **to be ~** glänzen; **~ magazine** (Hochglanz)magazin *nt*.
[2] *n* (*inf*) (Hochglanz)magazin *nt*.

glottal [ˈglɒtl] *adj* Stimmritzen-, glottal (*spec*) ◆ **~ stop** (*Phon*) Knacklaut, Stimmritzenverschlußlaut *m*.

glottis [ˈglɒtɪs] *n* Stimmritze, Glottis (*spec*) *f*.

glove [glʌv] *n* (Finger)handschuh *m*; (*Sport*) Handschuh *m* ◆ **to fit (sb) like a ~** (jdm) wie angegossen passen; (*job*) wie für jdn geschaffen sein; **with the ~s off** (*fig*) schonungslos, ohne Rücksicht auf Verluste (*inf*); **the ~s are off** mit der Rücksichtnahme ist es vorbei, die Schonzeit ist vorbei.

glove box *n* **(a)** (*Tech*) Handschuh-Schutzkasten *m*. **(b)** (*also* **glove compartment**) (*Aut*) Handschuhfach *nt*.

gloved [glʌvd] *adj* behandschuht.

glove puppet *n* Handpuppe *f*.

glover [ˈglʌvəʳ] *n* Handschuhmacher(in *f*) *m*.

glow [gləʊ] [1] *vi* glühen; (*colour, hands of clock*) leuchten; (*lamp also, candle*) scheinen ◆ **she/her cheeks ~ed with health** sie hatte ein blühendes Aussehen; **to ~ with pride/pleasure** vor Stolz glühen/vor Freude strahlen; **she ~ed with love** sie strahlte Liebe aus.
[2] *n* Glühen *nt*; (*of colour, clock hands*) Leuchten *nt*; (*of lamp, candle*) Schein *m*; (*of fire, sunset, passion*) Glut *f* ◆ **her face had a healthy ~, there was a ~ of health on her face** ihr Gesicht hatte eine blühende Farbe; **she felt a ~ of satisfaction/affection** sie empfand eine tiefe Befriedigung/Zuneigung; **radiant with the ~ of youth** blühende Jugend ausstrahlend; **there was a sort of ~ about her** sie strahlte so.

glower [ˈglaʊəʳ] [1] *vi* ein finsteres Gesicht machen ◆ **to ~ at sb** jdn finster ansehen.
[2] *n* finsterer Blick ◆ **angry ~** zorniger Blick; **there was a ~ on his face** ein finsterer Ausdruck lag auf seinem Gesicht.

glowering *adj*, **~ly** *adv* [ˈglaʊərɪŋ, -lɪ] finster.

glowing [ˈgləʊɪŋ] *adj* **(a)** glühend; *candle, colour, eyes* leuchtend; *cheeks, complexion* blühend.
(b) (*fig*) (*enthusiastic*) *account, description* begeistert; *words also* leidenschaftlich; *praise, report* überschwenglich; *pride, admiration, enthusiasm* glühend ◆ **to paint sth in ~ colours** (*fig*) etw in den leuchtendsten Farben schildern.

glowingly [ˈgləʊɪŋlɪ] *adv* (*fig*) begeistert; *describe* in glühenden Farben; *praise* überschwenglich.

glow-worm [ˈgləʊˌwɜːm] *n* Glühwürmchen *nt*.

glucose [ˈgluːkəʊs] *n* Glucose *f*, Traubenzucker *m*.

glue [gluː] [1] *n* Klebstoff *m*; (*from bones etc*) Leim *m* ◆ **to stick to sb/sth like ~** an jdm/etw kleben (*inf*).
[2] *vt* kleben; leimen ◆ **to ~ sth together** etw zusammenkleben/-leimen; **to ~ sth down/on** etw fest-/ankleben; **to ~ sth to sth** etw an etw (*acc*) kleben/ leimen, etw an etw (*dat*) festkleben/-leimen; **her ear was ~d to the keyhole** ihr Ohr klebte am Schlüsselloch; **to keep one's eyes ~d to sb/sth** jdn/etw nicht aus den Augen lassen; **always keep your eyes ~d to the road while you're driving** beim Autofahren müssen die Augen immer auf die Straße gerichtet sein; **his eyes were ~d to the screen/her cleavage** seine Augen hingen an der Leinwand/ihrem Ausschnitt; **he's ~d to the TV all evening** er hängt den ganzen Abend vorm Fernseher (*inf*); **he stood there as if ~d to the spot** er stand wie angewurzelt da.

glue: ~-pot *n* Leimtopf *m*; **~-sniffer** *n* (Klebstoff-)Schnüffler(in *f*) *m*; **~-sniffing** *n* (Klebstoff-)Schnüffeln *nt*.

gluey [ˈgluːɪ] *adj* klebrig.

glum [glʌm] *adj* (*+er*) niedergeschlagen, bedrückt; *atmosphere* gedrückt; *thoughts* schwarz ◆ **to feel ~** bedrückt sein.

glumly [ˈglʌmlɪ] *adv* niedergeschlagen, bedrückt.

glut [glʌt] [1] *vt* **(a)** (*Comm*) *market* (*manufacturer etc*) überschwemmen ◆ **sugar is ~ting the world market** der Weltmarkt wird mit Zucker überschwemmt.
(b) to ~ oneself (*with food*) schlemmen; **they ~ted themselves with strawberries** sie haben sich an den Erdbeeren gütlich getan; **that poor dog is ~ted with food** der arme Hund ist überfüttert.
[2] *n* Schwemme *f*; (*of manufactured goods also*) Überangebot *nt* (*of an +dat*) ◆ **a ~ of apples** eine Apfelschwemme.

gluteal [ˈgluːtɪəl] *adj* Gesäß-.

gluten [ˈgluːtən] *n* Kleber *m*, Gluten *nt*.

glutinous [ˈgluːtɪnəs] *adj* klebrig.

glutton [ˈglʌtn] *n* Vielfraß *m* (*also Zool*) ◆ **we ate like ~s** wir haben gegessen wie die Scheunendrescher (*inf*); **to be a ~ for work/punishment** ein Arbeitstier *nt* (*inf*)/Masochist *m* sein.

gluttonous [ˈglʌtənəs] *adj* (*lit, fig*) unersättlich; *person* gefräßig.

gluttony [ˈglʌtənɪ] *n* Völlerei, Fresserei (*inf*) *f*.

glycerin(e) [ˈglɪsəriːn] *n* Glyzerin, Glycerin (*spec*) *nt*.

glycerol [ˈglɪsərɒl] *n* Glyzerin *nt*.

glycol [ˈglaɪkɒl] *n* Glykol *nt*.

GM (*Brit*) *abbr of* **George Medal** *Tapferkeitsmedaille*.

gm *abbr of* **gram(s), gramme(s)** g.

G-man [ˈdʒiːmæn] *n, pl* **-men** [-men] (*US inf*) FBI-Mann *m*.

GMC (*Brit*) *abbr of* **General Medical Council**.

gms *abbr of* **gram(me)s** g.

GMT *abbr of* **Greenwich Mean Time** WEZ.

gnarled [nɑːld] *adj wood, tree* knorrig; *hand* knotig.

gnash [næʃ] *vt* **to ~ one's teeth** mit den Zähnen knirschen.

gnat [næt] *n* (Stech)mücke *f*; *see* **strain¹**.

gnaw [nɔː] [1] *vt* nagen an (*+dat*); *finger-nails also* kauen an (*+dat*); (*rust, disease*) fressen an (*+dat*); *hole* nagen; (*fig*) *conscience, sb* (*hunger, anxiety*) quälen; (*remorse*) verzehren ◆ **to ~ sth off** etw abnagen; **the box had been ~ed by the rats** die Ratten hatten die Kiste angenagt.
[2] *vi* nagen ◆ **to ~ at sth** an etw (*dat*) nagen; (*rust, disease*) sich durch etw fressen; **to ~ at sb** (*fig*) jdn quälen; **to ~ on sth** an etw (*dat*) nagen.

◆**gnaw away** [1] *vi* nagen (*at, on* an *+dat*).
[2] *vt sep* wegnagen.

gnawing [ˈnɔːɪŋ] *adj* (*lit*) *sound* nagend; (*fig*) quälend.

gneiss [naɪs] *n* Gneis *m*.

gnome [nəʊm] *n* Gnom *m*; (*in garden*) Gartenzwerg *m* ◆ **the ~s of Zurich** die Zürcher Gnome *pl*.

GNP *abbr of* **gross national product**.

gnu [nuː] *n* Gnu *nt*.

go [gəʊ] (*vb: pret* **went**, *ptp* **gone**) [1] *vi* **(a)** (*proceed, move*) gehen; (*vehicle, by vehicle*) fahren; (*plane*) fliegen; (*travel*) reisen; (*road*) führen ◆ **to ~ to France/ on holiday** nach Frankreich fahren/in Urlaub gehen; **I have to ~ to the doctor/London** ich muß zum Arzt (gehen)/nach London; **to ~ on a journey/course** verreisen, eine Reise/einen Kurs machen; **to ~ for a walk/ swim** spazierengehen/schwimmen gehen; **to ~ fishing/shopping/shooting** angeln/einkaufen/auf die Jagd gehen; **the dog/the doll ~es everywhere with her** der Hund geht überall mit ihr mit/sie nimmt die Puppe überallhin mit; **we can talk as we ~** wir können uns unterwegs unterhalten; **where do we ~ from here?** (*lit*) wo gehen wir anschließend hin?; (*fig*) und was (wird) jetzt?; **you're ~ing too fast for me** (*lit, fig*) du bist mir zu schnell; **the favourite is ~ing well** der Favorit liegt gut im Rennen; **to ~ looking for sb/sth** nach jdm/etw suchen; **to ~ for a doctor/newspaper** einen Arzt/eine Zeitung holen (gehen); **to ~ to sb for sth** (*ask sb*) jdn wegen etw fragen; (*fetch from sb*) bei jdm etw holen; **there he ~es!** da ist er ja!; **who ~es there?** (*guard*) wer da?; **you ~ first** geh du zuerst!; **you ~ next** du bist der nächste; **there you ~** (*giving sth*) bitte; (*I told you so*) na bitte; **there you ~ again!** (*inf*) du fängst ja schon wieder an!; **here we ~ again!** (*inf*) jetzt geht das schon wieder los! (*inf*); **to ~ to get sth, to ~ and get sth** etw holen gehen; **~ and shut the door/ tell him** mach mal die Tür zu/sag's ihm; **he's gone and lost his new watch** (*inf*) er hat seine neue Uhr verloren; **don't ~ telling him, don't ~ and tell him** geh jetzt bitte nicht hin und erzähl ihm das (*inf*); **don't ~ doing that!, don't ~ and do that!** mach das bloß nicht!

(b) *(attend)* gehen ◆ **to ~ to church/evening class** in die Kirche/in einen Abendkurs gehen, einen Abendkurs besuchen; **to ~ to work** zur Arbeit gehen; **he's ~ing as a pirate** er geht als Pirat; **what shall I ~ in?** was soll ich anziehen?
(c) *(depart)* gehen; *(vehicle, by vehicle also)* (ab)fahren; *(plane, by plane also)* (ab)fliegen ◆ **has he gone yet?** ist er schon weg?; **I must ~ now** ich muß jetzt gehen *or* weg; **after I ~** *or* **have gone** *or* **am gone** *(leave)* wenn ich weg bin; *(die)* wenn ich (einmal) nicht mehr (da) bin; **we must ~** *or* **be ~ing** *or* **get ~ing** *(inf)* wir müssen gehen *or* uns langsam auf den Weg machen *(inf)*; **time I was gone** Zeit, daß ich gehe; **be gone!** *(old)* hinweg mit dir *(old)*; **~!** *(Sport)* los!; **here ~es!** jetzt geht's los! *(inf)*.
(d) *(disappear, vanish)* verschwinden; *(pain, spot, mark etc also)* weggehen; *(be used up)* aufgebraucht werden; *(time)* vergehen ◆ **it is** *or* **has gone** *(disappeared)* es ist weg; *(used up, eaten etc)* es ist alle *(inf)*; **where has it gone?** wo ist es hin *or* geblieben?; **the trees have been gone for years** die Bäume sind schon seit Jahren nicht mehr da; **gone are the days when ...** die Zeiten sind vorbei, wo ...; **I don't know where the money ~es** ich weiß nicht, wo all das Geld bleibt; **all his money ~es on records** er gibt sein ganzes Geld für Schallplatten aus, sein ganzes Geld geht für Schallplatten drauf *(inf)*; **£50 a week ~es in** *or* **on rent** £ 50 die Woche sind für die Miete (weg); **the heat went out of the debate** die Debatte verlor an Hitzigkeit; **how is the time ~ing?** wie steht's mit der Zeit?; **it's just gone three** es ist gerade drei vorbei, es ist kurz nach drei; **two days to ~ till ...** noch zwei Tage bis ...; **only two more patients to ~** nur noch zwei Patienten; **two down and one to ~** zwei geschafft und noch eine(r, s) übrig; **there ~es another one!** und noch eine(r, s) weniger!
(e) *(be dismissed)* gehen; *(be got rid of)* verschwinden; *(be abolished)* abgeschafft werden ◆ **that minister will have to ~** der Minister wird gehen müssen; **that old settee will have to ~** das alte Sofa muß weg; **once that table has gone** wenn der Tisch erst einmal weg ist; **apartheid must ~!** weg mit der Apartheid!
(f) *(be sold)* **the hats aren't ~ing very well** die Hüte gehen nicht sehr gut (weg); **to ~ for nothing** umsonst sein; **to be ~ing cheap** billig sein; **it went for £5** es ging für £ 5 weg; **they are ~ing at 20p each** sie werden zu 20 Pence das Stück verkauft; **I won't let it ~ for less than that** billiger gebe ich es nicht her; **~ing, ~ing, gone!** zum ersten, zum zweiten, und zum dritten!
(g) *(have recourse to)* gehen ◆ **to ~ to the country** *(Brit Parl)* Wahlen ausrufen; **to ~ to law/war** vor Gericht gehen/Krieg führen *(over* wegen).
(h) *(prize, 1st place etc)* gehen *(to* an *+acc)*; *(inheritance)* zufallen *(to sb* jdm).
(i) *(extend)* gehen ◆ **the garden ~es down to the river** der Garten geht bis zum Fluß hinunter; **the difference between them ~es deep** der Unterschied zwischen ihnen geht tief; **I'll ~ to £100** ich gehe bis £ 100.
(j) *(run, function) (watch)* gehen; *(car, machine also)* laufen; *(workers)* arbeiten ◆ **to ~ slow** *(workers)* im Bummelstreik sein; *(watch)* nachgehen; **to get ~ing** in Schwung *or* Fahrt kommen; **to get sth ~ing, to make sth ~** etw in Gang bringen; *party* etw in Fahrt bringen; *business* etw auf Vordermann bringen; **to get sb ~ing** jdn in Fahrt bringen; **to get ~ing on** *or* **with sth** etw in Angriff nehmen; **once you get ~ing on it** wenn man erst mal damit angefangen hat; **to keep ~ing** *(person)* weitermachen; *(machine, engine etc)* weiterlaufen; *(car)* weiterfahren; *(business)* weiter laufen; **keep ~ing!** weiter!; **to keep a factory ~ing** eine Fabrik in Betrieb halten; **to keep the fire ~ing** das Feuer anbehalten; **she needs these pills/his friendship to keep her ~ing** sie braucht diese Pillen/seine Freundschaft, um durchzuhalten; **this medicine/prospect kept her ~ing** dieses Medikament/diese Aussicht hat sie durchhalten lassen; **here's £50/some work to keep you ~ing** hier hast du erst mal £ 50/ etwas Arbeit; **to keep sb ~ing in food** jdn mit Essen versorgen.
(k) *(happen, turn out) (project, things)* gehen; *(event, evening)* verlaufen; *(voting, election)* ausgehen ◆ **I've forgotten how the words ~** ich habe den Text vergessen; **how does the story/tune ~?** wie war die Geschichte doch noch mal/wie geht die Melodie?; **how does his theory ~?** welche Theorie hat er?, was ist seine Theorie?; **the story** *or* **rumour ~es that ...** es geht das Gerücht, daß ...; **the election/decision went in his favour/against him** die Wahl/Entscheidung fiel zu seinen Gunsten/Ungunsten aus; **how's it ~ing?, how ~es it?** *(inf)* wie geht's (denn so)? *(inf)*; **how did it ~?** wie war's?; **how did the exam/your holiday ~?** wie ging's in der Prüfung/wie war der Urlaub?; **how's the essay ~ing?** was macht der Aufsatz?; **everything is ~ing well (with us)** alles läuft gut, bei uns läuft alles gut; **if everything ~es well** wenn alles gutgeht; **all went well for him until ...** alles ging gut, bis ...; **we'll see how things ~** *(inf)* wir werden sehen, wie es läuft *(inf) or* geht; **you know the way things ~** Sie wissen ja, wie das so ist *or* geht; **the way things are ~ing I'll ...** so wie es aussieht, werde ich ...; **things have gone well/badly** es ist gut/schlecht gelaufen; **as things ~ today that's not very expensive** für heutige Verhältnisse ist das nicht teuer; **she has a lot ~ing for her** sie ist gut dran.
(l) *(fail, break, wear out) (material, mechanism, bulb, zip etc)* kaputtgehen; *(through rust)* (durch)rosten; *(health, strength, eyesight etc)* nachlassen; *(brakes, steering)* versagen; *(button)* abgehen ◆ **the jumper has gone at the elbows** der Pullover ist an den Ärmeln durch *(inf)*; **his mind is ~ing** er läßt geistig sehr nach; **there ~es another bulb/button!** schon wieder eine Birne kaputt/ein Knopf ab!
(m) *(be accepted: behaviour, dress etc)* gehen *(inf)* ◆ **anything ~es!** alles ist erlaubt; **what I say ~es!** was ich sage, gilt *or* wird gemacht!; **that ~es for me too** *(that applies to me)* das gilt auch für mich; *(I agree with that)* das meine ich auch.
(n) *(be available)* **there are several houses/jobs ~ing** es sind mehrere Häuser/Stellen zu haben; **is there any tea ~ing?** gibt es Tee?; **I'll have whatever is ~ing** ich nehme, was es gibt; **what do you want? — anything that's ~ing** was möchtest du? — was da ist; **the best beer ~ing** das beste Bier, das es gibt.
(o) *(be, become)* werden ◆ **to ~ deaf/mad/grey** taub/verrückt/grau werden; **to ~ hungry** hungern; **I went cold** mir wurde kalt; **to ~ in rags** in Lumpen gehen; **to ~ to sleep/ruin** einschlafen/zerfallen; **to ~ Japanese/ethnic** auf japanisch/auf Folklore machen *(inf)*; **to ~ Labour** Labour wählen.
(p) *(be contained, fit)* gehen, passen; *(belong, be placed)* hingehören; *(in drawer, cupboard etc)* (hin)kommen ◆ **it won't ~ in the box** es geht *or* paßt nicht in die Kiste; **the books ~ in that cupboard** die Bücher kommen *or* gehören in den Schrank dort; **4 into 12 ~es 3** 4 geht in 12 dreimal; **4 into 3 won't ~** 3 durch 4 geht nicht.
(q) *(match)* dazu passen ◆ **to ~ with sth** zu etw passen.
(r) *(contribute)* **the money ~es to help the poor** das Geld soll den Armen helfen; **the money will ~ towards a new car/the holiday** das ist Geld für ein neues Auto/den Urlaub; **the qualities that ~ to make a great man** die Eigenschaften, die einen großen Mann ausmachen.
(s) *(make a sound or movement)* machen ◆ **to ~ bang/shh/tick-tock** peng/pst/ticktack machen; **~ like that (with your left foot)** mach so (mit deinem linken Fuß); **there ~es the bell** es klingelt.
(t) *(US)* **food to ~** Essen zum Mitnehmen.
(u) **he's not bad as boys ~** verglichen mit anderen Jungen ist er nicht übel.
[2] *aux vb (forming future tense)* **I'm/I was/I had been ~ing to do it** ich werde/ich wollte es tun/ich habe es tun wollen; **I wasn't ~ing to do it (anyway)** ich hätte es sowieso nicht gemacht; **it's ~ing to rain** es wird wohl regnen; **he knew that he wasn't ~ing to see her again** er wußte, daß er sie nicht wiedersehen würde; **there's ~ing to be trouble** es wird Ärger geben.
[3] *vt* **(a)** *route, way* gehen; *(vehicle, by vehicle)* fahren.
(b) *(Cards etc)* **£5** gehen bis, mithalten bis.
(c) *(inf)* **to ~ it** *(~fast)* ein tolles Tempo draufhaben *(inf)*; *(live hard)* es toll treiben *(inf)*; *(work hard)* sich hineinknien *(inf)*; **to ~ it alone** sich selbständig machen.
(d) **my mind went a complete blank** ich hatte ein Brett vor dem Kopf *(inf)*.
(e) *(inf)* **I could ~ a beer** ich könnte ein Bier vertragen.
[4] *n, pl* **-es (a)** *(inf) (energy)* Schwung *m* ◆ **to be full of ~** unternehmungslustig sein.
(b) **to be on the ~** auf Trab sein *(inf)*; **to keep sb on the ~** jdn auf Trab halten; **he's got two women/books on the ~** er hat zwei Frauen gleichzeitig/er schreibt an zwei Büchern gleichzeitig; **it's all ~** es ist immer was los *(inf)*.
(c) *(attempt)* Versuch *m* ◆ **it's your ~** du bist dran *(inf) or* an der Reihe; **you've had your ~** du warst schon dran *(inf) or* an der Reihe; **miss one ~** einmal aussetzen; **to have a ~** es versuchen, es probieren; **have a ~!** versuch's *or* probier's *(inf)* doch mal!; **he's had several ~es at the exam** er hat schon mehrere Anläufe auf das Examen genommen; **to have a ~ at sb** *(criticize)* jdn runterputzen *(inf)*; *(fight)* es mit jdm aufnehmen; **the public were warned not to have a ~ (at him)** die Öffentlichkeit wurde gewarnt, nichts (gegen ihn) zu unternehmen; **to have a ~ at doing sth** versuchen *or* probieren, etw zu tun; **at the first/second ~** auf Anhieb *(inf)*/beim zweiten Mal *or* Versuch; **at** *or* **in one ~** auf einen Schlag *(inf)*; *(drink)* in einem Zug *(inf)*; **she asked for a ~ on his bike** sie wollte mal sein Fahrrad ausprobieren; **can I have a ~?** darf ich mal?
(d) *(bout: of illness etc)* Anfall *m* ◆ **I had a bad ~ of flu** ich hatte eine üble Grippe *(inf)*.
(e) *(success)* **to make a ~ of sth** in etw *(dat)* Erfolg haben; **(it's) no ~** *(inf)* das ist nicht drin *(inf)*, da ist nichts zu machen; **it's all the ~** *(inf)* das ist der große Hit *(inf) or* große Mode.
(f) **from the word ~** von Anfang an.
[5] *adj (esp Space)* **you are ~ for take-off/landing** alles klar zum Start/zur Landung; **all systems (are) ~** (es ist) alles klar.

◆**go about** [1] *vi* **(a)** *(move from place to place)* herumgehen, herumlaufen *(inf)*; *(by vehicle)* herumfahren; *(in old clothes etc)* herumlaufen ◆ **to ~ ~ in gangs** in Banden durch die Gegend ziehen; **to ~ ~ with sb** mit jdm zusammensein *or* herumziehen *(pej inf)*; **she's ~ing ~ with John** sie geht mit John *(inf)*; **you shouldn't ~ ~ doing that kind of thing** solche Sachen solltest du nicht machen.
(b) *(be current: rumour, flu etc)* umgehen.
(c) *(Naut: change direction)* wenden.
[2] *vi +prep obj* **(a)** *(set to work at) task, problem* anpacken ◆ **we must ~ ~ it carefully** wir müssen vorsichtig vorgehen; **how does one ~ ~ getting seats/finding a job?** wie bekommt man Plätze/eine Stelle?
(b) *(be occupied with) work, jobs* erledigen ◆ **to ~ ~ one's business** sich um seine eigenen Geschäfte kümmern.

◆**go across** [1] *vi +prep obj* überqueren; *street etc also* gehen über *(+acc)*; *river also* fahren über *(+acc)* ◆ **to ~ ~ the sea to Ireland** übers Meer nach Irland fahren.
[2] *vi* hinübergehen; *(by vehicle)* hinüberfahren; *(by plane)* hinüberfliegen; *(to the enemy etc)* überlaufen *(to* zu*)* ◆ **to ~ ~ to the other side** auf die andere Seite hinübergehen/hinüberfahren/zur anderen Seite überwechseln *or* übergehen; **to ~ ~ to a neighbour/the pub** zu Nachbars/in die Kneipe hinübergehen.

◆**go after** *vi +prep obj* **(a)** *(follow)* nachgehen *(+dat)*, nachlaufen *(+dat)*; *(in vehicle)* nachfahren *(+dat)* ◆ **the police went ~ the escaped criminal** die Polizei hat den entkommenen Verbrecher gejagt.

(b) (*try to win or obtain*) anstreben, es abgesehen haben auf (*+acc*) (*inf*); *job* sich bemühen um, aussein auf (*+acc*) (*inf*); *goal* verfolgen, anstreben; (*Sport*) *record* einstellen wollen; *personal best* anstreben; *girl* sich bemühen um, nachstellen (*+dat*) (*pej*) ◆ **when he decides what he wants he really ~es ~ it** wenn er weiß, was er will, tut er alles, um es zu bekommen.

◆**go against** *vi +prep obj* **(a)** (*be unfavourable to*) (*luck*) sein gegen; (*events*) ungünstig verlaufen für; (*evidence, appearance*) sprechen gegen.
(b) (*be lost by*) **the verdict went ~ her** das Urteil fiel zu ihren Ungunsten aus; **the battle/first rounds went ~ him** er hat die Schlacht/die ersten Runden verloren.
(c) (*contradict, be contrary to*) im Widerspruch stehen zu; *principles, conscience* gehen gegen; (*oppose: person*) handeln gegen, sich widersetzen (*+dat*).

◆**go ahead** *vi* **(a)** (*go in front*) vorangehen; (*in race*) sich an die Spitze setzen; (*go earlier*) vorausgehen; (*in vehicle*) vorausfahren ◆ **to ~ ~ of sb** vor jdm gehen; sich vor jdn setzen; jdm vorausgehen/-fahren.
(b) (*proceed*) (*person*) es machen; (*work, project*) vorangehen ◆ **he just went ~ and did it** er hat es einfach gemacht; **~ ~!** nur zu!; **to ~ ~ with sth** etw durchführen.

◆**go along** *vi* **(a)** (*walk along*) entlanggehen, entlangspazieren (*inf*) ◆ **as one ~es ~** (*while walking*) unterwegs; (*bit by bit*) nach und nach; (*at the same time*) nebenbei, nebenher; **~ ~ with you!** (*inf*) jetzt hör aber auf! (*inf*).
(b) (*accompany*) mitgehen, mitkommen (*with* mit) ◆ **the furniture ~es ~ with the flat** die Möbel gehören zur Wohnung.
(c) (*agree*) zustimmen (*with dat*); (*not object*) sich anschließen (*with dat*).

◆**go around** *vi see* **go about 1 (a, b), go round.**

◆**go at** *vi +prep obj* (*inf: attack*) *person* losgehen auf (*+acc*) (*inf*); *task* sich machen an (*+acc*) ◆ **to ~ ~ it** loslegen (*inf*).

◆**go away** *vi* (weg)gehen; (*for a holiday*) wegfahren; (*from wedding*) abreisen, wegfahren ◆ **they went ~ together** (*illicitly*) sie sind miteinander durchgebrannt (*inf*); **"gone ~"** (*on letter*) „verzogen"; **the smell still hasn't gone ~** der Geruch ist immer noch nicht weg; **~ing-~ dress** *Kleid, das die Braut trägt, wenn sie den Hochzeitsempfang verläßt.*

◆**go back** *vi* **(a)** (*return*) zurückgehen; (*to a subject*) zurückkommen (*to* auf *+acc*); (*revert: to habits, methods etc*) zurückkehren (*to* zu) ◆ **they have to ~ ~ to Germany/school next week** nächste Woche müssen sie wieder nach Deutschland zurück/wieder zur Schule; **when do the schools ~ ~?** wann fängt die Schule wieder an?; **to ~ ~ to the beginning** wieder von vorn anfangen; **you can't ~ ~ now** du kannst jetzt nicht zurück; **there's no ~ing ~ now** jetzt gibt es kein Zurück mehr; **I'll ~ ~ there for a holiday** da gehe *or* fahre ich noch mal in Urlaub hin; **he went ~ for his hat** er ging zurück, um seinen Hut zu holen.
(b) (*be returned*) (*faulty goods*) zurückgehen; (*library books*) zurückgebracht werden.
(c) (*date back*) zurückgehen, zurückreichen (*to* bis zu) ◆ **we ~ ~ a long way** wir kennen uns schon ewig.
(d) (*clock: be put back*) zurückgestellt werden.
(e) (*extend back: cave, garden etc*) zurückgehen, zurückreichen (*to* bis zu).

◆**go back on** *vi +prep obj* zurücknehmen; *decision* rückgängig machen; *friend* im Stich lassen ◆ **I never ~ ~ ~ my promises** was ich versprochen habe, halte ich auch.

◆**go before** [1] *vi* (*live before*) in früheren Zeiten leben; (*happen before*) vorangehen ◆ **those who have gone ~ (us)** unsere Vorfahren; **everything that had gone ~** alles Vorhergehende.
[2] *vi +prep obj* **to ~ ~ the court/headmaster/committee** vor Gericht erscheinen/zum Rektor/vor den Ausschuß kommen.

◆**go below** *vi* (*Naut*) unter Deck gehen.

◆**go beyond** *vi +prep obj* (*exceed*) hinausgehen über (*+acc*); *orders, instructions also* überschreiten; *hopes, expectations also* übertreffen.

◆**go by** [1] *vi* (*person, opportunity*) vorbeigehen (*prep obj* an *+dat*); (*procession*) vorbeiziehen (*prep obj* an *+dat*); (*vehicle*) vorbeifahren (*prep obj* an *+dat*); (*time*) vergehen ◆ **as time went ~** mit der Zeit; **in days gone ~** in längst vergangenen Tagen.
[2] *vi +prep obj* **(a)** (*base judgement or decision on*) gehen nach; (*be guided by*) *compass, watch etc, sb's example* sich richten nach; (*stick to*) *rules* sich halten an (*+acc*) ◆ **if that's anything to ~ ~** wenn man danach gehen kann; **~ing ~ what he said** nach dem, was er sagte; **that's not much to ~ ~** das will nicht viel heißen.
(b) to ~ ~ the name of X X heißen.

◆**go down** *vi* **(a)** hinuntergehen (*prep obj acc*); (*by vehicle, lift*) hinunterfahren (*prep obj acc*); (*sun, moon: set*) untergehen; (*Theat: curtain*) fallen; (*fall*) (*boxer etc*) zu Boden gehen; (*horse*) stürzen ◆ **to ~ ~ on one's knees** sich hinknien; (*to apologize, propose*) auf die Knie fallen; **this wine/cake ~es ~ rather well** dieser Wein/der Kuchen schmeckt gut; **it will help the tablet ~ ~** dann rutscht die Tablette besser (hinunter); **to ~ ~ on sb** (*inf: have oral sex with*) es jdm mit dem Mund machen (*inf*).
(b) (*ship, person: sink*) untergehen; (*be defeated*) geschlagen werden (*to* von); (*fail examination*) durchfallen; *see* **fight 2.**
(c) (*Brit Univ*) die Universität verlassen; (*for vacation*) in die Semesterferien gehen.
(d) (*inf: go to prison*) eingelocht werden (*inf*).
(e) (*be accepted, approved*) ankommen (*with* bei) ◆ **that won't ~ ~ well with him** das wird er nicht gut finden; **he went ~ big in the States** (*inf*) in den Staaten kam er ganz groß heraus (*inf*).
(f) (*be reduced, lessen*) (*floods, temperature, fever, supplies, swelling*) zurückgehen; (*taxes, value*) sich verringern, weniger werden; (*prices*) sinken, runtergehen (*inf*); (*barometer*) fallen; (*wind*) nachlassen; (*sea*) sich beruhigen; (*balloon, tyre*) Luft verlieren; (*deteriorate: neighbourhood*) herunterkommen ◆ **he has gone ~ in my estimation** er ist in meiner Achtung gesunken; *see* **world.**
(g) (*go as far as*) gehen (*to* bis) ◆ **I'll ~ ~ to the bottom of the page** ich werde die Seite noch fertig machen.
(h) (*be noted, remembered*) vermerkt werden ◆ **to ~ ~ to posterity/in history** der Nachwelt überliefert werden/in die Geschichte eingehen.
(i) (*Bridge*) den Kontrakt nicht erfüllen ◆ **they went five ~** sie blieben fünf unter dem gebotenen Kontrakt.
(j) (*become ill*) **to ~ ~ with a cold** eine Erkältung bekommen.
(k) (*Mus inf: lower pitch*) heruntergehen (*inf*), tiefer singen/spielen.

◆**go for** *vi +prep obj* **(a)** (*inf: attack*) *person* losgehen auf (*+acc*) (*inf*); (*verbally*) herziehen über (*+acc*) ◆ **these cigarettes went ~ my throat** ich habe die Zigaretten im Hals gespürt; **~ ~ him!** (*to dog*) faß!
(b) (*inf: admire, like*) gut finden, stehen auf (*+acc*) (*inf*) ◆ **I could ~ ~ her/that** ich finde sie/das gut.
(c) (*aim at*) zielen auf (*+acc*); (*fig*) aussein auf (*+acc*) (*inf*); (*in claim etc*) fordern ◆ **~ ~ it!** nichts wie ran! (*inf*); **if I were you I'd ~ ~ it** an deiner Stelle würde ich zugreifen; **he was obviously ~ing ~ the ball** er hatte es offensichtlich auf den Ball abgesehen.

◆**go forth** *vi* (*old, liter*) (*person*) hingehen; (*order*) ergehen (*liter*) ◆ **to ~ ~ into battle** in den Kampf ziehen.

◆**go forward** *vi* **(a)** (*make progress: work etc*) vorangehen. **(b)** (*proceed, go ahead*) **to ~ ~ with sth** etw durchführen, etw in die Tat umsetzen. **(c)** (*be put forward: suggestion etc*) vorgelegt werden (*to dat*).

◆**go in** *vi* **(a)** (*enter*) hineingehen; (*Cricket*) nach „innen" gehen ◆ **I must ~ ~ now** ich muß jetzt hinein(gehen); **when does school/the theatre ~ ~?** wann fängt die Schule/das Theater an?; **~ ~ and win!** (*inf*) jetzt zeig's ihnen aber! (*inf*).
(b) (*sun, moon: go behind clouds*) weggehen, verschwinden.
(c) (*fit in*) hineingehen, hineinpassen.
(d) (*sink in, be assimilated*) jdm eingehen.

◆**go in for** *vi +prep obj* **(a)** (*enter for*) teilnehmen an (*+dat*).
(b) (*approve of, be interested in, practise*) zu haben sein für; (*as career*) sich entschieden haben für, gewählt haben ◆ **to ~ ~ ~ sports/tennis** (*play oneself*) Sport treiben/Tennis spielen; (*be interested in*) sich für Sport/Tennis interessieren; **he's gone ~ ~ growing vegetables/breeding rabbits** *etc* er hat sich auf den Gemüseanbau/die Kaninchenzucht *etc* verlegt; **he ~es ~ ~ a very strange style of writing** er hat einen ziemlich eigenartigen Stil; **he ~es ~ ~ all these big words** all diese großartigen Wörter haben es ihm angetan.

◆**go into** *vi +prep obj* **(a)** *drawer, desk etc* kramen in (*+dat*); *a house, hospital, politics, the grocery trade* gehen in (*+acc*); *the army, navy etc* gehen zu ◆ **to ~ ~ digs** *or* **lodgings** sich (*dat*) ein Zimmer nehmen; **to ~ ~ publishing** ins Verlagswesen gehen; **to ~ ~ teaching/parliament/the Church** Lehrer/Abgeordneter/Geistlicher werden; **it's ~ing ~ its second year** das geht jetzt schon ins zweite Jahr.
(b) (*crash into*) *car* (hinein)fahren in (*+acc*); *wall* fahren gegen.
(c) (*embark on*) *explanation, description etc* von sich (*dat*) geben, vom Stapel lassen (*inf*); *routine* verfallen in (*+acc*).
(d) *trance, coma* fallen in (*+acc*); *convulsions, fit* bekommen ◆ **to ~ ~ hysterics** hysterisch werden; **to ~ ~ peals of/a fit of laughter** laut loslachen/einen Lachanfall bekommen; **to ~ ~ mourning for sb** um jdn trauern.
(e) (*start to wear*) *long trousers, mourning* tragen.
(f) (*look into*) sich befassen mit; (*treat, explain at length*) abhandeln ◆ **I don't want to ~ ~ that now** darauf möchte ich jetzt nicht (näher) eingehen; **this matter is being gone ~** man befaßt sich im Moment mit dieser Angelegenheit.

◆**go in with** *vi +prep obj* sich zusammentun *or* zusammenschließen mit.

◆**go off** [1] *vi* **(a)** (*leave*) weggehen; (*by vehicle*) abfahren, wegfahren (*on* mit); (*Theat*) abgehen ◆ **he went ~ to the States** er fuhr in die Staaten; **to ~ ~ with sb/sth** mit jdm/etw weggehen; (*illicitly*) mit jdm/etw auf und davon gehen (*inf*).
(b) (*stop operating*) (*light*) ausgehen; (*water, electricity, gas*) wegbleiben; (*telephones*) nicht funktionieren.
(c) (*gun, bomb, alarm*) losgehen; (*alarm clock*) klingeln.
(d) to ~ ~ into fits of laughter in schallendes Gelächter ausbrechen.
(e) (*go bad*) (*food*) schlecht werden; (*milk also*) sauer werden; (*butter also*) ranzig werden; (*fig*) (*person, work, performance*) nachlassen, sich verschlechtern; (*sportsman, writer, actor*) abbauen (*inf*), schlechter werden.
(f) (*inf*) (*go to sleep*) einschlafen; (*into trance*) in Trance verfallen.
(g) (*take place*) verlaufen ◆ **to ~ ~ well/badly** gut/schlecht gehen.
[2] *vi +prep obj* **(a)** (*lose liking for*) nicht mehr mögen; *hobby also* das Interesse verlieren an (*+dat*) ◆ **I've gone ~ him/that** ich mache mir nichts mehr aus ihm/daraus, ich mag ihn/es nicht mehr; **it's funny how you ~ ~ people** so schnell kann einem jemand unsympathisch werden.
(b) to ~ ~ the gold standard vom Goldstandard abgehen.

◆**go on** [1] *vi* **(a)** (*fit*) passen (*prep obj* auf *+acc*) ◆ **my shoes won't ~ ~** ich komme nicht in meine Schuhe.
(b) (*begin to operate*) (*light, power*) angehen.
(c) (*walk on etc*) weitergehen; (*by vehicle*) weiterfahren; (*ahead of others*) vorausgehen.
(d) (*carry on, continue*) (*talks, problems, war etc*) weitergehen; (*person*) weitermachen ◆ **it ~es ~ and on** es hört nicht mehr auf; **to ~ ~ with sth** etw fortsetzen, mit etw weitermachen; **to ~ ~ working/coughing/hoping/trying**

weiterarbeiten/weiterhusten/weiter hoffen/es weiter(hin) versuchen; **~ ~ with your work** arbeitet *or* macht weiter; **I want to ~ ~ being a teacher** *etc* ich möchte Lehrer *etc* bleiben; **to ~ ~ speaking** weitersprechen; (*after a pause*) fortfahren; **~ ~, tell me/try!** na, sag schon/na, versuch's doch!; **~ ~ (with you)!** (*iro inf*) na komm, komm! (*iro inf*); **to have enough/something to ~ ~ with** *or* **to be ~ing ~ with** fürs erste genug/mal etwas haben; **to ~ ~ to another matter** zu einer anderen Sache übergehen; **he went ~ to say that ...** dann sagte er, daß ...; **I can't ~ ~** ich kann nicht mehr; (*I'm stuck*) ich weiß nicht mehr weiter.
(e) (*talk incessantly*) wie ein Buch (*inf*) *or* unaufhörlich reden; (*nag, harp on*) darauf herumhacken (*inf*) ♦ **she just ~es ~ and on** sie redet und redet; **don't ~ ~ (about it)** nun hör aber (damit) auf; **you do ~ ~ a bit** du weißt manchmal nicht, wann du aufhören solltest; **to ~ ~ about sb/sth** (*talk a lot*) stundenlang von jdm/etw erzählen; (*complain*) dauernd über jdn/etw klagen; **to ~ ~ at sb** an jdm herumnörgeln, auf jdm herumhacken (*inf*).
(f) (*happen*) passieren, vor sich gehen; (*party, argument etc*) im Gange sein ♦ **this has been ~ing ~ for a long time** das geht schon lange so; **what's ~ing ~ here?** was geht hier vor?
(g) (*time: pass*) vergehen ♦ **as time ~es ~** im Laufe der Zeit.
(h) (*pej: behave*) sich aufführen ♦ **what a way to ~ ~!** wie kann man sich nur so aufführen!
(i) (*Theat: appear*) auftreten; (*Sport*) dran sein (*inf*), an der Reihe sein.
[2] *vi +prep obj* (a) (*ride on*) *bus, bike, roundabout etc* fahren mit; *tour* machen; *horse, donkey etc* reiten auf (*+dat*) ♦ **to ~ ~ the swings/slide** schaukeln/rutschen.
(b) (*be guided by*) gehen nach, sich verlassen auf (*+acc*); *evidence* sich stützen auf (*+acc*) ♦ **what have you to ~ ~?** worauf stützt du dich dabei?, wovon gehst du dabei aus?; **we've got nothing to ~ ~** wir haben keine Anhaltspunkte.
(c) **to ~ ~ short time/the dole** kurzarbeiten/stempeln gehen (*inf*); **to ~ ~ a diet/the pill** eine Schlankheitskur machen/die Pille nehmen.
(d) (*sl: like*) stehen auf (*+acc*) (*inf*); *see* **gone**.
(e) (*approach*) *fifty etc* zugehen auf (*+acc*).
♦**go on for** *vi +prep obj fifty, one o'clock* zugehen auf (*+acc*) ♦ **there were ~ing ~ ~ twenty people there** es waren fast zwanzig Leute da.
♦**go out** *vi* (a) (*leave*) hinausgehen ♦ **to ~ ~ of a room** aus einem Zimmer gehen.
(b) (*shopping etc*) weggehen; (*socially, to theatre etc*) ausgehen; (*with girl-/boyfriend*) gehen ♦ **to ~ ~ riding** ausreiten; **to ~ ~ for a meal** essen gehen; **John has been ~ing ~ with Susan for months** John geht schon seit Monaten mit Susan.
(c) (*be extinguished: fire, light*) ausgehen.
(d) (*become unconscious*) das Bewußtsein verlieren, wegsein (*inf*); (*fall asleep*) einschlafen, wegsein (*inf*).
(e) (*become outmoded*) (*fashion*) unmodern werden; (*custom*) überholt sein.
(f) **to ~ ~ cleaning/to work** putzen/arbeiten gehen.
(g) (*Pol: leave office*) abgelöst werden.
(h) (*emigrate, go overseas*) **the family went ~ to Australia** die Familie ging nach Australien.
(i) (*strike*) streiken ♦ **to ~ ~ on strike** in den Streik treten.
(j) (*tide*) zurückgehen.
(k) **my heart went ~ to him** ich fühlte mit ihm mit; **all our sympathy ~es ~ to you** wir teilen Ihr Leid.
(l) (*Sport: be defeated*) ausscheiden, herausfliegen (*inf*).
(m) (*strive*) **to ~ all ~** sich ins Zeug legen (*for* für).
(n) (*be issued*) (*pamphlet, circular*) (hinaus)gehen; (*Rad, TV: programme*) ausgestrahlt werden.
(o) (*year, month: end*) enden, zu Ende gehen.
(p) (*US: be a candidate for*) **to ~ ~ for** antreten für; (*Ftbl etc also*) spielen für.
♦**go over** [1] *vi* (a) (*cross*) hinübergehen, rübergehen (*inf*); (*by vehicle*) hinüberfahren, rüberfahren (*inf*).
(b) (*change allegiance, habit, diet etc*) übergehen (*to* zu); (*to another party*) überwechseln (*to* zu) ♦ **to ~ ~ to the other side/to a pipe** zur anderen Seite überwechseln/zur Pfeife übergehen.
(c) (*TV, Rad: to news desk, another studio*) umschalten.
(d) (*vehicle etc: be overturned*) umkippen.
(e) (*be received: play, remarks etc*) ankommen.
[2] *vi +prep obj* (a) (*examine, check over*) *accounts, report* durchgehen; *house, luggage* durchsuchen; *person, car* untersuchen; (*see over*) *house etc* sich (*dat*) ansehen, besichtigen.
(b) (*repeat, rehearse, review*) *lesson, role, facts* durchgehen ♦ **to ~ ~ sth in one's mind** etw durchdenken *or* überdenken; **to ~ ~ the ground** es durchsprechen.
(c) (*wash, dust etc*) *windows, room* schnell saubermachen.
(d) (*redraw*) *outlines etc* nachzeichnen.
♦**go past** *vi* vorbeigehen (*prep obj* an *+dat*); (*vehicle*) vorbeifahren (*prep obj* an *+dat*); (*procession*) vorbeiziehen (*prep obj* an *+dat*); (*time*) vergehen, verfließen.
♦**go round** *vi* (a) (*turn, spin*) sich drehen ♦ **my head is ~ing ~** mir dreht sich alles.
(b) (*make a detour*) außen herumgehen; (*by vehicle*) außen herumfahren ♦ **to ~ ~ sth** um etw herumgehen/-fahren; **to ~ ~ the long way** ganz außen herumgehen/-fahren; **we went ~ by Winchester** wir fuhren bei Winchester herum.
(c) (*visit, call round*) vorbeigehen (*to* bei).
(d) (*tour: round museum etc*) herumgehen (*prep obj* in *+dat*).
(e) (*be sufficient*) langen, (aus)reichen ♦ **there's enough food to ~ ~ (all these people)** es ist (für all diese Leute) genügend zu essen da; **to make the money ~ ~** mit dem Geld auskommen.
(f) *+prep obj* (*encircle, reach round*) herumgehen um.
(g) *see* **go about 1 (a, b)**.
♦**go through** [1] *vi* (*lit, fig*) durchgehen; (*business deal*) abgeschlossen werden; (*divorce*) durchkommen.
[2] *vi +prep obj* (a) *hole, door, customs etc* gehen durch.
(b) (*suffer, endure*) durchmachen.
(c) (*examine, discuss, rehearse*) *list, subject, play, mail, lesson* durchgehen.
(d) (*search*) *pocket, suitcase* durchsuchen.
(e) (*use up*) aufbrauchen; *money* ausgeben, durchbringen (*inf*); *shoes* durchlaufen (*inf*); *food, ice-cream* aufessen ♦ **he has gone ~ the seat of his trousers** er hat seine Hose durchgesessen; **this book has already gone ~ 13 editions** das Buch hat schon 13 Auflagen erlebt.
(f) *formalities, apprenticeship, initiation* durchmachen; *course* absolvieren; *funeral, matriculation* mitmachen ♦ **they went ~ the programme in two hours** sie haben das Programm in zwei Stunden durchgezogen; **to ~ ~ the marriage ceremony** sich trauen lassen.
♦**go through with** *vi +prep obj plan* durchziehen (*inf*); *crime* ausführen ♦ **she realized that she had to ~ ~ ~ it** sie sah, daß es kein Zurück gab *or* daß sich das nicht mehr vermeiden ließ; **she couldn't ~ ~ ~ it** sie brachte es nicht fertig.
♦**go to** *vi +prep obj* (*make an effort*) **to ~ ~ it** sich ranhalten (*inf*); **~ ~ it!** los, ran! (*inf*), auf geht's! (*inf*).
♦**go together** *vi* (a) (*harmonize: colours, ideas, people*) zusammenpassen. (b) (*go hand in hand: events, conditions*) zusammen auftreten. (c) (*go out together*) miteinander gehen.
♦**go under** [1] *vi* (*sink: ship, person*) untergehen; (*fail*) (*businessman*) scheitern (*because of* an *+dat*); (*company*) eingehen (*inf*) ♦ **to ~ ~ to a disease** einer Krankheit (*dat*) zum Opfer fallen; **to ~ ~ to sb** jdm unterliegen.
[2] *vi +prep obj* (a) (*pass under*) durchgehen unter (*+dat*); (*fit under*) gehen *or* passen unter (*+acc*).
(b) **to ~ ~ the name of X** als X bekannt sein.
♦**go up** *vi* (a) (*rise: price, temperature etc*) steigen ♦ **to ~ ~ (and up) in price** (immer) teurer werden.
(b) (*climb*) (*up stairs, hill*) hinaufgehen, hinaufsteigen (*prep obj acc*); (*up ladder*) hinaufsteigen (*prep obj acc*); (*up tree*) hinaufklettern (*prep obj* auf *+acc*) ♦ **to ~ ~ to bed** nach oben gehen.
(c) (*lift*) hochfahren; (*balloon*) aufsteigen; (*Theat: curtain*) hochgehen; (*be built: new flats etc*) gebaut werden.
(d) (*travel*) (*to the north*) hochfahren; (*to London*) fahren ♦ **to ~ ~ (to university)** (*Brit*) auf die Universität gehen.
(e) (*explode, be destroyed*) hochgehen (*inf*), in die Luft gehen ♦ **to ~ ~ in flames** in Flammen aufgehen.
♦**go with** *vi +prep obj* (a) *sb* gehen mit. (b) (*go hand in hand with*) Hand in Hand gehen mit. (c) (*be included or sold with*) gehören zu. (d) (*harmonize with*) passen zu.
♦**go without** [1] *vi +prep obj* nicht haben ♦ **to ~ ~ food/breakfast** nichts essen/nicht frühstücken; **to have to ~ ~ sth** ohne etw auskommen müssen, auf etw (*acc*) verzichten müssen; **to manage to ~ ~ sth** ohne etw auskommen; **he doesn't like to ~ ~ the luxuries of life** er verzichtet nicht gern auf den Luxus im Leben.
[2] *vi* darauf verzichten.
goad [gəʊd] [1] *n* (*stick*) Stachelstock *m*; (*fig*) (*spur*) Ansporn *m*; (*taunt*) aufstachelnde Bemerkung.
[2] *vt* (*taunt*) aufreizen ♦ **to ~ sb into sth** jdn zu etw anstacheln *or* treiben.
♦**goad on** *vt sep cattle* antreiben; (*fig*) anstacheln, aufstacheln.
go-ahead ['gəʊəhed] [1] *adj* fortschrittlich, progressiv.
[2] *n* **to give sb/sth the ~** jdm/für etw grünes Licht *or* freie Fahrt geben.
goal [gəʊl] *n* (a) (*Sport*) Tor *nt* ♦ **to keep ~, to play in ~** im Tor stehen, im Tor spielen, das Tor hüten; **to score/kick a ~** ein Tor erzielen/schießen. (b) (*aim, objective*) Ziel *nt*.
goal area *n* Torraum *m*.
goalie ['gəʊlɪ] *n* (*inf*) Tormann *m*.
goal: ~keeper *n* Torwart, Torhüter *m*; **~-kick** *n* Abstoß *m* (vom Tor); **~-line** *n* Torlinie *f*; **~mouth** *n* unmittelbarer Torbereich; **~post** *n* Torpfosten *m*; **to move the ~posts** (*fig inf*) die Spielregeln (ver)ändern.
goanna [gəʊ'ænə] *n* (*Zool*) Waran *m*.
goat [gəʊt] *n* Ziege *f*; (*inf*) (*silly person*) (*man*) Esel *m* (*inf*); (*woman*) Ziege *f* (*inf*); (*lecher*) Bock *m* (*inf*) ♦ **to act the ~** (*inf*) herumalbern; **to get sb's ~** (*inf*) jdn auf die Palme bringen (*inf*).
goatee (beard) [gəʊ'tiː(,biːəd)] *n* Spitzbart *m*.
goat: ~herd *n* Ziegenhirte *m*; **~skin** *n* Ziegenleder *nt*.
goat's milk *n* Ziegenmilch *f* ♦ **~ yoghurt** Joghurt *m or nt* aus Ziegenmilch.
gob[1] [gɒb] *n* (*lump*) Klumpen *m*.
gob[2] *n* (*Brit sl: mouth*) Schnauze *f* (*sl*) ♦ **shut your ~!** halt die Schnauze! (*sl*).
gob[3] *n* (*US sl: sailor*) blauer Junge (*inf*), Blaujacke *f* (*inf*).
gobbet ['gɒbɪt] *n* Brocken *m* ♦ **~s of cotton wool** Wattebäusche *pl*.
gobble ['gɒbl] [1] *vt* verschlingen.
[2] *vi* (a) (*eat noisily*) schmatzen. (b) (*turkey*) kollern.
[3] *n* (*of turkey*) Kollern *nt*.
♦**gobble down** *vt sep* hinunterschlingen.
♦**gobble up** *vt sep* (*lit, fig*) verschlingen; (*company*) schlucken.

gobbledegook, gobbledygook ['gɒbldɪˌguːk] *n (inf)* Kauderwelsch *nt.*
gobbler ['gɒbləʳ] *n* Truthahn *m.*
go-between ['gəʊbɪˌtwiːn] *n, pl* -s Vermittler(in *f*), Mittelsmann *m.*
Gobi Desert ['gəʊbɪ'dezət] *n* Wüste *f* Gobi.
goblet ['gɒblɪt] *n* Pokal *m*; *(esp of glass)* Kelchglas *nt.*
goblin ['gɒblɪn] *n* Kobold *m.*
gob-smacked ['gɒbsmækt] *adj (inf: amazed)* platt *(inf).*
gobstopper ['gɒbˌstɒpəʳ] *n (Brit) Riesenbonbon m or nt mit verschiedenen Farbschichten,* ≃ Dauerlutscher *m.*
goby ['gəʊbɪ] *n (fish)* Meergrundel *f.*
GOC *n abbr of* **General Officer Commanding** Oberbefehlshaber.
go: ~-by *n (inf)* **to give sb the ~-by** jdn schneiden, jdn links liegenlassen *(inf)*; **~-cart** *n (child's cart)* Seifenkiste *f*; *(Sport: kart)* Go-Kart *m*; *(US: walker)* Laufstuhl *m*; *(US: pushchair)* Sportwagen *m.*
god [gɒd] *n* **(a)** **G~** Gott *m*; **now he lies in G~'s (green) acre** *(euph)* nun deckt ihn der grüne Rasen *(euph)*, nun liegt er auf dem Gottesacker *(old)*; **G~ willing** so Gott will; **G~ forbid** *(inf)* Gott behüte *or* bewahre; **would to G~ that** *(form)* ich hoffe zu Gott, daß *(geh)*; **G~ (only) knows** *(inf)* wer weiß; **do you think he'll succeed? — G~ knows!** glaubst du, daß er Erfolg haben wird? — das wissen die Götter!; **(my) G~!, good G~!, G~ almighty!** *(all inf)* O Gott! *(inf)*, großer Gott! *(inf)*; **be quiet, for G~'s sake!** sei still, verdammt noch mal *(sl) or* Herrgott noch mal! *(inf)*; **for G~'s sake!** *(inf)* um Gottes *or* Himmels willen *(inf)*; **what in G~'s name ...?** um Himmels willen, was ...?
(b) *(non-Christian)* Gott *m* ◆ **Mars, the ~ of war** Mars, der Kriegsgott; **to play ~** Gott *or* den Herrgott spielen; **the commander was a ~ to his men** der Kommandant wurde von seinen Leuten wie ein (Ab)gott verehrt; **money is his ~** das Geld ist sein Gott *or* Götze.
(c) *(Brit Theat inf)* **the ~s** die Galerie, der Olymp *(inf).*
god: ~awful *adj (inf)* beschissen *(sl)*; **~child** *n* Patenkind *nt*; **~dam(ned)** *adj (inf)* Scheiß- *(sl)*, gottverdammt *(inf)*; **it's no ~dam use!** *(inf)* es hat keinen Zweck, verdammt noch mal *(sl)*; **~daughter** *n* Patentochter *f.*
goddess ['gɒdɪs] *n* Göttin *f.*
god: ~father *n (lit, fig)* Pate *m*; **my ~father** mein Patenonkel *m*; **~-fearing** *adj* gottesfürchtig; **~forsaken** *adj (inf)* gottverlassen; **~head** *n* Gottheit *f*; **the G~head** Gott *m*; **~less** *adj* gottlos; **~lessness** *n* Gottlosigkeit *f*; **~like** *adj* göttergleich; *attitude* gottähnlich; **he looked ~like** er sah aus wie ein junger Gott.
godliness ['gɒdlɪnɪs] *n* Frömmigkeit, Gottesfürchtigkeit *f.*
godly ['gɒdlɪ] *adj (+er)* fromm, gottesfürchtig.
god: ~mother *n* Patin *f*; **my ~mother** meine Patentante *f*; *see* **fairy ~mother**; **~parent** *n* Pate *m*, Patin *f*; **~send** *n* Geschenk *nt* des Himmels; **G~ slot** *n (Brit TV inf)* religiöse Sendungen *pl*, ≃ Wort *nt* zum Sonntag; **~son** *n* Patensohn *m*; **~speed** *interj (old)* behüt dich/euch Gott *(old)*, geh/geht mit Gott *(old)*; **to wish sb ~speed** jdn mit den besten Segenswünschen auf die Reise schicken.
goer ['gəʊəʳ] *n* **(a)** *(horse, runner)* Geher *m* ◆ **to be a good/sweet ~** gut laufen. **(b)** *(Austral inf: good idea)* **to be a ~** was taugen *(inf).*
-goer *n suf* -besucher(in *f*) *m.*
goes [gəʊz] *3rd pers sing present of* **go.**
gofer ['gəʊfəʳ] *n (inf)* Mädchen *nt* für alles *(inf).*
go-getter ['gəʊ'getəʳ] *n (inf)* Tatmensch, Ellbogentyp *(pej inf) m.*
goggle ['gɒgl] *vi (person)* staunen, starren, glotzen *(pej inf)*; *(eyes)* weit aufgerissen sein ◆ **to ~ at sb/sth** jdn/etw anstarren *or* anglotzen *(pej inf)*, auf jdn/etw starren *or* glotzen *(pej inf).*
goggle: ~-box *n (Brit inf)* Glotzkiste *(inf)*, Glotze *f (inf)*; **~-eyed** *adj* mit Kulleraugen, kulleräugig; **he stared at him/it ~-eyed** er starrte *or* glotzte *(pej inf)* ihn/es an; **a ~-eyed stare** ein starrer Blick.
goggles ['gɒglz] *npl* Schutzbrille *f*; *(inf: glasses)* Brille *f.*
go-go ['gəʊgəʊ]: **~-dancer** *n* Go-go-Tänzerin *f*, Go-go-girl *nt*; **~-dancing** *n* Go-go *nt.*
going ['gəʊɪŋ] [1] *n* **(a)** *(departure)* Weggang *m*, (Weg)gehen *nt.*
(b) *(pace, conditions)* **it's slow ~** es geht nur langsam; **that is good** *or* **fast ~** das ist ein flottes Tempo; **the ~ is good/soft/hard** *(in racing)* die Bahn ist gut/weich/hart; **the road was heavy/rough ~** man kam auf der Straße nur schwer/mit Mühe voran; **it's heavy ~ talking to him** es ist sehr mühsam, sich mit ihm zu unterhalten; **while the ~ is good** solange es noch geht; **to go while the ~ is good** sich rechtzeitig absetzen.
[2] *adj attr* **(a)** *(viable) business* gutgehend ◆ **to sell sth as a ~ concern** etw als ein bestehendes Unternehmen verkaufen.
(b) *(current) price, rate* gängig.
going-over [ˌgəʊɪŋ'əʊvəʳ] *n* **(a)** *(examination)* Untersuchung *f* ◆ **to give a contract/painting/patient/house a good ~** einen Vertrag gründlich prüfen/ein Gemälde/einen Patienten gründlich untersuchen/ein Haus gründlich durchsuchen.
(b) *(inf: beating-up)* Abreibung *f (inf)* ◆ **to give sb a good ~** jdm eine tüchtige Abreibung verpassen *(inf).*
goings-on [ˌgəʊɪŋ'zɒn] *npl (inf: happenings)* Dinge *pl* ◆ **there have been strange ~** da sind seltsame Dinge passiert; **fine ~!** schöne Geschichten!; **the ~ at home** was zu Hause passiert.
goitre, *(US)* **goiter** ['gɔɪtəʳ] *n* Kropf *m.*
go-kart ['gəʊˌkɑːt] *n* Go-Kart *m.*
gold [gəʊld] [1] *n* **(a)** Gold *nt*; *(wealth)* Geld *nt*; *(inf: ~ medal)* Goldmedaille *f*; *see* **glitter. (b)** *(colour)* Goldton *m.*
[2] *adj* golden; *(made of ~ also)* Gold-.
gold: ~ braid *n* Goldtresse *or* -litze *f*; **~brick** *(US)* [1] *n* **(a)** *(inf) (gilded metal bar)* falscher Goldbarren; *(worthless object)* schöner Schund; **to sell sb a ~brick** jdm etwas andrehen *(inf)*; **(b)** *(sl: shirker)* Drückeberger *m (inf)*; [2] *vi (sl)* sich drücken *(inf)*; **~bricker** *n (US sl) see* **~brick 1 (b)**; **G~ Coast** *n* Goldküste *f*; **~-coloured** *adj* goldfarben; **~crest** *n* Goldhähnchen *nt*; **~-digger** *n* Goldgräber *m*; **she's a real little ~-digger** *(inf)* sie ist wirklich nur aufs Geld aus *(inf)*; **~ dust** *n* Goldstaub *m.*
golden ['gəʊldən] *adj (lit, fig)* golden; *opportunity* einmalig ◆ **~ yellow/brown** goldgelb/goldbraun; **~ boy/girl** Goldjunge *m*/Goldmädchen *nt*; **to follow the ~ mean** die goldene Mitte wählen.
golden: ~ age *n (Myth)* Goldenes Zeitalter; *(fig)* Blütezeit *f*; **the ~ calf** *n* das Goldene Kalb; **G~ Delicious** *n* Golden Delicious *m*; **~ eagle** *n* Steinadler *m*; **G~ Fleece** *n*: **the G~ Fleece** das Goldene Vlies; **~ goal** *n (Ftbl)* Golden goal *nt*; **~ handcuffs** *npl Vergünstigungen pl für leitende Angestellte, um diese längerfristig an ein Unternehmen zu binden*; **~ handshake** *n (inf)* Abstandssumme *f*; **the director got a ~ handshake of £50,000** der Direktor hat zum Abschied £ 50.000 bekommen; **~ hello** *n (inf)* Einstellungsprämie *f*; **~ jubilee** *n* goldenes Jubiläum; **~ labrador** *n* Goldener Labrador; **~ oldie** *n (inf: tune, record)* (Golden) Oldie *m (inf)*; **~ oriole** *n* Pirol *m*; **~ pheasant** *n* Goldfasan *m*; **~rod** *n* Goldrute *f*; **~ rule** *n* goldene Regel; **I make it a ~ rule never to ...** ich mache es mir zu Regel, niemals zu ...; **~ syrup** *n (Brit)* (gelber) Sirup; **~ wedding (anniversary)** *n* goldene Hochzeit.
gold: ~ fever *n* Goldfieber *nt*; **~field** *n* Goldfeld *nt*; **~finch** *n (European)* Stieglitz, Distelfink *m*; *(US)* Amerikanischer Fink; **~fish** *n* Goldfisch *m*; **~fish bowl** *n* Goldfischglas *nt*; **it's like living in a ~fish bowl** da ist man wie auf dem Präsentierteller; **~ foil** *n* Goldfolie *f*; **~ leaf** *n* Blattgold *nt*; **~ medal** *n* Goldmedaille *f*; **~ mine** *n* Goldbergwerk *nt*, Goldgrube *f (also fig)*; **~ plate** *n (plating)* Goldüberzug *m*; *(plated articles)* vergoldetes Gerät; *(gold articles)* goldenes Gerät; **~-plate** *vt* vergolden; **~ reserves** *npl* Goldreserven *pl*; **~ rush** *n* Goldrausch *m*; **~smith** *n* Goldschmied *m*; **~ standard** *n* Goldstandard *m.*
golf [gɒlf] [1] *n* Golf *nt.*
[2] *vi* Golf spielen.
golf: ~ bag *n* Golftasche *f*; **~ball** *n* **(a)** Golfball *m*; **(b)** *(on typewriter)* Kugelkopf *m*; **~ball printer** Kugelkopfdrucker *m*; **~ club** *n (instrument)* Golfschläger *m*; *(association)* Golfklub *m*; **~ course** *n* Golfplatz *m.*
golfer ['gɒlfəʳ] *n* Golfer(in *f*), Golfspieler(in *f*) *m.*
golf links *npl* Golfplatz *m.*
Goliath [gəʊ'laɪəθ] *n (lit, fig)* Goliath *m.*
golliwog ['gɒlɪwɒg] *n* Negerpuppe *f* ◆ **to look like a ~** eine Negerkrause haben.
golly[1] ['gɒlɪ] *n (Brit inf) see* **golliwog.**
golly[2] *interj (inf)* Menschenskind *(inf).*
goloshes [gə'lɒʃəz] *npl see* **galoshes.**
Gomorrah, Gomorrha [gə'mɒrə] *n* Gomorr(h)a *nt.*
gonad ['gəʊnæd] *n* Gonade *f.*
gondola ['gɒndələ] *n* **(a)** *(in Venice, of balloon, cable car etc)* Gondel *f.* **(b)** *(US Rail: also* **~ car***)* offener Güterwagen. **(c)** *(in supermarket)* Gondel *f.*
gondolier [ˌgɒndə'lɪəʳ] *n* Gondoliere *m.*
gone [gɒn] [1] *ptp of* **go.**
[2] *adj pred* **(a)** *(inf: enthusiastic)* **to be ~ on sb/sth** von jdm/etw (ganz) weg sein *(inf)*; **I'm not ~ on ...** ich bin nicht verrückt auf *(+acc)* ... *(inf).* **(b)** *(inf: pregnant)* **she was 6 months ~** sie war im 7. Monat. **(c)** *see* **far.**
[3] *prep* **it's just ~ three** es ist gerade drei Uhr vorbei.
goner ['gɒnəʳ] *n (inf)* **to be a ~** *(car etc)* kaputt sein *(inf)*; *(patient)* es nicht mehr lange machen; *(socially, professionally: person, company)* weg vom Fenster sein *(inf)*; **if you pull out the whole plan's a ~** wenn du nicht mitmachst, wird aus der ganzen Sache nichts.
gong [gɒŋ] *n* **(a)** Gong *m.* **(b)** *(Brit sl: medal)* Blech *nt (inf)* ◆ **~s** Lametta *nt (inf).*
gonk [gɒŋk] *n (toy)* Stoffpuppe *f.*
gonna ['gɒnə] *(incorrect)* = **going to** ◆ **I'm not ~ tell you** das sage ich dir nicht.
gonorrhoea [ˌgɒnə'rɪə] *n* Gonorrhöe *f*, Tripper *m.*
goo [guː] *n (inf) (sticky stuff)* Papp *m (inf)*, Schmiere *f (inf)*; *(fig: sentimentality)* Schmalz *m (inf).*
goober ['guːbəʳ] *n (US inf)* Erdnuß *f.*
▼ **good** [gʊd] [1] *adj, comp* **better**, *superl* **best** **(a)** gut ◆ **that's a ~ one!** *(joke)* der ist gut!, das ist ein guter Witz *(also iro)*; *(excuse)* wer's glaubt, wird selig! *(inf)*; **you've done a ~ day's work** there da hast du gute Arbeit (für einen Tag) geleistet; **it's no ~ doing it like that** es hat keinen Sinn, das so zu machen; **that's no ~** das ist nichts; **a ~ fire was burning in the hearth** im Ofen brannte ein ordentliches *or* tüchtiges Feuer; **it's a ~ firm to work for** in der Firma läßt es sich gut arbeiten; **to be ~ at sport/languages** gut im Sport/in Sprachen sein; **to be ~ at sewing/typing** gut nähen/maschineschreiben können; **I'm not very ~ at that** das kann ich nicht besonders gut; **he's ~ at telling stories** er kann gut Geschichten erzählen; **he tells a ~ story** er erzählt gut; **to be ~ for sb** jdm guttun; *(be healthy also)* gesund sein; **to be ~ for toothache/one's health** gut gegen Zahnschmerzen/für die Gesundheit sein; **it's bound to be ~ for something** das muß doch zu *or* für etwas gut sein; **to drink more than is ~ for one** mehr trinken, als einem guttut; **she looks ~ enough to eat** *(hum)* sie sieht zum Anbeißen aus *(inf)*; **to be ~ with people** mit Menschen umgehen können; **~ fortune** Glück *nt*; **~ nature** Gutmütigkeit *f*; **you've never had it so ~!** es ist euch noch nie so gut gegangen, ihr habt es noch nie so gut gehabt; **it's too ~ to be true** es ist zu schön, um wahr zu sein; **to feel ~** sich wohl fühlen; **I don't feel too ~** mir ist nicht gut, ich fühle mich nicht wohl; **I don't feel too ~ about that** mir ist nicht ganz

➤ LANGUAGE IN USE: **good: 1a** → 11.2, 16.4, 23.5, 24.3

wohl dabei; **to come in a ~ third** einen guten dritten Platz belegen; **that's (not) ~ enough** das reicht (nicht); **is his work ~? — not ~ enough, I'm afraid/~ enough, I suppose** ist seine Arbeit gut? — leider nicht gut genug/es geht; **that's not ~ enough, you'll have to do better than that** das geht so nicht, du mußt dich schon etwas mehr anstrengen; **if he gives his word, that's ~ enough for me** wenn er sein Wort gibt, reicht mir das; **it's just not ~ enough!** so geht das nicht!; **his attitude/work/behaviour is just not ~ enough** er hat einfach nicht die richtige Einstellung/seine Arbeit ist einfach nicht gut genug/sein Benehmen ist nicht akzeptabel; **she felt he wasn't ~ enough for her** er war ihr nicht gut genug.
(b) (*favourable, opportune*) *moment, chance, opportunity* günstig, gut ◆ **a ~ day for a picnic** ein guter Tag für ein Picknick; **it's a ~ thing** *or* **job I was there** (nur) gut, daß ich dort war.
(c) (*enjoyable*) *holiday, evening* schön ◆ **the ~ life** das süße Leben; **to have a ~ time** sich gut amüsieren; **have a ~ time!** viel Spaß *or* Vergnügen!; **did you have a ~ day?** wie war's heute?, wie ging's (dir) heute?
(d) (*kind*) gut, lieb; *Samaritan* barmherzig ◆ **to be ~ to sb** gut *or* lieb zu jdm sein; **that's very ~ of you** das ist sehr lieb *or* nett von Ihnen; **(it was) ~ of you to come** nett, daß Sie gekommen sind; **would you be ~ enough to tell me ...** könnten Sie mir bitte sagen ..., wären Sie so nett, mir zu sagen ... (*also iro*); **she was ~ enough to help us** sie war so gut und hat uns geholfen; **with every ~ wish** mit den besten Wünschen.
(e) (*virtuous, honourable*) *name, manners, behaviour* gut; (*well-behaved, obedient*) artig, brav (*inf*) ◆ **the G~ Book** das Buch der Bücher; **the G~ Shepherd** der Gute Hirte; **(as) ~ as gold** mustergültig; **be a ~ girl/boy** sei artig *or* lieb *or* brav (*inf*); **be a ~ girl/boy and ...** sei so lieb und ...; **all ~ men and true** alle wackeren und aufrechten Männer (*old*); **your ~ man/lady** (*dated*) Ihr werter Gemahl/Ihre werte Gemahlin (*geh*); **my ~ man** (*dated*) mein Guter (*old*), mein guter Mann (*dated*); **~ man!** sehr löblich!; gut gemacht!; **~ girl/boy!** das ist lieb!; (*well done*) gut!; **~ old Charles!** der gute alte Charles!; **the ~ ship Santa Maria** die Santa Maria; **if you can't be ~, be careful** wenn du es schon tun mußt, sei wenigstens vorsichtig.
(f) (*valid*) *advice, excuse* gut; *reason also* triftig; *ticket* gültig; (*Comm: sound*) *debt* gedeckt; *risk* sicher ◆ **is his credit ~?** ist er kreditfähig?; **what** *or* **how much is he ~ for?** (*will he give us*) mit wieviel kann man bei ihm rechnen?; (*does he have*) wieviel hat er?; (*Comm*) wieviel Kredit hat er?; **he's ~ for £10,000** bei ihm kannst du mit £ 10.000 rechnen/er hat gut und gern £ 10.000/er hat bis zu £ 10.000 Kredit; **he/the car is ~ for another few years** mit ihm kann man noch ein paar Jahre rechnen/das Auto hält *or* tut's (*inf*) noch ein paar Jahre; **I'm ~ for another 5 miles** (*inf*) ich schaffe noch 5 Meilen (*inf*).
(g) (*handsome*) *looks, figure, features* gut; *legs also* schön ◆ **a ~ appearance** eine gute Erscheinung, ein gepflegtes Äußeres; **you look ~ in that** du siehst gut darin aus, das steht dir gut.
(h) (*thorough*) gut, gründlich, tüchtig (*inf*) ◆ **to give sb a ~ scolding** jdn gründlich *or* tüchtig ausschimpfen; **to give sth a ~ clean** etw gut *or* gründlich reinigen; **to have a ~ cry/laugh** sich ausweinen/ordentlich *or* so richtig lachen (*inf*); **to take a ~ look at sth** sich (*dat*) etw gut ansehen; **to have a ~ grounding in sth** gute Grundkenntnisse in etw (*dat*) haben.
(i) (*considerable, not less than*) *hour, while* gut; *amount, distance, way also* schön ◆ **it's a ~ distance** es ist ein ganz schönes Stück (*inf*) *or* eine ganz schöne Strecke; **it's a ~ 8 km** es sind gute 8 km; **a ~ deal of effort/money** beträchtliche Mühe/ziemlich viel Geld; **he ate a ~ half of the chocolates at once** er hat gut und gern die Hälfte der Pralinen auf einmal gegessen; **a ~ many/few people** ziemlich viele/nicht gerade wenig Leute.
(j) as ~ as so gut wie; **as ~ as new/settled** so gut wie neu/abgemacht; **he was as ~ as his word** er hat sein Wort gehalten; **he as ~ as called me a liar/invited me to come** er nannte mich praktisch einen Lügner/er hat mich praktisch eingeladen.
(k) (*in greetings*) gut ◆ **~ morning** guten Morgen.
(l) (*in exclamations*) gut, prima ◆ **that's ~!** gut!, prima!; **(it's) ~ to see you/to be here** (es ist) schön, dich zu sehen/hier zu sein; **~, I think that'll be all** gut *or* fein, ich glaube das reicht; **~ enough!** (*OK*) schön!; **~ heavens** *or* **Lord** *or* **God!** um Himmels willen! (*inf*); **~ grief** *or* **gracious!** ach du liebe *or* meine Güte! (*inf*); **very ~, sir** jawohl, sehr wohl (*old*); **~ for** *or* **on** (*Austral*) **you/him** *etc!* gut!, prima!; (*iro also*) das ist ja toll!
[2] *adv* **(a)** schön ◆ **a ~ strong stick/old age** ein schön(er) starker Stock/ein schön(es) hohes Alter; **~ and hard/proper/strong** (*inf*) ganz schön fest/ganz anständig/schön stark (*inf*).
(b) (*incorrect for* **well**) gut.
[3] *n* **(a)** (*what is morally right*) Gute(s) *nt* ◆ **~ and evil** Gut(es) und Böse(s); **to do ~** Gutes tun; **there's some ~ in everybody** in jedem steckt etwas Gutes; **to be up to no ~** (*inf*) etwas im Schilde führen (*inf*), nichts Gutes im Schilde führen (*inf*).
(b) (*advantage, benefit*) Wohl *nt* ◆ **the common ~** das Gemeinwohl; **for the ~ of the nation** zum Wohl(e) der Nation; **to stick to sb for ~ or ill** jdm in guten wie in schlechten Zeiten beistehen; **it's done now, for ~ or ill** es ist nun einmal geschehen; **I did it for your own ~** ich meine es nur gut mit dir, es war nur zu deinem Besten; **for the ~ of one's health** *etc* seiner Gesundheit *etc* zuliebe; **we were 5 glasses/£5 to the ~** wir hatten 5 Glas zuviel/£ 5 plus; **that's all to the ~** auch gut!; **he'll come to no ~** mit ihm wird es noch ein böses Ende nehmen.
(c) (*use*) **what's the ~ of hurrying?** wozu eigentlich die Eile?; **he's no ~ to us** er nützt uns (*dat*) nichts; **it's no ~ complaining to me** es ist sinnlos *or* es nützt nichts, sich bei mir zu beklagen; **it would be some ~** es wäre ganz nützlich; **if that is any ~ to you** wenn es dir hilft; **the applicant was no ~** der Bewerber war nicht gut; **he wasn't any ~ for the job** er eignete sich nicht für die Arbeit; **I'm no ~ at things like that** ich bin nicht gut in solchen Dingen.
(d) to do (some) ~ (etwas) helfen *or* nützen; **to do sb (some) ~** jdm helfen; (*rest, drink, medicine etc*) jdm guttun; **what ~ will that do you?** was hast du davon?; **much ~ may it do you** (*iro inf*) na, dann viel Vergnügen! (*iro inf*); **that won't do much/any ~** das hilft auch nicht viel/nichts; **that won't do you much/any ~** das hilft dir auch nicht viel/nichts; (*will be unhealthy etc*) das ist nicht gut für dich; **a (fat) lot of ~ that will do!** (*iro inf*) als ob das viel helfen würde! (*iro*); **a (fat) lot of ~ that will do you!** (*iro inf*) und wie dir das guttun wird! (*iro inf*).
(e) (*for ever*) **for ~ (and all)** für immer (und ewig).
(f) (*pl: people of virtue*) **the ~** die Guten *pl*.

good: ~bye, (*US*) **~by** [1] *n* Abschied *m*, Lebewohl *nt* (*geh*); **to say ~bye, to make one's ~byes** sich verabschieden, Lebewohl sagen (*geh*); **to wish sb ~bye, to say ~bye to sb** sich von jdm verabschieden, von jdm Abschied nehmen; **to say ~bye to sth** einer Sache (*dat*) Lebewohl sagen; **well, it's ~bye to all that** damit ist es jetzt vorbei; **when all the ~byes were over** als das Abschiednehmen vorbei war; [2] *interj* auf Wiedersehen, lebe wohl (*geh*); [3] *adj attr* Abschieds-; **~-for-nothing** [1] *n* Nichtsnutz, Taugenichts *m*; [2] *adj* nichtsnutzig; **his ~-for-nothing brother** sein Nichtsnutz von Bruder; **G~ Friday** *n* Karfreitag *m*; **~-hearted** *adj* gutherzig; **~-humoured,** (*US*) **~-humored** *adj* gut gelaunt; (*good-natured*) gutmütig.

goodish ['gʊdɪʃ] *adj* (*quite good*) ganz gut, anständig (*inf*); (*considerable*) ganz schön.

good: ~-looker *n* (*inf*) **to be a real ~-looker** wirklich gut *or* klasse (*inf*) aussehen; **~-looking** *adj* gutaussehend.

goodly ['gʊdlɪ] *adj* ansehnlich, stattlich (*geh*).

good: ~-natured *adj* gutmütig; *joke* harmlos; **~-naturedly** *adv* gutmütig.

goodness ['gʊdnɪs] *n* **(a)** Güte *f*; (*of person also*) Gütigkeit *f*; (*of food also*) Nährgehalt *m* ◆ **~ of heart** Herzensgüte *f*; **would you have the ~ to ...** (*form*) hätten Sie bitte die Güte, zu ... (*geh*).
(b) (*in exclamations etc*) **~ knows** weiß der Himmel (*inf*); **for ~' sake** um Himmels willen (*inf*); **I wish to ~ I had gone** wenn ich doch bloß gegangen wäre!; **(my) ~!** meine Güte! (*inf*); **~ gracious** *or* **me!** ach du liebe *or* meine Güte! (*inf*).

goodnight [gʊd'naɪt] *adj attr* Gutenacht-.

goods [gʊdz] *npl* Güter *pl* (*also Comm*); (*merchandise also*) Waren *pl*; (*possessions also*) Gut *nt* (*geh*), Habe *f* (*geh, liter*) ◆ **leather/manufactured ~** Leder-/Fertigwaren *pl*; **canned ~** Konserven *pl*; **stolen ~** gestohlene Waren *pl*, Diebesgut *nt*; **~ depot/train/wagon/yard** Güterdepot *nt*/-zug *m*/-wagen *m*/-bahnhof *m*; **one's ~ and chattels** sein Hab und Gut (*also Jur*), seine Siebensachen (*inf*); **to send sth ~** etw als Frachtgut schicken; **it's the ~** (*esp US inf*) das ist große Klasse (*inf*); **to get/have the ~ on sb** (*esp US inf*) gegen jdn etwas in die Hand bekommen/in der Hand haben; **if we don't produce the ~ on time** (*inf*) wenn wir es nicht rechtzeitig schaffen.

good: ~-sized *adj* ziemlich groß; *building, room also* geräumig; **~-tempered** *adj person* verträglich; *animal* gutartig; *smile, look* gutmütig; **~-time Charlie** *n* (*US inf*) Luftikus, (Bruder) Leichtfuß *m*; **~-time girl** *n* Playgirl *nt*; (*prostitute*) Freudenmädchen *nt*; **~will** *n* Wohlwollen *nt*; (*between nations, Comm*) Goodwill *m*; **a gesture of ~will** ein Zeichen seines/ihres *etc* guten Willens; **to gain sb's ~will** jds Gunst gewinnen; **~will mission/tour** Goodwillreise *f*/-tour *f*.

goody ['gʊdɪ] (*inf*) [1] *interj* toll, prima ◆ **~, ~ gumdrops!** (*hum*) juchhei, juchhe!
[2] *n* **(a)** (*person*) Gute(r) *m*. **(b)** (*delicacy*) gute Sache (*inf*), Leckerbissen *m*; (*sweet*) Süßigkeit *f*. **(c)** (*inf: good joke etc*) guter Witz/gute Geschichte *etc* ◆ **that's a ~!** der/das ist gut!

goody-goody ['gʊdɪ,gʊdɪ] (*inf*) [1] *n* Tugendlamm, Musterkind (*inf*) *nt*.
[2] *adj* tugendhaft, superbrav (*pej inf*); *attitude, behaviour also* musterhaft; (*pretending*) scheinheilig.

gooey ['gu:ɪ] *adj* (*+er*) (*inf*) **(a)** (*sticky*) klebrig; *pudding* pappig, matschig; *toffees, centres of chocolates* weich und klebrig; *cake* üppig. **(b)** (*sentimental*) schnulzig (*inf*), rührselig ◆ **a ~ song** eine Schnulze.

goof [gu:f] (*inf*) [1] *n* **(a)** (*esp US: idiot*) Dussel (*inf*), Doofie (*inf*) *m*. **(b)** (*mistake*) Schnitzer *m* (*inf*), dicker Hund (*sl*).
[2] *vi* **(a)** (*blunder*) sich (*dat*) etwas leisten (*inf*), danebenhauen (*inf*). **(b)** (*US: loiter*) (*also* **~ around**) (herum)trödeln, bummeln ◆ **to ~ over/off** herüberschlendern *or* -zockeln (*inf*)/abzwitschern (*inf*).

◆**goof up** *vt sep* (*inf*) vermasseln (*inf*), vermurksen (*inf*).

goofball ['gu:fbɔ:l] *n* (*esp US sl*) Schnellmacher *m* (*sl*).

goofy ['gu:fɪ] *adj* (*+er*) (*inf*) dämlich (*inf*), doof (*inf*).

googly ['gu:glɪ] *n* (*Cricket*) gedrehter Ball.

goon [gu:n] *n* **(a)** (*inf: idiot*) Idiot, Dussel (*inf*) *m*. **(b)** (*US sl: hired thug*) Schlägertyp *m* (*sl*).

goose [gu:s] [1] *n, pl* **geese** (*lit, inf*) Gans *f* ◆ **silly little ~!** (*inf*) dummes Gänschen! (*inf*); **all his geese are swans** bei ihm ist immer alles besser; **to kill the ~ that lays the golden eggs** das Huhn schlachten, das die goldenen Eier legt.
[2] *vt* (*inf*) einen Klaps auf den Hintern geben (+ *dat*) (*inf*).

gooseberry ['gʊzbərɪ] *n* (*plant, fruit*) Stachelbeere *f* ◆ **~ bush** Stachelbeerstrauch *m*; **to play ~** (*inf*) Anstandswauwau spielen (*inf*), das fünfte Rad am Wagen sein.

goose: ~flesh *n see* **~pimples**; **~-neck lamp** *n* Bogenleuchte *f*; **~pimples** *npl* Gänsehaut *f*; **to come out in ~pimples** eine Gänsehaut bekommen; **that**

➤ LANGUAGE IN USE: goods → 20.5

gives me ~pimples da(bei) bekomme ich eine Gänsehaut; **~-step** [1] *n* Stechschritt *m;* [2] *vi* im Stechschritt marschieren.

GOP *(US Pol) abbr of* **Grand Old Party.**

gopher ['gəʊfə^r] *n* Taschenratte *f; (squirrel)* Ziesel *m.*

gorblimey [ˌgɔː'blaɪmɪ] *interj (Brit inf)* ach du grüne Neune *(inf)*, ich denk' mich laust der Affe *(inf)*.

Gordian ['gɔːdɪən] *adj* gordisch ◆ **to cut the ~ knot** den gordischen Knoten durchhauen.

gore¹ [gɔː^r] *n (liter: blood)* Blut *nt.*

gore² *vt* aufspießen, durchbohren ◆ **~d to death by a bull** durch die Hörner eines Stiers tödlich verletzt.

gore³ *n (panel)* Bahn *f; (in sail)* Gehren *m.*

gored [gɔːd] *adj* mit Bahnen ◆ **~ skirt** Bahnenrock *m.*

gorge [gɔːdʒ] [1] *n* **(a)** *(Geog)* Schlucht *f.* **(b)** *(old: gullet)* Schlund *m* ◆ **it stuck in my ~ to ...** *(fig)* es war mir zuwider, zu ...; **it makes my ~ rise** *(fig: make angry)* dabei kommt mir die Galle hoch.
[2] *vr* schlemmen, sich vollessen; *(animal)* gierig fressen, schlingen ◆ **to ~ oneself on** *or* **with sth** etw in sich *(acc)* hineinschlingen, etw verschlingen.
[3] *vt* **they were ~d** sie hatten sich reichlich gesättigt *(with* an *+dat)*; *(animals)* sie hatten sich vollgefressen *(with* an *+dat)*.

gorgeous ['gɔːdʒəs] *adj* herrlich, großartig, sagenhaft *(inf)*; *(beautiful also) woman* hinreißend; *(richly coloured)* prächtig.

gorgeously ['gɔːdʒəslɪ] *adv see adj* ◆ **~ dressed in silks** in (farben)prächtigen Seidengewändern.

gorgeousness ['gɔːdʒəsnɪs] *n* Großartigkeit, Pracht *f; (beauty)* hinreißende Schönheit; *(colourfulness)* (Farben)pracht *f.*

Gorgon ['gɔːgən] *n (Myth)* Gorgo *f; (inf)* Drachen *m (inf)*.

gorgonzola [ˌgɔːgən'zəʊlə] *n* Gorgonzola *m.*

gorilla [gə'rɪlə] *n* Gorilla *m.*

gormless ['gɔːmlɪs] *adj (Brit inf)* doof *(inf)*.

gorse [gɔːs] *n* Stechginster *m* ◆ **~ bush** Stechginsterstrauch *m.*

gory ['gɔːrɪ] *adj (+er) battle etc* blutig; *person* blutbesudelt ◆ **all the ~ details** all die blutrünstigen Einzelheiten; *(fig)* die peinlichsten Einzelheiten.

gosh [gɒʃ] *interj* Mensch *(inf)*, Mann *(sl)*.

goshawk ['gɒshɔːk] *n* (Hühner)habicht *m.*

gosling ['gɒzlɪŋ] *n* junge Gans, Gänschen *nt.*

go-slow ['gəʊsləʊ] *n* Bummelstreik *m.*

gospel ['gɒspəl] *n* **(a)** *(Bibl)* Evangelium *nt* ◆ **the G~s** das Evangelium, die Evangelien *pl;* **the G~ according to St John** das Evangelium nach Johannes; **St John's G~** das Johannesevangelium; **the G~ for today** das heutige Evangelium.
(b) *(fig: doctrine)* Grundsätze, Prinzipien *pl; (of ideology, religion)* Lehre *f* ◆ **to preach/spread the ~ of temperance** Abstinenz predigen/sich für Abstinenz einsetzen; **she's a firm believer in the ~ of soap and water** sie ist eine überzeugte Anhängerin von Wasser und Seife; **to take sth for** *or* **as ~** etw für bare Münze nehmen *(inf)*; **what he said was always ~ to her** alles, was er sagte, war für sie (ein) Evangelium.
(c) *(Mus)* Gospel *m.*

gospeller ['gɒspələ^r] *n see* **hot ~.**

gospel: ~ song *n* Gospel(lied) *nt;* **~ truth** *n (inf)* reine Wahrheit.

gossamer ['gɒsəmə^r] [1] *n* **(a)** Spinnfäden, Marienfäden *pl.* **(b)** *(Tex)* hauchdünne Gaze.
[2] *adj* hauchdünn.

gossip ['gɒsɪp] [1] *n* **(a)** Klatsch, Tratsch *(inf) m; (chat)* Schwatz *m* ◆ **to have a ~ with sb** mit jdm schwatzen *or* plauschen *(inf) or* klönen *(N Ger)*; **it started a lot of ~** es gab Anlaß zu vielem Gerede *or* Klatsch *or* Tratsch *(inf)*; **office ~** Bürotratsch *m (inf)*. **(b)** *(person)* Klatschbase *f.*
[2] *vi* schwatzen, plauschen *(inf)*, klönen *(N Ger)*; *(maliciously)* klatschen, tratschen *(inf)*.

gossip: ~ column *n* Klatschkolumne *or* -spalte *f;* **~ columnist** *n* Klatschkolumnist(in *f*) *m.*

gossiping ['gɒsɪpɪŋ] [1] *adj* geschwätzig, schwatzhaft; *(malicious)* klatschsüchtig ◆ **to have a ~ tongue** ein Klatschmaul sein *(inf)*; **her ~ tongue will get her into trouble** ihre Klatschsucht wird ihr noch einmal Unannehmlichkeiten einbringen.
[2] *n* Geschwätz *nt; (malicious)* Geklatsche, Getratsche *(inf) nt* ◆ **there's too much ~ and not enough work in this office** in diesem Büro wird zuviel geschwatzt und zuwenig gearbeitet.

gossip: ~monger *n* Klatschmaul *nt (inf)*; **~mongering** *n* Klatscherei, Tratscherei *(inf) f.*

gossipy ['gɒsɪpɪ] *adj person* geschwätzig; *book, letter* im Plauderton geschrieben ◆ **a long ~ phone call** ein langer Schwatz *or* Tratsch am Telefon *(inf)*; **~ style** Plauderton *m.*

got [gɒt] *pret, ptp of* **get.**

Goth [gɒθ] *n* Gote *m.*

Gothic ['gɒθɪk] [1] *adj* **(a)** *people, language* gotisch. **(b)** *architecture etc* gotisch; *(fig)* vorsintflutlich ◆ **~ revival** Neugotik *f;* **~ novel** *(Liter)* Schauerroman *m.*
(c) *(Typ)* gotisch; *(US)* grotesk.
[2] *n* **(a)** *(language)* Gotisch *nt.*
(b) *(type)* Gotisch *nt; (US)* Grotesk *f.*

gotten ['gɒtn] *(esp US) ptp of* **get.**

gouache [gʊ'ɑːʃ] *n* Guasch, Gouache *f.*

gouge [gaʊdʒ] [1] *n (tool)* Hohlmeißel *or* -beitel *m; (groove)* Rille, Furche *f.*
[2] *vt* bohren ◆ **the river ~d a channel in the mountainside** der Fluß grub sich *(dat)* sein Bett in den Berg.

◆**gouge out** *vt sep* herausbohren ◆ **to ~ sb's eyes ~** jdm die Augen ausstechen.

goulash ['guːlæʃ] *n* Gulasch *nt.*

gourd [gʊəd] *n* Flaschenkürbis *m; (dried)* Kürbisflasche *f.*

gourmand ['gʊəmənd] *n* Schlemmer, Gourmand *m.*

gourmet ['gʊəmeɪ] *n* Feinschmecker, Gourmet *m.*

gout [gaʊt] *n (Med)* Gicht *f.*

gouty ['gaʊtɪ] *adj (+er) person* gichtkrank; *limb, joint also* gichtisch; *symptoms* Gicht-.

Gov *abbr of* **governor.**

govern ['gʌvən] [1] *vt* **(a)** *(rule) country* regieren; *province, colony, school etc* verwalten.
(b) *(control) (rules, laws etc)* bestimmen; *(legislation)* regeln; *(determine, influence) choice, decision also, development, person, actions* beeinflussen; *life* beherrschen ◆ **regulations ~ing the sale of spirits** Bestimmungen über den Verkauf von Spirituosen; **to be ~ed by sb's wishes** sich nach jds Wünschen richten.
(c) *(hold in check) passions etc* beherrschen; *(Mech) speed, engine* regulieren ◆ **to ~ one's temper** sich beherrschen.
(d) *(Gram) case* regieren ◆ **the number of the verb is ~ed by the subject** das Verb richtet sich in der Zahl nach dem Subjekt.
[2] *vi (Pol)* regieren, an der Regierung sein.

governable ['gʌvənəbl] *adj* regierbar.

governess ['gʌvənɪs] *n* Gouvernante, Hauslehrerin *f.*

governing ['gʌvənɪŋ] *adj* **(a)** *(ruling)* regierend ◆ **the ~ party** die Regierungspartei; **~ body** Vorstand *m.* **(b)** *(guiding, controlling)* beherrschend, entscheidend ◆ **~ principle** Leitgedanke *m;* **money was the ~ passion of his life** die Geldgier beherrschte sein Leben.

government ['gʌvən mənt] *n* **(a)** *(action of governing, body of administrators)* Regierung *f* ◆ **strong ~ is difficult in a democracy** es ist schwierig, in einer Demokratie mit fester Hand zu regieren; **to form a ~** eine Regierung bilden.
(b) *(system)* Regierungsform *f.*

government *in cpds* Regierungs-, der Regierung; *agency* staatlich ◆ **~ action** Maßnahmen *pl* der Regierung; *(intervention)* staatlicher Eingriff.

governmental [ˌgʌvən'mentl] *adj* Regierungs- ◆ **~ publication** Veröffentlichung *f* der Regierung.

government: ~ backing *n* staatliche Unterstützung; **~ department** *n* Ministerium *nt;* **~ grant** *n* (staatliche) Subvention; **G~ House** *n* Gouverneursresidenz *f;* **~ intervention** *n* staatlicher Eingriff; **~ loan** *n* Staatsanleihe *f;* **~ monopoly** *n* Staatsmonopol *nt,* staatliches Monopol; **~ securities** *npl* Staatsanleihen *pl;* **~ spending** *n* öffentliche Ausgaben *pl;* **~ stocks** *npl (Fin)* Staatspapiere *or* -anleihen *pl.*

governor ['gʌvənə^r] *n* **(a)** *(of colony, state etc)* Gouverneur *m* ◆ **~-general** *(Brit)* Generalgouverneur *m.*
(b) *(esp Brit: of bank, prison)* Direktor *m; (of school)* ≃ Mitglied *nt* des Schulbeirats ◆ **the (board of) ~s** der Vorstand; *(of bank also)* das Direktorium; *(of school)* ≃ der Schulbeirat.
(c) *(Brit inf) (boss)* Chef *m (inf)*; *(father)* alter Herr *(inf)*.
(d) *(Mech)* Regler *m.*

governorship ['gʌvənəʃɪp] *n (office)* Gouverneursamt *nt; (period)* Amtszeit *f* als Gouverneur.

govt *abbr of* **government** Reg.

gown [gaʊn] [1] *n* **(a)** Kleid *nt; (evening ~)* Robe *f,* Abendkleid *nt; (dressing ~)* Morgenmantel *m.* **(b)** *(academic ~)* Robe *f; (of clergyman, judge)* Talar *m; see* **town.**
[2] *vt* kleiden ◆ **to be ~ed by sb** von jdm eingekleidet werden.

GP *(Brit) abbr of* **general practitioner.**

GPO *abbr of* **General Post Office.**

gr [1] *n abbr of* **gross¹** Gr.
[2] *adj abbr of* **gross²** btto.

grab [græb] [1] *n* **(a)** Griff *m* ◆ **to make a ~ at** *or* **for sth** nach etw greifen *or* schnappen *(inf)*.
(b) *(Mech)* Greifer *m.*
(c) *(inf)* **to be up for ~s** zu haben sein *(inf)*; **~ bag** *(US)* Glücksbeutel, Krabbelsack *m.*
[2] *vt* **(a)** *(seize)* packen; *(greedily also)* sich *(dat)* schnappen *(inf)*; *(take, obtain)* wegschnappen *(inf)*; *money* raffen; *(inf: catch) person* schnappen *(inf)*; *chance* beim Schopf ergreifen *(inf)* ◆ **he ~bed my sleeve** er packte mich am Ärmel; **to ~ sth away from sb** jdm etw wegreißen; **the job was ~bed from under his nose** die Stelle wurde ihm vor der Nase weggeschnappt *(inf)*.
(b) *(inf: appeal to)* anmachen *(inf)* ◆ **it didn't ~ me** das hat mich nicht angemacht *(inf)*; **how does that ~ you?** wie findest du das?, was meinst du dazu?
[3] *vi* (hastig) zugreifen *or* zupacken ◆ **to ~ at** greifen *or* grapschen *(inf)* nach, packen *(+acc)*; **he ~bed at the chance of promotion** er ließ sich die Chance, befördert zu werden, nicht entgehen; **help yourselves, children, but don't ~** greift zu, Kinder, aber nicht so hastig.

grabby ['græbɪ] *adj (inf) (wanting possessions)* raffgierig, raffsüchtig; *(wanting more)* gierig ◆ **the baby's going through a ~ phase** das Baby grapscht nach allem, was es sieht *(inf)*.

grace [greɪs] [1] *n* **(a)** *no pl (gracefulness, graciousness)* Anmut *f; (of movement also)* Grazie *f; (of monarch etc)* Würde *f* ◆ **written with ~ and charm** reizend und charmant geschrieben; **to do sth with good/bad ~** etw anstandslos/widerwillig *or* unwillig tun; **he bore his defeat with good/bad ~** er nahm

seine Niederlage mit Fassung *or* anstandslos hin/man sah ihm seinen Ärger über die Niederlage an; **he took it with good/bad ~** er machte gute Miene zum bösen Spiel/er war sehr ungehalten darüber; **he had/didn't even have the ~ to apologize** er war so anständig/brachte es nicht einmal fertig, sich zu entschuldigen.
(b) *(pleasing quality)* (angenehme) Eigenschaft ◆ **social ~s** (gesellschaftliche) Umgangsformen *pl*; **a young woman with many ~s** eine sehr kultivierte junge Dame.
(c) *(favour)* **to be in sb's good/bad ~s** bei jdm gut/schlecht angeschrieben sein.
(d) *(respite)* *(for payment)* Zahlungsfrist *f* ◆ **a day's ~** ein Tag *m* Aufschub; **to give sb a few days' ~** jdm ein paar Tage Zeit lassen; **days of ~** *(Comm)* Respekttage *pl*.
(e) *(prayer)* Tischgebet *nt* ◆ **to say ~** das Tischgebet sprechen.
(f) *(mercy)* Gnade *f* ◆ **act of ~** Gnadenakt *m*; **by the ~ of God** durch die Gnade Gottes; **by the ~ of God Queen ...** Königin ... von Gottes Gnaden; **in this year of ~ 1978** im Jahre des Heils 1978; **in a state of ~** *(Eccl)* im Zustand der Gnade; **to fall from ~** in Ungnade fallen.
(g) *(title)* *(duke, duchess)* Hoheit *f*; *(archbishop)* Exzellenz *f* ◆ **Your G~** Euer Gnaden.
(h) *(Myth)* **the G~s** die Grazien *pl*.
(i) *(Mus)* Verzierung *f*, Ornament *nt* ◆ **~ note** Verzierung *f*.
[2] *vt* **(a)** *(adorn)* zieren *(geh)*.
(b) *(honour)* beehren *(with* mit); *performance also, event etc* zieren *(geh)*, sich *(dat)* die Ehre geben bei *(+dat)* ◆ **to ~ the occasion with one's presence** sich *(dat)* die Ehre geben.

graceful ['greɪsfʊl] *adj* anmutig; *outline, appearance also, behaviour* gefällig; *dancer also* graziös; *compliment* charmant, reizend; *letter* reizend ◆ **with a ~ bow** mit einer eleganten *or* charmanten Verbeugung; **he made a ~ apology** er entschuldigte sich auf sehr charmante *or* nette Art.

gracefully ['greɪsfəlɪ] *adv see adj* ◆ **he gave in ~** er gab großzügig(erweise) nach; **we cannot ~ refuse** wir haben keine annehmbare Entschuldigung.

gracefulness ['greɪsfʊlnɪs] *n* Anmut(igkeit) *f*; *(of movement also)* Grazie *f*.

graceless ['greɪslɪs] *adj* **(a)** *(Eccl)* ruchlos, gottlos. **(b)** *(rude)* schroff; *person, behaviour also* ungehobelt; *(lacking charm) teenager* linkisch.

gracious ['greɪʃəs] [1] *adj (kind)* liebenswürdig; *(condescending)* huldvoll; *(lenient, merciful)* gütig, gnädig; *living, way of life, age* kultiviert ◆ **our ~ Queen** unsere gnädige Königin; **by the ~ consent of** mit der gütigen Erlaubnis von; **Lord be ~ unto him** Herr sei ihm gnädig.
[2] *interj* **(good) ~!, ~ me!** du meine Güte!, lieber Himmel!

graciously ['greɪʃəslɪ] *adv see adj*.

graciousness ['greɪʃəsnɪs] *n see adj* Liebenswürdigkeit *f* *(towards* gegenüber *+dat)*; huldvolle Art; Güte, Gnädigkeit *f*; Kultiviertheit *f*.

gradate [grə'deɪt] *vt* abstufen.

gradation [grə'deɪʃən] *n* **(a)** *(step, degree)* Abstufung *f*; *(mark on thermometer etc)* Gradeinteilung *f* ◆ **~s of madness** Stufen *or* Grade des Wahnsinns; **the ~s of public opinion ran from sympathy to anger** die Skala der öffentlichen Meinung reichte von Sympathie bis zu Zorn. **(b)** *(gradual change)* Abstufung *f*.

grade [greɪd] [1] *n* **(a)** *(level, standard)* Niveau *nt*; *(of goods)* (Güte)klasse *f* ◆ **high-/low-~ goods** hoch-/minderwertige Ware; **this is ~ A** *(inf)* das ist I a *(inf)*; **to make the ~** *(fig)* es schaffen *(inf)*.
(b) *(job ~)* Position, Stellung *f*; *(Mil)* Rang, (Dienst)grad *m* *(auch von Beamten)*; *(salary ~)* Klasse, Stufe *f* ◆ **what ~ is your job?** in welcher Gehaltsklasse *or* -stufe sind Sie?
(c) *(Sch)* *(mark)* Note *f*; *(esp US: class)* Klasse *f*.
(d) *(US) see* **gradient**.
(e) *(US)* **at ~** auf gleicher Ebene; **an apartment at ~ (level)** eine Wohnung zu ebener Erde.
[2] *vt* **(a)** *wool, milk, animals* klassifizieren; *eggs, goods also* sortieren; *colours* abstufen; *students* einstufen. **(b)** *(Sch: mark)* benoten. **(c)** *(level) road, slope* ebnen.

◆**grade down** *vt sep (put in lower grade)* niedriger einstufen; *exam paper* schlechter benoten.

◆**grade up** *vt sep* höher einstufen; *exam paper* höher benoten.

grade: ~ crossing *n (US)* Bahnübergang *m*; **~ school** *n (US)* ≃ Grundschule *f*.

gradient ['greɪdɪənt] *n* Neigung *f*; *(upward also)* Steigung *f*; *(downward also)* Gefälle *nt* ◆ **a ~ of 1 in 10** eine Steigung/ein Gefälle von 10%; **what is the ~?** wie groß ist die Steigung/das Gefälle?; **what is the ~ of the hill?** welche Steigung/welches Gefälle hat der Berg?

gradual ['grædjʊəl] *adj* allmählich; *slope* sanft.

gradually ['grædjʊəlɪ] *adv* nach und nach, allmählich; *slope* sanft.

graduate[1] ['grædjʊɪt] *n (Univ)* (Hochschul)absolvent(in *f*) *m*; *(person with degree)* Akademiker(in *f*) *m*; *(US Sch)* Schulabgänger(in *f*) *m* ◆ **high-school ~** ≃ Abiturient(in *f*) *m*.

graduate[2] ['grædjʊeɪt] [1] *vt* **(a)** *(mark)* einteilen, graduieren *(form)*. **(b)** *colours* abstufen. **(c)** *(US Sch)* als Absolventen haben; *(Univ also)* graduieren *(form)*.
[2] *vi* **(a)** *(Univ)* graduieren; *(US Sch)* die Abschlußprüfung bestehen *(from* an *+dat)* ◆ **to ~ from a hard school** *(fig)* eine harte Lehre durchmachen.
(b) *(change by degrees)* allmählich übergehen.

graduate ['grædʊɪt-] *in cpds* für Akademiker; *unemployment* unter den Akademikern; **~ course** *n Kurs m für Studenten mit abgeschlossenem Studium*.

graduated ['grædjʊeɪtɪd] *adj markings, flask* Meß-; *scale* mit Meßeinteilung, graduiert *(form)*; *salary scale, tax* abgestuft.

graduate student ['grædʊɪt-] *n Student(in f) m mit abgeschlossenem Studium*, Jungakademiker(in *f*) *m*.

graduation [,grædjʊ'eɪʃən] *n* **(a)** *(mark)* (Maß)einteilung *f*. **(b)** *(Univ, US Sch: ceremony)* (Ab)schlußfeier *f (mit feierlicher Überreichung der Zeugnisse)* ◆ **his ~ was delayed by illness** wegen Krankheit wurde ihm sein Zeugnis erst später überreicht.

graduation *in cpds* Abschluß-; **~ day** *n* Tag *m* der Abschlußfeier (und Überreichung der Zeugnisse).

graffiti [grə'fi:tɪ] *npl* Graffiti, Wandschmierereien *(pej) pl* ◆ **~ artist** Graffitikünstler(in *f*) *m*; **a (piece of) ~** eine Wandschmiererei, ein Graffito *nt*.

graft [grɑ:ft] [1] *n* **(a)** *(Bot)* (Pfropf)reis *nt*; *(Med)* Transplantat *nt*. **(b)** *(inf: corruption)* Mauschelei *(inf)*, Schiebung *f*. **(c)** *(inf: hard work)* Schufterei *(inf)*, Plackerei *(inf) f*.
[2] *vt (Bot)* (auf)pfropfen *(on* auf *+acc)*; (ein)pfropfen *(in* in *+acc)*; *(Med)* übertragen *(on* auf *+acc)*, einpflanzen *(in* in *+acc)*; *(fig: incorporate)* einbauen *(onto* in *+acc)*; *(artificially)* aufpfropfen *(onto dat)*.
[3] *vi (inf: work hard)* schuften *(at* an *+dat) (inf)*.

◆**graft on** *vt sep see* **graft 2**.

grafter ['grɑ:ftəʳ] *n (inf)* **(a)** Gauner, Halunke *m*. **(b)** *(hard worker)* Arbeitstier *nt (inf)*, Malocher *m (inf)*.

graham ['greɪəm] *adj (US)* Graham-, Weizenschrot- ◆ **~ flour** Weizenschrot(mehl) *nt*.

grail [greɪl] *n* Gral *m*.

grain [greɪn] [1] *n* **(a)** *no pl* Getreide, Korn *nt*.
(b) *(of corn, salt, sand etc)* Korn *nt*; *(fig)* *(of sense, malice)* Spur *f*; *(of truth also)* Körnchen *nt*; *(of hope also)* Funke *m* ◆ **that's a ~ of comfort** das ist wenigstens ein kleiner Trost.
(c) *(of leather)* Narben *m*; *(of cloth)* Strich *m*; *(of meat)* Faser *f*; *(of wood, marble)* Maserung *f*; *(of stone)* Korn, Gefüge *nt*; *(Phot)* Korn *nt* ◆ **it goes against the ~ (with sb)** *(fig)* es geht jdm gegen den Strich.
(d) *(weight)* Gran *nt*.
[2] *vt wood* masern; *leather, paper* narben.

grain: ~ alcohol *n* Äthylalkohol *m*; **~ elevator** *n* Getreideheber *m*.

grainy ['greɪnɪ] *adj (+er)* **(a)** *(granular) texture* körnig; *surface* gekörnt. **(b)** *leather* genarbt; *wood* maserig, gemasert.

gram, gramme [græm] *n* Gramm *nt*.

grammar ['græməʳ] *n* **(a)** *(subject, book)* Grammatik, Sprachlehre *f* ◆ **your ~ is terrible** von Grammatik hast du keine Ahnung; **that is bad ~** das ist grammat(ikal)isch falsch. **(b)** *(inf) see* **~ school**.

grammar book *n* Grammatik(buch *nt*) *f*, Sprachlehrbuch *nt*.

grammarian [grə'mɛərɪən] *n* Grammatiker(in *f*) *m*.

grammar school *n (Brit)* ≃ Gymnasium *nt*; *(US)* ≃ Mittelschule *f (Stufe f zwischen Grundschule und Höherer Schule)*.

grammatical [grə'mætɪkəl] *adj* grammat(ikal)isch; *rules, mistakes also* Grammatik- ◆ **this is not ~** das ist grammatisch *or* grammatikalisch falsch; **to speak ~ English** grammat(ikal)isch richtiges Englisch sprechen.

grammaticality [grə,mætɪ'kælɪtɪ] *n* Grammatikalität *f*.

grammatically [grə'mætɪkəlɪ] *adv* grammat(ikal)isch; *write, speak* grammat(ikal)isch richtig.

gramme *n see* **gram**.

Grammy ['græmɪ] *n (award)* Grammy *m (Schallplattenpreis)*.

gramophone ['græməfəʊn] *n (Brit old)* Grammophon *nt (dated)* ◆ **~ record** Schallplatte *f*.

grampus ['græmpəs] *n* Rundkopf- *or* Rissosdelphin, Grampus *(spec) m* ◆ **to puff/snort like a ~** *(inf)* wie eine Lokomotive schnaufen *(inf)*.

gran [græn] *n (inf)* Oma *(inf)*, Omi *(inf) f*.

granary ['grænərɪ] *n* Kornkammer *f (also fig)*, Kornspeicher *m*.

grand [grænd] [1] *adj (+er)* **(a)** *(magnificent, imposing)* großartig *(also pej)*; *building, display* prachtvoll; *(lofty) idea* großartig, hochfliegend; *(dignified) air, person* feierlich, hoheitsvoll, würdevoll; *(posh) dinner party, person* vornehm, protzig *(pej)*; *(important, great) person* groß, bedeutend ◆ **to live in ~ style** in großem Stil *or* großartig leben; **the ~ old man** der große Alte; **the G~ Old Party** *(US Pol: abbr* **GOP**) die Republikanische Partei; *see* **manner**.
(b) *(main) question, room* groß; *staircase also* Haupt-.
(c) *(complete, final) total, result, design* Gesamt-.
(d) *(inf: splendid, fine)* fabelhaft, phantastisch *(inf)* ◆ **to have a ~ time** sich glänzend amüsieren.
(e) *(in titles)* Groß- ◆ **~ master** Großmeister *m*.
[2] *n* **(a)** *(sl)* ≃ Riese *m (inf) (1000 Dollar/Pfund)* ◆ **50 ~** 50 Riesen *(inf)*. **(b)** *(piano)* Flügel *m*.

grand: G~ Canary *n* Gran Canaria *nt*; **G~ Canyon** *n* Grand Canyon *m*; **~child** *n* Enkel(kind *nt*) *m*; **~(d)ad** *n (inf)*, Opa *(inf)* Opi *(inf) m*; **~daughter** *n* Enkelin *f*.

grandee [græn'di:] *n (of Spain)* Grande *m*; *(fig)* Fürst *m (inf)* ◆ **the local ~s** die lokalen Honoratioren *pl (hum inf)*.

grandeur ['grændjəʳ] *n* Größe *f*; *(of scenery, music also)* Erhabenheit *f (of manner also)* Würde, Vornehmheit *f*.

grand: ~father *n* Großvater *m*; **~father clock** *n* Standuhr, Großvateruhr *f*; **~fatherly** *adj* großväterlich; **~ finale** *n* großes Finale.

grandiloquence [græn'dɪləkwəns] *n (of speech, style)* Schwülstigkeit *f*; *(of person)* gewählte *or* geschraubte Ausdrucksweise.

grandiloquent *adj*, **~ly** *adv* [græn'dɪləkwənt, -lɪ] hochtrabend.

grandiose ['grændɪəʊz] *adj (impressive) house, idea, speech* grandios (*also pej*), großartig; (*pej: pompous*) *person, style* schwülstig, bombastisch (*inf*); *idea* grandios, hochfliegend.
grandiosely ['grændɪəʊzlɪ] *adv see adj.*
grand: ~ jury *n* (*US Jur*) Großes Geschworenengericht; **~ larceny** *n* schwerer Diebstahl.
grandly ['grændlɪ] *adv* großartig; *decorated, built, situated* prachtvoll; (*with dignity*) feierlich, hoheitsvoll, würdevoll; (*in style*) vornehm ♦ **he had been thinking ~ of** ... er hatte die großartige *or* hochfliegende Idee, zu ...
grand: ~ma *n* (*inf*) Oma (*inf*), Omi (*inf*) *f*; **~mother** *n* Großmutter *f*; **~motherly** *adj* großmütterlich; **G~ National** *n* Grand National *nt* (*bedeutendes Pferderennen in GB*).
grandness ['grændnɪs] *n see adj (a)* Großartigkeit *f*; Pracht *f*; Feierlichkeit, Würde *f*; Vornehmheit, Protzigkeit (*pej*) *f*; Größe, Bedeutung *f*.
grand: ~ opera *n* große Oper; **~pa** *n* (*inf*) Opa (*inf*), Opi (*inf*) *m*; **~parent** *n* Großelternteil *m* (*form*), Großvater *m*/-mutter *f*; **~parents** *npl* Großeltern *pl*; **~ piano** *n* Flügel *m*; **G~ Prix** *n* Grand Prix *m*; **~ slam** *n* (*Bridge*) Großschlemm *m*; **to win the ~ slam** (*Sport*) alle Wettbewerbe gewinnen; **~son** *n* Enkel(sohn) *m*; **~stand** *n* Haupttribüne *f*; **a ~stand finish** eine Entscheidung auf den letzten Metern; **to have a ~stand view of sth** (direkten) Blick auf etw (*acc*) haben; **~ tour** *n* (*old*) Kavalierstour *f* (*old*).
grange [greɪndʒ] *n* Bauernhof *m*, (kleiner) Gutshof.
granite ['grænɪt] *n* Granit *m*.
granny, grannie ['grænɪ] *n* **(a)** (*inf*) Oma (*inf*), Omi (*inf*) *f*. **(b)** (*also* **~ knot**) Altweiberknoten *m*.
granny: G~ bonds *npl* (*Brit Fin inf*) *indexgebundene staatliche Sparbriefe*; **~ flat** *n* (*Brit*) Einliegerwohnung *f*; **~ glasses** *npl* randlose Brille; **G~ Smith** *n* (*apple*) Granny Smith *m*.
grant [grɑːnt] 1 *vt* **(a)** gewähren (*sb* jdm); *period of grace, privilege also* zugestehen (*sb* jdm); *prayer* erhören; *honour* erweisen (*sb* jdm); *permission* erteilen (*sb* jdm); *request* stattgeben (+*dat*) (*form*); *land, pension* zusprechen, bewilligen (*sb* jdm); *wish* (*give*) gewähren, freistellen (*sb* jdm); (*fulfil*) erfüllen ♦ **I beg your pardon — ~ed** ich bitte (vielmals) um Entschuldigung — sie sei dir gewährt (*hum, form*).
(b) (*admit, agree*) zugeben, zugestehen ♦ **it must be ~ed that** ... man muß zugeben, daß ...; **~ing** *or* **~ed that this is true** ... angenommen, das ist wahr ...; **I ~ you that** da gebe ich dir recht, das gebe ich zu; **to take sb/sb's love/one's wealth for ~ed** jdn/jds Liebe/seinen Reichtum als selbstverständlich hinnehmen; **to take it for ~ed that** ... es selbstverständlich finden *or* als selbstverständlich betrachten, daß ...; **you take too much for ~ed** für dich ist (zu) vieles (einfach) selbstverständlich.
2 *n* (*of money*) Subvention *f*; (*for studying etc*) Stipendium *nt*.
grant: ~-aided *adj student* gefördert; *theatre, school, programme* subventioniert; **~-in-aid** *n* Zuschuß *m*, Beihilfe *f*.
granular ['grænjʊləʳ] *adj* körnig, gekörnt, granular (*spec*); *leather* genarbt, narbig ♦ **if the sugar becomes ~** wenn der Zucker auskristallisiert.
granulated sugar ['grænjʊleɪtɪd'ʃʊgəʳ] *n* Zuckerraffinade *f*.
granule ['grænjuːl] *n* Körnchen *nt*.
grape [greɪp] *n* (Wein)traube, Weinbeere *f* ♦ **a pound of ~s** ein Pfund (Wein)trauben; **a bunch of ~s** eine (ganze)Weintraube; **the juice of the ~** (*liter*) der Rebensaft (*liter*).
grape: ~fruit *n* Grapefruit, Pampelmuse *f*; **~fruit juice** *n* Grapefruitsaft *m*; **~ harvest** *n* Weinlese *f*; **~ hyacinth** *n* Traubenhyazinthe *f*; **~ juice** *n* Traubensaft *m*; **~-shot** *n* (*Hist*) Kartätsche *f*; **~-sugar** *n* Traubenzucker *m*; **~vine** *n* Weinstock *m*; (*inf*) Nachrichtendienst *m* (*inf*); **I heard it on the ~vine** es ist mir zu Ohren gekommen.
graph [grɑːf] *n* Diagramm, Schaubild *nt*; (*Math: of a function*) Graph *m*, Schaubild *nt* ♦ **~ paper** Millimeterpapier *nt*.
grapheme ['græfiːm] *n* Graphem *nt*.
graphic ['græfɪk] *adj* **(a)** grafisch, graphisch ♦ **~ arts** Grafik, Graphik *f*; **~ designer** Grafiker(in *f*), Graphiker(in *f*) *m*; **~ equalizer** (Graphic) Equalizer *m*. **(b)** (*vivid*) *description* plastisch, anschaulich.
graphical ['græfɪkəl] *adj* grafisch, graphisch.
graphically ['græfɪkəlɪ] *adv see adj.*
graphical user interface *n* (*Comput*) grafische Benutzeroberfläche.
graphics ['græfɪks] 1 *n* **(a)** *sing* (*subject*) Zeichnen *nt*, zeichnerische *or* graphische Darstellung. **(b)** *pl* (*drawings*) Zeichnungen, (graphische) Darstellungen *pl*. **(c)** *pl* (*Comput*) Grafik *f* ♦ **can your computer do ~?** ist Ihr Computer grafikfähig?
2 *adj attr* (*Comput*) *software etc* Grafik- ♦ **~ card** Grafikkarte *f*; **~ mode** Grafik-Mode *m*; **~ printer** Grafikdrucker *m*.
graphite ['græfaɪt] *n* Graphit *m*.
graphologist [græ'fɒlədʒɪst] *n* Graphologe *m*, Graphologin *f*.
graphology [græ'fɒlədʒɪ] *n* Graphologie, Handschriftendeutung *f*.
-graphy [-grəfɪ] *n suf* -graphie *f*.
grapnel ['græpnəl] *n* **(a)** (*anchor*) (Dregg)anker, Draggen (*spec*) *m*. **(b)** *see* **grappling iron**.
grapple ['græpl] 1 *n see* **grappling iron**.
2 *vi* (*lit*) ringen, kämpfen ♦ **to ~ with a problem/situation** sich mit einem Problem/einer Situation herumschlagen; **the wrestlers ~d with each other** die Ringer hielten sich in enger Umklammerung.
3 *vt* festhaken; *enemy boat* die Enterhaken verwenden bei ♦ **the boats were ~d together** die Boote waren durch Haken verbunden.
grappling ['græplɪŋ] *n* (*Sport inf*) Ringen *nt*.
grappling iron *n* Haken, Greifer *m*; (*Naut*) Enterhaken *m*.

➤ LANGUAGE IN USE: **grateful: a** → 2.1, 4, 20.1, 22 **gratitude** → 22, 24.4

grasp [grɑːsp] 1 *n* **(a)** (*hold*) Griff *m* ♦ **he held my arm in a strong ~** er hielt meinen Arm mit festem Griff; **just when safety/fame was within his ~** gerade als Sicherheit/Ruhm greifbar nahe war *or* in greifbare Nähe gerückt war.
(b) (*fig: understanding*) Verständnis *nt* ♦ **to have a good ~ of sth** etw gut beherrschen; **her ~ of the language/subject is not very good** sie beherrscht die Sprache/das Gebiet nicht sehr gut; **it is beyond/within his ~** das geht über seinen Verstand/das kann er verstehen *or* begreifen.
2 *vt* **(a)** (*catch hold of*) ergreifen, greifen nach; (*hold tightly*) festhalten ♦ **he ~ed the bundle in his arms** er hielt das Bündel in den Armen; **to ~ a chance/sb's hand** eine Gelegenheit ergreifen/nach jds Hand greifen.
(b) (*fig: understand*) begreifen, erfassen.
3 *vi* **to ~ at sth** (*lit*) nach etw greifen; (*fig*) sich auf etw (*acc*) stürzen; **to ~ at an excuse/an opportunity** eine Entschuldigung begierig aufgreifen/eine Gelegenheit beim Schopfe packen.
grasping ['grɑːspɪŋ] *adj* (*fig*) habgierig.
grass [grɑːs] 1 *n* **(a)** (*plant*) Gras *nt* ♦ **wheat is a ~** der Weizen gehört zu den Gräsern; **blade of ~** Grashalm *m*; **to go to ~** verwildern, von Gras überwuchert werden; **to let the ~ grow under one's feet** etwas/die Sache auf die lange Bank schieben; **the ~ is always greener on the other side of the hill** (*Prov*) auf des Nachbars Feld steht das Korn immer besser (*Prov*), die Kirschen in Nachbars Garten ... (*Prov*).
(b) *no pl* (*lawn*) Rasen *m*; (*pasture*) Weide(land *nt*) *f* ♦ **to play on ~** (*Sport*) auf (dem) Rasen spielen; **the cattle are out at ~** das Vieh ist auf der Weide; **to put** *or* **turn out to ~** *cattle* auf die Weide führen *or* treiben; *old horses* das Gnadenbrot geben (+*dat*); (*inf*) *employee* aufs Abstellgleis schieben (*inf*).
(c) (*sl: marijuana*) Gras *nt* (*sl*).
(d) (*Brit sl: informer*) Spitzel, Singvogel (*sl*) *m*.
2 *vt* (*also* **~ over**) *ground* mit Gras bepflanzen.
3 *vi* (*Brit sl*) singen (*sl*) (*to* bei) ♦ **to ~ on sb** jdn verpfeifen (*inf*).
grass: ~-green *adj* grasgrün; **~hopper** *n* Heuschrecke *f*, Grashüpfer *m* (*inf*); **~land** *n* Grasland *nt*; **~-roots** 1 *npl* Volk *nt*; (*of a party*) Basis *f*, Fußvolk *nt* (*hum inf*); 2 *adj attr* des kleinen Mannes, an der Basis; *democracy* Basis-; **at ~-roots level** an der Basis; **a ~-roots movement to block planning permission** eine Bürgerinitiative zur Verhinderung der Baugenehmigung; **~ seed** *n* Grassamen *m*; **~ skirt** *n* Bastrock *m*; **~ snake** *n* Ringelnatter *f*; **~ widow** *n* Strohwitwe *f*; (*US*) (*divorced*) geschiedene Frau; (*separated*) (von ihrem Mann) getrennt lebende Frau; **~ widower** *n* Strohwitwer *m*; (*US*) (*divorced*) geschiedener Mann; (*separated*) (von seiner Frau) getrennt lebender Mann.
grassy ['grɑːsɪ] *adj* (+*er*) grasig; *slope also* Gras-.
grate¹ [greɪt] *n* (*grid*) Gitter *nt*; (*in fire*) (Feuer)rost *m*; (*fireplace*) Kamin *m*.
grate² 1 *vt* **(a)** (*Cook*) reiben; *vegetables also* raspeln.
(b) (*bottom of car, boat etc: scrape*) streifen; (*person: make a grating noise with*) kratzen mit; *one's teeth* knirschen mit.
2 *vi* (*scrape*) streifen (*against acc*); (*make a noise*) kratzen; (*rusty door*) quietschen; (*feet on gravel*) knirschen; (*fig*) weh tun (*on sb* jdm), krank machen (*on sb* jdn) ♦ **to ~ on sb's nerves/ears** jdm auf die Nerven gehen, jds Nerven/Ohren angreifen.
➤ **grateful** ['greɪtfʊl] *adj* **(a)** dankbar (*to sb* jdm) ♦ **with ~ thanks** mit tiefer *or* aufrichtiger Dankbarkeit. **(b)** (*liter: causing gratitude*) wohltuend, willkommen.
gratefully ['greɪtfəlɪ] *adv* dankbar.
grater ['greɪtəʳ] *n* Reibe *f*; (*for vegetable also*) Raspel *f*.
gratification [,grætɪfɪ'keɪʃən] *n* **(a)** (*pleasure*) Genugtuung *f* ♦ **it is a source of great ~ to me** ich empfinde große Genugtuung darüber. **(b)** (*satisfying: of desires etc*) Befriedigung *f*.
gratify ['grætɪfaɪ] *vt* **(a)** (*give pleasure*) erfreuen ♦ **to be gratified at** *or* **by** *or* **with sth** über etw (*acc*) hoch erfreut sein; **I was gratified to hear that** ... ich habe mit Genugtuung gehört, daß ... **(b)** (*satisfy*) befriedigen, zufriedenstellen.
gratifying ['grætɪfaɪɪŋ] *adj* (sehr) erfreulich ♦ **it is ~ to learn that** ... es ist erfreulich zu erfahren, daß ...
gratifyingly ['grætɪfaɪɪŋlɪ] *adv* erfreulich ♦ **he was ~ pleased** es war erfreulich zu sehen, wie er sich freute.
grating¹ ['greɪtɪŋ] *n* Gitter *nt*.
grating² 1 *adj* kratzend; *sound* (*squeaking*) quietschend; (*rasping*) knirschend; (*on nerves*) auf die Nerven gehend; *voice* schrill.
2 *n* Kratzen *nt*; (*of rusty door*) Quietschen *nt*; (*of teeth, feet on gravel*) Knirschen *nt*.
gratis ['grætɪs] *adj, adv* gratis.
➤ **gratitude** ['grætɪtjuːd] *n* Dankbarkeit *f* (*to* gegenüber).
gratuitous [grə'tjuːɪtəs] *adj* überflüssig, unnötig; (*unasked-for*) unerwünscht.
gratuitously [grə'tjuːɪtəslɪ] *adv* unnötig ♦ **quite ~** ohne ersichtlichen Grund.
gratuity [grə'tjuːɪtɪ] *n* Gratifikation, (Sonder)zuwendung *f*; (*form: tip*) Trinkgeld *nt*.
grave¹ [greɪv] *n* (*lit, fig*) Grab *nt* ♦ **silent as the ~** totenstill; **the house was like a ~** es herrschte Totenstille im Haus; **to turn in one's ~** sich im Grabe herumdrehen; **from beyond the ~** aus dem Jenseits; **to be brought to an early ~** einen frühen Tod finden; **to rise from the ~** von den Toten auferstehen; **to dig one's own ~** (*fig*) sein eigenes Grab graben *or* schaufeln.
grave² *adj* (+*er*) (*earnest, solemn*) ernst; (*serious, important*) schwer; *danger, risk* groß; *error* ernst, gravierend; *situation, matter* ernst, bedenklich; *symptoms* bedenklich, ernstzunehmend; *news* schlimm.
grave³ [grɑːv] 1 *adj* **~ accent** Gravis, Accent grave *m*; (*in Greek*) Gravis *m*; **e**

~, ~ e e Accent grave.
[2] n Gravis m.
grave-digger ['greɪv,dɪgəʳ] n Totengräber m.
gravel ['grævəl] [1] n (a) Kies m; (*large chippings*) Schotter m. **(b)** (*Med*) Nierensand *or* -grieß m; (*in bladder*) Harngrieß m.
[2] *adj attr* Kies- ◆ ~ **path** Kiesweg m; ~ **pit** Kiesgrube f.
[3] *vt path, lane* mit Kies bestreuen; schottern.
gravelled, (*US*) **graveled** ['grævəld] *adj path* Kies-.
gravelly ['grævəlɪ] *adj road* kiesbedeckt; schotterbedeckt; *soil* steinig; (*fig*) *voice* rauh.
gravely ['greɪvlɪ] *adv* ernst; *be mistaken* schwer.
grave mound n Grabhügel m.
graven ['greɪvən] *adj* (*old, liter*) gehauen (*on, in* in +*acc*) ◆ ~ **image** Götzenbild *nt*; **to be ~ on one's memory** sich in jds Gedächtnis (*acc*) eingegraben haben (*geh*).
grave: ~ robber n Grabschänder m; **~side** n **at the ~side** am Grabe; **a ~side service** ein Gottesdienst am Grabe; **~stone** n Grabstein m; **~yard** n Friedhof m; **that ministry is a ~yard of political reputations** in diesem Ministerium hat schon mancher sein politisches Ansehen zu Grabe getragen; **~yard shift** n (*esp US*) Nachtschicht f.
graving dock ['greɪvɪŋ,dɒk] n Trockendock *nt*.
gravitate ['grævɪteɪt] *vi* (*lit*) gravitieren (*form*) (*to(wards)* zu, auf +*acc*), angezogen werden (*to(wards)* von); (*fig*) hingezogen werden (*to(wards)* zu), angezogen werden (*to(wards)* von).
gravitation [,grævɪ'teɪʃən] n (*Phys*) Gravitation, Schwerkraft f; (*fig*) Hinneigung f (*to* zu) ◆ **the hippies' ~ to San Francisco** die Anziehungskraft, die San Francisco auf die Hippies ausübt.
gravitational [,grævɪ'teɪʃənl] *adj* Gravitations- ◆ ~ **field** Gravitations- *or* Schwerefeld *nt*; ~ **force** Schwerkraft f; (*Space*) Andruck m; ~ **pull** Anziehungskraft f.
gravity ['grævɪtɪ] n (a) (*Phys*) Schwere, Schwerkraft f ◆ **the law of ~** das Gravitationsgesetz; **centre of ~** Schwerpunkt m; **force of ~** Schwerkraft f; **~ feed** Fall- *or* Schwerkraftspeisung f; **specific ~** spezifisches Gewicht.
(b) (*seriousness*) *see* **grave²** Ernst m; Schwere f; Größe f; Bedenklichkeit f ◆ **the ~ of the news** die schlimmen Nachrichten.
gravlax ['grævlæks] n *Art Räucherlachs*.
gravy ['greɪvɪ] n (a) (*Cook*) (*juice*) Fleisch- *or* Bratensaft m; (*sauce*) Soße f ◆ ~ **boat** Sauciere, Soßenschüssel f. **(b)** (*US inf*) (*perks*) Spesen *pl*; (*corrupt money*) Schmiergelder *pl* (*inf*) ◆ **to get on the ~ train** auch ein Stück vom Kuchen abbekommen (*inf*); **to ride the ~ train** locker Geld machen (*inf*).
gray *n, adj, vti* (*esp US*) *see* **grey**.
graze¹ [greɪz] [1] *vi* (*cattle etc*) grasen, weiden.
[2] *vt meadow, field* abgrasen, abweiden; *cattle* weiden lassen.
graze² [1] *vt* (*touch lightly*) streifen; (*scrape skin off*) aufschürfen ◆ **to ~ one's knees/oneself** sich (*dat*) die Knie aufschürfen/sich (auf)schürfen.
[2] *vi* streifen ◆ **the car ~d against/along the wall** das Auto hat die Mauer gestreift/ist an der Mauer entlanggestreift.
[3] n Abschürfung, Schürfwunde f.
grazier ['greɪzɪəʳ] n (*esp Brit*) Viehzüchter m.
grazing ['greɪzɪŋ] n Weideland *nt* ◆ **this land offers good ~** dies ist gutes Weideland; **~ land** Weideland *nt*; **~ rights** Weiderechte *pl*.
GRE n (*US Univ*) *abbr of* **Graduate Record Examination** *Zulassungsprüfung f für ein weiterführendes Studium*.
grease [gri:s] [1] n (a) Fett *nt*; (*lubricant also*) Schmierfett *nt*, Schmiere f. **(b)** (*also* **~ wool**) Schweißwolle f.
[2] *vt* fetten; *skin* einfetten, einschmieren (*inf*); (*Aut, Tech*) schmieren ◆ **to ~ back one's hair** sich (*dat*) die Haare mit Pomade nach hinten frisieren; **to ~ sb's palm** (*inf*) jdm etwas zustecken (*inf*), jdn schmieren (*inf*); **like ~d lightning** (*inf*) wie ein geölter Blitz.
grease: ~-gun n Fettspritze *or* -presse f; **~ mark** n Fettfleck m; **~ monkey** n (*inf*) Mechanikerlehrling m; **~ nipple** n Schmiernippel m; **~paint** n (*Theat*) (Fett)schminke f; **~proof** *adj* fettdicht; **~proof paper** Pergamentpapier *nt*.
greaser ['gri:səʳ] n (a) (*sl: motorcyclist*) Motorradfahrer m; (*gang member*) Rocker m (*inf*). **(b)** (*US pej: Latin American*) Latino m (*inf*). **(c)** (*inf: motor mechanic*) Automechaniker m.
grease remover n Fettlösungsmittel *nt*, Entfetter m.
greasiness ['gri:sɪnɪs] n (a) Fettigkeit f; (*of hands etc with engine grease*) Schmierigkeit f; (*slipperiness*) Schlüpfrigkeit f. **(b)** (*pej inf: of manner*) Schmierigkeit f (*pej inf*).
greasy ['gri:sɪ] *adj* (+*er*) **(a)** fettig; (*containing grease*) *food* fett; (*smeared with engine grease*) *machinery, axle* ölig, schmierig; *hands, clothes* schmierig, ölbeschmiert; (*slippery*) *road* glitschig, schlüpfrig ◆ ~ **spoon** (*US sl*) billiges Freßlokal (*sl*). **(b)** (*fig pej*) *person* schmierig; *speech* salbungsvoll.
▼ **great** [greɪt] [1] *adj* (+*er*) **(a)** groß ◆ ~ **big** (*inf*) riesig, Mords- (*inf*); **a ~ friend of ours** ein guter Freund von uns; **of no ~ importance** ziemlich unwichtig; **a ~ deal of** sehr viel; **it annoyed her a ~ deal** es hat sie sehr geärgert; **a ~ number of, a ~ many** eine große Anzahl, sehr viele; **at a ~ pace** sehr schnell, in *or* mit schnellem Tempo; **he lived to a ~ age** er erreichte ein hohes Alter; **to be in ~ favour with sb** bei jdm hoch angeschrieben sein; **~ good fortune** großes Glück; **with ~ good humour** sehr gut gelaunt; **in ~ detail** ganz ausführlich; **with ~ care** ganz vorsichtig; **to take a ~ interest** in sich sehr interessieren für; **she has a ~ heart** sie hat ein gutes Herz; **~ with child** (*old*) gesegneten Leibes (*old, Bibl*).
(b) (*in achievement, character, importance*) *master, writer, statesman* groß; *mind* genial ◆ **Frederick/Alexander the G~** Friedrich/Alexander der Große; **he sat there thinking ~ thoughts** er saß da und hatte geniale Gedanken; **one of his ~est plays** eines seiner bedeutendsten *or* größten Stücke; **one of the ~ minds of our times** einer der großen Geister unserer Zeit; **the G~ Powers** (*Pol*) die Großmächte; **~ landowner/industrialist** Großgrundbesitzer m/Großindustrielle(r) m; **to live in ~ style** auf großem Fuß leben; **the ~ thing is** ... das Wichtigste ist ...; **~ minds think alike** (*inf*) große Geister denken gleich.
▼ **(c)** (*inf: splendid, excellent*) prima (*inf*), Klasse (*inf*), Spitze (*sl*) ◆ **to be ~ at football/at singing/on jazz** ein großer Fußballspieler/Sänger/Jazzkenner sein; **he's a ~ one for cathedrals** Kathedralen sind sein ein und alles; **he's a ~ one for criticizing others** im Kritisieren anderer ist er (ganz) groß; **G~ Scott!** (*old*) großer Gott! (*dated*), lieber Himmel!
[2] n (a) *usu pl* (~ *person*) Größe f.
(b) (*Brit Univ*) **G~s** ≃ Klassische Philologie.
great: ~-aunt n Großtante f; **G~ Barrier Reef** n Großes Barriereriff; **G~ Bear** n Großer Bär; **G~ Britain** n Großbritannien *nt*; **~coat** n Überzieher, Paletot m; **G~ Dane** n Deutsche Dogge; **G~ Divide** n Rocky Mountains *pl*; (*fig: death*) Schwelle f des Todes (*liter*); **the ~ divide between** ... der Abgrund zwischen ... (*dat*).
greater ['greɪtəʳ] *adj, comp of* **great** größer ◆ **to pay ~ attention** besser aufpassen; **of ~ importance is** ... noch wichtiger ist ...; **one of the ~ painters** einer der bedeutenderen Maler; **~ and ~** immer größer; **G~ London** Groß-London *nt*.
greatest ['greɪtɪst] *adj, superl of* **great** größte(r, s) ◆ **with the ~ (of) pleasure** mit dem größten Vergnügen; **he's the ~** (*inf*) er ist der Größte; **it's the ~** (*inf*) das ist das Größte (*sl*), das ist einsame Klasse (*sl*).
great: ~-grandchild n Urenkel(in f) m; **~-grandparents** *npl* Urgroßeltern *pl*; **~-great-grandchild** n Ururenkel(in f) m; **~-great-grandparents** *npl* Urgroßeltern *pl*; **~-hearted** *adj* (*brave*) beherzt; (*generous*) hochherzig; **G~ Lakes** *npl*: **the G~ Lakes** die Großen Seen *pl*.
greatly ['greɪtlɪ] *adv* außerordentlich, sehr; *admired also* stark; *annoyed also* höchst; *improved* bedeutend; *superior* bei weitem ◆ **it is ~ to be feared** es ist stark zu befürchten.
great-nephew ['greɪt,nefju:] n Großneffe m.
greatness ['greɪtnɪs] n Größe f; (*of size, height, degree etc also*) Ausmaß *nt*; (*importance also*) Bedeutung f ◆ **~ of heart** Hochherzigkeit, Großmut f; **~ of mind** Geistesgröße f.
great: ~-niece n Großnichte f; **~ tit** n Kohlmeise f; **~-uncle** n Großonkel m; **G~ Wall of China** n Chinesische Mauer; **G~ War** n: **the G~ War** der Erste Weltkrieg.
grebe [gri:b] n (See)taucher m.
Grecian ['gri:ʃən] *adj* griechisch.
Greco- ['grekəʊ-] *pref* Gräko-, gräko-.
Greece [gri:s] n Griechenland *nt*.
greed [gri:d] n Gier f (*for* nach +*dat*); (*for material wealth also*) Habsucht, Habgier f; (*gluttony*) Gefräßigkeit f ◆ **~ for money/power** Geldgier f/Machtgier f; **the look of ~ in his eyes** der gierige Blick in seinen Augen.
greedily ['gri:dɪlɪ] *adv* gierig.
greediness ['gri:dɪnɪs] n Gierigkeit f; (*gluttony*) Gefräßigkeit f.
greedy ['gri:dɪ] *adj* (+*er*) gierig (*for* auf +*acc*, nach); (*for material wealth also*) habgierig; (*gluttonous*) gefräßig ◆ **~ for power/money** machtgierig/geldgierig; **to be ~ for praise** nach Lob gieren; **don't be so ~!** sei nicht so unbescheiden; **you ~ thing!** du Nimmersatt! (*inf*).
Greek [gri:k] [1] *adj* griechisch ◆ **~ Orthodox Church** griechisch-orthodoxe Kirche.
[2] n (a) Grieche m, Griechin f. **(b)** (*language*) Griechisch *nt* ◆ **it's all ~ to me** (*inf*) das sind böhmische Dörfer für mich (*inf*).
green [gri:n] [1] *adj* (+*er*) **(a)** (*in colour*) grün ◆ **~ beans/peas/salad/vegetables** grüne Bohnen *pl*/Erbsen *pl*/grüner Salat/Grüngemüse *nt*; **to turn ~** (*lit*) grün werden; (*fig: person*) (ganz) grün im Gesicht werden; (*with envy*) blaß *or* grün *or* gelb vor Neid werden.
(b) (*unripe*) *fruit, bacon, wood* grün; *meat* nicht abgehangen; *cheese* jung, unreif ◆ **~ corn** frische Maiskolben *pl*.
(c) (*fig*) (*inexperienced*) grün; (*gullible*) naiv, dumm ◆ **I'm not as ~ as I look** (*inf*) ich bin nicht so dumm, wie ich aussehe.
(d) (*new, fresh*) *memory* frisch.
(e) (*Pol*) *issues etc* grün.
[2] n (a) (*colour*) Grün *nt* ◆ **dressed in ~** grün gekleidet; **decorated in ~s and blues** ganz in Grün und Blau gehalten.
(b) (*piece of land*) Rasen m, Grünfläche f; (*Sport*) Rasen, Platz m; (*Golf*) Grün *nt*; (*village ~*) (Dorf)wiese f, Anger m (*old*).
(c) **~s** *pl* (*Cook*) Grüngemüse *nt*; (*US: greenery*) Grün *nt*; (*foliage*) grüne Zweige *pl*.
(d) (*Pol: person*) Grüne(r) *mf* ◆ **the G~s** die Grünen *pl*.
[3] *adv* (*Pol*) *vote, think* grün.
green: ~back n (*US sl*) Lappen (*sl*), Geldschein m; **~ belt** n Grüngürtel m; **G~ Berets** *npl* (*US Mil*) Kommandotruppe f der US-Streitkräfte; **~ card** n (*Mot Insur*) grüne Karte.
greenery ['gri:nərɪ] n Grün *nt*; (*foliage*) grünes Laub, grüne Zweige *pl*.
green: ~-eyed *adj* (*lit*) grünäugig; (*fig*) scheel(äugig), mißgünstig; **the ~-eyed monster** (*fig*) der blasse Neid; **~field** *adj land etc* unerschlossen; **~field site** unerschlossenes Bauland; **~finch** n Grünfink m; **~ fingers** *npl* gärtnerisches Geschick; **to have ~ fingers** eine Hand für Pflanzen haben; **~fly** n Blattlaus f; **~gage** n Reneklode, Reineclaude f; **~grocer** n (*esp Brit*) (Obst- und) Gemüsehändler m; **at the ~grocer's (shop)** im Gemüseladen; **~grocery** n (*esp Brit*) (*shop*) Obst- und Gemüsehandlung f; (*trade*) Obst-

➤ LANGUAGE IN USE: great: 1a → 3.2, 24.4, 26.1 1c → 13

und Gemüsehandel *m*; (*articles*) Obst und Gemüse *nt*; **~horn** *n* (*inf*) (*inexperienced*) Greenhorn *nt*; (*gullible*) Einfaltspinsel *m*; **~house** *n* Gewächshaus, Treibhaus *nt*; **~house effect** *n* Treibhauseffekt *m*; **~house gas** *n* Treibhausgas *nt*.

greenish ['gri:nɪʃ] *adj* grünlich.

green keeper *n* (*Sport*) Platzwart *m*.

Greenland ['gri:nlənd] *n* Grönland *nt*.

Greenlander ['gri:nləndəʳ] *n* Grönländer(in *f*) *m*.

green: ~ light *n* grünes Licht; **to give sb the ~ light** jdm grünes Licht *or* freie Fahrt geben; **~ man** *n* (*at street crossing*) grünes Licht; (*as said to children*) grünes Männchen.

greenness ['gri:nnɪs] *n see adj* **(a)** Grün *nt*. **(b)** Grünheit *f*; Unabgehangenheit *f*; Unreife *f*. **(c)** Grünheit *f*; Naivität, Dummheit *f*. **(d)** Frische *f*.

green: G~ Paper *n* (*Brit Pol*) Vorlage *f* für eine Parlaments-debatte; **G~ Party** *n*: **the G~ Party** die Grünen *pl*; **G~peace** *n* Greenpeace *nt*; **~ pepper** *n* (grüne) Paprikaschote; **~-room** *n* (*Theat*) Garderobe *f*; **~stick fracture** *n* Grünholzbruch *m*; **~ tea** *n* grüner Tee; **~ thumb** *n* (*US*) *see* **~ fingers**.

Greenwich (Mean) Time ['grenɪdʒ('mi:n),taɪm] *n* westeuropäische Zeit, Greenwicher Zeit *f*.

greenwood ['gri:nwʊd] *n* grüner Wald.

greet [gri:t] *vt* (*welcome*) begrüßen; (*receive, meet*) empfangen; (*say hallo to*) grüßen; *news, decision* aufnehmen ◆ **a terrible sight ~ed his eyes/him** ihm bot sich ein fürchterlicher Anblick; **to ~ sb's ears** an jds Ohr (*acc*) dringen.

greeting ['gri:tɪŋ] *n* Gruß *m*; (*act*) (*welcoming*) Begrüßung *f*; (*receiving, meeting*) Empfang *m* ◆ **we had a friendly ~ from the crowd** die Menge bereitete uns einen freundlichen Empfang; **~s** Grüße *pl*; (*congratulations also*) Glückwünsche *pl*; **~s card/telegram** Grußkarte *f*/-telegramm *nt*; **to send ~s to sb** Grüße an jdn senden; (*through sb else*) jdn grüßen lassen; **please give my ~s to them** bitte grüße sie von mir.

gregarious [grɪ'gɛərɪəs] *adj animal, instinct* Herden-; *person* gesellig.

Gregorian [grɪ'gɔ:rɪən] *adj* Gregorianisch ◆ **~ calendar/chant** Gregorianischer Kalender/Choral *or* Gesang.

gremlin ['gremlɪn] *n* (*hum*) böser Geist, Maschinenteufel *m* (*hum*).

Grenada [gre'neɪdə] *n* Grenada *nt*.

grenade [grɪ'neɪd] *n* Granate *f*.

Grenadian [gre'neɪdɪən] 1 *adj* grenadisch.
2 *n* Grenader(in *f*) *m*.

grenadier [,grenə'dɪəʳ] *n* Grenadier *m*.

grenadine ['grenədi:n] *n* Grenadine *f*.

grew [gru:] *pret of* **grow**.

grey, (*esp US*) **gray** [greɪ] 1 *adj* (*+er*) (*lit, fig*) grau; *day, outlook, prospect etc also* trüb; *life also* öd(e) ◆ **to go** *or* **turn ~** grau werden, ergrauen (*geh*); **little ~ cells** (*inf*) kleine graue Zellen *pl* (*inf*); **a ~ area** (*fig*) eine Grauzone.
2 *n* (*colour*) Grau *nt*; (*horse*) Grauschimmel *m* ◆ **shades of ~** (*Comput*) Graustufen *pl*.
3 *vt* grau werden lassen; *hair, person also* ergrauen lassen (*geh*).
4 *vi* grau werden; (*hair, person also*) ergrauen (*geh*) ◆ **his ~ing hair** sein angegrautes Haar.

grey: ~beard *n* Graubart *m*; **G~ Friar** *n* Franziskanermönch *m*; **~-haired** *adj* grauhaarig; **~hound** *n* Windhund *m*, Windspiel *nt*; **~hound racing** *n* Windhundrennen *nt*.

greyish ['greɪɪʃ] *adj* gräulich.

grey: ~lag (goose) *n* Graugans, Wildgans *f*; **~ matter** *n* (*Med, inf*) graue Zellen *pl*.

greyness ['greɪnɪs] *n* (*lit*) Grau *nt*; (*fig*) Trübheit *f*; (*of life*) Öde *f*.

grey: ~ parrot *n* Graupapagei *m*; **~ squirrel** *n* Grauhörnchen *nt*.

grid [grɪd] *n* **(a)** (*grating*) Gitter *nt*; (*in fireplace, on barbecue*) Rost *m* ◆ **~ system** (*in road-building*) Rechteckschema *nt*.
(b) (*on map*) Gitter, Netz *nt*.
(c) (*electricity, gas network*) Verteilernetz *nt* ◆ **the (national) ~** (*Elec*) das Überland(leitungs)netz.
(d) (*Motor-racing: starting ~*) Start(platz) *m*; (*US Ftbl*) Spielfeld *nt* ◆ **they're on the ~** sie sind auf den Startplätzen.
(e) (*Elec: electrode*) Gitter *nt*.
(f) (*Theat*) Schnürboden *m*.

griddle ['grɪdl] *n* (*Cook*) *gußeiserne Platte zum Pfannkuchenbacken* ◆ **~-cake** kleiner Pfannkuchen.

gridiron ['grɪd,aɪən] *n* **(a)** (*Cook*) (Brat)rost *m*. **(b)** (*US Ftbl*) Spielfeld *nt*.

gridlocked ['grɪdlɒkt] *adj* (*esp US*) **(a)** *road* völlig verstopft ◆ **traffic is ~ in the cities** der Verkehr in den Städten ist zum völligen Stillstand gekommen. **(b)** (*fig: Congress*) festgefahren.

grief [gri:f] *n* Leid *nt*, Kummer, Gram (*geh*) *m*; (*because of loss*) große Trauer, Schmerz, Gram (*geh*) *m* ◆ **to be a cause of ~ to sb** jdn zutiefst betrüben; (*death, loss also*) jdm großen Schmerz bereiten; (*failure, sb's behaviour also*) jdm großen Kummer bereiten; **to come to ~** Schaden erleiden; (*be hurt, damaged*) zu Schaden kommen; (*fail*) scheitern.

grief-stricken ['gri:f,strɪkən] *adj* untröstlich, tieftraurig; *look, voice* schmerzerfüllt, gramgebeugt (*geh*).

grievance ['gri:vəns] *n* Klage *f*; (*resentment*) Groll *m* ◆ **~ procedure** Beschwerdeweg *m*; **I've no ~s against him** (*no cause for complaint*) ich habe an ihm nichts auszusetzen; (*no resentment*) ich nehme ihm nichts übel; **to harbour a ~ against sb for sth** jdm etw übelnehmen; **to air one's ~s** seine Beschwerden vorbringen, sich offen beschweren, sich beklagen.

grieve [gri:v] 1 *vt* Kummer bereiten (*+dat*), betrüben ◆ **it ~s me to see that** ... ich sehe mit Schmerz *or* Kummer, daß ...
2 *vi* sich grämen (*geh*), trauern (*at, about* über *+acc*) ◆ **to ~ for sb/sth** um jdn/etw trauern; **to ~ for sb** (*sympathize with*) zutiefst mit jdm mitfühlen, jds Schmerz teilen; **my heart ~s for you** mir blutet das Herz; **to ~ over sb/sth** sich über jdn/etw grämen (*geh*), über jdn/etw zutiefst bekümmert sein; **she sat grieving over his body** sie saß trauernd bei seinem Leichnam.

grievous ['gri:vəs] *adj* (*severe*) *injury, blow, crime* schwer; *fault, error also* schwerwiegend; *wrong also* groß; (*distressing*) *news* betrüblich, schmerzlich; *pain* groß, schlimm; (*sorrowful*) *cry etc* schmerzlich, schmerzerfüllt ◆ **~ bodily harm** (*Jur*) schwere Körperverletzung.

grievously ['gri:vəslɪ] *adv* schwer; *cry* schmerzlich ◆ **he was ~ at fault in ...** er lud eine schwere Schuld auf sich (*acc*), als ...

griffin ['grɪfɪn], **griffon, gryphon** *n* (*Myth*) (Vogel) Greif *m*.

griffon ['grɪfən] *n* **(a)** (*bird*) (Gänse)geier *m*. **(b)** (*dog*) Griffon, Affenpinscher *m*. **(c)** (*Myth*) *see* **griffin**.

grift [grɪft] (*US sl*) 1 *n* (*money*) ergaunertes *or* erschwindeltes Geld ◆ **to make money on the ~** auf die krumme Tour zu Geld kommen (*sl*).
2 *vi* krumme Dinger drehen (*sl*).

grifter ['grɪftəʳ] *n* (*US sl: swindler*) Gauner, Schwindler *m*.

grig [grɪg] *n*: **merry as a ~** lustig und fidel.

grill [grɪl] 1 *n* **(a)** (*Cook*) (*on cooker etc*) Grill *m*; (*gridiron also*) (Brat)rost *m*; (*food*) Grillgericht *nt*, Grillade *f*; (*restaurant*) Grill(room) *m*. **(b)** *see* **grille**.
2 *vt* **(a)** (*Cook*) grillen. **(b)** (*inf: interrogate*) in die Zange nehmen (*inf*) ◆ **to ~ sb about sth** jdn über etw (*acc*) ausquetschen (*inf*) *or* ins Verhör nehmen.
3 *vi* **(a)** (*food*) auf dem Grill liegen, gegrillt werden. **(b)** (*inf: in sun*) schmoren (*inf*) ◆ **the ~ing heat of the sun** die sengende Sonne(nhitze).

grille [grɪl] *n* Gitter *nt*; (*on window*) Fenstergitter *nt*; (*to speak through*) Sprechgitter *nt*; (*Aut*) Kühlergrill *m*.

grilling ['grɪlɪŋ] *n* strenges Verhör ◆ **to give sb a ~/a ~ about sth** jdn in die Zange *or* die Kur nehmen (*inf*)/jdn über etw (*acc*) ausquetschen (*inf*) *or* ins Verhör nehmen.

grillroom ['grɪlru:m] *n* Grillroom *m*.

grilse [grɪls] *n* junger Lachs.

grim [grɪm] *adj* (*+er*) **(a)** (*cruel, fierce*) *battle, struggle* verbissen, erbittert, unerbittlich; *warrior* erbarmungslos, ingrimmig (*old*); (*stern*) *face, smile, silence* grimmig; *master, teacher* unerbittlich, hart; (*fig*) *landscape, town, prospects* trostlos; *news, joke, tale, task, job* grauenhaft, grausig (*inf*); *winter* hart; *weather* erbarmungslos; *times* hart, schwer; *determination, silence* eisern; *industriousness* verbissen; *necessity, truth* hart, bitter ◆ **a ~ sense of humour** Galgenhumor *m*, ein grimmiger Humor; **to look ~** (*person*) ein grimmiges Gesicht machen; (*things, prospects*) schlimm *or* trostlos aussehen; **to hold on (to sth) like ~ death** sich verbissen (an etw *dat*) festhalten, sich verzweifelt (an etw *dat*) festklammern.
(b) (*inf: unpleasant*) grausig (*inf*), schlimm.

grimace ['grɪməs] 1 *n* Grimasse *f* ◆ **to make a ~** eine Grimasse machen *or* schneiden; (*with disgust, pain also*) das Gesicht verziehen.
2 *vi* Grimassen machen *or* schneiden; (*with disgust, pain etc also*) das Gesicht verziehen.

grime [graɪm] *n* Dreck, Schmutz *m*; (*sooty*) Ruß *m*.

grimly ['grɪmlɪ] *adv fight, struggle, hold on* verbissen; (*sternly*) mit grimmiger Miene; *smile, silent* grimmig; *bleak, barren* trostlos; *depressing* grauenhaft ◆ **~ determined** verbissen.

grimness ['grɪmnɪs] *n see adj (a)* Verbissenheit, Erbittertheit, Unerbittlichkeit *f*; Erbarmungslosigkeit *f*; Grimmigkeit *f*; Härte *f*; Trostlosigkeit *f*; Grauenhaftigkeit *f*.

grimy ['graɪmɪ] *adj* (*+er*) schmutzig; *buildings also* verrußt; (*sooty also*) rußig.

grin [grɪn] 1 *n see vi* Lächeln, Strahlen *nt*; Grinsen *nt*.
2 *vi* (*with pleasure*) lächeln, strahlen; (*in scorn, stupidly, cheekily*) grinsen ◆ **to ~ and bear it** gute Miene zum bösen Spiel machen; (*tolerate pain*) die Zähne zusammenbeißen; **to ~ at sb** jdn anlächeln/angrinsen; **to ~ from ear to ear** über das ganze Gesicht strahlen; **to ~ like a Cheshire cat** wie ein Honigkuchenpferd grinsen *or* strahlen.

grind [graɪnd] (*vb: pret, ptp* **ground**) 1 *vt* **(a)** (*crush*) zerkleinern, zermahlen; *corn, coffee, pepper, flour* mahlen; (*in mortar*) zerstoßen ◆ **to ~ sth to a powder** etw fein zermahlen/zerstoßen; **to ~ one's teeth** mit den Zähnen knirschen.
(b) (*polish, sharpen*) *gem, lens* schleifen; *knife also* wetzen.
(c) (*turn*) *handle, barrel organ* drehen ◆ **to ~ one's cigarette butt/heel into the earth** den Zigarettenstummel in die Erde treten/den Absatz in die Erde bohren.
(d) ground down by poverty von Armut (nieder)gedrückt; **the tyrant ground the people into the dust** der Tyrann hat das Volk zu Tode geschunden.
2 *vi* **(a)** (*mill*) mahlen; (*brakes, teeth, gears*) knirschen ◆ **the metal ground against the stone** das Metall knirschte auf dem Stein; **the ship ground against the rocks** das Schiff lief knirschend auf die Felsen auf; **to ~ to a halt** *or* **standstill** (*lit*) quietschend zum Stehen kommen; (*fig*) stocken; (*production etc*) zum Erliegen kommen; (*negotiations*) sich festfahren; **the process ~s slowly on** das Verfahren schleppt sich hin.
(b) (*inf: study*) büffeln (*inf*).
3 *n* **(a)** (*sound*) Knirschen *nt*; *see* **bump**. **(b)** (*fig inf: drudgery*) Schufterei *f* (*inf*); (*US inf: swot*) Streber(in *f*) *m* (*inf*) ◆ **the daily ~** der tägliche Trott; **it's a real ~** das ist ganz schön mühsam (*inf*).

◆**grind away** *vi* schuften (*inf*) ◆ **to ~ ~ at sth** an etw (*dat*) schuften (*inf*); **to ~ away at Latin** Latein büffeln.

◆**grind down** *vt sep* (*lit*) (*mill*) *pepper etc* zermahlen; (*sea*) *rocks* abschleifen; (*fig*) *people, resistance* zermürben.
◆**grind on** *vi* (*enemy, invasion*) unaufhaltsam vorrücken; (*fig: bureaucracy etc*) unaufhaltsam sein ◆ **to ~ ~ towards sth** einer Sache (*dat*) unaufhaltsam entgegengehen.
◆**grind out** *vt sep article, essay* sich (*dat*) abquälen; *propaganda* ausspucken (*inf*); *tune* orgeln (*inf*).
◆**grind up** *vt sep* zermahlen.
grinder ['graɪndəʳ] *n* **(a)** (*meat~*) Fleischwolf *m*; (*coffee~*) Kaffeemühle *f*; (*for sharpening*) Schleifmaschine *f*; (*stone*) Schleifstein *m*. **(b)** (*person*) Messer-/Glasschleifer(in *f*) *m*. **(c)** (*tooth*) Backenzahn *m*; (*of animals also*) Mahlzahn *m*.
grinding ['graɪndɪŋ] *adj* knirschend; *poverty* drückend ◆ **to come to a ~ halt** quietschend zum Stehen kommen.
grinding wheel *n* Schleifscheibe *f*, Schleifstein *m*.
grindstone ['graɪndstəʊn] *n*: **to keep one's/sb's nose to the ~** hart arbeiten/jdn hart arbeiten lassen; **back to the ~** wieder in die Tretmühle (*hum*).
gringo ['grɪŋgəʊ] *n* (*esp US*) Gringo *m*.
grip [grɪp] [1] *n* **(a)** Griff *m*; (*on rope also, on road*) Halt *m* ◆ **to get a ~ on the road/rope** auf der Straße/am Seil Halt finden; **to get a ~ on oneself** (*inf*) sich zusammenreißen (*inf*); **he had a good ~ on himself** er hatte sich gut im Griff *or* in der Gewalt; **to have a good ~ of a subject/on an audience** ein Thema/ein Publikum im Griff haben; **to let go** *or* **release one's ~** loslassen (*on sth* etw); **to lose one's ~** (*lit*) den Halt verlieren; (*fig*) nachlassen; **the chairman is losing his ~ (on the company)** dem Vorsitzenden entgleiten die Zügel; **I must be losing my ~** mit mir geht's bergab; **to lose one's ~ on reality** den Bezug zur Wirklichkeit verlieren; **to lose one's ~ on a situation** eine Situation nicht mehr im Griff haben; **to lose one's ~ on an audience** ein Publikum aus dem Griff verlieren; **to have sb in one's ~** jdn in seiner Gewalt haben; **to be in the ~ of rage/terror** *etc* von Wut/Angst *etc* erfaßt sein; **the country is in the ~ of a general strike** das Land ist von einem Generalstreik lahmgelegt; **the country is in the ~ of winter** der Winter hat im Land seinen Einzug gehalten; **to get** *or* **come to ~s with sth** mit etw klarkommen (*inf*), etw in den Griff bekommen; **to get** *or* **come to ~s with sb** jdm zu Leibe rücken, zum Angriff gegen jdn übergehen.
(b) (*handle*) Griff *m*.
(c) (*hair~*) Klemmchen *nt*.
(d) (*travelling-bag*) Reisetasche *f*.
[2] *vt* packen; *hand also, (fig: fear etc also)* ergreifen; (*film, story etc also*) fesseln ◆ **the car/tyre ~s the road well** der Wagen liegt gut auf der Straße/der Reifen greift gut; **fear ~ped his heart** Furcht ergriff *or* packte ihn.
[3] *vi* greifen.
gripe [graɪp] [1] *vt* (*US inf: annoy*) aufregen, fuchsen (*inf*).
[2] *vi* (*inf: grumble*) meckern (*inf*), nörgeln ◆ **to ~ at sb** jdn anmeckern (*inf*), jdn anmotzen (*inf*).
[3] *n* **(a) the ~s** *pl* Kolik *f*, Bauchschmerzen *pl* ◆ **~ water** Kolikmittel *nt*. **(b)** (*inf: complaint*) Meckerei *f* (*inf*) ◆ **have you any more ~s?** sonst hast du nichts zu meckern? (*inf*).
grippe [grɪp] *n* (*dated US*) Grippe *f*.
gripping ['grɪpɪŋ] *adj story* spannend, packend, fesselnd.
grisly ['grɪzlɪ] *adj* (*+er*) grausig, gräßlich.
grist [grɪst] *n* **it's all ~ to his/the mill** das kann er/man alles verwerten; (*for complaint*) das ist Wasser auf seine Mühle.
gristle ['grɪsl] *n* Knorpel *m*.
gristly ['grɪslɪ] *adj* (*+er*) knorpelig.
grit [grɪt] [1] *n* **(a)** (*dust, in eye*) Staub *m*; (*gravel*) Splitt *m*, feiner Schotter; (*for roads in winter*) Streusand *m*. **(b)** (*courage*) Mut, Mumm (*inf*) *m*. **(c)** (*US*) **~s** *pl* Grütze *f*.
[2] *vt* **(a)** *road etc* streuen. **(b) to ~ one's teeth** die Zähne zusammenbeißen.
gritter ['grɪtəʳ] *n* Streuwagen *m*.
gritty ['grɪtɪ] *adj* (*+er*) **(a)** Splitt-, Schotter-; *path also* mit Splitt *or* feinem Schotter bedeckt; (*like grit*) *coal, sweets* grobkörnig ◆ **~ sandwiches** sandige Sandwiches. **(b)** (*inf: brave*) tapfer; *person also* mit Mumm (*inf*).
grizzle ['grɪzl] *vi* (*Brit inf*) quengeln.
grizzled ['grɪzld] *adj hair* ergraut; *person also* grauhaarig.
grizzly ['grɪzlɪ] *n* (*also* **~ bear**) Grisly(bär), Grizzly(bär) *m*.
groan [grəʊn] [1] *n* Stöhnen *nt no pl*; (*of pain also, of gate, planks etc*) Ächzen *nt no pl* ◆ **to let out** *or* **give a ~** (auf)stöhnen.
[2] *vi* stöhnen (*with* vor *+dat*); (*with pain also, gate, planks*) ächzen (*with* vor *+dat*) ◆ **the table ~ed under** *or* **beneath the weight** der Tisch ächzte unter der Last; **the country ~ed under** *or* **beneath his rule** das Land ächzte unter seiner Herrschaft.
groat [grəʊt] *n* (*Brit Hist*) *Silbermünze f im Wert von 4 alten Pence* ◆ **I haven't a ~** (*dated*) ich habe keinen roten Heller.
groats [grəʊts] *npl* Schrot *nt or m*; (*porridge*) Grütze *f*.
grocer ['grəʊsəʳ] *n* Lebensmittelhändler, Kaufmann *m* ◆ **at the ~'s** beim Lebensmittelhändler *or* Kaufmann.
grocery ['grəʊsərɪ] *n* **(a)** (*business, shop*) Lebensmittelgeschäft *nt*. **(b) groceries** *pl* (*goods*) Lebensmittel *pl*.
grog [grɒg] *n* Grog *m*.
groggily ['grɒgɪlɪ] *adv* (*inf*) groggy (*inf*); *shake one's head, answer* schwach.
groggy ['grɒgɪ] *adj* (*+er*) (*inf*) angeschlagen (*inf*), groggy *pred inv* (*inf*).
groin [grɔɪn] *n* **(a)** (*Anat*) Leiste *f* ◆ **to kick sb in the ~** jdn in den Unterleib *or* die Leistengegend treten. **(b)** (*Archit*) Grat *m*. **(c)** *see* **groyne**.
grommet ['grɒmɪt] *n* Öse *f*; (*Naut*) Taukranz *m*.
groom [gru:m] [1] *n* **(a)** (*in stables*) Stallbursche, Pferde- *or* Reitknecht *m*. **(b)** (*bride~*) Bräutigam *m*.
[2] *vt* **(a)** *horse* striegeln, putzen ◆ **to ~ oneself** (*birds, animals*) sich putzen; (*people*) sich pflegen; **well/badly ~ed** gepflegt/ungepflegt.
(b) (*prepare*) **he's being ~ed for the job of chairman/for the Presidency** er wird als zukünftiger Vorsitzender/Präsidentschaftskandidat aufgebaut; **to ~ sb for stardom** jdn als Star lancieren; **he is ~ing him as his successor** er zieht sich (*dat*) ihn als Nachfolger heran.
grooming ['gru:mɪŋ] *n* ein gepflegtes Äußeres.
groove [gru:v] [1] *n* Rille *f*; (*in rock also*) Rinne, Furche *f*; (*in face*) Furche *f*; (*fig*) altes Gleis ◆ **to be in the ~** (*dated sl*) in Stimmung sein (*inf*); **his thoughts run in the same old ~s** seine Gedanken bewegen sich immer in denselben Bahnen.
[2] *vt* Rillen machen in (*+acc*), rillen; (*water*) *stone* aushöhlen, Rinnen *pl or* Furchen *pl* machen in (*+acc*); *face* furchen.
[3] *vi* (*dated sl*) einen losmachen (*sl*), sich reinhängen (*sl*).
groover ['gru:vəʳ] *n* (*dated sl*) (*man*) irrer *or* starker Typ (*sl*); (*woman*) irre *or* starke Frau (*sl*).
groovy ['gru:vɪ] *adj* (*+er*) (*sl*) irr (*sl*), stark (*sl*).
grope [grəʊp] [1] *vi* (*also* **~ around** *or* **about**) (herum)tasten (*for* nach); (*for words*) suchen (*for* nach) ◆ **to be groping in the dark** im dunkeln tappen; (*try things at random*) vor sich (*acc*) hin wursteln (*inf*); **groping hands** tastende Hände *pl*.
[2] *vt* tasten nach; (*inf*) *girlfriend* befummeln (*inf*) ◆ **to ~ one's way** sich vorwärtstasten; **to ~ (one's way) in/out** sich hinein-/hinaustasten; **they are groping their way towards a new theory** sie machen tastende Versuche, eine neue Theorie zu entwickeln.
[3] *n* (*inf*) **to have a ~** fummeln (*inf*).
gropingly ['grəʊpɪŋlɪ] *adv* tastend.
grosgrain ['grəʊgreɪn] *n* grob geripptes Seidentuch.
gross[1] [grəʊs] *n no pl* Gros *nt*.
gross[2] [1] *adj* (*+er*) **(a)** (*fat*) *person* dick, fett, plump.
(b) (*coarse, vulgar*) *person, language, joke, indecency* grob, derb; *manners, tastes* roh; *food* grob; *eater, appetite* unmäßig.
(c) (*extreme, flagrant*) kraß; *crime, impertinence* ungeheuerlich; *error, mistake also, negligence* grob.
(d) (*luxuriant*) *vegetation* üppig.
(e) (*total*) brutto; *income, weight* Brutto- ◆ **he earns £2,500 ~** er verdient brutto £ 2.500, er hat einen Bruttolohn von £ 2.500; **~ national product** Bruttosozialprodukt *nt*; **~ ton** Bruttoregistertonne *f*.
[2] *vt* brutto verdienen; (*shop also*) brutto einnehmen.
grossly ['grəʊslɪ] *adv* **(a)** (*coarsely*) *behave, talk* derb, rüde ◆ **to eat ~** essen wie ein Schwein. **(b)** (*extremely*) *indecent, fat, vulgar* ungeheuer, schrecklich; *exaggerated also* grob.
grossness ['grəʊsnɪs] *n see adj (a-d)* **(a)** Körperfülle, Dicke, Fettheit *f*. **(b)** Grobheit *f*; Derbheit *f*; Roheit *f*; Unmäßigkeit *f*. **(c)** Kraßheit *f*; Ungeheuerlichkeit *f*; (*of negligence*) ungeheures Ausmaß. **(d)** Üppigkeit *f*.
grotesque [grəʊ'tesk] [1] *adj* grotesk.
[2] *n* **(a)** (*Art*) Groteske *f*; (*figure*) groteske Figur. **(b)** (*Typ*) Grotesk *f*.
grotesquely [grəʊ'tesklɪ] *adv see adj* ◆ **~ enough he had ...** groteskerweise hatte er ...; **he's ~ wrong** er irrt sich so gewaltig, daß es schon grotesk ist.
grotesqueness [grəʊ'tesknɪs] *n* **the ~ of the shape/this answer/his appearance** diese groteske Form/Antwort/seine groteske Erscheinung.
grotto ['grɒtəʊ] *n, pl* **-(e)s** Grotte, Höhle *f* ◆ **fairy ~** Märchenhöhle *f*.
grotty ['grɒtɪ] *adj* (*+er*) (*inf*) grausig (*inf*); *person, pub, town, job also* mies (*inf*).
grouch [graʊtʃ] [1] *n* **(a)** (*complaint*) Klage *f* ◆ **to have a ~** (*grumble*) schimpfen (*about* über *+acc*); **to have a ~ against sb** jdm grollen, auf jdn böse sein. **(b)** (*inf: person*) Miesepeter, Muffel *m* (*inf*).
[2] *vi* schimpfen, meckern (*inf*).
grouchiness ['graʊtʃɪnɪs] *n* schlechte Laune, Miesepetrigkeit (*inf*) *f*.
grouchy ['graʊtʃɪ] *adj* (*+er*) griesgrämig, miesepetrig (*inf*).
▼ **ground[1]** [graʊnd] [1] *n* **(a)** (*soil, terrain, fig*) Boden *m* ◆ **snow on high ~** Schnee in höheren Lagen; **hilly ~** hügeliges Gelände; **how much ~ do you own?** wieviel Grund und Boden *or* wieviel Land besitzen Sie?; **there is common ~ between us** uns verbindet einiges; **they found common ~ in the fact that ...** die Tatsache, daß ..., verband sie; **to be on dangerous/firm** *or* **sure ~** (*fig*) sich auf gefährlichem Boden bewegen/festen *or* sicheren Boden unter den Füßen haben; **to meet sb on his own ~** zu jdm kommen; **to be beaten on one's own ~** auf dem eigenen Gebiet geschlagen werden; **to cut the ~ from under sb** *or* **sb's feet** jdm den Boden unter den Füßen wegziehen; **to gain/lose ~** Boden gewinnen/verlieren; (*disease, rumour*) um sich greifen/im Schwinden begriffen sein; **to lose ~ to sb/sth** gegenüber jdm/etw an Boden verlieren; **to give ~ to sb/sth** vor jdm/etw zurückweichen; **to regain the ~ lost to sb** seine Position jdm gegenüber zurückerobern; **to break new** *or* **fresh ~** (*lit, fig*) neue Gebiete erschließen; (*person*) sich auf ein neues *or* unbekanntes Gebiet begeben; **to go over the ~** (*fig*) alles durchgehen; **to cover the/a lot of ~** (*lit*) die Strecke/eine weite Strecke zurücklegen; (*fig*) das Thema/eine Menge Dinge behandeln; **that covers the ~** das umreißt das Thema; **to hold** *or* **keep** *or* **stand one's ~** (*lit*) nicht von der Stelle weichen; (*fig*) seinen Mann stehen, sich nicht unterkriegen lassen; **to shift one's ~** (*fig*) seine Haltung ändern.
(b) (*surface*) Boden *m* ◆ **above/below ~** über/unter der Erde; (*Min*) über/unter Tage; (*fig*) unter den Lebenden/unter der Erde; **to fall to the ~** (*lit*) zu Boden fallen; (*fig: plans*) ins Wasser fallen, sich zerschlagen; **to sit on the ~** auf der Erde *or* dem Boden sitzen; **our hopes were dashed to the ~** unsere

Hoffnungen wurden am Boden zerstört; **to burn/raze sth to the ~** etw niederbrennen/etw dem Erdboden gleichmachen; **it suits me down to the ~** das ist ideal für mich; **to get off the ~** *(plane etc)* abheben; *(plans, project etc)* sich realisieren; **to go to ~** *(fox)* im Bau verschwinden; *(person)* untertauchen *(inf)*; **to run sb/sth to ~** jdn/etw aufstöbern, jdn/etw ausfindig machen; **to run sb/oneself into the ~** *(inf)* jdn/sich selbst fertigmachen *(inf)*; **to run a car into the ~** *(inf)* ein Auto schrottreif fahren; **opinion on the ~ is turning against him** die Meinung der Masse wendet sich gegen ihn.
(c) *(pitch)* Feld *nt*, Platz *m*; *(parade ~, drill~)* Platz *m* ◆ **recreation ~** Spiel- *or* Sportplatz *m*; **hunting ~s** Jagdgebiete *pl*; **fishing ~s** Fischgründe *pl*.
(d) **~s** *pl (premises, land)* Gelände *nt*; *(gardens)* Anlagen *pl* ◆ **a house standing in its own ~s** ein von Anlagen umgebenes Haus.
(e) **~s** *pl (sediment)* Satz *m* ◆ **let the ~s settle** warten Sie, bis sich der Kaffee/die Flüssigkeit *etc* gesetzt hat.
(f) *(background)* Grund *m* ◆ **on a blue ~** auf blauem Grund.
(g) *(US Elec)* Erde *f*.
(h) *(sea-bed)* Grund *m*.
▼**(i)** *(reason)* Grund *m* ◆ **to have ~(s) for sth** Grund zu etw haben; **to be ~(s) for sth** Grund für *or* zu etw sein; **to give sb ~(s) for sth** jdm Grund zu etw geben; **~(s) for divorce** Scheidungsgrund *m*; **~s for suspicion** Verdachtsmomente *pl*; **on the ~(s) of/that ...** aufgrund *(+gen)*, auf Grund von/mit der Begründung, daß ...; **on health ~s** aus gesundheitlichen Gründen.
[2] *vt* **(a)** *ship* auflaufen lassen, auf Grund setzen ◆ **to be ~ed** aufgelaufen sein.
(b) *(Aviat) plane (for mechanical reasons)* aus dem Verkehr ziehen; *pilot* sperren, nicht fliegen lassen ◆ **to be ~ed by bad weather/a strike** wegen schlechten Wetters/eines Streiks nicht starten *or* fliegen können.
(c) *(US Elec)* erden.
(d) *(base)* **to be ~ed on sth** sich auf etw *(acc)* gründen, auf etw *(dat)* basieren.
(e) **to ~ sb in a subject** jdm die Grundlagen eines Faches beibringen; **to be well ~ed in English** gute Grundkenntnisse im Englischen haben.
[3] *vi (Naut)* auflaufen.
ground[2] [1] *pret, ptp of* **grind**.
[2] *adj glass* matt; *coffee* gemahlen ◆ **~ rice** Reismehl *nt*.
ground: ~ attack *n* Bodenangriff *m*; **~bait** *n* Grundköder *m*; **~ bass** *n* Grundbaß *m*; **~breaking** *adj* umwälzend; *(research etc)* bahnbrechend; **~ colour** *n* Untergrund *m*; *(undercoat)* Grundierfarbe *f*; **~ control** *n (Aviat)* Bodenkontrolle *f*; **~ cover** *n (Hort)* Bodenvegetation *f*; **~ crew** *n* Bodenpersonal *nt*.
grounder ['graʊndəʳ] *n (US Sport)* Bodenball *m*.
ground: ~ floor *n* Erdgeschoß *nt*; **to get in on the ~ floor** *(fig)* gleich zu Anfang einsteigen *(inf)*; **~ frost** *n* Bodenfrost *m*; **~hog** *n (US)* Waldmurmeltier *nt*.
grounding ['graʊndɪŋ] *n* **(a)** *(basic knowledge)* Grundwissen *nt* ◆ **to give sb a ~ in English** jdm die Grundlagen *pl* des Englischen beibringen.
(b) *(Aviat) (of plane)* Startverbot *nt* (of für); *(due to strike, bad weather)* Hinderung *f* am Start; *(of pilot)* Sperren *nt*.
ground: ~ ivy *n* Gundelrebe *f*, Gundermann *m*; **~keeper** *n (US) see* **groundsman**; **~-launched** *adj missile* bodengestützt; **~less** *adj* grundlos, unbegründet; **~ level** *n* Boden *m*; **below ~ level** unter dem Boden; **~nut** *n* Erdnuß *f*; **~ plan** *n* Grundriß *m*; **~ rent** *n* Grundrente *f*; **~ rules** *npl* Grundregeln *pl*.
groundsel ['graʊnsl] *n* Kreuzkraut *nt*.
groundsheet ['graʊndʃiːt] *n* Zeltboden(plane *f*) *m*.
groundsman ['graʊndzmən] *n, pl* **-men** [-mən] *(esp Brit)* Platzwart *m*.
ground: ~ speed *n* Bodengeschwindigkeit *f*; **~ squirrel** *n* Erdhörnchen *nt*; **~ staff** *n* Bodenpersonal *nt*; **~ stroke** *n (Tennis)* nicht aus der Luft gespielter Ball; **~swell** *n* Dünung *f*; *(fig)* Anschwellen *nt*, Zunahme *f*; **there was a growing ~swell of public opinion against him** die Öffentlichkeit wandte sich zunehmend gegen ihn; **~-to-air missile** *n* Boden-Luft-Rakete *f*; **~-to-~ missile** *n* Boden-Boden-Flugkörper *m*; **~ water** *n* Grundwasser *nt*; **~wire** *n (US Elec)* Erdleitung *f*; **~work** *n* Vorarbeit *f*; **to do the ~work for sth** die Vorarbeit für etw leisten.
group [gruːp] [1] *n* Gruppe *f*; *(Comm also)* Konzern *m*; *(theatre ~ also)* Ensemble *nt* ◆ **a ~ of people/houses/trees** eine Gruppe Menschen/eine Häusergruppe/eine Baumgruppe.
[2] *attr* Gruppen-; *discussion, living, activities* in der Gruppe *or* Gemeinschaft.
[3] *vt* gruppieren ◆ **to ~ together** *(in one ~)* zusammentun; *(in several ~s)* in Gruppen einteilen *or* anordnen; **it's wrong to ~ all criminals together** es ist nicht richtig, alle Verbrecher über einen Kamm zu scheren *or* in einen Topf zu werfen *(inf)*; **~ the blue ones with the red ones** ordnen Sie die blauen bei den roten ein, tun Sie die blauen mit den roten zusammen; **they ~ed themselves round him** sie stellten sich um ihn (herum) auf, sie gruppierten sich um ihn; **to ~ sth around sth** etw um etw herum anordnen; **the books were ~ed on the shelf according to subject** die Bücher standen nach Sachgruppen geordnet im Regal.
group: ~ booking *n* Gruppenbuchung *or* -reservierung *f*; **~ captain** *n (Aviat)* Oberst *m*; **~ dynamics** *n* **(a)** *pl (relationships)* Gruppendynamik *f*; **(b)** *sing (subject)* Gruppendynamik *f*.
groupie ['gruːpɪ] *n* Groupie *nt (sl)*.
grouping ['gruːpɪŋ] *n* Gruppierung *f*; *(group of things also)* Anordnung *f*.
group: ~ insurance *n* Gruppenversicherung *f*; **~ practice** *n* Gemeinschaftspraxis *f*; **to be in a ~ practice** in einem Ärztekollektiv arbeiten; **~ therapy** *n* Gruppentherapie *f*.

grouse[1] [graʊs] *n, pl* - Waldhuhn, Rauhfußhuhn *nt*; *(red ~)* Schottisches Moor(schnee)huhn ◆ **~ shooting** Moorhuhnjagd *f*.
grouse[2] *(inf)* [1] *n (complaint)* Klage *f* ◆ **to have a good ~** sich ausschimpfen *(inf)*.
[2] *vi* schimpfen, meckern *(inf) (about* über *+acc)*.
grouser ['graʊsəʳ] *n (inf)* Meckerfritze *m*/-liese *f (inf)*.
grout [graʊt] [1] *vt tiles* verfugen, verkitten; *bricks* mit Mörtel ausgießen.
[2] *n* Vergußmaterial *nt*, Fugenkitt *m*; Mörtel *m*.
grove [grəʊv] *n* Hain *m*, Wäldchen *nt*.
grovel ['grɒvl] *vi* kriechen ◆ **to ~ at sb's feet** vor jdm kriechen; *(dog)* sich um jdn herumdrücken; **to ~ to *or* before sb** *(fig)* vor jdm kriechen; *(in apology)* vor jdm zu Kreuze kriechen.
groveller ['grɒvələʳ] *n* Kriecher *(inf)*, Speichellecker *(inf) m*.
grovelling ['grɒvəlɪŋ] [1] *adj* kriecherisch *(inf)*, unterwürfig.
[2] *n* Kriecherei *(inf)*, Speichelleckerei *(inf) f*.
grow [grəʊ] *pret* **grew**, *ptp* **grown** [1] *vt* **(a)** *plants* ziehen; *(commercially) potatoes, wheat, coffee etc* anbauen, anpflanzen; *(cultivate) flowers* züchten. **(b)** **to ~ one's beard/hair** sich *(dat)* einen Bart/die Haare wachsen lassen.
[2] *vi* **(a)** wachsen; *(person, baby also)* größer werden; *(hair also)* länger werden; *(in numbers)* zunehmen; *(in size also)* sich vergrößern; *(fig: become more mature)* sich weiterentwickeln ◆ **to ~ in stature/wisdom/authority** an Ansehen/Weisheit/Autorität zunehmen; **to ~ in popularity** immer beliebter werden; **to ~ in beauty** schöner werden; **my, how you've ~n** du bist aber groß geworden!; **it'll ~ on you** das wird dir mit der Zeit gefallen, du wirst schon noch Geschmack daran finden; **the habit grew on him** es wurde ihm zur Gewohnheit.
(b) *(become)* werden ◆ **to ~ to do/be sth** allmählich etw tun/sein; **to ~ to hate/love sb** jdn hassen/lieben lernen; **to ~ to enjoy sth** langsam Gefallen an etw *(dat)* finden; **I've ~n to expect him to be late** ich erwarte schon langsam, daß er zu spät kommt; **to ~ used to sth** sich an etw *(acc)* gewöhnen; **to ~ like sb** jdm immer ähnlicher werden.
◆**grow apart** *vi (fig)* sich auseinanderentwickeln.
◆**grow away** *vi (fig)* **to ~ ~ from sb** sich jdm entfremden.
◆**grow from** *vi +prep obj see* **grow out of (b)**.
◆**grow in** *vi (hair)* nachwachsen; *(teeth)* kommen; *(toenail)* einwachsen.
◆**grow into** *vi +prep obj* **(a)** *clothes, job* hineinwachsen in *(+acc)*. **(b)** *(become)* sich entwickeln zu, werden zu ◆ **to ~ ~ a man/woman** zum Mann/zur Frau heranwachsen; **to ~ ~ a scandal** sich zum Skandal auswachsen *or* entwickeln.
◆**grow out** *vi (perm, colour)* herauswachsen.
◆**grow out of** *vi +prep obj* **(a)** *clothes* herauswachsen aus ◆ **to ~ ~ ~ a habit** eine Angewohnheit ablegen; **to ~ ~ ~ one's friends** seinen Freunden entwachsen *(geh)*, sich von seinen Freunden entfernen. **(b)** *(arise from)* entstehen aus, erwachsen aus *(geh)*.
◆**grow together** *vi (lit, fig)* zusammenwachsen.
◆**grow up** *vi (spend childhood)* aufwachsen; *(become adult)* erwachsen werden; *(fig) (custom, hatred)* aufkommen; *(city)* entstehen ◆ **what are you going to do when you ~ ~?** was willst du mal werden, wenn du groß bist?; **to ~ ~ into a liar/beauty** sich zu einem Lügner/einer Schönheit entwickeln; **when are you going to ~ ~?** werde endlich erwachsen!
grow bag *n* Tüte *f* mit Komposterde.
grower ['grəʊəʳ] *n* **(a)** *(plant)* **to be a fast/good ~** schnell/gut wachsen. **(b)** *(person) (of fruit, vegetables)* Anbauer *m*; *(of flowers)* Züchter *m*; *(of tobacco, coffee)* Pflanzer *m*.
growing ['grəʊɪŋ] [1] *adj (lit, fig)* wachsend; *child* heranwachsend, im Wachstum befindlich *(form)*; *importance, interest, number etc also* zunehmend ◆ **he's still a ~ boy** er steckt noch *(inf) or* befindet sich noch im Wachstum.
[2] *n* Wachstum, Wachsen *nt* ◆ **~ pains** *(Med)* Wachstumsschmerzen *pl*; *(fig)* Kinderkrankheiten, Anfangsschwierig keiten *pl*; **~ season** Zeit *f* des Wachstums, Vegetationszeit *f (spec)*.
growl [graʊl] [1] *n* Knurren *nt no pl*; *(of bear)* (böses) Brummen *no pl*.
[2] *vi* knurren; *(bear)* böse brummen ◆ **to ~ at sb** jdn anknurren/anbrummen.
[3] *vt answer* knurren.
grown [grəʊn] [1] *ptp of* **grow**.
[2] *adj* erwachsen ◆ **fully ~** ausgewachsen; **they have a ~ family** sie haben schon erwachsene Kinder.
grown: ~ over *adj* überwachsen; *garden also* überwuchert; **~-up** [1] *adj* erwachsen; *clothes, shoes* Erwachsenen-, wie Erwachsene, wie Große *(inf)*; [2] *n* Erwachsene(r) *mf*.
growth [grəʊθ] *n* **(a)** Wachstum *nt*; *(of person also)* Entwicklung *f*; *(of plant also)* Wuchs *m*; *(increase in quantity, fig: of love, interest etc)* Zunahme *f*, Anwachsen *nt*; *(increase in size also)* Vergrößerung *f*; *(of capital etc)* Zuwachs *m*; *(of business also)* Erweiterung *f* ◆ **to reach full ~** seine/ihre volle Größe erreichen; **~ industry/stock** Wachstumsindustrie *f*/Wachstumsaktien *pl*; **rate of export ~** Wachstums- *or* Zuwachsrate *f* im Export.
(b) *(plants)* Vegetation *f*; *(of one plant)* Triebe *pl* ◆ **covered with a thick ~ of weeds** von Unkraut überwuchert *or* überwachsen; **cut away the old ~** schneiden Sie die alten Blätter und Zweige aus; **a thick ~ of beard** dichter Bartwuchs; **with a two days' ~ on his face** mit zwei Tage alten Bartstoppeln.
(c) *(Med)* Gewächs *nt*, Wucherung *f*.
groyne [grɔɪn] *n* Buhne *f*.
grub [grʌb] [1] *n* **(a)** *(larva)* Larve *f*. **(b)** *(inf: food)* Fressalien *pl (hum inf)*, Futterage *f (inf)* ◆ **~('s) up!** antreten zum Essenfassen *(inf)*.
[2] *vt (animal) ground, soil* aufwühlen, wühlen in *(+dat)*.

➤ LANGUAGE IN USE: **ground**[1]: **1i** → 15.2, 26.1

3 *vi* (*also* ~ **about** *or* **around**) (*pig*) wühlen (*in* in +*dat*); (*person*) (herum)kramen, (herum)wühlen (*in* in +*dat*, *for* nach).

◆**grub out** *vt sep* ausgraben.

◆**grub up** *vt sep weeds* jäten; *potatoes, bush etc* ausgraben; *soil* wühlen in (+*dat*); (*bird*) *worms* aus dem Boden ziehen; (*fig*) *information, people* auftreiben, zusammensammeln.

grubbily ['grʌbɪlɪ] *adv* schmuddelig (*inf*).

grubbiness ['grʌbɪnɪs] *n* Schmuddeligkeit *f* (*inf*).

grubby ['grʌbɪ] *adj* (+*er*) schmuddelig (*inf*); *hands* dreckig (*inf*).

grudge [grʌdʒ] 1 *n* Groll *m* (*against* gegen) ◆ **to bear sb a ~, to have a ~ against sb** jdm böse sein, jdm grollen, einen Groll gegen jdn hegen (*geh*); **I bear him no ~** ich trage ihm das nicht nach, ich nehme ihm das nicht übel; **to bear ~s** nachtragend sein; **to pay off a ~** eine alte Rechnung begleichen.

2 *vt* **to ~ sb sth** jdm etw nicht gönnen, jdm etw neiden (*geh*); **I don't ~ you your success** ich gönne Ihnen Ihren Erfolg; **to ~ doing sth** etw äußerst ungern tun, etw mit Widerwillen tun; **I don't ~ doing it** es macht mir nichts aus, das zu tun; **I ~ spending money/time on it** es widerstrebt mir *or* es geht mir gegen den Strich, dafür Geld auszugeben/Zeit aufzuwenden; **I don't ~ the money/time** es geht mir nichts ums Geld/um die Zeit; **I do ~ the money/time for things like that** das Geld/meine Zeit für solche Dinge tut mir leid.

grudge match *n* (*inf*: *Sport, fig*) erbitterter Zweikampft (*von Mannschaften oder Persönlichkeiten, zwischen denen eine offene Feindschaft besteht*).

grudging ['grʌdʒɪŋ] *adj person, attitude* unwirsch; *contribution, gift* widerwillig gegeben; *admiration, praise, support* widerwillig ◆ **in a ~ tone of voice** widerwillig; **to be ~ in one's support/praise for sth** etw nur widerwillig unterstützen/loben.

grudgingly ['grʌdʒɪŋlɪ] *adv* widerwillig.

gruel [grʊəl] *n* Haferschleim *m*, Schleimsuppe *f*.

gruelling, (*US*) **grueling** ['grʊəlɪŋ] *adj task, day etc* aufreibend, zermürbend; *march, climb, race* äußerst strapaziös, mörderisch (*inf*).

gruesome ['gru:səm] *adj* grausig, schauerlich, schaurig; *sense of humour* schaurig, makaber.

gruesomely ['gru:səmlɪ] *adv* schauerlich.

gruff [grʌf] *adj* (+*er*) *voice, manner, reply* barsch, schroff.

gruffly ['grʌflɪ] *adv see adj*.

gruffness ['grʌfnɪs] *n* Barschheit, Schroffheit *f*.

grumble ['grʌmbl] 1 *n* (*complaint*) Murren, Schimpfen *nt no pl*; (*noise: of thunder, guns*) Grollen *nt* ◆ **his chief ~ is that ...** worüber er am meisten murrt *or* schimpft ist, daß ...; **all his ~s** sein ständiges Schimpfen *or* Gemecker (*inf*); **to do sth without a ~** etw ohne Murren *or* Widerspruch tun.

2 *vi* murren, schimpfen (*about, over* über +*acc*); (*thunder, gunfire*) grollen ◆ **to ~ at sb** jdm gegenüber schimpfen *or* klagen; **grumbling appendix** gereizter Blinddarm.

grumbler ['grʌmbləʳ] *n* Nörgler(in *f*) *m*, Brummbär *m* (*inf*).

grummet ['grʌmɪt] *n see* **grommet**.

grumpily ['grʌmpɪlɪ] *adv see adj*.

grumpy ['grʌmpɪ] *adj* (+*er*) brummig, mürrisch, grantig; *child* quengelig (*inf*), unleidlich.

grungy ['grʌndʒɪ] *adj* (*esp US inf*) mies (*inf*).

grunt [grʌnt] 1 *n* (*of pig, person*) Grunzen *nt no pl*; (*of pain, in exertion*) Ächzen *nt no pl*, Ächzer *m* (*inf*) ◆ **to give a ~** grunzen (*of* vor +*dat*); ächzen (*of* vor +*dat*).

2 *vi* (*animal, person*) grunzen; (*with pain, exertion*) ächzen, aufseufzen; (*in irritation also*) knurren.

3 *vt reply* brummen, knurren.

gryphon ['grɪfən] *n see* **griffin**.

GS *abbr of* **General Staff**.

gsm *abbr of* **gram(me)s per square metre** g/m².

G-string ['dʒi:strɪŋ] *n* **(a)** (*Mus*) G-Saite *f* ◆ **Bach's Air on a ~** Bachs Air *nt*. **(b)** (*clothing*) Minislip *m*, Tangahöschen *nt*.

GT *abbr of* **gran turismo** GT.

Gt *abbr of* **Great**.

Guadeloupe [,gwɑ:də'lu:p] *n* Guadalupe, Guadelupe *nt*.

guano ['gwɑ:nəʊ] *n* Guano *m*.

guarantee [,gærən'ti:] 1 *n* **(a)** (*Comm*) Garantie *f*; (~ *slip also*) Garantieschein *m* ◆ **to have** *or* **carry a 6-month ~** 6 Monate Garantie haben; **there is a year's ~ on this watch** auf der Uhr ist ein Jahr Garantie; **while it is under ~** solange noch Garantie darauf ist; **to sell sth with a money-back ~** volles Rückgaberecht beim Verkauf von etw garantieren.

(b) (*promise*) Garantie *f* (*of* für) ◆ **that's no ~ that ...** das heißt noch lange nicht, daß ...; **it will be sent today, I give you my ~** *or* **you have my ~** es wird heute noch abgeschickt, das garantiere ich Ihnen.

(c) (*Jur*) *see* **guaranty**.

2 *vt* **(a)** (*Comm*) garantieren ◆ **to be ~d for three months** drei Monate Garantie haben; **to ~ sth against theft/fire** etw gegen Diebstahl/Feuer absichern.

(b) (*promise, ensure*) garantieren (*sb sth* jdm etw); (*take responsibility for*) garantieren für ◆ **I can't ~ (that) he will be any good** ich kann nicht dafür garantieren, daß er gut ist; **I ~ to come tomorrow** ich komme garantiert morgen.

(c) (*Jur*) garantieren, gewährleisten; *loan, debt* bürgen für.

guaranteed [,gærən'ti:d] *adj* garantiert ◆ **to be ~ pure gold/not to rust** garantiert echt Gold/nichtrostend sein; **~ price** Garantiepreis *m*; **that's a ~ success** das wird garantiert ein Erfolg.

guarantor [,gærən'tɔ:ʳ] *n* Garant *m*; (*Jur also*) Bürge *m* ◆ **to stand ~ for sb** für jdn eine Bürgschaft übernehmen.

guaranty ['gærəntɪ] *n* (*Jur*) Garantie *f*; (*pledge of obligation*) Bürgschaft *f*; (*security*) Sicherheit *f*.

guard [gɑ:d] 1 *n* **(a)** (*Mil*) Wache *f*; (*single soldier also*) Wachtposten *m*; (*no pl: squad also*) Wachmannschaft *f* ◆ **the G~s** (*Brit*) die Garde, das Garderegiment; **~ of honour** Ehrenwache *f*; **to change ~** Wachablösung machen.

(b) (*security* ~) Sicherheitsbeamte(r) *m*, Sicherheitsbeamtin *f*; (*at factory gates, in park etc*) Wächter(in *f*) *m*; (*esp US: prison* ~) Gefängniswärter(in *f*); (*Brit Rail*) Schaffner(in *f*), Zugbegleiter(in *f*) *m*.

(c) (*watch, also Mil*) Wache *f* ◆ **under ~** unter Bewachung; **to be under ~** bewacht werden; (*person also*) unter Bewachung *or* Aufsicht stehen; **to keep sb/sth under ~** jdn/etw bewachen; **to be on ~, to stand** *or* **keep** *or* **mount ~** Wache halten *or* stehen; **to keep** *or* **stand** *or* **mount ~ over sth** etw bewachen; **to go on/off ~** die Wache übernehmen/übergeben; **to put a ~ on sb/sth** jdn/etw bewachen lassen.

(d) (*Boxing, Fencing*) Deckung *f* ◆ **on ~!** (*Fencing*) en garde!; **to take ~** in Verteidigungsstellung gehen; (*Cricket*) in Schlagstellung gehen; **to drop** *or* **lower one's ~** (*lit*) seine Deckung vernachlässigen; (*fig*) seine Reserve aufgeben; **to have one's ~ down** (*lit*) nicht gedeckt sein; (*fig*) nicht auf der Hut sein; **he caught his opponent off his ~** er hat seinen Gegner mit einem Schlag erwischt, auf den er nicht vorbereitet *or* gefaßt war; **I was off my ~/he caught me off my ~ when he mentioned that** ich war nicht darauf gefaßt *or* vorbereitet, daß er das erwähnen würde/er hat mich völlig überrumpelt, als er das erwähnte; **to be on/off one's ~ (against sth)** (*lit*) gut/schlecht gedeckt sein; (*fig*) (vor etw *dat*) auf der/nicht auf der Hut sein; **to put sb on his ~ (against sth)** jdn (vor etw *dat*) warnen; **to throw** *or* **put sb off his ~** (*lit*) jdn seine Deckung vernachlässigen lassen; (*fig*) jdn einlullen.

(e) (*safety device, for protection*) Schutz *m* (*against* gegen); (*on machinery also*) Schutzvorrichtung *f*; (*fire* ~) Schutzgitter *nt*; (*on foil*) Glocke *f*; (*on sword etc*) Korb *m*.

(f) (*in basketball*) Verteidigungsspieler *m*.

2 *vt prisoner, place, valuables* bewachen; *treasure also, secret, tongue* hüten; *machinery* beaufsichtigen; *luggage* aufpassen auf (+*acc*); (*protect*) (*lit*) *person, place* schützen (*from, against* vor +*dat*), abschirmen (*from, against* gegen); *one's life* schützen; *one's reputation* achten auf (+*acc*); (*fig*) *child etc* behüten, beschützen (*from, against* vor +*dat*).

◆**guard against** *vi* +*prep obj* (*take care to avoid*) *suspicion, being cheated etc* sich in acht nehmen vor (+*dat*); *hasty reaction, bad habit, scandal also* sich hüten vor (+*dat*); (*take precautions against*) *illness, misunderstandings* vorbeugen (+*dat*); *accidents* verhüten ◆ **you must ~ ~ catching cold** Sie müssen aufpassen *or* sich in acht nehmen, daß Sie sich nicht erkälten; **they shut the door to ~ ~ being overheard** sie machten die Tür zu, um nicht belauscht zu werden; **in order to ~ ~ this** um (dem) vorzubeugen.

guard: ~ dog *n* Wachhund *m*; **~ duty** *n* Wachdienst *m*; **to be on ~ duty** auf Wache sein, Wache haben (*inf*).

guarded ['gɑ:dɪd] *adj reply* vorsichtig, zurückhaltend; *smile* zurückhaltend, reserviert; (*under guard*) *prisoner* bewacht; *machinery* geschützt, abgesichert ◆ **to be ~ in one's remarks** sich sehr vorsichtig *or* zurückhaltend ausdrücken.

guardedly ['gɑ:dɪdlɪ] *adv* vorsichtig, zurückhaltend ◆ **to be ~ optimistic** vorsichtigen Optimismus zeigen.

guardedness ['gɑ:dɪdnɪs] *n* Vorsichtigkeit *f*; (*of smile*) Reserviertheit *f*.

guardhouse ['gɑ:dhaʊs] *n* (*Mil*) (*for soldiers*) Wachlokal *nt*, Wachstube *f*; (*for prisoners*) Arrestlokal *nt*, Bunker *m* (*sl*).

guardian ['gɑ:dɪən] *n* Hüter, Wächter *m*; (*Jur*) Vormund *m* ◆ **~ of law and order** Hüter *m* des Gesetzes; **~ angel** Schutzengel *m*.

guardianship ['gɑ:dɪənʃɪp] *n* Wachen *nt* (*of* über +*acc*); (*Jur*) Vormundschaft *f* (*of* über +*acc*).

guard: ~rail *n* Schutzgeländer *nt*; (*around machinery*) Schutzleiste *f*; (*Rail*) Schutzschiene, Zwangsschiene *f*; **~room** *n* (*used by guard*) Wachstube *f*; **to put sb in the ~room** jdn unter Bewachung stellen.

guardsman ['gɑ:dzmən] *n*, *pl* **-men** [-mən] Wache *f*, Wachtposten *m*; (*member of guards regiment*) Gardist *m*; (*US: in National Guard*) Nationalgardist *m*.

guard's van ['gɑ:dzvæn] *n* (*Brit Rail*) Schaffnerabteil *nt*, Dienstwagen *m*.

Guatemala [,gwɑ:tɪ'mɑ:lə] *n* Guatemala *nt*.

Guatemalan [,gwɑ:tɪ'mɑ:lən] 1 *adj* guatemaltekisch, aus Guatemala.

2 *n* Guatemalteke *m*, Guatemaltekin *f*.

guava ['gwɑ:və] *n* Guave *f*; (*tree also*) Guavenbaum *m*.

gubbins ['gʌbɪnz] *n* (*Brit dated inf*) (*things*) Zeug *nt* (*inf*); (*person*) Dussel *m* (*inf*).

gubernatorial [,gu:bənə'tɔ:rɪəl] *adj* (*esp US Pol*) Gouverneurs-.

guddle ['gʌdl] (*Scot*) 1 *vt fish* mit den Händen fangen.

2 *n* (*inf: mess*) Durcheinander *nt* ◆ **this room's a ~** in diesem Zimmer herrscht das reinste Durcheinander (*inf*).

gudgeon ['gʌdʒən] *n* Gründling *m*.

guelder rose ['geldə,rəʊz] *n* (*Bot*) Schneeball *m*.

guer(r)illa [gə'rɪlə] 1 *n* Guerilla *mf*, Guerillakämpfer(in *f*) *m* ◆ **Palestinian ~s** palästinensische Freischärler *or* Guerillas *pl*.

2 *attr* Guerilla- ◆ **~ war/warfare** Guerillakrieg *m*.

Guernsey ['gɜ:nzɪ] *n* **(a)** Guernsey *nt*. **(b)** (*sweater: also* **g~**) dicker Pullover (*von Fischern getragen*).

guess [ges] 1 *n* Vermutung, Annahme *f*; (*estimate*) Schätzung *f* ◆ **to have** *or*

make a ~ (at sth) (etw) raten; *(estimate)* (etw) schätzen; **it was just a ~** ich habe nur geraten; **his ~ was nearly right** er hat es fast erraten; er hat es gut geschätzt; **it's a good ~** gut geraten *or* geschätzt *or* getippt; **it was just a lucky ~** das war nur gut geraten, das war ein Zufallstreffer *m*; **I'll give you three ~es** dreimal darfst du raten; **50 people, at a ~** schätzungsweise 50 Leute; **at a rough ~** grob geschätzt, über den Daumen gepeilt *(inf)*; **my ~ is that ...** ich tippe darauf *(inf)* *or* schätze *or* vermute, daß ...; **your ~ is as good as mine!** *(inf)* da kann ich auch nur raten!; **it's anybody's ~** *(inf)* das wissen die Götter *(inf)*.

2 *vi* **(a)** raten ◆ **how did you ~?** wie hast du das bloß erraten?; *(iro)* du merkst auch alles!; **to keep sb ~ing** jdn im ungewissen lassen; **he's only ~ing when he says they'll come** das ist eine reine Vermutung von ihm, daß sie kommen; **you'll never ~!** das wirst du nie erraten; **to ~ at sth** etw raten.

(b) *(esp US)* **I ~ not** wohl nicht; **he's right, I ~** er hat wohl recht; **is he coming? — I ~ so** kommt er? — (ich) schätze ja *(inf)*, ich glaube schon; **shall we go? — I ~ (so)** sollen wir gehen? — (ich) schätze ja *(inf)*, na gut; **that's all, I ~** das ist wohl alles, (ich) schätze, das ist alles *(inf)*.

3 *vt* **(a)** *(surmise)* raten; *(surmise correctly)* erraten; *(estimate) weight, numbers, amount* schätzen ◆ **I ~ed as much** das habe ich mir schon gedacht; **to ~ sb to be 20 years old/sth to be 10 lbs** jdn auf 20/etw auf 10 Pfund schätzen; **you'll never ~ who/what ...** das errätst du nie, wer/was ...; **~ who!** *(inf)* rat mal, wer!; **~ what!** *(inf)* stell dir vor! *(inf)*, denk nur! *(inf)*.

(b) *(esp US)* schätzen *(inf)*, vermuten, annehmen ◆ **I ~ we'll buy it** wir werden es wohl *or* wahrscheinlich kaufen.

guessable ['gesəbl] *adj answer* erratbar, zu erraten *pred*; *age also, number* schätzbar, zu schätzen *pred*.

guessing game ['gesɪŋ,geɪm] *n (lit, fig)* Ratespiel *nt*.

guesstimate ['gestɪmɪt] *n* grobe Schätzung.

guesswork ['geswɜːk] *n* (reine) Vermutung ◆ **there's too much ~ in historical essays** in historischen Aufsätzen wird zuviel vermutet; **they did it all by ~** sie haben nur geraten; **it's all ~** das sind doch nur Vermutungen, das ist doch alles nur geraten.

guest [gest] *n* Gast *m* ◆ **~ of honour** Ehrengast *m*; **be my ~** *(inf)* nur zu! *(inf)*.

guest *in cpds* Gast-; **~ appearance** *n* Gastauftritt *m*; **to make a ~ appearance** als Gast auftreten; **~ artist** *n* Gast(star), Gastkünstler(in *f*) *m*; *(Theat)* Gastspieler(in *f*) *m*; **~-house** *n* Gästehaus *nt*; *(boarding house)* (Fremden)pension *f*; **~ list** *n* Gästeliste *f*; **~-night** *n* Gästeabend *m*; **~-room** *n* Gästezimmer *nt*.

guff [gʌf] *n (sl)* Quark *(inf)*, Käse *(inf) m*.

guffaw [gʌ'fɔː] 1 *n* schallendes Lachen *no pl* ◆ **~s of laughter** Lachsalven *pl*; **to give a ~** schallend lachen.

2 *vi* schallend (los)lachen.

GUI ['guːɪ] *(Comput) abbr of* **graphical user interface** GUI.

Guiana [gaɪ'ænə] *n* Guayana *nt*.

guidance ['gaɪdəns] *n (direction)* Führung, Leitung *f*; *(counselling)* Beratung *f* *(on* über *+acc)*; *(from superior, parents, teacher etc)* Anleitung *f* ◆ **spiritual ~** geistiger Rat; **for your ~** zu Ihrer Orientierung *or* Hilfe; **to give sb ~ on sth** jdn bei etw beraten; **to pray for ~** um Erleuchtung bitten.

guidance: ~ system *n (on rocket)* Steuerungssystem *nt*; **~ teacher** *n (Scot)* Verbindungslehrer(in *f*) *m*.

guide [gaɪd] 1 *n* **(a)** *(person)* Führer(in *f*) *m*; *(fig: indication, pointer)* Anhaltspunkt *m* *(to* für*)*; *(model)* Leitbild *nt* ◆ **let reason/your conscience be your ~** lassen Sie sich von der Vernunft/Ihrem Gewissen leiten; **they used the star as their ~** sie ließen sich von dem Stern leiten; **he is my spiritual ~** er ist mein geistiger Berater.

(b) *(Tech)* Leitvorrichtung *f*.

(c) *(Brit: girl ~)* Pfadfinderin *f*.

(d) *(instructions)* Anleitung *f*; *(manual)* Leitfaden *m*, Handbuch *nt* *(to gen)*; *(travel ~)* Führer *m* ◆ **let this dictionary/this piece of work be your ~** orientieren Sie sich an diesem Wörterbuch/dieser Arbeit.

2 *vt people, blind man etc* führen; *discussion also* leiten; *missile, rocket, sb's behaviour, studies, reading* lenken ◆ **to ~ a plane in** ein Flugzeug einweisen; **to be ~d by sb/sth** *(person)* sich von jdm/etw leiten lassen; **his life was ~d by his father's example** sein Leben war vom Vorbild seines Vaters bestimmt; **to ~ sb on his way** jdm den Weg zeigen *or* weisen.

guide-book ['gaɪdbʊk] *n* (Reise)führer *m* *(to* von*)*.

guided missile [,gaɪdɪd'mɪsaɪl] *n* ferngelenktes Geschoß, Lenkwaffe *f*.

guide-dog ['gaɪddɒg] *n* Blindenhund *m*.

guided tour [,gaɪdɪd'tʊəʳ] *n* Führung *f* *(of* durch*)*.

guide: ~line *n* Richtlinie, Richtschnur *no pl f*; *(Typ, for writing)* Leitlinie *f*; **~post** *n* Wegweiser *m*.

guider ['gaɪdəʳ] *n (Brit)* Pfadfinderinnenführerin *f*.

guide-rope ['gaɪdrəʊp] *n* Schlepptau *nt*.

guiding ['gaɪdɪŋ]: **~ hand** *n* leitende Hand; **~ principle** *n* Leitmotiv *nt*; **~ star** *n* Leitstern *m*.

guild [gɪld] *n (Hist)* Zunft, Gilde *f*; *(association)* Verein *m*.

guilder ['gɪldəʳ] *n* Gulden *m*.

guile [gaɪl] *n* Tücke, (Arg)list *f* ◆ **to have great ~** sehr tückisch *or* arglistig sein; **without ~** ohne Arg, ohne Falsch *(liter)*.

guileful ['gaɪlfʊl] *adj* hinterhältig, tückisch, arglistig.

guileless ['gaɪllɪs] *adj* arglos, harmlos, unschuldsvoll.

guillemot ['gɪlɪmɒt] *n* Lumme *f*.

guillotine [,gɪlə'tiːn] 1 *n* **(a)** Guillotine *f*, Fallbeil *nt*.

(b) *(for paper)* (Papier)schneidemaschine *f*.

(c) *(Parl)* Beschränkung *f* der Diskussionszeit ◆ **to put a ~ on a bill** die Diskussionszeit für ein Gesetz einschränken.

2 *vt* **(a)** *person* mit der Guillotine *or* dem Fallbeil hinrichten. **(b)** *paper* schneiden. **(c)** *(Parl) bill* die Diskussionszeit einschränken für.

guilt [gɪlt] *n* Schuld *f* *(for, of* an *+dat)* ◆ **to feel ~ about sth** sich wegen etw schuldig fühlen, wegen etw Schuldgefühle haben; **~ complex** Schuldkomplex *m*.

guiltily ['gɪltɪlɪ] *adv* schuldbewußt; *act* verdächtig.

guiltiness ['gɪltɪnɪs] *n* Schuld *f*; *(feeling)* Schuldbewußtsein *nt*.

guiltless ['gɪltlɪs] *adj* schuldlos, unschuldig *(of* an *+dat)* ◆ **he is ~ of any crime** er ist keines Verbrechens schuldig.

guilty ['gɪltɪ] *adj (+er)* **(a)** schuldig *(of gen)* ◆ **the ~ person/party** der/die Schuldige/die schuldige Partei; **verdict of ~** Schuldspruch *m*; **to find sb ~/not ~ (of a crime)** jdn (eines Verbrechens) für schuldig/nicht schuldig befinden; **~/not ~!** *(Jur)* schuldig/nicht schuldig!; *(fig)* das war ich/das war ich nicht.

(b) *look, voice* schuldbewußt; *conscience, thought* schlecht; *intent, thought* böse.

(c) *(in phrases)* **we're all ~ of neglecting the problem** uns trifft alle Schuld, daß das Problem vernachlässigt wurde; **he was ~ of taking the book without permission** er hat das Buch ohne Erlaubnis genommen; **I've been ~ of that myself** den Fehler habe ich auch schon begangen; **I feel very ~ (about ...)** ich habe ein sehr schlechtes Gewissen(, daß ...).

Guinea ['gɪnɪ] *n* Guinea *nt*.

guinea ['gɪnɪ] *n (Brit old)* Guinee, Guinea *f* *(21 Shilling)*.

guinea: ~-fowl *n* Perlhuhn *nt*; **~-pig** *n* Meerschweinchen *nt*; *(fig)* Versuchskaninchen *nt*.

guise [gaɪz] *n (disguise)* Gestalt *f*; *(pretence)* Vorwand *m* ◆ **in the ~ of a clown/swan** als Clown verkleidet/in Gestalt eines Schwans; **in human ~** in Menschengestalt; **under the ~ of friendship** unter dem Deckmantel der Freundschaft.

guitar [gɪ'tɑːʳ] *n* Gitarre *f*.

guitarist [gɪ'tɑːrɪst] *n* Gitarrist(in *f*) *m*.

gulch [gʌlʃ] *n (US)* Schlucht *f*.

gulf [gʌlf] *n* **(a)** *(bay)* Golf, Meerbusen *m* ◆ **G~ Stream** Golfstrom *m*; **the G~ of Mexico/Bothnia** der Golf von Mexico/der Bottnische Meerbusen; **the (Persian) G~** der (Persische) Golf; **the G~ States** die Golfstaaten *pl*. **(b)** *(lit, fig: chasm)* tiefe Kluft.

gull[1] [gʌl] *n (sea~)* Möwe *f*.

gull[2] *(liter)* 1 *n* Spielball *m* *(of gen)*.

2 *vt* übertölpeln ◆ **to ~ sb out of his money** jdm sein Geld ablisten; **to be ~ed into sth** durch eine üble List dazu gebracht werden, etw zu tun.

gullet ['gʌlɪt] *n* Speiseröhre, Kehle *f* ◆ **that really stuck in my ~** *(fig)* das ging mir sehr gegen den Strich *(inf)*.

gullibility [,gʌlɪ'bɪlɪtɪ] *n* Leichtgläubigkeit *f*.

gullible *adj*, **-bly** *adv* ['gʌlɪbl, -ɪ] leichtgläubig.

gull: ~ wing door *n (Aut)* Flügeltür *f*; **~-winged** *adj car* mit Flügeltüren.

gully ['gʌlɪ] *n (ravine)* Schlucht *f*; *(narrow channel)* Rinne *f*.

gulp [gʌlp] 1 *n* Schluck *m* ◆ **at a/one ~** auf einen Schluck; **..., he said with a ~** ..., sagte er und schluckte.

2 *vt* (*also* **~ down**) *drink* runterstürzen; *food* runterschlingen; *medicine* hinunterschlucken ◆ **to ~ back one's tears/a reply** die Tränen/eine Antwort hinunterschlucken; **what?, he ~ed** was?, preßte er hervor.

3 *vi (try to swallow)* würgen; *(eat fast)* schlingen; *(drink fast)* hastig trinken; *(from emotion)* trocken schlucken ◆ **to drink with loud ~ing noises** gluckernd trinken.

gum[1] [gʌm] *n (Anat)* Zahnfleisch *nt no pl*.

gum[2] 1 *n* **(a)** Gummi *nt*; *(~-tree)* Gummibaum *m*; *(glue)* Klebstoff *m*. **(b)** *(chewing ~)* Kaugummi *m*; *(sweet)* Weingummi *m*. **(c)** *(US inf) see* **gum-shoe**.

2 *vt (stick together)* kleben; *(spread ~ on)* gummieren.

◆**gum down** *vt sep label* aufkleben; *envelope* zukleben.

◆**gum up** *vt sep* verkleben ◆ **to ~ ~ the works** *(inf)* alles verkleben; *(fig)* die Sache vermasseln *(inf)*; **to get ~med up** verkleben.

gum[3] *n (dated sl)*: **by ~!** Teufel noch mal! *(dated sl)*.

gum arabic *n* Gummiarabikum *nt*.

gumbo ['gʌmbəʊ] *n* Gumbo *m*.

gum: ~boil *n* Zahnfleischabszeß *m*; **~boot** *n* Gummistiefel *m*; **~drop** *n* Weingummi *m*.

gummy ['gʌmɪ] *adj (+er)* gummiert; *(sticky)* klebrig.

gumption ['gʌmpʃən] *n (inf)* Grips *m (inf)* ◆ **to have the ~ to do sth** geistesgegenwärtig genug sein, etw zu tun.

gum: ~-shield *n* Zahnschutz *m*; **~-shoe** *(US)* 1 *n* **(a)** *(overshoe)* Überschuh *m*, Galosche *f*; *(gym shoe)* Turnschuh *m*; **(b)** *(sl: detective)* Schnüffler *m (inf)*; 2 *vi (sl: move stealthily)* schleichen; **~-tree** *n* Gummibaum *m*; **to be up a ~-tree** *(Brit inf)* aufgeschmissen sein *(inf)*.

gun [gʌn] 1 *n* **(a)** *(cannon etc)* Kanone *f*, Geschütz *nt*; *(rifle)* Gewehr *nt*; *(pistol etc)* Pistole *f*, Kanone *f (sl)*, Schießeisen *nt (sl)* ◆ **to carry a ~** (mit einer Schußwaffe) bewaffnet sein, eine Schußwaffe tragen *(form)*; **to draw a ~ on sb** jdn mit einer Schußwaffe bedrohen; **to fire a 21-~ salute** 21 Salutschüsse abgeben; **the big ~s** die schweren Geschütze; **big ~** *(fig inf)* hohes *or* großes Tier *(inf)* *(in* in *+dat)*; **to stick to one's ~s** nicht nachgeben, festbleiben; **to jump the ~** *(Sport)* Frühstart machen; *(fig)* voreilig sein *or* handeln; **to be going great ~s** *(inf)* *(team, person)* toll in Schwung *or* Fahrt sein *(inf)*; *(car)* wie geschmiert laufen *(inf)*; *(business)* gut in Schuß sein *(inf)*.

(b) *(spray ~)* Pistole *f* ◆ **grease ~** Schmierpresse, Fettpresse *f*.

(c) *(person)* Schütze *m*; *(Hunt also)* Jäger *m*; *(inf esp US: ~man)* Pistolenheld *m* (*inf*) ◆ **he's the fastest ~ in the West** (*inf*) er zieht am schnellsten im ganzen Westen (*inf*).

2 *vt* (a) (*kill: also* **~ down**) *person* erschießen, zusammenschießen; *pilot, plane* abschießen.
(b) (*sl: rev*) *engine* aufheulen lassen.
3 *vi* (a) (*inf*) **to be ~ning for sb** (*lit*) Jagd auf jdn machen; (*fig*) jdn auf dem Kieker haben (*inf*); *for opponent* jdn auf die Abschußliste gesetzt haben. (b) (*sl: speed*) schießen (*inf*).

gun: ~ barrel *n* (*on cannon*) Kanonen- *or* Geschützrohr *nt*; (*on rifle*) Gewehrlauf *m*; (*on pistol*) Pistolenlauf *m*; **~boat** *n* Kanonenboot *nt*; **~boat diplomacy** Kanonenbootdiplomatie *f*; **~ carriage** *n* Lafette *f*; **~cotton** *n* Schießbaumwolle *f*; **~ crew** *n* Geschützbedienung *f*; **~ dog** *n* Jagdhund *m*; **~-fight** *n* Schießerei *f*; (*Mil*) Feuergefecht *nt*, Schußwechsel *m*; **~-fighter** *n* Revolverheld *m*; **~fire** *n* Schießerei *f*, Schüsse *pl*; (*Mil*) Geschützfeuer, Artilleriefeuer *nt*.

gunge [gʌndʒ] *n* (*Brit inf*) klebriges *or* schmieriges Zeug (*inf*).

gungho ['gʌŋ'həʊ] *adj* (*inf*) übereifrig.

gungy ['gʌndʒɪ] *adj* (+*er*) (*inf*) schmierig.

gunk [gʌŋk] *n* (*US sl*) *see* **gunge**.

gun: ~man *n* (mit einer Schußwaffe) Bewaffnete(r) *m*; **they saw the ~man** sie haben den Schützen gesehen; **~metal** 1 *n* Geschützmetall *nt*, Geschützbronze *f*; (*colour*) metallisches Blaugrau; 2 *adj attr* aus Geschützmetall *or* -bronze; *grey, colour* metallisch.

gunnel ['gʌnəl] *n see* **gunwale**.

gunner ['gʌnəʳ] *n* (*Mil*) Artillerist *m*; (*title*) Kanonier *m*; (*Naut*) Geschützführer *m*; (*in plane*) Bordschütze *m* ◆ **to be in the ~s** (*Mil*) bei der Artillerie sein.

gunnery ['gʌnərɪ] *n* Schießkunst *f* ◆ **~ officer** Artillerieoffizier *m*.

gunny ['gʌnɪ] *n* Sackleinen *nt*.

gun: ~point *n* **to hold sb at ~point** jdn mit einer Pistole/einem Gewehr bedrohen; **to force sb to do sth at ~point** jdn mit vorgehaltener Pistole/vorgehaltenem Gewehr zwingen, etw zu tun; **to surrender at ~point** sich, von einer Pistole/einem Gewehr bedroht, ergeben; **~powder** *n* Schießpulver *nt*; **G~powder Plot** (*Hist*) Pulververschwörung *f*; **~room** *n* Waffenkammer *f*; (*Naut*) Kadettenmesse *f*; **~runner** *n* Waffenschmuggler *or* -schieber *m*; **~running** *n* Waffenschmuggel *m*, Waffenschieberei *f* (*inf*); **~ ship** *n*: **helicopter ~ship** Kampfhubschrauber *m*; **~shot** *n* Schuß *m*; (*range*) Schußweite *f*; **~shot wound** Schußwunde *f*; **~-slinger** *n* (*inf*) Pistolenheld *m* (*inf*); **~smith** *n* Büchsenmacher *m*; **~ turret** *n* Geschützturm *m*; **~wale** ['gʌnl] *n* Dollbord *nt*.

guppy ['gʌpɪ] *n* Guppy, Millionenfisch *m*.

gurgle ['gɜːgl] 1 *n* (*of liquid*) Gluckern *nt no pl*; (*of brook also*) Plätschern *nt no pl*; (*of baby*) Glucksen *nt no pl* ◆ **to give ~s of pleasure/laughter** vor Vergnügen/Lachen glucksen.
2 *vi* (*liquid*) gluckern; (*brook also*) plätschern; (*person*) glucksen (*with* vor +*dat*).

guru ['gʊruː] *n* (*lit, fig*) Guru *m*.

gush [gʌʃ] 1 *n* (a) (*of liquid*) Strahl, Schwall *m*; (*of words*) Schwall *m*; (*of emotion*) Ausbruch *m*.
(b) (*inf: ~ing talk*) Geschwärme *nt* (*inf*).
2 *vi* (a) (*also* **~ out**) (*water*) herausschießen, heraussprudeln; (*smoke, blood, tears*) hervorquellen; (*flames*) herausschlagen.
(b) (*inf: talk*) schwärmen (*inf*) (*about, over* von); (*insincerely*) sich ergehen (*about, over* über +*acc*).
3 *vt* (*liter*) (*volcano*) ausstoßen ◆ **the wound ~ed blood** aus der Wunde schoß *or* quoll Blut; **what a delightful hat, she ~ed** welch entzückender Hut, sagte sie überschwenglich.

gusher ['gʌʃəʳ] *n* (*oil well*) (natürlich sprudelnde) Ölquelle.

gushing ['gʌʃɪŋ] *adj* (a) *water* sprudelnd, (heraus)schießend. (b) (*fig*) überschwenglich; *talk also* schwärmerisch.

gushingly ['gʌʃɪŋlɪ] *adv* überschwenglich.

gusset ['gʌsɪt] *n* (*in garment*) Keil, Zwickel *m*.

gust [gʌst] 1 *n* (*of wind*) Stoß *m*, Bö(e) *f*; (*of rain*) Böe *f*; (*fig: of emotion*) Anfall *m* ◆ **a ~ of smoke/flames** eine Rauchwolke/Stichflamme; **a ~ of laughter** eine Lachsalve.
2 *vi* böig *or* stürmisch wehen.

gustily ['gʌstɪlɪ] *adv* böig, stürmisch.

gusto ['gʌstəʊ] *n* Begeisterung *f* ◆ **to do sth with ~** etw mit Genuß tun.

gusty ['gʌstɪ] *adj* (+*er*) *wind, day, rain* böig, stürmisch.

gut [gʌt] 1 *n* (a) (*alimentary canal*) Darm *m*; (*stomach, paunch*) Bauch *m*.
(b) *usu pl* (*inf: stomach*) Eingeweide *nt*; (*fig*) (*essence: of problem, matter*) Kern *m*; (*contents*) Substanz *f* ◆ **to sweat** *or* **work one's ~s out** (*inf*) wie blöd schuften (*inf*); **to hate sb's ~s** (*inf*) jdn auf den Tod nicht ausstehen können (*inf*); **I'll have his ~s for garters!** (*inf*) den mache ich zur Minna (*inf*) *or* zur Schnecke (*inf*); **~ reaction** rein gefühlsmäßige Reaktion.
(c) (*inf: courage*) **~s** *pl* Mumm (*inf*), Schneid (*inf*) *m*; **his style has got ~s/no ~s** sein Stil ist knallhart/windelweich (*inf*).
(d) (*cat~*) Darm *m*; (*for racket, violin*) Darmsaiten *pl*.
2 *vt* (a) *animal, chicken, fish* ausnehmen.
(b) (*fire*) ausbrennen; (*remove contents*) ausräumen ◆ **it was completely ~ted by the fire** es war völlig ausgebrannt.

gutless ['gʌtlɪs] *adj* (*fig inf*) feige.

guts [gʌts] *n* (*Brit inf: greedy person*) Freßsack *m* (*inf*).

gutsy ['gʌtsɪ] *adj* (+*er*) (*inf*) (a) (*greedy*) verfressen (*inf*).
(b) (*fig*) *prose, music, player* rasant; *resistance* hart, mutig.

gutta-percha [ˌgʌtə'pɜːtʃə] *n* Guttapercha *f or nt*.

gutted ['gʌtɪd] *adj* (*Brit inf: disappointed*) am Boden (zerstört) (*inf*) ◆ **I was ~** ich war total am Boden (*inf*).

gutter ['gʌtəʳ] 1 *n* (*on roof*) Dachrinne *f*; (*in street*) Gosse *f* (*also fig*), Rinnstein *m* ◆ **to be born in the ~** aus der Gosse kommen; **the language of the ~** die Gassensprache.
2 *vi* (*candle, flame*) flackern.

guttering ['gʌtərɪŋ] 1 *n* Regenrinnen *pl*.
2 *adj* flackernd.

gutter: ~-press *n* Boulevardpresse *f*; **~snipe** *n* Gassenkind *nt*.

guttural ['gʌtərəl] 1 *n* Guttural(laut), Kehllaut *m*.
2 *adj* guttural, kehlig.

guv [gʌv], **guv'nor** ['gʌvnəʳ] *n* (*Brit inf*) Chef *m* (*inf*).

guy[1] [gaɪ] 1 *n* (a) (*inf: man*) Typ (*inf*), Kerl (*inf*) *m* ◆ **hey you ~s** he Leute (*inf*); **great ~s** dufte Typen *pl* (*inf*); **I'll ask the ~ next door** ich werde (den Typ von) nebenan fragen (*inf*); **are you ~s ready?** seid ihr fertig?
(b) (*Brit: effigy*) (Guy-Fawkes-)Puppe *f*; (*inf: sight*) Schießbudenfigur *f* (*inf*) ◆ **G~ Fawkes day** *Jahrestag m der Pulververschwörung (5. November)*; **a penny for the ~** Geld *nt* für das (Guy Fawkes) Feuerwerk.
2 *vt* (*ridicule*) sich lustig machen über (+*acc*).

guy[2] *n* (*also* **~-rope**) Haltetau *or* -seil *nt*; (*for tent*) Zeltschnur *f*.

Guyana [gaɪ'ænə] *n* Guyana (*form*), Guayana *nt*.

Guyanese [ˌgaɪə'niːz] *n* Guayaner(in *f*) *m*.

guzzle ['gʌzl] *vti* (*eat*) futtern (*inf*); (*drink*) schlürfen.

gym [dʒɪm] *n* (*gymnasium*) Turnhalle *f*; (*gymnastics*) Turnen *nt*.

gymkhana [dʒɪm'kɑːnə] *n* Reiterfest *nt*.

gymnasium [dʒɪm'neɪzɪəm] *n*, *pl* **-s** *or* (*form*) **gymnasia** [dʒɪm'neɪzɪə] Turnhalle *f*.

gymnast ['dʒɪmnæst] *n* Turner(in *f*) *m*.

gymnastic [dʒɪm'næstɪk] *adj ability* turnerisch; *training, exercise also* Turn-.

gymnastics [dʒɪm'næstɪks] *n* (a) *sing* (*discipline*) Gymnastik *f no pl*; (*with apparatus*) Turnen *nt no pl*. (b) *pl* (*exercises*) Übungen *pl* ◆ **verbal ~** Wortakrobatik *f*.

gym: ~ shoe *n* (*Brit*) Turnschuh *m*; **~slip** *n* (*Brit*) Schulträgerrock *m*; **~ teacher** *n* Turnlehrer(in *f*) *m*.

gynaecological, (*US*) **gynecological** [ˌgaɪnɪkə'lɒdʒɪkəl] *adj* gynäkologisch ◆ **~ illness** Frauenleiden *nt*, gynäkologisches Leiden.

gynaecologist, (*US*) **gynecologist** [ˌgaɪnɪ'kɒlədʒɪst] *n* Gynäkologe *m*, Gynäkologin *f*, Frauenarzt *m*/-ärztin *f*.

gynaecology, (*US*) **gynecology** [ˌgaɪnɪ'kɒlədʒɪ] *n* Gynäkologie, Frauenheilkunde *f*.

gyp [dʒɪp] *n* (a) (*sl: swindle*) Gaunerei *f* (*inf*). (b) (*sl: swindler*) Gauner *m*. (c) (*Brit Univ inf*) Putzfrau *f*. (d) (*inf*) **to give sb ~** jdn plagen (*inf*).

gypsum ['dʒɪpsəm] *n* Gips *m*.

gypsy *n, adj attr* (*esp US*) *see* **gipsy**.

gyrate [ˌdʒaɪə'reɪt] *vi* (*whirl*) (herum)wirbeln; (*rotate*) sich drehen, kreisen; (*dancer*) sich drehen und winden.

gyration [ˌdʒaɪə'reɪʃən] *n see vi* Wirbeln *nt no pl*; Drehung *f*, Kreisen *nt no pl*; Drehung und Windung *f usu pl*.

gyratory [ˌdʒaɪə'reɪtərɪ] *adj* (*whirling*) wirbelnd; (*revolving*) kreisend.

gyrocompass ['dʒaɪərəʊ'kʌmpəs] *n* Kreisel-Magnetkompaß *m*.

gyroscope ['dʒaɪərəˌskəʊp] *n* Gyroskop *nt*.

H, h [eɪtʃ] *n* H, h *nt*; *see* **drop.**
H *abbr of* **hard** (*on pencil*) H.
h *abbr of* **hour(s)** h.
ha [hɑː] *interj* ha.
habeas corpus ['heɪbɪəs'kɔːpəs] *n* (*Jur*) Habeaskorpusakte *f* ◆ **to issue a writ of ~** einen Vorführungsbefehl erteilen; **the lawyer applied for ~** der Rechtsanwalt verlangte, daß sein Klient einem Untersuchungsrichter vorgeführt wurde.
haberdasher ['hæbədæʃəʳ] *n* (*Brit*) Kurzwarenhändler(in *f*) *m*; (*US*) Herrenausstatter *m*.
haberdashery [ˌhæbə'dæʃərɪ] *n* (*Brit*) (*articles*) Kurzwaren *pl*; (*shop*) Kurzwarengeschäft *nt or* -handlung *f*; (*US*) (*articles*) Herrenbekleidung *f*; Herrenartikel *pl*; (*shop*) Herrenmodengeschäft *nt*.
habiliments [hə'bɪlɪmənts] *npl* (*form*) Ornat *nt* (*form*).
habit ['hæbɪt] *n* **(a)** Gewohnheit *f*; (*esp undesirable also*) Angewohnheit *f* ◆ **to be in the ~ of doing sth** die Angewohnheit haben, etw zu tun, etw gewöhnlich tun; **... as was his ~** ... wie es seine Gewohnheit war; **it became a ~** es wurde zur Gewohnheit; **out of** *or* **by (sheer) ~** aus (reiner) Gewohnheit, (rein) gewohnheitsmäßig; **from (force of) ~** aus Gewohnheit; **I don't make a ~ of asking strangers in** (für) gewöhnlich bitte ich Fremde nicht herein; **don't make a ~ of it** lassen Sie (sich *dat*) das nicht zur Gewohnheit werden; **to get into/to get sb into the ~ of doing sth** sich/jdm angewöhnen *or* sich/jdn daran gewöhnen, etw zu tun; **I'd got into the ~ of seeing you in uniform** ich war gewöhnt, Sie in Uniform zu sehen; **to get** *or* **fall into bad ~s** schlechte Gewohnheiten annehmen; **to get out of/to get sb out of the ~ of doing sth** sich/jdm abgewöhnen, etw zu tun; **you must get out of the ~ of biting your nails** du mußt dir das Nägelkauen abgewöhnen; **to have a ~ of doing sth** die Angewohnheit haben, etw zu tun; **he has a strange ~ of staring at you** er hat die merkwürdige Art, einen anzustarren.
(b) (*costume*) Gewand *nt*; (*monk's also*) Habit *nt or m* ◆ **(riding) ~** Reitkleid *nt*.
habitable ['hæbɪtəbl] *adj* bewohnbar.
habitat ['hæbɪtæt] *n* Heimat *f*; (*of animals also*) Lebensraum *m*.
habitation [ˌhæbɪ'teɪʃən] *n* (Be)wohnen *nt*; (*place*) Wohnstätte, Behausung *f* ◆ **to show signs of ~** bewohnt aussehen; **unfit for human ~** menschenunwürdig, für Wohnzwecke nicht geeignet.
habit-forming ['hæbɪtˌfɔːmɪŋ] *adj* **to be ~** zur Gewohnheit werden; **are those ~ drugs?** wird man davon abhängig?
habitual [hə'bɪtjʊəl] *adj* gewohnt; *smoker, drinker, gambler* Gewohnheits-, gewohnheitsmäßig; *liar* gewohnheitsmäßig, notorisch ◆ **his ~ courtesy/cheerfulness** *etc* die ihm eigene Höflichkeit/Heiterkeit *etc*.
habitually [hə'bɪtjʊəlɪ] *adv* ständig.
habituate [hə'bɪtjʊeɪt] *vt* gewöhnen (*sb to sth* jdn an etw (*acc*), *sb to doing sth* jdn daran, etw zu tun).
habitué [hə'bɪtjʊeɪ] *n* regelmäßiger Besucher, regelmäßige Besucherin, Habitué (*geh, Aus*) *m*; (*in pubs etc*) Stammgast *m*.
hacienda ['hæsɪəndə] *n* Hazienda *f*.
hack[1] [hæk] [1] *n* **(a)** (*cut*) (Ein)schnitt *m*, Kerbe *f*; (*action*) Hieb *m* ◆ **to take a ~ at sth** mit der Axt *etc* auf etw (*acc*) schlagen; (*in rage*) auf etw (*acc*) einhacken.
(b) (*kick*) Tritt *m* ◆ **he had a ~ at his opponent's ankle** er versetzte seinem Gegner einen Tritt gegen den Knöchel; **he got a ~ on the shin** er bekam einen Tritt gegen das Schienbein.
(c) (*cough*) trockener Husten.
[2] *vt* **(a)** (*cut*) schlagen, hacken ◆ **don't ~ your meat, cut it** du mußt das Fleisch nicht hacken, sondern schneiden; **to ~ sb/sth to pieces** (*lit*) jdn zerstückeln/etw (in Stücke) (zer)hacken *or* schlagen; (*fig*) jdn/etw zerfetzen; **he was brutally ~ed to death** er ist brutal (mit einem Beil *etc*) erschlagen worden; **to ~ one's way out** sich einen Weg freischlagen; **to ~ one's way through (sth)** sich (*dat*) einen Weg (durch etw) schlagen, sich (durch etw) durchhauen.
(b) (*Sport*) *ball* treten gegen, einen Tritt versetzen (+*dat*) ◆ **to ~ sb on the shin** jdn vors *or* gegen das Schienbein treten.
[3] *vi* **(a)** (*chop*) hacken ◆ **he ~ed at the branch with his axe** er schlug mit der Axt auf den Ast; **don't ~ at it** hack nicht daran herum. **(b)** (*cough*) trocken husten. **(c)** (*Sport*) **he was booked for ~ing** er wurde wegen Holzerei verwarnt. **(d)** (*Comput*) hacken ◆ **to ~ into a mainframe** in einen Mainframe eindringen.
◆**hack about** *vt sep* (*fig*) *text etc* zerstückeln.
◆**hack down** *vt sep bushes etc* abhacken; *people also* niedermetzeln; *tree* umhauen.
◆**hack off** *vt sep* abhacken, abschlagen ◆ **to ~ sth ~ sth** etw von etw abhacken *or* abschlagen.
◆**hack out** *vt sep clearing* schlagen; *hole* heraushacken.
◆**hack up** *vt sep* zerhacken; *meat, wood, furniture also* kleinhacken; *bodies* zerstückeln.
hack[2] [1] *n* **(a)** (*hired horse*) Mietpferd *nt*; (*worn-out horse*) Gaul, Klepper *m*. **(b)** (*pej: literary ~*) Schreiberling *m*; (*of cheap novels also*) Schundliterat(in *f*) *m*; (*journalist also*) Schmierfink *m* ◆ **the newspaper ~s** die Zeitungsschreiber *pl*; **paid ~** Soldschreiber *m*. **(c)** (*pej inf*) **(party) ~** (Partei)heini (*inf*) *or* -typ (*inf*) *m*. **(d)** (*US: taxi*) Taxi *nt*.
[2] *adj attr* (*pej*) *writing* stumpfsinnig ◆ **~ writer** *see* **hack**[2] **1 (b).**
[3] *vi* einen Spazierritt machen ◆ **to go ~ing** ausreiten.
hacker ['hækəʳ] *n* (*Comput*) Hacker *m*.
hackie ['hækɪ] *n* (*US inf*) Taxifahrer(in *f*) *m*.
hacking ['hækɪŋ] [1] *adj* **(a) ~ cough** trockener Husten. **(b) ~ jacket** Sportsakko *m or nt*; (*for riding*) Reitjacke *f*.
[2] *n* (*Comput*) Hacken *nt*.
hackle ['hækl] *n* (*Orn*) lange Nackenfeder; (*plumage also*) Nackengefieder *nt*; (*pl: of dog etc*) Fell *nt* im Nacken ◆ **the dog's ~s rose** dem Hund sträubte sich das Fell; **his ~s rose at the very idea** bei dem bloßen Gedanken sträubte sich alles in ihm; **to get sb's ~s up** jdn reizen, jdn auf die Palme bringen (*inf*); **to have one's ~s up** auf (hundert)achtzig sein (*inf*).
hackney carriage ['hæknɪˌkærɪdʒ] *n* (*horse-drawn*) (Pferde)droschke *f*; (*form: taxi*) (Kraft)droschke *f* (*form*).
hackneyed ['hæknɪd] *adj subject* abgedroschen, abgegriffen; *metaphor, turn of phrase also* abgenutzt.
hack: ~saw *n* Metallsäge *f*; **~work** *n* (*trivial writing*) Schmiererei *f* (*inf*); (*mindless editing*) Routinearbeit *f*.
had [hæd] *pret, ptp of* **have.**
haddock ['hædək] *n* Schellfisch *m*.
Hades ['heɪdiːz] *n* (*Myth*) Hades *m*.
hadn't ['hædnt] *contr of* **had not.**
Hadrian ['heɪdrɪən] *n* Hadrian *m* ◆ **~'s Wall** Hadrianswall *m*.
haematologist, (*US*) **hematologist** [ˌhiːmə'tɒlədʒɪst] *n* Hämatologe *m*, Hämatologin *f*.
haematology, (*US*) **hematology** [ˌhiːmə'tɒlədʒɪ] *n* Hämatologie *f*.
haemoglobin, (*US*) **hemoglobin** [ˌhiːməʊ'gləʊbɪn] *n* Hämoglobin *nt*, roter Blutfarbstoff.
haemophilia, (*US*) **hemophilia** [ˌhiːməʊ'fɪlɪə] *n* Bluterkrankheit, Hämophilie (*spec*) *f*.
haemophiliac, (*US*) **hemophiliac** [ˌhiːməʊ'fɪlɪæk] *n* Bluter *m*.
haemorrhage, (*US*) **hemorrhage** ['hemərɪdʒ] [1] *n* Blutung, Hämorrhagie (*spec*) *f*.
[2] *vi* bluten.
haemorrhoids, (*US*) **hemorrhoids** ['hemərɔɪdz] *npl* Hämorrhoiden *pl*.
hafnium ['hæfnɪəm] *n* (*Chem*) Hafnium *nt*.
haft [hɑːft] *n* (*of knife*) Heft *nt*; (*of sword*) Griff *m*.
hag [hæg] *n* Hexe *f*.
haggard ['hægəd] *adj* ausgezehrt; (*from tiredness*) abgespannt; (*from worry*) abgehärmt, verhärmt ◆ **he had a very ~ expression throughout the trial** er wirkte während der ganzen Verhandlung sehr mitgenommen.
haggis ['hægɪs] *n schottisches Gericht aus gehackten Schafsinnereien und Haferschrot, im Schafsmagen gekocht.*
haggish ['hægɪʃ] *adj* zänkisch, garstig.
haggle ['hægl] *vi* (*bargain*) feilschen (*about or over* um); (*argue also*) sich (herum)streiten (*over* um *or* wegen) ◆ **let's stop haggling over who's going to pay** hören wir doch auf mit dem Hin und Her (darüber), wer nun bezahlt.
haggling ['hæglɪŋ] *n* Feilschen, Gefeilsche *nt*, Feilscherei *f*.
hagiographer [ˌhægɪ'ɒgrəfəʳ] *n* (*form*) Hagiograph *m* (*form*).
hagiography [ˌhægɪ'ɒgrəfɪ] *n* (*form*) Heiligengeschichte, Hagiographie (*spec*) *f*.
hagiology [ˌhægɪ'ɒlədʒɪ] *n* (*form*) Hagiologie *f* (*spec*).

hag-ridden ['hægrɪdn] *adj (worried)* vergrämt, verhärmt; *atmosphere* drückend ◆ **to be ~** *(hum: tormented by women)* unter Weiberherrschaft stehen.

Hague [heɪg] *n* **the ~** Den Haag *nt*; **in the ~** in Den Haag.

ha-ha ['hɑː'hɑː] [1] *interj* ha-ha.
[2] *n (fence)* versenkter Grenzzaun.

hail[1] [heɪl] [1] *n* Hagel *m* ◆ **a ~ of rocks/blows/curses** ein Steinhagel *m or* Hagel *m* von Steinen/Schlägen/Flüchen; **in a ~ of bullets** im Kugel- *or* Geschoßhagel.
[2] *vi* hageln.

◆**hail down** [1] *vi (stones etc)* niederprasseln, niederhageln *(on sb/sth* auf jdn/etw) ◆ **the blows ~ed ~ (on him)** es hagelte Schläge (auf ihn nieder).
[2] *vt sep blows* niederprasseln lassen ◆ **she ~ed ~ curses on him** sie überschüttete ihn mit einem Schwall von Flüchen.

hail[2] [1] *vt* **(a)** zujubeln *(+dat)*, bejubeln ◆ **to ~ sb/sth as sth** jdn/etw als etw feiern.
(b) *(call loudly)* zurufen *(+dat)*; *ship* anrufen, preien *(spec)*; *taxi (by calling)* rufen; *(by making sign also)* anhalten, herbeiwinken, winken *(+dat)* ◆ **within ~ing distance** in Rufweite.
[2] *vi* **a ship ~ing from London** ein Schiff *nt* mit (dem) Heimathafen London; **where does that boat ~ from?** was ist der Heimathafen dieses Schiffs?; **they ~ from all parts of the world** sie kommen *or* stammen aus allen Teilen der Welt; **where do you ~ from?** wo stammen Sie her?
[3] *interj (obs, liter)* sei gegrüßt *(liter)* heil *(+dat) (liter)* ◆ **~ Caesar** heil dir Cäsar; **the H~ Mary** das Ave Maria.
[4] *n* (Zu)ruf *m* ◆ **within ~** in Rufweite.

hail-fellow-well-met ['heɪlfeləʊ,wel'met] *adj* plump-vertraulich ◆ **he tries to be ~ with everyone** er versucht, sich bei allen anzubiedern.

hail: ~stone *n* Hagelkorn *nt*; **~storm** *n* Hagel(schauer) *m*.

hair [hɛəʳ] [1] *n* **(a)** *(collective: on head)* Haare *pl*, Haar *nt* ◆ **a fine head of ~** schönes volles Haar, schöne volle Haare; **to do one's ~** sich frisieren, sich *(dat)* die Haare (zurecht)machen *(inf)*; **to have one's ~ cut/done** sich *(dat)* die Haare schneiden/frisieren lassen; **her ~ is always very well done** sie ist immer sehr gut frisiert; **to let one's ~ down** *(lit)* sein Haar aufmachen *or* lösen *(geh)*; *(fig)* aus sich *(dat)* herausgehen; **keep your ~ on!** *(inf)* ruhig Blut!; **to get in sb's ~** *(inf)* jdm auf den Wecker *or* auf die Nerven gehen *(inf)*; **that film really made my ~ stand on end** bei dem Film lief es mir eiskalt den Rücken herunter.
(b) *(single ~)* Haar *nt* ◆ **not a ~ of his head was harmed** ihm wurde kein Haar gekrümmt; **not a ~ out of place** *(fig)* wie aus dem Ei gepellt; **to win/lose by a ~** ganz knapp gewinnen/verlieren; *see* **turn, split.**
(c) *(on body)* Haar(e *pl*) *nt*; *(total body ~)* Behaarung *f* ◆ **body ~** Körperbehaarung *f*.
(d) *(of animal, plant)* Haar *nt*; *(of pig)* Borste *f* ◆ **the best cure for a hangover is the ~ of the dog (that bit you)** einen Kater kuriert man am besten, wenn man mit dem anfängt, womit man aufgehört hat.
[2] *attr mattress, sofa* Roßhaar-.

hair: ~ ball *n* Haarknäuel *nt*; **~-band** *n* Haarband *nt*; **~-breadth, ~'s breadth** *n* Haaresbreite *f*; **by a ~'s breadth** um Haaresbreite; **to be within a ~'s breadth of ruin** am Rande des Ruins stehen; **he was within a ~'s breadth of dying** er wäre um ein Haar gestorben; **to escape by a ~'s breadth** mit knapper Not entkommen; **~brush** *n* Haarbürste *f*; **~ clip** *n* Clip *m*; *(for pony-tail etc)* Haarspange *f*; **~-clippers** *npl* elektrische Haarschneidemaschine; **~ conditioner** *n* Pflegespülung *f*; **~ cream** *n* Haarcreme, Pomade *f*; **~ curler** *n* Lockenwickler *m*; **~cut** *n* Haarschnitt *m*; *(act also)* Haarschneiden *nt*; *(hairdo)* Frisur *f*; **to have** *or* **get a ~cut** sich *(dat)* die Haare schneiden lassen; **I need a ~cut** ich muß zum Friseur, ich muß mir die Haare schneiden lassen; **~do** *n (inf)* Frisur *f*; **~dresser** *n* Friseur *m*, Friseuse *f*; **the ~dresser's** der Friseur; **~dressing** *n* Frisieren *nt*; *(tonic)* Haarwasser *nt*; **~dressing salon** *n* Friseursalon *m*; **~-drier** *n* Haartrockner *m*; *(hand-held also)* Fön ® *m*; *(over head also)* Trockenhaube *f*.

-haired [hɛəd] *adj suf* -haarig.

hair: ~ follicle *n* Haarfollikel *nt*, Haarbalg *m*; **~-grip** *n* Haarklemme *f*, Klemmchen *nt*.

hairiness ['hɛərɪnɪs] *n* Behaartheit *f* ◆ **is ~ a sign of virility?** ist starker Haarwuchs ein Zeichen von Männlichkeit?

hair: ~ lacquer *n* Haarspray *m or nt*; **~less** *adj* unbehaart; *plant* haarlos; **~line** *n* **(a)** Haaransatz *m*; **(b)** *(thin line)* haarfeine Linie; *(in telescope, on sight)* Faden *m*; *(Typ)* senkrechter Strich; **~-lines** Fadenkreuz *nt*; **~-line crack** *n* Haarriß *m*; **~net** *n* Haarnetz *nt*; **~ oil** *n* Haaröl *nt*; **~-piece** *n* Haarteil *nt*; *(for men)* Toupet *nt*; **~pin** *n* Haarnadel *f*; **~pin (bend)** *n* Haarnadelkurve *f*; **~-raiser** *n (inf) (experience)* haarsträubendes *or* entsetzliches Erlebnis; *(film, story)* Horror- *or* Gruselfilm *m*/-geschichte *f*, Schocker *m (inf)*; **~-raising** *adj* haarsträubend; **~ remover** *n* Haarentferner *m*, Haarentfernungsmittel *nt*; **~ restorer** *n* Haarwuchsmittel *nt*; **~ roller** *n* Lockenwickler *m*; **~'s breadth** *n see* **~-breadth**; **~ shirt** *n* härenes Gewand *(old, liter)*; **~ slide** *n* Haarspange *f*; **~ space** *n (Typ)* Haarspatium *nt*; **~-splitter** *n* Haarspalter *m*; **~-splitting** [1] *n* Haarspalterei *f*; [2] *adj* haarspalterisch; **~spray** *n* Haarspray *m or nt*; **~spring** *n* Spiralfeder *f*; **~style** *n* Frisur *f*; **~ stylist** *n* Coiffeur *m*, Coiffeuse *f*, Haarkünstler(in *f*) *m*; **~ transplant** *n* Haartransplantation *f*; **~ trigger** *n* Stecher *m*.

hairy ['hɛərɪ] *adj (+er)* **(a)** stark behaart; *parts of body also, monster* haarig ◆ **the cat makes everything all ~** die Katze hinterläßt überall Haare; **some ~ freak** so ein behaarter Typ. **(b)** *(Bot)* behaart. **(c)** *(sl)* gefährlich, haarig *(inf)*; *bridge, corner, driving* kriminell *(sl)*; *situation also* brenzlig *(inf)*.

Haiti ['heɪtɪ] *n* Haiti *nt*.

Haitian ['heɪʃɪən] [1] *adj* haitianisch, haitisch.
[2] *n* **(a)** Haitianer(in *f*) *m*. **(b)** *(language)* Haitisch *nt*.

hake [heɪk] *n* See- *or* Meerhecht, Hechtdorsch *m*.

halberd ['hælbəd] *n* Hellebarde *f*.

halberdier [,hælbə'dɪəʳ] *n* Hellebardier *m*.

halcyon ['hælsɪən] *adj*: **~ days** glückliche Tage *pl*.

hale [heɪl] *adj (+er)* kräftig; *old man* rüstig ◆ **~ and hearty** gesund und munter.

half [hɑːf] [1] *n, pl* **halves** **(a)** Hälfte *f* ◆ **two halves make a whole** zwei Halbe machen ein Ganzes; **to cut in ~** halbieren; *(with knife also)* in zwei Hälften *or* Teile schneiden; *salary etc* um *or* auf die Hälfte kürzen; **to break/tear sth in ~** etw durchbrechen/ durchreißen; **~ of it/them** die Hälfte davon/von ihnen; **~ the book/money/my life** die Hälfte des Buches/Geldes/meines Lebens *or* das halbe Buch/Geld/mein halbes Leben; **he gave me ~** er gab mir die Hälfte; **~ a cup/an hour/a lifetime** eine halbe Tasse/Stunde/ein halbes Leben; **he's only ~ a man** er ist nur ein halber Mensch; **he's not ~ the man he used to be** er ist längst nicht mehr das, was er einmal war; **~ a second!** (einen) Augenblick mal!; **I'll be round in ~ a second** *(inf)* ich komme gleich (mal) hin; **to listen with ~ an ear** nur mit halbem Ohr zuhören; **to take ~ of sth** die Hälfte von etw nehmen; **to go halves (with sb on sth)** (mit jdm mit etw) halbe-halbe machen *(inf)*; **that's only ~ the story** das ist nur die halbe Geschichte; **have ~ of my apple** willst du einen halben Apfel von mir haben?; **bigger by ~** anderthalbmal so groß; **he is too clever by ~** *(inf)* das ist ein richtiger Schlaumeier; **he's too cocky by ~** *(inf)* er hält sich für wer weiß was *(inf)*; **not ~ enough** bei weitem nicht *or* längst nicht genug; **one and a ~** eineinhalb, anderthalb; **an hour and a ~** eineinhalb *or* anderthalb Stunden; **not to do things by halves** keine halben Sachen machen; **~ and ~** halb und halb; **that's a hill and a ~!** *(inf)* das ist vielleicht ein Berg!; **that's not the ~ of it** *(inf)*, **I haven't told you the ~ of it yet** *(inf)* und das ist noch nicht einmal die Hälfte *(inf)*.
(b) *(Sport) (of match)* (Spiel)hälfte, Halbzeit *f*; *(player)* Läufer(in *f*) *m*.
(c) *(of ticket)* Abschnitt *m* der Fahrkarte; *(travel, admission fee)* halbe Karte *(inf)* ◆ **return ~** Abschnitt *m* für die Rückfahrt; **two adults and one ~, please** zwei Erwachsene und ein Kind, bitte; **two and a ~ (to London)** zweieinhalb(mal London).
(d) *(beer)* kleines Bier, Halbe *f (dial)*, Halbe(s), Kleine(s) *nt*; *(Scot: whisky)* einfacher Whisky, Einfache(r) *m*.
[2] *adj* halb ◆ **a ~ cup** eine halbe Tasse; **with ~ his usual strength** nur mit halber Kraft; **~ one thing ~ another** halb und halb, halb das eine und halb das andere; **~ man ~ beast** halb Mensch, halb Tier; **it's neither opera nor operetta but sort of ~ and ~** es ist so ein Zwischending *nt* zwischen Oper und Operette.
[3] *adv* **(a)** halb ◆ **I ~ thought** ... ich hätte fast gedacht ...; **I was ~ afraid that** ... ich habe fast befürchtet, daß ...; **~ melted** halbgeschmolzen *attr*, halb geschmolzen *pred*; **the work is only ~ done** die Arbeit ist erst halb *or* zur Hälfte erledigt; **that's ~ right** das ist zur Hälfte richtig; **~ laughing, ~ crying** halb lachend, halb weinend; **~ laughing, ~ crying he told me** ... mit einem lachenden und einem weinenden Auge erzählte er mir ...; **he ~ rose to his feet** er erhob sich halb; **I ~ think** ich habe beinahe den Eindruck; **he only ~ understands** er begreift *or* versteht nur die Hälfte.
(b) *(Brit inf)* **he's not ~ stupid/rich** *etc* er ist vielleicht *or* unheimlich dumm/reich *etc*; **it didn't ~ rain/he didn't ~ yell** es *hat* vielleicht geregnet/er *hat* vielleicht gebrüllt; **not ~ bad** gar nicht schlecht; **not ~!** und wie! und ob!
(c) **it's ~ past three** *or* **~ three** es ist halb vier.
(d) **he is ~ as big as his sister** er ist halb so groß wie seine Schwester; **~ as big again** anderthalbmal so groß; **he earns ~ as much as you** er verdient halb so viel wie Sie; **he earns ~ as much again as you** er verdient die Hälfte mehr als du *or* anderthalbmal soviel wie du; **give me ~ as much again** gib mir noch die Hälfte dazu.

half: ~-a-crown *n see* **~-crown**; **~-a-dozen** *n, adj see* **~-dozen**; **~ back** *n (Sport)* Läufer(in *f*) *m*; **~-baked** *adj (fig) person, plan* blödsinnig; **~-binding** *n (of book)* Halbband *m*; **~-bred** *adj* Mischlings-; *(esp Red Indian)* Halbblut-; **~-breed** [1] *n (person)* Mischling *m*; *(esp Red Indian)* Halbblut *nt*; *(animal)* Rassenmischung *f*; *(horse)* Halbblut *nt*, Halbblüter *m*; [2] *adj animal* gekreuzt; *horse* Halbblut-; **a ~-breed dog** eine Mischrasse, eine Rassenmischung; *see also* **~-bred**; **~ brother** *n* Halbbruder *m*; **~-caste** [1] *n* Mischling *m*; *(esp Red Indian)* Halbblut *nt*; [2] *adj* Mischlings-; *(esp Red Indian)* Halbblut-; **a ~-caste American** ein amerikanischer Mischling; **~-circle** *n* Halbkreis *m*; **~-closed** *adj* halbgeschlossen *attr*, halb geschlossen *pred*; **~-cock** *n*: **to go off at ~-cock** *(inf)* ein Reinfall *m* sein *(inf)*, ein Schuß *m* in den Ofen sein *(sl)*; **~-cocked** *adj pistol* in Vorderraststellung; **~-cooked** *adj* halbgar *attr*, halb gar *pred*; **~ cracked** *adj (Brit sl: crazy)* beknackt *(sl)*, bescheuert *(sl)*; **~-crown** *n (in old Brit system)* Half Crown *f*, Zweieinhalbschillingstück *nt*; **~-cup brassière** *n* Büstenhalter *m* mit Halbschalen; **~-cut** *adj (Brit sl: drunk)* besoffen *(sl)*; **~-day** *(holiday) n* halber freier Tag; **we've got a ~-day (holiday)** wir haben einen halben Tag frei; **~-dead** *adj (lit, fig)* halbtot *(with* vor *+dat)*; **~-dollar** *n* halber Dollar; **~-dozen** *n* halbes Dutzend; **~-dressed** *adj* halbbekleidet *attr*, halb bekleidet *pred*; **~-empty** [1] *adj* halbleer *attr*, halb leer *pred*; [2] *vt* zur Hälfte leeren *or* leermachen; **~-fare** [1] *n* halber Fahrpreis; [2] *adv* zum halben Preis; **~-fill** *vt* halb füllen; **~-forgotten** *adj* fast vergessen; **~-frame camera** *n* Halbformatkamera *f*; **~-full** *adj* halbvoll *attr*, halb voll *pred*; **~-hearted** *adj* halbherzig; *attempt also* lustlos; *manner* lustlos, lau; *noises of approval also* lau; **he was rather ~-hearted about accepting** er nahm ohne rechte Lust an; **he seems very ~-hearted about it** er scheint sich dafür nicht so recht begeistern zu können; **~-heartedly** *adv* *agree* halben Herzens, mit halbem Herzen; **to do sth ~-heartedly** etw ohne rechte Überzeugung *or* Lust tun; **~-heartedness** *n* Halbherzigkeit, Lustlosigkeit *f*; **the ~-heartedness of his attempts** seine halbherzigen *or* lustlosen Versuche *pl*; **~-holiday** *n* halber Urlaubstag/Feiertag; **we've got a ~-holiday tomorrow morning** wir haben morgen vormittag frei; **~-hour** *n* halbe Stunde; **~-an-hour's** *or* **a ~-hour interval** eine halbstündige Pause, eine halbe Stunde Pause; **it strikes on the ~-hour** sie schlägt die halben Stunden; **~-hourly** [1] *adv* jede *or* alle halbe Stunde, halbstündlich; [2] *adj* halbstündlich; **~-landing** *n* Treppenabsatz *m*; **~-length** *adj* **~-length portrait** Brustbild *nt*; **~-life** *n* (*Phys*) Halbwertszeit *f*; **~-light** *n* Dämmerlicht, Halbdunkel *nt*; **~-mast** *n*: **at ~-mast** (*also hum*) (auf) halbmast; **with his trousers at ~-mast** (*too short*) mit Hochwasserhosen; **~-measure** *n* halbe Maßnahme; Stehenbleiben *nt no pl* auf halbem Weg; **we don't do things by ~-measures** wir machen keine halben Sachen, wir begnügen uns nicht mit Halbheiten; **~-monthly** [1] *adj* zweiwöchentlich, vierzehntäglich; *publication* zweimal im Monat erscheinend; [2] *adv* zweimal im Monat; **~-moon** *n* (**a**) Halbmond *m*; (**b**) (*of fingernails*) Mond *m*; **~-naked** *adj* halbnackt *attr*, halb nackt *pred*; **~ nelson** *n* (*Wrestling*) Halbnelson *m*; **~-note** *n* (*US Mus*) halbe Note; **~-open** [1] *adj* halboffen *attr*, halb offen *pred*; [2] *vt* halb öffnen *or* aufmachen; **~-pay** *n* halber Lohn; halbes Gehalt; **to be on ~-pay/to be put on ~-pay** den halben Lohn *etc* bekommen/auf halben Lohn gesetzt werden; **~pence** *n* halber Penny; **~penny** ['heɪpnɪ] (*Brit old*) [1] *n* halber Penny; [2] *attr stamp* Halbpenny-; **~-pint** *n* (**a**) ≃ Viertelliter *m or nt*; (*of beer also*) kleines Bier; (**b**) (*inf: person*) halbe Portion (*inf*), Knirps *m* (*inf*); **~-price** [1] *n* **at ~-price** zum halben Preis; **reduced to ~-price** auf den halben Preis heruntergesetzt; [2] *adj* zum halben Preis; **~ rest** *n* (*US Mus*) halbe Pause; **~-seas over** *adj* (*dated inf*) bezecht, leicht hinüber (*inf*); **~-serious** *adj* **I was only ~-serious about it** ich habe das nicht ganz ernst gemeint; **actually, I was ~-serious about it** ich habe das nicht nur im Scherz gesagt; **~-sister** *n* Halbschwester *f*; **~-size** [1] *n* Zwischengröße *f*; [2] *adj* halb so groß; **~-size plate** kleiner Teller; **a ~-size model of sth** ein Modell *nt* von etw in halber Größe; **~-term** *n* (*Brit*) Ferien *pl* in der Mitte des Trimesters; **we get three days for ~-term** wir haben drei Tage Ferien in der Mitte des Trimesters; **~-timbered** *adj* Fachwerk-; **~-timbering** *n* Fachwerkbauweise *f*; **~-time** [1] *n* (**a**) (*Sport*) Halbzeit *f*; **at ~-time** bei *or* zur Halbzeit; (**b**) (*Ind*) **to be/to be put on ~-time** auf Kurzarbeit sein/gesetzt werden; [2] *attr whistle, score* Halbzeit-, zur Halbzeit; [3] *adv* **to work ~-time** halbtags arbeiten *or* beschäftigt sein; **~-title** *n* Schmutztitel *m*; **~-tone** *n* (*Art, Phot, US Mus*) Halbton *m*; (*Phot*) (*process*) Halbtonverfahren *nt*; (*picture*) Halbtonbild *nt*; **~-tone screen** *n* (*Typ*) Raster *m*; **~-track** *n* (*vehicle*) Halbkettenfahrzeug *nt*; **~-truth** *n* Halbwahrheit *f*; **~-volley** (*Tennis*) [1] *n* Halfvolley, Halbflugball *m*; [2] *vt ball* als Halfvolley schlagen.

halfway ['hɑːfˌweɪ] [1] *adj attr measures* halb ◆ **at a ~ stage** in einem Zwischenstadium; **when we reached the ~ stage on our journey** als wir die Hälfte der Reise hinter uns (*dat*) hatten; **the project is at the ~ stage** das Projekt ist zur Hälfte abgeschlossen; **he was at the ~ stage of his musical career** er befand sich in der Mitte seiner musikalischen Karriere; **we're past the ~ stage** wir haben die Hälfte geschafft; **it is a sort of ~ stage between democracy and ...** das ist eine Art Zwischenstadium zwischen Demokratie und ...; (*non temporal*) es nimmt eine Art Zwischenstellung zwischen Demokratie und ... ein.
[2] *adv* **her hair reached ~ down her back** die Haare gingen ihr bis weit über die Schultern; **~ to** auf halbem Weg nach; **we drove ~ to London** wir fuhren die halbe Strecke *or* den halben Weg nach London; **~ between two points** (in der Mitte *or* genau) zwischen zwei Punkten; **I live ~ up the hill** ich wohne auf halber Höhe des Berges; **we went ~ up the hill** wir gingen den Berg halb hinauf; **~ through a book** halb durch ein Buch (durch); **to go ~** (*lit*) die halbe Strecke *or* die Hälfte des Weges zurücklegen; **this money will go ~ towards paying ...** diese Summe wird die Hälfte der Kosten für ... decken; **to meet sb ~** (*lit, fig*) jdm (auf halbem Weg) entgegenkommen.
[3] *attr* **~ house** Gasthaus *nt* auf halbem Weg; (*hostel*) offene Anstalt; (*fig*) Zwischending *nt*; **we could stop off at the King's Head, that's a ~ house** wir können im „King's Head" einkehren, das liegt auf halbem Wege.

half: ~-wit *n* Schwachsinnige(r) *mf*; (*fig*) Schwachkopf *m*; **~-witted** ['hɑːfˌwɪtɪd] *adj* schwachsinnig; **~-year** *n* Halbjahr *nt*; **~-yearly** [1] *adj* halbjährlich; [2] *adv* halbjährlich, jedes halbe Jahr.

halibut ['hælɪbət] *n* Heilbutt *m*.

halitosis [ˌhælɪ'təʊsɪs] *n* schlechter Mundgeruch.

hall [hɔːl] *n* (**a**) (*entrance ~ of house*) Diele *f*, Korridor *m*.
(**b**) (*large building*) Halle *f*; (*large room*) Saal *m*; (*Brit: of college*) Speisesaal *m*; (*Brit: college mealtime*) Essen *nt*; (*dance-* ~) Tanzdiele *f*; (*village* ~) Gemeindehalle *f*, Gemeindehaus *nt*; (*school assembly* ~) Aula *f* ◆ **he will join the ~ of fame of ...** (*fig*) er wird in die Geschichte des ... eingehen, er wird in die Ruhmeshalle des ... aufgenommen (*liter*).
(**c**) (*mansion*) Herrensitz *m*, Herrenhaus *nt*; (*students' residence: also ~ of residence*) Studenten(wohn)heim *nt* ◆ **to live in ~** im Wohnheim wohnen; **Ruskin ~** Haus Ruskin *nt*.

hallelujah [ˌhælɪ'luːjə] [1] *interj* halleluja.
[2] *n* Halleluja *nt*.

hallmark [ˌhɔːlmɑːk] [1] *n* (**a**) (*on gold, silver*) (Feingehalts)stempel *m*, Repunze *f*.
(**b**) (*fig*) Kennzeichen *nt* (*of gen*, für) ◆ **a ~ of good quality** ein Gütesiegel *nt*; **this is the ~ of a true genius** daran erkennt man das wahre Genie.
[2] *vt gold, silver* stempeln.

hallo [hə'ləʊ] *interj, n see* **hello**.

halloo [hə'luː] [1] *interj* hallo; (*Hunt*) horrido, hallo.
[2] *n* Halloruf *m*; (*Hunt*) Horrido, Hallo *nt*.
[3] *vi* (hallo) rufen; (*Hunt*) die Hunde hetzen.

hallow ['hæləʊ] *vt* heiligen; (*consecrate*) weihen ◆ **~ed be Thy name** (*Bibl*) geheiligt werde Dein Name.

Hallowe'en [ˌhæləʊ'iːn] *n* der Tag vor Allerheiligen.

hall: ~ porter *n* Portier *m*; **~-stand** *n* (Flur)garderobe *f*; (*tree-like*) Garderobenständer *m*.

hallucinate [hə'luːsɪneɪt] *vi* halluzinieren, Wahnvorstellungen haben.

hallucination [həˌluːsɪ'neɪʃən] *n* (**a**) Halluzination, Wahnvorstellung *f*. (**b**) (*inf: false idea*) Wahnvorstellung *f*.

hallucinatory [hə'luːsɪnətərɪ] *adj* halluzinatorisch; (*causing hallucinations*) Halluzinationen hervorrufend.

hallucinogenic [həˌluːsɪnə'dʒenɪk] *adj* Halluzinationen hervorrufend *attr*, halluzinogen (*spec*) ◆ **LSD is ~** LSD ist ein Halluzinogen *nt*.

hallway ['hɔːlweɪ] *n* Flur, Korridor *m*.

halo ['heɪləʊ] [1] *n, pl* **-(e)s** (*of saint, fig iro*) Heiligenschein *m*; (*Astron*) Hof, Halo (*spec*) *m* ◆ **his ~ never slips** nichts kann seinen Heiligenschein trüben.
[2] *vt* (*fig*) umrahmen.

halogen ['hæləʊdʒɪn] *n* Halogen *nt* ◆ **~ lamp** Halogenlampe *f*; (*Aut*) Halogenscheinwerfer *m*.

halt[1] [hɔːlt] [1] *n* (**a**) (*stop*) Pause *f*; (*Mil*) Halt *m*; (*in production*) Stopp *m* ◆ **the officer ordered a ~** der Offizier befahl Halt; **five minutes' ~** fünf Minuten Pause; **to come to a ~** zum Stillstand kommen; **to call a ~ to sth** einer Sache (*dat*) ein Ende machen *or* bereiten; **he called a ~ to the discussion** er beendete die Diskussion; **shall we call a ~ now, gentlemen?** wollen wir jetzt Schluß machen, meine Herren?; **~ sign** Stoppschild *nt*.
(**b**) (*small station*) Haltepunkt *m*.
[2] *vi* zum Stillstand kommen; (*person*) anhalten, stehenbleiben; (*Mil*) halten ◆ **he was going to ... but then ~ed** er wollte ..., aber hielt dann inne; **we ~ed briefly before attempting the summit** wir hielten kurz an *or* machten kurz halt, bevor wir den Gipfel in Angriff nahmen.
[3] *vt* anhalten; *production, vehicles, traffic also* zum Stehen *or* Stillstand bringen; *troops* halten lassen.
[4] *interj* halt; (*traffic sign*) stop.

halt[2] [1] *vi* (*obs*) hinken; (*in speech*) stockend sprechen.
[2] *n* (*Bibl*) **the ~ and the lame** die Krummen und die Lahmen.

halter ['hɔːltəʳ] *n* (**a**) (*horse's*) Halfter *nt*. (**b**) (*for hanging*) Schlinge *f*.

halter-neck ['hɒltənek] [1] *n* rückenfreies Kleid/Top *nt* mit Nackenband.
[2] *adj* rückenfrei mit Nackenverschluß.

halting ['hɔːltɪŋ] *adj walk* unsicher; *speech* stockend; *admission* zögernd; *verse* holp(e)rig.

haltingly ['hɔːltɪŋlɪ] *adv see adj*.

halve [hɑːv] *vt* (**a**) (*separate in two*) halbieren; (*Math also*) durch zwei teilen.
(**b**) (*reduce by one half*) auf die Hälfte reduzieren, halbieren.

halves [hɑːvz] *pl of* **half**.

halyard ['hæljəd] *n* (*Naut*) Fall *nt*; (*for flag*) Flaggleine *f*.

ham [hæm] [1] *n* (**a**) (*Cook*) Schinken *m* ◆ **~ sandwich** Schinkenbrot *nt*.
(**b**) (*Anat*) **~s** (hintere) Oberschenkel *pl*; (*of animal*) (Hinter)keulen *pl* ◆ **to squat on one's ~s** hocken, in der Hocke sitzen.
(**c**) (*Theat*) Schmierenkomödiant(in *f*) *m*.
(**d**) (*Rad inf*) Funkamateur *m*.
[2] *adj attr acting* übertrieben, zu dick aufgetragen ◆ **~ actor** Schmierenkomödiant(in *f*) *m*.
[3] *vi* (*Theat*) chargieren, übertrieben spielen.

◆**ham up** *vt sep* (*inf*) übertreiben ◆ **to ~ it ~** zu dick auftragen.

hamburger ['hæmˌbɜːgəʳ] *n* (flache) Frikadelle *f*; (*with bread*) Hamburger *m*.

ham: ~-fisted, ~-handed *adj* ungeschickt; *efforts, person also* tolpatschig (*inf*).

Hamitic [hæ'mɪtɪk] *adj* hamitisch.

hamlet ['hæmlɪt] *n* Weiler *m*, kleines Dorf.

hammer ['hæməʳ] [1] *n* (*generally*) Hammer *m*; (*of gun*) Hahn *m* ◆ **to go at it ~ and tongs** (*inf*) sich ins Zeug legen (*inf*), schwer rangehen (*sl*); (*work also*) schuften, daß die Fetzen fliegen (*inf*); (*quarrel*) sich in die Wolle kriegen (*inf*), sich streiten, daß die Fetzen fliegen; **my heart was going like a ~** das Herz schlug mir bis zum Hals; **to come under the ~** (*auction*) unter den Hammer kommen; **throwing the ~** (*Sport*) Hammerwerfen *nt*; **in the ~ (throwing)** (*Sport*) im Hammerwurf.
[2] *vt* (**a**) *nail, metal* hämmern ◆ **to ~ a nail into a wall** einen Nagel in die Wand schlagen; **to ~ sth into shape** *metal* etw zurechthämmern; (*fig*) *agreement* etw ausarbeiten; **to ~ sth into sb** *or* **sb's head** (*inf*) jdm etw einbleuen (*inf*).
(**b**) (*inf: defeat badly*) eine Schlappe beibringen +*dat* (*inf*) ◆ **Chelsea were ~ed 6-1** Chelsea mußte eine 6:1-Schlappe einstecken (*inf*).
(**c**) (*St Ex sl*) *stockbroker* für zahlungsunfähig erklären.
[3] *vi* hämmern ◆ **to ~ at the door** an die Tür hämmern.

◆**hammer away** *vi* (darauflos)hämmern ◆ **to ~ ~ at a problem** sich (*dat*) über ein Problem den Kopf zerbrechen; **to ~ ~ at the door** an die Tür hämmern; **the boxer ~ed ~ at him** der Boxer hämmerte auf ihn ein; **his heart was ~ing ~** sein Herz hämmerte nur so; **the pianist ~ed ~ at the keys** der Pianist hämmerte auf die Tasten.

◆**hammer down** *vt sep* festhämmern; *nail* einschlagen; *bump* flachhämmern.

◆**hammer home** *vt sep* (**a**) *nail* fest hineinschlagen. (**b**) *argument, point etc* Nachdruck verleihen (+*dat*), untermauern ◆ **he tried to ~ it ~ to the pupils**

that ... er versuchte, den Schülern einzubleuen (*inf*) *or* einzuhämmern, daß ...

◆**hammer in** *vt sep* **(a)** *nail etc* einschlagen, einhämmern. **(b)** *door* einschlagen. **(c)** (*fig*) *fact* einhämmern, einbleuen (*inf*).

◆**hammer out** *vt sep* **(a)** *metal* hämmern; *nail, bricks* (her)ausschlagen *or* -klopfen; *dent* ausbeulen. **(b)** (*fig*) *plan, agreement, solution* ausarbeiten, aushandeln; *difficulties* beseitigen, bereinigen; *verse* schmieden; *tune* hämmern.

hammer and sickle *n sing* Hammer und Sichel *pl*.

hammer: ~ beam *n* Stichbalken *m*; **~ drill** *n* Schlagbohrmaschine *f*; **~head** *n* (*shark*) Hammerhai *m*; (*of hammer*) Hammerkopf *m*.

hammering ['hæmərɪŋ] *n* **(a)** Hämmern, Klopfen *nt*. **(b)** (*inf: defeat*) Schlappe *f* (*inf*) ◆ **our team took a ~** unsere Mannschaft mußte eine Schlappe einstecken.

hammer toe *n* Hammerzehe *f or* -zeh *m*.

hammock ['hæmək] *n* Hängematte *f*.

hamper[1] ['hæmpəʳ] *n* (*basket*) Korb *m*; (*as present*) Geschenkkorb *m*.

hamper[2] *vt* behindern; *movement also* erschweren; *person also* Schwierigkeiten bereiten (+*dat*) ◆ **to be ~ed** gehandikapt sein; **the police were ~ed in their search by the shortage of clues** der Mangel an Hinweisen erschwerte der Polizei die Suche.

hamster ['hæmstəʳ] *n* Hamster *m*.

hamstring ['hæmstrɪŋ] (*vb: pret, ptp* **hamstrung** ['hæmstrʌŋ]) [1] *n* (*Anat*) Kniesehne *f*; (*of animal*) Achillessehne *f*.

[2] *vt* **(a)** (*lit*) *person, animal* die Kniesehne/Achillessehne durchschneiden (+*dat*).

(b) (*fig*) *attempt etc* vereiteln, unterbinden; *person* handlungsunfähig machen ◆ **to be hamstrung** aufgeschmissen sein (*inf*); (*project, undertaking*) lahmgelegt sein, lahmliegen.

▼ **hand** [hænd] [1] *n* **(a)** Hand *f*; (*of clock*) Zeiger *m* ◆ **on ~s and knees** auf allen vieren; **he felt he held victory in his ~** (*fig*) er glaubte, den Sieg schon in Händen zu haben; **to take/lead sb by the ~** jdn an die *or* bei der Hand nehmen/an der Hand führen; **~s up!** Hände hoch!; (*Sch*) meldet euch!; **~s up who knows the answer/who wants to go** wer es weiß, meldet sich *or* hebt die Hand/Hand hoch, wer gehen will; **~s off** (*inf*) Hände weg!; **keep your ~s off my wife** laß die Finger *or* Pfoten (*inf*) von meiner Frau!; **done** *or* **made by ~** handgearbeitet; **this sewing was done by ~** dies ist von Hand genäht worden; **to send a letter by ~** einen Brief durch (einen) Boten schicken; **"by ~"** „durch Boten"; **to raise an animal by ~** ein Tier von Hand *or* mit der Flasche aufziehen; **pistol in ~** mit vorgehaltener Pistole, mit der Pistole in der Hand; **to climb ~ over ~** Hand über Hand klettern; **to live from ~ to mouth** von der Hand in den Mund leben; **I give you my ~ on it** ich gebe dir die Hand darauf, ich verspreche es dir in die Hand; **with a heavy/firm ~** (*fig*) mit harter/fester *or* starker Hand; *see* **hold, shake**.

▼ **(b)** (*side, direction, position*) Seite *f* ◆ **on the right ~** auf der rechten Seite, rechts, rechter Hand; **on my right ~** rechts von mir, zu meiner Rechten (*geh*); **on every ~, on all ~s** auf allen Seiten, ringsum(her); **surrounded on all ~s** von allen Seiten umringt; **on the one ~ ... on the other ~ ...** einerseits *or* auf der einen Seite ..., andererseits *or* auf der anderen Seite ...

(c) (*agency, possession etc*) **it's the ~ of God/fate** das ist die Hand Gottes/des Schicksals; **your life is in your own ~s** Sie haben Ihr Leben (selbst) in der Hand; **it's in your own ~s what you do now** Sie haben es selbst in der Hand, was Sie jetzt tun; **to put sth into sb's ~s** jdm etw in die Hand geben, etw in jds Hände legen; **to leave sb/sth in sb's ~s** jdn in jds Obhut lassen/jdm etw überlassen; **to put oneself in(to) sb's ~s** sich jdm anvertrauen, sich in jds Hände begeben (*geh*); **my life is in your ~s** mein Leben ist *or* liegt in Ihren Händen; **to fall into the ~s of sb** jdm in die Hände fallen; **to be in good ~s** in guten Händen sein; **I received some pretty rough treatment at her ~s** ich bin von ihr ganz schön grob behandelt worden; **he suffered terribly at the ~s of the enemy** er machte in den Händen des Feindes Schreckliches durch; **he has too much time on his ~s** er hat zuviel Zeit zur Verfügung; **he has this problem/a lot of work/five children on his ~s** er hat ein Problem/viel Arbeit/fünf Kinder am Hals (*inf*); **I've got enough on my ~s already** ich habe ohnehin schon alle Hände voll zu tun, ich habe schon genug um die Ohren (*inf*) *or* am Hals (*inf*); **I like to have a lot on my ~s** es macht mir Spaß, wenn ich viel zu tun *or* um die Ohren (*inf*) habe; **to get sb/sth off one's ~s** jdn/etw loswerden; **to take sb/sth off sb's ~s** jdm jdn/etw abnehmen; **goods left on our ~s** (*Comm*) nicht abgesetzte Waren; *see* **die, change, free**.

(d) (*applause*) Applaus, Beifall *m* ◆ **they gave him a big ~** sie gaben ihm großen Applaus, sie klatschten ihm großen Beifall; **let's give a big ~ to our guest** und nun großen Beifall für unseren Gast.

(e) (*worker*) Arbeitskraft *f*, Arbeiter *m*; (*Naut*) Besatzungsmitglied *nt* ◆ **to take on ~s** Leute einstellen; (*Naut*) Leute anheuern; **~s** Leute *pl*, Belegschaft *f*; **(ship's) ~s** Besatzung, Mannschaft *f*; **all ~s on deck!** alle Mann an Deck!; **lost with all ~s** mit der ganzen Besatzung untergegangen.

(f) (*expert*) **to be a good ~ at sth/doing sth** (ein) Geschick *nt* für etw haben/ein Geschick dafür haben, etw zu tun; **to be an old ~ (at sth)** ein alter Hase (in etw *dat*) sein; *see* **dab**[3].

(g) (*Measure: of horse*) ≃ 10 cm.

(h) (*handwriting*) Handschrift *f* ◆ **he writes a good ~** er hat eine gute (Hand)schrift.

(i) (*Cards*) Blatt *nt*; (*person*) Mann *m*; (*game*) Runde *f* ◆ **3 ~s** (*people*) 3 Mann; **a ~ of bridge** eine Runde Bridge; **to show one's ~** seine Karten sehen lassen *or* aufdecken; (*fig*) sich (*dat*) in die Karten sehen lassen.

(j) summer/Christmas *etc* **is (close) at ~** der Sommer/Weihnachten *etc* steht vor der Tür, es ist bald Sommer/Weihnachten *etc*; **at first/second ~** aus erster/zweiter Hand; **according to the information at** *or* **on ~** gemäß *or* laut der vorhandenen *or* vorliegenden Informationen; **we have little information at** *or* **on ~** wir haben kaum Informationen *pl* (zur Verfügung); **to keep sth at ~** etw in Reichweite haben; **it's quite close at ~** es ist ganz in der Nähe; **he had the situation well in ~** er hatte die Situation im Griff; **she took the child in ~** sie nahm die Erziehung des Kindes in die Hand; **to take sb in ~** (*discipline*) jdn in die Hand nehmen; (*look after*) jdn in Obhut nehmen, nach jdm sehen; **stock in ~** (*Comm*) Warenlager *nt*; **what stock have you in ~?** welche Waren haben Sie am Lager?; **he still had £600/a couple of hours in ~** er hatte £ 600 übrig/noch zwei Stunden Zeit; **the matter in ~** die vorliegende *or* (*in discussion*) die zur Debatte stehende Angelegenheit; **work in ~** Arbeit, die zur Zeit erledigt wird; **we've got quite a lot of work in** *or* **on ~** wir haben sehr viel Arbeit anstehen *or* zu erledigen; **a matter/project** *etc* **is in ~** eine Sache/ein Projekt *nt etc* wird bearbeitet *or* ist in Bearbeitung; **to put sth in ~** zusehen, daß etw erledigt wird; **the children got out of ~** die Kinder waren nicht mehr zu bändigen *or* gerieten außer Rand und Band; **the party got out of ~** die Party ist ausgeartet; **the horse got out of ~** er hat/ich habe *etc* die Kontrolle über das Pferd verloren; **matters got out of ~** die Dinge sind außer Kontrolle geraten; **he has enough money to ~** ihm steht genügend Geld zur Verfügung; **I don't have the letter to ~** ich habe den Brief gerade nicht zur Hand; **your letter has come to ~** (*Comm*) wir haben Ihren Brief erhalten; **I don't know where it is right now but I'm sure it'll come to ~ before too long** ich weiß nicht, wo es im Augenblick ist, aber es wird sicherlich über kurz oder lang auftauchen; **he seized the first weapon to ~** er ergriff die erstbeste Waffe; *see* **palm**[2], **cash**.

(k) (*phrases*) **to keep one's ~ in** in Übung bleiben; **to eat out of sb's ~** (*lit, fig*) jdm aus der Hand fressen; **to force sb's ~** jdn zwingen, auf jdn Druck ausüben; **to wait on sb ~ and foot** jdn von vorne und hinten bedienen; **he never does a ~'s turn** er rührt keinen Finger, er macht keinen Finger krumm; **to have a ~ in sth** (*in decision*) an etw (*dat*) beteiligt sein; (*in crime*) die Hand bei etw im Spiel haben; **I had no ~ in it** ich hatte damit nichts zu tun; **to take a ~ in sth** an etw (*dat*) teilnehmen, sich an etw (+*dat*) beteiligen; **to lend** *or* **give sb a ~** jdm behilflich sein, jdm zur Hand gehen; **give me a ~!** hilf mir mal!; **to give sb a ~ up** jdm hochhelfen; **give me a ~ down** helfen Sie mir mal herunter/hinunter; **to be ~ in glove with sb** mit jdm unter einer Decke stecken, mit jdm gemeinsame Sache machen; **to have one's ~s full with sth** mit etw alle Hände voll zu tun haben; **to win ~s down** mühelos *or* spielend gewinnen; **to hold** *or* **stay one's ~** abwarten; **he is making money ~ over fist** er scheffelt das Geld nur so; **to spend money ~ over fist** in rauhen Mengen Geld ausgeben; **we're losing money/staff ~ over fist** wir verlieren massenweise Geld/Personal; **the inflation rate is rising ~ over fist** die Inflationsrate steigt rasend schnell; **to have the upper ~** die Oberhand behalten; **to get** *or* **gain the upper ~ (of sb)** (über jdn) die Oberhand gewinnen; **to ask for a lady's ~ (in marriage)** um die Hand einer Dame anhalten.

[2] *vt* **(a)** (*give*) reichen, geben (*sth to sb, sb sth* jdm etw) ◆ **you've got to ~ it to him** (*fig*) das muß man ihm lassen (*inf*).

(b) he ~ed the lady into/out of the carriage er half der Dame in die/aus der Kutsche.

◆**hand back** *vt sep* zurückgeben.

◆**hand down** *vt sep* **(a)** (*lit*) herunter-/hinunterreichen *or* -geben (*to sb* jdm).

(b) (*fig*) weitergeben; *tradition, belief also* überliefern; *heirloom etc* vererben (*to dat*); *clothes also* vererben (*inf*) (*to dat*); *story* (*from sb to sb*) überliefern (*to an* +*acc*), weitergeben (*to an* +*acc*) ◆ **all his clothes were ~ed ~ from his elder brothers** er mußte die Kleidung seiner älteren Brüder auftragen.

(c) (*Jur*) *sentence* fällen.

◆**hand in** *vt sep* abgeben; *forms, thesis also, resignation* einreichen.

◆**hand off** *vt sep* (*Rugby*) (mit der Hand) wegstoßen.

◆**hand on** *vt sep* weitergeben (*to an* +*acc*).

◆**hand out** *vt sep* austeilen, verteilen (*to sb* an jdn); *advice* geben, erteilen (*to sb* jdm); *heavy sentence* verhängen, austeilen ◆ **the Spanish boxer was really ~ing it ~** *or* **~ing ~ the punishment** (*inf*) der spanische Boxer hat wirklich ganz schön zugeschlagen *or* ausgeteilt (*inf*).

◆**hand over** [1] *vt sep* (*pass over*) (herüber-/hinüber)reichen (*to dat*); (*hand on*) weitergeben (*to an* +*acc*); (*give up*) (her)geben (*to dat*); (*to third party*) (ab)geben (*to dat*); *criminal, prisoner* übergeben (*to dat*); (*from one state to another*) ausliefern; *leadership, authority, powers* abgeben, abtreten (*to an* +*acc*); *the controls, property, business* übergeben (*to dat, an* +*acc*) ◆ **~ ~ that gun!** Waffe her!; **I now ~ you ~ to our political correspondent** ich gebe nun weiter *or* übergebe nun an unseren (politischen) Korrespondenten.

[2] *vi* **when the Conservatives ~ed ~ to Labour** als die Konservativen die Regierung an Labour abgaben; **when the chairman ~ed ~ to his successor** ... als der Vorsitzende das Amt an seinen Nachfolger abgab; **come on, ~ ~, I saw you take it** gib schon her, ich habe gesehen, wie du's genommen hast; **I now ~ ~ to our sports correspondent** ... ich übergebe nun an unseren Sportberichterstatter ...; **he ~ed ~ to the co-pilot** er übergab an den Kopiloten.

◆**hand round** *vt sep* herumreichen; *bottle also* herumgehen lassen; (*distribute*) *papers* austeilen, verteilen.

◆**hand up** *vt sep* hinauf-/heraufreichen.

hand: ~bag *n* Handtasche *f*; **~ baggage** *n* Handgepäck *nt*; **~ball** [1] *n* **(a)** (*game*) Handball *m*; **(b)** (*Ftbl: foul*) Handspiel *nt*, Hand *f*; [2] *interj* (*Ftbl*) Hand; **~barrow** *n* Schubkarre *f*; **~ basin** *n* Handwaschbecken *nt*; **~ bell** *n* Schelle *f*, Glocke *f* (mit Stiel); **~bill** *n* Flugblatt *nt*, Handzettel *m*; **~book** *n* Handbuch *nt*; (*tourist's*) Reiseführer *m*; **~brake** *n* (*Brit*) Handbremse *f*.

➤ LANGUAGE IN USE: **hand: 1b** → 26.2, 26.3

h & c *abbr of* **hot and cold (water)** k.u.w., kalt und warm.

hand: ~car *n (Rail)* Draisine *f*; **~cart** *n* Handwagen *m*; **~clasp** *n (US)* Händedruck *m*; **~ controls** *npl (Aut)* Handbedienung *f*; **~cuff** *vt* Handschellen anlegen (+*dat*); **he ~cuffed himself to the railings** er machte sich mit Handschellen am Geländer fest; **to be ~cuffed** Handschellen angelegt bekommen; **the accused was ~cuffed to a police officer** der Angeklagte war (mit Handschellen) an einen Polizisten gefesselt; **~cuffs** *npl* Handschellen *pl*; **~ drier** *n* Händetrockner *m*; **~-eye coordination** *n* visuell-motorische Koordination.

handfeed ['hænd,fiːd] *pret, ptp* **handfed** ['hænd,fed] *vt animal* mit der Flasche aufziehen.

handful ['hændfʊl] *n* **(a)** Handvoll *f*; *(of hair, fur)* Büschel *nt* ◆ **a ~ of soil** eine Handvoll Erde; **by the ~, in ~s** händeweise; büschelweise.
(b) *(small number)* Handvoll *f*.
(c) *(fig)* **those children are a ~** die Kinder können einen ganz schön in Trab halten; **his new girl's quite a ~** *(hum)* an seiner neuen Freundin ist ganz hübsch was dran *(inf)*.

hand: ~ grenade *n* Handgranate *f*; **~grip** *n* (Hand)griff *m*; *(handshake)* Händedruck *m*; **~ gun** *n* Handfeuerwaffe *f*; **~-held** *adj* **taken with a ~-held camera** aus der (freien) Hand aufgenommen; **~hold** *n* Halt *m*.

handicap ['hændɪkæp] **1** *n* **(a)** *(Sport)* Handikap *nt*; *(in horse racing, golf also)* Vorgabe *f*; *(race)* Vorgaberennen *nt* ◆ **a ~ of 5lbs** eine (Gewichts)vorgabe von 5 Pfund.
(b) *(disadvantage)* Handikap *nt*; *(for specific purpose also)* Nachteil *m*; *(physical, mental also)* Behinderung *f* ◆ **to be under a great ~** sehr im Nachteil sein, stark gehandikapt sein.
2 *vt* ein Handikap *nt* darstellen für; *(for a specific purpose also)* benachteiligen; *chances* beeinträchtigen ◆ **he has always been ~ped by his accent** sein Akzent war immer ein Nachteil *m* für ihn; **to be (physically/mentally) ~ped** (körperlich/geistig) behindert sein; **~ped children** behinderte Kinder *pl*.

handicraft ['hændɪkrɑːft] *n* **(a)** *(work)* Kunsthandwerk *nt*; *(needlework etc)* Handarbeit *f*; *(woodwork, modelling etc)* Werken *nt*, Bastelarbeit *f*. **(b)** *(skill)* Geschick *nt*, Handfertigkeit, Geschicklichkeit *f*.

handily ['hændɪlɪ] *adv* **(a)** *situated* günstig. **(b)** *(US: easily) win* mit Leichtigkeit.

handiness ['hændɪnɪs] *n* **(a)** *(skill)* Geschick *nt*, Geschicklichkeit *f*. **(b)** *(nearness, accessibility: of shops etc)* günstige Lage. **(c)** *(convenience, usefulness: of tool, car etc)* Nützlichkeit *f*; *(easiness to handle)* Handlichkeit *f*.

hand-in-hand ['hændɪn'hænd] *adv (lit, fig)* Hand in Hand.

handiwork ['hændɪwɜːk] *n, no pl* **(a)** *(lit)* Arbeit *f*; *(Sch: subject)* Werken *nt*; *(needlework etc)* Handarbeit *f* ◆ **examples of the children's ~** Werkarbeiten *pl*/ Handarbeiten *pl* der Kinder; **to do ~** werken, handarbeiten; *(at home)* basteln.
(b) *(fig)* Werk *nt*; *(pej)* Machwerk *nt* ◆ **that looks like the ~ of the Gillies gang** das sieht ganz nach der Gillies-Bande aus.

handkerchief ['hæŋkətʃɪf] *n* Taschentuch *nt*.

hand-knitted ['hænd,nɪtɪd] *adj* handgestrickt.

handle ['hændl] **1** *n* **(a)** Griff *m*; *(of door also)* Klinke *f*; *(esp of broom, comb, saucepan)* Stiel *m*; *(esp of basket, bucket, casserole, cup, jug etc)* Henkel *m*; *(of handbag also)* Bügel *m*; *(of pump)* Schwengel *m*; *(of car: starting ~)* (Anlaß- or Start)kurbel *f* ◆ **to fly off the ~** *(inf)* an die Decke gehen *(inf)*; **to have/get a ~ on sth** *(US inf)* etw im Griff haben/etw in den Griff bekommen.
(b) *(fig: pretext)* Handhabe *f*.
(c) *(inf)* Titel *m* ◆ **to have a ~ to one's name** ein „von und zu" sein *(inf)*.
2 *vt* **(a)** *(touch, use hands on)* anfassen, berühren; *(Ftbl) ball* mit der Hand berühren ◆ **be careful how you ~ that** gehen Sie vorsichtig damit um; **please do not ~ the goods** Waren bitte nicht berühren; **"~ with care"** „Vorsicht — zerbrechlich"; „Vorsicht Glas/Blumen/lebende Tiere *etc*".
(b) *(deal with) person, animal, plant, tool, weapon, machine, words, numbers etc* umgehen mit; *legal or financial matters* erledigen; *legal case* handhaben, bearbeiten; *applicant, matter, problem* sich befassen mit; *material for essay etc* bearbeiten, verarbeiten; *(tackle) problem, interview etc* anfassen, anpacken; *(succeed in coping with) child, drunk, situation, problem* fertig werden mit; *(resolve) matter* erledigen; *vehicle, plane, ship* steuern ◆ **how would you ~ the situation?** wie würden Sie sich in der Situation verhalten?; **you have to ~ that situation/your employees very carefully** in dieser Situation müssen Sie sehr behutsam vorgehen/Sie müssen Ihre Angestellten sehr vorsichtig behandeln; **a car that is easy to ~** ein Auto, das leicht zu fahren *or* zu steuern ist; **I can't ~ these fast balls** ich komme mit diesen schnellen Bällen nicht zurecht; **six children are too much for one woman to ~** mit sechs Kindern kann eine Frau allein nicht fertigwerden; **there's a salesman at the door — I'll ~ him** ein Vertreter ist an der Tür — ich werde ihn abfertigen; **you keep quiet, I'll ~ this** sei still, laß mich mal machen; **the accused decided to ~ his own defence** der Angeklagte beschloß, seine eigene Verteidigung zu übernehmen; **who's handling the publicity for this?** wer macht die Öffentlichkeitsarbeit dafür?; **could you ~ these interviews for me?** könnten Sie diese Interviews für mich machen?
(c) *(Comm) types of goods, items* handeln mit *or* in (+*dat*); *orders* bearbeiten; *prescriptions* ausführen; *shares, securities* handeln; *financial affairs* besorgen ◆ **airport workers refused to ~ goods for Uganda** die Flughafenarbeiter weigerten sich, Waren nach Uganda abzufertigen; **we ~ tax problems for several big companies** wir bearbeiten die Steuerangelegenheiten mehrerer großer Firmen; **the millionaire has several secretaries to ~ his business** der Millionär hat mehrere Sekretäre, die seine Geschäfte für ihn führen; **this department ~s all the export business** diese Abteilung bearbeitet den gesamten Export.
3 *vi (ship, plane)* sich steuern lassen; *(car, motorbike)* sich fahren *or* lenken lassen; *(gun)* sich handhaben lassen.
4 *vr* **he ~s himself well in a fight** er kann sich in einer Schlägerei behaupten; **if you live round here you have to know how to ~ yourself** wer in dieser Gegend wohnt, muß seine Fäuste zu gebrauchen wissen.

handle: ~bar moustache *n* Schnauzbart, Schnäuzer *(inf) m*; **~bar(s)** *n(pl)* Lenkstange *f*.

handler ['hændlə^r] *n (dog-~)* Hundeführer *m*.

handling ['hændlɪŋ] *n* **(a)** *(touching)* Berühren *nt*.
(b) *(of plant, animal, matter, problem)* Behandlung *f*; *(of person, patient etc also, tool, weapon, machine, vehicle, plane, ship, drug, explosive)* Umgang *m* (of mit); *(of tool, weapon, machine)* Handhabung *f*; *(of writer's material)* Verarbeitung, Bearbeitung *f*; *(of legal or financial matters)* Erledigung *f*; *(official ~ of matters, of legal case)* Bearbeitung *f* ◆ **his skilful ~ of the class/troops/Senate** seine geschickte Art, mit der Klasse/den Truppen/dem Senat umzugehen; **the policeman's tactful ~ of the drunk/crowd/situation** das taktvolle Verhalten des Polizisten gegenüber dem Betrunkenen/der Menge/in der Situation; **his ~ of the matter/situation** die Art, wie er die Angelegenheit/die Situation angefaßt *or* behandelt hat; **his successful ~ of the difficulty/task** seine Bewältigung der Schwierigkeit/der Aufgabe; **the car/this parcel needs careful ~** man muß mit dem Auto vorsichtig umgehen/dieses Paket muß vorsichtig behandelt werden; **these goods were damaged in ~** *(Comm)* diese Waren wurden beschädigt; **his expert ~ of the deal** sein Geschick beim Abschluß des Geschäfts; **~ charge** *(management fee)* Bearbeitungsgebühr *f*; *(in warehouse)* Umladekosten *pl*; *(in banking)* Kontoführungsgebühren *pl*.
(c) *(of vehicle)* **what's its ~ like?** wie fährt es sich?; **a car not renowned for its easy ~** ein Auto, das sich nicht gerade durch leichte Lenkung auszeichnet.

hand: ~-loom *n* Handwebstuhl *m*; **~-loom carpet** handgewebter Teppich; **~-loom weaving** Handweben *nt*; **~ lotion** *n* Handlotion *f*; **~ luggage** *n* Handgepäck *nt*; **~-made** *adj* handgearbeitet; **this is ~-made** das ist Handarbeit; **~maid** *n (obs)* Zofe *f (old)*; *(Bibl)* Magd *f*; **~-me-down** *n (inf)* abgelegtes Kleidungsstück; **~-mirror** *n* Handspiegel *m*; **~-off** *n (Rugby)* Wegstoß(en *nt*) *m* (mit der Hand); **~-operated** *adj* von Hand bedient *or* betätigt, handbedient, handbetrieben; **~out** *n (inf: money)* Unterstützung, (Geld)zuwendung *f*; *(leaflet)* Flugblatt *nt*; *(with several pages)* Broschüre *f*; *(in school)* Arbeitsblatt *nt*; *(publicity ~out)* Reklamezettel *m*; **budget ~out** Zuwendung *f* or Geschenk *nt* aus dem Etat; **Christmas ~outs** Weihnachtsgeld *nt*, Weihnachtsgratifikation *f*; **~over** *n (Pol)* Übergabe *f*; **~over of power** Machtübergabe *f*; **~-picked** *adj* von Hand geerntet; *(specially selected, fig)* handverlesen; **~rail** *n (of stairs etc)* Geländer *nt*; *(of ship)* Reling *f*; *(for bath etc)* Haltegriff *m*; **~ saw** *n* Handsäge *f*, Fuchsschwanz *m*; **~ set** **1** *n (Telec)* Hörer *m*; **2** *vt (Typ)* (von Hand) setzen; **~shake** *n* **(a)** Händedruck *m*; **(b)** *(Comput)* Handshake, Quittungsaustausch *m*; **~shaking** *n* Händeschütteln *nt*.

hands-off ['hændz'ɒf] *adj approach etc* passiv ◆ **a ~ manager** ein Geschäftsführer, der die Zügel gern locker läßt.

handsome ['hænsəm] *adj* **(a)** gutaussehend; *furniture* schön; *building* schön, ansehnlich ◆ **he is ~/he has a ~ face** er sieht gut aus; **she is a ~ woman for her age** für ihr Alter sieht sie gut aus.
(b) *(noble, generous)* großzügig, nobel *(inf)*; *conduct* großmütig, nobel *(inf)*; *apology* anständig ◆ **~ is as ~ does** *(Prov)* edel ist, wer edel handelt.
(c) *(considerable) fortune, profit, price, inheritance etc* ansehnlich, stattlich, beträchtlich.

handsomely ['hænsəmlɪ] *adv* **(a)** *(elegantly)* elegant; *dressed also* gut ◆ **he grinned ~ at the camera** er setzte für den Fotografen sein schönes Lächeln auf. **(b)** *(generously)* großzügig; *apologize* anständig ◆ **they were ~ rewarded for their patience** ihre Geduld wurde reichlich belohnt.

handsomeness ['hænsəmnɪs] *n (of looks)* gutes Aussehen; *(generosity)* Großzügigkeit *f*.

hands-on ['hændz'ɒn] *adj experience, approach etc* aktiv ◆ **a ~ manager** ein Geschäftsführer, der die Zügel gern fest in der Hand hält.

hand: ~spring *n* (Handstand)überschlag *m*; **~-stand** *n* Handstand *m*; **to do a ~-stand** (einen) Handstand machen; **~-stitched** *adj* handgenäht; **~ to ~** **1** *adv* im Nahkampf, Mann gegen Mann; **2** *adj* **~-to-~ fight/fighting** Nahkampf *m*; **~-to-mouth** *adj existence* kümmerlich, armselig; **to lead a ~-to-mouth existence** von der Hand in den Mund leben; **~ towel** *n* Händehandtuch *nt*; **~work** *n* Handarbeit *f*; **~-woven** *adj* handgewebt; **~writing** *n* Handschrift *f*; **~written** *adj* handgeschrieben, von Hand geschrieben.

handy ['hændɪ] *adj (+er)* **(a)** *person* geschickt, praktisch ◆ **to be ~ at doing sth** ein Geschick *nt* für etw haben; **to be ~ with a gun** gut mit einer Pistole umgehen können; **he's pretty ~ with his fists** er kann seine Fäuste gut gebrauchen.
(b) *pred (close at hand)* in der Nähe ◆ **to have** *or* **keep sth ~** etw griffbereit *or* zur Hand haben; **my apartment is ~ for the shops** meine Wohnung ist ganz in der Nähe der Geschäfte.
(c) *(convenient, useful)* praktisch; *(easy to handle also)* handlich ◆ **living here is handier for work** es ist praktischer, hier in der Nähe des Arbeitsplatzes zu wohnen; **that would come in ~ for ...** das könnte man gut für ... gebrauchen; **the new salary increase comes in ~** die neue Gehaltserhöhung kommt sehr gelegen; **my experience as a teacher comes in ~** meine Lehrerfahrung erweist sich als nützlich *or* kommt mir zugute; **he's a very ~ person to have around** man kann ihn gut (ge)brauchen *(inf)*; **he's very ~ about the house** er

kann im Hause alles selbst erledigen.

handyman ['hændımæn] *n, pl* **-men** [-mən] (*servant*) Faktotum *nt*, Mädchen *nt* für alles (*inf*); (*do-it-yourself*) Bastler, Heimwerker *m* ◆ **I'm not much of a ~ myself** ich bin kein großer Bastler, Basteln ist nicht gerade meine Stärke.

hang [hæŋ] (*vb: pret, ptp* **hung**) 1 *vt* **(a)** hängen; *painting* aufhängen; *door, gate* einhängen; (*Cook*) *game* abhängen lassen; *wallpaper* kleben ◆ **to ~ wallpaper** tapezieren; **to ~ sth from sth** etw an etw (*dat*) aufhängen; **to ~ sth on a hook** etw an einen Haken hängen.
(b) the rooms of the castle were hung with priceless pictures kostbare Gemälde hingen in den Räumen des Schlosses; **the walls were hung with tapestries** die Wände waren mit Gobelins behängt; **they hung the windows/streets with bunting** sie schmückten die Fenster/Straßen mit Fahnen.
(c) to ~ one's head den Kopf hängen lassen.
(d) to ~ fire (*lit: guns*) das Feuer einstellen; (*fig*) (*people*) zögern; **I think we should ~ fire a little longer** ich glaube, wir sollten noch etwas (zu)warten.
(e) *pret, ptp* **hanged** *criminal* hängen, aufhängen, henken (*form*) ◆ **hung, drawn and quartered** gehängt, gestreckt und gevierteilt; **to ~ oneself** sich erhängen *or* aufhängen (*inf*).
(f) (*inf*) **~ him!** zum Kuckuck mit ihm (*inf*); **(I'm) ~ed if I will** den Teufel werd' ich ... (*inf*); **(I'm) ~ed if I know** weiß der Henker (*inf*); **~ it!** so ein Mist (*inf*), verflixt (noch mal) (*inf*).
2 *vi* **(a)** hängen (*on* an (+*dat*), *from* von); (*drapery, clothes, hair*) fallen; (*inelegantly*) (herunter)hängen; (*pheasant etc*) abhängen.
(b) (*gloom, fog etc*) hängen (*over* über +*dat*) ◆ **to ~ in the air** (*fig*) in der Schwebe sein; **the hawk hung motionless in the sky** der Falke stand bewegungslos in der Luft; **time ~s heavy on my hands** die Zeit wird mir sehr lang.
(c) (*criminal*) gehängt werden, hängen.
(d) it/he can go ~! (*inf*) es/er kann mir gestohlen bleiben (*inf*).
3 *n* **(a)** (*of drapery*) Fall *m*; (*of suit*) Sitz *m*.
(b) *no pl* (*inf*) **to get the ~ of sth** den (richtigen) Dreh (bei etw) herauskriegen *or* -finden (*inf*); **to get the ~ of doing sth** den Dreh herausbekommen, wie man etw macht (*inf*).
(c) (*inf: damn*) **I don't give** *or* **care a ~** es ist mir völlig egal *or* Wurst (*inf*).

◆**hang about** *or* **around** 1 *vi* **(a)** (*inf*) (*wait*) warten; (*loiter*) sich herumtreiben (*inf*), herumlungern ◆ **to keep sb ~ing ~** jdn warten lassen; **of course she wants to get married, you can't keep her ~ing ~** natürlich will sie heiraten, du kannst sie doch nicht ewig hinhalten (*inf*).
(b) (*Brit sl: wait*) warten ◆ **~ about, I'm just coming** wart mal, ich komm ja schon; **now ~ about, I didn't say that** Moment mal (*inf*) *or* halt mal die Luft an (*sl*), das habe ich nicht gesagt.
(c) (*sl*) **this car/he doesn't ~ ~** das Auto zieht ganz schön ab (*sl*)/er ist einer von der schnellen Truppe.
2 *vi +prep obj* **to ~ ~ sb/a place** um jdn herumstreichen/sich an einem Ort herumtreiben (*inf*), an einem Ort herumlungern.

◆**hang back** *vi* (*lit*) sich zurückhalten; (*fig: hesitate*) zögern ◆ **one little boy was ~ing ~ at the edge of the group** ein kleiner Junge hielt sich immer im Hintergrund; **don't ~ ~, go and ask her** worauf wartest du denn, frag sie doch; **he hung ~ from suggesting that ...** er zögerte *or* konnte sich nicht entschließen, den Vorschlag zu machen, daß ...

◆**hang behind** *vi* zurückbleiben; (*dawdle*) (hinterher)bummeln *or* -trödeln.

◆**hang down** 1 *vi* herunter-/hinunterhängen ◆ **his clothes hung ~ in rags** seine Kleider hingen ihm in Fetzen vom Leib.
2 *vt sep* hinunter-/herunterhängen lassen.

◆**hang in** *vi* (*US sl*) **just ~ ~ there!** bleib am Ball (*inf*).

◆**hang on** 1 *vi* **(a)** (*hold*) sich festhalten, sich festklammern (*to sth* an etw *dat*); (*wallpaper etc*) halten, kleben (bleiben).
(b) (*hold out*) durchhalten; (*Telec*) am Apparat bleiben; (*inf: wait*) warten ◆ **~ ~ (a minute)** wart mal, einen Augenblick (mal); **~ ~ tight, we're off!** festhalten, es geht los!
2 *vi +prep obj* **(a) to ~ ~ sb's arm** an jds Arm (*dat*) hängen; **to ~ ~ sb's words** *or* **lips** an jds Lippen hängen; **he ~s ~ her every word** er hängt an ihren Lippen.
(b) (*depend on*) **everything ~s ~ his decision/getting the cash** alles hängt von seiner Entscheidung ab/alles hängt davon ab, ob man das Geld bekommt.

◆**hang on to** *vi +prep obj* **(a)** *hope* sich klammern an (+*acc*); *ideas* festhalten an (+*dat*). **(b)** (*keep*) behalten ◆ **could you ~ ~ ~ my seat until I get back?** können Sie mir den Platz so lange freihalten, bis ich zurück bin?

◆**hang out** 1 *vi* **(a)** (*tongue, shirt tails etc*) heraushängen ◆ **my tongue was ~ing ~ for a beer** ich lechzte nach einem Bier.
(b) (*inf*) sich aufhalten; (*live also*) hausen, wohnen; (*be usually found also*) sich herumtreiben (*inf*), zu finden sein.
(c) (*resist, endure*) nicht aufgeben ◆ **they hung ~ for more pay** sie hielten an ihrer Lohnforderung fest; **the soldiers hung ~ for three more days** die Soldaten hielten noch drei Tage durch.
(d) (*sl*) **to let it all ~ ~** die Sau rauslassen (*sl*); **come on now, let it all ~ ~** laß jucken (*sl*).
2 *vt sep* hinaushängen; *washing also* (draußen) aufhängen.

◆**hang over** *vi* (*continue*) andauern.

◆**hang together** *vi* (*people*) zusammenhalten; (*argument*) folgerichtig *or* zusammenhängend sein; (*alibi*) keinen Widerspruch aufweisen *or* enthalten; (*story, report etc*) gut verknüpft *or* zusammenhängend sein; (*statements*) zusammenpassen, keine Widersprüche *pl* aufweisen.

◆**hang up** 1 *vi* (*Telec*) auflegen; aufhängen ◆ **he hung ~ on me** er legte einfach auf.
2 *vt sep hat, picture* aufhängen; *telephone receiver* auflegen; aufhängen; *see* **hung-up**.

◆**hang upon** *vi +prep obj see* **hang on 2 (b)**.

hangar ['hæŋəʳ] *n* Hangar *m*, Flugzeughalle *f*.

hangdog ['hæŋdɒg] *adj look, expression* (*abject*) niedergeschlagen, trübsinnig; (*ashamed*) zerknirscht, Armsünder-.

hanger ['hæŋəʳ] *n* (*for clothes*) (Kleider)bügel *m*; (*loop on garment*) Aufhänger *m*.

hanger-on [,hæŋər'ɒn] *n, pl* **hangers-on** (*to celebrity*) Trabant, Satellit *m* ◆ **the film crew turned up with all its ~s-on** die Filmmannschaft erschien mit ihrem ganzen Anhang; **the celebrity was accompanied by his usual crowd of ~s-on** die Berühmtheit kam mit dem üblichen Schwarm von Gefolgsleuten *or* zog den üblichen Kometenschweif von Gefolgsleuten hinter sich her.

hang: ~-glide *vi* drachenfliegen; **~-glider** *n* (*device*) Drachen *m*; (*person*) Drachenflieger(in *f*) *m*; **~-gliding** *n* Drachenfliegen *nt*.

hanging ['hæŋıŋ] 1 *n* **(a)** (*of criminal*) Tod *m* durch den Strang, Erhängen *nt*; (*event*) Hinrichtung *f* (durch den Strang) ◆ **he deserves ~** er sollte aufgehängt werden; **to bring back ~** die Todesstrafe wiedereinführen.
(b) (*of wallpaper*) Anbringen, Kleben *nt*; (*of door*) Einhängen *nt*; (*of pictures*) (Auf)hängen *nt* ◆ **the ~ of the wallpaper** das Tapezieren.
(c) (*curtains etc*) **~s** *pl* Vorhänge *pl*; (*on wall*) Tapete *f*; (*tapestry*) Wandbehang *m or* -behänge *pl*; **bed ~s** Vorhänge *pl* des Himmelbetts.
2 *attr* **(a)** hängend; *bridge* Hänge-; *staircase* freischwebend; *sleeve* Flügel- ◆ **~ basket** Blumen- *or* Hängeampel *f*; **~ door** (*of garage*) Schwingtor *nt*; (*sliding*) Schiebetür *f*; **the ~ gardens of Babylon** die Hängenden Gärten der Semiramis.
(b) ~ judge Richter, der (zu) leicht das Todesurteil fällt; **it's a ~ matter** darauf steht der Galgen.
(c) ~ committee (*Art*) Hängekommission *f*.

hang: ~man *n* Henker *m*; (*game*) Galgen *m*; **~nail** *n* Niednagel *m*; **~-out** *n* (*inf*) (*place where one lives*) Bude *f* (*inf*); (*pub, café etc*) Stammlokal *nt*; (*of group*) Treff *m* (*inf*); **that disco is his favourite ~-out** er hängt mit Vorliebe in dieser Diskothek herum (*inf*); **~over** *n* **(a)** Kater *m* (*inf*); **(b)** (*sth left over*) Überbleibsel *nt*; **~up** *n* (*inf*) Komplex *m* (*about* wegen); (*obsession*) Fimmel *m* (*inf*); **he has this ~up about people smoking** er stellt sich furchtbar an, wenn Leute rauchen (*inf*).

hank [hæŋk] *n* (*of wool etc*) Strang *m*; (*of hair, fur*) Büschel *nt*.

hanker ['hæŋkəʳ] *vi* sich sehnen, Verlangen haben (*for or after sth* nach etw) ◆ **to ~ after glory** ruhmsüchtig sein.

hankering ['hæŋkərıŋ] *n* Verlangen *nt*, Sehnsucht *f* ◆ **to have a ~ for sth** Verlangen *or* Sehnsucht nach etw haben; **she always had a ~ for the stage** es hat sie schon immer zur Bühne gezogen.

hankie, hanky ['hæŋkı] *n* (*inf*) Taschentuch *nt*.

hanky-panky ['hæŋkı'pæŋkı] *n* (*inf*) **(a)** (*dishonest dealings*) Mauscheleien *pl* (*inf*), Tricks *pl* (*inf*) ◆ **there's some ~ going on** hier ist was faul (*inf*); **there's quite a lot of ~ behind the scenes** hinter den Kulissen wird ziemlich gemauschelt (*inf*).
(b) (*love affair*) Techtelmechtel *nt* (*inf*).
(c) (*sexy behaviour*) Gefummel *nt* (*sl*), Knutscherei *f* (*inf*) ◆ **they were having a bit of ~ on the sofa** sie haben auf dem Sofa ein bißchen geknutscht (*inf*) *or* gefummelt (*sl*).

Hanover ['hænəʊvəʳ] *n* Hannover *nt*.

Hanoverian [,hænəʊ'vıərıən] 1 *adj* hannover(i)sch ◆ **the ~ dynasty** das Haus Hannover.
2 *n* Hannoveraner(in *f*) *m*.

Hansard ['hænsɑːd] *n* der Hansard, die britischen Parlamentsberichte.

Hanseatic [,hænzı'ætık] *adj towns* Hanse- ◆ **~ League** Hanse *f*, Hansebund *m*.

hansom ['hænsəm] *n* (zweirädriger) Einspänner, Hansom *m*.

Hants [hænts] *abbr of* **Hampshire**.

hap [hæp] *vi* (*obs*) *see* **happen**[1].

ha'pence ['heıpəns] *n* (*Brit old*) halber Penny.

haphazard [,hæp'hæzəd] *adj* willkürlich, planlos ◆ **the whole thing was very ~** das Ganze war ziemlich zufällig *or* planlos; **the universe is neither ordered nor ~** das Universum hat weder eine feste noch eine ganz zufällige *or* willkürliche Ordnung; **in a ~ way** planlos, wahllos; **to choose in a ~ way** aufs Geratewohl *or* auf gut Glück (aus)wählen; **at a ~ guess I should say ...** auf gut Glück geschätzt würde ich sagen ...

haphazardly [,hæp'hæzədlı] *adv* wahllos, (ganz) willkürlich, planlos ◆ **decisions are made ~** Entscheidungen werden willkürlich *or* aufs Geratewohl *or* auf gut Glück getroffen; **a ~ organized reception/company** ein völlig ungeplanter Empfang/eine völlig systemlos aufgebaute Firma.

hapless ['hæplıs] *adj* glücklos ◆ **yet another misfortune in this ~ man's life** noch ein Unglück im Leben dieses vom Pech verfolgten Menschen.

ha'p'orth ['heıpəθ] *n contr of* **halfpennyworth** ◆ **a ~ of sweets** Bonbons für einen halben Penny; **to spoil the ship for a ~ of tar** (*Prov*) am falschen Ende sparen.

happen[1] ['hæpən] *vi* **(a)** geschehen; (*somewhat special or important event also*) sich ereignen; (*esp unexpected, unintentional or unpleasant event also*) passieren; (*process also*) vor sich gehen ◆ **it all ~ed like this ...** das Ganze geschah *or* war so ...; **nothing ever ~s here** hier ereignet sich *or* geschieht *or* passiert (doch) überhaupt nie etwas; **the match/party/meeting never ~ed** das Spiel/die Party/das Treffen fand (gar) nicht statt; **it's all ~ing here today** heute ist

hier ganz schön was los (*inf*); **where's it all ~ing tonight, where's the party?** wo ist denn heute abend etwas los, wo ist die Party?; **what's ~ing?** was läuft? (*inf*), was ist los?; **you can't just let things ~** du kannst die Dinge nicht einfach laufen lassen; **it's broken, how did it ~?** es ist kaputt, wie ist denn das passiert?; **it just ~ed all by itself** es ist ganz von allein passiert *or* gekommen; **as if nothing had ~ed** als ob nichts geschehen *or* gewesen wäre; **worse things have ~ed** es ist schon Schlimmeres passiert *or* vorgekommen; **don't let it ~ again** daß das nicht noch mal vorkommt *or* passiert!; **these things ~** so was kommt (schon mal) vor; **what has ~ed to him?** was ist ihm passiert *or* geschehen?; (*what have they done to him*) was ist mit ihm passiert?; (*what's wrong with him*) was ist mit ihm los?; (*what has become of him*) was ist aus ihm geworden?; **what's ~ed to your leg?** was ist mit deinem Bein los *or* passiert?; **if anything should ~ to me** wenn mir etwas zustoßen *or* passieren sollte; **accidents always ~ to other people** es sind immer die anderen, denen Unfälle passieren *or* zustoßen; **it all ~ed so quickly** es ging alles so schnell.
(b) (*chance*) **how does it ~ that ...?** (*cause*) wie kommt es, daß ...?; (*possibility*) wie ist es möglich, daß ...?; **it might ~ that you will be asked such a question** es könnte passieren *or* sein, daß Ihnen solch eine Frage gestellt wird; **how do you ~ to know?** wie kommt es, daß du das weißt?; **to ~ to do sth** zufällig(erweise) etw tun; **do you ~ to know whether ...?** wissen Sie vielleicht *or* zufällig, ob ...?; **I just ~ed to come along when ...** ich kam zufällig (gerade) vorbei, als ...; **he ~ed to see me just as I ...** muß er mich doch gerade in dem Augenblick sehen, als ich ...; **it so ~s** *or* **as it ~s I (don't) like that kind of thing** so etwas mag ich nun einmal (nicht); **as it ~s I've been there too** zufällig(erweise) bin ich auch dort gewesen; **as it ~s I'm going there today** zufällig(erweise) gehe ich heute (dort)hin; **you don't want to come, do you? — it so ~s, I do** du möchtest doch sicher nicht kommen, oder? — doch, natürlich; **when he first ~ed into this world** als er das Licht der Welt erblickte (*geh*).

◆**happen along** *vi* zufällig (an)kommen.

◆**happen (up)on** *vi +prep obj* zufällig stoßen auf (+*acc*); *person* zufällig treffen *or* sehen.

happen² ['æpn] *adv* (*N Eng inf: perhaps*) vielleicht.

happening ['hæpnɪŋ] *n* **(a)** Ereignis *nt*; (*not planned*) Vorfall *m* ◆ **there have been some peculiar ~s in that house** in dem Haus sind sonderbare Dinge vorgegangen; **such ~s cannot be tolerated** so etwas kann nicht geduldet werden, man kann derartige Vorkommnisse nicht einfach hinnehmen.
(b) (*Theat*) Happening *nt*.

happenstance ['hæpənstæns] *n* (*US inf*) Zufall *m*.

happily ['hæpɪlɪ] *adv* **(a)** glücklich; (*cheerfully also*) fröhlich, vergnügt, heiter; (*contentedly also*) zufrieden ◆ **they lived ~ ever after** (*in fairy-tales*) und wenn sie nicht gestorben sind, dann leben sie heute noch; **his dream was to get married and live ~ ever after** sein Wunschtraum war, zu heiraten und dann glücklich und zufrieden zu leben.
(b) (*fortunately*) glücklicherweise, zum Glück.
(c) (*felicitously*) glücklich, treffend ◆ **~ worded** glücklich formuliert.

happiness ['hæpɪnɪs] *n* **(a)** Glück *nt*; (*feeling of contentment also*) Zufriedenheit *f*; (*disposition*) Heiterkeit, Fröhlichkeit *f*. **(b)** (*of words*) glückliche Formulierung.

➤ **happy** ['hæpɪ] *adj* (+*er*) **(a)** glücklich; (*cheerful also*) fröhlich, vergnügt, heiter; (*glad about sth*) froh; (*contented also*) zufrieden; (*causing joy*) *thought, scene etc* erfreulich, freudig (*geh*) ◆ **is she ~?** ist sie glücklich?; **did you have a ~ Christmas/birthday?** hast du schöne Weihnachten/einen schönen Geburtstag gehabt *or* verlebt?; **to celebrate the ~ birth of a son** die glückliche Geburt eines Sohnes feiern; **a ~ event** ein frohes *or* freudiges Ereignis; **~ families** (*game*) Quartett *nt*; **that's all right, ~ to help** schon gut, ich helfe (doch) gern; **yes, I'd be (only too) ~ to** ja, sehr gern(e) *or* das würde mich freuen; **to be ~ to do sth** sich freuen, etw tun zu können *or* dürfen; **I am ~ to be here tonight** ich freue *or* es freut mich, heute abend hier zu sein; **(I'm) ~ to be of service** es freut *or* ich freue mich, helfen zu können; **I/the government would be only too ~ to do this, but ...** ich/die Regierung würde das ja gerne tun, aber ...; **not to be ~ with/about sth** mit etw nicht zufrieden sein/über etw (*acc*) nicht glücklich sein; **we are not entirely ~ with the plan** wir sind nicht so ganz glücklich über den Plan *or* zufrieden mit dem Plan; **the ~ few** die wenigen (Aus)erwählten.
(b) (*fortunate*) *solution* glücklich.
(c) (*felicitous*) *phrase, words* glücklich, gut getroffen; *gesture* geglückt.
(d) (*inf: slightly drunk*) angeheitert, beschwipst (*inf*).
➤ **(e) ~ anniversary** herzlichen Glückwunsch zum Hochzeitstag; **~ birthday!** herzlichen Glückwunsch *or* alles Gute zum Geburtstag!; **~ Easter** fröhliche *or* frohe Ostern; **~ New Year** ein glückliches *or* frohes neues Jahr.

-happy *adj suf* (*inf*) **trigger-~/strike-~** schießfreudig/streikfreudig (*inf*); **gold-~** goldgierig (*inf*).

happy: ~-go-lucky ['hæpɪgəʊ'lʌkɪ] *adj* unbekümmert, sorglos; **to do sth in a ~-go-lucky way** etw unbekümmert tun; **I wish you wouldn't be so ~-go-lucky about things** ich wollte, du wärest nicht bei allem so sorglos *or* würdest nicht alles so lässig nehmen (*inf*); **the preparations were very ~-go-lucky** die Vorbereitungen waren mehr oder weniger dem Zufall überlassen worden; **~ hour** *n* (*in pubs etc*) *Zeit f, in der Getränke zu ermäßigten Preisen angeboten werden*; **~ hunting ground** *n* **(a)** (*Myth*) ewige Jagdgründe *pl*; **(b)** (*fig*) Paradies *nt*.

harakiri [ˌhærə'kɪrɪ] *n* Harakiri *nt*.

harangue [hə'ræŋ] **1** *n* (*scolding*) (Straf)predigt *f*, Sermon *m*; (*lengthy also*) Tirade *f*; (*encouraging*) Appell *m* ◆ **to give sb a ~** jdm eine (Straf)predigt *etc* halten; einen Appell an jdn richten.
2 *vt see n person* eine (Straf)predigt *or* einen Sermon halten (+*dat*); eine Tirade loslassen auf (+*acc*) (*inf*); anfeuern, einen Appell richten an (+*acc*) ◆ **I don't like being ~d** ich kann es nicht leiden, wenn mir jemand lange Reden hält; **stop haranguing me about how lucky other men's wives are** hör auf, mir dauernd vorzuhalten *or* mir damit in den Ohren zu liegen (*inf*), wie gut es die Frauen anderer Männer haben.

harass ['hærəs] *vt* belästigen; (*mess around*) schikanieren; (*Mil*) *the enemy* Anschläge verüben auf (+*acc*), immer wieder überfallen ◆ **to ~ sb with complaints** jdn mit Klagen belästigen; **don't ~ me** dräng *or* hetz (*inf*) mich doch nicht so!; **they eventually ~ed him into resigning** sie setzten ihm so lange zu, bis er schließlich zurücktrat; **constant ~ing of the goalie eventually made him lose his nerve** der Torwart wurde ständig so hart bedrängt, daß er schließlich die Nerven verlor; **the landlord was ~ing me about the rent** der Hauswirt belästigte mich ständig wegen der Miete; **a lot of these people are ~ed by the police** viele dieser Leute werden ständig von der Polizei schikaniert; **a salesman should never seem to ~ a potential customer** ein Vertreter sollte einem potentiellen Kunden gegenüber niemals aufdringlich werden.

harassed ['hærəst] *adj* abgespannt, angegriffen, mitgenommen; (*worried*) von Sorgen gequält ◆ **a ~ family man** ein (viel)geplagter Familienvater; **she was very ~ that day** an dem Tag wußte sie nicht, wo ihr der Kopf stand; **he wiped his brow in a ~ manner** er wischte sich (*dat*) gequält die Stirn.

harassment ['hærəsmənt] *n* (*act*) Belästigung, Bedrängung *f*; (*messing around*) Schikanierung *f*; (*state*) Bedrängnis *f*; (*Mil*) Kleinkrieg *m* ◆ **if we can't win him over by argument we'll defeat him by ~** wenn wir ihn nicht im Guten überreden können, müssen wir ihm eben so lange zusetzen, bis er aufgibt; **constant ~ of the enemy** ständiger Kleinkrieg gegen den Feind; **police ~** Schikane *f* von seiten der Polizei.

harbinger ['hɑːbɪndʒəʳ] *n* (*liter*) Herold (*liter*), (Vor)bote *m*.

harbour, (*US*) **harbor** ['hɑːbəʳ] **1** *n* Hafen *m*.
2 *vt* **(a)** *criminal etc* beherbergen, Unterschlupf gewähren (+*dat*); *goods* (bei sich) aufbewahren.
(b) *suspicions, grudge* hegen.
(c) (*conceal, contain*) **its fur ~s a lot of fleas** in seinem Fell nisten die Flöhe in Scharen; **dirt ~s germs** Schmutz ist eine Brutstätte für Krankheitserreger.

harbour: ~ bar *n* Sandbank *f* vor dem Hafen; **~ dues** *npl* Hafengebühr(en *pl*) *f*; **~ master** *n* Hafenmeister *m*.

hard [hɑːd] **1** *adj* (+*er*) **(a)** (*generally*) hart; *see* **nail**.
(b) (*difficult*) schwer; (*complicated also*) schwierig; (*~ to endure*) hart ◆ **~ of hearing** schwerhörig; **I find it ~ to believe that ...** es fällt mir schwer zu glauben *or* ich kann es kaum glauben, daß ...; **these conditions are ~ to accept** mit diesen Bedingungen kann man sich nur schwer abfinden; **it's ~ to accept that anyone would change so much** es ist kaum zu glauben, daß jemand sich so verändern kann; **I know it's ~ for** *or* **on you, but ...** ich weiß, es ist schwer *or* hart für Sie, aber ...; **he is ~ to get on with** es ist schwer *or* schwierig, mit ihm auszukommen; **learning Japanese is ~ going** Japanisch zu lernen ist eine Schinderei *or* Plackerei; **this novel is ~ going** durch diesen Roman muß man sich mühsam durchbeißen; **chatting her up is ~ going** es ist gar nicht so einfach, die anzumachen; **he had a ~ time of it** er hat es nicht leicht gehabt; (*in negotiations, boxing match etc*) es hat ihn einen harten Kampf gekostet; **she pulled through after the operation but she had a ~ time of it** sie erholte sich von der Operation, aber es war eine schwere Zeit für sie; **~ luck!, ~ lines!** (so ein) Pech!; **it was ~ luck** *or* **lines that ...** es war (ein) Pech, daß ...; *see* **cheese**.
(c) (*severe, harsh*) hart; *voice, tone also* schroff, barsch; *frost* streng ◆ **a ~ man** ein harter Mann; (*esp ruthless*) ein knallharter Typ (*sl*); **he thinks he's a ~ man** (*inf*) er kommt sich unheimlich hart vor (*inf*); **don't be ~ on the boy** sei nicht zu hart *or* streng zu dem Jungen; **he was (very) ~ on his staff** er war seinem Personal gegenüber sehr hart; **I'm all for speaking the truth but you were a bit ~ on her** ich bin dafür, die Wahrheit zu sagen, aber Sie sind ein bißchen zu hart mit ihr ins Gericht gegangen.
(d) (*strenuous*) *fight, match, worker, work* hart ◆ **getting on with him is ~ work** (*inf*) es gehört schon etwas dazu, mit ihm auszukommen (*inf*); **he's ~ work** (*inf*) er ist ziemlich anstrengend (*inf*); (*difficult to know or persuade*) er ist ein harter Brocken (*inf*); **it was ~ work for me not to swear at him** es hat mich große Mühe gekostet, ihn nicht zu beschimpfen.
(e) to put the ~ word on sb (*Austral sl*) jdn um etw anhauen (*inf*).
2 *adv* (+*er*) **(a)** mit aller Kraft; (*with neg*) stark; (*violently*) heftig; *pull, push, hit also* kräftig; *hold also* fest; *drive* hart; *run* so schnell man kann; *breathe* schwer; *work* hart, schwer ◆ **he worked ~ at clearing his name** er versuchte mit allen Mitteln, seinen Namen reinzuwaschen; **to listen ~** genau hinhören; **he stood outside the door listening ~** er stand vor der Tür und horchte angestrengt; **think ~** denk mal scharf *or* gut nach; **you're not thinking ~ enough** du denkst nicht angestrengt genug *or* richtig nach; **think ~er** denk mal ein bißchen besser nach; **he was obviously thinking ~** er dachte (offen)sichtlich scharf *or* angestrengt nach; **he has obviously thought ~ about this** er hat es sich (*dat*) offensichtlich gut *or* genau überlegt; **think ~ before you ...** überlegen Sie sich's gut, bevor Sie ...; **if you try ~ you can ...** wenn du dich richtig bemühst *or* anstrengst, kannst du ...; **try ~er to please her** gib dir doch ein bißchen mehr Mühe *or* bemühe dich doch etwas mehr, sie zufriedenzustellen; **you're not trying ~ enough** du strengst dich nicht genügend an; **he was really trying ~ to win** er bemühte sich wirklich ernsthaft zu gewinnen; **you're trying too ~** du bemühst dich zu sehr *or* zu krampfhaft; **he tried as ~ as he could** er hat sein Bestes getan *or* sich nach

➤ LANGUAGE IN USE: **happy: a** → 3.1, 3.2, 14, 24.1, 24.1, 24.3, 25.2 **e** → 23.2, 23.3

Kräften bemüht; **to look ~ at sb/sth** sich jdn/etw genau ansehen; (*critically*) jdn/etw scharf ansehen; **to be ~ at it** (*inf*) schwer am Werk *or* dabei sein (*inf*); **~ a port!** (*Naut*) hart Backbord!; **he threw the wheel ~ over** er schlug das Steuerrad hart herum.

(b) (*in, with difficulty*) **to be ~ put to it to do sth** es sehr schwer finden *or* große Schwierigkeiten (damit) haben, etw zu tun; **I'd be ~ put to it ...** es würde mir schwerfallen ...; **to be ~ up** (*inf*) knapp bei Kasse sein (*inf*); **he's ~ up for ...** (*inf*) es fehlt ihm an (*+dat*) ...; **to be ~ up for something to fill one's day** (*inf*) nicht wissen, was man mit seiner Zeit anfangen soll; **it will go ~ with him if he carries on this way** er wird noch Schwierigkeiten kriegen, wenn er so weitermacht; **it'll go ~ with him if he's found out** es kann ihn teuer zu stehen kommen, wenn das herauskommt; **to be ~ done by** übel dran sein; **he reckons he's ~ done by having to work on Saturdays** er findet es hart, daß er samstags arbeiten muß; **he took it pretty ~** es ging ihm ziemlich nahe, es traf ihn schwer; **old traditions die ~** alte Traditionen sterben nur langsam.

(c) *rain, snow* stark ◆ **it was freezing ~** es herrschte strenger Frost, es fror Stein und Bein.

(d) (*close*) **~ by the mill** ganz nahe bei *or* ganz in der Nähe der Mühle; **there's a mill ~ by** ganz in der Nähe ist eine Mühle.

hard: ~ and fast *adj* fest; *rules also* bindend, verbindlich; **~-back** [1] *adj* (*also* **~backed**) *book* gebunden; [2] *n* gebundene Ausgabe; **~ball** *n* (*US*) **(a)** (*Baseball*) Hardball *m*; **(b)** (*fig*) **to play ~ball** rücksichtslos sein *or* vorgehen; **~-bitten** *adj person* abgebrüht; *manager* knallhart (*inf*); **~board** *n* Hartfaser- *or* Preßspanplatte *f*; **~-boiled** *adj* **(a)** *egg* hartgekocht; **(b)** (*fig: shrewd*) gerissen, ausgekocht (*inf*), mit allen Wassern gewaschen (*inf*); **(c)** (*fig: unsentimental*) kaltschnäuzig (*inf*); **(d)** (*fig: realistic*) *approach, appraisal etc* nüchtern, sachlich; **~ cash** *n* Bargeld, Bare(s) (*inf*) *nt*; **~ copy** *n* Ausdruck *m*, Hardcopy *f*; **~ core** *n* **(a)** (*for road*) Schotter *m*; **(b)** (*fig*) harter Kern; (*pornography*) harter Porno (*inf*); **~-core** *adj pornography* hart; **~-core magazine** hartes Pornoheft; **~ court** *n* Hartplatz *m*; **~ currency** *n* harte Währung; **~ disk** *n* (*Comput*) Festplatte *f*; **~ disk computer** *n* Festplattencomputer *m*; **~ disk drive** *n* Festplattenlaufwerk *nt*; **~ drink** *n* hartes Getränk; **~ drinker** *n* starker Trinker; **~ drug** *n* harte Droge; **~-earned** *adj wages* sauer verdient; *reward* redlich verdient; *victory* hart erkämpft.

harden ['hɑːdn] [1] *vt steel* härten; *body, muscles* kräftigen, stählen (*geh*); *person* (*physically*) abhärten; (*emotionally*) verhärten (*pej*), abstumpfen (*pej*); *clay* hart werden lassen ◆ **this ~ed his attitude** dadurch hat sich seine Haltung verhärtet; **to ~ oneself to sth** (*physically*) sich gegen etw abhärten; (*emotionally*) gegen etw unempfindlich werden; **war had ~ed the soldiers to death and killing** der Krieg hatte die Soldaten gegen den Tod und das Töten abgestumpft; **to ~ one's heart to sb** sein Herz gegen jdn verhärten (*geh*); *see* **hardened**.

[2] *vi* (*substance*) hart werden; (*fig: attitude*) sich verhärten; (*St Ex*) (*cease to fluctuate*) sich festigen, sich stabilisieren; (*rise*) anziehen ◆ **his voice ~ed** seine Stimme wurde hart *or* bekam einen harten Klang.

◆**harden off** *vt sep plants* widerstandsfähig machen.

◆**harden up** [1] *vi* (*concrete, glue etc*) hart werden.

[2] *vt sep* (*make hard*) härten, hart machen; (*fig: toughen*) abhärten.

hardened ['hɑːdnd] *adj steel* gehärtet; *criminal* Gewohnheits-; *troops* zäh, abgehärtet; *sinner* verstockt ◆ **to be ~ to** *or* **against the cold/the climate/sb's insensitivity/life** gegen die Kälte/das Klima abgehärtet sein/an jds Gefühllosigkeit (*acc*) gewöhnt sein/vom Leben hart gemacht sein; **you become ~ to it after a while** daran gewöhnt man sich mit der Zeit.

hardening ['hɑːdnɪŋ] *n* (*of steel*) (Er)härten *nt*, Härtung *f*; (*fig*) Verhärten *nt*, Verhärtung *f*; (*St Ex*) Versteifung, Festigung *f*; (*rise*) Anziehen *nt* ◆ **I noticed a ~ of his attitude** ich habe bemerkt, daß sich seine Einstellung verhärtet; **~ of the arteries** Arterienverkalkung *f*.

hard: ~-featured *adj person* mit harten Gesichtszügen; **~-fought** *adj battle* erbittert; *boxing match, competition, game* hart; **a ~-fought election** eine (erbitterte) Wahlschlacht; **~ hat** *n* Schutzhelm *m*; (*construction worker*) Bauarbeiter *m*; **~-headed** *adj* nüchtern; **~-hearted** *adj* hartherzig (*towards sb* jdm gegenüber); **~-heartedness** *n* Hartherzigkeit *f*.

hardihood ['hɑːdɪhʊd] *n* Kühnheit *f*; (*courage also*) Mut *m*; (*audacity also*) Dreistigkeit *f*.

hardiness ['hɑːdɪnɪs] *n* **(a)** (*toughness*) Zähigkeit, Widerstandsfähigkeit *f*; (*Bot also*) Frostunempfindlichkeit *f*; (*of people also*) Ausdauer *f*. **(b)** (*courage*) Mut *m*.

hard: ~ labour *n* Zwangsarbeit *f*; **~ line** *n* harte Haltung, harte Linie; **to take a ~ line** eine harte Haltung einnehmen, eine harte Linie verfolgen; **~-liner** *n* Vertreter(in *f*) *m* der harten Linie, Hardliner *m* (*esp Pol*); **~ liquor** *n* Schnaps *m*.

hardly ['hɑːdlɪ] *adv* **(a)** (*scarcely*) kaum ◆ **you've ~ eaten anything** du hast (ja) kaum etwas gegessen; **I need ~ tell you** ich muß Ihnen wohl kaum sagen; **I ~ know any French, I know ~ any French** ich kann kaum Französisch; **~ ever** kaum jemals, fast nie; **he had ~ gone** *or* **~ had he gone when ...** er war kaum gegangen, als ...; **he would ~ have said that** das hat er wohl kaum gesagt; **~!** (wohl) kaum; **you don't agree, do you? — ~** Sie sind damit nicht einverstanden, oder? — nein, eigentlich nicht.

(b) (*rare: harshly*) hart, streng.

hardness ['hɑːdnɪs] *n* **(a)** (*generally*) Härte *f*; (*of winter also*) Strenge *f*. **(b)** *see adj (b)* Schwere *f*, Schwierigkeit *f*, Härte *f* ◆ **~ of hearing** Schwerhörigkeit *f*. **(c)** *see adj (c)* Härte *f*, Schroffheit, Barschheit *f*, Strenge *f* ◆ **the ~ of his heart** seine Hartherzigkeit. **(d)** (*St Ex*) Festigung *f*, (*rise*) Anziehen *nt*.

hard: ~-on *n* (*sl*) Ständer *m* (*sl*); **to have a ~-on** einen hoch *or* stehen haben (*sl*); **~-packed** *adj snow* festgetreten; **~pad** *n* (*Vet*) Hartballenkrankheit *f*; **~pan** *n* (*Geol*) Ortgestein *nt*; **~-pressed** *adj troops etc* hart bedrängt; (*with work*) stark beansprucht; **to be ~-pressed** unter großem Druck stehen *or* sein, in harter Bedrängnis sein (*geh*); **the ~-pressed minister attempted to answer his critics** in die Enge getrieben, versuchte der Minister, seinen Kritikern zu antworten; **to be ~-pressed for money** in Geldnot sein, knapp bei Kasse sein (*inf*); **~ rock** *n* (*Mus*) Hardrock *m*; **~ sell** [1] *n* aggressive Verkaufstaktik, Hardsell *m*; [2] *attr* aggressiv, Hardsell-.

hardship ['hɑːdʃɪp] *n* (*condition*) Not *f*, Elend *nt*; (*instance*) Härte *f*; (*deprivation*) Entbehrung *f* ◆ **a temporary ~** eine vorübergehende Notlage; **to suffer great ~s** große Not leiden; **the ~s of war** das Elend/die Entbehrungen des Kriegs; **is that such a great ~?** ist das wirklich ein solches Unglück?; **if it's not too much (of a) ~ for you ...** wenn es dir nichts ausmacht *or* nicht zuviel Mühe macht ...; **the ~(s) of living in the country** die Entbehrungen *pl* des Landlebens.

hard: ~ shoulder *n* (*Brit*) Seitenstreifen *m*; **~tack** *n* Schiffszwieback *m*; **~top** *n* Hardtop *nt or m*; **~ware** [1] *n* **(a)** Eisenwaren *pl*; (*household goods*) Haushaltswaren *pl*; **(b)** (*Comput*) Hardware *f*; **(c)** (*Mil*) (Wehr)material *nt*; **(d)** (*US sl: gun*) Schießeisen *nt* (*sl*), Kanone *f* (*sl*); [2] *attr* **(a) ~ware dealer** Eisenwarenhändler *m*; (*including household goods*) Haushalt- und Eisenwarenhändler *m*; **~ware shop** *or* **store** Eisenwarenhandlung *f*; (*including household goods*) Haushalt- und Eisenwarengeschäft *nt*; **(b)** (*Comput*) Hardware-; **~-wearing** *adj* widerstandsfähig; *cloth, clothes* strapazierfähig; **~-wired** *adj* (*Comput*) festverdrahtet; **~-won** *adj battle, fight, victory* hart *or* schwer erkämpft; **~wood** *n* Hartholz *nt*; **~-working** *adj person* fleißig; *engine* leistungsfähig.

hardy ['hɑːdɪ] *adj* (*+er*) **(a)** (*tough*) zäh; *person also* abgehärtet; *plant* (frost)unempfindlich, winterhart; *tree* widerstandsfähig, kräftig ◆ **that's pretty ~ of you not to wear a coat** du mußt ganz schön abgehärtet sein, daß du keinen Mantel anziehst; **~ annual/perennial** winterharte einjährige/mehrjährige Pflanze; **nationalization, that ~ annual of Labour congresses** Verstaatlichung, ein Thema, das jedes Jahr beim Labour-Parteitag wieder auftaucht *or* akut wird.

(b) (*bold*) *person* kühn, unerschrocken.

hare [hɛəʳ] [1] *n* (Feld)hase *m* ◆ **~ and hounds** (*game*) Schnitzeljagd *f*; **to run with the ~ and hunt with the hounds** (*prov*) es mit niemandem verderben wollen; **to start a ~** (*fig*) vom Thema ablenken; *see* **mad**.

[2] *vi* (*inf*) sausen, flitzen (*inf*).

hare: ~bell *n* Glockenblume *f*; **~-brained** *adj person, plan* verrückt, behämmert (*inf*); **~lip** *n* Hasenscharte *f*.

harem [hɑːˈriːm] *n* Harem *m*.

haricot ['hærɪkəʊ] *n* **~ (bean)** Gartenbohne *f*.

hark [hɑːk] *vi* **to ~ to sth** (*liter*) einer Sache (*dat*) lauschen (*liter*); **~!** (*liter*) horch(t)! (*liter*), höret!; **~ at him!** (*inf*) hör ihn dir nur an!, hör sich einer den an! (*inf*).

◆**hark back** *vi* zurückkommen (*to* auf *+acc*) ◆ **this custom ~s ~ to the days when ...** dieser Brauch geht auf die Zeit zurück, als ...; **he's always ~ing ~ to the good old days** er fängt immer wieder von der guten alten Zeit an; **the author is ~ing ~ to former times** der Autor geht auf vergangene Zeiten zurück.

Harlequin ['hɑːlɪkwɪn] [1] *n* (*Theat*) Harlekin, Hanswurst *m*.

[2] *attr costume* Harlekin(s)-.

harlot ['hɑːlət] *n* (*old*) Metze (*old*), Hure *f*.

harm [hɑːm] [1] *n* (*bodily*) Verletzung *f*; (*material damage, to relations, psychological*) Schaden *m* ◆ **to do ~ to sb** jdm eine Verletzung zufügen/jdm schaden *or* Schaden zufügen; **to do ~ to sth** einer Sache (*dat*) schaden; **you could do somebody/yourself ~ with that axe** mit der Axt können Sie jemanden/sich verletzen; **the blow didn't do him any ~** der Schlag hat ihm nichts getan *or* ihn nicht verletzt; **he didn't do himself any ~ in the crash** er wurde bei dem Unfall nicht verletzt, er erlitt keinerlei Verletzungen bei dem Unfall; **he did himself quite a lot of ~** *or* **he did quite a lot of ~ to himself with his TV broadcast** er hat sich (*dat*) (selbst) mit diesem Fernsehauftritt ziemlich geschadet; **you will come to no ~** es wird Ihnen nichts geschehen; **it will do more ~ than good** es wird mehr schaden als nützen; **it will do you no/won't do you any ~** es wird dir nicht schaden; **I see no ~ in the odd cigarette** ich finde nichts dabei, wenn man ab und zu eine Zigarette raucht; **to mean no ~** es nicht böse meinen; **I don't mean him any ~** ich meine es nicht böse mit ihm; (*bodily, not offend*) ich will ihm nicht weh tun; **there's no ~ in asking/trying** es kann nicht schaden, zu fragen/es zu versuchen; **there's no ~ in me putting a word in for him, is there?** es kann doch nichts schaden, wenn ich ein gutes Wort für ihn einlege, oder?; **where's** *or* **what's the ~ in that?** was kann denn das schaden?, **to keep** *or* **stay out of ~'s way** die Gefahr meiden, der Gefahr (*dat*) aus dem Weg gehen; **you stay here out of ~'s way** du bleibst schön hier, in Sicherheit; **I've put those tablets in the cupboard out of ~'s way** ich habe die Tabletten im Schrank in Sicherheit gebracht.

[2] *vt person* verletzen; *thing* schaden (*+dat*); *sb's interests, relations, reputation etc* schaden (*+dat*), abträglich sein (*+dat*) ◆ **don't ~ the children** tu den Kindern nichts (an); **it wouldn't ~ you to be a little more polite** es würde nicht(s) schaden, wenn du ein bißchen höflicher wärest.

harmful ['hɑːmfʊl] *adj* schädlich (*to* für); *remarks* verletzend ◆ **~ to one's health** gesundheitsschädlich.

harmless ['hɑːmlɪs] *adj* **(a)** harmlos; *animal, toy, weapon etc also* ungefährlich; *drugs also* unschädlich ◆ **to make** *or* **render a bomb ~** eine Bombe entschärfen. **(b)** (*innocent*) harmlos; *conversation, question also* unverfänglich.

harmlessly ['hɑːmlɪslɪ] *adv* harmlos, in aller Harmlosigkeit.

harmlessness ['hɑːmlɪsnɪs] *n see adj* Harmlosigkeit *f*; Ungefährlichkeit *f*; Unschädlichkeit *f*; Unverfänglichkeit *f*.

harmonic [hɑː'mɒnɪk] [1] *n* (*Mus*) Oberton *m*.
[2] *adj* (*Mus, Phys*) harmonisch.

harmonica [hɑː'mɒnɪkə] *n* Harmonika *f*.

harmonics [hɑː'mɒnɪks] *n sing* Harmonik *f*.

harmonious *adj*, **~ly** *adv* [hɑː'məʊnɪəs, -lɪ] (*Mus, fig*) harmonisch.

harmonium [hɑː'məʊnɪəm] *n* Harmonium *nt*.

harmonization [ˌhɑːmənaɪ'zeɪʃən] *n* (*Mus, fig*) Harmonisierung *f*.

harmonize ['hɑːmənaɪz] [1] *vt* (*Mus, fig*) harmonisieren; *ideas etc also* miteinander in Einklang bringen; *plans, colours also* aufeinander abstimmen (*sth with sth* etw auf etw *acc*).
[2] *vi* **(a)** (*notes, colours, people etc*) harmonieren; (*facts*) übereinstimmen. **(b)** (*sing in harmony*) mehrstimmig singen.

harmony ['hɑːmənɪ] *n* Harmonie *f*; (*of colours also*) harmonisches Zusammenspiel; (*fig: harmonious relations*) Eintracht *f* ◆ **to live in perfect ~ with sb** in Harmonie *or* Eintracht mit jdm leben; **to be in/out of ~ with** (*lit*) harmonieren/nicht harmonieren mit; (*fig also*) in Einklang/nicht in Einklang stehen *or* sein mit; **to sing in ~** mehrstimmig singen; (*in tune*) rein singen; **his ideas are out of ~ with the age** seine Vorstellungen sind nicht zeitgemäß *or* passen nicht in die Zeit.

harness ['hɑːnɪs] [1] *n* **(a)** Geschirr *nt* ◆ **to get back into ~** (*fig*) sich wieder an die Arbeit machen, wieder in den täglichen Trott verfallen; **to be back in ~** (*fig*) wieder bei der Arbeit *or* im gewohnten Trott sein; **to work in ~** (*fig*) zusammenarbeiten; **to die in ~** (*fig*) (*often hum*) in den Sielen sterben.
(b) (*of parachute*) Gurtwerk *nt*; (*for baby*) Laufgurt *m*.
(c) (*Elec*) Kabelbaum *m*.
[2] *vt* **(a)** *horse* anschirren, aufzäumen ◆ **a horse that has never been ~ed** ein Pferd, das nie im Geschirr gegangen ist; **to ~ a horse to a carriage** ein Pferd vor einen Wagen spannen.
(b) (*utilize*) *river etc* nutzbar machen; *resources* (aus)nutzen.

harp [hɑːp] *n* Harfe *f*.

◆**harp on** *vi* (*inf*) **to ~ ~ sth** auf etw (*dat*) herumreiten; **he's always ~ing ~ about the need for ...** er spricht ständig von der Notwendigkeit *+gen ...*; **she's always ~ing ~ about her troubles** sie lamentiert ständig über ihre Probleme, sie jammert einem dauernd die Ohren voll mit ihren Problemen (*inf*); **she is always ~ing ~ the same string** es ist immer die alte Leier *or* das alte Lied bei ihr.

harpist ['hɑːpɪst] *n* Harfenspieler(in *f*), Harfenist(in *f*) *m*.

harpoon [hɑː'puːn] [1] *n* Harpune *f* ◆ **~ gun** Harpunenkanone *f*.
[2] *vt* harpunieren.

harpsichord ['hɑːpsɪkɔːd] *n* Cembalo *nt*.

harpy ['hɑːpɪ] *n* Harpyie *f*; (*shrewish woman*) Hexe *f*; (*grasping person*) Hyäne *f*.

harpy eagle *n* Harpyie *f*.

harridan ['hærɪdən] *n* Vettel *f*, Drache *m*.

harrier ['hærɪəʳ] *n* **(a)** (*Sport*) Querfeldeinläufer(in *f*), Geländeläufer(in *f*) *m*. **(b)** (*Orn*) Weih *m*. **(c)** (*dog*) *Hund m für die Hasenjagd*.

harrow ['hærəʊ] [1] *n* Egge *f*.
[2] *vt* **(a)** eggen. **(b)** (*fig: usu pass*) **to ~ sb** jdn quälen *or* peinigen (*geh*).

harrowed ['hærəʊd] *adj look* gequält.

harrowing ['hærəʊɪŋ] *adj story* entsetzlich, erschütternd, grauenhaft; *experience* qualvoll, grauenhaft.

Harry ['hærɪ] *n, dim of* **Henry** ◆ **old ~** (*Devil*) der Leibhaftige; **to play old ~ with sth** etw vollständig durcheinanderbringen; *with sb's lungs etc* etw kaputtmachen (*inf*).

harry ['hærɪ] *vt* **(a)** bedrängen, zusetzen (*+dat*). **(b)** (*old*) *country* plündern.

harsh [hɑːʃ] *adj* (*+er*) **(a)** rauh; *colour, contrast, light, sound* grell, hart; *taste* herb ◆ **it was ~ to the touch/taste/ear** es fühlte sich rauh an/es schmeckte herb/es gellte in den Ohren.
(b) (*severe*) hart; *words, tone of voice also* barsch, schroff; *treatment also* rauh; (*too strict*) streng ◆ **to be ~ with** *or* **on sb** jdn hart anfassen; **don't be too ~ with him** sei nicht zu streng *or* hart mit ihm.

harshly ['hɑːʃlɪ] *adv see adj*.

harshness ['hɑːʃnɪs] *n see adj* **(a)** Rauheit *f*; Grelle, Härte *f*; Herbheit *f*. **(b)** Härte *f*; Barschheit, Schroffheit *f*; Rauheit *f*; Strenge *f*.

hart [hɑːt] *n* Hirsch *m*.

harum-scarum ['hɛərəm'skɛərəm] [1] *adj* unbesonnen, unbedacht.
[2] *n* unbedachter Tollkopf.

harvest ['hɑːvɪst] [1] *n* Ernte *f*; (*of wines, berries also*) Lese *f*; (*of the sea*) Ausbeute *f*, Ertrag *m*; (*fig*) Frucht *f*, Ertrag *m* ◆ **the ~ of their efforts** die Früchte *pl* ihrer Arbeit *or* Anstrengungen; **a large ~ of apples** eine reiche Apfelernte.
[2] *vt* (*reap, also fig*) ernten; *vines also* lesen; (*bring in*) einbringen.
[3] *vi* ernten.

harvester ['hɑːvɪstəʳ] *n* (*person*) Erntearbeiter(in *f*) *m*; (*machine*) Mähmaschine *f*; (*cuts and binds*) Mähbinder, Bindemäher *m*; (*combine ~*) Mähdrescher *m*.

harvest: ~ festival *n* Erntedankfest *nt*; **~ home** *n* (*festival*) Erntefest *nt*; (*service*) Erntedankfest *nt*; **~ moon** *n* Herbstmond *m*, *heller Vollmond im September*; **~ time** *n* Erntezeit *f*.

has [hæz] *3rd pers sing present of* **have**.

has-been ['hæzbiːn] *n* (*pej*) vergangene *or* vergessene Größe ◆ **every comedian must dread finishing up a ~** jeder Komiker muß befürchten, (im Alter) in Vergessenheit zu geraten.

hash [hæʃ] [1] *n* **(a)** (*Cook*) Haschee *nt*.
(b) (*fig: mess*) Durcheinander *nt*, Kuddelmuddel *m* (*inf*); (*bad work*) Pfusch(erei *f*) *m* (*inf*) ◆ **to make a ~ of sth** etw verpfuschen *or* vermasseln (*inf*); **I'll soon settle his ~** (*inf*) ich werde ihm (mal kurz) den Kopf zurechtsetzen *or* waschen (*inf*); **that settled his ~** (*inf*) das hat ihn kuriert (*inf*).
(c) (*inf: hashish*) Hasch *nt* (*inf*).
[2] *vt* (*Cook*) hacken.

◆**hash up** *vt sep* **(a)** (*Cook*) hacken, zerkleinern. **(b)** (*inf: mess up*) verpfuschen, vermasseln (*inf*).

hashish ['hæʃɪʃ] *n* Haschisch *nt*.

hasn't ['hæznt] *contr of* **has not**.

hasp [hɑːsp] *n* (*for chest, door etc*) Überfall *m*; (*for book covers*) (Verschluß)spange, Schließe *f*.

hassle ['hæsl] (*inf*) [1] *n* Auseinandersetzung *f*; (*bother, trouble*) Mühe *f*, Theater *nt* (*inf*) ◆ **we had a real ~ getting these tickets for tonight** es war ein richtiges Theater (*inf*) *or* es hat uns (*dat*) viel Mühe gemacht, diese Karten für heute abend zu bekommen; **getting there is such a ~** es ist so umständlich, dorthin zu kommen; **it's always such a ~ getting him to do anything** es ist immer ein solches Theater, ihn dazu zu bringen, etwas zu tun (*inf*); **it's too much ~ cooking for myself** es ist mir zu umständlich *or* mühsam, für mich allein zu kochen; **all this security ~** dieser ganze Zirkus mit den Sicherheitsmaßnahmen (*inf*); **don't give me any ~** mach kein Theater (*inf*); **this job is just constant ~** bei diesem Job ist man ständig im Streß (*inf*).
[2] *vt* **(a)** (*mess around*) schikanieren. **(b)** (*keep on at*) bedrängen ◆ **keep hassling them till they pay** bleib ihnen auf den Fersen, bis sie bezahlen; **I'm feeling a bit ~d** ich fühle mich etwas unter Druck *or* im Streß (*inf*); **she gets easily ~d** sie läßt sich leicht unter Druck setzen.
[3] *vi* **keep hassling** bleib ihm/ihnen *etc* auf den Fersen; **in a job like this you have to be prepared to ~** in diesem Job muß man (anderen) Dampf machen können.

hassler ['hæsləʳ] *n* aufdringlicher Typ ◆ **we need someone who is a bit of a ~** wir brauchen einen, der Dampf machen kann.

hassock ['hæsək] *n* Betkissen, Kniekissen *nt*.

hast [hæst] (*obs*) *2nd pers sing present of* **have**.

haste [heɪst] *n* Eile *f*; (*nervous*) Hast *f* ◆ **to do sth in ~** etw in Eile tun; **to be in ~ to do sth** sich beeilen, etw zu tun; **in great ~** in großer Eile; **to make ~ to do sth** sich beeilen, etw zu tun; **make ~!** (*old*) spute dich (*old*); **more ~ less speed** (*Prov*) eile mit Weile (*Prov*).

hasten ['heɪsn] [1] *vi* sich beeilen ◆ **he ~ed to add that ...** er fügte schnell hinzu, daß ..., er beeilte sich, hinzuzufügen, daß ...; **I ~ to add that ...** ich muß allerdings hinzufügen, daß ...; **she ~ed down the stairs** sie eilte *or* hastete die Treppe hinunter.
[2] *vt* beschleunigen ◆ **the strain of office ~ed his death** die Belastung seines Amtes trug zu seinem vorzeitigen Tod bei; **to ~ sb's departure** jdn zum Aufbruch drängen.

◆**hasten away** *vi* forteilen *or* -hasten, eilig weggehen.

◆**hasten back** *vi* eilig *or* schnell zurückkehren, zurückeilen.

◆**hasten off** *vi* weg- *or* forteilen.

hastily ['heɪstɪlɪ] *adv* **(a)** (*hurriedly*) hastig, eilig. **(b)** (*rashly*) vorschnell.

hastiness ['heɪstɪnɪs] *n* **(a)** (*hurriedness*) Eile *f* ◆ **his ~ in resorting to violence** daß er so schnell gewalttätig wird.
(b) (*rashness*) Voreiligkeit, Unbesonnenheit *f*.
(c) (*dated: hot temper*) Hitzigkeit (*dated*), Heftigkeit *f*.

hasty ['heɪstɪ] *adj* (*+er*) **(a)** (*hurried*) hastig, eilig ◆ **they made a ~ exit** sie eilten hinaus, sie machten, daß sie hinauskamen (*inf*); **don't be so ~** nicht so hastig!; **I only had time for a ~ meal** ich hatte nur Zeit, hastig *or* schnell etwas zu essen.
(b) (*rash*) vorschnell ◆ **he's a bit ~ in his judgements** er urteilt etwas vorschnell.
(c) (*dated: hot-tempered*) hitzig, heftig.

hasty pudding *n* (*US*) Maismehlbrei *m*.

hat [hæt] *n* **(a)** Hut *m*; (*of cook*) Mütze *f* ◆ **to put on one's ~** den *or* seinen Hut aufsetzen; **to take one's ~ off** den Hut abnehmen; (*for greeting also*) den Hut ziehen (*to sb* vor jdm); **~s off!** Hut ab!; **my ~!** (*dated inf*) daß ich nicht lache! (*inf*).
(b) (*fig phrases*) **he's a bad ~** (*dated inf*) er ist ein übler Patron (*dated inf*); **I'll eat my ~ if ...** ich fresse einen Besen, wenn ... (*inf*); **I take my ~ off to him** Hut ab vor ihm!; **to talk through one's ~** (*inf*) dummes Zeug reden; **to keep sth under one's ~** (*inf*) etw für sich behalten; **at the drop of a ~** auf der Stelle, ohne weiteres; **to toss one's ~ in the ring** sich am politischen Reigen beteiligen; (*non-political*) sich einschalten; **that's old ~** (*inf*) das ist ein alter Hut (*inf*); **they're all pretty old ~** (*inf*) das sind doch alles olle Kamellen (*inf*); **to pass round the ~ for sb** für jdn sammeln *or* den Hut rumgehen lassen (*inf*); **with my accountant's ~ on I would say ...** (*inf*) als Buchhalter würde ich sagen ...; **he wears several different ~s** (*inf*) er übt mehrere Funktionen aus.

hat: ~band *n* Hutband *nt*; **~box** *n* Hutschachtel *f*.

hatch[1] [hætʃ] [1] *vt* (*also ~ out*) ausbrüten; (*fig*) *plot, scheme also* aushecken.
[2] *vi* (*also ~ out*) (*bird*) ausschlüpfen ◆ **when will the eggs ~?** wann schlüpfen die Jungen aus?
[3] *n* (*act of ~ing*) Ausbrüten *nt*; (*brood*) Brut *f*.

hatch[2] *n* **(a)** (*Naut*) Luke *f*; (*in floor, ceiling*) Bodenluke *f*; (*half-door*) Halbtür, Niedertür *f*; (*turret ~*) Ausstiegsluke *f* (*in Turm*); *see* **batten down**. **(b)** **(service) ~** Durchreiche *f*. **(c) down the ~!** (*inf*) hoch die Tassen! (*inf*).

hatch[3] *vt* (*Art*) schraffieren.

hatchback ['hætʃbæk] *n* Hecktürmodell *nt*; (*door*) Hecktür *f*.

hatchery ['hætʃərɪ] *n* Brutplatz *m or* -stätte *f.*

hatchet ['hætʃɪt] *n* Beil *nt*; (*tomahawk*) Kriegsbeil *nt* ◆ **to bury the ~** das Kriegsbeil begraben.

hatchet: ~ face *n* scharfgeschnittenes Gesicht; (*inf: person*) Raubvogelgesicht *nt*; **~-faced** *adj* mit scharfen Gesichtszügen; **~ job** *n* (*inf*) **to do a ~ job on sb** jdn fertigmachen (*inf*); **~ man** *n* (*hired killer*) gedungener Mörder; (*fig*) Vollstreckungsbeamte(r) *m.*

hatching ['hætʃɪŋ] *n* (*Art*) Schraffur, Schraffierung *f.*

hatchway ['hætʃweɪ] *n see* **hatch² (a).**

▼ **hate** [heɪt] [1] *vt* hassen; (*detest also*) verabscheuen, nicht ausstehen können (*inf*); (*dislike also*) nicht leiden können ◆ **to ~ the sound of sth** etw nicht hören können; **to ~ to do sth** *or* **doing sth** es hassen, etw zu tun; (*weaker*) etw äußerst ungern tun; **I ~ seeing her in pain** ich kann es nicht ertragen, sie leiden zu sehen; **I ~ the idea of leaving** der Gedanke, wegzumüssen, ist mir äußerst zuwider; **I ~ to bother you** es ist mir sehr unangenehm, daß ich Sie belästigen muß; **I ~ having to say it but ...** es fällt mir sehr schwer, das sagen zu müssen, aber ...; **I ~ being late** ich hasse es, zu spät zu kommen, ich komme äußerst ungern zu spät; **you'll ~ yourself for not thinking of the answer** du wirst dich schwarz ärgern, daß du nicht auf die Antwort gekommen bist (*inf*); **you'll ~ me for this but ...** du wirst es mir vielleicht übelnehmen, aber...; **don't ~ me for telling you the truth** nimm es mir nicht übel *or* sei mir nicht böse, daß ich dir die Wahrheit sage; **I should ~ to keep you waiting** ich möchte Sie auf keinen Fall warten lassen.

[2] *n* **(a)** Haß *m* (*for, of* auf *+acc*) ◆ **~ campaign** Hetzkampagne *f*; **~ mail** beleidigende Briefe *pl.*

(b) (*object of hatred*) **one of his pet ~s is chrome furniture/having to queue up** Stahlmöbel sind/Schlangestehen ist ihm ein Greuel *or* gehören/gehört zu den Dingen, die er am meisten haßt *or* verabscheut; **spiders are my pet ~** ich kann Spinnen auf den Tod nicht ausstehen *or* leiden (*inf*).

hated ['heɪtɪd] *adj* verhaßt.

hateful ['heɪtfʊl] *adj* abscheulich; *remarks also* häßlich; *person* unausstehlich ◆ **sth is ~ to sb** jd findet etw abscheulich/etw ist jdm verhaßt; **it was ~ of you to do that** es war häßlich *or* abscheulich von dir, das zu tun.

hatefully ['heɪtfəlɪ] *adv* abscheulich.

hat: ~less *adj* ohne Hut; **~pin** *n* Hutnadel *f*; **~ rack** *n* Hutablage *f.*

hatred ['heɪtrɪd] *n* Haß *m* (*for* auf *+acc*); (*of spinach, spiders etc*) Abscheu *m* (*of* vor *+dat*).

hatter ['hætəʳ] *n* Hutmacher(in *f*) *m*; (*seller*) Hutverkäufer(in *f*) *m*; *see* **mad.**

hat: ~ stand, ~ tree (*US*) *n* Garderobenständer *m*; (*for hats only*) Hutständer *m*; **~-trick** *n* Hattrick, Hat-Trick *m*; **to get a ~-trick** einen Hattrick erzielen; **with two divorces already behind her this looks like making the ~-trick** nachdem sie nun schon zweimal geschieden ist, denkt sie wohl, aller guten Dinge sind drei.

haughtily ['hɔːtɪlɪ] *adv see adj* hochmütig, hochnäsig (*inf*), überheblich ◆ **she stalked ~ out of the room** stolz erhobenen Hauptes verließ sie das Zimmer.

haughtiness ['hɔːtɪnɪs] *n see adj* Hochmut *m*, Hochnäsigkeit *f* (*inf*); Überheblichkeit *f.*

haughty ['hɔːtɪ] *adj* (*+er*) hochmütig, hochnäsig (*inf*); (*towards people*) überheblich ◆ **with a ~ toss of her head** mit hochmütig zurückgeworfenem Kopf.

haul [hɔːl] [1] *n* **(a)** (*hauling*) **a truck gave us a ~** ein Lastwagen schleppte uns ab *or* (*out of mud etc*) zog uns heraus; **they gave a good strong ~ at the rope** sie zogen mit aller Kraft am Seil.

(b) (*journey*) Strecke *f* ◆ **it's a long ~ to** es ist ein weiter Weg (bis) nach; **short/long/medium ~ aircraft** Kurz-/Lang-/Mittelstreckenflugzeug *nt*; **long-~ truck-driver** Fernfahrer *m*; **the project has been a long ~** das Projekt hat sich lang hingezogen; **the long ~ through the courts** der lange Weg durch die Instanzen.

(c) (*Fishing*) (Fisch)fang *m*; (*fig: booty, from robbery*) Beute *f*; (*inf: of presents*) Ausbeute *f* (*inf*) ◆ **our ~ on the last trawl was 500 kg of herring** bei unserer letzten Fahrt hatten wir eine Ausbeute von 500 kg Hering; **I got quite a ~ for Christmas** bei mir hat es zu Weihnachten ganz hübsch was gegeben (*inf*).

[2] *vt* **(a)** ziehen; *heavy objects also* schleppen; *see* **coal.**

(b) (*transport by lorry*) befördern, transportieren.

(c) (*Naut*) den Kurs (*+gen*) ändern ◆ **to ~ a boat into the wind** an den Wind segeln.

[3] *vi* (*Naut: also* **~ round**) den Kurs ändern ◆ **the yacht ~ed into the wind** die Jacht segelte an den Wind.

◆**haul away** *vi* (*pull*) mit aller Kraft ziehen (*at, on* an *+dat*); (*rowers*) sich in die Riemen legen ◆ **~ ~!** hau ruck!

◆**haul down** *vt sep* **(a)** *flag, sail* ein- *or* niederholen. **(b)** (*with effort*) herunterschleppen; (*pull down*) herunterzerren.

◆**haul in** *vt sep* einholen; *rope* einziehen.

◆**haul off** *vi* (*Naut*) (ab)drehen, den Kurs ändern.

◆**haul round** *vi* (*Naut*) (*ship*) den Kurs ändern; (*wind*) drehen.

◆**haul up** *vt sep* **(a)** (*carry*) hinauf- *or* hochschleppen; (*pull up*) hochzerren, hochziehen; *flag, sail* hissen; (*aboard ship*) (an Bord) hieven, hochziehen; (*onto beach*) schleppen, ziehen ◆ **the dinghies were lying ~ed ~ on the beach for the winter** man hatte die Jollen für den Winter an Land gezogen.

(b) (*fig inf*) **to ~ sb ~ before the magistrate/headmaster/brigadier** jdn vor den Kadi/Schulleiter/Brigadeführer schleppen (*inf*); **he's been ~ed ~ on a drugs charge** er wurde wegen einer Rauschgiftsache vor den Kadi gebracht.

haulage ['hɔːlɪdʒ] *n* **(a)** (*road transport*) Transport *m* ◆ **~ business** (*firm*) Transport- *or* Fuhrunternehmen *nt*, Spedition(sfirma) *f*; (*trade*) Speditionsbranche *f*, Fuhrwesen *nt*; **~ contractor** (*firm*) Transportunternehmen *nt*, Spedition(sfirma) *f*; (*person*) Transport- *or* Fuhrunternehmer, Spediteur *m.*

(b) (*transport charges*) Speditions- *or* Transportkosten *pl.*

haulier ['hɔːlɪəʳ] *n* Spediteur, Fuhrunternehmer *m*; (*company*) Spedition *f* ◆ **firm of ~s** Spedition(sfirma) *f*, Transportunternehmen *nt.*

haulm [hɔːm] *n* (*single*) Stengel *m*; (*collectively*) Stroh *nt*; (*grain, grass also*) Halm *m.*

haunch [hɔːntʃ] *n* (*of person*) Hüfte *f*; (*hip area*) Hüftpartie *f*; (*of animal*) (*hindquarters*) Hinterbacke *f*, (*top of leg*) Keule *f*; (*Cook*) Keule *f*, Lendenstück *nt* ◆ **~es** Gesäß *nt*; (*of animal*) Hinterbacken *pl*; **to go down on one's ~es** in die Hocke gehen; **the dog/he was sitting on his ~es** der Hund saß auf den Hinterbeinen/er saß in der Hocke; **~ of venison** (*Cook*) Rehkeule *f.*

haunt [hɔːnt] [1] *vt* **(a)** (*ghost*) *house, place* spuken in (*+dat*), umgehen in (*+dat*).

(b) *person* verfolgen; (*memory also*) nicht loslassen; (*fear also*) quälen ◆ **the nightmares which ~ed him** die Alpträume, die ihn heimsuchten.

(c) (*frequent*) verkehren in (*+dat*), frequentieren, häufig besuchen; (*animal*) vorkommen, auftreten.

[2] *n* (*of person*) (*pub etc*) Stammlokal *nt*; (*favourite resort*) Lieblingsort *or* -platz *m*; (*of criminals*) Treff(punkt) *m*; (*of animal*) Heimat *f* ◆ **the riverbank is the ~ of a variety of animals** eine Vielzahl von Tieren lebt an Flußufern; **to revisit the ~s of one's youth** die Stätten seiner Jugend wiederaufsuchen; **a ~ of tax dodgers** ein Refugium *nt* für Steuerflüchtlinge; **an evil ~** ein Ort *m* des Lasters (*geh*); **what are his ~s?** wo hält er sich vorwiegend *or* vorzugsweise auf?

haunted ['hɔːntɪd] *adj* **(a)** Spuk- ◆ **a ~ house** ein Spukhaus *nt*, ein Haus *nt*, in dem es spukt; **this place is ~** hier spukt es; **is it ~?** spukt es da?

(b) *look* gehetzt, gequält; *person* ruhelos.

haunting ['hɔːntɪŋ] *adj doubt* quälend, nagend; *tune, visions, poetry* eindringlich; *music* schwermütig ◆ **these ~ final chords** diese Schlußakkorde, die einen nicht loslassen.

hauntingly ['hɔːntɪŋlɪ] *adv* eindringlich.

hauteur [əʊ'tɜːʳ] *n* (*liter*) Hochmütigkeit *f.*

Havana [hə'vænə] *n* **(a)** Havanna *nt.* **(b)** Havanna(zigarre) *f.*

▼ **have** [hæv] *pret, ptp* **had,** *3rd pers sing present* **has** [1] *aux vb* **(a)** haben; (*esp with vbs of motion*) sein ◆ **to ~ been** gewesen sein; **to ~ seen/heard/eaten** gesehen/gehört/gegessen haben; **to ~ gone/run** gegangen/gelaufen sein; **I ~ /had been** ich bin/war gewesen; **I ~ /had seen** ich habe/hatte gesehen; **I ~ not/had not** *or* **I've not/I'd not** *or* **I ~n't/I hadn't seen him** ich habe/hatte ihn nicht gesehen; **had I seen him, if I had seen him** hätte ich ihn gesehen, wenn ich ihn gesehen hätte; **having seen him** (*since*) da *or* weil ich ihn gesehen habe/hatte; (*after*) als ich ihn gesehen hatte; **after having said that he left** nachdem *or* als er das gesagt hatte, ging er; **I ~ lived** *or* **~ been living here for 10 years/since January** ich wohne *or* lebe schon 10 Jahre/seit Januar hier; **you *have* grown** du bist aber gewachsen.

(b) (*in tag questions etc*) **you've seen her, ~n't you?** du hast sie gesehen, oder nicht?; **you ~n't seen her, ~ you?** du hast sie nicht gesehen, oder?; **you ~n't seen her — yes, I ~** du hast sie nicht gesehen — doch *or* wohl (*inf*); **you've made a mistake — no I ~n't** du hast einen Fehler gemacht — nein(, hab' ich nicht *inf*); **you've dropped your book — so I ~** dir ist dein Buch hingefallen — stimmt *or* tatsächlich *or* wahrhaftig; **~ you been there? if you ~/~n't ...** sind Sie schon mal da gewesen? wenn ja/nein *or* nicht, ...; **I ~ seen a ghost — ~ you?** ich habe ein Gespenst gesehen — wahrhaftig *or* tatsächlich?; **I've lost it — you ~n't** (*disbelieving*) ich habe es verloren — nein!

▼ [2] *modal aux* (*+infin: to be obliged*) **I ~ to do it, I ~ got to do it** (*Brit*) ich muß es tun *or* machen; **I don't ~ to do it, I ~n't got to do it** (*Brit*) ich muß es nicht tun, ich brauche es nicht zu tun; **do you ~ to go now?, ~ you got to go now?** (*Brit*) müssen Sie jetzt (wirklich) unbedingt gehen?; **do you ~ to make such a noise?** müssen Sie (unbedingt) so viel Lärm machen?; **you didn't ~ to tell her** das mußten Sie ihr nicht unbedingt sagen, das hätten Sie ihr nicht unbedingt sagen müssen *or* brauchen; **he doesn't ~ to work, he hasn't got to work** (*Brit*) er braucht nicht zu arbeiten, er muß nicht arbeiten; **she was having to get up at 6 each morning** sie mußte jeden Morgen um 6 Uhr aufstehen; **we've had to go and see her twice this week** wir mußten diese Woche schon zweimal zu ihr (hin); **the letter will ~ to be written tomorrow** der Brief muß morgen unbedingt geschrieben werden; **it's got to be** *or* **it has to be the biggest scandal this year** das ist todsicher der (größte) Skandal des Jahres; **I'm afraid it has to be** das muß leider sein.

[3] *vt* **(a)** (*possess*) haben ◆ **she has (got** *esp Brit***) blue eyes** sie hat blaue Augen; **~ you (got** *esp Brit***)** *or* **do you ~ a suitcase?** hast du einen Koffer?; **I ~n't (got** *esp Brit***)** *or* **I don't ~ a pen** ich habe keinen Kugelschreiber; **I must ~ more time** ich brauche mehr Zeit; **~ you (got** *esp Brit***)** *or* **do you have a cigarette?** hast du (mal) eine Zigarette?; **I ~ (got** *esp Brit***) no German** ich kann kein (Wort) Deutsch; **he had her on the sofa** er nahm sie auf dem Sofa; **I ~ it!** ich hab's!; **what time do you ~?** (*US*) wieviel Uhr hast du? (*inf*), wie spät hast du es?; **judge Smith has it ...** Kampfrichter Smith bewertet es mit ...

(b) to ~ breakfast/lunch/dinner frühstücken/zu Mittag essen/zu Abend essen; **to ~ tea with sb** mit jdm (zusammen) Tee trinken; **will you ~ tea or coffee/a drink/a cigarette?** möchten Sie lieber Tee oder Kaffee/möchten Sie etwas zu trinken/eine Zigarette?, hätten Sie lieber Tee oder Kaffee/gern etwas zu trinken/gern eine Zigarette?; **what will you ~? — I'll ~ the steak** was möchten *or* hätten Sie gern(e)? — ich hätte *or* möchte gern das Steak; **he had a cigarette/a drink/a steak** er rauchte eine Zigarette/trank etwas/aß ein Steak; **how do you ~ your eggs?** wie hätten *or* möchten Sie die Eier gern(e)?; **will you ~ some more?** möchten Sie *or* hätten Sie gern(e) (noch etwas) mehr?; **~ another one** nimm noch eine/einen/eines; trink noch einen; rauch noch eine; **he likes to ~ his steak medium** er hat sein Steak gern(e) halb durch(gebraten).

(c) (*receive, obtain, get*) haben ◆ **to ~ news from sb** von jdm hören; **I ~ it from my sister that ...** ich habe von meiner Schwester gehört *or* erfahren, daß ...; **to let sb ~ sth** jdm etw geben; **I must ~ something to eat at once** ich brauche dringend etwas zu essen, ich muß dringend etwas zu essen haben; **there are no newspapers to be had** es sind keine Zeitungen zu haben; **it's nowhere to be had** es ist nirgends zu haben *or* kriegen (*inf*); **it's to be had at the chemist's** es ist in der Apotheke erhältlich, man bekommt es in der Apotheke.

(d) (*maintain, insist*) **he will ~ it that Paul is guilty** er besteht darauf, daß Paul schuldig ist; **he won't ~ it that Paul is guilty** er will nichts davon hören, daß Paul schuldig ist; **as gossip has it** dem Hörensagen nach; **as the Bible/ Shakespeare has it** wie es in der Bibel steht/wie Shakespeare sagt; **as Professor James would ~ it** (*according to*) laut Professor James; (*as he would put it*) um mit Professor James zu sprechen.

(e) (*neg: refuse to allow*) **I won't ~ this nonsense** dieser Unsinn kommt (mir) nicht in Frage!; **I won't ~ this sort of behaviour!** diese Art (von) Benehmen lasse ich mir ganz einfach nicht bieten; **I won't ~ it!** das lasse ich mir nicht bieten!; **I won't ~ him insulted** ich lasse es nicht zu *or* dulde es nicht, daß man ihn beleidigt; **I won't ~ him insult his mother** ich lasse es nicht zu, daß er seine Mutter beleidigt; **we won't ~ women in our club** in unserem Klub sind Frauen nicht zugelassen; **I'm not having any of that!** (*inf*) mit mir nicht! (*inf*); **but she wasn't having any** (*sl*) aber sie wollte nichts davon wissen.

(f) (*hold*) (gepackt) haben ◆ **he had (got) me by the throat/the hair** er hatte *or* hielt mich am Hals/bei den Haaren gepackt; **I ~ (got) him where I want him** ich habe ihn endlich soweit, ich habe ihn endlich (da), wo ich will; **the champion had him now** der Meister hatte ihn jetzt fest im Griff *or* in der Tasche (*inf*); **he ought to ~ the fight by the third round** er sollte den Kampf eigentlich bis zur dritten Rund im Griff *or* unter Kontrolle haben; **I'll ~ you** (*inf*) dich krieg ich (beim Kragen); **you ~ me there** da bin ich überfragt.

(g) to ~ a child ein Kind bekommen; **she is having a baby in April** sie bekommt *or* kriegt (*inf*) im April ein Kind; **she had twins** sie hat Zwillinge bekommen *or* geboren *or* gekriegt (*inf*); **our cat has had kittens** unsere Katze hat Junge bekommen *or* gekriegt (*inf*).

(h) (*wish*) mögen ◆ **which one will you ~?** welche(n, s) möchten Sie haben *or* hätten Sie gern?; **what more would you ~?** was wollen Sie mehr?, was will man mehr?; **as fate would ~ it, ...** wie es das Schicksal so wollte, ...; **what would you ~ me say?** was soll ich dazu sagen?

(i) (*causative*) **to ~ sth done** etw tun lassen; **to ~ one's hair cut/a suit made** sich (*dat*) die Haare schneiden lassen/einen Anzug machen lassen; **I had my luggage brought up** ich habe (mir) das Gepäck nach oben bringen lassen; **~ it mended** geben Sie es in Reparatur, lassen Sie es reparieren; **to ~ sb do sth** jdn etw tun lassen; **they had him shot** sie ließen ihn erschießen; **I'd ~ you understand** ... Sie müssen nämlich wissen ...; **she nearly had the table over** sie hätte den Tisch beinahe umgekippt *or* zum Umkippen gebracht; **I had him in such a state that** ... er war in einer solchen Verfassung, daß ...; **he had the audience in hysterics** das Publikum kugelte sich vor Lachen; **he had the police baffled** die Polizei stand vor einem Rätsel.

(j) (*experience, suffer*) **he had his car stolen** man hat ihm sein Auto gestohlen; **he had his arm broken** er hat/hatte einen gebrochenen Arm; **I've had three windows broken** (bei) mir sind drei Fenster eingeworfen worden; **I had my friends turn against me** ich mußte es erleben, wie *or* daß sich meine Freunde gegen mich wandten.

(k) (*+n = vb identical with n*) **to ~ a walk** einen Spaziergang machen, spazierengehen; **to ~ a dream** träumen.

(l) *party* geben, machen; *meeting* abhalten ◆ **are you having a reception?** gibt es einen Empfang?; **we decided not to ~ a reception** wir haben uns gegen einen Empfang entschieden.

(m) (*phrases*) **let him ~ it!** gib's ihm! (*inf*); **he/that coat has had it** (*inf*) der ist weg vom Fenster (*inf*)/der Mantel ist im Eimer (*inf*); **if I miss the last bus, I've had it** (*inf*) wenn ich den letzten Bus verpasse, bin ich geliefert (*inf*) *or* ist der Ofen aus (*inf*); **~ it your own way** machen Sie es *or* halten Sie es, wie Sie wollen; **I didn't know he had it in him** ich hätte ihn dazu nicht für fähig gehalten; **to ~ a good time/a pleasant evening** Spaß haben, sich amüsieren/einen netten Abend verbringen; **~ a good time!** viel Spaß!; **you've been had!** (*inf*) da hat man dich übers Ohr gehauen (*inf*); **I'll ~ the sofa in this room** das Sofa möchte *or* werde ich in dieses Zimmer stellen; **thanks for having me** vielen Dank für Ihre Gastfreundschaft.

◆**have around** *vt always separate* **(a)** (bei sich) zu Besuch haben; (*invite*) einladen. **(b) he's a useful man to ~ ~** es ist ganz praktisch, ihn zur Hand zu haben.

◆**have at** *vi +prep obj* (*old*) angreifen ◆ **she had ~ me with her umbrella** sie ging mit ihrem Regenschirm auf mich los.

◆**have away** *vt always separate*: **to ~ it ~ with sb** (*sl*) es mit jdm treiben (*inf*).

◆**have back** *vt sep* zurückhaben.

◆**have down** [1] *vt sep people, guests* (bei sich) zu Besuch haben.

[2] *vt always separate* (*take down*) *scaffolding* herunterhaben; (*knock down*) *buildings* abreißen; *vase* herunterwerfen; (*put down*) *carpets* verlegen.

◆**have in** *vt always separate* **(a)** im Haus haben ◆ **we've (got** *esp Brit*) **the decorators ~ all week** wir haben die ganze Woche (über) die Anstreicher im Haus.

(b) to ~ it ~ for sb (*inf*) jdn auf dem Kieker haben (*inf*).

(c) (*make come in*) hereinrufen ◆ **can we ~ the next interviewee ~?** können wir den nächsten Kandidaten haben?

(d) (*put in*) **he had the new engine ~ in a couple of hours** er hatte den neuen Motor in ein paar Stunden drin (*inf*).

◆**have off** *vt always separate* **(a) to ~ it ~ with sb** (*sl*) es mit jdm treiben (*inf*). **(b)** (*take off*) **he had the top ~ in a second** er hatte den Deckel in Sekundenschnelle (he)runter; **he had to ~ his arm ~** sein Arm mußte abgenommen werden.

◆**have on** [1] *vt sep* (*wear*) anhaben; *radio* anhaben.

[2] *vt always separate* **(a)** (*have arranged*) vorhaben; (*be busy with*) zu tun haben ◆ **we've got a big job ~** wir haben ein großes Projekt in Arbeit.

(b) (*inf: deceive, trick*) übers Ohr hauen (*inf*); (*tease*) auf den Arm nehmen (*inf*).

(c) to ~ nothing ~ sb gegen jdn nichts in der Hand haben; **they've got nothing ~ me!** mir kann keiner! (*inf*).

(d) (*put on*) **they had the new tyres ~ in no time** sie hatten die neuen Reifen im Nu drauf (*inf*); **they still haven't got the roof ~** das Dach ist immer noch nicht drauf.

◆**have out** *vt always separate* **(a)** herausgenommen bekommen ◆ **he was having his tonsils ~** er bekam seine Mandeln herausgenommen. **(b)** (*discuss*) ausdiskutieren. **to ~ it ~ with sb** etw mit jdm ausdiskutieren; **I'll ~ it ~ with him** ich werde mit ihm reden, ich werde mich mit ihm aussprechen.

◆**have over** *or* **round** *vt always separate* (bei sich) zu Besuch haben; (*invite*) (zu sich) einladen.

◆**have up** *vt always separate* **(a)** (*inf: cause to appear in court*) drankriegen (*inf*) ◆ **that's the second time he's been had ~ for drunken driving** jetzt haben sie ihn schon zum zweiten Mal wegen Trunkenheit am Steuer drangekriegt (*inf*); **he's been had ~ again** er war schon wieder vor dem Kadi (*inf*).

(b) (*put up*) **when we had the tent/shelves ~** als wir das Zelt aufgestellt/die Regale an der Wand hatten.

haven ['heɪvən] *n* (*fig*) Zufluchtsstätte *f*.

haven't ['hævnt] *contr of* **have not**.

haves [hævz] *npl* (*inf*) **the ~** die Betuchten (*inf*), die Begüterten *pl*; **the ~ and the have-nots** die Betuchten und die Habenichtse.

havoc ['hævək] *n* verheerender Schaden; (*devastation also*) Verwüstung *f*; (*chaos*) Chaos *nt* ◆ **to wreak ~ in** *or* **with sth, to play ~ with sth** bei etw verheerenden Schaden anrichten; (*physical damage also*) etw verwüsten, etw verheerend zurichten; (*with health, part of the body*) für etw üble *or* schlimme Folgen haben, sich übel auf etw (*acc*) auswirken; **the tornado wreaked ~ all along the coast** der Tornado richtete entlang der ganzen Küste große Verwüstungen an; **the sudden rise in oil prices wreaked ~ with India's five-year plan** der plötzliche Anstieg der Ölpreise hat Indiens Fünfjahresplan vollständig über den Haufen geworfen (*inf*); **his sense of guilt played ~ with his imagination** er stellte sich (*dat*) aufgrund seiner Schuldgefühle alles mögliche vor.

haw[1] [hɔː] *n* (*Bot*) Mehlfäßchen *nt*, Mehlbeere *f*.

haw[2] *see* **hum**.

Hawaii [hə'waɪiː] *n* Hawaii *nt*; (*state also*) die Hawaii-Inseln *pl*.

Hawaiian [hə'waɪjən] [1] *adj* hawaiisch, Hawaii- ◆ **~ guitar** Hawaiigitarre *f*.

[2] *n* **(a)** Hawaiianer(in *f*) *m*. **(b)** (*language*) Hawaiisch *nt*.

hawfinch ['hɔːfɪntʃ] *n* (*Orn*) Kernbeißer *m*.

hawk[1] [hɔːk] [1] *n* **(a)** (*Orn*) Habicht *m*; (*sparrow ~*) Sperber *m*; (*falcon*) Falke *m*. **(b)** (*fig: politician*) Falke *m* ◆ **the ~s and the doves** die Falken und die Tauben.

[2] *vi* mit Falken jagen.

hawk[2] *vi* (*with phlegm*) sich räuspern.

hawk[3] *vt* hausieren (gehen) mit; (*in street*) verkaufen, feilhalten, feilbieten; (*by shouting out*) ausschreien.

◆**hawk about** *vi sep gossip etc* verbreiten, herumtratschen (*inf*).

◆**hawk up** *vt sep phlegm* aushusten.

hawker ['hɔːkə[r]] *n* **(a)** (*hunter*) Falkner *m*. **(b)** (*pedlar*) (*door-to-door*) Hausierer(in *f*) *m*; (*in street*) Straßenhändler(in *f*) *m*; (*at market*) Marktschreier(in *f*) *m*.

hawk-eyed ['hɔːkaɪd] *adj* scharfsichtig, adleräugig ◆ **to be ~** Adleraugen haben.

hawking ['hɔːkɪŋ] *n* (Falken)beize, Falkenjagd *f*.

hawkmoth ['hɔːkmɒθ] *n* Schwärmer *m*.

hawser ['hɔːzə[r]] *n* (*Naut*) Trosse *f*.

hawthorn ['hɔːθɔːn] *n* (*also* **~ bush/tree**) Weiß- *or* Rot- *or* Hagedorn *m* ◆ **~ hedge** Weiß- *or* Rotdornhecke *f*.

hay [heɪ] *n* Heu *nt* ◆ **to make ~** Heu machen, heuen; **to hit the ~** (*inf*) sich in die Falle hauen (*sl*); **to make ~ while the sun shines** (*Prov*) das Eisen schmieden, solange es heiß ist (*Prov*).

hay: ~cock *n* Heuhaufen *m*; **~ fever** *n* Heuschnupfen *m*; **~fork** *n* Heugabel *f*; (*motor-driven*) Heuwender *m*; **~loft** *n* Heuboden *m*; **~maker** *n* **(a)** Heumacher(in *f*) *m*; **(b)** (*Boxing inf*) knallharter Schlag, Schwinger *m*; **~making** *n* Heuen *nt*, Heuernte *f*; **~rack** *n* (*for fodder*) (Heu)raufe *f*; (*US: on wagon*) Heuwagenaufbau *m*; **~rick, ~stack** *n* Heuhaufen *m*.

haywire ['heɪwaɪə[r]] *adj pred* (*inf*) **to be (all) ~** (vollständig) durcheinander *or* ein Wirrwarr (*inf*) sein; **her life's all ~ again** ihr Leben ist wieder ein einziges Kuddelmuddel (*inf*) *or* totales Chaos (*inf*); **to go ~** (*go crazy*) durchdrehen (*inf*); (*plans, arrangements*) durcheinandergeraten, über den Haufen geworfen werden (*inf*); (*machinery*) verrückt spielen (*inf*).

hazard ['hæzəd] [1] *n* **(a)** (*danger*) Gefahr *f*; (*risk*) Risiko *nt* ◆ **a typical translating ~** eine typische Gefahr beim Übersetzen; **the ~s of war** die Gefahren

des Krieges; **it's a fire ~** es ist feuergefährlich, es stellt eine Feuergefahr dar.
(b) *(chance)* **by ~** durch Zufall; **game of ~** Glücksspiel *nt*.
(c) *(Sport: Golf, Show-jumping)* Hindernis *nt*.
(d) ~s *pl (Aut: also* **~ (warning) lights***)* Warnblinklicht *nt*.
2 *vt* **(a)** *(risk) life, reputation* riskieren, aufs Spiel setzen.
(b) *(venture to make)* wagen, riskieren ◆ **if I might ~ a remark/suggestion** wenn ich mir eine Bemerkung/einen Vorschlag erlauben darf; **to ~ a guess** (es) wagen, eine Vermutung anzustellen.

hazardous ['hæzədəs] *adj (dangerous)* gefährlich, risikoreich, gefahrvoll; *(risky)* gewagt, riskant; *(exposed to risk)* unsicher ◆ **~ waste** Sondermüll *m*.

haze [heɪz] *n* **(a)** Dunst *m* ◆ **a ~ of exhaust fumes** ein Dunstschleier *m* von Abgasen.
(b) *(fig)* **I/his mind was in a ~** *(daze)* ich/er war wie im Tran; *(confusion of thought)* ich/er war vollkommen verwirrt.

hazel **1** *n (Bot)* Haselnußstrauch, Haselbusch *m*.
2 *adj (colour)* haselnuß- *or* hellbraun.

hazelnut ['heɪzlnʌt] *n* Haselnuß *f*.

hazily ['heɪzɪlɪ] *adv* **(a) the island/hills loomed ~ through the mist** die Insel zeichnete/die Berge zeichneten sich verschwommen im Dunst ab. **(b)** *(vaguely) remember* vage.

haziness ['heɪzɪnɪs] *n* **(a) the ~ of the weather** das dunstige *or* diesige Wetter. **(b)** *(of ideas etc)* Verschwommenheit, Unklarheit *f*.

hazy ['heɪzɪ] *adj (+er)* **(a)** dunstig, diesig; *mountains* im Dunst (liegend). **(b)** *(unclear)* unklar, verschwommen ◆ **I'm ~ about what happened** ich kann mich nur vage *or* verschwommen daran erinnern, was geschah; **he's still a bit ~** *(after anaesthetic etc)* er ist immer noch ein wenig benommen.

HB *abbr, adj (on pencil)* HB.

H-bomb ['eɪtʃbɒm] *n* H-Bombe *f*.

HE *abbr of* **His Excellency** S.E.; **His Eminence** S.E.

he [hi:] **1** *pers pron* **(a)** er ◆ **it is ~** *(form)* er ist es, es ist er; **if I were ~** *(form)* wenn ich er wäre; **~ didn't do it, I did it** nicht er hat das getan, sondern ich; **so ~'s the one** der *(inf) or* er ist es also!; **Harry Rigg? who's ~?** Harry Rigg? wer ist das denn?
(b) ~ who *(liter) or* **that** *(liter)* ... derjenige, der ...; *(in proverbs)* wer ...
2 *n (of animal)* Männchen *nt* ◆ **it's a ~** *(inf: of newborn baby)* es ist ein Er.
3 *pref* männlich; *(of animals also)* -männchen *nt*.

head [hed] **1** *n* **(a)** *(Anat)* Kopf *m*, Haupt *nt (geh)* ◆ **from ~ to foot** von Kopf bis Fuß; **~ downwards** mit dem Kopf nach unten; **to stand on one's ~** auf dem Kopf stehen, einen Kopfstand machen; **to stand sth on its ~** etw auf den Kopf stellen; **you could do it standing on your ~** *(inf)* das kann man ja im Schlaf machen; **to stand** *or* **be ~ and shoulders above sb** *(lit)* jdn um Haupteslänge überragen; *(fig)* jdm haushoch überlegen sein; **he can hold his ~ (up) high in any company** er kann sich in jeder Gesellschaft sehen lassen; **the condemned man held his ~ high as he went to the scaffold** der Verurteilte ging erhobenen Hauptes zum Schafott; **to turn** *or* **go ~ over heels** einen Purzelbaum machen *or* schlagen; **to fall ~ over heels in love with sb** sich bis über beide Ohren in jdn verlieben; **to fall ~ over heels down the stairs** kopfüber die Treppe herunterfallen; **to fall ~ over heels over sth** über etw *(acc)* stolpern und fallen; **to keep one's ~ above water** *(lit)* den Kopf über Wasser halten; *(fig)* sich über Wasser halten; **to talk one's ~ off** *(inf)* reden wie ein Wasserfall *(inf) or* wie ein Buch *(inf)*; **to laugh one's ~ off** *(inf)* sich fast totlachen; **to shout one's ~ off** *(inf)* sich *(dat)* die Lunge aus dem Leib schreien *(inf)*; **to scream one's ~ off** *(inf)* aus vollem Halse schreien; **I've got some ~ this morning** *(inf)* ich habe einen ziemlichen Brummschädel heute morgen *(inf)*; **to give a horse its ~** einem Pferd die Zügel schießen lassen; **to give sb his ~** jdn machen lassen; **on your (own) ~ be it** auf Ihre eigene Verantwortung *or* Kappe *(inf)*; **you need a good ~ for heights** Sie müssen schwindelfrei sein; **she has no ~ for heights** sie ist nicht schwindelfrei; **he gave orders over my ~** er hat über meinen Kopf (hin)weg Anordnungen gegeben; **to go over sb's ~** etw über jds Kopf *(acc)* (hin)weg tun; **to be promoted over sb's ~** vor jdm bevorzugt befördert werden; **to go to one's ~** *(whisky, power)* einem in den *or* zu Kopf steigen; **I can't make ~ nor tail of it** daraus werde ich nicht schlau.
(b) *(measure of length)* Kopf *m*; *(Racing also)* Kopflänge *f* ◆ **taller by a ~** (um) einen Kopf größer; **by a short ~** *(Horseracing, fig)* um Nasenlänge.
(c) *(mind, intellect)* Kopf, Verstand *m* ◆ **use your ~** streng deinen Kopf an; **to get sth into one's ~** etw begreifen; **he won't get it into his ~ that** ... es will ihm nicht in den Kopf, daß ...; **get this into your ~** schreib dir das hinter die Ohren; **I can't get it into his ~** ich kann ihm das nicht begreiflich machen; **to take it into one's ~ to do sth** sich *(dat)* in den Kopf setzen, etw zu tun; **it never entered his ~ that** ... es kam ihm nie in den Sinn, daß ...; **what put that idea into his ~?** wie kommt er denn darauf?; *(unrealistic wish also)* wer hat ihm denn den Floh ins Ohr gesetzt? *(inf)*; **to put** *or* **get sth out of one's ~** sich *(dat)* etw aus dem Kopf schlagen; **don't put ideas into his ~** bring ihn bloß nicht auf dumme Gedanken!; *(unrealistic wish etc)* setz ihm bloß keinen Floh ins Ohr!; **he has a good ~ for mathematics** er ist mathematisch begabt; **he has a good business ~** er hat einen ausgeprägten Geschäftssinn; **he has a good ~ on his shoulders** er ist ein heller *or* kluger Kopf; **he has an old ~ on young shoulders** er ist sehr reif für sein Alter; **two ~s are better than one** *(prov)* besser zwei als einer allein; *(in spotting things)* vier Augen sehen mehr als zwei; **we put our ~s together** wir haben unsere Köpfe zusammengesteckt; **to be above** *or* **over sb's ~** über jds Horizont *(acc)* gehen; **he talked above** *or* **over their ~s** er hat über ihre Köpfe weg geredet; **to keep one's ~** den Kopf nicht verlieren; **to lose one's ~** den Kopf verlieren; **he is off his ~** *(inf)* er ist (ja) nicht (ganz) bei Trost *(inf)*, er hat ja den Verstand verloren; **to be weak** *or* **soft in the ~** *(inf)* einen (kleinen) Dachschaden haben *(inf)*.
(d) twenty ~ of cattle zwanzig Stück Vieh; **to pay 10 marks a** *or* **per ~** 10 Mark pro Kopf bezahlen.
(e) *(of flower, lettuce, cabbage, asparagus, hammer, nail, page, pier)* Kopf *m*; *(of celery)* Staude *f*; *(of arrow, spear)* Spitze *f*; *(of bed)* Kopf(ende *nt*) *m*; *(on beer)* Blume *f*; *(of cane)* Knauf, Griff *m*; *(of corn)* Ähre *f*; *(Archit: of column)* Kapitell *nt*; *(of stream) (upper area)* Oberlauf *m*; *(source)* Ursprung *m*; *(Med: of abscess etc)* Eiterpfropf *m* ◆ **~ of steam/water** *(pressure)* Dampf-/Wasserdruck *m*; **at the ~ of the lake** am Zufluß des Sees; **at the ~ of the page/stairs** oben auf der Seite/an der Treppe; **at the ~ of the list** oben auf der Liste; **at the ~ of the table** oben am Tisch, am Kopf(ende) des Tisches; **at the ~ of the queue/army** an der Spitze der Schlange/des Heeres.
(f) *(fig: crisis)* Krise *f*, Höhepunkt *m* ◆ **the illness has come to a ~** die Krise (der Krankheit) ist eingetreten; **to bring matters to a ~** die Sache auf die Spitze treiben; *(to decision)* die Entscheidung herbeiführen; **if things come to a ~** wenn sich die Sache zuspitzt.
(g) *(of family)* Oberhaupt *nt*; *(of business, organization)* Chef, Boss *(inf) m*; *(of department also)* Leiter *m*; *(of office, sub-department also)* Vorsteher *m*; *(Sch inf)* Schulleiter *m*; *(of secondary school also)* Direx *m (sl)*; *(of primary school also)* Rex *m (sl)* ◆ **~ of department** *(in business)* Abteilungsleiter *m*; *(Sch, Univ)* Fachbereichsleiter(in *f*) *m*; **~ of state** Staatsoberhaupt *nt*.
(h) *(~ing, division in essay etc)* Rubrik *f* ◆ **listed under several main ~s** in verschiedenen Rubriken eingetragen; **they should be treated/examined under separate ~s** sie müssen in verschiedenen Abschnitten behandelt werden/unter verschiedenen Aspekten untersucht werden.
(i) *(of coin)* Kopfseite *f* ◆ **~s or tails?** Kopf oder Zahl?; **~s I win** bei Kopf gewinne ich.
(j) *(Naut) (bow)* Bug *m*; *(of mast)* Topp *m*; *(toilet)* Pütz *f*.
(k) *(on tape-recorder)* Tonkopf *m*; *(Comput: read/write ~)* Kopf *m*.
(l) *(sl)* Junkie *m (sl)*.
2 *vt* **(a)** *(lead)* anführen; *(be in charge of also)* führen; *list, poll also* an oberster Stelle *or* an der Spitze stehen von.
(b) *(direct)* steuern, lenken *(towards, for* in Richtung).
(c) *(give a ~ing)* überschreiben, eine/die Überschrift geben *(+dat)* ◆ **in the chapter ~ed** ... in dem Kapitel mit der Überschrift ...; **he ~s each chapter with a quotation** er stellt jedem Kapitel ein Zitat voran; **~ed writing paper** Schreibpapier *nt* mit Briefkopf.
(d) *(Ftbl)* köpfen.
3 *vi* gehen; fahren ◆ **where are you ~ing** *or* **~ed** *(inf)*? wo gehen/fahren Sie hin?; **are you ~ing my way?** gehen/fahren Sie in der gleichen Richtung wie ich?; **and the meteorite was ~ing my way** und der Meteorit kam auf mich zu.

◆**head back** *vi* zurückgehen/-fahren ◆ **to be ~ing ~** auf dem Rückweg sein; **it's time we started ~ing ~ now** es ist Zeit, umzukehren *or* sich auf den Rückweg zu machen.

◆**head for** *vi +prep obj* **(a)** *place, person* zugehen/zufahren auf *(+acc)*; *town, country, direction* gehen/fahren in Richtung *(+gen)*; *(with continuous tense also)* auf dem Weg sein zu/nach; *pub, bargain counter, prettiest girl also* zusteuern auf *(+acc) (inf)*; *(ship also)* Kurs halten auf *(+acc)* ◆ **where are you ~ing** *or* **~ed ~?** wo gehen/fahren *or* steuern *(inf)* Sie hin?
(b) *(fig)* zusteuern auf *(+acc)*, auf dem Weg sein zu ◆ **you're ~ing ~ trouble** du bist auf dem besten Weg, Ärger zu bekommen; **he is ~ing ~ a fall** er rennt in sein Verderben.

◆**head in** **1** *vt sep ball* hineinköpfen ◆ **to ~ the ball ~to the net** den Ball ins Netz köpfen.
2 *vi* köpfen.

◆**head off** *vt sep* **(a)** abfangen. **(b)** *(avert) quarrel, war, strike* abwenden; *person asking questions* ablenken; *questions* abbiegen.

◆**head up** *vt sep committee, delegation* führen, leiten.

head *in cpds (top, senior)* Ober-; **~ache** *n* Kopfweh *nt*, Kopfschmerzen *pl*; *(inf: problem)* Problem *nt*; **this is a bit of a ~ache** das macht mir/uns ziemliches Kopfzerbrechen; **~band** *n* Stirnband *nt*; **~-banger** *n (sl: crazy person)* Bekloppte(r) *mf (sl)*; **~board** *n* Kopfteil *nt*; **~ boy** *n vom Schulleiter bestimmter Schulsprecher*; **~butt** **1** *n* Kopfstoß *m*; **2** *vt* mit dem Kopf stoßen; **~case** *n (Brit inf)* Spinner(in) *m(f)*; **~cheese** *n (US)* Schweinskopfsülze *f*; **~ clerk** *n (Comm)* Bürovorsteher(in *f*) *m*; *(Jur)* Kanzleivorsteher(in *f*) *m*; **~ cold** *n* Kopfgrippe *f*; **~-count** *n* **to have a ~-count** abzählen; **~crash** *n (Comput)* Headcrash *m*, Aufsitzen *nt or* Kratzen *nt* des Kopfes; **~dress** *n* Kopfschmuck *m*.

-headed [-hedɪd] *adj suf* -köpfig ◆ **a curly-~ child** ein lockiges Kind, ein Kind mit lockigen Haaren.

header ['hedəʳ] *n* **(a)** *(dive)* Kopfsprung, Köpfer *(inf) m* ◆ **to take a ~ into the water** einen Kopfsprung ins Wasser machen; *(fall)* kopfüber ins Wasser fallen. **(b)** *(Ftbl)* Kopfstoß, Kopfball *m* ◆ **he's a good ~ of the ball** er köpft gut. **(c)** *(Typ)* Kopfzeile *f*.

head: ~first *adv (lit, fig)* kopfüber; **~gate** *n* (oberes) Schleusentor; **~gear** *n* Kopfbedeckung *f*; *(of horse: bridle)* Zaumzeug *nt*; **~ girl** *n vom Schulleiter bestimmte Schulsprecherin*; **~guard** *n* Kopfschutz *m*; **~hunt** **1** *vt* abwerben; **I've been ~hunted** ich bin abgeworben worden; *(have been approached)* man hat versucht, mich abzuwerben; **2** *vi* **we'll have to go out and ~hunt** wir werden Mitarbeiter von anderen Firmen abwerben müssen; **~-hunter** *n (lit, fig)* Kopfjäger *m*.

headiness ['hedɪnɪs] *n* **this wine is known for its ~** dieser Wein ist dafür bekannt, daß er einem schnell zu Kopf(e) steigt; **the ~ of this intellectual**

atmosphere diese geistesgeladene Atmosphäre.

heading ['hedıŋ] *n* **(a)** Überschrift *f*; (*on letter, document*) Kopf *m*; (*in encyclopedia*) Stichwort *nt* ◆ **under the ~ of anthropology** unter dem Stichwort Anthropologie. **(b)** (*Ftbl*) Köpfen *nt*.

head: ~lamp, ~light *n* Scheinwerfer *m*; **~land** *n* Landspitze *f*; **~less** *adj* ohne Kopf; (*fig, old*) kopflos; **~line** *n* (*Press*) Schlagzeile *f*; **he is always in the ~lines** er macht immer Schlagzeilen; **to hit** *or* **make the ~lines** Schlagzeilen machen; **the news ~lines** Kurznachrichten *pl*, das Wichtigste in Kürze; **~line rate** *n* (*Econ*) **~line rate of inflation** Inflationsrate *f* (*unter Einbeziehung von Variablen wie Hypothekenzinssätzen etc*); **~long** *adj, adv fall* mit dem Kopf voran; *rush* überstürzt, Hals über Kopf; **~man** *n* (*of tribe*) Häuptling *m*, Stammesoberhaupt *nt*; **~master** *n* Schulleiter *m*; (*of secondary school also*) Direktor *m*; (*of primary school also*) Rektor *m*; **~mistress** *n* Schulleiterin *f*; (*of secondary school also*) Direktorin *f*; (*of primary school also*) Rektorin *f*; **~ office** *n* Zentrale *f*; **~-on** [1] *adj collision* frontal; *confrontation* direkt; [2] *adv collide* frontal; **to tackle a problem ~-on** ein Problem geradewegs angehen; **~phones** *npl* Kopfhörer *pl*; **~ post office** *n* Hauptpostamt *nt*; **~quarters** *n sing or pl* (*Mil*) Hauptquartier *nt*; (*of business*) Hauptstelle, Zentrale *f*; (*of political party*) Parteizentrale *f*, Hauptquartier *nt*; **police ~quarters** Polizeipräsidium *nt*; **~race** *n* Gerinne *nt*; **~rest** *n* Kopfstütze *f*; **~ restraint** *n* Kopfstütze *f*; **~room** *n* lichte Höhe; (*in car*) Kopfraum *m*; **15 ft ~room** (lichte) Höhe 15 Fuß; **~scarf** *n* Kopftuch *nt*; **~set** *n* Kopfhörer *pl*; **~ship** *n* Schulleiterstelle, Direktoren-/Rektorenstelle *f*; **under his ~ship** unter ihm als Schulleiter; **~shrinker** *n* (*lit*) Schrumpfkopfindianer *m*; (*sl: psychiatrist*) Seelenmasseur *m* (*inf*); **~square** *n* Kopftuch *nt*; **~ start** *n* Vorsprung *m* (*on sb* jdm gegenüber); **~stone** *n* (*on grave*) Grabstein *m*; **~strong** *adj* eigensinnig, dickköpfig; **~ teacher** *n* (*Brit*) *see* **~master, ~mistress**; **~ waiter** *n* Oberkellner *m*; **~ waitress** *n* Oberkellnerin *f*; **~waters** *npl* Quellflüsse *pl*; **~way** *n* **to make ~way** (*lit, fig*) vorankommen; **did you make any ~way with the unions?** haben Sie bei den Gewerkschaften etwas erreicht?; **~wind** *n* Gegenwind *m*; **~word** *n* Anfangswort *nt*; (*in dictionary*) Stichwort *nt*.

heady ['hedı] *adj* (+*er*) *scent, wine,* (*fig*) *atmosphere* berauschend; *person* impulsiv, unbedacht (*pej*); *atmosphere* geistesgeladen ◆ **in those ~ days** in jenen Tagen der Begeisterung.

heal [hi:l] [1] *vi* (*Med, fig*) heilen.
[2] *vt* **(a)** (*Med*) heilen; *person also* gesund machen ◆ **time ~s all wounds** (*Prov*) die Zeit heilt alle Wunden (*Prov*). **(b)** (*fig*) *differences etc* beilegen; (*third party*) schlichten.

◆**heal over** *vi* zuheilen.

◆**heal up** [1] *vi* zuheilen.
[2] *vt sep* zuheilen lassen.

healer ['hi:ləʳ] *n* Heiler(in *f*) *m* (*geh*); (*herb etc*) Heilmittel *nt*.

healing ['hi:lıŋ] [1] *n* Heilung *f*; (*of wound*) (Zu)heilen *nt*.
[2] *adj* (*Med*) Heil-, heilend, heilsam (*old*); (*fig*) besänftigend.

health [helθ] *n* **(a)** Gesundheit *f*; (*state of ~*) Gesundheitszustand *m* ◆ **in good/poor ~** gesund/nicht gesund, bei guter/schlechter Gesundheit; **state of ~** Gesundheitszustand *m*, Befinden *nt*; **how is his ~?** wie geht es ihm gesundheitlich?; **to regain one's ~** wieder gesund werden; **to enjoy good ~/to have poor** *or* **bad ~** sich guter Gesundheit (*gen*) erfreuen/kränklich sein; **to be good/bad for one's ~** gesund/ungesund *or* gesundheitsschädlich sein, der Gesundheit (*dat*) zuträglich/nicht zuträglich sein; **~ and safety regulations** Arbeitsschutzvorschriften *pl*; **Ministry of H~** Gesundheitsministerium *nt*; **I'm not just doing it for the good of my ~** (*inf*) ich mache das doch nicht bloß aus Spaß (*inf*).
(b) (*fig*) Gesundheit *f*.
(c) to drink (to) sb's ~ auf jds Wohl (*acc*) *or* Gesundheit (*acc*) trinken; **your ~!, good ~!** zum Wohl!, auf Ihre Gesundheit!

health: ~ authority *n* Gesundheitsbehörde *f*; **~ care** *n* Gesundheitsfürsorge *f*; **~ centre** *n* **(a)** (*Med*) Ärztezentrum *nt*; **(b)** (*keep-fit*) Fitness-Center *nt*; **~ certificate** *n* Gesundheitszeugnis *nt*; **~ club** *n* Keep-fit-Verein *m*; (*place also*) Fitness-Center *nt*; **~ education** *n* Hygiene *f*; **~ farm** *n* Gesundheitsfarm *f*; **~ food** *n* Reformkost *f*; **~ food shop** (*Brit*) *or* **store** (*esp US*) *n* Reformhaus *nt*, Bioladen, Naturkostladen *m*.

healthful ['helθfʊl], **healthgiving** ['helθ,gıvıŋ] *adj* gesund.

health hazard *n* Gefahr *f* für die Gesundheit.

healthily ['helθılı] *adv* gesund ◆ **we felt ~ tired** wir fühlten eine gesunde Müdigkeit.

healthiness ['helθınıs] *n* Gesundheit *f*.

health: ~ inspector *n* Sozialarbeiter(in *f*) *m* (*in der Gesundheitsfürsorge*); **~ insurance** *n* Krankenversicherung *f*; **~ problem** *n* Gesundheitsgefährdung *f*; **he retired because of a ~ problem** er trat aus gesundheitlichen Gründen in den Ruhestand; **~ resort** *n* Kurort *m*; (*spa also*) Kurbad, Heilbad *nt*; **H~ Service** *n* (*Brit*) **the H~ Service** das Gesundheitswesen; **H~ Service doctor** Kassenarzt *m*/-ärztin *f*; **~ studio** *n* Fitness-Studio *nt*; **~ visitor** *n* Sozialarbeiter(in *f*) *m* (*in der Gesundheitsfürsorge*).

healthy ['helθı] *adj* (+*er*) (*lit, fig*) gesund ◆ **it's not ~ to mix with that sort of person** es ist nicht ratsam *or* es kann einem schlecht bekommen, mit so jemandem zu verkehren; **it's not a ~ relationship** es ist eine ungesunde Beziehung.

heap [hi:p] [1] *n* **(a)** Haufen *m*; (*inf: old car*) Klapperkiste *f* (*inf*) ◆ **(to be piled) in a ~** auf einem Haufen (liegen); **the building was reduced to a ~ of rubble** das Haus sank in Schutt und Asche; **I was struck all of a ~** (*inf*) ich war wie vom Donner gerührt (*inf*); **he fell in a ~ on the floor** er sackte zu Boden.
(b) ~s of (*inf*) ein(en) Haufen (*inf*); **it happens ~s of times** (*inf*) das kommt andauernd vor; **do you have any glasses? — yes, ~s** haben Sie Gläser? — (ja,) jede Menge (*inf*).
[2] *adv* **~s** (*inf*) (unheimlich) viel.
[3] *vt* häufen ◆ **he ~ed his clothes together** er warf seine Kleider auf einen Haufen; **to ~ praises on sb/sth** über jdn/etw voll des Lobes sein (*geh*), jdn/etw über den grünen Klee loben (*inf*); (*in addressing*) jdn mit Lob überschütten; **to ~ insults on sb** sich über jdn sehr beleidigend äußern; (*in addressing*) jdm Beleidigungen an den Kopf werfen; (*cursing*) jdn mit einer Flut von Schimpfwörtern überschütten; **~ed spoonful** gehäufter Löffel.

◆**heap up** [1] *vt sep* aufhäufen ◆ **he ~ed ~ the litter into piles/a pile** er machte aus dem Abfall Haufen/einen Haufen.
[2] *vi* sich häufen.

▼ **hear** [hıəʳ] *pret, ptp* **heard** [1] *vt* **(a)** (*also learn*) hören ◆ **I ~d him say that ...** ich habe ihn sagen hören, daß ...; **I ~d somebody come in** ich habe jemanden (herein)kommen hören; **no sound was ~d** es war kein Laut zu hören, man hörte keinen Laut; **he was ~d to say that ...** man hat ihn sagen hören, daß ...; **to make oneself ~d** sich (*dat*) Gehör verschaffen; **you're not going, do you ~ me!** du gehst nicht, hörst du (mich)!; **now ~ this!** Achtung, Achtung!; **to ~ him speak you'd think ...** wenn man ihn so reden hört, könnte man meinen, ...; **I've often ~d say** *or* **it said that ...** ich habe oft gehört *or* sagen hören, daß ...; **you play chess, I ~** ich höre, Sie spielen Schach; **have you ~d the one about ...?** (haben Sie) den schon gehört von ...?; **I ~ tell you're going away** ich höre, Sie gehen weg; **I've ~d tell of monsters in the lake** ich habe von Ungeheuern in dem See gehört; **I've been ~ing things about you** von dir hört man ja schöne Dinge; **I must be ~ing things** ich glaube, ich höre nicht richtig.
(b) (*listen to*) *lecture, programme etc* hören ◆ **to ~ a case** (*Jur*) einen Fall verhandeln; **Lord, ~ our prayer/us** Herr, (er)höre unser Gebet/wir bitten dich, erhöre uns; **let's ~ your prayers before you go to sleep** wir wollen beten, bevor du schläfst.
▼ [2] *vi* **(a)** hören ◆ **he does not** *or* **cannot ~ very well** er hört nicht sehr gut ◆ **~, ~!** (sehr) richtig!; (*Parl*) hört!, hört!
▼ **(b)** (*get news*) hören ◆ **he's left his wife — yes, so I ~** er hat seine Frau verlassen — ja, ich habe es gehört; **I ~ from my daughter every week** ich höre jede Woche von meiner Tochter; **you'll be ~ing from me!** (*threatening*) Sie werden noch von mir hören!; **to ~ about sth** von etw hören *or* erfahren; **have you ~d about John? he's getting married** haben Sie gehört? John heiratet; **never ~d of him/it** nie (von ihm/davon) gehört; **I've ~d of him** ich habe schon von ihm gehört; **he wasn't ~d of for a long time** man hat lange Zeit nichts von ihm gehört; **he was never ~d of again** man hat nie wieder etwas von ihm gehört; **I've never ~d of such a thing!** das ist ja unerhört!; **I ~ of nothing else but that!** ich höre überhaupt nichts anderes mehr!

◆**hear of** *vi* +*prep obj* (*fig: allow*) hören wollen von ◆ **I won't ~ ~ it** ich will davon (gar) nichts hören.

◆**hear out** *vt sep person* ausreden lassen; *story* zu Ende hören.

heard [hɜ:d] *pret, ptp of* **hear**.

hearer ['hıərəʳ] *n* Hörer(in *f*) *m*.

hearing ['hıərıŋ] *n* **(a)** Gehör *nt* ◆ **to have a keen sense of ~** ein gutes Gehör haben.
(b) within/out of ~ (distance) in/außer Hörweite; **he said that in/out of my ~** ich war in Hörweite/nicht in Hörweite, als er das sagte.
(c) (*Pol*) Hearing *nt*, Anhörung *f*; (*Jur*) Verhandlung *f* ◆ **preliminary ~** Voruntersuchung *f*; **~ of witnesses** (*Jur*) Zeugenvernehmung *f*; **he was refused a ~** er wurde nicht angehört; **he didn't get a fair ~** man hörte ihn nicht richtig an; (*Jur*) er bekam keinen fairen Prozeß; **the Minister gave the petitioners a ~** der Minister hörte die Überbringer der Petition an; **to condemn sb without a ~** jdn verurteilen, ohne ihn (an)gehört zu haben; (*Jur*) jdn ohne Anhörung verurteilen.

hearing aid *n* Hörgerät *nt*, Hörhilfe *f*.

hearken ['hɑ:kn] *vi* (*old, liter*) horchen (*to* auf +*acc*).

hearsay ['hıəseı] *n* Gerüchte *pl* ◆ **to have sth from** *or* **by** *or* **on ~** etw vom Hörensagen wissen *or* haben.

hearsay: ~ account *n* Bericht *m* aus zweiter Hand; **~ evidence** *n* Zeugenaussage, die auf Hörensagen beruht.

hearse [hɜ:s] *n* Leichenwagen *m*.

heart [hɑ:t] *n* **(a)** (*Anat*) Herz *nt*.
(b) (*fig: for emotion, courage etc*) Herz *nt* ◆ **to break sb's ~** jdm das Herz brechen; **to break one's ~ over sth** sich über etw (*acc*) zu Tode grämen; **she thought her ~ would break** sie meinte, ihr würde das Herz brechen; **you're breaking my ~** (*iro*) ich fang' gleich an zu weinen (*iro*); **after my own ~** ganz nach meinem Herzen; **to have a change of ~** sich anders besinnen, seine Meinung ändern; **to learn/know/recite sth by ~** etw auswendig lernen/kennen/aufsagen; **to know sth by ~** (*through acquaintance*) etw (in- und) auswendig wissen; **in my ~ of ~s** im Grunde meines Herzens; **with all my ~** von ganzem Herzen; **from the bottom of one's ~** aus tiefstem Herzen; **~ and soul** mit Leib und Seele; **to put ~ and soul into sth** sich mit Leib und Seele einer Sache (*dat*) hingeben; **to take sth to ~** sich (*dat*) etw zu Herzen nehmen; **we have your interests at ~** Ihre Interessen liegen uns am Herzen; **to set one's ~ on sth** sein Herz an etw (*acc*) hängen (*geh*); **it did my ~ good** es wurde mir warm ums Herz; **to set sb's ~ at rest** jds Gemüt *or* jdn beruhigen; **to one's ~'s content** nach Herzenslust; **most men are boys at ~** die meisten Männer sind im Grunde (ihres Herzens) noch richtige Kinder; **I couldn't find it in my ~ to say no** ich konnte es nicht übers Herz bringen, nein zu sagen; **his ~ isn't in his work/in it** er ist nicht mit dem Herzen bei der Sache/dabei; **he's putting/not putting his ~ into his work** er geht in seiner Arbeit völlig auf/er

➤ LANGUAGE IN USE: **hear: 1a** → 12.2, 26.1 **2a** → 11.1 **2b** → 21.1, 24.3

ist nur mit halbem Herzen bei seiner Arbeit; **to lose ~** den Mut verlieren; **to lose one's ~ (to sb/sth)** sein Herz (an jdn/etw) verlieren; **to take ~** Mut fassen; **he took ~ from his brother's example** das Beispiel seines Bruders machte ihm Mut; **they've taken him to their ~s** sie haben ihn ins Herz geschlossen; **to put new ~ into sb/sth** jdn mit neuem Mut erfüllen/etw mit neuem Leben füllen; **to be in good ~** (*liter*) guten Mutes sein (*geh*); **be of good ~** (*liter*) sei guten Mutes (*geh*); **to have one's ~ in the right place** (*inf*) das Herz auf dem rechten Fleck haben (*inf*); **to have a ~ of stone** ein Herz aus Stein haben; **to wear one's ~ on one's sleeve** (*prov*) das Herz auf der Zunge tragen (*prov*); **my ~ was in my mouth** (*inf*) mir schlug das Herz bis zum Hals; **his ~ was in his boots** (*inf*) ihm ist das Herz in die Hose(n) gerutscht (*inf*); **have a ~!** (*inf*) gib deinem Herzen einen Stoß! (*inf*); **not to have the ~ to do sth** es nicht übers Herz bringen, etw zu tun; **she has a ~ of gold** sie hat ein goldenes Herz; **my ~ sank** (*with apprehension*) mir wurde bang ums Herz (*liter*), mir rutschte das Herz in die Hose(n) (*inf*); (*with sadness*) das Herz wurde mir schwer; (*I was discouraged*) mein Mut sank.

(c) (*centre: of town, country, cabbage etc*) Herz *nt* ◆ **in the ~ of winter/the forest** im tiefsten *or* mitten im Winter/Wald; **the ~ of the matter** der Kern der Sache; **the ~ of the tree** das Mark des Baumes; **artichoke ~** Artischockenboden *m*.

(d) yes, my ~ (*liter*) ja, mein Herz (*liter*); **dear ~** (*old, liter*) liebes Herz (*liter*).

(e) (*Cards*) **~s** *pl* Herz *nt*; (*Bridge*) Coeur *nt* ◆ **queen of ~s** Herz-/Coeurdame *f*.

heart: ~ache *n* Kummer *m*, Herzeleid (*old liter*), Herzweh (*geh*) *nt*; **~ attack** *n* Herzanfall *m*; (*thrombosis*) Herzinfarkt *m*; **I nearly had a ~ attack** (*fig inf*) (*shock*) ich habe fast einen Herzschlag gekriegt (*inf*); (*surprise also*) da hat mich doch fast der Schlag getroffen (*inf*); **~beat** *n* Herzschlag *m*; **~break** *n* großer Kummer, Leid *nt*; **I've had my share of ~breaks** ich habe meinen Teil an Kummer gehabt; **it was a ~break for him** es brach ihm (beinahe) das Herz; **~breaking** *adj* herzzerreißend; **it was ~breaking to see him with crutches** es brach einem das Herz, ihn an Krücken zu sehen; **it's a ~breaking job** es bricht einem das Herz; **~broken** *adj* untröstlich, todunglücklich; **she was ~broken about it** sie war darüber todunglücklich; (*because of love, death etc also*) es hat ihr das Herz gebrochen; **don't look so ~broken** schau (doch) nicht so unglücklich drein; **~burn** *n* Sodbrennen *nt*; **~-case** *n* Herzpatient(in *f*) *m*; **~ complaint** *n* Herzbeschwerden *pl*; **~ condition** *n* Herzleiden *nt*; **he has a ~ condition** er ist herzleidend, er hat's am Herzen (*inf*); **~ disease** *n* Herzkrankheit *f*.

-hearted [-hɑːtɪd] *adj suf* -herzig.

hearten [ˈhɑːtn] *vt* ermutigen.

heartening [ˈhɑːtnɪŋ] *adj news* ermutigend.

heart: ~ failure *n* Herzversagen *nt*; **~felt** *adj* von Herzen *or* tief empfunden; *sympathy* herzlichst.

hearth [hɑːθ] *n* Feuerstelle *f*; (*whole fireplace*) Kamin *m*; (*fig: home*) (häuslicher) Herd ◆ **the kettle was keeping hot on the ~** der Kessel wurde auf dem Herd warm gehalten; **~ and home** Haus und Herd.

hearth: ~ brush *n* Kaminbesen *m*; **~rug** *n* Kaminvorleger *m*.

heartily [ˈhɑːtɪlɪ] *adv* **(a)** *laugh, welcome* herzlich; *sing* kräftig; *eat* herzhaft, kräftig ◆ **I ~ agree** ich stimme von Herzen *or* voll und ganz zu. **(b)** (*very*) äußerst, herzlich.

heartland [ˈhɑːtlænd] *n* Herzland *nt*, Herz *nt* des Landes ◆ **in the Tory ~s** in den Hochburgen der Konservativen.

heart: ~less *adj* herzlos; (*cruel also*) grausam; **~lessness** *n see adj* Herzlosigkeit *f*; Grausamkeit *f*; **~-lung machine** *n* Herz-Lungen-Maschine *f*; **~ murmur** *n* Herzgeräusche *pl*; **~rending** *adj* herzzerreißend; **~-searching** *n* Selbstprüfung *f*; **~-shaped** *adj* herzförmig; **~sick** *adj* (*liter*) **to be ~sick** Herzeleid haben (*old liter*); **~strings** *npl* **to pull** *or* **tug at the/sb's ~strings** einen/jdn zu Tränen rühren, auf die/bei jdm auf die Tränendrüsen drücken (*inf*); **to play on sb's ~strings** mit jds Gefühlen spielen; **~-throb** *n* (*inf*) Schwarm *m* (*inf*); **~-to-~** [1] *adj* ganz offen; **to have a ~-to-~ talk with sb** sich mit jdm ganz offen aussprechen; [2] *n* offene Aussprache; **it's time we had a ~-to-~** es ist Zeit, daß wir uns einmal offen aussprechen; **~ transplant** *n* Herztransplantation, Herzverpflanzung *f*; **~-trouble** *n* Herzbeschwerden *pl*; **~-warming** *adj* herzerfreuend.

hearty [ˈhɑːtɪ] [1] *adj* (*+er*) herzlich; *kick, slap also, meal, appetite* herzhaft, kräftig; *dislike* tief; *person* (*robust*) kernig; (*cheerful*) laut und herzlich, derbherzlich ◆ **he is a ~ eater** er hat einen gesunden Appetit, er langt kräftig zu (*inf*); *see* **hale**.

[2] *n* **(a)** (*Naut inf*) **me hearties!** Jungs! (*inf*), Leute!
(b) (*Brit Univ sl*) Sportskamerad *or* -freund (*inf*) *m*.

heat [hiːt] [1] *n* **(a)** Hitze *f*; (*pleasant, Phys*) Wärme *f*; (*of curry etc*) Schärfe *f*; (*~ing*) Heizung *f* ◆ **I don't mind the ~** mir macht (die) Hitze nichts aus; **in the ~ of the day** wenn es heiß ist; **at (a) low ~** bei schwacher Hitze; **to regulate the ~** (*in oven*) die Hitze regulieren; (*on fire*) die Wärme regulieren.

(b) (*fig: of argument, discussion*) Hitze *f* ◆ **in the ~ of the moment** in der Hitze des Gefechts; (*when upset*) in der Erregung; **the discussion generated quite a lot of ~** die Diskussion erhitzte die Gemüter; **to take the ~ out of the situation/an argument** die Situation/Diskussion entschärfen.

(c) (*inf: pressure*) Druck *m* ◆ **to put the ~ on** Druck machen (*inf*); **to put the ~ on sb** jdn unter Druck setzen; **the ~ is off** der Druck ist weg (*inf*); (*danger is past*) die Gefahr ist vorbei.

(d) (*Sport*) Vorlauf *m*; (*Boxing etc*) Vorkampf *m* ◆ **final ~** Ausscheidungskampf *m*.

(e) (*Zool*) Brunst *f*; (*Hunt*) Brunft *f*; (*of dogs, cats*) Läufigkeit *f* ◆ **on ~** brünstig; brunftig; läufig, heiß; (*inf: woman*) heiß (*inf*).

[2] *vt* erhitzen; *food also* aufwärmen, heiß *or* warm machen; *house, room* heizen; *pool* beheizen; (*provide with ~*) *house, town* beheizen.

[3] *vi* (*room etc*) sich erwärmen, warm werden; (*get very hot*) sich erhitzen, heiß werden ◆ **your dinner is ~ing in the oven** dein Essen steht (im Backofen) warm.

◆**heat up** [1] *vi* sich erwärmen, warm werden; (*get very hot*) sich erhitzen; (*engine also*) heißlaufen ◆ **your soup will soon ~ ~** deine Suppe ist gleich warm.

[2] *vt sep* erwärmen; *food* aufwärmen, warm *or* heiß machen; (*fig*) *discussion* anheizen.

heat death *n* Wärmetod *m*.

heated [ˈhiːtɪd] *adj* **(a)** (*lit*) geheizt; *pool* beheizt. **(b)** (*fig*) *words, debate, discussion* hitzig, erregt ◆ **to get ~** hitzig werden; **things got rather ~** die Gemüter erhitzten sich sehr.

heatedly [ˈhiːtɪdlɪ] *adv* hitzig.

heater [ˈhiːtə^r] *n* Ofen *m*; (*electrical also*) Heizgerät *nt*; (*in car*) Heizung *f*; (*for fondue*) Rechaud *m*; (*US sl: gun*) Knarre *f* (*sl*) ◆ **what sort of ~s do you have?** was für eine Heizung haben Sie?; **turn the ~ on** stell die Heizung an.

heat: ~ exchanger *n* Wärme(aus)tauscher *m*; **~ exhaustion** *n* Hitzeschäden *pl*; **~ flash** *n* Hitzeblitz *m*.

heath [hiːθ] *n* **(a)** (*moorland*) Heide *f*; (*type of country also*) Heideland *nt*. **(b)** (*plant*) Heidekraut *nt*, Erika *f*.

heat haze *n* Hitzeflimmern *nt*.

heathen [ˈhiːðən] [1] *adj* heidnisch, Heiden-; (*fig*) unkultiviert, unzivilisiert.
[2] *n* Heide *m*, Heidin *f*; (*fig*) unkultivierter *or* unzivilisierter Mensch ◆ **the ~** (*collectively*) (*lit*) die Heiden; (*fig*) die Barbaren.

heathenism [ˈhiːðənɪzəm] *n* Heidentum *nt*.

heather [ˈheðə^r] *n* Heidekraut *nt*, Erika, Heide *f*.

Heath Robinson [ˌhiːθˈrɒbɪnsən] *adj* (*inf*) *gadget, machine* fantastisch (*inf*).

heating [ˈhiːtɪŋ] *n* Heizung *f*; (*act*) (*of room, house*) (Be)heizen *nt*; (*of substances*) Erwärmen, Erhitzen *nt* ◆ **what sort of ~ do you have?** was für eine Heizung haben Sie?

heating: ~ apparatus *n* Heizapparat *m*; **~ element** *n* Heizelement *nt*; **~ engineer** *n* Heizungsinstallateur *m*; **~ system** *n* Heizungssystem *nt*; (*apparatus*) Heizungsanlage *f*.

heat: ~ loss *n* Wärmeverlust *m*; **~proof** *adj* hitzebeständig; **~ pump** *n* Wärmepumpe *f*; **~ rash** *n* Hitzeausschlag *m*, Hitzepocken *pl*; **~-resistant, ~-resisting** *adj* hitzebeständig; **~-seeking** *adj* wärmesuchend; **~-sensitive** *adj* wärmeempfindlich **~ shield** *n* (*protection*) Hitzeschild *m*; (*to retain heat*) Wärmeschutz *m*; **~ spot** *n* Hitzebläschen *nt*; **~stroke** *n* Hitzschlag *m*; **~ treatment** *n* (*Metal, Med*) Wärmebehandlung *f*; **~wave** *n* Hitzewelle *f*.

heave [hiːv] [1] *vt* **(a)** (*lift*) (hoch)hieven, (hoch)heben, wuchten (*onto* auf *+acc*); (*drag*) schleppen ◆ **he ~d himself out of bed** er hievte sich aus dem Bett (*inf*); **to ~ coal** Kohlen schleppen.
(b) (*throw*) werfen, schmeißen (*inf*).
(c) *sigh, sob* ausstoßen.
(d) *pret, ptp* **hove** (*Naut*) wenden ◆ **to ~ anchor** den Anker lichten.

[2] *vi* **(a)** (*pull*) ziehen, hieven.
(b) sich heben und senken; (*sea, waves, bosom also*) wogen (*liter*); (*stomach*) sich umdrehen; (*body*) sich krümmen ◆ **whales heaving and wallowing in the waves** Wale, die sich in den Wogen auf und ab wälzen; **the earthquake made the ground ~** bei dem Beben hob sich die Erde.
(c) *pret, ptp* **hove** (*Naut*) **to ~ in(to) sight** in Sicht kommen; **to ~ alongside** längsseits gehen.

[3] *n* (*of sea, waves*) Auf und Ab, Wogen (*geh*) *nt*; (*of bosom, chest*) Wogen *nt* ◆ **to lift/throw sth with a great ~** etw mit großer Anstrengung hochhieven *or* hochwuchten/etw mit großer Wucht werfen.

◆**heave to** (*Naut*) [1] *vi* beidrehen.
[2] *vt sep ship* stoppen.

◆**heave up** [1] *vi* (*inf: vomit*) brechen.
[2] *vt sep* **(a)** hochhieven, hochwuchten; (*push up also*) hochstemmen. **(b)** (*inf: vomit*) ausbrechen, von sich geben (*inf*).

heave ho *interj* hau ruck.

heaven [ˈhevn] *n* **(a)** (*lit, fig inf*) Himmel *m* ◆ **in ~** im Himmel; **to go to ~** in den Himmel kommen; **he is in (his seventh) ~** er ist im siebten Himmel; **to move ~ and earth** Himmel und Hölle in Bewegung setzen; **it was ~** es war einfach himmlisch; **the ~s opened** der Himmel öffnete seine Schleusen.
(b) (*inf*) **(good) ~s!** (du) lieber Himmel! (*inf*), du liebe Zeit! (*inf*); **would you like to? — (good) ~s no!** möchten Sie? — um Gottes *or* Himmels willen, bloß nicht!; **did he say so? — (good) ~ no!** hat er das gesagt? — ach wo, um Gottes Willen!; **~ knows what ...** weiß Gott *or* der Himmel, was ... (*inf*); **~ forbid!** bloß nicht, um Himmels willen! (*inf*); **~ forbid that I should end up the same** daß ich um Himmels willen nicht auch so werde! (*inf*); **for ~'s sake!** um Himmels *or* Gottes willen!

heavenly [ˈhevnlɪ] *adj* **(a)** himmlisch, Himmels- ◆ **~ body** Himmelskörper *m*; **~ host** himmlische Heerscharen *pl*. **(b)** (*inf: delightful*) himmlisch, traumhaft.

heaven-sent [ˈhevnˌsent] *adj opportunity* ideal ◆ **it was ~** das kam wie gerufen.

heavenward(s) [ˈhevnwəd(z)] *adv* zum Himmel, gen Himmel (*liter*) ◆ **to raise one's eyes ~** die Augen zum Himmel erheben.

heaves [hiːvz] *n sing* (*Vet*) Dämpfigkeit *f* ◆ **to have the ~** dämpfig sein.

heavily [ˈhevɪlɪ] *adv* **(a)** *loaded, weigh (also fig), fall, breathe* schwer; *move, walk* schwerfällig ◆ **~ built** kräftig gebaut; **time hung ~ on his hands** die Zeit verging ihm nur langsam.

(b) *rain, smoke, drink, concentrate, rely, wooded, populated, disguised, influenced, overdrawn, in debt* stark; *defeated* schwer; *underlined* dick, fett; *lose, tax* hoch; *sleep* tief; *buy* in großem Umfang ◆ **to be ~ drugged** unter starkem Drogeneinfluß stehen; **~ committed** stark engagiert; **too ~ fished** überfischt; **to be ~ subscribed** viele Abonnenten haben.

heaviness ['hevɪnɪs] *n see adj* (a) Schwere *f*; Grobheit *f* ◆ **~ of heart** schweres Herz; **~ of spirit** gedrückte Stimmung, Niedergeschlagenheit *f*. (b) Schwere *f*; Stärke *f*; Höhe *f*; (*of buying*) Umfang *m*; Dicke *f*; Tiefe *f*; Reichheit *f*. (c) Schwerfälligkeit *f*. (d) Schwüle *f*; Bedecktheit *f* ◆ **the ~ of the silence** die bedrückende Stille. (e) Schwere *f*. (f) Schwere *f*, Ernst *m*.

heavy ['hevɪ] 1 *adj* (+*er*) (a) (*of great weight, Phys, fig*) schwer; *features* grob ◆ **with a ~ heart** schweren Herzens, mit schwerem Herzen; **~ with young** (*Zool*) trächtig; **~ with incense/pollen/scent** mit Weihrauch/Pollen geschwängert (*geh*)/duftgeschwängert (*geh*); **~ with sleep** *person* schläfrig; *eyes also* schwer; **~ with wine** voll des süßen Weines (*liter*); **~ goods vehicle** Lastkraftwagen *m*; **~ industry** Schwerindustrie *f*; **~ artillery** (*Mil*) schwere Artillerie.

(b) *tread, blow, gunfire, casualties, fog, clouds, sea, odour, music, book, wine, meal, sarcasm* schwer; *rain, cold also, traffic, eater, drinker, smoker* stark; *defeat, losses also, expenses, taxes* hoch; *buying* groß; *line* dick; *sleep* tief; *crop* reich ◆ **~ buyer** Großabnehmer *m*; **~ type** (*Typ*) Fettdruck *m*; **to be ~ on petrol** viel Benzin brauchen.

(c) (*~-handed*) *manner, style, sense of humour* schwerfällig.

(d) (*oppressive*) *silence* bedrückend; *weather, air* drückend, schwül; *sky* bedeckt.

(e) (*difficult*) *task, work, day* schwer ◆ **the going was ~** wir kamen nur schwer voran; **the conversation was ~ going** die Unterhaltung war mühsam; **this book is very ~ going** das Buch liest sich schwer.

(f) (*Theat*) *part* schwer, ernst.

(g) (*inf: strict*) streng (*on* mit) ◆ **to play the ~ father** den gestrengen Vater spielen.

(h) (*dated US sl*) prima (*inf*), dufte (*inf*).

2 *adv* schwer ◆ **his guilt weighs** *or* **lies ~ on him** seine Schuld lastet schwer auf ihm.

3 *n* (a) (*inf: thug*) Schlägertyp *m*.

(b) (*Theat: villain*) Schurke *m*.

(c) (*Scot: beer*) *dunkleres, obergäriges Bier.*

heavy: ~-duty *adj clothes, tyres etc* strapazierfähig; *boots* Arbeits-; *machine* Hochleistungs-; **~-footed** *adj* schwerfällig; **~-handed** *adj* schwerfällig, ungeschickt; **~-hearted** *adj* mit schwerem Herzen, bedrückt; **~-laden** *adj* (*also Bibl*) schwer beladen; **the air was ~-laden with incense** die Luft war von Weihrauch geschwängert (*geh*); **~ metal** *n* (a) Schwermetall *nt*; (b) (*Mus*) Heavy Metal *m*; **~ water** *n* schweres Wasser; **~ water reactor** *n* Schwerwasserreaktor *m*; **~weight** 1 *n* (*Boxing*) Schwergewicht *nt*; (*fig inf*) großes Tier (*inf*), Große(r) *m*; **the literary ~weights** die literarischen Größen; 2 *adj attr* Schwergewichts-.

hebdomadal [heb'dɒmədl] *adj* (*form*) wöchentlich.

Hebrew ['hi:bru:] 1 *adj* hebräisch.

2 *n* (a) Hebräer(in *f*) *m*. (b) (*language*) Hebräisch *nt*; *see also* **English**.

Hebridean [ˌhebrɪ'di:ən] *adj* Hebriden-, der Hebriden.

Hebrides ['hebrɪdi:z] *npl* Hebriden *pl*.

heck [hek] *interj* (*inf*) **oh ~!** zum Kuckuck! (*inf*); **ah, what the ~!** ach, was soll's! (*inf*); **what the ~ do you mean?** was zum Kuckuck soll das heißen? (*inf*); **I've a ~ of a lot to do** ich habe irrsinnig viel zu tun (*inf*).

heckle ['hekl] 1 *vt speaker* (durch Zwischenrufe) stören.

2 *vi* stören, Zwischenrufe machen.

heckler ['heklə^r] *n* Zwischenrufer, Störer (*pej*) *m*.

heckling ['heklɪŋ] *n* Zwischenrufe *pl*.

hectare ['hektɑ:^r] *n* Hektar *m or nt*.

hectic ['hektɪk] *adj* hektisch.

hectogramme, (*US*) **hectogram** ['hektəʊgræm] *n* Hektogramm *nt*.

hectolitre, (*US*) **hectoliter** ['hektəʊˌli:tə^r] *n* Hektoliter *m*.

hector ['hektə^r] *vt* (*liter: bully*) tyrannisieren.

hectoring ['hektərɪŋ] *adj* herrisch, tyrannisch.

he'd [hi:d] *contr of* **he would; he had.**

hedge [hedʒ] 1 *n* Hecke *f*; (*fig: protection*) Schutz *m*.

2 *vi* Fragen ausweichen, kneifen (*inf*) (*at* bei) ◆ **stop hedging and say what you think** weich nicht immer aus, sag, was du denkst!

3 *vt* (a) *investment* absichern ◆ **to ~ one's bets** (*lit, fig*) sich absichern, auf Nummer Sicher gehen (*inf*). (b) *field, garden* (mit einer Hecke) umgeben.

◆**hedge about** *or* **around** *vt sep* (a) (*with restrictions etc*) *life* einengen; *procedure* erschweren, behindern. (b) (*rare: lit*) (mit einer Hecke) einfassen.

◆**hedge in** *or* **round** *vt sep* (a) *field* mit einer Hecke umgeben *or* einfassen. (b) (*fig*) *procedure* behindern, erschweren ◆ **to ~ sb ~** jdn in seiner Freiheit einengen *or* beschränken.

◆**hedge off** *vt sep* mit einer Hecke abgrenzen *or* abtrennen.

hedgehog ['hedʒhɒg] *n* Igel *m*.

hedge: ~hop *vi* tief fliegen; **~row** *n* Hecke *f*, Knick *m* (*N Ger*); **~ sparrow** *n* Heckenbraunelle *f*.

hedonism ['hi:dənɪzəm] *n* Hedonismus *m*.

hedonist ['hi:dənɪst] 1 *n* Hedonist(in *f*) *m*.

2 *adj* hedonistisch.

hedonistic ['hi:dənɪstɪk] *adj* hedonistisch.

heebie-jeebies ['hi:bɪ'dʒi:bɪz] *npl* (*sl*) Gänsehaut *f* (*inf*) ◆ **it/he gives me the ~** dabei/wenn ich ihn sehe, bekomm' ich eine Gänsehaut (*inf*).

heed [hi:d] 1 *n* Beachtung *f* ◆ **to take ~** achtgeben, aufpassen; **to give** *or* **pay ~/no ~ to sb/sth, to take ~/no ~ of sb/sth** jdn/etw beachten/nicht beachten, jdm/einer Sache Beachtung/keine Beachtung schenken; **to take ~ to do sth** darauf achten, etw zu tun.

2 *vt* beachten, Beachtung schenken (+*dat*) ◆ **just ~ what your father says** hör auf deinen Vater; **he never ~s my advice** er hört nie auf meinen Rat.

heedful ['hi:dfʊl] *adj* **to be ~ of sb's warning/advice** auf jds Warnung (*acc*)/Rat (*acc*) hören.

heedless ['hi:dlɪs] *adj* rücksichtslos; *extravagance* leichtsinnig ◆ **to be ~ of sth** etw nicht beachten, auf etw (*acc*) nicht achten; **~ of their complaints** ohne sich um ihre Beschwerden zu kümmern, ohne Rücksicht auf ihre Beschwerden.

heedlessly ['hi:dlɪslɪ] *adv* rücksichtslos.

heehaw ['hi:hɔ:] 1 *n* Iah *nt*.

2 *vi* iahen.

heel[1] [hi:l] 1 *n* (a) Ferse *f*; (*of shoe*) Absatz *m* ◆ **with his dog/the children at his ~s** gefolgt von seinem Hund/de n Kindern; **to be right on sb's ~s** jdm auf den Fersen folgen; (*fig: chase*) jdm auf den Fersen sein; **to follow hard upon sb's ~s** jdm dicht auf den Fersen sein, sich an jds Fersen (*acc*) heften (*geh*); **winter followed hard upon autumn's ~s** (*liter*) der Herbst mußte dem Winter weichen (*liter*); **panic buying came on the ~s of the government's announcement** Hamsterkäufe folgten der Erklärung der Regierung auf dem Fuße; **to be down at ~** (*person*) abgerissen *or* heruntergekommen sein; (*shoes*) schiefe Absätze haben, abgelaufen sein; **to take to one's ~s** sich aus dem Staub(e) machen, Fersengeld geben (*dated, hum*); **to show sb a clean pair of ~s** (*escape*) vor jdm davonlaufen, jdm die Fersen zeigen (*geh*); (*leave behind*) jdm weit voraus sein, jdn weit hinter sich lassen; **~!** (*to dog*) (bei) Fuß!; **he brought the dog to ~** er befahl dem Hund, bei Fuß zu gehen; **to bring sb to ~** jdn an die Kandare nehmen (*inf*); **to turn on one's ~** auf dem Absatz kehrtmachen; **to cool** *or* **kick one's ~s** (*inf*) (*wait*) warten; (*do nothing*) Däumchen drehen; **~ bar** Absatzbar *f*.

(b) (*of golf club*) Ferse *f*; (*of loaf*) Kanten *m*; (*of mast*) Fuß *m*.

(c) (*pej sl: person*) Schwein *nt* (*sl*), Scheißkerl *m* (*sl*).

2 *vt* (a) **to ~ shoes** auf Schuhe neue Absätze machen; **the shoes need ~ing** die Schuhe brauchen neue Absätze; **to be well ~ed** (*inf*) betucht sein (*inf*), sich gut stehen (*inf*).

(b) (*Rugby*) *ball* hakeln.

heel[2] (*Naut*) 1 *vi* (*ship: also* **~ over**) krängen (*spec*), sich (auf die Seite) legen *or* neigen ◆ **to ~ hard over** sich stark auf die Seite legen, stark krängen (*spec*).

2 *vt* krängen lassen (*spec*), sich seitlich überlegen lassen.

3 *n* (seitliches) Überlegen, Seitenneigung *f*.

heft [heft] 1 *vt* (*US inf*) (*lift*) (hoch)heben; (*assess weight*) abwägen, das Gewicht (ab)schätzen von.

2 *n* Gewicht *nt*; (*strength*) (Muskel)kraft *f*.

hefty ['heftɪ] *adj* (+*er*) (*inf*) kräftig; *person also* gut beieinander (*inf*); *woman also* drall; *child also* stramm; *book* (*extensive*) dick; *object, workload* (schön) schwer; *stroke, blow also* saftig (*inf*); *sum of money, amount* saftig (*inf*), ganz schön (*inf*).

Hegelian [heɪ'geɪlɪən] 1 *adj* Hegelsch; (*in ~ tradition*) hegelianisch.

2 *n* Hegelianer(in *f*) *m*.

hegemony [hɪ'gemənɪ] *n* Hegemonie *f*.

hegira [he'dʒaɪərə] *n* Hedschra *f*.

Heidelberg man ['haɪdlbɜ:g'mæn] *n* Homo Heidelbergensis *m*.

heifer ['hefə^r] *n* Färse *f*.

heigh [heɪ] *interj* **~-ho!** nun ja!

height [haɪt] *n* (a) (*of building, mountain etc, altitude*) Höhe *f*; (*of person*) Größe *f* ◆ **to be six feet in ~** sechs Fuß groß *or* (*wall etc*) hoch sein; **what ~ are you?** wie groß sind Sie?; **he pulled himself up to his full ~** er richtete sich zu voller Größe auf; **you can raise the ~ of the saddle** du kannst den Sattel höher stellen.

(b) (*high place*) **~s** *pl* Höhen *pl* ◆ **to scale the ~s of Everest** den Mount Everest besteigen; **fear of ~s** Höhenangst *f*; **to be afraid of ~s** nicht schwindelfrei sein.

(c) (*fig*) Höhe *f*; (*of success, power, stupidity also*) Gipfel *m* ◆ **at the ~ of his power** auf der Höhe seiner Macht; **that is the ~ of folly** das ist der Gipfel der Torheit; **the ~ of glory** der höchste Ruhm; **that is the ~ of ill-manners!** das ist doch die Höhe!, das ist der Gipfel der Unverschämtheit!; **it is the ~ of ill-manners to ...** es verstößt gegen jede Etikette, zu ...; **at the ~ of the season** in der Hauptsaison; **at the ~ of the storm** als der Sturm am heftigsten war; **dressed in the ~ of fashion** nach der neuesten Mode gekleidet; **the ~ of fashion** der letzte Schrei, große Mode; **at the ~ of summer** im Hochsommer.

heighten ['haɪtn] 1 *vt* (*raise*) höher stellen *or* machen; (*emphasize*) *colour etc* hervorheben; (*Med*) *fever* steigen lassen, erhöhen; *intensity* steigern; *colour, feelings, anger, love, ambition* verstärken; *passions, fear, fitness, effect* verstärken, erhöhen ◆ **with ~ed colour** mit (hoch)rotem Gesicht.

2 *vi* (*fig: increase*) wachsen, größer *or* stärker werden.

heinous ['heɪnəs] *adj* abscheulich, verabscheuungswürdig.

heinously ['heɪnəslɪ] *adv* auf abscheuliche Weise.

heinousness ['heɪnəsnɪs] *n* Abscheulichkeit *f*.

heir [ɛə^r] *n* Erbe *m* (*to gen*) ◆ **~ apparent** gesetzlicher Erbe; **~ to the throne** Thronfolger *m*.

heiress ['ɛəres] *n* Erbin *f*.

heirloom ['ɛəlu:m] *n* Erbstück *nt*.

heist [haɪst] (*esp US sl*) 1 *n* Raubüberfall *m*.

2 *vt* rauben.

held [held] *pret, ptp of* **hold**.

Helen ['helın] *n* Helene *f;* (*Myth*) Helena *f* ◆ **~ of Troy** die Schöne Helena.

helical ['helıkəl] *adj gear* Schnecken-, Schrägverzahnungs-.

helicopter ['helıkɒptəʳ] [1] *n* Hubschrauber *m.*
[2] *vt* **he was ~ed out of the area** er wurde per Hubschrauber aus dem Gebiet abtransportiert.

Heligoland ['helıgəʊlænd] *n* Helgoland *nt.*

heliocentric [,hiːlıəʊ'sentrık] *adj* heliozentrisch.

heliograph ['hiːlıəʊgrɑːf] [1] *n* Heliograph *m.*
[2] *vt* heliographisch übermitteln.

heliotrope ['hiːlıətrəʊp] [1] *n* (*Bot, colour*) Heliotrop *nt.*
[2] *adj* heliotrop(isch).

heliotropic [,hiːlıəʊ'trəʊpık] *adj* heliotrop(isch).

helipad ['helıpæd] *n* Hubschrauber-Landeplatz *m.*

heliport ['helıpɔːt] *n* Hubschrauberflugplatz, Heliport *m.*

helium ['hiːlıəm] *n* Helium *nt.*

helix ['hiːlıks] *n* (räumliche) Spirale, Helix *f.*

hell [hel] *n* **(a)** Hölle *f* ◆ **to go to ~** (*lit*) in die Hölle kommen, zur Hölle fahren (*liter*).
(b) (*fig uses*) **all ~ was let loose** die Hölle war los; **it's ~ working there** es ist die reine Hölle, dort zu arbeiten; **it was ~ in the trenches** es war die reine Hölle in den Schützengräben; **life was ~ on earth** das Leben dort war die reinste Hölle *or* die Hölle auf Erden; **life became ~** das Leben wurde zur Hölle; **she made his life ~** sie machte ihm das Leben zur Hölle; **to give sb ~** (*inf*) (*tell off*) jdm die Hölle heiß machen; (*make life unpleasant*) jdm das Leben zur Hölle machen; **you'll get ~ if he finds out** (*inf*) der macht dich zur Schnecke (*inf*) *or* Sau (*sl*), wenn er das erfährt; **there'll be (all) ~ when he finds out** wenn er das erfährt, ist der Teufel los (*inf*); **to play ~ with sth** etw total durcheinanderbringen; **I did it for the ~ of it** (*inf*) ich habe es nur zum Spaß *or* aus Jux gemacht; **~ for leather** was das Zeug hält; *run also* was die Beine hergeben.
(c) (*inf: intensifier*) **a ~ of a noise** ein Höllen- *or* Heidenlärm *m* (*inf*); **to work like ~** arbeiten, was das Zeug hält, wie wild arbeiten (*inf*); **to run like ~** laufen, was die Beine hergeben; **we had a ~ of a time** (*bad, difficult*) es war grauenhaft; (*good*) wir haben uns prima amüsiert (*inf*); **a ~ of a lot** verdammt viel (*inf*); **she's a** *or* **one ~ of a girl** die ist schwer in Ordnung (*inf*), das ist ein klasse Mädchen (*inf*); **that's one** *or* **a ~ of a problem/difference/bruise/climb** das ist ein verdammt (*inf*) *or* wahnsinnig (*inf*) schwieriges Problem/wahnsinniger (*inf*) Unterschied/Bluterguß/eine wahnsinnige (*inf*) Kletterei; **to ~ with you/him** hol dich/ihn der Teufel (*inf*), du kannst/der kann mich mal (*sl*); **to ~ with it!** verdammt noch mal (*inf*); **to ~ with your problems!** deine Probleme können mir gestohlen bleiben (*inf*); **go to ~!** scher dich *or* geh zum Teufel! (*inf*); **what the ~ do you want?** was willst du denn, verdammt noch mal? (*inf*); **like ~ he will!** den Teufel wird er tun (*inf*); **pay that price for a meal? like ~** so viel für ein Essen bezahlen? ich bin doch nicht verrückt!; **he knows the Queen? — like ~!** er und die Königin kennen? — wer's glaubt!; **~!** so'n Mist! (*inf*), verdammt noch mal! (*inf*); **~'s bells!** (*euph*) *or* **teeth!** (*euph*) (*surprise*) heiliger Strohsack (*inf*) *or* Bimbam (*inf*)!; (*anger*) zum Kuckuck noch mal! (*inf*); **where the ~ is it?** wo ist es denn, verdammt noch mal? (*inf*).

he'll [hiːl] *contr of* **he shall; he will**.

hell: ~-bent *adj* versessen (on auf +*acc*); **to be ~-bent on vengeance** unerbittlich auf Rache sinnen; **~-cat** *n* Giftziege *f* (*inf*).

hellebore ['helıbɔː] *n* (*Bot*) Nieswurz *f.*

Hellenic [he'liːnık] *adj* hellenisch ◆ **a ~ cruise** eine Hellas-Kreuzfahrt.

hell: ~-fire *n* Höllenfeuer *nt;* (*punishment*) Höllenqualen *pl;* **~hole** *n* gräßliches Loch; **the trenches were a real ~hole** die (Schützen)gräben waren die reine Hölle.

hellish ['helıʃ] *adj* (*inf*) höllisch (*inf*) ◆ **the exams were ~** die Prüfungen waren verteufelt schwer (*inf*); **it's ~ not having any money** es ist schrecklich, wenn man kein Geld hat.

hellishly ['helıʃlı] *adv* (*inf*) verteufelt (*inf*), verdammt (*inf*).

▼ **hello** [hə'ləʊ] [1] *interj* (*all senses*) hallo ◆ **say ~ to your aunt** sag deiner Tante mal schön „guten Tag!"; **say ~ to your parents (from me)** grüß deine Eltern (von mir); **~, ~, ~! what's going on here?** nanu *or* he! was ist denn hier los?
[2] *n* Hallo *nt.*

hell's angels *npl* Hell's Angels *pl.*

helluva ['heləvə] *adj, adv* (*sl*) = **hell of a**; *see* **hell (c)**.

helm [helm] *n* **(a)** (*Naut*) Ruder, Steuer *nt* ◆ **to be at the ~** (*lit, fig*) am Ruder sein. **(b)** (*obs: helmet*) Helm *m.*

helmet ['helmıt] *n* Helm *m;* (*Fencing*) Maske *f.*

helmeted ['helmıtıd] *adj* behelmt.

helmsman ['helmzmən] *n, pl* **-men** [-mən] Steuermann *m.*

▼ **help** [help] [1] *n, no pl* Hilfe *f;* (*person: with pl*) Hilfe *f* ◆ **with his brother's ~** mit (der) Hilfe seines Bruders; **his ~ with the project** seine Mithilfe an dem Projekt; **with the ~ of a knife** mit Hilfe eines Messers; **we need all the ~ we can get** wir brauchen jede nur mögliche Hilfe; **he is beyond ~/beyond medical ~** ihm ist nicht mehr zu helfen/ihm kann kein Arzt mehr helfen; **to give ~** Hilfe leisten; **to go/come to sb's ~** jdm zu Hilfe eilen/kommen; **to be of ~ to sb** jdm helfen; (*person also*) jdm behilflich sein; (*thing also*) jdm nützen; **he isn't much ~ to me** er ist mir keine große Hilfe; **you're a great ~!** (*iro*) du bist mir eine schöne Hilfe!; **we are short of ~ in the shop** wir haben nicht genügend (Hilfs)kräfte im Geschäft; **there's no ~ for it** da ist nichts zu machen.
[2] *vt* **(a)** helfen (+*dat*) ◆ **to ~ sb (to) do sth** jdm (dabei) helfen, etw zu tun; **to ~ sb with the washing-up/his bags** jdm beim Abwaschen/mit seinen Taschen helfen; **~!** Hilfe!, zu Hilfe! (*old*); **so ~ me God!** so wahr mir Gott helfe!; **can I ~ you?** kann ich (Ihnen) helfen *or* behilflich sein?; (*in shop also*) womit kann ich dienen?; **that won't ~ you** das wird Ihnen nichts nützen; **this will ~ the pain/your headache** das wird gegen die Schmerzen/gegen Ihr Kopfweh helfen; **it will ~ the wound to heal** das wird die Heilung (der Wunde) fördern; **it will ~ the crops to grow** es wird das Wachstum des Getreides fördern; **God ~s those who ~ themselves** (*Prov*) hilf dir selbst, so hilft dir Gott (*Prov*); **a man is ~ing the police with their enquiries** (*form euph*) ein Mann wird zur Zeit von der Polizei vernommen.
(b) (*with particle*) **to ~ sb down** jdm hinunter-/herunterhelfen; **take some water to ~ the pill down** trinken Sie etwas Wasser, damit die Tablette besser rutscht; **to ~ sb off with his coat** jdm aus dem Mantel helfen; **he ~ed her out of the car/a jam** er half ihr aus dem Auto/einer Klemme; **to ~ sb over the street** jdm über die Straße helfen; **to ~ sb through a difficult time** (*belief, hope, pills etc*) jdm in einer schwierigen Zeit durchhelfen; (*person also*) jdm in einer schwierigen Zeit beistehen; **to ~ sb up** (*from floor, chair etc*) jdm aufhelfen *or* (*up stairs etc*) hinaufhelfen; **to ~ sb up with a suitcase** jdm helfen, den Koffer hochzuheben.
(c) she ~ed him to potatoes/meat sie gab ihm Kartoffeln/legte ihm Fleisch auf; **to ~ oneself to sth** sich mit etw bedienen; **to ~ oneself to vegetables** sich (*dat*) Gemüse nehmen; **~ yourself!** nehmen Sie sich doch!; **I'll ~ the children first** (*inf*) ich gebe den Kindern zuerst.
▼ **(d)** (*with can or cannot*) **he can't ~ it, he was born with it** er kann nichts dafür, das ist angeboren; **he can't ~ it!** (*hum inf: he's stupid*) (d)er ist nun mal so (doof); **I can't ~ being so clever** (ich kann nichts dafür,) ich bin nun mal ein Genie *or* so schlau (*inf*); **he can't ~ the way he is** das ist nun mal (so) seine Art; **don't say more than you can ~** sagen Sie nicht mehr als unbedingt nötig; **not if I can ~ it** nicht, wenn es nach mir geht; **I couldn't ~ thinking/laughing** ich konnte mir nicht helfen, ich mußte (einfach) glauben/lachen, ich konnte nicht umhin zu glauben/lachen (*geh*); **I had to do it, I couldn't ~ it** *or* **myself** ich konnte mir nicht helfen, ich mußte es einfach tun; **one cannot ~ wondering whether ...** man muß sich wirklich fragen, ob ...; **it can't be ~ed** das läßt sich nicht ändern, das ist nun mal so; **I can't ~ it if he always comes late** ich kann nichts dafür, daß er immer zu spät kommt.
[3] *vi* helfen ◆ **and forgetting to lock the door didn't ~ either** und daß die Tür nicht abgeschlossen wurde, hat natürlich die Sache auch nicht besser gemacht; **it ~s to fight pollution** es trägt zur Bekämpfung der Umweltverschmutzung bei; **it all ~s** Kleinvieh macht auch Mist (*inf*).

◆**help out** [1] *vi* aushelfen (*with* bei).
▼ [2] *vt sep* helfen (+*dat*) (*with* mit); (*in crisis also*) aufhelfen (+*dat*) (*with* bei) ◆ **will £3 ~ you ~?** helfen Ihnen £ 3 weiter?

helper ['helpəʳ] *n* Helfer(in *f*) *m;* (*assistant*) Gehilfe *m,* Gehilfin *f.*

▼ **helpful** ['helpfʊl] *adj person* hilfsbereit, gefällig, hilfreich (*old*); (*useful*) *gadget, remark, knowledge* nützlich; *advice* nützlich, hilfreich ◆ **you have been most ~ to me** Sie haben mir sehr geholfen; **you'll find these tablets most ~** diese Tabletten werden Ihnen sehr helfen *or* guttun.

helpfully ['helpfəlı] *adv* hilfreich ◆ **~, the instructions were written in three languages** es war eine große Hilfe, daß die Gebrauchsanweisung in drei Sprachen war; **the rear doors are ~ fitted with child-proof locks** es ist sehr nützlich *or* von Vorteil, daß die hinteren Türen kindersichere Schlösser haben.

helpfulness ['helpfʊlnıs] *n see adj* Hilfsbereitschaft, Gefälligkeit *f;* Nützlichkeit *f.*

help function *n* (*Comput*) Hilfefunktion *f.*

helping ['helpıŋ] [1] *n* (*at table*) Portion *f* ◆ **to take a second ~ of sth** sich (*dat*) noch einmal von etw nehmen; **he even had a third ~** er nahm sich (*dat*) sogar noch eine dritte Portion.
[2] *adj attr* **to give** *or* **lend a ~ hand to sb** jdm helfen, jdm behilflich sein; **if you want a ~ hand ...** wenn Sie Hilfe brauchen, ...

helpless ['helplıs] *adj* hilflos ◆ **are you ~!** bist du aber hilflos!; **I was ~ to avoid the collision** ich konnte nichts tun, um den Zusammenstoß zu verhindern; **she was ~ with laughter** sie konnte sich vor Lachen kaum halten.

helplessly ['helplıslı] *adv see adj.*

helplessness ['helplısnıs] *n* Hilflosigkeit *f.*

help: ~line *n* (*for emergencies*) Notruf *m;* (*for information*) Informationsdienst *m;* **~mate** (*old*), **~meet** (*obs*) *n* Gefährte *m* (*geh*), Gefährtin *f* (*geh*); (*helper*) Gehilfe *m* (*old*), Gehilfin *f* (*old*); **~ screen** *n* (*Comput*) Hilfsbildschirm *m.*

helter-skelter ['heltə'skeltəʳ] [1] *adv* Hals über Kopf (*inf*).
[2] *adj* wirr, wild.
[3] *n* **(a)** (*confusion*) Tohuwabohu *nt,* (wildes) Durcheinander. **(b)** (*Brit: on fairground*) Rutschbahn *f.*

hem[1] [hem] *interj see* **hum 2 (c)**.

hem[2] [1] *n* Saum *m.*
[2] *vt* säumen.

◆**hem about** *or* **around** *vt sep* umgeben.

◆**hem in** *vt sep troops etc* einschließen, umgeben; (*fig*) einengen.

he-man ['hiːmæn] *n, pl* **-men** [-men] (*inf*) He-man *m,* sehr männlicher Typ, echter *or* richtiger Mann ◆ **he fancies himself as a ~** er kommt sich unheimlich männlich vor (*inf*).

hematite ['hiːmətaıt] *n* Hämatit *m.*

hematology *n* (*US*) *see* **haematology**.

hemidemisemiquaver [,hemıdemı'semı,kweıvəʳ] *n* (*Mus*) Vierundsechzigstel(note *f*) *nt.*

hemiplegia [ˌhemɪˈpliːdʒɪə] *n* halbseitige Lähmung.
hemiplegic [ˌhemɪˈpliːdʒɪk] *adj* halbseitig gelähmt.
hemisphere [ˈhemɪsfɪəʳ] *n* Halbkugel, Hemisphäre *f*; (*of brain*) Hemisphäre, Gehirnhälfte *f* ◆ **in the northern ~** auf der nördlichen Halbkugel, in der nördlichen Hemisphäre.
hemline [ˈhemlaɪn] *n* Saum *m* ◆ **~s are lower this year** der Rocksaum ist dieses Jahr etwas tiefer gerutscht.
hemlock [ˈhemlɒk] *n* (*Bot: poisonous plant*) Schierling *m*; (*tree*) Schierlings- *or* Hemlocktanne *f*; (*poison*) Schierling(saft) *m* ◆ **Socrates drank the ~** Sokrates trank den Schierlingsbecher.
hemo- *in cpds* (*US*) *see* **haemo-**.
hemp [hemp] *n* **(a)** (*Bot*) Hanf *m* ◆ **~ seed** Hanfsamen *pl*. **(b)** (*drug*) Hanf *m*. **(c)** (*fibre*) Hanf(faser *f*) *m*.
hem-stitch [ˈhemstɪtʃ] **1** *vt* in Hohlsaum nähen.
2 *n* Hohlsaum *m*.
hen [hen] *n* **(a)** Huhn *nt*, Henne *f*. **(b)** (*female bird, lobster*) Weibchen *nt*. **(c)** (*inf*) (*also* **mother ~**) Glucke *f* (*inf*).
hen: ~bane *n* Bilsenkraut *nt*; **~ bird** *n* (Vogel)weibchen *nt*.
hence [hens] *adv* **(a)** (*for this reason*) also ◆ **~ the name** daher der Name. **(b)** (*from now*) **two years ~** in zwei Jahren. **(c)** (*obs, liter: from here*) von hier ◆ **(get thee) ~!** hinweg (mit dir)! (*liter*); **get thee ~, Satan!** weiche, Satan! (*liter*); **I must ~** ich muß von hinnen scheiden (*obs*).
henceforth [ˌhensˈfɔːθ], **henceforward** [ˌhensˈfɔːwəd] *adv* (*from that time on*) von da an, fortan (*liter*); (*from this time on*) von nun an, künftig.
henchman [ˈhentʃmən] *n, pl* **-men** [-mən] (*pej*) Spießgeselle, Kumpan *m*.
hen-coop [ˈhenkuːp] *n* Hühnerstall *m*.
henhouse [ˈhenhaʊs] *n* Hühnerhaus *nt*, Hühnerstall *m*.
henna [ˈhenə] **1** *n* Henna *f*.
2 *vt* mit Henna färben.
hen: ~-party *n* (*inf*) Damenkränzchen *nt*, ≃ Kaffeeklatsch *m* (*inf*), reine Weibergesellschaft (*pej, inf*); (*before wedding*) *für die Braut vor der Hochzeit arrangierte Damengesellschaft*; **~peck** *vt* unterm Pantoffel haben (*inf*); **a ~pecked husband** ein Pantoffelheld *m* (*inf*); **he is ~pecked** er steht unterm Pantoffel (*inf*); **he's started to look ~pecked** es sieht langsam so aus, als ob er unterm Pantoffel steht (*inf*); **~-run** *n* Hühnerhof *m*.
Henry [ˈhenrɪ] *n* Heinrich *m*.
hep [hep] *adj* (*US sl*) *see* **hip**[4].
hepatitis [ˌhepəˈtaɪtɪs] *n* Hepatitis *f*.
heptagon [ˈheptəgən] *n* Siebeneck, Heptagon *nt*.
heptathlon [hepˈtæθlɒn] *n* Siebenkampf *m*.
her [hɜːʳ] **1** *pers pron* **(a)** (*dir obj, with prep +acc*) sie; (*indir obj, with prep +dat*) ihr; (*when she is previously mentioned in clause*) sich ◆ **with her books about ~** mit ihren Büchern um sich. **(b)** (*emph*) sie ◆ **it's ~** sie ist's; **who, ~?** wer, sie?
2 *poss adj* ihr; *see also* **my**.
Heraclitean [ˌherəˈklaɪtɪən] *adj* Heraklitisch.
Heraclitus [ˌherəˈklaɪtəs] *n* Heraklit *m*.
herald [ˈherəld] **1** *n* **(a)** (*Hist*) Herold *m*; (*in newspaper titles*) Bote *m*. **(b)** (*fig*) (Vor)bote *m* (*geh*) ◆ **~ of spring** Frühlingsbote *m*. **(c)** (*Her*) **College of H~s** Heroldsamt *nt*.
2 *vt arrival of summer* ankündigen, Vorbote(n) sein für ◆ **to ~ (in) a new age** den Beginn eines neuen Zeitalters ankündigen.
heraldic [heˈrældɪk] *adj* heraldisch, Wappen- ◆ **~ arms** Wappen *pl*.
heraldry [ˈherəldrɪ] *n* **(a)** (*science*) Wappenkunde, Heraldik *f*. **(b)** (*heraldic signs*) Wappen *pl*. **(c)** (*ceremonial*) traditioneller höfischer Prunk.
herb [hɜːb] *n* Kraut *nt* ◆ **~ garden** Kräutergarten *m*.
herbaceous [hɜːˈbeɪʃəs] *adj* krautig ◆ **~ border** Staudenrabatte *f*.
herbage [ˈhɜːbɪdʒ] *n* Grünpflanzen *pl*; (*leaves and stems*) Grünzeug *nt*; (*pasturage*) Weide(land *nt*) *f*.
herbal [ˈhɜːbəl] **1** *adj* Kräuter-.
2 *n* Kräuterbuch *nt*.
herbalist [ˈhɜːbəlɪst] *n* Kräutersammler(in *f*) *m*; (*healer*) Naturheilkundige(r) *mf*.
herbarium [hɜːˈbɛərɪəm] *n* Herbarium *nt*.
herbicide [ˈhɜːbɪsaɪd] *n* Herbizid *nt*.
herbivorous [hɜːˈbɪvərəs] *adj* (*form*) pflanzenfressend.
herculean [ˌhɜːkjʊˈliːən] *adj* herkulisch; *strength* Bären-, Riesen-, herkulisch (*liter*); *proportions* riesenhaft; *effort* übermenschlich ◆ **a ~ task** eine Herkulesarbeit.
Hercules [ˈhɜːkjuliːz] *n* (*lit, fig*) Herkules *m*.
herd [hɜːd] **1** *n* (*of cattle etc*) Herde *f*; (*of deer*) Rudel *nt*; (*fig pej: of people*) Herde, Schar *f* ◆ **the common ~** die breite Masse.
2 *vt* **(a)** (*drive*) *cattle, prisoners* treiben. **(b)** (*tend*) *cattle* hüten.
◆**herd together** **1** *vi* sich zusammendrängen.
2 *vt sep* zusammentreiben.
herd: ~ instinct *n* Herdentrieb *m*; **~sman** *n* Hirt, Hirte *m*.
here [hɪəʳ] **1** *adv* **(a)** hier; (*with motion*) hierher, hierhin ◆ **~!** (*at roll call*) hier!; (*to dog*) hierher!; **~ I am** da *or* hier bin ich; **spring is ~** der Frühling ist da; **this man ~** dieser Mann (hier) ...; **John ~ reckons ...** John hier meint ...; **this ~ notice** (*incorrect*) dieser Anschlag da (*inf*); **~ and now** auf der Stelle, jetzt sofort; **this one ~** der/die/das hier *or* da; **I won't be ~ for lunch** ich bin zum Mittagessen nicht da; **shall we wait till he gets ~?** sollen wir warten, bis er hier *or* da ist?; **~ and there** hier und da; **~, there and everywhere** überall; **around/about ~** hier herum, ungefähr hier; **near ~** (hier) in der Nähe; **up/down to ~** bis hierher *or* hierhin; **it's in/over ~** es ist hier (drin)/hier drüben; **put it in/over ~** stellen Sie es hier herein/hierüber *or* hier herüber *or* hierher; **come in/over ~** kommen Sie hier herein/hierüber *or* hier herüber *or* hierher; **from ~ on in** (*esp US*) von jetzt *or* nun an.
(b) (*in phrases*) **~ you are** (*giving sb sth*) hier (,bitte); (*on finding sb*) da bist du ja!, ach, hier bist du!; (*on finding sth*) da *or* hier ist es ja; **~ we are, home again** so, da wären wir also wieder zu Hause; **~ we are again, confronted by yet another crisis** so, da hätten wir also wieder eine neue Krise; **~ he comes** da kommt *or* ist er ja; **look out, ~ he comes** Vorsicht, er kommt!; **~ comes trouble** jetzt geht's los (*inf*); **~ goes!** (*before attempting sth*) dann mal los; **~, try this one** hier, versuch's mal damit; **~, let me do that** komm, laß mich das mal machen; **~!** he!; **~'s to you!** (*in toasts*) auf Ihr Wohl!; **~'s to the success of the venture!** auf den Erfolg des Vorhabens!; **it's neither ~ nor there** es spielt keine Rolle, tut nichts zur Sache.
2 *n* **the ~ and now** das Hier und Heute; (*Rel, Philos*) das Diesseits.
here: ~abouts [ˈhɪərəbaʊts] *adv* hier herum, in dieser Gegend; **~after** **1** *adv* (*in books, contracts: following this*) im folgenden; (*in the future also*) künftig, in Zukunft; (*after death*) im Jenseits; **during my lifetime and ~after** zu meinen Lebzeiten und danach; **2** *n* **the ~after** das Jenseits; **~by** *adv* (*form*) hiermit.
hereditable [həˈredɪtəbl] *adj* (*Jur*) vererbbar; (*Med also*) (ver)erblich.
hereditary [hɪˈredɪtərɪ] *adj* erblich, Erb- ◆ **~ enemies** Erbfeinde *pl*; **~ disease** Erbkrankheit *f*; **to be ~** (*also hum*) erblich sein.
heredity [hɪˈredɪtɪ] *n* Vererbung *f* ◆ **the title is his by ~** er hat den Titel geerbt/wird den Titel erben.
here: ~in *adv* (*form*) hierin, darin; **~inafter** *adv* (*form*) im folgenden; **~of** *adv* (*form*) hiervon (*form*); **the house and the inhabitants ~of** das Haus und die Bewohner desselben (*form*).
heresy [ˈherəsɪ] *n* Ketzerei, Häresie (*spec*) *f* ◆ **heresies** Ketzereien, ketzerische Lehren *pl*.
heretic [ˈherətɪk] *n* Ketzer(in *f*), Häretiker(in *f*) (*spec*) *m*.
heretical [hɪˈretɪkəl] *adj* ketzerisch, häretisch (*spec*).
here: ~to *adv* (*form*) **the documents attached ~to** die beigefügten Dokumente; **his reply ~to** seine Antwort darauf/hierauf; **he gave his signature ~to** er setzte seine Unterschrift hinzu; **~tofore** *adv* (*form*) (*up to this time*) bisher; (*up to that time*) bis dahin; **~unto** *adv* (*form*) *see* **hereto**; **~upon** *adv* daraufhin; **~with** *adv* (*form*) hiermit.
heritable [ˈherɪtəbl] *adj* **(a)** erblich. **(b)** (*Jur*) *person* erbfähig.
heritage [ˈherɪtɪdʒ] *n* (*lit, fig*) Erbe *nt*, Erbschaft *f*.
heritage centre *n* (*Brit*) *auf ein bestimmtes Gebiet spezialisiertes (Heimat)museum*.
hermaphrodite [hɜːˈmæfrədaɪt] **1** *n* Zwitter, Hermaphrodit (*geh*) *m*.
2 *adj* zwittrig, hermaphroditisch (*geh*); *plants also* gemischtgeschlechtig.
hermetic [hɜːˈmetɪk] *adj* hermetisch.
hermetically [hɜːˈmetɪkəlɪ] *adv see adj* ◆ **~ sealed** hermetisch verschlossen *or* (*fig*) abgeriegelt.
hermit [ˈhɜːmɪt] *n* Einsiedler (*also fig*), Eremit *m*.
hermitage [ˈhɜːmɪtɪdʒ] *n* (*lit, fig*) Einsiedelei, Klause *f*.
hermit crab *n* Einsiedlerkrebs *m*.
hernia [ˈhɜːnɪə] *n* (Eingeweide)bruch *m*, Hernie *f* (*spec*).
hero [ˈhɪərəʊ] *n, pl* **-es** Held, Heros (*geh*) *m*; (*fig: object of hero-worship also*) Idol *nt*; (*Liter: of novel etc*) Held *m* ◆ **the ~ of the hour** der Held des Tages; **the ~ of the rescue** der mutige *or* beherzte Retter.
Herod [ˈherəd] *n* Herodes *m*.
heroic [hɪˈrəʊɪk] **1** *adj* mutig, heldenhaft, heldenmütig; *behaviour, action, decision also* heroisch; (*daring*) kühn; *proportions, size* mächtig, gewaltig; *effort* gewaltig; *words* heroisch ◆ **~ age/deed** Heldenzeitalter *nt*/Heldentat *f*; **~ couplet** Heroic Couplet *nt*, *Reimpaar nt aus fünffüßigen Jamben*; **~ verse** heroischer Vers; **~ tenor** Heldentenor *m*.
2 *n* **~s** *pl* hochtrabende *or* große Worte *pl* ◆ **the actor's ~s** das übertriebene Pathos des Schauspielers; **the goalkeeper's ~s** (*inf*) die Heldentaten des Torwarts (*inf*).
heroically [hɪˈrəʊɪkəlɪ] *adv see adj* ◆ **a ~ worded speech** eine pathetische Rede.
heroin [ˈherəʊɪn] *n* Heroin *nt* ◆ **~ addict** Heroinsüchtige(r) *mf*.
heroine [ˈherəʊɪn] *n* Heldin *f*; (*Theat also*) Heroine *f*.
heroism [ˈherəʊɪzəm] *n* Heldentum *nt*; (*heroic conduct*) (Helden)mut, Heroismus *m*; (*daring*) Kühnheit *f* ◆ **I'm not one for ~** ich bin kein Held.
heron [ˈherən] *n* Reiher *m*.
hero-worship [ˈhiːrəʊˌwɜːʃɪp] **1** *n* Verehrung *f* (*of gen*); (*in ancient tribe etc*) Heldenverehrung *f*; (*of popstar etc*) Schwärmerei *f* (*of* für) ◆ **the ~ of a boy for his older brother** die blinde Bewunderung eines Jungen für seinen älteren Bruder.
2 *vt* anbeten, verehren; *popstar etc* schwärmen für.
herpes [ˈhɜːpiːz] *n* (*Med*) Herpes *m*.
herring [ˈherɪŋ] *n* Hering *m* ◆ **~-gull** Silbermöwe *f*; **~-pond** (*hum inf*) großer Teich (*hum*); *see* **red ~**.
herringbone [ˈherɪŋbəʊn] **1** *n* **(a)** (*pattern*) Fischgrät *m*. **(b)** (*Ski*) Grätenschritt *m*.
2 *adj attr* **~ pattern** Fischgrät(en)muster *nt*; **~ stitch** Hexenstich *m*; **~ suit** Anzug *m* mit Fischgrätmuster.
hers [hɜːz] *poss pron* ihre(r, s) ◆ **~** (*on towels etc*) sie; *see also* **mine**[1].
herself [hɜːˈself] **1** *pers pron* **(a)** (*dir and indir obj, with prep*) sich; *see also* **myself**. **(b)** (*emph*) (sie) selbst.
2 *n* (*Ir inf*) **it was ~ who told me** sie selbst hat es mir gesagt.
Herts [hɑːts] *abbr of* **Hertfordshire**.
he's [hiːz] *contr of* **he is**; **he has**.

hesitancy ['hezɪtənsɪ] *n* Zögern, Zaudern (*geh*) *nt*.

hesitant ['hezɪtənt] *adj answer, smile* zögernd; *person also* unentschlossen, unschlüssig ◆ **he was so ~ that ...** er zögerte so lange, bis ...; **he was very ~ to accept** er zögerte lange *or* war sich (*dat*) sehr unschlüssig, ob er annehmen sollte.

hesitantly ['hezɪtəntlɪ] *adj accept* zögernd, zaudernd (*geh*).

hesitate ['hezɪteɪt] *vi* zögern, zaudern (*geh*); (*in speech*) stocken ◆ **if they don't stop hesitating we'll be lost** wenn sie noch länger zögern, sind wir verloren; **he who ~s is lost** (*Prov*) dem Feigen kehrt das Glück den Rücken (*Prov*); **I ~ to ask him over** ich bin mir nicht schlüssig, ob ich ihn herüberbitten soll; **I'd ~ to take** *or* **at taking on such a task** ich würde es mir gut überlegen, ob ich so eine Aufgabe übernehmen würde; **I ~d at the expenditure/about having a child at my age** ich hatte Bedenken wegen der Ausgabe/ich hatte Bedenken, in meinem Alter ein Kind zu bekommen; **even he would ~ at murder** selbst er hätte bei einem Mord Bedenken; **he ~s at nothing** er macht vor nichts halt, er schreckt vor nichts zurück; **I am still hesitating about what I should do** ich bin mir immer noch nicht schlüssig, was ich tun soll; **I ~ to say it, but ...** es widerstrebt mir, das zu sagen, aber ...; **if I did think that, I wouldn't ~ to say so** wenn ich wirklich der Meinung (*gen*) wäre, hätte ich keine Hemmungen, es zu sagen; **don't ~ to ask me** fragen Sie ruhig; (*more formally*) zögern Sie nicht, mich zu fragen.

hesitation [ˌhezɪ'teɪʃən] *n* Zögern, Zaudern (*geh*) *nt* ◆ **a moment's ~** ein Augenblick des Zögerns; **without the slightest ~** ohne auch nur einen Augenblick zu zögern; **I have no ~ in saying that ...** ich kann ohne weiteres sagen, daß ...

hessian ['hesɪən] 1 *n* Sackleinwand *f*, Rupfen *m*.
2 *attr* Rupfen-.

hetero ['hetərəʊ] *n* (*sl*) Hetero *m* (*inf*), Heterosexuelle(r) *mf* ◆ **he's a good straight ~** er ist sexuell total normal (*inf*), er ist einwandfrei hetero (*sl*).

heterodox ['hetərədɒks] *adj* heterodox, andersgläubig.

heterodoxy ['hetərədɒksɪ] *n* Heterodoxie, Andersgläubigkeit *f*.

heterogeneity [ˌhetərəʊdʒɪ'neɪtɪ] *n* Heterogenität *f*.

heterogeneous [ˌhetərəʊ'dʒiːnɪəs] *adj* heterogen.

heterosexual [ˌhetərəʊ'seksjʊəl] 1 *adj* heterosexuell.
2 *n* Heterosexuelle(r) *mf*.

heterosexuality [ˌhetərəʊˌseksjʊ'ælɪtɪ] *n* Heterosexualität *f*.

het up ['hetˌʌp] *adj* (*inf*) aufgeregt ◆ **to get ~ about/over sth** sich über etw (*acc*)/wegen einer Sache (*gen*) aufregen.

heuristic [hjʊə'rɪstɪk] 1 *adj* heuristisch.
2 *n* **~s** *sing* Heuristik *f*.

hew [hjuː] *pret* **~ed**, *ptp* **hewn** *or* **~ed** *vt* hauen; (*shape*) behauen ◆ **to ~ into pieces/logs** in Stücke hauen/zu Klötzen hacken; **they ~ed their captives to pieces** sie zerstückelten ihre Gefangenen.

◆**hew down** *vt sep trees* fällen, umhauen; *persons* niederhauen; (*with machine gun also*) niedermähen.

◆**hew off** *vt sep* abhauen, abhacken, abschlagen.

◆**hew out** *vt sep* heraushauen, herausschlagen (*of* aus) ◆ **he's ~n ~ a career for himself** er hat sich (*dat*) seine Karriere erkämpft; **they ~ed ~ a formula for peace** sie schmiedeten eine Friedensformel.

◆**hew up** *vt sep* zerstückeln; *wood* zerhacken.

hewer ['hjuːəʳ] *n* (*Min*) Hauer *m* ◆ **~s of wood** Holzhauer *pl*.

hex [heks] (*esp US inf*) 1 *n* Fluch *m* ◆ **there must be a ~ on this project** dieses Unternehmen muß verhext sein (*inf*); (*more serious*) auf dem Unternehmen muß ein Fluch liegen; **to put a ~ on sth** etw verhexen.
2 *vt* verhexen.

hexadecimal [ˌheksə'desɪməl] *adj* hexadezimal.

hexagon ['heksəgən] *n* Sechseck, Hexagon *nt*.

hexagonal [hek'sægənəl] *adj* sechseckig, hexagonal.

hexameter [hek'sæmɪtəʳ] *n* Hexameter *m*.

hex code *n* (*Comput*) Hexadezimalzahl *f*.

hey [heɪ] *interj* (*to attract attention*) he (Sie/du); (*in surprise*) he, Mensch (*inf*) ◆ **~ presto** Hokuspokus (Fidibus).

heyday ['heɪdeɪ] *n* Glanzzeit, Blütezeit *f* ◆ **in the ~ of its power** auf dem Höhepunkt seiner Macht; **in his ~** in seiner Glanzzeit.

Hezbollah [ˌhezbə'lɑː] *n see* **Hizbollah**.

HGV (*Brit*) *abbr of* **heavy goods vehicle** LKW *m*.

HH *abbr, adj* (*on pencil*) HH, 2H.

hi [haɪ] *interj* hallo.

hiatus [haɪ'eɪtəs] *n* Lücke *f*; (*Gram, Poet*) Hiatus *m*.

hibernate ['haɪbəneɪt] *vi* Winterschlaf halten *or* machen.

hibernation [ˌhaɪbə'neɪʃən] *n* (*lit, fig*) Winterschlaf *m*.

Hibernian [hɪ'bɜːnɪən] *adj* (*Poet*) hibernisch.

hibiscus [hɪ'bɪskəs] *n* Hibiskus, Eibisch *m*.

hiccough, hiccup ['hɪkʌp] 1 *n* Schluckauf *m*; (*fig inf: problem*) Problemchen *nt* (*inf*) ◆ **to have the ~s** den Schluckauf haben; **to let out/give a ~** hick machen (*inf*), hicksen (*dial*); **the computer had a slight ~** (*fig inf*) der Computer spielte leicht verrückt (*inf*); **without any ~s** ohne Störungen.
2 *vi* hicksen (*dial*) ◆ **he started ~ing** er bekam den Schluckauf.

hick [hɪk] *n* (*US inf*) Hinterwäldler *m* (*inf*); (*female*) Landpomeranze *f* (*inf*).

hickory ['hɪkərɪ] *n* (*tree*) Hickory(nußbaum) *m*; (*wood*) Hikkory(holz) *nt*.

hide¹ [haɪd] (*vb: pret* **hid** [hɪd], *ptp* **hidden** ['hɪdn] *or* **hid**) 1 *vt* verstecken (*from* vor +*dat*); *truth, tears, grief, feelings, face* verbergen (*from* vor +*dat*); (*obstruct from view*) *moon, rust* verdecken ◆ **hidden from view** nicht zu sehen, dem Blick *or* den Blicken entzogen; **he's hiding something in his pocket** er hat etwas in seiner Tasche versteckt; **I have nothing to ~** ich habe nichts zu verbergen; **his words had a hidden meaning** seine Worte hatten eine verborgene *or* versteckte Bedeutung; **you're hiding something from me** (*truth etc*) Sie verheimlichen mir etwas, Sie verbergen etwas vor mir.
2 *vi* sich verstecken, sich verbergen (*from sb* vor jdm) ◆ **quick! ~ in the cupboard** schnell, versteck dich im Schrank!; **he was hiding in the cupboard** er hielt sich im Schrank versteckt *or* verborgen; **he's just hiding behind his boss/his reputation** er versteckt sich bloß hinter seinem Chef/Ruf.
3 *n* Versteck *nt*.

◆**hide away** 1 *vi* sich verstecken, sich verbergen.
2 *vt sep* verstecken.

◆**hide out** *or* **up** *vi* sich verstecken; (*to be hiding also*) sich versteckt *or* verborgen halten.

hide² *n* (*of animal*) Haut *f*; (*on furry animal*) Fell *nt*; (*processed*) Leder *nt*; (*fig: of person*) Haut *f*, Fell *nt* ◆ **the bags are made out of the finest ~** die Taschen sind aus feinstem Leder; **to save one's own ~** die eigene Haut retten; **I haven't seen ~ nor hair of him for weeks** (*inf*) den habe ich in den letzten Wochen nicht mal von weitem gesehen.

hide: ~-and-seek *n* Versteckspiel *nt*; **to play ~-and-seek** Verstecken spielen; **~away** *n* Versteck *nt*; (*refuge*) Zufluchtsort *m*; **~bound** *adj person, views* engstirnig; **an officer of the old school, ~bound by convention** ein Offizier der alten Schule, der den Konventionen verhaftet ist.

hideous ['hɪdɪəs] *adj* grauenhaft, scheußlich; *colour also, day, disappointment* schrecklich.

hideousness ['hɪdɪəsnɪs] *n see adj* Grauenhaftigkeit, Scheußlichkeit *f*; Schrecklichkeit *f*.

hideout ['haɪdaʊt] *n* Versteck *nt*.

hiding¹ ['haɪdɪŋ] *n* **to be in ~** sich versteckt halten; **to go into ~** untertauchen, sich verstecken; **he came out of ~** er tauchte wieder auf, er kam aus seinem Versteck; **~ place** Versteck *nt*.

hiding² *n* **(a)** (*beating*) Tracht *f* Prügel ◆ **to give sb a good ~** jdm eine Tracht Prügel geben. **(b)** (*inf: defeat*) Schlappe *f* (*inf*) ◆ **the team got a real ~** die Mannschaft mußte eine schwere Schlappe einstecken (*inf*).

hie [haɪ] *vr* (*old, hum*) eilends laufen ◆ **~ thee hence!** hebe dich hinweg (*old, hum*).

hierarchic(al) [ˌhaɪə'rɑːkɪk(əl)] *adj*, **hierarchically** [ˌhaɪə'rɑːkɪkəlɪ] *adv* hierarchisch.

hierarchy ['haɪərɑːkɪ] *n* Hierarchie *f*.

hieroglyph ['haɪərəglɪf] *n* Hieroglyphe *f*.

hieroglyphic [ˌhaɪərə'glɪfɪk] 1 *adj* hieroglyphisch.
2 *n* **~s** *pl* Hieroglyphen(schrift *f*) *pl*.

hi-fi ['haɪˌfaɪ] 1 *n* **(a)** Hi-Fi *nt*. **(b)** (*system*) Hi-Fi-Anlage *f*.
2 *adj* Hi-Fi- ◆ **~ equipment** Hi-Fi-Geräte *pl*.

higgledy-piggledy ['hɪgldɪ'pɪgldɪ] 1 *adv* durcheinander, wie Kraut und Rüben (*inf*).
2 *adj* durcheinander; (*confused*) wirr.

high [haɪ] 1 *adj* (*+er*) **(a)** *mountain, wall, forehead, building* hoch *pred*, hohe(r, s) *attr* ◆ **a building 80 metres ~** ein 80 Meter hohes Gebäude; **a ~ dive** ein Kopfsprung *m* aus großer Höhe; **the ~er flats are more expensive** die oberen Wohnungen sind teurer; **on one of the ~er floors** in einem der oberen Stockwerke; **he lives on a ~er floor** er wohnt weiter oben; **the ~est flat/floor** die oberste Wohnung/Etage; **at ~ tide** *or* **water** bei Flut *or* Hochwasser; **the river is quite ~** der Fluß führt ziemlich viel Wasser; **~ and dry** (*boat*) auf dem Trockenen; **he left her ~ and dry with four little children** er hat sie mit vier kleinen Kindern sitzen lassen; **to be left ~ and dry** auf dem Trockenen sitzen (*inf*); **I knew him when he was only so ~** ich kannte ihn, als er nur *so* groß war *or* noch so klein war.
(b) (*important, superior*) hoch *pred*, hohe(r, s) *attr* ◆ **~ office** hohes Amt; **on the ~est authority** von höchster Stelle; **to be** *or* **act ~ and mighty** erhaben tun; **to be on one's ~ horse** (*fig*) auf dem hohen Roß sitzen; **O Lord most ~** (*Bibl*) erhabener Gott.
(c) (*considerable, extreme, great*) *opinion, speed, temperature, fever, pressure, salary, price, rate, density, sea* hoch *pred*, hohe(r, s) *attr*; *altitude* groß; *wind* stark; *complexion, colour* (hoch)rot ◆ **in the ~ latitudes** in fernen Breiten; **to pay a ~ price for sth** (*lit, fig*) etw teuer bezahlen; **to set a ~ value on sth** etw hoch einschätzen; **the ~est common factor** der größte gemeinsame Teiler; **in the ~est degree** im höchsten Grad *or* Maß; **in (very) ~ spirits** in Hochstimmung, in äußerst guter Laune; **to have a ~ old time** (*inf*) sich prächtig amüsieren, mächtig Spaß haben (*inf*); **it was ~ drama** es war hochdramatisch.
(d) (*good, admirable*) *ideals* hoch ◆ **a ~ calling** ein Ruf zu Höherem; **a man of ~ character** ein Mann von Charakter.
(e) (*of time*) **~ noon** zwölf Uhr mittags; **it's ~ time you went home/understood** es ist *or* wird höchste Zeit, daß du nach Hause gehst/endlich begreifst.
(f) *sound, note* hoch; (*shrill*) schrill.
(g) (*sl*) (*on drugs*) high (*sl*); (*on drink*) blau (*sl*).
(h) *meat* angegangen; *game also* anbrüchig (*spec*).
(i) (*Cards*) hoch *pred*, hohe(r, s) *attr* ◆ **aces ~** As ist die höchste (Stich)karte.
2 *adv* (*+er*) **(a)** hoch ◆ **~ up** (*position*) hoch oben; (*motion*) hoch hinauf; **one floor ~er** ein Stockwerk höher.
(b) to go as ~ as £200 bis zu £ 200 (hoch)gehen; **the sea is running ~** das Meer ist sehr stürmisch; **feelings ran ~** die Gemüter erhitzten sich; **to search ~ and low** überall suchen.
3 *n* **(a) God on ~** Gott in der Höhe *or* im Himmel; **the orders have come from on ~** (*hum inf*) der Befehl kommt von oben.

(b) **unemployment has reached a new ~** die Arbeitslosenziffern haben einen neuen Höchststand erreicht.
(c) (*Met*) Hoch *nt.*
(d) (*sl: on drugs*) **he's still got his ~** er ist immer noch high.
(e) (*US Aut: top gear*) **in ~** im höchsten Gang; **he moved into ~** er schaltete hoch *or* in den vierten/fünften Gang.
(f) (*US inf: high school*) Penne *f* (*inf*).

high: ~ altar *n* Hochaltar *m*; **~ball** *n* (*US*) Highball *m*; **~ beam** *n* (*Aut*) Fernlicht *nt*; **~born** *adj* von hoher Geburt, von edler Abkunft (*liter*); **~ boy** *n* (*US*) hohe Kommode; **~brow** [1] *n* Intellektuelle(r) *mf*; [2] *adj interests* intellektuell, hochgestochen (*pej*); *tastes, music* anspruchsvoll; **~chair** *n* Hochstuhl *m*; **H~ Church** [1] *n* Hochkirche *f*; [2] *adj* der Hochkirche; **to be very H~ Church** streng hochkirchlich eingestellt sein; **~-class** *adj* hochwertig; *shop* Qualitäts-; **~-class prostitute** Edelnutte *f* (*inf*); **~ comedy** *n* Gesellschaftskomödie *f*; **~ commission** *n* Hochkommissariat *nt*; **~ commissioner** *n* Hochkommissar *m*; **~ court** *n* oberstes *or* höchstes Gericht; (*institution also*) oberster Gerichtshof; **~ court judge** *n* Richter *m* am obersten Gerichtshof; **~-density** *adj* **(a)** *housing* dicht; **(b)** (*Comput*) *disk* mit hoher Schreibdichte; **~ diving** *n* Turmspringen *nt*; **~-energy** *adj particle, food* energiereich.

higher [ˈhaɪəʳ] [1] *adj* **(a)** *comp of* **high**. **(b)** *mathematics, education* höher; *animals, life-forms* höher (entwickelt) ◆ **H~ National Certificate** (*Brit*) ≃ Berufsschulabschluß *m*; **H~ National Diploma** (*Brit*) *Qualifikationsnachweis m in technischen Fächern.*
[2] *n* **H~** (*Scot*) ≃ Abschluß *m* der Sekundarstufe 2 ◆ **to take one's H~s** ≃ das Abitur machen; **3 H~s** ein Schulabschluß *m* in drei Fächern.

higher-up [ˈhaɪərʌp] *n* (*inf*) höheres Tier (*inf*).

▼ **high: ~ explosive** *n* hochexplosiver Sprengstoff; **~-explosive shell** *n* Sprenggranate *f*, Brisanzgeschoß *nt*; **~-falutin** [ˌhaɪfəˈluːtɪn], **~-faluting** [ˌhaɪfəˈluːtɪŋ] *adj* (*inf*) *language, behaviour* hochtrabend, geschwollen; *people* aufgeblasen, hochgestochen; **~-fibre** *adj diet* ballaststoffreich; **~-fidelity** [1] *n* High-Fidelity, Tontreue *f*; [2] *adj* High-Fidelity-; **~ flier** *n* (*inf*) (*successful person*) Senkrechtstarter *m*; (*ambitious*) Ehrgeizling *m* (*pej*); **he's a ~ flier** er ist ein Erfolgstyp (*inf*); **~-flown** *adj style, speech* hochtrabend, geschwollen; *ambitions* hochgesteckt; *ideas, plans* hochfliegend; **~-flying** *adj aircraft* mit großer Flughöhe; (*fig*) *businessman* erfolgreich; *lifestyle* exklusiv; **~ frequency** [1] *n* Hochfrequenz *f*; [2] *adj* Hochfrequenz-; **H~ German** *n* Hochdeutsch *nt*; **~-grade** *adj* hochwertig; *ore* gediegen; **~-handed** *adj* eigenmächtig; *character* überheblich; **~-hat** (*US inf*) [1] *adj* hochnäsig (*inf*); [2] *n* hochnäsiger Typ (*inf*); [3] *vt* herablassend behandeln, von oben herab behandeln; **~-heeled** *adj* mit hohen Absätzen, hochhackig; **~ heels** *npl* hohe Absätze *pl*; **~jack** *vt, n see* **hijack**; **~jacker** *n see* **hijacker**; **~ jinks** *npl* (*inf*) **they were having ~ jinks** bei denen war Highlife (*inf*); **~ jump** *n* (*Sport*) Hochsprung *m*; **to be for the ~ jump** (*fig inf*) dran sein (*inf*); **~land** *adj* Hochland-, hochländisch; **H~lander** *n* Bewohner(in *f*) *m* des schottischen Hochlands; **H~land fling** *n schottischer Volkstanz*; **H~land Games** *npl schottisches Volksfest mit traditionellen Wettkämpfen*; **H~lands** *npl* schottisches Hochland; (*generally*) Berg- *or* Hochland *nt*; **~-level** *adj talks, discussion* auf höchster Ebene; *road* Hoch-; (*Comput*) *language* höher; **~ life** *n* Highlife
▼ *nt*, Leben *nt* in großem Stil; **~light** [1] *n* **(a)** (*Art, Phot*) Glanzlicht *nt*; (*in hair*) Strähne *f*; **~lights** (*in hair*) Strähnchen *pl*; **(b)** (*fig*) Höhepunkt *m*; [2] *vt* **(a)** *need, problem* ein Schlaglicht werfen auf (+*acc*), hervorheben; **(b)** *text* (*with ~lighter*) hervorheben, markieren; (*on computer screen*) markieren; *hair* Strähnen machen in (+*acc*); **~lighter** *n* **(a)** (*pen*) Leuchtstift, Textmarker *m*; **(b)** (*for hair*) Aufheller *m*; (*cosmetic*) Töner *m*; **~ living** *n* flottes *or* (*pej*) ausschweifendes Leben.

highly [ˈhaɪlɪ] *adv* hoch- ◆ **~ spiced dishes** stark *or* (*hot*) scharf gewürzte Gerichte; **to be ~ paid** hoch bezahlt werden; **to think ~ of sb** eine hohe Meinung von jdm haben, große Stücke auf jdn halten; **to speak ~ of sb** sich sehr positiv über jdn äußern.

highly: ~-charged *adj atmosphere* aufgeladen; *debate* hitzig; **~-coloured** *adj* (*lit*) farbenfroh, sehr bunt; (*fig*) *report, description* (*one-sided*) stark gefärbt; (*detailed*) ausgeschmückt; **~-strung** *adj* nervös.

high: H~ Mass *n* Hochamt *nt*; **~-minded** *adj* hochgeistig; *ideals* hoch; **~-necked** *adj* hochgeschlossen.

highness [ˈhaɪnɪs] *n* **(a)** Höhe *f* ◆ **~ of ideals** hohe Ideale *pl.* **(b)** **Her/Your H~** Ihre/Eure Hoheit; **yes, Your H~** ja, Hoheit.

high: ~-octane *adj* mit einer hohen Oktanzahl; **~-performance** *adj* Hochleistungs-; **~-pitched** *adj* **(a)** *sound* hoch; **(b)** (*Archit*) *roof* steil; **~ point** *n* Höhepunkt *m*; **~-powered** *adj* **(a)** *car* stark(motorig), Hochleistungs-; **(b)** (*fig*) *businessman, politician* Vollblut-; *academic* Spitzen-; *conversation* sehr anspruchsvoll, hochintellektuell; **our new ~-powered professor** unser neuer Professor, der wirklich was auf dem Kasten hat (*inf*); **~-pressure** *adj* **(a)** (*Tech, Met*) Hochdruck-; **~-pressure area** Hochdruckgebiet *nt*; **a ~-pressure area over the Atlantic** ein Hoch(druckgebiet) über dem Atlantik, ein atlantisches Hoch; **(b)** (*fig*) *salesman* aufdringlich; *sales technique* aggressiv; **~-priced** *adj* teuer; **~ priest** *n* (*lit, fig*) Hohepriester *m*; **a ~ priest** ein Hoherpriester *m*; **of the ~ priest** des Hohenpriesters; **~-profile** *adj* profiliert; **~-protein** *adj* eiweißreich; **~-ranking** *adj* hoch(rangig), von hohem Rang; **~ relief** *n* Hochrelief *nt*; **~-resolution** *adj screen, graphics* hochauflösend; **~-rise** *adj* Hochhaus-; **~-rise flats** *npl* (Wohn)hochhaus *nt*; **~-risk** *adj* risikoreich; **~-risk group/patient** Risikogruppe *f*/-patient(in *f*) *m*; **~road** *n* (*old*) Landstraße *f*; **the ~road to success** der sichere Weg zum Erfolg; **~ school** *n* (*US*) Oberschule *f*; **~ seas** *npl* **the ~ seas** die Meere *pl*; **on the ~ seas** auf hoher See, auf offenem Meer; **~-security prison** *n* Hochsicherheitsgefängnis *nt*; **~-security wing** *n* Hochsicherheitstrakt *m*; **~ society** *n* High-Society *f*; **~-sounding** *adj* klangvoll; **~-speed** *adj* Schnell-; *printer also, train* Hochgeschwindigkeits-; *drill* mit hoher Umdrehungszahl; **~-speed lens** hochlichtstarkes Objektiv, lichtstarke Linse; **~-speed film** hoch(licht)empfindlicher Film; **~-spirited** *adj* temperamentvoll, lebhaft; **~ spirits** *npl* Hochstimmung *f*; **youthful ~ spirits** jugendlicher Übermut; **~ spot** *n* Höhepunkt *m*; **to hit the ~ spots** (*inf*) auf den Putz hauen (*inf*); **~ street** *n* (*Brit*) Hauptstraße *f*; **~ street banks** *npl* Geschäftsbanken *pl*; **~ street shops** *npl* Geschäfte *pl* in der Innenstadt; **~-strung** *adj* (*US*) nervös; **~ summer** *n* Hochsommer *m*; **~ table** *n* (*Sch*) Lehrertisch *m*; (*Univ*) Tisch *m* für Professoren und Dozenten.

hightail [ˈhaɪteɪl] *vi* (*US sl*) **to ~ (it) out of a place** (aus einem Ort) abhauen (*inf*), (von *or* aus einem Ort) verduften (*sl*).

high: ~ tea *n* (frühes) Abendessen; **~tech** [ˈhaɪˌtek] *n, adj see* **hitech**; **~ technology** *n* Hochtechnologie, Spitzentechnologie *f*; **~-tension** *adj* (*Elec*) Hochspannungs-; **~ treason** *n* Hochverrat *m*; **~-up** [1] *adj person* hochgestellt; [2] *n* (*inf*) hohes Tier (*inf*); **~-water mark** *n* (*lit*) Hochwasserstandsmarke *f*; (*fig*) höchster Stand; **~way** *n* Landstraße *f*; **public ~way** öffentliche Straße; **the ~ways and byways** Straßen und Wege; **he knows all the ~ways and byways of Dorset** er kennt Weg und Steg in Dorset; **~way code** *n* Straßenverkehrsordnung *f*; **~wayman** *n* Räuber, Wegelagerer, Strauchdieb *m*; **~way robbery** *n* Straßenraub *m*; (*fig inf*) Nepp *m* (*inf*); **H~ways Department** *n* Tiefbauamt *nt*; **~ wire** *n* Drahtseil *nt*; **~-yield** *adj* (*Agr*) Hochleistungs-.

hijack [ˈhaɪdʒæk] [1] *vt* entführen; (*rob*) *lorry* überfallen.
[2] *n see vt* Entführung *f*; Überfall *m* (*of* auf +*acc*).

hijacker [ˈhaɪdʒækəʳ] *n see vt* Entführer *m*; Räuber *m*.

hike [haɪk] [1] *vi* wandern.
[2] *n* **(a)** Wanderung *f*. **(b)** (*in interest rates*) Erhöhung *f*.

◆**hike up** *vt sep* hochziehen.

hiker [ˈhaɪkəʳ] *n* Wanderer *m*, Wanderin *f*.

hiking [ˈhaɪkɪŋ] *n* Wandern *nt* ◆ **~ boots** Wanderstiefel *pl*.

hilarious [hɪˈlɛərɪəs] *adj* sehr komisch *or* lustig, urkomisch (*inf*); (*loud and happy*) *mood* ausgelassen, übermütig.

hilariously [hɪˈlɛərɪəslɪ] *adv* **~ funny** zum Schreien.

hilarity [hɪˈlærɪtɪ] *n* (*of person, party etc*) übermütige Ausgelassenheit; (*of film*) Komik *f* ◆ **his statement caused some ~** seine Behauptung löste einige Heiterkeit aus.

Hilary [ˈhɪlərɪ] *n* (*Oxford Univ*) Frühjahrstrimester *nt*; (*Jur*) Frühjahrssitzungsperiode *f*.

hill [hɪl] *n* **(a)** Hügel *m*; (*higher*) Berg *m*; (*incline*) Hang *m* ◆ **the castle stands on a ~** das Schloß steht auf einem Berg; **the houses on the ~ beneath the castle** die Häuser am Schloßberg; **these flats are built on a ~** diese Wohnungen sind am Hang *or* Berg gebaut; **to park on a ~** am Berg parken; **up ~ and down dale** bergauf und bergab; **over ~ and dale** über Berg und Tal; **this car takes the ~s beautifully** dieses Auto nimmt Steigungen mühelos; **as old as the ~s** steinalt, uralt; **that joke's as old as the ~s** der Witz hat ja so einen langen Bart; **to take to the ~s** sich in die Berge flüchten; **to be over the ~** (*fig inf*) seine beste Zeit *or* die besten Jahre hinter sich (*dat*) haben.
(b) *see* **anthill, molehill** *etc.*

hillbilly [ˈhɪlbɪlɪ] (*US inf*) [1] *n* Hinterwäldler *m* (*pej*); (*female*) Landpomeranze *f* (*inf*).
[2] *adj* hinterwäldlerisch (*pej*) ◆ **~ music** Hillbilly *no art*, Hillbilly-Musik *f*.

hilliness [ˈhɪlɪnɪs] *n* Hügeligkeit *f*; (*higher*) Bergigkeit *f* ◆ **the ~ of the terrain** das hügelige *or* (*higher*) bergige Gelände.

hillock [ˈhɪlək] *n* Hügel *m*, Anhöhe *f*.

hill: ~side *n* Hang *m*; **~top** *n* Gipfel *m*; **~-walker** *n* Bergwanderer *m*, Bergwanderin *f*; **~-walking** *n* Bergwandern *nt*.

hilly [ˈhɪlɪ] *adj* (+*er*) hüg(e)lig; (*higher*) bergig.

hilt [hɪlt] *n* Heft *nt*; (*of dagger*) Griff *m* ◆ **up to the ~** (*fig*) voll und ganz; (*involved, in debt also*) bis über beide Ohren (*inf*); **I'll back you up to the ~** ich stehe voll und ganz hinter Ihnen.

him [hɪm] *pers pron* **(a)** (*dir obj, with prep* +*acc*) ihn; (*indir obj, with prep* +*dat*) ihm; (*when he is previously mentioned in clause*) sich ◆ **with his things around ~** mit seinen Sachen um sich. **(b)** (*emph*) er ◆ **it's ~** er ist's; **who, ~?** wer, er?

Himalayan [ˌhɪməˈleɪən] *adj* Himalaya-, des Himalaya.

Himalayas [ˌhɪməˈleɪəz] *npl* Himalaya *m*.

himself [hɪmˈself] [1] *pers pron* **(a)** (*dir and indir obj, with prep*) sich; *see also* **myself**. **(b)** (*emph*) (er) selbst.
[2] *n* (*Ir inf*) **it was ~ who told me** er selbst hat es mir gesagt.

hind¹ [haɪnd] *n* (*Zool*) Hirschkuh, Hindin (*poet*) *f*.

hind² *adj, superl* **hindmost** hintere(r, s) ◆ **~ legs** Hinterbeine *pl*; **to get up on one's ~ legs** (*inf: speak in public*) den Mund aufmachen (*inf*); **she could talk the ~ legs off a donkey** (*inf*) sie redet wie ein Buch (*inf*).

hinder [ˈhɪndəʳ] *vt* **(a)** (*obstruct, impede*) behindern; (*delay*) *person* aufhalten; *arrival* verzögern. **(b)** (*stop, prevent from happening*) **to ~ sb from doing sth** jdn daran hindern *or* davon abhalten, etw zu tun.

Hindi [ˈhɪndiː] *n* Hindi *nt*.

hind: ~most *adj superl of* **hind²** hinterste(r, s); **~quarters** *npl* Hinterteil *nt*; (*of carcass*) Hinterviertel *nt*; (*of horse*) Hinterhand *f*.

hindrance [ˈhɪndrəns] *n* Behinderung *f* ◆ **the rules/children are a ~** die Regeln/Kinder sind hinderlich; **it was a serious ~ to progress** es behinderte den Fortschritt sehr; **he/it is more of a ~ than a help** er/es hindert mehr, als daß er/es hilft; *see* **let¹**.

➤ LANGUAGE IN USE: **highlight : 1a → 26.3**

hindsight ['haɪndsaɪt] *n*: **now with the benefit/wisdom of ~** jetzt, hinterher *or* im nachhinein ist man ja immer schlauer; **with ~ it's easy to criticize** hinterher *or* im nachhinein ist es leicht zu kritisieren.

Hindu ['hɪnduː] [1] *adj customs, religion* hinduistisch, Hindu- ◆ **~ people** Hindu(s) *pl*.
[2] *n* Hindu *m*.

Hinduism ['hɪnduːɪzəm] *n* Hinduismus *m*.

Hindustan [,hɪndʊ'stɑːn] *n* Hindustan, Hindostan *nt*.

Hindustani [,hɪndʊ'stɑːnɪ] [1] *adj* hindustanisch.
[2] *n* **(a)** Bewohner(in *f*) *m* Hindustans. **(b)** (*language*) Hindustani *nt*.

hinge [hɪndʒ] [1] *n* **(a)** (*of door*) Angel *f*; (*of box etc*) Scharnier *nt*; (*of limb, shell*) Gelenk *nt*; (*fig*) Angelpunkt *m* ◆ **the door/lid is off its ~s** die Tür ist aus den Angeln/das Scharnier des Deckels ist ab; **take the door off its ~s** häng die Tür aus!
(b) (*also* **stamp ~**) (Klebe)falz *m*.
[2] *vt* **to ~ sth** etw mit Angeln/einem Scharnier an etw (*dat*) befestigen.
[3] *vi* (*fig*) abhängen (*on* von), ankommen (*on* auf +*acc*).

hinged [hɪndʒd] *adj* Scharnier-; *door* eingehängt; *lid also, box* mit einem Scharnier versehen.

hint [hɪnt] [1] *n* **(a)** (*intimation, suggestion*) Andeutung *f*, Hinweis *m* ◆ **to give a/no ~ of sth** etw ahnen lassen *or* andeuten/nicht ahnen lassen *or* andeuten; **to give** *or* **drop sb a ~** jdm einen Wink geben, jdm gegenüber eine Andeutung machen; **he was given a gentle ~ about attention to detail** man hat ihm leise angedeutet *or* den leisen Wink gegeben, auf Details zu achten; **to throw out** *or* **let fall** *or* **drop a ~** eine Andeutung machen, eine Bemerkung fallenlassen; **to know how to take a ~** einen Wink verstehen; **OK, I can take a ~** schon recht, ich verstehe *or* ich habe den Wink mit dem Zaunpfahl verstanden (*inf*); **I've almost run out of this perfume, ~, ~** ich habe fast nichts mehr von dem Parfüm, hörst du?
(b) (*trace*) Spur *f* ◆ **a ~ of garlic/irony** eine Spur Knoblauch/ein Hauch *m* von Spott; **with just a ~ of sadness in his smile** mit einem leichten Anflug von Traurigkeit in seinem Lächeln; **with the ~ of a smile** mit dem Anflug eines Lächelns; **not a ~ of tiredness** keine Spur von Müdigkeit.
(c) (*tip, piece of advice*) Tip *m* ◆ **~s for travellers** Reisetips *pl*.
[2] *vt* andeuten (*to* gegenüber) ◆ **what are you ~ing?** was wollen Sie damit sagen *or* andeuten?

◆**hint at** *vi +prep obj* **he ~ed ~ changes in the cabinet** er deutete an, daß es Umbesetzungen im Kabinett geben würde; **he ~ed ~ my involvement in the affair** er spielte auf meine Rolle in der Affäre an.

hinterland ['hɪntəlænd] *n* Hinterland *nt*.

hip[1] [hɪp] *n* Hüfte *f* ◆ **with one's hands on one's ~s** die Arme in die Hüften gestemmt.

hip[2] *n* (*Bot*) Hagebutte *f*.

hip[3] *interj*: **~! ~!, hurrah!** hipp hipp, hurra!

hip[4] *adj* (*sl*) **she is really ~** sie steigt voll durch (*sl*); (*artist etc*) sie ist wirklich *or* echt Spitze (*sl*); **to be ~ to sth** in etw (*dat*) voll durchsteigen (*sl*); **they played to some really ~ audiences** sie spielten vor wirklich Spitze Publikum (*sl*); **she really gets ~ to the Stones** wenn sie die Stones hört, ist sie weg (*sl*).

hip *in cpds* Hüft-; **~ bath** *n* Sitzbad *nt*; **~bone** *n* (*Anat*) Hüftbein *nt*, Hüftknochen *m*; **~-flask** *n* Taschenflasche *f*, Flachmann *m* (*inf*); **~ joint** *n* (*Anat*) Hüftgelenk *nt*; **~ measurement** *n* Hüftweite *f*, Hüftumfang *m*.

-hipped [-hɪpt] *adj suf* -hüftig ◆ **a big-~ woman** eine Frau mit breiten Hüften, eine breithüftige Frau.

hippie *n see* **hippy**.

hippo ['hɪpəʊ] *n* (*inf*) Nilpferd *nt*.

hip pocket *n* Gesäßtasche *f*.

Hippocratic oath [,hɪpəʊ,krætɪk'əʊθ] *n* hippokratischer Eid, Eid *m* des Hippokrates.

hippodrome ['hɪpədrəʊm] *n* Hippodrom *m or nt*; (*dated: music hall*) Varieté(theater) *nt*.

hippopotamus [,hɪpə'pɒtəməs] *n, pl* **-es** *or* **hippopotami** [,hɪpə'pɒtəmaɪ] Nilpferd, Flußpferd *nt*.

hippy, hippie ['hɪpɪ] *n* Hippie *m*.

hip replacement *n* Hüftoperation *f*; (*device*) Hüftprothese *f*.

hipster ['hɪpstə^r] [1] *n* **(a)** (*sl: one who is hip*) Hipster *m* (*sl*). **(b) ~s** *pl* (*trousers*) Hüfthose(n *pl*) *f*.
[2] *adj* Hüft-.

hire [haɪə^r] [1] *n* **(a)** Mieten *nt*; (*of car also, suit*) Leihen *nt*; (*of servant*) Einstellen *nt* ◆ **to have sth for ~** etw vermieten/verleihen; **for ~** (*taxi*) frei; **it's on ~** es ist geliehen/gemietet; **to let sth (out) on ~** etw vermieten.
(b) (*wages*) Lohn *m*; (*of sailor*) Heuer *f*.
[2] *vt* **(a)** mieten; *cars also, suits* leihen; *staff, person* einstellen ◆ **~d assassin** gedungener Mörder; **~d car** Mietwagen, Leihwagen *m*; **~d gun** gedungener Mörder, bezahlter Killer (*inf*); **~d hand** Lohnarbeiter *m*.
(b) *see* **hire out 1**.

◆**hire out** [1] *vt sep* vermieten, verleihen.
[2] *vi* (*US*) sich verdingen.

hireling ['haɪəlɪŋ] *n* (*pej*) Mietling *m* (*old pej*).

hire purchase *n* (*Brit*) Ratenkauf, Teilzahlungskauf *m* ◆ **on ~** auf Raten *or* Teilzahlung; **~ agreement** Teilzahlungs(kauf)vertrag *m*.

hirsute ['hɜːsjuːt] *adj* stark behaart.

his [hɪz] [1] *poss adj* sein; *see also* **my**.
[2] *poss pron* seine(r, s) ◆ **~** (*on towels etc*) er; *see also* **mine**[1].

Hispanic [hɪs'pænɪk] [1] *adj* hispanisch; *community* spanisch.
[2] *n* Hispano-Amerikaner(in *f*) *m*.

hiss [hɪs] [1] *vi* zischen; (*cat*) fauchen.
[2] *vt actor, speaker* auszischen ◆ **come here, he ~ed** komm her, zischte er.
[3] *n* Zischen *nt*; (*of cat*) Fauchen *nt*.

histamine ['hɪstəmiːn] *n* (*Med*) Histamin *nt*.

histology [hɪs'tɒlədʒɪ] *n* Histologie *f*.

historian [hɪs'tɔːrɪən] *n* Historiker(in *f*) *m*; (*in ancient times*) Geschichtsschreiber(in *f*) *m*.

historic [hɪs'tɒrɪk] *adj* (*also Gram*) historisch.

historical [hɪs'tɒrɪkəl] *adj* historisch; *studies, investigation, method also* geschichtlich, Geschichts- ◆ **places of ~ interest** historisch *or* geschichtlich interessante Stätten *pl*.

historically [hɪs'tɒrɪkəlɪ] *adv* historisch, aus historischer Sicht.

historicism [hɪs'tɒrɪsɪzəm] *n* Historizismus *m*.

historicity [hɪstə'rɪsɪtɪ] *n* Geschichtlichkeit, Historizität *f*.

historiography [,hɪstɒrɪ'ɒgrəfɪ] *n* Geschichtsschreibung, Historiographie *f*.

history ['hɪstərɪ] *n* **(a)** Geschichte *f*; (*study of ~ also*) Geschichtswissenschaft *f* ◆ **~ will be our judge** die Geschichte wird ihr Urteil fällen; **~ has taught us that ...** die Geschichte lehrt uns, daß ...; **to make ~** Geschichte machen; **that's all ~ now** (*fig*) das gehört jetzt alles der Vergangenheit an.
(b) (*personal record*) Geschichte *f* ◆ **he has a ~ of violence** er hat eine Vorgeschichte als Gewalttäter; **the family/he has a ~ of heart disease** Herzleiden liegen in der Familie/er hat schon lange ein Herzleiden.
(c) (*background*) Vorgeschichte *f* ◆ **to know the inner ~ of an affair** die inneren Zusammenhänge einer Affäre kennen; **bring me the ~ on this from the files** bringen Sie mir die Akten dazu.

histrionic [,hɪstrɪ'ɒnɪk] *adj* **(a)** (*overdone, affected*) theatralisch. **(b)** (*relating to acting*) Schauspieler-; *art* Schauspiel-; *ability* schauspielerisch.

histrionics [,hɪstrɪ'ɒnɪks] *npl* **(a)** theatralisches Getue ◆ **to indulge in ~** sich theatralisch aufführen. **(b)** Schauspielkunst *f*.

hit [hɪt] (*vb: pret, ptp* ~) [1] *n* **(a)** (*blow*) Schlag *m*; (*on target, Fencing*) Treffer *m*; (*Baseball*) Schlag *m*; *see* **score**.
(b) (*success, also Theat*) Erfolg, Knüller (*inf*) *m*; (*song*) Hit *m* ◆ **to be** *or* **make a ~ with sb** bei jdm gut ankommen.
(c) (*of sarcasm etc*) Spitze *f* ◆ **that's a ~ at me** das ist eine Spitze gegen mich; (*indirect also*) das ist auf mich gemünzt.
(d) (*sl: murder*) Mord *m*.
[2] *vt* **(a)** (*strike*) schlagen; (*Comput*) *key* drücken ◆ **to ~ sb a blow** jdm einen Schlag versetzen; **he ~ him a blow over the head** er gab ihm einen Schlag auf den Kopf; **to ~ one's head against sth** sich (*dat*) den Kopf an etw (*dat*) stoßen; **he ~ his head on the pavement** er schlug mit dem Kopf auf dem Pflaster auf; **the car ~ a tree** das Auto fuhr gegen einen Baum; **he was ~ by a stone** er wurde von einem Stein getroffen, ihn traf ein Stein; **the house was ~ by a shell** das Haus wurde von einer Granate getroffen; **to ~ one's way out of trouble** sich freischlagen; (*Tennis*) sich freispielen; (*Boxing*) sich freiboxen; **we're going to ~ the enemy with everything we've got** wir werden mit allen verfügbaren Mitteln gegen den Feind vorgehen; **the commandos ~ the town at dawn** die Kommandos griffen die Stadt im Morgengrauen an; **if I catch them taking bribes I'm going to ~ them hard** wenn ich sie dabei erwische, daß sie Bestechungsgelder nehmen, werde ich ganz scharf durchgreifen; **it ~s you (in the eye)** (*fig*) das fällt *or* springt einem ins Auge; **he didn't know what had ~ him** (*inf*) er wußte nicht, wie ihm geschah; **you won't know what has ~ you** (*inf*) du wirst dein blaues Wunder erleben (*inf*).
(b) (*wound*) treffen ◆ **he's been ~ in the leg** es hat ihn am Bein getroffen, er ist am Bein getroffen worden; **I've been ~!** ich bin getroffen worden, mich hat's erwischt (*inf*).
(c) *mark, target,* (*Fencing*) treffen ◆ **that ~ home** (*fig*) das hat getroffen, das saß (*inf*); **now you've ~ it** (*fig*) du hast es getroffen.
(d) (*affect adversely*) betreffen ◆ **the crops were ~ by the rain** der Regen hat der Ernte geschadet; **to be hard ~ by sth** von etw schwer getroffen werden; **how will this tax ~ you?** wie wird sich diese Steuer auf Sie auswirken?
(e) (*achieve, reach*) *likeness, top C* treffen; *speed, level, top form etc* erreichen.
(f) (*news, story*) **to ~ the papers** in die Zeitungen kommen; **the news ~ us/Wall Street like a bombshell** die Nachricht schlug bei uns/in Wall Street wie eine Bombe ein.
(g) (*occur to*) **to ~ sb** jdm aufgehen; **has it ever ~ you how alike they are?** ist es Ihnen schon mal aufgefallen, wie ähnlich sie sich sind?
(h) (*come to, arrive at*) *beaches etc* erreichen ◆ **to ~ town** (*inf*) die Stadt erreichen; **we eventually ~ the right road** schließlich haben wir den richtigen Weg gefunden *or* erwischt (*inf*); **we're going to ~ the rush hour** wir geraten *or* kommen direkt in den Stoßverkehr; **the driver ~ a patch of ice** der Fahrer geriet auf eine vereiste Stelle; **to ~ trouble/a problem** auf Schwierigkeiten/ein Problem stoßen.
(i) (*score*) schlagen ◆ **to ~ a century** hundert Läufe machen.
(j) (*sl: murder*) killen (*sl*), umlegen (*sl*).
(k) (*US inf*) **to ~ sb for $50** jdn um $ 50 anhauen (*inf*).
(l) (*fig inf phrases*) **to ~ the bottle** zur Flasche greifen; **to ~ the ceiling** *or* **roof** an die Decke *or* in die Luft gehen (*inf*); **to ~ the deck** sich zu Boden werfen, sich hinwerfen; **the vase ~ the deck and shattered** die Vase schlug *or* knallte (*inf*) auf den Boden und zerschellte; **to ~ the road** *or* **trail** sich auf den Weg *or* die Socken (*inf*) machen.
[3] *vi* **(a)** (*strike*) schlagen ◆ **he ~s hard** er schlägt hart zu. **(b)** (*collide*) zusammenstoßen. **(c)** (*attack, go in*) losschlagen.

◆**hit back** [1] *vi* (*lit, fig*) zurückschlagen ◆ **to ~ ~ at the enemy** zurück-

schlagen; **he ~ ~ at his critics** er gab seinen Kritikern Kontra.
[2] *vt sep* zurückschlagen.

◆**hit off** *vt sep* **(a) to ~ ~ a likeness** jdn/etw sehr gut treffen; **he ~ him ~ beautifully** er hat ihn ausgezeichnet getroffen.
(b) to ~ it ~ with sb (*inf*) sich gut mit jdm verstehen, prima mit jdm auskommen (*inf*); **they ~ it ~** sie haben sich von Anfang an gut verstanden.

◆**hit out** *vi* (*lit*) einschlagen, losschlagen (*at sb* auf jdn); (*fig*) scharf angreifen, attackieren (*at or against sb* jdn).

◆**hit (up)on** *vi +prep obj* stoßen auf (+*acc*), finden.

hit-and-run ['hɪtən'rʌn] [1] *n* **there was a ~ here last night** hier hat heute nacht jemand einen Unfall gebaut und Fahrerflucht begangen.
[2] *adj* **~ raid** (*Mil*) Blitzüberfall *m*; **~ accident/incident** Unfall *m* mit Fahrerflucht; **~ cases** Fälle von Fahrerflucht; **~ driver** unfallflüchtiger Fahrer, Fahrer, der Unfall- *or* Fahrerflucht begangen hat/begeht.

hitch [hɪtʃ] [1] *n* **(a)** (*snag*) Haken *m*; (*in plan, proceedings, programme*) Schwierigkeit *f*, Problem *nt* ◆ **without a ~** reibungslos, ohne Schwierigkeiten; **but there's one ~** aber die Sache hat einen Haken; **there's been a ~** es haben sich Schwierigkeiten ergeben, da ist ein Problem aufgetaucht.
(b) (*quick pull*) Ruck *m* ◆ **she gave it a quick ~** sie zog kurz daran.
(c) (*knot*) Knoten *m*; (*Naut*) Ste(e)k *m*.
(d) (*inf: lift*) **I got a ~ all the way to London** ich bin in einem Rutsch bis London (durch)getrampt (*inf*).
[2] *vt* **(a)** (*fasten*) festmachen, anbinden (*sth to sth* etw an etw +*dat*) ◆ **~ing post** Pfosten *m* (*zum Anbinden von Pferden*).
(b) (*inf*) **to get ~ed** heiraten, vor Anker gehen (*hum*); **why don't we get ~ed?** warum heiraten wir (eigentlich) nicht?
(c) to ~ a lift trampen, per Anhalter fahren; **she ~ed a lift from a lorry** ein Lastwagen nahm sie mit.
[3] *vi* trampen, per Anhalter fahren; *see also* **~-hike**.

◆**hitch up** *vt sep* **(a)** *horses, oxen* anschirren, anspannen ◆ **we ~ed ~ the horses to the wagon** wir spannten die Pferde vor den Wagen. **(b)** *trousers* hochziehen.

hitcher ['hɪtʃəʳ] *n* (*inf*) Anhalter(in *f*), Tramper(in *f*) *m*.

hitch: ~-hike *vi* per Anhalter fahren; **he's been away ~-hiking** er war per Anhalter unterwegs; **~-hiker** *n* Anhalter(in *f*), Tramper(in *f*) *m*; **~-hiking** *n* Trampen *nt*.

hitech ['haɪˌtek] [1] *n* Spitzentechnologie *f*, Hi-tech *nt*, Computertechnik *f*.
[2] *adj* Hi-tech-.

hither ['hɪðəʳ] *adv* (*obs*) hierher ◆ **~ and thither** (*liter*) hierhin und dorthin.

hitherto [ˌhɪðə'tuː] *adv* bisher, bis jetzt.

hit: ~list *n* (*lit, fig*) Abschußliste *f*; **~man** *n* (*sl*) Killer *m* (*sl*); **~-or-miss** *adj* auf gut Glück *pred*, aufs Geratewohl *pred*; *methods, planning* schlampig, schludrig (*inf*); **it was a rather ~-or-miss affair** das ging alles aufs Geratewohl; **~ parade** *n* Hitparade *f*; **~ record** *n* Hit *m*; **~ show** *n* erfolgreiche Show, Publikumserfolg *m*; **~ single** *n* Hit-Single *f*; **~ song** *n* Hit *m*; **~ squad, ~ team** *n* Killerkommando *nt*; **~ tune** *n* Schlagermelodie *f*.

HIV *abbr of* **human immunodeficiency virus** HIV ◆ **~ positive/negative** HIV-positiv/negativ.

hive [haɪv] [1] *n* **(a)** (*bee~*) Bienenkorb, Bienenstock *m*; (*bees in a ~*) (Bienen)schwarm *m*, (Bienen)volk *nt*.
(b) (*fig*) **what a ~ of industry** das reinste Bienenhaus; **the office was a ~ of activity** das Büro glich einem Bienenhaus.
[2] *vt bees, swarm* einfangen, in den Stock bringen.
[3] *vi* (*swarm*) in den (Bienen)stock (ein)fliegen, den/einen Stock beziehen.

◆**hive off** [1] *vt sep department* ausgliedern, abspalten; *work* vergeben (*to* an +*acc*).
[2] *vi* **(a)** (*branch out*) sich absetzen. **(b)** (*sl: slip away*) abschwirren (*sl*).

hives [haɪvz] *npl* (*Med*) Nesselausschlag *m*, Nesselsucht *f*.

hiya ['haɪjə] *interj* hallo.

Hizbollah [ˌhɪzbə'lɑː] *n* Hisb Allah *f*, Hisbollah *f*.

HM *abbr of* **His/Her Majesty** S.M./I.M.

HMG *abbr of* **His/Her Majesty's Government**.

HMI (*Brit*) *abbr of* **His/Her Majesty's Inspector** ≃ Schulrat *m*, Schulrätin *f*.

HMSO (*Brit*) *abbr of* **His/Her Majesty's Stationery Office** *Druckerei f für staatliche Drucksachen*.

HNC (*Brit*) *abbr of* **Higher National Certificate**.

HND (*Brit*) *abbr of* **Higher National Diploma**.

hoar [hɔːʳ] *n* Reif *m*.

hoard [hɔːd] [1] *n* Vorrat *m*; (*treasure*) Schatz, Hort *m* ◆ **a ~ of weapons** ein Waffenlager *nt*; **the miser's ~** der Schatz des Geizhalses; **~ of money** Schatz *m*, gehortetes Geld.
[2] *vt* (*also* **~ up**) *food etc* hamstern; *money* horten ◆ **a squirrel ~s nuts for the winter** ein Eichhörnchen hortet Nüsse für den Winter.

hoarder ['hɔːdəʳ] *n* (*animal*) *Tier nt, das Vorräte anlegt*; (*person*) Hamsterer *m*.

hoarding[1] ['hɔːdɪŋ] *n* (*of food etc*) Hamstern *nt*; (*of capital*) Anhäufen *nt*, Anhäufung *f*.

hoarding[2] *n* (*Brit*) (*fence, board*) Bretterzaun *m*; (*at building sites also*) Bauzaun *m* ◆ **(advertisement) ~** Plakatwand *f*.

hoarfrost ['hɔː'frɒst] *n* (Rauh)reif *m*.

hoarse [hɔːs] *adj* (+*er*) heiser ◆ **he shouted himself ~** er schrie sich heiser; **you sound rather ~** deine Stimme klingt heiser.

hoarsely ['hɔːslɪ] *adv* mit heiserer Stimme.

hoarseness ['hɔːsnɪs] *n* (*of person*) Heiserkeit *f* ◆ **the ~ of his voice** seine heisere Stimme.

hoary ['hɔːrɪ] *adj* (+*er*) **(a)** *hair, old man etc* ergraut. **(b)** (*fig: old*) uralt, altehrwürdig ◆ **a ~ old joke** ein alter Hut, ein Witz mit (einem langen) Bart.

hoax [həʊks] [1] *n* (*practical joke*) Streich *m*; (*trick etc*) Trick *m*; (*false alarm*) blinder Alarm ◆ **to play a ~ on sb** jdm einen Streich spielen; **~ caller** *see* **hoaxer**; **~ story** Zeitungsente *f*.
[2] *vt* anführen, hereinlegen (*inf*) ◆ **to ~ sb into believing sth** jdm etw weismachen; **he ~ed him into paying money** er hat ihm Geld abgeschwindelt *or* abgeluchst (*inf*); **we were completely ~ed** wir ließen uns anführen, wir fielen darauf herein.

hoaxer ['həʊksəʳ] *n* (*in bomb scares etc*) *jd, der einen blinden Alarm auslöst*.

hob [hɒb] *n* Kamineinsatz (zum Warmhalten) *m*; (*on modern cooker*) Kochfeld *nt*.

hobble ['hɒbl] [1] *vi* humpeln, hinken ◆ **to ~ in** herein-/hineinhumpeln.
[2] *vt horse* Fußfesseln anlegen (+*dat*), die Vorderbeine fesseln (+*dat*).
[3] *n* (*for horses*) Fußfessel *f*.

hobbledehoy ['hɒbldɪ'hɔɪ] *n* (*old*) Tolpatsch *m*.

hobby ['hɒbɪ] *n* Hobby, Steckenpferd (*dated*) *nt*.

hobby-horse ['hɒbɪhɔːs] *n* (*lit, fig*) Steckenpferd *nt*; (*lit: rocking horse*) Schaukelpferd *nt* ◆ **to be on one's ~** (*fig*) bei seinem Lieblingsthema sein; **don't get him on his ~** (*fig*) bring ihn (bloß) nicht auf sein Lieblingsthema.

hobgoblin ['hɒbˌgɒblɪn] *n* Kobold, Butzemann *m*; (*bogey*) schwarzer Mann, Butzemann *m*.

hobnail ['hɒbneɪl] *n* Schuhnagel *m*, Schuhzwecke *f*.

hobnailed ['hɒbneɪld] *adj* genagelt ◆ **~ boots** genagelte Schuhe, Nagelschuhe *pl*.

hobnob ['hɒbnɒb] *vi* **of course I'm not used to ~bing with the aristocracy** ich stehe *or* bin natürlich nicht mit dem Adel auf du und du; **she's been seen ~bing with some rather peculiar types** sie ist mit ein paar ziemlich merkwürdigen Typen durch die Gegend gezogen (*inf*); **he shouldn't still be ~bing with his bachelor friends** er sollte nicht immer noch mit seinen Freunden aus der Junggesellenzeit zusammenstecken; **who was that you were ~bing with last night?** mit wem hast du da gestern zusammengesessen?

hobo ['həʊbəʊ] *n* (*US*) **(a)** (*tramp*) Penner *m* (*inf*). **(b)** (*worker*) Wanderarbeiter *m*.

Hobson's choice ['hɒbsəns'tʃɔɪs] *n* **it's a case of ~** da habe ich (wohl) keine andere Wahl.

hock[1] [hɒk] *n* (*Anat: of animal*) Sprunggelenk *nt*.

hock[2] *n* (*wine*) weißer Rheinwein.

hock[3] (*sl*) [1] *vt* (*pawn*) versetzen, verpfänden.
[2] *n* **in ~** verpfändet, versetzt, im Leihhaus; **to get sth out of ~** etw auslösen.

hockey ['hɒkɪ] *n* Hockey *nt*; (*US*) Eishockey *nt* ◆ **~ pitch** Hockeyfeld *nt*; **~ player** Hockeyspieler(in *f*) *m*; (*US*) Eishockeyspieler *m*; **~ stick** Hockeyschläger *m*.

hocus-pocus ['həʊkəs'pəʊkəs] *n* **(a)** (*inf: trickery*) faule Tricks *pl* (*inf*), Hokuspokus *m*. **(b)** (*formula*) Hokuspokus *m*.

hod [hɒd] *n* **(a)** (*for bricks, mortar etc*) Tragmulde *f*. **(b)** (*also coal ~*) Kohlenschütte(r *m*) *f*.

hodgepodge ['hɒdʒpɒdʒ] *n see* **hotchpotch**.

hoe [həʊ] [1] *n* Hacke *f*.
[2] *vti* hacken.

hoedown ['həʊdaʊn] *n* (*US*) Schwof *m* (*inf*).

hog [hɒg] [1] *n* **(a)** (Mast)schwein *nt*; (*US: pig*) Schwein *nt*.
(b) (*pej inf: person*) Schwein *nt* (*inf*); (*greedy*) Vielfraß *m* (*inf*); (*selfish*) Saukerl *m* (*sl*); (*dirty*) Sau *f* (*sl*), Ferkel *nt* (*inf*); *see* **roadhog, whole ~**.
[2] *vt* (*inf*) sich (*dat*) aneignen, in Beschlag nehmen ◆ **he ~ged all the biscuits for himself** er grapschte sich (*dat*) alle Kekse (*inf*); **she ~ged his attention all evening** sie belegte ihn den ganzen Abend lang mit Beschlag; **a lot of drivers ~ the middle of the road** viele Fahrer meinen, sie hätten die Straßenmitte gepachtet (*inf*).

Hogmanay [ˌhɒgmə'neɪ] *n* (*Scot*) Silvester *nt*.

hogshead ['hɒgzhed] *n* großes Faß; (*measure*) Oxhoft *nt* (*obs*), *Flüssigkeitsmaß zwischen 200-250 l*.

hog: ~tie *vt* (*US*) an allen vieren fesseln; (*inf*) handlungsunfähig machen; **we're ~tied** uns (*dat*) sind Hände und Füße gebunden; **~wash** *n* **(a)** (*swill*) Schweinefutter *nt*; **(b)** (*inf: nonsense*) Quatsch, Quark *m* (*inf*), blödes Zeug (*inf*).

hoi polloi [ˌhɔɪpə'lɔɪ] *n* (*pej*) Volk *nt*, Pöbel, Plebs *m*.

hoist [hɔɪst] [1] *vt* hochheben, hieven (*inf*); (*pull up*) hochziehen, hieven (*inf*); *flag* hissen; *sails* aufziehen, hissen ◆ **to be ~ with one's own petard** (*prov*) in die eigene Falle gehen.
[2] *n* **(a)** Hebezeug *nt*, Hebevorrichtung *f*; (*in ships also*) Hebewerk *nt*; (*lift*) (Lasten)aufzug *m*; (*block and tackle*) Flaschenzug *m*; (*winch*) Winde *f*; (*crane*) Kran *m*.
(b) (*act of ~ing*) **to give sb a ~ (up)** jdn hochheben; (*pull up*) jdm hinauf-/heraufhelfen.

hoity-toity ['hɔɪtɪ'tɔɪtɪ] (*inf*) [1] *adj* hochnäsig, eingebildet ◆ **she's gone all ~** sie markiert die feine Dame (*inf*); **oh ~, are we?** wohl zu fein für unsereins?
[2] *interj* sieh mal einer an (*inf*).

hokum ['həʊkəm] *n* (*US inf*) **(a)** (*nonsense*) Quatsch (*inf*), Mumpitz *m*. **(b)** (*cheap sentiment*) Gefühlsduselei *f* (*inf*).

▼ **hold** [həʊld] (*vb: pret, ptp* **held**) [1] *n* **(a)** Griff *m*; (*fig*) Einfluß *m* (*over* auf +*acc*), Gewalt *f* (*over* über +*acc*) ◆ **to seize** *or* **grab ~ of sb/sth** (*lit*) jdn/etw fassen *or* packen; **to get (a) ~ of sth** sich an etw (*dat*) festhalten; **get ~ of my**

hand faß mich bei der Hand; **he lost his ~ on the rope** er konnte sich nicht mehr am Seil festhalten; **to have/catch ~ of sth** (*lit*) etw festhalten/etw fassen *or* packen; **to keep ~ of sth** etw nicht loslassen; (*keep*) etw behalten; **to get ~ of sb** (*fig*) jdn finden *or* auftreiben (*inf*); (*on phone etc*) jdn erreichen; **to get** *or* **lay ~ of sth** (*fig*) etw finden *or* auftreiben (*inf*); **where did you get ~ of that idea?** wie kommst du denn auf die Idee?; **to have a firm ~ on sb** (*lit*) jdn festhalten; (*fig*) jdn fest im Griff haben; **he hasn't got any ~ on** *or* **over me** (*fig*) er kann mir nichts anhaben; **to have a ~ over** *or* **on sb** (*fig*) (großen) Einfluß auf jdn ausüben; *audience, followers* jdn in seiner Gewalt haben; **to get (a) ~ of oneself** (*fig*) sich in den Griff bekommen; **get (a) ~ of yourself!** reiß dich zusammen!

(b) (*Mountaineering*) Halt *m no pl* ◆ **he lost his ~ and fell** er verlor den Halt und stürzte ab; **the face offers few ~s to climbers** die Wand bietet dem Bergsteiger wenig Halt.

(c) (*Wrestling*) Griff *m* ◆ **no ~s barred** (*lit*) alle Griffe (sind) erlaubt; **when those two have a row, there are no ~s barred** (*fig*) wenn die beiden sich streiten, dann kennen sie nichts mehr (*inf*) *or* kein Pardon (*inf*).

(d) (*Naut, Aviat*) Laderaum, Frachtraum *m*.

(e) (*Telec*) **to put sb on ~** jdn auf Wartestellung schalten; (*in larger organizations*) jdn auf die Warteschlange legen; **to be on ~** warten.

(f) (*fig*) **to put sth on ~** *decision etc* etw auf Eis legen; **to be on ~** auf Eis liegen; **let's put these applications on ~** legen wir diese Bewerbungen vorerst zur Seite; **can we put this discussion on ~?** können wir diese Diskussion unterbrechen?

▼ **2** *vt* **(a)** (*grasp, grip*) halten ◆ **to ~ hands** sich an der Hand halten, sich anfassen; (*lovers, children etc*) Händchen halten; **to walk along ~ing hands** angefaßt gehen; **to ~ one's sides with laughter** sich (*dat*) den Bauch vor Lachen halten; **to ~ sb/sth tight** jdn/etw (ganz) festhalten; **the frightened children held each other tight** die verängstigten Kinder klammerten sich aneinander; **this car ~s the road well** dieses Auto hat eine gute Straßenlage; **he held the corner well** er hat die Kurve gut genommen; **to ~ sth in place** etw (fest)halten.

(b) (*carry, maintain*) halten ◆ **to ~ oneself upright** sich gerade *or* aufrecht halten; **to ~ oneself/sth ready** *or* **in readiness** sich/etw bereithalten.

(c) (*contain*) enthalten; (*have capacity etc of: bottle, tank etc*) fassen; (*have room for: bus, plane, hall etc*) Platz haben für ◆ **this room ~s twenty people** in diesem Raum haben zwanzig Personen Platz; **the box will ~ all my books** in der Kiste ist Platz für alle meine Bücher; **this ~s the radar equipment** dies enthält die Radarausrüstung; **my head can't ~ so much information at one time** soviel kann ich nicht auf einmal behalten; **what does the future ~?** was bringt *or* birgt (*geh*) die Zukunft?; **life ~s no fears/mystery for them** das Leben hat *or* birgt (*geh*) nichts Beängstigendes/Geheimnisvolles für sie.

(d) (*believe*) meinen; (*maintain also*) behaupten ◆ **to ~ sth to be true/false/immoral** *etc* etw für wahr/falsch/unmoralisch *etc* halten; **to ~ the belief that ...** glauben, daß...; **to ~ the view that ...** die Meinung vertreten, daß ...

(e) (*consider*) **she held her youngest grandchild dear** ihr jüngstes Enkelkind bedeutete ihr sehr viel *or* war ihr teuer (*liter*); **she held the memory of her late husband dear** sie hielt das Andenken an ihren verstorbenen Mann hoch.

(f) (*restrain, retain, keep back*) *train* aufhalten; *one's breath* anhalten; *suspect, hostages etc* festhalten; *parcel, confiscated goods etc* zurückhalten; (*discontinue*) *fire* einstellen ◆ **~ your fire!** (*don't shoot*) nicht schießen!; **to ~ sb (prisoner)** jdn gefangenhalten; **if she wants to leave you, you can't ~ her** wenn sie dich verlassen will, kannst du sie nicht (zurück)halten; **do you find it difficult to ~ staff?** finden Sie es schwierig, das Personal zu halten?; **there's no ~ing him** er ist nicht zu bremsen (*inf*); **~ hard, ~ your horses** (*inf*) immer mit der Ruhe, immer sachte mit den jungen Pferden! (*inf*); **~ it!** (*inf*) Momentchen (*inf*), Moment mal (*inf*); **~ everything!** (*inf*) stop!; **~ it!** (*when taking photograph*) so ist gut; **~ it right there, buster** (*inf*) keine Bewegung, Freundchen (*inf*).

(g) (*possess, occupy*) *post, position* innehaben, bekleiden (*form*); *passport, permit* haben; (*Fin*) *shares* besitzen; (*Sport*) *record* halten; (*Mil*) *position* halten; (*against attack*) behaupten, halten; (*Eccl*) *living* innehaben ◆ **the family ~s most of the shares** die meisten Aktien sind *or* befinden sich in den Händen *or* im Besitz der Familie; **when Spain held vast territories in South America** als Spanien riesige Besitzungen in Südamerika hatte; **she ~s the key to the mystery** sie hat den Schlüssel zu dem Geheimnis; *see* **stage**.

▼ **(h)** (*keep, not let go*) **to ~ its value** seinen Wert behalten; **to ~ one's ground** *or* **own** sich behaupten (können); **to ~ course for** (*Naut*) Kurs halten auf (+*acc*); **to ~ one's course** die Richtung beibehalten; **I'll ~ you to your promise** *or* **that!** ich werde Sie beim Wort nehmen; **to ~ a note** (*Mus*) einen Ton halten.

(i) **he can't ~ his whisky/liquor** er verträgt keinen Whisky/nichts; **she can ~ her drink** sie verträgt was; **a man can always ~ his water** ein richtiger Mann kann sein Wasser halten.

(j) *meeting, session, debate* abhalten; (*Eccl*) *service* (ab)halten ◆ **services are held every Sunday at 11 am** Gottesdienst findet jeden Sonntag um 11 Uhr statt; **to ~ a check on sb/sth** jdn/etw kontrollieren; **to ~ a conversation** eine Unterhaltung führen *or* haben, sich unterhalten.

3 *vi* **(a)** (*rope, nail etc*) halten ◆ **to ~ firm** *or* **fast** halten.

(b) **~ still!** halt (doch mal) still!; **~ tight!** festhalten!

(c) (*continue*) **will the weather ~?** wird sich das Wetter wohl halten?; **if his luck ~s** wenn ihm das Glück treu bleibt.

(d) (*be valid, apply to*) gelten ◆ **to ~ good** (*rule, promise etc*) gelten.

◆**hold against** *vt always separate* **to ~ sth ~ sb** jdm etw übelnehmen *or* verübeln; *criminal record, past failings* jdm etw anlasten *or* zur Last legen.

◆**hold back** **1** *vi* (*stay back, hesitate, not perform fully*) sich zurückhalten; (*fail to act*) zögern ◆ **I think he's ~ing ~, he knows more** ich glaube, er weiß mehr und rückt nur nicht mit der Sprache heraus; **I held ~ from telling him just what I thought of him** ich unterließ es, ihm meine Meinung zu sagen.

2 *vt sep* **(a)** zurückhalten; *river, floods* (auf)stauen; *tears also* unterdrücken; *emotions* verbergen, unterdrücken ◆ **to ~ sb ~ from doing sth** jdn daran hindern, etw zu tun.

(b) (*prevent from making progress*) daran hindern, voranzukommen ◆ **he would let nothing ~ him ~ from getting his way** nichts kann ihn daran hindern, seinen Willen durchzusetzen; **nothing can ~ him ~ now** jetzt ist er nicht mehr aufzuhalten.

(c) (*withhold*) verheimlichen, verbergen; *information, report* geheimhalten; *pay increase* verzögern ◆ **he was ~ing something ~ from me** er verheimlichte *or* verbarg mir etwas.

◆**hold down** *vt sep* **(a)** (*keep on the ground*) niederhalten, unten halten; (*keep in its place*) (fest)halten; (*oppress*) *country, people* unterdrücken; (*keep in check*) unter Kontrolle haben; (*keep low*) *prices, costs, numbers, pressure* niedrig halten ◆ **to ~ one's head ~** den Kopf senken.

(b) *job* haben ◆ **he can't ~ any job ~ for long** er kann sich in keiner Stellung lange halten.

◆**hold forth** **1** *vi* sich ergehen (*geh*), sich auslassen (*on* über +*acc*).

2 *vt sep* (*form: offer*) bieten.

◆**hold in** *vt sep stomach* einziehen; *emotions* zurückhalten; *horse* zurückhalten, zügeln ◆ **to ~ ~ one's temper** seinen Ärger unterdrücken; **to ~ oneself ~** (*stomach*) den Bauch einziehen; (*emotionally*) sich beherrschen, an sich halten.

◆**hold off** **1** *vi* **(a)** (*keep away*) sich fernhalten (*from* von); (*not act*) warten; (*enemy*) nicht angreifen ◆ **they held ~ where they should have intervened** sie hätten eingreifen sollen, haben sich aber zurückgehalten; **she ~s ~ from all close friendships** sie vermeidet enge Freundschaften.

(b) (*rain, storm*) ausbleiben ◆ **I hope the rain ~s ~** ich hoffe, daß es nicht regnet.

2 *vt sep* (*keep back, resist*) *enemy, attack* abwehren; *inflation* eindämmen ◆ **how much longer can she go on ~ing him ~?** wie lange kann sie ihn wohl noch hinhalten?

◆**hold on** **1** *vi* (*lit: maintain grip*) sich festhalten; (*endure, resist*) durchhalten, aushalten; (*wait*) warten ◆ **~ ~!** Moment!; (*Telec*) einen Moment bitte!; **now ~ ~ a minute!** Moment mal!

2 *vt sep* (fest)halten ◆ **to be held ~ by sth** mit etw befestigt sein; **this sellotape won't ~ it ~** mit dem Tesafilm hält das nicht.

◆**hold on to** *vi +prep obj* **(a)** festhalten ◆ **here, ~ ~ ~ this!** halt das mal (fest)!; **he was ~ing ~ ~ the ledge** er hielt *or* klammerte sich am Felsvorsprung fest; **they firmly held ~ ~ each other** sie klammerten sich aneinander.

(b) *hope* nicht aufgeben; *idea* festhalten an (+*dat*).

(c) (*keep*) behalten; *position* beibehalten ◆ **to ~ ~ ~ the lead** in Führung bleiben.

◆**hold out** **1** *vi* **(a)** (*supplies etc*) reichen.

(b) (*endure, resist*) aushalten, durchhalten; (*refuse to yield*) nicht nachgeben ◆ **to ~ ~ against sb/sth** sich gegen jdn/etw behaupten; **to ~ ~ for sth** auf etw (*dat*) bestehen.

2 *vt sep* **(a)** vorstrecken, ausstrecken ◆ **to ~ ~ sth to sb** jdm etw hinhalten· **to ~ ~ one's hand** die Hand ausstrecken; **~ your hand ~** halt die Hand auf; **she held ~ her arms** sie breitete die Arme aus.

(b) (*fig: offer*) *prospects* bieten; *offer* machen ◆ **I held ~ little hope of his still being alive** ich hatte nur noch wenig Hoffnung, daß er noch lebte; **his case ~s ~ little hope** in seinem Fall besteht wenig Hoffnung.

◆**hold out on** *vi +prep obj* (*inf*) **you've been ~ing ~ ~ me** du verheimlichst mir doch was (*inf*).

◆**hold over** *vt sep question, matter* vertagen; *meeting also, decision* verschieben (*until* auf +*acc*).

◆**hold to** *vi +prep obj* festhalten an (+*dat*); bleiben bei ◆ **I ~ ~ my belief that ...** ich bleibe dabei, daß ...; **you should ~ ~ the assurance you gave them** Sie sollten Ihr Wort ihnen gegenüber einhalten.

◆**hold together** *vti* zusammenhalten.

◆**hold under** *vt sep country, race* unterdrücken, knechten.

◆**hold up** **1** *vi* **(a)** (*tent, wall etc*) stehen bleiben; (*light fitting, tile etc*) halten.

(b) (*belief*) standhalten; (*theory*) sich halten lassen.

2 *vt sep* **(a)** hochheben, hochhalten; *face* nach oben wenden ◆ **~ ~ your hand** heb die Hand; **to ~ sth ~ to the light** etw gegen das Licht halten.

(b) (*support*) (*from above*) halten; (*from the side*) stützen; (*from beneath*) tragen.

(c) **to ~ sb/sth ~ to ridicule/scorn** jdn/etw lächerlich/verächtlich machen; **to ~ sb ~ as an example** jdn als Beispiel hinstellen; **I don't want to ~ him ~ as the perfect statesman/goalkeeper** *etc* **but ...** ich möchte ihn nicht als den perfekten Politiker/Torwart *etc* hinstellen, aber ...

(d) (*stop*) anhalten; (*delay*) *people* aufhalten; *traffic, production* ins Stocken bringen; *talks, delivery* verzögern ◆ **my application was held ~ by the postal strike** durch den Poststreik hat sich meine Bewerbung verspätet.

(e) (*robbers*) *bank, person, vehicle* überfallen.

◆**hold with** *vi +prep obj* (*inf*) **I don't ~ ~ that** ich bin gegen so was (*inf*).

holdall ['həʊldɔːl] *n* Reisetasche *f*.

holder ['həʊldəʳ] *n* **(a)** (*person*) Besitzer(in *f*), Inhaber(in *f*) *m*; (*of title, office, record, passport*) Inhaber(in *f*) *m*; (*of farm*) Pächter(in *f*) *m*. **(b)** (*object*) Halter *m*; (*cigarette-~*) Spitze *f*; (*flowerpot-~*) Übertopf *m*.

➤ LANGUAGE IN USE: **hold: 2a** → 5.3 **2h** → 27.3

holding ['həʊldɪŋ] *n* **(a)** *(Boxing)* Festhalten *nt.* **(b)** *(land)* Land *nt; (with buildings)* Gut *nt* ◆ **~s** (Grund- *or* Land)besitz *m* ◆ Gutsbesitz *m.* **(c)** *(Fin)* **~s** *pl* Anteile *pl; (stocks)* Aktienbesitz *m* ◆ **~ company** Dach- *or* Holdinggesellschaft *f.* **(d)** *(Aviat)* **~ pattern** Warteschleife *f.*

hold-up ['həʊldʌp] *n* **(a)** *(delay)* Verzögerung *f; (of traffic)* Stockung *f* ◆ **what's the ~?** warum dauert das so lange?; **the strike caused a two-week ~ in production** der Streik brachte die Produktion zwei Wochen lang ins Stocken; **there's been a (bit of a) ~ in our plans** unsere Pläne haben sich verzögert.

(b) *(armed robbery)* bewaffneter Raubüberfall ◆ **this is a ~!** Hände hoch, das ist ein Überfall!

hole [həʊl] 1 *n* **(a)** Loch *nt* ◆ **to make a ~ in sb's savings** ein Loch in jds Ersparnisse reißen; **the argument is full of ~s** Ihre Argumentation weist viele Mängel auf; **he's talking through a ~ in his head** *(inf)* er quatscht lauter Blödsinn *(inf)*; **I need that like I need a ~ in the head** *(inf)* das ist das letzte, was ich gebrauchen kann.

(b) *(inf: awkward situation)* Klemme *(inf)*, Patsche *(inf) f* ◆ **to be in a ~** in der Patsche *or* Klemme sitzen *(inf)*; **to get sb out of a ~** jdm aus der Patsche *or* Klemme helfen *(inf)*.

(c) *(rabbit's, fox's)* Bau *m*, Höhle *f; (mouse's)* Loch *nt.*

(d) *(pej inf)* Loch *nt (inf); (town)* Kaff *(inf)*, Nest *(inf) nt.*

(e) *(Golf)* Loch *nt* ◆ **an 18-~ course** ein 18-Löcher-Platz *m;* **~-in-one** Hole in One *nt.*

2 *vt* **(a)** ein Loch machen in *(+acc)* ◆ **to be ~d** ein Loch bekommen; **the ship was ~d by an iceberg** der Eisberg schlug das Schiff leck.

(b) *ball (Golf)* einlochen, versenken; *(Billiards)* versenken.

3 *vi* **(a)** *(socks etc)* Löcher bekommen.

(b) *(Golf)* einlochen.

◆**hole out** *vi (Golf)* das/ein Loch spielen ◆ **to ~ ~ in one** ein Hole in One spielen.

◆**hole up** *vi (animal)* sich verkriechen; *(inf: gang etc) (hide)* sich verkriechen *(inf) or* verstecken; *(barricade themselves in)* sich verschanzen.

hole-and-corner ['həʊlən'kɔːnə^r] *adj* obskur, zwielichtig.

hole-in-the-heart 1 *n* Loch *nt* in der Herzscheidewand.

2 *adj attr operation* Herzfehler- ◆ **~ baby** Baby *nt* mit (angeborenem) Herzfehler.

hole-in-the-wall *adj attr (Brit inf) cash machine* in die Wand eingebaut.

holey ['həʊlɪ] *adj (inf)* löchrig.

holiday ['hɒlədɪ] 1 *n* **(a)** *(day off)* freier Tag; *(public ~)* Feiertag *m* ◆ **to take a ~** einen Tag frei nehmen.

(b) *(esp Brit: period) often pl* Urlaub *m (esp for working people)*, Ferien *pl; (Sch)* Ferien *pl* ◆ **on ~** in den Ferien; auf *or* im Urlaub; **to go on ~** Ferien/Urlaub machen; **where are you going for your ~(s)?** wo fahren Sie in den Ferien/im Urlaub hin?, wo machen Sie Ferien/Urlaub?; **to take a ~** Urlaub nehmen *or* machen; **I need a ~** ich bin ferienreif; **to take a month's ~** einen Monat Urlaub nehmen; **~ with pay/paid ~s** bezahlter Urlaub; **it was no ~, I can tell you** ich kann dir sagen, das war alles andere als eine Erholung.

2 *vi (esp Brit)* Ferien *or* Urlaub machen.

holiday *in cpds* Ferien-; Urlaubs-; **~ camp** *n* Feriendorf *nt;* **~ clothes** *npl* Urlaubskleidung *f;* **~ destination** *n* Ferien- *or* Reiseziel *nt;* **~ entitlement** *n* Urlaubsanspruch *m;* **~ feeling** *n* Urlaubs-/Ferienstimmung *f;* **~ guest** *n (esp Brit)* Feriengast *m;* **~ home** *n* Ferienhaus *nt*/-wohnung *f;* **~maker** *n (esp Brit)* Urlauber(in *f*) *m;* **~ mood** *n* Urlaubs-/Ferienstimmung *f;* **~ resort** *n* Ferienort *m;* **~ season** *n* Urlaubszeit *f;* **~ traffic** *n* Reiseverkehr *m.*

holier-than-thou ['həʊlɪəðən'ðaʊ] *adj attitude* selbstgerecht, selbstgefällig.

holiness ['həʊlɪnɪs] *n* Heiligkeit *f* ◆ **His/Your H~** *(Eccl)* Seine/Eure Heiligkeit.

holism ['həʊlɪzəm] *n* Holismus *m.*

holistic [həʊ'lɪstɪk] *adj* holistisch.

Holland ['hɒlənd] *n* Holland *nt.*

Hollander ['hɒləndə^r] *n (Typ)* Holländer *m.*

holler ['hɒlə^r] *(inf)* 1 *n* Schrei *m.*

2 *vti (also* **~ out**) brüllen.

hollow ['hɒləʊ] 1 *adj (+er)* **(a)** hohl ◆ **I feel ~** ich habe ein Loch im Bauch *(inf); (emotionally empty)* ich fühle mich ausgehöhlt *or* (innerlich) leer.

(b) *sound* hohl, dumpf; *voice* hohl, Grabes-.

(c) *(fig)* hohl; *laughter also* unecht; *person* innerlich hohl; *life* inhaltslos, leer; *sympathy, praise* unaufrichtig; *promise* leer; *victory* wertlos.

(d) *cheeks* hohl, eingefallen; *eyes* tiefliegend.

2 *adv sound* hohl ◆ **they beat us ~** *(inf)* sie haben uns haushoch geschlagen, sie haben uns fertiggemacht *(inf)*.

3 *n (of tree)* hohler Teil, Hohlung *f; (in ground)* Vertiefung, Mulde *f; (valley)* Senke *f* ◆ **a wooded ~** eine bewaldete Niederung; **the ~ of one's hand** die hohle Hand; **the ~ of one's back** das Kreuz; **in the ~ between two waves** im Wellental.

◆**hollow out** *vt sep* aushöhlen.

hollow-eyed ['hɒləʊaɪd] *adj* hohläugig.

hollowly ['hɒləʊlɪ] *adv laugh* hohl.

holly ['hɒlɪ] *n* **(a)** *(tree)* Stechpalme *f*, Ilex *m* ◆ **~ berry** Stechpalmenfrucht *f.*

(b) *(foliage)* Stechpalme(nzweige *pl*) *f.*

hollyhock ['hɒlɪhɒk] *n* Malve *f.*

holmium ['hɒlmɪəm] *n (Chem)* Holmium *nt.*

holm oak ['həʊm'əʊk] *n* Steineiche *f.*

holocaust ['hɒləkɔːst] *n* **(a)** Inferno *nt* ◆ **nuclear ~** Atominferno *nt.* **(b)** *(mass extermination)* Massenvernichtung *f; (in Third Reich)* Holocaust *m.*

hologram ['hɒləgræm] *n* Hologramm *nt.*

holograph ['hɒləgrɑːf] 1 *n* handschriftliches Dokument.

2 *adj* eigenhändig geschrieben, holographisch *(form)*.

holography [hɒ'lɒgrəfɪ] *n* Holographie *f.*

hols [hɒlz] *abbr of* **holidays.**

holster ['həʊlstə^r] *n* (Pistolen)halfter *nt or f.*

holy ['həʊlɪ] 1 *adj (+er)* **(a)** heilig; *chastity, poverty* gottgefällig; *bread, ground* geweiht ◆ **~ water** Weihwasser *nt;* **the H~ Bible** die Bibel; **the H~ City** die Heilige Stadt; **H~ Communion** Heilige Kommunion; **H~ Father** Heiliger Vater; **H~ Ghost** *or* **Spirit** Heiliger Geist; **H~ Land** Heiliges Land; **H~ Trinity** Heilige Dreieinigkeit; **H~ Oil** geweihtes Öl; **H~ Week** Karwoche, Passionswoche *f;* **H~ Scripture(s)** die Heilige Schrift; **H~ Saturday** Karsamstag *m;* **H~ Office** Inquisition *f.*

(b) *(inf)* **~ smoke** *or* **cow** *or* **Moses!** heiliger Strohsack *or* Bimbam!, Kruzitürken! *(all inf)*; **that child is a ~ terror** das Kind ist eine Nervensäge *(inf) or* eine Plage.

2 *n* **the H~ of Holies** *(lit)* das Allerheiligste; *(fig)* ein Heiligtum.

homage ['hɒmɪdʒ] *n* Huldigung *f; (for elders)* Ehrerbietung *f* ◆ **to pay** *or* **do ~ to sb** jdm huldigen; jdm seine Ehrerbietung erweisen; **to pay ~ to the dead king** um dem König die letzte Ehre zu erweisen; **a speech in ~ to the president/the victims of the disaster** eine Rede als Hommage für den Präsidenten/als Ehrerbietung für die Opfer der Katastrophe; **they stood there in silent ~** sie standen in stummer Ehrerbietung da.

homburg ['hɒmbɜːg] *n* Homburg *m.*

home [həʊm] 1 *n* **(a)** *(house)* Heim *nt; (country, area etc)* Heimat *f* ◆ **gifts for the ~** Geschenke *pl* für das Haus *or* die Wohnung; **a useful gadget to have in your ~** ein sehr praktisches Gerät für den Haushalt; **his ~ is in Brussels** er ist in Brüssel zu Hause; **Bournemouth is his second ~** Bournemouth ist seine zweite Heimat (geworden); **haven't you got a ~ to go to?** hast du kein Zuhause?; **he invited us round to his ~** er hat uns zu sich (nach Hause) eingeladen; **away from ~** von zu Hause weg; **a long way from ~** weit von zu Hause weg *or* entfernt; *(in different country also)* weit von der Heimat entfernt; **to live away from ~** nicht zu Hause wohnen; **he worked away from ~** er hat auswärts gearbeitet; **hasn't this hammer got a ~?** gehört der Hammer nicht irgendwohin?; **to have a ~ of one's own** ein eigenes Heim *or* Zuhause haben; **to find a ~ for sb/an animal/an object** ein Zuhause für jdn/ein Tier finden/einen Gegenstand irgendwo unterbringen; **I'll give that picture a ~** bei mir wird das Bild einen guten Platz finden *or* haben; **it's a ~ from ~** es ist wie zu Hause; **at ~** zu Hause; *(Comm)* im Inland; *(Sport)* auf eigenem Platz; **the next match will be at ~** das nächste Spiel ist ein Heimspiel; **Miss Hooper is not at ~ to anyone today** Frau Hooper *or* die gnädige Frau ist heute für niemanden zu Hause *or* zu sprechen; **to be** *or* **feel at ~ with sb** sich in jds Gegenwart *(dat)* wohl fühlen; **he doesn't feel at ~ in English** er fühlt sich im Englischen nicht sicher *or* zu Hause; **he is at ~ on anything to do with economics** er kennt sich bei allem aus, was mit Volkswirtschaft zu tun hat; **I don't feel at ~ with this new theory yet** ich komme mit dieser neuen Theorie noch nicht ganz zurecht; **to make oneself at ~** es sich *(dat)* gemütlich *or* bequem machen; **to make sb feel at ~** es jdm gemütlich machen; **to leave ~** von zu Hause weggehen; **Scotland is the ~ of the haggis** Schottland ist die Heimat des Haggis, das Haggis ist in Schottland zu Hause; **there's no place like ~** *(Prov)* daheim ist daheim *(prov)*, eigner Herd ist Goldes wert *(Prov)*; **~ sweet ~** *(Prov)* trautes Heim, Glück allein *(Prov)*.

(b) *(institution)* Heim *nt; (for orphans also)* Waisenhaus *nt; (for blind also)* Anstalt *f; see* **nursing ~.**

(c) *(Zool, Bot)* Heimat *f.*

(d) *(Sport: base)* Mal *nt; (Racing)* Ziel *nt.*

2 *adv* **(a)** *(position)* zu Hause, daheim; *(with verb of motion)* nach Hause, heim ◆ **to go ~** *(to house)* nach Hause gehen/fahren, heimgehen/heimfahren; *(to country)* heimfahren; **on the way ~** auf dem Heim- *or* Nachhauseweg; **the first runner ~ will .../was Fred** wer als erster durchs Ziel geht .../Fred ging als erster durchs Ziel; **to get ~** nach Hause kommen, heimkommen; *(in race)* durchs Ziel gehen; **I have to get ~ before ten** ich muß vor zehn zu Hause *or* daheim sein; **to return ~ from abroad** aus dem Ausland zurückkommen.

(b) *(to the mark)* **to drive a nail ~** einen Nagel einschlagen; **to bring** *or* **get sth ~ to sb** jdm etw klarmachen *or* beibringen; **it got ~ to him that ...** es wurde ihm klar, daß ...; **his words went ~** seine Worte hatten ihren Effekt; **to strike ~** ins Schwarze treffen, sitzen *(inf)*; *see* **drive ~, hammer ~, hit, press, push.**

3 *vi (pigeons)* heimkehren.

◆**home in** *vi (missiles)* sich ausrichten *(on sth* auf etw *acc)* ◆ **the missile will ~ ~** das Geschoß findet sein Ziel; **to ~ ~ on a target** ein Ziel finden *or* selbständig ansteuern; **he immediately ~d ~ on the essential point** er hat sofort den wichtigsten Punkt herausgegriffen.

home: ~ address *n* Heimatadresse *or* -anschrift *f; (as opposed to business address)* Privatanschrift *f;* **~-baked** *adj* selbstgebacken; **~ banking** *n* Homebanking *nt;* **~ base** *n (Baseball)* Heimbase *nt;* **~ birth** Hausgeburt *f;* **~boy** *n (US inf)* Einheimischer(r) *m;* **~-brew** *n* selbstgebrautes Bier, Selbstgebraute(s) *nt;* **~-brewed** *adj* selbstgebraut; **~ comforts** *npl* häuslicher Komfort; **~-coming** *n* Heimkehr *f;* **~ computer** *n* Homecomputer, Heimcomputer *m;* **~ computing** *n* Computern *nt;* **~ cooking** *n* häusliche Küche, Hausmannskost *f;* **H~ Counties** *npl Grafschaften, die an London angrenzen;* **~-cured** *adj* selbstgebeizt; **~ economics** *n sing* Hauswirtschaft(slehre) *f;* **~ exercise machine** *n* Hometrainer *m;* **~ front** *n* on the **~ front** *(Mil, Pol)* im eigenen Land; *(in business contexts)* im eigenen Betrieb; *(in personal, family contexts)* zu Hause; **~ game** *n (Sport)* Heimspiel *nt;* **~girl** *n (US inf)* Einheimische *f;* **~ ground** *n (Sport)* eigener Platz; **to be on ~ ground**

(*fig*) sich auf vertrautem Terrain bewegen; **~-grown** *adj vegetables* selbstgezogen; (*not imported*) einheimisch; **H~ Guard** *n* Bürgerwehr *f*; **~ help** *n* Haushaltshilfe *f*; **~ improvement** *n* Hausverbesserung *f*; **~ improvements loan** *n* Modernisierungsdarlehen *nt*; **~ key** *n* (*Comput*) Home-Taste *f*; **~land** *n* Heimat(land *nt*) *f*, Vaterland *nt*; **~less** *adj* heimatlos; *tramp, vagrant etc* obdachlos; **~lessness** *n see adj* Heimatlosigkeit *f*; Obdachlosigkeit *f*; **~ life** *n* Familienleben *nt*; **~like** *adj* heimelig, wie daheim; **~ loan** *n* Hypothek *f*; **~-loving** *adj* häuslich.

homely ['həʊmlɪ] *adj* (+*er*) **(a)** *food* Hausmacher-, bürgerlich; *person* (*home-loving*) häuslich, hausbacken (*pej*); *atmosphere* heimelig, gemütlich, behaglich; *style* anspruchslos, hausbacken (*pej*); *advice* einfach. **(b)** (*US: plain*) *person* unscheinbar; *face* reizlos.

home: ~-made *adj* selbstgemacht; **~maker** *n* (*US*) (*housewife*) Hausfrau, Hausmutter *f*; (*social worker*) Familienfürsorger(in *f*) *m*; **~ market** *n* Inlandsmarkt *m*, inländischer Markt; **~ match** *n* (*Sport*) Heimspiel *nt*; **~ news** *n* Meldungen *pl* aus dem Inland; **H~ Office** *n* (*Brit*) Innenministerium *nt*; (*with relation to aliens*) Einwanderungsbehörde *f*.

homeopath *etc* (*US*) *see* **homoeopath** *etc*.

home: ~-owner *n* Haus-/Wohnungseigentümer(in *f*) *m*; **~-ownership** *n* Eigenbesitz *m* von Häusern/Wohnungen; **~ plate** *n* (*Baseball*) Ausgangsbase *nt*; **~ page** *n* (*Comput*) Homepage *f*; **~ port** *n* Heimathafen *m*.

homer ['həʊmə^r] *n* **(a)** (*homing pigeon*) Brieftaube *f*. **(b)** (*Brit inf: job*) Nebenjob *m* (*inf*) ◆ **to do sth as a ~** etw privat *or* nebenher machen.

Homer ['həʊmə^r] *n* Homer *m*.

Homeric [həʊ'merɪk] *adj* homerisch.

home: H~ Rule *n* Selbstbestimmung, Selbstverwaltung *f*; (*in British contexts also*) Homerule *f*; **~ run** *n* (*Baseball*) Lauf *m* um alle vier Male; **~ sales** *npl* Inlandsumsatz *m*; **H~ Secretary** *n* (*Brit*) Innenminister *m*; **~ shopping** *n* Home-Shopping *nt*; **a ~-shopping TV programme** eine Teleshopping-Sendung; **~sick** *adj* heimwehkrank; **to be ~sick** Heimweh haben (*for* nach); **~sickness** *n* Heimweh *nt* (*for* nach); **~ side** *n* (*Sport*) Gastgeber *pl*, Heimmannschaft *f*; **~spun** [1] *adj* **(a)** *cloth* selbst- *or* handgesponnen; **(b)** (*fig: simple*) einfach; (*pej*) hausbacken; **~spun remedies** Hausmittel *pl*; **~spun philosophies** Lebensweisheiten *pl*; **~spun advice** altbewährter Rat; [2] *n* (*cloth*) Homespun *nt* (*grober, genoppter Wollstoff*); **~stead** *n* **(a)** Heimstätte *f*; **(b)** (*US*) Heimstätte *f* für Siedler; **~steader** *n* **(a)** Heimstättenbesitzer *m*; **(b)** (*US*) Heimstättensiedler *m*; **~ straight, ~ stretch** *n* (*Sport*) Zielgerade *f*; **we're on the ~ straight now** (*fig inf*) das Ende ist in Sicht; **~ team** *n* (*Sport*) Gastgeber *pl*, Heimmannschaft *f*, Platzherren *pl* (*inf*); **~ town** *n* Heimatstadt *f*; **~ truth** *n* bittere Wahrheit; **to tell sb some ~ truths** jdm die Augen öffnen.

homeward ['həʊmwəd] *adj journey, flight* Heim- ◆ **in a ~ direction** heim(wärts); (*to country also*) in Richtung Heimat; **we are ~-bound** es geht Richtung Heimat.

homeward(s) ['həʊmwəd(z)] *adv* nach Hause, heim; (*to country also*) in Richtung Heimat.

home: ~ waters *npl* (*Naut*) heimatliche Gewässer *pl*; **~work** *n* (*Sch*) Hausaufgaben, Schulaufgaben *pl*; **to give sb sth for ~work** jdm etw aufgeben; **what have you got for ~work?** was hast du auf?; **the minister had not done his ~work** (*inf*) der Minister hatte sich mit der Materie nicht vertraut gemacht; **~worker** *n* Heimarbeiter(in *f*) *m*; **~working** *n* Heimarbeit *f*.

homey ['həʊmɪ] *adj* (+*er*) (*US inf*) gemütlich; *atmosphere also* heimelig, behaglich.

homicidal [ˌhɒmɪ'saɪdl] *adj* gemeingefährlich; *mood also* Mord- ◆ **in his ~ fury** in seinem Mordrausch.

homicide ['hɒmɪsaɪd] *n* **(a)** Totschlag *m* ◆ **culpable ~** Mord *m*; **~ (squad)** Mordkommission *f*. **(b)** (*person*) Mörder(in *f*) *m*; Totschläger(in *f*) *m*.

homily ['hɒmɪlɪ] *n* Predigt *f*; (*fig also*) Sermon *m* (*pej*).

homing ['həʊmɪŋ] *adj missile* mit Zielsucheinrichtung ◆ **~ pigeon** Brieftaube *f*; **~ instinct** Heimfindevermögen *nt*; **~ device** Zielfluggerät *nt*, Zielsucheinrichtung *f*.

homo ['həʊməʊ] *n* (*dated sl*) Homo *m* (*inf*).

homoeopath, (*US*) **homeopath** ['həʊmɪəʊpæθ] *n* Homöopath(in *f*) *m*.

homoeopathic, (*US*) **homeopathic** [ˌhəʊmɪəʊ'pæθɪk] *adj* homöopathisch.

homoeopathy, (*US*) **homeopathy** [ˌhəʊmɪ'ɒpəθɪ] *n* Homöopathie *f*.

homogeneity [ˌhɒməʊdʒə'niːɪtɪ] *n* Homogenität *f*.

homogeneous [ˌhɒmə'dʒiːnɪəs] *adj* homogen.

homogenize [hə'mɒdʒənaɪz] *vt milk* homogenisieren.

homogenous [hə'mɒdʒɪnəs] *adj* homogen.

homograph ['hɒməʊgrɑːf] *n* Homograph *nt*.

homologous [hə'mɒləgəs] *adj* homolog.

homonym ['hɒmənɪm] *n* Homonym *nt*.

homonymous [hə'mɒnɪməs] *adj* homonym.

homophobe ['hɒməfəʊb] *n* Homophobe(r) *mf*.

homophone ['hɒməfəʊn] *n* Homophon *nt*.

Homo sapiens [ˌhəʊməʊ'sæpɪəns] *n* Homo sapiens *m*.

homosexual [ˌhɒməʊ'seksjʊəl] [1] *adj* homosexuell.
[2] *n* Homosexuelle(r) *mf*.

homosexuality [ˌhɒməʊseksjʊ'ælɪtɪ] *n* Homosexualität *f*.

homunculus [hɒ'mʌŋkjʊləs] *n* Homunkulus *m*.

homy *adj* (+*er*) (*US inf*) *see* **homey**.

Hon *abbr of* **(a)** honorary. **(b)** Honourable.

Honduran [hɒn'djʊərən] [1] *adj* honduranisch.
[2] *n* Honduraner(in *f*) *m*.

Honduras [hɒn'djʊərəs] *npl* Honduras *nt*.

hone [həʊn] [1] *n* Schleifstein, Wetzstein *m*.
[2] *vt blade* schleifen; (*fig*) schärfen.

◆**hone down** *vt sep* (*fig*) (zurecht)feilen (*to* auf +*acc*).

honest ['ɒnɪst] [1] *adj* **(a)** ehrlich; (*respectable*) redlich; (*not cheating*) *businessman* redlich; *business, action also* anständig; *truth* rein ◆ **be ~ with yourself** sei ehrlich gegen dich selbst, mach dir nichts vor (*inf*); **to be ~ with you, this is not good enough** um ehrlich zu sein, das ist nicht gut genug; **they are good ~ people** sie sind gute, rechtschaffene Leute; **~ to goodness** *or* **God!** (also) ehrlich! (*inf*); **he made an ~ woman of her** (*inf*) er machte sie zu seinem angetrauten Weibe (*hum*).
(b) *money, profit* ehrlich *or* redlich erworben ◆ **to earn an ~ penny** sein Geld ehrlich *or* redlich verdienen; **after an ~ day's work** nach einem ordentlichen Tagewerk; **he's never done an ~ day's work in his life** er ist in seinem ganzen Leben noch keiner ordentlichen Arbeit nachgegangen.
[2] *adv* (*inf*) ehrlich (*inf*), Ehrenwort (*inf*).

honest broker *n* (*esp Pol*) Vermittler(in) *m*(*f*).

honestly ['ɒnɪstlɪ] *adv* **(a)** *answer* ehrlich, aufrichtig; *earn money* ehrlich, auf ehrliche Weise. **(b)** (*inf: really*) ehrlich (*inf*); (*in exasperation*) also ehrlich ◆ **~, I don't care** das ist mir ehrlich (*inf*) *or* wirklich ganz egal; **~, it's terrible** das ist wirklich furchtbar.

honest-to-goodness ['ɒnɪstə'gʊdnɪs] *adj* (*inf: genuine*) echt; *person, expression* waschecht.

honesty ['ɒnɪstɪ] *n* **(a)** *see adj* Ehrlichkeit *f*; Redlichkeit *f*; Anständigkeit *f* ◆ **in all ~** ganz ehrlich; **one must admit, in all ~, ...** man muß ehrlicherweise zugeben, ...; **~ is the best policy** (*Prov*) ehrlich währt am längsten (*Prov*).
(b) (*Bot*) Mondviole *f*, Silberblatt *nt*, Judassilberling *m* (*inf*).

honey ['hʌnɪ] *n* **(a)** Honig *m*. **(b)** (*inf: dear*) Schätzchen *nt* ◆ **his little daughter is an absolute ~** seine kleine Tochter ist einfach süß (*inf*); **she's a ~** sie ist ein (Gold)schatz (*inf*).

honey: ~-bee *n* (Honig)biene *f*; **~bunch** *n* (*inf*) Schätzchen *nt*; **~comb** [1] *n* (Bienen)wabe *f*; (*filled with honey also*) Honigwabe *f*; [2] *vt usu pass* durchlöchern; **the mountain was ~combed with caves** der Berg war von Höhlen durchsetzt; **~dew** *n* Honigtau *m*; **~dew melon** Honigmelone *f*.

honeyed ['hʌnɪd] *adj words* honigsüß.

honeymoon ['hʌnɪmuːn] [1] *n* Flitterwochen *pl*; (*trip*) Hochzeitsreise *f* ◆ **to be on one's ~** in den Flitterwochen/auf Hochzeitsreise sein; **where did you go for your ~?** wo habt ihr eure Flitterwochen verbracht?; wohin habt ihr eure Hochzeitsreise gemacht?; **six months in the jungle was no ~** sechs Monate im Dschungel war kein Zuckerlecken; **the ~ is over** (*fig inf*) jetzt werden andere Saiten aufgezogen (*inf*), die Schonzeit ist vorbei; **~ couple** Flitterwöchner *pl*; **~ period** (*fig*) Schonzeit *f*.
[2] *vi* seine Hochzeitsreise machen ◆ **they are ~ing in Spain** sie sind in Spanien auf Hochzeitsreise.

honey: ~mooner ['hʌnɪˌmuːnə^r] *n* Hochzeitsreisende(r) *mf*; (*man also*) Flitterwöchner *m* (*hum*); **~suckle** *n* Geißblatt *nt*.

Hong Kong ['hɒŋ'kɒŋ] *n* Hongkong *nt*.

honk [hɒŋk] [1] *n* (*of car*) Hupen *nt*; (*of goose etc*) Schrei *m*.
[2] *interj* **~ ~** tut-tut, tüt, tüt.
[3] *vi* **(a)** (*car*) hupen, tuten. **(b)** (*geese*) schreien.
[4] *vt horn* drücken auf (+*acc*).

honky ['hɒŋkɪ] *n* (*negro pej sl*) Weiße(r) *mf*.

honky-tonk [ˌhɒŋkɪ'tɒŋk] [1] *n* (*US sl: night-club*) Schuppen *m* (*sl*).
[2] *adj music, piano* schräg.

Honolulu [ˌhɒnə'luːluː] *n* Honolulu *nt*.

honor *etc* (*US*) *see* **honour** *etc*.

honorarium [ˌɒnə'reərɪəm] *n, pl* **honoraria** [ˌɒnə'reərɪə] Honorar *nt*.

honorary ['ɒnərərɪ] *adj secretary* ehrenamtlich; *member, president* Ehren- ◆ **~ degree** *ehrenhalber verliehener akademischer Grad*; **~ doctor** Ehrendoktor, Doktor h.c.

honour, (*US*) **honor** ['ɒnə^r] [1] *n* **(a)** Ehre *f* ◆ **sense of ~** Ehrgefühl *nt*; **he made it a point of ~** er betrachtete es als Ehrensache; **he decided to make it a point of ~ never to ...** er schwor sich (*dat*), nie zu ...; **there is ~ among thieves** es gibt so etwas wie Ganovenehre; **~ where ~ is due** Ehre, wem Ehre gebührt; **on my ~!** (*old*) bei meiner Ehre (*old*); **I promise on my ~** ich gebe mein Ehrenwort; **you're on your ~** Sie haben Ihr Ehrenwort gegeben; **to put sb on his ~** jdm vertrauen; **he's put me on my ~ not to tell** ich habe ihm mein Ehrenwort gegeben, daß ich nichts sage; **man of ~** Ehrenmann *m*; **to lose one's ~** (*old*) seine Ehre verlieren (*old*); **to do ~ to sb** (*at funeral*) jdm die letzte Ehre erweisen; (*action, thought etc*) jdm zur Ehre gereichen; **to do ~ to sth, to be an ~ to sth** einer Sache (*dat*) Ehre machen; **in ~ of sb/sth** zu jds Ehren, zu Ehren von jdm/etw; (*of dead person, past thing*) in ehrendem Andenken an jdn/etw; **may I have the ~ of accompanying you?** (*form*) ich bitte um die Ehre, Sie begleiten zu dürfen (*geh*); **may I have the ~ (of the next dance)?** (*form*) darf ich (um den nächsten Tanz) bitten?; **if you would do me the ~ of accepting** (*form*) wenn Sie mir die Ehre erweisen würden anzunehmen (*geh*); **to whom do I have the ~ of speaking?** (*form, hum*) mit wem habe ich die Ehre? (*geh, hum*); **he is ~ bound to do it** es ist Ehrensache für ihn, das zu tun.
(b) (*title*) **Your H~** Hohes Gericht; **His H~** das Gericht; **the case was up before His H~ Sir Charles** der Fall wurde unter dem Vorsitz des vorsitzenden Richters Sir Charles verhandelt.
(c) (*distinction, award*) **~s** Ehren *pl*, Auszeichnung(en *pl*) *f* ◆ **with full military ~s** mit militärischen Ehren; **New Year's H~** Titelverleihung *f* am Neujahrstag.

(d) to do the ~s *(inf)* die Honneurs machen; *(on private occasions also)* den Gastgeber spielen.
(e) *(Univ)* **~s** *(also* **~s degree***)* *akademischer Grad mit Prüfung im Spezialfach;* **to do/take ~s in English** Englisch belegen, um den „Honours Degree" zu erwerben; **to get first-class ~s** das Examen mit Auszeichnung *or* „sehr gut" bestehen.
(f) *(Golf)* **it's his ~** er hat die Ehre.
(g) *(Cards) eine der (in bridge) 5 or (in whist) 4 höchsten Karten einer Farbe.*
[2] *vt* **(a)** *person* ehren ◆ **to ~ sb with a title** jdm einen Titel verleihen; **I should be (deeply) ~ed if you ...** ich würde mich (zutiefst) geehrt fühlen, wenn Sie ...; **we are ~ed by your visit** *(also iro)* wir fühlen uns durch Ihren Besuch geehrt; **he ~ed us with his presence** *(also iro)* er beehrte uns mit seiner Gegenwart; **it's Angelika, we *are* ~ed** *(iro)* es ist Angelika, welche Ehre.
(b) *cheque* annehmen, einlösen; *debt* begleichen; *bill of exchange* respektieren; *obligation* nachkommen *(+dat)*; *commitment* stehen zu; *credit card* anerkennen.

honourable, *(US)* **honorable** ['ɒnərəbl] *adj* **(a)** ehrenhaft; *person also* ehrenwert *(geh)*; *peace, discharge* ehrenvoll ◆ **to receive ~ mention** rühmend *or* lobend erwähnt werden.
(b) *(Parl) Anrede f von Abgeordneten innerhalb des Parlaments* ◆ **the H~ member for X** der (Herr) Abgeordnete für X; **the H~ member is wrong** der geschätzte *or* ehrenwerte *(iro)* (Herr) Kollege täuscht sich.
(c) *(title) Titel m der jüngeren Söhne von Grafen und der Kinder von Freiherren und Baronen* ◆ **I didn't know he was an H~** ich wußte nicht, daß er adelig *or* ein „von" *(inf)* ist.

honourably, *(US)* **honorably** ['ɒnərəblɪ] *adv* in Ehren; *behave* ehrenhaft, wie ein Ehrenmann; *settle peace* ehrenvoll; *mention* rühmend, lobend.

honours ['ɒnəz-]: **~ board** *n* Ehrentafel *f*; **~ degree** *n see* **honour 1 (e)**; **~ list** *n* Liste *f* der Titel- und Rangverleihungen(*, die zweimal im Jahr veröffentlicht wird*); *(Univ) Liste der Kandidaten, die den „Honours Degree" verliehen bekommen.*

hooch [hu:tʃ] *n (US sl)* Getränke *pl*, Stoff *m (sl)*.

hood [hʊd] [1] *n* **(a)** Kapuze *f*; *(thief's)* Maske *f*; *(hawk's)* Kappe *f*.
(b) *(Aut: roof)* Verdeck *nt*; *(US Aut)* (Motor)haube *f*; *(on fireplace etc)* Abzug *m*; *(on cooker)* Abzugshaube *f*.
(c) *(of cobra)* Brillenzeichnung *f*.
(d) *(esp US sl)* Gangster *(inf)*, Ganove *(inf) m*; *(young ruffian)* Rowdy, Rüpel *m*.
[2] *vt* eine Kapuze aufsetzen *(+dat)*; *hawk* eine Kappe aufsetzen *(+dat)*.

hooded ['hʊdɪd] *adj* **the ~ executioner/monk/robber** der Scharfrichter/Mönch mit seiner Kapuze/der maskierte Räuber; **their ~ heads** ihre Köpfe mit den Kapuzen; **~ crow** Nebelkrähe *f*; **~ eyes** Augen mit schweren Lidern.

hoodlum ['hu:dləm] *n* Rowdy *m*; *(member of gang)* Ganove *(inf)*, Gangster *(inf) m* ◆ **you young ~** du Rowdy, du Rüpel.

hoodoo ['hu:du:] *n* Unglück *nt*; *(person, thing)* Unglücksbote *m*.

hoodwink ['hʊdwɪŋk] *vt (inf)* (he)reinlegen *(inf)* ◆ **to ~ sb into doing sth** jdn dazu verleiten, etw zu tun; **they ~ed him into signing the contract** er ließ sich von ihnen (dazu) verleiten, den Vertrag zu unterschreiben; **I was ~ed into buying an imitation** man hat mir eine Imitation angedreht *(inf)*.

hooey ['hu:ɪ] *n (US sl)* Gelabere *nt (sl)*, Quatsch *m (inf)*.

hoof [hu:f] [1] *n, pl* **-s** *or* **hooves** Huf *m* ◆ **hooves** *(hum inf: feet)* Quadratlatschen *pl (sl)*; **cattle on the ~** Vieh *nt*.
[2] *vt:* **to ~ it** *(inf) (go on foot)* latschen *(inf)*; *(dance on stage)* tingeln *(inf)*.

hoofbeat ['hu:fbi:t] *n* Hufschlag *m*.

hoofed [hu:ft] *adj* Huf-.

hook [hʊk] [1] *n* **(a)** Haken *m*.
(b) *(Boxing)* Haken *m*; *(Golf)* Kurvball *m (nach links)*.
(c) *(Geog)* (gekrümmte) Landzunge.
(d) *(fig uses)* **he swallowed the story ~, line and sinker** er hat die Geschichte tatsächlich mit Stumpf und Stiel geschluckt *(inf)*; **he fell for it/her ~, line and sinker** er ging auf den Leim/er war ihr mit Haut und Haaren verfallen; **she took the bait ~, line and sinker** sie fuhr voll darauf ab *(inf)*; **by ~ or by crook** auf Biegen und Brechen; **to get sb off the ~** *(inf)* jdn herausreißen *(inf)*; *(out of trouble also)* jdn herauspauken *(inf)*; **that gets him off the ~ every time** damit kommt er jedesmal wieder davon; **to get oneself off the ~** sich aus der Schlinge ziehen; **that lets me off the ~** *(inf)* damit bin ich aus dem Schneider *(inf)*; **to leave the phone off the ~** nicht auflegen.
[2] *vt* **(a)** *(fasten with ~)* **he ~ed the door back/open** er hakte die Tür fest/er öffnete die Tür und hakte sie fest; **the old man ~s the rowing boats and pulls them in** der alte Mann zieht die Ruderboote mit einem Haken ans Ufer; **to ~ a trailer to a car** einen Anhänger an ein Auto hängen; **the bull had ~ed him on his horns** der Stier hatte ihn auf die Hörner genommen.
(b) to ~ one's arm/feet around sth seinen Arm/seine Füße um etw schlingen; **the trapeze artist ~s his legs over the bar** der Trapezkünstler hängt sich mit den Beinen an der Stange ein; **his car got its bumper ~ed around mine** sein Auto hat sich mit der Stoßstange in meiner verhakt.
(c) *fish* an die Angel bekommen; *husband* sich *(dat)* angeln ◆ **to be ~ed** an der Angel hängen; **the helicopter ~ed him clean out of the water** der Hubschrauber zog *or* angelte *(inf)* ihn aus dem Wasser.
(d) *(Boxing)* einen Haken versetzen *(+dat) or* geben *(+dat)*.
(e) to be/get ~ed (on sth) *(sl: addicted) (on drugs)* (von etw) abhängig sein/werden; *(on film, food, place etc)* auf etw *(acc)* stehen *(sl)*; **he's ~ed on the idea** er ist von der Idee besessen; **don't get ~ed on the idea** versteif dich nicht zu sehr auf den Gedanken.
(f) *(Rugby)* hakeln.
(g) *(Sport) ball* einen Linksdrall geben *(+dat)*.
(h) *(sl: clear off)* **to ~ it** Mücke machen *(sl)*.
[3] *vi (dress etc)* zugehakt werden.

◆**hook on** [1] *vi* (an)gehakt werden *(to* an *+acc)*; *(with tow-bar)* angekoppelt *or* angehängt werden *(to* an *+acc)*; *(burrs etc)* sich festhaken *(to* an *+dat)* ◆ **he ~ed ~ to him** *(fig)* er hängte *or* klammerte sich an ihn.
[2] *vt sep* anhaken *(to* an *+acc)*, mit Haken/einem Haken befestigen *(to* an *+dat)*; *(with tow-bar)* ankoppeln, anhängen ◆ **to ~ sth ~to sth** etw an etw *(acc)* (an)haken; **the gliders were ~ed ~ behind the tow-plane** die Segelflugzeuge waren hinten an das Schleppflugzeug angehängt *or* angekoppelt.

◆**hook up** [1] *vi* **(a)** *(dress)* mit Haken zugemacht werden. **(b)** *(Rad, TV)* gemeinsam ausstrahlen. **to ~ ~ with sb** sich jdm anschließen.
[2] *vt sep* **(a)** *dress etc* zuhaken ◆ **~ me** *or* **the dress ~, please** mach mir bitte die Haken zu, mach an dem Kleid bitte die Haken zu. **(b)** *(Rad, TV)* anschließen *(with* an *+acc)*. **(c)** *trailer, caravan* ankoppeln, anhängen; *broken-down car* abschleppen; *(by recovery vehicle)* auf den Haken nehmen.

hookah ['hʊka:] *n* Wasserpfeife, Huka *f*.

hook and eye *n* Haken und Öse *no art, pl vb*.

hooked [hʊkt] *adj* **(a)** *beak* Haken-, gebogen ◆ **~ nose** Hakennase *f*. **(b)** *(equipped with hooks)* mit Haken versehen.

hooker[1] ['hʊkə[r]] *n (US inf)* Nutte *f (inf)*.

hooker[2] *n (Rugby)* Hakler *m*.

hook: ~-nosed *adj* mit einer Hakennase, hakennasig; **~-up** *n (Rad, TV)* gemeinsame Ausstrahlung; **there will be a ~-up between the major European networks** die größeren europäischen Sender übertragen gemeinsam; **~worm** *n* Hakenwurm *m*; *(disease)* Hakenwurmkrankheit *f*.

hooky ['hʊkɪ] *n (US inf)* Schuleschwänzen *nt (inf)* ◆ **to play ~** (die) Schule schwänzen *(inf)*.

hooligan ['hu:lɪgən] *n* Rowdy *m*.

hooliganism ['hu:lɪgənɪzəm] *n* Rowdytum *nt*.

hoop [hu:p] [1] *n* Reifen *m*; *(in croquet)* Tor *nt*; *(on bird's plumage)* Kranz *m*; *(on animal)* Ring *m* ◆ **to go through the ~s** *(fig inf)* durch die Mangel gedreht werden *(inf)*; **to put sb through the ~s** *(fig inf)* jdn durch die Mangel drehen *(inf)*.
[2] *vt barrel* bereifen ◆ **~(ed) skirt** Reifrock *m*.

hoop-la ['hu:pla:] *n* Ringwerfen *nt*.

hoopoe ['hu:pu:] *n* Wiedehopf *m*.

hooray [hə'reɪ] *interj see* **hurrah**.

Hooray Henry *n junger Angehöriger der Oberschicht mit auffälligem Gehabe.*

hoosegow ['hu:sgaʊ] *n (US sl: jail)* Knast *m (sl)*.

hoot [hu:t] [1] *n* **(a)** *(of owl)* Ruf, Schrei *m* ◆ **~s of derision** verächtliches Gejohle; **~s of laughter** johlendes Gelächter; **I don't care a ~** *or* **two ~s** *(inf)* das ist mir piepegal *(inf) or* völlig schnuppe *(inf)*; **to be a ~** *(inf) (person, event etc)* zum Schreien (komisch) sein, zum Schießen sein *(inf)*.
(b) *(Aut)* Hupen *nt no pl*; *(of train, hooter)* Pfeifen *nt no pl*.
[2] *vi* **(a)** *(owl)* schreien, rufen; *(person: derisively)* johlen, buhen ◆ **to ~ with derision** verächtlich johlen; **to ~ with laughter** in johlendes Gelächter ausbrechen.
(b) *(Aut)* hupen; *(train, factory hooter)* pfeifen.
[3] *vt actor, speaker* auspfeifen, ausbuhen ◆ **he was ~ed off the stage** er wurde mit Buhrufen von der Bühne verjagt.

◆**hoot down** *vt sep* niederschreien.

hootchy-kootchy ['hu:tʃɪ'ku:tʃɪ] *n (US sl)* Bauchtanz *m*.

hootenanny ['hu:tə'nænɪ] *n* Hootenanny *f*.

hooter ['hu:tə[r]] *n* **(a)** *(Aut)* Hupe *f*; *(at factory)* Sirene *f*. **(b)** *(Brit sl: nose)* Zinken *m (sl)*.

hoover ® ['hu:və[r]] [1] *n* Staubsauger *m*.
[2] *vt* (staub)saugen; *carpet also* (ab)saugen.
[3] *vi* (staub)saugen.

hoovering ['hu:vərɪŋ] *n* **to do the ~** (staub)saugen.

hooves [hu:vz] *pl of* **hoof**.

hop[1] [hɒp] [1] *n* **(a)** (kleiner) Sprung; *(of bird, insect also)* Hüpfer *m*; *(of deer, rabbit also)* Satz *m*; *(of person also)* Hüpfer, Hopser *(inf) m* ◆ **to catch sb on the ~** *(fig inf)* jdn überraschen *or* überrumpeln; **to keep sb on the ~** *(fig inf)* jdn in Trab halten.
(b) *(inf: dance)* Tanz *m*, Hopserei *f (pej inf)*.
(c) *(Aviat inf)* Sprung, Satz *(inf) m* ◆ **a short ~** ein kleiner Satz *(inf)*, ein Katzensprung *m (inf)*.
[2] *vi (animal)* hüpfen, springen; *(rabbit)* hoppeln; *(person)* (auf einem Bein) hüpfen, hopsen *(inf)* ◆ **~ in, said the driver** steigen Sie ein, sagte der Fahrer; **she'd ~ into bed with anyone** die steigt mit jedem ins Bett *(inf)*; **to ~ off** aussteigen; *(from moving vehicle)* abspringen; **to ~ off the train** aus dem Zug aussteigen; *(while moving)* vom Zug abspringen; **he ~ped off his bicycle** er sprang vom Fahrrad; **to ~ on** aufsteigen; *(onto moving vehicle)* aufspringen; **to ~ on a train** in einen Zug einsteigen; *(while moving)* auf einen Zug aufspringen; **he ~ped on his bicycle** er schwang sich auf sein Fahrrad; **to ~ out** heraushüpfen; **he ~ped over the wall** er sprang über die Mauer.
[3] *vt* **(a)** *ditch* springen über *(+acc)*; *train* schwarzfahren in *(+dat) or* mit.
(b) *(inf)* **~ it!** verschwinde, zieh Leine *(inf)*; **I ~ped it quick** ich habe mich schnell aus dem Staub gemacht *(inf)*.

◆**hop off** *vi (inf)* sich verdrücken *(inf)*, sich aus dem Staub machen *(inf) (with sth* mit etw).

hop[2] *n (Bot)* Hopfen *m* ◆ **~ picker** Hopfenpflücker(in *f*) *m*; **~ picking**

Hopfenernte *f*, Hopfenpflücken *nt*; **~-picking season** Hopfenernte *f*; **~ garden** Hopfengarten *m*.

▼ **hope** [həʊp] [1] *n* (*also person*) Hoffnung *f* ◆ **past** *or* **beyond all ~** hoffnungslos, aussichtslos; **the patient is beyond all ~** für den Patienten besteht keine Hoffnung mehr; **to be full of ~** hoffnungsvoll *or* voller Hoffnung sein; **my ~ is that ...** ich hoffe nur, daß ...; **in the ~ of doing sth** in der Hoffnung, etw zu tun; **to have ~s of doing sth** hoffen, etw zu tun; **to live in ~ of sth** in der Hoffnung auf etw (*acc*) leben; **well, we live in ~** nun, wir hoffen eben (weiter); **to place one's ~ in sb/sth** seine Hoffnungen in *or* auf jdn/etw setzen; **there is no ~ of him having survived** es besteht keine Hoffnung, daß er überlebt hat; **we have some ~ of success** es besteht die Hoffnung, daß wir Erfolg haben; **there's no ~ of that** da braucht man sich gar keine Hoffnungen zu machen; **where there's life there's ~** es ist noch nicht aller Tage Abend; (*said of invalid*) solange er/sie sich noch regt, besteht auch noch Hoffnung; **to lose ~ of doing sth** die Hoffnung aufgeben, etw zu tun; **what a ~!** (*inf*), **some ~(s)!** (*inf*) schön wär's! (*inf*); **~ springs eternal** (*prov*) wenn die Hoffnung nicht wäre!

▼[2] *vi* hoffen (*for* auf +*acc*) ◆ **to ~ for the best** das Beste hoffen; **you can't ~ for anything else from him** man kann sich doch von ihm nichts anderes erhoffen; **one might have ~d for something better** man hätte (eigentlich) auf etwas Besseres hoffen dürfen, man hätte sich eigentlich Besseres erhoffen dürfen; **I ~ so/not** hoffentlich/hoffentlich nicht, ich hoffe es/(es) nicht; **to ~ against hope that ...** trotz allem die Hoffnung nicht aufgeben, daß ..., wider alle Hoffnung hoffen, daß ...

[3] *vt* hoffen ◆ **I ~ to see you** hoffentlich sehe ich Sie, ich hoffe, daß ich Sie sehe; **hoping to hear from you** ich hoffe, von Ihnen zu hören, in der Hoffnung (*form*), von Ihnen zu hören.

hope chest *n* (*US*) Aussteuertruhe *f*.

hopeful ['həʊpfʊl] [1] *adj* (a) hoffnungsvoll ◆ **don't be too ~** machen Sie sich (*dat*) keine zu großen Hoffnungen; **they weren't very ~** sie hatten keine große Hoffnung; **they continue to be ~** sie hoffen weiter, sie geben die Hoffnung nicht auf; **to be ~ that ...** hoffen, daß ...; **I'm ~ of a recovery** ich hoffe auf Besserung; **you think they'll agree? boy, you're ~** du glaubst, sie sind einverstanden? du bist vielleicht ein Optimist (*inf*).

(b) *situation, response, sign* vielversprechend, aussichtsreich ◆ **it looks ~** es sieht vielversprechend aus.

[2] *n* (*inf*) **a young ~** (*seems likely to succeed*) eine junge Hoffnung; (*hopes to succeed*) ein hoffnungsvoller junger Mensch.

hopefully ['həʊpfəlɪ] *adv* (a) hoffnungsvoll. (b) hoffentlich ◆ **~ it won't rain** hoffentlich regnet es nicht.

hopeless ['həʊplɪs] *adj situation, outlook* aussichtslos, hoffnungslos; *liar, drunkard etc* unverbesserlich; *weather, food* unmöglich (*inf*) ◆ **you're ~** du bist ein hoffnungsloser Fall; **he's ~ at maths/a ~ teacher** in Mathematik/als Lehrer ist er ein hoffnungsloser Fall.

hopelessly ['həʊplɪslɪ] *adv* hoffnungslos ◆ **we were ~ lost** wir hatten uns hoffnungslos verirrt; **I'm ~ bad at maths** in Mathematik bin ich ein hoffnungsloser Fall.

hopelessness ['həʊplɪsnɪs] *n* (*of situation*) Hoffnungslosigkeit *f*; (*of task*) Aussichtslosigkeit *f*.

hoplite ['hɒplaɪt] *n* Hoplit *m*.

hop-o'-my-thumb ['hɒpəmaɪ'θʌm] *n* Knirps, Stöpsel (*inf*) *m*.

hopper ['hɒpəʳ] *n* (a) (*Tech*) Einfülltrichter *m*; (*for coal also*) Speisetrichter *m*. (b) (*young locust*) junge Heuschrecke.

hopping mad ['hɒpɪŋ'mæd] *adj* (*inf*) fuchsteufelswild (*inf*).

hop: ~scotch *n* Himmel-und-Hölle(-Spiel) *nt*, Hopse *f* (*inf*); **~, step** *or* **skip and jump** *n* Dreisprung *m*.

Horace ['hɒrɪs] *n* Horaz *m*.

Horatian [hə'reɪʃən] *adj* horazisch.

horde [hɔːd] *n* (a) (*of nomads, wild animals*) Horde *f*; (*of insects*) Schwarm *m*. (b) (*inf*) Masse *f*; (*of football fans, children etc*) Horde *f* (*pej*) ◆ **~s of books** massenhaft Bücher (*inf*).

horizon [hə'raɪzn] *n* Horizont *m*; (*fig*) Horizont, Gesichtskreis *m no pl* ◆ **on the ~** am Horizont; (*fig*) in Sicht; **the ship went over** *or* **beneath the ~** das Schiff verschwand am Horizont.

horizontal [ˌhɒrɪ'zɒntl] *adj* waag(e)recht, horizontal ◆ **~ line** Waag(e)rechte, Horizontale *f*.

horizontal: ~ bar *n* Reck *nt*; **~ hold** *n* (*TV*) Zeilenfang, Bildfang *m*.

horizontally [ˌhɒrɪ'zɒntəlɪ] *adv see adj*.

hormonal [hɔː'məʊnəl] *adj* hormonal, hormonell.

hormone ['hɔːməʊn] *n* Hormon *nt* ◆ **~ treatment** Hormonbehandlung *f*.

horn [hɔːn] [1] *n* (a) (*of cattle, substance, container, Mus*) Horn *nt*; (*sl: trumpet, saxophone etc*) Kanne (*sl*), Tüte (*sl*) *f* ◆ **~s** (*of deer*) Geweih *nt*; (*fig: of cuckold*) Hörner *pl*; **caught on the ~s of a dilemma** in einer Zwickmühle; **that is the other ~ of the dilemma** das ist die andere Gefahr; **~ of plenty** Füllhorn *nt*; **to lock ~s** (*lit*) beim Kampf die Geweihe verhaken; (*fig*) die Klingen kreuzen.

(b) (*Aut*) Hupe *f*; (*Naut*) (Signal)horn *nt* ◆ **to sound** *or* **blow the ~** (*Aut*) hupen, auf die Hupe drücken (*inf*); (*Naut*) tuten, das Horn ertönen lassen.

(c) (*of snail, insect*) Fühler *m* ◆ **to draw in one's ~s** (*fig*) einen Rückzieher machen; (*spend less*) den Gürtel enger schnallen.

(d) (*of crescent moon*) Spitze *f* (der Mondsichel).

[2] *vt* (*gore*) mit den Hörnern aufspießen; (*butt*) auf die Hörner nehmen.

◆**horn in** *vi* (*sl*) (*interfere*) mitmischen (*inf*) (*on* bei); (*muscle in*) sich hineindrängen (*on* in +*acc*) ◆ **dozens of entrepreneurs started ~ing ~** zig Unternehmer versuchten, auch ein Stück vom Kuchen zu bekommen (*inf*).

horn *in cpds* Horn-; **~beam** *n* (*Bot*) Hain- *or* Weißbuche *f*; **~bill** *n* (*Orn*) (Nas)hornvogel *m*.

horned [hɔːnd] *adj* gehörnt, mit Hörnern ◆ **~ owl** Ohreule *f*; **~ toad** Krötenechse *f*.

hornet ['hɔːnɪt] *n* Hornisse *f* ◆ **to stir up a ~'s nest** (*fig*) in ein Wespennest stechen.

hornless ['hɔːnlɪs] *adj* ohne Hörner, hornlos.

horn: ~pipe *n englischer Seemannstanz*; **~-rimmed** *adj spectacles* Horn-.

horny ['hɔːnɪ] *adj* (+*er*) (a) (*like horn*) hornartig; *hands etc* schwielig; *soles* hornig. (b) (*inf: randy*) scharf (*inf*), geil (*inf*).

horology [hɔː'rɒlədʒɪ] *n* (*measuring time*) Zeitmessung *f*; (*watchmaking*) Uhrmacherkunst *f*.

horoscope ['hɒrəskəʊp] *n* Horoskop *nt*.

horrendous [hɒ'rendəs] *adj crime* abscheulich, entsetzlich; *prices, lie* horrend.

horrendously [hɒ'rendəslɪ] *adv* abscheulich, entsetzlich; *expensive* horrend.

horrible ['hɒrɪbl] *adj* fürchterlich, schrecklich ◆ **don't be ~ to your sister** sei nicht so gemein zu deiner Schwester (*inf*).

horribly ['hɒrɪblɪ] *adv see adj*.

horrid ['hɒrɪd] *adj* entsetzlich, fürchterlich, schrecklich ◆ **don't be so ~** sei nicht so gemein (*inf*).

horridly ['hɒrɪdlɪ] *adv see adj*.

horrific [hɒ'rɪfɪk] *adj* entsetzlich, schrecklich; *documentary* erschreckend; *price increase also* horrend.

horrify ['hɒrɪfaɪ] *vt* entsetzen ◆ **he was horrified by** *or* **at the suggestion** er war über den Vorschlag entsetzt; **it horrifies me to think what ...** ich denke (nur) mit Entsetzen daran, was ...; **he likes to ~ people** er schockiert gern.

horrifying *adj*, **~ly** *adv* ['hɒrɪfaɪɪŋ, -lɪ] schrecklich, fürchterlich, entsetzlich.

horror ['hɒrəʳ] [1] *n* (a) Entsetzen, Grauen *nt*; (*strong dislike*) Horror *m* (*of* vor +*dat*) ◆ **to have a ~ of doing sth** einen Horror davor haben, etw zu tun; **he has a ~ of growing old** er hat eine panische Angst vor dem Altwerden, ihm graut vor dem Altwerden; **she shrank back in ~** sie fuhr entsetzt zurück; **a scene of ~** ein Bild des Grauens.

(b) *usu pl* (*horrifying thing; of war etc*) Schrecken, Greuel *m*.

(c) (*inf*) **to be a real ~** furchtbar sein (*inf*); **you little ~!** du kleines Ungeheuer! (*inf*).

(d) (*inf usages*) **to have the ~s** (*in delirium tremens*) weiße Mäuse sehen (*inf*); **that gives me the ~s** da läuft's mir kalt den Rücken runter (*inf*); **~ of ~s** (*referring to an actual event*) oh Schreck (*inf*); **if, ~ of ~s, ...** wenn, Gott behüte, ...

[2] *attr books, comics, films* Horror-.

horror: ~-stricken, ~-struck *adj* von Entsetzen *or* Grauen gepackt ◆ **I was ~-stricken** *or* **-struck when he told me** mir grauste es *or* ich war hell entsetzt, als er es mir erzählte; **~ trip** *n* (*inf*) Horrortrip *m*.

hors de combat ['ɔːdə'kɒmbɑː] *adj* (*lit, fig*) außer Gefecht gesetzt, kampfunfähig.

hors d'oeuvre [ɔː'dɜːv] *n* Hors d'oeuvre *nt*, Vorspeise *f*.

horse [hɔːs] *n* (a) Pferd, Roß (*liter, pej*) *nt*.

(b) (*fig usages*) **wild ~s would not drag me there** keine zehn Pferde würden mich dahin bringen; **to eat like a ~** wie ein Scheunendrescher *m* essen *or* fressen (*inf*); **I could eat a ~** ich könnte ein ganzes Pferd essen; **to work like a ~** wie ein Pferd arbeiten; **information straight from the ~'s mouth** Informationen *pl* aus erster Hand; **to back the wrong ~** aufs falsche Pferd setzen; **but that's a ~ of a different colour** aber das ist wieder was anderes.

(c) (*Gymnastics*) Pferd *nt*; (*saw~*) Sägebock *m*.

(d) (*Mil*) *collective sing* Reiterei, Kavallerie *f* ◆ **light ~** leichte Kavallerie; **a thousand ~** tausend Reiter *or* Berittene.

◆**horse about** *or* **around** *vi* (*inf*) herumalbern (*inf*).

horse: ~-artillery *n* berittene Artillerie; **~back** *n* **on ~back** zu Pferd, zu Roß (*liter*); **to go/set off on ~back** reiten/wegreiten; **~-box** *n* (*van*) Pferdetransporter *m*; (*trailer*) Pferdetransportwagen *m*; (*in stable*) Box *f*; **~ brass** *n* Zaumzeugbeschlag *m*; **~ breeder** *n* Pferdezüchter *m*; **~ chestnut** *n* (*tree, fruit*) Roßkastanie *f*; **~-doctor** *n* (*inf*) Viehdoktor *m* (*inf*); **~-drawn** *adj* von Pferden gezogen; *hearse, milk-cart* pferdebespannt *attr*; **~-drawn cart** Pferdewagen *m*; **~flesh** *n* (*meat of horse*) Pferdefleisch *nt*; (*horses collectively*) Pferde *pl*; **a good judge of ~flesh** ein guter Pferdekenner; **~fly** *n* (Pferde)bremse *f*; **H~ Guards** *npl* berittene Garde, Gardekavallerie *f*; **~hair** [1] *n* Roßhaar *nt*; [2] *adj attr* Roßhaar-; **~ latitudes** *npl* Roßbreiten *pl*; **~-laugh** *n* wieherndes Lachen *or* Gelächter; **~less** *adj* ohne Pferd; **~less carriage** *n* (*old: motorcar*) selbstfahrender Wagen; **~man** *n* Reiter *m*; **~manship** *n* Reitkunst *f*; **~meat** *n* Pferdefleisch *nt*; **~ opera** *n* (*hum inf: Film*) Western *m*; **~play** *n* Alberei, Balgerei *f*; **to have a bit of ~play with sb** mit jdm herumbalgen; **~power** *n* Pferdestärke *f*; **a twenty ~power car** ein Auto mit zwanzig PS *or* Pferdestärken; **~-race** *n* Pferderennen *nt*; **~-racing** *n* Pferderennsport *m*; (*races*) Pferderennen *pl*; **~radish** *n* Meerrettich *m*; **~-riding** *n* Reiten *nt*; **~-sense** *n* gesunder Menschenverstand; **~shit** *n* (*fig sl: nonsense*) Scheiß *m* (*sl*); **~shoe** [1] *n* Hufeisen *nt*; [2] *attr* hufeisenförmig, Hufeisen-; **~ show** *n* Pferdeschau *f*; **~-trading** *n* (*fig*) Kuhhandel *m*; **~whip** [1] *n* Reitpeitsche *f*; [2] *vt* auspeitschen; **~woman** *n* Reiterin *f*.

hors(e)y ['hɔːsɪ] *adj* (+*er*) (*inf*) (*fond of horses*) pferdenärrisch; *appearance* pferdeähnlich ◆ **~ people** Pferdenarren *pl*; **~ face** Pferdegesicht *nt*; **she is going through a ~ stage** sie hat gerade einen Pferdefimmel (*inf*).

hortative ['hɔːtətɪv] *adj* anspornend.

horticultural [ˌhɔːtɪ'kʌltʃərəl] *adj* Garten(bau)- ◆ **~ show** Gartenschau, Gartenbauausstellung *f*.

horticulture ['hɔːtɪkʌltʃəʳ] *n* Gartenbau(kunst *f*) *m*.

➤ LANGUAGE IN USE: **hope: 2 → 8.4**

horticulturist [ˌhɔːtɪ'kʌltʃərɪst] *n* Gärtner(in *f*) *m*.

hosanna [həʊ'zænə] [1] *interj* hos(i)anna.
[2] *n* Hos(i)anna *nt*.

hose¹ [həʊz] [1] *n* (*also* **~pipe**) Schlauch *m*.
[2] *vt* (*also* **~ down**) abspritzen.

◆**hose out** *vt sep* ausspritzen.

hose² *n, no pl* **(a)** (*Comm: stockings*) Strümpfe, Strumpfwaren *pl*. **(b)** (*Hist: for men*) (Knie)hose *f*.

hosier ['həʊʒəʳ] *n* Strumpfwarenhändler *m*.

hosiery ['həʊʒərɪ] *n* Strumpfwaren *pl*.

hospice ['hɒspɪs] *n* **(a)** (*for terminally ill*) Pflegeheim *nt* (*für unheilbar Kranke*). **(b)** (*for travellers*) Hospiz *nt*.

hospitable *adj*, **-bly** *adv* [hɒs'pɪtəbl, -ɪ] gastfreundlich, gastlich.

hospital ['hɒspɪtl] *n* Krankenhaus *nt*, Klinik *f*, Hospital *nt* (*old, Sw*) ◆ **in** *or* (*US*) **in the ~** im Krankenhaus; **he's got to go to** *or* (*US*) **the ~** er muß ins Krankenhaus (gehen).

hospital *in cpds* Krankenhaus-; **~ administration** *n* Krankenhausverwaltung *f*; **~ administrator** *n* Krankenhausverwalter(in *f*) *m*; **~ bed** *n* Krankenhausbett *nt*; **~ case** *n* Fall, der im Krankenhaus behandelt werden muß; **~ facilities** *npl* (*equipment*) Krankenhauseinrichtung(en *pl*) *f*; (*hospitals*) Kranken(heil)anstalten *pl*.

hospitality [ˌhɒspɪ'tælɪtɪ] *n* Gastfreundschaft, Gastlichkeit *f*.

hospitalization [ˌhɒspɪtəlaɪ'zeɪʃən] *n* **(a)** Einweisung *f* ins Krankenhaus; (*stay in hospital*) Krankenhausaufenthalt *m*. **(b)** (*US: ~ insurance*) Versicherung *f* für Krankenhauspflege.

hospitalize ['hɒspɪtəlaɪz] *vt* ins Krankenhaus einweisen ◆ **he was ~d for three months** er lag drei Monate lang im Krankenhaus.

hospital: ~ nurse *n* Krankenschwester *f* (im Krankenhaus); **~ porter** *n* Pfleger(in *f*) *m*; (*doorman*) Pförtner(in *f*) *m* (im Krankenhaus); **~ ship** *n* Lazarett- *or* Krankenschiff *nt*; **~ train** *n* Lazarettzug *m*.

host¹ [həʊst] [1] *n* **(a)** Gastgeber *m*; (*in own home also*) Hausherr *m* ◆ **to be ~ to sb** jds Gastgeber sein; (*in own home also*) jdn zu Besuch *or* Gast haben; **~ country** Gastland *nt*.
(b) (*in hotel etc*) Wirt *m*, Herr *m* des Hauses (*form*) ◆ **your ~s are Mr and Mrs X** Ihre Wirtsleute sind Herr und Frau X; **mine ~** (*obs, hum*) der Herr Wirt.
(c) (*Bot*) Wirt(spflanze *f*) *m*; (*Zool*) Wirt(stier *nt*) *m*.
(d) (*on TV programme etc*) Gastgeber *m*.
(e) (*also* **~ computer**) Host(-Rechner) *m*.
[2] *vt TV programme, games* Gastgeber sein bei.

host² *n* **(a)** Menge, Masse (*inf*) *f* ◆ **he has a ~ of friends** er hat massenweise (*inf*) *or* eine Menge Freunde; **a whole ~ of reasons** eine ganze Menge *or* Anzahl von Gründen.
(b) (*obs, liter*) Heerschar *f* (*obs, liter*) ◆ **a ~ of angels** eine Engelschar; **the Lord of H~s** der Herr der Heerscharen.

Host [həʊst] *n* (*Eccl*) Hostie *f*.

hostage ['hɒstɪdʒ] *n* Geisel *f* ◆ **to take sb ~** jdn als Geisel nehmen; **to take ~s** Geiseln nehmen.

hostage: ~-taker *n* Geiselnehmer(in *f*); **~-taking** *n* Geiselnahme *f*.

hostel ['hɒstəl] [1] *n* (*for students, workers etc*) (Wohn)heim *nt* ◆ **Youth H~** Jugendherberge *f*.
[2] *vi*: **to go ~ling** in Jugendherbergen übernachten.

hosteller ['hɒstələʳ] *n* Heimbewohner(in *f*) *m*; (*in Youth Hostel*) Herbergsgast *m*.

hostelry ['hɒstəlrɪ] *n* (*obs*) Herberge *f* (*liter*).

hostess ['həʊstes] *n* **(a)** (*person*) Gastgeberin *f*; (*in own home also*) Hausherrin *f* ◆ **to be ~ to sb** jds Gastgeberin sein; (*in own home also*) jdn zu Besuch *or* Gast haben.
(b) (*in hotels etc*) Wirtin *f*.
(c) (*in night-club*) Hosteß *f*.
(d) (*air-~*) Stewardeß *f*; (*at exhibition etc*) Hosteß *f*.
(e) (*on TV programme etc*) Gastgeberin *f*.

hostile ['hɒstaɪl] *adj* **(a)** (*of an enemy*) feindlich. **(b)** (*showing enmity*) feindlich (gesinnt); *reception, looks* feindselig; *takeover bid* feindlich ◆ **to be ~ to sb** sich jdm gegenüber feindselig verhalten; **to be ~ to sth** einer Sache (*dat*) feindlich gegenüberstehen; **~ to technology** technikfeindlich.

hostility [hɒs'tɪlɪtɪ] *n* **(a)** Feindseligkeit *f*; (*between people*) Feindschaft *f* ◆ **to show ~ to sb** sich jdm gegenüber feindselig verhalten; **to show ~ to sth** einer Sache (*dat*) feindlich gegenüberstehen; **feelings of ~** feindselige Gefühle *pl*; **he feels no ~ towards anybody** er ist niemandem feindlich gesinnt; **~ to foreigners** Ausländerfeindlichkeit *f*.
(b) hostilities *pl* (*warfare*) Feindseligkeiten *pl*.

hostler ['ɒsləʳ] *n see* **ostler**.

hot [hɒt] [1] *adj* (+*er*) **(a)** heiß; *meal, tap, drink* warm ◆ **I am** *or* **feel ~** mir ist (es) heiß; **with ~ and cold water** mit warm und kalt Wasser; **it was a ~ and tiring climb** der Aufstieg machte warm und müde; **the weather is ~** es ist heißes Wetter; **in the ~ weather** bei dem heißen Wetter, wenn es so heiß ist; **Africa is a ~ country** in Afrika ist es heiß; **to get ~** (*things*) heiß werden; **I'm getting ~** mir wird (es) warm; **you're getting ~** (*fig: when guessing*) jetzt wird's schon wärmer (*inf*).
(b) (*to taste*) *curry, spices etc* scharf.
(c) (*inf: radioactive material*) radioaktiv, heiß (*inf*).
(d) (*sl*) *stolen goods* heiß (*inf*) ◆ **it's too ~ to sell** so heiße Ware läßt sich nicht verkaufen (*inf*).
(e) (*inf: in demand*) *product* zugkräftig.
(f) (*inf: good, competent*) stark (*inf*); *person also* fähig ◆ **he/it isn't (all) that ~** so umwerfend ist er/das auch wieder nicht (*inf*); **he's pretty ~ at maths** in Mathe ist er ganz schön stark (*inf*); **I'm not feeling too ~** mir geht's nicht besonders (*inf*).
(g) (*fig*) **to be (a) ~ favourite** hoch favorisiert sein, der große Favorit sein; **~ tip** heißer Tip; **~ jazz** Hot Jazz *m*; **~ news** das Neuste vom Neuen; **~ from the press** gerade erschienen; **the pace was so ~** das Tempo war so scharf; **she has a ~ temper** sie braust leicht auf, sie hat ein hitziges Wesen; **she's too ~ to handle** (*inf*) mit der wird keiner fertig (*inf*); **it's too ~ to handle** (*inf*) (*stolen goods*) das ist heiße Ware (*inf*); (*political issue, in journalism*) das ist ein heißes Eisen; **to get into ~ water** in Schwulitäten kommen (*inf*), in (des) Teufels Küche kommen (*inf*); **to be/get (all) ~ and bothered** (*inf*) ganz aufgeregt sein/werden (*about* wegen); **to look/feel ~ and bothered** (*inf*) ganz aufgeregt aussehen/ins Schwitzen kommen (*inf*); **to get ~ under the collar about sth** wegen etw in Rage geraten; (*embarrassed*) wegen etw verlegen werden; **I went ~ and cold all over** (*inf*) (*illness*) mir wurde abwechselnd heiß und kalt; (*emotion*) mir wurde es ganz anders (*inf*); **things started getting ~ in the tenth round/the discussion** (*inf*) in der zehnten Runde wurde es langsam spannend *or* ging's los (*inf*)/bei der Diskussion ging's heiß her (*inf*); **to make a place** *or* **things too ~ for sb** (*inf*) jdm die Hölle heiß machen (*inf*), jdm einheizen (*inf*); **it's getting too ~ for me here** (*inf*) hier wird mir der Boden unter den Füßen zu heiß; *see* **trail 1 (b)**.
[2] *adv* (+*er*) **the engine's running ~** der Motor läuft heiß; **he keeps blowing ~ and cold** er sagt einmal hü und einmal hott.
[3] *n* **to have the ~s for sb** (*inf*) auf jdn scharf sein (*inf*).

◆**hot up** (*inf*) [1] *vi* **the pace is ~ting ~** das Tempo wird schneller; **things are ~ting ~ in the Middle East** die Lage im Nahen Osten spitzt sich zu *or* verschärft sich; **things are ~ting ~** es geht langsam los (*inf*); (*party also*) die Sache kommt in Schwung.
[2] *vt sep* (*fig*) *music* verpoppen (*inf*); *pace* steigern; *engine* frisieren.

hot: ~ air *n* (*fig*) leeres Gerede, Gewäsch *nt*; **~-air** *adj attr balloon* Heißluft-; **~bed** *n* **(a)** (*fig*) Brutstätte *f*, Nährboden *m* (*of* für); **(b)** (*Hort*) Mist- *or* Frühbeet *nt*; **~-blooded** *adj* heißblütig.

hotchpotch ['hɒtʃpɒtʃ] *n* Durcheinander *nt*, Mischmasch *m*.

hot: ~ cross bun *n Rosinenbrötchen nt mit kleinem Teigkreuz, wird in der Karwoche gegessen*; **~ dog** *n* Hot dog *m or nt*; **~dogging** *n* (*Ski*) Freestyle *nt*.

hotel [həʊ'tel] *n* Hotel *nt*.

hotelier [həʊ'telɪəʳ] *n* Hotelier *m*.

hotel: ~ industry *n* Hotelgewerbe *nt*, Hotellerie *f*; **~ keeper** *n* Hotelier, Hotelbesitzer *m*; **~ manager** *n* Hoteldirektor(in *f*) *m*; **~ porter** *n* Haus- *or* Hoteldiener *m*; **~ room** *n* Hotelzimmer *nt*.

hot: ~foot [1] *adv* eilig; [2] *vt* (*inf*) **he ~footed it back home/out of town** er ging schleunigst nach Hause/er verließ schleunigst die Stadt; **~ gospeller** *n* Erweckungsprediger *m*; **~head** *n* Hitzkopf *m*; **~headed** *adj* hitzköpfig, unbeherrscht; **~house** [1] *n* (*lit, fig*) Treibhaus *nt*; [2] *adj attr* (*lit*) *plant* Treibhaus-; (*fig*) *atmosphere* spannungsgeladen, angespannt; **~ line** *n* (*Pol*) heißer Draht; (*TV etc*) Hotline *f*; **to get on the ~ line** (*Pol*) sich an den heißen Draht hängen (*inf*).

hotly ['hɒtlɪ] *adv contested* heiß; *say, argue, deny* heftig ◆ **he was ~ pursued by two policemen** zwei Polizisten waren ihm dicht auf den Fersen; **she blushed ~** sie wurde über und über rot.

hot: ~ metal (*Typ*) [1] *n* Blei *nt*; (*setting*) Bleisatz *m*; [2] *adj attr setting* Blei-; **~ pants** *npl* heiße Höschen, Hot Pants *pl*; **~plate** *n* **(a)** (*of stove*) Koch- *or* Heizplatte *f*; **(b)** (*plate-warmer*) Warmhalteplatte, Wärmplatte *f*; **~pot** *n* (*esp Brit Cook*) Fleischeintopf *m* mit Kartoffeleinlage; **~ potato** *n* (*fig inf*) heißes Eisen; **~ pursuit** *n* (*Mil*) Nacheile *f*; **to set off/be in ~ pursuit of sb/sth** jdm/einer Sache nachjagen; **in ~ pursuit of the thief** in wilder Jagd auf den Dieb; **~rod** *n* (*Aut*) hochfrisiertes Auto; **~ seat** *n* Schleudersitz *m*; (*US sl: electric chair*) elektrischer Stuhl; **to be in the ~ seat** auf dem Schleudersitz sein; (*in quiz etc*) auf dem Armsünderbänkchen sitzen (*hum*); **to take the ~ seat** auf den Schleudersitz kommen; (*in quiz*) sich auf das Armsünderbänkchen setzen (*hum*); **~ shoe** *n* (*Phot*) Steckschuh *m*; **~shot** (*US sl*) [1] *n* Kanone *f* (*inf*), As *nt* (*inf*); [2] *adj attr* Spitzen- (*inf*), erstklassig; **~ spot** *n* (*Pol*) Krisenherd *m*; **~ spring** *n* heiße Quelle, Thermalquelle *f*; **~ stuff** *n* (*inf*) **it's ~ stuff** (*very good*) das ist große Klasse (*inf*); (*provocative*) das ist Zündstoff; **she's/he's ~ stuff** (*very good*) sie/er ist große Klasse (*inf*) *or* eine Kanone (*inf*); (*very sexy*) das ist eine Klassefrau (*inf*) *or* scharfe Frau (*sl*)/das ist ein scharfer Typ (*sl*); **~-tempered** *adj* leicht aufbrausend, jähzornig.

Hottentot ['hɒtəntɒt] [1] *n* **(a)** Hottentotte *m*, Hottentottin *f*. **(b)** (*language*) Hottentottisch *nt*.
[2] *adj* hottentottisch.

hot-water bottle [ˌhɒt'wɔːtəˌbɒtl] *n* Wärmflasche *f*.

hoummos, houm(o)us ['huːməs] *n orientalische Creme aus Kichererbsen, Sesam und Knoblauch*.

hound [haʊnd] [1] *n* **(a)** (*Hunt*) (Jagd)hund *m* ◆ **the ~s lost the scent** die Meute verlor die Spur; **to ride to ~s** (*person*) mit der Meute jagen. **(b)** (*any dog*) Hund *m*, Tier *nt*.
[2] *vt* hetzen, jagen ◆ **to be/feel ~ed** gehetzt sein/sich gehetzt fühlen.

◆**hound down** *vt sep* Jagd machen auf (+*acc*), niederhetzen (*form*); (*criminal also*) zur Strecke bringen.

◆**hound out** *vt sep* verjagen, vertreiben (*of* aus).

hound's-tooth (check) ['haʊndztuːθ(ˌtʃek)] *n* Hahnentritt(muster *nt*) *m*.

hour ['aʊəʳ] *n* **(a)** Stunde *f*; (*time of day also*) Zeit *f* ◆ **half an ~, a half ~** eine halbe Stunde; **three-quarters/a quarter of an ~** eine dreiviertel Stunde, dreiviertel Stunden/eine Viertelstunde; **an ~ and a half** anderthalb *or* eineinhalb Stunden; **it's two ~s' walk from here** von hier geht man zwei

Stundem, von hier sind es zu Fuß zwei Stunden; **two ~s' walk from here there is ...** nach einem Weg von zwei Stunden kommt man an (*+acc*) *or* zu ...; **at 1500/1530 ~s,** (*spoken*) **at fifteen hundred/fifteen thirty ~s** um 15[00]/15[30] Uhr, (*gesprochen*) um fünfzehn Uhr/fünfzehn Uhr dreißig; **~ by ~** mit jeder Stunde, stündlich; **on the ~** zur vollen Stunde; **every ~ on the ~** jede volle Stunde; **20 minutes past the ~** 20 Minuten nach; **at the ~ of his death** in der Stunde seines Todes, in seiner Todesstunde; **at an early/a late ~** früh/spät, zu früher/später Stunde (*geh*); **at all ~s (of the day and night)** zu jeder (Tages- und Nacht)zeit; **what! at this ~ of the night!** was! zu dieser nachtschlafenden Zeit!; **what is the ~?** (*old*) wieviel Uhr ist es?; **to walk/drive at 10 kilometres an ~** zu Fuß 10 Kilometer in der Stunde zurücklegen/10 Kilometer in der Stunde *or* 10 Stundenkilometer fahren; **a 30 mile(s) an** *or* **per ~ limit** eine Geschwindigkeitsbegrenzung von 30 Meilen in der Stunde; **to be paid by the ~** stundenweise bezahlt werden; **she is paid £6 an ~** sie bekommt £ 6 pro Stunde.

(b) ~s *pl* (*inf: a long time*) Stunden *pl* ◆ **for ~s** stundenlang; **~s and ~s** Stunden und aber Stunden; **I/the train was ~s late** ich war sehr spät dran (*inf*), ich hatte mich um Stunden verspätet/der Zug hatte Stunden Verspätung; **he took ~s to do it** er brauchte ewig lang (*inf*) *or* stundenlang dazu.

(c) ~s *pl* (*of banks, shops etc*) Geschäftszeit(en *pl*) *f*; (*of shops also, pubs, park etc*) Öffnungszeiten *pl*; (*of post office*) Schalterstunden *pl*; (*office ~s*) Dienststunden *pl*; (*working ~s etc*) Arbeitszeit *f*; (*of doctor etc*) Sprechstunde *f* ◆ **out of/after ~s** (*in pubs*) außerhalb der gesetzlich erlaubten Zeit/nach der Polizeistunde; (*in shops etc*) außerhalb der Geschäftszeit(en)/nach Laden- *or* Geschäftsschluß; (*in office etc*) außerhalb der Arbeitszeit/nach Dienstschluß; (*of doctor etc*) außerhalb/nach der Sprechstunde; **what are your ~s?** (*shops, pubs etc*) wann haben Sie geöffnet *or* offen?; (*employee*) wie ist Ihre Arbeitszeit?; **to work long ~s** einen langen Arbeitstag haben; (*doctors, nurse, policeman etc*) lange Dienststunden haben.

(d) (*fig*) **his ~ has come** seine Stunde ist gekommen; (*death also*) sein (letztes) Stündchen hat geschlagen; **in the ~ of danger** in der Stunde der Gefahr; **the man of the ~** der Mann der Stunde; **the problems of the ~** die aktuellen Probleme.

hour: ~ glass [1] *n* Sanduhr *f*, Stundenglas *nt* (*old*); [2] *adj figure* kurvenreich; **~ hand** *n* Stundenzeiger *m*, kleiner Zeiger.

houri ['huːrɪ] *n* (*Rel*) Huri *f*; (*fig*) orientalische Schönheit.

hourly ['aʊəlɪ] [1] *adj* stündlich ◆ **at ~ intervals** jede Stunde, stündlich; **~ rate/wage** Stundensatz/-lohn *m*.

[2] *adv* stündlich, jede Stunde; (*hour by hour*) mit jeder Stunde.

house [haʊs] [1] *n, pl* **houses** ['haʊzɪz] **(a)** Haus *nt*; (*household also*) Haushalt *m* ◆ **at/to my ~** bei mir (zu Hause)/zu mir (nach Hause); **to set up ~** einen eigenen Hausstand gründen; (*in particular area*) sich niederlassen; **they set up ~ together** sie gründeten einen gemeinsamen Hausstand; **to put** *or* **set one's ~ in order** (*fig*) seine Angelegenheiten in Ordnung bringen; **he's getting on like a ~ on fire** (*inf*) (*in new job etc*) er macht sich prächtig (*inf*); (*with building, project etc*) er kommt prima *or* prächtig voran (*inf*); **he gets on with her like a ~ on fire** (*inf*) er kommt ausgezeichnet *or* prima (*inf*) mit ihr aus; **they get on like a ~ on fire** (*inf*) sie kommen ausgezeichnet miteinander aus; **as safe as ~s** (*Brit*) bombensicher (*inf*); **H~ of God** *or* **the Lord** Haus Gottes, Gotteshaus *nt*; **a ~ of worship** ein Ort des Gebets, ein Haus der Andacht.

(b) (*Pol*) **the upper/lower ~** das Ober-/Unterhaus; **H~ of Commons/Lords** (*Brit*) (britisches) Unter-/Oberhaus; **the H~** (*Brit inf*) das Parlament; (*as address also*) das Hohe Haus; **H~ of Representatives** (*US*) Repräsentantenhaus *nt*; **the H~s of Parliament** das Parlament(sgebäude).

(c) (*family, line*) Haus, Geschlecht *nt* ◆ **the H~ of Bourbon** das Haus Bourbon, das Geschlecht der Bourbonen.

(d) (*firm*) Haus *nt* ◆ **on the ~** auf Kosten des Hauses; (*on the company*) auf Kosten der Firma; **can I give you something for the phone call/meal? — oh no, it's on the ~** kann ich dir etwas für das Telefon/Essen geben? — nein, nein, das geht auf Kosten des Hauses/das spendiere ich dir.

(e) (*Theat*) Haus *nt*; (*performance*) Vorstellung *f* ◆ **to bring the ~ down** (*inf*) ein Bombenerfolg (beim Publikum) sein (*inf*).

(f) (*in boarding school*) Gruppenhaus *nt*; (*in day school*) *eine von mehreren Gruppen verschiedenaltriger Schüler, die z.B. in Wettkämpfen gegeneinander antreten*.

(g) (*in debate*) **H~** Versammlung *f*; **the motion before the H~** das Diskussionsthema, das zur Debatte *or* Diskussion stehende Thema; **this H~ believes capital punishment should be reintroduced** wir stellen die Frage zur Diskussion, ob die Todesstrafe wieder eingeführt werden sollte; (*in conclusion*) die Anwesenden sind der Meinung, daß die Todesstrafe wieder eingeführt werden sollte.

(h) full ~ (*Cards*) Full House *nt*; (*bingo*) volle Karte.

(i) (*Astrol*) Haus *nt*.

[2] [hauz] *vt people, goods* unterbringen; (*Tech also*) einbauen ◆ **this building ~s three offices/ten families** in diesem Gebäude sind drei Büros/zehn Familien untergebracht, dieses Gebäude beherbergt drei Büros/zehn Familien.

house *in cpds* Haus-; **~ arrest** *n* Hausarrest *m*; **~boat** *n* Hausboot *nt*; **~bound** *adj* ans Haus gefesselt; **~boy** *n* Boy *m*; **~breaker** *n* Einbrecher *m*; **~breaking** *n* Einbruch(sdiebstahl) *m*; **~-broken** *adj* (*US: house-trained*) stubenrein; **~ captain** *n* (*Brit Sch*) (*in boarding school*) Haussprecher(in *f*) *m*, Hausälteste(r) *mf*; (*in day school*) Gruppensprecher(in *f*) *m*, Gruppenälteste(r) *mf*; **~coat** *n* Morgenrock *or* -mantel *m*; **~-dog** *n* Haushund *m*; **~dress** *n* (*US*) Schürzenkleid *nt*; **~fly** *n* Stubenfliege *f*; **~guest** *n* (Haus)gast *m*.

household ['haʊshəʊld] [1] *n* Haushalt *m* ◆ **H~ Cavalry** Gardekavallerie *f*.

[2] *attr* Haushalts-; *furniture* Wohn- ◆ **~ chores** häusliche Pflichten *pl*, Hausarbeit *f*.

householder ['haʊs,həʊldə^r] *n* Haus-/Wohnungsinhaber(in *f*) *m*.

household: ~ god *n* Hausgott *m*; **the telly has become the ~ god in many homes** der Fernseher ist in vielen Familien zum Götzen geworden; **~ goods** *npl* Hausrat *m*; **~ linen** *n* Tisch- und Bettwäsche, Weißwäsche (*dated*) *f*; **~ name** *n* **to be/become a ~ name** ein Begriff sein/zu einem Begriff werden; **~ word** *n* Begriff *m*; **to be/become a ~ word for sth** ein (In)begriff für etw sein/zu einem (In)begriff für etw werden.

house: ~-hunt *vi* auf Haussuche sein; **they have started ~-hunting** sie haben angefangen, nach einem Haus zu suchen; **~-hunting** *n* Haussuche *f*; **~husband** *n* Hausmann *m*; **~ journal** *n* Hausnachrichten *pl*; **~keeper** *n* Haushälterin, Wirtschafterin *f*; (*in institution also*) Wirtschaftsleiterin *f*; **his wife is a good ~keeper** seine Frau ist eine gute Hausfrau; **~keeping** *n* **(a)** Haushalten *nt*; **(b)** (*also* **~keeping money**) Haushalts- *or* Wirtschaftsgeld *nt*; **~lights** *npl* Lichter *pl* im Saal; **~ magazine** *n see* **~ journal**; **~maid** *n* Dienstmädchen *nt*; **~maid's knee** *n* Schleimbeutelentzündung *f*; **~man** *n* (*Brit*) Assistenzarzt *m*; **~ martin** *n* Mehlschwalbe *f*; **~master/~mistress** *n* (*Brit*) Erzieher(in *f*) *m*; (*on teaching staff*) Lehrer(in *f*) *m*, *der/die für ein Gruppenhaus zuständig ist*; **~ parent** *n* Hausvater *m*/-mutter *f*; **~ parents** *pl* Hauseltern *pl*; **~ party** *n* mehrtägige Einladung; (*group invited*) Gesellschaft *f*; **~ physician** *n* im (Kranken)haus wohnender Arzt; (*in private clinic etc*) Haus- *or* Anstaltsarzt *m*/-ärztin *f*; **~-proud** *adj* **she is ~-proud** sie ist eine penible Hausfrau; **~room** *n*: **I wouldn't give it ~room** (*inf*) das wollte ich nicht geschenkt haben; **~ rule** *n* (Bestimmung der) Hausordnung *f*; **~sit** *vi* **to ~sit for sb** *während jds Abwesenheit in dessen Haus/Wohnung einziehen, um darauf aufzupassen*; **~ sparrow** *n* Haussperling *m*; **~ style** *n* Stil *m* des Hauses; **~ surgeon** *n* im (Kranken)haus wohnender Chirurg; (*in private clinic*) Haus- *or* Anstaltschirurg *m*; **~-to-~** *adj collection* Haus-; **a ~-to-~ search** eine Suche *or* Fahndung von Haus zu Haus; **to conduct ~-to-~ enquiries** von Haus zu Haus gehen und fragen; **~top** *n* (Haus)dach *nt*; **~-train** *vt* stubenrein machen; **~-trained** *adj* stubenrein; **~ warming (party)** *n* Einzugsparty *f*; **to have a ~ warming (party)** Einzug feiern; **~wife** *n* **(a)** (*person*) Hausfrau *f*; **(b)** ['hʌzɪf] (*dated: sewing case*) Nähetui, Nähzeug *nt*; **~wifely** *adj* hausfraulich; **~work** *n* Hausarbeit *f*.

housey-housey ['haʊsɪ'haʊsɪ] *n* (*dated*) Lotto *nt*.

housing ['haʊzɪŋ] *n* **(a)** (*act*) Unterbringung *f*. **(b)** (*houses*) Wohnungen *pl*; (*temporary*) Unterkunft *f*. **(c)** (*provision of houses*) Wohnungsbeschaffung *f*; (*building of houses*) Wohnungsbau *m*. **(d)** (*Tech*) Gehäuse *nt*.

housing *in cpds* Wohnungs-; **~ association** *n* Wohnungsbaugesellschaft *f*; **~ benefit** *n* Wohngeld *nt*; **~ conditions** *npl* Wohnbedingungen *or* -verhältnisse *pl*; **~ development** *or* (*Brit also*) **estate** *n* Wohnsiedlung *f*; **~ programme** *n* Wohnungsbeschaffungsprogramm *nt*; **~ scheme** *n* (*estate*) Siedlung *f*; (*project*) Siedlungsbauvorhaben *nt*.

hove [həʊv] *pret, ptp of* **heave 1 (d), 2 (c).**

hovel ['hɒvəl] *n* armselige Hütte; (*fig pej*) Bruchbude *f*, Loch *nt* (*inf*) ◆ **my humble ~** (*hum*) meine bescheidene Hütte.

hover ['hɒvə^r] *vi* **(a)** schweben; (*bird also*) stehen.

(b) (*fig*) **a smile ~ed on her lips** ein Lächeln lag auf ihren Lippen; **she ~ed on the verge of tears/of a decision** sie war den Tränen nahe/sie schwankte in ihrer Entscheidung; **danger was ~ing all around them** ringsum lauerte Gefahr; **to ~ on the brink of disaster** am Rande des Ruins stehen; **he ~ed between two alternatives** er schwankte zwischen zwei Alternativen; **he was ~ing between life and death** er schwebte zwischen Leben und Tod.

(c) (*fig: stand around*) herumstehen ◆ **to ~ over sb** jdm nicht von der Seite weichen; **don't ~ over me** geh endlich weg; **he's always ~ing over me** ich habe ihn ständig auf der Pelle (*inf*); **a waiter ~ed at his elbow, waiting to refill his glass** ein Kellner schwebte herum und wartete nur darauf, nachzuschenken.

◆**hover about** *or* **around** [1] *vi* (*persons*) herumlungern, herumhängen; (*helicopter, bird etc*) (in der Luft) kreisen ◆ **he was ~ing ~, waiting for us to ask him to join us** er strich um uns herum und wartete offensichtlich darauf, daß wir ihn einluden.

[2] *vi +prep obj* **to ~ ~ sb/sth** um jdn/etw herumschleichen *or* -streichen, sich um jdn/etw herumdrücken; **the hostess ~ed ~ her guests** die Gastgeberin umsorgte ihre Gäste mit (über)- großer Aufmerksamkeit.

hover: ~craft *n* Luftkissenfahrzeug, Hovercraft *nt*; **~port** *n* Anlegestelle *f* für Hovercrafts; **~train** *n* Schwebezug *m*.

how¹ [haʊ] *adv* **(a)** (*in what way*) wie ◆ **~ will we ever survive?** wie sollen *or* können wir nur *or* bloß überleben?; **~ so?, ~'s that?, ~ come?** (*inf*) wieso (denn das)?, wie kommt (denn) das?; **~ is it that we** *or* **~ come** (*inf*) **we earn less?** wieso *or* warum verdienen wir denn weniger?; **~ is it that ...?** wie kommt es, daß ...?; **I see ~ it is** ich verstehe (schon); **~ do you know that?** woher wissen Sie das?; **to learn/know ~ to do sth** lernen/wissen, wie man etw macht; **I'd like to learn ~ to swim/drive** *etc* ich würde gerne schwimmen/Auto fahren *etc* lernen.

(b) (*in degree, quantity etc*) wie ◆ **~ much** (*+n, adj, adv*) wieviel; (*+vb*) wie sehr; (*+vbs of physical action*) wieviel; **~ much do you visit them/go out?** wie oft besuchen Sie sie/gehen Sie aus?; **~ many** wieviel, wie viele.

(c) (*regarding health, general situation etc*) **~ do you do?** (*on introduction*) Guten Tag/Abend!, angenehm! (*form*); **~ are you?** wie geht es Ihnen?; **~'s work/the pound?** *etc* was macht die Arbeit/das Pfund? *etc* (*inf*); **~ are things at school/in the office?** *etc* wie geht's in der Schule/im Büro? *etc*.

(d) ~ about ...? wie wäre es mit ...?; ~ about it? (*about suggestion*) wie wäre es damit?; ~ about going for a walk? wie wär's mit einem Spaziergang?
(e) and ~! und ob *or* wie!; ~ he's grown! er ist aber *or* vielleicht groß geworden; look ~ he's grown! sieh mal, wie groß er geworden ist.
(f) (*that*) daß ◆ she told me ~ she had seen him there sie sagte mir, daß sie ihn dort gesehen hat.

how[2] *interj* (*Indian greeting*) hugh.

howdah ['haʊdɑː] *n* Sänfte *f* (*auf Elefanten*).

howdy ['haʊdɪ] *interj* (*esp US inf*) Tag (*inf*).

how-d'ye-do ['haʊdjədu:] (*inf*) [1] *interj* Tag (*inf*), Tagchen (*inf*).
[2] *n* (*palaver, fuss*) Theater *nt*; (*argument also*) Krach *m* ◆ a fine *or* pretty ~ eine schöne Bescherung (*inf*).

howe'er [haʊ'ɛər] *conj, adv* (*poet*) *contr of* however.

▼ **however** [haʊ'evər] [1] *conj* (a) jedoch, aber ◆ ~, we finally succeeded wir haben es schließlich doch noch geschafft.
(b) (*inf: oh well*) na ja (*inf*), nun ja (*inf*).
[2] *adv* (a) (*no matter how*) wie ... auch, egal wie (*inf*); (*in whatever way*) wie ◆ ~ strong he is wie stark er auch ist, egal wie stark er ist (*inf*); ~ you do it wie immer du es machst, wie du es auch machst; do it ~ you like mach's, wie du willst; buy it ~ expensive it is kaufen Sie es, egal, was es kostet; ~ much you cry und wenn du noch so weinst, wie sehr du auch weinst; ~ that may be wie dem auch sei.
(b) (*in question*) wie ... bloß *or* nur ◆ ~ did you manage it? wie hast du das bloß *or* nur geschafft?

howitzer ['haʊɪtsər] *n* Haubitze *f*.

howl [haʊl] [1] *n* (a) Schrei *m*; (*of animal, wind*) Heulen *nt no pl* ◆ the dog let out a ~ der Hund heulte auf *or* jaulte; a ~ of pain ein Schmerzensschrei; ~s of excitement/rage aufgeregtes/wütendes Geschrei *or* Gebrüll; ~s of laughter brüllendes Gelächter; ~s (of protest) Protestgeschrei *nt*.
(b) (*from loudspeaker*) Pfeifen *nt no pl*, Rückkopp(e)lung *f*.
[2] *vi* (a) (*person*) brüllen, schreien; (*animal*) heulen, jaulen; (*wind*) heulen ◆ to ~ with laughter in brüllendes Gelächter ausbrechen.
(b) (*weep noisily*) heulen; (*baby*) schreien, brüllen (*inf*).
(c) (*Elec: loudspeaker etc*) rückkoppeln, pfeifen.
[3] *vt* hinausbrüllen, hinausschreien ◆ they ~ed their disapproval sie äußerten lautstark ihr Mißfallen.

◆**howl down** *vt sep* niederbrüllen, niederschreien.

howler ['haʊlər] *n* (*inf*) Hammer (*sl*), Schnitzer (*inf*) *m* ◆ he made a real ~ da hat er sich (*dat*) einen Hammer geleistet (*sl*); stylistic ~ Stilblüte *f* (*hum*).

howling ['haʊlɪŋ] [1] *n* (*of person*) Gebrüll, Geschrei *nt*; (*noisy crying, of animal*) Heulen, Geheul *nt*; (*of wind*) Heulen *nt* ◆ stop that child's ~! bring das Kind zum Schweigen!
[2] *adj* (a) (*lit*) heulend. (b) (*inf: tremendous*) enorm; *success also* Riesen-.

howsoever [,haʊsəʊ'evər] *adv* (*old, form*) wie auch immer.

hoy [hɔɪ] *interj* he.

hoyden ['hɔɪdn] *n* wilde Range (*dated*), Wildfang *m* (*dated*).

hoydenish ['hɔɪdənɪʃ] *adj* rangenhaft (*dated*), wild, ungestüm.

HP, hp *abbr of* (a) hire purchase. (b) horse power PS.

HQ *abbr of* headquarters.

HRH *abbr of* His/Her Royal Highness S.M./I.M.

ht *abbr of* height.

hub [hʌb] *n* (a) (*of wheel*) (Rad)nabe *f*. (b) (*fig*) Zentrum *nt*, Mittelpunkt *m* ◆ the ~ of the universe der Nabel der Welt.

hubble-bubble ['hʌbl'bʌbl] *n* (a) (*pipe*) Wasserpfeife *f*. (b) (*noise*) Brodeln *nt*.

hubbub ['hʌbʌb] *n* Tumult *m* ◆ a ~ (of noise) ein Radau *m*; a ~ of voices ein Stimmengewirr *nt*.

hubby ['hʌbɪ] *n* (*inf*) Mann *m*.

hubcap ['hʌbkæp] *n* Radkappe *f*.

hubris ['hju:brɪs] *n* (*liter*) Anmaßung *f*; (*esp in Greek drama*) Hybris *f*.

huckleberry ['hʌklbərɪ] *n* amerikanische Heidelbeere.

huckster ['hʌkstər] *n* (a) (*hawker*) Straßenhändler(in *f*) *m*. (b) (*US inf*) Reklamefritze *m* (*inf*).

huddle ['hʌdl] [1] *n* (wirrer) Haufen *m*; (*of people*) Gruppe *f* ◆ in a ~ dicht zusammengedrängt; to go into a ~ (*inf*) die Köpfe zusammenstecken.
[2] *vi* (*also* to be ~d) (sich) kauern.

◆**huddle down** *vi* sich kuscheln.

◆**huddle together** *vi* sich aneinanderkauern ◆ to be ~d ~ aneinanderkauern.

◆**huddle up** *vi* sich zusammenkauern ◆ to be ~d ~ zusammenkauern; to ~ ~ against sb/sth sich an jdn/etw kauern.

hue[1] [hju:] *n* (*colour*) Farbe *f*; (*shade*) Schattierung *f*; (*fig: political leaning*) Schattierung, Färbung, Couleur (*geh*) *f*.

hue[2] *n*: ~ and cry Zeter und Mordio (*against* gegen); to set up *or* raise a ~ and cry Zeter und Mordio schreien.

huff [hʌf] [1] *n* to be/go off in a ~ beleidigt *or* eingeschnappt sein/abziehen (*inf*); to get into a ~ einschnappen (*inf*), den Beleidigten spielen; his ~s never last long er ist nie lange beleidigt.
[2] *vi* to ~ and puff (*inf*) schnaufen und keuchen.

huffily ['hʌfɪlɪ] *adv* beleidigt.

huffiness ['hʌfɪnɪs] *n* Beleidigtsein *nt*; (*touchiness*) Empfindlichkeit *f* ◆ the ~ in his voice sein beleidigter Ton.

huffy ['hʌfɪ] *adj* (+*er*) (*in a huff*) beleidigt; (*touchy*) empfindlich ◆ to get/be ~ about sth wegen etw eingeschnappt (*inf*) *or* beleidigt sein; he's a rather ~ kind of person er ist leicht beleidigt *or* eingeschnappt (*inf*).

➤ LANGUAGE IN USE: **however: 1a** → 26.1, 26.2, 26.3

hug [hʌg] [1] *n* Umarmung *f* ◆ to give sb a ~ jdn umarmen.
[2] *vt* (a) (*hold close*) umarmen; (*bear etc also*) umklammern; (*fig*) *hope, belief* sich klammern an (+*acc*) ◆ to ~ sb/sth to oneself jdn/etw an sich (*acc*) pressen *or* drücken.
(b) (*keep close to*) sich dicht halten an (+*acc*); (*car, ship etc also*) dicht entlangfahren an (+*dat*).
[3] *vr* (a) to ~ oneself to keep warm die Arme verschränken, damit einem warm ist. (b) to ~ oneself about sth (*fig*) sich zu etw beglückwünschen.

huge [hju:dʒ] *adj* (+*er*) riesig, gewaltig; *cheek, lie, mistake, appetite, thirst, town also* Riesen-.

hugely ['hju:dʒlɪ] *adv* ungeheuer; *enjoy, be pleased also* riesig.

hugeness ['hju:dʒnɪs] *n* Größe *f*, (gewaltiges/riesiges) Ausmaß.

Huguenot ['hju:gənəʊ] [1] *adj* hugenottisch, Hugenotten-.
[2] *n* Hugenotte *m*, Hugenottin *f*.

huh [hʌ] *interj* was; (*derision*) haha.

hula ['hu:lə] *n* Hula(-Hula) *m or f* ◆ to do the ~(~) Hula(-Hula) tanzen; ~ hoop Hula-Hoop-Reifen *m*; ~ skirt Bastrock *m*.

hulk [hʌlk] *n* (a) (*Naut: body of ship*) (Schiffs)rumpf *m*. (b) (*inf: person*) Klotz *m* (*inf*). (c) (*wrecked vehicle*) Wrack *nt*; (*building etc*) Ruine *f*.

hulking ['hʌlkɪŋ] *adj*: ~ great, great ~ massig; a great ~ wardrobe ein Ungetüm *nt* von einem Kleiderschrank; a ~ great brute (of a man/dog) ein grobschlächtiger, brutaler Kerl/ein scheußliches Ungetüm von einem Hund.

hull[1] [hʌl] *n* (*Naut*) Schiffskörper *m*; (*Aviat*) Rumpf *m* ◆ ship ~ down on the horizon Schiff in Sicht am Horizont.

hull[2] [1] *n* Hülse *f*; (*of peas also*) Schote *f*; (*of barley, oats also*) Spelze *f*; (*of strawberries etc*) Blättchen *nt*.
[2] *vt* schälen; *beans, peas* enthülsen, ausmachen (*inf*); *strawberries etc* entstielen.

hullabaloo [,hʌləbə'lu:] *n* (*inf*) Spektakel *m*; (*noise also*) Radau *m*.

hullo [hʌ'ləʊ] *interj see* hello.

hum [hʌm] [1] *n* (a) *see vi* (*a*) Summen *nt*; Brausen *nt*; Brummen *nt*; Surren *nt*; (*of voices*) Gemurmel *nt*.
(b) (*inf: smell*) Gestank *m* (*inf*) ◆ to give off a ~ stinken (*inf*).
[2] *vi* (a) (*insect, person*) summen; (*traffic*) brausen; (*engine, electric tool, wireless, top etc*) brummen; (*small machine, camera etc*) surren ◆ the lines were/the office was ~ming with the news (*fig*) die Drähte liefen heiß/im Büro sprach man von nichts anderem.
(b) (*fig inf: party, concert etc*) in Schwung kommen ◆ to make things/the party ~ die Sache/die Party in Schwung bringen; the headquarters was ~ming with activity im Hauptquartier ging es zu wie in einem Bienenstock.
(c) to ~ and haw (*inf*) herumdrucksen (*inf*) (*over, about* um).
(d) (*inf: smell*) stinken (*inf*).
[3] *vt music, tune* summen.
[4] *interj* hm.

human ['hju:mən] [1] *adj* menschlich ◆ you can't do that, it's not ~ das kannst du nicht tun, das ist unmenschlich; ~ race menschliche Rasse, Menschengeschlecht *nt* (*liter*); these footprints certainly aren't ~ diese Fußspuren sind *or* stammen sicher nicht von Menschen; she's only ~ sie ist auch nur ein Mensch; that's only ~ das ist doch menschlich; ~ interest die menschliche Seite; a ~ interest story on the front page eine Geschichte aus dem Leben auf der ersten Seite; ~ chain Menschenkette *f*; ~ nature die menschliche Natur; that's (only) ~ nature das liegt (nun einmal) in der Natur des Menschen; ~ sacrifice Menschenopfer *nt*; the ~ touch die menschliche Wärme; to lack the ~ touch nichts Menschliches haben; ~ rights Menschenrechte *pl*; this is a ~ rights issue das ist eine Frage der Menschenrechte; ~ rights activist Menschenrechtler(in *f*) *m*.
[2] *n* (*also* ~ being) Mensch *m*.

humane [hju:'meɪn] *adj* human, menschlich ◆ ~ killer Mittel *nt* zum schmerzlosen Töten; ~ society *Gesellschaft f zur Verhinderung von Grausamkeiten an Mensch und Tier.*

humanely [hju:'meɪnlɪ] *adv see adj* ◆ the dog was put down very ~ der Hund wurde auf humane Weise getötet.

human interest *n* (*in newspaper story etc*) Emotionalität *f* ◆ a ~ story eine ergreifende Story.

humanism ['hju:mənɪzəm] *n* Humanismus *m*.

humanist ['hju:mənɪst] [1] *n* Humanist *m*.
[2] *adj* humanistisch.

humanistic [,hju:mə'nɪstɪk] *adj* humanistisch.

humanitarian [hju:,mænɪ'tɛərɪən] [1] *n* Vertreter(in *f*) *m* des Humanitätsgedankens.
[2] *adj* humanitär.

humanitarianism [,hju:mænɪ'tɛərɪənɪzəm] *n* Humanitarismus *m*; (*of individual*) humanitäre Gesinnung.

humanity [hju:'mænɪtɪ] *n* (a) (*mankind*) die Menschheit. (b) (*human nature*) Menschlichkeit, Menschenhaftigkeit *f*. (c) (*humaneness*) Humanität, Menschlichkeit *f* ◆ to treat sb with ~ jdn human behandeln. (d) humanities *pl* Geisteswissenschaften *pl*; (*Latin and Greek*) Altphilologie *f*.

humanize ['hju:mənaɪz] *vt* humanisieren.

humankind [,hju:mən'kaɪnd] *n* die Menschheit.

humanly ['hju:mənlɪ] *adv* menschlich ◆ to do all that is ~ possible alles menschenmögliche tun.

humble ['hʌmbl] [1] *adj* (+*er*) (*unassuming*) bescheiden; (*meek, submissive, Rel*) demütig; *apology also* zerknirscht; (*lowly*) einfach, bescheiden ◆ my ~ apologies! ich bitte inständig um Verzeihung!; of ~ birth *or* origin von niedriger Geburt *or* Herkunft; my ~ self meine Wenigkeit; in my ~ opinion meiner bescheidenen Meinung nach; **to eat ~ pie** klein beigeben, zu Kreuze kriechen (*inf*); *see* **servant.**

[2] *vt* demütigen ◆ **to ~ oneself** sich demütigen *or* erniedrigen.

humble-bee ['hʌmbl,biː] *n* Hummel *f.*

humbleness ['hʌmblnɪs] *n* Bescheidenheit *f;* (*lowliness also*) Einfachheit *f;* (*meekness, submissiveness*) Demut *f.*

humbly ['hʌmblɪ] *adv* (*unassumingly, with deference*) demütig (*esp Rel*), bescheiden; (*in a lowly way*) einfach, bescheiden ◆ **I ~ submit this little work** in aller Bescheidenheit überreiche ich diese kleine Arbeit; **~ born** von niedriger Geburt; **he ~ apologized/agreed that he was wrong** er entschuldigte sich zerknirscht/er gab kleinlaut zu, daß er unrecht hatte.

humbug ['hʌmbʌg] *n* **(a)** (*Brit: sweet*) Pfefferminzbonbon *m or nt.* **(b)** (*inf: talk*) Humbug, Mumpitz *m* (*inf*). **(c)** (*inf: person*) Gauner, Halunke *m.*

humdinger ['hʌmdɪŋəʳ] *n* (*sl: person, thing*) **to be a ~** Spitze *or* große Klasse sein (*sl*); **a ~ of a job/girl** *etc* ein klasse Job/Mädchen *etc* (*sl*); **he hit him with a real ~ of a left hook** er landete einen erstklassigen linken Haken bei ihm (*inf*).

humdrum ['hʌmdrʌm] *adj* stumpfsinnig.

humerus ['hjuːmərəs] *n* Oberarmknochen *m.*

humid ['hjuːmɪd] *adj* feucht.

humidifier [hjuː'mɪdɪfaɪəʳ] *n* Luftbefeuchter *m;* (*humidification system*) Luftbefeuchtungsanlage *f.*

humidify [hjuː'mɪdɪfaɪ] *vt* befeuchten.

humidity [hjuː'mɪdɪtɪ] *n* (Luft)feuchtigkeit *f.*

humidor ['hjuːmɪdɔːʳ] *n* Feuchtraum *m.*

humiliate [hjuː'mɪlɪeɪt] *vt see n* demütigen, erniedrigen; beschämen.

humiliation [hjuː,mɪlɪ'eɪʃən] *n* Demütigung, Erniedrigung *f;* (*because of one's own actions*) Beschämung *f no pl* ◆ **much to my ~** sehr zu meiner Schande *or* Beschämung; **she couldn't hide her ~** sie konnte das Gefühl der Demütigung/Beschämung nicht verbergen.

humility [hjuː'mɪlɪtɪ] *n* Demut *f;* (*unassumingness*) Bescheidenheit *f.*

humming ['hʌmɪŋ] *n see vi 2 (a)* Summen *nt;* Brausen *nt;* Brummen *nt;* Surren *nt;* (*of voices*) Murmeln, Gemurmel *nt.*

humming: ~bird *n* Kolibri *m;* **~-top** *n* Brummkreisel *m.*

hummock ['hʌmək] *n* (kleiner) Hügel.

hummus ['hʊməs] *n see* **hoummos.**

humongous [hjuː'mʌŋgəs] *adj* (*inf*) wahnsinnig groß (*inf*), Riesen- ◆ **she's a ~ star** sie ist ein Riesenstar; **we had a ~ row** wir hatten einen Riesenkrach.

humor *etc* (*US*) *see* **humour** *etc.*

humorist ['hjuːmərɪst] *n* Humorist(in *f*) *m.*

humorous ['hjuːmərəs] *adj person* humorvoll; *book, story etc also, situation* lustig, komisch; *speech also* launig; *idea, thought* witzig; *smile, programme* lustig, heiter.

humorously ['hjuːmərəslɪ] *adv* humorvoll, witzig; *reflect, smile* heiter.

humour, (*US*) **humor** ['hjuːməʳ] [1] *n* **(a)** Humor *m* ◆ **a sense of ~** (Sinn *m* für) Humor *m;* **a story full of ~** eine humorvolle Geschichte; **I don't see the ~ in that** ich finde das gar nicht komisch; **this is no time for ~** jetzt ist nicht die Zeit für Witze.

(b) (*mood*) Stimmung, Laune *f* ◆ **to be in a good/in high ~** in guter/ausgezeichneter Stimmung sein, gute/glänzende *or* ausgezeichnete Laune haben; **with good ~** gutgelaunt; **to be out of ~** schlechte Laune haben, schlecht gelaunt sein.

(c) (*old Med*) Körpersaft *m.*

[2] *vt* **to ~ sb** jdm seinen Willen lassen *or* tun; **do it just to ~ him** tu's doch, damit er seinen Willen hat; **to ~ sb's wishes** sich jds Wünschen fügen, jdm seinen Willen lassen; **to ~ sb's whims/demands** jds Launen/Forderungen (*dat*) nachgeben.

-humoured, (*US*) **-humored** ['hjuːməd] *adj suf* -gelaunt.

humourless, (*US*) **humorless** ['hjuːməlɪs] *adj* humorlos, ohne jeden Humor; *speech, book etc also* trocken.

humourlessly, (*US*) **humorlessly** ['hjuːməlɪslɪ] *adv* humorlos, ohne jeden Humor.

hump [hʌmp] [1] *n* **(a)** (*Anat*) Buckel *m;* (*of camel*) Höcker *m.*

(b) (*hillock*) Hügel, Buckel (*esp S Ger*) *m* ◆ **we're over the ~ now** (*fig*) wir sind jetzt über den Berg.

(c) (*Brit inf*) **he's got the ~** er ist sauer (*inf*); **he/that gives me the ~** er/das fällt mir auf den Wecker (*inf*).

[2] *vt* **(a) to ~ one's back** einen Buckel machen.

(b) (*inf: carry*) schleppen; (*on back, shoulders*) auf dem Rücken/den Schultern tragen *or* schleppen ◆ **to ~ sth onto one's back/shoulders** sich (*dat*) etw auf den Rücken *or* Buckel (*inf*)/auf die Schultern laden *or* wuchten (*inf*).

hump: ~back *n* (*person*) Buck(e)lige(r) *mf;* (*back*) Buckel *m;* **~backed** *adj person* buck(e)lig; *bridge* gewölbt.

humph [mm] *interj* hm.

humpy ['hʌmpɪ] *adj* (*+er*) *country* hügelig, buckelig (*esp S Ger*).

humungous [hjuː'mʌŋgəs] *adj* (*inf*) *see* **humongous.**

humus ['hjuːməs] *n* Humus *m.*

Hun [hʌn] *n* **(a)** (*Hist*) Hunne *m,* Hunnin *f.* **(b)** (*pej inf*) Teutone *m* (*pej*), Teutonin *f* (*pej*), Boche *m* (*pej*).

hunch [hʌntʃ] [1] *n* **(a)** (*hump on sb's back*) Buckel *m.*

(b) (*premonition*) Gefühl *nt,* Ahnung *f* ◆ **to have a ~ that ...** den (leisen *inf*) Verdacht *or* das (leise) Gefühl haben, daß ...

[2] *vt* (*also* **~ up**) *back* krümmen; *shoulders* hochziehen ◆ **to ~ (up) one's back** einen Buckel machen, den Rücken krümmen; **he was ~ed (up) over his desk** er saßüber seinen Schreibtisch gebeugt; **~ed up with pain** vor Schmerzen gekrümmt.

hunch: ~back *n* (*person*) Buck(e)lige(r) *mf;* (*back*) Buckel *m;* **The H~back of Notre Dame** der Glöckner von Notre-Dame; **~backed** *adj* buck(e)lig.

hundred ['hʌndrɪd] [1] *adj* hundert ◆ **a** *or* **one ~ years** (ein)hundert Jahre; **two/several ~ years** zweihundert/mehrere hundert Jahre; **a** *or* **one ~ and one** (*lit*) (ein)hundert(und)eins; (*fig*) tausend; **a** *or* **one ~ and two/ten** (ein)hundert(und)zwei/-zehn; **(one) ~ and first/second** *etc* hundert(und)erste(r, s)/-zweite(r, s) *etc;* **a** *or* **one ~ thousand** (ein)hunderttausend; **a ~-mile walk** ein Hundertmeilenmarsch; **a** *or* **one ~ per cent** hundert Prozent; **a (one) ~ per cent increase** eine hundertprozentige Erhöhung, eine Erhöhung von *or* um hundert Prozent; **I'm not a** *or* **one ~ per cent fit** ich bin nicht hundertprozentig fit; **a** *or* **one ~ per cent inflation** eine Inflationsrate von hundert Prozent; **the H~ Years' War** (*Hist*) der Hundertjährige Krieg; **never in a ~ years!** nie im Leben!

[2] *n* hundert *num;* (*written figure*) Hundert *f* ◆ **~s** (*lit, fig*) Hunderte *pl;* (*Math: figures in column*) Hunderter *pl;* **to count in ~s/up to a** *or* **one ~** in Hunderten/bis hundert zählen; **the ~s column** (*Math*) die Hunderterspalte; **one in a ~** einer unter hundert; **eighty out of a ~** achtzig von hundert; **an audience of a** *or* **one/two ~** hundert/zweihundert Zuschauer; **~s of times** hundertmal, Hunderte von Malen; **~s and ~s** Hunderte und aber Hunderte; **~s of** *or* **and thousands** Hunderttausende *pl;* **~s and thousands** (*Cook*) Liebesperlen *pl;* **he earned nine ~ a year** er verdiente neunhundert im Jahr; **I'll lay (you) a ~ to one** ich wette hundert gegen eins; **to sell sth by the ~** (*lit, fig*) etw im Hundert verkaufen; **it'll cost you a ~** das wird dich einen Hunderter kosten; **to live to be a ~** hundert Jahre alt werden; **they came in (their) ~s** *or* **by the ~** sie kamen zu Hunderten.

hundredfold ['hʌndrɪdfəʊld] *adj, adv* hundertfach ◆ **to increase a ~** um das Hundertfache steigern.

hundredth ['hʌndrɪdθ] [1] *adj* (*in series*) hundertste(r, s); (*of fraction*) hundertstel.

[2] *n* Hundertste(r, s) *decl as adj;* (*fraction*) Hundertstel *nt; see also* **sixth.**

hundredweight ['hʌndrɪdweɪt] *n* Zentner *m;* (*Brit*) 50,8 kg; (*US*) 45,4 kg.

hung [hʌŋ] [1] *pret, ptp of* **hang.**

[2] *adj* **(a) ~ parliament** Parlament *nt* ohne klare Mehrheitsverhältnisse; **the election resulted in a ~ parliament** die Wahl führte zu einem parlamentarischen Patt. **(b) the way he's ~** (*inf: sexually*) wie er ausgestattet ist (*inf*).

Hungarian [hʌŋ'gɛərɪən] [1] *adj* ungarisch.

[2] *n* **(a)** (*person*) Ungar(in *f*) *m.* **(b)** (*language*) Ungarisch *nt.*

Hungary ['hʌŋgərɪ] *n* Ungarn *nt.*

hunger ['hʌŋgəʳ] [1] *n* **(a)** (*lit*) Hunger *m* ◆ **to die of ~** verhungern; **to go on (a) ~ strike** in (den) Hungerstreik treten; **~ march** Hungermarsch *m.* **(b)** (*fig*) Hunger *m* (*for* nach).

[2] *vi* (*old, liter*) hungern.

◆**hunger after** *or* **for** *vi +prep obj* (*liter*) hungern nach; *news* sehnsüchtig warten auf (*+acc*).

hung over *adj* **to be ~** einen Kater haben (*inf*); **to look ~** verkatert aussehen (*inf*).

hungrily ['hʌŋgrɪlɪ] *adv* (*lit, fig*) hungrig.

hungry ['hʌŋgrɪ] *adj* (*+er*) **(a)** (*lit*) hungrig ◆ **to be** *or* **feel/get ~** Hunger haben/bekommen; **to go ~** hungern.

(b) (*fig*) hungrig; *soil* mager, karg ◆ **~ for knowledge/love/power/adventure/success** bildungs-/liebes-/macht-/abenteuer-/erfolgshungrig; **to be ~ for news** sehnsüchtig auf Nachricht warten; **to be ~ for fame/riches/company** sich nach Ruhm/Reichtum/Gesellschaft sehnen.

hung-up [,hʌŋ'ʌp] *adj* (*inf*) **to be/get ~ (about sth)** (*be neurotic*) (wegen etw) einen Knacks weghaben (*inf*)/(wegen etw) durchdrehen (*inf*); (*have complex*) Komplexe (wegen etw) haben/kriegen; **he's really ~ about things like that** wenn es darum geht, hat er einen richtigen Knacks weg (*inf*); **to be ~ about being old/single** *etc* einen Komplex haben, weil man alt/nicht verheiratet *etc* ist; **he's ~ on drugs** (*sl*) er kommt von den Drogen nicht mehr los; **he's ~ on her** (*sl*) er steht auf sie (*sl*).

hunk [hʌŋk] *n* **(a)** Stück *nt.* **(b)** (*fig inf: man*) **a gorgeous ~ (of a man)** ein Mann! (*inf*).

hunky-dory ['hʌŋkɪ'dɔːrɪ] *adj* (*inf*) **that's ~** das ist in Ordnung.

hunt [hʌnt] [1] *n* Jagd *f;* (*huntsmen*) Jagd(gesellschaft) *f;* (*fig: search*) Suche *f* ◆ **tiger ~** Tigerjagd *f;* **~ ball** Jagdball *m;* **the ~ is on** *or* **up** die Suche hat begonnen; **to have a ~ for sth** nach etw fahnden (*inf*), eine Suche nach etw veranstalten; **to be on the ~ for sth** (*for animal*) etw jagen, auf etw (*acc*) Jagd machen; (*fig*) auf der Suche *or* Jagd nach etw sein (*inf*).

[2] *vt* **(a)** (*Hunt*) jagen; (*search for*) *criminal also* fahnden nach; *missing article etc* suchen; *missing person* suchen, fahnden nach ◆ **~ the slipper/thimble** Pantoffel-/Fingerhutverstecken *nt.*

(b) to ~ a horse/hounds zu Pferd/mit Hunden jagen.

[3] *vi* **(a)** (*Hunt*) jagen ◆ **to go ~ing** jagen, auf die Jagd gehen.

(b) (*to search*) suchen (*for, after* nach) ◆ **to ~ for an animal** auf ein Tier Jagd machen.

◆**hunt about** *or* **around** *vi* herumsuchen *or* -kramen (*for* nach).

◆**hunt down** *vt sep animal, person* (unerbittlich) Jagd machen auf (*+acc*); (*capture*) zur Strecke bringen.

◆**hunt out** *vt sep* heraussuchen, hervorkramen (*inf*); *person, facts* ausfindig machen, aufstöbern (*inf*).

◆**hunt up** *vt sep history, origins* Nachforschungen anstellen über (*+acc*), forschen nach (*+dat*); *person also, facts* auftreiben (*inf*), ausfindig machen; *old clothes, records etc* kramen nach (*+dat*), hervorkramen ◆ **~ him ~ for me, would you?** sieh mal bitte nach, ob du ihn irgendwo auftreiben kannst.

hunter [ˈhʌntəʳ] *n* **(a)** *(person)* Jäger *m*; *(horse)* Jagdpferd *nt*; *(dog)* Jagdhund *m*. **(b)** *(watch)* Sprungdeckeluhr *f*. **(c)** *(Astron)* **the H~** Orion *m*.

hunter-killer *n* Jagd-U-Boot *nt*.

hunting [ˈhʌntɪŋ] *n* **(a)** die Jagd, das Jagen ◆ **there's good ~ in these woods** diese Wälder sind ein gutes Jagdgebiet. **(b)** *(fig: search)* Suche *f* *(for* nach) ◆ **after a lot of ~** ... nach langer Suche ...

hunting *in cpds* Jagd-; **~ box** *n* Jagdhütte *f*; **~ lodge** *n* Jagdhütte *f*; *(larger)* Jagdschloß *nt*; **~ pink** *n (colour)* Rot *nt (des Reitrockes)*; *(clothes)* roter (Jagd)rock.

huntress [ˈhʌntrɪs] *n* Jägerin *f*.

huntsman [ˈhʌntsmən] *n, pl* **-men** [-mən] Jagdreiter *m*.

huntswoman [ˈhʌntswʊmən] *n, pl* **-women** [-wɪmɪn] Jagdreiterin *f*.

hurdle [ˈhɜːdl] [1] *n (Sport, fig)* Hürde *f* ◆ **~s** *sing (race)* Hürdenlauf *m*; *(Horseracing)* Hürdenrennen *nt*; **the 100m ~s** (die) 100 m Hürden, (der) 100-m-Hürdenlauf; **to fall at the first ~** *(fig)* (schon) über die erste *or* bei der ersten Hürde stolpern.
[2] *vt fence* nehmen.
[3] *vi* Hürdenlauf machen ◆ **hurdling** der Hürdenlauf.

hurdler [ˈhɜːdləʳ] *n (Sport)* Hürdenläufer(in *f*) *m*.

hurdy-gurdy [ˈhɜːdɪˌgɜːdɪ] *n* Leierkasten *m*, Drehorgel *f*.

hurl [hɜːl] *vt* schleudern ◆ **to ~ oneself at sb/into the fray** sich auf jdn/in das Getümmel stürzen; **they ~ed back their attackers** sie warfen ihre Angreifer zurück; **to ~ insults at sb** jdm Beleidigungen entgegenschleudern.

hurly-burly [ˈhɜːlɪˈbɜːlɪ] *n* Getümmel *nt*, Rummel *m (inf)* ◆ **the ~ of politics** der Rummel der Politik.

hurrah [hʊˈrɑː], **hurray** [hʊˈreɪ] *interj* hurra ◆ **~ for the king!** ein Hoch dem König!

hurricane [ˈhʌrɪkən] *n* Orkan *m*; *(tropical)* Hurrikan *m* ◆ **~ force** Orkanstärke *f*; **~ lamp** Sturmlaterne *f*.

hurried [ˈhʌrɪd] *adj* eilig; *letter, essay* eilig *or* hastig geschrieben; *ceremony* hastig durchgeführt, abgehaspelt *(inf)*; *work* in Eile gemacht; *(with little preparation) departure, wedding etc* überstürzt ◆ **to eat a ~ meal** hastig etwas essen.

hurriedly [ˈhʌrɪdlɪ] *adv* eilig.

hurry [ˈhʌrɪ] [1] *n* Eile *f* ◆ **it was rather a ~ (for us) to be ready** es war eine ziemliche Hetze, bis wir fertig waren; **in my ~ to get it finished** ... vor lauter Eile, damit fertig zu werden ...; **to do sth in a ~** etw schnell *or (too fast)* hastig tun; **I need it in a ~** ich brauche es schnell *or* eilig *or* dringend; **to be in a ~** es eilig haben, in Eile sein; **I won't do that again in a ~!** *(inf)* das mache ich so schnell nicht wieder!; **what's the/your ~?** was soll die Eile *or* Hast/warum (hast du's) so eilig?; **is there any ~ for it?** eilt es damit?, eilt das?; **there's no ~** es eilt nicht, es hat Zeit.
[2] *vi* sich beeilen; *(run/go quickly)* laufen, eilen *(geh)* ◆ **there's no need to ~** kein Grund zur Eile; **can't you make her ~?** kannst du sie nicht zur Eile antreiben?; **don't ~!** laß dir Zeit!, immer mit der Ruhe! *(inf)*; **I must ~ back** ich muß schnell zurück.
[3] *vt person (make act quickly)* (zur Eile) antreiben; *(make move quickly)* scheuchen *(inf)*; *work etc* beschleunigen, schneller machen; *(do too quickly)* überstürzen ◆ **troops were hurried to the spot** es wurden schleunigst Truppen dorthin gebracht; **don't ~ me** hetz mich nicht so!; **don't ~ your meals** schling das Essen nicht so runter!

◆**hurry along** [1] *vi* sich beeilen ◆ **~ ~ there, please!** schnell weitergehen, bitte!; **she hurried ~ to her friend** sie lief schnell zu ihrer Freundin; **to ~ ~ the road** die Straße entlanglaufen.
[2] *vt sep person* weiterdrängen; *(with work etc)* zur Eile antreiben; *things, work etc* vorantreiben, beschleunigen.

◆**hurry away** *or* **off** [1] *vi* schnell weggehen, forteilen *(geh)*.
[2] *vt sep* schnell wegbringen ◆ **they hurried him ~ to the waiting car** sie brachten ihn schnell zu dem wartenden Wagen.

◆**hurry on** [1] *vi* weiterlaufen; *(verbally, with work)* weitermachen.
[2] *vt sep person* weitertreiben; *(with work)* antreiben.

◆**hurry out** [1] *vi* hinauslaufen *or* -eilen.
[2] *vt sep* schnell hinausbringen *or* -treiben.

◆**hurry up** [1] *vi* sich beeilen ◆ **~ ~!** Beeilung!, beeil dich!; **can't you make him ~ ~?** kannst du nicht dafür sorgen, daß er sich beeilt?
[2] *vt sep person* zur Eile antreiben; *work etc* vorantreiben, beschleunigen.

hurry-scurry [ˈhʌrɪˈskʌrɪ] [1] *n* Gewühl, Gewimmel *nt*.
[2] *vi* (hin- und her)hasten, herumschwirren; *(children, insects)* wuseln.

hurt [hɜːt] *(vb: pret, ptp ~)* [1] *vt* **(a)** *(lit, fig) (cause pain) person, animal* weh tun (*+dat*); *(injure)* verletzen ◆ **to ~ oneself** sich *(dat)* weh tun; **to ~ one's arm** sich *(dat)* am Arm weh tun; *(injure)* sich *(dat)* den Arm verletzen; **my arm is ~ing me** mein Arm tut mir weh, mir tut der Arm weh; **if you go on like that someone is bound to get ~** wenn ihr so weitermacht, verletzt sich bestimmt noch jemand.
(b) *(harm)* schaden (*+dat*) ◆ **it won't ~ him to wait** es schadet ihm gar nicht(s), wenn er etwas wartet *or* warten muß; **walking on the grass doesn't ~ it** es schadet dem Gras nicht, wenn man darauf (herum)läuft; **those most ~ by this measure** die von dieser Maßnahme am stärksten Betroffenen.
[2] *vi* **(a)** *(be painful)* weh tun; *(fig also)* verletzend sein ◆ **that ~s!** *(lit, fig)* das tut weh!; **nothing ~s like the truth** nichts schmerzt mehr *or* tut mehr weh als die Wahrheit.
(b) *(do harm)* schaden ◆ **but surely a little drink won't ~** aber ein kleines Gläschen kann doch wohl nicht schaden.
[3] *n* Schmerz *m*; *(baby-talk)* Wehweh *nt*; *(to feelings)* Verletzung *f (to gen)*; *(to reputation etc)* Schädigung *f (to gen)*.
[4] *adj limb, feelings* verletzt; *tone, look* gekränkt.

hurtful [ˈhɜːtfʊl] *adj words, action* verletzend ◆ **it was very ~ to him/his feelings** es verletzte ihn/seine Gefühle sehr.

hurtfully [ˈhɜːtfəlɪ] *adv see adj* ... **she said ~** ... sagte sie in verletzendem Ton.

hurtle [ˈhɜːtl] *vi* rasen ◆ **the car was hurtling along** das Auto sauste *or* brauste dahin; **it ~d against/into the wall** es sauste gegen die Mauer; **he came hurtling round the corner** er kam um die Ecke gerast.

husband [ˈhʌzbənd] [1] *n* Ehemann *m* ◆ **my/her** *etc* **~** mein/ihr *etc* Mann; **give my best wishes to your ~** grüßen Sie Ihren Mann *or* Gatten *(form)* von mir.
[2] *vt strength, resources* haushalten mit, sparsam umgehen mit.

husbandry [ˈhʌzbəndrɪ] *n* **(a)** *(management)* Haushalten, Wirtschaften *nt*. **(b)** *(farming)* Landwirtschaft *f*.

hush [hʌʃ] [1] *vt person* zum Schweigen bringen; *(soothe) fears etc* beschwichtigen.
[2] *vi* still sein.
[3] *n* Stille *f*.
[4] *interj* pst.

◆**hush up** *vt sep* vertuschen.

hushed [hʌʃt] *adj voices* gedämpft; *words* leise ◆ **in ~ tones** mit gedämpfter Stimme, in gedämpftem Ton.

hush-hush [ˈhʌʃˈhʌʃ] *adj (inf)* streng geheim.

hush-money [ˈhʌʃmʌnɪ] *n* Schweigegeld *nt*.

husk [hʌsk] [1] *n* Schale *f*; *(of wheat)* Spelze *f*; *(of maize)* Hüllblatt *nt*; *(of rice also)* Hülse *f*.
[2] *vt* schälen.

huskily [ˈhʌskɪlɪ] *adv* mit rauher Stimme; *(hoarsely)* heiser, mit heiserer Stimme.

huskiness [ˈhʌskɪnɪs] *n* Rauheit *f*; *(hoarseness)* Heiserkeit *f*.

husky[1] [ˈhʌskɪ] *adj (+er)* **(a)** rauh, belegt; *singer's voice also* rauchig; *(hoarse)* heiser ◆ **a voice made ~ with emotion** eine vor Erregung heisere Stimme. **(b)** *(sturdy) person* stämmig.

husky[2] *n (dog)* Schlittenhund *m*.

hussar [hʊˈzɑːʳ] *n* Husar *m*.

hussy [ˈhʌsɪ] *n (pert girl)* Fratz *m (inf)*, (freche) Göre *(inf)*; *(whorish woman)* Flittchen *nt (pej)*.

hustings [ˈhʌstɪŋz] *npl (Brit) (campaign)* Wahlkampf *m*; *(meeting)* Wahlveranstaltung *f* ◆ **on the ~** im Wahlkampf; *(at election meeting)* in *or* bei einer Wahlveranstaltung.

hustle [ˈhʌsl] [1] *n (jostling)* Gedränge *nt*; *(hurry)* Hetze, Eile *f* ◆ **the ~ (and bustle) of the city centre** das geschäftige Treiben *or* das Gewühl *(inf)* in der Innenstadt.
[2] *vt* **(a) to ~ sb into a room** *etc*/**out of the building** jdn schnell in einen Raum *etc*/aus einem Gebäude bringen *or* befördern *(inf)*; **she ~d her way through the crowd** sie drängelte sich durch die Menge.
(b) *(fig)* drängen ◆ **I won't be ~d into a decision** ich lasse mich nicht zu einer Entscheidung drängen; **to ~ things (on** *or* **along)** die Dinge vorantreiben *or* beschleunigen.
[3] *vi* **(a)** hasten, eilen; *(through crowd etc)* sich (durch)drängeln. **(b)** *(solicit)* auf den Strich gehen *(inf)* ◆ **to ~ for custom** nach Freiern Ausschau halten *(inf)*. **(c)** *(US inf: work quickly)* sich ins Zeug legen *(inf)*.

hustler [ˈhʌsləʳ] *n* **(a)** *(prostitute)* Straßenmädchen, Strichmädchen *(inf) nt*; *(male)* Strichjunge *m (inf)*. **(b)** *(US inf: hard worker)* Arbeitstier *nt (inf)*.

hustling [ˈhʌslɪŋ] *n* (Straßen)prostitution *f*, der Strich *(inf)*.

hut [hʌt] *n* Hütte *f*; *(Mil)* Baracke *f*.

hutch [hʌtʃ] *n* Verschlag, Stall *m*.

hyacinth [ˈhaɪəsɪnθ] *n* Hyazinthe *f*.

hyaena, hyena [haɪˈiːnə] *n* Hyäne *f* ◆ **to laugh like a ~** wiehernd lachen.

hybrid [ˈhaɪbrɪd] [1] *n (Ling)* hybride Bildung *or* Form; *(Bot, Zool)* Kreuzung *f*, Hybride *mf (form)*; *(fig)* Mischform *f*.
[2] *adj (Ling)* hybrid *(spec)*; *(Bot, Zool)* Misch-.

hybridism [ˈhaɪbrɪdɪzəm] *n (lit, fig)* Hybridismus *m*.

hybridization [ˌhaɪbrɪdaɪˈzeɪʃən] *n (Ling)* Hybridisation *f (spec)*; *(Bot, Zool also)* Kreuzung *f*; *(fig)* Mischung *f*, Zwitter *m*.

hybridize [ˈhaɪbrɪdaɪz] *vt (Ling)* hybridisieren *(spec)*; *(Bot, Zool also)* kreuzen; *(fig)* mischen, kreuzen.

hydra [ˈhaɪdrə] *n (Zool, Myth)* Hydra *f*.

hydrangea [haɪˈdreɪndʒə] *n* Hortensie *f*.

hydrant [ˈhaɪdrənt] *n* Hydrant *m*.

hydrate [ˈhaɪdreɪt] [1] *n* Hydrat *nt*.
[2] [haɪˈdreɪt] *vt* hydratisieren.

hydrated [haɪˈdreɪtɪd] *adj* wasserhaltig.

hydraulic [haɪˈdrɒlɪk] *adj* hydraulisch.

hydraulics [haɪˈdrɒlɪks] *n sing* Hydraulik *f*.

hydro [ˈhaɪdrəʊ] *n* Kurhotel *nt (mit Hydrotherapie)*.

hydro- [ˈhaɪdrəʊ-] *pref (concerning water)* Hydro-, hydro-, Wasser-, wasser-; *(Chem)* (+*n*) -wasserstoff *m*. **~carbon** *n* Kohlenwasserstoff *m*; **~cephalic** [ˌhaɪdrəʊseˈfælɪk] *adj* wasserköpfig, mit einem Wasserkopf; **~cephalus** [ˌhaɪdrəʊˈsefələs] *n* Wasserkopf *m*; **~chloric acid** *n* Salzsäure *f*; **~dynamics** *n sing or pl* Hydrodynamik *f*; **~electric** *adj* hydroelektrisch; **~electric power** *n* durch Wasserkraft erzeugte Energie; **~electric power station** *n* Wasserkraftwerk *nt*; **~electricity** *n* durch Wasserkraft erzeugte Energie; **~foil** *n (boat)* Tragflächen- *or* Tragflügelboot *nt*; *(fin)* Tragfläche *f or* -flügel *m*.

hydrogen [ˈhaɪdrɪdʒən] *n* Wasserstoff *m*, Hydrogenium *nt (spec)* ◆ **~ bomb**

Wasserstoffbombe *f;* ~ **bond** Wasserstoffbrücke(nbindung) *f;* ~ **sulphide** (*gas*) Schwefelwasserstoff *m.*

hydrography [haɪ'drɒgrəfɪ] *n* Gewässerkunde *f.*

hydrology [haɪ'drɒlədʒɪ] *n* Hydrologie *f.*

hydrolysis [haɪ'drɒlɪsɪs] *n* Hydrolyse *f.*

hydrometer [haɪ'drɒmɪtə^r] *n* Hydrometer *nt.*

hydro-: ~pathic [,haɪdrəʊ'pæθɪk] *adj* hydrotherapeutisch; **~phobia** *n* Hydrophobie (*spec*), Wasserscheu *f;* (*rabies*) Tollwut *f;* **~phobic** *adj* hydrophob; **~plane** *n* **(a)** (*Aviat: aircraft*) Wasserflugzeug, Flugboot *nt;* (*float*) Schwimmer *m;* **(b)** (*Naut*) (*boat*) Gleitboot *nt;* (*of submarine*) Tiefenruder *nt;* **~ponics** [,haɪdrəʊ'pɒnɪks] *n sing* Hydrokultur *f;* **~therapeutics** *n sing* Wasserheilkunde, Hydrotherapeutik (*spec*) *f;* **~therapy** *n* Wasserbehandlung, Hydrotherapie (*spec*) *f.*

hydroxide [haɪ'drɒksaɪd] *n* Hydroxyd, Hydroxid *nt.*

hyena [haɪ'iːnə] *n see* **hyaena.**

hygiene ['haɪdʒiːn] *n* Hygiene *f* ◆ **personal ~** Körperpflege *f.*

hygienic *adj,* **~ally** *adv* [haɪ'dʒiːnɪk, -əlɪ] hygienisch.

hygienics [haɪ'dʒiːnɪks] *n sing* Hygiene, Gesundheitslehre *f.*

hygro- ['haɪgrəʊ-] *pref* Hygro-, hygro-, (Luft)feuchtigkeits- ◆ **~meter** ['haɪ'grɒmɪtə^r] Hygrometer *nt.*

hymen ['haɪmen] *n* Hymen (*spec*), Jungfernhäutchen *nt.*

hymenopterous [,haɪmə'nɒptərəs] *adj* **~ insect** Hautflügler *m.*

hymn [hɪm] [1] *n* Kirchenlied *nt* ◆ **~ of praise** (*fig*) Lobeshymne *f.*
[2] *vt* (*old*) besingen; (*Eccl*) (lob)preisen.

hymnal ['hɪmnəl] *n* Gesangbuch *nt.*

hymnbook ['hɪmbʊk] *n* Gesangbuch *nt.*

hymn-singing ['hɪm,sɪŋɪŋ] *n* Singen *nt* (von Chorälen) ◆ **we had ~ once a week** wir hatten einmal in der Woche Choralsingen.

hype [haɪp] (*inf*) [1] *n* Publicity *f* ◆ **the concept is largely ~** das Konzept beruht im wesentlichen auf Publicity; **all this ~ about ...** dieser ganze Rummel um ... (*inf*).
[2] *vt* (*also* **~ up**) *product etc* Publicity machen für.

hyped up ['haɪpt'ʌp] *adj* (*sl: on drugs*) high (*sl*), unter Strom (*sl*).

hyper- ['haɪpə^r] *pref* Hyper-, hyper-, Über-, über-, Super-, super-. **~acidity** *n* Übersäuerung, Hyperazidität (*spec*) *f;* **~active** *adj* überaktiv, sehr *or* äußerst aktiv; **a ~active thyroid** eine Überfunktion der Schilddrüse.

hyperbola [haɪ'pɜːbələ] *n* (*Math*) Hyperbel *f.*

hyperbole [haɪ'pɜːbəlɪ] *n* (*Liter*) Hyperbel *f.*

hyperbolic(al) [,haɪpə'bɒlɪk(əl)] *adj* (*Liter, Math*) hyperbolisch; (*Math also*) Hyperbel-.

hyper-: ~critical *adj* übertrieben kritisch; **~market** *n* Verbrauchermarkt *m;* **~sensitive** *adj* überempfindlich; **~tension** *n* Hypertonie *f,* erhöhter Blutdruck; **~hypertext** *n* (*Comput*) Hypertext *m;* **~thyroidism** *n* Überfunktion *f* der Schilddrüse, **~trophy** *n* Hypertrophie *f;* **~ventilate** *vi* hyperventilieren.

hyphen ['haɪfən] *n* Bindestrich, Divis (*spec*) *m;* (*at end of line*) Trenn(ungs)-strich *m;* (*Typ*) Divis *nt.*

hyphenate ['haɪfəneɪt] *vt* mit Bindestrich schreiben; (*Typ*) koppeln (*spec*) ◆ **~d word** Bindestrich- *or* (*Typ*) Koppelwort *nt.*

hyphenation [,haɪfə'neɪʃən] *n* Silbentrennung *f.*

hypno- [hɪpnəʊ-] *pref* Hypno-, hypno-.

hypnosis [hɪp'nəʊsɪs] *n* Hypnose *f* ◆ **under ~** unter *or* in Hypnose, in hypnotisiertem Zustand.

hypnotherapy [,hɪpnəʊ'θerəpɪ] *n* Hypnotherapie *f.*

hypnotic [hɪp'nɒtɪk] [1] *adj* hypnotisch; (*hypnotizing, fig*) hypnotisierend.
[2] *n* **(a)** (*drug*) Hypnotikum (*spec*), Schlafmittel *nt.* **(b)** (*person*) (*easily hypnotized*) leicht hypnotisierbarer Mensch; (*under hypnosis*) Hypnotisierte(r) *mf.*

hypnotism ['hɪpnətɪzəm] *n* Hypnotismus *m;* (*act*) Hypnotisierung *f.*

hypnotist ['hɪpnətɪst] *n* Hypnotiseur *m,* Hypnotiseuse *f.*

hypnotize ['hɪpnətaɪz] *vt* hypnotisieren.

hypo- [haɪpəʊ-] *pref* Hypo-, hypo.

hypochondria *n* Hypochondrie *f.*

hypochondriac [,haɪpəʊ'kɒndrɪæk] [1] *n* Hypochonder *m.*
[2] *adj* (*also* **~al** [-əl]) hypochondrisch.

hypocrisy [hɪ'pɒkrɪsɪ] *n* (*hypocritical behaviour*) Heuchelei *f;* (*sanctimony*) Scheinheiligkeit *f.*

hypocrite ['hɪpəkrɪt] *n* Heuchler(in *f*) *m;* Scheinheilige(r) *mf.*

hypocritical *adj,* **~ly** *adv* [,hɪpə'krɪtɪkəl, -ɪ] heuchlerisch, scheinheilig.

hypodermic [,haɪpə'dɜːmɪk] [1] *adj injection* subkutan ◆ **~ syringe/needle** Subkutanspritze *f*/-nadel *f;* (*loosely*) Spritze *f*/Nadel *f.*
[2] *n* **(a)** (*syringe*) subkutane Spritze. **(b)** (*injection*) subkutane Injektion.

hypoglycaemia, (*US*) **hypoglycemia** [,haɪpəʊglaɪ'siːmɪə] *n* (*Med*) Hypoglykämie *f,* Unterzuckerung *f.*

hypoglycaemic, (*US*) **hypoglycemic** [,haɪpəʊglaɪ'siːmɪk] *adj* (*Med*) *symptoms* hypoglykämisch, Unterzuckerungs-; *person* hypoglykämisch, an Unterzuckerung leidend.

hypotenuse [haɪ'pɒtɪnjuːz] *n* Hypotenuse *f* ◆ **the square on the ~** das Quadrat über der Hypotenuse.

hypothalamus [,haɪpə'θæləməs] *n, pl* **-mi** [-maɪ] (*Anat*) Hypothalamus *m.*

hypothermia [,haɪpəʊ'θɜːmɪə] *n* Unterkühlung *f;* Kältetod *m.*

hypothesis [haɪ'pɒθɪsɪs] *n, pl* **hypotheses** [haɪ'pɒθɪsiːz] Hypothese, Annahme *f* ◆ **working ~** Arbeitshypothese *f.*

hypothesize [haɪ'pɒθɪsaɪz] [1] *vi* Hypothesen/eine Hypothese aufstellen.
[2] *vt* annehmen.

hypothetical [,haɪpəʊ'θetɪkəl] *adj* hypothetisch, angenommen ◆ **purely ~** reine Hypothese.

hypothetically [,haɪpəʊ'θetɪkəlɪ] *adv* hypothetisch.

hysterectomy [,hɪstə'rektəmɪ] *n* Hysterektomie (*spec*), Totaloperation *f.*

hysteria [hɪ'stɪərɪə] *n* Hysterie *f* ◆ **mass ~** Massenhysterie *f.*

hysterical [hɪ'sterɪkəl] *adj* hysterisch; (*inf: very funny*) wahnsinnig komisch (*inf*).

hysterically [hɪ'sterɪkəlɪ] *adv* hysterisch ◆ **to laugh ~** hysterisch lachen; (*fig*) vor Lachen brüllen; **~ funny** (*inf*) irrsinnig komisch (*inf*).

hysterics [hɪ'sterɪks] *npl* Hysterie *f,* hysterischer Anfall ◆ **to stop sb's ~** jds Hysterie (*dat*) ein Ende machen; **to go into ~** hysterisch werden, einen hysterischen Anfall bekommen; (*fig inf: laugh*) sich totlachen, sich nicht mehr halten können vor Lachen; **we were in ~ about it** (*inf*) wir haben uns darüber (halb) totgelacht (*inf*).

Hz *abbr of* **hertz** Hz.

I

I[1], i [aɪ] *n* I, i *nt; see* **dot.**
I[2] *abbr of* **Island, Isle.**
I[3] *pers pron* ich ◆ **it is ~** *(form)* ich bin es.
IAAF *abbr of* **International Amateur Athletic Federation** IAAF.
iambic [aɪ'æmbɪk] [1] *adj* jambisch ◆ **~ pentameter** fünffüßiger Jambus.
[2] *n* Jambus *m.*
IATA [aɪ'ɑːtə] *abbr of* **International Air Transport Association** IATA *f.*
iatrogenic [ˌjætrəʊ'dʒenɪk, aɪˌætrəʊ-] *adj* iatrogen.
IBA *(Brit) abbr of* **Independent Broadcasting Authority** *Aufsichtsgremium nt der Fernsehanstalt ITV.*
Iberia [aɪ'bɪərɪə] *n* Iberien *nt.*
Iberian [aɪ'bɪərɪən] [1] *adj* iberisch ◆ **~ Peninsula** Iberische Halbinsel.
[2] *n* **(a)** Iberer(in *f*) *m.* **(b)** *(language)* Iberisch *nt.*
ibex ['aɪbeks] *n* Steinbock *m.*
ib(id) *abbr of* **ibidem** ib., ibd.
ibis ['aɪbɪs] *n* Ibis *m.*
i/c, I/C *abbr of* **in charge** v.D., vom Dienst.
ICBM *abbr of* **intercontinental ballistic missile** Interkontinentalrakete *f.*
ice [aɪs] [1] *n* **(a)** Eis *nt; (on roads)* (Glatt)eis *nt* ◆ **to be as cold as ~** eiskalt sein; **my hands are like ~** ich habe eiskalte Hände; **"Cinderella on I~"** „Aschenputtel auf dem Eis"; **to keep** *or* **put sth on ~** *(lit)* etw kalt stellen; *(fig)* etw auf Eis legen; **to break the ~** *(fig)* das Eis brechen; **to be** *or* **be treading** *or* **be skating on thin ~** *(fig)* sich aufs Glatteis begeben/begeben haben; **you are (skating) on thin ~ there** da begibst du dich aufs Glatteis; **to cut no ~ with sb** *(inf)* auf jdn keinen Eindruck machen; **that cuts no ~ with me** *(inf)* das kommt bei mir nicht an.
(b) *(Brit: ice-cream)* (Speise)eis *nt,* Eiskrem *f.*
(c) *no pl (US sl: diamond)* Klunker *m (sl).*
[2] *vt* **(a)** *(make cold)* (mit Eis) kühlen; *(freeze)* tiefkühlen.
(b) *cake* glasieren, mit Zuckerguß überziehen.
◆**ice over** *vi* zufrieren; *(windscreen)* vereisen.
◆**ice up** *vi (aircraft wings, rail points, windscreen)* vereisen; *(pipes etc)* einfrieren.
ice *in cpds* Eis-; **~ age** *n* Eiszeit *f;* **~ axe** *n* Eispickel *m;* **~berg** *n (lit, fig)* Eisberg *m;* **~-blue** *adj* eisblau; **~boat** *n* **(a)** *(Sport)* Segelschlitten *m;* **(b)** *see* **~breaker;** **~bound** *adj port* zugefroren, vereist; *ship* vom Eis eingeschlossen; *road* vereist; **~box** *n (Brit: in refrigerator)* Eisfach *nt; (US)* Eisschrank *m; (insulated box)* Eisbox, Kühltasche *f;* **this room is like an ~box** dieses Zimmer ist der reinste Eiskeller; **~breaker** *n* Eisbrecher *m;* **~ bucket** *n* Eiskühler *m;* **~cap** *n* Eisdecke, Eisschicht *f; (polar)* Eiskappe *f;* **~-cold** *adj* eiskalt; **~-cream** *n* Eis *nt,* Eiskrem *f;* **~-cream parlour** *n* Eisdiele *f;* **~-cream soda** *n Eisbecher m mit Sirup, Marmelade, Früchten, Milch und Ingwerlimonade;* **~ cube** *n* Eiswürfel *m.*
iced [aɪst] *adj* **(a)** *(cooled)* eisgekühlt; *(covered with ice)* vereist, mit Eis bedeckt ◆ **~ coffee** Eiskaffee *m;* **~ water** Eiswasser *nt.* **(b)** *cake* glasiert, mit Zuckerguß überzogen.
ice: ~ floe *n* Eisscholle *f;* **~ hockey** *n* Eishockey *nt;* **~house** *n* Eiskeller *m.*
Iceland ['aɪslənd] *n* Island *nt.*
Icelander ['aɪsləndə^r] *n* Isländer(in *f*) *m.*
Icelandic [aɪs'lændɪk] [1] *adj* isländisch.
[2] *n (language)* Isländisch *nt.*
ice: ~ lolly *n (Brit)* Eis *nt* am Stiel; **~man** *n (US)* Eisverkäufer *m;* **~ pack** *n* Packeis *nt; (on head)* Eisbeutel *m;* **~ pick** *n* Eispickel *m;* **~ rink** *n* (Kunst)eisbahn, Schlittschuhbahn *f;* **~ sheet** *n* Eisschicht *f;* **~-skate** *vi* Schlittschuh laufen *or* fahren; **~skate** *n* Schlittschuh *m;* **~-skating** *n* Eislauf *m,* Schlittschuhlaufen *nt; (figure-skating)* Eiskunstlauf *m;* **~-tray** *n* Eisschale *f.*
ichneumon fly [ɪk'njuːmən,flaɪ] *n* Schlupfwespe *f.*
ichthyology [ˌɪkθɪ'ɒlədʒɪ] *n* Fischkunde, Ichthyologie *f.*
icicle ['aɪsɪkl] *n* Eiszapfen *m.*
icily ['aɪsɪlɪ] *adv (lit, fig)* eisig ◆ **the wind blew ~** es wehte ein eisiger Wind; **to look ~ at sb** jdm einen eisigen Blick zuwerfen.
iciness ['aɪsɪnɪs] *n* Eiseskälte *f,* eisige Kälte; *(of road etc)* Vereisung *f.*
icing ['aɪsɪŋ] *n* **(a)** *(Cook)* Zuckerguß *m* ◆ **~ sugar** *(Brit)* Puderzucker *m.* **(b)** *(on aircraft, rail points)* Eisbildung, Vereisung *f.*
icon ['aɪkɒn] *n* **(a)** Ikone *f.* **(b)** *(Comput)* Ikon *nt,* ikonisches Zeichen.
iconoclasm [aɪ'kɒnəklæzəm] *n (lit, fig)* Bilderstürmerei *f.*
iconoclast [aɪ'kɒnəklæst] *n (lit, fig)* Bilderstürmer, Ikonoklast *(liter) m.*
iconoclastic [aɪˌkɒnə'klæstɪk] *adj (fig)* bilderstürmerisch.
iconographic [aɪˌkɒnə'græfɪk] *adj* ikonographisch.
icy ['aɪsɪ] *adj (+er) (lit, fig)* eisig; *(covered with ice) road* vereist; *ground* gefroren.
I'd [aɪd] *contr of* **I would; I had.**
id [ɪd] *n (Psych)* Es *nt.*
ID *n (abbr of* **identification; identity) do we have an ~ for him yet?** haben wir ihn schon identifiziert?; **~ card** Ausweis *m; (state-issued)* Personalausweis *m.*
▼ **idea** [aɪ'dɪə] *n* **(a)** Idee *f (also Philos); (sudden also)* Einfall *m* ◆ **good ~!** gute Idee!; **that's not a bad ~** das ist keine schlechte Idee; **what an ~!** so eine *or* was für eine Idee!; **who thought of that ~?** wer hat sich *(dat)* denn das einfallen lassen?; **he's our new ~s man** *(inf)* er ist hier der Mann mit den neuen Ideen; **history of ~s** Geistesgeschichte *f;* **man of ~s** Denker *m;* **the very ~!** (nein,) so was!; **the very ~ of eating horsemeat revolts me** der bloße Gedanke an Pferdefleisch ekelt mich; **the ~ never entered my head!** auf den Gedanken bin ich überhaupt nicht gekommen; **he is full of (bright) ~s** ihm fehlt es nie an (guten) Ideen; **to hit upon the ~ of doing sth** den plötzlichen Einfall haben, etw zu tun; **that gives me an ~, we could ...** da fällt mir ein, wir könnten ...; **he got the ~ for his novel while he was having a bath** die Idee zu seinem Roman kam ihm in der Badewanne; **to lack ~s** phantasielos *or* einfallslos sein; **whose bright ~ was that?** *(iro)* wer hat denn diese glänzende Idee gehabt?; **he hasn't an ~ in his head** er ist völlig ideenlos; **he's somehow got the ~ into his head that ...** er bildet sich *(dat)* irgendwie ein, daß ...; **don't get ~s** *or* **don't you go getting ~s about promotion** machen Sie sich *(dat)* nur keine falschen Hoffnungen auf eine Beförderung; **don't get** *or* **go getting any ~s about that fur coat** bilde dir nur nicht ein, du würdest den Pelzmantel bekommen; **to put ~s into sb's head** jdm einen Floh ins Ohr setzen, jdn auf dumme Gedanken bringen.
(b) *(purpose)* **the ~ was to meet at 6** wir wollten uns um 6 treffen; **what's the ~ of keeping him waiting?** was soll denn das, ihn warten zu lassen?; **what's the big ~?** *(inf)* was soll das denn?; **the ~ is to ...** es ist beabsichtigt, zu ...; **that's the ~** so ist es richtig, genau (das ist's)!; **you're getting the ~** Sie verstehen langsam, worum es geht.
(c) *(opinion)* Meinung, Ansicht *f; (conception)* Vorstellung *f* ◆ **if that's your ~ of fun** wenn Sie das lustig finden, wenn das Ihre Vorstellung von Spaß ist; **he has some very strange ~s** er hat manchmal merkwürdige Vorstellungen; **according to his ~** seiner Meinung *or* Ansicht nach; **he has no ~ of right and wrong** er kann zwischen Gut und Böse nicht unterscheiden; **his ~ of a pleasant evening is ...** seine Vorstellung von einem angenehmen Abend ist ...
▼ **(d)** *(knowledge)* Ahnung *f* ◆ **you've no ~ how worried I've been** du kannst dir nicht vorstellen, welche Sorgen ich mir gemacht habe; **to have some ~ of art** ein bißchen von Kunst verstehen; **(I've) no ~** (ich habe) keine Ahnung; **I haven't the least** *or* **slightest** *or* **faintest ~** ich habe nicht die leiseste *or* geringste Ahnung; **I have an ~ that ...** ich habe so das Gefühl, daß ...; **I had no ~ that ...** ich hatte ja keine Ahnung, daß ...; **just to give me an ~ of how long** damit ich so ungefähr weiß, wie lange; **could you give me an ~ of how long ...?** könnten Sie mir ungefähr sagen, wie lange ...?; **to give you an ~ of how difficult it is** um Ihnen eine Vorstellung davon zu vermitteln, wie schwierig es ist.
ideal [aɪ'dɪəl] [1] *adj* ideal, vollkommen ◆ **in an ~ world** im Idealfall; *(philosophical statement)* in einer vollkommenen *or* idealen Welt.
[2] *n* Idealvorstellung *f,* Ideal *nt (also Philos).*
idealism [aɪ'dɪəlɪzəm] *n* Idealismus *m.*
idealist [aɪ'dɪəlɪst] *n* Idealist(in *f*) *m.*
idealistic [aɪˌdɪə'lɪstɪk] *adj* idealistisch.
idealize [aɪ'dɪəlaɪz] *vt* idealisieren.
ideally [aɪ'dɪəlɪ] *adv* ideal ◆ **they are ~ suited for each other** sie passen ausgezeichnet zueinander; **~, the house should have four rooms** idealerweise *or* im Idealfall sollte das Haus vier Zimmer haben.
identical [aɪ'dentɪkəl] *adj (exactly alike)* identisch, (völlig) gleich; *(same)* derselbe/dieselbe/dasselbe ◆ **can you be sure this is the ~ man you saw?** sind Sie auch wirklich sicher, daß dies der Mann ist, den Sie gesehen haben?; **~ twins** eineiige Zwillinge *pl;* **we have ~ views** wir haben die gleichen Ansichten.
identically [aɪ'dentɪkəlɪ] *adv* identisch, gleich.
identifiable [aɪ'dentɪˌfaɪəbl] *adj* erkennbar; *(esp in scientific contexts)*

➤ LANGUAGE IN USE: **idea: a** → 1.1, 8.2, 8.3, 26.2 **d** → 6.2, 6.3

identifizierbar ◆ **he is ~ by his red hair** er ist an seinem roten Haar zu erkennen; **that makes him/it ~** daran kann man ihn/es erkennen.

identification [aɪˌdentɪfɪˈkeɪʃən] *n* **(a)** (*of criminal, dead person etc*) Identifizierung *f*, Feststellung *f* der Identität ◆ **a system of fingerprint ~** ein erkennungsdienstliches System auf der Basis von Fingerabdrücken.
(b) (*papers*) Ausweispapiere *pl*, Legitimation *f* ◆ **because he had no (means of) ~** weil er sich nicht ausweisen konnte.
(c) (*considering as identical, equation*) Gleichsetzung, Identifizierung *f*.
(d) (*association*) Identifikation *f* ◆ **a politician who has any form of ~ with a criminal group** ein Politiker, der irgendwie mit einer kriminellen Gruppe in Verbindung gebracht wird.

identification: ~ papers *npl* Ausweispapiere *pl*; **~ parade** *n* Gegenüberstellung *f* (zur Identifikation des Täters); **~ tag** *n* (*US*) Erkennungsmarke *f*.

identifier [aɪˈdentɪfaɪəʳ] *n* (*Comput*) Kennzeichnung *f*.

identify [aɪˈdentɪfaɪ] **1** *vt* **(a)** (*establish identity of*) identifizieren, die Identität (*+gen*) feststellen; *plant, species etc* bestimmen; (*mark identity of*) kennzeichnen; (*recognize, pick out*) erkennen ◆ **to ~ sb/sth by sth** jdn/etw an etw (*dat*) erkennen.
(b) (*consider as the same*) gleichsetzen (*with* mit).
(c) (*associate with*) assoziieren.
2 *vr* **(a) to ~ oneself** sich ausweisen.
(b) to ~ oneself with sb/sth sich mit jdm/etw identifizieren.
3 *vi* (*with film hero etc*) sich identifizieren (*with* mit).

Identikit ® [aɪˈdentɪkɪt] *n*: **~ (picture)** Phantombild *nt*.

identity [aɪˈdentɪtɪ] *n* **(a)** Identität *f* ◆ **to prove one's ~** sich ausweisen; **a driving licence will be accepted as proof of ~** ein Führerschein genügt, um sich auszuweisen; **proof of ~** (*permit*) Legitimation *f*; *see* **mistaken**.
(b) (*identicalness*) Gleichheit, Übereinstimmung, Identität *f* ◆ **~ of interest** Interessengleichheit *f*.

identity: ~ bracelet *n* Identitätsarmband *nt*; **~ card** *n* Ausweis *m*; (*state-issued*) Personalausweis *m*; **~ crisis** *n* Identitätskrise *f*; **~ disc** *n* (*Mil*) Erkennungsmarke *f*; (*for dogs*) Hundemarke *f*; **~ papers** *npl* Ausweispapiere *pl*; **~ parade** *n* Gegenüberstellung *f*.

ideogram [ˈɪdɪəʊgræm], **ideograph** [ˈɪdɪəʊgrɑːf] *n* Ideogramm *nt*.

ideological *adj*, **~ly** *adv* [ˌaɪdɪəˈlɒdʒɪkəl, -ɪ] weltanschaulich, ideologisch (*often pej*).

ideologist [ˌaɪdɪˈɒlədʒɪst] *n* Ideologe *m*, Ideologin *f*.

ideology [ˌaɪdɪˈɒlədʒɪ] *n* Weltanschauung, Ideologie *f*.

ides [aɪdz] *npl* Iden *pl* ◆ **the ~ of March** die Iden *pl* des März.

idiocy [ˈɪdɪəsɪ] *n* **(a)** *no pl* Idiotie *f*, Schwachsinn *m*. **(b)** (*stupid act, words*) Dummheit, Blödheit *f*.

idiolect [ˈɪdɪəʊlekt] *n* Idiolekt *m*.

idiom [ˈɪdɪəm] *n* **(a)** (*special phrase, group of words*) idiomatische Wendung, Redewendung *f*. **(b)** (*language*) Sprache *f*, Idiom *nt*; (*of region*) Mundart *f*, Dialekt *m*; (*of author*) Ausdrucksweise, Diktion *f* ◆ **... to use the modern ~ ...** um es modern auszudrücken.

idiomatic [ˌɪdɪəˈmætɪk] *adj* idiomatisch ◆ **to speak ~ German** idiomatisch richtiges Deutsch sprechen; **an ~ expression** eine Redensart, eine idiomatische Redewendung.

idiomatically [ˌɪdɪəˈmætɪkəlɪ] *adv see adj*.

idiomaticity [ˌɪdɪəʊməˈtɪsɪtɪ] *n* Idiomatik *f* ◆ **his language lacked ~** er drückte sich nicht sehr idiomatisch aus.

idiosyncrasy [ˌɪdɪəˈsɪŋkrəsɪ] *n* Eigenheit, Eigenart, Besonderheit *f*; (*Ling, Med*) Idiosynkrasie *f*.

idiosyncratic [ˌɪdɪəsɪŋˈkrætɪk] *adj* eigenartig; (*Ling, Med*) idiosynkratisch ◆ **he has a very ~ way of ...** er hat eine eigene Art zu ...

idiot [ˈɪdɪət] *n* Idiot, Dummkopf, Schwachkopf *m*; (*old Med*) Idiot(in *f*) *m*, Schwachsinnige(r) *mf* ◆ **what an ~!** so ein Idiot *or* Dummkopf!; **you (stupid) ~!** du Idiot!; **where's that ~ waiter?** wo ist dieser blöde Ober, wo ist dieser Idiot von Ober?; **this ~ brother of mine** dieser Schwachkopf *or* Dummkopf *or* Idiot von meinem Bruder; **you're speaking like an ~** du redest völligen Blödsinn; **what an ~ I am/was!** ich Idiot!

idiot card *n* (*TV*) Neger *m*.

idiotic [ˌɪdɪˈɒtɪk] *adj* blöd(sinnig), idiotisch ◆ **don't be ~!** sei nicht so blöd!; **what an ~ price to pay!** idiotisch, so viel dafür zu bezahlen!

idiotically [ˌɪdɪˈɒtɪkəlɪ] *adv* blödsinnig, idiotisch; *expensive* lachhaft, absurd; *exaggerated* lächerlich ◆ **~, I had ...** blödsinniger- *or* idiotischerweise hatte ich ...

idle [ˈaɪdl] **1** *adj* **(a)** (*not working*) *person* müßig, untätig ◆ **the ~ rich** die reichen Müßiggänger; **in my ~ moments** in ruhigen *or* stillen Augenblicken; **~ life** faules Leben; **money lying ~** totes Kapital; **we don't want to let the money lie ~** wir wollen das Geld nicht ungenutzt liegen lassen; **his car was lying ~ most of the time** sein Auto stand meistens unbenutzt herum.
(b) (*lazy*) faul, träge.
(c) (*in industry*) *person* unbeschäftigt; *machine* stillstehend *attr*, stilliegend *attr*, außer Betrieb ◆ **500 men have been made ~ by the strike** durch den Streik mußten 500 Leute ihre Arbeit einstellen; **the whole factory stood ~** die ganze Fabrik hatte die Arbeit eingestellt; **the machine stood ~** die Maschine stand still *or* arbeitete nicht *or* war außer Betrieb; **~ capacity** freie *or* brachliegende Kapazität; **~ time** Brachzeit, Leerzeit *f*; **~ money** totes *or* brachliegendes Kapital.
(d) *promise, threat, words* leer; *speculation, talk* müßig; (*useless*) nutzlos, vergeblich, eitel (*old*) ◆ **it would be ~ to go on trying** es wäre nutzlos *or* zwecklos, (es) weiter zu versuchen; **~ curiosity** pure *or* bloße Neugier; **~ fear** grundlose *or* unbegründete Angst; **~ wish** Wunschtraum *m*; **the ~ pleasures of this worldly life** die eitlen Vergnügungen dieses Erdenlebens.
2 *vi* **(a)** (*person*) untätig sein, faulenzen, nichts tun ◆ **a day spent idling on the river** ein Tag, den man untätig auf dem Wasser verbringt. **(b)** (*engine*) leerlaufen. **when the engine is idling** wenn der Motor im Leerlauf ist.

◆**idle about** *or* **around** *vi* herumtrödeln, bummeln; (*loiter*) herumlungern ◆ **we were idling ~ on the beach** wir faulenzten am Strand; **don't ~ ~** trödle nicht herum!, bummle nicht!

◆**idle away** *vt sep one's time etc* vertrödeln, verbummeln.

idleness [ˈaɪdlnɪs] *n* **(a)** (*state of not working*) Untätigkeit *f*; (*pleasurable*) Muße *f*, Müßiggang (*liter*) *m* ◆ **to live in ~** ein untätiges Leben führen, ein Leben der Muße führen (*liter*); **a life of blissful ~** ein Leben voller köstlicher Muße.
(b) (*laziness*) Faulheit, Trägheit *f*.
(c) *see adj (d)* Leere *f*; Müßigkeit *f*; Nutzlosigkeit, Vergeblichkeit, Eitelkeit *f*.

idler [ˈaɪdləʳ] *n* **(a)** (*person not working*) Müßiggänger(in *f*) *m*; (*lazy person*) Faulenzer(in *f*) *m*, Faulpelz *m*. **(b)** (*Tech*) (*wheel*) Zwischenrad *nt*; (*pulley*) Spannrolle *f*.

idly [ˈaɪdlɪ] *adv* **(a)** (*without working*) untätig; (*pleasurably*) müßig ◆ **to stand ~ by** untätig herumstehen. **(b)** (*lazily*) faul, träge. **(c)** (*without thinking*) *say, suggest* ohne sich/mir *etc* etwas dabei zu denken; (*vainly*) *speculate* müßig.

idol [ˈaɪdl] *n* (*lit*) Götze *m*, Götzenbild *nt*; (*fig*) Idol *nt*, Abgott *m*; (*Film, TV etc*) Idol *nt*.

idolater [aɪˈdɒlətəʳ] *n* Götzendiener *m*.

idolatress [aɪˈdɒlətrɪs] *n* Götzendienerin *f*.

idolatrous [aɪˈdɒlətrəs] *adj* (*lit*) Götzen-; (*fig*) abgöttisch.

idolatry [aɪˈdɒlətrɪ] *n* (*lit*) Götzendienst *m*, Götzenverehrung *f*; (*fig*) Vergötterung *f*, abgöttische Verehrung.

idolize [ˈaɪdəlaɪz] *vt* abgöttisch lieben *or* verehren, vergöttern ◆ **to ~ wealth** Reichtum anbeten.

I'd've [ˈaɪdəv] *contr of* **I would have**.

idyll [ˈɪdɪl] *n* **(a)** (*Liter*) Idylle *f*. **(b)** (*fig*) Idyll *nt*.

idyllic *adj*, **~ally** *adv* [ɪˈdɪlɪk, -lɪ] idyllisch.

i.e. *abbr of* **id est** i.e., d.h.

▼ **if** [ɪf] **1** *conj* wenn; (*in case also*) falls, für den Fall, daß ...; (*whether, in direct clause*) ob ◆ **I would be pleased ~ you could do it** wenn Sie das tun könnten, wäre ich sehr froh; **~ it rains tomorrow** wenn es *or* falls es morgen regnet; **I wonder ~ he'll come** ich bin gespannt, ob er kommt; **do you know ~ they have gone?** wissen Sie, ob sie gegangen sind?; **I'll let you know when or ~ I come to a decision** ich werde Ihnen mitteilen, ob und wenn ich mich entschieden habe; **where will you live when you get married? — ~ we get married!** wo wollt ihr wohnen, wenn ihr heiratet? — wenn wir überhaupt heiraten!; **~ I asked him he helped me** er half mir immer, wenn ich ihn darum bat; **(even) ~** auch wenn; **it's a good film (even) ~ rather long** es ist ein guter Film, auch wenn er etwas lang ist; **(even) ~ they are poor, at least they are happy** sie sind zwar arm, aber wenigstens glücklich; **~ only** wenn (doch) nur; **~ only I had known!** wenn ich das nur gewußt hätte!; **I would like to see him, ~ only for a few hours** ich würde ihn gerne sehen, wenn auch nur für ein paar Stunden; **as ~** als ob; **he acts as ~ he were** *or* **was** (*inf*) **rich** er tut so, als ob er reich wäre; **as ~ by chance** wie zufällig; **he stood there as ~ he were dumb** er stand wie stumm da; **~ necessary** falls nötig, im Bedarfsfall; **~ so** wenn ja; **~ not** falls nicht; **~ not, why not?** falls nicht, warum?; **~ I were you/him** wenn ich Sie/er wäre, an Ihrer/seiner Stelle; **~ anything this one is bigger** wenn überhaupt, dann ist dieses hier größer; **~ I know Pete, he'll ...** so wie ich Pete kenne, wird er ...; **well, ~ he didn't try to steal my bag!** (*inf*) wollte der doch tatsächlich meine Tasche klauen (*inf*); **well, ~ it isn't old Jim!** (*inf*) ich werd' verrückt, das ist doch der Jim (*inf*).
2 *n* Wenn *nt* ◆ **it's a big ~** das ist noch sehr fraglich, das ist die große *or* noch sehr die Frage; **~s and buts** Wenn und Aber *nt*.

iffy [ˈɪfɪ] *adj* (*+er*) (*inf*) strittig, fraglich, zweifelhaft ◆ **he was a bit ~ about it** er hat sich sehr vage ausgedrückt.

igloo [ˈɪgluː] *n* Iglu *m or nt*.

igneous [ˈɪgnɪəs] *adj* (*Geol*) **~ rock** Eruptivgestein *nt*.

ignite [ɪgˈnaɪt] **1** *vt* entzünden, anzünden; (*Aut*) zünden.
2 *vi* sich entzünden, Feuer fangen; (*Aut*) zünden.

ignition [ɪgˈnɪʃən] *n* **(a)** Entzünden, Anzünden *nt*. **(b)** (*Aut*) Zündung *f* ◆ **we have ~** (*of rocket*) „Zündung".

ignition (*Aut*) *in cpds* Zünd-; **~ coil** *n* Zündspule *f*; **~ key** *n* Zündschlüssel *m*; **~ lock** *n* Zündschloß *nt*.

ignoble [ɪgˈnəʊbl] *adj* schändlich, unwürdig, unehrenhaft ◆ **~ peace** schmachvoller Frieden.

ignominious [ˌɪgnəˈmɪnɪəs] *adj* schmachvoll, entwürdigend, schmählich; *behaviour* schändlich, unehrenhaft.

ignominiously [ˌɪgnəˈmɪnɪəslɪ] *adv see adj*.

ignominy [ˈɪgnəmɪnɪ] *n* Schmach, Schande *f*, Schimpf *m* (*old*).

ignoramus [ˌɪgnəˈreɪməs] *n* Nichtswisser, Ignorant *m*.

ignorance [ˈɪgnərəns] *n* (*general lack of knowledge, education*) Unwissenheit *f*, Mangel *m* an Bildung, Ignoranz *f*; (*of particular subject, language, plan etc*) Unkenntnis *f* ◆ **to keep sb in ~ of sth** jdn in Unkenntnis über etw (*acc*) lassen, jdn etw nicht wissen lassen; **to be in ~ of sth** etw nicht wissen *or* kennen; **~ (of the law) is no excuse** Unkenntnis schützt vor Strafe nicht.

ignorant [ˈɪgnərənt] *adj* **(a)** (*generally uneducated*) unwissend, ungebildet, ignorant; (*of particular subject*) unwissend; (*of plan, requirements etc*) nicht informiert (*of* über *+acc*) ◆ **to be ~ of geography** sich in Geographie nicht auskennen; **I am not exactly ~ of what has been going on** es ist nicht so, als wüßte ich nicht, was los ist; **to be ~ of the facts** die Tatsachen nicht kennen; **they are ~ of** *or* **about what happened** sie wissen nicht, was ge-

➤ LANGUAGE IN USE: **if: 1** → 1.1, 2.2, 17.1

schehen ist.
(b) (*ill-mannered*) unhöflich, ungeschliffen, ungehobelt ◆ **you ~ fool** du ungehobelter Patron.

ignorantly ['ɪgnərəntlɪ] *adv* unwissentlich; *behave* unhöflich, ungeschliffen, ungehobelt.

ignore [ɪg'nɔːʳ] *vt* ignorieren; (*deliberately overlook also*) hinwegsehen über (+*acc*); (*pass over, pay no attention to*) nicht beachten, unbeachtet lassen; *remark also* überhören, übergehen; *person also* übersehen, nicht beachten ◆ **I'll ~ that** ich habe nichts gehört/gesehen; **but I can't ~ the fact that ...** aber ich kann mich der Tatsache nicht verschließen, daß ...

iguana [ɪ'gwɑːnə] *n* Leguan *m*.

ikon ['aɪkɒn] *n see* **icon**.

ILEA ['ɪlɪə] *abbr of* **Inner London Education Authority** *Londoner Schulaufsichtsbehörde f.*

ilex ['aɪleks] *n* **(a)** (*holm oak*) Steineiche, Immergrüneiche *f.* **(b)** (*holly*) Ilex, Stechpalme *f.*

Iliad ['ɪlɪæd] *n* Ilias, Iliade *f.*

ilk [ɪlk] *n* **people of that ~** solche Leute; **all things of that ~** dergleichen Dinge; **and others of that ~** und dergleichen, und ihresgleichen.

ill¹ *abbr of* **illustrated; illustration** Abb., Abbildung *f.*

ill² [ɪl] [1] *adj* **(a)** *pred* (*sick*) krank ◆ **to fall** *or* **take** (*inf*) *or* **be taken ~** erkranken (*with sth* an etw *dat*), krank werden; **to feel ~** sich unwohl *or* krank fühlen; **I feel (terribly) ~** mir ist gar nicht gut; **he is ~ with fever/a cold** er hat Fieber/eine Erkältung; **~ with anxiety/jealousy** krank vor Angst/Eifersucht.
(b) *comp* **worse**, *superl* **worst** (*bad*) schlecht, schlimm, übel ◆ **~ feeling** böses Blut; **no ~ feeling?** ist es wieder gut?; **no ~ feeling!** ist schon vergessen; **due to ~ health** aus Gesundheitsgründen; **~ humour** *or* (*US*) **humor** schlechte Laune; **~ luck** Pech *nt*; **as ~ luck would have it** wie es der Teufel so will; **~ nature** Übellaunigkeit *f*; **~ will** böses Blut; **I don't bear them any ~ will** ich trage ihnen nichts nach; **it's an ~ wind (that blows nobody any good)** (*Prov*) so hat alles seine guten Seiten.
[2] *n* **(a) to think ~ of sb** schlecht *or* Schlechtes von jdm *or* über jdn denken; **to speak ~ of sb** schlecht über jdn reden.
(b) ~s *pl* (*misfortunes*) Mißstände, Übel *pl*; (*miseries*) Mißgeschicke *pl* ◆ **to do ~** (*old*) Böses *or* Unrecht tun.
[3] *adv* schlecht ◆ **to take sth ~** (*old*) etw übelnehmen; **things went ~ with him** (*liter*) es erging ihm nicht gut, es ward ihm kein Glück beschieden (*old*); **he can ~ afford to refuse** er kann es sich (*dat*) schlecht leisten abzulehnen; **it ~ becomes you** (*form*) es steht Ihnen (*dat*) nicht an (*form*).

I'll [aɪl] *contr of* **I will; I shall.**

ill: ~-advised *adj person* unklug; *action also* unratsam; **you would be ~-advised to trust her** Sie wären schlecht beraten, wenn Sie ihr trauten; **~-assorted** *adj group, bunch* schlecht zusammenpassend; **~-at-ease** *adj* unbehaglich; **I always felt ~-at-ease in his presence** ich habe mich in seiner Gegenwart nie wohl gefühlt; **~-bred** *adj* ungezogen, schlecht erzogen; **~-breeding** *n* schlechte Erziehung, Unerzogenheit *f*; **it's a sign of ~-breeding to ...** es ist ein Zeichen für eine schlechte Kinderstube, wenn man ...; **~-considered** *adj action, words* unüberlegt, unbedacht; **~-disposed** *adj* **to be ~-disposed to(wards) sb** jdm übel gesinnt sein.

illegal [ɪ'liːgəl] *adj* unerlaubt; (*against a specific law*) gesetzwidrig; *trade, immigration, possession etc* illegal; (*Sport*) regelwidrig.

illegality [ˌɪliː'gælɪtɪ] *n see adj* Ungesetzlichkeit *f*; Gesetzwidrigkeit *f*; Illegalität *f.*

illegally [ɪ'liːgəlɪ] *adv* **~ imported** illegal eingeführt; **you're ~ parked** Sie stehen im Parkverbot; **to act ~** sich gesetzwidrig verhalten.

illegibility [ɪˌledʒɪ'bɪlɪtɪ] *n* Unleserlichkeit *f.*

illegible *adj*, **-bly** *adv* [ɪ'ledʒəbl, -ɪ] unleserlich.

illegitimacy [ˌɪlɪ'dʒɪtɪməsɪ] *n see adj* **(a)** Unehelichkeit *f.* **(b)** Unzulässigkeit *f*; Unrechtmäßigkeit *f.* **(c)** Unzulässigkeit *f.*

illegitimate [ˌɪlɪ'dʒɪtɪmɪt] *adj* **(a)** *child* unehelich.
(b) (*contrary to law*) unzulässig, unerlaubt; *government* unrechtmäßig ◆ **~ use of the verb** regelwidriger Gebrauch des Verbs; **the ~ use of drugs** (der) Drogenmißbrauch.
(c) *argument, conclusion, inference* unzulässig, nicht folgerichtig, illegitim.

illegitimately [ˌɪlɪ'dʒɪtɪmɪtlɪ] *adv see adj* **(a)** unehelich.
(b) unzulässig, unerlaubt; *parked* an verbotener Stelle; *use* unrechtmäßigerweise, unzulässigerweise.
(c) unzulässig, nicht folgerichtig.

ill: ~-fated *adj* **(a)** (*unfortunate, unlucky*) *person* vom Unglück verfolgt, unglücklich; **(b)** (*doomed, destined to fail*) unglückselig, verhängnisvoll; **the ~-fated Titanic** die unglückselige Titanic; **~-favoured** *adj* (*liter: ugly*) ungestalt (*liter*), häßlich, unschön; **~-founded** *adj* unbegründet, unerwiesen, fragwürdig; **~-gotten gains** *npl* unrechtmäßiger Gewinn, Sündengeld *nt* (*hum*); **~-humoured**, (*US*) **~-humored** *adj* schlecht *or* übel gelaunt, schlecht aufgelegt, verstimmt.

illiberal [ɪ'lɪbərəl] *adj* **(a)** (*narrow-minded*) engstirnig, intolerant, engherzig. **(b)** (*niggardly*) knauserig, geizig.

illicit [ɪ'lɪsɪt] *adj* verboten; (*illegal also*) illegal; *spirits* schwarz hergestellt *or* gebrannt ◆ **~ trade** *or* **sale** Schwarzhandel *m.*

illicitly [ɪ'lɪsɪtlɪ] *adv* verbotenerweise; (*illegally*) illegal(erweise) ◆ **~ acquired** unrechtmäßig erworben.

illimitable [ɪ'lɪmɪtəbl] *adj* grenzenlos, unbegrenzt ◆ **the ~ ocean** der unendliche Ozean.

ill-informed ['ɪlɪn,fɔːmd] *adj person* schlecht informiert *or* unterrichtet; *attack, criticism, speech* wenig sachkundig.

illiteracy [ɪ'lɪtərəsɪ] *n* Analphabetentum *nt* ◆ **~ rate** Analphabetismus *m.*

illiterate [ɪ'lɪtərət] [1] *adj* des Schreibens und Lesens unkundig; (*badly-educated, uncultured*) *person* ungebildet, unwissend; (*handwriting*) ungeübt, krakelig (*inf*); *letter* voller Fehler ◆ **he's ~** er ist Analphabet.
[2] *n* Analphabet(in *f*) *m.*

ill: ~-judged *adj* unklug, wenig bedacht; **~-mannered** *adj* unhöflich; **~-matched** *adj* nicht zusammenpassend; **they're ~-matched** die beiden passen nicht zueinander; **~-natured** *adj*, **~-naturedly** *adv* bösartig.

illness ['ɪlnɪs] *n* Krankheit *f.*

illogical *adj*, **~ly** *adv* [ɪ'lɒdʒɪkəl, -ɪ] unlogisch.

illogicality [ɪˌlɒdʒɪ'kælɪtɪ] *n* mangelnde Logik, Unlogik *f* ◆ **the illogicalities in his argument** die logischen Fehler in seiner Argumentation.

ill: ~-omened ['ɪl,əʊmənd] *adj* unter einem unglücklichen Stern *or* unter einem Unstern stehend; **~-prepared** *adj* schlecht vorbereitet; **~-starred** *adj person* vom Unglück *or* Pech verfolgt; *day, undertaking etc* unter einem ungünstigen Stern (stehend), Unglücks-; **~-suited** *adj* (*to one another*) nicht zusammenpassend; (*to sth*) ungeeignet (*to* für); **they are ~-suited** sie passen nicht zueinander; **~-tempered** *adj* (*habitually*) mißmutig, übellaunig; (*on particular occasion*) schlecht gelaunt *pred*; (*violently*) schlechtgelaunt *attr*; **~-timed** *adj* ungelegen, unpassend; *move, speech* zeitlich schlecht abgestimmt; **~-treat** *vt* schlecht behandeln, mißhandeln; **~-treatment** *n* Mißhandlung *f*, schlechte Behandlung.

illuminate [ɪ'luːmɪneɪt] *vt* **(a)** (*light up*) *room, building* erhellen, erleuchten, beleuchten; (*spotlight etc*) anstrahlen; (*decorate with lights*) festlich beleuchten, illuminieren ◆ **~d sign** Leuchtzeichen *nt.* **(b)** (*Art*) *manuscript* illuminieren ◆ **~d letters** (verzierte) Initialen *pl.* **(c)** (*fig*) *subject* erhellen, erläutern.

illuminating [ɪ'luːmɪneɪtɪŋ] *adj* (*instructive*) aufschlußreich.

illumination [ɪˌluːmɪ'neɪʃən] *n* **(a)** (*of street, room, building*) Beleuchtung *f* ◆ **source of ~** Lichtquelle *f.* **(b)** (*decorative lights*) **~s** *pl* festliche Beleuchtung, Illumination *f.* **(c)** (*Art: of manuscript*) Illumination *f*; (*subject also*) Buchmalerei *f.* **(d)** (*fig*) Erläuterung *f.*

illuminator [ɪ'luːmɪneɪtəʳ] *n* (*Art: of manuscript*) Buchmaler, Illuminator *m.*

illumine [ɪ'luːmɪn] *vt* (*liter, fig*) erhellen.

ill-use [ˌɪl'juːz] *vt* schlecht behandeln, schlecht umgehen mit; (*physically*) mißhandeln.

illusion [ɪ'luːʒən] *n* Illusion *f*; (*hope also*) trügerische Hoffnung; (*misperception*) Täuschung *f* ◆ **to be under an ~** einer Täuschung (*dat*) unterliegen, sich (*dat*) Illusionen machen; **to be under the ~ that ...** sich (*dat*) einbilden, daß ...; **to have** *or* **be under no ~s** sich (*dat*) keine Illusionen machen, sich (*dat*) nichts vormachen (*about* über +*acc*); **it gives the ~ of space** es vermittelt die Illusion von räumlicher Weite; *see* **optical.**

illusionist [ɪ'luːʒənɪst] *n* Illusionist(in *f*) *m.*

illusive [ɪ'luːsɪv], **illusory** [ɪ'luːsərɪ] *adj* illusorisch, trügerisch.

illustrate ['ɪləstreɪt] *vt* **(a)** *book, story* illustrieren, bebildern ◆ **his lecture was ~d by coloured slides** er veranschaulichte seinen Vortrag mit Farbdias; **~d (magazine)** Illustrierte *f.* **(b)** (*fig*) erläutern, veranschaulichen, illustrieren.

illustration [ˌɪləs'treɪʃən] *n* **(a)** (*picture*) Abbildung *f*, Bild *nt*, Illustration *f.*
(b) (*fig*) (*of problem, subject*) Erklärung, Erläuterung *f*; (*of rule*) (*act*) Veranschaulichung *f*; (*thing*) Beispiel *nt* ◆ **by way of ~** als Beispiel.

illustrative ['ɪləstrətɪv] *adj* veranschaulichend, erläuternd, verdeutlichend ◆ **~ of** bezeichnend *or* beispielhaft für.

illustrator ['ɪləstreɪtəʳ] *n* Illustrator *m.*

illustrious [ɪ'lʌstrɪəs] *adj* glanzvoll, gefeiert; *deeds* glorreich.

ILO *abbr of* **International Labour Organization** Internationale Arbeitsorganisation.

I'm [aɪm] *contr of* **I am.**

image ['ɪmɪdʒ] *n* **(a)** (*carved, sculpted figure*) Standbild *nt*, Figur *f*; (*painted figure*) Bild, Bildnis (*geh*) *nt.*
(b) (*likeness*) Ebenbild, Abbild *nt* ◆ **he is the living** *or* **spitting ~ of his father** (*inf*) er ist sein Vater, wie er leibt und lebt, er ist seinem Vater wie aus dem Gesicht geschnitten; **God created man in his own ~** Gott (er)schuf den Menschen nach seinem Bilde.
(c) (*Opt*) Bild *nt* ◆ **~ converter** (*Elec*) Bildwandler *m*; **~ enhancement** Bildverstärkung *f*; **~ processing** Bildverarbeitung *f.*
(d) (*mental picture*) Vorstellung *f*, Bild *nt.*
(e) (*public face*) Image *nt* ◆ **brand ~** Markenimage *nt*; **~ maker** Imagemacher *m.*
(f) (*Liter*) **to speak in ~s** in Bildern *or* Metaphern sprechen; **a style full of ~s** ein bilderreicher *or* metaphorischer Stil.

imager ['ɪmɪdʒəʳ] *n* **thermal ~** Thermograph *m*; **magnetic resonance ~** Kernspin-Tomograph *m.*

imagery ['ɪmɪdʒərɪ] *n* Metaphorik *f* ◆ **visual ~** Bildersymbolik *f.*

imaginable [ɪ'mædʒɪnəbl] *adj* vorstellbar, denkbar, erdenklich ◆ **the best thing ~** das denkbar Beste; **the easiest/fastest way ~** der denkbar einfachste/schnellste Weg.

imaginary [ɪ'mædʒɪnərɪ] *adj danger* eingebildet, imaginär; *characters* frei ersonnen, erfunden ◆ **an ~ case** ein konstruierter Fall; **~ number** imaginäre Zahl.

imagination [ɪˌmædʒɪ'neɪʃən] *n* (*creative*) Phantasie, Vorstellungskraft, Einbildungskraft *f*; (*self-deceptive*) Einbildung *f* ◆ **to have (a lively** *or* **vivid) ~** (eine lebhafte *or* rege) Phantasie haben; **use your ~** lassen Sie Ihre Phantasie spielen; **in order to encourage children to use their ~(s)** um die Phantasie von Kindern anzuregen; **to lack ~** phantasielos *or* einfallslos

➤ LANGUAGE IN USE: **illustrate: b → 26.2**

sein; **it's only (your) ~!** das bilden Sie sich (*dat*) nur ein!; **it's all in your ~** das ist alles Einbildung.

imaginative *adj*, **~ly** *adv* [ɪ'mædʒɪnətɪv, -lɪ] phantasievoll.

imaginativeness [ɪ'mædʒɪnətɪvnɪs] *n* Phantasiereichtum *m*; (*of person also*) Phantasie *f*.

imagine [ɪ'mædʒɪn] *vt* **(a)** (*picture to oneself*) sich (*dat*) vorstellen, sich (*dat*) denken ◆ **~ yourself rich** stellen Sie sich mal vor, Sie wären reich; **you can ~ how I felt** Sie können sich vorstellen *or* denken, wie mir zumute war; **you can't ~ how ...** Sie machen sich kein Bild *or* Sie können sich nicht vorstellen *or* denken, wie ...; **just ~ my surprise** stellen Sie sich nur meine Überraschung vor; **you can't ~ it!** Sie machen sich keine Vorstellungen!; **as may (well) be ~d** wie man sich (leicht) denken *or* vorstellen kann.
(b) (*be under the illusion that*) sich (*dat*) einbilden ◆ **don't ~ that ...** bilden Sie sich nur nicht ein, daß ..., denken Sie nur nicht, daß ...; **he is always imagining things** (*inf*) er leidet ständig an Einbildungen; **you're (just) imagining things** (*inf*) Sie bilden sich das alles nur ein.
(c) (*suppose, conjecture*) annehmen, vermuten ◆ **are you tired? — well, what do you ~!** bist du müde? — na, was glaubst du wohl?; **is it time now? — I would ~ so** ist es soweit? — ich denke schon; **I would never have ~d he would have done that** ich hätte nie gedacht, daß er das tun würde.

imbalance [ɪm'bæləns] *n* Unausgeglichenheit *f*.

imbecile ['ɪmbəsiːl] **1** *adj* **(a)** *person* beschränkt, schwachsinnig, geistig minderbemittelt (*inf*); *laugh, trick, book* schwachsinnig, dumm, blöd(e); *idea, word* dumm, töricht.
(b) (*Med*) schwachsinnig, geistesschwach, imbezil (*spec*).
2 *n* **(a)** Dummkopf, Idiot, Schwachkopf *m* ◆ **to behave like an ~** sich völlig blödsinnig *or* wie ein Idiot benehmen.
(b) (*Med*) Schwachsinnige(r) *mf*.

imbecilic [ˌɪmbə'sɪlɪk] *adj see* **imbecile 1 (a)**.

imbecility [ˌɪmbə'sɪlɪtɪ] *n* **(a)** Beschränktheit, Idiotie *f*, Schwachsinn *m*. **(b)** (*Med*) Schwachsinn *m*.

imbibe [ɪm'baɪb] **1** *vt* **(a)** (*form, hum*) trinken, bechern (*hum*). **(b)** (*fig*) *ideas, information* in sich (*acc*) aufnehmen.
2 *vi* (*hum: drink*) viel trinken ◆ **will you ~?** ein Gläschen?; **I don't ~** ich trinke nicht.

imbroglio [ɪm'brəʊlɪəʊ] *n* (*liter*) verwickelte Lage, Verwirrung *f*.

imbue [ɪm'bjuː] *vt* (*fig*) durchdringen, erfüllen.

IMF *abbr of* **International Monetary Fund** IWF *m*.

imitable ['ɪmɪtəbl] *adj* nachahmbar, imitierbar.

imitate ['ɪmɪteɪt] *vt* **(a)** (*copy*) *person, accent etc* imitieren, nachmachen, nachahmen ◆ **children learn by imitating their parents** Kinder lernen dadurch, daß sie ihre Eltern nachahmen. **(b)** (*counterfeit*) nachmachen, imitieren.

imitation [ˌɪmɪ'teɪʃən] **1** *n* Imitation, Nachahmung *f* ◆ **to do an ~ of sb** jdn imitieren *or* nachmachen *or* nachahmen.
2 *adj* unecht, künstlich, falsch ◆ **~ gold/pearl/brick** Gold-/Perlen-/Ziegelimitation *f*; **~ leather** Lederimitation *f*, Kunstleder *nt*; **~ jewellery** unechter Schmuck; **~ fur** Webpelz *m*.

imitative ['ɪmɪtətɪv] *adj* nachahmend, imitierend ◆ **children are naturally ~** Kinder machen von Natur aus alles nach.

imitator ['ɪmɪteɪtə^r] *n* Nachahmer, Imitator *m*.

immaculate [ɪ'mækjʊlɪt] *adj* **(a)** untadelig, tadellos, picobello *inv* (*inf*); *behaviour* tadellos, mustergültig; *manuscript etc* fehlerfrei, einwandfrei. **(b)** (*Eccl*) **the I ~ Conception** die Unbefleckte Empfängnis.

immaculately [ɪ'mækjʊlɪtlɪ] *adv* tadellos; *behave also* untadelig.

immanence ['ɪmənəns] *n* Immanenz *f*.

immanent ['ɪmənənt] *adj* innewohnend, immanent (*also Philos*) ◆ **to be ~ in sth** einer Sache (*dat*) eigen sein *or* innewohnen.

immaterial [ˌɪmə'tɪərɪəl] *adj* **(a)** (*unimportant*) *objection, question* nebensächlich, unwesentlich, bedeutungslos ◆ **it is quite ~ to me (whether) ...** es ist für mich ohne Bedeutung *or* unwichtig, (ob) ...; **that's (quite) ~** das spielt keine Rolle, das ist egal.
(b) (*Philos etc*) immateriell ◆ **ghosts are ~** Gespenster sind körperlos.

immature [ˌɪmə'tjʊə^r] *adj* (*lit, fig*) unreif; *wine* nicht ausreichend gelagert; *plans, ideas etc also* unausgegoren ◆ **don't be so ~** sei nicht so kindisch!

immaturely [ˌɪmə'tjʊəlɪ] *adv react, behave* unreif.

immaturity [ˌɪmə'tjʊərɪtɪ] *n* Unreife *f*.

immeasurable [ɪ'meʒərəbl] *adj* unermeßlich, grenzenlos; *amount, distances* unmeßbar, riesig.

immeasurably [ɪ'meʒərəblɪ] *adv* unermeßlich, grenzenlos.

immediacy [ɪ'miːdɪəsɪ] *n* Unmittelbarkeit, Direktheit *f*; (*urgency*) Dringlichkeit *f*.

immediate [ɪ'miːdɪət] *adj* **(a)** *successor, knowledge, future, object, need* unmittelbar; *cause, successor also* direkt; *neighbour, vicinity also* nächste ◆ **only the ~ family were invited** nur die engste Familie wurde eingeladen; **our ~ plan is to go to France** wir fahren zuerst einmal nach Frankreich.
(b) (*instant*) *reply, reaction* sofortig, umgehend, prompt; *thought, conclusion* unmittelbar ◆ **to take ~ action** sofort handeln; **this had the ~ effect of ...** das hatte prompt zur Folge, daß ...; **for ~ delivery** zur sofortigen Lieferung.

immediately [ɪ'miːdɪətlɪ] **1** *adv* **(a)** (*at once*) sofort, gleich; *reply, return, depart also* umgehend ◆ **~ after/before that** unmittelbar danach/davor; **that's not ~ obvious** das ist nicht sofort *or* unmittelbar klar. **(b)** (*directly*) direkt, unmittelbar.
2 *conj* (*Brit*) sobald, sofort, als ...

immemorial [ˌɪmɪ'mɔːrɪəl] *adj* uralt ◆ **from time ~** seit undenklichen Zeiten, seit Urzeiten.

immense [ɪ'mens] *adj difficulty, fortune, sum of money, possibilities* riesig, enorm, immens; *problem, difference also, ocean, heat* gewaltig *self-confidence, success* ungeheuer, enorm; *achievement* großartig.

immensely [ɪ'menslɪ] *adv* unheimlich (*inf*), enorm ◆ **to enjoy oneself ~** sich ausgezeichnet *or* unheimlich (*inf*) *or* köstlich amüsieren; **~ grateful** äußerst dankbar.

immensity [ɪ'mensɪtɪ] *n* ungeheure Größe, Unermeßlichkeit *f* ◆ **the ~ of this task** das gewaltige Ausmaß dieser Aufgabe; **the ~ of space** die Unendlichkeit des (Welt)alls.

immerse [ɪ'mɜːs] *vt* **(a)** eintauchen (*in* in +acc) ◆ **to ~ one's head in water** den Kopf ins Wasser tauchen; **to be ~d in water** unter Wasser sein.
(b) (*fig*) **to ~ oneself in one's work** sich in seine Arbeit vertiefen *or* stürzen (*inf*); **to ~ oneself in a language** sich vollkommen in eine Sprache vertiefen; **to be ~d in one's work** in seine Arbeit vertieft sein; **to be ~d in one's reading** in seine Lektüre versunken *or* vertieft sein.
(c) (*Eccl*) untertauchen.

immersion [ɪ'mɜːʃən] *n* **(a)** Eintauchen, Untertauchen *nt* ◆ **after two hours' ~ in this solution** nach zwei Stunden in dieser Flüssigkeit; **~ heater** (*Brit*) Boiler, Heißwasserspeicher *m*; (*for jug etc*) Tauchsieder *m*. **(b)** (*fig*) Vertieftsein, Versunkensein *nt* ◆ **~ course** Intensivkurs *m*. **(c)** (*Eccl*) Taufe *f* durch Untertauchen.

immigrant ['ɪmɪgrənt] **1** *n* Einwanderer *m*, Einwanderin *f*, Immigrant(in *f*) *m*.
2 *attr* **~ labour/workers** ausländische Arbeitnehmer *pl*; (*esp in Germany*) Gastarbeiter *pl*; (*in Switzerland*) Fremdarbeiter *pl*; **the ~ population** die Einwanderer *pl*; **... has an ~ population of 50,000** ... hat einen ausländischen Bevölkerungsanteil von 50.000; **~ schools** Schulen mit hohem Anteil an Ausländern.

immigrate ['ɪmɪgreɪt] *vi* einwandern, immigrieren (*to* in +dat).

immigration [ˌɪmɪ'greɪʃən] *n* Einwanderung, Immigration *f*; (*at airport etc*) Einwanderungsstelle *f* ◆ **~ authorities/department** Einwanderungsbehörde *f*; **~ officer** Beamte(r) *m* der Einwanderungsbehörde; (*at customs*) Grenzbeamte(r) *m*.

imminence ['ɪmɪnəns] *n* nahes Bevorstehen ◆ **he hadn't appreciated the ~ of the danger/of war** er war sich (*dat*) nicht bewußt, daß die Gefahr/der Krieg so unmittelbar bevorstand.

imminent ['ɪmɪnənt] *adj* nahe bevorstehend ◆ **to be ~** nahe bevorstehen; **I think an announcement is ~** ich glaube, es steht eine Ankündigung bevor.

immobile [ɪ'məʊbaɪl] *adj* (*not moving*) unbeweglich; (*not able to move*) *person* (*through injury etc*) bewegungslos; (*through lack of transport*) unbeweglich, immobil ◆ **the car was completely ~** das Auto rührte sich nicht (von der Stelle); **to make** *or* **render a car ~** ein Auto benutzungsunfähig machen; **in space the rocket looks as though it's ~** im Weltraum sieht die Rakete aus, als würde sie sich nicht bewegen.

immobiliser [ɪ'məʊbɪlaɪzə^r] *n* (*Aut*) Wegfahrsperre *f*.

immobility [ˌɪməʊ'bɪlɪtɪ] *n see adj* Unbeweglichkeit *f*, Bewegungslosigkeit *f*; Immobilität *f*.

immobilize [ɪ'məʊbɪlaɪz] *vt traffic* lahmlegen, zum Erliegen bringen; *car, broken limb* stillegen; *army* bewegungsunfähig machen; *enemy tanks* außer Gefecht setzen; (*Fin*) *capital* festlegen.

immoderate [ɪ'mɒdərɪt] *adj desire, appetite* übermäßig, unmäßig, maßlos; *views* übertrieben, übersteigert, extrem ◆ **to be ~ in one's demands** maßlose Forderungen stellen.

immoderately [ɪ'mɒdərɪtlɪ] *adv see adj*.

immodest [ɪ'mɒdɪst] *adj* unbescheiden; (*indecent*) unanständig.

immodestly [ɪ'mɒdɪstlɪ] *adv see adj*.

immodesty [ɪ'mɒdɪstɪ] *n see adj* Unbescheidenheit *f*; Unanständigkeit *f*.

immolate ['ɪməʊleɪt] *vt* (*liter*) opfern, zum Opfer bringen.

immoral [ɪ'mɒrəl] *adj action* unmoralisch; *behaviour also* unsittlich; *person also* sittenlos ◆ **~ earnings** (*Jur*) Einkünfte *pl* aus gewerbsmäßiger Unzucht.

immorality [ˌɪmə'rælɪtɪ] *n* Unmoral *f*; (*of behaviour also*) Unsittlichkeit *f*; (*of person also*) Sittenlosigkeit *f*; (*immoral act*) Unsittlichkeit *f*.

immorally [ɪ'mɒrəlɪ] *adv see adj*.

immortal [ɪ'mɔːtl] **1** *adj person, God* unsterblich; *fame also* unvergänglich, ewig; *life* ewig.
2 *n* Unsterbliche(r) *mf*.

immortality [ˌɪmɔː'tælɪtɪ] *n see adj* Unsterblichkeit *f*, Unvergänglichkeit, Ewigkeit *f*.

immortalize [ɪ'mɔːtəlaɪz] *vt* verewigen ◆ **the film which ~d her** der Film, der sie unsterblich machte.

immovable [ɪ'muːvəbl] *adj* **(a)** (*lit*) unbeweglich; (*fig*) *obstacle* unüberwindlich, unbezwinglich. **(b)** (*fig: steadfast*) fest.

immune [ɪ'mjuːn] *adj* **(a)** (*Med*) immun (*against, from, to* gegen) ◆ **~ system** Immunsystem *nt*; **~ deficiency syndrome** Immunschwächekrankheit *f*.
(b) (*fig*) sicher (*from* vor +dat); (*from temptation etc also*) geschützt, gefeit (*from* gegen); (*not susceptible: to criticism etc*) unempfindlich, immun (*to* gegen) ◆ **nobody was ~ from his outbursts** keiner war vor seinen Wutanfällen sicher.

immunity [ɪ'mjuːnɪtɪ] *n* **(a)** (*Med, diplomatic*) Immunität *f* (*to, against* gegen).
(b) (*fig*) *see adj* **(b)** Sicherheit *f*, Geschütztheit, Gefeitheit *f*, Unempfindlichkeit, Immunität *f*.

immunization [ˌɪmjʊnaɪ'zeɪʃən] *n* Immunisierung *f*.

immunize ['ɪmjʊnaɪz] *vt* immunisieren, immun machen.

immunodeficiency [ˌɪmjʊnəʊdɪ'fɪʃənsɪ] *n* (*Med*) Immunschwäche *f*.

immunoglobulin [ˌɪmjʊnəʊˈglɒbjʊlɪn] *n* Immunglobulin *nt.*
immunological [ˌɪmjʊnəʊˈlɒdʒɪkəl] *adj (Med)* immunologisch.
immunologist [ˌɪmjʊˈnɒlədʒɪst] *n (Med)* Immunologe *m*, Immunologin *f.*
immunology [ˌɪmjʊˈnɒlədʒɪ] *n (Med)* Immunologie *f.*
immure [ɪˈmjʊəʳ] *vt* einkerkern.
immutability [ɪˌmjuːtəˈbɪlɪtɪ] *n* Unveränderlichkeit, Unwandelbarkeit *f.*
immutable [ɪˈmjuːtəbl] *adj* unveränderlich, unwandelbar.
imp [ɪmp] *n* Kobold *m*; *(inf: child also)* Racker *m (inf).*
impact [ˈɪmpækt] *n* Aufprall *m (on, against* auf *+acc)*; *(of two moving objects)* Zusammenprall *m*, Aufeinanderprallen *nt*; *(of bomb) (on house, factory)* Einschlag *m (on* in *+acc)*; *(on roof, ground)* Aufschlag *m (on* auf *+dat)*; *(of light, rays)* Auftreffen *nt (on* auf *+acc)*; *(force)* Wucht *f*; *(fig)* (Aus)wirkung *f (on* auf *+acc)* ◆ **on ~ (with)** beim Aufprall (auf *+acc*)/Zusammenprall (mit) *etc*; **he staggered under the ~ of the blow** er taumelte unter der Wucht des Schlages; **his speech had a great ~ on his audience** seine Rede machte großen Eindruck auf seine Zuhörer; **you can imagine the ~ of this on a four-year old** Sie können sich vorstellen, wie sich das auf einen Vierjährigen auswirkt.
◆**impact on** *vi +prep obj* einwirken auf (*+acc*).
impacted [ɪmˈpæktɪd] *adj* eingeklemmt, eingekeilt; *tooth also* impaktiert *(spec).*
impact printer *n* Impact-Drucker *m.*
impair [ɪmˈpɛəʳ] *vt* beeinträchtigen; *hearing, sight also* verschlechtern; *relations also, health* schaden (*+dat*).
impala [ɪmˈpɑːlə] *n* Impala *f.*
impale [ɪmˈpeɪl] *vt* aufspießen *(on* auf *+dat).*
impalpable [ɪmˈpælpəbl] *adj (lit)* nicht fühlbar; *(fig)* nicht greifbar, vage.
impanel [ɪmˈpænl] *vt* als Geschworenen einsetzen.
imparity [ɪmˈpærɪtɪ] *n* Ungleichheit *f.*
impart [ɪmˈpɑːt] *vt* **(a)** *(make known) information, news* mitteilen, übermitteln; *knowledge* vermitteln; *secret* preisgeben. **(b)** *(bestow)* verleihen, geben *(to dat).*
impartial [ɪmˈpɑːʃəl] *adj person, attitude* unparteiisch, unvoreingenommen; *decision, judgement also* gerecht.
impartiality [ɪmˌpɑːʃɪˈælɪtɪ], **impartialness** [ɪmˈpɑːʃəlnɪs] *n see adj* Unparteilichkeit, Unvoreingenommenheit *f*; Gerechtigkeit *f.*
impartially [ɪmˈpɑːʃəlɪ] *adv see adj.*
impassable [ɪmˈpɑːsəbl] *adj* unpassierbar.
impasse [ɪmˈpɑːs] *n (fig)* Sackgasse *f* ◆ **to have reached an ~** sich festgefahren haben, einen toten Punkt erreicht haben.
impassioned [ɪmˈpæʃnd] *adj* leidenschaftlich.
impassive *adj*, **~ly** *adv* [ɪmˈpæsɪv, -lɪ] gelassen.
impassiveness [ɪmˈpæsɪvnɪs], **impassivity** [ɪmpæˈsɪvɪtɪ] *n* Gelassenheit *f.*
impatience [ɪmˈpeɪʃəns] *n* Ungeduld *f*; *(intolerance)* Unduldsamkeit *f.*
impatient [ɪmˈpeɪʃənt] *adj* ungeduldig; *(intolerant)* unduldsam *(of* gegenüber) ◆ **to be ~ to do sth** unbedingt etw tun wollen.
impatiently [ɪmˈpeɪʃəntlɪ] *adv see adj.*
impeach [ɪmˈpiːtʃ] *vt* **(a)** *(Jur: accuse) public official* (eines Amtsvergehens) anklagen; *(US) president also* ein Impeachment einleiten gegen ◆ **to ~ sb for** *or* **with sth/for doing sth** jdn wegen einer Sache anklagen/jdn anklagen, etw getan zu haben.
(b) *(challenge) sb's character, motives* in Frage stellen, anzweifeln; *witness's testimony also* anfechten ◆ **to ~ a witness** die Glaubwürdigkeit eines Zeugen anzweifeln *or* anfechten.
impeachable [ɪmˈpiːtʃəbl] *adj person* (eines Amtsvergehens) anzuklagen; *action* als Amtsvergehen verfolgbar.
impeachment [ɪmˈpiːtʃmənt] *n see vt* **(a)** *(Jur)* Anklage *f* (wegen eines Amtsvergehens); Impeachment *nt.* **(b)** Infragestellung, Anzweiflung *f*; Anfechtung *f.*
impeccable *adj*, **-bly** *adv* [ɪmˈpekəbl, -ɪ] untadelig, tadellos.
impecunious [ˌɪmpɪˈkjuːnɪəs] *adj* mittellos, unbemittelt.
impede [ɪmˈpiːd] *vt person* hindern; *action, success* behindern, erschweren; *movement, traffic* behindern.
impediment [ɪmˈpedɪmənt] *n* **(a)** Hindernis *nt.* **(b)** *(Med)* Behinderung *f* ◆ **speech ~** Sprachfehler *m*, Sprachstörung *f.*
impedimenta [ɪmˌpedɪˈmentə] *npl* **(a)** *(inf)* (unnötiges) Gepäck. **(b)** *(Mil)* Troß *m.*
impel [ɪmˈpel] *vt* **(a)** *(force)* nötigen ◆ **to ~ sb to do sth** jdn (dazu) nötigen, etw zu tun. **(b)** *(drive on)* (voran)treiben.
impend [ɪmˈpend] *vi* bevorstehen; *(threaten)* drohen.
impending [ɪmˈpendɪŋ] *adj* bevorstehend; *death also* nahe; *storm also* heraufziehend; *(threatening)* drohend.
impenetrability [ɪmˌpenɪtrəˈbɪlɪtɪ] *n see adj* Undurchdringlichkeit *f*; Uneinnehmbarkeit *f*; Undurchlässigkeit *f*; Unergründlichkeit *f*; Undurchschaubarkeit, Undurchsichtigkeit *f.*
impenetrable [ɪmˈpenɪtrəbl] *adj* undurchdringlich; *fortress* uneinnehmbar; *enemy lines* undurchlässig; *mind, character also, mystery* unergründlich; *theory* undurchschaubar, undurchsichtig.
impenitence [ɪmˈpenɪtəns] *n* Reuelosigkeit *f.*
impenitent [ɪmˈpenɪtənt] *adj* reuelos ◆ **he remained quite ~** er zeigte keine Reue, er bereute es gar nicht; **to die ~** sterben, ohne bereut zu haben.
impenitently [ɪmˈpenɪtəntlɪ] *adv* ohne Reue.
imperative [ɪmˈperətɪv] [1] *adj* **(a)** *need, desire* dringend ◆ **to be ~** unbedingt nötig *or* erforderlich sein. **(b)** *manner* gebieterisch, befehlend, herrisch; *order* strikt. **(c)** *(Gram)* imperativisch, Imperativ-, befehlend, Befehls-.
[2] *n (Gram)* Imperativ, Befehl *m* ◆ **in the ~** im Imperativ, in der Befehlsform.
imperceptible [ˌɪmpəˈseptəbl] *adj* nicht wahrnehmbar; *difference, movement also* unmerklich; *sight also* unsichtbar; *sound also* unhörbar.
imperceptibly [ˌɪmpəˈseptəblɪ] *adv see adj* kaum wahrnehmbar; unmerklich; unsichtbar; unhörbar.
imperfect [ɪmˈpɜːfɪkt] [1] *adj* **(a)** *(faulty)* unvollkommen, mangelhaft; *(Comm) goods* fehlerhaft. **(b)** *(incomplete)* unvollständig, unvollkommen. **(c)** *(Gram)* Imperfekt-, Vergangenheits-.
[2] *n (Gram)* Imperfekt *nt*, Vergangenheit *f.*
imperfection [ˌɪmpəˈfekʃən] *n* **(a)** *no pl see adj* Unvollkommenheit, Mangelhaftigkeit *f*; Fehlerhaftigkeit *f*; Unvollständigkeit *f.* **(b)** *(fault, defect)* Mangel *m.*
imperfectly [ɪmˈpɜːfɪktlɪ] *adv see adj.*
imperial [ɪmˈpɪərɪəl] *adj* **(a)** *(of empire)* Reichs-; *(of emperor)* kaiserlich, Kaiser- ◆ **~ Rome** das Rom der Kaiserzeit; **His I~ Highness** Seine Kaiserliche Majestät.
(b) *(of British Empire)* Empire-, des Empire.
(c) *(lordly, majestic)* majestätisch, gebieterisch.
(d) *weights, measures* englisch.
imperialism [ɪmˈpɪərɪəlɪzəm] *n* Imperialismus *m (often pej)*, Weltmachtpolitik *f.*
imperialist [ɪmˈpɪərɪəlɪst] *n* Imperialist(in *f*) *m.*
imperialistic [ɪmˌpɪərɪəˈlɪstɪk] *adj* imperialistisch.
imperially [ɪmˈpɪərɪəlɪ] *adv* majestätisch, gebieterisch.
imperil [ɪmˈperɪl] *vt* gefährden, in Gefahr bringen.
imperious *adj*, **~ly** *adv* [ɪmˈpɪərɪəs, -lɪ] herrisch, gebieterisch.
imperishable [ɪmˈperɪʃəbl] *adj (lit)* unverderblich; *(fig)* unvergänglich.
impermanence [ɪmˈpɜːmənəns] *n* Unbeständigkeit *f.*
impermanent [ɪmˈpɜːmənənt] *adj* unbeständig.
impermeable [ɪmˈpɜːmɪəbl] *adj* undurchlässig, impermeabel *(spec).*
impersonal [ɪmˈpɜːsnl] *adj* unpersönlich *(also Gram).*
impersonality [ɪmˌpɜːsəˈnælɪtɪ] *n* Unpersönlichkeit *f.*
impersonate [ɪmˈpɜːsəneɪt] *vt* **(a)** *(pretend to be)* sich ausgeben als *(+nom).* **(b)** *(take off)* imitieren, nachahmen.
impersonation [ɪmˌpɜːsəˈneɪʃən] *n see vt* **(a)** Verkörperung *f* ◆ **his ~ of an officer** sein Auftreten *nt* als Offizier. **(b)** Imitation, Nachahmung *f* ◆ **he does ~s of politicians/females** er imitiert Politiker/spielt Frauen.
impersonator [ɪmˈpɜːsəneɪtəʳ] *n (Theat)* Imitator(in *f*) *m.*
impertinence [ɪmˈpɜːtɪnəns] *n* Unverschämtheit, Impertinenz *(dated) f* ◆ **what ~!, the ~ of it!** so eine Unverschämtheit!
impertinent [ɪmˈpɜːtɪnənt] *adj* **(a)** *(impudent)* unverschämt *(to* zu, gegenüber), impertinent *(dated) (to* gegenüber). **(b)** *(form: irrelevant)* irrelevant.
impertinently [ɪmˈpɜːtɪnəntlɪ] *adv see adj.*
imperturbability [ˈɪmpəˌtɜːbəˈbɪlɪtɪ] *n* Unerschütterlichkeit *f.*
imperturbable [ˌɪmpəˈtɜːbəbl] *adj* unerschütterlich ◆ **he is completely ~** er ist durch nichts zu erschüttern.
impervious [ɪmˈpɜːvɪəs] *adj* **(a)** *substance* undurchlässig ◆ **~ to rain/water** regen-/wasserundurchlässig; *coat, material* regen-/wasserdicht.
(b) *(fig)* unzugänglich *(to* für); *(to people's feelings also, criticism)* unberührt *(to* von) ◆ **he is ~ to reason** ihm ist mit Verstand nicht beizukommen.
impetigo [ˌɪmpɪˈtaɪgəʊ] *n (Med)* Eiterflechte, Impetigo *f.*
impetuosity [ɪmˌpetjʊˈɒsɪtɪ] *n* **(a)** *see adj* Ungestüm *nt*; Impulsivität *f*; Stürmische(s) *nt.* **(b)** *(impetuous behaviour)* ungestümes Handeln.
impetuous [ɪmˈpetjʊəs] *adj act, person* ungestüm, stürmisch; *decision* impulsiv; *(liter) attack, wind* stürmisch.
impetuously [ɪmˈpetjʊəslɪ] *adv see adj.*
impetuousness [ɪmˈpetjʊəsnɪs] *n see* **impetuosity.**
impetus [ˈɪmpɪtəs] *n (lit, fig)* Impuls *m*; *(force)* Kraft *f*; *(momentum)* Schwung, Impetus *(geh) m* ◆ **the ~ behind this increase in activity** die treibende Kraft hinter dieser zunehmenden Aktivität; **to give an ~ to sth** *(fig)* einer Sache *(dat)* Impulse geben.
impiety [ɪmˈpaɪətɪ] *n* **(a)** *see* **impious** Gottlosigkeit, Ungläubigkeit *f*; Pietätlosigkeit *f*; Ehrfurchtslosigkeit *f*; Respektlosigkeit *f.* **(b)** *(act)* Pietätlosigkeit *f*; Respektlosigkeit *f.*
impinge [ɪmˈpɪndʒ] *vi* **(a)** *(have effect: on sb's life, habits)* sich auswirken *(on* auf *+acc)*, beeinflussen *(on acc)*; *(infringe: on sb's rights etc also)* einschränken *(on acc)* ◆ **to ~ on sb/sb's consciousness** *or* **mind** jdm zu Bewußtsein kommen. **(b)** *(strike)* (auf)treffen, fallen *(on* auf *+acc).*
impingement [ɪmˈpɪndʒmənt] *n* **(a)** Auswirkung *f*, Einfluß *m (on* auf *+acc).* **(b)** *(striking)* Auftreffen *nt (on* auf *+dat).*
impious [ˈɪmpɪəs] *adj (not pious)* gottlos, ungläubig; *(irreverent)* pietätlos; *(to God)* ehrfurchtslos; *(to superior etc)* respektlos.
impiously [ˈɪmpɪəslɪ] *adv see adj.*
impish [ˈɪmpɪʃ] *adj remark* schelmisch; *smile, look also* verschmitzt; *child also* lausbübisch.
impishly [ˈɪmpɪʃlɪ] *adv see adj.*
impishness [ˈɪmpɪʃnɪs] *n see adj* Schelmische(s) *nt*; Verschmitztheit *f*; Lausbubenhaftigkeit *f.*
implacable [ɪmˈplækəbl] *adj opponent, enemy, hatred* unerbittlich, erbittert.
implacably [ɪmˈplækəblɪ] *adv see adj* ◆ **he was ~ opposed to capital punishment** er war ein erbitterter Gegner der Todesstrafe.
implant [ɪmˈplɑːnt] [1] *vt* **(a)** *(fig)* einimpfen *(in sb* jdm) ◆ **to be deeply ~ed in sb** (tief) in jdm verwurzelt sein. **(b)** *(Med)* implantieren, einpflanzen.
[2] [ˈɪmplɑːnt] *n (Med)* Implantat *nt.*

implantation [ˌɪmplɑːnˈteɪʃən] *n see vt* Einpflanzung *f*; Implantation, Einpflanzung *f*.
implausibility [ɪmˌplɔːzəˈbɪlɪtɪ] *n see adj* mangelnde Plausibilität; Unglaubhaftigkeit, Unglaubwürdigkeit *f*; Ungeschicktheit *f*.
implausible [ɪmˈplɔːzəbl] *adj* nicht plausibel; *story, tale, excuse also* unglaubhaft, unglaubwürdig; *lie* wenig überzeugend, ungeschickt.
implement [ˈɪmplɪmənt] 1 *n* **(a)** Gerät *nt*; (*tool also*) Werkzeug *nt*. **(b)** (*fig: agent*) Werkzeug *nt*.
2 [ɪmplɪˈment] *vt law* vollziehen; *contract, promise* erfüllen; (*carry out, put into effect*) *plan etc* durchführen, ausführen.
implementation [ˌɪmplɪmenˈteɪʃən] *n see vt* Vollzug *m*; Erfüllung *f*; Ausführung, Durchführung *f*.
implicate [ˈɪmplɪkeɪt] *vt* **to ~ sb in sth** jdn in etw verwickeln.
implication [ˌɪmplɪˈkeɪʃən] *n* **(a)** Implikation *f*; (*of law, agreement etc also*) Auswirkung *f*; (*of events also*) Bedeutung *f no pl* ◆ **the ~ of your statement is that ...** Ihre Behauptung impliziert, daß ...; **the possible ~s of his decision** die ganze Tragweite seiner Entscheidung; **by ~** implizit. **(b)** (*in crime*) Verwicklung *f* (*in* in +*acc*).
implicit [ɪmˈplɪsɪt] *adj* **(a)** (*implied*) implizit; *threat also* indirekt, unausgesprochen; *agreement, recognition also* stillschweigend ◆ **to be ~ in sth** durch etw impliziert werden; (*in contract etc*) in etw (*dat*) impliziert sein; **a threat was ~ in his action** in seiner Handlungsweise lag eine indirekte Drohung.
(b) (*unquestioning*) *belief, confidence* absolut, unbedingt.
implicitly [ɪmˈplɪsɪtlɪ] *adv see adj.*
implied [ɪmˈplaɪd] *adj* impliziert; *threat also* indirekt.
implode [ɪmˈpləʊd] 1 *vi* implodieren.
2 *vt* (*Ling*) als Verschlußlaut *or* Explosivlaut sprechen.
implore [ɪmˈplɔːʳ] *vt person* anflehen, inständig bitten; *forgiveness etc* erbitten, erflehen ◆ **do it, I ~ you!** ich flehe Sie an, tun Sie es!
imploring *adj*, **~ly** *adv* [ɪmˈplɔːrɪŋ, -lɪ] flehentlich, flehend.
implosion [ɪmˈpləʊʒən] *n* Implosion *f*.
imply [ɪmˈplaɪ] *vt* **(a)** andeuten, implizieren ◆ **are you ~ing** *or* **do you mean to ~ that ...?** wollen Sie damit vielleicht sagen *or* andeuten, daß ...? **it implies that he has changed his mind** das deutet darauf hin, daß er es sich (*dat*) anders überlegt hat.
(b) (*indicate, lead to conclusion*) schließen lassen auf (+*acc*).
(c) (*involve*) bedeuten.
impolite *adj*, **~ly** *adv* [ˌɪmpəˈlaɪt, -lɪ] unhöflich.
impoliteness [ˌɪmpəˈlaɪtnɪs] *n* Unhöflichkeit *f*.
impolitic [ɪmˈpɒlɪtɪk] *adj* unklug.
imponderable [ɪmˈpɒndərəbl] 1 *adj* unberechenbar, unwägbar.
2 *n* unberechenbare *or* unwägbare Größe ◆ **~s** Unwägbarkeiten, Imponderabilien (*geh*) *pl*.
import [ˈɪmpɔːt] 1 *n* **(a)** (*Comm*) Import *m*, Einfuhr *f*. **(b)** (*of speech, document etc*) (*meaning*) Bedeutung *f*; (*significance also*) Wichtigkeit *f*.
2 [ɪmˈpɔːt] *vt* **(a)** (*Comm*) *goods* einführen, importieren. **(b)** (*mean, imply*) bedeuten, beinhalten. **(c)** (*Comput*) importieren.
importable [ɪmˈpɔːtəbl] *adj* einführbar.
▼ **importance** [ɪmˈpɔːtəns] *n* Wichtigkeit *f*; (*significance also*) Bedeutung *f*; (*influence also*) Einfluß *m* ◆ **I don't see the ~ of that** ich verstehe nicht, warum das wichtig sein soll; **to be of no (great) ~** nicht (besonders) wichtig sein; **to be without ~** unwichtig sein; **to attach the greatest ~ to sth** einer Sache (*dat*) größten Wert *or* größte Wichtigkeit beimessen; **a man of ~** ein wichtiger *or* einflußreicher Mann; **to be full of one's own ~** ganz von seiner eigenen Wichtigkeit erfüllt sein.
important [ɪmˈpɔːtənt] *adj* wichtig; (*significant also*) bedeutend; (*influential*) einflußreich, bedeutend ◆ **that's not ~** das ist unwichtig; **it's not ~** (*doesn't matter*) das macht nichts; **to try to look ~** sich (*dat*) ein gewichtiges Aussehen geben.
importantly [ɪmˈpɔːtəntlɪ] *adv* **(a)** (*usu pej*) wichtigtuerisch (*pej*). **(b) it is ~ different** das ist entscheidend anders.
importation [ˌɪmpɔːˈteɪʃən] *n* Einfuhr *f*, Import *m*.
import *in cpds* Einfuhr-, Import-; **~ duty** *n* Einfuhrzoll, Importzoll *m*.
imported [ɪmˈpɔːtɪd] *adj* importiert, eingeführt, Import-.
importer [ɪmˈpɔːtəʳ] *n* Importeur(in *f*) *m* (*of* von); (*country also*) Importland *nt* (*of* für).
import: ~-export trade *n* Import-Export-Handel *m*, Ein- und Ausfuhr *f*; **~ licence** *n* Einfuhrlizenz, Importlizenz *f*; **~ permit** *n* Einfuhr- *or* Importerlaubnis *f*.
importunate [ɪmˈpɔːtjʊnɪt] *adj* aufdringlich; *salesman also, creditor, demand* hartnäckig, beharrlich.
importunately [ɪmˈpɔːtjʊnɪtlɪ] *adv see adj.*
importunateness [ɪmˈpɔːtjʊnɪtnɪs] *n see adj* Aufdringlichkeit *f*; Hartnäckigkeit, Beharrlichkeit *f*.
importune [ˌɪmpɔːˈtjuːn] *vt* belästigen; (*creditor, with questions*) zusetzen (+*dat*); (*visitor*) zur Last fallen (+*dat*).
importunity [ˌɪmpɔːˈtjuːnɪtɪ] *n* **(a)** *see* **importunateness**. **(b)** (*demand, request*) unverschämte Bitte.
impose [ɪmˈpəʊz] 1 *vt* **(a)** *task, conditions* aufzwingen, auferlegen (*on sb* jdm); *sanctions, fine, sentence* verhängen (*on* gegen); *tax* erheben ◆ **to ~ a tax on sth** etw mit einer Steuer belegen, etw besteuern. **(b) to ~ oneself** *or* **one's presence on sb** sich jdm aufdrängen; **he ~d himself on them for three months** er ließ sich einfach drei Monate bei ihnen nieder.
2 *vi* zur Last fallen (*on sb* jdm) ◆ **to ~ on sb's kindness** jds Freundlichkeit ausnützen *or* mißbrauchen; **I don't wish to ~** ich möchte Ihnen nicht zur Last fallen.
imposing [ɪmˈpəʊzɪŋ] *adj* beeindruckend, imponierend; *person, appearance, building also* stattlich, imposant.
imposition [ˌɪmpəˈzɪʃən] *n* **(a)** *no pl see vt (a)* Aufzwingen *nt*, Auferlegung *f*; Verhängung *f*; Erhebung *f*.
(b) (*tax*) Steuer *f* (*on* für, auf +*dat*).
(c) (*taking advantage*) Zumutung *f* (*on* für) ◆ **I'd love to stay if it's not too much of an ~** ich würde liebend gern bleiben, wenn ich Ihnen nicht zur Last falle; **if it's not too much of an ~ on your generosity** wenn das Ihre Großzügigkeit nicht zu sehr beansprucht.
impossibility [ɪmˌpɒsəˈbɪlɪtɪ] *n* Unmöglichkeit *f* ◆ **that's an ~** das ist unmöglich *or* ein Ding der Unmöglichkeit.
▼ **impossible** [ɪmˈpɒsəbl] 1 *adj* unmöglich ◆ **~!** ausgeschlossen!, unmöglich!; **it is ~ for him to leave/do that** er kann unmöglich gehen/das unmöglich tun.
2 *n* Unmögliche(s) *nt* ◆ **to ask for the ~** Unmögliches verlangen; **to do the ~** (*in general*) Unmögliches tun; (*in particular case*) das Unmögliche tun.
impossibly [ɪmˈpɒsəblɪ] *adv* unmöglich.
impostor [ɪmˈpɒstəʳ] *n* Betrüger(in *f*), Schwindler(in *f*) *m*; (*assuming higher position also*) Hochstapler(in *f*) *m*.
imposture [ɪmˈpɒstʃəʳ] *n see* **impostor** Betrug *m*, Schwindelei *f*; Hochstapelei *f*.
impotence [ˈɪmpətəns] *n see adj* Schwäche, Kraftlosigkeit *f*; Impotenz *f*; Schwäche, Machtlosigkeit *f*; Ohnmacht *f*.
impotent [ˈɪmpətənt] *adj* (*physically*) schwach, kraftlos; (*sexually*) impotent; (*fig*) schwach, machtlos; *grief, rage* ohnmächtig.
impound [ɪmˈpaʊnd] *vt* **(a)** (*seize*) *goods, contraband* beschlagnahmen. **(b)** *cattle* einsperren; *car* abschleppen (lassen).
impoverish [ɪmˈpɒvərɪʃ] *vt person, country* in Armut bringen, verarmen lassen; *soil* auslaugen, erschöpfen; (*fig*) *culture* verkümmern *or* verarmen lassen.
impoverished [ɪmˈpɒvərɪʃt] *adj* arm; *person, conditions also* ärmlich; (*having become poor*) verarmt; *soil* ausgelaugt, erschöpft; *supplies* erschöpft; (*fig*) dürftig.
impoverishment [ɪmˈpɒvərɪʃmənt] *n see vt* Verarmung *f*; Auslaugung, Erschöpfung *f*; Verkümmerung *f*.
impracticability [ɪmˌpræktɪkəˈbɪlɪtɪ] *n see adj* Impraktikabilität *f*; Unbrauchbarkeit *f*; schlechte Befahrbarkeit.
impracticable [ɪmˈpræktɪkəbl] *adj* impraktikabel; *plan also* in der Praxis nicht anwendbar, praktisch unmöglich; *design, size* unbrauchbar; *road* schwer befahrbar.
impractical [ɪmˈpræktɪkəl] *adj* unpraktisch; *scheme also* unbrauchbar.
impracticality [ɪmˌpræktɪˈkælɪtɪ] *n* (*of person*) unpraktische Art; (*of scheme, idea*) Unbrauchbarkeit *f*.
imprecation [ˌɪmprɪˈkeɪʃən] *n* Verwünschung *f*, Fluch *m*.
imprecise *adj*, **~ly** *adv* [ˌɪmprɪˈsaɪs, -lɪ] ungenau, unpräzis(e).
imprecision [ˌɪmprɪˈsɪʒən] *n* Ungenauigkeit *f*.
impregnable [ɪmˈpregnəbl] *adj* (*Mil*) *fortress, defences* uneinnehmbar; (*fig*) *position* unerschütterlich; *argument* unwiderlegbar, unumstößlich.
impregnate [ˈɪmpregneɪt] *vt* **(a)** (*saturate*) tränken. **(b)** (*fig*) erfüllen; *person also* durchdringen. **(c)** (*Biol: fertilize*) befruchten; *humans also* schwängern.
impregnation [ˌɪmpregˈneɪʃən] *n see vt* Tränkung *f*; Erfüllung *f*; Durchdringung *f*; Befruchtung *f*; Schwängerung *f*.
impresario [ˌɪmpreˈsɑːrɪəʊ] *n* Impresario *m*; Theater-/ Operndirektor *m*.
▼ **impress** [ɪmˈpres] 1 *vt* **(a)** beeindrucken; (*favourably, memorably also*) Eindruck machen auf (+*acc*); (*arouse admiration in*) imponieren (+*dat*) ◆ **how does it ~ you?** wie finden Sie das?; **he/it ~ed me favourably/unfavourably** er/das hat einen/keinen guten *or* günstigen Eindruck auf mich gemacht; **I am not ~ed** das beeindruckt mich nicht, das imponiert mir gar nicht; **he is not easily ~ed** er läßt sich nicht so leicht beeindrucken.
(b) (*fix in mind of*) einschärfen (*on sb* jdm); *idea, danger, possibility* (deutlich) klarmachen (*on sb* jdm).
(c) (*press to make mark*) **to ~ a pattern** *etc* **onto/into sth** ein Muster *etc* auf etw (*acc*) aufdrücken *or* aufprägen/in etw (*acc*) eindrücken *or* einprägen; **his parting words ~ed themselves on my mind** seine Abschiedsworte haben sich mir eingeprägt.
2 *vi* Eindruck machen; (*person: deliberately*) Eindruck schinden (*inf*).
3 [ˈɪmpres] *n* Abdruck *m*.
▼ **impression** [ɪmˈpreʃən] *n* **(a)** Eindruck *m* ◆ **to make a good/bad ~ on sb** einen guten/schlechten Eindruck auf jdn machen; **his words made an ~** seine Worte machten Eindruck; **he created an ~ of power** er erweckte den Eindruck von Macht; **first ~s are usually right** der erste Eindruck ist gewöhnlich richtig.
▼ **(b)** (*idea*) Eindruck *m*; (*feeling*) Gefühl *nt* ◆ **to give sb the ~ that ...** jdm den Eindruck vermitteln, daß ...; **I was under the ~ that ...** ich hatte den Eindruck, daß ...; **that gives an ~ of light/warmth** das vermittelt den Eindruck von Licht/ein Gefühl der Wärme; **he had the ~ of falling** er hatte das Gefühl, zu fallen.
(c) (*on wax etc*) Abdruck *m*; (*of engraving*) Prägung *f*.
(d) (*of book etc*) Nachdruck *m* ◆ **first ~** Erstdruck *m*.
(e) (*take-off*) Nachahmung, Imitation *f* ◆ **to do an ~ of sb** jdn imitieren *or* nachahmen.
impressionable [ɪmˈpreʃnəbl] *adj* für Eindrücke empfänglich, leicht zu beeindrucken *pred* (*pej*) ◆ **at an ~ age** in einem Alter, in dem man für Eindrücke besonders empfänglich ist.

➤ LANGUAGE IN USE: **importance** → 7.5 **impossible: 1** → 16.1 **impress: 1a** → 13 **impression: b** → 6.2

impressionism [ɪm'preʃənɪzəm] *n* Impressionismus *m*.
impressionist [ɪm'preʃənɪst] *n* Impressionist(in *f*) *m*.
impressionistic [ɪm,preʃə'nɪstɪk] *adj* impressionistisch; (*fig*) *story, account also* in groben Zügen (geschildert).
impressive [ɪm'presɪv] *adj* beeindruckend; *performance, speech, ceremony, personality also* eindrucksvoll; (*in size*) *building, person also* imposant.
impressively [ɪm'presɪvlɪ] *adv see adj.*
imprint [ɪm'prɪnt] [1] *vt* **(a)** (*mark*) *leather* prägen; *paper* bedrucken; *seal, paper etc* aufprägen (*on* auf *+acc*); (*on paper*) aufdrucken (*on* auf *+acc*) ◆ **the document was ~ed with the seal of ...** das Dokument trug das Siegel *+gen or* von ...
(b) (*fig*) einprägen (*on sb* jdm) ◆ **to ~ itself on sb's mind/ memory** sich jdm/sich in jds Gedächtnis (*acc*) einprägen.
[2] ['ɪmprɪnt] *n* **(a)** (*lit*) (*on leather, wax etc*) Abdruck *m*; (*on paper*) (Auf)druck *m*; (*fig*) Spuren, Zeichen *pl*, bleibender Eindruck.
(b) (*Typ*) Impressum *nt* ◆ **under the Collins ~** mit dem Collins-Impressum.
imprison [ɪm'prɪzn] *vt* (*lit*) inhaftieren, einsperren (*inf*); (*fig*) gefangenhalten ◆ **to be/keep ~ed** (*lit, fig*) gefangen sein/gefangenhalten.
imprisonment [ɪm'prɪznmənt] *n* (*action*) Einsperren *nt* (*inf*), Inhaftierung *f*; (*state*) Gefangenschaft *f* ◆ **to sentence sb to one month's/life ~** jdn zu einem Monat Gefängnis *or* Freiheitsstrafe/zu lebenslänglicher Freiheitsstrafe verurteilen; **to serve a sentence** *or* **term of ~** eine Freiheitsstrafe verbüßen.
improbability [ɪm,prɒbə'bɪlɪtɪ] *n* Unwahrscheinlichkeit *f*.
improbable [ɪm'prɒbəbl] *adj* unwahrscheinlich.
impromptu [ɪm'prɒmptju:] [1] *adj* improvisiert.
[2] *adv* improvisiert; *perform* aus dem Stegreif ◆ **to speak/sing/act ~** improvisieren.
[3] *n* (*Mus*) Impromptu *nt*.
improper [ɪm'prɒpəʳ] *adj* (*unsuitable*) unpassend, unangebracht; (*unseemly*) unschicklich; (*indecent*) unanständig; (*wrong*) *diagnosis, interpretation* unzutreffend; *use* unsachgemäß; (*dishonest*) *practice* unlauter; (*not professional*) *conduct* unehrenhaft ◆ **it is ~ to do that** es gehört sich nicht, das zu tun; **~ use of tools/drugs/one's position** Zweckentfremdung *f* von Geräten/Drogen-/Amtsmißbrauch *m*.
improperly [ɪm'prɒpəlɪ] *adv see adj.*
impropriety [,ɪmprə'praɪətɪ] *n* Unschicklichkeit *f*; (*of behaviour etc, language, remark*) Ungehörigkeit *f*; (*indecency: of jokes etc*) Unanständigkeit *f* ◆ **to behave with ~** sich ungehörig benehmen.
improve [ɪm'pru:v] [1] *vt* **(a)** verbessern; *area, appearance* ver- schönern; *sauce, food etc also* verfeinern; *production, value also* erhöhen, steigern; *knowledge also* erweitern; *low salaries also* aufbessern ◆ **to ~ one's mind** sich weiterbilden.
(b) to ~ the shining hour (*liter*) die Gelegenheit beim Schopfe packen.
[2] *vi see vt* sich verbessern, sich bessern; schöner werden; sich erhöhen, steigen ◆ **he has ~d in maths** er hat sich in Mathematik gebessert; **to ~ with use** mit Gebrauch besser werden; **wine ~s with age** je älter der Wein desto besser; **the invalid is improving** dem Kranken geht es besser; **I'll try to ~** ich werde versuchen, mich zu bessern; **things are improving** es sieht schon besser aus, die Lage bessert sich langsam; **this book ~s on re-reading** das Buch gewinnt beim zweiten Lesen; **his style has ~d in precision** sein Stil hat an Genauigkeit gewonnen, sein Stil ist genauer geworden.
[3] *vr* **to ~ oneself** an sich (*dat*) arbeiten.
◆**improve (up)on** *vi +prep obj* **(a)** übertreffen, besser machen ◆ **that can't be ~d** das kann man nicht übertreffen. **(b)** (*Comm, Fin*) *offer* überbieten, gehen über (*+acc*).
improved [ɪm'pru:vd] *adj* besser, verbessert; *offer also* höher.
improvement [ɪm'pru:vmənt] *n see vt* Verbesserung *f*, Besserung *f*; Verschönerung *f*; Verfeinerung *f*; Erhöhung, Steigerung *f*; Erweiterung *f*; Aufbesserung *f*; (*in health*) Besserung *f*; (*in studies also*) Fortschritte *pl* ◆ **an ~ in pay** eine Gehaltsaufbesserung; **~ of one's mind** Weiterbildung *f*; **to be open to ~** verbesserungsfähig sein; **an ~ on the previous one** eine Verbesserung/Besserung *etc* gegenüber dem Früheren; **to make ~s** Verbesserungen machen *or* durchführen (*to* an *+dat*); **to carry out ~s to a house** Ausbesserungs- *or* (*to appearance*) Verschönerungsarbeiten an einem Haus vornehmen.
improvidence [ɪm'prɒvɪdəns] *n* mangelnde Vorsorge (*of* für), Sorglosigkeit *f* (*of* in bezug auf *+acc*).
improvident [ɪm'prɒvɪdənt] *adj* sorglos ◆ **he was ~ of the future** er sorgte nicht für die Zukunft vor.
improvidently [ɪm'prɒvɪdəntlɪ] *adv see adj.*
improving [ɪm'pru:vɪŋ] *adj* informativ, lehrreich; *book, also* bildend; (*morally ~*) erbaulich.
improvisation [,ɪmprəvaɪ'zeɪʃən] *n* Improvisation, Improvisierung *f*; (*object improvised*) Provisorium *nt*.
improvise ['ɪmprəvaɪz] *vti* improvisieren.
imprudence [ɪm'pru:dəns] *n* Unklugheit *f*.
imprudent *adj*, **~ly** *adv* [ɪm'pru:dənt, -lɪ] unklug.
impudence ['ɪmpjʊdəns] *n* Unverschämtheit, Frechheit *f* ◆ **what ~!** so eine Unverschämtheit *or* Frechheit!; **he had the ~ to ask me** er hatte die Stirn *or* er besaß die Frechheit, mich zu fragen.
impudent *adj*, **~ly** *adv* ['ɪmpjʊdənt, -lɪ] unverschämt, dreist.
impugn [ɪm'pju:n] *vt person* angreifen; *sb's behaviour etc also* scharfe Kritik üben an (*+dat*); *sb's honesty, motives* in Zweifel ziehen, Zweifel hegen an (*+dat*); *statement, evidence, veracity of witness* bestreiten, anfechten.
impulse ['ɪmpʌls] *n* Impuls *m*; (*driving force*) (Stoß- *or* Trieb)kraft *f* ◆ **nerve ~** nervöser Reiz *or* Impuls; **to give an ~ to business** dem Handel neue Impulse geben; **creature/man of ~** impulsives Wesen/impulsiver Mensch; **to yield to a sudden** *or* **rash ~** einem Impuls nachgeben *or* folgen; **on ~** aus einem Impuls heraus, impulsiv; **~ buying** impulsives *or* spontanes Kaufen; **an ~ buy** *or* **purchase** ein Impulsivkauf *m*; **I had an ~ to hit him** ich hatte den (unwiderstehlichen) Drang *or* das plötzliche Verlangen, ihn zu schlagen; **he is ruled by his ~s** er läßt sich von seinen spontanen Regungen leiten.
impulsion [ɪm'pʌlʃən] *n* (*lit: act of impelling*) Antrieb *m*; (*lit, fig: driving force also*) Antriebskraft *f*; (*fig*) (*impetus*) Impuls *m*; (*compulsion*) Trieb, Drang *m*.
impulsive [ɪm'pʌlsɪv] *adj* **(a)** impulsiv; *action, remark also* spontan. **(b)** (*Phys, Tech*) *force* Trieb-, (an)treibend.
impulsively [ɪm'pʌlsɪvlɪ] *adv see adj (a).*
impulsiveness [ɪm'pʌlsɪvnɪs] *n see adj (a)* Impulsivität *f*; Spontaneität *f*.
impunity [ɪm'pju:nɪtɪ] *n* Straflosigkeit *f* ◆ **with ~** ungestraft.
impure [ɪm'pjʊəʳ] *adj water, drugs* unrein; *food* verunreinigt; *thoughts, mind also, motives* unsauber; *style* nicht rein.
impurity [ɪm'pjʊərɪtɪ] *n see adj* Unreinheit *f*; Verunreinigung *f*; Unsauberkeit *f*; Unreinheit *f* ◆ **the impurities in the liquid** die Verunreinigungen in der Flüssigkeit.
imputation [,ɪmpjʊ'teɪʃən] *n* (*of crime*) Bezichtigung *f*; (*of lie also*) Unterstellung *f*.
impute [ɪm'pju:t] *vt* zuschreiben (*to sb/sth* jdm/einer Sache) ◆ **to ~ a crime/lie to sb** jdn eines Verbrechens bezichtigen/jdm eine Lüge unterstellen, jdn einer Lüge bezichtigen.
in [ɪn] [1] *prep* **(a)** (*position*) in (*+dat*); (*with motion*) in (*+acc*) ◆ **it was ~ the lorry/pocket/car** es war auf dem Lastwagen/in der Tasche/im Auto; **he put it ~ the lorry/car/pocket** er legte es auf den Lastwagen/ins Auto/steckte es in die Tasche; **~ here/there** hierin/darin, hier/da drin (*inf*); (*with motion*) hier/da hinein/ herein, hier/da rein (*inf*); **go ~ that direction** gehen Sie in diese *or* dieser Richtung; **~ the street** auf der/die Straße; **~ Thompson Street** in der Thompsonstraße; **he lives ~ a little village** er wohnt auf *or* in einem kleinen Dorf; **sitting ~ the window** am Fenster sitzend; **a flag hung ~ the window** eine Flagge hing im Fenster; **~ (the) church** in der Kirche; **to stay ~ the house** im Haus *or* (*at home*) zu Hause bleiben; **~ bed/prison/town** im Bett/Gefängnis/in der Stadt; **~ Germany/Iran/Switzerland /the United States** in Deutschland/im Iran/in der Schweiz/in den Vereinigten Staaten; **the best ~ the class** der Beste der Klasse, der Klassenbeste.
(b) (*people, works*) bei ◆ **we find it ~ Dickens** wir finden das bei Dickens *or* in Dickens' Werken; **rare ~ a child of that age** selten bei einem Kind in diesem Alter; **you have a great leader ~ him** in ihm habt ihr einen großen Führer.
(c) (*time: with dates etc, during*) in (*+dat*) ◆ **~ 1974** (im Jahre) 1974; **~ the sixties** in den sechziger Jahren; **~ June** im Juni; **~ (the) spring** im Frühling; **~ the morning(s)** morgens, am Morgen, am Vormittag; **~ the afternoon** nachmittags, am Nachmittag; **~ the daytime** tagsüber, während des Tages; **~ the evening** abends, am Abend; **three o'clock ~ the afternoon** drei Uhr nachmittags; **~ those days** damals, zu jener Zeit; **~ the beginning** am Anfang, anfangs; **once ~ a lifetime** (nur) einmal im Leben.
(d) (*time: interval*) in (*+dat*); (*within*) innerhalb von ◆ **~ a moment** *or* **minute** sofort, gleich; **~ a short time** in kurzer Zeit; **~ a week('s time)** in einer Woche; **I haven't seen him ~ years** ich habe ihn seit Jahren *or* jahrelang nicht mehr gesehen.
(e) (*manner, state, condition*) **to speak ~ a loud/soft voice** mit lauter/leiser Stimme sprechen, laut/leise sprechen; **to speak ~ a whisper** flüstern, flüsternd sprechen; **to speak ~ German** Deutsch *or* deutsch reden; **the background is painted ~ red** der Hintergrund ist rot (gemalt) *or* in Rot gehalten; **to pay ~ dollars** mit *or* in Dollar bezahlen; **to stand ~ a row/~ groups** in einer Reihe/in Gruppen *or* gruppenweise stehen; **~ this way** so, auf diese Weise; **packed ~ hundreds** zu Hunderten abgepackt; **to walk ~ twos** zu zweit *or* zu zweien gehen; **to count ~ fives** in Fünfern zählen; **she squealed ~ delight** sie quietschte vor Vergnügen; **~ anger** im Zorn; **to be ~ a rage** wütend *or* zornig sein; **~ a good state** in gutem Zustand; **to live ~ luxury/poverty** im Luxus/in Armut leben.
(f) (*dress*) in (*+dat*) ◆ **~ one's best clothes** in Sonntagskleidung; **~ his shirt/shirt sleeves/slippers** im Hemd/in Hemdsärmeln, hemdsärmelig/in Hausschuhen; **dressed ~ white** weiß gekleidet; **the lady ~ green** die Dame in Grün.
(g) (*substance, material*) **upholstered ~ silk** mit Seide bezogen; **she was dressed ~ silk** sie war in Seide gekleidet; **to paint ~ oils** in Öl malen; **to write ~ ink/pencil** mit Tinte/Bleistift schreiben; **~ marble** in Marmor, marmorn; **a sculptor who works ~ marble** ein Bildhauer, der mit Marmor arbeitet.
(h) (*ratio*) **there are 12 inches ~ a foot** ein Fuß hat 12 Zoll; **one (man) ~ ten** einer von zehn, jeder zehnte; **one book/child ~ ten** jedes zehnte Buch/Kind, ein Buch/Kind von zehn; **fifteen pence ~ the pound discount** fünfzehn Prozent Rabatt.
(i) (*degree, extent*) **~ large/small quantities** in großen/ kleinen Mengen; **~ some measure** in gewisser Weise, zu einem gewissen Grad; **~ part** teilweise, zum Teil; **to die ~ hundreds** zu Hunderten sterben.
(j) (*in respect of*) **blind ~ the left eye** auf dem linken Auge *or* links blind; **weak ~ maths** in Mathematik schwach; **a rise ~ prices** ein Preisanstieg *m*, ein Anstieg *m* der Preise; **ten feet ~ height by thirty ~ length** zehn Fuß hoch auf dreißig Fuß lang; **to be too long ~ the leg** zu lange Beine haben; **five ~ number** fünf an der Zahl; **the latest thing ~ hats** der letzte Schrei bei Hüten.
(k) (*occupation, activity*) **he is ~ the army** er ist beim Militär; **he is ~ banking/the motor business** er ist im Bankwesen/in der Autobranche (tätig); **he travels ~ ladies' underwear** er reist in Damenunterwäsche.
(l) (*+prp*) **~ saying this, I ...** wenn ich das sage, ... ich; **~ trying to escape**

beim Versuch zu fliehen, beim Fluchtversuch; **but ~ saying this** aber indem ich dies sage; **~ making a fortune** im Streben nach Reichtum; **he made a mistake ~ saying that** es war ein Fehler von ihm, das zu sagen.
(m) ~ that insofern als.
[2] *adv* **(a)** da; (*at home also*) zu Hause ◆ **there is nobody ~** es ist niemand da/zu Hause; **the train is ~** der Zug ist da *or* angekommen; **the harvest is ~** die Ernte ist eingebracht; **our team is ~** (*Cricket*) unsere Mannschaft ist am Schlag; **we were asked ~** wir wurden hereingebeten; *see vbs.*
(b) (*fig*) **strawberries are ~** es ist Erdbeerzeit; **miniskirts are ~** Miniröcke sind in (*inf*) *or* in Mode; **the Socialists are ~** die Sozialisten sind an der Regierung; **our candidate is ~** unser Kandidat ist gewählt *or* reingekommen (*inf*); **the fire is still ~** das Feuer ist noch an *or* brennt noch.
(c) (*phrases*) **he's ~ for a surprise/disappointment** ihm steht eine Überraschung/Enttäuschung bevor, er kann sich auf eine Überraschung/Enttäuschung gefaßt machen; **we are ~ for rain/a cold spell** uns (*dat*) steht Regen/eine Kältewelle bevor; **he's ~ for it!** der kann sich auf was gefaßt machen (*inf*), der kann sich freuen (*iro*); **you don't know what you are ~ for/letting yourself ~ for** Sie wissen nicht, was Ihnen bevorsteht/auf was Sie sich da einlassen; **are you ~ for the race?** machen Sie bei dem Rennen mit?; **he is ~ for the post of manager** er hat sich um die Stelle des Managers beworben; **he hasn't got it ~ him** er hat nicht das Zeug dazu; **it's not ~ him to ...** er hat einfach nicht das Zeug dazu, zu ...; **to have it ~ for sb** (*inf*) es auf jdn abgesehen haben (*inf*); **to be ~ on sth** an einer Sache beteiligt sein; (*on secret etc*) über etw (*acc*) Bescheid wissen; **he likes to be ~ on things** er mischt gern (überall) mit (*inf*); **to be (well) ~ with sb** sich gut mit jdm verstehen; **my luck is ~** ich habe einen Glückstag.
[3] *adj attr* **(a) "~" door** Eingangstür *f*; *see* **in-patient** *etc.*
(b) (*inf*) in *inv* (*inf*) ◆ **an ~ subject** ein Modefach *nt*; **the ~ thing is to ...** es ist zur Zeit in (*inf*) *or* Mode, zu ...
[4] *n* **(a) to know the ~s and outs of a matter** bei einer Sache genau Bescheid wissen.
(b) (*US Pol*) **the ~s** die Regierungspartei.

inability [ˌɪnəˈbɪlɪtɪ] *n* Unfähigkeit *f*, Unvermögen *nt* ◆ **~ to pay** Zahlungsunfähigkeit *f*.

inaccessibility [ˈɪnækˌsesəˈbɪlɪtɪ] *n see adj* Unzugänglichkeit *f*; Unerreichbarkeit *f*.

inaccessible [ˌɪnækˈsesəbl] *adj information, person* unzugänglich; *place also* unerreichbar.

inaccuracy [ɪnˈækjʊrəsɪ] *n see adj* Ungenauigkeit *f*; Unrichtigkeit *f*.

inaccurate [ɪnˈækjʊrɪt] *adj* (*lacking accuracy*) ungenau; (*not correct*) unrichtig ◆ **she was ~ in her judgement of the situation** ihre Beurteilung der Lage traf nicht zu.

inaccurately [ɪnˈækjʊrɪtlɪ] *adv see adj.*

inaction [ɪnˈækʃən] *n* Untätigkeit, Tatenlosigkeit *f*.

inactive [ɪnˈæktɪv] *adj* untätig; *person, life, hands also* müßig (*geh*); *mind* träge, müßig (*geh*); *volcano* erloschen, untätig ◆ **don't have money lying ~ in the bank** lassen Sie (Ihr) Geld nicht auf der Bank brachliegen.

inactivity [ˌɪnækˈtɪvɪtɪ] *n* Untätigkeit *f*; (*of mind*) Trägheit *f*; (*Comm*) Stille, Flaute *f*.

inadequacy [ɪnˈædɪkwəsɪ] *n see adj* Unzulänglichkeit *f*; Unangemessenheit *f*.

inadequate [ɪnˈædɪkwɪt] *adj* unzulänglich, inadäquat (*geh*); *supplies, resources, punishment, reasons, proposals also* unzureichend; *measures* unangemessen ◆ **he is ~ for such a job/responsibility** er ist für eine solche Stelle nicht geeignet/er ist einer solchen Verantwortung nicht gewachsen; **she makes him feel ~** sie gibt ihm das Gefühl der Unzulänglichkeit.

inadequately [ɪnˈædɪkwɪtlɪ] *adv* unzulänglich, inadäquat (*geh*); *equipped, explained, documented also* unzureichend.

inadmissibility [ˈɪnədˌmɪsəˈbɪlɪtɪ] *n* Unzulässigkeit *f*.

inadmissible [ˌɪnədˈmɪsəbl] *adj* unzulässig.

inadvertence [ˌɪnədˈvɜːtəns] *n* Ungewolltheit *f* ◆ **through ~** versehentlich, aus Versehen.

inadvertent [ˌɪnədˈvɜːtənt] *adj* unbeabsichtigt, ungewollt.

inadvertently [ˌɪnədˈvɜːtəntlɪ] *adv* versehentlich.

inadvisability [ˈɪnədˌvaɪzəˈbɪlɪtɪ] *n* Unratsamkeit *f* (*of doing sth* etw zu tun).

▼ **inadvisable** [ˌɪnədˈvaɪzəbl] *adj* unratsam, nicht zu empfehlen *pred*, nicht zu empfehlend *attr.*

inalienable [ɪnˈeɪlɪənəbl] *adj rights* unveräußerlich.

inane [ɪˈneɪn] *adj* dumm; *suggestion also* hirnverbrannt.

inanely [ɪˈneɪnlɪ] *adv* dumm ◆ **he suggested ~ that ...** er machte den hirnverbrannten Vorschlag, zu ...

inanimate [ɪnˈænɪmɪt] *adj* leblos, tot; *nature* unbelebt.

inanition [ˌɪnəˈnɪʃən] *n* Auszehrung *f*.

inanity [ɪˈnænɪtɪ] *n see adj* Dummheit *f*; Hirnverbranntheit *f*.

inappetency [ɪnˈæpɪtənsɪ] *n* (*fig liter*) Lustlosigkeit, Unlust *f*.

inapplicable [ɪnˈæplɪkəbl] *adj answer* unzutreffend; *laws, rules* nicht anwendbar (*to sb* auf jdn).

inapposite [ɪnˈæpəzɪt] *adj* unpassend, unangebracht.

inappropriate [ˌɪnəˈprəʊprɪɪt] *adj* unpassend, unangebracht; *action also* unangemessen; *time* unpassend, ungelegen, ungünstig ◆ **this translation is rather ~** das ist keine angemessene Übersetzung; **you have come at a most ~ time** Sie kommen sehr ungelegen.

inappropriately [ˌɪnəˈprəʊprɪɪtlɪ] *adv see adj.*

inappropriateness [ˌɪnəˈprəʊprɪɪtnɪs] *n see adj* Unpassende(s) *nt*, Unangebrachtheit *f*; Unangemessenheit *f*; Ungünstigkeit *f*.

inapt [ɪnˈæpt] *adj* ungeschickt; *remark also* unpassend.

inaptitude [ɪnˈæptɪtjuːd] *n* (*of person*) Unfähigkeit *f*; (*for work etc*) Untauglichkeit *f*; (*of remark*) Ungeschicktheit *f*.

inarticulate [ˌɪnɑːˈtɪkjʊlɪt] *adj* **(a)** *essay* schlecht *or* unklar ausgedrückt, inartikuliert (*geh*); *speech also* schwerfällig ◆ **she's very ~** sie kann sich kaum *or* nur schlecht ausdrücken; **a brilliant but ~ scientist** ein glänzender, aber wenig wortgewandter Wissenschaftler; **~ with rage** sprachlos vor Zorn; **just a string of ~ grunts** nur eine Reihe unverständlicher Grunzlaute.
(b) (*Zool*) nicht gegliedert.

inartistic *adj*, **~ally** *adv* [ˌɪnɑːˈtɪstɪk, -əlɪ] unkünstlerisch; *work also* kunstlos.

inasmuch [ɪnəzˈmʌtʃ] *adv*: **~ as** da, weil; (*to the extent that*) insofern als.

inattention [ˌɪnəˈtenʃən] *n* Unaufmerksamkeit *f* ◆ **~ to detail** Ungenauigkeit *f* im Detail.

inattentive *adj*, **~ly** *adv* [ˌɪnəˈtentɪv, -lɪ] unaufmerksam.

inattentiveness [ˌɪnəˈtentɪvnɪs] *n* Unaufmerksamkeit *f*.

inaudibility [ɪnˌɔːdəˈbɪlɪtɪ] *n* Unhörbarkeit *f*.

inaudible *adj*, **-bly** *adv* [ɪnˈɔːdəbl, -ɪ] unhörbar.

inaugural [ɪˈnɔːgjʊrəl] [1] *adj lecture* Antritts-; *meeting, address, speech* Eröffnungs-.
[2] *n* (*speech*) Antritts-/Eröffnungsrede *f*.

inaugurate [ɪˈnɔːgjʊreɪt] *vt* **(a)** *president, official* (feierlich) in sein/ihr Amt einsetzen *or* einführen, inaugurieren (*geh*); *pope, king, bishop also* inthronisieren (*geh*). **(b)** *policy* einführen; *building* einweihen; *exhibition* eröffnen; *era* einleiten.

inauguration [ɪˌnɔːgjʊˈreɪʃən] *n see vt* **(a)** Amtseinführung, Inauguration (*geh*) *f*; Inthronisierung *f* (*geh*). **(b)** Einführung *f*; Einweihung *f*; Eröffnung *f*; Beginn, Anfang *m*.

inauspicious [ˌɪnɔːsˈpɪʃəs] *adj* unheilverheißend; *circumstances, omen also* unheilträchtig.

inauspiciously [ˌɪnɔːsˈpɪʃəslɪ] *adv see adj.*

in-between [ɪnbɪˈtwiːn] (*inf*) [1] *n*: **the ~s** wer/was dazwischenliegt *or* -kommt.
[2] *adj* Mittel-, Zwischen- ◆ **it is sort of ~** es ist so ein Mittelding; **~ stage** Zwischenstadium *nt*; **~ weather** Übergangswetter *nt*; **~ times** *adv* zwischendurch, dazwischen.

inboard [ˈɪnbɔːd] (*Naut*) [1] *adj* Innenbord-.
[2] *adv* binnenbords.
[3] *n* Innenbordmotor *m*.

inborn [ˈɪnˈbɔːn] *adj* angeboren.

inbred [ˈɪnˈbred] *adj* **(a) they look very ~** sie sehen nach Inzucht aus; **to stop them becoming ~** um die Inzucht bei ihnen aufzuhalten; **the royal family became very ~** in der Königsfamilie herrschte Inzucht. **(b)** *quality* angeboren.

inbreeding [ˈɪnˈbriːdɪŋ] *n* Inzucht *f*.

inbuilt [ˈɪnbɪlt] *adj safety features, error detection etc* integriert; *dislike, fear* angeboren, instinktiv; *predisposition, fondness* natürlich.

Inc (*US*) *abbr of* **Incorporated.**

Inca [ˈɪŋkə] [1] *n* Inka *mf*.
[2] *adj* (*also* **~n**) Inka-, inkaisch.

incalculable [ɪnˈkælkjʊləbl] *adj* **(a)** *amount* unschätzbar, unermeßlich; *damage, harm also, consequences* unabsehbar. **(b)** (*Math*) nicht berechenbar. **(c)** *character, mood* unberechenbar, unvorhersehbar.

incandescence [ˌɪnkænˈdesns] *n* (Weiß)glühen *nt*, (Weiß)glut *f*.

incandescent [ˌɪnkænˈdesnt] *adj* (*lit*) (weiß)glühend; (*fig liter*) hell leuchtend, strahlend ◆ **~ lamp** Glühlampe, Glühbirne *f*.

incantation [ˌɪnkænˈteɪʃən] *n* Zauber(spruch) *m*, Zauberformel *f*; (*act*) Beschwörung *f*.

incapability [ɪnˌkeɪpəˈbɪlɪtɪ] *n* Unfähigkeit *f*, Unvermögen *nt* (*of doing sth* etw zu tun).

▼ **incapable** [ɪnˈkeɪpəbl] *adj* **(a)** *person* unfähig; (*physically*) hilflos ◆ **to be ~ of doing sth** unfähig *or* nicht imstande sein, etw zu tun, etw nicht tun können; **drunk and ~** volltrunken; **he was completely ~** (*because drunk*) er war volltrunken; **~ of working** arbeitsunfähig; **~ of tenderness** zu Zärtlichkeit nicht fähig; **do it yourself, you're not ~** (*inf*) mach es doch selbst, du bist nicht so hilflos.
(b) (*form*) **~ of proof** nicht beweisbar; **~ of measurement** nicht meßbar; **~ of improvement** nicht verbesserungsfähig.

incapacitate [ˌɪnkəˈpæsɪteɪt] *vt* **(a)** unfähig machen (*for* für, *from doing sth* etw zu tun) ◆ **physically ~d** körperlich behindert; **somewhat ~d by his broken ankle** durch seinen gebrochenen Knöchel ziemlich behindert. **(b)** (*Jur*) entmündigen.

incapacity [ˌɪnkəˈpæsɪtɪ] *n* **(a)** Unfähigkeit *f* (*for* für) ◆ **~ for work** Arbeitsunfähigkeit *f*. **(b)** (*Jur*) mangelnde Berechtigung (*for* zu) ◆ **~ to inherit** Erbunfähigkeit *f*; **~ of a minor** Geschäftsunfähigkeit *f* eines Minderjährigen.

in-car [ˈɪnkɑːʳ] *adj attr phone, hi-fi* Auto-; *entertainment* während der Fahrt.

incarcerate [ɪnˈkɑːsəreɪt] *vt* einkerkern.

incarceration [ɪnˌkɑːsəˈreɪʃən] *n* (*act*) Einkerkerung *f*; (*period*) Kerkerhaft *f*.

incarnate [ɪnˈkɑːnɪt] [1] *adj* (*Rel*) fleischgeworden, menschgeworden; (*personified*) leibhaftig *attr*, in Person ◆ **to become ~** Fleisch werden, Mensch werden; **the word I~** das fleischgewordene Wort; **he's the devil ~** er ist der leibhaftige Teufel *or* der Teufel in Person.
[2] [ˈɪnkɑːneɪt] *vt* (*make real*) Gestalt *or* Form geben (+*dat*); (*be embodiment of*) verkörpern.

incarnation [ˌɪnkɑːˈneɪʃən] *n* (*Rel*) Inkarnation (*geh*), Menschwerdung,

➤ LANGUAGE IN USE: **inadvisable** → 2.2 **incapable: a** → 16.4

Fleischwerdung *f*; (*fig*) Inbegriff *m*, Verkörperung, Inkarnation (*geh*) *f*.
incautious *adj*, **~ly** *adv* [ɪn'kɔːʃəs, -lɪ] unvorsichtig, unbedacht.
incendiary [ɪn'sendɪərɪ] 1 *adj* (a) (*lit*) *bomb* Brand- ◆ **~ device** Brandsatz *m*. (b) (*fig*) *speech* aufwiegelnd, aufhetzend.
2 *n* (a) (*bomb*) Brandbombe *f*. (b) (*person*) (*lit*) Brandstifter(in *f*) *m*; (*fig*) Aufrührer(in *f*), Unruhestifter(in *f*) *m*.
incense[1] [ɪn'sens] *vt* wütend machen, erbosen, erzürnen ◆ **~d** wütend, erbost (*at, by* über *+acc*).
incense[2] ['ɪnsens] *n* (*Eccl*) Weihrauch *m*; (*fig*) Duft *m*.
incense: **~ bearer** *n* Weihrauchschwenker *or* -träger *m*; **~ burner** *n* Weihrauchschwenker *m*, Räucherpfanne *f*.
incentive [ɪn'sentɪv] *n* Anreiz *m* ◆ **it'll give them a bit of ~** das wird ihnen einen gewissen Anreiz *or* Ansporn geben; **~ bonus** Leistungszulage *f*; **~ scheme** (*Ind*) Anreizsystem *nt*.
inception [ɪn'sepʃən] *n* Beginn, Anfang *m* ◆ **from/at its ~** von Anbeginn an/zu Anbeginn.
incertitude [ɪn'sɜːtɪtjuːd] *n* Ungewißheit, Unsicherheit *f*.
incessant [ɪn'sesnt] *adj* unaufhörlich, unablässig; *complaints also* nicht abreißend; *noise* ununterbrochen.
incessantly [ɪn'sesntlɪ] *adv see adj*.
incest ['ɪnsest] *n* Inzest *m*, Blutschande *f*.
incestuous [ɪn'sestjʊəs] *adj* blutschänderisch, inzestuös (*geh*).
inch [ɪntʃ] 1 *n* Zoll, Inch *m* ◆ **3.5 ~ disk** 3,5-Zoll-Diskette *f*; **because of his lack of ~es** weil er ein bißchen klein ist/war; **she's gained a few ~es** sie hat in der Taille ein paar Zentimeter zugenommen; **she's grown a few ~es** sie ist ein paar Zentimeter gewachsen; **~ by ~** Zentimeter um Zentimeter; **he came within an ~ of winning/victory** er hätte um ein Haar *or* beinahe gewonnen; **he came within an ~ of being killed** er ist dem Tod um Haaresbreite entgangen; **he was within an ~ of death** sein Leben stand auf des Messers Schneide; **he missed being run over by ~es** er wäre um ein Haar überfahren worden; **the lorry missed me by ~es** der Lastwagen hat mich um Haaresbreite verfehlt; **he knows every ~ of the area** er kennt die Gegend wie seine Westentasche; **he is every ~ a soldier** er ist jeder Zoll ein Soldat; **we will not surrender one ~ of our territory** wir werden keinen Zentimeter unseres Gebiets abtreten; **they searched every ~ of the room** sie durchsuchten das Zimmer Zentimeter für Zentimeter; **he couldn't see an ~ in front of him** er konnte die Hand nicht vor den Augen sehen; **give him an ~ and he'll take a mile** (*prov*) wenn man ihm den kleinen Finger gibt, nimmt er die ganze Hand (*prov*).
2 *vi* **to ~ forward/out/in** sich millimeterweise *or* stückchenweise vorwärts-/hinaus-/heraus-/hinein-/hereinschieben; **because prices are ~ing up** weil die Preise allmählich ansteigen; **the Dutch swimmer is ~ing ahead** der holländische Schwimmer schiebt sich langsam an die Spitze.
3 *vt* langsam manövrieren ◆ **he ~ed his way forward** er schob sich langsam vorwärts.
inchoate ['ɪnkəʊeɪt] *adj* (*liter*) unausgeformt.
incidence ['ɪnsɪdəns] *n* (a) (*Opt*) Einfall *m* ◆ **angle of ~** Einfallswinkel *m*. (b) (*of crime, disease*) Häufigkeit *f* ◆ **a high ~ of crime** eine hohe Verbrechensquote.
incident ['ɪnsɪdənt] 1 *n* (a) (*event*) Ereignis *nt*, Begebenheit *f*, Vorfall *m* ◆ **a life full of ~s** ein ereignisreiches Leben; **an ~ from his childhood** ein Kindheitserlebnis *nt*.
(b) (*diplomatic etc*) Zwischenfall *m*; (*disturbance in pub etc*) Vorfall *m* ◆ **without ~** ohne Zwischenfälle; **~ room** Einsatzzentrale *f*.
(c) (*in book, play*) Episode *f*.
2 *adj* (a) **~ to** (*form*) verbunden mit.
(b) (*Opt*) *ray* einfallend.
incidental [ˌɪnsɪ'dentl] 1 *adj* (a) **dangers ~ to foreign travel** (*liter*) mit Auslandsreisen verbundene Gefahren; **~ music** Begleitmusik *f*; **~ expenses** Nebenkosten *pl*. (b) (*unplanned*) *event* zufällig. (c) (*secondary etc*) nebensächlich; *remark* beiläufig.
2 *n* Nebensächlichkeit, Nebensache *f* ◆ **~s** (*expenses*) Nebenausgaben *pl*.
▼ **incidentally** [ˌɪnsɪ'dentəlɪ] *adv* übrigens ◆ **it's only ~ important** das ist nur von nebensächlicher Bedeutung.
incinerate [ɪn'sɪnəreɪt] *vt* verbrennen; (*cremate*) einäschern.
incineration [ɪnsɪnə'reɪʃən] *n see vt* Verbrennung *f*, Einäscherung *f*.
incinerator [ɪn'sɪnəreɪtə[r]] *n* (Müll)verbrennungsanlage *f*; (*garden ~*) Verbrennungsofen *m*; (*in crematorium*) Feuerbestattungsofen, Verbrennungsofen *m*.
incipience [ɪn'sɪpɪəns] *n* Anfang, Beginn *m*.
incipient [ɪn'sɪpɪənt] *adj* anfangend, beginnend; *disease, difficulties also* einsetzend.
incise [ɪn'saɪz] *vt* (a) (ein)schneiden (*into* in *+acc*). (b) (*Art*) (*in wood*) (ein)schnitzen; (*in metal, stone*) eingravieren, einritzen.
incision [ɪn'sɪʒən] *n* Schnitt *m*; (*Med*) Einschnitt *m*.
incisive [ɪn'saɪsɪv] *adj style, tone, words* prägnant; *criticism* treffend, scharfsinnig; *mind* scharf; *person* scharfsinnig.
incisively [ɪn'saɪsɪvlɪ] *adv speak, formulate, put* prägnant; *argue, criticize, reason* treffend, scharfsinnig.
incisiveness [ɪn'saɪsɪvnɪs] *n see adj* Prägnanz *f*, Treffende *nt*, Scharfsinnigkeit *f*, Schärfe *f*.
incisor [ɪn'saɪzə[r]] *n* Schneidezahn *m*.
incite [ɪn'saɪt] *vt* aufhetzen; *masses also* aufwiegeln; *racial hatred* aufhetzen zu ◆ **to ~ the masses/sb to violence** die Massen/jdn zu Gewalttätigkeiten aufhetzen.

➤ LANGUAGE IN USE: **incidentally** → 26.2

incitement [ɪn'saɪtmənt] *n* (a) *no pl see vt* Aufhetzung *f*; Aufwieg(e)lung *f*. (b) (*incentive*) Anreiz, Ansporn *m* (*to* zu).
incivility [ˌɪnsɪ'vɪlɪtɪ] *n* Unhöflichkeit *f*.
incl *abbr of* **inclusive(ly)** incl., inkl.; **including** incl., inkl.
inclemency [ɪn'klemənsɪ] *n see adj* Rauheit, Unfreundlichkeit *f*; Unbarmherzigkeit, Unerbittlichkeit *f*.
inclement [ɪn'klemənt] *adj weather, wind* rauh, unfreundlich; *judge, attitude* unbarmherzig, unerbittlich.
inclination [ˌɪnklɪ'neɪʃən] *n* (a) (*tendency, wish etc*) Neigung *f* ◆ **he follows his (own) ~s** er tut das, wozu er Lust hat; **what are his natural ~s?** welches sind seine Neigungen?; **my (natural) ~ is to carry on** ich neige dazu, weiterzumachen; **~ to stoutness** Anlage *or* Neigung *f* zu Korpulenz; **to have an ~ towards rudeness** zur Unhöflichkeit neigen; **I have no ~ to see him again** ich habe keinerlei Bedürfnis, ihn wiederzusehen; **my immediate ~ was to refuse** mein erster Gedanke war abzulehnen; **he showed no ~ to leave** er schien nicht gehen zu wollen.
(b) (*of head, body*) Neigung *f*.
(c) (*of hill, slope etc*) Neigung *f*, Gefälle, Abfallen *nt*.
incline [ɪn'klaɪn] 1 *vt* (a) *head, body, roof* neigen ◆ **this ~s me to think that he must be lying** das läßt mich vermuten, daß er lügt.
(b) (*dispose*) veranlassen, bewegen ◆ **the news ~s me to stay** aufgrund der Nachricht würde ich gern bleiben; *see* **inclined**.
2 *vi* (a) (*slope*) sich neigen; (*ground also*) abfallen.
(b) (*be disposed, tend towards*) neigen ◆ **to ~ to a point of view** zu einer Ansicht neigen *or* tendieren; **he's beginning to ~ towards our point of view** er beginnt unserer Ansicht zuzuneigen.
3 ['ɪnklaɪn] *n* Neigung *f*; (*of hill*) Abhang *m*; (*gradient: Rail etc*) Gefälle *nt*.
inclined [ɪn'klaɪnd] *adj* (a) **to be ~ to do sth** (*feel that one wishes to*) Lust haben, etw zu tun, etw tun wollen; (*have tendency to*) dazu neigen, etw zu tun; **they are ~ to be late** sie kommen gern zu spät, sie neigen zum Zuspätkommen; **I am ~ to think that ...** ich neige zu der Ansicht, daß ...; **if you feel ~** wenn Sie Lust haben *or* dazu aufgelegt sind; **to be well ~ towards sb** jdm geneigt *or* gewogen sein; **if you're ~ that way** wenn Ihnen so etwas liegt; **I'm ~ to disagree** ich möchte da doch widersprechen; **I am not ~ to approve of this** ich bin nicht geneigt, das gutzuheißen; **I'm ~ to believe you** ich möchte Ihnen gern glauben; **it's ~ to break** das bricht leicht.
(b) *plane* geneigt, schräg.
inclose [ɪn'kləʊz] *vt see* **enclose**.
include [ɪn'kluːd] *vt* einschließen, enthalten; (*on list, in group etc*) aufnehmen, einbeziehen ◆ **your name is not ~d on the list** Ihr Name ist nicht auf der Liste; **the tip is not ~d in the bill** Trinkgeld ist in der Rechnung nicht inbegriffen; **all ~d** alles inklusive *or* inbegriffen; **the invitation ~s everybody** die Einladung betrifft alle; **they were all ~d in the accusation** die Anschuldigung bezog sich auf alle; **the children ~d** mit(samt) den Kindern, einschließlich der Kinder; **does that ~ me?** gilt das auch für mich?; **shut up! you ~d** *or* **that ~s you** Ruhe! Sie sind auch gemeint; **to ~ sb in one's prayers** jdn in sein Gebet einschließen; **in which category would you ~ this?** in welche Kategorie würden Sie das aufnehmen?; **I think we should ~ a chapter on ...** ich finde, wir sollten auch ein Kapitel über ... dazunehmen; **the book ~s two chapters on grammar** das Buch enthält auch zwei Grammatikkapitel.
◆**include out** *vt sep* (*hum inf*) auslassen ◆ **~ me ~** ohne mich.
including [ɪn'kluːdɪŋ] *prep* einschließlich, inklusive, inbegriffen, mit ◆ **that makes seven ~ you** mit Ihnen sind das sieben; **that comes to 200 marks ~ packing** das kommt auf 200 DM inklusive *or* einschließlich Verpackung; **there were six rooms ~ kitchen** mit Küche waren es sechs Zimmer, es waren sechs Zimmer einschließlich Küche; **~ the service charge** inklusive Bedienung, Bedienung (mit) inbegriffen; **not ~ service** exklusive Bedienung, Bedienung nicht inbegriffen *or* eingeschlossen; **up to and ~ chapter V** bis inklusive *or* einschließlich Kapitel V; **up to and ~ March 4th** bis einschließlich 4. März.
inclusion [ɪn'kluːʒən] *n* Aufnahme *f* ◆ **with the ~ of John that makes seven** mit John macht das sieben.
inclusive [ɪn'kluːsɪv] *adj* inklusive, einschließlich; *price* Inklusiv-, Pauschal- ◆ **~ sum** Pauschale, Pauschalsumme *f*; **~ terms** Pauschalpreis *m*; **to be ~ of** einschließlich (*+gen*) sein, einschließen (*+acc*); **to the fifth page ~** bis einschließlich der fünften Seite, bis Seite fünf einschließlich; **from 1st to 6th May ~** vom 1. bis einschließlich *or* inklusive 6. Mai, vom 1. bis 6. Mai inklusive.
inclusively [ɪn'kluːsɪvlɪ] *adv* inklusive, einschließlich ◆ **from 7 to 10 ~** von 7 bis einschließlich *or* inklusive 10.
incognito [ˌɪnkɒg'niːtəʊ] 1 *adv* inkognito.
2 *n* Inkognito *nt*.
3 *adj traveller* Inkognito- ◆ **to remain ~** inkognito bleiben.
incoherence [ˌɪnkəʊ'hɪərəns] *n* (*of style, prose*) Zusammenhanglosigkeit *f*, mangelnder Zusammenhang ◆ **with each further drink his ~ grew** seine Worte wurden mit jedem Glas wirrer *or* zusammenhangloser.
incoherent [ˌɪnkəʊ'hɪərənt] *adj style, argument* zusammenhanglos, unzusammenhängend, inkohärent (*geh*); *speech, conversation also* wirr; *person* sich unklar *or* undeutlich ausdrückend; *drunk etc* schwer verständlich ◆ **he was ~ with rage** seine wütenden Worte waren kaum zu verstehen.
incoherently [ˌɪnkəʊ'hɪərəntlɪ] *adv talk, write* zusammenhanglos, unzusammenhängend, wirr.
incombustible [ˌɪnkəm'bʌstəbl] *adj* unbrennbar.
income ['ɪnkʌm] *n* Einkommen *nt*; (*receipts*) Einkünfte *pl* ◆ **to live within/beyond one's ~** seinen Verhältnissen entsprechend/über seine Ver-

hältnisse leben.

income: ~ bracket *n* Einkommensklasse *f*; **~ group** *n* Einkommensgruppe *f*.

incomer ['ɪn,kʌmə^r] *n* (*new arrival*) Neuankömmling *m*; (*successor*) Nachfolger(in *f*) *m*.

income: ~s policy *n* Lohnpolitik *f*; **~ tax** *n* Lohnsteuer *f*; (*on private ~*) Einkommensteuer *f*; **~ tax return** *n* Steuererklärung *f*.

incoming ['ɪn,kʌmɪŋ] *adj* ankommend; *train also* einfahrend; *ship also* einlaufend; (*succeeding*) *president etc* nachfolgend, neu; *mail, orders etc* eingehend ◆ **~ tide** Flut *f*.

incomings ['ɪn,kʌmɪŋz] *npl* Einkünfte, Einnahmen *pl*.

incommensurable [,ɪnkə'menʃərəbl] *adj* nicht zu vergleichend *attr*, nicht vergleichbar; (*Math*) inkommensurabel.

incommensurate [,ɪnkə'menʃərɪt] *adj* **(a) to be ~ with sth** in keinem Verhältnis zu etw stehen. **(b)** (*inadequate*) unzureichend (*to* für).

incommode [,ɪnkə'məʊd] *vt* (*form*) lästig sein (*+dat*) ◆ **I don't wish to ~ you but could you/but could I** ... ich möchte Sie nicht behelligen, aber könnten Sie vielleicht .../würde es Sie sehr stören, wenn ich ...

incommodious [,ɪnkə'məʊdɪəs] *adj* (*form*) lästig, unbequem; (*cramped*) beengt.

incommunicado [,ɪnkəmjʊnɪ'kɑːdəʊ] *adj pred* ohne jede Verbindung zur Außenwelt, abgesondert ◆ **he was held ~** er hatte keinerlei Verbindung zur Außenwelt; **to be ~** (*fig*) für niemanden zu sprechen sein.

incomparable [ɪn'kɒmpərəbl] *adj* nicht vergleichbar (*with* mit); *beauty, skill* unvergleichlich.

incomparably [ɪn'kɒmpərəblɪ] *adv* unvergleichlich.

incompatibility ['ɪnkəm,pætə'bɪlɪtɪ] *n see adj* Unvereinbarkeit *f*; Unverträglichkeit *f* ◆ **divorce on grounds of ~** Scheidung aufgrund der Unvereinbarkeit der Charaktere der Ehepartner.

incompatible [,ɪnkəm'pætəbl] *adj characters, ideas, propositions, temperaments* unvereinbar; *technical systems* nicht kompatibel; *drugs, blood groups, colours* nicht miteinander verträglich ◆ **the drugs are ~** die Arzneimittel vertragen sich nicht miteinander; **we are ~, she said** wir passen überhaupt nicht zusammen *or* zueinander, sagte sie; **the possession of great wealth is surely ~ with genuine Marxist beliefs** der Besitz großer Reichtümer läßt sich wohl kaum mit echtem Marxismus vereinbaren.

incompetence [ɪn'kɒmpɪtəns], **incompetency** [ɪn'kɒmpɪtənsɪ] *n* **(a)** Unfähigkeit *f*; (*for job*) Untauglichkeit *f*. **(b)** (*Jur*) Unzuständigkeit, Inkompetenz *f*.

incompetent [ɪn'kɒmpɪtənt] **1** *adj* **(a)** *person* unfähig; (*for sth*) untauglich; *piece of work* unzulänglich ◆ **to be ~ in business** nicht geschäftstüchtig sein; **to be ~ to teach music** unfähig sein, Musik zu unterrichten, zum Musiklehrer untauglich sein.
(b) (*Jur*) unzuständig, nicht zuständig, inkompetent.
2 *n* Nichtskönner *m*, Niete *f* (*inf*).

incompetently [ɪn'kɒmpɪtəntlɪ] *adv* schlecht, stümperhaft.

incomplete [,ɪnkəm'pliːt] *adj collection, series* unvollkommen, unvollständig; (*referring to numbers*) unvollständig, nicht vollzählig; (*not finished also*) *painting, novel* unfertig.

incompletely [,ɪnkəm'pliːtlɪ] *adv see adj*.

incompleteness [,ɪnkəm'pliːtnɪs] *n see adj* Unvollkommenheit *f*; Unvollständigkeit *f*; Unfertigkeit *f*.

incomprehensible [ɪn,kɒmprɪ'hensəbl] *adj* unverständlich; *act also* unbegreiflich, unfaßbar ◆ **people like that are just ~** solche Leute kann ich einfach nicht begreifen.

incomprehensibly [ɪn,kɒmprɪ'hensəblɪ] *adv see adj*.

inconceivability ['ɪnkən,siːvə'bɪlɪtɪ] *n see adj* Unvorstellbarkeit *f*; Unfaßbarkeit, Unbegreiflichkeit *f*.

inconceivable [,ɪnkən'siːvəbl] *adj* unvorstellbar, undenkbar; (*hard to believe also*) unfaßbar, unbegreiflich.

inconceivably [,ɪnkən'siːvəblɪ] *adv see adj*.

inconclusive [,ɪnkən'kluːsɪv] *adj* (*not decisive*) *result* unbestimmt, zu keiner Entscheidung führend; *action, discussion, investigation* ohne (schlüssiges) Ergebnis, ergebnislos; (*not convincing*) *evidence, argument* nicht überzeugend, nicht schlüssig, nicht zwingend.

inconclusively [,ɪnkən'kluːsɪvlɪ] *adv* (*without result*) ergebnislos; *argue* nicht überzeugend, nicht schlüssig, nicht zwingend ◆ **his speech ended rather ~** seine Rede kam zu keinem überzeugenden Schluß.

incongruity [,ɪnkɒŋ'gruːɪtɪ] *n* **(a)** *no pl* (*of remark, sb's presence*) Unpassende(s), Unangebrachtsein *nt*; (*of dress*) Unangemessenheit *f*, Mißverhältnis *nt* (*of sth with sth* zwischen etw *dat* und etw *dat*); (*of juxtaposition, mixture*) Mißklang *m* ◆ **such was the ~ of his remark/his presence** seine Bemerkung war so unangebracht *or* unpassend/er war so fehl am Platz; **the film relies on the ~ of these images** der Film lebt von der inneren Widersprüchlichkeit dieser Bilder; **he commented on the ~ of the Rolls parked in the slums** er bemerkte, wie fehl am Platz sich der im Slum geparkte Rolls Royce ausmachte; **because of the ~ of this Spanish-style villa in a Scottish setting** weil diese Villa im spanischen Stil so gar nicht in die schottische Landschaft paßte/paßt.
(b) (*incongruous thing*) Unstimmigkeit *f*.

incongruous [ɪn'kɒŋgrʊəs] *adj couple, juxtaposition, mixture* wenig zusammenpassend *attr*, *thing to do, remark* unpassend; (*out of place*) fehl am Platz ◆ **he uses these ~ images** er benutzt diese unstimmigen Bilder; **it seems ~ that** ... es scheint abwegig *or* widersinnig, daß ...; **how ~ that he should have been chosen!** eigenartig, daß sie ausgerechnet ihn ausgewählt haben!

inconsequent [ɪn'kɒnsɪkwənt] *adj* unlogisch, nicht folgerichtig; *remark* nicht zur Sache gehörend *attr*, beziehungslos.

inconsequential [ɪn,kɒnsɪ'kwenʃəl] *adj* beziehungslos, irrelevant; (*not logical*) unlogisch, nicht folgerichtig; (*unimportant*) unbedeutend, unwichtig.

inconsequentially [ɪn,kɒnsɪ'kwenʃəlɪ] *adv* unlogisch.

inconsiderable [,ɪnkən'sɪdərəbl] *adj* unbedeutend, unerheblich ◆ **a not ~ amount** ein nicht unbedeutender Betrag.

inconsiderate [,ɪnkən'sɪdərɪt] *adj* rücksichtslos; (*in less critical sense, not thinking*) unaufmerksam.

inconsiderately [,ɪnkən'sɪdərɪtlɪ] *adv see adj*.

inconsistency [,ɪnkən'sɪstənsɪ] *n* **(a)** (*contradictoriness*) Widersprüchlichkeit, Ungereimtheit *f*. **(b)** (*unevenness: of work, in quality etc*) Unbeständigkeit *f*.

inconsistent [,ɪnkən'sɪstənt] *adj* **(a)** (*contradictory*) *action, speech* widersprüchlich, ungereimt ◆ **to be ~ with sth** zu etw im Widerspruch stehen, mit etw nicht übereinstimmen.
(b) (*uneven, irregular*) *work* unbeständig, ungleich; *person* inkonsequent ◆ **but you're ~, sometimes you say** ... aber da sind Sie nicht konsequent, manchmal sagen Sie ...

inconsistently [,ɪnkən'sɪstəntlɪ] *adv* **(a)** *argue* widersprüchlich ◆ **he is behaving ~ with his beliefs** sein Verhalten steht im Widerspruch zu seinen Auffassungen; **he then maintains, ~ with his initial posit, that** ... und dann behauptet er, im Widerspruch zu seiner anfänglichen Behauptung, daß ...
(b) *work, perform* unbeständig, ungleichmäßig.

inconsolable [,ɪnkən'səʊləbl] *adj* untröstlich.

inconspicuous [,ɪnkən'spɪkjʊəs] *adj* unauffällig ◆ **to make oneself ~** so wenig Aufsehen wie möglich erregen, sich klein machen (*inf*); **an ~ little man** ein unscheinbarer kleiner Mann.

inconspicuously [,ɪnkən'spɪkjʊəslɪ] *adv* unauffällig.

inconstancy [ɪn'kɒnstənsɪ] *n see adj* Unbeständigkeit *f*; Wankelmut *m*; Unstetigkeit *f*; Veränderlichkeit *f*.

inconstant [ɪn'kɒnstənt] *adj person* (*in friendship*) unbeständig, wankelmütig; (*in love*) unstet, wankelmütig; (*variable*) *weather, quality* veränderlich, unbeständig.

incontestable [,ɪnkən'testəbl] *adj* unbestreitbar, unanfechtbar ◆ **it is ~ that** ... es ist unbestritten, daß ...

incontestably [,ɪnkən'testəblɪ] *adv see adj*.

incontinence [ɪn'kɒntɪnəns] *n* (*Med*) Inkontinenz *f* (*spec*), Unfähigkeit *f*, Stuhl und/oder Harn zurückzuhalten; (*of desires*) Zügellosigkeit, Hemmungslosigkeit *f*.

incontinent [ɪn'kɒntɪnənt] *adj* (*Med*) unfähig, Stuhl und/oder Harn zurückzuhalten; *desires* zügellos, hemmungslos.

incontrovertible [ɪn,kɒntrə'vɜːtəbl] *adj* unstreitig, unbestreitbar, unwiderlegbar.

inconvenience [,ɪnkən'viːnɪəns] **1** *n* **(a)** Unannehmlichkeit *f* ◆ **there are ~s to living in the country** das Leben auf dem Land bringt Unannehmlichkeiten mit sich; **it was something of an ~ not having a car** es war eine ziemlich lästige *or* leidige Angelegenheit, kein Auto zu haben.
(b) *no pl* Unannehmlichkeit(en *pl*) *f* (*to sb* für jdn) ◆ **she complained about the ~ of having no shops nearby** sie beklagte sich darüber, wie unbequem *or* beschwerlich es sei, keine Geschäfte in der Nähe zu haben; **I don't want to cause you any ~** ich möchte Ihnen keine Umstände bereiten *or* machen; **to put sb to great ~** jdm große Umstände bereiten; **he went to a great deal of ~ to help** er machte sich viele Unannehmlichkeiten, um zu helfen; **at considerable personal ~** trotz beträchtlicher persönlicher Unannehmlichkeiten; **because of the ~ of the time/date** weil die Uhrzeit/der Termin ungelegen war.
2 *vt* Unannehmlichkeiten *or* Umstände bereiten (*+dat*); (*with reference to time*) ungelegen kommen (*+dat*) ◆ **don't ~ yourself** machen Sie keine Umstände.

▼ **inconvenient** [,ɪnkən'viːnɪənt] *adj time* ungelegen, ungünstig; *house, design* unbequem, unpraktisch; *location* ungünstig; *shops* ungünstig *or* ungeschickt gelegen; *journey* beschwerlich, lästig ◆ **3 o'clock is very ~ for me** 3 Uhr kommt mir sehr ungelegen *or* ist sehr ungünstig für mich; **you couldn't have chosen a more ~ time** einen ungünstigeren Zeitpunkt hätten Sie kaum wählen können; **it's very ~ of you to come so early** es kommt mir wirklich sehr ungelegen, daß Sie so früh kommen; **it's very ~ of you to live so far out** es ist wenig rücksichtsvoll von Ihnen, so weit außerhalb zu wohnen.

inconveniently [,ɪnkən'viːnɪəntlɪ] *adv see adj*.

inconvertibility ['ɪnkən,vɜːtɪ'bɪlɪtɪ] *n* (*Fin*) Uneinlösbarkeit, Inkonvertibilität *f*.

inconvertible [,ɪnkən'vɜːtəbl] *adj* uneinlösbar, inkonvertibel.

incorporate [ɪn'kɔːpəreɪt] *vt* **(a)** (*integrate*) aufnehmen, einbauen, integrieren (*into* in *+acc*) ◆ **the chemicals are ~d with** *or* **in the blood** die Chemikalien werden ins Blut aufgenommen; **Hanover was ~d into Prussia in 1886** Hannover wurde 1886 Preußen angegliedert *or* mit Preußen vereinigt.
(b) (*contain*) (in sich *dat*) vereinigen, enthalten ◆ **the tax is ~d in the price** (die) Steuer ist im Preis enthalten; **a new James Bond film incorporating all the ingredients of** ... ein neuer James-Bond-Film, der alle Bestandteile von ... verbindet *or* in sich (*dat*) vereinigt; **all the tribes are now ~d in one state** alle Stämme sind jetzt zu einem Staat zusammengeschlossen.
(c) (*Jur, Comm*) gesellschaftlich organisieren; (*US*) (amtlich) als

➤ LANGUAGE IN USE: **inconvenient → 14**

Aktiengesellschaft eintragen, registrieren ♦ **to ~ a company** eine Gesellschaft gründen; **~d company** (*US*) (handelsgerichtlich) eingetragene Gesellschaft.

incorporation [ɪn,kɔ:pə'reɪʃən] *n see vt* **(a)** Aufnahme, Einfügung, Integration *f* (*into, in* in *+acc*). **(b)** Verbindung, Vereinigung *f*. **(c)** (*Jur, Comm*) Gründung, Errichtung *f*.

incorporeal [,ɪnkɔ:'pɔ:rɪəl] *adj* nicht körperlich, körperlos.

incorrect [,ɪnkə'rekt] *adj* **(a)** (*wrong*) falsch; *wording, calculation also* fehlerhaft; *statement, assessment also* unzutreffend, unrichtig, unwahr; *opinion also* irrig; *text* ungenau, fehlerhaft ♦ **you are ~** Sie irren sich, Sie haben unrecht; **that is ~** das stimmt nicht, das ist nicht richtig *or* wahr; **you are ~ in thinking that ...** Sie haben unrecht, wenn Sie denken, daß ...
(b) (*improper*) *behaviour* inkorrekt, nicht einwandfrei; *dress* inkorrekt, falsch ♦ **it is ~ to ...** es ist nicht korrekt, zu ...

incorrectly [,ɪnkə'rektlɪ] *adv see adj* ♦ **I had ~ assumed that ...** ich hatte fälschlich(erweise) angenommen, daß ...

incorrigible [ɪn'kɒrɪdʒəbl] *adj* unverbesserlich.

incorruptible [,ɪnkə'rʌptəbl] *adj* **(a)** *person* charakterstark; (*not bribable*) unbestechlich ♦ **she's ~** man kann sie nicht verderben. **(b)** *material, substance* unzerstörbar.

increase [ɪn'kri:s] **[1]** *vi* zunehmen; (*taxes*) erhöht werden; (*pain also*) stärker werden; (*amount, number, noise, population also*) anwachsen; (*possessions, trade, riches also*) sich vermehren, (an)wachsen; (*pride also, strength, friendship*) wachsen; (*price, sales, demand*) steigen; (*supply, joy, rage*) sich vergrößern, größer werden; (*business firm, institution, town*) sich vergrößern, wachsen; (*rain, wind*) stärker werden ♦ **to ~ in volume/weight** umfangreicher/schwerer werden, an Umfang/Gewicht zunehmen; **to ~ in width/size/number** sich erweitern/vergrößern/vermehren, weiter/größer/mehr werden; **to ~ in height** höher werden.
[2] *vt* vergrößern; *rage, sorrow, joy, possessions, riches also* vermehren; *darkness, noise, love, resentment also, effort* verstärken; *trade, sales, business firm also* erweitern; *numbers, taxes, price, speed, demand* erhöhen ♦ **he ~d his efforts** er strengte sich mehr an, er machte größere Anstrengungen; **then to ~ our difficulties** was die Dinge noch schwieriger machte, was unsere Schwierigkeiten noch vergrößerte; **~d demand** erhöhte *or* verstärkte Nachfrage; **~d standard of living** höherer Lebensstandard; **~d efficiency** Leistungssteigerung *f*; **we ~d output to ...** wir erhöhten den Ausstoß auf ...
[3] *n* Zunahme, Erhöhung, Steigerung *f*; (*in size*) Vergrößerung, Erweiterung *f*; (*in number*) Vermehrung *f*, Zuwachs *m*, Zunahme *f*; (*in speed*) Erhöhung, Steigerung *f* (*in gen*); (*of business*) Erweiterung, Vergrößerung *f*; (*in sales*) Aufschwung *m*; (*in expenses*) Vermehrung, Steigerung *f* (*in gen*); (*of effort etc*) Vermehrung, Steigerung, Verstärkung *f*; (*of demand*) Verstärkung *f*, Steigen *nt*; (*of work*) Mehr *nt* (*of* an *+dat*), Zunahme *f*; (*of violence*) Zunahme *f*, Anwachsen *nt*; (*of salary*) Gehaltserhöhung *or* -aufbesserung *f*; (*of noise*) Zunahme, Verstärkung *f* ♦ **an ~ in the population of 10% per year** eine jährliche Bevölkerungszunahme *or* ein jährlicher Bevölkerungszuwachs von 10%; **to get an ~ of £5 per week** £ 5 pro Woche mehr bekommen, eine Lohnerhöhung von £ 5 pro Woche bekommen; **to be on the ~** ständig zunehmen; **~ in value** Wertzuwachs *m*, Wertsteigerung *f*; **rent ~** Mieterhöhung *f*.

increasing [ɪn'kri:sɪŋ] *adj* zunehmend, steigend, (an)wachsend ♦ **an ~ number of people are changing to ...** mehr und mehr Leute steigen auf (*+acc*) ... um.

increasingly [ɪn'kri:sɪŋlɪ] *adv* zunehmend, immer mehr ♦ **he became ~ angry** er wurde immer *or* zunehmend ärgerlicher; **~, people are finding that ...** man findet in zunehmendem Maße, daß ...; **this is ~ the case** dies ist immer häufiger der Fall.

incredible [ɪn'kredəbl] *adj* unglaublich; (*inf: amazing also*) unwahrscheinlich (*inf*) ♦ **this music is ~** diese Musik ist sagenhaft (*inf*); **you're ~** du bist wirklich unschlagbar.

incredibly [ɪn'kredəblɪ] *adv* unglaublich, unwahrscheinlich ♦ **~, he wasn't there** unglaublicherweise war er nicht da.

incredulity [,ɪnkrɪ'dju:lɪtɪ] *n* Ungläubigkeit, Skepsis *f*.

incredulous *adj*, **~ly** *adv* [ɪn'kredjʊləs, -lɪ] ungläubig, skeptisch; *look also* zweifelnd.

increment ['ɪnkrɪmənt] *n* Zuwachs *m*, Steigerung *f*; (*in salary*) Gehaltserhöhung *or* -zulage *f*; (*on scale*) Stufe *f*.

incriminate [ɪn'krɪmɪneɪt] *vt* belasten.

incriminating [ɪn'krɪmɪneɪtɪŋ], **incriminatory** [ɪn'krɪmɪneɪtərɪ] *adj* belastend.

incrimination [ɪn,krɪmɪ'neɪʃən] *n* Belastung *f*.

incrust [ɪn'krʌst] *vt see* **encrust**.

incubate ['ɪnkjʊbeɪt] **[1]** *vt egg* ausbrüten; *bacteria* züchten; *plan, idea* ausbrüten (*inf*), ausreifen lassen.
[2] *vi* (*lit*) ausgebrütet *or* bebrütet werden; (*fig*) (aus)reifen, sich formen.

incubation [,ɪnkjʊ'beɪʃən] *n see vb* Ausbrüten *nt*; Züchten *nt*; Ausreifen *nt* ♦ **~ period** (*Med*) Inkubationszeit *f*.

incubator ['ɪnkjʊbeɪtə^r^] *n* (*for babies*) Brutkasten, Inkubator *m*; (*for chicks*) Brutapparat *m*; (*for bacteria*) Brutschrank *m*.

incubus ['ɪŋkjʊbəs] *n* **(a)** (*demon*) Alp *m*. **(b)** (*burden*) Alptraum *m*, drückende Last.

inculcate ['ɪnkʌlkeɪt] *vt* einimpfen, einprägen (*in sb* jdm).

inculcation [,ɪnkʌl'keɪʃən] *n* Einimpfen *nt*, Einimpfung *f*.

incumbency [ɪn'kʌmbənsɪ] *n* **(a)** (*Eccl*) Pfründe *f*. **(b)** (*form: tenure of office*) Amtszeit *f*. **(c)** (*form: obligation*) Obliegenheit (*form*), Verpflichtung *f*.

incumbent [ɪn'kʌmbənt] (*form*) **[1]** *adj* **(a) to be ~ upon sb** jdm obliegen (*form*), jds Pflicht sein (*to do sth* etw zu tun). **(b) the ~ mayor** der amtshabende *or* amtierende Bürgermeister.
[2] *n* Amtsinhaber *m*; (*Eccl*) Inhaber *m* einer Pfarrstelle.

incunabula [,ɪnkjʊ'næbjʊlə] *npl* Inkunabeln, Wiegendrucke *pl*.

incur [ɪn'kɜ:^r^] *vt* **(a)** *anger, injury, displeasure* sich (*dat*) zuziehen, auf sich (*acc*) ziehen; *risk* eingehen, laufen ♦ **the disadvantages which you will ~** die Nachteile, die Ihnen erwachsen. **(b)** (*Fin*) *loss* erleiden; *debts, expenses* machen ♦ **other expenses ~red** weitere Auslagen *or* Ausgaben *pl*.

incurable [ɪn'kjʊərəbl] **[1]** *adj* (*Med*) unheilbar; (*fig*) unverbesserlich.
[2] *n* (*Med*) unheilbar Kranke(r) *mf*.

incurably [ɪn'kjʊərəblɪ] *adv see adj*.

incurious [ɪn'kjʊərɪəs] *adj* (*not curious*) nicht wißbegierig, nicht neugierig; (*uninterested*) gleichgültig, uninteressiert.

incursion [ɪn'kɜ:ʃən] *n* Einfall *m*, Eindringen *nt* (*into* in *+acc*); (*fig*) Ausflug *m* (*into* in *+acc*); (*of darkness*) Einbruch *m*.

indebted [ɪn'detɪd] *adj* **(a)** (*fig*) verpflichtet ♦ **to be ~ to sb for sth** jdm für etw (zu Dank) verpflichtet sein, für etw in jds Schuld (*dat*) stehen; **he's obviously greatly ~ to Matisse/Steinbeck** er hat offensichtlich Matisse/Steinbeck viel zu verdanken; **thank you very much, I am most ~ to you** vielen Dank, ich stehe zutiefst in Ihrer Schuld (*geh*).
(b) (*Fin*) verschuldet (*to sb* bei jdm).

indebtedness [ɪn'detɪdnɪs] *n* (*fig*) Verpflichtung *f* (*to* gegenüber); (*Fin*) Verschuldung *f* ♦ **we can see his obvious ~ to Matisse** wir können sehen, daß er Matisse viel zu verdanken hat.

indecency [ɪn'di:snsɪ] *n* Unanständigkeit, Anstößigkeit *f* ♦ **act of ~** (*Jur*) unsittliches Verhalten.

indecent [ɪn'di:snt] *adj* unanständig, anstößig; (*Jur*) *act* unsittlich, unzüchtig; *joke* schmutzig, unanständig, zotig ♦ **with ~ haste** mit ungebührlicher Eile *or* Hast; *see* **assault**.

indecently [ɪn'di:sntlɪ] *adv see adj*.

indecipherable [,ɪndɪ'saɪfərəbl] *adj* nicht zu entziffern *pred*, nicht zu entziffernd *attr*; *handwriting* unleserlich.

indecision [,ɪndɪ'sɪʒən] *n* Unentschlossenheit, Unschlüssigkeit *f*.

indecisive [,ɪndɪ'saɪsɪv] *adj* **(a)** *person, manner* unschlüssig, unentschlossen. **(b)** *discussion* ergebnislos; *argument, battle* nicht(s) entscheidend *attr*.

indecisively [,ɪndɪ'saɪsɪvlɪ] *adv see adj*.

indeclinable [,ɪndɪ'klaɪnəbl] *adj* (*Gram*) nicht deklinierbar, unbeugbar, beugungsunfähig.

indecorous *adj*, **~ly** *adv* [ɪn'dekərəs, -lɪ] unschicklich, ungehörig.

indecorum [,ɪndɪ'kɔ:rəm] *n* Unschicklichkeit, Ungehörigkeit *f*.

indeed [ɪn'di:d] *adv* **(a)** (*really, in reality, in fact*) tatsächlich, wirklich, in der Tat ♦ **~ I am tired** ich bin wirklich *or* tatsächlich *or* in der Tat müde; **I feel, ~ I know he is right** ich habe das Gefühl, ja ich weiß (sogar), daß er recht hat; **who else? — ~, who else?** wer anders? — in der Tat *or* ganz recht, wer sonst?
(b) (*confirming*) **isn't that wrong? — ~** ist das nicht falsch? — allerdings; **are you coming? — ~ I am!** kommst du? — aber sicher *or* natürlich; **may I open the window? — you may ~/~ you may not** darf ich das Fenster öffnen? — ja bitte, aber gern doch!/das dürfen Sie nicht; **are you pleased? — yes, ~ or ~, yes!** bist du zufrieden? — oh ja, das kann man wohl sagen!; **is that Charles? — ~** ist das Charles? — ganz recht.
(c) (*as intensifier*) wirklich ♦ **very ... ~** wirklich sehr ...; **thank you very much ~** vielen herzlichen Dank.
(d) (*showing interest, irony, surprise*) wirklich, tatsächlich ♦ **did you/is it ~?** nein wirklich?, tatsächlich?; **his wife, ~!** seine Frau ..., daß ich nicht lache!; **who is she ~!** na, wer wohl *or* schon!; **what ~!** was wohl!; **~?** ach so?, ach wirklich?
(e) (*admittedly*) zwar ♦ **there are ~ mistakes in it, but ...** es sind zwar Fehler darin, aber ...
(f) (*expressing possibility*) **if ~ ...** falls ... wirklich; **if ~ he were wrong** falls er wirklich unrecht haben sollte; **I may ~ come** es kann gut sein, daß ich komme.

indefatigable *adj*, **-bly** *adv* [,ɪndɪ'fætɪgəbl, -ɪ] unermüdlich, rastlos.

indefensible [,ɪndɪ'fensəbl] *adj* **(a)** *behaviour, remark etc* unentschuldbar, nicht zu rechtfertigend *attr or* rechtfertigen *pred*. **(b)** *town etc* nicht zu verteidigend *attr or* verteidigen *pred*, unhaltbar. **(c)** *cause, theory* unhaltbar, unvertretbar.

indefinable [,ɪndɪ'faɪnəbl] *adj word, colour, charm* unbestimmbar, undefinierbar; *feeling, impression* unbestimmt ♦ **she has a certain ~ something** sie hat das gewisse Etwas.

indefinite [ɪn'defɪnɪt] *adj* **(a)** *number, length*, (*Gram*) unbestimmt ♦ **~ leave** unbeschränkter *or* unbegrenzter Urlaub, Urlaub *m* auf unbestimmte Zeit.
(b) (*vague*) unklar, undeutlich. **he was very ~ about it** er war sehr unbestimmt *or* vage in dieser Sache.

indefinitely [ɪn'defɪnɪtlɪ] *adv* **(a)** *wait etc* unbegrenzt (lange), unendlich lange, endlos; *postpone* auf unbestimmte Zeit ♦ **we can't go on like this ~** wir können nicht endlos *or* immer so weitermachen. **(b)** (*vaguely*) unklar, undeutlich.

indelible [ɪn'deləbl] *adj stain* nicht zu entfernen; *ink also* wasserunlöslich; (*fig*) *impression* unauslöschlich ♦ **~ ink** Wäschetinte *f*; **~pencil** Kopierstift, Tintenstift *m*.

indelibly [ɪn'delɪblɪ] *adv* (*fig*) unauslöschlich.

indelicacy [ɪn'delɪkəsɪ] *n* Taktlosigkeit, Ungehörigkeit *f*; (*of person*) Mangel *m* an Feingefühl, Taktlosigkeit *f*; (*crudity*) Geschmacklosigkeit *f*.

indelicate [ɪn'delɪkət] *adj person* taktlos; *act, remark also* ungehörig; (*crude*) geschmacklos.

indelicately [ɪn'delɪkətlɪ] *adv see adj* taktlos; ungehörig; (*crudely*) geschmacklos.

indemnification [ɪn,demnɪfɪ'keɪʃən] *n* **(a)** (*compensation*) Schadensersatz *m*, Entschädigung *f* (*for* für); (*sum received*) Schadensersatz(summe *f*) *m*, Entschädigung(ssumme) *f*; (*for expenses*) Erstattung *f* (*for gen*). **(b)** (*for against gegen*) (*safeguard*) Absicherung *f*; (*insurance*) Versicherung *f*.

indemnify [ɪn'demnɪfaɪ] *vt* **(a)** (*compensate*) entschädigen, Schadensersatz *m* leisten (*for* für); (*for expenses*) erstatten (*sb for sth* jdm etw). **(b)** (*safeguard*) absichern (*from, against* gegen); (*insure*) versichern (*against, from* gegen).

indemnity [ɪn'demnɪtɪ] *n* **(a)** (*compensation*) (*for damage, loss etc*) Schadensersatz *m*, Entschädigung, Abfindung *f*; (*after war*) Wiedergutmachung *f*. **(b)** (*insurance*) Versicherung(sschutz *m*) *f* ◆ **deed of ~** (*Jur*) ≃ Versicherungspolice *f*.

indent [ɪn'dent] **1** *vt border, edge* einkerben; *coast* zerklüften, einbuchten; (*Typ*) *word, line* einrücken, einziehen; (*leave dent in*) *metal etc* einbeulen.
2 *vi* **to ~ on sb for sth** (*Brit Comm*) etw bei jdm ordern.
3 ['ɪndent] *n* (*in border etc*) Einkerbung, Kerbe *f*; (*in coast*) Einbuchtung *f*; (*Typ: of line*) Einrückung *f*, Einzug *m*; (*dent: in metal etc*) Beule, Delle *f*.

indentation [,ɪnden'teɪʃən] *n* **(a)** *no pl see vt* Einkerben *nt*; Zerklüften *nt*; Einrücken, Einziehen *nt*; Einbeulen *nt*.
(b) (*notch, dent*) (*in border, edge*) Kerbe *f*, Einschnitt *m*; (*in coast*) Einbuchtung *f*; (*Typ*) Einrückung *f*, Einzug *m*; (*in metal etc*) Delle, Vertiefung *f*.

indenture [ɪn'dentʃə^r] **1** *n* **(a) ~s** *pl* (*of apprentice*) Ausbildungs- *or* Lehrvertrag *m*.
(b) (*Jur*) *Vertrag m in zwei oder mehreren Ausführungen mit bestimmter Kanteneinkerbung zur Identifizierung.*
2 *vt apprentice* in die Lehre nehmen ◆ **he was ~d with Hobson's** er ging bei Hobson in die Lehre.

independence [,ɪndɪ'pendəns] *n* Unabhängigkeit *f* (*of* von); (*of person: in attitude, spirit also*) Selbständigkeit *f* ◆ **to achieve ~** die Unabhängigkeit erlangen; **I~ Day** (*US*) der Unabhängigkeitstag.

independent [,ɪndɪ'pendənt] **1** *adj* **(a)** unabhängig (*of* von) (*also Pol*); *person* (*in attitude, spirit also*) selbständig; *school* frei, unabhängig (vom Staat); *income* eigen, privat ◆ **he has a car, so he is ~ of buses** er hat ein Auto und ist nicht auf Busse angewiesen; **she is a very ~ young lady** sie ist eine sehr selbständige junge Dame; **a man of ~ means** eine Person mit Privateinkommen, ein Privatmann *m*.
(b) (*unconnected, unrelated to work of others*) *reports, research, thinker etc* unabhängig ◆ **they reached the summit by ~ routes** sie erreichten den Gipfel auf getrennten *or* gesonderten Wegen; **the two explosions were ~** die beide Explosionen hatten nichts miteinander zu tun *or* keine gemeinsame Ursache; **~ suspension** (*Aut*) Einzel(rad)aufhängung *f*.
(c) ~ clause (*Gram*) übergeordneter Satz, Hauptsatz *m*.
2 *n* (*Pol*) Unabhängige(r) *mf*.

independently [,ɪndɪ'pendəntlɪ] *adv* unabhängig; (*in attitude, spirit also*) selbständig; (*on own initiative also*) von allein(e) ◆ **quite ~ he offered to help** er bot von sich aus seine Hilfe an; **they each came ~ to the same conclusion** sie kamen unabhängig voneinander zur gleichen Schlußfolgerung.

in-depth ['ɪndepθ] *adj* eingehend, gründlich.

indescribable [,ɪndɪ'skraɪbəbl] *adj* unbeschreiblich; (*inf: terrible*) fürchterlich, schrecklich, unglaublich ◆ **a certain ~ something** ein unbeschreibliches Etwas.

indescribably [,ɪndɪ'skraɪbəblɪ] *adv see adj.*

indestructibility ['ɪndɪ,strʌktə'bɪlɪtɪ] *n* Unzerstörbarkeit *f*.

indestructible *adj*, **-bly** *adv* [,ɪndɪ'strʌktəbl, -ɪ] unzerstörbar.

indeterminable [,ɪndɪ'tɜːmɪnəbl] *adj* unbestimmbar, nicht zu bestimmend *attr or* bestimmen *pred*.

indeterminate [,ɪndɪ'tɜːmɪnɪt] *adj amount, length* unbestimmt; *duration also* ungewiß; *meaning, concept* unklar, vage ◆ **of ~ sex** von unbestimmbarem *or* nicht bestimmbarem Geschlecht.

indeterminately [,ɪndɪ'tɜːmɪnɪtlɪ] *adv see adj* ◆ **it continued ~** es ging auf unbestimmte Zeit weiter.

indetermination ['ɪndɪ,tɜːmɪ'neɪʃən] *n* (*indecisiveness*) Entschlußlosigkeit, Unschlüssigkeit, Unentschiedenheit *f*.

index ['ɪndeks] **1** *n* **(a)** *pl* **-es** (*in book*) Register *nt*, Index *m*; (*of sources*) Quellenverzeichnis *nt*; (*in library*) (*of topics*) (Schlagwort)katalog *m*; (*of authors*) (Verfasser)katalog *m*; (*card ~*) Kartei *f* ◆ **I~** (*Eccl*) Index *m*.
(b) *pl* **indices** (*pointer*) (*Typ*) Hinweiszeichen, Handzeichen *nt*; (*on scale*) (An)zeiger *m*, Zunge *f* ◆ **this is a good ~ to** *or* **of his character** das zeigt deutlich seinen Charakter, das läßt deutlich auf seinen Charakter schließen; **to provide a useful ~ to** *or* **of the true state of affairs** nützlichen Aufschluß über den wahren Stand der Dinge geben.
(c) *pl* **-es** *or* **indices** (*number showing ratio*) Index *m*, Meßzahl, Indexziffer *f* ◆ **cost-of-living ~** Lebenshaltungskosten-Index *m*.
(d) *pl* **indices** (*Math*) Index *m*; (*exponent*) Wurzelexponent *m*.
2 *vt* mit einem Register *or* Index versehen; *word* in das Register *or* in den Index aufnehmen ◆ **the book is well ~ed** das Buch hat ein gutes Register *or* einen guten Index.

index card *n* Karteikarte *f*.

indexed ['ɪndekst] *adj* (*Econ*) dynamisch.

index: ~ finger *n* Zeigefinger *m*; **~-linked** *adj rate, salaries* der Inflationsrate (*dat*) angeglichen; *pensions* dynamisch.

India ['ɪndɪə] *n* Indien *nt* ◆ **~ ink** (*US*) Tusche *f*; **~man** Indienfahrer *m*.

Indian ['ɪndɪən] **1** *adj* **(a)** indisch. **(b)** (*American ~*) indianisch, Indianer- ◆ **~ Ocean** Indischer Ozean.
2 *n* **(a)** Inder(in *f*) *m*. **(b)** (*American ~*) Indianer(in *f*) *m*.

Indian: ~ club *n* Keule *f*; **~ corn** *n* Mais *m*; **~ file** *n* Gänsemarsch *m*; **in ~ file** im Gänsemarsch; **~ giver** *n* (*US inf*) *jd, der etwas Geschenktes zurückfordert*; **~ ink** *n* Tusche *f*; **~ summer** *n* Altweibersommer, Spät- *or* Nachsommer *m*; (*fig*) zweiter Frühling; **~ wrestling** *n* Armdrücken *nt*.

India: ~ paper *n* Dünndruckpapier *nt*; **~ rubber** **1** *n* Gummi, Kautschuk *m*; (*eraser*) Radiergummi *m*; **2** *attr* Gummi-.

indicate ['ɪndɪkeɪt] **1** *vt* **(a)** (*point out, mark*) zeigen, bezeichnen, deuten auf (*+acc*) ◆ **large towns are ~d in red** Großstädte sind rot eingezeichnet *or* gekennzeichnet.
(b) (*person: gesture, express*) andeuten, zeigen, zu verstehen geben ◆ **to ~ one's feelings** seine Gefühle zeigen *or* zum Ausdruck bringen; **~ your intention to turn right** zeigen Sie Ihre Absicht an, nach rechts abzubiegen.
(c) (*be a sign of, suggest*) erkennen lassen, schließen lassen auf (*+acc*), (hin)deuten auf (*+acc*) ◆ **what does it ~ to you?** was erkennen Sie daraus, welche Schlüsse ziehen Sie daraus?
(d) (*register and display*) *temperature, speed* (an)zeigen.
(e) (*Med*) *treatment* indizieren; *illness* Anzeichen sein für, anzeigen.
2 *vi* (*Aut*) (Richtungswechsel) anzeigen (*form*), blinken, den Blinker setzen ◆ **to ~ right** rechts blinken, Richtungswechsel nach rechts anzeigen (*form*).

▼ **indication** [,ɪndɪ'keɪʃən] *n* **(a)** (*sign*) (An)zeichen *nt* (*also Med*) (*of* für), Hinweis *m* (*of* auf *+acc*) ◆ **there is every/no ~ that he is right** alles/nichts weist darauf hin *or* läßt darauf schließen, daß er recht hat; **he gave a clear ~ of his intentions** er zeigte seine Absichten deutlich, er ließ seine Absichten deutlich erkennen; **what are the ~s that it will happen?** was deutet darauf hin *or* spricht dafür *or* welchen Hinweis gibt es dafür, daß es geschieht?; **we had no ~ that ...** es gab kein Anzeichen dafür, daß ...; **that is some ~ of what we can expect** das gibt uns einen Vorgeschmack auf das, was wir zu erwarten haben; **if you could give me a rough ~ of ...** wenn Sie mir eine ungefähre Vorstellung davon geben könnten ...
(b) (*showing, marking*) (*by gesturing, facial expression*) Anzeigen, Erkennenlassen *nt*; (*by pointing, drawing*) Anzeigen, Bezeichnen *nt* ◆ **~ of the boundaries on this map is very poor** die Grenzen sind auf dieser Karte sehr undeutlich bezeichnet.
(c) (*on gauge*) Anzeige *f* ◆ **what is the pressure ~?** wie ist die Druck- *or* Manometeranzeige?

indicative [ɪn'dɪkətɪv] **1** *adj* **(a)** bezeichnend (*of* für) ◆ **to be ~ of sth** auf etw (*acc*) schließen lassen, auf etw (*acc*) hindeuten; *of sb's character* für etw bezeichnend sein.
(b) (*Gram*) indikativisch ◆ **~ mood** Indikativ *m*, Wirklichkeitsform *f*.
2 *n* (*Gram*) Indikativ *m*, Wirklichkeitsform *f* ◆ **in the ~** im Indikativ, in der Wirklichkeitsform.

indicator ['ɪndɪkeɪtə^r] *n* (*instrument, gauge*) Anzeiger *m*; (*needle*) Zeiger *m*; (*Aut*) Richtungsanzeiger *m* (*form*); (*flashing*) Blinker *m*; (*Chem*) Indikator *m*; (*fig: of economic position etc*) Meßlatte *f* ◆ **altitude/pressure ~** Höhen-/Druckmesser *m*; **(arrival/departure) ~ board** (*Rail, Aviat*) Ankunfts-/Abfahrts(anzeige)tafel *f*.

indices ['ɪndɪsiːz] *pl of* **index**.

indict [ɪn'daɪt] *vt* (*charge*) anklagen, beschuldigen (*on a charge of sth* einer Sache *gen*), unter Anklage stellen; (*US Jur*) Anklage erheben gegen (*for* wegen *+gen*) ◆ **to ~ sb as a murderer** jdn unter Mordanklage stellen, jdn des Mordes anklagen.

indictable [ɪn'daɪtəbl] *adj person* strafrechtlich verfolgbar; *offence* strafbar.

indictment [ɪn'daɪtmənt] *n* (*of person*) (*accusation*) Beschuldigung, Anschuldigung *f*; (*charge sheet*) Anklage *f* (*for, on a charge of* wegen); (*US: by grand jury*) Anklageerhebung *f* ◆ **to bring an ~ against sb** gegen jdn Anklage erheben, jdn unter Anklage stellen; **to draw up a bill of ~** eine Anklageschrift verfassen; **to be an ~ of sth** (*fig*) ein Armutszeugnis *nt* für etw sein.

indifference [ɪn'dɪfrəns] *n see adj* **(a)** Gleichgültigkeit, Indifferenz (*geh*) *f* (*to, towards* gegenüber) ◆ **it's a matter of complete ~ to me** das ist mir völlig egal *or* gleichgültig. **(b)** Mittelmäßigkeit, Durchschnittlichkeit *f*.

indifferent [ɪn'dɪfrənt] *adj* **(a)** (*lacking interest*) gleichgültig, indifferent (*geh*) (*to, towards* gegenüber) ◆ **he is quite ~ about it/to her** es/sie ist ihm ziemlich gleichgültig; **~ to her despair** ungerührt von ihrer Verzweiflung. **(b)** (*mediocre*) mittelmäßig, durchschnittlich.

indifferently [ɪn'dɪfrəntlɪ] *adv* **(a)** *see adj (a)*. **(b)** (*mediocrely*) (mittel)mäßig (gut), nicht besonders (gut).

indigence ['ɪndɪdʒəns] *n* Bedürftigkeit, Armut *f*.

indigenous [ɪn'dɪdʒɪnəs] *adj* einheimisch (*to* in *+dat*); *customs* landeseigen; *language* Landes- ◆ **plants ~ to Canada** in Kanada heimische *or* beheimatete Pflanzen; **~ tribes** einheimische *or* eingeborene Volksstämme.

indigent ['ɪndɪdʒənt] *adj* bedürftig, arm, ärmlich.

indigestible [,ɪndɪ'dʒestəbl] *adj* (*Med*) unverdaulich; (*fig*) schwer verdaulich, schwer zu ertragend *attr or* ertragen *pred*.

indigestion [,ɪndɪ'dʒestʃən] *n* Magenverstimmung *f*.

indignant [ɪn'dɪgnənt] *adj* entrüstet, empört (*at, about, with* über *+acc*), unwillig (*at, about* wegen) ◆ **to be ~ with sb** über jdn empört sein; **to make sb ~** jds Unwillen *or* Entrüstung erregen; **it's no good getting ~** es hat keinen Zweck, sich zu entrüsten *or* sich aufzuregen.

indignantly [ɪn'dɪgnəntlɪ] *adv see adj.*

indignation [,ɪndɪg'neɪʃən] *n* Entrüstung *f* (*at, about, with* über *+acc*), Unwillen *m* (*at, about* wegen).

indignity [ɪn'dɪgnɪtɪ] *n* Demütigung, Schmach (*liter*) *f* ◆ **oh, the ~ of it!** also,

➤ LANGUAGE IN USE: **indication: a → 26.3**

das ist doch der Gipfel!

indigo ['ɪndɪgəʊ] **1** *n* Indigo *nt or m.*
2 *adj* indigofarben ♦ ~ **blue** indigoblau.

indirect [ˌɪndɪ'rekt] *adj* **(a)** indirekt; *consequence, result etc also* mittelbar ♦ **by ~ means** auf Umwegen; **by an ~ route/path/ road** auf Umwegen *or* einem Umweg; **to make an ~ reference to sb/sth** auf jdn/etw anspielen *or* indirekt Bezug nehmen.
(b) *(Gram)* indirekt ♦ ~ **object** Dativobjekt *nt;* ~ **speech** *or (US)* **discourse** indirekte Rede.

indirectly [ˌɪndɪ'rektlɪ] *adv see adj (a).*

indirectness [ˌɪndɪ'rektnɪs] *n* Indirektheit *f.*

indiscernible [ˌɪndɪ'sɜːnəbl] *adj* nicht erkennbar *or* sichtbar; *improvement, change etc also* unmerklich; *noise* nicht wahrnehmbar ♦ **to be almost ~** kaum zu erkennen sein; *(noise)* kaum wahrzunehmen sein.

indiscernibly [ˌɪndɪ'sɜːnɪblɪ] *adv see adj.*

indiscipline [ɪn'dɪsɪplɪn] *n* Mangel *m* an Disziplin, Undiszipliniertheit, Disziplinlosigkeit *f.*

indiscreet [ˌɪndɪ'skriːt] *adj* indiskret; *(tactless)* taktlos, ohne Feingefühl ♦ **he is too ~ ever to be a successful diplomat** wegen seiner Neigung zu Indiskretionen wird er nie ein erfolgreicher Diplomat werden.

indiscreetly [ˌɪndɪ'skriːtlɪ] *adv see adj.*

indiscreetness [ˌɪndɪ'skriːtnɪs] *n see* **indiscretion.**

indiscretion [ˌɪndɪ'skreʃən] *n see adj* Indiskretion *f;* Taktlosigkeit *f*, Mangel *m* an Feingefühl; *(affair)* Abenteuer *nt*, Affäre *f* ♦ **his youthful ~s** seine jugendliche Unvernunft, sein jugendlicher Leichtsinn.

indiscriminate [ˌɪndɪ'skrɪmɪnɪt] *adj* wahllos; *spending also* unüberlegt; *reading also* kritiklos, unkritisch; *mixture also* kunterbunt; *choice* willkürlich; *reader, shopper* kritiklos, unkritisch; *tastes* unausgeprägt ♦ **you shouldn't be so ~ in the friends you make** du solltest dir deine Freunde etwas sorgfältiger aussuchen; **he was completely ~ in whom he punished** er verteilte seine Strafen völlig wahllos *or* willkürlich.

indiscriminately [ˌɪndɪ'skrɪmɪnɪtlɪ] *adv see adj.*

indiscriminating [ˌɪndɪ'skrɪmɪneɪtɪŋ] *adj* unkritisch, kritiklos.

indispensability ['ɪndɪˌspensɪ'bɪlɪtɪ] *n* Unentbehrlichkeit *f*, unbedingte Notwendigkeit *(to* für).

indispensable [ˌɪndɪ'spensəbl] *adj* unentbehrlich, unbedingt notwendig *or* erforderlich *(to* für) ♦ ~ **to life** lebensnotwendig; **to make oneself ~ to sb** sich für jdn unentbehrlich machen.

indispensably [ˌɪndɪ'spensəblɪ] *adv* **it is ~ necessary to them** es ist unbedingt notwendig *or* erforderlich für sie; **that is necessarily and ~ a part of our system** das ist notwendiger und unverzichtbarer Bestandteil unseres Systems.

indisposed [ˌɪndɪ'spəʊzd] *adj* **(a)** *(unwell)* unwohl, indisponiert *(geh)*, unpäßlich *(geh)*. **(b)** *(disinclined)* **to be ~ to do sth** nicht gewillt *or* geneigt sein, etw zu tun.

indisposition [ˌɪndɪspə'zɪʃən] *n see adj* **(a)** Unwohlsein *nt*, Indisposition *(geh)*, Unpäßlichkeit *(geh) f.* **(b)** Unwilligkeit *f* ♦ ~ **to work** Arbeitsunwilligkeit *f*, Mangel *m* an Arbeitswilligkeit.

indisputability ['ɪndɪˌspjuːtə'bɪlɪtɪ] *n* Unbestreitbarkeit, Unstrittigkeit *f.*

indisputable [ˌɪndɪ'spjuːtəbl] *adj* unbestreitbar, unstrittig, nicht zu bestreitend *attr or* bestreiten *pred; evidence* unanfechtbar.

▼ **indisputably** [ˌɪndɪ'spjuːtəblɪ] *adv* unstrittig, unbestreitbar.

indissolubility ['ɪndɪˌsɒljʊ'bɪlɪtɪ] *n (Chem)* Unlöslichkeit, Unlösbarkeit *f; (fig)* Unauflöslichkeit, Unauflösbarkeit *f.*

indissoluble *adj*, **-bly** *adv* [ˌɪndɪ'sɒljʊbl, -ɪ] *(Chem)* unlöslich, unlösbar; *(fig)* unauflöslich, unauflösbar, unlöslich.

indistinct [ˌɪndɪ'stɪŋkt] *adj object, shape, words* verschwommen, unklar, undeutlich; *noise* schwach, unklar; *memory* undeutlich; *voice* undeutlich, unklar.

indistinctly [ˌɪndɪ'stɪŋktlɪ] *adv* nicht deutlich, verschwommen; *speak* undeutlich; *remember* schwach, dunkel.

indistinguishable [ˌɪndɪ'stɪŋgwɪʃəbl] *adj* **(a)** nicht unterscheidbar, nicht zu unterscheidend *attr or* unterscheiden *pred (from* von) ♦ **the twins are ~ (one from the other)** man kann die Zwillinge nicht (voneinander) unterscheiden.
(b) *(indiscernible)* nicht erkennbar *or* sichtbar; *improvement, change, difference etc also* unmerklich; *noise* nicht wahrnehmbar.

individual [ˌɪndɪ'vɪdjʊəl] **1** *adj* **(a)** *(separate)* einzeln ♦ ~ **cases** Einzelfälle *pl;* **to give ~ help** jedem einzeln helfen, Einzelhilfe leisten; ~ **tastes differ** jeder hat einen eigenen *or* individuellen Geschmack, die Geschmäcker sind verschieden.
(b) *(own)* eigen; *(for one person) portion etc* einzeln, Einzel- ♦ **our own ~ plates** unsere eigenen Teller; ~ **portions cost 55p** eine Einzelportion kostet 55 Pence.
(c) *(distinctive, characteristic)* eigen, individuell.
2 *n* Individuum *nt*, Einzelne(r) *mf*, Einzelperson *f; (inf)* Individuum *nt*, Mensch *m*, Person *f* ♦ **the freedom of the ~** die Freiheit des einzelnen, die individuelle Freiheit; *see* **private.**

individualism [ˌɪndɪ'vɪdjʊəlɪzəm] *n* Individualismus *m.*

individualist [ˌɪndɪ'vɪdjʊəlɪst] *n* Individualist(in *f*) *m.*

individuality ['ɪndɪˌvɪdjʊ'ælɪtɪ] *n* Individualität *f*, (eigene) Persönlichkeit.

individualize [ˌɪndɪ'vɪdjʊəlaɪz] *vt* individualisieren; *(treat separately)* einzeln behandeln; *(give individuality to) book, author's style, performance* eine persönliche *or* individuelle *or* eigene Note verleihen (+*dat*).

individually [ˌɪndɪ'vɪdjʊəlɪ] *adv* individuell; *(separately)* einzeln ♦ ~ **styled suit** Modellanzug *m.*

indivisible *adj*, **-bly** *adv* [ˌɪndɪ'vɪzəbl, -ɪ] unteilbar *(also Math)*, untrennbar.

Indo- ['ɪndəʊ-] *pref* Indo- ♦ **~-China** *n* Indochina *nt.*

indoctrinate [ɪn'dɒktrɪneɪt] *vt* indoktrinieren.

indoctrination [ɪnˌdɒktrɪ'neɪʃən] *n* Indoktrination *f.*

Indo: **~-European** **1** *adj* indogermanisch, indoeuropäisch; **2** *n* **(a)** Indogermane *m*, Indogermanin *f*, Indoeuropäer(in *f*) *m;* **(b)** *(language)* Indogermanisch, Indoeuropäisch *nt;* **~-Germanic** *(old) adj, n see* **~-European 1, 2 (b).**

indolence ['ɪndələns] *n* Trägheit, Indolenz *(rare) f.*

indolent *adj*, **-ly** *adv* ['ɪndələnt, -lɪ] träge, indolent *(rare).*

indomitable [ɪn'dɒmɪtəbl] *adj person, courage* unbezähmbar, unbezwingbar; *will* unbeugsam, eisern, unerschütterlich ♦ **his ~ pride** sein nicht zu brechender Stolz.

Indonesia [ˌɪndəʊ'niːzɪə] *n* Indonesien *nt.*

Indonesian [ˌɪndəʊ'niːzɪən] **1** *adj* indonesisch.
2 *n* **(a)** Indonesier(in *f*) *m.* **(b)** *(language)* Indonesisch *nt.*

indoor ['ɪndɔːʳ] *adj aerial* Zimmer-, Innen-; *plant* Zimmer-, Haus-; *clothes* Haus-; *photography* Innen-; *sport* Hallen-; *swimming pool* Hallen-; *(private)* überdacht ♦ ~ **work** Arbeit, die nicht im Freien ausgeführt wird; ~ **games** Spiele *pl* fürs Haus, Haus- *or* Zimmerspiele *pl; (Sport)* Hallenspiele *pl.*

indoors [ɪn'dɔːz] *adv* drin(nen) *(inf)*, innen; *(at home)* zu Hause ♦ **what's the house like ~?** wie sieht das Haus innen aus?; **to stay ~** im Haus bleiben, drin bleiben *(inf);* **go and play ~** geh im Haus *or* drinnen spielen; **to go ~** ins Haus gehen, nach drinnen gehen; ~ **and outdoors** im und außer Haus, drinnen und draußen, im Haus und im Freien.

indubitable [ɪn'djuːbɪtəbl] *adj* zweifellos, unzweifelhaft.

indubitably [ɪn'djuːbɪtəblɪ] *adv* zweifellos, zweifelsohne.

induce [ɪn'djuːs] *vt* **(a)** *(persuade)* dazu bewegen *or* bringen *or* veranlassen.
(b) *reaction, hypnosis* herbeiführen, bewirken, hervorrufen; *sleep* herbeiführen; *illness* verursachen, führen zu; *labour, birth* einleiten ♦ **this drug ~s sleep** dieses Mittel hat eine einschläfernde Wirkung; **she had to be ~d** die Geburt mußte eingeleitet werden; **(artificially) ~d sleep** künstlicher Schlaf.
(c) *(Philos)* induktiv *or* durch Induktion erarbeiten.
(d) *(Elec) current, magnetic effect* induzieren.

inducement [ɪn'djuːsmənt] *n* **(a)** *(no pl: persuasion)* Überredung *f; (motive, incentive)* Anreiz *m*, Ansporn *m no pl* ♦ **he can't work without ~s** er kann nicht arbeiten, ohne daß man ihn dazu anspornt; **cash ~s** finanzielle Anreize *pl.* **(b)** *see* **induction (b).**

induct [ɪn'dʌkt] *vt* **(a)** *bishop, president etc* in sein Amt einsetzen *or* einführen.
(b) *(US Mil)* einziehen, einberufen.

inductee [ɪndʌk'tiː] *n (US Mil)* (zum Wehrdienst) Eingezogene(r) *or* Einberufene(r) *m.*

induction [ɪn'dʌkʃən] *n* **(a)** *(of bishop, president etc)* Amtseinführung *f; (US Mil)* Einberufung, Einziehung *f* ♦ ~ **course** Einführungskurs *m.* **(b)** *(of sleep, reaction etc)* Herbeiführen *nt; (of labour, birth)* Einleitung *f.* **(c)** *(Philos, Math, Elec)* Induktion *f* ♦ ~ **coil** *(Elec)* Induktionsspule *f;* ~ **loop** Induktionsschleife *f.*

inductive *adj*, **-ly** *adv* [ɪn'dʌktɪv, -lɪ] *(all senses)* induktiv.

indulge [ɪn'dʌldʒ] **1** *vt* **(a)** *appetite, desires etc* nachgeben (+*dat*); *person also* nachsichtig sein mit; *(over~) children* verwöhnen, verhätscheln; *one's imagination* frönen (+*dat*) ♦ **to ~ oneself in sth** sich *(dat)* etw gönnen, in etw schwelgen.
(b) *debtor* Zahlungsaufschub gewähren (+*dat*).
2 *vi* **to ~ in sth** sich *(dat)* etw gönnen *or* genehmigen *(inf); (in vice, drink, daydreams)* einer Sache *(dat)* frönen, sich einer Sache *(dat)* hingeben; **to ~ in sth to excess** etw bis zum Exzeß treiben; **dessert came, but I didn't ~** *(inf)* der Nachtisch kam, aber ich konnte mich beherrschen; **will you ~?** *(inf) (offering drink etc)* genehmigen Sie sich auch einen/eine *etc? (inf);* **I don't ~** ich trinke/rauche *etc* nicht.

indulgence [ɪn'dʌldʒəns] *n* **(a)** Nachsicht *f; (of appetite etc)* Nachgiebigkeit *f (of* gegenüber); *(over~)* Verwöhnung, Verhätschelung *f* ♦ **the ~ of his wishes** das Erfüllen seiner Wünsche; **too much ~ of your children's wishes is bad for their character** wenn man den Wünschen seiner Kinder zu oft nachgibt, ist das schlecht für ihre charakterliche Entwicklung.
(b) *(in activity, drink etc)* ~ **in drink** übermäßiges Trinken; **he regards ~ in any unconventional sexual activity with horror** jede Art von unkonventioneller sexueller Betätigung ist ihm ein Graus; **excessive ~ in vice led to the collapse of the Roman Empire** die Lasterhaftigkeit der Römer führte zum Untergang ihres Reiches; **too much ~ in sport is bad for your studies** übermäßiges Sporttreiben wirkt sich schlecht auf das Lernen aus.
(c) *(thing indulged in)* Luxus *m; (food, drink, pleasure)* Genuß *m* ♦ **such are his little ~s** das sind die kleinen Genüsse, die er sich *(dat)* gönnt.
(d) *(form: permission)* Einwilligung, Zustimmung *f.*
(e) *(Eccl)* Ablaß *m.*

indulgent [ɪn'dʌldʒənt] *adj (to* gegenüber) nachsichtig; *mother etc also* nachgiebig; *(to one's own desires etc)* zu nachgiebig.

indulgently [ɪn'dʌldʒəntlɪ] *adv see adj.*

industrial [ɪn'dʌstrɪəl] **1** *adj production, designer, diamond, worker, equipment, state, archeology* Industrie-; *production also, expansion* industriell; *research, training, medicine, experience, accident* Betriebs-; *medicine, psychology* Arbeits- ♦ ~ **action** Arbeitskampfmaßnahmen *pl;* **to take ~ action** in den Ausstand treten; ~ **democracy** Demokratie *f* im Betrieb; ~ **dispute** Auseinandersetzungen *pl* zwischen Arbeitgebern und Arbeitnehmern; *(about*

➤ LANGUAGE IN USE: **indisputably** → 26.3

pay also) Tarifkonflikt *m*; (*strike*) Streik *m*; **~ estate** (*Brit*) Industriegebiet *nt*; **~ fabric** Industriefasern *pl*; **~ growth** Industriewachstum *nt*; **~ injury** Arbeitsunfall *m*; **~ insurance** Unfallversicherung *f*; **~ park** (*US*) Industriegelände *nt*; **~ relations** Beziehungen *pl* zwischen Arbeitgebern und Gewerkschaften; **I~ Revolution** Industrielle Revolution; **~ robot** Industrieroboter *m*; **~ tribunal** Arbeitsgericht *nt*; **~ trouble** *or* **unrest** Arbeitsunruhen *pl*; **~ waste** Industrieabfälle *pl*, Industriemüll *m*.
[2] *npl* **~s** (*St Ex*) Industrieaktien *pl*.

industrialism [ɪn'dʌstrɪəlɪzəm] *n* Industrie *f*.

industrialist [ɪn'dʌstrɪəlɪst] *n* Industrielle(r) *mf*.

industrialization [ɪn,dʌstrɪəlaɪ'zeɪʃən] *n* Industrialisierung *f*.

industrialize [ɪn'dʌstrɪəlaɪz] *vti* industrialisieren.

industrious *adj*, **~ly** *adv* [ɪn'dʌstrɪəs, -lɪ] arbeitsam, fleißig.

industriousness [ɪn'dʌstrɪəsnɪs] *n* Arbeitsamkeit *f*, Fleiß *m*.

industry ['ɪndəstrɪ] *n* **(a)** (*trade, branch of* ~) Industrie *f* ♦ **heavy/light ~** Schwer-/Leichtindustrie *f*; **hotel ~** Hotelgewerbe *nt*; **tourist ~** Touristik, Tourismusbranche *or* -industrie *f*; **in certain industries** in einigen Branchen. **(b)** (*industriousness*) Fleiß *m*.

inebriate [ɪ'ni:brɪɪt] [1] *n* (*form*) Trinker(in *f*) *m*.
[2] *adj see* **inebriated (a)**.
[3] [ɪ'ni:brɪeɪt] *vt* (*lit*) betrunken machen; (*fig*) trunken machen; (*success, popularity etc*) berauschen.

inebriated [ɪ'ni:brɪeɪtɪd] *adj* **(a)** (*form*) betrunken, unter Alkoholeinfluß (*form*). **(b)** (*fig*) berauscht, trunken (*liter*).

inebriation [ɪ,ni:brɪ'eɪʃən],

inebriety [,ɪni:'braɪətɪ] *n* (*form*) betrunkener Zustand.

inedible [ɪn'edɪbl] *adj* nicht eßbar; (*unpleasant*) *meal etc* ungenießbar.

ineducable [ɪn'edjʊkəbl] *adj* bildungsunfähig.

ineffable *adj*, **-bly** *adv* [ɪn'efəbl, -ɪ] (*liter*) unsäglich (*liter*), unsagbar, unaussprechlich.

ineffective [,ɪnɪ'fektɪv] *adj* unwirksam, ineffektiv; *attempt also* fruchtlos, nutzlos; *person* unfähig, untauglich.

ineffectively [,ɪnɪ'fektɪvlɪ] *adv see adj*.

ineffectiveness [,ɪnɪ'fektɪvnɪs] *n see adj* Unwirksamkeit, Ineffektivität *f*; Fruchtlosigkeit, Nutzlosigkeit *f*; Unfähigkeit, Untauglichkeit *f*.

ineffectual [,ɪnɪ'fektjʊəl] *adj* ineffektiv.

inefficacious [,ɪnefɪ'keɪʃəs] *adj* unwirksam, wirkungslos, ohne Wirkung; *policy* erfolglos, fruchtlos.

inefficacy [ɪn'efɪkəsɪ] *n see* **inefficacious** Unwirksamkeit, Wirkungslosigkeit *f*; Erfolglosigkeit, Fruchtlosigkeit *f*.

inefficiency [,ɪnɪ'fɪʃənsɪ] *n see* **inefficient** Unfähigkeit, Ineffizienz (*geh*) *f*; Inkompetenz *f*; Leistungsunfähigkeit *f*; Unproduktivität *f*.

inefficient [,ɪnɪ'fɪʃənt] *adj person* unfähig, ineffizient (*geh*); *worker, secretary also* inkompetent; *machine, engine, factory, company* leistungsunfähig; *method, organization* unrationell, unproduktiv, ineffizient (*geh*) ♦ **to be ~ at doing sth** etw schlecht machen; **the ~ working of a mechanism** das schlechte Funktionieren eines Mechanismus.

inefficiently [,ɪnɪ'fɪʃəntlɪ] *adv* schlecht ♦ **he works very ~** er ist ineffizient *or* inkompetent.

inelastic [,ɪnɪ'læstɪk] *adj* (*lit*) unelastisch; (*fig*) starr, nicht flexibel.

inelasticity [,ɪnılæs'tɪsɪtɪ] *n* (*lit*) Mangel *m* an Elastizität; (*fig*) Mangel *m* an Flexibilität, Starrheit *f*.

inelegance [ɪn'elɪgəns] *n see adj* Uneleganz *f*; Mangel *m* an Schick *or* Eleganz; Schwerfälligkeit, Unausgewogenheit *f*; Ungeschliffenheit, Plumpheit *f*; Derbheit, Unschönheit *f*.

inelegant [ɪn'elɪgənt] *adj* unelegant; *clothes also* ohne Schick *or* Eleganz; *person also* ohne Eleganz; *style also* schwerfällig, unausgewogen; *prose, phrase also* ungeschliffen, plump, schwerfällig; *dialect* derb, unschön, schwerfällig.

inelegantly [ɪn'elɪgəntlɪ] *adv see adj* ♦ **she walks very ~** ihr Gang ist ohne Eleganz, sie hat einen wenig eleganten Gang.

ineligibility [ɪn,elɪdʒə'bɪlɪtɪ] *n see adj* Nichtberechtigtsein *nt*; Unwählbarkeit *f*; mangelnde Eignung, Untauglichkeit *f*.

ineligible [ɪn'elɪdʒəbl] *adj* (*for benefits, grant*) nicht berechtigt (*for* zu Leistungen *+gen*); (*for election*) nicht wählbar; (*for job, office, as husband*) ungeeignet, untauglich ♦ **~ for military service** wehruntauglich; **you are ~ for social security benefits** Sie sind nicht zu Leistungen der Sozialversicherung berechtigt; **to be ~ for a pension** nicht pensionsberechtigt sein.

ineloquent [ɪn'eləkwənt] *adj* nicht wortgewandt.

ineluctable [,ɪnɪ'lʌktəbl] *adj* (*liter*) unausweichlich, unabwendbar (*liter*).

inept [ɪ'nept] *adj behaviour* ungeschickt, linkisch, unbeholfen; *remark* unpassend, unangebracht, ungeschickt; *compliment, refusal, attempt* plump; *comparison* ungeeignet, unpassend; *person* (*clumsy*) ungeschickt, ungelehrig, unbeholfen; (*slow at learning*) begriffsstutzig, unverständig.

ineptitude [ɪ'neptɪtju:d], **ineptness** [ɪ'neptnɪs] *n see adj* Ungeschicktheit, Unbeholfenheit *f*; Unangebrachtheit *f*; Plumpheit *f*; Ungeeignetheit *f*; Ungeschick *nt*, Ungelehrigkeit *f*; Begriffsstutzigkeit *f* ♦ **full of stylistic ~s** voller Stilbrüche.

inequality [,ɪnɪ'kwɒlɪtɪ] *n* (*lack of equality*) Ungleichheit *f*; (*instance of* ~) Unterschied *m* ♦ **great inequalities in wealth** große Unterschiede *pl* in der Verteilung von Reichtum; **~ of opportunity** Chancenungleichheit *f*; **~ of opportunity in education** Ungleichheit *f* der Bildungschancen.

inequitable [ɪn'ekwɪtəbl] *adj* ungerecht.

inequity [ɪn'ekwɪtɪ] *n* Ungerechtigkeit *f*.

ineradicable [,ɪnɪ'rædɪkəbl] *adj mistake, failing* unabänderlich, unwiderruflich; *feeling of guilt, hatred* tiefsitzend, unauslöschlich; *disease, prejudice* unausrottbar.

inert [ɪ'nɜ:t] *adj* unbeweglich; (*Phys*) *matter* träge; (*Chem*) *substance* inaktiv ♦ **~ gas** Edelgas *nt*.

inertia [ɪ'nɜ:ʃə] *n* (*lit, fig*) Trägheit *f* ♦ **~-reel seat belt** Automatikgurt *m*.

inescapable [,ɪnɪs'keɪpəbl] *adj* unvermeidlich; *consequence also* unausweichlich; *conclusion also* zwangsläufig.

inescapably [,ɪnɪs'keɪpəblɪ] *adv see adj*.

inessential [,ɪnɪ'senʃəl] [1] *adj* unwesentlich, unerheblich, unwichtig.
[2] *n* Unwesentliche(s) *nt no pl*, Nebensächlichkeit *f*.

inestimable [ɪn'estɪməbl] *adj* unschätzbar.

inevitability [ɪn,evɪtə'bɪlɪtɪ] *n* Unvermeidlichkeit *f*.

▼ **inevitable** [ɪn'evɪtəbl] *adj* unvermeidlich, unvermeidbar; *result also* zwangsläufig ♦ **victory/defeat seemed ~** der Sieg/die Niederlage schien unabwendbar; **a tourist with his ~ camera** ein Tourist mit dem unvermeidlichen Fotoapparat.

inevitably [ɪn'evɪtəblɪ] *adv* **if it's ~ the case that ...** wenn es notgedrungenerweise *or* zwangsläufig so sein muß, daß ...; **~ rising prices** zwangsläufig steigende Preise; **~, he got drunk/was late** es konnte ja nicht ausbleiben, daß er sich betrank/zu spät kam; **as ~ happens on these occasions** wie es bei solchen Anlässen immer ist.

inexact *adj*, **~ly** *adv* [,ɪnɪg'zækt, -lɪ] ungenau.

inexactitude [,ɪnɪg,zæktɪtju:d] *n* Ungenauigkeit *f*.

inexcusable *adj*, **-bly** *adv* [,ɪnɪks'kju:zəbl, -ɪ] unverzeihlich, unverzeihbar, unentschuldbar.

inexhaustible [,ɪnɪg'zɔ:stəbl] *adj* unerschöpflich; *source, spring also* nie versiegend; *curiosity* unstillbar, unendlich; *person, talker* unermüdlich.

inexorable [ɪn'eksərəbl] *adj* (*relentless*) erbarmungslos, unerbittlich; (*not to be stopped*) unaufhaltsam; *truth, facts* unumstößlich.

inexorably [ɪn'eksərəblɪ] *adv see adj*.

inexpediency [,ɪnɪk'spi:dɪənsɪ] *n see adj* Ungeeignetheit, Unzweckmäßigkeit *f*; Unratsamkeit, Unklugheit *f*.

inexpedient [,ɪnɪk'spi:dɪənt] *adj plan, measures, action, decision* ungeeignet, unzweckmäßig; *policy* unratsam, unklug ♦ **that was rather ~ of you** das war ziemlich unklug von Ihnen.

inexpensive [,ɪnɪk'spensɪv] *adj* billig, preisgünstig.

inexpensively [,ɪnɪk'spensɪvlɪ] *adv* billig; *live also* ohne große Kosten.

inexperience [,ɪnɪk'spɪərɪəns] *n* Unerfahrenheit *f*, Mangel *m* an Erfahrung ♦ **his ~ with our techniques** seine mangelnde Vertrautheit mit unseren Methoden.

inexperienced [,ɪnɪk'spɪərɪənst] *adj* unerfahren; *woodworker, skier etc* ungeübt, nicht so versiert ♦ **to be ~ in doing sth** wenig Erfahrung mit etw haben, in etw (*dat*) wenig geübt sein.

inexpert [ɪn'ekspɜ:t] *adj* unfachmännisch, laienhaft; *treatment also* unsachgemäß; (*untrained*) ungeübt ♦ **to be ~ in doing sth** ungeübt darin sein, etw zu tun.

inexpertly [ɪn'ekspɜ:tlɪ] *adv see adj*.

inexpertness [ɪn'ekspɜ:tnɪs] *n see adj* Laienhaftigkeit *f*; Unsachgemäßheit *f*; Ungeübtheit *f*.

inexplicability [,ɪnɪksplɪkə'bɪlɪtɪ] *n* Unerklärlichkeit, Unerklärbarkeit *f*.

inexplicable [,ɪnɪk'splɪkəbl] *adj* unerklärlich, unerklärbar.

inexplicably [,ɪnɪk'splɪkəblɪ] *adv* (*+adj*) unerklärlich; (*+vb*) unerklärlicherweise.

inexplicit [ɪnɪk'splɪsɪt] *adj* unklar, ungenau.

inexpressible [,ɪnɪk'spresəbl] *adj thoughts, feelings* unbeschreiblich, unbeschreibbar; *pain, joy also* unsagbar.

inexpressive [,ɪnɪk'spresɪv] *adj face* ausdruckslos; *word* blaß, nichtssagend; *style* blaß, ohne Ausdruckskraft.

inextinguishable [,ɪnɪk'stɪŋgwɪʃəbl] *adj fire* unlöschbar; *love, hope* unerschütterlich, beständig; *passion* unbezwinglich.

inextricable [,ɪnɪk'strɪkəbl] *adj tangle* unentwirrbar; *confusion* unüberschaubar; *difficulties* verwickelt, unlösbar.

inextricably [,ɪnɪk'strɪkəblɪ] *adv entangled* unentwirrbar; *linked* untrennbar ♦ **he has become ~ involved with her** er kommt nicht mehr von ihr los.

infallibility [ɪn,fælə'bɪlɪtɪ] *n* Unfehlbarkeit *f* (*also Eccl*).

infallible [ɪn'fæləbl] *adj* unfehlbar (*also Eccl*).

infallibly [ɪn'fæləblɪ] *adv* unfehlbar; *work* fehlerfrei.

infamous ['ɪnfəməs] *adj* (*notorious*) berüchtigt, verrufen; (*shameful*) *person* niederträchtig, gemein, ruchlos (*old, liter*); *deed, conduct* niederträchtig, infam, schändlich (*geh*).

infamy ['ɪnfəmɪ] *n* **(a)** *see adj* Verrufenheit *f*; Niedertracht, Gemeinheit *f*; Infamie, Schändlichkeit (*geh*) *f*. **(b)** (*public disgrace*) Schande *f*.

infancy ['ɪnfənsɪ] *n* frühe Kindheit, Kindesalter *nt*; (*Jur*) Minderjährigkeit *f*; (*fig*) Anfangsstadium *nt* ♦ **data processing is no longer in its ~** die Datenverarbeitung steckt nicht mehr in den Kinderschuhen *or* ist den Kinderschuhen entwachsen.

infant ['ɪnfənt] *n* (*baby*) Säugling *m*; (*young child*) Kleinkind *nt*; (*Jur*) Minderjährige(r) *mf* ♦ **~ class** (*Brit*) *erste und zweite Grundschulklasse*; **~ mortality** Säuglingssterblichkeit *f*; **~ school** (*Brit*) *Grundschule f für die ersten beiden Jahrgänge*; **she teaches ~s** sie unterrichtet Grundschulkinder.

infanta [ɪn'fæntə] *n* Infantin *f*.

infante [ɪn'fæntɪ] *n* Infant *m*.

infanticide [ɪn'fæntɪsaɪd] *n* Kindesmord *m*, Kindestötung *f*; (*person*) Kindesmörder(in *f*) *m*.

infantile ['ɪnfəntaɪl] *adj* **(a)** (*childish*) kindisch, infantil. **(b)** (*Med*) Kinder- ♦ **~**

➤ LANGUAGE IN USE: **inevitable** → 15.1

paralysis (*dated*) Kinderlähmung *f*.
infantry ['ɪnfəntrɪ] *n* (*Mil*) Infanterie, Fußtruppe (*Hist*) *f*.
infantryman ['ɪnfəntrɪmən] *n*, *pl* **-men** [-mən] Infanterist, Fußsoldat (*Hist*) *m*.
infarction [ɪn'fɑːkʃən] *n* Infarkt *m*.
infatuated [ɪn'fætjʊeɪtɪd] *adj* vernarrt, verknallt (*inf*) (*with* in +*acc*) ◆ **to become ~ with sb** sich in jdn vernarren; **he's ~ with his own importance** er hält sich für den Nabel der Welt.
infatuation [ɪn,fætjʊ'eɪʃən] *n* (**a**) (*state*) Vernarrtheit *f* (*with* in +*acc*). (**b**) (*object of ~*) Angebetete(r) *mf* ◆ **tidiness has become an ~ with her** Ordnung ist bei ihr zur Leidenschaft geworden.
infect [ɪn'fekt] *vt* (**a**) *wound* infizieren; (*lit*) *person also* anstecken; *water* verseuchen, verunreinigen; *meat* verderben ◆ **to be ~ed with** *or* **by an illness** sich mit einer Krankheit infiziert *or* angesteckt haben; **his wound became ~ed** seine Wunde entzündete sich; **her cold ~ed all her friends** sie steckte alle ihre Freunde mit ihrer Erkältung an.
(**b**) (*fig*) (*with enthusiasm etc*) anstecken.
infection [ɪn'fekʃən] *n* (**a**) (*illness*) Infektion, Entzündung *f*. (**b**) (*act of infecting*) Infektion *f*; (*of person also*) Ansteckung *f*; (*of water*) Verseuchung, Verunreinigung *f*.
infectious [ɪn'fekʃəs] *adj* (**a**) (*Med*) *disease* ansteckend, infektiös ◆ **are you still ~?** besteht bei dir noch Ansteckungsgefahr? (**b**) (*fig*) *enthusiasm, laugh* ansteckend; *idea* zündend.
infectiousness [ɪn'fekʃəsnɪs] *n* (**a**) (*Med*) **the ~ of this disease** die Ansteckungs- *or* Infektionsgefahr bei dieser Krankheit.
(**b**) (*fig*) **the ~ of these views** das Ansteckende an diesen Anschauungen; **the ~ of his laughter/enthusiasm** sein ansteckendes Lachen/seine mitreißende Begeisterung.
infelicitous [,ɪnfɪ'lɪsɪtəs] *adj* unglücklich; *remark etc* unangebracht, unpassend.
infelicity [,ɪnfɪ'lɪsɪtɪ] *n* (*form*) **the ~ of the expression** der unglücklich *or* ungeschickt gewählte Ausdruck; **several infelicities of style** einige sehr ungeschickte Stilfehler.
infer [ɪn'fɜːʳ] *vt* (**a**) schließen, folgern (*from* aus) ◆ **nothing can be ~red from this** daraus kann man nichts schließen *or* folgern. (**b**) (*imply*) andeuten, zu verstehen geben.
inferable [ɪn'fɜːrəbl] *adj* ableitbar, zu folgern *pred*, zu schließen *pred*.
inference ['ɪnfərəns] *n* Schluß(folgerung *f*) *m* ◆ **he was intelligent enough to realize by ~ from what I said that ...** er war intelligent genug, um aus dem, was ich sagte, den Schluß zu ziehen, daß ...; **by ~ he said that ...** implizit sagte er, daß ...
inferential [,ɪnfə'renʃəl] *adj* schlußfolgernd; *proof* Indizien-.
inferior [ɪn'fɪərɪəʳ] [1] *adj* (**a**) (*in quality*) minderwertig; *quality also* minder, geringer; *person* unterlegen; (*in rank*) untergeordnet, niedriger; *court* untergeordnet ◆ **an ~ workman** ein weniger guter Handwerker; **to be ~ to sth** (*in quality*) von minderer *or* geringerer Qualität sein als etw, gegen etw abfallen *or* nicht ankommen; **to be ~ to sb** jdm unterlegen sein; (*in rank*) jdm untergeordnet *or* nachgestellt sein; **he feels ~** er kommt sich (*dat*) unterlegen *or* minderwertig vor.
(**b**) (*Typ*) **~ letter** tiefstehender Buchstabe.
(**c**) (*Biol*) *order, species* niedriger.
[2] *n* **one's ~s** (*in social standing*) Leute *or* Personen *pl* aus einer niedrigeren Schicht; (*in rank*) seine Untergebenen *pl*.
inferiority [ɪn,fɪərɪ'ɒrɪtɪ] *n* (*in quality*) Minderwertigkeit *f*; (*of person*) Unterlegenheit *f* (*to* gegenüber); (*in rank*) untergeordnete Stellung, niedrigere Stellung, niedrigerer Rang (*to* als) ◆ **~ complex** Minderwertigkeitskomplex *m*.
infernal [ɪn'fɜːnl] *adj* (*lit*) Höllen-; (*fig*) *cruelty, scheme* teuflisch; *weather* gräßlich; (*inf*) *impudence, nuisance* verteufelt; *noise* höllisch.
infernally [ɪn'fɜːnəlɪ] *adv* (*inf*) teuflisch, verdammt (*inf*).
inferno [ɪn'fɜːnəʊ] *n* (*hell*) Hölle *f*, Inferno *nt*; (*blazing house etc*) Flammenmeer *nt* ◆ **a blazing ~** ein flammendes Inferno; **it's like an ~ in here** (*fig*) hier ist es wie in einem Brutofen.
infertile [ɪn'fɜːtaɪl] *adj soil, womb* unfruchtbar; *mind* unergiebig, ideenlos.
infertility [,ɪnfɜː'tɪlɪtɪ] *n see adj* Unfruchtbarkeit *f*; Unergiebigkeit, Ideenlosigkeit *f*.
infest [ɪn'fest] *vt* (*rats, lice*) herfallen über (+*acc*); (*plague also*) befallen; (*fig: unwanted people*) heimsuchen, verseuchen ◆ **to be ~ed with disease/rats** verseucht/mit Ratten verseucht sein; **to be ~ed** (*with lice etc*) mit Ungeziefer verseucht sein.
infestation [,ɪnfes'teɪʃən] *n* Verseuchung *f* ◆ **an ~ of rats** eine Rattenplage.
infidel ['ɪnfɪdəl] *n* (*Hist, Rel*) Ungläubige(r) *mf*.
infidelity [,ɪnfɪ'delɪtɪ] *n* Untreue *f*.
in-fighting ['ɪnfaɪtɪŋ] *n* (*Boxing*) Nahkampf *m*; (*fig*) interner Machtkampf.
infill ['ɪnfɪl] *n* (*Build*) Füllmaterial *nt*, Ausfüllung *f*.
infiltrate ['ɪnfɪltreɪt] [1] *vt* (**a**) *troops* infiltrieren; *enemy lines also* eindringen in (+*acc*); (*Pol*) *organization also* unterwandern; *spies, informer* einschleusen.
(**b**) (*liquid*) einsickern in (+*acc*), durchsickern in (+*acc*), durchdringen ◆ **to ~ a liquid into a substance** eine Flüssigkeit in eine Substanz einsickern *or* eindringen lassen.
[2] *vi* (**a**) (*Mil*) eindringen (*into* in +*acc*); (*spy, informer also*) sich einschleusen (*into* in +*acc*), unterwandern (*into acc*); (*fig: ideas*) infiltrieren, eindringen (*into* in +*acc*).
(**b**) (*liquid*) **to ~ into a substance** in eine Substanz eindringen *or* einsickern; **to ~ through sth** durch etw durchsickern.
infiltration [,ɪnfɪl'treɪʃən] *n* (**a**) (*Mil*) Infiltration *f*; (*Pol also*) Unterwanderung *f* ◆ **the ~ of spies** das Einschleusen von Spionen; **by ~ of the enemy's lines** durch Eindringen in die feindlichen Linien, durch Infiltration der feindlichen Linien.
(**b**) (*of liquid*) Eindringen, Durchsickern, Einsickern *nt*.
infiltrator ['ɪnfɪl,treɪtəʳ] *n* (*Mil*) Eindringling *m*; (*Pol*) Unterwanderer *m* ◆ **~s** (*Mil*) Sickertruppe *f*.
infinite ['ɪnfɪnɪt] [1] *adj* (*lit*) unendlich; (*fig also*) *care, trouble, joy, pleasure* grenzenlos; *knowledge* grenzenlos, unendlich groß ◆ **an ~ amount of time/money/space** unendlich viel Zeit/Geld/unbegrenzt *or* unbeschränkt viel Platz.
[2] *n*: **the ~** (*space*) das Unendliche; (*God*) der Unendliche.
infinitely ['ɪnfɪnɪtlɪ] *adv* unendlich; (*fig also*) grenzenlos; *improved* ungeheuer; *better, worse* unendlich viel.
infinitesimal [,ɪnfɪnɪ'tesɪməl] *adj* unendlich klein, winzig; (*Math*) infinitesimal, unendlich klein ◆ **~ calculus** Infinitesimalrechnung *f*.
infinitesimally [,ɪnfɪnɪ'tesɪməlɪ] *adv smaller, better, different* nur ganz geringfügig; *small* zum Verschwinden.
infinitive [ɪn'fɪnɪtɪv] (*Gram*) [1] *adj* Infinitiv-, infinitivisch.
[2] *n* Infinitiv *m*, Grundform *f* ◆ **in the ~** im Infinitiv.
infinitude [ɪn'fɪnɪtjuːd] *n* (*infinite number*) unbegrenztes Maß (*of* an +*dat*); (*of facts, possibilities etc*) unendliches Maß (*of* an +*dat*); (*of space*) unendliche Weite (*of gen*).
infinity [ɪn'fɪnɪtɪ] *n* (*lit*) Unendlichkeit *f*; (*fig also*) Grenzenlosigkeit *f*; (*Math*) das Unendliche ◆ **to ~** (bis) ins Unendliche; **in ~** in der Unendlichkeit/im Unendlichen; **to focus on ~** (*Phot*) (auf) Unendlich einstellen; **I have an ~ of things to do** ich habe unendlich viel zu tun; **composed of an ~ of parts** aus unendlich vielen Teilen *or* einer Unzahl von Teilen zusammengesetzt.
infirm [ɪn'fɜːm] *adj* gebrechlich, schwach ◆ **~ of purpose** (*liter*) willensschwach, wenig zielstrebig.
infirmary [ɪn'fɜːmərɪ] *n* (*hospital*) Krankenhaus *nt*; (*in school etc*) Krankenzimmer *nt or* -stube *f*; (*in prison, barracks*) (Kranken)revier *nt*, Krankenstation *f*.
infirmity [ɪn'fɜːmɪtɪ] *n* Gebrechlichkeit *f* ◆ **the infirmities of old age** die Altersgebrechen *pl*; **his ~ of purpose** (*liter*) seine Willensschwäche, sein Mangel *m* an Zielstrebigkeit.
infix [1] [ɪn'fɪks] *vt idea* einprägen; (*Ling*) einfügen ◆ **the idea is ~ed in his mind** diese Idee hat sich bei ihm festgesetzt.
[2] ['ɪnfɪks] *n* (*Ling*) Infix *nt*, Einfügung *f*.
infixation [,ɪnfɪk'seɪʃən] *n* (*of idea*) Einprägen, Festsetzen *nt*; (*Ling*) Einfügung *f*.
in flagrante delicto [,ɪnflə'græntɪdɪ'lɪktəʊ] *adv* in flagranti.
inflame [ɪn'fleɪm] *vt* (**a**) (*Med*) entzünden ◆ **her eyes were ~d with crying** ihre Augen waren vom Weinen gerötet; **to become ~d** (*wound, eyes etc*) sich entzünden.
(**b**) *person* erzürnen, aufbringen; *feelings* entflammen, entfachen; *anger* erregen, entfachen ◆ **his speech ~d the people** seine Rede brachte die Menge in Harnisch *or* auf; **they were ~d by the news** die Nachricht brachte sie in Harnisch *or* auf; **~d with rage** wutentbrannt; **~d with passion he ...** von glühender Leidenschaft erfaßt, ... er ...; **he was ~d with rage/desire** *etc* er glühte vor Zorn/Begierde *etc*.
inflammable [ɪn'flæməbl] [1] *adj* (*lit*) feuergefährlich, (leicht) entzündbar, inflammabel (*form*); (*fig*) *temperament* explosiv, leicht reizbar; *situation* brisant, gereizt ◆ **"highly ~"** „Vorsicht Feuergefahr", „feuergefährlich".
[2] *n* feuergefährlicher *or* leicht brennbarer Stoff.
inflammation [,ɪnflə'meɪʃən] *n* (**a**) (*Med*) Entzündung *f*. (**b**) (*fig: of passion, anger etc*) Aufstacheln *nt*, Aufstachelung *f*.
inflammatory [ɪn'flæmətərɪ] *adj speech, pamphlet* aufrührerisch, aufwieglerisch, Hetz-.
inflatable [ɪn'fleɪtɪbl] [1] *adj* aufblasbar; *dinghy* Schlauch-.
[2] *n* (*boat*) Gummiboot *nt*.
inflate [ɪn'fleɪt] [1] *vt* (**a**) aufpumpen; (*by mouth*) aufblasen.
(**b**) (*Econ*) *prices, bill* steigern, hochtreiben ◆ **to ~ the currency** die Inflation anheizen, den Geldumlauf steigern.
(**c**) (*fig*) steigern, erhöhen; *sb's ego etc also* aufblähen ◆ **~d with pride** mit *or* vor Stolz geschwollen.
[2] *vi* sich mit Luft füllen.
inflated [ɪn'fleɪtɪd] *adj prices* überhöht, inflationär; *pride* übersteigert, übertrieben; *style, rhetoric* geschwollen, hochtrabend ◆ **to have an ~ opinion of oneself** ein übertriebenes Selbstbewußtsein haben.
inflation [ɪn'fleɪʃən] *n* (**a**) (*Econ*) Inflation *f* ◆ **to fight ~** die Inflation bekämpfen. (**b**) (*act of inflating*) *see vt* Aufpumpen *nt*; Aufblasen *nt*; Steigern, Hochtreiben *nt*; Steigern, Erhöhen *nt*; Aufblähen *nt*.
inflationary [ɪn'fleɪʃənərɪ] *adj politics, demands* inflationär, inflationistisch (*pej*); *spiral* Inflations-.
inflationism [ɪn'fleɪʃənɪzəm] *n* Inflationspolitik *f*.
inflation-proof [ɪn'fleɪʃən,pruːf] *adj* inflationssicher, inflationsgeschützt.
inflect [ɪn'flekt] [1] *vt* (**a**) (*Gram*) flektieren, beugen. (**b**) *voice* modulieren.
[2] *vi* (*Gram*) flektierbar *or* veränderlich sein, gebeugt werden.
inflected [ɪn'flektɪd] *adj word* flektiert, gebeugt; *language* flektierend.
inflection [ɪn'flekʃən] *n see* **inflexion**.
inflexibility [ɪn,fleksɪ'bɪlɪtɪ] *n* (*lit*) Unbiegsamkeit, Starrheit *f*; (*fig*) Unbeugsamkeit, Sturheit (*pej*) *f*.
inflexible [ɪn'fleksəbl] *adj* (*lit*) *substance, object* unbiegsam, starr; (*fig*) *person, attitude, opinion* unbeugsam, inflexibel, stur (*pej*).

inflexion [ɪn'flekʃən] *n* **(a)** (*Gram: of word, language*) Flexion, Beugung *f*. **(b)** (*of voice*) Tonfall *m*.

inflexional [ɪn'flekʃənl] *adj* (*Gram*) *ending* Flexions-.

inflict [ɪn'flɪkt] *vt punishment, fine* verhängen (*on, upon* gegen), auferlegen (*on or upon sb* jdm); *suffering* zufügen (*on or upon sb* jdm); *wound* zufügen, beibringen (*on or upon sb* jdm) ◆ **to ~ oneself** *or* **one's company on sb** sich jdm aufdrängen; **he always has to ~ all his troubles on us** er muß uns immer mit seinen Problemen behelligen.

infliction [ɪn'flɪkʃən] *n* **(a)** (*act*) *see vt* Verhängung (*on, upon* gegen), Auferlegung *f*; Zufügen *nt*; Beibringen *nt*. **(b)** (*misfortune*) Plage *f*, Kreuz *nt* ◆ **the ~s of the poor** die Leiden *or* Nöte *pl* der Armen.

in-flight ['ɪnflaɪt] *adj entertainment* während des Fluges.

inflorescence [ˌɪnflɔː'resəns] *n* Blütenstand *m*.

inflow ['ɪnfləʊ] *n* **(a)** (*of water, air*) (*action*) Zustrom *m*, Einfließen, Zufließen *nt*; (*quantity*) Zufluß(menge *f*), Einfluß(menge *f*) *m*; (*place*) Zufluß *m* ◆ **~ pipe** Zuflußrohr *nt*.

(b) (*fig*) (*of foreign currency, goods*) Zustrom *m*; (*of people also*) Andrang *m*; (*of ideas etc*) Eindringen *nt*.

influence ['ɪnfluəns] [1] *n* Einfluß *m* (*over* auf *+acc*) ◆ **to have an ~ on sb/sth** (*person*) Einfluß auf jdn/etw haben; (*fact, weather etc also*) Auswirkungen *pl* auf jdn/etw haben; **the weather had a great ~ on the number of voters** das Wetter beeinflußte die Zahl der Wähler stark; **to have a great deal of ~ with sb** großen Einfluß bei jdm haben; **he was a great ~ in ...** er war ein bedeutender Faktor bei ...; **he's been a bad ~ on you** er war ein schlechter Einfluß für Sie; **to bring ~ to bear on sb, to exert an ~ on sb** Einfluß auf jdn ausüben; **you have to have ~ to get a job here** Sie müssen schon einigen Einfluß haben, wenn Sie hier eine Stelle haben wollen; **a man of ~** eine einflußreiche Person; **under the ~ of drink/drugs** unter Alkohol-/Drogeneinfluß, unter Alkohol-/Drogeneinwirkung; **under the ~** (*inf*) betrunken; **the changes were due to American ~** die Veränderungen sind auf amerikanische Einflüsse zurückzuführen; **one of my early ~s was Beckett** einer der Schriftsteller, die mich schon früh beeinflußt haben, war Beckett.

[2] *vt* beeinflussen ◆ **to be easily ~d** leicht beeinflußbar *or* zu beeinflussen sein.

influential [ˌɪnflu'enʃəl] *adj* einflußreich ◆ **these factors were ~ in my decision** diese Faktoren haben meine Entscheidung beeinflußt.

influenza [ˌɪnflu'enzə] *n* Grippe *f*.

influx ['ɪnflʌks] *n* **(a)** (*of capital, shares, foreign goods*) Zufuhr *f*; (*of people*) Zustrom, Andrang *m*; (*of ideas etc*) Zufluß *m*. **(b)** *see* **inflow (a)**.

info ['ɪnfəʊ] *n* (*inf*) *see* **information**.

infomercial ['ɪnfəʊmɜːʃəl] *n als Informationssendung getarntes Werbevideo*, Infomercial *nt*.

▼ **inform** [ɪn'fɔːm] [1] *vt* **(a)** *person* benachrichtigen, informieren (*about* über *+acc*); unterrichten ◆ **to ~ sb of sth** jdn von etw unterrichten, jdn über etw informieren; **I am pleased to ~ you that** ... ich freue mich, Ihnen mitteilen zu können *or* Sie davon in Kenntnis setzen zu können (*form*), daß ...; **to ~ the police** die Polizei verständigen *or* benachrichtigen *or* informieren; **to keep sb/oneself ~ed** jdn/sich auf dem laufenden halten (*of* über *+acc*); **to ~ oneself about sth** sich über etw (*acc*) informieren; **until we are better ~ed** bis wir Näheres wissen *or* besser Bescheid wissen *or* genauer informiert sind; **why was I not ~ed?** warum wurde mir das nicht mitgeteilt?, warum wurde ich nicht (darüber) informiert?; **I should like to be ~ed just as soon as he arrives** unterrichten Sie mich bitte sofort von seiner Ankunft, informieren Sie mich bitte sofort über seine Ankunft.

(b) (*liter: permeate*) durchdringen, erfüllen.

[2] *vi* **to ~ against** *or* **on sb** jdn anzeigen *or* denunzieren (*pej*).

informal [ɪn'fɔːməl] *adj* (*esp Pol: not official*) *meeting, talks* nicht formell, nicht förmlich; *visit* inoffiziell, nicht förmlich; *arrangement* inoffiziell; (*simple, without ceremony*) *meeting, gathering, party* zwanglos, ungezwungen; *manner, tone also* leger; *language, speech* ungezwungen, informell; *restaurant* gemütlich ◆ **the ~ use of "du"** die vertraute Anrede „du"; **"dress ~"** „zwanglose Kleidung"; **he is very ~** er ist sehr leger.

informality [ˌɪnfɔː'mælɪtɪ] *n see adj* nicht formeller *or* förmlicher Charakter; inoffizieller Charakter; Zwanglosigkeit *f*; Ungezwungenheit *f*; informeller Charakter *or* Ton; Gemütlichkeit *f*; legere Art ◆ **the ~ of his behaviour** sein legeres Benehmen.

informally [ɪn'fɔːməlɪ] *adv* (*unofficially*) inoffiziell; (*casually, without ceremony*) zwanglos, ungezwungen.

informant [ɪn'fɔːmənt] *n* Informant, Gewährsmann *m* ◆ **according to my ~ the book is out of print** wie man mir mitteilt *or* berichtet, ist das Buch vergriffen.

informatics [ˌɪnfə'mætɪks] *n sing* Informatik *f*.

information [ˌɪnfə'meɪʃən] *n* **(a)** Auskunft *f*, Informationen *pl* ◆ **a piece of ~** eine Auskunft *or* Information; **for your ~** zu Ihrer Information *or* Kenntnisnahme (*form*); (*indignantly*) damit Sie es wissen; **his ~ on the subject is most extensive** sein Wissen auf diesem Gebiet ist äußerst umfassend; **to give sb ~ about** *or* **on sb/sth** jdm Auskunft *or* Informationen über jdn/etw geben; **to get ~ about** *or* **on sb/sth** sich über jdn/etw informieren, über jdn/etw Erkundigungen einziehen; **to ask for ~ on** *or* **about sb/sth** um Auskunft *or* Informationen über jdn/etw bitten; **"~"** „Auskunft"; **we have no ~ about that** wir wissen darüber nicht Bescheid; **until further ~ is available** bevor wir nichts Näheres wissen; **what ~ do we have on Kowalsky?** welche Informationen besitzen wir über Kowalsky?; **where did you get your ~?** woher haben Sie diese Kenntnisse *or* Informationen?; **detailed ~** Einzelheiten *pl*.

(b) (*Comput*, *~ content*) Information *f*.

informational [ˌɪnfə'meɪʃənl] *adj* informationell ◆ **~ needs** Informationsbedürfnisse *pl*; **~ programme** (*TV*) Informationssendung *f*.

information: ~ bureau *n* Auskunft(sbüro *nt*) *f*, Verkehrsbüro *nt*; **~ content** *n* Informationsgehalt *m*; **~ officer** *n* Auskunftsbeamte(r) *m*; **~ processing** *n* Informationsverarbeitung *f*; **~ retrieval** *n* Informations- *or* Datenabruf *m*; **~ sciences** *npl* Informatik *f*; **~ scientist** *n* Informatiker(in *f*) *m*; **~ storage** *n* Datenspeicherung *f*; **~ superhighway** *n* Datenautobahn *f*; **~ technology** *n* Informationstechnik *f*; **~ theory** *n* Informationstheorie *f*.

informative [ɪn'fɔːmətɪv] *adj* aufschlußreich, informativ (*geh*); *book, lecture also* lehrreich ◆ **he's not very ~ about his plans** er ist nicht sehr mitteilsam, was seine Pläne betrifft.

informed [ɪn'fɔːmd] *adj* (*having information*) *observers* informiert, (gut) unterrichtet; (*educated*) gebildet.

informer [ɪn'fɔːmə^r] *n* Informant, Denunziant (*pej*) *m* ◆ **police ~** Polizeispitzel *m*; **to turn ~** seine Mittäter verraten.

infotainment [ɪnfəʊ'teɪnmənt] *n* (*Brit TV*) Infotainment *nt*.

infra dig ['ɪnfrə'dɪg] *adj* (*inf*) unter meiner/seiner *etc* Würde.

infra-red ['ɪnfrə'red] *adj* infrarot.

infrastructure ['ɪnfrəˌstrʌktʃə^r] *n* Infrastruktur *f*.

infrequency [ɪn'friːkwənsɪ] *n* Seltenheit *f*.

infrequent [ɪn'friːkwənt] *adj* selten ◆ **at ~ intervals** in großen Abständen; **her mistakes are so ~** sie macht so selten Fehler.

infrequently [ɪn'friːkwəntlɪ] *adv see adj*.

infringe [ɪn'frɪndʒ] [1] *vt* verstoßen gegen; *law also* verletzen, übertreten; *copyright also* verletzen.

[2] *vi* **to ~ (up)on sb's rights/privacy** in jds Rechte/Privatsphäre (*acc*) eingreifen, jds Rechte/Privatsphäre verletzen.

infringement [ɪn'frɪndʒmənt] *n* **(a) an ~ (of a rule)** ein Regelverstoß *m*; **~ of the law** Gesetzesverletzung *or* -übertretung *f*; **~ of a patent/copyright** Patentverletzung *f*/Verletzung *f* des Urheberrechts. **(b)** (*of privacy*) Eingriff *m* (*of* in *+acc*).

infuriate [ɪn'fjʊərɪeɪt] *vt* wütend *or* rasend machen, zur Raserei bringen ◆ **to be/get ~d** wütend *or* rasend sein/werden.

infuriating [ɪn'fjʊərɪeɪtɪŋ] *adj* (äußerst) ärgerlich ◆ **an ~ habit** eine Unsitte; **an ~ person** ein Mensch, der einen zur Raserei bringen kann *or* der einen rasend *or* wütend machen kann.

infuriatingly [ɪn'fjʊərɪeɪtɪŋlɪ] *adv* aufreizend ◆ **she's ~ slow** sie ist zum Verzweifeln langsam.

infuse [ɪn'fjuːz] [1] *vt* **(a)** *courage, enthusiasm etc* einflößen, geben (*into sb* jdm) ◆ **~d with new hope** von neuer Hoffnung erfüllt. **(b)** (*Cook*) *tea, herbs* aufbrühen, aufgießen.

[2] *vi* ziehen.

infuser [ɪn'fjuːzə^r] *n* Tee-Ei *nt*.

infusion [ɪn'fjuːʒən] *n* **(a)** (*of hope etc*) Einflößen *nt*. **(b)** (*Cook*) Aufguß *m*; (*tea-like*) Tee *m* ◆ **an ~ of rose-hip tea** Hagebuttentee *m*. **(c)** (*Med*) Infusion *f*.

ingenious [ɪn'dʒiːnɪəs] *adj* genial; *person also* erfinderisch, geschickt, findig; *idea, method also* glänzend, ingeniös (*geh*); *device, instrument also* raffiniert, geschickt.

ingeniously [ɪn'dʒiːnɪəslɪ] *adv* genial, glänzend.

ingeniousness [ɪn'dʒiːnɪəsnɪs] *n see* **ingenuity**.

ingénue [ˌænʒeɪ'njuː] *n* naives Mädchen; (*Theat*) Naive *f*.

ingenuity [ˌɪndʒɪ'njuːɪtɪ] *n* Genialität *f*; (*of person also*) Einfallsreichtum *m*, Findigkeit *f*; (*of idea, method also*) Brillanz *f*; (*of device, instrument also*) Raffiniertheit *f*.

ingenuous [ɪn'dʒenjʊəs] *adj* **(a)** (*candid*) offen, aufrichtig, unbefangen. **(b)** (*naive*) naiv.

ingenuously [ɪn'dʒenjʊəslɪ] *adv see adj*.

ingenuousness [ɪn'dʒenjʊəsnɪs] *n see adj* **(a)** Offenheit, Aufrichtigkeit, Unbefangenheit *f*. **(b)** Naivität *f*.

ingest [ɪn'dʒest] *vt* (*Biol*) zu sich nehmen, aufnehmen.

ingestion [ɪn'dʒestʃən] *n* (*Biol*) Nahrungsaufnahme *f*.

inglenook ['ɪŋgəlnʊk] *n* Kaminecke *f*.

inglorious [ɪn'glɔːrɪəs] *adj* unrühmlich, unehrenhaft; *defeat* schmählich, ruhmlos.

ingoing ['ɪngəʊɪŋ] *adj mail* eingehend, einlaufend ◆ **~ tenant** neuer Mieter, Nachmieter *m*.

ingot ['ɪŋgət] *n* Barren *m* ◆ **steel ~** Stahlblock *m*.

ingrained [ˌɪn'greɪnd] *adj* **(a)** (*fig*) *habit* fest, eingefleischt; *prejudice* tief verwurzelt *or* eingewurzelt; *belief* fest verankert, unerschütterlich ◆ **to be ~** fest verwurzelt sein.

(b) *dirt* tief eingedrungen, tiefsitzend (*attr*) ◆ **the dirt was deeply ~ in the carpet** der Schmutz hatte sich tief im Teppich festgesetzt; **hands ~ with dirt** Hände, bei denen sich der Schmutz in den Poren festgesetzt hat.

ingrate ['ɪngreɪt] *n* undankbarer Mensch, Undankbare(r) *mf* (*old, liter*).

ingratiate [ɪn'greɪʃɪeɪt] *vr* **to ~ oneself with sb** sich bei jdm einschmeicheln.

ingratiating [ɪn'greɪʃɪeɪtɪŋ] *adj person, speech* schmeichlerisch, schöntuerisch; *smile* schmeichlerisch süßlich.

ingratiatingly [ɪn'greɪʃɪeɪtɪŋlɪ] *adv see adj*.

ingratitude [ɪn'grætɪtjuːd] *n* Undank *m* ◆ **sb's ~** jds Undankbarkeit *f*.

ingredient [ɪn'griːdɪənt] *n* Bestandteil *m*, Ingredienz *f* (*spec*); (*for recipe*) Zutat *f* ◆ **all the ~s of success** alles, was man zum Erfolg braucht; **the ~s of a man's character** alles, was den Charakter eines Menschen ausmacht.

➤ LANGUAGE IN USE: **inform: 1a** → 12.3, 24.4

ingress ['ɪngres] *n (form)* Zutritt, Eintritt *m* ◆ **no right of ~** Zutritt verboten; **to have free ~** Recht auf freien Zugang haben.
in-group ['ɪngruːp] *n* maßgebliche Leute *pl*, Spitze *f*; *(Sociol)* In-Group *f*.
ingrowing ['ɪngrəʊɪŋ] *adj (Med) toenail* eingewachsen.
inguinal ['ɪŋgwɪnəl] *adj (Med)* Leisten-, inguinal *(spec)*.
inhabit [ɪn'hæbɪt] *vt* bewohnen; *(animals)* leben in (+*dat*).
inhabitable [ɪn'hæbɪtəbl] *adj* bewohnbar.
inhabitant [ɪn'hæbɪtənt] *n (of house, burrow etc)* Bewohner(in *f*) *m*; *(of island, town also)* Einwohner(in *f*) *m*.
inhalation [ˌɪnhə'leɪʃən] *n (Med)* Inhalation *f*.
inhalator ['ɪnhəleɪtə^r] *n* Inhalationsapparat *m*.
inhale [ɪn'heɪl] **1** *vt* einatmen; *(Med)* inhalieren.
2 *vi (in smoking)* Lungenzüge machen, inhalieren ◆ **do you ~?** rauchen Sie auf Lunge?
inhaler [ɪn'heɪlə^r] *n* Inhalationsapparat *m*.
inharmonious [ˌɪnhɑː'məʊnɪəs] *adj* unharmonisch.
inhere [ɪn'hɪə^r] *vi* **to ~ in sth** einer Sache *(dat)* innewohnen.
inherent [ɪn'hɪərənt] *adj* innewohnend, eigen, inhärent *(esp Philos) (to, in dat)* ◆ **the ~ hardness of diamonds** die den Diamanten eigene Härte; **instincts ~ in all animals** allen Tieren inhärente *or* eigene Instinkte.
inherently [ɪn'hɪərəntlɪ] *adv* von Natur aus.
inherit [ɪn'herɪt] **1** *vt (lit, fig)* erben ◆ **the problems which we ~ed from the last government** die Probleme, die uns die letzte Regierung hinterlassen *or* vererbt hat.
2 *vi* erben ◆ **to ~ from sb** jdn beerben.
inheritable [ɪn'herɪtəbl] *adj (lit, fig)* erblich; *goods, shares* vererbbar.
inheritance [ɪn'herɪtəns] *n* Erbe *nt (also fig)*, Erbschaft *f* ◆ **he got it by ~** er hat es durch eine Erbschaft bekommen.
inherited [ɪn'herɪtɪd] *adj qualities, disease* ererbt.
inhibit [ɪn'hɪbɪt] *vt* hemmen *(also Psych, Sci)* ◆ **to ~ sb from doing sth** jdn daran hindern, etw zu tun; **don't let me ~ you** haben Sie meinetwegen keine Hemmungen; **don't let my presence ~ the discussion** lassen Sie sich durch meine Anwesenheit in Ihrer Diskussion nicht stören.
inhibited [ɪn'hɪbɪtɪd] *adj* gehemmt ◆ **to be ~** Hemmungen haben, gehemmt sein.
inhibition [ˌɪnhɪ'bɪʃən] *n* Hemmung *f (also Psych, Sci)* ◆ **a feeling of ~** Hemmungen *pl*; **he has no ~s about speaking French** er hat keine Hemmungen, Französisch zu sprechen.
inhibitory [ɪn'hɪbɪtərɪ] *adj (Psych)* hemmend; *(Physiol also)* behindernd.
inhospitable [ˌɪnhɒ'spɪtəbl] *adj* ungastlich; *climate, region* unwirtlich.
inhospitably [ˌɪnhɒ'spɪtəblɪ] *adv* ungastlich.
inhospitality ['ɪnˌhɒspɪ'tælɪtɪ] *n* Ungastlichkeit *f*, mangelnde Gastfreundschaft; *(of climate)* Unwirtlichkeit *f*.
in-house ['ɪnhaʊs] **1** *adj jobs, work* im Hause zu erledigend *attr or* zu erledigen *pred*; *project* intern.
2 [ɪn'haʊs] *adv* im Hause; intern.
inhuman [ɪn'hjuːmən] *adj (lit) monster, shape* nicht menschlich; *(fig)* unmenschlich.
inhumane [ˌɪnhjuː'meɪn] *adj* inhuman; *(to people also)* menschenunwürdig.
inhumaneness [ˌɪnhjuː'meɪnnɪs] *n see adj* Inhumanität *f*; Menschenunwürdigkeit *f*.
inhumanity [ˌɪnhjuː'mænɪtɪ] *n* Unmenschlichkeit *f* ◆ **the ~ of man to man** die Unmenschlichkeit der Menschen untereinander.
inhumation [ˌɪnhjuː'meɪʃən] *n (form)* Beisetzung *f (form)*.
inhume [ɪn'hjuːm] *vt (form)* beisetzen *(form)*.
inimical [ɪ'nɪmɪkəl] *adj (hostile)* feindselig *(to* gegen); *(injurious)* abträglich *(to dat)*.
inimitable [ɪ'nɪmɪtəbl] *adj* unnachahmlich.
iniquitous [ɪ'nɪkwɪtəs] *adj* ungeheuerlich.
iniquity [ɪ'nɪkwɪtɪ] *n (no pl: wickedness)* Ungeheuerlichkeit *f*; *(sin)* Missetat *f*; *(crime)* Greueltat *f*; *see* **den**.
initial [ɪ'nɪʃəl] **1** *adj* **(a)** anfänglich, Anfangs- ◆ **my ~ reaction** meine anfängliche Reaktion; **in the ~ stages** im Anfangsstadium. **(b)** *(Ling)* Anlaut-, anlautend. **(c)** *(Typ)* **~ letter** Anfangsbuchstabe *m*, Initiale *f*.
2 *n* Initiale *f*; *(Typ also)* Anfangsbuchstabe *m* ◆ **to sign a letter with one's ~s** seine Initialen *or (Pol)* Paraphe unter einen Brief setzen; *(Comm)* einen Brief abzeichnen *or* mit seinem Namenszeichen versehen.
3 *vt letter, document* mit seinen Initialen unterzeichnen; *(Comm)* abzeichnen; *(Pol)* paraphieren.
initialization [ɪˌnɪʃəlaɪ'zeɪʃən] *n (Comput)* Initialisierung *f*.
initialize [ɪ'nɪʃəlaɪz] *vt (Comput)* initialisieren.
initially [ɪ'nɪʃəlɪ] *adv* anfangs, zu *or* am Anfang; *(Ling)* im Anlaut.
initiate [ɪ'nɪʃɪeɪt] **1** *vt* **(a)** *(set in motion)* den Anstoß geben zu, initiieren; *negotiations also* einleiten; *legislation* einbringen ◆ **to ~ proceedings against sb** *(Jur)* gegen jdn einen Prozeß anstrengen.
(b) *(formally admit: into club etc)* feierlich aufnehmen; *(in tribal society) adolescents* initiieren.
(c) *(instruct: in knowledge, skill)* einweihen.
2 *n (in club etc)* Neuaufgenommene(r) *mf*; *(in tribal society)* Initiierte(r) *mf*; *(in knowledge)* Eingeweihte(r) *mf*.
initiation [ɪˌnɪʃɪ'eɪʃən] *n* **(a)** *(of project, fashion etc)* Initiierung *f*; *(of negotiations also)* Einleitung *f*. **(b)** *(into society)* Aufnahme *f*; *(as tribal member)* Initiation *f* ◆ **~ ceremony** Aufnahmezeremonie *f*; **~ rite** Initiationsritus *m*. **(c)** *(into branch of knowledge)* Einweihung *f*.
initiative [ɪ'nɪʃətɪv] *n* Initiative *f* ◆ **to take the ~** die Initiative ergreifen; **on one's own ~** aus eigener Initiative; **to have ~** Initiative haben.
initiator [ɪ'nɪʃɪeɪtə^r] *n* Initiator(in *f*) *m*.
inject [ɪn'dʒekt] *vt* (ein)spritzen; *(fig) comment* einwerfen; *money into economy* pumpen ◆ **to ~ sb with sth** *(Med)* jdm etw spritzen *or* injizieren; **to ~ sb with enthusiasm, to ~ enthusiasm into sb** jdn mit Begeisterung erfüllen; **he ~ed new life into the club** er brachte neues Leben in den Verein.
injection [ɪn'dʒekʃən] *n (act)* Einspritzung *f*; *(of gas)* Einblasen *nt*; *(that injected)* Injektion, Spritze *f* ◆ **to give sb an ~** jdm eine Injektion *or* Spritze geben; **the ~ of more money into the economy** eine größere Finanzspritze für die Wirtschaft; **the team needed an ~ of new life** die Mannschaft brauchte frisches Blut; **~ moulding** Spritzguß *m*.
injector [ɪn'dʒektə^r] *n* Einspritzpumpe *f*.
injudicious *adj*, **~ly** *adv* [ˌɪndʒʊ'dɪʃəs, -lɪ] unklug.
injunction [ɪn'dʒʌŋkʃən] *n* Anordnung *f*; *(Jur)* gerichtliche Verfügung.
injure ['ɪndʒə^r] *vt* **(a)** *(lit)* verletzen ◆ **to ~ one's leg** sich *(dat)* das Bein verletzen, sich *(acc)* am Bein verletzen; **the horse was ~d** das Pferd verletzte sich; **how many were ~d?, how many ~d were there?** wie viele Verletzte gab es?; **the ~d** die Verletzten *pl*.
(b) *(fig) (offend) sb, sb's feelings* verletzen, kränken; *(damage) reputation* schaden (+*dat*) ◆ **his ~d reputation** sein geschädigter Ruf; **the ~d party** *(Jur)* der/die Geschädigte.
injurious [ɪn'dʒʊərɪəs] *adj* schädlich ◆ **to be ~ to sb/sth** jdm/einer Sache schaden *or* schädlich sein; **~ to health** gesundheitsschädigend *or* -schädlich.
injury ['ɪndʒərɪ] *n* Verletzung *f (to gen)*; *(fig also)* Kränkung *f (to gen)* ◆ **to do sb/oneself an ~** jdn/sich verletzen; **to play ~ time** *(Brit Sport)* nachspielen, Nachspielzeit haben; **they are into ~ time** *(Brit Sport)* das ist Nachspielzeit.
injustice [ɪn'dʒʌstɪs] *n (unfairness, inequality)* Ungerechtigkeit *f*; *(violation of sb's rights)* Unrecht *nt no pl* ◆ **to do sb an ~** jdm Unrecht tun; **if a real ~ has been done to you ...** wenn Ihnen wirklich Unrecht geschehen ist ...
ink [ɪŋk] **1** *n* Tinte *(also Zool) f*; *(Art)* Tusche *f*; *(Typ)* Druckfarbe *f*; *(for newsprint)* Druckerschwärze *f* ◆ **written in ~** mit Tinte geschrieben; **a sketch in ~** eine Tuschzeichnung.
2 *vt* mit Tinte beschmieren; *(Typ)* einfärben.
◆**ink in** *vt sep outline, writing* mit Tinte *or (Art)* Tusche ausziehen *or* nachziehen; *(fill in) shape* mit Tinte *or (Art)* Tusche ausmalen *or* ausfüllen.
◆**ink out** *vt sep* mit Tinte übermalen.
◆**ink over** *vt sep* mit Tinte *or (Art)* Tusche nachzeichnen.
ink *in cpds* Tinten-; *(Art)* Tusch-; **~ bag** *n (Zool)* Tintenbeutel *m*; **~ blot** *n* Tintenklecks *m*; **~ blot test** *(Psych)* Rorschachtest *m*; **~-bottle** *n* Tintenfaß *nt*; **~ eraser** *n* Tintenradiergummi, Tintenradierer *(inf) m*; **~-jet (printer)** *n* Tintenstrahldrucker *m*.
inkling ['ɪŋklɪŋ] *n (vague idea)* dunkle Ahnung ◆ **he hadn't an ~** er hatte nicht die leiseste Ahnung *or* keinen blassen Schimmer *(inf)*; **to give sb an ~** jdm eine andeutungsweise Vorstellung geben; **there was no ~ of the disaster to come** nichts deutete auf die bevorstehende Katastrophe hin.
ink: ~ pad *n* Stempelkissen *nt*; **~pot** *n* Tintenfaß *nt*; **~stain** *n* Tintenfleck *m*; **~stained** *adj* tintenbeschmiert; **~stand** *n* Tintenfaß *nt (mit Halter für Federn etc)*; **~well** *n (in eine Tischplatte eingelassenes)* Tintenfaß *nt*.
inky ['ɪŋkɪ] *adj (+er)* **(a)** *(lit)* tintenbeschmiert, voller Tinte, tintig; *fingers also* Tinten-. **(b)** *(fig) darkness* tintenschwarz; *blue, black* tintig.
inlaid [ɪn'leɪd] **1** *ptp of* **inlay**.
2 *adj* eingelegt *(with* mit) ◆ **~ table** Tisch mit Einlegearbeit; **~ work** Einlegearbeit *f*.
inland ['ɪnlænd] **1** *adj* **(a)** *waterway, navigation, sea* Binnen- ◆ **~ town** Stadt *f* im Landesinneren.
(b) *(domestic) mail* Inland(s)-; *trade* Binnen- ◆ **~ produce** inländisches Erzeugnis, inländische Erzeugnisse *pl*, Inlandserzeugnis(se *pl*) *nt*; **I~ Revenue** *(Brit)* ≃ Finanzamt *nt*.
2 *adv* landeinwärts.
inlaw ['ɪnlɔː] *n* angeheirateter Verwandter, angeheiratete Verwandte ◆ **~s** *(parents-in-law)* Schwiegereltern *pl*.
inlay [ɪn'leɪ] *(vb: pret, ptp* **inlaid**) **1** *n (in table, box)* Einlegearbeit *f*, Intarsien *pl*; *(Dentistry)* Plombe, Füllung *f*; *(of gold etc)* Inlay *nt*.
2 *vt* einlegen *(with* mit).
inlet ['ɪnlet] *n* **(a)** *(of sea)* Meeresarm *m*; *(of river)* Flußarm *m*. **(b)** *(Tech)* Zuleitung *f*; *(of ventilator)* Öffnung *f*.
inlet: ~ pipe *n* Zuleitung(srohr *nt*) *f*; **~ valve** *n* Einlaßventil *nt*.
inmate ['ɪnmeɪt] *n* Insasse *m*, Insassin *f*.
inmost ['ɪnməʊst] *adj see* **innermost**.
inn [ɪn] *n* **(a)** Gasthaus *nt*; *(old: hotel)* Herberge *f (old)*; *(old: tavern)* Schenke *f*. **(b)** *(Jur)* **the I~s of Court** die vier englischen Juristenverbände.
innards ['ɪnədz] *npl* Innereien *pl (also fig)*, Eingeweide *pl*.
innate [ɪ'neɪt] *adj* angeboren ◆ **man's ~ desire for happiness** das dem Menschen angeborene Streben nach Glück.
inner ['ɪnə^r] **1** *adj* **(a)** innere(r, s); *side, surface, door, court, city, (Anat) ear also* Innen- ◆ **~ harbour** Innenbecken *nt*.
(b) *(fig) emotions* innere(r, s); *meaning* verborgen; *life* Seelen- ◆ **his ~ circle of friends** sein engster Freundeskreis; **he wasn't one of the ~ circle** er gehörte nicht zum engeren Kreise; **the ~ man** *(soul)* das Innere; **the needs of the ~ man** die inneren Bedürfnisse; **to satisfy the ~ man** für sein leibliches Wohl sorgen.
2 *n (Archery)* Schwarze(s) *nt*.
inner-city ['ɪnə'sɪtɪ] *adj attr* Innenstadt-; *housing* in der Innenstadt; *(of cities generally)* in den Innenstädten; *decay, renewal, problem* der Innenstadt/der

Innenstädte.

innermost ['ɪnəməʊst] *adj* innerst ◆ **~ in sb** zuinnerst in jdm; **in the ~ recesses of the mind** in den hintersten Winkeln des Gehirns; **in the ~ depths of the forest** im tiefsten Wald.

inner tube *n* Schlauch *m*.

inning ['ɪnɪŋ] *n* (*Baseball*) Inning *nt*.

innings ['ɪnɪŋz] *n* (*Cricket*) Innenrunde *f* ◆ **to have one's ~** (*fig inf*) an der Reihe sein; **he has had a long** *or* **a good ~** (*fig inf*) er war lange an der Reihe; (*life*) er hatte ein langes, ausgefülltes Leben.

innkeeper ['ɪn,ki:pə^r] *n* (Gast)wirt *m*.

innocence ['ɪnəsəns] *n* **(a)** Unschuld *f* ◆ **to pretend ~** vorgeben, unschuldig zu sein, unschuldig tun; **in all ~** in aller Unschuld. **(b)** (*liter: ignorance*) Unkenntnis *f*.

innocent ['ɪnəsənt] [1] *adj* **(a)** unschuldig; *mistake, misrepresentation* unabsichtlich ◆ **she is ~ of the crime** sie ist an dem Verbrechen unschuldig; **to put on an ~ air** eine Unschuldsmiene aufsetzen; **as ~ as a newborn babe** unschuldig wie ein Lamm; **he is ~ about night life in a big city** er ist die reine Unschuld, was das Nachtleben in einer Großstadt angeht.
(b) ~ of (*liter: ignorant*) nicht vertraut mit; (*devoid of*) frei von, ohne.
[2] *n* Unschuld *f* ◆ **he's a bit of an ~** er ist eine rechte Unschuld; **massacre of the Holy I~s** (*Rel*) der Kindermord zu Bethlehem; **Holy I~s' Day** das Fest der Unschuldigen Kinder.

innocently ['ɪnəsəntlɪ] *adv* unschuldig; (*in all innocence*) in aller Unschuld.

innocuous *adj*, **~ly** *adv* [ɪ'nɒkjʊəs, -lɪ] harmlos.

innovate ['ɪnəʊveɪt] [1] *vt* neu einführen ◆ **the new techniques which he ~d** die neuen Techniken, die er einführte.
[2] *vi* Neuerungen einführen.

innovation [,ɪnəʊ'veɪʃən] *n* Innovation *f*; (*introduction also*) Neueinführung *f* (*of gen*); (*thing introduced also*) Neuerung *f*.

innovative [ɪnə'veɪtɪv] *adj* auf Neuerungen aus, innovativ.

innovator ['ɪnəʊveɪtə^r] *n* Neuerer *m*; (*of reform*) Begründer *m*.

innuendo [,ɪnjʊ'endəʊ] *n, pl* **-es** versteckte Andeutung ◆ **to make ~es about sb** über jdn Andeutungen fallenlassen.

innumerable [ɪ'nju:mərəbl] *adj* unzählig.

innumeracy [ɪ'nju:mərəsɪ] *n* Nicht-Rechnen-Können *nt*.

innumerate [ɪ'nju:mərɪt] *adj* **to be ~** nicht rechnen können.

inoculate [ɪ'nɒkjʊleɪt] *vt person* impfen (*against* gegen) ◆ **to ~ sb with a virus** jdm einen Virus einimpfen.

inoculation [ɪ,nɒkjʊ'leɪʃən] *n* Impfung *f* ◆ **to give sb an ~ (against smallpox)** jdn (gegen Pocken) impfen.

inoffensive [,ɪnə'fensɪv] *adj* harmlos.

inoperable [ɪn'ɒpərəbl] *adj disease, tumour* inoperabel, nicht operierbar; *policy* undurchführbar.

inoperative [ɪn'ɒpərətɪv] *adj* **(a)** (*ineffective*) *law, rule* außer Kraft, ungültig ◆ **to become ~** außer Kraft treten, ungültig werden. **(b)** (*not working*) **to be ~** (*machine, radio*) nicht funktionieren; **to render sth ~** etw außer Betrieb setzen.

inopportune [ɪn'ɒpətju:n] *adj* inopportun; *demand, visit, moment also* ungelegen; *words* unpassend, nicht angebracht ◆ **to be ~** ungelegen *or* zur Unzeit kommen; **it's very ~ that ...** es kommt sehr ungelegen, daß ...

inopportunely [ɪn'ɒpətju:nlɪ] *adv* zur Unzeit.

inordinate [ɪ'nɔ:dɪnɪt] *adj* unmäßig; *number of people, size, sum of money* ungeheuer.

inordinately [ɪ'nɔ:dɪnɪtlɪ] *adv* unmäßig; *large* ungeheuer.

inorganic [,ɪnɔ:'gænɪk] *adj* anorganisch; (*fig*) unorganisch.

in-patient ['ɪnpeɪʃnt] *n* stationär behandelter Patient/behandelte Patientin.

input ['ɪnpʊt] [1] *n* **(a)** (*into computer*) Eingabe *f*, Input *m or nt*; (*of capital*) Investition *f*; (*of manpower*) (Arbeits)aufwand *m*; (*power* **~**) Energiezufuhr *f*; (*of project etc*) Beitrag *m* ◆ **their ~ into the project** ihr Beitrag zum Projekt; **~ port** (*Comput*) Eingabeport *m*. **(b)** (*point of* **~**, **~** *terminal*) Eingang *m*.
[2] *vt* (*Comput*) *data, text* eingeben.

inquest ['ɪnkwest] *n* (*into death*) gerichtliche Untersuchung der Todesursache; (*fig*) Manöverkritik *f*.

inquietude [ɪn'kwaɪətju:d] *n* (*liter*) Unruhe *f*.

inquire [ɪn'kwaɪə^r] *etc* (*esp US*) *see* **enquire** *etc*.

inquisition [,ɪnkwɪ'zɪʃən] *n* **(a)** (*Hist Eccl*) **the I~** die Inquisition. **(b)** (*Jur*) Untersuchung *f*. **(c)** (*fig*) Inquisition *f*, Verhör *nt*.

inquisitive [ɪn'kwɪzɪtɪv] *adj* neugierig; (*for knowledge*) wißbegierig ◆ **he's very ~ about my friends** er will alles über meine Freunde wissen.

inquisitively [ɪn'kwɪzɪtɪvlɪ] *adv see adj*.

inquisitiveness [ɪn'kwɪzɪtɪvnɪs] *n* (*of person*) Neugier *f*; (*for knowledge*) Wißbegier (de) *f* ◆ **the ~ of her look/questions** *etc* ihr neugieriger Blick/ihre neugierigen Fragen *etc*.

inquisitor [ɪn'kwɪzɪtə^r] *n* (*Hist Eccl, fig*) Inquisitor *m*.

inquisitorial [ɪn,kwɪzɪ'tɔ:rɪəl] *adj* inquisitorisch ◆ **after an ~ session with the headmaster** nachdem ihn der Rektor streng verhört hatte *or* ins Verhör genommen hatte.

inroad ['ɪnrəʊd] *n* **(a)** (*Mil*) Einfall *m* (*into* in +*acc*).
(b) (*fig*) **to make ~s upon** *or* **into sb's rights** in jds Rechte (*acc*) eingreifen; **the Japanese are making ~s into the British market** die Japaner dringen in den britischen Markt ein; **these expenses are making heavy ~s into my bank account** diese Ausgaben greifen mein Bankkonto stark an; **extra work has made ~s (up)on** *or* **into my spare time** zusätzliche Arbeit hat meine Freizeit sehr eingeschränkt.

inrush ['ɪnrʌʃ] *n* Zustrom *m*; (*of water*) Einbruch *m* ◆ **there was a sudden ~ of tourists** die Touristen kamen plötzlich in Strömen.

ins *abbr of* **(a) insurance** Vers. **(b) inches.**

insalubrious [,ɪnsə'lu:brɪəs] *adj* unzuträglich.

insane [ɪn'seɪn] [1] *adj* **(a)** geisteskrank, wahnsinnig; (*fig*) wahnsinnig, irrsinnig ◆ **you must be ~!** du bist wohl geisteskrank *or* wahnsinnig!; **that's ~!** das ist Wahnsinn *or* Irrsinn! **(b)** (*esp US*) **~ asylum/ward** Anstalt *f*/ Abteilung *f* für Geisteskranke.
[2] *npl* **the ~** die Geisteskranken *pl*.

insanely [ɪn'seɪnlɪ] *adv* irr; (*fig*) verrückt; *jealous* irrsinnig.

insanitary [ɪn'sænɪtərɪ] *adj* unhygienisch.

insanity [ɪn'sænɪtɪ] *n* Geisteskrankheit *f*, Wahnsinn *m*; (*fig*) Irrsinn, Wahnsinn *m*.

insatiability [ɪn,seɪʃə'bɪlɪtɪ] *n see adj* Unersättlichkeit *f*; Unstillbarkeit *f*.

insatiable [ɪn'seɪʃəbl], **insatiate** [ɪn'seɪʃɪɪt] (*liter*) *adj* unersättlich; *curiosity, desire also* unstillbar.

inscribe [ɪn'skraɪb] *vt* **(a)** (*sth on sth* etw in etw *acc*) *words, symbols etc* (*engrave*) (*on ring etc*) eingravieren; (*on rock, stone, wood*) einmeißeln; (*on tree*) einritzen.
(b) *book* eine Widmung schreiben in (+*acc*).
(c) to ~ sth in sb's memory etw in jds Gedächtnis (*dat*) verankern.
(d) (*Math*) einbeschreiben (*in a circle etc* einem Kreis *etc*).
(e) (*Fin*) **~d stock** Namensaktien *pl*.

inscription [ɪn'skrɪpʃən] *n* **(a)** (*on monument etc*) Inschrift *f*, (*on coin*) Aufschrift *f*. **(b)** (*in book*) Widmung *f*.

inscrutability [ɪn,skru:tə'bɪlɪtɪ] *n* Unergründlichkeit *f*.

inscrutable [ɪn'skru:təbl] *adj* unergründlich ◆ **~ face** undurchdringlicher Gesichtsausdruck; **don't pretend to be so ~** tu nicht so geheimnisvoll.

insect ['ɪnsekt] *n* Insekt *nt*.

insect: ~ bite *n* Insektenstich *m*; **~ eater** *n* Insektenfresser *m*; **~-eating plant** *n* fleischfressende Pflanze.

insecticide [ɪn'sektɪsaɪd] *n* Insektengift, Insektizid (*form*) *nt*.

insectivorous [,ɪnsek'tɪvərəs] *adj* insektenfressend.

insect: ~-powder *n* Insektenpulver *nt*; **~-repellent** [1] *adj* insektenvertreibend; [2] *n* Insektenbekämpfungsmittel *nt*.

insecure [,ɪnsɪ'kjʊə^r] *adj* unsicher ◆ **if they feel ~ in their jobs** wenn sie sich in ihrem Arbeitsplatz nicht sicher fühlen.

insecurely [,ɪnsɪ'kjʊəlɪ] *adv fastened* nicht sicher.

insecurity [,ɪnsɪ'kjʊərɪtɪ] *n* Unsicherheit *f*.

inseminate [ɪn'semɪneɪt] *vt* inseminieren (*spec*), befruchten; *cattle* besamen; (*fig*) *beliefs* einimpfen.

insemination [ɪn,semɪ'neɪʃən] *n see vt* Insemination (*spec*), Befruchtung *f*; Besamung *f*; Einimpfung *f*; (*fig: of knowledge*) Vermittlung *f*.

insensate [ɪn'senseɪt] *adj* (*liter*) **(a)** *matter, stone* leblos, tot. **(b)** (*fig: unfeeling*) gefühllos ◆ **she flew into an ~ fury** ein unmäßiger Zorn bemächtigte sich ihrer (*liter*).

insensibility [ɪn,sensə'bɪlɪtɪ] *n* **(a)** (*bodily*) Unempfindlichkeit *f* (*to* gegenüber); (*unconsciousness*) Bewußtlosigkeit *f*. **(b)** (*lack of feeling*) Gefühllosigkeit *f* (*to* gegenüber) ◆ **artistic ~** Unempfänglichkeit *f* für Künstlerisches.

insensible [ɪn'sensəbl] *adj* **(a)** (*bodily*) unempfindlich (*to* gegen); (*unconscious*) bewußtlos ◆ **he seems to be ~ to the cold** er scheint kälteunempfindlich zu sein; **his hands became ~ to any feeling** seine Hände verloren jegliches Gefühl.
(b) (*liter: of beauty, music*) unempfänglich (*of, to* für).
(c) (*liter: unaware*) **~ of** *or* **to sth** einer Sache (*gen*) nicht bewußt.
(d) (*form: imperceptible*) unmerklich, nicht wahrnehmbar.

insensitive [ɪn'sensɪtɪv] *adj* **(a)** (*emotionally*) gefühllos.
(b) (*unappreciative*) unempfänglich ◆ **to be ~ to the beauties of nature** *etc* für Schönheiten der Natur *etc* unempfänglich sein.
(c) (*physically*) unempfindlich ◆ **~ to pain/light** schmerz-/ lichtunempfindlich.

insensitivity [ɪn,sensɪ'tɪvɪtɪ] *n* **(a)** (*emotional*) Gefühllosigkeit *f* (*towards* gegenüber).
(b) (*unappreciativeness*) Unempfänglichkeit *f* (*to* für) ◆ **his ~ towards the reasons behind the demands** seine Verständnislosigkeit *or* sein Unverständnis für die Gründe, die hinter den Forderungen stehen.
(c) (*physical*) Unempfindlichkeit *f*.

inseparability [ɪn,sepərə'bɪlɪtɪ] *n see adj* Untrennbarkeit *f*; Unzertrennlichkeit *f*.

inseparable [ɪn'sepərəbl] *adj* untrennbar; *friends* unzertrennlich ◆ **these two questions are ~** diese beiden Fragen sind untrennbar miteinander verbunden.

inseparably [ɪn'sepərəblɪ] *adv* untrennbar.

insert [ɪn'sɜ:t] [1] *vt* (*stick into*) hineinstecken; (*place in*) hineinlegen; (*place between*) einfügen; *zip, pocket* einsetzen; *thermometer, suppository* einführen; *coin* einwerfen; *injection needle* einstechen; (*Comput*) *disk* einlegen; *text* einfügen ◆ **to ~ sth in sth** etw in etw (*acc*) stecken; **to ~ an extra paragraph in a chapter** einen weiteren Absatz in ein Kapitel einfügen; **to ~ an advert in a paper** eine Anzeige in eine Zeitung setzen, in einer Zeitung inserieren; **he managed to ~ himself between two other students on the crowded benches** es gelang ihm, sich auf den überfüllten Bänken zwischen zwei andere Studenten zu zwängen; **~ mode** (*Comput*) Einfügemodus *m*.
[2] ['ɪnsɜ:t] *n* (*in book*) Einlage *f*, (*word*) Beifügung, Einfügung *f*, (*in magazine*) Beilage *f*, (*advertisement*) Inserat *nt*.

insertion [ɪn'sɜ:ʃən] *n* **(a)** *see vt* Hineinstecken *nt*; Hineinlegen *nt*; Einfügen *nt*; Einsetzen *nt*; Einführen *nt*; Einwerfen *nt*; Einstechen *nt*; (*of an advert*) Aufgeben *nt*; (*by printer*) Einrücken *nt*. **(b)** *see* **insert 2. (c)** (*Sew*) Einsatz *m*.

in-service ['ɪn,sɜːvɪs] *adj attr* **~ training** (berufsbegleitende) Fortbildung; (*in firm also*) innerbetriebliche Fortbildung; (*course also*) Fortbildungslehrgang *m*.

inset ['ɪnset] (*vb: pret, ptp* ~) **1** *vt map, illustration* einfügen; (*Sew*) einsetzen.
2 [ɪn'set] *n* **(a)** (*pages*) Einlage, Beilage *f*; (*also* **~ map**) Nebenkarte *f*; (*on diagram*) Nebenbild *nt*. **(b)** (*Sew*) Einsatz *m*.

inshore ['ɪn'ʃɔːʳ] **1** *adj* Küsten- ◆ **~ fishing** Küstenfischerei *f*.
2 *adv fish, be* in Küstennähe; *blow, flow* auf die Küste zu.

inside ['ɪn'saɪd] **1** *n* **(a)** Innere(s) *nt*; (*of pavement*) Innenseite *f* ◆ **keep to the ~ of the road** halte dich am Straßenrand; **the car overtook on the ~** das Auto überholte innen; **it's painted on the ~** es ist innen bemalt; **you'll have to ask someone on the ~** Sie müssen einen Insider *or* Eingeweihten fragen; **to know a company from the ~** interne Kenntnisse über eine Firma haben; **he's seen politics from the ~** er kennt die Politik von innen; **locked from** *or* **on the ~** von innen verschlossen.
(b) the wind blew the umbrella ~ out der Wind hat den Schirm umgestülpt; **your jumper's ~ out** du hast deinen Pullover links *or* verkehrt herum an; **to turn sth ~ out** etw umdrehen; (*fig*) *flat etc* etw auf den Kopf stellen; **to know sth ~ out** etw in- und auswendig kennen.
(c) (*inf*) (*stomach: also* **~s**) Eingeweide, Innere(s) *nt* ◆ **to have pains in one's ~s** Bauch- *or* Leibschmerzen haben.
2 *adj* Innen-, innere(r, s) ◆ **~ information** Insider-Informationen *pl*, interne Informationen *pl*; **it is an ~ job** (*done in office etc*) das wird betriebsintern gemacht; **it looks like an ~ job** (*crime*) es sieht nach dem Werk von Insidern aus (*inf*); **~ lane** (*Sport*) Innenbahn *f*; (*Aut*) Innenspur *f*; **~ leg measurement** innere Beinlänge; **~ pocket** Innentasche *f*; **~ seat** Platz *m* an der Wand/am Fenster, Fensterplatz *m*; **~ story** (*Press*) Inside-Story *f*; **~ track** Innenbahn *f*; **~ forward** Halbstürmer *m*; **~ left** Halblinke(r) *m*; **~ right** Halbrechte(r) *m*.
3 *adv* innen; (*indoors*) drin(nen); (*direction*) nach innen, hinein/herein ◆ **look ~** sehen Sie hinein; (*search*) sehen Sie innen nach; **come ~!** kommen Sie herein!; **let's go ~** gehen wir hinein; **he passed the ball ~** er spielte nach innen ab; **there is something ~** es ist etwas (innen) drin; **to be ~** (*inf*) (*in prison*) sitzen (*inf*).
4 *prep* (*also esp US:* **~ of**) **(a)** (*place*) innen in (*+dat*); (*direction*) in (*+acc*) ... (hinein) ◆ **don't let him come ~ the house** lassen Sie ihn nicht ins Haus (herein); **he was waiting ~ the house** er wartete im Haus; **once ~ the door he** ... wenn er erst einmal im Haus ist/war ...
(b) (*time*) innerhalb ◆ **he's well ~ a record time** er liegt noch gut unter der Rekordzeit; **he was 5 secs ~ the record** er ist 5 Sekunden unter dem Rekord geblieben.

insider [ɪn'saɪdəʳ] *n* Insider, Eingeweihte(r) *m* ◆ **~ dealing** (*Fin*) Insiderhandel *m*.

insidious *adj*, **~ly** *adv* [ɪn'sɪdɪəs, -lɪ] heimtückisch.

insight ['ɪnsaɪt] *n* **(a)** *no pl* Verständnis *nt* ◆ **he lacks ~** ihm fehlt das Verständnis; **his ~ into my problems** sein Verständnis für meine Probleme; **~ into human nature** Menschenkenntnis *f*.
(b) Einblick *m* (*into* in *+acc*) ◆ **to gain an ~ into sth** in etw (einen) Einblick gewinnen *or* bekommen.

insignia [ɪn'sɪgnɪə] *npl* Insignien *pl*.

insignificance [,ɪnsɪg'nɪfɪkəns] *n see adj* Belanglosigkeit *f*; Geringfügigkeit *f*; Unscheinbarkeit *f*.

insignificant [,ɪnsɪg'nɪfɪkənt] *adj* belanglos; *sum, difference also* unbedeutend; *little man, person* unscheinbar.

insincere [,ɪnsɪn'sɪəʳ] *adj* unaufrichtig; *person, smile also* falsch.

insincerely [,ɪnsɪn'sɪəlɪ] *adv see adj*.

insincerity [,ɪnsɪn'serɪtɪ] *n see adj* Unaufrichtigkeit *f*; Falschheit *f*.

insinuate [ɪn'sɪnjʊeɪt] *vt* **(a)** (*hint, suggest*) andeuten (*sth to sb* etw jdm gegenüber) ◆ **what are you insinuating?** was wollen Sie damit sagen?; **are you insinuating that I am lying?** willst du damit sagen, daß ich lüge? **(b) to ~ oneself into sb's favour** sich bei jdm einschmeicheln.

insinuating [ɪn'sɪnjʊeɪtɪŋ] *adj remark* anzüglich; *article also* voller Anzüglichkeiten; *tone of voice* spitz, bedeutungsvoll ◆ **he said it in such an ~ way** er sagte es auf eine so anzügliche Art.

insinuation [ɪn,sɪnjʊ'eɪʃən] *n* Anspielung *f* (*about* auf *+acc*) ◆ **he objected strongly to any ~ that** ... er wehrte sich heftig gegen jede Andeutung, daß ...

insipid [ɪn'sɪpɪd] *adj* fad; *person, novel, lyrics also* geistlos.

insipidity [,ɪnsɪ'pɪdɪtɪ] *n see adj* Fadheit *f*; Geistlosigkeit *f*.

insist [ɪn'sɪst] *vti* bestehen ◆ **I ~!** ich bestehe darauf!; **but he still ~ed that** ... aber er beharrte *or* bestand trotzdem darauf, daß ...; **if you ~** wenn Sie darauf bestehen; (*if you like*) wenn's unbedingt sein muß; **I must ~ that you stop** ich muß darauf bestehen, daß Sie aufhören; **I must ~ that I am right** ich muß doch nachdrücklich betonen, daß ich recht habe; **he ~s on his innocence** *or* **that he is innocent** er behauptet beharrlich, unschuldig zu sein; **to ~ (up)on a point** auf einem Punkt beharren; **to ~ on silence** auf absoluter Ruhe bestehen; **I ~ on the best** ich bestehe auf bester Qualität; **to ~ on doing sth/on sb doing sth** darauf bestehen, etw zu tun/daß jd etw tut; **he will ~ on calling her by the wrong name** er redet sie beharrlich beim falschen Namen an; **if you will ~ on smoking that foul tobacco** wenn Sie schon unbedingt diesen scheußlichen Tabak rauchen müssen.

insistence [ɪn'sɪstəns] *n* Bestehen *nt* (*on* auf *+dat*) ◆ **the accused's ~ on his innocence** die Unschuldsbeteuerungen des Angeklagten; **in spite of his ~ that he was right** trotz seiner beharrlichen Behauptung, recht zu haben; **I did it at his ~** ich tat es auf sein Drängen, ich tat es, weil er darauf bestand; **I can't understand his ~ on the use of oil** ich kann nicht verstehen, warum er darauf besteht, daß Öl benutzt wird.

insistent [ɪn'sɪstənt] *adj* **(a)** *person* beharrlich, hartnäckig; *salesman etc* aufdringlich ◆ **I didn't want to but he was ~** ich wollte eigentlich nicht, aber er bestand *or* beharrte darauf; **he was most ~ about it** er beharrte *or* bestand hartnäckig darauf.
(b) (*urgent*) *demand, tone, rhythm* nachdrücklich, penetrant (*pej*).

insistently [ɪn'sɪstəntlɪ] *adv* mit Nachdruck.

insofar [,ɪnsəʊ'fɑːʳ] *adv*: **~ as** soweit.

insole ['ɪnsəʊl] *n* Einlegesohle *f*; (*part of shoe*) Brandsohle *f*.

insolence ['ɪnsələns] *n* Unverschämtheit, Frechheit *f* ◆ **the ~ of it!** so eine Unverschämtheit *or* Frechheit!

insolent *adj*, **~ly** *adv* ['ɪnsələnt, -lɪ] unverschämt, frech.

insolubility [ɪn,sɒljʊ'bɪlɪtɪ] *n see adj* **(a)** Unlöslichkeit *f*. **(b)** Unlösbarkeit *f*.

insoluble [ɪn'sɒljʊbl] *adj* **(a)** *substance* unlöslich. **(b)** *problem* unlösbar.

insolvency [ɪn'sɒlvənsɪ] *n* Zahlungsunfähigkeit, Insolvenz (*geh*) *f*.

insolvent [ɪn'sɒlvənt] *adj* zahlungsunfähig, insolvent (*geh*).

insomnia [ɪn'sɒmnɪə] *n* Schlaflosigkeit *f*.

insomniac [ɪn'sɒmnɪæk] *n* **to be an ~** an Schlaflosigkeit leiden.

insomuch [,ɪnsəʊ'mʌtʃ] *adv see* **inasmuch**.

insouciance [ɪn'suːsɪəns] *n* (*liter*) Unbekümmertheit, Sorglosigkeit *f*.

inspect [ɪn'spekt] *vt* **(a)** (*examine*) kontrollieren, prüfen ◆ **to ~ sth for sth** etw auf etw (*acc*) (hin) prüfen *or* kontrollieren. **(b)** (*Mil etc: review*) inspizieren.

inspection [ɪn'spekʃən] *n* **(a)** Kontrolle, Prüfung *f*; (*medical*) Untersuchung *f*; (*of school*) Inspektion *f* ◆ **on ~** bei näherer Betrachtung *or* Prüfung; **customs ~** Zollkontrolle *f*; **for your ~** zur Prüfung *or* (*documents also*) Einsicht; **~ copy** Ansichtsexemplar *nt*. **(b)** (*Mil*) Inspektion *f*.

inspector [ɪn'spektəʳ] *n* (*factory* ~, *on buses, trains*) Kontrol- leur(in *f*) *m*; (*of schools*) Schulrat *m*, Schulrätin *f*; (*of police*) Polizeiinspektor *m*; (*higher*) Kommissar *m*; (*of taxes*) Steuerinspektor *m* ◆ **customs ~** Zollinspektor(in *f*) *m*.

inspectorate [ɪn'spektərɪt] *n* Inspektion *f*.

inspiration [,ɪnspə'reɪʃən] *n* Inspiration (*for* zu *or* für), Eingebung (*for* zu) *f* ◆ **he gets his ~ from** ... er läßt sich von ... inspirieren; **you give me ~** Sie inspirieren mich; **I haven't had any ~ for months** seit Monaten habe ich keine Inspirationen mehr; **to have a sudden ~** eine plötzliche Inspiration *or* Erleuchtung haben; **you are my ~** du inspirierst mich; **his courage has been an ~ to us all** sein Mut hat uns alle inspiriert.

inspirational [,ɪnspə'reɪʃənl] *adj* inspirativ.

inspire [ɪn'spaɪəʳ] *vt* **(a)** *respect, trust, awe* einflößen (*in sb* jdm); *hope, confidence etc* (er)wecken (*in* in *+dat*); *hate* hervorrufen (*in* bei) ◆ **to ~ sb with hope/confidence/hate/respect** jdn mit Hoffnung/Vertrauen/Haß/ Respekt erfüllen.
(b) (*be inspiration to*) *person* inspirieren ◆ **to ~ sb with an idea** jdn zu einer Idee inspirieren; **I was ~d by his example/courage** sein Vorbild/Mut hat mich inspiriert; **whatever ~d you to change it?** (*iro*) was hat dich bloß dazu inspiriert, es zu ändern?

inspired [ɪn'spaɪəd] *adj* genial; *work also* voller Inspiration; *author also* inspiriert ◆ **in an ~ moment** in einem Augenblick der Inspiration; (*iro*) in einem lichten Moment; **it was an ~ guess** das war genial geraten.

inspiring [ɪn'spaɪərɪŋ] *adj speech* inspirierend ◆ **this subject/translation isn't particularly ~** (*inf*) dieses Thema/diese Übersetzung reißt einen nicht gerade vom Stuhl (*inf*).

Inst *abbr of* **Institute** Inst.

inst *abbr of* **instant** d.M.

instability [,ɪnstə'bɪlɪtɪ] *n* Instabilität *f*; (*of character also*) Labilität *f*.

install [ɪn'stɔːl] *vt* installieren; *telephone also* anschließen; *bathroom, fireplace* einbauen; *person also* (in ein Amt) einsetzen *or* einführen; *priest* investieren ◆ **to have electricity ~ed** ans Elektrizitätsnetz angeschlossen werden; **when you've ~ed yourself in your new office** wenn Sie sich in Ihrem neuen Büro installiert *or* eingerichtet haben; **he ~ed himself in the best armchair** (*inf*) er pflanzte sich auf den besten Sessel (*inf*).

installation [,ɪnstə'leɪʃən] *n* **(a)** *see vt* Installation *f*; Anschluß *m*; Einbau *m*; Amtseinsetzung *or* -einführung *f*; Investitur *f* ◆ **~ program** (*Comput*) Installationsprogramm *nt*.
(b) (*machine etc*) Anlage, Einrichtung *f*.
(c) military ~ militärische Anlage.

installment plan *n* (*US*) Ratenzahlung *f* ◆ **to buy on the ~** auf Raten kaufen.

instalment, (*US*) **installment** [ɪn'stɔːlmənt] *n* **(a)** (*of story, serial*) Fortsetzung *f*; (*Rad, TV*) (Sende)folge *f*. **(b)** (*Fin, Comm*) Rate *f* ◆ **monthly ~** Monatsrate *f*; **to pay in** *or* **by ~s** in Raten *or* ratenweise bezahlen.

instance ['ɪnstəns] **1** *n* **(a)** (*example*) Beispiel *nt*; (*case*) Fall *m* ◆ **for ~** zum Beispiel; **as an ~ of** als (ein) Beispiel für; **in many ~s** in vielen Fällen; **there have been many ~s of people refusing** es hat viele Fälle gegeben, in denen Leute abgelehnt haben; **in the first ~** zuerst *or* zunächst (einmal); **the appointment will be for two years in the first ~** die Anstellung ist zunächst auf zwei Jahre befristet; **this is a good ~ of the way** ... das ist ein gutes Beispiel dafür, wie ...
(b) at the ~ of (*form*) auf Ersuchen *or* Betreiben (*+gen*) (*form*), auf Veranlassung von.
(c) (*Jur*) **court of first ~** erste Instanz.
2 *vt* **(a)** (*exemplify*) Beispiele anführen für.
(b) (*cite*) *cost, example* anführen.

instant ['ɪnstənt] 1 *adj* **(a)** unmittelbar; *relief, result, reply, success also* sofortig *attr* ◆ ~ **camera** Sofortbildkamera *f*; ~ **replay** *(TV)* Wiederholung *f*.
(b) *(Cook)* Instant- ◆ ~ **coffee** Pulver- *or* Instantkaffee *m*; ~ **milk** Trockenmilch *f*; ~ **food** Schnellgerichte *pl*; ~ **potatoes** fertiger Kartoffelbrei.
(c) *(Comm)* dieses Monats ◆ **your letter of the 10th inst(ant)** Ihr Schreiben vom 10. dieses Monats.
2 *n* Augenblick *m* ◆ **this (very)** ~ sofort, auf der Stelle; **I'll be ready in an** ~ ich bin sofort fertig; **he left the ~ he heard the news** er ging sofort, als er die Nachricht hörte; **at that very** ~ ... genau in dem Augenblick ...

instantaneous [,ɪnstən'teɪnɪəs] *adj* unmittelbar ◆ **death was** ~ der Tod trat sofort *or* unmittelbar ein; **the reaction was almost** ~ die Reaktion erfolgte fast sofort.

instantaneously [,ɪnstən'teɪnɪəslɪ] *adv* sofort, unverzüglich.

instanter [ɪn'stæntəʳ] *adv* stante pede, stehenden Fußes *(geh)*.

instantly ['ɪnstəntlɪ] *adv* sofort.

instead [ɪn'sted] 1 *prep* ~ **of** statt *(+gen or (inf) +dat)*, anstelle von ◆ ~ **of going to school** (an)statt zur Schule zu gehen; ~ **of that** statt dessen; **his brother came ~ of him** sein Bruder kam an seiner Stelle *or* statt ihm *(inf)*; **he accidentally hit Jim ~ of John** er traf aus Versehen Jim (an)statt John; **this is ~ of a Christmas present** das ist anstelle eines Weihnachtgeschenks.
2 *adv* statt dessen, dafür ◆ **if he doesn't want to go, I'll go** ~ wenn er nicht gehen will, gehe ich (statt dessen); **if he doesn't come here, I shall go there** ~ wenn er nicht herkommt, gehe ich statt dessen hin.

instep ['ɪnstep] *n* **(a)** *(Anat)* Spann, Rist *m* ◆ **to have high ~s** einen hohen Rist haben. **(b)** *(of shoe)* Blatt *nt*.

instigate ['ɪnstɪgeɪt] *vt* anstiften; *rebellion, strike also* anzetteln; *new idea, reform etc* initiieren.

instigation [,ɪnstɪ'geɪʃən] *n see vt* Anstiftung *f*; Anzettelung *f*; Initiierung *f* ◆ **at sb's** ~ auf jds Betreiben *or* Veranlassung.

instigator ['ɪnstɪgeɪtəʳ] *n (of crime etc)* Anstifter(in *f*) *m*; *(of new idea, reform etc)* Initiator(in *f*) *m*.

instil [ɪn'stɪl] *vt* einflößen, einprägen *(into sb* jdm); *knowledge, attitudes* beibringen *(into sb* jdm).

instinct ['ɪnstɪŋkt] 1 *n* Instinkt *m* ◆ **the sex/survival** ~ der Geschlechtstrieb/Überlebenstrieb; **by** *or* **from** ~ instinktiv; **to have an ~ for business, to have a good business** ~ einen ausgeprägten Geschäftssinn *or* -instinkt haben.
2 [ɪn'stɪŋkt] *adj (liter)* ~ **with** erfüllt von.

instinctive [ɪn'stɪŋktɪv] *adj* instinktiv; *behaviour also* Instinkt-, instinktgesteuert.

instinctively [ɪn'stɪŋktɪvlɪ] *adv* instinktiv.

institute ['ɪnstɪtjuːt] 1 *vt* **(a)** *new laws, custom, reforms* einführen; *(found) organization etc* einrichten; *search* einleiten ◆ **a newly ~d post** eine neu eingerichtete Stelle.
(b) *(Jur) enquiry* einleiten; *an action* einleiten *(against sb* gegen jdn); *proceedings* anstrengen *(against* gegen) ◆ **to ~ divorce proceedings** die Scheidung einreichen.
2 *n* Institut *nt*; *(home)* Anstalt *f* ◆ **I ~ of Technology/Education** technische Hochschule/pädagogische Hochschule; **educational** ~ pädagogische Einrichtung; **women's** ~ Frauenverein *m*.

institution [,ɪnstɪ'tjuːʃən] *n see vt* **(a)** Einführung *f*; Einrichtung *f*; Einleitung *f*.
(b) Einleitung *f*; Anstrengung *f*; Einreichung *f*.
(c) *(organization)* Institution, Einrichtung *f*.
(d) *(building, home etc)* Anstalt *f*.
(e) *(custom)* Institution *f* ◆ **he's been here so long he's become an** ~ er ist schon so lange hier, daß er zur Institution geworden ist.

institutional [,ɪnstɪ'tjuːʃənl] *adj* **(a)** *life etc* Anstalts- ◆ ~ **care in hospital/an old folk's home** stationäre Versorgung *or* Pflege im Krankenhaus/in einem Altenheim. **(b)** *(US)* ~ **advertising** Prestigewerbung *f*. **(c)** *(Fin)* ~ **buying** Käufe *pl* durch institutionelle Anleger; ~ **investors** institutionelle Anleger *pl*.

institutionalize [,ɪnstɪ'tjuːʃənəlaɪz] *vt (all senses)* institutionalisieren.

in-store ['ɪnstɔːʳ] *adj attr* im Laden ◆ ~ **surveillance system** geschäftsinternes Überwachungssystem.

instruct [ɪn'strʌkt] *vt* **(a)** *(teach) person* unterrichten ◆ **to ~ sb in the use of a machine** jdn in der Handhabung einer Maschine unterweisen.
(b) *(tell, direct) person* anweisen; *(command)* die Anweisung erteilen *(+dat)*; *(Brit Jur) solicitor (give information to)* unterrichten, instruieren; *(appoint) lawyer* beauftragen; *jury* instruieren, belehren ◆ **I've been ~ed to report to you** ich habe (An)weisung, Ihnen Meldung zu erstatten; **what were you ~ed to do?** welche Instruktionen *or* Anweisungen haben Sie bekommen?
(c) *(form: inform)* in Kenntnis setzen.

instruction [ɪn'strʌkʃən] *n* **(a)** *(teaching)* Unterricht *m* ◆ **course of** ~ Lehrgang *m*; **to give sb ~ in fencing** jdm Fechtunterricht erteilen.
(b) *(order, command)* Anweisung, Instruktion *f*; *(of jury)* Belehrung, Instruktion *f* ◆ **what were your ~s?** welche Instruktionen *or* Anweisungen hatten Sie?; **on whose ~s did you do that?** auf wessen Anweisung *or* Anordnung haben Sie das getan?; **~s for use** Gebrauchsanweisung, Gebrauchsanleitung *f*; ~ **manual** *(Tech)* Bedienungsanleitung *f*.

instructive [ɪn'strʌktɪv] *adj* instruktiv, aufschlußreich; *(of educational value)* lehrreich.

instructor [ɪn'strʌktəʳ] *n (also Sport)* Lehrer *m*; *(US)* Dozent *m*; *(Mil)* Ausbilder *m*.

instructress [ɪn'strʌktrɪs] *n (also Sport)* Lehrerin *f*; *(US)* Dozentin *f*; *(Mil)* Ausbilderin *f*.

instrument ['ɪnstrʊmənt] 1 *n* **(a)** *(Mus, Med, Tech)* Instrument *nt*; *(domestic)* Gerät *nt* ◆ **to fly an aircraft by** *or* **on ~s** ein Flugzeug nach den (Bord)instrumenten fliegen. **(b)** *(person)* Werkzeug *nt*. **(c)** *(Jur)* Urkunde *f*, Dokument *nt*.
2 ['ɪnstrʊ,ment] *vt* **(a)** *(Mus)* instrumentieren.
(b) *(put into effect)* durch- *or* ausführen.

instrument *in cpds (Aviat)* Instrumenten-.

instrumental [,ɪnstrʊ'mentl] 1 *adj* **(a) he was ~ in getting her the job** er hat ihr zu dieser Stelle verholfen; **he was ~ in bringing about the downfall of the government** er war am Sturz der Regierung beteiligt. **(b)** *(Mus) music, accompaniment* Instrumental- ◆ ~ **performer** Instrumentalist(in *f*) *m*.
2 *n (Mus)* Instrumentalstück *nt*.

instrumentalist [,ɪnstrʊ'mentəlɪst] *n* Instrumentalist(in *f*) *m*.

instrumentality [,ɪnstrʊmen'tælɪtɪ] *n* **through** *or* **by the ~ of sb** durch jds Vermittlung *or* Eingreifen.

instrumentation [,ɪnstrʊmen'teɪʃən] *n* Instrumentation *f*.

instrument board *or* **panel** *n (Aviat, Aut)* Armaturenbrett *nt*.

insubordinate [,ɪnsə'bɔːdənɪt] *adj* aufsässig.

insubordination ['ɪnsə,bɔːdɪ'neɪʃən] *n* Aufsässigkeit *f*; *(Mil)* Gehorsamsverweigerung, Insubordination *(dated) f*.

insubstantial [,ɪnsəb'stænʃəl] *adj* wenig substantiell; *fear, hopes, accusation also* gegenstandslos; *dreams* immateriell; *ghost* nicht körperhaft *or* wesenhaft; *amount* gering(fügig); *meal, plot also* dürftig.

insufferable *adj*, **-bly** *adv* [ɪn'sʌfərəbl, -ɪ] unerträglich.

insufficiency [,ɪnsə'fɪʃənsɪ] *n (of supplies)* Knappheit *f*, unzureichende Menge; *(of sb's work)* Unzulänglichkeit *f*.

insufficient [,ɪnsə'fɪʃənt] *adj* nicht genügend, ungenügend *pred*; *work, insulation also* unzulänglich.

insufficiently [,ɪnsə'fɪʃəntlɪ] *adv* ungenügend; unzulänglich.

insular ['ɪnsjələʳ] *adj* **(a)** *(narrow)* engstirnig. **(b)** *administration, climate* Insel-, insular.

insularity [,ɪnsjʊ'lærɪtɪ] *n see adj* **(a)** Engstirnigkeit *f*. **(b)** insulare Lage, Insellage, Insularität *f*.

insulate ['ɪnsjʊleɪt] *vt* **(a)** *room, (Elec)* isolieren ◆ **in this anorak you're well ~d against the cold** in diesem Anorak sind Sie gut gegen Kälte geschützt; **~d pliers** Isolierzange *f*. **(b)** *(fig: from unpleasantness etc)* abschirmen *(from* gegen).

insulating ['ɪnsjʊleɪtɪŋ]: ~ **material** *n (Brit)* Isoliermaterial *nt*; ~ **tape** *n (Brit)* Isolierband *nt*.

insulation [,ɪnsjʊ'leɪʃən] *n* **(a)** Isolation *f*; *(material also)* Isoliermaterial *nt*.
(b) *(fig)* Geschütztheit *f (from* gegen).

insulator ['ɪnsjʊleɪtəʳ] *n (Elec: device)* Isolator *m*; *(material also)* Isolierstoff *m*; *(for heat)* Wärmeschutzisolierung *f*.

insulin ['ɪnsjʊlɪn] *n* Insulin *nt*.

insult [ɪn'sʌlt] 1 *vt* beleidigen; *(by words also)* beschimpfen.
2 ['ɪnsʌlt] *n* Beleidigung *f*; *(with words also)* Beschimpfung *f* ◆ **an ~ to the profession** eine Beleidigung für den ganzen Berufsstand; **an ~ to my intelligence** eine Beleidigung meiner Intelligenz; **that's not a salary, it's an ~!** das ist doch kein Gehalt, das ist blanker Hohn *or* eine Beleidigung!; **to add ~ to injury** das Ganze noch schlimmer machen.

insulting [ɪn'sʌltɪŋ] *adj* beleidigend; *question* unverschämt ◆ **to use ~ language to sb** jdm gegenüber beleidigende Äußerungen machen, jdn beschimpfen; **he was very ~ to her** er hat sich ihr gegenüber sehr beleidigend geäußert.

insultingly [ɪn'sʌltɪŋlɪ] *adv* beleidigend; *behave* in beleidigender *or* unverschämter Weise.

insuperable [ɪn'suːpərəbl] *adj* unüberwindlich.

insuperably [ɪn'suːpərəblɪ] *adv* **it was ~ difficult** es hat unüberwindliche Schwierigkeiten bereitet.

insupportable [,ɪnsə'pɔːtəbl] *adj* unerträglich.

insurable [ɪn'ʃʊərəbl] *adj* versicherbar.

insurance [ɪn'ʃʊərəns] *n* Versicherung *f*; *(amount paid out)* Versicherungssumme *f or* -betrag *m* ◆ **to take out** ~ eine Versicherung abschließen *(against* gegen).

insurance: ~ **agent** *n* Versicherungsvertreter(in *f*) *m*; ~ **broker** *n* Versicherungsmakler *m*; ~ **company** *n* Versicherungsgesellschaft *f*; ~ **cover** *n* Versicherungsschutz *m*; ~ **office** *n* Versicherungsanstalt *f*/-büro *nt*; ~ **policy** *n* Versicherungspolice *f*; *(fig)* Sicherheitsvorkehrung *f*; **to take out an ~ policy** eine Versicherung abschließen; *(fig)* Sicherheitsvorkehrungen treffen; **as an ~ policy** *(fig)* für alle Fälle, sicherheitshalber; ~ **premium** *n* Versicherungsprämie *f*; ~ **scheme** *n* Versicherung(smöglichkeit) *f*; ~ **stamp** *n (Brit)* Versicherungsmarke *f*.

insure [ɪn'ʃʊəʳ] *vt car, house* versichern (lassen) ◆ **to ~ oneself** *or* **one's life** eine Lebensversicherung abschließen; **to ~ oneself against poverty/failure** *etc (fig)* sich gegen Armut/einen Fehlschlag *etc* (ab)sichern.

insured [ɪn'ʃʊəd] 1 *adj* versichert.
2 *n* **the ~ (party)** der/die Versicherungsnehmer(in), der/die Versicherte.

insurer [ɪn'ʃʊərəʳ] *n* Versicherer, Versicherungsgeber *m*.

insurgent [ɪn'sɜːdʒənt] 1 *adj* aufständisch.
2 *n* Aufständische(r) *mf*.

insurmountable [,ɪnsə'maʊntəbl] *adj* unüberwindlich.

insurrection [,ɪnsə'rekʃən] *n* Aufstand *m*.

insurrectionary [,ɪnsə'rekʃənərɪ] 1 *adj* aufständisch.
2 *n* Aufständische(r) *mf*.

insurrectionist [ˌɪnsəˈrekʃənɪst] *n* Aufständische(r) *mf*.

intact [ɪnˈtækt] *adj* (*not damaged*) unversehrt, intakt; (*whole, in one piece*) intakt ◆ **not one window was left ~** kein einziges Fenster blieb ganz *or* heil; **his confidence remained ~** sein Vertrauen blieb ungebrochen *or* unerschüttert.

intake [ˈɪnteɪk] *n* **(a)** (*act*) (*of water, electric current*) Aufnahme *f*; (*of steam*) Ansaugen *nt*; (*amount*) (*of water, electricity*) Aufnahme *f*, aufgenommene Menge; (*of steam*) angesaugte *or* einströmende Menge; (*pipe*) (*for water*) Zuflußrohr, Einführungsrohr *nt*; (*for steam*) Einströmungsöffnung, Ansaugöffnung *f*, Einführungsrohr *nt* ◆ **air ~** Luftzufuhr *f*; **food ~** Nahrungsaufnahme *f*.
(b) (*Sch*) Aufnahme *f*; (*Mil*) Rekrutierung *f* ◆ **what is your yearly ~?** (*Sch*) wie viele neue Schüler nehmen Sie im Jahr auf?; (*Mil*) wie viele Männer rekrutieren Sie im Jahr?

intake: ~ class *n* (*Sch*) Anfängerklasse *f*; **~ valve** *n* Ansaug-/Einlaß-/Einströmventil *nt*.

intangible [ɪnˈtændʒəbl] *adj* **(a)** nicht greifbar. **(b)** *fears, longings* unbestimmbar. **(c)** (*Jur, Comm*) **~ property** immaterielle Güter *pl*; **~ assets** immaterielle Werte *pl*.

integer [ˈɪntɪdʒəʳ] *n* ganze Zahl.

integral [ˈɪntɪgrəl] [1] *adj* **(a)** *part* wesentlich, integral (*geh*). **(b)** (*whole*) vollständig, vollkommen. **(c)** (*Math*) *calculus* Integral-.
[2] *n* (*Math*) Integral *nt*.

integrate [ˈɪntɪgreɪt] [1] *vt* (*all senses*) integrieren ◆ **to ~ sth into sth** etw in etw (*acc*) integrieren; **to ~ sth with sth** etw auf etw (*acc*) abstimmen; **to ~ a school/college** (*US*) eine Schule/ein College auch für Schwarze *etc* zugänglich machen.
[2] *vi* (*US: schools etc*) auch für Schwarze *etc* zugänglich werden.

integrated [ˈɪntɪgreɪtɪd] *adj plan* einheitlich; *piece of work* einheitlich, ein organisches Ganzes bildend; *school, town* ohne Rassentrennung ◆ **a fully ~ personality** eine in sich ausgewogene Persönlichkeit; **~ circuit** integrierter Schaltkreis.

integration [ˌɪntɪˈgreɪʃən] *n* (*all senses*) Integration *f* (*into* in +*acc*) ◆ **(racial) ~** Rassenintegration *f*.

integrationist [ˌɪntɪˈgreɪʃənɪst] *n* (*US*) Vertreter(in *f*) *m* der Rassenintegration.

integrity [ɪnˈtegrɪtɪ] *n* **(a)** (*honesty*) Integrität *f*. **(b)** (*wholeness*) Einheit *f*.

integument [ɪnˈtegjʊmənt] *n* Integument *nt* (*spec*).

intellect [ˈɪntɪlekt] *n* **(a)** Intellekt *m* ◆ **a man of such ~** ein Mann mit einem solchen Intellekt; **his powers of ~** seine intellektuellen Fähigkeiten. **(b)** (*person*) großer Geist.

intellectual [ɪntɪˈlektjʊəl] [1] *adj* intellektuell; *interests also* geistig ◆ **something a little more ~** etwas geistig Anspruchsvolleres.
[2] *n* Intellektuelle(r) *mf*.

intellectualism [ɪntɪˈlektjʊəlɪzəm] *n* Intellektualismus *m*.

intellectualize [ɪntɪˈlektjʊəlaɪz] *vt* intellektualisieren.

intellectually [ɪntɪˈlektjʊəlɪ] *adv* intellektuell ◆ **he always approaches emotional problems much too ~** er geht an Gefühlsprobleme immer viel zu verstandesmäßig heran.

intelligence [ɪnˈtelɪdʒəns] *n* **(a)** Intelligenz *f* ◆ **hedgehogs don't have much ~** Igel haben keine große Intelligenz; **a man of little ~** ein Mensch von geringer Intelligenz; **if he hasn't got the ~ to wear a coat** wenn er nicht gescheit genug ist, einen Mantel anzuziehen.
(b) (*news, information*) Informationen *pl* ◆ **according to our latest ~** unseren letzten Meldungen *or* Informationen zufolge; **shipping ~** Meldungen *pl* für die Schiffahrt; **enemy shipping ~** Informationen *pl* über Feindschiffe.
(c) (*Mil etc*) Geheim- *or* Nachrichtendienst *m*.

intelligence: ~ corps *n* (*Mil*) Geheim- *or* Nachrichtend ienst *m*; **~ officer** *n* (*Mil*) Nachrichtenoffizier *m*; **~ quotient** *n* Intelligenzquotient *m*; **~ service** *n* (*Pol*) Geheim- *or* Nachrichtendienst *m*; **~ test** *n* Intelligenztest *m*.

intelligent [ɪnˈtelɪdʒənt] *adj* intelligent, klug; *machine* intelligent ◆ **are there ~ beings on Mars?** gibt es auf dem Mars vernunftbegabte *or* intelligente Lebewesen?

intelligently [ɪnˈtelɪdʒəntlɪ] *adv* intelligent.

intelligentsia [ɪnˌtelɪˈdʒentsɪə] *n* Intelligenz, Intelligenzija *f*.

intelligibility [ɪnˌtelɪdʒəˈbɪlɪtɪ] *n* Verständlichkeit *f*; (*of handwriting*) Leserlichkeit *f*.

intelligible [ɪnˈtelɪdʒəbl] *adj* zu verstehen *pred*, verständlich; *handwriting* leserlich (*to sb* für jdn).

intelligibly [ɪnˈtelɪdʒəblɪ] *adv* deutlich.

intemperance [ɪnˈtempərəns] *n* (*lack of moderation*) Maßlosigkeit, Unmäßigkeit *f*; (*drunkenness*) Trunksucht *f*.

intemperate [ɪnˈtempərɪt] *adj* **(a)** *person* (*lacking moderation*) unmäßig, maßlos; (*addicted to drink*) trunksüchtig. **(b)** *climate* extrem; *wind* heftig; *zeal, haste* übermäßig.

▼ **intend** [ɪnˈtend] *vt* **(a)** (+*n*) beabsichtigen, wollen ◆ **I ~ him to go with me** ich beabsichtige *or* habe vor, ihn mitzunehmen; (*insist*) er soll mir mitkommen; **I ~ed no harm** es war (von mir) nicht böse gemeint; (*with action*) ich hatte nichts Böses beabsichtigt; **did you ~ that?** hatten Sie das beabsichtigt?, war das Ihre Absicht?; **I didn't ~ it as an insult** das sollte keine Beleidigung sein; **it was ~ed as a compliment** das sollte ein Kompliment sein; **I wondered what he ~ed by that remark** ich fragte mich, was er mit dieser Bemerkung beabsichtigte; **the meaning which he ~ed was not the same as that which came across** er meinte das nicht so, wie es aufgefaßt wurde; **he is ~ed for the diplomatic service** er soll einmal in den diplomatischen Dienst; **this park is ~ed for the general public** dieser Park ist für die Öffentlichkeit gedacht *or* bestimmt; **that remark was ~ed for you** diese Bemerkung war auf Sie gemünzt, mit dieser Bemerkung waren Sie gemeint; **this water is not ~ed for drinking** dieses Wasser ist nicht zum Trinken (gedacht); **games ~ed for young children** Spiele, die für kleine Kinder gedacht sind.
▼ **(b)** (+*vb*) beabsichtigen, fest vorhaben ◆ **he ~s to win** er hat fest vor, zu gewinnen; **I ~ to leave next year** ich beabsichtige *or* habe vor, nächstes Jahr zu gehen; **if you don't change your mind then you should know that I ~ to leave you!** laß dir gesagt sein, wenn du es dir nicht anders überlegst, mache ich ernst und verlasse dich; **what do you ~ to do about it?** was beabsichtigen Sie, dagegen zu tun?; **I fully ~ to punish him** ich habe fest vor *or* bin fest entschlossen, ihn zu bestrafen; **you are ~ed to help me** Sie sollen mir helfen; **did you ~ that to happen?** hatten Sie das beabsichtigt?

intended [ɪnˈtendɪd] [1] *adj* **(a)** *effect* beabsichtigt, geplant ◆ **what is the ~ meaning of that remark?** was ist mit dieser Bemerkung gemeint? **(b)** *husband, wife* zukünftig, in spe *pred*.
[2] *n* **my ~** (*inf*) mein Zukünftiger (*inf*)/meine Zukünftige (*inf*).

intense [ɪnˈtens] *adj* **(a)** intensiv; *joy, anxiety, disappointment* äußerst groß. **(b)** *person* ernsthaft; *study, life* intensiv ◆ **he suddenly looked very ~** er sah plötzlich ganz ernst aus.

intensely [ɪnˈtenslɪ] *adv cold, hot, disappointed, angry, difficult* äußerst; *study* intensiv, ernsthaft ◆ **he spoke so ~ that none could doubt his sincerity** er sprach mit einer solchen Intensität, daß niemand an seiner Aufrichtigkeit zweifeln konnte.

intenseness [ɪnˈtensnɪs] *n see* **intensity**.

intensification [ɪnˌtensɪfɪˈkeɪʃən] *n* Intensivierung *f*; (*Phot*) Verstärkung *f*.

intensifier [ɪnˈtensɪfaɪəʳ] *n* (*Gram*) Verstärkungspartikel *f* ◆ **image ~** (*Phys*) Bildverstärker *m*.

intensify [ɪnˈtensɪfaɪ] [1] *vt* intensivieren; *meaning* verstärken.
[2] *vi* zunehmen; (*pain, heat also*) stärker werden; (*fighting also*) sich verschärfen.

intensity [ɪnˈtensɪtɪ] *n* Intensität *f*; (*of feeling, storm also*) Heftigkeit *f* ◆ **~ of a negative** (*Phot*) Dichte *f* eines Negativs.

intensive [ɪnˈtensɪv] *adj* intensiv, Intensiv- ◆ **to be in ~ care** (*Med*) auf der Intensivstation sein; **~ care unit** Intensivstation *f*; **they came under ~ fire** sie kamen unter heftigen Beschuß.

intensively [ɪnˈtensɪvlɪ] *adv* intensiv.

intent [ɪnˈtent] [1] *n* Absicht *f* ◆ **with good ~** in guter Absicht; **to all ~s and purposes** im Grunde; **with ~ to** (*esp Jur*) in der Absicht *or* mit dem Vorsatz zu; **to do sth with ~** etw vorsätzlich tun; *see* **loiter**.
[2] *adj* **(a)** *look* durchdringend, forschend.
(b) to be ~ on achieving sth fest entschlossen sein, etw zu erreichen; **he was so ~ on catching the bus that he didn't notice the lorry coming** er war so darauf bedacht, den Bus zu kriegen, daß er den Lastwagen nicht kommen sah; **to be ~ on one's work** auf seine Arbeit konzentriert sein.

▼ **intention** [ɪnˈtenʃən] *n* **(a)** Absicht, Intention *f* ◆ **what was your ~ in saying that?** mit welcher Absicht haben Sie das gesagt?; **it is my ~ to punish you severely** ich beabsichtige, Sie streng zu bestrafen; **I have every ~ of doing that** ich habe die feste Absicht, das zu tun; **to have no ~ of doing sth** nicht die Absicht haben, etw zu tun; **I have no** *or* **haven't the least** *or* **the slightest ~ of staying!** ich habe nicht die geringste Absicht hierzubleiben, ich denke nicht daran hierzubleiben; **with good ~s** mit guten Vorsätzen; **with the best of ~s** in der besten Absicht; **with the ~ of ...** in der Absicht zu ..., mit dem Vorsatz zu ...; **his ~s are good, but he seldom carries them out** er hat immer gute Vorsätze *pl*, aber er führt sie selten aus.
(b) ~s (*inf*) (Heirats)absichten *pl* ◆ **his ~s are honourable** er hat ehrliche Absichten *pl*.

intentional [ɪnˈtenʃənl] *adj* absichtlich, vorsätzlich (*esp Jur*) ◆ **it wasn't ~** das war keine Absicht, es war unabsichtlich.

intentionally [ɪnˈtenʃnəlɪ] *adv* absichtlich.

intently [ɪnˈtentlɪ] *adv listen, gaze* konzentriert.

inter [ɪnˈtɜːʳ] *vt* (*form*) bestatten.

inter- [ˈɪntəʳ-] *pref* zwischen-, Zwischen-.

interact [ˌɪntərˈækt] *vi* aufeinander wirken; (*Phys*) wechselwirken; (*Psychol, Sociol*) interagieren.

interaction [ˌɪntərˈækʃən] *n see vi* gegenseitige Einwirkung, Wechselwirkung *f* (*also Phys*); Interaktion *f*.

interactive [ˌɪntərˈæktɪv] *adj* interaktiv; **~ television** *n* interaktives Fernsehen.

inter alia [ˈɪntərˈeɪlɪə] *adv* unter anderem.

interbank [ˈɪntəˈbæŋk] *adj* (*Fin*) **~ deposits** Bank-bei-Bank-Einlagen *pl*; **~ loan** Bank-an-Bank-Kredit *m*.

interbreed [ˈɪntəˈbriːd] [1] *vt* kreuzen.
[2] *vi* (*crossbreed*) sich kreuzen; (*inbreed*) sich untereinander vermehren.

intercede [ˌɪntəˈsiːd] *vi* sich einsetzen, sich verwenden (*with* bei, *for, on behalf of* für); (*in argument*) vermitteln.

intercellular [ˌɪntəˈseljʊləʳ] *adj* interzellular.

intercept [ˌɪntəˈsept] *vt message, person, plane, pass* abfangen; (*Math*) abschneiden ◆ **they ~ed the enemy** sie schnitten dem Feind den Weg ab.

interception [ˌɪntəˈsepʃən] *n see vt* Abfangen *nt*; Sektion *f* ◆ **point of ~** (*Math*) Schnittpunkt *m*.

interceptor [ˌɪntəˈseptəʳ] *n* (*Aviat*) Abfangjäger *m*.

intercession [ˌɪntəˈseʃən] *n* Fürsprache *f*; (*in argument*) Vermittlung *f*.

➤ LANGUAGE IN USE: **intend: b** → 8.1, 8.2, 8.3 **intention: a** → 8.2, 8.3

interchange [ˈɪntəˌtʃeɪndʒ] 1 *n* (a) (*of roads*) Kreuzung *f*; (*of motorways*) (Autobahn)kreuz *nt*. (b) (*exchange*) Austausch *m*.
2 [ˌɪntəˈtʃeɪndʒ] *vt* (a) (*switch round*) (miteinander) vertauschen, (aus)tauschen. (b) *ideas etc* austauschen (*with* mit).
interchangeable [ˌɪntəˈtʃeɪndʒəbl] *adj* austauschbar ◆ **the front wheels are ~ with the back ones** Vorder- und Hinterräder sind austauschbar.
interchangeably [ˌɪntəˈtʃeɪndʒəblɪ] *adv* austauschbar ◆ **they are used ~** sie können ausgetauscht werden.
inter-city [ˌɪntəˈsɪtɪ] *adj* Intercity- ◆ **~ train** Intercityzug *m*.
intercollegiate [ˈɪntəkəˈliːdʒɪt] *adj* zwischen Colleges.
intercom [ˈɪntəkɒm] *n* (Gegen)sprechanlage *f*; (*in ship, plane*) Bordverständigungsanlage *f*; (*in schools etc*) Lautsprecheranlage *f*.
intercommunicate [ˌɪntəkəˈmjuːnɪkeɪt] *vi* (*departments, people*) miteinander in Verbindung stehen; (*rooms*) miteinander verbunden sein.
intercommunication [ˈɪntəkəˌmjuːnɪˈkeɪʃən] *n* gegenseitige Verbindung, Verbindung *f* untereinander.
intercommunion [ˌɪntəkəˈmjuːnɪən] *n* Beziehungen *pl*.
interconnect [ˌɪntəkəˈnekt] 1 *vt* miteinander verbinden; *parts* schlüssig verbinden; *loudspeakers, circuits also* zusammenschalten ◆ **~ed facts/results/events** *etc* zueinander in Beziehung stehende Tatsachen *pl*/Ergebnisse *pl*/Ereignisse *pl etc*; **are these events ~ed in any way?** besteht irgendein Zusammenhang zwischen diesen Vorfällen?
2 *vi* (*parts*) sich schlüssig verbinden; (*rooms*) miteinander verbunden sein; (*facts, events*) in Zusammenhang stehen ◆ **~ing rooms** miteinander verbundene Zimmer *pl*.
interconnection [ˌɪntəkəˈnekʃən] *n* Verbindung *f*; (*of parts*) schlüssige Verbindung; (*of circuits etc*) Zusammenschaltung *f*; (*of facts, events etc*) Verbindung *f*, Zusammenhang *m*.
intercontinental [ˈɪntəˌkɒntɪˈnentl] *adj* interkontinental, Interkontinental-.
intercourse [ˈɪntəkɔːs] *n* (a) Verkehr *m* ◆ **commercial ~** Handelsbeziehungen *pl*; **human/social ~** Verkehr *m* mit Menschen/gesellschaftlicher Verkehr.
(b) **(sexual) ~** (Geschlechts)verkehr *m*; **did ~ take place?** hat (Geschlechts)verkehr *or* Beischlaf stattgefunden?
interdenominational [ˈɪntədɪˌnɒmɪˈneɪʃənl] *adj* interkonfessionell.
interdepartmental [ˈɪntəˌdiːpɑːtˈmentl] *adj relations, quarrel* zwischen den Abteilungen; *conference, projects* mehrere Abteilungen betreffend.
interdependence [ˌɪntədɪˈpendəns] *n* wechselseitige Abhängigkeit, Interdependenz *f* (*geh*).
interdependent [ˌɪntədɪˈpendənt] *adj* wechselseitig voneinander abhängig, interdependent (*geh*).
interdict [ˈɪntədɪkt] 1 *vt* (a) (*Jur*) untersagen, verbieten. (b) (*Eccl*) *person, place* mit dem Interdikt belegen; *priest* suspendieren.
2 *n* (a) (*Jur*) Verbot *nt*. (b) (*Eccl*) Interdikt *nt*.
interdiction [ˌɪntəˈdɪkʃən] *n* (*Jur*) Verbot *nt*, Untersagung *f*; (*Eccl*) Interdikt *nt*.
▼ **interest** [ˈɪntrɪst] 1 *n* (a) Interesse *nt* ◆ **do you have any ~ in chess?** interessieren Sie sich für Schach?, haben Sie Interesse an Schach (*dat*)?; **to take/feel an ~ in sb/sth** sich für jdn/etw interessieren; **to take a sympathetic ~ in sth** an etw (*dat*) Anteil nehmen; **after that he took no further ~ in us/it** danach war er nicht mehr an uns (*dat*)/daran interessiert; **to show (an) ~ in sb/sth** Interesse für jdn/etw zeigen; **is it of any ~ to you?** (*do you want it*) sind Sie daran interessiert?; **just for ~** nur aus Interesse, nur interessehalber; **he has lost ~** er hat das Interesse verloren; **what are your ~s?** was sind Ihre Interessen(gebiete)?; **his ~s are ...** er interessiert sich für ...
(b) (*importance*) Interesse *nt* (*to* für) ◆ **matters of vital ~ to the economy** Dinge *pl* von lebenswichtiger Bedeutung *or* lebenswichtigem Interesse für die Wirtschaft.
(c) (*advantage, welfare*) Interesse *nt* ◆ **to act in sb's/one's own ~(s)** in jds/im eigenen Interesse handeln; **in the ~(s) of sb/sth** in jds Interesse (*dat*)/im Interesse einer Sache (*gen*); **the public ~** das öffentliche Wohl; **in the public ~** im öffentlichen Interesse.
(d) (*Fin*) Zinsen *pl* ◆ **~ on an investment** Zinsen aus einer Kapitalanlage; **rate of ~, ~ rate** Zinssatz *m*; **to bear ~ at 4%** 4% Zinsen tragen, mit 4% verzinst sein; **loan with ~** verzinstes Darlehen; **to repay a loan with ~** ein Darlehen mit Zins und Zinseszins zurückzahlen; **to return sb's kindness with ~** (*fig*) jds Freundlichkeit vielfach erwidern; **I'll pay him back with ~** (*fig*) ich werde es ihm mit Zinsen heimzahlen.
(e) (*Comm*) (*share, stake*) Anteil *m*; (*~ group*) Kreise *pl*, Interessentengruppe *f* ◆ **shipping/oil ~s** (*shares*) Reederei-/Ölanteile *pl*; (*people*) Reeder, Reedereikreise *pl*/Vertreter *pl* von Ölinteressen; **the landed ~(s)** die Landbesitzer *pl*, die Gutsbesitzer *pl*; **he has a financial ~ in the company** er ist finanziell an der Firma beteiligt; **British trading ~s** britische Handelsinteressen *pl*; **German ~s in Africa** deutsche Interessen *pl* in Afrika.
▼ 2 *vt* interessieren (*in* für, an *+dat*) ◆ **to ~ sb in doing sth** jdn dafür interessieren, etw zu tun; **can I ~ you in a little drink?** kann ich Sie zu etwas Alkoholischem überreden?; **to ~ a pupil in maths** das Interesse eines Schülers an *or* für Mathematik wecken, einen Schüler für Mathematik interessieren; **to ~ oneself in sb/sth** sich für jdn/etw interessieren.
interest-bearing [ˈɪntrɪstˌbeərɪŋ] *adj loan* verzinslich; *account, investment* mit Zinsertrag, zinsbringend.
interested [ˈɪntrɪstɪd] *adj* (a) interessiert (*in* an *+dat*) ◆ **I'm not ~** ich habe kein Interesse (daran), ich bin nicht (daran) interessiert; **... and I'm not even ~ either** ... und es interessiert mich auch gar nicht; **to be ~ in sb/sth** sich für jdn/etw interessieren, an jdm/etw interessiert sein; **would you be ~ in a game of cards?** hätten Sie Interesse, Karten zu spielen?; **I'm going to the cinema, are you ~ (in coming)?** ich gehe ins Kino, haben Sie Interesse daran *or* Lust mitzukommen?; **I'm selling my car, are you ~?** ich verkaufe meinen Wagen, sind Sie interessiert?; **the company is ~ in expanding its sales** die Firma hat Interesse daran *or* ist daran interessiert, ihren Absatz zu vergrößern; **I'd be ~ to know how ...** es würde mich ja schon interessieren, wie ...; **she was ~ to see what he would do** sie war gespannt, was er wohl tun würde; **I was ~ to hear that** es interessierte mich, das zu hören.
(b) (*having personal or financial interest*) befangen; (*involved*) beteiligt ◆ **he is an ~ party** er ist befangen/daran beteiligt.
interest-free [ˈɪntrɪstˌfriː] *adj, adv* zinslos, zinsfrei.
interest group *n* Interessengruppe *f*.
interesting [ˈɪntrɪstɪŋ] *adj* interessant ◆ **she's in an ~ condition** (*euph*) sie ist in anderen Umständen.
interestingly [ˈɪntrɪstɪŋlɪ] *adv see adj* ◆ **~ enough, I saw him yesterday** interessanterweise habe ich ihn gestern gesehen.
interface [ˈɪntəfeɪs] 1 *n* Grenzfläche, Grenzschicht *f*; (*Comput*) Schnittstelle *f*, Interface *nt* ◆ **there's a bigger ~ between these two fields than I thought** diese beiden Gebiete haben mehr Berührungspunkte, als ich gedacht hätte; **the man/machine ~ in society** die Interaktion von Mensch und Maschine in der Gesellschaft.
2 [ɪntəˈfeɪs] *vt* koppeln.
interfacing [ˈɪntəfeɪsɪŋ] *n* (*Sew*) Einlage *f*.
interfere [ˌɪntəˈfɪəʳ] *vi* (a) (*meddle*) (*in argument, sb's affairs*) sich einmischen (*in* in *+acc*); (*with machinery, sb's property*) sich zu schaffen machen (*with* an *+dat*); (*euph: sexually*) sich vergehen (*with* an *+dat*) ◆ **don't ~ with the machine** laß die Finger von der Maschine; **who's been interfering with my books?** wer war an meinen Büchern?; **the body has been ~d with** jemand hatte sich an der Leiche zu schaffen gemacht; (*sexually*) die Leiche zeigte Spuren eines Sittlichkeitsverbrechens.
(b) (*thing, event: disrupt, obstruct*) **to ~ with sth** etw stören (*also Rad*); **to ~ with sb's plans** jds Pläne durchkreuzen.
interference [ˌɪntəˈfɪərəns] *n* (a) (*meddling*) Einmischung *f* ◆ **I don't want any ~ with my books/papers** ich will nicht, daß jemand an meine Bücher/Papiere geht. (b) (*disruption, Rad, TV*) Störung *f* (*with gen*).
interfering [ˌɪntəˈfɪərɪŋ] *adj person* sich ständig einmischend ◆ **his ~ ways annoy me** es ärgert *or* stört mich, wie er sich immer einmischt; **don't be so ~** misch dich nicht immer ein.
interferon [ˌɪntəˌfɪərɒn] *n* (*Chem*) Interferon *nt*.
intergalactic [ˌɪntəgəˈlæktɪk] *adj* intergalaktisch.
interim [ˈɪntərɪm] 1 *n* Zwischenzeit *f*, Interim *nt* (*geh*) ◆ **in the ~** in der Zwischenzeit.
2 *adj* vorläufig; *agreement, arrangements, solution also* Übergangs-, Interims- (*geh*); *report, payment* Zwischen-; *government* Übergangs-, Interims- (*geh*) ◆ **~ dividend** (*Fin*) Abschlagsdividende *f*.
interior [ɪnˈtɪərɪəʳ] 1 *adj* (*inside*) Innen-; (*inland*) Binnen-; (*domestic*) Inlands-, Binnen-.
2 *n* (*of country*) Innere(s) *nt*; (*Art*) Interieur *nt*; (*of house*) Innenausstattung *f*, Interieur *nt* (*geh*); (*Phot*) Innenaufnahme *f* ◆ **deep in the ~** tief im Landesinneren; **Department of the I~** (*US*) Innenministerium *nt*; **the ~ of the house has been newly decorated** das Haus ist innen neu gemacht.
interior: ~ angle *n* Innenwinkel *m*; **~ decoration** *n* Innenausstattung *f*; (*decor also*) Interieur *nt*; **~ decorator** *n* Innenausstatter(in *f*) *m*; **~ design** *n* Innenarchitektur *f*; **~ designer** *n* Innenarchitekt(in *f*) *m*; **~ monologue** *n* innerer Monolog; **~-sprung** *adj mattress* Federkern-.
interject [ˌɪntəˈdʒekt] *vt remark, question* einwerfen ◆ **..., he ~ed ...,** rief er dazwischen.
interjection [ˌɪntəˈdʒekʃən] *n* (*exclamation*) Ausruf *m*; (*Ling also*) Interjektion *f*; (*remark*) Einwurf *m*.
interlace [ˌɪntəˈleɪs] 1 *vt threads etc* verflechten; (*in cloth also*) verweben; *cloth* (*with thread*) durchwirken; *fingers* verschlingen; (*fig*) *scenes, styles* verflechten.
2 *vi* sich ineinander verflechten; (*twigs*) verschlungen sein.
interlacing [ˈɪntəleɪsɪŋ] 1 *adj* verflochten; *branches also* verschlungen.
2 *n* Flechtwerk *nt*.
interlard [ˌɪntəˈlɑːd] *vt* **to ~ a speech with facetious comments** witzige Kommentare in eine Rede einflechten; **a speech ~ed with jokes** eine mit Witzen gespickte Rede.
interleave [ˌɪntəˈliːv] *vt* mit Zwischenblättern versehen, durchschießen (*spec*).
inter-library loan [ˈɪntəˌlaɪbrərɪˈləʊn] *n* Fernleihe *f* ◆ **to have a book on ~** ein Buch über die Fernleihe (ausgeliehen) haben.
interline [ˌɪntəˈlaɪn] *vt* (a) (*Typ*) *corrections, translation* interlinear einfügen. (b) (*Sew*) mit einer Einlage versehen.
interlinear [ˌɪntəˈlɪnɪəʳ] *adj* Interlinear-, interlinear.
interlink [ˌɪntəˈlɪŋk] 1 *vt* ineinanderhängen; (*fig*) *theories etc* miteinander verknüpfen *or* verbinden.
2 *vi* ineinanderhängen; (*fig: theories etc*) zusammenhängen.
interlock [ˌɪntəˈlɒk] 1 *vt* (fest) zusammen- *or* ineinanderstecken.
2 *vi* ineinandergreifen; (*one piece*) fest stecken *or* sitzen (*with* in *+dat*); (*antlers, chariot wheels etc*) sich verfangen; (*antlers*) sich verhaken; (*fig: destinies*) verkettet sein.
interlocutor [ˌɪntəˈlɒkjʊtəʳ] *n* Gesprächspartner(in *f*) *m*; (*asking questions*) Fragesteller(in *f*) *m*.

➤ LANGUAGE IN USE: **interest: 1a** → 19.3 **2** → 2.2, 7.5

interloper ['ɪntələʊpəʳ] *n* Eindringling *m*.
interlude ['ɪntəlu:d] *n* Periode *f*; (*Theat*) (*interval*) Pause *f*; (*performance*) Zwischenspiel *nt*; (*Mus*) Interludium *nt*; (*episode*) Intermezzo *nt*, Episode *f* ◆ **a brief ~ of peace** eine kurze Zeit *or* Periode des Friedens; **a peaceful ~ in his busy life** eine friedliche Unterbrechung seines geschäftigen Lebens.
intermarriage [,ɪntə'mærɪdʒ] *n* (*between groups*) Mischehen *pl*; (*within the group*) Heirat *f* untereinander.
intermarry [,ɪntə'mærɪ] *vi* (*marry within the group*) untereinander heiraten; (*two groups: marry with each other*) sich durch Heirat vermischen, Mischehen eingehen.
intermediary [,ɪntə'mi:dɪərɪ] [1] *n* (Ver)mittler(in *f*) *m*, Mittelsperson *f*, Mittelsmann *m*.
[2] *adj* (*intermediate*) Zwischen-; (*mediating*) Vermittlungs-, vermittelnd.
intermediate [,ɪntə'mi:dɪət] *adj* Zwischen-; *French, maths etc* für fortgeschrittene Anfänger ◆ **an ~ student** ein fortgeschrittener Anfänger; **~-range missile** Mittelstreckenrakete *f*.
interment [ɪn'tɜ:mənt] *n* Beerdigung, Bestattung *f*.
intermezzo [,ɪntə'metsəʊ] *n* Intermezzo *nt*.
interminable [ɪn'tɜ:mɪnəbl] *adj* endlos ◆ **after what seemed an ~ journey** nach einer Reise, die nicht enden zu wollen schien.
interminably [ɪn'tɜ:mɪnəblɪ] *adv* endlos, ewig.
intermingle [,ɪntə'mɪŋgl] [1] *vt* vermischen.
[2] *vi* sich mischen (*with* unter +*acc*) ◆ **people from many countries ~d at the conference** Menschen aus vielen Ländern bekamen bei der Konferenz Kontakt miteinander.
intermission [,ɪntə'mɪʃən] *n* **(a)** Unterbrechung, Pause *f*. **(b)** (*Theat, Film*) Pause *f*.
intermittent [,ɪntə'mɪtənt] *adj* periodisch auftretend; (*Tech*) intermittierend ◆ **~ fever** Wechselfieber *nt*.
intermittently [,ɪntə'mɪtəntlɪ] *adv* periodisch; (*Tech*) intermittierend.
intermix [,ɪntə'mɪks] [1] *vt* vermischen.
[2] *vi* sich vermischen.
intern¹ [ɪn'tɜ:n] *vt person* internieren; *ship etc* festhalten.
intern² ['ɪntɜ:n] (*US*) [1] *n* Assistenzarzt *m*/-ärztin *f*.
[2] *vi* das Medizinalpraktikum absolvieren.
internal [ɪn'tɜ:nl] *adj* (*inner*) innere(r, s); (*Math*) *angle, diameter* Innen-; (*within country also*) *trade etc* Binnen-, im Inland; (*within organization*) *policy, mail examination, examiner* intern; *telephone* Haus- ◆ **~ combustion engine** Verbrennungsmotor *m*; **~ medicine** Innere Medizin; **~ market** (*Econ*) Binnenmarkt *m*; (*in health service etc, within organization*) marktwirtschaftliche Struktur; **~ rhyme** Binnenreim *m*; **I~ Revenue Service** (*US*) Steueramt, Finanzamt *nt*; **~ affairs** innere Angelegenheiten *pl*, Inneres *nt*.
internalize [ɪn'tɜ:nəlaɪz] *vt* verinnerlichen, internalisieren (*spec*).
internally [ɪn'tɜ:nəlɪ] *adv* innen, im Inneren; (*in body*) innerlich; (*in country*) landesintern; (*in organization*) intern ◆ **he is bleeding ~** er hat innere Blutungen *pl*; **"not to be taken ~"** „nicht zur inneren Anwendung", „nicht zum Einnehmen".
international [,ɪntə'næʃnəl] [1] *adj* international ◆ **I~ Court of Justice** Internationaler Gerichtshof; **~ date line** Datumsgrenze *f*; **~ law** Völkerrecht *nt*, internationales Recht; **I~ Monetary Fund** Internationaler Währungsfonds; **~ money order** Auslandsanweisung *f*; **I~ Olympic Committee** Internationales Olympisches Komitee.
[2] *n* **(a)** (*Sport*) (*match*) Länderspiel *nt*; (*player*) Nationalspieler(in *f*) *m*. **(b)** (*Pol*) **I~** Internationale *f*.
Internationale [,ɪntə,næʃə'nɑ:l] *n* Internationale *f*.
internationalism [,ɪntə'næʃnəlɪzəm] *n* Internationalismus *m*.
internationalist [,ɪntə'næʃnəlɪst] *n* Internationalist(in *f*) *m*.
internationalize [,ɪntə'næʃnəlaɪz] *vt* internationalisieren.
internationally [,ɪntə'næʃnəlɪ] *adv* international.
interne *n, vi see* **intern²**.
internecine [,ɪntə'ni:saɪn] *adj* (*mutually destructive*) für beide Seiten verlustreich; (*bloody*) mörderisch ◆ **~ war** gegenseitiger Vernichtungskrieg; **~ strife** innere Zerrissenheit.
internee [,ɪntɜ:'ni:] *n* Internierte(r) *mf*.
Internet ['ɪntənet] *n* **the ~** das Internet; **to surf the ~** im Internet surfen.
internist [ɪn'tɜ:nɪst] *n* (*US*) Internist(in *f*) *m*.
internment [ɪn'tɜ:nmənt] *n* Internierung *f* ◆ **~ camp** Internierungslager *nt*.
internship ['ɪntɜ:nʃɪp] *n* (*US*) Medizinalpraktikum *nt*.
internuncio [,ɪntə'nʌnsɪəʊ] *n* Internuntius *m*.
interplanetary [,ɪntə'plænɪtərɪ] *adj* interplanetar.
interplay ['ɪntəpleɪ] *n* Zusammenspiel *nt*.
Interpol ['ɪntəpɒl] *n* Interpol *f*.
interpolate [ɪn'tɜ:pəleɪt] *vt remark* einwerfen; *matter into book etc* interpolieren, einfügen; (*Math*) interpolieren.
interpolation [ɪn,tɜ:pə'leɪʃən] *n* (*of remark*) Einwerfen *nt*; (*remark made*) Einwurf *m*; (*in text*) Interpolation, Einfügung *f*; (*Math*) Interpolation *f*.
interpose [,ɪntə'pəʊz] [1] *vt* **(a)** *object* dazwischenbringen *or* -stellen/-legen ◆ **to ~ sth between two things** etw zwischen zwei Dinge bringen *or* stellen/legen; **to be ~d between two things** zwischen zwei Dingen stehen/liegen; **to ~ oneself between two people** sich zwischen zwei Leute stellen.
(b) (*interject*) *remark, question* einwerfen; *objection* vorbringen (*into* in +*dat*).
[2] *vi* (*intervene*) eingreifen.
interpret [ɪn'tɜ:prɪt] [1] *vt* **(a)** (*translate orally*) dolmetschen. **(b)** (*explain, understand*) auslegen, interpretieren; *omen, dream* deuten; (*Theat, Mus*) interpretieren ◆ **how would you ~ what he said?** wie würden Sie seine Worte verstehen *or* auffassen?
[2] *vi* dolmetschen.
interpretation [ɪn,tɜ:prɪ'teɪʃən] *n* **(a)** *see vt (b)* Auslegung, Interpretation *f*; Deutung *f*; Interpretation *f* ◆ **what ~ do they put on his speech?** wie legen sie seine Rede aus?, wie interpretieren sie seine Rede?; **the speech can be given several ~s** die Rede kann verschieden ausgelegt *or* interpretiert werden; **an ~ of a poem** eine Gedichtinterpretation. **(b)** (*Admin: interpreting*) Dolmetschen *nt*.
interpretative [ɪn'tɜ:prɪtətɪv] *adj* interpretierend.
interpreter [ɪn'tɜ:prɪtəʳ] *n* **(a)** Dolmetscher(in *f*) *m*; (*Theat, Mus*) Interpret(in *f*) *m*; (*of dreams*) Traumdeuter(in *f*) *m*. **(b)** (*Comput*) Interpreter *m*.
interpretive [ɪn'tɜ:prɪtɪv] *adj see* **interpretative**.
interracial [,ɪntə'reɪʃəl] *adj* (*between races*) zwischen den *or* verschiedenen Rassen; (*multiracial*) gemischtrassig ◆ **~ tensions** Rassenspannungen *pl*.
interregnum [,ɪntə'regnəm] *n, pl* **-s** *or* **interregna** [,ɪntə'regnə] Interregnum *nt*.
interrelate [,ɪntərɪ'leɪt] *vt two things* zueinander in Beziehung bringen, eine Beziehung herstellen zwischen (+*dat*) ◆ **to ~ one thing with another** eine Sache in Beziehung zu einer anderen bringen; **to be ~d** zueinander in Beziehung stehen, zusammenhängen; **~d facts** zusammenhängende Tatsachen *pl*.
interrelation [,ɪntərɪ'leɪʃən] *n* Beziehung *f* (*between* zwischen +*dat*).
interrogate [ɪn'terəgeɪt] *vt* verhören; (*father, headmaster etc*) regelrecht verhören.
interrogation [ɪn,terə'geɪʃən] *n* Verhör *nt* ◆ **why should I submit to your ~?** warum soll ich mich von dir verhören lassen?; **~ room** Vernehmungsraum *m or* -zimmer *nt*.
interrogative [,ɪntə'rɒgətɪv] [1] *adj look, tone* fragend; (*Gram*) Frage-, Interrogativ-.
[2] *n* (*Gram*) (*pronoun*) Interrogativpronomen, Fragefürwort *nt*; (*mood*) Interrogativ *m*, Frageform *f* ◆ **in the ~** in der Frageform.
interrogatively [,ɪntə'rɒgətɪvlɪ] *adv* fragend; (*Gram also*) interrogativ.
interrogator [ɪn'terəgeɪtəʳ] *n* Vernehmungsbeamte(r) *mf* (*form*) ◆ **my/his ~s** die, die mich/ihn verhörten/verhören.
interrogatory [,ɪntə'rɒgətərɪ] *adj* fragend.
interrupt [,ɪntə'rʌpt] [1] *vt* (*break the continuity of*) unterbrechen (*also Elec*); (*in conversation: rudely also*) ins Wort fallen (+*dat*); *activity, work also* stören; *traffic flow also* aufhalten, stören; (*obstruct*) *view* versperren ◆ **~ function** (*Comput*) Unterbrechungsfunktion *f*.
[2] *vi* (*in conversation*) unterbrechen; (*~ sb's work etc*) stören ◆ **stop ~ing!** fall mir/ihm *etc* nicht dauernd ins Wort!
interrupter [,ɪntə'rʌptəʳ] *n* (*Elec*) Unterbrecher *m*.
interruption [,ɪntə'rʌpʃən] *n* Unterbrechung *f*; (*of work, activity, traffic flow also*) Störung *f*; (*of view*) Versperrung *f* ◆ **without ~** ohne Unterbrechung, ununterbrochen.
intersect [,ɪntə'sekt] [1] *vt* durchschneiden; (*Geometry*) schneiden.
[2] *vi* sich kreuzen; (*Geometry, in set theory*) sich schneiden ◆ **~ing sets** Schnittmengen *pl*.
intersection [,ɪntə'sekʃən] *n* (*crossroads*) Kreuzung *f*; (*Geometry*) Schnittpunkt *m* ◆ **point of ~** Schnittpunkt *m*.
intersperse [,ɪntə'spɜ:s] *vt* (*scatter*) verteilen ◆ **~d with sth** mit etw dazwischen; **a speech ~d with quotations** eine mit Zitaten gespickte Rede; **boredom ~d with periods of ...** Langeweile und dazwischen *or* zwischendurch ...
interstate [,ɪntə'steɪt] *adj* (*US*) zwischen den (US-Bundes)staaten, zwischenstaatlich ◆ **~ highway** Bundesautobahn *f*, Interstate Highway *m*.
interstellar [,ɪntə'steləʳ] *adj* interstellar.
interstice [ɪn'tɜ:stɪs] *n* Zwischenraum *m*; (*in wall etc also*) Sprung, Riß *m*; (*between panels also*) Fuge *f*.
intertextuality [,ɪntətekstjʊ'ælɪtɪ] *n* (*Liter*) Intertextualität *f*.
intertribal [,ɪntə'traɪbl] *adj* zwischen den *or* verschiedenen Stämmen ◆ **~ war** Stammeskrieg *m*.
intertwine [,ɪntə'twaɪn] [1] *vt* verschlingen; (*fig*) *destinies also* verknüpfen; *stories* verweben.
[2] *vi* (*branches, arms etc*) sich ineinander verschlingen; (*threads*) verschlungen sein; (*fig: destinies*) sich verbinden.
interurban [,ɪntə'ɜ:bən] *adj* (*US*) *railroad* städteverbindend.
interval ['ɪntəvəl] *n* **(a)** (*space, time*) Abstand *m*, Intervall *nt* (*form*) ◆ **at ~s** in Abständen; **sunny ~s** (*Met*) Aufheiterungen *pl*. **(b)** (*Sch, Theat etc*) Pause *f*. **(c)** (*Mus*) Intervall *nt*.
intervene [,ɪntə'vi:n] *vi* (*person*) einschreiten (*in* bei), intervenieren; (*event, fate*) dazwischenkommen ◆ **if nothing ~s** wenn nichts dazwischenkommt; **twelve years ~ between these events** zwölf Jahre liegen zwischen den Ereignissen.
intervening [,ɪntə'vi:nɪŋ] *adj period of time* dazwischenliegend ◆ **in the ~ weeks** in den Wochen dazwischen, in den dazwischenliegenden Wochen; **the ~ meetings were less well attended** die Versammlungen dazwischen *or* die dazwi schen stattfindenden Versammlungen waren weniger gut besucht.
intervention [,ɪntə'venʃən] *n* Eingreifen *nt*, Eingriff *m*, Intervention *f*.
interventionist [,ɪntə'venʃənɪst] [1] *n* Interventionist(in *f*) *m*.
[2] *adj* interventionistisch.
➤ **interview** ['ɪntəvju:] [1] *n* **(a)** (*for job*) Vorstellungsgespräch *nt*; (*with authorities, employer etc*) Gespräch *nt*; (*for grant*) Auswahlgespräch *nt*. **(b)** (*Press, TV etc*) Interview *nt*. **(c)** (*formal talk*) Gespräch *nt*, Unterredung *f*.
[2] *vt* **(a)** *job applicant* ein/das Vorstellungsgespräch führen mit; *applicant for*

➤ LANGUAGE IN USE: **interview: 1a** → 19.3, 19.5

grant etc Fragen stellen (*+dat*) ◆ **he is being ~ed on Monday for the job** er hat am Montag sein Vorstellungsgespräch. **(b)** (*Press, TV etc*) interviewen.
[3] *vi* **(a)** das Vorstellungsgespräch/die Vorstellungsgespräche führen. **(b)** (*Press, TV etc*) interviewen.
interviewee [ˌɪntəvjuːˈiː] *n* (*for job*) Kandidat(in *f*) *m* (für die Stelle); (*Press, TV etc*) Interviewte(r) *mf*.
interviewer [ˈɪntəvjuːəʳ] *n* (*for job*) Leiter(in *f*) *m* des Vorstellungsgesprächs; (*Press, TV etc*) Interviewer(in *f*) *m*.
interwar [ˈɪntəˈwɔːʳ] *adj years* zwischen den Weltkriegen.
interweave [ˌɪntəˈwiːv] [1] *vt* (*lit, fig*) verweben; *branches, fingers* verschlingen, ineinanderschlingen.
[2] *vi* sich verweben; (*branches*) sich ineinanderschlingen.
intestate [ɪnˈtestɪt] *adj* (*Jur*) nicht testamentarisch vermacht ◆ **to die ~** ohne Testament sterben.
intestinal [ɪnˈtestɪnl] *adj* Darm-, intestinal (*form*).
intestine [ɪnˈtestɪn] *n* Darm *m* ◆ **small/large ~** Dünn-/Dickdarm *m*.
intimacy [ˈɪntɪməsɪ] *n* Vertrautheit, Intimität *f*; (*euph: sexual* ~) Intimität *f* ◆ **acts of ~** Vertraulichkeiten *pl*; **~ took place** (*form euph*) es kam zu Intimitäten.
intimate[1] [ˈɪntɪmɪt] [1] *adj* **(a)** *friend* eng, vertraut, intim (*geh*); (*sexually*) intim ◆ **we're friends but we are not ~** wir sind befreundet, stehen aber nicht auf so vertraulichem Fuß; **to be on ~ terms with sb** mit jdm auf vertraulichem Fuß stehen; **he was a bit too ~ with my wife** er war ein bißchen zu vertraulich mit meiner Frau; **to be/become ~ with sb** mit jdm vertraut sein/werden; (*sexually*) mit jdm intim sein/werden.
(b) (*fig*) intim (*geh*); *feelings, thoughts also* geheim; *connection also* eng; *knowledge* gründlich.
(c) *freshness* intim, im Intimbereich ◆ **~ deodorant** Intimspray *m or nt*.
[2] *n* Vertraute(r) *mf*.
intimate[2] [ˈɪntɪmeɪt] *vt* andeuten ◆ **he ~d to them that they should stop** er gab ihnen zu verstehen, daß sie aufhören sollten.
intimately [ˈɪntɪmɪtlɪ] *adv acquainted* bestens; *behave, speak* vertraulich; *related, connected* eng; *know* genau, gründlich ◆ **we know each other but not ~** wir kennen uns, aber nicht besonders gut; **he is ~ involved in local politics** er ist tief in Lokalpolitik verwickelt.
intimation [ˌɪntɪˈmeɪʃən] *n* Andeutung *f*.
intimidate [ɪnˈtɪmɪdeɪt] *vt* einschüchtern ◆ **they ~d him into not telling the police** sie schüchterten ihn so ein, daß er der Polizei nichts erzählte; **we won't be ~d** wir lassen uns nicht einschüchtern.
intimidation [ɪnˌtɪmɪˈdeɪʃən] *n* Einschüchterung *f*.
into [ˈɪntʊ] *prep* **(a)** in (*+acc*); (*against*) *crash, drive* gegen ◆ **to translate sth ~ French** etw ins Französische übersetzen; **to divide 3 ~ 9** 9 durch 3 teilen *or* dividieren; **3 ~ 9 goes 3** 3 geht dreimal in 9; **they worked far ~ the night** sie arbeiteten bis tief in die Nacht hinein; **it turned ~ a nice day** es wurde ein schöner Tag.
(b) (*inf*) **to be ~ sb/sth** (*like*) auf jdn/etw (*acc*) stehen (*inf*); (*be interested in*) sich für jdn/etw interessieren; **to be ~ sth** (*use*) *drugs etc* etw nehmen; **I'm not really ~ the job yet** ich bin noch nicht ganz drin im Job (*inf*); **he's ~ local politics in a big way** (*actively involved*) er ist schwer in der Lokalpolitik aktiv (*inf*); **she's ~ getting up early/health food** sie ist passionierte Frühaufsteherin/sie steht auf Gesundheitskost (*inf*); **he's ~ wine** (*likes*) er ist Weinliebhaber; (*is expert*) er ist Weinkenner; **he's ~ computers** er ist Computerfan (*inf*); **we're ~ IT at work** (*use it*) wir haben im Büro Informationstechnik eingeführt; **well if that's what you're ~ ...** also, wenn das dein Fall ist ...; **I'm not ~ that** darauf stehe ich nicht (*inf*).
intolerable *adj*, **-bly** *adv* [ɪnˈtɒlərəbl, -ɪ] unerträglich.
intolerance [ɪnˈtɒlərəns] *n* **(a)** Intoleranz *f* (*of* gegenüber). **(b)** (*esp Med*) Überempfindlichkeit *f* (*to, of* gegen).
intolerant [ɪnˈtɒlərənt] *adj* intolerant (*of* gegenüber); (*Med*) überempfindlich (*to, of* gegen).
intolerantly [ɪnˈtɒlərəntlɪ] *adv* intolerant; *refuse* intoleranterweise.
intonate [ˈɪntəʊneɪt] *vt* (*Ling*) intonieren.
intonation [ˌɪntəʊˈneɪʃən] *n* Intonation *f*; (*Ling also*) Satzmelodie *f* ◆ **~ pattern** Intonationsmuster *nt*.
intone [ɪnˈtəʊn] *vt* intonieren.
in toto [ɪnˈtəʊtəʊ] *adv* im ganzen, in toto (*geh*).
intoxicant [ɪnˈtɒksɪkənt] *n* Rauschmittel *nt*.
intoxicate [ɪnˈtɒksɪkeɪt] *vt* (*lit, fig*) berauschen.
intoxicated [ɪnˈtɒksɪkeɪtɪd] *adj* betrunken, berauscht (*also fig*), im Rausch (*also fig*) ◆ **~ by drugs/with success** im Drogenrausch/vom Erfolg berauscht.
intoxication [ɪnˌtɒksɪˈkeɪʃən] *n* Rausch *m* (*also fig*), (Be)trunkenheit *f*; (*Med: poisoning*) Vergiftung *f* ◆ **in a state of ~** (*form*) in (be)trunkenem Zustand, im Rausch.
intra- [ˌɪntrə-] *pref* intra-.
intractable [ɪnˈtræktəbl] *adj metal* unnachgiebig; *problem, illness* hartnäckig; *child* widerspenstig; *temper* unlenksam.
intramural [ˌɪntrəˈmjʊərəl] *adj* (*esp Univ*) (*course*) innerhalb der Universität; *activities* studienspezifisch.
intransigence [ɪnˈtrænsɪdʒəns] *n* Unnachgiebigkeit *f*.
intransigent [ɪnˈtrænsɪdʒənt] *adj* unnachgiebig.
intransitive [ɪnˈtrænsɪtɪv] [1] *adj verb* intransitiv, Intransitiv-.
[2] *n* Intransitiv *nt*.
intrastate [ˌɪntrəˈsteɪt] *adj* (*US*) innerhalb des (Bundes)staates.
intra-uterine device [ˌɪntrəˈjuːtəraɪndɪˌvaɪs] *n* Intrauterinpessar *nt*.
intravenous [ˌɪntrəˈviːnəs] *adj* intravenös.
in-tray [ˈɪntreɪ] *n* Ablage *f* für Eingänge.
intrepid *adj*, **~ly** *adv* [ɪnˈtrepɪd, -lɪ] unerschrocken, kühn.
intrepidity [ˌɪntrɪˈpɪdɪtɪ] *n* Unerschrockenheit, Kühnheit *f*.
intricacy [ˈɪntrɪkəsɪ] *n* Kompliziertheit *f*; (*intricate part: of law, chess etc*) Feinheit *f*.
intricate [ˈɪntrɪkɪt] *adj* kompliziert; (*involved also*) verwickelt.
intricately [ˈɪntrɪkɪtlɪ] *adv* kompliziert.
intrigue [ɪnˈtriːg] [1] *vi* intrigieren.
[2] *vt* (*arouse interest of*) faszinieren; (*arouse curiosity of*) neugierig machen ◆ **I would be ~d to know why ...** es würde mich schon interessieren, warum ...
[3] [ˈɪntriːg] *n* **(a)** (*plot*) Intrige *f*; (*no pl: plotting*) Intrigen(spiel *nt*) *pl*. **(b)** (*dated: love affair*) Liaison, Liebschaft *f*.
intriguer [ɪnˈtriːgəʳ] *n* Intrigant(in *f*), Ränkeschmied *m*.
intriguing [ɪnˈtriːgɪŋ] [1] *adj* faszinierend, interessant.
[2] *n* Intrigen(spiel *nt*) *pl*.
intriguingly [ɪnˈtriːgɪŋlɪ] *adv* auf faszinierende Weise.
intrinsic [ɪnˈtrɪnsɪk] *adj merit, value* immanent; (*essential*) wesenhaft, wesentlich ◆ **is this form ~ to the poem?** ist dies eine dem Gedicht innewohnende Form? (*geh*).
intrinsically [ɪnˈtrɪnsɪkəlɪ] *adv* an sich.
intro [ˈɪntrəʊ] *n see* **introduction**.
introduce [ˌɪntrəˈdjuːs] *vt* **(a)** (*make acquainted*) (*to person*) vorstellen (*to sb* jdm), bekannt machen (*to* mit); (*butler*) ankündigen; (*to subject*) einführen (*to* in *+acc*) ◆ **have you two been ~d?** hat man Sie bekannt gemacht?; **I don't think we've been ~d** ich glaube nicht, daß wir uns kennen; **to ~ oneself** sich vorstellen; **he was ~d to drink at an early age** er hat schon früh Bekanntschaft mit dem Alkohol gemacht; **who ~d him to heroin?** durch wen ist er ans Heroin geraten?; **he was ~d to flying by a friend** er ist durch einen Freund zum Fliegen gekommen; **to ~ sb/sth into sb's presence** jdn/etw vor jdn bringen.
(b) *fashion, practice, reform, invention* einführen; (*Parl*) *bill* einbringen; *mood* bringen (*into* in *+acc*); *book, subject, era* einleiten; (*announce*) *speaker* vorstellen, ankündigen; *programme* ankündigen ◆ **to ~ sth onto the market** etw auf den Markt bringen, etw auf dem Markt einführen.
(c) (*insert*) einführen (*into* in *+acc*).
introduction [ˌɪntrəˈdʌkʃən] *n* **(a)** (*to person*) Vorstellung *f* ◆ **since his ~ to Lord X** seit er Lord X vorgestellt worden ist; **to make** *or* **perform the ~s** die Vorstellung übernehmen; **letter of ~** Einführungsbrief *m or* -schreiben *nt*.
(b) (*introductory part*) (*to book, music*) Einleitung *f* (*to* zu).
(c) (*elementary course, book*) Einführung *f* ◆ **an ~ to French** eine Einführung ins Französische.
(d) (*introducing, being introduced*) (*to subject*) Einführung *f* (*to* in *+acc*); (*to habit, hobby*) Bekanntschaft *f* (*to* mit); (*of fashion, practice, reform etc*) Einführung *f*; (*of bill*) Einbringen *nt*; (*announcing*) (*of speaker*) Vorstellung, Ankündigung *f*; (*of programme*) Ankündigung *f*; (*bringing or carrying in*) Einführung *f* (*into* in *+dat*); (*insertion*) Einführung *f* (*into* in *+acc*) ◆ **our next guest needs no ~** unser nächster Gast braucht nicht vorgestellt zu werden.
introductory [ˌɪntrəˈdʌktərɪ] *adj page, paragraph, chapter* einleitend; *words, remarks* einführend; *talk* Einführungs-.
introit [ˈɪntrɔɪt] *n* Introitus *m*.
introspection [ˌɪntrəʊˈspekʃən] *n* Selbstbeobachtung, Introspektion (*geh*) *f*.
introspective [ˌɪntrəʊˈspektɪv] *adj person* selbstbeobachtend, introspektiv (*geh*); *novel, remarks* introspektiv.
introspectiveness [ˌɪntrəʊˈspektɪvnɪs] *n* (*of novel, remarks*) introspektiver Charakter; (*of person*) Neigung *f* zur Selbstbeobachtung *or* Introspektion (*geh*).
introversion [ˌɪntrəʊˈvɜːʃən] *n* (*Psych*) Introversion *f*.
introvert [ˈɪntrəʊvɜːt] [1] *n* (*Psych*) Introvertierte(r) *mf* ◆ **to be an ~** introvertiert sein.
[2] *vt* (*Psych*) nach innen wenden; (*Biol*) nach innen stülpen.
introverted [ˈɪntrəʊvɜːtɪd] *adj* introvertiert, in sich gekehrt.
intrude [ɪnˈtruːd] [1] *vi* sich eindrängen ◆ **to ~ in sb's affairs** sich in jds Angelegenheiten (*acc*) einmischen; **am I intruding?** störe ich?; **to ~ on sb's privacy/grief** jds Privatsphäre verletzen/jdn in seinem Kummer stören; **to ~ on a conversation** sich in eine Unterhaltung (ein)mischen; **to ~ on sb's leisure time** jds Freizeit in Anspruch nehmen.
[2] *vt remark* einwerfen ◆ **the thought ~d itself into my mind** der Gedanke drängte sich mir auf; **to ~ oneself** *or* **one's presence/one's views upon sb** sich jdm/jdm seine Ansichten aufdrängen; **to ~ oneself into sb's affairs** sich in jds Angelegenheiten (*acc*) mischen.
intruder [ɪnˈtruːdəʳ] *n* Eindringling *m*.
intrusion [ɪnˈtruːʒən] *n* **(a)** Störung *f*; (*on sb's privacy also*) Verletzung, *f* (*on gen*) ◆ **forgive the ~, I just wanted to ask ...** entschuldigen Sie, wenn ich hier so eindringe, ich wollte nur fragen ...; **the ~ of his work on his free time** daß seine Arbeit immer mehr von seiner Freizeit beanspruchte; **the sudden ~ of reality on his dreams** das plötzliche Eindringen der Wirklichkeit in seine Träume; **they regarded her advice as an ~** sie betrachteten ihren Rat als eine Einmischung.
(b) (*forcing: of opinions, advice, one's presence*) Aufdrängen *nt*.
intrusive [ɪnˈtruːsɪv] *adj person* aufdringlich; (*Phon*) intrusiv.
intuition [ˌɪntjuːˈɪʃən] *n* Intuition *f*; (*of future events etc*) (Vor)ahnung *f* (*of* von) ◆ **to know sth by ~** etw intuitiv wissen.
intuitive [ɪnˈtjuːɪtɪv] *adj* intuitiv; *guess, feeling, assessment* instinktiv.
intuitively [ɪnˈtjuːɪtɪvlɪ] *adv* intuitiv ◆ **~ I'd say 50** ich hätte instinktiv 50 gesagt.

inundate ['ɪnʌndeɪt] *vt* (*lit, fig*) überschwemmen, überfluten; (*with work*) überhäufen ◆ **have you a lot of work? — I'm ~d** haben Sie viel Arbeit? — ich ersticke darin.

inundation [ˌɪnʌn'deɪʃən] *n* (*lit, fig*) (*with invitations, offers etc*) Überschwemmung *f*; (*with work*) Überhäufung *f* ◆ **an ~ of tourists/letters** eine Flut von Touristen/Briefen.

inure [ɪn'jʊəʳ] *vt* gewöhnen (*to an +acc*); (*physically*) abhärten (*to* gegen); (*to danger*) stählen (*to* gegen) ◆ **to become ~d to sth** sich an etw (*acc*) gewöhnen/sich gegen etw abhärten/stählen.

invade [ɪn'veɪd] *vt* (*Mil*) *country* einmarschieren in (+*acc*); (*fig*) überfallen, heimsuchen; *privacy* eindringen in (+*acc*), stören.

invader [ɪn'veɪdəʳ] *n* (*Mil*) Invasor *m*; (*fig*) Eindringling *m* (*of* in +*acc*); (*of privacy*) Eindringling (*of* in +*acc*), Störer *m* (*of gen*).

invading [ɪn'veɪdɪŋ] *adj* einmarschierend; *Huns, Vikings etc* einfallend; *army, troops also* Invasions-.

invalid¹ ['ɪnvəlɪd] [1] *adj* (a) krank; (*disabled*) invalide, körperbehindert. **(b)** (*for invalids*) Kranken-; Invaliden- ◆ **~ chair** Roll- *or* Krankenstuhl *m*; **~ car** Invaliden(kraft)fahrzeug *nt*.
[2] *n* Kranke(r) *mf*; (*disabled person*) Invalide, Körperbehinderte(r) *mf* ◆ **he's been an ~ all his life** er hat sein ganzes Leben lang ein körperliches Leiden gehabt.

◆**invalid out** *vt sep* dienstuntauglich *or* -unfähig schreiben *or* erklären ◆ **to be ~ed ~ of the army** wegen Dienstuntauglichkeit aus dem Heer entlassen werden.

invalid² [ɪn'vælɪd] *adj* (*esp Jur*) ungültig; *deduction, argument* nicht schlüssig *or* stichhaltig; *assumption* nicht zulässig ◆ **it makes the argument ~** es entkräftet das Argument.

invalidate [ɪn'vælɪdeɪt] *vt* ungültig machen; *theory* entkräften.

invalidation [ɪnˌvælɪ'deɪʃən] *n* (*of document*) Ungültigmachung *f*; (*of theory*) Entkräftung *f*.

invalidism ['ɪnvəlɪdɪzəm] *n* körperliches Leiden; (*disability*) Körperbehinderung, Invalidität *f*.

invalidity [ɪnvə'lɪdɪtɪ] *n see* **invalid²** Ungültigkeit *f*; mangelnde Schlüssigkeit *or* Stichhaltigkeit; Unzulässigkeit *f*.

invaluable [ɪn'væljʊəbl] *adj* unbezahlbar; *service, role* unschätzbar; *jewel, treasure* von unschätzbarem Wert ◆ **to be ~ (to sb)** (für jdn) von unschätzbarem Wert sein.

invariable [ɪn'vɛərɪəbl] [1] *adj* (*also Math*) unveränderlich; *bad luck* konstant, ständig.
[2] *n* (*Math*) Konstante *f*.

invariably [ɪn'vɛərɪəblɪ] *adv* ständig, unweigerlich; (*not changing*) unveränderlich ◆ **do you trust his judgement? — ~!** trauen Sie seinem Urteil? — ausnahmslos!

invasion [ɪn'veɪʒən] *n* (*lit, fig*) Invasion *f*; (*of privacy etc*) Eingriff *m* (*of* in +*acc*) ◆ **the Viking ~** der Einfall der Wikinger; **the German ~ of Poland** der Einmarsch *or* Einfall (*pej*) der Deutschen in Polen.

invasive [ɪn'veɪsɪv] *adj* (a) (*Med*) invasiv. **(b)** (*Mil*) *war* Invasions-.

invective [ɪn'vektɪv] *n* Beschimpfungen (*against gen*), Schmähungen (*geh*) (*against* gegen), Invektiven (*liter*) *pl*.

inveigh [ɪn'veɪ] *vi* **to ~ against sb/sth** (*liter*) jdn/etw schmähen (*liter*), sich in Schimpfreden gegen jdn/etw ergehen (*geh*).

inveigle [ɪn'viːgl] *vt* (*liter*) verleiten (*into* zu); (*lure*) locken ◆ **to ~ sb into doing sth** jdn dazu verleiten *or* verlocken, etw zu tun.

invent [ɪn'vent] *vt* erfinden.

invention [ɪn'venʃən] *n* (a) Erfindung *f* ◆ **of one's own ~** selbsterfunden. **(b)** (*inventiveness*) Phantasie *f*.

inventive [ɪn'ventɪv] *adj* (*creative*) *powers, skills, mind* schöpferisch; *novel, design* einfallsreich; (*resourceful*) erfinderisch ◆ **games which encourage a child to be ~** Spiele, die die Phantasie des Kindes anregen.

inventiveness [ɪn'ventɪvnɪs] *n* Einfallsreichtum *m*.

inventor [ɪn'ventəʳ] *n* Erfinder(in *f*) *m*.

inventory ['ɪnvəntrɪ] [1] *n* Inventar *nt*, Bestandsaufnahme *f* ◆ **to make** *or* **take an ~ of sth** Inventar von etw *or* den Bestand einer Sache (*gen*) aufnehmen; **~ control** Bestandskontrolle *f*.
[2] *vt* (*Comm*) inventarisieren.

inverse ['ɪn'vɜːs] [1] *adj* umgekehrt, entgegengesetzt ◆ **in ~ order** in umgekehrter Reihenfolge; **to be in ~ proportion to ...** im umgekehrten Verhältnis zu ... stehen; (*Math*) umgekehrt proportional zu ... sein.
[2] *n* Gegenteil *nt*.

inversion [ɪn'vɜːʃən] *n* Umkehrung *f*; (*Mus also, Gram*) Inversion *f*; (*fig: of roles, values*) Verkehrung, Umkehrung *f*.

invert [ɪn'vɜːt] *vt* umkehren; *object also* auf den Kopf stellen; *order also* umdrehen; (*Gram*) *subject and object* umstellen; *word order* umkehren ◆ **~ed commas** (*Brit*) Anführungszeichen *pl*; **that's just ~ed snobbery** das ist auch eine Art Snobismus.

invertebrate [ɪn'vɜːtɪbrɪt] [1] *n* Wirbellose(r), Invertebrat (*spec*) *m*.
[2] *adj* wirbellos.

invert sugar ['ɪnvɜːt'ʃʊgəʳ] *n* Invertzucker *m*.

invest [ɪn'vest] [1] *vt* (a) (*Fin, fig*) investieren (*in* in +*acc or dat*); (*Fin also*) anlegen (*in* in +*dat*).
(b) (*form: with rank or authority*) *president etc* einsetzen, investieren (*old*) ◆ **to ~ sb/sth with sth** jdm/einer Sache etw verleihen; **the event was ~ed with an air of mystery** das Ereignis war von etwas Geheimnisvollem umgeben.
(c) (*Mil: besiege*) belagern.
[2] *vi* investieren, Geld anlegen (*in* in +*acc or dat, with* bei) ◆ **to ~ in shares** in Aktien investieren, sein Geld in Aktien anlegen; **to ~ in a new car** sich (*dat*) ein neues Auto anschaffen.

investigate [ɪn'vestɪgeɪt] [1] *vt* untersuchen; (*doing scientific research also*) erforschen; *sb's political beliefs, an insurance claim, business affairs* überprüfen; *complaint* nachgehen (+*dat*); *motive, reason* erforschen; *crime* untersuchen; (*by police also*) Ermittlungen anstellen über (+*acc*) ◆ **to ~ a case** in einem Fall ermitteln *or* Ermittlungen anstellen.
[2] *vi* nachforschen; (*police*) ermitteln, Ermittlungen anstellen.

investigation [ɪnˌvestɪ'geɪʃən] *n* (a) (*to determine cause*) Untersuchung *f* (*into gen*); (*official enquiry also*) Ermittlung *f* ◆ **on ~ it turned out that ...** bei näherer Untersuchung stellte (es) sich heraus, daß ...
(b) (*looking for sth*) Nachforschung *f*; (*by police*) Ermittlungen *pl*; (*of affairs, applicants, political beliefs etc*) Überprüfung *f* ◆ **to be under ~** überprüft werden; **he is under ~** (*by police*) gegen ihn wird ermittelt; **new methods of criminal ~** neue polizeiliche Ermittlungsmethoden; **(private) ~ agency** Detektei *f*, Detektivbüro *nt*.
(c) (*scientific research*) (*in field*) Forschung *f*; (*of bacteria, object etc*) Erforschung *f* (*into gen*) ◆ **recent scientific ~ has shown ...** die neuesten wissenschaftlichen Untersuchungen haben gezeigt ...

investigative [ɪn'vestɪgətɪv] *adj journalism* Enthüllungs-; *technique* Forschungs-; *mind* Forscher-.

investigator [ɪn'vestɪgeɪtəʳ] *n* Ermittler *m*; (*private ~*) (Privat)detektiv *m*; (*insurance ~*) (Schadens)ermittler(in *f*) *m*; (*from government department*) Untersuchungs- *or* Ermittlungsbeamte(r) *m* ◆ **a team of ~s** ein Untersuchungsausschuß *m*, eine Untersuchungskommission.

investiture [ɪn'vestɪtʃəʳ] *n* (*of president etc*) (feierliche) Einsetzung, Amtseinführung *f*; (*of royalty*) Investitur *f*; (*of honour*) Verleihung *f*; (*occasion*) Auszeichnungsfeier *f* ◆ **after his ~ with the VC, ...** nachdem ihm das Viktoriakreuz verliehen worden war, ...

investment [ɪn'vestmənt] *n* (a) (*Fin*) Investition *f*; (*act also*) Anlage *f* ◆ **industry needs more ~** die Industrie braucht mehr Investitionen; **to make an ~** investieren (*of sth* etw); **oil/this company is a good ~** Öl/diese Firma ist eine gute (Kapital)anlage; **learning languages is a good ~** es macht sich bezahlt, wenn man Sprachen lernt.
(b) (*investiture*) (*as sth*) (Amts)einsetzung *f*; (*with sth*) Verleihung *f* (+*gen*).
(c) (*Mil: blockade*) Belagerung *f*.

investment: ~ company *n* Investmentgesellschaft *f*; **~ incentive** *n* Investitionsanreiz *m*; **~ income** *n* Kapitalerträge *pl*; **~ management** *n* Vermögensverwaltung *f*; **~ trust** *n* Investmenttrust *m*.

investor [ɪn'vestəʳ] *n* Kapitalanleger, Investor *m* ◆ **the small ~** die Kleinanleger *pl*.

inveterate [ɪn'vetərɪt] *adj dislike, hatred* tief verwurzelt, abgrundtief; *opposition, prejudice* hartnäckig; *enemies, hatred* unversöhnlich; *criminal, smoker* Gewohnheits-; *liar, gambler* unverbesserlich.

invidious [ɪn'vɪdɪəs] *adj remark* gehässig, boshaft; *task, position* unerfreulich, unangenehm; *behaviour, conduct* gemein; *distinctions, comparison* ungerecht ◆ **it would be ~ to ...** es wäre ungerecht, zu ...

invigilate [ɪn'vɪdʒɪleɪt] (*Brit*) [1] *vt exam* Aufsicht führen bei.
[2] *vi* Aufsicht führen.

invigilation [ɪnˌvɪdʒɪ'leɪʃən] *n* (*Brit*) Aufsicht *f* ◆ **to do the ~** Aufsicht führen.

invigilator [ɪn'vɪdʒɪleɪtəʳ] *n* (*Brit*) Aufsicht *f*, Aufsichtführende(r) *mf*, Aufsichtsperson *f*.

invigorate [ɪn'vɪgəreɪt] *vt* beleben; (*tonic, cure*) kräftigen.

invigorating [ɪn'vɪgəreɪtɪŋ] *adj climate* gesund; *sea air, shower* erfrischend, belebend; *tonic, cure* kräftigend, stärkend; (*fig*) *attitude, frankness* (herz)erfrischend ◆ **he found the American business world very ~** die amerikanische Geschäftswelt stimulierte ihn.

invincibility [ɪnˌvɪnsɪ'bɪlɪtɪ] *n* Unbesiegbarkeit *f*.

invincible [ɪn'vɪnsəbl] *adj army etc* unbesiegbar, unschlagbar; *courage, determination* unerschütterlich.

inviolability [ɪnˌvaɪələ'bɪlɪtɪ] *n see adj* Unantastbarkeit *f*; Unverletzlichkeit *f*; Heiligkeit *f*.

inviolable [ɪn'vaɪələbl] *adj* unantastbar; *frontiers also* unverletzlich; *law, oath* heilig.

inviolate [ɪn'vaɪəlɪt] *adj* (*form*) *honour* unbeschadet; *rights* unangetastet; *virgin* unberührt.

invisibility [ɪnˌvɪzə'bɪlɪtɪ] *n* Unsichtbarkeit *f*.

invisible [ɪn'vɪzəbl] *adj* unsichtbar ◆ **~ earnings/exports** (*Econ*) unsichtbare Einkünfte *pl*/Exporte *pl*; **~ ink** Geheimtinte *f*; **~ mending** Kunststopfen *nt*; **~ thread** Nylonfaden *m*; **~ to the naked eye** mit dem bloßen Auge nicht erkennbar.

invisibly [ɪn'vɪzəblɪ] *adv* unsichtbar ◆ **you should have it ~ mended** du solltest es kunststopfen lassen.

▼ **invitation** [ˌɪnvɪ'teɪʃən] *n* Einladung *f* ◆ **by ~ (only)** nur auf Einladung; **at sb's ~** auf jds Aufforderung (*acc*) (hin); **an ~ to burglars** eine Aufforderung zum Diebstahl; **~ card** Einladungskarte *f*.

invite [ɪn'vaɪt] [1] *vt* (a) *person* einladen ◆ **to ~ sb to do sth** jdn auffordern *or* bitten, etw zu tun; **he ~d me to try for myself** er bot mir an, es doch selbst zu versuchen.
(b) (*ask for, attract*) *suggestions, questions* bitten um; (*behaviour*) *ridicule, contempt, trouble* auslösen, führen zu ◆ **written in such a way as to ~ further discussion** so geschrieben, daß es zu weiteren Diskussionen auffordert; **it ~s comparison with another theory** der Vergleich mit einer anderen Theorie drängt sich auf; **you're inviting defeat/an accident by ...** das muß ja zu einer Niederlage/einem Unglück führen, wenn du ...; **you're inviting ridicule/**

➤ LANGUAGE IN USE: **invitation** → 25.1, 25.2

criticism du machst dich lächerlich/setzt dich der Kritik aus; **he just seems to ~ trouble** wo er auftaucht, gibt es meistens Unannehmlichkeiten; **there's no need to ~ trouble** man muß es ja nicht auf Ärger anlegen.
[2] ['ɪnvaɪt] *n (inf)* Einladung *f*.

◆**invite in** *vt sep* hereinbitten, ins Haus bitten ◆ **could I ~ you ~ for (a) coffee?** möchten Sie auf eine Tasse Kaffee hereinkommen?

◆**invite out** *vt sep* einladen ◆ **I ~d her ~** ich habe sie gefragt, ob sie mit mir ausgehen möchte; **to ~ sb ~ for a meal** jdn in ein Restaurant einladen.

◆**invite round** *vt sep* (zu sich) einladen.

◆**invite up** *vt sep* heraufbitten.

inviting [ɪn'vaɪtɪŋ] *adj* einladend; *prospect, idea, meal* verlockend.

invitingly [ɪn'vaɪtɪŋlɪ] *adv* einladend; *(temptingly)* verlockend.

in vitro [ɪn'viːtrəʊ] *(Biol)* [1] *adj* künstlich, In-vitro-(*spec*).
[2] *adv fertilize* künstlich, in vitro (*spec*).

invocation [,ɪnvəʊ'keɪʃən] *n* Beschwörung *f*; *(Eccl)* Invokation *f* ◆ **an ~ to the muses** *(Liter)* eine Anrufung der Musen.

▼ **invoice** ['ɪnvɔɪs] [1] *n (bill)* (Waren)rechnung *f*; *(list)* Lieferschein *m*.
[2] *vt goods* in Rechnung stellen, berechnen ◆ **to ~ sb for sth** jdm für etw eine Rechnung ausstellen; **has he been ~d for these yet?** hat er dafür schon eine Rechnung bekommen?; **we'll ~ you** wir senden Ihnen die Rechnung; **~ clerk** Fakturist(in *f*) *m*.

invoicing ['ɪnvɔɪsɪŋ] *n* Fakturierung *f*; *(of goods also)* Berechnung, Inrechnungstellung *f*; *(invoiced sales)* Fakturierungen *pl*.

invoke [ɪn'vəʊk] *vt* **(a)** *(appeal to, call for) God, the law, muse* anrufen; *evil spirits* beschwören ◆ **to ~ the name of Marx** Marx ins Feld führen; **to ~ God's blessing/help from God** Gottes Segen erbitten/Gott um Hilfe anflehen.
(b) *(call into operation) treaty etc* sich berufen auf (+*acc*) ◆ **to ~ sb's help** an jds Hilfsbereitschaft (*acc*) appellieren.

involuntarily [ɪn'vɒləntərɪlɪ] *adv* unbeabsichtigt, unabsichtlich; *(automatically)* unwillkürlich ◆ **he found himself ~ involved** er sah sich unfreiwilligerweise verwickelt.

involuntary [ɪn'vɒləntərɪ] *adj* unbeabsichtigt, ungewollt; *muscle movement etc* unwillkürlich ◆ **I found myself an ~ listener/agent of their plot** ich wurde zum unfreiwilligen Zuhörer/Werkzeug ihres Komplotts.

involute ['ɪnvəluːt] *adj (liter: complex)* verwickelt.

▼ **involve** [ɪn'vɒlv] *vt* **(a)** *(entangle)* verwickeln *(sb in sth* jdn in etw *acc)*; *(include)* beteiligen *(sb in sth* jdn an etw *dat)*; *(concern)* betreffen ◆ **to ~ sb in a quarrel** jdn in einen Streit verwickeln *or* hineinziehen; **don't ~ yourself in any unnecessary expense** machen Sie sich keine unnötigen Ausgaben; **to ~ sb in expense** jdm Kosten verursachen; **the book doesn't ~ the reader** das Buch fesselt *or* packt den Leser nicht; **I was watching TV but I wasn't really ~d in it** ich habe ferngesehen, war aber gar nicht richtig dabei; **it wouldn't ~ you at all** du hättest damit gar nichts zu tun; **to be ~d in sth** etwas mit etw zu tun haben; *(have part in also)* an etw (*dat*) beteiligt sein; *(in sth bad also)* in etw (*acc*) verwickelt sein; **to get ~d in sth** in etw (*acc*) verwickelt werden; *(in quarrel, crime etc also)* in etw (*acc*) hineingezogen werden; **I didn't want to get ~d** ich wollte damit/mit ihm *etc* nichts zu tun haben; **I didn't want to get too ~d** ich wollte mich nicht zu sehr engagieren; **a matter of principle is ~d** es ist eine Frage des Prinzips, es geht ums Prinzip; **the person ~d** die betreffende Person; **we are all ~d in the battle against inflation** der Kampf gegen die Inflation geht uns alle an; **to be/get ~d with sth** etwas mit etw zu tun haben; *(have part in)* an etw (*dat*) beteiligt sein; *(work etc)* mit etw beschäftigt sein; **he got ~d with local politics** er hat sich lokalpolitisch engagiert; **to be ~d with sb** mit jdm zu tun haben; *(sexually)* mit jdm ein Verhältnis haben; **he's very ~d with her** er hat sich bei ihr sehr stark engagiert; **he's ~d with some shady characters** er hat Umgang mit einigen zwielichtigen Gestalten; **to get ~d with sb** mit jdm Kontakt bekommen, sich mit jdm einlassen (*pej*); **I don't want to get ~d with them** ich will mit ihnen nichts zu tun haben; **he got ~d with a girl** er hat eine Beziehung mit einem Mädchen angefangen; **she doesn't want to get ~d** sie will sich nicht engagieren *or* enger binden.
(b) *(entail)* mit sich bringen, zur Folge haben; *(encompass)* umfassen; *(mean)* bedeuten ◆ **what does your job ~?** worin besteht Ihre Arbeit?; **this problem ~s many separate issues** dieses Problem umfaßt viele verschiedene Punkte *or* schließt viele verschiedene Punkte ein; **to ~ considerable expense/a lot of hard work** beträchtliche Kosten/viel Arbeit mit sich bringen *or* zur Folge haben; **it's involving too much of my time** es beansprucht zuviel Zeit, es kostet mich zuviel Zeit; **he doesn't understand what's ~d in this sort of work** er weiß nicht, worum es bei dieser Arbeit geht; **do you realize what's ~d in raising a family?** weißt du denn, was es bedeutet, eine Familie großzuziehen?; **about £1,000 was ~d** es ging dabei um etwa £ 1.000; **the job ~d 50 workmen** für die Arbeit wurden 50 Arbeiter gebraucht; **it would ~ moving to Germany** das würde bedeuten, nach Deutschland umzuziehen; **finding the oil ~d the use of a special drill** um das Öl zu finden, brauchte man einen Spezialbohrer.

involved [ɪn'vɒlvd] *adj* kompliziert; *regulations also* verwirrend; *story also* verwickelt; *style* komplex, umständlich (*pej*) ◆ **long ~ sentences** umständliche Schachtelsätze *pl*.

involvement [ɪn'vɒlvmənt] *n (being concerned with)* Beteiligung *f (in* an +*dat)*; *(in quarrel, crime etc)* Verwicklung *f (in* in +*acc)*; *(commitment)* Engagement *nt*; *(sexually)* Verhältnis *nt*; *(complexity)* Kompliziertheit, Verworrenheit (*pej*) *f* ◆ **his ~ with shady characters** sein Umgang *m* mit zwielichtigen Gestalten; **the extent of his ~ with her/his work** das Maß, in dem er sich bei ihr/bei seiner Arbeit engagiert hat; **we don't know the extent of his ~ in the plot/plan** wir wissen nicht, wie weit er an dem Komplott/Plan beteiligt ist/war; **there is no ~ of the reader in the novel** der Leser fühlt sich von dem Roman nicht angesprochen.

invulnerability [ɪn,vʌlnərə'bɪlɪtɪ] *n see adj* Unverwundbarkeit, Unverletzbarkeit *f*; Uneinnehmbarkeit *f*; Unangreifbarkeit *f*.

invulnerable [ɪn'vʌlnərəbl] *adj* unverwundbar, unverletzbar; *fortress* uneinnehmbar; *(lit, fig) position* unangreifbar ◆ **~ to attack** unbezwingbar.

inward ['ɪnwəd] *adj* **(a)** *(inner)* innere(r, s); *smile, life* innerlich; *thoughts* innerste(r, s). **(b)** *curve* nach innen gehend; *mail* eintreffend. **(c)** *(Fin)* **~ investment** Investitionen *pl* aus dem Ausland.

inward-looking ['ɪnwəd'lʊkɪŋ] *adj* in sich gekehrt, beschaulich.

inwardly ['ɪnwədlɪ] *adv* innerlich, im Inneren.

inwardness ['ɪnwədnɪs] *n* Innerlichkeit *f*.

inward(s) ['ɪnwəd(z)] *adv* nach innen ◆ **his thoughts turned ~** er versank in Selbstbetrachtung.

in-your-face, in-yer-face ['ɪnjə'feɪs] *(sl) adj attitude etc* provokativ.

I/O *abbr of* **input/output**.

IOC *abbr of* **International Olympic Committee** IOK *nt*.

iodine ['aɪədiːn] *n* Jod *nt*.

ion ['aɪən] *n* Ion *nt*.

Ionian [aɪ'əʊnɪən] *adj* **~ Sea** Ionisches Meer.

Ionic [aɪ'ɒnɪk] *adj* ionisch.

ionic [aɪ'ɒnɪk] *adj* Ionen-.

ionization [,aɪənaɪ'zeɪʃən] *n* Ionisierung *f*.

ionize ['aɪənaɪz] *vti* ionisieren.

ionosphere [aɪ'ɒnəsfɪəʳ] *n* Ionosphäre *f*.

iota [aɪ'əʊtə] *n* Jota *nt* ◆ **not an** *or* **one ~** nicht ein Jota; **not an ~ of truth** kein Funke *m or* Körnchen *nt* Wahrheit.

IOU [,aɪəʊ'juː] *abbr of* **I owe you** Schuldschein *m* ◆ **to give sb an ~** jdm einen Schuldschein ausschreiben.

IPA *abbr of* **International Phonetic Alphabet** internationale Lautschrift.

ipso facto ['ɪpsəʊ'fæktəʊ] *adv* eo ipso.

IQ *abbr of* **intelligence quotient** IQ, Intelligenzquotient *m* ◆ **~ test** Intelligenztest, IQ-Test *m*.

IRA *abbr of* **Irish Republican Army** IRA *f*.

Iran [ɪ'rɑːn] *n* (der) Iran.

Iranian [ɪ'reɪnɪən] [1] *adj* iranisch.
[2] *n* **(a)** Iraner(in *f*) *m*. **(b)** *(language)* Iranisch *nt*.

Iraq [ɪ'rɑːk] *n* (der) Irak.

Iraqi [ɪ'rɑːkɪ] [1] *adj* irakisch.
[2] *n* **(a)** Iraker(in *f*) *m*. **(b)** *(dialect)* Irakisch *nt*.

irascibility [ɪ,ræsɪ'bɪlɪtɪ] *n* Reizbarkeit *f*, Jähzorn *m*.

irascible [ɪ'ræsɪbl] *adj* reizbar, erregbar, jähzornig; *temperament also* jähzornig, heftig, aufbrausend.

irascibly [ɪ'ræsɪblɪ] *adv* gereizt.

irate [aɪ'reɪt] *adj* zornig; *crowd* wütend.

irately [aɪ'reɪtlɪ] *adv* zornig.

ire [aɪəʳ] *n (liter)* Zorn *m*.

Ireland ['aɪələnd] *n* Irland *nt* ◆ **Northern ~** Nordirland *nt* ◆ **Republic of ~** Republik *f* Irland.

iridescence [,ɪrɪ'desəns] *n see adj (liter)* Irisieren *nt*; Schillern *nt*; Schimmern *nt*.

iridescent [,ɪrɪ'desənt] *adj (liter)* irisierend; *plumage also, water* schillernd; *opals etc, silk* schimmernd.

iris ['aɪərɪs] *n* **(a)** *(of eye)* Regenbogenhaut, Iris *f*. **(b)** *(Bot)* Iris, Schwertlilie *f*.

Irish ['aɪərɪʃ] [1] *adj* **(a)** irisch ◆ **~ coffee** Irish Coffee *m*; **~ Free State** irischer Freistaat; **~ joke** Irenwitz, ≃ Ostfriesenwitz *m*; **~man** Ire, Irländer *m*; **~ Republican Army** Irisch-Republikanische Armee; **~ Sea** Irische See; **~ setter** Irish Setter *m*; **~ stew** Irish Stew *nt*; **~woman** Irin, Irländerin *f*.
(b) *(hum inf: illogical)* unlogisch, blödsinnig.
[2] *n* **(a)** *pl* **the ~** die Iren, die Irländer *pl*.
(b) *(language)* Irisch *nt*, irisches Gälisch.

irk [ɜːk] *vt* verdrießen (*geh*), ärgern.

irksome ['ɜːksəm] *adj* lästig.

iron ['aɪən] [1] *n* **(a)** Eisen *nt* ◆ **old ~** Alteisen *nt*; **~ tablets** *pl* Eisentabletten *pl*; **a man of ~** ein stahlharter Mann; **a will of ~** ein eiserner Wille; **to rule with a rod of ~** mit eiserner Rute *or* Hand herrschen.
(b) *(electric ~, flat~)* Bügeleisen, Plätteisen (*dial*) *nt* ◆ **to have more than one ~ in the fire** *(fig)* mehrere Eisen im Feuer haben; **he has too many ~s in the fire** er macht zuviel auf einmal; **to strike while the ~ is hot** *(Prov)* das Eisen schmieden, solange es heiß ist (*Prov*).
(c) *(Golf)* Eisen *nt*.
(d) *(fetters)* **~s** *pl* Hand- und Fußschellen *pl* ◆ **to put a man in ~s** jdn in Eisen legen.
[2] *adj* **(a)** *(Chem)* Eisen-; *(made of ~)* Eisen-, eisern, aus Eisen ◆ **~ pyrites** Eisenkies, Pyrit *m*.
(b) *(fig) constitution, hand* eisern; *will* eisern, stählern; *rule* streng, unbarmherzig ◆ **to rule with an ~ hand** mit eiserner Faust regieren; **the I~ Chancellor** der Eiserne Kanzler; **they soon discovered that here was an ~ fist in a velvet glove** es wurde ihnen bald klar, daß mit ihm *etc* nicht zu spaßen war, obwohl er *etc* so sanft wirkte.
[3] *vt clothes* bügeln, plätten (*dial*).
[4] *vi (person)* bügeln; *(cloth)* sich bügeln lassen.

◆**iron out** *vt sep (lit, fig)* ausbügeln; *differences also* ausgleichen; *problems, difficulties also* aus dem Weg räumen.

iron: I~ Age *n* Eisenzeit *f*; **I~ Chancellor** *n* Eiserne(r) Kanzler; **~clad** [1] *adj*

➤ LANGUAGE IN USE: **invoice: 1 → 20.7**

gepanzert; [2] n (obs) Panzerschiff nt; **I~ Curtain** n Eiserne(r) Vorhang; **the I~ Curtain countries** die Länder hinter dem Eisernen Vorhang; **I~ Duke** n Wellington m; ~ **horse** n (old: train) Dampfroß nt (old hum).

ironic(al) [aɪˈrɒnɪk(əl)] adj ironisch; smile also spöttisch; position paradox, witzig (inf) ◆ **it's really ~** das ist wirklich witzig (inf); **it's really ~ that now he's got a car he's not allowed to drive** es ist doch paradox or wirklich witzig (inf), daß er jetzt, wo er ein Auto hat, nicht fahren darf.

ironically [aɪˈrɒnɪkəlɪ] adv ironisch ◆ **and then, ~ enough, he turned up** komischerweise or witzigerweise (inf) tauchte er dann auf; **and then, ~, it was he himself who ...** und dann hat ausgerechnet er ..., und dann hat paradoxerweise er ...

ironing [ˈaɪənɪŋ] n (process) Bügeln, Plätten (dial) nt; (clothes) Bügelwäsche, Plättwäsche (dial) f ◆ **to do the ~** (die Wäsche) bügeln; ~ **board** Bügelbrett, Plättbrett (dial) nt.

iron: I~ Lady n (Brit Pol) eiserne Lady; ~ **lung** n eiserne Lunge; **~monger** n (Brit) Eisen(waren)händler(in f) m; **~monger's (shop)** n (Brit) Eisen- und Haushaltswarenhandlung f; **~mongery** n (Brit) (shop) Eisen- und Haushaltswarenhandlung f; (goods) Eisenwaren pl; ~ **ore** n Eisenerz nt; ~ **rations** npl eiserne Ration; **~work** n Eisen nt; (on chest, cart etc) Eisenbeschläge pl; **to do ~work** Eisenarbeiten machen; **ornamental ~work** Eisenverzierungen pl; **~works** n sing or pl Eisenhütte f.

irony [ˈaɪərənɪ] n Ironie f no pl ◆ **the ~ of it is that ...** das Ironische daran ist, daß ..., die Ironie liegt darin, daß ...; **one of the ironies of fate** die Ironie des Schicksals; **life's ironies** die Ironie des Lebens.

irradiate [ɪˈreɪdɪeɪt] vt (a) (emit) heat, light rays ausstrahlen. (b) (liter: illumine) erhellen (liter). (c) (treat by irradiating) bestrahlen ◆ **~d food** strahlungsbehandelte Lebensmittel pl.

irrational [ɪˈræʃənl] adj (a) (illogical, Math, Psych) irrational; fear, belief also unsinnig; (not sensible) unvernünftig ◆ **if you maintain X, then it is ~ to deny Y** wenn Sie X behaupten, ist es widersinnig or unlogisch, Y zu leugnen.
(b) (not having reason) animal vernunftlos.

irrationality [ɪˌræʃəˈnælɪtɪ] n see adj Irrationalität f; Unsinnigkeit f; Unvernünftigkeit f.

irrationally [ɪˈræʃnəlɪ] adv irrational; (not sensibly) unvernünftig ◆ **quite ~, he believed ...** er glaubte gegen jede Vernunft or völlig unsinnigerweise ...

irreconcilable [ɪˌrekənˈsaɪləbl] adj (a) enemy, hatred unversöhnlich. (b) belief, opinion, differences unvereinbar.

irreconcilably [ɪˌrekənˈsaɪləblɪ] adv see adj.

irrecoverable [ˌɪrɪˈkʌvərəbl] adj endgültig or für immer verloren, unwiederbringlich verloren; loss unersetzlich, unersetzbar; debt nicht eintreibbar, uneinbringlich ◆ **the company's losses are ~** die Verluste der Firma können nicht mehr wettgemacht werden.

irrecoverably [ˌɪrɪˈkʌvrəblɪ] adv ~ **lost** für immer verloren.

irredeemable [ˌɪrɪˈdiːməbl] adj (a) currency, pawned object nicht einlösbar; bonds unkündbar, untilgbar; annuity, debt nicht ablösbar.
(b) (fig) sinner (rettungslos) verloren; loss unwiederbringlich; fault unverbesserlich; transgression unverzeihlich ◆ ~ **disaster** völlige Katastrophe; **a period of ~ gloom** eine Zeit völliger Hoffnungslosigkeit.

irredeemably [ˌɪrɪˈdiːməblɪ] adv lost rettungslos; confused hoffnungslos ◆ **he's an ~ wicked man** er ist ein von Grund auf böser or ein abgrundtief böser Mensch.

irreducible [ˌɪrɪˈdjuːsəbl] adj (Chem, Math) nicht reduzierbar ◆ **the ~ minimum** das Allermindeste.

irrefragable [ɪˈrefrəgəbl] adj (form) unwiderlegbar.

irrefutability [ˌɪrɪfjuːtəˈbɪlɪtɪ] n Unwiderlegbarkeit f.

irrefutable [ˌɪrɪˈfjuːtəbl] adj unwiderlegbar, unbestreitbar.

irrefutably [ˌɪrɪˈfjuːtɪblɪ] adv unwiderlegbar; demonstrate also eindeutig.

irregular [ɪˈregjʊləʳ] [1] adj (a) (uneven) unregelmäßig; intervals, teeth also, shape, coastline ungleichmäßig; surface uneben ◆ **to be ~ in one's attendance** unregelmäßig erscheinen; **the windows are deliberately ~** die Fenster sind bewußt uneinheitlich; **to keep ~ hours** ein ungeregeltes Leben führen, keine festen Zeiten haben; **he's been a bit ~ recently** (inf) er hat in letzter Zeit ziemlich unregelmäßigen Stuhlgang.
(b) (not conforming) unstatthaft; (contrary to rules) unvorschriftsmäßig; (contrary to law) ungesetzlich; marriage ungültig; behaviour ungebührlich, ungehörig ◆ **well, it's a bit ~, but I'll ...** eigentlich dürfte ich das nicht tun, aber ich ...; **it's a most ~ request, but ...** das ist ein höchst unübliches Ersuchen, aber ...; **this is most ~!** das ist äußerst ungewöhnlich!; **because of ~ procedures, the contract was not valid** wegen einiger Formfehler war der Vertrag ungültig.
(c) (Gram) unregelmäßig.
(d) troops irregulär.
[2] n (Mil) Irreguläre(r) m ◆ **the ~s** die irreguläre Truppe.

irregularity [ɪˌregjʊˈlærɪtɪ] n see adj (a) Unregelmäßigkeit f; Ungleichmäßigkeit f; Unebenheit f; Uneinheitlichkeit f; Ungeregeltheit f.
(b) Unstatthaftigkeit f; Unvorschriftsmäßigkeit f; Ungesetzlichkeit f; (of marriage) unvorschriftsmäßige Durchführung; Ungebührlichkeit, Ungehörigkeit f ◆ **a slight ~ in the proceedings** ein kleiner Formfehler; **a slight ~ with one of his pupils/the chambermaid** eine kleine Entgleisung mit einem seiner Schüler/dem Zimmermädchen.
(c) (Gram) Unregelmäßigkeit f.

irregularly [ɪˈregjʊləlɪ] adv see adj (a) unregelmäßig; ungleichmäßig; uneben. (b) unstatthaft; unvorschriftsmäßig; ungesetzlich; ungebührlich, ungehörig ◆ **the business has been conducted rather ~** es wurden ziemlich ungewöhnliche Geschäftsmethoden angewandt.

irrelevance [ɪˈreləvəns], **irrelevancy** [ɪˈrelɪvənsɪ] n Irrelevanz f no pl; (of details also) Unwesentlichkeit, Nebensächlichkeit f; (of titles, individuals) Bedeutungslosigkeit f ◆ **his speech was full of irrelevancies** vieles in seiner Rede war irrelevant or nebensächlich or unwesentlich; **it's become something of an ~** es ist ziemlich irrelevant geworden.

irrelevant [ɪˈreləvənt] adj irrelevant; details also, information unwesentlich, nebensächlich; titles etc bedeutungslos ◆ **it is ~ whether he agrees or not** es ist irrelevant or belanglos, ob er zustimmt; **it's ~ to the subject** das ist für das Thema irrelevant; **don't be ~** (in discussion) bleib bei der Sache; (in essay writing) bleiben Sie beim Thema.

irrelevantly [ɪˈreləvəntlɪ] adv belanglos ◆ **..., he said ~ ...**, sagte er, obwohl das gar nicht zur Sache gehörte; **he rambled on ~** er schwafelte irrelevantes or belangloses Zeug.

irreligious [ˌɪrɪˈlɪdʒəs] adj unreligiös, irreligiös; youth, savages gottlos; (lacking respect) pietätlos.

irremediable [ˌɪrɪˈmiːdɪəbl] adj character defects, errors nicht behebbar; situation nicht mehr zu retten pred or rettend attr.

irremediably [ˌɪrɪˈmiːdɪəblɪ] adv hoffnungslos.

irreparable [ɪˈrepərəbl] adj damage irreparabel, nicht wiedergutzumachen pred or wiedergutzumachend attr; loss unersetzlich; harm also bleibend.

irreparably [ɪˈrepərəblɪ] adv irreparabel ◆ **his reputation was ~ damaged** sein Ruf war unwiderruflich zerstört.

irreplaceable [ˌɪrɪˈpleɪsəbl] adj unersetzlich.

irrepressible [ˌɪrɪˈpresəbl] adj urge, curiosity unbezähmbar; optimism unerschütterlich, unverwüstlich; person nicht unter- or kleinzukriegen; child sonnig; delight unbändig ◆ **his ~ high spirits** sein sonniges Gemüt; **he has an ~ disposition** er ist eine Frohnatur; **you're ~** du bist nicht kleinzukriegen.

irreproachable [ˌɪrɪˈprəʊtʃəbl] adj manners tadellos, einwandfrei; conduct also untadelig.

irreproachably [ˌɪrɪˈprəʊtʃəblɪ] adv tadellos.

irresistible [ˌɪrɪˈzɪstəbl] adj unwiderstehlich.

irresistibly [ˌɪrɪˈzɪstəblɪ] adv unwiderstehlich ◆ **it's ~ funny** es ist von unwiderstehlicher Komik.

irresolute [ɪˈrezəluːt] adj unentschlossen, unentschieden.

irresolutely [ɪˈrezəluːtlɪ] adv unentschlossen, unschlüssig.

irresoluteness [ɪˈrezəluːtnɪs], **irresolution** [ɪˌrezəˈluːʃən] n Unentschiedenheit, Unentschlossenheit f.

irrespective [ˌɪrɪˈspektɪv] adj: ~ **of** ungeachtet (+gen), unabhängig von; **candidates should be chosen ~ of sex** bei der Auswahl der Kandidaten sollte das Geschlecht keine Rolle spielen; **~ of whether they want to or not** egal or gleichgültig, ob sie wollen oder nicht.

irresponsibility [ˈɪrɪˌspɒnsəˈbɪlɪtɪ] n see adj Unverantwortlichkeit f; Verantwortungslosigkeit f.

irresponsible [ˌɪrɪˈspɒnsəbl] adj action, behaviour unverantwortlich; person verantwortungslos.

irresponsibly [ˌɪrɪˈspɒnsəblɪ] adv unverantwortlich; behave also verantwortungslos.

irretrievable [ˌɪrɪˈtriːvəbl] adj nicht mehr wiederzubekommen; past, happiness etc unwiederbringlich; loss unersetzlich ◆ **the erased information is ~** die gelöschte Information kann nicht mehr abgerufen werden; **~ breakdown of marriage** (unheilbare) Zerrüttung der Ehe.

irretrievably [ˌɪrɪˈtriːvəblɪ] adv ~ **lost** für immer verloren; ~ **broken down** (unheilbar) zerrüttet.

irreverence [ɪˈrevərəns] n see adj Unehrerbietigkeit f; Respektlosigkeit, Despektierlichkeit f; Pietätlosigkeit f.

irreverent [ɪˈrevərənt] adj behaviour unehrerbietig; remark respektlos, despektierlich; novel, author respektlos; (towards religion, the dead) pietätlos.

irreverently [ɪˈrevərəntlɪ] adv see adj.

irreversible [ˌɪrɪˈvɜːsəbl] adj nicht rückgängig zu machen; judgment unwiderruflich; (Med, Phys, Chem) irreversibel; damage bleibend; decision unumstößlich.

irrevocable adj, **-bly** adv [ɪˈrevəkəbl, -ɪ] unwiderruflich.

irrigate [ˈɪrɪgeɪt] vt (a) land, crop bewässern. (b) (Med) spülen.

irrigation [ˌɪrɪˈgeɪʃən] n (a) (Agr) Bewässerung f ◆ ~ **canal** Bewässerungskanal m. (b) (Med) Spülung, Irrigation f.

irritability [ˌɪrɪtəˈbɪlɪtɪ] n Reizbarkeit f; Gereiztheit f.

irritable [ˈɪrɪtəbl] adj (as characteristic) reizbar; (on occasion) gereizt ◆ **don't be so ~** sei doch nicht so gereizt.

irritably [ˈɪrɪtəblɪ] adv gereizt.

irritant [ˈɪrɪtənt] n (Med) Reizerreger m; (person) Nervensäge f (inf); (noise etc) Ärgernis nt.

irritate [ˈɪrɪteɪt] vt (a) (annoy) ärgern, aufregen; (deliberately) reizen; (get on nerves of) irritieren ◆ **to get ~d** ärgerlich werden; **she's easily ~d** sie ist sehr reizbar or schnell verärgert; **I get ~d at or with him** er reizt or ärgert mich, er regt mich auf. (b) (Med) reizen.

irritating [ˈɪrɪteɪtɪŋ] adj ärgerlich; cough lästig ◆ **I find his jokes most ~** seine Witze regen mich wirklich auf; **you really are the most ~ person** du kannst einem wirklich auf die Nerven gehen; **how ~ for you!** wie ärgerlich!

irritatingly [ˈɪrɪteɪtɪŋlɪ] adv ärgerlich ◆ **he very ~ changed his mind** ärgerlicherweise hat er seine Meinung geändert.

irritation [ˌɪrɪˈteɪʃən] n (a) (state) Ärger m, Verärgerung f; (act) Ärgern nt; (deliberate) Reizen nt; (thing that irritates) Ärgernis nt, Unannehmlichkeit f ◆ **the noise is a source of ~** der Lärm irritiert einen; **to avoid the ~ of a long delay** um eine ärgerliche or lästige Verzögerung zu vermeiden.
(b) (Med) Reizung f.

irrupt [ɪ'rʌpt] *vi* eindringen, hereinstürzen; (*water also*) hereinbrechen.

irruption [ɪ'rʌpʃən] *n* Eindringen, Hereinstürzen *nt*; (*of water also*) Hereinbrechen *nt*.

Is *abbr of* **Island(s), Isle(s).**

is [ɪz] *3rd person sing present of* **be**.

Isaiah [aɪ'zaɪə] *n* Jesaja *m*.

ISBN *abbr of* **International Standard Book Number** ISBN-Nummer *f*.

-ise [-aɪz] *vb suf* -isieren.

-ish [-ɪʃ] *adj suf* (+*adj*) -lich; (+*n*) -haft; (*esp Brit: approximately*) um ... herum, zirka ◆ **green~** grünlich; **cold~** ziemlich kalt; **boy~** jungenhaft; **forty~** um vierzig herum, zirka vierzig.

isinglass ['aɪzɪŋglɑːs] *n* Fischleim *m*.

Islam ['ɪzlɑːm] *n* (*religion*) der Islam; (*Moslems collectively*) Mohammedaner *pl*.

Islamic [ɪz'læmɪk] *adj* islamisch.

island ['aɪlənd] *n* (*lit, fig*) Insel *f*.

islander ['aɪləndəʳ] *n* Insulaner(in *f*), Inselbewohner(in *f*) *m*.

isle [aɪl] *n* (*poet*) Eiland *nt* (*poet*) ◆ **the I~ of Man** die Insel Man.

islet ['aɪlɪt] *n* kleines Eiland (*poet*), Inselchen *nt*.

ism ['ɪzəm] *n* (*inf*) Ismus *m* (*inf*).

isn't ['ɪznt] *contr of* **is not**.

isobar ['aɪsəʊbɑːʳ] *n* Isobare *f*.

isolate ['aɪsəʊleɪt] *vt* **(a)** (*separate*) absondern, isolieren; (*Med, Chem*) isolieren ◆ **the causes of crime cannot be ~d from social conditions** man kann die Gründe für kriminelles Verhalten nicht von den gesellschaftlichen Verhältnissen gesondert *or* isoliert betrachten.
(b) (*cut off*) abschneiden, isolieren ◆ **to ~ oneself from other people** sich (von anderen) abkapseln; **to ~ oneself from the world** sich isolieren, sich von der Welt zurückziehen.
(c) (*pinpoint*) herausfinden; *problem also, essential factor* herauskristallisieren.

isolated ['aɪsəʊleɪtɪd] *adj* **(a)** (*cut off*) abgeschnitten, isoliert; (*remote*) abgelegen; *existence* zurückgezogen; (*Med*) isoliert. **(b)** (*single*) einzeln ◆ **~ instances** Einzelfälle *pl*.

isolating ['aɪsəʊleɪtɪŋ] *adj*: **~ language** isolierende Sprache.

isolation [ˌaɪsəʊ'leɪʃən] *n* **(a)** (*act*) (*separation, cutting-off*) Absonderung, Isolierung (*esp Med, Chem*) *f*; (*pinpointing*) Herausfinden *nt*; (*of problem also, of essential factor*) Herauskristallisierung *f*.
(b) (*state*) Isoliertheit, Abgeschnittenheit *f*; (*remoteness*) Abgelegenheit, Abgeschiedenheit *f* ◆ **his ~ from the world** seine Abgeschiedenheit von der Welt; **this deliberate and self-imposed social ~** diese absichtliche und selbstauferlegte gesellschaftliche Isolation; **spiritual ~** geistige Isolation; **he felt a sense of ~** er fühlte sich isoliert; **Splendid I~** (*Hist*) Splendid Isolation *f*; **he lived in splendid ~ in a bedsitter in the suburbs** (*iro*) er wohnte, weitab vom Schuß (*inf*) *or* jenseits von Gut und Böse (*hum*), in einem möblierten Zimmer am Stadtrand; **to keep a patient in ~** einen Patienten isolieren; **to live in ~** zurückgezogen leben; **to consider sth in ~** etw gesondert *or* isoliert betrachten; **it doesn't make much sense in ~** ohne Zusammenhang *or* isoliert ist es ziemlich unverständlich.

isolation hospital *n* Isolierspital *nt*.

isolationism [ˌaɪsəʊ'leɪʃənɪzəm] *n* Isolationismus *m*.

isolationist [ˌaɪsəʊ'leɪʃənɪst] 1 *adj* isolationistisch.
2 *n* Isolationist(in *f*) *m*.

isolation ward *n* Isolierstation *f*.

isomer ['aɪsəʊməʳ] *n* (*Chem*) Isomer(e) *nt*.

isomeric [ˌaɪsəʊ'merɪk] *adj* (*Chem*) isomer.

isometrics [ˌaɪsəʊ'metrɪks] *n sing* Isometrie *f*.

isomorphic [ˌaɪsəʊ'mɔːfɪk] *adj* (*form*) isomorph.

isosceles [aɪ'sɒsɪliːz] *adj*: **~ triangle** gleichschenkliges Dreieck.

isotherm ['aɪsəʊθɜːm] *n* (*Met*) Isotherme *f*.

isotope ['aɪsəʊtəʊp] *n* Isotop *nt*.

Israel ['ɪzreɪl] *n* Israel *nt*.

Israeli [ɪz'reɪlɪ] 1 *adj* israelisch.
2 *n* Israeli *mf*.

Israelite ['ɪzrɪəlaɪt] *n* (*Bibl*) Israelit(in *f*) *m*.

issue ['ɪʃuː] 1 *vt* **(a)** (*give, send out*) *passport, documents, certificate, driving licence* ausstellen; *tickets, library books* ausgeben; *shares, banknotes* ausgeben, emittieren; *stamps* herausgeben; *coins* ausgeben; *order, warning* ergehen lassen (*to* an +*acc*), erteilen (*to dat*); *warning* aussprechen; *proclamation* erlassen; *details* bekanntgeben ◆ **the issuing authorities** die ausstellende Behörde; **to ~ sb with a visa, to ~ a visa to sb** jdm ein Visum ausstellen; **a warrant for his arrest was ~d** gegen ihn wurde Haftbefehl erlassen; **~d capital** (*Fin*) ausgegebenes Kapital.
(b) (*publish*) *book, newspaper* herausgeben.
(c) (*supply*) *rations, rifles, ammunition* ausgeben ◆ **to ~ sth to sb/to ~ sb with sth** etw an jdn ausgeben; **all troops are ~d with ...** alle Truppen sind mit ... ausgerüstet.
2 *vi* (*liquid, gas*) austreten; (*smoke*) (heraus)quellen; (*sound*) (hervor- *or* heraus)dringen; (*people etc*) (heraus)strömen ◆ **his actions ~ from a desire to help** seine Handlungen entspringen dem Wunsch zu helfen; **the sewage/river ~s into the sea** das Abwasser fließt/der Fluß mündet ins Meer.
3 *n* **(a)** (*question*) Frage *f*; (*matter also*) Angelegenheit *f*; (*problematic*) Problem *nt* ◆ **the factual ~s** die Tatsachen *pl*; **the ~ is whether** ... es geht darum *or* die Frage ist, ob ...; **the whole future of the country is at ~** es geht um die Zukunft des Landes; **what is at ~?** worum geht es?; **that's not at ~** das steht nicht zur Debatte; **to join ~ with sb over sth** jdn in einer Sache aufgreifen; **to take ~ with sb over sth** jdm in etw (*dat*) widersprechen; **this has become something of an ~** das ist zu einem Problem geworden; **to make an ~ of sth** etw aufbauschen; **to evade the ~** ausweichen; **do you want to make an ~ of it?** (*inf*) du willst dich wohl mit mir anlegen?; **to avoid the ~** ausweichen; (*in reply also*) ausweichend antworten.
(b) (*outcome, result*) Ergebnis *nt* ◆ **that decided the ~** das war entscheidend *or* ausschlaggebend; **to bring sth to an ~** eine Entscheidung in etw (*dat*) herbeiführen; **to force the ~** eine Entscheidung erzwingen.
(c) (*giving out, that given out*) (*of banknotes, shares, coins, stamps etc*) Ausgabe *f*; (*of shares also*) Emission *f* ◆ **place of ~** (*of tickets*) Ausgabestelle *f*; (*of passports*) Ausstellungsort *m*; **date of ~** (*of tickets*) Ausstellungsdatum *nt*; (*of stamps*) Ausgabetag *m*; **~ desk** Ausgabe(schalter *m*) *f*.
(d) (*handing-out*) Ausgabe *f*; (*supplying, thing supplied*) Lieferung *f* ◆ **the ~ of blankets/guns to the troops** die Versorgung der Truppen mit Decken/die Ausrüstung der Truppen mit Gewehren; **this rifle is the latest ~** dieses Gewehr ist das neueste Modell; **it's part of the clothing ~** es ist Teil der Ausstattung.
(e) (*of book etc*) Herausgabe *f*; (*book etc*) Ausgabe *f*.
(f) (*of liquid, gas*) Ausströmen *nt* ◆ **~ of pus** Eiterabsonderung *f*; **an ~ of blood from the cut** eine Blutung der Wunde.
(g) (*Jur: offspring*) Nachkommenschaft *f*.

Istanbul [ˌɪstæn'buːl] *n* Istanbul *nt*.

isthmus ['ɪsməs] *n* Landenge *f*, Isthmus *m*.

IT *abbr of* **information technology.**

it¹ [ɪt] 1 *pron* **(a)** (*when replacing German noun*) (*subj*) er/sie/es; (*dir obj*) ihn/sie/es; (*indir obj*) ihm/ihr/ihm ◆ **of ~** davon; **behind/over/under** *etc* **~** dahinter/darüber/darunter *etc*; **who is ~? — ~'s me** *or* **I** (*form*) wer ist da? — ich (bin's); **who is ~? — ~'s the Browns!** wer ist da? — die Browns!; **what is ~?** was ist es *or* das?; (*matter*) was ist los?; **that's not ~** (*not the trouble*) das ist es (gar) nicht; (*not the point*) darum geht's gar nicht; **the cheek of ~!** so eine Frechheit!; **the worst of ~ is that ...** das Schlimmste daran ist, daß ...
(b) (*indef subject*) es ◆ **~'s raining** es regnet; **yes, ~ is a problem** ja, das ist ein Problem; **~ seems simple to me** mir scheint das ganz einfach; **if ~ hadn't been for her, we would have come** wenn sie nicht gewesen wäre, wären wir gekommen; **why is ~ always me who has to ...?** warum muß (ausgerechnet) immer ich ...?; **why is ~ always him who can't ...?** warum ist es immer er, der nicht ... kann?; **~ wasn't me** *ich* war's nicht; **~ was the Italians/10 miles** es waren die Italiener/10 Meilen; **I don't think ~ (is) wise of you ...** ich halte es für unklug, wenn du ...
(c) (*emph*) **~ was him** *or* **he** (*form*) **who asked her** *er* hat sie gefragt; **~ was a cup that he dropped and not ...** er hat eine *Tasse* fallen lassen und nicht ...; **~'s his appearance I object to** ich habe nur etwas gegen sein Äußeres; **~ was for his sake that she lied** nur um seinetwillen hat sie gelogen; **~'s the other one I like** ich mag den *anderen*/das *andere etc*.
(d) (*inf phrases*) **that's ~!** (*agreement*) ja, genau!; (*annoyed*) jetzt reicht's mir!; **that's ~ (then)!** (*achievement*) (so,) das wär's!, geschafft!; (*disappointment*) ja, das war's dann wohl; **this is ~!** (*before action*) jetzt geht's los!; *see* **at, in, with-it.**
2 *n* (*inf*) **(a)** (*in children's games*) **you're ~!** du bist!
(b) this is really ~! das ist genau das richtige, *das* ist es; **he really thinks he's ~** er bildet sich (*dat*) ein, er sei sonst wer.
(c) my cat's an ~ meine Katze ist ein Neutrum.
(d) (*dated: sex appeal*) Sex-Appeal *m*.

it² *n* (*dated sl*): **gin and ~** Gin mit italienischem Wermut.

ITA (*dated Brit*) *abbr of* **Independent Television Authority.**

ita *abbr of* **initial teaching alphabet** *Lautschrift f für den Anfangsunterricht im Lesen*.

Italian [ɪ'tæljən] 1 *adj* italienisch.
2 *n* **(a)** Italiener(in *f*) *m*. **(b)** (*language*) Italienisch *nt*.

Italianate [ɪ'tæljəneɪt] *adj* nach italienischer Art ◆ **the ~ style of the church/painting** der von der italienischen Schule beeinflußte Stil der Kirche/des Gemäldes.

italic [ɪ'tælɪk] 1 *adj* kursiv ◆ **~ type** Kursivdruck *m*; **~ script** Kurrentschrift *f*.
2 *n* **~s** *pl* Kursivschrift, Kursive *f* ◆ **in ~s** kursiv (gedruckt); **my ~s** Hervorhebung von mir.

italicize [ɪ'tælɪsaɪz] *vt* kursiv schreiben/drucken.

Italy ['ɪtəlɪ] *n* Italien *nt*.

ITC (*Brit*) *abbr of* **Independent Television Commission.**

itch [ɪtʃ] 1 *n* **(a)** Jucken *nt*, Juckreiz *m* ◆ **I have an ~** mich juckt es, ich habe einen Juckreiz.
(b) (*inf: urge*) Lust *f* ◆ **I have an ~ to do sth/for sth** es reizt *or* juckt (*inf*) mich, etw zu tun/etw reizt *or* juckt (*inf*) mich.
2 *vi* **(a)** jucken ◆ **my back ~es** mein Rücken juckt (mich), mir *or* mich juckt der Rücken; **that rash made me ~ all over** der Ausschlag juckte am ganzen Körper.
(b) (*inf*) **he is ~ing to ...** es reizt *or* juckt (*inf*) ihn, zu ...; **he's ~ing for a fight** er ist auf Streit aus.

itching ['ɪtʃɪŋ] 1 *adj* juckend ◆ **to have an ~ palm** (*fig*) gern die Hand aufhalten (*inf*).
2 *n* Jucken *nt*, Juckreiz *m* ◆ **~ powder** Juckpulver *nt*.

itchy ['ɪtʃɪ] *adj* (+*er*) **(a)** (*itching*) juckend ◆ **it is ~** es juckt; **I've got ~ feet** (*inf*) ich will hier weg (*inf*); (*want to travel also*) mich packt das Fernweh; **he's got ~ fingers/an ~ palm** (*inf*) er macht lange Finger/er hält gern die Hand auf (*inf*).
(b) (*causing itching*) *cloth* kratzig.

it'd ['ɪtəd] *contr of* **it would; it had.**

-ite [-aɪt] *n suf (follower of)* -anhänger(in *f*) *m*.

▼ **item** ['aɪtəm] *n* **(a)** *(in programme, on agenda etc)* Punkt *m*; *(Comm: in account book)* (Rechnungs)posten *m*; *(article)* Stück, Ding *nt*, Gegenstand *m*; *(in catalogue etc)* Artikel *m*; *(Brit: in variety show)* Nummer *f* ◆ **~s of furniture** Möbelstücke *pl*; **he went through it ~ by ~** er ging die Sache Punkt für Punkt durch; **petrol is one of the most expensive ~s I have to buy** Benzin gehört zu den teuersten Dingen, die ich kaufe.
(b) *(of news)* Bericht *m*; *(short, Rad, TV also)* Meldung *f* ◆ **a short news ~** eine Zeitungsnotiz/eine Kurzmeldung.

itemization [ˌaɪtəmaɪ'zeɪʃən] *n* detaillierte Aufstellung, Einzelaufführung *f*.

itemize ['aɪtəmaɪz] *vt* spezifizieren, einzeln aufführen ◆ **~d account** spezifizierte Rechnung; **to ~ a bill** die Rechnungsposten einzeln aufführen, die Rechnung spezifizieren.

iterate ['ɪtəreɪt] *vt (form)* wiederholen.

iteration [ɪtə'reɪʃən] *n (form)* Wiederholung *f*.

iterative ['ɪtərətɪv] *adj (Gram)* iterativ.

itinerant [ɪ'tɪnərənt] *adj* umherziehend, wandernd, Wander-; *preacher* Wander-; *minstrel* fahrend; *worker* Saison-, Wander-; *judge* Reise- ◆ **~ theatre group** Wandertruppe *f*.

itinerary [aɪ'tɪnərərɪ] *n (route)* (Reise)route *f*; *(map)* Straßenkarte *f*, Wegeverzeichnis *nt*.

it'll ['ɪtl] *contr of* **it will; it shall.**

ITN *(Brit) abbr of* **Independent Television News** *Nachrichtendienst m der Fernsehanstalt ITV*.

its [ɪts] *poss adj* sein(e)/ihr(e)/sein(e).

it's [ɪts] *contr of* **it is; it has** *(as aux)*.

itself [ɪt'self] *pron* **(a)** *(reflexive)* sich.
(b) *(emph)* selbst ◆ **and now we come to the text ~** und jetzt kommen wir zum Text selbst; **the frame ~ is worth £1,000** der Rahmen allein *or* schon der Rahmen ist £ 1.000 wert; **in ~, the actual amount is not important** der Betrag an sich ist unwichtig; **enthusiasm is not enough in ~** Begeisterung allein genügt nicht.
(c) by ~ *(alone)* allein; *(automatically)* von selbst, selbsttätig; **seen by ~** einzeln betrachtet; **the bomb went off by ~** die Bombe ging von selbst los.

ITV *(Brit) abbr of* **Independent Television** *britische Fernsehanstalt*.

IUD *abbr of* **intra-uterine device.**

I've [aɪv] *contr of* **I have.**

ivied ['aɪvɪd] *adj* efeuumrankt.

ivory ['aɪvərɪ] [1] *n* **(a)** *(also colour)* Elfenbein *nt*. **(b)** *(Art)* Elfenbeinschnitzerei *f*. **(c)** *(inf)* **ivories** *(piano keys)* Tasten *pl*; *(billiard balls)* Billardkugeln *pl*; *(dice)* Würfel *pl*; *(dated: teeth)* Beißer *pl (inf)*.
[2] *adj* **(a)** elfenbeinern. **(b)** *colour* elfenbeinfarben.

Ivory Coast *n* Elfenbeinküste *f*.

ivory tower [1] *n (fig)* Elfenbeinturm *m*.
[2] *adj attr* weltfremd.

ivy ['aɪvɪ] *n* Efeu *m*.

Ivy League *n (US)* Eliteuniversitäten *pl* der USA.

-ize [-aɪz] *vb suf* -isieren.

➤ LANGUAGE IN USE: **item: a** → 20.3, 20.6

J

J, j [dʒeɪ] *n* J, j *nt.*

jab [dʒæb] [1] *vt* **(a)** *(with stick, elbow etc)* stoßen; *(with knife also)* stechen ◆ **he ~bed his elbow into my side** er stieß mir den *or* mit dem Ellbogen in die Seite; **she ~bed the jellyfish with a stick** sie pik(s)te mit einem Stock in die Qualle (hinein) *(inf)*; **he ~bed his finger** er stach sich *(dat)* in den Finger; **he ~bed his finger at the map** er tippte mit dem Finger auf die Karte; **a sharp ~bing pain** ein scharfer, stechender Schmerz.
(b) *(inf: give injection to)* eine Spritze geben *or* verpassen *(inf)* *(+dat)*.
[2] *vi* stoßen *(at sb with sth* mit etw nach jdm); *(Boxing)* eine (kurze) Gerade schlagen *(at* auf *+acc)*.
[3] *n* **(a)** *(with stick, elbow)* Stoß *m*; *(with needle, knife)* Stich *m* ◆ **he gave the jellyfish a ~ with a stick** er stieß *or* pik(s)te *(inf)* mit dem Stock in die Qualle (hinein); **he got a nasty ~ in the eye when she opened her umbrella** sie stach ihn ins Auge, als sie den Regenschirm öffnete.
(b) *(inf: injection)* Spritze *f.*
(c) *(Boxing)* (kurze) Gerade.

jabber ['dʒæbəʳ] [1] *vt* (daher)plappern *(inf)*; *poem, prayers* herunterrasseln, abhaspeln *(inf)*.
[2] *vi (also ~* **away)** plappern, schwätzen, quasseln *(inf)* ◆ **they sat there ~ing away in Spanish** sie saßen da und quasselten *(inf)* Spanisch.
[3] *n* Geplapper, Gequassel *(inf)*, Geschnatter *nt.*

jabbering ['dʒæbərɪŋ] *n* Geplapper, Plappern, Geschnatter *nt.*

jacaranda [ˌdʒækə'rændə] *n* Jakaranda(baum) *m*; *(wood)* Jakarandaholz *nt*, Palisander(holz *nt*) *m.*

Jack [dʒæk] *n dim of* **John** Hans *m* ◆ **I'm all right ~** das kann mich überhaupt nicht jucken *(inf)*; **his attitude of I'm all right ~** seine Einstellung „das kann mich überhaupt nicht jucken".

jack [dʒæk] *n* **(a)** Hebevorrichtung *f*; *(Aut)* Wagenheber *m.*
(b) *(Cards)* Bube *m.*
(c) *(Naut: flag)* Gösch, Bugflagge *f*; *see* **Union J~**.
(d) *(Bowling)* Zielkugel *f.*
(e) *(boot~)* Stiefelknecht *m.*
(f) every man ~ (of them) *(inf)* alle ohne Ausnahme, (alle) geschlossen; **every man ~ of them voted against it** sie stimmten alle ohne Ausnahme *or* geschlossen dagegen.

◆**jack in** *vt sep (sl) university, job etc* stecken *(sl)*, aufgeben; *girlfriend* Schluß machen mit *(inf)* ◆ **~ it ~!** *(stop it)* hör auf damit!, steck's *(sl)*.

◆**jack up** *vt sep* **(a)** *car* aufbocken. **(b)** *(sl) prices, wages* (in die Höhe) treiben.

jackal ['dʒækɔːl] *n* Schakal *m.*

jackanapes ['dʒækəneɪps] *n, pl - (old) (man)* Fant *m (old)*, (eingebildeter) Laffe *(old)*; *(child)* Racker *m (old)*.

jackass ['dʒækæs] *n (donkey)* Eselhengst *m*; *(inf: person)* Esel *(inf)*, Dummkopf *(inf) m.*

jackboot ['dʒækbuːt] *n* Schaftstiefel *m.*

jackdaw ['dʒækdɔː] *n* Dohle *f.*

jacket ['dʒækɪt] *n* **(a)** *(garment)* Jacke *f*; *(man's tailored ~ also)* Jackett *nt*; *(life ~)* Schwimmweste *f.* **(b)** *(of book)* Schutzumschlag *m*, Buchhülle *f*; *(US: of record)* Plattenhülle *f.* **(c)** *(esp US: for papers etc)* Umschlag *m.* **(d) ~ potatoes, potatoes (baked) in their ~s** (in der Schale) gebackene Kartoffeln *pl.* **(e)** *(Tech: of boiler etc)* Mantel *m*, Ummantelung *f.*

jack: J~ Frost *n* der Frost, der Reif *(personifiziert)*; **J~ Frost has been, J~ Frost has painted the window** es sind Eisblumen am Fenster; **~-in-office** *n* Beamtenseele *f*; **~-in-the-box** *n* Schachtel- *or* Kastenteufel *m*; **he was up and down like a ~-in-the-box** er sprang immer wieder auf, der reinste Hampelmann.

jackknife ['dʒæknaɪf] [1] *n* **(a)** (großes) Taschenmesser. **(b)** *(also ~* **dive)** gehechteter Sprung.
[2] *vi* **the lorry ~d** der Auflieger *or* Anhänger hat sich quergestellt.

jack: ~-of-all-trades *n* Alleskönner *m*; **to be (a) ~-of-all-trades (and master of none)** *(prov)* ein Hansdampf *m* in allen Gassen sein; **~-o'-lantern** *n* Kürbislaterne *f*; *(will-o'-the-wisp)* Irrlicht *nt*; **~ plane** *n (Tech)* Schropp- *or* Doppelhobel *m*; **~ plug** *n* Bananenstecker *m*; *(for telephone)* Klinkenstecker *m.*

jackpot ['dʒækpɒt] *n* Pott *m (inf)*; *(Cards also)* Jackpot *m*; *(in lottery etc)* Hauptgewinn *m* ◆ **the ~ this week stands at £20,000** diese Woche ist der Höchstgewinn £ 20.000; **to hit the ~** *(lit)* einen Treffer haben; *(in lottery)* den Hauptgewinn bekommen; *(fig)* das große Los ziehen.

jack: ~ rabbit *n* Eselhase *m*; **J~ Robinson** [ˌdʒæk'rɒbɪnsən] *n*: **before you could say J~ Robinson** *(inf)* im Nu, im Handumdrehen.

jacks [dʒæks] *n sing (game) Kinderspiel nt mit kleinem Gummiball und Metallsternchen.*

jackstraws ['dʒækˌstrɔːz] *n sing* Mikado *nt.*

Jack Tar *n (Naut inf)* Seebär *m (inf)*.

Jacob ['dʒeɪkəb] *n* Jakob *m.*

Jacobean [ˌdʒækə'biːən] *adj* aus der Zeit Jakobs I.

Jacobite ['dʒækəbaɪt] *n* Jakobit *m.*

jacuzzi [dʒə'kuːzɪ] *n* Whirlpool *m.*

jade¹ [dʒeɪd] [1] *n (stone)* Jade *m or f*; *(colour)* Jadegrün *nt.*
[2] *adj* Jade-; *(colour)* jadegrün ◆ **~ green** jadegrün.

jade² *n (old)* **(a)** *(horse)* Schindmähre *f (old)*, Klepper *m (old)*. **(b)** *(loose woman)* Weibsbild, Weibsstück *nt*; *(pert girl)* freches *or* keckes Weibsbild.

jaded ['dʒeɪdɪd] *adj (physically)* matt, abgespannt; *(permanently)* verbraucht, abgelebt; *(mentally dulled)* stumpfsinnig, abgestumpft; *(from overindulgence etc)* übersättigt; *appearance* verlebt, verbraucht; *palate* abgestumpft.

jag [dʒæg] *n* **(a)** *(of rock)* Zacke, Spitze *f*; *(of saw)* Zacke *f.* **(b) to go on a ~** *(sl)* einen draufmachen *(sl)*. **(c)** *(Scot inf: injection)* Spritze *f.*

Jag [dʒæg] *n (inf: car)* Jaguar *m* ®.

jagged ['dʒægɪd] *adj* zackig; *edge, hole also* schartig, (aus)gezackt; *wound, tear* ausgefranst; *coastline* zerklüftet.

jaguar ['dʒægjʊəʳ] *n* Jaguar *m.*

jail [dʒeɪl] [1] *n* Gefängnis *nt* ◆ **in ~** im Gefängnis; **after 2 years ~** nach zwei Jahren Gefängnis, nach zweijähriger Haft; **to go to ~** eingesperrt werden, ins Gefängnis kommen.
[2] *vt* einsperren, ins Gefängnis sperren.

jail: ~bait *n (inf)* **she's ~bait** die ist noch minderjährig, laß lieber die Finger von ihr *(inf)*; **~bird** *n (inf)* Knastbruder *m (inf)*; **~break** *n* Ausbruch *m (aus dem Gefängnis)*; **~breaker** *n* Ausbrecher *m.*

jailer ['dʒeɪləʳ] *n* Gefängniswärter(in *f*) *or* -aufseher(in *f*) *m.*

jail house *n (US)* Gefängnis *nt.*

jalop(p)y [dʒə'lɒpɪ] *n (inf)* alte (Klapper)kiste *or* Mühle *(inf)*.

jalousie ['ʒælu(ː)ziː] *n* Jalousie *f.*

jam¹ [dʒæm] *n* Marmelade, Konfitüre *f* ◆ **you want ~ on it too, do you?** *(Brit inf)* du kriegst wohl nie genug *or* den Hals voll *(inf)*?

jam² [1] *n* **(a)** *(crowd)* Gedränge, Gewühl *nt.*
(b) *(traffic ~)* (Verkehrs)stau *m*, Stauung *f.*
(c) *(blockage in machine, of logs etc)* Stockung, Stauung *f* ◆ **there's a ~ in the pipe** das Rohr ist verstopft.
(d) *(inf: tight spot)* Klemme *(inf)*, Patsche *(inf) f* ◆ **to be in a ~** in der Klemme *or* Patsche sitzen *(inf)*; **to get into a ~** ins Gedränge kommen *(inf)*; **to get into a ~ with sb/sth** mit jdm/etw Schwierigkeiten haben; **to get sb out of a ~** jdm aus der Klemme helfen *(inf)*, jdn aus der Patsche ziehen *(inf)*.
[2] *vt* **(a)** *(make stick) window, drawer etc* verklemmen, verkanten; *gun, brakes etc* blockieren; *(wedge) (to stop rattles etc)* festklemmen; *(between two things)* einklemmen ◆ **be careful not to ~ the lock** paß auf, daß sich das Schloß nicht verklemmt; **they had him ~med up against the wall** sie hatten ihn gegen die Wand gedrängt; **it's ~med** es klemmt; **the ship was ~med in the ice** das Schiff saß im Eis fest; **he got his finger ~med** *or* **he ~med his finger in the door** er hat sich *(dat)* den Finger in der Tür eingeklemmt.
(b) *(cram, squeeze) (into* in *+acc) things* stopfen, hineinzwängen, quetschen; *people* quetschen, pferchen ◆ **to be ~med together** *(things)* zusammengezwängt sein; *(people)* zusammengedrängt sein; *(in train etc also)* zusammengepfercht sein; **why ~ all the facts into one article?** warum zwängen *or* quetschen *(inf)* Sie alle Fakten in einen Artikel?
(c) *(crowd, block) street, town etc* verstopfen, blockieren; *(people also)* sich drängen in *(+dat)* ◆ **a street ~med with cars** eine verstopfte Straße; **the passage was ~med with people** Menschen verstopften *or* versperrten den Durchgang.
(d) *(move suddenly)* **to ~ one's foot on the brake** eine Vollbremsung machen, auf die Bremse steigen *(inf) or* latschen *(inf)*; **he ~med his knees into the donkey's flanks** er preßte dem Esel die Knie in die Flanken; *see also* **~ on**.
(e) *(Rad) station, broadcast* stören.
[3] *vi* **(a) the crowd ~med into the bus** die Menschenmenge zwängte sich in

den Bus.
(b) *(become stuck)* *(brake)* sich verklemmen; *(gun)* Ladehemmung haben; *(door, window etc)* klemmen.

◆jam in [1] *vt sep* **(a)** *(wedge in)* einkeilen ◆ **he was ~med ~ by the crowd** er war in der Menge eingekeilt. **(b)** *(press in)* (herein)stopfen in *(+acc)*.
[2] *vi* *(crowd in)* sich herein-/hineindrängen.

◆jam on [1] *vt sep* **(a) to ~ ~ the brakes** eine Vollbremsung machen, voll auf die Bremse latschen *(inf)*. **(b) to ~ ~ one's hat** sich *(dat)* den Hut aufstülpen.
[2] *vi* *(brakes)* klemmen.

◆jam up *vt sep* **(a)** *see* **jam[2] 2 (a)**. **(b)** *(block) roads, entrance etc* blockieren, versperren; *drain, pipe* verstopfen, blockieren.

Jamaica [dʒəˈmeɪkə] *n* Jamaika *nt.*

Jamaican [dʒəˈmeɪkən] [1] *adj* jamaikanisch ◆ **~ rum** Jamaikarum *m.*
[2] *n* Jamaikaner(in *f*) *m.*

jamb [dʒæm] *n* (Tür-/Fenster)pfosten *m.*

jamboree [ˌdʒæmbəˈriː] *n* *(Scouts')* Jamboree, (Pfadfinder)treffen *nt*; *(dated: party)* Rummel *m* *(inf)* ◆ **village ~** Dorffest *nt.*

James [dʒeɪmz] *n* Jakob *m.*

jam: ~-full *adj container* vollgestopft, gepfropft voll; *room, bus* überfüllt, knallvoll *(inf)*, proppenvoll *(inf)*; **~-full of people** vollgestopft mit Leuten; **~ jar** *n* Marmeladenglas *nt.*

jamming [ˈdʒæmɪŋ] *n* *(Rad)* Störung *f* ◆ **~ station** Störsender *m.*

jammy [ˈdʒæmɪ] *adj (+er)* *(Brit sl: lucky)* Glücks- ◆ **a ~ shot** ein Glückstreffer *m*; **the ~ bugger won three in a row** der mit seinem Schweineglück *or* der verdammte Glückspilz hat dreimal nacheinander gewonnen *(inf)*.

jam: ~-packed *adj* überfüllt, proppenvoll *(inf)*; **~-packed with tourists** voller Touristen; **~ pot** *n* Marmeladentöpfchen *nt*; **~ puff** *n* Blätterteigteilchen *nt* mit Marmelade; **~ roll** *n* Biskuitrolle *f*; **~ session** *n* Jam Session *f.*

Jan *abbr of* **January** Jan.

Jane [dʒeɪn] *n* **(a)** *see* **plain. (b) j~** *(US sl: woman)* Weib *nt* *(inf)*.

jangle [ˈdʒæŋgl] [1] *vi* *(keys, money)* klimpern *(inf)*; *(bells)* bimmeln *(inf)*; *(chains, harness)* klirren, rasseln.
[2] *vt money* klimpern mit; *bell* bimmeln lassen; *keys also, chains* rasseln mit ◆ **it ~d my nerves** das ist mir durch Mark und Bein gegangen.
[3] *n see* **jangling 2.**

jangling [ˈdʒæŋglɪŋ] [1] *adj keys, money* klimpernd; *bells* bimmelnd; *chains, harness* klirrend, rasselnd.
[2] *n see vi* Klimpern, Geklimper *(inf)* *nt*; Bimmeln *nt*; Klirren, Rasseln *nt.*

janitor [ˈdʒænɪtə[r]] *n* Hausmeister *m*; *(of block of flats also)* Hauswart *m.*

janitress [ˈdʒænɪtrɪs] *n* Hausmeisterin *f.*

jankers [ˈdʒæŋkəz] *npl* *(Mil sl: prison)* Bau *m* *(Mil sl)*.

January [ˈdʒænjʊərɪ] *n* Januar *m*; *see also* **September.**

Janus [ˈdʒeɪnəs] *n* Janus *m.*

Jap [dʒæp] *n* *(pej inf)* Japs(e) *m* *(pej)*.

japan [dʒəˈpæn] [1] *n* schwarzer Lack, Japanlack *m.*
[2] *vt* mit Japanlack überziehen.

Japan [dʒəˈpæn] *n* Japan *nt.*

Japanese [ˌdʒæpəˈniːz] [1] *adj* japanisch.
[2] *n* **(a)** Japaner(in *f*) *m.* **(b)** *(language)* Japanisch *nt.*

jape [dʒeɪp] [1] *n* *(old)* Spaß, Scherz *m*; *(trick)* Streich *m.*
[2] *vi* spaßen, scherzen.

japonica [dʒəˈpɒnɪkə] *n* japanische Quitte.

jar[1] [dʒɑː[r]] *n* **(a)** *(for jam etc)* Glas *nt*; *(without handle)* Topf *m*, Gefäß *nt*; *(with handle)* Krug *m.* **(b)** *(inf: drink)* Bierchen *nt* *(inf)* ◆ **fancy a ~?** kommst du (mit) auf ein Bierchen? *(inf)*.

jar[2] [1] *n* **(a)** *(jolt)* Ruck *m* ◆ **he/his neck got quite a ~ in the accident** er/sein Hals hat bei dem Autounfall einen schweren Stoß abbekommen. **(b)** *(fig)* Schock *m.*
[2] *vi* **(a)** *(grate: metal etc)* kreischen, quietschen ◆ **to ~ on** *or* **against sth** auf etw *(dat)* quietschen *or* kreischen.
(b) *(be out of harmony)* *(note)* schauerlich klingen; *(colours, patterns)* sich beißen *(inf)*, nicht harmonieren *(with* mit*)*; *(ideas, opinions)* sich nicht vertragen, nicht harmonieren *(with* mit*)* ◆ **this ~s stylistically** das fällt stilmäßig aus dem Rahmen.
[3] *vt building etc* erschüttern; *back, knee* sich *(dat)* stauchen; *(jolt continuously)* durchrütteln; *(fig)* einen Schock versetzen *(+dat)* ◆ **he must have ~red the camera** er muß mit dem Photoapparat gewackelt haben; **someone ~red my elbow** jemand hat mir an den *or* mich am Ellbogen gestoßen.

◆jar (up)on *vi +prep obj* Schauer über den Rücken jagen *(+dat)* ◆ **this noise ~s ~ my nerves** dieser Lärm geht mir auf die Nerven; **her voice ~s ~ my ears** ihre Stimme geht mir durch und durch.

jardinière [ˌʒɑːdɪnɪˈɛə[r]] *n* Blumenbank *f.*

jargon [ˈdʒɑːgən] *n* Jargon *m* *(pej)*, Fachsprache *f.*

jarring [ˈdʒɑːrɪŋ] *adj sound* gellend, kreischend; *accent* störend; *colour, pattern* sich beißend *attr* *(inf)*, nicht zusammenpassend *attr.*

jasmin(e) [ˈdʒæzmɪn] *n* Jasmin *m* ◆ **winter ~** gelber Jasmin.

Jason [ˈdʒeɪsən] *n* Jason *m.*

jasper [ˈdʒæspə[r]] *n* Jaspis *m.*

jaundice [ˈdʒɔːndɪs] *n* Gelbsucht *f.*

jaundiced [ˈdʒɔːndɪst] *adj* **(a)** *(lit)* gelbsüchtig. **(b)** *attitude* verbittert, zynisch ◆ **to take a ~ view of sth** in bezug auf etw *(acc)* zynisch sein.

jaunt [dʒɔːnt] *n* Trip *m*, Spritztour *f* ◆ **to go for** *or* **on a ~** einen Ausflug *or* eine Spritztour machen; **on his last ~ through Europe** auf seiner letzten Europatour, auf seinem letzten Trip durch Europa.

jauntily [ˈdʒɔːntɪlɪ] *adv* munter, fröhlich, unbeschwert; *walk also* schwungvoll ◆ **with his hat perched ~ over one ear** den Hut keck aufgesetzt, den Hut keck auf einem Ohr.

jauntiness [ˈdʒɔːntɪnɪs] *n* Unbeschwertheit, Sorglosigkeit *f*; *(of singing)* Munterkeit, Fröhlichkeit, Heiterkeit *f* ◆ **the ~ of his step** sein schwungvoller *or* munterer Gang.

jaunty [ˈdʒɔːntɪ] *adj (+er)* munter, fröhlich; *tune also, hat* flott; *attitude* unbeschwert, sorglos; *steps also* schwungvoll ◆ **he wore his hat at a ~ angle** er hatte den Hut keck aufgesetzt.

Java [ˈdʒɑːvə] *n* Java *nt.*

Javanese [ˌdʒɑːvəˈniːz] [1] *adj* *(also* **Javan***)* javanisch.
[2] *n* **(a)** Javaner(in *f*) *m.* **(b)** *(language)* Javanisch *nt.*

javelin [ˈdʒævlɪn] *n* Speer *m* ◆ **in the ~** *(Sport)* beim Speerwerfen; **throwing the ~, ~ throwing** Speerwerfen *nt*; **~ thrower** Speerwerfer(in *f*) *m.*

jaw [dʒɔː] [1] *n* **(a)** Kiefer *m*, Kinnlade *f* ◆ **the lion opened its ~s** der Löwe riß seinen Rachen auf; **with its prey between its ~s** mit der Beute im Maul.
(b) ~s *pl* *(fig)* *(of valley etc)* Mündung, Öffnung *f* ◆ **the ~s of death** die Klauen *pl* des Todes; **the company charged into the ~s of death** die Kompanie ging in den sicheren Tod; **snatched from the very ~s of death** den Klauen des Todes entrissen; **like walking into the ~s of death** wie ein Gang zum Schafott.
(c) *(of pincer, vice)* (Klemm)backe *f.*
(d) *(inf)* *(chatting)* Gerede, Geschwätz *nt*; *(chat)* Schwatz *m*, Schwätzchen *nt.*
(e) *(inf)* *(sermonizing)* (Moral)predigen *nt* *(inf)*; *(sermon)* Moralpredigt *f* *(inf)*.
[2] *vi* **(a)** *(inf: chat)* quatschen *(inf)*, quasseln *(inf)*.
(b) *(inf: moralize)* predigen *(inf)*.

jaw: ~bone *n* Kieferknochen *m*, Kinnbacke *f*; **~breaker** *n* *(inf)* Zungenbrecher *m.*

jay [dʒeɪ] *n* Eichelhäher *m.*

jay: ~walk *vi* sich als Fußgänger unachtsam verhalten; **~walker** *n* unachtsamer Fußgänger; **~walking** *n* Unachtsamkeit *f* (eines Fußgängers) im Straßenverkehr.

jazz [dʒæz] [1] *n* **(a)** *(Mus)* Jazz *m.*
(b) *(inf: talk)* Getön *(inf)*, Gewäsch *(pej)* *nt* ◆ **he gave me a lot of ~ about his marvellous job** er schwärmte mir was von seinem tollen Job vor *(inf)*; **... and all that ~** ... und all so 'n Zeug *(inf)*, ... und das ganze Drum und Dran *(inf)*.
[2] *attr band, music* Jazz-.
[3] *vi* *(dated: play ~)* jazzen, Jazz machen.

◆jazz up *vt sep* aufmöbeln *(inf)*, aufpeppen *(inf)* ◆ **to ~ ~ the classics** klassische Musik verjazzen.

jazzman [ˈdʒæzmæn] *n, pl* **-men** [-men] Jazzer *m.*

jazzy [ˈdʒæzɪ] *adj (+er)* *colour* knallig *(inf)*, auffallend, schreiend *(pej)*; *pattern* wild, stark gemustert, auffallend; *dress, tie* poppig *(inf)*, knallig *(inf)*.

JC *abbr of* **Jesus Christ** J. Chr.

JCB ® [dʒeɪsiːˈbiː] *n* Erdräummaschine *f.*

jealous [ˈdʒeləs] *adj* **(a)** *husband, lover, child etc* eifersüchtig; *(envious: of sb's possessions, success etc)* neidisch, mißgünstig ◆ **to be ~ of sb** auf jdn eifersüchtig sein/jdn beneiden; **I'm not at all ~ of his success** ich bin nicht neidisch auf seinen Erfolg, ich beneide ihn nicht um seinen Erfolg.
(b) *(watchful, careful)* sehr besorgt *(of* um*)*, bedacht *(of* auf *+acc)* ◆ **~ guardian** strenger Wächter *or* Hüter; **to keep a ~ watch over** *or* **a ~ eye on sb** jdn mit Argusaugen bewachen.
(c) *(Bibl)* **a ~ God** ein eifersüchtiger Gott.

jealously [ˈdʒeləslɪ] *adv* **(a)** *see adj (a)*. **(b)** *(carefully)* sorgsam, sorgfältig.

jealousy [ˈdʒeləsɪ] *n see adj (of* auf *+acc)* Eifersucht *f*; Neid *m*, Mißgunst *f* ◆ **their small-minded, petty jealousies** ihre engstirnigen, kleinlichen Eifersüchteleien *pl.*

jeans [dʒiːnz] *npl* Jeans *pl* ◆ **a pair of ~** (ein Paar) Jeans *pl.*

jeep [dʒiːp] *n* Jeep *m.*

jeepers (creepers) [ˈdʒiːpəz(ˈkriːpəz)] *interj* *(US inf)* Mensch *(inf)*.

jeer [dʒɪə[r]] [1] *n* *(remark)* höhnische Bemerkung; *(shout, boo)* Buhruf *m*, Johlen *nt no pl*; *(laughter)* Hohngelächter *nt.*
[2] *vi see n* höhnische Bemerkungen machen, höhnen *(old, geh)*; johlen, buhen; höhnisch lachen ◆ **to ~ at sb** jdn (laut) verhöhnen; **he's doing his best, don't ~** er versucht sein Bestes, also spotte nicht.

jeering [ˈdʒɪərɪŋ] *see* **jeer 1** [1] *adj* höhnisch; johlend; höhnisch lachend.
[2] *n* höhnische Bemerkungen *pl*; Johlen, Gejohle *nt*; Hohngelächter *nt.*

Jehovah [dʒɪˈhəʊvə] *n* Jehova, Jahwe *m* ◆ **~'s witness** Zeuge *m*/Zeugin *f* Jehovas.

jejune [dʒɪˈdʒuːn] *adj* *(liter)* *(dull)* fade, langweilig; *(naive, simple)* simpel.

jell [dʒel] *vi see* **gel.**

jello [ˈdʒeləʊ] *n* *(US)* Wackelpeter *m* *(inf)*.

jelly [ˈdʒelɪ] [1] *n* **(a)** Gelee *nt*; *(esp Brit: dessert)* (rote) Grütze, Wackelpeter *m* *(inf)*; *(esp US: jam)* Marmelade *f*; *(round meat etc)* Aspik, Gallert(e *f*) *m* ◆ **it forms a kind of ~** es bildet eine gelee- *or* gallertartige Masse. **(b)** *(sl: gelignite)* Dynamit *nt.*
[2] *vt* in Aspik einlegen ◆ **jellied eels** Aal in Aspik, Sülzaale *pl.*

jelly: ~baby *n* *(Brit)* Gummibärchen *nt*; **~bean** *n* Geleebonbon *m or nt*; **~fish** *n* Qualle *f.*

jemmy [ˈdʒemɪ], *(US)* **jimmy** *n* Brecheisen, Stemmeisen *nt.*

jenny [ˈdʒenɪ] *n* *(donkey)* Eselin *f*; *(mule)* weibliches Maultier; *(spinning ~)* (frühe) Feinspinnmaschine ◆ **~ wren** Zaunkönigweibchen *nt*; *(in children's stories)* Frau Zaunkönig.

jeopardize [ˈdʒepədaɪz] *vt* gefährden, in Gefahr bringen.

jeopardy [ˈdʒepədɪ] *n* Gefahr *f* ◆ **in ~** in Gefahr, gefährdet; **to put sb/sth in ~**

jdn/etw gefährden *or* in Gefahr bringen; **to be in ~ of one's life** in Lebensgefahr schweben *or* sein.

jerbil *n see* **gerbil.**

jeremiad [ˌdʒerɪ'maɪəd] *n (liter)* Jeremiade *f (liter)*, Klagelied *nt.*

Jeremiah [ˌdʒerɪ'maɪə] *n* Jeremia(s) *m.*

Jericho ['dʒerɪkəʊ] *n* Jericho *nt.*

jerk [dʒɜːk] [1] *n* **(a)** Ruck *m; (jump)* Satz *m; (spasm, twitch)* Zuckung *f*, Zucken *nt no pl* ◆ **to give sth a ~** einer Sache *(dat)* einen Ruck geben; *rope, fishing line* an etw *(dat)* ruckartig ziehen; **to give a ~** *(car)* rucken, einen Satz machen; *(twitch) (person)* zusammenzucken; *(knee etc)* zucken; *(head)* zurückzucken; **the train stopped with a ~/a series of ~s** der Zug hielt mit einem Ruck/ruckweise an; **to move in a series of ~s** sich ruckartig bewegen.
(b) *see* **physical ~s.**
(c) *(sl: person)* Trottel *(inf)*, Dämlack *(inf) m.*
[2] *vt* rucken *or* ruckeln *(inf)* an *(+dat)* ◆ **the impact ~ed his head forward/back** beim Aufprall wurde sein Kopf nach vorn/hinten geschleudert; **he ~ed the fish out of the water** er zog den Fisch mit einem Ruck aus dem Wasser; **he ~ed his head back to avoid the punch** er riß den Kopf zurück, um dem Schlag auszuweichen; **he ~ed the book away/out of my hand** er riß das Buch weg/er riß mir das Buch aus der Hand; **he ~ed himself free** er riß sich los; **to ~ out one's words** die Worte hervorstoßen.
[3] *vi (rope, fishing line)* rucken; *(move jerkily)* ruckeln *(inf)*; *(body, muscle)* zucken, zusammenzucken; *(head)* zurückzucken ◆ **he ~ed away from me** er sprang mit einem Satz von mir weg; **his head ~ed forward** sein Kopf wurde nach vorne geschleudert; **the car ~ed forward** der Wagen machte einen Satz *or* Ruck nach vorn; **the car ~ed to a stop** das Auto hielt ruckweise an; **to ~ out/open** heraus-/aufspringen.

◆**jerk off** *vi (sl: masturbate)* sich *(dat)* einen runterholen *(sl).*

jerkily ['dʒɜːkɪlɪ] *adv* ruckartig; *(over cobbles etc)* holpernd, rüttelnd; *write, speak* holprig.

jerkin ['dʒɜːkɪn] *n* Jacke *f; (Hist)* (Leder)wams *nt.*

jerkwater ['dʒɜːk,wɔːtə^r] *adj attr (US inf)* Provinz- ◆ **a ~ town** ein Kaff *(inf)*, ein (Provinz)nest *(inf) nt.*

jerky ['dʒɜːkɪ] *adj (+er)* **(a)** ruckartig; *way of speaking also* abgehackt; *style* sprunghaft, abgehackt ◆ **a ~ ride over cobbles/in an old bus** eine holprige Fahrt über Kopfsteinpflaster/in einem alten Bus. **(b)** *(sl: foolish)* trottelig *(inf)*, blöd *(inf).*

jeroboam [ˌdʒerɪ'bəʊəm] *n* Doppelmagnum(flasche) *f.*

Jerome [dʒə'rəʊm] *n* Hieronymus *m.*

jerry ['dʒerɪ] *n (Brit sl: chamberpot)* Pott *(inf)*, Thron *(inf) m.*

Jerry ['dʒerɪ] *n (esp Mil sl) (German soldier)* deutscher Soldat, Deutsche(r) *m*; *(the Germans)* die Deutschen *pl.*

jerry: ~-builder *n* schlampiger Bauunternehmer; **~-building** *n* schlampige Bauweise; **~-built** *adj* schlampig gebaut; **~ can** *n* großer (Blech)kanister.

jersey ['dʒɜːzɪ] *n* Pullover *m; (Cycling, Ftbl etc)* Trikot *nt; (cloth)* Jersey *m* ◆ **~ wool** Wolljersey *m.*

Jersey ['dʒɜːzɪ] *n* **(a)** Jersey *nt.* **(b)** *(cow)* Jersey(rind) *nt.*

Jerusalem [dʒə'ruːsələm] *n* Jerusalem *nt* ◆ **~ artichoke** Jerusalem- *or* Erdartischocke *f*, Topinambur *m.*

jessamine ['dʒesəmɪn] *n* Jasmin *m.*

jest [dʒest] [1] *n (no pl: fun)* Spaß *m; (joke also)* Scherz, Witz *m* ◆ **in ~** im Spaß.
[2] *vi* scherzen, spaßen ◆ **you ~, sir!** *(old)* Sie belieben zu scherzen, mein Herr! *(old)*; **she's not a woman to ~ with** sie läßt nicht mit sich spaßen; **to ~ about sth** über etw *(acc)* Scherze *or* Witze machen.

jester ['dʒestə^r] *n* **(a)** *(Hist)* Narr *m* ◆ **the King's ~** der Hofnarr. **(b)** *(joker)* Spaßvogel, Witzbold *(inf) m.*

jesting ['dʒestɪŋ] [1] *adj* spaßend, scherzhaft ◆ **it's no ~ matter** darüber macht man keine Späße.
[2] *n* Spaßen, Scherzen *nt.*

jestingly ['dʒestɪŋlɪ] *adv* im Spaß, scherzhaft.

Jesuit ['dʒezjʊɪt] *n* Jesuit *m.*

Jesuitic(al) [ˌdʒezjʊ'ɪtɪk(əl)] *adj* jesuitisch, Jesuiten-.

Jesus ['dʒiːzəs] [1] *n* Jesus *m* ◆ **~ Christ** Jesus Christus.
[2] *interj (sl)* Mensch *(inf)* ◆ **~ Christ!** Herr Gott, (noch mal)! *(inf)*; *(surprised)* Menschenskind! *(inf).*

jet[1] [dʒet] [1] *n* **(a)** *(of water, vapour)* Strahl *m* ◆ **a thin ~ of water** ein dünner Wasserstrahl; **a ~ of gas** (aus einer Düse) austretendes Gas. **(b)** *(nozzle)* Düse *f.* **(c)** *(engine)* Düsentriebwerk, Strahltriebwerk *nt*; *(also* **~ plane***)* Düsenflugzeug *nt*, Jet *m.*
[2] *vi* **(a)** *(water etc)* schießen. **(b)** *(Aviat)* jetten *(inf).*
[3] *attr (Aviat)* Düsen-.

◆**jet off** *vi (inf)* düsen *(inf) (to* nach).

jet[2] *n (Miner)* Jet(t) *m or nt*, Gagat *m* ◆ **~ black** kohl(pech)rabenschwarz, pechschwarz.

jet: ~ engine *n* Düsentriebwerk, Strahltriebwerk *nt*; **~-engined** *adj* Düsen-, mit Düsenantrieb; **~ fighter** *n* Düsenjäger *m*; **~foil** *n* Tragflügelboot *nt*; **~lag** *n* Jet-lag *nt*, Schwierigkeiten *pl* durch den Zeitunterschied; **he's suffering from ~lag** er hat Jet-lag, er ist durch den Zeitunterschied völlig aus dem Rhythmus gekommen; **~lagged** *adj* **to be ~lagged** an Jet-lag leiden; **~ plane** *n* Düsenflugzeug *nt*; **~-powered, ~-propelled** *adj* mit Strahl- *or* Düsenantrieb, Düsen-; **~ propulsion** *n* Düsen- *or* Strahlantrieb *m.*

jetsam ['dʒetsəm] *n* über Bord geworfenes Gut; *(on beach)* Strandgut *nt*; *see* **flotsam.**

jet: ~ set *n* Jet-set *m*; **~-set** *vi* **he ~-setted off to Rio** er ist im Jet nach Rio gedüst; **~-setter** *n* **he has become a real ~-setter** der ist voll in den Jet-set eingestiegen *(inf)*; **~-setting** *n* Jet-set-Leben *nt*; **~ ski** [1] *n* Wassermotorrad *nt*; [2] *vi* Wassermotorrad fahren.

jettison ['dʒetɪsn] *vt* **(a)** *(Naut, Aviat)* (als Ballast) abwerfen *or* über Bord werfen. **(b)** *(fig) plan* über Bord werfen; *person* abhängen, aufgeben; *unwanted articles* wegwerfen.

jetty ['dʒetɪ] *n (breakwater)* Mole *f*, Hafendamm *m*; *(landing pier)* Landesteg, Pier *m*, Landungsbrücke *f.*

Jew [dʒuː] *n* **(a)** Jude *m*, Jüdin *f* ◆ **~-baiting** Judenverfolgung, Judenhetze *f.* **(b)** *(pej inf)* Geizkragen, Geizhals *(inf) m.*

jewel ['dʒuːəl] *n* **(a)** *(gem)* Edelstein *m*, Juwel *nt (geh)*; *(piece of jewellery)* Schmuckstück *nt* ◆ **~ box, ~ case** Schmuckkästchen *nt*, Schmuckkasten *m*; **a case full of ~s** ein Koffer voll Juwelen *or* wertvoller Schmuckstücke. **(b)** *(of watch)* Stein *m.* **(c)** *(fig: person)* Juwel, Goldstück *(inf) nt.*

jewelled, (US) jeweled ['dʒuːəld] *adj* mit Juwelen *(geh) or* Edelsteinen besetzt; *watch* mit Steinen.

jeweller, (US) jeweler ['dʒuːələ^r] *n* Juwelier, Schmuckhändler *m*; *(making jewellery)* Goldschmied *m* ◆ **at the ~'s (shop)** beim Juwelier, im Juwelierladen.

jewellery, (US) jewelry ['dʒuːəlrɪ] *n* Schmuck *m no pl* ◆ **a piece of ~** ein Schmuckstück *nt.*

Jewess ['dʒuːɪs] *n* Jüdin *f.*

Jewish ['dʒuːɪʃ] *adj* jüdisch; *(pej inf: mean)* knickerig *(inf).*

Jewry ['dʒʊərɪ] *n* die Juden *pl*, das jüdische Volk.

jew's-harp ['dʒuːz'hɑːp] *n* Maultrommel *f*, Brummeisen *nt.*

Jezebel ['dʒezəbel] *n (Bibl)* Isebel *f*; *(fig)* verruchtes Weib.

jib [dʒɪb] [1] *n* **(a)** *(of crane)* Ausleger, Dreharm *m.* **(b)** *(Naut)* Klüver *m* ◆ **~-boom** Klüverbaum *m.* **(c)** *(dated inf)* **until I see the cut of his ~** bis ich weiß, was für ein Mensch er ist; **I don't like the cut of his ~** seine Nase gefällt mir nicht.
[2] *vi (horse)* scheuen, bocken *(at* vor *+dat)* ◆ **to ~ at sth** *(person)* sich gegen etw sträuben.

jibe [dʒaɪb] *n, vi see* **gibe.**

jiffy ['dʒɪfɪ], **jiff** [dʒɪf] *n (inf)* Minütchen *nt (inf)* ◆ **I won't be a ~** ich komme sofort *or* gleich; *(back soon)* ich bin sofort *or* gleich wieder da; **half a ~/wait a ~!** Augenblick(chen)! *(inf)*; **in a ~** sofort, gleich.

Jiffy bag ® ['dʒɪfɪ,bæg] *n* (gepolsterte) Versandtasche.

jig [dʒɪg] [1] *n* **(a)** *(dance) lebhafter Volkstanz* ◆ **she did a little ~** *(fig)* sie vollführte einen Freudentanz.
(b) *(Tech)* Spannvorrichtung *f.*
[2] *vi (dance)* tanzen; *(fig: also* **~ about***)* herumhüpfen ◆ **to ~ up and down** Sprünge machen, herumspringen.
[3] *vt* **he was ~ging his foot up and down** er wippte mit dem Fuß; **to ~ a baby up and down on one's knees** ein Kind auf den Knien reiten lassen *or* schaukeln.

jigger ['dʒɪgə^r] *n* **(a)** *(sieve)* Schüttelsieb *nt.* **(b)** *(US: measure) Meßbecher m für Alkohol:* $1\frac{1}{2}$ *Unzen.* **(c)** *(sandflea)* Sandfloh *m.*

jiggered ['dʒɪgəd] *adj (inf)* **well, I'm ~!** da bin ich aber platt *(inf) or* baff *(inf)*; **I'm ~ if I'll do it** den Teufel werde ich tun *(inf)*; **to be ~** *(tired)* kaputt sein *(inf).*

jiggery-pokery ['dʒɪgərɪ'pəʊkərɪ] *n (inf)* Schmu *m (inf)* ◆ **I think there's been some ~ going on here** ich glaube, hier geht es nicht ganz hasenrein zu *(inf) or* hier ist was faul *(inf).*

jiggle ['dʒɪgl] *vt* wackeln mit; *door handle* rütteln an *(+dat).*

jigsaw ['dʒɪgsɔː] *n* **(a)** *(Tech)* Tischler-Bandsäge *f.* **(b)** *(also* **~ puzzle***)* Puzzle(spiel) *nt.*

jilt [dʒɪlt] *vt lover* den Laufpaß geben *(+dat)*; *girl* sitzenlassen ◆ **~ed** verschmäht.

Jim [dʒɪm] *n dim of* **James.**

Jim Crow [1] *n (pej: negro)* Nigger *(pej)*, Schwarze(r) *m*; *(discrimination)* Rassendiskriminierung *f.*
[2] *attr law, policy* (gegen Schwarze) diskriminierend; *saloon etc* Neger-.

jim-dandy ['dʒɪm'dændɪ] *adj (US inf)* prima *(inf)*, klasse *(inf).*

jiminy ['dʒɪmɪnɪ] *interj (US)* Menschenskind *(inf).*

jim-jams ['dʒɪmdʒæmz] *n (sl)* **(a)** *(nervousness)* **it gives me the ~** da kriege ich Muffensausen *(sl).* **(b)** *(the creeps)* **he gives me the ~** bei dem kriege ich das große Grausen *(inf).*

jimmy ['dʒɪmɪ] *n (US) see* **jemmy.**

Jimmy ['dʒɪmɪ] *n dim of* **James.**

jingle ['dʒɪŋgl] [1] *n* **(a)** *(of keys, coins etc)* Geklimper, Klimpern *nt*; *(of bells)* Bimmeln *nt.* **(b)** *(catchy verse)* Spruch *m*, *(for remembering)* Merkvers *m* ◆ **(advertising) ~** Jingle *m.*
[2] *vi (keys, coins etc)* klimpern; *(bells)* bimmeln.
[3] *vt keys, coins* klimpern mit; *bells* bimmeln lassen.

jingly ['dʒɪŋglɪ] *adj* klingelnd, bimmelnd.

jingo ['dʒɪŋgəʊ] *n, pl* **-es (a)** Hurrapatriot, Chauvinist *m.* **(b)** *(dated inf)* **by ~!** Tod und Teufel! *(old)*, Teufel, Teufel! *(inf).*

jingoism ['dʒɪŋgəʊɪzəm] *n* Hurrapatriotismus, Chauvinismus *m.*

jingoistic [ˌdʒɪŋgəʊ'ɪstɪk] *adj* hurrapatriotisch, chauvinistisch.

jinks [dʒɪŋks] *npl (inf) see* **high ~.**

jinn [dʒɪn] *n* Dschinn *m.*

jinx [dʒɪŋks] *n* **there must be** *or* **there's a ~ on it** das ist verhext; **he's been a ~ on us** er hat uns nur Unglück gebracht; **to put a ~ on sth** etw verhexen.

jinxed [dʒɪŋkst] *adj* verhext.

jitney ['dʒɪtnɪ] *n (US sl)* Fünfcentmünze *f*; *(bus)* billiger Bus.

jitterbug ['dʒɪtəbʌg] [1] *n* **(a)** *(dance)* Jitterbug *m*. **(b)** *(inf: panicky person)* Nervenbündel *nt (inf)*.
[2] *vi* Jitterbug tanzen.

jitters ['dʒɪtəz] *npl (inf)* **the ~** das große Zittern *(inf) or* Bibbern *(inf)*; **his ~** sein Bammel *m (inf)*; **he had (a bad case of) the ~ about the exam** er hatte wegen der Prüfung das große Zittern *(inf)*; **to give sb the ~** jdn ganz rappelig machen *(inf)*.

jittery ['dʒɪtərɪ] *adj (inf)* nervös, rappelig *(inf)*.

jiujitsu [dʒuː'dʒɪtsuː] *n* Jiu-Jitsu *nt*.

jive [dʒaɪv] [1] *n* **(a)** *(dance)* Swing *m*. **(b)** *(US inf: nonsense)* **don't give me that ~** hör bloß mit dem Quatsch auf *(inf)*.
[2] *vi* swingen, Swing tanzen.

Joan [dʒəʊn] *n* Johanna *f* ◆ **~ of Arc** Johanna von Orleans, Jeanne d'Arc.

Job [dʒəʊb] *n (Bibl)* Hiob, Job *m* ◆ **the Book of ~** das Buch Hiob; **he/that would try the patience of ~** bei ihm/da muß man eine Engelsgeduld haben; **~'s comforter** *jemand, der durch seinen Trost die Situation nur verschlimmert*; **you're a real ~'s comforter** du bist vielleicht ein schöner *or* schwacher Trost.

▼ **job** [dʒɒb] [1] *n* **(a)** *(piece of work)* Arbeit *f*; *(Comput)* Job *m* ◆ **I have a ~ to do** ich habe zu tun; **I have several ~s to do** ich habe verschiedene Sachen zu erledigen; **I have a little ~ for you** ich habe da eine kleine Arbeit *or* Aufgabe für Sie; **it's quite a ~ to paint the house** das ist vielleicht eine Arbeit *or* eine Heidenarbeit *(inf)*, das Haus zu streichen; **the car's in for a spray ~** *(inf)* der Wagen ist zum Lackieren in der Werkstatt; **the plumbers have a lot of ~s on just now** die Klempner haben zur Zeit viele Aufträge; **to be paid by the ~** für (die) geleistete Arbeit bezahlt werden, pro Auftrag bezahlt werden; **he's on the ~** *(inf: at work)* er ist bei *or* an der Arbeit; *(sl: having sex)* er ist am Ball *(inf) or* zu Gange *(inf)*; **to make a good/bad ~ of sth** bei etw gute/schlechte Arbeit leisten; **he knows his ~** er versteht sein Handwerk; *see* **odd**.
▼ **(b)** *(employment)* Stelle *f*, Job *m (inf)* ◆ **the nice thing about a teaching ~ is ...** das Schöne am Lehrberuf *or* an einer Anstellung als Lehrer ist ...; **he had a vacation ~** *or* **a ~ for the vacation** er hatte eine Ferienarbeit *or* einen Ferienjob *(inf)*; **500 ~s lost** 500 Arbeitsplätze verlorengegangen; **to bring new ~s to a region** in einer Gegend neue Arbeitsplätze schaffen.
(c) *(duty)* Aufgabe *f* ◆ **that's not my ~** dafür bin ich nicht zuständig; **it's not my ~ to tell him** es ist nicht meine Aufgabe, ihm das zu sagen; **I'll do my ~ and you do yours** ich mache meine Arbeit, und Sie Ihre; **I had the ~ of breaking the news to her** es fiel mir zu, ihr die Nachricht beizubringen; **he's not doing his ~** er erfüllt seine Aufgabe(n) nicht; **I'm only doing my ~** ich tue nur meine Pflicht.
(d) that's a good ~! so ein Glück; **what a good ~** *or* **it's a good ~ I brought my cheque book, I brought my cheque book and a good ~ too!** nur gut, daß ich mein Scheckbuch mitgenommen habe; **it's a bad ~** schlimme Sache *(inf)*; **to give sb/sth up as a bad ~** jdn/etw aufgeben; **that should do the ~** das müßte hinhauen *(inf)*; **this is just the ~** das ist goldrichtig *or* genau das richtige; **a holiday in the sun would be just the ~** Ferien in der Sonne, das wäre jetzt genau das richtige; **double whisky? — just the ~** einen doppelten Whisky? — prima Idee *(inf)*.
(e) *(difficulty)* **I had a ~ doing it** *or* **to do it** das war gar nicht so einfach; **you'll have a ~** das wird gar nicht so einfach sein; **she has a ~ getting up the stairs** es ist gar nicht einfach für sie, die Treppe raufzukommen; **it was quite a ~** das war ganz schön schwer *(inf) or* schwierig.
(f) *(sl: crime)* Ding *nt (sl)* ◆ **we're going to do a ~ next week** wir drehen nächste Woche ein Ding *(sl)*; **remember that bank ~?** erinnerst du dich an das große Ding in der Bank? *(sl)*.
(g) *(inf: person, thing)* Ding *nt* ◆ **his new car's a lovely little ~** sein neues Auto ist wirklich große Klasse *(inf) or* eine Wucht *(inf)*; **that blonde's a gorgeous little ~** die Blondine (da) sieht wirklich klasse aus *(inf)*.
(h) *(baby-talk)* **to do a (big/little) ~** ein (großes/kleines) Geschäft machen *(inf)*, Aa/Pipi machen *(baby-talk)*.
[2] *vi* **(a)** *(do casual work)* Gelegenheitsarbeiten tun *or* verrichten, jobben *(sl)* ◆ **a graphic designer who ~s for various advertising firms** ein Graphiker, der für verschiedene Werbeagenturen Aufträge *or* Arbeiten ausführt.
(b) *(St Ex)* als Makler tätig sein, Maklergeschäfte betreiben.
(c) *(profit from public position)* sein Amt (zu privatem Nutzen) mißbrauchen.
[3] *vt (also* **~ out)** *work* in Auftrag geben, auf Kontrakt *or* auf feste Rechnung vergeben.

-job *suf (inf: operation)* -korrektur *f* ◆ **chin/eye/nose-job** Kinn-/Augen-/Nasenkorrektur *f*.

job advertisement *n* Stellenanzeige *f*.

jobber ['dʒɒbər] *n* **(a)** *(St Ex)* Makler, Börsenhändler, Effektenhändler *m*. **(b)** *(casual worker)* Gelegenheitsarbeiter *m*.

jobbing ['dʒɒbɪŋ] [1] *adj worker, gardener* Gelegenheits-; *printer* Akzidenz-.
[2] *n* **(a)** *(casual work)* Gelegenheitsarbeit *f*. **(b)** *(St Ex)* Börsen- *or* Effektenhandel *m*.

job: ~ centre *n (Brit)* Arbeitsamt *nt*; **~ creation** *n* Arbeitsbeschaffung *f*; **~ creation scheme** Beschäftigungsprogramm *nt*; **~ cuts** *npl* Arbeitsplatzabbau *m*; **~ description** *n* Tätigkeitsbeschreibung *f*; **~ evaluation** *n* Arbeitsplatzbewertung *f*; **~ holder** *n* Arbeitnehmer(in *f*) *m*; **~ hopper** *n (inf) jd, der häufig seine Arbeitsstelle wechselt*; **~ hunter** *n* Arbeitssuchende(r) *mf*; **~ hunting** *n* Arbeitssuche, Stellenjagd *(inf) f*; **to be ~ hunting** auf Arbeitssuche *or* Stellenjagd *(inf)* sein; **~less** [1] *adj* arbeitslos, stellungslos; [2] *n* **the ~less** *pl* die Arbeitslosen *pl*; **~ loss** *n* **there were 1,000 ~ losses** 1 000 Arbeitsplätze gingen verloren; **~ lot** *n (Comm)* (Waren)posten *m*; **~ printer** *n* Akzidenzdrucker *m*; **~ profile** *n* Stellenbeschreibung *f*, Stellenprofil *nt*; **~ satisfaction** *n* Zufriedenheit *f* am Arbeitsplatz; **I've got ~ satisfaction** ich bin mit meiner Arbeit zufrieden; **~ security** *n* Sicherheit *f* des Arbeitsplatzes; **we can offer no ~ security guarantees** wir können die Sicherheit des Arbeitsplatzes/der Arbeitsplätze nicht garantieren; **~ seeker** *n* Arbeitssuchende(r) *mf*; **~ seeker's allowance** *n (Brit)* ≃ Arbeitslosengeld *nt*; **~-sharer** *n jd, der seinen Arbeitsplatz mit anderen teilt*; **~-sharing** [1] *n* Arbeitsplatzteilung *f*, Job-sharing *nt*; [2] *attr scheme* zur Arbeitsplatzteilung.

Jock [dʒɒk] *n (inf)* Schotte *m*.

jockey ['dʒɒkɪ] [1] *n* Jockei, Jockey, Rennreiter(in *f*) *m*.
[2] *vi* **to ~ for position** *(lit)* sich in eine gute Position zu drängeln versuchen, sich gut plazieren wollen; *(fig)* rangeln; **they were all ~ing for office in the new government** sie rangelten alle um ein Amt in der neuen Regierung.
[3] *vt (force by crafty manoeuvres)* **to ~ sb into doing sth** jdn dazu bringen, etw zu tun; **he felt he had been ~ed into it** er hatte das Gefühl, daß man ihn da reinbugsiert hatte *(inf)*; **to ~ sb out of a job** jdn aus seiner Stellung hinausbugsieren *(inf)*.

jockstrap ['dʒɒkstræp] *n* Suspensorium *nt*.

jocose [dʒə'kəʊs] *adj* scherzend, launig *(geh)*.

jocular ['dʒɒkjʊlər] *adj* lustig, spaßig, witzig ◆ **to be in a ~ mood** zu Scherzen *or* Späßen aufgelegt sein.

jocularity [,dʒɒkjʊ'lærɪtɪ] *n* Spaßigkeit, Witzigkeit, Scherzhaftigkeit *f*.

jocularly ['dʒɒkjʊləlɪ] *adv* scherzhaft; *(as a joke)* im Scherz.

jocund ['dʒɒkənd] *adj* heiter, fröhlich, frohsinnig *(geh)*.

jodhpurs ['dʒɒdpəz] *npl* Reithose(n *pl*) *f*.

Joe [dʒəʊ] *n dim of* **Joseph** Sepp *(S Ger)*, Jupp *(dial) m*.

Joe Bloggs [,dʒəʊ'blɒgz] *n (inf: ordinary person)* Otto Normalverbraucher *m (inf)*.

joey ['dʒəʊɪ] *n (Austral inf)* junges Känguruh.

jog [dʒɒg] [1] *vt* stoßen an *(+acc) or* gegen; *person* anstoßen ◆ **he ~ged the child up and down on his knee** er ließ das Kind auf seinem Knie reiten; **he was being ~ged up and down on the horse** das Pferd schüttelte ihn durch; **to ~ sb's memory** jds Gedächtnis *(dat)* nachhelfen *or* auf die Sprünge helfen.
[2] *vi* trotten, zuckeln *(inf)*; *(Sport)* Dauerlauf machen, joggen ◆ **to ~ up and down** auf und ab hüpfen.
[3] *n* **(a)** *(push, nudge)* Stoß, Schubs, Stups *m* ◆ **to give sb's memory a ~** jds Gedächtnis *(dat)* nachhelfen.
(b) *(run)* trabender Lauf, Trott *m*; *(Sport)* Dauerlauf *m* ◆ **he broke into a ~** er fing an zu traben; **he came back at a gentle ~** er kam langsam zurückgetrabt *or* zurückgetrottet; **to go for a ~** *(Sport)* einen Dauerlauf machen, joggen (gehen).

◆**jog about** *or* **around** [1] *vi* hin und her gerüttelt werden.
[2] *vt sep* durchschütteln, durchrütteln.

◆**jog along** *vi* **(a)** *(go along: person, vehicle)* entlangzuckeln. **(b)** *(fig) (person, worker, industry)* vor sich *(acc)* hin wursteln *(inf)*; *(work)* seinen Gang gehen.

jogger ['dʒɒgər] *n* **(a)** *(person)* Jogger(in *f*) *m*. **(b)** *(shoe)* Joggingschuh, Freizeitstiefel *m*.

jogging ['dʒɒgɪŋ] *n* Jogging, Joggen *nt* ◆ **~ suit** Jogging-Anzug *m*.

joggle ['dʒɒgl] [1] *vt* schütteln, rütteln.
[2] *n* Schütteln, Rütteln *nt*.

jog-trot ['dʒɒgtrɒt] *n* Trott *m*.

John [dʒɒn] *n* Johannes *m* ◆ **~ the Baptist** Johannes der Täufer; **~ Barleycorn** der Gerstensaft; **~ Bull** ein typischer Engländer, John Bull *m*; *(the English)* die Engländer *pl*; **~ Doe** *(US)* Otto Normalverbraucher *m (inf)*.

john [dʒɒn] *n (esp US inf) (toilet)* Klo *nt (inf)*; *(prostitute's customer)* Freier *m (inf)*.

Johnny ['dʒɒnɪ] *n dim of* **John** Hänschen *nt*, Hänsel *m (old)* ◆ **j~** *(Brit sl) (man)* Typ *m (inf)*; *(condom)* Pariser *m (inf)*.

joie de vivre [,ʒwædə'viːvr] *n* Lebensfreude, Lebenslust *f*.

▼ **join** [dʒɔɪn] [1] *vt* **(a)** *(lit, fig: connect, unite)* verbinden *(to* mit); *(attach also)* anfügen *(to* an *+acc)* ◆ **to ~ two things together** zwei Dinge (miteinander) verbinden; *(attach also)* zwei Dinge zusammenfügen *or* aneinanderfügen; **to ~ battle (with the enemy)** den Kampf mit dem Feind aufnehmen; **to ~ hands** *(lit, fig)* sich *(dat) or* einander die Hände reichen; **~ed in marriage** durch das heilige Band der Ehe verbunden *or* vereinigt; **we ~ our prayers to theirs** wir stimmen in ihre Gebete ein.
(b) *(become member of) army* gehen zu; *one's regiment* sich anschließen *(+dat)*, sich begeben zu; *political party, club* beitreten *(+dat)*, Mitglied werden von *or* bei *or* in *(+dat)*, eintreten in *(+acc)*; *religious order* eintreten in *(+acc)*, beitreten *(+dat)*; *university (as student)* anfangen an *(+dat)*; *(as staff) firm* anfangen bei; *group of people, procession* sich anschließen *(+dat)* ◆ **to ~ the queue** sich in die Schlange stellen *or* einreihen; **he has been ordered to ~ his ship at Liverpool** er hat Order bekommen, sich in Liverpool auf seinem Schiff einzufinden *or* zu seinem Schiff zu begeben; **Dr Morris will be ~ing us for a year as guest professor** Dr Morris wird ein Jahr bei uns Gastprofessor sein.
▼ **(c) he ~ed us in France** er stieß in Frankreich zu uns; **I ~ed him at the station** wir trafen uns am Bahnhof, ich traf mich mit ihm am Bahnhof; **I'll ~ you in five minutes** ich bin in fünf Minuten bei Ihnen; *(follow you)* ich komme in fünf Minuten nach; **may I ~ you?** kann ich mich Ihnen anschließen?; *(sit with you)* darf ich Ihnen Gesellschaft leisten?, darf ich mich zu Ihnen setzen?; *(in game, plan etc)* kann ich mitmachen?; **will you ~ us?** machen Sie mit, sind Sie dabei?; *(sit with us)* wollen Sie uns nicht Gesellschaft leisten?, wollen Sie sich (nicht) zu uns setzen?; *(come with us)* kommen Sie mit?; **do ~ us for lunch** wollen Sie nicht mit uns essen?; **will**

➤ LANGUAGE IN USE: **job: 1b** → 19.1, 19.2 **join: 1c** → 25.1

you ~ me in a drink? trinken Sie ein Glas mit mir?; **Paul ~s me in wishing you ...** Paul schließt sich meinen Wünschen für ... an; **they ~ed us in singing ...** sie sangen mit uns zusammen ...
(d) (*river*) *another river, the sea* einmünden *or* fließen in (+*acc*); (*road*) *another road* (ein)münden in (+*acc*) ◆ **his estates ~ ours** seine Ländereien grenzen an unsere (an).
2 *vi* **(a)** (*also* **~ together**) (*two parts*) (*be attached*) (miteinander) verbunden sein; (*be attachable*) sich (miteinander) verbinden lassen; (*grow together*) zusammenwachsen; (*meet, be adjacent*) zusammenstoßen, zusammentreffen; (*estates*) aneinander (an)grenzen; (*rivers*) zusammenfließen, sich vereinigen; (*roads*) sich treffen ◆ **let us all ~ together in the Lord's Prayer** wir wollen alle zusammen das Vaterunser beten; **he ~s with me in wishing you ...** er schließt sich meinen Wünschen für ... an; **to ~ together in doing sth** etw zusammen *or* gemeinsam tun; **the bones wouldn't ~ properly** die Knochen wollten nicht richtig zusammenheilen; **they all ~ed together to get her a present** sie taten sich alle zusammen, um ihr ein Geschenk zu kaufen.
(b) (*club member*) beitreten, Mitglied werden.
3 *n* Naht(stelle) *f*; (*in pipe, knitting*) Verbindungsstelle *f*.
◆**join in** *vi* (*in activity*) mitmachen (*prep obj* bei); (*in game also*) mitspielen (*prep obj* bei); (*in demonstration also, in protest*) sich anschließen (*prep obj* +*dat*); (*in conversation*) sich beteiligen (*prep obj* an +*dat*) ◆ **~ ~, everybody!** (*in song etc*) alle (mitmachen)!; **they all ~ed ~ in singing the chorus** sie sangen alle den Refrain mit; **everybody ~ed ~ the chorus** sie sangen alle zusammen den Refrain, alle fielen in den Refrain ein; **he didn't want to ~ ~ the fun** er wollte nicht mitmachen.
◆**join on** 1 *vi* (*be attachable*) sich verbinden lassen (*prep obj, -to* mit), sich anfügen lassen (*prep obj, -to* an +*acc*); (*be attached*) verbunden sein (*prep obj, -to* mit); (*people: in procession etc*) sich anschließen (*prep obj, -to* +*dat*, an +*acc*).
2 *vt sep* verbinden (*prep obj, -to* mit); (*extend with*) ansetzen (*prep obj, -to* an +*acc*).
◆**join up** 1 *vi* **(a)** (*Mil*) Soldat werden, zum Militär gehen. **(b)** (*meet: road etc*) sich treffen, aufeinanderstoßen; (*join forces*) sich zusammenschließen, sich zusammentun (*inf*).
2 *vt sep* (miteinander) verbinden.
joiner ['dʒɔɪnəʳ] *n* Tischler, Schreiner *m*.
joinery ['dʒɔɪnərɪ] *n* (*trade*) Tischlerei *f*, Tischlerhandwerk *nt*; (*piece of ~*) Tischlerarbeit *f*.
joint [dʒɔɪnt] 1 *n* **(a)** (*Anat, tool, in armour etc*) Gelenk *nt* ◆ **he's feeling a bit stiff in the ~s** (*inf*) er fühlt sich ein bißchen steif (in den Knochen); **the times are out of ~** (*fig liter*) die Zeit *or* Welt ist aus den Fugen; *see* **nose**.
(b) (*join*) (*in woodwork*) Fuge *f*; (*in pipe etc*) Verbindung(sstelle) *f*; (*welded etc*) Naht(stelle) *f*; (*junction piece*) Verbindungsstück *nt*.
(c) (*Cook*) Braten *m* ◆ **a ~ of beef** ein Rindsbraten *m*.
(d) (*sl: place*) Laden *m* (*inf*); (*for gambling*) Spielhölle *f*.
(e) (*sl: of marijuana*) Joint *m* (*sl*).
2 *vt* **(a)** (*Cook*) (in Stücke) zerlegen *or* zerteilen.
(b) *boards, pipes etc* verbinden.
3 *adj attr* gemeinsam; (*in connection with possessions also*) gemeinschaftlich; *action, work, decision also* Gemeinschafts-; (*co-*) *ruler, owner etc* Mit-; *rulers, owners etc* gemeinsam; (*total, combined*) *influence, strength* verein ◆ **~ account** gemeinsames Konto; **~ agreement** *Lohnabkommen nt mehrerer Firmen mit einer Gewerkschaft*; **~ committee** gemeinsamer *or* gemischter Ausschuß; **it was a ~ effort** das ist in Gemeinschaftsarbeit entstanden; **it took the ~ efforts of six strong men to move it** es waren die vereinten Anstrengungen *or* Kräfte von sechs starken Männern nötig, um es von der Stelle zu bewegen; **~ estate** Gemeinschaftsbesitz *m*; **~ heir** Miterbe *m*, Miterbin *f*; **they were ~ heirs** sie waren gemeinsame Erben; **~ life insurance** wechselseitige (Über)lebensversicherung; **~ ownership** Miteigentum *nt*, Mitbesitz *m*; **~ partner** Teilhaber *m*; **~ plaintiff/plaintiffs** Nebenkläger *m*/ gemeinsame Kläger *pl*; **~ resolution** (*US Pol*) gemeinsamer Beschluß (beider gesetzgebender Versammlungen); **~ stock** Aktienkapital *nt*; **~ stock company/bank** Aktiengesellschaft *f*/-bank *f*; **~ venture** Gemeinschaftsunternehmen, Joint-venture (*Comm*) *nt*.
jointed ['dʒɔɪntɪd] *adj* (*articulated*) mit Gelenken versehen, gegliedert ◆ **a ~ doll** eine Gliederpuppe; **a ~ fishing rod** eine zerlegbare Angel.
jointly ['dʒɔɪntlɪ] *adv* gemeinsam; *decide, work, rule also* zusammen, miteinander.
jointure ['dʒɔɪntʃəʳ] *n* (*Jur*) Wittum *nt*.
joist [dʒɔɪst] *n* Balken *m*; (*of metal, concrete*) Träger *m*.
joke [dʒəʊk] 1 *n* Witz *m*; (*hoax*) Scherz *m*; (*prank*) Streich *m*; (*inf: pathetic person or thing*) Witz *m*; (*laughing stock*) Gespött, Gelächter *nt* ◆ **for a ~** zum Spaß, zum *or* aus Jux (*inf*); **I don't see the ~** ich möchte wissen, was daran so lustig ist *or* sein soll; **he treats the school rules as a big ~** für ihn sind die Schulregeln ein Witz; **he can/can't take a ~** er versteht Spaß/keinen Spaß; **what a ~!** zum Totlachen! (*inf*), zum Schießen! (*inf*); **it's no ~** das ist nicht witzig; **the ~ is that ...** das Witzige *or* Lustige daran ist, daß ...; **it's beyond a ~** das ist kein Spaß *or* Witz mehr, das ist nicht mehr lustig; **this is getting beyond a ~** das geht (langsam) zu weit; **the ~ was on me** der Spaß ging auf meine Kosten; **why do you have to turn everything into a ~?** warum müssen Sie über alles Ihre Witze machen *or* alles ins Lächerliche ziehen?; **I'm not in the mood for ~s** ich bin nicht zu(m) Scherzen aufgelegt; **to play a ~ on sb** jdm einen Streich spielen; **to make a ~ about sb/sth** einen Witz über jdn/ etw machen *or* reißen (*inf*); **to make ~s about sb/sth** sich über jdn/etw lustig machen, über jdn/etw Witze machen *or* reißen (*inf*).
2 *vi* Witze machen, scherzen (*geh*) (*about* über +*acc*); (*pull sb's leg*) Spaß machen ◆ **I'm not joking** ich meine das ernst; **you must be joking!** das ist ja wohl nicht Ihr Ernst, das soll wohl ein Witz sein; **you're joking!** mach keine Sachen (*inf*) *or* Witze!; ..., **he ~d** ..., sagte er scherzhaft.
joker ['dʒəʊkəʳ] *n* **(a)** (*person*) Witzbold, Spaßvogel *m*. **(b)** (*sl*) Typ (*inf*), Kerl (*inf*) *m*. **(c)** (*Cards*) Joker *m*.
jokey *adj see* **joky**.
jokily ['dʒəʊkɪlɪ] *adv* lustig; *say* scherzhaft, im Scherz.
joking ['dʒəʊkɪŋ] 1 *adj tone* scherzhaft, spaßend ◆ **I'm not in a ~ mood** ich bin nicht zu Scherzen *or* Späßen aufgelegt.
2 *n* Witze *pl* ◆ **~ apart** *or* **aside** Spaß *or* Scherz beiseite.
jokingly ['dʒəʊkɪŋlɪ] *adv* im Spaß; *say, call also* scherzhaft.
joky ['dʒəʊkɪ] *adj* lustig.
jollification [,dʒɒlɪfɪ'keɪʃən] *n* (*hum*) Festivität *f* (*hum*); (*merrymaking: also ~s*) Festlichkeiten *pl*.
jollity ['dʒɒlɪtɪ] *n* Fröhlichkeit, Ausgelassenheit *f*.
jolly ['dʒɒlɪ] 1 *adj* (+*er*) **(a)** (*merry*) fröhlich, vergnügt.
(b) (*inf: tipsy*) angeheitert (*inf*).
2 *adv* (*Brit inf*) ganz schön (*inf*), vielleicht (*inf*); *nice, warm, happy, pleased* mächtig (*inf*) ◆ **you are ~ lucky** Sie haben vielleicht Glück *or* ein Mordsglück (*inf*); **~ good/well** prima (*inf*), famos (*dated inf*); **that's ~ kind of you** das ist furchtbar *or* unheimlich nett von Ihnen; **it's getting ~ late** es wird langsam spät; **you ~ well will go!** und ob du gehst!; **so you ~ well should be!** das will ich schwer meinen! (*inf*); **I should ~ well think so too!** das will ich auch gemeint haben!
3 *vt* **to ~ sb into doing sth** jdn bereden, etw zu tun; **to ~ sb along** jdm aufmunternd zureden; **to ~ sb up** jdn aufmuntern.
jolly: ~ boat *n* Beiboot *nt*; **J~ Roger** *n* Totenkopfflagge, Piratenflagge *f*.
jolt [dʒəʊlt] 1 *vi* (*vehicle*) holpern, rüttelnd fahren; (*give one ~*) einen Ruck machen ◆ **to ~ along** rüttelnd entlangfahren; **to ~ to a halt** ruckweise anhalten.
2 *vt* (*lit*) (*shake*) durchschütteln, durchrütteln; (*once*) einen Ruck geben *or* versetzen (+*dat*); (*fig*) aufrütteln ◆ **to ~ sb out of his complacency** jdn aus seiner Zufriedenheit aufrütteln *or* reißen; **it ~ed him into action** das hat ihn aufgerüttelt.
3 *n* **(a)** (*jerk*) Ruck *m*. **(b)** (*fig inf*) Schock *m* ◆ **he realized with a ~ ...** mit einem Schlag wurde ihm klar, ...; **it gave me a ~** das hat mir einen Schock versetzt.
jolting ['dʒəʊltɪŋ] *n* Rütteln, Schütteln, Holpern *nt* ◆ **we had a bit of a ~ on the way** wir sind auf der Fahrt ziemlich durchgeschüttelt worden.
jolty ['dʒəʊltɪ] *adj* (+*er*) *cart etc* holp(e)rig, rüttelnd; *road* holp(e)rig, uneben.
Jonah ['dʒəʊnə] *n* Jona(s) *m*.
jonquil ['dʒɒŋkwɪl] *n* Jonquille *f* (*Art von Narzisse*).
Jordan ['dʒɔːdn] *n* (*country*) Jordanien *nt*; (*river*) Jordan *m*.
Joseph ['dʒəʊzɪf] *n* Joseph, Josef *m*.
Josephine ['dʒəʊzɪfiːn] *n* Josephine *f*.
josh [dʒɒʃ] (*US inf*) 1 *vt* aufziehen, veräppeln, verulken (*all inf*).
2 *vi* Spaß machen (*inf*).
3 *n* Neckerei, Hänselei *f*.
Joshua ['dʒɒʃjʊə] *n* Josua *m*.
joss stick ['dʒɒsstɪk] *n* Räucherstäbchen *nt*.
jostle ['dʒɒsl] 1 *vi* drängeln ◆ **he ~d against me** er rempelte mich an; **the people jostling round the stalls** die Leute, die sich vor den Buden drängelten; *see* **position**.
2 *vt* anrempeln, schubsen ◆ **they ~d him out of the room** sie drängten *or* schubsten ihn aus dem Zimmer; **he was ~d along with the crowd** die Menge schob ihn mit sich.
3 *n* Gedränge *nt*, Rempelei *f*.
jot [dʒɒt] *n* (*inf*) (*of truth, sense*) Funken *m*, Fünkchen, Körnchen *nt* ◆ **it won't do a ~ of good** das nützt gar nichts *or* nicht das geringste bißchen; **not one ~ or tittle** (*inf*) aber auch nicht das kleinste bißchen (*inf*), keinen Deut.
◆**jot down** *vt sep* sich (*dat*) notieren, sich (*dat*) eine Notiz machen von ◆ **to ~ ~ notes** Notizen machen.
jotter ['dʒɒtəʳ] *n* (*note pad*) Notizblock *m*; (*notebook*) Notizheft(chen) *nt*.
jottings ['dʒɒtɪŋz] *npl* Notizen *pl*.
joule [dʒuːl] *n* (*Phys*) Joule *nt*.
journal ['dʒɜːnl] *n* **(a)** (*magazine*) Zeitschrift *f*; (*newspaper*) Zeitung *f*. **(b)** (*diary*) Tagebuch *nt* ◆ **to keep a ~** Tagebuch führen. **(c)** (*Naut*) Logbuch, Bordbuch *nt*; (*Comm*) Journal *nt*; (*daybook*) Tagebuch *nt*; (*Jur*) Gerichtsakten *pl*. **(d)** (*Mech*) Achszapfen, Achsschenkel *m*.
journalese [,dʒɜːnə'liːz] *n* Zeitungs- *or* Pressejargon *m*.
journalism ['dʒɜːnəlɪzəm] *n* Journalismus *m*.
journalist ['dʒɜːnəlɪst] *n* Journalist(in *f*) *m*.
journalistic [,dʒɜːnə'lɪstɪk] *adj* journalistisch.
journalistically [,dʒɜːnə'lɪstɪkəlɪ] *adv* im Zeitungsstil.
journey ['dʒɜːnɪ] 1 *n* Reise *f*; (*by car, train etc also*) Fahrt *f* ◆ **to go on a ~** eine Reise machen, verreisen; **they have gone on a ~** sie sind verreist; **to set out on one's/a ~** abreisen/eine Reise antreten; **it is a ~ of 50 miles** *or* **a 50 mile ~** es liegt 50 Meilen entfernt; **from X to Y is a ~ of 50 miles/two hours** es sind 50 Meilen/zwei Stunden (Fahrt) von X nach Y; **a two day ~** eine Zwei-Tage-Reise; **it's a two day ~ to get to ... from here** man braucht zwei Tage, um von hier nach ... zu kommen; **a bus/train ~** eine Bus-/Zugfahrt; **the ~ home** die Heimreise, die Heimfahrt; **he has quite a ~ to get to work** er muß ziemlich weit fahren, um zur Arbeit zu kommen; **to reach one's ~'s end**

(*liter*) am Ziel der Reise angelangt sein; **his ~ through life** sein Lebensweg *m*.
[2] *vi* reisen ◆ **to ~ on** weiterreisen.

journeyman ['dʒɜːnɪmən] *n, pl* **-men** [-mən] Geselle *m* ◆ **~ baker** Bäckergeselle *m*.

joust [dʒaʊst] [1] *vi* im Turnier kämpfen, turnieren (*obs*).
[2] *n* Zweikampf *m* im Turnier.

jousting ['dʒaʊstɪŋ] *n* Turnier(kämpfe *pl*) *nt*.

Jove [dʒəʊv] *n* Jupiter *m* ◆ **by ~**! (*dated*) Donnerwetter!; **have you/did he, by ~**! tatsächlich!

jovial ['dʒəʊvɪəl] *adj* fröhlich, jovial (*esp pej*); *welcome* freundlich, herzlich.

joviality [ˌdʒəʊvɪ'ælɪtɪ] *n see adj* Fröhlichkeit, Jovialität (*esp pej*) *f*; Herzlichkeit *f*.

jovially ['dʒəʊvɪəlɪ] *adv see adj*.

jowl [dʒaʊl] *n* (*jaw*) (Unter)kiefer *m*; (*often pl*) (*cheek*) Backe *f*; (*fold of flesh*) Hängebacke *f*; *see* **cheek**.

joy [dʒɔɪ] *n* **(a)** Freude *f* ◆ **to my great ~** zu meiner großen Freude; **she/the garden is a ~ to behold** *or* **to the eye** sie/der Garten ist eine Augenweide; **it's a ~ to hear him** es ist eine wahre Freude *or* ein Genuß, ihn zu hören; **to wish sb ~** jdm Glück (und Zufriedenheit) wünschen; **I wish you ~ (of it)**! (*iro*) na dann viel Spaß *or* viel Vergnügen!; **one of the ~s of this job is ...** eine der erfreulichen Seiten dieses Berufs ist ...; **that's the ~ of this system** das ist das Schöne an diesem System; *see* **jump**.
(b) *no pl* (*Brit inf: success*) Erfolg *m* ◆ **I didn't get much/any ~** ich hatte nicht viel/keinen Erfolg; **any ~?** hat es geklappt? (*inf*); **you won't get any ~ out of him** bei ihm werden Sie keinen Erfolg haben.

joyful ['dʒɔɪfʊl] *adj* freudig, froh.

joyfully ['dʒɔɪfəlɪ] *adv* freudig.

joyfulness ['dʒɔɪfʊlnɪs] *n* Fröhlichkeit *f*; (*of person also*) Frohsinn *m*, Heiterkeit *f*.

joyless ['dʒɔɪlɪs] *adj* freudlos; *person also* griesgrämig.

joyous ['dʒɔɪəs] *adj* (*liter*) freudig, froh.

joy: ~-ride *n* Spritztour *f*, Vergnügungsfahrt *f* (*in einem gestohlenen Auto*); **to go for a ~-ride** (ein Auto stehlen und damit) eine Spritztour *or* Vergnügungsfahrt machen; **~-rider** *n Autodieb, der den Wagen nur für eine Spritztour will*; **~riding** *n* Joyriding *nt*; **~stick** *n* (*Aviat*) Steuerknüppel *m*; (*Comput*) Joystick *m*.

JP (*Brit*) *abbr of* **Justice of the Peace**.

Jr *abbr of* **junior** jr., jun.

jubilant ['dʒuːbɪlənt] *adj* überglücklich; (*expressing joy*) jubelnd *attr*; *voice* jubelnd *attr*, frohlockend *attr*; *face* strahlend *attr*; (*at sb's failure etc*) triumphierend *attr* ◆ **they gave him a ~ welcome** sie empfingen ihn mit Jubel; **to be ~** überglücklich sein; jubeln; strahlen; triumphieren.

jubilation [ˌdʒuːbɪ'leɪʃən] *n* Jubel *m* ◆ **a cause for ~** ein Grund zum Jubel; **a sense of ~** ein Gefühl von Triumph.

jubilee ['dʒuːbɪliː] *n* Jubiläum *nt*.

Judaea [dʒuː'diːə] *n* Judäa *nt*.

Judah ['dʒuːdə] *n* Juda *m*.

Judaic [dʒuː'deɪɪk] *adj* judaisch.

Judaism ['dʒuːdeɪɪzəm] *n* Judaismus *m*.

Judas ['dʒuːdəs] *n* **(a)** (*Bibl, fig*) Judas *m*. **(b)** **j~ (hole)** Guckloch *nt*.

judder ['dʒʌdəʳ] (*Brit*) [1] *n* Erschütterung *f*; (*in car etc*) Ruckeln *nt* ◆ **to give a ~** *see vi*.
[2] *vi* erzittern; (*person*) zucken; (*car etc*) ruckeln ◆ **the train ~ed to a standstill** der Zug kam ruckartig zum Stehen.

Judea *n see* **Judaea**.

judge [dʒʌdʒ] [1] *n* **(a)** (*Jur*) Richter(in *f*) *m*; (*of competition*) Preisrichter(in *f*) *m*; (*Sport*) Punktrichter(in *f*), Kampfrichter(in *f*) *m* ◆ **~-advocate** (*Mil*) Beisitzer *m* bei einem Kriegsgericht, Kriegsgerichtsrat *m*.
(b) (*fig*) Kenner *m* ◆ **to be a good/bad ~ of character** ein guter/schlechter Menschenkenner sein; **to be a good/no ~ of wine/horses** ein/kein Weinkenner/Pferdekenner sein; **to be a good ~ of quality** Qualität gut beurteilen können; **I'll be the ~ of that** das müssen Sie mich schon selbst beurteilen lassen.
(c) (*Bibl*) **(the Book of) J~s** (das Buch der) Richter.
[2] *vt* **(a)** (*Jur*) *person* die Verhandlung führen über (+*acc*); *case* verhandeln; (*God*) richten.
(b) *competition* beurteilen, bewerten; (*Sport*) Punktrichter *or* Kampfrichter sein bei.
(c) (*fig: pass judgement on*) ein Urteil fällen über (+*acc*) ◆ **you shouldn't ~ people by appearances** Sie sollten Menschen nicht nach ihrem Äußeren beurteilen.
(d) (*consider, assess, deem*) halten für, erachten für (*geh*) ◆ **this was ~d to be the best way** dies wurde für die beste Methode gehalten *or* erachtet (*geh*); **you can ~ for yourself which is better/how upset I was** Sie können selbst beurteilen, was besser ist/Sie können sich (*dat*) denken, wie bestürzt ich war; **I can't ~ whether he was right or wrong** ich kann nicht beurteilen, ob er recht oder unrecht hatte; **I ~d from his manner that he was guilty** ich schloß aus seinem Verhalten, daß er schuldig war; **how would you ~ him?** wie würden Sie ihn beurteilen *or* einschätzen?
(e) (*estimate*) *speed, width, distance etc* einschätzen ◆ **he ~d the moment well** er hat den richtigen Augenblick abgepaßt.
[3] *vi* **(a)** (*Jur*) Richter sein; (*God*) richten; (*at competition*) Preisrichter sein; (*Sport*) Kampfrichter *or* Punktrichter sein.
(b) (*fig*) (*pass judgement*) ein Urteil fällen; (*form an opinion*) (be)urteilen ◆ **who am I to ~?** ich kann mir dazu kein Urteil erlauben; **as far as one can ~** soweit man (es) beurteilen kann; **judging by** *or* **from sth** nach etw zu urteilen; **judging by appearances** dem Aussehen nach; **to ~ by appearances** nach dem Äußeren urteilen; **(you can) ~ for yourself** beurteilen Sie das selbst; **he let me ~ for myself** er überließ es meinem Urteil.

judg(e)ment ['dʒʌdʒmənt] *n* **(a)** (*Jur*) (Gerichts)urteil *nt*; (*Eccl*) Gericht *nt*; Richterspruch *m*; (*divine punishment*) Strafe *f* Gottes ◆ **to await ~** (*Jur*) auf sein *or* das Urteil warten; (*Eccl*) auf das Gericht *or* den Richterspruch (Gottes) warten; **the Day of J~** der Tag des Jüngsten Gerichtes; **to pass** (*also fig*) *or* **give** *or* **deliver ~** ein Urteil fällen, das Urteil sprechen (*on* über +*acc*); **to sit in ~ on a case** Richter in einem Fall sein; **to sit in ~ on sb** über jdn zu Gericht sitzen; (*Jur also*) die Verhandlung über jdn führen; **I don't want to sit in ~ on you** ich möchte mich nicht zu Ihrem Richter aufspielen; **it's a ~ from above** das ist die Strafe Gottes; **it's a ~ on him for being so lazy** das ist die Strafe Gottes dafür, daß er so faul war/ist.
(b) (*opinion*) Meinung, Ansicht *f*, Urteil *nt*; (*moral ~, value ~*) Werturteil *nt*; (*estimation: of distance, speed etc*) Einschätzung *f* ◆ **to give one's ~ on sth** sein Urteil über etw (*acc*) abgeben, seine Meinung zu etw äußern; **an error of ~** eine falsche Einschätzung, eine Fehleinschätzung; **in my ~** meines Erachtens, meiner Meinung nach.
(c) (*discernment*) Urteilsvermögen *nt* ◆ **a man of ~** ein Mensch *m* mit gutem Urteilsvermögen; **to show ~** ein gutes Urteilsvermögen beweisen *or* zeigen; **it's all a question of ~** das ist Ansichtssache.

judg(e)mental [dʒʌdʒ'mentl] *adj* wertend ◆ **don't be so ~** nimm nicht immer gleich Wertungen vor, bewerte nicht immer gleich alles.

judg(e)ment: ~ call *n* (*esp US*) Gewissensentscheidung *f* ◆ **to make a judg(e)ment call** eine Gewissensentscheidung treffen; **J~ Day** *n* Tag *m* des Jüngsten Gerichts; **~ seat** *n* Gottes Richterstuhl *m*.

judicature ['dʒuːdɪkətʃəʳ] *n* (*judges*) Richterstand *m*; (*judicial system*) Gerichtswesen *nt*, Gerichtsbarkeit *f*.

judicial [dʒuː'dɪʃəl] *adj* **(a)** (*Jur*) gerichtlich, Justiz-; *power* richterlich ◆ **~ function** Richteramt *nt*; **to take ~ proceedings against sb** ein Gerichtsverfahren *nt* gegen jdn anstrengen *or* einleiten; **~ murder** Justizmord *m*; **~ separation** Gerichtsbeschluß *m* zur Aufhebung der ehelichen Gemeinschaft.
(b) (*critical*) *mind* klar urteilend *attr*, kritisch.

judiciary [dʒuː'dɪʃərɪ] *n* (*branch of administration*) Gerichtsbehörden *pl*; (*legal system*) Gerichtswesen *nt*; (*judges*) Richterstand *m*.

judicious *adj*, **~ly** *adv* [dʒuː'dɪʃəs, -lɪ] klug, umsichtig.

judo ['dʒuːdəʊ] *n* Judo *nt*.

Judy ['dʒuːdɪ] *n abbr of* **Judith**; (*in Punch and ~*) Gretel *f*.

jug¹ [dʒʌg] [1] *n* **(a)** (*for milk, coffee etc*) (*with lid*) Kanne *f*; (*without lid*) Krug *m*; (*small*) Kännchen *nt*.
(b) (*sl: prison*) Kittchen *nt* (*sl*), Knast *m* (*sl*) ◆ **in ~** hinter schwedischen Gardinen (*inf*), im Kittchen (*sl*) *or* Knast (*sl*).
[2] *vt* (*Cook*) schmoren ◆ **~ged hare** ≃ Hasenpfeffer *m*.

jug² *n* (*of nightingale*) Flöten *nt*.

juggernaut ['dʒʌgənɔːt] *n* **(a)** (*Brit: lorry*) Schwerlaster *m*.
(b) (*Rel*) **J~** Dschagannath, Jagannath *m*.
(c) (*fig: destructive force*) verheerende Gewalt ◆ **the ~ of war** der Moloch des Krieges; **Puritanism, like some huge ~, swept across the country** der Puritanismus rollte mit unaufhaltsamer Gewalt über das Land.

juggins ['dʒʌgɪnz] *n* (*Brit inf*) Depp (*S Ger*), Trottel (*inf*) *m*.

juggle ['dʒʌgl] [1] *vi* jonglieren ◆ **to ~ with the facts/figures** die Fakten/Zahlen so hindrehen, daß sie passen.
[2] *vt balls* jonglieren (mit); *facts, figures* so hindrehen, daß sie passen.

juggler ['dʒʌgləʳ] *n* **(a)** (*lit*) Jongleur *m*. **(b)** (*fig: trickster*) Schwindler *m* ◆ **~ with words** Wortverdreher *m*.

jugglery ['dʒʌglərɪ] *n see* **juggling**.

juggling ['dʒʌglɪŋ] *n* **(a)** (*lit*) Jonglieren *nt*.
(b) (*fig*) Verdrehen *nt* (*with* von) ◆ **~ with words/figures** Wort-/Zahlenakrobatik *f*; (*falsification*) Wortverdrehung *f*/Frisieren *nt* von Zahlen; **there is a bit of ~ here** das ist doch so hingedreht worden, daß es paßt, das ist doch nicht ganz hasenrein (*inf*).

juggling act *n* (*fig*) Balanceakt *m*.

Jugoslav ['juːgəʊˌslɑːv] [1] *adj* jugoslawisch.
[2] *n* Jugoslawe *m*, Jugoslawin *f*.

Jugoslavia [ˌjuːgəʊ'slɑːvɪə] *n* Jugoslawien *nt*.

jugular ['dʒʌgjʊləʳ] *adj*: **~ vein** Drosselvene, Jugularvene *f*.

juice [dʒuːs] *n* **(a)** (*of fruit, meat*) Saft *m*. **(b)** *usu pl* (*of body*) Körpersäfte *pl*. **(c)** (*sl: electricity, petrol*) Saft *m* (*sl*).

juiciness ['dʒuːsɪnɪs] *n* (*lit*) Saftigkeit *f*; (*fig*) Pikanterie, Schlüpfrigkeit *f*, gewisser Reiz; (*of scandal*) Saftigkeit *f* (*inf*).

juicy ['dʒuːsɪ] *adj* (+*er*) *fruit* saftig; (*inf*) *profit* saftig (*inf*); *squelch* schmatzend, quatschend; *story* pikant, schlüpfrig; *scandal* gepfeffert (*inf*), saftig (*inf*); (*inf*) *girl* knackig (*inf*) ◆ **a big ~ kiss** ein dicker Schmatz (*inf*).

jujitsu [ˌdʒuː'dʒɪtsuː] *n* Jiu-Jitsu *nt*.

jujube ['dʒuːdʒuːb] *n* (*Bot*) Jujube *f*; (*berry also*) Brustbeere *f*.

jukebox ['dʒuːkbɒks] *n* Musikbox *f*, Musikautomat *m*.

Jul *abbr of* **July**.

julep ['dʒuːlep] *n* **(a)** ≃ Sirup, Saft *m*. **(b)** *see* **mint²**.

Julian ['dʒuːlɪən] [1] *n* Julian *m*.
[2] *adj* julianisch ◆ **~ calendar** Julianischer Kalender.

Julius ['dʒuːlɪəs] *n* Julius *m* ◆ **~ Caesar** Julius Caesar *m*.

July [dʒuː'laɪ] *n* Juli *m*; *see also* **September**.

jumble ['dʒʌmbl] [1] *vt* (*also* **~ up**) **(a)** (*lit*) durcheinanderwerfen, kunterbunt

➤ LANGUAGE IN USE: **judge: 2d** → 6.3

vermischen ◆ **~d up** durcheinander, kunterbunt vermischt; **to ~ everything up** alles durcheinanderbringen *or* in Unordnung bringen; **his clothes are ~d together on his bed** seine Kleider liegen in einem unordentlichen Haufen auf dem Bett.
(b) *(fig) facts, details* durcheinanderbringen, verwirren.
2 *n* **(a)** Durcheinander *nt*; *(of ideas also)* Wirrwarr *m*.
(b) *no pl (for ~ sale)* gebrauchte Sachen *pl* ◆ **~ sale** *(Brit)* ≃ Flohmarkt *m (von Vereinen veranstalteter Verkauf von gebrauchten Sachen)*; *(for charity)* Wohltätigkeitsbasar *m*.

jumbo ['dʒʌmbəʊ] *n* **(a)** *(inf)* Jumbo *m (inf)*. **(b)** *(~ jet)* Jumbo(-Jet) *m*.

jump [dʒʌmp] **1** *n* **(a)** *(lit)* Sprung *m*; *(of animal also)* Satz *m*; *(with parachute)* Absprung *m*; *(on race-course)* Hindernis *nt* ◆ **this horse is no good over the ~s** dieses Pferd taugt bei den Hindernissen nichts.
(b) *(fig) (of prices)* (plötzlicher *or* sprunghafter) Anstieg; *(in narrative)* Sprung *m*, abrupter Übergang ◆ **to take a sudden ~** *(prices, temperature)* ruckartig *or* sprunghaft ansteigen *(to* auf *+acc)*, in die Höhe schnellen; **the movie is full of ~s** der Film ist sprunghaft; **he's always one ~ ahead** er ist immer einen Schritt voraus.
(c) *(start)* **to give sb a ~** jdn erschrecken, jdn zusammenzucken lassen; **you gave me such a ~** du hast mich aber erschreckt; **it gave him a ~** er zuckte zusammen.
(d) to have the ~ on sb *(sl)* jdm gegenüber im Vorteil sein.
2 *vi* **(a)** *(leap)* springen, einen Satz machen; *(Sport)* springen; *(parachutist)* (ab)springen ◆ **to ~ into a river** in einen Fluß springen; **this horse ~s well** dieses Pferd springt gut *or* nimmt die Hindernisse gut; **to ~ for joy** Freudensprünge *pl*/einen Freudensprung machen; *(heart)* vor Freude hüpfen; **to ~ up and down on the spot** auf der Stelle hüpfen; **they ~ed up and down on his stomach** sie hüpften auf seinem Bauch herum; **to ~ to conclusions** vorschnelle Schlüsse ziehen.
(b) *(typewriter)* Buchstaben überspringen *or* auslassen.
(c) *(fig)* springen, unvermittelt übergehen; *(prices, shares)* in die Höhe schnellen, sprunghaft ansteigen ◆ **~ to it!** los schon!, mach schon!; **the film suddenly ~s from the 18th into the 20th century** der Film macht plötzlich einen Sprung vom 18. ins 20. Jahrhundert; **if you keep ~ing from one thing to another** wenn Sie nie an einer Sache bleiben; **let's offer £200 and see which way they ~** *(inf)* machen wir ihnen doch (einfach) ein Angebot von £ 200 und sehen dann, wie sie darauf reagieren.
(d) *(start)* zusammenfahren, zusammenzucken ◆ **the shout made him ~** er zuckte *or* fuhr bei dem Schrei zusammen; **you made me ~** du hast mich (aber) erschreckt; **his heart ~ed when ...** sein Herz machte einen Satz, als ...
3 *vt* **(a)** *ditch etc* überspringen, hinüberspringen über *(+acc)*; *(horses also)* (hinüber)setzen über *(+acc)*.
(b) *horse* springen lassen ◆ **he ~ed his horse over the fence** er setzte mit seinem Pferd über den Zaun.
(c) *(skip)* überspringen, auslassen; *pages also* überblättern.
(d) *(pick-up) groove* überspringen ◆ **to ~ the rails** *(train)* entgleisen; **to ~ a man** *(Draughts)* einen überspringen.
(e) *(inf usages) (Jur)* **to ~ bail** abhauen *(inf) (während man auf Kaution freigelassen ist)*; **to ~ a claim** einen schon bestehenden Anspruch (auf Land *or* Rechte) übergehen; **to ~ the lights** bei Rot drüberfahren *(inf) or* über die Kreuzung fahren; **to ~ the queue** *(Brit)* sich vordrängeln; **to ~ ship** *(Naut) (passenger)* das Schiff vorzeitig verlassen; *(sailor)* heimlich abheuern; **to ~ a train** *(get on)* auf einen Zug aufspringen; *(get off)* von einem Zug abspringen; **they ~ed a train to Acapulco** sie fuhren schwarz nach Acapulco; **to ~ sb** jdn überfallen.

◆**jump about** *or* **around** *vi* herumhüpfen *or* -springen.

◆**jump at** *vi +prep obj person (lit)* anspringen; *(fig)* anfahren; *object* zuspringen auf *(+acc)*; *offer* sofort zugreifen bei, sofort ergreifen; *suggestion* sofort aufgreifen; *chance* sofort beim Schopf ergreifen.

◆**jump down** *vi* hinunter-/herunterhüpfen *or* -springen *(from* von) ◆ **to ~ ~ sb's throat** jdn anfahren, jdm dazwischenfahren *(inf)*; **~ ~!** spring *or* hüpf (runter)!

◆**jump in** *vi* hineinspringen/hereinspringen ◆ **~ ~!** *(to car)* steig ein!; *(at swimming pool etc)* spring *or* hüpf (hinein/herein)!

◆**jump off** *vi* **(a)** herunterspringen *(prep obj* von); *(from train, bus)* aussteigen *(prep obj* aus); *(when moving)* abspringen *(prep obj* von); *(from bicycle, horse)* absteigen *(prep obj* von). **(b)** *(Show-jumping)* den Wettbewerb durch ein Stechen entscheiden ◆ **they had to ~ ~ to decide the winner** der Sieger mußte durch ein Stechen ermittelt werden.

◆**jump on** **1** *vi (lit) (onto vehicle)* einsteigen *(prep obj, -to* in *+acc)*; *(onto moving train, bus)* aufspringen *(prep obj, -to* auf *+acc)*; *(onto bicycle, horse)* aufsteigen *(prep obj, -to* auf *+acc)* ◆ **to ~ ~(to) sb/sth** auf jdn/etw springen; **he ~ed ~(to) his bicycle** er schwang sich auf sein Fahrrad.
2 *vi +prep obj (inf) person* anfahren; *suggestion* kritisieren, heruntermachen *(inf)*.

◆**jump out** *vi* hinaus-/herausspringen; *(from vehicle)* aussteigen *(of* aus); *(when moving)* abspringen *(of* von) ◆ **to ~ ~ of bed** aus dem Bett springen; **to ~ ~ of the window** aus dem Fenster springen, zum Fenster hinausspringen.

◆**jump up** *vi* hochspringen; *(from sitting or lying position also)* aufspringen; *(onto sth)* hinaufspringen *(onto* auf *+acc)*.

jump ball *n* Schiedsrichterball *m*.

jumped-up ['dʒʌmpt'ʌp] *adj (inf)* **this new ~ manageress** dieser kleine Emporkömmling von einer Abteilungsleiterin.

jumper ['dʒʌmpəʳ] *n* **(a)** *(garment) (Brit)* Pullover *m*; *(US: dress)* Trägerkleid *nt*. **(b)** *(person, animal)* Springer *m*. **(c)** *(Comput)* Steckbrücke, Drahtbrücke *f*.

jumper cables *n (US) see* **jump leads**.

jumpiness ['dʒʌmpɪnɪs] *n see adj (inf)* Nervosität *f*; Schreckhaftigkeit *f*.

jumping jack ['dʒʌmpɪŋ'dʒæk] *n* Hampelmann *m*.

jumping-off place [ˌdʒʌmpɪŋ'ɒfpleɪs] *n (fig) (for negotiations)* Ausgangsbasis *f*; *(for job)* Sprungbrett *nt*.

jump: **~ jet** *n* Senkrechtstarter *m*; **~ leads** *npl (Brit Aut)* Starthilfekabel *nt*; **~-off** *n (Show-jumping)* Stechen *nt*; **~ seat** *n* Notsitz, Klappsitz *m*; **~ suit** *n* Overall *m*.

jumpy ['dʒʌmpɪ] *adj (+er)* **(a)** *(inf) person* nervös; *(easily startled)* schreckhaft; *market* unsicher. **(b)** *motion* ruckartig.

Jun *abbr of* **June; junior** jr., jun.

junction ['dʒʌŋkʃən] *n* **(a)** *(Rail)* Gleisanschluß *m*; *(of roads)* Kreuzung *f*; *(of rivers)* Zusammenfluß *m* ◆ **a very sharp ~** eine sehr scharfe Abzweigung; **Clapham J~** Claphamer Kreuz *nt*; **Hamm is a big railway ~** Hamm ist ein großer Eisenbahnknotenpunkt. **(b)** *(Elec)* Anschlußstelle *f*. **(c)** *(act)* Verbindung *f*.

junction box *n (Elec)* Verteilerkasten, Kabelkasten *m*.

juncture ['dʒʌŋktʃəʳ] *n*: **at this ~** zu diesem Zeitpunkt.

June [dʒuːn] *n* Juni *m*; *see also* **September**.

jungle ['dʒʌŋgl] *n* Dschungel *(also fig)*, Urwald *m* ◆ **~ juice** *(hum sl: alcohol)* Feuerwasser *nt (inf)*.

junior ['dʒuːnɪəʳ] **1** *adj* **(a)** *(younger)* jünger ◆ **he is ~ to me** er ist jünger als ich; **Hiram Schwarz, ~** Hiram Schwarz junior; **Smith, ~** *(at school)* Smith II, der kleine Smith; **the ~ miss** die kleine Dame; **~ classes** *(Sch)* Unterstufe *f*; **~ school** *(Brit)* Grundschule *f*; **~ college** *(US Univ) College, an dem man die ersten zwei Jahre eines 4-jährigen Studiums absolviert*; **~ high (school)** *(US)* ≃ Mittelschule *f*.
(b) *(subordinate) employee* untergeordnet; *officer* rangniedriger ◆ **to be ~ to sb** unter jdm stehen; **~ clerk** zweiter Buchhalter; **he's just some ~ clerk** er ist bloß ein kleiner Angestellter; **~ Minister** Staatssekretär *m*; **~ partner** jüngerer Teilhaber; *(in coalition)* kleinerer (Koalitions)partner.
(c) *(Sport)* Junioren-, der Junioren ◆ **~ team** Juniorenmannschaft *f*.
2 *n* **(a)** Jüngere(r) *mf*, Junior *m* ◆ **he is my ~ by two years, he is two years my ~** er ist zwei Jahre jünger als ich; **where's ~?** wo ist der Junior?
(b) *(Brit Sch) (at primary school)* Grundschüler(in *f*) *m*; *(at secondary school)* Unterstufenschüler(in *f*) *m*.
(c) *(US Univ) Student(in f) m im vorletzten Studienjahr.*
(d) *(Sport)* **the ~s** die Junioren *pl*.

juniper ['dʒuːnɪpəʳ] *n* Wacholder *m* ◆ **~ berry** Wacholderbeere *f*.

junk[1] [dʒʌŋk] *n* **(a)** *(discarded objects)* Trödel *m*, altes Zeug, Gerümpel *nt*. **(b)** *(inf: trash)* Ramsch, Plunder, Schund *m*. **(c)** *(sl: drugs)* Stoff *m (sl)*.

junk[2] *n (boat)* Dschunke *f*.

junk bond *n (Fin) niedrig eingestuftes Wertpapier mit hohen Ertragschancen bei erhöhtem Risiko.*

junket ['dʒʌŋkɪt] **1** *n* **(a)** *(Cook)* Dickmilch *f*. **(b)** *(old, hum: merrymaking)* Gelage, Fest *nt*, Lustbarkeit *f (old, hum)*.
2 *vi (old, hum)* ein Gelage abhalten.

junketing ['dʒʌŋkɪtɪŋ] *n* **(a)** *(old, hum: merrymaking)* Festivität(en *pl*) *(esp hum)*, Lustbarkeit *(old, hum) f*. **(b)** *(US: trip at public expense)* (Vergnügungs)reise *f* auf Staatskosten.

junk: **~ food** *n* Junk food(s *pl*) *nt (inf)*, ungesundes Essen ◆ **~ heap** *n (also inf: car)* Schrotthaufen *m (inf)*; **you'll end up on the ~ heap** du wirst in der Gosse landen.

junkie ['dʒʌŋkɪ] *n (sl)* Fixer(in *f*) *(sl)*, Junkie *(sl) m* ◆ **chocolate/ice-cream ~** Schokoladen-/Eisfreak *m (sl)*.

junk: **~ mail** *n* (Post)wurfsendungen *pl*, Reklame *f*; **~ room** *n* Rumpelkammer *f*; **~ shop** *n* Trödelladen *m*; **~ yard** *n (for metal)* Schrottplatz *m*; *(for discarded objects)* Schuttabladeplatz *m*; *(of rag and bone merchant)* Trödellager(platz *m*) *nt*.

junta ['dʒʌntə] *n* Junta *f*.

Jupiter ['dʒuːpɪtəʳ] *n* Jupiter *m*.

juridical [dʒʊə'rɪdɪkəl] *adj (of law)* juristisch, Rechts-; *(of court)* gerichtlich.

jurisdiction [ˌdʒʊərɪs'dɪkʃən] *n* Gerichtsbarkeit *f*; *(range of authority)* Zuständigkeit(sbereich *m*) *f* ◆ **matters that do not fall under the ~ of this court** Fälle, für die dieses Gericht nicht zuständig ist; **this court has no ~ over him** er untersteht diesem Gericht nicht; **that's not (in) my ~** dafür bin ich nicht zuständig.

jurisprudence [ˌdʒʊərɪs'pruːdəns] *n* Jura *nt*, Rechtswissenschaft, Jurisprudenz *(old) f*; *see* **medical**.

jurist ['dʒʊərɪst] *n* Jurist(in *f*), Rechtswissenschaftler(in *f*) *m*.

juror ['dʒʊərəʳ] *n* Schöffe *m*, Schöffin *f*; *(for capital crimes)* Geschworene(r) *mf*; *(in competition)* Preisrichter(in *f*) *m*, Jury-Mitglied *nt*.

jury ['dʒʊərɪ] *n* **(a)** *(Jur)* **the ~** die Schöffen *pl*; *(for capital crimes)* die Geschworenen *pl*; **they don't have juries there** da gibt's keine Schöffengerichte *or (for capital crimes)* Schwurgerichte; **to sit on the ~** Schöffe/Geschworener sein; **Gentlemen of the J~** meine Herren Schöffen/Geschworenen.
(b) *(for examination)* Prüfungsausschuß *m*; *(for exhibition, competition)* Jury *f*, Preisgericht *nt*.

jury: **~ box** *n* Schöffen-/Geschworenenbank *f*; **~man** *n* Schöffe *m*; Geschworene(r) *m*; **~ rig** *n (Naut)* Hilfstakelage, Nottakelage *f*; **~ service** *n* Schöffenamt *nt*; Amt *nt* des Geschworenen; **to do ~ service** Schöffe/Geschworener sein; **he's never been called for ~ service** er wurde nie als Schöffe/Geschworener berufen; **~ system** *n* Schöffengerichte *pl or (for capital crimes)* Schwurgerichte *pl*; **~woman** *n* Schöffin *f*, Geschworene *f*.

▼ **just**[1] [dʒʌst] *adv* **(a)** *(immediate past)* gerade, (so)eben ◆ **they have ~ left** sie

sind gerade *or* (so)eben gegangen; **she left ~ before I came** sie war, gerade *or* kurz bevor ich kam, weggegangen; **he's ~ been appointed** er ist gerade *or* eben erst ernannt worden; **I met him ~ after lunch** ich habe ihn direkt *or* gleich nach dem Mittagessen getroffen.
(b) (*at this/that very moment*) gerade ◆ **hurry up, he's ~ going** beeilen Sie sich, er geht gerade; **he's ~ coming** er kommt gerade *or* eben; **I'm ~ coming** ich komme ja schon; **I was ~ going to** ... ich wollte gerade ...; **~ as I was going** genau in dem Moment *or* gerade, als ich gehen wollte.
(c) (*barely, almost not*) gerade noch, mit knapper Not ◆ **he (only) ~ escaped being run over** er wäre um ein Haar überfahren worden; **it ~ missed** es hat fast *or* beinahe getroffen; **I've got only ~ enough to live on** mir reicht es gerade so *or* so eben noch zum Leben; **I arrived ~ in time** ich bin gerade (noch) zurecht gekommen.
(d) (*exactly*) genau, gerade ◆ **it is ~ five o'clock** es ist genau fünf Uhr; **that's ~ like you** das sieht dir ähnlich; **it's ~ on nine o'clock** es ist gerade neun Uhr; **it happened ~ as I expected** es passierte genau so, wie ich es erwartet hatte; **it's ~ because of that that he insists** gerade *or* eben deshalb besteht er darauf; **that's ~ it!** das ist's ja gerade *or* eben!; **that's ~ what I was going to say** genau das wollte ich (auch) sagen; **~ what do you mean by that?** was wollen Sie damit sagen?; **~ what does this symbol mean?** was bedeutet dieses Zeichen genau?; **it was ~ there** genau da war es; **~ so!** (*old*) genau, ganz recht; **everything has to be ~ so** es muß alles seine Ordnung haben.
(e) (*only, simply*) nur, bloß ◆ **I can stay ~ a minute** ich kann nur *or* bloß eine Minute bleiben; **~ you and me** nur wir beide, wir beide allein; **this is ~ to show you how it works** dies soll Ihnen lediglich zeigen, wie es funktioniert; **this is ~ to confirm** ... hiermit bestätigen wir, daß ...; **he's ~ a boy** er ist doch noch ein Junge; **why don't you want to/like it? — I ~ don't** warum willst du nicht/magst du es nicht? — ich will/mag's eben *or* halt (*inf*) nicht; **~ like that** (ganz) einfach so; **I don't know, I ~ don't** ich weiß (es) nicht, beim besten Willen nicht; **you can't ~ assume** ... Sie können doch nicht ohne weiteres annehmen ...; **it's ~ not good enough** es ist einfach nicht gut genug; **I ~ prefer it this way** ich find's eben *or* einfach besser so.
(f) (*a small distance, with position*) gleich ◆ **~ round the corner** gleich um die Ecke; **~ above the trees** direkt über den Bäumen; **put it ~ over there** stell's mal da drüben hin; **~ here** (genau) hier.
(g) (*absolutely*) einfach, wirklich ◆ **it was ~ fantastic** es war einfach prima; **it's ~ terrible** das ist ja schrecklich!
▼ **(h)** **~ as** genauso, ebenso; **the blue hat is ~ as nice as the red one** der blaue Hut ist genauso hübsch wie der rote; **she didn't understand you — it's ~ as well!** sie hat Sie nicht verstanden — das ist vielleicht auch besser so; **it's ~ as well you stayed at home, you didn't miss anything** es macht nichts, daß Sie zu Hause geblieben sind, Sie haben nichts verpaßt; **it's ~ as well you didn't go out** nur gut, daß Sie nicht weggegangen sind; **it would be ~ as well if you came** es wäre doch besser, wenn Sie kämen; **come ~ as you are** kommen Sie so, wie Sie sind; **it's ~ as you please** wie Sie wollen; **~ as I thought!** ich habe es mir doch gedacht!
(i) **~ about** in etwa, so etwa; **I am ~ about ready** ich bin so gut wie fertig; **it's ~ about here** es ist (so) ungefähr hier; **did he make it in time? — ~ about** hat er's (rechtzeitig) geschafft? — so gerade; **will this do? — ~ about** ist das recht so? — so in etwa; **I am ~ about fed up with it!** (*inf*) so langsam aber sicher hängt es mir zum Hals raus (*inf*); **that's ~ about the limit!** das ist doch die Höhe!
(j) im Moment ◆ **~ now** (*in past*) soeben (erst), gerade erst; **not ~ now** im Moment nicht; **~ now?** jetzt gleich?; **you can go, but not ~ now** Sie können gehen, aber nicht gerade jetzt.
(k) (*other uses*) **~ think** denk bloß; **~ listen** hör mal; **~ try** versuch's doch mal; **~ taste this** probier das mal; (*it's awful*) probier bloß das mal; **~ let me try** lassen Sie's mich doch mal versuchen; **~ shut up!** sei bloß still!; **~ wait here a moment** warten Sie hier mal (für) einen Augenblick; **~ a moment** *or* **minute!** Moment mal!; **I can ~ see him as a soldier** ich kann ihn mir gut als Soldat vorstellen; **I can ~ see you getting up so early** (*iro*) du — und so früh aufstehen!; **can I ~ finish this?** kann ich das eben noch fertigmachen?; **the possibilities ~ go on for ever** die Möglichkeiten sind ja unerschöpflich; **don't I ~!** und ob (ich ...); **~ watch it** nimm dich bloß in acht; **~ you dare** wehe, wenn du's wagst.

just[2] *adj* (*+er*) **(a)** *person, decision* gerecht (*to* gegenüber). **(b)** *punishment, reward* gerecht; *anger* berechtigt; *suspicion* gerechtfertigt, begründet ◆ **a ~ cause** eine gerechte Sache; **I had ~ cause to be alarmed** ich hatte guten Grund, beunruhigt zu sein; **as (it) is only ~** wie es recht und billig ist.

justice ['dʒʌstɪs] *n* **(a)** (*Jur*) (*quality*) Gerechtigkeit *f*; (*system*) Gerichtsbarkeit, Justiz *f* ◆ **British ~** britisches Recht; **is this the famous British ~?** ist das die berühmte britische Gerechtigkeit?; **to bring a thief to ~** einen Dieb vor Gericht bringen; **court of ~** Gerichtshof *m*, Gericht *nt*; **to administer ~** Recht sprechen; *see* **poetic**.
(b) (*fairness*) Gerechtigkeit *f*; (*of claims*) Rechtmäßigkeit *f* ◆ **to do him ~** um ihm gegenüber gerecht zu sein, um mal fair zu sein (*inf*); **this photograph doesn't do me ~** auf diesem Foto bin ich nicht gut getroffen; **she never does herself ~** sie kommt nie richtig zur Geltung; **that's not true, you're not doing yourself ~** das stimmt nicht, Sie unterschätzen sich; **you didn't do yourself ~ in the exams** Sie haben im Examen nicht gezeigt, was Sie können; **they did ~ to my dinner** sie wußten mein Essen zu würdigen; **and with ~** und (zwar) zu Recht; **there's no ~, is there?** das ist doch nicht gerecht.
(c) (*judge*) Richter *m* ◆ **Lord Chief J~** *oberster Richter in Großbritannien*; **J~ of the Peace** Friedensrichter *m*; **Mr J~ Plod** Richter Plod.

justifiable [ˌdʒʌstɪ'faɪəbl] *adj* gerechtfertigt, berechtigt.

justifiably [ˌdʒʌstɪ'faɪəblɪ] *adv* zu Recht, berechtigterweise.

justification [ˌdʒʌstɪfɪ'keɪʃən] *n* **(a)** Rechtfertigung *f* (*of gen, for* für) ◆ **it can be said in his ~ that** ... zu seiner Verteidigung *or* Entschuldigung kann gesagt werden, daß ...; **as a ~ for his action** zur Rechtfertigung *or* Verteidigung seiner Handlungsweise; **he had no ~ for lying** er hatte keine Rechtfertigung *or* Entschuldigung für seine Lüge.
(b) (*Typ*) Justieren *nt*; (*Comput*) Randausgleich *m*.

▼ **justify** ['dʒʌstɪfaɪ] *vt* **(a)** (*show to be right*) rechtfertigen, verteidigen (*sth to sb* etw vor jdm *or* jdm gegenüber) ◆ **you don't need to ~ yourself** Sie brauchen sich nicht zu rechtfertigen *or* verteidigen; **don't try to ~ your action** versuchen Sie nicht, Ihre Tat zu entschuldigen *or* verteidigen; **am I justified in thinking that ...?** gehe ich recht in der Annahme, daß ...?
▼ **(b)** (*be good reason for*) rechtfertigen, ein Grund sein für ◆ **the future could hardly be said to ~ great optimism** die Zukunft berechtigt wohl kaum zu großem Optimismus; **this does not ~ his being late** das ist kein Grund für sein Zuspätkommen; **he was justified in doing that** es war gerechtfertigt, daß er das tat; **you're not justified in talking to her like that** Sie haben kein Recht, so mit ihr zu reden.
(c) (*Typ*) justieren; (*Comput*) ausrichten ◆ **right/left justified** rechts-/linksbündig.

justly ['dʒʌstlɪ] *adv* zu Recht, mit Recht; *treat, try* gerecht; *condemn* gerechterweise.

justness ['dʒʌstnɪs] *n* (*of cause*) Gerechtigkeit, Billigkeit (*liter*) *f*; (*of character*) Gerechtigkeit *f*.

jut [dʒʌt] *vi* (*also* **~ out**) hervorstehen, hervorragen, herausragen ◆ **he saw a gun ~ting (out) from behind the wall** er sah ein Gewehr hinter der Mauer (her)vorragen; **the cliff ~s out into the sea** die Klippen ragen ins Meer hinaus; **to ~ out over the street** über die Straße vorstehen *or* hinausragen.

jute [dʒu:t] *n* Jute *f*.

Jutland ['dʒʌtlənd] *n* Jütland *nt*.

juvenile ['dʒu:vənaɪl] [1] *n* (*Admin*) Jugendliche(r) *mf*.
[2] *adj* (*youthful*) jugendlich; (*for young people*) Jugend-, für Jugendliche; (*pej*) kindisch, unreif.

juvenile: ~ court *n* Jugendgericht *nt*; **~ delinquency** *n* Jugendkriminalität *f*, Kriminalität *f* bei Jugendlichen; **~ delinquent** *n* jugendlicher Straftäter; **~ lead** *n* (*Theat*) Rolle *f* des jugendlichen Hauptdarstellers; (*actor*) jugendlicher Hauptdarsteller.

juxtapose ['dʒʌkstəˌpəʊz] *vt* nebeneinanderstellen; *ideas also* gegeneinanderhalten; *colours* nebeneinandersetzen.

juxtaposition [ˌdʒʌkstəpə'zɪʃən] *n* (*act*) Nebeneinanderstellung *f* ◆ **in ~** (direkt) nebeneinander.

➤ LANGUAGE IN USE: **just: h** → 5.4 **justify: b** → 26.1

K

K, k [keɪ] *n* K, k *nt.*
K *abbr* (*in salaries etc*) -tausend ◆ **15~** 15.000.
k *n* (*Comput*) *abbr of* **kilobyte** KB.
Kaffir ['kæfəʳ] *n* Kaffer *m.*
Kafkaesque [,kæfkə'esk] *adj* kafkaesk.
kagul *n see* **cagoule.**
kale, kail [keɪl] *n* Grünkohl *m.*
kaleidoscope [kə'laɪdəskəʊp] *n* Kaleidoskop *nt.*
kaleidoscopic [kə,laɪdə'skɒpɪk] *adj* kaleidoskopisch.
kamikaze [kæmɪ,kɑːzɪ] *n* Kamikaze *nt* ◆ **~ pilot** Kamikaze-Flieger *m.*
Kampuchea [,kæmpʊ'tʃɪə] *n* Kampuchea *nt.*
kangaroo [,kæŋgə'ruː] *n* Känguruh *nt* ◆ **~ court** inoffizielles Gericht, Femegericht *nt.*
kaolin ['keɪəlɪn] *n* Kaolin *m or nt,* Porzellanerde *f.*
kapok ['keɪpɒk] *n* Kapok *m.*
kaput [kə'pʊt] *adj* (*sl*) kaputt (*inf*).
karat ['kærət] *n see* **carat.**
karate [kə'rɑːtɪ] *n* Karate *nt* ◆ **~ chop** Karateschlag *or* -hieb *m.*
karma ['kɑːmə] *n* Karma *nt.*
kart [kɑːt] *n* Go-Kart *m.*
karting ['kɑːtɪŋ] *n* Go-Kart-Fahren *nt.*
Kashmir [kæʃ'mɪəʳ] *n* Kaschmir *nt.*
Kate [keɪt] *n dim of* **Catherine** Käthe, Kathi *f.*
katydid ['keɪtɪdɪd] *n* Laubheuschrecke *f.*
kayak ['kaɪæk] *n* Kajak *m or nt.*
KC (*Brit*) *abbr of* **King's Counsel.**
kc *abbr of* **kilocycle.**
kebab [kə'bæb] *n* Kebab *m.*
kedge [kedʒ] *n* (*Naut*) Warpauker *m.*
kedgeree [,kedʒə'riː] *n Reisgericht nt mit Fisch und Eiern.*
keel [kiːl] *n* (*Naut*) Kiel *m* ◆ **to be on an even ~ again** (*lit*) sich wieder aufgerichtet haben; **he put the business back on an even ~** er brachte das Geschäft wieder ins Lot *or* wieder auf die Beine (*inf*); **when things are more on an even ~** wenn sich alles besser eingespielt hat.
◆**keel over** *vi* (*ship*) kentern; (*fig inf*) umkippen ◆ **she ~ed ~ in a faint** sie klappte zusammen (*inf*), sie kippte um (*inf*).
keelhaul ['kiːlhɔːl] *vt* kielholen.
▼ **keen**[1] [kiːn] *adj* (+*er*) **(a)** (*sharp*) *blade, wind* scharf.
(b) (*acute, intense*) *appetite* kräftig; *interest* groß, stark; *pleasure* groß; *feeling* stark, tief; *desire, pain* heftig, stark; *sight, eye, hearing, ear* gut, scharf; *mind, wit* scharf; (*esp Brit*) *prices* günstig; *competition* scharf ◆ **he has a ~ sense of history** er hat ein ausgeprägtes Gefühl für Geschichte.
▼ **(c)** (*enthusiastic*) begeistert; *football fan, golf player also, supporter* leidenschaftlich; (*eager, interested*) *applicant, learner* stark interessiert; (*hardworking*) eifrig ◆ **~ to learn/know** lernbegierig/begierig zu wissen; **try not to seem too ~** versuchen Sie, Ihr Interesse nicht zu sehr zu zeigen; **if he's ~ we can teach him** wenn er wirklich interessiert ist *or* Interesse hat, können wir es ihm beibringen; **he is terribly ~** seine Begeisterung/sein Interesse/sein Eifer kennt kaum Grenzen; **to be ~ on sb** von jdm sehr angetan sein, scharf auf jdn sein (*inf*); *on pop group, actor, author* von jdm begeistert sein; **to be ~ on sth** etw sehr gern mögen; *classical music, Italian cooking also, football* sehr viel für etw übrig haben; **to be ~ on doing sth** (*like to do*) etw gern *or* mit Begeisterung tun; **to be ~ to do sth** (*want to do*) sehr darauf erpicht sein *or* scharf darauf sein (*inf*), etw zu tun; **to be ~ on mountaineering/dancing** begeisterter *or* leidenschaftlicher Bergsteiger/Tänzer sein, leidenschaftlich gern bergsteigen/tanzen; **he is very ~ on golf/tennis** *etc* er ist ein Golf-/ Tennis- *etc* -narr *m*; **to become ~ on sb/sth** sich für jdn/etw erwärmen; **I'm not very ~ on him/that idea** ich bin von ihm/dieser Idee nicht gerade begeistert; **he's very ~ on getting the job finished** ihm liegt sehr viel daran, daß die Arbeit fertig wird; **he's not ~ on her coming** er legt keinen (gesteigerten) Wert darauf, daß sie kommt; **he's very ~ that we should go** er legt sehr großen Wert darauf *or* ihm ist sehr daran gelegen, daß wir gehen.
(d) (*US sl: very good*) Spitze (*sl*).
keen[2] (*Ir*) **1** *n* Totenklage *f.*
2 *vi* die Totenklage halten.
keenly ['kiːnlɪ] *adv* **(a)** (*sharply*) scharf, schneidend. **(b)** (*intensely, acutely*) *feel* leidenschaftlich, tief, stark; *interested, wish, desire* stark, sehr, leidenschaftlich ◆ **the competition was ~ contested** im Wettbewerb wurde hart gekämpft. **(c)** (*enthusiastically*) mit Begeisterung.
keenness ['kiːnnɪs] *n* **(a)** (*of blade, mind, wind, sight*) Schärfe *f.* **(b)** *see adj (c)* Begeisterung *f*; Leidenschaftlichkeit *f*; starkes Interesse; Eifer *m* ◆ **his ~ to go is suspicious** daß er so unbedingt gehen will, ist verdächtig.
keep [kiːp] (*vb: pret, ptp* **kept**) **1** *vt* **(a)** (*retain*) behalten ◆ **to ~ one's temper** sich beherrschen; **to ~ sb/sth in mind** an jdn/etw denken; **please ~ me in mind for the job** bitte denken Sie an mich bei der Vergabe des Postens; **to ~ a place for sb** einen Platz für jdn freihalten; **to ~ one's place in a book** sich (*dat*) die Stelle im Buch markieren; **I can't ~ that number in my head** ich kann die Nummer nicht behalten *or* mir die Nummer nicht merken; **to ~ a note of sth** sich (*dat*) etw notieren; **Uncle Jim wanted to ~ him another week** Onkel Jim wollte ihn noch eine Woche bei sich behalten; **they wanted to ~ me for dinner** sie wollten, daß ich zum Essen bleibe; **you can ~ it!** (*inf*) das kannst du behalten *or* dir an den Hut stecken (*inf*).
(b) *shop, hotel, restaurant* haben, unterhalten, führen; *bees, pigs etc* halten ◆ **who kept your dog while you were on holiday?** wer hat Ihren Hund gehabt, während Sie in Urlaub waren?; **to ~ house for sb** jdm den Haushalt führen; **to ~ servants/a car** sich (*dat*) Diener/ein Auto halten.
(c) (*support*) versorgen, unterhalten ◆ **I earn enough to ~ myself** ich verdiene genug für mich (selbst) zum Leben; **I have six children to ~** ich habe sechs Kinder zu unterhalten; **he ~s a mistress** er hält sich (*dat*) eine Geliebte; **to ~ sb in clothing** (*person*) für jds Kleidung sorgen; **I couldn't afford to ~ you in drink** ich könnte deine Getränke nicht bezahlen.
(d) (*maintain in a certain state or place or position*) halten ◆ **to ~ one's dress clean** sein Kleid nicht schmutzig machen; **to ~ sb quiet** zusehen *or* dafür sorgen, daß jd still ist; **that'll ~ them quiet for a while** das wird für eine Weile Ruhe schaffen; **it kept her in bed for a week** sie mußte deswegen eine Woche im Bett bleiben; **he kept his hands in his pockets** er hat die Hände in der Tasche gelassen; **just to ~ her happy** damit sie zufrieden ist; **to ~ sb alive** jdn am Leben halten; **to ~ sb at work** jdn bei der Arbeit halten; **to ~ sb waiting** jdn warten lassen; **~ her hoping** lassen Sie ihr die Hoffnung; **can't you ~ him talking?** können Sie ihn nicht in ein Gespräch verwickeln?; **~ your hands to yourself!** nehmen Sie Ihre Hände weg!; **the garden was well kept** der Garten war (gut) gepflegt; **to ~ the traffic moving** den Verkehr in Fluß *or* am Fließen halten; **to ~ a machine running** eine Maschine laufen lassen; **to ~ the conversation going** das Gespräch in Gang halten.
(e) (*in a certain place, look after*) aufbewahren; (*put aside*) aufheben ◆ **where does he ~ his money?** wo bewahrt er sein Geld auf?; **where do you ~ your spoons?** wo sind die Löffel?; **I've been ~ing it for you** ich habe es für Sie aufgehoben.
(f) (*be faithful to, observe, fulfil*) *promise* halten; *law, rule* einhalten, befolgen; *treaty* einhalten; *obligations* nachkommen (+*dat*), erfüllen; *appointment* einhalten ◆ **to ~ a vow** einen Schwur halten, ein Gelübde erfüllen.
(g) (*celebrate*) **to ~ Lent/the Sabbath** das Fasten/die Sonntagsruhe *or* den Sabbat (ein)halten.
(h) (*guard, protect*) (be)hüten; *sheep etc* hüten, aufpassen auf (+*acc*) ◆ **God ~ you!** (*old*) Gott befohlen! (*old*); **to ~ goal** (*Ftbl*) im Tor sein *or* stehen, das Tor hüten; *see* **~ from 1 (b).**
(i) *accounts, diary etc* führen (*of* über +*acc*).
(j) (*Comm: stock*) führen, (zu verkaufen) haben.
(k) (*detain*) aufhalten, zurückhalten ◆ **I mustn't ~ you** ich will Sie nicht aufhalten; **what kept you?** wo waren Sie denn so lang?; **what's ~ing him?** wo bleibt er denn?; **illness kept her at home** Krankheit fesselte sie ans Haus; **to ~ sb prisoner** jdn gefangenhalten; **to ~ sb in prison** jdn in Haft halten.
(l) (*not disclose*) **can you ~ this from your mother?** können Sie das vor Ihrer Mutter geheimhalten *or* verbergen?; **~ it to yourself** behalten Sie das für sich; *see* **secret.**
(m) (*US: continue to follow*) *road, path* weitergehen *or* -fahren, folgen (+*dat*); *direction* einhalten ◆ **to ~ one's course** (den) Kurs (ein)halten.
(n) (*esp US: remain in*) **to ~ one's bed/one's room** im Bett/auf seinem Zimmer bleiben; **to ~ one's seat** sitzenbleiben.
(o) **to ~ late hours** lange aufbleiben.
2 *vi* **(a)** (*continue in a specified direction*) **to ~ (to the) left/right** sich links/rechts halten; **to ~ to the left** (*Aut*) auf der linken Seite bleiben, links

➤ LANGUAGE IN USE: **keen**[1]**: c** → 8.3

fahren; to ~ to the middle of the road immer in der Mitte der Straße fahren; ~ on this road bleiben Sie auf dieser Straße; ~ north gehen/fahren Sie immer Richtung Norden.
(b) (*continue*) to ~ doing sth (*not stop*) etw weiter tun; (*repeatedly*) etw immer wieder tun; (*constantly*) etw dauernd tun; to ~ walking weitergehen; he kept lying to her er hat sie immer wieder belogen; if you ~ complaining wenn Sie sich weiter beschweren; she ~s talking about you all the time sie redet dauernd von Ihnen; ~ going machen Sie weiter; I ~ hoping she's still alive ich hoffe immer noch, daß sie noch lebt; I ~ thinking ... ich denke immer ...
(c) (*remain in a certain state, position*) bleiben ◆ to ~ quiet still sein; to ~ silent schweigen; to ~ calm ruhig bleiben, Ruhe bewahren; she kept indoors for three days sie blieb drei Tage im Haus.
(d) (*food etc*) sich halten ◆ that meat won't ~ dieses Fleisch hält sich nicht *or* bleibt nicht gut.
(e) (*be in a certain state of health*) how are you ~ing? und wie geht es Ihnen denn so?; to ~ well gesund bleiben; to ~ fit fit bleiben, sich in Form halten; he's ~ing better now es geht ihm wieder besser; to ~ in good health sich guter Gesundheit erfreuen; to ~ alive sich am Leben halten.
(f) (*wait*) that business can ~ das kann warten; will it ~? kann das warten?
(g) (*dated Univ: reside*) wohnen.
[3] *n* (a) (*livelihood, food*) Unterhalt *m* ◆ I got £100 a week and my ~ ich bekam £ 100 pro Woche und freie Kost und Logis; he's not worth his ~ (*inf*) er ist sein Brot nicht wert, der bringt doch nichts (ein) (*inf*).
(b) (*in castle*) Bergfried *m*; (*as prison*) Burgverlies *nt*.
(c) for ~s (*inf*) für immer; he's playing for ~s ihm ist's ernst; it's yours for ~s das darfst du behalten.

◆**keep ahead** *vi* vorne bleiben ◆ to ~ ~ of one's rivals seinen Konkurrenten vorausbleiben; to ~ one step ~ of the others den anderen einen Schritt voraus sein.

◆**keep at** [1] *vi +prep obj* (a) (*continue with*) weitermachen mit ◆ ~ ~ it machen Sie weiter so. (b) (*nag*) herumnörgeln an (*+dat*) ◆ ~ ~ him until he says yes laß ihm so lange keine Ruhe, bis er ja sagt.
[2] *vt +prep obj* to ~ sb ~ a task jdn nicht mit einer Arbeit aufhören lassen; to ~ sb ~ it jdn hart hernehmen (*inf*), jdn an der Kandare haben.

◆**keep away** [1] *vi* (*lit*) wegbleiben; (*not approach*) nicht näher herankommen (*from* an *+acc*) ◆ ~ ~! nicht näherkommen!; ~ ~ from that place gehen Sie da nicht hin; he just can't ~ ~ from the pub es zieht ihn immer wieder in die Wirtschaft; I just can't ~ ~ es zieht mich immer wieder hin; ~ ~ from him lassen Sie die Finger von ihm; he just can't ~ ~ from her/drink er kann einfach nicht von ihr/vom Alkohol lassen.
[2] *vt always separate person, children, pet etc* fernhalten (*from* von) ◆ to ~ sth ~ from sth etw nicht an etw (*acc*) kommen lassen; ~ your hand ~ from the cutting edge kommen Sie mit Ihrer Hand nicht an die Schneide; ~ them ~ from each other halten Sie sie auseinander; business kept him ~ for three months er war aus geschäftlichen Gründen drei Monate weg; what's been ~ing you ~? wo waren Sie denn so lange?

◆**keep back** [1] *vi* zurückbleiben, nicht näherkommen ◆ ~ ~! bleiben Sie, wo Sie sind!, treten Sie zurück!; please ~ ~ from the edge bitte gehen Sie nicht zu nahe an den Rand.
[2] *vt sep* (a) (*hold back*) *person, hair, crowds, enemy* zurückhalten; *water* stauen; *tears* unterdrücken ◆ to ~ sb/sth ~ from sb jdn/etw von jdm abhalten.
(b) (*withhold*) *money, taxes* einbehalten; *information, facts etc* verschweigen (*from sb* jdm); (*from parent, husband etc*) verheimlichen, verschweigen (*from sb* jdm) ◆ I know you're ~ing something ~ ich weiß, daß du mir etwas verheimlichst *or* verschweigst; they are ~ing ~ the names of the victims die Namen der Opfer werden nicht bekanntgegeben.
(c) (*make late*) aufhalten; *pupil* dabehalten ◆ I don't want to ~ you ~ ich möchte Sie nicht aufhalten.
(d) (*hold up, slow down*) behindern ◆ being with the slower learners is ~ing him ~ weil er mit schwächeren Schülern zusammen ist, kommt er nicht so schnell voran.

◆**keep down** [1] *vi* unten bleiben ◆ ~ ~! duck dich!, bleib unten!
[2] *vt sep* (a) (*lit*) unten lassen; (*hold down*) unten halten; *head* ducken ◆ ~ your voices ~ reden Sie leise *or* nicht so laut.
(b) *people, revolt, one's anger* unterdrücken; *dog* bändigen; *rebellious person* im Zaum *or* unter Kontrolle halten; *rabbits, weeds etc* in Grenzen *or* unter Kontrolle halten ◆ you can't ~ a good man ~ der Tüchtige läßt sich nicht unterkriegen.
(c) *taxes, rates, prices* niedrig halten; *spending* einschränken ◆ to ~ one's weight ~ nicht zunehmen.
(d) *food etc* bei sich behalten.
(e) (*Sch*) wiederholen lassen ◆ he was kept ~ er mußte wiederholen.

◆**keep from** [1] *vt +prep obj* (a) *sb* hindern an (*+dat*); (*from going, doing sth also*) abhalten von ◆ I couldn't ~ him ~ doing it/going there ich konnte ihn nicht daran hindern *or* davon abhalten(, das zu tun)/, dort hinzugehen; to ~ sb ~ falling jdn am Fallen hindern; to ~ oneself ~ doing sth sich (davor) hüten, etw zu tun; the bells ~ me ~ sleeping die Glocken lassen mich nicht schlafen; to ~ sb ~ school jdn nicht in die Schule (gehen) lassen; ~ them ~ getting wet verhindern Sie es, daß sie naß werden; this will ~ the water ~ freezing das verhindert, daß das Wasser gefriert; you shouldn't ~ them ~ their work Sie sollten sie nicht von der Arbeit abhalten.
(b) (*protect*) to ~ sb ~ sth jdn vor etw (*dat*) bewahren.
(c) (*withhold*) to ~ sth ~ sb jdm etw verschweigen; *piece of news also* jdm etw vorenthalten.
[2] *vi +prep obj* to ~ ~ doing sth etw nicht tun; (*avoid doing also*) es vermeiden, etw zu tun; in order to ~ ~ becoming overworked um sich nicht zu überarbeiten; she couldn't ~ ~ laughing sie mußte einfach lachen.

◆**keep in** [1] *vt sep* (a) *fire* nicht ausgehen lassen; *feelings* zügeln. (b) *schoolboy* nachsitzen lassen ◆ I've been kept ~! ich mußte nachsitzen!; his mummy's kept him ~ seine Mutti hat ihn nicht weggelassen *or* gehen lassen. (c) *stomach* einziehen ◆ ~ your tummy ~! Bauch rein!
[2] *vi* (a) (*fire*) anbleiben ◆ it'll ~ ~ all night es brennt die ganze Nacht durch. (b) (*stay indoors*) drinnen bleiben. (c) (*with person*) he's just trying to ~ ~ er will sich lieb Kind machen.

◆**keep in with** *vi +prep obj* sich gut stellen mit.

◆**keep off** [1] *vi* (*person*) wegbleiben ◆ if the rain ~s ~ wenn es nicht regnet; "~ ~!" „Betreten verboten!"
[2] *vt sep* (a) *dog, person* fernhalten (*prep obj* von); *one's hands* wegnehmen, weglassen (*prep obj* von) ◆ this weather will ~ the crowds ~ dieses Wetter wird einen Massenandrang verhindern; "~ ~ the grass" „Betreten des Rasens verboten"; ~ him ~ me halten Sie ihn mir vom Leib; ~ your hands ~ Hände weg!; ~ the dog ~ the couch lassen Sie den Hund nicht aufs Sofa.
(b) *jacket etc* ausbehalten; *hat* abbehalten.
[3] *vi +prep obj* vermeiden ◆ ~ ~ the whisky lassen Sie das Whiskytrinken.

◆**keep on** [1] *vi* (a) weitermachen, nicht aufhören ◆ to ~ ~ doing sth etw weiter tun; (*repeatedly*) etw immer wieder tun; (*incessantly*) etw dauernd tun; he ~s ~ swearing er flucht dauernd; ~ ~ talking! reden Sie weiter!; if you ~ ~ like this wenn du so weitermachst; ~ ~ trying versuchen Sie es weiter; I ~ ~ telling you ich sage dir ja immer; the rain kept ~ all night es regnete die ganze Nacht durch; he kept ~ crying the whole night er hat die ganze Nacht unaufhörlich geweint.
(b) (*keep going*) weitergehen *or* -fahren ◆ ~ ~ past the church fahren Sie immer weiter an der Kirche vorbei; ~ straight ~ immer geradeaus.
(c) to ~ ~ at sb (*inf*) dauernd an jdm herummeckern (*inf*); they kept ~ at him until he agreed sie haben ihm so lange keine Ruhe gelassen, bis er zustimmte.
(d) to ~ ~ about sth (*inf*) unaufhörlich von etw reden; there's no need to ~ ~ so (*inf*) es ist wirklich nicht nötig, ewig darauf herumzuhacken (*inf*); don't ~ ~ so! (*inf*) hören Sie doch endlich auf damit!
[2] *vt sep* (a) *servant, employee* weiterbeschäftigen, behalten.
(b) *coat etc* anbehalten; *hat* aufbehalten.

◆**keep out** [1] *vi* (*of room, building*) draußen bleiben; (*of property, land, area*) etw nicht betreten ◆ ~ ~ of my room! geh/komm nicht in mein Zimmer; "~ ~" „Zutritt verboten"; to ~ ~ of the rain/cold/sun nicht in den Regen/die Kälte/die Sonne gehen; to ~ ~ of sight sich nicht zeigen; (*hiding*) in Deckung bleiben; to ~ ~ of danger Gefahr meiden; to ~ ~ of debt keine Schulden machen; that child can never ~ ~ of mischief das Kind stellt dauernd etwas an; to ~ ~ of a quarrel sich nicht in einen Streit einmischen, sich aus einem Streit heraushalten; you ~ ~ of this! halten Sie sich da *or* hier raus!
[2] *vt sep* (a) *person* nicht hereinlassen (*of* in *+acc*); *light, cold, rain, enemy etc* abhalten ◆ this screen ~s the sun ~ of your eyes diese Blende schützt Ihre Augen vor Sonne; how can I ~ the rabbits ~/~ of my garden? was kann ich tun, daß die Kaninchen nicht hereinkommen/nicht in meinen Garten kommen?
(b) to ~ sb ~ of danger/harm jdn vor Gefahr/Gefahren schützen; to ~ sb ~ of a quarrel jdn nicht mit in einen Streit hereinziehen; I wanted to ~ him ~ of this ich wollte nicht, daß er da mit hereingezogen wurde; to ~ sb's name ~ of the papers jds Namen nicht in der Zeitung erwähnen; ~ the plants ~ of the sun/cold schützen Sie die Pflanzen vor Sonne/Kälte; ~ him ~ of my way halte ihn mir vom Leib; they kept him ~ of their plans sie haben ihn von ihren Plänen ausgeschlossen.

◆**keep to** [1] *vi +prep obj* (a) to ~ ~ one's promise sein Versprechen halten, zu seinem Wort stehen; to ~ ~ one's bed/one's room im Bett/in seinem Zimmer bleiben; ~ ~ the main road bleiben Sie auf der Hauptstraße; to ~ ~ the schedule/plan den Zeitplan einhalten, sich an den Zeitplan/Plan halten; to ~ ~ the traditional way an der herkömmlichen Art festhalten; to ~ ~ the subject/point bei der Sache *or* beim Thema bleiben; to ~ ~ the text sich an den Text halten, am Text bleiben.
(b) to ~ (oneself) ~ oneself nicht sehr gesellig sein, ein Einzelgänger sein; they ~ (themselves) ~ themselves (*as a group*) sie bleiben unter sich.
[2] *vt +prep obj* to ~ sb ~ his word/promise jdn beim Wort nehmen; ~ them ~ the target sorgen Sie dafür, daß sie ihr Soll erfüllen; to ~ sth ~ a minimum etw auf ein Minimum beschränken.

◆**keep together** [1] *vi* (*stay together*) zusammenbleiben; (*as friends etc*) zusammenhalten; (*singers, oarsmen etc*) im Einklang *or* Takt sein.
[2] *vt sep* zusammen aufbewahren; (*fix together, unite*) *things, people* zusammenhalten; (*conductor*) *orchestra* im Takt halten.

◆**keep under** [1] *vt sep fire* unter Kontrolle halten; *anger, feelings, people, race* unterdrücken; *passions* zügeln; *subordinates* streng behandeln, an der Kandare haben; (*keep under anaesthetic*) unter Narkose halten ◆ you won't ~ him ~ der läßt sich nicht unterkriegen *or* kleinkriegen.
[2] *vi* (*under water etc*) unter Wasser bleiben.

◆**keep up** [1] *vi* (a) (*tent, pole*) stehen bleiben.
(b) (*rain*) (an)dauern; (*weather, hurricane etc*) anhalten; (*prices, output, standard*) gleich hoch bleiben; (*moral, strength, determination*) nicht nachlassen ◆ their spirits ~ ~ sie verzagen nicht, sie bleiben guten Muts.
(c) to ~ ~ (with sb/sth) (*in race, work, with prices*) (mit jdm/etw) Schritt halten, (mit jdm/etw) mithalten können (*inf*); (*in comprehension*) (jdm/einer

Sache) folgen können; **they bought it just to ~ ~ with the Joneses** sie kauften es nur, um den Nachbarn nicht nachzustehen; **to ~ ~ with the times** mit der Zeit gehen; **to ~ ~ with the news** sich auf dem laufenden halten; **I haven't kept ~ with my French** ich bin mit meinem Französisch ganz aus der Übung gekommen.
(d) (*keep in touch with*) **to ~ ~ with sb** mit jdm in Kontakt bleiben; **we haven't kept ~ at all since she went abroad** wir haben nichts mehr voneinander gehört, seit sie im Ausland ist.
2 *vt sep* **(a)** *pole, tent* aufrecht halten ◆ **the lifebelt kept him ~** der Rettungsring hielt ihn über Wasser; **to ~ his trousers ~** damit die Hose nicht herunterrutscht.
(b) (*not stop*) nicht aufhören mit; *study etc* fortsetzen, weitermachen; *quality, prices, output, friendship, tradition, custom* aufrechterhalten; *subscription* beibehalten; *payments etc* weiterbezahlen; *workrate, speed* (*maintain*) halten; (*endure*) durchhalten ◆ **I try to ~ ~ my Latin** ich versuche, mit meinem Latein nicht aus der Übung zu kommen; **to ~ ~ a correspondence** in Briefwechsel bleiben; **to ~ one's morale ~** den Mut nicht verlieren; **he kept their morale ~** er hat ihnen Mut gemacht; **~ it ~!** (machen Sie) weiter so!; **he couldn't ~ it ~** er hat schlappgemacht (*inf*); (*sexually*) er ist ihm weggeschlafft (*sl*).
(c) (*maintain*) *house* unterhalten; *road* in stand halten.
(d) (*prevent from going to bed*) am Schlafengehen hindern ◆ **that child kept me ~ all night** das Kind hat mich die ganze Nacht nicht schlafen lassen; **I was kept ~ pretty late last night** ich bin gestern abend ziemlich spät ins Bett gekommen.

keeper ['ki:pəʳ] *n* (*in asylum, zoo*) Wärter(in *f*), Pfleger(in *f*), Betreuer(in *f*) *m*; (*of museum*) Kustos *m*; (*guard*) Wächter(in *f*), Aufseher(in *f*), Aufpasser(in *f*) *m* ◆ **am I my brother's ~?** soll ich meines Bruders Hüter sein?

keeping ['ki:pɪŋ] *n* **(a)** (*care*) **to put sb in sb's ~** jdn in jds Obhut (*acc*) geben; **to put sth in sb's ~** jdm etw zur Aufbewahrung übergeben; *see* **safe-keeping.**
(b) (*of rule*) Beachten, Einhalten *nt*.
(c) in ~ with in Übereinstimmung *or* Einklang mit; **her behaviour was out of ~ with the dignity of the occasion** ihr Benehmen entsprach nicht der Feierlichkeit des Anlasses.

keepsake ['ki:pseɪk] *n* Andenken *nt*.

keg [keg] *n* **(a)** (*barrel*) kleines Faß, Fäßchen *nt*. **(b)** (*also* **~ beer**) Bier *nt* vom Faß.

kelp [kelp] *n* Seetang *m*.

ken [ken] **1** *n* **that is beyond** *or* **outside my ~** das entzieht sich meiner Kenntnis.
2 *vti* (*Scot*) *see* **know.**

kennel ['kenl] *n* **(a)** Hundehütte *f*. **(b) ~s** (*cage*) Hundezwinger *m*; (*for breeding*) Hundezucht *f*; (*boarding*) (Hunde)heim, Tierheim *nt*; **to put a dog in ~s** einen Hund in Pflege geben.

Kenya ['kenjə] *n* Kenia *nt*.

Kenyan ['kenjən] **1** *n* Kenianer(in *f*) *m*.
2 *adj* kenianisch.

kepi ['keɪpɪ] *n* Käppi *nt*.

kept [kept] **1** *pret, ptp of* **keep.**
2 *adj* **~ woman** Mätresse *f*; **she's a ~ woman** sie läßt sich aushalten.

kerb [kɜ:b] *n* (*Brit*) Bordkante *f*, Randstein *m*.

kerb: ~ crawler *n* Freier *m* im Autostrich (*inf*); **~ crawling** *n* Autostrich *m*; **~ crawling area** *n* Autostrich *m*; **~ drill** *n* Verkehrserziehung *f*; **~stone** *n* Bordstein, Randstein *m*.

kerchief ['kɜ:tʃɪf] *n* (*old*) Hals- *or* Kopftuch *nt*.

kerfuffle [kə'fʌfl] *n* (*Brit inf*) (*noise*) Lärm *m*, Gedöns *nt* (*inf*); (*fight*) Balgerei *f* (*inf*); (*trouble*) Theater *nt* (*inf*).

kernel ['kɜ:nl] *n* (*lit, fig*) Kern *m*.

kerning ['kɜ:nɪŋ] *n* (*Comput*) Kerning *nt*.

kerosene ['kerəsi:n] *n* Kerosin *nt* ◆ **~ lamp** Petroleum- *or* Paraffinlampe *f*.

kestrel ['kestrəl] *n* Turmfalke *m*.

ketch [ketʃ] *n* Ketsch *f*.

ketchup ['ketʃəp] *n* Ketchup *nt or m*.

kettle ['ketl] *n* Kessel *m* ◆ **I'll put the ~ on** ich stelle mal eben (Kaffee-/Tee)wasser auf; **the ~'s boiling** das Wasser kocht; **this is a pretty ~ of fish** (*inf*) das ist eine schöne Bescherung; **this is a different ~ of fish** (*inf*) das ist doch was ganz anderes.

kettledrum ['ketldrʌm] *n* (Kessel)pauke *f*.

key [ki:] **1** *n* **(a)** Schlüssel *m*.
(b) (*fig: solution*) Schlüssel *m* ◆ **education is the ~ to success** Bildung ist der Schlüssel zum Erfolg; **the ~ to the mystery** der Schlüssel zum Geheimnis, des Rätsels Lösung; **this was the ~ to the murderer's identity** das gab Aufschluß darüber *or* den Hinweis, wer der Mörder war.
(c) (*answers*) Lösungen *pl*, Schlüssel *m*; (*Sch*) Schlüssel *m*, Lehrerheft *nt*; (*Math etc*) Lösungsheft *nt*; (*for maps etc*) Zeichenerklärung *f*.
(d) (*of piano, typewriter, Comput*) Taste *f*.
(e) (*Mus*) Tonart *f* ◆ **to sing off ~** falsch singen; **change of ~** Tonartwechsel *m*, Modulation *f*; **in the ~ of C** in C-Dur/c-Moll.
(f) (*Build*) Untergrund *m*.
2 *adj attr* (*vital*) Schlüssel-, wichtigste(r, s) ◆ **~ industry** Schlüsselindustrie *f*; **~ man** Schlüsselfigur *f*; **~ point** springender Punkt; **~ position** Schlüsselposition *or* -stellung *f*; **~ question** Schlüsselfrage *f*; **~ role** Schlüsselrolle *f*.
3 *vt* **(a)** *speech etc* (*to or for one's audience*) (auf jdn) abstimmen *or* zuschneiden (*to, for* auf *+acc*), anpassen (*to, for dat*).
(b) (*Comput*) (*input*) *text, data* eingeben; (*hit*) *character, F7 etc* drücken.
4 *vi* (*Comput*) Text/Daten eingeben.

◆**key in** *vt sep* (*Comput*) eingeben.

◆**key up** *vt sep* **(a) she was (all) ~ed ~ about the interview** sie war wegen des Interviews ganz aufgedreht (*inf*); **he was all ~ed ~ for the big race** er hatte sich schon ganz auf das große Rennen eingestellt; **to ~ the crowds ~ for the big speech** die Menge auf die große Rede einstimmen. **(b)** (*Comput*) eingeben.

key: ~board 1 *n* (*of piano*) Klaviatur, Tastatur *f*; (*of organ*) Manual *nt*; (*of typewriter, Comput*) Tastatur *f*; **~board instrument** (*Mus*) Tasteninstrument *nt*; **~board operator** Texterfasser(in *f*) *m*; **~board template** Tastaturschablone *f*; **a genius on the ~board** (*Mus*) ein Klaviergenie *nt*; **2** *vti* (*Typ, Comput*) eingeben; **~boarder** *n* (*Typ, Comput*) Texterfasser(in *f*) *m*; **what's she like as a ~boarder?** wie ist sie bei der Texterfassung?; **~boarding** *n* (*Comput*) Texteingabe *f*; **~boarding skills** Fähigkeiten *pl* bei der Texterfassung; **~hole** *n* Schlüsselloch *nt*.

keying ['ki:ɪŋ] *n* (*Comput*) Texteingabe *f*.

key: ~ money *n* Provision *f*, Schlüsselgeld *nt*; **~ note** *n* (*Mus*) Grundton *m*; (*of a speech*) Leitgedanke, Tenor *m*; **~note speech** (*Pol etc*) programmatische Rede; **~pad** *n* (*Comput*) Tastenfeld *nt*; **~ ring** *n* Schlüsselring *m*; **~ signature** *n* (*Mus*) Tonartbezeichnung *f*; **~stone** *n* (*Archit*) Schlußstein *m*; (*fig*) Grundpfeiler *m*; **~ stroke** *n* Anschlag *m*.

KG (*Brit*) *abbr of* **Knight of the Garter.**

kg *abbr of* **kilogramme(s), kilogram(s)** kg.

KGB *n* KGB *m*.

khaki ['kɑ:kɪ] **1** *n* K(h)aki *nt*.
2 *adj* k(h)aki(braun *or* -farben).

Khmer Rouge [k'mɛə'ru:ʒ] *npl* Rote Khmer *pl*.

kibbutz [kɪ'bʊts] *n, pl* **-im** [ˌkɪbʊt'si:m] Kibbuz *m*.

kibosh ['kaɪbɒʃ] *n* (*sl*): **to put the ~ on sth** etw vermasseln (*inf*).

kick [kɪk] **1** *n* **(a)** (*act of ~ing*) Tritt, Stoß, Kick (*inf*) *m* ◆ **to take a ~ at sb/sth** nach jdm/etw treten; **he gave the ball a tremendous ~** er trat mit Wucht gegen den Ball; **a tremendous ~ by Beckenbauer** ein toller Schuß von Beckenbauer; **he hasn't much of a ~ with his left leg** links kann er nicht kräftig schießen *or* zutreten; **to give the door a ~** gegen die Tür treten; **give it a ~** tritt mal dagegen; **to get a ~ on the leg** einen Tritt ans Bein bekommen, gegen das *or* ans Bein getreten werden; **it's better than a ~ in the pants** (*inf*) das ist besser als ein Tritt in den Hintern (*inf*); **what he needs is a good ~ up the backside** (*inf*) er braucht mal einen kräftigen Tritt in den Hintern (*inf*).
(b) (*inf: thrill*) **she gets a ~ out of it** es macht ihr einen Riesenspaß (*inf*); (*physically*) sie verspürt einen Kitzel dabei; **to do sth for ~s** etw zum Spaß *or* Jux (*inf*) *or* Fez (*inf*) tun; **just for ~s** nur aus Jux und Tollerei (*inf*); **she just lives for ~s** sie lebt nur zu ihrem Vergnügen; **how do you get your ~s?** was machen Sie zu ihrem Vergnügen?
(c) *no pl* (*power to stimulate*) Feuer *nt*, Pep *m* (*inf*) ◆ **this drink has plenty of ~ in it** dieses Getränk hat es in sich; **this drink hasn't much ~ in it** dieses Getränk ist ziemlich zahm (*inf*).
(d) (*of gun*) Rückstoß *m*.
2 *vi* (*person*) treten; (*struggle*) um sich treten; (*baby, while sleeping*) strampeln; (*animal*) austreten, ausschlagen; (*dancer*) das Bein hochwerfen; (*gun*) zurückstoßen *or* -schlagen, Rückstoß haben; (*inf: engine*) stottern (*inf*) ◆ **he ~ed into third** (*sl*) er ging in den dritten (Gang).
3 *vt* **(a)** (*person, horse*) *sb* treten, einen Tritt versetzen (*+dat*); *door, ball* treten gegen; *ball* kicken (*inf*); *object* einen Tritt versetzen (*+dat*), mit dem Fuß stoßen ◆ **to ~ sb's behind** jdn in den Hintern treten; **to ~ a goal** ein Tor schießen; **to ~ the bucket** (*inf*) abkratzen (*inf*), ins Gras beißen (*inf*); **I could have ~ed myself** (*inf*) ich hätte mich ohrfeigen können, ich hätte mich selbst *or* mir in den Hintern treten können (*inf*).
(b) (*sl: stop*) **to ~ heroin** vom Heroin runterkommen (*sl*); **to ~ the habit** es sich (*dat*) abgewöhnen.

◆**kick about** *or* **around 1** *vi* (*sl*) (*person*) rumhängen (*sl*) (*prep obj* in *+dat*); (*thing*) rumliegen (*inf*) (*prep obj* in *+dat*).
2 *vt sep* **to ~ a ball ~** (herum)bolzen (*inf*), den Ball herumkicken (*inf*); **you shouldn't let them ~ you ~** Sie sollten sich nicht so herumschubsen lassen; **don't ~ that book ~** werfen Sie das Buch nicht so herum; **to ~ an idea ~** (*sl*) eine Idee durchdiskutieren.

◆**kick against** *vi +prep obj* treten gegen ◆ **to ~ ~ the pricks** sich widersetzen, wider *or* gegen den Stachel löcken (*geh*).

◆**kick at** *vi +prep obj* treten nach.

◆**kick away** *vt sep* wegstoßen; (*knock down*) niedertreten.

◆**kick back 1** *vi* **(a)** zurücktreten ◆ **if you annoy him he'll ~ ~** (*fig*) wenn Sie ihn ärgern, gibt er es Ihnen zurück. **(b)** (*gun*) zurückstoßen, einen Rückstoß haben.
2 *vt sep blanket* wegstrampeln; *ball* zurückspielen *or* -schießen *or* -kicken (*inf*).

◆**kick in** *vt sep door* eintreten ◆ **to ~ sb's teeth ~** jdm die Zähne einschlagen.

◆**kick off 1** *vi* (*Ftbl*) anstoßen; (*player also*) den Anstoß ausführen; (*fig inf*) losgehen (*inf*), beginnen ◆ **who's going to ~ ~?** (*fig inf*) wer fängt an?
2 *vt sep* wegtreten; *shoes* von sich schleudern.

◆**kick out 1** *vi* (*horse*) ausschlagen; (*person*) um sich treten ◆ **to ~ ~ at sb** nach jdm treten.
2 *vt sep* hinauswerfen (*of* aus) ◆ **he was ~ed ~ of the club** er ist aus dem Verein hinausgeworfen worden *or* geflogen (*inf*).

◆**kick over** *vi +prep obj*: **to ~ ~ the traces** über die Stränge schlagen.

◆**kick up** *vt sep* **(a)** *dust* aufwirbeln. **(b)** *(fig inf)* **to ~ ~ a row** *or* **a din** Krach machen *(inf)*; **to ~ ~ a fuss** Krach schlagen *(inf)*.
kick: ~back *n (inf) (reaction)* Auswirkung *f*; *(as bribe)* Provision *f*; *(perk)* Nebeneinnahme *f*; **~down** *n* Kickdown *m*.
kicker ['kɪkəʳ] *n Spieler, der Strafstöße etc ausführt*, Strafstoßexperte *m*.
kick: ~-off *n* **(a)** *(Sport)* Anpfiff, Anstoß *m* ◆ **the ~-off is at 3 o'clock** Anpfiff ist um 3 Uhr; **(b)** *(sl: of ceremony etc)* Start, Anfang *m* ◆ **the ~-off is at 3 o'clock** um 3 geht's los *(inf)*; **for a ~-off** *(to begin with)* erst mal, zunächst; **~-start(er)** *n* Kickstarter *m*; **~turn** *n (Ski)* Kehre *f*.
kid [kɪd] 1 *n* **(a)** *(young goat)* Kitz, Zicklein *(liter) nt*.
(b) *(leather)* Ziegen- *or* Glacéleder *nt*.
(c) *(inf: child)* Kind *nt* ◆ **when I was a ~** als ich klein war; **to get the ~s to bed** die Kleinen ins Bett bringen; **it's ~'s stuff** *(for children)* das ist was für kleine Kinder *(inf)*; *(easy)* das ist doch ein Kinderspiel.
(d) *(inf) (man)* Junge, Bursche *(inf) m*; *(woman)* Kleine *f (inf)* ◆ **listen ~, I didn't mean it** nun hör mir mal gut zu, ich hab's doch nicht so gemeint; **listen ~, you keep out of this** hör mal Kleiner, du hältst dich hier raus *(inf)*; **come on ~s!** los Jungs! *(inf)*; **she's some ~** die ist nicht ohne *(inf)*; *(clever)* die ist ganz schön clever *(inf)*; **he's done it already? some ~** was, er hat das schon gemacht? stark *(sl) or* tolle Leistung *(inf)*.
2 *adj attr* **~ brother** kleiner Bruder, Brüderchen *nt*; **~ gloves** Glacéhandschuhe *pl*; **to handle sb with ~ gloves** *(fig)* jdn mit Samthandschuhen *or* Glacéhandschuhen anfassen.
3 *vt (inf)* **to ~ sb (on)** *(tease)* jdn aufziehen *(inf)*; *(deceive)* jdm etw vormachen, jdn an der Nase rumführen *(inf)*; **you can't ~ me** mir kannst du doch nichts vormachen; **don't ~ yourself!** machen Sie sich doch nichts vor!; **I ~ you not** das ist mein Ernst, ganz ehrlich *(inf)*.
4 *vi (inf)* Jux machen *(inf)* ◆ **no ~ding** im Ernst, ehrlich *(inf)*.
◆**kid on** *vt sep see* **kid 3**.
kiddo ['kɪdəʊ] *n (sl) see* **kid 1 (d)**.
kiddy ['kɪdɪ] *n (inf)* Kleinchen *(inf)*, Kindchen *(inf) nt*.
kidnap ['kɪdnæp] *vt* entführen, kidnappen.
kidnapper ['kɪdnæpəʳ] *n* Entführer(in *f*), Kidnapper(in *f*) *m*.
kidnapping ['kɪdnæpɪŋ] *n* Entführung *f*, Kidnapping *nt*.
kidney ['kɪdnɪ] *n* **(a)** *(Anat, Cook)* Niere *f*. **(b)** *(fig: type, temperament)* **of the same ~** vom gleichen Schlag *or* Typ.
kidney: ~ bean *n* Gartenbohne *f*; **~ dish** *n* Nierenschale *f*; **~ machine** *n* künstliche Niere; **~-shaped** *adj* nierenförmig; **~ stone** *n (Med)* Nierenstein *m*.
kidology [kɪ'dɒlədʒɪ] *n (inf: bluffing)* Bluff *m (inf)*.
kill [kɪl] 1 *vt* **(a)** töten, umbringen; *(by beating)* totschlagen, erschlagen; *(by shooting)* erschießen, totschießen; *(by stabbing)* erstechen, erdolchen; *animals* töten; *(Hunt)* erlegen; *(slaughter)* schlachten; *(shock)* umbringen; *pains* beseitigen; *weeds* vernichten ◆ **to be ~ed in action/in battle/in the war** fallen/im Kampf fallen/im Krieg fallen; **too many people are being ~ed on the roads** zu viele Menschen sterben auf der Straße *or* kommen auf der Straße um; **last year's drought ~ed thousands of animals** bei der letztjährigen Trockenheit kamen Tausende von Tieren um; **her brother was ~ed in a car accident** ihr Bruder ist bei einem Autounfall ums Leben gekommen; **how many were ~ed?** wieviel Todesopfer gab es?; **smoking will ~ you** das Rauchen wird Sie (noch) das Leben kosten; **the frost has ~ed my geraniums** meine Geranien sind erfroren; **she ~ed herself** sie brachte sich um, sie nahm sich *(dat)* das Leben; **he was ~ed with this weapon** dies ist die Mord- *or* Tatwaffe; **please, don't ~ me** bitte, lassen Sie mich leben; **he was ~ed by cancer** er starb an Krebs; **many people were ~ed by the plague** viele Menschen sind der Pest zum Opfer gefallen; **he was ~ed with poison/a knife/a hammer** er wurde vergiftet/(mit einem Messer) erstochen/mit einem Hammer erschlagen; **each man ~s the thing he loves** jeder zerstört das, was er liebt; **I'll ~ him!** *(also fig)* den bring' ich um *(inf)*; **the bullet ~ed him** die Kugel traf ihn tödlich *or* tötete ihn.
(b) *(fig uses) feelings, love etc* töten, zerstören ◆ **to ~ time** die Zeit totschlagen; **we have two hours to ~** wir haben noch zwei Stunden übrig; **to ~ two birds with one stone** *(Prov)* zwei Fliegen mit einer Klappe schlagen *(Prov)*; **these stairs/the children are ~ing me** *(inf)* diese Treppe bringt/die Kinder bringen mich (noch mal) um *(inf)*; **my girdle is ~ing me** *(inf)* mein Hüfthalter bringt mich um *(inf)*; **she was ~ing herself (laughing)** *(inf)* sie hat sich totgelacht *or* kaputtgelacht *(inf)*; **this one'll ~ you** *(inf)* da lachst du dich tot *(inf)*; **this heat is ~ing me** *(inf)* ich vergehe vor Hitze; **my feet are ~ing me** *(inf)* mir brennen die Füße; **they're not exactly ~ing themselves** *(inf: overworking)* sie bringen sich nicht gerade um *(inf)*, sie reißen sich *(dat)* kein Bein aus; **don't ~ yourself** *(iro)* übernehmen Sie sich nicht.
(c) *(spoil the effect of) taste, performance* verderben, überdecken; *hopes* vernichten, zunichte machen ◆ **this red ~s the other colours** dieses Rot übertönt *or* erschlägt die anderen Farben.
(d) *(defeat) parliamentary bill, proposal* zu Fall bringen.
(e) *sound* schlucken ◆ **to ~ a ball** eine Bombe schlagen *(inf)*; **~ that light!** *(inf)* Licht aus!
(f) *(Press etc) paragraph, story* streichen, abwürgen *(sl)*.
(g) *(Tech) engine etc* abschalten, ausschalten; *(Elec) circuit* unterbrechen.
(h) *(inf) bottle* leermachen, auf den Kopf stellen *(inf)*.
2 *vi* töten ◆ **cigarettes can ~** Zigaretten können tödlich sein *or* tödliche Folgen haben; **he was dressed to ~** er hatte sich in Schale geworfen *(inf)*.
3 *n* **(a)** *(Hunt)* Erlegen *nt*, Abschuß *m*; *(at bullfight)* Todesstoß *m* ◆ **the wolves gathered round for the ~** die Wölfe kreisten die Beute ein, um sie zu erlegen; **the tiger has made a ~** der Tiger hat ein Opfer erlegt *or* geschlagen; **to be in at the ~** *(lit)* beim Abschuß dabei sein; *(fig)* den Schlußakt miterleben.
(b) *(Hunt etc: animals killed)* Beute *f no pl*.
◆**kill off** *vt sep* vernichten, töten; *whole race* ausrotten, vernichten; *cows, pigs, elephants* abschlachten; *weeds* vertilgen; *character in TV series* sterben lassen.
killer ['kɪləʳ] *n (person)* Mörder(in *f*), Killer *(inf) m* ◆ **this disease is a ~** diese Krankheit ist tödlich; **it's a ~** *(inf: race, job etc)* das ist der glatte Mord *(inf)*; *see* **lady-killer, weed-killer**.
killer: ~ instinct *n*: **the ~ instinct** *(lit)* der Tötungsinstinkt; **a boxer with the ~ instinct** ein Boxer, in dem der Killer wach wird *(inf)*; **a successful businessman needs the ~ instinct** ein erfolgreicher Geschäftsmann muß über Leichen gehen können; **~ satellite** *n* Killersatellit *m*; **~ whale** *n* Schwertwal, Mordwal *m*.
killing ['kɪlɪŋ] 1 *n* **(a)** *(of animals) (Hunt)* Erlegen *nt*; *(at abattoir)* (Ab)schlachten *nt*. **(b)** *(of person)* Töten *nt*, Tötung *f* ◆ **three more ~s in Belfast** drei weitere Morde *or* Todesopfer in Belfast. **(c)** *(fig)* **to make a ~** einen Riesengewinn machen.
2 *adj* **(a)** *blow etc* tödlich. **(b)** *(exhausting) work* mörderisch *(inf)*. **(c)** *(funny)* urkomisch *(inf)*.
killingly ['kɪlɪŋlɪ] *adv*: **~ funny** zum Totlachen *(inf)*.
killjoy ['kɪldʒɔɪ] *n* Spielverderber, Miesmacher *m*.
kiln [kɪln] *n (for baking, burning)* (Brenn)ofen *m*; *(for minerals)* Röst- *or* Kiesofen *m*; *(for drying bricks etc)* Trockenofen *m*; *(for hops etc)* Darre *f*, Darrofen *m*.
kilo ['kiːləʊ] *n* Kilo *nt*.
kilobyte ['kiːləʊbaɪt] *n* Kilobyte *nt*.
kilocycle ['kɪləʊ,saɪkl] *n* Kilohertz *nt*.
kilogramme, *(US)* **kilogram** ['kɪləʊgræm] *n* Kilogramm *nt*.
kilohertz ['kɪləʊhɜːts] *n* Kilohertz *nt*.
kilolitre, *(US)* **kiloliter** ['kɪləʊ,liːtəʳ] *n* Kiloliter *m*.
kilometre, *(US)* **kilometer** ['kɪləʊ,miːtəʳ] *n* Kilometer *m*.
kilowatt ['kɪləʊwɒt] *n* Kilowatt *nt* ◆ **~ hour** Kilowattstunde *f*.
kilt [kɪlt] *n* Kilt, Schottenrock *m*.
kimono [kɪ'məʊnəʊ] *n* Kimono *m*.
kin [kɪn] 1 *n* Familie *f*, Verwandte *pl*, Verwandschaft *f* ◆ **has he any ~?** hat er Verwandte *or* Familie?; *see* **kith, next of ~**.
2 *adj* verwandt *(to* mit).
kind¹ [kaɪnd] *n* **(a)** *(class, variety, nature)* Art *f*; *(of coffee, sugar, paint etc)* Sorte *f* ◆ **they differ in ~** sie sind verschiedenartig; **several ~s of flour** mehrere Mehlsorten; **this ~ of book** diese Art Buch; **what ~ of ...?** was für ein(e) ...?; **what ~ of people does he think we are?** für wen hält er uns denn?; **the only one of its ~** das einzige seiner Art; **a funny ~ of person** ein komischer Mensch *or* Typ; **he is not the ~ of man to refuse** er ist nicht der Typ, der nein sagt; **he's not that ~ of person** so ist er nicht; **I'm not that ~ of girl** so eine bin ich nicht; **they're two of a ~** die beiden sind vom gleichen Typ *or* von der gleichen Art; *(people)* sie sind vom gleichen Schlag; **I know your ~** deinen Typ kenne ich; **your ~ never do any good** Leute Ihres Schlags *or* Leute wie Sie tun nie gut; **this ~ of thing** so etwas; **you know the ~ of thing I mean** Sie wissen, was ich meine; **... of all ~s** alle möglichen ...; **something of the ~** so etwas ähnliches; **nothing of the ~** nichts dergleichen; **you'll do nothing of the ~** du wirst dich schwer hüten, du wirst das schön bleiben lassen!; **it was beef of a ~** *(pej)* es war Rindfleisch oder so was ähnliches *(inf)*; **it's not my ~ of holiday** solche Ferien sind nicht mein Fall *(inf) or* nach meinem Geschmack; **she's my ~ of woman** sie ist mein Typ.
(b) a ~ of ... eine Art ..., so ein(e) ...; **a ~ of box** so (etwas wie) eine Schachtel, eine Art Schachtel; **in a ~ of way I'm sorry** *(inf)* irgendwie tut es mir leid; **he was ~ of worried-looking** *(inf)* er sah irgendwie bedrückt aus; **I ~ of thought that he ...** *(inf) (and he didn't)* ich habe eigentlich gedacht, daß er ...; *(and he did)* ich habe es mir beinahe gedacht, daß er ...; **are you nervous? — ~ of** *(inf)* bist du nervös? — ja, schon *(inf)*.
(c) *(goods, as opposed to money)* Naturalien *pl*, Ware *f* ◆ **payment in ~** Bezahlung in Naturalien; **I shall pay you back in ~** *(fig)* ich werde es Ihnen in gleicher Münze zurückzahlen.
▼ **kind²** *adj (+er)* liebenswürdig, nett, freundlich *(to* zu) ◆ **he's ~ to animals** er ist gut zu Tieren; **would you be ~ enough to open the door** wären Sie (vielleicht) so nett *or* freundlich *or* lieb, die Tür zu öffnen; **he was so ~ as to show me the way** er war so nett *or* freundlich und zeigte mir den Weg; **it was very ~ of you to help me** es war wirklich nett *or* lieb von Ihnen, mir zu helfen.
kinda ['kaɪndə] *adv (incorrect)* = **kind of** irgendwie.
kindergarten ['kɪndə,gɑːtn] *n* Kindergarten *m*.
kind-hearted ['kaɪnd'hɑːtɪd] *adj* gutherzig, gütig.
kind-heartedness ['kaɪnd'hɑːtɪdnɪs] *n* Gutherzigkeit, Güte *f*.
kindle ['kɪndl] 1 *vt fire* entfachen, anzünden, entzünden; *passions, desire* entfachen, wecken.
2 *vi (fire, wood etc)* brennen; *(passions, enthusiasm etc)* entbrennen, aufflammen.
kindliness ['kaɪndlɪnɪs] *n* Freundlichkeit, Güte, Liebenswürdigkeit *f*.
kindling ['kɪndlɪŋ] *n (wood)* Anzündholz, Anmachholz *nt*.
kindly ['kaɪndlɪ] 1 *adv* **(a)** *speak, act* freundlich, nett; *treat* liebenswürdig, freundlich ◆ **they ~ put me up for a night** sie nahmen mich freundlicherweise für eine Nacht auf.
(b) will you ~ do it now tun Sie das sofort, wenn ich bitten darf; **~ shut the door** machen Sie doch bitte die Tür zu; **would you ~ shut up!** halten Sie doch endlich den Mund.
(c) I don't take ~ to his smoking sein Rauchen ist mir gar nicht angenehm;

➤ LANGUAGE IN USE: **kind²** → 4, 21.2

he won't take at all ~ to that das wird ihm gar nicht gefallen; I don't take ~ to not being asked es ärgert mich, wenn ich nicht gefragt werde; she didn't take ~ to the idea of going abroad sie konnte sich gar nicht mit dem Gedanken anfreunden, ins Ausland zu gehen; she didn't take it ~ when I said ... sie hat es nicht gut aufgenommen, als ich sagte ...
[2] *adj* (+er) *person* lieb, nett, freundlich; *advice* gut gemeint, freundlich; *voice* sanft, gütig.

kindness ['kaɪndnɪs] *n* **(a)** *no pl* Freundlichkeit, Liebenswürdigkeit *f* (*towards* gegenüber); (*goodness of heart*) Güte *f* (*towards* gegenüber) ◆ **thank you very much for all your ~** vielen Dank, daß Sie so freundlich *or* liebenswürdig waren; **to treat sb with ~, to show sb ~** freundlich *or* liebenswürdig zu jdm sein; **out of the ~ of one's heart** aus reiner Nächstenliebe; **would you have the ~ to ...?** hätten Sie die Freundlichkeit *or* Güte, zu ...?
(b) (*act of* ~) Gefälligkeit, Aufmerksamkeit *f* ◆ **to do sb a ~** jdm eine Gefälligkeit erweisen; **it would be a ~ to tell him** man würde ihm einen Gefallen tun, wenn man es ihm sagen würde; **thank you for all your many ~es** vielen Dank für alles, was Sie für mich getan haben.

kindred ['kɪndrɪd] [1] *n, no pl* (*relatives*) Verwandtschaft *f*.
[2] *adj* (*related*) verwandt ◆ **~ spirit** Gleichgesinnte(r) *mf*.

kinetic [kɪ'netɪk] *adj* kinetisch.

kinfolk ['kɪnfəʊk] *n see* **kinsfolk**.

king [kɪŋ] *n* **(a)** (*lit*) König *m* ◆ **~'s Bench** (*Jur*) *erste Kammer des Obersten Gerichts in Großbritannien*; **K~'s Counsel** (*Jur*) Kronanwalt *m* (*Staatsanwalt, der in höheren Strafsachen die Krone vertritt*); **the ~'s highway** (*old, form*) *eine öffentliche Straße*; **~'s messenger** (*Diplomacy*) königlicher Gesandter; **it must have cost a ~'s ransom** das muß eine stolze Summe *or* ein Vermögen gekostet haben.
(b) (*fig*) König *m* ◆ **an oil ~** ein Ölkönig *or* -magnat *m*.
(c) (*Chess, Cards*) König *m*; (*Draughts*) Dame *f*.

king: ~ bolt *n* (*US*) *see* **~pin**; **~cup** *n* (*buttercup*) Hahnenfuß *m*, Butterblume *f*; (*marsh marigold*) Sumpfdotterblume *f*.

kingdom ['kɪŋdəm] *n* **(a)** (*lit*) Königreich *nt*. **(b)** (*Rel*) **~ of heaven** Himmelreich *nt*; **to send sb to ~ come** (*inf*) jdn ins Jenseits befördern (*inf*); **you can go on doing that till ~ come** (*inf*) Sie können (so) bis in alle Ewigkeit weitermachen; **he's gone to ~ come** (*inf*) er hat das Zeitliche gesegnet (*hum inf*). **(c)** (*Zool, Bot*) Reich *nt*.

kingfisher ['kɪŋfɪʃəʳ] *n* Eisvogel *m* ◆ **~-blue** eisblau, gletscherblau.

kingly ['kɪŋlɪ] *adj* königlich, majestätisch.

king: ~maker *n* (*lit, fig*) Königsmacher *m*; **~pin** *n* (*Tech*) Königsbolzen, Drehzapfen *m*; (*Aut*) Achsschenkelbolzen *m*; (*fig: person*) Stütze *f*; **he's the ~pin of the whole organization** mit ihm steht und fällt die ganze Organisation; **~ship** *n* Königtum *nt*; **~-size(d)** *adj* (*inf*) in Großformat, großformatig; *cigarettes* King-size; *bed* extra groß; **I've got a ~-size(d) headache** (*hum*) ich hab' vielleicht einen Brummschädel (*inf*) *or* einen dicken Kopf (*inf*).

kink [kɪŋk] [1] *n* **(a)** (*in rope etc*) Knick *m*, Schlaufe *f*; (*in hair*) Welle *f*. **(b)** (*mental peculiarity*) Schrulle *f*, Tick *m* (*inf*); (*sexual*) abartige Veranlagung.
[2] *vi* (*rope*) Schlaufen bilden, sich verdrehen; (*hair*) sich wellen.

kinky ['kɪŋkɪ] *adj* (+er) **(a)** *hair* wellig. **(b)** (*inf*) *person, ideas, mind* verdreht (*inf*), schrullig, spleenig (*inf*); *boots, fashion* verrückt (*inf*), irr (*sl*); (*sexually*) abartig ◆ **~!** nein, so was! (*inf*), ist ja irre! (*sl*), lustig, lustig! (*inf*).

kinsfolk ['kɪnzfəʊk] *n* Verwandtschaft *f*, Verwandte(n) *pl*.

kinship ['kɪnʃɪp] *n* Verwandtschaft *f*.

kinsman ['kɪnzmən] *n, pl* **-men** [-mən] Verwandte(r) *m*.

kinswoman ['kɪnzwʊmən] *n, pl* **-women** [-wɪmɪn] Verwandte *f*.

kiosk ['kiːɒsk] *n* **(a)** Kiosk, Verkaufsstand *m*, Bude *f*. **(b)** (*Brit Telec*) (Telefon)zelle *f*.

kip [kɪp] (*Brit sl*) [1] *n* (*sleep*) Schläfchen *nt*, Ratzer(chen *nt*) *m* (*sl*) ◆ **I've got to get some ~** ich muß mal 'ne Runde pennen (*sl*); **I need a good ~** ich muß mal (wieder) richtig pennen (*sl*) *or* ratzen (*sl*).
[2] *vi* (*also* **~ down**) pennen (*sl*).

kipper ['kɪpəʳ] *n* Räucherhering, Bückling *m*.

kir [kiːəʳ] *n* Kir *m*.

kirk [kɜːk] *n* (*Scot*) Kirche *f* ◆ **the K~** *die Presbyterianische Kirche Schottlands*.

kiss [kɪs] [1] *n* Kuß *m* ◆ **~ of life** Mund-zu-Mund-Beatmung *f*; **that will be the ~ of death for them** das wird ihnen den Todesstoß versetzen; **~ curl** Schmachtlocke *f*.
[2] *vt* küssen; (*fig: touch gently*) sanft berühren ◆ **to ~ sb's cheek** jdn auf die Wange küssen; **to ~ sb's hand** jdm die Hand küssen; (*woman's hand: in greeting*) jdm einen Handkuß geben; **they ~ed each other** sie gaben sich einen Kuß, sie küßten sich; **to ~ sb back** jds Kuß (*acc*) erwidern, jdn wiederküssen; **to ~ sb good night/goodbye** jdm einen Gute-Nacht-Kuß/Abschiedskuß geben; **come here and I'll ~ it better** komm her, ich werde mal blasen, dann tut's nicht mehr weh.
[3] *vi* küssen; (*~ each other*) sich küssen ◆ **to ~ and make up** sich mit einem Kuß versöhnen.

◆**kiss away** *vt sep* **she ~ed ~ the child's tears** sie küßte dem Kind die Tränen fort.

kissable ['kɪsəbl] *adj mouth* zum Küssen einladend *attr* ◆ **a ~ girl** ein Mädchen, das man küssen möchte.

kiss-and-tell [,kɪsən'tel] *adj* **~ story** Enthüllungsstory *f* (*mit Details einer Affäre mit einer prominenten Person*).

kisser ['kɪsəʳ] *n* **(a) to be a good ~** gut küssen (können). **(b)** (*sl: mouth, face*) Fresse (*sl*), Schnauze (*sl*) *f*.

kissing gate ['kɪsɪŋ,geɪt] *n* Schwinggatter *nt* (*an Weidenzäunen und Hecken, das nur je eine Person durchläßt*).

kiss-off ['kɪsɒf] *n* (*US inf*) **to give sb the ~** jdn in die Wüste schicken (*inf*); (*boyfriend etc*) jdm den Laufpaß geben (*inf*).

kissogram ['kɪsəgræm] *n durch eine spärlich bekleidete Angestellte einer Agentur persönlich übermittelter Geburtstagsgruß etc.*

kissproof ['kɪspruːf] *adj* kußecht.

kit [kɪt] *n* **(a)** (*equipment*) (*for fishing, photography etc*) Ausrüstung *f*; (*Mil also*) Montur *f* (*old*) ◆ **~ inspection** (*Mil*) Bekleidungs- *or* Ausrüstungsappell *m*.
(b) (*Sport: clothes*) Ausrüstung *f*, Zeug *nt* (*inf*), Sachen *pl* (*inf*) ◆ **gym ~** Sportzeug *nt*, Sportsachen *pl*.
(c) (*belongings, luggage etc*) Sachen *pl*; *see* **caboodle**.
(d) (*set of items*) (*tools*) Werkzeug *nt*; (*in box*) Werkzeugkasten *m*; (*puncture repair ~*) Flickzeug *nt*.
(e) (*for self-assembly*) Bastelsatz *m*.

◆**kit out** *or* **up** *vt sep* ausrüsten (*esp Mil*), ausstatten; (*clothe*) einkleiden ◆ **he arrived ~ted ~ in oilskins** er erschien (ausgestattet) in Ölzeug.

kitbag ['kɪtbæg] *n* Seesack *m*.

kitchen ['kɪtʃɪn] [1] *n* Küche *f*.
[2] *attr* Küchen-; *scales also, soap* Haushalts-.

kitchenette [,kɪtʃɪ'net] *n* (*separate room*) kleine Küche; (*part of one room*) Kochnische *f*.

kitchen: ~ foil *n* Alufolie *f*; **~ garden** *n* Gemüsegarten, Küchengarten *m*; **~maid** *n* Küchenmagd *f*; **~ range** *n* Küchenherd *m*; **~ roll** *n* Küchenrolle *f*; **~ scissors** *npl* Küchenschere, Haushaltsschere *f*; **~ sink** *n* Spüle *f*, Ausguß, Spülstein *m*; **I've packed everything but the ~ sink** (*inf*) ich habe den ganzen Hausrat eingepackt; **~-sink drama** *n* Alltagsdrama, Wohnküchendrama *nt*; **~ unit** *n* Küchenschrank *m*; **~ware** *n* Küchengeräte *pl*.

kite [kaɪt] *n* **(a)** (*Orn*) Milan *m*. **(b)** (*toy*) Drachen *m* ◆ **K~ mark** (*Brit*) *dreieckiges Gütezeichen*; **to fly a ~** (*fig*) einen Versuchsballon steigen lassen. **(c)** (*Aviat sl*) Vogel *m* (*sl*).

kith [kɪθ] *n*: **~ and kin** Blutsverwandte *pl*; **we're ~ and kin with the British** wir sind mit den Briten blutsverwandt, die Briten sind unsere Blutsbrüder; **they came with ~ and kin** sie kamen mit Kind und Kegel.

kitsch [kɪtʃ] *n* Kitsch *m*.

kitschy ['kɪtʃɪ] *adj* (+er) kitschig.

kitten ['kɪtn] *n* kleine Katze, Kätzchen *nt* ◆ **to have ~s** (*fig inf*) Junge *or* Zustände kriegen (*inf*).

kittenish ['kɪtənɪʃ] *adj* verspielt; (*fig*) *woman* kokett.

kittiwake ['kɪtɪweɪk] *n* Dreizehenmöwe *f*.

kitty ['kɪtɪ] *n* **(a)** (*shared money*) (gemeinsame) Kasse; (*Cards etc also*) Spielkasse *f* ◆ **we'll have a ~ for the drinks** wir machen eine Umlage für die Getränke; **I've nothing left in the ~** die Kasse ist leer. **(b)** (*inf: cat*) Mieze *f*.

kiwi ['kiːwiː] *n* **(a)** Kiwi *m*. **(b)** (*also* **~ fruit**) Kiwi(frucht) *f*. **(c)** (*inf: New Zealander*) Neuseeländer(in *f*) *m*, Kiwi *mf* (*inf*).

KKK *abbr of* **Ku Klux Klan**.

klaxon ['klæksn] *n* Horn *nt*, Hupe *f*.

Kleenex ® ['kliːneks] *n* Tempo(taschentuch) ® *nt*.

kleptomania [,kleptəʊ'meɪnɪə] *n* Kleptomanie *f*.

kleptomaniac [,kleptəʊ'meɪnɪæk] [1] *n* Kleptomane *m*, Kleptomanin *f*.
[2] *adj* kleptomanisch.

km *abbr of* **kilometre(s)** km.

km/h, kmph *abbr of* **kilometres per hour** km/h.

knack [næk] *n* Trick, Kniff *m*; (*talent*) Talent, Geschick *nt* ◆ **there's a (special) ~ (to** *or* **in it)** da ist ein (gewisser) Trick *or* Kniff dabei; **there's a (special) ~ to opening it** da ist ein Trick *or* Kniff dabei, wie man das aufbekommt; **to learn** *or* **get the ~ of doing sth** (es) herausbekommen, wie man etw macht; **you'll soon get the ~ of it** Sie werden den Dreh bald rausbekommen *or* raushaben; **I've lost the ~** ich bekomme *or* kriege (*inf*) das nicht mehr hin *or* fertig; **she's got a ~ of saying the wrong thing** sie hat ein Geschick *or* Talent, immer das Falsche zu sagen.

knacker ['nækəʳ] *n* (*Brit*) (*of horses*) Abdecker, Schinder *m*; (*of boats, houses*) Abbruchunternehmer *m* ◆ **to send a horse to the ~'s (yard)** ein Pferd zum Abdecker *or* auf den Schindanger (*old*) bringen.

knackered ['nækəd] *adj* (*Brit sl*) kaputt (*inf*), ausgebufft (*sl*).

knapsack ['næpsæk] *n* Proviantbeutel, Tornister (*esp Mil*), Knappsack (*old*) *m*.

knave [neɪv] *n* **(a)** (*old*) Bube (*old*), Schurke *m*. **(b)** (*Cards*) Bube, Unter (*old*) *m*.

knavery ['neɪvərɪ] *n* (*old*) Bubenstück *nt* (*old*), Büberei *f* (*old*).

knavish ['neɪvɪʃ] *adj* (*old*) bübisch (*old*), schurkisch.

knead [niːd] *vt wax etc* kneten; (*massage*) *muscles* massieren, durchkneten (*inf*).

knee [niː] [1] *n* Knie *nt* ◆ **to be on one's ~s** (*lit, fig*) auf den Knien liegen; **on one's ~s, on bended ~(s)** (*liter, hum*) kniefällig; **to go (down) on one's ~s** (*lit*) niederknien, (sich) hinknien; (*fig*) sich auf die Knie werfen; **to go down on one's ~s to sb** (*lit, fig*) sich vor jdm auf die Knie werfen, vor jdm einen Kniefall machen; **to bow** *or* **bend the ~ (to sb)** (vor jdm) die Knie beugen; **to bring sb to his ~s** (*lit, fig*) jdn in die Knie zwingen; **he sank in up to the** *or* **his ~s** er sank knietief *or* bis zu den Knien ein; **at ~ level** in Kniehöhe; **I'll put you over my ~ in a minute** ich lege dich gleich übers Knie.
[2] *vt* mit dem Knie stoßen ◆ **he ~d his opponent in the chest** er hat seinem Gegner mit dem Knie eins gegen den Brustkasten gegeben (*inf*).

knee: ~ breeches *npl* Kniehose, Bundhose *f*; **~cap** [1] *n* Kniescheibe *f*; [2] *vt* die Kniescheibe(n) durchschießen (+ *dat*); **~-deep** *adj* knietief; **the water was ~-deep** das Wasser ging mir *etc* bis zum Knie *or* war knietief; **he was ~-deep in mud** er steckte knietief im Schlamm; **~-high** *adj* kniehoch, in

Kniehöhe; ~ **jerk** *n (Med)* Kniesehnenreflex *m*; **~-jerk reaction** *n* Kurzschlußreaktion *f*; ~ **joint** *n (Med, Tech)* Kniegelenk *nt*.

kneel [niːl] *pret, ptp* **knelt** *or* **~ed** *vi (before* vor *+dat)* knien; *(also* **~ down***)* niederknien, (sich) hinknien.

knee-length ['niːleŋθ] *adj skirt* knielang; *boots* kniehoch.

kneeler ['niːləʳ] *n* Kniepolster *nt*; *(stool)* Kniebank *f*.

knee: ~pad *n* Knieschützer *m*, Knieleder *nt*; ~ **reflex** *n* Kniesehnenreflex *m*.

knees-up ['niːzʌp] *n (Brit inf) (dance)* Tanz *m*; *(party)* Fete, Party *f*.

knell [nel] *n* Geläut *nt*, (Toten)glocke *f* ◆ **to sound the ~** die (Toten)glocke läuten.

knelt [nelt] *pret, ptp of* **kneel**.

knew [njuː] *pret of* **know**.

knickerbockers ['nɪkəbɒkəz] *npl* Knickerbocker *pl*.

knickers ['nɪkəz] *npl* **(a)** Schlüpfer *m* ◆ **to get one's ~ in a twist** *(sl)* sich *(dat)* ins Hemd machen *(sl)*; **don't get your ~ in a twist!** *(sl)* dreh nicht gleich durch! *(inf)*; **~!** *(sl) (rubbish)* Quatsch! *(inf)*; *(bother)* Mist! *(inf)*. **(b)** *(old) see* **knickerbockers**.

knick-knack ['nɪknæk] *n* nette Kleinigkeit, Kinkerlitzchen *nt* ◆ **~s** Krimskrams *m*; *(esp figurines)* Nippes, Nippsachen *pl*.

knife [naɪf] [1] *n, pl* **knives** Messer *nt* ◆ **~, fork and spoon** Besteck *nt*; **he's got his ~ into me** *(inf)* der hat es auf mich abgesehen *(inf)*; **to be/go under the ~** *(Med inf)* unterm Messer sein *(inf)*/unters Messer kommen *(inf)*; **to turn** *or* **twist the ~ (in the wound)** *(fig)* Salz in die Wunde streuen; **before you could say ~** *(inf)* eh' man sich's versah, im Nu; **it's war to the ~ between them** sie bekämpfen sich bis aufs Messer.

[2] *vt* einstechen auf *(+acc)*; *(fatally)* erstechen, erdolchen.

knife: ~ box *n* Besteckkasten *m*; ~ **edge** *n (lit)* (Messer)schneide *f*; **to be balanced on a ~ edge** *(fig)* auf Messers Schneide stehen; ~ **grinder** *n (person)* Scherenschleifer(in *f*) *m*; *(thing)* Schleifrad *nt or* -stein *m*; ~ **pleat** *n* einfache Falte; **~-point** *n* **to hold sb at ~-point** jdn mit einem Messer bedrohen; **to force sb to do sth at ~-point** jdn mit vorgehaltenem Messer zwingen, etw zu tun; ~ **rest** *n* Messerbänkchen *nt*; ~ **sharpener** *n* Messerschärfer *m*.

knifing ['naɪfɪŋ] *n* Messerstecherei *f*.

knight [naɪt] [1] *n (title, Hist)* Ritter *m*; *(Chess)* Springer *m*, Pferd(chen), Rössel *nt* ◆ **K~ of the Garter** Träger *m* des Hosenbandordens; **~ of the road** *(Brit hum)* Kapitän *m* der Landstraße *(hum)*.

[2] *vt* adeln, zum Ritter schlagen.

knight: ~ errant *n, pl* **~s errant** fahrender Ritter; **~-errantry** [naɪt'erəntrɪ] *n* fahrendes Rittertum; *(fig)* Ritterlichkeit *f*.

knighthood ['naɪthʊd] *n* **(a)** *(knights collectively)* Ritterschaft *f*. **(b)** *(rank)* Ritterstand *m* ◆ **to receive a ~** in den Adelsstand erhoben werden; **he's going for a ~** er hat es darauf abgesehen, in den Adelsstand erhoben zu werden.

knightly ['naɪtlɪ] *adj (+er)* ritterlich.

knit [nɪt] *pret, ptp* **~ted** *or* **~** [1] *vt* **(a)** stricken ◆ **the wool is then ~ted into ...** aus der Wolle wird dann ... gestrickt; **~ three, purl two** drei rechts, zwei links. **(b) to ~ one's brow** die Stirn runzeln.

[2] *vi* **(a)** stricken. **(b)** *(bones: also* **~ together, ~ up***)* verwachsen, zusammenwachsen.

◆**knit together** [1] *vt sep* **(a)** *stitches* zusammenstricken. **(b)** *(unite) threads of story* (miteinander) verknüpfen; *people* eng verbinden.

[2] *vi* **(a)** *see* **knit 2 (b)**. **(b)** *(unite)* miteinander verwachsen ◆ **they ~ well ~** sie harmonieren gut; *(through experience)* sie sind gut aufeinander eingespielt.

◆**knit up** [1] *vi* **(a)** *(wool)* sich stricken. **(b)** *see* **knit 2 (b)**.

[2] *vt sep jersey* stricken.

knitted ['nɪtɪd] *adj* gestrickt; *cardigan, dress etc* Strick- ◆ **~ goods** Strickwaren *or* -sachen *pl*.

knitter ['nɪtəʳ] *n* Stricker(in *f*) *m*.

knitting ['nɪtɪŋ] *n* **(a)** Stricken *nt*; *(material being knitted)* Strickzeug *nt*, Strickarbeit *f*; *(knitted goods)* Gestrickte(s) *nt*, Stricksachen *pl* ◆ **this cardigan is a nice piece of ~** die Jacke ist schön gestrickt; **she was doing her ~** sie strickte.

(b) *(of bones etc)* Verwachsen, Zusammenwachsen *nt*.

knitting: ~ machine *n* Strickmaschine *f*; ~ **needle** *n* Stricknadel *f*; ~ **wool** *n* (Strick)wolle *f*, Strickgarn *nt*.

knitwear ['nɪtwɛəʳ] *n* Strickwaren, Strick- *or* Wollsachen *pl*.

knives [naɪvz] *pl of* **knife**.

knob [nɒb] *n* **(a)** *(on walking stick)* Knauf *m*; *(on door also)* Griff *m*; *(on instrument etc)* Knopf *m* ◆ **and the same to you with (brass) ~s on** *(Brit sl)* das beruht auf Gegenseitigkeit. **(b)** *(swelling)* Beule *f*, Knubbel *m (inf)*; *(on tree)* Knoten, Auswuchs *m*. **(c)** *(small piece)* Stückchen *nt*.

knobbly ['nɒblɪ] *adj (+er) wood* knorrig, verwachsen; *surface* uneben, höckrig, knubbelig *(inf)* ◆ **~ knees** Knubbelknie *pl (inf)*.

knobby ['nɒbɪ] *adj (+er) wood, trunk* knorrig.

knock [nɒk] [1] *n* **(a)** *(blow)* Stoß *m*; *(esp with hand, tool etc)* Schlag *m* ◆ **to get a ~** einen Stoß/Schlag abbekommen; **my head got a ~, I got a ~ on the head** *(was hit)* ich habe einen Schlag auf den Kopf bekommen; *(hit myself)* ich habe mir den Kopf angeschlagen *or* angestoßen; **his knee got a ~** er hat sich *(dat)* das Knie angeschlagen; **he got a ~ from the swing** die Schaukel hat ihn getroffen; **he had a bit of a ~** er hat etwas abbekommen *(inf)*; **the car got a few ~s** das Auto ist ein paarmal gerammt worden, mit dem Auto hat es ein paarmal gebumst *(inf)*; **the gatepost got a ~ from the car** das Auto hat den Torpfosten gerammt; **the furniture has had a few ~s** die Möbel haben ein paar Schrammen abbekommen; **he gave himself a nasty ~** er hat sich böse angeschlagen *or* angestoßen; **he gave the car/lamppost a ~** er hat das Auto/den Laternenpfahl gerammt.

(b) *(noise)* Klopfen, Pochen *(liter) nt no pl*; *(in engine)* Klopfen *nt no pl*, Klopfgeräusch *nt* ◆ **there was a ~ at the door** es hat (an der Tür) geklopft; **I heard a ~** ich habe es klopfen hören; **I'll give you a ~ at 7 o'clock** *(Brit)* ich klopfe um 7 Uhr (an deine Tür).

(c) *(fig: setback)* (Tief)schlag *m* ◆ **~s** *(inf: criticism)* Kritik *f*; **to (have to) take a lot of ~s** viele Tiefschläge einstecken (müssen); *(be criticized)* unter starken Beschuß kommen; **to take a ~** *(self-confidence, pride etc)* erschüttert werden; *(person)* einen Tiefschlag erleben; **the company took a bit of a ~ as a result of the tax changes** die Steuerreform hat der Firma einen Schlag versetzt.

[2] *vt* **(a)** *(hit, strike)* stoßen; *(with hand, tool, racket etc)* schlagen; *one's knee, head etc* anschlagen, anstoßen *(on* an *+dat)*; *(nudge, jolt)* stoßen gegen; *(collide with) (car, driver)* rammen ◆ **to ~ one's head/elbow** *etc* sich *(dat)* den Kopf/Ellbogen *etc* anschlagen *or* anstoßen; **he ~ed his foot against a stone** er stieß mit dem Fuß gegen einen Stein; **to ~ sb on the head** jdn an *or* auf den Kopf schlagen; **that ~ed his plans on the head** *(inf)* das hat all seine Pläne über den Haufen geworfen *(inf)*; **to ~ sb to the ground** jdn zu Boden werfen; **to ~ sb unconscious** jdn bewußtlos werden lassen; *(person)* jdn bewußtlos schlagen; **he ~ed some holes in the side of the box** er machte ein paar Löcher in die Seite der Kiste; **to ~ holes in an argument** ein Argument zerpflücken; **to ~ sb/sth out of the way** jdn/etw beiseite stoßen; **he ~ed it as he went past** er ist beim Vorbeigehen dagegengestoßen; *(deliberately)* er hat ihm/ihr *etc* beim Vorbeigehen einen Stoß versetzt *or* gegeben; **she ~ed the glass to the ground** sie stieß gegen das Glas, und es fiel zu Boden; **don't ~ your glass off the table** werfen *or* stoßen Sie Ihr Glas nicht vom Tisch; **somebody ~ed the nose off the statue** jemand hat der Statue die Nase abgeschlagen; **to ~ the nonsense out of sb** jdm den Unsinn austreiben; **to ~ some sense into sb** *or* **sb's head** jdn zur Vernunft bringen.

(b) *(inf: criticize)* (he)runtermachen *(inf)* ◆ **if you don't know it, don't ~ it** verdamme doch nicht etwas, was du überhaupt nicht kennst.

[3] *vi* **(a)** klopfen, pochen *(liter)*; *(engine etc)* klopfen ◆ **to ~ at the door/window** an die Tür klopfen, anklopfen/gegen das Fenster klopfen; **~ before entering** bitte anklopfen; **he ~ed on the table** er schlug *or* klopfte auf den Tisch.

(b) *(bump, collide)* stoßen *(into, against* gegen*)* ◆ **he ~ed into** *or* **against the gatepost** er rammte den Türpfosten.

(c) his knees were ~ing ihm zitterten *or* schlotterten *(inf)* die Knie.

[4] *interj* **~ ~!** klopf, klopf.

◆**knock about** *or* **around** [1] *vi (inf)* **(a)** *(person)* herumziehen *(prep obj* in *+dat)* ◆ **to ~ ~ the house** im Haus rumgammeln *(inf)*; **he has ~ed ~ a bit** er ist schon (ganz schön) (he)rumgekommen *(inf)*.

(b) *(object)* herumliegen *(prep obj* in *+dat)*.

[2] *vt sep* **(a)** *(ill-treat)* verprügeln, schlagen ◆ **he was badly ~ed ~ in the crash** er ist beim Unfall ziemlich zugerichtet worden.

(b) *(damage)* ramponieren *(inf)*, beschädigen ◆ **the car/place was rather ~ed ~** das Auto/das Zimmer *etc* war ziemlich mitgenommen.

(c) to ~ a ball ~ ein paar Bälle schlagen.

◆**knock back** *vt sep (inf)* **(a) he ~ed ~ his whisky** er kippte sich *(dat)* den Whisky hinter die Binde *(inf)*; **come on, ~ it ~** nun trink schon (aus) *(inf)*.

(b) *(cost)* **this watch ~ed me ~ £20** ich habe für die Uhr £ 20 hingelegt, die Uhr hat mich £ 20 gekostet; **what did they ~ you ~ for it?** was mußten Sie dafür hinlegen *or* blechen? *(inf)*.

(c) *(shock)* schocken, erschüttern.

(d) *(reject)* zurückweisen.

◆**knock down** *vt sep* **(a)** *person, thing* umwerfen, zu Boden werfen; *opponent (by hitting)* niederschlagen; *(car, driver)* anfahren, umfahren; *(fatally)* überfahren; *building* abreißen, niederreißen; *tree* fällen, umhauen; *door* einschlagen; *obstacle, fence* niederreißen; *(car)* umfahren ◆ **she was ~ed ~ and killed** sie wurde überfahren; **he ~ed him ~ with one blow** er schlug *or* streckte *(geh)* ihn mit einem Schlag zu Boden.

(b) *price (buyer)* herunterhandeln *(to* auf *+acc)*; *(seller)* heruntergehen mit ◆ **I managed to ~ him ~ a pound** ich konnte ein Pfund herunterhandeln; **I ~ed him ~ to £15** ich habe es auf £ 15 heruntergehandelt; **he ~ed the price ~ by £5 for me** er hat mir £ 5 nachgelassen.

(c) *(at auction)* zuschlagen *(to sb* jdm*)* ◆ **to be ~ed ~ at £1** für ein Pfund versteigert werden.

(d) *machine, furniture* zerlegen, auseinandernehmen.

◆**knock in** *vt sep nail* einschlagen.

◆**knock off** [1] *vi (inf)* aufhören, Feierabend *or* Schluß machen *(inf)* ◆ **let's ~ ~ now** Schluß für heute *(inf)*; **to ~ ~ for lunch** Mittag machen.

[2] *vt sep* **(a)** *(lit) vase, cup, person etc* hinunterstoßen; *nose off statue etc* abschlagen; *insect* abschütteln; *high jump bar* reißen ◆ **the branch ~ed the rider ~ (his horse)** der Ast riß den Reiter vom Pferd.

(b) *(inf: reduce price by)* nachlassen *(for sb* jdm*)*, runtergehen *(inf)* ◆ **he ~ed £5 ~ the bill/price** er hat £ 5 von der Rechnung/vom Preis nachgelassen; **I got something ~ed ~** ich habe es billiger bekommen.

(c) *(inf: do quickly) essay, painting* hinhauen *(inf)*; *(with good result)* aus dem Ärmel schütteln *(inf)*.

(d) *(Brit sl: steal)* klauen *(inf)*.

(e) *(sl: kill)* umlegen *(inf)*.

(f) *(inf: stop)* aufhören mit; *smoking, criticizing* stecken *(sl)* ◆ **to ~ ~ work** Feierabend machen; **~ it ~!** nun hör schon auf!

◆**knock out** *vt sep* **(a)** *tooth* ausschlagen; *nail* herausschlagen *(of* aus*)*; *pipe*

ausklopfen; *contents* herausklopfen (*of* aus).
(b) (*stun*) bewußtlos werden lassen; (*by hitting*) bewußtlos schlagen, k.o. schlagen; (*Boxing*) k.o. schlagen; (*drink*) umhauen (*inf*) ◆ **he was ~ed ~** er wurde bewußtlos; (*Boxing*) er wurde k.o. geschlagen; ihn hat's umgehauen (*inf*).
(c) (*from competition*) besiegen (*of* in *+dat*) ◆ **to be ~ed ~** ausscheiden, rausfliegen (*inf*) (*of* aus).
(d) (*inf: stun, shock*) (*good news*) umwerfen, umhauen (*inf*); (*bad news, sb's death etc*) schocken.
(e) (*sl: bowl over*) hinreißen (*inf*), umhauen (*inf*) ◆ **that music really ~s me ~** die Musik ist wirklich irre (*sl*) *or* umwerfend.
(f) (*inf: exhaust*) schaffen (*inf*), kaputtmachen (*inf*).

◆**knock over** *vt sep* umwerfen, umstoßen; (*car*) anfahren; (*fatally*) überfahren.

◆**knock together** [1] *vi* **his knees were ~ing ~** seine Knie zitterten *or* schlotterten (*inf*).
[2] *vt sep* **(a)** (*make hurriedly*) *shelter, object* zusammenzimmern; *meal, snack* auf die Beine stellen (*inf*). **(b)** (*lit*) aneinanderstoßen ◆ **I'd like to ~ their heads ~** man sollte die beiden zur Räson bringen.

◆**knock up** [1] *vi* **(a)** (*Brit Sport*) sich einspielen, ein paar Bälle schlagen. **(b)** (*US sl*) bumsen (*inf*).
[2] *vt sep* **(a)** (*hit upwards*) hochschlagen.
(b) (*Brit: wake*) (auf)wecken.
(c) (*make hurriedly*) *meal* auf die Beine stellen (*inf*); *building* hochziehen, hinstellen; *shelter* zusammenzimmern.
(d) (*Brit sl: exhaust*) kaputtmachen (*inf*), schaffen (*inf*); (*experience, shock*) schaffen (*inf*).
(e) (*sl*) (*make pregnant*) ein Kind anhängen (*+dat*) (*inf*), ein Kind machen (*+dat*) (*inf*); (*US: have sex with*) bumsen mit (*inf*) ◆ **she's ~ed ~** die hat 'nen dicken Bauch (*sl*).
(f) (*Cricket*) **to ~ ~ 20 runs** 20 Läufe machen.
(g) (*inf: do*) *mileage* fahren; *overtime* machen.

knock: ~about [1] *adj* **~about comedy** (*Theat*) Klamaukstück *nt*; **~about clothes** gammelige Kleidung; [2] *n* (*Naut*) kleiner Einmaster; **~-down** *adj attr furniture etc* zerlegbar; **~-down price** Schleuderpreis *m*; (*at auction*) Mindestpreis *m*; **~-down blow** (*Boxing*) Niederschlag *m*.

knocker ['nɒkəʳ] *n* **(a)** (*door ~*) (Tür)klopfer *m*.
(b) **(pair of) ~s** (*Brit sl: breasts*) Vorbau *m* (*inf*); **what a pair of ~s!** toller Vorbau (*inf*), ganz schön Holz vor der Hütte (*sl*).
(c) (*inf: critic*) Kritikaster *m* (*inf*) ◆ **every good new idea is sure to have its ~s** bei jeder guten Idee gibt's jemanden, der was dran auszusetzen hat.

knock-for-knock ['nɒkfə'nɒk] *adj* (*Insur*) **~ agreement** *Vereinbarung, bei der jede Versicherungsgesellschaft den Schaden des von ihr versicherten Fahrzeugs übernimmt.*

knocking ['nɒkɪŋ] *n* **(a)** Klopfen, Pochen (*liter*) *nt*; (*in engine*) Klopfen *nt*. **(b)** (*inf*) Kritik *f* (*of an +dat*) ◆ **he has taken** *or* **had a lot of ~** er ist ziemlich unter Beschuß gekommen.

knocking: ~ copy *n* (*in advertising*) Negativwerbung *f*; **~-off time** *n* (*inf*) Feierabend *m*; **~ shop** *n* (*Brit sl*) Puff *m* (*inf*).

knock: ~-kneed [nɒk'ni:d] *adj* X-beinig; **to be ~-kneed** X-Beine haben; **~-on effect** *n* Folgewirkungen *pl* (*on* auf *+acc*); **~out** [1] *n* (*Boxing*) Knockout, K.o. *m*; (*inf: person, thing*) Wucht *f* (*inf*); [2] *attr* **(a)** (*Boxing, fig*) **~out blow** K.o.-Schlag *m*; **(b)** **~out competition** Ausscheidungskampf *m*; **~-up** *n* (*Brit Sport*) **to have a ~-up** ein paar Bälle schlagen.

knoll [nəʊl] *n* Hügel *m*, Kuppe *f*.

knot [nɒt] [1] *n* **(a)** (*in string, tie, fig*) Knoten *m*; (*in muscle*) Verspannung *f* ◆ **to tie/undo** *or* **untie a ~** einen Knoten machen/aufmachen *or* lösen; **marriage ~** Band *nt or* Bund *m* der Ehe (*geh*); **to tie the ~** (*fig*) den Bund fürs Leben schließen; **to tie oneself (up) in ~s** (*fig*) sich immer mehr verwickeln *or* tiefer verstricken; **his stomach was in a ~** sein Magen krampfte sich zusammen; **his muscles stood out in ~s** seine Muskeln traten vor *or* wölbten sich; **the whole matter is full of legal ~s** die ganze Sache ist rechtlich äußerst verwickelt.
(b) (*Naut: speed*) Knoten *m* ◆ **to make 20 ~s** 20 Knoten machen; *see* **rate**[1] **1 (a)**.
(c) (*in wood*) Ast *m*, Verwachsung *f*.
(d) (*group*) Knäuel *m* ◆ **a ~ of tourists** ein Touristenknäuel *m*.
[2] *vt* einen Knoten machen in (*+acc*); (*~ together*) verknoten, verknüpfen ◆ **to ~ sth to sth** etw mit etw verknoten; **get ~ted!** (*sl*) du kannst mich mal! (*inf*), rutsch mir den Buckel runter! (*inf*); **I told him to get ~ted** (*sl*) ich hab ihm gesagt, er kann mich mal (*inf*) *or* er kann mir den Buckel runterrutschen (*inf*).
[3] *vi* sich verknoten, Knoten bilden.

◆**knot together** *vt sep* verknoten.

knotty ['nɒtɪ] *adj* (*+er*) *wood* astreich, knorrig; *veins, rope* knotig; *problem* verwickelt, verzwickt (*inf*).

knout [naʊt] *n* Knute *f*.

▼ **know** [nəʊ] (*vb: pret* **knew**, *ptp* **known**) [1] *vti* **(a)** (*have knowledge about*) wissen; *answer, facts, dates, details, results etc also* kennen; *French, English etc* können ◆ **to ~ how to do sth** (*in theory*) wissen, wie man etw macht; (*in practice*) etw tun können; **he ~s a thing or two** (*inf*) er weiß Bescheid, er weiß ganz schön viel (*inf*); **she ~s all the answers** sie weiß Bescheid, sie kennt sich aus; (*pej*) sie weiß immer alles besser; **he thinks he ~s all the answers** *or* **everything** er meint, er wüßte alles; **do you ~ the difference between ...?** wissen Sie, was der Unterschied zwischen ... ist?; **to ~ that/why ...** wissen, daß/warum ...; **he knew himself (to be) guilty** er wußte, daß er schuldig war, er wußte sich schuldig (*liter*); **to let sb ~ sth** (*not keep back*) jdn etw wissen lassen; (*tell, inform*) jdm von etw Bescheid sagen *or* geben; **he soon let me ~ what he thought of it** er hat mich schnell wissen lassen, was er davon hielt; **when can you let me ~?** wann können Sie es mich wissen lassen?, wann können Sie mir Bescheid sagen?; **that's what *I'd* like to ~ (too)** das möchte ich auch wissen; ***that's* what I'd like to ~** das möchte ich wirklich wissen; **that's worth ~ing** das ist ja interessant; **that might be worth ~ing** es könnte interessant sein, das zu wissen; **as far as I ~** soviel ich weiß, meines Wissens; **he might even be dead for all I ~** vielleicht ist er sogar tot, was weiß ich; **not that I ~** nicht daß ich wüßte; **who ~s?** wer weiß?, weiß ich's; **there's no ~ing** (*inf*) das kann keiner sagen, das weiß niemand; **there's no ~ing what he'll do** man weiß nie, was er noch tut; **the channel was rough, as I well ~** *or* **as well I ~!** die Überfahrt war stürmisch, das kann ich dir sagen; **I'd have you ~ that ...** ich möchte doch sehr betonen, daß ...; **to ~ what one is talking about** wissen, wovon man redet; **to ~ one's own mind** wissen, was man will; **before you ~ where you are** ehe man sich's versieht; **I've been a fool and don't I ~ it!** (*inf*) ich seh's ja ein, ich war doof (*inf*), ich war vielleicht doof (*inf*); **she's angry! — don't I ~ it!** (*inf*) sie ist wütend! — wem sagst du das! (*inf*); **he just didn't want to ~** er wollte einfach nicht hören; **afterwards they just didn't want to ~** nachher wollten sie einfach nichts mehr davon wissen; **he didn't want to ~ me** er wollte nichts mit mir zu tun haben; **I ~!** ich weiß!, weiß ich (doch)!; (*having a good idea*) ich weiß was!, ich habe eine Idee!; **I don't ~** (das) weiß ich nicht; **I wouldn't ~** (*inf*) weiß ich (doch) nicht (*inf*); **don't you ~?** weißt du das denn nicht?; **how should I ~?** wie soll ich das wissen?; **what do you ~!** (*inf*) sieh mal einer an!; **what do you ~! I've just seen her!** (*inf*) stellen Sie sich vor, ich habe sie eben gesehen; **you never ~** man kann nie wissen.
(b) **you ~, we could/there is ...** weißt du, wir könnten/da ist ...; **he gave it away/he didn't come, you ~** er hat es nämlich weggegeben/er ist nämlich nicht gekommen; **if you come back later, she might be back, you ~** (wissen Sie,) wenn Sie später noch einmal kommen, ist sie vielleicht da; **it's raining, you ~** es regnet; **then there was this man, you ~, and ...** und da war dieser Mann, nicht (wahr), und ...; **and then we'll go to your place, you ~, and ...** und dann gehen wir zu dir, nicht (wahr), und ...; **it's long and purple and, you ~, sort of crinkly** es ist lang und lila und, na ja, so kraus.
(c) (*be acquainted with*) *people, places, book, author* kennen ◆ **I ~ Bavaria well** ich kenne Bayern gut, ich kenne mich gut in Bayern aus; **to get to ~ sb/sth** jdn/etw kennenlernen; **do you ~ him to speak to?** kennen Sie ihn näher?; **if I ~ John, he'll already be there** wie ich John kenne, ist er schon da; **~ thyself!** erkenne dich selbst!; *see* **name 1 (a)**, **sight 1 (b)**.
(d) **to get to ~ sb/a place** jdn/einen Ort kennenlernen; **to get to ~ sth** *methods, techniques, style, pronunciation etc* etw lernen; *habits, faults, shortcuts etc* etw herausfinden.
(e) (*recognize*) erkennen ◆ **to ~ sb by his voice/walk** *etc* jdn an der Stimme/am Gang *etc* erkennen; **would you ~ him again?** würden Sie ihn wiedererkennen?; **he ~s a good thing when he sees it** er weiß, was gut ist; **he ~s a bargain/good manuscript when he sees one** er weiß, was ein guter Kauf/ein gutes Manuskript ist.
(f) (*be able to distinguish*) unterscheiden können ◆ **don't you ~ your right from your left?** können Sie rechts und links nicht unterscheiden?; **you wouldn't ~ him from his brother** Sie könnten ihn nicht von seinem Bruder unterscheiden; **to ~ the difference between right and wrong, to ~ right from wrong** den Unterschied zwischen Gut und Böse kennen, Gut und Böse unterscheiden können; **he wouldn't ~ the difference** das merkt er nicht; **he doesn't ~ one end of a horse/hammer from the other** er hat keine Ahnung von Pferden/er hat keine Ahnung, was ein Hammer ist (*inf*).
(g) (*experience*) erleben ◆ **I've never ~n it to rain so heavily** so einen starken Regen habe ich noch nie erlebt; **I've never ~n him to smile** ich habe ihn noch nie lächeln sehen, ich habe es noch nie erlebt, daß er lächelt; **you have never ~n me to tell a lie** Sie haben mich noch nie lügen hören; **have you ever ~n such a thing to happen before?** haben Sie je schon so etwas erlebt?, ist Ihnen so etwas schon einmal vorgekommen?
(h) (*in passive*) **to be ~n (to sb)** (jdm) bekannt sein; **it is (well) ~n that ...** es ist (allgemein) bekannt, daß ...; **is he/that ~n here?** ist er/das hier bekannt?, kennt man ihn/das hier?; **he is ~n to have been here** man weiß, daß er hier war; **he is ~n as Mr X** man kennt ihn als Herrn X; **she wishes to be ~n as Mrs X** sie möchte Frau X genannt werden; **to make sb/sth ~n** jdn/etw bekanntmachen; **to make oneself ~n** sich melden (*to sb* bei jdm); (*introduce oneself*) sich vorstellen (*to sb* jdm); (*become well-known*) sich (*dat*) einen Namen machen; **to become ~n** bekannt werden; (*famous*) berühmt werden; **to make one's presence ~n** sich melden (*to* bei).
(i) **I ~ better than that** ich bin ja nicht ganz dumm; **I ~ better than to say something like that** ich werde mich hüten, so etwas zu sagen; **he ~s better than to eat into his capital** er ist nicht so dumm, sein Kapital anzugreifen; **he/you ought to have ~n better** das war dumm (von ihm/dir); **he ought to have** *or* **should have ~n better than to do that** es war dumm von ihm, das zu tun; **you ought to ~ better at your age** in deinem Alter müßte man das aber (besser) wissen; **they don't ~ any better** sie kennen's nicht anders; **he says he didn't do it, but I ~ better** er sagt, er war es nicht, aber ich weiß, daß das nicht stimmt; **mother always ~s best** Mutter weiß es am besten; **OK, you ~ best** o.k., Sie müssen's wissen.
(j) (*obs, Bibl: sexually*) erkennen.
[2] *n* (*inf*) **to be in the ~** eingeweiht sein, im Bild sein (*inf*), Bescheid wissen (*inf*); **the people in the ~ say ...** Leute, die darüber Bescheid wissen, sagen ...,

➤ LANGUAGE IN USE: **know: 1a** → 15.1, 15.4, 16.1, 16.4, 26.3

die Fachleute sagen ...

◆**know about** [1] *vi +prep obj (have factual knowledge, experience of) history, maths, politics* sich auskennen in (*+dat*); *Africa* Bescheid wissen über (*+acc*); *women, cars, horses* sich auskennen mit; (*be aware of, have been told about*) wissen von ◆ **I ~ ~ that** das weiß ich; **I didn't ~ ~ that** das wußte ich nicht; **I only knew ~ it yesterday** ich habe erst gestern davon gehört; **I'd rather not ~ ~ it** das möchte ich lieber nicht wissen; **did you ~ ~ Maggie?** weißt du über Maggie Bescheid?; **I ~ ~ John, but is anyone else absent?** John, das weiß ich, aber fehlt sonst noch jemand?; **to get to ~ ~ sb/sth** von jdm/etw hören; **I don't ~ ~ that** davon weiß ich nichts; (*don't agree*) da bin ich aber nicht so sicher; **that isn't ~n ~** davon weiß man nichts; **she's very clever, isn't she? — I don't ~ ~ clever, but she certainly knows how to use people** sie ist sehr klug, nicht wahr? — klug, na, ich weiß nicht, aber sie weiß Leute auszunutzen.
[2] *vt sep +prep obj* **to ~ a lot/nothing/something ~ sth** (*have factual knowledge*) viel/nichts/etwas über etw (*acc*) wissen; (*in history, maths etc*) in etw (*dat*) gut/nicht/etwas Bescheid wissen; (*about women, cars, horses etc*) viel/nichts/etwas von etw verstehen; (*be aware of, have been told about*) viel/nichts/etwas von etw wissen; **that was the first I knew ~ it** davon hatte ich nichts gewußt; **not much is ~n ~ that** darüber weiß man nicht viel; **I ~ all ~ that** da kenne ich mich aus; (*I'm aware of that*) das weiß ich; (*I've been told about it*) ich weiß Bescheid; **I ~ all ~ you** ich weiß über Sie Bescheid; **that's all you ~ ~ it!** (*iro*) das meinst auch nur du!

◆**know of** *vi +prep obj café, better method* kennen; (*have heard of*) *sb, sb's death* gehört haben von ◆ **I soon got to ~ ~ all the facts/all his hang-ups** ich war bald über alle Fakten/all seine Komplexe informiert; **not that I ~ ~** nicht, daß ich wüßte.

knowable ['nəʊəbl] *adj* der/die/das man wissen kann.

know: ~-all *n* Alleswisser, Besserwisser *m*; **~-how** *n* praktische Kenntnis, Know-how *nt*; **he hasn't got the ~-how for the job** er hat nicht die nötige Sachkenntnis für diese Arbeit.

knowing ['nəʊɪŋ] *adj look, smile* wissend; *person* verständnisvoll.

knowingly ['nəʊɪŋlɪ] *adv* **(a)** (*consciously*) bewußt, absichtlich, wissentlich. **(b)** *look, smile* wissend.

know-it-all ['nəʊɪtɔːl] *n* (*US*) *see* **know-all**.

▼ **knowledge** ['nɒlɪdʒ] *n* **(a)** (*understanding, awareness*) Wissen *nt*, Kenntnis *f* ◆ **to have ~ of** Kenntnis haben *or* besitzen von, wissen von; **to have no ~ of** keine Kenntnis haben von, nichts wissen von; **to (the best of) my ~** soviel ich weiß, meines Wissens; **to the best of my ~ and belief** nach bestem Wissen und Gewissen; **not to my ~** nicht, daß ich wüßte; **without his ~** ohne sein Wissen; **without the ~ of her mother** ohne Wissen ihrer Mutter, ohne daß ihre Mutter es wußte/weiß; **it has come to my ~ that ...** ich habe erfahren, daß ...
▼ **(b)** (*learning, facts learnt*) Kenntnisse *pl*, Wissen *nt* ◆ **my ~ of English** meine Englischkenntnisse *pl*; **my ~ of D.H. Lawrence** was ich von D.H. Lawrence kenne; **I have a thorough ~ of this subject** auf diesem Gebiet weiß ich gründlich Bescheid *or* besitze ich umfassende Kenntnisse; **the police have no ~ of him/his activities** die Polizei weiß nichts über ihn/seine Aktivitäten; **his ~ will die with him** sein Wissen wird mit ihm sterben; **the advance of ~** der Fortschritt der Wissenschaft.

knowledgeable ['nɒlɪdʒəbl] *adj person* kenntnisreich, bewandert; *report* gut fundiert ◆ **to be ~** viel wissen (*about* über *+acc*).

known [nəʊn] [1] *ptp of* **know**.
[2] *adj* bekannt; *expert also* anerkannt ◆ **it is a ~ fact that ...** es ist (allgemein) bekannt, daß ...; **~ quantity** bekannte Größe.

knuckle ['nʌkl] *n* (Finger)knöchel *m*; (*of meat*) Hachse, Haxe *f*; *see* **near 2 (a)**, **rap**.

◆**knuckle down** *vi* (*inf*) sich dahinterklemmen (*inf*), sich dranmachen (*inf*) ◆ **to ~ ~ to work** sich hinter die Arbeit klemmen (*inf*), sich an die Arbeit machen.

◆**knuckle under** *vi* (*inf*) spuren (*inf*), sich fügen.

knuckle: ~bone *n* Knöchelbein *nt*; **~bones** *npl see* **jacks**; **~duster** *n* Schlagring *m*; **~head** *n* (*inf*) Blödmann *m* (*inf*); **~ joint** *n* (*Anat*) Knöchel- *or* Fingergelenk *nt*; (*Tech*) Kardan- *or* Kreuzgelenk *nt*.

knurl [nɜːl] [1] *n* Einkerbung, Riffelung *f*; (*Tech*) Rändelrad *nt*.
[2] *vt* rändeln, kordieren.

KO [1] *n* K.o.(-Schlag) *m*.
[2] *vt* (*Boxing*) k.o. schlagen.

koala [kəʊ'ɑːlə] *n* (*also* **~ bear**) Koala(bär) *m*.

kookaburra ['kʊkə,bʌrə] *n* Rieseneisvogel *m*, Lachender Hans.

kooky ['kuːkɪ] *adj* (*+er*) (*US inf*) komisch (*inf*), verrückt (*inf*).

Koran [kɒ'rɑːn] *n* Koran *m*.

Korea [kə'rɪə] *n* Korea *nt*.

Korean [kə'rɪən] [1] *adj* koreanisch ◆ **~ war** Koreakrieg *m*.
[2] *n* **(a)** Koreaner(in *f*) *m*. **(b)** (*language*) Koreanisch *nt*.

kosher ['kəʊʃə^r] *adj* **(a)** koscher. **(b)** (*inf*) in Ordnung ◆ **to make everything ~** alles in Ordnung bringen; **there's something not quite ~ about that deal** an dem Geschäft ist etwas faul (*inf*).

kowtow ['kaʊtaʊ] *vi* einen Kotau machen, dienern ◆ **to ~ to sb** vor jdm dienern *or* katzbuckeln (*inf*) *or* einen Kotau machen.

kph *abbr of* **kilometres per hour** kph.

kraal [krɑːl] *n* Kral *m*.

kraken ['krækən] *n* Krake *m*.

Kraut [kraʊt] *n, adj als Schimpfwort gebrauchte Bezeichnung für Deutsche und Deutsches.*

Kremlin ['kremlɪn] *n*: **the ~** der Kreml.

kremlinologist [,kremlɪ'nɒlədʒɪst] *n* Kremlforscher(in *f*) *m*.

kremlinology [,kremlɪ'nɒlədʒɪ] *n* Kremlforschung *f*.

krypton ['krɪptɒn] *n* Krypton *nt*.

Kt (*Brit*) *abbr of* **Knight**.

kudos ['kjuːdɒs] *n* Ansehen *nt*, Ehre *f* ◆ **he only did it for the ~** er tat es nur der Ehre wegen.

Ku Klux Klan [,kjuːklʌks'klæn] *n* Ku-Klux-Klan *m*.

kumquat ['kʌmkwɒt] *n* Kumquat *f*, *kleine Orange*.

kung fu ['kʌŋ'fuː] *n* Kung-Fu *nt*.

Kurd [kɜːd] *n* Kurde *m*, Kurdin *f*.

Kurdish ['kɜːdɪʃ] [1] *adj* kurdisch.
[2] *n* Kurdisch *nt*.

Kuwait [kʊ'weɪt] *n* Kuwait *nt*.

Kuwaiti [kʊ'weɪtɪ] [1] *adj* kuwaitisch.
[2] *n* Kuwaiter(in *f*) *m*.

kw *abbr of* **kilowatt(s)** kW.

kWh, kwh *abbr of* **kilowatt hour(s)** kWh.

➤ LANGUAGE IN USE: **knowledge: b** → 19.2, 19.4

L

L, l [el] *n* L, l *nt.*
L *abbr of* **(a)** (*Brit Mot*) **Learner. (b) Lake. (c) large.**
l *abbr of* **(a) litre(s)** l. **(b) left** l.
LA *abbr of* **Los Angeles.**
lab [læb] *abbr of* **laboratory.**
Lab (*Brit Pol*) *abbr of* **Labour.**
label ['leɪbl] **1** *n* **(a)** Etikett *nt;* (*showing contents, instructions etc*) Aufschrift, Beschriftung *f;* (*on specimen, cage*) Schild *nt;* (*tied on*) Anhänger *m;* (*adhesive*) Aufkleber *m,* Aufklebeetikett *nt;* (*on parcel*) Paketadresse *f;* (*of record company*) Schallplattengesellschaft, Plattenfirma *f* ◆ **on the Pye ~** von Pye herausgegeben. **(b)** (*fig*) Etikett *nt* (*usu pej*).
2 *vt* **(a)** etikettieren, mit einem Schild/Anhänger/Aufkleber versehen; (*write on*) beschriften ◆ **the bottle was ~led "poison"** die Flasche trug die Aufschrift ,,Gift".
(b) (*fig*) *ideas* bezeichnen; (*pej*) abstempeln ◆ **to ~ sb (as) sth** jdn als etw abstempeln; **he got himself ~led as a troublemaker** er brachte sich (*dat*) den Ruf eines Unruhestifters ein.
labia ['leɪbɪə] *pl of* **labium.**
labial ['leɪbɪəl] **1** *adj* (*Anat, Phon*) labial, Lippen-.
2 *n* (*Phon*) Labial, Lippenlaut *m.*
labiodental [ˌleɪbɪəʊ'dentəl] (*Phon*) **1** *adj* labiodental.
2 *n* Labiodental *m.*
labium ['leɪbɪəm] *n, pl* **labia** (*Anat*) Schamlippe *f,* Labium *nt* (*spec*).
labor *etc* (*US*) *see* **labour** *etc* ◆ **~ union** (*US*) Gewerkschaft *f.*
laboratory [lə'bɒrətərɪ, (*US*) 'læbrəˌtɔːrɪ] *n* Labor(atorium) *nt* ◆ **~ assistant** Laborant(in *f*) *m;* **~ results** Laborwerte *pl;* **~ ship** Laborschiff *nt;* **the project was abandoned at the ~ stage** das Projekt wurde im Versuchsstadium abgebrochen.
laborious [lə'bɔːrɪəs] *adj task, undertaking* mühsam, mühselig; *style* schwerfällig, umständlich.
laboriously [lə'bɔːrɪəslɪ] *adv* mühsam; *speak* umständlich.
labour, (*US*) labor ['leɪbəʳ] **1** *n* **(a)** (*work in general*) Arbeit *f;* (*toil*) Anstrengung, Mühe *f* ◆ **after much ~ the job was at last completed** nach langen Mühen war die Arbeit endlich vollendet; **they succeeded by their own ~s** sie haben es aus eigener Kraft geschafft.
(b) (*task*) Aufgabe *f* ◆ **it was a ~ of love** ich/er *etc* tat es aus Liebe zur Sache; **the ~s of Hercules** die Arbeiten *pl* des Herkules; **a ~ of Hercules** eine Herkulesarbeit.
(c) (*Jur*) *see* **hard ~.**
(d) (*persons*) Arbeiter, Arbeitskräfte *pl* ◆ **to withdraw one's ~** die Arbeit verweigern; **organized ~** die organisierte Arbeiterschaft.
(e) (*Brit Pol*) **L~** die Labour Party; **this district is L~** dies ist ein Labourbezirk *m.*
(f) (*Med*) Wehen *pl* ◆ **to be in ~** in den Wehen liegen, die Wehen haben; **to go into ~** die Wehen bekommen.
2 *vt point, subject* auswalzen, breittreten (*inf*) ◆ **I won't ~ the point** ich will nicht darauf herumreiten.
3 *vi* **(a)** (*in fields etc*) arbeiten; (*work hard*) sich abmühen (*at, with* mit) ◆ **they ~ed hard to get the house finished on time** sie gaben sich die größte Mühe, das Haus rechtzeitig fertigzustellen; **to ~ for** *or* **in a cause** sich für eine Sache einsetzen; **to ~ under a delusion/misapprehension** sich einer Täuschung/Illusion (*dat*) hingeben; **to ~ under difficulties** mit Schwierigkeiten zu kämpfen haben.
(b) (*move etc with effort or difficulty*) sich quälen ◆ **the engine is ~ing** der Motor hört sich gequält an; (*in wrong gear*) der Motor läuft untertourig; **to ~ up a hill** sich einen Hügel hinaufquälen, mühsam den Berg hochkriechen; **his breathing became ~ed** er begann, schwer zu atmen.
labour: ~ camp *n* Arbeitslager *nt;* **L~ Day** *n* der Tag der Arbeit.
laboured, (*US*) labored ['leɪbəd] *adj* schwerfällig; *breathing* schwer.
labourer, (*US*) laborer ['leɪbərəʳ] *n* (Hilfs)arbeiter *m;* (*farm ~*) Landarbeiter *m;* (*day-~*) Tagelöhner *m* ◆ **a ~ in the cause of justice** ein Kämpfer *m* für die Gerechtigkeit.
labour: L~ Exchange *n* (*dated Brit*) Arbeitsamt *nt;* **~ force** *n* Arbeiterschaft *f;* (*of company*) Belegschaft *f.*
labouring, (*US*) laboring ['leɪbərɪŋ] *adj class* Arbeiter-, arbeitend; *job* Aushilfs-.
labour-intensive, (*US*) labor-intensive *adj* arbeitsintensiv.
labourite ['leɪbəraɪt] *n* (*pej*) Labour-Anhänger *m.*
labour: ~-market *n* Arbeitsmarkt *m;* **~ movement** *n* Arbeiterbewegung *f;* **~ pains** *npl* Wehen *pl;* **L~ Party** *n* Labour Party *f;* **~ relations** *npl* die Beziehungen *pl* zwischen Unternehmern und Arbeitern *or* Gewerkschaften; **~-saving** *adj* arbeitssparend; **~ shortage** *n* Arbeitskräftemangel *m;* **~ supply** *n* Angebot *nt* an Arbeitskräften; **~ ward** *n* Kreißsaal *m.*
Labrador ['læbrədɔːʳ] *n* Labradorhund *m.*
laburnum [lə'bɜːnəm] *n* Goldregen *m.*
labyrinth ['læbɪrɪnθ] *n* (*lit, fig*) Labyrinth *nt.*
labyrinthine [ˌlæbɪ'rɪnθaɪn] *adj* labyrinthisch (*also fig*), labyrinthähnlich.
lace [leɪs] **1** *n* **(a)** (*fabric*) Spitze *f;* (*as trimming*) Spitzenborte *f or* -besatz *m;* (*of gold, silver*) Tresse, Litze *f.*
(b) (*of shoe*) (Schuh)band *nt,* Schnürsenkel *m.*
2 *vt* **(a)** schnüren; *shoe also* zubinden; (*fig*) *fingers* ineinander verschlingen.
(b) **to ~ a drink** einen Schuß Alkohol in ein Getränk geben; **~d with brandy** mit einem Schuß Weinbrand; **a ~d drink** ein Getränk mit Schuß.
3 *vi* (*shoes etc*) (zu)geschnürt werden.
◆**lace into** *vi +prep obj* **to ~ ~ sb** (*verbally*) jdm eine Standpauke halten, jdn anschnauzen (*inf*); (*physically*) auf jdn losgehen, jdn verprügeln.
◆**lace up** **1** *vt sep* (zu)schnüren.
2 *vi* geschnürt werden.
lacerate ['læsəreɪt] *vt* **(a)** verletzen; (*by glass etc*) zerschneiden; (*by thorns*) zerkratzen, aufreißen; (*by claws, whip*) zerfetzen; *painting* aufschlitzen ◆ **he ~d his arm** er zog sich (*dat*) tiefe Wunden am Arm zu; **she ~d her wrist with a razor-blade** sie schlitzte sich (*dat*) die Pulsadern mit einer Rasierklinge auf; **her knee was badly ~d** sie hatte tiefe Wunden am Knie.
(b) (*fig*) *feeling, pride* zutiefst verletzen.
laceration [ˌlæsə'reɪʃən] *n* Verletzung, Fleischwunde *f;* (*tear*) Rißwunde *f;* (*from blow*) Platzwunde *f;* (*from whip*) Striemen *m;* (*from glass*) Schnittwunde *f;* (*from claws etc*) Kratzwunde *f.*
lace-up (shoe) ['leɪsʌp(ʃuː)] *n* Schnürschuh *m.*
lachrymal ['lækrɪml] *adj* Tränen-.
lachrymose ['lækrɪməʊs] *adj* (*liter*) *person* weinerlich; *story, film etc* rührselig, ergreifend.
lacing ['leɪsɪŋ] *n* (*of shoe*) Schnürsenkel, Schuhbänder *pl;* (*of corset*) Schnürung *f* ◆ **uniforms with gold ~** goldbetreßte Uniformen *pl;* **tea with a ~ of rum** Tee *m* mit einem Schuß Rum.
▼ **lack** [læk] **1** *n* Mangel *m* ◆ **for** *or* **through ~ of sth** aus Mangel an etw (*dat*); **they failed for** *or* **through ~ of support** sie scheiterten, weil es ihnen an Unterstützung fehlte *or* mangelte; **his absence was a real ~** er fehlte sehr; **~ of water/time** Wasser-/Zeitmangel *m;* **there is no ~ of money in that family** in dieser Familie fehlt es nicht an Geld.
2 *vt* **they ~ the necessary equipment/talent** es fehlt ihnen an der notwendigen Ausrüstung/am richtigen Talent; **we ~ time** uns fehlt die nötige Zeit.
3 *vi* **(a)** **to be ~ing** fehlen; **his sense of humour is sadly ~ing** mit seinem Sinn für Humor ist es nicht weit her.
(b) **he is ~ing in confidence** ihm fehlt es an Selbstvertrauen; **he is completely ~ing in any sort of decency** er besitzt überhaupt keinen Anstand.
(c) **he ~ed for nothing** es fehlte ihm an nichts.
lackadaisical [ˌlækə'deɪzɪkəl] *adj* (*lacking energy*) lustlos, desinteressiert; (*careless*) nachlässig, lasch.
lackey ['lækɪ] *n* (*lit, fig*) Lakai *m.*
lacking ['lækɪŋ] *adj* **(a)** **to be found ~** sich nicht bewähren, der Sache (*dat*) nicht gewachsen sein; **they were not found ~** sie waren der Sache (*dat*) gewachsen.
(b) (*inf*) geistig minderbemittelt (*inf*), beschränkt.
lacklustre ['lækˌlʌstəʳ] *adj surface* stumpf, glanzlos; *style* farblos, langweilig; *eyes also* trübe.
laconic [lə'kɒnɪk] *adj* lakonisch; *prose, style* knapp.
laconically [lə'kɒnɪkəlɪ] *adv* lakonisch; *write* knapp.
lacquer ['lækəʳ] **1** *n* Lack *m;* (*hair ~*) Haarspray *nt;* (*nail ~*) Nagellack *m.*
2 *vt* lackieren; *hair* sprayen.
lacquered ['lækəd] *adj* lackiert; *hair* gesprayt; *wood* Lack-.
lacrimal, lacrymal *adj see* **lachrymal.**

➤ LANGUAGE IN USE: **lack: 1 → 17.1**

lacrosse [lə'krɒs] *n* Lacrosse *nt.*
lactate ['lækteɪt] *vi* Milch absondern, laktieren (*spec*).
lactation [læk'teɪʃən] *n* Milchabsonderung, Laktation (*spec*) *f*; (*period*) Stillzeit, Laktationsperiode (*spec*) *f*.
lacteal ['læktɪəl] *adj* Milch-.
lactic ['læktɪk] *adj* **~ acid** Milchsäure *f*.
lactose ['læktəʊs] *n* Milchzucker *m*, Laktose *f*.
lacuna [lə'kju:nə] *n, pl* **-e** [lə'kju:ni:] Lakune *f*.
lacy ['leɪsɪ] *adj* (*+er*) Spitzen-; (*like lace*) spitzenartig.
lad [læd] *n* Junge *m*; (*in stable etc*) Bursche *m* ◆ **young ~** junger Mann; **listen, ~** hör mir mal zu, mein Junge!; **when I was a ~** als ich ein junger Bursche war; **he's only a ~** er ist (doch) noch jung, er ist (doch) noch ein Junge; **a simple country ~** ein einfacher Bauernjunge, ein einfacher Junge vom Land; **all together, ~s, push!** alle Mann anschieben!, alle zusammen, Jungs, anschieben!; **he's a bit of a ~** (*inf*) er ist ein ziemlicher Draufgänger; **he's a bit of a ~ with the girls** (*inf*) er ist ein ganz schöner Frauentyp (*inf*); **he likes a night out with the ~s** (*inf*) er geht gern mal mit seinen Kumpels weg (*inf*).
ladder ['lædə^r] [1] *n* **(a)** Leiter *f*.
(b) (*fig*) (Stufen)leiter *f* ◆ **social ~** Leiter des gesellschaftlichen Erfolges; **the climb up the social ~** der gesellschaftliche Aufstieg; **it's a first step up the ~** das ist ein Anfang; **a big step up the ~** ein großer Schritt nach vorn; *see* **top**.
(c) (*Brit: in stocking*) Laufmasche *f* ◆ **~proof** maschenfest, laufmaschensicher.
[2] *vt* (*Brit*) *stocking* zerreißen ◆ **I've ~ed my stocking** ich habe mir eine Laufmasche geholt.
[3] *vi* (*Brit: stocking*) Laufmaschen bekommen.
laddie ['lædɪ] *n* (*esp Scot*) Junge, Bub (*S Ger, Aus, Sw*) *m*.
lade [leɪd] *pret* **~d**, *ptp* **laden** [1] *vt ship* beladen; *cargo* verladen.
[2] *vi* Ladung übernehmen *or* an Bord nehmen.
laden ['leɪdn] *adj* (*lit, fig*) beladen (*with* mit) ◆ **bushes ~ with flowers** blütenschwere Büsche *pl*.
la-di-da ['lɑ:dɪ'dɑ:] *adj* (*inf*) affektiert, affig (*inf*).
lading ['leɪdɪŋ] *n* (*act*) Verladen *nt*; (*cargo*) Ladung *f*.
ladle ['leɪdl] [1] *n* (Schöpf- *or* Suppen)kelle *f*, Schöpflöffel *m*.
[2] *vt* schöpfen ◆ **he's ladling money into that business** er steckt *or* pumpt massenhaft Geld in das Geschäft.
◆**ladle out** *vt sep soup, praise* austeilen ◆ **he ~s ~ praise to everyone** er überschüttet jeden mit Lob.
ladleful ['leɪdlfʊl] *n* **one ~** eine Kelle (voll); **each pan holds ten ~s** in jeden Topf paßt der Inhalt von zehn Schöpfkellen.
lady ['leɪdɪ] *n* **(a)** Dame *f* ◆ **"Ladies"** (*lavatory*) „Damen"; **where is the ladies** *or* **the ladies' room?** wo ist die Damen toilette?; **ladies and gentlemen!** sehr geehrte *or* meine (sehr verehrten) Damen und Herren!; **ladies, ...** meine Damen, ...; **~ of the house** Dame des Hauses; **the minister and his ~** der Minister und seine Gattin; **your good ~** (*hum, form*) Ihre Frau Gemahlin (*hum, form*); **the old ~** (*inf*) (*mother*) die alte Dame (*inf*); (*wife*) meine/deine/seine Alte (*inf*) *or* Olle (*N Ger inf*); **young ~** junge Dame; (*scoldingly*) mein Fräulein; **his young ~** seine Freundin; **she's no ~** sie ist keine Dame; **ladies' man** Charmeur, Frauenheld *m*; **he's a bit of a ladies' man** er wirkt auf Frauen; **ladies' bicycle** Damen(fahr)rad *nt*.
(b) (*noble*) Adlige *f* ◆ **L~** (*as a title*) Lady *f*; **dinner is served, my ~** es ist angerichtet, Mylady *or* gnädige Frau; **to live like a ~** wie eine große Dame leben.
(c) Our L~ die Jungfrau Maria, Unsere Liebe Frau; **Church of Our L~** (Lieb)frauenkirche *f*.
lady: ~bird, (*US*) **~bug** *n* Marienkäfer *m*; **L~ chapel** *n* Marienkapelle *f*; **L~ Day** *n* Mariä Verkündigung *no art*; **~ doctor** *n* Ärztin *f*; **~ friend** *n* Dame *f*; **~-in-waiting** *n* Ehrendame, Hofdame *f*; **~-killer** *n* (*inf*) Herzensbrecher *m*; **~like** *adj* damenhaft, vornehm; **it's not ~like** es ist nicht ladylike, es gehört sich nicht für eine Dame/ein Mädchen; **~-love** *n* (*old*) Geliebte *f*, Feinsliebchen *nt* (*old*); **~ mayoress** *n Titel der Frau des Lord Mayor*, Frau *f* (Ober)bürgermeister (*dated*); **~ship** *n*: **Her/Your L~ship** Ihre Ladyschaft; **certainly, Your L~ship** gewiß, Euer Gnaden; **~'s maid** *n* (Kammer)zofe *f*.
lag^1 [læg] [1] *n* (*time-~*) Zeitabstand *m*, Zeitdifferenz *f*; (*delay*) Verzögerung *f* ◆ **there is too much of a ~** es vergeht zuviel Zeit; **after a ~ of 15 minutes** nach 15 Minuten, nachdem 15 Minuten vergangen *or* verstrichen waren; **there was a ~ of six months between buying the house and actually being able to move in** das Haus konnte erst sechs Monate nach dem Kauf bezogen werden; **the cultural ~ is very apparent** der kulturelle Rückstand ist offensichtlich.
[2] *vi* (*time*) langsam vergehen, dahinkriechen; (*in pace*) zurückbleiben.
◆**lag behind** *vi* zurückbleiben ◆ **we ~ ~ in space exploration** in der Raumforschung liegen wir (weit) zurück *or* hinken wir hinterher (*inf*); **why don't you walk beside me instead of always ~ging ~?** warum läufst du nicht neben mir, anstatt immer hinterherzutrödeln?
lag^2 *vt boiler, pipe* umwickeln, isolieren.
lag^3 *n* (*sl: also* **old ~**) (ehemaliger) Knacki (*sl*).
lager ['lɑ:gə^r] *n* helles Bier ◆ **a glass of ~** ein (Glas) Helles; **~ lout** (*Brit inf*) betrunkener Rowdy; (*causing damage also*) betrunkener Randalierer.
laggard ['lægəd] [1] *n* (*sb who has fallen behind*) Nachzügler(in *f*) *m*; (*idler*) Trödler *m* ◆ **he is a ~ in love** (*liter, hum*) er ist nicht so stürmisch.
[2] *adj student, worker* faul.
lagging ['lægɪŋ] *n* Isolierschicht *f*; (*material*) Isoliermaterial *nt*.
lagoon [lə'gu:n] *n* Lagune *f*.
laid [leɪd] *pret, ptp of* **lay^4**.
laid-back [,leɪd'bæk] *adj* (*inf*) gelassen, cool (*inf*).
lain [leɪn] *ptp of* **lie^2**.
lair [lɛə^r] *n* Lager *nt*; (*cave*) Höhle *f*; (*den*) Bau *m*.
laird [lɛəd] *n* (*Scot*) Gutsherr *m*.
laissez-faire ['leɪseɪ'fɛə^r] [1] *n* Laisser-faire *nt* ◆ **there's too much ~ here** hier geht es zu leger zu.
[2] *adj* (*Econ*) Laisser-faire-; (*fig*) leger, lax.
laity ['leɪɪtɪ] *n* **(a)** (*laymen*) Laienstand *m*, Laien *pl*. **(b)** (*those outside a profession*) Laien *pl*.
lake^1 [leɪk] *n* See *m*.
lake^2 *n* (*colour*) Karm(es)inrot *nt*.
lake: L~ District *n* Lake District *m* (*Seengebiet nt im NW Englands*); **~-dweller** *n* Pfahlbaubewohner *m*; **~-dwelling** *n* Pfahlbau *m*; **L~ Poets** *npl Dichter pl des Lake District: Wordsworth, Coleridge, Southey*; **~side** [1] *n* Seeufer *nt*; [2] *attr* am See.
lam^1 [læm] (*sl*) [1] *vt* vermöbeln (*sl*).
[2] *vi* **to ~ into sb** jdn zur Schnecke machen (*sl*); (*physically*) auf jdn eindreschen (*inf*).
lam^2 *n* (*US sl*) **he's on the ~** hinter dem sind sie her (*inf*); **he took it on the ~** er machte (die) Mücke (*sl*), er türmte (*inf*).
lama ['lɑ:mə] *n* (*Rel*) Lama *m*.
lamb [læm] [1] *n* **(a)** (*young sheep*) Lamm *nt*. **(b)** (*meat*) Lamm(fleisch) *nt*. **(c)** (*person*) Engel *m* ◆ **the little ~s** (*children*) die lieben Kleinen; **my poor ~!** mein armes Lämmchen!; **she took it like a ~** sie ertrug es geduldig wie ein Lamm; **like a ~ to the slaughter** wie das Lamm zur Schlachtbank, wie ein Opferlamm. **(d) the L~ of God** das Lamm Gottes.
[2] *vi* lammen ◆ **the ~ing season** die Lammungszeit.
lambast [læm'bæst], **lambaste** [læm'beɪst] *vt* fertigmachen (*inf*), es tüchtig geben (*+dat*) (*inf*).
lamb: ~ chop *n* Lammkotelett *nt*; **~skin** *n* Lammfell *nt*; **~'s lettuce** *n* Feldsalat *m*; **~'s tail** *n* (*Bot*) Haselkätzchen *nt*; **~swool** *n* Lammwolle *f*.
lame [leɪm] [1] *adj* (*+er*) **(a)** lahm; (*as result of stroke etc*) gelähmt ◆ **to be ~ in one foot** einen lahmen Fuß haben; **to be ~ in one leg** auf einem Bein lahm sein; **the horse went ~** das Pferd fing an zu lahmen. **(b)** (*fig*) *excuse* lahm, faul; *argument* schwach, wenig überzeugend; *metre* holprig ◆ **~ duck** Niete *f* (*inf*); **~ duck company** unwirtschaftliche Firma.
[2] *vt* lähmen; *horse* lahm machen.
lamé ['lɑ:meɪ] *n* Lamé *nt*.
lamely ['leɪmlɪ] *adv argue, say etc* lahm ◆ **to walk ~** hinken; (*of horse*) lahmen; **he limped ~ into the room** er humpelte ins Zimmer; **~ he mumbled an excuse** er murmelte eine lahme Entschuldigung vor sich hin.
lameness ['leɪmnɪs] *n* **(a)** Lähmung *f* (*in, of gen*) ◆ **his ~** sein Gelähmtsein *nt*. **(b)** (*fig*) *see adj (b)* Lahmheit *f*, Schwäche *f*, mangelnde Überzeugungskraft; Holprigkeit *f*.
lament [lə'ment] [1] *n* **(a)** Klage(n *pl*), Wehklage *f* ◆ **in ~** (weh)klagend ◆ **(b)** (*Liter, Mus*) Klagelied *nt*.
[2] *vt* beklagen; *misfortune etc also* bejammern ◆ **to ~ sb** jds Tod beklagen, um jdn trauern; **it is much to be ~ed that ...** es ist sehr zu beklagen, daß ...; **what will become of me now?, he ~ed** was soll nun aus mir werden?, klagte *or* jammerte er.
[3] *vi* (weh)klagen ◆ **to ~ for sb** um jdn trauern; **to ~ over sth** über etw (*acc*) jammern, etw bejammern *or* beklagen; **she ~ed over his dead body** sie wehklagte über seinem Leichnam.
lamentable ['læməntəbl] *adj* beklagenswert; *piece of work* jämmerlich schlecht, erbärmlich.
lamentably ['læməntəblɪ] *adv* erbärmlich, beklagenswert ◆ **he failed ~** er scheiterte kläglich; **~, this idea is not practicable** bedauerlicherweise läßt sich diese Idee nicht verwirklichen; **she was ~ ignorant of politics** es war traurig *or* zum Weinen, wie wenig sie von Politik wußte.
lamentation [,læmən'teɪʃən] *n* (Weh)klage *f*; (*act*) Klagen, Jammern *nt*; (*poem, song*) Klagelied *nt* ◆ **he cried out in ~** er brach in lautes Wehklagen aus.
laminated ['læmɪneɪtɪd] *adj* geschichtet; *windscreen* Verbundglas-; *book cover* laminiert ◆ **~ glass** Verbundglas *nt*; **~ wood** Sperrholz *nt*; **~ plastic** Resopal ® *nt*; **~ working surfaces** Arbeitsflächen aus Resopal.
lamp [læmp] *n* Lampe *f*; (*in street*) Laterne *f*; (*Aut, Rail*) Scheinwerfer *m*; (*rear~*) Rücklicht *nt*; (*torch*) Taschenlampe *f*; (*sun~*) Höhensonne *f*; (*fig*) Licht *nt*.
lamp: ~black *n* Farbruß *m*; **~ bracket** *n* Lampenhalterung *f*; **~ chimney, ~ glass** *n* Zylinder *m*; **~light** *n* Lampenlicht *nt*, Schein *m* der Lampe(n); (*in street*) Licht *nt* der Laterne(n); **by ~light** bei Lampenlicht; **in the ~light** im Schein der Lampe(n); **~lighter** *n* Laternenanzünder *m*.
lampoon [læm'pu:n] [1] *n* Spott- *or* Schmähschrift *f*.
[2] *vt* verspotten, verhöhnen.
lamppost ['læmppəʊst] *n* Laternenpfahl *m*.
lamprey ['læmprɪ] *n* Neunauge *nt*, Bricke *f*; (*sea ~*) Lamprete *f*.
lamp: ~shade *n* Lampenschirm *m*; **~-standard** *n see* **~post.**
LAN [læn] (*Comput*) *abbr of* **local area network** LAN *nt*.
lance [lɑ:ns] [1] *n* Lanze *f* ◆ **~-corporal** Obergefreite(r) *m*.
[2] *vt* (*Med*) öffnen, aufschneiden.
lancer ['lɑ:nsə^r] *n* Lanzenreiter, Ulan *m*.
lancers ['lɑ:nsəz] *n sing* (*dance*) Lancier *m*, Quadrille *f*.
lancet ['lɑ:nsɪt] *n* **(a)** (*Med*) Lanzette *f*. **(b)** (*Archit*) **~ arch** Spitzbogen *m*; **~ window** Spitzbogenfenster *nt*.
Lancs [læŋks] *abbr of* **Lancashire**.
land [lænd] [1] *n* **(a)** (*not sea*) Land *nt* ◆ **by ~** auf dem Landweg; **by ~ and by**

sea zu Land und zu Wasser; **as they approached ~** als sie sich dem Land näherten; **to see how the ~ lies** (*lit*) das Gelände erkunden *or* auskundschaften; (*fig*) die Lage sondieren *or* peilen; **the lay** *or* **lie of the ~** (*lit*) die Beschaffenheit des Geländes; **until I've seen the lay** *or* **lie of the ~** (*fig*) bis ich die Lage sondiert habe; **for ~'s sake** (*US inf*) um Himmels willen; *see* **dry land**.
(b) (*nation, region, fig*) Land *nt* ◆ **to be in the ~ of the living** unter den Lebenden sein.
(c) (*as property*) Grund und Boden *m*; (*estates*) Ländereien *pl* ◆ **to own ~** Land besitzen; **get off my ~!** verschwinden Sie von meinem Grundstück *or* Grund und Boden!
(d) (*Agr*) Land *nt*; (*soil*) Boden *m* ◆ **to return to the ~** zur Scholle zurückkehren; **to work on the ~** das Land bebauen; **the drift from the ~** die Landflucht; **to live off the ~** (*grow own food*) sich vom Lande ernähren, von den Früchten des Landes leben (*liter*); (*forage*) sich aus der Natur ernähren.
[2] *vt* **(a)** (*Naut*) *passengers* absetzen, von Bord gehen lassen; *troops* landen; *goods* an Land bringen, löschen; *fish at port* anlanden; *boat* an Land ziehen ◆ **he ~ed the boat on the beach** er zog das Boot an den Strand.
(b) (*Aviat*) *passengers* absetzen, von Bord gehen lassen; *troops* landen; *goods* abladen ◆ **to ~ a plane** (mit einem Flugzeug) landen; **the helicopter ~ed a doctor on the ship** der Hubschrauber setzte einen Arzt auf dem Schiff ab; **scientists will ~ a space probe on the moon** Wissenschaftler werden eine Raumsonde auf dem Mond landen.
(c) *fish on hook* an Land ziehen.
(d) (*inf: obtain*) kriegen (*inf*); *contract* sich (*dat*) verschaffen; *prize* (sich *dat*) holen (*inf*) ◆ **she finally ~ed him** sie hat sich (*dat*) ihn schließlich geangelt (*inf*).
(e) (*inf*) *blow* landen (*inf*) ◆ **he ~ed him one** *or* **a punch on the jaw** er versetzte ihm *or* landete (bei ihm) einen Kinnhaken.
(f) (*inf: place*) bringen ◆ **behaviour like that will ~ you in trouble/jail** bei einem solchen Betragen wirst du noch mal Ärger bekommen/im Gefängnis landen; **it ~ed me in a mess** dadurch bin ich in einen ganz schönen Schlamassel (*inf*) geraten *or* gekommen; **I've ~ed myself in a real mess** ich bin (ganz schön) in die Klemme geraten (*inf*); **I ~ed myself in an argument** ich habe mich auf einen Streit eingelassen.
(g) (*inf: lumber*) **to ~ sb with sth** jdm etw aufhalsen (*inf*) *or* andrehen (*inf*); **I got ~ed with the job** man hat mir die Arbeit aufgehalst (*inf*); **I got ~ed with him for two hours** ich hatte ihn zwei Stunden lang auf dem Hals.
[3] *vi* **(a)** (*from ship*) an Land gehen.
(b) (*Aviat*) landen; (*bird, insect*) landen, sich setzen ◆ **as it ~ed** (*Aviat*) bei der Landung; **we're coming in to ~** wir setzen zur Landung an.
(c) (*fall, be placed, strike*) landen ◆ **the bomb ~ed on the building** die Bombe fiel auf das Gebäude; **to ~ on one's feet** (*lit*) auf den Füßen landen; (*fig*) auf die Füße fallen; **to ~ on one's head** auf den Kopf fallen; **he ~ed awkwardly** er ist ungeschickt aufgekommen *or* gelandet (*inf*).
◆**land up** *vi* (*inf*) landen (*inf*) ◆ **you'll ~ ~ in trouble** du wirst noch mal Ärger bekommen; **I ~ed ~ with only £2** (*had left*) ich hatte noch ganze £ 2 in der Tasche (*inf*); (*obtained only*) ich habe nur £ 2 herausgeschlagen (*inf*); **he ~ed ~ being sacked from the job after all** er wurde schließlich doch entlassen.
land-agent ['lænd,eɪdʒənt] *n* Gutsverwalter(in *f*) *m*.
land army *n* Landstreitkräfte *pl*.
landau ['lændɔː] *n* Landauer *m*.
land: ~-based *adj missiles* landgestützt; **~-breeze** *n* Landwind *m*; **~ defences** *npl* Landwehr *f*.
landed ['lændɪd] *adj* **the ~ class** die Großgrundbesitzer *pl*; **~ gentry** Landadel *m*; **~ property** Grundbesitz *m*.
land: ~fall *n* Sichten *nt* von Land; (*land sighted*) gesichtetes Land; **to make ~fall** Land sichten; **~fill (site)** *n* Mülldeponie *f*; **~ forces** *npl* Landstreitkräfte *pl*; **~holder** *n* (*~-owner*) Grundbesitzer *m*; (*tenant*) Pächter *m*.
landing ['lændɪŋ] *n* **(a)** (*Naut*) (*of person*) Landung *f*; (*of ship also*) Anlegen *nt*; (*of goods*) Löschen *nt*. **(b)** (*Aviat*) Landung *f*. **(c)** (*on stairs*) (*inside house*) Flur, Gang *m*; (*outside flat door*) Treppenabsatz *m*; (*corridor outside flat doors*) Gang, Etagenabsatz *m*.
landing: ~-card *n* Einreisekarte *f*; **~-craft** *n* Landungsboot *nt*; **~-field** *n* Landeplatz *m*; **~-gear** *n* Fahrgestell *nt*; **~-net** *n* Kescher *m*; **~-party** *n* Landetrupp *m*; **~-place** *n* (*Naut*) Anlegeplatz *m*; **~-stage** *n* (*Naut*) Landesteg *m*, Landungsbrücke *f*; **~-strip** *n* Landebahn *f*; **~ wheels** *npl* (Lauf)räder *pl*.
land: ~lady *n* Vermieterin, Hauswirtin *f*; (*in pub*) Wirtin *f*; **~ law** *n* Bodenrecht *nt*; **~less** *adj* landlos; **~locked** *adj* von Land eingeschlossen; **a ~locked country** ein Land ohne Zugang zum Meer, ein Binnenstaat *m*; **~lord** *n* (*of land*) Grundbesitzer *m*; (*of flat etc*) Vermieter, Hauswirt *m*; (*of pub*) Wirt *m*; **~lord!** Herr Wirt!; **~lubber** ['lændlʌbəʳ] *n* Landratte *f* (*inf*); **~mark** *n* (*Naut*) Landmarke *f*; (*boundary mark*) Grenzstein, Grenzpfahl *m*; (*well-known thing*) Wahrzeichen *nt*; (*fig*) Meilenstein, Markstein *m*; **~mass** *n* Landmasse *f*; **~mine** *n* Landmine *f*; **~-owner** *n* Grundbesitzer *m*; **~ reform** *n* Boden(rechts)reform *f*; **~ register** *n* (*Brit*) Grundbuch *nt*; **~ route** *n* Landweg *m*; **by the ~ route** auf dem Landweg; **~scape** ['lændskeɪp] [1] *n* Landschaft *f*; [2] *vt big area, natural park* landschaftlich gestalten; *garden, grounds* gärtnerisch gestalten, anlegen; **~scape gardener** *n* (*for big areas etc*) Landschaftsgärtner(in *f*) *m*; (*for gardens etc*) Gartengestalter(in *f*) *m*; **~scape gardening** *n* Landschaftsgärtnerei *or* -gestaltung *f*; Gartengestaltung *f*; **~slide** *n* (*lit, fig*) Erdrutsch *m*; **a ~slide victory** ein überwältigender Sieg, ein Erdrutschsieg *m*; **~slip** *n* Erdrutsch *m*; **~ tax** *n* Grundsteuer *f*; **~ward** *adj view* zum (Fest)land; **they were sailing in a ~ward direction** sie fuhren in Richtung Land *or* auf das Land zu; **on the ~ward side** auf der Landseite, auf der dem Land zugekehrten Seite; **~ward(s)** *adv* landwärts; **to ~ward** in Richtung Land.
lane [leɪn] *n* (*in country*) (*for walking*) (Feld)weg *m*; (*for driving*) Sträßchen *nt*; (*in town*) Gasse *f*, Weg *m*; (*Sport*) Bahn *f*; (*motorway*) Spur *f*; (*shipping ~*) Schiffahrtsweg *m or* -linie *f*; (*air ~*) (Flug)route, Luftstraße *f* ◆ **~ markings** (*on road*) Spurmarkierungen *pl*; **"get in ~"** „bitte einordnen".
language ['læŋgwɪdʒ] *n* Sprache *f* ◆ **a book on ~** ein Buch über die Sprache; **philosophy of ~** Sprachphilosophie *f*; **the ~ of flowers** die Blumensprache; **to study ~s** Sprachen studieren; **your ~ is disgusting** deine Ausdrucksweise ist abscheulich, du drückst dich abscheulich aus; **that's no ~ to use to your mother!** so spricht man nicht mit seiner Mutter!; **it's a bloody nuisance! — ~!** verfluchter Mist! — na, so was sagt man doch nicht!; **bad ~** Kraftausdrücke *pl*; **strong ~** Schimpfwörter, derbe Ausdrücke *pl*; (*forceful ~*) starke Worte *pl*; **he used strong ~, calling them fascist pigs** er beschimpfte sie als Faschistenschweine; **the request/complaint was couched in rather strong ~** die Aufforderung/Beschwerde hörte sich ziemlich kraß an; **putting it into plain ~ ...** (*simply*) einfach ausgedrückt ...; (*bluntly*) um es ganz direkt *or* ohne Umschweife zu sagen, ...; **to talk sb's ~** jds Sprache sprechen; **to talk the same ~ (as sb)** die gleiche Sprache (wie jd) sprechen.
language: ~ course *n* Sprachkurs(us) *m*; **~ lab(oratory)** *n* Sprachlabor *nt*; **~-learning** [1] *n* Spracherlernung *f*; [2] *adj* Sprachlern-; **~ teacher** *n* Sprachlehrer(in *f*) *m*.
languid ['læŋgwɪd] *adj* träge; *gesture* müde, matt; *manner* lässig, gelangweilt; *walk* lässig, schlendernd; *voice* müde.
languidly ['læŋgwɪdlɪ] *adv* träge, lässig ◆ **is that all? she said ~** ist das alles?, sagte sie gelangweilt; **the model posed ~ against the sofa** das Modell lehnte sich in einer lässigen Pose gegen das Sofa; **~ she waved to the crowd** mit einer müden *or* matten Geste winkte sie der Menge zu; **the chords build up slowly and ~** die Akkorde bauen sich langsam und schleppend auf.
languidness ['læŋgwɪdnɪs] *n see adj* Trägheit *f*; Mattigkeit *f*; Lässigkeit *f* ◆ **the ~ of her voice** ihre müde Stimme.
languish ['læŋgwɪʃ] *vi* schmachten; (*flowers*) dahinwelken; (*pine*) sich sehnen (*for* nach) ◆ **he ~ed in hospital for months** er war monatelang ans Krankenbett gefesselt (*geh*); **the panda merely ~ed in its new home** der Panda wurde in seiner neuen Heimat immer apathischer *or* stumpfer; **the child ~ed during his mother's absence** das Kind verzehrte sich nach seiner Mutter (*geh*); **I ~ without you, he wrote** ich verzehre mich vor Sehnsucht nach dir, schrieb er; **I'm ~ing away in this boring town** ich verkümmere in dieser langweiligen Stadt.
languishing ['læŋgwɪʃɪŋ] *adj* schmachtend; *death* langsam und qualvoll.
languor ['læŋgəʳ] *n* (*indolence*) Trägheit, Schläfrigkeit *f*; (*weakness*) Mattigkeit, Schlappheit *f*; (*emotional*) Stumpfheit, Apathie *f* ◆ **the ~ of the tropical days** die schläfrige Schwüle der tropischen Tage.
languorous ['læŋgərəs] *adj* träge, schläfrig; *heat* schläfrig, wohlig; *feeling* wohlig; *music* schmelzend; *rhythm, metre* gleitend, getragen; *tone, voice* schläfrig ◆ **a ~ beauty** eine schwüle Schönheit.
languorously ['læŋgərəslɪ] *adv* träge; *speak* mit schläfriger Stimme ◆ **the soft, ~ sentimental mood of the poem** die weiche, schwül-sentimentale Stimmung des Gedichts; **she stretched out ~** sie räkelte sich verführerisch.
lank [læŋk] *adj person, body* dürr, hager; *hair* strähnig, kraftlos; *grass* dürr, mager.
lanky ['læŋkɪ] [1] *adj* (*+er*) schlaksig.
[2] *n* (*inf*) Lange(r) *mf* (*inf*).
lanolin(e) ['lænəʊlɪn] *n* Lanolin *nt*.
lantern ['læntən] *n* (*also Archit*) Laterne *f*; *see* **Chinese**.
lantern: ~-jawed *adj* hohlwangig; **~-slide** *n* Glasdiapositiv, Lichtbild *nt*.
lanyard ['lænjəd] *n* (*cord*) Kordel *f* (*an der Pfeife oder Messer getragen wird*); (*Naut*) Taljereep *nt*.
Laos [laʊs] *n* Laos *nt*.
Laotian ['laʊʃɪən] [1] *adj* laotisch.
[2] *n* Laote *m*, Laotin *f*.
lap¹ [læp] *n* Schoß *m* ◆ **on her ~** auf dem/ihrem Schoß; **his opponent's mistake dropped victory into his ~** durch den Fehler seines Gegners fiel ihm der Sieg in den Schoß; **it's in the ~ of the gods** es liegt im Schoß der Götter; **to live in the ~ of luxury** ein Luxusleben führen.
lap² (*over~*) [1] *n* Überlappung *f*.
[2] *vt* überlappen.
[3] *vi* sich überlappen ◆ **the meeting ~ped over into extra time** die Versammlung ging über die vorgesehene Zeit hinaus.
lap³ *vt* (*wrap*) wickeln.
lap⁴ (*Sport*) [1] *n* (*round*) Runde *f*; (*fig: stage*) Etappe, Strecke *f*, Abschnitt *m* ◆ **his time for the first ~** seine Zeit in der ersten Runde; **on the second ~** in der zweiten Runde; **~ of honour** Ehrenrunde *f*; **we're on the last ~ now** (*fig*) wir haben es bald geschafft.
[2] *vt* überrunden.
[3] *vi* **to ~ at 90 mph** mit einer Geschwindigkeit von 90 Meilen pro Stunde seine Runden drehen; **he's ~ping at 58 seconds** (*athlete*) er läuft die Runde in einer Zeit von 58 Sekunden.
lap⁵ [1] *n* (*lick*) Schlecken, Lecken *nt*; (*of waves*) Klatschen, Schlagen, Plätschern *nt* ◆ **the cat took a cautious ~ at the milk** die Katze leckte *or* schleckte vorsichtig an der Milch.
[2] *vt* **(a)** (*lick*) lecken, schlecken.
(b) (*water*) **the waves ~ped the shore** die Wellen rollten an *or* plätscherten an *or* klatschten gegen das Ufer.

3 vi (*waves, water*) plätschern (*against* an +*acc*), klatschen (*against* gegen) ◆ **to ~ over sth** schwappen über etw (*acc*).

◆**lap up** *vt sep* (a) *liquid* auflecken, aufschlecken, aufschlabbern (*inf*) ◆ **the children hungrily ~ped ~ their soup** die Kinder löffelten hungrig ihre Suppe.

(b) *praise, compliments* genießen; *nonsense* schlucken ◆ **she ~ped it ~** das ging ihr runter wie Honig (*inf*); **he ~ped ~ the compliments** die Komplimente gingen ihm wie Honig runter.

laparoscopy [ˌlæpəˈrɒskəpɪ] *n* Laparoskopie *f*.

laparotomy [ˌlæpəˈrɒtəmɪ] *n* Laparotomie *f*.

lap-dog [ˈlæpdɒg] *n* Schoßhund *m*.

lapel [ləˈpel] *n* Aufschlag *m*, Revers *nt or m*.

lapidary [ˈlæpɪdərɪ] 1 *adj* **~ art** (Edel)steinschneidekunst *f*; **~ inscription** in Stein gehauene Inschrift.

2 *n* Steinschneider *m*.

lapis lazuli [ˈlæpɪsˈlæzjʊlaɪ] *n* Lapislazuli *m*.

Lapland [ˈlæplænd] *n* Lappland *nt*.

Laplander [ˈlæplændə^r], **Lapp** [læp] *n* Lappländer(in *f*) *m*, Lappe *m*, Lappin *f*.

Lapp [læp] *n* (a) *see* **Laplander.** (b) *see* **Lappish.**

lapping [ˈlæpɪŋ] *n* (*of water*) Plätschern, Schlagen *nt*.

Lappish [ˈlæpɪʃ] *n* Lappländisch, Lappisch *nt*.

lapse [læps] 1 *n* (a) (*error*) Fehler *m*; (*moral*) Fehltritt *m*, Verfehlung *f* ◆ **~ of justice** Justizirrtum *m*; **he had a ~ of memory** es ist ihm entfallen; **to suffer from ~s of memory** an Gedächtnisschwäche leiden; **~ of good taste** Geschmacksverirrung *f*.

(b) (*decline*) Absinken, Abgleiten *nt no pl* ◆ **a ~ in confidence** ein Vertrauensschwund *m*; **~ in standards** Niveauabfall *m*.

(c) (*expiry*) Ablauf *m*; (*of claim*) Verfall *m*, Erlöschen *nt*; (*cessation*) Aussterben, Schwinden *nt*.

(d) (*of time*) Zeitspanne *f*, Zeitraum *m* ◆ **after a ~ of 4 months** nach (einem Zeitraum von) 4 Monaten; **there was a ~ in the conversation** es gab eine Gesprächspause.

2 *vi* (a) (*make mistake*) einen Fehler begehen, etwas falsch machen; (*morally*) fehlen (*liter*), einen Fehltritt begehen, Unrecht tun ◆ **to ~ from one's faith** von seinem Glauben abfallen, seinem Glauben abtrünnig werden; **to ~ from duty** seine Pflicht vernachlässigen.

(b) (*decline*) verfallen (*into* in +*acc*); abgleiten (*from sth into sth* von etw in etw *acc*) ◆ **his taste must have ~d when he bought that picture** er muß an Geschmacksverirrung gelitten haben, als er das Bild kaufte; **to ~ into one's old ways** wieder in seine alten Gewohnheiten verfallen; **he ~d into the vernacular** er verfiel (wieder) in seinen Dialekt; **he ~d into silence** er versank in Schweigen; **he ~d into a coma** er sank in ein Koma; **he/his work is lapsing** er/seine Arbeit läßt nach, mit ihm/seiner Arbeit geht es bergab.

(c) (*expire*) ablaufen; (*claims*) verfallen, erlöschen; (*cease to exist*) aussterben; (*friendship, correspondence*) einschlafen ◆ **the plan ~d because of lack of support** der Plan wurde mangels Unterstützung fallengelassen.

lapsed [læpst] *adj Catholic* abtrünnig, vom Glauben abgefallen; *insurance policy* abgelaufen, verfallen.

laptop [ˈlæptɒp] (*Comput*) 1 *n* Laptop *m*.

2 *attr* Laptop-.

lapwing [ˈlæpwɪŋ] *n* Kiebitz *m*.

larboard [ˈlɑːbəd] (*old*) 1 *adj* Backbord-.

2 *n* Backbord *nt*.

larceny [ˈlɑːsənɪ] *n* (*Jur*) Diebstahl *m*.

larch [lɑːtʃ] *n* (*also* **~ tree**) Lärche *f*; (*wood*) Lärche(nholz *nt*) *f*.

lard [lɑːd] 1 *n* Schweineschmalz *nt*.

2 *vt* mit Schweineschmalz bestreichen; (*with strips of bacon, fig*) spicken.

larder [ˈlɑːdə^r] *n* (*room*) Speisekammer *f*; (*cupboard*) Speiseschrank *m*.

lardy-cake [ˈlɑːdɪˌkeɪk] *n Schmalzkuchen m aus Brotteig mit Rosinen*.

large [lɑːdʒ] 1 *adj* (+*er*) (a) (*big*) groß; *person* stark, korpulent; *meal* reichlich, groß; *list* lang ◆ **a ~ land-owner** ein Großgrundbesitzer *m*; **she looks as ~ as life in that photograph** sie sieht auf dem Foto aus, wie sie leibt und lebt; **there he/it was as ~ as life** da war er/es in voller Lebensgröße.

(b) (*extensive*) *interests, power* weitreichend, bedeutend ◆ **his interests were on a ~ scale** er hatte weitreichende *or* breit gestreute Interessen; **taking the ~ view** global betrachtet.

(c) (*old: generous, tolerant*) großzügig ◆ **a ~ understanding** ein großes Verständnis.

2 *adv* groß ◆ **guilt was written ~ all over his face** die Schuld stand ihm deutlich im Gesicht geschrieben.

3 *n* (a) (*in general*) **at ~** im großen und ganzen, im allgemeinen; **people** *or* **the world at ~** die Allgemeinheit; **he wanted to tell his story to the world at ~** er wollte der ganzen Welt seine Geschichte erzählen.

(b) **to be at ~** (*free*) frei herumlaufen; **the goats wander at ~** die Ziegen laufen frei herum.

(c) **at ~** (*in detail, at length*) ausführlich, lang und breit.

(d) **strewn at ~** (*at random*) kreuz und quer verstreut; **scattering accusations at ~** mit Anschuldigungen um sich werfend.

(e) **ambassador at ~** Sonderbotschafter *m*.

large-hearted [ˈlɑːdʒˌhɑːtɪd] *adj* großherzig.

largely [ˈlɑːdʒlɪ] *adv* (*mainly*) zum größten Teil.

large-minded [ˈlɑːdʒˌmaɪndɪd] *adj* aufgeschlossen.

largeness [ˈlɑːdʒnɪs] *n see adj* (a) Größe *f*; Umfang *m*; Reichlichkeit *f*; Länge *f*. (b) Bedeutung *f*, Umfang *m*. (c) Großzügigkeit *f*.

large: ~-scale *adj* groß angelegt; *reception, party, changes* in großem Rahmen; **a ~-scale producer of food** ein Großhersteller *m* von Nahrungsmitteln; **~-scale rioting** Massenaufruhr *m*, Massenunruhen *pl*; **a ~-scale map** eine (Land)karte in großem Maßstab; **~-scale integration** (*Comput*) Großintegration *f*; **~-sized** *adj* groß.

largesse [lɑːˈʒes] *n* Großzügigkeit, Freigebigkeit; (*gift*) (großzügige) Gabe.

largish [ˈlɑːdʒɪʃ] *adj* ziemlich groß.

largo [ˈlɑːgəʊ] *n* Largo *nt*.

lariat [ˈlærɪət] *n* Lasso *nt or m*.

lark¹ [lɑːk] *n* (*Orn*) Lerche *f* ◆ **to get up with the ~** mit den Hühnern aufstehen; **as happy as a ~** quietschfidel.

lark² *n* (*inf*) (a) (*joke, fun, frolic*) Jux (*inf*), Spaß *m* ◆ **let's go to the party, it'll be a bit of a ~** gehen wir zu der Party, das wird bestimmt lustig; **that's the best ~ we've had for a long time!** soviel Spaß haben wir schon lange nicht mehr gehabt!; **what a ~!** das ist (ja) zum Schreien *or* Schießen!; **to do sth for a ~** etw (nur) zum Spaß *or* aus Jux machen; **to have a ~ with sb** mit jdm zusammen Spaß haben.

(b) (*business, affair*) **this whole agency ~ is ...** die ganze Geschichte mit der Agentur ist ... (*inf*); **he's got involved in the used-car ~** er ist ins Gebrauchtwagengeschäft eingestiegen (*inf*); **I wouldn't get involved in that ~** auf so was *or* so 'ne Sache würde ich mich nicht einlassen (*inf*); **politics and all that ~** Politik und der ganze Kram (*inf*); **this dinner-jacket ~** dieser Blödsinn mit dem Smoking (*inf*).

◆**lark about** *or* **around** *vi* (*inf*) herumblödeln, herumalbern ◆ **to ~ ~ with sth** mit etw herumspielen.

larkspur [ˈlɑːkspɜː^r] *n* Rittersporn *m*.

larva [ˈlɑːvə] *n*, *pl* **-e** [ˈlɑːvɪ] Larve *f*.

larval [ˈlɑːvəl] *adj* Larven-, larvenartig.

laryngeal [ləˈrɪndʒəl] *adj* Kehlkopf-.

laryngitis [ˌlærɪnˈdʒaɪtɪs] *n* Kehlkopfentzündung, Laryngitis (*spec*) *f*.

larynx [ˈlærɪŋks] *n* Kehlkopf, Larynx (*spec*) *m*.

lasagne, lasagna [ləˈzænjə] *n* Lasagne *pl*.

lascivious [ləˈsɪvɪəs] *adj* lasziv (*geh*); *movements, person, look, behaviour also* lüstern; *book* schlüpfrig.

lasciviously [ləˈsɪvɪəslɪ] *adv* lüstern ◆ **the dancer moved ~** die Bewegungen der Tänzerin waren lasziv.

lasciviousness [ləˈsɪvɪəsnɪs] *n see adj* Laszivität *f* (*geh*); Lüsternheit *f*; Schlüpfrigkeit *f*.

laser [ˈleɪzə^r] 1 *n* Laser *m*; (*Comput: printer*) Laserdrucker *m*.

2 *attr* Laser-.

laser: ~ beam *n* Laserstrahl *m*; **~ gun** *n* Laserkanone *f*; **~ printer** *n* Laserdrucker *m*; **~ show** *n* Laser-Show *f*; **~ surgery** *n* Laserchirurgie *f*; **~ technology** *n* Lasertechnik *f*; **~ weapon** *n* Laserwaffe *f*.

lash¹ [læʃ] *n* (*eye~*) Wimper *f* ◆ **she fluttered her ~es at him** sie machte ihm schöne Augen.

lash² 1 *n* (a) (*whip*) Peitsche *f*; (*thong*) Schnur *f*. (b) (*stroke, as punishment*) (Peitschen)schlag *m*. (c) (*~ing*) (*of tail*) Schlagen *nt*; (*of waves, rain also*) Peitschen *nt*. (d) (*fig*) Schärfe *f* ◆ **the ~ of her tongue** ihre scharfe Zunge.

2 *vt* (a) (*beat*) peitschen; (*as punishment*) auspeitschen; (*hail, rain, waves*) peitschen gegen; (*tail*) schlagen mit ◆ **the wind ~ed the sea into a fury** wütend peitschte der Wind die See; **the cow ~ed the flies with its tail** die Kuh schlug mit ihrem Schwanz nach den Fliegen; **to ~ the crowd into a fury** die Menge aufpeitschen; **he ~ed himself into a fury** er steigerte sich in seine Wut hinein; **his speech ~ed his audience into a passion of enthusiasm** seine Rede riß die Zuhörer zu Begeisterungsstürmen hin.

(b) (*fig: criticize*) heruntermachen (*inf*), abkanzeln.

(c) (*tie*) festbinden (*to* an +*dat*) ◆ **to ~ sth together** etw zusammenbinden.

3 *vi* **to ~ against** peitschen gegen.

◆**lash about** *or* **around** *vi* (wild) um sich schlagen.

◆**lash along** *vt sep see* **lash on.**

◆**lash around** *vi see* **lash about.**

◆**lash back** *vt sep* festbinden.

◆**lash down** 1 *vt sep* (*tie down*) festbinden *or* -zurren.

2 *vi* (*rain etc*) niederprasseln.

◆**lash into** *vi* +*prep obj* **to ~ ~ sb** (*physically*) auf jdn einschlagen; (*with words*) jdn anfahren *or* anbrüllen (*inf*).

◆**lash on** *or* **along** *vt sep horse, slaves* mit der Peitsche antreiben.

◆**lash out** 1 *vi* (a) (*physically*) (wild) um sich schlagen *or* hauen; (*horse*) ausschlagen ◆ **to ~ ~ at sb** auf jdn losgehen.

(b) (*in words*) vom Leder ziehen (*inf*) ◆ **to ~ ~ against** *or* **at sb/sth** gegen jdn/etw wettern; **"TUC boss ~es ~"** „Gewerkschaftsboß holt zum Schlag aus".

(c) (*inf: with money*) sich in Unkosten stürzen ◆ **to ~ ~ on sth** sich (*dat*) etw was kosten lassen (*inf*); **to ~ ~ on sb** spendabel gegenüber jdm sein (*inf*); **I'm going to ~ ~ on a new car** ich werde mir ein neues Auto leisten; **now we can really ~ ~** jetzt können wir uns wirklich mal etwas leisten.

2 *vt insep sum of money* springen lassen.

◆**lash up** *vt sep* verschnüren.

lashing [ˈlæʃɪŋ] *n* (a) (*beating*) Prügel *pl*; (*punishment*) Auspeitschung *f*.

(b) (*tying*) Verschnürung *f*; (*of prisoner*) Fesseln *pl*; (*Naut*) Tau *nt*, Zurring *m*.

(c) **~s** *pl* (*inf*) eine Unmenge (*inf*) ◆ **~s of money/cream** eine Unmenge *or* massenhaft Geld/Schlagsahne (*inf*).

lass [læs] *n* (junges) Mädchen, Mädel *nt* (*dial*); (*country ~*) Mädchen *nt* vom Land; (*sweetheart*) Freundin *f*, Schatz *m*.

lassie [ˈlæsɪ] *n* (*inf: esp Scot, N Engl*) *see* **lass.**

lassitude ['læsɪtjuːd] *n* Mattigkeit, Trägheit *f*.

lasso [læ'suː] 1 *n, pl* **-(e)s** Lasso *m or nt*.
2 *vt* mit dem Lasso einfangen.

last¹ [lɑːst] 1 *adj* (a) letzte(r, s) ◆ **he was ~ to arrive** er kam als letzter an; **the ~ person** der letzte; **the ~ but one, the second ~ (one)** der/die/das vorletzte; **the third ~ house** das drittletzte Haus; **(the) ~ one there buys the drinks!** der letzte *or* wer als letzter ankommt, zahlt die Getränke; **~ Monday, on Monday ~** letzten Montag; **~ year** letztes Jahr, im vorigen Jahr; **during the ~ 20 years, these ~ 20 years** in den letzten 20 Jahren; **~ but not least** nicht zuletzt, last not least.
(b) (*most unlikely, unsuitable etc*) **that's the ~ thing I worry about** das ist das letzte, worüber ich mir Sorgen machen würde; **that was the ~ thing I expected** damit hatte ich am wenigsten gerechnet; **that's the ~ thing I wanted to happen** das habe ich am wenigsten gewollt; **he's the ~ person I want to see** er ist der letzte, den ich sehen möchte; **you're the ~ person to be entrusted with it** du bist der letzte, dem man das anvertrauen kann.
2 *n* (a) (*final one or part, one before*) der/die/das letzte ◆ **he was the ~ of the visitors to leave** er ging als letzter der Besucher; **he withdrew the ~ of his money from the bank** er hob sein letztes Geld von der Bank ab; **each one is better than the ~** eins ist besser als das andere; **this is the ~ of the cake** das ist der Rest des Kuchens; **that's the ~ of the trouble** jetzt hat der Ärger ein Ende; **I hope this is the ~ we'll hear about it** ich hoffe, damit ist die Sache erledigt; **that was the ~ we saw of him** danach haben wir ihn nicht mehr gesehen; **the ~ we heard of him was ...** das letzte, was wir von ihm hörten, war ...; **that was the ~ we heard of it/him** seitdem haben wir nichts mehr darüber/von ihm gehört; **that's the ~ I want to hear about it** ich möchte davon nichts mehr hören; **I shall be glad to see the ~ of this/him** ich bin froh, wenn ich das hinter mir habe/wenn ich den los bin (*inf*) *or* nicht mehr sehe; **we shall never hear the ~ of it** das werden wir noch lange zu hören kriegen; **to look one's ~ on sth** den letzten Blick auf etw (*acc*) werfen; **my ~** (*Comm*) mein letztes Schreiben.
(b) **at ~** endlich; **at long ~** schließlich und endlich; **so you're ready at long ~!** du bist also endlich fertig geworden!; **to the ~** bis zum Schluß.
3 *adv* **when did you ~ have a bath** *or* **have a bath ~?** wann hast du das letztemal gebadet?; **I ~ heard from him a month ago** vor einem Monat habe ich das letztemal von ihm gehört; **he spoke ~** er sprach als letzter; **the horse came in ~** das Pferd ging als letztes durchs Ziel.

last² 1 *vt* **it will ~ me/a careful user a lifetime** das hält/bei vernünftiger Benutzung hält es ein Leben lang *or* ewig (*inf*); **the car has ~ed me eight years** das Auto hat acht Jahre (lang) gehalten; **these cigarettes will ~ me a week** diese Zigaretten reichen mir eine Woche.
2 *vi* (*continue*) dauern; (*remain intact: cloth, flowers, marriage*) halten ◆ **it can't ~** es hält nicht an; **it won't ~** es wird nicht lange anhalten *or* so bleiben; **it's too good to ~** das ist zu schön, um wahr zu sein; **he'll stay as long as the beer ~s** er bleibt, solange Bier da ist; **will this material ~?** ist dieses Material haltbar *or* dauerhaft?; **none of his girlfriends ~s for long** bei ihm hält sich keine Freundin lange; **he won't ~ long in this job** er wird in dieser Stelle nicht alt werden (*inf*); **the previous boss ~ed only a week** der letzte Chef blieb nur eine Woche.

◆**last out** 1 *vt sep* ausreichen für; (*people*) durchhalten.
2 *vi* (*money, resources*) ausreichen; (*person*) durchhalten.

last³ *n* Leisten *m* ◆ **cobbler, stick to your ~!** Schuster, bleib bei deinem Leisten!

last: L~ Day *n* **the L~ Day** der Jüngste Tag; **~-ditch** *adj* allerletzte(r, s); *attempt etc* in letzter Minute.

lasting ['lɑːstɪŋ] *adj relationship* dauerhaft; *material also* haltbar; *shame etc* anhaltend.

Last Judgement *n* **the ~** das Jüngste *or* Letzte Gericht.

lastly ['lɑːstlɪ] *adv* schließlich, zum Schluß.

last: ~-minute *adj* in letzter Minute; **~ number redial** *n* (*Telec*) Letztnummernspeicher *m*; **~ post** *n* Zapfenstreich *m*; **~ rites** *npl* Letzte Ölung; **L~ Supper** *n* **the L~ Supper** das (Letzte) Abendmahl; **~ word** *n* **the ~ word** (*in fashion*) der letzte Schrei; **to have the ~ word** das letzte Wort haben; **the ~ word on biochemistry/on this subject** das maßgebende Werk über Biochemie/auf diesem Gebiet.

Lat *abbr of* **Latin** lat, Lat.

lat *abbr of* **latitude** Br.

latch [lætʃ] 1 *n* Riegel *m* ◆ **to be on the ~** nicht verschlossen sein, nur eingeklinkt sein; **to leave the door on the ~** die Tür nur einklinken; **to drop the ~** den Riegel vorschieben, die Tür verriegeln.
2 *vt* verriegeln.

◆**latch on** *vi* (*inf*) (a) (*get hold*) sich festhalten; (*with teeth*) sich festbeißen (*to sth* an etw *dat*) ◆ **he ~ed ~ to the idea of coming with us** er hat es sich (*dat*) in den Kopf gesetzt, mitzukommen.
(b) (*attach oneself*) sich anschließen (*to dat*) ◆ **she ~ed ~ to me at the party** sie hängte sich auf der Party an mich (*inf*).
(c) (*understand*) kapieren (*inf*).

latchkey ['lætʃ,kiː] *n* Haus-/Wohnungsschlüssel *m* ◆ **~ child** Schlüsselkind *nt*.

late [leɪt] 1 *adj* (*+er*) (a) spät ◆ **to be ~ (for sth)** (zu etw) zu spät kommen; **the trains tend to be ~** die Züge haben oft Verspätung; **dinner will be ~ tonight** wir essen heute abend später; (*in hotels*) es wird heute abend später serviert; **I was ~ in getting up this morning** ich bin heute morgen zu spät aufgestanden; **he is ~ with his rent** er hat seine Miete noch nicht bezahlt; **he is always ~ with his rent** er bezahlt seine Miete immer zu spät; **my period is ~, I am ~** meine Periode ist noch nicht da; **I don't want to make you ~** ich möchte Sie nicht aufhalten; **you'll make me ~** Ihretwegen werde ich mich verspäten; **that made me ~ for work** dadurch bin ich zu spät zur Arbeit gekommen; **I don't want to make you ~ for work** ich möchte nicht, daß du zu spät zur Arbeit kommst; **that made the coach ~** dadurch hatte der Bus Verspätung; **that made the harvest ~** dadurch verzögerte sich die Ernte; **due to the ~ arrival of ...** wegen der verspäteten Ankunft ... (*+gen*).
(b) **it's ~** es ist spät; **it's getting ~** es ist schon spät; **is it as ~ as that?** ist es schon so spät?
(c) *hour* spät; *opening hours* lang; *bus, train* Spät- ◆ **at this ~ hour** zu so später Stunde, so spät; **at a ~ hour** zu später *or* vorgerückter Stunde; **he keeps very ~ hours** er geht sehr spät ins Bett; **the night was cold and the hour ~** die Nacht war kalt, und es war sehr spät; **they had a ~ dinner yesterday** sie haben gestern spät zu Abend gegessen; **there is no ~ delivery of post on Saturdays** sonnabends gibt es keine zweite Zustellung; **~ night club** Nachtbar *f*; **~ potato/summer/edition/programme** Spätkartoffel *f*/-sommer *m*/-ausgabe *f*/-programm *nt*; **~ entrants to the examination will be charged £10 extra** für Nachmeldungen zur Prüfung wird eine Gebühr von £ 10 erhoben; **this essay was a ~ entry for the competition** dieser Aufsatz wurde verspätet für den Wettbewerb eingereicht; (*last-minute*) dieser Aufsatz wurde in letzter Minute eingereicht; **it happened in the ~ eighties** es geschah Ende der achtziger Jahre; **a man in his ~ eighties** ein Mann hoch in den Achtzigern, ein Endachtziger; **in the ~ morning** am späten Vormittag; **a ~ 18th-century building** ein Gebäude aus dem späten 18. Jahrhundert; **he came in ~ June** er kam Ende Juni; **L~ Stone Age** Jungsteinzeit *f*; **L~ Latin** Spätlatein *nt*; **Easter is ~ this year** Ostern liegt *or* ist dieses Jahr spät; **spring is ~ this year** wir haben dieses Jahr einen späten Frühling.
(d) *attr* (*deceased*) verstorben ◆ **the ~ John F. Kennedy** John F. Kennedy.
(e) (*former*) **the ~ Prime Minister** der frühere *or* vorige Premierminister.
(f) (*recent*) jüngst ◆ **in the ~ war** im letzten Krieg.
(g) **~ of No 13 White St** ehemals *or* bis vor kurzem White St Nr. 13; **~ of the Diplomatic Service** ehemals *or* bis vor kurzem im diplomatischen Dienst tätig.
2 *adv* spät ◆ **to come ~** zu spät kommen; **I'll be home ~ today** ich komme heute spät nach Hause, es wird heute spät; **the train arrived eight minutes ~** der Zug hatte acht Minuten Verspätung; **better ~ than never** lieber *or* besser spät als gar nicht; **to sit** *or* **stay up ~** lange aufbleiben; **don't wait up ~ for me** warte nicht zu lange auf mich; **to work ~ at the office** länger im Büro arbeiten; **~ at night** spät abends; **~ in the night** spät in der Nacht; **~ into the night** bis spät in die Nacht; **~ in the afternoon** am späten Nachmittag; **~ last century/in the year** (gegen) Ende des letzten Jahrhunderts/Jahres; **he took up the piano rather ~ in life** er begann ziemlich spät mit dem Klavierspielen; **Goethe was still active even ~ in life** Goethe war auch im hohen Alter noch aktiv; **of ~** in letzter Zeit; **until as ~ as 1900** noch bis 1900; **it was as ~ as 1900 before child labour was abolished** erst 1900 wurde die Kinderarbeit abgeschafft.

latecomer ['leɪtkʌməʳ] *n* Zuspätkommende(r) *mf*, Nachzügler(in *f*) *m* (*inf*) ◆ **the firm is a ~ to the industry** die Firma ist neu in der Industrie.

lateen sail [lə'tiːn'seɪl] *n* Lateinsegel *nt*.

late lamented *adj* kürzlich verstorben *or* verschieden (*geh*) ◆ **my ~ boss** (*iro*) mein heißgeliebter ehemaliger Chef (*iro*).

lately ['leɪtlɪ] *adv* in letzter Zeit ◆ **till ~** bis vor kurzem.

latency ['leɪtənsɪ] *n* Latenz *f* ◆ **the ~ of his artistic abilities** seine verborgenen *or* latenten künstlerischen Fähigkeiten.

lateness ['leɪtnɪs] *n* (*being late at work etc*) Zuspätkommen *nt*; (*of train, payments*) Verspätung *f*; (*of meal*) späte Zeit; (*of harvest, seasons*) spätes Eintreten ◆ **the ~ of the hour** die so späte Stunde.

latent ['leɪtənt] *adj* latent; *strength also* verborgen; *artistic talent, ability also* verborgen, versteckt; *heat also* gebunden; *energy* ungenutzt; (*Med*) *period* Latenz- ◆ **the evil which is ~ in all men** das in jedem Menschen latent vorhandene Böse.

later ['leɪtəʳ] 1 *adj* später ◆ **at a ~ hour, at a ~ time** später, zu einer späteren Zeit; **this version is ~ than that one** diese Version ist neuer als die andere; **in his ~ years** in vorgerücktem Alter, in seinem späteren Leben.
2 *adv* später ◆ **Mr Smith, ~ to become Sir John** Mr Smith, der spätere Sir John; **the weather cleared up ~ in the day** das Wetter klärte sich im Laufe des Tages auf; **~ that night/week/day** später in der Nacht/Woche/an dem Tag; **a moment ~** einen Augenblick später, im nächsten Augenblick; **see you ~!** bis nachher, bis später; **I saw him no ~ than yesterday** ich habe ihn (erst) gestern noch gesehen; **come at 7 o'clock and no ~** komm um 7 Uhr und nicht *or* keine Minute später; **not ~ than 1995** spätestens 1995; **~ on** nachher.

lateral ['lætərəl] *adj* seitlich; *view, window* Seiten- ◆ **~ line** (*of fish*) Seitenlinie *f*; **~ thinking** spielerisches Denken.

laterally ['lætərəlɪ] *adv* seitlich.

latest ['leɪtɪst] 1 *adj* (a) späteste(r,s) ◆ **what is the ~ date you can come?** wann kannst du spätestens kommen?
(b) (*most recent*) *fashion, version* neu(e)ste(r, s) ◆ **the ~ news** das Neu(e)ste.
(c) *people* letzte(r, s) ◆ **the ~ men to resign** die letzten, die zurückgetreten sind; **he was the ~ to arrive** er kam als letzter.
2 *adv* am spätesten ◆ **he came ~** er kam zuletzt *or* als letzter.
3 *n* (a) **what's the ~ (about John)?** was gibt's Neues (über John)?; **wait till you hear the ~!** warte, bis du das Neueste gehört hast!; **have you seen John's ~?** (*girl*) hast du Johns Neu(e)ste schon gesehen?; **have you heard John's ~?** (*joke*) hast du Johns Neuesten schon gehört?

(b) at the (very) ~ spätestens.
latex ['leɪteks] *n* Latex (*spec*), Milchsaft *m*.
lath [læθ] *n* Latte *f* ♦ ~s *pl* (*structure*) Lattenwerk *nt*.
lathe [leɪð] *n* Drehbank *f* ♦ ~ **operator** Dreher *m*.
lather ['lɑːðəʳ] 1 *n* (Seifen)schaum *m*; (*sweat*) Schweiß *m* ♦ **work the soap into a rich ~** die Seife zum Schäumen bringen; **the horse/athlete was in a ~** das Pferd/der Sportler war schweißnaß; **to get into a ~ (about sth)** (*inf*) sich (über etw *acc*) aufregen, (wegen etw *dat*) durchdrehen (*inf*).
2 *vt* einschäumen.
3 *vi* schäumen.
Latin ['lætɪn] 1 *adj* (a) (*Roman*) *civilization, world* römisch; *poets, literature also* lateinisch ♦ ~ **language** lateinische Sprache; (*of ancient Latium*) latinische Sprache.
(b) (*of Roman origin*) romanisch; *temperament, charm* südländisch ♦ ~ **Quarter** Quartier Latin *nt*.
(c) (*Rel*) römisch-katholisch.
2 *n* (a) (*inhabitant of ancient Latium*) Latiner(in *f*) *m*; (*Roman*) Römer(in *f*) *m*; (*a member of any Latin race*) Südländer(in *f*), Romane *m*, Romanin *f*.
(b) (*language*) Latein(isch) *nt*.
Latin America *n* Lateinamerika *nt*.
Latin-American ['lætɪnə'merɪkən] 1 *adj* lateinamerikanisch.
2 *n* Lateinamerikaner(in *f*) *m*.
latinism ['lætɪnɪzəm] *n* Latinismus *m*.
latinist ['lætɪnɪst] *n* Latinist *m*.
latinity [lə'tɪnɪtɪ] *n* (*rare*) Latinität *f*.
latinize ['lætɪnaɪz] *vt* latinisieren.
latish ['leɪtɪʃ] 1 *adj* ziemlich spät; *applicant, letter* verspätet; *amendment* neuer, später.
2 *adv* ziemlich spät.
latitude ['lætɪtjuːd] *n* Breite *f*; (*fig*) Freiheit *f*, Spielraum *m*.
latitudinal [,lætɪ'tjuːdɪnl] *adj* Breiten- ♦ ~ **lines** Breitengrade *pl*.
latrine [lə'triːn] *n* Latrine *f*.
➤ **latter** ['lætəʳ] 1 *adj* (a) (*second of two*) letztere(r, s).
(b) (*at the end*) **the ~ part of the book/story is better** gegen Ende wird das Buch/die Geschichte besser; **the ~ part/half of the week/year/century** die zweite Hälfte der Woche/des Jahres/des Jahrhunderts; **in the ~ years** in den letzten Jahren; **in his ~ years** in den späteren Jahren seines Lebens.
➤ 2 *n* **the ~** der/die/das/letztere; die letzteren.
latter-day ['lætə'deɪ] *adj* modern ♦ **the L~ Saints** die Heiligen der Letzten Tage.
latterly ['lætəlɪ] *adv* in letzter Zeit.
lattice ['lætɪs] *n* Gitter *nt* ♦ **~-work** Gitterwerk *nt*.
latticed ['lætɪst] *adj* vergittert.
Latvia ['lætvɪə] *n* Lettland *nt*.
Latvian ['lætvɪən] 1 *adj* lettisch.
2 *n* (a) Lette *m*, Lettin *f*. (b) (*language*) Lettisch *nt*.
laud [lɔːd] *vt* (*old*) preisen (*geh*).
laudable ['lɔːdəbl] *adj* lobenswert.
laudably ['lɔːdəblɪ] *adv* lobenswerterweise ♦ ~ **unselfish remarks** lobenswert selbstlose Worte *pl*.
laudanum ['lɔːdnəm] *n* Laudanum *nt*.
laudatory ['lɔːdətərɪ] *adj* lobend ♦ **a ~ speech** eine Lobrede *or* Laudatio (*geh*).
laugh [lɑːf] 1 *n* (a) Lachen *nt* ♦ **no, she said, with a ~** nein, sagte sie lachend; **she let out** *or* **gave a loud ~** sie lachte laut auf; **that woman has a ~ like a hyena** die Frau gackert wie ein Huhn; **what a ~ (she's got)!** die hat vielleicht 'ne Lache! (*inf*); **to have a good ~ over** *or* **about sth** sich köstlich über etw (*acc*) amüsieren; **you'll have a good ~ about it one day** eines Tages wirst du darüber lachen können; **give us a ~!** (*inf*) bring uns mal zum Lachen!; **it'll give us a ~** (*inf*) das wird lustig; **the ~ was on me** der Witz ging auf meine Kosten; **to have the last ~ (over** *or* **on sb)** es jdm zeigen (*inf*); **I'll have the last ~** ich werd's dir schon noch zeigen (*inf*); **to play for ~s** Lacherfolge haben wollen; **he played Hamlet for ~s** er machte aus Hamlet eine komische Figur; **they played "Othello" for ~s** sie machten aus „Othello" eine Komödie.
(b) (*inf: fun*) **what a ~** (das ist ja) zum Totlachen *or* zum Schreien (*inf*)!; **just for a ~** nur (so) aus Spaß; **it'll be a good ~** es wird bestimmt lustig; **we didn't achieve much, but we had a good ~** wir haben nicht viel geschafft, aber es war trotzdem lustig; **he's a ~** er ist urkomisch *or* zum Schreien (*inf*); **to be good for a ~** ganz lustig sein.
2 *vi* lachen (*about, at, over* über +*acc*) ♦ **to ~ at sb** sich über jdn lustig machen; **to ~ up one's sleeve** sich (*dat*) ins Fäustchen lachen; **she's ~ing up her sleeve at us** sie macht sich heimlich über uns lustig; **it's nothing to ~ about** das ist nicht zum Lachen; **it's all very well for you to ~** du hast gut lachen; **you'll be ~ing on the other side of your face soon** dir wird das Lachen noch vergehen; **to ~ out loud** laut auflachen; **to ~ in sb's face** jdm ins Gesicht lachen; **he who ~s last ~s longest** (*Prov*) wer zuletzt lacht, lacht am besten (*Prov*); **don't make me ~!** (*iro inf*) daß ich nicht lache! (*inf*); **you've got your own house, you're ~ing** (*inf*) du hast ein eigenes Haus, du hast es gut.
3 *vt* **to ~ oneself silly** sich tot- *or* kaputtlachen (*inf*); **he was ~ed out of court** er wurde ausgelacht; **the idea was ~ed out of court** die Idee wurde verlacht.
◆**laugh away** 1 *vt sep* mit Humor tragen, sich lachend hinwegsetzen über (+*acc*) ♦ **my father ~ed ~ my fears** mein Vater nahm mir mit einem Lachen die Angst.
2 *vi* **he sat there ~ing ~** er saß da und lachte und lachte.

➤ LANGUAGE IN USE: **latter: 2** → 26.2

◆**laugh down** *vt sep* auslachen, mit Gelächter übertönen ♦ **the audience ~ed him/his reply ~** er/seine Antwort ging im Gelächter des Publikums unter.
◆**laugh off** *vt* (a) *always separate* **to ~ one's head ~** sich tot- *or* kaputtlachen (*inf*). (b) *sep* (*dismiss*) lachen über (+*acc*), mit einem Lachen abtun.
laughable ['lɑːfəbl] *adj* lachhaft, lächerlich ♦ **if it wasn't so serious, it would be almost ~** wenn es nicht so ernst wäre, könnte man fast darüber lachen.
laughably ['lɑːfəblɪ] *adv* lächerlich.
laughing ['lɑːfɪŋ] 1 *adj* lachend ♦ **it's no ~ matter** das ist nicht zum Lachen, das ist gar nicht komisch.
2 *n* Lachen *nt* ♦ **the sound of hysterical ~** der Klang hysterischen Gelächters.
laughing: ~ gas *n* Lachgas *nt*; ~ **hy(a)ena** *n* Tüpfel- *or* Fleckenhyäne *f*; ~ **jackass** *n* Rieseneisvogel *m*.
laughingly ['lɑːfɪŋlɪ] *adv see adj*.
laughing stock *n* Witzfigur *f* ♦ **his visionary ideas made him a ~** mit seinen phantastischen Ideen machte er sich lächerlich *or* zum allgemeinen Gespött.
laughter ['lɑːftəʳ] *n* Gelächter *nt* ♦ **~ broke out among the audience** das Publikum brach in Gelächter aus; **children's ~** Kinderlachen *nt*; **he shook with silent ~** er schüttelte sich vor Lachen; **at this there was ~** das rief Gelächter hervor.
launch [lɔːntʃ] 1 *n* (a) (*vessel*) Barkasse *f*.
(b) (*~ing*) (*of ship*) Stapellauf *m*; (*of lifeboat*) Aussetzen *nt*; (*of rocket*) Abschuß *m*.
(c) (*~ing*) (*of company*) Gründung, Eröffnung *f*; (*of new product*) Einführung *f*; (*with party, publicity: of film, play, book*) Lancierung *f*; (*bringing out*) (*of film, play*) Premiere *f*; (*of book*) Herausgabe *f*; (*of shares*) Emission *f*.
2 *vt* (a) *new vessel* vom Stapel lassen; (*christen*) taufen; *lifeboat* zu Wasser lassen, aussetzen; *rocket* abschießen; *plane* katapultieren ♦ **Lady X ~ed the new boat** der Stapellauf fand in Anwesenheit von Lady X statt; **the rocket was ~ed into space** die Rakete wurde in den Weltraum geschossen.
(b) *company, newspaper* gründen; *new product* einführen, auf den Markt bringen; (*with party, publicity*) *film, play, book* lancieren; (*bring out*) *film* anlaufen lassen; *play* auf die Bühne bringen; *book* herausbringen; *plan* in die Wege leiten; *programme, trend* einführen; *policy* in Angriff nehmen; *shares* emittieren, ausgeben ♦ **to ~ an offensive** *or* **an attack against the enemy** zum Angriff gegen den Feind übergehen; **the attack was ~ed at 15.00 hours** der Angriff fand um 15^{00} Uhr statt; **to ~ sb into society** jdn in die Gesellschaft einführen; **to ~ pupils into the world** Schüler ins Leben entlassen; **to ~ sb on his way** jdm einen guten Start geben; **he helped ~ his son into the City** er brachte seinen Sohn in Finanzkreisen unter; **once he is ~ed on this subject** ... wenn er einmal mit diesem Thema angefangen hat *or* bei diesem Thema gelandet ist, ...; **now that he's ~ed himself on this long description** da er jetzt mit dieser langen Beschreibung losgelegt hat (*inf*).
(c) (*hurl*) schleudern ♦ **he ~ed himself into the crowd** er stürzte sich in die Menge.
◆**launch forth** *vi see* **launch out (a, d)**.
◆**launch into** *vi +prep obj* (*question, attack etc vigorously*) angreifen ♦ **the author ~es straight ~ his main theme** der Autor kommt gleich zum Hauptthema.
◆**launch out** *vi* (a) (*also ~ forth*) **the astronauts ~ed ~ into the unknown** die Astronauten starteten ins Unbekannte.
(b) (*diversify*) sich verlegen (*in* auf +*acc*) ♦ **the company ~ ed ~ in several new directions** die Firma stieg in einige neue Branchen ein.
(c) (*inf: spend a lot*) **to ~ ~** sich in Unkosten stürzen; **now we can afford to ~ ~ a bit** jetzt können wir es uns leisten, etwas mehr auszugeben (*on* für).
(d) (*start: also ~ forth*) anfangen (*into sth* mit etw, etw *acc*) ♦ **to ~ ~ into a new career** eine neue Karriere starten; **he ~ed ~ into a violent attack on the government** er ließ wütende Angriffe gegen die Regierung vom Stapel (*inf*) *or* los (*inf*); **he ~ed ~ into a description of** ... er legte mit einer Schilderung der/des ... los (*inf*).
launching ['lɔːntʃɪŋ] *n see* **launch 1 (b, c)**.
launching: ~ pad *n* Start- *or* Abschußrampe *f*; (*fig*) Sprungbrett *nt*; ~ **party** *n* (*of film, play*) Premierenfeier *f*; ~ **site** *n* Abschußbasis *f*.
launch: ~ pad *n see* **launching pad**; ~ **vehicle** *n* (*Space*) Booster *m*, Startrakete *f*.
launder ['lɔːndəʳ] 1 *vt* waschen und bügeln; (*fig*) *money* waschen.
2 *vi* waschen und bügeln ♦ **modern fabrics ~ easily** moderne Gewebe lassen sich leicht reinigen *or* sind pflegeleicht.
launderette [,lɔːndə'ret] *n* Waschsalon *m*.
laundress ['lɔːndrɪs] *n* Waschfrau, Wäscherin *f*.
laundromat ['lɔːndrəʊmæt] *n* (*US*) Waschsalon *m*.
laundry ['lɔːndrɪ] *n* (*establishment*) Wäscherei *f*; (*clothes*) (*dirty*) schmutzige Wäsche; (*washed*) Wäsche *f* ♦ **to do the ~** (Wäsche) waschen; ~ **basket** Wäschekorb *m*; **~man** Wäschemann *m* (*inf*).
laureate ['lɔːrɪɪt] *n*: **poet ~** Hofdichter, Poeta laureatus *m*.
laurel ['lɒrəl] *n* Lorbeer *m* ♦ **to look to one's ~s** sich behaupten (müssen); **to rest on one's ~s** sich auf seinen Lorbeeren ausruhen; **to win** *or* **gain one's ~s** Lorbeeren ernten.
lav [læv] *n* (*Brit inf*) Klo *nt* (*inf*).
lava ['lɑːvə] *n* Lava *f* ♦ ~ **bed** Lavadecke *f*.
lavatory ['lævətrɪ] *n* Toilette *f* ♦ ~ **attendant** Toilettenfrau *f*/-mann *m*; ~ **seat** Toilettensitz *m*, Brille *f* (*inf*).
lavender ['lævɪndəʳ] 1 *n* (*flower*) Lavendel *m*; (*colour*) Lavendel *nt*.
2 *adj* (*colour*) lavendelfarben ♦ **eyes of ~ blue** lavendelblaue Augen *pl*.

lavender: ~ bag *n* Lavendelsäckchen *nt;* **~ water** *n* Lavendelwasser *nt.*

lavish ['lævɪʃ] [1] *adj gifts* großzügig, üppig; *praise, affection* überschwenglich; *banquet* üppig; *party* feudal; *(pej)* verschwenderisch; *expenditure* verschwenderisch ♦ **to be ~ in** *or* **with sth** mit etw verschwenderisch sein *or* umgehen; **he was ~ in his help to others** er half anderen großzügig; **he's ~ in giving money to good causes** für gute Zwecke spendet er großzügig Geld; **you were very ~ with the cream** du hast ja mit der Sahne nicht gespart; **to be ~ with one's money** das Geld mit vollen Händen ausgeben.
[2] *vt* **to ~ sth on sb** jdn mit etw überhäufen *or* überschütten; **she ~ed food and drink on them** sie bewirtete sie fürstlich; **to ~ care on sth** viel Sorgfalt auf etw *(acc)* verwenden.

lavishly ['lævɪʃlɪ] *adv give* großzügig; *praise* überschwenglich; *put paint on, spread* reichlich; *entertain* üppig, reichlich ♦ **they entertain ~** sie geben feudale Feste; **~ furnished** luxuriös *or* aufwendig eingerichtet; **to spend (money) ~** das Geld mit vollen Händen ausgeben *(on* für); **he is ~ extravagant in his hospitality** seine Gastfreundschaft kennt keine Grenzen.

lavishness ['lævɪʃnɪs] *n (of gifts)* Großzügigkeit, Üppigkeit *f; (of praise, affection)* Überschwenglichkeit *f; (of banquet)* Üppigkeit *f; (of person)* Großzügigkeit *f; (pej)* Verschwendungssucht *f* ♦ **the ~ of the party** die feudale Party.

law [lɔː] *n* **(a)** *(rule, Jewish, Sci)* Gesetz *nt* ♦ **~ of nature** Naturgesetz *nt;* **it's the ~** das ist Gesetz; **his word is ~** sein Wort ist Gesetz; **to become ~** rechtskräftig werden; **is there a ~ against it?** ist das verboten?; **there is no ~ against asking, is there?** *(inf)* man darf doch wohl noch fragen, oder?; **he/his behaviour is a ~ unto himself/itself** er macht, was er will, er/sein Benehmen ist (recht) eigenwillig.
(b) *(body of laws)* Gesetz *nt no pl; (system)* Recht *nt* ♦ **in** *or* **under French ~** nach französischem Recht; **he is above/outside the ~** er steht über dem Gesetz/außerhalb des Gesetzes; **what is the ~ on drugs?** wie sind die Drogengesetze?; **to keep within the ~** sich im Rahmen des Gesetzes bewegen; **in ~** vor dem Gesetz; **ignorance is no defence in ~** Unwissenheit schützt vor Strafe nicht; **by ~** gesetzlich; **the ~ as it relates to property** die gesetzlichen Bestimmungen über das Eigentum.
(c) *(as study)* Jura *no art,* Recht(swissenschaft *f) nt.*
(d) *(Sport)* Regel *f; (Art)* Gesetz *nt* ♦ **the ~s of harmony** die Harmonielehre; **one of the basic ~s of harmony** eins der grundlegenden Prinzipien der Harmonielehre.
(e) *(operation of ~)* **to practise ~** eine Anwaltspraxis haben; **to go to ~** vor Gericht gehen, den Rechtsweg beschreiten; **to take sb to ~, to go to ~ with** *or* **against sb** gegen jdn gerichtlich vorgehen, jdn vor Gericht bringen; **to take a case against sb to ~** in einer Sache gegen jdn gerichtlich vorgehen; **to take the ~ into one's own hands** das Recht selbst in die Hand nehmen; **~ and order** Ruhe *or* Recht und Ordnung, Law and Order; **the forces of ~ and order** die Ordnungskräfte *pl.*
(f) the ~ *(inf)* die Polente *(sl);* **I'll have the ~ on you** ich hole die Polizei; **he got the ~ on to me** er hat mir die Polizei auf den Hals gehetzt *(inf).*

law: ~-abiding *adj* gesetzestreu; **~breaker** *n* Rechtsbrecher *m;* **~ court** *n* Gerichtshof *m,* Gericht *nt;* **~ enforcement** *n* **the duty of the police is ~ enforcement** Aufgabe der Polizei ist es, dem Gesetz Geltung zu verschaffen; **~ enforcement officer** *n* Polizeibeamte(r) *m.*

lawful ['lɔːfʊl] *adj* rechtmäßig ♦ **~ wedded wife** rechtmäßig angetraute Frau; **will you take this man to be your ~ wedded husband?** willst du mit diesem Mann den Bund der Ehe eingehen?

lawfully ['lɔːfəlɪ] *adv see adj* ♦ **he is ~ entitled to compensation** er hat einen Rechtsanspruch *or* rechtmäßigen Anspruch auf Entschädigung; **he was careful to carry on his activities ~** er achtete darauf, daß seine Handlungen im Rahmen des Gesetzes blieben.

lawgiver ['lɔːgɪvəʳ] *n* Gesetzgeber *m.*

lawless ['lɔːlɪs] *adj act* gesetzwidrig; *person* gesetzlos; *country* ohne Gesetzgebung.

lawlessness ['lɔːlɪsnɪs] *n* Gesetzwidrigkeit *f* ♦ **~ among young people** gesetzwidriges Verhalten unter Jugendlichen; **after the coup, the country reverted to ~** nach dem Staatsstreich fiel das Land in einen Zustand der Gesetzlosigkeit zurück.

Law Lord *n (Brit) Mitglied nt des Oberhauses mit besonderem Verantwortungsbereich in Rechtsfragen.*

lawn[1] [lɔːn] *n (grass)* Rasen *m no pl* ♦ **the ~s in front of the houses** der Rasen vor den Häusern.

lawn[2] *n (Tex)* Batist, Linon *m.*

lawn: ~mower *n* Rasenmäher *m;* **~ tennis** *n* Rasentennis, Lawn-Tennis *nt.*

lawrencium [lɔː'rensɪəm] *n (Chem)* Lawrencium *nt.*

law: ~ reports *npl* Entscheidungs- *or* Fallsammlung *f; (journal)* Gerichtszeitung *f;* **~ school** *n (US)* juristische Fakultät; **~ student** *n* Jurastudent(in *f*) *m,* Student(in *f*) *m* der Rechte *(form);* **~suit** *n* Prozeß *m,* Klage *f;* **he brought a ~suit for damages** er strengte eine Schadenersatzklage an.

lawyer ['lɔːjəʳ] *n* (Rechts)anwalt *m,* (Rechts)anwältin *f.*

lax [læks] *adj (+er)* **(a)** lax; *discipline also* lasch; *morals also* locker, lose ♦ **she is rather ~ in her relations with men** sie hat ein recht lockeres Verhältnis zu Männern; **to be ~ about sth** etw vernachlässigen; **he's ~ about washing/imposing discipline** er nimmt's mit dem Waschen/der Disziplin nicht so genau; **I've been rather ~ about replying to your letters** ich habe mir mit der Beantwortung Ihrer Briefe reichlich viel Zeit gelassen; **things are very ~ at the school** in der Schule geht es sehr lax *or* undiszipliniert zu.
(b) ~ bowels dünner Stuhl(gang).

laxative ['læksətɪv] [1] *adj* abführend, laxativ *(spec).*
[2] *n* Abführmittel, Laxativ(um) *(spec) nt.*

laxity ['læksɪtɪ], **laxness** ['læksnɪs] *n (lack of vigour, discipline)* Laxheit *f; (carelessness also)* Nachlässigkeit *f* ♦ **his moral ~** seine lockeren *or* laxen moralischen Einstellungen; **sexual ~** lockere Sitten *pl,* sexuelle Freizügigkeit.

lay[1] [leɪ] *n (Liter, Mus)* Ballade *f,* Lied *nt.*

lay[2] *adj* Laien- ♦ **~ opinion** die öffentliche Meinung, die Öffentlichkeit; **a ~ opinion** die Meinung eines Laien.

lay[3] *pret of* **lie.**

lay[4] *(vb: pret, ptp* **laid)** [1] *n* **(a)** Lage *f; see* **land 1(a).**
(b) *(sl)* **she's an easy ~** sie läßt jeden ran *(sl);* **she's a good ~** sie ist gut im Bett *(inf);* **that's/she is the best ~ I ever had** das war die beste Nummer, die ich je gemacht habe *(sl)*/sie hat's bisher am besten gebracht *(sl).*
[2] *vt* **(a)** *(place, put)* legen *(sth on sth* etw auf etw *acc)* ♦ **to ~ (one's) hands on** *(get hold of)* erwischen, fassen; *(find)* finden; **to ~ a hand on sb** jdm etwas tun, Hand an jdn legen *(geh);* **I never laid a hand on him** ich habe ihn überhaupt nicht angefaßt *or* ihm nichts getan; **he grabs all the money he can ~ his hands on** er rafft alles Geld an sich, das ihm unter die Finger kommt.
(b) *bricks, foundations, track* legen; *concrete* gießen; *cable, mains, pipes* verlegen; *road* bauen, anlegen; *carpet, lino* (ver)legen ♦ **to ~ a floor with carpets** einen Boden mit Teppichen auslegen.
(c) *(prepare) fire* herrichten; *(Brit) table* decken; *mines, ambush* legen; *trap* aufstellen; *plans* schmieden ♦ **to ~ breakfast/lunch** den Frühstücks-/Mittagstisch decken; **to ~ a trap for sb** jdm eine Falle stellen.
(d) *(non-material things) burden* auferlegen *(on sb* jdm) ♦ **to ~ the blame for sth on sb/sth** jdm/einer Sache die Schuld an etw *(dat)* geben; **to ~ responsibility for sth on sb** jdn für etw verantwortlich machen; **the importance which he ~s on it** die Bedeutung, die er dieser Sache *(dat)* beimißt; **the stress which he ~s on it** der Nachdruck, den er darauf legt.
(e) *(bring forward) complaint* vorbringen *(before* bei); *accusation* erheben ♦ **the police laid a charge of murder against him** die Polizei erstattete gegen ihn Anzeige wegen Mordes; **he laid his case before them** er trug ihnen seinen Fall vor.
(f) *dust* binden; *ghost* austreiben; *fear* zerstreuen; *doubts* beseitigen ♦ **he laid him sprawling** er schlug ihn nieder *or* zu Boden; **to ~ waste** verwüsten; *see* **low**[1]**, open** *etc.*
(g) *eggs (hen)* legen; *(fish, insects)* ablegen.
(h) *bet* abschließen; *money* setzen ♦ **to ~ a bet on sth** auf etw *(acc)* wetten; **I ~ you a fiver on it!** ich wette mit dir um 5 Pfund!; **I'll ~ you that ...** ich wette mit dir, daß ...; **I'll ~ you anything ...** ich gehe mit dir jede Wette ein ...
(i) *(sl)* **to ~ a woman** eine Frau aufs Kreuz legen *(sl);* **he just wants to get laid** er will nur bumsen *(inf).*
[3] *vi (hen)* legen.

♦**lay about** [1] *vi* um sich schlagen.
[2] *vt sep* losschlagen gegen.

♦**lay aside** *or* **away** *vt sep, work etc* weglegen, zur Seite legen; *(keep in reserve, save)* beiseite *or* auf die Seite legen; *(cast away)* ablegen; *doubts* aufgeben; *plans etc* auf Eis legen.

♦**lay back** *vt sep ears* anlegen; *person* zurücklegen.

♦**lay before** *vt +prep obj* **to ~ sth ~ sb** *plan* jdm etw vorlegen; *ideas also* jdm etw unterbreiten; *claim, complaint* etw bei jdm vorbringen.

♦**lay by** *vt sep* beiseite *or* auf die Seite legen.

♦**lay down** *vt sep* **(a)** *book, pen etc* hinlegen ♦ **he laid his bag ~ on the table** er legte seine Tasche auf den Tisch; **she laid herself ~ to sleep** *(liter)* sie begab sich zur Ruhe.
(b) *(give up) burden* ablegen; *office* niederlegen ♦ **to ~ ~ one's arms** die Waffen niederlegen; **to ~ ~ one's life** sein Leben geben *or* opfern.
(c) *(impose, establish) condition* festsetzen *or* -legen; *policy* festsetzen, bestimmen; *rules* aufstellen, festlegen; *price* festsetzen, vorschreiben ♦ **it is laid ~ that** es wurde festgelegt, daß; **to ~ ~ the law** *(inf)* Vorschriften machen *(to sb* jdm).
(d) *(store)* lagern.
(e) *ship* auf Stapel legen.
(f) *deposit* hinterlegen.

♦**lay in** *vt sep food etc* einlagern; *supplies also* anlegen ♦ **they have laid ~ plenty of water** sie haben (sich *dat*) einen großen Wasservorrat angelegt.

♦**lay into** *vi +prep obj (inf)* **to ~ ~ sb** auf jdn losgehen; *(verbally)* jdn fertigmachen *(inf) or* runterputzen *(inf).*

♦**lay off** [1] *vi (inf: stop)* aufhören *(prep obj* mit) ♦ **~ ~, will you?** hör (mal) auf, ja?; **~ ~ it!** hör auf damit!, laß das!; **you'll have to ~ ~ smoking** du wirst das Rauchen aufgeben müssen *(inf);* **I wish you'd ~ ~ coming here every day** ich wünschte, du würdest nicht mehr jeden Tag hierherkommen; **~ ~ my little brother, will you!** laß bloß meinen kleinen Bruder in Ruhe!
[2] *vt sep workers* Feierschichten machen lassen; *(permanently)* entlassen ♦ **to be laid ~** Feierschichten einlegen müssen; entlassen werden.

♦**lay on** *vt sep* **(a)** *(apply) paint* auftragen; *see* **thick.**
(b) *(prepare, offer) hospitality* bieten *(for sb* jdm); *(supply) entertainment* sorgen für; *excursion* veranstalten; *extra buses* einsetzen; *water, electricity* anschließen ♦ **if you ~ ~ the drinks I'll get the food** wenn du die Getränke stellst, besorge ich das Essen; **she had laid ~ a lot of food** sie hatte sehr viel zu essen aufgetischt; **an extra flight was laid ~** eine Sondermaschine wurde eingesetzt *or* bereitgestellt.
(c) *(impose)* **to ~ a tax ~ sth** etw mit einer Steuer belegen, etw besteuern.
(d) he laid it ~ me *(esp US sl: tell off)* er hat mich zur Sau gemacht *(sl).*

♦**lay out** [1] *vt sep* **(a)** ausbreiten ♦ **the vast plain laid ~ before us** die weite Ebene, die sich vor uns ausbreitete.

(b) *(prepare)* *clothes* zurechtlegen; *corpse* (waschen und) aufbahren.
(c) *(design, arrange)* anlegen, planen; *garden also* gestalten; *room* aufteilen; *rooms in house* verteilen, anordnen; *office* aufteilen, anordnen; *book* gestalten; *page* umbrechen; *(in magazines)* das Layout (+*gen*) machen.
(d) *money (spend)* ausgeben; *(invest)* investieren.
(e) *(knock out)* **to ~ sb ~** jdn k.o. schlagen; **three whiskies were enough to ~ him ~** nach drei Whiskys war er erledigt *(inf)*; **he laid himself ~ cold when he fell downstairs** er verlor das Bewußtsein, als er die Treppe hinunterfiel.
[2] *vr (dated: take trouble)* sich bemühen, sich *(dat)* Mühe geben ◆ **to ~ oneself ~ to please** sich Mühe geben, zu gefallen.
◆**lay over** *vi (US)* Aufenthalt haben.
◆**lay to** *vi (Naut)* beidrehen.
◆**lay up** *vt sep* **(a)** *(store)* lagern; *supply* anlegen; *(amass, save)* anhäufen, ansammeln ◆ **he's ~ing ~ trouble for himself in the future** er wird später noch (viel) Ärger bekommen.
(b) *(immobilize)* *ship* auflegen; *boat* aufbocken; *car* still(l)egen, einmotten *(inf)* ◆ **to be laid ~ (in bed)** auf der Nase *(inf) or* im Bett liegen; **you'd better take it easy or you'll ~ yourself ~** Sie müssen etwas langsamer treten, sonst liegen Sie nachher flach *or* auf der Nase *(inf)*.
lay: ~about *n* Nichtstuer, Arbeitsscheue(r) *m*; **~ brother** *n* Laienbruder *m*; **~by** *n (Brit) (in town)* Parkbucht *f*; *(in country)* Parkplatz *m*; *(big)* Rastplatz *m*.
layer ['leɪəʳ] [1] *n* **(a)** Schicht *(also Geol)*, Lage *f* ◆ **to arrange the meat in ~s** das Fleisch lagenweise anordnen; **we climbed through ~ upon ~ of cloud** wir stiegen durch eine Wolkenschicht nach der anderen auf; **the cake was covered with ~ upon ~ of chocolate** der Kuchen war mit vielen Schokoladenschichten überzogen; **~ cake** Schichttorte *f*.
(b) *(Hort)* Ableger *m*.
(c) *(hen)* Legehenne *f*.
[2] *vt* **(a)** *(Hort)* absenken. **(b)** *hair* abstufen.
layette [leɪ'et] *n* Babyausstattung *f*.
lay figure *n* Gliederpuppe *f*; *(fig)* Marionette *f*.
laying ['leɪɪŋ] *n*: **~ on of hands** Handauflegen *nt*.
lay: ~man *n* Laie *m*; **~-off** *n* **further ~-offs were unavoidable** weitere Arbeiter mußten Feierschichten einlegen *or (permanent)* mußten entlassen werden; **during the ~-off period** während der Feierschichten; **~out** *n* Anordnung, Anlage *f*; *(Typ)* Layout *nt*; **the standard ~out of German stations** wie deutsche Bahnhöfe normalerweise angelegt sind; **we have changed the ~out of this office** wir haben dieses Büro anders aufgeteilt; **our house has a different ~out** unser Haus hat eine andere Zimmerverteilung *or* ist anders angelegt; **~over** *n (US)* Aufenthalt *m*; **~person** *n* Laie *m*; **~ reader** *n* Vorbeter, Hilfsdiakon *m*; **~ sister** *n* Laienschwester *f*; **~woman** *n* Laie *m*.
laze [leɪz] [1] *n* **to have a ~** faulenzen; **to have a long ~ in bed** lange faul im Bett (liegen) bleiben.
[2] *vi* faulenzen.
◆**laze about** *or* **around** *vi* faulenzen, auf der faulen Haut liegen ◆ **stop lazing ~** steh/sitz *etc* nicht so faul herum!
◆**laze away** *vt sep* verbummeln.
lazily ['leɪzɪlɪ] *adv* faul; *(languidly, unhurriedly)* träge.
laziness ['leɪzɪnɪs] *n* Faulheit *f*; *(languor)* Trägheit *f*.
lazy ['leɪzɪ] *adj (+er) (not inclined to work)* faul; *(slow-moving)* langsam, träge; *(lacking activity)* träge ◆ **~ little streams** träge fließende kleine Bäche *pl*; **we had a ~ holiday** wir haben im Urlaub nur gefaulenzt; **I enjoy a ~ day at home** ich mache mir gerne einen faulen *or* gemütlichen Tag zu Hause; **~ Susan** *(US inf)* drehbare Tisch-Menage.
lazybones ['leɪzɪ,bəunz] *n sing (inf)* Faulpelz *m*, Faultier *nt*.
lb *n (weight)* ≃ Pfd.
lbw *abbr of* **leg before wicket.**
lc *(Typ) abbr of* **lower case.**
LCD *abbr of* **liquid crystal display** LCD *nt* ◆ **~ screen** LCD-Bildschirm *m*.
LEA *(Brit) abbr of* **Local Education Authority.**
lea [liː] *n (poet)* Au(e) *f (poet)*, Wiesengrund *m (liter)*.
leach [liːtʃ] *vt* (durch)filtern; *(extract)* auslaugen.
lead¹ [led] [1] *n* **(a)** *(metal)* Blei *nt* ◆ **they filled him full of ~** *(inf)* sie pumpten ihn mit Blei voll *(sl)*. **(b)** *(in pencil)* Graphit *nt*; *(single ~)* Mine *f*. **(c)** *(Naut)* Lot *nt*. **(d) ~s** *pl (on roof)* Bleiplatten *pl*; *(in window)* Bleifassung *f*.
[2] *vt (weight with ~)* mit Blei beschweren.
▼ **lead**² [liːd] *(vb: pret, ptp* **led***)* [1] *n* **(a)** *(front position)* Spitzenposition *f*; *(leading position, Sport)* Führung, Spitze *f*; *(in league etc)* Tabellenspitze *f* ◆ **to be in the ~** führend sein, in Führung liegen; *(Sport)* in Führung *or* vorn liegen, führen; **to take the ~, to move into the ~** in Führung gehen, die Führung übernehmen; *(in league)* Tabellenführer werden; **he took the ~ from the German runner** er ging vor dem deutschen Läufer in Führung; **Japan took the ~ from Germany in exports** Japan lief Deutschland auf dem Exportmarkt den Rang ab.
(b) *(distance, time ahead)* Vorsprung *m* ◆ **to have two minutes' ~ over sb** zwei Minuten Vorsprung vor jdm haben.
(c) *(example)* Beispiel *nt* ◆ **to give sb a ~** jdm etw vormachen; **to take the ~, to show a ~** mit gutem Beispiel vorangehen.
(d) *(clue)* Indiz *nt*, Anhaltspunkt *m*; *(in guessing etc)* Hinweis, Tip *m* ◆ **the police have a ~** die Polizei hat eine Spur; **it gave the police a ~** das brachte die Polizei auf die Spur.
(e) *(Cards)* **it's my ~** ich fange an.
(f) *(Theat) (part)* Hauptrolle *f*; *(person)* Hauptdarsteller(in *f*) *m* ◆ **to sing the ~** die Titelpartie *or* die tragende Partie singen.
(g) *(leash)* Leine *f* ◆ **on a ~** an der Leine.

➤ LANGUAGE IN USE: **lead²: 2f** → 26.1

(h) *(Elec)* Leitung(skabel *nt*) *f*, Kabel *nt*; *(from separate source)* Zuleitung *f (form)*.
[2] *vt* **(a)** *(conduct)* *person, animal* führen; *water* leiten ◆ **that road will ~ you back to the station** auf dieser Straße kommen Sie zum Bahnhof zurück; **to ~ the way** *(lit, fig)* vorangehen; *(fig: be superior)* führend sein; **all this talk is ~ing us nowhere** dieses ganze Gerede bringt uns nicht weiter; **the argument led us round in a circle** unsere Argumentation drehte sich im Kreis.
(b) *(be the leader of, direct)* (an)führen; *expedition, team* leiten; *regiment* führen; *movement, revolution* anführen; *orchestra (conductor)* leiten; *(first violin)* führen ◆ **to ~ a government** an der Spitze einer Regierung stehen, Regierungschef sein; **to ~ a party** Parteivorsitzender sein, den Parteivorsitz führen.
(c) *(be first in)* anführen ◆ **they led us by 30 seconds** sie lagen mit 30 Sekunden vor uns *(dat)*; **Britain ~s the world in textiles** Großbritannien ist auf dem Gebiet der Textilproduktion führend in der Welt.
(d) *card* ausspielen.
(e) *life* führen ◆ **to ~ a life of luxury/misery** in Luxus/im Elend leben, ein Luxusleben/elendes Leben führen; **to ~ sb a wretched life** jdm das Leben schwermachen.
▼ **(f)** *(influence)* **to ~ sb to do sth** jdn dazu bringen, etw zu tun; **what led him to change his mind?** wie kam er dazu, seine Meinung zu ändern?; **to ~ sb to believe that ...** jdm den Eindruck vermitteln, daß ..., jdn glauben machen, daß ... *(geh)*; **I am led to believe that ...** ich habe Grund zu der Annahme, daß ...; **to ~ sb into error** jdn irreleiten *or* fehlleiten; **to ~ sb into trouble** jdn in Schwierigkeiten bringen; **he is easily led** er läßt sich leicht beeinflussen; *(deceive)* er läßt sich leicht täuschen *or* sich *(dat)* leicht etwas weismachen; **this led me to the conclusion that ...** daraus schloß ich, daß ...; **I am led to the conclusion that ...** ich komme zu dem Schluß, daß ...; **what ~s you to think that?** woraus schließen Sie das?
(g) *wire, flex* legen, entlangführen.
[3] *vi* **(a)** *(go in front)* vorangehen; *(in race)* in Führung liegen ◆ **to ~ by 10 metres** einen Vorsprung von 10 Metern haben, mit 10 Metern in Führung liegen; **he easily ~s** er liegt klar in Führung; **he always follows where his brother ~s** er macht alles nach, was sein Bruder macht; **the "Times" led with a story about the financial crisis** die „Times" berichtete auf der ersten Seite ausführlich über die Finanzkrise; **he ~s with his right** *(Boxing)* er ist Rechtsausleger.
(b) *(be a leader, also in dancing)* führen ◆ **he had shown the ability to ~** er hat gezeigt, daß er Führungsqualitäten besitzt.
(c) *(Cards)* ausspielen *(with sth* etw) ◆ **who ~s?** wer spielt aus?, wer fängt an?
(d) *(street etc)* führen, gehen ◆ **it ~s into that room** es führt zu diesem Raum; **this road ~s nowhere** diese Straße führt nirgendwohin *or* geht nicht weiter.
(e) *(result in, cause)* führen *(to* zu) ◆ **all this talk is ~ing nowhere** dieses ganze Gerede führt zu nichts; **remarks like that could ~ to trouble** solche Bemerkungen können unangenehme Folgen haben; **what will all these strikes ~ to?** wo sollen all diese Streiks hinführen?
◆**lead along** *vt sep* führen ◆ **he led him ~ the street** er führte ihn die Straße entlang.
◆**lead aside** *vt sep* auf die Seite *or* beiseite nehmen.
◆**lead away** [1] *vt sep* wegführen *or* -bringen; *criminal, prisoner* abführen ◆ **we must not allow this argument to ~ us ~ from the matter in hand** wir dürfen uns durch dieses Argument nicht vom eigentlichen Thema abbringen lassen.
[2] *vi* wegführen ◆ **this is ~ing ~ from the subject** das führt vom Thema ab.
◆**lead off** [1] *vt sep* abführen ◆ **a policeman led the drunk man ~ the pitch** ein Polizist führte den Betrunkenen vom Platz.
[2] *vi* **(a)** *(go off from)* abgehen ◆ **several streets led ~ the square** mehrere Straßen gingen von dem Platz ab.
(b) *(start)* beginnen ◆ **my partner led ~ with the ten of hearts** mein Partner spielte die Herz-Zehn aus.
◆**lead on** [1] *vi usu imper* **~ ~, sergeant!** führen Sie an, Feldwebel!; **~ ~, John!** geh vor, John!
[2] *vt sep (deceive)* anführen *(inf)*, hinters Licht führen; *(tease)* aufziehen, auf den Arm nehmen *(inf)* ◆ **he led us ~ to believe that we would get the money** er hat uns vorgemacht, wir würden das Geld bekommen; **she's just ~ing him ~** sie hält ihn nur zum Narren *or* führt ihn nur an der Nase herum.
◆**lead out** [1] *vt sep* hinausführen ◆ **he led his wife ~ onto the dance floor** er führte seine Frau auf die Tanzfläche.
[2] *vi* hinausgehen.
◆**lead up** [1] *vt sep* hinaufführen *(to* auf *+acc)*; *(lead across)* führen *(to* zu) ◆ **to ~ sb ~ the garden path** *(fig)* jdm etwas vormachen, jdn an der Nase herumführen.
[2] *vi* **(a)** *(come before)* **the events/years that led ~ to the war** die Ereignisse/Jahre, die dem Krieg voran- *or* vorausgingen.
(b) *(introduce)* **he was obviously ~ing ~ to an important announcement** er schickte sich offensichtlich an, etwas Wichtiges anzukündigen; **his speech was obviously ~ing ~ to an important announcement** seine Rede war offensichtlich die Einleitung zu einer wichtigen Ankündigung; **what are you ~ing ~ to?** worauf willst du hinaus?; **what's all this ~ing ~ to?** was soll das Ganze?
lead acetate [led-] *n* Bleiacetat *nt*.
leaded ['ledɪd] *adj window* bleiverglast, Bleiglas-; *petrol* verbleit.
leaden ['ledn] *adj* **(a)** *(old: of lead)* bleiern *(geh)*, Blei-. **(b)** *sky, colour* bleiern

(*geh*); *heart, limbs* bleischwer.

leader ['li:dəʳ] *n* **(a)** Führer *m*; (*of union, party also*) Vorsitzende(r) *mf*; (*military also*) Befehlshaber *m*; (*of gang, rebels*) Anführer *m*; (*of expedition, project*) Leiter(in *f*) *m*; (*Sport*) (*in league*) Tabellenführer *m*; (*in race*) der/die/das Erste; (*Mus*) (*of orchestra*) Konzertmeister *m*; (*of choir*) Leiter *m*; (*of band*) erster Bläser; (*of jazz band, pop group*) Leader *m* ◆ **to be the ~** (*in race, competition*) in Führung liegen; **the ~s** (*in race, competition*) die Spitzengruppe; **~ of the opposition** Oppositionsführer(in *f*) *m*; **the ~s of fashion** die Modemacher *pl*; **the product is a ~ in its field** dieses Produkt ist auf diesem Gebiet führend; **we are still the ~s in biochemical research** wir sind auf dem Gebiet der biochemischen Forschung immer noch führend; **has he the qualities to be a ~ of men?** hat er Führungsqualitäten?

(b) (*Brit Press*) Leitartikel *m* ◆ **~ writer** Leitartikler *m*.

leaderless ['li:dəlɪs] *adj* führerlos, ohne Führer; *party, union* führungslos.

leadership ['li:dəʃɪp] *n* **(a)** Führung, Leitung *f*; (*office also*) Vorsitz *m* ◆ **under the ~ of** unter (der) Führung von; **a crisis in the ~** eine Führungskrise. **(b)** (*quality*) Führungsqualitäten *pl* ◆ **the country is looking for ~** das Land ruft nach einer straffen Führung.

lead-free ['ledfri:] [1] *adj* bleifrei; *petrol also* unverbleit.

[2] *n* (*petrol*) unverbleites *or* bleifreies Benzin.

lead guitar ['li:d-] *n* Leadgitarre *f*.

lead-in ['li:dɪn] *n* Einführung, Einleitung *f* (*to* in *+acc*).

leading[1] ['ledɪŋ] *n* (*Typ*) Durchschuß *m*.

leading[2] ['li:dɪŋ] *adj* **(a)** (*first*) vorderste(r, s); *runner, horse, car also* führend ◆ **the ~ car in the procession** das die Kolonne anführende Auto.

(b) (*most important*) *person, company* führend; *sportsman, product* Spitzen-; *issue* Haupt-, wichtigste(r, s); *part, role* (*Theat*) tragend, Haupt-; (*fig*) führend ◆ **we are a ~ company in ...** unsere Firma ist führend auf dem Gebiet ... (*+gen*).

leading: ~ article *n* Leitartikel *m*; **~ edge** *n* (*Aviat*) (Flügel)vorderkante *f*; **~-edge** *adj company, technology* Spitzen-; (*in hi-tech*) Hi-Tech-; **~ lady** *n* Hauptdarstellerin *f*; **~ light** *n* Nummer eins *f*; (*person also*) großes Licht, Leuchte *f*; **~ man** *n* Hauptdarsteller *m*; **~ question** *n* Suggestivfrage *f*.

lead [led-]: **~ paint** *n* Bleifarbe *f*; **~ pencil** *n* Bleistift *m*; **~-poisoning** *n* Bleivergiftung *f*; **~ shot** *n* Schrot *m or nt*.

lead ['li:d]: **~ singer** *n* Leadsänger(in *f*) *m*; **~ story** *n* Hauptartikel *m*; **~ time** *n* (*for production*) Produktionszeit *f*; (*for delivery*) Lieferzeit *f*; **~-up** *n* Vorfeld *nt* (*to* +gen) ◆ **in the ~-up to the election** im Vorfeld der Wahl.

leaf [li:f] [1] *n, pl* **leaves (a)** Blatt *nt* ◆ **to be in ~** grün sein; **to come into ~** grün werden, ausschlagen (*poet*); **he swept the leaves into a pile** er fegte das Laub auf einen Haufen.

(b) (*of paper*) Blatt *nt* ◆ **to take a ~ out of sb's book** sich (*dat*) von jdm eine Scheibe abschneiden; **to turn over a new ~** einen neuen Anfang machen; **it's time you turned over a new ~, said the teacher** es wird Zeit, daß du dich änderst, sagte der Lehrer.

(c) (*of table*) Ausziehplatte *f* ◆ **pull the leaves out** zieh den Tisch aus!

(d) (*of metal*) Folie *f* ◆ **gold/silver ~** Blattgold/-silber *nt*.

[2] *vi* **to ~ through a book** ein Buch durchblättern.

leaf: ~ bud *n* Blattknospe *f*; **~less** *adj* blattlos, kahl.

leaflet ['li:flɪt] [1] *n* **(a)** Prospekt *m*; (*single page*) Hand- *or* Reklamezettel *m*; (*with instructions*) Merkblatt *nt*; (*handout*) Flugblatt *nt*; (*brochure for information*) Broschüre *f*, Informationsblatt *nt*. **(b)** (*young leaf*) Blättchen *nt*.

[2] *vt area* Flugblätter verteilen in (*+dat*); (*Comm*) Werbematerial verteilen in (*+dat*).

leafleting ['li:flətɪŋ] *n* Flugblattaktionen *pl*; (*Comm*) Verteilen *nt* von Werbematerial ◆ **~ campaign** Flugblattaktion *f*.

leaf: ~-mould, (*US*) **~ mold** *n* (Laub)kompost *m*; **~ spring** *n* Blattfeder *f*.

leafy ['li:fɪ] *adj branch, tree* grün, belaubt; *bower, lane* grün.

league[1] [li:g] *n* (*measure*) Wegstunde *f*.

league[2] *n* **(a)** (*treaty*) Bündnis *nt*, Bund *m*; (*organization*) Verband *m*, Liga *f* ◆ **L~ of Nations** Völkerbund *m*; **to enter into a ~** einen Bund schließen; **to be in ~ with sb** mit jdm gemeinsame Sache machen; **to be in ~ with the devil** mit dem Teufel im Bunde sein; **these two boys must be in ~ with each other** diese beiden Jungen stecken sicher unter einer Decke (*inf*); **to be in ~ against sb** sich gegen jdn verbündet haben.

(b) (*Sport*) Liga *f* ◆ **the club is top of the ~** der Klub ist Tabellen- *or* Ligaführer; **he was not in the same ~** (*fig*) er hatte nicht das gleiche Format; **Peter's car is not in the same ~ as Wendy's** Peters Auto ist eine Nummer kleiner als Wendys.

league: ~ game *n* Ligaspiel *nt*; **~ leaders** *npl* Tabellenführer *m*; **~ table** *n* Tabelle *f*.

leak [li:k] [1] *n* **(a)** (*hole*) undichte Stelle; (*in container*) Loch *nt*; (*Naut*) Leck *nt* ◆ **to have a ~** undicht sein; (*bucket etc*) laufen, lecken; **my biro has a ~** mein Kugelschreiber läuft aus *or* ist nicht dicht; **there's a ~ in the gas pipe** die Gasleitung ist undicht; **the rain is coming in through a ~ in the roof** es regnet durchs Dach herein.

(b) (*escape of liquid*) Leck *nt* ◆ **a gas ~** eine undichte Stelle in der Gasleitung; **the tunnel was flooded because of the ~s** der Tunnel wurde vom eindringenden Wasser überflutet; **a faulty joint caused a ~ of gas** durch die fehlerhafte Verbindung strömte Gas aus.

(c) (*fig*) undichte Stelle ◆ **there was a ~ of information** es sind Informationen durchgesickert; **a security/news ~** eine undichte Stelle; **the news ~ may have been the result of carelessness** die Nachricht kann aufgrund einer Unachtsamkeit durchgesickert sein; **a ~ to the press** eine Indiskretion der Presse gegenüber; **they wanted to break the news gently by a series of ~s to the press** sie wollten die Nachricht langsam an die Presse durchsickern lassen.

(d) (*sl*) **to go for** *or* **have a ~** pissen gehen (*sl*).

[2] *vt* **(a)** durchlassen ◆ **that tank is ~ing acid** aus diesem Tank läuft Säure aus.

(b) (*fig*) *information, story, plans* zuspielen (*to sb* jdm).

[3] *vi* **(a)** (*ship, receptacle, pipe*) lecken; (*roof*) undicht *or* nicht dicht sein; (*pen*) auslaufen, undicht sein.

(b) (*gas*) ausströmen, entweichen; (*liquid*) auslaufen; (*ooze out*) tropfen (*from* aus) ◆ **water is ~ing (in) through the roof** Wasser tropft *or* sickert durch das Dach, es regnet durch (das Dach durch); **to ~ away** auslaufen.

◆**leak out** [1] *vt sep news* zuspielen (*to sb* jdm).

[2] *vi* **(a)** (*liquid*) auslaufen, durchsickern. **(b)** (*news*) durchsickern.

leakage ['li:kɪdʒ] *n* **(a)** (*act*) Auslaufen *nt*; (*of body fluids*) Austreten *nt* ◆ **there's a ~ of water into the oil** da läuft *or* tropft Wasser ins Öl; **there's still a slight ~** es ist immer noch etwas undicht; **the ground was polluted by a ~ of chemicals** der Boden war durch auslaufende Chemikalien verunreinigt.

(b) (*fig*) **~ of information** (*act*) Durchsickern *nt* von Informationen; **the government was worried by repeated security ~s** die Regierung war besorgt, weil wiederholt Informationen durchgesickert waren.

leakproof ['li:kpru:f] *adj* dicht, lecksicher (*spec*) ◆ **we'll have to make the department ~** (*fig*) wir müssen undichte Stellen in der Abteilung beseitigen.

leaky ['li:kɪ] *adj* (*+er*) undicht; *boat also* leck ◆ **the ministry has become rather ~** (*fig inf*) aus dem Ministerium sickert inzwischen einiges durch.

lean[1] [li:n] [1] *adj* (*+er*) **(a)** (*thin*) mager, dünn; *face, person* schmal; (*through lack of food*) hager; *meat* mager ◆ **to grow ~** schlank *or* schmal werden. **(b)** *year, harvest* mager.

[2] *n* mageres Fleisch.

lean[2] (*vb: pret, ptp* **~ed** *or* **leant**) [1] *n* Neigung *f*.

[2] *vt* **(a)** (*put in sloping position*) lehnen (*against* gegen, an *+acc*) ◆ **to ~ one's head on sb's shoulder** seinen Kopf an jds Schulter (*acc*) lehnen.

(b) (*rest*) aufstützen (*on* auf *+dat or acc*) ◆ **to ~ one's elbow on sth** sich mit dem Ellbogen auf etw (*acc*) stützen.

[3] *vi* **(a)** (*be off vertical*) sich neigen (*to* nach); (*trees*) sich biegen ◆ **the box was ~ing dangerously on its side** die Kiste neigte sich gefährlich auf die Seite; **he ~t across the counter** er beugte sich über den Ladentisch; **a motorcyclist should ~ into the corner** ein Motorradfahrer sollte sich in die Kurve legen.

(b) (*rest*) sich lehnen ◆ **to ~ against sth** sich gegen etw lehnen; **~ing against the bar** an die Bar gelehnt; **she ~t on my arm** sie stützte sich auf meinen Arm; **he ~t on the edge of the table** er stützte sich auf die Tischkante; **to ~ on one's elbow** sich mit dem Ellbogen aufstützen.

(c) (*tend in opinion etc*) **to ~ towards the left/socialism** nach links/zum Sozialismus tendieren; **to ~ towards sb's opinion** zu jds Ansicht neigen *or* tendieren; **which way does he ~?** in welche Richtung tendiert er?; **he started to ~ away from the party line** er entfernte sich allmählich von der Parteilinie; **at least they're ~ing in the direction of reform** sie neigen immerhin Reformen (*dat*) zu.

◆**lean back** *vi* sich zurücklehnen.

◆**lean forward** *vi* sich vorbeugen.

◆**lean on** *vi* **(a)** (*depend*) **to ~ ~ sb** sich auf jdn verlassen. **(b)** (*inf: put pressure on*) **to ~ ~ sb** jdn bearbeiten (*inf*) *or* beknien (*inf*); **they ~t ~ him too hard** sie haben ihn zu sehr unter Druck gesetzt (*inf*).

◆**lean out** *vi* sich hinauslehnen (*of* aus).

◆**lean over** *vi* **(a)** (*be off vertical*) sich (vor)neigen.

(b) sich vorbeugen ◆ **they ~t ~ the side of the bridge** sie beugten sich über das Brückengeländer; **he ~t ~ her shoulder** er beugte sich über ihre Schulter; *see* **backwards**.

lean-burn ['li:nbɜ:n] *adj* **~ engine** Magermotor *m*.

leaning ['li:nɪŋ] [1] *adj* schräg, schief ◆ **the L~ Tower of Pisa** der Schiefe Turm von Pisa.

[2] *n* Hang *m*, Neigung *f* ◆ **he had a ~ towards the left** er hatte einen Hang nach links; **what are his ~s?** was sind seine Neigungen?; **artistic ~s** künstlerische Neigungen *pl*.

leanness ['li:nnɪs] *n* Magerkeit *f* ◆ **the ~ of his face** sein schmales Gesicht; (*through lack of food*) sein hageres Gesicht.

leant [lent] *pret, ptp of* **lean**[2].

lean-to ['li:ntu:] [1] *n* Anbau *m*; (*shelter*) Wetterschutz *m or* -schirm *m*.

[2] *adj* angebaut.

leap [li:p] (*vb: pret, ptp* **~ed** *or* **leapt**) [1] *n* Sprung, Satz (*inf*) *m* ◆ **in one ~, at a ~** mit einem Satz; **to take a ~ at sth** einen Satz über etw (*acc*) machen, über etw (*acc*) setzen; **a great ~ forward** (*fig*) ein großer Sprung nach vorn; **a ~ in the dark** (*fig*) ein Sprung ins Ungewisse; **by ~s and bounds** (*fig*) sprunghaft.

[2] *vt* springen *or* setzen über (*+acc*) ◆ **he ~t the horse across the ditch** er ließ das Pferd über den Graben springen.

[3] *vi* springen ◆ **my heart ~ed (with joy)** mein Herz hüpfte vor Freude (*geh*), mein Herz machte vor Freude einen Sprung; **to ~ about** herumspringen; **to ~ for joy** vor Freude hüpfen, Freudensprünge machen; **try to ~ over to the other side** versuch mal, auf die andere Seite zu springen *or* hinüberzuspringen; **to ~ to one's feet** aufspringen; **he ~t to her assistance** er sprang ihr zu Hilfe; **the house ~t into view** das Haus kam plötzlich in Sicht *or* tauchte plötzlich auf; *see* **look**.

◆**leap at** *vt insep* **to ~ ~ a chance** eine Gelegenheit beim Schopf packen, sofort zugreifen; **to ~ ~ an offer** sich (förmlich) auf ein Angebot stürzen.

◆**leap out** *vi* **(a)** (*jump out*) hinaus-/herausspringen (*of* aus +*dat*) ◆ **he ~t ~ of the car** er sprang aus dem Auto.
(b) (*colours*) ins Auge springen, hervorstechen ◆ **the bright colours ~ ~ at you** die hellen Farben springen einem ins Auge.

◆**leap up** *vi* (*person, animals*) aufspringen; (*flames*) hochschlagen; (*prices*) sprunghaft ansteigen, emporschnellen ◆ **he ~t ~ from behind the wall** er sprang hinter der Mauer hervor; **to ~ ~ into the air** in die Höhe springen.

leapfrog ['li:pfrɒg] [1] *n* Bockspringen *nt* ◆ **to play ~** Bockspringen spielen *or* machen (*inf*).
[2] *vi* bockspringen ◆ **the children ~ged over one another** die Kinder spielten *or* machten (*inf*) Bocksprünge.
[3] *vt* **he ~ged him** er machte einen Bocksprung über ihn; **he ~ged his way to the top of the company** er machte in der Firma eine Blitzkarriere.

leap of faith *n* Vertrauensvorschuß *m* ◆ **to take** *or* **make a ~** einen Vertrauensvorschuß gewähren; **it takes a considerable ~ to believe that ...** man muß schon eine Menge Vertrauen aufbringen, um zu glauben, daß ...

leap year *n* Schaltjahr *nt.*

leapt [lept] *pret, ptp of* **leap**.

learn [lɜ:n] *pret, ptp* **~ed** *or* **learnt** [1] *vt* **(a)** (*gain knowledge, skill etc*) lernen; *language also* erlernen ◆ **where did you ~ that habit?** wo hast du dir das angewöhnt?; **I ~t (how) to swim** ich habe schwimmen gelernt.
(b) (*be informed*) erfahren.
[2] *vi* **(a)** (*gain knowledge etc*) lernen ◆ **I can't play the piano, but I'm hoping to ~** ich kann nicht Klavier spielen, aber ich hoffe, es zu lernen; **he'll never ~!** er lernt es nie!; **some people never ~!** manche lernen's nie!; **to ~ from experience** aus der *or* durch Erfahrung lernen.
(b) (*find out*) hören, erfahren (*about, of* von).

◆**learn off** *vt sep* lernen.

◆**learn up** *vt sep* (*learn by study*) lernen, pauken (*inf*); (*memorize*) (auswendig) lernen.

learned ['lɜ:nɪd] *adj* gelehrt; *book also, journal* wissenschaftlich; *society also, profession* akademisch ◆ **a ~ man** ein Gelehrter *m*; **my ~ colleague** mein geschätzter Kollege.

learnedly ['lɜ:nɪdlɪ] *adv* gelehrt.

learner ['lɜ:nə^r] *n* Anfänger(in *f*), Lerner(in *f*) (*esp Ling*) *m*; (*student*) Lernende(r) *mf*; (*~ driver*) Fahrschüler(in *f*) *m* ◆ **~s of languages** Sprachschüler *or* -studenten *pl*; **special classes for slow ~s** Sonderklassen *pl* für lernschwache Schüler.

learning ['lɜ:nɪŋ] *n* **(a)** (*act*) Lernen *nt* ◆ **difficulties encountered during the ~ of geometry/English** Schwierigkeiten beim Erlernen der Geometrie/beim Englischlernen.
(b) (*erudition*) Gelehrsamkeit, Gelehrtheit *f* ◆ **a man of ~** ein Gelehrter *m*; **the ~ contained in these volumes** das in diesen Bänden enthaltene Wissen; **seat of ~** Stätte *f* der Gelehrsamkeit.

learning curve *n* Lernkurve *f* ◆ **we're back on the ~** wir müssen mit dem Lernen wieder von vorn anfangen; **life is a constant ~** man lernt immer noch dazu.

learnt [lɜ:nt] *pret, ptp of* **learn**.

lease [li:s] [1] *n* (*of land, farm, business premises etc*) Pacht *f*; (*contract*) Pachtvertrag *m*; (*of house, flat, office*) Miete *f*; (*contract*) Mietvertrag *m*; (*of equipment*) Leasing *nt*; (*contract*) Leasing-Vertrag *m* ◆ **the ~ was prematurely terminated** die Pacht *or* das Pachtverhältnis/das Mietverhältnis wurde vorzeitig beendet; **to take a ~ on a house** ein Haus mieten; **to take a ~ on business premises** ein Geschäft(sgrundstück) *nt* pachten; **to occupy a house on a 99-year ~** ein Haus auf 99 Jahre pachten; **you can buy the ~ for a period of 99 years** Sie können einen Pachtvertrag für 99 Jahre abschließen; **we have the house/farm on a ~** wir haben das Haus gemietet/den Bauernhof gepachtet; **to let sth out on ~** etw in Pacht geben, etw verpachten/vermieten; **to give sb/sth a new ~ of life** jdm/einer Sache (neuen) Aufschwung geben.
[2] *vt* (*take*) pachten (*from* von), in Pacht nehmen (*from* bei); mieten (*from* von); mieten, leasen (*from von*); (*give: also* **~ out**) verpachten (*to* an +*acc*), in Pacht geben (*to sb* jdm); vermieten (*to* an +*acc*); vermieten, leasen (*to* an +*acc*).

lease: ~back [1] *n* Verkauf und Rückmiete *pl*; [2] *attr arrangement* Rückmiet-; **~hold** [1] *n* (*property*) Pachtbesitz *m*; (*land also*) Pachtgrundstück *nt*; (*building also*) gepachtetes Gebäude; (*contract, tenure*) Pachtvertrag *m*; **who has the ~hold on the property?** wer hat das Land/Gebäude gepachtet?; **we own the house on ~hold** wir haben das Haus langfristig gepachtet; **~hold reform** Mietrechtsreform *f*; [2] *adj* gepachtet, in Pacht; *property* Pacht-; **~holder** *n* Pächter *m*.

leash [li:ʃ] *n* Leine *f* ◆ **on a ~** an der Leine; *see* **strain**[1].

▼ **least** [li:st] [1] *adj* **(a)** (*slightest, smallest*) geringste(r, s).
(b) (*with uncountable nouns*) wenigste(r, s) ◆ **he has the ~ money** er hat am wenigsten Geld.
[2] *adv* **(a)** (+*vb*) am wenigsten ◆ **~ of all would I wish to offend him** auf gar keinen Fall möchte ich ihn beleidigen.
(b) (+*adj*) **~ possible expenditure** möglichst geringe Kosten; **the ~ expensive car** das billigste *or* preiswerteste Auto; **the ~ important matter** das Unwichtigste; **of all my worries that's the ~ important** *das* ist meine geringste Sorge; **the ~ talented player** der am wenigsten talentierte Spieler; **the ~ known** der/die/das Unbekannteste; **the ~ interesting** der/die/das Uninteressanteste; **he's the ~ aggressive of men** er ist nicht im mindesten aggressiv; **not the ~ bit drunk** kein bißchen *or* nicht im geringsten betrunken.
▼ [3] *n* **the ~** der/die/das Geringste *or* Wenigste; **that's the ~ of my worries** darüber mache ich mir die wenigsten Sorgen; **I have many worries, and money is the ~ of them** ich habe viele Sorgen, und Geld kümmert mich am wenigsten; **it's the ~ one can do** es ist das wenigste, was man tun kann; **you gave yourself the ~** du hast dir (selbst) am wenigsten gegeben; **at ~, I think so** ich glaube wenigstens; **at ~ it's not raining** wenigstens *or* zumindest regnet es nicht; **we can at ~ try** wir können es wenigstens versuchen; **there were eight at ~** es waren mindestens acht da; **we need at ~ three** wir brauchen wenigstens *or* mindestens drei; **we need three at the very ~** allermindestens brauchen wir drei; **there must have been twenty at the very ~** es waren mindestens zwanzig da; **at the very ~ you could apologize** du könntest dich wenigstens *or* zumindest entschuldigen; **and that's the ~ of it** und das ist noch das wenigste; **not in the ~!** nicht im geringsten!, ganz und gar nicht!; **he was not in the ~ upset** er war kein bißchen *or* nicht im geringsten verärgert; **to say the ~** um es milde zu sagen; **the ~ said, the better, ~ said, soonest mended** (*Prov*) je weniger man darüber spricht, desto besser.

leastways ['li:stweɪz] *adv* (*inf*) zumindest, wenigstens.

leather ['leðə^r] [1] *n* Leder *nt* ◆ **~neck** (*US sl*) Ledernacken *m*.
[2] *adj* Leder-, ledern.
[3] *vt* (*inf*) versohlen (*inf*), ein paar überziehen (+*dat*) (*inf*).

leatherette [,leðə'ret] *n* Kunstleder *nt*.

leathering ['leðərɪŋ] *n* (*inf*) Tracht *f* Prügel.

leathery ['leðərɪ] *adj material* lederartig; *smell* Leder-; *skin* ledern; *meat* zäh.

leave [li:v] (*vb: pret, ptp* **left**) [1] *n* **(a)** (*permission*) Erlaubnis *f* ◆ **by your ~** (*form*) mit Ihrer (gütigen) Erlaubnis (*form*); **to ask sb's ~ to do sth** jdn um Erlaubnis bitten, etw zu tun; **he borrowed my car without so much as a by your ~** er hat sich (*dat*) so einfach *or* so mir nichts, dir nichts mein Auto geliehen.
(b) (*permission to be absent, Mil*) Urlaub *m* ◆ **to be on ~** auf Urlaub sein, Urlaub haben; **to be on ~ from sth** von etw beurlaubt sein; **I've got ~ to attend the conference** ich habe freibekommen, um an der Konferenz teilzunehmen; **a two-day ~** zwei Tage Urlaub; **~ of absence** Beurlaubung *f*; **to be on ~ of absence** beurlaubt sein.
(c) **to take one's ~** sich verabschieden; **to take ~ of one's senses** den Verstand verlieren; **~-taking** Abschied *m*; (*act*) Abschiednehmen *nt*.
[2] *vt* **(a)** (*depart from, quit*) *place, person* verlassen ◆ **the train left the station** der Zug fuhr aus dem Bahnhof; **when the plane left Rome** als das Flugzeug von Rom abflog; **when he left Rome** als er von Rom wegging/wegfuhr/abflog *etc*; **you may ~ us** Sie können gehen; **please sir, may I ~ the room?** Herr X, darf ich mal raus?; **to ~ home** von zu Hause weggehen/wegfahren; (*permanently*) von zu Hause weggehen; **she left her parents' home** sie verließ ihr Elternhaus; **to ~ school** die Schule verlassen; (*prematurely also*) (von der Schule) abgehen; **to ~ the table** vom Tisch aufstehen; **to ~ one's job** seine Stelle aufgeben; **to ~ the road** (*crash*) von der Straße abkommen; (*turn off*) von der Straße abbiegen; **to ~ the rails** entgleisen; **the rocket left the ground** die Rakete hob (vom Boden) ab; **I'll ~ you at the station** am Bahnhof trennen wir uns dann; (*in car*) ich setze dich am Bahnhof ab.
(b) (*allow or cause to remain*) lassen; *bad taste, dirty mark, message, scar, impression* hinterlassen ◆ **I'll ~ my address with you** ich lasse Ihnen meine Adresse da; **I'll ~ the key with the neighbours** ich hinterlege *or* lasse den Schlüssel bei den Nachbarn; **to ~ one's supper** sein Abendessen stehenlassen; **the postman left three letters for you** der Briefträger hat drei Briefe für dich gebracht.
(c) (*~ in a certain condition*) lassen ◆ **who left the window open?** wer hat das Fenster offengelassen?; **to ~ two pages blank** zwei Seiten freilassen; **this ~s me free for the afternoon/free to go shopping** dadurch habe ich den Nachmittag frei/Zeit zum Einkaufen; **this new development ~s us with a problem** diese neue Entwicklung stellt uns vor ein Problem; **the death of her uncle left her with no financial worries** nach dem Tod ihres Onkels hatte sie keine finanziellen Probleme mehr; **~ the dog alone** laß den Hund in Ruhe; **~ me alone!** laß mich (in Ruhe)!; **to ~ well alone** die Finger davonlassen (*inf*); **to ~ sb to himself** jdn allein lassen; **to ~ go** *or* **hold of** loslassen; **let's ~ it at that** lassen wir es dabei (bewenden); **if we ~ it so that he'll contact us** wenn wir dabei verbleiben, daß er sich mit uns in Verbindung setzt; **how did he ~ things at the last meeting?** wobei hat er es beim letzten Treffen belassen?
(d) (*forget*) liegen- *or* stehenlassen.
(e) (*after death*) *person, money* hinterlassen ◆ **he left his wife very badly off** er ließ seine Frau fast mittellos zurück.
(f) **to be left** (*remain, be over*) übrigbleiben; **all I have left** alles, was ich noch habe; **how many are there left?** wie viele sind noch da *or* übrig?; **3 from 10 ~s 7** 10 minus 3 ist *or* (ist) gleich 7; **what does that ~?** wieviel bleibt übrig?; (*Math*) wieviel gibt *or* ist das?; **nothing was left for me but to sell it** mir blieb nichts anderes übrig, als es zu verkaufen.
(g) (*entrust*) überlassen (*up to sb* jdm) ◆ **~ it to me** laß mich nur machen; **I ~ it to you to judge** es bleibt dir überlassen, zu urteilen; **to ~ sth to chance** etw dem Zufall überlassen.
(h) (*stop*) **let's ~ this now** lassen wir das jetzt mal.
[3] *vi* (weg)gehen; abfahren; abfliegen; (*train, bus, ship*) abfahren; (*plane*) abfliegen ◆ **we ~ for Sweden tomorrow** wir fahren morgen nach Schweden; **which flight did he ~ on?** welchen Flug hat er genommen?

◆**leave about** *or* **around** *vt sep* herumliegen lassen.

◆**leave aside** *vt sep* beiseite lassen.

◆**leave behind** *vt sep* **(a)** *the car, the children* dalassen, zurücklassen ◆ **we've left all that ~ us** das alles liegt hinter uns; **we've left all our worries ~ us** (*settled*) wir sind alle Sorgen los; (*forgotten*) wir haben all unsere Sorgen ver-

➤ LANGUAGE IN USE: **least: 3** → 26.3

gessen.
(b) (*outstrip*) hinter sich (*dat*) lassen ◆ **he left all his fellow-students ~** er stellte alle seine Kommilitonen in den Schatten.
(c) (*forget*) liegen- *or* stehenlassen.
◆**leave in** *vt sep sentence, scene in play etc* lassen, nicht herausnehmen, drinlassen (*inf*) ◆ **don't ~ the dog ~ all day** lassen Sie den Hund nicht den ganzen Tag im Haus; **how long should the meat be left ~?** wie lange muß das Fleisch im Ofen bleiben *or* gelassen werden?
◆**leave off** [1] *vt sep clothes* nicht anziehen; *lid* nicht darauftun, ablassen (*inf*); *radio, lights* auslassen; *umlaut* weglassen ◆ **you can ~ your coat ~** du brauchst deinen Mantel nicht anzuziehen; **don't ~ the top ~ your pen** laß den Füllhalter nicht offen *or* ohne Kappe liegen; **you left her name ~ the list** Sie haben ihren Namen nicht in die Liste aufgenommen.
[2] *vi +prep obj* (*inf*) aufhören ◆ **we left ~ work after lunch** wir haben nach dem Mittagessen Feierabend gemacht; **~ ~ doing that, will you!** hör auf damit, ja?
[3] *vi* (*inf*) aufhören ◆ **~ ~!** laß das!
◆**leave on** *vt sep clothes* anbehalten, anlassen (*inf*); *lights, fire etc* anlassen ◆ **we left the wall-paper ~ and painted over it** wir haben die Tapete drangelassen (*inf*) *or* nicht entfernt und sie überstrichen.
◆**leave out** *vt sep* (a) (*not bring in*) draußen lassen.
(b) (*omit*) auslassen; (*exclude*) *people* ausschließen (*of* von) ◆ **he was instructed to ~ ~ all references to politics** er bekam Anweisung, alle Hinweise auf Politik wegzulassen; **he had been left ~ in the restructuring** er wurde bei der Neugliederung nicht berücksichtigt; **you ~ my wife/politics ~ of this** lassen Sie meine Frau/die Politik aus dem Spiel; **he got left ~ of things at school** er wurde in der Schule nie mit einbezogen.
(c) (*leave available*) dalassen ◆ **I'll ~ the books ~ on my desk** ich lasse die Bücher auf meinem Schreibtisch; **will you ~ the tools ~ ready?** legen Sie bitte das Werkzeug zurecht.
(d) (*not put away*) nicht wegräumen, liegen lassen.
◆**leave over** *vt sep* (a) (*leave surplus*) übriglassen ◆ **to be left ~** übrig(geblieben) sein. (b) (*postpone*) verschieben, vertagen.
leaven ['levn] [1] *n* (*also* **~ing** [-ɪŋ]) Treibmittel *nt*; (*fermenting dough*) Sauerteig *m*; (*fig*) Auflockerung *f* ◆ **even his most serious speeches had a ~ of humour** auch seine ernstesten Reden waren mit Humor gewürzt.
[2] *vt* (auf)gehen lassen, treiben; (*fig*) auflockern.
leaves [li:vz] *pl of* **leaf**.
leaving ['li:vɪŋ] *n* Fortgang, Weggang *m* ◆ **~ was very difficult (for him)** das Weggehen fiel ihm schwer.
leaving: ~ certificate *n* Abgangszeugnis *nt*; **~ day** *n* (*Sch*) Schuljahrsabschluß *m*, letzter Schultag; **~-party** *n* Abschiedsfeier *or* -party *f*; **~ present** *n* Abschiedsgeschenk *nt*.
leavings ['li:vɪŋz] *npl* (*food*) (Über)reste *pl*; (*rubbish*) Abfälle *pl*.
Lebanese [,lebə'ni:z] [1] *adj* libanesisch.
[2] *n* Libanese *m*, Libanesin *f*.
Lebanon ['lebənən] *n* **the ~** der Libanon.
lecher ['letʃəʳ] [1] *n* Lüstling, Wüstling *m*; (*hum*) Lustmolch *m*.
[2] *vi* lüstern sein ◆ **to ~ after sb** (*chase*) jdm nachstellen; (*in mind*) sich lüsterne Vorstellungen *pl* über jdn machen.
lecherous ['letʃərəs] *adj* lüstern; *man, behaviour also* geil.
lecherously ['letʃərəslɪ] *adv* lüstern.
lechery ['letʃərɪ] *n* Lüsternheit, Geilheit *f* ◆ **his reputation for ~** sein Ruf *m* als Wüstling.
lectern ['lektɜ:n] *n* Pult *nt*.
lector ['lektəʳ] *n* (*Univ: foreign language assistant*) Lektor(in *f*) *m*.
lecture ['lektʃəʳ] [1] *n* (a) Vortrag *m*; (*Univ*) Vorlesung *f* ◆ **to give a ~** einen Vortrag/eine Vorlesung halten (*to* für, *on sth* über etw *acc*); **I asked for a short explanation and got a ~** ich wollte nur eine kurze Erklärung und bekam einen Vortrag zu hören.
(b) (*scolding*) (Straf)predigt *f* ◆ **to give sb a ~** jdm eine Strafpredigt *or* Standpauke (*inf*) halten (*about* wegen).
[2] *vt* (a) (*give a ~*) **to ~ sb on sth** jdm einen Vortrag/eine Vorlesung über etw (*acc*) halten; **he ~s us in French** wir hören bei ihm (Vorlesungen in) Französisch.
(b) (*scold*) tadeln, abkanzeln ◆ **to ~ sb** jdm eine Strafpredigt halten (*on* wegen).
[3] *vi* einen Vortrag halten; (*Univ*) (*give ~*) eine Vorlesung halten; (*give ~ course*) lesen, Vorlesungen halten (*on* über *+acc*) ◆ **he ~s in English** er ist Dozent für Anglistik; **he ~s on Victorian poetry** er liest über Viktorianische Dichtung; **have you ever heard him ~?** hast du schon mal eine Vorlesung bei ihm gehört?; **he ~s at Princeton** er lehrt in Princeton; **he ~s well** seine Vorlesungen sind gut.
lecture: ~ course *n* Vorlesungs-/Vortragsreihe *f*; **~ hall** *n* Hörsaal *m*; **~ notes** *npl* (*professor's*) Manuskript *nt*; (*student's*) Aufzeichnungen *pl*; (*handout*) Vorlesungsskript *nt*.
lecturer ['lektʃərəʳ] *n* Dozent(in *f*) *m*; (*speaker*) Redner(in *f*) *m* ◆ **assistant ~** ≃ Assistent(in *f*) *m*; **senior ~** *Dozent(in f) m in höherer Position*.
lecture room *n* Hörsaal *m*.
lectureship ['lektʃəʃɪp] *n* Stelle *f* als Dozent, Lehrauftrag *m*.
lecture: ~ theatre *n* Hörsaal *m*; **~ tour** *n* Vortragsreise *f*.
LED *abbr of* **light-emitting diode**.
led [led] *pret, ptp of* **lead²**.
ledge [ledʒ] *n* (a) Leiste, Kante *f*; (*along wall*) Leiste *f*; (*of window*) (*inside*) Fensterbrett *nt*; (*outside*) (Fenster)sims *nt or m*; (*shelf*) Ablage *f*, Bord *nt*; (*mountain ~*) (Fels)vorsprung *m*. (b) (*ridge of rocks*) Riff *nt*.
ledger ['ledʒəʳ] *n* Hauptbuch *nt* ◆ **~ line** (*Mus*) Hilfslinie *f*.
lee [li:] [1] *adj* Lee-.
[2] *n* (a) (*Naut*) Lee *f*. (b) (*shelter*) Schutz, Windschatten *m*.
leech [li:tʃ] *n* Blutegel *m*; (*fig*) Blutsauger *m*.
leek [li:k] *n* Porree, Lauch *m*.
leer [lɪəʳ] [1] *n* (*knowing, sexual*) anzügliches Grinsen; (*evil*) heimtückischer Blick.
[2] *vi* anzüglich grinsen; einen heimtückischen *or* schrägen Blick haben ◆ **he ~ed at the girl** er warf dem Mädchen lüsterne Blicke zu.
lees [li:z] *npl* Bodensatz *m*.
leeward ['li:wəd] [1] *adj* Lee-.
[2] *adv* leewärts ◆ **the ship was anchored ~ of the island** das Schiff ankerte an der Leeseite der Insel.
[3] *n* Lee(seite) *f* ◆ **to ~** an der Leeseite; **steer to ~** nach der Leeseite steuern, leewärts steuern.
Leeward Isles ['li:wəd,aɪlz] *npl* Leeward-Inseln *pl* (*nördlicher Teil der Inseln über dem Winde*).
leeway ['li:weɪ] *n* (a) (*Naut*) Abtrift *f*, Leeweg *m*.
(b) (*fig*) (*flexibility*) Spielraum *m*; (*time lost*) Zeitverlust *m* ◆ **to make up ~** den Zeitverlust aufholen; **there's a lot of ~ to make up** es gibt viel nachzuarbeiten, ein großer Rückstand muß aufgeholt werden.
left¹ [left] *pret, ptp of* **leave**.
left² [1] *adj* (*also Pol*) linke(r, s) ◆ **no ~ turn** Linksabbiegen verboten; **he's got two ~ hands** (*inf*) er hat zwei linke Hände (*inf*).
[2] *adv* links (*of* von) ◆ **turn ~** (*Aut*) links abbiegen; **keep ~** sich links halten, links fahren; **move ~ a little** rücken Sie ein bißchen nach links; **~, right, ~, right** links, rechts, links, rechts; **~ turn!** (*Mil*) links um!
[3] *n* (a) Linke(r, s) ◆ **on the ~** links (*of* von), auf der linken Seite (*of +gen*); **on** *or* **to your ~** links (von Ihnen), auf der linken Seite; **his wife sat on my ~** seine Frau saß links von mir *or* zu meiner Linken (*form*); **to keep to the ~** sich links halten; links fahren; **to fall to the ~** nach links fallen.
(b) (*Pol*) Linke *f* ◆ **to be on the ~** links stehen; **he's further to the ~ than I am** er steht weiter links als ich; **to be on** *or* **to the ~ of the party** dem linken Flügel der Partei angehören.
(c) (*Boxing*) Linke *f*.
left: ~ back *n* linker Verteidiger; **~ half** *n* linker Vorstopper; **~-hand** *adj* **~-hand drive** Linkssteuerung *f*; **~-hand side** linke Seite; **he stood on the ~-hand side of the king** er stand zur Linken des Königs; **~-hand turn** linke Abzweigung; **take the ~-hand turn** bieg links ab; **~-handed** *adj* linkshändig; *tool* für Linkshänder; (*fig*) *compliment* zweifelhaft; **both the children are ~-handed** beide Kinder sind Linkshänder; **a ~-handed blow** ein linker Treffer; **~-hander** *n* Linkshänder(in *f*) *m*.
leftie ['leftɪ] *n* (*pej*) linker Typ (*pej*), Rote(r) *mf* (*pej inf*).
leftish ['leftɪʃ] *adj* linksliberal, links angehaucht (*inf*) ◆ **his views are ~** er ist links angehaucht (*inf*).
leftist ['leftɪst] [1] *adj* linke(r, s), linksgerichtet ◆ **his views are ~** er ist linksgerichtet, er steht links.
[2] *n* Linke(r) *mf*.
left: ~-luggage (office) *n* Gepäckaufbewahrung *f*; **is there anywhere for ~-luggage in this station?** kann man auf diesem Bahnhof irgendwo sein Gepäck zur Aufbewahrung geben?; **~-luggage locker** *n* Gepäckschließfach *nt*; **~-over** [1] *adj* übriggeblieben; [2] *n* **~-overs** (Über)reste *pl*; **~-wing** [1] *adj* (*Pol*) linke(r, s); *politician also* linksgerichtet; [2] *n* **~ wing** linker Flügel (*also Sport*); (*player*) Linksaußen *m*; **~-winger** *n* (*Pol*) Linke(r) *mf*; (*Sport*) Linksaußen *m*.
leg [leg] [1] *n* (a) (*also of trousers*) Bein *nt* ◆ **to be all ~s** staksig sein; **the newly-born calf seemed to be all ~s** das neugeborene Kalb schien nur aus Beinen zu bestehen; **to be on one's last ~s** in den letzten Zügen liegen (*inf*); (*person*) auf dem letzten Loch pfeifen (*inf*); **this dress/carpet is on its last ~s** dieses Kleid/dieser Teppich hält *or* macht's (*inf*) nicht mehr lange; **he hasn't a ~ to stand on** (*fig*) (*no excuse*) er kann sich nicht herausreden; (*no proof*) das kann er nicht belegen; **to walk one's ~s off** sich (*dat*) die Füße wund laufen; **to walk sb's ~s off** jdn (ganz schön) scheuchen (*inf*), jdm davonlaufen; **you've walked my ~s off** du bist mir zu schnell gelaufen; **to run sb's ~s off** (*fig*) jdn herumscheuchen (*inf*); **he ran the other athletes' ~s off** er rannte den anderen Läufern davon; **he ran the dog's ~s off** er gab dem Hund Auslauf; **I'll take the children to the park and run their ~s off** ich gehe mit den Kindern in den Park, da können sie sich austoben; **to be out ~ before wicket** (*Cricket*) aus sein, weil sein vor dem Mal stehendes Bein von einem Wurf getroffen wurde; **to get one's ~ over** (*sl*) bumsen (*inf*).
(b) (*as food*) Keule, Hachse *f* ◆ **~ of lamb** Lammkeule *f*.
(c) (*of furniture*) Bein *nt*; (*of bed also*) Fuß *m*.
(d) (*stage*) Etappe *f*.
[2] *vt*: **to ~ it** (*inf: go on foot*) laufen, zu Fuß gehen.
legacy ['legəsɪ] *n* (*lit, fig*) Erbschaft *f*, Vermächtnis *nt*; (*fig also*) Erbe *nt*; (*fig pej*) Hinterlassenschaft *f* ◆ **our ~ to future generations must not be a polluted world** wir dürfen den zukünftigen Generationen keine verschmutzte Welt hinterlassen.
legal ['li:gl] *adj* (a) (*lawful*) legal, rechtlich zulässig; *claim* Rechts-, rechtmäßig; (*according to the law*) *tender, restrictions, obligation, limit* gesetzlich; (*allowed by law*) *fare, speed* zulässig; (*valid before law*) *will, purchase* rechtsgültig ◆ **to become ~** rechtskräftig werden; **to make sth ~** etw legalisieren; **the ~ age for marriage** das gesetzliche Heiratsalter, die Ehemündigkeit; **it is not ~ to sell drink to children** es ist gesetzlich verboten, Alkohol an Kinder zu ver-

kaufen; ~ **separation** gesetzliche Trennung; ~ **rights** gesetzlich verankerte Rechte *pl*; **they don't know what their ~ rights are** sie kennen ihre eigenen Rechte nicht; **the ~ custody of the children** das Sorgerecht für die Kinder; **women had no ~ status** Frauen waren nicht rechtsfähig; **he made ~ provision for his ex-wife** er hat die Versorgung seiner geschiedenen Frau rechtlich geregelt.
(**b**) (*relating to the law*) *matters, affairs* juristisch, rechtlich, Rechts-; *advice, journal, mind* juristisch; *fees, charges* Gerichts-; *dictionary, act, protection, adviser* Rechts-; *decision* richterlich, Gerichts-; *inquiry, investigation* gerichtlich ◆ ~ **action** Klage *f*; **to take ~ action against sb** gegen jdn Klage erheben, jdn verklagen; **from a ~ point of view** aus juristischer Sicht, rechtlich gesehen; **what's his ~ position?** wie ist seine rechtliche Stellung?; ~ **aid** Rechtshilfe *f*; **to take ~ advice** juristischen Rat einholen; ~ **department** Rechtsabteilung *f*, juristische Abteilung; ~ **offence** strafbare Handlung; **drug-peddling is a ~ offence** der Handel mit Drogen ist strafbar; **the ~ profession** der Anwaltsstand, die Anwaltschaft; (*including judges*) die Juristenschaft; ~ **representative** gesetzlicher Vertreter; (*counsel*) (Rechts)anwalt, Verteidiger *m*.

legalese [ˌliːgəˈliːz] *n* (*pej*) Juristensprache *f* or -jargon *m*; Juristendeutsch *nt*.

legalistic [ˌliːgəˈlɪstɪk] *adj* legalistisch.

legality [liːˈgælɪtɪ] *n* Legalität *f*; (*of claim*) Rechtmäßigkeit *f*; (*of tender*) Gesetzlichkeit *f*; (*of restrictions, obligation*) Gesetzmäßigkeit *f*; (*of fare, speed*) Zulässigkeit *f*; (*of contract also, of will, marriage, purchase, decision, limit*) rechtliche Gültigkeit, Rechtsgültigkeit *f*.

legalization [ˌliːgəlaɪˈzeɪʃən] *n* Legalisierung *f*.

legalize [ˈliːgəlaɪz] *vt* legalisieren.

legally [ˈliːgəlɪ] *adv* (*lawfully*) *transacted* legal; *married* rechtmäßig; *guaranteed, obliged, set down* gesetzlich; (*relating to the law*) *advise* juristisch; *indefensible* rechtlich ◆ **what's the position ~?** wie ist die Lage rechtlich gesehen?; ~, **there was no objection** rechtlich *or* juristisch gesehen gab es keine Einwände; ~ **speaking** vom rechtlichen Standpunkt aus, juristisch gesehen; **it's wrong — ~ or morally?** es ist nicht richtig — aus rechtlicher oder moralischer Sicht?; ~ **responsible** vor dem Gesetz verantwortlich; **to be ~ entitled to sth** einen Rechtsanspruch auf etw (*acc*) haben; ~ **binding** rechtsverbindlich; ~, **he can only stay for 3 months** legal(erweise) kann er nur 3 Monate bleiben; ~ **valid** rechtsgültig.

legate [ˈlegɪt] *n* Legat *m*.

legatee [ˌlegəˈtiː] *n* Vermächtnisnehmer(in *f*) *m*.

legation [lɪˈgeɪʃən] *n* (*diplomats*) Gesandtschaft, Vertretung *f*; (*building*) Gesandtschaftsgebäude *nt*.

legend [ˈledʒənd] *n* (**a**) Legende *f*; (*fictitious*) Sage *f* ◆ **heroes of Greek ~** griechische Sagenhelden *pl*; **Robin Hood is a figure of ~ rather than of fact** die Figur Robin Hoods beruht eher auf Legenden als auf Tatsachen; **to become a ~ in one's lifetime** schon zu Lebzeiten zur Legende werden.
(**b**) (*inscription, caption*) Legende *f*.

legendary [ˈledʒəndərɪ] *adj* (**a**) legendär; *person also* sagenumwoben. (**b**) (*famous*) berühmt.

legerdemain [ˌledʒədəˈmeɪn] *n* Taschenspielerei *f*.

-legged [-ˈlegd, -ˈlegɪd] *adj suf* -beinig ◆ **bare-~** ohne Strümpfe.

leggings [ˈlegɪŋz] *npl* (hohe *or* lange) Gamaschen *pl*; (*fireman's, yachtsman's*) Beinlinge *f*; (*trousers*) Überhose *f*; (*baby's*) Gamaschenhose *f*.

leggy [ˈlegɪ] *adj* (+*er*) langbeinig; (*gawky*) staksig.

Leghorn [ˈleghɔːn] *n* (*Geog*) Livorno *nt*.

legibility [ˌledʒɪˈbɪlɪtɪ] *n* Lesbarkeit *f*; Leserlichkeit *f*.

legible [ˈledʒɪbl] *adj* lesbar; *handwriting also* leserlich.

legibly [ˈledʒɪblɪ] *adv* lesbar; *write* leserlich.

legion [ˈliːdʒən] *n* (**a**) Armee *f*; (*Foreign L~*) Legion *f*.
(**b**) (*Roman*) Legion *f*.
(**c**) (*organization*) **L~** Legion *f*; **American/British L~** American/British Legion *f* (*Verband m der Kriegsteilnehmer des 1. Weltkrieges*); **L~ of Honour** Ehrenlegion *f*.
(**d**) (*fig: large number*) Legion *f* ◆ **they are ~** ihre Zahl ist Legion; **his supporters are ~** seine Anhänger sind Legion.

legionary [ˈliːdʒənərɪ] [1] *adj* Legions-.
[2] *n* (*also* **legionnaire**) Legionär *m*.

legionnaire [ˌliːdʒəˈnɛəʳ] *n* Legionär *m* ◆ **~'s disease** Legionärskrankheit *f*.

legislate [ˈledʒɪsleɪt] [1] *vi* (**a**) Gesetze/ein Gesetz erlassen ◆ **parliament's job is to ~** die Aufgabe des Parlaments ist die Gesetzgebung ◆ (**b**) (*fig*) **to ~ for sth** etw berücksichtigen; (*give ruling on*) für etw Regeln aufstellen.
[2] *vt* **to ~ sth out of existence** etw durch Gesetz aus der Welt schaffen; **attempts to ~ the trade unions into submission** Versuche *pl*, die Gewerkschaften durch Gesetz zu unterwerfen.

legislation [ˈledʒɪsˈleɪʃən] *n* (*making laws*) Gesetzgebung, Legislatur (*geh*) *f*; (*laws*) Gesetze *pl*.

legislative [ˈledʒɪslətɪv] *adj* gesetzgebend, legislativ (*geh*) ◆ ~ **reforms** Gesetzesreformen *pl*.

legislator [ˈledʒɪsleɪtəʳ] *n* Gesetzgeber *m*.

legislature [ˈledʒɪsleɪtʃəʳ] *n* Legislative *f*.

legit [lɪˈdʒɪt] *adj* (*sl*) O.K. (*inf*).

legitimacy [lɪˈdʒɪtɪməsɪ] *n* Rechtmäßigkeit, Legitimität *f*; (*of birth*) Ehelichkeit *f*; (*of conclusion*) Berechtigung *f* ◆ **I don't doubt the ~ of your excuse/reason** ich bezweifle nicht, daß Ihre Entschuldigung/Ihr Grund gerechtfertigt ist.

legitimate [lɪˈdʒɪtɪmət] *adj* (**a**) (*lawful*) rechtmäßig, legitim ◆ **how ~ is his claim?** wie legitim ist sein Anspruch? (**b**) (*reasonable*) berechtigt; *excuse* begründet ◆ **his use of the company car was not ~** er war nicht berechtigt, den Firmenwagen zu benutzen. (**c**) (*born in wedlock*) ehelich.

legitimately [lɪˈdʒɪtɪmətlɪ] *adv* (*lawfully*) legitim; (*with reason*) berechtigterweise, mit Recht ◆ **he argues, quite ~, that** ... er führt das berechtigte Argument an, daß ...; **it can ~ be expected of people that** ... man kann mit Recht von den Leuten erwarten, daß ...

legitimatize [lɪˈdʒɪtɪmətaɪz], **legitimize** [lɪˈdʒɪtɪmaɪz] *vt* legitimieren; *children* für ehelich erklären.

leg: ~less *adj* (*without legs*) ohne Beine; (*sl: drunk*) sternhagelvoll (*sl*); **~man** *n* (*US*) *kleiner Reporter, der Informationsquellen abklappert*; (*who runs errands*) Laufbursche, Bote *m*; **~-pull** *n* (*inf*) Scherz, Bluff (*inf*) *m*; **what he said to us was only a ~-pull** damit wollte er uns nur auf den Arm nehmen; **~room** *n* Platz *m* für die Beine, Beinfreiheit *f*; **~-show** *n* (*inf*) Revue *f*.

legume [ˈlegjuːm] *n* (*species*) Hülsenfrüchtler *m*; (*fruit*) Hülsenfrucht *f*.

leguminous [leˈgjuːmɪnəs] *adj* Hülsenfrucht-.

leg: ~ up *n* **to give sb a ~ up** jdm hochhelfen; **~warmer** *n* Legwarmer *m*; **~work** *n* Lauferei *f*.

Leics *abbr of* **Leicestershire**.

leisure [ˈleʒəʳ] *n* Freizeit *f* ◆ **a gentleman of ~** ein Privatier *m* (*dated*); **she decided to give up her job and become a lady of ~** sie entschloß sich, ihren Beruf aufzugeben und in Muße zu leben; **to lead a life of ~** ein Leben in *or* der Muße führen (*geh*), sich dem (süßen) Nichtstun ergeben; **the problem of what to do with one's ~** das Problem der Freizeitgestaltung; **the Prime Minister is seldom at ~** der Premierminister hat selten Zeit für sich *or* hat selten freie Zeit; **do it at your ~** (*in own time*) tun Sie es, wenn Sie Zeit *or* Ruhe dazu haben; (*at own speed*) lassen Sie sich (*dat*) Zeit damit; **to have the ~ to do sth** die Zeit *or* Muße haben, etw zu tun; **~ hours** Freizeit *f*.

leisure: ~ activities *npl* Hobbys, Freizeitbeschäftigungen *pl*; **~ centre** *n* Freizeitzentrum *nt*; **~ clothes** *npl* Freizeitkleidung *f*.

leisured [ˈleʒəd] *adj* **the ~ classes** die feinen Leute.

leisurely [ˈleʒəlɪ] *adj* geruhsam ◆ **to walk at a ~ pace** gemächlich *or* langsam gehen.

leisure: ~ suit *n* Jogginganzug *m*; **~ time** *n* Freizeit *f*; **~wear** *n* Freizeitbekleidung *f*.

lemma [ˈlemə] *pl* **-s** *or* **-ta** [ˈlemətə] *n* (*Ling*) Lemma *nt*.

lemmatization [ˌlemətaɪˈzeɪʃən] *n* (*Ling*) Lemmatisierung *f*.

lemming [ˈlemɪŋ] *n* Lemming *m*.

lemon [ˈlemən] [1] *n* (**a**) Zitrone *f*; (*colour*) Zitronengelb *nt*; (*tree*) Zitrone(nbaum *m*) *f*. (**b**) (*inf: fool*) Dussel *m* (*inf*). (**c**) (*US inf: poor-quality product*) schlechte Ware ◆ **I bought a ~** sie haben mir was angedreht (*inf*).
[2] *adj* Zitronen- ◆ **~ paint** zitronengelbe Farbe; **~ yellow** Zitronengelb *nt*.

lemonade [ˌleməˈneɪd] *n* Limonade *f*; (*with lemon flavour*) Zitronenlimonade *f*.

lemon: ~ cheese *or* **curd** *n zähflüssiger Brotaufstrich mit Zitronengeschmack*; **~ juice** *n* Zitronensaft *m*; **~ meringue pie** *n mit Baisermasse gedeckter Mürbeteig mit einer Zitronencremefüllung*; **~ sole** *n* Seezunge *f*; **~ squash** *n* Zitronensaft *m*; (*in bottle*) Zitronensirup *m*; **~ squeezer** *n* Zitronenpresse *f*; **~ tea** *n* Zitronentee *m*.

lemur [ˈliːməʳ] *n* Lemur, Maki *m*.

lend [lend] *pret, ptp* **lent** [1] *vt* (**a**) (*loan*) leihen (*to sb* jdm); (*banks*) *money* verleihen (*to* an +*acc*).
(**b**) (*fig: give*) verleihen (*to dat*); *name* geben ◆ **I am not going to ~ my name to this** dafür gebe ich meinen (guten) Namen nicht her; **to ~ a hand** helfen, mit anfassen.
[2] *vr* **to ~ oneself to sth** sich für etw hergeben; (*be suitable*) sich für etw eignen.

◆**lend out** *vt sep* verleihen; *books also* ausleihen.

lender [ˈlendəʳ] *n* (*professional*) Geldverleiher *m* ◆ **he returned the £100 to the ~** er gab die £ 100 an den zurück, der sie ihm geliehen hatte.

lending [ˈlendɪŋ] *adj library* Leih- ◆ **~ bank** kreditierende Bank; **~ business** Kreditgeschäft *nt*; **~ country** Gläubigerland *nt*; **~ policy** (*of bank etc*) Kreditpolitik *f*; **~ rate** (Darlehens)zinssatz *m*; **~ rights** Verleihrecht *nt*; (*for author*) Anspruch *m* auf Leihbücherei-Tantiemen.

lend-lease [ˈlendˈliːs] *n*: **~ agreement** Leih-Pacht-Abkommen *nt*.

length [leŋθ] *n* (**a**) Länge *f* ◆ **a journey of incredible ~** eine unglaublich lange *or* weite Reise; **to be 4 metres in ~** 4 Meter lang sein; **what ~ is it?** wie lang ist es?; **what ~ do you want it?** wie lang hätten Sie es gerne?; **of some ~** ziemlich lang; **the river, for most of its ~, meanders through meadows** der Fluß schlängelt sich in seinem Verlauf größtenteils durch Wiesen; **along the whole ~ of the river/lane** den ganzen Fluß/Weg entlang; **the pipe, for most of its ~**, ... fast das ganze Rohr ...; **it turns in its own ~** es kann sich um die eigene Achse drehen; **over all the ~ and breadth of England** in ganz England; (*travelling*) kreuz und quer durch ganz England; **the ~ of skirts** die Rocklänge; **at full ~** in voller Länge.
(**b**) (*section*) (*of cloth, rope, pipe*) Stück *nt*; (*of wallpaper*) Bahn *f*; (*of road*) Abschnitt *m*; (*of pool*) Bahn, Länge *f*.
(**c**) (*of time*) Dauer *f*; (*great ~*) lange Dauer ◆ **of some ~** ziemlich lange, von einiger Dauer; **we didn't stay any (great) ~ of time** wir sind nicht lange geblieben; **the ~ of time needed** die Zeit, die man dazu braucht; **in that ~ of time I could have** ... in dieser Zeit hätte ich ...; **for any ~ of time** für längere Zeit; **for what ~ of time?** für wie lange?; **~ of life** (*of people*) Lebenserwartung *f*; (*of animals*) Lebensalter *nt*; (*of machine*) Lebensdauer *f*; **~ of service with a company** Betriebszugehörigkeit *f*; **~ of service with the army** Dienstjahre *pl* bei der Armee; **at ~** (*finally*) schließlich; (*for a long time*) lange, ausführlich, lang und breit (*pej*).
(**d**) (*Phon, Poet, Sport*) Länge *f* ◆ **~ mark** Längenzeichen *nt*; **to win by half a ~**

mit einer halben Länge siegen.
(e) **to go to any ~s to do sth** vor nichts zurückschrecken, um etw zu tun; **to go to great ~s** sich (*dat*) sehr viel Mühe geben, alles mögliche versuchen; **to go to the ~ of ...** so weit gehen, daß ...

lengthen [ˈleŋθən] **1** *vt* verlängern; *clothes* länger machen.
2 *vi* länger werden.

lengthily [ˈleŋθɪlɪ] *adv* ausführlich, langatmig (*pej*).

lengthways [ˈleŋθweɪz], **lengthwise** [ˈleŋθwaɪz] **1** *adj* Längen-, Längs- ◆ **~ measurement** Längenmessung *f*; **~ cut** Längsschnitt *m*.
2 *adv* der Länge nach.

lengthy [ˈleŋθɪ] *adj* (*+er*) lange; (*dragging on*) langwierig; *speech* ausführlich, langatmig (*pej*).

lenience [ˈliːnɪəns], **leniency** [ˈliːnɪənsɪ] *n see adj* Nachsicht *f*; Milde *f*.

lenient [ˈliːnɪənt] *adj* nachsichtig (*towards* gegenüber); *judge, attitude* milde.

leniently [ˈliːnɪəntlɪ] *adv* nachsichtig; *judge* milde.

Leninism [ˈlenɪnɪzəm] *n* Leninismus *m*.

Leninist [ˈlenɪnɪst] **1** *adj* leninistisch.
2 *n* Leninist(in *f*) *m*.

lens [lenz] *n* (*Anat, Opt, Phot*) Linse *f*; (*in spectacles*) Glas *nt*; (*camera part containing ~*) Objektiv *nt*; (*eyeglass*) Klemmlupe *f*; (*for stamps etc*) Vergrößerungsglas *nt*, Lupe *f*.

lens: ~ cap *n* Schutzkappe *f*; **~ hood** *n* Sonnenblende, Gegenlichtblende *f*.

lent [lent] *pret, ptp of* **lend**.

Lent [lent] *n* Fastenzeit *f*.

Lenten [ˈlentən] *adj* Fasten- ◆ **~ fast** Fasten *nt* (zur Fastenzeit).

lentil [ˈlentl] *n* Linse *f* ◆ **~ soup** Linsensuppe *f*.

Leo [ˈliːəʊ] *n* (*Astrol*) Löwe *m*.

leonine [ˈliːənaɪn] *adj* Löwen-, löwenartig ◆ **the ~ bust of Karl Marx** die Büste von Karl Marx mit seiner Löwenmähne.

leopard [ˈlepəd] *n* Leopard *m* ◆ **the ~ never changes its spots** (*Prov*) die Katze läßt das Mausen nicht (*Prov*).

leotard [ˈliːətɑːd] *n* Trikot *nt*; (*Gymnastics*) Gymnastikanzug *m*.

leper [ˈlepəʳ] *n* Leprakranke(r), Lepröse(r) (*spec*), Aussätzige(r) (*old, fig*) *mf* ◆ **~ colony** Leprasiedlung *f*, Lepradorf *nt*.

lepidoptera [ˌlepɪˈdɒptərə] *npl* Falter, Lepidopteren (*spec*) *pl*.

leprechaun [ˈleprəkɔːn] *n* Gnom, Kobold *m*.

leprosy [ˈleprəsɪ] *n* Lepra *f*, Aussatz *m* (*old*).

leprous [ˈleprəs] *adj* leprös, Lepra-, aussätzig (*old*).

lesbian [ˈlezbɪən] **1** *adj* lesbisch.
2 *n* Lesbierin, Lesbe (*inf*) *f*.

lesbianism [ˈlezbɪənɪzəm] *n* (*in general*) lesbische Liebe; (*of one person*) Lesbiertum *nt*.

lèse-majesté, lese majesty [ˈleɪzˈmæʒəsteɪ] *n* (*high treason*) Hochverrat *m*; (*insult to dignity*) (Majestäts)beleidigung *f*.

lesion [ˈliːʒən] *n* Verletzung *f*; (*structural change*) krankhafte Gewebsveränderung ◆ **~s in the brain** Gehirnverletzungen *pl*.

Lesotho [lɪˈsəʊtəʊ] *n* Lesotho *nt*.

▼ **less** [les] **1** *adj, adv, n* weniger ◆ **of ~ importance** von geringerer Bedeutung, weniger bedeutend; **~ noise, please!** nicht so laut, bitte!; **no ~ a person than the bishop** kein Geringerer als der Bischof; **he did it in ~ time** er hat es in kürzerer Zeit *or* schneller getan; **to grow ~** weniger werden; (*grow at slow rate*) langsamer wachsen; (*decrease*) abnehmen; **his problem is ~ one of money than of enthusiasm** sein Problem ist weniger das Geld als vielmehr mangelnde Begeisterung; **~ and ~** immer weniger; **she saw him ~ and ~ (often)** sie sah ihn immer seltener; **a sum ~ than £1** eine Summe unter £ 1; **it's nothing ~ than disgraceful/than a disaster** es ist wirklich eine Schande/ein Unglück *nt*; **this is nothing ~ than blackmail** das ist ja direkt Erpressung; **it was little ~ than blackmail** das war schon fast *or* so gut wie Erpressung; **he was ~ frightened than angry** er war nicht so sehr ängstlich, sondern eher ärgerlich; **~ beautiful** nicht so schön; **~ quickly** nicht so schnell; **he works ~ than I (do)** er arbeitet weniger als ich; **still** *or* **even ~** noch weniger; **none the ~** trotzdem, nichtsdestoweniger; **I didn't find the film any the ~ interesting** ich fand den Film nicht weniger interessant; **I don't love her any the ~** ich liebe sie nicht weniger; **their apology did not make him any the ~ angry** ihre Entschuldigung konnte seinen Ärger nicht besänftigen; **can't you let me have it for ~?** können Sie es mir nicht etwas billiger lassen?; **I hope you won't think (any the) ~ of me** ich hoffe, du denkst nicht schlecht von mir; **~ of that!** komm mir nicht so!
2 *prep* weniger; (*Comm*) abzüglich ◆ **a year ~ 4 days** ein Jahr weniger 4 Tage; **6 ~ 4 is 2** 6 weniger *or* minus 4 ist 2.

-less [-lɪs] *adj suf* -los ◆ **hat~** ohne Hut; **sun~** ohne Sonne.

lessee [leˈsiː] *n* Pächter *m*; (*of house, flat*) Mieter *m*; (*of equipment*) Leasingnehmer *m*.

lessen [ˈlesn] **1** *vt* (a) (*make less*) verringern; *cost* senken, vermindern; *effect* vermindern, abschwächen.
(b) (*make seem less important etc*) herabsetzen, herabwürdigen; *a person's contribution, services also* schmälern.
2 *vi* nachlassen; (*danger, wind, enthusiasm, difficulty also*) abnehmen; (*value of money*) sich verringern, abnehmen.

lessening [ˈlesnɪŋ] *n* Nachlassen *nt* (*in sth +gen*) ◆ **~ of value** Wertabnahme *f*; **a ~ in the rate of inflation** ein Rückgang *m or* eine Verringerung der Inflationsrate.

lesser [ˈlesəʳ] *adj* geringer; (*in names*) klein ◆ **to a ~ extent** in geringerem Maße; **a ~ amount** ein kleinerer Betrag; **the ~ weight** das leichtere Gewicht; **which is the ~ crime?** welches Verbrechen ist weniger schlimm?; **he is a ~ man than his brother** (*less good*) er ist kein so guter Mensch wie sein Bruder; (*less great*) er ist weniger bedeutend als sein Bruder.

lesson [ˈlesn] *n* (a) (*Sch etc*) Stunde *f*; (*unit of study*) Lektion *f* ◆ **~s** Unterricht *m*; (*homework*) (Haus)aufgaben *pl*; **his ~s are boring** sein Unterricht ist *or* seine Stunden sind langweilig; **~s begin at 9** der Unterricht *or* die Schule beginnt um 9; **he's not very good at his ~s** er ist kein besonders guter Schüler; **a French ~** eine Französischstunde; **a driving ~** eine Fahrstunde; **to give** *or* **teach a ~** eine Stunde geben, unterrichten; **we're having a French ~ now** wir haben jetzt Französisch.
(b) (*fig*) Lehre *f* ◆ **to be a ~ to sb** jdm eine Lehre sein; **he has learnt his ~** er hat seine Lektion gelernt; **to teach sb a ~** jdm eine Lektion erteilen; **what ~ can we learn from this story?** was können wir von dieser Geschichte lernen?; **he had not learned the big ~ of life that ...** er hatte die goldene Lebensregel nicht begriffen, daß ...
(c) (*Eccl*) Lesung *f* ◆ **to read the ~** die Lesung halten.

lessor [leˈsɔːʳ] *n* (*form*) Verpächter *m*; (*of flat etc*) Vermieter *m*; (*of equipment*) Leasinggeber *m*.

lest [lest] *conj* (*form*) (a) (*for fear that*) aus Furcht, daß; (*in order that ... not*) damit ... nicht; (*in case*) für den Fall, daß ◆ **I didn't do it ~ somebody should object** ich habe es aus Furcht, daß jemand dagegen sein könnte, nicht getan; **~ we forget** damit wir nicht vergessen.
(b) (*after fear, be afraid etc*) daß ◆ **I was frightened ~ he should fall** ich hatte Angst, daß er fallen könnte.

let[1] [let] *n* (a) (*Tennis*) Netz(ball *m*) *nt*. (b) **without ~ or hindrance** (*Jur*) ungehindert.

let[2] *n* **they are looking for a ~ in this area** sie wollen eine Wohnung/ein Haus in dieser Gegend mieten; **I have this house on a long ~** ich habe dieses Haus für längere Zeit gemietet.

▼ **let**[3] *pret, ptp* **~** *vt* (a) (*permit*) lassen ◆ **to ~ sb do sth** jdn etw tun lassen; **she ~ me borrow the car** sie lieh mir das Auto, ich durfte ihr Auto nehmen; **we can't ~ that happen** wir dürfen das nicht zulassen; **he wants to but I won't ~ him** er möchte gern, aber ich lasse ihn nicht *or* erlaube es ihm nicht; **the particle wants to escape but the magnetic force won't ~ it** das Teilchen möchte sich freimachen, aber die magnetische Kraft verhindert es; **oh please ~ me** bitte, bitte, laß mich doch (mal)!; **~ me help you** darf ich Ihnen helfen *or* behilflich sein?; **~ me know what you think** sagen Sie mir (Bescheid) *or* lassen Sie mich wissen (*form*), was Sie davon halten; **to ~ oneself be seen** sich sehen lassen; **to ~ sb be** jdn (in Ruhe) lassen; **to ~ sb/sth go, to ~ go of sb/sth** jdn/etw loslassen; **to ~ sb go** (*depart*) jdn gehen lassen; **~ me go!** lassen Sie mich los!, loslassen!; **to ~ oneself go** (*neglect oneself*) sich gehenlassen; (*relax*) aus sich herausgehen; **to ~ sth go** (*neglect*) etw vernachlässigen; **to ~ oneself go on a subject** sich über ein Thema auslassen; **to ~ it go at that** es dabei bewenden lassen; **to ~ sb pass** jdn vorbeilassen; **we'll ~ it pass** *or* **go this once** (*disregard*) *error* wir wollen es mal durchgehen lassen; *see* **drop, fly**[2], **slip**.
(b) (*old: causative*) lassen ◆ **~ the bells be rung** lasset die Glocken ertönen (*liter*); **~ it be known by all citizens, that ...** allen Bürgern sei kundgetan, daß ... (*old*); **~ it be known, that ...** alle sollen wissen, daß ...
(c) **to ~ sb/sth alone** jdn/etw in Ruhe lassen; **we can't improve it any more, we'd better ~ it alone** wir können es nicht mehr verbessern, also lassen wir es lieber so; **we'd better ~ well alone** wir lassen besser die Finger davon; **please ~ me by/past** bitte, lassen Sie mich vorbei/durch; **to ~ sb/sth through** jdn/etw durchlassen.
(d) **~ alone** (*much less*) geschweige denn.
▼ (e) **~'s go home** komm, wir gehen nach Hause; **~'s go!** gehen wir!; **~'s get out of here** bloß weg von hier!; **yes, ~'s** oh ja!; **it's late, but yes ~'s** es ist spät, aber na ja, einverstanden; **~'s not** lieber nicht; **don't ~'s** *or* **~'s not fight** wir wollen uns doch nicht streiten; **~'s be happy** laß uns glücklich sein; **~'s be friends** wir wollen Freunde sein; **~'s all be a bit more friendly** seien wir doch alle ein bißchen freundlicher; **~ him try (it)!** das soll er nur *or* mal versuchen!; **~ me think** *or* **see, where did I put it?** warte mal *or* Moment mal, wo habe ich das nur hingetan?; **~ their need be never so great** mag ihre Not auch noch so groß sein; **~ X be 60** X sei 60; **~ there be music** laßt Musik erklingen; **~ there be peace** es soll Friede sein; **~ there be light** es werde Licht; **~ us pray** laßt uns beten; **~ us suppose ...** nehmen wir (mal) an, daß ...
(f) (*esp Brit: hire out*) vermieten ◆ **"to ~"** „zu vermieten"; **we can't find a house to ~** wir können kein Haus finden, das zu mieten ist.
(g) **to ~ blood** einen Aderlaß machen; **they ~ so much of his blood** sie nahmen ihm so viel Blut ab.

◆**let away** *vt sep* **to ~ sb (get) ~ with sth** jdm etw durchgehen lassen; **I'll ~ you (get) ~ with it just this once** diesmal drücke ich noch ein Auge zu (*inf*).

◆**let down** *vt sep* (a) (*lower*) *rope, person* hinunter-/herunterlassen; *seat* herunterklappen; *hair, window* herunterlassen ◆ **to ~ sb ~ gently** (*fig*) jdm etw/das schonend beibringen.
(b) (*lengthen*) *dress* länger machen.
(c) (*deflate*) **to ~ a tyre ~** die Luft aus einem Reifen lassen.
(d) (*fail to help*) **to ~ sb ~** jdn im Stich lassen (*over* mit); **the weather ~ us ~** das Wetter machte uns einen Strich durch die Rechnung; **to ~ the side ~** die anderen im Stich lassen.
(e) (*disappoint*) enttäuschen ◆ **to feel ~ ~** enttäuscht sein.
(f) **to ~ the school/oneself ~** die Schule/sich blamieren *or* in Verruf bringen; **you'd be ~ting yourself ~ if you only got 5 out of 10** es wäre unter deinem Niveau, nur 5 von 10 Punkten zu bekommen.

◆**let in** **1** *vt sep* (a) *water* durchlassen.
(b) (*admit*) *air, cat, visitor* hereinlassen; (*to club etc*) zulassen (*to* zu) ◆ **he ~**

➤ LANGUAGE IN USE: **less: 1** → 5.1, 5.3, 7.3, 26.3 **let**[3]**: a** → 9.3 **e** → 26.1

himself ~ (with his key) er schloß die Tür auf und ging hinein; **he ~ himself ~to the flat** er ging in die Wohnung hinein; **just ~ yourself ~** geh einfach hinein; **I was just ~ting myself ~** ich schloß gerade die Tür auf.
(c) (*involve in*) **to ~ sb ~ for a lot of work** jdm eine Menge Arbeit aufhalsen; **see what you've ~ me ~ for now** da hast du mir aber was eingebrockt! (*inf*); **to ~ oneself ~ for sth** sich auf etw (*acc*) einlassen; **to ~ oneself/sb ~ for trouble** sich/jdm Ärger einbringen *or* einhandeln; **I got ~ ~ for £50** ich bin £ 50 losgeworden (*inf*).
(d) (*allow to know*) **to ~ sb ~ on sth, to ~ sb ~to sth** jdn in etw (*acc*) einweihen; **she ~ me ~ on the secret** sie hat es mir verraten.
(e) (*Sew*) **to ~ ~ a panel** eine Bahn einsetzen.
2 *vi* (*shoes, tent*) Wasser durchlassen, undicht sein.
◆**let off** 1 *vt sep* (a) *also vt* (*fire*) *arrow* abschießen; *gun, shot* abfeuern.
(b) (*explode*) *firework, bomb* hochgehen lassen.
(c) (*emit*) *vapour* von sich geben; *gases* absondern; *smell* verbreiten ◆ **to ~ ~ steam** (*lit*) Dampf ablassen; (*fig also*) sich abreagieren.
(d) (*forgive*) **to ~ sb ~** jdm etw durchgehen lassen; **I'll ~ you ~ this time** diesmal drücke ich noch ein Auge zu; **OK, I'll ~ you ~, you're quite right** ich will dir mal ausnahmsweise recht geben; **to ~ sb ~ sth** jdm etw erlassen; **to ~ sb ~ with a warning/fine** jdn mit einer Verwarnung/Geldstrafe davonkommen lassen; **to ~ sb ~ lightly** mit jdm glimpflich verfahren; **to be ~ ~ lightly** glimpflich davonkommen; **he's been ~ ~** man hat ihn laufenlassen.
(e) (*allow to go*) gehen lassen ◆ **we were ~ ~ early** wir durften früher gehen.
(f) (*from car etc*) herauslassen (*inf*), aussteigen lassen.
2 *vi* (*inf: fart*) einen fahren lassen (*inf*).
◆**let on** *vi* (a) *also vt* (*inf: tell, give away*) **don't ~ ~ you know** laß dir bloß nicht anmerken, daß du das weißt; **he ~ ~ that he had known all the time** er kam damit heraus (*inf*), daß er es schon die ganze Zeit gewußt hatte; **don't ~ ~ about our meeting with John** sag nichts über unser Treffen mit John.
(b) (*pretend*) **to ~ ~ that ...** vorgeben, daß ...
◆**let out** *vt sep* (a) (*allow to go out*) *cat, smell, air* hinaus-/herauslassen; (*from car*) absetzen ◆ **to ~ oneself ~** sich (*dat*) die Tür aufmachen; **I'll ~ myself ~** ich finde alleine hinaus.
(b) *prisoner* entlassen, rauslassen (*inf*); (*divulge*) *news* bekanntgeben *or* -machen; *secret* verraten, ausplaudern (*inf*).
(c) (*emit*) *yell* ausstoßen ◆ **to ~ ~ a laugh** auflachen; **to ~ ~ a yawn** (laut) gähnen; **to ~ ~ a groan** (auf)stöhnen.
(d) (*make larger*) *dress* weiter machen, auslassen.
(e) *fire* ausgehen lassen.
(f) (*free from responsibility*) **that ~s me ~ (of it)** da komme ich (schon mal) nicht in Frage.
(g) (*rent*) vermieten.
◆**let up** *vi* (a) (*cease*) aufhören ◆ **he never ~s ~ about his money** er redet unaufhörlich *or* pausenlos von seinem Geld. (b) (*ease up*) nachlassen. (c) **to ~ ~ on sb** jdn in Ruhe lassen; **the trainer didn't ~ ~ on them until they were perfect** der Trainer hat so lange nicht locker gelassen, bis sie perfekt waren.
-let [-lɪt] *suf* -lein, -chen.
let-down ['letdaʊn] *n* (*inf: disappointment*) Enttäuschung *f*.
lethal ['li:θəl] *adj* tödlich ◆ **a ~-looking knife** ein gefährlich aussehendes Messer.
lethargic [lɪ'θɑ:dʒɪk] *adj* (a) *appearance, person* träge, lethargisch; *atmosphere also* schläfrig; *animal* träge; *pace of music* schleppend; (*uninterested*) lethargisch, teilnahmslos, lustlos ◆ **a ~-looking child** ein teilnahmslos aussehendes Kind.
(b) (*Med*) schlafsüchtig, lethargisch.
lethargically [lɪ'θɑ:dʒɪkəlɪ] *adv see adj*.
lethargy ['leθədʒɪ] *n* (a) Lethargie, Trägheit *f* ◆ **an atmosphere of ~** eine schläfrige *or* träge Atmosphäre. (b) (*Med*) Schlafsucht, Lethargie *f*.
Letraset ® ['letrə,set] *n* Letraset ® *nt*.
let's [lets] *contr of* **let us**.
Lett [let] *adj, n see* **Latvian**.
▼ **letter** ['letə^r] 1 *n* (a) (*of alphabet*) Buchstabe *m* ◆ **the ~ of the law** der Buchstabe des Gesetzes; **to the ~** buchstabengetreu, genau; **did he do it? — to the ~** hat er es getan? — ganz nach Vorschrift.
▼ (b) (*written message*) Brief *m*; (*Comm etc*) Schreiben *nt* (*form*) (*to an +acc*) ◆ **by ~** schriftlich, brieflich; **~ of credit** Kreditbrief *m*, Akkreditiv *nt*; **~s patent** Patent(urkunde *f*) *nt*.
(c) (*Liter*) **~s** Literatur *f* ◆ **man of ~s** Belletrist *m*; (*writer*) Literat *m*.
(d) (*US: award*) *als Auszeichnung verliehenes Schulabzeichen*.
2 *vt sign, label* beschriften ◆ **he ~ed the invitations in gold** er ließ die Einladungen in Gold(buchstaben) drucken.
letter: ~ bomb *n* Briefbombe *f*; **~box** *n* Briefkasten *m*; **~-card** *n* Briefkarte *f*.
lettered ['letəd] *adj* (a) (*rare*) *person* gelehrt. (b) *object* beschriftet ◆ **~ in gold** in Goldschrift.
letterhead ['letəhed] *n* Briefkopf *m*; (*writing paper*) Geschäfts(brief)papier *nt*.
lettering ['letərɪŋ] *n* Beschriftung *f*.
letter: ~press *n* Hochdruck *m*; **~ quality** *n* Korrespondenz- *or* Briefqualität, Schönschrift *f*; **~-quality** *adj printer* Schönschreib-; *script* korrespondenzfähig; *printout* in Korrespondenz- *or* Briefqualität.
letting ['letɪŋ] *n* Vermieten *nt* ◆ **he's in the ~ business** er ist in der Wohnungsbranche.
Lettish ['letɪʃ] *adj, n see* **Latvian**.

➤ LANGUAGE IN USE: **letter: 1b** → 21.1

lettuce ['letɪs] *n* Kopfsalat *m*; (*genus*) Lattich *m*.
let-up ['letʌp] *n* (*inf*) Pause *f*; (*easing up*) Nachlassen *nt* ◆ **if there is a ~ in the rain** wenn der Regen aufhört/nachläßt.
leucocyte, leukocyte ['lu:kəʊsaɪt] *n* (*form*) Leukozyt *m*.
leukaemia, leukemia [lu:'ki:mɪə] *n* Leukämie *f*.
Levant [lɪ'vænt] *n* Levante *f*.
Levantine ['levəntaɪn] 1 *adj* levantinisch.
2 *n* (*person*) Levantiner(in *f*) *m*.
levee¹ ['levɪ] *n* (*Hist*) (*on awakening*) Lever *nt*; (*at British court*) Nachmittagsempfang *m*.
levee² ['levɪ] *n* Damm, Deich *m*.
level ['levl] 1 *adj* (a) (*flat*) *ground, surface, floor* eben; *spoonful* gestrichen ◆ **try to keep the boat ~** versuchen Sie, das Boot waagerecht zu halten; **the glider maintained a ~ course** das Segelflugzeug behielt die gleiche Flughöhe bei.
(b) (*at the same height*) auf gleicher Höhe (*with* mit); (*parallel*) parallel (*with* zu) ◆ **the bedroom is ~ with the ground** das Schlafzimmer liegt ebenerdig *or* zu ebener Erde.
(c) (*equal*) *race* Kopf-an-Kopf-; (*fig*) gleich gut ◆ **the two runners are absolutely** *or* **dead ~** die beiden Läufer liegen *or* sind genau auf gleicher Höhe; **Jones was almost ~ with the winner** Jones kam fast auf gleiche Höhe mit dem Sieger; **the two teams are ~ in the league** die beiden Mannschaften haben den gleichen Tabellenstand.
(d) (*steady*) *tone of voice* ruhig; (*well-balanced*) ausgeglichen; *judgement* ab- *or* ausgewogen; *head* kühl ◆ **to have/keep a ~ head** einen kühlen Kopf haben/bewahren.
(e) **I'll do my ~ best** ich werde mein möglichstes tun.
2 *adv* **~ with** in Höhe (*+gen*); **it should lie ~ with ...** es sollte gleich hoch sein wie ...; **the pipe runs ~ with the ground** das Rohr verläuft zu ebener Erde; (*parallel*) das Rohr verläuft parallel zum Boden; **they're running absolutely ~** sie laufen auf genau gleicher Höhe; **the value of the shares stayed ~ for some time** der Wert der Aktien blieb für einige Zeit gleich; **to draw ~ with sb** jdn einholen, mit jdm gleichziehen; (*in league etc*) punktegleich mit jdm sein; **the two runners drew ~ on the last lap** in der letzten Runde zogen die beiden Läufer gleich.
3 *n* (a) (*instrument*) Wasserwaage *f*.
(b) (*altitude*) Höhe *f* ◆ **on a ~ (with)** auf gleicher Höhe (mit); **water always finds its own ~** Wasser kehrt immer in die Waagerechte zurück; **at eye ~** in Augenhöhe; **the trees were very tall, almost at roof ~** die Bäume waren sehr hoch, sie reichten fast bis zum Dach; **to be on a ~ with the ground** in Bodenhöhe *or* zu ebener Erde sein *or* liegen.
(c) (*flat place*) ebene Fläche, ebenes Stück.
(d) (*storey*) Geschoß *nt*.
(e) (*position on scale*) Niveau *nt*, Ebene *f* ◆ **they're on a different ~** sie haben ein unterschiedliches Niveau; **to descend** *or* **sink** *or* **come down to that ~** auf ein so tiefes Niveau absinken; **he expects everyone to come down to his ~** er erwartet von jedem, daß er sich auf sein Niveau herabbegibt; **she tried to go above her own natural ~** sie versuchte, ihre natürlichen Grenzen zu überschreiten; **to be on a ~ with** auf gleichem Niveau sein wie; **they are on a ~ as far as salaries are concerned** sie bekommen das gleiche Gehalt; **he tried to raise the ~ of the conversation** er versuchte, der Unterhaltung etwas mehr Niveau zu geben; **if profit keeps on the same ~** wenn sich der Gewinn auf dem gleichen Stand hält; **he maintains his high ~ of excellence** er hält sein äußerst hohes Niveau; **a high ~ of intelligence** ein hoher Intelligenzgrad; **the very high ~ of production** das hohe Produktionsniveau; **a low ~ of sales** ein sehr geringer Absatz; **a high ~ of civilization** eine hohe Kulturstufe; **the higher ~s of academic research** die höheren Stufen der wissenschaftlichen Forschung; **the talks were held at a very high ~** die Gespräche fanden auf hoher Ebene statt; **the varying ~s of abilities** die verschiedenen Fähigkeitsgrade; **to reduce sth to a more comprehensible ~** etw auf eine etwas verständlichere Ebene bringen; **he reduces everything to the commercial ~** er reduziert alles auf eine rein kommerzielle Basis; **on the moral ~** aus moralischer Sicht; **on a purely personal ~** rein persönlich, auf rein persönlicher Ebene.
(f) (*amount, degree*) **a high ~ of hydrogen** ein hoher Wasserstoffanteil *or* Anteil an Wasserstoff; **the ~ of alcohol in the blood** der Alkoholspiegel im Blut; **what sort of ~ of mistakes can you tolerate?** welche Fehlerquote können Sie dulden?
(g) (*inf: straightforward, honest*) **it's on the ~** (*business*) es ist reell; (*proposition*) es ist ehrlich gemeint; **I guess you're on the ~** du bist wohl schon in Ordnung (*inf*); **is he on the ~?** meint er es ehrlich?; **to be on the ~ with sb** jdm gegenüber ehrlich *or* aufrichtig sein.
4 *vt* (a) *ground, site etc* einebnen, planieren; *building* abreißen; *town* dem Erdboden gleichmachen ◆ **to ~ sth to** *or* **with the ground** etw dem Erdboden gleichmachen.
(b) *blow* versetzen, verpassen (*inf*) (*at sb* jdm); *weapon* richten (*at* auf *+acc*); *accusation* erheben (*at* gegen); *remark* richten (*at* gegen) ◆ **to ~ a charge against sb** Anklage gegen jdn erheben, jdn anklagen.
5 *vi* (*sl*) **to ~ with sb** jdm keinen Quatsch *or* Scheiß erzählen (*sl*); **I'll ~ with you** ich werd ehrlich mit dir sein (*inf*).
◆**level down** *vt sep* (*lit*) einebnen; (*fig*) auf ein tieferes Niveau bringen *or* herabsetzen; *salaries* nach unten angleichen.
◆**level out** 1 *vi* (*also ~ off*) (a) (*ground*) eben *or* flach werden; (*fig*) sich ausgleichen, sich einpendeln. (b) (*Aviat*) (*pilot*) das Flugzeug abfangen; (*plane*) sich fangen; (*after rising*) horizontal fliegen.
2 *vt sep site* planieren, einebnen; (*fig*) *differences* ausgleichen.

◆**level up** *vt sep (lit)* ausgleichen; *salaries* angleichen; *(fig)* auf ein höheres Niveau bringen ◆ **you sit on the other side of the boat and that'll ~ it ~** du setzt dich auf die andere Seite des Bootes, dann ist das Gleichgewicht (wieder)hergestellt.

level: ~ crossing *n (Brit)* (beschrankter) Bahnübergang; **~-headed** *adj person* ausgeglichen; *attitude, reply, decision* ausgewogen; *reply, decision also* überlegt.

leveller ['levləʳ] *n* Gleichmacher *m* ◆ **death is a great ~** der Tod macht alle (Menschen) gleich.

levelly ['levəlɪ] *adv (calmly)* ruhig; *gaze* gerade.

level pegging ['levl'pegɪŋ] *adj* punktgleich ◆ **with 30 votes each they are ~** mit jeweils 30 Stimmen liegen sie auf gleicher Höhe; **it's ~ as they go round the final bend** sie liegen in der letzten Kurve auf gleicher Höhe.

lever ['li:vəʳ, *(US)* 'levəʳ] [1] *n* Hebel *m*; *(crowbar)* Brechstange *f*; *(fig)* Druckmittel *nt* ◆ **that should give us a ~** das können wir als Druckmittel benutzen.

[2] *vt* (hoch)stemmen, mit einem Hebel/einer Brechstange (an- *or* hoch)heben ◆ **he ~ed the machine-part into place** er hob das Maschinenteil durch Hebelwirkung an seinen Platz; **he ~ed the box open** er stemmte die Kiste auf; **he ~ed himself onto the ledge** er hievte sich auf den Felsvorsprung (hoch); **he seems to have ~ed himself into a position of power** er scheint sich in eine Machtposition manövriert zu haben.

◆**lever out** *vt sep* herausstemmen *or* -brechen ◆ **we'll never ~ him ~ of such a comfortable job** aus diesem bequemen Job werden wir ihn nie herausholen *or* -lotsen können *(inf)*; **he ~ed himself ~ of the armchair** er hievte sich aus dem Sessel (hoch).

◆**lever up** *vt sep* mit einem Hebel/einer Brechstange hochheben, aufstemmen.

leverage ['li:vərɪdʒ] *n* Hebelkraft *f*; *(fig)* Einfluß *m* ◆ **this spanner can exert considerable ~** dieser Schraubenschlüssel kann eine beträchtliche Hebelwirkung ausüben; **to use sth as ~** *(fig)* etw als Druckmittel benutzen; *(to one's own advantage)* etw zu seinem Vorteil ausnützen; **this gave us a bit of ~ with the authorities** dadurch konnten wir etwas Druck auf die Behörden ausüben; **his approval gives us a bit of ~ with them** seine Zustimmung verstärkt unsere Position ihnen gegenüber; **~ buyout** *Aufkauf m einer Kapitalgesellschaft durch das eigene Management mit Hilfe externer Finanzierung.*

lever-arch file ['li:vərɑ:tʃ'faɪl] *n* Leitz-Ordner ® *m.*

leveret ['levərɪt] *n* junger Hase, Häschen *nt.*

leviathan [lɪ'vaɪəθən] *n* Leviathan *m*, Meerungeheuer *nt*; *(fig)* Gigant *m*; *(state)* Leviathan *m.*

Levis, levis ® ['li:vaɪz] *npl* Levis ® *f*, Jeans *pl.*

levitate ['levɪteɪt] [1] *vt* schweben lassen.

[2] *vi* schweben.

levitation [,levɪ'teɪʃən] *n* Levitation *f*, freies Schweben.

Levite ['li:vaɪt] *n* Levit(e) *m.*

levity ['levɪtɪ] *n* Leichtfertigkeit *f* ◆ **sounds of ~** Gelächter *nt.*

levy ['levɪ] [1] *n (act)* (Steuer)einziehung *or* -eintreibung *f*; *(tax)* Steuer *f*, Abgaben *pl*; *(Mil)* Aushebung *f*; *(of supplies)* Einziehung, Beschlagnahme *f* ◆ **there were 100 men in the first ~** 100 Männer wurden bei der ersten Aushebung eingezogen.

[2] *vt* **(a)** *(raise) tax* einziehen, erheben; *fine* auferlegen *(on sb* jdm); *(Mil) army, troops* ausheben; *supplies* einziehen, beschlagnahmen ◆ **to ~ a tax on beer** Bier mit einer Steuer belegen, Steuern *pl* auf Bier erheben.

(b) *(wage) war* führen *(against, on* gegen).

lewd [lu:d] *adj (+er)* unanständig; *(lustful)* lüstern; *remark* anzüglich; *joke, song* unanständig, anstößig, anzüglich; *imagination* schmutzig ◆ **don't be ~** werd nicht anzüglich.

lewdly ['lu:dlɪ] *adv* anzüglich ◆ **he spoke ~ about his amorous adventures** er erzählte lüstern *or* in anzüglicher Weise von seinen amourösen Abenteuern.

lewdness ['lu:dnɪs] *n (being indecent)* Anstößigkeit, Unanständigkeit *f*; *(being lustful)* Lüsternheit *f*; *(of remark)* Anzüglichkeit *f*; *(of imagination)* Schmutzigkeit *f.*

lexical ['leksɪkəl] *adj* lexikalisch.

lexicalize ['leksɪkəlaɪz] *vt* lexikalisieren.

lexicographer [,leksɪ'kɒgrəfəʳ] *n* Lexikograph(in *f*) *m.*

lexicographic(al) [,leksɪkəʊ'græfɪk(əl)] *adj* lexikographisch.

lexicography [,leksɪ'kɒgrəfɪ] *n* Lexikographie *f.*

lexicology [,leksɪ'kɒlədʒɪ] *n* Lexikologie *f.*

lexicon ['leksɪkən] *n* Wörterbuch, Lexikon *nt*; *(in linguistics)* Lexikon *nt.*

lexis ['leksɪs] *n (Ling)* Lexik *f.*

Leyden jar ['laɪdn'dʒɑ:ʳ] *n* Leidener Flasche *f.*

l.h.d. *abbr of* **left-hand drive.**

liability [,laɪə'bɪlɪtɪ] *n* **(a)** *(burden)* Belastung *f.*

(b) *(being subject to)* **one's ~ for tax** jds Steuerpflicht *f*; **he has a tax ~ of £1,000** er muß £ 1000 Steuern bezahlen; **~ to pay damages** Schadensersatzpflicht *f.*

(c) *(proneness)* Anfälligkeit *f (to* für) ◆ **our economy's ~ to inflation** die Inflationsanfälligkeit unserer Wirtschaft.

(d) *(responsibility)* Haftung *f* ◆ **we accept no ~ for ...** wir übernehmen keine Haftung für ...; **his ~ for his wife's debts** seine Haftung *or* Haftbarkeit für die Schulden seiner Frau; **that is not my ~** dafür hafte ich nicht.

(e) *(Fin)* **liabilities** Verbindlichkeiten, Verpflichtungen *pl.*

liable ['laɪəbl] *adj* **(a)** *(subject to)* **to be ~** unterliegen *(for sth* einer Sache *dat)*; **to be ~ for tax** *(things)* besteuert werden; *(person)* steuerpflichtig sein; **people earning over £X are ~ for surtax** wer mehr als £ X verdient, unterliegt einer Zusatzsteuer *or* ist zusatzsteuerpflichtig; **~ to penalty** strafbar; **you'll make yourself ~ to a heavy fine** Sie können zu einer hohen Geldstrafe verurteilt werden.

(b) *(prone to)* anfällig ◆ **he's always been ~ to bronchitis** er war schon immer anfällig für Bronchitis; **~ to inflation** inflationsanfällig.

(c) *(responsible)* **to be ~** haften, haftbar sein; **to be ~ for** haftbar sein *or* haften für, aufkommen müssen für.

(d) *(likely to)* **we are ~ to get shot here** wir können hier leicht beschossen werden; **the pond is ~ to freeze** der Teich friert leicht zu; **is he ~ to come?** ist anzunehmen, daß er kommt?; **he's ~ to tell the police** es wäre ihm zuzutrauen, daß er es der Polizei meldet; **if you don't write it down I'm ~ to forget it** wenn Sie das nicht aufschreiben, kann es durchaus sein, daß ich es vergesse; **the plan is ~ to changes** der Plan wird möglicherweise geändert; **I don't think it's ~ to happen tonight** ich halte es für nicht wahrscheinlich, daß es heute nacht passiert; **the car is ~ to run out of petrol any minute** dem Auto kann jede Minute das Benzin ausgehen; **if you tell him that, he's ~ to lose his temper** wenn Sie ihm das sagen, wird er bestimmt wütend.

liaise [li:'eɪz] *vi (be the contact person)* als Verbindungsperson fungieren; *(get in contact)* sich in Verbindung setzen *(with* mit) ◆ **he has a sort of liaising job** er ist eine Art Verbindungsmann.

liaison [li:'eɪzɒn] *n* **(a)** *(coordination)* Verbindung, Zusammenarbeit *f*; *(person)* Verbindungsmann, V-Mann *(inf) m*; *(Mil)* Verbindung *f*; *(person)* Verbindungsmann *or* -offizier *m.* **(b)** *(affair)* Liaison *f.*

liaison officer *n* Verbindungsmann *m*; *(Mil)* Verbindungsoffizier *m* ◆ **the firm's ~** der Firmensprecher.

liar ['laɪəʳ] *n* Lügner(in *f*) *m.*

lib [lɪb] *n abbr of* **liberation.**

Lib *(Pol) abbr of* **Liberal.**

libation [laɪ'beɪʃən] *n* **(a)** *(offering)* Trankopfer *nt.* **(b)** *(inf: drinking session)* **~s** Trinkgelage, Saufgelage *(inf) nt.*

libel ['laɪbəl] [1] *n* (schriftlich geäußerte) Verleumdung *(on gen)* ◆ **to utter/publish a ~ against sb** jdn verleumden; **it's a ~ on all of us** das ist eine Verleumdung, die uns alle trifft.

[2] *vt* verleumden.

libellous, (US) libelous ['laɪbələs] *adj* verleumderisch.

liberal ['lɪbərəl] [1] *adj* **(a)** *(generous) offer, supply* großzügig; *helping of food* reichlich. **(b)** *(broad-minded)* liberal. **(c) ~ education** Allgemeinbildung *f*; **the ~ arts** die geisteswissenschaftlichen Fächer. **(d)** *(Pol)* liberal.

[2] *n (Pol:* **L~**) Liberale(r) *mf* ◆ **he's a ~ in social matters** er hat eine liberale Einstellung in sozialen Angelegenheiten.

Liberal Democrat(ic) Party *n (Brit)* Liberaldemokratische Partei.

liberalism ['lɪbərəlɪzəm] *n* Liberalität *f*; *(Pol:* **L~**) der Liberalismus.

liberality [,lɪbə'rælɪtɪ] *n* **(a)** *(generosity)* Großzügigkeit *f.* **(b)** *see* **liberal-mindedness.**

liberalization [,lɪbərəlaɪ'zeɪʃən] *n* Liberalisierung *f.*

liberalize ['lɪbərəlaɪz] *vt* liberalisieren.

liberally ['lɪbərəlɪ] *adv* liberal; *(generously)* großzügig ◆ **he applies the paint very ~** er trägt die Farbe dick *or* reichlich auf.

liberal: ~-minded *adj person* liberal (eingestellt); *views* liberal; **~-mindedness** *n (of person)* liberale Einstellung *or* Gesinnung; *(of views)* Liberalität *f.*

liberate ['lɪbəreɪt] *vt* **(a)** *(free) prisoner, country* befreien. **(b)** *gas etc* freisetzen. **the experiment ~d a poisonous gas** bei dem Experiment wurde ein giftiges Gas frei(gesetzt).

liberated ['lɪbəreɪtɪd] *adj women, times* emanzipiert.

liberation [,lɪbə'reɪʃən] *n* Befreiung *f*; *(of gases)* Freisetzung *f.*

liberator ['lɪbəreɪtəʳ] *n* Befreier *m.*

Liberia [laɪ'bɪərɪə] *n* Liberia *nt.*

Liberian [laɪ'bɪərɪən] [1] *adj* liberianisch, liberisch.

[2] *n* Liberianer(in *f*), Liberier(in *f*) *m.*

libertine ['lɪbəti:n] *n* Wüstling, Libertin *(geh) m.*

liberty ['lɪbətɪ] *n* **(a)** Freiheit *f* ◆ **~ of conscience** Gewissensfreiheit *f*; **basic liberties** Grundrechte *pl*; **to restore sb to ~** jdm die Freiheit wiedergeben; **to be at ~** *(criminal etc)* frei herumlaufen; *(having time)* Zeit haben; **to be at ~ to do sth** *(be permitted)* etw tun dürfen; **I am not at ~ to comment** es ist mir nicht gestattet, darüber zu sprechen; **you are at ~ to go** es steht Ihnen frei zu gehen; **is he at ~ to come?** darf er kommen?

(b) *(presumptuous action, behaviour)* **I have taken the ~ of giving your name** ich habe mir erlaubt, Ihren Namen anzugeben; **to take liberties with a text** einen Text sehr frei bearbeiten; **to take liberties with sb** sich jdm gegenüber Freiheiten herausnehmen; **what a ~!** *(inf)* so eine Frechheit.

liberty bodice *n* Leibchen *nt.*

libidinous [lɪ'bɪdɪnəs] *adj* lüstern; *person, behaviour also* triebhaft; *(Psych)* libidinös.

libido [lɪ'bi:dəʊ] *n* Libido *f.*

LIBOR ['li:bɔʳ] *n abbr of* **London Inter-Bank Offer Rate** *bankeninterner Wechselkurs.*

Libra ['li:brə] *n* Waage *f.*

Libran ['li:brən] *n* Waage(mensch *m*) *f.*

librarian [laɪ'breərɪən] *n* Bibliothekar(in *f*) *m.*

librarianship [laɪ'breərɪənʃɪp] *n* **(a)** *(subject)* Bibliothekswesen *nt or* -lehre *f.* **(b)** *(job)* Bibliothekarsstelle *f.*

library ['laɪbrərɪ] *n* **(a)** *(public)* Bibliothek, Bücherei *f.* **(b)** *(private)* Bibliothek *f.* **(c)** (*collection of books/records*) (Bücher)sammlung/(Schallplatten)sammlung *f.* **(d)** (*series of books*) Buchreihe, Bibliothek *f.*

library: ~ book *n* Leihbuch *nt*; **~ edition** *n* Leihbuchausgabe *f*; **~ science** *n* Bibliothekswissenschaften *pl*; **~ ticket** *n* Leserausweis *m.*

librettist [lɪ'bretɪst] *n* Librettist *m.*

libretto [lɪ'bretəʊ] *n* Libretto *nt.*

Libya ['lɪbɪə] *n* Libyen *nt.*

Libyan ['lɪbɪən] [1] *adj* libysch.
[2] *n* Libyer(in *f*) *m.*

lice [laɪs] *pl of* **louse.**

licence, (*US*) **license** ['laɪsəns] *n* **(a)** (*permit*) Genehmigung, Erlaubnis *f*; (*by authority*) behördliche Genehmigung, Konzession *f*; (*Comm*) Lizenz *f*; (*driving ~*) Führerschein *m*; (*road ~*) Kfz-Steuer *f*; (*gun ~*) Waffenschein *m*; (*hunting ~*) Jagdschein *m*; (*marriage ~*) Eheerlaubnis *f*; (*radio ~, television ~*) (Rundfunk-/Fernseh)genehmigung *f*; (*dog ~*) Hundemarke *f* ◆ **he hasn't paid his (dog) ~** er hat seine Hundesteuer nicht bezahlt; **you have to have a (television) ~** man muß Fernsehgebühren bezahlen; **a ~ to practise medicine** die Approbation, die staatliche Zulassung als Arzt; **the restaurant has lost its ~ (to sell drinks)** das Restaurant hat seine Schankerlaubnis *or* Konzession verloren; **we'll get a late ~ for the reception** für den Empfang bekommen wir eine Genehmigung für verlängerte Ausschankzeiten; **a ~ to kill** ein Freibrief *m* zum Töten; **to manufacture sth under ~** etw in Lizenz herstellen.
(b) (*freedom*) Freiheit *f* ◆ **translated with a good deal of ~** sehr frei übersetzt; **the editor altered the text with too great a degree of ~** der Lektor erlaubte sich bei der Änderung des Textes zu große Freiheiten.
(c) (*excessive freedom*) Zügellosigkeit *f* ◆ **there is too much ~ in sexual matters/the cinema nowadays** in sexuellen Dingen/im Kino geht es heutzutage zu freizügig zu.

licence: ~ number *n* (*Aut*) Kraftfahrzeug- *or* Kfz-Kennzeichen *nt*; **~ plate** *n* (*Aut*) Nummernschild *nt.*

license ['laɪsəns] [1] *n* (*US*) *see* **licence.**
[2] *vt* eine Lizenz/Konzession vergeben an (*+acc*) ◆ **a car must be ~d every year** die Kfz-Steuer muß jedes Jahr bezahlt werden; **to ~ a pub** einer Gaststätte Schankerlaubnis *or* eine Schankkonzession erteilen; **to be ~d to do sth** die Genehmigung haben, etw zu tun; **he is ~d to practise medicine** er ist approbierter Arzt, er ist als Arzt zugelassen; **we're not ~d for dancing** wir haben keine Tanzgenehmigung; **we are not ~d to sell alcohol** wir haben keine Schankerlaubnis *or* Konzession; **secret agents are ~d to kill** Geheimagenten dürfen Leute totschießen.

licensed ['laɪsənst] *adj* **~ house/premises** Lokal *nt* mit Schankerlaubnis; **fully ~** mit voller Schankkonzession *or* -erlaubnis; **~ trade** (konzessionierter) Alkoholhandel; **I used to be in the ~ trade** ich war früher Gastwirt; **~ victualler** *Lebensmittelhändler m mit einer Konzession für den Verkauf von Alkohol.*

licensee [ˌlaɪsən'siː] *n see* **licence** Konzessions-/Lizenzinhaber(in *f*) *m*; Inhaber(in *f*) *m* eines Waffenscheins *etc*; (*of bar*) Inhaber(in *f*) *m* einer Schankerlaubnis ◆ **the ~ of our local pub** der Wirt unserer Stammkneipe; **postage paid by ~** Gebühr bezahlt Empfänger.

licensing ['laɪsənsɪŋ] *adj* **~ agreement** Lizenzabkommen *nt*; **~ hours** Ausschankzeiten *pl*; **after ~ hours** über die Polizeistunde *or* Sperrzeit hinaus; **~ laws** Schankgesetze *pl*, Gesetz *nt* über den Ausschank und Verkauf alkoholischer Getränke.

licentiate [laɪ'senʃɪɪt] *n* Lizentiat *m*; (*degree*) Lizentiat *nt.*

licentious [laɪ'senʃəs] *adj* ausschweifend, lasterhaft; *behaviour* unzüchtig; *book* sehr freizügig; *look* lüstern.

licentiousness [laɪ'senʃəsnɪs] *n* Unmoral, Unzüchtigkeit *f*; (*of book*) Freizügigkeit *f*; (*of look*) Lüsternheit *f.*

lichen ['laɪkən] *n* Flechte *f.*

lichgate, lychgate ['lɪtʃgeɪt] *n* überdachter Kirchhofseingang.

licit ['lɪsɪt] *adj* erlaubt, gesetzlich.

lick [lɪk] [1] *n* **(a)** (*with tongue*) Lecken, Schlecken (*dial*) *nt* ◆ **to give sth a ~** an etw (*dat*) lecken.
(b) (*salt ~*) (Salz)lecke *f*; (*artificial*) Leckstein *m.*
(c) (*inf: small quantity*) **it's time we gave the kitchen a ~ of paint** die Küche könnte auch mal wieder etwas Farbe vertragen (*inf*); **to give oneself a ~ and a promise** Katzenwäsche machen.
(d) (*inf: pace*) **the project is coming along at a good ~** das Projekt geht ganz gut voran (*inf*); **to go/drive at a good ~** einen (ganz schönen) Zahn drauf haben (*inf*); **he rushed to the station at full ~** er raste mit Volldampf zum Bahnhof (*inf*).
[2] *vt* **(a)** (*with tongue*) lecken ◆ **he ~ed the stamp** er leckte an der Briefmarke; **he ~ed the ice-cream** er leckte am Eis; **to ~ one's lips** sich (*dat*) die Lippen lecken; (*fig*) sich (*dat*) die Finger lecken; **to ~ one's wounds** (*fig*) seine Wunden lecken; **to ~ sb's boots** (*fig*) vor jdm kriechen (*inf*), jds Stiefel lecken; **to ~ sb into shape** (*fig*) jdn auf Vordermann bringen (*inf*).
(b) (*waves*) plätschern an (*+acc*); (*flames*) züngeln an (*+dat*).
(c) (*inf: beat, defeat*) in die Pfanne hauen (*sl*), einseifen (*inf*) ◆ **this ~s everything!** das haut dem Faß den Boden aus! (*inf*); **I think we've got it ~ed** ich glaube, wir haben die Sache jetzt im Griff.
[3] *vi* **to ~ at sth** an etw (*dat*) lecken; **flames ~ed round the building** Flammen züngelten an dem Gebäude empor.

◆**lick off** *vt sep* ablecken ◆ **to ~ ~ sth ~ sth** etw von etw ablecken.

◆**lick up** *vt sep* auflecken.

lickety-split ['lɪkɪtɪ'splɪt] *adv* (*US inf*) blitzschnell, mit Volldampf (*inf*).

licking ['lɪkɪŋ] *n* (*inf*) (*beating*) Tracht *f* Prügel; (*defeat*) Niederlage *f* ◆ **to give sb a ~** (*beating*) jdm eine Abreibung geben (*inf*); (*defeat*) jdn in die Pfanne hauen (*sl*) *or* einseifen (*inf*).

licorice *n see* **liquorice.**

lid [lɪd] *n* **(a)** Deckel *m* ◆ **that puts the (tin) ~ on it** (*inf*) das ist doch die Höhe, das schlägt dem Faß den Boden aus; **a documentary that really takes the ~ off Hollywood** ein Dokumentarfilm, der das wahre Gesicht Hollywoods zeigt; **the press took the ~ off the whole plan** die Presse hat den Plan enthüllt *or* aufgedeckt.
(b) (*eye~*) Lid *nt.*
(c) (*sl: hat*) Deckel *m* (*inf*).

lidless ['lɪdlɪs] *adj* **(a)** ohne Deckel. **(b)** *eyes* ohne Lider.

lido ['liːdəʊ] *n* Freibad *nt.*

lie[1] [laɪ] [1] *n* Lüge *f* ◆ **it's a ~!** das ist eine Lüge!, das ist gelogen!; **to tell a ~** lügen; **to give the ~ to sb** jdn der Lüge bezichtigen *or* beschuldigen; **to give the ~ to a report** die Unwahrheit eines Berichtes zeigen *or* beweisen, einen Bericht Lügen strafen (*geh*); **~ detector** Lügendetektor *m.*
[2] *vi* lügen ◆ **to ~ to sb** jdn belügen *or* anlügen.
[3] *vt* **to ~ one's way out of sth** sich aus etw herauslügen.

lie[2] (*vb: pret* **lay,** *ptp* **lain**) [1] *n* (*position*) Lage, Position *f.*
[2] *vi* **(a)** (*in horizontal or resting position*) liegen; (*~ down*) sich legen ◆ **he lay where he had fallen** er blieb liegen, wo er hingefallen war; **~ on your back** leg dich auf den Rücken; **obstacles ~ in the way of our success** unser Weg zum Erfolg ist mit Hindernissen verstellt; **the snow didn't ~** der Schnee blieb nicht liegen; **to ~ with sb** (*Bibl, old*) bei jdm liegen (*Bibl, old*).
(b) (*be buried*) ruhen ◆ **to ~ at rest** zur letzten Ruhe gebettet sein (*geh*).
(c) (*be situated*) liegen ◆ **the runner who is lying third** der Läufer, der auf dem dritten Platz liegt; **Uganda ~s far from the coast** Uganda liegt weit von der Küste ab *or* entfernt; **our road lay along the river** unsere Straße führte am Fluß entlang; **our futures ~ in quite different directions** unsere zukünftigen Wege führen in verschiedene Richtungen; **you are young and your life ~s before you** du bist jung, und das Leben liegt noch vor dir.
(d) (*be, remain in a certain condition*) liegen ◆ **to ~ asleep** (daliegen und) schlafen; **to ~ helpless** hilflos daliegen; **to ~ dying** im Sterben liegen; **to ~ resting** ruhen; **he lay resting on the sofa** er ruhte sich auf dem Sofa aus; **the snow lay deep** es lag tiefer Schnee; **the book lay unopened** das Buch lag ungeöffnet da; **to ~ low** untertauchen, sich nicht mehr sehen lassen; **how do things ~?** wie steht die Sache?; **to ~ heavy on the stomach** schwer im Magen liegen; **to ~ heavy on the conscience** schwer auf dem Gewissen lasten.
(e) (*immaterial things*) liegen ◆ **where does the difficulty ~?** wo liegt die Schwierigkeit?; **it ~s with you to solve the problem** es liegt bei dir, das Problem zu lösen; **his interests ~ in music** seine Interessen liegen auf dem Gebiet der Musik *or* gelten der Musik; **he did everything that lay in his power to help us** er tat alles in seiner Macht stehende, um uns zu helfen; **that responsibility ~s with your department** dafür ist Ihre Abteilung verantwortlich.

◆**lie about** *or* **around** *vi* herumliegen.

◆**lie back** *vi* **(a)** (*recline*) sich zurücklehnen.
(b) (*fig: take no action*) es sich gemütlich machen, sich ausruhen ◆ **we can't afford to ~ ~ and relax until the job's finished** wir können uns (*dat*) keine Ruhe gönnen, bis die Arbeit erledigt ist.

◆**lie down** *vi* **(a)** sich hinlegen ◆ **he lay ~ on the bed** er legte sich aufs Bett; **~ ~!** (*to a dog*) leg dich!, hinlegen!
(b) (*fig: accept, submit*) **to ~ ~ under sth** sich (*dat*) etw gefallen *or* bieten lassen; **he won't take that lying ~!** das läßt er sich nicht gefallen *or* bieten!; **he didn't take defeat lying ~** er nahm die Niederlage nicht tatenlos hin.

◆**lie in** *vi* **(a)** (*stay in bed*) im Bett bleiben. **(b)** (*old: childbirth*) im Wochenbett liegen.

◆**lie off** *vi* (*Naut: be anchored nearby*) vor Anker liegen ◆ **the ship lay ~ Aberdeen** das Schiff lag vor Aberdeen vor Anker.

◆**lie over** *vi* vertagt *or* zurückgestellt werden.

◆**lie to** *vi* (*Naut*) **(a)** (*be anchored*) vor Anker liegen, ankern. **(b)** (*come into a position for anchoring*) beidrehen.

◆**lie up** *vi* **(a)** (*rest after illness etc*) im Bett bleiben. **(b)** (*hide*) untertauchen ◆ **the robbers are lying ~** die Räuber sind untergetaucht. **(c)** (*be out of use*) nicht benutzt werden, unbenutzt stehen; (*car*) abgestellt sein.

lie-abed ['laɪəbed] *n* Langschläfer(in *f*) *m.*

Liechtenstein ['liːxtənˌʃtaɪn] *n* Liechtenstein *nt.*

lie-down ['laɪdaʊn] *n* (*inf*) Schläfchen (*inf*), Nickerchen (*inf*) *nt* ◆ **to have a ~** ein Schläfchen *or* Nickerchen machen (*inf*).

lief [liːf] *adv* (*old*) **I would as ~** ich würde ebenso gern; **I would as ~ ... as anything** ich würde nichts lieber tun als ...

liege [liːdʒ] *n* (*old*) **(a)** (*also* **~ lord**) Lehnsherr *m* ◆ **my ~** Euer Gnaden. **(b)** (*also* **~ man**) Lehnsmann, Vasall *m.*

lie-in ['laɪɪn] *n* (*inf*) **to have a ~** (sich) ausschlafen.

lien [lɪən] *n* Zurückbehaltungsrecht, Pfandrecht *nt.*

lieu [luː] *n* (*form*) **money in ~** statt dessen Geld; **in ~ of X** an Stelle von X; **in ~ of that** statt dessen.

Lieut. (*Mil*) *abbr of* **lieutenant** Lt.

lieutenancy [lef'tenənsɪ, (*US*) luː'tenənsɪ] *n* Leutnantsrang *m* ◆ **he gained his ~** er ist zum Leutnant befördert worden.

lieutenant [lef'tenənt, (*US*) luː'tenənt] *n* **(a)** Leutnant *m*; (*Brit*) Oberleutnant *m* ◆ **first** (*US*)/**second ~** Oberleutnant/Leutnant. **(b)** (*governor*) Statthalter, Gouverneur *m.*

lieutenant: ~-colonel *n* Oberstleutnant *m*; **~-commander** *n*

Fregattenkapitän *m*; **~-general** *n* Generalleutnant *m*; **~-governor** *n* Vizegouverneur *m*.

life [laɪf] *n, pl* **lives (a)** Leben *nt* ◆ **bird/plant ~** die Vogel-/Pflanzenwelt; **there is not much insect ~ here** hier gibt es nicht viele Insekten; **drawn from ~** lebensnah; **to the ~** lebensecht; **the battle resulted in great loss of ~** bei der Schlacht kamen viele ums Leben; **this is a matter of ~ and death** hier geht es um Leben und Tod; **a ~ and death struggle** ein Kampf auf Leben und Tod; **~ begins at 40** das Leben fängt mit 40 (erst richtig) an; **to bring sb back to ~** jdn wiederbeleben, jdn ins Leben zurückrufen; **his book brings history to ~** sein Buch läßt die Geschichte lebendig werden; **to come to ~** (*fig*) lebendig werden; **I'm the sort of person who comes to ~ in the evenings** ich bin ein Typ, der erst abends munter wird; **after half an hour the discussion came to ~** nach einer halben Stunde kam Leben in die Diskussion; **to put new ~ into sb** jdm wieder Auftrieb geben; **for dear ~** verzweifelt; **they swam for dear ~** sie schwammen um ihr Leben; **they looked at him in the oxygen tent fighting for dear ~** sie sahen, wie er im Sauerstoffzelt um sein Leben kämpfte; **at my time of ~** in meinem Alter; **marriage should be for ~** eine Ehe sollte fürs Leben geschlossen werden; **he's got a job for ~** er hat eine Stelle auf Lebenszeit; **the murderer was imprisoned for ~** der Mörder wurde zu lebenslänglicher Freiheitsstrafe verurteilt; **he's doing ~** (*inf*) er ist ein Lebenslänglicher (*inf*); **he got ~** (*inf*) er hat lebenslänglich gekriegt (*inf*).
(b) (*individual life*) **how many lives were lost?** wie viele (Menschen) sind ums Leben gekommen?; **the lives of the prisoners** das Leben der Gefangenen; **to take sb's ~** jdn umbringen; **to take one's own ~** sich (*dat*) das Leben nehmen; **to save sb's ~** (*lit*) jdm das Leben retten; (*fig*) jdn retten; **the suspected murderer is on trial for his ~** für den Mordverdächtigen geht es bei dem Prozeß um Leben und Tod; **early/later in ~, in early/later ~** in frühen Jahren/in späteren Jahren *or* später im Leben; **she began (her working) ~ as a teacher** sie begann ihr Berufsleben als Lehrerin; **all his ~** sein ganzes Leben lang; **I've never been to London in my ~** ich war in meinem ganzen Leben noch nicht in London; **run for your lives!** rennt um euer Leben!; **I can't for the ~ of me ...** (*inf*) ich kann beim besten Willen nicht ...; **never in my ~ have I heard such nonsense** ich habe mein Lebtag noch nicht *or* noch nie im Leben so einen Unsinn gehört; **not on your life!** (*inf*) ich bin doch nicht verrückt! (*inf*); **would you ever disobey him? — not on your ~!** (*inf*) würdest du je seine Befehle mißachten? — nie im Leben!; **he is a good/bad ~** (*Insur*) er ist ein hohes/niedriges Risiko.
(c) (*the world, social activity*) **to see ~** die Welt sehen; **there isn't much ~ here in the evenings** hier ist abends nicht viel Leben *or* nicht viel los.
(d) (*liveliness*) Leben *nt* ◆ **those children are full of ~!** diese Kinder stecken voller Leben *or* sind sehr lebhaft!; **the performance of the play was full of ~** die Aufführung war sehr lebendig; **he's still got so much ~ in him** er ist noch so vital *or* steckt noch voller Leben; **there's ~ in the old girl yet** (*inf*) sie ist noch schwer aktiv (*inf*); (*of car*) die Kiste bringt's noch (*sl*); **he is the ~ and soul of every party** er bringt Leben in jede Party; **wherever John goes, he wants to be the ~ and soul of the party** John will überall im Mittelpunkt stehen.
(e) (*way of life*) Leben *nt* ◆ **village ~** das Leben auf dem Dorf; **this is the ~!** ja, ist das ein Leben!; **what a ~!** was für ein Leben!; **such is ~** so ist das Leben; **to lead the ~ of Riley** wie Gott in Frankreich leben; **it's a good ~** es ist ein schönes Leben; **the good ~** das süße Leben.
(f) (*useful or active life of sth*) Lebensdauer *f* ◆ **during the ~ of the present Parliament** während der Legislaturperiode des gegenwärtigen Parlaments; **there's not much ~ left in the battery** die Batterie macht's nicht mehr lange (*inf*).
(g) (*book*) (*biography*) Biographie *f*; (*of saint, king etc*) Lebensbeschreibung *f*.

life: ~ annuity *n* Leib- *or* Lebensrente *f*; **~ assurance** *n* Lebensversicherung *f*; **~belt** *n* Rettungsgürtel *m*; **~blood** *n* Blut *nt*; (*fig*) Lebensnerv *m*; **to drain away sb's ~blood** (*fig*) jdn ausbluten lassen; **~boat** *n* (*from shore*) Rettungsboot *nt*; (*from ship also*) Beiboot *nt*; **~buoy** *n* Rettungsring *m*; **~ cycle** *n* Lebenszyklus *m*; **~ expectancy** *n* Lebenserwartung *f*; **~ force** *n* Lebenskraft *f*; **~-giving** *adj* lebenspendend; **~-giving aid to poor countries** lebensnotwendige Hilfe für arme Länder; **~guard** *n* **(a)** (*on beach*) Rettungsschwimmer *m*; (*in baths*) Bademeister *m*; **(b)** (*Mil*) Leibwache *f*; **~ history** *n* Lebensgeschichte *f*; (*Biol*) Entwicklungsgeschichte *f*; **~ imprisonment** *n* lebenslängliche Freiheitsstrafe; **~ insurance** *n see* **~ assurance**; **~ jacket** *n* Schwimmweste *f*.

lifeless [ˈlaɪflɪs] *adj* **(a)** (*inanimate*) leblos, tot; *planet* unbelebt, ohne Leben. **(b)** (*dead, as if dead*) leblos. **(c)** (*fig*) (*listless, dull*) lahm (*inf*), langweilig; *people also* teilnahmslos.

lifelessly [ˈlaɪflɪslɪ] *adv* leblos; (*fig*) teilnahmslos.

lifelessness [ˈlaɪflɪsnɪs] *n* Leblosigkeit *f*; (*fig*) Teilnahmslosigkeit *f*.

life: ~like *adj* lebensecht; *imitation also* naturgetreu; **~line** *n* **(a)** Rettungsleine *f*; (*of diver*) Signalleine *f*; (*fig*) Rettungsanker *m*; **the telephone is a ~line for many old people** das Telefon ist für viele alte Leute lebenswichtig; **in doing this they risked severing their financial ~line** dadurch haben sie riskiert, daß ihnen der Geldhahn zugedreht wird; **(b)** (*Palmistry*) Lebenslinie *f*; **~long** *adj* lebenslang; **they are ~long friends** sie sind schon ihr Leben lang Freunde; **he's my ~long friend** er war schon immer mein Freund; **we became ~long friends** wir wurden Freunde fürs Leben; **his ~long devotion to the cause** die Sache, in deren Dienst er sein Leben gestellt hat; **her ~long fear of water** ihre angeborene Angst vor Wasser; **~ membership** *n* Mitgliedschaft *f* auf Lebenszeit; **~ peer** *n* Peer *m* auf Lebenszeit; **~ preserver** *n* **(a)** (*Brit*) Totschläger *m*; **(b)** (*US*) Schwimmweste *f*.

lifer [ˈlaɪfəʳ] *n* (*sl*) Lebenslängliche(r) *mf* (*inf*).

life: ~ raft *n* Rettungsfloß *nt*; **~saver** *n* **(a)** Lebensretter(in *f*) *m*; (*lifeguard*) Rettungsschwimmer(in *f*) *m*; **(b)** (*fig*) Retter *m* in der Not; **it was a real ~saver!** das hat mich gerettet; **~-saving** [1] *n* Lebensrettung *f*; (*saving people from drowning*) Rettungsschwimmen *nt*; [2] *adj techniques, apparatus* Rettungs-; *phone call, drug* lebensrettend; *drop of whisky* rettend; **~-saving certificate** Rettungsschwimmabzeichen *nt*; **~ science** *n Medizin, Biologie etc*; **~ sentence** *n* lebenslängliche Freiheitsstrafe; **~-size(d)** *adj* in Lebensgröße, lebensgroß; **~span** *n* (*of people*) Lebenserwartung *f*; (*of animals, plants*) Leben(sdauer *f*) *nt*; **~ story** *n* Lebensgeschichte *f*; **~style** *n* Lebensstil *m*; **~ support system** *n* Lebenserhaltungssystem *nt*; **~-threatening** *adj* lebensbedrohend; **~time** *n* **(a)** Lebenszeit *f*; (*of battery, machine, animal*) Lebensdauer *f*; **once in a ~time** einmal im Leben; **during** *or* **in my ~time** während meines Lebens; **in his ~time there were no buses** zu seiner Zeit gab es keine Busse; **the chance of a ~time** eine einmalige Chance, *die* Chance (*inf*); **a ~time's devotion to charity** ein Leben, das der Wohltätigkeit gewidmet ist; **the work of a ~time** ein Lebenswerk *nt*; **(b)** (*fig*) Ewigkeit *f*; **~work** *n* Lebenswerk *nt*.

lift [lɪft] [1] *n* **(a)** (*~ing*) Heben *nt* ◆ **the haughty ~ of her head** ihre hochmütige Kopfhaltung; **give me a ~ up** heb mich mal hoch; **give me a ~ with this trunk** hilf mir, den Koffer hochzuheben.
(b) (*Weightlifting*) **that was a good ~** das war eine gute Leistung; **his next ~ is 100 kg** beim nächsten Versuch will er 100 kg heben; **different types of ~** mehrere verschiedene Hebearten *pl*.
(c) (*emotional uplift*) **to give sb a ~** jdn aufmuntern; (*drug*) jdn aufputschen; (*prospect*) jdm Auftrieb geben.
(d) (*in car etc*) Mitfahrgelegenheit *f* ◆ **to give sb a ~** (*take along*) jdn mitnehmen; (*as special journey*) jdn fahren; **to get a ~ from sb** von jdm mitgenommen werden/von jdm gefahren werden; **don't take ~s from strangers** laß dich nicht von Fremden mitnehmen; **want a ~?** möchten Sie mitkommen/soll ich dich fahren?
(e) (*Brit: elevator*) Fahrstuhl, Aufzug, Lift *m*; (*for goods*) Aufzug *m* ◆ **he took the ~** er fuhr mit dem Fahrstuhl *etc*.
(f) (*Aviat*) Auftrieb *m*.
[2] *vt* **(a)** (*also* **~ up**) hochheben; *window* hochschieben; *feet, head* heben; *eyes* aufschlagen; *hat* lüften, ziehen; *potatoes etc* ernten; *child etc* hochheben ◆ **to ~ the baby out of his pram** das Baby aus dem Kinderwagen heben; **to ~ one's hand to sb** die Hand gegen jdn erheben.
(b) (*fig also* **~ up**) heben; *voice* erheben ◆ **~ (up) your hearts to God** erhebt eure Herzen zu Gott; **the news ~ed him out of his depression** durch die Nachricht verflog seine Niedergeschlagenheit; **his new job ~ed him far above his humble origins** seine neue Stellung war für ihn ein Aufstieg aus seiner bescheidenen Herkunft; **the excellence of his style ~s him far above his contemporaries** sein ausgezeichneter Stil stellt ihn weit über seine Zeitgenossen.
(c) (*remove*) *restrictions etc* aufheben.
(d) (*inf: steal*) mitgehen lassen (*inf*), klauen (*inf*); (*plagiarize*) abschreiben, klauen (*sl*).
(e) **to have one's face ~ed** sich (*dat*) das Gesicht straffen *or* liften lassen.
(f) (*sl: arrest*) schnappen (*inf*).
[3] *vi* **(a)** (*be lifted*) sich hochheben lassen ◆ **that chair is too heavy (for you) to ~** dieser Stuhl ist zu schwer zum Hochheben. **(b)** (*mist*) sich lichten. **(c)** (*rocket, plane*) abheben ◆ **it ~ed slowly into the sky** es stieg langsam zum Himmel auf.

◆**lift down** *vt sep* herunterheben.

◆**lift off** *vti sep* abheben.

◆**lift up** [1] *vt sep see* **lift 2 (a, b)** ◆ **to ~ ~ one's head** (*fig*) den Kopf hochhalten; **I'll never ~ ~ my head again** ich kann niemandem mehr in die Augen blicken.
[2] *vi* hochgeklappt werden.

lift: ~ attendant *n* (*Brit*) Fahrstuhlführer *m*; **~boy** *n* (*Brit*) Liftboy *m*; **~ cage** *n* Fahrstuhl *m*; **~man** *n* (*Brit*) *see* **~ attendant**; **~-off** *n* (*Space*) Abheben *nt*, Start *m*; **we have ~-off** der Start ist erfolgt; **~ -off correction tape** *n* (*for typewriter*) (Lift-off-)Korrekturband *nt*; **~shaft** *n* Aufzugsschacht *m*.

ligament [ˈlɪgəmənt] *n* Band, Ligament *nt* ◆ **he's torn a ~ in his shoulder** er hat einen Bänderriß in der Schulter.

ligature [ˈlɪgətʃəʳ] *n* (*Med, Mus, Typ*) Ligatur *f*; (*bandage*) Binde *f*; (*Med: thread or cord*) Abbindungsschnur *f*/-draht *m*.

light[1] [laɪt] (*vb: pret, ptp* **lit** *or* **~ed**) [1] *n* **(a)** (*in general*) Licht *nt* ◆ **~ and shade** Licht und Schatten; **at first ~** bei Tagesanbruch; **hang the picture in a good ~** häng das Bild ins richtige Licht; **to cast** *or* **shed** *or* **throw ~ on sth** (*lit*) etw beleuchten; (*fig also*) Licht in etw (*acc*) bringen; **the moon cast its silvery ~ on ...** der Mond beleuchtete ... silbern *or* warf sein silbernes Licht auf (+*acc*) ...; **to cast a new** *or* **fresh ~ on sth** neues Licht auf etw (*acc*) werfen; **to stand in sb's ~** (*lit*) jdm im Licht stehen; **in the cold ~ of day** (*fig*) bei Licht besehen; **this story shows his character in a bad ~** diese Geschichte wirft ein schlechtes Licht auf seinen Charakter; **it revealed him in a different ~** es ließ ihn in einem anderen Licht erscheinen; **I don't see things in that ~** ich sehe die Dinge anders *or* in einem anderen Licht; **to see sth in a new ~** etw mit anderen Augen betrachten; **in the ~ of** angesichts (+*gen*); **the theory, seen in the ~ of recent discoveries** die Theorie im Licht(e) der neuesten Entdeckungen betrachtet; **in the ~ of what you say** in Anbetracht dessen, was Sie sagen; **to bring to ~** ans Tageslicht bringen; **to come to ~** ans Tageslicht kommen; **to see the ~** (*liter: be born*) das Licht der Welt erblicken (*liter*); (*liter: be made public*) veröffentlicht werden; **finally I saw the ~** (*inf*) endlich ging

mir ein Licht auf (*inf*); (*morally*) endlich wurden mir die Augen geöffnet; **to go out like a ~** sofort weg sein (*inf*).
(b) Licht *nt*; (*lamp*) Lampe *f*; (*fluorescent ~*) Neonröhre *f* ◆ **put out the ~/~s before you go to bed** mach das Licht aus, bevor du ins Bett gehst; **all the ~s went out during the storm** während des Sturms gingen alle Lichter aus; **(traffic) ~s** Ampel *f*; **the ~s** (*of a car*) die Beleuchtung; **all ships must show a ~ while at sea** alle Schiffe müssen auf See Lichter führen; **~s out** (*Mil*) Zapfenstreich *m*; **~s out for the boys was at 8 pm** um 20 Uhr mußten die Jungen das Licht ausmachen; **~s out!** Licht aus(machen)!; **to hide one's ~ under a bushel** (*prov*) sein Licht unter den Scheffel stellen (*prov*).
(c) (*flame*) **have you a ~?** haben Sie Feuer?; **to put a ~ to sth, to set ~ to sth** etw anzünden.
(d) (*Archit*) (Dach)fenster *nt*; (*skylight*) Oberlicht *nt* ◆ **leaded ~s** in Blei gefaßte Fensterscheiben.
(e) (*in eyes*) Leuchten *nt* ◆ **the ~ went out of her eyes** das Strahlen erlosch in ihren Augen.
(f) (*standards*) **according to his ~s** nach bestem Wissen und Gewissen.
[2] *adj* (*+er*) hell ◆ **a ~ green dress** ein hellgrünes Kleid; **it is ~ now** es ist jetzt hell *or* Tag.
[3] *vt* **(a)** (*illuminate*) beleuchten; *lamp, light* anmachen ◆ **electricity ~s the main streets** die Hauptstraßen werden elektrisch beleuchtet; **a smile lit her face** ein Lächeln erhellte ihr Gesicht; **to ~ the way for sb** jdm leuchten; (*fig*) jdm den Weg weisen; **his pioneering work lit the way for a whole generation of scholars** seine Pionierarbeit war wegweisend für eine ganze Gelehrtengeneration.
(b) anzünden; *cigarette also* anstecken; *fire also* anmachen.
[4] *vi* (*begin to burn*) brennen ◆ **this fire won't ~** das Feuer geht nicht an.

◆**light up** [1] *vi* **(a)** (*be lit*) aufleuchten ◆ **the shop signs ~ ~ after dark** die Leuchtreklamen werden nach Einbruch der Dunkelheit eingeschaltet; **the room/whole house suddenly lit ~** plötzlich ging das Licht im Zimmer an/ plötzlich gingen die Lichter im Haus an.
(b) (*face*) sich erhellen; (*eyes*) aufleuchten ◆ **his face lit ~ with joy** sein Gesicht strahlte vor Freude.
(c) (*smoke*) **the men took out their pipes and lit ~** die Männer holten ihre Pfeifen hervor und zündeten sie an.
[2] *vt sep* **(a)** (*illuminate*) beleuchten; (*from inside also*) erhellen; *lights* anmachen ◆ **a smile lit ~ his face** ein Lächeln erhellte sein Gesicht; **Piccadilly Circus was all lit ~** der Piccadilly Circus war hell erleuchtet.
(b) *cigarette etc* anzünden.
(c) (*fig sl*) **to be lit ~** angesäuselt (*inf*) *or* beduselt (*sl*) sein.

◆**light (up)on** *vi + prep obj* (*inf*) entdecken, stoßen auf (*+acc*).

light[2] [1] *adj* (*+er*) leicht; *taxes* niedrig; *punishment* milde ◆ **~ lorry/railway** Kleinlastwagen *m*/Kleinbahn *f*; **to give sb ~ weight** jdm zuwenig abwiegen; **she has a very ~ touch on the piano** sie hat einen sehr weichen Anschlag; **to be a ~ eater** wenig essen, kein großer Esser sein; **~ comedy** Lustspiel *nt*, Schwank *m*; **~ opera** Operette *f*; **~ reading** Unterhaltungslektüre *f*; **a ~ and cheerful approach to life** eine unbeschwerte, fröhliche Einstellung zum Leben; **with a ~ heart** leichten Herzens; **as ~ as air** *or* **a feather** federleicht; **a bit ~ in the head** (*crazy*) nicht ganz richtig im Kopf; (*tipsy*) angeheitert; (*dizzy*) benommen; **to be ~ on one's feet** sich leichtfüßig bewegen; **to make ~ of one's difficulties** seine Schwierigkeiten auf die leichte Schulter nehmen; **you shouldn't make ~ of her problems** du solltest dich über ihre Probleme nicht lustig machen; **to make ~ work of** spielend fertigwerden mit.
[2] *adv* **to travel ~** mit wenig *or* leichtem Gepäck reisen.

light[3] *vi pret, ptp* **~ed** *or* **lit** (*liter*) sich niederlassen.

light: ~-armed *adj* leichtbewaffnet; **~ bulb** *n* Glühlampe *or* -birne *f*; **~-coloured** *adj, comp* **~er-coloured,** *superl* **~est-coloured** hell; **~-emitting diode** *n* Leuchtdiode *f*.

lighten[1] ['laɪtn] [1] *vt* erhellen; *colour, hair* aufhellen; *gloom* aufheitern.
[2] *vi* hell werden, sich aufhellen ◆ **to thunder and ~** (*Met*) donnern und blitzen.

lighten[2] [1] *vt load* leichter machen ◆ **to ~ a ship/a ship's cargo** ein Schiff leichtern; **to ~ sb's burden** jds Lage erleichtern; **to ~ sb's workload** jdm etwas Arbeit abnehmen; **the good news ~ed her cares/heart** die gute Nachricht befreite sie von ihren Sorgen/machte ihr das Herz leichter.
[2] *vi* (*load*) leichter werden ◆ **her heart ~ed** ihr wurde leichter ums Herz.

lighter[1] ['laɪtə^r] *n* Feuerzeug *nt*.

lighter[2] *n* (*Naut*) Leichter *m*.

light: ~-fingered [,laɪt'fɪŋgəd] *adj, comp* **~er-fingered,** *superl* **~est-fingered** langfingerig; **~ fitting, ~ fixture** *n* (*~bulb holder*) Fassung *f*; (*bracket*) (Lampen)halterung *f*; **~-footed** *adj, comp* **~er-footed,** *superl* **~est-footed** leichtfüßig; **~-haired** *adj, comp* **~er-haired,** *superl* **~est-haired** hellhaarig; *animals also* mit hellem Fell; **~-headed** *adj, comp* **~er-headed,** *superl* **~est-headed** benebelt (*inf*); (*dizzy also*) benommen; (*tipsy also*) angeheitert; (*with fever*) wirr (im Kopf); (*frivolous*) oberflächlich, leichtfertig; **I felt quite ~-headed when I heard I'd passed the exam** ich wurde ganz ausgelassen *or* übermütig, als ich hörte, daß ich die Prüfung bestanden hatte; **wine makes me ~-headed** Wein steigt mir in den Kopf; **~-headedness** *n see adj* Benommenheit *f*; angeheiterter Zustand; Verwirrtsein *nt*; Oberflächlichkeit, Leichtfertigkeit *f*; Ausgelassenheit *f*, Übermut *m*; **~-hearted** *adj* unbeschwert, unbekümmert; *chat* zwanglos; *reply* scherzhaft; *book, film* fröhlich, vergnüglich; *look at life* heiter, unbekümmert; *comedy* leicht; **~-heartedly** *adv* unbekümmert, leichten Herzens; *reply* scherzhaft; **~-heartedness** *n see adj* Unbeschwertheit, Unbekümmertheit *f*; Zwanglosigkeit *f*; Scherzhaftigkeit *f*; Fröhlichkeit, Vergnüglichkeit *f*; Heiterkeit *f*; **~ heavyweight** *n* Halbschwergewicht *nt*; (*boxer*) Halbschwergewichtler *m*; **~house** *n* Leuchtturm *m*; **~house keeper** *n* Leuchtturmwärter *m*.

lighting ['laɪtɪŋ] *n* Beleuchtung *f*.

lighting-up time [,laɪtɪŋ'ʌptaɪm] *n Zeitpunkt m, zu dem Straßen- und Fahrzeugbeleuchtung eingeschaltet werden muß* ◆ **when is ~?** wann wird die Beleuchtung angemacht?

lightish ['laɪtɪʃ] *adj colour* hell ◆ **a ~ brown** ein helleres Braun.

lightless ['laɪtlɪs] *adj* dunkel, lichtlos.

lightly ['laɪtlɪ] *adv* **(a)** *touch, rain, eat, wounded, stressed* leicht; *walk, tread* leise ◆ **to sleep ~** einen leichten Schlaf haben; **~ clad (in sth)** leicht (mit etw) bekleidet; **they are ~ taxed** sie haben niedrige Steuern; **to get off ~** glimpflich davonkommen; **to touch ~ on a subject** ein Thema nur berühren *or* streifen.
(b) (*casually*) *say* leichthin ◆ **to speak ~ of sb/sth** sich abfällig *or* geringschätzig über jdn/etw äußern; **he spoke ~ of his illness** er nahm seine Krankheit auf die leichte Schulter; **don't take her problems so ~** nimm ihre Probleme etwas ernster; **to treat sth too ~** etw nicht ernst genug nehmen; **she referred ~ to the fact that ...** sie erwähnte leichthin, daß ...; **a responsibility not to be ~ undertaken** eine Verantwortung, die man nicht unüberlegt auf sich nehmen sollte; **it's not a job I'd ~ do again** die Arbeit würde ich so leicht nicht wieder tun.

light: ~ meter *n* Belichtungsmesser *m*; **~-minded** *adj* oberflächlich, leichtfertig.

lightness[1] ['laɪtnɪs] *n* Helligkeit *f*.

lightness[2] *n* **(a)** geringes Gewicht, Leichtheit *f*; (*of task, step, movements*) Leichtigkeit *f*; (*of taxes*) Niedrigkeit *f*; (*of punishment*) Milde *f*; (*of soil, cake*) Lockerheit *f* ◆ **the ~ of the breeze/wound/music** *etc* die leichte Brise/ Verletzung/Musik *etc*; **a feeling of ~ came over him** ein Gefühl der Erleichterung überkam ihn; **there was a certain ~ in her attitude to life** ihre Einstellung zum Leben hatte etwas Unbeschwertes.
(b) (*lack of seriousness*) mangelnder Ernst ◆ **a certain ~ in your attitude towards the authorities** eine gewisse Leichtfertigkeit den Behörden gegenüber.

lightning ['laɪtnɪŋ] [1] *n* Blitz *m* ◆ **a flash of ~** ein Blitz *m*; (*doing damage*) ein Blitzschlag *m*; **struck by ~** vom Blitz getroffen; **what causes ~?** wie entstehen Blitze?; **we had some ~ an hour ago** vor einer Stunde hat es geblitzt; **as quick as ~, like (greased) ~** wie der Blitz, wie ein geölter Blitz; **~ conductor** *or* (*US*) **rod** Blitzableiter *m*.
[2] *attr* blitzschnell, Blitz- ◆ **~ attack** Überraschungs- *or* Blitzangriff *m*; **~ strike** spontaner Streik; **with ~ speed** blitzschnell, mit Blitzesschnelle.

light pen *n* (*Comput*) Lichtgriffel, Lichtstift *m*.

lights [laɪts] *npl* (*Anat*) Tierlunge *f*.

light: ~ship *n* Feuerschiff *nt*; **~-skinned** *adj, comp* **~er-skinned,** *superl* **~est-skinned** hellhäutig; **~ water reactor** *n* Leichtwasserreaktor *m*; **~ wave** *n* (Licht)welle *f*; **~weight** [1] *adj* leicht; (*boxer*) Leichtgewichts-; (*fig*) schwach; **the ~weight boxing championship** die Boxmeisterschaft im Leichtgewicht; [2] *n* Leichtgewicht *nt*; (*boxer*) Leichtgewichtler *m*; (*fig*) Leichtgewicht *nt*; **he is regarded as a ~weight in academic circles** er wird in akademischen Kreisen nicht für voll genommen; **~-year** *n* Lichtjahr *nt*.

ligneous ['lɪgnɪəs] *adj* hölzern, holzartig.

lignite ['lɪgnaɪt] *n* Lignit *m*.

likable *adj see* **lik(e)able.**

▼ **like**[1] [laɪk] [1] *adj* **(a)** (*similar*) ähnlich ◆ **the two boys are very ~** die beiden Jungen sind sich (*dat*) sehr ähnlich.
(b) (*same*) **of ~ origin** gleicher Herkunft.
▼ [2] *prep* wie ◆ **to be ~ sb** jdm ähnlich sein; **they are very ~ each other** sie sind sich (*dat*) sehr ähnlich; **who(m) is he ~?** wem sieht er ähnlich?, wem gleicht er?; **what's he ~?** wie ist er?; **what's your new coat ~?** wie sieht dein neuer Mantel aus?; **she was ~ a sister to me** sie war wie eine Schwester zu mir; **that's just ~ him!** das sieht ihm ähnlich!, das ist typisch!; **it's not ~ him** es ist nicht seine Art; **I never saw anything ~ it** so (et)was habe ich noch nie gesehen; **that's just ~ a woman!** typisch Frau!; **that's more ~ it!** so ist es schon besser!; **that hat's nothing ~ as nice as this one** der Hut ist bei weitem nicht so hübsch wie dieser; **there's nothing ~ a nice cup of tea!** es geht nichts über eine schöne Tasse Tee!; **there's nothing ~ it** das ist einmalig; **is this what you had in mind? — it's something/nothing ~ it** hattest du dir so etwas vorgestellt? — ja, so ähnlich/nein, überhaupt nicht; **that's something ~ a steak!** das ist vielleicht ein Steak!, das nenne ich ein Steak!; **the Americans are ~ that** so sind die Amerikaner; **people ~ that** solche Leute; **a car ~ that** so ein Auto, ein solches Auto; **I found one ~ it** ich habe ein ähnliches gefunden; **one exactly ~ it** eines, das genau gleich ist; **it will cost something ~ £10** es wird etwa *or* so ungefähr £ 10 kosten; **I was thinking of something ~ a doll** ich habe an so etwas wie eine Puppe gedacht; **that sounds ~ a good idea** das hört sich gut an; **~ a man** wie ein Mann; **~ mad** (*inf*), **~ anything** (*inf*) wie verrückt (*inf*) *or* wild (*inf*); **~ that** so; **it wasn't ~ that at all** so war's doch gar nicht; **he thinks ~ us** er denkt wie wir; **A, ~ B, thinks that ...** A wie (auch) B meinen, daß ...
[3] *adv* (*inf*) **it's nothing ~** es ist nichts dergleichen; **as ~ as not, very ~, ~ enough** höchst wahrscheinlich, sehr wahrscheinlich; **I found this money, ~** (*dial*) ich hab da das Geld gefunden, nich (*sl*) *or* wa (*dial*) *or* gell (*S Ger*).
[4] *conj* (*strictly incorrect*) **~ I said** wie ich schon sagte, wie gesagt; **it's just ~ I say** das sage ich ja immer; **~ we used to (do)** wie früher; **do it ~ I do** mach es so wie ich.

➤ LANGUAGE IN USE: **like**[1]**: 2** → 5.1, 7.2, 17.2

[5] *n* (*equal etc*) **we shall not see his ~ again** einen Mann *or* so etwas (*inf*) wie ihn bekommen wir nicht wieder; **did you ever see the ~?** (*inf*) hast du so was schon gesehen?; **and the ~, and such ~** und dergleichen; **I've met the ~s of you before** solche wie dich kenne ich schon; **I've no time for the ~s of him** (*inf*) mit solchen Leuten gebe ich mich nicht ab (*inf*).

▼ **like²** [1] *n usu pl* (*taste*) Geschmack *m* ◆ **she tried to find out his ~s and dislikes** sie wollte herausbekommen, was er mochte und was nicht; **when it comes to food he has far too many ~s and dislikes** beim Essen ist er viel zu wählerisch.

[2] *vt* (**a**) *person* mögen, gern haben ◆ **don't you ~ me a little bit?** magst du mich nicht ein kleines bißchen?; **how do you ~ him?** wie gefällt er dir?; **I don't ~ him** ich kann ihn nicht leiden, ich mag ihn nicht; **he is well ~d here** er ist hier sehr beliebt.

▼ (**b**) (*find pleasure in*) **I ~ black shoes** ich mag *or* mir gefallen schwarze Schuhe; **I ~ it** das gefällt mir; **I ~ chocolate** ich mag Schokolade, ich esse gern Schokolade; **I ~ football** (*playing*) ich spiele gerne Fußball; (*watching*) ich finde Fußball gut; **I ~ dancing** ich tanze gern; **I ~ this translation** ich finde diese Übersetzung gut; **we ~ it here** es gefällt uns hier; **how do you ~ your coffee?** wie trinken Sie Ihren Kaffee?; **I ~ wine but wine doesn't ~ me** (*inf*) ich trinke gern Wein, aber er bekommt mir nicht; **how do you ~ Cádiz?** wie gefällt Ihnen Cádiz?; **how would you ~ a walk?** was hältst du von einem Spaziergang?; **how would you ~ a black eye?** du willst dir wohl ein blaues Auge holen!; **your father won't ~ it** deinem Vater wird das nicht gefallen; **well, I ~ that!** (*inf*) das ist ein starkes Stück! (*inf*); **(well) how do you ~ that?** (*inf*) wie findest du denn das? (*inf*); **I ~ your nerve!** (*inf*) du hast Nerven! (*inf*).

▼ (**c**) (*wish, wish for*) **I should ~ more time** ich würde mir gerne noch etwas Zeit lassen; **they should have ~d to come** sie wären gern gekommen; **I should ~ to know why** ich wüßte (gerne), warum; **I should ~ you to do it** ich möchte, daß du es tust; **I ~ to be obeyed** ich erwarte Gehorsam; **whether he ~s it or not** ob es ihm paßt oder nicht, ob er will oder nicht; **I didn't ~ to disturb him** ich wollte ihn nicht stören; **what would you ~?** was hätten *or* möchten Sie gern?, was darf es sein?; **would you ~ a drink?** möchten Sie etwas trinken?; **would you ~ to go to Seville?** würden Sie gern nach Sevilla fahren?

▼ [3] *vi* **he is free to act as he ~s** es steht ihm frei, zu tun, was er will; **as you ~** wie Sie wollen; **if you ~** wenn Sie wollen.

-like *adj suf* -ähnlich, -artig.

lik(e)able ['laɪkəbl] *adj* sympathisch, liebenswert.

lik(e)ableness ['laɪkəblnɪs] *n* liebenswertes Wesen ◆ **there's a certain ~ about him** er hat etwas Sympathisches *or* Liebenswertes an sich.

likelihood ['laɪklɪhʊd] *n* Wahrscheinlichkeit *f* ◆ **in all ~** aller Wahrscheinlichkeit nach; **there is no ~ of that** das ist nicht wahrscheinlich; **there is little ~ that ...** es ist kaum anzunehmen, daß ...; **is there any ~ of him coming?** besteht die Möglichkeit, daß er kommt?; **what's the ~ of their getting married?** wie wahrscheinlich ist es *or* wie groß ist die Wahrscheinlichkeit, daß die beiden heiraten?; **what's the ~ of you coming out with me tonight?** wie sind die Chancen, daß du heute abend mit mir ausgehst?

likely ['laɪklɪ] [1] *adj* (*+er*) (**a**) (*probable*) wahrscheinlich ◆ **he is not ~ to come** es ist unwahrscheinlich, daß er kommt; **is it ~ that I would do that?** trauen Sie mir das zu?; **the plan most ~ to succeed** der erfolgversprechendste Plan; **an incident ~ to cause trouble** ein Zwischenfall, der möglicherweise Ärger nach sich zieht; **a ~ explanation** eine mögliche *or* wahrscheinliche Erklärung; (*iro*) wer's glaubt, wird selig! (*inf*); **this is a ~ place for him to stay** es ist gut möglich, daß er sich hier aufhält; **a ~ story!** (*iro*) das soll mal einer glauben!

(**b**) (*inf: suitable*) **a ~ spot for a picnic** ein geeignetes *or* prima (*inf*) Plätzchen für ein Picknick; **he is a ~ person for the job** er kommt für die Stelle in Frage; **~ candidates** aussichtsreiche Kandidaten; **a ~ lad** ein vielversprechender junger Mann.

[2] *adv* **not ~!** (*inf*) wohl kaum (*inf*); **as ~ as not** höchstwahrscheinlich; **very ~ they've lost it** höchstwahrscheinlich haben sie es verloren; **they'll ~ be late** (*dial*) sie kommen wahrscheinlich zu spät; **it's more ~ to be early than late** es wird eher früh als spät werden.

like-minded ['laɪk'maɪndɪd] *adj* gleichgesinnt ◆ **~ people** Gleichgesinnte *pl*.

liken ['laɪkən] *vt* vergleichen (*to* mit).

▼ **likeness** ['laɪknɪs] *n* (*resemblance*) Ähnlichkeit *f*; (*portrait*) Bild(nis) *nt* ◆ **the ghost appeared in the ~ of a monk** der Geist erschien in der Gestalt eines Mönchs; **the god took on the ~ of a bull** der Gott nahm die Form eines Stiers an.

likewise ['laɪkwaɪz] *adv* ebenso, gleichermaßen ◆ **he did ~** er machte es ebenso, er tat das gleiche; **have a nice weekend — ~** schönes Wochenende! — danke gleichfalls!; **I'm going to the cinema tonight — ~** ich gehe heute abend ins Kino — ich auch.

liking ['laɪkɪŋ] *n* (**a**) (*for particular person*) Zuneigung *f*; (*for types*) Vorliebe *f* ◆ **to have a ~ for sb** Zuneigung für jdn empfinden, jdn gern haben; **she took a ~ to him** sie mochte ihn (gut leiden), er war ihr sympathisch.

(**b**) (*for thing*) Vorliebe *f* ◆ **to take a ~ to sth** eine Vorliebe für etw bekommen; **to be to sb's ~** nach jds Geschmack *nt* sein.

lilac ['laɪlək] [1] *n* (**a**) (*plant*) Flieder *m*. (**b**) (*colour*) (Zart)lila *nt*.

[2] *adj* fliederfarben, (zart)lila.

Lilliput ['lɪlɪpʌt] *n* Liliput *nt*.

Lilliputian [ˌlɪlɪ'pju:ʃɪən] [1] *adj* (*lit*) Liliputaner-; (*fig*) winzig, liliputanerhaft.

[2] *n* (*lit, fig*) Liliputaner(in *f*) *m*.

lilo ® ['laɪˌləʊ] *n* Luftmatratze *f*.

lilt [lɪlt] [1] *n* (**a**) (*of song*) munterer Rhythmus; (*of voice*) singender Tonfall ◆ **she spoke with a Welsh ~** sie sprach mit dem singenden Tonfall der Waliser.

(**b**) (*song*) fröhliches *or* munteres Lied.

[2] *vt song* trällern.

[3] *vi* **I love the way her voice ~s** ich mag ihren singenden Tonfall; **the tune ~s merrily along** die Melodie plätschert munter dahin.

lilting ['lɪltɪŋ] *adj accent* singend; *ballad, tune, melody* beschwingt, munter.

liltingly ['lɪltɪŋlɪ] *adv see adj*.

lily ['lɪlɪ] *n* Lilie *f*; (*water ~*) Seerose *f* ◆ **~ of the valley** Maiglöckchen *nt*.

lily: ~-livered ['lɪlɪˌlɪvəd] *adj* feige; **~ pad** *n* Seerosenblatt *nt*; **~-white** *adj* schnee- *or* blütenweiß; (*fig*) tugendhaft.

limb [lɪm] *n* (**a**) (*Anat*) Glied *nt* ◆ **~s** *pl* Glieder, Gliedmaßen *pl*; **the lower ~s** die unteren Gliedmaßen; **to rest one's tired ~s** seine müden Glieder *or* Knochen (*inf*) ausruhen; **to tear sb ~ from ~** jdn in Stücke reißen; **life and ~** Leib und Leben.

(**b**) (*of tree*) Ast *m* ◆ **to be out on a ~** (*fig*) (ganz) allein (da)stehen; **those ideas of John's put him out on a ~** mit diesen Ideen steht John allein auf weiter Flur; **he had left himself out on a ~** er hatte sich in eine prekäre Lage gebracht.

(**c**) (*of cross*) Balken *m*; (*of organization etc*) Glied *nt*.

-limbed [-lɪmd] *adj suf* -glied(e)rig.

limber¹ ['lɪmbə^r] *n* (*Mil*) Protze *f*.

limber² *adj* beweglich, gelenkig.

◆**limber up** *vi* Lockerungsübungen machen; (*fig*) sich vorbereiten ◆ **~ ~ with a few easy exercises** machen Sie sich mit ein paar einfachen Übungen warm; **he ~s (himself) ~ with exercises every morning** er bringt sich jeden Morgen mit Gymnastik in Schwung.

limbless ['lɪmlɪs] *adj tree* astlos ◆ **a ~ person** ein Versehrter; (*with no limbs*) ein Mensch *m* ohne Gliedmaßen.

limbo¹ ['lɪmbəʊ] *n* (**a**) (*Rel*) Vorhölle *f*, Limbus *m* (*spec*).

(**b**) (*fig*) Übergangs- *or* Zwischenstadium *nt* ◆ **our expansion plans are in ~ because of lack of money** unsere Erweiterungspläne sind wegen Geldmangels in der Schwebe; **a sort of ~ for retired politicians** eine Art Abstellgleis für zurückgetretene Politiker; **I'm in a sort of ~** ich hänge in der Luft (*inf*).

limbo² *n* (*dance*) Limbo *m*.

lime¹ [laɪm] [1] *n* (**a**) (*Geol*) Kalk *m*. (**b**) (*bird~*) (Vogel)leim *m*.

[2] *vt* mit Kalk düngen.

lime² *n* (*Bot: linden, also* ~ **tree**) Linde(nbaum *m*) *f*.

lime³ [1] *n* (*Bot: citrus fruit*) Limone(lle) *f*; (*tree*) Limonenbaum *m* ◆ **~ juice** Limonensaft *m*.

[2] *adj* (*colour*) hellgrün.

lime-green ['laɪmgri:n] *adj* hellgrün.

lime kiln *n* Kalkofen *m*.

limelight ['laɪmlaɪt] *n* Rampenlicht *nt* ◆ **to be in the ~** im Rampenlicht *or* im Licht der Öffentlichkeit stehen; **he never sought the ~** er stand nie gern im Rampenlicht *or* im Licht der Öffentlichkeit.

limerick ['lɪmərɪk] *n* Limerick *m*.

limestone ['laɪmstəʊn] *n* Kalkstein *m*.

limey ['laɪmɪ] *n* (*US sl*) Engländer(in *f*) *m*.

limit ['lɪmɪt] [1] *n* (**a**) Grenze *f*; (*limitation*) Beschränkung, Begrenzung *f*; (*speed ~*) Geschwindigkeitsbegrenzung *f*; (*Comm*) Limit *nt* ◆ **the city ~s** die Stadtgrenzen *pl*; **a 40-mile ~** eine Vierzigmeilengrenze; (*speed ~*) eine Geschwindigkeitsbegrenzung von 40 Meilen pro Stunde; **is there any ~ on the size?** gibt es irgendwelche Größenbeschränkungen?, ist die Größe begrenzt *or* beschränkt?; **to put a ~ on sth, to set a ~ to** *or* **on sth** etw begrenzen, etw beschränken; **within the spatially restricted ~s of the office** innerhalb der räumlich begrenzten Möglichkeiten des Büros; **that's beyond my financial ~s** das übersteigt meine finanziellen Möglichkeiten; **I am at the ~ of my patience** meine Geduld ist am Ende; **we're constantly working at the ~s of our abilities** unsere Arbeit bringt uns ständig an die Grenzen unserer Leistungsfähigkeit; **there's a ~!** alles hat seine Grenzen!; **there is a ~ to what one person can do** ein Mensch kann nur so viel tun und nicht mehr; **there's a ~ to the time you should spend** Sie sollten nicht allzuviel Zeit darauf verwenden; **there is no ~ to his stupidity** seine Dummheit kennt keine Grenzen; **there's a ~ to the amount of money we can spend** unseren Ausgaben sind Grenzen gesetzt, wir können nicht unbegrenzt Geld ausgeben; **there are ~s!** es gibt (schließlich) Grenzen!; **it is true within ~s** es ist bis zu einem gewissen Grade richtig; **without ~s** unbegrenzt, unbeschränkt; **off ~s to military personnel** Zutritt für Militär verboten, für Militär gesperrt; **to go to the ~ to help sb** bis zum Äußersten gehen, um jdm zu helfen; **to know no ~s** keine Grenzen kennen; **over the ~** zuviel; (*in time*) zu lange; **you are** *or* **your baggage is over the ~** Ihr Gepäck hat Übergewicht; **you shouldn't drive, you're over the ~** du solltest dich nicht ans Steuer setzen, du hast zuviel getrunken; **he had more than the legal ~ (of alcohol) in his blood** er hatte mehr Promille als gesetzlich erlaubt; **top C is my ~** höher als bis zum hohen C komme ich nicht; **I'll offer £400, that's my ~** ich biete £ 400, das ist mein Limit *or* höher kann ich nicht gehen; **50 pages per week is my ~** 50 Seiten pro Woche sind mein Limit.

(**b**) (*inf*) **it's the (very) ~!** das ist die Höhe (*inf*) *or* das letzte (*inf*); **that child is the ~!** dieses Kind ist eine Zumutung! (*inf*); **he's the ~!, isn't he the ~?** das ist 'ne Type! (*inf*).

➤ LANGUAGE IN USE: **like²: 2b** → 7.2, 7.3, 7.4 **2c** → 3.3, 8.4, 13, 25.2 **3** → 3.1 **likeness** → 5.5

2 *vt* begrenzen, beschränken; *freedom, spending, possibilities* einschränken; *imagination* hemmen ◆ to ~ sth to sth etw auf etw (*acc*) beschränken; are you ~ed for time? ist Ihre Zeit begrenzt?; to ~ oneself to a few remarks sich auf einige (wenige) Bemerkungen beschränken; time is the ~ing factor wir sind zeitlich gebunden; what are the ~ing factors? wodurch sind uns (*dat*) Grenzen gesetzt?

limitation [ˌlɪmɪ'teɪʃən] *n* Beschränkung *f*; (*of freedom, spending*) Einschränkung *f* ◆ poor education is a great ~ eine schlechte Schulbildung ist ein großes Handikap; there is no ~ on exports of coal es gibt keine Beschränkungen für den Kohleexport; the ~s of a bilingual dictionary die beschränkten Möglichkeiten eines zweisprachigen Wörterbuchs; to have one's/its ~s seine Grenzen haben.

limited ['lɪmɪtɪd] *adj improvement, knowledge* begrenzt; *edition, means also* beschränkt; *intelligence, knowledge also* mäßig; *person* beschränkt ◆ in a more ~ sense in engerem Sinn; this is only true in a ~ sense dies ist nur in gewissem Maße wahr; ~ liability company (*Brit*) Gesellschaft *f* mit beschränkter Haftung; ~ partner Kommanditist(in *f*) *m*.

limitless ['lɪmɪtlɪs] *adj* grenzenlos.

limo ['lɪməʊ] *n* (*inf: limousine*) Limousine *f*.

limousine ['lɪməziːn] *n* Limousine *f*.

limp¹ [lɪmp] 1 *n* Hinken, Humpeln *nt* ◆ to walk with a ~ hinken, humpeln; the accident left him with a ~ seit dem Unfall hinkt er; he has a bad ~ er hinkt *or* humpelt sehr stark.

2 *vi* hinken, humpeln ◆ the ship managed to ~ into port das Schiff kam gerade noch *or* mit Müh und Not in den Hafen.

limp² *adj* (*+er*) schlapp, schlaff; *flowers* welk; *material, cloth* weich; *voice* matt, müde; (*of homosexual etc*) süßlich ◆ he's a ~ sort of character er hat einen schwachen Charakter; let your body go ~ alle Muskeln entspannen, alles locker lassen.

limpet ['lɪmpɪt] *n* Napfschnecke *f* ◆ to stick to sb like a ~ (*inf*) wie eine Klette an jdm hängen; ~ mine Haftmine *f*.

limpid ['lɪmpɪd] *adj* klar; *liquid also* durchsichtig.

limply ['lɪmplɪ] *adv* schlapp, schlaff ◆ ~ bound in calfskin in weiches Kalbsleder gebunden; ..., he said ~ ..., sagte er mit matter Stimme; (*of homosexual etc*) ..., flötete er (*inf*).

limpness ['lɪmpnɪs] *n see adj* Schlaffheit, Schlappheit *f*; Welkheit *f*; Weichheit *f*; Mattigkeit *f*; Süßlichkeit *f*.

limp-wristed ['lɪmp'rɪstɪd] *adj* (*inf: gay*) schwul (*inf*), warm (*inf*).

limy ['laɪmɪ] *adj* (*+er*) kalkhaltig.

linchpin ['lɪntʃpɪn] *n* Achs(en)nagel *m*, Lünse *f*; (*fig*) Stütze *f* ◆ accurate timing is the ~ of the entire operation das ganze Unternehmen steht und fällt mit genauer Zeiteinteilung.

linden ['lɪndən] *n* (*also* ~ tree) Linde(nbaum *m*) *f*.

line¹ [laɪn] 1 *n* (a) (*rope etc, washing* ~, *fishing* ~) Leine *f*.

(b) (*Math etc, on tennis court etc, on paper, palm*) Linie *f*; (*on face*) Falte *f* ◆ drawn in a few bold ~s mit wenigen kühnen Strichen gezeichnet; his drawings show great delicacy of ~ seine Zeichnungen weisen eine sehr feine Linienführung auf; all along the ~ (*fig*) auf der ganzen Linie; *see* hard.

(c) (*boundary, outline*) the ~ die Linie, der Äquator; the state ~ die Staatsgrenze; the ~ between right and wrong die Grenze zwischen Recht und Unrecht; the snow/tree ~ die Schnee-/Baumgrenze; the ship's graceful ~s die schnittigen Linien des Schiffes.

(d) (*row*) Reihe *f*; (*of people, cars also*) Schlange *f*; (*of hills*) Kette *f*; (*Sport*) Linie *f* ◆ in (a) ~ in einer Reihe; in a straight ~ geradlinig; a ~ of soldiers eine Reihe Soldaten; a ~ of traffic eine Autoschlange; a single ~ of traffic einspuriger Verkehr; John is next in ~ for promotion John ist als nächster mit der Beförderung an der Reihe; to be in ~ (*buildings etc*) geradlinig sein; to be out of ~ nicht geradlinig sein; to be out of ~ with sb/sth (*fig*) mit jdm/etw nicht übereinstimmen *or* in Einklang stehen; to be in ~ (with) (*fig*) in Einklang stehen (mit), übereinstimmen (mit); to bring sb into ~ with sth (*fig*) jdn auf die gleiche Linie wie etw (*acc*) bringen; it's time these rebels were brought into ~ es wird Zeit, daß die Rebellen zurückgepfiffen werden; to fall *or* get into ~ (*abreast*) sich in Reih und Glied aufstellen; (*behind one another*) sich hintereinander *or* in einer Reihe aufstellen; the policemen fell into ~ six abreast die Polizisten stellten sich in Sechserreihen auf; he refused to fall into ~ with the new proposals er weigerte sich, mit den neuen Vorschlägen konform zu gehen; it's time these rebels fell into ~ es ist Zeit, daß sich diese Rebellen anpassen *or* daß diese Rebellen spuren (*inf*); to keep the party in ~ die Einheit der Partei wahren; to step out of ~ (*lit*) aus der Reihe treten; (*fig*) aus der Reihe tanzen; he was stepping out of ~ telling the director what to do es war anmaßend von ihm, dem Direktor zu sagen, was er zu tun hätte; if he steps out of ~ again wenn er sich noch einmal etwas zuschulden kommen läßt.

(e) (*US: queue*) Schlange *f* ◆ to stand in ~ Schlange stehen.

(f) (*in factory*) Band *nt*.

(g) (*company: of aircraft, liners, buses*) Gesellschaft, Linie *f*; (*shipping company also*) Reederei *f*.

(h) (*of descent*) in the male ~ in der männlichen Linie; he was descended from a long ~ of farmers er stammte aus einem alten Bauerngeschlecht; royal ~ königliche Familie; in an unbroken ~ in ununterbrochener Folge; who is fourth in ~ to the throne? wer steht an vierter Stelle der Thronfolge?

(i) (*Rail*) (*in general*) Strecke, Bahnlinie *f*; (*section of track*) Strecke *f* ◆ ~s *pl* Gleise *pl*; to reach the end of the ~ (*fig*) am Ende sein.

(j) (*Telec: cable*) Leitung *f* ◆ the firm has 52 ~s die Firma hat 52 Anschlüsse; this is a very bad ~ die Verbindung ist sehr schlecht; to be on the ~ to sb mit jdm telefonieren; get off the ~! gehen Sie aus der Leitung!; hold the ~ bleiben Sie am Apparat!; can you get me a ~ to Chicago? können Sie mir eine Verbindung nach Chicago geben?

(k) (*written*) Zeile *f* ◆ ~s (*Sch*) Strafarbeit *f*; the teacher gave me 200 ~s der Lehrer ließ mich 200mal ... schreiben; ~s (*Theat*) Text *m*; I don't get any good ~s in this part der Text für diese Rolle *or* diese Partie ist sehr dürftig; what a ~! you don't expect me to say that! Sie können doch nicht erwarten, daß ich so einen Text spreche *or* so etwas sage!; he gets all the funny ~s er bekommt immer die lustigen Stellen; the poem "~s to a skylark" das Gedicht „An die Lerche"; to drop sb a ~ jdm ein paar Zeilen *or* Worte schreiben; to read between the ~s zwischen den Zeilen lesen.

(l) (*direction, course*) we tried a new ~ of approach to the problem wir versuchten, an das Problem anders heranzugehen; ~ of argument Argumentation *f*; ~ of attack (*fig*) Taktik *f*; what's your ~ of attack? wie wollen Sie an die Sache herangehen?; the police refused to reveal their ~s of inquiry die Polizei weigerte sich zu sagen, in welcher Richtung sie ermittelte; ~ of thought Denkrichtung *f*; ~ of vision Blickrichtung *f*; I can't see if you stand in my ~ of vision ich kann nichts sehen, wenn du mir die Sicht versperrst; to be on the right ~s (*fig*) auf dem richtigen Weg sein, richtig liegen (*inf*); a possible ~ of development eine mögliche Entwicklungsrichtung; we must take a firm *or* strong ~ with these people wir müssen diesen Leuten gegenüber sehr bestimmt auftreten; the government will take a strong ~ over inflation die Regierung wird gegen die Inflation energisch vorgehen; he took a strong/moderate ~ in the discussion er vertrat in der Diskussion einen festen/gemäßigten Standpunkt; the ~ of least resistance der Weg des geringsten Widerstandes; he took the ~ that ... er vertrat den Standpunkt, daß ...; I've heard that ~ before (*inf*) die Platte kenn' ich schon (*inf*); what sort of ~ do you think I should take when I see him? wie meinen Sie, soll ich mich verhalten, wenn ich ihn sehe?; what ~ is your thesis going to take? in welcher Richtung wollen Sie in Ihrer Doktorarbeit argumentieren?; to be along the ~s of ungefähr so etwas wie ... sein; to be on the same ~s as in der gleichen Richtung liegen wie; the essay is written along the ~s of the traditional theory der Aufsatz ist in Richtung der herkömmlichen Lehre verfaßt; along rather general ~s in ziemlich groben Zügen; the story developed along these ~ die Geschichte hat sich so *or* folgendermaßen entwickelt; along these ~s ungefähr so; something along these ~s etwas in dieser Richtung *or* Art; I was thinking along the same ~s ich hatte etwas ähnliches gedacht; on *or* along rather expressionistic ~s auf ziemlich expressionistische Art; it's all in the ~ of duty das gehört zu meinen/seinen *etc* Pflichten; things you do in the ~ of duty dienstliche Pflichten *pl*.

(m) (*Mil*) ~ of battle Kampflinie *f*; to draw up the ~s of battle (*fig*) (Kampf)stellung beziehen; enemy ~s feindliche Stellungen *or* Linien *pl*; ~s of communication Verbindungswege *pl*; ~ of retreat Rückzugslinie *f*; to keep one's ~s of retreat open sich (*dat*) den Rückzug offenhalten; *see* fire.

(n) (*fig: business*) Branche *f* ◆ what ~ is he in?, what's his ~? was ist er von Beruf?, was macht er beruflich?; that's not in my ~ of business damit habe ich nichts zu tun; we're in the same ~ of business wir sind in der gleichen Berufssparte *or* Branche tätig; that's not in my ~ das liegt mir nicht; fishing's more in my ~ Angeln liegt mir mehr *or* gefällt mir besser.

(o) (*range of items*) the best in its ~ das beste seiner Art; we have a new ~ in spring hats wir haben eine neue Kollektion Frühjahrshüte; that ~ did not sell at all dieses Modell ließ sich überhaupt nicht verkaufen; he has a good ~ in patter (*inf*) das ist eine gute Masche, wie er die Leute anquatscht (*inf*).

(p) (*clue, information*) to give sb a ~ on sth jdm einen Hinweis auf etw (*acc*) geben; can you give me a ~ on it? können Sie mir darüber etwas sagen?; the police eventually managed to get a ~ on him die Polizei konnte ihm schließlich etwas nachweisen; once a journalist has got a ~ on a story ... wenn ein Journalist einer Geschichte erst einmal auf der Spur ist ...

(q) (*inf*) to lay it on the ~ (*inf*) die Karten auf den Tisch legen (*inf*); they laid it on the ~ to the government, that ... sie erklärten der Regierung klipp und klar, daß ... (*inf*); to lay it on the ~ to sb jdm reinen Wein einschenken (*inf*).

(r) to put one's life/job *etc* on the ~ (*inf*) sein Leben/seine Stelle *etc* riskieren.

2 *vt* (a) (*cross with* ~s) linieren, liniieren ◆ worry had ~d his face sein Gesicht war von Sorgen gezeichnet.

(b) *streets* säumen ◆ an avenue ~d with trees eine von Bäumen gesäumte Straße; the streets were ~d with cheering crowds eine jubelnde Menge säumte die Straßen; the crew ~d the sides of the ship die Mannschaft hatte sich auf beiden Seiten des Schiffes aufgestellt; portraits ~d the walls an den Wänden hing ein Porträt neben dem andern.

◆**line up** 1 *vi* (*stand in line*) sich aufstellen, antreten; (*queue*) sich anstellen ◆ the teams ~d ~ like this die Mannschaften hatten folgende Aufstellung; the party ~d ~ behind their leader (*fig*) die Partei stellte sich hinter ihren Vorsitzenden.

2 *vt sep* (a) *troops, pupils, prisoners* antreten lassen; *boxes, books etc* in einer Reihe *or* nebeneinander aufstellen ◆ the police ~d the gang ~ with their backs to the wall die Polizei befahl der Bande, sich mit dem Rücken zur Wand aufzustellen; they ~d the prisoners ~ along the wall die Gefangenen mußten sich an der Wand entlang aufstellen.

(b) (*prepare, arrange*) *entertainment* sorgen für, auf die Beine stellen (*inf*); *speakers* bekommen, verpflichten; *support* mobilisieren ◆ what have you got ~d ~ for me today? was haben Sie heute für mich geplant?; I've ~d ~ a meeting with the directors ich habe ein Treffen mit den Direktoren arrangiert; I've got a meeting with John ~d ~ for 10 o'clock um 10 Uhr steht

➤ LANGUAGE IN USE: **line¹: 1j** → 27.3, 27.5, 27.7

ein Treffen mit John auf dem Programm; **I've got a nice little date ~d ~ for this evening** ich habe für heute abend eine nette Verabredung arrangiert.

line² *vt clothes* füttern; *pipe* auskleiden, innen beziehen; *floor of attic* auslegen ◆ **~ the box with paper** den Karton mit Papier auskleiden *or* ausschlagen; **to ~ brakes** Bremsbeläge *pl* erneuern (lassen); **the membranes which ~ the stomach** die Schleimhäute, die den Magen auskleiden *or* innen überziehen; **to ~ one's own pockets** (*fig*) sich bereichern, in die eigene Tasche arbeiten *or* wirtschaften (*inf*).

lineage ['lɪnɪdʒ] *n* (*descent*) Abstammung *f*; (*descendants*) Geschlecht *nt*.

lineal ['lɪnɪəl] *adj descent* direkt.

lineament ['lɪnɪəmənt] *n* (*form*) Lineament *nt* (*rare*) ◆ **~s** *pl* (*of face*) Gesichtszüge *pl*.

linear ['lɪnɪəʳ] *adj motion* linear, geradlinig; *design* Linien-; *measure* Längen- ◆ **~ B** Linear B *f*.

line command *n* (*Comput*) Zeilenbefehl *m*.

lined [laɪnd] *adj face etc* (*of old people*) faltig; (*through worry, tiredness etc*) gezeichnet; *paper* liniert, liniiert ◆ **to become ~ with age** Altersfalten bekommen.

line: ~ drawing *n* Zeichnung *f*; **~ editor** *n* (*Comput*) Zeileneditor *m*; **~ feed** *n* (*Comput*) Zeilenvorschub *m*; **~ judge** *n* (*Tennis*) Linienrichter(in *f*) *m*; **~ manager** *m* leitender Angestellter, leitende Angestellte.

linen ['lɪnɪn] [1] *n* Leinen *nt*; (*table ~*) Tischwäsche *f*; (*sheets, garments etc*) Wäsche *f* ◆ **~ closet, ~ cupboard** Wäscheschrank *m*.
[2] *adj* Leinen-.

line: ~-out *n* (*Rugby*) Gasse *f*; **~ printer** *n* (*Comput*) Zeilendrucker *m*; **~ printout** *n* (*Comput*) Zeilenausdruck *m*.

liner ['laɪnəʳ] *n* (*ship*) Passagierschiff *nt*, Liniendampfer *m*; (*plane*) Verkehrsflugzeug *nt*.

linesman ['laɪnzmən], (*US also*) **lineman** ['laɪnmən] *n*, *pl* **-men** [-mən] (*Sport*) Linienrichter *m*; (*Rail*) Streckenwärter *m*; (*Elec, Telec*) Leitungsmann *m*; (*for faults*) Störungssucher *m*.

line spacing *n* Zeilenabstand *m*.

line-up ['laɪnʌp] *n* (*Sport*) Aufstellung *f*; (*cast*) Besetzung *f*; (*alignment*) Gruppierung *f*; (*US: queue*) Schlange *f* ◆ **she picked the thief out of the ~** sie erkannte den Dieb bei der Gegenüberstellung.

line width *n* Zeilenlänge *f*.

ling¹ [lɪŋ] *n* (*Zool*) Leng(fisch) *m*.

ling² *n* (*Bot*) Heidekraut *nt*.

linger ['lɪŋgəʳ] *vi* **(a)** (*also* **~ on**) (zurück)bleiben, verweilen (*liter*); (*in dying*) zwischen Leben und Tod schweben; (*custom*) fortbestehen, sich halten; (*doubts, suspicions*) zurückbleiben; (*feeling, emotion, pain*) anhalten, bleiben; (*memory*) fortbestehen, bleiben; (*chords*) nachklingen; (*scent*) sich halten ◆ **the party was over, but many of the guests ~ed in the hall** die Party war vorbei, aber viele Gäste standen noch im Flur herum; **it was incredible how Franco ~ed on** es war erstaunlich, wie fest Franco am Leben hielt.
(b) (*delay*) sich aufhalten, verweilen (*liter*) ◆ **I mustn't ~ or I'll miss the bus** ich darf mich nicht lange aufhalten, sonst verpasse ich den Bus.
(c) (*dwell*) **to ~ on a subject** bei einem Thema verweilen (*geh*); **I let my eyes ~ on the scene** ich ließ meinen Blick auf der Szene ruhen; **to ~ over a meal** sich (*dat*) bei einer Mahlzeit Zeit lassen, sich bei einer Mahlzeit lange aufhalten; **we ~ed over a glass of wine** wir tranken gemächlich ein Glas Wein.

lingerie ['lænʒəriː] *n* (Damen)unterwäsche *f*.

lingering ['lɪŋgərɪŋ] *adj* lang, ausgedehnt; *death* langsam; *illness* langwierig, schleppend; *doubt* zurückbleibend; *look* sehnsüchtig; *chords* lange (nach)klingend; *kiss* innig ◆ **the lovers took a ~ farewell of each other** der Abschied der Liebenden wollte kein Ende nehmen; **I've still got one ~ doubt** es bleibt noch ein Zweifel (zurück); **the customs officer gave him a long ~ look** der Zollbeamte sah ihn lange prüfend an.

lingo ['lɪŋgəʊ] *n* (*inf*) Sprache *f*; (*specialist jargon*) Kauderwelsch *nt* (*inf*).

lingua franca ['lɪŋgwə'fræŋkə] *n* Verkehrssprache, Lingua franca *f*; (*official language*) Amtssprache *f*.

lingual ['lɪŋgwəl] *adj* Zungen-.

linguist ['lɪŋgwɪst] *n* **(a)** (*speaker of languages*) Sprachkundige(r) *mf* ◆ **he's a good ~** er ist sehr sprachbegabt; **I'm no ~** ich bin nicht sprachbegabt. **(b)** (*specialist in linguistics*) Linguist(in *f*), Sprachforscher(in *f*) *m*.

linguistic [lɪŋ'gwɪstɪk] *adj* **(a)** (*concerning language*) sprachlich; *competence* Sprach-. **(b)** (*of science*) linguistisch, sprachwissenschaftlich.

linguistically [lɪŋ'gwɪstɪkəlɪ] *adv see adj* sprachlich; linguistisch ◆ **~ aware** sprachbewußt.

linguistics [lɪŋ'gwɪstɪks] *n sing* Linguistik, Sprachwissenschaft *f*.

liniment ['lɪnɪmənt] *n* Einreibemittel, Liniment (*spec*) *nt*.

lining ['laɪnɪŋ] *n* (*of clothes etc*) Futter *nt*; (*~ material*) Futterstoff *m*; (*of brake*) (Brems)belag *m*; (*of pipe*) Auskleidung *f*; (*of attic floor*) Belag *m* ◆ **the ~ of the stomach** die Magenschleimhaut.

link [lɪŋk] [1] *n* **(a)** (*of chain, fig*) Glied *nt*; (*person*) Verbindungsmann *m*, Bindeglied *nt*.
(b) (*connection*) Verbindung *f* ◆ **a new rail ~ for the village** eine neue Zug- *or* Bahnverbindung zum Dorf; **photographs give you a ~ with the past** Fotos verbinden einen mit der Vergangenheit; **cultural ~s** kulturelle Beziehungen *pl*; **this is the first cultural ~ between our two countries** das ist der Anfang der kulturellen Beziehungen zwischen unseren beiden Ländern; **the strong ~s between Britain and Australia** die starken Bindungen *or* engen Beziehungen zwischen Großbritannien und Australien; **the ~ of friendship** freundschaftliche Bindungen *pl*; **are there any ~s between the two phenomena?** besteht zwischen diesen beiden Phänomenen ein Zusammenhang *or* eine Beziehung *or* eine Verbindung?
(c) (*Measure*) Link *nt*.
[2] *vt* verbinden; *spaceships also* aneinanderkoppeln ◆ **to ~ arms** sich unterhaken (*with* bei); **the police ~ed arms** die Polizisten bildeten einen Kordon; **we are ~ed by telephone to ...** wir sind telefonisch verbunden mit ...; **the two companies are now ~ed** die beiden Firmen haben sich zusammengeschlossen; **do you think these two murders are ~ed?** glauben Sie, daß zwischen den beiden Morden eine Verbindung besteht?; **success in business is closely ~ed with self-confidence** Erfolg im Beruf hängt eng mit Selbstvertrauen zusammen; **his name is closely ~ed with several reforms** sein Name ist mit mehreren Reformen eng verbunden.
[3] *vi* **to ~ (together)** (*parts of story*) sich zusammenfügen lassen; (*parts of machine*) verbunden werden; (*railway lines*) sich vereinigen, zusammenlaufen.

◆**link up** [1] *vi* zusammenkommen; (*people*) sich zusammentun; (*facts*) übereinstimmen, zusammenpassen; (*companies*) sich zusammenschließen ◆ **to ~ ~ in space** ein Kopplungsmanöver im Weltraum durchführen; **how does that ~ ~ with what Freud says?** wie hängt das mit dem zusammen, was Freud sagt?
[2] *vt sep* miteinander verbinden; *bits of evidence* miteinander in Verbindung bringen; *spaceships* koppeln.

link man *n*, *pl* **-men** [-men] Verbindungsmann *m*; (*Rad, TV*) Moderator *m*.

links [lɪŋks] *npl* **(a)** Dünen *pl*. **(b)** (*golf course*) Golfplatz *m*.

link-up ['lɪŋkʌp] *n* (*Telec, general*) Verbindung *f*; (*of spaceships*) Kopplung(smanöver *nt*) *f*.

linnet ['lɪnɪt] *n* (Blut)hänfling *m*.

lino ['laɪnəʊ] *n* Linoleum *nt* ◆ **~ cut** Linolschnitt *m*.

linoleum [lɪ'nəʊlɪəm] *n* Linoleum *nt*.

linotype ® ['laɪnəʊtaɪp] *n* Linotype ®, Zeilengieß- *or* Setzmaschine *f*.

linseed ['lɪnsiːd] *n* Leinsamen *m* ◆ **~ oil** Leinöl *nt*.

lint [lɪnt] *n* Scharpie *f*, Mull *m*.

lintel ['lɪntl] *n* (*Archit*) Sturz *m*.

lint-free ['lɪnt,friː] *adj* flusenfrei.

lion ['laɪən] *n* Löwe *m* ◆ **he was one of the literary ~s of his day** er war einer der bedeutendsten *or* größten Schriftsteller seiner Zeit; **social ~** Salonlöwe *m*; **the ~'s share** der Löwenanteil.

lioness ['laɪənɪs] *n* Löwin *f*.

lionhearted ['laɪən,hɑːtɪd] *adj* unerschrocken, furchtlos.

lionize ['laɪənaɪz] *vt* **to ~ sb** jdn zum Helden machen.

lip [lɪp] *n* **(a)** (*Anat*) Lippe *f* ◆ **he wouldn't open his ~s** er wollte den Mund nicht aufmachen; **to hang on sb's ~s** an jds Lippen (*dat*) hängen; **to keep a stiff upper ~** Haltung bewahren; **to lick** *or* **smack one's ~s** sich (*dat*) die Lippen lecken.
(b) (*of jug*) Schnabel *m*; (*of cup, crater*) Rand *m*.
(c) (*inf: cheek*) Frechheit(en *pl*) *f* ◆ **to give sb a lot of ~** jdm gegenüber eine (dicke *or* freche) Lippe riskieren (*inf*); **any more of your ~ and there'll be trouble** wenn du weiterhin so eine (dicke *or* freche) Lippe riskierst, gibt's Ärger (*inf*); **none of your ~!** sei nicht so frech.

lip gloss *n* Lip-Gloss *m*.

liposuction ['lɪpəʊ,sʌkʃən] *n* Fettabsaugung *f*.

-lipped [-lɪpt] *adj suf* -lippig.

lip: ~read [1] *vt* **I could ~read what he said** ich konnte ihm von den Lippen *or* vom Mund ablesen, was er sagte; [2] *vi* von den Lippen *or* vom Mund ablesen; **~reading** *n* **deaf people use/learn ~reading** Taube lesen vom Mund ab/lernen, vom Mund abzulesen; **~ salve** *n* Lippen-Fettstift *m*; **~ service** *n* **to pay ~ service to an idea** ein Lippenbekenntnis zu einer Idee ablegen; **~stick** *n* Lippenstift *m*.

liquefaction [,lɪkwɪ'fækʃən] *n* Verflüssigung *f*.

liquefy ['lɪkwɪfaɪ] [1] *vt* verflüssigen.
[2] *vi* sich verflüssigen.

liqueur [lɪ'kjʊəʳ] *n* Likör *m*.

liquid ['lɪkwɪd] [1] *adj* **(a)** flüssig; *measure* Flüssigkeits-; (*fig*) *eyes* blank, glänzend; (*fig*) *notes, song* perlend.
(b) (*Comm*) *asset* (frei) verfügbar, flüssig.
(c) (*Phon*) **~ consonant** Liquida *f*, Fließlaut *m*.
[2] *n* **(a)** Flüssigkeit *f* ◆ **she can only take ~s** sie kann nur Flüssiges zu sich nehmen. **(b)** (*Phon*) Liquida *f*, Fließlaut *m*.

liquidate ['lɪkwɪdeɪt] *vt* **(a)** (*Comm*) liquidieren; *assets also* flüssig machen; *company also* auflösen ◆ **to ~ a debt** eine Schuld/Schulden tilgen. **(b)** *enemy etc* liquidieren.

liquidation [,lɪkwɪ'deɪʃən] *n* **(a)** (*Comm*) Liquidation, Liquidierung *f*; (*of company also*) Auflösung *f*; (*of debts*) Tilgung *f* ◆ **to go into ~** in Liquidation gehen. **(b)** Liquidierung *f*.

liquidator ['lɪkwɪdeɪtəʳ] *n* Liquidator, Abwickler *m*.

liquid-crystal ['lɪkwɪd'krɪstəl] *adj* Flüssigkristall- ◆ **~ display** Flüssigkristall-Anzeige *f*.

liquidity [lɪ'kwɪdɪtɪ] *n* Liquidität *f*.

liquidize ['lɪkwɪdaɪz] *vt* (im Mixer) pürieren *or* zerkleinern.

liquidizer ['lɪkwɪdaɪzəʳ] *n* Mixgerät *nt*.

liquor ['lɪkəʳ] *n* **(a)** (*whisky, brandy etc*) Spirituosen *pl*; (*alcohol*) Alkohol *m* ◆ **people who drink hard ~** Leute, die scharfe Sachen trinken, Schnapstrinker *pl*; **a powerful ~** ein hochprozentiges Getränk; **the local ~** der am Ort hergestellte Schnaps; **he can't take his ~** er verträgt nichts.
(b) (*juice*) Flüssigkeit *f* ◆ **potato ~** Kartoffelwasser *nt*.

◆**liquor up** *vt sep* (*US sl*) **to get ~ed ~** sich besaufen (*sl*); **to be ~ed ~** besoffen sein (*sl*).

liquorice, licorice ['lɪkərɪs] *n* (*plant*) Süßholz *nt*; (*root*) Süßholzwurzel *f*; (*flavouring, sweetmeat*) Lakritze *f*.

liquor store *n* (*US*) ≃ Wein- und Spirituosengeschäft *nt*.

lira ['lɪərə] *n* Lira *f* ◆ **500 ~(s)** 500 Lire.

Lisbon ['lɪzbən] *n* Lissabon *nt*.

lisle [laɪl] *n* (*also* **~ thread**) Florgarn *nt* ◆ **~ stockings** Baumwollstrümpfe *pl*.

lisp [lɪsp] [1] *n* Lispeln *nt* ◆ **to speak with a ~, to have a ~** lispeln.
[2] *vti* lispeln.

lissom(e) ['lɪsəm] *adj* geschmeidig; *person also* gelenkig.

list[1] [lɪst] [1] *n* **(a)** Liste *f*; (*shopping* ~) Einkaufszettel *m* ◆ **it's not on the ~** es steht nicht auf der Liste; **~ of names** Namensliste *f*; (*esp in book*) Namensregister, Namensverzeichnis *nt*; **~ of prices** Preisliste *f*, Preisverzeichnis *nt*; **~ of applicants** Bewerberliste *f*; **there's a long ~ of people waiting for houses** für Häuser besteht eine lange Warteliste; **it's on my ~ for tomorrow** es steht für morgen auf dem Programm.
(b) (*publisher's* ~) Programm *nt* ◆ **we'd like to start an educational ~** wir würden gern Lehrbücher in unser Programm aufnehmen.
[2] *vt* aufschreiben, notieren; *single item* in die Liste aufnehmen; (*verbally*) aufzählen ◆ **it is not ~ed** es ist nicht aufgeführt.

list[2] (*Naut*) [1] *n* Schlagseite, Krängung (*spec*) *f* ◆ **to have a bad ~** schwere Schlagseite haben; **to have a ~ of 20°** sich um 20° auf die Seite neigen; **a ~ to port** Schlagseite nach Backbord.
[2] *vi* Schlagseite haben, krängen (*spec*) ◆ **to ~ badly** schwere Schlagseite haben.

list[3] *vi* (*obs*) lauschen (*old*).

list[4] *vi* (*obs, poet*) **the wind bloweth where it ~eth** der Wind bläst, wo er will.

listed ['lɪstɪd] *adj* (*Brit*) *building* unter Denkmalschutz (stehend *attr*) ◆ **it's a ~ building** es steht unter Denkmalschutz.

listen ['lɪsn] *vi* **(a)** (*hear*) hören (*to sth* etw *acc*) ◆ **to ~ to the radio** Radio hören; **if you ~ hard, you can hear the sea** wenn du genau horchst *or* hinhörst, kannst du das Meer hören; **she ~ed carefully to everything he said** sie hörte ihm genau zu; **to ~ for sth** auf etw (*acc*) horchen; **the boys are ~ing for the bell at the end of the lesson** die Jungen warten auf das Klingeln am Ende der Stunde; **to ~ for sb** horchen *or* hören, ob jd kommt.
(b) (*heed*) zuhören ◆ **~ to me!** hör mir zu!; **~, I know what we'll do** paß auf, ich weiß, was wir machen; **~, I'm warning you** hör mal, ich warne dich!; **don't ~ to him** hör nicht auf ihn; **if he suggests anything, don't ~** hör nicht darauf, wenn er etwas vorschlägt; **he wouldn't ~** er wollte nicht hören.

◆**listen in** *vi* (im Radio) hören (*to sth* etw *acc*); (*listen secretly*) mithören (*on sth* etw *acc*) ◆ **I'd like to ~ ~ on** *or* **to your discussion** ich möchte mir Ihre Diskussion mit anhören.

listener ['lɪsnə^r] *n* Zuhörer(in *f*) *m*; (*Rad*) Hörer(in *f*) *m* ◆ **to be a good ~** gut zuhören können.

listening ['lɪsnɪŋ] *n* **good ~!** gute Unterhaltung!; **~ post** (*Mil, fig*) Horchposten *m*.

listeria [lɪs'tɪərɪə] *n* Listeriose *f*.

listing ['lɪstɪŋ] *n* Auflistung *f*, Verzeichnis *nt*.

listing paper *n* (*Comput*) Endlospapier *nt*.

listless ['lɪstlɪs] *adj* lustlos; *patient* teilnahmslos.

listlessly ['lɪstlɪslɪ] *adv see adj*.

listlessness ['lɪstlɪsnɪs] *n see adj* Lustlosigkeit *f*; Teilnahmslosigkeit *f*.

list price *n* Listenpreis *m*.

lists [lɪsts] *npl* (*Hist*) Schranken *pl* ◆ **to enter the ~** (*fig*) in die Schranken treten (*liter*), zum Kampf antreten; **he entered the ~ after the first ballot** er trat nach dem ersten Wahlgang in den Wahlkampf ein.

lit [lɪt] *pret, ptp of* **light**[1], **light**[3].

litany ['lɪtənɪ] *n* Litanei *f*.

lit crit ['lɪt'krɪt] *n* (*Brit inf*) *abbr of* **literary criticism**.

liter *n* (*US*) *see* **litre**.

literacy ['lɪtərəsɪ] *n* Fähigkeit *f*, lesen und schreiben zu können ◆ **~ campaign** Kampagne *f* gegen das Analphabetentum, Alphabetisierungskampagne *f*; **the ~ rate in Slobodia is only 30%** die Analphabetenquote in Slobodia beträgt 70%; **~ is low in Slobodia** Slobodia hat eine hohe Analphabetenquote; **~ test** Lese- und Schreibtest *m*.

literal ['lɪtərəl] [1] *adj* **(a)** (*esp Typ*) **~ error** Schreib-/Tipp-/Druck- fehler *m*.
(b) *translation* wörtlich; *meaning, sense also* eigentlich.
(c) (*real*) **that is the ~ truth** das ist die reine Wahrheit; **it was a ~ disaster** es war im wahrsten Sinne des Wortes eine Katastrophe; **the ~ impossibility of working there** die völlige *or* buchstäbliche Unmöglichkeit, dort zu arbeiten.
(d) (*prosaic*) nüchtern, prosaisch ◆ **he has a very ~ mind** *or* **is very ~-minded** er denkt sehr nüchtern, er ist sehr prosaisch.
[2] *n* Schreib-/Tipp-/Druckfehler *m*.

literally ['lɪtərəlɪ] *adv* **(a)** (*word for word, exactly*) (wort)wörtlich ◆ **to take sth ~** etw wörtlich nehmen.
(b) (*really*) buchstäblich, wirklich ◆ **the best meal I've ever had, ~** wirklich das Beste, was ich je gegessen habe; **it was ~ impossible to work there** es war wirklich *or* einfach unmöglich, dort zu arbeiten; **he was ~ a giant** er war im wahrsten Sinne des Wortes ein Riese.

literariness ['lɪtərərɪnɪs] *n* literarische Stilebene.

literary ['lɪtərərɪ] *adj* literarisch ◆ **he has ~ tastes** er interessiert sich für Literatur; **a ~ man** ein Literaturkenner *m*; (*author*) ein Literat *or* Autor *m*; **~ criticism** (*as subject*) Literaturwissenschaft *f*; (*reviews*) Literaturkritik *f*; **~ historian** Literaturhistoriker(in *f*) *m*.

literate ['lɪtərɪt] *adj* **(a) to be ~** lesen und schreiben können; **they aim to achieve a ~ population in one generation** sie wollen die Bevölkerung in einer Generation alphabetisieren.
(b) (*well-educated*) gebildet ◆ **his style is not very ~** er schreibt einen ungeschliffenen Stil.

literati [ˌlɪtə'rɑːtiː] *npl* Literaten *pl*.

literature ['lɪtərɪtʃə^r] *n* Literatur *f*; (*inf: brochures etc*) Informationsmaterial *nt*; (*specialist* ~) (Fach)literatur *f*.

lithe [laɪð] *adj* (*+er*) geschmeidig; *person, body also* gelenkig.

lithium ['lɪθɪəm] *n* Lithium *nt*.

litho ['laɪθəʊ] *n* (*inf*) Litho *nt*.

lithograph ['lɪθəʊgrɑːf] [1] *n* Lithographie *f*, Steindruck *m*.
[2] *vt* lithographieren.

lithographer [lɪ'θɒgrəfə^r] *n* Lithograph(in *f*) *m*.

lithographic [ˌlɪθəʊ'græfɪk] *adj* lithographisch, Steindruck-.

lithography [lɪ'θɒgrəfɪ] *n* Lithographie *f*, Steindruck(verfahren *nt*) *m*.

Lithuania [ˌlɪθjʊ'eɪnɪə] *n* Litauen *nt*.

Lithuanian [ˌlɪθjʊ'eɪnɪən] [1] *adj* litauisch.
[2] *n* **(a)** Litauer(in *f*) *m*. **(b)** (*language*) Litauisch *nt*.

litigant ['lɪtɪgənt] *n* prozeßführende Partei ◆ **the ~s** die Prozeßgegner *pl*, die prozeßführenden Parteien.

litigate ['lɪtɪgeɪt] *vi* einen Prozeß führen *or* anstrengen.

litigation [ˌlɪtɪ'geɪʃən] *n* Prozeß, Rechtsstreit *m* ◆ **he threatened them with ~** er drohte ihnen mit einem Prozeß.

litigious [lɪ'tɪdʒəs] *adj* prozeßsüchtig ◆ **a ~ person** jd, der ständig Prozesse führt, ein Prozeßhansel *m* (*inf*).

litmus ['lɪtməs] *n* Lackmus *m or nt* ◆ **~ paper** Lackmuspapier *nt*; **~ test** (*lit*) Lackmustest *m*; (*fig*) entscheidender Test.

litotes [laɪ'təʊtiːz] *n* Litotes *f*.

litre, (*US*) **liter** ['liːtə^r] *n* Liter *m or nt*.

litter ['lɪtə^r] [1] *n* **(a)** Abfälle *pl*; (*papers, wrappings*) Papier *nt* ◆ **the park was strewn with ~** der Park war mit Papier und Abfällen übersät; **a ~ of books** ein Haufen *m* Bücher.
(b) (*Zool*) Wurf *m*.
(c) (*vehicle*) Sänfte *f*; (*Med*) Tragbahre, Trage *f*.
(d) (*bedding for animals*) Streu *f*, Stroh *nt*; (*for plants*) Stroh *nt*; (*cat* ~) Katzenstreu *f*.
[2] *vt* **(a) to be ~ed with sth** (*lit, fig*) mit etw übersät sein; **old cans ~ed the countryside** alte Dosen verschandelten die Landschaft; **to ~ a room with papers** Papier(e) im Zimmer verstreuen.
(b) (*give birth to*) werfen.
(c) *plant* abdecken; *animal* Streu geben (*+dat*).
[3] *vi* **(a)** (*have young*) werfen. **(b)** (*esp US*) Abfall wegwerfen.

litter: ~ basket *n* Abfallkorb *m*; **~ bin** *n* Abfalleimer *m*; (*hooked on*) Abfallkorb *m*; (*bigger*) Abfalltonne *f*; **~ bug** (*inf*), **~ lout** (*inf*) *n* Dreckspatz (*inf*), Schmutzfink (*inf*) *m*.

little ['lɪtl] [1] *adj* klein ◆ **a ~ house** ein Häuschen *nt*, ein kleines Haus; **a funny ~ nose** ein lustiges (kleines) Näschen; **the ~ ones** die Kleinen *pl*; **a nice ~ profit** ein hübscher Gewinn; **the ~ people** *or* **folk** die Elfen; **he will have his ~ joke** er will auch einmal ein Witzchen machen; **to worry about ~ things** sich (*dat*) über Kleinigkeiten Gedanken machen; **he has a ~ mind** er ist ein Kleingeist; **~ things please ~ minds** so kann man auch mit kleinen Sachen Kindern eine Freude machen; **a L~ Englander** *Gegner m des Imperialismus im 19. Jahrhundert*, Isolationist *m*; **a ~ while ago** vor kurzem, vor kurzer Zeit; **it's only a ~ while till I ...** es ist nicht mehr lange, bis ich ...; **in a ~ while** bald.
[2] *adv, n* **(a)** wenig ◆ **of ~ importance/interest** von geringer Bedeutung/geringem Interesse; **he knows ~ Latin and less Greek** er kann (nur) wenig Latein und noch weniger Griechisch; **~ better than** kaum besser als; **~ more than a month ago** vor kaum einem Monat; **~ short of** fast schon, beinahe; **~ did I think that ...** ich hätte kaum gedacht, daß ...; **~ does he know that ...** er hat keine Ahnung, daß ...; **they ~ realize what will happen to them** sie sind sich (*dat*) wohl kaum darüber im klaren, was mit ihnen geschehen wird; **to think ~ of sb/sth** nicht viel von jdm/etw halten; **I walk as ~ as possible** ich laufe so wenig wie möglich; **to spend ~ or nothing** so gut wie (gar) nichts ausgeben; **every ~ helps** Kleinvieh macht auch Mist (*Prov*); **please donate, every ~ helps** auch die kleinste Spende hilft; **he had ~ to say** er hatte nicht viel zu sagen; **I see very ~ of her nowadays** ich sehe sie in letzter Zeit sehr selten; **there was ~ we could do** wir konnten nicht viel tun; **the ~ of his book that I have read** das wenige *or* bißchen, was ich von seinem Buch gelesen habe; **she did what ~ she could** sie tat das Wenige, das sie tun konnte; **~ by ~** nach und nach; **~ by ~, he dragged himself across the room** Stückchen für Stückchen schleppte er sich durch das Zimmer; **to make ~ of sth** etw herunterspielen *or* bagatellisieren; **I could make ~ of this book** ich konnte mit diesem Buch nicht viel anfangen.
(b) a ~ ein wenig, ein bißchen; **a ~ hot/better** etwas *or* ein bißchen heiß/besser, ein wenig besser; **with a ~ effort** mit etwas Anstrengung; **I'll give you a ~ advice** ich gebe dir einen kleinen Tip; **a ~ after five** kurz nach fünf; **we were not a ~ worried** wir waren recht besorgt; **I was not a ~ surprised** ich war einigermaßen überrascht; **we walked on for a ~** wir liefen noch ein bißchen *or* Stück *or* Weilchen weiter; **after a ~** nach einer Weile; **for a ~** für ein Weilchen.

littleness ['lɪtlnɪs] *n* Kleinheit *f*, geringe Größe; (*of contribution*) Geringfügigkeit *f*; (*of mind*) Beschränktheit *f*.

littoral ['lɪtərəl] (*form*) [1] *adj* litoral (*spec*), Litoral- (*spec*); (*of lake also*) Ufer-; (*of sea also*) Küsten-.

[2] *n* Litorale *nt;* Uferland *nt;* Küstenstrich *m or* -region *f.*
liturgical [lɪ'tɜːdʒɪkəl] *adj* liturgisch.
liturgy ['lɪtədʒɪ] *n* Liturgie *f.*
livable, liveable ['lɪvəbl] *adj life* erträglich.
livable: ~-in *adj (inf)* **the house is ~-in** in dem Haus kann man *or* läßt es sich wohnen; **~-with** *adj (inf)* **John's too moody to be ~-with** John ist zu launisch, mit ihm kann man nicht zusammen leben; **arthritis can't be cured, but it can be made ~-with** Arthritis ist unheilbar, kann aber erträglich gemacht werden.
live¹ [lɪv] [1] *vt life* führen ◆ **to ~ a part** in einer Rolle aufgehen; **he had been living a lie** sein Leben war eine Lüge; **to ~ one's own life** sein eigenes Leben leben.
[2] *vi* **(a)** leben ◆ **there is no man living who can equal him** es gibt niemanden, der es ihm gleichtun könnte; **will he ~, doctor?** wird er (über)leben, Herr Doktor?; **don't worry, you'll ~, it's only a broken ankle** reg dich nicht auf, du stirbst schon nicht, du hast nur einen gebrochenen Knöchel; **long ~ Queen Anne!** lang lebe Königin Anne!; **we ~ and learn** man lernt nie aus; **to ~ and let ~** leben und leben lassen; **to ~ like a king** *or* **lord** fürstlich *or* wie Gott in Frankreich leben; **not many people ~ to be a hundred** nicht viele Menschen werden hundert (Jahre alt); **to ~ to a ripe old age** ein hohes Alter erreichen; **his spirit ~s** sein Geist lebt weiter; **his name will ~ for ever** sein Ruhm wird nie vergehen; **his poetry will ~ for ever** seine Dichtung ist unvergänglich; **we will ~ again after death** wir werden nach dem Tode wiedergeboren werden; **if the spirit of the Renaissance should ever ~ again** wenn der Geist der Renaissance je wiedererwachen sollte; **it was as though the father were living again in the son** es war, als lebte der Vater im Sohn weiter; **to ~ by one's wits** sich (so) durchschlagen; **to ~ by one's pen** von seinen Büchern *or* vom Schreiben leben; **he ~d through two wars** er hat zwei Kriege miterlebt; **to ~ through an experience** eine Erfahrung durchmachen; **the patient was not expected to ~ through the night** man rechnete nicht damit, daß der Patient die Nacht überstehen *or* überleben würde; **I would rather like to ~ to the end of the century** ich möchte die Jahrhundertwende noch miterleben; **to ~ within/beyond one's income** nicht über/über seine Verhältnisse leben; **you'll ~ to regret it** das wirst du noch bereuen.
(b) *(experience real living)* **I want to ~** ich will leben *or* was erleben *(inf)*; **that's existing, not living** das ist doch kein Leben; **you've never skied? you haven't ~d!** du bist noch nie Ski gefahren? du weißt gar nicht, was du versäumt hast!; **you've never ~d until you've discovered Crete** wer Kreta nicht kennt, hat noch nicht gelebt; **before she met him she hadn't ~d** sie begann erst zu leben, als sie ihn kennenlernte.
(c) *(reside)* wohnen; *(in town, in country also, animals)* leben ◆ **he ~s at 19 Marktstraße** er wohnt in der Marktstraße Nr. 19; **he ~s in Gardner St/on the High St** er wohnt in der Gardner St/auf der *or* in der Hauptstraße; **who ~s in that big house?** wer bewohnt das große Haus?, wer wohnt in dem großen Haus?; **he ~s with his parents** er wohnt bei seinen Eltern; **a house not fit to ~ in** ein unbewohnbares Haus, ein Haus, in dem man nicht wohnen kann; **this house is not fit for a human being to ~ in** dies ist eine menschenunwürdige Behausung.
(d) *(inf: belong)* **where does this jug ~?** wo gehört der Krug hin?; **the knives ~ in this drawer** die Messer gehören in diese Schublade.
(e) **the other athletes couldn't ~ with him/the pace** die anderen Läufer konnten mit ihm/mit dem Tempo nicht mithalten.
◆**live down** *vt sep scandal, humiliation* hinwegkommen über *(+acc)*, verwinden; *(actively) scandal, mistake* Gras wachsen lassen über *(+acc)* ◆ **he'll never ~ it ~** das wird man ihm nie vergessen.
◆**live in** *vi* im Haus/im Wohnheim *etc* wohnen, nicht außerhalb wohnen.
◆**live off** *vi +prep obj* **to ~ ~ one's estates** von seinem Besitz leben; **to ~ ~ one's relations** auf Kosten seiner Verwandten leben.
◆**live on** [1] *vi (continue to live)* weiterleben.
[2] *vi +prep obj* **to ~ ~ eggs** sich von Eiern ernähren, von Eiern leben; **he doesn't earn enough to ~ ~** er verdient nicht genug, um davon zu leben; **to ~ ~ hope** (nur noch) von der Hoffnung leben; **to ~ ~ one's reputation** von seinem Ruf zehren.
◆**live out** [1] *vi* außerhalb (des Hauses/des Wohnheims *etc*) wohnen.
[2] *vt sep life* verbringen; *winter* überleben ◆ **he ~d ~ a life of poverty in the country** er lebte bis an sein Ende in Armut auf dem Land.
◆**live together** *vi (cohabit)* zusammenleben; *(share a room, flat etc)* zusammenwohnen.
◆**live up** *vt always separate*: **to ~ it ~** *(inf)* die Puppen tanzen lassen *(inf)*; *(extravagantly)* in Saus und Braus leben *(inf)*; **in my young days we really knew how to ~ it ~** in meiner Jugend wußten wir noch, wie man sich so richtig auslebt.
◆**live up to** *vi +prep obj* **the holidays ~d ~ ~ expectations/the advertiser's claims** der Urlaub hielt, was ich *etc* mir davon versprochen hatte/was die Werbung versprochen hatte; **to ~ ~ ~ standards/one's reputation** den Anforderungen/seinem Ruf gerecht werden; **the reality never ~s ~ ~ the anticipation** die Wirklichkeit kommt nie an die Erwartungen heran; **the holiday didn't ~ ~ ~ our hopes** der Urlaub entsprach nicht dem, was wir uns *(dat)* erhofft hatten; **he's got a lot to ~ ~ ~** in ihn werden große Erwartungen gesetzt; **if he wants to emulate his father he's got a lot to ~ ~ ~** er hat sich *(dat)* ein hohes Ziel gesteckt, wenn er seinem Vater nacheifern will; **you should ~ ~ ~ your father's principles** du solltest die Grundsätze deines Vaters anstreben; **I doubt whether he can ~ ~ ~ his brother** ich bezweifle, daß er seinem Bruder das Wasser reichen kann.
live² [laɪv] [1] *adj* **(a)** *(alive)* lebend; *issue, question* aktuell ◆ **a real ~ duke** ein waschechter Herzog; **~ births** Lebendgeburten *pl;* **~-cell therapy** Frischzellentherapie *f.*
(b) *(having power or energy) coal* glühend; *match* ungebraucht; *cartridge, shell* scharf; *(Elec)* geladen ◆ **"danger, ~ wires!"** „Vorsicht Hochspannung!"; **she's a real ~ wire** *(fig)* sie ist ein richtiges Energiebündel.
(c) *(Rad, TV)* live ◆ **a ~ programme** eine Livesendung.
[2] *adv (Rad, TV)* live, direkt.
liveable ['lɪvəbl] *adj see* **livable.**
lived-in ['lɪvdɪn] *adj feel* gemütlich, behaglich.
live-in ['lɪvɪn] *adj cook, maid* in Haus wohnend.
livelihood ['laɪvlɪhʊd] *n* Lebensunterhalt *m* ◆ **rice is their ~** sie verdienen ihren Lebensunterhalt mit Reis; **to earn a ~** sich *(dat)* seinen Lebensunterhalt verdienen; **they earned a ~ from farming** sie lebten von der Landwirtschaft.
liveliness ['laɪvlɪnɪs] *n see adj* Lebhaftigkeit *f;* Lebendigkeit *f;* Dynamik *f;* Schnelligkeit *f;* Aufgewecktheit *f.*
livelong ['lɪvlɒŋ] *adj*: **all the ~ day/night** den lieben langen Tag, den ganzen Tag über/die ganze Nacht durch.
lively ['laɪvlɪ] *adj (+er)* lebhaft; *scene, account* lebendig; *campaign* dynamisch; *pace* flott; *mind* wach, aufgeweckt ◆ **things are getting ~** es geht hoch her *(inf)*; **at 8 things will start to get ~** um 8 wird es dann lebhafter; **we had a ~ time** es war viel los *(inf)*; **he's having a ~ time of it in his new job** in seiner neuen Stelle kann er sich über Langeweile nicht beklagen; **to look ~** *(speed up)* schnell machen.
liven up ['laɪvən'ʌp] [1] *vt sep* beleben, Leben bringen in *(+acc) (inf).*
[2] *vi* in Schwung kommen; *(person)* aufleben.
liver¹ ['lɪvəʳ] *n* **clean ~** solider Mensch; **he's a fast ~** er führt ein flottes Leben *(inf).*
liver² *n (Anat, Cook)* Leber *f* ◆ **~ pâté** Leberpastete *f;* **~ sausage, ~ wurst** Leberwurst *f.*
liveried ['lɪvərɪd] *adj* livriert.
liverish ['lɪvərɪʃ] *adj* **(a) to be ~** etwas mit der Leber haben; **I felt a bit ~ after the party** mir ging es nach der Party ziemlich mies *(inf).* **(b)** *(bad-tempered)* mürrisch.
Liverpudlian [ˌlɪvə'pʌdlɪən] [1] *n* Liverpooler(in *f*) *m.*
[2] *adj* Liverpooler.
liverwort ['lɪvəwɜːt] *n (Bot)* Lebermoos *nt; (hepatica)* Leberblümchen *nt.*
livery ['lɪvərɪ] *n* Livree *f; (fig liter)* Kleid *nt.*
livery: ~ company *n* Zunft *f;* **~ stable** *n* Mietstall *m.*
lives [laɪvz] *pl of* **life.**
livestock ['laɪvstɒk] *n* Vieh *nt; (number of animals)* Viehbestand *m.*
livid ['lɪvɪd] *adj* **(a)** *(inf)* wütend, fuchsteufelswild *(inf)* ◆ **to be ~ with rage** wütend sein; **he got ~ with us** er hatte eine Stinkwut auf uns *(inf).* **(b)** bleifarben ◆ **the sky was a ~ grey** der Himmel war blaugrau.
living ['lɪvɪŋ] [1] *adj* lebend; *example, faith* lebendig ◆ **a ~ creature** ein Lebewesen *nt;* **not a ~ soul** keine Menschenseele; **(with)in ~ memory** seit Menschengedenken; **he is ~ proof of ...** er ist der lebende Beweis für ...; **her existence was a ~ death** ihr Leben war eine einzige Qual; **~ or dead** tot oder lebendig.
[2] *n* **(a) the ~** *pl* die Lebenden *pl.*
(b) *(way of ~)* **the art of ~** Lebenskunst *f;* **he is fond of good ~** er lebt gern gut; **gracious ~** die vornehme Lebensart; **loose ~** lockerer Lebenswandel; *see* **standard.**
(c) *(livelihood)* Lebensunterhalt *m* ◆ **to earn** *or* **make a ~** sich *(dat)* seinen Lebensunterhalt verdienen; **he sells brushes for a ~** er verkauft Bürsten, um sich *(dat)* seinen Lebensunterhalt zu verdienen; **they made a bare ~ out of the soil** sie hatten mit dem Ertrag des Bodens ihr Auskommen; **to work for one's ~** arbeiten, um sich *(dat)* seinen Lebensunterhalt zu verdienen; **some of us have to work for a ~** es gibt auch Leute, die arbeiten müssen.
(d) *(Eccl)* Pfründe *f.*
living: ~ conditions *npl* Wohnverhältnisse *pl;* **~ room** *n* Wohnzimmer *nt;* **~ space** *n (in house)* Wohnraum *m; (for a nation)* Lebensraum *m;* **~ wage** *n* ausreichender Lohn; **£65 a week is not a ~ wage** von £ 65 pro Woche kann man nicht leben.
Livy ['lɪvɪ] *n* Livius *m.*
lizard ['lɪzəd] *n* Eidechse *f; (including larger forms also)* Echse *f.*
ll *abbr of* **lines** Z.
llama ['lɑːmə] *n* Lama *nt.*
LlB *abbr of* **Bachelor of Laws.**
LLD *abbr of* **Doctor of Laws** Dr. jur.
LMT *(US) abbr of* **local mean time** Ortszeit *f.*
LNG *n abbr of* **liquefied natural gas** LNG *nt,* Flüssiggas *nt.*
lo [ləʊ] *interj (old)* siehe *(old)* ◆ **~ and behold!** und siehe da.
loach [ləʊtʃ] *n* Schmerle *f.*
load [ləʊd] [1] *n* **(a)** *(sth carried, burden)* Last *f; (cargo)* Ladung *f; (on girder, axle etc, fig)* Belastung, Last *f* ◆ **what sort of ~ was the ship/lorry carrying?** was hatte das Schiff/der Lastwagen geladen?; **to put a ~ on sth** etw belasten; **to put too heavy a ~ on sth** etw überlasten; **the maximum ~ for that bridge is 10 tons** die maximale Tragkraft *or* -fähigkeit dieser Brücke beträgt 10 Tonnen; **an arm-~ of shopping** ein Armvoll Einkäufe; **a train-~ of passengers** ein Zug voll Reisender; **(work) ~** (Arbeits)pensum *nt;* **he has a heavy teaching ~ this term** er hat in diesem Semester eine hohe Stundenzahl; **he carries a heavy ~ of responsibility** er trägt eine schwere Verantwortung; **that's a ~ off my mind!** da fällt mir ein Stein vom Herzen!; **to take a ~ off sb's mind** jdm eine

Last von der Seele nehmen.
(b) *(Elec) (supplied)* Leistung *f*; *(carried)* Spannung *f*.
(c) *(inf usages)* **~s of, a ~ of** massenhaft *(inf)*, jede Menge *(inf)*; **thanks, we have ~s** danke, wir haben jede Menge *(inf)*; **it's a ~ of old rubbish** das ist alles Blödsinn *(inf) or* Quatsch *(inf)*; *(film, book, translation)* das ist alles Mist! *(inf)*; **to take on a ~** (ganz schön) einen heben *(inf)*; **get a ~ of this!** *(listen)* hör dir das mal an!; *(look)* guck dir das mal an! *(inf)*.
[2] *vt* **(a)** *goods* laden; *lorry etc* beladen ◆ **the ship was ~ed with bananas** das Schiff hatte Bananen geladen.
(b) *(burden, weigh down)* beladen ◆ **the branch was ~ed with pears** der Ast war mit Birnen überladen.
(c) *(fig)* überhäufen ◆ **to ~ sb with honours** jdn mit Ehrungen überschütten *or* -häufen; **the whole matter is ~ed with problems** die Angelegenheit steckt voller Probleme; **they ~ed themselves with debts** sie haben sich in Schulden gestürzt.
(d) *gun* laden ◆ **to ~ a camera** einen Film (in einen Fotoapparat) einlegen; **is this camera ~ed?** ist ein Film im Apparat?
(e) *dice* fälschen, präparieren ◆ **to ~ the dice** *(fig)* mit gezinkten Karten spielen; **to ~ the dice against sb** *(fig)* jdn übervorteilen; **the dice had been ~ed against him** *(fig)* es war Schiebung *(inf) or* ein abgekartetes Spiel.
(f) *(Comput)* laden.
[3] *vi* **(a)** laden ◆ **~ing bay** Ladeplatz *m*; **"~ing and unloading"** „Be- und Entladen".
(b) (~ *gun*) laden; (~ *camera*) einen Film einlegen ◆ **~!** Gewehr(e) laden!; **how does this gun/camera ~?** wie lädt man dieses Gewehr?/wie legt man einen Film in diesen Apparat ein?
(c) *(Comput)* laden.
◆**load down** *vt sep* (schwer) beladen; *(fig)* überladen ◆ **the poor animal was ~ed ~ by its burden** das arme Tier wurde von seiner Last niedergedrückt; **he is ~ed ~ with sorrows** Sorgen lasten schwer auf ihm *or* drücken ihn.
◆**load up** [1] *vi* aufladen.
[2] *vt sep* **(a)** lorry beladen; *goods* aufladen. **(b)** *(Comput)* laden.
loadable ['ləʊdəbl] *adj (Comput)* ladbar.
load: ~-bearing *adj wall* tragend; **~ capacity** *n (Elec)* Belastung(sfähigkeit) *f*; *(of lorry)* maximale Nutzlast.
loaded ['ləʊdɪd] *adj* beladen; *dice* falsch, präpariert; *camera* mit eingelegtem Film; *gun* geladen ◆ **a ~ question** eine Fangfrage; **he's ~** *(inf: rich)* er ist stink- *or* steinreich *(inf)*, er schwimmt im Geld *(inf)*; *(sl: drunk)* der hat ganz schön geladen *(inf)*.
load: ~ line *n* Ladelinie *f*; **~star** *n see* **lodestar**; **~stone** *n see* **lodestone**.
loaf [ləʊf] *n, pl* **loaves** Brot *nt*; *(unsliced)* (Brot)laib *m*; *(meat ~)* Hackbraten *m* ◆ **a ~ of bread** ein (Laib) Brot; **a small white ~** ein kleines Weißbrot; **half a ~ is better than none** *or* **than no bread** *(Prov)* (wenig ist) besser als gar nichts; **use your ~!** *(sl)* streng deinen Grips an *(inf)*; **use your ~, show some tact** *(sl)* denk mal ein bißchen, und sei etwas taktvoller *(inf)*.
◆**loaf about** *or* **around** *vi (inf)* faulenzen ◆ **he ~ed ~ the house all day** er hing den ganzen Tag zu Hause herum *(inf)*.
loafer ['ləʊfəʳ] *n* **(a)** *(inf: idler)* Faulenzer, Nichtstuer *m*. **(b)** *(US: casual shoe)* Halbschuh, Trotteur *m*.
loam [ləʊm] *n* Lehmerde *f*.
loamy ['ləʊmɪ] *adj (+er)* lehmig ◆ **~ soil** Lehmboden *m*.
loan [ləʊn] [1] *n* **(a)** *(thing lent)* Leihgabe *f*; *(from bank etc)* Darlehen *nt*; *(public ~)* Anleihe *f* ◆ **my friend let me have the money as a ~** mein Freund hat mir das Geld geliehen; **it's not a gift, it's a ~** es ist nicht geschenkt, sondern nur geliehen; **government ~s** Regierungsdarlehen *nt*; *(borrowings)* Staatsanleihen *pl*.
(b) **I asked for the ~ of the bicycle** ich bat darum, das Fahrrad ausleihen zu dürfen; **he gave me the ~ of his bicycle** er hat mir sein Fahrrad geliehen; **conditions governing the ~ of this book** Leihbedingungen *pl* für dieses Buch; **it's on ~** es ist geliehen; *(out on ~)* es ist verliehen *or* ausgeliehen; **the machinery is on ~ from the American government** die Maschinen sind eine Leihgabe der amerikanischen Regierung; **to have sth on ~** etw geliehen haben *(from* von).
[2] *vt* leihen *(to sb* jdm).
loan: ~ account *n* Darlehenskonto, Kreditkonto *nt*; **~-back facility** *n (Insur)* Beleihungsmöglichkeit *f*; **~ capital** *n* Anleihekapital *nt*; **~ collection** *n* Leihgaben *pl*; **~ shark** *n (inf)* Kredithai *m (inf)*; **~ word** *n* Lehnwort *nt*.
loath, loth [ləʊθ] *adj* **to be ~ to do sth** etw ungern tun; **~ as I am to leave** so ungern ich auch gehe; **he was ~ for us to go** er ließ uns ungern gehen; **nothing ~** *(old)* bereitwillig(st).
loathe [ləʊð] *vt thing, person* verabscheuen; *modern art, spinach, jazz etc* nicht ausstehen können ◆ **I ~ doing it** *(in general)* ich hasse es, das zu tun; *(on particular occasion)* es ist mir zuwider, das zu tun.
loathing ['ləʊðɪŋ] *n* Abscheu *m*.
loathsome ['ləʊðsəm] *adj thing, person* abscheulich, widerlich; *task* verhaßt; *deformity* abstoßend; *wound* ekelerregend.
loathsomeness ['ləʊðsəmnɪs] *n see adj* Abscheulichkeit, Widerlichkeit *f*; Verhaßtheit *f*; abstoßender Anblick.
loaves [ləʊvz] *n, pl of* **loaf**.
lob [lɒb] [1] *n (Tennis)* Lob *m*.
[2] *vt ball* im Lob spielen, lobben ◆ **he ~bed the grenade over the wall** er warf die Granate im hohen Bogen über die Mauer; **to ~ sth over to sb** jdm etw zuwerfen; **~ it over!** wirf es herüber!
[3] *vi (Tennis)* lobben.
lobby ['lɒbɪ] [1] *n (entrance hall)* Vor- *or* Eingangshalle *f*; *(of hotel, theatre)* Foyer *nt*; *(corridor)* Flur, Korridor *m*; *(anteroom, waiting room)* Vorzimmer *nt*; *(place in Parliament)* Lobby *f*; *(Pol)* Lobby, Interessengruppe *f or* -verband *m* ◆ **the railway ~** die Eisenbahnlobby.
[2] *vt* **to ~ one's Member of Parliament** auf seinen Abgeordneten Einfluß nehmen; **to ~ a bill through parliament** als Interessengruppe ein Gesetz durchs Parlament bringen.
[3] *vi* auf die Abgeordneten Einfluß nehmen, Lobbyist sein ◆ **they are ~ing for this reform** die Lobbyisten versuchen, diese Reform durchzubringen; **the farmers are ~ing for higher subsidies** die Bauernlobby will höhere Subventionen durchsetzen.
lobbying ['lɒbɪɪŋ] *n* Beeinflussung *f* von Abgeordneten (durch Lobbies) ◆ **the Prime Minister refused to be influenced by ~** der Premierminister wollte sich nicht von Lobbies *or* Interessenverbänden beeinflussen lassen.
lobbyist ['lɒbɪɪst] *n* Lobbyist *m*.
lobe [ləʊb] *n (Anat) (of ear)* Ohrläppchen *nt*; *(of lungs, brain)* Lappen, Lobus *(spec) m*; *(of leaf)* Ausbuchtung *f*.
lobed [ləʊbd] *adj* gelappt.
lobelia [ləʊ'bi:lɪə] *n* Lobelie *f*.
lobotomy [ləʊ'bɒtəmɪ] *n (Med)* Lobotomie *f*.
lobster ['lɒbstəʳ] *n* Hummer *m* ◆ **~ pot** Hummer(fang)korb *m*.
local ['ləʊkəl] [1] *adj* **(a)** Orts-, örtlich; *(in this area)* hiesig; *(in that area)* dortig; *radio station* Regional-; *newspaper also* Lokal-; *train* Nahverkehrs-; *politician* Kommunal-; *anaesthetic* lokal, örtlich ◆ **all the ~ residents** alle Ortsansässigen *pl*; **he's a ~ man** er ist ein Ortsansässiger, er ist von hier *(inf)*; **~ authorities** städtische Behörden *pl*; *(council)* Gemeindeverwaltung *f*; Stadtverwaltung *f*; Stadt- und Kreisverwaltung *f*; **~ government** Kommunal- *or* Gemeindeverwaltung *f*; Kreisverwaltung *f*; **he is in ~ government** er arbeitet bei der Stadtverwaltung, er ist bei der Stadt *(inf)*; **reform of ~ government** Gemeindereform *f*; **~ opinion is against the change** die öffentliche Meinung am Ort ist gegen die Änderung; **the latest ~ gossip** der neueste Klatsch (hier/dort); **~ bus** Stadtbus *m*; *(serving the immediate locality)* Nahverkehrsbus *m*; **~ colour** Lokalkolorit *nt*; **go into your ~ branch** gehen Sie zu Ihrer Zweigstelle; **vote for your ~ candidate** wählen Sie den Kandidaten Ihres Wahlkreises; **accents with the usual ~ variations** Dialekte mit den üblichen regionalen Unterschieden; **one of our ~ sons** einer der Söhne unserer Gemeinde/Stadt; **we used the ~ shops when we were in Spain** wir haben in den Läden der Einheimischen eingekauft, als wir in Spanien waren; **our village hasn't got a ~ butcher** unser Dorf hat keinen eigenen Schlachter; **there are two ~ grocers** es gibt zwei Lebensmittelhändler am Ort; **the ~ shops aren't very good** die dortigen/hiesigen Geschäfte sind nicht sehr gut; **our ~ doctor back home in Canada** unser Arzt zu Hause in Kanada; **what are their main ~ products there?** was wird dort hauptsächlich erzeugt?; **our best ~ wine** der beste hiesige Wein; **the ~ wine over there will make you sick** von dem dortigen Wein wird es einem schlecht.
(b) **~ area network** *(Comput)* lokales Rechnernetz, LAN *nt*.
[2] *n* **(a)** *(pub)* **the ~** *(in village)* der Dorfkrug, die Dorfkneipe *(inf)*; *(in community)* das Stammlokal; **our ~** unsere Stammkneipe *(inf)*, unser Stammlokal *nt*.
(b) *(born in)* Einheimische(r) *mf*; *(living in)* Einwohner(in *f*) *m*.
locale [ləʊ'kɑ:l] *n* Schauplatz *m*.
locality [ləʊ'kælɪtɪ] *n* Gegend *f* ◆ **in the ~ of the crime** am Ort des Verbrechens.
localize ['ləʊkəlaɪz] *vt* **(a)** *(detect)* lokalisieren. **(b)** **this custom, once widespread, has now become very ~d** die einst weitverbreitete Sitte ist jetzt auf wenige Orte begrenzt.
locally ['ləʊkəlɪ] *adv* am Ort; *(Med)* örtlich ◆ **houses are dear ~** Häuser sind hier teuer; **I prefer to shop ~** ich kaufe lieber im Ort ein; **the shops are situated ~** die Geschäfte befinden sich in günstiger Lage; **do you live ~?** wohnen Sie am Ort?; **I work in Glasgow but I don't live ~** ich arbeite in Glasgow, wohne aber nicht hier/da; **was she well-known ~?** war sie in dieser Gegend sehr bekannt?; **if each district is ~ governed** wenn jeder Bezirk regional regiert wird; **the plant grows ~** die Pflanze wächst in dieser Gegend.
locate [ləʊ'keɪt] *vt* **(a)** *(position)* legen; *headquarters* einrichten; *(including act of building)* bauen, errichten; *sportsground, playground* anlegen; *road* bauen, anlegen ◆ **to be ~d at** *or* **in** sich befinden in *(+dat)*; **the hotel is centrally ~d** das Hotel liegt zentral; **where shall we ~ the new branch?** wohin sollen wir die neue Zweigstelle legen?
(b) *(find)* ausfindig machen; *submarine, plane* orten.
location [ləʊ'keɪʃən] *n* **(a)** *(position, site)* Lage *f*; *(of building also)* Standort *m*; *(of road)* Führung *f*; *(of ship)* Position *f* ◆ **this would be an ideal ~ for the road/airport** das wäre ein ideales Gelände für die Straße/den Flughafen; **they shifted the ~ of the factory** sie verlegten die Fabrik; **the precise ~ of the earthquake** wo das Erdbeben genau stattgefunden hat; **the doctors haven't determined the precise ~ of the tumour** die Ärzte haben den Tumor noch nicht genau lokalisiert; **that shop is in a good ~** dieses Geschäft hat eine gute Lage.
(b) *(positioning, siting)* *(of building, road)* Bau *m*; *(of park)* Anlage *f*; *(of headquarters)* *(removal)* Einrichtung *f*; *(building)* Errichtung *f* ◆ **they discussed the ~ of the road/airport** sie diskutierten, wo die Straße/der Flughafen gebaut werden soll.
(c) *(finding)* Auffinden *nt*; *(of tumour)* Lokalisierung *f*; *(of star, ship)* Ortung, Positionsbestimmung *f* ◆ **the ~ of oil in the North Sea** die Entdeckung von Erdöl in der Nordsee.

(d) *(Film)* Drehort *m* ◆ **to be on ~ in Mexico** *(person)* bei Außenaufnahmen in Mexiko sein; **part of the film was done on ~ in Mexico** Außenaufnahmen für den Film wurden in Mexiko gedreht; **we had a lot of ~ work** wir mußten viele Außenaufnahmen machen.

locative ['lɒkətɪv] *n* Lokativ *m.*

loc cit ['lɒk'sɪt] *abbr of* **loco citato** l.c., a.a.O.

loch [lɒx] *n (Scot)* See *m*; *(sea ~)* Meeresarm *m.*

loci ['lɒkiː] *pl of* **locus.**

lock[1] [lɒk] *n (of hair)* Locke *f.*

lock[2] [1] *n* **(a)** *(on door, box, gun)* Schloß *nt* ◆ **to put sb/sth under ~ and key** jdn hinter Schloß und Riegel bringen/etw wegschließen; **to keep money under ~ and key** Geld unter Verschluß halten; **he offered me the house ~, stock and barrel** er bot mir das Haus mit allem Drum und Dran an *(inf)*; **they destroyed it ~, stock and barrel** sie haben es total zerstört; **to condemn sth ~, stock and barrel** etw in Grund und Boden verdammen; **they rejected the idea ~, stock and barrel** sie lehnten die Idee in Bausch und Bogen ab; **he swallowed my story ~, stock and barrel** er hat mir die Geschichte voll und ganz abgenommen; **it is finished ~, stock and barrel** es ist ganz und gar fertig.
(b) *(canal ~)* Schleuse *f.*
(c) *(hold)* Fesselgriff *m.*
(d) *(Aut)* Wendekreis *m* ◆ **the steering wheel was on** *or* **at full ~** das Lenkrad war voll eingeschlagen.
[2] *vt door etc* ab- *or* zuschließen; *steering wheel* sperren, arretieren; *wheel* blockieren; *(Comput) keyboard* verriegeln ◆ **to ~ sb in a room** jdn in einem Zimmer einschließen; **the armies were ~ed in combat** die Armeen waren in Kämpfe verwickelt; **they were ~ed in each other's arms** sie hielten sich fest umschlungen; **he ~ed my arm in a firm grip** er umklammerte meinen Arm mit festem Griff; **this bar ~s the wheel in position** diese Stange hält das Rad fest; **the chains were ~ed round his arms** die Ketten waren an seinen Armen festgemacht; *see* **stable[2].**
[3] *vi* schließen; *(wheel)* blockieren ◆ **a suitcase that ~s** ein verschließbarer Koffer, ein Koffer, der sich abschließen läßt; **his jaw had ~ed fast** er hatte Mundsperre; **the lion's jaws ~ed round his arm** der Kiefer des Löwen schloß sich fest um seinen Arm.

◆**lock away** *vt sep* wegschließen; *person* einsperren ◆ **he ~ed the money ~ in his safe** er schloß das Geld in seinem Safe ein.

◆**lock in** *vt sep* **(a)** einschließen ◆ **to be ~ed ~** eingesperrt sein. **(b) we're ~ed ~ to this supplier** wir sind an diesen Lieferanten gebunden; **I don't want to get myself ~ed ~** ich will mich nicht zu sehr binden.

◆**lock on** [1] *vi (spaceship etc)* gekoppelt werden *(to* mit*)* ◆ **the radio automatically ~s ~ to a channel** das Radio hat automatische Feineinstellung; **the missile ~s ~ to its target** das Geschoß richtet sich auf das Ziel; **his mind has ~ed ~ to one way of thinking** er hat sich auf eine Denkart festgefahren.
[2] *vt sep radio, scanner* einstellen *(to auf +acc)* ◆ **with a padlock he ~ed the extra piece ~** er befestigte das zusätzliche Stück mit einem Anhängeschloß.

◆**lock out** *vt sep* aussperren.

◆**lock together** [1] *vi (rockets)* (miteinander) gekoppelt werden; *(pieces of jigsaw)* sich zusammenstecken lassen.
[2] *vt sep rockets* (miteinander) koppeln; *pieces of jigsaw* zusammenstecken ◆ **~ed ~ in a passionate embrace** in einer leidenschaftlichen Umarmung fest umschlungen.

◆**lock up** [1] *vt sep* **(a)** *thing, house* abschließen; *person* einsperren ◆ **to ~ sth ~ in sth** etw in etw *(dat)* einschließen; **he ought to be ~ed ~!** den müßte man einsperren! **(b)** *(Comm) capital* fest anlegen.
[2] *vi* abschließen.

locker ['lɒkəʳ] *n* Schließfach *nt*; *(Naut, Mil)* Spind *m* ◆ **~ room** Umkleideraum *m.*

locket ['lɒkɪt] *n* Medaillon *nt.*

lock: ~ gate *n* Schleusentor *nt*; **~jaw** *n* Wundstarrkrampf *m*; **~ keeper** *n* Schleusenwärter *m*; **~nut** *n* Gegenmutter *f*; **~out** *n* Aussperrung *f*; **~smith** *n* Schlosser *m*; **~stitch** *n* Steppstich *m*; **~-up** *n* **(a)** *(shop)* Laden *m*, Geschäft *nt*; *(garage)* Garage *f*; **(b)** *(prison)* Gefängnis *nt.*

loco[1] *n (Rail inf)* Lok *f (inf).*

loco[2] *adj (esp US sl)* bekloppt *(sl)* ◆ **he's gone ~** der spinnt *(inf).*

loco citato [ˌlɒkəʊsɪ'tɑːtəʊ] *see* **loc cit.**

locomotion [ˌləʊkə'məʊʃən] *n* Fortbewegung *f* ◆ **means of ~** Fortbewegungsmittel *nt.*

locomotive [ˌləʊkə'məʊtɪv] [1] *adj* Fortbewegungs- ◆ **~ power** Fortbewegungsfähigkeit *f.*
[2] *n* Lokomotive *f.*

locum (tenens) ['ləʊkəm('tenenz)] *n* Vertreter(in *f*) *m.*

locus ['lɒkəs] *n, pl* **loci** geometrischer Ort.

locust ['ləʊkəst] *n* Heuschrecke *f* ◆ **~ tree** Robinie *f.*

locution [lə'kjuːʃən] *n* Ausdrucksweise *f*; *(expression)* Ausdruck *m* ◆ **a set ~** eine feste *or* feststehende Redewendung.

lode [ləʊd] *n* Ader *f.*

lode: ~star *n* Leitstern *m*; Polarstern *m*; *(fig) (person)* Leitbild *nt*; *(principle)* Leitstern *m*; **~stone** *n* Magnetit, Magneteisenstein *m.*

lodge [lɒdʒ] [1] *n (in grounds)* Pförtnerhaus *nt*; *(of Red Indian)* Wigwam *m*; *(shooting ~, skiing ~ etc)* Hütte *f*; *(porter's ~)* Pförtnerloge *f*; *(in school, Univ)* Pedellzimmer *nt*; *(masonic ~)* Loge *f*; *(of beaver)* Bau *m.*
[2] *vt* **(a)** *person* unterbringen.
(b) *complaint* einlegen *(with* bei*)*; *charge* einreichen.
(c) *(insert) spear* stoßen ◆ **to be ~d** (fest)stecken.
(d) *jewellery, money* deponieren, hinterlegen.
[3] *vi* **(a)** *(live)* (zur *or* in Untermiete) wohnen *(with sb, at sb's* bei jdm*)*; *(at boarding house)* wohnen *(in* in *+dat)*.
(b) *(object, bullet)* steckenbleiben.

lodger ['lɒdʒəʳ] *n* Untermieter(in *f*) *m* ◆ **I was a ~ there once** ich habe dort einmal zur *or* in Untermiete gewohnt; **she takes ~s** sie vermietet (Zimmer), sie nimmt Untermieter auf.

lodging ['lɒdʒɪŋ] *n* **(a)** Unterkunft *f* ◆ **they gave me a night's ~** sie gaben mir Unterkunft *or* ein Zimmer für die Nacht.
(b) ~s *pl* ein möbliertes Zimmer; möblierte Zimmer *pl* ◆ **where are your ~s?** wo wohnen Sie?; **we took ~s with Mrs B** wir mieteten uns bei Frau B ein; **~ house** Pension *f.*

loess ['ləʊɪs] *n* Löß *m.*

loft [lɒft] [1] *n* **(a)** Boden, Speicher *m*; *(hay~)* Heuboden *m* ◆ **in the ~** auf dem Boden *or* Speicher. **(b)** *(organ ~, choir ~)* Empore *f.*
[2] *vt (Sport)* hochschlagen ◆ **he ~ed the ball over the fence** er schlug den Ball im hohen Bogen über den Zaun.

loftily ['lɒftɪlɪ] *adv* hoch; *say, speak* stolz, hochmütig.

loftiness ['lɒftɪnɪs] *n* **(a)** *(of tree, mountain)* Höhe *f.* **(b)** *(of sentiments)* Erhabenheit *f*; *(of prose)* erlesener *or* gehobener *or* hochtrabender *(pej)* Stil ◆ **the ~ of his ambitions/ideals** seine hochfliegenden Ambitionen/seine hohen *or* hochfliegenden Ideale. **(c)** *(haughtiness)* Hochmütigkeit *f.*

lofty ['lɒftɪ] [1] *adj (+er)* **(a)** *(high)* hoch. **(b)** *(noble) ideals* hoch(fliegend); *ambitions* hochfliegend; *sentiments* erhaben; *prose, style* erlesen, gehoben, hochtrabend *(pej)*. **(c)** *(haughty)* stolz, hochmütig.
[2] *n (inf)* Lange(r) *mf (inf).*

log[1] [lɒg] *n* Baumstamm *m*; *(short length of tree trunk)* Block, Klotz *m*; *(for a fire)* Scheit *nt* ◆ **to sleep like a ~** wie ein Stein schlafen; **~ cabin** Blockhaus *nt or* -hütte *f*; **~ rolling** *(Pol)* Kuhhandel *m (inf)*; *(Sport) Wettkampf m, bei dem zwei Gegner auf einem im Wasser schwimmenden Baumstamm stehen und sich durch Drehen desselben zum Fallen bringen.*

log[2] [1] *n* **(a)** *(Naut: apparatus)* Log *nt.* **(b)** *(record)* Aufzeichnungen *pl*; *(Naut)* Logbuch *nt* ◆ **to make** *or* **keep a ~ of sth** über etw *(acc)* Buch führen.
[2] *vt* **(a)** Buch führen über *(+acc)*; *(Naut)* (ins Logbuch) eintragen. **(b)** *(travel)* zurücklegen.

◆**log in** *vi (Comput)* einloggen.

◆**log off** *(Comput)* [1] *vi* ausloggen.
[2] *vt* ausloggen, abmelden.

◆**log on** *(Comput)* [1] *vi* einloggen.
[2] *vt* einloggen, anmelden.

◆**log out** *vi (Comput)* ausloggen.

◆**log up** *vt sep (Naut)* (ins Logbuch) eintragen; *(clock up) distance* zurücklegen; *(fig) successes* einheimsen *(inf).*

log[3] *abbr of* **logarithm** log ◆ **~ tables** Logarithmentafel *f.*

loganberry ['ləʊgənbərɪ] *n (fruit)* Loganbeere *f*; *(bush)* Loganbeerbusch *m.*

logarithm ['lɒgərɪθəm] *n* Logarithmus *m.*

logarithmic [ˌlɒgə'rɪθmɪk] *adj* logarithmisch.

log book *n (Naut)* Logbuch *nt*; *(Aviat)* Bordbuch *nt*; *(of lorries)* Fahrtenbuch *nt*; *(Aut: registration book)* Kraftfahrzeug- *or* Kfz-Brief *m*; *(in hospitals, police stations etc)* Dienstbuch *nt.*

loggerheads ['lɒgəhedz] *npl*: **to be at ~ (with sb)** Streit (mit jdm) haben, sich *(dat)* (mit jdm) in den Haaren liegen *(inf)*; **they were constantly at ~ with the authorities** sie standen mit den Behörden dauernd auf Kriegsfuß; **his views are at ~ with the traditional theory** seine Auffassungen vertragen sich überhaupt nicht mit der herkömmlichen Lehre.

loggia ['lɒdʒɪə] *n* Loggia *f.*

logging ['lɒgɪŋ] *n* Holzfällen *nt.*

logic ['lɒdʒɪk] *n* Logik *f* ◆ **there's no ~ in that** das ist völlig unlogisch; **~ analyzer** *(Comput)* Logikanalysator *m.*

logical ['lɒdʒɪkəl] *adj* logisch; *conclusion also* folgerichtig ◆ **he has a ~ mind** er denkt logisch.

logically ['lɒdʒɪkəlɪ] *adv think, argue* logisch ◆ **~, he may be right** logisch gesehen könnte er recht haben.

logician [lɒ'dʒɪʃən] *n* Logiker(in *f*) *m.*

logistic [lɒ'dʒɪstɪk] *adj* logistisch.

logistics [lɒ'dʒɪstɪks] *n sing* Logistik *f.*

logo ['ləʊgəʊ, 'lɒgəʊ] *n* Logo, Emblem *nt.*

loin [lɔɪn] *n* Lende *f* ◆ **~ cloth** Lendenschurz *m*; *see* **gird up.**

loiter ['lɔɪtəʳ] [1] *vt* **to ~ away the time** die Zeit verbummeln *(inf).*
[2] *vi* **(a)** *(waste time)* trödeln, bummeln.
(b) *(hang around suspiciously)* sich herumtreiben, herumlungern ◆ **"no ~ing"** „unberechtigter Aufenthalt verboten"; **to ~ with intent** sich verdächtig machen, sich auffällig verhalten.

◆**loiter about** *or* **around** *vi* herumlungern.

loiterer ['lɔɪtərəʳ] *n* Herumtreiber(in *f*), Herumlungerer *m*; *(straggler)* Nachzügler(in *f*), Bummelant *m (inf).*

loll [lɒl] *vi* lümmeln ◆ **stand up straight, don't ~** stell dich gerade hin, laß dich nicht so hängen *(inf)*; **he was ~ing in an easy chair** er hing *(inf) or* räkelte sich im Sessel; **to ~ against sth** sich (lässig) gegen *or* an etw *(acc)* lehnen.

◆**loll about** *or* **around** *vi* herumlümmeln, herumhängen *(inf).*

◆**loll back** *vi* sich zurücklehnen.

◆**loll out** *vi* heraushängen ◆ **the dog's tongue was ~ing ~** dem Hund hing die Zunge heraus.

lollipop ['lɒlɪpɒp] *n* Lutscher *m*; *(iced ~)* Eis *nt* am Stiel ◆ **~ man/woman** *(Brit* *inf)* ≃ Schülerlotse *m.*

lollop ['lɒləp] *vi* (*also* **~ along**) (*animal*) trotten, zotteln; (*puppy, rabbit*) hoppeln; (*person*) zockeln ◆ **he ran with a ~ing stride** er rannte in großen, schlaksigen Sätzen.

lolly ['lɒlɪ] *n* **(a)** (*inf: lollipop*) Lutscher *m* ◆ **an ice(d) ~** ein Eis *nt* am Stiel. **(b)** (*sl: money*) Mäuse (*sl*), Piepen (*sl*) *pl.*

Lombard ['lɒmbɑːd] [1] *adj* lombardisch.
[2] *n* Lombarde *m*, Lombardin *f.*

Lombardy ['lɒmbədɪ] *n* Lombardei *f.*

London ['lʌndən] [1] *n* London *nt.*
[2] *adj* Londoner.

Londoner ['lʌndənə^r] *n* Londoner(in *f*) *m.*

lone [ləʊn] *adj* einzeln, einsam; (*only*) einzig ◆ **he prefers to play a ~ hand** er macht lieber alles im Alleingang; **~ wolf** (*fig*) Einzelgänger *m.*

loneliness ['ləʊnlɪnɪs] *n* Einsamkeit *f.*

lonely ['ləʊnlɪ] *adj* (*+er*) einsam ◆ **~ hearts ad** Kontaktanzeige *f.*

loner ['ləʊnə^r] *n* Einzelgänger(in *f*) *m.*

lonesome ['ləʊnsəm] *adj* (*esp US*) einsam.

long[1] *abbr of* **longitude** L.

long[2] [lɒŋ] [1] *adj* (*+er*) **(a)** (*in size*) lang; *glass* hoch; *journey* weit ◆ **it is 6 metres ~** es ist 6 Meter lang; **to be ~ in the leg** lange Beine haben; **to pull a ~ face** ein langes Gesicht machen; **it's a ~ way** das ist weit; **it's a ~ way to Hamburg** nach Hamburg ist es weit; **to have a ~ memory** ein gutes Gedächtnis haben; **to be ~ in the tooth** (*inf*) nicht mehr der/die Jüngste sein; **surely he is a bit ~ in the tooth to be climbing Everest** ist er nicht schon ein bißchen (zu) alt, um den Everest zu besteigen?
(b) (*in time*) lang; *job* langwierig ◆ **it's a ~ time since I saw her** ich habe sie schon lange *or* seit längerer Zeit nicht mehr gesehen; **will you need it for a ~ time?** brauchen Sie es lange?; **he's been here (for) a ~ time** er ist schon lange hier; **she was abroad for a ~ time** sie war lange *or* (eine) lange Zeit im Ausland; **well hullo, it's been a ~ time** hallo, schon lange nicht mehr gesehen; **~ time no see** (*inf*) sieht man dich auch mal wieder? (*inf*); **to take a ~ look at sth** etw lange *or* ausgiebig betrachten; **how ~ is the film?** wie lange dauert der Film?; **a year is 12 months ~** ein Jahr hat 12 Monate; **how ~ are your holidays?** wie lange haben Sie Urlaub?; **to take the ~ view** etw auf lange Sicht betrachten.
(c) (*Poet, Phon*) *vowel, syllable* lang.
(d) a ~ drink (*mixed*) ein Longdrink *m*; (*beer*) ein Bier *nt*; **a ~ gin** ein Gin mit Tonic und Eis *etc*; **I'd like something ~ and cool** ich möchte einen kühlen Longdrink.
[2] *adv* **(a)** lang(e) ◆ **to be ~ in** *or* **about doing sth** lange zu etw brauchen; **don't be ~!** beeil dich!; **don't be too ~ about it** laß dir nicht zuviel Zeit, mach nicht zu lange (*inf*); **don't be too ~ about phoning me** ruf mich bald (mal) an; **I shan't be ~** (*in finishing*) ich bin gleich fertig; (*in returning*) ich bin gleich wieder da; **two months without you, it's been too ~** zwei Monate ohne dich, das war zu lang(e); **he drank ~ and deep** er nahm einen langen, tiefen Schluck; **all night ~** die ganze Nacht; **~ ago** vor langer Zeit; **not ~ ago** vor kurzem; **~ before** lange vorher; **~ before now** viel früher; **~ before they arrived** lange bevor sie ankamen; **not ~ before I met you** kurz bevor ich dich kennenlernte; **not ~ before that** kurz davor; **those days are ~ (since) past** diese Tage sind schon lange vorbei; **at the ~est** höchstens; **as ~ as** so lange wie; **we waited as ~ as we could** wir haben gewartet, solange wir konnten; **as ~ as, so ~ as** (*provided that*) solange; *see also* **ago, since.**
(b) (*in comp*) **how much ~er can you stay?** wie lange können Sie noch bleiben?; **I can't wait any ~er** (*from then*) länger kann ich nicht warten; (*from now*) ich kann nicht mehr länger warten; **if that noise goes on any ~er** wenn der Lärm weitergeht; **no ~er** (*not any more*) nicht mehr; **I'll wait no ~er** ich warte nicht länger; **I'll insist no ~er** ich werde nicht weiter darauf bestehen.
(c) so ~! (*inf*) tschüs! (*inf*), bis später!
[3] *n* **(a) the ~ and the short of it is that ...** kurz gesagt ..., der langen Rede kurzer Sinn, ...; **that's the ~ and the short of it** und damit hat sich's (*inf*); **before ~** bald; **are you going for ~?** werden Sie länger weg sein?; **I won't stay for ~** ich bleibe nicht lange; **it won't take ~** das dauert nicht lange; **it won't take ~ before ...** es wird nicht lange dauern, bis ...; **I won't take ~** ich brauche nicht lange (dazu). **(b)** (*Poet*) lange Silbe.

long[3] *vi* sich sehnen (*for* nach); (*less passionately*) herbeisehnen, kaum erwarten können (*for sth* etw *acc*) ◆ **he ~ed for his love to return** er wartete sehnsüchtig auf die Rückkehr seiner Liebsten; **I'm ~ing for him to resign** ich warte ungeduldig auf seinen Rücktritt; **the children were ~ing for the bell to ring** die Kinder warteten sehnsüchtig auf das Klingeln *or* konnten das Klingeln kaum erwarten; **he is ~ing for me to make a mistake** er möchte zu gern, daß ich einen Fehler mache; **I'm ~ing to see my native hills** ich sehne mich danach, die heimatlichen Berge zu sehen; **I am ~ing to go abroad** ich brenne darauf, ins Ausland zu gehen; **he ~ed to know what was happening** er hätte zu gerne gewußt, was vorging; **I'm ~ing to see my cat again** ich möchte meine Katze so gern wiedersehen; **I'm ~ing to see that film** ich will den Film unbedingt sehen; **I'm ~ing to hear his reaction** ich bin sehr auf seine Reaktion gespannt; **how I ~ for a cup of tea/a shower** wie ich mich nach einer Tasse Tee/einer Dusche sehne; **~ed-for** ersehnt; **the much ~ed-for cup of tea** die heißersehnte Tasse Tee.

long: ~boat *n* großes Beiboot; (*of Vikings*) Wikingerboot *nt*; **~bow** *n* (Lang)bogen *m*; **~-case clock** *n* Großvateruhr *f*; **~-distance** [1] *adj lorry, call* Fern-; *flight also, race, runner* Langstrecken-; **~-distance bus** (Fern)reisebus, Überlandbus *m*; [2] *adv* **to call ~-distance** ein Ferngespräch führen; **~ division** *n* schriftliche Division; **~-drawn-out** *adj speech, argument* langatmig; *meeting* ausgedehnt, in die Länge gezogen.

longevity [lɒn'dʒevɪtɪ] *n* Langlebigkeit *f.*

long: ~-forgotten *adj* längst vergessen; **~-haired** *adj person* langhaarig; *dog etc* Langhaar-; **~-haired cow** Kuh *f* mit langhaarigem Fell; **~hand** [1] *n* Langschrift *f*; [2] *adv* in Langschrift; **~-headed** *adj* (*fig*) klug, weitblickend; **~horn** *n* Longhorn *nt.*

longing ['lɒŋɪŋ] [1] *adj look* sehnsüchtig; *eyes* sehnsuchtsvoll.
[2] *n* Sehnsucht *f* (*for* nach) ◆ **this sense of ~** diese Sehnsucht; **his great ~ in life** sein sehnsüchtigster Wunsch; **to have a ~ to do sth** sich danach sehnen, etw zu tun.

longingly ['lɒŋɪŋlɪ] *adv* sehnsüchtig.

longish ['lɒŋɪʃ] *adj* ziemlich lang.

longitude ['lɒŋgɪtjuːd] *n* Länge *f* ◆ **lines of ~** Längengrade *pl.*

longitudinal [ˌlɒŋgɪ'tjuːdɪnəl] *adj* Längen-; *stripes, cut* Längs-.

longitudinally [ˌlɒŋgɪ'tjuːdɪnəlɪ] *adv* der Länge nach.

long: ~ johns *npl* (*inf*) lange Unterhosen *pl*; **~ jump** *n* Weitsprung *m*; **~ jumper** *n* Weitspringer(in *f*) *m*; **~-legged** *adj* langbeinig; **~-life** *adj battery etc* mit langer Lebensdauer; **~-life milk** H-Milch *f*; **~-limbed** *adj* lang-glied(e)rig; **~-lived** ['lɒŋlɪvd] *adj* langlebig; *success* dauerhaft, von Dauer; *anger* anhaltend, von Dauer; **~-lived trees** Bäume, die lange leben; **~-lost** *adj person* verloren geglaubt; *ideals, enthusiasm etc* verlorengegangen; **~-playing** *adj* Langspiel-; **~-range** *adj gun* weittragend; *missile, aircraft* Langstrecken-; *forecast, plane* langfristig; **~-range study** Langzeitstudie *f*; **~ship** *n* Wikingerboot *nt*; **~shoreman** *n* (*US*) Hafenarbeiter *m*; **~ shot** *n* **(a)** (*Phot*) Fernaufnahme *f*; **(b)** (*inf*) **it's a ~ shot, but it may pay off** es ist gewagt, aber es könnte sich auszahlen; **it was a ~ shot, but it proved to be true** die Vermutung war weit hergeholt, hat sich aber als wahr erwiesen; **that horse is a ~ shot** auf das Pferd zu setzen, ist gewagt; **not by a ~ shot** bei weitem nicht, noch lange nicht; **~-sight** *n see* **~-sightedness**; **~-sighted** *adj* (*lit, fig*) weitsichtig; **~-sightedness** *n* Weitsichtigkeit *f*; (*fig*) Weitsicht *f*; **~-standing** [1] *adj* alt; *friendship also* langjährig; *interest, invitation* schon lange bestehend; [2] *n* **of ~ standing** *see adj*; **~-suffering** *adj* schwer geprüft; **~ suit** *n* (*Cards*) lange Reihe; (*fig*) Trumpf *m*; **~-tailed** *adj* langschwänzig; **~-term** *adj plans, investment* langfristig; *memory, effect* Langzeit-; **the ~-term unemployed** die Langzeitarbeitslosen *pl*; **~ term** *n* **in the ~ term** langfristig gesehen; **to plan for the ~ term** auf lange Sicht planen; **~ vacation** *n* (*Univ*) (Sommer)semesterferien *pl*; (*Sch*) große Ferien *pl*; **~-wave** [1] *adj* Langwellen-; [2] *n* Langwelle *f.*

longways ['lɒŋweɪz] *adv* der Länge nach, längs.

long: ~-winded *adj* umständlich; *story* langatmig; **~-windedness** *n* Langatmigkeit *f.*

loo [luː] *n* (*Brit inf*) Klo *nt* (*inf*) ◆ **to go to the ~** aufs Klo gehen (*inf*); **in the ~** auf dem Klo (*inf*).

loofah ['luːfə] *n* Luffa *f*; (*as sponge*) Luffa(schwamm) *m.*

look [lʊk] [1] *n* **(a)** (*glance*) Blick *m* ◆ **she gave me a dirty ~, I got a dirty ~ from her** sie warf mir einen vernichtenden Blick zu; **she gave me a ~ of disbelief** sie sah mich ungläubig an; **he gave me such a ~!** er hat mir (vielleicht) einen Blick zugeworfen!; **we got some very odd ~s** wir wurden komisch angesehen; **to have** *or* **take a ~ at sth** sich (*dat*) etw ansehen; **he had a quick ~ at his watch** er sah kurz auf die Uhr; **can I have a ~?** darf ich mal sehen *or* gucken (*inf*)?; **have a ~ at this!** sieh *or* guck (*inf*) dir das mal an!; **is it in the dictionary? — have a ~ (and see)** steht das im Wörterbuch? — sieh *or* guck (*inf*) mal nach; **let's have a ~** laß mal sehen, zeig mal her; **let's have a ~ at it/you** laß mal sehen, zeig mal/laß dich mal ansehen; **do you want a ~?** willst du mal sehen?; (*at the paper*) willst du mal hineinsehen *or* einen Blick hineinwerfen?; **to take a good ~ at sth** sich (*dat*) etw genau ansehen; **take** *or* **have a good ~** sehen *or* gucken (*inf*) Sie genau hin; **to have a ~ for sth** sich nach etw umsehen; **I can't find it — have another ~** ich finde es nicht — sieh *or* guck (*inf*) noch mal nach; **to have a ~ round** sich umsehen; **shall we have a ~ round the town?** sollen wir uns (*dat*) die Stadt ansehen?
(b) (*air, appearances*) Aussehen *nt* ◆ **there was a ~ of despair in his eyes** ein verzweifelter Blick war in seinen Augen; **he put on a serious ~** er machte ein ernstes Gesicht; **he had the ~ of a sailor** er sah wie ein Seeman aus; **I don't like the ~ of him/this wound** er/die Wunde gefällt mir gar nicht; **by the ~ of him** so, wie er aussieht; **judging by the ~ of the sky** wenn man sich (*dat*) den Himmel ansieht, so, wie der Himmel aussieht; **to give sth a new ~** einer Sache (*dat*) ein neues Aussehen verleihen *or* Gesicht geben; **the town has now taken on a new ~** die Stadt hat ein neues Gesicht bekommen.
(c) ~s *pl* Aussehen *nt* ◆ **good ~s** gutes Aussehen; **~s aren't everything** auf das Aussehen allein kommt es nicht an; **you can't go by ~s alone** man kann nicht nur nach dem Aussehen *or* Äußeren gehen; **she began to lose her ~s** sie verlor allmählich ihr gutes Aussehen.
[2] *vt* **he is ~ing his age** man sieht ihm sein Alter an; **he's not ~ing himself these days** er sieht in letzter Zeit ganz verändert aus; **he's ~ing his old self again** er ist wieder ganz der alte; **to ~ one's best** sehr vorteilhaft aussehen; **I want to ~ my best tonight** ich möchte heute abend besonders gut aussehen; **she ~s her best in red** Rot steht ihr am besten; **he ~ed death in the face** er sah dem Tod ins Angesicht (*geh*) *or* Auge; **~ what you've done!** sieh *or* guck (*inf*) dir mal an, was du da angestellt hast!; **~ what you've done, now she's offended** jetzt hast du's geschafft, nun ist sie beleidigt; **~ what you've made me do** (sieh *or* schau (*dial*) *or* guck (*inf*) mal,) daran bist du schuld; **can't you ~ what you're doing!** kannst du nicht aufpassen, was du machst?; **~ where you're going!** paß auf, wo du hintrittst!; **just ~ where he's put the car!** sieh *or* schau (*dial*) *or* guck (*inf*) dir bloß mal an, wo er das Auto abge-

stellt hat!; **~ who's here!** guck (*inf*) *or* schau (*dial*) mal *or* sieh doch, wer da ist!

3 *vi* **(a)** (*see, glance*) gucken, schauen (*liter, dial*); (*with prep etc also*) sehen ◆ **to ~ round** sich umsehen; **he ~ed in(to) the chest** er sah *or* schaute (*dial*) *or* guckte (*inf*) in die Kiste (hinein); **to ~ carefully** genau hinsehen *etc*; **to ~ and see** nachsehen *etc*; **~ here!** hör (mal) zu!; **now ~ here, it wasn't my fault** Moment mal, das war aber nicht meine Schuld; **~, I know you're tired, but** ... ich weiß ja, daß du müde bist, aber ...; **~, there's a much better solution** da gibt es doch eine wesentlich bessere Lösung; **just ~!** guck mal!; **to ~ over sb's shoulder** jdm über die Schulter sehen; **~ before you leap** (*Prov*) erst wägen, dann wagen (*Prov*).

(b) (*search*) suchen, nachsehen.

(c) (*seem*) aussehen ◆ **it ~s all right to me** es scheint mir in Ordnung zu sein; **it ~s suspicious to me** es kommt mir verdächtig vor, es sieht verdächtig aus; **how does it ~ to you?** was meinst du dazu?; **I think the cake is done, how does it ~ to you?** ich glaube, der Kuchen ist fertig, was meinst du?; **the car ~s about 10 years old** das Auto sieht so aus, als ob es 10 Jahre alt wäre; **it ~s well on you** es steht dir gut.

(d) to ~ like aussehen wie; **the picture doesn't ~ like him** das Bild sieht ihm nicht ähnlich; **it ~s like rain, it ~s as if it will rain** es sieht nach Regen aus; **it ~s like cheese to me** (ich finde,) das sieht wie Käse aus; **it ~s as if we'll be late** es sieht (so) aus, als würden wir zu spät kommen; **the festival ~s like being lively** auf dem Festival wird es wahrscheinlich hoch hergehen.

(e) (*face*) gehen nach ◆ **this window ~s (towards the) north** dieses Fenster geht nach Norden; **the village ~s towards the forest** das Dorf liegt dem Wald zugewendet.

◆**look about** *vi* sich umsehen (*for sth* nach etw) ◆ **to ~ ~ one** sich umsehen; **if we ~ ~ we might find some more examples** wenn wir suchen, finden wir vielleicht noch ein paar Beispiele.

◆**look after** *vi +prep obj* **(a)** (*take care of*) sich kümmern um ◆ **to ~ ~ oneself** (*cook etc*) für sich selbst sorgen, sich selbst versorgen; (*be capable, strong etc*) auf sich (*acc*) aufpassen; **he's only ~ing ~ his own interests** (*acc*) er handelt nur im eigenen Interesse. **(b)** (*temporarily*) sehen nach; *children also* aufpassen auf (+*acc*). **(c)** (*follow with eyes*) nachsehen (+*dat*).

◆**look ahead** *vi* **(a)** nach vorne sehen *or* gucken (*inf*).

(b) (*fig*) vorausschauen ◆ **when we ~ ~ to the next 30 years/the future of this country** wenn wir die nächsten 30 Jahre/die Zukunft dieses Landes betrachten; **a good manager is one who can ~ ~** ein guter Manager muß Weitblick haben.

◆**look around** *vi* **(a)** sich umsehen. **(b)** (*in shop etc*) sich umsehen; (+*prep obj*) sich (*dat*) ansehen *or* angucken (*inf*).

◆**look at** *vi +prep obj* **(a)** ansehen, anschauen (*dial*), angucken (*inf*) ◆ **just ~ ~ him!** sieh *etc* dir den mal an!; **he ~ed ~ his watch** er sah *etc* auf die Uhr; **~ ~ the blackboard** schau(t) an *or* auf die Tafel; **don't ~ directly ~ the sun** sehen *etc* Sie nicht direkt in die Sonne; **I can't ~ ~ him without feeling** ... wenn ich ihn ansehe *etc*, habe ich immer das Gefühl, daß ...; **he/it isn't much to ~ ~** (*not attractive*) er/es sieht nicht besonders (gut) aus; (*nothing special*) er/es sieht nach nichts aus; **to ~ ~ him** ... wenn man ihn sieht ...

(b) (*examine*) sich (*dat*) ansehen *or* -schauen (*dial*) *or* -gucken (*inf*); *offer* prüfen ◆ **we'll have to ~ ~ the financial aspect** wir müssen die finanzielle Seite betrachten; **has the manuscript been ~ed ~ yet?** ist das Manuskript schon durchgesehen worden?

(c) (*view*) betrachten, sehen ◆ **they ~ ~ life in a different way** sie haben eine andere Einstellung zum Leben, sie sehen das Leben von einer anderen Warte aus.

(d) (*consider*) *possibilities* sich (*dat*) überlegen; *suggestions, offer* in Betracht ziehen.

◆**look away** *vi* **(a)** wegsehen. **(b) the house ~s ~ from the sea** das Haus liegt vom Meer abgewendet.

◆**look back** *vi* sich umsehen; (*fig*) zurückblicken (*on sth, to sth* auf etw *acc*) ◆ **he's never ~ed ~** (*inf*) es ist ständig mit ihm bergauf gegangen.

◆**look down** *vi* hinunter-/heruntersehen *or* -schauen (*dial*) *or* -gucken (*inf*) ◆ **we ~ed ~ the hole** wir sahen *etc* ins Loch hinunter; **~ ~ on the valley beneath** sieh *etc* ins Tal hinunter.

◆**look down on** *vi +prep obj* herabsehen auf (+*acc*) ◆ **you shouldn't ~ ~ ~ his attempts to help** du solltest ihn nicht belächeln, wenn er versucht zu helfen.

◆**look for** *vi +prep obj* **(a)** (*seek*) suchen ◆ **he's ~ing ~ trouble** er wird sich (*dat*) Ärger einhandeln; (*actively*) er sucht Streit. **(b)** (*expect*) erwarten.

◆ **look forward to** *vi +prep obj* sich freuen auf (+*acc*) ◆ **I'm so ~ing ~ ~ seeing you again** ich freue mich so darauf, dich wiederzusehen; **I ~ ~ ~ hearing from you** ich hoffe, bald von Ihnen zu hören.

◆**look in** *vi* **(a)** hinein-/hereinsehen *or* -schauen (*dial*) *or* -gucken (*inf*). **(b)** (*visit*) vorbeikommen (*on sb* bei jdm) ◆ **would you ~ ~ at Smith's and collect my dress?** kannst du bei Smith vorbeigehen und mein Kleid abholen? **(c)** (*watch TV*) fernsehen.

◆**look into** *vi +prep obj* untersuchen; *complaint etc* prüfen.

◆**look on** *vi* **(a)** (*watch*) zusehen, zugucken (*inf*).

(b) to ~ ~to (*window*) (hinaus)gehen auf (+*acc*); (*building*) liegen an (+*dat*).

(c) *+prep obj* (*also* **look upon**) betrachten, ansehen ◆ **to ~ ~ sb as a friend** jdn als Freund betrachten; **I ~ ~ him as a good doctor** ich halte ihn für einen guten Arzt; **to ~ ~ sb with respect** Achtung *or* Respekt vor jdm haben.

◆**look out** 1 *vi* **(a)** hinaus-/heraussehen *or* -schauen (*dial*) *or* -gucken (*inf*) ◆ **to ~ ~ (of) the window** zum Fenster hinaussehen *etc*, aus dem Fenster sehen *etc*. **(b)** (*building etc*) **to ~ ~ on** *or* **over sth** einen Blick auf etw (*acc*) haben. **(c)** (*take care*) aufpassen.

2 *vt sep* heraussuchen.

◆**look out for** *vi +prep obj* **(a)** (*keep watch for*) **we'll ~ ~ ~ you at the station/after the meeting** wir werden auf dem Bahnhof/nach der Versammlung nach dir Ausschau halten; **~ ~ ~ pickpockets/his left hook** nimm dich vor Taschendieben/seinem linken Haken in acht, paß auf Taschendiebe/auf seinen linken Haken auf; **the bouncers were told to ~ ~ ~ troublemakers** die Rausschmeißer sollten auf Unruhestifter achten *or* achtgeben; **you must ~ ~ ~ spelling mistakes/snakes** Sie müssen auf Rechtschreibfehler/Schlangen achten.

(b) (*seek*) *new job* sich umsehen nach; *new staff also, ideas* suchen.

◆**look over** *vt sep papers, notes etc* durchsehen; *house* sich (*dat*) ansehen.

◆**look round** *vi see* **look around.**

◆**look through** 1 *vi* durchsehen *or* -schauen (*dial*) *or* -gucken (*inf*) (*prep obj* durch) ◆ **he stopped at the window and ~ed ~** er blieb am Fenster stehen und sah *etc* hinein/herein; **he ~ed ~ the window** er sah *etc* zum Fenster hinein/herein/hinaus/heraus; **to ~ straight ~ sb** durch jdn hindurchgucken.

2 *vt sep* (*examine*) durchsehen.

◆**look to** *vi +prep obj* **(a)** (*look after*) sich kümmern um ◆ **~ ~ it that** ... sieh zu, daß ...

(b) (*rely on*) sich verlassen auf (+*acc*) ◆ **they ~ed ~ him to solve the problem** sie verließen sich darauf, daß er das Problem lösen würde; **we ~ ~ you for support/to lead the country** wir rechnen auf Ihre *or* mit Ihrer Hilfe/wir rechnen damit *or* zählen darauf, daß Sie das Land führen; **there's no point in ~ing ~ him for help** es ist sinnlos, von ihm Hilfe zu erwarten; **we ~ ~ you for guidance** wir wenden uns an Sie um Rat.

◆**look up** 1 *vi* **(a)** aufsehen *or* -blicken ◆ **don't ~ ~** guck nicht hoch (*inf*). **(b)** (*improve*) besser werden; (*shares, prices*) steigen ◆ **things are ~ing ~** es geht bergauf.

2 *vt sep* **(a) to ~ sb ~ and down** jdn von oben bis unten ansehen *or* mustern. **(b)** (*visit*) **to ~ sb ~** bei jdm vorbeischauen, jdn besuchen. **(c)** (*seek*) *word* nachschlagen.

◆**look upon** *vi +prep obj see* **look on (c).**

◆**look up to** *vi +prep obj* **to ~ ~ ~ sb** zu jdm aufsehen; **he was always ~ed ~ ~** andere haben immer zu ihm aufgesehen.

look: ~alike *n* Doppelgänger(in *f*) *m*; **a Rupert Murdoch ~alike** ein Doppelgänger von Rupert Murdoch; **it's not just another ~alike** es sieht nicht wie all die anderen aus; **~-around** *n* **to have** *or* **take a ~-around** sich umsehen.

looked-for ['lʊktfɔːʳ] *adj* (*expected*) (lang)ersehnt.

looker ['lʊkəʳ] *n* (*inf*) **to be a (good** *or* **real) ~** klasse aussehen (*inf*).

looker-on ['lʊkəʳ(r)ɒn] *n* Zuschauer(in *f*) *m*, Schaulustige(r) *mf* (*pej*).

look-in ['lʊkɪn] *n* (*inf*) Chance *f* ◆ **he didn't get a ~** er hatte keine Chance.

-looking [-'lʊkɪŋ] *adj suf* aussehend ◆ **she/it is not bad-~** sie/es sieht nicht schlecht aus.

looking glass *n* Spiegel *m*.

look: ~-out *n* **(a)** (*tower etc*) (*Mil*) Ausguck *m*; **~-out post/station/tower** Beobachtungsposten *m*/-station *f*/-turm *m*; **(b)** (*person*) (*Mil*) Wacht- *or* Beobachtungsposten *m*; **the thieves had a ~-out on the building opposite** einer der Diebe stand auf dem gegenüberliegenden Gebäude Wache *or* Schmiere (*inf*); **(c) to be on the ~-out for, to keep a ~-out for** *see* **look out for**; **(d)** (*prospect*) Aussichten *pl*; **it's a grim ~-out for us** es sieht schlecht aus für uns; **(e)** (*inf: worry*) **that's his ~-out!** das ist sein Problem!; **~-see** *n* (*inf*) **to have a ~-see** nachgucken (*inf*) *or* -schauen (*dial*) *or* -sehen; **~-through** *n* (*inf*) Durchsicht *f*; **would you have a ~-through?** können Sie sich das mal durchsehen?; **to give sth a quick ~-through** etw kurz durchsehen.

loom¹ [luːm] *n* Webstuhl *m*.

loom² *vi* (*also* **~ ahead** *or* **up**) (*lit, fig*) sich abzeichnen; (*storm*) heraufziehen; (*disaster*) sich zusammenbrauen; (*danger*) drohen; (*difficulties*) sich auftürmen; (*exams*) bedrohlich näherrücken ◆ **the ship ~ed (up) out of the mist** das Schiff tauchte undeutlich/bedrohlich aus dem Nebel (auf); **the threat of unemployment was ~ing on the horizon** Arbeitslosigkeit zeichnete sich drohend ab; **the fear of a sudden attack ~ed in their thoughts** sie schwebten in Angst vor einem plötzlichen Angriff; **to ~ large** eine große Rolle spielen; **the skyscraper ~s over the city** der Wolkenkratzer ragt über die Stadt.

loon¹ [luːn] *n* (*Orn*) Seetaucher *m*.

loon² *n* (*sl*) Blödmann *m* (*sl*).

loony ['luːnɪ] (*sl*) 1 *adj* (+*er*) bekloppt (*sl*).

2 *n* Verrückte(r) (*inf*), Irre(r) *mf* ◆ **~ bin** Klapsmühle *f* (*sl*).

loony left (*Brit Pol pej inf*) 1 *n* **the loony left** die radikale Linke.

2 *adj attr* linksradikal.

loop [luːp] 1 *n* **(a)** (*curved shape*) Schlaufe *f*; (*of wire*) Schlinge *f*; (*of river, Rail*) Schleife *f*; (*Med*) Spirale *f*.

(b) (*Aviat*) Looping *m* ◆ **to ~ the ~** einen Looping machen.

(c) (*Comput*) Schleife *f*.

2 *vt rope etc* schlingen (*round* um) ◆ **to ~ a rope through a ring** ein Seil durch einen Ring ziehen.

3 *vi* (*rope etc*) sich schlingen; (*line, road etc*) eine Schleife machen ◆ **the road ~s round the fields** die Straße schlängelt sich um die Felder.

◆**loop back** 1 *vt sep* **the wire ~ around the lid** biegen Sie den Draht zurück um den Deckel.

2 *vi* **(a)** (*road*) eine Schleife machen; (*person*) in einem Bogen zurückkehren ◆ **this wire has to ~ ~** dieser Draht muß zurückgebogen werden. **(b)** (*Comput*) **the program then ~s ~ to** ... die Programmschleife

➤ LANGUAGE IN USE: **look: 3c** → 15.2, 15.3 **look forward to** → 20.7, 21.2

wird dann ab ... nochmals durchlaufen.

loop: ~hole *n* (*Mil*) Schießscharte *f*; (*fig*) Hintertürchen *nt*; **a ~-hole in the law** eine Lücke im Gesetz; **~line** *n* (*Rail*) Schleife *f*.

loopy ['lu:pɪ] *adj* (*+er*) (*sl*) bekloppt (*sl*).

loose [lu:s] 1 *adj* (*+er*) **(a)** (*not tight, movable*) *board, button* lose; *dress, collar* weit; *tooth, bandage, knot, screw, soil, weave* locker; *limbs* beweglich, locker ◆ **~ change** Kleingeld *nt*; **he kept his change ~ in his pocket** er hatte sein Kleingeld lose in der Tasche; **a ~ connection** (*Elec*) ein Wackelkontakt *m*; **to come** *or* **work ~** (*screw, handle etc*) sich lockern; (*sole, cover etc*) sich (los)lösen; (*button*) abgehen; **to hang ~** lose herunterhängen; **her hair hung ~** sie trug ihr Haar offen; **to have ~ bowels** Durchfall haben; **just hang ~** (*sl*) bleib cool (*sl*).

(b) (*free*) **to break** *or* **get ~** (*person, animal*) sich losreißen (*from* von); (*ship*) sich (von der Vertäuung) losreißen; (*from group of players etc*) sich trennen, sich lösen; (*break out*) ausbrechen; (*from commitment, parental home etc*) sich freimachen (*from* von); **to run ~** frei herumlaufen; (*of children*) unbeaufsichtigt herumlaufen; **to be at a ~ end** (*fig*) nichts mit sich anzufangen wissen; **to turn** *or* **let** *or* **set ~** frei herumlaufen lassen; *prisoner* freilassen; *imagination* freien Lauf lassen (*+dat*); **to tie up the ~ ends** (*fig*) ein paar offene *or* offenstehende Probleme lösen.

(c) (*not exact, vague*) *translation* frei; *account, thinking, planning* ungenau; *connection* lose.

(d) (*too free, immoral*) *conduct* lose; *morals* locker; *person* unmoralisch, lose ◆ **a ~ life** ein lockerer Lebenswandel; **a ~ woman** eine Frau mit lockerem Lebenswandel; **in that bar you get ~ women** in der Bar findest du lose Mädchen; **do you think that's being ~?** meinst du, das ist unmoralisch?; **to have a ~ tongue** nichts für sich behalten können.

2 *n* (*inf*) **to be on the ~** (*prisoners, dangerous animals*) frei herumlaufen; **he was on the ~ in Paris** er machte Paris unsicher; **the troops were on the ~ in the city** die Truppen wüteten in der Stadt; **oh dear, when these two are on the ~** wehe, wenn sie losgelassen!

3 *vt* **(a)** (*free*) befreien. **(b)** (*untie*) losmachen. **(c)** (*slacken*) lockern.

◆**loose off** 1 *vt sep* loslassen; *shot, bullet* abfeuern.

2 *vi* Feuer eröffnen (*at* auf *+acc*) ◆ **to ~ ~ at sb** (*fig inf*) eine Schimpfkanonade auf jdn loslassen (*inf*).

loose: ~box *n* Box *f*; **~ cannon** *n* (*inf*) unberechenbares Element; **he's a ~ cannon** er ist unberechenbar; **~ covers** *npl* Überzüge *pl*; **~-fitting** *adj* weit; **~-leaf binder** *n* Ringbuch *nt*; **~-leaf book** *n* Loseblattausgabe *f*; **~-leaf pad** *n* Ringbucheinlage *f*; **~-limbed** *adj* (*lithe*) gelenkig, beweglich; (*gangling*) schlaksig; **~-living** *adj* verkommen, lose.

loosely ['lu:slɪ] *adv* **(a)** lose, locker ◆ **in hot countries it's better to be ~ dressed in robes** in warmen Ländern trägt man besser weitgeschnittene *or* lose hängende Kleider; **his hands dangled ~ from his wrists** er ließ seine Hände locker baumeln; **he held her hand ~ in his** er hielt ihre Hand locker in der seinen.

(b) ~ speaking grob gesagt; **~ translated** frei übersetzt; **I was using the word rather ~** ich habe das Wort ziemlich frei gebraucht; **they are ~ connected** sie hängen lose zusammen.

(c) *behave* unmoralisch ◆ **he lives ~** er führt ein loses *or* lockeres Leben.

loosen ['lu:sn] 1 *vt* **(a)** (*free*) befreien; *tongue* lösen. **(b)** (*untie*) losmachen, lösen. **(c)** (*slacken*) lockern; *belt also* weitermachen; *soil* auflockern; *collar* aufmachen.

2 *vi* sich lockern.

◆**loosen up** 1 *vt sep muscles* lockern; *soil* auflockern.

2 *vi* (*muscles*) locker werden; (*athlete*) sich (auf)lockern; (*relax*) auftauen.

looseness ['lu:snɪs] *n* Lockerheit *f*; (*of clothes*) Weite *f*; (*of thinking*) Ungenauigkeit *f*; (*of translation*) Freiheit *f* ◆ **~ of the bowels** zu rege Darmtätigkeit; **the ~ of her conduct** ihr loses *or* unmoralisches Benehmen; **the ~ of this way of life** ein solch lockerer Lebenswandel.

loot [lu:t] 1 *n* Beute *f*; (*inf: money*) Zaster *m* (*sl*).

2 *vti* plündern.

looter ['lu:tə^r] *n* Plünderer *m*.

lop [lɒp] *vt* (*also* **~ off**) abhacken.

lope [ləʊp] *vi* in großen Sätzen springen; (*hare*) hoppeln ◆ **he ~d along by her side** er lief mit großen Schritten neben ihr her; **to ~ off** davonspringen.

lop-eared ['lɒp,ɪəd] *adj* mit Hängeohren.

lop ears *npl* Hänge- *or* Schlappohren (*inf*) *pl*.

lopsided ['lɒp'saɪdɪd] *adj* schief; (*fig*) einseitig ◆ **the balance of the committee is ~** der Ausschuß ist sehr einseitig besetzt.

loquacious [lə'kweɪʃəs] *adj* redselig.

loquacity [lə'kwæsɪtɪ] *n* Redseligkeit *f*.

lord [lɔ:d] 1 *n* **(a)** (*master, ruler*) Herr *m* ◆ **~ and master** Herr und Meister *m*; (*hum: husband*) Herr und Gebieter *m*; **tobacco ~s** Tabakkönige *pl*.

(b) (*Brit: nobleman*) Lord *m* ◆ **the (House of) L~s** das Oberhaus; **my ~** (*to bishop*) Exzellenz; (*to noble*) (*in English contexts*) Mylord; (*to baron*) Herr Baron; (*to earl, viscount*) Euer Erlaucht; (*to judge*) Euer Ehren.

(c) (*Brit: important official*) **First L~ of the Admiralty** Stabschef *m* der Marine; **L~ Chancellor** Lordsiegelbewahrer, Lordkanzler *m*; **L~ Mayor** ≃ Oberbürgermeister *m*; **L~ Justice** *Richter m an einem Berufungsgericht*.

(d) (*Rel*) **L~** Herr *m*; **the L~ (our) God** Gott, der Herr; **the L~'s day** der Tag des Herrn; **the L~'s prayer** das Vaterunser; **the L~'s supper** das (Heilige) Abendmahl; **(good) L~!** (*inf*) ach, du lieber Himmel! (*inf*), (ach,) du meine Güte! (*inf*); (*annoyed*) mein Gott! (*inf*); **L~ help him!** (*inf*) (dann) Gnade ihm Gott!; **L~ knows** (*inf*) wer weiß; **L~ knows I've tried often enough** ich hab's weiß Gott oft genug versucht.

2 *vt* **to ~ it** das Zepter schwingen; **to ~ it over sb** jdn herumkommandieren.

lordliness ['lɔ:dlɪnɪs] *n* Vornehmheit *f*; (*haughtiness*) Überheblichkeit, Arroganz *f*.

lordly ['lɔ:dlɪ] *adj* (*+er*) **(a)** (*magnificent*) vornehm; *house also* (hoch)herrschaftlich. **(b)** (*proud, haughty*) hochmütig, arrogant; *tone of voice* herrisch, gebieterisch.

lordship ['lɔ:dʃɪp] *n* (*Brit: title*) Lordschaft *f* ◆ **his/your ~** seine/Eure Lordschaft; (*to bishop*) seine/Eure Exzellenz; (*to judge*) seine/Euer Ehren *or* Gnaden.

lore [lɔ:^r] *n* Überlieferungen *pl* ◆ **in local ~** nach hiesiger Überlieferung; **gypsy ~** Sagengut *nt or* Überlieferungen *pl* der Zigeuner; **plant ~** Pflanzenkunde *f*.

lorgnette [lɔ:'njet] *n* Lorgnette *f*.

lorry ['lɒrɪ] *n* (*Brit*) Last(kraft)wagen, Lkw, Laster (*inf*) *m* ◆ **it fell off the back of a ~** (*hum inf*) ich hab/er hat *etc* das „gefunden" (*hum inf*); **~ driver** Last(kraft)wagenfahrer(in *f*), Lkw-Fahrer(in *f*) *m*.

lose [lu:z] *pret, ptp* **lost** 1 *vt* **(a)** verlieren; *pursuer* abschütteln; *one's French* vergessen, verlernen; *prize* nicht bekommen ◆ **many men ~ their hair** vielen Männern gehen die Haare aus; **the cat has lost a lot of hair** die Katze hat viel Haar verloren; **the shares have lost 15% in a month** die Aktien sind in einem Monat um 15% gefallen; **you will ~ nothing by helping them** es kann dir nicht schaden, wenn du ihnen hilfst; **that mistake lost him his job/her friendship/the game** dieser Fehler kostete ihn die Stellung/ihre Freundschaft/den Sieg; **he lost himself in his work** er ging ganz in seiner Arbeit auf; **he likes to ~ himself in his memories** er verliert sich gern in Erinnerungen; **to ~ no time in doing sth** etw sofort tun.

(b) my watch lost three hours meine Uhr ist drei Stunden nachgegangen.

(c) you've lost me now with all this abstract argument bei dieser abstrakten Argumentation komme ich nicht mehr mit.

(d) (*not catch*) *train, opportunity* verpassen; *words* nicht mitbekommen ◆ **to ~ the post** die (Briefkasten)leerung verpassen.

(e) (*passive usages*) **to be lost** (*things*) verschwunden sein; (*people*) sich verlaufen haben; (*fig*) verloren sein; (*words*) untergehen; **I can't follow the reasoning, I'm lost** ich kann der Argumentation nicht folgen, ich verstehe nichts mehr; **he was soon lost in the crowd** er hatte sich bald in der Menge verloren; **to be lost at sea** auf See geblieben sein; (*of ship*) auf See vermißt sein; **the ship was lost with all hands** das Schiff war mit der ganzen Besatzung untergegangen; **all is lost!** alles verloren!; **to get lost** sich verlaufen; **I got lost after the second chapter** nach dem zweiten Kapitel kam ich nicht mehr mit; **get lost!** (*inf*) verschwinde! (*inf*); **to look lost** (ganz) verloren aussehen; (*fig*) ratlos *or* hilflos aussehen; **you look (as though you're) lost, can I help you?** haben Sie sich verlaufen *or* verirrt, kann ich Ihnen behilflich sein?; **to give sb/sth up for lost** jdn verloren geben/etw abschreiben; **the motion was lost** der Antrag wurde abgelehnt; **he was lost to science** er war für die Wissenschaft verloren; **he is lost to all finer feelings** er hat keinen Sinn für höhere Gefühle; **I'm lost without my watch** ohne meine Uhr bin ich verloren *or* aufgeschmissen (*inf*); **classical music is lost on him** er hat keinen Sinn für klassische Musik; **good wine is lost on him** er weiß guten Wein nicht zu schätzen; **the joke/remark was lost on her** der Witz/die Bemerkung kam bei ihr nicht an.

2 *vi* verlieren; (*watch*) nachgehen ◆ **you can't ~** du kannst nichts verlieren; **the novel ~s a lot in the film** der Roman verliert in der Verfilmung sehr; **you will not ~ by helping him** es kann dir nicht schaden, wenn du ihm hilfst.

◆**lose out** *vi* (*inf*) schlecht wegkommen (*inf*), den kürzeren ziehen (*on* bei).

loser ['lu:zə^r] *n* Verlierer(in *f*) *m* ◆ **he's a born ~** er ist der geborene Verlierer.

losing ['lu:zɪŋ] *adj team* Verlierer-; (*causing to lose*) die Niederlage entscheidend, verhängnisvoll ◆ **a ~ battle** ein aussichtsloser Kampf; **to be on the ~ side** verlieren.

loss [lɒs] *n* **(a)** Verlust *m* ◆ **~ of memory** Gedächtnisverlust *m*; **progressive ~ of memory** Gedächtnisschwund *m*; **the ~ of the last three games upset the team** die letzten drei Niederlagen brachten die Mannschaft aus der Fassung; **~ of speed/time** *etc* Geschwindigkeits-/Zeitverlust *m etc*; **he felt her ~ very deeply** ihr Tod war ein schwerer Verlust für ihn; **there was a heavy ~ of life** viele kamen ums Leben.

(b) (*amount, sth lost*) Verlust *m* ◆ **how many ~es has the team had so far?** wieviele Spiele hat die Mannschaft bis jetzt verloren?; **the army suffered heavy ~es** die Armee erlitt schwere Verluste; **his business is running at a ~** er arbeitet mit Verlust; **to sell sth at a ~** etw mit Verlust verkaufen; **it's your ~** es ist deine Sache; **he's no ~** er ist kein (großer) Verlust; **you're a great ~ to the civil service** (*should have been a civil servant*) an dir ist ein Beamter verlorengegangen; **a dead ~** (*inf*) ein böser Reinfall (*inf*); (*person*) ein hoffnungsloser Fall (*inf*); **total ~** Totalverlust *m*.

(c) to be at a ~ nicht mehr weiterwissen; **we are at a ~ with this problem** wir stehen dem Problem ratlos gegenüber; **we are at a ~ what to do** wir wissen nicht mehr aus noch ein; **to be at a ~ to explain sth** etw nicht erklären können; **we are at a ~ to say why** wir haben keine Ahnung, warum; **to be at a ~ for words** nicht wissen, was man sagen soll; **he's never at a ~ for words/an excuse** er ist nie um Worte/eine Ausrede verlegen.

loss: ~ leader *n* Lockvogelangebot *nt*; **~-making** *adj* **a ~-making company** ein Unternehmen, das mit Verlust arbeitet.

lost [lɒst] 1 *pret, ptp of* **lose**.

2 *adj* verloren; *art* ausgestorben; *cause* aussichtslos; *child* verschwunden, vermißt; *civilisation* untergegangen, versunken; *opportunity* verpaßt ◆ **he is mourning his ~ wife** er betrauert den Verlust seiner Frau; **~-and-found**

(department) (*US*), **~ property (office)** Fundbüro *nt.*

lot¹ [lɒt] *n* **(a)** (*for deciding*) Los *nt* ◆ **by ~** durch Losentscheid, durch das Los; **to cast** *or* **draw ~s** losen, Lose ziehen; **to cast** *or* **draw ~s for sth** etw verlosen; **to cast** *or* **draw ~s for a task** eine Aufgabe auslosen; **they drew ~s to see who would begin** sie losten aus, wer anfangen sollte.
(b) (*destiny*) Los *nt* ◆ **failure was his ~ in life** es war sein Los, immer zu versagen; **it falls to my ~ to tell him** mir fällt die Aufgabe zu, es ihm zu sagen; **to throw in one's ~ with sb** sich mit jdm zusammentun.
(c) (*plot*) Parzelle *f*; (*Film*) Filmgelände *nt* ◆ **building ~** Bauplatz *m*; **parking ~** (*US*) Parkplatz *m.*
(d) (*articles of same kind*) Posten *m*; (*at auction*) Los *nt.*
(e) (*group of things*) **where shall I put this ~?** wo soll ich das hier *or* das Zeug (*inf*) hintun?; **can you carry that ~ by yourself?** kannst du das (alles) alleine tragen?; **divide the books up into three ~s** teile die Bücher in drei Teile *or* Stapel ein; **we moved the furniture in two ~s** wir haben die Möbel in zwei Fuhren befördert; **I'd just finished marking the papers when he gave me another ~** ich war gerade mit dem Korrigieren fertig, da gab er mir einen neuen Packen *or* Stoß *or* noch eine Ladung (*inf*); **we bought a new ~ of cutlery** wir haben uns (ein) neues Besteck gekauft.
(f) he/she is a bad ~ (*inf*) er/sie taugt nichts, er/sie ist eine miese Type (*sl*); **they are a bad ~** (*inf*) das ist ein übles Pack.
(g) (*inf: group*) Haufen *m* ◆ **that ~ in the next office** die *or* die Typen (*sl*) vom Büro nebenan (*inf*); **I'm fed up with you ~** ich hab' die Nase voll von euch allen (*inf*) *or* von euch Bande (*inf*); **are you ~ coming to the pub?** kommt ihr (alle) in die Kneipe?; **bring your ~ with you** bring die ganze Mannschaft mit.
(h) the ~ (*inf*) alle; alles; **that's the ~** das ist alles, das wär's (*inf*); **the whole ~ of them** sie alle; (*people also*) die ganze Mannschaft (*inf*); **he's eaten the ~** er hat alles aufgegessen; **big ones, little ones, the ~!** Große, Kleine, alle!

lot² [1] *n* **a ~, ~s** viel; **a ~ of money** viel *or* eine Menge Geld; **a ~ of books, ~s of books** viele *or* eine Menge Bücher; **such a ~** so viel; **what a ~!** was für eine Menge!; **what a ~ of time you take** wie lange du nur brauchst!; **what a ~ you've got** du hast aber viel; **how much has he got? — ~s** *or* **a ~** wieviel hat er? — jede Menge (*inf*) *or* viel; **quite a ~ of books** ziemlich viele *or* eine ganze Menge Bücher; **such a ~ of books** so viele Bücher; **an awful ~ of things to do** furchtbar viel zu tun; **he made ~s and ~s of mistakes** er hat eine Unmenge Fehler gemacht; **I want ~s and ~s** ich will jede Menge (*inf*); **we see a ~ of John these days** wir sehen John in letzter Zeit sehr oft; **I'd give a ~ to know ...** ich würde viel drum geben, wenn ich wüßte ...
[2] *adv*: **a ~, ~s** viel; **things have changed a ~** es hat sich vieles geändert; **he disappointed me a ~** er hat mich sehr enttäuscht; **I feel ~s** *or* **a ~ better** es geht mir sehr viel besser; **a ~ you care!** dich interessiert das überhaupt nicht!

loth *adj see* **loath.**

lotion ['ləʊʃən] *n* Lotion *f.*

lottery ['lɒtərɪ] *n* Lotterie *f* ◆ **life is a ~** das Leben ist ein Glücksspiel.

lotus ['ləʊtəs] *n* Lotos *m* ◆ **~-eater** Lotophage, Lotosesser(in *f*) *m*; (*fig*) Müßiggänger *m*; **~ position** Lotossitz *m.*

loud [laʊd] [1] *adj* (+*er*) **(a)** laut ◆ **he was ~ in his praise of the concert** er lobte das Konzert überschwenglich; **~ and clear** laut und deutlich. **(b)** *behaviour* aufdringlich; *colour* grell, schreiend; (*in bad taste*) auffällig.
[2] *adv* laut ◆ **to say sth out ~** etw laut sagen.

loudhailer [,laʊd'heɪləʳ] *n* Megaphon *nt*, Flüstertüte *f* (*inf*); (*not hand-held*) Lautsprecher *m.*

loudly ['laʊdlɪ] *adv see adj* ◆ **he was ~ dressed in blue** er war in ein grelles Blau gekleidet.

loud: ~-mouth *n* (*inf*) Großmaul *nt* (*inf*); **~-mouthed** ['laʊd,maʊðd] *adj* (*inf*) großmäulig (*inf*).

loudness ['laʊdnɪs] *n see adj* Lautstärke *f*; Aufdringlichkeit *f*; Grellheit *f*; Auffälligkeit *f* ◆ **the ~ of his voice** seine laute Stimme.

loudspeaker [,laʊd'spiːkəʳ] *n* Lautsprecher *m*; (*of hi-fi also*) Box *f.*

lough [lɒx] *n* (*Ir*) See *m*; (*sea ~*) Meeresarm *m.*

lounge [laʊndʒ] [1] *n* (*in house*) Wohnzimmer *nt*; (*in hotel*) Gesellschaftsraum *m*; (*~ bar, on liner etc*) Salon *m*; (*at airport*) Warteraum *m* ◆ **TV ~** Fernsehraum *m.*
[2] *vi* faulenzen ◆ **to ~ about** *or* **around** herumliegen/-sitzen/-stehen; **to ~ against a wall** sich lässig gegen eine Mauer lehnen; **to ~ back in a chair** sich in einem Stuhl zurücklehnen; **to ~ up to sb** auf jdn zuschlendern.

lounge: ~ bar *n* Salon *m* (*vornehmerer Teil einer Gaststätte*); **~ lizard** *n* Salonlöwe *m.*

lounger ['laʊndʒəʳ] *n* Nichtstuer, Faulenzer *m.*

lounge suit *n* Straßenanzug *m.*

lour, lower ['laʊəʳ] *vi* (*person*) ein finsteres Gesicht machen; (*clouds*) sich türmen ◆ **a threatening sky ~ed above us** der Himmel war bedrohlich dunkel *or* überzogen; **to ~ at sb** jdn finster *or* drohend ansehen.

louring ['laʊərɪŋ] *adj* finster.

louse [laʊs] [1] *n, pl* **lice (a)** (*Zool*) Laus *f.* **(b)** (*sl*) fieser Kerl (*sl*) ◆ **he behaved like a real ~ to her** er war richtig fies zu ihr (*sl*), er hat sich richtig fies benommen (*sl*).
[2] *vt* (*sl*) **to ~ sth up** etw vermasseln (*sl*); *friendship* kaputtmachen (*inf*).

lousy ['laʊzɪ] *adj* **(a)** verlaust ◆ **he is ~ with money** (*sl*) er hat Geld wie Dreck (*sl*).
(b) (*sl: very bad*) saumäßig (*sl*), beschissen (*sl*); *trick etc* fies (*sl*) ◆ **I'm ~ at arithmetic** in Mathe bin ich miserabel (*inf*) *or* saumäßig (*sl*); **a ~ $3** popelige *or* lausige 3 Dollar (*inf*).

lout [laʊt] *n* Rüpel, Flegel *m.*

loutish ['laʊtɪʃ] *adj* rüpelhaft, flegelhaft.

louvre, louver ['luːvəʳ] *n* Jalousie *f* ◆ **~ door** Lamellentür *f.*

louvred, louvered ['luːvəd] *adj* Jalousie- ◆ **~ blinds** Jalousie *f.*

lovable ['lʌvəbl] *adj* liebenswert.

▼ **love** [lʌv] [1] *n* **(a)** (*affection*) Liebe *f* ◆ **~ is ...** die Liebe ist ...; **the ~ he has for his wife** die Liebe, die er für seine Frau empfindet; **to have a ~ for** *or* **of sb/sth** jdn/etw sehr lieben; **he has a great ~ of swimming** er schwimmt sehr gerne; **~ of learning** Freude *f* am Lernen; **~ of adventure** Abenteuerlust *f*; **~ of books** Liebe *f* zu Büchern; **the ~ of God for his creatures** die Liebe Gottes zu seinen Geschöpfen; **the ~ of God ruled his life** die Liebe zu Gott bestimmte sein Leben; **~ of (one's) country** Vaterlandsliebe *f*; **for ~** aus Liebe; (*free*) umsonst; (*without stakes*) nur zum Vergnügen; **for ~ nor money** nicht für Geld und gute Worte; **for the ~ of** aus Liebe zu; **for the ~ of God!** um Himmels willen!; **he studies history for the ~ of it** er studiert Geschichte aus Liebe zur Sache; **to be in ~ (with sb)** (in jdn) verliebt sein; **to fall in ~ (with sb)** sich (in jdn) verlieben; **there is no ~ lost between them** sie können sich nicht ausstehen; **to make ~** (*dated: flirt*) flirten (*to sb* mit jdm); (*dated: court*) den Hof machen (*dated*) (*to sb* jdm); (*sexually*) sich lieben, miteinander schlafen; **to make ~ to sb** (*sexually*) mit jdm schlafen; **I've never made ~** ich habe noch mit keinem/keiner geschlafen; **make ~ to me** liebe mich; **he's good at making ~** er ist gut in der Liebe; **make ~ not war** Liebe, nicht Krieg, make love not war.
▼ **(b)** (*greetings, in letters etc*) **with my ~** mit herzlichen Grüßen; **give him my ~** grüß ihn von mir; **to send one's ~ to sb** jdn grüßen lassen; **he sends his ~** er läßt grüßen.
(c) (*sb/sth causing fondness*) Liebe *f* ◆ **yes, (my) ~** ja, Liebling *or* Schatz; **he sent some roses to his ~** (*dated*) er schickte seiner Liebsten (*dated*) ein paar Rosen; **the child is a little ~** das Kind ist ein kleiner Schatz.
(d) (*inf: form of address*) mein Lieber/meine Liebe ◆ **I'm afraid the bus is full, ~** der Bus ist leider voll.
(e) (*Tennis*) null ◆ **fifteen ~** fünfzehn null; **Rosewall lost 3 ~ games** Rosewall verlor 3 Spiele zu null.
▼ [2] *vt* lieben; (*like*) *thing* gern mögen ◆ **I ~ tennis** ich mag Tennis sehr gern; (*to play*) ich spiele sehr gern Tennis; **he ~s swimming, he ~s to swim** er schwimmt sehr *or* für sein Leben gern; **don't be sad, you know we all ~ you** sei nicht traurig, du weißt doch, daß wir dich alle sehr gern haben; **I'd ~ to be with you all the time** ich wäre so gerne die ganze Zeit mit dir zusammen; **I'd ~ a cup of tea** ich hätte (liebend) gern(e) eine Tasse Tee; **I'd ~ to come** ich würde sehr *or* liebend gerne kommen; **I should ~ to!** sehr *or* liebend gerne!; **we'd all ~ you to come with us** wir würden uns alle sehr freuen, wenn du mitkommen würdest.
[3] *vi* lieben.

love: ~ affair *n* Liebschaft *f*, Verhältnis *nt*; **~bird** *n* (*Orn*) Unzertrennliche(r) *m*; (*fig inf*) Turteltaube *f*; **~ bite** *n* Knutschfleck *m* (*inf*); **~ child** *n* (*dated*) Kind *nt* der Liebe (*dated*); **~ game** *n* (*Tennis*) Zu-Null-Spiel *nt*; **~ handles** *npl* (*inf*) Rettungsring *m* (*hum inf*); **~-hate relationship** *n* Haßliebe *f*; **they have a ~-hate relationship** zwischen ihnen besteht eine Haßliebe; **~less** *adj* ohne Liebe; *home also* lieblos; **~ letter** *n* Liebesbrief *m*; **~ life** *n* Liebesleben *nt.*

loveliness ['lʌvlɪnɪs] *n* Schönheit *f*; (*of weather, view also*) Herrlichkeit *f.*

lovelorn ['lʌvlɔːn] *adj* (*liter*) *person* liebeskrank (*liter*); *song, poem* liebesweh (*liter*).

lovely ['lʌvlɪ] [1] *adj* (+*er*) (*beautiful*) schön; *object also* hübsch; *baby* niedlich, reizend; (*delightful*) herrlich, wunderschön; *joke* herrlich; (*charming, likeable*) liebenswürdig, nett ◆ **we had a ~ time** es war sehr schön; **it's ~ and warm in this room** es ist schön warm in diesem Zimmer; **it's been ~ to see you** es war schön, dich zu sehen; **how ~ of you to remember!** wie nett *or* lieb, daß Sie daran gedacht haben; **what a ~ thing to say!** wie nett, so was zu sagen!
[2] *n* (*inf: person*) Schöne *f* ◆ **yes, my ~** ja, mein schönes Kind.

love: ~-making *n* (*sexual*) Liebe *f*; (*dated: flirtation*) Flirt *m*; (*dated: courting*) Liebeswerben *nt* (*dated*); **oriental ~-making** orientalische Liebeskunst; **his expert ~-making** sein gekonntes Liebesspiel; **~ match** *n* Liebesheirat *f*; **~ nest** *n* Liebesnest *nt*; **~ philtre** (*old*), **~ potion** *n* Liebestrank *m.*

lover ['lʌvəʳ] *n* **(a)** Liebhaber, Geliebte(r) (*old, liter*) *m*, Geliebte *f* ◆ **the ~s** die Liebenden *pl*, das Liebespaar; **we were ~s for two years** wir waren zwei Jahre lang eng *or* intim befreundet; **Romeo and Juliet were ~s** Romeo und Julia liebten sich; **so she took a ~** da nahm sie sich (*dat*) einen Liebhaber.
(b) a ~ of books ein Bücherfreund *m*, ein Liebhaber *m* von Büchern; **a ~ of good food** ein Freund *m or* Liebhaber *m* von gutem Essen; **music ~** Musikliebhaber *or* -freund *m*; **football ~s** Fußballanhänger *or* -begeisterte *pl.*

loverboy ['lʌvəbɔɪ] *n* (*sl*) unser Freund hier (*inf*); (*boyfriend*) Freund *m* ◆ **listen, ~** hör mal zu, mein Freund(chen) (*inf*).

love: ~ seat *n* S-förmiges Sofa, Tête-à-Tête *nt*; **~ set** *n* (*Tennis*) Zu-Null-Satz *m*; **~sick** *adj* liebeskrank; **to be ~sick** Liebeskummer *m* haben; **~song** *n* Liebeslied *nt*; **~ story** *n* Liebesgeschichte *f.*

loving ['lʌvɪŋ] *adj* liebend; *look, disposition* liebevoll ◆ **~ kindness** Herzensgüte *f*; (*of God*) Barmherzigkeit *f*; **~ cup** Pokal *m*; **your ~ son ...** in Liebe Euer Sohn ...

lovingly ['lʌvɪŋlɪ] *adv* liebevoll.

low¹ [ləʊ] [1] *adj* (+*er*) **(a)** niedrig; *form of life, musical key* nieder; *bow, note* tief; *density, intelligence* gering; *food supplies* knapp; *pulse* schwach; *quality* gering; (*pej*) minderwertig (*pej*); *light* gedämpft, schwach; (*Ling*) *vowel* offen; (*Math*) *denominator* klein ◆ **the lamp was ~** die Lampe brannte schwach; **the sun was ~ in the sky** die Sonne stand tief am Himmel; **her dress was ~ at the**

➤ LANGUAGE IN USE: **love: 1b** → 21.1, 23.1 **2** → 8.4

neck ihr Kleid hatte einen tiefen Ausschnitt; **~ blow** *or* **punch** Tiefschlag *m*; **that punch was a bit ~** der Schlag war etwas tief; **the river is ~** der Fluß hat *or* führt wenig Wasser; **a ridge of ~ pressure** ein Tiefdruckkeil *m*; **a ~-calorie diet** eine kalorienarme Diät; **~ density housing** aufgelockerte Bauweise; **activity on the stock exchange is at its ~est** die Börsentätigkeit hat ihren Tiefstand erreicht; **to be ~ in funds** knapp bei Kasse sein (*inf*).

(b) (*not loud or shrill*) **to speak in a ~ voice** leise sprechen.

(c) (*socially inferior, vulgar*) *birth* nieder, niedrig; *rank, position also* untergeordnet; *tastes, manners* gewöhnlich, ordinär (*pej*); *character, company* schlecht; *joke, song* geschmacklos; *trick* gemein ◆ **I really felt ~ having to tell him that** ich kam mir richtig gemein vor, daß ich ihm das sagen mußte; **how ~ can you get!** wie kann man nur so tief sinken!; **~ life** niederes Milieu; **~ cunning** Gerissenheit *f*.

(d) (*weak in health or spirits*) *resistance* schwach, gering; *morale* schlecht ◆ **the patient is rather ~ today** der Patient ist heute nicht auf der Höhe; **to be in ~ health** bei schlechter Gesundheit sein; **to be in ~ spirits** in gedrückter Stimmung sein, bedrückt *or* niedergeschlagen sein; **to feel ~** sich nicht wohl *or* gut fühlen; (*emotionally*) niedergeschlagen sein; **to make sb feel ~** (*events*) jdn mitnehmen, jdm zu schaffen machen; (*people*) jdn mitnehmen *or* bedrücken.

[2] *adv aim* nach unten; *speak, sing* leise; *fly, bow* tief ◆ **they turned the lamps down ~** sie drehten die Lampen herunter; **a dress cut ~ in the back** ein Kleid mit tiefem Rückenausschnitt; **to fall ~** (*morally*) tief sinken; **I would never sink so ~ as to ...** so tief würde ich nie sinken, daß ich ...; **share prices went so ~ that ...** die Aktienkurse fielen so sehr, daß ...; **to buy ~ and sell high** billig kaufen und teuer verkaufen; **to lay sb ~** (*punch*) jdn zu Boden strecken; (*disease*) jdn befallen; **he's been laid ~ with the flu** er liegt mit Grippe im Bett; **to play ~** (*Cards*) um einen niedrigen *or* geringen Einsatz spielen; **to run** *or* **get ~** knapp werden; **we are getting ~ on petrol** uns (*dat*) geht das Benzin aus.

[3] *n* **(a)** (*Met*) Tief *nt*; (*fig also*) Tiefpunkt, Tiefstand *m* ◆ **to reach a new ~** einen neuen Tiefstand erreichen; **this represents a new ~ in deceit** das ist ein neuer Gipfel der Falschheit.

(b) (*Aut: ~ gear*) niedriger Gang.

low² [1] *n* (*of cow*) Muh *nt*.

[2] *vi* muhen.

low: ~-alcohol *adj* alkoholarm; **~born** *adj* von niedriger Geburt; **~boy** *n* (*US*) niedrige Kommode; **~bred** *adj* gewöhnlich, ordinär (*pej*); **~brow** [1] *adj* (geistig) anspruchslos; *person also* ungebildet; [2] *n* Kulturbanause *m* (*inf*); **~-budget** *adj film etc* mit kleinem Budget produziert; **~-cal, ~-calorie** *adj* kalorienarm; **L~ Church** *n reformierter, puritanischer Teil der Anglikanischen Kirche*; **~ comedy** *n* Schwank *m*, Klamotte *f* (*pej*); **~-cost** *adj* preiswert; **L~ Countries** *npl*: **the L~ Countries** die Niederlande *pl*; **~-cut** *adj dress* tief ausgeschnitten; **~-down** (*inf*) [1] *n* Informationen *pl*; **what's the ~-down on Kowalski?** was wissen *or* haben (*inf*) wir über Kowalski?; **he gave me the ~-down on it** er hat mich darüber aufgeklärt; **to get the ~-down on sth** über etw (*acc*) aufgeklärt werden; [2] *adj* (*esp US*) gemein, fies (*sl*).

lower¹ [ˈləʊəʳ] [1] *adj see* **low¹** niedriger; tiefer *etc*; (*Geog*) *Austria etc* Nieder-; *jaw, arm* Unter-; *limbs, storeys, latitudes* untere(r, s) ◆ **the ~ school** die unteren Klassen, die Unter- und Mittelstufe; **the ~ reaches of the river** der Unterlauf des Flusses; **the ~ parts of the hill** die tiefer gelegenen Teile des Berges; **hemlines are ~ this year** die Röcke sind dieses Jahr länger; **the ~ classes** die unteren Schichten; **the ~ deck** das Unterdeck; (*men*) Unteroffiziere und Mannschaft.

[2] *adv* tiefer; leiser ◆ **~ down the mountain** weiter unten am Berg; **~ down the list** weiter unten auf der Liste.

[3] *vt* **(a)** (*let down*) *boat, injured man, load* herunter-/hinunterlassen; *eyes, gun* senken; *mast* umlegen; *sail, flag* einholen; *bicycle saddle* niedriger machen ◆ **"~ the life-boats!"** „Rettungsboote aussetzen!"; **"~ away!"** „holt ein!".

(b) (*reduce*) *pressure* verringern; *voice, price, tone* senken; *morale, resistance* schwächen; *standard* herabsetzen ◆ **~ your voice** sprich leiser; **that is no excuse for ~ing your standard of behaviour** das ist keine Entschuldigung dafür, dich gehenzulassen; **his behaviour ~ed him in my opinion** sein Benehmen ließ ihn in meiner Achtung sinken; **to ~ oneself** sich hinunterlassen; (*socially*) sich unter sein Niveau begeben; **he ~ed himself into an armchair/his sports car** er ließ sich in einen Sessel nieder/stieg in seinen Sportwagen; **to ~ oneself to do sth** sich herablassen, etw zu tun.

[4] *vi* sinken, fallen.

lower² [ˈlaʊəʳ] *vi see* **lour**.

lower: L~ Austria *n* Niederösterreich *nt*; **~ case** [1] *n* Kleinbuchstaben, Gemeine (*spec*) *pl*; [2] *adj* klein, gemein (*spec*); **L~ Chamber** *n* Unterhaus *nt*, zweite Kammer; **~-class** *adj* Unterschicht-; *pub, habit, vocabulary* der unteren *or* niederen Schichten; **~-class people** Leute *pl* der Unterschicht *or* unteren Schicht(en).

lowering [ˈlaʊərɪŋ] *adj see* **louring**.

Lower Saxony *n* Niedersachsen *nt*.

low: ~-flying *adj* tieffliegend; **~-flying plane** Tiefflieger *m*; **~ frequency** *n* Niederfrequenz *f*; **L~ German** *n* Platt(deutsch) *nt*; (*Ling*) Niederdeutsch *nt*; **~-grade** *adj* minderwertig; **~-grade petrol** *n* Benzin mit niedriger Oktanzahl; **~-heeled** *adj shoes* mit flachem *or* niedrigem Absatz.

lowing [ˈləʊɪŋ] *n* Muhen *nt*.

low: ~ key [1] *n* zurückhaltender Ton; [2] *adj approach* gelassen; *handling* besonnen; *production, film's treatment* einfach gehalten, unaufdringlich; *reception* reserviert; *colours* gedämpft; **~land** [1] *n* Flachland *nt*; **the L~lands of Scotland** das schottische Tiefland; **the ~lands of Northern Europe** die Tiefebenen *pl* Mitteleuropas; [2] *adj* Flachland-; (*of Scotland*) Tiefland-; **~lander** *n* Flachlandbewohner(in *f*) *m*; **L~lander** *n* (*in Scotland*) Bewohner(in *f*) *m* des schottischen Tieflandes; **L~ Latin** *n* nichtklassisches Latein; **~-level** *adj infection* leicht; *radioactivity* mit niedrigem Strahlungswert; (*Comput*) *language* nieder; **~lights** *npl* **(a)** (*in hair*) dunkle Strähnchen *pl*. **(b)** (*usu hum: of event*) Tiefpunkt *m*.

lowliness [ˈləʊlɪnɪs] *n* Bescheidenheit *f*; (*of position, birth also*) Niedrigkeit *f*.

low-loader [ˈləʊˌləʊdəʳ] *n* Tieflader *m*.

lowly [ˈləʊlɪ] *adj* (*+er*) *see n* bescheiden; niedrig.

low: ~-lying *adj* tiefgelegen; **L~ Mass** *n* (einfache) Messe; **~-minded** *adj* gemein; **~-necked** *adj* tief ausgeschnitten.

lowness [ˈləʊnɪs] *n see* **low¹ (a)** Niedrigkeit *f*; Tiefe *f*; Knappheit *f*; Schwäche *f*; Minderwertigkeit *f*; Gedämpftheit *f*; (*of sun, shares*) niedriger Stand ◆ **~ of neckline** tiefer Ausschnitt; **~ of a river** niedriger Wasserstand eines Flusses; **~ of intelligence** geringer Grad an Intelligenz.

(b) the ~ of her voice ihre leise Stimme.

(c) Niedrigkeit *f*; Gewöhnlichkeit *f*; Schlechtheit, Schlechtigkeit *f*; Geschmacklosigkeit *f*; Gemeinheit *f*.

(d) Schwäche *f* ◆ **his present ~, the present ~ of his spirits** seine gegenwärtige Niedergeschlagenheit.

low: ~-pitched *adj* tief; **~-pressure** *adj* (*Tech*) Niederdruck-; (*Met*) Tiefdruck-; **~-priced** *adj* günstig; **~-profile** *adj* wenig profiliert; **a deliberately ~-profile sort of person** ein Mensch, der sich bewußt im Hintergrund hält; **~-rise** *attr* niedrig (gebaut); **~ season** *n* Nebensaison *f*; **~-slung** *adj* **to have ~-slung hips** kurze Beine haben; **~-spirited** *adj*, **~-spiritedly** *adv* niedergeschlagen; **~-tech** *adj* nicht mit Hi-Tech ausgestattet; **it's pretty ~-tech** es ist nicht gerade hi-tech; **~-tension** *adj* (*Elec*) Niederspannungs-; **~ tide, ~ water** *n* Niedrigwasser *nt*; **at ~ water** bei Niedrigwasser; **~-water mark** *n* Niedrigwassergrenze *f*.

loyal [ˈlɔɪəl] *adj* (*+er*) **(a)** treu ◆ **he was very ~ to his friends** er hielt (treu) zu seinen Freunden. **(b)** (*without emotional involvement*) loyal. **he's too ~ to say anything against the party/his colleague** er ist zu loyal, um etwas gegen seine Partei/seinen Kollegen zu sagen.

loyalist [ˈlɔɪəlɪst] [1] *n* Loyalist *m* ◆ **the ~s in the army** die regierungstreuen Teile der Armee.

[2] *adj* loyal; *army, troops* regierungstreu.

loyally [ˈlɔɪəlɪ] *adv see adj* **(a)** treu. **(b)** loyal ◆ **he ~ refused to give the names** er war zu loyal, um die Namen zu verraten.

loyalty [ˈlɔɪəltɪ] *n see adj* **(a)** Treue *f* ◆ **conflicting loyalties** nicht zu vereinbarende Treuepflichten; **torn between ~ to X and ~ to Y** hin- und hergerissen in der Treue zu X und der zu Y.

(b) Loyalität *f* ◆ **his changing political loyalties** seine wechselnden politischen Bekenntnisse.

lozenge [ˈlɒzɪndʒ] *n* **(a)** (*Med*) Pastille *f*. **(b)** (*shape*) Raute *f*, Rhombus *m*.

LP *abbr of* **long player, long-playing record** LP *f*.

L-plate [ˈelpleɪt] *n Schild nt mit der Aufschrift „L" (für Fahrschüler)*.

LRAM (*Brit*) *abbr of* **Licentiate of the Royal Academy of Music.**

LSD *abbr of* **lysergic acid diethylamide** LSD *nt*.

lsd *n* (*old Brit inf: money*) Geld *nt*, Pinke *f* (*inf*).

LSE (*Brit*) *abbr of* **London School of Economics.**

Lt *abbr of* **Lieutenant** Lt.

LTA *abbr of* **Lawn Tennis Association.**

Ltd *abbr of* **Limited** GmbH.

lubricant [ˈluːbrɪkənt] [1] *adj* Schmier-; (*Med*) Gleit-.

[2] *n* Schmiermittel *nt*; (*Med*) Gleitmittel *nt*.

lubricate [ˈluːbrɪkeɪt] *vt* (*lit, fig*) schmieren, ölen ◆ **~d sheath** Kondom *m* mit Gleitsubstanz; **well-~d** (*hum*) bezecht; **to ~ the wheels of commerce** den Handel reibungslos gestalten.

lubrication [ˌluːbrɪˈkeɪʃən] *n* Schmieren, Ölen *nt*; (*fig*) reibungslose Gestaltung.

lubricator [ˈluːbrɪkeɪtəʳ] *n* Schmiervorrichtung *f*.

lubricity [luːˈbrɪsɪtɪ] *n* (*liter: lewdness*) Schlüpfrigkeit *f*.

Lucerne [luːˈsɜːn] *n* Luzern *nt* ◆ **Lake ~** Vierwaldstätter See *m*.

lucid [ˈluːsɪd] *adj* (*+er*) **(a)** (*clear*) klar; *account, statement also* präzise; *explanation* einleuchtend, anschaulich. **(b)** (*sane*) **~ intervals** lichte Augenblicke; **he was ~ for a few minutes** ein paar Minuten lang war er bei klarem Verstand.

lucidity [luːˈsɪdɪtɪ] *n* Klarheit *f*; (*of explanation*) Anschaulichkeit *f*.

lucidly [ˈluːsɪdlɪ] *adv* klar; *explain* einleuchtend, anschaulich; *write* verständlich.

Lucifer [ˈluːsɪfəʳ] *n* Luzifer *m*.

▼ **luck** [lʌk] *n* Glück *nt* ◆ **his life was saved by ~** sein Leben wurde durch einen glücklichen Zufall gerettet; **bad ~** Unglück, Pech *nt*; **bad ~!** so ein Pech!; **bad ~, that's your own fault** Pech (gehabt), da bist du selbst schuld; **good ~** Glück *nt*; **good ~!** viel Glück!; **good ~ to them!** (*iro*), **and the best of (British) ~!** (*iro*) na dann viel Glück!; **it was his good ~ to be chosen** er hatte das Glück, gewählt zu werden; **here's ~!** (*toast*) auf glückliche Zeiten!; **no such ~!** schön wär's! (*inf*); **just my ~!** Pech (gehabt), wie immer!; **it's just his ~ to miss the train** es mußte ihm natürlich wieder passieren, daß er den Zug verpaßt hat; **it's the ~ of the draw** man muß es eben nehmen, wie's kommt; **with any ~** mit etwas Glück; **worse ~!** leider, wie schade; **better ~ next time!** vielleicht klappt's beim nächsten Mal!; **to be in ~** Glück haben; **to be out of ~** kein Glück haben; **he was a bit down on his ~** er hatte eine Pechsträhne; **tramps and others who are down on their ~** Landstreicher und

➤ LANGUAGE IN USE: **luck** → 23.5

andere, die kein Glück im Leben haben; **to bring sb bad ~** jdm Unglück bringen; **as ~ would have it** wie es der Zufall wollte; **for ~** als Glücksbringer *or* Talisman; **Bernstein kisses his cufflinks for ~** Bernstein küßt seine Manschettenknöpfe, damit sie ihm Glück bringen; **to keep sth for ~** etw als Glücksbringer aufheben; **one for ~** und noch eine(n, s); **to try one's ~** sein Glück versuchen.

◆**luck out** *vi* (*US inf*) Schwein haben (*inf*).

luckily ['lʌkɪlɪ] *adv* glücklicherweise ◆ **~ for me** zu meinem Glück.

luckless ['lʌklɪs] *adj* glücklos; *attempt also* erfolglos.

lucky ['lʌkɪ] *adj* (*+er*) **(a)** (*having luck*) Glücks- ◆ **a ~ shot** ein Glückstreffer *m*; **that was a ~ move** der Zug war Glück; **you ~ thing!, ~ you!** du Glückliche(r) *mf*; **who's the ~ man?** wer ist der Glückliche?; **to be ~** Glück haben; **I was ~ enough to meet him** ich hatte das (große) Glück, ihn kennenzulernen; **you are ~ to be alive** du kannst von Glück sagen, daß du noch lebst; **you were ~ to catch him** du hast Glück gehabt, daß du ihn erwischt hast; **he's a ~ man to have a wife like that** mit dieser Frau hat er das große Los gezogen (*inf*); **you're a ~ man** du bist ein Glückspilz; **you'll be ~ to make it in time** wenn du das noch schaffst, hast du (aber) Glück; **I want another £500 — you'll be ~!** ich will nochmal £ 500 haben — viel Glück!; **to be ~ at cards** Glück im Spiel haben; **to be born ~** ein Glücks- *or* Sonntagskind sein; **to be ~ in that** ... Glück haben, daß ...

(b) (*bringing luck*) *star, day, number* Glücks- ◆ **~ charm** Glücksbringer, Talisman *m*; **~ dip** ≈ Glückstopf *m*; **it must be my ~ day** ich habe wohl heute meinen Glückstag; **to be ~** Glück bringen.

(c) (*happening fortunately*) *coincidence* glücklich ◆ **it was ~ I stopped him in time** ein Glück, daß ich ihn rechtzeitig aufgehalten habe, zum Glück habe ich ihn rechtzeitig aufgehalten; **it's ~ for you I remembered the number** dein Glück, daß ich die Nummer noch wußte; **that was very ~ for you** da hast du aber Glück gehabt; **they had a ~ escape from the fire** sie waren dem Feuer glücklich entkommen; **he had a ~ escape in the accident** bei dem Unfall ist er glücklich *or* noch einmal davongekommen; **that was a ~ escape** da habe ich/hast du *etc* noch mal Glück gehabt.

lucrative ['luːkrətɪv] *adj* einträglich, lukrativ.

lucrativeness ['luːkrətɪvnɪs] *n* Einträglichkeit *f*.

lucre ['luːkə^r] *n* **filthy ~** schnöder Mammon.

Lucretius [luː'kriːʃəs] *n* Lukrez *m*.

lucubration [ˌluːkjʊ'breɪʃən] *n* (*form*) geistige Arbeit.

Luddite ['lʌdaɪt] (*Hist, fig*) [1] *n* Maschinenstürmer *m*.

[2] *adj* maschinenstürmerisch.

ludicrous ['luːdɪkrəs] *adj* grotesk; *sight, words also* lächerlich; *suggestion also* haarsträubend; *prices, wages* (*low*), *speed* (*slow*) lächerlich, lachhaft; *prices, wages* (*high*), *speed* (*fast*) haarsträubend ◆ **don't be ~, I can't do it that fast** das ist ja grotesk, so schnell kann ich das nicht (machen); **I've done the most ~ thing!** mir ist etwas Haarsträubendes passiert!

ludicrously ['luːdɪkrəslɪ] *adv see adj* grotesk; lächerlich; haarsträubend ◆ **it takes me ~ long to** ... ich brauche lachhaft lange dazu, zu ...; **~ expensive** absurd teuer; **prices are ~ high/low** die Preise sind haarsträubend *or* absurd hoch/lächerlich *or* grotesk niedrig.

ludicrousness ['luːdɪkrəsnɪs] *n see adj* Groteskheit *f*; Lächerlichkeit *f*; Lachhaftigkeit *f*; Absurdität *f*.

ludo ['luːdəʊ] *n* Mensch, ärgere dich nicht *nt*.

luff [lʌf] (*Naut*) [1] *n* Vorliek *nt*.

[2] *vti* (an)luven.

lug[1] [lʌg] *n* **(a)** (*earflap*) Klappe *f*; (*Tech*) Haltevorrichtung *f*. **(b)** (*sl: ear*) Ohr *nt* ◆ **~-hole** (*sl*) Ohr *nt*, Löffel *pl* (*inf*).

lug[2] *n see* **lugsail**.

lug[3] *vt* schleppen; (*towards one*) zerren ◆ **to ~ sth about with one** etw mit sich herumschleppen; **to ~ sth along behind one** etw hinter sich (*dat*) herschleppen.

luggage ['lʌgɪdʒ] *n* (*esp Brit*) Gepäck *nt*.

luggage: ~ carrier *n* Gepäckträger *m*; **~ locker** *n* Gepäckschließfach *nt*; **~ rack** *n* (*Rail etc*) Gepäcknetz *nt or* -ablage *f*; (*Aut*) Gepäckträger *m*; **~ trolley** *n* Kofferkuli *m*; **~ van** *n* (*Rail*) Gepäckwagen *m*.

lugger ['lʌgə^r] *n* Logger *m*.

lugsail ['lʌgsl] *n* Loggersegel *nt*.

lugubrious [luː'guːbrɪəs] *adj person, song* schwermütig; *smile, tune* wehmütig; *face, expression* kummervoll.

lugubriously [luː'guːbrɪəslɪ] *adv* traurig, kummervoll.

Luke [luːk] *n* Lukas *m*.

lukewarm ['luːkwɔːm] *adj* (*lit, fig*) lauwarm; *applause, support also* lau, mäßig; *friendship* lau, oberflächlich ◆ **he's ~ on the idea** er ist von der Idee nur mäßig begeistert.

lull [lʌl] [1] *n* Pause *f*; (*Comm*) Flaute *f* ◆ **a ~ in the wind** eine Windstille; **we heard the scream during a ~ in the storm** wir hörten den Schrei, als der Sturm für einen Augenblick nachließ; **a ~ in the conversation** eine Gesprächspause.

[2] *vt baby* beruhigen; (*fig*) einlullen; *fears etc* zerstreuen, beseitigen ◆ **to ~ a baby to sleep** ein Baby in den Schlaf wiegen; **he ~ed them into a sense of false security** er wiegte sie in trügerische Sicherheit.

lullaby ['lʌləbaɪ] *n* Schlaflied, Wiegenlied *nt*.

lumbago [lʌm'beɪgəʊ] *n* Hexenschuß *m*, Lumbago *f* (*spec*).

lumbar ['lʌmbə^r] *adj* Lenden-, lumbal (*spec*).

lumber[1] ['lʌmbə^r] [1] *n* **(a)** (*timber*) (Bau)holz *nt*.

(b) (*junk*) Gerümpel *nt*.

[2] *vt* **(a)** (*also* **~ up**) *space, room* vollstopfen *or* -pfropfen.

(b) (*Brit inf*) **to ~ sb with sth** jdm etw aufhalsen (*inf*); **he got ~ed with the job** man hat ihm die Arbeit aufgehalst (*inf*); **I got ~ed with her for the evening** ich hatte sie den ganzen Abend auf dem Hals (*inf*); **what a job! you've really been ~ed!** was für eine Arbeit! da hat man dir aber was aufgehalst! (*inf*).

(c) (*US*) *hillside, forest* abholzen.

[3] *vi* Holz fällen, holzen.

lumber[2] *vi* (*cart*) rumpeln; (*tank*) walzen; (*elephant, person*) trampeln; (*bear*) tapsen ◆ **a big fat man came ~ing into the room** ein dicker, fetter Mann kam ins Zimmer gewalzt; **she went ~ing about the room** sie trampelte im Zimmer herum.

lumbering[1] ['lʌmbərɪŋ] *adj see* **lumber[2]** rumpelnd; trampelnd; tapsig; *tank* schwer, klobig; *gait* schwerfällig.

lumbering[2] *n* Holzfällen *nt*, Holzfällerei *f*.

lumber: ~jack, ~man *n* Holzfäller *m*; **~ jacket** *n* Lumberjack *m*; **~ mill** *n* Sägemühle *f or* -werk *nt*; **~ room** *n* Rumpelkammer *f*; **~yard** *n* (*US*) Holzlager *nt*.

luminary ['luːmɪnərɪ] *n* **(a)** (*form*) Himmelskörper *m*, Gestirn *nt*. **(b)** (*fig*) Koryphäe, Leuchte (*inf*) *f*.

luminosity [ˌluːmɪ'nɒsɪtɪ] *n* (*form*) Helligkeit *f*; (*emission of light*) Leuchtkraft *f*; (*fig*) Brillanz *f*.

luminous ['luːmɪnəs] *adj* **(a)** leuchtend; *paint, dial* Leucht-. **(b)** (*fig liter*) *writings* brillant, luzid (*liter*).

lummox ['lʌməks] *n* (*US inf*) Trottel *m* (*inf*).

lummy, lumme ['lʌmɪ] *interj* (*Brit*) ach, du Schreck!

lump [lʌmp] [1] *n* **(a)** Klumpen *m*; (*of sugar*) Stück *nt*.

(b) (*swelling*) Beule *f*; (*inside the body*) Geschwulst *f*; (*in breast*) Knoten *m*; (*on surface*) Huppel *m* (*inf*), kleine Erhebung ◆ **with a ~ in one's throat** (*fig*) mit einem Kloß im Hals, mit zugeschnürter Kehle; **I get a ~ in my throat** mir ist die Kehle wie zugeschnürt, ich habe einen Kloß im Hals.

(c) (*inf: person*) Klotz *m*, Trampel *mf or nt* (*inf*) ◆ **a big** *or* **great fat ~ (of a man)** ein Fettkloß *m* (*inf*); **a great fat ~ of a dog** ein fetter Brocken (*inf*).

(d) you can't judge them in the ~ like that du kannst sie doch nicht so pauschal beurteilen *or* alle über einen Kamm scheren; **taken in the ~, they're not bad** alles in allem sind sie nicht schlecht; **to pay money in a ~** (*at once*) auf einmal bezahlen; (*covering different items*) pauschal bezahlen.

[2] *vt* (*inf: put up with*) **to ~ it** sich damit abfinden; **if he doesn't like it he can ~ it** wenn's ihm nicht paßt, hat er eben Pech gehabt (*inf*).

[3] *vi* (*sauce, flour*) klumpen.

◆**lump together** *vt sep* **(a)** (*put together*) zusammentun; *books* zusammenstellen; *expenses, money* zusammenlegen. **(b)** (*judge together*) *persons, topics* in einen Topf werfen, über einen Kamm scheren ◆ **he ~ed all the soldiers ~ as traitors** er urteilte all die Soldaten pauschal als Verräter ab.

lumpish ['lʌmpɪʃ] *adj person* klobig, plump.

lump: ~ payment *n* (*at once*) einmalige Bezahlung; (*covering different items*) Pauschalbezahlung *f*; **~ sugar** *n* Würfelzucker *m*; **~ sum** *n* Pauschalbetrag *m or* -summe *f*; **to pay sth in a ~ sum** etw pauschal bezahlen.

lumpy ['lʌmpɪ] *adj* (*+er*) *liquid etc, mattress, cushion* klumpig; *figure* pummelig, plump.

lunacy ['luːnəsɪ] *n* Wahnsinn *m* ◆ **it's sheer ~!** das ist reiner Wahnsinn!; **lunacies** *pl* Verrücktheiten *pl*.

lunar ['luːnə^r] *adj* Mond-, lunar (*spec*).

lunatic ['luːnətɪk] [1] *adj* verrückt, wahnsinnig ◆ **~ fringe** Extremisten *pl*, radikale *or* extremistische Randgruppe.

[2] *n* Wahnsinnige(r), Irre(r) *mf* ◆ **~ asylum** Irrenanstalt *f*.

lunch [lʌntʃ] [1] *n* Mittagessen *nt* ◆ **to have** *or* **take ~** (zu) Mittag essen; **to give sb ~** jdn zum Mittagessen einladen; **how long do you get for ~?** wie lange haben Sie Mittagspause?; **when do you have ~ in the office?** wann haben *or* machen Sie im Büro Mittag?; **he's at ~** er ist beim Mittagessen; **to have ~ out** auswärts *or* im Restaurant (zu Mittag) essen; **out to ~** (*sl: crazy*) weggetreten (*inf*).

[2] *vt* zum Mittagessen einladen.

[3] *vi* (zu) Mittag essen ◆ **we ~ed on a salad** zum (Mittag)essen gab es einen Salat.

◆**lunch out** *vi* auswärts *or* im Restaurant (zu) Mittag essen.

lunch break *n* Mittagspause *f*.

luncheon ['lʌntʃən] *n* (*form*) Lunch *nt or m*, Mittagessen *nt*.

luncheon: ~ meat *n* Frühstücksfleisch *nt*; **~ voucher** *n* Essen(s)bon *m or* -marke *f*.

lunch: ~ hour *n* Mittagsstunde *f*; (*~ break*) Mittagspause *f*; **~room** *n* (*US*) Imbißstube *f*; (*canteen*) Kantine *f*; **~time** *n* Mittagspause *f*; **they arrived at ~time** sie kamen um die Mittagszeit *or* gegen Mittag an.

lung [lʌŋ] *n* Lunge *f*; (*iron ~*) eiserne Lunge ◆ **that baby has plenty of ~ power** das Baby hat eine kräftige Lunge; **he has weak ~s** er hat keine gute Lunge; **~ cancer** Lungenkrebs *m*.

lunge [lʌndʒ] [1] *n* Satz *m* nach vorn; (*esp Fencing*) Ausfall *m* ◆ **he made a ~ at his opponent** er stürzte sich auf seinen Gegner; (*Fencing*) er machte einen Ausfall.

[2] *vi* (sich) stürzen; (*esp Fencing*) einen Ausfall machen ◆ **to ~ at sb** sich auf jdn stürzen; **the exhausted boxer could only ~ at his opponent** der erschöpfte Boxer schlug nur noch wahllos nach seinem Gegner.

◆**lunge out** *vi* ausholen ◆ **to ~ ~ at sb** sich auf jdn stürzen.

lupin, (*US*) **lupine** ['luːpɪn] *n* Lupine *f*.

lupine ['luːpaɪn] *adj* wölfisch.

lurch[1] [lɜːtʃ] *n*: **to leave sb in the ~** (*inf*) jdn im Stich lassen, jdn hängenlassen (*inf*).

lurch² [1] *n* Ruck *m*; (*of boat*) Schlingern *nt* ◆ **with a drunken ~ he started off down the road** betrunken taumelte er die Straße hinunter; **to give a ~** einen Ruck machen; (*boat*) schlingern.
[2] *vi* **(a)** *see* **to give a ~**.
(b) (*move with ~es*) ruckeln, sich ruckartig bewegen; (*boat*) schlingern; (*person*) taumeln, torkeln ◆ **the train ~ed to a standstill** der Zug kam mit einem Ruck zum Stehen; **to ~ about** hin und her schlingern/hin und her taumeln *or* torkeln; **the bus ~ed off down the bumpy track** der Bus ruckelte den holprigen Weg hinunter; **to ~ along** dahinruckeln/entlang torkeln *or* -taumeln; **the economy still manages to ~ along** die Wirtschaft schlittert gerade so eben dahin.

lure [ljʊəʳ] [1] *n* (*bait*) Köder *m*; (*person, for hawk*) Lockvogel *m*; (*general*) Lockmittel *nt*; (*fig: of city, sea etc*) Verlockungen *pl* ◆ **the ~ of the wild** der lockende Ruf der Wildnis; **she used her beauty as a ~** sie benutzte ihre Schönheit als Lockmittel; **he resisted all her ~s** er widerstand all ihren Verführungskünsten.
[2] *vt* anlocken ◆ **to ~ sb away from sth** jdn von etw weg- *or* fortlocken; **to ~ sb/an animal into a trap** jdn/ein Tier in eine Falle locken; **to ~ sb on to destruction** jdn ins Verderben stürzen; **to ~ sb/an animal out** jdn/ein Tier herauslocken.

◆**lure on** *vt sep* (*inf*) spielen mit.

lurid ['ljʊərɪd] *adj* (*+er*) **(a)** *colour, sky* grell; *dress* grellfarben, in grellen Farben; *posters also* schreiend ◆ **a ~ sunset of pinks and oranges** ein Sonnenuntergang in grellen Rosa- und Orangetönen; **her taste in clothes is rather ~** sie mag Kleider in ziemlich grellen *or* schreienden Farben.
(b) (*fig*) *language* reißerisch, blutrünstig; *account* reißerisch aufgemacht, sensationslüstern; *detail* blutig, grausig; (*sordid*) widerlich, peinlich ◆ **~ tale** Horrorgeschichte *f*; **all the love scenes are presented in ~ detail** die Liebesszenen werden bis in die allerletzten Einzelheiten dargestellt; **~ details of their quarrels** peinliche Einzelheiten ihrer Streitereien.

luridly ['ljʊərɪdlɪ] *adv* **(a)** grell ◆ **the sky glowed ~** der Himmel leuchtete in grellen Farben. **(b)** reißerisch.

luridness ['ljʊərɪdnɪs] *n see adj* **(a)** Grellheit *f*.
(b) (*of account*) reißerische *or* sensationslüsterne Aufmachung; (*of details*) grausige/peinliche Darstellung ◆ **the ~ of his language** seine reißerische Sprache; **the ~ of this tale** diese blutrünstige *or* grausige Geschichte.

lurk [lɜːk] *vi* lauern ◆ **a nasty suspicion ~ed at the back of his mind** er hegte einen fürchterlichen Verdacht; **the fears which still ~ in the unconscious** Ängste, die noch im Unterbewußtsein lauern; **a doubt still ~ed in his mind** ein Zweifel plagte ihn noch.

◆**lurk about** *or* **around** *vi* herumschleichen.

lurking ['lɜːkɪŋ] *adj* heimlich; *doubt also* nagend.

luscious ['lʌʃəs] *adj* köstlich, lecker; *fruit also* saftig; *colour* satt; *girl* zum Anbeißen (*inf*), knusprig (*inf*); *figure* (*full*) üppig; (*pleasing*) phantastisch.

lusciously ['lʌʃəslɪ] *adv* köstlich ◆ **~ coated in thick cream** mit einer köstlich dicken Sahneschicht; **with custard poured ~ all over** reichlich mit köstlicher Vanillesoße übergossen.

lusciousness ['lʌʃəsnɪs] *n* Köstlichkeit *f*; (*of fruit also*) Saftigkeit *f*; (*of colour*) Sattheit *f*; (*of girl*) knuspriges *or* appetitliches Aussehen (*inf*); (*of figure*) Üppigkeit *f*.

lush [lʌʃ] [1] *adj grass, meadows* saftig, satt; *vegetation* üppig.
[2] *n* (*US sl*) Säufer(in *f*) *m* (*inf*).

lushness ['lʌʃnɪs] *n see adj* Saftigkeit *f*; Üppigkeit *f*.

lust [lʌst] [1] *n* (*inner sensation*) Wollust, Sinneslust *f*; (*wanting to acquire*) Begierde *f* (*for* nach); (*greed*) Gier *f* (*for* nach) ◆ **rape is an act of ~** Vergewaltigungen entspringen triebhafter Gier; **the ~s of the flesh** die fleischlichen (Ge)lüste, die Fleischeslust; **~ for power** Machtgier *f*; **his uncontrollable ~** seine ungezügelte Gier/fleischliche Begierde.
[2] *vi* **to ~ after, to ~ for** (*old, hum: sexually*) begehren (*+acc*); (*greedily*) gieren nach.

luster *n* (*US*) *see* **lustre**.

lusterless *adj* (*US*) *see* **lustreless**.

lustful *adj*, **~ly** *adv* ['lʌstfʊl, -fəlɪ] lüstern.

lustfulness ['lʌstfʊlnɪs] *n* Lüsternheit, Begierde *f*.

lustily ['lʌstɪlɪ] *adv* kräftig; *work* mit Schwung und Energie; *eat* herzhaft; *sing* aus voller Kehle; *cry* aus vollem Hals(e).

lustre ['lʌstəʳ] *n* **(a)** Schimmer *m*, schimmernder Glanz; (*in eyes*) Glanz *m*.
(b) (*fig*) Glanz, Ruhm *m*.

lustreless ['lʌstəlɪs] *adj* glanzlos; *eyes, hair also* stumpf.

lustrous ['lʌstrəs] *adj* schimmernd, glänzend.

lusty ['lʌstɪ] *adj* (*+er*) *person* gesund und munter, voller Leben; *man also, life* kernig, urwüchsig; *appetite* herzhaft, kräftig; *cheer, cry* laut, kräftig; *push, kick etc* kräftig, kraftvoll.

lute [luːt] *n* Laute *f*.

lutenist ['luːtənɪst] *n* Lautenist(in *f*), Lautenspieler(in *f*) *m*.

lutetium [lʊ'tiːʃɪəm] *n* (*Chem*) Lutetium *nt*.

Luther ['luːθəʳ] *n* Luther *m*.

Lutheran ['luːθərən] [1] *adj* lutherisch.
[2] *n* Lutheraner(in *f*) *m*.

Lutheranism ['luːθərənɪzəm] *n* Luthertum *nt*.

lux *abbr of* **luxury**.

Luxembourg ['lʌksəmbɜːg] [1] *n* Luxemburg *nt*.
[2] *adj attr* Luxemburger.

Luxembourger ['lʌksəmbɜːgəʳ] *n* Luxemburger(in *f*) *m*.

luxuriance [lʌg'zjʊərɪəns] *n* Üppigkeit *f*; (*of hair also*) Fülle, Pracht *f*.

luxuriant *adj*, **~ly** *adv* [lʌg'zjʊərɪənt, -lɪ] üppig.

luxuriate [lʌg'zjʊərɪeɪt] *vi* **to ~ in sth** (*people*) sich in etw (*dat*) aalen; (*plants*) in etw (*dat*) prächtig gedeihen.

luxurious [lʌg'zjʊərɪəs] *adj* luxuriös, Luxus-; *carpet, seats, hotel also* feudal; *food* üppig ◆ **he is a man of ~ habits/tastes** er hat einen luxuriösen Lebensstil/einen Hang zum Luxus.

luxuriously [lʌg'zjʊərɪəslɪ] *adv* luxuriös ◆ **to live ~** ein Luxusleben *or* ein Leben im Luxus führen; **he sank back ~ into the cushions** er ließ sich genüßlich in die Kissen sinken.

luxury ['lʌkʃərɪ] [1] *n* **(a)** (*in general*) Luxus *m*; (*of car, house etc*) luxuriöse *or* feudale Ausstattung, Komfort *m* ◆ **to live a life of ~** ein Luxusleben *or* ein Leben im Luxus führen.
(b) (*article*) Luxus *m no pl* ◆ **we can't allow ourselves many luxuries** wir können uns (*dat*) nicht viel Luxus leisten; **little luxuries** Luxus *m*; (*to eat*) kleine Genüsse *pl*.
[2] *adj* (*cruise, tax*) Luxus-.

LV (*Brit*) *abbr of* **luncheon voucher**.

LW *abbr of* **long wave** LW.

lychee ['laɪtʃiː] *n* Litschi *f*.

lychgate *n see* **lichgate**.

lye [laɪ] *n* Lauge *f*.

lying ['laɪɪŋ] [1] *adj* lügnerisch, verlogen.
[2] *n* Lügen *nt* ◆ **that would be ~** das wäre gelogen.

lying-in ['laɪɪŋ'ɪn] *n* (*old Med*) Wochenbett *nt* (*dated*) ◆ **during her ~** im Wochenbett (*dated*); **~ ward** Wöchnerinnenstation *f* (*dated*).

lymph [lɪmf] *n* Lymphe, Gewebsflüssigkeit *f* ◆ **~ node/gland** Lymphknoten *m*/-drüse *f*.

lymphatic [lɪm'fætɪk] [1] *adj* lymphatisch, Lymph-.
[2] *n* Lymphgefäß *nt*.

lymphocyte ['lɪmfəʊˌsaɪt] *n* Lymphozyt *m*.

lynch [lɪntʃ] *vt* lynchen.

lynching ['lɪntʃɪŋ] *n* Lynchen *nt* ◆ **there'll be a ~ soon** er *etc* wird bestimmt gelyncht werden.

lynch law *n* Lynchjustiz *f*.

lynx [lɪŋks] *n* Luchs *m*.

lynx-eyed ['lɪŋksˌaɪd] *adj* mit Luchsaugen ◆ **the ~ teacher** der Lehrer, der Augen wie ein Luchs hatte.

lyre ['laɪəʳ] *n* Leier, Lyra (*geh*) *f* ◆ **~-bird** Leierschwanz *m*.

lyric ['lɪrɪk] [1] *adj* lyrisch.
[2] *n* (*poem*) lyrisches Gedicht; (*genre*) Lyrik *f*; (*often pl: words of pop song*) Text *m*.

lyrical ['lɪrɪkəl] *adj* lyrisch; (*fig*) schwärmerisch ◆ **to get** *or* **wax ~ about sth** über etw (*acc*) ins Schwärmen geraten.

lyrically ['lɪrɪkəlɪ] *adv* lyrisch; (*fig*) schwärmerisch; *sing* melodisch.

lyricism ['lɪrɪsɪzəm] *n* Lyrik *f*.

lyricist ['lɪrɪsɪst] *n* **(a)** (*poet*) Lyriker(in *f*) *m*. **(b)** (*Mus*) Texter(in *f*) *m*.

lysergic acid diethylamide [laɪ'sɜːdʒɪkˌæsɪdˌdaɪə'θɪləmaɪd] *n* Lysergsäurediäthylamid *nt*.

lysol ® ['laɪsɒl] *n* Lysol ® *nt*.

M

M, m [em] *n* M, m *nt.*
M *abbr of* **medium.**
m *abbr of* **million(s)** Mill., Mio.; **metre(s)** m; **mile(s); minute(s)** min; **married** verh.; **masculine** m.
MA *abbr of* **Master of Arts** M.A.
ma [mɑː] *n* (*inf*) Mama (*inf*), Mutti (*inf*) *f.*
ma'am [mæm] *n* gnä' Frau *f* (*form*); *see* **madam (a).**
mac¹ [mæk] *n* (*Brit inf*) Regenmantel *m.*
mac² *n* (*esp US inf*) Kumpel *m* (*inf*).
macabre [mə'kɑːbrə] *adj* makaber.
macadam [mə'kædəm] *n* Schotter, Splitt *m*, Makadam *m or nt* ◆ **~ road** Schotterstraße *f.*
macadamize [mə'kædəmaɪz] *vt* schottern, makadamisieren (*spec*).
macaroni [,mækə'rəʊnɪ] *n* Makkaroni *pl* ◆ **~ cheese** Käsemakkaroni *pl.*
macaronic [,mækə'rɒnɪk] *adj* makkaronisch.
macaroon [,mækə'ruːn] *n* Makrone *f.*
macaw [mə'kɔː] *n* Ara *m.*
mace¹ [meɪs] *n* (*weapon*) Streitkolben *m*, Keule *f*; (*mayor's*) Amtsstab *m* ◆ **~bearer** Träger *m* des Amtsstabes.
mace² *n* (*spice*) Muskatblüte *f*, Mazis *m.*
Macedonia [,mæsɪ'dəʊnɪə] *n* Makedonien, Mazedonien *nt.*
Macedonian [,mæsɪ'dəʊnɪən] 1 *n* Makedonier(in *f*), Mazedonier(in *f*) *m.*
2 *adj* makedonisch, mazedonisch.
macerate ['mæsəreɪt] 1 *vt* aufweichen, einweichen.
2 *vi* aufweichen, weich werden.
Mach [mæk] *n* Mach *nt* ◆ **~ number** Mach-Zahl *f*; **the jet was approaching ~ 2** das Flugzeug näherte sich (einer Geschwindigkeit von) 2 Mach.
machete [mə'tʃeɪtɪ] *n* Machete *f*, Buschmesser *nt.*
Machiavelli [,mækɪə'velɪ] *n* Machiavelli *m.*
Machiavellian [,mækɪə'velɪən] *adj* machiavellistisch.
machination [,mækɪ'neɪʃən] *n usu pl* Machenschaften *pl.*
machine [mə'ʃiːn] 1 *n* Maschine *f*, Apparat *m*; (*vending ~*) Automat *m*; (*car*) Wagen *m*; (*cycle, plane*) Maschine *f*; (*Pol*) Partei-/Regierungsapparat *m*; (*fig: person*) Maschine *f*, Roboter *m.*
2 *vt* (*Tech*) maschinell herstellen; (*treat with ~*) maschinell bearbeiten; (*Sew*) mit der Maschine nähen.
machine: ~ age *n*: **the ~ age** das Maschinenzeitalter; **~ code** *n* Maschinencode *m*; **~ gun** 1 *n* Maschinengewehr *nt*; 2 *vt* mit dem Maschinengewehr beschießen/erschießen; **~ gunner** *n* Soldat *m*/Polizist *m etc* mit Maschinengewehr; **~ intelligence** *n* künstliche Intelligenz; **~ language** *n* (*Comput*) Maschinensprache *f*; **~-made** *adj* maschinell hergestellt; **~ operator** *n* Maschinenarbeiter *m*; (*skilled*) Maschinist *m*; **~-readable** *adj* (*Comput*) maschinenlesbar.
machinery [mə'ʃiːnərɪ] *n* (*machines*) Maschinen *pl*, Maschinerie *f*; (*mechanism*) Mechanismus *m*; (*fig*) Maschinerie *f* ◆ **the ~ of government** der Regierungsapparat.
machine: ~ shop *n* Maschinensaal *m*; **~ stitch** *vt* maschinell *or* mit der Maschine nähen; **~ time** *n* Betriebszeit *f*; (*computing time*) Rechenzeit *f*; **the relationship between cost and ~ time** das Verhältnis der Kosten zur Betriebszeit der Maschine(n); **~ tool** *n* Werkzeugmaschine *f*; **~ translation** *n* maschinelle Übersetzung; **~-washable** *adj* waschmaschinenfest.
machinist [mə'ʃiːnɪst] *n* (*Tech*) (*operator*) Maschinist *m*; (*constructor, repairer*) Maschinenschlosser *m*; (*Sew*) Näherin *f.*
machismo [mæ'kɪzməʊ, mæ'tʃɪzməʊ] *n* Machismo *m.*
macho ['mætʃəʊ] 1 *adj* macho *pred*, Macho- ◆ **a ~ type/man** ein Macho *m.*
2 *n* Macho *m.*
mackerel ['mækrəl] *n* Makrele *f.*
mackintosh ['mækɪntɒʃ] *n* Regenmantel *m.*
macramé [mə'krɑːmɪ] *n* Makramee *nt.*
macro ['mækrəʊ] *n* (*Comput*) Makro *nt.*
macro- *pref* makro-, Makro-.
macrobiotic ['mækrəʊbaɪ'ɒtɪk] *adj* makrobiotisch.
macrocosm ['mækrəʊ,kɒzəm] *n* Makrokosmos *m* ◆ **the ~ of Italian society** die italienische Gesellschaft als ganzes *or* in ihrer Gesamtheit.
macroeconomics [,mækrəʊ,iːkə'nɒmɪks] *n sing or pl* Makroökonomie *f.*
macron ['mækrɒn] *n* (*Typ*) Querbalken *m*, Längezeichen *nt.*

mad [mæd] 1 *adj* (*+er*) **(a)** wahnsinnig, verrückt; *dog* tollwütig; *idea* verrückt ◆ **to go ~** verrückt *or* wahnsinnig werden; **to drive sb ~** jdn wahnsinnig *or* verrückt machen; **it's enough to drive you ~** es ist zum Verrücktwerden; **he has a ~ look in his eye** er hat einen irren Blick; **he's as ~ as a hatter** *or* **a March hare** (*prov*) er ist ein komischer Vogel *or* Kauz; **are you raving ~?** bist du total verrückt geworden?; **you must be ~!** du bist ja wahnsinnig!; **I must have been ~ to believe him** ich war wohl von Sinnen, ihm zu glauben; **~ cow disease** Rinderwahnsinn *m.*
(b) (*inf: angry*) böse, sauer (*inf*) ◆ **to be ~ at sb** auf jdn böse *or* sauer (*inf*) sein; **to be ~ about** *or* **at sth** über etw (*acc*) wütend *or* sauer (*inf*) sein; **he makes me so ~** er macht mich so wütend; **don't get ~ at** *or* **with me** sei nicht böse *or* sauer (*inf*) auf mich.
(c) (*stupid, rash*) verrückt ◆ **you ~ fool!** du bist ja wahnsinnig *or* verrückt!; **it's a ~ hope** es ist verrückt, darauf zu hoffen; **that was a ~ thing to do** das war Wahnsinn (*inf*).
(d) (*inf: very keen*) **to be ~ about** *or* **on sth** auf etw (*acc*) verrückt sein; **I'm not exactly ~ about this job** ich bin nicht gerade versessen auf diesen Job; **I'm (just) ~ about you** ich bin (ganz) verrückt nach dir!
(e) (*wild*) wahnsinnig ◆ **they made a ~ rush** *or* **dash for the door** sie stürzten zur Tür; **the prisoner made a ~ dash for freedom** der Gefangene unternahm einen verzweifelten Ausbruchsversuch; **to be ~ with joy** sich wahnsinnig freuen.
2 *adv* (*inf*) **to be ~ keen on sb/sth** ganz scharf auf jdn/etw sein (*inf*); **to be ~ keen to do sth** ganz versessen darauf sein, etw zu tun; **like ~** wie verrückt; **he ran like ~** er rannte wie wild.
Madagascan [,mædə'gæskən] 1 *adj* madegassisch.
2 *n* Madegasse *m*, Madegassin *f.*
Madagascar [,mædə'gæskə^r] *n* Madagaskar *nt.*
madam ['mædəm] *n* **(a)** gnädige Frau (*old, form*) ◆ **~, would you kindly desist!** würden Sie das bitte unterlassen! (*form*); **yes, ~** sehr wohl, gnädige Frau (*old, form*), ja (wohl); **can I help you, ~?** kann ich Ihnen behilflich sein?; **dear ~** sehr geehrte gnädige Frau; **Dear Sir or M~** Sehr geehrte Damen und Herren.
(b) (*inf: girl*) kleine Prinzessin.
(c) (*of brothel*) Bordellwirtin, Puffmutter (*inf*) *f.*
madcap ['mædkæp] 1 *adj idea* versponnen; *youth* stürmisch; *tricks* toll.
2 *n* impulsiver Mensch.
madden ['mædn] *vt* (*make mad*) verrückt machen; (*make angry*) ärgern, fuchsen (*inf*) ◆ **it ~s me to think of the opportunity we missed** ich könnte mich schwarz ärgern (*inf*), wenn ich daran denke, was für eine Chance wir vertan haben.
maddening ['mædnɪŋ] *adj* unerträglich, zum Verrücktwerden; *delay also* lästig; *habit* aufreizend ◆ **isn't it ~?** ist das nicht ärgerlich?; **this is ~!** das ist (ja) zum Verrücktwerden!
maddeningly ['mædnɪŋlɪ] *adv* unerträglich ◆ **the train ride was ~ slow** es war zum Verrücktwerden, wie langsam der Zug fuhr.
madder ['mædə^r] *n* (*plant*) Krapp *m*, Färberröte *f*; (*dye*) Krapprot *nt*, Krappfarbstoff *m.*
made [meɪd] *pret, ptp of* **make.**
Madeira [mə'dɪərə] *n* Madeira *nt*; (*wine*) Madeira *m* ◆ **~ cake** Sandkuchen *m.*
made-to-measure ['meɪdtə'meʒə^r] *adj* maßgeschneidert ◆ **~ suit** Maßanzug *m*; **~ clothes** Maßkonfektion *f.*
made-up ['meɪd'ʌp] *adj story* erfunden; *face* geschminkt.
madhouse ['mædhaʊs] *n* (*lit, fig*) Irrenhaus *nt.*
madly ['mædlɪ] *adv* **(a)** wie verrückt ◆ **he worked ~ for weeks on end** er arbeitete wochenlang wie besessen *or* verrückt.
(b) (*inf: extremely*) wahnsinnig ◆ **to be ~ in love (with sb)** bis über beide Ohren (in jdn) verliebt sein, total (in jdn) verschossen sein (*inf*); **I'm not ~ keen to go** ich bin nicht wahnsinnig scharf (*inf*) *or* erpicht darauf (zu gehen).
madman ['mædmən] *n, pl* **-men** [-mən] Irre(r), Verrückte(r) *m.*
▼ **madness** ['mædnɪs] *n* Wahnsinn *m* ◆ **it's sheer ~!** das ist heller *or* reiner Wahnsinn!; **what ~!** das ist doch Wahnsinn!
Madonna [mə'dɒnə] *n* Madonna *f*; (*picture also*) Madonnenbild *nt*; (*statue also*) Madonnenfigur *f.*
Madrid [mə'drɪd] *n* Madrid *nt.*

➤ LANGUAGE IN USE: **madness** → 2.3

madrigal ['mædrɪgəl] *n* Madrigal *nt.*
Maecenas [miː'siːnəs] *n* Maecenas *m*; (*fig*) Mäzen *m.*
maelstrom ['meɪlstrəʊm] *n* (*lit rare*) Malstrom *m*; (*fig*) Malstrom (*liter*), Sog *m* ♦ **he returned to the ~ of public life** er kehrte in den Trubel des öffentlichen Lebens zurück.
maestro ['maɪstrəʊ] *n* Maestro *m.*
Mae West [,meɪ'west] *n* (*hum*) Schwimmweste *f.*
Mafia ['mæfɪə] *n* Maf(f)ia *f.*
mafioso [,mæfɪ'əʊsəʊ] *n, pl* **-sos** *or* **-si** Mafioso *m.*
mag [mæg] *n* (*inf*) Magazin *nt*; (*glossy also*) Illustrierte *f* ♦ **porn ~** Pornoheft *nt.*
magazine [,mægə'ziːn] *n* **(a)** (*journal*) Zeitschrift *f*, Magazin *nt.* **(b)** (*in gun*) Magazin *nt.* **(c)** (*Mil: store*) Magazin (*Hist*), Depot *nt.*
magenta [mə'dʒentə] **1** *n* Fuchsin *nt.*
2 *adj* tiefrot.
maggot ['mægət] *n* Made *f.*
maggoty ['mægətɪ] *adj* madig ♦ **the cheese has gone all ~** der Käse wimmelt von Maden.
Magi ['meɪdʒaɪ] *npl*: **the ~** die Heiligen Drei Könige, die drei Weisen aus dem Morgenland.
magic ['mædʒɪk] **1** *n* **(a)** Magie, Zauberei, Zauberkunst *f* ♦ **the witch doctor tried ~ to cure the woman** der Medizinmann versuchte, die Frau durch Magie zu heilen; **he entertained them with a display of ~** er unterhielt sie mit ein paar Zauberkunststücken; **he made the spoon disappear by ~** er zauberte den Löffel weg; **you don't expect the essay to write itself by ~?** glaubst du, daß der Aufsatz sich von alleine schreibt?; **as if by ~** wie durch Zauberei, wie durch ein Wunder; **it worked like ~** (*inf*) es klappte *or* lief wie am Schnürchen (*inf*).
(b) (*mysterious charm*) Zauber *m.*
2 *adj* **(a)** Zauber-; *powers* magisch; *moment* zauberhaft ♦ **the witch cast a ~ spell on her** die Hexe verzauberte sie; **the ~ word** (*having special effect*) das Stichwort; (*making sth possible*) das Zauberwort; **the ~ touch** ein geschicktes Händchen; **a pianist who really had the ~ touch** ein begnadeter Pianist; **he gave it his ~ touch and it worked** er hat es nur angefaßt, und schon funktionierte es; **"The M~ Flute"** „Die Zauberflöte".
(b) (*sl: fantastic*) toll (*inf*).
magical ['mædʒɪkəl] *adj* magisch ♦ **the effect was ~** das wirkte (wahre) Wunder.
magically ['mædʒɪkəlɪ] *adv* wunderbar ♦ **~ transformed** auf wunderbare Weise verwandelt; **her headache disappeared ~** ihre Kopfschmerzen waren auf einmal wie weggeblasen.
magic: ~ carpet *n* fliegender Teppich; **~ circle** *n* Gilde *f* der Zauberkünstler; **~ eye** *n* magisches Auge.
magician [mə'dʒɪʃən] *n* Magier, Zauberer *m*; (*conjuror*) Zauberkünstler *m* ♦ **I'm not a ~!** ich kann doch nicht hexen!
magic: ~ lantern *n* Laterna magica *f*; **~ wand** *n* Zauberstab *m.*
magisterial [,mædʒɪ'stɪərɪəl] *adj* **(a)** (*lit*) *powers, office, robes* eines Friedensrichters. **(b)** (*imperious*) gebieterisch.
magisterially [mædʒɪ'stɪərɪəlɪ] *adv* gebieterisch.
magistracy ['mædʒɪstrəsɪ] *n* (*position*) Amt *nt* des Friedensrichters; (*judges*) Friedensrichter *pl.*
magistrate ['mædʒɪstreɪt] *n* Friedensrichter, Schiedsmann *m* ♦ **~s' court** Friedens- *or* Schiedsgericht *nt.*
magnanimity [,mægnə'nɪmɪtɪ] *n* Großherzigkeit, Großmut *f* ♦ **he acted with great ~** er handelte sehr großherzig.
magnanimous *adj*, **~ly** *adv* [mæg'nænɪməs, -lɪ] großmütig, großherzig.
magnate ['mægneɪt] *n* Magnat *m.*
magnesia [mæg'niːʃə] *n* Magnesia *f.*
magnesium [mæg'niːzɪəm] *n* Magnesium *nt.*
magnet ['mægnɪt] *n* (*lit, fig*) Magnet *m.*
magnetic [mæg'netɪk] *adj* (*lit*) magnetisch; *charms* unwiderstehlich ♦ **he has a ~ personality** er hat eine große Ausstrahlung *or* ein sehr anziehendes Wesen; **this perfume has a ~ effect on men** dieses Parfüm übt eine magnetische Wirkung auf Männer aus.
magnetically [mæg'netɪkəlɪ] *adv* magnetisch.
magnetic: ~ attraction *n* magnetische Anziehungskraft; **~ card reader** *n* Magnetkartenleser *m*; **~ compass** *n* Magnetkompaß *m*; **~ disk** *n* (*Comput*) Magnetplatte *f*; **~ field** *n* Magnetfeld *nt*; **~ mine** *n* Magnetmine *f*; **~ needle** *n* Magnetnadel *f*; **~ north** *n* nördlicher Magnetpol; **~ pole** *n* Magnetpol *m*; **~ storm** *n* (erd)magnetischer Sturm; **~ strip, ~ stripe** *n* Magnetstreifen *m*; **~ tape** *n* Magnetband *nt.*
magnetism ['mægnɪtɪzəm] *n* Magnetismus *m*; (*fig: of person*) Anziehungskraft, Ausstrahlung *f.*
magnetize ['mægnɪtaɪz] *vt* magnetisieren ♦ **the audience was ~d by this incredible performance** das Publikum folgte dieser unglaublichen Darstellung wie gebannt.
magneto [mæg'niːtəʊ] *n* Magnetzünder *m.*
magnification [,mægnɪfɪ'keɪʃən] *n* Vergrößerung *f* ♦ **high/low ~** starke/geringe Vergrößerung; **seen at 300 ~s** in 300facher Vergrößerung, 300fach vergrößert.
magnificence [mæg'nɪfɪsəns] *n* **(a)** (*excellence*) Großartigkeit, Größe *f.* **(b)** (*splendid appearance*) Pracht *f*, Glanz *m.* **(c)** **his M~** Seine Magnifizenz.
magnificent [mæg'nɪfɪsənt] *adj* **(a)** (*wonderful, excellent*) großartig; *food, meal* hervorragend, ausgezeichnet. **(b)** (*of splendid appearance*) prachtvoll, prächtig.
magnificently [mæg'nɪfɪsəntlɪ] *adv see adj* **(a)** großartig ♦ **you did ~** das hast du großartig gemacht; **a ~ rousing finale** ein glanzvolles (und) mitreißendes Finale. **(b)** prachtvoll, prächtig.
magnify ['mægnɪfaɪ] *vt* **(a)** vergrößern ♦ **to ~ sth 7 times** etw 7fach vergrößern; **~ing glass** Vergrößerungsglas *nt*, Lupe *f.*
(b) (*exaggerate*) aufbauschen.
(c) (*obs, liter: praise*) *the Lord* lobpreisen (*old, liter*).
magniloquence [mæg'nɪləkwəns] *n* (*liter*) Wortgewalt *f* (*liter*).
magniloquent [mæg'nɪləkwənt] *adj* (*liter*) wortgewaltig (*liter*).
magnitude ['mægnɪtjuːd] *n* **(a)** Ausmaß *nt*, Größe *f*; (*importance*) Bedeutung *f* ♦ **I didn't appreciate the ~ of the task** ich war mir über den Umfang der Aufgabe nicht im klaren; **in operations of this ~** bei Vorhaben dieser Größenordnung; **a matter of the first ~** eine Angelegenheit von äußerster Wichtigkeit; **a fool of the first ~** ein Narr erster Güte.
(b) (*Astron*) Größenklasse *f.*
magnolia [mæg'nəʊlɪə] *n* Magnolie *f*; (*also* **~ tree**) Magnolienbaum *m.*
magnum ['mægnəm] *n* ≃ Anderthalbliterflasche *f* (*esp von Sekt*) ♦ **~ opus** Hauptwerk *nt.*
magpie ['mægpaɪ] *n* Elster *f.*
Magyar ['mægjɑːʳ] **1** *adj* madjarisch, magyarisch.
2 *n* Madjar(in *f*), Magyar(in *f*) *m.*
maharajah [,mɑːhə'rɑːdʒə] *n* Maharadscha *m.*
maharani [,mɑːhə'rɑːniː] *n* Maharani *f.*
maharishi [,mɑːhɑː'rɪʃɪ] *n* Maharischi *m.*
mahogany [mə'hɒgənɪ] **1** *n* Mahagoni *nt*; (*tree*) Mahagonibaum *m.*
2 *adj* Mahagoni-; (*colour*) mahagoni(farben).
Mahomet [mə'hɒmɪt] *n* Mohammed, Mahomet (*liter*) *m.*
Mahometan [mə'hɒmɪtən] **1** *adj* mohammedanisch.
2 *n* Mohammedaner(in *f*) *m.*
mahout [mə'haʊt] *n* Mahaut, Elefantenführer *m.*
maid [meɪd] *n* **(a)** (*servant*) (Dienst)mädchen *nt*, Hausangestellte *f*; (*in hotel*) Zimmermädchen *nt*; (*lady's ~*) Zofe *f.* **(b)** (*old*) (*maiden*) Jungfer (*obs*), Maid (*old, poet*) *f*; (*young girl*) Mägdelein *nt* (*poet*) ♦ **the M~ of Orleans** die Jungfrau von Orleans. **(c)** *see* **old ~.**
maiden ['meɪdn] **1** *n* (*liter*) Maid *f* (*old, poet*), Mädchen *nt.*
2 *adj flight, voyage etc* Jungfern-.
maiden: ~ aunt *n* unverheiratete, ältere Tante; **~hair** *n* Frauenhaar *nt*; **~head** *n* (*Anat*) Jungfernhäutchen *nt*; **she lost her ~head** (*liter*) sie hat ihre Unschuld verloren; **~hood** *n* Jungfräulichkeit, Unschuld *f*; (*time*) Jungmädchenzeit *f.*
maidenly ['meɪdnlɪ] *adj* jungfräulich; (*modest*) mädchenhaft.
maiden: ~ name *n* Mädchenname *m*; **~ over** *n* (*Cricket*) *6 Würfe ohne einen Lauf*; **~ speech** *n* Jungfernrede *f.*
maid: ~-of-all-work *n* (*person*) Mädchen *nt* für alles; (*machine*) Allzweckgerät *nt*; **~ of honour** *n* Brautjungfer *f*; **~servant** *n* Hausangestellte *f*, Hausmädchen *nt.*
mail[1] [meɪl] **1** *n* Post *f* ♦ **to send sth by ~** etw mit der Post versenden *or* schicken; **is there any ~ for me?** ist Post für mich da?
2 *vt* aufgeben; (*put in letterbox*) einwerfen; (*send by ~*) mit der Post schicken ♦ **~ing list** Anschriftenliste *f.*
mail[2] **1** *n* (*Mil*) Kettenpanzer *m.*
2 *vt* **the ~ed fist of imperialism** die gepanzerte Faust des Imperialismus.
mail: ~bag *n* Postsack *m*; **~boat** *n* Postdampfer *m*; **~ bomb** *n* (*US*) Briefbombe *f*; **~box** *n* **(a)** (*US*) Briefkasten *m*; **(b)** (*Comput*) Mailbox *f*, (elektronischer) Briefkasten; **~ car** *n* (*US Rail*) Postwagen *m*; **~ coach** *n* (*Hist*) Postkutsche *f*; (*Rail*) Postwagen *m*; **~ drop** *n* (*US*) Briefeinwurf (*form*), Briefschlitz *m*; **M~gram** ® *n* (*US*) *auf elektronischem Wege an ein Postamt im Bezirk des Empfängers übermittelte Nachricht, die dann als normale Briefsendung zugestellt wird.*
mailing ['meɪlɪŋ] *n* Rundschreiben *nt* ♦ **~ list** Anschriftenliste *f.*
mail: ~man *n* (*US*) Briefträger, Postbote *m*; **~ merge** *n* (*Comput*) Mailmerge *nt*; **~ merge program** Dateimischprogramm *nt*; **~-order catalogue** *n* Versandhauskatalog *m*; **~-order firm, ~-order house** *n* Versandhaus, Versandgeschäft *nt*; **~shot** **1** *n* Direktwerbung *f* (per Post); **to send out a ~shot** Werbebriefe verschicken; **2** *vt* Werbebriefe verschicken an (+*acc*); **~ train** *n* Postzug *m*; **~ van** *n* (*on roads*) Postauto *nt*; (*Brit Rail*) Postwagen *m.*
maim [meɪm] *vt* (*mutilate*) verstümmeln; (*cripple*) zum Krüppel machen ♦ **the wounded and the ~ed** die Verletzten und Versehrten; **he will be ~ed for life** er wird sein Leben lang ein Krüppel bleiben; **he was ~ed in the bomb attack** der Bombenanschlag machte ihn zum Krüppel.
main [meɪn] **1** *adj attr* Haupt- ♦ **the ~ idea in this book** der Haupt- *or* Leitgedanke in diesem Buch; **what is the ~ thing in life?** was ist die Hauptsache im Leben?; **the ~ thing is to ...** die Hauptsache ist, daß ...; **the ~ thing is you're still alive** Hauptsache, du lebst noch; *see* **part.**
2 *n* **(a)** (*pipe*) Hauptleitung *f* ♦ **the ~s** (*of town*) das öffentliche Versorgungsnetz; (*electricity*) das Stromnetz; (*of house*) der Haupthahn; (*for electricity*) der Hauptschalter; **the machine is run directly off the ~s** das Gerät wird direkt ans Stromnetz angeschlossen; **~s operated** für Netzbetrieb, mit Netzanschluß; **the water/gas/electricity was switched off at the ~s** der Haupthahn/Hauptschalter für Wasser/Gas/Elektrizität wurde abgeschaltet.
(b) (*poet*) **the ~** das offene Meer, die hohe See.
(c) **in the ~** im großen und ganzen.
(d) *see* **might**[2].
main: ~brace *n* Großbrasse *f*; **to splice the ~brace** Rum an die Mannschaft ausgeben; **~ course** *n* Hauptgericht *nt*; **~ deck** *n* Hauptdeck *nt*; **~ force** *n*

rohe Gewalt; **~frame (computer)** *n* Großrechner, Mainframe *m*; **~land** *n* Festland *nt*; **on the ~land of Europe** auf dem europäischen Festland; **~line** [1] *n* Hauptstrecke *f*; **~line train** Schnellzug *m*; [2] *vi* (*sl*) fixen (*sl*).

mainly ['meɪnlɪ] *adv* hauptsächlich, in erster Linie ◆ **the meetings are held ~ on Tuesdays** die Besprechungen finden meistens dienstags statt; **the climate is ~ wet** das Klima ist vorwiegend *or* überwiegend feucht.

main: ~mást *n* Haupt- *or* Großmast *m*; **~ road** *n* Hauptstraße *f*; **~sail** *n* Haupt- *or* Großsegel *nt*; **~spring** *n* (*Mech, fig*) Triebfeder *f*; **~stay** *n* (*Naut*) Haupt- *or* Großstag *nt*; (*fig*) Stütze *f*; **~stream** [1] *n* **(a)** Hauptrichtung *f*; **to be in the ~stream of sth** der Hauptrichtung (*+gen*) angehören; **(b)** (*Jazz*) Mainstream *m*; [2] *adj* **(a)** *politician* der Mitte (*gen*); *philosophy etc* vorherrschend; **(b)** *jazz* Mainstream-.

▼ **maintain** [meɪn'teɪn] *vt* **(a)** (*keep up*) aufrechterhalten; *law and order, peace etc also* wahren; *quality also, speed, attitude* beibehalten; *prices* halten; *life* erhalten.
(b) (*support*) *family* unterhalten.
(c) (*keep in good condition*) *machine* warten; *roads, building* instand halten; *car* pflegen ◆ **this old car is too expensive to ~** dieses alte Auto ist im Unterhalt zu teuer.
▼ **(d)** (*claim*) behaupten ◆ **he still ~ed he was innocent** er beteuerte immer noch seine Unschuld.
(e) (*defend*) *theory* vertreten; *rights* verteidigen.

maintenance ['meɪntɪnəns] *n see vt* **(a)** Aufrechterhaltung *f*; Wahrung *f*; Beibehaltung *f*; Erhaltung *f*.
(b) (*of family*) Unterhalt *m*; (*social security*) Unterstützung *f* ◆ **he has to pay ~** er ist unterhaltspflichtig.
(c) Wartung *f*; Instandhaltung *f*; Pflege *f*; (*cost*) Unterhalt *m* ◆ **his hobby is car ~** er bastelt gern an Autos herum.

maintenance: ~ contract *n* Wartungsvertrag *m*; **~ costs** *npl* Unterhaltskosten *pl*; **~ crew** *n* Wartungsmannschaft *f*.

maintop ['meɪntɒp] *n* Großmars *m*.

maisonette [,meɪzə'net] *n* (*small flat*) Appartement *nt*; (*small house*) Häuschen *nt*.

maître d' [,metrə,diː] *n* (*US: head waiter*) Oberkellner *m*.

maize [meɪz] *n* Mais *m*.

Maj *abbr of* **major**.

majestic [mə'dʒestɪk] *adj* majestätisch; *proportions* stattlich; *movement* gemessen; *music* getragen; (*not slow*) erhaben.

majestically [mə'dʒestɪkəlɪ] *adv move* majestätisch ◆ **~ proportioned buildings** Gebäude von stattlichen Ausmaßen; **the music ends ~** die Musik kommt zu einem erhabenen *or* grandiosen Schluß.

majesty ['mædʒɪstɪ] *n* (*stateliness*) Majestät *f*; (*of movements etc*) Würde *f* ◆ **the ~ of the mountains** die Majestät *or* Erhabenheit der Bergwelt; **music full of ~ and grace** Musik voller Erhabenheit und Anmut; **His/Her M~** Seine/Ihre Majestät; **Your M~** Eure Majestät.

Maj Gen *abbr of* **major general**.

major ['meɪdʒəʳ] [1] *adj* **(a)** Haupt-; (*of great importance*) bedeutend; (*of great extent*) groß ◆ **a ~ road** eine Hauptverkehrsstraße; **a ~ poet** ein bedeutender Dichter; **matters of ~ interest** Angelegenheiten *pl* von großem *or* größerem Interesse; **of ~ importance** von großer *or* größerer Bedeutung; **~ premise** erste Prämisse, Obersatz *m*; **a ~ operation** eine größere Operation; **a ~ work of art** ein bedeutendes Kunstwerk.
(b) (*Mus*) *key, scale* Dur- ◆ **A/A flat/G sharp ~** A-/As-/Gis-Dur *nt*; **~ third** große Terz.
(c) **Jenkins M~** Jenkins der Ältere.
[2] *n* **(a)** (*Mil*) Major *m*.
(b) (*Mus*) Dur *nt* ◆ **in the ~** in Dur.
(c) (*Jur*) **to become a ~** volljährig *or* mündig werden.
(d) (*US*) (*subject*) Hauptfach *nt* ◆ **he's a psychology ~** Psychologie ist/war sein Hauptfach.
[3] *vi* (*US*) **to ~ in French** Französisch als Hauptfach studieren, das Examen mit Französisch im Hauptfach ablegen.

Majorca [mə'jɔːkə] *n* Mallorca *nt*.

Majorcan [mə'jɔːkən] [1] *adj* mallorquinisch.
[2] *n* Mallorquiner(in *f*) *m*.

major domo [,meɪdzə'dəʊməʊ] *n* Haushofmeister, Majordomus *m*.

majorette [,meɪdʒə'ret] *n* Majorette *f*.

major general *n* Generalmajor *m*.

majority [mə'dʒɒrɪtɪ] *n* **(a)** Mehrheit *f* ◆ **the ~ of cases** die Mehrheit *or* Mehrzahl der Fälle; **to be in a ~** in der Mehrzahl sein; **to be in a ~ of 3** eine Mehrheit von 3 Stimmen haben; **to have/get a ~** die Mehrheit haben/bekommen; **to have a ~ of 10** eine Mehrheit von 10 Stimmen haben; **what was his ~?** wie groß war seine Mehrheit?; **a two-thirds ~** die Zweidrittelmehrheit; **by a small ~** mit knapper Mehrheit.
(b) (*Jur*) Volljährigkeit, Mündigkeit *f* ◆ **to attain one's ~, to reach the age of ~** volljährig *or* mündig werden.

majority: ~ decision *n* Mehrheitsbeschluß *m*; **~ holding** *n* (*Fin*) Mehrheitsbeteiligung *f*; **~ rule** *n* Mehrheitsregierung *f*.

make [meɪk] (*vb: pret, ptp* **made**) [1] *vt* **(a)** (*produce, prepare*) machen; *bread* backen; *cars* herstellen; *dress* nähen; *coffee* kochen; *house* bauen; *peace* stiften; *the world* erschaffen ◆ **she made it into a suit** sie machte einen Anzug daraus; **it's made of gold** es ist aus Gold; **made in Germany** in Deutschland hergestellt, made in Germany; **he's as clever as they ~ 'em** (*inf*) der ist ein ganz gerissener Hund (*inf*); **to show what one is made of** zeigen, was in einem steckt; **the job is made for him** die Arbeit ist wie für ihn geschaffen; **they're made for each other** sie sind wie geschaffen füreinander; **this car wasn't made to carry 8 people** dieses Auto ist nicht dazu gedacht, 8 Leute zu transportieren; **I'm not made for running** ich bin nicht zum Laufen *or* zum Läufer geschaffen.
(b) (*do, execute*) *bow, journey, mistake, attempt, plan, remarks, suggestions etc* machen; *speech* halten; *choice, arrangements* treffen; *decision* fällen, treffen ◆ **to ~ an application/a guess** sich bewerben/raten; **to ~ sb a present of sth** jdm etw schenken *or* zum Geschenk machen (*geh*).
(c) (*cause to be or become*) machen; (*appoint*) machen zu ◆ **to ~ sb happy/angry** *etc* jdn glücklich/wütend *etc* machen; **does that ~ you happy?** bist du jetzt endlich zufrieden?; **to ~ sb one's wife** jdn zu seiner Frau machen; **to ~ one's voice heard** mit seiner Stimme durchdringen; **he was made a judge** man ernannte ihn zum Richter; **they'll never ~ a soldier of him** *or* **out of him** aus ihm wird nie ein Soldat; **I'll ~ it easy for you** ich mache es dir leicht *or* es leicht für dich; **to ~ a success/a mess of a job** etw glänzend erledigen/etw vermasseln (*inf*); **he ~s Macbeth very evil** er läßt Macbeth sehr böse erscheinen; **it ~s the room look smaller** es läßt den Raum kleiner wirken; **to ~ good one's/sb's losses** seine Verluste wettmachen/jdm seine Verluste ausgleichen *or* ersetzen; **we decided to ~ a day/night of it** wir beschlossen, den ganzen Tag dafür zu nehmen/(die Nacht) durchzumachen; **let's ~ it Monday** sagen wir Montag; **do you want to ~ something of it?** (*inf*) hast du was dagegen? (*inf*), stört's dich etwa? (*inf*).
(d) (*cause to do or happen*) lassen, (dazu) bringen; (*compel*) zwingen ◆ **it all ~s me think that ...** das alles läßt mich denken, daß ...; **to ~ sb laugh** jdn zum Lachen bringen; **onions ~ your eyes water** von Zwiebeln tränen einem die Augen; **what ~s you say that?** warum sagst du das?; **I'll ~ him suffer for this** dafür soll er mir büßen!; **he ~s his heroine die** er läßt seine Heldin sterben; **to ~ sb do sth** jdn dazu bringen *or* veranlassen (*geh*), etw zu tun; (*force*) jdn zwingen, etw zu tun; **you can't ~ me!** mich kann keiner zwingen!; **~ me!** (*challenging*) versuch mal, mich zu zwingen!; **I'll ~ him** den zwing ich!; **to ~ sth do, to ~ do with sth** sich mit etw begnügen; **to ~ do with less money/on a small income** mit weniger Geld/einem niedrigen Gehalt auskommen; **you can't ~ things happen** man kann die Dinge nicht zwingen; **I wish I could ~ the rain stop** wenn ich nur machen (*inf*) *or* bewirken könnte, daß der Regen aufhört; **how can I ~ you understand?** wie kann ich es Ihnen verständlich machen?; **that made the cloth shrink** dadurch ging der Stoff ein; **what ~s the engine go?** was treibt den Motor an?, wie wird der Motor angetrieben?; **what made it explode?** was hat die Explosion bewirkt?; **that certainly made him think again** das hat ihm bestimmt zu denken gegeben; **what ~s you think you can do it?** was macht Sie glauben, daß Sie es schaffen können?; **the chemical ~s the plant grow faster** die Chemikalie bewirkt, daß die Pflanze schneller wächst; **that will ~ the pain go** dies wird den Schmerz vertreiben; **if I could ~ your doubts disappear** wenn ich (nur) Ihre Zweifel beseitigen könnte; **what made you come to this town?** was hat Sie dazu veranlaßt, in diese Stadt zu kommen?; **what will ~ you change your mind?** was wird Sie dazu bringen, Ihre Meinung zu ändern?; **what finally made me drop the idea was ...** was mich am Ende dazu veranlaßt hat, den Gedanken fallenzulassen, war ...
(e) (*earn*) *money* verdienen; *profit, loss, fortune* machen (*on* bei); *name, reputation* sich (*dat*) verschaffen; *name* sich (*dat*) machen ◆ **how much do you stand to ~?** wieviel verdienst du (dabei)?, was bringt dir das ein? (*inf*).
(f) (*reach, achieve, also Sport*) schaffen (*inf*), erreichen; *train, plane etc also* erwischen (*inf*); *connection* schaffen; *summit, top, shore etc* es schaffen zu (*inf*); (*ship*) *20 knots* machen ◆ **to ~ land/port** (*Naut*) anlegen/in den Hafen einlaufen; **we made good time** wir kamen schnell voran; **he just made it** er hat es gerade noch geschafft; **sorry I couldn't ~ your party last night** tut mir leid, ich habe es gestern abend einfach nicht zu deiner Party geschafft; **his first record didn't ~ the charts** seine erste Platte schaffte es nicht bis in die Hitparade; **to ~ it** *or* **~ good (as a writer)** es (als Schriftsteller) schaffen (*inf*) *or* zu etwas bringen; **we've made it!** wir haben es geschafft!; **he'll never ~ it through the winter** er wird den Winter nie überstehen; **we'll never ~ the airport in time** wir schaffen es garantiert nicht mehr zum Flughafen; **he made colonel in one year** er brachte es in einem Jahr zum Obersten; **he was out to ~ the top** er wollte es ganz nach oben schaffen; **he made university/the first eleven** er schaffte es, an die Universität/in die erste Mannschaft zu kommen; **the story made the front page** die Geschichte kam auf die Titelseite.
(g) (*cause to succeed*) *stars etc* berühmt machen, zum Erfolg verhelfen (*+dat*) ◆ **this film made her** mit diesem Film schaffte sie es (*inf*) *or* den Durchbruch; **his performance ~s the play** das Stück lebt von seiner schauspielerischen Leistung; **you'll be made for life** Sie werden ausgesorgt haben; **he's got it made** (*inf*) er hat ausgesorgt; **he's a made man** er ist ein gemachter Mann; **but what really made the evening was ...** die eigentliche Krönung des Abends war ...; **that ~s my day!** das freut mich unheimlich!; (*iro*) das hat mir gerade noch gefehlt!; **seeing the Queen made her day** sie war selig, als sie die Königin gesehen hatte; **you've made my day** ich könnte dir um den Hals fallen! (*inf*); **the weather will ~ or mar the parade** der Festzug steht und fällt mit dem Wetter; **he can ~ or break you** er hat dein Schicksal in der Hand.
(h) (*equal*) sein, (er)geben; (*constitute also*) machen, (ab)geben ◆ **2 plus 2 ~s 4** 2 und 2 ist 4; **1760 yards ~ 1 mile** 1760 Yards sind eine Meile; **this ~s the fifth time** das ist nun das fünfte Mal; **that ~s £55 you owe me** Sie schulden mir damit (nun) £ 55; **how much does that ~ altogether?** was macht das insgesamt?; **to ~ a fourth at bridge** den vierten Mann beim Bridge machen; **it ~s good television/publicity** es ist sehr fernsehwirksam/werbewirksam; **he**

➤ LANGUAGE IN USE: **maintain: d** → 26.2

made a good father er gab einen guten Vater ab; **he'll never ~ a soldier/an actor** aus dem wird nie ein Soldat/Schauspieler; **you'd ~ someone a good wife** Sie würden eine gute Ehefrau abgeben; **she made him a good wife** sie war ihm eine gute Frau; **he'd ~ a fantastic Hamlet/a good teacher** er wäre ein fantastischer Hamlet/guter Lehrer, er gäbe einen fantastischen Hamlet/guten Lehrer ab; **they ~ a good/an odd couple** sie sind ein gutes/ungleiches Paar; **it made a very strange sight** es war ein sehr merkwürdiger Anblick.

(i) *(estimate) distance, total* schätzen auf ◆ **what time do you ~ it?, what do you ~ the time?** wie spät hast du es?, wie spät ist es bei dir?; **I ~ it 3.15** ich habe 3^{15}, auf meiner Uhr ist es 3^{15}; **I ~ the total 107** ich kriege insgesamt 107 heraus; **I ~ it 3 miles** ich schätze 3 Meilen; **how many do you ~ it?** wie viele sind es nach deiner Zählung?; **things aren't as bad as he ~s them** es ist nicht so schlimm, wie er es hinstellt.

(j) *(Cards) (fulfil) contract* erfüllen; *(win) trick* machen; *(shuffle) pack* mischen; *see* **bid**.

(k) *(Elec) circuit* schließen; *contact* herstellen.

(l) *(inf)* **to ~ a woman** mit einer Frau schlafen; **~ me, she sighed** nimm mich, seufzte sie; **to ~ it (with sb)** mit jdm schlafen; **they were making it all night** sie liebten sich die ganze Nacht.

(m) *(Naut: signal)* senden, funken ◆ **~ (the following message) to HMS Victor** machen Sie die folgende Meldung an HMS Victor.

[2] *vi* **(a)** *(go)* **to ~ towards a place** auf einen Ort zuhalten; *(ship)* Kurs auf einen Ort nehmen; **to ~ after sb** jdm nachsetzen; **he made at me with a knife** er ging mit einem Messer auf mich los; *see* **~ for, ~ off.**

(b) to ~ on a deal bei einem Geschäft verdienen.

(c) *(begin)* **to ~ as if to do sth** Anstalten machen, etw zu tun; *(as deception)* so tun, als wolle man etw tun; **I made to run** ich machte Anstalten loszulaufen, ich wollte loslaufen.

(d) *(sl)* **to ~ like** so tun, als ob; **he made like he was dying** er tat so, als ob er am Sterben wäre, er markierte *(inf) or* spielte den Sterbenden; **he's started making like a big-shot** er hat angefangen, den starken Mann zu spielen *or* zu markieren *(inf)*.

[3] *vr* **(a) to ~ oneself useful** sich nützlich machen; **to ~ oneself comfortable** es sich *(dat)* bequem machen; **~ yourself small** mach dich klein; **to ~ oneself conspicuous** auffallen; **you'll ~ yourself ill!** du machst dich damit krank!; **he made himself Emperor for life** er krönte *or* machte sich selbst zum Kaiser auf Lebenszeit; **to ~ oneself heard/understood** sich *(dat)* Gehör verschaffen/sich verständlich machen.

(b) to ~ oneself do sth sich dazu zwingen, etw zu tun.

[4] *n* **(a)** *(brand)* Marke *f*, Fabrikat *nt* ◆ **what ~ of car do you run?** welche (Auto)marke fahren Sie?; **it's a good ~** das ist eine gute Marke; **these are my own ~** die sind selbstgemacht *or* Eigenfabrikat *(hum)*; **chocolates of their own/of Belgian ~** Pralinen eigener/belgischer Herstellung.

(b) *(pej inf)* **on the ~** *(for profit)* profitgierig *(inf)*, auf Profit aus; *(ambitious)* karrieresüchtig *(inf)*, auf Karriere aus; *(sexually)* sexhungrig *(inf)*, auf sexuelle Abenteuer aus.

◆**make away** *vi see* **make off.**

◆**make away with** *vi +prep obj* **to ~ ~ ~ sb/oneself** jdn beseitigen, jdn/sich umbringen.

◆**make for** *vi +prep obj* **(a)** *(head for)* zuhalten auf (+*acc*); *(crowd also)* zuströmen (+*dat*, auf +*acc*); *(attack)* losgehen auf (+*acc*); *(vehicle)* losfahren auf (+*acc*) ◆ **where are you making ~?** wo willst du hin?; **we are making ~ London** wir wollen nach London; *(by vehicle also)* wir fahren Richtung London; *(by ship also)* wir halten Kurs auf London.

(b) *(promote)* führen zu; *happy marriage, successful parties* den Grund legen für ◆ **such tactics don't ~ ~ good industrial relations** solche Praktiken wirken sich nicht gerade günstig auf das Arbeitsklima aus; **the trade figures ~ ~ optimism** die Handelsziffern geben Anlaß zum Optimismus.

◆**make of** *vi +prep obj* halten von ◆ **I didn't ~ much ~ it** ich konnte nicht viel dabei finden; **well, what do you ~ ~ that?** nun, was halten Sie davon?, was sagen Sie dazu?; **don't ~ too much ~ it** überbewerten Sie es nicht.

◆**make off** *vi* sich davonmachen *(with sth* mit etw).

◆**make out** [1] *vt sep* **(a)** *(write out) cheque, receipt* ausstellen *(to* auf +*acc*); *list, bill* aufstellen, zusammenstellen; *(fill out) form* ausfüllen ◆ **to ~ ~ a case for sth** für etw argumentieren.

(b) *(see, discern)* ausmachen; *(decipher)* entziffern; *(understand)* verstehen; *person, actions* schlau werden aus ◆ **I can't ~ ~ what he wants** ich komme nicht dahinter, was er will; **how do you ~ that ~?** wie kommst du darauf?

(c) *(claim)* behaupten.

(d) *(imply)* **to ~ ~ that ...** es so hinstellen, als ob ...; **he made ~ that he was hurt** er tat, als sei er verletzt; **to ~ sb ~ to be clever/a genius** jdn als klug/Genie hinstellen; **she's not as rich as he ~s ~** sie ist nicht so reich, wie er es hinstellt; **he tried to ~ ~ it was my fault** er versuchte, es so hinzustellen, als wäre ich daran schuld; **Jesus is made ~ to be a Communist** Jesus wird zum Kommunisten gemacht.

[2] *vi* **(a)** *(inf) (get on)* zurechtkommen; *(with people)* auskommen; *(succeed)* es schaffen ◆ **he didn't ~ ~ with her** er ist bei ihr nicht gelandet *(inf)*; **he eventually made ~** er hat es schließlich geschafft.

(b) *(US inf: pet)* knutschen *(inf)*, fummeln *(inf)*.

◆**make over** *vt sep* **(a)** *(assign)* überschreiben *(to sb dat)*; *(bequeath) property, money* vermachen *(to sb dat)*. **(b)** *(convert)* umändern, umarbeiten; *house* umbauen ◆ **the gardens have been made ~ into a parking lot** man hat die Anlagen in einen Parkplatz umgewandelt.

◆**make up** [1] *vt sep* **(a)** *(constitute)* bilden ◆ **to be made ~ of** bestehen aus, sich zusammensetzen aus; **he made ~ the four at bridge** er war der vierte Mann zum *or* beim Bridge.

(b) *(put together) food, medicine, bed* zurechtmachen; *parcel also* zusammenpacken; *list, accounts* zusammenstellen, aufstellen; *team* zusammenstellen; *(Typ) page* umbrechen; *(design layout)* aufmachen ◆ **to ~ material ~ into sth** Material zu etw verarbeiten; **they made the daffodils ~ into bunches** sie banden die Osterglocken zu Sträußen.

(c) *quarrel* beilegen, begraben ◆ **to ~ it ~ (with sb)** sich (mit jdm) wieder vertragen, sich (mit jdm) aussöhnen; **come on, let's ~ it ~** komm, wir wollen uns wieder vertragen.

(d) *face, eyes* schminken ◆ **the way she's made ~** wie sie geschminkt ist.

(e) to ~ ~ one's mind (to do sth) sich (dazu) entschließen(, etw zu tun); **~ ~ your mind!** entschließ dich!; **my mind is quite made ~** mein Entschluß steht fest; **once his mind is made ~, that's it** wenn er einmal einen Entschluß gefaßt hat, bleibt es dabei; **I can't ~ ~ your mind for you** ich kann das nicht für dich entscheiden; **to ~ ~ one's mind about sb/sth** sich *(dat)* eine Meinung über jdn/etw bilden; **I can't ~ ~ my mind about him** ich weiß nicht, was ich von ihm halten soll.

(f) *(invent)* erfinden, sich *(dat)* ausdenken ◆ **you're making that ~!** jetzt schwindelst du aber! *(inf)*; **he ~s it ~ as he goes along** *(storyteller)* er macht das aus dem Stegreif; *(child playing)* er macht das, wie es ihm gerade einfällt; *(making excuses, telling lies)* er saugt sich *(dat)* das nur so aus den Fingern; **it was all made ~** das war alles nur erfunden.

(g) *(complete) crew* vollständig *or* komplett *(inf)* machen ◆ **I'll ~ ~ the other £20** ich komme für die restlichen £ 20 auf; **he made the gift ~ to £50** er rundete das Geschenk auf £ 50 auf; **add water to ~ it ~ to one litre** mit Wasser auf einen Liter auffüllen.

(h) *(compensate for) loss* ausgleichen; *time* einholen, aufholen; *sleep* nachholen ◆ **to ~ it ~ to sb (for sth)** *(compensate)* jdn (für etw) entschädigen; *(emotionally, return favour etc)* jdm etw wiedergutmachen.

(i) *fire* (wieder) anschüren *or* anfachen.

[2] *vi* **(a)** *(after quarrelling)* sich versöhnen, sich wieder vertragen ◆ **let's kiss and ~ ~** komm, gib mir einen Kuß und wir vertragen uns wieder.

(b) *(material)* **this material will ~ ~ nicely/into a nice coat** dieser Stoff wird sich gut verarbeiten lassen/wird sich als Mantel gut machen.

(c) *(catch up)* aufholen ◆ **to ~ ~ on sb** jdn einholen, an jdn herankommen; **you've a lot of making ~ to do** du hast viel nachzuholen *or* aufzuarbeiten.

◆**make up for** *vi +prep obj* **to ~ ~ ~ sth** etw ausgleichen; **to ~ ~ ~ lost time** verlorene Zeit aufholen; **to ~ ~ ~ the loss of sb/lack of sth** jdn/etw ersetzen; **that still doesn't ~ ~ ~ the fact that you were very rude** das macht noch lange nicht ungeschehen, daß du sehr unhöflich warst.

◆**make up to** *vi +prep obj (inf)* sich heranmachen an (+*acc*).

◆**make with** *vi +prep obj (esp US sl)* **he started making ~ his trumpet** er legte mit seiner Trompete los *(inf)*; **OK, let's ~ ~ the paint brushes** na dann, schnappen wir uns die Pinsel *(inf)*; **just ~ ~ the scissors** mach schon los mit der Schere *(inf)*.

make-believe ['meɪkbɪ,li:v] [1] *adj attr* Phantasie-, imaginär; *world also* Schein-.

[2] *n* Phantasie *f* ◆ **a world of ~** eine Phantasiewelt; **don't be afraid, it's only ~** hab keine Angst, das ist doch nur eine Geschichte.

[3] *vt* sich *(dat)* vorstellen.

make-or-break ['meɪkɔ:'breɪk] *adj attr (inf)* kritisch, entscheidend.

maker ['meɪkə^r] *n (manufacturer)* Hersteller *m* ◆ **our M~** unser Schöpfer *m*; **to go to meet one's M~** zum Herrn eingehen *(geh)*.

-maker *n suf (hat-~, clock~)* -macher(in *f*) *m*.

make: ~-ready *n (Typ)* Zurichtung *f*; **~-ready time** *n (Ind)* Vorbereitungszeit *f*; **~shift** [1] *adj* improvisiert; *repairs* Not-, behelfsmäßig; [2] *n* Übergangslösung *f*, Notbehelf *m*; *see* **shift 1 (d)**; **~-up** *n* **(a)** Make-up *nt*; *(cosmetics also)* Schminke *f*; *(Theat also)* Maske *f*; **the star does his own ~-up** der Star schminkt sich selbst/macht seine Maske selbst; **she spends hours on her ~-up** sie braucht Stunden zum Schminken; **(b)** *(composition) (of team, party etc)* Zusammenstellung *f*; *(character)* Veranlagung *f*; **psychological ~-up** Psyche *f*; **loyalty is part of his ~-up** er ist loyal veranlagt; **it's part of their national ~-up** das gehört zu ihrem Nationalcharakter; **(c)** *(Typ)* Umbruch *m*; *(layout)* Aufmachung *f*; **~-up bag** *n* Kosmetiktasche *f*; **~-up girl** *n* Maskenbildnerin *f*; **~-up kit** *n* Schminkset *nt*; **~-up man** *n* Maskenbildner *m*; **~-up mirror** *n* Schminkspiegel *m*; **~weight** *n* **(a)** *(lit)* **he added a few more as ~weights** er gab noch ein paar dazu, um das Gewicht vollzumachen; **(b)** *(fig: person)* Lückenbüßer *m*; **to use sth as a ~weight** etw in die Waagschale werfen.

making ['meɪkɪŋ] *n* **(a)** *(production)* Herstellung *f*; *(of food)* Zubereitung *f* ◆ **in the ~** im Werden, im Entstehen; **his reputation was still in the ~** er war noch dabei, sich *(dat)* einen Ruf zu schaffen; **here you can see history in the ~** hier hat man den Finger am Puls der Geschichte *(liter)*; **it's a civil war in the ~** hier ist ein Bürgerkrieg im Entstehen; **the mistake was not of my ~** der Fehler war nicht mein Werk; **it was the ~ of him** das hat ihn zum Mann gemacht; *(made him successful)* das hat ihn zu dem gemacht, was er (heute) ist.

(b) ~s *pl* Voraussetzungen *(of zu) pl*; **he has the ~s of an actor/a general** *etc* er hat das Zeug zu einem Schauspieler/General *etc*; **the situation has all the ~s of a strike** die Situation bietet alle Voraussetzungen für einen Streik.

maladjusted [,mælə'dʒʌstɪd] *adj (Psych, Sociol)* verhaltensgestört ◆ **psychologically ~** verhaltensgestört; **socially ~** verhaltensgestört, umweltgestört; **~ youths** fehlangepaßte *or* nicht angepaßte Jugendliche *pl*.

maladjustment [,mælə'dʒʌstmənt] *n (Psych, Sociol)* Verhaltensstörung *f* ◆ **her social ~** ihr soziales Fehlverhalten.

maladministration ['mæləd,mınıs'treıʃən] *n* schlechte Verwaltung.
maladroit *adj*, **~ly** *adv* [,mælə'drɔıt, -lı] ungeschickt.
maladroitness [,mælə'drɔıtnıs] *n* Ungeschicklichkeit *f*.
malady ['mælədı] *n* Leiden *nt*, Krankheit *f* ◆ **social ~** gesellschaftliches Übel.
malaise [mæ'leız] *n* Unwohlsein *nt*; (*fig*) Unbehagen *nt* ◆ **I have a vague feeling of ~ about the future** mich überkommt ein leises Unbehagen, wenn ich an die Zukunft denke.
malapropism ['mæləprɒpızəm] *n* Malapropismus *m*.
malaria [mə'lεərıə] *n* Malaria *f*.
malarial [mə'lεərıəl] *adj* Malaria-.
malarkey [mə'lɑ:kı] *n* (*sl*) (*messing about*) Blödelei *f* (*inf*); (*nonsense*) Hokuspokus *m* (*sl*); (*goings-on*) faule Dinger *pl* (*sl*).
Malawi [mə'lɑ:wı] *n* Malawi *nt*.
Malay [mə'leı] [1] *adj* malaiisch.
[2] *n* (a) Malaie *m*, Malaiin *f*. (b) (*language*) Malaiisch *nt*.
Malaya [mə'leıə] *n* Malaya *nt*.
Malayan [mə'leıən] [1] *adj* malaiisch.
[2] *n* Malaie *m*, Malaiin *f*.
Malaysia [mə'leızıə] *n* Malaysia *nt*.
Malaysian [mə'leızıən] [1] *adj* malaysisch.
[2] *n* Malaysier(in *f*) *m*.
malcontent ['mælkən,tent] [1] *adj* unzufrieden.
[2] *n* Unzufriedene(r) *mf*.
Maldive Islands ['mɔ:ldaıv'aıləndz], **Maldives** ['mɔ:ldaıvz] *npl* Malediven *pl*.
male [meıl] [1] *adj* (a) männlich ◆ **~ child** Junge *m*; **a ~ doctor** ein Arzt *m*; **~ nurse** Krankenpfleger *m*; **~ sparrow/crocodile** Spatzen-/Krokodilmännchen *nt*; **~ chauvinism** Chauvinismus *m*; **~ chauvinist pig** (*inf pej*) Chauvi (*inf*), Chauvinistenschwein *nt* (*pej*); **~ menopause** (*hum*) Wechseljahre *pl* (des Mannes).
(b) *choir, voice* Männer- ◆ **an all-~ club** ein reiner Männerverein; **that's a typical ~ attitude** das ist typisch männlich.
(c) (*manly*) männlich.
(d) (*Mech*) **~ screw** Schraube *f*; **~ plug** Stecker *m*.
[2] *n* (*animal*) Männchen *nt*; (*inf: man*) Mann *m*, männliches Wesen ◆ **the ~ of the species** das männliche Tier, das Männchen; **that's typical of a ~** (*inf*) das ist typisch Mann (*inf*).
malediction [,mælı'dıkʃən] *n* Fluch *m*, Verwünschung *f*.
malefactor ['mælıfæktə^r] *n* Übeltäter, Missetäter *m*.
malevolence [mə'levələns] *n* Boshaftigkeit *f*; (*of action*) Böswilligkeit *f* ◆ **to feel ~ towards sb** einen Groll gegen jdn hegen.
malevolent [mə'levələnt] *adj* boshaft; *gods* übelwollend; *action* böswillig.
malformation [,mælfɔ:'meıʃən] *n* Mißbildung *f*.
malformed [mæl'fɔ:md] *adj* mißgebildet.
malfunction [,mæl'fʌŋkʃən] [1] *n* (*of liver etc*) Funktionsstörung *f*; (*of machine*) Defekt *m* ◆ **a ~ of the carburettor** ein Defekt im Vergaser, ein defekter Vergaser; **a ~ in management** ein Versagen *nt* der Betriebsleitung.
[2] *vi* (*liver etc*) nicht richtig arbeiten; (*machine etc*) defekt sein, nicht richtig funktionieren; (*system*) versagen, nicht richtig funktionieren ◆ **the ~ing part** das defekte Teil.
malice ['mælıs] *n* (a) Bosheit, Bösartigkeit *f*; (*of action*) Böswilligkeit *f* ◆ **a look of ~** ein boshafter Blick; **out of ~** aus Bosheit; **to bear sb ~** einen Groll gegen jdn hegen; **I bear him no ~** ich bin ihm nicht böse. (b) (*Jur*) **with ~ aforethought** in böswilliger Absicht, vorsätzlich.
malicious [mə'lıʃəs] *adj* (a) *person, words* boshaft; *behaviour* bösartig, böswillig; *crime* gemein, arglistig; *slander* böswillig. (b) (*Jur*) *damage* mutwillig, böswillig.
maliciously [mə'lıʃəslı] *adv see adj*.
malign [mə'laın] [1] *adj* (*liter*) *intent* böse; *influence* unheilvoll; *see also* **malignant**.
[2] *vt* verleumden; (*run down*) schlechtmachen ◆ **to ~ sb's character** jdm Übles nachsagen; **without wishing in any way to ~ her/her character** ... ich will ihr ja nichts (Schlechtes) nachsagen, aber ...
malignancy [mə'lıgnənsı] *n* Bösartigkeit *f*; (*Med also*) Malignität *f* (*form*); (*fig: evil thing*) Übel *nt*.
malignant [mə'lıgnənt] *adj* bösartig; (*Med also*) maligne (*spec*) ◆ **he took a ~ delight in our misfortunes** unser Unglück bereitete ihm ein hämisches Vergnügen; **a ~ growth** (*Med, fig*) ein bösartiges Geschwür.
malignity [mə'lıgnıtı] *n* Bösartigkeit *f*; (*Med also*) Malignität *f* (*spec*).
malinger [mə'lıŋgə^r] *vi* simulieren, krank spielen.
malingerer [mə'lıŋgərə^r] *n* Simulant *m*.
mall [mɔ:l, mæl] *n* (*US: also* **shopping ~**) Einkaufszentrum *nt*.
mallard ['mælɑ:d] *n* Stockente *f*.
malleability [,mælıə'bılıtı] *n* Formbarkeit *f*; (*of clay, wax also*) Geschmeidigkeit *f*.
malleable ['mælıəbl] *adj* formbar (*also fig*), weich; (*of clay, wax also*) geschmeidig.
mallet ['mælıt] *n* Holzhammer *m*; (*croquet*) (Krocket)hammer *m*; (*polo*) (Polo)schläger *m*.
mallow ['mæləʊ] *n* Malve *f*.
malmsey ['mɑ:lmzı] *n* Malvasier(wein) *m*.
malnutrition [,mælnjʊ'trıʃən] *n* Unterernährung *f*.
malodorous [mæl'əʊdərəs] *adj* (*form*) übelriechend.
malpractice [,mæl'præktıs] *n* Berufsvergehen *nt*, Verstoß *m* gegen das Berufsethos, Amtsvergehen *nt* (*eines Beamten*) ◆ **minor ~s common in the profession** kleinere Unregelmäßigkeiten, wie sie in diesem Berufszweig häufig sind.
malt [mɔ:lt] [1] *n* Malz *nt* ◆ **~ extract** Malzextrakt *m*; **~ liquor** *aus Malz gebrautes alkoholisches Getränk*; (*US: beer*) Starkbier *nt*; **~ loaf** ≃ Rosinenbrot *nt*; **~ whisky** Malt Whisky *m*.
[2] *vt barley* malzen, mälzen; *drink etc* mit Malz versetzen *or* mischen ◆ **~ed milk** Malzmilch *f*.
Malta ['mɔ:ltə] *n* Malta *nt*.
Maltese [,mɔ:l'ti:z] [1] *adj* maltesisch ◆ **~ cross** Malteserkreuz *nt*.
[2] *n* (a) Malteser(in *f*) *m*. (b) (*language*) Maltesisch *nt*.
maltreat [,mæl'tri:t] *vt* schlecht behandeln; (*using violence*) mißhandeln.
maltreatment [,mæl'tri:tmənt] *n* schlechte Behandlung; Mißhandlung *f*.
mamba ['mæmbə] *n* Mamba *f*.
mambo ['mæmbəʊ] *n* Mambo *m*.
mam(m)a [mə'mɑ:] *n* (*inf*) Mama *f* (*inf*).
mammal ['mæməl] *n* Säugetier *nt*, Säuger *m*.
mammalian [mæ'meılıən] *adj* Säugetier-, der Säugetiere.
mammary ['mæmərı] *adj* Brust- ◆ **~ gland** Brustdrüse *f*.
mammogram ['mæməgræm] *n* (*Med*) Mammographie *f*.
mammon ['mæmən] *n* Mammon, Reichtum *m* ◆ **M~** der Mammon.
mammoth ['mæməθ] [1] *n* Mammut *nt*.
[2] *adj* Mammut-; *cost, enterprise* kolossal.
mammy ['mæmı] *n* (*inf*) Mami *f* (*inf*); (*US*) (schwarze) Kinderfrau, Negermami (*inf*) *f*.
man [mæn] [1] *n, pl* **men** (a) (*adult male*) Mann *m* ◆ **be a ~!** sei ein Mann!; **to make a ~ out of sb** einen Mann aus jdm machen; **this incident made a ~ out of him** dieses Ereignis hat ihn zum Mann gemacht; **we'll never make a ~ out of him** aus ihm wird nie ein Mann; **he's only half a ~** er ist kein richtiger Mann; **I'm only half a ~ without you** ohne dich bin ich nur ein halber Mensch; **he took it like a ~** er hat es wie ein Mann *or* mannhaft ertragen; **that's just like a ~** das ist typisch Mann; **her ~** (*inf*) ihr Mann; **~ and boy** von Kindheit/Jugend an; **they are ~ and wife** sie sind Mann und Frau; **the ~ in the street** der Mann auf der Straße, der kleine Mann; **~ of God** Mann *m* Gottes; **~ of letters** (*writer*) Schriftsteller, Literat *m*; (*scholar*) Gelehrter *m*; **~ of property** vermögender Mann; **you're a ~ about town, you know where ...** du kennst dich aus, du weißt, wo ...; **he used to be something of a ~ about town** er hatte früher ein reges gesellschaftliches Leben; **a suit for the ~ about town** ein Anzug für den feinen Herrn; **a ~ of the world** ein Mann *m* von Welt; **well done, that ~!** gut gemacht, alter Junge! (*inf*); **~'s bicycle/jacket** Herrenfahrrad *nt*/-jacke *f*; **old ~** (*dated*) alter Junge (*dated*) *or* Knabe (*dated*); *see* **good**.
(b) (*human race: also* **M~**) der Mensch; die Menschen.
(c) (*person*) man ◆ **no ~** keiner, niemand; **any ~** jeder; **any ~ who believes that ...** wer das glaubt, ...; **sometimes a ~ needs a change** (*inf*) manchmal braucht man einfach etwas Abwechslung; **men say that ...** die Leute sagen, daß ...; **that ~!** dieser Mensch!; **that ~ Jones** dieser *or* der Jones!; **the strong ~ of the government** der starke Mann (in) der Regierung; **as one ~** geschlossen, wie ein Mann; **they are communists to a ~** sie sind allesamt Kommunisten.
(d) (*type*) **the right/wrong ~** der Richtige/Falsche; **you've come to the right ~** da sind *or* liegen (*inf*) Sie bei mir richtig; **then I am your ~** dann bin ich genau der Richtige (für Sie); **he's not the ~ for the job** er ist nicht der Richtige für diese Aufgabe; **he's not the ~ to make a mistake like that** so etwas würde ihm bestimmt nicht passieren; **he's not a ~ to ...** er ist nicht der Typ, der ...; **he's not a ~ to meddle with** mit ihm ist nicht gut Kirschen essen; **he is a Cambridge ~** er hat in Cambridge studiert; **medical ~** Mediziner *m*; **family ~** Familienvater *m*; **he's a family ~** (*home-loving*) er ist sehr häuslich; **it's got to be a local ~** es muß jemand von hier *or* aus dieser Gegend sein; **I'm not a drinking ~** ich bin kein großer Trinker; **I'm a whisky ~ myself** ich bin mehr für Whisky; **I'm not a football ~** ich mache mir nicht viel aus Fußball; **he's a 4-pint ~** mehr als 4 Halbe verträgt er nicht; unter 4 Halben tut er's nicht.
(e) (*sl: interj*) Mensch (*inf*), Mann (*inf*) ◆ **you can't do that, ~** Mensch *or* Mann, das kannst du doch nicht machen! (*inf*); **fantastic, ~!** dufte, Mann! (*sl*); **see you, ~!** bis später; **are you coming with us, ~?** du, kommst du noch mit?
(f) (*employee, soldier etc*) Mann *m*; (*servant also*) Bedienstete(r) *m* ◆ **she has a ~ to do the garden** sie hat jemanden, der den Garten macht; **officers and men** Offiziere und Mannschaften; **follow me, men!** mir nach, Leute!
(g) (*Chess*) Figur *f*; (*in draughts*) Stein *m*.
(h) **the M~** (*US sl*) (*boss*) der Boß (*inf*), der Alte (*inf*); (*police*) die Bullen *pl* (*sl*); (*white man*) die Weißen *pl*.
[2] *vt ship* bemannen; *fortress* besetzen; *power station, pump, gun, telephone etc* bedienen ◆ **the ship is ~ned by a crew of 30** das Schiff hat 30 Mann Besatzung; **a fully ~ned ship** ein vollbemanntes Schiff; **he left 10 soldiers behind to ~ the fortress** er ließ 10 Soldaten als Besatzung für die Festung zurück; **~ the guns/pumps!** an die Geschütze/Pumpen!; **the captain gave the signal to ~ the guns** der Kapitän gab das Zeichen zur Besetzung der Geschütze.
manacle ['mænəkl] [1] *n usu pl* Handfesseln, Ketten *pl*.
[2] *vt person* in Ketten legen; *hands* (mit Ketten) fesseln ◆ **they were ~d together** sie wurden/waren aneinandergekettet; **he was ~d to the wall** er war an die Wand gekettet.
manage ['mænıdʒ] [1] *vt* (a) *company, organization* leiten; *property* verwalten; *affairs* in Ordnung halten, regeln; *football team, pop group* managen ◆ **he ~d the election** er war Wahlleiter; **the election was ~d** (*pej*) die Wahl war

manipuliert; **~d fund** Investmentfonds *m mit gelegentlicher Umschichtung des Aktienbestandes.*
(b) *(handle, control) person, child, animal* zurechtkommen mit, fertigwerden mit; *car, ship* zurechtkommen mit, handhaben ◆ **the car is too big for her to ~** sie kommt mit dem großen Auto nicht zurecht; **she can't ~ children** sie kann nicht mit Kindern umgehen; **I can ~ him** mit dem werde ich schon fertig.
(c) *task* bewältigen, zurechtkommen mit; *another portion* bewältigen, schaffen *(inf)* ◆ **£5 is the most I can ~** ich kann mir höchstens £ 5 leisten; **I'll ~ it** das werde ich schon schaffen; **he ~d it very well** er hat das sehr gut gemacht; **you'll ~ it next time** nächstes Mal schaffst du's; **I'll do that as soon as I can ~ it** ich mache das, sobald ich kann *or* sobald ich es schaffe; **he should take some exercise as soon as he can ~ it** er sollte sich so bald wie möglich Bewegung verschaffen; **can you ~ the cases?** kannst du die Koffer (allein) tragen?; **thanks, I can ~ them** danke, das geht schon; **she can't ~ the stairs** sie kommt die Treppe nicht hinauf/hinunter; **can you ~ two more in the car?** kriegst du noch zwei Leute in dein Auto? *(inf)*; **can you ~ 8 o'clock?** 8 Uhr, ginge *or* geht das?; **could you ~ (to be ready by) 8 o'clock?** kannst du um 8 Uhr fertig sein?; **can you ~ another cup?** darf's noch eine Tasse sein?; **could you ~ another whisky?** schaffst du noch einen Whisky?; **I think I could ~ another cake** ich glaube, ich könnte noch ein Stück Kuchen vertragen; **I couldn't ~ another thing** ich könnte keinen Bissen mehr runterbringen.
(d) to ~ to do sth es schaffen, etw zu tun; **we have ~d to reduce our costs** es ist uns gelungen, die Kosten zu senken; **do you think you'll ~ to do it?** meinen Sie, Sie können *or* schaffen das?; **I hope you'll ~ to come** ich hoffe, Sie können kommen; **how did you ~ to get a salary increase?** wie hast du es geschafft *or* angestellt, eine Gehaltserhöhung zu bekommen?; **he ~d to control himself** es gelang ihm, sich zu beherrschen; **he ~d not to get his feet wet** es ist ihm gelungen, keine nassen Füße zu bekommen; **how did you ~ to miss that?** wie konnte Ihnen das nur entgehen?; **how could you possibly ~ to do that?** wie hast du denn das fertiggebracht?; **how could anybody possibly ~ to be so stupid?** wie kann ein Mensch nur so dumm sein?; **could you possibly ~ to close the door?** *(iro)* wäre es vielleicht möglich, die Tür zuzumachen?
[2] *vi* zurechtkommen, es schaffen ◆ **can you ~?** geht es?; **thanks, I can ~** danke, es geht schon *or* ich komme schon zurecht; **I thought I could cope with things, but I can't ~** ich dachte, ich käme zurecht, aber ich schaffe es nicht *or* ich bringe es nicht fertig; **she ~s well enough** sie kommt ganz gut zurecht; **how do you ~?** wie schaffen *or* machen Sie das bloß?; **to ~ without sth** ohne etw auskommen, sich *(dat)* ohne etw behelfen; **we'll just have to ~ without** dann müssen wir uns *(dat)* eben so behelfen, dann müssen wir eben so auskommen; **to ~ without sb** ohne jdn auskommen *or* zurechtkommen; **I can ~ by myself** ich komme (schon) allein zurecht; **how do you ~ on £20 a week?** wie kommen Sie mit £ 20 pro Woche aus?

manageable ['mænɪdʒəbl] *adj child* folgsam, fügsam; *horse* fügsam; *amount, job* zu bewältigen; *hair* leicht frisierbar, geschmeidig; *number* überschaubar; *car* leicht zu handhaben ◆ **since the treatment he's been less violent, more ~** seit der Behandlung ist er nicht mehr so gewalttätig, man kann besser mit ihm umgehen *or* zurechtkommen; **the children are no longer ~ for her** sie wird mit den Kindern nicht mehr fertig; **is that ~ for you?** schaffen Sie das?; **this company is just not ~** es ist unmöglich, dieses Unternehmen (erfolgreich) zu leiten; **you should try and keep the book within ~ limits** Sie sollten versuchen, das Buch in überschaubaren Grenzen zu halten; **pieces of a more ~ size** Stücke, die leichter zu handhaben sind, Stücke *pl* in handlicher Größe; **a job of ~ size** eine überschaubare Aufgabe; **the staircase isn't ~ for an old lady** die Treppe ist für eine alte Dame zu beschwerlich.

management ['mænɪdʒmənt] *n* **(a)** *(act) (of company)* Leitung, Führung *f*, Management *nt*; *(of non-commercial organization)* Leitung *f*; *(of estate, assets, money)* Verwaltung *f*; *(of affairs)* Regelung *f* ◆ **losses due to bad ~** Verluste, die auf schlechtes Management zurückzuführen sind; **crisis ~** Krisenmanagement *nt*.
(b) *(persons)* Unternehmensleitung *f*; *(of single unit or smaller factory)* Betriebsleitung *f*; *(non-commercial)* Leitung *f*; *(Theat)* Intendanz *f* ◆ **"under new ~"** „neuer Inhaber"; *(shop)* „neu eröffnet"; *(pub)* „unter neuer Bewirtschaftung".

management: ~ accounting *n* Kosten- und Leistungsrechnung *f*; **~ accounts** *npl* Geschäftsbilanz *f*; **~ buy-out** *n Aufkauf m eines Unternehmens durch Mitglieder der Geschäftsleitung*, Management-buyout *nt*; **~ consultancy** *n* Unternehmensberatung *f*; **~ consultant** *n* Unternehmensberater(in *f*) *m*; **~ course** *n* Managerkurs *m*; **~ fee** *n* Verwaltungsgebühr *f*; **~ skills** *npl* Führungsqualitäten *pl*; **~ studies** *n* Betriebswirtschaft *f*; **~ style** *n* Führungsstil *m*.

manager ['mænɪdʒəʳ] *n (Comm etc)* Geschäftsführer, Manager *m*; *(of restaurant)* Geschäftsführer *m*; *(of smaller firm or factory)* Betriebsleiter *m*; *(of bank, chain store)* Filialleiter *m*; *(of department)* Abteilungsleiter *m*; *(of estate etc)* Verwalter *m*; *(Theat)* Intendant *m*; *(of private theatre)* Theaterdirektor *m*; *(of pop group, boxer etc)* Manager *m*; *(of team)* Trainer *m* ◆ **sales/publicity ~** Verkaufsleiter *m*/Werbeleiter *m*; **business ~** *(for theatre)* Verwaltungsdirektor *m*; *(of pop star etc)* Manager *m*.

manageress [,mænɪdʒə'res] *n* Geschäftsführerin *f*, Leiterin *f* eines Unternehmens/Hotels *etc*; *(of department)* Abteilungsleiterin *f*; *(of chain store)* Filialleiterin *f*.

managerial [,mænə'dʒɪərɪəl] *adj* geschäftlich; *(executive)* Management-; *post* leitend ◆ **at ~ level** auf der Führungsebene; **he has no ~ skills** er ist für leitende Funktionen ungeeignet.

managing director ['mænɪdʒɪŋdɪ'rektəʳ] *n* Geschäftsführer(in *f*) *m*.

man-at-arms [,mænət'ɑːmz] *n, pl* **men-at-arms** [,menət'ɑːmz] Soldat, Krieger *(old) m*.

manatee [,mænə'tiː] *n* (Rundschwanz)seekuh *f*.

Manchuria [mæn'tʃʊərɪə] *n* die Mandschurei.

Manchurian [mæn'tʃʊərɪən] [1] *adj* mandschurisch.
[2] *n* **(a)** Mandschu *m*. **(b)** *(language)* Mandschu *nt*.

Mancunian [mæŋ'kjuːnɪən] [1] *n* Bewohner(in *f*) *m* Manchesters ◆ **he's a ~** er kommt *or* ist aus Manchester.
[2] *adj* aus Manchester.

mandarin ['mændərɪn] *n* **(a)** *(Chinese official)* Mandarin *m*; *(official)* hoher Funktionär, Bonze *m (pej)*. **(b)** *(language)* **M~** Hochchinesisch *nt*. **(c)** *(fruit)* Mandarine *f*.

mandate ['mændeɪt] [1] *n* Auftrag *m*; *(Pol also)* Mandat *nt*; *(territory)* Mandat(sgebiet) *nt* ◆ **to give sb a ~ to do sth** jdm den Auftrag geben *or* jdn damit beauftragen, etw zu tun; **we have a clear ~ from the country to ...** wir haben den eindeutigen Wählerauftrag, zu ...
[2] *vt* **to ~ a territory to sb** ein Gebiet jds Verwaltung *(dat)* unterstellen *or* als Mandat an jdn vergeben.

mandated ['mændeɪtɪd] *adj territory* Mandats-.

mandatory ['mændətərɪ] *adj* obligatorisch; *(Pol)* mandatorisch ◆ **the ~ nature of this ruling** der Zwangscharakter dieser Regelung; **union membership is ~** Mitgliedschaft in der Gewerkschaft ist Pflicht.

man-day ['mæn'deɪ] *n* Manntag *m*.

mandible ['mændɪbl] *n (of vertebrates)* Unterkiefer(knochen) *m*, Mandibel *f (spec)* ◆ **~s** *(of insects)* Mundwerkzeuge, Mundgliedmaßen *pl*, Mandibel *f (spec)*; *(of birds)* Schnabel *m*.

mandolin(e) ['mændəlɪn] *n* Mandoline *f*.

mandrake ['mændreɪk] *n* Mandragore *f* ◆ **~ root** Alraune *f*.

mandrill ['mændrɪl] *n* Mandrill *m*.

mane [meɪn] *n (lit, fig)* Mähne *f*.

man: ~eater *n* Menschenfresser *m*; *(shark)* Menschenhai *m*; *(inf: woman)* männermordendes Weib *(inf)*; **~-eating shark** *n* Menschenhai *m*; **~-eating tiger** *n* Menschenfresser *m*.

maneuver *n, vti (US) see* **manoeuvre**.

manful *adj*, **~ly** *adv* ['mænfʊl, -fəlɪ] mannhaft *(geh)*, mutig, beherzt.

manganese [,mæŋgə'niːz] *n* Mangan *nt*.

mange [meɪndʒ] *n* Räude *f*; *(of man)* Krätze *f*.

mangel(-wurzel) ['mæŋgl(,wɜːzl)] *n* Runkel- *or* Futterrübe *f*.

manger ['meɪndʒəʳ] *n* Krippe *f*.

mangetout ['mɑ̃ːʒ'tuː] *n (also* **~ pea***)* Zuckererbse *f*.

mangle¹ ['mæŋgl] [1] *n* Mangel *f*.
[2] *vt clothes* mangeln.

mangle² *vt (also* **~ up***)* (übel) zurichten.

mango ['mæŋgəʊ] *n (fruit)* Mango *f*; *(tree)* Mangobaum *m*.

mangold(-wurzel) ['mæŋgəld(,wɜːzl)] *n see* **mangel(-wurzel)**.

mangrove ['mæŋgrəʊv] *n* Mangrove(n)baum *m* ◆ **~ swamp** Mangrove *f*.

mangy ['meɪndʒɪ] *adj (+er) dog* räudig; *carpet* schäbig; *hotel* schäbig, heruntergekommen.

man: ~handle *vt* **(a)** grob *or* unsanft behandeln; **he was ~handled into the back of the van** er wurde recht unsanft *or* gewaltsam in den Laderaum des Wagens verfrachtet; **(b)** *piano etc* hieven; **~hole** *n* Kanal- *or* Straßenschacht *m*; *(in boiler etc)* Mannloch *nt*, Einsteigöffnung *f*.

manhood ['mænhʊd] *n* **(a)** *(state)* Mannesalter *nt*. **(b)** *(manliness)* Männlichkeit *f*. **(c)** *(men)* Männer *pl*.

man: ~-hour *n* Arbeitsstunde *f*; **~hunt** *n* Fahndung *f*; *(for criminal also)* Verbrecherjagd *f*; *(hum: of woman)* Männerfang *m*.

mania ['meɪnɪə] *n* **(a)** *(madness)* Manie *f* ◆ **persecution ~** Verfolgungswahn *m*.
(b) *(inf: enthusiasm)* Manie *f*, Tick *(inf)*, Fimmel *(inf) m* ◆ **this ~ for nationalization** diese Verstaatlichungsmanie; **this current ~ for the 1920's** die derzeitige Manie für die 20er Jahre; **he has a ~ for collecting old matchboxes** er hat den Tick *or* Fimmel, alte Streichholzschachteln zu sammeln *(inf)*; **he has this ~ for collecting stuff** er hat einen Sammeltick *(inf) or* -fimmel *(inf)*; **~ for cleanliness** Sauberkeitstick *(inf)*, Reinlichkeitsfimmel *(inf) m*; **it has become a ~ with him** das ist bei ihm zur Manie geworden.

maniac ['meɪnɪæk] [1] *adj* wahnsinnig.
[2] *n* **(a)** Wahnsinnige(r), Irre(r) *mf*. **(b)** *(fig)* **these sports ~s** diese Sportfanatiker *pl*; **you ~** du bist ja wahnsinnig!

maniacal [mə'naɪəkəl] *adj* wahnsinnig.

manic-depressive ['mænɪkdɪ'presɪv] [1] *adj* manisch-depressiv.
[2] *n* Manisch-Depressive(r) *mf* ◆ **he is a ~** er ist manisch-depressiv.

manicure ['mænɪ,kjʊəʳ] [1] *n* Maniküre *f* ◆ **~ set** Nagelnecessaire, Nagel- *or* Maniküreetui *nt*.
[2] *vt* maniküren ◆ **his well-~d hands** seine gepflegten *or* sorgfältig manikürten Hände.

manicurist ['mænɪ,kjʊərɪst] *n* Handpflegerin *f*.

manifest ['mænɪfest] [1] *adj* offenkundig, offenbar; *(definite also)* eindeutig ◆ **I think it's ~ that ...** es liegt doch wohl auf der Hand, daß ...; **to make sth ~** etw klar *or* deutlich machen; **he made it ~ that ...** er machte klar *or* deutlich, daß ...
[2] *n (Naut)* Manifest *nt*.
[3] *vt* zeigen, bekunden.
[4] *vr* sich zeigen; *(Sci, Psych etc)* sich manifestieren; *(ghost)* erscheinen; *(guilt etc)* sich offenbaren, offenbar werden.

manifestation [ˌmænɪfeˈsteɪʃən] *n* (*act of showing*) Ausdruck *m*, Manifestierung, Bekundung *f*; (*sign*) Anzeichen *nt*, Manifestation *f*; (*of spirit*) Erscheinung *f*.

manifestly [ˈmænɪfestlɪ] *adv* eindeutig, offensichtlich ♦ **it's so ~ obvious** es ist so völlig offensichtlich.

manifesto [ˌmænɪˈfestəʊ] *n, pl* **-(e)s** Manifest *nt*.

manifold [ˈmænɪfəʊld] 1 *adj* mannigfaltig (*geh*), vielfältig ♦ **~ uses** vielseitige Anwendung; **it's a ~ subject** das ist ein sehr komplexes Thema; **his ~ experience** seine reichhaltigen Erfahrungen.
2 *n* (*Aut*) (*inlet ~*) Ansaugrohr *nt*; (*exhaust ~*) Auspuffrohr *nt*.

manikin [ˈmænɪkɪn] *n* (*dwarf*) Männchen *nt*, Knirps *m*; (*Art*) Modell *nt*, Gliederpuppe *f*.

manila, manilla [məˈnɪlə] *n* **(a)** (*~ paper*) Hartpapier *nt* ♦ **~ envelopes** braune Umschläge. **(b)** (*~ hemp*) Manilahanf *m*.

manioc [ˈmænɪɒk] *n* Maniok *m*.

manipulate [məˈnɪpjʊleɪt] *vt* **(a)** *machine etc* handhaben, bedienen; *bones* einrenken; (*after fracture*) zurechtrücken. **(b)** *public opinion, person, prices* manipulieren; *accounts, figures also* frisieren (*inf*).

manipulation [məˌnɪpjʊˈleɪʃən] *n* Manipulation *f*.

manipulator [məˈnɪpjʊleɪtəʳ] *n* Manipulator, Manipulant *m* ♦ **he's a skilled ~ of public opinion** er versteht es, die öffentliche Meinung geschickt zu manipulieren.

mankind [mænˈkaɪnd] *n* die Menschheit.

manlike [ˈmænlaɪk] *adj* menschlich; (*like a male*) männlich; *robot* menschenähnlich.

manliness [ˈmænlɪnɪs] *n* Männlichkeit *f*.

manly [ˈmænlɪ] *adj* (*+er*) männlich ♦ **to behave in a ~ fashion** sich als Mann erweisen.

man-made [ˈmænˈmeɪd] *adj* künstlich, Kunst- ♦ **~ fibres** Kunstfasern, synthetische Fasern *pl*.

manna [ˈmænə] *n* Manna *nt*.

manned [mænd] *adj satellite etc* bemannt.

mannequin [ˈmænɪkɪn] *n* (*fashion*) Mannequin *nt*; (*Art*) Modell *nt*; (*dummy*) Gliederpuppe *f*.

manner [ˈmænəʳ] *n* **(a)** (*mode*) Art, Weise, Art und Weise *f* ♦ **in** *or* **after this ~** auf diese Art und Weise; **in** *or* **after the ~ of Petrarch** im Stile Petrarcas; **in the Spanish ~** im spanischen Stil; **in like ~** (*form*) auf die gleiche Weise, ebenso; **in such a ~ that** ... so ..., daß ...; **a painter in the grand ~** ein Maler der alten Schule; **a ball in the grand ~** ein Ball alten Stils *or* im alten Stil; **in a ~ of speaking** sozusagen, gewissermaßen; **in a ~ of speaking, the job's finished** die Arbeit ist sozusagen *or* gewissermaßen fertig; **it's just a ~ of speaking** (*of idiom*) das ist nur so eine Redensart; **I didn't mean to insult him, it was just a ~ of speaking** das sollte keine Beleidigung sein, ich habe das nur so gesagt; **as to the ~ born** als sei er/sie dafür geschaffen; **a horseman as to the ~ born** ein geborener Reiter.
(b) (*behaviour etc*) Art *f* ♦ **he has a very kind ~** er hat ein sehr freundliches Wesen; **his ~ to his parents** sein Verhalten gegenüber seinen Eltern; **I don't like his ~** ich mag seine Art nicht; **there's something odd about his ~** er benimmt sich irgendwie komisch.
(c) **~s** *pl* (*good, bad etc*) Manieren *pl*, Benehmen *nt*, Umgangsformen *pl* ♦ **road ~s** Verhalten *nt* im Straßenverkehr; **he hasn't got any road ~s** er ist ein sehr unhöflicher *or* rücksichtsloser Fahrer; **that's bad ~s** das *or* so etwas gehört sich nicht, das ist unanständig; **~s!** benimm dich!; **it's bad ~s to ...** es gehört sich nicht *or* es ist unanständig, zu ...; **to have bad ~s** schlechte Manieren haben; **he has no ~s** er hat keine Manieren, er kann sich nicht benehmen; **have you forgotten your ~s?** wo hast du denn deine Manieren gelassen?; **now, don't forget your ~s!** du weißt doch, was sich gehört!; **to teach sb some ~s** jdm Manieren beibringen.
(d) **~s** *pl* (*of society*) Sitten (und Gebräuche) *pl* ♦ **a novel/comedy of ~s** ein Sittenroman *m*/eine Sittenkomödie.
(e) (*class, type*) Art *f* ♦ **all ~ of birds** die verschiedensten Arten von Vögeln; **we saw all ~ of interesting things** wir sahen allerlei Interessantes *or* so manches Interessante; **I've got all ~ of things to do yet** ich habe noch allerlei *or* tausenderlei zu tun; **by no ~ of means** keineswegs, in keinster Weise (*inf*); **what ~ of man is he?** (*liter*) was ist er für ein Mensch?

mannered [ˈmænəd] *adj style* manieriert; *friendliness, subservience etc* betont, prononciert (*geh*).

-mannered *adj suf* mit ... Manieren.

mannerism [ˈmænərɪzəm] *n* **(a)** (*in behaviour, speech*) Angewohnheit, Eigenheit *f*. **(b)** (*of style*) Manieriertheit *f* ♦ **his ~s** seine Manierismen.

mannerliness [ˈmænəlɪnɪs] *n* Wohlerzogenheit *f*.

mannerly [ˈmænəlɪ] *adj* wohlerzogen.

mannish [ˈmænɪʃ] *adj woman, clothes* männlich wirkend.

manoeuvrability [məˌnuːvrəˈbɪlɪtɪ] *n* Manövrierfähigkeit, Wendigkeit *f*.

manoeuvrable [məˈnuːvrəbl] *adj* manövrierfähig, wendig ♦ **easily ~** leicht zu manövrieren.

manoeuvre, (*US*) **maneuver** [məˈnuːvəʳ] 1 *n* **(a)** (*Mil*) Feldzug *m* ♦ **in a well-planned ~** durch einen geschickt geplanten Feldzug.
(b) (*Mil*) **~s** Manöver *nt or pl*, Truppenübung *f* ♦ **the troops were out on ~s** die Truppen befanden sich im Manöver.
(c) (*clever plan*) Manöver *nt*, Winkelzug, Schachzug *m* ♦ **rather an obvious ~** ein ziemlich auffälliges Manöver.
2 *vt* manövrieren ♦ **he ~d his troops out onto the plain** er dirigierte *or* führte seine Truppen hinaus auf die Ebene; **to ~ a gun into position** ein Geschütz in Stellung bringen; **to ~ sb into doing sth** jdn dazu bringen, etw zu tun; **he ~d his brother into a top job** er manövrierte *or* lancierte seinen Bruder in eine Spitzenposition.
3 *vi* manövrieren; (*Mil*) (ein) Manöver durchführen ♦ **to ~ for position** (*lit, fig*) sich in eine günstige Position manövrieren; **room to ~** Spielraum *m*, Manövrierfähigkeit *f*.

man-of-war [ˌmænəvˈwɔːʳ] *n, pl* **men-of-war** [ˌmenəvˈwɔːʳ] (*old*) *see* **Portuguese**.

manor [ˈmænəʳ] *n* Gut(shof *m*), Landgut *nt* ♦ **lord/lady of the ~** Gutsherr *m*/-herrin *f*; **~ house** Herrenhaus *nt*.

manpower [ˈmænˌpaʊəʳ] *n* Leistungs- *or* Arbeitspotential *nt*; (*Mil*) Stärke *f* ♦ **we haven't got the ~** wir haben dazu nicht genügend Personal *or* Arbeitskräfte *pl*; **M~ Services Commission** (*Brit*) *Behörde f für Arbeitsbeschaffung, Arbeitsvermittlung und Berufsausbildung.*

manqué [ˈmɒŋkeɪ] *adj pred* (*failed*) gescheitert; (*unfulfilled*) verkannt ♦ **an artist ~** ein verkannter Künstler; **he's a novelist ~** an ihm ist ein Schriftsteller verlorengegangen.

manse [mæns] *n* Pfarrhaus *nt*.

manservant [ˈmænsɜːvənt] *n, pl* **menservants** [ˈmensɜːvənts] Diener *m*.

mansion [ˈmænʃən] *n* Villa *f*; (*of ancient family*) Herrenhaus *nt*.

man: ~-sized *adj steak* Riesen-; **~slaughter** *n* Totschlag *m*.

manta (ray) [ˈmæntə(reɪ)] *n* Teufelsrochen, Manta *m*.

mantelpiece [ˈmæntlpiːs] *n*, **mantelshelf** [ˈmæntlʃelf] *n, pl* **-shelves** [-ʃelvz] (*above fireplace*) Kaminsims *nt or m*; (*around fireplace*) Kaminverkleidung *or* -einfassung *f*.

mantilla [mænˈtɪlə] *n* Mantille, Mantilla *f*.

mantis [ˈmæntɪs] *n see* **praying ~**.

mantle [ˈmæntl] 1 *n* **(a)** Umhang *m*; (*fig*) Deckmantel *m* ♦ **a ~ of snow** eine Schneedecke. **(b)** (*gas ~*) Glühstrumpf *m*.
2 *vt* (*liter*) bedecken.

man: ~-to-~ *adj, adv* von Mann zu Mann; **a ~-to-~ talk** ein Gespräch *nt* von Mann zu Mann; **~trap** *n* Fußangel *f*.

manual [ˈmænjʊəl] 1 *adj* manuell; *control also* von Hand; *work also* Hand-; *labour* körperlich ♦ **~ labourer** Schwerarbeiter *m*; **~ worker** (manueller *or* Hand)arbeiter *m*; **~ skill** Handwerk *nt*; **he was trained in several ~ skills** er hatte verschiedene Handwerksberufe *pl* erlernt; **~ gear change** Schaltgetriebe *nt*, Schaltung *f* von Hand.
2 *n* **(a)** (*book*) Handbuch *nt*. **(b)** (*Mus*) Manual *nt*. **(c)** (*~ operation*) Handbetrieb *m*, manueller Betrieb ♦ **to run on ~** im Handbetrieb laufen; **to put a machine on ~** eine Maschine auf Handbetrieb stellen.

manually [ˈmænjʊəlɪ] *adv* von Hand, manuell.

manufacture [ˌmænjʊˈfæktʃəʳ] 1 *n* (*act*) Herstellung *f*; (*pl: products*) Waren, Erzeugnisse *pl* ♦ **articles of foreign ~** ausländische Erzeugnisse *pl*.
2 *vt* **(a)** herstellen ♦ **~d goods** Fertigware *f*, Fertigerzeugnisse *pl*. **(b)** (*fig*) *excuse* erfinden.
3 *vi* **we started manufacturing** ... wir begannen mit der Herstellung ...

manufacturer [ˌmænjʊˈfæktʃəʳəʳ] *n* Hersteller *m* ♦ **this country/firm has always been a big ~ of** ... dieses Land/Unternehmen hat schon immer eine bedeutende Rolle bei der Herstellung von ... gespielt.

manufacturing [ˌmænjʊˈfæktʃərɪŋ] 1 *adj techniques* Herstellungs-; *capacity* Produktions-; *industry* verarbeitend.
2 *n* Erzeugung, Herstellung *f*.

manure [məˈnjʊəʳ] 1 *n* Dung, Mist *m*; (*esp artificial*) Dünger *m* ♦ **liquid ~** Jauche *f*; **artificial ~** Kunstdünger *m*.
2 *vt field* düngen.

manuscript [ˈmænjʊskrɪpt] *n* Manuskript *nt*; (*ancient also*) Handschrift *f* ♦ **the novel is still in ~** der Roman ist noch in Manuskriptform; **I read it first in ~ form** ich habe es zuerst als Manuskript gelesen.

Manx [mæŋks] 1 *adj* der Insel Man ♦ **~ cat** Manx-Katze *f* (*stummelschwänzige Katze*).
2 *n* (*language*) Manx *nt*.

Manxman [ˈmæŋksmən] *n, pl* **-men** [-mən] Bewohner *m* der Insel Man.

many [ˈmenɪ] 1 *adj, pron* viele ♦ **~ people** viele (Menschen *or* Leute); **she has ~** sie hat viele (davon); **he hasn't got ~** er hat nicht viele (davon); **there were as ~ as 20** es waren sogar 20 da; **fifty went to France and as ~ to Germany** fünfzig gingen nach Frankreich und ebenso viele nach Deutschland; **as ~ again** noch einmal so viele; **they are just so ~ cowards** das sind lauter Feiglinge; **there's one too ~** einer ist zuviel; **he's had one too ~** er hat einen zuviel *or* einen über den Durst getrunken; **they were too ~ for us** sie waren zu viele *or* zu zahlreich für uns; **he made one mistake too ~** er hat einen Fehler zuviel gemacht; **a good/great ~ houses** eine (ganze) Reihe *or* Anzahl Häuser; **~ a good soldier** so mancher gute Soldat; **~ a time** so manches Mal; **she waited ~ a long year** (*liter*) sie wartete gar manches lange Jahr (*liter*); **~'s the time I've heard that old story** ich habe diese alte Geschichte so manches Mal gehört.
2 *n* **the ~** die (große) Masse.

many: ~-coloured *adj* bunt, vielfarbig; **~-sided** *adj* vielseitig; *figure also* vieleckig; **it's a ~-sided problem** das Problem hat sehr viele verschiedene Aspekte.

Maoist [ˈmaʊɪst] *n* Maoist(in *f*) *m*.

Maori [ˈmaʊrɪ] 1 *adj* Maori-.
2 *n* **(a)** Maori *mf*. **(b)** (*language*) Maori *nt*.

map [mæp] 1 *n* (Land)karte *f*; (*of streets, town*) Stadtplan *m*; (*showing specific item*) Karte *f* ♦ **a ~ of the stars/rivers** eine Stern-/Flußkarte; **is it on the ~?** ist das auf der Karte (eingezeichnet)?; **this will put Cheam on the ~** (*fig*) das wird Cheam zu einem Namen verhelfen; **it's right off the ~** (*fig*) das liegt

(ja) am Ende der Welt *or* hinter dem Mond (*inf*); **entire cities were wiped off the ~** ganze Städte wurden ausradiert.
[2] *vt* (*measure*) vermessen; (*make a map of*) eine Karte anfertigen von ◆ **the history of her suffering was ~ped on her face** ihr Gesicht war von Leid gezeichnet.
◆**map out** *vt sep* **(a)** (*lit*) *see* **map 2.**
(b) (*fig: plan*) entwerfen ◆ **the essay is well ~ped ~** der Aufsatz ist gut angelegt; **our holiday schedule was all ~ped ~ in advance** der Zeitplan für unsere Ferien war schon im voraus genau festgelegt; **he has ~ped ~ what he will do** er hat bereits geplant, was er tun wird.
maple ['meɪpl] *n* (*wood, tree*) Ahorn *m*.
maple: ~ leaf *n* Ahornblatt *nt*; **~ sugar** *n* Ahornzucker *m*; **~ syrup** *n* Ahornsirup *m*.
map: ~maker *n* Kartograph *m*; **~making** *n* Kartographie *f*.
mapping ['mæpɪŋ] *n* (*Comput*) Abbildung *f*, Mapping *nt*.
map: ~reader *n* Kartenleser(in *f*) *m*; **~reading** *n* Kartenlesen *nt*.
Mar *abbr of* **March** Mrz.
mar [mɑːʳ] *vt* verderben; *happiness* trüben; *beauty* mindern ◆ **not a cloud to ~ the sky** kein Wölkchen trübte den Himmel; **his essay was ~red by careless mistakes** durch seine Flüchtigkeitsfehler verdarb er (sich) den ganzen Aufsatz; *see* **make.**
marabou ['mærəbuː] *n* Marabu *m*.
maraca [mə'rækə] *n* Rassel, Maracá *f*.
maraschino [ˌmærə'skiːnəʊ] *n* (*drink*) Maraschino *m*; (*~ cherry*) Maraschinokirsche *f*.
marathon ['mærəθən] [1] *n* **(a)** (*lit*) Marathon(lauf) *m*. **(b)** (*fig*) Marathon *nt*. **this film is a real ~** das ist wirklich ein Marathonfilm *m*.
[2] *adj speech, film, meeting* Marathon-.
maraud [mə'rɔːd] *vti* plündern ◆ **they went ~ing about the countryside** sie zogen plündernd durch die Lande.
marauder [mə'rɔːdəʳ] *n* Plünderer *m*; (*animal*) Räuber *m*.
marauding [mə'rɔːdɪŋ] *adj* plündernd ◆ **the deer fled from the ~ wolf** das Reh floh vor dem beutesuchenden Wolf.
marble ['mɑːbl] [1] *n* **(a)** Marmor *m*. **(b)** (*work in ~*) Marmorplastik *f*. **(c)** (*glass ball*) Murmel *f*, Klicker *m* (*inf*) ◆ **he hasn't got all his ~s** (*inf*) er hat nicht mehr alle Tassen im Schrank (*inf*).
[2] *adj* Marmor-.
marble cake *n* Marmorkuchen *m*.
marbled ['mɑːbld] *adj surface, pages* marmoriert.
March [mɑːtʃ] *n* März *m*; *see also* **September.**
march¹ [mɑːtʃ] [1] *n* **(a)** (*Mil, Mus*) Marsch *m*; (*demonstration*) Demonstration *f*; (*fig: long walk*) Weg *m* ◆ **to move at a good stiff ~** mit strammen Schritten *or* stramm marschieren; **we had been five days on the ~** wir waren fünf Tage lang marschiert; **it's two days' ~** es ist ein Zwei-Tage-Marsch; **he went for a good ~ across the moors** er ist durchs Moorland marschiert.
(b) (*of time, history, events*) Lauf *m*.
(c) **to steal a ~ on sb** jdm zuvorkommen.
[2] *vt soldiers* marschieren lassen; *distance* marschieren ◆ **to ~ sb off** jdn abführen.
[3] *vi* marschieren ◆ **forward ~!** vorwärts(, marsch)!; **quick ~!** im Laufschritt, marsch!; **to ~ in** einmarschieren; **she just ~ed into the room** sie marschierte einfach (ins Zimmer) hinein; **time ~es on** die Zeit bleibt nicht stehen; **to ~ out** abmarschieren, ausrücken; **to ~ past sb** an jdm vorbeimarschieren; **she ~ed straight up to him** sie marschierte schnurstracks auf ihn zu.
march² *n* (*Hist*) Grenzmark *f* ◆ **the Welsh ~es** das Grenzland zwischen England und Wales.
marcher ['mɑːtʃə] *n* (*in demo*) Demonstrant(in *f*) *m*.
marching ['mɑːtʃɪŋ]: **~ orders** *npl* (*Mil*) Marschbefehl *m*; (*inf*) Entlassung *f*; **the new manager got his ~ orders** der neue Manager ist gegangen worden (*inf*); **she gave him his ~ orders** sie hat ihm den Laufpaß gegeben; **~ song** *n* Marschlied *nt*.
marchioness ['mɑːʃənɪs] *n* Marquise *f*.
march past *n* Vorbeimarsch, Aufmarsch *m*, Defilee *nt*.
Mardi gras ['mɑːdɪ'grɑː] *n* Karneval *m*.
mare [mɛəʳ] *n* (*horse*) Stute *f*; (*donkey*) Eselin *f*.
mare's nest ['mɛəznest] *n* Windei *nt*, Reinfall *m*.
Margaret ['mɑːgərɪt] *n* Margarete *f*.
margarine [ˌmɑːdʒə'riːn], **marge** [mɑːdʒ] (*inf*) *n* Margarine *f*.
margin ['mɑːdʒɪn] *n* **(a)** (*on page*) Rand *m* ◆ **a note (written) in the ~** eine Randbemerkung, eine Bemerkung am Rand.
(b) (*extra amount*) Spielraum *m* ◆ **~ of error** Fehlerspielraum *m*; **to allow for a ~ of error** etwaige Fehler mit einkalkulieren; **he left a safety ~ of one hour** sicherheitshalber kalkulierte er einen Spielraum von einer Stunde ein; **by a narrow ~** knapp; **it's within the safety ~** das ist noch sicher.
(c) (*Comm: also* **profit ~**) Gewinnspanne, Verdienstspanne *f*.
(d) (*liter: edge*) Rand, Saum (*liter*) *m* ◆ **the grassy ~ of the lake** das grüne Seeufer.
marginal ['mɑːdʒɪnl] *adj* **(a)** *note* Rand-. **(b)** *improvement, difference* geringfügig, unwesentlich; *constituency, seat* mit knapper Mehrheit ◆ **this is a ~ constituency for the Tories** die Tories haben in diesem Wahlkreis nur eine knappe Mehrheit.
marginalization [ˌmɑːdʒɪnəlaɪ'zeɪʃən] *n* Marginalisierung *f* (*geh*).
marginalize ['mɑːdʒɪnəlaɪz] *vt* marginalisieren (*geh*).
marginally ['mɑːdʒɪnəlɪ] *adv* geringfügig, unwesentlich, nur wenig ◆ **is that better? — ~** ist das besser? — etwas *or* ein wenig; **but only just ~** nur ganz knapp; **it's only ~ useful** es hat nur sehr begrenzte Anwendungsmöglichkeiten *pl*.
margin: ~ release *n* Randlöser *m*; **~ stop** *n* Randsteller *m*.
marguerite [ˌmɑːgə'riːt] *n* Margerite *f*.
marigold ['mærɪgəʊld] *n* (*African or French ~*) Tagetes, Studentenblume *f*; (*common or pot ~*) Ringelblume *f*.
marihuana, marijuana [ˌmærɪ'hwɑːnə] *n* Marihuana *nt*.
marina [mə'riːnə] *n* Yacht- *or* Jachthafen *m*.
marinade [ˌmærɪ'neɪd] *n* Marinade *f*.
marinate ['mærɪneɪt] *vt* marinieren.
marine [mə'riːn] [1] *adj* Meeres-, See- ◆ **~ insurance** Seeversicherung *f*; **~ underwriter** Seeversicherer *m*; **~ life** Meeresfauna und -flora *f*.
[2] *n* **(a)** (*fleet*) Marine *f* ◆ **merchant ~** Handelsmarine *f*.
(b) (*person*) Marineinfanterist *m* ◆ **the ~s** die Marineinfanterie, die Marinetruppen *pl*; **tell that to the ~s!** (*inf*) das kannst du mir nicht weismachen, das kannst du deiner Großmutter erzählen! (*inf*).
mariner ['mærɪnəʳ] *n* Seefahrer, Seemann *m*.
marionette [ˌmærɪə'net] *n* Marionette *f*.
marital ['mærɪtl] *adj* ehelich ◆ **~ status** Familienstand *m*; **~ vows** Ehegelübde *nt*; **~ bliss** Eheglück *nt*; **they lived together in ~ bliss** sie genossen ein glückliches Eheleben.
maritime ['mærɪtaɪm] *adj warfare, law* See- ◆ **~ regions** Küstenregionen *pl*.
marjoram ['mɑːdʒərəm] *n* Majoran *m*.
Mark [mɑːk] *n* Markus *m* ◆ **~ Antony** Mark Anton.
mark¹ [mɑːk] *n* (*Fin*) Mark *f*.
mark² [1] *n* **(a)** (*stain, spot etc*) Fleck *m*; (*scratch*) Kratzer *m*, Schramme *f* ◆ **to make a ~ on sth** einen Fleck auf etw (*acc*) machen/etw beschädigen; **dirty ~s** Schmutzflecken *pl*; **with not a ~ on it** in makellosem Zustand; **will the operation leave a ~?** wird die Operation Spuren *or* Narben hinterlassen?; **the ~s of violence** die Spuren der Gewalt; **he left the ring without a ~ on him/his body** er verließ den Ring, ohne auch nur eine Schramme abbekommen zu haben; **the corpse didn't have a ~ on it** die Leiche wies keine Verletzungen auf.
(b) (*~ing*) (*on animal*) Fleck *m*; (*on person*) Mal *nt*; (*on plane, football pitch etc*) Markierung *f*; (*sign: on monument etc*) Zeichen *nt*.
(c) (*in exam*) Note *f* ◆ **high** *or* **good ~s** gute Noten *pl*; **the ~s are out of 100** insgesamt kann/konnte man 100 Punkte erreichen; **you get no ~s at all as a cook** (*fig*) in puncto Kochen bist du ja nicht gerade eine Eins (*inf*); **there are no ~s for guessing** (*fig*) das ist ja wohl nicht schwer zu erraten; **he gets full ~s for punctuality** (*fig*) in Pünktlichkeit verdient er eine Eins.
(d) (*sign, indication*) Zeichen *nt* ◆ **he had the ~s of old age** er war vom Alter gezeichnet; **it bears the ~s of genius** das trägt geniale Züge; **it's the ~ of a gentleman** daran erkennt man den Gentleman.
(e) (*instead of signature*) **to make one's ~** drei Kreuze (als Unterschrift) machen.
(f) (*level*) **expenses have reached the £100 ~** die Ausgaben haben die 100-Pfund-Grenze erreicht; **the temperature reached the 35° ~** die Temperatur stieg bis auf 35° an.
(g) **Cooper M~ II** Cooper, II; **the new secretary, a sort of Miss Jones ~ 2** die neue Sekretärin, eine zweite Ausführung von Fräulein Jones.
(h) (*phrases*) **to be quick off the ~** (*Sport*) einen guten Start haben; (*fig*) blitzschnell handeln *or* reagieren; **you were quick off the ~** du warst aber fix!; **he was quickest off the ~** er war der Schnellste; **to be slow off the ~** (*Sport*) einen schlechten Start haben; (*fig*) nicht schnell genug schalten *or* reagieren; (*as characteristic*) eine lange Leitung haben (*inf*); **to be up to the ~** den Anforderungen entsprechen; **his work is not up to the ~** seine Arbeit ist unter dem Strich; **I'm not feeling quite up to the ~** ich bin *or* fühle mich nicht ganz auf dem Posten; **to leave one's ~ (on sth)** einer Sache (*dat*) seinen Stempel aufdrücken; **to make one's ~** sich (*dat*) einen Namen machen; **on your ~s!** auf die Plätze!; **to be wide of the ~** (*shooting*) danebentreffen, danebenschießen; (*fig: in guessing, calculating*) danebentippen, sich verhauen (*inf*); **your calculations were wide of the ~** mit deiner Kalkulation hast du dich ganz schön verhauen (*inf*); **to hit the ~** (*lit, fig*) ins Schwarze treffen.
(i) (*Rugby*) Freifang *m* ◆ **"~!"** „Marke!"
[2] *vt* **(a)** (*adversely*) beschädigen; (*stain*) schmutzig machen, Flecken machen auf (+*acc*); (*scratch*) zerkratzen ◆ **the other boxer was not ~ed at all** der andere Boxer hatte nicht eine Schramme *or* überhaupt nichts abbekommen; **her face was ~ed for life** sie hat bleibende Narben im Gesicht zurückbehalten; **the experience ~ed him for life** das Erlebnis hat ihn für sein Leben gezeichnet.
(b) (*for recognition, identity*) markieren, bezeichnen; (*label*) beschriften; (*price*) auszeichnen; *playing cards* zinken ◆ **~ed with the name and age of the exhibitor** mit Namen und Alter des Ausstellers versehen; **the bottle was ~ed "poison"** die Flasche trug die Aufschrift „Gift"; **the chair is ~ed at £2** der Stuhl ist mit £ 2 ausgezeichnet; **the picture/cage isn't ~ed** das Bild ist ohne Angaben/der Käfig hat keine Aufschrift; **~ where you have stopped in your reading** machen Sie sich (*dat*) ein Zeichen, bis wohin Sie gelesen haben; **to ~ sth with an asterisk** etw mit einem Sternchen versehen; **X ~s the spot** X markiert *or* bezeichnet die Stelle; **the teacher ~ed him absent** der Lehrer trug ihn als fehlend ein; **it's not ~ed on the map** es ist nicht auf der Karte eingezeichnet; **it's ~ed with a blue dot** es ist mit einem blauen Punkt gekennzeichnet; **he ~ed his own books with a secret sign** er kennzeichnete seine eigenen Bücher mit einem Geheimzeichen.
(c) (*characterize*) kennzeichnen ◆ **a decade ~ed by violence** ein Jahrzehnt, das im Zeichen der Gewalt stand; **the new bill ~s a change of policy** das

neue Gesetz deutet auf einen politischen Kurswechsel hin; **it ~ed the end of an era** damit ging eine Ära zu Ende; **it ~s him as a future star** daran zeigt sich, daß er eine große Karriere vor sich (*dat*) hat; **a month ~ed by inactivity** ein Monat, der sich durch Untätigkeit auszeichnete.
(d) (*usu pass*) zeichnen ◆ **~ed with grief** von Schmerz gezeichnet; **a beautifully ~ed bird** ein schön gezeichneter Vogel.
(e) *exam, paper* korrigieren (und benoten) ◆ **to ~ a paper A** eine Arbeit mit (einer) Eins benoten; **to ~ a candidate** einem Kandidaten eine Note geben; **the candidate was ~ed ...** der Kandidate erhielt die Note ...; **we ~ed him A** wir haben ihm eine Eins gegeben; **to ~ sth wrong** etw anstreichen.
(f) (*heed*) hören auf (+*acc*) ◆ **~ my words** eins kann ich dir sagen; (*threatening, warning also*) lassen Sie sich das gesagt sein!; **~ you, he may have been right** er könnte gar nicht so unrecht gehabt haben; **~ you, I didn't believe him** ich habe ihm natürlich nicht geglaubt.
(g) (*old: notice*) bemerken ◆ **did you ~ where it fell?** hast du dir gemerkt, wo es hingefallen ist?
(h) (*Sport*) *player, opponent* decken.
(i) **to ~ time** (*Mil, fig*) auf der Stelle treten.
[3] *vi* (a) (*get dirty*) schmutzen, schmutzig werden; (*scratch*) Kratzer bekommen. (b) **her skin ~s easily** sie bekommt leicht blaue Flecken. (c) (*Sport*) decken.

◆**mark down** *vt sep* (a) (*note down*) (sich *dat*) notieren. (b) *prices* herab- *or* heruntersetzen.

◆**mark off** *vt sep* kennzeichnen; *boundary* markieren; *football pitch etc* abgrenzen; *danger area etc* absperren ◆ **these characteristics ~ him ~ from the others** durch diese Eigenschaften unterscheidet er sich von den anderen.

◆**mark out** *vt sep* (a) *tennis court etc* abstecken.
(b) (*note*) bestimmen (*for* für) ◆ **he's been ~ed ~ for promotion** er ist zur Beförderung vorgesehen; **the area has been ~ed ~ for special government grants** für das Gebiet sind besondere staatliche Zuschüsse vorgesehen.
(c) (*identify*) **his speeches have ~ed him ~ as a communist** aus seinen Reden geht hervor *or* kann man schließen, daß er Kommunist ist; **what ~s this example ~ as being different?** worin unterscheidet sich dieses Beispiel?

◆**mark up** *vt sep* (a) (*write up*) notieren (*on* auf +*dat*); (*Typ*) auszeichnen. (b) *price* heraufsetzen, erhöhen.

marked [mɑːkt] *adj* (a) *contrast* merklich, deutlich; *accent* stark, deutlich; *improvement* spürbar, merklich ◆ **it is becoming more ~** es wird immer deutlicher *or* tritt immer deutlicher zutage. (b) **he's a ~ man** er steht auf der schwarzen Liste.

markedly [ˈmɑːkɪdlɪ] *adv* merklich ◆ **it is ~ better** es ist wesentlich *or* bedeutend besser; **not ~ so** nicht, daß es auffallen würde; **they are not ~ different** es besteht kein besonderer *or* großer Unterschied zwischen ihnen.

marker [ˈmɑːkəʳ] *n* (a) Marke *f*; (*to turn at*) Wendemarke *f*, Wendepunkt *m*; (*on road*) Schild *nt*, Wegweiser *m*; (*in book*) Lesezeichen *nt*. (b) (*for exams*) Korrektor(in *f*) *m*; (*scorekeeper in games*) Punktezähler *m* ◆ **will you be the ~?** schreibst du (die Punkte) auf? (c) (*Ftbl*) Beschatter *m*. (d) (*pen*) Markierstift, Marker *m*.

market [ˈmɑːkɪt] [1] *n* (a) Markt *m* ◆ **when is the next ~?** wann ist wieder Markt(tag)?; **he took his sheep to ~** er brachte seine Schafe zum Markt; **at the ~** auf dem Markt; **to go to ~** auf den/zum Markt gehen.
(b) (*trade*) Markt *m* ◆ **world ~** Weltmarkt *m*; **open ~** offener Markt; **to be in the ~ for sth** an etw (*dat*) interessiert sein; **to be on the ~** auf dem Markt sein; **to come on(to) the ~** auf den Markt kommen; **to put on the ~** auf den Markt bringen; *house* zum Verkauf anbieten.
(c) (*area, demand*) (Absatz)markt *m*; (*area also*) Absatzgebiet *nt* ◆ **to create a ~** Nachfrage erzeugen; **to find a ready ~** guten Absatz finden.
(d) (*stock ~*) Börse *f* ◆ **to play the ~** (an der Börse) spekulieren.
[2] *vt* vertreiben ◆ **to ~ a (new) product** ein (neues) Produkt auf den Markt bringen; **it's a nice idea, but we can't ~ it** das ist eine gute Idee, sie läßt sich nur nicht verkaufen *or* vermarkten; **the reason it didn't sell was simply that it wasn't properly ~ed** es fand wegen unzureichenden Marketings keinen Absatz.
[3] *vi* sich verkaufen, Absatz finden, gehen (*inf*).

marketability [ˌmɑːkɪtəˈbɪlɪtɪ] *n* Marktfähigkeit *f*.

marketable [ˈmɑːkɪtəbl] *adj* absetzbar, marktfähig.

market: ~ analysis *n* Marktanalyse *f*; **~ behaviour** *n* Marktverhalten *nt*; **~ day** *n* Markttag *m*.

marketeer [ˌmɑːkəˈtɪəʳ] *n* (*Pol*) **(Common) M~** Anhänger *or* Befürworter *m* der EG; **black ~** Schwarzhändler *m*.

market: ~ forces *npl* Marktkräfte *pl*; **~ garden** *n* Gemüseanbaubetrieb *m*, Gärtnerei *f*; **~ gardener** *n* Gärtner(in *f*) *m*; **~ gardening** *n* (gewerbsmäßiger) Anbau von Gemüse.

marketing [ˈmɑːkɪtɪŋ] *n* Marketing *nt* ◆ **~ manager** Marketing-manager(in *f*) *m*.

market: ~ leader *n* Marktführer *m*; **~ niche** *n* Marktnische *f*; **~place** *n* Marktplatz *m*; (*world of trade*) Markt *m*; **in/on the ~place** auf dem Markt(platz); **~ price** *n* Marktpreis *m*; **~ research** *n* Marktforschung *f*; **~ researcher** *n* Marktforscher(in *f*) *m*; **~ share** *n* Marktanteil *m*; **~ square** *n* Marktplatz *m*; **~ survey** *n* Marktuntersuchung *f*; **~ town** *n* Marktstädtchen *nt*; **~ trends** *npl* Markttendenzen *pl*; **~ value** *n* Marktwert *m*.

marking [ˈmɑːkɪŋ] *n* (a) Markierung *f*; (*on aeroplane also*) Kennzeichen *nt*; (*on animal*) Zeichnung *f* ◆ **~ ink** Wäschetinte *f*. (b) (*of exams*) (*correcting*) Korrektur *f*; (*grading*) Benotung *f*. (c) (*Sport*) Decken *nt*, Deckung *f*.

marksman [ˈmɑːksmən] *n, pl* **-men** [-mən] Schütze *m*; (*police etc*) Scharfschütze *m*.

marksmanship [ˈmɑːksmənʃɪp] *n* Treffsicherheit *f*.

mark-up [ˈmɑːkʌp] *n* (a) Handelsspanne *f*; (*amount added*) Preiserhöhung *f or* -aufschlag *m* ◆ **~ price** Verkaufspreis *m*. (b) (*Typ*) Auszeichnung *f*.

marl [mɑːl] *n* Mergel *m*.

marlin [ˈmɑːlɪn] *n* Fächerfisch, Marlin *m*.

marlinspike [ˈmɑːlɪnspaɪk] *n* Marlspieker *m*, Splißeisen *nt*.

marmalade [ˈmɑːməleɪd] *n* Marmelade *f* aus Zitrusfrüchten ◆ **(orange) ~** Orangenmarmelade *f*.

marmoreal [mɑːˈmɔːrɪəl] *adj* marmorn, aus Marmor; (*resembling marble*) marmorartig.

marmoset [ˈmɑːməʊzet] *n* Krallenaffe *m*, Pinseläffchen *nt*.

marmot [ˈmɑːmət] *n* Murmeltier *nt*.

maroon¹ [məˈruːn] [1] *adj* kastanienbraun, rötlichbraun.
[2] *n* (*colour*) Kastanienbraun *nt*; (*firework*) Leuchtkugel *f*.

maroon² *vt* aussetzen ◆ **~ed** von der Außenwelt abgeschnitten; **~ed by floods** vom Hochwasser eingeschlossen.

marque [mɑːk] *n* (*brand*) Marke *f*.

marquee [mɑːˈkiː] *n* (a) Festzelt *nt*. (b) (*US: of theatre etc*) Vordach, Canopy *nt* ◆ **his name's on all the ~s** sein Name ist auf allen Anzeigetafeln zu sehen.

marquess [ˈmɑːkwɪs] *n* Marquis *m*.

marquetry [ˈmɑːkɪtrɪ] *n* Marketerie, Einlegearbeit *f*.

marquis [ˈmɑːkwɪs] *n see* **marquess**.

marram grass [ˈmærəm,grɑːs] *n* Strandhafer *m*, Dünengras *nt*.

▼ **marriage** [ˈmærɪdʒ] *n* (a) (*state*) die Ehe; (*wedding*) Hochzeit, Heirat *f*; (*~ ceremony*) Trauung *f* ◆ **civil ~** Zivilehe *f*/standesamtliche Trauung; **~ of convenience** Vernunftehe *f*; **relations by ~** angeheiratete Verwandte; **to be related by ~** (*in-laws*) miteinander verschwägert sein; (*others*) miteinander verwandt sein; **to give sb in ~ to sb** jdn jdm zur Frau geben; **to give sb in ~** jdn verheiraten; **an offer of ~** ein Heiratsantrag *m*.
(b) (*fig*) Verbindung *f* ◆ **a ~ of two minds** eine geistige Ehe.

marriageable [ˈmærɪdʒəbl] *adj* heiratsfähig ◆ **of ~ age** im heiratsfähigen Alter.

marriage: ~-bed *n* Ehebett *nt*; **~ ceremony** *n* Trauzeremonie *f*; **~ certificate** *n* Heiratsurkunde *f*; **~ guidance** *n* Eheberatung *f*; **~ guidance counsellor** *n* Eheberater(in *f*) *m*; **~ licence** *n* Eheerlaubnis *f*; **~ lines** *npl* (*inf*) Trauschein *m*; **~ portion** *n* (*old*) Mitgift *f*; **~ settlement** *n* Ehevertrag *m*; **~ vow** *n* Ehegelübde *nt*.

married [ˈmærɪd] *adj life, state* Ehe-; *man, woman* verheiratet ◆ **~ couple** Ehepaar *nt*; **~ quarters** Unterkünfte für Eheleute; **he/she is a ~ man/woman** er/sie ist verheiratet.

marrow [ˈmærəʊ] *n* (a) (*Anat*) (Knochen)mark *nt* ◆ **~bone** Markknochen *m*; **he's a Scot to the ~** er ist durch und durch Schotte; **to be frozen to the ~** völlig durchgefroren sein. (b) (*fig: of statement etc*) Kern *m*, Wesentliche(s) *nt*. (c) (*Bot*) (*also* **vegetable ~**) Gartenkürbis *m*.

▼ **marry** [ˈmærɪ] [1] *vt* (a) heiraten ◆ **to ~ money** reich heiraten; **will you ~ me?** willst du mich heiraten?
(b) (*priest*) trauen.
(c) (*father*) verheiraten ◆ **he married all his daughters into very rich families** er hat zugesehen, daß alle seine Töchter in reiche Familien einheirateten.
▼[2] *vi* (a) (*also* **get married**) heiraten, sich verheiraten; (*of couple*) heiraten, sich vermählen (*geh*) ◆ **to ~ into a rich family** in eine reiche Familie einheiraten; **to ~ into money** reich heiraten; **he married into a small fortune** durch die Heirat ist er an ein kleines Vermögen gekommen; **he's not the ~ing kind** er ist nicht der Typ, der heiratet; **~ in haste, repent at leisure** (*prov*) Heiraten in Eile bereut man in Weile (*prov*).
(b) (*fig: of two pieces of wood etc*) ineinanderpassen.

◆**marry off** *vt sep* an den Mann/die Frau bringen (*inf*); *girl also* unter die Haube bringen (*inf*) ◆ **he has married ~ his daughter to a rich young lawyer** er hat dafür gesorgt, daß seine Tochter einen reichen jungen Anwalt heiratet.

Mars [mɑːz] *n* Mars *m*.

Marseillaise [ˌmɑːsəˈleɪz] *n*: **the ~** die Marseillaise.

Marseilles [mɑːˈseɪlz] *n* Marseille *nt*.

marsh [mɑːʃ] *n* Sumpf *m*.

marshal [ˈmɑːʃəl] [1] *n* (*Mil, of royal household*) Marschall *m*; (*at sports meeting etc*) Platzwärter *m*; (*at demo etc*) Ordner *m*; (*US*) Bezirkspolizeichef *m*.
[2] *vt facts, arguments* ordnen; *soldiers* antreten lassen; (*lead*) geleiten, führen.

marshalling yard [ˈmɑːʃəlɪŋˈjɑːd] *n* Rangier- *or* Verschiebebahnhof *m*.

marsh: ~ gas *n* Methangas, Sumpf- *or* Grubengas *nt*; **~land** *n* Marschland *nt*; **~mallow** *n* (*sweet*) Marshmallow *nt*; (*Bot*) Eibisch *m*; **~ marigold** *n* Sumpfdotterblume *f*.

marshy [ˈmɑːʃɪ] *adj* (+*er*) sumpfig ◆ **a ~ district** ein Sumpfgebiet *nt*.

marsupial [mɑːˈsuːpɪəl] [1] *adj* **~ animal** Beuteltier *nt*.
[2] *n* Beuteltier *nt*.

mart [mɑːt] *n* (*old*) Markt *m*.

marten [ˈmɑːtɪn] *n* Marder *m*.

martial [ˈmɑːʃəl] *adj music* kriegerisch, Kampf-; *bearing* stramm, soldatisch ◆ **the ~ arts** die Kampfkunst; **the ~ art of judo** der Kampfsport Judo; **~ law** Kriegsrecht *nt*; **the state was put under ~ law** über den Staat wurde (das) Kriegsrecht verhängt.

Martian [ˈmɑːʃɪən] [1] *adj atmosphere, exploration* des Mars; *invaders* vom Mars.
[2] *n* Marsbewohner(in *f*), Marsmensch *m*.

martin [ˈmɑːtɪn] *n* Schwalbe *f*.

➤ LANGUAGE IN USE: **marriage: a** → 24.3 **marry: 2a** → 24.3

martinet [ˌmɑːtɪˈnet] *n* (strenger) Zuchtmeister ◆ **he's a real ~** er führt ein strenges Regiment.
martini [mɑːˈtiːnɪ] *n* Martini *m.*
Martinique [ˌmɑːtɪˈniːk] *n* Martinique *nt.*
Martinmas [ˈmɑːtɪnməs] *n* Martinstag *m*, Martini *nt.*
martyr [ˈmɑːtəʳ] 1 *n* Märtyrer(in *f*) *m* ◆ **he was a ~ to the cause of civil rights** er wurde zum Märtyrer für die Sache der Bürgerrechtsbewegung; **to be a ~ to arthritis** entsetzlich unter Arthritis zu leiden haben; **there's no need to make a ~ of yourself** (*inf*) du brauchst hier nicht den Märtyrer zu spielen (*inf*).
2 *vt* martern, (zu Tode) quälen ◆ **thousands of Christians were ~ed** Tausende von Christen starben den Märtyrertod.
martyrdom [ˈmɑːtədəm] *n* (*suffering*) Martyrium *nt*; (*death*) Märtyrertod *m.*
marvel [ˈmɑːvəl] 1 *n* Wunder *nt* ◆ **the ~s of modern science** die Wunder der modernen Wissenschaft; **this medicine is a ~** diese Medizin wirkt Wunder; **if he ever gets there it will be a ~** (*inf*) wenn er jemals dort ankommt, ist das ein Wunder; **it's a ~ to me that he escaped unhurt** es kommt mir wie ein Wunder vor, daß er ohne Verletzungen davonkam; **it's a ~ to me how he does it** (*inf*) es ist mir einfach unerklärlich *or* schleierhaft, wie er das macht; **her desk is a ~ of tidiness** ihr Schreibtisch ist ein Muster an Ordnung; **you're a ~!** (*inf*) du bist ein Engel!; (*clever*) du bist ein Genie!
2 *vi* staunen (*at* über +*acc*) ◆ **to ~ at a sight** einen Anblick bestaunen; **they ~led at her beauty** (*liter*) sie bewunderten ihre Schönheit.
marvellous, (*US*) **marvelous** [ˈmɑːvələs] *adj* wunderbar, phantastisch, fabelhaft ◆ **isn't it ~?** ist das nicht herrlich?; (*iro*) gut, nicht! (*iro*).
marvellously, (*US*) **marvelously** [ˈmɑːvələslɪ] *adv* (*with adj*) herrlich; (*with vb*) großartig, fabelhaft.
Marxian [ˈmɑːksɪən] *adj* Marxisch.
Marxism [ˈmɑːksɪzəm] *n* der Marxismus.
Marxist [ˈmɑːksɪst] 1 *adj* marxistisch.
2 *n* Marxist(in *f*) *m.*
Mary [ˈmɛərɪ] *n* Maria *f.*
marzipan [ˌmɑːzɪˈpæn] *n* Marzipan *nt or m.*
mascara [mæˈskɑːrə] 1 *n* Wimperntusche, Maskara *f.*
2 *vt* tuschen.
mascot [ˈmæskət] *n* Maskottchen *nt.*
masculine [ˈmæskjʊlɪn] 1 *adj* männlich; *woman* maskulin.
2 *n* (*Gram*) Maskulinum *nt.*
masculinity [ˌmæskjʊˈlɪnɪtɪ] *n* Männlichkeit *f.*
mash [mæʃ] 1 *n* Brei *m*; (*for animals*) Futterbrei *m*, Schlempe *f*; (*potatoes*) Püree *nt*; (*in brewing*) Maische *f.*
2 *vt* zerstampfen.
MASH *n* (*US*) *abbr of* **Mobile Army Surgical Hospital** mobiles Lazarett.
mashed [mæʃt] *adj* **~ potatoes** Kartoffelbrei *m or* -püree *nt.*
masher [ˈmæʃəʳ] *n* Stampfer *m*; (*for potatoes*) Kartoffelstampfer *m.*
mask [mɑːsk] 1 *n* (*lit, fig, Comput*) Maske *f* ◆ **the ~ slipped** (*fig*) er/sie *etc* ließ die Maske fallen; **surgeon's ~** Mundschutz *m.*
2 *vt* maskieren; (*clouds, trees etc*) verdecken; *feelings* verbergen; *intentions* maskieren.
masked [mɑːskt] *adj* maskiert ◆ **~ ball** Maskenball *m.*
masochism [ˈmæsəʊkɪzəm] *n* Masochismus *m.*
masochist [ˈmæsəʊkɪst] *n* Masochist(in *f*) *m.*
masochistic [ˌmæsəʊˈkɪstɪk] *adj* masochistisch.
mason [ˈmeɪsn] *n* **(a)** (*builder*) Steinmetz *m*; (*in quarry*) Steinhauer *m*; *see* **monumental**. **(b)** (*free~*) Freimaurer *m.*
masonic [məˈsɒnɪk] *adj* Freimaurer-.
masonry [ˈmeɪsnrɪ] *n* **(a)** (*stonework*) Mauerwerk *nt.* **(b)** (*free~*) Freimaurerei *f*, Freimaurertum *nt.*
masque [mɑːsk] *n* Maskenspiel *nt.*
masquerade [ˌmæskəˈreɪd] 1 *n* Maskerade *f* ◆ **that's just a ~, she's not really like that at all** (*fig*) das ist alles nur Theater, in Wirklichkeit ist sie gar nicht so.
2 *vi* **to ~ as ...** sich verkleiden als ...; (*fig*) sich ausgeben als ..., vorgeben, ... zu sein; **this cheap rubbish masquerading as literature** dieser Schund, der als Literatur ausgegeben wird.
mass¹ [mæs] *n* (*Eccl*) Messe *f* ◆ **high ~** Hochamt *nt*; **to go to ~** zur Messe gehen; **to hear ~** die Messe feiern; **to say ~** die *or* eine Messe lesen.
mass² 1 *n* **(a)** (*general, Phys*) Masse *f*; (*of people*) Menge *f* ◆ **a ~ of snow/rubble** eine Schneemasse/ein Schutthaufen *m*; **the ~ of rubble** der Haufen Schutt; **a ~ of cold air** eine kalte Luftmasse; **a ~ of red hair** ein Wust roter Haare; **a ~ of flames** ein einziges Flammenmeer; **this confused ~ of thoughts** dieser wirre Gedankenwust; **the essay is one great ~ of spelling mistakes** der Aufsatz wimmelt nur so von Schreibfehlern; **he's a ~ of bruises** er ist voller blauer Flecken; **the garden is a ~ of yellow/colour** der Garten ist ein Meer *nt* von Gelb/ein Farbenmeer *nt*; **the ~es** die Masse(n *pl*); **the great ~ of the population** die (breite) Masse der Bevölkerung; **the nation in the ~** die breite(n) Volksmasse(n); **people, in the ~, prefer ...** die breite Masse (der Menschen) zieht es vor, ...
(b) (*bulk*) **the great ~ of the mountains** das riesige Bergmassiv; **the huge ~ of the ship loomed up out of the night** die riesige Form des Schiffes tauchte aus der Nacht auf.
(c) (*inf*) **~es** massenhaft, eine Masse (*inf*); **he has ~es of money/time** er hat massenhaft *or* massig (*inf*) *or* eine Masse (*inf*) Geld/Zeit; **the factory is producing ~es of cars** die Fabrik produziert Unmengen von Autos; **I've got ~es of things to do** ich habe noch massig (*inf*) zu tun.
2 *vt troops* massieren, zusammenziehen ◆ **the ~ed bands of the Royal Navy** die vereinigten Militärkapellen der königlichen Marine.
3 *vi* (*Mil*) sich massieren; (*Red Indians etc*) sich versammeln; (*clouds*) sich (zusammen)ballen ◆ **they're ~ing for an attack** sie sammeln sich zum Angriff.
mass *in cpds* Massen-.
massacre [ˈmæsəkəʳ] 1 *n* Massaker *nt.*
2 *vt* niedermetzeln, massakrieren ◆ **last Saturday they ~d us 6-0** (*inf*) letzten Samstag haben sie uns mit 6:0 fertiggemacht (*inf*).
massage [ˈmæsɑːʒ] 1 *n* Massage *f* ◆ **~ parlour** Massagesalon *m.*
2 *vt* massieren.
masseur [mæˈsɜːʳ] *n* Masseur *m.*
masseuse [mæˈsɜːz] *n* Masseuse *f.*
massif [mæˈsiːf] *n* (*Geog*) (Gebirgs)massiv *nt.*
massive [ˈmæsɪv] *adj* riesig, enorm; *structure, wall* massiv, wuchtig; *forehead* breit, wuchtig; *boxer* wuchtig, massig; *task* gewaltig; *support, heart attack* massiv ◆ **the ship was designed on a ~ scale** das Schiff hatte riesenhafte Ausmaße; **the symphony is conceived on a ~ scale** die Symphonie ist ganz groß angelegt; **space research is financed on a ~ scale** Raumforschung wird in ganz großem Rahmen finanziert.
massively [ˈmæsɪvlɪ] *adv* wuchtig ◆ **a ~ built man** ein Schrank *m* von einem Mann; **~ in debt** enorm verschuldet.
massiveness [ˈmæsɪvnɪs] *n* (*of expanse of land, plane, ship, hotel etc*) riesige *or* gewaltige Ausmaße *pl*; (*of fortune, expenditure, orchestra*) enorme Größe; (*of structure, wall*) Wuchtigkeit, Massivität *f*; (*of boxer, forehead*) Wuchtigkeit *f* ◆ **the ~ of the task** die gewaltige Aufgabe.
mass: ~ marketing *n* massenweise Vermarktung; **~ media** *npl* Massenmedien *pl*; **~ meeting** *n* Massenveranstaltung *f*; (*in company*) Betriebsversammlung *f*; (*of trade union*) Vollversammlung *f*; (*Pol*) Massenkundgebung *f*; **~ murderer** *n* Massenmörder(in *f*) *m*; **~ murders** *npl* Massenmord *m*; **~ number** *n* (*Phys*) Massenzahl *f*; **~-produce** *vt* in Massenproduktion herstellen; *cars, engines etc* serienweise herstellen; **~-produced** *adj* **~-produced items** Massenartikel *pl*; **it looks as though it was ~-produced** das sieht sehr nach Massenware aus; **~-production** *n* Massenproduktion *f*; **~ psychology** *n* Massenpsychologie *f*; **~ storage (device)** *n* (*Comput*) Massenspeicher *m*; **~ unemployment** *n* Massenarbeitslosigkeit *f.*
mast¹ [mɑːst] *n* (*Naut*) Mast(baum) *m*; (*Rad etc*) Sendeturm *m* ◆ **10 years before the ~** 10 Jahre auf See.
mast² *n* (*Bot*) Mast *f.*
mastectomy [mæˈstektəmɪ] *n* Brustamputation *f.*
-masted [-mɑːstɪd] *adj suf* mastig ◆ **a three-~ vessel** ein Dreimaster *m.*
master [ˈmɑːstəʳ] 1 *n* **(a)** (*of the house, dog, servants*) Herr *m* ◆ **M~** (*Christ*) der Herr; (*in address*) Meister; **I am (the) ~ now** jetzt bin ich der Herr; **to be ~ in one's own house** (*also fig*) Herr im Hause sein; **to be one's own ~** sein eigener Herr sein.
(b) (*Naut*) Kapitän *m* ◆ **~'s certificate** Kapitänspatent *nt.*
(c) (*musician, painter etc*) Meister *m.*
(d) (*teacher*) Lehrer *m*; (*of apprentice*) Meister *m.*
(e) to be ~ of sth etw beherrschen; **to be ~ of the situation** Herr *m* der Lage sein; **to be the ~ of one's fate** sein Schicksal in der Hand haben; *see* **grand, past ~**.
(f) (*boy's title*) Master, Meister (*old*) *m.*
(g) (*of college*) Leiter, Rektor *m.*
(h) (*~ copy*) Original *nt.*
2 *vt* meistern; *one's emotions* unter Kontrolle bringen; *technique, method* beherrschen ◆ **to ~ the violin** das Geigenspiel beherrschen; **to ~ one's temper** sich beherrschen, sein Temperament zügeln.
master *in cpds* (*with trades*) -meister *m*; **~-at-arms** *n* Bootsmann *m* mit Polizeibefugnis; **~ bedroom** *n* großes Schlafzimmer; **~ builder** *n* Baumeister *m*; **~ copy** *n* Original *nt*; **~ disk** *n* Hauptplatte *f*; **~ file** *n* (*Comput*) Stammdatei *f.*
masterful [ˈmɑːstəfʊl] *adj* meisterhaft; *ball control* gekonnt; (*dominating*) *personality* gebieterisch ◆ **he's got a ~, yet polite attitude** er hat eine bestimmte, aber trotzdem höfliche Art; **he said in a ~ tone** sagte er in bestimmtem Ton; **we were amazed at his ~ control of the meeting** wir staunten darüber, wie überlegen *or* souverän er die Sitzung in der Hand hatte.
masterfully [ˈmɑːstəfəlɪ] *adv* meisterhaft; *control* überlegen, souverän; *play, kick etc* gekonnt.
master key *n* Haupt- *or* Generalschlüssel *m.*
masterly [ˈmɑːstəlɪ] *adj* meisterhaft, gekonnt ◆ **in a ~ fashion** meisterhaft, gekonnt.
master: ~ mariner *n* Kapitän *m*; **~ mason** *n* Steinmetzmeister *m*; **~mind** 1 *n* (führender) Kopf; **who's the ~mind who planned all these operations?** wer ist der Kopf, der hinter der Planung dieser Unternehmungen steckte?; 2 *vt* **who ~minded the robbery?** wer steckt hinter dem Raubüberfall?; **M~ of Arts/Science** *n* ≃ Magister *m* (der philosophischen/naturwissenschaftlichen Fakultät); **~ of ceremonies** *n* (*at function*) Zeremonienmeister *m*; (*on stage*) Conférencier *m*; (*on TV*) Showmaster *m*; **~ of (fox)hounds** *n* Master *m*; **~piece** *n* Meisterwerk *nt*; **~ race** *n* Herrenvolk *nt*; **~ sergeant** *n* (*US*) Oberfeldwebel *m*; **~ stroke** *n* Meister- *or* Glanzstück *nt*; **~ switch** *n* Hauptschalter *m*; **~ tape** *n* Originalband *nt*; (*Comput*) Stammband *nt*; **~work** *n* Meisterwerk *nt.*
mastery [ˈmɑːstərɪ] *n* (*control: of language, technique, instrument etc*) Beherr-

schung *f*; (*skill*) Können *nt*; (*over competitors etc*) Oberhand *f* ◆ **~ of the seas** Herrschaft *f* über die Meere; **the painter's ~ of colour and form** des Malers meisterhafter Gebrauch von Form und Farbe; **to gain the ~ of sth** etw beherrschen.

masthead ['mɑːsthed] *n* (*Naut*) Mars, Mastkorb *m*; (*US: in magazines etc*) Impressum *nt*.

mastic ['mæstɪk] *n* (*Build*) Mastix *m*.

masticate ['mæstɪkeɪt] *vti* kauen; (*for young*) vorkauen.

mastication [ˌmæstɪ'keɪʃən] *n* Kauen *nt*; Vorkauen *nt*.

mastiff ['mæstɪf] *n* Dogge *f*.

mastitis [mæ'staɪtɪs] *n* Brust(drüsen)entzündung, Mastitis *f*.

mastodon ['mæstədɒn] *n* Mastodon *nt*.

mastoid ['mæstɔɪd] 1 *adj* warzenförmig, mastoid (*spec*).
2 *n* Warzenfortsatz *m*, Mastoid *nt* (*spec*).

masturbate ['mæstəbeɪt] *vi* masturbieren, onanieren.

masturbation [ˌmæstə'beɪʃən] *n* Masturbation, Onanie *f*.

mat¹ [mæt] 1 *n* Matte *f*; (*door* ~) Fußmatte *f*; (*on table*) Untersetzer *m*; (*of cloth*) Deckchen *nt*; (*of hair*) Gewirr *nt* ◆ **place ~** Set *nt*.
2 *vt* **the sea-water had ~ted his hair** durch das Salzwasser waren seine Haare verfilzt geworden.
3 *vi* verfilzen.

mat² *adj see* **matt**.

matador ['mætədɔːʳ] *n* Matador *m*.

match¹ [mætʃ] *n* Streich- *or* Zündholz *nt*.

▼ **match²** 1 *n* (**a**) (*sb/sth similar, suitable etc*) **to be** *or* **make a good ~** gut zusammenpassen; **the skirt is a good ~ for the jumper** der Rock paßt gut zum Pullover; **I want a ~ for this yellow paint** ich möchte Farbe in diesem Gelbton; **this chair is a ~ for that one** dieser Stuhl ist das Gegenstück zu dem.
▼ (**b**) (*equal*) **to be a/no ~ for sb** (*be able to compete with*) sich mit jdm messen/nicht messen können; (*be able to handle*) jdm gewachsen/nicht gewachsen sein; **he's a ~ for anybody** er kann es mit jedem aufnehmen; **A was more than a ~ for B** A war B weit überlegen; **to meet one's ~** seinen Meister finden.
(**c**) (*marriage*) Heirat *f* ◆ **who thought up this ~?** wer hat die beiden zusammengebracht?; **she made a good ~** sie hat eine gute Partie gemacht; **he's a good ~** er ist eine gute Partie.
(**d**) (*Sport*) (*general*) Wettkampf *m*; (*team game*) Spiel *nt*; (*Tennis*) Match *nt*, Partie *f*; (*Boxing, Fencing*) Kampf *m*; (*quiz*) Wettkampf, Wettbewerb *m* ◆ **athletics ~** Leichtathletikkampf *m*; **I'll give you a ~** ich werde einmal gegen Sie spielen; **we must have another ~ some time** wir müssen wieder einmal gegeneinander spielen; **that's ~** (*Tennis*) Match!, damit ist das Match entschieden.
2 *vt* (**a**) (*pair off*) **they're well ~ed as man and wife** die beiden passen gut zusammen; **the two boxers were well ~ed** die beiden Boxer waren einander ebenbürtig; **the teams are well ~ed** die Mannschaften sind gleichwertig; **~ each diagram with its counterpart** ordnen Sie die Schaubilder einander zu.
▼ (**b**) (*equal*) gleichkommen (*+dat*) (*in an +dat*) ◆ **A doesn't quite ~ B in originality** A kann es an Originalität nicht mit B aufnehmen; **nobody can ~ him in argument** niemand kann so gut argumentieren wie er; **a quality that has never been ~ed since** eine Qualität, die bislang unerreicht ist *or* noch ihresgleichen sucht (*geh*); **no knight could ~ him in battle** kein Ritter konnte sich mit ihm messen; **I can't ~ him in chess** im Schach kann ich es mit ihm nicht aufnehmen; **that sort of easy self-confidence which is not ~ed by any great degree of intelligence** jene Selbstsicherheit, die nicht mit der entsprechenden Intelligenz gepaart ist; **~ that if you can!** das soll erst mal einer nachmachen, das macht so leicht keiner nach!; **three kings! ~ that!** drei Könige! kannst du da noch mithalten?; **this climate/whisky can't be ~ed anywhere in the world** so ein Klima/so einen Whisky gibt es nicht noch einmal.
(**c**) (*correspond to*) entsprechen (*+dat*) ◆ **the results did not ~ our hopes** die Ergebnisse entsprachen nicht unseren Hoffnungen.
(**d**) (*clothes, colours*) passen zu ◆ **she ~ed the carpet with some nice curtains** sie fand nette, zum Teppich passende Vorhänge; **can you ~ this fabric?** haben Sie etwas, das zu diesem Stoff paßt?; **to ~ colours and fabrics so that ...** Farben und Stoffe so aufeinander abstimmen, daß ...; **the colour of his face ~ed the red of his jumper** sein Gesicht war so rot wie sein Pullover.
(**e**) (*pit*) **he decided to ~ his team against** *or* **with the champions** er beschloß, seine Mannschaft gegen die Meister antreten zu lassen; **to be ~ed against sb** gegen jdn antreten; **to ~ one's wits/strength against sb** sich geistig mit jdm messen/seine Kräfte mit jdm messen.
3 *vi* zusammenpassen ◆ **it doesn't ~** das paßt nicht (zusammen); **with a skirt to ~** mit (dazu) passendem Rock.

◆**match up** 1 *vi* (**a**) (*correspond*) zusammenpassen. (**b**) (*be equal*) **he ~ed ~ to the situation** er war der Situation gewachsen.
2 *vt sep colours* aufeinander abstimmen ◆ **to ~ sth ~ with sth** das Passende zu etw finden.

matchbox ['mætʃbɒks] *n* Streichholzschachtel *f*.

matching ['mætʃɪŋ] *adj* (dazu) passend ◆ **they form a ~ pair** sie passen *or* gehören zusammen; **a ~ set of wine glasses** ein Satz *m* Weingläser; **~ funds** (*US*) *Geldmittel pl, die von der Regierung oder einem Unternehmen zur Verfügung gestellt werden, um von privater Seite aufgebrachte Spenden etc zu verdoppeln.*

matchless ['mætʃlɪs] *adj* einzigartig, unvergleichlich.

match: ~lock *n* Luntenschloß *nt*; **~maker** *n* Ehestifter(in *f*), Kuppler(in *f*) (*pej*) *m*; **~making** *n* **she loves ~making** sie verkuppelt die Leute gern (*inf*); **~ point** *n* (*Tennis*) Matchball *m*; **~stick** *n* Streichholz *nt*; **~wood** *n Holz nt zur Herstellung von Streichhölzern*; **smashed to ~wood** (*fig*) zu Kleinholz gemacht (*inf*).

mate¹ [meɪt] (*Chess*) 1 *n* Matt *nt*.
2 *vt* matt setzen.
3 *vi* **white ~s in two** Weiß setzt den Gegner in zwei Zügen matt.

mate² 1 *n* (**a**) (*fellow worker*) Arbeitskollege, Kumpel *m*.
(**b**) (*helper*) Gehilfe, Geselle *m*.
(**c**) (*Naut*) Maat *m*.
(**d**) (*of animal*) (*male*) Männchen *nt*; (*female*) Weibchen *nt* ◆ **his ~** das Weibchen.
(**e**) (*inf: friend*) Freund(in *f*), Kamerad(in *f*) *m* ◆ **listen, ~** hör mal, Freundchen! (*inf*); **got a light, ~?** hast du Feuer, Kumpel? (*inf*).
(**f**) (*hum inf: husband, wife*) Mann *m*/Frau *f*.
(**g**) (*of pair*) **here's one sock, where's its ~?** hier ist eine Socke, wo ist die andere *or* zweite?
2 *vt animals* paaren; *female animal* decken lassen; (*fig hum*) verkuppeln ◆ **they ~d their mare with our stallion** sie haben ihre Stute von unserem Hengst decken lassen.
3 *vi* (*Zool*) sich paaren.

mater ['meɪtəʳ] *n* (*Brit inf*) Mama *f*.

material [mə'tɪərɪəl] 1 *adj* (**a**) (*of matter, things*) materiell ◆ **~ damage** Sachschaden *m*.
(**b**) (*of physical needs*) *needs, comforts* materiell.
(**c**) (*esp Jur: important*) *evidence, witness* wesentlich; *difference also* grundlegend ◆ **that's not ~** das ist nicht relevant.
2 *n* (**a**) Material *nt*; (*for report, novel etc*) Stoff *m*; (*esp documents etc*) Material *nt* ◆ **~s** Material *nt*; **building ~s** Baustoffe *pl or* -material *nt*; **raw ~s** Rohstoffe *pl*; **writing ~s** Schreibzeug *nt*; **he's good editorial ~** er hat das Zeug zum Redakteur; **this group would be good ~ for our show** diese Band wäre für unsere Show ganz brauchbar.
(**b**) (*cloth*) Stoff *m*, Material *nt*.

materialism [mə'tɪərɪəlɪzəm] *n* der Materialismus.

materialist [mə'tɪərɪəlɪst] *n* Materialist(in *f*) *m*.

materialistic *adj*, **~ally** *adv* [məˌtɪərɪə'lɪstɪk, -əlɪ] materialistisch.

materialize [mə'tɪərɪəlaɪz] *vi* (**a**) (*idea, plan*) sich verwirklichen; (*promises, hopes etc*) wahr werden ◆ **this idea will never ~** aus dieser Idee wird nie etwas; **the meeting never ~d** das Treffen kam nie zustande; **if this deal ever ~s** wenn aus diesem Geschäft je etwas wird, wenn dieses Geschäft je zustande kommt; **the money he'd promised me never ~d** von dem Geld, das er mir versprochen hatte, habe ich nie etwas gesehen.
(**b**) (*ghost*) erscheinen; (*indistinct object also*) auftauchen.

materially [mə'tɪərɪəlɪ] *adv* grundlegend, wesentlich ◆ **they are not ~ different** sie unterscheiden sich nicht wesentlich.

matériel [məˌtɪərɪ'el] *n* (*US*) Ausrüstung *f*.

maternal [mə'tɜːnl] *adj* mütterlich ◆ **~ grandfather** Großvater mütterlicherseits; **~ affection** Mutterliebe *f*; **~ instincts** Mutterinstinkte, mütterliche Instinkte *pl*.

maternity [mə'tɜːnɪtɪ] *n* Mutterschaft *f* ◆ **the idea of ~ never appealed to her** sie konnte sich nicht mit dem Gedanken befreunden, Mutter zu werden.

maternity: ~ benefit *n* Mutterschaftsgeld *nt*; **~ dress** *n* Umstandskleid *nt*; **~ home, ~ hospital** *n* Entbindungsheim *nt*; **~ leave** *n* Mutterschaftsurlaub *m*; **~ unit** *n* Entbindungs- *or* Wöchnerinnenstation *f*; **~ ward** *n* Entbindungsstation *f*.

matey ['meɪtɪ] (*Brit inf*) 1 *adj* (*+er*) *person* freundlich, kollegial; (*pej*) vertraulich; *atmosphere* freundschaftlich, kollegial; *gathering* vertraulich ◆ **careful what you say, he's ~ with the director** sei vorsichtig mit dem, was du sagst, er steht mit dem Direktor auf du und du; **he was getting just a bit too ~ with my wife** er wurde ein wenig zu vertraulich mit meiner Frau.
2 *n* Kumpel *m*; (*warningly*) Freundchen *nt* (*inf*).

math [mæθ] *n* (*US inf*) Mathe *f* (*inf*).

mathematical *adj*, **~ly** *adv* [ˌmæθə'mætɪkəl, -ɪ] mathematisch.

mathematician [ˌmæθəmə'tɪʃən] *n* Mathematiker(in *f*) *m*.

mathematics [ˌmæθə'mætɪks] *n* (**a**) *sing* Mathematik *f*. (**b**) *pl* **the ~ of this are complicated** das ist mathematisch kompliziert.

maths [mæθs] *n sing* (*Brit inf*) Mathe *f* (*inf*).

matinée ['mætɪneɪ] *n* Matinee *f*; (*in the afternoon also*) Frühvorstellung *f* ◆ **~ coat** (*for baby*) Ausfahrjäckchen *nt*.

mating ['meɪtɪŋ] *n* Paarung *f*.

mating: ~ call *n* Lockruf *m*; (*of birds also*) Balzlaut *m*; (*of deer also*) Brunstschrei *m*; **~ dance** *n* Paarungstanz *m*; **~ season** *n* Paarungszeit *f*.

matins ['mætɪnz] *n sing* (*Catholic*) Matutin *f*, Morgenlob *nt*; (*Anglican*) Morgenandacht *f*.

matriarch ['meɪtrɪɑːk] *n* Matriarchin *f*.

matriarchal [ˌmeɪtrɪ'ɑːkl] *adj* matriarchalisch.

matriarchy ['meɪtrɪɑːkɪ] *n* Matriarchat *nt*.

matric [mə'trɪk] *n* (*inf*) *see* **matriculation**.

matrices ['meɪtrɪsiːz] *pl of* **matrix**.

matricide ['meɪtrɪsaɪd] *n* (*act*) Muttermord *m*; (*person*) Muttermörder(in *f*) *m*.

matriculate [mə'trɪkjʊleɪt] 1 *vi* sich immatrikulieren.
2 *vt* immatrikulieren.

matriculation [məˌtrɪkjʊ'leɪʃən] *n* Immatrikulation *f*; (*ceremony*) Immatrikulationsfeier *f*.

➤ LANGUAGE IN USE: **match²: 1b** → 5.3 **2b** → 5.3

matrimonial [ˌmætrɪˈməʊnɪəl] *adj vows, problems* Ehe-.
matrimony [ˈmætrɪmənɪ] *n (form)* Ehe *f* ◆ **to enter into holy ~** in den heiligen Stand der Ehe treten.
matrix [ˈmeɪtrɪks] *n, pl* **matrices** *or* **-es** (a) *(mould)* Matrize, Mater *f*. (b) *(Geol, Math)* Matrix *f* ◆ **~ printer** Matrixdrucker *m*.
matron [ˈmeɪtrən] *n* (a) *(in hospital)* Oberin, Oberschwester *f*; *(in school)* Schwester *f*. (b) *(married woman)* Matrone *f*.
matronly [ˈmeɪtrənlɪ] *adj* matronenhaft.
matron-of-honour [ˈmeɪtrənəvˈɒnəʳ] *n, pl* **matrons-of-honour** *verheiratete Frau, die als Brautjungfer fungiert.*
matt [mæt] *adj* matt, mattiert ◆ **a paint with a ~ finish** ein Mattlack *m*.
matted [ˈmætɪd] *adj* verfilzt.
matter [ˈmætəʳ] [1] *n* (a) *(substance, not mind)* die Materie ◆ **organic/inorganic ~** organische/anorganische Stoffe *pl*.
(b) *(particular kind)* Stoff *m* ◆ **advertising ~** Reklame, Werbung *f*; **printed ~** Drucksache(n *pl*) *f*; **colouring ~** Farbstoff(e *pl*) *m*; **vegetable ~** pflanzliche Stoffe *pl*.
(c) *(Med: pus)* Eiter *m*.
(d) *(Typ) (copy)* Manuskript *nt*; *(type set up)* Satz *m*.
(e) *(content)* Inhalt *m* ◆ **the main ~ of his speech was ...** (der) Hauptgegenstand seiner Rede war ...
(f) *(question, affair)* Sache, Angelegenheit *f*; *(topic)* Thema *nt*, Stoff *m* ◆ **can I talk to you on a ~ of great urgency?** kann ich Sie in einer äußerst dringenden Angelegenheit sprechen?; **this is a ~ I know little about** darüber weiß ich wenig; **in the ~ of ...** was ... *(+acc)* anbelangt, hinsichtlich ... *(+gen)*; **in the ~ of clothes** *etc* in puncto Kleidung *etc*; **there's the ~ of my expenses** da ist (noch) die Sache *or* Frage mit meinen Ausgaben; **it's no great ~** das macht nichts, das ist nicht so wichtig; **that's quite another ~** das ist etwas (ganz) anderes; **that's another ~ altogether, that's a very different ~** das ist etwas völlig anderes; **it will be no easy ~ (to)** ... es wird nicht einfach sein, zu ...; **it's a serious ~** das ist eine ernste Angelegenheit, die Sache ist ernst; **the ~ is closed** die Sache *or* der Fall ist erledigt.
(g) **~s** *pl* Angelegenheiten *pl* ◆ **business ~s** geschäftliche Angelegenheiten *or* Dinge *pl*, Geschäftliche(s) *nt*; **money ~s** Geldangelegenheiten *or* -fragen *pl*; **as ~s stand** wie die Dinge liegen; **to make ~s worse** zu allem Unglück (noch).
(h) **for that ~** eigentlich; **I haven't seen him for weeks, nor for that ~ has anybody else** ich habe ihn seit Wochen schon nicht mehr gesehen, und eigentlich hat ihn sonst auch niemand gesehen; **he wants to complain about it and for that ~, so do I** er will sich darüber beschweren und ich eigentlich auch.
(i) **a ~ of** eine Frage *(+gen)*, eine Sache von; **it's a ~ of form/time** das ist eine Formsache/Zeitfrage *or* Frage der Zeit; **it's a ~ of taste/opinion** das ist Geschmacks-/Ansichtssache; **it's a ~ of adjusting this part exactly** es geht darum, dieses Teil genau einzustellen; **it will be a ~ of a few weeks** es wird ein paar Wochen dauern; **it's a ~ of 10 miles from ...** es sind 10 Meilen von ...; **it's a ~ of a couple of hours** das ist eine Sache von ein paar Stunden; **if it's just a ~ of another 10 minutes, then I'll wait** wenn es sich nur noch um 10 Minuten handelt, dann warte ich so lange; **in a ~ of minutes** innerhalb von Minuten; **it's a ~ of great concern to us** die Sache ist für uns von großer Bedeutung; **it's not just a ~ of increasing the money supply** es ist nicht damit getan, die Geldzufuhr zu erhöhen; **it's just a ~ of trying harder** man muß sich ganz einfach etwas mehr anstrengen; **as a ~ of course** selbstverständlich; **it's a ~ of course with us** für uns ist das eine Selbstverständlichkeit; **you should always take your passport with you as a ~ of course** es sollte für Sie eine Selbstverständlichkeit sein, stets Ihren Paß bei sich zu haben; **earthquakes happen as a ~ of course in that part of the world** Erdbeben sind in der Gegend an der Tagesordnung.
(j) **no ~!** macht nichts; **I've decided to leave tomorrow, no ~ what** ich gehe morgen, egal was passiert; **no ~ how/what/when/where** *etc* ... egal, wie/was/wann/wo *etc* ...; **no ~ how you do it** wie du es auch machst, egal, wie du es machst; **no ~ how hot it was** auch *or* selbst bei der größten Hitze; **no ~ how hard he tried** so sehr er sich auch anstrengte.
(k) **sth is the ~ with sb/sth** etw ist mit jdm/etw los; *(ill)* etw fehlt jdm; **what's the ~?** was ist (denn) los?, was ist (denn)?; **what's the ~ with you this morning? — nothing's the ~** was ist denn heute morgen mit dir los? *or* was hast du denn heute morgen? — gar nichts; **what's the ~ with having a little fun?** was ist denn schon dabei, wenn man ein bißchen Spaß hat?; **something's the ~ with the lights** mit dem Licht ist irgend etwas nicht in Ordnung; **as if nothing was the ~** als ob nichts (los) wäre.
[2] *vi* **it doesn't ~** (es *or* das) macht nichts, ist schon gut; **what does it ~?** was macht das schon?; **I forgot it, does it ~? — yes, it does** ich hab's vergessen, ist das schlimm? — ja, das ist schlimm; **does it ~ to you if I go?** macht es dir etwas aus, wenn ich gehe?; **doesn't it ~ to you at all if I leave you?** macht es dir denn gar nichts aus, wenn ich dich verlasse?; **why should it ~ to me?** warum sollte mir das etwas ausmachen?; **why should it ~ to me if people are starving?** was geht es mich an, wenn Menschen verhungern?; **it doesn't ~ to me what you do** es ist mir (ganz) egal, was du machst; **some things ~ more than others** es ist aber nicht alles gleich wichtig; **the things which ~ in life** was im Leben wichtig ist *or* zählt; **poverty ~s** Armut geht jeden etwas an.
matter-of-fact [ˈmætərəvˈfækt] *adj* sachlich, nüchtern ◆ **he was very ~ about it** er blieb sehr sachlich *or* nüchtern.
Matthew [ˈmæθjuː] *n* Matthias *m*; *(Bibl)* Matthäus *m*.
matting [ˈmætɪŋ] *n* Matten *pl*; *(material)* Mattenmaterial *nt*.

mattock [ˈmætək] *n* Breithacke *f*.
mattress [ˈmætrɪs] *n* Matratze *f*.
maturation [ˌmætjʊˈreɪʃən] *n* Reifeprozeß *m*, Reifung *f*.
mature [məˈtjʊəʳ] [1] *adj (+er)* (a) *person, mind* reif; *child* verständig, vernünftig ◆ **his mind is very ~** geistig ist er schon sehr reif; **of ~ years** im reiferen *or* vorgerückten Alter.
(b) *wine* ausgereift; *sherry, port, cheese* reif; *fruit* reif, ausgereift; *plant* ausgewachsen; *plans* ausgereift ◆ **after ~ deliberation** nach reiflicher Überlegung; **his ~r poems** seine reiferen Gedichte.
(c) *(Comm) bill, debt* fällig.
[2] *vi* (a) *(person)* heranreifen *(geh)*, reifer werden; *(animal)* auswachsen ◆ **his character ~d during the war years** der Krieg ließ ihn reifer werden *or* machte ihn reifer. (b) *(wine, cheese)* reifen, reif werden. (c) *(Comm)* fällig werden.
[3] *vt* (a) *person* reifer machen. (b) *wine, cheese* reifen lassen.
maturely [məˈtjʊəlɪ] *adv behave* verständig, vernünftig ◆ **a more ~ conceived novel** ein ausgereifterer Roman.
maturity [məˈtjʊərɪtɪ] *n* (a) Reife *f* ◆ **to reach ~** *(person)* erwachsen werden; *(legally)* volljährig werden; *(animal)* ausgewachsen sein; **poems of his ~** Gedichte *pl* seiner reiferen Jahre; **he's somewhat lacking in ~** ihm fehlt die nötige Reife. (b) *(Comm)* Fälligkeit *f*; *(date)* Fälligkeitsdatum *nt*.
maudlin [ˈmɔːdlɪn] *adj story* rührselig; *person* sentimental, gefühlsselig.
maul [mɔːl] *vt* übel zurichten; *(fig) writer, play etc* verreißen.
Maundy [ˈmɔːndɪ] *n*: **~ money** *Almosen, die an Gründonnerstag verteilt werden*; **~ Thursday** Gründonnerstag *m*.
Mauritius [məˈrɪʃəs] *n* Mauritius *nt*.
mausoleum [ˌmɔːsəˈlɪəm] *n* Mausoleum *nt*.
mauve [məʊv] [1] *adj* mauve, malvenfarben.
[2] *n* Mauvein *nt*.
maverick [ˈmævərɪk] *n* (a) *(US Agr)* herrenloses Kalb/Rind *nt* ohne Brandzeichen. (b) *(dissenter)* Abtrünnige(r) *m*. (c) *(independent person)* Alleingänger, Einzelgänger *m*.
maw [mɔː] *n* (a) *(Anat)* Magen *m*; *(of cow)* (Lab)magen *m*; *(of bird)* Hals *m*. (b) *(liter)* Maul *nt*; *(fig)* Rachen, Schlund *m*.
mawkish [ˈmɔːkɪʃ] *adj* rührselig, kitschig; *taste* unangenehm *or* widerlich süß, süßlich.
mawkishness [ˈmɔːkɪʃnɪs] *n see adj* Rührseligkeit, Sentimentalität *f*; widerliche Süße.
max *abbr of* **maximum** max.
maxi [ˈmæksɪ] *n (dress)* Maxirock *m*/-kleid *nt*/-mantel *m*.
maxim [ˈmæksɪm] *n* Maxime *f*.
maximal [ˈmæksɪməl] *adj* maximal.
maximization [ˌmæksɪmaɪˈzeɪʃən] *n* Maximierung *f*.
maximize [ˈmæksɪmaɪz] *vt* maximieren.
maximum [ˈmæksɪməm] [1] *adj attr* Höchst-; *size, height, costs, length* maximal ◆ **he scored ~ points** er hat die höchste Punktzahl erreicht; **a ~ speed of ...** eine Höchstgeschwindigkeit von ...; **we are producing at ~ speed** wir produzieren mit maximaler Geschwindigkeit; **5 is the ~ number allowed in a taxi** maximal *or* höchstens 5 Leute dürfen in ein Taxi; **~ security wing/prison** Hochsicherheitstrakt *m*.
[2] *n, pl* **-s** *or* **maxima** [ˈmæksɪmə] Maximum *nt* ◆ **up to a ~ of £8** bis zu maximal *or* höchstens £ 8; **temperatures reached a ~ of 34°** die Höchsttemperatur betrug 34°; **is that the ~ you can offer?** ist das Ihr höchstes Angebot?; **my salary is now at its ~** ich bin jetzt in der höchsten *or* obersten Gehaltsstufe.
maxiskirt [ˈmæksɪˌskɜːt] *n* Maxirock *m*.
May [meɪ] [1] *n* Mai *m*.
[2] *vi*: **to go m~ing** den Mai feiern.
▼ **may** [meɪ] *vi pret* **might** *(see also* **might**[1]*)* (a) *(possibility: also* **might***)* können ◆ **it ~ rain** es könnte regnen, vielleicht regnet es; **it ~ be that ...** vielleicht ..., es könnte sein, daß ...; **although it ~ have been useful** obwohl es hätte nützlich sein können; **he ~ not be hungry** vielleicht hat er keinen Hunger; **I ~ have said so** es kann *or* könnte sein, daß ich das gesagt habe; **you ~ be right** Sie könnten recht haben; **~ there ~ not be a next time** vielleicht gibt's gar kein nächstes Mal; **they ~ be brothers for all I know** es kann *or* könnte sein, daß sie Brüder sind; **yes, I ~** ja, das ist möglich *or* das kann sein; **I ~ just do that** vielleicht tue ich das wirklich; **that's as ~ be** *(not might)* das mag ja sein, (aber ...); **one ~ well wonder why ...** die Frage wäre wohl berechtigt, warum ...; **you ~ well ask** das kann man wohl fragen.
▼ (b) *(permission)* dürfen ◆ **~ I go now?** darf ich jetzt gehen?; **yes, you ~** ja, Sie dürfen.
(c) **I hope he ~ succeed** ich hoffe, daß es ihm gelingt; **I had hoped he might succeed this time** ich hatte gehofft, es würde ihm diesmal gelingen; **such a policy as ~** *or* **might bring peace** eine Politik, die zum Frieden führen könnte; **we ~** *or* **might as well go** ich glaube, wir können (ruhig) gehen; **you ~** *or* **might as well go now** du kannst jetzt ruhig gehen; **if they don't have it we ~** *or* **might as well go to another firm** wenn sie es nicht haben, gehen wir am besten zu einer anderen Firma; **if they won't help we ~** *or* **might just as well give up** wenn sie uns nicht helfen, können wir (ja) gleich aufgeben.
(d) *(in wishes)* **~ you be successful!** (ich wünsche Ihnen) viel Erfolg!; **~ your days be full of joy** mögen Ihnen glückliche Tage beschieden sein; **~ you be very happy together** ich wünsche euch, daß ihr sehr glücklich miteinander werdet; **~ the Lord have mercy on your soul** der Herr sei deiner Seele gnädig; **~ you be forgiven** *(inf)* so was tut man doch nicht!; **~ I be struck dead if I lie!** ich will auf der Stelle tot umfallen, wenn das nicht stimmt.
(e) *(in questions)* **who ~** *or* **might you be?** und wer sind Sie?, wer sind Sie

➤ LANGUAGE IN USE: **may: a** → 15.2, 26.3 **b** → 3.3, 9.1

denn?

Maya ['meɪjə] *n* **(a)** Maya *mf.* **(b)** *(language)* Maya *nt,* Mayasprache *f.*

Mayan ['meɪjən] [1] *adj* Maya-.
[2] *n* **(a)** Maya *mf.* **(b)** *(language)* Maya(sprache *f*) *nt.*

▼ **maybe** ['meɪbi:] *adv* vielleicht, kann sein(, daß ...).

May: **~ Day** *n* der 1. Mai, der Maifeiertag; **~day** *n (distress call)* Maydaysignal *nt,* SOS-Ruf *m; (said)* Mayday.

mayest ['meɪəst] *(obs),* **mayst** *(obs) 2nd pers sing of* **may.**

mayfly ['meɪflaɪ] *n* Eintagsfliege *f.*

mayhem ['meɪhem] *n* **(a)** *(US Jur)* (schwere) Körperverletzung. **(b)** *(havoc)* Chaos *nt.*

mayn't [meɪnt] *contr of* **may not.**

mayo ['meɪəʊ] *n (US inf)* Mayonnaise, Mayo *(inf) f.*

mayonnaise [,meɪə'neɪz] *n* Mayonnaise *f.*

mayor [mɛə^r] *n* Bürgermeister(in *f*) *m.*

mayoral ['mɛərəl] *adj* des Bürgermeisters.

mayoralty ['mɛərəltɪ] *n (office)* Bürgermeisteramt *nt,* Amt *nt* des Bürgermeisters ◆ **during his ~** ... als er Bürgermeister war ..., während seiner Zeit als Bürgermeister ...

mayoress ['mɛəres] *n* Frau *f* Bürgermeister; Tochter *f* des Bürgermeisters; *(lady mayor)* Bürgermeisterin *f.*

may: **~pole** *n* Maibaum *m;* **M~ queen** *n* Maikönigin *f.*

mayst [meɪst] *(obs) see* **mayest.**

maze [meɪz] *n* Irrgarten *m; (puzzle)* Labyrinth *nt; (fig)* Wirrwarr *m,* Gewirr *nt* ◆ **the ~ of streets** das Gewirr der Straßen.

mazurka [mə'zɜ:kə] *n* Mazurka *f.*

MB *abbr of* **Bachelor of Medicine.**

MBA *abbr of* **Master of Business Administration** ◆ **he's doing/he has an ~** er studiert Betriebswirtschaft/er ist Betriebswirt.

MBE *abbr of* **Member of the Order of the British Empire** *britischer Verdienstorden.*

MC *abbr of* **(a) Master of Ceremonies. (b) Military Cross.**

MCC *abbr of* **Marylebone Cricket Club.**

McCoy [mə'kɔɪ] *n see* **real.**

MCP *abbr of* **male chauvinist pig.**

MD *abbr of* **(a) Doctor of Medicine** Dr. med. **(b) managing director.**

m.d. *abbr of* **mentally deficient.**

me [mi:] *pron* **(a)** *(dir obj, with prep +acc)* mich; *(indir obj, with prep +dat)* mir ◆ **with my books about ~** mit meinen Büchern um mich herum; **he's older than ~** er ist älter als ich. **(b)** *(emph)* ich. **who, ~?** wer, ich?; **it's ~** ich bin's.

mead[1] [mi:d] *n (drink)* Met *m.*

mead[2] *n (old, poet)* Aue *f.*

meadow ['medəʊ] *n* Wiese, Weide *f* ◆ **in the ~** auf der Wiese *etc.*

meadow: **~land** *n* Weideland *nt;* **~sweet** *n* Mädesüß *nt.*

meagre, *(US)* **meager** ['mi:gə^r] *adj* **(a)** spärlich; *amount* kläglich; *meal* dürftig, kärglich. **(b)** *(liter: lean)* hager.

meagrely, *(US)* **meagerly** ['mi:gəlɪ] *adv* spärlich; *live* kärglich.

meagreness, *(US)* **meagerness** ['mi:gənɪs] *n see adj* Spärlichkeit *f;* Kläglichkeit *f;* Dürftigkeit, Kärglichkeit *f.*

meal[1] [mi:l] *n* Schrot(mehl *nt*) *m.*

meal[2] *n* Mahlzeit *f; (food)* Essen *nt* ◆ **come round for a ~** komm zum Essen (zu uns); **to go for a ~** essen gehen; **to have a (good) ~** (gut) essen; **hot ~s** warme Mahlzeiten *pl,* warmes Essen; **I haven't had a ~ for two days** ich habe seit zwei Tagen nichts Richtiges mehr gegessen; **to make a ~ of sth** *(inf)* etw auf sehr umständliche Art machen; **don't make a ~ of it** *(inf)* nun übertreib's mal nicht *(inf).*

meal: **~s on wheels** *n* Essen *nt* auf Rädern; **~-ticket** *n (US: lit)* Essensbon *m or* -marke *f;* **that letter of introduction was his ~-ticket for the next few months** dank des Empfehlungsschreibens konnte er sich die nächsten paar Monate über Wasser halten; **a boyfriend is just a ~-ticket to a lot of girls** viele Mädchen haben nur einen Freund, um sich von ihm aushalten zu lassen; **~time** *n* Essenszeit *f;* **you shouldn't smoke at ~times** Sie sollten während des Essens nicht rauchen.

mealy ['mi:lɪ] *adj* mehlig.

mealy-mouthed ['mi:lɪ'maʊðd] *adj* unaufrichtig; *politician* schönfärberisch ◆ **let's not be ~ about it** wir wollen doch mal nicht so um den heißen Brei herumreden.

mean[1] [mi:n] *adj (+er)* **(a)** *(miserly)* geizig, knauserig ◆ **don't be ~!** sei doch nicht so geizig *or* knauserig!; **you ~ thing!** du Geizhals *or* Geizkragen!
(b) *(unkind, spiteful)* gemein ◆ **don't be ~!** sei nicht so gemein *or* fies! *(inf);* **you ~ thing!** du gemeines *or* fieses *(sl)* Stück!, du Miststück! *(sl);* **it made me feel ~** ich kam mir richtig schäbig *or* gemein vor.
(c) *(base, inferior) birth, motives* niedrig ◆ **the ~est citizen** der Geringste unter den Bürgern *(old).*
(d) *(shabby, unimpressive) shack, house* schäbig, armselig.
(e) *(vicious)* bösartig; *look* gehässig, hinterhältig; *criminal* niederträchtig, abscheulich.
(f) **he is no ~ player** er ist ein beachtlicher Spieler; **that's no ~ feat** diese Aufgabe ist nicht zu unterschätzen *or* nicht von Pappe *(inf);* **a sportsman/politician of no ~ ability** ein sehr fähiger Sportler/Politiker.

mean[2] [1] *n (middle term)* Durchschnitt *m; (Math)* Durchschnitt, Mittelwert *m,* Mittel *nt* ◆ **the golden** *or* **happy ~** die goldene Mitte.
[2] *adj* mittlere(r, s) ◆ **~ sea level** Normalnull *nt.*

▼ **mean[3]** *pret, ptp* **meant** *vt* **(a)** bedeuten; *(person: refer to, have in mind)* meinen ◆ **what do you ~ by that?** was willst du damit sagen?; **the name ~s nothing to me** der Name sagt mir nichts; **it ~s starting all over again** das bedeutet *or* das heißt, daß wir wieder ganz von vorne anfangen müssen; **this will ~ great changes** dies wird bedeutende Veränderungen zur Folge haben; **a pound ~s a lot to her** für sie ist ein Pfund eine Menge Geld; **your friendship/he ~s a lot to me** deine Freundschaft/er bedeutet mir viel; **you ~ everything to me** du bist alles für mich.
▼ **(b)** *(intend)* beabsichtigen ◆ **to ~ to do sth** etw tun wollen; *(do on purpose)* etw absichtlich tun; **to be ~t for sb/sth** für jdn/etw bestimmt sein; **to ~ sb to do sth** wollen, daß jd etw tut; **sth is ~t to be sth** etw soll etw sein; **what do you ~ to do?** was wirst du tun?, was hast du vor?; **I only ~t to help** ich wollte nur helfen; **of course it hurt, I ~t it to** *or* **it was ~t to** natürlich tat das weh, das war Absicht; **without ~ing to sound rude** ich möchte nicht unverschämt klingen(, aber ...); **I ~t it as a joke** das sollte ein Witz sein; **I ~t you to have it** das solltest du haben; **I was ~t to do that** ich hätte das tun sollen; **you are ~t to be on time** du solltest pünktlich sein; **he wasn't ~t to be a leader** er war nicht zum Führer bestimmt; **I thought it was ~t to be hot in the south** ich dachte immer, daß es im Süden so heiß sei; **I ~ to be obeyed** ich verlange, daß man mir gehorcht; **I ~ to have it** ich bin fest entschlossen, es zu bekommen; **this pad is ~t for drawing** dieser Block ist zum Zeichnen gedacht *or* da *(inf);* **if he ~s to be awkward ...** wenn er vorhat, Schwierigkeiten zu machen, ...; **this present was ~t for you** dieses Geschenk sollte für dich sein *or* war für dich gedacht; *see* **business, mischief.**
(c) *(be serious about)* ernst meinen ◆ **I ~ it!** das ist mein Ernst!, ich meine das ernst!; **do you ~ to say you're not coming?** willst du damit sagen *or* soll das heißen, daß du nicht kommst?; **I ~ what I say** ich sage das im Ernst; **do you really ~ it this time?** ist es dir diesmal Ernst damit?
(d) **he ~s well/no harm** er meint es gut/nicht böse; **to ~ well by sb** es gut mit jdm meinen; **to ~ sb no harm** es gut mit jdm meinen, jdm nichts Böses wollen; *(physically)* jdm nichts tun; *(in past tense)* jdm nichts tun wollen; **I ~t no harm by what I said** was ich da gesagt habe, war nicht böse gemeint.

meander [mɪ'ændə^r] *vi (river)* sich (dahin)schlängeln, mäandern; *(person)* wirr sein; *(go off subject)* (vom Thema) abschweifen; *(walking)* schlendern.

meanderings [mɪ'ændərɪŋz] *npl (of river)* Windungen *pl,* Mäander *m; (talk)* Gefasel *nt; (off subject)* Abschweifungen, Exkurse *pl* ◆ **the ~ of his mind** seine verworrenen Gedankengänge.

meanie ['mi:nɪ] *n (inf) (miserly person)* Geizhals *or* -kragen *m; (nasty person)* Miststück *nt (sl); (male also)* Schuft *m.*

meaning ['mi:nɪŋ] [1] *adj look etc* vielsagend, bedeutsam.
[2] *n* Bedeutung *f; (sense: of words, poem etc also)* Sinn *m* ◆ **a look full of ~** ein bedeutungsvoller *or* bedeutsamer Blick; **what's the ~ of (the word) "hick"?** was soll das Wort „hick" heißen *or* bedeuten?; **to mistake sb's ~** jdn mißverstehen; **do you get my ~?** haben Sie mich (richtig) verstanden?; **you don't know the ~ of love/hunger** du weißt ja gar nicht, was Liebe/Hunger ist *or* bedeutet; **what's the ~ of this?** was hat denn das zu bedeuten?, was soll denn das (heißen)?

meaningful ['mi:nɪŋfʊl] *adj* **(a)** *(semantically) word, symbol* mit Bedeutung, sinntragend; *(Ling) unit* bedeutungstragend; *poem, film* bedeutungsvoll ◆ **to be ~** eine Bedeutung haben; **the statistics only become ~ when ...** die Zahlen ergeben nur dann einen Sinn, wenn ...
(b) *(purposeful) job, negotiations* sinnvoll; *relationship* tiefergehend.

meaningless ['mi:nɪŋlɪs] *adj* **(a)** *(semantically) word, symbol etc* ohne Bedeutung, bedeutungslos. **(b)** sinnlos ◆ **my life is ~** mein Leben hat keinen Sinn.

meanness ['mi:nnɪs] *n see adj* **(a)** Geiz *m,* Knauserigkeit *f.* **(b)** Gemeinheit *f.* **(c)** Niedrigkeit *f.* **(d)** Schäbigkeit, Armseligkeit *f.* **(e)** Bösartigkeit *f;* Gehässigkeit, Hinterhältigkeit *f;* Niedertracht *f.*

▼ **means** [mi:nz] *n* **(a)** *sing (method)* Möglichkeit *f; (instrument)* Mittel *nt* ◆ **a ~ of transport** ein Beförderungsmittel *nt;* **a ~ of escape** eine Fluchtmöglichkeit; **a ~ to an end** ein Mittel *nt* zum Zweck; **I have/there is no ~ of doing it** es ist mir/es ist unmöglich, das zu tun; **is there any ~ of doing it?** ist es irgendwie möglich, das zu tun?; **there must be a ~ of doing it** es muß doch irgendwie *or* auf irgendeine Art und Weise zu machen sein; **we've no ~ of knowing** wir können nicht wissen; **he was the ~ of sending it** man ließ es durch ihn überbringen; **they used him as the ~ of getting the heroin across the border** sie benutzten ihn, um das Heroin über die Grenze zu bringen; **all known ~ have been tried** man hat alles Mögliche versucht; **by ~ of sth** durch etw, mittels einer Sache *(gen) (form);* **by ~ of doing sth** dadurch, daß man etw tut; **by this ~** dadurch, auf diese Weise; **by some ~ or other** auf irgendeine Art und Weise, irgendwie.
(b) *sing* **by all ~!** (aber) selbstverständlich *or* natürlich!; **by all ~ take one** nehmen Sie sich ruhig (eins); **by no ~, not by any ~** keineswegs, durchaus nicht; *(under no circumstances)* auf keinen Fall.
(c) *pl (wherewithal)* Mittel *pl; (financial ~ also)* Gelder *pl* ◆ **a man of ~** ein vermögender Mann; **private ~** private Mittel; **that is within/beyond my ~** das kann ich mir leisten/nicht leisten; **to live beyond/within one's ~** über seine Verhältnisse leben/seinen Verhältnissen entsprechend leben; **~ test** Einkommens- *or* Vermögensveranlagung *f.*

meant [ment] *pret, ptp of* **mean[3].**

meantime ['mi:ntaɪm] [1] *adv* inzwischen.
[2] *n* **for the ~** vorerst, im Augenblick, einstweilen; **in the ~** in der Zwischenzeit, inzwischen.

meanwhile ['mi:nwaɪl] *adv* inzwischen.

measles ['mi:zlz] *n sing* Masern *pl.*

measly ['mi:zlɪ] *adj (+er) (inf)* mick(e)rig *(inf),* poplig *(inf).*

measurable ['meʒərəbl] *adj* meßbar; *(perceptible)* erkennbar.

➤ LANGUAGE IN USE: **maybe** → 2.2, 4 **mean[3]:** **a** → 6.3, 16.1, 26.3 **b** → 8.2 **means:** **a** → 17.1

measurably ['meʒərəblɪ] *adv see adj* meßbar; deutlich.
measure ['meʒəʳ] [1] *n* **(a)** *(unit of measurement)* Maß(einheit *f*) *nt* ♦ **a ~ of length** ein Längenmaß *nt*; **beyond ~** grenzenlos; **her joy was beyond** *or* **knew no ~** ihre Freude kannte keine Grenzen; *see* **weight**.
(b) *(object for measuring)* Maß *nt*; *(graduated for length)* Maßstab *m*; *(graduated for volume)* Meßbecher *m*.
(c) *(amount ~d)* Menge *f* ♦ **a small ~ of flour** ein wenig Mehl; **wine is sold in ~s of 1/4 litre** Wein wird in Vierteln ausgeschenkt; **to give sb full/short ~** *(barman)* richtig/zuwenig ausschenken; *(grocer)* richtig/zu wenig abwiegen; **in full ~** in höchstem Maße; **for good ~** zur Sicherheit, sicherheitshalber; ... **and another one for good ~** ... und noch eines obendrein.
(d) *(fig: yardstick)* Maßstab *m* *(of* für) ♦ **can we regard this exam as a ~ of intelligence?** kann diese Prüfung als Intelligenzmaßstab gelten?; **MacLeod's approval is the ~ of a good whisky** MacLeods Urteil in bezug auf Whisky ist (für mich) maßgebend *or* ausschlaggebend; **please consider this as a ~ of my esteem for ...** bitte betrachten Sie dies als Ausdruck meiner Anerkennung für ...; **it gave us some ~ of the difficulty** es gab uns einen Begriff von der Schwierigkeit; **it's a ~ of his skill as a writer that ...** seine schriftstellerischen Fähigkeiten lassen sich daran beurteilen, daß ...; **words cannot always give the ~ of one's feelings** Worte können Gefühle nicht immer angemessen ausdrücken.
(e) *(extent)* **in some ~** in gewisser Hinsicht *or* Beziehung; **some ~ of** ein gewisses Maß an; **to a** *or* **in large ~** in hohem Maße; **to get the ~ of sb/sth** jdn/etw (richtig) einschätzen.
(f) *(step)* Maßnahme *f* ♦ **to take ~s to do sth** Maßnahmen ergreifen, um etw zu tun.
(g) *(Poet)* Versmaß *nt*.
(h) *(US Mus)* Takt *m*.
(i) *(old: dance)* Tanz *m* ♦ **to tread a ~ with sb** mit jdm ein Tänzchen wagen.
[2] *vt* messen; *length also* abmessen; *room also* ausmessen; *(take sb's measurements)* Maß nehmen bei; *(fig)* beurteilen, abschätzen; *words* abwägen ♦ **a ~d mile** genau eine Meile; **to ~ one's length** *(fig)* der Länge nach hinfallen.
[3] *vi* messen ♦ **what does it ~?** wieviel mißt es?, wie groß ist es?
♦**measure off** *vt sep area, length of cloth* abmessen.
♦**measure out** *vt sep* abmessen; *weights also* abwiegen.
♦**measure up** [1] *vt sep* **(a)** *(take measurements of) wood, room etc* abmessen; *person for suit etc* Maß nehmen bei.
(b) *(fig: assess) situation* abschätzen; *person* einschätzen.
[2] *vi* **(a)** *(be good enough, compare well)* **he didn't ~ ~** er hat enttäuscht; **to ~ ~ to sth** an etw *(acc)* herankommen; **visually he ~d ~ (to the description)** vom Aussehen her paßte er (auf die Beschreibung); **it's a hard job, but he should ~ ~** das ist eine schwierige Aufgabe, aber er sollte ihr gewachsen sein.
(b) *(take measurements)* Maß nehmen, messen.
measured ['meʒəd] *adj tread* gemessen *(liter)*; *tone* bedacht, bedächtig; *words* wohlüberlegt, durchdacht ♦ **he walked with ~ steps** er ging gemessenen Schrittes *(liter)*.
measureless ['meʒəlɪs] *adj* unermeßlich.
measurement ['meʒəmənt] *n* **(a)** *(act)* Messung *f* ♦ **the metric system of ~** das metrische Maßsystem. **(b)** *(measure)* Maß *nt*; *(figure)* Meßwert *m*; *(fig)* Maßstab *m* ♦ **to take sb's ~s** an *or* bei jdm Maß nehmen.
measuring ['meʒərɪŋ] *n* Messen *nt* ♦ **to take ~s of sth** etw messen; **~ jug** Meßbecher *m*.
meat [mi:t] *n* **(a)** Fleisch *nt* ♦ **cold ~** kalter Braten; *(sausage)* Wurst *f*; **assorted cold ~s** Aufschnitt *m*.
(b) *(old: food)* Essen *nt*, Speise *f (liter)* ♦ **~ and drink** Speise und Trank; **one man's ~ is another man's poison** *(Prov)* des einen Freud, des andern Leid *(Prov)*.
(c) *(fig: of argument, book)* Substanz *f* ♦ **a book with some ~ in it** ein aussagestarkes Buch.
meat *in cpds* Fleisch-; **~ball** *n* Fleischkloß *m*; **~head** *n (US sl)* Dummkopf *m*; **~ loaf** *n* ≃ Fleischkäse *m*; **~ products** *npl* Fleisch- und Wurstwaren *pl*; **~-safe** *n* Fliegenschrank *m*.
meaty ['mi:tɪ] *adj (+er)* **(a)** *taste* Fleisch-. **(b)** *(fig) book* aussagestark.
Mecca ['mekə] *n (lit, fig)* Mekka *nt*.
mechanic [mɪ'kænɪk] *n* Mechaniker *m*.
mechanical [mɪ'kænɪkəl] *adj (lit, fig)* mechanisch; *toy* technisch ♦ **~ engineer/engineering** Maschinenbauer *or* -bauingenieur *m*/Maschinenbau *m*; **a ~ device** ein Mechanismus *m*.
mechanically [mɪ'kænɪkəlɪ] *adv (lit, fig)* mechanisch ♦ **~-minded** technisch begabt.
mechanics [mɪ'kænɪks] *n* **(a)** *sing (subject) (engineering)* Maschinenbau *m*; *(Phys)* Mechanik *f* ♦ **home ~ for the car-owner** kleine Maschinenkunde für den Autobesitzer.
(b) *pl (technical aspects)* Mechanik *f*, Mechanismus *m*; *(fig: of writing etc)* Technik *f* ♦ **there is something wrong with the ~ of the car** das Auto ist mechanisch nicht in Ordnung; **I don't understand the ~ of parliamentary procedure** ich verstehe den Mechanismus parlamentarischer Abläufe nicht.
mechanism ['mekənɪzəm] *n* Mechanismus *m*.
mechanistic *adj*, **~ally** *adv* [ˌmekə'nɪstɪk, -əlɪ] mechanistisch.
mechanization [ˌmekənaɪ'zeɪʃən] *n* Mechanisierung *f*.
mechanize ['mekənaɪz] *vt* mechanisieren.
med *abbr of* **medium**.
medal ['medl] *n* Medaille *f*; *(decoration)* Orden *m*.
medalist *n (US) see* **medallist**.
medallion [mɪ'dæljən] *n* Medaillon *nt*; *(medal)* Medaille *f*.
medallist, *(US)* **medalist** ['medəlɪst] *n* Medaillengewinner(in *f*) *m*.
meddle ['medl] *vi (interfere)* sich einmischen *(in* in *+acc)*; *(tamper)* sich zu schaffen machen, herumfummeln *(inf) (with* an *+dat)* ♦ **to ~ with sb** sich mit jdm einlassen; **he's not a man to ~ with** mit ihm ist nicht gut Kirschen essen; **he's always meddling** er mischt sich in alles ein.
meddler ['medləʳ] *n* **he's a terrible ~** er muß sich immer in anderer Leute Angelegenheiten *or* in alles einmischen.
meddlesome ['medlsəm] *adj*, **meddling** ['medlɪŋ] *adj attr* **she's a ~ old busybody** sie mischt sich dauernd in alles ein.
media ['mi:dɪə] *n, pl of* **medium** Medien *pl* ♦ **he works in the ~** er ist im Mediensektor tätig *or* beschäftigt; **~ studies** Medienwissenschaft *f*; **~ event** Medienereignis *nt*; **~ coverage** Berichterstattung *f* in den Medien; **to get too much ~ coverage** zuviel Publicity bekommen.
mediaeval *adj see* **medieval**.
mediaevalist *n see* **medievalist**.
medial ['mi:dɪəl] *adj (situated in the middle)* mittlere(r, s) ♦ **in (word) ~ position** *(Ling)* im Inlaut.
median ['mi:dɪən] [1] *adj* mittlere(r, s) ♦ **~ strip** *(US)* Mittelstreifen *m*.
[2] *n (Math)* Zentralwert *m*.
mediaperson ['mi:dɪəˌpɜ:sn] *n, pl* **mediapeople** ['mi:dɪəˌpi:pl] *(well-known)* Medienstar *m*.
mediate¹ ['mi:dɪət] *adj (rare)* mittelbar.
mediate² ['mi:dɪeɪt] [1] *vi* vermitteln.
[2] *vt settlement* aushandeln, herbeiführen.
mediation [ˌmi:dɪ'eɪʃən] *n* Vermittlung *f*.
mediator ['mi:dɪeɪtəʳ] *n* Vermittler, Mittelsmann *m*.
mediatory ['mi:dɪətərɪ] *adj* vermittelnd, des Vermittlers ♦ **in a ~ capacity** als Vermittler.
medic ['medɪk] *n (inf)* Mediziner *m (inf)*.
Medicaid ['medɪˌkeɪd] *n (US) staatliche Krankenversicherung und Gesundheitsfürsorge für Einkommensschwache in den USA*.
medical ['medɪkəl] [1] *adj* medizinisch; *(in military contexts)* Sanitäts-; *test, examination, treatment* ärztlich; *authority, board, inspector* Gesundheits-; *student* Medizin- ♦ **~ school** ≃ medizinische Fakultät; **the ~ world** die Ärzteschaft; **I'm not a ~ man** ich bin kein Arzt *or* Doktor; **her ~ history** ihre Krankengeschichte; **that made ~ history** das hat in der Medizin Geschichte gemacht; **~ card** *(Brit)* Krankenversicherungsschein *m*; **~ jurisprudence** Gerichtsmedizin *f*; **~ ward** Innere Abteilung.
[2] *n* (ärztliche) Untersuchung ♦ **have you had your ~?** bist du zur Untersuchung gewesen?, hast du dich untersuchen lassen?
medically ['medɪkəlɪ] *adv* medizinisch; *examine* ärztlich.
medicament [me'dɪkəmənt] *n* Medikament, Mittel *nt*.
Medicare ['medɪˌkɛəʳ] *n (US) staatliche Krankenversicherung und Gesundheitsfürsorge für ältere Bürger in den USA*.
medicate ['medɪkeɪt] *vt* (medizinisch) behandeln ♦ **~d** medizinisch.
medication [ˌmedɪ'keɪʃən] *n (act)* (medizinische) Behandlung; *(drugs etc)* Verordnung *f*, Medikamente *pl*.
medicinal [me'dɪsɪnl] *adj* Heil-, heilend ♦ **for ~ purposes** zu medizinischen Zwecken; **the ~ properties of various herbs** die Heilkraft verschiedener Kräuter.
medicinally [me'dɪsɪnəlɪ] *adv use, take* zu Heilzwecken, zu medizinischen Zwecken; *valuable* medizinisch.
medicine ['medsɪn, 'medɪsɪn] *n* **(a)** Arznei, Medizin *(inf) f*; *(one particular preparation)* Medikament *nt* ♦ **to take one's ~** *(lit)* seine Arznei einnehmen; *(fig)* die bittere Pille schlucken, in den sauren Apfel beißen; **now we'll see how you like a taste of your own ~** jetzt werden wir sehen, wie es dir schmeckt, wenn dir das passiert; **to give sb a taste of his own ~** *(fig)* es jdm mit gleicher Münze heim- *or* zurückzahlen.
(b) *(science)* Medizin *f* ♦ **to practise ~** den Arztberuf ausüben.
medicine: ~ ball *n* Medizinball *m*; **~ chest** *n* Hausapotheke *f*, Arzneischränkchen *nt*; **~-man** *n* Medizinmann *m*.
medico ['medɪkəʊ] *n (dated inf)* Medikus *m (dated, hum)*.
medieval [ˌmedɪ'i:vəl] *adj* mittelalterlich.
medievalist [ˌmedɪ'i:vəlɪst] *n* Mediävist(in *f*) *m*.
mediocre [ˌmi:dɪ'əʊkəʳ] *adj* mittelmäßig.
mediocrity [ˌmi:dɪ'ɒkrɪtɪ] *n* **(a)** *(quality)* Mittelmäßigkeit *f*. **(b)** *(person)* kleines Licht.
meditate ['medɪteɪt] [1] *vt*: **to ~ revenge** auf Rache sinnen *(liter)*.
[2] *vi* nachdenken *(upon, on* über *+acc)*; *(Rel, Philos)* meditieren.
meditation [ˌmedɪ'teɪʃən] *n* Nachdenken *nt*; *(Rel, Philos)* Meditation *f* ♦ **"A M~ on Life"** „Betrachtungen über das Leben".
meditative ['medɪtətɪv] *adj* nachdenklich; *(Rel, Philos)* Meditations-.
meditatively ['medɪtətɪvlɪ] *adv see adj* nachdenklich; meditierend.
Mediterranean [ˌmedɪtə'reɪnɪən] [1] *n* Mittelmeer *nt* ♦ **in the ~** *(in sea)* im Mittelmeer; *(in region)* am Mittelmeer, im Mittelmeerraum.
[2] *adj climate, nations* Mittelmeer-; *scenery, character, person* südländisch ♦ **the ~ Sea** das Mittelmeer; **~ fruit** Südfrüchte *pl*; **~ types** Südländer *pl*.
medium ['mi:dɪəm] [1] *adj quality, size etc* mittlere(r, s); *steak* halbdurch, medium; *brown, sized etc* mittel- ♦ **of ~ height/difficulty** mittelgroß/-schwer.
[2] *n, pl* **media** *or* **-s** **(a)** *(means)* Mittel *nt*; *(TV, Rad, Press)* Medium *nt*; *(Art, Liter)* Ausdrucksmittel *nt* ♦ **~ of exchange** Tauschmittel *nt*; **through the ~ of the press** durch die Presse; **advertising ~** Werbeträger *m*.

(b) *(surrounding substance) (Phys)* Medium *nt*; *(environment)* Umgebung *f*; *(air, water etc)* Element *nt*.
(c) *(midpoint)* Mitte *f* ♦ **happy ~** goldener Mittelweg; **to strike a happy ~** den goldenen Mittelweg finden.
(d) *(spiritualist)* Medium *nt*.

medium *in cpds* mittel-; **~-dry** *adj wine, sherry* halbtrocken; **~-priced** *adj* **a ~-priced hotel/whisky** ein Hotel *nt*/ein Whisky *m* mittlerer Preislage; **in the ~-priced range** mittlerer *or* in der mittleren Preislage; **~-range** *adj rocket, missile, aircraft* Mittelstrecken-; **~-rare** *adj* rosa, englisch; **~-sized** *adj* mittelgroß; **~ wave** *n* Mittelwelle *f*.

medley ['medlɪ] *n* Gemisch *nt*; *(Mus)* Potpourri, Medley *nt* ♦ **~ relay** *Staffellauf m, bei dem die einzelnen Teilnehmer über verschieden lange Strecken laufen, z.B. Schwedenstaffel, Olympische Staffel*; *(Swimming)* Lagenstaffel *f*.

medulla [me'dʌlə] *n* Mark *nt*; *(of spine)* Rückenmark *nt*; *(renal ~)* Nierenmark *nt*.

meek [miːk] *adj (+er)* sanft(mütig), lammfromm *(inf)*; *(pej)* duckmäuserisch; *(uncomplaining)* duldsam, geduldig ♦ **don't be so ~ and mild** laß dir doch nicht (immer) alles gefallen!

meekly ['miːklɪ] *adv* sanft, lammfromm *(inf)*; *(pej)* duckmäuserisch; *agree* widerspruchslos.

meekness ['miːknɪs] *n see adj* Sanftmut *f*; *(pej)* Duckmäuserei *f*; Duldsamkeit *f*.

meerschaum ['mɪəʃəm] *n* Meerschaum *m*; *(pipe)* Meerschaumpfeife *f*.

meet[1] [miːt] *adj (obs)* geziemend *(liter)* ♦ **it is ~ that** ... es ist billig *or* (ge)ziemt sich *(liter, old)*, daß ...; **to be ~ for** sich (ge)ziemen für *(liter, old)*.

meet[2] *(vb: pret, ptp* **met***)* [1] *vt* **(a)** *(encounter) person* treffen, begegnen *(+dat)*; *(by arrangement)* treffen, sich treffen mit; *difficulty* stoßen auf *(+acc)*; *(Sport)* treffen auf *(+acc)* ♦ **I'll ~ you outside** ich treffe euch draußen; **he met his guests at the door** er empfing seine Gäste an der Tür; **he met him in a duel** er duellierte sich mit ihm; **he met his death in 1800** im Jahre 1800 fand er den Tod; **to ~ death calmly** dem Tod gefaßt entgegentreten; **to arrange to ~ sb** sich mit jdm verabreden; **to ~ a challenge** sich einer Herausforderung *(dat)* stellen; **the last time Rangers met Celtic there was a riot** bei der letzten Begegnung zwischen Rangers und Celtic kam es zu heftigen Auseinandersetzungen; **his eyes** *or* **gaze met mine** unsere Blicke trafen sich; **she refused to ~ his eyes** *or* **gaze** sie wich seinem Blick aus; **I could not ~ his eye** ich konnte ihm nicht in die Augen sehen; **there's more to it than ~s the eye** da steckt mehr dahinter, als man auf den ersten Blick meint.
(b) *(get to know)* kennenlernen; *(be introduced to)* bekannt gemacht werden mit ♦ **you don't know him? come and ~ him** du kennst ihn nicht? komm, ich mache dich mit ihm bekannt; **pleased to ~ you!** guten Tag/Abend, sehr angenehm! *(form)*.
(c) *(await arrival, collect)* abholen *(at* an *+dat*, von*)*; *(connect with) train, boat etc* Anschluß haben an *(+acc)* ♦ **I'll ~ your train** ich hole dich vom Zug ab; **the car will ~ the train** der Wagen wartet am Bahnhof *or* steht am Bahnhof bereit.
(d) *(join, run into)* treffen *or* stoßen auf *(+acc)*; *(converge with)* sich vereinigen mit; *(river)* münden *or* fließen in *(+acc)*; *(intersect)* schneiden; *(touch)* berühren ♦ **where East ~s West** *(fig)* wo Ost und West sich treffen.
(e) *expectations, target, obligations, deadline* erfüllen; *requirement, demand, wish* entsprechen *(+dat)*, gerecht werden *(+dat)*; *deficit, expenses, needs* decken; *debt* bezahlen, begleichen; *charge, objection, criticism* begegnen *(+dat)*.
[2] *vi* **(a)** *(encounter) (people)* sich begegnen; *(by arrangement)* sich treffen; *(society, committee etc)* zusammenkommen, tagen; *(Sport)* aufeinandertreffen; *(in duel)* sich duellieren ♦ **keep it until we ~ again** behalten Sie es, bis wir uns mal wieder sehen; **until we ~ again!** bis zum nächsten Mal!; **to ~ halfway** einen Kompromiß schließen.
(b) *(become acquainted)* sich kennenlernen; *(be introduced)* bekannt gemacht werden ♦ **we've met before** wir kennen uns bereits; **haven't we met before somewhere?** sind wir uns nicht schon mal begegnet?, kennen wir uns nicht irgendwoher?
(c) *(join etc) see vt (d)* sich treffen, aufeinanderstoßen; sich vereinigen; ineinanderfließen; sich schneiden; sich berühren; *(fig: come together)* sich treffen ♦ **our eyes met** unsere Blicke trafen sich; **the skirt wouldn't ~ round her waist** der Rock ging an der Taille nicht zu.
[3] *n (Hunt)* Jagd(veranstaltung) *f*; *(US Sport)* Sportfest *nt* ♦ **swimming ~** Schwimmfest *nt*.

♦**meet up** *vi* sich treffen.

♦**meet with** *vi +prep obj* **(a)** *(encounter, experience) hostility, opposition, problems* stoßen auf *(+acc)*; *success, accident* haben; *disaster, loss, shock* erleiden; *setback* erleben; *approval, encouragement, an untimely death* finden ♦ **to ~ ~ praise/blame** gelobt/getadelt werden; **to ~ ~ kindness/a warm welcome** freundlich behandelt/herzlich empfangen werden.
(b) *person* treffen; *(esp US: have a meeting with)* (zu einer Unterredung) zusammenkommen mit.

meeting ['miːtɪŋ] *n* **(a)** Begegnung *f*, Zusammentreffen *nt*; *(arranged)* Treffen *nt*; *(business ~)* Besprechung, Konferenz *f* ♦ **the minister had a ~ with the ambassador** der Minister traf zu Gesprächen mit dem Botschafter zusammen.
(b) *(of committee, board of directors, council)* Sitzung *f*; *(of members, employees, citizens)* Versammlung *f*, Meeting *nt* ♦ **at the last ~** bei der letzten Sitzung; **the committee has three ~s a year** der Ausschuß tagt dreimal im Jahr; **Mr Jones is at/in a ~** Herr Jones ist (gerade) in einer Sitzung; **~ of creditors** Gläubigerversammlung *f*.
(c) *(Sport)* Veranstaltung *f*; *(between teams, opponents)* Begegnung *f*, Treffen *nt*.
(d) *(of rivers)* Zusammenfluß *m* ♦ **at the ~ of the X and the Y** wo X und Y zusammenfließen.

meeting: ~ house *n* Gemeindehaus *nt* (der Quäker); **~ place** *n* Treffpunkt *m*; **~ point** *n* Treffpunkt *m*; *(of rivers)* Zusammenfluß *m*; *(of lines)* Schnitt-/Berührungspunkt *m*; **at the ~ point of the two roads/cultures** wo die beiden Straßen zusammentreffen/wo sich die beiden Kulturen treffen.

mega- ['megə-] *pref* Mega-; **~bucks** *n (inf)* **he's making ~bucks** er verdient ein Schweinegeld *(inf)*, er macht schwer Moos *(sl)*

megabyte ['megəˌbaɪt] *n (Comput)* Megabyte *nt* ♦ **a 40-~ memory** ein 40-Megabyte-Speicher *m*.

megalith ['megəlɪθ] *n* Megalith *m*.

megalithic [ˌmegə'lɪθɪk] *adj* megalithisch.

megalomania [ˌmegələʊ'meɪnɪə] *n* Größenwahn *m*, Megalomanie *f (spec)*.

megalomaniac [ˌmegələʊ'meɪnɪæk] *n* Größenwahnsinnige(r) *mf* ♦ **he's a ~** er leidet an Größenwahn, er ist größenwahnsinnig.

megaphone ['megəfəʊn] *n* Megaphon *nt*.

mega: ~volt *n* Megavolt *nt*; **~watt** *n* Megawatt *nt*.

meiosis [maɪ'əʊsɪs] *n, pl* **-ses** [-siːz] *(Biol)* Meiose *f*.

melamine ['meləmiːn] *n* Melamin *nt*.

melancholia [ˌmelən'kəʊlɪə] *n* Schwermut, Melancholie *f*.

melancholic [ˌmelən'kɒlɪk] *adj* melancholisch, schwermütig.

melancholy ['melənkəlɪ] [1] *adj* melancholisch, schwermütig; *duty, sight etc* traurig.
[2] *n* Melancholie, Schwermut *f*.

Melba toast ['melbə'təʊst] *n* dünner, harter Toast.

mêlée ['meleɪ] *n (confused struggle)* Gedränge, Gewühl *nt*; *(fighting)* Handgemenge *nt*.

mellifluous [me'lɪflʊəs] *adj* wohltönend *or* -klingend.

mellifluously [me'lɪflʊəslɪ] *adv* klangvoll ♦ **..., he said ~** ..., sagte er mit wohltönender *or* klangvoller Stimme.

mellow ['meləʊ] [1] *adj (+er)* **(a)** *fruit* ausgereift, saftig; *wine* ausgereift, lieblich; *colour, light* warm; *sound* voll, rund, weich; *voice* weich, sanft ♦ **a ~ instrument** ein Instrument mit einem vollen *or* weichen Klang.
(b) *person* abgeklärt, gesetzt; *(fig: slightly drunk)* heiter, angeheitert ♦ **in the ~ later years** im gesetzteren Alter.
[2] *vt* reifen, heranreifen lassen; *(relax)* heiter stimmen; *sounds, colours* dämpfen, abschwächen; *taste* mildern.
[3] *vi (wine, fruit)* reif werden, (heran)reifen; *(colours, sounds)* weicher werden; *(person) (become gentler)* abgeklärter *or* gesetzter werden; *(relax)* umgänglicher werden.

mellowness ['meləʊnɪs] *n see adj* **(a)** Ausgereiftheit, Saftigkeit *f*; lieblicher Geschmack; Wärme *f*; Weichheit *f*; weicher *or* sanfter Klang. **(b)** Abgeklärtheit, Gesetztheit *f*; heitere *or* angeheiterte Stimmung.

melodic [mɪ'lɒdɪk] *adj* melodisch.

melodious [mɪ'ləʊdɪəs] *adj* melodiös, melodisch, wohlklingend ♦ **a ~ tune** eine harmonische Melodie.

melodiously [mɪ'ləʊdɪəslɪ] *adv* melodiös, melodisch.

melodiousness [mə'ləʊdɪəsnɪs] *n* Wohlklang *m*, Melodik *f*.

melodrama ['meləʊˌdrɑːmə] *n* Melodrama *nt*.

melodramatic *adj*, **~ally** *adv* [ˌmeləʊdrə'mætɪk, -əlɪ] melodramatisch.

melody ['melədɪ] *n* Melodie *f*; *(fig: of poetry etc)* Melodik *f*.

melon ['melən] *n* Melone *f*.

melt [melt] [1] *vt* **(a)** schmelzen; *snow also* zum Schmelzen bringen; *butter* zergehen lassen, zerlassen; *sugar, grease* auflösen. **(b)** *(fig) heart etc* erweichen ♦ **her tears ~ed my anger** beim Anblick ihrer Tränen verflog mein Zorn.
[2] *vi* **(a)** schmelzen; *(butter also)* zergehen; *(sugar, grease)* sich (auf)lösen ♦ **it just ~s in the mouth** es zergeht einem nur so auf der Zunge. **(b)** *(fig) (person)* dahinschmelzen; *(anger)* verfliegen ♦ **... and then his heart ~ed** ... und dann ließ er sich erweichen; **to ~ into tears** in Tränen zerfließen *(liter)*.

♦**melt away** *vi* **(a)** *(lit)* (weg)schmelzen. **(b)** *(fig)* sich auflösen; *(person)* dahinschmelzen; *(anger, anxiety)* verfliegen; *(suspicion, money)* zerrinnen.

♦**melt down** [1] *vt sep* einschmelzen.
[2] *vi (reactor core)* schmelzen.

meltdown ['meltdaʊn] *n* Kernschmelze *f*.

melting ['meltɪŋ]: **~ point** *n* Schmelzpunkt *m*; **what is the ~ point of iron?** welchen Schmelzpunkt hat Eisen?; **~ pot** *n (lit, fig)* Schmelztiegel *m*; **to be in the ~ pot** in der Schwebe sein.

member ['membəʳ] *n* **(a)** Mitglied *nt*; *(of tribe, species)* Angehörige(r) *mf* ♦ **"~s only"** „nur für Mitglieder"; **~ of the family** Familienmitglied *nt*; **if any ~ of the audience** ... falls einer der Zuschauer/Zuhörer ...; **you have to be a ~** Sie müssen Mitglied sein; **the ~ countries/states** die Mitgliedsstaaten *pl*.
(b) *(Parl)* Abgeordnete(r) *mf* ♦ **~ of parliament** Parlamentsmitglied *nt*; *(in GB)* Abgeordnete(r) *mf* des Unterhauses; *(in BRD)* Bundestagsabgeordnete(r) *mf*; **the ~ for Woodford** der/die Abgeordnete für den Wahlkreis Woodford.
(c) *(Math, Logic)* Glied *nt*.

membership ['membəʃɪp] *n* Mitgliedschaft *f (of* in *+dat)*; *(number of members)* Mitgliederzahl *f* ♦ **when I applied for ~ of the club** als ich mich um die Clubmitgliedschaft bewarb; **~ list** Mitgliederkartei *f*.

membrane ['membreɪn] *n* Membran(e) *f*.

membranous [mem'breɪnəs] *adj* membranartig.

memento [mə'mentəʊ] *n, pl* **-(e)s** Andenken *nt (of* an *+acc)*.

memo ['meməʊ] *n abbr of* **memorandum** Mitteilung, Notiz *f*, Memo *nt* ♦ **~ pad** Notizblock *m*.

memoir ['memwɑːʳ] *n* **(a)** Kurzbiographie *f.* **(b) ~s** *pl* Memoiren *pl.*
memorable ['memərəbl] *adj* unvergeßlich; (*important*) denkwürdig.
memorably ['memərəblɪ] *adv* bemerkenswert.
memorandum [ˌmemə'rændəm] *n, pl* **memoranda** [ˌmemə'rændə] **(a)** (*in business*) Mitteilung *f;* (*personal reminder*) Notiz *f,* Vermerk *m.* **(b)** (*Pol*) Memorandum *nt.*
memorial [mɪ'mɔːrɪəl] 1 *adj plaque, service* Gedenk- ◆ ~ **park** (*US: cemetery*) Friedhof *m.*
2 *n* Denkmal *nt* (*to* für) ◆ **M~ Day** (*US*) ≃ Volkstrauertag *m.*
memorize ['meməraɪz] *vt* sich (*dat*) einprägen.
memory ['memərɪ] *n* **(a)** Gedächtnis *nt;* (*faculty*) Erinnerungsvermögen *nt* ◆ **from ~** aus dem Kopf; **to commit sth to ~** sich (*dat*) etw einprägen; *poem* etw auswendig lernen; **I have a bad ~ for faces/names** ich habe ein schlechtes Personengedächtnis/Namensgedächtnis; **if my ~ serves me right** wenn ich mich recht entsinne; *see* **living.**
(b) (*that remembered*) Erinnerung *f* (*of* an +*acc*) ◆ **I have no ~ of it** ich kann mich nicht daran erinnern; **to take a trip** *or* **to walk down ~ lane** in Erinnerungen schwelgen.
(c) (*Comput*) Speicher *m.*
(d) to honour sb's ~ jds Andenken *nt* ehren; **in ~ of** zur Erinnerung *or* zum Gedenken (*form*) an (+*acc*); *see* **blessed.**
memory (*Comput*): ~ **bank** *n* Datenbank *f;* ~ **chip** *n* Speicherchip *m;* ~ **expansion card** *n* Speichererweiterungskarte *f;* ~ **management** *n* Speicherverwaltung *f;* ~**-resident** *adj* speicherresident.
men [men] *pl of* **man.**
menace ['menɪs] 1 *n* **(a)** Bedrohung *f* (*to gen*); (*issued by a person*) Drohung *f;* (*imminent danger*) drohende Gefahr ◆ **to demand money with ~s** unter Androhung von Gewalt Geld fordern. **(b)** (*inf: nuisance*) (Land)plage *f* ◆ **she's a ~ on the roads** sie gefährdet den ganzen Verkehr.
2 *vt* bedrohen.
menacing ['menɪsɪŋ] *adj* drohend.
menacingly ['menɪsɪŋlɪ] *adv see adj* ◆ ..., **he said ~** ..., sagte er mit drohender Stimme.
ménage [me'nɑːʒ] *n* Haushalt *m* ◆ ~ **à trois** Dreiecksverhältnis *nt.*
menagerie [mɪ'nædʒərɪ] *n* Menagerie *f.*
mend [mend] 1 *n* (*in shoe*) reparierte Stelle; (*in piece of metal, cloth etc also*) Flickstelle *f;* (*in roof, fence etc also*) ausgebesserte Stelle ◆ **the ~ is almost invisible** man sieht kaum, daß es repariert/geflickt/ausgebessert worden ist; **to be on the ~** (*lit: person, fig*) sich (langsam) erholen, sich auf dem Wege der Besserung befinden (*form*); **the fracture is on the ~** der Bruch heilt schon wieder *or* ist am Verheilen (*inf*).
2 *vt* **(a)** (*repair*) reparieren; *roof, fence also* ausbessern; *hole, clothes* flicken ◆ **my shoes need ~ing** ich muß meine Schuhe reparieren *or* machen (*inf*) lassen.
(b) (*improve*) **you'd better ~ your ways** das muß aber anders werden mit dir/Ihnen!; **to ~ one's ways** sich bessern; **to ~ matters** eine Angelegenheit bereinigen; **that won't ~ matters** das macht die Sache auch nicht besser.
3 *vi* (*bone*) (ver)heilen ◆ **the patient is ~ing nicely** der Patient macht gute Fortschritte; **make do and ~** (*prov*) aus alt mach neu (*prov*).
mendacious [men'deɪʃəs] *adj* lügnerisch, verlogen.
mendaciously [men'deɪʃəslɪ] *adv* unwahrheitsgemäß.
mendacity [men'dæsɪtɪ] *n* Verlogenheit *f.*
Mendelian [men'diːlɪən] *adj* Mendelsch.
mendicant ['mendɪkənt] 1 *adj* bettelnd; *order, monk* Bettel-.
2 *n* (*beggar*) Bettler(in *f*) *m;* (*monk*) Bettelmönch *m.*
mending ['mendɪŋ] *n* (*articles to be mended*) Flickarbeit *f.*
menfolk ['menfəʊk] *npl* Männer *pl,* Mannsvolk *nt* (*old*).
menial ['miːnɪəl] 1 *adj* niedrig, untergeordnet ◆ **she regards no task as too ~ for her** sie betrachtet keine Arbeit für unter ihrer Würde; **the ~ staff** die (unteren) Dienstboten, das Gesinde.
2 *n* (*pej*) Dienstbote *m.*
meningitis [ˌmenɪn'dʒaɪtɪs] *n* Hirnhautentzündung, Meningitis *f.*
meniscus [mɪ'nɪskəs] *n, pl* **menisci** [mɪ'nɪsaɪ] Meniskus *m.*
menopause ['menəʊpɔːz] *n* Wechseljahre *pl,* Menopause *f* (*spec*).
menorrhagia [ˌmenɔː'reɪdʒɪə] *n* (*Med*) überhöhte Menstruationsblutung.
menses ['mensiːz] *npl* (*rare*) Menses *pl* (*dated*).
men's room ['menzruːm] *n* (*esp US*) Herrentoilette *f.*
menstrual ['menstrʊəl] *adj* Menstruations-, menstrual (*spec*) ◆ ~ **bleeding** Monatsblutung *f.*
menstruate ['menstrʊeɪt] *vi* menstruieren (*spec*), die Menstruation haben.
menstruation [ˌmenstrʊ'eɪʃən] *n* die Menstruation *or* Periode.
mental ['mentl] *adj* **(a)** geistig; *cruelty* seelisch ◆ **he has a ~ age of ten** er ist auf dem geistigen Entwicklungsstand eines Zehnjährigen; **to make a ~ note of sth** sich (*dat*) etw merken; ~ **blackout** Bewußtseinsstörung *f;* **to have a ~ blackout** eine Bewußtseinsstörung haben, geistig weggetreten sein (*inf*); (*due to alcohol*) einen Filmriß haben (*inf*); (*in exam*) ein Brett vor dem Kopf haben (*inf*); ~ **breakdown** Nervenzusammenbruch *m;* ~ **arithmetic** Kopfrechnen *nt;* ~ **health** Geisteszustand *m;* ~ **home** (Nerven)heilanstalt *f;* ~ **hospital** psychiatrische Klinik, Nervenklinik *f;* ~ **illness** Geisteskrankheit *f;* ~ **patient** Geisteskranke(r) *mf;* ~ **process** geistiger *or* gedanklicher Prozeß, Denkvorgang *m;* ~ **reservation** (stille) Bedenken, Vorbehalte *pl;* **the causes are ~ not physical** die Ursachen sind eher psychischer als physischer Natur; **he still shows great ~ agility** er ist geistig noch immer sehr rege.
(b) (*sl: mad*) übergeschnappt (*inf*).
mentality [men'tælɪtɪ] *n* Mentalität *f* ◆ **they have a very aggressive ~** sie haben eine sehr aggressive Art; **how can we change this materialistic ~?** wie können wir diese materialistische Einstellung *or* Auffassung ändern?
mentally ['mentəlɪ] *adv* **(a)** geistig ◆ ~ **handicapped/deficient** geistig behindert/geistesschwach; **he is ~ ill** er ist geisteskrank. **(b)** (*in one's head*) im Kopf.
menthol ['menθɒl] *n* Menthol *nt* ◆ ~ **cigarettes** Mentholzigaretten *pl.*
mentholated ['menθəleɪtɪd] *adj* Menthol-, mit Menthol.
➤ **mention** ['menʃən] 1 *n* Erwähnung *f* ◆ **to get** *or* **receive a ~** erwähnt werden; **he received a ~ for bravery** er erhielt eine Auszeichnung *or* Belobigung für seine Tapferkeit; **to give sth a ~** etw erwähnen; **there is a/no ~ of it** es wird erwähnt/nicht erwähnt; **I can't find any ~ of his name** ich kann seinen Namen nirgendwo finden; **his contribution certainly deserves ~** sein Beitrag verdient gewiß, erwähnt zu werden; ~ **should also be made of ...** ... sollte Erwähnung finden (*form*); **it's hardly worth a ~** es ist kaum erwähnenswert, es lohnt sich kaum, das zu erwähnen; **at the ~ of his name/the police** ... als sein Name/das Wort Polizei fiel *or* erwähnt wurde ...
➤ 2 *vt* erwähnen (*to sb* jdm gegenüber) ◆ **he was ~ed in several dispatches** er wurde mehrfach lobend erwähnt; **not to ~** ... nicht zu vergessen ..., geschweige denn ...; **France and West Germany, not to ~ Holland** Frankreich und die Bundesrepublik, von Holland ganz zu schweigen *or* ganz abgesehen von Holland; **too numerous to ~** zu zahlreich, um sie einzeln erwähnen zu können; **don't ~ it!** (das ist doch) nicht der Rede wert!, (bitte,) gern geschehen!; **if I may ~ it** wenn ich das einmal sagen darf; **it hardly needs ~ing that we're very grateful** es versteht sich wohl von selbst, daß wir sehr dankbar sind; **to ~ sb in one's will** jdn in seinem Testament berücksichtigen; ~ **me to your parents!** empfehlen Sie mich Ihren Eltern! (*form*), viele Grüße an Ihre Eltern!
mentor ['mentɔːʳ] *n* Mentor *m.*
menu ['menjuː] *n* **(a)** (*bill of fare*) Speisekarte *f;* (*dishes served*) Menü *nt* ◆ **may we see the ~?** können *or* würden Sie uns bitte die Karte bringen?, können wir bitte die Karte sehen?; **what's on the ~?** was steht heute auf dem Speisezettel?, was gibt es heute (zu essen)?; **they have a very good ~ there** man kann dort ausgezeichnet essen; **the typical British ~ consists of ...** ein typisches britisches Essen besteht aus ...
(b) (*Comput*) Menü *nt.*
menu (*Comput*): ~**-driven** *adj* menügesteuert; ~ **line** *n* Menüzeile *f.*
meow *n, vi see* **miaow.**
MEP *abbr of* **Member of the European Parliament** Mitglied *nt* des Europäischen Parlaments.
mercantile ['mɜːkəntaɪl] *adj* Handels-; *nation also* handeltreibend ◆ **the ~ marine** die Handelsmarine.
mercantilism ['mɜːkəntɪlɪzəm] *n* Merkantilismus *m.*
mercenary ['mɜːsɪnərɪ] 1 *adj* **(a)** *person* geldgierig ◆ **his motives were purely ~** er tat es nur des Geldes wegen; **don't be so ~** sei doch nicht so hinter dem Geld her (*inf*); **he's got a rather ~ attitude** bei ihm spielt nur das Geld eine Rolle. **(b)** (*Mil*) *troops* Söldner-.
2 *n* Söldner *m.*
mercerized ['mɜːsəraɪzd] *adj thread* merzerisiert.
merchandise ['mɜːtʃəndaɪz] *n* (Handels)ware *f* ◆ **"please do not handle the ~"** ,,das Berühren der Ware(n) ist verboten".
merchandiser ['mɜːtʃəndaɪzəʳ] *n* Verkaufsförderungsexperte *m.*
merchandising ['mɜːtʃəndaɪzɪŋ] *n* Verkaufsförderung *f.*
merchant ['mɜːtʃənt] *n* **(a)** Kaufmann *m* ◆ **corn/fruit/diamond ~** Getreide-/Obst-/Diamantenhändler *m.* **(b)** (*Brit sl*) Typ *m* (*sl*) ◆ **he's a real speed ~** der fährt wie der Henker (*sl*); **gossip ~** Klatschmaul *nt* (*inf*); (*woman also*) Klatschtante *f* (*inf*).
merchant *in cpds* Handels-; ~ **bank** *n* Handelsbank *f;* ~**man** *n* Handelsschiff *nt;* ~ **navy** *n* Handelsmarine *f;* ~ **prince** *n* reicher Kaufmann, Handelsboss (*inf*) *m;* ~ **seaman** *n* Matrose *m* in der Handelsmarine; ~ **ship** *n* Handelsschiff *nt.*
merciful ['mɜːsɪfʊl] *adj* gnädig ◆ **o ~ Lord** gütiger Gott; **O Lord be ~!** Gott, sei uns (*dat*) gnädig!; **his death was a ~ release from pain** sein Tod war für ihn eine Erlösung; ~ **heavens!** (*dated*) barmherziger Himmel! (*dated*).
mercifully ['mɜːsɪfəlɪ] *adv act* barmherzig; *treat sb* gnädig; (*fortunately*) glücklicherweise ◆ **his suffering was ~ short** es war eine Gnade, daß er nicht lange leiden mußte.
merciless ['mɜːsɪlɪs] *adj* unbarmherzig, erbarmungslos; *destruction* schonungslos.
mercilessly ['mɜːsɪlɪslɪ] *adv* erbarmungslos.
mercurial [mɜː'kjʊərɪəl] *adj* (*Chem*) Quecksilber-; (*containing mercury*) quecksilberhaltig; (*fig*) (*volatile*) sprunghaft, wechselhaft; (*lively*) quicklebendig.
Mercury ['mɜːkjʊrɪ] *n* Merkur *m.*
mercury ['mɜːkjʊrɪ] *n* Quecksilber *nt.*
mercy ['mɜːsɪ] *n* **(a)** *no pl* (*feeling of compassion*) Erbarmen *nt;* (*action, forbearance from punishment*) Gnade *f;* (*God's ~*) Barmherzigkeit *f* ◆ **to beg for ~** um Gnade bitten *or* flehen; **to have ~/no ~ on sb** mit jdm Erbarmen/kein Erbarmen haben; **have ~!** Gnade!, Erbarmen!; **Lord have ~ upon us** Herr, erbarme dich unser; **to show sb ~/no ~** Erbarmen/kein Erbarmen mit jdm haben; **to throw oneself on sb's ~** sich jdm auf Gnade und Ungnade ausliefern; **to be at the ~ of sb** jdm (auf Gedeih und Verderb) ausgeliefert sein; **to be at the ~ of sth** einer Sache (*dat*) ausgeliefert sein; **we're at your ~** wir sind in Ihrer Gewalt *or* Hand; **at the ~ of the elements** dem Spiel der Elemente preisgegeben; **a mission of ~** eine Hilfsaktion.
(b) (*inf: blessing*) Segen *m,* Glück *nt* ◆ **it's a ~ nobody was hurt** man kann von

➤ LANGUAGE IN USE: **mention: 1** → 26.3 **2** → 19.4, 26.2

Glück sagen, daß niemand verletzt wurde; **we must be thankful for small mercies** man muß schon mit wenigem zufrieden *or* für weniges dankbar sein.

mercy: ~ killing *n* Euthanasie *f*, Töten *nt* aus Mitleid; **~ seat** *n* Gnadenthron *or* -stuhl *m*.

mere¹ [mɪəʳ] *n (poet)* See *m*.

mere² *adj* bloß; *formality also, nonsense* rein ◆ **he's a ~ clerk** er ist bloß ein kleiner Angestellter; **a ~ 3%/2 hours** bloß *or* lediglich 3%/2 Stunden; **a ~ nothing** eine (bloße) Lappalie; **but she's a ~ child** aber sie ist doch noch ein Kind!

merely ['mɪəlɪ] *adv* lediglich, bloß ◆ **it's not ~ broken, it's ruined** es ist nicht bloß kaputt, es ist völlig ruiniert.

meretricious [,merɪ'trɪʃəs] *adj* trügerisch.

merge [mɜːdʒ] 1 *vi* **(a)** zusammenkommen; *(colours)* ineinander übergehen; *(roads)* zusammenlaufen *or* -führen ◆ **to ~ with sth** mit etw verschmelzen, sich mit etw vereinen; *(colour)* in etw *(acc)* übergehen; *(road)* in etw *(acc)* einmünden; **to ~ (in) with/into the crowd** in der Menge untergehen/untertauchen; **to ~ into sth** in etw *(acc)* übergehen; **the bird ~d into** *or* **in with its background of leaves** der Vogel verschmolz mit dem Laubwerk im Hintergrund; **this question ~s into that bigger one** diese Frage geht in dem größeren Fragenkomplex auf; **"motorways ~"** „Autobahneinmündung".
(b) *(Comm)* fusionieren, sich zusammenschließen.
2 *vt* **(a)** miteinander vereinen *or* verbinden *or* verschmelzen; *colours also* ineinander übergehen lassen; *metals* legieren; *(Comput) files* mischen ◆ **to ~ sth with sth** etw mit etw vereinen *or* verbinden *or* verschmelzen; etw in etw *(acc)* übergehen lassen.
(b) *(Comm)* zusammenschließen, fusionieren ◆ **they were ~d into one company** sie wurden zu einer Firma zusammengeschlossen; **they were ~d with ...** sie haben mit ... fusioniert.

merger ['mɜːdʒəʳ] *n (Comm)* Fusion *f*.

meridian [mə'rɪdɪən] *n (Astron, Geog)* Meridian *m*; *(fig)* Höhepunkt, Gipfel *m*.

meringue [mə'ræŋ] *n* Meringe *f*, Baiser *nt*.

merino [mə'riːnəʊ] *n* **(a)** *(sheep)* Merino(schaf *nt*) *m*. **(b)** *(wool)* Merinowolle *f*.

merit ['merɪt] 1 *n (achievement)* Leistung *f*, Verdienst *nt*; *(advantage)* Vorzug *m* ◆ **to look** *or* **inquire into the ~s of sth** etw auf seine Vorteile *or* Vorzüge untersuchen; **men of ~** verdiente Leute *pl*; **a work of great literary ~** ein Werk von großem literarischem Wert; **what are the particular ~s of Greek drama?** wodurch zeichnet sich das griechische Drama besonders aus?; **she won the election on ~ alone** sie gewann die Wahl aufgrund persönlicher Fähigkeiten; **judged on ~ alone** ausschließlich nach Leistung(en) *or* ihren Verdiensten beurteilt; **I don't see any ~ in being rich** ich betrachte Reichtum als kein besonderes Verdienst; **there's no particular ~ in coming early** es ist keine besondere Leistung *or* kein besonderes Verdienst, früh zu kommen; **to treat a case on its ~s** einen Fall für sich selbst *or* gesondert behandeln; **to pass an exam with ~** ein Examen mit Auszeichnung bestehen.
2 *vt* verdienen ◆ **it ~s your consideration** das ist es wert, daß Sie sich damit beschäftigen.

meritocracy [,merɪ'tɒkrəsɪ] *n* Leistungsgesellschaft, Meritokratie *(geh) f*.

meritocratic [,merɪtə'krætɪk] *adj* leistungsorientiert.

meritorious *adj*, **~ly** *adv* [,merɪ'tɔːrɪəs, -lɪ] lobenswert.

mermaid ['mɜːmeɪd] *n* Nixe, See- *or* Meerjungfrau *f*.

merman ['mɜːmæn] *n, pl* **-men** [-men] Nix, Wassergeist *m*.

merrily ['merɪlɪ] *adv* vergnügt.

merriment ['merɪmənt] *n* Heiterkeit, Fröhlichkeit *f*; *(laughter)* Gelächter *nt* ◆ **at this there was much ~** das erregte allgemeine Heiterkeit, das rief großes Gelächter hervor.

▼ **merry** ['merɪ] *adj (+er)* **(a)** *(cheerful)* fröhlich, vergnügt, lustig; *song, tune* fröhlich ◆ **to make ~** lustig und vergnügt sein; **M~ Christmas!** Fröhliche *or* Frohe Weihnachten!; **M~ England** das gute alte England; **to give sb ~ hell** *(inf)* jdm einheizen *(inf)*.
(b) *(inf: tipsy)* beschwipst, angeheitert *(inf)* ◆ **to get ~** sich *(dat)* einen anpicheln *(inf)*.

merry: ~-go-round *n* Karussell *nt*; **~maker** *n* Festgast *m*, Feiernde(r) *mf*; **~making** *n* Feiern *nt*, Belustigung, Lustbarkeit *(liter) f*; **after the ~making had finished** nach Beendigung des Festes *or* der Lustbarkeiten *(liter)*.

mesa ['meɪsə] *n* Tafelberg *m*.

mescalin(e) ['meskəlɪn] *n* Meskalin *nt*.

mesh [meʃ] 1 *n* **(a)** *(hole)* Masche *f*; *(size of hole)* Maschenweite *f* ◆ **caught in the fine ~ of the net** in den feinen Maschen des Netzes gefangen; **fine ~ stockings** feinmaschige Strümpfe *pl*; **the broad ~ of this material makes it ideal** die Grobmaschigkeit dieses Materials ist ideal; **a 5mm ~ screen** ein 5 mm Maschendraht; **the ~ is big enough to see through** es ist großmaschig genug, um durchzusehen.
(b) *(material)* *(wire ~)* Maschendraht *m*; *(network of wires)* Drahtgeflecht *nt*; *(Tex)* Gittergewebe *nt*.
(c) *(Mech)* **out of/in ~** nicht im/im Eingriff; **the tight ~ of the cogwheels** die enge Verzahnung der Räder.
(d) *(fig)* **to catch** *or* **entangle sb in one's ~es** jdn umgarnen, jdn in sein Netz locken; **to be caught in sb's ~es** jdm ins Netz gegangen sein; **he was entangled in the ~es of his own intrigues** er verfing sich im Netz seiner eigenen Intrigen.
2 *vi* **(a)** *(Mech)* eingreifen *(with* in *+acc)* ◆ **the gears ~ (together)** die Zahnräder greifen ineinander.
(b) *(fig: views, approach)* sich vereinen lassen ◆ **he tried to make the departments ~ (together)** er versuchte, die einzelnen Abteilungen miteinander zu koordinieren.
3 *vt see* **enmesh**.

meshugge [mɪ'ʃʊgə] *adj (sl)* meschugge *(inf)*.

mesmeric [mez'merɪk] *adj* hypnotisch; *movement* hypnotisierend.

mesmerism ['mezmərɪzəm] *n* hypnotische Wirkung; *(old)* Mesmerismus *m*.

mesmerize ['mezməraɪz] *vt* hypnotisieren; *(fig)* faszinieren, fesseln ◆ **the audience sat ~d** die Zuschauer saßen wie gebannt.

meson ['miːzɒn] *n (Phys)* Meson *nt*.

Mesopotamia [,mesəpə'teɪmɪə] *n* Mesopotamien *nt*.

mess¹ [mes] 1 *n* **(a)** Durcheinander *nt*; *(untidy also)* Unordnung *f*; *(dirty)* Schweinerei *f* ◆ **to be (in) a ~** unordentlich sein, in einem fürchterlichen Zustand sein; *(disorganized)* ein einziges Durcheinander sein; *(fig: one's life, marriage, career etc)* verkorkst sein *(inf)*; **to be a ~** *(piece of work)* eine Schweinerei sein; *(disorganized)* ein einziges *or* heilloses Durcheinander sein; *(person)* *(in appearance)* unordentlich aussehen; *(psychologically)* verkorkst sein *(inf)*; **to look a ~** *(person)* unmöglich aussehen; *(untidy also)* schlampig *or* unordentlich aussehen; *(dirty also)* völlig verdreckt sein; *(room, piece of work)* unordentlich *or* schlimm aussehen; **to make a ~** *(be untidy)* Unordnung machen; *(be dirty)* eine Schweinerei machen; **to make a ~ of sth** *(make untidy)* etw in Unordnung bringen, etw durcheinanderbringen; *(make dirty)* etw verdrecken; *(bungle, botch)* etw verpfuschen, bei etw Mist bauen *(inf)*; *one's life* etw verkorksen *(inf) or* verpfuschen; **I made a ~ of sewing it on** ich habe beim Annähen Mist gebaut *(inf)*; **you've really made a ~ of things** du hast alles total vermasselt *(inf)*; **a fine ~ you've made of that** da hast du was Schönes angerichtet; **what a ~!** wie sieht das denn aus!, das sieht ja vielleicht aus!; *(fig)* ein schöner Schlamassel! *(inf)*; **I'm not tidying up your ~** ich räume nicht für dich auf; **a ~ of beer cans/pots and pans** ein Haufen Bierdosen/Töpfe und Pfannen.
(b) *(awkward predicament)* Schwierigkeiten *pl*, Schlamassel *m (inf)* ◆ **cheating got him into a ~** durch seine Mogelei ist er in ziemliche Schwierigkeiten geraten; **he got into a ~ with the police** er hat Ärger mit der Polizei bekommen; **when he forgot his lines he panicked and got into a ~** als er seinen Text vergaß, geriet er in Panik und verhedderte sich völlig *(inf)*.
(c) *(euph: excreta)* Dreck *m* ◆ **the cat/baby has made a ~ on the carpet** die Katze/das Baby hat auf den Teppich gemacht.
2 *vi see* **~ about 2 (c, d)**.

◆**mess about** *or* **around** *(inf)* 1 *vt sep (fiddle, tinker with)* herumpfuschen an *(+dat) (inf)*; *plans* durcheinanderbringen; *person* an der Nase herumführen *(inf)*; *(boss, person in authority)* herumschikanieren; *(by delaying decision)* hinhalten.
2 *vi* **(a)** *(play the fool)* herumalbern *or* -blödeln *(inf)*.
(b) *(do nothing in particular)* herumgammeln *(inf)* ◆ **he enjoys ~ing ~ on the river** er gondelt gern (im Boot) auf dem Fluß herum.
(c) *(tinker, fiddle)* herumfummeln *(inf) or* -spielen *(with* an *+dat)*; *(as hobby etc)* herumbasteln *(with* an *+dat) (inf)* ◆ **that'll teach you to ~ ~ with explosives** das soll dir eine Lehre sein, nicht mit Sprengkörpern herumzuspielen; **I don't like film directors ~ing ~ with my scripts** ich kann es nicht haben, wenn Regisseure an meinen Drehbüchern herumändern.
(d) to ~ ~ with sb *(associate with)* sich mit jdm einlassen *or* abgeben; *(not take seriously)* jdn zum Narren haben.

◆**mess up** *vt sep* durcheinanderbringen; *(make dirty)* verdrecken; *(botch, bungle)* verpfuschen, verhunzen *(inf)*; *marriage* kaputtmachen *(inf)*, ruinieren; *life, person* verkorksen *(inf)*; *person (as regards looks)* übel zurichten ◆ **missing the connection ~ed ~ the whole journey** dadurch, daß wir den Anschluß verpaßten, lief die ganze Reise schief; **her visit really ~ed me ~** *(inf)* ihr Besuch hat mir wirklich alles vermasselt *(inf)*; **that's really ~ed things ~** das hat wirklich alles verdorben *or* vermasselt *(inf)*.

mess² *(Mil)* 1 *n* Kasino *nt*; *(on ships)* Messe *f*; *(food)* Essen *nt*.
2 *vi* essen, das Essen einnehmen.

▼ **message** ['mesɪdʒ] *n* **(a)** Mitteilung, Nachricht, Botschaft *(old, form) f*; *(radio ~)* Funkspruch *m or* -meldung *f*; *(report, police ~)* Meldung *f* ◆ **to take a ~ to sb** jdm eine Nachricht überbringen; **to give sb a ~** *(verbal)* jdm etwas ausrichten; *(written)* jdm eine Nachricht geben; **would you give John a ~ (for me)?** könnten Sie John etwas (von mir) ausrichten?; **have you given him my ~ yet?** hast du es ihm schon ausgerichtet?; **to send a ~ to sb** jdn benachrichtigen; **to leave a ~ for sb** *(written)* jdm eine Nachricht hinterlassen; *(verbal)* jdm etwas ausrichten lassen; **can I take a ~ (for him)?** *(on telephone)* kann ich (ihm) etwas ausrichten?; **the Queen's ~ to the people** die (Fernseh)ansprache der Königin.
(b) *(moral)* Botschaft *f* ◆ **the ~ of the play is ...** die Aussage des Stückes ist ..., das Stück will folgendes sagen ...; **a pop song with a ~** ein Schlagertext, der einem etwas zu sagen hat.
(c) to get the ~ *(fig inf)* kapieren *(inf)*; **I got the ~** ich habe schon verstanden *or* kapiert *(inf)*.
(d) *(Scot: errand)* Einkauf *m* ◆ **to do** *or* **get one's ~s** einkaufen.

message switching *n (Comput)* Speichervermittlung *f*.

messaging ['mesɪdʒɪŋ] *n* Datentransfer *m*.

mess deck *n* Speisedeck *nt*.

messenger ['mesɪndʒəʳ] *n* Bote *(old, form)*, Überbringer(in *f*) *m* (einer Nachricht); *(Mil)* Kurier *m* ◆ **~ boy** Botenjunge, Laufbursche *m*; **bank/post office ~** Bank-/Postbote *m*.

➤ LANGUAGE IN USE: **merry: a → 23.2** **message: a → 27.6**

mess hall *n* Kasino *nt*.
Messiah [mɪ'saɪə] *n* Messias *m*.
messianic [ˌmesɪ'ænɪk] *adj* messianisch.
mess: ~ **jacket** *n* Affenjäckchen *nt* (*inf*); ~ **kit** *n* (*Brit*) *Uniform f für gesellschaftliche Anlässe*; (*US*) Eßgeschirr *nt*; ~ **mate** *n* **they were ~ mates** sie waren Kameraden bei der Armee.
Messrs ['mesəz] *pl of* **Mr** *abbr of* **Messieurs** ◆ **to ~** ... an die Herren ...
mess tin *n* Eß- *or* Kochgeschirr *nt*.
mess-up ['mesʌp] *n* Kuddelmuddel *nt* (*inf*) ◆ **there's been a bit of a ~** da ist etwas schiefgelaufen (*inf*).
messy ['mesɪ] *adj* (+*er*) (*dirty*) dreckig, schmutzig; (*untidy*) unordentlich; (*confused*) durcheinander; (*fig: unpleasant*) unschön ◆ ~ **writing** fürchterliche Klaue (*inf*); **he's a ~ eater** er kann nicht ordentlich essen, er ißt wie ein Schwein.
met[1] [met] *pret, ptp of* **meet**[2].
met[2] *abbr of* **meteorological.**
meta- ['metə-] *pref* meta-, Meta-.
metabolic [ˌmetə'bɒlɪk] *adj* Stoffwechsel-, metabolisch.
metabolism [me'tæbəlɪzəm] *n* Stoffwechsel, Metabolismus *m*.
metacarpal [ˌmetə'kɑːpl] *n* Mittelhandknochen *m*.
metal ['metl] [1] *n* Metall *nt*; (*Brit: on road*) Asphalt *m* ◆ **~s** *pl* (*Rail*) Schienen *pl*.
[2] *vt road* asphaltieren ◆ **~led road** Asphaltstraße *f*.
metallic [mɪ'tælɪk] *adj* metallisch.
metallurgic(al) [ˌmetə'lɜːdʒɪk(əl)] *adj* metallurgisch.
metallurgist [me'tælədʒɪst] *n* Metallurg(in *f*) *m*.
metallurgy [me'tælədʒɪ] *n* Hüttenkunde, Metallurgie *f*.
metal *in cpds* Metall-; ~ **plating** *n* Metallschicht *f*; (*act*) Plattierung *f*; ~ **polish** *n* Metallpolitur *f*; **~work** *n* Metall *nt*; **we did ~work at school** wir haben in der Schule Metallarbeiten gemacht; **~worker** *n* Metallarbeiter *m*.
metamorphose [ˌmetə'mɔːfəʊz] [1] *vt* verwandeln; (*Sci*) umwandeln.
[2] *vi* sich verwandeln; (*Sci*) sich umwandeln.
metamorphosis [ˌmetə'mɔːfəsɪs] *n, pl* **metamorphoses** [ˌmetə'mɔːfəsiːz] Metamorphose *f*; (*fig*) Verwandlung *f*.
metaphor ['metəfəʳ] *n* Metapher *f*.
metaphorical [ˌmetə'fɒrɪkəl] *adj* metaphorisch.
metaphorically [ˌmetə'fɒrɪkəlɪ] *adv see adj* ◆ ~ **speaking** metaphorisch ausgedrückt, bildlich gesprochen.
metaphysical *adj*, **~ly** *adv* [ˌmetə'fɪzɪkəl, -ɪ] metaphysisch.
metaphysician [ˌmetəfɪ'zɪʃn] *n* Metaphysiker(in *f*) *m*.
metaphysics [ˌmetə'fɪzɪks] *n sing* Metaphysik *f*.
metastasis [mɪ'tæstəsɪs] *n, pl* **metastases** [mɪ'tæstəsiːz] *n* Metastasenbildung, Metastasierung *f*.
metatarsal [ˌmetə'tɑːsl] *adj* Mittelfuß-, metatarsal (*spec*).
metathesis [me'tæθəsɪs] *n, pl* **metatheses** [me'tæθəsiːz] Metathese, Metathesis *f*.
metazoan [metə'zəʊən] [1] *n* Metazoon *nt* (*spec*), Vielzeller *m*.
[2] *adj* vielzellig, metazoisch (*spec*).
mete [miːt] *vt*: **to ~ out** zuteil werden lassen (*to sb* jdm); *praise* austeilen; *rewards* verteilen; **to ~ out a punishment to sb** jdn bestrafen; **the function of the courts is to ~ out justice** es ist Aufgabe der Gerichte zu richten; **justice was ~d out to them** es wurde über sie gerichtet *or* Gericht gesessen.
metempsychosis [ˌmetəmsaɪ'kəʊsɪs] *n, pl* **metempsychoses** [ˌmetəmsaɪ'kəʊsiːz] Metempsychose *f*.
meteor ['miːtɪəʳ] *n* Meteor *m* ◆ ~ **shower** Meteorregen *m*.
meteoric [ˌmiːtɪ'ɒrɪk] *adj* meteorisch; (*fig*) kometenhaft.
meteorite ['miːtɪəraɪt] *n* Meteorit *m*.
meteoroid ['miːtɪərɔɪd] *n* Sternschnuppe *f*.
meteorological [ˌmiːtɪərə'lɒdʒɪkəl] *adj* Wetter-, meteorologisch ◆ **the M~ Office** (*Brit*) das Wetteramt.
meteorologist [ˌmiːtɪə'rɒlədʒɪst] *n* Meteorologe *m*, Meteorologin *f*.
meteorology [ˌmiːtɪə'rɒlədʒɪ] *n* Meteorologie, Wetterkunde *f*.
meter[1] ['miːtəʳ] [1] *n* Zähler *m*; (*gas ~ also*) Gasuhr *f*; (*water ~*) Wasseruhr *f*; (*parking ~*) Parkuhr *f*; (*exposure or light ~*) Belichtungsmesser *m*; (*slot ~*) Münzzähler *m* ◆ **the ~ has run out** die Parkuhr ist abgelaufen/es ist kein Geld mehr im Zähler.
[2] *vt* messen.
meter[2] *n* (*US*) *see* **metre.**
meter maid *n* (*inf*) Politesse *f*.
methane ['miːθeɪn] *n* Methan *nt*.
methinks [mɪ'θɪŋks] *pret* **methought** [mɪ'θɔːt] *vi impers* (*obs*) mich deucht (*obs*), mir *or* mich dünkt (*old*).
method ['meθəd] *n* Methode *f*; (*process*) Verfahren *nt*; (*Cook*) Zubereitung *f*; (*in experiment*) Vorgehens- *or* Verfahrensweise *f* ◆ **a man of ~** ein Mensch mit Methode; ~ **of payment/application** Zahlungs-/Anwendungsweise *f*; **there's ~ in his madness** sein Wahnsinn hat Methode; ~ **acting** *Schauspielen nt nach dem System Stanislawski*.
methodical *adj*, **~ly** *adv* [mɪ'θɒdɪkəl, -ɪ] methodisch.
Methodism ['meθədɪzəm] *n* Methodismus *m*.
Methodist ['meθədɪst] [1] *adj* methodistisch.
[2] *n* Methodist(in *f*) *m*.
methodology [ˌmeθə'dɒlədʒɪ] *n* Methodik, Methodologie *f*.
meths [meθs] *n sing abbr of* **methylated spirits** Spiritus *m* ◆ ~ **drinker** ≃ Fuseltrinker *m*.
Methuselah [mə'θuːzələ] *n* Methusalem *m* ◆ **as old as ~** so alt wie Methusalem.
methyl alcohol ['miːθaɪl'ælkəhɒl] *n* Methylalkohol *m*.
methylated spirits ['meθɪleɪtɪd'spɪrɪts] *n sing* Äthylalkohol, (Brenn)spiritus *m*.
meticulous [mɪ'tɪkjʊləs] *adj* sorgfältig, (peinlich) genau, exakt ◆ **to be ~ about sth** es mit etw sehr genau nehmen; **with ~ attention to detail** mit besonderer Sorgfalt für das Detail.
meticulously [mɪ'tɪkjʊləslɪ] *adv see adj* ◆ ~ **clean** peinlich sauber.
métier ['meɪtɪeɪ] *n* Metier *nt*.
Met Office ['metˌɒfɪs] *n* (*Brit*) Wetteramt *nt*.
metonymy [mə'tɒnɪmɪ] *n* Metonymie *f*.
metre, (*US*) **meter** ['miːtəʳ] *n* **(a)** (*Measure*) Meter *m or nt*. **(b)** (*Poet*) Metrum *nt*.
metric ['metrɪk] *adj* metrisch ◆ **the ~ system** das metrische Maßsystem; ~ **ton** Metertonne *f*; **to go ~** auf das metrische Maßsystem umstellen.
metrical ['metrɪkəl] *adj* (*Poet*) metrisch.
metrication [ˌmetrɪ'keɪʃən] *n* Umstellung *f* auf das metrische Maßsystem.
metronome ['metrənəʊm] *n* Metronom *nt*.
metropolis [mɪ'trɒpəlɪs] *n* Metropole, Weltstadt *f*; (*capital*) Hauptstadt *f*.
metropolitan [ˌmetrə'pɒlɪtən] [1] *adj* weltstädtisch, weltoffen; der Hauptstadt; (*Eccl*) Metropolitan-; *diocese* Erz-; *bishop* Diözesan- ◆ **a ~ city** eine Weltstadt; **M~ Police** Londoner/New Yorker Polizei.
[2] *n* Weltbürger(in *f*) *m*; (*citizen*) Großstädter(in *f*) *m*; Hauptstädter(in *f*) *m*; (*Eccl*) Metropolit *m*.
mettle ['metl] *n* (*spirit*) Courage *f*, Stehvermögen *nt*; (*of horse*) Zähigkeit *f*; (*temperament*) Feuer *nt* ◆ **a man of ~** ein Mann von echtem Schrot und Korn; **to show one's ~** zeigen, was in einem steckt; **to test sb's ~** herausfinden, was in jdm steckt; **to be on one's ~** auf dem Posten sein; **to put sb on his ~** jdn fordern.
mettlesome ['metlsəm] *adj person* couragiert, schneidig; *horse* feurig.
mew [mjuː] [1] *n* Miau(en) *nt*.
[2] *vi* miauen.
mewl [mjuːl] *vi* (*cat*) maunzen, mauzen; (*baby*) wimmern.
mews [mjuːz] *n sing or pl* (*houses*) *Siedlung f ehemaliger zu modischen Wohnungen umgebauter Kutscherhäuschen*; (*street*) Gasse *f*; (*old: stables*) Stall(ungen *pl*) *m* ◆ **a ~ cottage** ein ehemaliges Kutscherhäuschen.
Mexican ['meksɪkən] [1] *adj* mexikanisch.
[2] *n* Mexikaner(in *f*) *m*.
Mexico ['meksɪkəʊ] *n* Mexiko *nt* ◆ ~ **City** Mexiko City *nt*.
mezzanine ['mezəniːn] *n* Mezzanin *nt*.
mezzo-soprano [ˌmetsəʊsə'prɑːnəʊ] *n* Mezzosopran *m*.
mezzotint ['metsəʊˌtɪnt] *n* Mezzotint *nt*.
mfd *abbr of* **manufactured** hergest.
mg *abbr of* **milligram(s), milligramme(s)** mg.
MI *abbr of* **machine intelligence.**
MI5 (*Brit*) *abbr of* **Military Intelligence, section 5** *Spionageabwehrdienst m der britischen Regierung*.
MI6 (*Brit*) *abbr of* **Military Intelligence, section 6** *britischer Geheimdienst*.
miaow [miː'aʊ] [1] *n* Miau(en) *nt*.
[2] *vi* miauen.
miasma [mɪ'æzmə] *n, pl* **-ta** [mɪ'æzmətə] *or* **miasmas** [mɪ'æzməz] Miasma *nt*.
mica ['maɪkə] *n* Muskovit *m*.
mice [maɪs] *pl of* **mouse.**
Michaelmas ['mɪklməs] *n* Michaeli(s) *nt* ◆ ~ **daisy** Herbstaster *f*; ~ **Day** Michaelis(tag *m*) *nt*.
mickey ['mɪkɪ] *n* (*sl*): **to take the ~ (out of sb)** jdn auf den Arm *or* auf die Schippe nehmen (*inf*), jdn veräppeln (*inf*); **are you taking the ~?** du willst mich/ihn *etc* wohl veräppeln *etc* (*inf*).
Mickey Finn ['mɪkɪ'fɪn] *n* (*inf*) Betäubungsmittel *nt*; (*drink*) präparierter Drink ◆ **they slipped him a ~** sie haben ihm was in den Drink getan (*inf*).
Mickey Mouse [1] *n* Micky-Maus *f*.
[2] *adj attr* (*inf*) *company etc* lachhaft, Witz- (*inf*).
micro ['maɪkrəʊ] *n* (*Comput*) Mikro(computer) *m*.
micro- *pref* mikro-, Mikro-.
microbe ['maɪkrəʊb] *n* Mikrobe *f*.
micro: **~biology** *n* Mikrobiologie *f*; **~channel architecture** *n* (*Comput*) Microchannel-Architektur *f*; **~chip** *n* Mikrochip *nt*; **~circuit** *n* Mikroschaltung *f*; **~circuitry** *n* Mikroschaltung(saufbau *m*) *f*; **~computer** *n* Mikrorechner, Mikrocomputer *m*; **~cosm** *n* Mikrokosmos *m*; **~diskette** *n* Mikrofloppy, Mikrodiskette *f*; **~dot** *n* Mikrobild *nt*; **~economics** *n* Mikroökonomie *f*; **~electronics** *n* Mikroelektronik *f*; **~fiche** *n* Mikrofiche *m or nt*, Mikrokarte *f*; **~film** [1] *n* Mikrofilm *m*; [2] *vt* auf Mikrofilm aufnehmen; **~gravity** *n* (*Phys*) Mikrogravitation *f*; **~light** *n* Ultraleichtflugzeug *nt*; **~meter** [maɪ'krɒmɪtəʳ] *n* (*gauge*) Mikrometerschraube, Meßschraube *f*; **~metre,** (*US*) **~meter** *n* Mikrometer *m or nt*.
micron ['maɪkrɒn] *n* Mikron, Mikrometer *nt*.
micro: **~organism** *n* Mikroorganismus *m*; **~phone** *n* Mikrophon *nt*; **~processor** *n* Mikroprozessor *m*; **~scope** *n* Mikroskop *nt*.
microscopic [ˌmaɪkrə'skɒpɪk] *adj details, print* mikroskopisch ◆ ~ **creature** mikroskopisch kleines Lebewesen.
microscopically [ˌmaɪkrə'skɒpɪkəlɪ] *adv* mikroskopisch.
micro: **~second** *n* Mikrosekunde *f*; **~spacing** *n* (*Comput*) Feinausgleich *m*; **~structural** *adj* mikrostrukturell; **~surgery** *n* Mikrochirurgie *f*; **~surgical** *adj* mikrochirurgisch; **~transmitter** *n* Mikrosender *m*.

microwave ['maɪkrəʊ,weɪv] *n* Mikrowelle *f* ◆ **~ oven** Mikrowellenherd *m*.
micturate ['mɪktjʊreɪt] *vi* (*Med: urinate*) urinieren, harnen (*form*).
micturition [,mɪktjʊ'rɪʃən] *n* (*Med: urinating*) Urinieren *nt*, Miktion *f* (*spec*).
mid [mɪd] 1 *prep* (*poet*) *see* **amid(st)**.
2 *adj* mittel-, Mittel- ◆ **in ~ January/June** Mitte Januar/Juni; **in the ~ 1950s** Mitte der fünfziger Jahre; **in the ~ 20th century** Mitte des 20. Jahrhunderts; **temperatures in the ~ eighties** Temperaturen um 85° Fahrenheit; **in ~ morning/afternoon** am Vormittag/Nachmittag; **a ~-morning/-afternoon break** eine Frühstücks-/Nachmittagspause; **a ~-morning/-afternoon snack** ein zweites Frühstück/ein Imbiß *m* am Nachmittag; **~-Atlantic** *accent etc* anglo-amerikanisch; **in ~ channel** in der Mitte des Kanals; **in ~ ocean** mitten auf dem Meer; **in ~ air** in der Luft; **~-flight course corrections** Kurskorrekturen während des Flugs; **in ~ course** mittendrin (*inf*).
Midas ['maɪdəs] *n* Midas *m* ◆ **the ~ touch** eine glückliche Hand, Glück *nt*; **he has the ~ touch** er macht aus Dreck Geld (*inf*).
midday ['mɪd'deɪ] 1 *n* Mittag *m* ◆ **at ~** mittags, gegen Mittag, um die Mittagszeit.
2 *adj attr* mittäglich ◆ **~ meal** Mittagessen *nt*; **~ sun/heat** Mittagssonne/-hitze *f*.
midden ['mɪdn] *n* (*Archeol*) Muschelhaufen *m*; (*dial*) (*dustbin*) Mülleimer *m*; (*rubbish dump*) Müll *m*.
middle ['mɪdl] 1 *n* Mitte *f*; (*central section: of book, film etc*) Mittelteil *m*, mittlerer Teil; (*inside of fruit, nut etc*) Innere(s) *nt*; (*stomach*) Bauch, Leib *m*; (*waist*) Taille *f* ◆ **in the ~ of the table** mitten auf dem Tisch; (*in exact centre*) in der Mitte des Tisches; **he passed the ball to the ~ of the field** er spielte den Ball zur (Feld)mitte; **in the ~ of the night/morning** mitten in der Nacht/am Vormittag; **in the ~ of the day** mitten am Tag; (*around midday*) gegen Mittag; **in the ~ of nowhere** j.w.d. (*inf*), am Ende der Welt; **in the ~ of summer/winter** mitten im Sommer/Winter; (*height of summer season*) im Hochsommer; **in** *or* **about the ~ of May** Mitte Mai; **in the ~ of the century** um die Jahrhundertmitte, Mitte des Jahrhunderts; **we were in the ~ of lunch** wir waren mitten beim Essen; **in the ~ of my back** im Kreuz; **to be in the ~ of doing sth** mitten dabei sein, etw zu tun; **I'm in the ~ of reading it** ich bin mittendrin; **down the ~** in der Mitte; **he parts/she parted his hair down the ~** er hat einen Mittelscheitel/sie scheitelte sein Haar in der Mitte.
2 *adj* mittlere(r, s); *part, point, finger* Mittel- ◆ **the ~ house** das mittlere Haus, das Haus in der Mitte.
middle *in cpds* Mittel-, mittel-; **~ age** *n* mittleres Lebensalter; **~-aged** *adj* in den mittleren Jahren, mittleren Alters; *feeling, appearance* alt; *attitudes* spießig (*pej*), altmodisch; **M~ Ages** *npl* Mittelalter *nt*; **M~ America** *n* (a) (*Geog*) Mittelamerika *nt*; (b) (*class*) die amerikanische Mittelschicht; **~brow** 1 *adj* für den (geistigen) Normalverbraucher; *tastes* Durchschnitts-, des Normalverbrauchers; 2 *n* (geistiger) Normalverbraucher; **~ C** *n* (eingestrichenes) C; **~-class** *adj* bürgerlich, spießig (*pej*); (*Sociol*) Mittelstands-, mittelständisch; **he's so typically ~-class** er ist ein typischer Vertreter der Mittelklasse, er ist ein richtiger Spießer (*pej*); **~ class(es)** *n* Mittelstand *m or* -schicht *f*; **~ distance** *n* mittlere Entfernung; (*Art*) Mittelgrund *m*; **~ distance runner** *n* Mittelstreckenläufer *m*; **~ distance running** *n* Mittelstreckenlauf *m*; **~ distance running is ...** der Mittelstreckenlauf ist ...; **~ ear** *n* Mittelohr *nt*; **M~ East** *n* Naher Osten; **M~ England** *n* (*fig: middle classes*) die englische Mittelschicht; **M~ English** *n* Mittelenglisch *nt*; **M~ High German** *n* Mittelhochdeutsch *nt*; **M~ Low German** *n* Mittelniederdeutsch *nt*; **~man** *n* Mittelsmann *m*; (*Comm*) Zwischenhändler *m*; **~ management** *n* mittlere(s) Management; **~ name** *n* zweiter (Vor)name; **modesty is my ~ name** (*fig*) ich bin die Bescheidenheit in Person; **~-of-the-road** *adj* gemäßigt; *policy, politician* der gemäßigten Mitte; **~-of-the-roader** *n* Vertreter(in *f*) *m* der gemäßigten Mitte; **~ watch** *n* Mittelwache *f*; **~weight** (*Sport*) 1 *n* Mittelgewicht *nt*; (*person also*) Mittelgewichtler *m*; 2 *adj* Mittelgewichts-; **~weight champion** Meister *m* im Mittelgewicht.
middling ['mɪdlɪŋ] 1 *adj* mittelmäßig; (*of size*) mittlere(r, s) ◆ **how are you? — ~** wie geht es dir? — einigermaßen; **what was the weather like? — ~** wie war das Wetter? — so lala (*inf*) *or* durchwachsen.
2 *adv* (*inf: fairly*) **~ good** mittelprächtig (*inf*).
Middx *abbr of* **Middlesex**.
midfield [,mɪd'fi:ld] 1 *n* Mittelfeld *nt*.
2 *adj player* Mittelfeld-.
midge [mɪdʒ] *n* Mücke *f*.
midget ['mɪdʒɪt] 1 *n* kleiner Mensch, Liliputaner *m*; (*child*) Knirps *m*.
2 *adj* winzig; *submarine* Kleinst-.
midi (system) ['mɪdɪ(,sɪstəm)] *n* Midi-System *nt or* -Anlage *f*.
mid: ~land 1 *adj attr* im Landesinneren (gelegen); 2 *n* Landesinnere(s) *nt*; **the M~lands** die Midlands; **~life crisis** *n* Midlife-crisis *f*, Krise *f* in der Mitte des Lebens; **he's having his ~life crisis** er befindet sich in der Midlife-crisis; **~night** 1 *n* Mitternacht *f*; **at ~night** um Mitternacht; 2 *adj attr* mitternächtlich; *walk also, feast, hour* Mitternachts-; **the ~night sun** die Mitternachtssonne; **~point** *n* mittlerer Punkt; (*Geom*) Mittelpunkt *m*; **to reach ~point** die Hälfte hinter sich (*dat*) haben.
midriff ['mɪdrɪf] *n* Taille *f* ◆ **a punch to the ~** ein Schlag in die Magengegend *or* -grube.
mid: ~shipman *n* Fähnrich *m* zur See; **~ships** *adv* mittschiffs.
midst [mɪdst] 1 *n* Mitte *f* ◆ **in the ~ of** mitten in; **in the ~ of her tears** unter Tränen; **and in the ~ of our troubles Grandpa died** und zu allem Unglück starb noch Großvater; **in our ~** unter uns, in unserer Mitte (*geh*).
2 *prep* (*old poet*) *see* **amid(st)**.
mid: ~stream *n* **in ~stream** (*lit*) in der Mitte des Flusses; (*fig*) auf halber Strecke, mittendrin; **~summer** 1 *n* Hochsommer *m*; **M~summer's Day** Sommersonnenwende *f*, Johanni(stag *m*) *nt*; 2 *adj days, nights* Hochsommer-; **"A M~summer Night's Dream"** „Ein Sommernachtstraum"; **~summer madness** Sommerkoller *m* (*inf*); **that was ~summer madness** das war eine Schnapsidee (*inf*); **~-term** 1 *n* **in ~-term** mitten im Trimester/Schulhalbjahr; **by ~-term** bis zur Trimesterhälfte/bis zur Mitte des Schulhalbjahres; **it was ~-term before ...** das halbe Trimester/Schulhalbjahr war schon vorbei, bevor ...; 2 *adj* **~-term elections** (*Pol*) Zwischenwahlen *pl*; **~-term examinations** *Prüfungen in der Mitte eines Trimesters/Schulhalbjahres*; **~way** 1 *adv* auf halbem Weg; **~way through sth** mitten in etw (*dat*); **we are now ~way** die Hälfte haben wir hinter uns (*dat*); 2 *adj* **X is the ~way point between A and B** X liegt auf halbem Wege zwischen A und B; **we've now reached the ~way point/stage in the project** das Projekt ist jetzt zur Hälfte fertig; 3 *n* (*US: at fair*) *Mittelweg m eines Jahrmarkts, an dem sich die Hauptattraktionen befinden*; **~week** 1 *adv* mitten in der Woche; **by ~week** Mitte der Woche; 2 *adj attr* Mitte der Woche; **he booked a ~week flight** er buchte einen Flug für Mitte der Woche; **M~west** *n* Mittelwesten *m*; **M~western** *adj* mittelwestlich; *songs, dialect etc also* des Mittelwestens.
midwife ['mɪdwaɪf] *n, pl* **-wives** Hebamme *f*.
midwifery [,mɪd'wɪfərɪ] *n* Geburtshilfe *f*.
midwinter [,mɪd'wɪntə^r] 1 *n* Mitte *f* des Winters, Wintermitte *f*.
2 *adj* um die Mitte des Winters, mittwinterlich.
midwives ['mɪdwaɪvz] *pl of* **midwife**.
mien [mi:n] *n* (*liter*) Miene *f*.
miff [mɪf] *vt* (*inf*) **to be ~ed at sth** (*annoyed*) über etw (*acc*) verärgert sein; (*offended*) sich wegen etw auf den Schlips getreten fühlen (*inf*); **to get ~ed at sth** sich über etw (*acc*) erhitzen.
➤ **might**[1] [maɪt] *pret of* **may** ◆ **they ~ be brothers, they look so alike** sie könnten Brüder sein, sie sehen sich so ähnlich; **as you ~ expect** wie zu erwarten war; **how old ~ he be?** wie alt er wohl ist?; **~ I smoke?** dürfte ich wohl rauchen?; **you ~ try Smith's** Sie könnten es ja mal bei Smiths versuchen; **he ~ at least have apologized** er hätte sich wenigstens entschuldigen können; **she was thinking of what ~ have been** sie dachte an das, was hätte sein können.
might[2] *n* Macht *f* ◆ **with ~ and main** mit aller Macht; **with all one's ~** mit aller Kraft; **superior ~** Übermacht, Überlegenheit *f*; **~ is right** (*Prov*) Macht geht vor Recht (*Prov*).
mightily ['maɪtɪlɪ] *adv* (a) mit aller Macht; (*fig: majestically, imposingly*) gewaltig. (b) (*inf: extremely*) mächtig (*inf*) ◆ **a ~ improved team** eine stark verbesserte Mannschaft.
mightiness ['maɪtɪnɪs] *n* Macht *f*; (*of wave, shout, scream*) Gewalt *f*; (*of warrior, noise, cheer*) Stärke *f*; (*of ship, tree etc*) gewaltige Ausmaße *pl*.
mightn't ['maɪtnt] *contr of* **might not**.
mighty ['maɪtɪ] 1 *adj* (*+er*) gewaltig; (*wielding power*) mächtig; *warrior* stark.
2 *adv* (*inf*) mächtig (*inf*).
mignonette [,mɪnjə'net] *n* Reseda, Resede *f*.
migraine ['mi:greɪn] *n* Migräne *f*.
migrant ['maɪgrənt] 1 *adj* Wander- ◆ **~ bird** Zugvogel *m*; **~ worker** Wanderarbeiter *m*; (*esp in EC*) Gastarbeiter *m*.
2 *n* Zugvogel *m*; Wanderarbeiter *m*; Gastarbeiter *m*.
migrate [maɪ'greɪt] *vi* (*animals, workers*) (ab)wandern; (*birds*) nach Süden ziehen; (*fig: townsfolk etc*) ziehen ◆ **do these birds ~?** sind das Zugvögel?
migration [maɪ'greɪʃən] *n* (a) Wanderung *f*; (*of birds also*) (Vogel)zug *m*; (*fig: of people*) Abwanderung *f*; (*seasonal*) Zug *m*. (b) (*number*) Schwarm *m*.
migratory [maɪ'greɪtərɪ] *adj life* Wander- ◆ **~ birds** Zugvögel; **~ instinct** Wandertrieb *m*; **~ worker** Wanderarbeiter *m*; **~ creatures** Tiere, die auf Wanderung gehen.
mike [maɪk] *n* (*inf*) Mikro (*inf*), Mikrophon *nt*.
Mike [maɪk] *n dim of* **Michael** ◆ **for the love of ~!** (*inf*) um Himmels willen (*inf*).
milady [mɪ'leɪdɪ] *n* Mylady *f*, gnädige Frau.
milage *n see* **mileage**.
Milan [mɪ'læn] *n* Mailand *nt*.
mild [maɪld] 1 *adj* (*+er*) (a) (*gentle*) *climate, weather, punishment, spring day* mild; *breeze, criticism, rebuke* leicht, sanft; *medicine* leicht; *person, character* sanft ◆ **a detergent which is ~ to your hands** ein Waschmittel, das Ihre Hände schont.
(b) (*in flavour*) *taste, cigar, cheese* mild; *cigarettes also, whisky* leicht ◆ **this cheese has a very ~ taste** der Käse ist sehr mild (im Geschmack); **~ ale** leichtes dunkles Bier.
(c) (*slight*) leicht.
2 *n* (*beer*) leichtes dunkles Bier.
mildew ['mɪldju:] 1 *n* Schimmel *m*; (*on plants*) Mehltau *m*.
2 *vi* verschimmeln, Schimmel ansetzen; (*plants*) von Mehltau befallen sein ◆ **they are all ~ed with age** sie sind im Laufe der Jahre ganz verschimmelt.
mildewy ['mɪldju:ɪ] *adj* schimmelig, verschimmelt; *plants* von Mehltau befallen ◆ **to get ~** schimmelig werden, verschimmeln.
mildly ['maɪldlɪ] *adv* leicht; *scold, say* sanft; *scold, rebuke* milde ◆ **to put it ~** gelinde gesagt; **... and that's putting it ~** ... und das ist noch milde ausgedrückt; **they seemed ~ interested** sie machten einen leicht interessierten Eindruck.
mildness ['maɪldnɪs] *n see adj* (a) Milde *f*; Sanftheit *f*; Leichtigkeit *f*; Sanftmütigkeit *f*. (b) Milde *f*; Leichtigkeit *f*.
mile [maɪl] *n* Meile *f* ◆ **how many ~s per gallon does your car do?** wieviel ver-

➤ LANGUAGE IN USE: **might**[1] → 15.2, 15.3

braucht Ihr Auto?; **a fifty-~ journey** eine Fahrt von fünfzig Meilen; **~s (and ~s)** (*inf*) meilenweit; **~ upon ~ of yellow beaches** meilenweite Sandstrände *pl*; **they live ~s away** sie wohnen meilenweit weg; **you can tell it a ~ off/it stands** *or* **sticks out a ~** das sieht ja ein Blinder (mit Krückstock) (*inf*); **it smelled for ~s around** das roch 10 Kilometer gegen den Wind (*inf*); **you were ~s off the target** du hast meilenweit danebengetroffen; **he's ~s better at tennis than she is** er spielt hundertmal besser Tennis als sie (*inf*); **not a hundred ~s from here** (*fig*) in nächster Nähe, gar nicht weit weg.

mileage ['maılıdʒ] *n* Meilen *pl*; (*on odometer*) Meilenstand *m*, Meilenzahl *f* ◆ **what ~ did you do yesterday?** wie viele Meilen seid ihr gestern gefahren?; **~ per gallon** Benzinverbrauch *m*; **you get a much better ~ (per gallon) from this car if ...** dieser Wagen ist viel sparsamer im Verbrauch, wenn ...; **~ allowance** ≃ Kilometerpauschale *f*; **~ recorder** Meilenzähler, ≃ Kilometerzähler *m*; **we got a lot of ~ out of it** (*fig inf*) das war uns (*dat*) sehr dienlich; **it's still got a lot of ~ left in it** (*fig inf*) da steckt noch einiges drin (*inf*).

mileometer [maı'lɒmıtəʳ] *n* ≃ Kilometerzähler *m*.

milepost ['maılpəʊst] *n* Meilenanzeiger *or* -pfosten *m*.

miler ['maıləʳ] *n* 1500-Meter-Läufer(in *f*) *m*.

milestone ['maılstəʊn] *n* (*lit, fig*) Meilenstein *m*.

milieu ['mi:ljɜ:] *n* Milieu *nt*.

militant ['mılıtənt] 1 *adj* militant.
2 *n* militantes Mitglied/militanter Student/Gewerkschaftler/Politiker ◆ **the ~s among the trade unionists** die militanten Gewerkschaftler.

militarily ['mılıtrılı] *adv* militärisch (gesehen), auf militärischem Gebiet.

militarism ['mılıtərızəm] *n* Militarismus *m*.

militarist ['mılıtərıst] 1 *adj* militaristisch.
2 *n* Militarist *m*.

militaristic [,mılıtə'rıstık] *adj* militaristisch.

militarize ['mılıtəraız] *vt* militarisieren ◆ **fully ~d** hochmilitarisiert.

military ['mılıtərı] 1 *adj* militärisch; *government, band* Militär- ◆ **~ police** Militärpolizei *f*; **~ service** Militärdienst, Wehrdienst *m*; **to do one's ~ service** seinen Wehr- *or* Militärdienst ableisten *or* machen (*inf*); **he's doing his ~ service** er ist gerade beim Militär *or* (*BRD inf*) Bund; **the top ~ men** die führenden Militärs; **the ~-industrial complex** (*US*) der militärisch-industrielle Komplex.
2 *n*: **the ~** das Militär.

militate ['mılıteıt] *vi* **to ~ against/in favour of sth** für/gegen etw sprechen.

militia [mı'lıʃə] *n* Miliz, Bürgerwehr *f*.

militiaman [mı'lıʃəmən] *n, pl* **-men** [-mən] Milizsoldat *m*.

milk [mılk] 1 *n* Milch *f* ◆ **~ of magnesia** Magnesiamilch *f*; **the land of** *or* **flowing with ~ and honey** das Land, wo Milch und Honig fließt; **the ~ of human kindness** die Milch der frommen Denk(ungs)art (*liter*); **she was not exactly flowing over with the ~ of human kindness** sie strömte nicht gerade über vor Freundlichkeit; **it's** *or* **there's no use crying over spilt ~** (*prov*) was passiert ist, ist passiert.
2 *vt* (*lit, fig*) melken ◆ **the little old lady was ~ed dry by some heartless swindler** die alte Frau wurde von einem gewissenlosen Betrüger nach Strich und Faden ausgenommen (*inf*).
3 *vi* Milch geben, milchen (*dial*).

milk *in cpds* Milch-; **~-and-water** *adj* (*fig*) seicht, verwässert; **~ bar** *n* Milchbar *f*; **~ chocolate** *n* Vollmilchschokolade *f*; **~ churn** *n* Milchkanne *f*; **~ float** *n* Milchauto *nt*.

milkiness ['mılkınıs] *n* Milchigkeit *f*.

milking ['mılkıŋ] *n* Melken *nt* ◆ **~ machine** Melkmaschine *f*; **~ stool** Melkschemel *m*.

milk: ~maid *n* Milchmädchen *nt*; **~man** *n* Milchmann *m*; **~ product** *n* Milchprodukt *nt*; **~ pudding** *n* Milchspeise *f*; **~ run** *n* (*Aviat inf*) Routineflug *m*; **~shake** *n* Milchmixgetränk *nt*, Milchshake *m*; **~sop** *n* Milchbart *m*, Milchgesicht *nt*; **~ tooth** *n* Milchzahn *m*; **~weed** *n* (*US*) Schwalbenwurzgewächs *nt*; **~-white** *adj* milchig-weiß, milchweiß.

milky ['mılkı] *adj* (*+er*) milchig ◆ **~ coffee** Milchkaffee *m*; **rich ~ chocolate** sahnige Vollmilchschokolade.

Milky Way [,mılkı'weı] *n* Milchstraße *f*.

mill [mıl] 1 *n* **(a)** (*building*) Mühle *f*.
(b) (*machine*) Mühle *f* ◆ **the poor man really went through the ~** (*inf*) der Arme hat wirklich viel durchmachen müssen; (*was questioned hard*) der Arme wurde wirklich durch die Mangel gedreht (*inf*); **in training you're really put through the ~** (*inf*) im Training wird man ganz schön hart rangenommen (*inf*).
(c) (*paper, steel ~ etc*) Fabrik *f*; (*cotton ~*) (*for thread*) Spinnerei *f*; (*for cloth*) Weberei *f* ◆ **saw ~** Sägemühle *f or* -werk *nt*.
2 *vt flour, coffee etc* mahlen; *metal, paper* walzen; (*with milling machine*) *metal* fräsen; *coin* rändeln.

◆**mill about** *or* **around** *vi* umherlaufen ◆ **people were ~ing ~ the office** es herrschte ein Kommen und Gehen im Büro; **the crowds ~ing ~ the stalls in the market place** die Menschenmenge, die sich zwischen den Marktständen einherschob.

milled [mıld] *adj grain* gemahlen; *coin, edge* gerändelt.

millenarian [mılı'nɛərıən] *adj* (*Rel*) millenaristisch, chiliastisch.

millennial [mı'lenıəl] *adj* tausendjährig.

millennium [mı'lenıəm] *n, pl* **-s** *or* **millennia** [mı'lenıə] (*1,000 years*) Jahrtausend, Millennium *nt*; (*state of perfection*) Tausendjähriges Reich, Millennium *nt*.

Millennium Fund *n* (*Brit*) *Fonds m für die Finanzierung von Projekten zur Feier der Jahrtausendwende.*

millepede ['mılıpi:d] *n see* **millipede.**

miller ['mıləʳ] *n* Müller *m*.

millet ['mılıt] *n* Hirse *f*.

milli- ['mılı-] *pref* Milli-.

milliard ['mılıɑ:d] *n* (*Brit*) Milliarde *f*.

milli: ~bar *n* Millibar *nt*; **~gram(me)** *n* Milligramm *nt*; **~litre,** (*US*) **~liter** *n* Milliliter *m or nt*; **~metre,** (*US*) **~meter** *n* Millimeter *m or nt*.

milliner ['mılınəʳ] *n* Hutmacher *m*, Hut- *or* Putzmacherin, Modistin *f* ◆ **at the ~'s (shop)** im Hutgeschäft *or* -laden.

millinery ['mılınərı] *n* (*trade*) Hut- *or* Putzmacherhandwerk *nt*; (*articles*) Hüte *pl*.

milling machine ['mılıŋmə,ʃi:n] *n* (*for coins*) Rändel(eisen) *nt*; (*for metal*) Fräse, Fräsmaschine *f*.

million ['mıljən] *n* Million *f* ◆ **4 ~ people** 4 Millionen Menschen; **for ~s and ~s of years** für Millionen und aber Millionen von Jahren; **the starving ~s** die Millionen, die Hunger leiden; **she's one in a ~** (*inf*) so jemanden wie sie findet man sobald nicht wieder, sie ist einsame Klasse (*sl*); **it will sell a ~** (*inf*) das wird ein Millionenerfolg; **I've done it ~s of times** (*inf*) das habe ich schon tausendmal gemacht; **to feel like a ~ dollars** (*inf*) sich pudelwohl fühlen.

millionaire [,mıljə'nɛəʳ] *n* Millionär *m*.

millionairess [,mıljə'nɛəres] *n* Millionärin *f*.

millionth ['mıljənθ] 1 *adj* (*fraction*) millionstel; (*in series*) millionste(r, s).
2 *n* Millionstel *nt*.

millipede ['mılıpi:d] *n* Tausendfüßler *m*.

mill: ~pond *n* Mühlteich *m*; **~race** *n* Mühlbach *or* -graben *m*; **~stone** *n* Mühlstein, Mahlstein *m*; **she's/it's a ~stone round his neck** sie/das ist für ihn ein Klotz am Bein; **~stream** *n* Mühlbach *m*; **~wheel** *n* Mühlrad *nt*.

milord [mı'lɔ:d] *n* (*person*) Mylord, Lord *m*; (*as address*) Mylord *m* ◆ **like some English ~** wie ein englischer Lord.

milt [mılt] *n* (*Fishing*) Milch *f*.

mime [maım] 1 *n* (*acting*) Pantomime *f*; (*actor*) Pantomime *m*; (*ancient play, actor*) Mimus *m* ◆ **the art of ~** die Pantomimik, die Kunst der Pantomime; **to do a ~** eine Pantomime darstellen.
2 *vt* pantomimisch darstellen.
3 *vi* Pantomimen spielen.

mimeograph ['mımıəgrɑ:f] 1 *n* Vervielfältigungsapparat *m*.
2 *vt* vervielfältigen, abziehen (*inf*).

mimic ['mımık] 1 *n* Imitator *m* ◆ **he's a very good ~** er kann sehr gut Geräusche/andere Leute nachahmen *or* -machen.
2 *vt* nachahmen *or* -machen; (*ridicule*) nachäffen.

mimicry ['mımıkrı] *n* Nachahmung *f*; (*Biol*) Mimikry *f* ◆ **protective ~** Schutzfärbung, Tarnfarbe *f*; **his talent for ~** sein Talent dafür, andere nachzuahmen.

mimosa [mı'məʊzə] *n* Mimose *f*.

Min *abbr of* **Minister** Min; **Ministry** Min.

min *abbr of* **minute(s)** min; **minimum** min.

minaret [,mınə'ret] *n* Minarett *nt*.

mince [mıns] 1 *n* (*Brit*) Hackfleisch, Gehackte(s) *nt*.
2 *vt meat* hacken, durch den Fleischwolf drehen ◆ **he doesn't ~ his words** er nimmt kein Blatt vor den Mund; **not to ~ matters ...** um es mal ganz deutlich *or* brutal (*inf*) zu sagen ...
3 *vi* (*walk*) tänzeln, trippeln, scharwenzeln; (*behave/speak*) sich geziert benehmen/ausdrücken.

mince: ~meat *n süße Gebäckfüllung aus Dörrobst und Sirup*; **to make ~meat of sb** (*inf*) (*physically*) Hackfleisch aus jdm machen (*inf*); (*verbally*) jdn zur Schnecke machen (*inf*); **to make ~meat of sth** (*inf*) keinen guten Faden an etw (*dat*) lassen; **~ pie** *n mit Mincemeat gefülltes Gebäck.*

mincer ['mınsəʳ] *n* Fleischwolf *m*.

mincing ['mınsıŋ] *adj* geziert; *steps* tänzelnd, trippelnd.

▼ **mind** [maınd] 1 *n* **(a)** (*intellect*) Geist (*also Philos*), Verstand *m* ◆ **things of the ~** Geistiges; **a phenomenon of ~ over matter** ein Phänomen des willentlichen Einflusses auf die Materie; **it's a question of ~ over matter** es ist eine Willenssache *or* -frage; **a triumph of ~ over matter** ein Triumph des Geistes *or* Willens über den Körper; **the conscious and unconscious ~** das Bewußte und das Unbewußte; **it's all in the ~** das ist alles Einbildung; **in one's ~'s eye** vor seinem geistigen Auge, im Geiste; **to blow sb's ~** (*sl*) jdn umwerfen (*inf*); (*drugs*) jdn high machen (*sl*); *see* **close², cross¹, improve, open, boggle.**
(b) (*person*) Geist *m* ◆ **one of the finest ~s of our times** einer der großen Geister unserer Zeit; *see* **great, two.**
(c) (*type of ~*) Geist, Kopf *m*; (*way of thinking*) Denkweise *f* ◆ **to have a good ~** ein heller Kopf sein; **he has that kind of ~** er ist so veranlagt; **to have a literary/logical** *etc* **~** literarisch/logisch *etc* veranlagt sein; **to the child's/Victorian ~** in der Denkweise des Kindes/der viktorianischen Zeit; **the female ~** was im Kopf von Frauen vorgeht; **the public ~** das Empfinden der Öffentlichkeit; **state** *or* **frame of ~** (seelische) Verfassung, (Geistes)zustand *m*.
(d) (*thoughts*) Gedanken *pl* ◆ **to be clear in one's ~ about sth** sich (*dat*) über etw im klaren sein; **he had something on his ~** ihn beschäftigte etwas; **you are always on my ~** ich denke ständig an dich; **to put** *or* **set** *or* **give one's ~ to sth** (*try to do*) sich anstrengen, etw zu tun; (*think about sth*) sich auf etw (*acc*) konzentrieren; **if you put** *or* **set your ~ to it** wenn du dich anstrengst; **keep your ~ on the job** bleib mit den Gedanken *or* dem Kopf bei der Arbeit; **she**

couldn't get *or* **put the song/him out of her ~** das Lied/er ging ihr nicht aus dem Kopf; **you can put that idea out of your ~!** den Gedanken kannst du dir aus dem Kopf schlagen!; **to take sb's ~ off things/sth** jdn auf andere Gedanken bringen/jdn etw vergessen lassen; **don't let your ~ dwell on the problem** grüble nicht über dieses Problem nach; **he can't keep his ~ off sex** er denkt nur an Sex *or* an nichts anderes als Sex; **the idea never entered my ~** daran hatte/hätte ich überhaupt nicht gedacht; **it's been going through my ~** es ging mir im Kopf herum.

(e) (*memory*) Gedächtnis *nt* ♦ **to bear** *or* **keep sth in ~** etw nicht vergessen; *facts also, application* etw im Auge behalten; **to bear** *or* **keep sb in ~** an jdn denken; *applicant also* jdn im Auge behalten; **it went right out of my ~** daran habe ich überhaupt nicht mehr gedacht; **that quite put it out of my ~** dadurch habe ich es vergessen; **to bring** *or* **call sth to ~** etw in Erinnerung rufen, an etw (*acc*) erinnern; **it puts me in ~ of sb/sth** es weckt in mir Erinnerungen an jdn/etw; *see* **sight, slip.**

(f) (*inclination*) Lust *f*; (*intention*) Sinn *m*, Absicht *f* ♦ **to have sb/sth in ~** an jdn/etw denken; **to have in ~ to do sth** vorhaben *or* im Sinn haben, etw zu tun; **to have it in ~ to do sth** beabsichtigen *or* sich (*dat*) vorgenommen haben, etw zu tun; **I've half a ~/a good ~ to ...** ich hätte Lust/große *or* gute Lust, zu ...; **to be of a ~ to do sth** geneigt sein, etw zu tun (*geh*); **nothing was further from my ~** nichts lag mir ferner; **his ~ is set on that** er hat sich (*dat*) das in den Kopf gesetzt; **he guessed what was in my ~** er erriet meine Gedanken; *see* **read[1]**.

▼ **(g)** (*opinion*) Meinung, Ansicht *f* ♦ **to change one's ~** seine Meinung ändern (*about* über +*acc*), es sich (*dat*) anders überlegen; **to be in two ~s about sth** sich (*dat*) über etw (*acc*) nicht im klaren sein; **to be of one** *or* **the same ~** eines Sinnes (*geh*) *or* gleicher Meinung sein; **I'm of the same ~ as you** ich denke wie du, ich bin deiner Meinung; **with one ~** wie ein Mann; **to my ~ he's wrong** meiner Ansicht nach *or* nach meiner Meinung irrt er sich; **to have a ~ of one's own** (*person*) (*think for oneself*) eine eigene Meinung haben; (*not conform*) seinen eigenen Kopf haben; (*hum: machine etc*) seine Mucken haben (*inf*); *see* **know, make up, piece, speak.**

(h) (*sanity*) Verstand *m*, Sinne *pl* ♦ **his ~ is wandering** er ist nicht ganz klar im Kopf; **to go out of** *or* **lose one's ~** verrückt werden, den Verstand verlieren; **to drive sb out of his ~** jdn um den Verstand bringen, jdn wahnsinnig machen; **to be out of one's ~** verrückt *or* nicht bei Verstand sein; (*with worry etc*) ganz *or* völlig aus dem Häuschen sein (*inf*); **nobody in his right ~** kein normaler Mensch; **while the balance of his ~ was disturbed** (*Jur*) wegen Verlusts des seelischen Gleichgewichts.

[2] *vt* **(a)** (*look after*) aufpassen auf (+*acc*); *sb's chair, seat* freihalten ♦ **I'm ~ing the shop** (*fig*) ich sehe nach dem Rechten.

(b) (*be careful of*) aufpassen (auf +*acc*); (*pay attention to*) achten auf (+*acc*); (*act in accordance with*) beachten ♦ **~ what you're doing!** paß (doch) auf!; **~ what you're doing with that car** paß auf das Auto auf; **~ what I say!** laß dir das gesagt sein; (*do as I tell you*) hör auf das, was ich dir sage; **~ your language!** drück dich anständig aus!; **~ the step!** Vorsicht Stufe!; **~ your head!** Kopf einziehen (*inf*), Vorsicht! niedrige Tür/Decke *etc*; **~ your feet!** (*when sitting*) zieh die Füße ein!; (*when moving*) paß auf, wo du hintrittst!; **~ your own business** kümmern Sie sich um Ihre eigenen Angelegenheiten; **~ you do it!** sieh zu, daß du das tust.

(c) (*care, worry about*) sich kümmern um; (*object to*) etwas haben gegen ♦ **she ~s/doesn't ~ it** es macht ihr etwas/nichts aus; (*is/is not bothered, annoyed by*) es stört sie/stört sie nicht; (*is not/is indifferent to*) es ist ihr nicht egal/ist ihr egal; **I don't ~ the cold** die Kälte macht mir nichts aus; **I don't ~ what he does** es ist mir egal, was er macht; **I don't ~ four but six is too many** ich habe nichts gegen vier, aber sechs sind zuviel; **do you ~ coming with me?** würde es dir etwas ausmachen mitzukommen?; **would you ~ opening the door?** wären Sie so freundlich, die Tür aufzumachen?; **do you ~ my smoking?** macht es Ihnen etwas aus *or* stört es Sie *or* haben Sie etwas dagegen, wenn ich rauche?; **I hope you don't ~ my asking you/sitting here** ich hoffe, Sie nehmen es mir nicht übel, wenn ich frage/ich hoffe, Sie haben nichts dagegen, daß ich hier sitze; **never ~ the expense** (es ist) egal, was es kostet; **never ~ that now** das ist jetzt nicht wichtig, laß das doch jetzt; **never ~ him** kümmere dich *or* achte nicht auf ihn; **never ~ your back, I'm worried about ...** dein Rücken ist mir doch egal, ich mache mir Sorgen um ...; **don't ~ me** laß dich (durch mich) nicht stören; (*iro*) nimm auf mich keine Rücksicht; **I wouldn't ~ a cup of tea** ich hätte nichts gegen eine Tasse Tee.

[3] *vi* **(a)** (*be careful*) aufpassen ♦ **~ and see if ...** sieh zu, ob ...; **~ you get that done** sieh zu, daß du das fertigbekommst.

(b) ~ you allerdings; **~ you, I'd rather not go** ich würde eigentlich *or* allerdings lieber nicht gehen; **it was raining at the time, ~ you** allerdings hat es da geregnet; **~ you, he did try/ask** er hat es immerhin versucht/hat immerhin gefragt; **he's quite good, ~ you** er ist eigentlich ganz gut; **I'm not saying I'll do it, ~** ich will damit aber nicht sagen, daß ich es tue; **he's not a bad lad, ~, just ...** er ist eigentlich kein schlechter Junge, nur ...; **he didn't do it, ~** er hat es (ja) nicht getan.

▼ **(c)** (*care, worry*) sich kümmern, sich (*dat*) etwas daraus machen; (*object*) etwas dagegen haben ♦ **he doesn't seem to ~ about anything** ihn scheint nichts zu kümmern; **I wish he ~ed a little** ich wünschte, es würde ihm etwas ausmachen *or* ihn ein bißchen kümmern; **nobody seemed to ~** es schien keinem etwas auszumachen, niemand schien etwas dagegen zu haben; **do you ~?** macht es Ihnen etwas aus?; **do you ~!** (*iro*) na hör mal!, ich möchte doch sehr bitten!; **do you ~ if I open** *or* **would you ~ if I opened the window?** macht es Ihnen etwas aus, wenn ich das Fenster öffne?; **I don't ~ if I do** ich hätte nichts dagegen; **never you ~!** kümmere du dich mal nicht darum; (*none of your business*) das geht dich überhaupt nichts an!

(d) never ~ macht nichts, ist doch egal; (*in exasperation*) ist ja auch egal, schon gut; **never ~, you'll find another** mach dir nichts draus, du findest bestimmt einen anderen; **I've hurt my knee — never ~, I'll kiss it better** ich habe mir das Knie weh getan — ist nicht so schlimm, ich werde blasen; **oh, never ~, I'll do it myself** ach, laß (es) *or* schon gut, ich mache es selbst; **never ~ about that now!** laß das doch jetzt!, das ist doch nicht wichtig; **never ~ about what you said to him, what did he say to you?** es ist doch egal *or* unwichtig, was du zu ihm gesagt hast, was hat er zu dir gesagt?; **never ~ about that mistake** mach dir nichts aus dem Fehler; **never ~ about your back** (*in exasperation*) dein Rücken ist mir doch egal.

♦**mind out** *vi* aufpassen (*for* auf +*acc*) ♦ **~ ~!** paß (doch) auf!

mind: ~-bending, ~-blowing *adj* (*sl*) irre (*sl*); **~-boggling** *adj* (*inf*) irrsinnig (*inf*), verrückt (*inf*).

minded ['maɪndɪd] *adj* gesonnen (*geh*), gewillt ♦ **if you are so ~** wenn Ihnen der Sinn danach steht (*geh*).

-minded *adj suf* **romantically-~** romantisch veranlagt; **nasty-~** übel gesinnt; **an industrially-~ nation** ein auf Industrie ausgerichtetes Land; **I'm not really opera-~** ich mache mir nichts aus Opern (*inf*).

minder ['maɪndəʳ] *n* (*inf*) Aufpasser(in *f*) *m*.

mind-expanding ['maɪndiks,pændɪŋ] *adj* bewußtseinserweiternd.

mindful ['maɪndfʊl] *adj* **to be ~ of sth** etw berücksichtigen *or* bedenken; **ever ~ of the risks, she ...** weil sie sich (*dat*) der Risiken bewußt war, ... sie ...; **ever ~ of her feelings** immer an ihre Gefühle denkend.

mind: ~ game *n* psychologisches Spiel ♦ **to play ~ games with sb** jdn verunsichern; **~less** *adj* (*stupid*) hirnlos, ohne Verstand; (*senseless*) *destruction, crime* sinnlos; *occupation* geistlos; **~-reader** *n* Gedankenleser(in *f*) *m*; **I'm not a ~-reader** ich bin doch kein Gedankenleser.

mine[1] [maɪn] [1] *poss pron* meine(r, s) ♦ **this car is ~** das ist *mein* Auto, dieses Auto gehört mir; **is this ~?** gehört das mir?, ist das meine(r, s)?; **his friends and ~** seine und meine Freunde; **a friend of ~** ein Freund von mir; **will you be ~?** (*old*) willst du die Meine werden? (*old*); **~ is a rather different job** meine Arbeit ist ziemlich anders; **that cook of ~!** dieser Koch!; **no advice of ~ could ...** keiner meiner Ratschläge konnte ...; **a favourite expression of ~** einer meiner Lieblingsausdrücke.

[2] *adj* (*obs*) mein(e).

mine[2] [1] *n* **(a)** (*Min*) Bergwerk *nt*; (*copper ~, gold~, silver-~ also*) Mine *f*; (*coal~ also*) Grube, Zeche *f* ♦ **to work down the ~s** unter Tage arbeiten.

(b) (*Mil, Naut etc*) Mine *f* ♦ **to lay ~s** Minen legen.

(c) (*fig*) **the book is a ~ of information** das Buch ist eine wahre Fundgrube; **he is a ~ of information** er ist ein wandelndes Lexikon (*inf*); **he's a ~ of information about history** er besitzt ein schier unerschöpfliches Geschichtswissen.

[2] *vt* **(a)** *coal, metal* fördern, abbauen; *area* Bergbau betreiben *or* Bodenschätze abbauen in (+*dat*).

(b) (*Mil, Naut*) *channel, road* verminen; *ship* eine Mine befestigen an (+*dat*); (*blow up*) (mit einer Mine) sprengen.

[3] *vi* Bergbau betreiben ♦ **to ~ for sth** nach etw graben; **they ~d deep down into the mountain** sie trieben einen Stollen bis tief in den Berg hinein.

mine: ~-detector *n* Minensuchgerät *nt*; **~field** *n* Minenfeld *nt*; **to enter a (political) ~field** sich auf (politisch) gefährliches Terrain begeben; **it's an absolute ~field!** das ist Sprengstoff!; **~hunter** *n* Minensuchboot *nt*; **~layer** *n* Minenleger *m*.

miner ['maɪnəʳ] *n* Bergarbeiter, Bergmann *m* ♦ **~'s lamp** Grubenlampe *f*.

mineral ['mɪnərəl] [1] *n* Mineral *nt*.

[2] *adj* mineralisch; *deposit, resources, kingdom* Mineral- ♦ **~ ores** Erze *pl*.

mineralogical [,mɪnərə'lɒdʒɪkəl] *adj* mineralogisch.

mineralogist [,mɪnə'rælədʒɪst] *n* Mineraloge *m*, Mineralogin *f*.

mineralogy [,mɪnə'rælədʒɪ] *n* Mineralogie *f*.

mineral: ~ oil *n* Mineralöl *nt*; **~ water** *n* Mineralwasser *nt*.

mineshaft ['maɪnʃa:ft] *n* Schacht *m*.

minestrone [,mɪnɪ'strəʊnɪ] *n* Minestrone, Gemüsesuppe *f*.

mine: ~sweeper *n* Minenräumboot *or* -suchboot *nt or* -sucher *m*; **~ workings** *npl* Stollen *pl*.

Ming [mɪŋ] *adj* Ming-.

mingle ['mɪŋgl] [1] *vi* sich vermischen; (*people, groups*) sich untereinander vermischen ♦ **he ~d with people of all classes** er hatte Umgang mit Menschen aller gesellschaftlichen Schichten; **to ~ with the crowd** sich unters Volk mischen.

[2] *vt* mischen (*with* mit); (*liter*) *waters* vermischen ♦ **love ~d with hate** mit Haß ver- *or* gemischte Liebe.

mingy ['mɪndʒɪ] *adj* (+*er*) (*Brit inf*) knickerig (*inf*); *amount* lumpig (*inf*), mickerig (*inf*).

mini- ['mɪnɪ-] *pref* Mini-.

miniature ['mɪnɪtʃəʳ] [1] *n* Miniatur- *or* Kleinausgabe *f*; (*Art*) Miniatur *f*; (*bottle*) Miniflasche *f* ♦ **in ~** en miniature, im kleinen; **he's got his father's face in ~** er hat das Gesicht seines Vaters in Kleinformat.

[2] *adj attr* Miniatur-.

miniature: ~ camera *n* Kleinbildkamera *f*; **~ golf** *n* Mini- *or* Kleingolf *nt*; **~ poodle** *n* Zwergpudel *m*; **~ railway** *n* Liliputbahn *f*; **~ submarine** *n* Kleinst-U-Boot *nt*.

miniaturist ['mɪnɪtʃərɪst] *n* Miniaturmaler(in *f*) *m*.

miniaturize ['mɪnɪtʃəraɪz] *vt* verkleinern.

mini: ~-budget *n Etat m, der nur Teilbereiche bzw. nur einen Teil des Rechnungsjahres abdeckt*, Zwischenetat *m*; **~bus** *n* Kleinbus *m*; **~cab** *n*

➤ LANGUAGE IN USE: **mind: 1g** → 8.2 **3c** → 4, 9.1

Minicar *m*, Kleintaxi *nt*; **~cassette** *n* Minikassette *f*; **~computer** *n* Minicomputer, Kleinrechner *m*.

minim ['mɪnɪm] *n* (*Brit Mus*) halbe Note.

minimal *adj*, **~ly** *adv* ['mɪnɪml, -ɪ] minimal.

minimalism ['mɪnɪməlɪzəm] *n* Minimalismus *m*.

minimalist ['mɪnɪməlɪst] *adj* minimalistisch.

minimize ['mɪnɪmaɪz] *vt* **(a)** (*reduce*) *expenditure, time lost etc* auf ein Minimum reduzieren, minimieren (*form*). **(b)** (*belittle, underestimate*) schlechtmachen, herabsetzen.

minimum ['mɪnɪməm] **1** *n* Minimum *nt* ♦ **the temperature reached a ~ of 5 degrees** die Tiefsttemperatur betrug 5 Grad; **with a ~ of inconvenience** mit einem Minimum an Unannehmlichkeiten; **what is the ~ you will accept?** was ist für Sie das Minimum *or* der Mindestbetrag?; **a ~ of 2 hours/£50/10 people** mindestens 2 Stunden/£ 50/10 Leute; **to reduce sth to a ~** etw auf ein Minimum *or* Mindestmaß reduzieren.

2 *adj attr* Mindest- ♦ **to achieve maximum possible profits from ~ possible expenditure** möglichst hohe Gewinne mit möglichst geringen Ausgaben erzielen; **the ~ expenditure will be ...** das wird mindestens ... kosten; **~ temperature** Tiefsttemperatur *f*; **~ wage** Mindestlohn *m*; **~ lending rate** Diskontsatz *m*.

mining ['maɪnɪŋ] *n* **(a)** (*Min*) Bergbau *m*; (*work at the face*) Arbeit *f* im Bergwerk. **(b)** (*Mil*) (*of area*) Verminen *nt*; (*of ship*) Befestigung *f* einer Mine (*of an +dat*); (*blowing-up*) Sprengung *f* (mit einer Mine).

mining: ~ area *n* Bergbaugebiet, Revier *nt*; **~ disaster** *n* Grubenunglück *nt*; **~ engineer** *n* Berg(bau)ingenieur *m*; **~ industry** *n* Bergbau *m*; **~ town** *n* Bergarbeiterstadt *f*.

minion ['mɪnɪən] *n* (*old*) Günstling *m*; (*fig*) Trabant *m*.

mini: ~pill *n* Minipille *f*; **~skirt** *n* Minirock *m*.

minister ['mɪnɪstə^r] **1** *n* **(a)** (*Pol*) Minister *m*.

(b) (*Eccl*) Pfarrer, Pastor *m*, protestantischer Geistlicher ♦ **good morning, ~** guten Morgen, Herr Pfarrer *or* Herr Pastor.

2 *vi* **to ~ to sb** sich um jdn kümmern; **to ~ to sb's needs/wants** jds Bedürfnisse/Wünsche (*acc*) befriedigen; **a ~ing angel** (*liter*) ein barmherziger Engel.

ministerial [ˌmɪnɪ'stɪərɪəl] *adj* (*Pol*) ministeriell, Minister- ♦ **~ post** Ministerposten *m*; **his ~ duties** seine Pflichten als Minister; **those of ~ rank** diejenigen, die im Rang eines Ministers stehen (*form*) *or* die einen Ministerposten innehaben.

ministration [ˌmɪnɪ'streɪʃən] *n usu pl* Pflege, Fürsorge *f*.

ministry ['mɪnɪstrɪ] *n* **(a)** (*Pol*) Ministerium *nt* ♦ **~ of defence/agriculture** Verteidigungs-/Landwirtschaftsministerium; **during his ~** in *or* während seiner Amtszeit (als Minister); **during the ~ of X** als X Minister war.

(b) (*Eccl*) geistliches Amt ♦ **to join** *or* **enter** *or* **go into the ~** Pfarrer *or* Geistlicher werden; **to train for the ~** Theologie studieren, um Geistlicher zu werden.

(c) (*ministering*) Sendungsbewußtsein *nt* ♦ **her ~ to the sick** ihr Dienst an den Kranken; **Christ's ~ here on earth** das Wirken Christi auf Erden.

miniver ['mɪnɪvə^r] *n* Hermelin *m*.

mink [mɪŋk] *n* Nerz *m* ♦ **~ coat** Nerzmantel *m*.

minnow ['mɪnəʊ] *n* Elritze *f*.

Minoan [mɪ'nəʊən] *adj* minoisch.

minor ['maɪnə^r] **1** *adj* **(a)** (*of lesser extent*) kleiner; (*of lesser importance*) unbedeutend, unwichtig; *offence, operation, injuries* leicht; *interest, importance* geringer; *poet, position* unbedeutend; *prophet, planet* klein; *road* Neben- ♦ **a ~ role** eine Nebenrolle, eine kleinere Rolle; **he only played a ~ role in the company** er spielte in der Firma nur eine untergeordnete *or* ganz kleine Rolle; **I have one or two ~ criticisms of the hotel** ich habe an dem Hotel nur ein paar Kleinigkeiten auszusetzen; **~ premise** Untersatz *m*.

(b) (*Mus*) *key, scale* Moll- ♦ **G/E flat/C sharp ~** g-/es-/cis-Moll *nt*; **~ third** kleine Terz; **the novel ends in a ~ key** *or* **on a ~ note** der Roman endet mit einer traurigen Note.

(c) (*Sch sl*) **Smith ~** Smith der Jüngere.

2 *n* **(a)** (*Mus*) **the ~** Moll *nt*; **the music shifts to the ~** die Musik wechselt nach Moll über *or* geht in die Molltonart über.

(b) (*Jur*) Minderjährige(r) *mf*.

(c) (*US Univ*) Nebenfach *nt*.

3 *vi* (*US Univ*) im Nebenfach studieren (*in acc*).

Minorca [mɪ'nɔːkə] *n* Menorca *nt*.

Minorcan [mɪ'nɔːkən] **1** *adj* menorkinisch.

2 *n* Menorkiner(in *f*) *m*.

minority [maɪ'nɒrɪtɪ] **1** *n* **(a)** Minderheit, Minorität *f* ♦ **to be in a ~** in der Minderheit sein; **you are in a ~ of one** Sie stehen allein da. **(b)** (*Jur*) Minderjährigkeit *f*.

2 *adj attr* Minderheits- ♦ **~ group** Minderheit, Minorität *f*; **~ programme** (*Rad, TV*) Programm, das nur einen kleinen Hörerkreis/Zuschauerkreis anspricht; **~ holding, ~ interest** (*Fin*) Minderheitsbeteiligung *f*.

Minotaur ['maɪnətɔː^r] *n* Minotaur(us) *m*.

minster ['mɪnstə^r] *n* Münster *nt*.

minstrel ['mɪnstrəl] *n* (*medieval*) Spielmann *m*; (*wandering*) (fahrender) Sänger; (*ballad-singer*) Bänkelsänger *m*; (*singer of love songs*) Minnesänger *m*; (*esp US: modern*) *weißer, als Neger zurechtgemachter Sänger und Komiker*.

mint[1] [mɪnt] **1** *n* Münzanstalt *or* -stätte, Münze *f* ♦ **(Royal) M~** (Königlich-) Britische Münzanstalt; **to be worth a ~** Gold wert *or* unbezahlbar sein; **he earns a ~ (of money)** er verdient ein Heidengeld (*inf*); **his father made a ~** sein Vater hat einen Haufen Geld gemacht (*inf*).

2 *adj stamp* postfrisch, ungestempelt ♦ **in ~ condition** in tadellosem Zustand.

3 *vt coin, phrase* prägen.

mint[2] *n* (*Bot*) Minze *f*; (*sweet*) Pfefferminz *nt* ♦ **~ julep** *Whisky m mit Eis und frischer Minze*; **~ sauce** Minzsoße *f*.

minuet [ˌmɪnjʊ'et] *n* Menuett *nt*.

minus ['maɪnəs] **1** *prep* **(a)** minus, weniger ♦ **£100 ~ taxes** £ 100 abzüglich (der) Steuern.

(b) (*without, deprived of*) ohne ♦ **he returned from the war ~ an arm** er kam mit einem Arm weniger aus dem Krieg zurück.

2 *adj quantity, value* negativ; *sign* Minus-, Subtraktions-; *temperatures* Minus-, unter Null ♦ **~ three degrees centigrade** drei Grad minus; **an alpha ~** (*in grading*) eine Eins minus.

3 *n* (*sign*) Minus(zeichen) *nt* ♦ **2 ~es make a plus** minus mal minus gibt plus; **if the result is a ~ ...** wenn das Ergebnis negativ *or* eine negative Größe ist ...

minuscule ['mɪnɪskjuːl] *adj* winzig.

minute[1] ['mɪnɪt] **1** *n* **(a)** (*of time, degree*) Minute *f* ♦ **in a ~** gleich, sofort; **this (very) ~!** auf der Stelle!; **at this very ~** gerade jetzt *or* in diesem Augenblick; **I shan't be a ~, it won't take a ~** es dauert nicht lang; **any ~** jeden Augenblick; **tell me the ~ he comes** sag mir sofort Bescheid, wenn er kommt; **let me know the ~ it stops** sagen Sie mir Bescheid, sobald es aufhört; **at 6 o'clock to the ~** genau um 6 Uhr, um Punkt 6 Uhr, um 6 Uhr auf die Minute; **have you got a ~?** hast du mal eine Minute *or* einen Augenblick Zeit?; **it won't take 5 ~s/a ~** es dauert keine 5 Minuten/keine Minute; **I enjoyed every ~ of it** ich habe es von Anfang bis Ende genossen; **at the last ~** in letzter Minute.

(b) (*official note*) Notiz *f* ♦ **~s** Protokoll *nt*; **to take the ~s** das Protokoll führen.

2 *vt meeting* protokollieren; *remark, fact* zu Protokoll nehmen.

minute[2] [maɪ'njuːt] *adj* (*small*) winzig; *resemblance* ganz entfernt; (*detailed, exact*) minuziös; *detail* kleinste(r, s).

minute[3] ['mɪnɪt]: **~ book** *n* Protokollbuch *nt*; **~ hand** *n* Minutenzeiger *m*.

minutely [maɪ'njuːtlɪ] *adv* (*by a small amount*) ganz geringfügig; (*in detail*) genauestens ♦ **anything ~ resembling a fish** alles, was auch nur annähernd nach Fisch aussieht; **a ~ detailed account** eine sehr detaillierte Schilderung.

minute-man ['mɪnɪtmæn] *n, pl* **-men** [-men] (*US*) *Freiwilliger im Unabhängigkeitskrieg, der auf Abruf bereitstand*.

minuteness [maɪ'njuːtnɪs] *n* (*size*) Winzigkeit *f*; (*of account, description*) Ausführlichkeit *f*; (*of detail*) Genauigkeit *f*.

minute steak ['mɪnɪt-] *n* Minutensteak *nt*.

minutiae [mɪ'njuːʃiː] *npl* genaue Einzelheiten *pl* ♦ **the ~ of one's day-to-day affairs** die tägliche Kleinarbeit.

minx [mɪŋks] *n* Biest *nt* (*inf*).

miracle ['mɪrəkəl] *n* Wunder *nt* ♦ **to work** *or* **perform ~s** (*lit*) Wunder tun *or* wirken *or* vollbringen; **I can't work ~s** ich kann nicht hexen *or* zaubern; **by a ~, by some ~** (*fig*) wie durch ein Wunder; **it will be a ~ if ...** das wäre ein Wunder, wenn...; **it's a ~ he ...** es ist ein Wunder, daß er ...; **her recovery/his victory was a ~** es war ein Wunder, daß sie wieder gesund geworden ist/er gewonnen hat; **it'll take a ~ for us** *or* **we'll need a ~ to be finished on time** da müßte schon ein Wunder geschehen, wenn wir noch rechtzeitig fertig werden sollen.

miracle: ~ drug *n* Wunderdroge *f*; **~ play** *n* Mirakelspiel *nt*, geistliches Drama; **~ worker** *n* Wundertäter *m*.

miraculous [mɪ'rækjʊləs] *adj* wunderbar, wundersam (*liter*); *powers* Wunder- ♦ **there was a ~ change in her appearance** es war kaum zu fassen, wie sie sich verändert hatte; **that is nothing short of ~** das grenzt an ein Wunder.

miraculously [mɪ'rækjʊləslɪ] *adv* (*lit*) auf wunderbare Weise; (*fig*) wie durch ein Wunder ♦ **she was somehow ~ changed** es war nicht zu fassen, wie verändert sie war.

mirage ['mɪrɑːʒ] *n* Fata Morgana, Luftspiegelung *f*; (*fig*) Trugbild *nt*, Illusion *f*.

mire ['maɪə^r] *n* Morast (*also fig*), Schlamm *m* ♦ **the football pitch was an absolute ~** der Fußballplatz war ein einziges Schlammfeld; **to drag sb through the ~** (*fig*) jds Namen in den Schmutz ziehen.

mirror ['mɪrə^r] **1** *n* Spiegel *m* ♦ **a ~ of 19th century life** ein Spiegel(bild) des Lebens im 19. Jahrhundert; **to hold a ~ up to sb/sth** jdm den Spiegel vorhalten/etw widerspiegeln; **~ image** Spiegelbild *nt*; **~ writing** Spiegelschrift *f*.

2 *vt* widerspiegeln, spiegeln ♦ **the trees ~ed in the lake** die Bäume, die sich im See (wider)spiegelten.

mirth [mɜːθ] *n* Freude *f*, Frohsinn *m*; (*laughter*) Heiterkeit *f* ♦ **sounds of ~ coming from the classroom** frohes *or* fröhliches Lachen, das aus dem Klassenzimmer drang.

mirthful ['mɜːθfʊl] *adj* froh, heiter, fröhlich.

mirthless ['mɜːθlɪs] *adj* freudlos; *laughter* unfroh.

mirthlessly ['mɜːθlɪslɪ] *adv* unfroh.

miry ['maɪərɪ] *adj* morastig, schlammig.

misadventure [ˌmɪsəd'ventʃə^r] *n* Mißgeschick *nt* ♦ **death by ~** Tod *m* durch Unfall; **he's had a ~** ihm ist ein Mißgeschick passiert.

misalliance [ˌmɪsə'laɪəns] *n* Mesalliance *f*.

misanthrope ['mɪzənθrəʊp], **misanthropist** [mɪ'zænθrəpɪst] *n* Misanthrop, Menschenfeind *m*.

misanthropic [ˌmɪzən'θrɒpɪk] *adj* misanthropisch, menschenfeindlich.

misanthropy [mɪ'zænθrəpɪ] *n* Misanthropie, Menschenfeindlichkeit *f.*
misapply ['mɪsə'plaɪ] *vt* falsch anwenden; *funds* falsch verwenden; *one's energy* verschwenden.
misapprehend ['mɪs,æprɪ'hend] *vt* mißverstehen.
misapprehension ['mɪs,æprɪ'henʃən] *n* Mißverständnis *nt* ◆ **I think you are under a ~** ich glaube, bei Ihnen liegt (da) ein Mißverständnis vor; **he was under the ~ that ...** er hatte fälschlicherweise *or* irrtümlicherweise angenommen, daß ...
misappropriate ['mɪsə'prəʊprɪeɪt] *vt* entwenden; *money* veruntreuen.
misappropriation ['mɪsə,prəʊprɪ'eɪʃən] *n see vt* Entwendung *f*; Veruntreuung *f.*
misbegotten ['mɪsbɪ'gɒtn] *adj* (*liter: illegitimate*) unehelich; (*fig: ill-conceived*) schlecht konzipiert.
misbehave ['mɪsbɪ'heɪv] *vi* sich schlecht *or* unanständig benehmen; (*child also*) ungezogen sein ◆ **I saw him misbehaving with my wife** ich habe ihn in einer unmißverständlichen *or* eindeutigen Situation mit meiner Frau gesehen.
misbehaviour, (*US*) **misbehavior** ['mɪsbɪ'heɪvjə^r] *n* schlechtes Benehmen; (*of child also*) Ungezogenheit *f* ◆ **sexual ~** sexuelles Fehlverhalten.
misbelief ['mɪsbɪ'li:f] *n* irrige Annahme; (*Rel*) Irrglaube *m.*
miscalculate ['mɪs'kælkjʊleɪt] [1] *vt* falsch berechnen; (*misjudge*) falsch einschätzen ◆ **to ~ a distance/a jump** sich in der Entfernung/bei einem Sprung verschätzen.
[2] *vi* sich verrechnen; (*estimate wrongly*) sich verkalkulieren; (*misjudge*) sich verschätzen.
miscalculation ['mɪs,kælkjʊ'leɪʃən] *n* Rechenfehler *m*; (*wrong estimation*) Fehlkalkulation *f*; (*misjudgement*) Fehleinschätzung *f* ◆ **to make a ~ in sth** bei etw einen Rechenfehler machen/etw falsch kalkulieren/etw falsch einschätzen.
miscall ['mɪs'kɔ:l] *vt* (*Sport*) *shot* falsch bewerten *or* aufrufen.
miscarriage ['mɪs,kærɪdʒ] *n* **(a)** (*Med*) Fehlgeburt *f.* **(b) ~ of justice** Justizirrtum *m.* **(c)** (*form: of letter*) Fehlleitung *f.*
miscarry [,mɪs'kærɪ] *vi* **(a)** (*Med*) eine Fehlgeburt haben. **(b)** (*fail: plans*) fehllaufen *or* -schlagen. **(c)** (*form: letter, goods*) fehlgeleitet werden.
miscast ['mɪs'kɑ:st] *pret, ptp* ~ *vt play* falsch *or* schlecht besetzen, fehlbesetzen ◆ **the actor was clearly ~ in this role** mit diesem Schauspieler war die Rolle eindeutig fehlbesetzt.
miscegenation [,mɪsɪdʒɪ'neɪʃən] *n* Rassenmischung *f.*
miscellanea [,mɪsə'leɪnɪə] *npl* Verschiedenes *nt*; (*of literary compositions, objects*) (bunte) Sammlung.
miscellaneous [,mɪsɪ'leɪnɪəs] *adj* verschieden; *poems* vermischt, verschiedenerlei; *collection, crowd* bunt ◆ **"~"** „Verschiedenes"; **a ~ section** Vermischtes.
miscellaneously [,mɪsɪ'leɪnɪəslɪ] *adv* verschieden; *grouped, collected* bunt, wahllos.
miscellany [mɪ'selənɪ] *n* (*collection*) (bunte) Sammlung, (buntes) Gemisch; (*variety*) Vielfalt *f*; (*of writings*) vermischte Schriften *pl*; (*of poems, articles*) Sammelband *m*, Auswahl *f.*
mischance [,mɪs'tʃɑ:ns] *n* unglücklicher Zufall ◆ **by some ~** durch einen unglücklichen Zufall.
mischief ['mɪstʃɪf] *n* **(a)** (*roguery*) Schalk *m*, Verschmitztheit *f*; (*naughty, foolish behaviour*) Unsinn, Unfug *m* ◆ **she's full of ~** sie hat nur Unfug im Kopf; **he's up to some ~** er führt etwas im Schilde; **there's some ~ going on** irgend etwas geht hier vor; **he's always getting into ~** er stellt dauernd etwas an; **to keep sb out of ~** aufpassen, daß jd keine Dummheiten macht; **to keep out of ~** keinen Unfug machen; **that'll keep you out of ~** dann kannst du wenigstens nichts anstellen *or* kommst du wenigstens auf keine dummen Gedanken.
(b) (*trouble*) **to mean/make ~** Unfrieden stiften wollen/stiften; **to make ~ for sb** jdm Unannehmlichkeiten bereiten, jdn in Schwierigkeiten bringen; **~-maker** Unruhestifter *m.*
(c) (*damage, physical injury*) Schaden *m* ◆ **to do sb a ~** jdm Schaden zufügen; (*physically*) jdm etwas (an)tun, jdn verletzen; **to do ~ to sth** Schaden bei etw anrichten.
(d) (*person*) Schlawiner *m*; (*child, puppy also*) Racker *m.*
mischievous ['mɪstʃɪvəs] *adj* **(a)** (*roguish, playful*) *expression, smile* schelmisch, verschmitzt, spitzbübisch ◆ **a ~ person/child** ein Schlawiner/Schlingel *or* Racker; **her son is really ~** ihr Sohn ist ein Schlingel *or* hat nur Unfug im Sinn; **what ~ pranks are you up to now?** welche üblen Streiche heckst du jetzt aus?; **a ~ elf** eine Elfe, die Schabernack treibt.
(b) (*troublemaking*) *rumour* bösartig; *person* boshaft; *strike* schädlich; (*physically disabling*) *blow* verletzend.
mischievously ['mɪstʃɪvəslɪ] *adv see adj* **(a)** *smile, say* schelmisch, verschmitzt, spitzbübisch ◆ **to behave ~** Unfug anstellen, Schabernack treiben. **(b)** bösartig; boshaft.
mischievousness ['mɪstʃɪvəsnɪs] *n* (*roguery*) Verschmitztheit *f.*
miscible ['mɪsɪbl] *adj* (*form*) mischbar.
misconceive ['mɪskən'si:v] *vt* (*understand wrongly*) verkennen, eine falsche Vorstellung haben von; (*base on false assumption*) von einer falschen Voraussetzung ausgehen bei.
misconception ['mɪskən'sepʃən] *n* fälschliche *or* irrtümliche Annahme; (*no pl: misunderstanding*) Verkennung *f.*
misconduct [,mɪs'kɒndʌkt] [1] *n* **(a)** (*improper behaviour*) schlechtes Benehmen; (*professional*) Berufsvergehen *nt*; Verfehlung *f* im Amt; (*sexual*) Fehltritt *m.*
(b) (*mismanagement*) schlechte Verwaltung.
[2] [,mɪskən'dʌkt] *vt* schlecht verwalten.
[3] [,mɪskən'dʌkt] *vr* **to ~ oneself** sich schlecht benehmen; (*professionally*) sich falsch verhalten.
misconstruction ['mɪskən'strʌkʃən] *n* falsche Auslegung, Fehlinterpretation, Mißdeutung *f* ◆ **he put a deliberate ~ on my words** er hat meine Worte absichtlich mißverstanden.
misconstrue ['mɪskən'stru:] *vt* mißverstehen, mißdeuten, falsch auslegen ◆ **you have ~d my meaning** Sie haben mich falsch verstanden; **to ~ sth as sth** etw irrtümlicherweise für etw halten.
miscount ['mɪs'kaʊnt] [1] *n* **there was a ~** da hat sich jemand verzählt.
[2] *vt* falsch (aus)zählen.
[3] *vi* sich verzählen.
miscreant ['mɪskrɪənt] *n* (*old*) Bösewicht (*old*), Schurke *m.*
misdate [,mɪs'deɪt] *vt letter* falsch datieren.
misdeal ['mɪs'di:l] *pret, ptp* **misdealt** ['mɪs'delt] [1] *vt cards* falsch (aus)geben.
[2] *vi* sich vergeben, falsch geben.
misdeed ['mɪs'di:d] *n* Missetat *f* (*old*).
misdemeanour, (*US*) **misdemeanor** [,mɪsdɪ'mi:nə^r] *n* schlechtes Betragen *or* Benehmen; (*Jur*) Vergehen *nt*, Übertretung *f* ◆ **she was guilty of a slight ~ at the party** sie benahm sich auf der Party leicht daneben.
misdirect ['mɪsdɪ'rekt] *vt* **(a)** *letter* falsch adressieren; *energies* falsch einsetzen, vergeuden; *person* (*send astray*) in die falsche Richtung schicken; (*misinform*) falsch informieren, eine falsche Auskunft geben (*+dat*); (*Jur*) *jury* falsch belehren.
(b) *campaign, operation* schlecht durchführen.
misdirection ['mɪsdɪ'rekʃən] *n see vt* **(a)** falsche Adressierung; falscher Einsatz, Vergeudung *f*; falsche Richtungsweisung; falsche Information; falsche Unterrichtung. **(b)** schlechte Durchführung.
mise-en-scène [,mi:zɑ̃n'seɪn] *n* (*Theat, fig*) Kulisse *f.*
miser ['maɪzə^r] *n* Geizhals *or* -kragen *m.*
miserable ['mɪzərəbl] *adj* **(a)** (*unhappy*) unglücklich; *colour* trist ◆ **I feel ~ today** ich fühle mich heute elend *or* miserabel; **~ with hunger/cold** elend vor Hunger/Kälte; **to make sb ~** jdm Kummer machen *or* bereiten, jdn unglücklich machen; **to make life ~ for sb** jdm das Leben schwer machen.
(b) (*wretched, causing distress*) *headache, cold, weather* gräßlich, fürchterlich; *existence, hovels, spectacle* erbärmlich, elend, jämmerlich ◆ **he died a ~ death** er ist elend *or* jämmerlich zugrunde gegangen.
(c) (*contemptible*) miserabel, jämmerlich, erbärmlich; *person* gemein, erbärmlich; *treatment, behaviour* gemein; *failure* kläglich, jämmerlich ◆ **a ~ £3** miese £ 3 (*inf*); **you ~ little wretch!** du mieses kleines Biest!, du Miststück! (*inf*).
miserably ['mɪzərəblɪ] *adv* **(a)** (*unhappily*) unglücklich; *say also* kläglich.
(b) (*wretchedly, distressingly*) *hurt, ache, rain* gräßlich, fürchterlich; *live, die* elend, jämmerlich; *poor* erbärmlich.
(c) (*contemptibly*) *pay, feed* miserabel; *play also* erbärmlich; *fail* kläglich, jämmerlich; *treat, behave* gemein.
misericord ['mɪzərɪkɔ:d] *n* Miserikordie *f.*
miserliness ['maɪzəlɪnɪs] *n* Geiz *m.*
miserly ['maɪzəlɪ] *adj* geizig; *hoarding* kleinlich.
misery ['mɪzərɪ] *n* **(a)** (*sadness*) Kummer *m*, Trauer *f* ◆ **she looked the picture of ~** sie war ein Bild des Jammers.
(b) (*suffering*) Qualen *pl*; (*wretchedness*) Elend *nt* ◆ **the ~ caused by war** das Elend des Krieges; **a life of ~** ein erbärmliches *or* jämmerliches *or* elendes Leben; **to make sb's life a ~** jdm das Leben zur Qual *or* zur Hölle machen; **to put an animal out of its ~** ein Tier von seinen Qualen erlösen; **to put sb out of his ~** (*fig*) jdn nicht länger auf die Folter spannen.
(c) (*inf: person*) Miesepeter *m* (*inf*) ◆ **~-guts** (*inf*) Miesmacher *m* (*inf*).
misfire ['mɪs'faɪə^r] *vi* (*engine*) fehlzünden, eine Fehlzündung haben; (*plan*) fehlschlagen; (*joke, trick*) danebengehen.
misfit ['mɪsfɪt] *n* (*person*) Außenseiter(in *f*) *m*; (*social ~ also*) Nichtangepaßte(r) *mf* ◆ **society's ~s** die Außenseiter der Gesellschaft; **he's a real ~** er ist ein sehr schwieriger Fall; **he's always been a ~ here** er hat nie richtig hierher gepaßt, er hat sich hier nie angepaßt; **I felt a ~** ich fühlte mich fehl am Platze.
misfortune [mɪs'fɔ:tʃu:n] *n* (*ill fortune, affliction*) (schweres) Schicksal *or* Los *nt*; (*bad luck*) Pech *nt no pl*; (*unlucky incident*) Mißgeschick *nt* ◆ **companion in ~** Leidensgenosse *m*/-genossin *f*; **it was my ~** *or* **I had the ~ to ...** ich hatte das Pech, zu ...; **a life of disaster and ~** ein von Katastrophen und Mißgeschick(en) begleitetes Leben; **a victim of ~** ein Unglücksrabe *or* Pechvogel *m*; **financial ~s** finanzielle Fehlschläge *pl.*
▼ **misgiving** [mɪs'gɪvɪŋ] *n* Bedenken *pl* ◆ **I had (certain) ~s about the scheme/about lending him the money** mir war bei dem Vorhaben/dem Gedanken, ihm das Geld zu leihen, nicht ganz wohl.
misgovern ['mɪs'gʌvən] *vt* schlecht regieren, schlecht verwalten.
misgovernment ['mɪs'gʌvənmənt] *n* Mißwirtschaft *f* (*of* in *+dat*).
misguided ['mɪs'gaɪdɪd] *adj* töricht; *decision also, opinions* irrig; (*misplaced*) *kindness, enthusiasm, solicitude* unangebracht, fehl am Platz ◆ **I think it was ~ of you** *or* **you were ~ to accept his proposal** meiner Ansicht nach waren Sie schlecht beraten *or* war es töricht, seinen Vorschlag anzunehmen.
misguidedly ['mɪs'gaɪdɪdlɪ] *adv* töricht; *teach, believe* irrigerweise.
mishandle ['mɪs'hændl] *vt case* falsch *or* schlecht handhaben.
mishap ['mɪshæp] *n* Mißgeschick *nt* ◆ **without (further) ~** ohne (weitere) Zwischenfälle; **he's had a slight ~** ihm ist ein kleines Mißgeschick *or*

➤ LANGUAGE IN USE: **misgiving** → 26.3

Malheur passiert.

mishear ['mɪs'hɪəʳ] *pret, ptp* **misheard** ['mɪs'hɜːd] [1] *vt* falsch hören.
[2] *vi* sich verhören.

mishmash ['mɪʃmæʃ] *n* Mischmasch *m.*

misinform ['mɪsɪn'fɔːm] *vt* falsch informieren *or* unterrichten ◆ **you've been ~ed** man hat Sie *or* Sie sind falsch informiert; **does the press ~ the public?** verbreitet die Presse falsche Informationen?

misinterpret ['mɪsɪn'tɜːprɪt] *vt* falsch auslegen *or* deuten; *play, novel* fehlinterpretieren, falsch auslegen; (*interpreter*) falsch wiedergeben *or* verdolmetschen ◆ **it could easily be ~ed as implying ingratitude** es könnte (mir/dir *etc*) leicht als Undankbarkeit ausgelegt werden; **he ~ed her silence as agreement** er deutete ihr Schweigen fälschlich als Zustimmung.

misinterpretation ['mɪsɪn,tɜːprɪ'teɪʃən] *n* Fehldeutung *f*, falsche Auslegung; (*of play, novel*) Fehlinterpretation *f*, falsche Auslegung; (*by interpreter*) falsche Wiedergabe.

misjudge ['mɪs'dʒʌdʒ] *vt* falsch einschätzen, sich verschätzen in (*+dat*); *person also* falsch beurteilen.

misjudgement [,mɪs'dʒʌdʒmənt] *n* Fehleinschätzung *f*; (*of person also*) falsche Beurteilung.

mislay [,mɪs'leɪ] *pret, ptp* **mislaid** [,mɪs'leɪd] *vt* verlegen.

mislead [,mɪs'liːd] *pret, ptp* **misled** *vt* **(a)** (*give wrong idea*) irreführen ◆ **you have been misled** Sie irren *or* täuschen sich, Sie befinden sich im Irrtum (*form*); **don't be misled by appearances** lassen Sie sich nicht durch Äußerlichkeiten täuschen; **your description misled me into thinking that ...** aufgrund Ihrer Beschreibung nahm ich (irrtümlich) an, daß ...
(b) (*lead into bad ways*) verleiten (*into* zu).
(c) (*in guiding*) in die Irre *or* falsche Richtung führen.

misleading [,mɪs'liːdɪŋ] *adj* irreführend ◆ **the ~ simplicity of his style** die täuschende Einfachheit seines Stils.

misleadingly [,mɪs'liːdɪŋlɪ] *adv* irreführenderweise.

misled [,mɪs'led] *pret, ptp of* **mislead.**

mismanage ['mɪs'mænɪdʒ] *vt company, finances* schlecht verwalten; *affair, deal* schlecht abwickeln *or* handhaben.

mismanagement ['mɪs'mænɪdʒmənt] *n* Mißwirtschaft *f* ◆ **his ~ of the matter** seine schlechte Abwicklung der Angelegenheit.

misname ['mɪs'neɪm] *vt* unzutreffend benennen.

misnomer ['mɪs'nəʊməʳ] *n* unzutreffende Bezeichnung.

misogamist [mɪ'sɒgəmɪst] *n* Misogam *m.*

misogamy [mɪ'sɒgəmɪ] *n* Misogamie *f.*

misogynist [mɪ'sɒdʒɪnɪst] *n* Frauenfeind, Misogyn (*geh*) *m.*

misogyny [mɪ'sɒdʒɪnɪ] *n* Frauenhaß *m*, Misogynie *f* (*geh*).

misplace ['mɪs'pleɪs] *vt* **(a)** *document, file etc* falsch einordnen; (*mislay*) verlegen. **(b) to be ~d** (*confidence, trust, affection*) fehl am Platz *or* unangebracht sein; **her ~d affection/trust** ihre törichte Zuneigung/ihr törichtes Vertrauen.

misplay [,mɪs'pleɪ] *vt* verschießen.

misprint ['mɪsprɪnt] [1] *n* Druckfehler *m.*
[2] [,mɪs'prɪnt] *vt* verdrucken.

mispronounce ['mɪsprə'naʊns] *vt* falsch aussprechen.

mispronunciation ['mɪsprə,nʌnsɪ'eɪʃən] *n* falsche *or* fehlerhafte Aussprache.

misquotation ['mɪskwəʊ'teɪʃən] *n* falsches Zitat ◆ **his constant ~ of Shakespeare** daß er Shakespeare ständig falsch zitiert/zitiert hat.

misquote ['mɪs'kwəʊt] *vt* falsch zitieren ◆ **he was ~d as having said ...** man unterstellte ihm, gesagt zu haben ...

misread ['mɪs'riːd] *pret, ptp* **misread** ['mɪs'red] *vt* falsch *or* nicht richtig lesen; (*misinterpret*) falsch verstehen.

misrepresent ['mɪs,reprɪ'zent] *vt* falsch darstellen; *facts also* verdrehen; *ideas* verfälschen ◆ **he was ~ed in the papers** seine Worte *etc* wurden von der Presse verfälscht *or* entstellt wiedergegeben; **he was ~ed as being for the strike** er wurde zu Unrecht als Befürworter des Streiks hingestellt; **he was ~ed as having said ...** ihm wurde unterstellt, gesagt zu haben ...

misrepresentation ['mɪs,reprɪzen'teɪʃən] *n* falsche Darstellung; (*of facts also*) Verdrehung *f*; (*of theory*) Verfälschung *f* ◆ **to be accused of ~** der Verdrehung (*gen*) von Tatsachen beschuldigt werden.

misrule ['mɪs'ruːl] [1] *n* schlechte Regierung; (*by government also*) Mißwirtschaft *f.*
[2] *vt* schlecht regieren.

miss¹ [mɪs] [1] *n* **(a)** (*shot*) Fehltreffer *or* -schuß *m*; (*failure*) Mißerfolg *m*, Pleite *f* (*inf*), Reinfall *m* (*inf*) ◆ **his first shot was a ~** sein erster Schuß ging daneben; **it was a near ~** das war eine knappe Sache; (*shot*) das war knapp daneben; **it was a near ~ with that car** das Auto haben wir aber um Haaresbreite verfehlt; **the sales department voted it a ~** in der Verkaufsabteilung räumte man dem keine Chance ein; **a ~ is as good as a mile** (*prov*) knapp vorbei ist auch daneben.
(b) to give sth a ~ (*inf*) sich (*dat*) etw schenken.
[2] *vt* **(a)** (*fail to hit, catch, reach, find, attend etc*) (*by accident*) verpassen; *chance, appointment, bus, concert also* versäumen; (*deliberately not attend*) nicht gehen zu *or* in (*+acc*); (*not hit, find*) *target, ball, way, step, vocation, place, house* verfehlen; (*shot, ball*) verfehlen, vorbeigehen an (*+dat*) ◆ **to ~ breakfast** nicht frühstücken; (*be too late for*) das Frühstück verpassen; **you haven't ~ed much!** da hast du nichts *or* nicht viel verpaßt *or* versäumt!; **they ~ed each other in the crowd** sie verpaßten *or* verfehlten sich in der Menge; **to ~ the boat** *or* **bus** (*fig*) den Anschluß verpassen; **he ~ed school for a week** er hat eine Woche lang die Schule versäumt; **~ a turn** einmal aussetzen; **have I ~ed my turn?** bin ich übergangen worden?; **if you ~ a pill** wenn Sie vergessen, eine Pille zu nehmen.
(b) (*fail to experience*) verpassen; (*deliberately*) sich (*dat*) entgehen lassen; (*fail to hear or perceive also*) nicht mitbekommen; (*deliberately*) überhören/-sehen ◆ **I ~ed that** das ist mir entgangen; **he doesn't ~ much** (*inf*) ihm entgeht so schnell nichts; **I wouldn't have ~ed it for anything** das hätte ich mir nicht entgehen lassen wollen.
(c) (*fail to achieve*) *prize* nicht bekommen *or* schaffen (*inf*) ◆ **he narrowly ~ed being first/becoming president** er wäre beinahe auf den ersten Platz gekommen/Präsident geworden.
(d) (*avoid*) *obstacle* (noch) ausweichen können (*+dat*); (*escape*) entgehen (*+dat*) ◆ **to ~ doing sth** etw fast *or* um ein Haar tun; **the car just ~ed the tree** das Auto wäre um ein Haar gegen den Baum gefahren; **we narrowly ~ed having an accident** wir hätten um ein Haar einen Unfall gehabt.
(e) (*leave out*) auslassen; (*overlook, fail to deal with*) übersehen ◆ **my heart ~ed a beat** mir stockte das Herz.
(f) (*notice or regret absence of*) (*person*) *people, things* vermissen ◆ **I ~ him/my old car** er/mein altes Auto fehlt mir; **he won't be ~ed** keiner wird ihn vermissen; **he'll never ~ it** er wird es nie merken(, daß es ihm fehlt).
[3] *vi* **(a)** nicht treffen; (*punching also*) danebenschlagen; (*shooting also*) danebenschießen; (*not catch*) danebengreifen; (*not be present, not attend*) fehlen; (*ball, shot, punch also*) danebengehen; (*Aut: engine*) aussetzen.
(b) (*inf: fail*) **you can't ~** da kann nichts schiefgehen; **he never ~es** er schafft es immer.

◆**miss out** [1] *vt sep* auslassen; (*accidentally not see*) übersehen; *last line or paragraph etc* weglassen ◆ **my name was ~ed ~ from the list** mein Name fehlte auf der Liste.
[2] *vi* (*inf*) zu kurz kommen ◆ **to ~ ~ on sth** etw verpassen; (*get less*) bei etw zu kurz kommen; **he's been ~ing ~ on life** er ist im Leben zu kurz gekommen.

miss² *n* **(a) M~** Fräulein *nt*, Frl. *abbr*; **M~ Germany 1980** (die) Miß Germany von 1980.
(b) (*girl*) **a proper little ~** ein richtiges Dämchen *or* kleines Fräulein; **look here, you cheeky little ~!** hör mal, mein (kleines) Fräulein!; **these saucy young ~es** diese frechen (jungen) Dinger.
(c) (*term of address*) mein Fräulein; (*to waitress etc*) Fräulein; (*to teacher*) Fräulein *or* Frau X.

missal ['mɪsəl] *n* Meßbuch, Missale *nt.*

misshapen ['mɪs'ʃeɪpən] *adj* mißgebildet; *plant, tree also* verwachsen; *chocolates* unförmig, mißraten.

missile ['mɪsaɪl] *n* **(a)** (*stone, javelin etc*) (Wurf)geschoß *nt.*
(b) (*rocket*) Rakete *f*, Flugkörper *m* (*form*) ◆ **~ base** *or* **site** Raketenbasis *f*; **~ defence system** Raketenabwehrsystem *nt*; **~ launcher** Abschuß- *or* Startrampe *f*; (*vehicle*) Raketenwerfer *m.*

missilry ['mɪsɪlrɪ] *n* (*science*) Raketentechnik *f*; (*missiles*) Raketen(waffen) *pl.*

missing ['mɪsɪŋ] *adj* (*not able to be found*) *person, soldier, aircraft, boat* vermißt; *object* verschwunden; (*not there*) fehlend ◆ **to be ~/to have gone ~** fehlen; (*mountaineer, aircraft, boat etc*) vermißt werden; **the coat has two buttons ~** an dem Mantel fehlen zwei Knöpfe; **we are £50 ~** uns (*dat*) fehlen £ 50; **the ~ clue to his identity** der Schlüssel zu seiner Identität; **~ in action** vermißt; **~ person** Vermißte(r) *mf*; **~ link** fehlendes Glied; (*Biol*) Missing link *nt*, Übergangs- *or* Zwischenform *f.*

mission ['mɪʃən] *n* **(a)** (*business, task*) Auftrag *m*; (*calling*) Aufgabe, Berufung *f*; (*Mil*) Befehl *m*; (*operation*) Einsatz *m* ◆ **what is their ~?** welchen Auftrag haben sie?; wie lauten ihre Befehle?; **our ~ is to ...** wir sind damit beauftragt, zu ...; **the soldiers' ~ was to ...** die Soldaten hatten den Befehl erhalten, zu ...; **to send sb on a secret ~** jdn mit einer geheimen Mission beauftragen; **he's on a secret ~** er ist in geheimer Mission unterwegs; **sense of ~** Sendungsbewußtsein *nt*; **~ accomplished** (*Mil, fig*) Befehl ausgeführt; (*without military overtones*) Auftrag ausgeführt; **~ statement** (*of company*) Firmenphilosophie *f.*
(b) (*journey*) Mission *f* ◆ **trade ~** Handelsreise *f*; **~ of inquiry** Erkundungsreise *f*; **Henry Kissinger's ~ to the Middle East** Kissingers Nahostmission; **~ control** (*Space*) Kontrollzentrum *nt*, Flugleitung *f*; **~ controller** (*Space*) Flugleiter(in *f*) *m.*
(c) (*people on ~*) Gesandtschaft, Delegation *f*; (*Pol*) Mission *f* ◆ **trade ~** Handelsdelegation *f.*
(d) (*Rel*) Mission *f* ◆ **~ hut** Mission(sstation) *f.*

missionary ['mɪʃənrɪ] [1] *n* Missionar(in *f*) *m.*
[2] *adj* missionarisch ◆ **~ position** (*fig inf*) Missionarsstellung *f.*

missis ['mɪsɪz] *n* (*Brit inf*) (*wife*) bessere Hälfte (*hum inf*), Alte (*pej inf*), Olle (*sl*) *f*; (*mistress of household*) Frau *f* des Hauses ◆ **yes, ~** ja(wohl).

Mississippi [mɪsɪ'sɪpɪ] *n* Mississippi *m.*

missive ['mɪsɪv] *n* (*form, old*) Schreiben *nt* (*form*).

Missouri [mɪ'zʊərɪ] *n* (*river*) Missouri *m*; (*state*) Missouri *nt.*

misspell ['mɪs'spel] *pret, ptp* **~ed** *or* **misspelt** *vt* verkehrt *or* falsch schreiben.

misspelling ['mɪs'spelɪŋ] *n* (*act*) falsches Schreiben; (*spelling mistake*) Rechtschreib(e)fehler *m.*

misspelt ['mɪs'spelt] *pret, ptp of* **misspell.**

misspent [,mɪs'spent] *adj* vergeudet, verschwendet ◆ **I regret my ~ youth** ich bedaure es, in meiner Jugend so ein liederliches Leben geführt zu haben; (*wasted youth*) ich bedaure es, meine Jugend so vergeudet *or* vertan zu haben.

misstate ['mɪs'steɪt] *vt* falsch darlegen *or* darstellen.

misstatement ['mɪs'steɪtmənt] *n* falsche Darstellung.
missus ['mɪsɪz] *n (inf) see* **missis.**
missy ['mɪsɪ] *n (inf)* Fräuleinchen *nt (inf)*, kleines Fräulein.
mist [mɪst] *n* **(a)** Nebel *m*; *(in liquid)* Trübung *f*; *(haze)* Dunst *m*; *(on glass etc)* Beschlag *m*.
(b) *(fig)* **through a ~ of tears** durch einen Tränenschleier; **it is lost in the ~s of time/antiquity** das liegt im Dunkel der Vergangenheit; **the ~s of confusion surrounding the affair** das undurchsichtige Dunkel, in das die Angelegenheit gehüllt ist.
◆**mist over** [1] *vi (become cloudy)* sich trüben; *(glass, mirror: also* **mist up***)* (sich) beschlagen ◆ **her eyes ~ed ~ with tears** Tränen verschleierten ihren Blick *(liter)*.
[2] *vt sep* **the condensation is ~ing ~ the windows** durch den Dampf beschlagen die Fensterscheiben.
mistakable [mɪ'steɪkəbl] *adj* **the twins are easily ~** man kann die Zwillinge leicht miteinander verwechseln.
mistake [mɪ'steɪk] [1] *n* Fehler *m* ◆ **to make a ~** *(in writing, calculating etc)* einen Fehler machen; *(be mistaken)* sich irren; **you're making a big ~ in marrying him** Sie machen *or* begehen *(form)* einen schweren Fehler, wenn Sie ihn heiraten; **to make the ~ of asking too much** den Fehler machen *or* begehen *(form)*, zuviel zu verlangen; **what a ~ (to make)!** wie kann man nur (so einen Fehler machen)!; **by ~** aus Versehen, versehentlich; **there must be some ~** da muß ein Fehler *or* Irrtum vorliegen; **the ~ is mine** der Fehler liegt bei mir; **there's no ~ about it,** ... (es besteht) kein Zweifel, ...; **let there be no ~ about it, make no ~ (about it)** ein(e)s *or* das steht fest: ...; **make no ~, I mean what I say** damit wir uns nicht falsch verstehen: mir ist es Ernst; **it's freezing and no ~!** *(inf)* (ich kann dir sagen,) das ist vielleicht eine Kälte! *(inf)*.
[2] *vt pret* **mistook,** *ptp* **mistaken (a)** *words, meaning, remarks etc* falsch auffassen *or* verstehen; *seriousness, cause* verkennen, nicht erkennen; *house, road, time of train* sich irren *or* vertun *(inf)* in *(+dat)* ◆ **to ~ sb's meaning** jdn falsch verstehen; **I mistook you** *or* **what you meant** ich habe Sie falsch *or* nicht richtig verstanden; **there's no mistaking the urgency of the situation** die Dringlichkeit der Situation steht außer Frage; **there's no mistaking her writing** ihre Schrift ist unverkennbar *or* nicht zu verkennen; **there's no mistaking what he meant** er hat sich unmißverständlich ausgedrückt; **there was no mistaking his anger** er war eindeutig wütend.
(b) to ~ A for B A mit B verwechseln, A für B halten; **it cannot possibly be ~n for anything else** das ist doch unverkennbar!, das kann man doch gar nicht verwechseln!
(c) to be ~n sich irren; **you are badly ~n there** da irren Sie sich aber gewaltig!; **if I am not ~n** ... wenn mich nicht alles täuscht ..., wenn ich mich nicht irre ...
▼ **mistaken** [mɪ'steɪkən] *adj (wrong) idea* falsch; *(misplaced) loyalty, kindness* unangebracht, fehl am Platz; *affection, trust* töricht ◆ **a case of ~ identity** eine Verwechslung.
mistakenly [mɪ'steɪkənlɪ] *adv* fälschlicherweise, irrtümlicherweise; *(by accident)* versehentlich.
mister ['mɪstəʳ] *n* **(a)** *(abbr* **Mr***)* Herr *m*; *(on envelope)* Herrn; *(with politicians' names etc) not translated.* **(b)** *(inf: sir) not translated* ◆ **please, ~, can you tell me ...?** können Sie mir bitte sagen ...?; **now listen here, ~** hören Sie mal her.
mistime ['mɪs'taɪm] *vt* **(a)** *(act)* einen ungünstigen Zeitpunkt wählen für ◆ **a badly ~d political announcement** eine politische Erklärung, die zu einem denkbar ungünstigen Zeitpunkt kommt. **(b)** *race* falsch *or* fehlerhaft stoppen.
mistle thrush ['mɪsl,θrʌʃ] *n* Misteldrossel *f*.
mistletoe ['mɪsltəʊ] *n* Mistel *f*; *(sprig)* Mistelzweig *m*.
mistook [mɪ'stʊk] *pret of* **mistake.**
mistral [mɪ'strɑːl] *n* Mistral *m*.
mistranslate ['mɪstrænz'leɪt] *vt* falsch übersetzen.
mistranslation ['mɪstrænz'leɪʃ ən] *n (act)* falsche Übersetzung; *(error also)* Übersetzungsfehler *m*.
mistreat [,mɪs'triːt] *vt* schlecht behandeln; *(violently)* mißhandeln.
mistreatment [,mɪs'triːtmənt] *n* schlechte Behandlung; *(violent)* Mißhandlung *f*.
mistress ['mɪstrɪs] *n* **(a)** *(of house, horse, dog)* Herrin *f* ◆ **she is now ~ of the situation** sie ist jetzt Herr der Lage. **(b)** *(lover)* Geliebte, Mätresse *(old) f*. **(c)** *(teacher)* Lehrerin *f*. **(d)** *(old: Mrs)* Frau *f*.
mistrial [,mɪs'traɪəl] *n* **it was declared a ~** das Urteil wurde wegen Verfahrensmängeln aufgehoben.
mistrust ['mɪs'trʌst] [1] *n* Mißtrauen *nt (of* gegenüber).
[2] *vt* mißtrauen *(+dat)*.
mistrustful [,mɪs'trʌstfʊl] *adj* mißtrauisch ◆ **to be ~ of sb/sth** jdm/einer Sache mißtrauen *or* gegenüber mißtrauisch sein.
misty ['mɪstɪ] *adj (+er)* **(a)** *day, morning* neblig; *(hazy)* dunstig; *mountain peaks* in Nebel/Dunst gehüllt; *colour* gedeckt ◆ **~ weather** Nebel(wetter *nt*) *m*; **a ~ view of the valley** ein Blick auf das (nebel)verhangene *or* dunstige Tal.
(b) *(fig) memory* verschwommen ◆ **her eyes grew ~, a ~ look came into her eyes** ihr Blick verschleierte sich; **~-eyed** mit verschleiertem Blick.
(c) *glasses (misted up)* beschlagen; *(opaque)* milchig; *liquid* trübe ◆ **the window is getting ~** das Fenster beschlägt.
misunderstand ['mɪsʌndə'stænd] *pret, ptp* **misunderstood** [1] *vt* falsch verstehen, mißverstehen ◆ **don't ~ me** ... verstehen Sie mich nicht falsch ...
[2] *vi* **I think you've misunderstood** ich glaube, Sie haben das mißverstanden *or* falsch verstanden.

misunderstanding ['mɪsʌndə'stændɪŋ] *n* **(a)** Mißverständnis *nt* ◆ **there must be some ~** da muß ein Mißverständnis vorliegen; **so that no ~ is possible** um Mißverständnissen vorzubeugen; **let there be no ~ (about it)** ... damit keine Mißverständnisse entstehen: ..., damit wir uns nicht mißverstehen: ...
(b) *(disagreement)* Meinungsverschiedenheit *f*.
misunderstood ['mɪsʌndə'stʊd] [1] *ptp of* **misunderstand.**
[2] *adj* unverstanden; *artist, playwright* verkannt.
misuse ['mɪs'juːs] [1] *n* Mißbrauch *m*; *(of words)* falscher Gebrauch; *(of funds)* Zweckentfremdung *f* ◆ **~ of power/authority** Macht-/Amtsmißbrauch *m*.
[2] ['mɪs'juːz] *vt see n* mißbrauchen; falsch gebrauchen; zweckentfremden.
misword ['mɪs'wɜːd] *vt contract etc* falsch formulieren.
MIT *(US) abbr of* **Massachusetts Institute of Technology.**
mite[1] [maɪt] *n (Zool)* Milbe *f*.
mite[2] [1] *n* **(a)** *(Hist: coin)* Scherf, Heller *m* ◆ **to contribute one's ~ to sth** sein Scherflein zu etw beitragen.
(b) *(small amount)* bißchen *nt* ◆ **well, just a ~ then** na gut, ein (ganz) kleines bißchen.
(c) *(child)* Würmchen *nt (inf)* ◆ **poor little ~!** armes Wurm!
[2] *adv (inf)* **a ~ surprised/disappointed/early** etwas *or* ein bißchen überrascht/enttäuscht/früh dran; **could you wait a ~ longer?** können Sie noch ein Momentchen warten? *(inf)*.
miter *n (US) see* **mitre.**
mitigate ['mɪtɪgeɪt] *vt pain* lindern; *punishment* mildern ◆ **mitigating circumstances** mildernde Umstände *pl*.
mitigation [,mɪtɪ'geɪʃən] *n see vt* Linderung *f*; Milderung *f* ◆ **to say a word in ~** etwas zu jds/seiner Verteidigung anführen; **have you anything to say in ~ of this accusation?** haben Sie irgend etwas zu Ihrer Entlastung vorzubringen?
mitre, *(US)* **miter** ['maɪtəʳ] [1] *n* **(a)** *(Eccl)* Mitra *f*. **(b)** *(Tech: also* **~-joint***)* Gehrung, Gehrfuge *f*.
[2] *vt (Tech)* gehren.
mitt [mɪt] *n* **(a)** *see* **mitten (a). (b)** *(baseball glove)* Fang- *or* Baseballhandschuh *m*. **(c)** *(sl: hand)* Pfote *f (inf)*.
mitten ['mɪtn] *n* **(a)** Fausthandschuh, Fäustling *m*; *(with bare fingers)* Handschuh *m* ohne Finger *or* mit halben Fingern. **(b) ~s** *pl (Boxing)* Boxhandschuhe *pl*.
mix [mɪks] [1] *n* Mischung *f* ◆ **a good social ~ at the party** ein gutgemischtes Publikum; **cake ~** Backmischung *f*; **product ~** Produktspanne *f*.
[2] *vt* **(a)** (ver)mischen; *drinks (prepare)* mischen, mixen; *(Cook) ingredients* verrühren; *dough* zubereiten; *salad* untermengen, wenden ◆ **you shouldn't ~ your drinks** man sollte nicht mehrere Sachen durcheinander trinken; **to ~ sth into sth** etw unter etw *(acc)* mengen *or* mischen.
(b) *(confuse)* durcheinanderbringen ◆ **to ~ sb/sth with sb/sth** jdn/etw mit jdm/etw verwechseln.
(c) to ~ it *(sl)* sich prügeln *or* kloppen *(sl)*; **the gangs were really ~ing it** die Banden haben sich eine ganz schöne Schlägerei geliefert *(inf)*.
[3] *vi* **(a)** sich mischen lassen; *(chemical substances, races)* sich vermischen.
(b) *(go together)* zusammenpassen ◆ **business and pleasure don't ~** Arbeit und Vergnügen lassen sich nicht verbinden.
(c) *(people) (get on)* miteinander auskommen; *(mingle)* sich vermischen; *(associate)* miteinander verkehren ◆ **to ~ with sb** mit jdm auskommen; sich unter jdn mischen; mit jdm verkehren; **he finds it hard to ~** er ist nicht sehr gesellig *or* kontaktfreudig; **to ~ well** kontaktfreudig *or* gesellig sein; **he ~es in high society** er verkehrt in den besseren Kreisen.
◆**mix in** *vt sep egg, water* unterrühren.
◆**mix up** *vt sep* **(a)** vermischen; *ingredients* verrühren; *medicine* mischen.
(b) *(get in a muddle)* durcheinanderbringen; *(confuse with sb/sth else)* verwechseln.
(c) *(involve)* **to ~ sb ~ in sth** jdn in etw *(acc)* hineinziehen; *(in crime etc also)* jdn in etw *(acc)* verwickeln; **to be ~ed ~ in sth** in etw *(acc)* verwickelt sein; **he's got himself ~ed ~ with the police/that bunch** er hat Scherereien mit der Polizei bekommen/sich mit der Bande eingelassen.
(d) to ~ it ~ *(US inf)* sich prügeln *(with* mit); *(non-physically)* sich anlegen *(with* mit).
mixed [mɪkst] *adj* **(a)** *(assorted)* gemischt ◆ **~ nuts/biscuits** Nuß-/Keksmischung *f*.
(b) *(both sexes) choir, bathing, school* gemischt.
(c) *(varied)* gemischt; *(both good and bad)* unterschiedlich ◆ **a ~ set of people** eine bunt zusammengewürfelte Gruppe; **I have ~ feelings about him/it** ich habe ihm gegenüber zwiespältige Gefühle/ich betrachte die Sache mit gemischten Gefühlen.
mixed: ~ blessing *n* **it's a ~ blessing** das ist ein zweischneidiges Schwert; **children are a ~ blessing** Kinder sind kein reines Vergnügen; **~ doubles** *npl (Sport)* gemischtes Doppel; **~ economy** *n* gemischte Wirtschaftsform; **~ farming** *n* Ackerbau und Viehzucht *(+pl vb)*; **~ grill** *n* Grillteller *m*; **~ marriage** *n* Mischehe *f*; **~ metaphor** *n* gemischte Metapher, Bildervermengung *f*; **~ pickles** *npl* Mixed Pickles, Mixpickles *pl*; **~-up** *adj* durcheinander *pred*; *(muddled) person also, ideas* konfus; **I'm all ~-up** ich bin völlig durcheinander; **she's just a crazy ~-up kid** sie ist total verdreht.
mixer ['mɪksəʳ] *n* **(a)** *(food ~)* Mixer *m*, Mixgerät *nt*; *(cement ~)* Mischmaschine *f*.
(b) *(for drink) Cola, Ginger Ale, Tonic etc zum Auffüllen von alkoholischen Mixgetränken.*
(c) *(Rad) (person)* Toningenieur, Mixer *m*; *(thing)* Mischpult *nt*.

➤ LANGUAGE IN USE: **mistaken** → 12.1

(d) (*sociable person*) **to be a good ~** kontaktfreudig sein; **David's not much of a ~** David ist ziemlich kontaktarm *or* verschlossen.
(e) (*US inf*) Party *f* zum Kennenlernen; (*for new students*) Erstsemesterfete *f*.
mixer tap *n* (*Brit*) Mischbatterie *f*.
mixture ['mɪkstʃəʳ] *n* Mischung *f*; (*Med*) Mixtur *f*; (*Cook*) Gemisch *nt*; (*cake ~, dough*) Teig *m* ◆ **~ of tobaccos/teas** Tabak-/Teemischung *f*; **~ of gases** Gasgemisch *nt*; **I've had quite a ~ of drinks tonight** ich habe heute abend ziemlich viel durcheinander getrunken; **a ~ of comedy and tragedy** eine Mischung aus Komödie und Tragödie.
mix-up ['mɪksʌp] *n* Durcheinander *nt* ◆ **we got in a ~ with the trains** mit unseren Zugverbindungen ging alles schief *or* durcheinander; **there seemed to be some ~ about which train** ... es schien völlig unklar, welchen Zug ...; **there must have been a ~** da muß irgend etwas schiefgelaufen sein (*inf*).
MLR (*Brit*) *abbr of* **minimum lending rate**.
mm *abbr of* **millimetre(s)** mm.
mnemonic [nɪ'mɒnɪk] [1] *adj* **(a)** Gedächtnis- ◆ **~ trick** *or* **device** Gedächtnisstütze *f*; **~ rhyme** Eselsbrücke *f* (*inf*). **(b)** (*Comput*) mnemotechnisch.
[2] *n* Gedächtnisstütze *or* -hilfe, Eselsbrücke (*inf*) *f*.
MO *abbr of* **(a) money order. (b) medical officer. (c) modus operandi.**
mo [məʊ] *n* (*inf*) *abbr of* **moment.**
moan [məʊn] [1] *n* **(a)** (*groan*) Stöhnen *nt*; (*of wind*) Seufzen, Raunen (*geh*) *nt*; (*of trees etc*) Raunen *nt* (*geh*).
(b) (*grumble*) Gejammer *nt no pl* (*inf*) ◆ **to have a ~ about sth** über etw (*acc*) jammern *or* schimpfen.
[2] *vi* **(a)** (*groan*) stöhnen; (*wind, trees*) raunen (*geh*).
(b) (*grumble*) jammern, schimpfen (*about* über +*acc*) ◆ **~, ~, ~, that's all she does** sie ist ständig am Maulen (*inf*).
[3] *vt* **..., he ~ed** ... stöhnte er; **he ~ed a sigh of relief** er stöhnte erleichtert auf; **he ~ed a confession** er brachte das Geständnis stöhnend *or* unter Stöhnen heraus.
moaner ['məʊnəʳ] *n* (*inf*) Miesepeter *m* (*inf*); Mäkelliese *f* (*inf*).
moaning ['məʊnɪŋ] *n* **(a)** Stöhnen *nt*; (*of wind also*) Seufzen *nt*; (*of trees etc*) Raunen *nt* (*geh*). **(b)** (*grumbling*) Gestöhn(e) *nt*.
moat [məʊt] *n* Wassergraben *m*; (*of castle also*) Burggraben *m*.
moated ['məʊtɪd] *adj* von einem Wassergraben umgeben.
mob [mɒb] [1] *n* **(a)** (*crowd*) Horde, Schar *f*; (*riotous, violent*) Mob *m no pl* ◆ **an undisciplined ~** ein undisziplinierter Haufen; **~s gathered to burn the houses** der Mob *or* Pöbel lief zusammen, um die Häuser zu verbrennen; **the crowd became a ~** das Volk wurde zur wütenden Menge; **they went in a ~ to the town hall** sie stürmten zum Rathaus.
(b) (*inf*) (*criminal gang*) Bande *f*; (*fig: clique*) Haufen *m*, Bande *f* ◆ **which ~ were you in?** (*Mil*) bei welchem Haufen warst du denn? (*inf*).
(c) the ~ (*pej: the masses*) die Masse(n *pl*).
[2] *vt* herfallen über (+*acc*), sich stürzen auf (+*acc*); *actor, pop star also* belagern ◆ **the prisoner was ~bed** die Menge fiel über den Gefangenen her.
mobcap ['mɒbkæp] *n* (*Hist*) (Spitzen)haube *f*.
mobile ['məʊbaɪl] [1] *adj* **(a)** *person* beweglich, mobil; (*having means of transport*) beweglich, motorisiert; (*Sociol*) mobil ◆ **the patient is ~ already** der Patient kann schon aufstehen.
(b) *X-ray unit etc* fahrbar ◆ **~ canteen** Kantine *f* auf Rädern, mobile Küche; **~ home** Wohnwagen *m*; **~ library** Fahrbücherei *f*; **~ phone** Mobiltelefon *nt*, Handy *nt*; **~ shop** (*Brit*) Verkaufswagen *m*; **~ walkway** (*US*) Rollsteg *m*.
(c) *mind* wendig, beweglich; *face, expression, features* lebhaft, beweglich.
[2] *n* **(a)** (*also* **~ phone**) Handy *nt*. **(b)** (*decoration*) Mobile *nt*.
mobility [məʊ'bɪlɪtɪ] *n* (*of person*) Beweglichkeit *f*; (*of work force, Sociol*) Mobilität *f*; (*of mind also*) Wendigkeit *f*; (*of features, face etc also*) Lebhaftigkeit *f* ◆ **a car gives you ~** ein Auto macht Sie beweglicher.
mobilization [ˌməʊbɪlaɪ'zeɪʃən] *n* Mobilisierung *f*; (*Mil also*) Mobilmachung *f*.
mobilize ['məʊbɪlaɪz] [1] *vt* mobilisieren; (*Mil also*) mobil machen.
[2] *vi* mobil machen.
mob rule *n* Herrschaft *f* des Pöbels.
mobster ['mɒbstəʳ] *n* (*esp US*) Gangster, Bandit *m*.
mob violence *n* Massenausschreitungen *pl*.
moccasin ['mɒkəsɪn] *n* Mokassin *m*.
mocha ['mɒkə] *n* Mokka *m*.
mock [mɒk] [1] *n* **to make a ~ of sth** etw ad absurdum führen; (*put an end to*) etw vereiteln *or* zunichte machen.
[2] *adj attr emotions* gespielt; *attack, battle, fight* Schein-; *crash, examination* simuliert; *Tudor, Elizabethan* Pseudo-.
[3] *vt* **(a)** (*ridicule*) sich lustig machen über (+*acc*), verspotten. **(b)** (*mimic*) nachmachen *or* -äffen. **(c)** (*defy*) trotzen (+*dat*); *law* sich hinwegsetzen über (+*acc*); (*set at nought*) *plans, efforts* vereiteln, zunichte machen.
[4] *vi* **to ~ at sb/sth** sich über jdn/etw lustig machen *or* mokieren; **don't ~** mokier dich nicht!, spotte nicht! (*geh*).
mocker ['mɒkəʳ] *n* **(a)** Spötter(in *f*) *m*, spöttischer Mensch. **(b) to put the ~s on sth** (*Brit sl*) etw vermasseln (*inf*).
mockery ['mɒkərɪ] *n* **(a)** (*derision*) Spott *m*.
(b) (*object of ridicule*) Gespött *nt* ◆ **they made a ~ of him** sie machten ihn zum Gespött der Leute; **to make a ~ of sth** etw lächerlich machen; (*prove its futility*) etw ad absurdum führen; **inflation will make a ~ of our budget** durch die Inflation wird unser Haushaltsplan zur Farce.
(c) this is a ~ of justice das spricht jeglicher Gerechtigkeit hohn; **it was a ~ of a trial** der Prozeß war eine einzige Farce; **what a ~ (this is)!** das ist doch glatter *or* der reinste Hohn!
mock: ~-heroic *adj* (*Liter*) heroisch-komisch; **~-heroic poem** komisches Epos; **~-heroics** *npl* (*Liter*) heroisch-komische Passage(n *pl*).
mocking ['mɒkɪŋ] [1] *adj* spöttisch.
[2] *n* Spott *m*.
mockingbird ['mɒkɪŋˌbɜːd] *n* Spottdrossel *f*.
mockingly ['mɒkɪŋlɪ] *adv* spöttisch, voller Spott ◆ **she ~ repeated his words** sie äffte seine Worte nach.
mock: ~ orange *n* falscher Jasmin, Pfeifenstrauch *m*; **~ turtle soup** *n* Mockturtlesuppe *f*; **~-up** *n* Modell *nt* in Originalgröße.
MOD (*Brit*) *abbr of* **Ministry of Defence.**
mod [mɒd] (*dated sl*) [1] *adj* modern, pop(p)ig (*inf*).
[2] *n modisch gekleideter Halbstarker in den 60er Jahren.*
modal ['məʊdl] *adj* modal ◆ **~ verb** Modalverb *nt*.
modality [məʊ'dælɪtɪ] *n* Modalität *f*.
mod cons ['mɒd'kɒnz] *abbr of* **modern conveniences** mod. Komf., (moderner) Komfort.
mode [məʊd] *n* **(a)** (*Gram*) Modus *m*; (*Mus*) Tonart *f*; (*Philos*) Modalität *f*. **(b)** (*way*) Art *f* (und Weise); (*form*) Form *f* ◆ **~ of transport** Transportmittel *nt*; **~ of life** Lebensweise *f*; (*Biol*) Lebensform *f*. **(c)** (*Fashion*) Mode *f*. **to be the ~** in Mode sein. **(d)** (*Comput*) Modus, Mode *m*.
model ['mɒdl] [1] *n* **(a)** Modell *nt* ◆ **to make sth on the ~ of sth** etw (*acc*) einer Sache (*dat*) nachbilden; **it is built on the ~ of the Doge's Palace** es ist eine Nachbildung des Dogenpalastes; **our democracy is based on the ~ of Greece** unsere Demokratie ist nach dem Vorbild Griechenlands aufgebaut.
(b) (*perfect example*) Muster *nt* (*of an* +*dat*) ◆ **this book is a ~ of clear expression** dieses Buch ist beispielhaft für klare Ausdrucksweise; **to hold sb up as a ~** jdn als Vorbild hinstellen.
(c) (*artist's, photographer's*) Modell *nt*; (*fashion ~*) Mannequin *nt*; (*male ~*) Dressman *m*.
(d) (*of car, dress, machine etc*) Modell *nt*.
[2] *adj* **(a)** *railway, town* Modell-; *house, home* Muster-.
(b) (*perfect*) vorbildlich, Muster-, mustergültig.
[3] *vt* **(a) to ~ X on Y** Y als Vorlage *or* Muster für X benützen; **X is ~led on Y** Y dient als Vorlage *or* Muster für X; **this building is ~led on the Parthenon** dieses Gebäude ist dem Parthenon nachgebildet; **the system was ~led on the American one** das System war nach amerikanischem Muster aufgebaut; **this poem is ~led on Shakespeare's sonnets** dieses Gedicht ist Shakespeares Sonetten nachempfunden; **it's not ~led on anything** es ist frei entstanden, dafür gibt es keine Vorlage; **students nowadays all seem to be ~led on one pattern** die heutigen Studenten scheinen alle einen Typ zu verkörpern; **to ~ oneself/one's life on sb** sich (*dat*) jdn zum Vorbild nehmen.
(b) (*make a ~*) modellieren, formen ◆ **her delicately ~led features** (*fig*) ihre feingeschnittenen Gesichtszüge.
(c) *dress etc* vorführen.
[4] *vi* **(a)** (*make ~s*) modellieren.
(b) (*Art, Phot*) als Modell arbeiten *or* beschäftigt sein; (*fashion*) als Mannequin/Dressman arbeiten ◆ **to ~ for sb** jdm Modell stehen/jds Kreationen vorführen.
modelling, (US) modeling ['mɒdlɪŋ] *n* **(a)** (*of statue etc*) Modellieren *nt*; (*fig: of features*) Schnitt *m*. **(b) to do some ~** (*Phot, Art*) als Modell arbeiten; (*Fashion*) als Mannequin/Dressman arbeiten.
modem ['məʊdem] *n* Modem *nt* ◆ **~ card** Modem-Karte *f*.
moderate ['mɒdərɪt] [1] *adj* gemäßigt (*also Pol*); *language also, appetite, enjoyment, lifestyle, speed* mäßig; *demands also, price* vernünftig, angemessen; *drinker, eater* maßvoll; *income, success* (mittel)mäßig, bescheiden; *punishment, winter* mild ◆ **a ~ amount** einigermaßen viel; **~-sized, of ~ size** mittelgroß.
[2] *n* (*Pol*) Gemäßigte(r) *mf*.
[3] ['mɒdəreɪt] *vt* **(a)** mäßigen ◆ **the climate is ~d by the Gulf Stream** das Klima wird durch den Golfstrom gemäßigter; **to have a moderating influence on sb** mäßigend auf jdn wirken. **(b)** *meeting, discussion* den Vorsitz führen bei; (*TV, Rad*) moderieren.
[4] ['mɒdəreɪt] *vi* **(a)** nachlassen, sich mäßigen; (*wind etc*) nachlassen, sich abschwächen; (*demands*) gemäßigter werden. **(b)** den Vorsitz führen; (*TV, Rad*) moderieren.
moderately ['mɒdərɪtlɪ] *adv* einigermaßen ◆ **a ~ expensive suit** ein nicht allzu *or* übermäßig teurer Anzug; **the house was ~ large** das Haus war mäßig groß.
moderation [ˌmɒdə'reɪʃən] *n* Mäßigung *f* ◆ **in ~** mit Maß(en).
moderator ['mɒdəreɪtəʳ] *n* (*Eccl*) Synodalpräsident *m*.
modern ['mɒdən] [1] *adj* modern (*also Art, Liter*); *times, world also* heutig; *history* neuere und neueste ◆ **~ languages** neuere Sprachen, moderne Fremdsprachen *pl*; (*Univ*) Neuphilologie *f*; **M~ Greek** *etc* Neugriechisch *etc nt*; **~ studies** Gegenwartskunde und Kulturwissenschaft; **~ French studies** französische Sprache und Landeskunde.
[2] *n* Anhänger(in *f*) *m* der Moderne.
modernism ['mɒdənɪzəm] *n* Modernismus *m*.
modernist ['mɒdənɪst] [1] *adj* modernistisch.
[2] *n* Modernist *m*.
modernistic [ˌmɒdə'nɪstɪk] *adj* modernistisch.
modernity [mɒ'dɜːnɪtɪ] *n* Modernität *f*.
modernization [ˌmɒdənaɪ'zeɪʃən] *n* Modernisierung *f*.
modernize ['mɒdənaɪz] *vt* modernisieren.
modernly ['mɒdənlɪ] *adv* (*fashionably*) modern ◆ **more ~ known as ...** in

neuerer Zeit als ... bekannt.

modernness ['mɒdənnɪs] *n see* **modernity.**

modest ['mɒdɪst] *adj* **(a)** *(unboastful)* bescheiden ◆ **to be ~ about one's successes** nicht mit seinen Erfolgen prahlen.
(b) *(moderate)* bescheiden; *person also* genügsam; *requirements also* gering; *price* mäßig ◆ **a ~ crowd turned out for the occasion** die Veranstaltung war (nur) mäßig besucht.
(c) *(chaste, proper)* schamhaft; *(in one's behaviour)* anständig, sittsam *(geh)*, züchtig *(old)* ◆ **to be ~ in one's dress** sich unauffällig *or* dezent kleiden.

modestly ['mɒdɪstlɪ] *adv* **(a)** *(unassumingly, moderately)* bescheiden. **(b)** *(chastely, properly)* schamhaft; *behave* anständig, züchtig *(old)*; *dress* unauffällig, dezent.

modesty ['mɒdɪstɪ] *n see adj* **(a)** Bescheidenheit *f* ◆ **in all ~** bei aller Bescheidenheit; **the ~ of the man!** *(iro)* der ist ja überhaupt nicht von sich eingenommen! *(iro inf)*.
(b) Bescheidenheit *f*; Genügsamkeit *f*; Mäßigkeit *f*.
(c) Schamgefühl *nt*; Anstand *m*, Sittsamkeit *(geh)*, Züchtigkeit *(old) f*; Unauffälligkeit, Dezentheit *f*.

modicum ['mɒdɪkəm] *n* ein wenig *or* bißchen ◆ **with a ~ of luck** mit ein (klein) wenig *or* einem Quentchen Glück; **a ~ of hope/decorum/confidence** ein Funke (von) Hoffnung/Anstand/Vertrauen; **a ~ of truth** ein Körnchen Wahrheit.

modifiable ['mɒdɪfaɪəbl] *adj* modifizierbar.

modification [,mɒdɪfɪ'keɪʃən] *n* (Ver)änderung *f*; *(of design)* Abänderung *f*; *(of terms, contract, wording)* Modifizierung, Modifikation *f* ◆ **to make ~s to sth** (Ver)änderungen an etw *(dat)* vornehmen; etw abändern; etw modifizieren; **the suggested ~s to his design** die Änderungsvorschläge *pl* zu seinem Entwurf.

modifier ['mɒdɪfaɪəʳ] *n (Gram)* Bestimmungswort *nt*, nähere Bestimmung.

modify ['mɒdɪfaɪ] *vt* **(a)** *(change)* (ver)ändern; *design* abändern; *terms, contract, wording* modifizieren. **(b)** *(moderate)* mäßigen. **(c)** *(Gram)* näher bestimmen.

modish ['məʊdɪʃ] *adj (fashionable)* modisch; *(stylish)* schick ◆ **it is very ~ to ...** es ist große Mode, zu ...

modishly ['məʊdɪʃlɪ] *adv see adj* ◆ **he ~ professed his solidarity with the working classes** er folgte dem herrschenden Trend und bekannte sich mit der Arbeiterklasse solidarisch.

modiste [məʊ'di:st] *n* Modistin *f*.

modular ['mɒdjʊləʳ] *adj* aus Elementen zusammengesetzt; *(Comput)* modular ◆ **the ~ design of their furniture** ihre als Bauelemente konzipierten Möbel.

modulate ['mɒdjʊleɪt] *vti (Mus, Rad)* modulieren ◆ **the key ~d from major to minor** die Tonart wechselte von Dur nach Moll.

modulation [,mɒdjʊ'leɪʃən] *n (Mus, Rad)* Modulation *f*.

module ['mɒdju:l] *n* (Bau)element *nt*; *(in education)* Kurs *m*; *(Comput)* Modul *nt*; *(Space)* Raumkapsel *f* ◆ **command ~** Kommandokapsel *f*; **lunar ~** Mondlandefähre *f or* -fahrzeug *nt*; **service ~** Betriebseinheit *f*.

modus operandi ['məʊdəs,ɒpə'rændɪ] *n* Modus operandi *m*.

modus vivendi ['məʊdəs,vɪ'vendɪ] *n* Modus vivendi *m*; *(way of life)* Lebensstil *m or* -weise *f*.

moggy ['mɒgɪ] *n (Brit inf)* Mieze *f (inf)*.

mogul ['məʊgəl] *n* Mogul *m*.

MOH *abbr of* **Medical Officer of Health.**

mohair ['məʊhɛəʳ] *n* Mohair *m*.

Mohammed [məʊ'hæmed] *n* Mohammed *m*.

Mohammedan [məʊ'hæmɪdən] [1] *adj* mohammedanisch.
[2] *n* Mohammedaner(in *f*) *m*.

Mohammedanism [mə'hæmədənɪzəm] *n* Islam *m*.

Mohican [məʊ'hi:kən] *n* **(a)** Mohikaner(in *f*) *m*. **(b) m~** *(haircut)* Irokesenschnitt *m*.

moiety ['mɔɪtɪ] *n (Jur: half)* Hälfte *f*; *(liter) (small amount)* Hauch *m (geh)* (of an +*dat*); *(small share)* Bruchteil *m*.

moist [mɔɪst] *adj (+er)* feucht *(from, with* vor +*dat)*.

moisten ['mɔɪsn] [1] *vt* anfeuchten ◆ **to ~ sth with sth** etw mit etw befeuchten.
[2] *vi* feucht werden.

moistness ['mɔɪstnɪs] *n* Feuchtigkeit *f*.

moisture ['mɔɪstʃəʳ] *n* Feuchtigkeit *f* ◆ **drops of ~** Wasser-/Schweißtropfen *pl*.

moisturize ['mɔɪstʃəraɪz] *vt skin* mit einer Feuchtigkeitscreme behandeln; *(cosmetic)* geschmeidig machen, Feuchtigkeit verleihen (+*dat*); *air* befeuchten.

moisturizer ['mɔɪstʃəraɪzəʳ], **moisturizing cream** ['mɔɪstʃəraɪzɪŋ'kri:m] *n* Feuchtigkeitscreme *f*.

moke [məʊk] *n (Brit sl)* Esel *m*.

molar (tooth) ['məʊləʳ(,tu:θ)] *n* Backenzahn *m*.

molasses [məʊ'læsɪz] *n* Melasse *f* ◆ **to be as slow as ~ (in winter)** *(US inf)* eine (fürchterliche) Transuse sein *(inf)*.

mold *etc (US) see* **mould** *etc.*

molt *n, vti (US) see* **moult.**

mole[1] [məʊl] *n (Anat)* Pigmentmal *nt (form)*, Leberfleck *m*.

mole[2] *n (Zool)* Maulwurf *m*; *(inf: secret agent)* Spion(in *f*) *m*.

mole[3] *n (Naut)* Mole *f*.

molecular [məʊ'lekjʊləʳ] *adj* molekular, Molekular-.

molecule ['mɒlɪkju:l] *n* Molekül *nt*.

mole: ~hill *n* Maulwurfshaufen *or* -hügel *m*; **~skin** *n (fur)* Maulwurfsfell *nt*; *(garment)* Mantel/Jacke *etc* aus Maulwurfsfell; *(fabric)* Moleskin *m or nt*.

molest [məʊ'lest] *vt* belästigen.

molestation [,məʊles'teɪʃən] *n* Belästigung *f*.

moll [mɒl] *n (sl)* Gangsterbraut *f*.

mollify ['mɒlɪfaɪ] *vt* besänftigen, beschwichtigen ◆ **he was somewhat mollified by this** daraufhin beruhigte er sich etwas.

mollusc ['mɒləsk] *n* Molluske *f (spec)*, Weichtier *nt*.

mollycoddle ['mɒlɪ,kɒdl] [1] *vt* verhätscheln, verpäppeln, verzärteln ◆ **to ~ oneself** sich päppeln.
[2] *n* Weichling *m*.

Moloch ['məʊlɒk] *n* Moloch *m*.

Molotov cocktail ['mɒlətɒf'kɒkteɪl] *n* Molotowcocktail *m*.

molten ['məʊltən] *adj* geschmolzen; *glass, lava* flüssig.

mom [mɒm] *n (US inf) see* **mum[2].**

mom-and-pop store ['mɒmən'pɒp,stɔ:ʳ] *n (US inf)* Tante-Emma-Laden *m (inf)*.

moment ['məʊmənt] *n* **(a)** Augenblick, Moment *m* ◆ **there were one or two ~s when I thought** ... ein paarmal dachte ich ...; **from ~ to ~** zusehends, von Minute zu Minute; **any ~ now, (at) any ~** jeden Augenblick; **at any ~** *(any time)* jederzeit; **at the ~** im Augenblick, momentan; **at the ~ when** ... zu dem Zeitpunkt, als ...; **not at the** *or* **this ~** im Augenblick *or* zur Zeit nicht; **at the ~ of impact** beim Aufprall, im Augenblick des Aufpralls; **at the last ~** im letzten Augenblick; **at this (particular) ~ in time** momentan, augenblicklich; **for the ~** im Augenblick, vorläufig; **for a ~** (für) einen Moment; **for one ~ it seemed to have stopped** einen Augenblick lang schien es aufgehört zu haben; **not for a** *or* **one ~** ... nie(mals) ...; **I didn't hesitate for a ~** ich habe keinen Augenblick gezögert; **in a ~** gleich; **in a ~ of madness** in einem Anflug von geistiger Umnachtung; **it was all over in a ~** *or* **a few ~s** das ganze dauerte nur wenige Augenblicke *or* war im Nu geschehen; **to leave things until the last ~** alles erst im letzten Moment erledigen *or* machen *(inf)*; **half a ~/one ~!** Momentchen/einen Moment!; **just a ~!, wait a ~!** Moment mal!; **I shan't be a ~** ich bin gleich wieder da; *(nearly ready)* ich bin gleich soweit; **do it this very ~!** tu das auf der Stelle!; **I have just this ~ heard of it** ich habe es eben *or* gerade erst erfahren; **we haven't a ~ to lose** wir haben keine Minute zu verlieren; **not a ~ too soon** keine Minute zu früh, in letzter Minute; **not a ~'s peace** *or* **rest** keine ruhige Minute; **the ~ it happened** (in dem Augenblick,) als es passierte; **the ~ I saw him I knew** ... als ich ihn sah, wußte ich sofort ...; **the ~ he arrives there's trouble** sobald er auftaucht, gibt es Ärger; **tell me the ~ he comes** sagen Sie mir sofort Bescheid, wenn er kommt; **the ~ of truth** die Stunde der Wahrheit; **he is the man of the ~** er ist der Mann des Tages.
(b) *(Phys)* Moment *nt* ◆ **~ of acceleration/inertia** Beschleunigungs-/Trägheitsmoment *nt*.
(c) *(importance)* Bedeutung *f* ◆ **of little ~** bedeutungslos, unwichtig.

momentarily ['məʊməntərɪlɪ] *adv* **(a)** (für) einen Augenblick *or* Moment. **(b)** *(US) (very soon)* jeden Augenblick *or* Moment; *(from moment to moment)* zusehends.

momentary ['məʊməntərɪ] *adj* kurz; *glimpse also* flüchtig ◆ **there was a ~ silence** einen Augenblick lang herrschte Stille.

momentous [məʊ'mentəs] *adj (memorable, important)* bedeutsam, bedeutungsvoll; *(of great consequence)* von großer Tragweite ◆ **of ~ significance** von entscheidender Bedeutung.

momentousness [məʊ'mentəsnɪs] *n* Bedeutsamkeit *f*; *(of decision)* Tragweite *f*.

momentum [məʊ'mentəm] *n (of moving object)* Schwung *m*; *(at moment of impact)* Wucht *f*; *(Phys)* Impuls *m*; *(fig)* Schwung *m* ◆ **the rock's ~ carried it through the wall** der Felsbrocken hatte eine solche Wucht, daß er die Mauer durchschlug; **he let the car go under its own ~** er ließ das Auto von allein weiterrollen; **to gather** *or* **gain ~** *(lit)* sich beschleunigen, in Fahrt kommen *(inf)*; *(fig: idea, movement, plan)* in Gang kommen; **that idea is now gathering** *or* **gaining ~** diese Idee gewinnt an Boden; **to keep going under its own ~** *(lit)* sich aus eigener Kraft weiterbewegen; *(fig)* eine Eigendynamik entwickelt haben; **to lose ~** *(lit, fig)* Schwung verlieren.

Mon *abbr of* **Monday** Mo.

Monaco ['mɒnəkəʊ] *n* Monaco *nt*.

monarch ['mɒnək] *n* Monarch(in *f*), Herrscher(in *f*) *m*; *(fig)* König *m* ◆ **absolute ~** Alleinherrscher *m*.

monarchic(al) [mɒ'nɑ:kɪk(əl)] *adj* monarchisch; *(favouring monarchy)* monarchistisch.

monarchism ['mɒnəkɪzəm] *n (system)* Monarchie *f*; *(advocacy of monarchy)* Monarchismus *m*.

monarchist ['mɒnəkɪst] [1] *adj* monarchistisch.
[2] *n* Monarchist(in *f*) *m*, Anhänger(in *f*) *m* der Monarchie.

monarchy ['mɒnəkɪ] *n* Monarchie *f*.

monastery ['mɒnəstərɪ] *n* (Männer- *or* Mönchs)kloster *nt*.

monastic [mə'næstɪk] *adj* mönchisch, klösterlich; *architecture* Kloster-; *life* Ordens-, Kloster- ◆ **~ vows** Ordensgelübde *nt*; **he leads a ~ existence** *(fig)* er lebt wie ein Mönch.

monasticism [mə'næstɪsɪzəm] *n* Mönch(s)tum *nt*.

Monday ['mʌndɪ] *n* Montag *m*; *see also* **Tuesday.**

Monegasque [mɒnə'gæsk] [1] *n* Monegasse *m*, Monegassin *f*.
[2] *adj* monegassisch.

monetarism ['mʌnɪtərɪzəm] *n* Monetarismus *m*.

monetarist ['mʌnɪtərɪst] [1] *n* Monetarist(in *f*) *m*.

[2] *adj* monetaristisch.
monetary ['mʌnɪtərɪ] *adj* **(a)** *(pertaining to finance or currency)* währungspolitisch, monetär; *talks, policy, reform, system* Währungs-; *reserves, institutions* Geld-; *unit* Geld-, Währungs-. **(b)** *(pecuniary)* Geld-; *considerations* geldlich.
money ['mʌnɪ] *n* Geld *nt*; *(medium of exchange)* Zahlungsmittel *nt* ◆ **they use these stones as ~** sie benutzen diese Steine als Zahlungsmittel *or* anstelle von Geld; **to make ~** *(person)* (viel) Geld verdienen; *(business)* etwas einbringen, sich rentieren; **to lose ~** *(person)* Geld verlieren; *(business)* Verluste machen *or* haben; **~ talks** *(Pol)* Währungsgespräche *pl*; **there's ~ in it** das ist sehr lukrativ; **if you help me, there's ~ in it** wenn du mir hilfst, springt für dich auch etwas dabei heraus *(inf)*; **it's a bargain for the ~** das ist eine günstige Anschaffung; **what can you expect for the ~?** was kann man bei dem Preis schon verlangen?; **that's the one for my ~!** ich tippe auf ihn/sie *etc*; **it's ~ for jam** *(inf) or* **old rope** *(inf)* da wird einem das Geld ja nachgeworfen *(inf)*; **to be in the ~** *(inf)* Geld wie Heu haben; **what's the ~ like in this job?** wie wird der Job bezahlt?; **to earn good ~** gut verdienen; **to get one's ~'s worth** etwas für sein Geld bekommen; **I've really had my ~'s worth** *or* **~ out of that car** der Wagen hat sich wirklich bezahlt gemacht *or* war wirklich sein Geld wert; **to keep sb in ~** jdn (finanziell) unterstützen; **do you think I'm made of ~?** *(inf)* ich bin doch kein Krösus!; **that's throwing good ~ after bad** das ist rausgeschmissenes Geld *(inf)*; **your ~ or your life!** Geld oder Leben!; **to put one's ~ where one's mouth is** *(inf)* (nicht nur reden, sondern) Taten sprechen lassen; **~ talks** *(inf)* mit Geld geht alles; **~ isn't everything** *(prov)* Geld (allein) macht nicht glücklich *(prov)*.
money: ~ bag *n* Geldsack *m*; **~bags** *n sing (inf)* Geldsack *m*; **~ belt** *n* ≃ Gürteltasche *f (mit Geldfächern)*; **~box** *n* Sparbüchse *f*; **~changer** *n* (Geld)wechsler *m*.
moneyed ['mʌnɪd] *adj* begütert.
money: ~grubber *n* Raffke *m (inf)*; **~grubbing** [1] *adj* geld- *or* raffgierig; [2] *n* Geld- *or* Raffgier *f*; **~lender** *n* Geld(ver)leiher *m*; **~lending** *n* Geldverleih *m*; **~maker** *n (idea)* einträgliche Sache; *(product)* Verkaufserfolg *m*; *(company)* gewinnbringendes *or* gutgehendes Unternehmen; **~making** [1] *adj idea, plan* gewinnbringend, einträglich; [2] *n* Geldverdienen *nt*; **~ market** *n* Geldmarkt *m*; **~ matters** *npl* Geldangelegenheiten *or* -dinge *pl*; **~ order** *n* Post- *or* Zahlungsanweisung *f*; **~ prize** *n* Geldpreis *m*; **~ spider** *n kleine Spinne*; **~spinner** *n (inf)* Verkaufsschlager *(inf) or* -hit *(inf) m*; **~ supply** *n* Geldvolumen *nt*.
Mongol ['mɒŋgəl] [1] *adj* **(a)** mongolisch. **(b)** *(Med)* **m~** mongoloid.
[2] *n* **(a)** *see* **Mongolian 2. (b)** *(Med)* **he's a m~** er ist mongoloid.
Mongolia [mɒŋ'gəʊlɪə] *n* Mongolei *f*.
Mongolian [mɒŋ'gəʊlɪən] [1] *adj* mongolisch; *features, appearance* mongolid.
[2] *n* **(a)** Mongole *m*, Mongolin *f*. **(b)** *(language)* Mongolisch *nt*.
mongolism ['mɒŋgəlɪzəm] *n (Med)* Mongolismus *m*.
Mongoloid ['mɒŋgəlɔɪd] *adj* **(a)** mongolid. **(b)** *(Med)* **m~** mongoloid.
mongoose ['mɒŋgu:s] *n, pl* **-s** Mungo *m*.
mongrel ['mʌŋgrəl] [1] *adj race* Misch-.
[2] *n (also* **~ dog**) Promenadenmischung *f*; *(pej)* Köter *m*; *(pej: person)* Mischling *m*.
moni(c)ker ['mɒnɪkə^r] *n (Brit sl: signature)* Name, (Friedrich) Wilhelm *(inf) m*.
monitor ['mɒnɪtə^r] [1] *n* **(a)** *(Sch) Schüler(in f) m mit besonderen Pflichten* ◆ **stationery/book ~** Schreibwaren-/Bücherwart *m*.
(b) *(TV, Tech: screen)* Monitor *m*.
(c) *(control, observer)* Überwacher *m*; *(of telephone conversations)* Abhörer *m*; *(Rad)* Mitarbeiter(in *f*) *m* am Monitor-Dienst.
(d) *(also* **~ lizard**) Waran(echse *f*) *m*.
[2] *vt* **(a)** *foreign station, telephone conversation* abhören; *TV programme* mithören. **(b)** *(control, check)* überwachen; *personal expenditure etc* kontrollieren.
monitoring ['mɒnɪtərɪŋ] [1] *n see vt* Abhören *nt*; Mithören *nt*; Überwachung *f*; Kontrolle *f*.
[2] *adj attr function* Überwachungs-, Kontroll- ◆ **~ body** Kontrollorgan *nt*.
monk [mʌŋk] *n* Mönch *m*.
monkey ['mʌŋkɪ] [1] *n* Affe *m*; *(fig: child)* Strolch, Schlingel *m* ◆ **to make a ~ out of sb** *(inf)* jdn verhohnepipeln *(inf)*; **well, I'll be a ~'s uncle** *(inf)* (ich glaub,) mich laust der Affe *(inf)*; **to have a ~ on one's back** *(US sl)* an der Nadel hängen *(sl)*; **I don't give a ~'s (fart)** *(sl)* das ist mir scheißegal *(sl) or* schnurzpiepe *(hum inf)*.
[2] *vi* **to ~ about** *(inf)* herumalbern; **to ~ about with sth** an etw *(dat)* herumspielen *or* -fummeln *(inf)*.
monkey: ~ business *n (inf)* **no ~ business!** mach(t) mir keine Sachen! *(inf)*; **there's some ~ business going on here** da ist doch irgend etwas faul *(inf)*; **what ~ business have you been up to?** was hast du jetzt schon wieder angestellt?; **~ jacket** *n* Affenjäckchen *nt (inf)*; **~-nut** *n* Erdnuß *f*; **~-puzzle (tree)** *n* Andentanne, Araukarie *(spec) f*; **~ suit** *n (inf: tails)* Frack *m*; **he was all done up in his ~ suit** er hatte sich in volle Montur *or* in Schale geworfen *(inf)*; **~-tricks** *npl* Unfug *m*, dumme Streiche *pl*; **none of your ~-tricks!** mach(t) mir keinen Unfug!; **I bet he's up to some ~-tricks again!** der hat doch sicher wieder irgendwas ausgeheckt *(inf)*; **~-wrench** *n* verstellbarer Schraubenschlüssel, Engländer *m*; **to throw a ~-wrench into the works** *(US inf)* jdm einen Knüppel zwischen die Beine werfen *(inf)*.
monkish ['mʌŋkɪʃ] *adj* mönchisch; *(fig pej)* pastorenhaft ◆ **he leads a ~ life** er führt ein Leben wie ein Mönch.
mono ['mɒnəʊ] [1] *n* Mono *nt*.
[2] *adj* mono- *attr*; *record also* in Mono *pred*.
mono- *pref* Mono-, mono-.
monochrome ['mɒnəkrəʊm] [1] *adj* monochrom, einfarbig; *television* Schwarzweiß-; *(Comput)* monochrom, monochromatisch ◆ **~ screen** Monochrom-Bildschirm *m*.
[2] *n (Art)* monochrome *or* in einer Farbe gehaltene Malerei; *(TV)* Schwarzweiß *nt*.
monocle ['mɒnəkəl] *n* Monokel *nt*.
monogamous [mɒ'nɒgəməs] *adj* monogam.
monogamy [mɒ'nɒgəmɪ] *n* Monogamie *f*.
monogram ['mɒnəgræm] *n* Monogramm *nt*.
monogrammed ['mɒnəgræmd] *adj* mit Monogramm.
monograph ['mɒnəgrɑ:f] *n* Monographie *f*.
monokini [,mɒnə'ki:ni:] *n* Minikini, Monokini *m*.
monolingual [,mɒnə'lɪŋgwəl] *adj* einsprachig.
monolith ['mɒnəʊlɪθ] *n* Monolith *m*.
monolithic [,mɒnəʊ'lɪθɪk] *adj (lit)* monolithisch; *(fig)* gigantisch, riesig.
monologue ['mɒnəlɒg] *n* Monolog *m*.
mono: ~mania *n* Monomanie *f*; **~plane** *n* Eindecker *m*.
monopolist [mə'nɒpəlɪst] *n* Monopolist *m*.
monopolization [mə,nɒpəlaɪ'zeɪʃən] *n (lit)* Monopolisierung *f*; *(fig) (of bathroom, best seat etc)* Beschlagnahme *f*; *(of person, sb's time etc)* völlige Inanspruchnahme; *(of conversation etc)* Beherrschung *f*.
monopolize [mə'nɒpəlaɪz] *vt (lit) market* monopolisieren, beherrschen; *(fig) person, place, sb's time etc* mit Beschlag belegen, in Beschlag nehmen; *conversation, discussion* beherrschen, an sich *(acc)* reißen ◆ **to ~ the supply/distribution of ...** eine Monopolstellung für die Lieferung/den Vertrieb von ... haben; **she wants to ~ his affections** sie möchte seine Zuneigung *or* ihn ganz für sich haben.
monopoly [mə'nɒpəlɪ] *n* **(a)** *(lit)* Monopol *nt* ◆ **~ position** Monopolstellung *f*; **coal is a government ~** der Staat hat das Kohlenmonopol *or* das Monopol für Kohle; **Monopolies and Mergers Commission** *(Brit) britisches Kartellamt*.
(b) *(fig)* **to have the** *or* **a ~ on** *or* **of sth** etw für sich gepachtet haben *(inf)*; **you haven't got a ~ on me** ich bin doch nicht dein Eigentum.
(c) M~ ® *(game)* Monopoly ® *nt*.
mono: ~rail *n* Einschienenbahn *f*; **~syllabic** *adj (lit, fig)* einsilbig, monosyllabisch *(Ling)*; **~syllable** *n* einsilbiges Wort, Einsilber *m*; **to speak/answer in ~syllables** einsilbig sein/antworten, einsilbige Antworten geben; **~theism** *n* Monotheismus *m*; **~theistic** *adj* monotheistisch.
monotone ['mɒnətəʊn] *n* monotoner Klang; *(voice)* monotone Stimme.
monotonous [mə'nɒtənəs] *adj (lit, fig)* eintönig, monoton ◆ **her ~ complaints** ihre sich ständig wiederholenden Klagen; **it's getting ~** es wird allmählich langweilig.
monotony [mə'nɒtənɪ] *n (lit, fig)* Eintönigkeit, Monotonie *f* ◆ **the sheer ~ of it!** dieses ewige Einerlei!; *(of work, routine etc also)* dieser Stumpfsinn!
monotype ® ['mɒnəʊtaɪp] *n* Monotype-Verfahren ® *nt* ◆ **~ machine** Monotype ® *f*.
monoxide [mɒ'nɒksaɪd] *n* Monoxyd *nt*.
Monsignor [mɒn'si:njə^r] *n* Monsignore *m*.
monsoon [mɒn'su:n] *n* Monsun *m* ◆ **the ~ rains** der Monsunregen; **in the ~s** *or* **the ~ season** in der Monsunzeit.
monster ['mɒnstə^r] [1] *n* **(a)** *(big animal, thing)* Ungetüm, Monstrum *nt*; *(animal also)* Ungeheuer *nt* ◆ **a real ~ of a fish** ein wahres Monstrum *or* Ungeheuer von (einem) Fisch; **a ~ of a book** ein richtiger Schinken *(inf)*, ein Mammutwerk; **a ~ of greed** ein (hab)gieriges Monster.
(b) *(abnormal animal)* Ungeheuer, Monster, Monstrum *nt*; *(legendary animal)* (groteskes) Fabelwesen.
(c) *(cruel person)* Unmensch *m*, Ungeheuer *nt*.
[2] *attr* **(a)** *(enormous)* Riesen-; *film* Mammut-.
(b) *(to do with ~s)* Monster-.
monstrance ['mɒnstrəns] *n (Eccl)* Monstranz *f*.
monstrosity [mɒn'strɒsɪtɪ] *n (quality)* Ungeheuerlichkeit, Monstrosität *f*; *(thing)* Monstrosität *f*; *(cruel deed)* Greueltat *f* ◆ **it's a ~ that ...** es ist unmenschlich *or* schändlich, daß ...
monstrous ['mɒnstrəs] *adj* **(a)** *(huge)* ungeheuer (groß), riesig. **(b)** *(shocking, horrible)* abscheulich; *crime, thought, colour also* gräßlich; *suggestion* ungeheuerlich ◆ **it's ~ that ...** es ist einfach ungeheuerlich *or* schändlich, daß ...; **how ~ of him!** das war schändlich (von ihm)!
monstrously ['mɒnstrəslɪ] *adv* schrecklich, fürchterlich.
montage [mɒn'tɑ:ʒ] *n* Montage *f*.
month [mʌnθ] *n* Monat *m* ◆ **in the ~ of October** im Oktober; **six ~s** ein halbes Jahr, sechs Monate; **in** *or* **for ~s** seit langem; **it went on for ~s** es hat sich monatelang hingezogen; **in the early ~s of the war** in den ersten Kriegsmonaten; **one ~'s salary** ein Monatsgehalt; **paid by the ~** monatlich bezahlt.
monthly ['mʌnθlɪ] [1] *adj* monatlich; *magazine, ticket, instalment* Monats- ◆ **they have ~ meetings** sie treffen sich einmal im Monat.
[2] *adv* monatlich ◆ **twice ~** zweimal im *or* pro Monat.
[3] *n* Monats(zeit)schrift *f*.
monument ['mɒnjʊmənt] *n* Denkmal *nt*; *(big also)* Monument *nt*; *(small, on grave etc)* Gedenkstein *m*; *(fig)* Zeugnis *nt (to gen)* ◆ **his great trilogy survives as a ~ to his talent** seine große Trilogie legt Zeugnis von seinem Talent ab.
monumental [,mɒnjʊ'mentl] *adj* **(a)** **~ inscription** Grabinschrift *f*; **~ mason** Steinmetz, Steinbildhauer *m*; **~ sculptures** Steinfiguren *pl*. **(b)** *(very great)* enorm, monumental *(geh)*; *proportions, achievement* gewaltig; *ignorance,*

stupidity, error kolossal, ungeheuer.

moo [muː] [1] *n* **(a)** Muhen *nt* ◆ **the cow gave a ~** die Kuh muhte *or* machte ,,muh" (*inf*); **~cow** (*baby-talk*) Muhkuh *f* (*baby-talk*). **(b)** (*sl: woman*) Kuh *f* (*inf*).
[2] *vi* muhen, ,,muh" machen (*inf*).

mooch [muːtʃ] (*inf*) [1] *vi* tigern (*inf*) ◆ **I spent all day just ~ing about** *or* **around the house** ich habe den ganzen Tag zu Hause herumgegammelt (*inf*).
[2] *vt* (*US inf*) abstauben (*inf*).

mood¹ [muːd] *n* **(a)** (*of party, town etc*) Stimmung *f*; (*of one person also*) Laune *f* ◆ **he was in a good/bad/foul ~** er hatte gute/schlechte/eine fürchterliche Laune, er war gut/schlecht/fürchterlich gelaunt; **to be in a cheerful ~** gut aufgelegt sein; **to be in a festive/forgiving ~** feierlich/versöhnlich gestimmt sein; **to be in a generous ~** in Geberlaune sein; **in one of his crazy** *or* **mad ~s** aus einer plötzlichen Laune heraus, in einer seiner Anwandlungen; **I'm in no laughing ~** *or* **in no ~ for laughing** mir ist nicht nach *or* zum Lachen zumute; **to be in the ~ for sth/to do sth** zu etw aufgelegt sein/dazu aufgelegt sein, etw zu tun; **I'm not in the ~ for work** *or* **to work/for chess** ich habe keine Lust zum Arbeiten/zum Schachspielen; **I'm not in the ~ for this type of music** ich bin nicht in der Stimmung für diese Musik; **I'm not in the ~** ich bin nicht dazu aufgelegt; (*to do sth also*) ich habe keine Lust; (*for music etc also*) ich bin nicht in der richtigen Stimmung; **~ music** stimmungsvolle Musik.
(b) (*bad ~*) schlechte Laune ◆ **he's in one of his ~s** er hat mal wieder eine seiner Launen; **he's in a ~** er hat schlechte Laune; **he has ~s** er ist sehr launisch; **he is a man of ~s** er ist sehr starken Gemüts- *or* Stimmungsschwankungen unterworfen.

mood² *n* (*Gram*) Modus *m* ◆ **indicative/imperative/subjunctive ~** Indikativ/Imperativ/Konjunktiv *m*.

moodily [ˈmuːdɪlɪ] *adv see adj*.

moodiness [ˈmuːdɪnɪs] *n see adj* Launenhaftigkeit *f*; schlechte Laune; Verdrossenheit *f* ◆ **his ~** sein launisches Wesen.

moody [ˈmuːdɪ] *adj* (*+er*) launisch, launenhaft; (*bad-tempered*) schlechtgelaunt *attr*, schlecht gelaunt *pred*; *look, answer* verdrossen, übellaunig.

moola(h) [ˈmuːlɑː] *n* (*dated US sl: money*) Kohle *f* (*inf*).

moon [muːn] [1] *n* Mond *m* ◆ **is there a ~ tonight?** scheint heute der Mond?; **the man in the ~** der Mann im Mond; **you're asking for the ~!** du verlangst Unmögliches!; **to promise sb the ~** jdm das Blaue vom Himmel versprechen; **to be over the ~** (*inf*) überglücklich sein.
[2] *vi* **(a)** (vor sich *acc* hin) träumen. **(b)** (*sl: with backside*) seinen nackten Hintern herausstrecken.

◆**moon about** *or* **around** *vi* (vor sich *acc* hin) träumen ◆ **to ~ ~ (in) the house** zu Hause hocken.

◆**moon away** *vt sep time* verträumen.

moon *in cpds* Mond-; **~beam** *n* Mondstrahl *m*; **~boots** *npl* Moonboots *pl*; **~buggy** *n* Mondauto *or* -fahrzeug *nt*; **~calf** *n* (*dated*) Schwachsinnige(r) *mf*; (*inf*) Mondkalb *nt*; **~-faced** [ˈmuːnˌfeɪst] *adj* mit einem Mondgesicht, mondgesichtig.

Moonie [ˈmuːnɪ] *n* (*inf*) Anhänger(in *f*) *m* der Mun-Sekte, Moonie *m* (*inf*).

moon: ~ landing *n* Mondlandung *f*; **~less** *adj night* mondlos; **~light** [1] *n* Mondlicht *nt or* -schein *m*; **it was ~light** der Mond schien; **a ~light walk** ein Mondscheinspaziergang *m*; *see* **flit**; [2] *vi* (*inf*) schwarzarbeiten; **~lighter** *n* (*inf*) Schwarzarbeiter(in *f*) *m*; **~lighting** *n* (*inf*) Schwarzarbeit *f*; **~lit** *adj object* mondbeschienen; *night, landscape, lawn* mondhell; **~shine** *n* **(a)** (*~light*) Mondschein *m*; **(b)** (*inf: nonsense*) Unsinn *m*; **(c)** (*inf: illegal whisky*) *illegal gebrannter Whisky*; **~shiner** *n* (*inf*) Schwarzbrenner *m*; **~shot** *n* Mondflug *m*; **~stone** *n* Mondstein *m*; **~struck** *adj* (*mad*) mondsüchtig; (*fig*) vernarrt.

moony [ˈmuːnɪ] *adj* (*+er*) (*inf: dreamy*) verträumt.

Moor [mʊəʳ] *n* Maure *m*; (*old: black man*) Moor *m*.

moor¹ [mʊəʳ] *n* (Hoch- *or* Heide)moor *nt*; (*Brit: for game*) Moorjagd *f* ◆ **a walk on the ~s** ein Spaziergang *m* übers Moor.

moor² [1] *vt* festmachen, vertäuen; (*at permanent moorings*) muren.
[2] *vi* festmachen, anlegen.

moorage [ˈmʊərɪdʒ] *n* (*place*) Anlegeplatz *m*; (*charge*) Anlegegebühren *pl*.

moorhen [ˈmʊəhen] *n* Teichhuhn *nt*.

mooring [ˈmʊərɪŋ] *n* (*act of ~*) Anlegen *nt*; (*place*) Anlegeplatz *m* ◆ **~s** (*ropes, fixtures*) Verankerung, Muring *f*; **~ buoy** Muringsboje *f*.

Moorish [ˈmʊərɪʃ] *adj* maurisch; *invasion* der Mauren.

moorland [ˈmʊələnd] *n* Moor- *or* Heideland(schaft *f*) *nt*.

moose [muːs] *n, pl* - Elch *m*.

moot [muːt] [1] *adj*: **a ~ point** *or* **question** eine fragliche Sache; **it's a ~ point** *or* **question whether** ... es ist noch fraglich *or* die Frage (*inf*), ob ...
[2] *vt* aufwerfen; *suggestion* vorbringen ◆ **it has been ~ed whether** ... es wurde zur Debatte gestellt, ob ...

mop [mɒp] [1] *n* (*floor ~*) (Naß)mop *m*; (*dish ~*) Spülbürste *f*; (*sponge ~*) Schwammop *m*; (*inf: hair*) Mähne *f*, Zotteln *pl* (*inf*) ◆ **her ~ of hair/curls** ihre Mähne/ihr Wuschelkopf.
[2] *vt floor, kitchen* wischen ◆ **to ~ one's face** sich (*dat*) den Schweiß vom Gesicht wischen.

◆**mop down** *vt sep walls* abwischen; *floor* wischen.

◆**mop up** [1] *vt sep* **(a)** aufwischen. **(b)** (*Mil*) säubern (*inf*) ◆ **to ~ ~ (what's left of) the enemy** ein Gebiet von feindlichen Truppen säubern (*inf*); **~ping-~ operations** Säuberungsaktion *f*; (*hum*) Aufräumungsarbeiten *pl*.
[2] *vi* (auf)wischen.

mopboard [ˈmɒpbɔːd] *n* (*US*) Scheuerleiste *f*.

mope [məʊp] *vi* Trübsal blasen (*inf*).

◆**mope about** *or* **around** *vi* mit einer Jammermiene herumlaufen ◆ **to ~ ~ the house** zu Hause hocken und Trübsal blasen (*inf*).

moped [ˈməʊped] *n* Moped *nt*; (*very small*) Mofa *nt*.

mopes [məʊps] *npl* (*inf*) **to have (a fit of) the ~** seinen *or* den Moralischen haben (*inf*).

mopy [ˈməʊpɪ] *adj* (*+er*) (*inf*) trübselig ◆ **I'm feeling a bit ~ today** ich bin heute etwas in Tiefstimmung (*inf*).

moraine [mɒˈreɪn] *n* Moräne *f*.

moral [ˈmɒrəl] [1] *adj* **(a)** moralisch, sittlich; *principles, philosophy* Moral-; *support, victory, obligation* moralisch ◆ **~ values** sittliche Werte, Moralvorstellungen *pl*; **~ code** (*of individual*) Auffassung *f* von Moral; (*of society*) Sitten- *or* Moralkodex *m*; **~ standards** Moral *f*; **~ sense** Gefühl *nt* für Gut und Böse, moralisches Bewußtsein; **~ courage** Charakter *m*; **~ lecture** Moralpredigt *f*; **M~ Rearmament** Moralische Aufrüstung; **M~ Majority** (*US Pol*) Moralische Mehrheit.
(b) (*virtuous*) integer, moralisch einwandfrei; (*sexually*) tugendhaft; (*moralizing*) *story, book* moralisch.
(c) it's a ~ certainty that ... es ist mit Sicherheit anzunehmen, daß ...; **to have a ~ right to sth** jedes Recht auf etw (*acc*) haben.
[2] *n* **(a)** (*lesson*) Moral *f* ◆ **to draw a ~ from sth** eine Lehre aus etw ziehen.
(b) ~s *pl* (*principles*) Moral *f* ◆ **his ~s are different from mine** er hat ganz andere Moralvorstellungen als ich; **she's a girl of loose ~s** sie hat eine recht lockere Moral; **do your ~s allow you to do this?** kannst du das moralisch vertreten?

morale [mɒˈrɑːl] *n* Moral *f* ◆ **to boost sb's ~** jdm (moralischen) Auftrieb geben; **to destroy sb's ~** jdn entmutigen.

moralist [ˈmɒrəlɪst] *n* (*Philos, fig*) Moralist *m*.

moralistic [ˌmɒrəˈlɪstɪk] *adj* moralisierend; (*Philos*) moralistisch.

morality [məˈrælɪtɪ] *n* Moralität *f*; (*moral system*) Moral, Ethik *f* ◆ **~ play** Moralität *f*.

moralize [ˈmɒrəlaɪz] *vi* moralisieren ◆ **to ~ about** *or* **upon sb/sth** sich über jdn/etw moralisch entrüsten; **stop your moralizing!** hör mit deinen Moralpredigten auf!

morally [ˈmɒrəlɪ] *adv* **(a)** (*ethically*) moralisch. **(b)** (*virtuously*) integer, moralisch einwandfrei; (*sexually*) tugendhaft.

morass [məˈræs] *n* Morast, Sumpf (*also fig*) *m* ◆ **to sink** *or* **be sucked into the ~ (of vice)** sich immer tiefer (im Laster) verstricken; **a ~ of problems/figures** ein Gewirr *nt or* Wust *m* von Problemen/ein Zahlengewirr *nt or* -wust *m*.

moratorium [ˌmɒrəˈtɔːrɪəm] *n* Stopp *m*; (*Mil*) Stillhalteabkommen *nt*; (*on treaty etc*) Moratorium *nt*; (*Fin*) Zahlungsaufschub *m* ◆ **a ~ on nuclear armament** ein Atomwaffenstopp *m*; **to declare a ~ on sth** etw (vorläufig) mit einem Stopp belegen; in der Frage einer Sache (*gen*) ein Moratorium beschließen; **there's been a ~ on new transplant techniques** neue Transplantationstechniken wurden vorläufig gestoppt.

morbid [ˈmɔːbɪd] *adj* **(a)** *idea, thought, jealousy etc* krankhaft; *interest, attitude also* unnatürlich; *imagination, mind also, sense of humour, talk etc* makaber; (*gloomy*) *outlook, thoughts* düster; *person* trübsinnig; (*pessimistic*) schwarzseherisch; *poet, novel, music etc* morbid ◆ **that's ~!, that's a ~ thought** *or* **idea!** das ist ja makaber; **don't be so ~!** sieh doch nicht alles so schwarz!; **he's such a ~ little boy** er hat einen Hang zum Makaberen.
(b) (*Med*) morbid; *growth* krankhaft.

morbidity [mɔːˈbɪdɪtɪ] *n see adj* **(a)** Krankhaftigkeit *f*; Unnatürlichkeit *f*; Düsterkeit *f*; Hang *m* zu düsteren Gedanken; Morbidität *f* ◆ **the ~ of the story put me off** ich fand diese makabre Geschichte wirklich abstoßend.
(b) Morbidität *f*; Krankhaftigkeit *f*.

morbidly [ˈmɔːbɪdlɪ] *adv* **to talk/think ~** krankhafte *or* düstere *or* morbide (*geh*) Gedanken äußern/haben; **a ~ humorous story** eine Geschichte von makabrem Humor; **he is ~ interested in bad crashes** er hat ein krankhaftes Interesse an schweren Unfällen; **staring ~ out of the window** trübsinnig *or* düster aus dem Fenster schauend; **maybe I'll be dead then, he said ~** vielleicht bin ich dann schon tot, sagte er düster.

mordacious [mɔːˈdeɪʃəs] *adj see* **mordant**.

mordacity [mɔːˈdæsɪtɪ], **mordancy** [ˈmɔːdənsɪ] *n* beißender Humor ◆ **the ~ of his wit** sein beißender Humor.

mordant [ˈmɔːdənt] *adj* beißend, ätzend.

▼ **more** [mɔːʳ] [1] *n, pron* **(a)** (*greater amount*) mehr; (*a further or additional amount*) noch mehr; (*of countable things*) noch mehr *or* welche ◆ **~ and ~** immer mehr; **I want a lot ~** ich will viel mehr; (*in addition*) ich will noch viel mehr; **three/a few ~** noch drei/noch ein paar; **a little ~** etwas mehr; (*in addition*) noch etwas mehr; **many/much ~** viel mehr; **not many/much ~** nicht mehr viele/viel; **no ~** nichts mehr; (*countable*) keine mehr; **some ~** noch etwas; (*countable*) noch welche; **any ~?** noch mehr *or* etwas?; (*countable*) noch mehr *or* welche?; **there isn't/aren't any ~** mehr gibt es nicht; (*here, at the moment, left over*) es ist nichts mehr da/es sind keine mehr da; **is/are there any ~?** gibt es noch mehr?; (*left over*) ist noch etwas da/sind noch welche da?; **even ~** noch mehr; **I shall have ~ to say about this** dazu habe ich noch etwas zu sagen; **let's say no ~ about it** reden wir nicht mehr darüber; **we shall hear/see ~ of you** wir werden öfter von dir hören/dich öfter sehen; **there's ~ to come** da kommt noch etwas, das ist noch nicht alles; **what ~ do you want?** was willst du denn noch?; **what ~ could one want?** mehr kann man sich doch nicht wünschen; **there's ~ to it** da steckt (noch) mehr dahinter; **there's ~ to bringing up children than just** ... zum Kindererziehen gehört mehr als nur ...; **and what's ~, he** ... und außerdem

➤ LANGUAGE IN USE: **more: 1a → 12.2**

or obendrein hat er ... (noch) ...; **they are ~ than we are** sie sind in der Mehrzahl; **there's ~ where that came from** davon gibt's noch mehr.
(b) (all) the ~ um so mehr; **the ~ you give him, the ~ he wants** je mehr du ihm gibst, desto mehr verlangt er; **it makes me (all) the ~ ashamed** das beschämt mich um so mehr; **the ~ the merrier** je mehr, desto *or* um so (*inf*) besser.
[2] *adj* mehr; (*in addition*) noch mehr ◆ **two/five ~ bottles** noch zwei/fünf Flaschen; **one ~ day, one day ~** noch ein Tag; **~ and ~ money/friends** immer mehr Geld/Freunde; **a lot/a little ~ money** viel/etwas mehr Geld; (*in addition*) noch viel/noch etwas mehr Geld; **a few ~ friends/weeks** noch ein paar Freunde/Wochen; **you won't have many ~ friends/much ~ money left** du hast nicht mehr viele Freunde/nicht mehr viel Geld übrig; **no ~ money/friends** kein Geld mehr/keine Freunde mehr; **no ~ singing/quarrelling!** Schluß mit der Singerei/mit dem Zanken!; **do you want some ~ tea/books?** möchten Sie noch etwas Tee/noch ein paar Bücher?; **is there any ~ wine in the bottle?** ist nöch (etwas) Wein in der Flasche?; **there isn't any ~ wine** es ist kein Wein mehr da; **there aren't any ~ books** mehr Bücher gibt es nicht; (*here, at the moment*) es sind keine Bücher mehr da; **(the) ~ fool you!** du bist ja vielleicht ein Dummkopf!; **the ~ fool you for giving him** *or* **to give him the money** daß du auch so dumm bist, und ihm das Geld gibst.
➤ [3] *adv* **(a)** mehr ◆ **~ and ~** immer mehr; **it will weigh/grow a bit ~** es wird etwas mehr wiegen/noch etwas wachsen; **will it weigh/grow any ~?** wird es mehr wiegen/noch wachsen?; **it'll grow ~ if you ...** es wächst besser, wenn du ...; **to like/want sth ~** etw lieber mögen/wollen; **~ than** mehr als; **£5/2 hours ~ than I thought** £ 5 mehr/2 Stunden länger, als ich dachte; **it will ~ than meet the demand** das wird die Nachfrage mehr als genügend befriedigen; **he's ~ lazy than stupid** er ist eher faul als dumm; **no ~ than** nicht mehr als; **no ~ a duchess than I am** genausowenig eine Herzogin wie ich (eine bin); **nothing ~ than ignorance** reine Unkenntnis; **no ~ do I** ich auch nicht; **he has resigned — that's no ~ than I expected** er hat gekündigt — das habe ich ja erwartet.
(b) (*again*) **once ~** noch einmal, noch mal (*inf*); **never ~** nie mehr *or* wieder.
(c) (*longer*) mehr ◆ **no ~, not any ~** nicht mehr; **to be no ~** (*person*) nicht mehr sein *or* leben; (*thing*) nicht mehr existieren; **if he comes here any ~ ...** wenn er noch weiter *or* länger hierher kommt ...
(d) (*to form comp of adj, adv*) -er (*than* als) ◆ **~ beautiful/beautifully** schöner; **~ and ~ beautiful** immer schöner; **no ~ stupid than I am** (auch) nicht dümmer als ich.
(e) ~ or less mehr oder weniger; **neither ~ nor less, no ~, no less** nicht mehr und nicht weniger.

moreish ['mɔːrɪʃ] *adj* (*inf*) **these biscuits are very ~** diese Plätzchen schmecken nach mehr (*inf*).
morello [mɒ'reləʊ] *n* Sauerkirsche, Morelle *f*.
➤ **moreover** [mɔː'rəʊvə^r] *adv* überdies, zudem, außerdem.
mores ['mɔːreɪz] *npl* Sittenkodex *m*.
morganatic [ˌmɔːgə'nætɪk] *adj* morganatisch.
morgue [mɔːg] *n* **(a)** (*mortuary*) Leichenschauhaus *nt* ◆ **to be like a ~** wie ausgestorben sein. **(b)** (*Press*) Archiv *nt*.
MORI ['mɔːrɪ] (*Brit*) *abbr of* **Market and Opinion Research Institute** *britisches Meinungsforschungsinstitut* ◆ **~ poll** Meinungsumfrage *f*.
moribund ['mɒrɪbʌnd] *adj person* todgeweiht (*geh*), moribund (*spec*); *species* im Aussterben begriffen; (*fig*) *plan, policy* zum Scheitern verurteilt; *customs, way of life* zum Aussterben verurteilt ◆ **the empire was in a ~ state** das Weltreich stand vor dem Untergang *or* ging seinem Untergang entgegen.
Mormon ['mɔːmən] [1] *adj* mormonisch, Mormonen-; *doctrine* der Mormonen.
[2] *n* Mormone *m*, Mormonin *f*.
Mormonism ['mɔːmənɪzəm] *n* Mormonentum *nt*.
morn [mɔːn] *n* (*poet*) Morgen *m*.
mornay ['mɔːneɪ] *adj sauce* Käse- ◆ **cauliflower/eggs ~** Blumenkohl/hartgekochte Eier in Käsesoße.
morning ['mɔːnɪŋ] [1] *n* Morgen *m*; (*as opposed to afternoon also*) Vormittag *m*; (*fig*) (*of life*) Frühling *m* (*liter*); (*of an era*) Anfänge *pl*, Beginn *m* ◆ **~ dawned** der Morgen *or* es dämmerte; **in the ~** morgens, am Morgen; vormittags, am Vormittag; (*tomorrow*) morgen früh; **early in the ~** früh(morgens), in der Frühe, am frühen Morgen; (*tomorrow*) morgen früh; **very early in the ~** in aller Frühe, ganz früh (am Morgen); (*tomorrow*) morgen ganz früh; **late (on) in the ~** am späten Vormittag, gegen Mittag; **(at) 7 in the ~** (um) 7 Uhr morgens *or* früh; (*tomorrow*) morgen (früh) um 7; **this/yesterday/tomorrow ~** *adv* heute morgen/gestern morgen/morgen früh, heute/gestern/morgen vormittag; **on the ~ of November 28th** am Morgen des 28. November, am 28. November morgens; **the ~ after** am nächsten *or* anderen Tag *or* Morgen; **the ~ after the night before, the ~-after feeling** der Katzenjammer *or* die Katerstimmung am nächsten Morgen.
[2] *attr* Morgen-; (*regularly in the ~*) morgendlich; *train, service etc* Vormittags-; (*early ~*) *train, news* Früh- ◆ **what time is ~ coffee?** (*at work*) wann ist morgens die Kaffeepause?; (*in café*) ab wann wird vormittags Kaffee serviert?
morning: ~ coat *n* Cut(away) *m*; **~ dress** *n, no pl* Cut(away) *m*; (*dark*) Stresemann *m*; **~ glory** *n* Winde *f*; **~ gown** *n* Hauskleid *nt*; **M~ Prayer** *n* Morgenandacht *f*, Frühgottesdienst *m*; **~-room** *n* Frühstückszimmer *nt*; **~ sickness** *n* (Schwangerschafts)übelkeit *f*; **~ star** *n* Morgenstern *m*; **~ suit** *n* Cut(away) *m*; (*dark*) Stresemann *m*.
Moroccan [mə'rɒkən] [1] *adj* marokkanisch.
[2] *n* Marokkaner(in *f*) *m*.
Morocco [mə'rɒkəʊ] *n* Marokko *nt*.
morocco [mə'rɒkəʊ] *n* (*also* **~ leather**) Maroquin *nt*.
moron ['mɔːrɒn] *n* (*Med*) Geistesschwache(r), Debile(r) (*spec*) *mf*; (*inf*) Trottel (*inf*), Schwachkopf (*inf*) *m*.
moronic [mə'rɒnɪk] *adj* (*Med*) geistesschwach, debil (*spec*); (*inf*) idiotisch (*inf*).
morose *adj*, **~ly** *adv* [mə'rəʊs, -lɪ] verdrießlich, mißmutig.
moroseness [mə'rəʊsnɪs] *n* Verdrießlichkeit *f*, Mißmut *m*.
morpheme ['mɔːfiːm] *n* Morphem *nt*.
morphia ['mɔːfɪə], **morphine** ['mɔːfiːn] *n* Morphium, Morphin (*spec*) *nt*.
morphing ['mɔːfɪŋ] *n* (*Film, TV*) Morphing *nt*.
morphological [ˌmɔːfə'lɒdʒɪkəl] *adj* morphologisch.
morphology [mɔː'fɒlədʒɪ] *n* Morphologie *f*.
morris dance ['mɒrɪs'dɑːns] *n* Moriskentanz *m*, *alter englischer Volkstanz*.
morrow ['mɒrəʊ] *n* (*old*) **the ~** der kommende *or* folgende Tag; **on the ~** tags darauf; **good ~!** (*old*) guten Morgen!
morse [mɔːs] *n* (*also* **M~ code**) Morsezeichen *pl*, Morseschrift *f* ◆ **~ alphabet** Morsealphabet *nt*; **do you know ~** *or* **(the) M~ code?** können Sie morsen?
morsel ['mɔːsl] *n* (*of food*) Bissen, Happen *m*; (*fig*) bißchen *nt*; (*of information*) Brocken *m* ◆ **not a ~ of food** kein Bissen zu essen; **a ~ of comfort** ein kleiner Trost.
mortal ['mɔːtl] [1] *adj* **(a)** (*liable to die*) sterblich; (*causing death*) *injury, combat* tödlich. **(b)** (*extreme*) *agony, fear* tödlich, Todes-; *sin, enemy* Tod-; (*inf*) *hurry* irrsinnig (*inf*). **(c)** (*inf: conceivable*) **no ~ use** überhaupt kein Nutzen. **(d)** (*inf: tedious*) *hours, boredom* tödlich (*inf*).
[2] *n* Sterbliche(r) *mf* ◆ **ordinary ~** (*inf*) Normalsterbliche(r) *mf* (*inf*).
mortality [mɔː'tælɪtɪ] *n* **(a)** (*mortal state*) Sterblichkeit *f*.
(b) (*number of deaths*) Todesfälle *pl*; (*rate*) Sterblichkeit(sziffer), Mortalität (*form*) *f* ◆ **~ rate, rate of ~** Sterbeziffer, Sterblichkeitsziffer, Mortalität (*form*) *f*.
mortally ['mɔːtəlɪ] *adv* (*fatally*) tödlich; (*fig: extremely*) *shocked etc* zu Tode; *wounded* zutiefst; *offended* tödlich.
mortar[1] ['mɔːtə^r] *n* **(a)** (*bowl*) Mörser *m*. **(b)** (*cannon*) Minenwerfer *m*.
mortar[2] [1] *n* (*cement*) Mörtel *m*.
[2] *vt* mörteln.
mortarboard ['mɔːtəˌbɔːd] *n* **(a)** (*Univ*) Doktorhut *m*. **(b)** (*Build*) Mörtelbrett *nt*.
mortgage ['mɔːgɪdʒ] [1] *n* Hypothek *f* (*on* auf +*acc/dat*) ◆ **a ~ for £50,000/for that amount** eine Hypothek über *or* von £ 50.000/über diesen Betrag; **~ rate** Hypothekenzinssatz *m*.
[2] *vt house, land* hypothekarisch belasten ◆ **to ~ one's future** (*fig*) sich (*dat*) die *or* seine Zukunft verbauen.
mortgagee [ˌmɔːgə'dʒiː] *n* Hypothekar *m*.
mortgagor [ˌmɔːgə'dʒɔː^r] *n* Hypothekenschuldner *m*.
mortice *n, vt see* **mortise**.
mortician [ˌmɔː'tɪʃən] *n* (*US*) Bestattungsunternehmer *m*.
mortification [ˌmɔːtɪfɪ'keɪʃən] *n* **(a)** Beschämung *f*; (*embarrassment*) äußerste Verlegenheit; (*humiliation*) Demütigung *f* ◆ **much to his ~, she ...** er empfand es als sehr beschämend, daß sie ...; (*embarrassment*) es war ihm äußerst peinlich, daß sie ...; (*humiliation*) er empfand es als eine Schmach, daß sie ...; **I discovered to my ~ that I had made a mistake** ich stellte zu meiner größten Verlegenheit fest, daß ich einen Fehler gemacht hatte; **because of her ~ at what had happened** weil ihr das, was geschehen war, so überaus peinlich war; **oh the ~ of it all!** diese Schande!; **he felt great ~ at being rejected** er empfand es als eine Schmach *or* Schande, daß er nicht angenommen wurde.
(b) (*Rel*) Kasteiung *f*.
(c) (*Med*) Brand *m*.
mortify ['mɔːtɪfaɪ] [1] *vt usu pass* **(a)** beschämen; (*embarrass*) äußerst peinlich sein (+*dat*) ◆ **he was mortified** er empfand das als beschämend; (*embarrassed*) es war ihm äußerst peinlich; **embarrassed? I was mortified!** peinlich?, ich wäre am liebsten im Boden versunken!; **his brother's success mortified him** er empfand den Erfolg seines Bruders als eine Schmach; **a mortified look** ein äußerst betretener Gesichtsausdruck.
(b) (*Rel*) kasteien.
(c) (*Med*) absterben lassen ◆ **to be mortified** abgestorben sein.
[2] *vi* (*Med*) absterben.
mortifying *adj*, **~ly** *adv* ['mɔːtɪfaɪɪŋ, -lɪ] beschämend; (*embarrassing*) peinlich.
mortise, mortice ['mɔːtɪs] [1] *n* Zapfenloch *nt* ◆ **~ lock** (Ein)steckschloß *nt*.
[2] *vt* verzapfen (*into* mit).
mortuary ['mɔːtjʊərɪ] *n* Leichenhalle *f*.
Mosaic [məʊ'zeɪɪk] *adj* mosaisch.
mosaic [məʊ'zeɪɪk] [1] *n* Mosaik *nt*.
[2] *attr* Mosaik-.
Moscow ['mɒskəʊ] *n* Moskau *nt*.
Moselle [məʊ'zel] *n* Mosel *f*; (*also* **~ wine**) Mosel(wein) *m*.
Moses ['məʊzɪz] *n* Mose(s) *m* ◆ **~ basket** Körbchen *nt*.
Moslem ['mɒzlem] [1] *adj* mohammedanisch.
[2] *n* Moslem *m*.
mosque [mɒsk] *n* Moschee *f*.
mosquito [mɒ'skiːtəʊ] *n, pl* **-es** Stechmücke *f*; (*in tropics*) Moskito *m* ◆ **~ net** Moskitonetz *nt*.
moss [mɒs] *n* Moos *nt*.

➤ LANGUAGE IN USE: **more: 3a** → 7.3 **moreover** → 26.1

mossy ['mɒsɪ] *adj* (+er) (*moss-covered*) moosbedeckt, bemoost; *lawn* vermoost; (*mosslike*) moosig, moosartig.

most [məʊst] 1 *adj superl* **(a)** meiste(r, s); (*greatest*) *satisfaction, pleasure etc* größte(r, s); (*highest*) *speed etc* höchste(r, s) ◆ **who has (the) ~ money?** wer hat am meisten *or* das meiste Geld?; **that gave me (the) ~ pleasure** das hat mir am meisten Freude *or* die größte Freude gemacht; **for the ~ part** größtenteils, zum größten Teil; (*by and large*) im großen und ganzen.
(b) (*the majority of*) die meisten ◆ **~ men/people** die meisten (Menschen/Leute); **he's better than ~ people** er ist besser als die meisten anderen.
2 *n, pron* (*uncountable*) das meiste; (*countable*) die meisten ◆ **~ of it/them** das meiste/die meisten; **~ of the money/his friends** das meiste Geld/die meisten seiner Freunde; **~ of the winter/day** fast den ganzen Winter/Tag über; **~ of the time** die meiste *or* fast die ganze Zeit; (*usually*) meist(ens); **do the ~ you can** machen Sie soviel (wie) Sie können; **at (the) ~/the very ~** höchstens/allerhöchstens; **to make the ~ of sth** (*make good use of*) etw voll ausnützen; (*enjoy*) etw in vollen Zügen genießen; **to make the ~ of a story/an affair** soviel wie möglich aus einer Geschichte/Affäre machen; **to make the ~ of one's looks** *or* **oneself** das Beste aus sich machen; **the girl with the ~** (*inf*) die Superfrau (*inf*); **it's the ~!** (*dated sl*) das ist dufte! (*dated sl*).
3 *adv* **(a)** *superl* (+*vbs*) am meisten; (+*adj*) -ste(r, s); (+*adv*) am -sten ◆ **the ~ beautiful/difficult** *etc* der/die/das schönste/schwierigste *etc*; **which one did it ~ easily?** wem ist es am leichtesten gefallen?; **what ~ displeased him ..., what displeased him ~ ...** was ihm am meisten mißfiel ...; **~ of all** am allermeisten; **~ of all because ...** vor allem, weil ...
(b) (*very*) äußerst, überaus ◆ **~ likely** höchstwahrscheinlich; **he added ~ unnecessarily ...** er sagte noch völlig unnötigerweise ...; **he had told you ~ explicitly** er hat Ihnen doch ganz eindeutig gesagt ...
(c) (*old, dial: almost*) fast, so ziemlich (*inf*), schier (*old, S Ger*).

most-favoured-nation clause [,məʊst'feɪvəd'neɪʃn,klɔːz] *n* (*Pol*) Meistbegünstigungsklausel *f*.

mostly ['məʊstlɪ] *adv* (*principally*) hauptsächlich; (*most of the time*) meistens; (*by and large*) zum größten Teil ◆ **they are ~ women/over fifty** die meisten sind Frauen/über fünfzig; **~ because ...** hauptsächlich, weil ...

MOT (*Brit*) **(a)** *abbr of* **Ministry of Transport. (b) ~ (test)** ≃ TÜV *m* ◆ **it failed its ~** es ist nicht durch den TÜV gekommen.

mote [məʊt] *n* (*old*) Staubkorn, Stäubchen *nt* ◆ **to see the ~ in one's neighbour's eye (and not the beam in one's own)** den Splitter im Auge des anderen (und nicht den Balken im eigenen Auge) sehen.

motel [məʊ'tel] *n* Motel *nt*.

motet [məʊ'tet] *n* Motette *f*.

moth [mɒθ] *n* Nachtfalter *m*; (*wool-eating*) Motte *f* ◆ **the clothes had got ~s** in den Kleidern waren die Motten.

moth: ~ball *n* Mottenkugel *f*; **to put in ~balls** (*lit, fig*) einmotten; *ship* stillegen, außer Dienst stellen; **~-eaten** *adj* (*lit*) mottenzerfressen; (*fig*) ausgedient, vermottet (*inf*).

mother ['mʌðəʳ] 1 *n* **(a)** Mutter *f*; (*animal also*) Muttertier *nt*; (*address to elderly lady*) Mütterchen ◆ **M~ of God** Muttergottes, Mutter Gottes *f*; **M~'s Day** Muttertag *m*; **~'s help** Haus(halts)hilfe *f*; **a ~'s love** Mutterliebe *f*; **I had the ~ and father of a headache** (*inf*) ich hatte vielleicht Kopfschmerzen!; **shall I be ~?** (*inf*) (*pour tea*) soll ich eingießen?; (*serve food*) soll ich austeilen?
(b) (*US vulg*) Saftsack *m* (*vulg*) ◆ **a real ~ of a ...** ein/eine Scheiß- ... (*sl*).
2 *attr church, plant* Mutter-; *bear, bird etc* -mutter *f* ◆ **~ hen** Glucke *f*; **~ plane** Mutterflugzeug *nt*.
3 *vt* (*care for*) *young* auf- *or* großziehen; (*give birth to*) zur Welt bringen; (*cosset*) bemuttern.

mother: ~board *n* (*Comput*) Mutterplatine, Hauptplatine *f*; **~ country** *n* (*native country*) Vaterland *nt*, Heimat *f*; (*head of empire*) Mutterland *nt*; **~craft** *n* Kinderpflege *f*; **M~ Earth** *n* Mutter *f* Erde; **~ figure** *n* Mutterfigur *f*; **~-fucker** *n* (*US vulg*) Saftsack *m* (*vulg*), Arschloch *nt* (*vulg*); **~-fucking** *adj* (*US vulg*) Scheiß- (*vulg*); **~hood** *n* Mutterschaft *f*.

Mothering Sunday ['mʌðərɪŋ'sʌndɪ] *n* ≃ Muttertag *m*.

mother: ~-in-law *n, pl* **~s-in-law** Schwiegermutter *f*; **~land** *n* (*native country*) Vaterland *nt*, Heimat *f*; (*ancestral country*) Land *nt* der Väter *or* Vorfahren; **~less** *adj* mutterlos; **he was left ~less at the age of 2** er verlor mit 2 Jahren seine Mutter; **~ love** *n* Mutterliebe *f*.

motherly ['mʌðəlɪ] *adj* mütterlich.

mother: ~-of-pearl 1 *n* Perlmutt *nt*, Perlmutter *f*; 2 *adj* Perlmutt-; **~ ship** *n* Mutterschiff *nt*; **M~ Superior** *n* Mutter Oberin *f*; **~-to-be** *n, pl* **~s-to-be** werdende Mutter; **~ tongue** *n* Muttersprache *f*; **~ wit** *n* Mutterwitz *m*.

moth: ~-hole *n* Mottenloch *nt*; **~-proof** 1 *adj* mottenfest; 2 *vt* mottenfest machen.

motif [məʊ'tiːf] *n* (*Art, Mus*) Motiv *nt*; (*Sew*) Muster *nt*.

motion ['məʊʃən] 1 *n* **(a)** *no pl* (*movement*) Bewegung *f* ◆ **to be in ~** sich bewegen; (*engine, machine etc*) laufen; (*train, bus etc*) fahren; **to set** *or* **put sth in ~** etw in Gang bringen *or* setzen.
(b) (*gesture*) Bewegung *f* ◆ **to go through the ~s (of doing sth)** (*because protocol, etiquette etc demands it*) etw pro forma *or* der Form halber tun; (*pretend*) so tun, als ob (man etw täte), den Anschein erwecken(, etw zu tun); (*do mechanically*) etw völlig mechanisch tun.
(c) (*proposal*) Antrag *m* ◆ **to propose** *or* **make** (*US*) **a ~** einen Antrag stellen.
(d) (*in debate*) Thema *nt*.
(e) (*bowel ~*) Stuhlgang *m*; (*faeces*) Stuhl *m* ◆ **to have a ~** Stuhlgang haben.
2 *vti* **to ~ (to) sb to do sth** jdm bedeuten, etw zu tun (*geh*), jdm ein Zeichen geben, daß er etw tun solle; **he ~ed me to a chair** er wies mir einen Stuhl an; **he ~ed me in/away** er winkte mich herein/er gab mir ein Zeichen, wegzugehen.

motion: ~less *adj* unbeweglich, reg(ungs)los; **~ picture** *n* Film *m*; **~-picture** *attr* Film-.

motivate ['məʊtɪveɪt] *vt* motivieren ◆ **he's just not ~d enough** es fehlt ihm einfach die nötige Motivation.

motivation [,məʊtɪ'veɪʃən] *n* Motivation *f*.

motivational [,məʊtɪ'veɪʃənəl] *adj* motivational.

motive ['məʊtɪv] 1 *n* **(a)** (*incentive, reason*) Motiv *nt*, Beweggrund *m*; (*for crime*) (Tat)motiv *nt* ◆ **the profit ~** Gewinnstreben *nt*; **my ~s were of the purest** ich hatte die besten Absichten. **(b)** *see* **motif.**
2 *adj power, force* Antriebs-, Trieb-.

motiveless ['məʊtɪvlɪs] *adj* grundlos, ohne Motiv, unmotiviert.

mot juste ['məʊ'ʒuːst] *n* passender *or* treffender Ausdruck.

motley ['mɒtlɪ] 1 *adj* kunterbunt; (*varied also*) bunt(gemischt); (*multicoloured also*) bunt (gescheckt).
2 *n* Narrenkostüm *or* -kleid *nt* ◆ **on with the ~!** lache, Bajazzo!

motocross ['məʊtəkrɒs] *n* Moto-Cross *nt*.

motor ['məʊtəʳ] 1 *n* **(a)** Motor *m*. **(b)** (*inf: car*) Auto *nt*.
2 *vi* (*dated*) (mit dem Auto) fahren.
3 *attr* **(a)** (*Physiol*) motorisch. **(b)** (*~-driven*) Motor-.

motor: ~-assisted *adj* mit Hilfsmotor; **~bike** *n* Motorrad *nt*; **~boat** *n* Motorboot *nt*.

motorcade ['məʊtə,keɪd] *n* Fahrzeug- *or* Wagenkolonne *f*.

motor: ~car *n* (*dated, form*) Automobil (*dated*), Kraftfahrzeug (*form*) *nt*; **~ coach** *n* (*dated*) Autobus *m*; **~-cycle** *n* Motorrad, Kraftrad (*form*) *nt*; **~-cycle combination** Motorrad mit Beiwagen; **~-cycling** *n* Motorradfahren *nt*; (*Sport*) Motorradsport *m*; **~-cyclist** *n* Motorradfahrer(in *f*) *m*; **~-driven** *adj* Motor-, mit Motorantrieb.

-motored [-'məʊtəd] *adj suf* -motorig.

motoring ['məʊtərɪŋ] 1 *adj attr accident, offence* Verkehrs-; *news, correspondent* Auto- ◆ **~ skills** Fahrkünste *pl*; **the ~ public** die Autofahrer *pl*.
2 *n* Autofahren *nt* ◆ **school of ~** Fahrschule *f*.

motorist ['məʊtərɪst] *n* Autofahrer(in *f*) *m*.

motorization [,məʊtəraɪ'zeɪʃən] *n* Motorisierung *f*.

motorize ['məʊtəraɪz] *vt* motorisieren ◆ **to be ~d** motorisiert sein; (*private person also*) ein Auto haben.

motor: ~man *n* (*of train*) Zugführer *m*; (*of tram*) Straßenbahnfahrer *m*; **~ mechanic** *n* Kraftfahrzeugmechaniker, Kfz-Mechaniker *m*; **~ nerve** *n* motorischer Nerv; **~ race** *n* (Auto)rennen *nt*; **~ racing** *n* Rennsport *m*; **he did a lot of ~ racing** er hat an vielen Autorennen teilgenommen; **~ road** *n* Fahrstraße *f*; **~ scooter** *n* (*form*) Motorroller *m*; **~ show** *n* Automobilausstellung *f*; **~ sport** *n* Motorsport *m*; (*with cars also*) Automobilsport *m*; **~ truck** *n* (*US*) Lastwagen *m*; **~ vehicle** *n* (*form*) Kraftfahrzeug *nt*; **~way** *n* (*Brit*) Autobahn *f*; **~way madness** Geschwindigkeitsrausch *m*; **~way driving** das Fahren auf der Autobahn, das Autobahnfahren.

mottled ['mɒtld] *adj* gesprenkelt; *complexion* fleckig ◆ **~ brown and white** braun und weiß gesprenkelt.

motto ['mɒtəʊ] *n, pl* **-es** Motto *nt*, Wahlspruch *m*; (*personal also*) Devise *f*; (*Her also*) Sinnspruch *m*; (*in cracker, on calendar*) Spruch *m* ◆ **the school ~** das Motto der Schule.

mould[1], (*US*) **mold** [məʊld] 1 *n* **(a)** (*hollow form*) (Guß)form *f*; (*Typ also*) Mater *f*; (*shape, Cook*) Form *f*.
(b) (*jelly, blancmange*) Pudding, Wackelpeter (*inf*) *m*.
(c) (*fig: character, style*) **to be cast in the same/a different ~** (*people*) vom gleichen/von einem anderen Schlag sein, aus dem gleichen/einem anderen Holz geschnitzt sein; (*novel characters*) nach demselben/einem anderen Muster geschaffen sein; **the two painters/novelists** *etc* **are cast in the same/a different ~** die beiden Maler/Schriftsteller *etc* verbindet viel/wenig miteinander; **his younger sister cast him in a heroic ~** für seine jüngere Schwester verkörperte er den Typ des Helden; **to break the ~** (*fig*) mit der Tradition brechen; **to fit sb/sth into a ~** jdn/etw in ein Schema zwängen.
2 *vt* **(a)** (*lit*) (*fashion*) formen (*into* zu); (*cast*) gießen.
(b) (*fig*) *character, person* formen ◆ **to ~ sb into sth** etw aus jdm machen; **it/the hero is ~ed on ...** es orientiert sich an (+*dat*)/der Held ist nach dem Vorbild (+*gen*) geschaffen.
3 *vr* **to ~ oneself on sb** sich (*dat*) jdn zum Vorbild nehmen; **to ~ oneself on an ideal** sich an einem Ideal orientieren.

mould[2], (*US*) **mold** *n* (*fungus*) Schimmel *m*.

mould[3], (*US*) **mold** *n* (*soil*) Humus(boden *m or* -erde *f*) *m*.

moulder[1], (*US*) **molder** ['məʊldəʳ] *n* (*Tech*) Former, (Form)gießer *m*.

moulder[2], (*US*) **molder** *vi* (*lit*) vermodern; (*leaves also*) verrotten; (*food*) verderben; (*carcass*) verwesen; (*fig*) (*mental faculties, building*) zerfallen; (*equipment*) vermodern, vergammeln (*inf*); (*person*) verkümmern.

mouldiness, (*US*) **moldiness** ['məʊldɪnɪs] *n* Schimmel *m* (*of* auf +*dat*), Schimmligkeit *f* ◆ **a smell of ~** ein Modergeruch *m*.

moulding, (*US*) **molding** ['məʊldɪŋ] *n* **(a)** (*act*) Formen *nt*; (*of metals*) Gießen *nt*. **(b)** (*cast*) Abdruck *m*; (*of metal*) (Ab)guß *m*; (*ceiling ~*) Deckenfries *or* -stuck *m*. **(c)** (*fig*) Formen *nt*.

mouldy, (*US*) **moldy** ['məʊldɪ] *adj* (+er) **(a)** (*covered with mould*) verschimmelt, schimmelig; (*musty*) mod(e)rig. **(b)** (*dated inf*) (*pathetic, contemptible*) miserabel (*inf*); (*mean*) *person* schäbig; *amount* lumpig (*inf*).

moult, (*US*) **molt** [məʊlt] 1 *n* (*of birds*) Mauser *f* (*also Comput*); (*of mammals*) Haarwechsel *m*; (*of snakes*) Häutung *f*.
2 *vt hairs* verlieren; *feathers, skin* abstreifen.
3 *vi* (*bird*) sich mausern; (*mammals*) sich haaren; (*snake*) sich häuten.

mound [maʊnd] *n* **(a)** (*hill, burial* ~) Hügel *m*; (*earthwork*) Wall *m*; (*Baseball*) Wurfmal *nt*. **(b)** (*pile*) Haufen *m*; (*of books, letters*) Stoß, Stapel *m*.

mount¹ [maʊnt] *n* **(a)** (*poet: mountain, hill*) Berg *m*. **(b)** (*in names*) **M~ Etna/Kilimanjaro** *etc* der Ätna/Kilimandscharo *etc*; **M~ Everest** Mount Everest *m*; **on M~ Sinai** auf dem Berg(e) Sinai.

mount² [1] *n* **(a)** (*horse etc*) Reittier, Roß (*old, liter*) *nt*.
(b) (*support, base*) (*of machine*) Sockel, Untersatz *m*; (*of colour slide*) Rahmen *m*; (*of microscope slide*) Objektträger *m*; (*of jewel*) Fassung *f*; (*of photo, picture*) Passepartout *nt*; (*backing*) Unterlage *f*, Rücken *m*; (*stamp* ~) Falz *m*.
[2] *vt* **(a)** (*climb onto*) besteigen, steigen auf (+*acc*).
(b) (*place in/on* ~) montieren; *picture, photo* mit einem Passepartout versehen; (*on backing*) aufziehen; *colour slide* rahmen; *microscope slide, specimen, animal* präparieren; *jewel* (ein)fassen; *stamp* aufkleben.
(c) (*organize*) *play* inszenieren; *attack, expedition, exhibition* organisieren, vorbereiten; *army* aufstellen.
(d) to ~ a guard eine Wache aufstellen (*on* vor +*dat*); **to ~ guard** Wache stehen *or* halten (*on* vor +*dat*).
(e) (*mate with*) bespringen; (*birds, inf: person*) besteigen.
(f) (*provide with horse*) mit Pferden/einem Pferd versorgen.
[3] *vi* **(a)** (*get on*) aufsteigen; (*on horse also*) aufsitzen.
(b) (*increase: also* ~ **up**) sich häufen.

mountain ['maʊntɪn] *n* (*lit, fig*) Berg *m* ♦ **in the ~s** im Gebirge, in den Bergen; **to make a ~ out of a molehill** aus einer Mücke einen Elefant(en) machen (*inf*).

mountain *in cpds* Berg-; (*alpine, Himalayan etc*) Gebirgs-; ~ **ash** *n* Eberesche *f*; ~ **bike** *n* Mountain-Bike *nt*; ~ **chain** *n* Berg- *or* Gebirgskette *f*, Gebirgszug *m*; ~ **dew** *n* (*inf*) *illegal gebrannter Whisky*.

mountaineer [,maʊntɪ'nɪəʳ] [1] *n* Bergsteiger(in *f*) *m*.
[2] *vi* bergsteigen.

mountaineering [,maʊntɪ'nɪərɪŋ] [1] *n* Bergsteigen *nt*.
[2] *attr* Bergsteiger- ♦ ~ **skill** bergsteigerisches Können; **learn ~ skills with ...** erlernen Sie das Bergsteigen mit ...; **in ~ circles** unter Bergsteigern.

mountain lion *n* Puma, Silberlöwe *m*.

mountainous ['maʊntɪnəs] *adj* bergig, gebirgig; (*fig: huge*) riesig.

mountain: ~ range *n* Gebirgszug *m or* -kette *f*; ~ **sheep** *n* Dickhornschaf *nt*; ~ **sickness** *n* Höhen- *or* Bergkrankheit *f*; **~side** *n* (Berg)hang *m*.

mountebank ['maʊntɪbæŋk] *n* Quacksalber, Scharlatan *m*.

mounted ['maʊntɪd] *adj* (*on horseback*) beritten; (*Mil: with motor vehicles*) motorisiert.

Mountie ['maʊntɪ] *n* (*inf*) *berittener kanadischer Polizist*.

mounting ['maʊntɪŋ] *n* **(a)** *see* **mount² 2 (b)** Montage *f*, Versehen *nt* mit einem Passepartout; Aufziehen *nt*; Rahmen *nt*; Präparieren *nt*; (Ein)fassen *nt*; Aufkleben *nt*. **(b)** (*frame etc*) *see* **mount² 1 (b)**. **engine ~s** Motoraufhängung *f*.

mourn [mɔːn] [1] *vt person* trauern um, betrauern; *sb's death* beklagen, betrauern; (*with wailing*) beklagen; (*fig*) nachtrauern (+*dat*) ♦ **who is she ~ing?** um wen trauert sie?; (*wear ~ing for*) warum trägt sie Trauer?; **what is to become of us?, she ~ed** was soll aus uns werden?, klagte sie.
[2] *vi* trauern; (*wear ~ing*) Trauer tragen, in Trauer gehen ♦ **to ~ for** *or* **over sb/sth** um jdn trauern, jds Tod (*acc*) betrauern/einer Sache (*dat*) nachtrauern.

mourner ['mɔːnəʳ] *n* Trauernde(r) *mf*; (*non-relative at funeral*) Trauergast *m*.

mournful ['mɔːnfʊl] *adj* (*sad*) *person, occasion, atmosphere* traurig, trauervoll; *person* (*as character trait*), *voice* weinerlich; *look also* jammervoll, Jammer-; *sigh, appearance* kläglich, jämmerlich; *sound, cry* klagend.

mournfully ['mɔːnfəlɪ] *adv see adj*.

mournfulness ['mɔːnfʊlnɪs] *n see adj* Traurigkeit *f*; Weinerlichkeit *f*; Jämmerlichkeit *f*; klagender Laut.

mourning ['mɔːnɪŋ] *n* (*act*) Trauer *f*, Trauern *nt* (*of* um); (*with wailing*) Wehklage *f*; (*period etc*) Trauerzeit *f*; (*dress*) Trauer(kleidung) *f* ♦ **to be in ~ for sb** um jdn trauern; (*wear* ~) Trauer tragen; **to come out of ~** die Trauer ablegen; **to go into ~** trauern; (*wear* ~) Trauer anlegen; **next Tuesday has been declared a day of national ~** für den kommenden Dienstag wurde Staatstrauer angeordnet.

mouse [maʊs] [1] *n, pl* **mice (a)** Maus *f* (*also Comput*). **(b)** (*inf: person*) (*shy*) schüchternes Mäuschen; (*nondescript*) graue Maus.
[2] *vi* Mäuse fangen, mausen ♦ **to go mousing** auf Mäusejagd gehen.

mouse *in cpds* Mause-; **~-coloured** *adj* mausgrau.

mouser ['maʊsəʳ] *n* Mäusefänger(in *f*) *or* -jäger(in *f*) *m*.

mousetrap ['maʊstræp] *n* Mausefalle *f*.

mousey *adj see* **mousy**.

moussaka [mʊ'sɑːkə] *n* Moussaka *f*.

mousse [muːs] *n* **(a)** Creme(speise) *f*. **(b)** (*also* **styling ~**) Schaumfestiger *m*.

moustache, (*US*) **mustache** [mə'stɑːʃ] *n* Schnurrbart *m*.

mousy, mousey ['maʊsɪ] *adj* (+*er*) (*timid, shy*) schüchtern; (*nondescript*) farblos, unscheinbar; *colour, hair* mausgrau.

mouth [maʊθ] [1] *n* (*of person*) Mund *m*; (*of animal*) Maul *nt*; (*of bird*) Rachen *m*; (*of bottle, cave, vice etc*) Öffnung *f*; (*of river*) Mündung *f*; (*of harbour*) Einfahrt *f* ♦ **to be down in the ~** (*inf*) deprimiert *or* niedergeschlagen sein; **to keep one's (big) ~ shut** (*inf*) den Mund *or* die Klappe (*inf*) halten; **to have a foul ~** ein grobes *or* ungewaschenes Maul haben (*inf*); **he has three ~s to feed** er hat drei Mäuler zu ernähren *or* stopfen (*inf*); *see* **word**.
[2] [maʊð] *vt* (*say affectedly*) (über)deutlich artikulieren; (*articulate soundlessly*) mit Lippensprache sagen.

mouthful ['maʊθfʊl] *n* (*of drink*) Schluck *m*; (*of food*) Bissen, Happen (*inf*) *m*; (*fig*) (*difficult word*) Zungenbrecher *m*; (*long word*) Bandwurm *m* ♦ **the diver gulped in great ~s of air** der Taucher machte ein paar tiefe Atemzüge; **I got a ~ of salt water** ich habe einen ganzen Schwall Salzwasser geschluckt; **you said a ~** (*US inf*) das kann man wohl sagen.

mouth *in cpds* Mund-; **~-organ** *n* Mundharmonika *f*; **~piece** *n* Mundstück *nt*; (*of telephone*) Sprechmuschel *f*; (*fig: spokesman, publication*) Sprachrohr *nt*; **~-to-~** *adj* Mund-zu-Mund-; **~-to-~ resuscitation** *n* Mund-zu-Mund-Beatmung *f*; **~wash** *n* Mundwasser *nt*; **~-watering** *adj* lecker; **that smells/looks really ~-watering** da läuft einem ja das Wasser im Mund(e) zusammen!; **~-wateringly** *adv* appetitlich.

movability [,muːvə'bɪlɪtɪ] *n see adj* Beweglichkeit *f*; Transportfähigkeit *f*.

movable ['muːvəbl] [1] *adj* beweglich (*auch Jur, Eccl*); (*transportable*) transportierbar, transportfähig ♦ **not easily ~** schwer zu bewegen/transportieren.
[2] *n* **(a)** (*portable object*) bewegliches Gut ♦ **~s** Mobiliar *nt*, Mobilien *pl*. **(b)** *usu pl* (*Jur*) bewegliches Vermögen, Mobiliarvermögen *nt*.

move [muːv] [1] *n* **(a)** (*in game*) Zug *m*; (*fig*) (*step, action*) Schritt *m*; (*measure taken*) Maßnahme *f* ♦ **it's my** *etc* **~** (*lit, fig*) ich *etc* bin am Zug *or* dran (*inf*); **to have first/to make a ~** (*lit*) den ersten Zug/einen Zug machen; **to make a/the first ~** (*fig*) etwas *or* Schritte unternehmen/den ersten Schritt tun; **that was a false** *or* **bad/good/clever ~** (*lit*) das war ein schlechter/guter/raffinierter Zug; (*fig*) das war taktisch falsch *or* unklug/das war ein guter/geschickter Schachzug.
(b) (*movement*) Bewegung *f* ♦ **to be on the ~** (*things, people*) in Bewegung sein; (*fig: things, developments*) im Fluß sein; (*person: in different places*) unterwegs *or* auf Achse (*inf*) sein; (*vehicle*) fahren; (*country, institutions etc*) sich im Umbruch befinden; **to watch sb's every ~** jdn nicht aus den Augen lassen; **to get a ~ on (with sth)** (*inf*) (*hurry up*) zumachen (*inf*) *or* sich beeilen (mit etw); (*make quick progress*) (mit etw) vorankommen; **get a ~ on!** nun mach schon! (*inf*), mach mal zu! (*inf*); **to make a ~ to do sth** (*fig*) Anstalten machen, etw zu tun; **nobody had made a ~ (towards going)** keiner hatte Anstalten gemacht zu gehen; **it's time we made a ~** es wird Zeit, daß wir gehen *or* daß wir uns auf den Weg machen.
(c) (*of house etc*) Umzug *m*; (*to different job*) Stellenwechsel *m*; (*to different department*) Wechsel *m*.
[2] *vt* **(a)** (*make sth* ~) *leaves, pointer, part* bewegen; *wheel, windmill etc* (an)treiben; (*shift*) *objects, furniture* woanders hinstellen; (~ *away*) wegstellen; (*shift about*) umstellen, umräumen; *chest, chair* rücken; *vehicle* (*engine*) von der Stelle bewegen; (*driver*) wegfahren; (*transport*) befördern; (*remove*) *soil, dirt, rubble* wegschaffen; *obstacle* aus dem Weg räumen; *rock* von der Stelle bewegen; *chess piece etc* ziehen mit, einen Zug machen mit; (*out of the way*) wegnehmen ♦ **to ~ sth to a different place** etw an einen anderen Platz stellen; **to be unable to ~ sth** (*lift*) etw nicht von der Stelle *or* vom Fleck (*inf*) bringen; *screw, nail* etw nicht losbekommen; **I can't ~ this lid/handle** der Deckel/Griff läßt sich nicht bewegen; **you'll have to ~ these books/your car (out of the way)** Sie müssen diese Bücher wegräumen/Ihr Auto wegfahren; **don't ~ anything, said the detective** verändern Sie nichts *or* lassen Sie alles so, wie es ist, sagte der Detektiv; **you must have ~d the camera** da haben Sie wahrscheinlich gewackelt; **recent events have ~d the share index upwards/downwards** infolge der jüngsten Ereignisse sind die Aktien gestiegen/gefallen.
(b) *parts of body* bewegen; (*take away*) *arm* wegnehmen; *one's foot, hand* wegziehen ♦ **not to ~ a muscle** sich nicht rühren; **could you ~ your head a little to the side?** können Sie vielleicht Ihren Kopf ein wenig zur Seite drehen?; **he ~d his face a little closer** er ging mit dem Gesicht etwas näher heran; **~ yourself, can't you?** können Sie nicht mal etwas Platz machen?; **to ~ the** *or* **one's bowels** (*form*) Stuhlgang haben; **this mixture will help to ~ the bowels** dieses Mittel regt die Verdauung an *or* ist verdauungsfördernd.
(c) (*change location of*) *offices, troops, production* verlegen; (*Comput*) *text block* verschieben ♦ **to ~ house/office** umziehen/(in ein anderes Büro) umziehen; **the removal men are moving us on Friday** die Spediteure machen am Freitag unseren Umzug; **we've been ~d to a new office** wir mußten in ein anderes Büro umziehen.
(d) *enemy, demonstrators* vertreiben; *patient* bewegen; (*transport*) transportieren; (*transfer*) verlegen; *refugees* transportieren; (*out of area*) evakuieren; *employee* (*to different department etc*) versetzen; (*upgrade*) befördern (*to* zu); *pupil* (*by authorities*) versetzen ♦ **~ those people** schicken Sie die Leute da weg; **to ~ sb to a hospital** jdn ins Krankenhaus einliefern; **to ~ soldiers into the city** in der Stadt Soldaten einsetzen; **I'm going to ~ you to sales manager/goalkeeper** *etc* ich werde Sie jetzt als Verkaufsleiter/Torwart *etc* einsetzen; **his parents ~d him to another school** seine Eltern haben ihn in eine andere Schule getan *or* gegeben.
(e) (*fig: sway*) **to ~ sb from an opinion** *etc* jdn von einer Meinung *etc* abbringen; **to ~ sb to do sth** jdn veranlassen *or* bewegen (*geh*) *or* dazu bringen, etw zu tun; **I am not to be ~d, I shall not be ~d** ich bleibe hart, ich bleibe dabei.
(f) (*cause emotion in*) rühren, bewegen; (*upset*) erschüttern, ergreifen ♦ **his speech really ~d them** sie waren von seiner Rede tief bewegt; **to be ~d** gerührt sein; erschüttert sein; **I'm not easily ~d, but ...** ich bin ja sonst nicht so schnell gerührt/leicht zu erschüttern, aber ...; **to ~ sb to tears/anger/pity** jdn zu Tränen rühren/jds Zorn/Mitleid erregen; **to ~ sb to action** jdn veranlassen, etwas zu unternehmen.
(g) (*form: propose*) beantragen ♦ **she ~d an amendment to the motion** sie stellte einen Abänderungsantrag; **I ~ that we adjourn** ich beantrage eine Vertagung.

(h) (*Comm: sell*) absetzen.
[3] *vi* (a) sich bewegen ◆ **nothing/nobody ~d** nichts/niemand rührte sich; **the wheel/vehicle began to ~** das Rad/Fahrzeug setzte sich in Bewegung; **how does a caterpillar ~?** wie bewegt sich eine Raupe fort?; **she ~s gracefully/like a cat** ihre Bewegungen sind anmutig/katzenhaft; **don't ~!** stillhalten!; **don't ~ or I'll shoot** keine Bewegung, oder ich schieße!
(b) (*not be stationary*) (*vehicle, ship*) fahren; (*traffic*) vorankommen ◆ **to keep moving** nicht stehenbleiben; **to keep sb/sth moving** jdn/etw in Gang halten; **keep those people moving!** sorgen Sie dafür, daß die Leute weitergehen!; **things are moving at last** endlich kommen die Dinge in Gang *or* geschieht etwas; **~!** na los, wird's bald! (*inf*).
(c) (*~ house*) umziehen ◆ **we ~d to London/to a bigger house** wir sind nach London/in ein größeres Haus umgezogen; **they ~d from London** sie sind von London weggezogen.
(d) (*change place*) gehen; (*in car etc*) fahren ◆ **let's ~ into the garden** gehen wir in den Garten; **he has ~d to room 52** er ist jetzt in Zimmer 52; **he has ~d to another department/a different company** er hat die Abteilung/Firma gewechselt; **he used to sit here, has he ~d?** das war doch sein Platz, sitzt er nicht mehr da?; **he has ~d to Brown's** er ist zu Brown gegangen; **have the troops ~d?** sind die Truppen abgezogen?; **the troops ~d to another base** die Truppen zogen zu einem anderen Stützpunkt weiter; **~!** weitergehen!; (*go away*) verschwinden Sie!; **don't ~** gehen Sie nicht weg; **I won't ~ from here** ich rühre mich nicht von der Stelle; **it's time we were moving** *or* **we ~d** es wird Zeit, daß wir gehen.
(e) (*progress*) **to ~ (away) from/closer to** *or* **towards sth** sich von etw entfernen/sich einer Sache (*dat*) nähern; **which way are events/is civilization moving?** in welche Richtung entwickeln sich die Dinge/entwickelt sich unsere Zivilisation?; **scientific progress ~s at an ever faster rate** die Wissenschaft macht immer raschere Fortschritte; **to ~ with the times** mit der Zeit gehen.
(f) (*inf*) (*go fast*) einen Zahn *or* ein Tempo draufhaben (*inf*); (*hurry up*) zumachen (*inf*), einen Zahn zulegen (*sl*) ◆ **he can ~** der ist unheimlich schnell (*inf*); **150? that's moving!** 150? das ist aber ein ganz schönes Tempo! (*inf*).
(g) **to ~ in high society/in yachting circles** *etc* in den besseren Kreisen/in Seglerkreisen *etc* verkehren.
(h) (*in games*) (*make a ~*) einen Zug machen, ziehen; (*have one's turn*) am Zug sein, ziehen.
(i) (*fig: act*) etwas unternehmen, Maßnahmen ergreifen ◆ **they must ~ first** sie müssen den ersten Schritt tun; **a general must ~ swiftly** ein General muß rasch handeln (können).
(j) (*form: propose, request*) **to ~ for sth** etw beantragen.
(k) (*sell*) sich absetzen lassen, gehen (*inf*).

◆**move about** [1] *vt sep* (*place in different positions*) umarrangieren; *furniture, ornaments etc* umstellen, umräumen; *parts of body* (hin und her) bewegen; (*fiddle with*) herumspielen mit; *employee* versetzen; (*make travel*) umher- *or* herumschicken ◆ **the families of servicemen get ~d ~ a lot** die Familien von Militärpersonal müssen oft umziehen.
[2] *vi* sich (hin und her) bewegen; (*fidget*) herumzappeln; (*travel*) unterwegs sein; (*move house*) umziehen ◆ **I can hear him moving ~** ich höre ihn herumlaufen; **the car/stick will help her to ~ ~** mit dem Auto/Stock ist sie beweglicher.

◆**move along** [1] *vt sep* weiterrücken; *car* vorfahren; *bystanders etc* zum Weitergehen veranlassen.
[2] *vi* (*along seat etc*) auf- *or* durchrücken; (*along pavement, bus etc*) weitergehen; (*cars*) weiterfahren ◆ **I'd better be moving ~** (*inf*) ich glaube, ich muß weiter *or* los (*inf*).

◆**move around** *vti sep see* **move about.**

◆**move aside** [1] *vt sep* zur Seite *or* beiseite rücken *or* schieben; *person* beiseite drängen.
[2] *vi* zur Seite gehen, Platz machen.

◆**move away** [1] *vt sep* wegräumen; *car* wegfahren; *person* wegschicken; (*to different town, job etc*) versetzen; *troops* abziehen; *pupil* wegsetzen ◆ **to ~ sb ~ from sb/sth** jdn von jdm/etw entfernen.
[2] *vi* (a) (*move aside*) aus dem Weg gehen, weggehen; (*leave*) (*people*) weggehen; (*vehicle*) losfahren; (*move house*) fort- *or* wegziehen (*from* aus, von); (*firm*) wegziehen (*from* von, aus), verziehen; (*person*) (*from department*) verlassen (*from acc*); (*from job*) wechseln (*from acc*).
(b) (*fig*) abkommen (*from* von); (*from policy, aims etc also*) sich entfernen (*from* von).

◆**move back** [1] *vt sep* (a) (*to former place*) zurückstellen; *people* zurückbringen; (*into old house, town*) wieder unterbringen (*into* in +*dat*); (*to job*) zurückversetzen; *soldiers* zurückbeordern ◆ **they'll ~ you ~ when the danger is past** Sie werden zurückgeschickt, wenn die Gefahr vorbei ist.
(b) (*to the rear*) *things* zurückschieben *or* -rücken; *car* zurückfahren; *chess piece* zurückziehen, zurückgehen mit; *people* zurückdrängen; *troops* zurückziehen.
[2] *vi* (a) (*to former place*) zurückkommen; (*into one's house*) wieder einziehen (*into* in +*acc*); (*into old job*) zurückgehen (*to* zu); (*fig: to theory, ideology*) zurückkehren (*to* zu).
(b) (*to the rear*) zurückweichen; (*troops*) sich zurückziehen; (*car*) zurückfahren ◆ **~ ~, please!** bitte zurücktreten!

◆**move down** [1] *vt sep* (*downwards*) (weiter) nach unten stellen; (*along*) (weiter) nach hinten stellen; (*Sch*) zurückstufen; (*Sport*) absteigen lassen ◆ **~ that item further ~ the list** führen Sie diesen Punkt weiter unten auf der Liste auf; **to ~ sb ~ (the line/the bus)** jdn weiter hinten hinstellen/jdn (im Bus) aufrücken lassen; **he ~d the cows/soldiers ~ to the plains** er trieb die Kühe/beorderte die Soldaten ins Flachland hinunter.
[2] *vi* (*downwards*) nach unten rücken *or* rutschen; (*along*) weiterrücken *or* -rutschen; (*in bus etc*) nach hinten aufrücken; (*Sch*) zurückgestuft werden; (*team etc*) absteigen, zurückfallen (*to* auf +*acc*) ◆ **~ (right) ~ the bus, please!** rücken Sie bitte (ans hintere Ende des Busses) auf!; **to ~ ~ the social scale** gesellschaftlich absteigen; **he had to ~ ~ a year** (*Sch*) er mußte eine Klasse zurück; **when the nomads/cows ~d ~ to the plain** als die Nomaden/Kühe ins Flachland herunterkamen.

◆**move forward** [1] *vt sep* (a) *person* vorgehen lassen; *chair, table etc* vorziehen *or* -rücken; *chess piece* vorziehen, vorgehen mit; *car* vorfahren; *troops* vorrücken lassen.
(b) (*fig: advance*) *event, date* vorverlegen ◆ **to ~ the hands of a clock ~** den Zeiger *or* die Uhr vorstellen.
[2] *vi* (*person*) vorrücken; (*crowd*) sich vorwärts bewegen; (*car*) vorwärtsfahren; (*troops*) vorrücken; (*hands of clock*) vor- *or* weiterrücken.

◆**move in** [1] *vt sep* (a) *police, troops, extra staff* einsetzen (*-to* in +*dat*); (*march/drive in*) einrücken lassen (*-to* in +*acc*); (*take inside*) *luggage etc* herein-/hineinstellen (*-to* in +*acc*); *car* hineinfahren (*-to* in +*acc*).
(b) **the council/removal firm hasn't ~d us ~ (to the house) yet** die Stadt hat uns noch nicht im Haus untergebracht/die Spedition hat unseren Umzug noch nicht gemacht.
[2] *vi* (a) (*into accommodation*) einziehen (*-to* in +*acc*).
(b) (*come closer*) sich nähern (*on dat*), näher herankommen (*on* an +*acc*); (*camera*) näher herangehen (*on* an +*acc*); (*police, troops*) anrücken; (*start operations*) (*workers*) (an)kommen, anfangen; (*hooligans, firms etc*) auf den Plan treten ◆ **to ~ ~ on sb** (*police, troops*) gegen jdn vorrücken; (*guests*) jdm auf den Leib rücken; **the big concerns ~d ~ on the market/the casinos** die großen Konzerne etablierten sich auf dem Markt/im Kasinogeschäft; **the troops ~d ~to the town** die Truppen rückten in die Stadt ein.

◆**move off** [1] *vt sep people* wegschicken ◆ **~ her ~!** (*car, train etc*) (*inf*) fahr los!
[2] *vi* (a) (*go away*) (*people*) weggehen; (*troops*) abziehen.
(b) (*start moving*) sich in Bewegung setzen; (*train, car also*) los- *or* abfahren.

◆**move on** [1] *vt sep hands of clock* vorstellen ◆ **the policeman ~d them ~** der Polizist forderte sie auf weiterzugehen/weiterzufahren; **he ~d the discussion ~ to the next point** er leitete die Diskussion zum nächsten Punkt über.
[2] *vi* (*people*) weitergehen; (*vehicles*) weiterfahren ◆ **it's about time I was moving ~** (*fig*) es wird Zeit, daß ich (mal) etwas anderes mache; **to ~ ~ to higher things** sich Höherem zuwenden; **to ~ ~ to a more responsible job** zu einem verantwortungsvolleren Posten aufsteigen; **I've got to be moving ~ or I'll miss my train** ich muß unbedingt weiter, sonst verpasse ich noch den Zug; **they ~d ~ to discuss the future of the company** als nächstes besprachen sie die Zukunft der Firma; **let's ~ ~ to the next point** gehen wir zum nächsten Punkt über; **time is moving ~** die Zeit vergeht.

◆**move out** [1] *vt sep* (a) *car* herausfahren (*of* aus) ◆ **we had to ~ ~ the furniture** wir mußten die Möbel hinausräumen *or* -stellen; **~ the table ~ of the corner** stellen *or* rücken Sie den Tisch von der Ecke weg; **she ~d it ~ from under the bed** sie zog es unter dem Bett (her)vor.
(b) (*withdraw*) *troops* abziehen ◆ **they are being ~d ~ (of their house)** sie müssen (aus ihrem Haus) ausziehen; **the council ~s ~ all bad tenants** die Stadt zwingt alle schlechten Mieter, ihre Wohnung zu räumen; **they ~d everybody ~ of the danger zone** alle mußten die Gefahrenzone verlassen *or* räumen; **the removal men are moving us ~ tomorrow** die Spediteure machen morgen unseren Umzug.
[2] *vi* (a) (*leave accommodation*) ausziehen; (*withdraw: troops*) abziehen ◆ **to ~ ~ of an area** ein Gebiet räumen.
(b) (*leave: train etc*) abfahren.

◆**move over** [1] *vt sep* herüber-/hinüberschieben ◆ **~ your bottom ~** (*inf*) rück *or* rutsch mal ein Stück zur Seite (*inf*); **he ~d the car ~ to the side** er fuhr an die Seite heran.
[2] *vi* zur Seite rücken *or* rutschen ◆ **~ ~, we all want to sit down** rück *or* rutsch mal ein Stück, wir wollen uns auch hinsetzen (*inf*); **~ ~ to your side of the bed** leg dich in deine Hälfte des Betts; **he ~d ~ to his own side of the bed** er rückte herüber in seine Betthälfte.

◆**move up** [1] *vt sep* (a) (weiter) nach oben stellen; (*promote*) befördern; (*Sch*) versetzen; (*Sport*) aufsteigen lassen ◆ **~ that ~ to the top of the list** stellen Sie das ganz oben an die Liste, führen Sie das ganz oben auf; **they ~d him ~ two places** sie haben ihn zwei Plätze vorgerückt; **they ~d the cows ~ to the pastures** sie trieben die Kühe auf die Alm (hinauf); **the general ~d his men ~ onto the hill** der General beorderte seine Leute auf den Hügel hinauf; **to ~ sb ~ (the line/the bus)** jdn weiter nach vorne stellen/jdn (im Bus) aufrücken lassen.
(b) *troops etc* (*into battle area*) aufmarschieren lassen; (*to front line*) vorrücken lassen; *guns, artillery* auffahren.
[2] *vi* (a) (*fig*) aufsteigen; (*shares, rates etc*) steigen; (*be promoted*) befördert werden; (*Sch*) versetzt werden ◆ **the tribe ~d ~ to the hills for the summer** der Stamm zog den Sommer über in die Berge hinauf; **to ~ ~ the social scale** die gesellschaftliche Leiter hinaufklettern.
(b) (*move along*) auf- *or* weiterrücken ◆ **~ ~ the bus!** rücken Sie auf *or* weiter!

moveable *adj, n see* **movable.**

movement ['muːvmənt] *n* (a) (*motion*) Bewegung *f*; (*fig: trend*) Trend *m* (*towards* zu); (*of events*) Entwicklung *f*; (*of prices/rates*) Preis-/Kursbewegung *f*; (*of troops etc*) Truppenbewegung *f* ◆ **a slight downward/upward ~** eine leichte Abwärts-/Aufwärtsbewegung; **the novel lacks ~** dem Roman fehlt

die Handlung; ~ **(of the bowels)** *(Med)* Stuhlgang *m;* **there was a ~ towards the door** alles drängte zur Tür; **a marked ~ to the right** ein merklicher *or* deutlicher Rechtsruck; **the jumpy/flowing ~ of the piece** *(Mus)* der hüpfende/fließende Rhythmus des Stückes.
(b) *(political, artistic etc ~)* Bewegung *f.*
(c) *(transport: of goods etc)* Beförderung *f.*
(d) *(Mus)* Satz *m.*
(e) *(mechanism)* Antrieb(smechanismus) *m,* Getriebe *nt;* *(of clock)* Uhrwerk *nt.*

mover ['mu:vəʳ] *n* **(a)** *(of proposition)* Antragsteller *m.* **(b)** *(remover)* Möbelpacker *m.* **(c)** *(walker, dancer etc)* **he is a good/poor** *etc* ~ seine Bewegungen sind schön/plump *etc.* **(d) to be a fast ~** *(inf)* von der schnellen Truppe sein *(inf).*

movie ['mu:vɪ] *n (esp US)* Film *m* ◆ **(the) ~s** der Film; **to go to the ~s** ins Kino gehen.

movie *in cpds* Film-; ~ **camera** *n* Filmkamera *f;* **~goer** *n* Kinogänger(in *f*) *m;* **~-house** *n* Kino, Filmtheater *nt;* ~ **star** *n* Filmstar *m;* ~ **theater** *n (US)* Kino *nt.*

moving ['mu:vɪŋ] *adj* **(a)** *(that moves)* beweglich ◆ ~ **staircase** *or* **stairs** Rolltreppe *f;* ~ **pavement** *(esp Brit) or* **walk** *(US)* Rollsteg *m.* **(b)** *(Tech: motive) power etc* Antriebs-; *(fig: instigating) force* treibend. **(c)** *(causing emotion)* ergreifend; *movement also* bewegend; *tribute* rührend.

movingly ['mu:vɪŋlɪ] *adv* ergreifend.

mow[1] [məʊ] *pret* **~ed,** *ptp* **mown** *or* **~ed** *vti* mähen.

◆**mow down** *vt sep* abmähen; *(fig: slaughter)* niedermähen.

mow[2] *n (US)* Heuhaufen *m;* *(storing place)* Heuboden *m.*

mower ['məʊəʳ] *n (person)* Mäher, Schnitter *(old) m;* *(machine) (on farm)* Mähmaschine *f;* *(lawn~)* Rasenmäher *m.*

mowing ['məʊɪŋ] *n* Mähen *nt* ◆ ~ **machine** Mähmaschine *f.*

mown [məʊn] *ptp of* **mow**[1].

Mozambique [,məʊzəm'bi:k] *n* Mozambique, Moçambique *nt.*

MP *abbr of* **(a) Member of Parliament. (b) Military Police. (c) Metropolitan Police.**

mpg *abbr of* **miles per gallon.**

mph *abbr of* **miles per hour.**

MPhil *abbr of* **Master of Philosophy.**

Mr ['mɪstəʳ] *abbr of* **Mister** Herr *m.*

MRP *abbr of* **manufacturer's recommended price** empf. Preis.

Mrs ['mɪsɪz] *abbr of* **Mistress** Frau *f.*

MS *n abbr of* **multiple sclerosis.**

Ms [mɪz] *n* Frau *f (auch für Unverheiratete).*

ms *abbr of* **manuscript** Ms, Mskr.

MSc *abbr of* **Master of Science.**

MSC *(Brit) abbr of* **Manpower Services Commission.**

Msg *abbr of* **Monsignor** Msgr., Mgr.

Mt *abbr of* **Mount.**

MT *abbr of* **machine translation.**

much [mʌtʃ] **[1]** *adj, n* **(a)** viel *inv* ◆ **how ~** wieviel *inv;* **not ~** nicht viel; **that ~** so viel; **but that ~ I do know** aber *das* weiß ich; **~ of this is true** viel *or* vieles daran ist wahr; **we don't see ~ of each other** wir sehen uns nicht oft *or* nur selten; **he/it isn't up to ~** *(inf)* er/es ist nicht gerade berühmt *(inf);* **I'm not ~ of a musician/cook/player** ich bin nicht sehr musikalisch/keine große Köchin/kein (besonders) guter Spieler; **not ~ of a gain** kein großer Gewinn; **that wasn't ~ of a dinner/party** das Essen/die Party war nicht gerade besonders; **I find that a bit (too) ~ after all I've done for him** nach allem was ich für ihn getan habe, finde ich das ein ziemlich starkes Stück *(inf).*
(b) too ~ *(in quantity, money, etc, inf: more than one can take)* zuviel *inv;* *(with emphatic too)* zu viel; *(sl) (marvellous, hilarious)* Spitze *(sl);* *(ridiculous)* das Letzte *(inf);* **to be too ~ for sb** *(in quantity)* zuviel für jdn sein; *(too expensive)* jdm zuviel *or* zu teuer sein; **that insult was too ~ for me** die Beleidigung ging mir zu weit; **that jazz concert/the sight of her face was too ~ for me** *(inf)* ich fand das Jazzkonzert Spitze *(sl)*/ihr Gesicht war zum Schreien *(inf);* **these children are/this job is too ~ for me** ich bin den Kindern/der Arbeit nicht gewachsen; **he'd be too ~ for anybody** er wäre für jeden eine Zumutung; **he doesn't do too ~** er tut nicht übermäßig viel; **far too ~, too ~ by half** viel zu viel.
(c) (just) as ~ ebensoviel *inv,* genausoviel *inv;* **about/not as ~** ungefähr/nicht soviel; **three times as ~** dreimal soviel; **I have twice** *or* **three times as ~ as I can eat** das kann ich nie im Leben aufessen; **as ~ as you want/can** *etc* soviel du willst/kannst *etc;* **he spends as ~ as he earns** er gibt (genau)soviel aus, wie er verdient; **as ~ again** noch einmal soviel; **I feared/thought** *etc* **as ~** (genau) das habe ich befürchtet/mir gedacht *etc;* **it's as ~ as I can do to stand up** es fällt mir schwer genug aufzustehen; **as ~ as to say ...** was soviel heißt *or* bedeutet wie ...
(d) so ~ soviel *inv;* *(emph so, with following that)* so viel; **it's not so ~ a problem of modernization as ...** es ist nicht so sehr ein Problem der Modernisierung, als ...; **at so ~ a pound** zu soundsoviel Mark/Pfund *etc* pro Pfund; **you know so ~** du weißt so viel; *see also* **so.**
(e) to make ~ of sb/sth viel Wind um jdn/etw machen; **Glasgow makes ~ of its large number of parks** Glasgow rühmt sich seiner vielen Parks; **I couldn't make ~ of that chapter** mit dem Kapitel konnte ich nicht viel anfangen *(inf).*
[2] *adv* **(a)** *(with adj, adv)* viel; *(with vb)* sehr; *(with vb of physical action) drive, sleep, think, talk, laugh etc* viel; *come, visit, go out etc* oft, viel *(inf)* ◆ **a ~-admired/-married woman** eine vielbewunderte/oft verheiratete Frau; **he was ~ dismayed/embarrassed** *etc* er war sehr bestürzt/verlegen *etc;* **so ~/too ~** soviel/zuviel; so sehr/zu sehr; **I like it very/so ~** es gefällt mir sehr gut/so gut *or* so sehr; **I don't like him/it too ~** ich kann ihn/es nicht besonders leiden; **thank you very/(ever) so ~** vielen Dank/ganz *or* vielen herzlichen Dank; **I don't ~ care** *or* **care ~** es ist mir ziemlich egal; **however ~ he tries** sosehr *or* wie sehr er sich auch bemüht; **~ to my astonishment** sehr zu meinem Erstaunen; **~ as I should like to** so gern ich möchte; **~ as I like him** sosehr ich ihn mag; *see also* **so.**
(b) *(by far)* weitaus, bei weitem ◆ **~ the biggest** weitaus *or* bei weitem der/die/das größte, der/die/das weitaus größte; **I would ~ prefer to** *or* **~ rather stay** ich würde viel lieber bleiben.
(c) *(almost)* beinahe ◆ **they are ~ of an age** *or* **~ the same age** sie sind fast *or* beinahe gleichaltrig; **they're (fairly) ~ the same size** sie sind beinahe *or* so ziemlich gleich groß.

muchness ['mʌtʃnɪs] *n* **they're much of a ~** *(inf) (things)* das ist eins wie das andere; *(people)* sie sind einer wie der andere.

muck [mʌk] *n* **(a)** *(dirt)* Dreck *m;* *(euph: cat's/dog's ~)* Kot *m;* *(manure)* Dung, Mist *m;* *(liquid manure)* Jauche *f* ◆ **where there's ~, there's brass** *or* **money** *(Prov)* Dreck und Geld liegen nahe beisammen *(prov).*
(b) *(fig) (rubbish)* Mist *m;* *(obscenities)* Schund *m;* *(food etc)* Zeug *nt (inf)* ◆ **Lord/Lady ~** Graf Rotz *(inf)*/die feine Dame.

◆**muck about** *or* **around** *(inf)* **[1]** *vt sep* **(a) to ~ sb ~** mit jdm machen, was man will, jdn verarschen *(sl);* *(by not committing oneself)* jdn hinhalten; **that applicant/the travel agents really ~ed us ~** das war ein ewiges Hin und Her mit dem Bewerber/dem Reisebüro *(inf);* **stop ~ing me ~!** sag mir endlich, woran ich bin *or* was los ist!
(b) *(fiddle around with, spoil)* herumpfuschen an (+*dat*) *(inf)* ◆ **to ~ things ~** alles durcheinanderbringen.
[2] *vi* **(a)** *(lark about)* herumalbern *or* -blödeln *(inf);* *(do nothing in particular)* herumgammeln *(inf)* ◆ **to ~ ~ in boats** sich mit Booten beschäftigen; **to ~ ~ at sth/(at) doing sth** Zeit mit etw vertrödeln *(inf)*/Zeit damit vertrödeln, etw zu tun.
(b) *(tinker with)* herumfummeln *(with* an +*dat).*
(c) to ~ ~ with sb jdn an der Nase herumführen *(inf).*

◆**muck in** *vi (inf)* mit anpacken *(inf).*

◆**muck out** *vti sep* (aus)misten.

◆**muck up** *vt sep (inf)* **(a)** *(dirty)* dreckig machen *(inf)* ◆ **you've really ~ed ~ this place** ihr habt hier ja eine (ganz) schöne Schweinerei angerichtet! **(b)** *(spoil)* vermasseln *(inf);* *person (emotionally)* verkorksen *(inf)* ◆ **that's really ~ed me/my plans ~** das hat mir alles/meine Pläne vermasselt *(inf).*

muckiness ['mʌkɪnɪs] *n* Schmutzigkeit *f.*

muck: ~-rake *vi (fig inf)* im Schmutz wühlen; **~-raker** *n (fig inf)* Sensationshai *m (inf);* **~-raking [1]** *n (fig inf)* Sensationsmache(rei) *f (inf);* **[2]** *adj (fig inf) person* sensationslüstern; **a ~-raking newspaper** ein Skandalblatt *nt;* **~-spread** *vi* Mist streuen *or* (aus)breiten; **~-spreading** *n* Miststreuen *nt;* **~-up** *n (inf)* Durcheinander *nt;* *(fiasco)* Katastrophe *f;* **there's been a ~-up with the invitations** bei den Einladungen hat jemand/habe ich *etc* Mist gemacht *(inf).*

mucky ['mʌkɪ] *adj* (+*er*) dreckig *(inf),* schmutzig; *soil etc* matschig ◆ **to get oneself/sth all ~** sich/etw ganz dreckig *(inf) or* schmutzig machen; **you ~ thing** *or* **pup!** *(inf)* du Ferkel! *(inf).*

mucous ['mju:kəs] *adj* schleimig; *deposits, secretions etc* Schleim- ◆ ~ **membrane** Schleimhaut *f.*

mucus ['mju:kəs] *n* Schleim *m.*

mud [mʌd] *n* **(a)** Schlamm *m;* *(on roads etc)* Matsch *m* ◆ **(here's) ~ in your eye!** *(dated)* zum Wohl!, prösterchen! *(hum).*
(b) *(fig)* **his name is ~** *(inf)* er ist unten durch *(inf);* **to drag sb/sb's name** *or* **reputation through the ~** jdn/jds guten Namen in den Schmutz zerren *or* ziehen; **to throw** *or* **sling ~** im Schmutz *or* Dreck *(inf)* wühlen; **to throw** *or* **sling ~ at sb/sth** jdn mit Schmutz bewerfen/etw in den Dreck *(inf) or* Schmutz ziehen; **some of the ~ has stuck/is bound to stick** etwas ist hängengeblieben/bleibt immer hängen; **~ sticks** etwas bleibt immer hängen.

mud: ~-bath *n* Schlammbad *nt;* *(Med)* Moorbad *nt;* **~-coloured** *adj* schmutzig grau.

muddle ['mʌdl] **[1]** *n* Durcheinander *nt* ◆ **to get in(to) a ~** *(things)* durcheinandergeraten; *(person)* konfus werden; **to get in(to) a ~ with sth** mit etw nicht klarkommen *(inf);* **how did things get into such a ~?** wie ist denn dieses Durcheinander entstanden?; **to get sb/sth in(to) a ~** jdn/etw völlig durcheinanderbringen; **to be in a ~** völlig durcheinander sein; **this room is (in) a real ~** in diesem Zimmer herrscht ein einziges Durcheinander; **to make a ~ of/with/over sth** etw völlig durcheinanderbringen.
[2] *vt* durcheinanderbringen; *two things or people also* verwechseln; *(make confused) person also* verwirren, konfus machen ◆ **you're only muddling the issue** du machst die Sache nur verworrener.

◆**muddle along** *or* **on** *vi* vor sich *(acc)* hinwursteln *(inf).*

◆**muddle through** *vi* durchkommen, sich (irgendwie) durchwursteln *(inf) or* durchschlagen.

◆**muddle up** *vt sep see* **muddle 2.**

muddled ['mʌdld] *adj* konfus; *person also* durcheinander *pred;* *thoughts, ideas also* verworren, wirr ◆ **set out in a ~ way** ziemlich konfus angelegt; **he has/this is a rather ~ way of doing things** er macht alles/das ist ja ziemlich kompliziert; **in a ~ way it does make sense** es ist zwar verworren, ergibt aber doch einen Sinn.

muddle-headed ['mʌdl,hedɪd] *adj person* zerstreut; *ideas* konfus, ver-

worren.
muddler ['mʌdlər] *n (person)* Tölpel, Dussel *(inf) m.*
muddy ['mʌdɪ] [1] *adj (+er)* **(a)** *floor, shoes, hands etc* schmutzig, schlammbeschmiert; *road, ground etc* schlammig, matschig; *liquid* schlammig, trübe ◆ **to get** *or* **make sb/oneself/sth ~** jdn/sich/etw schmutzig machen *or* mit Schlamm beschmieren.
(b) *(fig) complexion* gräulich schimmernd; *style* verworren.
[2] *vt* schmutzig machen, mit Schlamm beschmieren ◆ **his explanation only helped to ~ the waters** durch seine Erklärung ist die Sache nur noch verworrener geworden.
mud: ~flap *n* Schmutzfänger *m;* **~flat** *n* Watt(enmeer) *nt no pl;* **~guard** *n (on cycles)* Schutzblech *nt; (on cars)* Kotflügel *m;* **~ hut** *n* Lehmhütte *f;* **~ pack** *n* Schlammpackung *f;* **~ pie** *n* Kuchen *m (aus Sand, Erde etc);* **~-slinger** *n* Dreckschleuder *f (inf);* **~-slinging** [1] *n* Schlechtmacherei *f;* **all that ~-slinging before every election** diese gegenseitige Verunglimpfung vor jeder Wahl; **we've had enough ~-slinging** es ist genug im Schmutz *or* Dreck *(inf)* gewühlt worden; **I'm not descending to this level of ~-slinging** ich werde nicht so tief sinken, daß ich andere mit Schmutz bewerfe; [2] *adj* **a ~-slinging politician/newspaper** ein Politiker, der/eine Zeitung, die andere mit Schmutz bewirft; **the election turned into a ~-slinging match** die Wahlen arteten zur reinsten Schlammschlacht aus; **~ wrestling** *n* Schlammringen *nt.*
muesli ['mju:zlɪ] *n* Müsli *nt.*
muezzin [mu:'ezɪn] *n* Muezzin *m.*
muff[1] [mʌf] *n* Muff *m.*
muff[2] *(inf)* [1] *n* **to make a ~ of sth** *see vt.*
[2] *vt* vermasseln *(inf),* verpatzen *(inf); exam also* verhauen *(inf); question* danebenhauen *or* sich verhauen bei *(inf); kick, shot, ball* danebensetzen *(inf); lines, text, passage* verpatzen *(inf)* ◆ **to ~ a catch** danebengreifen *(inf),* schlecht fangen; **he ~ed a few notes** er hat ein paarmal gepatzt *(inf).*
muffin ['mʌfɪn] *n (Brit) weiches, flaches Milchbrötchen, meist warm gegessen; (US) kleiner pfannkuchenartiger Fladen.*
muffle ['mʌfl] *vt* **(a)** *(wrap warmly: also ~ up) person* einmummen. **(b)** *(deaden) sound, shot etc* dämpfen; *noise* abschwächen; *shouts* ersticken; *bells, oars, drum* umwickeln.
muffled ['mʌfld] *adj sound etc* gedämpft; *shouts* erstickt; *drum, bells, oars* umwickelt.
muffler ['mʌflər] *n* **(a)** *(scarf)* (dicker) Schal. **(b)** *(Tech)* Schalldämpfer *m; (US Aut)* Auspuff(topf) *m.*
mufti ['mʌftɪ] *n (clothing)* Zivil(kleidung *f) nt* ◆ **in ~** in Zivil.
mug [mʌg] [1] *n* **(a)** *(cup)* Becher *m; (for beer)* Krug *m.*
(b) *(inf: dupe)* Trottel *m* ◆ **have you found some ~ to do that?** hast du einen Dummen dafür gefunden?; **I was left looking a real ~** ich stand dann blöd da *(inf);* **don't be such a ~** sei doch nicht so blöd *(inf);* **to take sb for a ~** jdn für blöd halten; **that's a ~'s game** das ist doch schwachsinnig.
(c) *(sl: face)* Visage *f (sl)* ◆ **~ shot** Verbrecherfoto *nt (inf).*
[2] *vt* **(a)** *(attack and rob)* überfallen.
(b) *(US sl: photograph)* fotografieren.
◆**mug up** *vt sep* **(a)** *(also: ~ ~ on) (inf)* **to ~ sth/one's French ~, to ~ ~ on sth/one's French** etw/Französisch pauken *(inf).* **(b) to ~ it ~** *(US inf)* zu dick auftragen.
mugger ['mʌgər] *n* Straßenräuber *m.*
mugging ['mʌgɪŋ] *n* Straßenraub *m no pl* ◆ **a lot of ~s** viele Überfälle auf offener Straße.
muggins ['mʌgɪnz] *n sing (Brit inf)* Blödmann *m (inf)* ◆ **while ~ does all the work** und ich bin mal wieder der/die Dumme und kann die ganze Arbeit allein machen *(inf);* **and ~ here forgot ...** und ich Blödmann vergesse *(inf)* ...; und der Blödmann hier vergißt *(inf)* ...; **he's a bit of a ~** er ist etwas bescheuert *(inf).*
muggy ['mʌgɪ] *adj (+er)* schwül; *heat* drückend.
mugwump ['mʌgwʌmp] *n (US Pol)* Unabhängige(r) *mf.*
Mujaheddin [,mu:dʒəhe'di:n] *n* Mudschaheddin *m.*
mulatto [mju:'lætəʊ] [1] *adj* Mulatten-; *features* eines Mulatten/einer Mulattin.
[2] *n, pl* **-es** Mulatte *m,* Mulattin *f.*
mulberry ['mʌlbərɪ] *n (fruit)* Maulbeere *f; (tree)* Maulbeerbaum *m; (colour)* Aubergine *nt,* dunkles Violett.
mulch [mʌltʃ] *(Hort)* [1] *n* Krümelschicht *f,* Mulch *m (spec).*
[2] *vt* mulchen *(spec),* abdecken.
mulct [mʌlkt] *vt* **(a)** *(fine)* mit einer Geldstrafe belegen *(form).* **(b)** *(defraud)* **to ~ sb of sth** jdm etw abschwindeln.
mule[1] [mju:l] *n* **(a)** *(of donkey and mare)* Maultier *nt; (of stallion and donkey)* Maulesel *m* ◆ **~ skinner** *(US inf)* Maultiertreiber *m.* **(b)** *(inf: person)* Maulesel *m* ◆ **(as) stubborn as a ~** (so) störrisch wie ein Maulesel. **(c)** *(Tech)* Selfaktor *m.*
mule[2] *n (slipper)* Schlappen *m (dial),* Pantoffel *m.*
muleteer [,mju:lɪ'tɪər] *n* Maultiertreiber *m.*
mulish ['mju:lɪʃ] *adj* stur, starrsinnig; *person also* störrisch.
mulishly ['mju:lɪʃlɪ] *adv* stur, starrsinnig.
mulishness ['mju:lɪʃnɪs] *n* Starrsinn *m,* Sturheit *f.*
mull [mʌl] *vt mit Zucker und Gewürzen ansetzen und erhitzen* ◆ **to ~ wine** Glühwein zubereiten; **~ed wine** Glühwein *m.*
◆**mull over** *vt sep* sich *(dat)* durch den Kopf gehen lassen.
Mullah ['mʌlə] *n* Mullah *m.*
mullet ['mʌlɪt] *n* Meeräsche *f.*
mulligatawny [,mʌlɪgə'tɔ:nɪ] *n* Currysuppe *f.*
mullion ['mʌlɪən] *n* Längs- *or* Zwischenpfosten *m* ◆ **~s** *(in Gothic Archit)* Stabwerk *nt.*
mullioned ['mʌlɪənd] *adj window* längs unterteilt.
multi ['mʌltɪ] *n (inf: company)* Multi *m (inf).*
multi- *pref* mehr-, Mehr-; *(with Latin stem in German)* Multi-, multi-.
multi: ~-access *adj (Comput) system etc* Mehrplatz-; **~-band** *adj (Telec)* Mehrband-; **~-cellular** *adj* viel- *or* mehrzellig; **~channel** *adj (TV)* mehrkanalig, Mehrkanal-; **~coloured** *adj* mehrfarbig; *material also, lights, decorations* bunt; *bird* buntgefiedert; *fish* buntschillernd; **~coloured pen** Mehrfarbenstift *m;* **~cultural** *adj* multikulturell; **~faceted** *adj* vielseitig.
multifarious [,mʌltɪ'fɛərɪəs] *adj* vielfältig, mannigfaltig ◆ **the ~ tribal languages** die Vielfalt der Stammessprachen.
multi: ~form *adj* vielgestaltig; **~-functional** *adj (Comput)* Multifunktions-; **~-functional keyboard** Multifunktionstastatur *f;* **~grade** *adj oil* Mehrbereichs-; **~hull** *n (Naut)* Mehrkörperschiff *nt;* **~lateral** *adj (Pol)* multilateral; *(Math)* mehrseitig; **~level** *adj shopping centre etc* terrassenartig angelegt; **~lingual** *adj* mehrsprachig; **~media** *adj aids, presentation (also Comput)* multimedial, Multimedia-; **~millionaire** *n* Multimillionär(in *f) m;* **~national** [1] *n* multinationaler Konzern, Multi *m (inf);* [2] *adj* multinational; **~-party** *adj* **(a)** *(Pol)* Mehrparteien-; **(b)** *(Telec)* Konferenz-.
multiple ['mʌltɪpl] [1] *adj* **(a)** *(with sing n: of several parts)* mehrfach ◆ **~ birth** Mehrlingsgeburt *f;* **~ choice** Multiple Choice *nt;* **~ collision** Massenkarambolage *f;* **~ cropping** mehrfache Bebauung; **~ personality** *(Psych)* alternierende Persönlichkeit, Persönlichkeitsspaltung *f;* **~ star** Sternhaufen *m;* **~-unit** *(train)* Triebwagen *m;* **~ voting** mehrfache Stimmberechtigung.
(b) *(with pl n: many)* mehrere.
[2] *n* **(a)** *(Math)* Vielfache(s) *nt* ◆ **eggs are usually sold in ~s of six** Eier werden gewöhnlich in Einheiten zu je sechs verkauft.
(b) *(Brit: also* **~ store***)* Ladenkette *f.*
multiple sclerosis *n* multiple Sklerose.
multiplexer, multiplexor ['mʌltɪpleksər] *n (Telec)* Multiplexer *m.*
multiplicand [,mʌltɪplɪ'kænd] *n* Multiplikand *m.*
multiplication [,mʌltɪplɪ'keɪʃən] *n* **(a)** *(Math)* Multiplikation *f; (act also)* Multiplizieren, Malnehmen *(inf) nt* ◆ **~ table** Multiplikationstabelle *f;* **he knows all his ~ tables** er kann das Einmaleins. **(b)** *(fig)* Vervielfachung, Vermehrung *f.*
multiplicity [,mʌltɪ'plɪsɪtɪ] *n* Vielzahl, Fülle *f* ◆ **for a ~ of reasons** aus vielerlei Gründen.
multiplier ['mʌltɪplaɪər] *n (Math)* Multiplikator *m.*
multiply ['mʌltɪplaɪ] [1] *vt* **(a)** *(Math)* multiplizieren, malnehmen *(inf)* ◆ **to ~ 8 by 7** 8 mit 7 multiplizieren *or* malnehmen *(inf);* **4 multiplied by 6 is 24** 4 mal 6 ist 24. **(b)** *(fig)* vervielfachen, vermehren.
[2] *vi* **(a)** *(Math) (person)* multiplizieren; *(numbers)* sich multiplizieren lassen. **(b)** *(fig)* zunehmen, sich vermehren *or* vervielfachen. **(c)** *(breed)* sich vermehren.
multi: ~-purpose *adj* Mehrzweck-; **~racial** *adj* gemischtrassig; **~racial policy** Politik *f* der Rassenintegration; **~racial school** Schule *f* ohne Rassentrennung; **~-stage** *adj* Mehrstufen-; **~-stor(e)y** *adj* mehrstöckig; **~-stor(e)y flats** (Wohn)hochhäuser *pl;* **~-stor(e)y car-park** *(Brit)* Park(hoch)haus *nt;* **~strike** *adj* **(a)** *ribbon* Multistrike-; **(b)** *(Mil)* **~strike capability** Fähigkeit *f* zum Angriff auf mehrere Ziele; **~tasking** *n (Comput)* Multitasking *nt;* **~track** *adj* mehrspurig; **~track recording** Mehrspuraufzeichnung *f.*
multitude ['mʌltɪtju:d] *n* Menge *f* ◆ **a ~ of** eine Vielzahl von, eine Menge; *(of people also)* eine Schar (von); **for a ~ of reasons** aus vielerlei Gründen; **they came in ~s** sie kamen scharenweise.
multitudinous [,mʌltɪ'tju:dɪnəs] *adj* zahlreich.
multi-user ['mʌltɪ'ju:zər] *adj (Comput) system* Mehrplatz-, Mehrbenutzer-.
mum[1] [mʌm] *n, adj (inf)* **~'s the word!** nichts verraten! *(inf);* **to keep ~** den Mund halten *(about* über *+acc) (inf).*
mum[2] *n (Brit inf: mother)* Mutter *f; (as address)* Mutti *f (inf).*
mum[3] *n (US inf: chrysanthemum)* Chrysantheme *f.*
mumble ['mʌmbl] [1] *n* Gemurmel, Murmeln *nt* ◆ **there was a ~ of discontent** ein Murren erhob sich; **he spoke in a ~** er nuschelte.
[2] *vt* murmeln ◆ **he ~d the words** er nuschelte.
[3] *vi* vor sich hin murmeln; *(speak indistinctly)* nuscheln ◆ **don't ~ (into your beard)** murm(e)le doch nicht so in deinen Bart.
mumbler ['mʌmblər] *n* **he's a real ~** er nuschelt so.
mumblingly ['mʌmblɪŋlɪ] *adv* undeutlich.
mumbo jumbo ['mʌmbəʊ'dʒʌmbəʊ] *n (empty ritual, superstition)* Hokuspokus *m; (gibberish)* Kauderwelsch *nt; (idol)* Wodugott *m.*
mummer ['mʌmər] *n (old)* Mime *m (old).*
mummery ['mʌmərɪ] *n (old)* Pantomimenspiel *nt; (fig)* Mummenschanz *m.*
mummification [,mʌmɪfɪ'keɪʃən] *n* Mumifizierung *f.*
mummify ['mʌmɪfaɪ] *vti* mumifizieren.
mummy[1] ['mʌmɪ] *n (corpse)* Mumie *f.*
mummy[2] *n (Brit inf: mother)* Mami, Mama *f (inf).*
mumps [mʌmps] *n sing* Mumps *m or f (inf) no art.*
mumsy ['mʌmzɪ] *adj (inf)* mütterlich.
munch [mʌntʃ] *vti* mampfen *(inf).*
◆**munch away** *vi* vor sich hin mampfen *(inf)* ◆ **he was ~ing ~ on** *or* **at an apple** er mampfte einen Apfel *or* an einem Apfel.
munchies ['mʌnʃɪz] *npl (US inf)* Knabberei *f (inf).*

mundane [ˌmʌnˈdeɪn] *adj* (*worldly*) weltlich, irdisch; (*fig*) schlicht und einfach; (*pej: humdrum*) profan, banal.

mundanely [ˌmʌnˈdeɪnlɪ] *adv* weltlich; (*in a down-to-earth way*) *remark, describe* nüchtern; *dressed* schlicht und einfach; (*pej*) banal ◆ **from the exotic to the ~ trivial** vom Außergewöhnlichen zum Banal-Trivialen.

mundaneness [ˌmʌnˈdeɪnnɪs] *n see adj* Weltlichkeit *f*; Schlichtheit *f*; Banalität *f*.

Munich [ˈmjuːnɪk] [1] *n* München *nt*.
[2] *adj attr* Münchner.

municipal [mjuːˈnɪsɪpəl] *adj* städtisch; *baths also* Stadt-; *administration, council, elections etc* Stadt-, Gemeinde-.

municipality [mjuːˌnɪsɪˈpælɪtɪ] *n* (*place*) Ort *m*, Gemeinde *f*; (*council*) Stadt, Gemeinde *f*.

municipalization [ˌmjuːnɪsɪpəlaɪˈzeɪʃən] *n* Übernahme *f* durch die Stadt *or* durch die Gemeinde.

municipalize [ˌmjuːˈnɪsɪpəlaɪz] *vt bus service, baths etc* unter städtische Verwaltung *or* Gemeindeverwaltung bringen.

municipally [mjuːˈnɪsɪpəlɪ] *adv* von der Stadt *or* Gemeinde ◆ **~ owned** im Besitz der Stadt *or* Gemeinde.

munificence [mjuːˈnɪfɪsns] *n* (*form*) Großzügigkeit, Generosität (*geh*) *f*.

munificent [mjuːˈnɪfɪsnt] *adj* (*form*) großzügig; *person also* generös (*geh*).

munificently [mjuːˈnɪfɪsntlɪ] *adv* (*form*) großzügig, generös (*geh*) ◆ **~ donated by ...** großzügigerweise gespendet von ...

muniments [ˈmjuːnɪmənts] *npl* (*Jur form*) Urkunde *f*.

munition [mjuːˈnɪʃən] *n usu pl* Kriegsmaterial *nt no pl*, Waffen *pl* und Munition *f* ◆ **~s dump** (Waffen- und) Munitionslager *or* -depot *nt*.

mural [ˈmjʊərəl] [1] *n* Wandgemälde *nt*.
[2] *adj* Wand-.

murder [ˈmɜːdəʳ] [1] *n* (**a**) Mord *m* ◆ **the ~ of John F. Kennedy** der Mord an John F. Kennedy, die Ermordung John F. Kennedys; **to stand accused of ~** unter Mordverdacht stehen; **~ trial** Mordprozeß *m*.
(**b**) (*fig inf*) **it was/it's ~** es war/ist mörderisch; **it'll be ~** es wird schrecklich werden; (*exhausting also*) das ist glatter Mord (*inf*); **to cry ~, to scream blue ~** Zeter und Mordio schreien, ein Mordsspektakel *or* -theater machen (*inf*); **to get away with ~** sich (*dat*) alles erlauben können.
[2] *vt* (**a**) ermorden, umbringen (*inf*); (*slaughter*) morden; (*inf*) *opponents* haushoch schlagen. (**b**) (*inf: ruin*) *music, play etc* verhunzen (*inf*).

murderer [ˈmɜːdərəʳ] *n* Mörder *m*.

murderess [ˈmɜːdərɪs] *n* Mörderin *f*.

murderous [ˈmɜːdərəs] *adj villain, soldiers etc* mordgierig, blutrünstig; *deed, intent, plot* Mord-; (*fig*) mörderisch ◆ **~ attack** Mordanschlag *m*; **a ~ type** ein brutaler Typ; **there was a ~ look about him** er hatte etwas Brutales an sich; **he gave me a ~ look** er erdolchte mich mit Blicken; **once he had started on this ~ course** als er erst einmal den Weg der Gewalt eingeschlagen hatte.

murderously [ˈmɜːdərəslɪ] *adv* mordgierig, blutdürstig; (*fig*) mörderisch ◆ **the knife glinted ~** das Messer blitzte tödlich; **a ~ cunning trap** eine teuflische Falle.

murk [mɜːk] *n* Düsternis *f*; (*in water*) trübes Wasser.

murkily [ˈmɜːkɪlɪ] *adv* trübe ◆ **the wreck could be seen ~ through the muddy water** das Wrack zeichnete sich undeutlich im schlammigen Wasser ab.

murkiness [ˈmɜːkɪnɪs] *n see adj* Trübheit, Unklarheit, Unschärfe *f*; Finsterkeit *f*; Dunkel *nt*.

murky [ˈmɜːkɪ] *adj* (*+er*) trübe; *fog* dicht; *photo, outline etc* unscharf, unklar; (*shady*) *character, deed* finster; *past* dunkel ◆ **it's really ~ outside** draußen ist es so düster.

murmur [ˈmɜːməʳ] [1] *n* (*soft speech*) Murmeln, Raunen (*liter*) *nt*; (*of discontent*) Murren *nt*; (*of water, wind, leaves, traffic*) Rauschen *nt* ◆ **there was a ~ of approval/disagreement** ein beifälliges/abfälliges Murmeln erhob sich; **a soft ~ of voices** gedämpftes Stimmengemurmel; **..., she said in a ~ ...,** murmelte sie; **not a ~** kein Laut; **without a ~** ohne zu murren.
[2] *vt* murmeln; (*with discontent*) murren.
[3] *vi* murmeln; (*with discontent*) murren (*about, against* über *+acc*); (*fig*) rauschen.

murmuring [ˈmɜːmərɪŋ] *n see vi* Murmeln *nt no pl*; Murren *nt no pl*; Rauschen *nt no pl* ◆ **~s (of discontent)** Unmutsäußerungen (*from gen*); **do I hear ~?** asked the chairman irgendwelche Unstimmigkeiten?, fragte der Vorsitzende.

Murphy's Law [ˈmɜːfɪzˌlɔː] *n* (*hum inf*) *„Gesetz" nt, demzufolge eine Sache, die schiefgehen kann, auch bestimmt schiefgehen wird.*

muscadel(le) [ˌmʌskəˈdel] *n see* **muscatel.**

muscat [ˈmʌskət] *n* (*grape*) Muskatellertraube *f*.

muscatel [ˌmʌskəˈtel] *n* (*wine*) Muskateller *m*.

muscle [ˈmʌsl] *n* Muskel *m*; (*fig: power*) Macht *f* ◆ **he's all ~** er besteht nur aus Muskeln *or* ist sehr muskulös (gebaut); **to have financial ~** finanzstark *or* -kräftig sein; **he never moved a ~** er rührte sich nicht.

◆**muscle in** *vi* (*sl*) mitmischen (*sl*) (*on* bei) ◆ **to ~ ~ on sb's territory** jdm dazwischenfunken (*inf*).

muscle: ~-bound *adj* (*inf: muscular*) muskulös; **to be ~-bound** eine überentwickelte Muskulatur haben; **~man** *n* Muskelmann *or* -protz (*pej*) *m*.

Muscovite [ˈmʌskəvaɪt] [1] *adj* Moskauer; (*Hist*) moskowitisch.
[2] *n* Moskauer(in *f*) *m*; (*Hist*) Moskowiter(in *f*) *m*.

Muscovy [ˈmʌskəvɪ] *n* (*Hist*) Moskauer Staat *m*.

muscular [ˈmʌskjʊləʳ] *adj* Muskel-, muskulär (*form*); (*having strong muscles*) muskulös ◆ **~ dystrophy** Muskeldystrophie *f*.

musculature [ˈmʌskjʊlətʃəʳ] *n* Muskulatur *f*.

Muse [mjuːz] *n* (*Myth*) Muse *f*.

muse [mjuːz] [1] *vi* nachgrübeln, nachsinnen (*liter*) (*about, on* über *+acc*).
[2] *vt* grüblerisch *or* sinnierend (*liter*) sagen.

museum [mjuːˈzɪəm] *n* Museum *nt* ◆ **~ piece** (*lit, hum*) Museumsstück *nt*.

mush [mʌʃ] *n* (**a**) Brei *m*; (*of fruit also*) Mus *nt* ◆ **the snow became a soft ~** der Schnee wurde matschig. (**b**) (*inf*) Schmalz *m* ◆ **he always sings such ~** er singt immer solche Schnulzen.

mushroom [ˈmʌʃrʊm] [1] *n* (eßbarer) Pilz; (*button ~*) Champignon *m*; (*atomic ~*) Pilz *m* ◆ **a great ~ of smoke** ein großer Rauchpilz; **to grow like ~s** wie die Pilze aus dem Boden schießen.
[2] *attr* (**a**) (*~-shaped*) pilzförmig ◆ **~ cloud** Atompilz *m*.
(**b**) (*made of ~s*) Pilz-; Champignon-.
(**c**) (*rapid and ephemeral*) *growth* sprunghaft; *fame, success* über Nacht erlangt, schlagartig ◆ **~ town** Stadt, die aus dem Boden geschossen ist.
[3] *vi* (**a**) **to go ~ing** in die Pilze gehen, Pilze sammeln (gehen).
(**b**) (*grow rapidly*) wie die Pilze aus dem Boden schießen ◆ **his fame/success ~ed** er wurde schlagartig berühmt/erfolgreich; **to ~ into sth** sich rasch zu etw entwickeln.
(**c**) (*become ~-shaped*) **the smoke ~ed in the still air** der Rauch breitete sich pilzförmig in der Luft aus.

mushy [ˈmʌʃɪ] *adj* (*+er*) (**a**) matschig; *liquid, consistency* breiig ◆ **~ snow** Schneematsch *m*; **~ peas** Erbsenmus *nt*. (**b**) (*inf: maudlin*) schmalzig.

music [ˈmjuːzɪk] *n* Musik *f*; (*of voice*) Musikalität *f*; (*written score*) Noten *pl* ◆ **do you use ~?** spielen/singen Sie nach Noten?; **to set** *or* **put sth to ~** etw vertonen; **~ of the spheres** Sphärenmusik *f*; **it was (like) ~ to my ears** das war Musik für mich *or* in meinen Ohren; **to face the ~** (*fig*) dafür gradestehen.

musical [ˈmjuːzɪkəl] [1] *adj* (**a**) (*of music*) musikalisch; *instrument, evening* Musik- ◆ **~ box** Spieluhr *or* -dose *f*; **~ chairs** *sing* Reise *f* nach Jerusalem. (**b**) (*tuneful*) melodisch. (**c**) (*musically-minded*) musikalisch.
[2] *n* Musical *nt*.

musicality [ˌmjuːzɪˈkælɪtɪ] *n* Musikalität *f*.

musically [ˈmjuːzɪkəlɪ] *adv* (**a**) musikalisch. (**b**) (*tunefully*) melodisch.

music *in cpds* Musik-; **~ box** *n* (*esp US*) Spieldose *or* -uhr *f*; **~ centre** *n* Kompaktanlage *f*, Musik-Center *nt*; **~ drama** *n* Musikdrama *nt*; **~ hall** *n* Varieté *nt*.

musician [mjuːˈzɪʃən] *n* Musiker(in *f*) *m*.

musicianship [mjuːˈzɪʃənʃɪp] *n* musikalisches Können.

musicological [ˌmjuːzɪkəˈlɒdʒɪkəl] *adj* musikwissenschaftlich.

musicologist [ˌmjuːzɪˈkɒlədʒɪst] *n* Musikwissenschaftler(in *f*) *m*.

musicology [ˌmjuːzɪˈkɒlədʒɪ] *n* Musikwissenschaft *f*.

music: ~-paper *n* Notenpapier *nt*; **~ stand** *n* Notenständer *m*; **~-stool** *n* Klavierstuhl *or* -hocker *m*.

musing [ˈmjuːzɪŋ] [1] *adj* grüblerisch, nachdenklich, sinnierend (*liter*); *philosopher, book, article* gedankenvoll.
[2] *n* Überlegungen *pl* (*on* zu).

musk [mʌsk] *n* (**a**) (*secretion, smell*) Moschus *m*. (**b**) (*Bot*) Moschuskraut *nt*.

musk deer *n* Moschustier *nt*, Moschushirsch *m*.

musket [ˈmʌskɪt] *n* Muskete *f*.

musketeer [ˌmʌskɪˈtɪəʳ] *n* Musketier *m*.

musketry [ˈmʌskɪtrɪ] *n* (*muskets*) Musketen *pl*; (*troops*) Musketiere *pl*.

musk: ~-melon *n* Zucker- *or* Gartenmelone *f*; **~-ox** *n* Moschusochse *m*; **~rat** *n* Bisamratte *f*; **~-rose** *n* Moschusrose *f*.

musky [ˈmʌskɪ] *adj* (*+er*) moschusartig; *smell* Moschus-; *aftershave etc* nach Moschus riechend.

Muslim [ˈmʊzlɪm] *adj, n see* **Moslem.**

muslin [ˈmʌzlɪn] [1] *n* Musselin *m*.
[2] *adj* Musselin-, aus Musselin.

musquash [ˈmʌskwɒʃ] *n* Bisamratte *f*.

muss [mʌs] (*US inf*) [1] *n* Durcheinander *nt* ◆ **to be in a ~** durcheinander (*inf*) *or* unordentlich sein.
[2] *vt* (*also ~ up*) in Unordnung bringen; *hair, room also* durcheinanderbringen (*inf*) ◆ **to get ~ed (up)** in Unordnung geraten.

mussel [ˈmʌsl] *n* (Mies)muschel *f* ◆ **~ bed** Muschelbank *f*.

Mussulman [ˈmʌslmən] *n, pl* **-mans** (*old*) Muselman(in *f*) *m*.

mussy [ˈmʌsɪ] *adj* (*+er*) (*US inf*) unordentlich, durcheinander *pred* (*inf*).

▼ **must**[1] [mʌst] [1] *vb aux present tense only* (**a**) müssen ◆ **you ~ (go and) see this church** Sie müssen sich (*dat*) diese Kirche unbedingt ansehen; **do it if you ~** tu, was du nicht lassen kannst; **~ you/I?** *etc* (*really?*) ja (wirklich)?; (*do you/I have to?*) muß das sein?; **we ~ away** (*old*) wir müssen fort.
▼ (**b**) (*in neg sentences*) dürfen ◆ **I ~n't forget that** ich darf das nicht vergessen.
▼ (**c**) (*be certain to*) **he ~ be there by now** er ist wohl inzwischen da; (*is bound to*) er ist inzwischen bestimmt da, er muß (wohl) inzwischen da sein; **he (surely) ~ be there by now** er *muß* doch inzwischen da sein; **I ~ have lost it** ich habe es wohl verloren, ich muß es wohl verloren haben; (*with stress on ~*) ich muß es verloren haben; **you ~ have heard of him** Sie haben bestimmt schon von ihm gehört; (*with stress on ~*) Sie müssen doch schon von ihm gehört haben; **there ~ have been five of them** es müssen fünf gewesen sein; (*about five*) es waren wohl etwa fünf; (*at least five*) es waren bestimmt fünf; **he ~ be older than that** er muß älter sein; **there ~ be a reason for it** es gibt bestimmt eine Erklärung dafür; (*with stress on ~*) es muß doch eine Erklärung dafür geben; **it ~ be about 3 o'clock** es wird wohl (so) etwa 3 Uhr sein, es muß so gegen 3 Uhr sein; **I ~ have been dreaming** da habe ich wohl geträumt; **I ~ have been mad** ich muß (wohl) wahnsinnig gewesen sein; **you ~ be crazy!** du bist ja *or* wohl wahnsinnig!
(**d**) (*showing annoyance*) müssen ◆ **he ~ come just now** natürlich muß er

➤ LANGUAGE IN USE: **must**[1]: **1a** → 4, 10.1, 15.1 **1b** → 9.5 **1c** → 15.2

gerade jetzt kommen.
[2] *n* (*inf*) Muß *nt* ◆ **a sense of humour/an umbrella is a ~** man braucht unbedingt Humor/einen Schirm, Humor/ein Schirm ist unerläßlich; **tighter security is a ~** bessere Sicherheitskontrollen sind unerläßlich; **this novel/programme is a ~ for everyone** diesen Roman/dieses Programm muß man einfach *or* unbedingt gelesen/gesehen haben.

must^{2} *n* (*mustiness*) Muffigkeit *f*.

must^{3} *n* (*Winemaking*) Most *m*.

must- *pref* (*inf*) **a ~see movie** ein Film, den man gesehen haben muß; **a ~read** ein Buch, das man gelesen haben muß; **it's a ~visit** dort muß man gewesen sein.

mustache *n* (*US*) *see* **moustache**.

mustachio [mʌˈstæʃɪəʊ] *n, pl* **-s** Schnauzbart *m*.

mustachioed [mʌˈstæʃɪəʊd] *adj* schnauzbärtig.

mustang [ˈmʌstæŋ] *n* Mustang *m*.

mustard [ˈmʌstəd] [1] *n* Senf *m*; (*colour*) Senfgelb *nt* ◆ **to be as keen as ~** Feuer und Flamme sein; **to cut the ~** (*US inf*) es bringen (*sl*).
[2] *attr flavour, smell* Senf-; (*yellow*) senffarben.

mustard *in cpds* Senf-; **~ plaster** *n* Senfpackung *f*; **~ yellow** [1] *n* Senfgelb *nt*; [2] *adj* senfgelb.

muster [ˈmʌstəʳ] [1] *n* (*esp Mil: assembly*) Appell *m*; (*cattle ~*) Zusammentreiben *nt* der Herde ◆ **to pass ~** (*fig*) den Anforderungen genügen.
[2] *vt* **(a)** (*summon*) versammeln, zusammenrufen; (*esp Mil*) antreten lassen; *cattle* zusammentreiben ◆ **the men were ~ed at 14.00** die Leute mußten um 14^{00} zum Appell antreten.
(b) (*manage to raise: also* **~ up**) zusammenbekommen, aufbringen; (*fig*) *intelligence, strength etc* aufbieten; *strength, courage* aufbringen; *all one's strength, courage* zusammennehmen.
[3] *vi* sich versammeln; (*esp Mil*) (zum Appell) antreten.

◆**muster in** *vt sep* (*US*) *troops, recruits* einziehen.

◆**muster out** *vt sep* (*US*) *troops* entlassen.

mustiness [ˈmʌstɪnɪs] *n* Muffigkeit *f*.

mustn't [ˈmʌsnt] *contr of* **must not**.

musty [ˈmʌstɪ] *adj* (*+er*) *air* muffig; *books* moderig.

mutability [ˌmjuːtəˈbɪlɪtɪ] *n* Wandlungsfähigkeit, Mutabilität (*spec*) *f*.

mutable [ˈmjuːtəbl] *adj* variabel, veränderlich; (*Biol*) mutabel.

mutant [ˈmjuːtənt] [1] *n* Mutante (*spec*), Mutation *f*.
[2] *adj* Mutations-.

mutate [mjuːˈteɪt] [1] *vi* sich verändern; (*Biol*) mutieren (*to* zu); (*Ling*) sich verwandeln (*to* in *+acc*).
[2] *vt* wandeln; (*Biol*) zu einer Mutation führen bei.

mutation [mjuːˈteɪʃən] *n* (*process*) Veränderung *f*; (*result*) Variante *f*; (*Biol*) Mutation *f*; (*Ling*) Wandel *m* (*to* zu).

mute [mjuːt] [1] *adj* stumm (*also Ling*); *amazement, rage* sprachlos ◆ **he was ~ with rage** er brachte vor Wut kein Wort heraus.
[2] *n* **(a)** (*dumb person*) Stumme(r) *mf*. **(b)** (*hired mourner*) Totenkläger *m*; (*woman*) Klageweib *nt*. **(c)** (*Mus*) Dämpfer *m*.
[3] *vt* dämpfen.

muted [ˈmjuːtɪd] *adj* gedämpft; (*fig*) *criticism etc* leise, leicht.

mutilate [ˈmjuːtɪleɪt] *vt person, animal, story, play* verstümmeln; *painting, building etc* verschandeln (*inf*).

mutilation [ˌmjuːtɪˈleɪʃən] *n see vt* Verstümmelung *f*; Verschandelung *f* (*inf*).

mutineer [ˌmjuːtɪˈnɪəʳ] *n* Meuterer *m*.

mutinous [ˈmjuːtɪnəs] *adj* (*Naut*) meuterisch, aufrührerisch; (*fig*) rebellisch.

mutiny [ˈmjuːtɪnɪ] (*Naut, fig*) [1] *n* Meuterei *f*.
[2] *vi* meutern.

mutism [ˈmjuːtɪzəm] *n* (*Psych*) Mutismus *m*.

mutt [mʌt] *n* (*pej sl*) (*dog*) Köter *m*; (*idiot*) Dussel *m* (*inf*).

mutter [ˈmʌtəʳ] [1] *n* Murmeln, Gemurmel *nt*; (*of discontent*) Murren *nt* ◆ **a ~ of voices** ein Stimmengemurmel; **a ~ of discontent** ein unzufriedenes Murren.
[2] *vt* murmeln, brummeln ◆ **they ~ed their discontent** sie murrten unzufrieden; **are you ~ing insults/threats at me?** höre ich Sie Beleidigungen/Drohungen (gegen mich) brummeln?
[3] *vi* murmeln; (*with discontent*) murren.

muttering [ˈmʌtərɪŋ] *n* (*act*) Gemurmel *nt*; (*with discontent*) Murren *nt*; (*remark*) Gemurmel *nt no pl*; Meckerei *f* (*inf*).

mutton [ˈmʌtn] *n* Hammel(fleisch *nt*) *m* ◆ **as dead as ~** mausetot (*inf*); **she's ~ dressed as lamb** (*inf*) sie macht auf jung (*inf*).

mutton: ~chops *npl* (*whiskers*) Koteletten *pl*; **~-head** *n* (*fig inf*) Schafskopf *m* (*inf*).

mutual [ˈmjuːtjʊəl] *adj* (*reciprocal*) *trust, respect, affection etc* gegenseitig; (*bilateral*) *troop withdrawals, efforts, détente, satisfaction* beiderseitig; (*shared, in common*) *friends, dislikes etc* gemeinsam ◆ **it would be for our ~ benefit** es wäre für uns beide von Vorteil *or* zu unser beider Nutzen (*form*); **the feeling is ~** das beruht (ganz) auf Gegenseitigkeit; **I hate you! — the feeling is ~** ich hasse dich! — ganz meinerseits (*inf*); **~ insurance** Versicherung *f* auf Gegenseitigkeit.

mutuality [ˌmjuːtjʊˈælɪtɪ] *n* Gegenseitigkeit *f*.

mutually [ˈmjuːtjʊəlɪ] *adv* beide; (*reciprocally*) *distrust* gegenseitig; *satisfactory, beneficial* für beide Seiten; *agreed, rejected* von beiden Seiten ◆ **a gentleman ~ known to us** ein Herr, den wir beide kennen.

muzak ® [ˈmjuːzæk] *n* Berieselungsmusik *f* (*inf*).

muzziness [ˈmʌzɪnɪs] *n see adj* Benommenheit *f*; Verschwommenheit *f*; Verzerrtheit *f*.

muzzle [ˈmʌzl] [1] *n* **(a)** (*snout, mouth*) Maul *nt*. **(b)** (*for dog etc*) Maulkorb *m*. **(c)** (*of gun*) Mündung *f*; (*barrel*) Lauf *m*.
[2] *vt animal* einen Maulkorb um- *or* anlegen (*+dat*); (*fig*) *critics, the press* mundtot machen; *criticism, protest* ersticken.

muzzle: ~-loader *n* Vorderlader *m*; **~-loading** *adj gun* mit Vorderladung; **~ velocity** *n* Mündungs- *or* Auffangsgeschwindigkeit *f*.

muzzy [ˈmʌzɪ] *adj* (*+er*) (*dizzy, dazed*) benommen, benebelt; (*blurred*) *view, memory etc* verschwommen; *noise* verzerrt.

MW *abbr of* **medium wave** MW.

my [maɪ] [1] *poss adj* mein ◆ **I've hurt ~ leg/arm** ich habe mir das Bein/den Arm verletzt; **~ father and mother** mein Vater und meine Mutter; **in ~ country** bei uns, in meinem Land (*form*).
[2] *interj* (*surprise*) (du) meine Güte, du liebe Zeit; (*delight*) ach, oh ◆ **~, ~, hasn't she grown!** nein so was, die ist vielleicht groß geworden.

Myanmar [ˈmaɪænmɑːʳ] *n* Myanmar *nt*.

myna(h) bird [ˈmaɪnəˌbɜːd] *n* Hirtenstar *m*.

myopia [maɪˈəʊpɪə] *n* Kurzsichtigkeit, Myopie (*spec*) *f*.

myopic [maɪˈɒpɪk] *adj* kurzsichtig.

myriad [ˈmɪrɪəd] [1] *n* Myriade *f* ◆ **a ~ of** Myriaden von.
[2] *adj* (*innumerable*) unzählige.

myrrh [mɜːʳ] *n* Myrrhe *f*.

myrtle [ˈmɜːtl] *n* Myrte *f* ◆ **~ green** moosgrün.

myself [maɪˈself] *pers pron* **(a)** (*dir obj, with prep +acc*) mich; (*indir obj, with prep +dat*) mir ◆ **I said to ~** ich sagte mir; **singing to ~** vor mich hin singend; **I wanted to see (it) for ~** ich wollte es selbst *or* selber sehen; **I tried it out on ~** ich habe es an mir selbst *or* selber ausprobiert; **I addressed the letter to ~** ich habe den Brief an mich selbst adressiert.
(b) (*emph*) (ich) selbst ◆ **my wife and ~** meine Frau und ich; **I did it ~** ich habe es selbst gemacht; **I thought so ~** das habe ich auch gedacht; **... if I say so or it ~** ... auch wenn ich es selbst sage; **(all) by ~** (ganz) allein(e); **I ~ believe** *or* **~, I believe that ...** ich persönlich *or* ich selbst bin der Ansicht, daß ...; **~, I doubt it** ich persönlich *or* ich für meinen Teil bezweifle das.
(c) (*one's normal self*) **I'm not (feeling) ~ today** mit mir ist heute etwas nicht in Ordnung *or* irgend etwas los; (*healthwise also*) ich bin heute nicht ganz auf der Höhe; **I didn't look ~ in that dress** das Kleid paßte überhaupt nicht zu mir; **I tried to be just ~** ich versuchte, mich ganz natürlich zu benehmen.

mysterious [mɪˈstɪərɪəs] *adj* (*puzzling*) rätselhaft, mysteriös; (*secretive*) geheimnisvoll; *atmosphere, stranger* geheimnisvoll ◆ **she is being quite ~ about it/him** sie macht ein großes Geheimnis daraus/um ihn; **why are you being so ~?** warum tust du so geheimnisvoll?

mysteriously [mɪˈstɪərɪəslɪ] *adv vague, unwilling, pleased* sonderbar; (*puzzlingly*) *vanish, change* auf rätselhafte *or* geheimnisvolle *or* mysteriöse Weise; *disappointed, missing* unerklärlicherweise; (*secretively*) geheimnisvoll.

mystery [ˈmɪstərɪ] *n* (*puzzle*) Rätsel *nt*; (*secret*) Geheimnis *nt* ◆ **to be shrouded** *or* **veiled** *or* **surrounded in ~** von einem Geheimnis umwittert *or* umgeben sein; **there's no ~ about it** da ist überhaupt nichts Geheimnisvolles dabei; **it's a ~ to me** das ist mir schleierhaft *or* ein Rätsel; **don't make a great ~ out of it!** mach doch kein so großes Geheimnis daraus!; **why all the ~?** was soll denn die Geheimnistuerei?

mystery: ~ novel *n see* **~ story**; **~ play** *n* Mysterienspiel *nt*; **~ story** *n* Kriminalgeschichte *f*, Krimi *m* (*inf*); **~ tour** *n* Fahrt *f* ins Blaue; **a ~ tour of the Black Forest** eine Entdeckungsreise durch den Schwarzwald; **~ writer** *n* Kriminalschriftsteller(in *f*) *m*.

mystic [ˈmɪstɪk] [1] *adj* mystisch; *writing, words, beauty also* geheimnisvoll.
[2] *n* Mystiker(in *f*) *m*.

mystical [ˈmɪstɪkəl] *adj* mystisch.

mysticism [ˈmɪstɪsɪzəm] *n* Mystizismus *m*; (*of poetry etc*) Mystik *f*, Mystische(s) *nt*.

mystification [ˌmɪstɪfɪˈkeɪʃən] *n* (*bafflement*) Verwunderung, Verblüffung *f*; (*act of bewildering*) Verwirrung *f* ◆ **he put an end to my ~ by explaining ...** das Rätsel löste sich für mich, als er mir erklärte ...

mystify [ˈmɪstɪfaɪ] *vt* vor ein Rätsel stellen ◆ **his explanation mystified us all** seine Erklärung blieb uns allen ein Rätsel; **I was completely mystified by the whole business** die ganze Sache war mir ein völliges Rätsel *or* völlig schleierhaft (*inf*); **the conjurer's tricks mystified the audience** die Kunststücke des Zauberers verblüfften das Publikum; **~ing** unerklärlich, rätselhaft.

mystique [mɪˈstiːk] *n* geheimnisvoller Nimbus ◆ **modern women have little ~, there is little ~ about modern women** die moderne Frau hat wenig Geheimnisvolles an sich.

myth [mɪθ] *n* Mythos *m*; (*fig*) Märchen *nt* ◆ **it's a ~** (*fig*) das ist doch ein Gerücht *or* Märchen.

mythical [ˈmɪθɪkəl] *adj* mythisch, sagenhaft; (*fig*) erfunden ◆ **~ figure/character** Sagengestalt *f*; **~ story** Mythos *m*, Sage *f*.

mythological [ˌmɪθəˈlɒdʒɪkəl] *adj* mythologisch.

mythology [mɪˈθɒlədʒɪ] *n* Mythologie *f*.

myxomatosis [ˌmɪksəʊməˈtəʊsɪs] *n* Myxomatose *f*.

N, n [en] *n* N, n *nt.*
N *abbr of* **north** N.
n (a) (*Math*) n. **(b)** **'n** (*inf*) = **and. (c)** (*inf: many*) x (*inf*) ◆ **~ times** x-mal (*inf*).
n *abbr of* **(a) noun** Subst. **(b) neuter** nt.
n/a *abbr of* **not applicable** entf.
NAACP (*US*) *abbr of* **National Association for the Advancement of Colored People** *Vereinigung f zur Förderung Farbiger.*
Naafi ['næfɪ] *abbr of* **Navy, Army and Air Force Institutes** (*shop*) *Laden m der britischen Armee;* (*canteen*) *Kantine f der britischen Armee.*
nab [næb] *vt* (*inf*) **(a)** (*catch*) erwischen; (*police also*) schnappen (*inf*) ◆ **the police ~bed him when he** ... die Polizei hat ihn dabei erwischt, wie er ...
(b) (*take for oneself*) sich (*dat*) grapschen (*inf*) ◆ **somebody had ~bed my seat** mir hatte jemand den Platz geklaut (*inf*).
nabob ['neɪbɒb] *n* Nabob *m;* (*fig also*) Krösus *m.*
nacelle [næ'sel] *n* **(a)** (*on aeroplane*) (Flugzeug)rumpf *m.* **(b)** (*gondola*) (*on airship*) (Luftschiff)gondel *f;* (*on balloon*) (Ballon)korb *m.*
nacre ['neɪkəʳ] *n* Perlmutter *f or nt,* Perlmutt *nt.*
nacreous ['neɪkriːəs] *adj* perlmutterartig, Perlmutt(er)-.
nadir ['neɪdɪəʳ] *n* **(a)** (*Astron*) Nadir, Fußpunkt *m.* **(b)** (*fig*) Tiefstpunkt *m* ◆ **the ~ of despair** tiefste Verzweiflung.
naff [næf] *adj* (*Brit sl*) **(a)** (*stupid*) *idea, thing to do, suggestion* blöd (*inf*). **(b)** (*not much use*) *management, company* lahm (*inf*); *computer, gadget etc also* nutzlos ◆ **this new monitor's a bit ~** dieser neue Monitor bringt's nicht (*inf*) *or* ist nicht das Wahre (*inf*). **(c)** (*not perceived as good style*) *colour, jacket, tie, decoration, design, book cover, car* ordinär ◆ **it looks a bit ~, doesn't it?** es sieht nicht gerade schick aus, oder?; **Japanese cars are really ~** wer fährt denn noch japanische Autos?
◆**naff off** *vi* (*Brit sl*) verschwinden (*inf*) ◆ **~ ~!** (*expressing refusal*) du spinnst wohl!
NAFTA ['næftə] *n abbr of* **North American Free Trade Agreement** NAFTA *f.*
nag[1] [næg] [1] *vt* (*find fault with*) herumnörgeln an (*+dat*); (*pester*) keine Ruhe lassen (*+dat*) (*for* wegen) ◆ **she's forever ~ging me** sie nörgelt immerzu an mir herum, sie hat dauernd etwas an mir auszusetzen; **don't ~ me** nun laß mich doch in Ruhe!; **to ~ sb to do sth** jdm schwer zusetzen *or* die Hölle heiß machen, damit er etw tut; **she kept on ~ging him until he did it** sie hat ihm solange zugesetzt *or* keine Ruhe gelassen, bis er es machte; **one thing that's been ~ging me for some time is** ... was mich schon seit einiger Zeit plagt *or* nicht in Ruhe läßt, ist ...
[2] *vi* (*find fault*) herumnörgeln, meckern (*inf*); (*be insistent*) keine Ruhe geben ◆ **to ~ at sb** an jdm herumnörgeln, jdm keine Ruhe lassen; **stop ~ging** hör auf zu meckern (*inf*).
[3] *n* (*fault-finder*) Nörgler(in *f*) *m;* (*woman also*) Meckerliese, Meckerziege *f* (*inf*); (*man also*) Meckerfritze *m* (*inf*); (*pestering*) Quälgeist *m* ◆ **don't be a ~** nun meckre nicht immer (*inf*).
nag[2] *n* (*old horse*) Klepper *m,* Mähre *f;* (*inf: horse*) Gaul *m.*
nagger ['nægəʳ] *n see* **nag**[1] **3.**
nagging ['nægɪŋ] [1] *adj* **(a)** *wife* meckernd (*inf*), nörglerisch; (*pestering*) ewig drängend. **(b)** *pain* dumpf; *worry, doubt* quälend.
[2] *n* (*fault-finding*) Meckern *nt* (*inf*), Nörgelei *f;* (*pestering*) ewiges Drängen.
NAHT (*Brit*) *abbr of* **National Association of Head Teachers.**
naiad ['naɪæd] *n* Najade, Wassernymphe *f.*
nail [neɪl] [1] *n* **(a)** (*Anat*) Nagel *m.*
(b) (*Tech*) Nagel *m* ◆ **as hard as ~s** knallhart (*inf*), (unheimlich) hart; (*physically*) zäh wie Leder; **on the ~** (*fig inf*) auf der Stelle, sofort; **cash on the ~** (*inf*) Bargeld *nt;* **to hit the ~ (right) on the head** (*fig*) den Nagel auf den Kopf treffen; **to drive a ~ into sb's coffin, to be a ~ in sb's coffin** (*fig*) ein Nagel zu jds Sarg sein.
[2] *vt* **(a)** (*fix with ~s, put ~s into*) nageln ◆ **to ~ sth to the floor/door/wall** etw an den Boden/an die Tür/Wand nageln, etw auf dem Boden/an der Tür/Wand festnageln; **~ this on here** nageln Sie das hier an *or* fest; **he ~ed his opponent to the canvas** er pinnte seinen Gegner auf die Matte (*inf*).
(b) (*fig*) *person* festnageln ◆ **fear ~ed him to the spot** er war vor Furcht wie auf der Stelle festgenagelt; **they ~ed the contract** sie haben den Vertrag unter Dach und Fach gebracht.
(c) (*inf*) **to ~ sb** sich (*dat*) jdn schnappen (*inf*); (*charge also*) jdn drankriegen (*inf*).
◆**nail down** *vt sep* **(a)** (*lit*) *box* zunageln; *carpet, lid* festnageln. **(b)** (*fig*) *person* festnageln (*to* auf *+acc*) ◆ **I ~ed him ~ to coming at 6 o'clock** ich nagelte ihn auf 6 Uhr fest.
◆**nail up** *vt sep picture etc* annageln; *door, window* vernageln; *box* zunageln; *goods* in Kisten verpacken und vernageln.
nail *in cpds* Nagel-; **~-biting** [1] *n* Nägelkauen *nt;* [2] *adj* (*inf*) *terror* atemberaubend; *suspense also* atemlos; *match* spannungsgeladen; **~-brush** *n* Nagelbürste *f;* **~-clippers** *npl* Nagelzwicker *m;* **~-file** *n* Nagelfeile *f;* **~ polish** *n* Nagellack *m;* **~ polish remover** *n* Nagellackentferner *m;* **~ scissors** *npl* Nagelschere *f;* **~ varnish** *n* (*Brit*) Nagellack *m.*
naïve [naɪ'iːv] *adj* (*+er*) naiv; *person, remark also* einfältig.
naïvely [naɪ'iːvlɪ] *adv* naiv ◆ **he ~ believed me** er war so naiv, mir zu glauben, in seiner Einfalt glaubte er mir.
naïveté [naɪ'iːvteɪ], **naïvety** [naɪ'iːvɪtɪ] *n* Naivität *f;* (*of person also*) Einfalt *f.*
naked ['neɪkɪd] *adj* **(a)** *person* nackt, unbekleidet, bloß (*liter*) ◆ **to go ~** nackt *or* nackend gehen; **I feel ~ without my wristwatch/make-up** ich fühle mich ohne meine Armbanduhr unangezogen/ohne Make-up nackt und bloß; **(as) ~ as nature intended** (*hum*) im Adams-/Evaskostüm (*hum*); **(as) ~ as the day (that) he was born** splitterfasernackt (*hum*).
(b) *branch* nackt, kahl; *countryside* kahl; *sword* bloß, blank, nackt; *flame, light* ungeschützt; *truth, facts* nackt ◆ **the ~ eye** das bloße Auge; **a room with one ~ light** ein Zimmer, in dem nur eine Glühbirne hing.
nakedness ['neɪkɪdnɪs] *n* Nacktheit, Blöße *f* (*liter*).
NALGO ['nælgəʊ] (*Brit*) *abbr of* **National and Local Government Officers' Association** *Gewerkschaft f der staatlichen und kommunalen Verwaltungsangestellten.*
Nam [næm] *n* (*US*) *abbr of* **Vietnam.**
namby-pamby ['næmbɪ'pæmbɪ] (*inf*) [1] *n* Mutterkind *nt;* (*boy also*) Muttersöhnchen *nt.*
[2] *adj person* verweichlicht, verzärtelt (*inf*); (*indecisive*) unentschlossen.
name [neɪm] [1] *n* **(a)** Name *m* ◆ **what's your ~?** wie heißen Sie?, wie ist Ihr Name? (*form*); **my ~ is** ... ich heiße ..., mein Name ist ... (*form*); **this man, Smith by ~** dieser Mann namens Smith; **a man by the ~ of Gunn** ein Mann namens *or* mit Namen Gunn; **I know him only by ~** ich kenne ihn nur dem Namen nach; **he knows all his customers by ~** er kennt alle seine Kunden bei Namen; **to refer to sb/sth by ~** jdn/etw namentlich *or* mit Namen nennen; **in ~ alone** *or* **only** nur dem Namen nach; **a marriage in ~ only** *or* **in ~ alone** eine nur auf dem Papier bestehende Ehe; **I won't mention any ~s** ich möchte keine Namen nennen; **he writes under the ~ of X** er schreibt unter dem Namen X; **fill in your ~(s) and address(es)** Namen und Adresse eintragen; **they married to give the child a ~** sie haben geheiratet, damit das Kind einen Namen hatte; **what ~ shall I say?** wie ist Ihr Name, bitte?; (*on telephone*) wer ist am Apparat?; (*before showing sb in*) wen darf ich melden?; **to have one's ~ taken** (*Ftbl, Police etc*) aufgeschrieben werden; **in the ~ of** im Namen (*+gen*); **stop in the ~ of the law** halt, im Namen des Gesetzes; **in the ~ of goodness/God** um Himmels/Gottes willen; **all the big ~s were there** alle großen Namen waren da; **I'll put my/your ~ down** (*on list, in register etc*) ich trage mich/dich ein; (*for school, class, excursion, competition etc*) ich melde mich/dich an (*for* zu, *for a school* in einer Schule); (*for tickets, goods etc*) ich lasse mich/dich vormerken; (*on waiting list*) ich lasse mich *or* meinen Namen/dich *or* deinen Namen auf die Warteliste setzen; **to put one's ~ down for a vacancy** sich um *or* für eine Stelle bewerben; **I'll put your ~ down, Sir/Madam** ich werde Sie vormerken, mein Herr/meine Dame; **to call sb ~s** jdn beschimpfen; **you can call me all the ~s you like** ... du kannst mich nennen, was du willst ...; **not to have a penny/cent to one's ~** völlig pleite sein (*inf*), keinen roten Heller haben (*dated*); **what's in a ~?** was ist *or* bedeutet schon ein Name?, Name ist Schall und Rauch (*Prov*); **in all but ~** praktisch; **that's the ~ of the game** (*inf*) darum geht es; **for these people survival is the ~ of the game** diesen Leuten geht es ums Überleben; **I'll do it or my ~'s not Bob Brown** ich mache das, so wahr ich Bob Brown heiße.
(b) (*reputation*) Name, Ruf *m* ◆ **to have a good/bad ~** einen guten/schlechten Ruf *or* Namen haben; **to get a bad ~** in Verruf kommen; **to give sb a bad ~** jdn in Verruf bringen; **to protect one's good ~** seinen Ruf *or* guten Namen wahren; **to make one's ~ as, to make a ~ for oneself as** sich (*dat*) einen Namen machen als; **to make one's ~** berühmt werden; **this book made his ~** mit diesem Buch machte er sich einen Namen; **to have a ~ for**

sth für etw bekannt sein.
[2] *vt* **(a)** (*call by a ~, give a ~ to*) *person* nennen; *plant, new star etc* benennen, einen Namen geben (*+dat*); *ship* taufen, einen Namen geben (*+dat*) ◆ **I ~ this child/ship X** ich taufe dieses Kind/Schiff auf den Namen X; **a person ~d Smith** jemand namens *or* mit Namen Smith; **the child is ~d Peter** das Kind hat den *or* hört auf den Namen Peter; **to ~ a child after** *or* (*US*) **for sb** ein Kind nach jdm nennen; **to ~ sb as a witness** jdn als Zeugen nennen; **he was ~d as the thief/culprit/victim** er wurde als der Dieb/der Schuldige/das Opfer genannt *or* bezeichnet; **to ~ names** Namen nennen.
(b) (*appoint, nominate*) ernennen ◆ **to ~ sb mayor/as leader** jdn zum Bürgermeister/Führer ernennen; **to ~ sb for the post of mayor** jdn für das Amt des Bürgermeisters vorschlagen; **he has been ~d as Nobel Prize winner** ihm wurde der Nobelpreis verliehen; **they ~d her as the winner of the award** sie haben ihr den Preis verliehen; **to ~ sb as an heir** jdn zu seinem Erben bestimmen.
(c) (*describe, designate*) **to ~ sb (as) sth** jdn als etw bezeichnen.
(d) (*specify, list*) nennen ◆ **~ the main plays by Shakespeare** nenne mir die wichtigsten Dramen Shakespeares; **~ your price** nennen Sie Ihren Preis; **to ~ the day** (*inf*) den Hochzeitstag festsetzen; **~ the date and I'll be there** bestimmen Sie den Tag, und ich werde da sein; **you ~ it, they have it/he's done it** es gibt nichts, was sie nicht haben/was er noch nicht gemacht hat.

name-calling [ˈneɪm,kɔːlɪŋ] *n* Beschimpfung(en *pl*), Schimpferei(en *pl*) *f*.

-named [-neɪmd] *adj suf* genannt ◆ **the first-/last-~** der erst-/letztgenannte, der zuerst/zuletzt genannte.

name: ~-day *n* Namenstag *m*; **~-drop** *vi* (*inf*) berühmte Bekannte in die Unterhaltung einfließen lassen; **she's always ~-dropping** sie muß dauernd erwähnen, wen sie alles kennt; **~-dropper** *n* (*inf*) **he's a terrible ~-dropper** er muß dauernd erwähnen, wen er alles kennt; **~-dropping** *n* (*inf*) Angeberei *f* mit berühmten Bekannten; **his constant ~-dropping is most tedious** es ist nicht auszuhalten, wie er ständig mit berühmten Namen um sich wirft; **~less** *adj* **(a)** (*unknown*) *person* unbekannt; *author also* namenlos; **(b)** (*undesignated*) namenlos; **a person who shall be/remain ~less** jemand, der nicht genannt werden soll/der ungenannt bleiben soll; **(c)** (*undefined*) *sensation, emotion* unbeschreiblich; *longing, terror, suffering also* namenlos; **(d)** (*shocking*) *vice, crime* unaussprechlich.

namely [ˈneɪmlɪ] *adv* nämlich.

name: ~-part *n* Titelrolle *f*; **~-plate** *n* Namensschild *nt*; (*on door also*) Türschild *nt*; (*on business premises*) Firmenschild *nt*; **~sake** *n* Namensvetter(in *f*) *m*; **~-tape** *n* Wäschezeichen *nt*.

Namibia [næˈmɪbɪə] *n* Namibia *nt*.

Namibian [næˈmɪbɪən] *adj* namibisch.

nan(a) [ˈnæn(ə)] *n* Oma *f* (*inf*).

nana [ˈnɑːnə] *n* (*inf*) Trottel *m* (*inf*).

nan bread [ˈnɑːnˈbred] *n warm serviertes, fladenförmiges Weißbrot als Beilage zu indischen Fleisch- und Gemüsegerichten.*

nancy-boy [ˈnænsɪ,bɔɪ] *n* (*dated Brit inf*) Schwule(r) *m*.

nankeen [nænˈkiːn] *n, no pl* (*cloth*) Nanking(stoff *m*) *m or nt*.

nanny [ˈnænɪ] *n* **(a)** Kindermädchen *nt*. **(b)** (*inf: also* **nana**) Oma, Omi *f* (*inf*). **(c)** (*also* **~-goat**) Geiß, Ziege *f*.

nanosecond [ˈnænəʊ,sekənd] *n* Nanosekunde *f*.

nanotechnology [ˈnænəʊtek,nɒlədʒɪ] *n* Nanotechnologie *f*.

nap[1] [næp] [1] *n* Schläfchen, Nickerchen *nt* ◆ **afternoon ~** Nachmittagsschläfchen *nt*; **to have** *or* **take a ~** ein Schläfchen *or* ein Nickerchen machen; **he always has** *or* **takes a 20/15 minute ~ after lunch** nach dem Mittagessen legt er sich immer 20 Minuten/eine Viertelstunde aufs Ohr *or* hin.
[2] *vi* **to catch sb ~ping** (*fig*) jdn überrumpeln.

nap[2] *n* (*Tex*) Flor *m*; (*Sew*) Strich *m*.

nap[3] (*Racing*) [1] *vt winner, horse* setzen auf (*+acc*).
[2] *n* Tip *m* ◆ **to select a ~** auf ein bestimmtes Pferd setzen.

napalm [ˈneɪpɑːm] [1] *n* Napalm *nt*.
[2] *vt* mit Napalm bewerfen.

napalm: ~ bomb *n* Napalmbombe *f*; **~ bombing** *n* Abwurf *m* von Napalmbomben.

nape [neɪp] *n* (*usu:* **~ of the/one's neck**) Nacken *m*, Genick *nt*.

naphtha [ˈnæfθə] *n* Naphtha *nt or f*.

naphthalene [ˈnæfθəliːn] *n* Naphthalin *nt*.

napkin [ˈnæpkɪn] *n* **(a)** (*table ~*) Serviette *f*, Mundtuch *nt* (*old*) ◆ **~ ring** Serviettenring *m*. **(b)** (*for baby*) Windel *f*; (*US: sanitary ~*) (Damen)binde *f*.

Naples [ˈneɪplz] *n* Neapel *nt*.

Napoleon [nəˈpəʊlɪən] *n* Napoleon *m*.

Napoleonic [nə,pəʊlɪˈɒnɪk] *adj* Napoleonisch.

nappy [ˈnæpɪ] *n* (*Brit*) Windel *f* ◆ **~ rash** Wundsein *nt*, Windeldermatitis *f* (*spec*); **little Jonathan's got ~ rash** der kleine Jonathan ist wund.

narc [nɑːk] *n* (*US sl*) Rauschgiftfahnder(in *f*) *m*.

narcissi [nɑːˈsɪsaɪ] *pl of* **narcissus (a)**.

narcissism [nɑːˈsɪsɪzəm] *n* Narzißmus *m*.

narcissistic [,nɑːsɪˈsɪstɪk] *adj* narzißtisch.

narcissus [nɑːˈsɪsəs] *n* **(a)** *pl* **narcissi** (*Bot*) Narzisse *f*. **(b)** (*Myth*) **N~** Narziß *m*.

narcosis [nɑːˈkəʊsɪs] *n* Narkose *f*.

narcotic [nɑːˈkɒtɪk] [1] *adj* **(a) ~ substance/drug** Rauschgift *nt*. **(b)** (*Med*) narkotisch.
[2] *n* **(a)** Rauschgift *nt* ◆ **~s agent** Rauschgiftfahnder(in *f*) *m*; **the ~s squad** das Rauschgiftdezernat. **(b)** (*Med*) Narkotikum *nt*.

nark [nɑːk] (*Brit*) [1] *vt* (*inf*) ärgern ◆ **to get/feel ~ed** wütend werden/sich ärgern.
[2] *n* (*sl*) Spitzel *m*.

narky [ˈnɑːkɪ] *adj* (*+er*) (*Brit inf*) gereizt.

narrate [nəˈreɪt] *vt* erzählen; *events, journey etc* schildern.

narration [nəˈreɪʃən] *n* Erzählung *f*; (*of events, journey*) Schilderung *f*.

narrative [ˈnærətɪv] [1] *n* **(a)** (*story*) Erzählung *f*; (*account*) Schilderung *f*; (*text*) Text *m* ◆ **writer of ~** erzählender Autor. **(b)** (*act of narrating*) Erzählen *nt*; (*of events, journey*) Schilderung *f*.
[2] *adj* erzählend; *ability etc* erzählerisch ◆ **~ poem** Ballade *f*; (*modern*) Erzählgedicht *nt*.

narrator [nəˈreɪtəʳ] *n* Erzähler(in *f*) *m* ◆ **a first-/third-person ~** ein Ich-/Er-Erzähler.

narrow [ˈnærəʊ] [1] *adj* (*+er*) **(a)** eng; *road, path, passage, valley also, shoulders, hips* schmal ◆ **to become ~** eng werden; (*road etc*) sich verengen.
(b) (*fig*) *person, attitudes, ideas* engstirnig, beschränkt; *views also, sense, meaning, interpretation* eng; *existence* beschränkt; *majority, victory* knapp; *scrutiny* peinlich genau ◆ **to have a ~ mind** engstirnig sein; **to have a ~ escape** mit knapper Not davonkommen, gerade noch einmal davonkommen; **that was a ~ escape/squeak** (*inf*) das war knapp, das wäre beinahe ins Auge gegangen (*inf*).
(c) (*Ling*) *vowel* geschlossen.
[2] *n* **~s** *pl* enge Stelle.
[3] *vt road etc* enger machen, verengen ◆ **to ~ the field** (*fig*) die Auswahl reduzieren (*to* auf *+acc*); **with ~ed eyes** mit zusammengekniffenen Augen.
[4] *vi* enger werden, sich verengen ◆ **the field ~ed to two candidates** die Auswahl war auf zwei Kandidaten zusammengeschrumpft.

◆**narrow down** (*to* auf *+acc*) [1] *vi* sich beschränken; (*be concentrated*) sich konzentrieren ◆ **the question ~s ~ to this** die Frage läuft darauf hinaus.
[2] *vt sep* (*limit*) beschränken, einschränken; *possibilities etc* beschränken; (*concentrate*) konzentrieren ◆ **that ~s it ~ a bit** dadurch wird die Auswahl kleiner.

narrow: ~ boat *n* Kahn *m*; **~casting** *n* (*TV*) Spartenfernsehen *nt*; **~-gauge** *adj* schmalspurig, Schmalspur-.

narrowly [ˈnærəʊlɪ] *adv* **(a)** (*by a small margin*) *escape* mit knapper Not ◆ **he ~ escaped being knocked down** er wäre um ein Haar *or* beinahe überfahren worden; **you ~ missed (seeing) him** du hast ihn gerade verpaßt. **(b)** *interpret* eng; *examine* peinlich genau ◆ **she looks at things/life much too ~** sie sieht die Dinge/das Leben viel zu eng.

narrow: ~-minded *adj*, **~-mindedly** *adv* engstirnig; **~-mindedness** *n* Engstirnigkeit *f*; **~ness** *n* Enge *f*; **~-shouldered** *adj* schmalschult(e)rig.

narwhal [ˈnɑːwəl] *n* Narwal *m*.

nary [ˈneərɪ] *adj* (*old*) **with ~ a word** ohne ein Wort zu sagen.

NASA [ˈnæsə] *abbr of* **National Aeronautics and Space Administration** NASA *f*.

nasal [ˈneɪzəl] [1] *adj* **(a)** (*Anat*) Nasen- ◆ **~ cavities** Nasenhöhle *f*. **(b)** *sound* nasal, Nasal-; *accent, voice, intonation* näselnd ◆ **to speak in a ~ voice** durch die Nase sprechen, näseln.
[2] *n* (*Ling*) Nasal(laut) *m*.

nasalization [,neɪzəlaɪˈzeɪʃən] *n* Nasalierung *f*.

nasalize [ˈneɪzəlaɪz] *vt* nasalieren.

nasally [ˈneɪzəlɪ] *adv pronounce* nasal; *speak* durch die Nase, näselnd.

nascent [ˈnæsnt] *adj* **(a)** (*liter*) *republic, world, culture* werdend, im Entstehen begriffen; *state* Entwicklungs-; *doubt, hope, pride* aufkommend. **(b)** (*Chem*) naszierend.

nastily [ˈnɑːstɪlɪ] *adv* **(a)** (*unpleasantly*) scheußlich; *speak, say* gehässig, gemein; *behave also* gemein ◆ **to speak ~ to sb** zu jdm gehässig sein, jdn angiften (*inf*). **(b)** (*awkwardly, dangerously*) *fall, cut oneself* böse, schlimm; *skid, veer* gefährlich.

nastiness [ˈnɑːstɪnɪs] *n, no pl* **(a)** *see adj (a)* Scheußlichkeit *f*; Ekelhaftigkeit *f*; Abscheulichkeit *f*; Schmutzigkeit *f*; Gefährlichkeit *f*.
(b) (*of behaviour etc*) Gemeinheit *f*; (*of person also*) Bosheit *f*; (*of remarks etc also*) Gehässigkeit *f*; (*behaviour*) gemeines *or* scheußliches Benehmen (*to* gegenüber); (*remarks*) Gehässigkeit(en *pl*) *f* (*to(wards)* gegenüber).
(c) *see adj (c)* Anstößigkeit *f*; Ekelhaftigkeit *f* ◆ **the ~ of his mind** seine üble/schmutzige Phantasie.

nasturtium [nəsˈtɜːʃəm] *n* (Kapuziner)kresse *f*, Kapuziner *m*.

nasty [ˈnɑːstɪ] *adj* (*+er*) **(a)** (*unpleasant*) scheußlich; *smell, taste also, medicine* ekelhaft, widerlich; *weather, habit also* abscheulich, übel; *surprise also* böse, unangenehm; (*serious*) *break, cough, wound also* böse, schlimm; (*objectionable*) *crime, behaviour, language, word, names* abscheulich; (*dirty*) schmutzig; (*dangerous*) *virus, disease* böse, gefährlich; *corner, bend, fog* böse, übel, gefährlich ◆ **that's a ~-looking sky/cut** der Himmel/der Schnitt sieht böse aus; **she had a ~ fall** sie ist böse *or* schlimm gefallen; **he had a ~ time of it** es ging ihm sehr schlecht *or* ganz übel; **he has a ~ look in his eyes** sein Blick verheißt nichts Gutes; **don't touch that, that's ~** pfui, faß das nicht an; **they pulled all his teeth out — ~!** sie haben ihm alle Zähne gezogen — wie scheußlich *or* unangenehm!; **to turn ~** (*situation, person*) unangenehm werden; (*animal*) wild werden; (*weather*) schlecht werden, umschlagen; **events took a ~ turn** die Dinge nahmen eine Wendung zum Schlechten.
(b) *person, behaviour* gemein, garstig (*dated*), fies (*inf*); *trick* gemein, übel; (*spiteful*) *remark, person also* gehässig; *rumour* gehässig, übel ◆ **he has a ~ temper** mit ihm ist nicht gut Kirschen essen; **don't say that, that's ~** pfui, so was sagt man doch nicht; **that was a ~ thing to say/do** das war gemein *or* fies (*inf*); **you ~ little boy (you)!** du böser Junge; **what a ~ man** was für ein ekelhafter Mensch; **he's a ~ bit** *or* **piece of work** (*inf*) er ist ein übler Kunde

(*inf*) *or* Typ (*inf*).
(c) (*offensive*) anstößig; *film, book also* ekelhaft, schmutzig ◆ **to have a ~ mind** eine üble Phantasie haben; (*obsessed with sex*) eine schmutzige Phantasie haben.
Nat *abbr of* **national.**
Natal [nəˈtæl] *n* Natal *nt*.
natal [ˈneɪtl] *adj* Geburts-.
natality [nəˈtælɪtɪ] *n* (*esp US*) Geburtenziffer *f*.
NATFHE (*Brit*) *abbr of* **National Association of Teachers in Further and Higher Education.**
nation [ˈneɪʃən] *n* Volk *nt*; (*people of one country*) Nation *f* ◆ **people of all ~s** Menschen aller Nationen; **the voice of the ~** die Stimme des Volkes; **in the service of the ~** im Dienste des Volkes; **to address the ~** zum Volk sprechen; **the whole ~ watched him do it** das ganze Land sah ihm dabei zu; **the Sioux ~** die Siouxindianer *pl*, das Volk der Sioux(indianer).
national [ˈnæʃənəl] [1] *adj* national; *problem, affairs also* das (ganze) Land betreffend, des Landes, des Staates; *interest, debt, income* Staats-, öffentlich; *strike, scandal* landesweit; *economy* Volks-; *security* Staats-; *character* National-; *defence, language, religion* Landes-; *custom, monument* Volks-; (*not local*) *agreement, radio station, press etc* überregional; (*in names*) Staats-, staatlich ◆ **~ status** Landeszugehörigkeit *f*.
[2] *n* (a) (*person*) Staatsbürger(in *f*) *m* ◆ **foreign ~** Ausländer(in *f*) *m*; **Commonwealth ~s** Angehörige *pl* des Commonwealth.
(b) (*inf: newspaper*) überregionale Zeitung.
(c) (*Sport*) *see* **Grand N~.**
national: ~ anthem *n* Nationalhymne *f*; **~ assistance** *n* Sozialhilfe *f*; **to be on ~ assistance** Sozialhilfe erhalten; **~ bank** *n* National- *or* Staatsbank *f*; **~ costume, ~ dress** *n* National- *or* Landestracht *f*; **~ flag** *n* National- *or* Landesflagge *f*; **N~ Front** *n* (*Brit*) *rechtsradikale Partei*; **N~ Guard** *n* (*esp US*) Nationalgarde *f*; **N~ Health** *adj attr* ≃ Kassen-; **N~ Health (Service)** *n* (*Brit*) Staatlicher Gesundheitsdienst; **I got it on the N~ Health** ≃ das hat die Krankenkasse bezahlt; **~ holiday** *n* gesetzlicher *or* staatlicher Feiertag; **~ insurance** *n* (*Brit*) Sozialversicherung *f*; **~ insurance benefits** Arbeitslosen- und Krankengeld *nt*.
nationalism [ˈnæʃnəlɪzəm] *n* Nationalismus *m* ◆ **feeling of ~** Nationalgefühl *nt*.
nationalist [ˈnæʃnəlɪst] [1] *adj* nationalistisch.
[2] *n* Nationalist(in *f*) *m*.
nationalistic [ˌnæʃnəˈlɪstɪk] *adj* nationalistisch.
nationality [ˌnæʃəˈnælɪtɪ] *n* Staatsangehörigkeit, Nationalität *f* ◆ **what ~ is he?** welche Staatsangehörigkeit hat er?; **she is of German ~** sie hat die deutsche Staatsangehörigkeit; **the many nationalities present** die Menschen verschiedener Nationalitäten, die anwesend sind/waren.
nationalization [ˌnæʃnəlaɪˈzeɪʃən] *n* Verstaatlichung *f*.
nationalize [ˈnæʃnəlaɪz] *vt industries etc* verstaatlichen.
National Lottery *n* (*Brit*) ≃ Lotto *nt*.
nationally [ˈnæʃnəlɪ] *adv* (*as a nation*) als Nation; (*nation-wide*) im ganzen Land, landesweit.
national: ~ park *n* Nationalpark *m*; **~ savings certificate** *n* (*Brit*) *festverzinsliches öffentliches Sparpapier*; **~ service** *n* Wehrdienst *m*; **N~ Socialism** *n* der Nationalsozialismus; **N~ Socialist** [1] *n* Nationalsozialist(in *f*) *m*; [2] *adj* nationalsozialistisch.
nationhood [ˈneɪʃənhʊd] *n* nationale Einheit *or* Geschlossenheit.
nation-wide [ˈneɪʃən,waɪd] *adj, adv* landesweit ◆ **the speech was broadcast ~** die Rede wurde im ganzen Land übertragen.
native [ˈneɪtɪv] [1] *adj* (a) *land, country, town* Heimat-; *language* Mutter-; *product, costume, customs, habits, plants* einheimisch; (*associated with natives*) *question, quarters, labour* Eingeborenen- ◆ **the ~ inhabitants** die Einheimischen *pl*; (*in colonial context*) die Eingeborenen *pl*; (*original inhabitants*) die Ureinwohner *pl*; **the ~ habitat of the tiger** die Heimat des Tigers; **my ~ Germany** mein Heimatland *nt or* meine Heimat Deutschland; **his ~ Berlin** seine Heimatstadt *or* Vaterstadt Berlin; **a ~ German** ein gebürtiger Deutscher, eine gebürtige Deutsche; **an animal/tree ~ to India** ein in Indien beheimatetes Tier/beheimateter Baum; **to go ~** wie die Eingeborenen leben.
(b) (*inborn*) *wit, quality* angeboren.
(c) *metal* gediegen.
[2] *n* (a) (*person*) Einheimische(r) *mf*; (*in colonial contexts*) Eingeborene(r) *mf*; (*original inhabitant*) Ureinwohner(in *f*) *m* ◆ **a ~ of Britain/Germany** ein gebürtiger Brite/Deutscher, eine gebürtige Britin/Deutsche.
(b) **to be a ~ of ...** (*plant, animal*) in ... beheimatet sein.
Native American [1] *adj* indianisch.
[2] *n* Indianer(in) *m(f)*.
native: ~-born *adj attr* gebürtig; **~ country** *n* Heimatland, Vaterland *nt*; **~ land** *n* Vaterland *nt*; **~ speaker** *n* Muttersprachler(in *f*) *m*; **I'm not a ~ speaker of English** Englisch ist nicht meine Muttersprache; **he speaks English like a ~ speaker** er spricht Englisch, als wäre es seine Muttersprache.
nativity [nəˈtɪvɪtɪ] *n* Geburt *f* ◆ **the N~** Christi Geburt *f*; (*picture*) die Geburt Christi; **~ play** Krippenspiel *nt*.
NATO [ˈneɪtəʊ] *abbr of* **North Atlantic Treaty Organization** NATO *f*.
natter [ˈnætəʳ] (*Brit inf*) [1] *vi* (*gossip*) schwatzen (*inf*); (*chatter also*) quasseln (*inf*) ◆ **to ~ away in German** deutsch quasseln (*inf*); **to ~ on about sth** über etw (*acc*) quasseln (*inf*).
[2] *n* Schwatz *m* (*inf*) ◆ **to have a ~** einen Schwatz halten (*inf*).
natty [ˈnætɪ] *adj* (*+er*) (a) (*neat*) *dress* schick, schmuck (*dated*); *person also* adrett ◆ **he's a ~ dresser** er zieht sich immer elegant *or* schmuck (*dated*) an.
(b) (*handy*) *tool, gadget* handlich.
natural [ˈnætʃrəl] [1] *adj* (a) natürlich; *rights* naturgegeben, Natur-; *laws, forces, phenomena, religion, silk, sponge* Natur- ◆ **it is ~ for you/him to think ...** es ist nur natürlich, daß Sie denken/er denkt ...; **~ resources** Naturschätze *pl*; **the ~ world** die Natur; **in its ~ state** im Naturzustand; **~ childbirth** natürliche Geburt; (*method*) die schmerzlose Geburt; **to die a ~ death** *or* **of ~ causes** eines natürlichen Todes sterben; **death from ~ causes** (*Jur*) Tod durch natürliche Ursachen; **to be imprisoned for the rest of one's ~ life** (*Jur*) eine lebenslängliche Gefängnisstrafe verbüßen; **a ~ son of Utah** in Utah geboren.
(b) (*inborn*) *gift, ability, quality* angeboren ◆ **to have a ~ talent for sth** eine natürliche Begabung für etw haben; **he is a ~ artist/comedian** er ist der geborene Künstler/Komiker; **it is ~ for birds to fly** Vögel können von Natur aus fliegen; **sth comes ~ to sb** etw fällt jdm leicht.
(c) (*unaffected*) *manner* natürlich, ungekünstelt.
(d) (*Math*) *number* natürlich.
(e) *parents* leiblich; (*old*) *child* natürlich.
[2] *n* (a) (*Mus*) (*sign*) Auflösungszeichen *nt*; (*note*) Note *f* ohne Vorzeichen; (*note with a ~ sign*) Note *f* mit Auflösungszeichen ◆ **B ~/D ~** H, h/D, d; **you played F sharp instead of a ~** Sie haben fis statt f gespielt; *see also* **major, minor.**
(b) (*inf: person*) Naturtalent *nt* ◆ **he's a ~ for this part** diese Rolle ist ihm wie auf den Leib geschrieben.
(c) (*inf: life*) Leben *nt* ◆ **I've never heard the like in all my ~** ich habe so was mein Lebtag noch nicht gehört (*inf*).
(d) (*old: idiot*) Einfaltspinsel *m*.
natural: ~ gas *n* Erdgas *nt*; **~ history** *n* Naturkunde *f*; (*concerning evolution*) Naturgeschichte *f*.
naturalism [ˈnætʃrəlɪzəm] *n* Naturalismus *m*.
naturalist [ˈnætʃrəlɪst] *n* (a) Naturforscher(in *f*) *m*. (b) (*Art, Liter*) Naturalist(in *f*) *m*.
naturalistic [ˌnætʃrəˈlɪstɪk] *adj* (*Art, Liter*) naturalistisch.
naturalization [ˌnætʃrəlaɪˈzeɪʃən] *n* Naturalisierung, Einbürgerung *f* ◆ **~ papers** Einbürgerungsurkunde *f*.
naturalize [ˈnætʃrəlaɪz] *vt* (a) *person* einbürgern, naturalisieren ◆ **to become ~d** eingebürgert werden. (b) *animal, plants* heimisch machen; *word* einbürgern ◆ **to become ~d** heimisch werden/sich einbürgern.
naturally [ˈnætʃrəlɪ] *adv* (a) von Natur aus ◆ **he is ~ artistic/lazy** er ist künstlerisch veranlagt/von Natur aus faul. (b) (*not taught*) natürlich, instinktiv. **it comes ~ to him** das fällt ihm leicht. (c) (*unaffectedly*) *behave, speak* natürlich, ungekünstelt. (d) (*of course*) natürlich.
naturalness [ˈnætʃrəlnɪs] *n* Natürlichkeit *f*.
natural: ~ philosophy *n* Naturwissenschaft, Naturlehre (*old*) *f*; **~ science** *n* Naturwissenschaft *f*; **the ~ sciences** die Naturwissenschaften *pl*; **~ selection** *n* natürliche Auslese; **~ wastage** *n* natürliche Personalreduzierung.
nature [ˈneɪtʃəʳ] *n* (a) Natur *f* ◆ **N~** die Natur; **laws of ~** Naturgesetze *pl*; **against ~** gegen die Natur; **in a state of ~** (*uncivilized, inf: naked*) im Naturzustand; **to return to ~** (*person*) zur Natur zurückkehren; (*garden*) in den Naturzustand zurückkehren; **to paint from ~** nach der Natur malen.
(b) (*of person*) Wesen(sart *f*) *nt*, Natur *f* ◆ **it is not in my ~ to say things like that** es entspricht nicht meiner Art *or* meinem Wesen, so etwas zu sagen; **cruel by ~** von Natur aus grausam.
(c) (*of object, material*) Beschaffenheit *f* ◆ **it's in the ~ of things** das liegt in der Natur der Sache; **the ~ of the case is such ...** der Fall liegt so ...
(d) (*type, sort*) Art *f* ◆ **things of this ~** derartiges; **something in the ~ of an apology** so etwas wie eine Entschuldigung; **... or something of that ~** ... oder etwas in der Art.
nature: ~ conservancy *n* Naturschutz *m*; **~ cure** *n* Naturheilverfahren *nt*.
-natured [-ˈneɪtʃəd] *adj suf things, animals* -artig; *person* mit einem ... Wesen ◆ **good~** gutmütig; **ill~** bösartig.
nature: ~-lover *n* Naturfreund *m*; **~ poet** *n* Naturdichter(in *f*) *m*; **~ reserve** *n* Naturschutzgebiet *nt*; **~ study** *n* Naturkunde *f*; **~ trail** *n* Naturlehrpfad *m*; **~ worship** *n* Naturreligion *f*.
naturism [ˈneɪtʃərɪzəm] *n* Freikörperkultur *f*, FKK *no art*.
naturist [ˈneɪtʃərɪst] [1] *n* Anhänger(in *f*) *m* der Freikörperkultur, FKK-Anhänger(in *f*) *m*.
[2] *adj* FKK-, Freikörperkultur-.
naught [nɔːt] *n* (*old, form*) *see* **nought (b).**
naughtily [ˈnɔːtɪlɪ] *adv* frech, dreist; (*esp of child*) *say, remark* ungezogen, frech; *behave* unartig, ungezogen ◆ **I very ~ opened your letter** ich war so frech und habe deinen Brief aufgemacht; **but he very ~ did it all the same** aber frecherweise hat er es trotzdem getan.
naughtiness [ˈnɔːtɪnɪs] *n see adj* (a) Frechheit, Dreistigkeit *f*; Unartigkeit *f*; Ungezogenheit *f*; Ungehorsam *m*. (b) Unanständigkeit *f*.
naughty [ˈnɔːtɪ] *adj* (*+er*) (a) frech, dreist; *child* unartig, ungezogen; *dog* unartig, ungehorsam ◆ **you ~ boy/dog!** du böser *or* unartiger Junge/Hund!; **it was ~ of him to break it** das war aber gar nicht lieb von ihm, daß er das kaputtgemacht hat; **I was ~ and ate a whole bar of chocolate** ich habe schwer gesündigt und eine ganze Tafel Schokolade gegessen; **~, ~!** aber, aber!; **how ~ of me/him!** das war ja gar nicht lieb!; **the kitten's been ~ on the carpet** (*inf*) das Kätzchen hat auf den Teppich gemacht.
(b) (*shocking*) *joke, word, story* unanständig ◆ **~!** nein, wie unanständig!; **the ~ nineties** die frechen neunziger Jahre.

nausea ['nɔːsɪə] *n (Med)* Übelkeit *f*; *(fig)* Ekel *m* ◆ **a feeling of ~** Übelkeit *f*; *(fig)* ein Gefühl *nt* des Ekels; **the very thought fills me with ~** bei dem Gedanken allein wird mir schon übel.

nauseate ['nɔːsɪeɪt] *vt* **to ~ sb** *(Med)* (bei) jdm Übelkeit verursachen, in jdm Übelkeit erregen; *(fig)* jdn anwidern.

nauseating ['nɔːsɪeɪtɪŋ] *adj sight, smell, violence, food* ekelerregend; *film, book, style* gräßlich; *overpoliteness* widerlich; *person* ekelhaft, widerlich ◆ **that is a ~ attitude** bei der Einstellung kann einem übel werden.

nauseatingly ['nɔːsɪeɪtɪŋlɪ] *adv* widerlich.

nauseous ['nɔːsɪəs] *adj* **(a)** *(Med)* **that made me (feel) ~** dabei wurde mir übel. **(b)** *(fig)* widerlich.

nautical ['nɔːtɪkəl] *adj* nautisch; *chart also* See-; *prowess, superiority* zur See, seefahrerisch; *distance* zur See; *stories* von der Seefahrt; *language, tradition, appearance* seemännisch ◆ **a ~ nation** eine Seefahrernation; **he is interested in ~ matters, he's a very ~ person** er interessiert sich für die Seefahrt; **the music/play has a ~ flavour** die Musik/das Stück beschwört die See herauf; **~ mile** Seemeile *f*.

nautically ['nɔːtɪkəlɪ] *adv superior* in bezug auf die Seefahrt.

nautilus ['nɔːtɪləs] *n* Nautilus *m*, Schiffsboot *nt*.

naval ['neɪvəl] *adj* Marine-; *base, agreement, parade* Flotten-; *battle, forces* See- ◆ **his interests are ~ not military** er interessiert sich für die Marine und nicht für das Heer.

naval: ~ academy *n* Marineakademie *f*; **~ architect** *n* Schiffsbauingenieur *m*; **~ architecture** *n* Schiffsbau *m*; **~ aviation** *n* Seeflugwesen *nt*; **~ power** *n* Seemacht *f*; **~ warfare** *n* Seekrieg *m*.

nave [neɪv] *n* **(a)** *(of church)* Haupt- *or* Mittel- *or* Längsschiff *nt*. **(b)** *(of wheel)* (Rad)nabe *f*.

navel ['neɪvəl] *n* **(a)** *(Anat)* Nabel *m*. **(b)** *(also* **~ orange***)* Navelorange *f*.

navel-gazing *n (pej)* Nabelschau *f*.

navigable ['nævɪgəbl] *adj* **(a)** schiffbar ◆ **in a ~ condition** *(ship)* seetüchtig. **(b)** *balloon, airship* lenkbar.

navigate ['nævɪgeɪt] [1] *vi (in plane, ship)* navigieren; *(in car)* den Fahrer dirigieren; *(in rally)* der Beifahrer sein ◆ **who was navigating?** *(in plane, ship)* wer war für die Navigation zuständig?; *(in car)* wer war der Beifahrer?; **I don't know the route, you'll have to ~** ich kenne die Strecke nicht, du mußt mir sagen, wie ich fahren muß *or* du mußt mich dirigieren.

[2] *vt* **(a)** *aircraft, ship, spaceship* navigieren ◆ **to ~ sth through sth** etw durch etw (hindurch)navigieren; *(fig)* etw durch etw hindurchschleusen; **he ~d his way through the crowd** er bahnte sich *(dat)* einen Weg durch die Menge.

(b) *(journey through)* durchfahren; *(plane, pilot)* durchfliegen.

navigation [,nævɪ'geɪʃən] *n* **(a)** *(act of navigating)* Navigation *f*. **(b)** *(shipping)* Schiffsverkehr *m*. **(c)** *(skill) (in ship, plane)* Navigation *f* ◆ **how's your ~?** *(in car)* bist du als Beifahrer gut zu gebrauchen?; **his ~ was lousy, we got lost** *(in car)* er hat mich so schlecht dirigiert, daß wir uns verirrt haben.

navigation: ~ law *n* Schiffahrtsregelung *f*; **~ light** *n* Positionslicht *nt or* -lampe *f*.

navigator ['nævɪgeɪtə^r] *n (Naut)* Navigationsoffizier *m*; *(Aviat)* Navigator *m*; *(Mot)* Beifahrer *m*.

navvy ['nævɪ] *n (Brit)* Bauarbeiter *m*; *(on road also)* Straßenarbeiter *m*.

navy ['neɪvɪ] [1] *n* **(a)** (Kriegs)marine *f* ◆ **to serve in the ~** in der Marine dienen; **N~ Department** *(US)* Marineministerium *nt*. **(b)** *(also* **~ blue***)* Marineblau *nt*.

[2] *adj* **(a)** *attr* Marine-. **(b)** *(also* **~ blue***)* marineblau.

nawab [nə'wɒb] *n see* **nabob**.

nay [neɪ] [1] *adv* **(a)** *(obs, dial)* nein. **(b)** *(liter)* **surprised, ~ astonished** überrascht, nein vielmehr verblüfft.

[2] *n* Nein *nt*, Neinstimme *f*; *see* **yea**.

Nazarene ['næzəriːn] *n* Nazaräer *m*.

Nazi ['nɑːtsɪ] [1] *n* Nazi *m*; *(fig pej)* Faschist *m*.

[2] *adj* Nazi-.

Nazism ['nɑːtsɪzəm] *n* Nazismus *m*.

NB *abbr of* **nota bene** NB.

NCB *(Brit old) abbr of* **National Coal Board** *Verband m der britischen Kohleindustrie*.

NCO *abbr of* **non-commissioned officer** Unteroffizier, Uffz. *m*.

NE *abbr of* **north-east** NO.

Neanderthal [nɪ'ændətɑːl] *adj* Neandertaler *attr* ◆ **~ man** der Neandertaler.

neap [niːp] *n (also* **~-tide***)* Nippflut, Nippzeit, Nipptide *(N Ger) f*.

Neapolitan [nɪə'pɒlɪtən] [1] *adj* neapolitanisch ◆ **~ ice-cream** Fürst-Pückler-Eis *nt*.

[2] *n* Neapolitaner(in *f*) *m*.

near [nɪə^r] *(+er)* [1] *adv* **(a)** *(close in space and time)* nahe ◆ **to be ~** *(person, object)* in der Nähe sein; *(event, departure, festival etc)* bevorstehen; *(danger, end, help etc)* nahe sein; **to be very ~** ganz in der Nähe sein; *(in time)* nahe *or* unmittelbar bevorstehen; *(danger etc)* ganz nahe sein; **to be ~er/~est** näher/am nächsten sein; *(event etc)* zeitlich näher liegen/zeitlich am nächsten liegen; **to be ~ at hand** zur Hand sein; *(shops)* in der Nähe sein; *(help)* ganz nahe sein; *(event)* unmittelbar bevorstehen; **when death is so ~** wenn man dem Tod nahe ist; **he lives quite ~** er wohnt ganz in der Nähe; **don't sit/stand so ~** setzen Sie sich/stehen Sie nicht so nahe (daran); **you live ~er/~est** du wohnst näher/am nächsten; **to move/come ~er** näherkommen; **could you get** *or* **move ~er together?** könnten Sie näher *or* enger *or* mehr zusammenrücken?; **to draw ~/~er** heranrücken/näher heranrücken; **his answer came ~er than mine/~est** seine Antwort traf eher zu als meine/traf die Sachlage am ehesten; **that was the ~est I ever got to seeing him** da hätte ich ihn fast gesehen; **this is the ~est I can get to solving the problem** besser kann ich das Problem nicht lösen; **that's the ~est I ever got to being fired** da hätte nicht viel gefehlt, und ich wäre rausgeworfen worden.

(b) *(closely, exactly, accurately)* genau ◆ **as ~ as I can judge** soweit ich es beurteilen kann; **they're the same length or as ~ as makes no difference** sie sind so gut wie gleich lang; **it's as ~ stopped as makes no difference** es hat so gut wie aufgehört; **(that's) ~ enough** so geht's ungefähr, das haut so ungefähr hin *(inf)*; **... no, but ~ enough ...** nein, aber es war nicht weit davon entfernt; **there were ~ enough 60 people at the party** es waren knapp 60 Leute auf der Party; **the same size as ~ as dammit** *(inf)* fast genau die gleiche Größe.

(c) *(almost)* fast, beinahe; *impossible also, dead* nahezu.

(d) it's nowhere *or* **not anywhere ~ enough/right** das ist bei weitem nicht genug/das ist weit gefehlt; **we're not any ~er (to)/nowhere ~ solving the problem** wir sind der Lösung des Problems kein bißchen nähergekommen/wir haben das Problem bei weitem nicht *or* noch nicht einmal annähernd gelöst; **we're nowhere** *or* **not anywhere ~ finishing the book** wir haben das Buch noch lange nicht fertig; **nowhere ~ as much** lange *or* bei weitem nicht soviel; **you are nowhere** *or* **not anywhere ~ the truth** das ist weit gefehlt, du bist weit von der Wahrheit entfernt; **he is nowhere** *or* **not anywhere ~ as clever as you** er ist lange *or* bei weitem nicht so klug wie du.

[2] *prep (also adv:* **~ to***)* **(a)** *(close to) (position)* nahe an (*+dat*), nahe (*+dat*); *(with motion)* nahe an (*+acc*); *(in the vicinity of)* in der Nähe von *or +gen*; *(with motion)* in die Nähe von *or +gen* ◆ **to be/get ~ (to) the church** in der Nähe der Kirche sein/in die Nähe der Kirche kommen; **he lives ~ (to) the border** er wohnt in der Nähe der Grenze *or* nahe der Grenze; **the hotel is very ~ (to) the station** das Hotel liegt ganz in der Nähe des Bahnhofs; **move the chair ~/~er (to) the table** rücken Sie den Stuhl an den/näher an den Tisch; **to come** *or* **get ~/~er (to) sb/sth** nahe/näher an jdn/etw herankommen; **to stand ~/~er (to) the table** am *or* neben dem *or* nahe am/näher am Tisch stehen; **he won't go ~ anything illegal** mit Ungesetzlichem will er nichts zu tun haben; **when we got ~ (to) the house** als wir an das Haus herankamen *or* in die Nähe des Hauses kamen; **when we are ~er home** wenn wir nicht mehr so weit von zu Hause weg sind; **keep ~ me** bleib in meiner Nähe; **~ here/there** hier/dort in der Nähe; **don't come ~ me** komm mir nicht zu nahe; **~ (to) where I had seen him** nahe der Stelle, wo ich ihn gesehen hatte; **to be ~est to sth** einer Sache *(dat)* am nächsten sein; **take the chair ~est (to) you/the table** nehmen Sie den Stuhl direkt neben Ihnen/dem Tisch; **that's ~er it** das trifft schon eher zu; **the adaptation is very ~ (to) the original** die Bearbeitung hält sich eng ans Original; **to be ~ (to) sb's heart** *or* **sb** jdm am Herzen liegen; **to be ~ the knuckle** *or* **bone** *(inf) (joke)* gewagt sein; *(remark)* hart an der Grenze sein.

(b) *(close in time: with time stipulated)* gegen ◆ **~ (to) death/her confinement** dem Tode/der Geburt nahe; **she is ~ her time** es ist bald so weit (bei ihr); **~ (to) the appointed time** um die ausgemachte Zeit herum; **phone again ~er (to) Christmas** rufen Sie vor Weihnachten noch einmal an; **come back ~er (to) 3 o'clock** kommen Sie gegen 3 Uhr wieder; **on the Wednesday ~est Easter** am Mittwoch (direkt) vor Ostern; **to be ~er/~est (to) sth** einer Sache *(dat)* zeitlich näher liegen/am nächsten liegen; **~ (to) the end of my stay/the play/book** gegen Ende meines Aufenthalts/des Stücks/des Buchs; **I'm ~ (to) the end of the book/my stay** ich habe das Buch fast zu Ende gelesen/mein Aufenthalt ist fast zu Ende *or* vorbei; **her birthday is ~ (to) mine** ihr und mein Geburtstag liegen nahe beieinander; **the sun was ~ (to) setting** die Sonne war am Untergehen; **the evening was drawing ~ (to) its close** *(liter)* der Abend ging zur Neige *(liter)*; **it is drawing ~ (to) Christmas** es geht auf Weihnachten zu; **as it drew ~/~er (to) his departure** als seine Abreise heranrückte/näher heranrückte.

(c) *(on the point of)* **to be ~ (to) doing sth** nahe daran sein, etw zu tun; **to be ~ (to) tears/despair** *etc* den Tränen/der Verzweiflung *etc* nahe sein; **she was ~ (to) laughing out loud** sie hätte beinahe laut gelacht; **the project is ~/~er (to) completion** das Projekt steht vor seinem Abschluß/ist dem Abschluß nähergekommen; **he came ~ to ruining his chances** er hätte sich seine Chancen beinahe verdorben, es hätte nicht viel gefehlt, und er hätte sich seine Chancen verdorben; **we were ~ to being drowned** wir waren dem Ertrinken nahe, wir wären beinahe ertrunken; **our hopes are ~ (to) fruition** unsere Hoffnungen werden bald in Erfüllung gehen.

(d) *(similar to)* ähnlich (*+dat*) ◆ **German is ~er (to) Dutch than English is** Deutsch ist dem Holländischen ähnlicher als Englisch; **it's the same thing or ~ it** es ist so ziemlich das gleiche; **nobody comes anywhere ~ him at swimming** *(inf)* im Schwimmen kann es niemand mit ihm aufnehmen *(inf)*.

[3] *adj* **(a)** *(close in space)* nahe ◆ **it looks very ~** es sieht so aus, als ob es ganz nah wäre; **our ~est neighbours are 5 miles away** unsere nächsten Nachbarn sind 5 Meilen entfernt; **these glasses make things look ~er** diese Brille läßt alles näher erscheinen.

(b) *(close in time)* nahe ◆ **these events are still very ~** diese Ereignisse liegen noch nicht lange zurück; **the hour is ~ (when ...)** *(old)* die Stunde ist nahe(, da ...) *(old)*; **her hour was ~** *(old)* ihre Stunde war nahe *(old)*.

(c) *(closely related, intimate) relation* nah; *friend* nah, vertraut ◆ **my ~est and dearest** meine Lieben *pl*; **a ~ and dear friend** ein lieber und teurer Freund.

(d) *escape* knapp; *resemblance* groß, auffallend ◆ **a ~ disaster/accident** beinahe ein Unglück *nt*/ein Unfall *m*; **a ~ race/contest** ein Rennen *nt*/Wettkampf *m* mit knappem Ausgang; **that was a ~ guess** Sie haben es beinahe erraten, das war nicht schlecht geraten; **to be in a state of ~ collapse/hysteria** am Rande eines Zusammenbruchs/der Hysterie sein; **round up the figure to the ~est pound** runden Sie die Zahl auf das nächste Pfund auf; **£50 or ~est offer** *(Comm)* Verhandlungsbasis £ 50; **we'll sell it for £50, or ~est offer** wir verkaufen es für £ 50 oder das nächstbeste Angebot; **the ~est in line to the throne** der unmittelbare Thronfolger; **this is the ~est equivalent** das kommt dem am nächsten; **this is the ~est translation you'll get** besser kann man es kaum übersetzen, diese Übersetzung trifft es noch am ehesten; **that is the ~est (thing) you'll get to a compliment/an answer** ein besseres Kompliment/eine bessere Antwort kannst du kaum erwarten.

[4] *vt place* sich nähern *(+dat)* ◆ **he was ~ing his end** sein Leben neigte sich dem Ende zu; **to be ~ing sth** *(fig)* auf etw *(acc)* zugehen; **to ~ completion** kurz vor dem Abschluß stehen.

nearby [nɪə'baɪ] [1] *adv (also* **near by***)* in der Nähe.
[2] *adj* nahe gelegen.

Near East *n* Naher Osten ◆ **in the ~** im Nahen Osten.

near letter-quality *n* Schönschrift, Korrespondenz- *or* Briefqualität *f.*

nearly ['nɪəlɪ] *adv* **(a)** *(almost)* beinahe, fast ◆ **I ~ laughed** ich hätte fast *or* beinahe gelacht; **she was ~ crying** *or* **in tears** sie war den Tränen nahe. **(b) not ~** bei weitem nicht, nicht annähernd; **not ~ enough** bei weitem nicht genug.

near miss *n (Aviat)* Beinahezusammenstoß *m; see also* **miss 1 (a)**.

nearness ['nɪənɪs] *n* Nähe *f.*

near: ~side [1] *adj* auf der Beifahrerseite, linke(r, s)/rechte(r, s); [2] *n* Beifahrerseite *f;* **~-sighted** *adj* kurzsichtig; **~-sightedness** *n* Kurzsichtigkeit *f;* **~ thing** *n* **that was a ~ thing** das war knapp.

neat [ni:t] *adj (+er)* **(a)** *(tidy) person, house, hair-style* ordentlich; *worker, work, handwriting, sewing also* sauber; *hair, appearance also* gepflegt ◆ **to make a ~ job of sth** etwas tadellos machen; **he made a very ~ job of repairing the window** er hat das Fenster tadellos repariert; *see* **pin**.
(b) *(pleasing)* nett; *clothes also* adrett; *person, figure also* hübsch; *ankles* schlank; *car, ship, house also* schmuck *(dated)* ◆ **she has a ~ figure** sie hat ein nettes Figürchen; **~ little suit** schmucker *or* netter Anzug.
(c) *(skilful) gadget, speech* gelungen; *style* gewandt; *solution* sauber, elegant; *trick* schlau ◆ **that's very ~** das ist sehr schlau.
(d) *(undiluted) spirits* pur; *wines* unverdünnt ◆ **to drink one's whisky ~** Whisky pur trinken.
(e) *(US inf: excellent)* prima *(inf)*, klasse *inv (inf)*.

neaten ['ni:tn] *vt (also* **~ up***)* in Ordnung bringen; *phrasing* glätten.

'neath [ni:θ] *prep (poet)* unter *(+dat)*, unterhalb *(+gen)*; *(with motion)* unter *(+acc)*.

neatly ['ni:tlɪ] *adv see adj (a-c)* **(a)** ordentlich; sauber. **(b)** nett; adrett; hübsch ◆ **a ~ turned ankle** eine hübsche schlanke Fessel. **(c)** gelungen; gewandt; sauber, elegant; schlau ◆ **~ put** treffend ausgedrückt; **~ turned phrases** gewandt formulierte Sätze *pl.*

neatness ['ni:tnɪs] *n see adj (a-c)* **(a)** Ordentlichkeit *f;* Sauberkeit *f.* **(b)** Nettheit *f,* nettes Aussehen; Adrettheit *f;* hübsches Aussehen; Schlankheit *f.* **(c)** Gelungenheit *f;* Gewandtheit *f;* Sauberkeit, Eleganz *f;* Schlauheit *f.*

nebula ['nebjʊlə] *n, pl* **-e** ['nebjʊli:] **(a)** *(Astron)* Nebel *m,* Nebelfleck *m.* **(b)** *(Med)* Trübung *f.*

nebulous ['nebjʊləs] *adj* **(a)** *(Astron)* Nebel-. **(b)** *(fig)* unklar, verworren, nebulös.

▼ **necessarily** ['nesɪsərɪlɪ] *adv* notwendigerweise *(also Logic)*, unbedingt ◆ **not ~** nicht unbedingt; **if that is true, then it is ~ the case that** ... wenn das wahr ist, dann folgt notwendigerweise daraus, daß ...; **we must ~ agree to these changes** wir müssen diesen Änderungen notgedrungen zustimmen.

necessary ['nesɪsərɪ] [1] *adj* **(a)** notwendig, nötig, erforderlich *(to, for* für) ◆ **it is ~ to ...** man muß ...; **is it ~ for me to come too?** muß ich auch kommen?; **it's not ~ for you to come** Sie brauchen nicht zu kommen; **it is ~ for him to be there** es ist nötig *or* notwendig, daß er da ist, er muß (unbedingt) da sein; **all the ~ qualifications** alle erforderlichen Qualifikationen; **~ condition** Voraussetzung *f;* *(Logic)* notwendige Voraussetzung; **to be/become ~ to sb** jdm unentbehrlich sein/werden; **to make it ~ for sb to do sth** es erforderlich machen, daß jd etw tut; **if ~** wenn nötig, nötigenfalls; **you were rude to him, was that ~?** du warst grob zu ihm, war das denn notwendig *or* nötig?; **to make the ~ arrangements** die erforderlichen *or* notwendigen Maßnahmen treffen; **to do everything ~, to do what is ~** alles Nötige tun; **good food is ~ to health** gutes Essen ist für die Gesundheit notwendig; **to do no more than is ~** nicht mehr tun, als unbedingt notwendig *or* nötig ist.
(b) *(unavoidable) conclusion, change, result* unausweichlich ◆ **we drew the ~ conclusions** wir haben die entsprechenden Schlüsse daraus gezogen; **a ~ evil** ein notwendiges Übel.
[2] *n* **(a)** *(inf: what is needed)* **the ~** das Notwendige; **will you do the ~?** wirst du das Notwendige *or* Nötige erledigen?
(b) *(inf: money)* **the ~** das nötige Kleingeld.
(c) *usu pl* **the ~** *or* **necessaries** das Notwendige.

necessitate [nɪ'sesɪteɪt] *vt* notwendig *or* erforderlich machen, erfordern *(form)* ◆ **the heat ~d our staying indoors** die Hitze zwang uns, im Haus zu bleiben.

necessitous [nɪ'sesɪtəs] *adj (old, form)* dürftig, armselig.

necessity [nɪ'sesɪtɪ] *n* **(a)** *no pl* Notwendigkeit *f* ◆ **from** *or* **out of ~** aus Not; **of ~** notgedrungen, notwendigerweise; **he did not realize the ~ for a quick decision** er hat nicht erkannt, wie wichtig *or* notwendig eine schnelle Entscheidung war; **it is a case of absolute ~** es ist unbedingt notwendig; **there is no ~ for you to do that** es besteht nicht die geringste Notwendigkeit, daß Sie das tun; **in case of ~** im Notfall; **~ is the mother of invention** *(Prov)* Not macht erfinderisch *(Prov)*.
(b) *no pl (poverty)* Not, Armut *f* ◆ **to live in ~** Not leiden, in Armut leben.
(c) *(necessary thing)* Notwendigkeit *f* ◆ **the bare necessities (of life)** das Notwendigste (zum Leben).

neck [nek] [1] *n* **(a)** Hals *m* ◆ **to break one's ~** sich *(dat)* das Genick *or* den Hals brechen; **but don't break your ~** *(inf)* bring dich nicht um *(inf)*; **to risk one's ~** Kopf und Kragen riskieren; **to save one's ~** seinen Hals aus der Schlinge ziehen; **a stiff ~** ein steifer Hals *or* Nacken; **to win by a ~** um eine Kopflänge gewinnen; **to have sb round one's ~** *(fig inf)* jdn auf dem *or* am Halse haben; **to be up to one's ~ in work** bis über den Hals *or* über die Ohren in der Arbeit stecken; **he's in it up to his ~** *(inf)* er steckt bis über den Hals drin; **to get it in the ~** *(inf)* eins aufs Dach bekommen *(inf)*; **to stick one's ~ out** seinen Kopf riskieren; **it's ~ or nothing** *(inf)* alles oder nichts; **in this ~ of the woods** *(inf)* in diesen Breiten; *see* **breathe**.
(b) *(Cook)* **~ of lamb** Halsstück *nt* vom Lamm.
(c) *(of bottle, vase, violin, bone)* Hals *m;* *(of land)* Landenge *f.*
(d) *(of dress etc)* Ausschnitt *m* ◆ **it has a high ~** es ist hochgeschlossen.
(e) *(also* **~ measurement***)* Halsweite *f.*
[2] *vi (inf)* knutschen *(inf)*, schmusen *(inf)*.

neck: ~ and ~ *(lit, fig)* [1] *adj attr* Kopf-an-Kopf-; [2] *adv* Kopf an Kopf; **~band** *n* Besatz *m;* *(of shirt)* Kragensteg *m;* *(of pullover)* Halsbündchen *nt;* **~cloth** *n (obs)* Halstuch *nt.*

neckerchief ['nekətʃi:f] *n* Halstuch *nt.*

necklace ['neklɪs] *n* (Hals)kette *f.*

necklet ['neklɪt] *n* Kettchen *nt.*

neck: ~line *n* Ausschnitt *m;* **~tie** *n (esp US)* Krawatte *f,* Binder, Schlips *m.*

necrology [ne'krɒlədʒɪ] *n (form)* Totenverzeichnis, Nekrologium *nt;* *(obituary)* Nachruf, Nekrolog *m.*

necromancer ['nekrəʊ,mænsə^r] *n* Toten- *or* Geisterbeschwörer(in *f*), Nekromant *m.*

necromancy ['nekrəʊ,mænsɪ] *n* Toten- *or* Geisterbeschwörung, Nekromantie *f.*

necrophilia [,nekrəʊ'fɪlɪə] *n* Leichenschändung, Nekrophilie *f.*

necropolis [ne'krɒpəlɪs] *n* Totenstadt, Nekropole, Nekropolis *f.*

nectar ['nektə^r] *n (lit, fig)* Nektar *m.*

nectarine ['nektərɪn] *n (fruit)* Nektarine *f;* *(tree)* Nektarine(nbaum *m*) *f.*

ned [ned] *n (inf)* Rowdy *m;* *(criminal type)* Halunke *m.*

NEDC ['nedɪ] *(Brit) abbr of* **National Economic Development Council** *Rat m für Wirtschaftsentwicklung.*

née [neɪ] *adj* **Mrs Smith, ~ Jones** Frau Smith, geborene Jones.

▼ **need** [ni:d] [1] *n* **(a)** *no pl (necessity)* Notwendigkeit *f (for gen)* ◆ **if ~ be** nötigenfalls, wenn nötig; **in case of ~** notfalls, im Notfall; **(there is) no ~ for sth** etw ist nicht nötig; **(there is) no ~ to do sth** etw braucht nicht *or* muß nicht unbedingt getan werden; **there is no ~ for sb to do sth** jd braucht etw nicht zu tun; **there is no ~ for tears** du brauchst nicht zu weinen; **there was no ~ to send it registered mail** es war nicht nötig, es eingeschrieben zu schicken; **there's no ~ to get angry** du brauchst nicht gleich wütend zu werden; **to be (badly) in ~ of sth** *(person)* etw (dringend) brauchen; **those most in ~ of help** diejenigen, die Hilfe am nötigsten brauchen; **to be in ~ of repair/an overhaul** reparaturbedürftig sein/(dringend) überholt werden müssen; **this window is in ~ of a coat of paint** dieses Fenster könnte ein wenig Farbe gut gebrauchen; **to have no ~ of sth** etw nicht brauchen; **to have no ~ to do sth** etw nicht zu tun brauchen.
(b) *no pl (misfortune)* Not *f* ◆ **in time(s) of ~** in schwierigen Zeiten, in Zeiten der Not; **do not fail me in my hour of ~** *(usu iro)* verlaß mich nicht in der Stunde der Not.
(c) *no pl (poverty)* Not *f* ◆ **to be in great ~** große Not leiden; **those in ~** die Notleidenden *pl.*
(d) *(requirement)* Bedürfnis *nt* ◆ **the body's ~ for oxygen** das Sauerstoffbedürfnis des Körpers; **my ~s are few** ich stelle nur geringe Ansprüche; **a list of all your ~s** eine Aufstellung all dessen, was Sie brauchen; **your ~ is greater than mine** Sie haben es nötiger als ich; **there is a great ~ for ...** es besteht ein großer Bedarf an *(+dat)* ...; **investment is one of the firm's greatest ~s** die Firma braucht dringend Investitionen.

▼ [2] *vt* **(a)** *(require)* brauchen ◆ **he ~ed no second invitation** man mußte ihn nicht zweimal bitten; **to ~ no introduction** keine spezielle Einführung brauchen; **much ~ed** dringend notwendig; **what I ~ is a good drink** ich brauche etwas zu trinken; **just what I ~ed** genau das richtige; **that's/you're all I ~ed** *(iro)* das hat/du hast mir gerade noch gefehlt; **this situation ~s some explanation** diese Situation bedarf einer Erklärung *(gen)*; **it ~s a service/a coat of paint/careful consideration** es muß gewartet/gestrichen/gründlich überlegt werden; **is a visa ~ed to enter the USA?** braucht man für die Einreise in die USA ein Visum?; **it ~ed a revolution to change that** es bedurfte einer Revolution *or* brauchte eine Revolution, um das zu ändern; **it ~ed an accident to make him drive carefully** er mußte erst einen Unfall haben, bevor er vernünftig fuhr.

▼ **(b)** *(in verbal constructions)* **sth ~s doing** *or* **to be done** etw muß gemacht werden; **he ~s watching/cheering up** man muß ihn beobachten/aufheitern, er muß beobachtet/aufgeheitert werden; **to ~ to do sth** *(have to)* etw tun müssen; **not to ~ to do sth** etw nicht zu tun brauchen; **he doesn't ~ to be told** man braucht es ihm nicht zu sagen; **you shouldn't ~ to be told** das müßte man dir nicht erst sagen müssen; **it doesn't ~ me to tell you that** das brauche ich dir ja wohl nicht zu sagen; **she ~s to have everything explained**

➤ LANGUAGE IN USE: **necessarily** → 16.1 **need: 2a** → 10.2 **2b** → 1.1, 9.4

to her man muß ihr alles erklären.
[3] v aux (a) (indicating obligation) (in positive contexts) müssen ◆ ~ he go? muß er gehen?; ~ I say more? mehr brauche ich ja wohl nicht zu sagen; I ~ hardly say that ... ich brauche wohl kaum zu erwähnen, daß ...; no-one ~ go or ~s to go home yet es braucht noch keiner nach Hause zu gehen; you only ~ed (to) ask du hättest nur (zu) fragen brauchen; one ~ only look ein Blick genügt.
(b) (indicating obligation) (in negative contexts) brauchen ◆ you ~n't wait du brauchst nicht (zu) warten; we ~n't have come/gone wir hätten gar nicht kommen/gehen brauchen; I/you ~n't have bothered das war nicht nötig.
(c) (indicating logical necessity) ~ that be true? ist das notwendigerweise wahr?; that ~n't be the case das muß nicht unbedingt der Fall sein; it ~ not follow that ... daraus folgt nicht unbedingt, daß ...

needful ['ni:dfʊl] [1] adj (old) notwendig, nötig (for, to für, zu).
[2] n (inf) (what is necessary) to do the ~ das Nötige tun; to supply the ~ (money) das nötige Kleingeld zur Verfügung stellen.

neediness ['ni:dɪnɪs] n Armut, Bedürftigkeit f.

needle ['ni:dl] [1] n (all senses) Nadel f ◆ it's like looking for a ~ in a haystack es ist, als ob man eine Stecknadel im Heuhaufen or Heuschober suchte; to give sb the ~ (inf) jdn reizen.
[2] vt (a) (inf: goad) ärgern, piesacken (inf) ◆ what's needling him? was ist ihm über die Leber gelaufen? (inf).
(b) (US inf) to ~ a drink einen Schuß Alkohol in ein Getränk geben.

needle: ~-book n Nadelheft nt; ~-case n Nadeletui nt; ~craft n handarbeitliches Geschick; ~ match n spannendes Spiel; ~-sharp adj (inf) clever (inf), schwer auf Zack (inf).

needless ['ni:dlɪs] adj unnötig; remark etc also überflüssig ◆ ~ to say, he didn't come er kam natürlich nicht.

needlessly ['ni:dlɪslɪ] adv unnötig(erweise), überflüssig(erweise) ◆ he was quite ~ rude er war ganz unnötig grob.

needlessness ['ni:dlɪsnɪs] n Unnötigkeit f.

needle: ~woman n Näherin f; ~work n Handarbeit f; a piece of ~work eine Handarbeit.

needs [ni:dz] adv (obs) I must ~ away/obey ich muß fort/notwendigerweise gehorchen; ~ must as the devil drives (prov) nolens volens.

needy ['ni:dɪ] [1] adj (+er) ärmlich, bedürftig.
[2] n the ~ die Bedürftigen pl.

ne'er [nɛəʳ] adv (old, poet: never) nie, niemals.

ne'er-do-well ['nɛədu:,wel] (dated) [1] n Tunichtgut, Taugenichts (dated) m.
[2] adj nichtsnutzig.

ne'ertheless [,nɛəðə'les] adv (old, poet) nichtsdestoweniger.

nefarious [nɪ'fɛərɪəs] adj verrucht, ruchlos (liter).

negate [nɪ'geɪt] vt (nullify) zunichte machen; (deny) verneinen (also Gram), negieren (geh).

negation [nɪ'geɪʃən] n Verneinung f; (of statement, negative form also) Negation f.

negative ['negətɪv] [1] adj negativ; answer verneinend; (Gram) form verneint ◆ ~ sign (Math) Minuszeichen nt, negatives Vorzeichen; ~ ion Anion nt; ~ cash flow (Fin) Überhang m der Zahlungsausgänge; I got a ~ reply to my request ich habe auf meinen Antrag einen abschlägigen Bescheid bekommen.
[2] n (a) (also Gram) Verneinung f ◆ to answer in the ~ eine verneinende Antwort geben; (say no) mit Nein antworten; (refuse) einen abschlägigen Bescheid geben; his answer was a curt ~ er antwortete mit einem knappen Nein; put this sentence into the ~ verneinen Sie diesen Satz; how do you express this statement in the ~? wie drückt man diesen Satz verneint or in der Verneinungsform aus?
(b) (Gram: word) Verneinungswort nt, Negation f; (Math) negative Zahl ◆ two ~s make a positive (Math) zweimal minus gibt plus.
(c) (Phot) Negativ nt.
(d) (Elec) negativer Pol.
[3] interj nein.

negatively ['negətɪvlɪ] adv negativ; (in the negative) verneinend.

negativity [negə'tɪvɪtɪ] n negative Einstellung.

neglect [nɪ'glekt] [1] vt vernachlässigen; promise nicht einhalten; opportunity versäumen; advice nicht befolgen ◆ to ~ to do sth es versäumen or unterlassen, etw zu tun.
[2] n see vt Vernachlässigung f; Nichteinhalten nt; Versäumen nt; Nichtbefolgung f; (negligence) Nachlässigkeit f ◆ ~ of one's duties Pflichtvergessenheit f, Pflichtversäumnis nt; to be in a state of ~ verwahrlost sein, völlig vernachlässigt sein; the garden suffered through (our) ~ der Garten hat darunter gelitten, daß wir ihn vernachlässigt haben.

neglected [nɪ'glektɪd] adj vernachlässigt; area, garden etc also verwahrlost ◆ to feel ~ sich vernachlässigt fühlen.

neglectful [nɪ'glektfʊl] adj nachlässig; father, government etc pflichtvergessen ◆ to be ~ of sb/sth sich nicht um jdn/etw kümmern, jdn/etw vernachlässigen.

neglectfully [nɪ'glektfəlɪ] adv see adj.

négligé(e) ['neglɪʒeɪ] n Negligé nt.

negligence ['neglɪdʒəns] n (carelessness) Nachlässigkeit f; (causing danger, Jur) Fahrlässigkeit f.

negligent ['neglɪdʒənt] adj (a) nachlässig; (causing danger, damage) fahrlässig ◆ to be ~ of sb/sth jdn/etw vernachlässigen; to be ~ of one's duties pflichtvergessen sein; both drivers were ~ beide Fahrer haben sich fahrlässig verhalten.
(b) (off-hand) lässig.

negligently ['neglɪdʒəntlɪ] adv see adj (a) nachlässig; fahrlässig ◆ he very ~ forgot in seiner Nachlässigkeit vergaß er es, nachlässig, wie er war, vergaß er es. (b) lässig.

negligible ['neglɪdʒəbl] adj unwesentlich, unbedeutend; quantity, amount, sum also geringfügig, unerheblich ◆ the opposition in this race is ~ in diesem Rennen gibt es keinen ernstzunehmenden Gegner.

negotiable [nɪ'gəʊʃɪəbl] adj (a) (Comm) (can be sold) verkäuflich, veräußerlich; (can be transferred) übertragbar ◆ not ~ nicht verkäuflich/übertragbar.
(b) these terms are ~ über diese Bedingungen kann verhandelt werden. (c) road befahrbar; river, mountain pass passierbar; obstacle, difficulty überwindbar.

negotiate [nɪ'gəʊʃɪeɪt] [1] vt (a) (discuss) verhandeln über (+acc); (bring about) aushandeln. (b) bend in road, (horse) fence nehmen; river, mountain, rapids passieren; obstacle, difficulty überwinden. (c) (Comm) shares handeln mit; sale tätigen (form).
[2] vi verhandeln (for über +acc).

negotiation [nɪ,gəʊʃɪ'eɪʃən] n (a) siehe vt (a) Verhandlung f; Aushandlung f ◆ the matter is still under ~ über diese Sache wird noch verhandelt; it's a matter for ~ darüber muß verhandelt werden; the price is a matter for ~ über den Preis kann verhandelt werden; by ~ auf dem Verhandlungsweg.
(b) usu pl (talks) Verhandlung f ◆ to begin ~s with sb Verhandlungen pl mit jdm aufnehmen; to be in ~(s) with sb mit jdm in Verhandlungen stehen.
(c) (of river, mountain, rapids) Passage f, Passieren nt; (of obstacle, difficulty) Überwindung f.

negotiator [nɪ'gəʊʃɪeɪtəʳ] n Unterhändler(in f) m.

Negress ['ni:gres] n Negerin f.

Negro ['ni:grəʊ] [1] adj Neger-.
[2] n Neger m.

Negroid ['ni:grɔɪd] adj negroid.

neigh [neɪ] [1] vi wiehern.
[2] n Wiehern nt.

neighbour, (US) neighbor ['neɪbəʳ] [1] n (a) Nachbar(in f) m; (at table) Tischnachbar(in f) m; see next-door.
(b) (Bibl) Nächste(r) mf.
[2] vt (adjoin) country, river angrenzen an (+acc).
[3] vi (a) to ~ on (adjoin) (an)grenzen an (+acc); (approach) grenzen an (+acc).
(b) (US inf) to ~ with sb gutnachbarliche Beziehungen pl zu jdm haben.

neighbourhood, (US) neighborhood ['neɪbəhʊd] n (district) Gegend f, Viertel nt; (people) Nachbarschaft f ◆ get to know your ~ lernen Sie Ihre nähere Umgebung or (people also) Ihre Nachbarschaft kennen; all the children from the ~ all die Kinder aus der Nachbarschaft or der Gegend; she is very popular with the whole ~ sie ist bei allen Nachbarn or in der ganzen Nachbarschaft sehr beliebt; in the ~ of sth in der Nähe von etw; (fig: approximately) um etw herum; ~ watch Vereinigung f von Bürgern, die durch Straßenwachen etc in ihrem Bezirk die Polizei bei der Verbrechensbekämpfung unterstützen.

neighbouring, (US) neighboring ['neɪbərɪŋ] adj house(s), village benachbart, angrenzend, Nachbar-; fields, community angrenzend, Nachbar-.

neighbourly, (US) neighborly ['neɪbəlɪ] adj person nachbarlich; action, relations gutnachbarlich ◆ they are ~ people sie sind gute Nachbarn; to behave in a ~ way sich als guter Nachbar erweisen.

neighing ['neɪɪŋ] n Wiehern nt.

neither ['naɪðəʳ] [1] adv ~ ... nor weder ... noch; he ~ knows nor cares er weiß es nicht und will es auch nicht wissen.
[2] conj auch nicht ◆ if you don't go, ~ shall I wenn du nicht gehst, gehe ich auch nicht; I'm not going — ~ am I ich gehe nicht — ich auch nicht; he didn't do it (and) ~ did his sister weder er noch seine Schwester haben es getan; I can't go, ~ do I want to ich kann und will auch nicht gehen.
[3] adj keine(r, s) (der beiden) ◆ ~ one of them keiner von beiden; in ~ case in keinem Fall, weder in dem einen noch in dem anderen Fall.
[4] pron keine(r, s) ◆ ~ of them keiner von beiden; which will you take? — ~ welches nehmen Sie? — keines (von beiden).

nelly ['nelɪ] n: not on your ~ (Brit hum inf) nie im Leben.

nelson ['nelsən] n (Wrestling) full ~ Doppelnelson m, doppelter Nackenheber; half ~ Nelson m, einfacher Nackenheber; to put a half/full ~ on sb den Nelson/Doppelnelson bei jdm ansetzen.

nem con [,nem'kɒn] adv ohne Gegenstimme.

nemesis ['nemɪsɪs] n Nemesis f (liter), die gerechte Strafe.

neo- ['ni:əʊ-] pref neo-, Neo- ◆ ~classical klassizistisch; ~classicism Klassizismus m; ~colonial neokolonialistisch; ~colonialism Neokolonialismus m.

neodymium [,ni:əʊ'dɪmɪəm] n (Chem) Neodym nt.

neo: ~fascism n Neofaschismus m; ~fascist [1] adj neofaschistisch; [2] n Neofaschist(in f) m.

neolithic [,ni:əʊ'lɪθɪk] adj jungsteinzeitlich, neolithisch.

neologism [nɪ'ɒlədʒɪzəm] n (Ling) (Wort)neubildung f, Neologismus m.

neon ['ni:ɒn] [1] n (Chem) Neon nt.
[2] adj attr lamp, lighting, tube Neon- ◆ ~ sign (name) Neon- or Leuchtschild nt; (advertisement) Neon- or Leuchtreklame f no pl.

neo-Nazi [,ni:əʊ'nɑ:tsɪ] [1] n Neonazi m.
[2] adj neonazistisch.

neophyte ['ni:əʊfaɪt] n Neubekehrte(r) mf, Neophyt(in f) m (spec); (in RC church) neugeweihter Priester.

Neo: ~-Platonic *adj* neuplatonisch; **~-Platonism** *n* Neuplatonismus *m*; **~-Platonist** *n* Neuplatoniker(in *f*) *m*.

Nepal [nɪ'pɔ:l] *n* Nepal *nt*.

Nepalese [ˌnepə'li:z], **Nepali** [nɪ'pɔ:lɪ] [1] *adj* nepalesisch, nepalisch.
[2] *n* **(a)** Nepalese *m*, Nepalesin *f*. **(b)** (*language*) Nepalesisch *nt*.

nephew ['nevju:, 'nefju:] *n* Neffe *m*.

nephritis [ne'fraɪtɪs] *n* Nierenentzündung, Nephritis (*spec*) *f*.

nepotism ['nepətɪzəm] *n* Vetternwirtschaft *f*, Nepotismus *m*.

Neptune ['neptju:n] *n* (*Astron, Myth*) Neptun *m*.

neptunium [nep'tju:nɪəm] *n* (*Chem*) Neptunium *nt*.

nerd [nɜ:d] *n* (*sl*) Schwachkopf *m*.

nereid ['nɪərɪɪd] *n* (*Myth*) Nereide, Meerjungfrau *f*.

nerve [nɜ:v] [1] *n* **(a)** (*Anat*) Nerv *m* ♦ **to suffer from ~s** nervös sein; **to have an attack** *or* **fit of ~s** in Panik geraten, durchdrehen (*inf*); (*before exam also*) Prüfungsangst haben; **to be in a terrible state of ~s** mit den Nerven völlig fertig *or* herunter sein; **it's only ~s** du bist/er ist *etc* nur nervös; **to be all ~s** ein Nervenbündel sein; **his ~s are bad** er hat schlechte Nerven; **to get on sb's ~s** (*inf*) jdm auf die Nerven gehen *or* fallen; **he doesn't know what ~s are** er hat die Ruhe weg (*inf*); **to live on one's ~s** nervlich angespannt sein, völlig überreizt sein; **to have ~s of steel** Nerven wie Drahtseile haben.
(b) *no pl* (*courage*) Mut *m* ♦ **to lose/keep one's ~** die Nerven verlieren/nicht verlieren; **to regain one's ~, to get one's ~ back** seine Angst überwinden; **his ~ failed him** ihn verließ der Mut, er bekam Angst; **to have the ~ to do sth** sich trauen, etw zu tun; **a test of ~** eine Nervenprobe.
(c) *no pl* (*inf: impudence*) Frechheit, Unverschämtheit *f* ♦ **to have the ~ to do sth** die Frechheit besitzen, etw zu tun; **he's got a ~!** der hat Nerven! (*inf*); **what a ~!, the ~ of it!** so eine Frechheit!
(d) (*Bot*) Ader *f*, Nerv *m*.
[2] *vtr* **to ~ oneself for sth/to do sth** sich seelisch und moralisch auf etw (*acc*) vorbereiten/darauf vorbereiten, etw zu tun; **I can't ~ myself to do it** ich bringe einfach den Mut nicht auf, das zu tun; **to ~ sb to do sth** jdm den Mut geben, etw zu tun.

nerve *in cpds* Nerven-; **~ cell** *n* Nervenzelle *f*; **~ centre** (*Brit*), **~ center** (*US*) *n* (*Anat*) Nervenzentrum *nt*; (*fig also*) Schaltstelle *or* -zentrale *f*; **~ ending** *n* Nervende *nt*; **~ gas** *n* Nervengas *nt*.

nerveless ['nɜ:vlɪs] *adj* **(a)** (*without nerves*) ohne Nerven; *plant also* ohne Adern, ungeädert. **(b)** (*confident*) *person* gelassen, seelenruhig.

nerve-racking ['nɜ:vrækɪŋ] *adj* nervenaufreibend.

nervous ['nɜ:vəs] *adj* **(a)** (*Anat*) *structure* Nerven-; (*related to the nerves*) *problem, disorder also* nervös (bedingt); *exhaustion, reflex* nervös ♦ **~ tension** Nervenanspannung *f*.
(b) (*apprehensive, timid*) nervös; (*overexcited, tense also*) aufgeregt ♦ **to feel ~** nervös sein; **you make me (feel) ~, I am** *or* **I feel ~ of you** du machst mich (noch) ganz nervös; **I am ~ about the exam/him** mir ist bange vor dem Examen/um ihn; **I was rather ~ about giving him the job** mir war nicht wohl bei dem Gedanken, ihm die Stelle zu geben; **I am rather ~ about diving** ich habe einen ziemlichen Bammel vor dem Tauchen (*inf*); **to be in a ~ state** nervös *or* aufgeregt sein.

nervous *in cpds* Nerven-; **~ breakdown** *n* Nervenzusammenbruch *m*; **~ energy** *n* Vitalität *f*; **after the exam I still had a lot of ~ energy** nach dem Examen war ich noch ganz aufgedreht.

nervously ['nɜ:vəslɪ] *adv* nervös; (*excitedly, tensely also*) aufgeregt.

nervous Nellie *n* (*US inf*) Flattermann *m* (*inf*).

nervousness ['nɜ:vəsnɪs] *n* Nervosität *f*; (*tension also*) Aufgeregtheit *f* ♦ **his ~ about flying** seine Angst vor dem Fliegen.

nervous: ~ system *n* Nervensystem *nt*; **~ wreck** *n* (*inf*) **to be/look a ~ wreck** mit den Nerven völlig am Ende *or* fertig sein.

nervy ['nɜ:vɪ] *adj* (+*er*) **(a)** (*Brit: tense*) nervös, unruhig. **(b)** (*US inf: cheeky*) frech, unverschämt.

nest [nest] [1] *n* **(a)** (*of birds, bees, ants*) Nest *nt* ♦ **to leave the ~** (*lit, fig*) das Nest verlassen.
(b) (*of boxes etc*) Satz *m* ♦ **a ~ of tables** ein Satz Tische *or* von Tischen.
(c) (*fig: den*) Schlupfwinkel *m* ♦ **a ~ of thieves/crime** ein Diebes-/Verbrechernest; **a ~ of machine-guns** eine Maschinengewehrstellung.
[2] *vi* **(a)** (*bird*) nisten ♦ **~ing instinct** (*lit, fig*) Nistinstinkt *or* -trieb *m*.
(b) to go ~ing Nester ausheben *or* ausnehmen.

nest-egg ['nesteg] *n* (*lit*) Nestei *nt*; (*fig*) Notgroschen *m* ♦ **to have a nice little ~** (*fig*) sich (*dat*) einen Notgroschen zurückgelegt haben.

nesting-box ['nestɪŋbɒks] *n* Nistkasten *m*.

nestle ['nesl] *vi* **to ~ down in bed** sich ins Bett kuscheln; **to ~ up to sb** sich an jdn schmiegen *or* kuscheln; **to ~ against sb's shoulder** sich an jds Schulter (*acc*) schmiegen; **the village nestling in the hills** das Dorf, das zwischen den Bergen eingebettet liegt; **a house nestling** *or* **~d among the trees** ein von Bäumen eingerahmtes Haus.

nestling ['neslɪŋ] *n* Nestling *m*.

Net *n* (*Comput inf*) **the ~** das Internet; **to surf the ~** im Internet surfen.

net¹ [net] [1] *n* **(a)** (*lit, fig*) Netz *nt* ♦ **to make ~s** Netze knüpfen; **to walk into the police ~** (*fig*) der Polizei ins Netz *or* Garn gehen; **to be caught in the ~** (*fig*) in die Falle gehen; **he felt the ~ closing round him** (*fig*) er fühlte, wie sich die Schlinge immer enger zog.
(b) (*Sport*) Netz *nt* ♦ **to come up to the ~** ans Netz gehen; **the ball's in the ~** der Ball ist im Tor *or* Netz; **the ~s** (*Cricket*) *von Netzen umspannter Übungsplatz*.
(c) (*Tex*) Netzgewebe *nt*; (*for curtains, clothes etc*) Tüll *m*.
[2] *vt* **(a)** *fish, game, butterfly* mit dem Netz fangen; (*fig*) *criminal* fangen ♦ **the police have ~ted the criminal** der Verbrecher ist der Polizei ins Netz gegangen.
(b) (*Sport*) *ball* ins Netz schlagen ♦ **to ~ a goal** ein Tor schießen *or* erzielen.

net² [1] *adj* **(a)** *price, income, weight* netto, Netto- ♦ **~ assets** Nettovermögen *nt*; **~ disposable income** verfügbares Nettoeinkommen; **~ profit** Reingewinn, Nettoertrag *m*; **it costs £15 ~** es kostet £ 15 netto.
(b) (*fig*) *result* End-, letztendlich.
[2] *vt* netto einnehmen; (*in wages, salary*) netto verdienen; (*show, deal etc*) einbringen ♦ **I ~ted a salary of £250 a month** ich bezog ein Gehalt von £ 250 netto im Monat, ich hatte ein monatliches Nettogehalt von £ 250.

net: ~ bag *n* (Einkaufs)netz *nt*; **~ball** *n* (*Brit*) Korbball *m*; **~ curtain** *n* Tüllgardine *f*, Store *m*.

nether ['neðə^r] *adj* (*liter*) untere(r, s) ♦ **~ regions** Unterwelt *f*.

Netherlander ['neðəˌlændə^r] *n* Niederländer(in *f*) *m*.

Netherlands ['neðələndz] *npl* **the ~** die Niederlande *pl*.

nethermost ['neðəməʊst] *adj* (*liter*) unterste(r, s) ♦ **in the ~ parts of the earth** in den tiefsten Tiefen der Erde (*liter*).

net: ~ play *n* (*Tennis*) Spiel *nt* am Netz; **~ stocking** *n* Netzstrumpf *m*.

nett *see* **net²**.

netting ['netɪŋ] *n* Netz *nt*; (*wire ~*) Maschendraht *m*; (*fabric*) Netzgewebe *nt*; (*for curtains etc*) Tüll *m*.

nettle ['netl] [1] *n* (*Bot*) Nessel *f* ♦ **to grasp the ~** (*fig*) in den sauren Apfel beißen.
[2] *vt* (*fig inf*) *person* ärgern, wurmen (*inf*), fuchsen (*inf*).

nettle: ~ rash *n* Nesselausschlag *m*; **~ sting** *n* Brennesselstich *m*; **her legs were covered in ~ stings** ihre Beine waren von den Brennesseln völlig zerstochen.

network ['netwɜ:k] [1] *n* **(a)** (*lit, fig*) Netz *nt*. **(b)** (*Rad, TV*) Sendenetz *nt*; (*Elec, Comput*) Netzwerk *nt* ♦ **~ card/driver/server** (*Comput*) Netzwerkkarte *f*/-treiber/-server *m*.
[2] *vt* (*inf*) *programme* im ganzen Netzbereich ausstrahlen.

networking ['netwɜ:kɪŋ] *n* (*Comput*) Rechnerverbund *m*.

neural ['njʊərəl] *adj* Nerven-.

neuralgia [njʊə'rældʒə] *n* Neuralgie *f*, Nervenschmerzen *pl*.

neurasthenia [ˌnjʊərəs'θi:nɪə] *n* Neurasthenie, Nervenschwäche *f*.

neurasthenic [ˌnjʊərəs'θenɪk] [1] *n* Neurastheniker(in *f*) *m*.
[2] *adj* neurasthenisch.

neuritis [njʊə'raɪtɪs] *n* Neuritis, Nervenentzündung *f*.

neuro- [njʊərəʊ-] *in cpds* Neuro-, neuro-; **~biology** *n* Neurobiologie *f*; **~chemistry** *n* Neurochemie *f*.

neurological [ˌnjʊərə'lɒdʒɪkəl] *adj* neurologisch.

neurologist [njʊə'rɒlədʒɪst] *n* Neurologe *m*, Neurologin *f*, Nervenarzt *m*/-ärztin *f*.

neurology [njʊə'rɒlədʒɪ] *n* Neurologie *f*.

neuron ['njʊərɒn] *n* Neuron *nt*.

neuropath ['njʊərəpæθ] *n* Nervenkranke(r) *mf*.

neuropathic [njʊərəʊ'pæθɪk] *adj* neuropathisch.

neuropathology [ˌnjʊərəʊpə'θɒlədʒɪ] *n* Neuropathologie *f*, Lehre *f* von den Nervenkrankheiten.

neurosis [njʊə'rəʊsɪs] *n*, *pl* **neuroses** [njʊə'rəʊsi:z] Neurose *f*.

neurosurgeon ['njʊərəʊˌsɜ:dʒən] *n* Neurochirurg(in *f*) *m*.

neurosurgery ['njʊərəʊˌsɜ:dʒərɪ] *n* Neurochirurgie *f*.

neurosurgical ['njʊərəʊˌsɜ:dʒɪkəl] *adj* neurochirurgisch.

neurotic [njʊə'rɒtɪk] [1] *adj* neurotisch ♦ **to be ~ about sth** (*inf*) in bezug auf etw (*acc*) neurotisch sein; **he's getting rather ~ about this problem** das Problem ist bei ihm schon zur Neurose geworden.
[2] *n* Neurotiker(in *f*) *m*.

neurotically [njʊə'rɒtɪkəlɪ] *adv* neurotisch.

neuter ['nju:tə^r] [1] *adj* **(a)** (*Gram*) sächlich ♦ **this word is ~** dieses Wort ist sächlich *or* ein Neutrum. **(b)** *animal, person* geschlechtslos; (*castrated*) kastriert; *plant* ungeschlechtlich.
[2] *n* **(a)** (*Gram*) Neutrum *nt*; (*noun also*) sächliches Hauptwort ♦ **in the ~** in der sächlichen Form, im Neutrum.
(b) (*animal*) geschlechtsloses Wesen; (*castrated*) kastriertes Tier; (*plant*) ungeschlechtliche Pflanze.
[3] *vt cat, dog* kastrieren; *female* sterilisieren.

neutral ['nju:trəl] [1] *adj* (*all senses*) neutral.
[2] *n* **(a)** (*person*) Neutrale(r) *mf*; (*country*) neutrales Land.
(b) (*Aut*) Leerlauf *m* ♦ **to be in ~** im Leerlauf sein; **to put the car/gears in ~** den Gang herausnehmen.

neutralism ['nju:trəlɪzəm] *n* Neutralismus *m*.

neutrality [nju:'trælɪtɪ] *n* Neutralität *f*.

neutralization [ˌnju:trəlaɪ'zeɪʃən] *n* Neutralisation *f*; (*fig*) Aufhebung *f*.

neutralize ['nju:trəlaɪz] *vt* neutralisieren; (*fig*) aufheben; *the force of an argument* die Spitze nehmen (+*dat*) ♦ **neutralizing agent** neutralisierender Wirkstoff.

neutrino [nju:'tri:nəʊ] *n* Neutrino *nt*.

neutron ['nju:trɒn] *n* Neutron *nt*.

neutron: ~ bomb *n* Neutronenbombe *f*; **~ star** *n* Neutronenstern *m*.

never ['nevə^r] *adv* **(a)** (*not ever*) nie, niemals (*geh*) ♦ **I ~ eat it** das esse ich nie; **I have ~ seen him** ich habe ihn (noch) nie gesehen; **~ again** nie wieder; **~ do that again** mach das bloß nie wieder *or* nicht noch einmal; **I'll ~ try that again** das werde ich nie wieder *or* nicht noch einmal versuchen; **~ again will I see my own country** ich werde meine Heimat nie wiedersehen; **~ before** noch nie; **I had ~ seen him before today** ich hatte ihn (vor heute)

➤ LANGUAGE IN USE: **never: a** → 6.3, 18.3

noch nie gesehen; **~ before have men climbed this peak** noch nie hatten *or* nie zuvor haben Menschen diesen Gipfel erklommen; **~ before had there been such a disaster** eine solche Katastrophe hatte es noch nie (zuvor) gegeben; **~ even** nicht einmal; **~ ever** gar *or* absolut *or* garantiert nie; **I have ~ ever been so insulted** ich bin noch nie so beleidigt worden; **I have ~ yet been able to find ...** ich habe ... bisher noch nicht finden können; **I ~ heard such a thing!** so etwas ist mir noch nie zu Ohren gekommen!
(b) (*emph: not*) **that will ~ do!** das geht ganz und gar nicht!; **I ~ slept a wink** ich habe kein Auge zugetan; **he ~ so much as smiled** er hat nicht einmal gelächelt; **he said ~ a word** er hat kein einziges Wort gesagt; **you've ~ left it behind!** (*inf*) du hast es doch wohl nicht etwa liegenlassen! (*inf*); **you've ~ done that!** hast du das wirklich gemacht?; **would you do it again? — ~!** würdest du das noch einmal machen? — bestimmt nicht; **Spurs were beaten — ~!** (*inf*) Spurs ist geschlagen worden — das ist doch nicht möglich *or* nein! *or* nein wirklich? (*iro*); **well I ~ (did)!** (*inf*) nein, so was!; **~ fear** keine Angst.

never: ~-ending *adj* endlos, unaufhörlich; *discussions, negotiations also* nicht enden wollend *attr*; **it seemed ~-ending** es schien kein Ende nehmen zu wollen; **a ~-ending job** eine Arbeit ohne Ende; **~-failing** *adj method etc* unfehlbar; *source, spring etc* unversieglich; **~more** *adv* (*liter*) nimmermehr (*liter*), niemals wieder; **he departed ~more to return** er ging und kehrte niemals wieder (*liter*); **~-never** *n* (*Brit inf*) **on the ~-never** auf Pump (*inf*); **~-never land** *n* Wunsch- *or* Traumwelt *f*.

▼ **nevertheless** [ˌnevəðə'les] *adv* trotzdem, dennoch, nichtsdestoweniger (*geh*).

never-to-be-forgotten ['nevətəbi:fə'gɒtn] *adj attr* unvergeßlich.

new [nju:] *adj* (+*er*) **(a)** neu ◆ **there's a ~ moon tonight** heute nacht ist Neumond; **the ~ people at number five** die Neuen in Nummer fünf; **that's nothing ~** das ist nichts Neues; **that's something ~** das ist wirklich ganz was Neues!; **what's ~?** (*inf*) was gibt's Neues? (*inf*); **to make sth (look) like ~** etw wie neu machen; **as ~** wie neu; **this system is ~ to me** dieses System ist mir neu; **he is a ~ man** (*fig*) er ist ein neuer Mensch; **that's a ~ one on me** (*inf*) das ist mir ja ganz neu; (*joke*) den kenne ich noch nicht; **a ~ kind of engine** ein neuartiger Motor.
(b) (*fresh*) *potatoes* neu; *wine* neu, jung; *bread* frisch.
(c) (*modern, novel*) modern; *fashion, style* neu ◆ **the ~ woman** die moderne Frau; **the ~ diplomacy** die neue Diplomatie; **the ~ look** (*Fashion*) der New Look.
(d) (*lately arrived, inexperienced*) *person, pupil, recruit* neu ◆ **the ~ boys/girls** die Neuen *pl*, die neuen Schüler; **the ~ rich** die Neureichen *pl*; **I'm quite ~ to this job/to the company** ich bin neu in dieser Stelle/Firma; **to be ~ to business** ein Neuling im Geschäftsleben sein; **are you ~ here?** sind Sie neu hier?; **I am ~ to this place** ich bin erst seit kurzem hier.

new: ~-born *adj* neugeboren; **the ~-born babies** die Neugeborenen; **~comer** *n* (*who has just arrived*) Neuankömmling *m*; (*in job, subject etc*) Neuling *m* (*to* in +*dat*); **they are ~comers to this town** sie sind neu in dieser Stadt, sie sind Zuzügler; **for the ~comers I will recap** für diejenigen, die neu dazugekommen sind, fasse ich kurz zusammen.

New Delhi [ˌnju:'delɪ] *n* Neu-Delhi *nt*.

newel ['nju:əl] *n* (*of spiral staircase*) Spindel *f*; (*supporting banister*) Pfosten *m*.

new: N~ England *n* Neuengland *nt*; **~ face** *n* neues Gesicht, Neuling *m*; **~-fangled** *adj* neumodisch; **~-fashioned** *adj* modisch, modern; **~-found** *adj friend, happiness* neu(gefunden); *confidence, hope* neugeschöpft; **N~foundland** ['nju:fəndlənd] [1] *n* Neufundland *nt*; [2] *adj attr* neufundländisch; **N~foundland dog** Neufundländer *m*; **N~foundlander** *n* Neufundländer(in *f*) *m*; **N~ Guinea** *n* Neuguinea *nt*.

newish ['nju:ɪʃ] *adj* ziemlich neu.

new: ~-laid *adj* frisch; **~-look** *adj* (*inf*) neu.

newly ['nju:lɪ] *adv* frisch ◆ **a ~-dug trench** ein frisch gezogener Graben; **~-made** ganz neu; *bread, cake etc* frisch gebacken; *road, gardens etc* neuangelegt; *grave* frisch.

newlyweds ['nju:lɪwedz] *npl* (*inf*) Neu- *or* Frischvermählte *pl*.

new: N~ Mexico *n* New Mexico *nt*; **~-mown** *adj* frisch gemäht.

newness ['nju:nɪs] *n* Neuheit *f*; (*of bread, cheese etc*) Frische *f* ◆ **his ~ to this job/the trade/this town** die Tatsache, daß er neu in dieser Arbeit ist/daß er Neuling ist/daß er erst seit kurzem in dieser Stadt ist.

New Orleans [ˌnju:ɔ:'li:nz] *n* New Orleans *nt*.

news [nju:z] *n, no pl* **(a)** (*report, information*) Nachricht *f*; (*recent development*) Neuigkeit(en *pl*) *f* ◆ **a piece of ~** eine Neuigkeit; **I have ~/no ~ of him** ich habe von ihm gehört/nicht von ihm gehört, ich weiß Neues/nichts Neues von ihm; **there is no ~** es gibt nichts Neues zu berichten; **have you heard the ~?** haben Sie schon (das Neueste) gehört?; **have you heard the ~ about Fred?** haben Sie schon das Neueste über Fred gehört?; **tell us your ~** erzähl uns die Neuigkeiten *or* das Neueste; **let us have** *or* **send us some ~ of yourself** lassen Sie mal von sich hören; **what's your ~?** was gibt's Neues?; **is there any ~?** gibt es etwas Neues?; **I have ~ for you** (*iro*) ich habe eine Überraschung für dich; **bad/sad/good ~** schlimme *or* schlechte/traurige/gute Nachricht(en); **that is good ~** das ist erfreulich zu hören, das sind ja gute Nachrichten; **that's bad ~ for English football** das ist ein schwerer Schlag für den englischen Fußball; **when the ~/the ~ of his death broke** als es/sein Tod bekannt wurde; **who will break the ~ to him?** wer wird es ihm sagen *or* beibringen?; **that is ~/no ~ (to me)!** das ist (mir) ganz/nicht neu!; **that isn't exactly ~** das ist nichts Neues; **it will be ~ to him that ...** er wird staunen, daß ...; **~ travels fast** wie sich doch alles herumspricht; **bad ~ travels fast** schlechte Nachrichten verbreiten sich schnell; **as far as party Head Office is concerned, he's bad ~** (*inf*) für die Parteizentrale bedeutet er (nichts als) Ärger; **no ~ is good ~** keine Nachricht ist gute Nachricht.
(b) (*Press, Film, Rad, TV*) Nachrichten *pl* ◆ **~ in brief** Kurznachrichten *pl*; **financial ~** Wirtschaftsbericht *m*; **sports ~** Sportnachrichten *pl*; **it was on the ~** das kam in den Nachrichten; **to be in the ~** von sich reden machen; **to make ~** Schlagzeilen machen; **that's not ~** damit kann man keine Schlagzeilen machen.

news: ~ agency *n* Nachrichtenagentur *f*, Nachrichtendienst *m*; **~agent** *n* (*Brit*) Zeitungshändler *m*; **~-boy** *n* (*US*) Zeitungsjunge *m*; **~ bulletin** *n* Bulletin *nt*; **~cast** *n* Nachrichtensendung *f*; **~caster** *n* Nachrichtensprecher(in *f*) *m*; **~ cinema** *n* Aktualitätenkino *nt*; **~copy** *n* (*Press, TV*) Bericht *m*; **~ dealer** *n* (*US*) Zeitungshändler *m*; **~ desk** *n* Nachrichtenredaktion *f*; **~ editor** *n* Nachrichtenredakteur(in *f*) *m*; **~flash** *n* Kurzmeldung *f*; **~hawk, ~ hound** *n* (*inf*) Zeitungsmann (*inf*), Reporter *m*; **~ headlines** *npl* Kurznachrichten *pl*; (*recap*) Nachrichten *pl* in Kürze; **~ item** *n* Neuigkeit, Nachricht *f*; **the three main ~ items today** die drei Hauptpunkte der Nachrichten; **a short ~ item** (*in paper*) eine Pressenotiz, eine Zeitungsnotiz; **~letter** *n* Rundschreiben, Mitteilungsblatt *nt*; **~maker** *n jd/etw, der/das Schlagzeilen macht*; **~monger** *n* Klatschmaul *nt*; (*in paper*) Klatschspaltenschreiber *m*.

New South Wales *n* Neusüdwales *nt*.

newspaper ['nju:zˌpeɪpəʳ] *n* Zeitung *f* ◆ **daily/weekly ~** Tageszeitung/Wochenzeitung; **he works on a ~** er ist bei einer Zeitung beschäftigt.

newspaper: ~ article *n* Zeitungsartikel *m*; **~ boy** *n* Zeitungsjunge *m*; **~ cutting** *n* Zeitungsausschnitt *m*; **~ man** *n* Zeitungsverkäufer, Zeitungsmann (*inf*) *m*; (*journalist*) Journalist *m*; **~ office** *n* Redaktion *f*; **~ report** *n* Zeitungsbericht *m*.

news: ~print *n* Zeitungspapier *nt*; **~reader** *n* Nachrichtensprecher(in *f*) *m*; **~reel** *n* Wochenschau *f*; **~room** *n* (*of newspaper*) Nachrichtenredaktion *f*; (*TV, Rad also*) Nachrichtenstudio *nt or* -zentrale *f*; **~ satellite** *n* Nachrichtensatellit *m*; **~ sheet** *n* Informationsblatt *nt*; **~ stand** *n* Zeitungsstand *m*; **~ story** *n* Bericht *m*; **~ theatre** *n* Aktualitätenkino *nt*.

new-style ['nju:staɪl] *adj* im neuen Stil ◆ **~ calendar** Kalender neuen Stils *or* nach neuer Zeitrechnung.

news: ~ vendor *n* Zeitungsverkäufer(in *f*) *m*; **~worthy** *adj* **to be ~worthy** Neuigkeitswert haben.

newsy ['nju:zɪ] *adj* (+*er*) (*inf*) voller Neuigkeiten.

newt [nju:t] *n* Wassermolch *m* ◆ **as drunk as a ~** voll wie eine Strandhaubitze.

new: N~ Testament [1] *n* **the N~ Testament** das Neue Testament; [2] *adj attr* des Neuen Testaments; **~ wave** [1] *n* (*in films*) neue Welle; [2] *adj attr* der neuen Welle; **N~ World** *n* **the N~ World** die Neue Welt.

▼ **New Year** *n* neues Jahr; (*~'s Day*) Neujahr *nt* ◆ **to bring in** *or* **see in the ~** das neue Jahr begrüßen; **Happy ~!** (ein) glückliches *or* gutes neues Jahr!; **over/at ~** über/an Neujahr; **~'s Day,** (*US also*) **~'s** Neujahr *nt*, Neujahrstag *m*; **~'s Eve** Silvester, Sylvester *nt*; **~ resolution** (guter) Vorsatz für das neue Jahr.

New: ~ York [1] *n* New York *nt*; [2] *adj attr* New Yorker; **~ Yorker** *n* New Yorker(in *f*) *m*; **~ Zealand** [1] *n* Neuseeland *nt*; [2] *adj attr* Neuseeländer *attr*, neuseeländisch; **~ Zealander** *n* Neuseeländer(in *f*) *m*.

next [nekst] [1] *adj* **(a)** (*in place*) nächste(r, s).
(b) (*in time*) nächste(r, s) ◆ **come back ~ week/Tuesday** kommen Sie nächste Woche/nächsten Dienstag wieder; **he came back the ~ day/week** er kam am nächsten Tag/in der nächsten Woche wieder; **(the) ~ time I see him** wenn ich ihn das nächste Mal sehe; **(the) ~ moment he was gone** im nächsten Moment war er weg; **from one moment to the ~** von einem Moment zum anderen; **this time ~ week** nächste Woche um diese Zeit; **the year/week after ~** übernächstes Jahr/übernächste Woche; **the ~ day but one** der übernächste Tag.
(c) (*order*) nächste(r, s) ◆ **who's ~?** wer ist der nächste?; **you're ~** Sie sind dran (*inf*) *or* an der Reihe; **~ please!** der nächste bitte!; **I come ~ after you** ich bin nach Ihnen an der Reihe *or* dran (*inf*); **I knew I was the ~ person to speak** ich wußte, daß ich als nächster sprechen sollte; **I'll ask the very ~ person (I see)** ich frage den nächsten(, den ich sehe); **my name is ~ on the list** mein Name kommt als nächster auf der Liste; **the ~ but one** der/die/das übernächste; **the ~ thing to do is (to) polish it** als nächstes poliert man (es); **the ~ size smaller/bigger** die nächstkleinere/nächstgrößere Größe.
[2] *adv* **(a)** (*the ~ time*) das nächste Mal; (*afterwards*) danach ◆ **what shall we do ~?** und was sollen wir als nächstes machen?; **when shall we meet ~?** wann treffen wir uns wieder *or* das nächste Mal?; **a new dress! what ~?** ein neues Kleid? sonst noch was?; **whatever ~?** (*in surprise*) Sachen gibt's! (*inf*); (*despairingly*) wo soll das nur hinführen?
(b) ~ to sb/sth neben jdm/etw; (*with motion*) neben jdn/etw; **the ~ to last row** die vorletzte Reihe; **he was ~ to last** er war der vorletzte; **the ~ to bottom shelf** das vorletzte Brett, das zweitunterste Brett; **~ to the skin** (direkt) auf der Haut; **~ to nothing/nobody** so gut wie nichts/niemand; **~ to impossible** nahezu unmöglich; **the thing ~ to my heart** (*most important*) was mir am meisten am Herzen liegt; (*dearest*) das mir liebste.
(c) the ~ best der/die/das nächstbeste; **the ~ tallest/oldest boy** (*second in order*) der zweitgrößte/zweitälteste Junge; **she is my ~ best friend** sie ist meine zweitbeste Freundin.
[3] *n* nächste(r) *mf*; (*child*) nächste(s) *nt*.
[4] *prep* (*old*) neben (+*dat*).

next door ['neks'dɔ:ʳ] *adv* nebenan ◆ **they live ~ to us** sie wohnen (direkt) neben uns *or* (gleich) nebenan; **we live ~ to each other** wir wohnen Tür an Tür; **the boy ~** der Junge von nebenan; **it's ~ to madness** das grenzt an

➤ LANGUAGE IN USE: **nevertheless** → 26.2 **New Year** → 23.2

Wahnsinn.

next-door ['neks'dɔːʳ] *adj* **the ~ neighbour/house** der direkte Nachbar/das Nebenhaus; **we are ~ neighbours** wir wohnen Tür an Tür.

next of kin *n, pl* - nächster Verwandter, nächste Verwandte; nächste Verwandte *pl*.

nexus ['neksəs] *n* Verknüpfung, Verkettung *f* ◆ **the ~ of ties between these countries** die Verflochtenheit dieser Länder.

NF *(Brit) abbr of* **National Front.**

NFL *(US) abbr of* **National Football League** *amerikanische Fußball-Nationalliga.*

NFU *(Brit) abbr of* **National Farmers' Union** *Bauerngewerkschaft f.*

NG *(US) abbr of* **National Guard.**

NHS *(Brit) abbr of* **National Health Service.**

niacin ['naɪəsɪn] *n* Nikotinsäure *f*, Niacin *nt (spec)*.

Niagara [naɪ'ægrə] *n* Niagara *m* ◆ **~ Falls** die Niagarafälle *pl*.

nib [nɪb] *n* Feder *f*; *(point of ~)* (Feder)spitze *f*.

nibble ['nɪbl] 1 *vt* knabbern; *(pick at) food* nur anessen, herumnagen an *(+dat) (inf)*.
2 *vi (at* an *+dat)* knabbern; *(pick at)* herumnagen; *(fig)* sich interessiert zeigen ◆ **to ~ at the bait/an offer** *(fig)* sich interessiert zeigen.
3 *n* **I think I've got a ~** ich glaube, bei mir beißt einer an; **I feel like a ~** *(inf)* ich habe Appetit auf etwas, ich brauche etwas zwischen die Zähne *(hum inf)*.

nibs [nɪbz] *n (hum inf)*: **his ~** der hohe Herr *(hum)*, Seine Herrlichkeit *(hum inf)*.

Nicaragua [,nɪkə'rægjʊə] *n* Nicaragua *nt*.

Nicaraguan [,nɪkə'rægjʊən] 1 *adj* nicaraguanisch.
2 *n* Nicaraguaner(in *f*) *m*.

nice [naɪs] *adj (+er)* **(a)** nett; *person, ways, voice also* sympathisch; *(~-looking) girl, dress, looks etc also* hübsch; *weather* schön, gut; *taste, smell, meal, whisky* gut; *warmth, feeling, car* schön; *food* gut, lecker; *(skilful) workmanship, work* gut, schön, fein ◆ **be ~ to him** sei nett zu ihm; **that's not ~!** das ist aber nicht nett; **be a ~ girl and ...** sei lieb und ...; **to have a ~ time** sich gut amüsieren; **I had a ~ rest** ich habe mich gut *or* schön ausgeruht; **it's ~ to be needed** es ist schön, gebraucht zu werden; **how ~ of you to ...** wie nett *or* lieb von Ihnen, zu ...; **that's a ~ one** der/die/das ist toll *(inf) or* prima *(inf)*; **he has a ~ taste in ties** er hat einen guten Geschmack, was Krawatten angeht.
(b) *(intensifier)* schön ◆ **a ~ long holiday** schön lange Ferien; **~ and warm/near/quickly** schön warm/nahe/schnell; **~ and easy** ganz leicht; **take it ~ and easy** überanstrengen Sie sich nicht; **~ and easy does it** immer schön sachte.
(c) *(respectable)* nett; *district* fein; *words* schön; *(refined) manners* gut, fein ◆ **not a ~ word/district/book** gar kein schönes Wort/Viertel/Buch.
(d) *(iro)* nett, schön, sauber *(all iro)* ◆ **here's a ~ state of affairs!** das sind ja schöne *or* nette Zustände!; **you're in a ~ mess** du sitzt schön im Schlamassel *(inf)*; **that's a ~ way to talk to your mother** das ist ja eine schöne Art, mit deiner Mutter zu sprechen, wie sprichst du denn mit deiner Mutter?
(e) *(subtle) distinction, shade of meaning* fein, genau ◆ **overly ~ distinctions** überfeine *or* subtile Unterscheidungen; **that was a ~ point** das war eine gute Bemerkung; **one or two ~ points** ein paar brauchbare *or* gute Gedanken.
(f) *(hard to please) person* anspruchsvoll, pingelig *(inf)*, heikel *(dial)* ◆ **to be ~ about one's food** in bezug aufs Essen wählerisch *or* pingelig *(inf) or* heikel *(dial)* sein.

nice-looking ['naɪs'lʊkɪŋ] *adj* schön; *woman also, man* gut aussehend; *face, dress etc* nett; *hotel, village also* hübsch ◆ **to be ~** gut aussehen.

nicely ['naɪslɪ] *adv* **(a)** *(pleasantly)* nett; *(well) go, speak, behave, placed* gut ◆ **to go ~** wie geschmiert laufen *(inf)*; **she thanked me ~** sie hat sich nett bei mir bedankt; **eat up/say thank you ~!** iß mal schön auf/sag mal schön danke!; **that will do ~** das reicht vollauf; **how's it going? — ~, thank you** wie geht es so? — danke, ganz gut; **a ~ situated home** ein hübsch gelegenes Haus; **to be ~ spoken** sich gepflegt ausdrücken; **he's such a ~ spoken young man** es ist eine Freude, diesem jungen Mann zuzuhören; **~ done** gut gemacht, prima *(inf)*; **when the engine's ~ warmed up** wenn der Motor schön warmgelaufen ist.
(b) *(carefully) distinguish* genau, fein.

niceness ['naɪsnɪs] *n* **(a)** *(pleasantness) (of person, behaviour)* Nettigkeit *f*; *(nice appearance)* nettes *or* hübsches Aussehen; *(skilfulness)* Qualität, Feinheit *f*.
(b) *(subtlety)* Feinheit, Genauigkeit *f*.
(c) *(fastidiousness)* anspruchsvolle Art, Pingeligkeit *(inf)*, Heikelkeit *(dial) f*.

nicety ['naɪsɪtɪ] *n* **(a)** *(subtlety)* Feinheit *f*; *(of judgement also)* Schärfe *f*; *(precision)* (peinliche) Genauigkeit ◆ **to a ~** äußerst *or* sehr genau; **a point/question of some ~** ein feiner *or* subtiler Punkt/eine subtile Frage. **(b) niceties** *pl* Feinheiten, Details *pl*.

niche [niːʃ] *n (Archit)* Nische *f*; *(fig)* Plätzchen *nt*.

Nicholas ['nɪkələs] *n* Nikolaus *m*.

Nick [nɪk] *n abbr of* **Nicholas** ◆ **Old ~** *(inf)* der Böse, der Leibhaftige *(old)*.

nick¹ [nɪk] 1 *n* **(a)** Kerbe *f* ◆ **I got a little ~ on my chin** ich habe mich leicht am Kinn geschnitten. **(b) in the ~ of time** gerade noch (rechtzeitig). **(c)** *(Brit inf: condition)* **in good/bad ~** gut/nicht gut in Schuß *(inf)*.
2 *vt* **(a)** *wood, stick* einkerben ◆ **to ~ oneself/one's chin** *(inf)* sich schneiden/sich am Kinn schneiden. **(b)** *(bullet) person, wall, arm* streifen.

nick² *(Brit)* 1 *vt (inf)* **(a)** *(arrest)* einsperren *(inf)*, einlochen *(inf)*; *(catch)* schnappen *(inf)* ◆ **he got ~ed** den haben sie sich *(dat)* gekascht *(sl) or* geschnappt *(inf)*.
(b) *(steal)* klauen *(inf)*, mitgehen lassen *(inf)*.
2 *n (sl) (prison)* Kittchen *nt (inf)*, Knast *m (sl)*; *(police station)* Wache *f*, Revier *nt*.

nick³ *vt (US sl)* **to ~ sb for sth** jdm etw abknöpfen *(inf)*.

nickel ['nɪkl] *n* **(a)** *(metal)* Nickel *nt* ◆ **~ silver** Neusilber *nt*. **(b)** *(US)* Nickel *m*, Fünfcentstück *nt*.

nickel-and-dime ['nɪklən'daɪm] *adj (US inf)* klein, Pfennig- *(inf)*.

nickelodeon [,nɪkəl'əʊdɪən] *n (US dated)* **(a)** (Film-/Varieté)theater *nt (mit Eintrittspreisen von 5 Cent)*. **(b)** *(juke-box)* Musikbox *f*.

nickel-plated ['nɪkl,pleɪtɪd] *adj* vernickelt.

nicker ['nɪkəʳ] *n, pl* - *(Brit sl: pound)* **50 ~** 50 Eier *(sl)*.

nickname ['nɪkneɪm] 1 *n* Spitzname *m*.
2 *vt person* betiteln, taufen *(inf)* ◆ **they ~d him Baldy** sie gaben ihm den Spitznamen Glatzköpfchen.

nicotine ['nɪkətiːn] *n* Nikotin *nt*.

nicotine: ~ poisoning *n* Nikotinvergiftung *f*; **~-stained** *adj* gelb von Nikotin; *fingers also* nikotingelb.

niece [niːs] *n* Nichte *f*.

Nielsen rating ['niːlsən,reɪtɪŋ] *n (US)* Zuschauerquote *f*.

niff [nɪf] *n (Brit inf)* Mief *m (inf)*.

niffy ['nɪfɪ] *adj (+er) (Brit inf)* muffig *(inf)*.

nifty ['nɪftɪ] *adj (+er) (inf) (smart)* flott *(inf)*; *gadget, tool* schlau *(inf)*; *(quick) person* flott *(inf)*, fix *(inf)* ◆ **a ~ piece of work** gute Arbeit; **he's pretty ~ with a gun** er hat ein lockeres Händchen mit dem Schießeisen *(inf)*; **you'd better be ~ about it!** und ein bißchen dalli *(inf)*; **a ~ little car** ein netter kleiner Flitzer *(inf)*.

Niger ['naɪdʒəʳ] *n* Niger *m*.

Nigeria [naɪ'dʒɪərɪə] *n* Nigeria *nt*.

Nigerian [naɪ'dʒɪərɪən] 1 *adj* nigerianisch.
2 *n* Nigerianer(in *f*) *m*.

niggardliness ['nɪgədlɪnɪs] *n see adj* Knaus(e)rigkeit *f*; Armseligkeit, Kümmerlichkeit *f*.

niggardly ['nɪgədlɪ] *adj person* knaus(e)rig; *amount, portion also* armselig, kümmerlich.

nigger ['nɪgəʳ] *n (pej)* Nigger *m (pej inf)* ◆ **so you're the ~ in the woodpile** Sie sind es also, der querschießt; **there's a ~ in the woodpile** irgend jemand schießt quer *(inf)*; *(snag)* da ist ein Haken dran *(inf)*.

niggle ['nɪgl] 1 *vi (complain)* (herum)kritteln *(inf)*, herumkritisieren *(about* an *+dat)*.
2 *vt (worry)* plagen, quälen, zu schaffen machen *(+dat)*.

niggling ['nɪglɪŋ] 1 *adj person* kritt(e)lig *(inf)*, überkritisch; *question, doubt, pain* bohrend, quälend; *detail* pingelig *(inf)*; *feeling* ungut.
2 *n* Kritteln, Meckern *(inf) nt*.

nigh [naɪ] 1 *adj (old, liter)* nahe.
2 *adv* **(a)** *(old, liter)* **to draw ~** sich nahen *(old, geh) (to dat)*. **(b) ~ on** nahezu *(geh)*; **well ~ impossible** nahezu unmöglich.
3 *prep (old, liter)* nahe *(+dat)*.

night [naɪt] 1 *n* **(a)** Nacht *f*; *(evening)* Abend *m* ◆ **~ is falling** die Nacht bricht herein; **I saw him last ~** ich habe ihn gestern abend gesehen; **I'll see him tomorrow ~** ich treffe ihn morgen abend; **I stayed with them last ~** ich habe heute *or* letzte Nacht bei ihnen übernachtet; **to stay four ~s with sb** vier Nächte lang bei jdm bleiben; **I'll stay with them tomorrow ~** ich übernachte morgen nacht bei ihnen; **on Friday ~** Freitag abend/nacht; **on the ~ of (Saturday) the 11th** am (Samstag, dem) 11. nachts; **11/6 o'clock at ~** 11 Uhr nachts/6 Uhr abends; **to travel/see Paris by ~** nachts reisen/Paris bei Nacht sehen; **far into the ~** bis spät in die Nacht, bis in die späte Nacht; **in/during the ~** in/während der Nacht; **the ~ before they were ...** am Abend/die Nacht zuvor waren sie ...; **the ~ before last they were ...** vorgestern abend/vorletzte Nacht waren sie ...; **to spend the ~ at a hotel** in einem Hotel übernachten; **to have a good/bad ~** *or* **~'s sleep** gut/schlecht schlafen; *(patient also)* eine gute/schlechte Nacht haben; **I need a good ~'s sleep** ich muß mal wieder ordentlich schlafen; **night-night!** *(inf)* gut Nacht! *(inf)*; **~ after ~** jede Nacht, Nacht um Nacht *(geh)*; **all ~ (long)** die ganze Nacht; **~ and day** *(lit, fig)* Tag und Nacht; **to have a ~ out** (abends) ausgehen; **a ~ out with the lads** ein Abend mit den Kumpeln; **to make a ~ of it** durchmachen *(inf)*; **to have/get a late/an early ~** spät/früh ins Bett kommen, spät/früh schlafen gehen; **too many late ~s!** zuwenig Schlaf!; **after your early ~** nachdem du so früh schlafen gegangen bist; **to work ~s** nachts arbeiten; **to be on ~s** Nachtdienst haben; *(shift worker)* Nachtschicht haben; **the ~ of the soul** *(fig)* die Nacht der Seele.
(b) *(Theat)* Abend *m* ◆ **last three ~s of ...** die letzten drei Abende von ...; **a Mozart ~** ein Mozartabend *m*; *see* **first ~**.
2 *adv* **~s** *(esp US)* nachts.

night *in cpds* Nacht-; **~-bird** *n* Nachtvogel *m*; *(fig)* Nachteule *f (inf)*, Nachtschwärmer *m*; **~-blindness** *n* Nachtblindheit *f*; **~cap** *n* **(a)** *(garment)* Nachtmütze *f*; *(for woman)* Nachthaube *f*; **(b)** *(drink)* Schlaftrunk *m (inf)*; **~clothes** *npl* Nachtzeug *nt*, Nachtwäsche *f (esp Comm)*; **~-club** *n* Nachtlokal *nt or* -klub *m*; **~dress** *n* Nachthemd *nt*; **~ editor** *n* Redakteur *m* vom Nachtdienst; **~fall** *n* Einbruch *m* der Dunkelheit; **at ~fall** bei Einbruch der Dunkelheit; **~fighter** *n* Nachtjäger *m*; **~ flight** *n* Nachtflug *m*; **~gown** *n* Nachthemd *nt*; **~-hawk** *n (US) (lit)* Amerikanischer Ziegenmelker; *(fig)* Nachtschwärmer *m*.

nightie ['naɪtɪ] *n (inf)* Nachthemd *nt*.

nightingale ['naɪtɪŋgeɪl] *n* Nachtigall *f*.

night: ~jar *n* Ziegenmelker *m*, Nachtschwalbe *f*; **~ letter** *n (US) (zu billigem Tarif gesandtes)* Nachttelegramm *nt*; **~-life** *n* Nachtleben *nt*; **~-light** *n* **(a)**

(*for child etc*) Nachtlicht *nt;* **(b)** (*for teapot etc*) Teelicht *nt;* **~long** *adj* sich über die ganze Nacht hinziehend; (*lasting several nights*) nächtelang; **after their ~long vigil** nachdem sie die ganze Nacht gewacht hatten.

nightly ['naɪtlɪ] [1] *adj* (*every night*) (all)nächtlich, Nacht-; (*every evening*) (all)abendlich, Abend- ◆ **~ performances** (*Theat*) allabendliche Vorstellung.
[2] *adv* (*every night*) jede Nacht/jeden Abend ◆ **performances/three performances ~** jeden Abend Vorstellung/drei Vorstellungen; **twice ~** zweimal pro Abend.

nightmare ['naɪtmɛəʳ] *n* (*lit, fig*) Alptraum *m* ◆ **that was a ~ of a journey** die Reise war ein Alptraum.

nightmare scenario *n* Alptraum- *or* Schreckensvision *f.*

nightmarish ['naɪtmɛərɪʃ] *adj* grauenhaft, alptraumhaft.

night: ~-nurse *n* Nachtschwester *f;* (*man*) Nachtpfleger *m;* **~owl** *n* (*inf*) Nachteule *f* (*inf*); **~-porter** *n* Nachtportier *m;* **~safe** *n* Nachtsafe *m;* **~school** *n* Abendschule *f.*

nightshade ['naɪtʃeɪd] *n* Nachtschatten *m;* *see* **deadly ~.**

night: ~-shift *n* Nachtschicht *f;* **to be** *or* **work on ~-shift** Nachtschicht haben *or* arbeiten; **~-shirt** *n* (Herren)nachthemd *nt;* **~ sky** *n* nächtlicher Himmel; **~-spot** *n* Nachtlokal *nt;* **~ stand** *n* (*US*) Nachttisch *m;* **~stick** *n* (*US*) Schlagstock *m;* **~-storage heater** *n* Nachtspeicherofen *m;* **~ table** *n* (*US*) Nachttisch *m;* **~-time** [1] *n* Nacht *f;* **at ~-time** nachts; **in the ~-time** während der Nacht, nachts; [2] *adj attr* nächtlich, Nacht-; **~ vision aid** *n* Nachtsichtgerät *nt;* **~-watch** *n* Nachtwache *f;* **~-watchman** *n* Nachtwächter *m;* **~wear** *n* Nachtzeug *nt,* Nachtwäsche *f* (*esp Comm*).

nihilism ['naɪɪlɪzəm] *n* Nihilismus *m.*

nihilist ['naɪɪlɪst] *n* Nihilist(in *f*) *m.*

nihilistic [ˌnaɪɪ'lɪstɪk] *adj* nihilistisch.

Nikkei average, Nikkei index ['nɪkeɪ] *n* Nikkei-(Durchschnitts)index *m.*

nil [nɪl] *n* (*zero*) null (*also Sport*); (*nothing*) nichts ◆ **the score was one-~** es stand eins zu null; **the response** *etc* **was ~** die Reaktion *etc* war gleich Null.

Nile [naɪl] *n* Nil *m.*

nimble ['nɪmbl] *adj* (*+er*) (*quick*) *fingers, feet* flink; *person also* behende (*geh*); (*agile*) gelenkig, wendig, beweglich; (*skilful*) geschickt; *mind* beweglich ◆ **as ~ as a goat** leichtfüßig (wie eine Gemse); **she is still ~** sie ist noch sehr rüstig.

nimble: ~-fingered *adj* fingerfertig; **~-footed** *adj* leichtfüßig.

nimbleness ['nɪmblnɪs] *n see adj* Flinkheit *f;* Behendigkeit *f* (*geh*); Gelenkigkeit, Wendigkeit, Beweglichkeit *f;* Geschicklichkeit *f,* Geschick *nt.*

nimble-witted ['nɪmblˌwɪtɪd] *adj* schlagfertig.

nimbly ['nɪmblɪ] *adv work, respond* flink; *dance* leicht(füßig); *jump, climb* gelenkig, behende (*geh*) ◆ **her fingers moved ~** ihre Finger bewegten sich leicht und flink.

nimbus ['nɪmbəs] *n* **(a)** (*Liter: halo*) Nimbus (*geh*), Heiligenschein *m.* **(b)** (*Met*) *see* **cumulonimbus.**

nincompoop ['nɪŋkəmpu:p] *n* (*inf*) Trottel (*inf*), Simpel (*inf*) *m.*

nine [naɪn] [1] *adj* neun ◆ **~ times out of ten** in neun Zehntel der Fälle, so gut wie immer; **to have ~ lives** ein zähes Leben haben; **a ~ days' wonder** eine Eintagsfliege (*inf*).
[2] *n* Neun *f* ◆ **dressed up to the ~s** in Schale (*inf*); *see also* **six.**

ninepins ['naɪnpɪnz] *n* (*game*) Kegeln *nt* ◆ **to go down like ~** (*fig*) wie die Fliegen umfallen (*inf*).

nineteen ['naɪn'ti:n] [1] *adj* neunzehn.
[2] *n* Neunzehn *f* ◆ **she talks ~ to the dozen** sie redet wie ein Wasserfall (*inf*); **they were talking ~ to the dozen** sie redeten, was das Zeug hielt (*inf*).

nineteenth ['naɪn'ti:nθ] [1] *adj* (*in series*) neunzehnte(r, s); (*as fraction*) neunzehntel ◆ **the ~ (hole)** (*Golf inf*) das neunzehnte Loch (*Bar im Clubhaus*).
[2] *n* Neunzehnte(r, s); Neunzehntel *nt;* *see also* **sixteenth.**

ninetieth ['naɪntɪɪθ] [1] *adj* (*in series*) neunzigste(r, s); (*as fraction*) neunzigstel.
[2] *n* Neunzigste(r, s); Neunzigstel *nt.*

nine-to-five [ˌnaɪntə'faɪv] *adj job, mentality* Büro-.

nine-to-fiver [ˌnaɪntə'faɪvəʳ] *n* (*US inf*) Büroangestellte(r) *mf,* Bürohengst *m* (*pej inf*).

ninety ['naɪntɪ] [1] *adj* neunzig.
[2] *n* Neunzig *f;* *see also* **sixty.**

ninny ['nɪnɪ] *n* (*inf*) Dussel *m* (*inf*).

ninth [naɪnθ] [1] *adj* (*in series*) neunte(r, s); (*as fraction*) neuntel.
[2] *n* Neunte(r, s); Neuntel *nt;* (*Mus*) None *f;* *see also* **sixth.**

niobium [naɪ'əʊbɪəm] *n* (*Chem*) Niob *nt.*

Nip [nɪp] *n* (*pej*) Japs(e) *m* (*pej inf*).

nip¹ [nɪp] [1] *n* **(a)** (*pinch*) Kniff *m;* (*bite from animal etc*) Biß *m* ◆ **to give sb a ~ in the arm** jdn in den Arm zwicken *or* kneifen; (*dog*) jdn in den Arm zwicken; **the dog gave him a ~** der Hund hat kurz zugeschnappt; **it was ~ and tuck** (*esp US inf*) das war eine knappe Sache; **they came up to the finishing line ~ and tuck** sie lagen vor dem Ziel praktisch auf gleicher Höhe.
(b) there's a ~ in the air today es ist ganz schön frisch heute.
[2] *vt* **(a)** (*bite*) zwicken; (*pinch also*) kneifen ◆ **the dog ~ped his ankle** der Hund hat ihn am Knöchel gezwickt; **to ~ oneself/one's finger in sth** sich (*dat*) den Finger in etw (*dat*) klemmen.
(b) (*Hort*) *bud, shoot* abknipsen ◆ **to ~ sth in the bud** (*fig*) etw im Keim ersticken.
(c) (*cold, frost etc*) *plants* angreifen ◆ **the cold air ~ped our faces** die Kälte schnitt uns ins Gesicht; **the plants had been ~ped by the frost** die Pflanzen hatten Frost abbekommen.
[3] *vi* (*Brit inf*) sausen (*inf*), flitzen (*inf*) ◆ **to ~ up(stairs)/down(stairs)** hoch-/runtersausen (*inf*) *or* -flitzen (*inf*); **I'll just ~ down to the shops** ich gehe mal kurz einkaufen (*inf*); **I'll just ~ round to his place** ich gehe mal kurz bei ihm vorbei (*inf*); **I'll ~ on ahead** ich gehe schon mal voraus (*inf*).

◆**nip along** *vi* (*Brit inf*) entlangsausen (*inf*) *or* -flitzen (*inf*) ◆ **~ ~ to Joan's house** lauf *or* saus mal schnell zu Joan rüber (*inf*).

◆**nip in** *vi* (*Brit inf*) hinein-/hereinsausen (*inf*); (*call in*) auf einen Sprung vorbeikommen/-gehen ◆ **I've just ~ped ~ for a minute** ich bin nur für ein Minütchen vorbeigekommen (*inf*); **he just ~ped ~to the pub for a drink** er ging auf einen Sprung *or* nur mal kurz in die Kneipe (*inf*); **to ~ ~ and out of the traffic** sich durch den Verkehr schlängeln.

◆**nip off** [1] *vi* (*Brit inf*) davonsausen (*inf*).
[2] *vt sep twig* abknicken; (*with clippers etc*) abzwicken ◆ **he ~ped ~ the end of his finger** er hat sich (*dat*) die Fingerspitze gekappt.

◆**nip out** *vi* (*Brit inf*) hinaus-/heraussausen (*inf*); (*out of house etc*) kurz weggehen (*inf*).

nip² *n* (*inf: drink*) Schlückchen *nt.*

nipper ['nɪpəʳ] *n* **(a)** (*Zool*) Schere, Zange *f.* **(b)** (*Brit inf: child*) Steppke *m* (*inf*).

nipple ['nɪpl] *n* **(a)** (*Anat*) Brustwarze *f,* Nippel *m* (*inf*); (*US: on baby's bottle*) Sauger, Schnuller (*inf*) *m.* **(b)** (*Tech*) Nippel *m.*

nippy ['nɪpɪ] *adj* (*+er*) **(a)** (*Brit inf*) flink, flott; *car, motor* spritzig ◆ **be ~ about it** ein bißchen zack zack (*inf*) *or* dalli dalli (*inf*). **(b)** (*sharp, cold*) *weather* frisch; *wind also* beißend.

Nirvana [nɪə'vɑ:nə] *n* Nirwana *nt.*

nisi ['naɪsaɪ] *conj see* **decree.**

Nissen hut ['nɪsnˌhʌt] *n* (*Brit*) Nissenhütte *f.*

nit [nɪt] *n* **(a)** (*Zool*) Nisse, Niß *f.* **(b)** (*Brit inf*) Dummkopf, Blödmann (*inf*) *m.*

niter *n* (*US*) *see* **nitre.**

nit-pick ['nɪtpɪk] *vi* (*inf*) kleinlich *or* pingelig (*inf*) sein.

nit-picker ['nɪtpɪkəʳ] *n* (*inf*) Kleinigkeitskrämer(in *f*) *m* (*inf*).

nit-picking ['nɪtpɪkɪŋ] *adj* (*inf*) kleinlich, pingelig (*inf*).

nitrate ['naɪtreɪt] *n* Nitrat *nt.*

nitration [naɪ'treɪʃən] *n* Nitrierung *f.*

nitre, (*US*) **niter** ['naɪtəʳ] *n* Salpeter *m or nt.*

nitric ['naɪtrɪk] *adj* (*of nitrogen*) Stickstoff-; (*of nitre*) Salpeter-.

nitric: ~ acid *n* Salpetersäure *f;* **~ oxide** *n* Stick(stoffmon)oxyd *nt.*

nitrogen ['naɪtrədʒən] *n* Stickstoff *m.*

nitrogen *in cpds* Stickstoff-.

nitroglycerin(e) ['naɪtrəʊ'glɪsəri:n] *n* Nitroglyzerin *nt.*

nitrous ['naɪtrəs]: **~ acid** *n* salpetrige Säure; **~ oxide** *n* Distickstoffmonoxyd, Lachgas *nt.*

nitty-gritty ['nɪtɪ'grɪtɪ] *n* (*inf*) **to get down to the ~** zur Sache kommen.

nitwit ['nɪtwɪt] *n* (*inf*) Dummkopf, Schwachkopf (*inf*) *m.*

nix [nɪks] [1] *n* (*sl*) nix (*inf*).
[2] *vt* (*US inf*) *proposal* über den Haufen werfen (*inf*).

NLQ *abbr of* **near letter-quality** NLQ ◆ **in ~ mode** im NLQ-Druckmodus.

NNE *abbr of* **north-north-east** NNO.

NNW *abbr of* **north-north-west** NNW.

No, no *abbr of* **(a) north** N. **(b) number** Nr.

no [nəʊ] [1] *adv* **(a)** (*negative*) nein ◆ **oh ~!** o nein!; **to answer ~** (*to question*) mit Nein antworten, verneinen; (*to request*) nein sagen; **she can't say ~** sie kann nicht nein sagen; **the answer is ~** da muß ich nein sagen; (*as emphatic reply also*) nein (und noch mal nein).
(b) (*not*) nicht ◆ **whether he comes or ~** ob er kommt oder nicht; **hungry or ~, you'll eat it** ob du Hunger hast oder nicht, das wird gegessen (*inf*).
(c) (*with comp*) nicht ◆ **I can bear it ~ longer** ich kann es nicht länger ertragen; **I have ~ more money** ich habe kein Geld mehr; **he has ~ more than anyone else** er hat auch nicht mehr als jeder andere; **I'm ~ less tired than you are** ich bin auch nicht weniger müde als du; **~ later than Monday** spätestens Montag; **~ longer ago than last week** erst letzte Woche.
[2] *adj* **(a)** (*not any: also with numerals and "other"*) kein ◆ **a person of ~ intelligence** ein Mensch ohne jede Intelligenz; **a person of ~ integrity** ein unredlicher Mensch; **~ one person could do it** keiner könnte das allein tun; **~ two men could be less alike** zwei verschiedenere Menschen könnte es nicht geben; **~ other man** kein anderer; **it's of ~ interest/importance** das ist belanglos/unwichtig; **it's ~ use** *or* **good** das hat keinen Zweck.
(b) (*forbidding*) **~ parking/smoking** Parken/Rauchen verboten; **~ surrender!** wir kapitulieren nicht!
(c) (*with gerund*) **there's ~ saying** *or* **telling what he'll do next** man kann nie wissen, was er als nächstes tun wird; **there's ~ denying it** es läßt sich nicht leugnen; **there's ~ pleasing him** ihm kann man es auch nie recht machen.
(d) (*emph*) **she's ~ genius/beauty** sie ist nicht gerade ein Genie/eine Schönheit; **president or ~ president** Präsident oder nicht; **this is ~ place for children** das ist hier nichts für Kinder; **I'm ~ expert, but ...** ich bin ja kein Fachmann, aber ...; **in ~ time** im Nu; **it's ~ small matter** das ist keine Kleinigkeit; **~ little difficulty was caused by her objections** ihre Einwände bereiteten einige Schwierigkeiten; **theirs is ~ easy task** sie haben keine leichte Aufgabe; **there is ~ such thing** so etwas gibt es nicht; **it was/we did ~ such thing** bestimmt nicht, nichts dergleichen; **I'll do ~ such thing** ich werde mich hüten.
[3] *n, pl* **-es** Nein *nt;* (*~ vote*) Neinstimme *f* ◆ **I won't take ~ for an answer** ich bestehe darauf, ich lasse nicht locker; **he's the type who won't take ~ for an answer** er läßt sich nicht mit einem Nein abspeisen; **the ~es have it** die Mehrheit ist dagegen.

no-account ['nəʊəˌkaʊnt] (*US inf*) [1] *adj* (*no use*) nutzlos; (*up to no good*) nichtsnutzig.

2 *n (no use)* Niete *f (inf)*; *(up to no good)* Nichtsnutz *m*.

Noah ['nəʊə] *n* Noah *m* ◆ **~'s ark** die Arche Noah.

nob¹ [nɒb] *n (inf)* einer der besseren Leute *(inf)* ◆ **all the ~s** all die besseren Leute *(inf)*, alles, was Rang und Namen hat; **he thinks he's a real ~** er meint, er sei was besseres *(inf)*.

nob² *n (inf: head)* Rübe *f (inf)*.

no-ball ['nəʊ'bɔːl] *n (Cricket) wegen Übertreten ungültiger Ball.*

nobble ['nɒbl] *vt (Brit inf)* **(a)** *horse, dog* lahmlegen *(inf)*. **(b)** *(catch)* sich *(dat)* schnappen *(inf)*. **(c)** *(obtain dishonestly) votes etc* (sich *dat*) kaufen; *money* einsacken *(inf)*.

nobelium [nəʊ'biːlɪəm] *n* Nobelium *nt*.

Nobel ['nəʊbel]: **~ peace prize** *n* Friedensnobelpreis *m*; **~ prize** *n* Nobelpreis *m*; **~ prize winner** Nobelpreisträger(in *f*) *m*.

nobility [nəʊ'bɪlɪtɪ] *n, no pl* **(a)** *(people)* (Hoch)adel *m* ◆ **she is one of the ~** sie ist eine Adlige.
(b) *(quality)* Adel *m*, Edle(s) *nt* ◆ **~ of mind/thought** geistiger Adel; **~ of feelings/sentiment** edle Gefühle *pl*/edles Gefühl.

noble ['nəʊbl] 1 *adj (+er)* **(a)** *(aristocratic) person, rank* adlig ◆ **to be of ~ birth** adlig sein, von edler *or* adliger Geburt sein.
(b) *(fine) person, deed, thought etc* edel, nobel; *appearance* vornehm; *soul, mind also* adlig; *(brave) resistance* heldenhaft, wacker ◆ **the ~ art of self-defence** die edle Kunst der Selbstverteidigung; **that was a ~ attempt** das war ein löblicher Versuch.
(c) *monument* stattlich, prächtig; *stag also* kapital.
(d) *(inf: selfless)* edel, großmütig, edelmütig ◆ **how ~ of you!** *(iro)* zu gütig.
(e) *metal* edel, Edel-.
2 *n* Adlige(r) *mf*, Edelmann *m (Hist)* ◆ **the ~s** die Adligen *or* Edelleute *(Hist)*.

noble: ~man *n* Adlige(r), Edelmann *(Hist) m*; **~-minded** *adj* edel gesinnt, vornehm.

nobleness ['nəʊblnɪs] *n* **(a)** *(of person)* Adligkeit *f*; *(of birth, rank)* Vornehmheit *f*.
(b) *(of deed, thought)* Vornehmheit *f*; *(of person)* edle *or* noble Gesinnung; *(of soul, mind also)* Adel *m*; *(braveness)* Heldenhaftigkeit *f*.
(c) *(impressiveness)* Stattlichkeit *f*.
(d) *(inf: selflessness)* Großmütigkeit *f*; *(of person also)* Großmut, Edelmut *m*.

noblesse oblige [nəʊ'blesəʊ'bliːʒ] Adel verpflichtet, noblesse oblige.

noblewoman ['nəʊblwʊmən] *n, pl* **-women** [-wɪmɪn] Adlige *f*; *(married also)* Edelfrau *f (Hist)*; *(unmarried also)* Edelfräulein *nt (Hist)*.

nobly ['nəʊblɪ] *adv* **(a)** *(aristocratically)* vornehm ◆ **~ born** von edler Geburt.
(b) *(finely)* edel, vornehm; *(bravely)* wacker, heldenhaft ◆ **you've done ~** du hast dich wacker geschlagen *(inf)*.
(c) *(impressively) proportioned* prächtig, prachtvoll.
(d) *(inf: selflessly)* nobel, edel(mütig), großmütig.

nobody ['nəʊbədɪ] 1 *pron* niemand, keiner ◆ **who saw him? — ~** wer hat ihn gesehen? — niemand; **~ knows better than I** niemand *or* keiner weiß besser als ich; **there was ~ else** da war niemand anderes *or* sonst niemand; **~ else could have done it** es kann niemand anders *or* kein anderer gewesen sein; **~ else but you can do it** nur du kannst das, außer dir kann das niemand; **~ else offered to give them money** sonst hat sich keiner *or* niemand angeboten, ihnen Geld zu geben; **like ~'s business** wie nichts; **the speed he works at is ~'s business** er arbeitet wie kein anderer, er arbeitet mit einem Affentempo *(inf)*; **he's ~'s fool** er ist nicht auf den Kopf gefallen.
2 *n* Niemand *m no pl*, Nichts *nt no pl* ◆ **he's a mere ~** er ist überhaupt nichts, er ist doch ein Niemand *or* Nichts; **to marry a ~** jdn heiraten, der nichts ist und nichts hat; **they are nobodies** sie sind doch niemand; **I worked with him when he was (a) ~** ich habe mit ihm gearbeitet, als er noch ein Niemand war.

no-claim(s) bonus ['nəʊ,kleɪm(z)'bəʊnəs] *n* Schadenfreiheitsrabatt *m*.

nocturnal [nɒk'tɜːnl] *adj* nächtlich; *sound also* der Nacht; *animal, bird* Nacht- ◆ **~ flowers** Nachtblüher *pl*.

nocturne ['nɒktɜːn] *n (Mus)* Nokturne *f*.

nod [nɒd] 1 *n* **(a)** Nicken *nt* ◆ **he gave a quick ~** er nickte kurz; **to give sb a ~** jdm zunicken; **to answer with a ~** (zustimmend) nicken; **a ~ is as good as a wink (to a blind man)** *(inf)* schon verstanden; das wird er schon verstehen; **to go through on the ~** *(inf)* ohne Einwände angenommen werden.
(b) *(inf: sleep)* **the land of N~** das Land der Träume.
2 *vi* **(a)** *(person, flowers)* nicken; *(plumes)* wippen ◆ **to ~ to sb** jdm zunicken; **to ~ in agreement/welcome** zustimmend/zur Begrüßung nicken; **he ~ded to me to leave** er gab mir durch ein Nicken zu verstehen, daß ich gehen sollte.
(b) *(doze)* ein Nickerchen machen *(inf)* ◆ **she was ~ding over a book** sie war über einem Buch eingenickt *(inf)*.
(c) even Homer ~s Irren ist menschlich *(Prov)*.
3 *vt* **(a) to ~ one's head** mit dem Kopf nicken; **to ~ one's agreement/approval** zustimmend nicken; **to ~ a greeting/welcome to sb** jdm zum Gruß/zur Begrüßung zunicken.
(b) *(Sport) ball* köpfen.

◆**nod off** *vi* einnicken *(inf)*.

nodal ['nəʊdl] *adj* knotenartig, Knoten-; *(fig) point* Knoten-.

nodding ['nɒdɪŋ] *adj* **to have a ~ acquaintance with sb** jdn flüchtig kennen.

noddle ['nɒdl] *n (Brit inf: head)* Dez *(inf)*, Schädel *(inf) m*.

node [nəʊd] *n (all senses)* Knoten *m*.

nodular ['nɒdjʊləʳ] *adj* knötchenartig, Knötchen-.

nodule ['nɒdjuːl] *n (Med, Bot)* Knötchen *nt*; *(Geol)* Klümpchen *nt*.

no-fault ['nəʊ,fɔːlt] *(US)* 1 *adj* **(a)** *divorce* in gegenseitigem Einvernehmen.
(b) *(Insur) coverage* mit garantierter Entschädigungssumme.
2 *n (also* **~ insurance***) Kraftfahrzeugversicherung f mit garantierter Auszahlung einer Entschädigungssumme ohne vorherige Klärung der Unfallschuld.*

no-frills ['nəʊ'frɪlz] *adj attr package, deal etc* ohne (alle) Extras; *style, decor etc* (schlicht und) einfach.

noggin ['nɒgɪn] *n* **(a)** *(inf: head)* Birne *f (inf)*. **(b)** *(Measure)* Becher *m (ca. 0,15 Liter)* ◆ **let's have a ~** *(inf)* wie wär's mit 'nem Gläschen? *(inf)*.

no-go area ['nəʊ,gəʊ'ɛərɪə] *n* Sperrgebiet *nt*.

no: ~-good 1 *adj person* nichtsnutzig; 2 *n (person)* Nichtsnutz *m*; **~-growth** *adj attr* nicht wachstumsorientiert; *(preventing growth)* wachstumshemmend; **the company's in a ~-growth situation** die Firma zeigt kein Wachstum; **~-hoper** *n (inf)* völlige Niete *(inf)*, Nulpe *f (dial inf)*; **~how** *adv (incorrect, hum)* **not never not ~how** nie und nimmer.

noise [nɔɪz] 1 *n* Geräusch *nt*; *(loud, irritating sound)* Lärm, Krach *m*; *(Elec: interference)* Rauschen *nt* ◆ **what was that ~?** was war das für ein Geräusch?; **a hammering ~** ein hämmerndes Geräusch; **the ~ of (the) jet planes** der Düsenlärm; **the ~ of the traffic/bells** der Straßenlärm/der Lärm der Glocken; **the ~ of horses coming up the street** Pferdegetrappel die Straße herauf; **~s in the ears** *(Med)* Ohrensausen *nt*; **the rain made a ~ on the roof** der Regen prasselte aufs Dach; **it made a lot of ~** es war sehr laut, es hat viel Krach gemacht; **don't make a ~!** sei leise!; **stop making such a (loud) ~** hör auf, solchen Lärm *or* Krach zu machen; **she made ~s about leaving early** sie wollte unbedingt früh gehen; **he's always making ~s about resigning** er redet dauernd davon, daß er zurücktreten will; **to make a lot of ~ about sth** *(inf)* viel Geschrei um etw machen; **to make a ~ in the world** Aufsehen erregen, von sich reden machen; **a big ~** *(fig inf)* ein großes Tier *(inf)*; **~ abatement** Lärmbekämpfung *f*; **~ level** Geräuschpegel *m*; **a low ~-level engine** ein geräuscharmer Motor; **~ pollution** Lärmbelästigung *f*; **~ prevention** Lärmbekämpfung *f*.
2 *vt* **to ~ sth abroad** *or* **about** *(old, hum)* etw verbreiten; **it was ~d about that** ... es ging das Gerücht (um), daß ...

noiseless ['nɔɪzlɪs] *adj* geräuschlos; *tread, step also* lautlos.

noiselessly ['nɔɪzlɪslɪ] *adv* geräuschlos; *move also* lautlos.

noisily ['nɔɪzɪlɪ] *adv see adj.*

noisiness ['nɔɪzɪnɪs] *n* Lärm *m*; *(of person)* laute Art; *(of children)* Krachmacherei *f (inf)*; *(of protest, welcome, debate)* Lautstärke *f* ◆ **the ~ of these pupils/this car** der Lärm *or* Krach, den diese Schüler machen/dieses Auto macht.

noisome ['nɔɪsəm] *adj* **(a)** *smell* widerlich, eklig. **(b)** *(noxious)* giftig, (gesundheits)schädlich.

noisy ['nɔɪzɪ] *adj (+er)* laut; *traffic, child also* lärmend; *machine, behaviour, work also* geräuschvoll; *protest, welcome, debate* lautstark ◆ **don't be so ~** sei nicht so laut, mach nicht so viel Lärm; **this is a ~ house** in dem Haus ist es laut.

no-jump ['nəʊdʒʌmp] *n* Fehlsprung *m*.

nomad ['nəʊmæd] *n* Nomade *m*, Nomadin *f*.

nomadic [nəʊ'mædɪk] *adj* nomadisch, Nomaden-; *tribe, race* Nomaden-.

no-man's-land ['nəʊmænzlænd] *n (lit, fig)* Niemandsland *nt*.

nom de plume ['nɒmdə'pluːm] *n* Pseudonym *nt*.

nomenclature [nəʊ'menklətʃəʳ] *n* Nomenklatur *f*.

nominal ['nɒmɪnl] *adj* **(a)** *(in name)* nominell ◆ **~ value** *(of shares)* Nenn- *or* Nominalwert *m*; **~ shares** Stamm- *or* Gründungsaktien *pl*. **(b)** *(small) salary, fee, amount, rent* nominell, symbolisch. **(c)** *(Gram)* Nominal-.

nominalism ['nɒmɪnəlɪzəm] *n (Philos)* Nominalismus *m*.

nominalize ['nɒmɪnəlaɪz] *vt (Gram)* nominalisieren; *word also* substantivieren.

nominally ['nɒmɪnəlɪ] *adv* nominell.

nominate ['nɒmɪneɪt] *vt* **(a)** *(appoint)* ernennen ◆ **he was ~d chairman** er wurde zum Vorsitzenden ernannt. **(b)** *(propose)* nominieren, aufstellen. **he was ~d for the presidency** er wurde als Präsidentschaftskandidat aufgestellt.

nomination [,nɒmɪ'neɪʃən] *n* **(a)** *(appointment)* Ernennung *f*. **(b)** *(proposal)* Nominierung *f*, Kandidatenvorschlag *m*.

nominative ['nɒmɪnətɪv] *(Gram)* 1 *n* Nominativ, Werfall *m*.
2 *adj* **(the) ~ case** der Nominativ, der Werfall.

nominee [,nɒmɪ'niː] *n* Kandidat(in *f*) *m*.

non- [nɒn-] *pref* nicht-.

non: ~-absorbent *adj* nicht absorbierend; **~-acceptance** *n (Comm, Fin)* Nichtannahme, Annahmeverweigerung *f*; **~-achiever** *n* Leistungsschwache(r) *mf*; **~-adjustable** *adj* nichtverstellbar *attr*, nicht verstellbar *pred*, unverstellbar; **~-affiliated** *adj (to an +acc) business, industry* nichtangeschlossen *attr*, nicht angeschlossen *pred*.

nonagenarian [,nɒnədʒɪ'nɛərɪən] 1 *n* Neunziger(in *f*) *m*.
2 *adj* in den Neunzigern.

non-aggression [nɒnə'greʃən] *n* Nichtangriff *m* ◆ **~ pact** Nichtangriffspakt *m*.

nonagon ['nɒnəgɒn] *n* Neuneck, Nonagon *nt*.

non: ~-alcoholic *adj* nichtalkoholisch, alkoholfrei; **~-aligned** *adj (Pol)* blockfrei, bündnisfrei; **~-alignment** *n (Pol)* Blockfreiheit, Bündnisfreiheit *f*; **~-alignment policy** Neutralitätspolitik *f*; **~-appearance** *n* Nichterscheinen *nt*; **~-arrival** *n* Ausbleiben *nt*; *(of train, plane, letter also)* Nichteintreffen *nt*; **~-attendance** *n* Nichtteilnahme *f (at an +dat)*; **~-availability** *n see adj* Unerhältlichkeit *f*, Unabkömmlichkeit *f*; **~-available** *adj* nicht erhältlich; *person* unabkömmlich; **~-belligerent** 1 *n* Kriegsunbeteiligte(r) *m*; **to be a ~-belligerent** nicht am Krieg teilnehmen; 2 *adj* nicht kriegführend, kriegsunbeteiligt; **~-breakable** *adj* unzerbrechlich, nicht zerbrechlich; **~-cash** *adj (Fin) payment* bargeldlos; **~-cash assets** Sachwerte *pl*.

nonce-word ['nɒnswɜːd] *n* Ad-hoc-Bildung *f.*
nonchalance ['nɒnʃələns] *n* Lässigkeit, Nonchalance *f.*
nonchalant *adj,* **~ly** *adv* ['nɒnʃələnt, -lɪ] lässig, nonchalant.
non: ~-Christian [1] *n* Nichtchrist(in *f*) *m;* [2] *adj* nichtchristlich; **~-collegiate** *adj university* nicht aus Colleges bestehend; **~-com** *n* (*Mil inf*) Uffz *m* (*sl*); **~-combatant** [1] *n* Nichtkämpfer, Nonkombattant (*spec*) *m;* [2] *adj* nicht am Kampf beteiligt; **~-combustible** [1] *adj* nicht brennbar; [2] *n* nicht brennbarer Stoff; **~-commissioned** *adj* (*Mil*): **~-commissioned officer** Unteroffizier *m;* **~-committal** *adj* zurückhaltend; *answer also* unverbindlich; **to be ~-committal about whether ...** sich nicht festlegen, ob ...; **he's so ~-committal** er legt sich nie fest; **~-committally** *adv answer, say* unverbindlich; **~-communicant** *n* (*Eccl*) Nichtkommunikant(in *f*) *m;* **~-completion** *n* Nichtbeendung *f;* (*of work also, contract*) Nichtabschluß *m;* **~-compliance** *n* (*with regulations etc*) Nichteinhaltung, Nichterfüllung *f* (*with gen*); (*with wishes, orders*) Zuwiderhandlung *f,* Zuwiderhandeln *nt* (*with gen*).
non compos mentis ['nɒn,kɒmpəs'mentɪs] *adj* nicht zurechnungsfähig, unzurechnungsfähig ◆ **to look/be ~** (*inf*) etwas geistesabwesend aussehen/ nicht ganz dasein (*inf*).
non: ~conformism *n* Nonkonformismus *m;* **his social ~conformism** seine mangelnde Anpassung an die Gesellschaft; **the ~conformism of his views** seine nonkonformistischen Ansichten; **~conformist** [1] *n* Nonkonformist(in *f*) *m;* [2] *adj* nonkonformistisch; **~conformity** *n* (*with rules*) Nichteinhaltung *f* (*with gen*), Nichtkonformgehen *nt* (*form*) (*with* mit); **~-contributory** *adj benefits, insurance, pension scheme* ohne Eigenbeteiligung; *member* beitragsfrei; **~-controversial** *adj* für alle annehmbar, nicht kontrovers; **to be ~-controversial** keinen Anlaß zu Kontroversen bieten; **~-convertible** *adj* (*Fin*) nicht konvertierbar; **~-cooperation** *n* unkooperative Haltung; **~-cooperative** *adj* unkooperativ; **~-delivery** *n* Nichtlieferung *f;* **~-denominational** *adj* bekenntnisfrei, konfessionslos; **~-departure** *n* (*of train, flight*) Ausfall *m.*
nondescript ['nɒndɪskrɪpt] *adj taste, colour* unbestimmbar; *person, appearance* unauffällig, unscheinbar (*pej*).
non: ~-detachable *adj handle, hood etc* nicht abnehmbar, fest angebracht; *lining* nicht ausknöpfbar; (*without zip*) nicht ausreißbar; **~-discrimination** *n* Nichtdiskriminierung *f* (*against, towards gen*); **~-discriminatory** *adj* nichtdiskriminierend; **~-drinker** *n* Nichttrinker(in *f*) *m;* **she is a ~-drinker** sie trinkt keinen Alkohol; **~-driver** *n* Nichtfahrer(in *f*) *m;* **~-drivers are ...** wer selbst nicht (Auto) fährt, ist ...; **~-dutiable** *adj* unverzollbar.
none [nʌn] [1] *pron* keine(r, s); keine; (*on form*) keine ◆ **~ of the boys/the chairs/them/the girls** keiner der Jungen/Stühle/von ihnen/keines der Mädchen; **~ of this/the cake** nichts davon/von dem Kuchen; **~ of this is any good** das ist alles nicht gut; **~ of this money is mine** von dem Geld gehört mir nichts; **do you have any bread/apples? — ~ (at all)** haben Sie Brot/ Äpfel? — nein, gar keines/keine; **there is ~ left** es ist nichts übrig; **money have I ~** (*liter*) Geld hab' ich keines; **~ but he/the best** nur er/nur das Beste; **their guest was ~ other than ...** ihr Gast war kein anderer als ...; **there is ~ better than him at climbing** niemand kann besser klettern als er; **but ~ of your silly jokes** aber laß bitte deine dummen Witze; **I want ~ of your excuses** und ich will keine Entschuldigungen hören; **(we'll have) ~ of that!** jetzt reicht's aber!; **I want ~ of this/this nonsense** ich will davon/von diesem Unsinn nichts hören; **I'll have ~ of your cheek** (*inf*) ich dulde diese Frechheit nicht; **he would have ~ of it** er wollte davon nichts wissen.
[2] *adv* **to be ~ the wiser** auch nicht *or* um nichts schlauer sein; **it's ~ too warm** es ist nicht *or* keineswegs zu warm; **~ too sure/easy** durchaus nicht sicher/einfach.
nonentity [nɒ'nentɪtɪ] *n* (*person*) Nullität *f,* unbedeutende Figur.
non-essential [nɒnɪ'senʃəl] [1] *adj* unnötig; *workers* nicht unbedingt nötig; *services* nicht lebenswichtig.
[2] *n* **~s** *pl* nicht (lebens)notwendige Dinge *pl.*
➤ **nonetheless** [,nʌnðə'les] *adv* nichtsdestoweniger, trotzdem.
non: ~-event *n* (*inf*) Reinfall *m* (*inf*), Pleite *f* (*inf*), Schlag *m* ins Wasser (*inf*); **~-executive** *adj* **in a ~-executive capacity** ohne Entscheidungsbefugnis; **~-executive director** ≃ Aufsichtsratsmitglied *nt* (*ohne Entscheidungsbefugnis*); **~-existence** *n* Nichtvorhandensein *nt;* (*Philos*) Nicht-Existenz *f;* **~-existent** *adj* nichtvorhanden *attr,* nicht vorhanden *pred;* (*Philos*) nicht existent; **his accent is practically ~-existent** er hat praktisch keinen Akzent; **~-fat** *adj diet* fettlos; **~-fat creamer** *n* milch- freier Kaffeeweißer; **~-fat milk** *n* Milchersatz *m auf pflanzlicher Basis;* **~-fattening** *adj* nicht dickmachend *attr;* **fruit is ~-fattening** Obst macht nicht dick; **~-ferrous** *adj* nicht eisenhaltig; **~-fiction** [1] *n* Sachbücher *pl;* [2] *adj* **~-fiction book/publication** Sachbuch *nt;* **~-fiction department** Sachbuchabteilung *f;* **~-finite** *adj* (*Gram*) infinit; **~-flammable** *adj* nichtentzündbar *attr,* nicht entzündbar *pred;* **~-flowering** *adj* nichtblühend; **~-hereditary** *adj* nichtvererbbar *attr,* nicht vererbbar *pred; disease also* nichtvererblich *attr,* nicht vererblich *pred;* **~-impact printer** *n* Non-impact-Drucker *m,* anschlagfreier Drucker; **~-infectious** *adj* nicht ansteckend, nicht infektiös (*form*); **~-inflammable** *adj* nicht feuergefährlich; **~-interference** *n* Nichteinmischung *f* (*in* in *+acc*); **~-intervention** *n* (*Pol etc*) Nichteinmischung *f,* Nichteingreifen *nt* (*in* in *+acc*); **~-interventionist** *adj policy* der Nichteinmischung; **~-iron** *adj* bügelfrei; **~-member** *n* Nichtmitglied *nt;* (*of society also*) Nichtangehörige(r) *mf;* **open to ~-members** Gäste willkommen; **~-migratory** *adj* **~-migratory bird** Standvogel, Nichtzieher (*spec*) *m;* **~-milk** *adj:* **~-milk fat(s)** nichttierische Fette *pl;* **~-negotiable** *adj ticket* nicht übertragbar.
no-no ['nəʊnəʊ] *n* (*inf*) **that's/she's a ~!** das/sie kommt nicht in Frage! (*inf*); **that's a ~!** (*you mustn't do it*) das gibt's nicht!
non: ~-obligatory *adj* freiwillig, nicht Pflicht *pred,* freigestellt *pred;* **~-observance** *n* Nicht(be)achtung *f.*
no-nonsense ['nəʊ,nɒnsəns] *adj* (kühl und) sachlich, nüchtern.
non: ~pareil [nɒnpə'reɪ] [1] *adj* (*liter*) unerreicht; [2] *n* (*liter*) (*thing*) Nonplusultra *nt;* (*person*) unerreichter Meister; **~-partisan** *adj* unparteiisch; **~-payment** *n* Nichtzahlung, Zahlungsverweigerung *f;* **~-perishable** *adj* dauerhaft, haltbar; **~-person** *n* Unperson *f.*
nonplus ['nɒn'plʌs] *vt* verblüffen ◆ **utterly ~sed** völlig verdutzt *or* verblüfft.
non: ~-poisonous *adj* nicht giftig, ungiftig; **~-political** *adj* nichtpolitisch; **~-polluting** *adj* umweltschonend; **~-porous** *adj* nichtporös *attr,* nicht porös *pred;* **~-productive** *adj* **~-productive industries** Dienstleistungssektor *m;* **~-productive worker** Angestellte(r) *mf* im Dienstleistungssektor; **~-profit** (*US*), **~-profit-making** *adj* keinen Gewinn anstrebend *attr; charity etc also* gemeinnützig; **~-proliferation** *n* Nichtverbreitung *f* von Atomwaffen; **~-proliferation treaty** Atomsperrvertrag *m;* **~-publication** *n* Nichterscheinen *nt;* **~-radioactive** *adj substance* nicht radioaktiv, strahlenfrei; **~-reader** *n* Analphabet(in *f*) *m;* **there are still five ~-readers in this class** in dieser Klasse können fünf Schüler noch nicht lesen; **~-recognition** *n* Nichtanerkennung *f;* **~-refillable** *adj* Wegwerf-; **~-resident** [1] *adj* nicht ansässig; (*in hotel*) nicht im Hause wohnend; [2] *n* Nicht(orts)ansässige(r) *mf;* (*in hotel*) nicht im Haus wohnender Gast; **open to ~-residents** auch für Nichthotelgäste; **~-returnable** *adj bottle* Einweg-; **~-run** *adj* laufmaschenfrei, maschenfest; **~-scheduled** *adj flight, train* außerplanmäßig; **~-sectarian** *adj* nichtkonfessionell; *assembly* nicht konfessionsgebunden.
nonsense ['nɒnsəns] *n, no pl* (*also as interjection*) Unsinn, Quatsch (*inf*), Nonsens (*geh*) *m;* (*verbal also*) dummes Zeug; (*silly behaviour*) Dummheiten *pl* ◆ **a piece of ~** ein Unsinn *or* Quatsch (*inf*) *m;* **that's a lot of ~!** das ist (ja) alles dummes Zeug!; **I've had enough of this ~** jetzt reicht's mir aber; **to make (a) ~ of sth** etw ad absurdum führen, etw unsinnig *or* sinnlos machen; **what's all this ~ about a salary reduction/about them not wanting to go?** was soll all das Gerede von einer Gehaltskürzung/was soll all das Gerede, daß sie nicht mitgehen wollen?; **no more of your ~!** Schluß mit dem Unsinn!; **and no ~** und keine Dummheiten; **I will stand** *or* **have no ~ from you** ich werde keinen Unsinn *or* keine Dummheiten dulden; **he will stand no ~ from anybody** er läßt nicht mit sich spaßen; **he won't stand any ~ over that** was das betrifft, verträgt er keinen Spaß; **a man with no ~ about him** ein nüchterner *or* kühler und sachlicher Mensch; *see* **stuff.**
nonsense verse *n* Nonsens-Vers, Unsinnsvers *m;* (*genre*) Nonsens-Verse, Unsinnsverse *pl.*
nonsensical [nɒn'sensɪkəl] *adj idea, action* unsinnig ◆ **don't be ~** sei nicht albern.
nonsensically [nɒn'sensɪkəlɪ] *adv argue etc* unsinnigerweise.
non sequitur [,nɒn'sekwɪtəʳ] *n* unlogische (Schluß)folgerung.
non: ~-shrink *adj* nichteinlaufend *attr;* **to be ~-shrink** nicht einlaufen; **~-skid** *adj* rutschsicher; **~-slip** *adj* rutschfest; **~-smoker** *n* **(a)** (*person*) Nichtraucher(in *f*) *m;* **(b)** (*Rail*) Nichtraucher(abteil *nt*) *m;* **~-smoking** *adj area* Nichtraucher-; **~-standard** *adj sizes* nicht der Norm entsprechend; (*of clothes, shoes*) Sonder-; (*not usually supplied*) *fittings* nicht üblich, Sonder-; **~-standard use of language** unüblicher *or* ungewöhnlicher Sprachgebrauch; **~-starter** *n* **(a)** (*in race*) (*person*) Nichtstartende(r) *mf;* (*horse*) nichtstartendes Pferd; **there were two ~-starters** zwei traten nicht an; **(b)** (*fig: person, idea*) Blindgänger *m;* **~-stick** *adj pan, surface* kunststoffbeschichtet, Teflon- ®; **~-stop** [1] *adj train* durchgehend; *journey* ohne Unterbrechung; *flight, performances* Nonstop-; [2] *adv talk* ununterbrochen; *fly* nonstop; *travel* ohne Unterbrechung, nonstop; **~-survival** *n* Aussterben *nt;* **~-swimmer** *n* Nichtschwimmer(in *f*) *m;* **~-taxable** *adj* nichtsteuerpflichtig; **~-technical** *adj language etc* für den Laien verständlich; *subject* nichttechnisch; **~-toxic** *adj* ungiftig; **~-U** *adj* (*Brit*) *charakteristisch für die Gewohnheiten, Sprechweise etc des Kleinbürgertums,* nicht vornehm; **~-union** *adj worker, labour* nichtorganisiert; **~-verbal** *adj communication* nichtverbal, wortlos, ohne Worte; **~-violence** *n* Gewaltlosigkeit *f;* **~-violent** *adj* gewaltlos; **~-vocational** *adj subject, course* nicht berufsorientiert; **~-volatile** *adj* (*Chem, Comput*) nicht- flüchtig; **~-voter** *n* Nichtwähler(in *f*) *m;* **~-voting** *adj* **~-voting shares** stimmrechtslose Aktien *pl;* **~-white** [1] *n* Farbige(r) *mf;* [2] *adj* farbig.
noodle ['nuːdl] *n* **(a)** (*Cook*) Nudel *f.* **(b)** (*dated inf: fool*) Dummerjan *m* (*dated inf*). **(c)** (*US inf: head*) Birne *f* (*inf*) ◆ **use your ~** streng deinen Grips an (*inf*).
nook [nʊk] *n* (*corner*) Ecke *f,* Winkel *m;* (*remote spot*) Winkel *m* ◆ **a shady ~** ein schattiges Fleckchen; **a cosy ~** ein gemütliches Eckchen; **in every ~ and cranny** in jedem Winkel.
nooky, nookie ['nʊkɪ] *n* (*inf*) **to have a bit of ~** bumsen (*inf*).
noon [nuːn] [1] *n* Mittag *m* ◆ **at ~** um 12 Uhr mittags.
[2] *adj* 12-Uhr-, Mittags- (*inf*).
noonday ['nuːndeɪ] *adj attr* Mittags-, mittäglich.
no-one ['nəʊwʌn] *pron see* **nobody 1.**
noon: ~time, ~tide (*liter*) *n* Mittagszeit, Mittagsstunde (*geh*) *f;* **at ~time** *or* **~tide** um die Mittagsstunde (*geh*).
noose [nuːs] *n* Schlinge *f* ◆ **to put one's head in the ~** (*prov*) den Kopf in die Schlinge stecken.
nope [nəʊp] *adv* (*inf*) ne(e) (*dial*), nein.
nor [nɔːʳ] *conj* **(a)** noch ◆ **neither ... ~** weder ... noch.
(b) (*and not*) und ... auch nicht ◆ **I shan't go, ~ will you** ich gehe nicht, und

➤ LANGUAGE IN USE: **nonetheless** → 26.3

du auch nicht; ~ **do/have/am I** ich auch nicht; ~ **was this all** und das war noch nicht alles.

Nordic ['nɔːdɪk] *adj* nordisch.

nor'-east [nɔː'riːst] *(Naut) see* **north-east.**

norm [nɔːm] *n* Norm *f* ◆ **our ~ is** ... unsere Norm liegt bei ...

normal ['nɔːməl] 1 *adj* **(a)** *person, situation, conditions* normal; *procedure, practice, routine also, customary* üblich ◆ **it's a perfectly** *or* **quite a ~ thing** das ist völlig normal; ~ **temperature/consumption/output** Normaltemperatur *f*/ -verbrauch *m*/-leistung *f*; **he is not his ~ self today** er ist heute so anders.
(b) *(Math)* senkrecht.
(c) *(Chem) solution* Normal-.
2 *n, no pl (of temperature)* Normalwert, Durchschnitt *m*; *(Math)* Senkrechte *f*; *(to tangent)* Normale *f* ◆ **temperatures below ~** Temperaturen unter dem Durchschnitt; **her temperature is above/below ~** sie hat erhöhte Temperatur/sie hat Untertemperatur; **when things/we are back to ~** wenn sich alles wieder normalisiert hat.

normalcy ['nɔːməlsɪ] *n see* **normality.**

normality [nɔː'mælɪtɪ] *n* Normalität *f* ◆ **the return to ~ after war** die Normalisierung (des Lebens) *or* die Wiederaufnahme eines normalen Lebens nach dem Krieg; **to return to ~** sich wieder normalisieren; **despite his apparent ~** obwohl er ganz normal zu sein scheint/schien.

normalization [ˌnɔːməlaɪ'zeɪʃən] *n* Normalisierung *f*.

normalize ['nɔːməlaɪz] *vt* normalisieren; *relations* wiederherstellen ◆ **to be ~d** sich normalisiert haben.

normally ['nɔːməlɪ] *adv (usually)* normalerweise, gewöhnlich; *(in normal way)* normal.

normal school *n (US old)* Pädagogische Hochschule.

Norman ['nɔːmən] 1 *adj* normannisch ◆ **the ~ Conquest** der normannische Eroberungszug.
2 *n* Normanne *m*, Normannin *f*.

Normandy ['nɔːməndɪ] *n* Normandie *f*.

normative ['nɔːmətɪv] *adj* normativ.

nor'-nor'-east [ˌnɔːnɔː'riːst] *(Naut) see* **north-north-east.**

nor'-nor'-west [ˌnɔːnɔː'west] *(Naut) see* **north-north-west.**

Norse [nɔːs] 1 *adj mythology* altnordisch.
2 *n (Ling)* **Old ~** Altnordisch *nt*.

Norseman ['nɔːsmən] *n, pl* **-men** [-mən] *(Hist)* Normanne, Wikinger *m*.

north [nɔːθ] 1 *n* **(a)** Norden *m* ◆ **in/from the ~** im/aus dem Norden; **to live in the ~** im Norden leben; **to the ~ of** nördlich von, im Norden von; **to veer/go to the ~** in nördliche Richtung *or* nach Norden drehen/gehen; **the wind is in the ~** es ist Nordwind; **to face (the) ~** nach Norden liegen; **the N~ (of Scotland/England)** Nordschottland/Nordengland *nt*.
(b) *(US Hist)* **the N~** der Norden, die Nordstaaten.
2 *adj attr* Nord-.
3 *adv (towards N~)* nach Norden, gen Norden *(liter)*, nordwärts *(liter, Naut)*; *(Met)* in nördliche Richtung ◆ ~ **of** nördlich *or* im Norden von.

north *in cpds* Nord-; **N~ Africa** *n* Nordafrika *nt*; **N~ African** 1 *adj* nordafrikanisch; 2 *n* Nordafrikaner(in *f*) *m*; **N~ America** *n* Nordamerika *nt*; **N~ American** 1 *adj* nordamerikanisch; 2 *n* Nordamerikaner(in *f*) *m*.

Northants [nɔː'θænts] *abbr of* **Northamptonshire.**

north: N~ Atlantic *n* Nordatlantik *m*; **~bound** *adj carriageway* nach Norden (führend); *traffic* in Richtung Norden; ~ **country** *n*: **the ~ country** Nordengland *nt*; **~-country** *adj* nordenglisch; **~-east** 1 *n* Nordosten, Nordost *(esp Naut) m*; **in/from the ~-east** im Nordosten/von Nordost; 2 *adj* Nordost-, nordöstlich; 3 *adv* nach Nordosten; **~-east of** nordöstlich von; **~-easterly** 1 *adj* nordöstlich; 2 *n (wind)* Nordostwind *m*; **~-eastern** *adj provinces* nordöstlich, im Nordosten; **~-eastwards** *adv* nordostwärts, nach Nordost(en).

northerly ['nɔːðəlɪ] 1 *adj wind, direction, latitude* nördlich.
2 *adv* nach Norden, nordwärts *(liter, Naut)*.
3 *n* Nordwind *m*.

northern ['nɔːðən] *adj hemisphere, counties* nördlich; *Germany, Italy etc* Nord- ◆ **the ~ lights** das Nordlicht; **N~ Ireland** Nordirland *nt*; **N~ Irish** nordirisch; **with a ~ outlook** mit Blick nach Norden.

northerner ['nɔːðənəʳ] *n* **(a)** Bewohner(in *f*) *m* des Nordens; Nordengländer(in *f*) *m*/-deutsche(r) *mf etc* ◆ **he is a ~** er kommt aus dem Norden des Landes. **(b)** *(US)* Nordstaatler(in *f*) *m*.

northernmost ['nɔːðənməʊst] *adj area* nördlichste(r, s).

north: N~ Korea *n* Nordkorea *nt*; **N~ Korean** 1 *adj* nordkoreanisch; 2 *n* Nordkoreaner(in *f*) *m*; **~-north-east** 1 *n* Nordnordosten, Nordnordost *(esp Naut) m*; 2 *adj* Nordnordost-, nordnordöstlich; 3 *adv* nach Nordnordost(en); **~-north-east of** nordnordöstlich von; **~-north-west** 1 *n* Nordnordwesten, Nordnordwest *(esp Naut) m*; 2 *adj* Nordnordwest-, nordnordwestlich; 3 *adv* nach Nordnordwest(en); **~-north-west of** nordnordwestlich von; **N~ Pole** *n* Nordpol *m*; **N~ Sea** 1 *n* Nordsee *f*; 2 *adj* Nordsee-; **N~ Sea gas/oil** Nordseegas *nt*/-öl *nt*; **~-south divide** *n* Nord-Süd-Gefälle *nt*; **N~ Star** *n* Nordstern *m*; **N~ Vietnam** *n* Nordvietnam *nt*; **N~ Vietnamese** 1 *adj* nordvietnamesisch; 2 *n* Nordvietnamese *m*/ -vietnamesin *f*; **~ward, ~wardly** 1 *adj* nördlich; **in a ~wardly direction** nach Norden, (in) Richtung Norden; 2 *adv (also* **~wards)** nach Norden, nordwärts; **~-west** 1 *n* Nordwesten, Nordwest *(esp Naut) m*; 2 *adj* Nordwest-, nordwestlich; **the N~-west Passage** die Nordwestliche Durchfahrt; 3 *adv* nach Nordwest(en); **~-west of** nordwestlich von; **~-westerly** 1 *adj* nordwestlich; 2 *n* Nordwestwind *m*.

Norway ['nɔːweɪ] *n* Norwegen *nt*.

Norwegian [nɔː'wiːdʒən] 1 *adj* norwegisch.
2 *n* **(a)** Norweger(in *f*) *m*. **(b)** *(language)* Norwegisch *nt*.

nor'-west [nɔː'west] *(Naut) see* **north-west.**

Nos., nos. *abbr of* **numbers** Nrn.

nose [nəʊz] 1 *n* **(a)** Nase *f* ◆ **to hold one's ~** sich *(dat)* die Nase zuhalten; **to speak through one's ~** durch die Nase sprechen; **the tip of one's ~** die Nasenspitze; **to bleed at the ~** aus der Nase bluten; **my ~ is bleeding** ich habe Nasenbluten; **follow your ~** immer der Nase nach; **she always has her ~ in a book** sie hat dauernd den Kopf in einem Buch (vergraben); **to do sth under sb's very ~** etw vor jds Augen tun; **to find sth under one's ~** praktisch mit der Nase auf etw *(acc)* stoßen; **it was right under his ~ all the time** er hatte es die ganze Zeit direkt vor der Nase; **I just followed my ~** ich bin immer der Nase nach gegangen; **she leads him by the ~** er tanzt ganz nach ihrer Pfeife *(inf)*; **don't let him lead you by the ~** laß dich von ihm nicht unterbuttern!; **to poke** *or* **stick one's ~ into sth** *(fig)* seine Nase in etw *(acc)* stecken; **you keep your ~ out of this** *(inf)* halt du dich da raus *(inf)*; **to cut off one's ~ to spite one's face** *(prov)* sich ins eigene Fleisch schneiden; **to look down one's ~ at sb/sth** auf jdn/etw herabblicken; **with one's ~ in the air** mit hocherhobenem Kopf, hochnäsig; **to pay through the ~** *(inf)* viel blechen *(inf)*, sich dumm und dämlich zahlen *(inf)*; **to win by a ~** *(horse)* um eine Nasenlänge gewinnen; **to put sb's ~ out of joint** jdn vor den Kopf stoßen; **his ~ is out of joint over this** er fühlt sich dadurch vor den Kopf gestoßen; **to keep one's ~ clean** *(inf)* sauber bleiben *(inf)*, eine saubere Weste behalten *(inf)*; **to pay on the ~** sofort bezahlen.
(b) *(sense of smell)* Nase *f*; *(fig also)* Riecher *m (inf)* ◆ **to have a ~ for sth** *(fig)* eine Nase *or* einen Riecher *(inf)* für etw haben.
(c) *(of wines)* Blume *f*.
(d) *(of plane)* Nase *f*; *(of car)* Schnauze *f*; *(of boat also)* Bug *m*; *(of torpedo)* Kopf *m* ◆ ~ **to tail** *(cars)* Stoßstange an Stoßstange.
2 *vti* **the car/ship ~d (its way) through the fog** das Auto/Schiff tastete sich durch den Nebel; **the car ~d (its way) into the stream of traffic** das Auto schob sich in den fließenden Verkehr vor; **to ~ into sb's affairs** *(fig)* seine Nase in jds Angelegenheiten *(acc)* stecken *(inf)*.

◆**nose about** *or* **around** *vi* herumschnüffeln *(inf)*; *(person also)* herumspionieren *(inf)*.

◆**nose out** 1 *vt sep* aufspüren; *secret, scandal* ausspionieren *(inf)*, ausschnüffeln *(inf)*.
2 *vi (car)* sich vorschieben.

nose: ~bag *n* Futtersack *m*; **~band** *n* Nasenriemen *m*; **~bleed** *n* Nasenbluten *nt*; **to have a ~bleed** Nasenbluten haben; ~ **cone** *n (Aviat)* Raketenspitze *f*.

-nosed [-nəʊzd] *adj suf* -nasig.

nose: ~dive 1 *n (Aviat)* Sturzflug *m*; **to go into a ~dive** zum Sturzflug ansetzen; **the car/he took** *or* **made a ~dive into the sea** das Auto stürzte vornüber/er stürzte kopfüber ins Meer; **the company's affairs took a ~dive** mit der Firma ging es rapide bergab; 2 *vi (plane)* im Sturzflug herabgehen; **to ~dive off sth** vornüber von etw stürzen; *(person)* kopfüber von etw stürzen; **~drops** *npl* Nasentropfen *pl*; **~-flute** *n* Nasenflöte *f*; **~gay** *n* (Biedermeier)sträußchen *nt*; ~ **job** *n (inf)* Nasenkorrektur *f*; **to have a ~ job** sich einer Nasenkorrektur unterziehen; ~ **ring** *n* Nasenring *m*; **~-wheel** *n* Bugrad *nt*.

nosey *adj see* **nosy.**

nosey parker [ˌnəʊzɪ'pɑːkəʳ] *n (inf)* Schnüffler(in *f*) *m (inf)* ◆ **I don't like ~s** ich mag Leute nicht, die ihre Nase in alles stecken *(inf)*; **~!** sei doch nicht so neugierig!

nosh [nɒʃ] *(Brit sl)* 1 *n (food)* Futter *nt (inf)*; *(meal)* Schmaus *m* ◆ **to have some ~** was essen *or* futtern *(inf)*.
2 *vi* futtern *(inf)*.

no-show ['nəʊʃəʊ] *n (Aviat)* No-show *m*, fehlender Flugpassagier.

nosh-up ['nɒʃʌp] *n (Brit sl)* Schmaus *m*, Freßgelage *nt (sl)*.

nostalgia [nɒ'stældʒɪə] *n* Nostalgie *f (for* nach) ◆ **to feel ~ for sth** sich nach etw zurücksehnen.

nostalgic [nɒ'stældʒɪk] *adj* nostalgisch, wehmütig ◆ **to feel/be ~ for sth** sich nach etw zurücksehnen.

no-strike ['nəʊstraɪk] *adj attr deal, agreement* Streikverzicht-.

nostril ['nɒstrəl] *n* Nasenloch *nt*; *(of horse, zebra etc)* Nüster *f*.

nostrum ['nɒstrəm] *n (old lit, fig)* Patentrezept *nt*.

nosy ['nəʊzɪ] *adj (+er) (inf)* neugierig.

not [nɒt] *adv* **(a)** nicht ◆ **he told me ~ to come/to do that** er sagte, ich solle nicht kommen/ich solle das nicht tun; **do ~** *or* **don't come** kommen Sie nicht; **that's how ~ to do it** so sollte man es nicht machen; **he was wrong in ~ making a protest** es war falsch von ihm, nicht zu protestieren; **~ wanting to be heard, he** ... da er nicht gehört werden wollte, ... er ...; **~ I!** ich nicht!; **fear ~!** *(old)* fürchte dich/fürchtet euch nicht!
(b) *(emphatic)* nicht ◆ **~ a sound/word** *etc* kein Ton/Wort *etc*, nicht *ein* Ton/Wort *etc*; **~ a bit** kein bißchen; **~ a sign of** ... keine Spur von ...; **~ one of them** kein einziger, nicht einer; **~ a thing** überhaupt nichts; **~ any more** nicht mehr; **~ yet** noch nicht; **~ so** *(as reply)* nein; **say ~ so** *(old)* sag, daß es nicht wahr ist.
(c) *(in tag or rhetorical questions)* **it's hot, isn't it** *or* **is it ~?** *(form)* es ist heiß, nicht wahr *or* nicht? *(inf)*; **isn't it hot?** (es ist) heiß, nicht wahr?, ist das vielleicht heiß!; **isn't he cheeky!** ist er nicht frech?, (er ist) ganz schön frech, nicht! *(inf)*; **you are coming, aren't you** *or* **are you ~?** Sie kommen doch, oder?; **you have got it, haven't you?** Sie haben es doch, oder?, Sie haben es, nicht wahr?; **you like it, don't you** *or* **do you ~?** *(form)* das gefällt

dir, nicht (wahr)?; **you are ~ angry, are you?** Sie sind nicht böse, oder?; **you are ~ angry — or are you?** Sie sind doch nicht etwa böse?
(d) (*as substitute for clause*) nicht ◆ **is he coming? — I hope/I believe ~** kommt er? — ich hoffe/glaube nicht; **it would seem** *or* **appear ~** anscheinend nicht; **he's decided not to do it — I should think/hope ~** er hat sich entschlossen, es nicht zu tun — das möchte ich auch meinen/hoffen.
(e) (*elliptically*) **are you cold? — ~ at all** ist dir kalt? — überhaupt *or* gar nicht; **thank you very much — ~ at all** vielen Dank — keine Ursache *or* gern geschehen; **~ in the least** überhaupt *or* gar nicht, nicht im geringsten; **~ that I care** nicht, daß es mir etwas ausmacht(e); **~ that I know of** nicht, daß ich wüßte; **it's ~ that I don't believe him** ich glaube ihm ja, es ist ja nicht so, daß ich ihm nicht glaube.

notability [ˌnəʊtəˈbɪlɪtɪ] *n* (a) (*person*) bedeutende Persönlichkeit ◆ **the notabilities of the town** die Honoratioren *pl* der Stadt. (b) (*eminence*) Berühmtheit, Bedeutung *f*.

notable [ˈnəʊtəbl] 1 *adj* (*eminent*) *person* bedeutend; (*worthy of note*) *success, fact, event also* bemerkenswert, beachtenswert, denkwürdig; (*big*) *difference, improvement* beträchtlich, beachtlich; (*conspicuous*) auffallend ◆ **he was ~ by his absence** er glänzte durch Abwesenheit.
2 *n see* **notability (a)**.

notably [ˈnəʊtəblɪ] *adv* (a) (*strikingly*) auffallend; *improved, different* beträchtlich ◆ **to be ~ absent** durch Abwesenheit glänzen. (b) (*in particular*) hauptsächlich, vor allem.

notarial [nəʊˈtɛərɪəl] *adj seal, deed, style* notariell; *fees* Notar-.

notarize [ˈnəʊtəraɪz] *vt* notariell beglaubigen.

notary (public) [ˈnəʊtərɪ(ˈpʌblɪk)] *n* Notar(in *f*) *m*.

notate [nəʊˈteɪt] *vt* (*Mus*) in Notenschrift schreiben.

notation [nəʊˈteɪʃən] *n* (a) (*system*) Zeichensystem *nt*, Notation *f* (*Sci*); (*symbols*) Zeichen *pl*; (*phonetic also*) Schrift *f*; (*Mus*) Notenschrift, Notation *f*. (b) (*note*) Notiz, Anmerkung *f*.

notch [nɒtʃ] 1 *n* Kerbe *f*; (*of handbrake, for adjustment etc*) Raste *f*; (*in belt*) Loch *nt*; (*on damaged blade etc*) Scharte *f*; (*US Geog*) Schlucht *f* ◆ **to cut a ~ into sth** eine Kerbe in etw (*acc*) machen; **our team is a ~ above theirs** unsere Mannschaft ist eine Klasse besser als ihre; *see* **top-notch**.
2 *vt* einkerben, einschneiden.

◆**notch up** *vt sep score, points* erzielen, einheimsen (*inf*); *record* erringen, verzeichnen; *success* verzeichnen können.

➤ **note** [nəʊt] 1 *n* (a) Notiz, Anmerkung *f*; (*foot~*) Anmerkung, Fußnote *f*; (*official: in file etc*) Vermerk *m*; (*diplomatic ~*) Note *f*; (*informal letter*) Briefchen *nt*, paar Zeilen *pl* ◆ **~s** (*summary*) Aufzeichnungen *pl*; (*plan, draft*) Konzept *nt*; **a few rough ~s** ein paar Stichworte *pl*; **lecture ~s** (*professor's*) Manuskript *nt*; (*student's*) Aufzeichnungen *pl*; (*handout*) Vorlesungsskript *nt*; **to speak without ~s** frei sprechen, ohne Vorlage sprechen; **to speak from ~s** (von einer Vorlage) ablesen; **"Author's N~"** „Anmerkung des Verfassers"; **exchange of ~s** (*Pol*) Notenaustausch *m*; **to send sb a ~** jdm ein paar Zeilen schicken; **to write a hasty ~** schnell ein paar Zeilen schreiben; **to take** *or* **make ~s** Notizen machen; (*in lecture also, in interrogation*) mitschreiben; **to make ~s on a text** (sich *dat*) Notizen zu einem Text machen; **to take** *or* **make a ~ of sth** sich (*dat*) etw notieren.
(b) *no pl* (*notice*) **to take ~ of sth** von etw Notiz nehmen, etw zur Kenntnis nehmen; (*heed*) einer Sache (*dat*) Beachtung schenken; **take no ~ of what he says** nehmen Sie keine Notiz von dem, was er sagt, achten Sie nicht darauf, was er sagt; **take ~ of what I tell you** hören Sie auf das, was ich zu sagen habe; **worthy of ~** beachtenswert, erwähnenswert.
(c) *no pl* (*importance*) **a man of ~** ein bedeutender Mann; **nothing of ~** nichts Beachtens- *or* Erwähnenswertes.
(d) (*Mus*) (*sign*) Note *f*; (*sound, on piano etc*) Ton *m*; (*song of bird etc*) Lied *nt*, Gesang *m* ◆ **to give the ~** den Ton angeben; **to play/sing the right/wrong ~** richtig/falsch spielen/singen; **to strike the right ~** (*fig*) den richtigen Ton treffen; **it struck a wrong** *or* **false ~** (*fig*) da hat er *etc* sich im Ton vergriffen; (*wasn't genuine*) es klang nicht echt.
(e) (*quality, tone*) Ton, Klang *m* ◆ **his voice had a ~ of desperation** aus seiner Stimme klang Verzweiflung, seine Stimme hatte einen verzweifelten Klang; **a ~ of nostalgia** eine nostalgische Note; **to sound** *or* **strike a ~ of warning/caution** warnen/zur Vorsicht mahnen; **there was a ~ of warning in his voice** seine Stimme hatte einen warnenden Unterton.
(f) (*Fin*) Note *f*, Schein *m* ◆ **a £5 ~, a five-pound ~** eine Fünfpfundnote, ein Fünfpfundschein *m*.
➤ 2 *vt* (a) bemerken; (*take note of*) zur Kenntnis nehmen; (*pay attention to*) beachten. (b) *see* **~ down**.

◆**note down** *vt sep* notieren, aufschreiben; (*as reminder*) sich (*dat*) notieren *or* aufschreiben.

note: ~book *n* Notizbuch *or* -heft *nt*; **~case** *n* Brieftasche *f*.

noted [ˈnəʊtɪd] *adj* bekannt, berühmt (*for* für, wegen).

note: ~pad *n* Notizblock *m*; **~paper** *n* Briefpapier *nt*.

noteworthy [ˈnəʊtwɜːðɪ] *adj* beachtenswert, erwähnenswert.

nothing [ˈnʌθɪŋ] 1 *n, pron, adv* (a) nichts ◆ **~ pleases him** nichts gefällt ihm, ihm gefällt nichts; **~ could be easier** nichts wäre einfacher; **it was reduced to ~** es blieb nichts davon übrig; **she is five foot ~** (*inf*) sie ist genau fünf Fuß.
(b) (*with vb*) nichts ◆ **she is** *or* **means ~ to him** sie bedeutet ihm nichts; **she is ~ (compared) to her sister** sie ist nichts im Vergleich zu ihrer Schwester; **that came to ~** da ist nichts draus geworden; **I can make ~ of it** das sagt mir nichts, ich werde daraus nicht schlau; **he thinks ~ of doing that** er findet nichts dabei(, das zu tun); **think ~ of it** keine Ursache!; **will you come? — ~ doing!** (*inf*) kommst du? — ausgeschlossen! *or* kein Gedanke (*inf*); **there was ~ doing at the club** (*inf*) im Club war nichts los; **I tried, but there's ~ doing** (*inf*) ich hab's versucht, aber da ist nichts drin (*sl*) *or* aber da ist nichts zu machen.
(c) (*with prep*) **all his fame was as ~** (*liter*) *or* **stood** *or* **counted for ~** sein Ruhm galt nichts; **for ~** (*free, in vain*) umsonst; **it's not for ~ that he's called X** er heißt nicht umsonst *or* ohne Grund X; **there's ~ (else) for it but to leave** da bleibt einem nichts übrig als zu gehen; **there's ~ (else) for it, we'll have to ...** da hilft alles nichts, wir müssen ...; **there was ~ in it for me** das hat sich für mich nicht gelohnt, ich hatte nichts davon; (*financially also*) dabei sprang nichts für mich heraus (*inf*); **there's ~ in the rumour** das Gerücht ist völlig unfundiert *or* aus der Luft gegriffen, an dem Gerücht ist nichts (Wahres); **that is ~ to you** für dich ist das doch gar nichts; (*isn't important*) das kümmert *or* berührt dich nicht, das ist dir egal; **there's ~ to it** (*inf*) das ist kinderleicht (*inf*).
(d) (*with adj, adv*) **~ but** nur; **he does ~ but eat** er ißt nur *or* ständig, er tut nichts anderes als essen; **~ else** sonst nichts; **~ more** sonst nichts; **I'd like ~ more than that** ich möchte nichts lieber als das; **I'd like ~ more than to go to Canada** ich würde (nur) zu gern nach Kanada gehen; **~ much** nicht viel; **~ less than** nur; **~ if not polite** äußerst *or* überaus höflich; **~ new** nichts Neues; **it was ~ like so big as we thought** es war lange nicht so groß, wie wir dachten.
(e) (*US inf*) **in ~ flat** in Null Komma nichts (*inf*); **you don't know from ~** du hast (überhaupt) keine Ahnung (*inf*); **he has ~ on her** (*also Brit*) er kann ihr nicht das Wasser reichen (*inf*).
2 *n* (a) (*Math*) Null *f*.
(b) (*thing, person of no value*) Nichts *nt* ◆ **it's a mere ~ compared to what he spent last year** im Vergleich zu dem, was er letztes Jahr ausgegeben hat, ist das gar nichts; **it was a mere ~** das war doch nicht der Rede wert, das war doch nur eine winzige Kleinigkeit; **don't apologize, it's ~** entschuldige dich nicht, es ist nicht der Rede wert; **what's wrong with you? — it's ~** was ist mit dir los? — nichts; **to whisper sweet ~s to sb** jdm Zärtlichkeiten ins Ohr flüstern.

nothingness [ˈnʌθɪŋnɪs] *n* Nichts *nt*.

no through road *n* **it's a ~** es ist keine Durchfahrt.

no-throw [ˈnəʊˈθrəʊ] *n* Fehlwurf *m*.

notice [ˈnəʊtɪs] 1 *n* (a) (*warning, communication*) Bescheid *m*, Benachrichtigung *f*; (*written notification*) Mitteilung *f*; (*of forthcoming event, film etc*) Ankündigung *f* ◆ **~ to pay** (*Comm*) Zahlungsaufforderung *f*; **final ~** letzte Aufforderung; **we need three weeks' ~** wir müssen drei Wochen vorher Bescheid wissen; **to give ~ of sth** von etw Bescheid geben; (*of film, change etc*) etw ankündigen; (*of arrival etc*) etw melden; **to give sb one week's ~ of sth** jdn eine Woche vorher von etw benachrichtigen, jdm eine Woche vorher über etw (*acc*) Bescheid geben; **to give sb ~ of sth** jdn von etw benachrichtigen, jdm etw mitteilen; **to give ~ of appeal** (*Jur*) Berufung einlegen; **we must give advance ~ of the meeting** wir müssen das Treffen ankündigen; **to give official ~ that ...** öffentlich bekanntgeben, daß ...; (*referring to future event*) öffentlich ankündigen, daß ...; **without ~** ohne Ankündigung; (*of arrival also*) unangemeldet; **~ is hereby given that ...** hiermit wird bekanntgegeben, daß ...; **he didn't give us much ~, he gave us rather short ~** er hat uns nicht viel Zeit gelassen *or* gegeben; **to have ~ of sth** von etw Kenntnis haben; **I must have ~** *or* **you must give me some ~ of what you intend to do** ich muß Bescheid wissen *or* Kenntnis davon haben (*form*), was Sie vorhaben; **to serve ~ on sb** (*Jur: to appear in court*) jdn vorladen; **at short ~** kurzfristig; **at a moment's ~** jederzeit, sofort; **at three days' ~** binnen drei Tagen, innerhalb von drei Tagen; **until further ~** bis auf weiteres.
(b) (*public announcement*) (*on ~-board etc*) Bekanntmachung *f*, Anschlag *m*; (*poster also*) Plakat *nt*; (*sign*) Schild *nt*; (*in newspaper*) Mitteilung, Bekanntmachung *f*; (*short*) Notiz *f*; (*of birth, wedding, vacancy etc*) Anzeige *f* ◆ **the ~ says ...** da steht ...; **to post a ~** einen Anschlag machen, ein Plakat *nt* aufhängen; **public ~** öffentliche Bekanntmachung; **birth/marriage/death ~** Geburts-/Heirats-/Todesanzeige *f*; **I saw a ~ in the paper about the concert** ich habe das Konzert in der Zeitung angekündigt gesehen.
(c) (*prior to end of employment, residence etc*) Kündigung *f* ◆ **~ to quit** Kündigung *f*; **to give sb ~** (*employer, landlord*) jdm kündigen; (*lodger, employee also*) bei jdm kündigen; **to give in one's ~** kündigen; **I am under ~ (to quit), I got my ~** mir ist gekündigt worden; **a month's ~** eine einmonatige Kündigungsfrist; **I have to give (my landlady) a week's ~** ich habe eine einwöchige Kündigungsfrist; **she gave me** *or* **I was given a month's ~** mir wurde zum nächsten Monat gekündigt.
(d) (*review*) Kritik, Rezension *f*.
(e) (*attention*) **to take ~ of sth** von etw Notiz nehmen; (*heed*) etw beachten, einer Sache (*dat*) Beachtung schenken; **I'm afraid I wasn't taking much ~ of what they were doing** ich muß gestehen, ich habe nicht aufgepaßt, was sie machten; **to take no ~ of sb/sth** jdn/etw ignorieren, von jdm/etw keine Notiz nehmen, jdm/etw keine Beachtung schenken; **take no ~!** kümmern Sie sich nicht darum!; **a lot of ~ he takes of me!** als ob er mich beachten würde!; **to attract ~** Aufmerksamkeit erregen; **that has escaped his ~** das hat er nicht bemerkt; **it might not have escaped your ~ that ...** Sie haben vielleicht bemerkt, daß ...; **to bring sth to sb's ~** jdn auf etw (*acc*) aufmerksam machen; (*in letter etc*) jdn von etw in Kenntnis setzen; **it came to his ~ that ...** er erfuhr, daß ..., es ist ihm zu Ohren gekommen, daß ...
2 *vt* bemerken; (*feel, hear, touch also*) wahrnehmen; (*recognize, acknowledge existence of*) zur Kenntnis nehmen; *difference* feststellen; (*realize also*) merken ◆ **~ the beautiful details** achten Sie auf die schönen Einzelheiten; **without**

➤ LANGUAGE IN USE: **note: 1a → 20.7 2a → 26.3**

my noticing it ohne daß ich etwas gemerkt *or* bemerkt habe, von mir unbemerkt; **did anybody ~ him leave?** hat jemand sein Gehen bemerkt?; **I ~d her hesitating** ich bemerkte *or* merkte, daß sie zögerte; **did he wave? — I never ~d** hat er gewinkt? — ich habe es nicht bemerkt *or* gesehen; **I ~ you have a new dress** ich stelle fest, du hast ein neues Kleid, wie ich sehe, hast du ein neues Kleid; **to get oneself ~d** Aufmerksamkeit erregen, auf sich (*acc*) aufmerksam machen; (*negatively*) auffallen.

noticeable ['nəʊtɪsəbl] *adj* erkennbar, wahrnehmbar; (*visible*) sichtbar; (*obvious, considerable*) deutlich; *relief, pleasure, disgust etc*) sichtlich, merklich ◆ **the stain is very ~** der Fleck fällt ziemlich auf; **his incompetence was very ~** seine Unfähigkeit trat klar zum Vorschein *or* zeigte sich deutlich; **the change was ~** man konnte eine Veränderung feststellen; **it is hardly ~, it isn't really ~** man merkt es kaum; (*visible also*) man sieht es kaum; **it is ~ that** ... man merkt, daß ...; **she was ~ because of her large hat** sie fiel durch ihren großen Hut auf.

noticeably ['nəʊtɪsəblɪ] *adv* deutlich, merklich; *relieved, pleased, annoyed etc* sichtlich.

notice-board ['nəʊtɪsbɔːd] *n* (*Brit*) Anschlagbrett *nt*; (*in school etc also*) Schwarzes Brett; (*sign*) Schild *nt*, Tafel *f*.

notifiable ['nəʊtɪfaɪəbl] *adj* meldepflichtig.

notification [ˌnəʊtɪfɪ'keɪʃən] *n* Benachrichtigung, Mitteilung *f*; (*of disease, crime, loss, damage etc*) Meldung *f*; (*written ~: of birth etc*) Anzeige *f* ◆ **~ of the authorities** (die) Benachrichtigung der Behörden; **to send written ~ of sth to sb** jdm etw schriftlich mitteilen.

notify ['nəʊtɪfaɪ] *vt person, candidate* benachrichtigen, unterrichten (*form*); *change of address, loss, disease etc* melden ◆ **to ~ sb of sth** jdn von etw benachrichtigen, jdm etw mitteilen; *authorities, insurance company* jdm etw melden; **to be notified of sth** über etw (*acc*) informiert werden, von etw benachrichtigt *or* unterrichtet (*form*) werden.

notion ['nəʊʃən] *n* **(a)** (*idea, thought*) Idee *f*; (*conception also*) Vorstellung *f*; (*vague knowledge also*) Ahnung *f*; (*opinion*) Meinung, Ansicht *f* ◆ **I haven't the foggiest** (*inf*) *or* **slightest ~ (of what he means)** ich habe keine Ahnung *or* nicht die leiseste Ahnung(, was er meint); **I have no ~ of time** ich habe überhaupt kein Zeitgefühl; **to give sb ~s, to put ~s into sb's head** jdn auf Gedanken *or* Ideen bringen; **that gave me the ~ of inviting her** das brachte mich auf die Idee *or* den Gedanken, sie einzuladen; **where did you get the ~** *or* **what gave you the ~ that I ...?** wie kommst du denn auf die Idee, daß ich ...?; **he got the ~ (into his head)** *or* **he somehow got hold of the ~ that she wouldn't help him** irgendwie hat er sich (*dat*) eingebildet, sie würde ihm nicht helfen; **I have a ~ that** ... ich habe den Verdacht, daß ...; **that's not my ~ of fun** unter Spaß stelle ich mir etwas anderes vor.
(b) (*whim*) Idee *f* ◆ **to get/have a ~ to do sth** Lust bekommen/haben, etw zu tun; **if he gets a ~ to do something, nothing can stop him** wenn er sich (*dat*) etwas in den Kopf gesetzt hat, kann ihn keiner davon abhalten; **she has some strange ~s** sie kommt manchmal auf seltsame Ideen *or* Gedanken; **I hit (up)on** *or* **suddenly had the ~ of going to see her** mir kam plötzlich die Idee, sie zu besuchen.
(c) (*esp US inf*) **~s** *pl* Kurzwaren *pl*.

notional ['nəʊʃənl] *adj* **(a)** (*hypothetical*) fiktiv, angenommen; (*nominal*) *payment* nominell, symbolisch. **(b)** (*esp US*) versponnen, verträumt. **(c)** (*Philos*) spekulativ.

notoriety [ˌnəʊtə'raɪətɪ] *n* traurige Berühmtheit.

notorious [nəʊ'tɔːrɪəs] *adj person, fact* berüchtigt, berühmt-berüchtigt; *place also* verrufen, verschrieen; (*well-known*) *gambler, criminal, liar* notorisch ◆ **a ~ woman** eine Frau von schlechtem Ruf; **to be ~ for sth** für etw berüchtigt sein; **it is a ~ fact that** ... es ist leider nur allzu bekannt, daß ...

notoriously [nəʊ'tɔːrɪəslɪ] *adv* notorisch ◆ **to be ~ inefficient/violent** *etc* für seine Untüchtigkeit/Gewalttätigkeit berüchtigt *or* bekannt sein.

no-trump ['nəʊ'trʌmp] (*Cards*) **1** *adj* Sans-Atout-, Ohne-Trumpf-.
2 *n* (*also* **~s**) Sans-Atout, Ohne-Trumpf-Spiel *nt*.

Notts [nɒts] *abbr of* **Nottinghamshire**.

notwithstanding [ˌnɒtwɪθ'stændɪŋ] (*form*) **1** *prep* ungeachtet (*+gen*) (*form*), trotz (*+gen*).
2 *adv* dennoch, trotzdem, nichtsdestotrotz (*form*).
3 *conj* **~ that** ... obwohl *or* obgleich ...

nougat ['nuːgɑː] *n* Nougat *m*.

nought [nɔːt] *n* **(a)** (*number*) Null *f* ◆ **~s and crosses** (*Brit*) *Kinderspiel nt mit Nullen und Kreuzen*. **(b)** (*liter: nothing*) Nichts *nt* ◆ **to come to ~** sich zerschlagen; **to bring to ~** zunichte machen.

noun [naʊn] *n* Substantiv(um), Hauptwort *nt* ◆ **proper/common/abstract/collective ~** Name *m*/Gattungsname *or* -begriff *m*/Abstraktum *nt*/Sammelbegriff *m*; **~ phrase** Nominalphrase *f*.

nourish ['nʌrɪʃ] **1** *vt* **(a)** nähren; *person also* ernähren; *leather* pflegen ◆ **a good diet ~ed her back to health** gute Ernährung brachte sie wieder zu Kräften. **(b)** (*fig*) *hopes etc* nähren, hegen ◆ **literature to ~ their minds** Literatur als geistige Nahrung.
2 *vi* nahrhaft sein.

nourishing ['nʌrɪʃɪŋ] *adj food, diet, drink* nahrhaft.

nourishment ['nʌrɪʃmənt] *n* (*food*) Nahrung *f* ◆ **you need some real ~** du brauchst gutes Essen.

nous [naʊs] *n* (*inf*) Grips *m* (*inf*).

nouveau riche [ˌnuːvəʊ'riːʃ] **1** *n, pl* **-x -s** [ˌnuːvəʊ'riːʃ] Neureiche(r) *mf*.
2 *adj* typisch neureich.

Nov *abbr of* **November** Nov.

nova ['nəʊvə] *n, pl* **-e** ['nəʊviː] *or* **-s** Nova *f*.

Nova Scotia ['nəʊvə'skəʊʃə] *n* Neuschottland *nt*.

Nova Scotian ['nəʊvə'skəʊʃən] **1** *adj* neuschottisch.
2 *n* Neuschotte *m*, Neuschottin *f*.

novel[1] ['nɒvəl] *n* Roman *m*.

novel[2] *adj* neu(artig).

novelette [ˌnɒvə'let] *n* (*pej*) Romänchen *nt*, Kitschroman *m*.

novelettish [ˌnɒvə'letɪʃ] *adj* (*pej*) *situation* rührselig, kitschig.

novelist ['nɒvəlɪst] *n* Romanschriftsteller(in *f*), Romancier *m*.

novelistic [nɒvə'lɪstɪk] *adj* Roman-.

novella [nə'velə] *n* Novelle *f*.

novelty ['nɒvəltɪ] *n* **(a)** (*newness*) Neuheit *f* ◆ **once the ~ has worn off** wenn der Reiz des Neuen *or* der Neuheit vorbei ist. **(b)** (*innovation*) Neuheit *f*, Novum *nt*. **it was quite a ~** das war etwas ganz Neues, das war ein Novum. **(c)** (*Comm: trinket*) Krimskrams *m*.

November [nəʊ'vembəʳ] *n* November *m*; *see also* **September**.

novena [nəʊ'viːnə] *n* Novene *f*.

novice ['nɒvɪs] *n* (*Eccl*) Novize *m*, Novizin *f*; (*fig*) Neuling, Anfänger(in *f*) *m* (*at* bei, in *+dat*).

noviciate, novitiate [nəʊ'vɪʃɪɪt] *n* (*Eccl*) **(a)** (*state*) Noviziat *nt*. **(b)** (*place*) Novizenhaus *nt*.

novocaine ® ['nəʊvəʊkeɪn] *n* Novokain, Novocain ® *nt*.

now [naʊ] **1** *adv* **(a)** jetzt, nun; (*immediately*) jetzt, sofort, gleich; (*at this very moment*) gerade, (so)eben; (*nowadays*) heute, heutzutage ◆ **she ~ realized why** ... nun *or* da erkannte sie, warum ...; **just ~** gerade; (*immediately*) gleich, sofort; **~ is the time to do it** jetzt ist der richtige Moment dafür; **I'll do it just** *or* **right ~** ich mache es jetzt gleich *or* sofort; **do it (right) ~** mach es jetzt (sofort); **it's ~ or never** jetzt oder nie; **even ~ it's not right** es ist immer noch nicht richtig; **~ for it** los!; **what is it ~?** was ist denn jetzt *or* nun schon wieder?; **by ~** (*present, past*) inzwischen, mittlerweile; **they have/had never met before ~** sie haben sich bis jetzt/sie hatten sich bis dahin noch nie getroffen; **before ~ it was thought** ... früher dachte man, daß ...; **we'd have heard before ~** das hätten wir (inzwischen) schon gehört; **I've been there before ~** ich war schon (früher) da; **for ~** (jetzt) erst einmal, im Moment, vorläufig; **even ~** auch *or* selbst jetzt noch; **from ~ on(wards)** von nun an; **between ~ and the end of the week** bis zum Ende der Woche; **in three days from ~** (heute) in drei Tagen; **from ~ until then** bis dahin; **up to ~, till ~, until ~** bis jetzt.
(b) (*alternation*) **~ ... ~** bald ... bald; **(every) ~ and then, ~ and again** ab und zu, von Zeit zu Zeit, gelegentlich.
2 *conj* **(a) ~ (that) you've seen him** jetzt, wo Sie ihn gesehen haben, nun, da Sie ihn gesehen haben (*geh*).
(b) (*in explanation etc*) nun.
3 *interj* also ◆ **~, ~!** na, na!; **well ~** also; **~ then** also (jetzt); **stop that ~!** Schluß jetzt!; **come ~, don't exaggerate** nun übertreib mal nicht; **~, why didn't I think of that?** warum habe ich bloß nicht daran gedacht?

nowadays ['naʊədeɪz] *adv* heute, heutzutage ◆ **heroes of ~** Helden von heute.

no way ['nəʊ'weɪ] *adv see* **way 1 (h)**.

nowhere ['nəʊwɛəʳ] *adv* nirgendwo, nirgends; (*with verbs of motion*) nirgendwohin ◆ **~ special** irgendwo; (*with motion*) irgendwohin; **it's ~ you know** du kennst den Ort nicht; **it's ~ you'll ever find it** es ist an einem Platz, wo du es bestimmt nicht findest; **to appear from** *or* **out of ~** ganz plötzlich *or* aus heiterem Himmel auftauchen; **to come ~** (*Sport*) unter „ferner liefen" kommen *or* enden; **to come from ~ and win** (*Sport*) überraschend siegen; **we're getting ~ (fast)** wir machen keine Fortschritte, wir kommen nicht weiter; **rudeness will get you ~** Grobheit bringt dir gar nichts ein, mit Grobheit bringst du es auch nicht weiter; *see* **near**.

nowt [naʊt] *n, pron, adv* (*Brit dial*) nix (*inf*), nischt (*dial, inf*).

noxious ['nɒkʃəs] *adj* schädlich; *habit* übel; *influence also* verderblich.

nozzle ['nɒzl] *n* Düse *f*; (*of syringe*) Kanüle *f*.

nr *abbr of* **near** b., bei.

NSB (*Brit*) *abbr of* **National Savings Bank** ≃ Postsparkasse *f*.

NSPCC (*Brit*) *abbr of* **National Society for the Prevention of Cruelty to Children** ≃ Kinderschutzbund *m*.

NT *abbr of* **New Testament** NT *nt*.

nth [enθ] *adj* **the ~ power** *or* **degree** die n-te Potenz; **for the ~ time** zum x-ten Mal (*inf*).

nuance ['njuːɑ̃ːns] *n* Nuance *f*; (*of colour also*) Schattierung *f*.

nub [nʌb] *n* **(a)** (*piece*) Stückchen, Klümpchen *nt*. **(b)** (*fig*) **the ~ of the matter** der springende Punkt, der Kernpunkt.

Nubia ['njuːbɪə] *n* Nubien *nt*.

Nubian ['njuːbɪən] **1** *adj* nubisch.
2 *n* Nubier(in *f*) *m*.

nubile ['njuːbaɪl] *adj girl* heiratsfähig; (*attractive*) gut entwickelt.

nuclear ['njuːklɪəʳ] *adj* Kern-, Atom- (*esp Mil*); *fusion, fission, reaction, research* Kern-; *fuel, disarmament* nuklear, atomar; *attack, test, testing* Kernwaffen-, Atomwaffen-; *propulsion* Atom-; *submarine, missile* atomgetrieben, Atom-.

nuclear: ~ deterrent *n* nukleares Abschreckungsmittel; **~ energy** *n see* **~ power**; **~ family** *n* Klein- *or* Kernfamilie *f*; **~-free** *adj* atomwaffenfrei; **~ physicist** *n* Kernphysiker(in *f*) *m*; **~ physics** *n* Kernphysik *f*; **~ pile** *n* Atommeiler *m*; **~ power** *n* Atomkraft, Kernenergie *f*; **~-powered** *adj* atomgetrieben; **~ power station** *n* Kern- *or* Atomkraftwerk *nt*; **~ reactor** *n* Kern- *or* Atomreaktor *m*; **~ submarine** *n* Atom-U-Boot *nt*; **~ war** *n* Atomkrieg *m*; **~ warfare** *n* Atomkrieg *m*; **~ warhead** *n* Atomsprengkopf *m*; **~ waste** *n* Atommüll *m*; **~ weapon** Atomwaffe *f*; **~ winter** *n* nu-

➤ LANGUAGE IN USE: **noticeable** → 26.3 **now: 1a** → 26.1 **nowadays** → 26.1

klearer Winter.

nuclei ['nju:klıaı] *pl of* **nucleus**.

nucleic acid [nju:'kleıık'æsıd] *n* Nukleinsäure *f*.

nucleus ['nju:klıəs] *n, pl* **nuclei** (*Phys, Astron, fig*) Kern *m*; (*Biol: of cell also*) Nukleus *m* ◆ **atomic ~** Atomkern *m*.

nude [nju:d] 1 *adj* nackt; (*Art*) Akt- ◆ **~ study** (*Art*) Akt(studie *f*) *m*; **~ figure/portrait** Akt *m*.
2 *n* (*person*) Nackte(r) *mf*; (*Art*) (*painting, sculpture etc*) Akt *m*; (*model*) Aktmodell *nt* ◆ **to paint from the ~** einen Akt malen; **in the ~** nackt.

nudge [nʌdʒ] 1 *vt* stupsen, anstoßen ◆ **to ~ sb's memory** (*fig*) jds Gedächtnis (*dat*) (ein wenig) nachhelfen.
2 *n* Stups *m*, kleiner Stoß ◆ **to give sb a ~** jdm einen Stups geben, jdn stupsen.

nudie ['nju:dı] *adj* (*inf*) *picture etc* Nackt- ◆ **~ magazine** Porno- *or* Nacktmagazin *nt*.

nudism ['nju:dızəm] *n* Freikörperkultur *f*, Nudismus *m*.

nudist ['nju:dıst] *n* Anhänger(in *f*) *m* der Freikörperkultur, FKK-Anhänger(in *f*), Nudist(in *f*) *m* ◆ **~ colony/camp/beach** FKK-Kolonie *f*/-platz *m*/-strand *m*, Nudistenkolonie *f*/-platz *m*/Nacktbadestrand *m*.

nudity ['nju:dıtı] *n* Nacktheit *f*.

nugatory ['nju:gətərı] *adj* (*liter*) belanglos, nichtig (*geh*).

nugget ['nʌgıt] *n* (*of gold etc*) Klumpen *m*; (*fig: of information, knowledge*) Brocken *m*, Bröckchen *nt*.

nuisance ['nju:sns] *n* **(a)** (*person*) Plage *f*; (*esp pestering*) Nervensäge *f*; (*esp child*) Quälgeist *m* ◆ **he can be a ~** er kann einen aufregen, er kann einem auf die Nerven *or* den Geist (*inf*) gehen; **to make a ~ of oneself** lästig werden; **to have ~ value** als Störfaktor wirken; **he's/that's good ~ value** er/das sorgt für Umtrieb.
(b) (*thing, event*) **to be a ~** lästig sein; (*annoying*) ärgerlich sein; **what a ~, having to do it again** wie ärgerlich *or* lästig, das noch einmal machen zu müssen; **to become a ~** lästig werden; **this wind is a ~** dieser Wind ist eine Plage.
(c) (*Jur*) **public ~** öffentliches Ärgernis; **to commit a (public) ~** (öffentliches) Ärgernis erregen.

NUJ (*Brit*) *abbr of* **National Union of Journalists** *Journalistengewerkschaft f*.

nuke [nju:k] (*US sl*) 1 *n* **(a)** (*power plant*) Kern- *or* Atomkraftwerk *nt*. **(b)** (*bomb*) Atombombe *f*.
2 *vt* (*attack*) mit Atomwaffen angreifen; (*destroy*) atomar vernichten.

null [nʌl] *adj* (*Jur*) *act, decree* (null und) nichtig, ungültig ◆ **to render sth ~ and void** etw null und nichtig machen.

nullification [,nʌlıfı'keıʃən] *n* **(a)** Annullierung, Aufhebung *f*. **(b)** (*US*) unterlassene Amts- *or* Rechtshilfe.

nullify ['nʌlıfaı] *vt* annullieren, für (null und) nichtig erklären.

nullity ['nʌlıtı] *n* (*Jur*) Ungültigkeit, Nichtigkeit *f*.

NUM (*Brit*) *abbr of* **National Union of Mineworkers** *Bergarbeitergewerkschaft f*.

numb [nʌm] 1 *adj* (+*er*) taub, empfindungslos, gefühllos; *feeling* taub; (*emotionally*) benommen, wie betäubt ◆ **hands ~ with cold** Hände, die vor Kälte taub *or* gefühllos sind; **~ with grief** starr *or* wie betäubt vor Schmerz.
2 *vt* (*cold*) taub *or* gefühllos machen; (*injection, fig*) betäuben ◆ **~ed with fear/grief** starr vor Furcht/Schmerz, vor Furcht erstarrt/wie betäubt vor Schmerz.

▼ **number** ['nʌmbəʳ] 1 *n* **(a)** (*Math*) Zahl *f*; (*numeral*) Ziffer *f* ◆ **the ~ of votes cast** die abgegebenen Stimmen.
(b) (*quantity, amount*) Anzahl *f* ◆ **a ~ of problems/applicants** eine (ganze) Anzahl von Problemen/Bewerbern; **large ~s of people/books** eine große Anzahl von Leuten, (sehr) viele Leute/eine ganze Menge Bücher; **on a ~ of occasions** des öfteren; **boys and girls in equal ~s** ebenso viele Jungen wie Mädchen, Jungen und Mädchen zu gleicher Zahl (*geh*); **in a small ~ of cases** in wenigen Fällen; **ten in ~** zehn an der Zahl; **they were few in ~** es waren nur wenige; **to be found in large ~s** zahlreich vorhanden sein, häufig zu finden sein; **in small/large ~s** in kleinen/großen Mengen; **many in ~** zahlreich; **a fair ~ of times** ziemlich oft; **times without ~** unzählige Male *pl*; **any ~ can play** beliebig viele Spieler können teilnehmen; **any ~ of cards** *etc* (*when choosing*) beliebig viele Karten *etc*; (*many*) sehr viele Karten *etc*; **I've told you any ~ of times** ich habe es dir zigmal *or* x-mal gesagt (*inf*); **to win by force of ~s** aufgrund zahlenmäßiger Überlegenheit gewinnen; **they have the advantage of ~s** sie sind zahlenmäßig überlegen; **they were defeated by superior ~s** sie wurden von einer zahlenmäßigen Übermacht geschlagen.
▼ **(c)** (*of house, room, phone*) Nummer *f*; (*of page*) Seitenzahl *f*; (*of car*) (Auto)nummer *f*; (*Mil: of soldier etc*) Kennummer *f* ◆ **at ~ 4** (in) Nummer 4; **N~ Ten (Downing Street)** Nummer zehn (Downing Street); **I've got the wrong ~** ich habe mich verwählt; **it was a wrong ~** ich/er *etc* war falsch verbunden; **the ~ one pop star/footballer** (*inf*) der Popstar/Fußballer Nummer eins (*inf*); **to take care of** *or* **look after ~ one** (*inf*) (vor allem) an sich (*acc*) selbst denken; **he's my ~ two** (*inf*) er ist mein Vize (*inf*) *or* Stellvertreter *m*; **I'm (the) ~ two in the department** ich bin die Nummer zwei in der Abteilung; **his ~'s up** (*inf*) er ist dran (*inf*); **to do ~ one/two** (*baby-talk*) klein/groß machen (*baby-talk*); **to get sb's ~** (*US inf*) jdn einschätzen *or* einordnen *or* durchschauen; **to do sth by (the** *US*) **~s** etw nach Schema F (*esp pej*) *or* rein mechanisch erledigen.
(d) (*song, act etc*) Nummer *f*; (*issue of magazine etc also*) Ausgabe *f*, Heft *nt*; (*dress*) Kreation *f* ◆ **the June ~** das Juniheft, die Juniausgabe *or* -nummer; **she's a nice little ~** das ist eine tolle Mieze (*inf*).
(e) (*Gram*) Numerus *m*.
(f) (*Eccl*) **The Book of N~s** das Vierte Buch Mose, Numeri *pl*.
(g) (*company*) **one of their/our ~** eine(r) aus ihren/unseren Reihen.
(h) **~s** *pl* (*arithmetic*) Rechnen *nt*.
2 *vt* **(a)** (*give a number to*) numerieren ◆ **~ed account** Nummernkonto *nt*.
(b) (*include*) zählen (*among* zu) ◆ **to be ~ed with the saints** zu den Heiligen gezählt werden *or* zählen.
(c) (*amount to*) zählen ◆ **the group ~ed 50** es waren 50 (Leute in der Gruppe); **the library ~s 30,000 volumes** die Bibliothek hat 30.000 Bände.
(d) (*count*) zählen ◆ **to be ~ed** (*limited*) begrenzt sein; **his days are ~ed** seine Tage sind gezählt.
3 *vi* (*Mil etc: also* **~ off**) abzählen.

number cruncher ['nʌmbə'krʌntʃəʳ] *n* (*Comput*) Number Cruncher, Supercomputer *m*.

number crunching ['nʌmbə'krʌntʃıŋ] *n* (*Comput*) Number Crunching *nt*.

numbering ['nʌmbərıŋ] *n* (*of houses etc*) Numerierung *f* ◆ **~ machine** Nummernstempel *m*; **~ system** Numeriersystem *nt*.

number: ~less *adj* zahllos, unzählig; **~-plate** *n* (*Brit*) Nummernschild, Kennzeichen *nt*; **~s game** *n* Zahlenspiel *nt* ◆ **to play the ~s game** Zahlenspielerei betreiben; **~s lock** *n* (*Comput*) Zahlenverriegelung *f*.

numbness ['nʌmnıs] *n* (*of limbs etc*) Taubheit, Starre *f*; (*fig: of mind, senses*) Benommenheit, Betäubung *f*.

num(b)skull ['nʌmskʌl] *n* (*inf*) Holzkopf *m* (*inf*).

numeracy ['nju:mərəsı] *n* Rechnen *nt* ◆ **his ~** seine rechnerischen Fähigkeiten.

numeral ['nju:mərəl] *n* Ziffer *f*.

numerate ['nju:mərıt] *adj* rechenkundig ◆ **to be (very) ~** (gut) rechnen können.

numeration [,nju:mə'reıʃən] *n* Numerierung *f*.

numerator ['nju:məreıtəʳ] *n* (*Math*) Zähler, Dividend *m*.

numeric [nju:'merık] *adj* **~ keypad** Zehnertastatur *f*, numerisches Tastenfeld.

numerical [nju:'merıkəl] *adj equation, order* numerisch; *symbols, value* Zahlen-; *superiority* zahlenmäßig.

numerically [nju:'merıkəlı] *adv* zahlenmäßig.

numerous ['nju:mərəs] *adj* zahlreich; *family* kinderreich.

numismatic [,nju:mız'mætık] *adj* numismatisch.

numismatics [,nju:mız'mætıks] *n sing* Münzkunde, Numismatik *f*.

numismatist [nju:'mızmətıst] *n* Numismatiker(in *f*) *m*.

numskull *n see* **num(b)skull**.

nun [nʌn] *n* Nonne *f*.

nunciature ['nʌnʃıətjʊəʳ] *n* Nuntiatur *f*.

nuncio ['nʌnʃıəʊ] *n* (*Papal ~*) Nuntius *m*.

nunnery ['nʌnərı] *n* (*old*) (Nonnen)kloster *nt*.

NUPE ['nju:pı] (*Brit*) *abbr of* **National Union of Public Employees** *Gewerkschaft f der Angestellten im öffentlichen Dienst*.

nuptial ['nʌpʃəl] 1 *adj bliss* ehelich, Ehe-; *feast, celebration* Hochzeits-; *vow* Ehe- ◆ **the ~ day** (*hum*) der Hochzeitstag.
2 *n* **the ~s** *pl* (*hum, liter*) die Hochzeit *f*.

NUR (*Brit*) *abbr of* **National Union of Railwaymen** *Eisenbahnergewerkschaft f*.

nurd *n* (*US sl*) *see* **nerd**.

Nuremberg ['njʊərəm,bɜ:g] *n* Nürnberg *nt*.

nurse [nɜ:s] 1 *n* Schwester *f*; (*as professional title*) Krankenschwester *f*; (*nanny*) Kindermädchen *nt*, Kinderfrau *f*; (*wet-~*) Amme *f* ◆ **male ~** Krankenpfleger *m*.
2 *vt* **(a)** pflegen; *plant also, (fig) plan* hegen; *hope, wrath etc* hegen, nähren (*geh*); *fire* bewachen; (*treat carefully*) schonen; *business* sorgsam verwalten ◆ **to ~ sb back to health** jdn gesundpflegen; **to ~ sb through an illness** jdn während *or* in einer Krankheit pflegen; **to ~ a cold** an einer Erkältung herumlaborieren (*inf*); **he stood there nursing his bruised arm** er stand da und hielt seinen verletzten Arm; **to ~ the economy** die Wirtschaft hegen und pflegen.
(b) (*suckle*) *child* stillen; (*cradle*) (in den Armen) wiegen.

nurseling ['nɜ:slıŋ] *n see* **nursling**.

nursemaid ['nɜ:smeıd] *n* (*nanny, hum: servant*) Kindermädchen *nt*.

nursery ['nɜ:sərı] *n* **(a)** (*room*) Kinderzimmer *nt*; (*in hospital*) Säuglingssaal *m*. **(b)** (*institution*) Kindergarten *m*; (*all-day*) Kindertagesstätte *f*, Hort *m*. **(c)** (*Agr, Hort*) (*for plants*) Gärtnerei *f*; (*for trees*) Baumschule *f*; (*fig*) Zuchtstätte *f*.

nursery: ~man *n* Gärtner *m*; **~ nurse** *n* Kindermädchen *nt*, Kinderfrau *f*; **~ rhyme** *n* Kinderreim *m*; **~ school** *n* Kindergarten *m*; **~ school teacher** *n* Kindergärtner(in *f*) *m*; **~ slope** *n* (*Ski*) Idiotenhügel (*hum*), Anfängerhügel *m*.

nursing ['nɜ:sıŋ] 1 *n* **(a)** (*care of invalids*) Pflege *f*, Pflegen *nt*.
(b) (*profession*) Krankenpflege *f* ◆ **she's going in for ~** sie will in der Krankenpflege arbeiten.
(c) (*feeding*) Stillen *nt*.
2 *adj attr staff* Pflege-; *abilities* pflegerisch ◆ **the ~ profession** die Krankenpflege; (*nurses collectively*) die pflegerischen Berufe.

nursing: ~ auxiliary *n* Schwesternhelferin *f*; **~ bottle** *n* (*US*) Flasche *f*, Fläschchen *nt*; **~ care** *n* Pflege *f*; **~ home** *n* Privatklinik *f*; (*Brit: maternity hospital*) Entbindungsklinik *f*; (*convalescent home*) Pflegeheim *nt*; **~ mother** *n* stillende Mutter; **~ officer** *n* (*Brit*) Oberpfleger *m*, Oberschwester *f*.

nursling ['nɜ:slıŋ] *n* Pflegling *m*.

nurture ['nɜ:tʃəʳ] 1 *n* (*nourishing*) Hegen *nt*; (*upbringing*) Erziehung, Bildung *f*.
2 *vt* **(a)** (*lit, fig*) **to ~ sb on sth** jdn mit etw aufziehen. **(b)** (*fig: train*) hegen und pflegen.

➤ LANGUAGE IN USE: **number: 1c** → 27.1, 27.3, 27.4, 27.7

NUS (*Brit*) *abbr of* **National Union of Students** *Studentengewerkschaft f*; **National Union of Seamen** *Seeleutegewerkschaft f.*

NUT (*Brit*) *abbr of* **National Union of Teachers.**

nut [nʌt] *n* **(a)** (*Bot*) Nuß *f*; (*of coal*) kleines Stück ◆ **a packet of ~s and raisins** eine Tüte Studentenfutter; **a hard ~ to crack** (*fig*) eine harte Nuß.
(b) (*inf: head*) Nuß (*inf*), Birne (*inf*) *f* ◆ **use your ~!** streng deinen Grips an! (*inf*); **to be off one's ~** nicht ganz bei Trost sein (*inf*), spinnen (*inf*); **to go off one's ~** durchdrehen (*inf*); **to do one's ~** (*Brit sl*) durchdrehen (*inf*); *see also* **nuts.**
(c) (*inf: person*) Spinner(in *f*) *m* (*inf*) ◆ **he's a tough ~** (*inf*) er ist ein harter *or* zäher Brocken (*inf*).
(d) (*Mech*) (Schrauben)mutter *f*; **the ~s and bolts of a theory** die Grundbestandteile einer Theorie.
(e) **~s** *pl* (*US sl: testicles*) Eier *pl* (*sl*).

nut: ~-brown *adj* nußbraun; **~-case** *n* (*inf*) Spinner(in *f*) *m* (*inf*); **~cracker(s** *pl*) *n* Nußknacker *m*; **~hatch** *n* Kleiber *m*; **~-house** *n* (*inf*) (*lit, fig*) Irrenhaus *nt* (*inf*); (*lit also*) Klapsmühle *f* (*inf*); **~meg** *n* (*spice*) Muskat(nuß *f*) *m*; (*also* **~meg tree**) Muskatnußbaum *m.*

nutrasweet ® ['nju:trəswi:t] *n* Süßstoff *m.*

nutrient ['nju:trɪənt] 1 *adj substance* nahrhaft; *properties* Nähr-.
2 *n* Nährstoff *m.*

nutriment ['nju:trɪmənt] *n* (*form*) Nahrung *f.*

nutrition [nju:'trɪʃən] *n* (*diet, science*) Ernährung *f.*

nutritional [nju:'trɪʃənl] *adj value, content* Nähr- ◆ **~ contents/information** Nährwertangaben *pl.*

nutritionist [nju:'trɪʃənɪst] *n* Ernährungswissenschaftler(in *f*) *m.*

nutritious [nju:'trɪʃəs] *adj* nahrhaft.

nutritiousness [nju:'trɪʃəsnɪs] *n* Nahrhaftigkeit *f.*

nutritive ['nju:trɪtɪv] *adj* nahrhaft.

nuts [nʌts] *adj pred* (*inf*) **to be ~** spinnen (*inf*); **to go ~** durchdrehen (*inf*), anfangen zu spinnen (*inf*); **to be ~ about sb/sth** ganz verrückt nach jdm/auf etw (*acc*) sein (*inf*); **~!** (*US*) Quatsch! (*inf*); (*in annoyance*) Mist (*inf*)!; **~ to him!** (*US*) er kann mich mal (gern haben)! (*inf*).

nutshell ['nʌtʃel] *n* Nußschale *f* ◆ **in a ~** (*fig*) kurz gesagt, mit einem Wort; **to put the matter in a ~** (*fig*) um es (ganz) kurz *or* kurz und bündig zu sagen.

nutter ['nʌtə^r] *n* (*Brit sl*) Spinner(in *f*) *m* (*inf*); (*dangerous*) Verrückte(r) *mf* ◆ **he's a ~** er hat einen Stich (*inf*) *or* Vogel (*inf*).

nutty ['nʌtɪ] *adj* (+*er*) **(a)** *flavour* Nuß-; *cake also* mit Nüssen. **(b)** (*inf: crazy*) bekloppt (*inf*) ◆ **to be ~ about sb/sth** ganz verrückt nach jdm/auf etw (*acc*) sein (*inf*).

nuzzle ['nʌzl] 1 *vt* (*pig*) aufwühlen; (*dog*) beschnüffeln, beschnuppern.
2 *vi* **to ~ (up) against sb, to ~ up to sb** (*person, animal*) sich an jdn schmiegen *or* drücken.

NVQ (*Brit*) *abbr of* **National Vocational Qualification.**

NW *abbr of* **north-west** NW.

NY *abbr of* **New York.**

Nyasaland [naɪ'æsəlænd] *n* Njassaland *nt.*

NYC *abbr of* **New York City.**

nylon ['naɪlɒn] 1 *n* **(a)** (*Tex*) Nylon *nt.* **(b)** **~s** *pl* Nylonstrümpfe *pl.*
2 *adj* Nylon- ◆ **~ material** Nylon *nt.*

nymph [nɪmf] *n* **(a)** (*Myth*) Nymphe *f.* **(b)** (*Zool*) Nymphe *f.*

nymphet [nɪm'fet] *n* Nymphchen *nt.*

nympho ['nɪmfəʊ] *n* (*inf*) Nymphomanin *f.*

nymphomania [ˌnɪmfəʊ'meɪnɪə] *n* Nymphomanie *f.*

nymphomaniac [ˌnɪmfəʊ'meɪnɪæk] *n* Nymphomanin *f.*

NYPD (*US*) *abbr of* **New York Police Department.**

NZ *abbr of* **New Zealand.**

O, o [əʊ] *n* **(a)** O, o *nt.* **(b)** [(*Brit*) əʊ, (*US*) 'zɪərəʊ] (*Telec*) Null *f.*

O *interj* **(a)** (*Poet*) o ◆ **~ my people** o du mein Volk!
(b) (*expressing feeling*) oh, ach ◆ **~ how wrong he was** wie hatte er sich (doch) da geirrt; **~ for a bit of fresh air!** ach, wenn es doch nur ein bißchen frische Luft gäbe!; **~ to be in France** (ach,) wäre ich nur in Frankreich!; *see also* **oh.**

o' [ə] *prep abbr of* **of.**

oaf [əʊf] *n, pl* **-s** *or* **oaves** Flegel, Lümmel *m* ◆ **you clumsy ~!** du altes Trampel! (*inf*).

oafish ['əʊfɪʃ] *adj* flegelhaft, lümmelhaft; (*clumsy*) tölpelhaft.

oak [əʊk] *n* Eiche *f*; (*wood also*) Eichenholz *nt* ◆ **he has a heart of ~** er hat ein unerschütterliches Gemüt; **dark ~** (*colour*) (in) dunkel Eiche.

oak *in cpds* Eichen-; **~ apple** *n* Gallapfel *m.*

oaken ['əʊkən] *adj* (*liter*) Eichen-, eichen.

oakum ['əʊkəm] *n* Werg *nt.*

OAP (*Brit*) *abbr of* **old-age pensioner.**

OAPEC [əʊ'eɪpek] *abbr of* **Organization of Arab Petroleum Exporting Countries.**

oar [ɔːʳ] *n* **(a)** Ruder *nt*, Riemen *m* (*spec*) ◆ **to pull at the ~s** sich in die Riemen legen; **to be** *or* **pull a good ~** ein guter Ruderer/eine gute Ruderin sein; **he always has to put his ~ in** (*fig inf*) er muß (aber auch) immer mitmischen (*inf*); **to rest on one's ~s** (*fig*) langsamer treten (*inf*).
(b) (*person*) Ruderer *m*, Ruderin *f.*

-oared [-ɔːd] *adj suf* -ruderig ◆ **four-~ boat** Boot *nt* mit vier Rudern.

oar: ~lock *n* (*US*) (Ruder)dolle *f*; **~sman** *n* Ruderer *m*; **~smanship** *n* Rudertechnik *or* -kunst *f.*

OAS *abbr of* **Organization of American States** OAS *f.*

oasis [əʊ'eɪsɪs] *n, pl* **oases** [əʊ'eɪsiːz] (*lit, fig*) Oase *f.*

oast [əʊst] *n* Darre *f*, Trockenboden *m* ◆ **~-house** Trockenschuppen *m or* -haus *nt.*

oat [əʊt] *n usu pl* Hafer *m* ◆ **~s** *pl* (*Cook*) Haferflocken *pl*; **to sow one's wild ~s** (*fig*) sich (*dat*) die Hörner abstoßen; **he's feeling his ~s** ihn sticht der Hafer; **to be off one's ~s** (*hum sl*) keinen Appetit haben; **he hasn't had his ~s for some time** (*hum sl*) der hat schon lange keine mehr vernascht (*hum sl*).

oatcake ['əʊtkeɪk] *n* Haferkeks *m.*

oath [əʊθ] *n* **(a)** Schwur *m*; (*Jur*) Eid *m* ◆ **to take** *or* **make** *or* **swear an ~** schwören; (*Jur*) einen Eid ablegen *or* leisten; **to declare under ~** *or* **on ~** (*Jur*) unter Eid aussagen; **to be under ~** (*Jur*) unter Eid stehen; **to break one's ~** seinen Schwur brechen; **to put sb on ~** (*Jur*) jdn vereidigen; **to take the ~** (*Jur*) vereidigt werden; **he refused to take the ~** (*Jur*) er verweigerte den Eid; **on my ~!** (*obs*) bei meiner Seele! (*obs*).
(b) (*curse, profanity*) Fluch *m.*

oatmeal ['əʊtmiːl] **1** *n, no pl* Haferschrot *m*, Hafermehl *nt.*
2 *adj colour, dress* hellbeige.

OAU *abbr of* **Organization of African Unity** OAU *f.*

oaves [əʊvz] *pl of* **oaf.**

ob *abbr of* **obiit** gest.

obbligato *n, adj see* **obligato.**

obduracy ['ɒbdjʊrəsɪ] *n see adj* Hartnäckigkeit *f*; Verstocktheit, Halsstarrigkeit *f*; Unnachgiebigkeit *f.*

obdurate ['ɒbdjʊrɪt] *adj* (*stubborn*) hartnäckig; *sinner* verstockt, halsstarrig; (*hardhearted*) unnachgiebig, unerbittlich.

OBE *abbr of* **Officer of the Order of the British Empire** *britischer Verdienstorden.*

obedience [ə'biːdɪəns] *n, no pl* Gehorsam *m* ◆ **in ~ to the law** dem Gesetz entsprechend; **in ~ to your wishes** (*form*) Ihren Wünschen gemäß; **to teach sb ~** jdn gehorchen lehren.

obedient [ə'biːdɪənt] *adj* gehorsam; *child, dog also* folgsam ◆ **to be ~** gehorchen (*to dat*); (*child, dog also*) folgen (*to dat*); (*steering, controls, car also*) reagieren, ansprechen (*to* auf *+acc*).

obediently [ə'biːdɪəntlɪ] *adv see adj* ◆ **the car responded ~** das Auto reagierte prompt.

obeisance [əʊ'beɪsəns] *n* **(a)** (*form: homage, respect*) Ehrerbietung, Reverenz (*geh*), Huldigung (*liter*) *f* ◆ **to do** *or* **make** *or* **pay ~ (to sb)** (jdm) seine Huldigung darbringen, jdm huldigen. **(b)** (*obs: deep bow*) Verbeugung, Verneigung *f.*

obelisk ['ɒbɪlɪsk] *n* **(a)** (*Archit*) Obelisk *m.* **(b)** (*Typ*) Kreuz *nt.*

obese [əʊ'biːs] *adj* fettleibig (*form, Med*), feist (*pej*).

obeseness [əʊ'biːsnɪs], **obesity** [əʊ'biːsɪtɪ] *n* Fettleibigkeit (*form, Med*), Feistheit (*pej*) *f.*

obey [ə'beɪ] **1** *vt* gehorchen (*+dat*); *conscience also,* (*child, dog also*) folgen (*+dat*); *law, rules* sich halten an (*+acc*), befolgen; *order* befolgen; (*Jur*) *summons* nachkommen (*+dat*), Folge leisten (*+dat*); (*machine, vehicle*) *controls* reagieren *or* ansprechen auf (*+acc*); *driver* gehorchen (*+dat*) ◆ **to ~ sb implicitly** jdm absoluten Gehorsam leisten; **he makes** *or* **can make himself ~ed** (bei) ihm gehorcht man; **I like to be ~ed** ich bin (es) gewohnt, daß man meine Anordnungen befolgt.
2 *vi* gehorchen; (*child, dog also*) folgen; (*machine, vehicle also*) reagieren ◆ **the troops refused to ~** die Truppen verweigerten den Gehorsam.

obfuscate ['ɒbfəskeɪt] *vt* (*liter*) *mind* verwirren, trüben; *issue* unklar *or* verworren machen, vernebeln.

obituary [ə'bɪtjʊərɪ] *n* Nachruf *m* ◆ **~ notice** Todesanzeige *f*; **I saw his ~ notice today** ich habe seinen Namen heute im Sterberegister gelesen; **~ column** Sterberegister *nt.*

object[1] ['ɒbdʒɪkt] *n* **(a)** (*thing*) Gegenstand *m*, Ding *nt*; (*Philos, abstract etc*) Objekt, Ding *nt* ◆ **he treats her like an ~** er behandelt sie wie ein Ding *or* Objekt; **she became an ~ of pity** mit ihr mußte man Mitleid haben; **he was an ~ of scorn** er war die Zielscheibe der Verachtung; **the cat is the sole ~ of her love** ihre ganze Liebe gilt ihrer Katze.
(b) (*aim*) Ziel *nt*, Absicht *f*, Zweck *m* ◆ **with this ~ in view** *or* **in mind** mit diesem Ziel vor Augen; **with the sole ~ (of doing)** mit dem einzigen Ziel *or* nur in der Absicht(, zu ...); **he has no ~ in life** er hat kein Ziel im Leben *or* kein Lebensziel; **what's the ~ (of staying here)?** wozu *or* zu welchem Zweck (bleiben wir hier)?; **the ~ of the exercise** der Zweck *or* (*fig also*) Sinn der Übung; **to defeat one's own ~** sich (*dat*) selber schaden, sich (*dat*) ins eigene Fleisch schneiden (*inf*); **that defeats the ~** das macht es sinnlos, das verfehlt seinen Sinn *or* Zweck; **he made it his ~ to ...** er setzte es sich (*dat*) zum Ziel, zu ...
(c) (*obstacle*) Hinderungsgrund *m* ◆ **money/distance (is) no ~** Geld/Entfernung spielt keine Rolle *or* (ist) nebensächlich.
(d) (*Gram*) Objekt *nt* ◆ **direct/indirect ~** direktes/indirektes Objekt, Akkusativ-/Dativobjekt.
(e) (*inf: odd thing*) Ding, Dings (*inf*) *nt*; (*odd person*) Subjekt *nt*, Vogel *m* (*inf*).

▼ **object[2]** [əb'dʒekt] **1** *vi* dagegen sein; (*make objection, protest*) protestieren; (*be against: in discussion etc*) Einwände haben (*to* gegen); (*raise objection*) Einwände erheben; (*disapprove*) Anstoß nehmen (*to* an *+dat*), sich stören (*to* an *+dat*) ◆ **to ~ to sth** (*disapprove*) etw ablehnen *or* mißbilligen; **I don't ~ to that** ich habe nichts dagegen (einzuwenden); **if you don't ~** wenn es (Ihnen) recht ist, wenn Sie nichts dagegen haben; **do you ~ to my smoking?** stört es (Sie), wenn ich rauche?, haben Sie etwas dagegen, wenn ich rauche?; **he ~s to my drinking** er nimmt daran Anstoß *or* er hat etwas dagegen, daß ich trinke; **I ~ to your tone/to people smoking in my living room** ich verbitte mir diesen Ton/ich verbitte mir, daß in meinem Wohnzimmer geraucht wird; **I ~ most strongly to his smoking** ich mißbillige es aufs äußerste, daß er raucht; **I ~ most strongly to what he says/to his argument** ich protestiere energisch gegen seine Behauptung/ich lehne seine Argumentation energisch ab; **I ~ to him bossing me around** ich wehre mich dagegen, daß er mich (so) herumkommandiert; **I ~ to orange curtains with green wallpaper** Vorhänge in Orange mit grünen Tapeten, da protestiere ich!; **she ~s to all that noise** sie stört sich an dem vielen Lärm; **he doesn't ~ to the odd little drink** er hat nichts gegen ein kleines Gläschen ab und zu (einzuwenden); **I ~!** ich protestiere!, ich erhebe Einspruch (*form*); **to ~ to a witness** (*Jur*) einen Zeugen ablehnen.
2 *vt* einwenden.

object: ~ clause *n* Objektsatz *m*; **~ deletion** *n* (*Gram*) Unterdrückung *f* des Objekts.

objection [əb'dʒekʃən] *n* **(a)** (*reason against*) Einwand *m* (*to* gegen) ◆ **to make** *or* **raise an ~** einen Einwand machen *or* erheben (*geh*); **I have no ~ to his going away** ich habe nichts dagegen (einzuwenden), daß er weggeht; **are there any ~s?** irgendwelche Einwände?; **I see no ~ to it** ich sehe nichts, was dagegen spricht; **what are your ~s to it/him?** was haben Sie dagegen/gegen ihn (einzuwenden)?, welche Einwände haben Sie dagegen/gegen ihn?; **~!** (*Jur*) Einspruch!

➤ LANGUAGE IN USE: **object[2]: 1** → 9.2, 12.1, 26.3

(b) (*dislike*) Abneigung *f*; (*disapproval*) Einspruch, Widerspruch *m* ◆ **I have a strong ~ to dogs** ich habe eine starke Abneigung gegen Hunde; **I have no ~ to him** (*as a person*) ich habe nichts gegen ihn; **that's bound to meet with your parents' ~** da erheben deine Eltern bestimmt Einspruch.

objectionable [əb'dʒekʃənəbl] *adj* störend; *conduct* anstößig, nicht einwandfrei; *remark, language* anstößig, unanständig; *smell* unangenehm, übel ◆ **he's a most ~ person** er ist unausstehlich *or* ekelhaft; **he became ~** er wurde unangenehm.

objectionably [əb'dʒekʃənəblɪ] *adv* unangenehm.

objective [əb'dʒektɪv] 1 *adj* (a) (*impartial*) *person, article* objektiv, sachlich. (b) (*real*) objektiv ◆ **~ fact** Tatsache *f*.
2 *n* (a) (*aim*) Ziel *nt*; (*esp Comm*) Zielvorstellung *f*; (*Mil*) Angriffsziel *nt* ◆ **in establishing our ~s** bei unserer Zielsetzung.
(b) (*Opt, Phot*) Objektiv *nt*.

objectively [əb'dʒektɪvlɪ] *adv* (a) (*unemotionally*) objektiv, sachlich. (b) (*in real life etc*) tatsächlich, wirklich.

objectivism [əb'dʒektɪvɪzəm] *n* Objektivismus *m*.

objectivity [ˌɒbdʒek'tɪvɪtɪ] *n* Objektivität *f*.

object lesson *n* (a) (*fig*) Paradebeispiel, Musterbeispiel *nt* (*in, on* für, *gen*). (b) (*Sch*) Anschauungsunterricht *m*.

objector [əb'dʒektə[r]] *n* Gegner(in *f*) *m* (*to gen*).

objet d'art ['ɒbʒeɪ'dɑː] *n* Kunstgegenstand *m*.

objurgate ['ɒbdʒɜːgeɪt] *vt* (*form*) rügen (*geh*), tadeln.

objurgation [ˌɒbdʒɜː'geɪʃən] *n* (*form*) Tadel *m*, Rüge *f*.

oblate[1] ['ɒbleɪt] *adj* (*Math*) abgeplattet.

oblate[2] *n* (*Eccl*) Oblate *m*.

oblation [əʊ'bleɪʃən] *n* (*Eccl*) Opfergabe *f*, Opfer *nt*.

obligate ['ɒblɪgeɪt] *vt* verpflichten (*sb to do sth* jdn, etw zu tun).

obligation [ˌɒblɪ'geɪʃən] *n* Verpflichtung, Pflicht *f* ◆ **to be under an ~ to do sth** verpflichtet sein *or* die Pflicht haben, etw zu tun; **to be under an ~ to sb** jdm verpflichtet sein; **you have placed us all under a great ~** wir sind Ihnen alle sehr verpflichtet; **without ~** (*Comm*) unverbindlich, ohne Obligo (*form*); **with no ~ to buy** ohne Kaufzwang.

obligato [ˌɒblɪ'gɑːtəʊ] 1 *n* (*part*) Obligato *nt*.
2 *adj* obligato.

obligatory [ɒ'blɪgətərɪ] *adj* obligatorisch; *rule* verbindlich; *subject* Pflicht- ◆ **biology is ~** Biologie ist Pflicht; **attendance is ~** Anwesenheit ist vorgeschrieben; **it's ~ to pay taxes** jeder ist steuerpflichtig; **to make it ~ to do sth/for sb to do sth** vorschreiben, daß etw getan wird/daß jd etw tut; **identity cards were made ~** Personalausweise wurden Vorschrift; **with the ~ piper** mit dem obligaten Dudelsackpfeifer.

▼ **oblige** [ə'blaɪdʒ] 1 *vt* (a) (*compel*) zwingen; (*because of duty*) verpflichten (*sb to do sth* jdn, etw zu tun); (*Jur*) vorschreiben (*sb to do sth* jdm, etw zu tun) ◆ **to feel ~d to do sth** sich verpflichtet fühlen, etw zu tun; **I was ~d to go** ich sah mich gezwungen zu gehen; **you are not ~d to do it** Sie sind nicht dazu verpflichtet; **you are not ~d to answer this question** Sie brauchen diese Frage nicht zu beantworten.
(b) (*do a favour to*) einen Gefallen tun (*+dat*), gefällig sein (*+dat*) ◆ **could you ~ me with a light?** wären Sie so gut, mir Feuer zu geben?; **please ~ me by opening a window** würden Sie mir bitte den Gefallen tun und ein Fenster öffnen?; **he ~d us with a song** er gab uns ein Lied zum besten; **would you ~ me by not interrupting** hätten Sie die Güte, mich nicht zu unterbrechen; **you would ~ me by shutting up!** würden Sie gefälligst Ruhe geben!; **anything to ~ a friend** was tut man nicht alles für einen Freund!
▼ (c) **much ~d!** herzlichen Dank!; **I am much ~d to you for this!** ich bin Ihnen dafür sehr verbunden *or* dankbar.
2 *vi* **she is always ready to ~** sie ist immer sehr gefällig *or* hilfsbereit; (*hum*) sie ist niemals abgeneigt; **they called for a song, but no-one ~d** sie verlangten nach einem Lied, aber niemand kam der Aufforderung nach; **anything to ~** stets zu Diensten!; **a prompt reply would ~** (*Comm*) wir bitten um baldige Antwort.

obliging [ə'blaɪdʒɪŋ] *adj* entgegenkommend, gefällig; *personality* zuvorkommend.

obligingly [ə'blaɪdʒɪŋlɪ] *adv* entgegenkommenderweise, freundlicherweise, liebenswürdigerweise.

oblique [ə'bliːk] 1 *adj* (a) *line* schief, schräg, geneigt; *angle* schief; (*Gram*) *case* abhängig ◆ **~ stroke** Schrägstrich *m*.
(b) (*fig*) *look* schief, schräg; *course* schräg; *method, style, reply* indirekt; *hint, reference* indirekt, versteckt ◆ **he achieved his goal by rather ~ means** er erreichte sein Ziel auf Umwegen *or* (*dishonestly*) auf krummen Wegen.
2 *n* Schrägstrich *m* ◆ **and ~ or** und Strich oder.

obliquely [ə'bliːklɪ] *adv* (a) schräg. (b) (*fig*) indirekt.

obliqueness [ə'bliːknɪs] *n* (a) Schiefe, Schräge, Neigung *f*. (b) (*fig: of means*) Indirektheit *f*.

obliterate [ə'blɪtəreɪt] *vt* (*erase, abolish*) auslöschen; *past, memory also* tilgen (*geh*); *city also, (inf) opposite team etc* vernichten; (*hide from sight*) *sun, view* verdecken ◆ **the coffee stain has ~d most of the design/text** der Kaffeefleck hat das Muster/den Text fast ganz unkenntlich/unleserlich gemacht; **a sculpture whose features were ~d by age** eine vom Alter unkenntlich gemachte Skulptur; **by the 19th century this disease had been completely ~d** im 19. Jahrhundert war dann diese Krankheit völlig ausgerottet.

obliteration [əˌblɪtə'reɪʃən] *n see vt* Auslöschen *nt*; Vernichtung *f*; Verdecken *nt*.

oblivion [ə'blɪvɪən] *n* (a) Vergessenheit *f*, Vergessen *nt* ◆ **to sink** *or* **fall into ~** in Vergessenheit geraten, der Vergessenheit anheimfallen (*geh*); **to rescue sb/sth from ~** jdn/etw wieder ins Bewußtsein *or* ans Tageslicht bringen; **he drank himself into ~** er trank bis zur Bewußtlosigkeit.
(b) (*unawareness*) *see* **obliviousness**.

oblivious [ə'blɪvɪəs] *adj* **to be ~ of sth** sich (*dat*) etw nicht bewußt machen, sich (*dat*) einer Sache (*gen*) nicht bewußt sein; **he was quite ~ of his surroundings** er nahm seine Umgebung gar nicht wahr; **~ of his surroundings** ohne Notiz von seiner Umgebung zu nehmen; **they are ~ of** *or* **to the beauty of their surroundings** sie haben für die Schönheit ihrer Umgebung keinen Sinn; **he was totally ~ of what was going on in his marriage** er (be)merkte gar nicht, was in seiner Ehe vor sich ging; **~ of the traffic lights** ohne die Ampel zu bemerken; **~ of the world** weltvergessen.

obliviously [ə'blɪvɪəslɪ] *adv* **to carry on ~** einfach (unbeirrt) weitermachen.

obliviousness [ə'blɪvɪəsnɪs] *n* **because of his ~ of the danger he was in** weil er sich (*dat*) nicht der Gefahr bewußt war, in der er schwebte; **because of his ~ of what was happening** weil er gar nicht bemerkte, was vorging; **a state of blissful ~ to the world** ein Zustand seliger Weltvergessenheit.

oblong ['ɒblɒŋ] 1 *adj* rechteckig.
2 *n* Rechteck *nt*.

obloquy ['ɒbləkwɪ] *n* (*liter*) (a) (*blame, abuse*) Schmähung (*liter*), Beschimpfung *f*. (b) (*disgrace*) Schande, Schmach *f*.

obnoxious [ɒb'nɒkʃəs] *adj* widerlich, widerwärtig; *person also, behaviour* unausstehlich ◆ **an ~ person** ein Ekel *nt* (*inf*); **don't be so ~ to her** sei nicht so gemein *or* fies (*inf*) zu ihr.

obnoxiously [ɒb'nɒkʃəslɪ] *adv see adj*.

obnoxiousness [ɒb'nɒkʃəsnɪs] *n see adj* Widerlichkeit, Widerwärtigkeit *f*; Unausstehlichkeit *f*.

oboe ['əʊbəʊ] *n* Oboe *f*.

oboist ['əʊbəʊɪst] *n* Oboist(in *f*) *m*.

obscene [əb'siːn] *adj* obszön; *word, picture, book also* unzüchtig; *language, joke also* zotig; *gesture, posture, thought also* schamlos, unzüchtig; (*non-sexually, repulsive*) ekelerregend; *prices, demands* unverschämt ◆ **this colour scheme is positively ~** diese Farbzusammenstellung widert mich an *or* ist widerlich.

obscenely [əb'siːnlɪ] *adv* obszön; (*repulsively*) ekelerregend.

obscenity [əb'senɪtɪ] *n* Obszönität *f* ◆ **the ~ of these crimes** diese ekelerregenden Verbrechen; **he used an ~** er benutzte *or* gebrauchte einen ordinären Ausdruck.

obscurantism [ˌɒbskjʊə'ræntɪzəm] *n* Obskurantismus *m*, Aufklärungsfeindlichkeit *f*.

obscurantist [ˌɒbskjʊə'ræntɪst] *n* Obskurant *m*, Feind *m* der Aufklärung.

obscure [əb'skjʊə[r]] 1 *adj* (*+er*) (a) (*hard to understand*) dunkel; *style* unklar, undurchsichtig; *argument* verworren; *book, poet, poem* schwer verständlich.
(b) (*indistinct*) *feeling, memory* dunkel, undeutlich, unklar ◆ **for some ~ reason** aus einem unerfindlichen Grund.
(c) (*unknown, little known, humble*) obskur; *poet, village also* unbekannt; *beginnings* (*humble*) unbedeutend; (*not known also*) dunkel; *life* wenig beachtenswert ◆ **of ~ birth** von unbekannter Herkunft; **he holds some ~ post in the Civil Service** er hat so ein obskures Pöstchen im Staatsdienst.
(d) (*rare: dark*) düster, finster.
2 *vt* (a) (*hide*) *sun, view* verdecken ◆ **the tree ~d the bay from our view** der Baum nahm uns (*dat*) die Sicht auf die Bucht.
(b) (*confuse*) verworren *or* unklar machen; *mind* verwirren.

obscurely [əb'skjʊəlɪ] *adv* (a) *written, presented, argued, remember* undeutlich, unklar. (b) **a movement which began ~ in the depths of Russia** eine Bewegung mit obskuren Anfängen im tiefsten Rußland. (c) *lit* schwach.

obscurity [əb'skjʊərɪtɪ] *n* (a) *no pl* (*of a wood, night*) Dunkelheit, Finsternis *f*, Dunkel *nt*.
(b) (*of style, ideas, argument*) Unklarheit, Unverständlichkeit, Verworrenheit *f* ◆ **to lapse into ~** verworren *or* unklar werden; **he threw some light on the obscurities of the text** er erhellte einige der unklaren Textstellen.
(c) *no pl* (*of birth, origins*) Dunkel *nt* ◆ **to live in ~** zurückgezogen leben; **to rise from ~** aus dem Nichts auftauchen; **in spite of the ~ of his origins** trotz seiner unbekannten Herkunft; **to sink into ~** in Vergessenheit geraten.

obsequies ['ɒbsɪkwɪz] *npl* (*form*) Beerdigungsfeier *f*, Leichenbegängnis *nt* (*liter*).

obsequious *adj*, **~ly** *adv* [əb'siːkwɪəs, -lɪ] unterwürfig, servil (*geh*) (*to(wards)* gegen, gegenüber).

obsequiousness [əb'siːkwɪəsnɪs] *n* Unterwürfigkeit, Servilität (*geh*) *f*.

observable [əb'zɜːvəbl] *adj* sichtbar, erkennbar ◆ **as is ~ in rabbits** wie bei Kaninchen zu beobachten ist *or* beobachtet wird; **a welcome improvement has recently become ~** in letzter Zeit zeichnet sich eine willkommene Verbesserung ab; **there has been no ~ change in his condition today** es wurde heute keine Veränderung seines Befindens beobachtet.

observance [əb'zɜːvəns] *n* (a) (*of law*) Befolgung, Beachtung *f*, Beachten *nt*.
(b) (*Eccl*) (*keeping of rites etc*) Einhalten *nt*, Einhaltung *f*, Beachten *nt*; (*celebration*) Kirchenfest *nt*; (*in a convent etc*) (Ordens)regel, Observanz *f* ◆ **~ of the Sabbath** Einhaltung *f* des Sabbats *or* (*non-Jewish*) des Sonntagsgebots; **religious ~s** religiöse *or* (*Christian also*) kirchliche Feste.

observant [əb'zɜːvənt] *adj* (a) (*watchful*) *person* aufmerksam, wach(sam), achtsam ◆ **that's very ~ of you** das hast du aber gut bemerkt; **if you'd been a little more ~** wenn du etwas besser aufgepaßt hättest.
(b) (*strict in obeying rules*) **you should be a little more ~ of the law** Sie sollten sich etwas mehr an das Gesetz halten.

observantly [əb'zɜːvəntlɪ] *adv* aufmerksam ◆ **... which he very ~ spotted ...**, wie er sehr gut bemerkt hat.

observation [ˌɒbzə'veɪʃən] *n* (a) Beobachtung *f*; (*act also*) Beobachten *nt*

➤ LANGUAGE IN USE: **oblige: 1c → 4**

◆ **to keep sb/sth under ~** jdn/etw unter Beobachtung halten; (*by police*) jdn/etw überwachen *or* observieren (*form*); **~ of nature** Naturbeobachtung *f*; **to take an ~** (*Naut*) das Besteck nehmen; **powers of ~** Beobachtungsgabe *f*; **he's in hospital for ~** er ist zur Beobachtung im Krankenhaus; **to escape sb's ~** (von jdm) unbemerkt bleiben, jdm entgehen.
(b) (*of rules, Sabbath*) Einhalten *nt*.
(c) (*remark*) Bemerkung, Äußerung *f* ◆ **~s on Kant** Betrachtungen über *or* zu Kant; **his ~s on the experiment** seine Versuchserläuterungen.

observational [ˌɒbzəˈveɪʃənəl] *adj* empirisch, auf Grund von Beobachtungen gewonnen.

observation: ~ car *n* (*US Rail*) Aussichtswagen, Panoramawagen *m*; **~ lounge** *n* Aussichtsrestaurant *nt*; **~ post** *n* Beobachtungsposten *m*; **~ tower** *n* Aussichtsturm *m*; **~ ward** *n* Beobachtungsstation *f*.

observatory [əbˈzɜːvətrɪ] *n* Observatorium *nt*, Sternwarte *f*; (*Met*) Observatorium *nt*, Wetterwarte *f*.

▼ **observe** [əbˈzɜːv] **1** *vt* **(a)** (*see, notice*) beobachten, bemerken; *difference, change also* wahrnehmen ◆ **did you actually ~ him do it?** haben Sie ihn wirklich dabei beobachtet?; **the thief was ~d to ...** der Dieb wurde dabei beobachtet, wie er ...
(b) (*watch carefully, study*) beobachten; (*by police*) überwachen.
▼ **(c)** (*remark*) bemerken, feststellen, äußern.
(d) (*obey*) achten auf (+*acc*); *rule, custom, ceasefire, Sabbath* einhalten; *anniversary etc* begehen, feiern ◆ **to ~ a minute's silence** eine Schweigeminute einlegen; **failure to ~ the law** ein Verstoß gegen das Gesetz.
2 *vi* **(a)** (*watch*) zusehen; (*act as an observer*) beobachten.
(b) (*remark*) bemerken, feststellen (*on* zu, über +*acc*) ◆ **you were about to ~ ...?** Sie wollten gerade sagen ...?

observer [əbˈzɜːvəʳ] *n* (*watcher*) Zuschauer(in *f*) *m*; (*Mil, Aviat, Pol*) Beobachter *m*.

obsess [əbˈses] *vt* **to be ~ed by** *or* **with sb/sth** von jdm/etw besessen sein; **sth ~es sb** jd ist von etw besessen; **his one ~ing thought** der ihn ständig verfolgende Gedanke; **don't become ~ed by it** laß das nicht zum Zwang *or* zur Manie werden.

obsession [əbˈseʃən] *n* **(a)** (*fixed idea*) fixe Idee, Manie *f*; (*fear etc*) Zwangsvorstellung, Obsession (*spec*) *f* ◆ **the cat was an ~ with her** die Katze war ihre ganze Leidenschaft; **it's an ~ with him** das ist eine fixe Idee von ihm; (*hobby etc*) er ist davon besessen; **watching TV is an ~ with him** Fernsehen ist bei ihm zur Sucht geworden.
(b) (*state*) Besessenheit (*with* von), Monomanie *f* ◆ **this ~ with order/tidiness/accuracy** dieser Ordnungs-/Aufräumungs-/Genauigkeitswahn *m*; **an unnatural ~ with detail** eine (ganz) unnatürliche Detailbesessenheit; **because of his ~ with her** weil er ihr gänzlich verfallen ist/war.

obsessive [əbˈsesɪv] *adj* zwanghaft, obsessiv (*spec*) ◆ **to become ~** zum Zwang *or* zur Manie werden; **an ~ thought/memory** ein Gedanke, der/eine Erinnerung, die einen nicht losläßt; **an ~ desire for wealth** eine Sucht nach Reichtum; **he is an ~ reader** er liest wie besessen, er hat die Lesewut (*inf*); **~ neurosis** (*Psych*) Zwangsneurose *f*.

obsessively [əbˈsesɪvlɪ] *adv* wie besessen ◆ **she is ~ preoccupied with cleanliness** sie huldigt einem Sauberkeitswahn.

obsolescence [ˌɒbsəˈlesns] *n* Veralten *nt*; *see* **planned**.

obsolescent [ˌɒbsəˈlesnt] *adj* allmählich außer Gebrauch kommend ◆ **to be ~** anfangen zu veralten; (*machine, process etc*) technisch (fast) überholt sein.

obsolete [ˈɒbsəliːt] *adj* veraltet, überholt, obsolet (*geh*) ◆ **to become ~** veralten.

obstacle [ˈɒbstəkl] *n* (*lit, fig*) Hindernis *nt* ◆ **~ course** Hindernisstrecke *f*; **getting from the desk to the door is a real ~ course** der Weg vom Schreibtisch zur Tür ist mit Hindernissen übersät; **~ race** (*Sport, fig*) Hindernisrennen *nt*; **to be an ~ to sb/sth** jdm/einer Sache im Weg(e) stehen, jdn/etw (be)hindern; **if they put any ~ in the way of our plans** wenn man uns Steine in den Weg legt *or* unsere Pläne behindert; **that's no ~ to our doing it** das wird uns nicht daran hindern; **all the ~s to progress/peace** *etc* alles, was den Fortschritt/Frieden *etc* behindert.

obstetric(al) [ɒbˈstetrɪk(əl)] *adj* (*Med*) *techniques etc* Geburtshilfe- ◆ **~ ward** Entbindungs- *or* Wöchnerinnenstation *f*; **~ clinic** Entbindungsheim *nt*, Geburtsklinik *f*.

obstetrician [ˌɒbstəˈtrɪʃən] *n* Geburtshelfer(in *f*) *m*.

obstetrics [ɒbˈstetrɪks] *n sing* Geburtshilfe, Obstetrik (*spec*) *f*; (*ward*) Wöchnerinnenstation *f*.

obstinacy [ˈɒbstɪnəsɪ] *n* **(a)** (*of person*) Hartnäckigkeit *f*, Starrsinn *m* ◆ **his ~ in doing sth** die Hartnäckigkeit, mit der er etw tut. **(b)** (*of illness*) Hartnäckigkeit *f*; (*of resistance also*) Verbissenheit *f*.

obstinate [ˈɒbstɪnɪt] *adj* **(a)** *person* hartnäckig, starrsinnig; *stain* hartnäckig; *nail etc* widerspenstig ◆ **to remain ~** stur bleiben; **he was ~ in insisting that ...** er bestand stur *or* hartnäckig darauf, daß ... **(b)** *resistance, illness* hartnäckig.

obstinately [ˈɒbstɪnɪtlɪ] *adv* hartnäckig, stur.

obstreperous [əbˈstrepərəs] *adj* aufmüpfig (*inf*); *child* aufsässig ◆ **the drunk became ~** der Betrunkene fing an zu randalieren; **it's not a real complaint, he's just being ~** es ist keine echte Beschwerde, er will nur Schwierigkeiten machen.

obstreperously [əbˈstrepərəslɪ] *adv see adj*.

obstreperousness [əbˈstrepərəsnɪs] *n see adj* Aufmüpfigkeit *f*, Aufsässigkeit *f*.

obstruct [əbˈstrʌkt] **1** *vt* **(a)** (*block*) blockieren; *passage, road also, view* versperren; (*Med*) *artery, pipe also* verstopfen ◆ **you're ~ing my view** Sie nehmen *or* versperren mir die Sicht.
(b) (*hinder*) (be)hindern; *navigation* behindern; *traffic, progress also* aufhalten, hemmen; (*Sport*) behindern; (*in possession of ball*) sperren ◆ **to ~ a bill** (*Parl*) einen Gesetzentwurf blockieren; **to ~ the course of justice** die Rechtsfindung behindern.
2 *vi* (*be obstructionist*) obstruieren, Obstruktion treiben; (*Sport*) sperren.

obstruction [əbˈstrʌkʃən] *n* **(a)** *see vt* (*a*) Blockierung *f*; (*of view*) Versperren *nt*; Verstopfung *f*.
(b) *see vt* (*b*) Behinderung *f*; Hemmung *f*; Sperren *nt* ◆ **to cause an ~** den Verkehr behindern.
(c) (*obstacle*) Hindernis, Hemmnis (*esp fig*) *nt* ◆ **there is an ~ in the pipe** das Rohr ist blockiert *or* verstopft; **all ~s to progress** alles, was den Fortschritt aufhält *or* hemmt.
(d) (*Pol*) Obstruktion, Behinderung *f*.

obstructionism [əbˈstrʌkʃənɪzəm] *n* Obstruktionspolitik *f*.

obstructionist [əbˈstrʌkʃənɪst] *n* Obstruktionspolitiker *m*.

obstructive [əbˈstrʌktɪv] *adj* obstruktiv (*esp Pol*), behindernd ◆ **~ politician** Obstruktionspolitiker(in *f*) *m*; **to be ~** (*person*) Schwierigkeiten machen, sich querstellen (*inf*); **to be ~ to progress** dem Fortschritt hinderlich sein.

obtain [əbˈteɪn] **1** *vt* erhalten, bekommen; *result, votes also* erzielen; *knowledge* erwerben ◆ **to ~ sth by hard work** etw durch harte Arbeit erreichen; *possession* sich (*dat*) etw mühsam erarbeiten; **can food be ~ed from seawater?** können aus Meer(es)wasser Nahrungsmittel gewonnen werden?; **to ~ sth for sb** jdm etw be- *or* verschaffen.
2 *vi* (*form*) gelten; (*rules also*) in Kraft sein; (*customs*) bestehen, herrschen.

obtainable [əbˈteɪnəbl] *adj* erhältlich.

obtrude [əbˈtruːd] **1** *vt* **(a) to ~ oneself (up)on others** sich anderen aufdrängen; **to ~ one's opinion(s) (up)on sb** jdm seine Meinung aufzwingen.
(b) (*push out*) hervorstrecken, hervorschieben.
2 *vi* **(a)** (*intrude*) sich aufdrängen ◆ **not to ~ upon sb's private grief** jdn nicht in seinem Schmerz belästigen.
(b) (*protrude*) (her)vorstehen; (*fig*) hervortreten.

obtrusion [əbˈtruːʒən] *n* **(a)** Aufdrängen *nt* ◆ **because of this ~ of himself/his ideas upon others** weil er sich/seine Ideen anderen aufdrängen will. **(b)** (*pushing out*) Hervorstrecken *nt*. **(c)** (*sticking out*) Herausragen *nt*.

obtrusive [əbˈtruːsɪv] *adj person* aufdringlich; *smell also* penetrant; *building, furniture* zu auffällig.

obtrusively [əbˈtruːsɪvlɪ] *adv see adj*.

obtrusiveness [əbˈtruːsɪvnɪs] *n see adj* Aufdringlichkeit *f*; Penetranz *f*; Auffälligkeit *f*.

obtuse [əbˈtjuːs] *adj* **(a)** (*Geometry*) stumpf. **(b)** *person* begriffsstutzig, beschränkt ◆ **are you just being ~?** tust du nur so beschränkt?

obtuseness [əbˈtjuːsnɪs] *n* Begriffsstutzigkeit, Beschränktheit *f*.

obverse [ˈɒbvɜːs] **1** *adj side* Vorder-.
2 *n* **(a)** (*of coin*) Vorderseite *f*. **(b)** (*of statement, truth*) andere Seite, Kehrseite *f*.

obviate [ˈɒbvɪeɪt] *vt* vermeiden, umgehen; *objection, need* vorbeugen (+*dat*).

obvious [ˈɒbvɪəs] *adj* offensichtlich, deutlich; (*visually also*) augenfällig; (*not subtle*) plump; *proof* klar, eindeutig; *difference, fact* eindeutig, offensichtlich, offenkundig; *statement* naheliegend, selbstverständlich; *reason* (leicht) ersichtlich; *dislike, reluctance, surprise* sichtlich ◆ **an ~ truth** eine offenkundige Tatsache; **because of the ~ truth of what he maintains** da es so eindeutig *or* offensichtlich wahr ist, was er sagt; **that's the ~ translation/solution** das ist die naheliegendste Übersetzung/Lösung; **he was the ~ choice** es lag nahe, ihn zu wählen; **it was ~ he didn't want to come** er wollte offensichtlich nicht kommen; **it's quite ~ he doesn't understand** man merkt doch (sofort) *or* es ist doch klar, daß er nicht versteht; **to make sth a little more ~** etw etwas deutlicher *or* eindeutiger machen; **there's no need to make it so ~** man braucht das (doch) nicht so deutlich werden zu lassen; **do I have to make it even more ~?** muß ich denn noch deutlicher werden?; **we must not be too ~ about it** wir dürfen es nicht zu auffällig machen; **I would have thought that was perfectly ~** das liegt doch auf der Hand; (*noticeable*) das springt doch ins Auge; **with the ~ exception of ...** natürlich mit Ausnahme von ...; **subtle? he's the most ~ person I know** raffiniert? ich kenne niemanden, der einfacher zu durchschauen wäre!; **even if I am stating the ~** selbst wenn ich hier etwas längst Bekanntes sage; **he has a gift for stating the ~** der merkt aber auch alles! (*inf*); **don't just state the ~, try to be original** sagen/schreiben Sie nicht, was sich von selbst versteht, sondern bemühen Sie sich um Originalität; **what's the ~ thing to do?** was ist das Naheliegendste?, was bietet sich am ehesten an?

obviously [ˈɒbvɪəslɪ] *adv* offensichtlich, offenbar; (*noticeably*) (offen)sichtlich ◆ **he's ~ French** er ist eindeutig ein Franzose; **~!** natürlich!, selbstverständlich!; **is he there? — well, ~ not** ist er da? — offensichtlich nicht; **~ he's not going to like it** das wird ihm natürlich nicht gefallen; **he's ~ not going to get the job** er bekommt die Stelle nicht, das ist ja klar (*inf*).

obviousness [ˈɒbvɪəsnɪs] *n* Offensichtlichkeit, Deutlichkeit *f* ◆ **amused by the ~ of his approach** belustigt über die Eindeutigkeit *or* Plumpheit seines Annäherungsversuchs.

OC *n abbr of* **Officer Commanding** (*Mil*) Oberbefehlshaber *m* ◆ **who's ~ paper supply in the office?** (*sl*) wer ist hier im Büro der Papier-UvD (*hum*) *or* Papierhengst? (*sl*).

ocarina [ˌɒkəˈriːnə] *n* Okarina *f*.

Occam's razor [ˈɒkəmzˈreɪzəʳ] *n* **to apply ~ (to sth)** etw komprimieren, etw auf das Wesentliche beschränken.

occasion [əˈkeɪʒən] **1** *n* **(a)** (*point in time*) Gelegenheit *f*, Anlaß *m* ◆ **on that ~**

➤ LANGUAGE IN USE: **observe: 1c → 26.2**

damals, bei *or* zu jener Gelegenheit *or* jenem Anlaß *(geh)*; **on another ~** ein anderes Mal, bei einer anderen Gelegenheit *etc*; **on several ~s** mehrmals, bei *or* zu mehreren Gelegenheiten *etc*; **(on) the first ~** beim ersten Mal, das erste Mal; **on ~** gelegentlich; *(if need be)* wenn nötig; **it does not befit the ~** es ist unpassend für diesen *or* zu diesem Anlaß; **to rise to the ~** sich der Lage gewachsen zeigen.

(b) *(special time)* Ereignis *nt* ◆ **~s of state** Staatsanlässe *pl*; **on the ~ of his birthday** anläßlich *or* aus Anlaß seines Geburtstages *(geh)*; **one's 21st birthday should be something of an ~** ein 21. Geburtstag sollte schon ein besonderes Ereignis sein.

(c) *(opportunity)* Gelegenheit, Möglichkeit *f* ◆ **I never had the ~ to congratulate him** es bot sich mir keine *or* nicht die Gelegenheit *or* ich hatte nicht die Möglichkeit, ihm zu gratulieren; **I would like to take this ~ to ...** *(form)* ich möchte diese Gelegenheit ergreifen, um ...

(d) *(reason)* Grund, Anlaß *m*, Veranlassung *f* ◆ **should the ~ arise** sollte es nötig sein *or* werden; **to give ~ to sth** *(form)* zu etw Anlaß geben; **if you have ~ to ...** sollten Sie Veranlassung haben, zu ...; **not an ~ for merriment** kein Grund zur Freude.

[2] *vt (form)* verursachen, Anlaß geben zu, zeitigen *(geh)* ◆ **to ~ sb to do sth** jdn dazu veranlassen, etw zu tun.

occasional [ə'keɪʒənl] *adj* **(a) he likes an** *or* **the ~ cigar** er raucht hin und wieder ganz gerne *or* gelegentlich ganz gern eine Zigarre.

(b) *(designed for special event) poem, music* zu der Gelegenheit *or* dem Anlaß verfaßt/komponiert ◆ **~ table** kleiner Wohnzimmertisch.

occasionally [ə'keɪʒənəlɪ] *adv* gelegentlich, hin und wieder, zuweilen *(geh)* ◆ **very ~** sehr selten, nicht sehr oft.

occident ['ɒksɪdənt] *n (liter)* Abendland *nt*, Okzident *m (geh)* ◆ **the O~** *(Pol)* der Westen.

occidental [,ɒksɪ'dentəl] [1] *adj (liter)* abendländisch.

[2] *n (rare)* Abendländer(in *f*) *m*.

occipital [ɒk'sɪpɪtəl] *adj (spec)* des Hinterkopfs.

occiput ['ɒksɪpʌt] *n (spec)* Hinterkopf *m*.

occlude [ɒ'klu:d] *(spec)* [1] *vt (Anat, Med) pores, artery* verschließen, verstopfen, okkludieren *(spec)*; *(Chem) gas* adsorbieren ◆ **~d front** *(Met)* Okklusion *f*.

[2] *vi (Dentistry)* eine normale Bißstellung haben.

occlusion [ɒ'klu:ʒən] *n (spec) (Med: of artery)* Verschluß *m*, Okklusion *f (spec)*; *(Dentistry)* Biß *m*, normale Bißstellung; *(Phon)* Verschluß *m*; *(Chem)* Adsorption *f*; *(Met)* Okklusion *f*.

occult [ɒ'kʌlt] [1] *adj* okkult; *(of occultism)* okkultistisch; *(secret)* geheimnisvoll.

[2] *n* Okkulte(s) *nt*.

occultism ['ɒkəltɪzəm] *n* Okkultismus *m*.

occultist [ɒ'kʌltɪst] *n* Okkultist(in *f*) *m*.

occupancy ['ɒkjʊpənsɪ] *n* Bewohnen *nt*; *(period)* Wohndauer *f* ◆ **a change of ~** ein Besitzerwechsel *m*; *(of rented property)* ein Mieterwechsel *m*; **multiple ~** Mehrfachbelegung *f* von Wohnraum; **levels of hotel ~** Übernachtungsziffern *pl*.

occupant ['ɒkjʊpənt] *n (of house)* Bewohner(in *f*) *m*; *(of post)* Inhaber(in *f*) *m*; *(of car)* Insasse *m*.

occupation [,ɒkjʊ'peɪʃən] [1] *n* **(a)** *(employment)* Beruf *m*, Tätigkeit *f* ◆ **what is his ~?** was ist er von Beruf?, welche Tätigkeit übt er aus?; **he is a joiner by ~** er ist Tischler von Beruf.

(b) *(pastime)* Beschäftigung, Betätigung, Tätigkeit *f*.

(c) *(Mil)* Okkupation *f*; *(act also)* Besetzung *f* (of von); *(state also)* Besatzung *f* (of in *+dat*) ◆ **army of ~** Besatzungsarmee *f*.

(d) *(of house etc)* Besetzung *f* ◆ **to be in ~ of a house** ein Haus bewohnen; **ready for ~** bezugsfertig, schlüsselfertig; **we found them already in ~** wir sahen, daß sie schon eingezogen waren.

[2] *adj attr troops* Besatzungs-, Okkupations-.

occupational [,ɒkjʊ'peɪʃənl] *adj* Berufs-, beruflich ◆ **~ accident** Berufsunfall *m*; **~ disease** Berufskrankheit *f*; **~ guidance** Berufsberatung *f*; **~ hazard** Berufsrisiko *nt*; **~ pension scheme** betriebliche Altersversorgung; **~ risk** *see* **~ hazard**; **~ therapy** Beschäftigungstherapie *f*; **~ therapist** Beschäftigungstherapeut(in *f*) *m*.

occupier ['ɒkjʊpaɪə^r] *n (of house, land)* Bewohner(in *f*) *m*; *(of post)* Inhaber(in *f*) *m*.

occupy ['ɒkjʊpaɪ] *vt* **(a)** *house* bewohnen; *seat, room* belegen, besetzen; *hotel room* belegen ◆ **is this seat occupied?** ist dieser Platz belegt?; **you ~ a special place in my memories** du hast einen besonderen Platz in meinem Herzen (inne).

(b) *(Mil etc)* besetzen; *country also* okkupieren.

(c) *post, position* innehaben, bekleiden *(geh)*.

(d) *(take up)* beanspruchen; *space also* einnehmen; *time also* in Anspruch nehmen; *(help pass)* ausfüllen; *attention also* in Anspruch nehmen ◆ **can't you find some better way of ~ing your time?** kannst du mit deiner Zeit nicht etwas Besseres anfangen?

(e) *(busy)* beschäftigen ◆ **to be occupied (with)** beschäftigt sein (mit); **to ~ oneself** sich beschäftigen; **to keep sb occupied** jdn beschäftigen; **that'll keep him occupied** dann hat er was zu tun *or* ist er beschäftigt; **he kept his mind occupied** er beschäftigte sich geistig; **a thought which has been ~ing my mind** ein Gedanke, der mich beschäftigt.

occur [ə'kɜ:^r] *vi* **(a)** *(take place) (event)* geschehen, sich ereignen, vorkommen; *(difficulty)* sich ergeben; *(change)* stattfinden ◆ **that doesn't ~ very often** das kommt nicht oft vor, das gibt es nicht oft; **don't let it ~ again** lassen Sie das nicht wieder vorkommen, daß das nicht wieder passiert!; **should the case ~** sollte der Fall eintreten; **if the opportunity ~s** wenn sich die Gelegenheit bietet *or* ergibt.

(b) *(be found: disease)* vorkommen.

(c) *(come to mind)* einfallen, in den Sinn kommen *(geh)* *(to sb* jdm) ◆ **if it ~s to you that he is wrong** falls es Ihnen so vorkommt, als habe er sich geirrt; **it ~s to me that ...** ich habe den Eindruck, daß ...; **the idea just ~red to me** es ist mir gerade eingefallen; **it never ~red to me** darauf bin ich noch nie gekommen; **it didn't even ~ to him to ask** er kam erst gar nicht auf den Gedanken, zu fragen; **did it ever ~ to you to apologize?** hast du eigentlich je daran gedacht, dich zu entschuldigen?

occurrence [ə'kʌrəns] *n* **(a)** *(event)* Ereignis, Begebenheit *f*. **(b)** *(presence, taking place)* Auftreten *nt*; *(of minerals)* Vorkommen *nt* ◆ **the ~ of typhoons in Dorset is rare** Taifune kommen in Dorset selten vor; **further ~s of this nature must be avoided** weitere Vorkommnisse dieser Art müssen vermieden werden.

ocean ['əʊʃən] *n* **(a)** Ozean *m*, Meer *nt*. **(b) an ~ of flowers** ein Blumenmeer *nt*; **~s of** *(inf)* jede Menge *(inf)*, massenhaft.

ocean: ~ bed *n* Meeresboden *or* -grund *m*; **~ chart** *n* Seekarte *f*; **~ climate** *n* Meeresklima *nt*, maritimes Klima; **~-going** *adj* hochseetauglich; **~-going tug** Hochseeschlepper *m*.

Oceania [,əʊʃɪ'eɪnɪə] *n* Ozeanien *nt*.

Oceanian [,əʊʃɪ'eɪnɪən] [1] *adj* ozeanisch.

[2] *n* Ozeanier(in *f*) *m*.

oceanic [,əʊʃɪ'ænɪk] *adj* Meeres-; *(fig)* riesenhaft.

ocean liner *n* Ozeandampfer *m*.

oceanographer [,əʊʃə'nɒgrəfə^r] *n* Ozeanograph(in *f*), Meereskundler(in *f*) *m*.

oceanography [,əʊʃə'nɒgrəfɪ] *n* Ozeanographie, Meereskunde *f*.

ocean: O~ State *n* **the O~ State** *(US)* Rhode Island *nt*; **~ voyage** *n* Schiffsreise, Seereise *f*.

ocelot ['ɒsɪlɒt] *n* Ozelot *m*.

och [ɒx] *interj (Scot)* ach was, ach wo ◆ **~ aye** ach ja.

ochre, (US) ocher ['əʊkə^r] [1] *n* Ocker *m or nt* ◆ **red ~** roter *or* rotes Ocker; **yellow ~** *(substance)* Ocker *m or nt*; *(colour)* Ocker(gelb *nt*) *m or nt*.

[2] *adj* ockerfarben.

o'clock [ə'klɒk] *adv* **(a) at 5 ~** um 5 Uhr; **it is 5 ~** es ist 5 Uhr; **what ~ is it?** *(obs)* was ist die Uhr? **(b) aircraft approaching at 5 ~** Flugzeug aus Südsüdost.

OCR *abbr of* **optical character reader; optical character recognition** ◆ **~ font** OCR-Schrift *f*.

Oct *abbr of* **October** Okt.

octagon ['ɒktəgən] *n* Achteck, Oktogon, Oktagon *nt*.

octagonal [ɒk'tægənl] *adj* achteckig, oktogonal.

octahedron [,ɒktə'hi:drən] *n* Oktaeder, Achtflächner *m*.

octane ['ɒkteɪn] *n* Oktan *nt* ◆ **high-~ petrol** Benzin mit hoher Oktanzahl; **~ number, ~ rating** Oktanzahl *f*.

octave ['ɒktɪv] *n* **(a)** *(Mus)* Oktave *f*. **(b)** *(of sonnet)* Oktett *nt*.

octavo [ɒk'teɪvəʊ] *n* Oktav(format) *nt*; *(also* **~ volume**) Oktavband *m*.

octet [ɒk'tet] *n (Mus, Poet)* Oktett *nt*.

October [ɒk'təʊbə^r] *n* Oktober *m* ◆ **the ~ Revolution** die Oktoberrevolution; *see also* **September**.

octogenarian [,ɒktəʊdʒɪ'neərɪən] [1] *n* Achtziger(in *f*) *m*, Achtzigjährige(r) *mf*.

[2] *adj* achtzigjährig.

octopus ['ɒktəpəs] *n* Tintenfisch *m*, Krake *f*.

ocular ['ɒkjʊlə^r] *adj (form)* Augen-.

oculist ['ɒkjʊlɪst] *n* Augenspezialist(in *f*) *m*.

OD *(sl)* [1] *n* Überdosis *f*.

[2] *vi* eine Überdosis nehmen ◆ **to ~ on heroin** eine Überdosis Heroin nehmen.

odalisque ['əʊdəlɪsk] *n* Odaliske *f*.

odd [ɒd] *adj (+er)* **(a)** *(peculiar)* merkwürdig, seltsam, sonderbar; *person, thing, idea also* eigenartig, absonderlich ◆ **how ~ that we should meet him** (wie) eigenartig *etc*, daß wir ihn trafen; **the ~ thing about it is that ...** das Merkwürdige *etc* daran ist, daß ...; **he's got some ~ ways** er hat eine schrullige *or* verschrobene Art.

(b) *number* ungerade.

(c) *(one of a pair or a set) shoe, glove* einzeln ◆ **he/she is (the) ~ man** *or* **one out** er/sie ist übrig *or* überzählig *or* das fünfte Rad am Wagen; *(in character)* er/sie steht (immer) abseits *or* ist ein Außenseiter/eine Außenseiterin; **in each group underline the word/picture which is the ~ man** *or* **one out** unterstreichen Sie in jeder Gruppe das nicht dazugehörige Wort/Bild.

(d) *(about)* **600 ~ marks** so um die 600 Mark, ungefähr *or* etwa 600 Mark.

(e) *(surplus, extra)* übrig, restlich, überzählig ◆ **the ~ one left over** der/die/das Überzählige.

(f) *(not regular or specific) moments, times* zeitweilig; *(Comm) size* ausgefallen ◆ **any ~ piece of wood** irgendein Stück(chen) Holz; **at ~ moments** *or* **times** ab und zu; **at ~ moments during the day** zwischendurch; **~ job** (gelegentlich) anfallende Arbeit; **he does all the ~ jobs** er macht alles, was an Arbeit anfällt; **~ job man** Mädchen *nt* für alles.

oddball ['ɒdbɔ:l] *(inf)* [1] *n* Spinner *m*; *(more harmless)* komischer Kauz; *(less harmless, weirdo)* Verrückte(r) *mf*.

[2] *adj ideas, friends* komisch.

oddbod ['ɒdbɒd] *n (inf)* komischer Kauz.

oddity ['ɒdɪtɪ] *n* **(a)** (*strangeness: of person*) Wunderlichkeit, Absonderlichkeit, Eigenartigkeit *f*; (*of thing*) Ausgefallenheit *f*. **(b)** (*odd person*) komischer Kauz *or* Vogel; (*who doesn't fit*) Kuriosität *f*; (*thing*) Kuriosität *f*.

oddly ['ɒdlɪ] *adv speak, behave* eigenartig, sonderbar, merkwürdig ◆ **I find her ~ attractive** ich finde sie auf (eine) seltsame Art anziehend; **they are ~ similar** sie sind sich seltsam *or* merkwürdig ähnlich; **~ enough she was at home** merkwürdigerweise *or* seltsamerweise war sie zu Hause; **~ enough you are right** Sie werden überrascht sein, aber das stimmt.

oddment ['ɒdmənt] *n usu pl* Restposten *m*; (*of cloth also*) Rest *m*; (*single piece also*) Einzelstück *nt*.

oddness ['ɒdnɪs] *n* Merkwürdigkeit, Seltsamkeit *f*.

odds [ɒdz] *npl* **(a)** (*Betting*) Gewinnquote *f*; (*Horseracing also*) Odds *pl* (*spec*); (*of bookmaker also*) (feste) Kurse *pl* ◆ **the ~ are 6 to 1** die Chancen stehen 6 zu 1 (*written*: 6:1); **long/short ~** geringe/hohe Gewinnchancen; **he won at long ~** er hat mit einer hohen Gewinnquote gewonnen; **fixed ~** feste Kurse; **to lay** *or* **give ~ of 2 to 1 (against/in favour of sb)** den Kurs mit 2 zu 1 (*written*: 2:1) (gegen/für jdn) angeben; **I'll lay ~ (of 3 to 1) that ...** (*fig*) ich wette (3 gegen 1), daß ...
(b) (*chances for or against*) Chance(n *pl*) *f* ◆ **the ~ were against us** alles sprach gegen uns; **in spite of the tremendous ~ against him ...** obwohl alles so völlig gegen ihn sprach *or* war ...; **the ~ were in our favour** alles sprach für uns; **against all the ~ he won** wider Erwarten *or* entgegen allen Erwartungen gewann er; **what are the ~ on/against ...?** wie sind *or* stehen die Chancen, daß .../daß ... nicht?; **to fight against heavy/overwhelming ~** (*Mil*) gegen eine große/überwältigende gegnerische Übermacht ankämpfen; **to struggle against impossible ~** so gut wie keine Aussicht auf Erfolg haben; **the ~ are that he will come** es sieht ganz so aus, als ob er käme *or* kommen würde.
(c) (*inf*) **to pay over the ~** einiges mehr bezahlen; **foreign buyers who are prepared to pay over the ~** Ausländer, die gewillt sind, Liebhaberpreise zu bezahlen.
(d) (*difference*) **what's the ~?** was macht das schon (aus)?; **it makes no ~** es spielt keine Rolle; **it makes no ~ to me** es ist mir (völlig) einerlei; **does it really make any ~ if I don't come?** macht es etwas aus, wenn ich nicht komme?
(e) (*variance*) **to be at ~ with sb over sth** mit jdm in etw (*dat*) nicht übereinstimmen; **we are at ~ as to the best solution** wir gehen nicht darin einig, wie das am besten gelöst werden soll; **to be at ~ with oneself** mit sich selbst nicht klarkommen.

odds and ends *npl* Krimskrams, Kram *m*; (*of food*) Reste *pl*; (*of cloth*) Reste, Flicken *pl* ◆ **bring all your ~** bringen Sie Ihren ganzen Kram *or* Ihre Siebensachen (*inf*).

odds and sods *npl* (*hum inf*) Kleinkram *m* ◆ **I've got a few ~ to tidy up** ich muß hier und da noch ein paar Sachen in Ordnung bringen; **a few ~** (*people*) ein paar Leute.

odds-on ['ɒdzɒn] **1** *adj* **the ~ favourite** der klare Favorit; **he's ~ favourite for the post** er hat die größten Aussichten, die Stelle zu bekommen.
2 *adv* **it's ~ that he'll come** es ist so gut wie sicher, daß er kommt.

ode [əʊd] *n* Ode *f* (*to, on* an +*acc*).

odious ['əʊdɪəs] *adj person* abstoßend, ekelhaft; *action* abscheulich, verabscheuenswürdig ◆ **an ~ person** ein Ekel *nt*; **what an ~ thing to say** wie abscheulich, so etwas zu sagen.

odium ['əʊdɪəm] *n* (*being hated*) Haß *m*; (*repugnance*) Abscheu *m*.

odometer [ɒ'dɒmɪtəʳ] *n* Kilometerzähler *m*.

odontologist [,ɒdɒn'tɒlədʒɪst] *n* Odontologe *m*, Odontologin *f*, Facharzt *m*/-ärztin *f* für Zahnheilkunde.

odontology [,ɒdɒn'tɒlədʒɪ] *n* Odontologie, Zahnheilkunde *f*.

odor *etc* (*US*) *see* **odour** *etc*.

odoriferous [,əʊdə'rɪfərəs] *adj* (*form*) wohlriechend, duftend.

odorous ['əʊdərəs] *adj* (*esp poet*) duftend, wohlriechend.

odour, (*US*) **odor** ['əʊdəʳ] *n* **(a)** (*lit, fig*) Geruch *m*; (*sweet smell*) Duft, Wohlgeruch *m*; (*bad smell*) Gestank *m*. **(b) to be in good/bad ~ with sb** gut/schlecht bei jdm angeschrieben sein.

odourless, (*US*) **odorless** ['əʊdəlɪs] *adj* geruchlos.

Odyssey ['ɒdɪsɪ] *n* (*Myth, fig*) Odyssee *f*.

OE *abbr of* **Old English**.

OECD *abbr of* **Organization for Economic Cooperation and Development** OECD *f*.

oecumenical [,i:kju:'menɪkəl] *adj see* **ecumenical**.

oedema, (*US*) **edema** [ɪ'di:mə] *n* Ödem *nt*.

Oedipus ['i:dɪpəs] *n* Ödipus *m* ◆ **~ complex** Ödipuskomplex *m*.

o'er ['əʊəʳ] *prep, adv* (*poet*) *contr of* **over**.

oesophagus, (*US*) **esophagus** [i:'sɒfəgəs] *n* Speiseröhre *f*.

of [ɒv, əv] *prep* **(a)** (*indicating possession or relation*) von (+*dat*), *use of gen* ◆ **the wife ~ the doctor** die Frau des Arztes, die Frau vom Arzt; **a friend ~ ours** ein Freund von uns; **a painting ~ the Queen** ein Gemälde der *or* von der Königin; **a painting ~ the Queen's** (*belonging to her*) ein Gemälde (im Besitz) der Königin; (*painted by her*) ein Gemälde (von) der Königin; **~ it** davon; **the first ~ May** der erste Mai; **the first ~ the month** der Erste (des Monats), der Monatserste; **that damn dog ~ theirs** ihr verdammter Hund; **it is very kind ~ you** es ist sehr freundlich von Ihnen.
(b) (*indicating separation in space or time*) **south ~ Paris** südlich von Paris; **within a month ~ his death** einen Monat nach seinem Tod; **a quarter ~ six** (*US*) Viertel vor sechs.
(c) (*indicating cause*) **he died ~ poison/cancer** er starb an Gift/Krebs; **he died ~ hunger** er verhungerte, er starb Hungers (*geh*); **it did not happen ~ itself** (*liter*) das ist nicht von selbst *or* von allein geschehen; **it tastes ~ garlic** es schmeckt nach Knoblauch; **she is proud ~ him** sie ist stolz auf ihn; **I am ashamed ~ it** ich schäme mich dafür.
(d) (*indicating deprivation, riddance*) **he was cured ~ the illness** er wurde von der Krankheit geheilt; **trees bare ~ leaves** Bäume ohne Blätter; **free ~ charge** kostenlos.
(e) (*indicating material*) aus ◆ **dress made ~ wool** Wollkleid *nt*, Kleid *nt* aus Wolle.
(f) (*indicating quality, identity etc*) **house ~ ten rooms** Haus *nt* mit zehn Zimmern; **man ~ courage** mutiger Mensch, Mensch *m* mit Mut; **girl ~ ten** zehnjähriges Mädchen, Mädchen *nt* von zehn Jahren; **a question ~ no importance** eine Frage ohne Bedeutung; **the city ~ Paris** die Stadt Paris; **person ~ swarthy complexion** dunkelhäutige Person; **a town ~ narrow streets** eine Stadt mit engen Straßen; **where is that rascal ~ a boy?** wo ist dieser verflixte Bengel?; **that idiot ~ a waiter** dieser Idiot von Kellner.
(g) (*objective genitive*) **fear ~ God** Gottesfurcht *f*; **his love ~ his father** die Liebe zu seinem Vater; **he is a leader ~ men** er hat die Fähigkeit, Menschen zu führen; **great eaters ~ fruit** große Obstesser *pl*; **writer ~ legal articles** Verfasser von juristischen Artikeln; **love ~ money** Liebe zum Geld.
(h) (*subjective genitive*) **love ~ God for man** Liebe Gottes zu den Menschen; **affection ~ a mother** Mutterliebe *f*.
(i) (*partitive genitive*) **the whole ~ the house** das ganze Haus; **half ~ the house** das halbe Haus; **how many ~ them do you want?** wie viele möchten Sie (davon)?; **many ~ them came** viele (von ihnen) kamen; **there were six ~ us** wir waren zu sechst, wir waren sechs; **he is not one ~ us** er gehört nicht zu uns; **one ~ the best** einer der Besten; **he asked the six ~ us to lunch** er lud uns sechs zum Mittagessen ein; **~ the ten only one was absent** von den zehn fehlte nur einer; **today ~ all days** ausgerechnet heute; **you ~ all people ought to know** gerade Sie sollten das wissen; **they are the best ~ friends** sie sind die besten Freunde; **the best ~ teachers** der (aller)beste Lehrer; **the bravest ~ the brave** der Mutigste der Mutigen; **he drank ~ the wine** (*liter*) er trank von dem Weine (*liter*).
(j) (*concerning*) **what do you think ~ him?** was halten Sie von ihm?; **what has become ~ him?** was ist aus ihm geworden?; **he warned us ~ the danger** er warnte uns vor der Gefahr; **doctor ~ medicine** Doktor der Medizin; **what ~ it?** ja und?
(k) (*obs, liter: by*) **forsaken ~ men** von allen verlassen; **beloved ~ all** von allen geliebt.
(l) (*in temporal phrases*) **he's become very quiet ~ late** er ist letztlich *or* seit neuestem so ruhig geworden; **they go out ~ an evening** (*inf*) sie gehen abends (schon mal) aus (*inf*); **he died ~ a Saturday morning** (*dial*) er starb an einem Samstagmorgen.

off [ɒf] **1** *adv* **(a)** (*distance*) **the house is 5 km ~** das Haus ist 5 km entfernt; **some way ~ (from here)** in einiger Entfernung (von hier); **it's a long way ~** das ist weit weg; (*time*) das liegt in weiter Ferne; **August isn't/the exams aren't very far ~** es ist nicht mehr lang bis August/bis zu den Prüfungen; **Christmas is only a week ~** es ist nur noch eine Woche bis Weihnachten; **noises ~** (*Theat*) Geräusche *pl* hinter den Kulissen.
(b) (*departure*) **to be/go ~** gehen; **he's ~ to school** er ist zur Schule gegangen; **(be) ~ with you!** fort mit dir!, mach, daß du wegkommst!; **~ with him!** fort *or* weg mit ihm!; **I must be ~** ich muß (jetzt) gehen *or* weg (*inf*); **it's time I was ~** es wird *or* ist (höchste) Zeit, daß ich gehe; **where are you ~ to?** wohin gehen Sie denn?, wohin geht's denn (*inf*)?; **~ we go!** los!, auf los geht's los!, na denn man los! (*inf*); **he's ~ playing tennis** *or* **he goes ~ playing tennis every evening** er geht jeden Abend Tennis spielen; **they're ~** (*Sport*) sie sind vom Start; **she's ~** (*inf: complaining etc*) sie legt schon wieder los (*inf*); *see vbs*.
(c) (*removal*) **he had his coat ~** er hatte den Mantel aus; **he helped me ~ with my coat** er half mir aus dem Mantel; **with his trousers ~** ohne Hose; **~ with those wet clothes!** raus aus den nassen Kleidern!; **the handle is ~** *or* **has come ~** der Griff ist ab (*inf*) *or* ist abgegangen; **there are two buttons ~** es fehlen zwei Knöpfe, da sind zwei Knöpfe ab (*inf*); **~ with his head!** herunter mit seinem Kopf!, Kopf ab!; **he had the back of the TV ~** er hatte die Rückwand des Fernsehers abgenommen; **the lid is ~** der Deckel ist nicht drauf.
(d) (*discount*) **3% ~** (*Comm*) 3% Nachlaß *or* Abzug; **3% ~ for cash** (*Comm*) 3% Skonto, bei Barzahlung 3%; **to give sb £5/something ~** jdm £ 5 Ermäßigung/eine Ermäßigung geben; **he let me have £5 ~** er gab es mir (um) £ 5 billiger.
(e) (*not at work*) **to have time ~ to do sth** (Zeit) freibekommen haben, um etw zu tun; **I've got a day ~** ich habe einen Tag frei(bekommen); **she's nearly always ~ on Tuesdays** dienstags hat sie fast immer frei; **to be ~ sick** wegen Krankheit fehlen.
(f) (*in phrases*) **~ and on, on and ~** ab und zu, ab und an; **it rained ~ and on** es regnete mit Unterbrechungen; **right** *or* **straight ~** gleich; **3 days straight ~** 3 Tage hintereinander.
2 *adj* **(a)** *attr* (*substandard*) *year, day etc* schlecht ◆ **I'm having an ~ day today** ich bin heute nicht in Form.
(b) *pred* (*not fresh*) verdorben, schlecht; *milk also* sauer; *butter also* ranzig.
(c) *pred* (*cancelled*) *match, party, talks* abgesagt; (*not available: in restaurant*) *chops, fish* aus ◆ **I'm afraid veal is ~ today/now** Kalbfleisch gibt es heute nicht/das Kalbfleisch ist aus; **the bet/agreement is ~** die Wette/Abmachung gilt nicht (mehr); **their engagement is ~** ihre Verlobung ist gelöst; **the play is ~** (*cancelled*) das Stück wurde abgesagt; (*no longer running*)

das Stück wurde abgesetzt.
(d) *TV, light, machine* aus(geschaltet); *tap* zu(gedreht) ◆ **the gas/electricity was ~** das Gas/der Strom war abgeschaltet; **the handbrake was ~** die Handbremse war gelöst.
(e) **they are badly** *or* **poorly/well** *or* **comfortably ~** sie sind nicht gut/(ganz) gut gestellt, sie stehen sich schlecht/(ganz) gut; **I am badly ~ for money/time** mit Geld/Zeit sieht es bei mir nicht gut aus; **how are we ~ for time?** wie sieht es mit der Zeit aus?, wieviel Zeit haben wir noch?; **he is better/worse ~ staying in England** er steht sich in England besser/schlechter.
(f) *pred (wide of the truth etc)* **you're ~ there** da irrst du gewaltig, da vertust du dich; **he was quite badly ~ in his calculations** er hatte sich in seinen Berechnungen ziemlich *or* schwer *(inf)* vertan; **the high notes were a bit ~** die hohen Töne waren etwas schief *(inf) or* unsauber.
(g) *pred (inf)* **that's a bit ~!** das ist ein dicker Hund! *(inf)*; **it's a bit ~ not letting me know** das ist ja nicht die feine Art, mir nicht Bescheid zu sagen; **his behaviour was rather ~** er hat sich ziemlich danebenbenommen; **she's been a bit ~ with me all week** sie hat sich die ganze Woche mir gegenüber etwas komisch verhalten; *(has been angry)* sie war die ganze Woche über etwas sauer auf mich *(inf)*.
[3] *prep* **(a)** *(indicating motion, removal etc)* von *(+dat)* ◆ **he jumped ~ the roof** er sprang vom Dach; **once you are ~ the premises** sobald Sie vom Gelände (herunter) sind; **he borrowed money ~ his father** *(inf)* er lieh sich *(dat)* von seinem Vater Geld; **they dined ~ a chicken** sie verspeisten ein Hühnchen; **I'll take something ~ the price for you** ich lasse Ihnen vom *or* im Preis etwas nach; **he got £2 ~ the shirt** er bekam das Hemd £ 2 billiger; **the lid had been left ~ the tin** jemand hatte den Deckel nicht wieder auf die Büchse getan; **the coat has two buttons ~ it** am Mantel fehlen zwei Knöpfe; **which coat is that button ~?** von welchem Mantel ist dieser Knopf?
(b) *(distant from)* ab(gelegen) von *(+dat)*; *(in a sidestreet from)* in einer Nebenstraße von *(+dat)*; *(Naut)* vor *(+dat)* ◆ **the house was ~/1 mile ~ the main road** das Haus lag von der Hauptstraße ab/lag eine Meile von der Hauptstraße weg *or* entfernt; **height ~ the ground** Höhe vom Boden (weg); **just ~ Piccadilly** in der Nähe von Piccadilly, gleich bei Piccadilly; **a road ~ Bank Street** eine Querstraße von *or* zu Bank Street.
(c) **~ the map** nicht auf der Karte; **I just want it ~ my hands** ich möchte das nur loswerden; *see* **duty, food** *etc.*
(d) **I'm ~ sausages/beer/him/German** *(don't like at the moment)* Wurst/Bier/er/Deutsch kann mich zur Zeit nicht reizen.

offal ['ɒfəl] *n, no pl* Innereien *pl*; *(fig)* Abfall, Ausschuß *m*.

off: ~beat [1] *adj* **(a)** *(unusual)* unkonventionell, ausgefallen, ungewöhnlich; **(b)** *jazz* synkopiert; [2] *n* unbetonte Taktzeit; **~-Broadway** [1] *adj in New York außerhalb des Broadway aufgeführt/gelegen*; [2] *adv in New York außerhalb des Broadway*; **~-centre,** *(US)* **~-center** *adj (lit)* nicht in der Mitte; *construction* asymmetrisch; **his translation/explanation was a bit ~-centre** seine Übersetzung/Erklärung war schief *or* ging an der Sache vorbei; **~-chance** *n* **I just did it on the ~-chance** ich habe es auf gut Glück getan; **to do sth on the ~-chance that ...** etw auf den Verdacht hin *or* in der unbestimmten Hoffnung tun, daß ...; **he bought it on the ~-chance that it would come in useful** er kaufte es, weil es vielleicht irgendwann mal nützlich sein könnte; **I came on the ~-chance of seeing her** ich kam in der Hoffnung, sie vielleicht zu sehen; **~-colour,** *(US)* **~-color** *adj* **(a)** *(unwell)* unwohl; **to feel/be ~-colour** sich nicht wohl fühlen, sich daneben fühlen *(inf)*; **(b)** *(indecent)* schlüpfrig, gewagt.

offence, *(US)* **offense** [ə'fens] *n* **(a)** *(Jur: crime)* Straftat *f*, Delikt *nt*; *(minor also)* Vergehen *nt* ◆ **to commit an ~** sich strafbar machen; **it is an ~ to ...** ... ist bei Strafe verboten; **first ~** erste Straftat, erstes Vergehen; **second ~** Rückfall *m*; **an ~ against ...** ein Verstoß *m* gegen ...
(b) *(fig)* **an ~ against good taste** eine Beleidigung des guten Geschmacks; **an ~ against common decency** eine Erregung öffentlichen Ärgernisses; **it is an ~ to the eye** das beleidigt das Auge.
(c) *no pl (to sb's feelings)* Kränkung, Beleidigung *f*; *(to sense of decency, morality etc)* Anstoß *m* ◆ **to cause** *or* **give ~ to sb** jdn kränken *or* beleidigen; **without giving ~** ohne kränkend zu sein; **to take ~ at sth** wegen etw gekränkt *or* beleidigt sein; **she is quick to take ~** sie ist leicht gekränkt *or* beleidigt; **I meant no ~** ich habe es nicht böse gemeint; **no ~ (meant)** nichts für ungut; **no ~ (taken)** ich nehme dir das nicht übel.
(d) *(Eccl: sin)* Sünde *f*.
(e) [ɒ'fens] *(attack, US: attacking part of team)* Angriff *m* ◆ **~ is the best defence** Angriff ist die beste Verteidigung.

offend [ə'fend] [1] *vt* **(a)** *(hurt feelings of)* kränken; *(be disagreeable to)* Anstoß erregen bei ◆ **don't be ~ed** seien Sie (doch) nicht beleidigt, nehmen Sie mir *etc* das nicht übel; **this novel would ~ a lot of people** dieser Roman würde bei vielen Leuten Anstoß erregen.
(b) *ear, eye* beleidigen; *reason* verstoßen gegen; *sense of justice* gehen gegen, verletzen.
[2] *vi* **(a)** *(give offence)* beleidigend sein.
(b) *(do wrong)* Unrecht tun.

◆**offend against** *vi +prep obj task, common sense* verstoßen gegen; *God* sündigen gegen.

offender [ə'fendəʳ] *n (law-breaker)* (Straf)täter(in *f*) *m*; *(against traffic laws)* Verkehrssünder(in *f*) *m* ◆ **young ~** jugendlicher Straffälliger *or* Straftäter; **home for young ~s** Jugendstrafanstalt *f*; **who left that here? — I'm afraid I was the ~** wer hat das da liegenlassen? — ich war der Übeltäter; *see* **first ~**.

offending [ə'fendɪŋ] *adj remark* kränkend, beleidigend ◆ **the ~ party** *(Jur)* die schuldige Partei; *(fig)* der/die Schuldige; **the ~ object** der Stein des Anstoßes.

offense *n (US) see* **offence.**

offensive [ə'fensɪv] [1] *adj* **(a)** *weapon (Jur)* Angriffs-; *(Mil also)* Offensiv- ◆ **~ play** *(Sport)* Offensivspiel *nt*.
(b) *(unpleasant) smell, sight* übel, abstoßend, widerlich; *language, film, book* anstößig, Anstoß erregend; *(insulting, abusive) remark, gesture, behaviour* beleidigend, unverschämt ◆ **his language was ~ to his parents** seine Ausdrucksweise erregte Anstoß bei seinen Eltern; **to find sb/sth ~** jdn/etw abstoßend finden; *behaviour, language* Anstoß an etw *(dat)* nehmen; **he was ~ to her** er beleidigte sie; **there's no need to get ~** kein Grund, ausfällig *or* ausfallend zu werden.
[2] *n (Mil, Sport)* Angriff *m*, Offensive *f* ◆ **to take the ~** in die Offensive gehen; **to go over to the ~** zum Angriff übergehen; **on the ~** in der Offensive.

offensively [ə'fensɪvlɪ] *adv* **(a)** *(unpleasantly)* übel, widerlich; *(in moral sense)* anstößig; *(abusively)* beleidigend, unverschämt; *(obscenely)* unflätig. **(b)** *(Mil, Sport)* offensiv.

offensiveness [ə'fensɪvnɪs] *n see adj (b)* Widerlichkeit *f*; Anstößigkeit *f*; Unverschämtheit *f*.

▼ **offer** ['ɒfəʳ] [1] *n* Angebot *nt*; *(also* **~ of marriage**) (Heirats)antrag *m* ◆ **the ~'s there** das Angebot gilt *or* steht; **did you have many ~s of help?** haben Ihnen viele Leute ihre Hilfe angeboten?; **any ~s?** ist jemand interessiert?; **to make an ~ of sth to sb** jdm etw anbieten; **he made me an ~ (of £50)** er machte mir ein Angebot (von £ 50); **an ~ I couldn't refuse** ein Angebot, zu dem ich nicht nein sagen konnte; **~s over £15,000** Angebote nicht unter £ 15.000; **on ~** *(Comm) (on special ~)* im Angebot; *(for sale also)* verkäuflich; *see* **near 3 (d).**
▼ [2] *vt* **(a)** anbieten; *reward, prize* aussetzen ◆ **to ~ to do sth** anbieten, etw zu tun; *(~ one's services)* sich bereit erklären, etw zu tun; **he ~ed to give me £5 for it** er bot mir dafür £ 5 an; **he ~ed to help** er bot seine Hilfe an; **to ~ one's services** sich anbieten; **he was ~ed the job** ihm wurde die Stelle angeboten; **did he ~ to?** hat er sich angeboten?; **he's got nothing to ~** er hat nichts zu bieten.
(b) *advice* anbieten; *plan, suggestion* unterbreiten; *remark* beisteuern; *excuse* vorbringen; *consolation* spenden; *condolences* aussprechen ◆ **to ~ an opinion** sich (dazu) äußern.
(c) *(present in worship or sacrifice) prayers, homage, sacrifice* darbringen; *one's life* opfern ◆ **nuns ~ their lives to God** Nonnen stellen ihr Leben in den Dienst Gottes.
(d) *(put up, attempt to inflict) resistance* bieten ◆ **to ~ violence** gewalttätig werden *(to* gegen); *see* **battle.**
▼ **(e)** *(afford, make available) sleeping accommodation etc* bieten ◆ **the bay ~ed a fine view** von der Bucht bot sich eine schöne Aussicht.
(f) *subject (for exam)* machen.
[3] *vi* **whenever the opportunity ~s** wann immer sich die Gelegenheit bietet *or* ergibt; **did he ~?** hat er es angeboten?

◆**offer up** *vt sep prayers, sacrifice* darbringen *(to sb* jdm) ◆ **to ~ oneself ~ to a life of public service** sein Leben in den Dienst der Öffentlichkeit stellen.

offering ['ɒfərɪŋ] *n* Gabe *f*; *(Rel) (collection)* Opfergabe *f*; *(sacrifice)* Opfer *nt*; *(iro: essay, play etc)* Vorstellung *f*.

offer price *n* Angebotspreis *m*.

offertory ['ɒfətərɪ] *n (Eccl) (part of service)* Opferung *f*, Offertorium *nt*; *(collection)* Kollekte, Geldsammlung *f* ◆ **~ hymn** Lied *nt* während der Opferung; **~ box** Opferstock *m*.

offhand [,ɒf'hænd] [1] *adj (also* **off-handed**) *(casual) remark, manner* lässig ◆ **to be ~ to sb** sich jdm gegenüber lässig benehmen; **to be ~ about sth** etw leichthin abtun.
[2] *adv* so ohne weiteres, aus dem Stand *(inf)* ◆ **I couldn't tell you ~** das könnte ich Ihnen auf Anhieb *or* so ohne weiteres nicht sagen.

offhandedly [,ɒf'hændɪdlɪ] *adv* lässig, leichthin.

offhandedness [,ɒf'hændɪdnɪs] *n* Lässigkeit *f*.

office ['ɒfɪs] *n* **(a)** Büro *nt*; *(of lawyer)* Kanzlei *f*; *(part of organization)* Abteilung *f*; *(branch also)* Geschäftsstelle *f* ◆ **at the ~** im Büro; **O~ of Fair Trading** *(Brit)* Behörde *f* gegen unlauteren Wettbewerb; **local government ~s** Gemeindeverwaltung *f*.
(b) *(public position)* Amt *nt* ◆ **to take ~** sein *or* das Amt antreten; *(political party)* die Regierung übernehmen, an die Regierung kommen; **to be in** *or* **hold ~** im Amt sein; *(party)* an der Regierung sein; **to be out of ~** nicht mehr an der Regierung sein; *(person)* nicht im Amt sein.
(c) *(duty)* Aufgabe, Pflicht *f*.
(d) *usu pl (attention, help)* **through his good ~s** durch seine guten Dienste; **through the ~s of ...** durch Vermittlung von ...
(e) *(Eccl)* Gottesdienst *m* ◆ **~ for the dead** Totenamt *nt*; *(RC)* Totenmesse *f*.
(f) *(Comm)* **"usual ~s"** „übliche Nebenräume".

office: ~ automation *n* Büroautomation *f*; **~ bearer** *n* Amtsträger(in *f*), Amtsinhaber(in *f*) *m*; **~ block** *n* Bürohaus *or* -gebäude *nt*; **~ boy** *n* Laufjunge *m*; **~ furniture** *n* Büromöbel *pl*; **~ hours** *npl* Arbeitsstunden *pl*, Dienstzeit *f*; *(on sign)* Geschäfts- *or* Öffnungszeiten *pl*; **to work ~ hours** normale Arbeitszeiten haben; **~ job** *n* Stelle *f* im Büro; **~ junior** *n* Bürogehilfe *m*/-gehilfin *f*; **~ manager(ess)** *n* Büroleiter(in *f*) *m*; **~ party** *n* Büroparty *f*.

officer ['ɒfɪsəʳ] *n* **(a)** *(Mil, Naut, Aviat)* Offizier *m* ◆ **~ of the day** diensthabender Offizier, Offizier *m* vom Dienst; **~s' mess** Offizierskasino *nt*; **O~s' Training Corps** *(Brit) Verband m zur Offiziersausbildung*.
(b) *(official)* Beamte(r) *m*, Beamtin *f*; *(police ~)* Polizeibeamte(r), Polizist *m*;

(*of club, society*) Vorstandsmitglied *nt*, Funktionär *m* ♦ **medical ~ of health** Amtsarzt *m*; (*Mil*) Stabsarzt *m*; **yes, ~** jawohl, Herr Wachtmeister.

office: ~ supplies *npl* Büroartikel *pl*, Bürobedarf *m*; **~-worker** *n* Büroangestellte(r) *mf*.

official [əˈfɪʃəl] [1] *adj* offiziell; *report, duties, meeting also* amtlich; *robes, visit* Amts-; *uniform* Dienst-; (*formal*) *ceremony, style* förmlich, formell ♦ **~ statement** amtliche Verlautbarung; **is that ~?** ist das amtlich?; (*publicly announced*) ist das offiziell?; **~ secret** Dienstgeheimnis, Amtsgeheimnis *nt*; **O~ Secrets Act** Gesetz *nt* zur amtlichen Schweigepflicht; **~ strike** offizieller Streik, gewerkschaftlich genehmigter Streik; **acting in one's ~ capacity** in Ausübung seiner Amtsgewalt; **~ seal** Dienstsiegel, Amtssiegel *nt*.
[2] *n* (*railway ~, post office ~ etc*) Beamte(r) *m*, Beamtin *f*; (*of club, at race-meeting*) Funktionär, Offizielle(r) (*inf*) *m*.

officialdom [əˈfɪʃəldəm] *n* (*pej*) Bürokratie *f*, Beamtentum *nt*.

officialese [ə,fɪʃəˈliːz] *n* Beamtensprache, Amtssprache *f*, Beamtenchinesisch *nt* (*pej*).

officially [əˈfɪʃəlɪ] *adv* offiziell ♦ **~ approved** offiziell anerkannt.

officiate [əˈfɪʃɪeɪt] *vt* amtieren, fungieren (*at* bei) ♦ **to ~ as president** als Präsident fungieren, das Amt des Präsidenten ausüben; **to ~ at a marriage** eine Trauung vornehmen.

officious [əˈfɪʃəs] *adj* (dienst)beflissen, übereifrig ♦ **to be ~** sich vor (Dienst)eifer überschlagen.

officiousness [əˈfɪʃəsnɪs] *n* (Dienst)beflissenheit *f*, Übereifer *m*.

offing [ˈɒfɪŋ] *n*: **in the ~** in Sicht; **there's a pay rise in the ~ for us** uns steht eine Gehaltserhöhung bevor, wir haben Aussicht auf eine Gehaltserhöhung.

off: ~-key *adj* (*Mus*) falsch; **~-licence** *n* (*Brit*) **(a)** (*shop*) Wein- und Spirituosenhandlung *f*; **(b)** (*permit*) Lizenz *f* zum Alkoholvertrieb *or* -verkauf; **~-line** (*Comput*) [1] *adj* Off-line-; [2] *adv* off line; **to go ~-line** auf Off-line-Betrieb schalten; **to put a printer ~-line** einen Drucker auf Off-line-Betrieb schalten; **~-load** *vt goods* ausladen, entladen; *passengers* aussteigen lassen; **~-peak** *adj* **~-peak central heating** Nacht(strom)-speicherheizung *f*; **~-peak electricity** Strom *m* außerhalb der Hauptabnahmezeit, Nachtstrom *m*; **~-peak charges** verbilligter Tarif; (*Elec*) ≃ Nachttarif *m*; **during ~-peak hours** außerhalb der Stoßzeiten; **~-peak ticket** verbilligte Fahrkarte/Flugkarte außerhalb der Stoßzeit; **~-piste** *adj, adv* abseits der Piste; **~print** *n* Sonderabdruck *m*; **~-putting** *adj* (*Brit*) *smell, behaviour* abstoßend; *sight also, meal* wenig einladend; *thought, idea, story* wenig ermutigend; (*daunting*) entmutigend; *interviewer* wenig entgegenkommend; *job* unsympathisch; **it can be rather ~-putting to see how sausages are made** es kann einem den Appetit verderben *or* die Lust am Essen nehmen, wenn man sieht, wie Wurst gemacht wird; **~-road** *adj driving, racing* im Gelände ♦ **~ vehicle** Geländefahrzeug *nt*; **~ sales** *n* (*Brit*) **(a)** *pl* Verkauf *m* aus dem Haus; **(b)** *sing see* **~-licence (a)**; **~-season** [1] *n* (*in tourism*) Nebensaison *f*; **in the ~-season** außerhalb der Saison; [2] *adj travel, prices* außerhalb der Saison.

offset [ˈɒfset] (*vb: pret, ptp* ~) [1] *vt* **(a)** (*financially, statistically etc*) ausgleichen; (*make up for*) wettmachen, aufwiegen.
(b) [ɒfˈset] (*place non-centrally*) versetzen.
[2] *n* **(a)** (*Typ*) **~ (lithography/printing)** Offsetdruck *m*.
(b) (*Hort*) Ableger *m*.
(c) (*fig: counterbalancing factor*) Ausgleich *m* ♦ **as an ~** zum Ausgleich, als Ausgleich (*to* für).

off: ~shoot *n* **(a)** (*of plant*) Ausläufer, Ableger *m*; (*of tree*) Schößling, Sproß *m*; **(b)** (*fig*) (*of family*) Nebenlinie *f*; (*of organization*) Nebenzweig *m*; (*of discussion, action etc*) Randergebnis *nt*; **~shore** [1] *adj fisheries* Küsten-; *island* küstennah; *wind* ablandig; *oilfield, installations etc* Off-shore-, im Meer; *investment* im Ausland; **~shore drilling rig** Bohrinsel *f*; **the ~shore industry/business** (*oil*) die Off-shore-Erdölindustrie; [2] *adv drill, explore* im Meer; *work, live* auf einer Bohrinsel; **the wind blew ~shore** der Wind kam vom Land; **the ship anchored ~shore** das Schiff ankerte vor der Küste; **50% of our oil comes from ~shore** 50% unseres Erdöls kommt *or* stammt aus dem Meer; **~side** [1] *adj* **(a)** (*Sport*) im Abseits; **to be ~side** im Abseits sein *or* stehen; **~side trap** Abseitsfalle *f*; **(b)** (*Aut*) auf der Fahrerseite, rechte(r, s)/linke(r, s); [2] *n* (*Aut*) Fahrerseite *f*; [3] *adv* (*Sport*) abseits, im Abseits; **~spring** *n* **(a)** *sing* Sprößling *m*, Kind *nt*, Abkömmling *m*; (*of animal*) Junge(s) *nt*; **(b)** *pl* (*form, hum: of people*) Nachwuchs *m* (*hum*), Nachkommen *pl*; (*of animals*) (die/ihre) Jungen *pl*; **how are your ~spring?** (*hum*) wie geht's dem Nachwuchs? (*hum*); **~stage** *adv* hinter den Kulissen, hinter der Bühne; **~-street parking** *n* **there isn't much ~-street parking in this area** in dieser Gegend gibt es wenige Parkhäuser und Parkplätze; **~-the-cuff** *adj remark, speech* aus dem Stegreif; **~-the-job training** *n* außerbetriebliche Weiterbildung; **~-the-peg** *attr*, **~ the peg** *pred* (*Brit*), **~-the-rack** *attr*, **~ the rack** *pred* (*US*) *dress, suit* von der Stange, Konfektions-; **~-the-wall** *adj* (*US inf: zany*) irre (*inf*), verrückt; **~-white** [1] *adj* gebrochen weiß; [2] *n* gebrochenes Weiß.

Ofgas [ˈɒfgæs] *n* (*Brit*) *abbr of* **Office of Gas Supply** *Regulierungsbehörde f für die Gasindustrie*.

Oflot [ˈɒflɒt] *n abbr* (*Brit*) *Regulierungsbehörde f für die britische Staatslotterie*.

oft [ɒft] *adv* (*liter*) oft ♦ **an ~-told story** eine gar oft erzählte Geschichte (*liter*).

Oftel [ˈɒftel] *n* (*Brit*) *abbr of* **Office of Telecommunications** *Regulierungsbehörde f für die Telekommunikationsindustrie*.

▼ **often** [ˈɒfən] *adv* oft, häufig ♦ **he went there ~, he ~ went there** er ging oft *or* häufig da hin; **you have been there as ~ as I have** Sie sind schon (eben)sooft wie ich dort gewesen; **do you go there as ~ as twice a week?** gehen Sie tatsächlich zweimal in der Woche dahin?; **not as ~ as twice a week** weniger als zweimal in der Woche; **as ~ as I ask you ...** jedesmal wenn *or* sooft ich Sie frage ...; **more ~ than not, as ~ as not** meistens; **every so ~** öfters, von Zeit zu Zeit; **he did it once too ~** er hat es einmal zu oft *or* zuviel getan; **how ~?** wie oft?; **it is not ~ that ...** es kommt selten vor, daß ..., es geschieht nicht oft, daß ...; **oft(en) times** (*obs*) oftmals, gar viele Male (*old*).

Ofwat [ˈɒfwɒt] *n* (*Brit*) *abbr of* **Office of Water Services** *Regulierungsbehörde f für die Wasserindustrie*.

ogle [ˈəʊgl] *vt* kein Auge lassen *or* wenden von, begaffen (*pej*); (*flirtatiously*) liebäugeln mit, schöne Augen machen (*+dat*); *legs, girls* schielen nach, beäuge(l)n (*esp hum*), beaugapfeln (*hum*); (*hum*) *cream cakes etc* schielen nach.

O grade [ˈəʊgreɪd] *n* (*Scot*) = **O level**.

ogre [ˈəʊgəʳ] *n* Menschenfresser *m*; (*fig*) Unmensch *m*.

ogress [ˈəʊgrɪs] *n* (*lit*) menschenfressende Riesin; (*fig*) Ungeheuer *nt*, Unmensch *m*.

oh [əʊ] *interj* ach; (*admiring, surprised, disappointed*) oh; (*questioning, disinterested, in confirmation*) tatsächlich, wahrhaftig ♦ **~ good!** au *or* Mensch prima! (*inf*); **~ well** na ja!; **~ bother/damn!** Mist! (*inf*)/verdammt! (*sl*); **~ dear!** o je!; **~ yes?** (*interested*) ach ja?; (*disbelieving*) so, so; **~ yes, that's right** ach ja, das stimmt; **~ yes, of course there'll be room** o ja, klar haben wir Platz; **~ my God!** o Gott!, ach du lieber Gott!

ohm [əʊm] *n* Ohm *nt* ♦ **O~'s law** Ohmsches Gesetz.

OHMS *abbr of* **On His/Her Majesty's Service** *Aufdruck auf amtlichen Postsendungen*.

OHP *abbr of* **overhead projector**.

oi(c)k [ɔɪk] *n* (*Brit pej sl*) Prolet *m*.

oil [ɔɪl] [1] *n* **(a)** Öl *nt* ♦ **to pour ~ on troubled waters** die Wogen glätten, Öl auf die Wogen gießen.
(b) (*petroleum*) (Erd)öl *nt* ♦ **to strike ~** (*lit*) auf Öl stoßen; (*fig*) einen guten Fund machen; (*get rich*) das große Los ziehen.
(c) (*Art*) (*painting*) Ölgemälde *nt* ♦ **to paint in ~s** in Öl malen; **a painting in ~s** ein Ölgemälde *nt*.
(d) (*sl: flattery*) Schmeicheleien *pl*.
[2] *vt* ölen, schmieren; *table, furniture* einölen ♦ **to ~ sb's tongue** (*fig*) jdm die Zunge ölen *or* schmieren; **to ~ the wheels** (*fig*) die Dinge erleichtern.

oil *in cpds* Öl-; **~-based** *adj* auf Ölbasis; **~-based paint** Ölfarbe *f*; **~-burning** *adj lamp, stove* Öl-; **~cake** *n* Ölkuchen *m*; **~can** *n* Ölkanne *f*; (*for lubricating also*) Ölkännchen *nt*; **~ change** *n* Ölwechsel *m*; **to do an ~ change** einen Ölwechsel machen *or* vornehmen; **I took the car in for an ~ change** ich habe den Wagen zum Ölwechsel(n) gebracht; **~cloth** *n* Wachstuch *nt*; **~ colours** *npl* Ölfarben *pl*; **~ company** *n* Ölkonzern *m*.

oiled [ɔɪld] *adj* **(a) ~ silk** Ölhaut *f*. **(b)** (*sl: drunk*) **he's well-~** der ist ganz schön voll (*inf*), der hat ganz schön getankt (*inf*).

oil: ~-exporting *adj* ölexportierend; **~field** *n* Ölfeld *nt*; **~-fired** *adj* Öl-, mit Öl befeuert; **~ industry** *n* Ölindustrie *f*.

oiliness [ˈɔɪlɪnɪs] *n* **(a)** ölige Beschaffenheit; (*of food*) Fettigkeit *f*. **(b)** (*fig*) (*of person*) aalglattes Wesen ♦ **the ~ of his voice/manners** seine aalglatte Stimme/sein aalglattes Benehmen.

oil: ~ lamp *n* Öllampe *f*; **~ level** *n* Ölstand *m*; **~man** *n* Öltyp (*inf*), Ölmensch (*inf*) *m*; (*trader*) Ölhändler *m*; **~ paint** *n* Ölfarbe *f*; **~ painting** *n* (*picture*) Ölgemälde *nt*; (*art*) Ölmalerei *f*; **she's no ~ painting** (*inf*) sie ist nicht gerade eine Schönheit; **~pan** *n* Ölwanne *f*; **~-producing** *adj* ölproduzierend; **~-rich** *adj* ölreich; **~ rig** *n* (Öl)bohrinsel *f*; **~ sheik** *n* Ölscheich *m*; **~skin** *n* (*cloth*) Öltuch *nt*; **~skins** *npl* (*clothing*) Ölzeug *nt*; **~ slick** *n* Ölteppich *m*; **~stone** *n* geölter Wetzstein; **~ stove** *n* Ölofen *m*; **~ tanker** *n* (*ship*) (Öl)tanker *m*, Tankschiff *nt*; (*lorry*) Tankwagen *m*; **~ terminal** *n* Ölhafen *m*; **~ well** *n* Ölquelle *f*.

oily [ˈɔɪlɪ] *adj* (*+er*) **(a)** ölig; *food* fettig; *clothes, fingers* voller Öl. **(b)** (*fig*) aalglatt, schleimig, ölig.

oink [ɔɪŋk] *interj* (*pig*) grunz.

ointment [ˈɔɪntmənt] *n* Salbe *f*.

OK, okay [ˈəʊˈkeɪ] (*inf*) [1] *interj* okay (*inf*); (*agreed also*) einverstanden, in Ordnung ♦ **~, ~!** ist ja gut! (*inf*), okay, okay! (*inf*); **I'll come too, ~?** ich komme auch, okay (*inf*) *or* einverstanden?
[2] *adj* in Ordnung, okay (*inf*) ♦ **that's ~ with** *or* **by me** (*that's convenient*) das ist mir recht, mir ist's recht; (*I don't mind that*) von mir aus, mir soll's recht sein; **is it ~ with you if ...?** macht es (dir) was aus, wenn ...?; **how's your mother? — she's ~** wie geht's deiner Mutter? — gut *or* (*not too well*) so la la (*inf*), so einigermaßen; **to be ~ (for time/money** *etc*) (noch) genug (Zeit/Geld *etc*) haben; **is your car ~?** ist Ihr Auto in Ordnung?; **is that ~?** geht das?, ist das okay? (*inf*); **what do you think of him? — he's ~** was halten Sie von ihm? — der ist in Ordnung (*inf*); **he's an ~ guy** (*esp US*) er ist ein prima Kerl (*inf*).
[3] *adv* **(a)** (*well*) gut; (*not too badly*) einigermaßen (gut); (*for sure*) schon ♦ **can you mend/manage it ~?** kannst du das reparieren/kommst du damit klar?; **he'll come ~** der kommt schon. **(b)** (*inf: admittedly*) **~ it's difficult but ...** zugegeben, es ist schwer, aber ...
[4] *vt order, plan, suggestion* gutheißen, billigen; *document, proposed expenses* genehmigen ♦ **you have to get the boss to ~ it, you have to ~ it with the boss** das muß der Chef bewilligen.
[5] *n* Zustimmung *f* ♦ **to give sth one's ~** seine Zustimmung zu etw geben; **if the boss gives his ~** wenn der Chef das bewilligt.

okapi [əʊˈkɑːpɪ] *n, pl* **-s**, *or* **-** Okapi *nt*.

okey-doke [ˈəʊkɪˈdəʊk], **okey-dokey** [ˈəʊkɪˈdəʊkɪ] *interj* (*inf*) okay (*inf*).

okra [ˈɒkrə] *n* Okra *f*.

➤ LANGUAGE IN USE: **often** → 26.1

old [əʊld] [1] *adj (+er)* **(a)** alt ◆ ~ **people** *or* **folk(s)** alte Leute, die Alten *pl*; **if I live to be that** ~ wenn ich (je) so alt werde; ~ **Mr Smith,** ~ **man Smith** *(esp US)* der alte (Herr) Smith; **he is 40 years** ~ er ist 40 (Jahre alt); **two-year-**~ Zweijährige(r) *mf*; **the** ~ **part of Ulm** die Ulmer Altstadt; **the** ~ **(part of) town** die Altstadt; **my** ~ **school** meine alte *or* ehemalige Schule.
(b) *(inf: as intensifier)* **she dresses any** ~ **how** die ist vielleicht immer angezogen *(inf)*; **any** ~ **thing** irgendwas, irgendein Dings *(inf)*; **any** ~ **bottle/blouse** *etc* irgendeine Flasche/Bluse *etc (inf)*; ~ **Mike** der Michael *(inf)*; **the same** ~ **excuse** die gleiche alte Entschuldigung; **we had a great** ~ **time** wir haben uns prächtig amüsiert; **funny** ~ **guy** komischer Typ *(inf)*.
[2] *n* **in days of** ~ in alten *or* früheren Zeiten; **the men of** ~ die Menschen früherer Zeiten; **I know him of** ~ ich kenne ihn von früher; **as of** ~ wie in alten Zeiten.

old: ~ **age** *n* das Alter; **to reach** ~ **age** ein hohes Alter erreichen; **in one's** ~ **age** im Alter, auf seine alten Tage *(also hum)*; ~**-age pension** *n* (Alters)rente *f*; ~**-age pensioner** *n* Rentner(in *f*) *m*; **O**~ **Bill** *npl (Brit sl)*: **the O**~ **Bill** die Bullen *pl (sl)*; ~ **boy** *n* **(a)** *(Brit Sch)* ehemaliger Schüler, Ehemalige(r) *m*; **the** ~**-boy network** Beziehungen *pl* (von der Schule her); **(b)** *(inf: old man)* **the** ~ **boy next door** der Alte von nebenan; **(c)** *(dated inf: as address)* alter Junge *(inf)*; ~ **country** *n* Mutterland *nt*, alte Heimat.

olden ['əʊldən] *adj (liter)* alt ◆ **in** ~ **times** *or* **days** früher, vordem *(liter)*, in alten Zeiten; **city of** ~ **times** Stadt vergangener Zeiten.

old: O~ **English** [1] *n* Altenglisch *nt*; [2] *adj* altenglisch; **O**~ **English sheepdog** *n* Bobtail *m*; ~**-established** *adj family, firm* alteingesessen; *custom* seit langem bestehend, alt.

olde-worlde ['əʊldɪ'wɜːldɪ] *adj* altertümlich; *(pej)* auf alt getrimmt *(inf) or* gemacht.

old: ~**-fashioned** ['əʊld'fæʃnd] [1] *adj* altmodisch; [2] *n (US: cocktail) Cocktail m aus Whiskey, Bitterlikör, Zucker und Früchten*; ~ **girl** *n (Brit Sch)* Ehemalige *f*, ehemalige Schülerin; **O**~ **Glory** *n (US)* die Flagge der USA; ~ **gold** *n* Altgold *nt*; ~ **guard** *n (fig)* alte Garde; **O**~ **High German** *n* Althochdeutsch *nt*.

oldie ['əʊldɪ] *n (inf) (joke)* alter Witz; *(song)* Oldie *m*; *(record)* alte Platte, Oldie *m* ◆ **the** ~**s** *(people)* die Alten *pl*, die Oldies *pl (inf)*; **that's a real** ~ *(joke)* der hat so einen Bart *(inf)*.

oldish ['əʊldɪʃ] *adj* ältlich.

old: ~ **lady** *n (inf)* **the/my** ~ **lady** *(wife)* die/meine Alte *(inf) or* Olle *(inf)*; *(mother)* die/meine alte Dame *(inf)*; ~**-line** *adj (following tradition)* der alten Schule; *(long-established)* alteingesessen; ~ **maid** *n* alte Jungfer; ~**-maidish** *adj* altjüngferlich, altbacken; ~ **man** *n (inf)* **my/the** ~ **man** *(husband)* mein/dein *etc* Alter *(inf) or* Oller *(inf)*; *(father)* mein Alter/der Alte *(inf)*, mein alter/der alte Herr *(inf)*; **the** ~ **man** *(boss etc)* der Alte; ~ **master** *n* alter Meister; ~ **people's home** *n* Altersheim *nt*; ~ **salt** *n* (alter) Seebär; ~ **school** *n (fig)* alte Schule; ~ **school tie** *n (lit)* Schulschlips *m*; *(fig) Gehabe, das von Ehemaligen einer Public School erwartet wird*; **O**~ **South** *m Südstaaten der USA vor dem amerikanischen Bürgerkrieg*; ~ **stager** *n (inf)* alter Hase *(inf)*.

oldster ['əʊldstə^r] *n (US inf)* älterer Mann ◆ **some of us** ~**s** einige von uns Alten.

old: ~**-style** *adj* im alten Stil; ~**-style calendar** Kalender *m* alten Stils *or* nach alter Zeitrechnung; **O**~ **Testament** *n* Altes Testament; ~**-timer** *n* Altgediente(r), Veteran *m*; ~ **wives' tale** *n* Ammenmärchen *nt*; ~ **woman** *n* **(a)** *see* ~ **lady**; **(b) he's an** ~ **woman** er ist wie ein altes Weib; ~**-womanish** *adj* tuntig *(inf)*; **O**~ **World** *n* alte Welt; ~**-world** *adj* **(a)** *(quaint) politeness, manners* altväterlich; *cottage, atmosphere* altehrwürdig, heimelig; **(b)** *(esp US: European etc)* zur alten Welt gehörend.

oleaginous [,əʊlɪ'ædʒɪnəs] *adj (form) consistency* ölig, Öl-; *(containing oil)* ölhaltig.

oleander [,əʊlɪ'ændə^r] *n* Oleander *m*.

oleo- ['əʊlɪəʊ-] *pref* Öl- ◆ ~**margarine** *(esp US)* Margarine *f*.

O level ['əʊlevl] *n (Brit)* Abschluß *m* der Sekundarstufe 1, ≃ mittlere Reife ◆ **to do one's** ~**s** ≃ die mittlere Reife machen; **to have English** ~ bis zur mittleren Reife Englisch gelernt haben; **he failed his English** ~ er fiel durch die O-level-Prüfung in Englisch; **3** ~**s** die mittlere Reife in 3 Fächern.

olfactory [ɒl'fæktərɪ] *adj* Geruchs-, olfaktorisch *(spec)*.

oligarchic(al) [,ɒlɪ'gɑːkɪk(əl)] *adj* oligarchisch.

oligarchy ['ɒlɪgɑːkɪ] *n* Oligarchie *f*.

olive ['ɒlɪv] [1] *n* **(a)** Olive *f*; *(also* ~ **tree)** Olivenbaum *m*; *(also* ~ **wood)** Olive(nholz *nt*) *f*. **(b)** *(colour)* Olive *nt*.
[2] *adj (also* ~**-coloured)** olivgrün; *complexion* dunkel.

olive: ~ **branch** *n (lit, fig)* Ölzweig *m*; **to hold out the** ~ **branch to sb** *(fig)* jdm seinen Willen zum Frieden bekunden; ~**-green** [1] *adj cloth* olivgrün; [2] *n* Olivgrün *nt*; ~ **grove** *n* Olivenhain *m*; ~ **oil** *n* Olivenöl *nt*.

Olympiad [əʊ'lɪmpɪæd] *n* Olympiade *f*.

Olympian [əʊ'lɪmpɪən] [1] *adj* olympisch.
[2] *n* **the** ~**s** die Olympier *pl*.

Olympic [əʊ'lɪmpɪk] [1] *adj games, stadium* olympisch ◆ ~ **champion** Olympiasieger(in *f*) *m*; ~ **flame** *or* **torch** olympisches Feuer.
[2] *n* **the** ~**s** *pl* die Olympiade, die Olympischen Spiele.

Olympus [əʊ'lɪmpəs] *n (also* **Mount** ~) der Olymp.

OM *abbr of* **Order of Merit.**

Oman [əʊ'mɑːn] *n* Oman *nt*.

Omani [əʊ'mɑːnɪ] [1] *adj* omanisch.
[2] *n* Omaner(in *f*) *m*.

omasum [əʊ'mɑːsəm] *n* Blättermagen *m*.

ombudsman ['ɒmbʊdzmən] *n, pl* **-men** [-mən] Ombudsmann *m*.

omega ['əʊmɪgə] *n* Omega *nt*.

omelette, *(US)* **omelet** ['ɒmlɪt] *n* Omelett(e) *nt* ◆ **you can't make an** ~ **without breaking eggs** *(Prov)* wo gehobelt wird, da fallen Späne *(Prov)*.

omen ['əʊmen] *n* Omen, Zeichen *nt* ◆ **it is an** ~ **of success** das bedeutet Erfolg; **a bird of ill** ~ ein Unglücksvogel *m*.

ominous ['ɒmɪnəs] *adj* bedrohlich; *event, appearance also* drohend; *look, voice also* unheilverkündend, unheilschwanger; *sign also* verhängnisvoll ◆ **that's** ~ das läßt nichts Gutes ahnen; **that sounds** ~ das verspricht nichts Gutes.

ominously ['ɒmɪnəslɪ] *adv* bedrohlich; *say* in einem unheilverkündenden Ton.

omission [əʊ'mɪʃən] *n (omitting: of word, detail etc)* Auslassen *nt*; *(word, thing etc left out)* Auslassung *f*; *(failure to do sth)* Unterlassung *f* ◆ **with the** ~ **of** ... unter Auslassung *(+gen)* ...; **sin of** ~ *(Eccl, fig)* Unterlassungssünde *f*.

omit [əʊ'mɪt] *vt* **(a)** *(leave out)* auslassen ◆ **please** ~ **all reference to me** bitte erwähnen Sie mich nicht, bitte unterlassen Sie jeden Hinweis auf mich.
(b) *(fail) (to do sth* etw zu tun) es unterlassen; *(accidentally also)* versäumen.

omnibus ['ɒmnɪbəs] [1] *n* **(a)** *(form: bus)* Omnibus, Autobus *m*. **(b)** *(book)* Sammelausgabe *f*, Sammelband *m*.
[2] *adj (esp US)* allgemein, umfassend ◆ ~ **bill** *(Parl)* Sammelgesetz *nt*.

omnidirectional [,ɒmnɪdɪ'rekʃənl] *adj* Rundstrahl-.

omnipotence [ɒm'nɪpətəns] *n, no pl* Allmacht, Omnipotenz *f*.

omnipotent [ɒm'nɪpətənt] [1] *adj* allmächtig, omnipotent.
[2] *n* **The O**~ der Allmächtige.

omnipresence ['ɒmnɪ'prezəns] *n* Allgegenwart *f*.

omnipresent ['ɒmnɪ'prezənt] *adj* allgegenwärtig.

omniscience [ɒm'nɪsɪəns] *n* Allwissenheit *f*.

omniscient [ɒm'nɪsɪənt] *adj* allwissend.

omnivore ['ɒmnɪ,vɔː^r] *n* Allesfresser, Omnivore *(spec) m*.

omnivorous [ɒm'nɪvərəs] *adj (lit)* allesfressend, omnivor *(spec)* ◆ **an** ~ **reader of books** ein Vielfraß *m*, was Bücher angeht.

on [ɒn] [1] *prep* **(a)** *(indicating place, position)* auf *(+dat)*; *(with vb of motion)* auf *(+acc)*; *(on vertical surface, part of body)* an *(+dat/acc)* ◆ **the book is** ~ **the table** das Buch ist auf dem Tisch; **he put the book** ~ **the table** er legte das Buch auf den Tisch; **it was** ~ **the blackboard** es stand an der Tafel; **he hung it** ~ **the wall/nail** er hängte es an die Wand/den Nagel; **a ring** ~ **his finger** ein Ring am Finger; **he hit his head** ~ **the table/**~ **the ground** er hat sich *(dat)* den Kopf am Tisch/auf dem *or* am Boden angeschlagen; **they came** ~**(to) the stage** sie kamen auf die Bühne; **they advanced** ~ **the fort** sie rückten zum Fort vor; **they made an attack** ~ **us** sie griffen uns an; **he turned his back** ~ **us** er kehrte uns *(dat)* den Rücken zu; ~ **the right** rechts; ~ **my right** rechts von mir, zu meiner Rechten; ~ **TV/the radio** im Fernsehen/Radio; **who's** ~ **his show tonight?** wer ist heute in seiner Show?; **I have no money** ~ **me** ich habe kein Geld bei mir; **to count sth** ~ **one's fingers** etw an den Fingern abzählen; **we had something to eat** ~ **the train** wir haben im Zug etwas gegessen; **a house** ~ **the coast/main road** ein Haus am Meer/an der Hauptstraße; ~ **the bank of the river** am Flußufer; *see also* **onto**.
(b) *(indicating means of travel)* **we went** ~ **the train/bus** wir fuhren mit dem Zug/Bus; ~ **a bicycle** mit dem (Fahr)rad; ~ **foot/horseback** zu Fuß/Pferd.
(c) *(indicating means)* **he lives** ~ **his income** er lebt von seinem Einkommen; **I could live** ~ **that** davon könnte ich leben; **they live** ~ **potatoes** sie ernähren sich von Kartoffeln; **the heating works** ~ **oil** die Heizung wird mit Öl betrieben.
(d) *(about, concerning)* über *(+acc)* ◆ **a book** ~ **German grammar** ein Buch über deutsche Grammatik; **we read Stalin** ~ **Marx** wir lasen Stalins Ausführungen zu Marx; **have you heard him** ~ **that?** haben Sie ihn zu diesem Thema gehört?
(e) *(in expression of time)* an *(+dat)* ◆ ~ **Sunday** (am) Sonntag; ~ **Sundays** sonntags; ~ **December the first** am ersten Dezember; **stars visible** ~ **clear nights** Sterne, die in klaren Nächten sichtbar sind; ~ **or about the twentieth** um den Zwanzigsten herum; ~ **and after the twentieth** am Zwanzigsten und danach; ~ **the minute** auf die Minute genau.
(f) *(at the time of)* bei *(+dat)* ◆ ~ **my arrival** bei meiner Ankunft; ~ **examination** bei der Untersuchung; ~ **request** auf Wunsch; ~ **hearing this he left** als er das hörte, ging er; ~ **(receiving) my letter** nach Erhalt meines Briefes.
(g) *(as a result of)* auf *(+acc)* ... hin ◆ ~ **receiving my letter** auf meinen Brief hin.
(h) *(indicating membership)* in *(+dat)* ◆ **he is** ~ **the committee/the board** er gehört dem Ausschuß/Vorstand an, er sitzt im Ausschuß/Vorstand; **he is** ~ **the "Evening News"** er ist bei der „Evening News"; **he is** ~ **the teaching staff** er gehört zum Lehrpersonal.
(i) *(engaged upon)* **I am working** ~ **a new project** ich arbeite gerade an einem neuen Projekt; **he was away** ~ **an errand** er war auf einem Botengang unterwegs; **I am** ~ **overtime** ich mache Überstunden; **we're** ~ **the past tense** *(Sch)* wir sind bei der Vergangenheit; **we were** ~ **page 72** wir waren auf Seite 72.
(j) *(at the expense of etc)* **this round is** ~ **me** diese Runde geht auf meine Kosten; **have it** ~ **me** das spendiere ich (dir/Ihnen), ich gebe (dir/Ihnen) das aus; *see* **house**.
(k) *(as against)* im Vergleich zu ◆ **prices are up** ~ **last year('s)** im Vergleich zum letzten Jahr sind die Preise gestiegen.
(l) *(Mus)* **he played (it)** ~ **the violin/trumpet** er spielte (es) auf der Geige/Trompete; ~ **drums/piano** am Schlagzeug/Klavier; **Roland Kirk** ~ **tenor sax** Roland Kirk, Tenorsaxophon.
(m) *(according to)* nach *(+dat)* ◆ ~ **your theory** Ihrer Theorie nach *or* zufolge, nach Ihrer Theorie.

(n) (*in phrases*) *see also n, vb etc* **he made mistake ~ mistake** er machte einen Fehler nach dem anderen; **I'm ~ £8,000 a year** ich bekomme £ 8.000 im Jahr; **he retired ~ a good pension** er trat mit einer guten Rente in den Ruhestand; **to be ~ a course** (*Sch, Univ*) an einem Kurs teilnehmen; **to be ~ drugs/pills** Drogen/Pillen nehmen; **he has nothing ~ me** (*not as good as*) er kann mir nicht das Wasser reichen; (*no hold over*) er hat nichts gegen mich in der Hand, er kann mir nichts anhaben.

[2] *adv see also vb + on* **(a)** (*indicating idea of covering*) **he put his hat ~** er setzte seinen Hut auf; **he put his coat ~** er zog seinen Mantel an; **he screwed the lid ~** er schraubte den Deckel drauf; **try it ~** probieren Sie es an; **she had nothing ~** sie hatte nichts an; **what did he have ~?** was hatte er an?; **he had his hat ~ crooked** er hatte den Hut schief auf.
(b) (*indicating advancing movement*) **move ~!** gehen Sie weiter!, weitergehen!; **~! ~!** weiter! weiter!; **to pass a message ~** eine Nachricht weitergeben.
(c) (*indicating time*) **from that day ~** von diesem Tag an; **later ~** später; **it was well ~ in the night** es war zu vorgerückter Stunde, es war spät in der Nacht; **well ~ in the morning/afternoon** später am Morgen/Nachmittag; **it was well ~ into September** es war spät im September; *see* **get ~**.
(d) (*indicating continuation*) **to keep ~ talking** immer weiterreden, in einem fort reden; **go ~ with your work** machen Sie Ihre Arbeit weiter; **life still goes ~** das Leben geht weiter; **they talked ~ and ~** sie redeten und redeten, sie redeten unentwegt; **the noise went ~ and ~** der Lärm hörte überhaupt nicht auf; **she went ~ and ~** sie hörte gar nicht mehr auf.
(e) (*indicating position towards one*) **put it this way ~** stellen/legen Sie es so herum (darauf); **lengthways ~** längs.
(f) (*in phrases*) **he's always ~ at me** er hackt dauernd auf mir herum, er meckert dauernd an mir herum (*inf*); **he's always (going) ~ at me to get my hair cut** er liegt mir dauernd in den Ohren, daß ich mir die Haare schneiden lassen soll; **he's been ~ at me about that several times** er ist mir ein paarmal damit gekommen; **she's always ~ about her experiences in Italy** sie kommt dauernd mit ihren Italienerfahrungen; **what's he ~ about?** wovon redet er nun schon wieder?

[3] *adj* **(a)** (*switched on*) *lights, TV, radio* an; *brake* angezogen; *electricity, gas* an(gestellt) ◆ **the ~ switch** der Einschalter; **in the ~ position** auf „ein" gestellt; **to leave the engine ~** den Motor laufen lassen; **it wasn't one of his ~ days** (*inf*) er war nicht gerade in Form.
(b) *pred* (*in place*) *lid, cover* drauf ◆ **his hat/tie was ~ crookedly** sein Hut saß/sein Schlips hing schief; **his hat/coat was already ~** er hatte den Hut schon auf/den Mantel schon an.
(c) to be ~ (*being performed*) (*in theatre, cinema*) gegeben *or* gezeigt werden; (*on TV, radio*) gesendet *or* gezeigt werden; **who's ~ tonight?** (*Theat, Film*) wer spielt heute abend?, wer tritt heute abend auf?; (*TV*) wer kommt heute abend (im Fernsehen)?; **you're ~ now** (*Theat, Rad, TV*) Ihr Auftritt!, Sie sind (jetzt) dran (*inf*); **is that programme still ~?** läuft das Programm immer noch?; **the play is still ~** (*running*) das Stück wird immer noch gegeben *or* gespielt; **what's ~ tonight?** was ist *or* steht heute abend auf dem Programm?; **tell me when the English team is ~** sagen Sie mir, wenn die englische Mannschaft dran ist *or* drankommt; **I have nothing ~ tonight** ich habe heute abend nichts vor; **there's a tennis match ~ tomorrow** morgen findet ein Tennismatch statt; **there's a tennis match ~ at the moment** ein Tennismatch ist gerade im Gang; **what's ~ in London?** was ist los in London?; **there's never anything ~ in this town** in dieser Stadt ist nie was los.
(d) (*valid*) **to be ~** (*bet, agreement*) gelten; **you're ~!** abgemacht!; **you're/he's not ~** (*inf*) das ist nicht drin (*inf*); **it's just not ~** (*not acceptable*) das ist einfach nicht drin (*inf*), das gibt es einfach nicht; **his behaviour was really not ~** sein Benehmen war unmöglich; **are you ~?** (*inf: are you with us*) bist du mit von der Partie? (*inf*), machst du mit?

onanism ['əʊnənɪzəm] *n* (*form*) Coitus interruptus *m*; (*masturbation*) Onanie, Masturbation *f*.

once [wʌns] [1] *adv* **(a)** (*on one occasion*) einmal ◆ **~ only** nur einmal; **~ again** *or* **more** noch einmal; **~ again we find that ...** wir stellen wiederum *or* erneut fest, daß ...; **~ or twice** (*lit*) ein- oder zweimal; (*fig*) nur ein paarmal; **~ and for all** ein für allemal; **(every) ~ in a while, ~ in a way** ab und zu mal; **you can come this ~** dieses eine Mal können Sie kommen; **for ~** ausnahmsweise einmal; **I never ~ wondered where you were** ich habe mich kein einziges Mal gefragt, wo Sie wohl waren; **if ~ you begin to hesitate** wenn Sie erst einmal anfangen zu zögern; **~ is enough** einmal reicht.
(b) (*in past*) einmal ◆ **he was ~ famous** er war früher einmal berühmt; **~ upon a time there was ...** es war einmal ...
(c) at ~ (*immediately*) sofort, auf der Stelle; (*at the same time*) auf einmal, gleichzeitig; **all at ~** auf einmal; (*suddenly*) ganz plötzlich; **they came all at ~** sie kamen alle zur gleichen Zeit; **don't spend it all at ~** gib es nicht alles auf einmal aus.

[2] *conj* wenn; (*with past tense*) als ◆ **~ you understand, it's easy** wenn Sie es einmal verstehen, ist es einfach; **~ learnt, it isn't easily forgotten** was man einmal gelernt hat, vergißt man nicht so leicht.

once-over ['wʌnsəʊvəʳ] *n* (*inf*) (*quick look*) flüchtige Überprüfung, kurze Untersuchung ◆ **to give sb/sth the** *or* **a ~** (*appraisal*) jdn/etw mal begucken (*inf*) *or* kurz überprüfen *or* inspizieren; (*clean*) mal kurz über etw (*acc*) gehen (*inf*); **to give sb the** *or* **a ~** (*beat up*) jdn in die Mache nehmen (*inf*).

oncologist [ɒŋ'kɒlədʒɪst] *n* Onkologe *m*, Onkologin *f*.

oncology [ɒŋ'kɒlədʒɪ] *n* Onkologie *f*.

oncoming ['ɒnkʌmɪŋ] [1] *adj car, traffic* entgegenkommend; *danger* nahend, drohend ◆ **the ~ traffic** der Gegenverkehr.

[2] *n* (*of winter etc*) Nahen, Kommen *nt*.

OND (*Brit*) *abbr of* **Ordinary National Diploma.**

one [wʌn] [1] *adj* **(a)** (*number*) ein/eine/ein; (*counting*) eins ◆ **~ man in a thousand** einer von tausend; **there was ~ person too many** da war einer zuviel; **~ girl was pretty, the other was ugly** das eine Mädchen war hübsch, das andere häßlich; **she was in ~ room, he was in the other** sie war im einen Zimmer, er im anderen; **the baby is ~ (year old)** das Kind ist ein Jahr (alt); **it is ~ (o'clock)** es ist eins, es ist ein Uhr; **~ hundred pounds** hundert Pfund; (*on cheque etc*) einhundert Pfund; **that's ~ way of doing it** so kann man's (natürlich) auch machen.
(b) (*indefinite*) **~ morning/day** *etc* **he realized ...** eines Morgens/Tages bemerkte er ...; **~ morning next week** nächste Woche einmal morgens; **~ day next week/soon** nächste Woche einmal/bald einmal; **~ sunny summer's day** an einem sonnigen Sommertag.
(c) (*a certain*) **~ Mr Smith** ein gewisser Herr Smith.
(d) (*sole, only*) **he is the ~ man to tell you** er ist der einzige, der es Ihnen sagen kann; **no ~ man could do it** niemand konnte es allein tun; **my ~ (and only) hope** meine einzige Hoffnung; **the ~ and only Brigitte Bardot** die unvergleichliche Brigitte Bardot.
(e) (*same*) **they all came in the ~ car** sie kamen alle in dem einen Auto; **they are ~ and the same person** das ist ein und dieselbe Person; **it is ~ and the same thing** das ist ein und dasselbe; **it's all ~** das ist einerlei.
(f) (*united*) **God is ~** Gott ist unteilbar; **are they ~ with us?** sind sie mit uns eins?; **we are ~ on the subject** wir sind uns über dieses Thema einig; **they were ~ in wanting that** sie waren sich darin einig, daß sie das wollten.

[2] *pron* **(a)** eine(r s) ◆ **the ~ who ...** der(jenige), der .../die(jenige), die .../das(jenige), das ...; **he/that was the ~** er/das war's; **do you have ~?** haben Sie einen/eine/ein(e)s?; **the red/big** *etc* **~** der/die/das rote/große *etc*; **he has very fine ~s** er hat sehr schöne; **my/his ~** (*inf*) meiner/meine/mein(e)s/seiner/seine/sein(e)s; **not (a single) ~ of them, never ~ of them** nicht eine(r, s) von ihnen, kein einziger/keine einzige/kein einziges; **no ~ of these people** keiner dieser Leute; **any ~** irgendeine(r, s); **every ~** jede(r, s); **this ~** diese(r, s); **that ~** der/die/das, jene(r, s) (*geh*); **which ~?** welche(r, s)?; **the little ~s** (*children*) die Kleinen *pl*; (*animals*) die Jungen *pl*; **my sweet ~** mein Süßer, meine Süße; **that's a good ~** (*inf*) der (Witz) ist gut; (*iro: excuse etc*) (das ist ein) guter Witz; **I'm not ~ to go out often** ich bin nicht der Typ, der oft ausgeht; **I'm not usually ~ to go out often, but today ...** ich gehe sonst nicht oft aus, aber heute ...; **I am not much of a ~ for cakes** (*inf*) ich bin kein großer Freund von Kuchen (*inf*), Kuchen ist eigentlich nicht mein Fall (*inf*); **she was never ~ to cry** Weinen war noch nie ihre Art; (*but she did*) sonst weinte sie nie; **he's never ~ to say no** er sagt nie nein; **what a ~ he is for the girls!** der ist vielleicht ein Schwerenöter! (*inf*); **he's a great ~ for discipline/turning up late** der ist ganz groß, wenn's um Disziplin/ums Zuspätkommen geht; **ooh, you are a ~!** (*inf*) oh, Sie sind mir vielleicht eine(r)! (*inf*); **she is a teacher, and he/her sister wants to be ~ too** sie ist Lehrerin, und er möchte auch gern Lehrer werden/ihre Schwester möchte auch gern eine werden; **I, for ~, think otherwise** ich, zum Beispiel, denke anders; **they came ~ and all** sie kamen alle (ohne Ausnahme); **~ by ~** einzeln; **~ after the other** eine(r, s) nach dem/der/dem anderen; **take ~ or the other** nehmen Sie das eine oder das andere/den einen oder den anderen/die eine oder die andere; **you can't have ~ without the other** Sie können das eine nicht ohne das andere haben; **~ or other of them will do it** der/die eine oder andere wird es tun; **he's not ~ of our group** er gehört nicht zu unserer Gruppe; **he is ~ of us** er ist einer von uns; **~ who knows the country** jemand, der das Land kennt; **in the manner of ~ who ...** in der Art von jemandem, der ...; **like ~ demented/possessed** wie verrückt/besessen.
(b) (*impers*) (*nom*) man; (*acc*) einen; (*dat*) einem ◆ **~ must learn to keep quiet** man muß lernen, still zu sein; **to hurt ~'s foot** sich (*dat*) den Fuß verletzen; **to wash ~'s face/hair** sich (*dat*) das Gesicht/die Haare waschen; **~ likes to see ~'s** *or* **his** (*US*) **friends happy** man sieht seine Freunde gern glücklich.

[3] *n* (*written figure*) Eins *f* ◆ **Chapter ~** Kapitel eins; **in ~s and twos** in kleinen Gruppen; **they became ~** sie wurden eins; **they were made ~** sie wurden vereint; **to be at ~ (with sb)** sich (*dat*) (mit jdm) einig sein; **he was at ~ with the world** er war mit der Welt im Einklang; **he is not at ~ with himself** er ist mit sich selbst nicht im reinen; **it was bedroom and sitting-room (all) in ~** es war Schlaf- und Wohnzimmer in einem; **the goods are sold in ~s** die Waren werden einzeln verkauft; **jumper and trousers all in ~** Pullover und Hose in einem Stück; **I landed him ~** (*inf*) dem habe ich eine(n) *or* eins verpaßt (*inf*); **to be ~ up on sb** (*inf*) (*know more*) jdm eins voraussein; (*have more*) jdm etwas voraushaben; **Rangers were ~ up after the first half** Rangers hatten nach der ersten Halbzeit ein Tor Vorsprung.

one-acter ['wʌn,æktəʳ], **one-act play** ['wʌnækt'pleɪ] *n* Einakter *m*.

one another = **each other**; *see* **each 2 (b)**.

one: ~-armed *adj* einarmig; **~-armed bandit** *n* (*inf*) einarmiger Bandit; **~-eyed** *adj* einäugig; **~-handed** [1] *adj person* einhändig; [2] *adv* mit einer Hand; **~-horse** *adj* **(a)** *vehicle* einspännig; **(b)** (*sl: inferior*) **~-horse town** Kuhdorf *nt* (*inf*); **~-legged** *adj person* einbeinig; **~-line** *adj message etc* einzeilig; **~-liner** *n* (*inf*) witzige Bemerkung; **~-man** *adj* Einmann-; **~-man band** Einmannkapelle *f*; (*fig inf*) Einmannbetrieb *m*; **~-man job** Arbeit *f* für einen einzelnen; **~-man show** (*Art*) Ausstellung *f* eines (einzigen) Künstlers; (*Theat etc*) Einmannshow *f*; **Rover's a ~-man dog** Rover (er)kennt nur einen Herrn (an); **she's a ~-man woman** ihr liegt nur an einem Mann etwas.

oneness ['wʌnnɪs] *n* Einheit *f*; (*of personality, thought*) Geschlossenheit *f*; (*concord: with nature, fellow men*) Einklang *m*.

one: ~-night stand *n* (*Theat*) einmalige Vorstellung; (*fig*) einmalige Angelegenheit; **he's just after a ~-night stand** er sucht nur eine für eine Nacht; **~-off** (*Brit inf*) [1] *adj* einmalig; [2] *n* **a ~-off** etwas Einmaliges; **that mistake** *etc* **was just a ~-off** dieser Fehler *etc* war eine Ausnahme; **~-one** *adj* (*US*) *see* **~-to-one**; **~-party** *adj* (*Pol*) *system* Einparteien-; **~-piece** [1] *adj* einteilig; [2] *n* (*bathing costume*) (einteiliger) Badeanzug, Einteiler *m*; **~-room** *attr*, **~-roomed** *adj* Einzimmer-.

onerous ['ɒnərəs] *adj responsibility* schwer(wiegend); *task, duty* beschwerlich, schwer.

oneself [wʌn'self] *pron* **(a)** (*dir and indir, with prep*) sich; (*~ personally*) sich selbst *or* selber. **(b)** (*emph*) (sich) selbst; *see also* **myself**.

one: ~-shot *adj, n* (*US*) *see* **~-off**; **~-sided** *adj* einseitig; *judgement, account also* parteiisch; **~-time** *adj* ehemalig; **~-to-one** *adj correspondence, correlation* sich Punkt für Punkt entsprechend, eins-zu-eins; **~-to-one teaching** Einzelunterricht *m*; **~-track** *adj* **he's got a ~-track mind** der hat immer nur das eine im Sinn *or* Kopf; **~-upmanship** [,wʌn'ʌpmənʃɪp] *n* **that's just a form of ~-upmanship** damit will er *etc* den anderen nur um eine Nasenlänge voraus sein; **the art of ~-upmanship** (*hum*) die Kunst, allen anderen um einen Schritt *or* eine Nasenlänge voraus zu sein; **~-way** *adj traffic, street* Einbahn-; **~-way ticket** (*US Rail*) einfache Fahrkarte.

ongoing ['ɒngəʊɪŋ] *adj* (*in progress*) *research, project* im Gang befindlich, laufend; (*long-term, continuing*) *development, relationship* andauernd.

onion ['ʌnjən] *n* Zwiebel *f* ◆ **he knows his ~s** (*Brit inf*) er kennt seinen Kram (*inf*).

onion: ~ dome *n* Zwiebelturm *m*; **~-shaped** *adj* zwiebelförmig; **~skin** *n* Zwiebelschale *f*; (*paper*) Florpost *f*; **~ soup** *n* Zwiebelsuppe *f*.

on-line ['ɒnlaɪn] [1] *adj* On-line-.
[2] [ɒn'laɪn] *adv* on line ◆ **to go ~** auf On-line-Betrieb schalten; **to put a printer ~** einen Drucker auf On-line-Betrieb schalten; **to be ~ to sb/sth** mit jdm/etw verbunden sein.

onlooker ['ɒnlʊkəʳ] *n* Zuschauer(in *f*) *m*.

only ['əʊnlɪ] [1] *adj attr* einzige(r, s) ◆ **he's an/my ~ child** er ist ein Einzelkind *nt*/mein einziges Kind; **the ~ one** *or* **person/ones** *or* **people** der/die einzige/die einzigen; **he was the ~ one to leave** *or* **who left** er ist als einziger gegangen; **the ~ thing** das einzige; **the ~ thing I could suggest would be to invite him too** ich könnte höchstens vorschlagen, daß wir *etc* ihn auch einladen; **that's the ~ thing for it/the ~ thing to do** das ist die einzige Möglichkeit; **the ~ thing I have against it is that ...** ich habe nur eins dagegen einzuwenden, nämlich, daß ...; **the ~ thing** *or* **problem is ...** nur ...; **the ~ thing is (that) it's too late** es ist bloß *or* nur schon zu spät; **my ~ wish/regret** das einzige, was ich mir wünsche/was ich bedaure; **the ~ real problem** das einzig wirkliche Problem; **her ~ answer was a grin** *or* **to grin** ihre Antwort bestand nur aus einem Grinsen; *see* **one 1 (d)**.
[2] *adv* **(a)** nur ◆ **it's ~ five o'clock** es ist erst fünf Uhr; **~ yesterday/last week** erst gestern/letzte Woche; **I ~ wanted to be with you** ich wollte nur mit dir zusammen sein; **I wanted ~ to be with you** (*esp liter*) ich wollte weiter nichts, als mit dir zusammen zu sein; **"members ~"** „(Zutritt) nur für Mitglieder"; **~ think of it!** stellen Sie sich das nur (mal) vor!; **~ to think of it made him ill** der bloße Gedanke *or* schon der Gedanke daran machte ihn krank.
(b) (*in constructions*) **~ too true/easy** *etc* nur (all)zu wahr/leicht *etc*; **I'd be ~ too pleased to help** ich würde nur zu gerne helfen; **if ~ that hadn't happened** wenn das bloß *or* nur nicht passiert wäre; **we ~ just caught the train** wir haben den Zug gerade noch gekriegt; **he has ~ just arrived** er ist gerade erst angekommen; **I've ~ just got enough** ich habe gerade genug; **not ~ ... but also ...** nicht nur ..., sondern auch ...
[3] *conj* bloß, nur ◆ **I would do it myself, ~ I haven't time** ich würde es selbst machen, ich habe bloß *or* nur keine Zeit.

ono *abbr of* **or near(est) offer**.

on-off switch ['ɒn'ɒfswɪtʃ] *n* Ein- und Ausschalter *m*.

onomatopoeia [,ɒnəʊmætəʊ'piːə] *n* Lautmalerei, Onomatopöie (*spec*) *f*.

onomatopoeic [,ɒnə,mætəʊ'piːɪk], **onomatopoetic** [,ɒnə,mætəpəʊ'etɪk] *adj* lautmalend, onomatopoetisch (*spec*).

onrush ['ɒnrʌʃ] *n* (*of people*) Ansturm *m*; (*of water*) Schwall *m*.

on-screen ['ɒnskriːn] [1] *adj attr* **(a)** (*Comput*) auf dem Bildschirm ◆ **read the ~ text** lesen Sie den Text auf dem Bildschirm; **~ display** Bildschirmanzeige *f*. **(b)** (*Film, TV*) *romance, kiss etc* Film-/Bildschirm-. **an ~ adventure** ein Film-/Bildschirmabenteuer *nt*.
[2] *adv* (*Film*) auf der Leinwand; (*TV*) auf dem Bildschirm.

onset ['ɒnset] *n* Beginn *m*; (*of cold weather also*) Einbruch *m*; (*of illness*) Ausbruch *m* ◆ **at the first ~ of winter** bei Einbruch *or* Beginn des Winters; **the ~ of this illness is quite gradual** diese Krankheit kommt nur allmählich zum Ausbruch; **with the ~ of old age he ...** als er alt zu werden begann ...

onshore ['ɒnʃɔːʳ] [1] *adj* Land-; *wind* See-, auflandig ◆ **to be ~** an Land sein.
[2] [ɒn'ʃɔːʳ] *adv* (*also* **on shore**) an Land; *blow* landwärts, küstenwärts.

onside [ɒn'saɪd] *adv* nicht im Abseits ◆ **to stay ~** nicht ins Abseits laufen.

on-site [ɒn'saɪt] *adj supervision, maintenance, personnel etc* Vor-Ort-.

onslaught ['ɒnslɔːt] *n* (*Mil*) (heftiger) Angriff (*on* auf *+acc*); (*fig also*) Attacke *f* (*on* auf *+acc*) ◆ **to make an ~ on sb/sth** (*fig*) (*verbally*) jdn/etw angreifen *or* attackieren; (*on work*) einer Sache (*dat*) zu Leibe rücken; **the initial ~ of the storm** das Losbrechen des Sturms.

on-the-job training ['ɒnðə,dʒɒb'treɪnɪŋ] *n* Ausbildung *f* am Arbeitsplatz, innerbetriebliche Ausbildung.

onto ['ɒntʊ] *prep* **(a)** (*upon, on top of*) auf (*+acc*); (*on sth vertical*) an (*+acc*) ◆ **to clip sth ~ sth** etw an etw (*acc*) anklemmen; **to get ~ the committee** in den Ausschuß kommen.
(b) (*in verbal expressions*) *see also vb + on* **to get/come ~ a subject** auf ein Thema zu sprechen kommen; **are you ~ the next chapter already?** sind Sie schon beim nächsten Kapitel?; **when will you get ~ the next chapter?** wann kommen Sie zum nächsten Kapitel?; **to be/get ~** *or* **on to sb** (*find sb out*) jdm auf die Schliche gekommen sein/kommen (*inf*); (*police*) jdm auf der Spur sein/jdm auf die Spur kommen.

ontological [,ɒntə'lɒdʒɪkəl] *adj* ontologisch.

ontology [ɒn'tɒlədʒɪ] *n* Ontologie *f*.

onus ['əʊnəs] *n, no pl* Pflicht *f*; (*burden*) Last, Bürde (*geh*) *f* ◆ **to shift the ~ for sth onto sb** jdm die Verantwortung für etw zuschieben; **the ~ to do it is on** *or* **lies with him** es liegt an ihm, das zu tun; **the ~ of proof rests with the prosecution** die Anklage trägt die Beweislast.

onward ['ɒnwəd] [1] *adj* **the ~ march of time/progress** das Fortschreiten der Zeit/der Vormarsch des Fortschritts; **the ~ path we must tread** der Weg nach vorn, den wir beschreiten müssen.
[2] *adv* (*also* **~s**) voran, vorwärts; *march* weiter ◆ **from today/this time ~** von heute/der Zeit an.
[3] *interj* (*also* **~s**) voran, vorwärts.

onyx ['ɒnɪks] [1] *n* Onyx *m*.
[2] *adj* Onyx-.

oodles ['uːdlz] *npl* (*inf*) jede Menge (*inf*) ◆ **~ and ~** Unmengen *pl* (*inf*); **~ (and ~) of money** Geld wie Heu (*inf*); **~ (and ~) of time** massenhaft Zeit (*inf*).

ooh [uː] [1] *interj* oh.
[2] *vi* **there was a lot of ~ing and ahing** es gab viele Ohs und Ahs.

oomph [ʊmf] *n* (*sl*) **(a)** (*energy*) Pep (*inf*), Schwung *m*. **(b)** (*sex appeal*) Sex *m* (*inf*) ◆ **to have ~** sexy sein (*inf*).

ooze [uːz] [1] *n* **(a)** (*of mud, glue, resin*) Quellen *nt*; (*of water, blood*) Sickern, Triefen *nt*. **(b)** (*mud*) Schlamm *m*.
[2] *vi* **(a)** triefen; (*water, blood also*) sickern; (*wound*) nässen; (*resin, mud, glue*) (heraus)quellen.
(b) (*fig*) **to ~ with sth** *see vt* **(b)**; **he stood there, sweat/charm oozing out of** *or* **from every pore** er stand da, förmlich triefend vor Schweiß/Liebenswürdigkeit.
[3] *vt* **(a)** (aus)schwitzen, absondern ◆ **my shoes were oozing water** das Wasser quoll mir aus den Schuhen.
(b) (*fig*) *kindness, charm, culture* triefen von (*pej*), verströmen; *vanity, pride* strotzen von; *money, wealth* stinken vor (*+dat*) (*inf*) ◆ **the house ~s money** *or* **wealth/culture** das Haus verströmt eine Atmosphäre von Reichtum/Kultur.

◆**ooze away** *vi* wegsickern; (*into ground*) versickern; (*fig*) (*courage, pride, affection etc*) schwinden.

◆**ooze out** *vi* herausquellen; (*water, blood etc*) heraussickern.

op[1] *abbr of* **opus** op.

op[2] [ɒp] *n* (*inf*) *see* **operation**.

opacity [əʊ'pæsɪtɪ] *n* **(a)** Undurchsichtigkeit, Lichtundurchlässigkeit *f*; (*of paint*) Deckkraft *f*. **(b)** (*fig: of essay, meaning etc*) Undurchsichtigkeit *f*.

opal ['əʊpəl] [1] *n* (*stone*) Opal *m*; (*colour*) beige-graue Farbe.
[2] *adj* Opal-; (*in colour*) opalen (*liter*), beige-grau schimmernd.

opalescence [,əʊpə'lesns] *n* Schimmern *nt*, Opaleszenz *f*.

opalescent [,əʊpə'lesnt] *adj* schimmernd, opaleszierend.

opaline ['əʊpəliːn] *adj* opalen (*liter*).

opaque [əʊ'peɪk] *adj* **(a)** opak; *glass also, liquid* trüb; *paper* undurchsichtig. **(b)** (*fig*) *essay, prose* undurchsichtig, unklar.

op art ['ɒp'ɑːt] *n* Op-art *f*.

op cit [ɒp'sɪt] *abbr of* **opere citato** op. cit.

OPEC ['əʊpek] *abbr of* **Organization of Petroleum Exporting Countries** OPEC *f*.

open ['əʊpən] [1] *adj* **(a)** *door, bottle, book, eye, flower etc* offen, auf *pred*, geöffnet; *circuit* offen; *lines of communication* frei; *wound etc* offen ◆ **to keep/hold the door ~** die Tür offen- *or* auflassen/offen- *or* aufhalten; **to fling** *or* **throw the door ~** die Tür aufstoßen *or* aufwerfen; **I can't keep my eyes ~** ich kann die Augen nicht offen- *or* aufhalten; **the window flew ~** das Fenster flog auf; **to lay sb's head ~** (*surgeon*) jds Schädel freilegen; **the thugs laid his head ~** die Schläger brachten ihm eine klaffende Wunde am Kopf bei; **his head was laid ~ when he fell** er schlug sich beim Fallen schwer den Kopf auf; **~ door policy** Politik *f* der offenen Tür; **a shirt ~ at the neck** ein am Hals offenes Hemd.
(b) (*~ for business: shop, bank etc*) geöffnet ◆ **the baker/baker's shop is ~** der Bäcker hat/der Bäckerladen ist *or* hat geöffnet *or* hat auf (*inf*) *or* hat offen (*inf*).
(c) (*not enclosed*) offen; *country, ground also, view* frei; *carriage, car also* ohne Verdeck ◆ **~ sandwich** belegtes Brot; **in the ~ air** im Freien; **on ~ ground** auf offenem *or* freiem Gelände; (*waste ground*) auf unbebautem Gelände.
(d) (*not blocked, Ling*) offen; *road, canal, pores also* frei (*to* für), geöffnet; *rail track, river* frei (*to* für); (*Mus*) *string* leer; *pipe* offen ◆ **~ note** Grundton *m*; **have you had your bowels ~ today?** (*Med form*) haben Sie heute Stuhlgang gehabt?; **~ to traffic/shipping** für den Verkehr/die Schiffahrt freigegeben; **"road ~ to traffic"** „Durchfahrt frei"; **~ cheque** (*Brit*) Barscheck *m*.
(e) (*officially in use*) *building* eingeweiht; *road, bridge also* (offiziell) freigegeben; *exhibition* eröffnet ◆ **to declare sth ~** etw einweihen/freigeben/für eröffnet erklären.
(f) (*not restricted, accessible*) *letter, scholarship* offen; *market, competition also* frei; (*public*) *meeting, trial* öffentlich ◆ **to be ~ to sb** (*competition, membership, possibility*) jdm offenstehen; (*admission*) jdm freistehen; (*place*) für jdn geöffnet sein; (*park*) jdm zur Verfügung stehen; **my house is always ~ to you** mein Haus steht dir immer offen; **~ day** Tag *m* der offenen Tür; **in ~ court** (*Jur*) in öffentlicher Verhandlung; **~ to the public** der Öffentlichkeit

zugänglich; **park ~ to the public** öffentlicher Park; **~ shop** (*Ind*) Open Shop *m*; **we have an ~ shop** wir haben keinen Gewerkschaftszwang; **~ forum** öffentliches Forum.
(g) to be ~ to advice/suggestions/ideas Ratschlägen/Vorschlägen/Ideen zugänglich sein *or* gegenüber offen sein; **I'm ~ to persuasion/correction** ich lasse mich gern überreden/verbessern; **I'm ~ to offers** ich lasse gern mit mir handeln *or* reden; **~ to bribes** Bestechungen zugänglich.
(h) (*not filled*) *evening, time* frei; *job, post also* offen.
(i) (*not concealed*) *campaign, secret, resistance* offen; *hostility also* unverhohlen, unverhüllt.
(j) (*not decided or settled*) *question* offen, ungeklärt, ungelöst ◆ **they left the matter ~** sie ließen die Angelegenheit offen *or* ungeklärt; **to keep an arrangement ~** es offen lassen; **to keep an ~ mind** alles offen lassen; (*judge, jury*) unvoreingenommen sein; **to have an ~ mind on sth** einer Sache (*dat*) aufgeschlossen gegenüberstehen; **keep your mind ~ to new suggestions** verschließen Sie sich neuen Vorschlägen nicht.
(k) (*exposed, not protected*) (*Mil*) *town* offen; *coast also* ungeschützt ◆ **a position ~ to attack** eine exponierte *or* leicht angreifbare Position; **~ to the elements** Wind und Wetter ausgesetzt; **to be ~/lay oneself ~ to criticism/attack** der Kritik/Angriffen ausgesetzt sein/sich der Kritik/Angriffen aussetzen; **a theory ~ to criticism** eine anfechtbare Theorie.
(l) *weave* locker; *fabric, pattern* durchbrochen.
(m) (*frank*) *character, face, person* offen, aufrichtig ◆ **he was ~ with us** er war ganz offen mit uns.
2 *n* **in the ~** (*outside*) im Freien; (*on ~ ground*) auf freiem Feld; **it's all out in the ~** nun ist alles heraus (*inf*), nun ist es alles zur Sprache gekommen; **to bring sth out into the ~** mit etw nicht länger hinterm Berg halten; **to come out into the ~** (*fig*) (*person*) Farbe bekennen, sich erklären; (*affair*) herauskommen; **he eventually came out into the ~ about what he meant to do** er rückte endlich mit der Sprache heraus (*inf*), was er tun wollte; **to force sb out into the ~** jdn zwingen, sich zu stellen; (*fig*) jdn zwingen, Farbe zu bekennen; **to force sth out into the ~** etw zur Sprache bringen.
3 *vt* **(a)** *door, mouth, bottle, letter etc* öffnen, aufmachen (*inf*); *book also, newspaper* aufschlagen; *throttle, circuit* öffnen ◆ **he didn't ~ his mouth once** er hat kein einziges Mal den Mund aufgemacht; **to ~ ranks** (*Mil*) weg- *or* abtreten.
(b) (*officially*) *exhibition* eröffnen; *building* einweihen; *motorway* (für den Verkehr) freigeben.
(c) *region* erschließen ◆ **they ~ed a road through the mountains** durch die Berge wurde eine Straße gebaut.
(d) (*reveal, unfold*) öffnen ◆ **to ~ one's heart to sb** sich jdm eröffnen (*geh*), jdm sein Herz aufschließen (*geh*); **~ your mind to new possibilities** öffnen Sie sich (*dat*) den Blick für neue Möglichkeiten; **it had ~ed new horizons for him** dadurch erschlossen sich ihm neue Horizonte.
(e) (*start*) *case, trial* eröffnen; *account also* einrichten; *debate, conversation etc also* beginnen.
(f) (*set up*) *shop* eröffnen, aufmachen (*inf*); *school* einrichten.
(g) (*Med*) *pores* öffnen ◆ **to ~ the bowels** (*person*) Stuhlgang haben; (*medicine*) abführen.
(h) to ~ fire (*Mil*) das Feuer eröffnen (*on* auf *+acc*).
4 *vi* **(a)** aufgehen; (*door, flower, book, wound, pores also*) sich öffnen ◆ **I couldn't get the bonnet/bottle to ~** ich habe die Motorhaube/Flasche nicht aufbekommen; **it won't ~** es geht nicht auf.
(b) (*shop, museum*) öffnen, aufmachen.
(c) (*afford access: door*) führen (*into* in *+acc*) ◆ **the two rooms ~ into one another** diese zwei Zimmer sind durch eine Tür verbunden; *see also* **~ on to.**
(d) (*start*) beginnen (*with* mit); (*Cards, Chess*) eröffnen ◆ **the play ~s next week** das Stück wird ab nächster Woche gegeben; **when we/the play ~ed in Hull** bei unserer ersten Vorstellung in Hull/als das Stück nach Hull kam.
◆**open on to** *vi +prep obj* (*window*) gehen auf (*+acc*); (*door also*) führen auf (*+acc*).
◆**open out** **1** *vi* **(a)** (*become wider: river, street*) sich verbreitern (*into* zu); (*valley also, view*) sich weiten, sich öffnen.
(b) (*flower*) sich öffnen, aufgehen.
(c) (*map*) sich ausfalten lassen.
(d) (*fig*) (*person*) aus sich herausgehen; (*business*) sich ausdehnen (*into* auf *+acc*); (*new horizons*) sich auftun.
2 *vt sep* **(a)** (*unfold*) *map, newspaper etc* auseinanderfalten, aufmachen (*inf*).
(b) (*make wider*) *hole* erweitern, vergrößern. **(c)** (*fig*) (*make expansive*) *person* aus der Reserve locken; (*develop*) *business* ausdehnen, erweitern.
◆**open up** **1** *vi* **(a)** (*flower*) sich öffnen, aufgehen; (*fig*) (*prospects*) sich eröffnen, sich ergeben, sich erschließen; (*field, new horizons*) sich auftun, sich erschließen.
(b) (*become expansive*) gesprächiger werden ◆ **to get sb to ~ ~** jdn zum Reden bringen; **to ~ ~ about sth** über etw (*acc*) sprechen *or* reden.
(c) (*inf: accelerate*) aufdrehen (*inf*).
(d) (*unlock doors: of house, shop etc*) aufschließen, aufmachen ◆ **~ ~!** aufmachen!
(e) (*start up: new shop*) aufmachen.
(f) (*start firing: guns, enemy*) das Feuer eröffnen.
(g) (*Sport: game*) sich auflockern.
2 *vt sep* **(a)** (*make accessible*) *territory, mine, prospects* erschließen; *new horizons, field of research etc also* auftun; (*unblock*) *disused tunnel etc* freimachen ◆ **to ~ ~ a country to trade** ein Land für den Handel erschließen.
(b) (*cut, make*) *passage* bauen; *gap* schaffen; *hole* machen; (*make wider*) *hole* größer *or* weiter machen, vergrößern.
(c) (*unlock*) *house, shop, car etc* aufschließen, aufmachen.
(d) (*start*) *business* eröffnen; *shop also* aufmachen.
(e) (*Sport*) *game* auflockern.
open: ~-air *adj* im Freien; **~-air swimming pool** *n* Freibad *nt*; **~-air theatre** *n* Freilichtbühne *f*, Freilichttheater *nt*; **~-and-shut** *adj* simpel; **it's an ~-and-shut case** es ist ein glasklarer Fall; **~-cast** *adj coal-mine* über Tage *pred*; **~-cast mining** Tagebau *m*; **~-ended** *adj* (*fig*) *contract* offen, zeitlich nicht begrenzt; *offer* unbegrenzt; *commitment* Blanko-; *discussion* alles offen lassend *attr*; *subject, category* endlos, uferlos; **this question/subject is ~-ended** über diese Frage/dieses Thema kann man endlos weiterdiskutieren; **~ enrollment** *n* (*US Univ*) *Einschreibung f ohne Zulassungsvoraussetzungen.*
opener ['əʊpnəʳ] *n* **(a)** Öffner *m*. **(b) for ~s** (*inf*) für den Anfang.
open: ~-eyed *adj* mit weit offenen Augen; **he stood in ~-eyed amazement** er stand da und staunte nur; **~-handed** *adj* freigebig, großzügig; **~-handedness** *n* Freigebigkeit, Großzügigkeit *f*; **~-hearted** *adj* offen, offenherzig; **~-hearth** *adj* (*Tech*) Herdofen-; *process* (Siemens-)Martin-; **~-heart surgery** *n* Eingriff *m* am offenen Herzen; **~ house** *n* **it's ~ house there** das ist ein gastfreundliches Haus, das ist ein Haus der offenen Tür; **to keep ~ house** ein offenes Haus führen; **~ housing** *n* (*US*) *Wohnraumvergabe f ohne (Rassen)diskriminierung.*
opening ['əʊpnɪŋ] **1** *n* **(a)** Öffnung *f*; (*in hedge, branches, clouds, wall etc also*) Loch *nt*; (*cleft also*) Spalt *m*; (*in traffic stream*) Lücke *f*; (*forest clearing*) Lichtung *f*; (*fig: in conversation*) Anknüpfungspunkt *m*.
(b) (*beginning, initial stages*) Anfang *m*; (*of debate, speech, trial also, Chess, Cards*) Eröffnung *f*.
(c) (*official ~*) (*of exhibition, stores*) Eröffnung *f*; (*of building also*) Einweihung *f*; (*of motorway*) Freigabe *f* (für den Verkehr) ◆ **O~ of Parliament** Parlamentseröffnung *f*.
(d) (*action*) (*of door, mouth, bottle, letter, pub, shop etc*) Öffnen *nt*; (*by sb also*) Öffnung *f*; (*of flower also*) Aufgehen *nt*; (*of account*) Eröffnung *f*; (*setting up: of shop, school etc*) Eröffnen, Aufmachen *nt* ◆ **hours of ~** Öffnungszeiten *pl*.
(e) (*opportunity*) Möglichkeit, Chance *f*; (*for career also*) Start *m*; (*job vacancy*) (freie) Stelle ◆ **he gave his adversary an ~** er bot seinem Gegner eine Blöße; **leave an ~ for negotiations** lassen Sie die Möglichkeit für Verhandlungen offen.
2 *attr* (*initial, first*) erste(r, s); *speech, move, gambit also* Eröffnungs-; *remarks* einführend.
opening: ~ ceremony *n* Eröffnungsfeierlichkeiten *pl*; **~ night** *n* Eröffnungsvorstellung *f* (am Abend); **~ price** *n* (*St Ex*) Eröffnungs- *or* Anfangskurs *m*; **~ time** *n* Öffnungszeit *f*; **what are the bank's ~ times?** wann hat die Bank geöffnet?; **when is ~ time on Sundays?** wann machen am Sonntag die Lokale auf?
openly ['əʊpənlɪ] *adv* (*without concealment*) offen; *speak also* freiheraus; (*publicly*) öffentlich.
open: ~-minded *adj* aufgeschlossen; **~-mindedness** *n* Aufgeschlossenheit *f*; **~-mouthed** [,əʊpn'maʊðd] *adj* (*in surprise or stupidity*) mit offenem Mund, baff *pred* (*inf*); **she stood in ~-mouthed amazement** sie sperrte vor Staunen den Mund auf; **~-necked** *adj shirt* mit offenem Kragen.
openness ['əʊpnnɪs] *n* **(a)** (*frankness*) Offenheit, Aufrichtigkeit *f*; (*publicness*) Öffentlichkeit, Offenheit *f*. **(b)** (*fig: of mind*) Aufgeschlossenheit *f* (*to* für). **(c)** (*of countryside, coast*) Offenheit *f*. **(d)** (*looseness: of weave*) Lockerheit *f*.
open: ~-plan *adj office* Großraum-; *stairs* Frei-, frei angelegt; *flat etc* offen angelegt; **~ prison** *n* offenes Gefängnis; **~ season** *n* (*Hunt*) Jagdzeit *f*; **~ shop** *n* Open Shop *m*; **we have an ~ shop** wir haben keinen Gewerkschaftszwang; **O~ University** *n* (*Brit*) Fernuniversität *f*; **to do an O~ University course** ein Fernstudium machen *or* absolvieren; **~work** **1** *n* (*Sew*) Durchbrucharbeit *f*; (*Archit*) Durchbruchmauerwerk *nt*; **2** *adj* durchbrochen.
opera ['ɒpərə] *n* Oper *f* ◆ **to go to the ~** in die Oper gehen.
operable ['ɒpərəbl] *adj* **(a)** (*Med*) operierbar, operabel. **(b)** (*practicable*) durchführbar, praktikabel.
opera *in cpds* Opern-; **~ glasses** *npl* Opernglas *nt*; **~ hat** *n* Chapeau claque *m*; **~ house** *n* Opernhaus *nt*.
operand ['ɒpə,rænd] *n* (*Math, Comput*) Operand *m*.
opera singer *n* Opernsänger(in *f*) *m*.
operate ['ɒpəreɪt] **1** *vi* **(a)** (*machine, mechanism*) funktionieren; (*be powered*) betrieben werden (*by, on* mit); (*be in operation*) laufen, in Betrieb sein; (*fig: worker*) arbeiten ◆ **how does it ~?** wie funktioniert es?; **to ~ at maximum efficiency** (*lit, fig*) Höchstleistung bringen.
(b) (*theory, plan, law*) sich auswirken; (*causes, factors also*) hinwirken (*on, for* auf *+acc*); (*organization, system*) arbeiten; (*medicine*) wirken ◆ **that law/plan is not operating properly** dieses Gesetz greift nicht richtig/der Plan funktioniert nicht richtig; **I don't understand how his mind ~s** ich verstehe seine Gedankengänge nicht; **to ~ against/in favour of sb/sth** gegen jdn/etw/zugunsten von jdm/etw wirken.
(c) (*carry on one's business*) operieren; (*company also*) Geschäfte tätigen; (*detective, spy also*) agieren; (*airport, station*) in Betrieb sein; (*buses, planes*) verkehren ◆ **I don't like the way he ~s** ich mag seine Methoden nicht; **that firm ~s by defrauding its customers** es gehört zu den (Geschäfts)methoden der Firma, die Kunden zu betrügen.
(d) (*Mil*) operieren.
(e) (*Med*) operieren (*on sb/sth* jdn/etw) ◆ **to be ~d on** operiert werden; **he ~d on him for appendicitis/a cataract** er operierte ihn am Blinddarm/auf grauen Star.
2 *vt* **(a)** (*person*) *machine, switchboard etc* bedienen; (*set in operation*) in Be-

trieb setzen; *small mechanism, brakes etc also* betätigen; (*lever, button etc*) betätigen; *small mechanism etc* betätigen, auslösen; (*electricity, batteries etc*) betreiben.
(b) (*manage*) *business* betreiben, führen.
(c) (*put into practice*) *system, law* anwenden, arbeiten nach; *policy also* betreiben.
(d) (*airline etc*) *route* bedienen; *bus etc service* unterhalten; *holiday, tours* veranstalten.

operatic [ˌɒpəˈrætɪk] *adj singer, music* Opern-.

operatics [ˌɒpəˈrætɪks] *n sing*: **(amateur)** ~ Amateuropern *pl*.

operating [ˈɒpəreɪtɪŋ] *adj attr* **(a)** (*Tech, Comm*) *altitude, pressure, cost, profit* Betriebs- ♦ ~ **statement** (*US*) Gewinn- und Verlustrechnung *f*; ~ **system** (*Comput*) Betriebssystem *nt*. **(b)** (*Med*) Operations- ♦ ~ **theatre** (*Brit*) *or* **room** Operationssaal, OP *m*.

operation [ˌɒpəˈreɪʃən] *n* **(a)** (*act of operating vi*) (*of machine, mechanism, system*) Funktionieren *nt*; (*of machine also*) Gang, Lauf *m*; (*of plan*) Durchführung *f*; (*of theory*) Anwendung *f*; (*method of functioning*) (*of machine, organization*) Arbeitsweise *f*; (*of system, organ*) Funktionsweise *f*; (*of law*) Wirkungsweise *f* ♦ **to be in** ~ (*machine*) in Betrieb sein; (*law*) in Kraft sein; (*plan*) durchgeführt werden; **to be out of** ~ außer Betrieb sein; (*fig: person*) nicht einsatzfähig sein; **to come into** ~ (*machine*) in Gang kommen; (*law*) in Kraft treten; (*plan*) zur Anwendung gelangen; **to bring** *or* **put a law into** ~ ein Gesetz in Kraft setzen.
(b) (*act of operating vt*) (*of machine etc*) Bedienung, Handhabung *f*; (*of small mechanism*) Betätigung *f*; (*of business*) Betreiben, Führen *nt*; (*of system, policy*) Anwendung *f*; (*of plan, law*) Durchführung *f*; (*of route*) Bedienung *f*; (*of bus service etc*) Unterhaltung *f*; (*of tours*) Veranstaltung *f*.
(c) (*Med*) Operation *f* (*on an +dat*) ♦ **to have an** ~ operiert werden ♦ **to have a serious/heart** ~ sich einer schweren Operation/Herzoperation unterziehen; **to have an** ~ **for a hernia** wegen eines Bruchs operiert werden.
(d) (*enterprise*) Unternehmen *nt*, Unternehmung, Operation *f*; (*task, stage in undertaking*) Arbeitsgang *m*; (*Math*) Rechenvorgang *m*, Operation *f* ♦ (**business**) **~s** Geschäfte *pl*; **to cease/resume ~s** den Geschäftsverkehr einstellen/wieder aufnehmen; **mental ~s** Denkvorgänge *pl*.
(e) (*esp Mil: campaign*) Operation *f*, Einsatz *m*, Unternehmen *nt*; (*in police force etc*) Einsatz *m* ♦ **~s room** Hauptquartier *nt*; **O~ Cynthia** Operation Cynthia.

operational [ˌɒpəˈreɪʃənl] *adj* **(a)** (*ready for use or action*) *machine, vehicle* betriebsbereit *or* -fähig; *army unit, aeroplane, tank etc*, (*fig*) *worker etc* einsatzfähig; (*in use or action*) *machine, vehicle etc* in Betrieb, in *or* im Gebrauch; *airport* in Betrieb; *army unit etc* im Einsatz.
(b) (*Tech, Comm*) *altitude, fault, costs* Betriebs- ♦ **the** ~ **range of radar/an aircraft** der Einflußbereich von Radar/der Flugbereich eines Flugzeugs.
(c) (*Mil*) *patrol, flight* Einsatz-; *base* Operations- ♦ **these submarines have never seen** ~ **service** diese U-Boote sind nie eingesetzt worden *or* kamen nie zum Einsatz.

operative [ˈɒpərətɪv] **1** *adj* **(a)** (*producing an effect*) *measure, laws* wirksam; *clause* maßgeblich, entscheidend; (*in effect*) *law* rechtsgültig, geltend ♦ **"if" being the** ~ **word** wobei ich „wenn" betone; **to become** ~ (*law*) in Kraft treten; (*system etc*) verbindlich eingeführt werden.
(b) (*Med*) *treatment* operativ.
(c) (*manual*) *skills* maschinentechnisch; *class* Arbeiter-.
2 *n* (*of machinery*) Maschinenarbeiter(in *f*) *m*; (*detective*) Detektiv *m*; (*spy*) Agent(in *f*) *m*.

operator [ˈɒpəreɪtəʳ] *n* **(a)** (*Telec*) ≃ Vermittlung *f* ♦ **a call through the** ~ ein handvermitteltes Gespräch.
(b) (*of machinery*) (Maschinen)arbeiter(in *f*) *m*; (*of vehicle, lift*) Führer(in *f*) *m*; (*of electrical equipment*) Bediener *m*; (*of computer etc*) Operator(in *f*) *m* ♦ **lathe** *etc* ~ Arbeiter(in *f*) *m* an der Drehbank *etc*.
(c) (*private company, company owner*) Unternehmer *m*; (*Fin*) (Börsen)makler *m*; (*tour* ~) Veranstalter *m*.
(d) (*inf*) (raffinierter) Kerl, Typ (*inf*) *m*; (*criminal*) Gauner *m* ♦ **to be a smooth/clever** ~ raffiniert vorgehen.

operetta [ˌɒpəˈretə] *n* Operette *f*.

ophthalmic [ɒfˈθælmɪk] *adj* Augen- ♦ ~ **optician** *approbierter Augenoptiker, der berechtigt ist, Sehhilfen zu verschreiben.*

ophthalmologist [ˌɒfθælˈmɒlədʒɪst] *n* Ophthalmologe *m*, Ophthalmologin *f*.

ophthalmology [ˌɒfθælˈmɒlədʒɪ] *n* Augenheilkunde, Ophthalmologie (*spec*) *f*.

ophthalmoscope [ɒfˈθælməskəʊp] *n* Augenspiegel *m*.

opiate [ˈəʊpɪɪt] **1** *n* Opiat *nt*; (*fig*) Beruhigungsmittel *nt*.
2 *adj* opiumhaltig.

opine [əʊˈpaɪn] *vt* (*liter*) dafürhalten (*geh*), meinen.

➤ **opinion** [əˈpɪnjən] *n* **(a)** (*belief, view*) Meinung, Ansicht *f* (*about, on* zu); (*political, religious*) Anschauung *f* ♦ **in my** ~ meiner Meinung *or* Ansicht nach, meines Erachtens; **in the** ~ **of certain experts** nach Ansicht gewisser Experten; **to be of the** ~ **that** ... der Meinung *or* Ansicht sein, daß ...; **to express** *or* **put forward an** ~ seine Meinung äußern *or* vorbringen; **to ask sb's** ~ jdn nach seiner Meinung fragen; **it is a matter of** ~ das ist Ansichtssache; **I have no** ~ **about it** *or* **on the matter** dazu habe ich keine Meinung.
(b) *no pl* (*estimation*) Meinung *f* ♦ **to have a good** *or* **high/low** *or* **poor** ~ **of sb/sth** eine gute *or* hohe/keine gute *or* eine schlechte Meinung von jdm/etw haben; **to form an** ~ **of sb/sth** sich (*dat*) eine Meinung über jdn/etw bilden.
(c) (*professional advice*) Gutachten *nt*; (*esp Med*) Befund *m* ♦ **it is the** ~ **of the court that** ... das Gericht ist zu der Auffassung *or* Ansicht gekommen, daß ...; **to seek** *or* **get a second** ~ (*esp Med*) ein zweites Gutachten *or* einen zweiten Befund einholen.

opinionated [əˈpɪnjəneɪtɪd] *adj* selbstherrlich, rechthaberisch.

opinion poll *n* Meinungsumfrage *f*.

opium [ˈəʊpɪəm] *n* (*lit, fig*) Opium *nt* ♦ **the** ~ **of the masses** Opium *nt* für das Volk.

opium *in cpds* Opium-; ~ **den** *n* Opiumhöhle *f*; ~ **fiend** *n* Opiumsüchtige(r) *mf*; ~ **poppy** *n* Schlafmohn *m*.

opossum [əˈpɒsəm] *n* Opossum *nt*.

opp *abbr of* **opposite** Gegent.

➤ **opponent** [əˈpəʊnənt] *n* Gegner(in *f*) *m*; (*in debate, battle of wits etc also*) Opponent *m*.

opportune [ˈɒpətjuːn] *adj time* gelegen, günstig; *remark* an passender Stelle; *action, event* rechtzeitig, opportun (*geh*).

opportunely [ˈɒpətjuːnlɪ] *adv* gelegen, günstig, opportun (*geh*); *remark* an passender Stelle.

opportunism [ˌɒpəˈtjuːnɪzəm] *n* Opportunismus *m*.

opportunist [ˌɒpəˈtjuːnɪst] **1** *n* Opportunist *m*.
2 *adj* opportunistisch.

opportunity [ˌɒpəˈtjuːnɪtɪ] *n* **(a)** Gelegenheit *f* ♦ **at the first** *or* **earliest** ~ bei der erstbesten Gelegenheit; **I have little/no** ~ **for listening** *or* **to listen to music** ich habe wenig/nie Gelegenheit, Musik zu hören; **to take/seize the** ~ **to do sth** *or* **of doing sth** die Gelegenheit nutzen/ergreifen, etw zu tun; **as soon as I get the** ~ sobald sich die Gelegenheit ergibt; ~ **makes the thief** (*Prov*) Gelegenheit macht Diebe (*Prov*).
(b) (*chance to better oneself*) Chance, Möglichkeit *f* ♦ **opportunities for promotion** Aufstiegsmöglichkeiten *or* -chancen *pl*; **equality of** ~ Chancengleichheit *f*.

oppose [əˈpəʊz] *vt* **(a)** (*be against*) ablehnen; (*fight against*) sich entgegenstellen *or* entgegensetzen (*+dat*), opponieren gegen (*form*); *leadership, orders, plans, decisions, sb's wishes* sich widersetzen (*+dat*); *government* sich stellen gegen ♦ **if you think he is the best I won't** ~ **you** wenn Sie meinen, daß er der beste ist, werde ich mich nicht dagegen stellen; **he ~s our coming** er ist absolut dagegen, daß wir kommen.
(b) (*stand in opposition: candidate*) kandidieren gegen.
(c) (*form*) (*against, to dat*) (*set up in opposition*) entgegensetzen, entgegenstellen; (*contrast*) gegenüberstellen.

➤ **opposed** [əˈpəʊzd] *adj* **(a)** *pred* (*hostile*) dagegen ♦ **to be** ~ **to sb/sth** gegen jdn/etw sein; **I am** ~ **to your going away** ich bin dagegen, daß Sie gehen.
(b) (*opposite, contrasted*) entgegengesetzt, gegensätzlich ♦ ~ **to all reason** entgegen aller Vernunft. **(c) as** ~ **to** im Gegensatz zu.

opposing [əˈpəʊzɪŋ] *adj team* gegnerisch; *army* feindlich; *characters* entgegengesetzt, gegensätzlich; *minority* opponierend ♦ ~ **party** (*Jur*) Gegenpartei *f*; ~ **counsel** (*Jur*) Anwalt *m* der Gegenpartei.

opposite [ˈɒpəzɪt] **1** *adj* **(a)** (*in place*) entgegengesetzt; (*facing*) gegenüberliegend *attr*, gegenüber *pred* ♦ **to be** ~ gegenüber liegen/stehen/sitzen *etc*; **on the** ~ **page** auf der Seite gegenüber, auf der gegenüberliegenden *or* anderen Seite.
(b) (*contrary*) entgegengesetzt (*to, from dat*, zu) ♦ **the** ~ **sex** das andere Geschlecht; ~ **number** Pendant *nt*; ~ **poles** (*Geog*) entgegengesetzte Pole *pl*; (*Elec also*) Gegenpole *pl*; (*fig*) zwei Extreme; **they've got quite** ~ **characters** sie sind ganz gegensätzliche Charaktere.
2 *n* Gegenteil *nt*; (*contrast: of pair*) Gegensatz *m* ♦ **black and white are ~s** Schwarz und Weiß sind Gegensätze; **quite the ~!** ganz im Gegenteil!; **she's quite the** ~ **of her husband** sie ist genau das Gegenteil von ihrem Mann.
3 *adv* gegenüber, auf der anderen *or* gegenüberliegenden Seite ♦ **they sat** ~ sie saßen uns/ihnen/sich *etc* gegenüber.
4 *prep* gegenüber (*+dat*) ♦ ~ **one another** sich gegenüber; **they live** ~ **us** sie wohnen uns gegenüber, sie wohnen gegenüber von uns; **to play** ~ **sb** (*Theat*) jds Gegenspieler sein, die Gegenrolle zu jdm spielen.

opposition [ˌɒpəˈzɪʃən] *n* **(a)** (*resistance*) Widerstand *m*, Opposition *f*; (*people resisting*) Opposition *f* ♦ **to offer** ~ **to sb/sth** jdm/einer Sache Widerstand entgegensetzen; **to act in** ~ **to sth** einer Sache (*dat*) zuwiderhandeln; **to start up a business in** ~ **to sb** ein Konkurrenzunternehmen zu jdm aufmachen; **without** ~ widerstandslos.
(b) (*contrast*) Gegensatz *m* ♦ **to be in** ~ **to sb** anderer Meinung als jd sein; **to be in** ~ **to sth** im Gegensatz zu etw stehen; **he found himself in** ~ **to the general opinion** er sah sich im Widerspruch zur allgemeinen Meinung.
(c) (*Astron*) Opposition *f*, Gegenschein *m* ♦ **planet in** ~ Planet *m* in Opposition *or* im Gegenschein.
(d) (*esp Brit Parl*) **O~** Opposition(spartei) *f*; **the O~, Her Majesty's O~** die Opposition; **leader of the O~** Oppositionsführer(in *f*) *m*; **O~ benches** Oppositionsbank *f*.

oppress [əˈpres] *vt* **(a)** (*tyrannize*) unterdrücken. **(b)** (*weigh down*) bedrücken, lasten auf (*+dat*); (*heat*) lasten auf (*+dat*) ♦ **the climate ~es me** das Klima macht mir schwer zu schaffen; **I feel ~ed by the heat** die Hitze lastet schwer auf mir.

oppression [əˈpreʃən] *n* **(a)** (*tyranny*) Unterdrückung *f*. **(b)** (*fig*) (*depression*) Bedrängnis, Bedrücktheit *f*; (*due to heat, climate*) bedrückende Atmosphäre ♦ **the** ~ **of his spirits** seine Bedrängtheit.

oppressive [əˈpresɪv] *adj* **(a)** (*tyrannical*) *regime, laws* repressiv; *taxes* (er)drückend. **(b)** (*fig*) drückend; *thought* bedrückend; *heat also* schwül.

oppressively [əˈpresɪvlɪ] *adv* **(a)** *rule* repressiv ♦ **to tax** ~ drückende Steuern *pl* erheben. **(b)** (*fig*) drückend.

➤ LANGUAGE IN USE: **opinion: a** → 1.1, 2.1, 6.1, 6.2, 6.3, 11.1, 13, 26.2 **opponent** → 14 **opposed: a** → 12.1, 14

oppressiveness [ə'presɪvnɪs] *n* **(a)** Unterdrückung *f* (*of* durch); (*of taxes*) (er)drückende Last. **(b)** (*fig*) bedrückende Atmosphäre; (*of thought*) schwere Last; (*of heat, climate*) Schwüle *f*.
oppressor [ə'presəʳ] *n* Unterdrücker *m*.
opprobrious [ə'prəʊbrɪəs] *adj invective, remark* verächtlich, schmähend; *conduct* schändlich, schandhaft, schimpflich.
opprobrium [ə'prəʊbrɪəm] *n* (*disgrace*) Schande, Schmach *f*; (*scorn, reproach*) Schmähung *f* ◆ **a term of ~** ein Schmähwort *nt*.
opt [ɒpt] *vi* **to ~ for sth/to do sth** sich für etw entscheiden/sich entscheiden, etw zu tun; **to ~ to belong to Britain** für Großbritannien optieren.
◆**opt in** *vi* beitreten (*+dat*).
◆**opt out** *vi* sich anders entscheiden; (*of awkward situation also*) abspringen (*of* bei); (*of responsibility, invitation*) ablehnen (*of acc*); (*give up membership, Rad, TV*) austreten (*of* aus); (*of insurance scheme*) kündigen (*of acc*) ◆ **he ~ed ~ of going to the party** er entschied sich, doch nicht zur Party zu gehen.
optative ['ɒptətɪv] **1** *n* Optativ *m*, Wunschform *f*.
2 *adj* optativ.
optic ['ɒptɪk] *adj nerve, centre* Seh-.
optical ['ɒptɪkəl] *adj* optisch ◆ **~ character reader** (*Comput*) optischer Klarschriftleser; **~ character recognition** (*Comput*) optische Zeichenerkennung; **~ disk** optische Platte; **~ fibre** (*material*) Glasfaser *f*; (*cable*) Glasfaserkabel *nt*; **~ illusion** optische Täuschung.
optician [ɒp'tɪʃən] *n* Augenarzt *m*, Augenärztin *f*, Optiker(in *f*) *m*.
optics ['ɒptɪks] *n sing* Optik *f*.
optima ['ɒptɪmə] *pl of* **optimum**.
optimal ['ɒptɪml] *adj* optimal.
optimism ['ɒptɪmɪzəm] *n* Optimismus *m*.
optimist ['ɒptɪmɪst] *n* Optimist(in *f*) *m*.
optimistic [ˌɒptɪ'mɪstɪk] *adj* optimistisch, zuversichtlich ◆ **to be ~ about sth** in bezug auf etw (*acc*) optimistisch sein; **I'm not very ~ about it** ich bin nicht sehr optimistisch.
optimistically [ˌɒptɪ'mɪstɪkəlɪ] *adv see adj*.
optimize ['ɒptɪmaɪz] *vt* optimieren.
optimum ['ɒptɪməm] **1** *adj* optimal; *conditions also* bestmöglich.
2 *n, pl* **optima** *or* **-s** Optimum *nt* ◆ **at an ~** optimal.
option ['ɒpʃən] *n* **(a)** (*choice*) Wahl *f no pl*; (*possible course of action also*) Möglichkeit *f* ◆ **since you've got the ~ of leaving or staying** da Sie die Wahl haben, ob Sie gehen oder bleiben wollen; **I have little/no ~** mir bleibt kaum eine/keine andere Wahl; **he had no ~ but to come** ihm blieb nichts anderes übrig, als zu kommen; **you have only two ~s (open to you)** es stehen Ihnen nur zwei Möglichkeiten zur Wahl; **that leaves us no ~** das läßt uns keine andere Wahl; **to leave one's ~s open** sich (*dat*) alle Möglichkeiten offenlassen; **imprisonment without the ~ of a fine** (*Jur*) Gefängnisstrafe *f* ohne Zulassung einer ersatzweisen Geldstrafe.
(b) (*Comm*) Option *f* (*on* auf *+acc*); (*on house, goods etc also*) Vorkaufsrecht *nt* (*on* an *+dat*); (*on shares*) Bezugsrecht *nt* (*on* für) ◆ **with an ~ to buy** mit einer Kaufoption *or* (*on shares*) Bezugsoption; (*on approval*) zur Ansicht; **to have a 20-day ~** eine Option mit einer Frist von 20 Tagen haben.
(c) (*Univ, Sch*) Wahlfach *nt*.
optional ['ɒpʃənl] *adj* (*not compulsory*) freiwillig; (*Sch, Univ*) *subject* Wahl-, wahlfrei, fakultativ; (*not basic*) *trim, mirror etc* auf Wunsch erhältlich ◆ **"evening dress ~"** „Abendkleidung nicht Vorschrift"; **~ extras** Extras *pl*; **the cigar lighter is an ~ extra** der Zigarettenanzünder wird auf Wunsch eingebaut.
optometrist [ɒp'tɒmətrɪst] *n* (*US: optician*) Optiker(in *f*) *m*.
opt-out ['ɒptaʊt] **1** *adj attr* **(a)** (*Brit*) *school, hospital* aus der Kontrolle der Kommunalverwaltung ausgetreten. **(b)** (*esp Brit*) **~ clause** Rücktrittsklausel *f*.
2 *n* **(a)** (*Brit: by school, hospital*) Austritt *m* aus der Kontrolle der Kommunalverwaltung. **(b)** (*from agreement, treaty*) Rücktritt *m*.
opulence ['ɒpjʊləns] *n, no pl see adj* Reichtum *m*; Wohlhabenheit *f*; Prunk *m*, Stattlichkeit *f*; Feudalität *f*; Üppigkeit *f*; Fülligkeit *f* ◆ **to live in ~** im Überfluß leben.
opulent ['ɒpjʊlənt] *adj* reich; *appearance* (*of person*) *also* wohlhabend; *clothes, building, room* prunkvoll, stattlich; *car, chairs, carpets* feudal; *décor also, lifestyle, vegetation* üppig; *figure* üppig, füllig.
opus ['əʊpəs] *n, pl* **opera** ['ɒpərə] *n* (*Mus*) Opus *nt*.
or¹ [ɔːʳ] *n* (*Her*) Gold *nt*.
▼ **or²** *conj* **(a)** oder; (*with neg*) noch ◆ **he could not read ~ write** er konnte weder lesen noch schreiben; **without tears ~ sighs** ohne Tränen oder Seufzer; **you'd better go ~ (else) you'll be late** gehen Sie jetzt besser, sonst kommen Sie zu spät; **you'd better do it ~ else!** tu das lieber, sonst ...!; **in a day/month ~ two** in ein bis *or* oder zwei Tagen/Monaten.
(b) (*that is*) (oder) auch ◆ **the Lacedaemonians, ~ Spartans** die Lazedämonier, (oder) auch Spartaner; **the Congo, ~ rather, Zaire** der Kongo, beziehungsweise Zaire.
oracle ['ɒrəkl] *n* **(a)** Orakel *nt*; (*person*) Seher(in *f*) *m*; (*fig*) Alleswisser *m* ◆ **Delphic ~** delphisches Orakel, Orakel zu Delphi. **(b) O~** ® *britisches Videotext-System*.
oracular [ɒ'rækjʊləʳ] *adj inscriptions, utterances* orakelhaft; *powers* seherisch; (*fig*) weise.
oral ['ɔːrəl] **1** *adj* **(a)** *consonant, phase etc* oral; *medicine also* Oral- (*spec*), zum Einnehmen; *cavity, hygiene, sex also* Mund-. **(b)** (*verbal*) mündlich ◆ **to improve one's ~ skills in a language** eine Sprache besser sprechen lernen.
2 *n* Mündliche(s) *nt*.
orally ['ɔːrəlɪ] *adv* **(a)** oral. **(b)** (*verbally*) mündlich.
orange ['ɒrɪndʒ] **1** *n* **(a)** (*fruit, tree*) Orange, Apfelsine *f*; (*drink*) Orangensaft *m*. **(b)** (*colour*) Orange *nt*.
2 *adj* **(a)** Orangen-. **(b)** (*in colour*) orange *inv*, orange(n)farben *or* -farbig.
orangeade ['ɒrɪndʒ'eɪd] *n* Orangeade, Orangenlimonade *f*.
orange: ~-blossom *n* Orangenblüte *f* (*wird von Bräuten zur Hochzeit getragen*); **~ box** *n* Obst- *or* Apfelsinenkiste *f*; **~-coloured** *adj* orange(n)farben *or* -farbig; **~ grove** *n* Orangenhain *m*; **~ juice** *n* Orangensaft, O-Saft (*inf*) *m*; **O~man** *n* Anhänger *m* der Orange Order; **O~ March** *n* Demonstration *f* der Orange Order; **O~ Order** *n protestantische Vereinigung, die den Namen Wilhelms von Oranien trägt*; **~ peel** *n* Orangen- *or* Apfelsinenschale *f*.
orangery ['ɒrɪndʒərɪ] *n* Orangerie *f*.
orange stick *n* Maniküstäbchen *nt*.
orang-outang, orang-utan [ɔːˌræŋuː'tæŋ, -n] *n* Orang-Utan *m*.
orate [ɒ'reɪt] *vi* Reden/eine Rede halten (*to* vor *+dat*).
oration [ɒ'reɪʃən] *n* Ansprache *f* ◆ **funeral ~** Grabrede *f*.
orator ['ɒrətəʳ] *n* Redner(in *f*), Orator (*rare, Hist*) *m*.
oratorical [ˌɒrə'tɒrɪkəl] *adj* oratorisch; *contest also* Redner-.
oratorio [ˌɒrə'tɔːrɪəʊ] *n* (*Mus*) Oratorium *nt*.
oratory¹ ['ɒrətərɪ] *n* (*art of making speeches*) Redekunst *f* ◆ **to go off into a flight of ~** sich in großen Reden ergehen.
oratory² *n* (*Eccl*) Oratorium *nt*.
orb [ɔːb] *n* **(a)** (*poet*) Ball *m*; (*star*) Gestirn *nt* (*geh*); (*eye*) Auge *nt*. **(b)** (*of sovereignty*) Reichsapfel *m*.
orbit ['ɔːbɪt] **1** *n* **(a)** (*Astron, Space*) (*path*) Umlaufbahn, Kreisbahn *f*, Orbit *m* (*spec*); (*single circuit*) Umkreisung *f*, Umlauf *m* ◆ **to be in/go into ~ (round the earth/moon)** in der (Erd-/Mond)umlaufbahn sein/in die (Erd-/Mond)umlaufbahn eintreten; **to put a satellite into ~** einen Satelliten in die Umlaufbahn schießen.
(b) (*fig*) Kreis *m*; (*sphere of influence*) (Macht)bereich *m*, Einflußsphäre *f*.
2 *vt* umkreisen.
3 *vi* kreisen.
orbital ['ɔːbɪtl] *adj* orbital; *velocity* Umlauf-.
orbiter ['ɔːbɪtəʳ] *n* (*Space*) Orbiter *m*, Raumflugkörper *m*.
orchard ['ɔːtʃəd] *n* Obstgarten *m*; (*commercial*) Obstplantage *f* ◆ **apple/cherry ~** Obstgarten *m* mit Apfel-/Kirschbäumen; (*commercial*) Apfel-/Kirschplantage *f*.
orchestra ['ɔːkɪstrə] *n* Orchester *nt*.
orchestral [ɔː'kestrəl] *adj* Orchester-, orchestral.
orchestrally [ɔː'kestrəlɪ] *adv* orchestral.
orchestra: ~ pit *n* Orchestergraben *m*; **~ stalls** *npl* Orchestersitze *pl*; **a seat in the ~ stalls** ein Orchestersitz *m*.
orchestrate ['ɔːkɪstreɪt] *vt* orchestrieren.
orchestration [ˌɔːkɪs'treɪʃən] *n* Orchestrierung, Orchesterbearbeitung *f*.
orchid ['ɔːkɪd] *n* Orchidee *f*.
ordain [ɔː'deɪn] *vt* **(a)** *sb* ordinieren; (*Eccl*) *a priest* weihen ◆ **to be ~ed priest/to the ministry** ordiniert werden; (*Catholic also*) zum Priester geweiht werden.
(b) (*destine: God, fate*) wollen, bestimmen ◆ **God has ~ed that man should die** Gott hat es gewollt *or* hat bestimmt, daß der Mensch sterbe; **fate ~ed that he should die, it was ~ed that he should die** das Schicksal hat es so gefügt *or* es war ihm vom Schicksal bestimmt, daß er sterben sollte.
(c) (*decree*) (*law*) bestimmen; (*ruler also*) verfügen.
ordeal [ɔː'diːl] *n* **(a)** Tortur *f*; (*stronger, long-lasting*) Martyrium *nt*; (*torment, emotional ~*) Qual *f*. **(b)** (*Hist: trial*) Gottesurteil *nt* ◆ **~ by fire/water** Feuer-/Wasserprobe *f*.
▼ **order** ['ɔːdəʳ] **1** *n* **(a)** (*sequence*) (Reihen)folge, (An)ordnung *f* ◆ **word ~** Wortstellung, Wortfolge *f*; **are they in ~/in the right ~?** sind sie geordnet/sind sie in der richtigen Reihenfolge?; **in ~ of preference/merit** *etc* in der bevorzugten/in der ihren Auszeichnungen entsprechenden Reihenfolge; **to put sth in (the right) ~** etw ordnen; **to be in the wrong ~** *or* **out of ~** durcheinander sein; (*one item*) nicht am richtigen Platz sein; **to get out of ~** durcheinandergeraten; (*one item*) an eine falsche Stelle kommen.
(b) (*system*) Ordnung *f* ◆ **there's no ~ in his work** seiner Arbeit fehlt die Systematik; **he has no sense of ~** er hat kein Gefühl für Systematik *or* Methode; **the ~ of the world** die Weltordnung; **it is in the ~ of things** es liegt in der Natur der Dinge.
(c) (*tidy or satisfactory state*) Ordnung *f* ◆ **his passport was in ~** sein Paß war in Ordnung; **to put** *or* **set one's life/affairs in ~** Ordnung in sein Leben/seine Angelegenheiten bringen.
(d) (*discipline*) (*in society*) Ordnung *f*; (*in school, team also*) Disziplin *f* ◆ **to keep ~** die Ordnung wahren; die Disziplin aufrechterhalten; **to keep the children in ~** die Kinder unter Kontrolle halten; **~ in court** (*Brit*) *or* **the courtroom!** (*US*) Ruhe im Gerichtssaal!; **~, ~!** Ruhe!
(e) (*working condition*) Zustand *m* ◆ **to be in good/bad ~** in gutem/schlechtem Zustand sein; (*work well/badly also*) in Ordnung/nicht in Ordnung sein; **to be out of/in ~** (*car, radio, telephone*) nicht funktionieren/funktionieren; (*machine, lift also*) außer/in Betrieb sein.
(f) (*command*) Befehl *m*, Order *f* (*old, hum*) ◆ **by ~ of the court** laut gerichtlicher Anweisung; **~s are ~s** Befehl ist Befehl; **"no parking/smoking by ~"** „Parken/Rauchen verboten!"; **"no parking — by ~ of the Town Council"** „Parken verboten — die Stadtverwaltung"; **by ~ of the minister** auf Anordnung des Ministers; **I don't take ~s from anyone** ich lasse mir von niemandem befehlen; **to be under ~s to do sth** Instruktionen haben, etw

➤ LANGUAGE IN USE: **or²: a → 26.2**

zu tun; **until further ~s** bis auf weiteren Befehl.
▼**(g)** *(in restaurant etc, Comm)* Bestellung *f*; *(contract to manufacture or supply)* Auftrag *m* ◆ **two ~s of French fries** *(US)* zwei Portionen Pommes frites; **made to ~** auf Bestellung (gemacht *or* hergestellt); **to give an ~ to** *or* **place an ~ with sb** eine Bestellung bei jdm aufgeben *or* machen; jdm einen Auftrag geben; **to put sth on ~** etw in Bestellung/Auftrag geben.
(h) *(Fin)* **cheque to ~** Orderscheck, Namensscheck *m*; **pay to the ~ of** zahlbar an (+*acc*); **pay X or O~** (zahlbar) an X oder dessen Order.
(i) in ~ to do sth um etw zu tun; **in ~ that** damit.
(j) *(correct procedure at meeting, Parl etc)* **a point of ~** eine Verfahrensfrage; **to be out of ~** gegen die Verfahrensordnung verstoßen; *(Jur: evidence)* unzulässig sein; *(fig)* aus dem Rahmen fallen; **to call sb/the meeting to ~** jdn ermahnen, sich an die Verfahrensordnung zu halten/die Versammlung zur Ordnung rufen; **an explanation/a drink would seem to be in ~** eine Erklärung/ein Drink wäre angebracht; **is it in ~ for me to go to Paris?** ist es in Ordnung, wenn ich nach Paris fahre?; **his demand is quite in ~** seine Forderung ist völlig berechtigt; **what's the ~ of the day?** was steht auf dem Programm *(also fig)* *or* auf der Tagesordnung?; *(Mil)* wie lautet der Tagesbefehl?
(k) *(Archit)* Säulenordnung *f*; *(Biol)* Ordnung *f*; *(fig: class, degree)* Art *f* ◆ **intelligence of a high** *or* **the first ~** hochgradige Intelligenz; **something in the ~ of ten per cent** in der Größenordnung von zehn Prozent; **something in the ~ of one in ten applicants** etwa einer von zehn Bewerbern.
(l) *(Mil: formation)* Ordnung *f*.
(m) *(social)* Schicht *f* ◆ **the higher/lower ~s** die oberen/unteren Schichten; **the ~ of baronets** der Freiherrnstand.
(n) *(Eccl: of monks etc)* Orden *m* ◆ **Benedictine ~** Benediktinerorden *m*.
(o) *(Eccl)* **(holy) ~s** *pl* Weihe(n *pl*) *f*; *(of priesthood)* Priesterweihe *f* ◆ **to take (holy) ~s** die Weihen empfangen; **he is in (holy) ~s** er gehört dem geistlichen Stand an.
(p) *(honour, society of knights)* Orden *m* ◆ **O~ of Merit** *(Brit)* Verdienstorden *m*.
2 *vt* **(a)** *(command, decree)* *sth* befehlen, anordnen; *(prescribe: doctor)* verordnen *(for sb* jdm) ◆ **to ~ sb to do sth** jdn etw tun heißen *(geh)*, jdm befehlen *or* *(doctor)* verordnen, etw zu tun; *(esp Mil)* jdn dazu beordern, etw zu tun; **he was ~ed to be quiet** man befahl ihm, still zu sein; *(in public)* er wurde zur Ruhe gerufen; **the army was ~ed to retreat** dem Heer wurde der Rückzug befohlen; **he ~ed his gun to be brought (to him)** er ließ sich *(dat)* sein Gewehr bringen; **to ~ sb out/home** *(call in etc)* jdn heraus-/heimbeordern *(form, hum)* *or* -rufen; *(send in etc)* jdn hinaus-/heimbeordern *(form, hum)* *or* -schicken.
(b) *(direct, arrange)* *one's affairs, life* ordnen ◆ **to ~ arms** *(Mil)* das Gewehr abnehmen.
(c) *(Comm etc)* *goods, dinner, taxi* bestellen; *(to be manufactured)* *ship, suit, machinery etc* in Auftrag geben *(from sb* bei jdm).
3 *vi* bestellen.

◆**order about** *or* **around** *vt sep* herumkommandieren.

order: ~ book *n (Comm)* Auftragsbuch *nt*; **the ~ books are full** die Auftragsbücher sind voll; **~ cheque** *n* Orderscheck, Namensscheck *m*; **~ form** *n* Bestellformular *nt*, Bestellschein *m*.

orderliness [ˈɔːdəlɪnɪs] *n* **(a)** Ordentlichkeit *f* ◆ **the ~ of his life** sein geregeltes Leben. **(b)** *(of group, demonstration)* Friedlichkeit, Gesittetheit *f*.

orderly [ˈɔːdəlɪ] **1** *adj* **(a)** *(tidy, methodical)* ordentlich, geordnet; *life also* geregelt; *person, mind* ordentlich, methodisch. **(b)** *group, demonstration* ruhig, friedlich, gesittet.
2 *n* **(a)** *(Mil)* *(attached to officer)* Bursche *m (dated)*. **(b) (medical) ~** Pfleger(in *f*) *m*; *(Mil)* Sanitäter *m*.

orderly: ~ officer *n* diensthabender Offizier, Offizier *m* vom Dienst; **~ room** *n* Schreibstube *f*.

order paper *n (esp Parl)* Tagesordnung *f*.

ordinal [ˈɔːdɪnl] *(Math)* **1** *adj* Ordnungs-, Ordinal-.
2 *n* Ordnungs- *or* Ordinalzahl, Ordinale *(spec) f*.

ordinance [ˈɔːdɪnəns] *n* **(a)** *(order)* *(of government)* Verordnung *f*; *(Jur)* Anordnung *f*; *(of fate)* Fügung *f (geh)*. **(b)** *(Eccl)* *(sacrament)* Sakrament *nt*; *(rite also)* Ritus *m*.

ordinand [ˈɔːdɪˌnænd] *n* Priesteramtskandidat *m*.

ordinarily [ˈɔːdnrɪlɪ] *adv* normalerweise, gewöhnlich; (+*adj*) normal, wie gewöhnlich ◆ **more than ~ stupid/intelligent** außergewöhnlich dumm/intelligent.

ordinary [ˈɔːdnrɪ] **1** *adj* **(a)** *(usual)* gewöhnlich, normal ◆ **to do sth in the ~ way** etw auf die normale *or* gewöhnliche Art und Weise tun; **in the ~ way I would ...** normalerweise *or* gewöhnlich würde ich ...; **~ use** normaler Gebrauch; **my ~ doctor** der Arzt, zu dem ich normalerweise gehe.
(b) *(average)* normal, durchschnittlich; *(nothing special, commonplace)* gewöhnlich; alltäglich ◆ **the ~ Englishman** der normale Engländer; **a very ~ kind of person** ein ganz gewöhnlicher Mensch; **this is no ~ car** dies ist kein gewöhnliches Auto.
2 *n* **(a) out of the ~** außergewöhnlich, außerordentlich; **nothing/something out of the ~** nichts/etwas Außergewöhnliches *or* Ungewöhnliches; **intelligence above the ~** überdurchschnittliche *or* außergewöhnliche Intelligenz.
(b) *(form)* **physician/painter in ~ to the king** Leibarzt *m* des Königs/königlicher Hofmaler.

ordinary: O~ grade *n see* **O grade**; **O~ level** *n see* **O level**; **O~ National Diploma** *n (Brit)* *Diplom nt einer Technischen Fachschule*; **~ seaman** *n* Maat *m*; **~ share** *n (Fin)* Stammaktie *f*.

ordination [ˌɔːdɪˈneɪʃən] *n* Ordination *f*.

ordnance [ˈɔːdnəns] *(Mil)* *n* **(a)** *(artillery)* (Wehr)material *nt*. **(b)** *(supply)* Material *nt*, Versorgung *f*; *(corps)* Technische Truppe; *(in times of war)* Nachschub *m*.

ordnance: ~ factory *n* Munitionsfabrik *f*; **O~ Survey** *n (Brit)* ≃ Landesvermessungsamt *nt (BRD)*, Abteilung *f* Vermessung (im Ministerium des Innern) *(DDR)*; **O~ Survey map** *n (Brit)* amtliche topographische Karte *(form)*, Meßtischblatt *nt*.

ordure [ˈɔːdjʊəʳ] *n (liter)* *(excrement)* Kot *m*; *(rubbish)* Unrat, Unflat *(geh) m*; *(fig)* Schmutz *m no pl*.

ore [ɔːʳ] *n* Erz *nt*.

oregano [ˌɒrɪˈgɑːnəʊ] *n* Origano, Oregano *m*.

organ [ˈɔːgən] *n* **(a)** *(Anat)* Organ *nt*; *(penis)* Geschlecht *nt* ◆ **~ of speech** Sprechorgan. **(b)** *(Mus)* Orgel *f* ◆ **to be at the ~** die Orgel spielen; **~ loft** Orgelempore, Orgelbühne *f*. **(c)** *(mouthpiece of opinion)* Sprachrohr *nt*; *(newspaper)* Organ *nt*. **(d)** *(means of action)* Organ *nt*.

organdie, *(US)* **organdy** [ˈɔːgəndɪ] **1** *n* Organdy *m*.
2 *attr* Organdy-.

organ-grinder [ˈɔːgənˈgraɪndəʳ] *n* Drehorgelspieler, Leierkastenmann *m* ◆ **I want to talk to the ~, not the monkey** *(inf)* ich will den sprechen, der das Sagen hat.

organic [ɔːˈgænɪk] *adj* **(a)** *(Sci)* organisch; *vegetables, farming* biodynamisch. **(b)** *(fig)* *whole, unity* organisch; *part of whole* substantiell; *fault* immanent.

organically [ɔːˈgænɪkəlɪ] *adv* **(a)** *(Sci)* organisch; *farm, grow* biodynamisch. **(b)** *(fig)* *integrated, connected etc* organisch.

organism [ˈɔːgənɪzəm] *n (Biol, fig)* Organismus *m*.

organist [ˈɔːgənɪst] *n* Organist(in *f*) *m*.

organization [ˌɔːgənaɪˈzeɪʃən] *n* **(a)** *(act)* Organisation *f (also Pol)*; *(of work also, of time)* Einteilung *f*. **(b)** *(arrangement)* *see vt (a)* Ordnung *f*; Organisation *f*; Einteilung *f*; Aufbau *m*; Planung *f*. **(c)** *(institution)* Organisation *f*; *(Comm)* Unternehmen *nt*.

organization: ~ chart *n* Diagramm *nt* der Unternehmensstruktur; **O~ for Economic Cooperation and Development** *n* Organisation *f* für wirtschaftliche Zusammenarbeit und Entwicklung; **O~ of African Unity** *n* Organisation *f* für afrikanische Einheit; **O~ of American States** *n* Organisation *f* amerikanischer Staaten; **O~ of Arab Petroleum Exporting Countries** *n* Organisation *f* der arabischen erdölexportierenden Länder; **O~ of Petroleum Exporting Countries** *n* Organisation *f* der erdölexportierenden Länder.

organize [ˈɔːgənaɪz] **1** *vt* **(a)** *(give structure to, systematize)* ordnen; *facts also* organisieren; *time* einteilen; *work* organisieren, einteilen; *essay* aufbauen; *one's/sb's life* planen ◆ **to get (oneself) ~d** *(get ready)* alles vorbereiten; *(to go out)* sich fertigmachen; *(for term, holiday etc)* sich vorbereiten; *(sort things out)* seine Sachen in Ordnung bringen; *(sort out one's life)* ein geregeltes Leben anfangen; **I'll have to get better ~d** ich muß das alles besser organisieren; **I'll come as soon as I've got (myself) ~d** ich komme, sobald ich so weit bin; **to get (oneself) ~d with a job/equipment** *etc* sich *(dat)* einen Job/eine Ausrüstung besorgen; **I've only just taken over the shop, but as soon as I've got ~d I'll contact you** ich habe den Laden gerade erst übernommen, aber sobald alles (richtig) läuft, melde ich mich bei Ihnen; **it took us quite a while to get ~d in our new house** wir haben eine ganze Zeit gebraucht, uns in unserem neuen Haus (richtig) einzurichten.
(b) *(arrange)* *party, meeting etc* organisieren; *food, music for party etc* sorgen für; *sports event also* ausrichten; *(into teams, groups)* einteilen ◆ **to ~ things so that ...** es so einrichten, daß ...; **organizing committee** Organisationskomitee *nt*.
(c) *(Pol: unionize)* organisieren.
2 *vi (Pol)* sich organisieren.

organized [ˈɔːgənaɪzd] *adj* **(a)** *(Sci)* organisch.
(b) *(structured, systematized)* organisiert; *life* geregelt ◆ **~ crime** organisiertes Verbrechen; **he isn't very ~** bei ihm geht alles drunter und drüber *(inf)*; **you have to be ~** du mußt planvoll *or* systematisch *or* mit System vorgehen; **as far as his work/social life is concerned, he's well ~** was seine Arbeit/sein gesellschaftliches Leben angeht, so läuft bei ihm alles sehr geregelt ab; **he's well ~** *(in new flat etc)* er ist bestens eingerichtet; *(well-prepared)* er ist gut vorbereitet.
(c) *(Pol: unionized)* organisiert.

organizer [ˈɔːgənaɪzəʳ] *n* **(a)** Organisator, Veranstalter *m*; *(of sports event)* Ausrichter *m*. **(b)** *see* **personal ~**.

organza [ɔːˈgænzə] *n* Organza *m*.

orgasm [ˈɔːgæzəm] *n (lit, fig)* Orgasmus *m* ◆ **to go into ~s** *(fig sl)* einen Orgasmus nach dem anderen kriegen *(inf)*; **to be having ~s** *(fig sl)* ganz außer sich sein.

orgasmic [ɔːˈgæzmɪk] *adj* orgasmisch.

orgiastic [ˌɔːdʒɪˈæstɪk] *adj* orgiastisch.

orgy [ˈɔːdʒɪ] *n (lit, fig)* Orgie *f* ◆ **drunken ~** Sauforgie *f*; **an ~ of killing** eine Blutorgie; **~ of spending** Kauforgie *f*; **an ~ of colour** eine orgiastische Farbenpracht.

oriel (window) [ˈɔːrɪəl(ˈwɪndəʊ)] *n* Erker(fenster *nt*) *m*.

orient [ˈɔːrɪənt] **1** *n (also* **O~***)* Orient *m*; *(poet also)* Morgenland *nt*.
2 *adj (poet)* *sun, moon* aufgehend.
3 *vt see* **orientate**.

oriental [ˌɔːrɪˈentl] **1** *adj* orientalisch; *languages also* östlich; *(Univ)* orientalistisch; *rug* Orient- ◆ **~ studies** *pl* Orientalistik *f*.
2 *n (person)* **O~** Orientale *m*, Orientalin *f*.

➤ LANGUAGE IN USE: **order: 1g** → 20.3, 20.4

orientate ['ɔːrɪənteɪt] [1] *vr* (*lit*) sich orientieren (*by an +dat, by the map* nach der Karte); (*fig also*) sich zurechtfinden.
[2] *vt* ausrichten (*towards* auf *+acc*); *new employees etc* einführen; *thinking* orientieren (*towards* an *+dat*) ◆ **money-~d** materiell ausgerichtet.

orientation [,ɔːrɪən'teɪʃən] *n* **(a)** (*getting one's bearing*) Orientierung *f*; (*fig also*) Ausrichtung *f*.
(b) (*position, direction*) (*lit: of boat, spaceship etc*) Kurs *m*; (*fig*) Orientierung *f*; (*attitude*) Einstellung *f* (*towards* zu); (*leaning*) Ausrichtung *f* (*towards* auf *+acc*).

orienteering [,ɔːrɪən'tɪərɪŋ] *n* Orientierungslauf *m*.

orifice ['ɒrɪfɪs] *n* Öffnung *f*.

origami [,ɒrɪ'gɑːmɪ] *n* Origami *nt*.

origin ['ɒrɪdʒɪn] *n* **(a)** Ursprung *m*, Herkunft *f*; (*of person, family*) Herkunft, Abstammung *f*; (*of world*) Entstehung *f*; (*of river*) Ursprung *m* (*geh*) ◆ **to have its ~ in sth** auf etw (*acc*) zurückgehen; (*river*) in etw (*dat*) entspringen; **his family had its ~ in France** seine Familie ist französischer Herkunft; **country of ~** Herkunftsland *nt*; **nobody knew the ~ of that rumour** niemand wußte, wie das Gerücht entstanden war; **what are his ~s?** was für eine Herkunft hat er?; **the ~s of the new state** die Anfänge des neuen Staates.
(b) (*Math*) Ursprung *m*.

original [ə'rɪdʒɪnl] [1] *adj* **(a)** (*first, earliest*) ursprünglich ◆ **~ sin** die Erbsünde; **~ inhabitants of a country** Ureinwohner *pl* eines Landes; **~ text/version** Urtext *m*/Urfassung *f*; **~ edition** Originalausgabe *f*.
(b) (*not imitative*) *painting* original; *idea, writer, play* originell ◆ **~ research** eigene Forschung; **~ document** (*Jur*) Originaldokument *nt*.
(c) (*unconventional, eccentric*) *character, person* originell.
[2] *n* **(a)** Original *nt*; (*of model*) Vorlage *f*.
(b) (*eccentric person*) Original *nt*.

originality [ə,rɪdʒɪ'nælɪtɪ] *n* Originalität *f*.

originally [ə'rɪdʒənəlɪ] *adv* **(a)** ursprünglich. **(b)** (*in an original way*) originell.

originate [ə'rɪdʒɪneɪt] [1] *vt* hervorbringen; *policy, company* ins Leben rufen; *product* erfinden ◆ **who ~d the idea?** von wem stammt die Idee?
[2] *vi* **(a)** entstehen ◆ **the legend ~d in ...** die Legende ist in (*+dat*) ... entstanden *or* hat ihren Ursprung in (*+dat*) ...; **to ~ from a country** aus einem Land stammen; **to ~ from** *or* **with sb** von jdm stammen; **the company ~d as a family concern** die Firma war ursprünglich *or* anfänglich ein Familienbetrieb.
(b) (*US: bus, train etc*) ausgehen (*in* von).

originator [ə'rɪdʒɪneɪtəʳ] *n* (*of plan, idea*) Urheber(in *f*) *m*; (*of company*) Gründer(in *f*) *m*; (*of product*) Erfinder(in *f*) *m*.

oriole ['ɔːrɪəʊl] *n* Pirol *m*.

Orkney Islands ['ɔːknɪ'aɪləndz], **Orkneys** ['ɔːknɪz] *npl* Orkneyinseln *pl*.

orlon ® ['ɔːlɒn] *n* Orlon ® *nt*.

ormolu ['ɔːməʊluː] [1] *n* (*alloy*) Messing *nt*; (*decoration*) Messingverzierungen *pl*; (*mountings*) Messingbeschläge *pl*.
[2] *adj* Messing-.

ornament ['ɔːnəmənt] [1] *n* **(a)** (*decorative object*) Schmuck(gegenstand) *m no pl*, Verzierung *f*, Ziergegenstand *m*; (*on mantelpiece etc*) Ziergegenstand *m*; (*fig*) Zierde *f* (*to gen*) ◆ **his secretary is just an ~** seine Sekretärin ist nur zur Verzierung *or* Dekoration da; **she has the house full of ~s** sie hat das Haus voller Nippes (*pej*) *or* Ziergegenstände; **altar ~s** (*Eccl*) Altarschmuck *m*.
(b) (*no pl: ornamentation*) Ornamente *pl*; (*decorative articles, on clothes etc*) Verzierungen *pl*, Zierat *m* (*geh*) ◆ **by way of ~, for ~** zur Verzierung; **the interior of the palace was rich in ~** das Innere des Palastes war prunkvoll ausgeschmückt.
(c) (*Mus*) Verzierung *f*, Ornament *nt*.
[2] [ɔːnə'ment] *vt* verzieren; *room* ausschmücken.

ornamental [,ɔːnə'mentl] *adj* dekorativ; *object, garden, plant etc also* Zier-; *detail* schmückend, zierend ◆ **to be purely ~** zur Verzierung *or* Zierde (da) sein; **~ lake** Zierteich *m*; **~ object** *or* **piece** Zier- *or* Schmuckgegenstand, Zierat (*geh*) *m*.

ornamentation [,ɔːnəmen'teɪʃən] *n* **(a)** (*ornamenting*) Verzieren *nt*, Verzierung *f*; (*of room*) Ausschmücken *nt*, Ausschmückung *f*. **(b)** (*ornamental detail*) Verzierungen *pl*, Zierat *m* (*geh*); (*Art, Archit*) Ornamentik *f*; (*ornaments: in room etc*) Schmuck *m*.

ornate [ɔː'neɪt] *adj* kunstvoll; (*of larger objects*) prunkvoll; *decoration also* aufwendig; *music* ornamentreich; *description* reich ausgeschmückt, umständlich (*pej*); *language, style* umständlich (*pej*), überladen (*pej*), reich.

ornately [ɔː'neɪtlɪ] *adv* kunstvoll; *describe* mit beredten Worten, umständlich (*pej*); *written* in reicher Sprache.

ornateness [ɔː'neɪtnɪs] *n* Verzierungsreichtum *m*; (*of baroque church, palace etc also*) Prunk *m*, Prachtentfaltung *f*; (*of music also*) ornamentaler Reichtum; (*of style*) Reichtum *m*; (*of description*) Wortreichtum *m*, Umständlichkeit *f* (*pej*); (*of decoration*) Reichtum *m*, Aufwendigkeit *f*.

ornithological [,ɔːnɪθə'lɒdʒɪkəl] *adj* ornithologisch, vogelkundlich.

ornithologist [,ɔːnɪ'θɒlədʒɪst] *n* Ornithologe *m*, Ornithologin *f*, Vogelkundler(in *f*) *m*.

ornithology [,ɔːnɪ'θɒlədʒɪ] *n* Ornithologie, Vogelkunde *f*.

orphan ['ɔːfən] [1] *n* Waise *f*, Waisenkind *nt* ◆ **the accident made** *or* **left him an ~** der Unfall machte ihn zur Waise *or* zum Waisenkind; **like ~ Annie** (*inf*) wie bestellt und nicht abgeholt.
[2] *adj child* Waisen-.
[3] *vt* zur Waise machen ◆ **to be ~ed** zur Waise werden; **he was ~ed by the war** er ist (eine) Kriegswaise; **~ed since the age of three** verwaist *or* eine Waise seit dem dritten Lebensjahr.

orphanage ['ɔːfənɪdʒ] *n* Waisenhaus *nt*.

Orpheus ['ɔːfjuːs] *n* (*Myth*) Orpheus *m*.

orthodontic [,ɔːθəʊ'dɒntɪk] *adj* kieferorthopädisch.

orthodontics [,ɔːθəʊ'dɒntɪks] *n sing* Kieferorthopädie *f*.

orthodox ['ɔːθədɒks] *adj* **(a)** (*Rel*) orthodox. **(b)** (*fig*) konventionell; *view, method, approach etc also* orthodox.

orthodoxy ['ɔːθədɒksɪ] *n* **(a)** Orthodoxie *f*. **(b)** *see adj* (*b*) Konventionalität *f*; Orthodoxie *f*. **(c)** (*orthodox belief, practice etc*) orthodoxe Konvention.

orthographic(al) [,ɔːθə'græfɪk(əl)] *adj* orthographisch, Rechtschreib(ungs)-.

orthography [ɔː'θɒgrəfɪ] *n* Rechtschreibung, Orthographie *f*.

orthopaedic, (*US*) **orthopedic** [,ɔːθəʊ'piːdɪk] *adj* orthopädisch.

orthopaedics, (*US*) **orthopedics** [,ɔːθəʊ'piːdɪks] *n sing* Orthopädie *f*.

orthopaedist, (*US*) **orthopedist** [,ɔːθəʊ'piːdɪst] *n* Orthopäde *m*, Orthopädin *f*.

OS *abbr of* **(a) ordinary seaman. (b) Ordnance Survey. (c) outsize.**

Oscar ['ɒskəʳ] *n* (*Film*) Oscar *m* ◆ **Dustin Hoffman in his ~-winning performance** Dustin Hoffman in der Rolle, für die er den Oscar bekam.

oscillate ['ɒsɪleɪt] *vi* (*Phys*) oszillieren, schwingen; (*compass needle etc*) schwanken; (*rapidly*) zittern; (*fig*) schwanken ◆ **the needle ~d violently** die Nadel schlug stark aus.

oscillating ['ɒsɪleɪtɪŋ] *adj* **(a)** (*Phys*) Schwing-, schwingend; *circuit* Schwing(ungs)-; *needle* ausschlagend; (*rapidly*) zitternd. **(b)** (*fig*) schwankend.

oscillation [,ɒsɪ'leɪʃən] *n see vi* Oszillation, Schwingung *f*; Schwanken *nt*; Zittern *nt*; (*individual movement etc*) Schwankung *f*.

oscillator ['ɒsɪleɪtəʳ] *n* Oszillator *m*.

oscillograph [ə'sɪləgræf] *n* Oszillograph *m*.

oscilloscope [ə'sɪləskəʊp] *n* Oszilloskop *nt*.

osier ['əʊzɪəʳ] [1] *n* Korbweide *f*; (*twig*) Weidenrute *or* -gerte *f*.
[2] *attr basket, branch etc* Weiden-; *chair etc* Korb-.

osmium ['ɒzmɪəm] *n* Osmium *nt*.

osmosis [ɒz'məʊsɪs] *n* Osmose *f*.

osmotic [ɒz'mɒtɪk] *adj* osmotisch.

osprey ['ɒspreɪ] *n* Fischadler *m*.

osseous ['ɒsɪəs] *adj* Knochen-, knöchern.

ossification [,ɒsɪfɪ'keɪʃən] *n* Verknöcherung, Ossifikation (*spec*) *f*.

ossify ['ɒsɪfaɪ] [1] *vt* (*lit*) verknöchern lassen; (*fig*) erstarren lassen; (*mind*) unbeweglich machen ◆ **to be/become ossified** (*lit*) verknöchert sein/verknöchern; (*fig*) erstarrt sein/erstarren; unbeweglich sein/werden (*by* durch).
[2] *vi* (*lit*) verknöchern; (*fig*) erstarren; (*mind*) unbeweglich werden.

ossuary ['ɒsjʊərɪ] *n* Ossarium *nt*; (*building also*) Beinhaus *nt*.

Ostend [ɒ'stend] *n* Ostende *nt*.

ostensible *adj*, **-bly** *adv* [ɒ'stensəbl, -ɪ] angeblich.

ostentation [,ɒsten'teɪʃən] *n* **(a)** (*pretentious display*) (*of wealth etc*) Pomp *m*; (*of skills etc*) Großtuerei *f* ◆ **his ~** seine Großspurigkeit. **(b)** (*obviousness*) aufdringliche *or* penetrante Deutlichkeit ◆ **with ~** demonstrativ, ostentativ; **with great ~** betont auffällig.

ostentatious [,ɒsten'teɪʃəs] *adj* **(a)** (*pretentious*) pompös, protzig (*inf*) ◆ **he is so ~ about his wealth** er stellt seinen Reichtum so aufdringlich zur Schau, er protzt so mit seinem Geld (*inf*). **(b)** (*conspicuous*) ostentativ, betont auffällig.

ostentatiously [,ɒsten'teɪʃəslɪ] *adv see adj* **(a)** pompös, protzig (*inf*); *live* pompös, in Pomp, auf großem Fuße. **(b)** ostentativ, betont auffällig.

ostentatiousness [,ɒsten'teɪʃəsnɪs] *n see* **ostentation**.

osteoarthritis ['ɒstɪəʊɑː'θraɪtɪs] *n* Arthrose *f*.

osteopath ['ɒstɪəpæθ] *n* Osteopath(in *f*) *m*.

osteopathy [,ɒstɪ'ɒpəθɪ] *n* Osteopathologie *f*.

ostler ['ɒsləʳ] *n* (*Hist*) Stallknecht *m*.

ostracism ['ɒstrəsɪzəm] *n* Ächtung *f*.

ostracize ['ɒstrəsaɪz] *vt* ächten; (*Hist*) verbannen.

ostrich ['ɒstrɪtʃ] *n* Strauß *m* ◆ **~ policy** Vogel-Strauß-Politik *f*.

OT *abbr of* **Old Testament** AT.

OTC *abbr of* **Officers' Training Corps.**

other ['ʌðəʳ] [1] *adj* **(a)** andere(r, s) ◆ **~ people** andere (Leute); **some ~ people will come later** später kommen noch ein paar; **there were 6 ~ people there as well** es waren auch noch 6 andere (Leute) da; **do you have any ~ questions?** haben Sie sonst noch Fragen?; **he had no ~ questions** er hatte sonst keine Fragen; **he could be no ~ than strict** er konnte nicht anders als streng sein, er konnte nur streng sein; **the ~ day** neulich; **the ~ world** das Jenseits, jene andere Welt (*liter*); **some ~ time** (*in future*) ein andermal; (*in past*) ein anderes Mal; **~ people's property** fremdes Eigentum; **to see how the ~ half lives** sehen, wie andere leben.
(b) every ~ (*alternate*) jede(r, s) zweite.
(c) ~ than (*except*) außer (*+dat*); (*different to*) anders als.
(d) some time or ~ irgendwann (einmal); **some writer/house** *etc* **or ~** irgend so ein *or* irgendein Schriftsteller *m*/Haus *nt etc.*
[2] *pron* andere(r, s) ◆ **he doesn't like hurting ~s** er mag niemanden verletzen, er mag niemandem weh tun; **there are 6 ~s** da sind noch 6 (andere); **are there any ~s there?** sind noch andere *or* sonst noch welche da?; **there were no ~s there** es waren sonst keine da; **something/someone or ~** irgend etwas/jemand; **one or ~ of them will come** einer (von ihnen) wird kommen; **can you tell one from the ~?** kannst du sie auseinanderhalten?; **he fancied a bit of the ~** (*inf*) ihm war nach ein bißchen - na ja, du weißt

schon (*inf*), er wollte ein bißchen bumsen (*inf*); *see* **each, one.**
[3] *adv* **he could do no ~ (than come)** er konnte nicht anders (als kommen), er konnte nichts anderes tun (als kommen); **I've never seen her ~ than with her husband** ich habe sie immer nur mit ihrem Mann gesehen; **somehow or ~** irgendwie, auf die eine oder andere Weise; **somewhere or ~** irgendwo.

other-directed ['ʌðədaɪ'rektɪd] *adj* fremdbestimmt.

otherness ['ʌðənɪs] *n* Anderssein *nt*, Andersartigkeit *f*.

other ranks *npl* (*Brit Mil*) *Angehörige pl der britischen Streitkräfte unterhalb des Offiziersrangs.*

▼ **otherwise** ['ʌðəwaɪz] [1] *adv* **(a)** (*in a different way*) anders ◆ **I am ~ engaged** (*form*) ich bin anderweitig beschäftigt; **except where ~ stated** (*form*) sofern nicht anders angegeben; **Richard I, ~ (known as) the Lionheart** Richard I., auch bekannt als Löwenherz, Richard I. oder auch Löwenherz; **you seem to think ~** Sie scheinen anderer Meinung zu sein.
(b) (*in other respects*) sonst, ansonsten, im übrigen.
▼[2] *conj* (*or else*) sonst, andernfalls.
[3] *adj pred* anders ◆ **poems tragic and ~** tragische und andere Gedichte.

other: ~-worldliness *n see adj* Weltferne *f*; Entrücktheit *f*; **~-worldly** *adj attitude* weltfern; *person also* nicht von dieser Welt; *smile, expression* entrückt.

otiose ['əʊfɪəʊs] *adj* (*liter*) müßig (*geh*).

OTT (*sl*) *abbr of* **over the top.**

otter ['ɒtə^r] *n* Otter *m*.

Ottoman ['ɒtəmən] [1] *adj* osmanisch, ottomanisch (*rare*).
[2] *n* Osmane *m*, Osmanin *f*, Ottomane *m* (*rare*), Ottomanin *f* (*rare*).

ottoman ['ɒtəmən] *n* Polstertruhe *f*.

ouch [aʊtʃ] *interj* autsch.

▼ **ought**[1] [ɔːt] *v aux* **(a)** (*indicating moral obligation*) **I ~ to do it** ich sollte *or* müßte es tun; **he ~ to have come** er hätte kommen sollen *or* müssen; **this ~ to have been done** das hätte man tun sollen *or* müssen; **~ I to go too? — yes, you ~ (to)/no, you ~n't (to)** sollte *or* müßte ich auch (hin)gehen? — ja doch/nein, das sollen Sie nicht; **he thought he ~ to tell you/you ~ to know** er meinte, er sollte Ihnen das sagen/Sie sollten das wissen; **people have come who ~ not to have done** es sind Leute gekommen, die nicht hätten kommen sollen; **~/~n't you to have left by now?** hätten Sie schon/hätten Sie nicht schon gehen müssen?; **cars are parked where they ~ not to be** Autos sind an Stellen geparkt, wo sie nicht hingehören; **he behaved just as he ~ (to have)** (*was well-behaved*) er hat sich völlig korrekt benommen; (*did the right thing*) er hat sich völlig richtig verhalten.
▼ **(b)** (*indicating what is right, advisable, desirable*) **you ~ to see that film** den Film sollten Sie sehen; **you ~ to have seen his face** sein Gesicht hätten Sie sehen müssen; **she ~ to have been a teacher** sie hätte Lehrerin werden sollen.
(c) (*indicating probability*) **he ~ to win the race** er müßte (eigentlich) das Rennen gewinnen; **come at six, that ~ to be early enough** komm (mal) um sechs, das sollte *or* müßte früh genug sein; **that ~ to do** das dürfte wohl *or* müßte reichen; **he ~ to be here soon** er müßte bald hier sein; **he ~ to have left by now** er müßte inzwischen gegangen/abgefahren sein; **... and I ~ to know!** ... und ich muß es doch wissen!

ought[2] *n see* **aught.**

ouija (board) ['wiːdʒə('bɔːd)] *n Buchstabenbrett nt für spiritistische Sitzungen.*

ounce [aʊns] *n* Unze *f* ◆ **there's not an ~ of truth in it** daran ist kein Fünkchen Wahrheit; **if he had an ~ of sense** wenn er nur einen Funken *or* für fünf Pfennig (*inf*) Verstand hätte.

our ['aʊə^r] *poss adj* unser ◆ **these are ~ own make** die stellen wir selbst her; **O~ Father** (*in prayer*) Vater unser; **the O~ Father** das Vaterunser *or* Unservater (*Sw*); *see also* **my 1.**

ours ['aʊəz] *poss pron* unsere(r, s) ◆ **~ not to reason why(, ~ but to do or die)** (*prov*) das wissen die Götter (*inf*), es ist nicht an uns, nach dem Warum zu fragen; *see also* **mine**[1].

ourself [ˌaʊə'self] *pers pron* (*form*) (wir) selbst.

ourselves [ˌaʊə'selvz] *pers pron* (*dir, indir obj +prep*) uns; (*emph*) selbst; *see also* **myself.**

oust [aʊst] *vt* (*get, drive out*) herausbekommen; *sth stuck also* freibekommen; *government* absetzen; *politician, colleague etc* ausbooten (*inf*), absägen (*inf*); *heckler, anglicisms* entfernen; *rivals* ausschalten; (*take place of*) verdrängen ◆ **to ~ sb from office/his post** jdn aus seinem Amt/seiner Stellung entfernen *or* (*by intrigue*) hinausmanövrieren; **to ~ sb from the market** jdn vom Markt verdrängen.

out [aʊt] [1] *adv* **(a)** (*not in container, car etc*) außen; (*not in building, room*) draußen; (*indicating motion*) (*seen from inside*) hinaus, raus (*inf*); (*seen from ~side*) heraus, raus (*inf*) ◆ **to be ~** weg sein; (*when visitors come*) nicht da sein; **they're ~ in the garden/~ playing** sie sind draußen im Garten/sie spielen draußen; **they are ~ fishing/shopping** sie sind zum Fischen/Einkaufen (gegangen), sie sind fischen/einkaufen; **he's ~ in his car** er ist mit dem Auto unterwegs; **she was ~ all night** sie war die ganze Nacht weg; **it's cold ~ here/there** es ist kalt hier/da *or* dort draußen; **~ you go!** hinaus *or* raus (*inf*) mit dir!; **~!** raus (hier)!; **~ with him!** hinaus *or* raus (*inf*) mit ihm!; **~ it goes!** hinaus damit, raus damit (*inf*); **everybody ~!** alle Mann *or* alles raus!; **he likes to be ~ and about** er ist gern unterwegs; **at weekends I like to be ~ and about** an den Wochenenden will ich (immer) raus; **we had a day ~ at the beach/in London** wir haben einen Tag am Meer/in London verbracht; **we had a day ~ at the shops** wir haben einen Einkaufsbummel gemacht; **the journey ~** die Hinreise; (*seen from destination*) die Herfahrt; **the goods were damaged on the journey ~** die Waren sind auf dem Transport beschädigt worden; **the book is ~** (*from library*) das Buch ist ausgeliehen *or* unterwegs (*inf*); **the Socialists are ~** die Sozialisten sind nicht mehr an der Regierung; **the workers are ~** (*on strike*) die Arbeiter streiken *or* sind im Ausstand; **school is ~** die Schule ist aus; **the tide is ~** es ist Ebbe; **the chicks should be ~ tomorrow** die Küken sollten bis morgen heraus sein.
(b) (*indicating distance*) **when he was ~ in Persia** als er in Persien war; **to go ~ to China** nach China fahren; **~ in the Far East** im Fernen Osten; **~ here in Australia** hier in Australien; **Wilton Street? isn't that ~ your way?** Wilton Street? ist das nicht da (hinten) bei euch in der Gegend?; **the boat was ten miles ~** das Schiff war zehn Meilen weit draußen; **five days ~ from Liverpool** (*Naut*) fünf Tage nach dem Auslaufen in/vor Liverpool; **five miles ~ from harbour** fünf Meilen vom Hafen weg, fünf Meilen vor dem Hafen.
(c) to be ~ (*sun*) (he)raus *or* draußen sein; (*stars, moon*) am Himmel stehen (*geh*), dasein; (*flowers*) blühen.
(d) (*in existence*) **the worst newspaper/best car ~** die schlechteste Zeitung/das beste Auto, die/das es zur Zeit gibt, die schlechteste Zeitung/das beste Auto überhaupt; **to be ~** (*be published*) herausgekommen sein; **when will it be ~?** wann kommt es heraus?; **there's a warrant ~ for him** es besteht Haftbefehl gegen ihn.
(e) (*not in prison*) **to be ~** draußen sein; (*seen from ~side also*) (he)raus sein; **to come ~** (he)rauskommen.
(f) (*in the open, known*) **their secret was ~** ihr Geheimnis war bekanntgeworden *or* herausgekommen; **it's ~ now** jetzt ist es heraus; **the results are ~** die Ergebnisse sind (he)raus; **the news will ~** die Neuigkeit will heraus; **~ with it!** heraus damit!, heraus mit der Sprache!
(g) (*to or at an end*) **before the day/month is/was ~** vor Ende des Tages/Monats, noch am selben Tag/im selben Monat.
(h) (*light, fire*) aus.
(i) (*not in fashion*) aus der Mode, passé, out (*sl*).
(j) (*Sport*) (*ball*) aus; (*player*) aus(geschlagen), out.
(k) (*~ of the question, not permissible*) ausgeschlossen, nicht drin (*inf*).
(l) (*worn ~*) **the jacket is ~ at the elbows** die Jacke ist an den Ellbogen durch.
(m) (*indicating error*) **he was ~ in his calculations, his calculations were ~** er lag mit seinen Berechnungen daneben (*inf*) *or* falsch, er hatte sich in seinen Berechnungen geirrt; **not far ~!** beinah(e) (richtig)!; **you're not far ~** Sie haben es fast (getroffen); **you're far** *or* **way ~!** weit gefehlt! (*geh*), da hast du dich völlig vertan (*inf*); **you're a little bit ~ there** das stimmt nicht ganz; **we were £5/20% ~** wir hatten uns um £ 5/20% verrechnet *or* vertan (*inf*); **that's £5/20% ~** das stimmt um £ 5/20% nicht; **the perspective is just a little bit ~** die Perspektive stimmt nicht ganz; **the post isn't quite vertical yet, it's still a bit ~** der Pfahl ist noch nicht ganz senkrecht, er ist noch etwas schief; **my clock is 20 minutes ~** meine Uhr geht 20 Minuten falsch *or* verkehrt.
(n) (*indicating loudness, clearness*) **speak ~ (loud)** sprechen Sie laut/lauter; **they shouted ~ (loud)** sie riefen laut (und vernehmlich).
(o) (*indicating purpose*) **to be ~ for sth** auf etw (*acc*) aussein; **to be ~ for a good time** sich amüsieren wollen; **to be ~ for trouble** Streit suchen; **she was ~ to pass the exam** sie war (fest) entschlossen, die Prüfung zu bestehen; **he's ~ for all he can get** er will haben, was er nur bekommen kann; **he's ~ to get her** er ist hinter ihr her; **he's just ~ to make money** er ist nur auf Geld aus, ihm geht es nur um Geld; **he was always ~ to make money** er wollte immer das große Geld machen; **she's ~ to find a husband** sie ist auf der Suche nach einem Mann.
(p) (*unconscious*) **to be ~** bewußtlos *or* weg (*inf*) sein; (*drunk*) weg *or* hinüber sein (*inf*); (*asleep*) weg (*inf*) *or* eingeschlafen sein; **she went straight ~** sie war sofort weg (*inf*).
(q) (*dirt, stain etc*) (he)raus.
(r) ~ and away weitaus, mit Abstand.
[2] *n* **(a)** *see* **in. (b)** (*esp US inf: way ~*) Hintertür *f*.
[3] *prep* aus (*+dat*) ◆ **to go ~ the door/window** zur Tür/zum Fenster hinausgehen; **from ~ the wood** (*poet*) aus dem Walde heraus; *see also* **~ of.**

out- *pref with vbs* **to ~-dance** *etc* **sb** jdn im Tanzen *etc* übertreffen, besser als jd tanzen *etc*.

outact [ˌaʊt'ækt] *vt* an die Wand spielen.

out-and-out ['aʊtən'aʊt] *adj liar* Erz-, ausgemacht; *fool* vollkommen, ausgemacht; *defeat* völlig, total ◆ **he is an ~ revolutionary** er ist ein Revolutionär durch und durch; **it's an ~ disgrace** das ist eine bodenlose Schande.

outargue [ˌaʊt'ɑːgjuː] *vt* in der Diskussion überlegen sein (*+dat*), argumentativ überlegen sein (*+dat*) (*geh*).

outback ['aʊtbæk] (*in Australia*) [1] *n*: **the ~** das Hinterland.
[2] *attr* **an ~ farm** eine Farm im Hinterland.

out: ~bid *pret, ptp* **~bid** *vt* überbieten; **~board** [1] *adj motor* Außenbord-; [2] *n* Außenborder *m* (*inf*); **~bound** *adj ship* auslaufend, ausfahrend; **~box** *vt sb* besser boxen als; **for once he was completely ~boxed** zum ersten Mal ließ ihn seine Technik völlig im Stich; **he was ~boxed by the younger man** der jüngere Boxer war ihm (technisch) überlegen.

outbreak ['aʊtbreɪk] *n* (*of war, hostility, disease*) Ausbruch *m* ◆ **a recent ~ of fire caused ...** ein Brand verursachte kürzlich ...; **if there should be an ~ of fire** wenn ein Brand *or* Feuer ausbricht; **~ of feeling/anger** Gefühls-/Zornesausbruch *m*; **at the ~ of war** bei Kriegsausbruch.

outbuilding ['aʊtbɪldɪŋ] *n* Nebengebäude *nt*.

outburst ['aʊtbɜːst] *n* (*of joy, anger*) Ausbruch *m* ◆ **~ of temper** *or* **anger** *etc*/**feeling** Wutanfall *m*/Gefühlsausbruch *m*; **and to what do we owe that little ~?** und warum dieser kleine Gefühlsausbruch, wenn ich mal fragen darf?

outcast ['aʊtkɑːst] [1] *n* Ausgestoßene(r) *mf* ◆ **social ~** Außenseiter *m* der

➤ LANGUAGE IN USE: **otherwise: 2** → 2.3 **ought**[1]**: a** → 1.1 **b** → 2.2

Gesellschaft; **he was treated as an ~** er wurde zum Außenseiter gestempelt; **one of the party's ~s** einer, den die Partei verstoßen hat.
[2] *adj* ausgestoßen, verstoßen.
outclass [ˌaʊtˈklɑːs] *vt* voraus *or* überlegen sein (*+dat*), in den Schatten stellen.
outcome [ˈaʊtkʌm] *n* Ergebnis, Resultat *nt* ◆ **what was the ~ of your meeting?** was ist bei eurem Treffen herausgekommen?; **what was the ~?** was ist dabei herausgekommen?; **I don't know whether there'll be any immediate ~** ich weiß nicht, ob es unmittelbar zu einem Ergebnis führen wird.
outcrop [ˈaʊtkrɒp] *n* **(a)** (*Geol*) **an ~ (of rock)** eine Felsnase. **(b)** (*fig: of riots etc*) (plötzlicher) Ausbruch.
outcry [ˈaʊtkraɪ] *n* Aufschrei *m* der Empörung (*against* über *+acc*); (*public protest*) Protestwelle *f* (*against* gegen) ◆ **to raise an ~ against sb/sth** gegen jdn/etw (lautstarken) Protest erheben; **there was a general ~ about the increase in taxes** eine Welle des Protests erhob sich wegen der Steuererhöhung.
out: ~dated *adj idea, theory* überholt; *machine, word, style, custom* veraltet; **~did** *pret of* **~do**; **~distance** *vt* hinter sich (*dat*) lassen, abhängen (*inf*); **Y was ~distanced by X** Y fiel hinter X (*dat*) zurück, Y wurde von X abgehängt (*inf*).
outdo [ˌaʊtˈduː] *pret* **outdid** [ˌaʊtˈdɪd], *ptp* **outdone** [ˌaʊtˈdʌn] *vt* übertreffen, überragen, überbieten (*sb in sth* jdn an etw *dat*) ◆ **he can ~ him in every sport** er ist ihm in jeder Sportart überlegen; **but Jimmy was not to be outdone** aber Jimmy wollte da nicht zurückstehen.
outdoor [ˈaʊtdɔːʳ] *adj* **~ games** Freiluftspiele *pl*, Spiele *pl* für draußen *or* im Freien; **~ shoes** Straßenschuhe *pl*; **~ clothes** wärmere Kleidung; **~ type** sportlicher Typ; **the ~ life** das Leben im Freien; **to lead an ~ life** viel im Freien sein; **~ swimming pool** Freibad *nt*; **~ shot** (*Film*) Außenaufnahme *f*.
outdoors [ˈaʊtˈdɔːz] [1] *adv live, play, sleep* draußen, im Freien ◆ **to go ~** nach draußen gehen, rausgehen (*inf*); **go ~ and play** geh draußen spielen.
[2] *n* **the great ~** (*hum*) die freie Natur.
outer [ˈaʊtəʳ] *adj attr* äußere(r, s); *door etc also* Außen- ◆ **~ garments** Oberbekleidung, Überkleidung *f*; **~ harbour** Außen- *or* Vorhafen *m*; **~ man** (*appearance*) äußere Erscheinung, Äußere(s) *nt*; **~ space** der Weltraum.
Outer Hebrides [ˌaʊtəˈhebrɪdiːz] *npl* Äußere Hebriden *pl*.
Outer Mongolia [ˌaʊtəmɒŋˈgəʊlɪə] *n* die Äußere Mongolei.
outermost [ˈaʊtəməʊst] *adj* äußerste(r, s).
out: ~fall [1] *n* (*of drain, sewer*) Ausfluß *m*; [2] *attr sewer, pipe* Ausfluß-; **~field** *n* (*Sport*) (*place*) Außenfeld *nt*; (*people*) Außenfeldspieler *pl*; **~fielder** *n* Außenfeldspieler *m*; **~fight** *pret, ptp* **~fought** *vt* besser kämpfen als; (*defeat*) bezwingen.
outfit [ˈaʊtfɪt] *n* **(a)** (*clothes*) Kleidung *f*, Kleider *pl*; (*Fashion*) Ensemble *nt*; (*fancy dress*) Kostüm *nt*; (*uniform*) Uniform *f*; (*of scout*) Kluft *f* ◆ **is that a new ~ you're wearing?** hast du dich neu eingekleidet?; **she has so many ~s** sie hat so viel anzuziehen; **her ~s range from ...** ihre Garderobe reicht von ...
(b) (*equipment*) Ausrüstung *f*.
(c) (*inf*) (*organization*) Laden (*inf*), Verein (*inf*) *m*; (*Mil*) Einheit, Truppe *f*.
outfitter [ˈaʊtfɪtəʳ] *n* (*of ships*) Ausrüster *m* ◆ **gentlemen's ~'s** Herrenausstatter *m*; **sports ~'s** Sport(artikel)geschäft *nt*.
out: ~flank *vt* **(a)** (*Mil*) *enemy* umfassen, von der Flanke/den Flanken angreifen; **~flanking movement** Umfassungsangriff *m or* -bewegung *f*; **(b)** (*fig: outwit*) überlisten; **~flow** *n* (*of gutter*) Ausfluß, Abfluß *m*; (*of water etc*) (*act*) Abfließen *nt*, Ausfluß *m*; (*amount*) Ausfluß(menge *f*) *m*; (*of lava*) Ausfließen *nt*; Ausfluß, Auswurf *m*; (*of gas*) Ausströmen *nt*; Ausströmungsmenge *f*; (*of money*) Abfließen *nt*; Abfluß *m*; **~fly** *pret* **~flew,** *ptp* **~flown** *vt* (fliegerisch) überlegen sein (*sb/sth* jdm/etw); **~fought** *pret, ptp of* **~fight**; **~fox** *vt* überlisten, austricksen (*inf*); **~general** *vt* taktisch überlegen sein (*+dat*); **~go** *n* (*US*) Ausgabe(n *pl*) *f*.
outgoing [ˌaʊtˈgəʊɪŋ] [1] *adj* **(a)** *tenant* ausziehend; *office-holder* scheidend; *train, boat* hinausfahrend; *flight* hinausgehend; *cable* wegführend, hinausführend ◆ **~ tide** ablaufendes Wasser, Ebbe *f*; **the ~ flight for New York** der Flug nach New York.
(b) *personality* aus sich herausgehend, kontaktfreudig.
[2] *npl* **~s** Ausgaben *pl*.
outgrow [ˌaʊtˈgrəʊ] *pret* **outgrew** [ˌaʊtˈgruː], *ptp* **outgrown** [ˌaʊtˈgrəʊn] *vt* **(a)** *clothes* herauswachsen aus.
(b) *habit* entwachsen (*+dat*), hinauswachsen über (*+acc*); *opinion* sich hinausentwickeln über (*+acc*) ◆ **he has ~n such childish pastimes** über solche Kindereien ist er hinaus.
(c) (*grow taller than*) (*tree*) hinauswachsen über (*+acc*); (*person*) über den Kopf wachsen (*+dat*).
outgrowth [ˈaʊtgrəʊθ] *n* (*offshoot*) Auswuchs *m*; (*fig*) Folge *f*.
out: ~-Herod *vt*: **to ~-Herod Herod** dem Teufel Konkurrenz machen; **~house** *n* Seitengebäude *nt*.
outing [ˈaʊtɪŋ] *n* Ausflug *m* ◆ **school/firm's ~** Schul-/Betriebsausflug *m*; **to go for an ~ in the car** eine Fahrt mit dem Auto machen; **to go on an ~** einen Ausflug machen.
outlandish [ˌaʊtˈlændɪʃ] *adj* absonderlich, sonderbar; *behaviour also* befremdend, befremdlich; *prose etc* eigenwillig; *name* ausgefallen, extravagant; *wallpaper, colour-combination etc* ausgefallen, eigenwillig; *prices* haarsträubend ◆ **such ~ nonsense** solch unglaublicher Unsinn.
outlandishly [ˌaʊtˈlændɪʃlɪ] *adv* sonderbar, absonderlich; *decorated, portrayed* eigenwillig; *expensive* haarsträubend.
outlandishness [ˌaʊtˈlændɪʃnɪs] *n see adj* Absonderlichkeit, Sonderbarkeit *f*; Befremdlichkeit *f*; Eigenwilligkeit *f*; Ausgefallenheit, Extravaganz *f*.
outlast [ˌaʊtˈlɑːst] *vt* (*person*) (*live longer*) überleben; (*endure longer*) länger aus- *or* durchhalten als; (*thing*) länger halten als; (*idea etc*) überdauern, sich länger halten als.
outlaw [ˈaʊtlɔː] [1] *n* Geächtete(r) *mf*; (*in western etc*) Bandit *m* ◆ **to declare sb an ~** jdn ächten.
[2] *vt* ächten; *newspaper, action etc* für ungesetzlich erklären, verbieten.
outlawry [ˈaʊtlɔːrɪ] *n* Ächtung *f*; (*defiance*) Gesetzlosigkeit *f*.
outlay [ˈaʊtleɪ] *n* (Kosten)aufwand *m*; (*recurring, continuous*) Kosten *pl* ◆ **the initial ~** die anfänglichen Aufwendungen; **capital ~** Kapitalaufwand *m*; **to recover one's ~** seine Auslagen wieder hereinholen *or* -bekommen; (*business*) die Unkosten hereinwirtschaften.
outlet [ˈaʊtlet] [1] *n* **(a)** (*for water etc*) Abfluß, Auslaß *m*; (*for steam etc*) Abzug *m*; (*of river*) Ausfluß *m*.
(b) (*Comm*) Absatzmöglichkeit *f or* -markt *m*; (*merchant*) Abnehmer *m*; (*shop*) Verkaufsstelle *f*.
(c) (*fig*) (*for talents etc*) Betätigungsmöglichkeit *f*; (*for emotion*) Ventil *nt*.
[2] *attr* (*Tech*) *drain, pipe* Auslaß-, Abfluß-; (*for steam etc*) Abzugs-; *valve* Auslaß-.
outline [ˈaʊtlaɪn] [1] *n* **(a)** (*of objects*) Umriß *m*; (*line itself*) Umrißlinie *f*; (*silhouette*) Silhouette *f*; (*of face*) Züge *pl* ◆ **he drew the ~ of a head** er zeichnete einen Kopf im Umriß; **to draw sth in ~** etw im Umriß *or* in Umrissen zeichnen; **~ drawing** Umrißzeichnung *f*.
(b) (*fig: summary*) Grundriß, Abriß *m* ◆ **in (broad) ~** in großen *or* groben Zügen; **just give (me) the broad ~s** umreißen *or* skizzieren Sie es (mir) grob; **~s of botany** Abriß *or* Grundriß *m or* Grundzüge *pl* der Botanik.
(c) (*Shorthand*) Kürzel, Sigel, Sigle *nt*.
[2] *attr drawing, map* Umriß-.
[3] *vt* **(a)** (*draw outer edge of*) umreißen, den Umriß *or* die Umrisse zeichnen (*+gen*) ◆ **the mountain was ~d against the sky** die Umrisse des Berges zeichneten sich gegen den Himmel ab; **she stood there ~d against the sunset** ihre Silhouette zeichnete sich gegen die untergehende Sonne ab.
(b) (*give summary of*) umreißen, skizzieren.
outlive [ˌaʊtˈlɪv] *vt* **(a)** (*live longer than*) *person* überleben; *century* überdauern ◆ **to have ~d one's day** nicht mehr der/die sein, der/die man einmal war; **to have ~d one's usefulness** ausgedient haben; (*method, system*) sich überlebt haben.
(b) (*come safely through*) *storm etc* überstehen; *disgrace etc* sich reinigen (können) von (*geh*), frei werden von.
outlook [ˈaʊtlʊk] *n* **(a)** (*view*) (Aus)blick *m*, Aussicht *f* (*over* über *+acc*, *on to* auf *+acc*).
(b) (*prospects*) (Zukunfts)aussichten *pl*; (*Met*) Aussichten *pl* ◆ **what's the ~ for the mining industry?** wie sind die (Zukunfts)aussichten im Bergbau?
(c) (*mental attitude*) Einstellung *f* ◆ **his ~ (up)on life** seine Lebensauffassung, seine Einstellung zum Leben; **what's his ~ on the matter?** wie steht er zu der Sache?; **his breadth of ~** sein weiter Horizont; **narrow ~** beschränkter Horizont, (geistige) Beschränktheit; **if you adopt such a narrow ~** wenn Sie die Dinge so eng sehen.
out: ~lying *adj* (*distant*) entlegen, abgelegen; (*outside the town boundary*) umliegend; *district* (*of town*) Außen-, äußere(r, s); **~lying suburbs** Außenbezirke, äußere Vororte *pl*; **~manoeuvre,** (*US*) **~maneuver** *vt* (*Mil, fig*) ausmanövrieren; (*in rivalry*) ausstechen; **~match** *vt* übertreffen, überlegen sein (*+dat*); **Y was ~matched by X** Y konnte gegen X nichts ausrichten; **~moded** *adj* unzeitgemäß, altmodisch; *design etc also* antiquiert; *technology etc also* überholt, veraltet; **~most** [1] *adj* äußerste(r, s); *regions etc also* entlegenste(r, s); [2] *n*: **at the ~most** äußerstenfalls, im äußersten Falle.
outnumber [ˌaʊtˈnʌmbəʳ] *vt* in der Mehrzahl *or* Überzahl sein gegenüber; (*in fight etc also*) zahlenmäßig überlegen sein (*+dat*); (*in survey, poll etc also*) in der Mehrheit sein gegenüber ◆ **we were ~ed (by them)** wir waren (ihnen gegenüber) in der Minderzahl; wir waren (ihnen) zahlenmäßig unterlegen; wir waren (ihnen gegenüber) in der Minderheit; **we were ~ed five to one** sie waren fünfmal so viele wie wir; wir waren (ihnen) zahlenmäßig fünffach unterlegen; wir waren im Verhältnis fünf zu eins in der Minderheit.
out of *prep* **(a)** (*outside, away from*) (*position*) nicht in (*+dat*), außerhalb (*+gen*); (*motion*) aus (*+dat*); (*fig*) außer (*+dat*) ◆ **I'll be ~ town all week** ich werde die ganze Woche (über) nicht in der Stadt sein; **to go/be ~ the country** außer Landes gehen/sein; **he was ~ the room at the time** er war zu dem Zeitpunkt nicht im Zimmer; **he walked ~ the room** er ging aus dem Zimmer (hinaus); **he went ~ the door** er ging zur Tür hinaus; **as soon as he was ~ the door** sobald er draußen war *or* zur Tür hinaus war; **to look ~ the window** aus dem Fenster sehen, zum Fenster hinaus-/herausgucken; **I saw him ~ the window** ich sah ihn durchs Fenster; **~ danger/sight** außer Gefahr/Sicht; **get ~ my sight!** geh mir aus den Augen!; **he's ~ the tournament** er ist aus dem Turnier ausgeschieden; **he feels ~ it** (*inf*) er kommt sich (*dat*) ausgeschlossen vor, er fühlt sich ausgeschlossen; **they were 150 miles ~ Hamburg** (*Naut*) sie waren 150 Meilen von Hamburg weg *or* vor Hamburg; **three days ~ port** drei Tage nach dem Auslaufen aus dem Hafen/vor dem Einlaufen in den Hafen; **he lives 10 miles ~ London** er wohnt 10 Meilen außerhalb Londons; **you're well ~ it** so ist es besser für dich.
(b) (*cause, motive*) aus (*+dat*) ◆ **~ curiosity** aus Neugier.
(c) (*indicating origins or source*) aus (*+dat*) ◆ **to drink ~ a glass** aus einem Glas trinken; **made ~ silver** aus Silber (gemacht); **a filly ~ the same mare** ein Fohlen *nt* von derselben Stute.
(d) (*from among*) von (*+dat*) ◆ **in seven cases ~ ten** in sieben von zehn Fällen; **one ~ every four smokers** einer von vier Rauchern; **he picked one ~**

the pile er nahm einen aus dem Stapel (heraus).
(e) (*without*) ~ **breath** außer Atem; **we are ~ money/petrol/bread** wir haben kein Geld/Benzin/Brot mehr, das Geld/Benzin/Brot ist alle (*inf*); *see other nouns.*

out: ~-of-date *adj, pred* ~ **of date** *methods, technology, ideas* überholt, veraltet; *clothes, records* altmodisch, unmodern; *customs* veraltet; **you're ~ of date** Sie sind nicht auf dem laufenden; **~-of-doors** *adv see* **outdoors 1**; **~-of-pocket** *adj, pred* ~ **of pocket** **~-of-pocket expenses** Barauslagen *pl*; **to be ~ of pocket** drauflegen, draufzahlen; **I was £5 ~ of pocket** ich habe £ 5 aus eigener Tasche bezahlt; **I'm still £2 ~ of pocket** ich habe immer noch £ 2 zuwenig; **~-of-the-way** *adj, pred* ~ **of the way** (*remote*) *spot* abgelegen, aus der Welt; (*unusual*) *theory* ungewöhnlich; (*not commonly known*) *facts* wenig bekannt; **~-of-towner** *n* (*US*) Auswärtige(r) *mf*; **~patient** *n* ambulanter Patient, ambulante Patientin; **~patients' (department)** Ambulanz *f*; **~patients' hospital** *or* **clinic** Poliklinik *f*; **~play** *vt* (*Sport*) besser spielen als, überlegen sein (*+dat*); **we were completely ~played (by them)** wir konnten (gegen sie) absolut nichts ausrichten, sie waren uns haushoch überlegen; **~point** *vt* auspunkten; **~post** *n* (*Mil, fig*) Vorposten *m*; **~pouring** *n often pl* Erguß *m* (*fig*).

output ['aʊtpʊt] *n* (*of machine, factory, person*) (*act*) Produktion *f*; (*quantity also*) Ausstoß *m*, Output *m or nt*; (*rate of ~ also*) (Produktions)leistung *f*, Output *m or nt*; (*quantity in agriculture also*) Ertrag *m*; (*Elec*) Leistung *f*; (~ *terminal*) Ausgang *m*; (*capacity of amplifier*) (Ausgangs)leistung *f*; (*of mine*) Förderung *f*; (*quantity*) Fördermenge, Förderung *f*; (*rate of ~*) Förderleistung, Förderung *f*; (*of computer*) Ausgabe *f*, Output *m or nt* ◆ ~ **device** (*Comput*) Ausgabegerät *nt*; **effective ~ of a machine** Nutzleistung *f* einer Maschine; **this factory has an ~ of 600 radios a day** diese Fabrik produziert täglich 600 Radios.

outrage ['aʊtreɪdʒ] **1** *n* **(a)** (*wicked, violent deed*) Schandtat, Untat (*geh*) *f*; (*cruel also*) Greueltat *f*; (*by police, demonstrators etc*) Ausschreitung *f* ◆ **bomb ~** verbrecherischer Bombenanschlag; **an ~ against the State** ein schändliches *or* ruchloses (*liter*) Verbrechen gegen den Staat.
(b) (*indecency, injustice*) Skandal *m* ◆ **it's an ~ to waste food** es ist ein Skandal *or* Frevel, Essen umkommen zu lassen; **an ~ against humanity** ein Verbrechen *nt* gegen die Menschlichkeit; **an ~ against common decency** eine empörende Verletzung des allgemeinen Anstandsgefühls; **an ~ against public morality** ein empörender Verstoß gegen die guten Sitten *or* die öffentliche Moral; **an ~ against good taste** eine unerhörte Geschmacklosigkeit, eine Geschmacklosigkeit sondergleichen; **a linguistic ~** ein Verbrechen *nt or* Frevel *m* an der Sprache.
(c) (*sense of ~*) Empörung, Entrüstung *f* (*at* über *+acc*) ◆ **he reacted with (a sense of) ~** er war empört *or* entrüstet.
2 [aʊt'reɪdʒ] *vt morals, conventions* ins Gesicht schlagen (*+dat*), hohnsprechen (*+dat*) (*geh*); *sense of decency* beleidigen; *ideals* mit Füßen treten; *person* empören, entrüsten ◆ **public opinion was ~d by this cruelty/injustice** die öffentliche Meinung war über diese Grausamkeit/Ungerechtigkeit empört; **he deliberately set out to ~ his critics** er hatte es darauf angelegt, seine Kritiker zu schockieren.

outrageous [aʊt'reɪdʒəs] *adj* **(a)** (*cruel, violent*) greulich, verabscheuenswürdig ◆ **murder, rape, and other ~ deeds** Mord, Vergewaltigung und andere Untaten.
(b) unerhört, empörend; *demand, insolence, arrogance etc also* unglaublich, unverschämt; *conduct, exaggeration, nonsense also* haarsträubend; *language* entsetzlich, unflätig; *lie* unerhört, unverschämt; *charge, defamation etc* ungeheuerlich; *clothes, make-up etc* ausgefallen, unmöglich (*inf*); (*indecent*) geschmacklos; *complexity, selfishness* unglaublich, unerhört ◆ ~ **colour** Schockfarbe *f*.

outrageously [aʊt'reɪdʒəslɪ] *adv* fürchterlich; *lie* schamlos; *exaggerate also* maßlos, haarsträubend; *made-up also, dressed* haarsträubend, unmöglich (*inf*) ◆ **he suggested/demanded quite ~ that ...** er machte den unerhörten Vorschlag/er stellte die unerhörte Forderung, daß ...; **an ~ low neckline** ein übertrieben tiefer Ausschnitt.

out: ~ran *pret of* **~run**; **~range** *vt* eine größere Reichweite haben als; **we were ~ranged** die anderen hatten/der Feind *etc* hatte eine größere Reichweite; **~rank** *vt* (*Mil*) rangmäßig stehen über (*+dat*); **he was ~ranked** er war rangniedriger.

outré ['u:treɪ] *adj* überspannt, extravagant.

out: ~ride *pret* **~rode**, *ptp* **~ridden** *vt* besser reiten als; (*on bike*) besser fahren als; (*outdistance*) davonreiten (*+dat*)/-fahren (*+dat*); **he was completely ~ridden** er konnte absolut nicht mithalten; **he can't be ~ridden** mit ihm kann keiner mithalten; **~rider** *n* (*on motorcycle*) Kradbegleiter *m*; **~rigger** *n* (*Naut*) Ausleger *m*; (*boat*) Auslegerboot *nt*.

outright [aʊt'raɪt] **1** *adv* **(a)** (*entirely*) **to buy sth ~** etw ganz kaufen; (*not on HP*) den ganzen Preis für etw sofort bezahlen.
(b) (*at once*) *kill* sofort, auf der Stelle, gleich ◆ **he felled him ~** er streckte ihn mit einem einzigen Schlag zu Boden.
(c) (*openly*) geradeheraus, unumwunden, ohne Umschweife.
2 ['aʊtraɪt] *adj* **(a)** (*complete*) ausgemacht; *deception, lie also* rein, glatt (*inf*); *nonsense also* total, absolut; *disaster, loss* völlig, vollkommen, total; *refusal, denial* total, absolut, glatt (*inf*); *defeat, error* gründlich, ausgesprochen, absolut ◆ **that's ~ arrogance/impertinence/deception/selfishness** das ist die reine Arroganz/Unverschämtheit/das ist reiner *or* glatter (*inf*) Betrug/reiner Egoismus; ~ **sale** (*Comm*) Verkauf *m* gegen sofortige Zahlung der Gesamtsumme.
(b) (*open*) *person* offen.

out: ~rode *pret of* **~ride**; **~run** *pret* **~ran**, *ptp* **~run** *vt* schneller laufen als; (*outdistance*) davonlaufen (*+dat*); (*in race also*) schlagen; (*fig*) übersteigen; **the white horse ~ran the rest of the field** der Schimmel ließ das übrige Feld hinter sich (*dat*); **~set** *n* Beginn, Anfang *m*; **at the ~set** zu *or* am Anfang; **from the ~set** von Anfang an, von Anbeginn (*geh*); **let me make it quite clear at the ~set that ...** lassen Sie mich von vornherein klarstellen, daß ...; **~shine** *pret, ptp* **~shone** *vt* überstrahlen (*geh*), heller sein als; (*fig*) in den Schatten stellen.

outside ['aʊt'saɪd] **1** *n* **(a)** (*of house, car, object*) Außenseite *f* ◆ **the ~ of the car is green** das Auto ist (von) außen grün; **to open the door from the ~** die Tür von außen öffnen; **to stay on the ~ of a group** sich in einer Gruppe im Hintergrund halten; **people on the ~ (of society)** Menschen außerhalb der Gesellschaft; **to overtake on the ~** außen überholen; **judging from the ~** (*fig*) wenn man es als Außenstehender beurteilt.
(b) (*extreme limit*) **at the (very) ~** im äußersten Falle, äußerstenfalls.
2 *adj* **(a)** (*external*) Außen-, äußere(r, s) ◆ ~ **aerial** Außenantenne *f*; **an ~ broadcast** eine nicht im Studio produzierte Sendung; **an ~ broadcast from Wimbledon** eine Sendung aus Wimbledon; **to get some ~ help** Hilfe von außen holen; ~ **influences** äußere Einflüsse, Einflüsse von außen; **the ~ lane** die äußere Spur, die Überholspur; ~ **seat** (*in a row*) Außensitz *m*, Platz *m* am Gang; ~ **toilet** Außentoilette *f*; ~ **work** Außendienst *m*; **I'm doing ~ work on the dictionary** ich arbeite freiberuflich am Wörterbuch mit; ~ **world** Außenwelt *f*.
(b) *price* äußerste(r, s) ◆ **at an ~ estimate** maximal.
(c) (*very unlikely*) **an ~ chance** eine kleine Chance.
3 *adv* (*on the outer side*) außen; (*of house, room, vehicle*) draußen ◆ **to be/go ~** draußen sein/nach draußen gehen; **seen from ~** von außen gesehen; **put the cat ~** bring die Katze raus (*inf*) *or* nach draußen; **I feel ~ it all** ich komme mir so ausgeschlossen vor.
4 *prep* (*also* ~ **of**) **(a)** (*on the outer side of*) außerhalb (*+gen*) ◆ **to be/go ~ sth** außerhalb einer Sache sein/aus etw gehen; **he went ~ the house** er ging aus dem/vors/hinters Haus, er ging nach draußen; **he is waiting ~ the door** er wartet vor der Tür; **the car ~ the house** das Auto vorm Haus.
(b) (*beyond limits of*) außerhalb (*+gen*) ◆ **it is ~ our agreement** es geht über unsere Vereinbarung hinaus; ~ **the Festival** außerhalb der Festspiele; **this falls ~ the scope of ...** das geht über den Rahmen (*+gen*) ... hinaus.
(c) (*apart from*) außer (*+dat*), abgesehen von (*+dat*).

outside: ~ half *n* (*Rugby*) äußerer Halb(spieler); **~ lane** *n* Überholspur *f*; **~ left** *n* (*Ftbl, Hockey*) Linksaußen(spieler) *m*; **~ line** *n* (*Tel*) Amtsanschluß *m*.

outsider [ˌaʊt'saɪdə^r] *n* Außenseiter(in *f*), Outsider *m*.

outside right *n* (*Ftbl, Hockey*) Rechtsaußen(spieler) *m*.

out: ~size *adj* **(a)** übergroß; **~size clothes** Kleidung *f* in Übergröße, Übergrößen *pl*; **the ~size department** die Abteilung für Übergrößen; **(b)** (*inf: enormous*) riesig; **~skirts** *npl* (*of town*) Außen- *or* Randgebiete *pl*, Stadtrand *m*; (*of wood*) Rand *m*; **~smart** *vt* (*inf*) überlisten, austricksen (*inf*).

outspoken [ˌaʊt'spəʊkən] *adj person, criticism, speech, book* freimütig; *remark* direkt; *answer also* unverblümt ◆ **he is ~** er nimmt kein Blatt vor den Mund; **there was no need for you to be so ~** so deutlich hättest du nicht zu sein brauchen.

outspokenly [ˌaʊt'spəʊkənlɪ] *adv* geradeheraus, unverblümt; *answer, write also* freimütig; *remark also* direkt.

outspokenness [ˌaʊt'spəʊkənnɪs] *n see adj* Freimütigkeit *f*; Direktheit *f*; Unverblümtheit *f*.

outspread ['aʊtspred] (*vb: pret, ptp* ~) **1** *adj* ausgebreitet.
2 *vt* ausbreiten.

outstanding [ˌaʊt'stændɪŋ] *adj* **(a)** (*exceptional*) hervorragend; *talent, beauty, brilliance* außerordentlich, überragend ◆ **of ~ ability** hervorragend *or* außerordentlich begabt; **work of ~ excellence** ganz ausgezeichnete Arbeit; **of ~ importance** von höchster Bedeutung.
(b) (*prominent, conspicuous*) *event* bemerkenswert; *detail* auffallend; *feature* hervorstechend, auffallend.
(c) (*Comm, Fin*) *business* unerledigt; *account, bill, interest* ausstehend ◆ **a lot of work is still ~** viel Arbeit ist noch unerledigt; **are there any problems still ~?** gibt es noch irgendwelche ungeklärten Probleme?; ~ **debts** Außenstände *pl*.

outstandingly [ˌaʊt'stændɪŋlɪ] *adv* hervorragend.

out: ~station *n* Vorposten *m*; **~stay** *vt* länger bleiben als; **I don't want to ~stay my welcome** ich will eure Gastfreundschaft nicht überbeanspruchen *or* nicht zu lange in Anspruch nehmen; **~stretched** *adj body* ausgestreckt; *arms also* ausgebreitet; **to welcome sb with ~stretched arms** jdn mit offenen Armen empfangen; **~strip** *vt* **(a)** überholen; **(b)** (*fig*) übertreffen (*in* an *+dat*); **~swim** *pret* **~swam**, *ptp* **~swum** *vt* **to ~swim sb** jdm davonschwimmen; **~take** *n für die endgültige Fassung nicht verwendete, herausgeschnittene Filmsequenz*, Nichtkopierer *m* (*spec*); **~-tray** *n* Ablage *f* für Ausgänge; **~vote** *vt* überstimmen.

outward ['aʊtwəd] **1** *adj* **(a)** (*of or on the outside*) *appearance, form* äußere(r, s); *beauty* äußerlich ◆ **that's only his ~ self** so erscheint er nur nach außen hin; **he spoke with an ~ show of confidence** er gab sich den Anstrich von Selbstsicherheit.
(b) (*going out*) *movement* nach außen führend *or* gehend; *freight* ausgehend; *journey, voyage* Hin- ◆ **the ~ flow of traffic** der Verkehr(sstrom) aus der Stadt heraus.
2 *adv* nach außen ◆ **the door opens ~** die Tür geht nach außen auf; **~ bound** (*ship*) auslaufend (*from* von, *for* mit Bestimmung, mit Kurs auf *+acc*); **O~ Bound course** Abenteuerkurs *m*.

outwardly ['aʊtwədlɪ] *adv* nach außen hin.
outwards ['aʊtwədz] *adv* nach außen.
out: ~wear *pret* **~wore,** *ptp* **~worn** *vt* **(a)** *(last longer than)* überdauern, länger halten als; **(b)** *(wear out) clothes* abtragen; *see also* **~worn**; **~weigh** *vt* überwiegen, mehr Gewicht haben als; **~wit** *vt* überlisten; *(in card games etc)* austricksen *(inf)*; **~work** *n (Mil)* Außenwerk *nt*; **~worn** *adj idea, subject, expression* abgedroschen, abgenutzt; *custom, doctrine* veraltet.
ouzo ['u:zəʊ] *n* Ouzo *m*.
ova ['əʊvə] *pl of* **ovum.**
oval ['əʊvəl] [1] *adj* oval ◆ **~-shaped** oval.
[2] *n* Oval *nt*.
Oval Office *n (US)* Oval Office *nt, Büro nt des US-Präsidenten.*
ovarian [əʊ'vɛərɪən] *adj* **(a)** *(Anat)* des Eierstocks/der Eierstöcke ◆ **~ cyst** Zyste *f* im Eierstock. **(b)** *(Bot)* des Fruchtknotens.
ovary ['əʊvərɪ] *n* **(a)** *(Anat)* Eierstock *m*. **(b)** *(Bot)* Fruchtknoten *m*.
ovation [əʊ'veɪʃən] *n* Ovation *f*, stürmischer Beifall ◆ **to give sb an ~** jdm eine Ovation darbringen, jdm stürmischen Beifall zollen; **to get an ~** stürmischen Beifall ernten; *see* **standing.**
oven ['ʌvn] *n (Cook)* (Back)ofen *m*; *(Tech) (for drying)* (Trocken)ofen *m*; *(for baking pottery etc)* (Brenn)ofen *m* ◆ **to put sth in the ~** etw in den Ofen tun *or* stecken; **put it in the ~ for two hours** backen Sie es zwei Stunden; *pottery* brennen Sie es zwei Stunden; **to cook in a hot** *or* **quick/moderate/slow ~** bei starker/mittlerer/schwacher Hitze backen; **it's like an ~ in here** hier ist ja der reinste Backofen.
oven: ~-cloth *n* Topflappen *m*; **~ door** *n* Ofentür, Ofenklappe *f*; **~-glove** *n (Brit)* Topfhandschuh *m*; **~proof** *adj dish* feuerfest, hitzebeständig; **~-ready** *adj* bratfertig; **~-to-table-ware** *n* feuerfestes Geschirr; **~ware** *n* feuerfeste Formen *pl*.
over ['əʊvəʳ] [1] *prep* **(a)** *(indicating motion)* über *(+acc)* ◆ **he spread the blanket ~ the bed** er breitete die Decke über das Bett; **he spilled coffee ~ it** er goß Kaffee darüber, er vergoß Kaffee darauf; **to hit sb ~ the head** jdm auf den Kopf schlagen.
(b) *(indicating position: above, on top of)* über *(+dat)* ◆ **if you hang the picture ~ the desk** wenn du das Bild über dem Schreibtisch aufhängst *or* über den Schreibtisch hängst; **with his hat ~ one ear** mit dem Hut über einem Ohr; **bent ~ one's books** über die Bücher gebeugt.
(c) *(on the other side of)* über *(+dat)*; *(to the other side of)* über *(+acc)* ◆ **to look ~ the wall** über die Mauer schauen; **the noise came from ~ the wall** der Lärm kam von der anderen Seite der Mauer; **it's ~ the page** es ist auf der nächsten Seite; **he looked ~ my shoulder** er sah mir über die Schulter; **the house ~ the way** das Haus gegenüber; **the family from ~ the way** die Familie von gegenüber; **it's just ~ the road from us** das ist von uns (aus) nur über die Straße; **the bridge ~ the river** die Brücke über den Fluß; **we're ~ the main obstacles now** wir haben jetzt die größten Hindernisse hinter uns *(dat)*; **when they were ~ the river** als sie über den Fluß hinüber/herüber waren; **they're all safely ~ the first fence** sie sind alle sicher über die erste Hürde gekommen.
(d) *(in or across every part of)* in *(+dat)* ◆ **it was raining ~ London** es regnete in (ganz) London; **they came from all ~ England** sie kamen aus allen Teilen Englands *or* aus ganz England; **I'll show you ~ the house** ich zeige Ihnen das Haus; **you've got ink all ~ you/your hands** Sie/Ihre Hände sind ganz voller Tinte; **a blush spread ~ her face** sie errötete über und über; **to be all ~ sb** *(inf)* ein Mordstheater um jdn machen *(inf)*.
(e) *(superior to)* über *(+dat)* ◆ **Mr X is ~ me in the business** Herr X steht im Geschäft über mir; **to have authority ~ sb** Autorität über jdn haben; **he has no control ~ his urges/his staff** er hat seine Triebe nicht in der Gewalt/seine Angestellten nicht unter Kontrolle; **he was promoted ~ me** er wurde über mich befördert; **we were all ~ them** *(inf)* wir waren ihnen haushoch überlegen.
(f) *(more than, longer than)* über *(+acc)* ◆ **~ and above that** darüber hinaus; **~ and above the expenses** über die Ausgaben hinaus; **that was well ~ a year ago** das ist gut ein Jahr her, das war vor gut einem Jahr; **she will not live ~ the winter** sie wird den Winter nicht überleben.
(g) *(in expressions of time)* über *(+acc)*; *(during)* während *(+gen)*, in *(+dat)* ◆ **can we stay ~ the weekend?** können wir übers Wochenende bleiben?; **~ the summer/Christmas** den Sommer über/über Weihnachten; **~ the summer we have been trying ...** während des Sommers haben wir versucht ...; **~ the (past) years I've come to realize ...** im Laufe der (letzten) Jahre ist mir klargeworden ...; **he has mellowed ~ the years** er ist mit den Jahren milder geworden; **the visits were spread ~ several months** die Besuche verteilten sich über mehrere Monate.
(h) they talked ~ a cup of coffee sie unterhielten sich bei *or* über einer Tasse Kaffee; **the speeches were made ~ coffee** die Reden wurden beim Kaffee gehalten; **let's discuss that ~ dinner/a beer** besprechen wir das beim Essen/bei einem Bier; **they'll be a long time ~ it** sie werden dazu lange brauchen; **to pause ~ a difficulty** bei *or* über einer Schwierigkeit verharren; **he dozed off ~ his work** er nickte über seiner Arbeit ein; **to get stuck ~ a difficulty** bei einer Schwierigkeit stecken bleiben.
(i) he told me ~ the phone er hat es mir am Telefon gesagt; **I heard it ~ the radio** ich habe es im Radio gehört; **a voice came ~ the intercom** eine Stimme kam über die Sprechanlage.
(j) *(about)* über *(+acc)* ◆ **it's not worth arguing ~** es lohnt (sich) nicht, darüber zu streiten; **that's nothing for you to get upset ~** darüber brauchst du dich nicht aufzuregen.
(k) what is 7 ~ 3? wieviel ist 7 durch 3?; **blood pressure of 150 ~ 120** Blutdruck *m* von 150 zu *or* über 120.
[2] *adv* **(a)** *(across)* *(away from speaker)* hinüber; *(towards speaker)* herüber; *(on the other side)* drüben ◆ **they swam ~ to us** sie schwammen zu uns herüber; **he took the fruit ~ to his mother** er brachte das Obst zu seiner Mutter hinüber; **when the first man is ~ the second starts to climb/to swim** wenn der erste drüben angekommen ist, klettert/schwimmt der zweite los; **come ~ tonight** kommen Sie heute abend vorbei; **I just thought I'd come ~** ich dachte, ich komme mal rüber *(inf)*; **he is ~ here/there** er ist hier/dort drüben; **~ to you!** Sie sind daran; **and now ~ to our reporter in Belfast** und nun schalten wir zu unserem Reporter in Belfast um; **and now ~ to Paris where ...** und nun (schalten wir um) nach Paris, wo ...; **he has gone ~ to America** er ist nach Amerika gefahren; **~ in America** drüben in Amerika; **he drove us ~ to the other side of town** er fuhr uns ans andere Ende der Stadt; **he went ~ to the enemy** er lief zum Feind über.
(b) he searched the house ~ er durchsuchte das (ganze) Haus; **famous the world ~** in der ganzen Welt berühmt; **I've been looking for it all ~** ich habe überall danach gesucht; **I am aching all ~** mir tut alles weh; **you've got dirt all ~** Sie sind voller Schmutz, Sie sind ganz schmutzig; **he was shaking all ~** er zitterte am ganzen Leib; **I'm wet all ~** ich bin völlig naß; **he was black all ~** er war von oben bis unten schwarz; **the dog licked him all ~** der Hund leckte ihn von oben bis unten ab; **that's him/Fred all ~** das ist typisch für ihn/Fred, typisch Fred; **it happens all ~** das gibt es überall.
(c) *(indicating movement from one side to another, from upright position)* **to turn an object ~ (and ~)** einen Gegenstand (immer wieder) herumdrehen; **he hit her and ~ she went** er schlug sie, und sie fiel um.
(d) *(ended)* *(film, first act, operation, fight etc)* zu Ende; *(romance, summer also)* vorbei; *(romance also)* aus ◆ **the rain is ~** der Regen hat aufgehört; **the pain will soon be ~** der Schmerz wird bald vorbei sein; **the danger was ~** die Gefahr war vorüber, es bestand keine Gefahr mehr; **when all this is ~** wenn das alles vorbei ist; **it's all ~ with him** es ist Schluß *or* aus mit ihm; **it's all ~ between us** es ist aus zwischen uns.
(e) *(indicating repetition)* **he counted them ~ again** er zählte sie noch einmal; **to start (all) ~ again** noch einmal (ganz) von vorn anfangen; **~ and ~ (again)** immer (und immer) wieder, wieder und wieder; **he did it five times ~** er hat es fünfmal wiederholt; **must I say everything twice ~!** muß ich denn immer alles zweimal sagen!
(f) *(excessively)* übermäßig, allzu ◆ **he has not done it ~ well** er hat es nicht gerade übermäßig gut gemacht; **he is not ~ healthy** er ist nicht allzu gesund; **there's not ~ much left** es ist nicht allzuviel übrig.
(g) *(remaining)* übrig ◆ **there was no/a lot of meat (left) ~** es war kein Fleisch mehr übrig/viel Fleisch übrig; **7 into 22 goes 3 and 1 ~** 22 durch 7 ist 3, Rest 1; **6 metres and a little ~** 6 Meter und ein bißchen; **after doing the books I was a few pounds ~** *(inf)* nach der Abrechnung war ich ein paar Pfund im Plus.
(h) *(more)* **children of 8 and ~** Kinder ab 8; **all results of 5.3 and ~** alle Ergebnisse ab 5,3 *or* von 5,3 und darüber; **if it takes three hours or ~** wenn es drei oder mehr Stunden dauert.
(i) *(Telec)* **come in, please, ~** bitte kommen, over; **~ and out** Ende der Durchsage; *(Aviat)* over and out.
[3] *n (Cricket) 6 aufeinanderfolgende Würfe.*
over- *pref* über-.
over: ~abundance *n* Überfülle *f (of* von); **~abundant** *adj* überreichlich, sehr reichlich; **to have an ~abundant supply of sth** überreichlich mit etw versorgt sein; **~-achieve** *vi* leistungsorientiert sein; **a society which encourages people to ~-achieve** ein Gesellschaftssystem, das vom Menschen immer größere Leistungen fordert; **~-achiever** *n* leistungsorientierter Mensch; **a chronic ~-achiever** ein typischer Erfolgsmensch; **~act** *(Theat)* [1] *vt role* übertreiben, übertrieben gestalten; [2] *vi* übertreiben *(also fig)*, chargieren; **~active** *adj* zu *or* übertrieben aktiv; **~active thyroid** *(Med)* Schilddrüsenüberfunktion *f*; **~-age** *adj* zu alt.
overage ['əʊvərɪdʒ] *n (US Comm)* Überschuß *m*.
overall[1] [,əʊvər'ɔ:l] [1] *adj* **(a)** *width, length, total* gesamt, Gesamt- ◆ **~ dimensions** *(Aut)* Außenmaße *pl*; **~ majority** absolute Mehrheit.
(b) *(general)* allgemein ◆ **there's been an ~ improvement recently in his work/health** sein Gesundheitszustand hat sich/seine Leistungen haben sich in letzter Zeit allgemein verbessert; **the ~ effect of this was to ...** dies hatte das Endergebnis, daß ...
[2] *adv* **(a)** insgesamt ◆ **what does it measure ~?** wie sind die Gesamtmaße?
(b) *(in general, on the whole)* im großen und ganzen.
overall[2] ['əʊvərɔ:l] *n (Brit)* Kittel *m*; *(for women also)* Kittelschürze *f*; *(for children)* Kittelchen *nt*.
overalls ['əʊvərɔ:lz] *npl* Overall, Arbeitsanzug *m*.
over: ~ambitious *adj* übertrieben *or* zu ehrgeizig; **~anxiety** *n* übersteigerte Angst; **~anxious** *adj* übertrieben besorgt; *(on particular occasion)* übermäßig aufgeregt, übermäßig nervös; **he was ~anxious to start and caused two false starts** er konnte den Start kaum abwarten *or* erwarten und verursachte so zwei Fehlstarts; **he's ~anxious to please** er überschlägt sich, um zu gefallen; **I'm not exactly ~anxious to go** ich bin nicht gerade scharf darauf zu gehen; **~arm** *adj, adv (Sport) throw* mit gestrecktem (erhobenem) Arm; *serve* über Kopf; **~ate** *pret of* **~eat**; **~awe** *vt (intimidate)* einschüchtern; *(impress)* überwältigen, tief beeindrucken; **~balance** [1] *vi (person, object)* aus dem Gleichgewicht kommen, Übergewicht bekommen, das Gleichgewicht verlieren; [2] *vt object* umwerfen, umstoßen; *boat* kippen; *person* aus dem Gleichgewicht bringen.
overbearing [,əʊvə'bɛərɪŋ] *adj* herrisch; *arrogance* anmaßend.

overbearingly [ˌəʊvəˈbɛərɪŋlɪ] *adv* herrisch ◆ **so ~ arrogant** von einer derartig anmaßenden Arroganz.

over: ~bid *pret, ptp* **~bid** [1] *vt* **(a)** (*at auction*) überbieten; **(b)** (*Cards*) überreizen; **to ~bid one's hand** zu hoch reizen; [2] *vi* **(a)** (*at auction*) mehr bieten, ein höheres Angebot machen; **(b)** (*Cards*) überreizen; **~blouse** *n* Überbluse *f*; **~blow** *pret* **~blew,** *ptp* **~blown** *vt* (*Mus*) überblasen; **~blown** *adj* **(a)** *flower* verblühend; **(b)** *prose, rhetoric* geschwollen, schwülstig, hochtrabend; **(c)** (*Mus*) *note* überblasen.

overboard [ˈəʊvəbɔːd] *adv* **(a)** (*Naut*) über Bord ◆ **to fall ~** über Bord gehen *or* fallen; **man ~!** Mann über Bord!; **to throw sb/sth ~** jdn/etw über Bord werfen; (*fig*) etw verwerfen.
(b) (*fig inf*) **to go ~** übers Ziel hinausschießen, zu weit gehen, es übertreiben; **to go ~ for sb** von jdm ganz hingerissen sein, Feuer und Flamme für jdn sein (*inf*); **there's no need to go ~ (about it)** übertreib es nicht, kein Grund zum Übertreiben.

over: ~bold *adj person, action* verwegen; **~book** [1] *vi* zu viele Buchungen vornehmen; [2] *vt* zu viele Buchungen vornehmen für; **~burden** *vt* (*lit*) überladen; (*fig*) überlasten; **~buy** *pret, ptp* **~bought** *vi* zuviel kaufen, über Bedarf einkaufen; **~call** (*Cards*) [1] *vt* überbieten; [2] *n* höheres Gebot; **~came** *pret of* **~come**; **~capacity** *n* Überkapazität *f*; **~capitalize** *vt* überkapitalisieren; **~careful** *adj* übervorsichtig; **~cast** *adj* **(a)** *weather* bedeckt; *sky also* bewölkt; **it's getting rather ~cast** es zieht sich zu; **(b)** (*Sew*) *stitch* Überwendlings-; **~cast seam** überwendliche Naht; **~cautious** *adj* übervorsichtig, übertrieben vorsichtig; **~cautiousness** *n* übertriebene Vorsicht.

overcharge [ˌəʊvəˈtʃɑːdʒ] [1] *vt* **(a)** *person* zuviel berechnen (+*dat*) *or* abverlangen (+*dat*) (*for* für) ◆ **you've been ~d** man hat dir zuviel berechnet; **they ~d me by £2** sie haben mir £ 2 zuviel berechnet. **(b)** *electric circuit* überlasten. **(c)** (*with detail, emotion*) *painting, style* überladen.
[2] *vi* zuviel verlangen (*for* für) ◆ **to ~ on a bill** zuviel berechnen *or* anrechnen.

overcoat [ˈəʊvəkəʊt] *n* Mantel, Überzieher *m*.

overcome [ˌəʊvəˈkʌm] *pret* **overcame** [ˌəʊvəˈkeɪm], *ptp* ~ [1] *vt enemy* überwältigen, bezwingen; *bad habit* sich (*dat*) abgewöhnen; *shyness, nerves, difficulty, anger, obstacle etc* überwinden; *temptation* widerstehen (+*dat*), bezwingen; *disappointment* hinwegkommen über (+*acc*) ◆ **he was ~ by the fumes** die giftigen Gase machten ihn bewußtlos *or* betäubten ihn; **~ by the cold** von der Kälte betäubt; **sleep overcame him** der Schlaf übermannte ihn; **he was ~ by the temptation** er erlag der Versuchung; **he was quite ~ by the song** er war sehr gerührt von dem Lied; **he was ~ by grief/by emotion** Schmerz/Rührung übermannte ihn; **he was ~ by remorse/a feeling of despair** Reue/ein Gefühl der Verzweiflung überkam ihn; **~ with fear** von Furcht ergriffen *or* übermannt; **~ (with emotion)** ergriffen, gerührt.
[2] *vi* siegen, siegreich sein ◆ **we shall ~** wir werden siegen.

over: ~compensate *vi* **to ~compensate for sth** etw überkompensieren; **~compensation** *n* Überkompensation *f*; **~confidence** *n see adj* **(a)** übersteigertes Selbstvertrauen *or* Selbstbewußtsein; **(b)** zu großer Optimismus; **(c)** blindes Vertrauen (*in* in +*acc*); **~confident** *adj* **(a)** (*extremely self-assured*) übertrieben selbstsicher *or* selbstbewußt; **(b)** (*too optimistic*) zu optimistisch; **he was ~confident of success** er war sich (*dat*) seines Erfolges zu sicher; **(c)** (*excessively trustful*) blind vertrauend (*in* auf +*acc*); **you are ~confident in him** Sie haben zu großes Vertrauen in ihn; **~consumption** *n* zu starker Verbrauch (*of* an +*dat*); **~cook** *vt* verbraten; (*boil*) verkochen; **~correct** [1] *vt* überkorrigieren; [2] *adj* überkorrekt; **~critical** *adj* zu kritisch; **~crowd** *vt* überladen; *bus etc also, room* (*with people*) überfüllen; **~crowded** *adj* (*with things*) überfüllt; *town also* überbevölkert; (*overpopulated*) überbevölkert; (*with things*) überladen; **~crowding** *n* (*of bus, room, flat, class-room*) Überfüllung *f*; (*of town*) Überbevölkerung *f*; **~dependent** *adj* zu abhängig (*on* von); **~developed** *adj* überentwickelt.

overdo [ˌəʊvəˈduː] *pret* **overdid** [ˌəʊvəˈdɪd], *ptp* **overdone** [ˌəʊvəˈdʌn] *vt* **(a)** (*exaggerate*) übertreiben ◆ **you are ~ing it** *or* **things** (*going too far*) Sie übertreiben, Sie gehen zu weit; (*tiring yourself*) Sie übernehmen *or* überlasten sich; **you've overdone the blue paint** Sie haben es mit der blauen Farbe übertrieben; **don't ~ the smoking/sympathy** übertreibe das Rauchen nicht/übertreibe es nicht mit dem Mitleid; **she rather overdid the loving wife** sie hat die liebevolle Ehefrau etwas zu dick aufgetragen; **gin? — please, but don't ~ the tonic** Gin? — ja bitte, aber nicht zu viel Tonic; **I'm afraid you've rather overdone the garlic** ich fürchte, du hast es mit dem Knoblauch etwas zu gut gemeint.
(b) (*cook too long*) verbraten; (*boil*) verkochen.

▼ **over: ~done** *adj* **(a)** (*exaggerated*) übertrieben; **(b)** *see vt (b)* verbraten; verkocht; **~dose** [1] *n* (*lit*) Überdosis *f*; (*fig*) Zuviel *nt* (*of* an +*dat*); **he died of an ~dose of sleeping pills** er starb an einer Überdosis Schlaftabletten; [2] *vt* überdosieren, eine Überdosis geben (+*dat*); [3] *vi* eine Überdosis nehmen; **~draft** *n* Konto-Überziehung *f*; **my bank manager wouldn't let me have a bigger ~draft** der Direktor meiner Bank wollte mir ein weiteres Überziehen meines Kontos nicht gestatten; **to have an ~draft of £10** sein Konto um £ 10 überzogen haben; **I've still got an ~draft** mein Konto ist immer noch überzogen; **~draft facility** *n* Überziehungs- *or* Dispositionskredit *m*; **~draw** *pret* **~drew,** *ptp* **~drawn** *vt one's account* überziehen; **I'm always ~drawn at the end of the month** mein Konto ist am Ende des Monats immer überzogen; **~dress** [1] [ˌəʊvəˈdres] *vti* (sich) übertrieben *or* zu fein kleiden; **do you think I'm ~dressed?** was meinst du, bin ich zu elegant angezogen?; [2] [ˈəʊvəˌdres] *n* Überkleid *nt*; **~drive** *n* (*Aut*) Schnellgang(getriebe *nt*), Schongang(getriebe *nt*) *m*; **~due** *adj* überfällig; **long ~due** schon seit langem fällig; **~due interest** Zinsrückstände *pl*; **he is ~due** er müßte schon lange da sein; **~eager** *adj* übereifrig; **he was ~eager to impress** er war (zu) sehr darauf aus, Eindruck zu machen; **he was ~eager to start** er konnte den Start kaum abwarten; **they're not exactly ~eager to learn** sie sind nicht gerade übermäßig lernbegierig; **~eagerness** *n* Übereifer *m*; **~eat** *pret* **~ate,** *ptp* **~eaten** *vi* zuviel essen, sich überessen; **~eating** *n* Überessen *nt*; **~elaborate** *adj design, style* manieriert, gekünstelt; *excuse, plan, scheme* (viel zu) umständlich, zu ausgeklügelt; *hairstyle, dress* überladen; **~emphasis** *n* Überbetonung *f*; **an ~emphasis on money** eine Überbewertung des Geldes; **~emphasize** *vt* überbetonen; **one cannot ~emphasize the importance of this** man kann nicht genug betonen, wie wichtig das ist; **~employed** *adj* (beruflich) überfordert; **~enthusiastic** *adj* übertrieben begeistert; **not exactly ~enthusiastic** nicht gerade hingerissen; ▼ **~estimate** [1] [ˌəʊvərˈestɪmeɪt] *vt* überschätzen; [2] [ˌəʊvərˈestɪmɪt] *n* (*of price*) Überbewertung *f*, zu hohe Schätzung; **~excite** *vt* zu sehr aufregen; **~excited** *adj person* überreizt, zu aufgeregt; *children* aufgedreht, zu aufgeregt; **~excitement** *n* Überreiztheit *f*, zu starke Aufregung; (*of children*) Aufgedrehtheit *f*; **~exercise** [1] *vt* übertrainieren; [2] *vi* übermäßig viel trainieren; **the dangers of ~exercising** die Gefahren übermäßigen Trainings; **~exert** *vt* überanstrengen; **~exertion** *n* Überanstrengung *f*; **~expose** *vt* (*Phot*) überbelichten; **~exposure** *n* (*Phot*) Überbelichtung *f*; (*in media etc: of topic*) Überbehandlung *f*; **the President's image is suffering from ~exposure (in the media)** das Image des Präsidenten leidet darunter, daß er zu oft in den Medien erscheint; **~familiar** *adj* **to be ~familiar with sb** etwas zu vertraulich *or* intim mit jdm sein; (*too pally also*) plumpvertraulich mit jdm sein; **I'm not ~familiar with their methods** ich bin nicht allzu vertraut mit ihren Methoden; **~feed** *pret, ptp* **~fed** *vt* überfüttern; **~flew** *pret of* **~fly**.

overflow [ˈəʊvəfləʊ] [1] *n* **(a)** (*act*) Überlaufen *nt*. **(b)** (*amount*) Übergelaufene(s), Übergeflossene(s) *nt*. **(c)** (*outlet*) Überlauf *m*. **(d)** (*excess: of people*) Überschuß *m* (*of* an +*dat*).
[2] [ˌəʊvəˈfləʊ] *vt area* überschwemmen; *container, tank* überlaufen lassen ◆ **the river has ~ed its banks** der Fluß ist über die Ufer getreten.
[3] [ˌəʊvəˈfləʊ] *vi* **(a)** (*liquid, river etc*) überlaufen, überfließen; (*container*) überlaufen; (*room, vehicle*) zum Platzen gefüllt sein, überfüllt sein (*with* mit) ◆ **full to ~ing** (*bowl, cup*) bis oben hin voll, zum Überlaufen voll; (*room*) überfüllt, zu voll; **the crowd at the meeting ~ed into the street** die Leute bei der Versammlung standen bis auf die Straße; **you'll have to open the doors and let the crowd ~ into the grounds** man wird die Türen öffnen müssen, damit die Leute in die Gartenanlagen ausweichen können.
(b) (*fig: be full of*) überfließen (*with* von) ◆ **his heart was ~ing with love** sein Herz lief *or* floß über vor Liebe; **he's not exactly ~ing with generosity/ideas** er überschlägt sich nicht gerade vor Großzügigkeit/er sprudelt nicht gerade über vor Ideen.

over: ~flow meeting *n* Parallelversammlung *f*; **~flow pipe** *n* Überlaufrohr *nt or* -leitung *f*; **~fly** *pret* **~flew,** *ptp* **~flown** *vt* **(a)** (*fly over*) *town* überfliegen; **(b)** (*fly beyond*) *runway, airport* hinausfliegen über (+*acc*); **~fond** *adj* **to be ~fond of sth/of doing sth** etw nur zu gern haben/tun; **he's ~fond of criticizing others** er kritisiert andere nur zu gern; **I'm not exactly ~fond of ...** ich bin nicht gerade begeistert von ...; **~full** *adj* übervoll (*with* von, mit); **~generous** *adj* zu *or* übertrieben großzügig; **she was ~generous in her praise** sie geizte nicht mit Lob, sie spendete überreichliches Lob; **he gave me an ~generous helping** er überhäufte meinen Teller; **~grow** *pret* **~grew,** *ptp* **~grown** *vt path, garden, wall* überwachsen, überwuchern; **~grown** *adj* **(a)** überwachsen, überwuchert (*with* von); **(b)** *child* aufgeschossen, zu groß; **he's just an ~grown schoolboy** er ist ein großes Kind; **you're just an ~grown baby** du bist der reinste Säugling; **~hand** *adj, adv* **(a)** (*Sport*) *see* **~arm**; **(b)** (*Naut*) **~hand knot** einfacher Knoten; **~hang** (*vb: pret, ptp* **~hung**) [1] *vt* hängen über (+*acc*); (*project over: rocks, balcony*) hinausragen über (+*acc*), vorstehen über (+*acc*); [2] *n* (*of rock, building*) Überhang *m*; (*Archit*) Überkragung *f*; **~hanging** *adj cliff, wall* überhängend; *balcony* vorstehend; **~hasty** *adj* voreilig, übereilt; **don't do anything ~hasty** übereilen Sie nichts, überstürzen Sie nichts; **am I being ~hasty?** bin ich da zu voreilig?; **~haul** [1] *n* Überholung *f*, Überholen *nt*; (*inf: of patient*) Generalüberholung *f* (*inf*); **the machine needs an ~haul** die Maschine muß überholt werden; [2] *vt* **(a)** *engine* überholen; *plans* revidieren, überprüfen; (*inf*) *patient* gründlich untersuchen; **(b)** (*pass*) überholen; (*catch up*) einholen.

overhead[1] [ˌəʊvəˈhed] [1] *adv* oben; (*in the sky: position*) am Himmel, in der Luft ◆ **the people ~** (*above us*) die Leute über uns; (*above them*) die Leute darüber; **a plane flew ~** ein Flugzeug flog über uns *etc* (*acc*) (hinweg).
[2] [ˈəʊvəhed] *adj cables, wires* Frei- ◆ **~ cable** Überlandleitung *f*; (*high voltage*) Hochspannungsleitung *f*; (*Rail*) Oberleitung *f*; **~ railway** Hochbahn *f*; **~ cam(shaft)** obenliegende Nockenwelle; **~ lighting** Deckenbeleuchtung *f*; **~ projector** Overheadprojektor *m*; **~ travelling crane** Laufkran *m*; **~-valve engine** obengesteuerter Motor; **~ valves** obengesteuerte Ventile *pl*; **~ volley** (*Sport*) Hochball *m*.

overhead[2] [ˈəʊvəhed] (*Comm*) [1] *adj* **~ charges** *or* **costs** *or* **expenses** allgemeine Unkosten *pl*.
[2] *n* **~s** (*Brit*), **~** (*US*) allgemeine Unkosten *pl* ◆ **company ~s** allgemeine Geschäftskosten *or* Betriebs(un)kosten *pl*.

overhear [ˌəʊvəˈhɪəʳ] *pret, ptp* **overheard** [ˌəʊvəˈhɜːd] *vt* zufällig mit anhören, zufällig mitbekommen ◆ **we don't want him to ~ us** wir wollen nicht, daß er uns zuhören kann *or* daß er mitbekommt, was wir sagen; **I ~d them plotting** ich hörte zufällig, wie sie etwas ausheckten; **things you ~**

➤ LANGUAGE IN USE: **overestimate : 2 → 26.1**

in bars Dinge, die man in Bars so mit anhört *or* mitbekommt; **the other day he was ~d to say that ...** neulich hat ihn jemand sagen hören, daß ...; **he was being ~d** jemand hörte mit.

over: ~heat [1] *vt engine* überhitzen; *room* überheizen; [2] *vi (engine)* heißlaufen; *(fig: economy)* sich überhitzen; **~heated** *adj* heißgelaufen; *room* überheizt; *discussion* erhitzt; **~hung** *pret, ptp of* **~hang.**

overindulge ['əʊvərɪn'dʌldʒ] [1] *vt* **(a)** *person* zu nachsichtig sein mit, zuviel durchgehen lassen (*+dat*).
(b) *fantasies etc* allzu freien Lauf lassen (*+dat*); *passion, sexual appetite also* zügellos frönen (*+dat*) ◆ **a writer who ~s himself** ein Schriftsteller, der seiner Phantasie allzu freien Lauf läßt.
[2] *vi* zuviel genießen; *(as regards eating also)* Völlerei betreiben ◆ **I ~d at the party** ich habe auf der Party ein bißchen zuviel das Guten gehabt; **to ~ in wine** zuviel Wein trinken.

overindulgence ['əʊvərɪn'dʌldʒəns] *n* **(a)** allzu große Nachsicht *or* Nachgiebigkeit (*of sb* jdm gegenüber).
(b) *(as regards eating)* Völlerei *f* ◆ **~ in wine** übermäßiger Weingenuß; **~ in cigarettes** zu starkes Rauchen; **this constant ~ of his sexual appetite** sein zügelloses Sexualleben; **the author's regrettable ~ in the use of metaphor** die bedauerlicherweise ungezügelte Vorliebe dieses Autors für Metaphern; **health ruined by ~ in ...** durch übermäßigen Genuß von ... geschädigte Gesundheit.

overindulgent ['əʊvərɪn'dʌldʒənt] *adj parent* zu nachsichtig, zu gutmütig (*to(wards) sb* jdm gegenüber, mit jdm) ◆ **should I have another or would that be ~?** soll ich mir noch einen nehmen, oder wäre das des Guten zuviel *or* Völlerei?

overjoyed [,əʊvə'dʒɔɪd] *adj* überglücklich, äußerst erfreut (*at, by* über *+acc*) ◆ **not exactly ~** nicht gerade erfreut.

over: ~kill *n (Mil)* Overkill *m*; *(fig: getting rid of too much, having wider than necessary consequences)* Rundumschlag, Kahlschlag *m*; **you didn't have to repaint the whole room, that's definitely ~kill** du mußtest nicht das ganze Zimmer neu streichen, das war des Guten zuviel *or* das war übertrieben; **~laden** *adj (lit, fig)* überladen (*with* mit); *lorry, circuit also* überlastet; **~laid** *pret, ptp of* **~lay**; **~land** [1] *adj journey* auf dem Landweg; **~land route** Route *f* auf dem Landweg; [2] *adv travel etc* über Land, auf dem Landweg.

overlap ['əʊvəlæp] [1] *n* Überschneidung *f*; *(spatial also)* Überlappung *f*, Überlapp *m*; *(of concepts)* teilweise Entsprechung *or* Deckung ◆ **3 inches' ~** 3 Zoll Überlapp(ung); **there is an ~ of two days between our holidays** unsere Ferien überschneiden sich um zwei Tage.
[2] [,əʊvə'læp] *vi* **(a)** *(tiles, boards)* einander überdecken, überlappen; *(teeth)* übereinander stehen ◆ **made of ~ping planks** aus (einander) überlappenden Brettern.
(b) *(visits, dates, responsibilities)* sich überschneiden; *(ideas, concepts, plans, work areas)* sich teilweise decken.
[3] [,əʊvə'læp] *vt* **(a)** *part* gehen über (*+acc*); liegen über (*+dat*); *(person)* überlappen ◆ **the tiles ~ each other** die Dachziegel überlappen sich *or* liegen übereinander.
(b) *holiday, visit etc* sich überschneiden mit; *idea etc* sich teilweise decken mit.
[4] *adj attr joint* Überlappungs-.

over: ~lay *(vb: pret, ptp* **~laid**) [1] [,əʊvə'leɪ] *vt* überziehen; *(with metal)* belegen; *wall* verkleiden; [2] ['əʊvəleɪ] *n* Überzug *m*; *(metal)* Auflage *f*; *(on map)* Auflegemaske *f*; *(Typ)* Zurichtung *f*, Zurichtebogen *m*; **~leaf** *adv* umseitig; **the illustration ~leaf** die umseitige Abbildung; **see ~leaf** siehe umseitig; **~load** [1] *n* Übergewicht *nt*, zu große Last, Überbelastung *f*; *(Elec)* Überlast *f*; [2] *vt* überladen; *car, lorry, animal also, (Elec, Mech)* überlasten; **~long** [1] *adj* überlang; [2] *adv* zu lang.

overlook [,əʊvə'lʊk] *vt* **(a)** *(have view onto)* überblicken ◆ **we had a room ~ing the park** wir hatten ein Zimmer mit Blick auf den Park; **the castle ~s the whole town** vom Schloß aus hat man Aussicht auf die ganze Stadt; **the garden is not ~ed** niemand kann in den Garten hineinsehen.
(b) *(fail to notice) detail* übersehen, nicht bemerken ◆ **it is easy to ~** man übersieht es leicht.
(c) *(ignore) mistake* hinwegsehen über (*+acc*), durchgehen lassen ◆ **I am prepared to ~ it this time** diesmal will ich noch ein Auge zudrücken.

over: ~lord *n (Hist)* Oberherr *m*; **~lordship** *n (Hist)* Oberherrschaft *f*.

overly ['əʊvəlɪ] *adv* übermäßig, allzu.

over: ~manned *adj* **to be ~manned** eine zu große Belegschaft haben; **~manning** *n* zu große Belegschaft(en *pl*); **~mantel** *n (Archit)* Kaminaufsatz *or* -aufbau *m*; **~much** [1] *adv* zuviel, übermäßig; **they're not paid ~much** sie bekommen nicht übermäßig viel bezahlt; [2] *adj* zuviel; **~nice** *adj distinction* spitzfindig, zu genau.

overnight ['əʊvə'naɪt] [1] *adv* **(a)** über Nacht ◆ **we drove ~** wir sind die Nacht durchgefahren; **to stay ~ (with sb)** bei jdm übernachten, (bei jdm) über Nacht bleiben.
(b) *(fig)* von heute auf morgen, über Nacht ◆ **the place had changed ~** der Ort hatte sich über Nacht verändert.
[2] *adj* **(a)** *journey* Nacht- ◆ **~ stay** Übernachtung *f*; **~ bag** Reisetasche *f*.
(b) *(fig: sudden)* ganz plötzlich ◆ **an ~ success** ein Blitzerfolg *m*; **the play was an ~ success** das Stück wurde über Nacht ein Erfolg.

over: ~paid *pret, ptp of* **~pay**; **~particular** *adj* zu genau, pingelig (*inf*); **he's not ~particular about what he eats** er ist nicht wählerisch *or* pingelig (*inf*), was (das) Essen angeht; **he wasn't ~particular about filling in his expenses form correctly** er nahm es mit dem Ausfüllen seines Spesenantrages nicht zu *or* so genau; **~pass** *n* Überführung *f*; **~pay** *pret, ptp* **~paid** *vt* überbezahlen, zuviel bezahlen (*+dat*); **he's been ~paid by about £5** man hat ihm etwa £ 5 zuviel bezahlt; **~payment** *n (act)* Überbezahlung *f*; *(amount)* zuviel bezahlter Betrag; **~play** *vt (overact)* übertrieben darstellen *or* spielen; **to ~play one's hand** *(fig)* es übertreiben, den Bogen überspannen; **~plus** *n (esp US)* Überschuß *m*, Mehr *nt* (*of* an *+dat*); **~populated** *adj* übervölkert; **~population** *n* Überbevölkerung *f*.

overpower [,əʊvə'paʊəʳ] *vt* **(a)** *(emotion, heat)* überwältigen, übermannen ◆ **he was ~ed by the drug** die Droge tat ihre Wirkung (bei ihm). **(b)** *(Mech)* **to be ~ed** übermotorisiert sein.

overpowering [,əʊvə'paʊərɪŋ] *adj* überwältigend; *smell* penetrant; *perfume* aufdringlich; *heat* glühend ◆ **I felt an ~ desire ...** ich fühlte den unwiderstehlichen Drang, ...; **he's a bit ~ at times** seine Art kann einem manchmal zuviel werden.

over: ~praise *vt* übertrieben *or* zu sehr loben; **~price** *vt* einen zu hohen Preis verlangen für; **if the public will pay for it then it's not ~priced** wenn es die Leute bezahlen, dann ist der Preis nicht zu hoch angesetzt; **at £50 it's ~priced** £ 50 ist zuviel dafür; **~print** [1] *vt* **(a)** *stamp, text* überdrucken; *(Phot)* überkopieren; **(b)** *(print too many copies of)* in zu großer Auflage drucken; [2] *n (on stamp)* Überdruck *m*; **~produce** *vi* überproduzieren, zuviel produzieren; **~production** *n* Überproduktion *f*; **~protect** *vt child* überbehüten, zu sehr behüten; **~protective** *adj parent* überängstlich; **~ran** *pret of* **~run**; **~rate** *vt* überschätzen; *book, play, system etc also* überbewerten; **to be ~rated** überschätzt werden; **~reach** *vi* sich übernehmen; **~react** *vi* übertrieben reagieren (*to* auf *+acc*); **~reaction** *n* übertriebene Reaktion (*to* auf *+acc*).

override [,əʊvə'raɪd] *pret* **overrode** [,əʊvə'rəʊd], *ptp* **overridden** [,əʊvə'rɪdn] *vt* **(a)** *(disregard)* sich hinwegsetzen über (*+acc*); *opinion, claims also* nicht berücksichtigen.
(b) *(prevail over, cancel out) order, decision, ruling* aufheben, außer Kraft setzen; *objection* ablehnen ◆ **I'm afraid I'll have to ~ you there, said the chairman** dazu muß ich leider nein sagen, sagte der Vorsitzende; **to ~ sb's authority** sich über jds Autorität (*acc*) hinwegsetzen.
(c) *horse* müde reiten.
(d) *(teeth)* gehen über (*+acc*).

overriding [,əʊvə'raɪdɪŋ] *adj principle* vorrangig, wichtigste(r, s); *priority* vordringlich; *desire* dringendste(r, s); *(Jur) act, clause* Aufhebungs- ◆ **matters of ~ importance** äußerst bedeutende Angelegenheiten; **my ~ ambition is to ...** mein allergrößter Ehrgeiz ist es, zu ...

over: ~ripe *adj* überreif; **~rode** *pret of* **~ride.**

overrule [,əʊvə'ru:l] *vt* ablehnen; *claim also* nicht anerkennen; *objection also* zurückweisen; *verdict, decision* aufheben ◆ **his objection was ~d** sein Einspruch wurde abgewiesen; **we were ~d** unser Vorschlag/Einspruch *etc* wurde abgelehnt; **he was ~d by the majority** er wurde überstimmt.

overrun [,əʊvə'rʌn] *pret* **overran** [,əʊvə'ræn], *ptp* **~** [1] *vt* **(a)** *(weeds)* überwuchern, überwachsen ◆ **the town was ~ with tourists/mice** die Stadt war von Touristen/Mäusen überlaufen.
(b) *(troops etc: invade) country, district* einfallen in (*+dat*), herfallen über (*+acc*); *enemy position* überrennen.
(c) *(go past) mark* hinauslaufen über (*+acc*); *(Rail) signal* überfahren; *(train) platform* hinausfahren über (*+acc*); *(plane) runway* hinausrollen über (*+acc*).
(d) *(go beyond) time* überziehen, überschreiten ◆ **the TV programme overran its time** das Fernsehprogramm überzog.
(e) *(overflow) banks* überfluten.
[2] *vi (in time: speaker, concert etc)* überziehen ◆ **you're ~ning** Sie überziehen (Ihre Zeit); **his speech overran by ten minutes** seine Rede dauerte zehn Minuten zu lang.

oversaw [,əʊvə'sɔ:] *pret of* **oversee.**

overseas ['əʊvə'si:z] [1] *adj country* überseeisch, in Übersee; *market, trade* Übersee-; *telegram* nach/aus Übersee; *(in Europe)* europäisch; *telegram* nach/aus Europa ◆ **our ~ office** unsere Zweigstelle in Übersee/Europa; **~ aid** Entwicklungshilfe *f*; **an ~ visitor** ein Besucher aus Übersee/Europa; **~ service** *(Mil)* Militärdienst in Übersee/Europa.
[2] *adv* **to be ~** in Übersee/Europa sein; **to go ~** nach Übersee/Europa gehen; **to be sent ~** nach Übersee/Europa geschickt werden; **from ~** aus Übersee/Europa.

over: ~see *pret* **~saw**, *ptp* **~seen** *vt (supervise) person, work* beaufsichtigen, überwachen; **~seer** *n* Aufseher(in *f*) *m*; *(foreman)* Vorarbeiter(in *f*) *m*; *(in coal-mine)* Steiger *m*; **~sell** *pret, ptp* **~sold** *vti* **(a)** *(sell too many)* **to ~sell (sth)** (von etw) mehr verkaufen, als geliefert werden kann; *concert, match etc* (für etw) zu viele Karten verkaufen; **(b)** *(promote too much)* zuviel Reklame machen für; **~sensitive** *adj* überempfindlich; **~sew** *pret* **~sewed**, *ptp* **~sewed** *or* **~sewn** *vt* umnähen; **~sexed** *adj* **to be ~sexed** einen übermäßig starken Sexualtrieb haben; **don't leave me alone with that ~sexed brother of yours** laß mich bloß mit deinem Lustmolch von Bruder nicht allein (*inf*); **you're ~sexed!** du bist unersättlich; **~shadow** *vt (lit, fig)* überschatten; **~shoe** *n* Überschuh *m*.

overshoot [,əʊvə'ʃu:t] *pret, ptp* **overshot** [,əʊvə'ʃɒt] [1] *vt target, runway* hinausschießen über (*+acc*); *production target etc* übertreffen ◆ **the golfer overshot the green** der Golfer schlug (den Ball) über das Grün hinaus; **to ~ the mark** *(lit, fig)* übers Ziel hinausschießen.
[2] *vi (plane)* durchstarten.

oversight ['əʊvəsaɪt] *n* **(a)** Versehen *nt* ◆ **by** *or* **through an ~** aus Versehen.
(b) *(supervision)* Aufsicht, Beaufsichtigung *f*.

over: ~simplification *n* (zu) grobe Vereinfachung; **~simplify** *vt* zu sehr vereinfachen, zu einfach darstellen; **~size(d)** *adj* übergroß; **~size(d)**

families zu kinderreiche Familien *pl*; **~sleep** *pret, ptp* **~slept** *vi* verschlafen; **~sold** *pret, ptp of* **~sell**; **~spend** *pret, ptp* **~spent** [1] *vi* zuviel ausgeben; **we've ~spent by £10** wir haben £ 10 zuviel ausgegeben; **~spending city councils** Stadträte *pl* mit zu hoher Ausgabenpolitik; [2] *vt* überschreiten; **~spending** *n* zu hohe Ausgaben *pl*; **~spill** *(Brit)* [1] [ˈəʊvəˌspɪl] *n* Bevölkerungsüberschuß *m*; **~spill town** Trabantenstadt *f*; [2] [ˌəʊvəˈspɪl] *vi see* **~flow 3 (a)**; **~staffed** *adj* überbesetzt; **this office is ~staffed** dieses Büro hat zuviel Personal; **~staffing** *n* zuviel Personal, Personalüberschuß *m*; **~staffing problems** Probleme aufgrund von Personalüberschuß; **~state** *vt facts, case* übertreiben, übertrieben darstellen; **~statement** *n* Übertreibung *f*, übertriebene Darstellung; **~stay** *vt see* **outstay**; **~steer** [1] *n* Übersteuern *nt*; [2] *vi* übersteuern; **~step** *vt* überschreiten; **to ~step the mark** zu weit gehen.

overstock [ˌəʊvəˈstɒk] [1] *vt farm, pond* zu hoch bestücken ◆ **the farm/pond is ~ed** der Hof/der Teich hat einen zu großen Vieh-/Fischbestand; **to ~ a shop** in einem Geschäft das Lager überfüllen; **the shop is ~ed** der Laden hat zu große Bestände.
[2] *vi (shop)* zu große (Lager)bestände haben, zuviel lagern; *(farm)* zu große (Vieh)bestände haben.

overstrain [ˌəʊvəˈstreɪn] *vt horse, person* überanstrengen, überfordern; *metal* überbelasten; *resources, strength, theory* überbeanspruchen ◆ **to ~ oneself** sich übernehmen, sich überanstrengen; **don't ~ yourself** *(iro)* übernimm dich bloß nicht; **to ~ one's heart** sein Herz überlasten.

over: ~strung *adj* **(a)** *person* überspannt; **(b)** *piano* kreuzsaitig; **~subscribe** *vt (Fin)* überzeichnen; **the zoo outing was ~subscribed** zu viele (Leute) hatten sich für den Ausflug in den Zoo angemeldet; **~supply** [1] *vt* überbeliefern; [2] *n* Überangebot *nt (of* an *+dat)*, Überversorgung *f (of* mit*)*.

overt [əʊˈvɜːt] *adj* offen; *hostility* unverhohlen.

overtake [ˌəʊvəˈteɪk] *pret* **overtook** [ˌəʊvəˈtʊk], *ptp* **overtaken** [ˌəʊvəˈteɪkən] [1] *vt* **(a)** einholen; *(pass) runner etc, (Brit) car* überholen. **(b)** *(take by surprise) (storm, night)* überraschen; *(fate)* ereilen *(geh)* ◆ **~n by fear** von Furcht befallen; **we were ~n by events, events have ~n us** wir waren auf die Entwicklung der Dinge nicht gefaßt.
[2] *vi (Brit)* überholen.

overtaking [ˌəʊvəˈteɪkɪŋ] *n (Brit)* Überholen *nt*.

over: ~tax *vt* **(a)** *(fig) person, heart* überlasten, überfordern; *patience* überfordern; **to ~tax one's strength** sich übernehmen; **don't ~tax my patience** stelle meine Geduld nicht auf die Probe; **(b)** *(lit: tax too heavily)* übermäßig besteuern; **~technical** *adj* zu fachspezifisch; *(regarding technology)* zu technisch; **~-the-counter** *adj drugs* nicht rezeptpflichtig; *sale* offen; **~throw** *(vb: pret* **~threw**, *ptp* **~thrown**) [1] [ˈəʊvəˌθrəʊ] *n* **(a)** Sieg *m (of* über *+acc)*; *(being ~thrown)* Niederlage *f*; *(of dictator, government, empire)* Sturz *m*; *(of country)* Eroberung *f*; **(b)** *(Cricket)* zu weiter Wurf; [2] [ˌəʊvəˈθrəʊ] *vt (defeat) enemy* besiegen; *government, dictator, general* stürzen, zu Fall bringen; *plans* umstoßen; *country* erobern.

overtime [ˈəʊvətaɪm] [1] *n* **(a)** Überstunden *pl* ◆ **I am on ~** *or* **doing ~** ich mache Überstunden; **he did four hours' ~** er hat vier (Stunden) Überstunden gemacht.
(b) *(US Sport)* Verlängerung *f* ◆ **we had to play ~** es gab eine Verlängerung.
[2] *adv* **to work ~** Überstunden machen; **my imagination was working ~** *(inf)* meine Phantasie lief auf Hochtouren *(inf)*; **his liver's been working ~ to keep up with all this alcohol** *(inf)* seine Leber mußte sich ganz schön ranhalten *(inf) or* lief auf Hochtouren *(inf)*, um all den Alkohol zu verkraften; **we shall have to work ~ to regain the advantage we have lost** *(fig)* wir müssen uns mächtig ranhalten, wenn wir den verlorenen Vorsprung wieder wettmachen wollen *(inf)*.
[3] [ˌəʊvəˈtaɪm] *vt (Phot) photo* überbelichten ◆ **the programme planners ~d the symphony** die Programmgestalter hatten zuviel Zeit für die Symphonie eingeplant.
[4] *adj attr* **~ ban** Überstundensperre *f*; **~ pay** Überstundenlohn *m*; **~ rates** Überstundentarif *m*.

overtired [ˌəʊvəˈtaɪəd] *adj* übermüdet.

overtly [əʊˈvɜːtlɪ] *adv* offen.

overtone [ˈəʊvətəʊn] *n* **(a)** *(Mus)* Oberton *m*. **(b)** *(fig)* Unterton *m* ◆ **unmistakable ~s of jealousy** ein unverkennbarer Unterton von Eifersucht; **political ~s** politische Untertöne *pl*; **what are the precise ~s of this speech/word?** was genau ist der Unterton dieser Rede/was klingt bei diesem Wort alles mit?

over: ~took *pret of* **~take**; **~top** *vt* überragen; **~train** *vti* zuviel *or* zu hart trainieren; **~trick** *n (Cards)* überzähliger Stich; **~trump** *vt* übertrumpfen.

overture [ˈəʊvətjʊəʳ] *n* **(a)** *(Mus)* Ouvertüre *f*. **(b)** *usu pl (approach)* Annäherungsversuch *m* ◆ **to make ~s to sb** Annäherungsversuche bei jdm machen; **peace ~s** Friedensannäherungen *pl*.

overturn [ˌəʊvəˈtɜːn] [1] *vt* **(a)** umkippen, umwerfen; *(capsize) boat also* zum Kentern bringen ◆ **the ship rocked violently ~ing chairs and tables** das Schiff schwankte so heftig, daß Tische und Stühle umkippten.
(b) *regime* stürzen; *philosophy, world view* umstürzen.
[2] *vi (chair)* umkippen; *(boat also)* kentern.
[3] [ˈəʊvətɜːn] *n (of government)* Sturz *m*; *(of world view etc)* Umsturz *m*.

over: ~use [1] [ˌəʊvəˈjuːs] *n* übermäßiger *or* zu häufiger Gebrauch; [2] [ˌəʊvəˈjuːz] *vt* übermäßig oft *or* zu häufig gebrauchen; **~value** *vt goods* zu hoch schätzen; *idea, object, person* überbewerten; **~view** *n* Überblick *m (of* über *+acc)*.

overweening [ˌəʊvəˈwiːnɪŋ] *adj* überheblich, anmaßend; *arrogance, pride, ambition* maßlos.

overweight [ˈəʊvəˈweɪt] [1] *adj thing* zu schwer; *person also* übergewichtig ◆ **this box is 5 kilos ~** diese Schachtel hat 5 Kilo Übergewicht; **~ luggage** Gepäck mit Übergewicht; **you're ~** Sie haben Übergewicht.
[2] *n* Übergewicht *nt*.

overwhelm [ˌəʊvəˈwelm] *vt* **(a)** *(overpower: strong feelings)* überwältigen ◆ **he was ~ed when they gave him the present** er war zutiefst gerührt, als sie ihm das Geschenk gaben; **Venice ~ed me** ich fand Venedig überwältigend; **you ~ me!** *(iro)* da bin ich aber sprachlos!
(b) *(ruin, crush) enemy* überwältigen; *country* besiegen; *(Sport) defence* überrennen.
(c) *(submerge: water)* überschwemmen, überfluten; *(earth, lava)* verschütten, begraben.
(d) *(fig) (with favours, praise)* überschütten, überhäufen; *(with questions)* bestürmen; *(with work)* überhäufen.

overwhelming [ˌəʊvəˈwelmɪŋ] *adj* überwältigend; *desire, power* unwiderstehlich; *misfortune* erschütternd.

overwhelmingly [ˌəʊvəˈwelmɪŋlɪ] *adv see adj* ◆ **he was quite ~ friendly** er war umwerfend freundlich; **they voted ~ for it** sie haben mit überwältigender Mehrheit dafür gestimmt.

over: ~wind *pret, ptp* **~wound** *vt watch* überdrehen; **~work** [1] *n* Überarbeitung, Arbeitsüberlastung *f*; **he is ill from ~work** er hat sich krank gearbeitet; [2] *vt horse etc* schinden; *person* überanstrengen; *image, idea, theme etc* überstrapazieren; **to ~work oneself** sich überarbeiten; [3] *vi* sich überarbeiten; **~write** *pret* **~wrote**, *ptp* **~written** *vti (Comput)* überschreiben; **~write mode** *n (Comput)* Überschreibmodus *m*; **~written** *adj (too flowery etc)* zu blumig (geschrieben); *(too strong)* zu stark formuliert; *(too rhetorical)* zu schwülstig.

overwrought [ˌəʊvəˈrɔːt] *adj* **(a)** *person* überreizt. **(b)** *(too elaborate) style* überfeinert, verkünstelt.

overzealous [ˌəʊvəˈzeləs] *adj* übereifrig.

Ovid [ˈɒvɪd] *n* Ovid *m*.

oviduct [ˈəʊvɪdʌkt] *n* Eileiter *m*.

oviform [ˈəʊvɪfɔːm] *adj (form)* eiförmig.

oviparous [əʊˈvɪpərəs] *adj* eierlegend, ovipar *(spec)*.

ovipositor [ˌəʊvɪˈpɒzɪtəʳ] *n* Legebohrer, Legestachel *m*.

ovoid [ˈəʊvɔɪd] *adj* eiförmig, ovoid.

ovulate [ˈɒvjʊleɪt] *vi* ovulieren.

ovulation [ˌɒvjʊˈleɪʃən] *n* Eisprung *m*, Ovulation *f*.

ovule [ˈɒvjuːl] *n (Zool)* Ovulum, Ei *nt*; *(Bot)* Samenanlage *f*.

ovum [ˈəʊvəm] *n, pl* **ova** Eizelle *f*, Ovum *nt*.

owe [əʊ] [1] *vt* **(a)** *money* schulden, schuldig sein *(sb sth, sth to sb* jdm etw*)* ◆ **can I ~ you the rest?** kann ich dir den Rest schuldig bleiben?; **I ~ him a meal** ich bin ihm noch ein Essen schuldig, ich schulde ihm noch ein Essen; **how much do I ~ you?** *(in shop etc)* was bin ich schuldig?
(b) *reverence, obedience, loyalty* schulden, schuldig sein *(to sb* jdm*)*; *allegiance* schulden *(to sb* jdm*)*.
(c) *(be under an obligation for)* verdanken *(sth to sb* jdm etw*)* ◆ **I ~ my life to him** ich verdanke ihm mein Leben; **to what do I ~ the honour of your visit?** *(iro)* und was verschafft mir die Ehre Ihres Besuches?; **we ~ it to them that we are alive today** wir haben es ihnen zu verdanken, daß wir heute noch leben; **he ~s it to himself to make a success of it** er ist es sich *(dat)* (selber) schuldig, daraus einen Erfolg zu machen; **you ~ it to yourself to keep fit** du bist es dir schuldig, fit zu bleiben; **he ~s his failure to himself** er hat sich sein Versagen selbst zuzuschreiben; **we ~ nothing to him, we ~ him nothing** wir sind ihm (gar) nichts schuldig; **I think you ~ me an explanation** ich glaube, du bist mir eine Erklärung schuldig.
[2] *vi* **to ~ sb for sth** jdm Geld für etw schulden; **can I ~ you for the rest?** kann ich Ihnen den Rest schuldig bleiben?; **I still ~ him for the meal** ich muß ihm das Essen noch bezahlen.

➤ **owing** [ˈəʊɪŋ] [1] *adj* unbezahlt ◆ **the amount ~ on the house** die Schulden, die auf dem Haus liegen; **how much is still ~?** wieviel steht noch aus?; **a lot of money is ~ to me** man schuldet mir viel Geld; **the money still ~ to us** *(Comm)* die Außenstände *pl*; **to pay what is ~** den ausstehenden Betrag bezahlen.
➤ [2] *prep* **~ to** wegen *(+gen or (inf) +dat)*, infolge *(+gen)*; **~ to the circumstances** umständehalber; **~ to his being foreign** weil er Ausländer ist/war; **and it's all ~ to him that we succeeded** und unser Erfolg ist ihm allein zuzuschreiben.

owl [aʊl] *n* Eule *f* ◆ **wise old ~** weise Eule.

owlet [ˈaʊlɪt] *n* junge Eule.

owlish [ˈaʊlɪʃ] *adj* **the glasses gave him a somewhat ~ look** die Brille ließ ihn ein wenig eulenhaft erscheinen; **his ~ face** sein Eulengesicht *nt*; **to look ~** wie eine Eule aussehen.

owlishly [ˈaʊlɪʃlɪ] *adv look, stare* wie eine Eule.

own[1] [əʊn] [1] *vt* **(a)** *(possess)* besitzen, haben ◆ **who ~s that?** wem gehört das?; **we used to rent the flat, now we ~ it** wir hatten die Wohnung vorher gemietet, jetzt gehört sie uns; **he looks as if he ~s the place** er sieht so aus, als wäre er hier zu Hause; **the tourists behaved as if they ~ed the hotel** die Touristen benahmen sich, als gehöre das Hotel ihnen; **you don't ~ me, she said** ich bin nicht dein Privateigentum, sagte sie; **if you're going to behave like that, I don't ~ you** *(inf)* wenn du dich so benimmst, gehörst du nicht zu mir.
(b) *(admit)* zugeben, zugestehen; *(recognize)* anerkennen ◆ **he ~ed that the claim was reasonable** er erkannte die Forderung als gerechtfertigt an, er gab zu, daß die Forderung gerechtfertigt war; **he ~ed himself defeated** er gab sich geschlagen; **to ~ a child** *(Jur)* ein Kind (als seines) anerkennen.

➤ LANGUAGE IN USE: **owing: 2** → 17.1, 21.4

[2] *vi* **to ~ to sth** etw eingestehen; *to debts* etw anerkennen; **he ~ed to having done it** er gestand, es getan zu haben; **he didn't ~ to having done it** er hat nicht zugegeben, daß er es getan hat.

◆**own up** *vi* es zugeben ◆ **come on, ~ ~** (nun) gib schon zu; **to ~ ~ to sth** etw zugeben; **he ~ed ~ to stealing the money** er gab zu *or* er gestand, das Geld gestohlen zu haben.

own² [1] *adj attr* eigen ◆ **his ~ car** sein eigenes Auto; **one's ~ car** ein eigenes Auto; **he's his ~ man** er geht seinen eigenen Weg; **he likes beauty for its ~ sake** er liebt die Schönheit um ihrer selbst willen; **he does (all) his ~ cooking** er kocht für sich selbst; **thank you, I'm quite capable of finding my ~ way out** danke, ich finde sehr gut alleine hinaus; **my ~ one is smaller** meine(r, s) ist kleiner; **my ~ one** (*liter, hum: beloved*) mein Einziger, meine Einzige.

[2] *pron* **(a) that's my ~** das ist mein eigenes; **those are my ~** die gehören mir; **my ~ is bigger** meine(r, s) ist größer; **my time is my ~** ich kann mit meiner Zeit machen, was ich will; **I can scarcely call my time my ~** ich kann kaum sagen, daß ich über meine Zeit frei verfügen kann; **his ideas were his ~** die Ideen stammten von ihm selbst; **I'd like a little house to call my ~** ich würde gern ein kleines Häuschen mein eigen nennen; **a house of one's ~** ein eigenes Haus; **I have money of my ~** ich habe selbst Geld; **it has a beauty all its ~** *or* **of its ~** es hat eine ganz eigene *or* eigenartige Schönheit; **for reasons of his ~** aus irgendwelchen Gründen; **he gave me one of his ~** er gab mir eins von seinen (eigenen).

(b) (*in phrases*) **can I have it for my (very) ~?** darf ich das ganz für mich allein behalten?; **to get one's ~ back (on sb)** es jdm heimzahlen; **he was determined to get his ~ back** er war entschlossen, sich zu revanchieren; **(all) on one's ~** (ganz) allein; (*without help also*) selbst; **on its ~** von selbst, von allein; **if I can get him on his ~** wenn ich ihn allein erwische.

own-brand ['əʊn,brænd] *adj* Hausmarken-.

owner ['əʊnəʳ] *n* Besitzer(in *f*), Eigentümer(in *f*) *m*; (*of shop, factory, firm etc*) Inhaber(in *f*) *m*; (*of dogs, car, slaves*) Halter *m* ◆ **who's the ~ of this umbrella?** wem gehört dieser Schirm?; **at ~'s risk** auf eigene Gefahr.

owner: ~-driver *n Fahrzeughalter, der sein eigenes Auto fährt*; **~-editor** *n* Redakteur *m* im eigenen Hause; **~less** *adj* herrenlos; **~-occupancy** *n* **there's a growing level of ~-occupancy** immer mehr Häuser/Wohnungen werden eigengenutzt *or* befinden sich im Besitz der Bewohner; **~-occupied** *adj house* vom Besitzer bewohnt; **~-occupier** *n* Bewohner *m* im eigenen Haus, Eigennutzer *m* (*form*).

ownership ['əʊnəʃɪp] *n* Besitz *m* ◆ **to establish the ~ of sth** den Besitzer einer Sache (*gen*) feststellen; **there are doubts as to the ~ of the property** es ist nicht klar, wer der Eigentümer dieses Grundstücks ist; **under his ~ the business flourished** das Geschäft blühte in der Zeit, als es sich in seinem Besitz befand; **under new ~** unter neuer Leitung; **since we've been under new ~** seit der Eigentümer gewechselt hat; **this certifies your ~ of ...** das weist Sie als Eigentümer von ... aus.

own goal *n* (*lit, fig*) Eigentor *nt* ◆ **to score an ~** (*lit, fig*) ein Eigentor schießen.

ownsome ['əʊnsəm] *n*: **on one's ~** (*inf*) mutterseelenallein.

owt [aʊt] *pron* (*N Engl*) *see* **anything 1**.

ox [ɒks] *n, pl* **-en** Ochse *m* ◆ **as strong as an ~** bärenstark.

oxalic [ɒk'sælɪk] *adj acid* Oxal-.

ox-bow lake ['ɒksbəʊ'leɪk] *n* toter Flußarm.

Oxbridge ['ɒksbrɪdʒ] [1] *n* Oxford und/oder Cambridge.

[2] *adj accent* wie in Oxford oder Cambridge; *people* der Universität (*gen*) Oxford oder Cambridge.

ox cart *n* Ochsenkarren *m*.

oxen ['ɒksən] *pl of* **ox**.

oxeye daisy ['ɒks,aɪ'deɪzɪ] *n* Margerite *f*.

Oxfam ['ɒksfæm] *n abbr of* **Oxford Committee for Famine Relief (a)** *britische karitative Vereinigung zur Hungerhilfe.* **(b)** (*also* **~ shop**) *Gebrauchtwarenladen m, dessen Verkaufserlös der Hungerhilfe zugute kommt,* ≃ Dritte-Welt-Laden *m*.

oxford ['ɒksfəd] *n see* **Oxford shoe**.

Oxford: ~ bags *npl* sehr weite Hosen *pl*; **~ blue** *n Mitglied eines Oxforder Studentensportclubs, das für die Universität angetreten ist*; **~ English** *n* Oxford-Englisch *nt*; **~ shoe** *n* geschnürter Halbschuh.

oxidation [,ɒksɪ'deɪʃən] *n* (*Chem*) Oxydation, Oxidation *f*.

oxide ['ɒksaɪd] *n* (*Chem*) Oxyd, Oxid *nt*.

oxidize ['ɒksɪdaɪz] *vti* oxydieren, oxidieren.

oxlip ['ɒkslɪp] *n* (*Bot*) hohe *or* weiße Schlüsselblume.

Oxon ['ɒksən] *abbr of* **(a) Oxfordshire. (b) Oxoniensis** der Universität Oxford.

Oxonian [ɒk'səʊnɪən] [1] *n* Oxfordstudent(in *f*) *m*.

[2] *adj* der Oxforder Universität angehörend.

ox: ~tail *n* Ochsenschwanz *m*; **~tail soup** *n* Ochsenschwanzsuppe *f*.

oxyacetylene ['ɒksɪə'setɪli:n] *adj* Azetylensauerstoff- ◆ **~ burner** *or* **lamp** *or* **torch** Schweißbrenner *m*; **~ welding** Autogenschweißen *nt*.

oxygen ['ɒksɪdʒən] *n* Sauerstoff *m*.

oxygenate [ɒk'sɪdʒəneɪt] *vt* oxygenieren, mit Sauerstoff behandeln *or* anreichern.

oxygenation [,ɒksɪdʒə'neɪʃən] *n* Oxygenierung *f*, Anreicherung *or* Behandlung *f* mit Sauerstoff.

oxygen: ~ bottle, ~ cylinder *n* Sauerstofflasche *f*; **~ mask** *n* Sauerstoff- *or* Atemmaske *f*; **~ tank** *n* Sauerstoffbehälter *m*; **~ tent** *n* Sauerstoffzelt *nt*.

oxymoron [,ɒksɪ'mɔ:rɒn] *n* Oxymoron *nt*.

oyez ['əʊjez] *interj* (*old*) Achtung, Achtung.

oyster ['ɔɪstəʳ] *n* Auster *f* ◆ **the world's his ~** die Welt steht ihm offen; **to shut up** *or* **clam up like an ~** kein Wort mehr sagen.

oyster: ~ bank, ~ bed *n* Austernbank *f*; **~-breeding** *n* Austernzucht *f*; **~catcher** *n* (*Orn*) Austernfischer *m*; **~ cracker** *n* (*US*) Kräcker *m*; **~ farm** *n* Austernpark *m*; **~ shell** *n* Austernschale *f*.

oz *abbr of* **ounce(s)**.

ozalid ['ɒzəlɪd] *n* (*Typ*) Blaukopie *f*.

ozone ['əʊzəʊn] *n* Ozon *nt* ◆ **~ layer** Ozonschicht *f*; **an ~ hole, a hole in the ~ layer** ein Ozonloch *nt*; **~-friendly** *spray etc* ohne Treibgas, FCKW-frei.

P, p [piː] *n* P, p *nt* ◆ **to mind one's P's and Q's** (*inf*) sich anständig benehmen.

p *abbr of* **(a) page** S. **(b) penny, pence.**

PA *abbr of* **(a) Press Association. (b) personal assistant. (c) public address (system).**

p.a. *abbr of* **per annum.**

pa [pɑː] *n* (*inf*) Papa, Papi, Vati *m* (*all inf*).

pace¹ ['peɪsɪ] *prep* ohne ... (*dat*) nahetreten zu wollen.

pace² [peɪs] 1 *n* **(a)** (*step*) Schritt *m*; (*of horse*) Gangart *f*; (*lifting both legs on same side*) Paßgang *m* ◆ **twelve ~s off** zwölf Schritt(e) entfernt; **to put a horse through its ~s** ein Pferd alle Gangarten machen lassen; **to put sb/a new car through his/its ~s** (*fig*) jdn/ein neues Auto auf Herz und Nieren prüfen.
(b) (*speed*) Tempo *nt* ◆ **the more leisurely ~ of life in those days** das geruhsamere Leben damals; **at a good** *or* **smart ~** recht schnell; **at an incredible ~** unglaublich schnell, mit *or* in unglaublichem Tempo; **at a slow ~** langsam; **we kept up a good ~ with the work** wir kamen mit der Arbeit gut voran; **the present ~ of development** die momentane Entwicklungsrate; **to keep ~** Schritt halten; (*in discussing*) mitkommen; **I can't keep ~ with events** ich komme mit den Ereignissen nicht mehr mit; **to make** *or* **set the ~** das Tempo angeben; **to quicken one's ~** seinen Schritt beschleunigen; (*working*) sein Tempo beschleunigen; **I'm getting old, I can't stand the ~ any more** (*inf*) ich werde alt, ich kann nicht mehr mithalten; **the change of ~ between the third and fourth acts** der Tempowechsel zwischen dem dritten und vierten Akt; **he has a good change of ~** (*runner*) er kann sein Tempo gut beschleunigen.
2 *vt* **(a)** (*measure*) *floor, room* mit Schritten ausmessen.
(b) (*in anxiety etc*) auf und ab gehen *or* schreiten in (*+dat*).
(c) *competitor* das Tempo angeben (*+dat*).
(d) *horse* im Paßgang gehen lassen.
3 *vi* **(a) to ~ around** hin und her laufen; **to ~ up and down** auf und ab gehen *or* schreiten.
(b) (*horse*) im Paßgang gehen.

◆**pace off** *or* **out** *vt sep distance* ausschreiten, mit Schritten ausmessen *or* abmessen.

pacemaker ['peɪsˌmeɪkəʳ] *n* (*in race, business, Med*) Schrittmacher *m*.

pacer ['peɪsəʳ], **pace-setter** ['peɪssetəʳ] *n* (*Sport*) Schrittmacher *m*.

pachyderm ['pækɪdɜːm] *n* Dickhäuter *m*.

Pacific [pə'sɪfɪk] *n* **the ~ (Ocean)** der Pazifische *or* Stille Ozean, der Pazifik; **the ~ Rim** der Pazifikgürtel, der pazifische Raum; **~ time** Pazifische Zeit; **the ~ islands** die Pazifischen Inseln; **a ~ island** eine Insel im Pazifik.

pacific [pə'sɪfɪk] *adj people, nation* friedliebend, friedfertig.

pacifically [pə'sɪfɪkəlɪ] *adv live* in Frieden.

pacification [ˌpæsɪfɪ'keɪʃən] *n* Versöhnung *f*; (*of area*) Befriedung *f* ◆ **attempts at ~** Friedensbemühungen *pl*.

pacifier ['pæsɪfaɪəʳ] *n* **(a)** (*peacemaker*) Friedensstifter(in *f*) *m*. **(b)** (*US: dummy*) Schnuller *m*.

pacifism ['pæsɪfɪzəm] *n* Pazifismus *m*.

pacifist ['pæsɪfɪst] 1 *adj* pazifistisch.
2 *n* Pazifist(in *f*) *m*.

pacify ['pæsɪfaɪ] *vt baby* beruhigen; *warring countries* miteinander aussöhnen; *area* befrieden ◆ **just to ~ the unions** nur damit die Gewerkschaften stillhalten.

pack [pæk] 1 *n* **(a)** (*bundle*) Bündel *nt*; (*on animal*) Last *f*; (*rucksack*) Rucksack *m*; (*Mil*) Gepäck *nt no pl*, Tornister *m* (*dated*).
(b) (*packet*) (*for cereal, washing powder, frozen food*) Paket *nt*; (*US: of cigarettes*) Packung, Schachtel *f* ◆ **towels/books sold in ~s of six** Handtücher/Bücher im Sechserpack.
(c) (*Hunt*) Meute *f*.
(d) (*of wolves, cubs*) Rudel *nt*; (*of submarines*) Gruppe *f*.
(e) (*pej: group*) Horde, Meute *f* ◆ **a ~ of thieves** eine Diebesbande; **he told us a ~ of lies** er tischte uns einen Sack voll Lügen auf; **it's all a ~ of lies** es ist alles erlogen; **you ~ of louts!** ihr Rabauken!
(f) (*of cards*) (Karten)spiel *nt* ◆ **52 cards make a ~** ein Blatt *nt* besteht aus 52 Karten.
(g) (*Rugby*) Stürmer *pl*.
(h) (*Med, cosmetic*) Packung *f*.
(i) (*of ice*) Scholle *f*.
2 *vt* **(a)** *crate, container etc* vollpacken; *fish, meat in tin etc* abpacken ◆ **~ed in dozens** im Dutzend abgepackt.
(b) *case, trunk* packen; *things in case, clothes etc* einpacken.
(c) (*wrap, put into parcel*) einpacken ◆ **it comes ~ed in polythene** es ist in Cellophan verpackt.
(d) (*crowd, cram*) packen; *container also* vollstopfen; *articles also* stopfen, pfropfen ◆ **the box was ~ed full of explosives** die Kiste war voll mit Sprengstoff; **the crowds that ~ed the stadium** die Menschenmassen, die sich im Stadium drängten; **the comedy was playing to ~ed houses** die Komödie lief vor ausverkauften Häusern; **to be ~ed** (*full*) gerammelt voll sein (*inf*); **all this information is ~ed into one chapter** all diese Informationen sind in einem Kapitel zusammengedrängt; **a holiday ~ed with excitement** Ferien voller aufregender Erlebnisse; **a speech ~ed with jokes** eine mit Witzen gespickte Rede; **a thrill-~ed film** ein packender Film; **the coast is ~ed with tourists** an der Küste wimmelt es von Touristen.
(e) (*make firm*) *soil etc* festdrücken.
(f) *jury* mit den eigenen Leuten besetzen.
(g) (*US inf: carry*) *gun* tragen, dabei haben ◆ **to ~ one's lunch** sich (*dat*) sein Mittagessen mitnehmen.
(h) (*inf*) **to ~ a (heavy) punch** kräftig zuschlagen; **he ~s a nasty left** er hat *or* schlägt eine ganz gemeine Linke (*inf*).
(i) *leak, pipe* (zu)stopfen.
3 *vi* **(a)** (*items*) passen ◆ **that won't all ~ into one suitcase** das paßt *or* geht nicht alles in einen Koffer; **it ~s (in) nicely** es läßt sich gut verpacken; **the boxes are designed to ~ into this container** die Kästen sind so gemacht, daß sie in diesen Behälter hineingehen.
(b) (*person*) packen ◆ **I'm still ~ing** ich bin noch beim Packen.
(c) (*crowd*) **the crowds ~ed into the stadium** die Menge drängte sich in das Stadion; **we can't all ~ into one Mini** wir können uns nicht alle in einen Mini zwängen; **they ~ed round the president** sie belagerten *or* umringten den Präsidenten.
(d) (*become firm*) fest werden ◆ **the snow had ~ed round the wheels** an den Rädern klebte eine feste Schneeschicht.
(e) (*inf*) **to send sb ~ing** jdn kurz abfertigen; **what would you do with a drunken husband like mine? — I'd send him ~ing** was würden Sie mit einem Trunkenbold wie meinem Mann machen? — ich würde ihn vor die Tür setzen.

◆**pack away** 1 *vt sep* **(a)** *clothes, boxes etc* wegpacken ◆ **~ your toys ~ before you go out** räum deine Spielsachen weg, bevor du rausgehst; **I've ~ed all your books ~ in the attic** ich habe alle deine Bücher auf den Boden geräumt; **he ~ed the deckchairs ~ for the winter** er räumte die Liegestühle für den Winter weg.
(b) (*inf*) *food* **he can really ~ it ~** er kann ganz schön was verdrücken (*inf*) *or* verputzen (*inf*).
2 *vi* **the bed ~s ~ into a wall-cupboard** man kann das Bett in einem Wandschrank verschwinden lassen.

◆**pack down** *vi* (*Rugby*) ein Gedränge *nt* bilden.

◆**pack in** 1 *vt sep* **(a)** *clothes etc* einpacken.
(b) *people* hineinpferchen in (*+acc*) ◆ **we can't ~ any more ~ here** (*people*) hier geht *or* paßt keiner mehr rein; (*things*) hier geht *or* paßt nichts mehr rein.
(c) (*play, actor etc*) in Scharen anziehen ◆ **this film is really ~ing them ~** (*inf*) dieser Film zieht die Leute in Scharen an.
(d) (*Brit inf*) (*give up*) *job* hinschmeißen (*inf*); *girlfriend* sausen lassen (*inf*); (*stop*) *noise* aufhören mit; *work, activity* Schluß *or* Feierabend (*inf*) machen mit ◆ **a footballer should know when it's time to ~ it ~** ein Fußballspieler sollte wissen, wann es Zeit ist, Schluß zu machen *or* aufzuhören; **~ it ~!** hör auf!, laß es gut sein!; (*job*) schmeiß die Sache hin!
2 *vi* **(a)** (*crowd in*) sich hineindrängen ◆ **we all ~ed ~ to his car** wir zwängten uns alle in sein Auto.
(b) (*inf: stop working*) (*engine*) seinen Geist aufgeben (*hum*); (*person*) zusammenpacken, Feierabend machen (*inf*).

◆**pack off** *vt sep* **she ~ed them ~ to bed/school** sie verfrachtete sie ins Bett/schickte sie in die Schule.

◆**pack out** *vt sep usu pass* **to be ~ed ~** (*hall, theatre etc*) gerammelt voll sein (*inf*), überfüllt sein.

◆**pack up** [1] *vt sep clothes etc* zusammenpacken.
[2] *vi* **(a)** (*prepare luggage*) packen ◆ **he just ~ed ~ and left** er packte seine Sachen und ging. **(b)** (*inf: stop working*) (*engine*) seinen Geist aufgeben (*hum*); (*person*) Feierabend machen (*inf*). **(c) the tent ~s ~ easily** das Zelt läßt sich gut verpacken.

package ['pækɪdʒ] [1] *n* **(a)** (*parcel, esp US: packet*) Paket *nt*; (*of cardboard*) Schachtel *f*. **(b)** (*esp Comm: group, set*) Paket, Bündel *nt* ◆ **software ~** Softwarepaket *nt*.
[2] *vt* **(a)** verpacken. **(b)** (*in order to enhance sales*) präsentieren.

package: ~ deal *n* Pauschalangebot *nt*; **~ holiday** *n* Pauschalreise *f*.

packager ['pækɪdʒəʳ] *n* (*for books*) Redaktionsbüro *nt*, Packager *m*; (*TV*) Produktionsfirma *f*.

package: ~ store *n* (*US*) Spirituosenhandlung *f*; **~ tour** *n see* **~ holiday**.

packaging ['pækɪdʒɪŋ] *n see vt* **(a)** Verpackung *f* ◆ **this is where they do the ~** hier werden die Sachen verpackt. **(b)** Präsentation *f* ◆ **the public don't buy the product, they buy the ~** die Leute kaufen nicht das Produkt, sondern die Verpackung.

pack: ~ animal *n* Packtier, Lasttier *nt*; **~ drill** *n* Strafexerzieren *nt* in gefechtsmäßiger Ausrüstung.

packer ['pækəʳ] *n* Packer(in *f*) *m* ◆ **he's a very untidy ~** er packt sehr unordentlich.

packet ['pækɪt] *n* **(a)** Paket *nt*; (*of cigarettes*) Päckchen *nt*, Schachtel, Packung *f*; (*small box*) Schachtel *f*. **(b)** (*Naut*) Paketboot *nt*. **(c)** (*Brit sl: lot of money*) **to make a ~** ein Schweinegeld verdienen (*sl*); **that must have cost a ~** das muß ein Heidengeld gekostet haben (*inf*).

packet: ~ boat *n* Paketboot *nt*; **~ switching** *n* (*Telec, Comput*) Paketvermittlung *f*.

pack: ~horse *n* Packpferd *nt*; **I'm not your ~horse!** ich bin nicht dein Packesel!; **~ice** *n* Packeis *nt*.

packing ['pækɪŋ] *n* **(a)** (*act*) (*in suitcases*) Packen *nt*; (*in factories etc*) Verpackung *f* ◆ **to do one's ~** packen. **(b)** (*material*) Verpackung *f*; (*for leak*) Dichtung *f*.

packing: ~ case *n* Kiste *f*; **~ house** *n* (*US*) Abpackbetrieb *m*; **~ list** *n* (*Comm*) Packliste *f*; **~ plant** *n* (*US*) *see* **~ house**.

pack: ~ rat *n* Buschschwanzratte *f*; **~sack** *n* (*US*) Rucksack *m*; **~-saddle** *n* Packsattel *m*; **~-thread** *n* Zwirn *m*; **~ train** *n* Tragtierkolonne *f*.

pact [pækt] *n* Pakt *m* ◆ **to make a ~ with sb** mit jdm einen Pakt schließen.

pad[1] [pæd] *vi* **to ~ about** umhertapsen; **to ~ along** entlangtrotten; **the panther ~ded up and down** der Panther trottete auf und ab; **the tiger ~ded off into the bushes** der Tiger trottete ins Gebüsch.

pad[2] [1] *n* **(a)** (*stuffing*) (*for comfort etc*) Polster *nt*; (*for protection*) Schützer *m*; (*in bra*) Einlage *f*; (*brake ~ etc*) Belag *m*.
(b) (*of paper*) Block *m*; (*of blotting paper*) Schreibunterlage *f*.
(c) (*for inking*) Stempelkissen *nt*.
(d) (*of animal's foot*) Ballen *m*.
(e) (*launching ~*) (Abschuß)rampe *f*.
(f) (*inf: room, home*) Bude *f* (*inf*) ◆ **at your ~** in deiner Bude, bei dir.
[2] *vt shoulders etc* polstern.

◆**pad out** *vt sep* **(a)** *shoulders* polstern. **(b)** *article, essay etc* auffüllen; *speech* ausdehnen, strecken.

padded ['pædɪd] *adj shoulders, armour, bra* wattiert; *dashboard* gepolstert ◆ **~ cell** Gummizelle *f*.

padding ['pædɪŋ] *n* **(a)** (*material*) Polsterung *f*. **(b)** (*fig: in essay etc*) Füllwerk *nt*, Füllsel *pl*.

paddle ['pædl] [1] *n* **(a)** (*oar*) Paddel *nt*.
(b) (*blade of wheel*) Schaufel *f*; (*wheel*) Schaufelrad *nt*.
(c) (*for mixing*) Rührschaufel *f*.
(d) Grandpa still enjoys a ~ Opa planscht noch gern durchs Wasser; **to go for a ~, to have a ~** durchs Wasser waten.
(e) (*US: in table tennis*) Schläger *m*.
[2] *vt* **(a)** *boat* paddeln.
(b) to ~ one's feet in the water mit den Füßen im Wasser planschen; **~ your feet and you'll stay afloat** du mußt mit den Füßen paddeln, dann gehst du nicht unter.
(c) (*US: spank*) verhauen, versohlen (*inf*).
[3] *vi* **(a)** (*in boat*) paddeln.
(b) (*with feet, swimming*) paddeln.
(c) (*walk in shallow water*) waten.

paddle: ~ boat *n* Raddampfer *m*; (*small, on pond*) Paddelboot *nt*; **~ box** *n* Radkasten *m*; **~ steamer** *n* Raddampfer *m*; **~ wheel** *n* Schaufelrad *nt*.

paddling pool ['pædlɪŋ,puːl] *n* Planschbecken *nt*.

paddock ['pædək] *n* (*field*) Koppel *f*; (*of racecourse*) Sattelplatz *m*; (*motor racing*) Fahrerlager *nt*.

Paddy ['pædɪ] *n* (*inf*) Paddy, *Spitzname der Iren*.

paddy[1] ['pædɪ] *n* **(a)** (*rice*) ungeschälter Reis. **(b)** (*also* **~ field**) Reisfeld *nt*.

paddy[2] *n* (*Brit inf*) Koller *m* (*inf*) ◆ **to get into a ~** einen Koller kriegen (*inf*); **to be in a ~** einen Koller haben (*inf*).

paddy wagon *n* (*US inf*) grüne Minna (*inf*).

paddywhack ['pædɪwæk] *n* (*inf*) **(a)** *see* **paddy**[2]. **(b)** (*spank*) Klaps *m*.

padlock ['pædlɒk] [1] *n* Vorhängeschloß *nt*.
[2] *vt* (mit einem Vorhängeschloß) verschließen.

padre ['pɑːdrɪ] *n* (*Mil*) Feldkaplan, Feldgeistliche(r) *m* ◆ **yes, ~** ja, Herr Kaplan.

paean ['piːən] *n* Lobrede *f*.

paediatric, (*US*) **pediatric** [,piːdɪ'ætrɪk] *adj* Kinder-, pädiatrisch (*spec*).

paediatrician, (*US*) **pediatrician** [,piːdɪə'trɪʃən] *n* Kinderarzt *m*/-ärztin *f*, Pädiater *m* (*spec*).

paediatrics, (*US*) **pediatrics** [,piːdɪ'ætrɪks] *n* Kinderheilkunde, Pädiatrie (*spec*) *f*.

paedological, (*US*) **pedological** [,piːdə'lɒdʒɪkəl] *adj* pädologisch.

paedology, (*US*) **pedology** [,piː'dɒlədʒɪ] *n* Pädologie *f*.

paedophile, (*US*) **pedophile** ['piːdəfaɪl] *n* Pädophile(r) *mf*.

paedophilia, (*US*) **pedophilia** [,piːdəʊ'fɪlɪə] *n* Pädophilie *f*.

paedophiliac, (*US*) **pedophiliac** [,piːdə'fɪlɪæk] [1] *n* Pädophile(r) *mf*.
[2] *adj* pädophil.

pagan ['peɪgən] [1] *adj* heidnisch.
[2] *n* Heide *m*, Heidin *f*.

paganism ['peɪgənɪzəm] *n* Heidentum *nt*.

page[1] [peɪdʒ] [1] *n* (*also* **~-boy**) Page *m*; (*of knight*) Page, Edelknabe *m*.
[2] *vt* **to ~ sb** jdn ausrufen lassen; **paging Mr Cousin** Herr Cousin, bitte!

page[2] [1] *n* **(a)** Seite *f* ◆ **on ~ 14** auf Seite 14; **write on both sides of the ~** beschreiben Sie beide Seiten.
(b) a glorious ~ of English history ein Ruhmesblatt *nt* in der Geschichte Englands; **to go down in the ~s of history** in die Geschichte *or* die Annalen der Geschichte eingehen.
[2] *vt* (*Typ*) paginieren, mit Seitenzahlen versehen.

pageant ['pædʒənt] *n* (*show*) historische Aufführung, Historienspiel *nt* ◆ **Christmas ~** Weihnachtsspiel *nt*; (*procession*) Festzug *m*; **a ~ of Elizabethan times** (*series of theatrical tableaux etc*) eine historische Darstellung des Elisabethanischen Zeitalters; (*procession*) ein Festzug *m or* festlicher Umzug im Stil des Elisabethanischen Zeitalters; **the whole ~ of life** die breite Fülle des Lebens.

pageantry ['pædʒəntrɪ] *n* Prunk *m*, Gepränge *nt* ◆ **all the ~ of history** die ganze Pracht der Geschichte; **the coronation was celebrated with great ~** die Krönung wurde sehr prunkvoll *or* mit großem Prunk *or* Gepränge gefeiert.

page: ~-boy *n* **(a)** Page *m*; **(b)** (*hairstyle*) Pagenkopf *m*; **~ break** *n* (*Comput*) Seitenwechsel *m*; **~ make-up** *n* (*Typ*) Umbruch *m*; **~ number** *n* Seitenzahl *f*; **~ preview** *n* (*Comput*) Preview *m*; **~ printer** *n* (*Comput*) Seitendrucker *m*; **~ proof** *n* Korrekturfahne *f*.

pager ['peɪdʒəʳ] *n* (*Telec*) Funkrufempfänger *m*.

paginate ['pædʒɪneɪt] *vt* paginieren.

pagination [,pædʒɪ'neɪʃən] *n* Paginierung *f*.

pagoda [pə'gəʊdə] *n* Pagode *f*.

paid [peɪd] [1] *pret, ptp of* **pay**.
[2] *adj official, work* bezahlt ◆ **to put ~ to sth** etw zunichte machen; **that's put ~ to my holiday** damit ist mein Urlaub geplatzt *or* gestorben (*inf*); **that's put ~ to him** damit ist für ihn der Ofen aus (*inf*), das war's dann wohl für ihn (*inf*).

paid-up ['peɪd'ʌp] *adj share* eingezahlt ◆ **a ~ membership of 500** 500 zahlende Mitglieder; **fully ~ member** Mitglied ohne Beitragsrückstände; **is he fully ~?** hat er alle Beiträge bezahlt?; **to make an insurance policy ~** eine Versicherung beitragsfrei stellen.

pail [peɪl] *n* Eimer *m*; (*child's*) Eimerchen *nt*.

pailful ['peɪlfʊl] *n* Eimer *m*.

paillasse ['pælɪæs] *n* Strohsack *m*.

pain [peɪn] [1] *n* **(a)** Schmerz *m* ◆ **is the ~ still there?** hast du noch Schmerzen?; **where is the ~ exactly?** wo tut es denn genau weh?; **this will help the ~** das ist gut gegen die Schmerzen; **to be in ~** Schmerzen haben; **you can't just leave him in ~** du kannst ihn nicht einfach leiden lassen; **he screamed in ~** er schrie vor Schmerzen; **do insects feel ~?** können Insekten Schmerz empfinden?; **a sharp ~** ein stechender Schmerz; **cucumber gives me a ~ in the stomach** von Gurken bekomme ich Magenschmerzen *pl*; **my ankle has been giving** *or* **causing me a lot of ~** mein Knöchel tut mir sehr weh; **I have a ~ in my leg** mein Bein tut mir weh, ich habe Schmerzen im Bein; **to put sb out of his ~** jdn von seinen Schmerzen erlösen.
(b) (*mental*) Qualen *pl* ◆ **the ~ of parting** der Abschiedsschmerz; **Werther: a soul in ~** Werther: eine gequälte Seele; **being so totally ignored like that was a source of great ~ to her** so vollkommen ignoriert zu werden, war für sie sehr schmerzlich; **he suffered great mental ~** er litt Seelenqualen; **the decision caused me a lot of ~** die Entscheidung war sehr schmerzlich für mich; **a look of ~ came over his face** sein Gesicht nahm einen schmerzlichen Ausdruck an.
(c) ~s *pl* (*efforts*) Mühe *f* ◆ **to be at (great) ~s to do sth** sich (*dat*) (große) Mühe geben, etw zu tun; **to take ~s over sth/to do sth** sich (*dat*) Mühe mit etw geben/sich (*dat*) Mühe geben, etw zu tun; **great ~s have been taken to ...** besondere Mühe wurde darauf verwendet ...; **she takes great ~s over her appearance** sie verwendet sehr viel Sorgfalt auf ihr Äußeres; **all he got for his ~s was a curt refusal** zum Dank für seine Mühe wurde er schroff abgewiesen; **see what you get for your ~s!** das hast du nun für deine Mühe!
(d) (*penalty*) **on ~ of death** bei Todesstrafe, bei Strafe des Todes (*old*), unter Androhung der Todesstrafe.
(e) (*inf: also* **~ in the neck** *or* **arse** *sl*) **to be a (real) ~** einem auf den Wecker (*inf*) *or* Geist (*inf*) gehen; **this job is getting to be a ~** dieser Job geht mir langsam auf den Wecker (*inf*).
[2] *vt* (*mentally*) schmerzen ◆ **it ~s me to see their ignorance** ihre Unwissenheit tut schon weh; **his behaviour ~ed his parents** mit seinem Benehmen bereitete er seinen Eltern (*dat*) großen Kummer; **it ~s me to have to tell you this but ...** es schmerzt mich, Ihnen dies mitteilen zu müssen, aber ...

pain barrier *n* Schmerzgrenze *f*.

pained [peɪnd] *adj expression, voice* schmerzerfüllt.

painful ['peɪnfʊl] *adj* **(a)** (*physically*) schmerzhaft ◆ **is it ~?** tut es weh?; **it's ~ to the touch** es tut weh, wenn man es berührt; **my arm was becoming ~** mein Arm fing an zu schmerzen.
(b) (*unpleasant*) *experience, memory* unangenehm ◆ **it is my ~ duty to tell you that** ... ich habe die traurige Pflicht, Ihnen mitteilen zu müssen, daß ...; **~ to behold** ein qualvoller Anblick.
(c) (*inf: terrible*) peinlich ◆ **~, isn't it?** das tut weh, was?; **I went to the party but it was really ~** (*boring*) ich war auf der Party, aber es war zum Sterben langweilig; (*embarrassing*) ich war auf der Party, eine äußerst peinliche Angelegenheit; **she gave a ~ performance** ihre Vorführung war mehr als peinlich.
painfully ['peɪnfəlɪ] *adv* **(a)** (*physically*) schmerzhaft ◆ **he dragged himself ~ along** er quälte sich mühsam weiter.
(b) (*inf: very*) schrecklich ◆ **it was ~ obvious** es war nicht zu übersehen; **he was being ~ overpolite** es war peinlich, wie betont höflich er sich benahm; **he became ~ aware that** ... ihm wurde schmerzlich bewußt, daß ...
pain: ~killer *n* schmerzstillendes Mittel; **~killing** *adj drug* schmerzstillend.
painless ['peɪnlɪs] *adj* schmerzlos ◆ **I promise you the interview will be quite ~** (*inf*) ich versichere Ihnen, daß das Interview kurz und schmerzlos wird (*inf*); **a procedure which makes paying completely ~** (*inf*) ein Verfahren, bei dem Sie von der Bezahlung überhaupt nichts merken; **don't worry, it's quite ~** (*inf*) keine Angst, es tut gar nicht weh.
painlessly ['peɪnlɪslɪ] *adv see adj.*
painstaking ['peɪnz,teɪkɪŋ] *adj person, piece of work* sorgfältig ◆ **with ~ accuracy** mit peinlicher Genauigkeit.
painstakingly ['peɪnz,teɪkɪŋlɪ] *adv* sorgfältig, gewissenhaft ◆ **one has to be so ~ precise** man muß äußerst genau sein.
paint [peɪnt] [1] *n* **(a)** Farbe *f*; (*on car, furniture also*) Lack *m*; (*make-up*) Schminke *f* ◆ **there's too much ~ on your face** du hast zu viel Farbe im Gesicht, du bist zu stark angemalt (*inf*).
(b) ~s *pl* Farben *pl* ◆ **box of ~s** Farb- *or* Malkasten *m*.
(c) (*US: piebald horse*) Schecke *m*.
[2] *vt* **(a)** streichen; *car* lackieren; *door also* lackieren ◆ **to ~ one's face** sich anmalen (*inf*); (*Theat*) sich schminken; **to ~ the town red** (*inf*) die Stadt unsicher machen (*inf*).
(b) *picture, person* malen ◆ **he ~ed a very convincing picture of life on the moon** er zeichnete ein sehr überzeugendes Bild vom Leben auf dem Mond; *see* **black**.
[3] *vi* malen; (*decorate*) (an)streichen.
◆**paint in** *vt sep* (*add*) dazumalen; (*fill in*) ausmalen.
◆**paint on** *vt sep* aufmalen.
◆**paint out** *or* **over** *vt sep* übermalen; (*on wall*) überstreichen.
◆**paint up** *vt sep building* neu *or* frisch anstreichen; *face* anmalen ◆ **she gets all ~ed ~ on a Friday night** freitags abends legt sie immer ihre Kriegsbemalung an (*inf*).
paint: ~box *n* Farb- *or* Malkasten *m*; **~brush** *n* Pinsel *m*.
painted woman ['peɪntɪd'wʊmən] *n* Flittchen *nt* (*inf*).
painter¹ ['peɪntəʳ] *n* (*Art*) Maler(in *f*) *m*; (*decorator also*) Anstreicher(in *f*) *m*.
painter² *n* (*Naut*) Fangleine *f*.
painting ['peɪntɪŋ] *n* **(a)** (*picture*) Bild, Gemälde *nt*. **(b)** *no pl* (*Art*) Malerei *f*. **(c)** *no pl* (*of flat etc*) Anstreichen *nt*.
paint: ~ pot *n* Farbtopf *m*; **~ roller** *n* Farbrolle *f*; **~ shop** *n* (*Ind*) Lackiererei *f*; **~ spray(er)** *n* Spritzpistole *f*; **~ stripper** *n* Abbeizmittel *nt*; **~work** *n* (*on car etc*) Lack *m*; (*on wall, furniture*) Anstrich *m*.
pair [pɛəʳ] [1] *n* **(a)** (*of gloves, shoes, people*) Paar *nt*; (*of animals, cards*) Pärchen *nt*; (*hum sl: breasts*) Vorbau *m* (*inf*), Dinger *pl* (*sl*) ◆ **I've lost the ~ to this glove** ich habe den anderen *or* zweiten Handschuh verloren; **a ~ of trousers** eine Hose; **six ~s of trousers** sechs Hosen; **a new ~** (*of trousers*) eine neue (Hose); (*of shoes*) (ein Paar) neue; **I've lost my scissors, could I borrow your ~?** ich habe meine Schere verloren, kannst du mir deine leihen?; **he has a useful ~ of hands** (*boxer*) er ist ein guter Boxer; **a huge ~ of eyes** ein riesiges Augenpaar; **in ~s** paarweise; *hunt, arrive, go out* zu zweit; *seated* in Zweiergruppen; **they're a ~ of rascals** das sind vielleicht zwei Lausejungen; **what a ~ of fools we are!** wir (beide) sind vielleicht dumm!; **you're a fine ~ you are!** (*iro*) ihr seid mir (vielleicht) ein sauberes Pärchen (*iro*); *see* **carriage**.
(b) the ~s *sing or pl* (*Skating*) Paarlauf *m*; (*Rowing*) Zweier *m*; **in the ~s** im Paarlauf/Zweier.
[2] *vt* in Paaren *or* paarweise anordnen ◆ **I was ~ed with Bob for the next round** in der nächsten Runde mußte ich mit Bob ein Paar bilden.
[3] *vi* (*Parl*) *mit einem Abgeordneten einer anderen Partei ein Abkommen für eine Wahl treffen.*
◆**pair off** [1] *vt sep* in Zweiergruppen einteilen ◆ **to ~ sb ~ with sb** (*find boyfriend etc for*) jdn mit jdm zusammenbringen *or* verkuppeln (*inf*); **she was ~ed ~ with Jean in the tournament** sie wurde beim Turnier mit Jean zusammengebracht; **~ ~ each word with its opposite** ordnen Sie jedem Wort den jeweiligen Gegensatz zu.
[2] *vi* Paare bilden ◆ **all the people at the party had ~ed ~** bei der Party hatten alle Pärchen gebildet.
pairing ['pɛərɪŋ] *n* Paarung *f*.
pair-skating ['pɛə,skeɪtɪŋ] *n* Paarlaufen *nt*.
paisley ['peɪzlɪ] [1] *n* türkisches Muster.
[2] *adj pattern* türkisch; *shirt* türkisch gemustert.
pajamas [pə'dʒɑːməz] *npl* (*US*) *see* **pyjamas**.
Paki ['pækɪ] (*inf*) [1] *n* **(a)** (*often pej: person*) Pakistani *mf*. **(b)** (*restaurant*) pakistanisches Restaurant; (*meal*) pakistanisches Gericht. **(c)** (*shop*) Lebensmittelladen *m* (*von Pakistanis geführt*).
[2] *adj* (*often pej*) pakistanisch.
Pakistan [,pɑːkɪs'tɑːn] *n* Pakistan *nt*.
Pakistani [,pɑːkɪs'tɑːnɪ] [1] *adj* pakistanisch.
[2] *n* Pakistani *mf*, Pakistaner(in *f*) *m*.
pal [pæl] *n* (*inf*) Kumpel *m* (*inf*) ◆ **OK, let's be ~s again** na gut, vertragen wir uns wieder!; **be a ~!** sei so nett!; **help me with this, there's a ~** sei doch so nett und hilf mir dabei.
◆**pal up** *vi* (*inf*) sich anfreunden (*with* mit).
palace ['pælɪs] *n* (*lit, fig*) Palast *m* ◆ **bishop's ~** bischöfliches Palais, bischöfliche Residenz; **royal ~** (Königs)schloß *nt*; **the PM was summoned to the ~** der Premierminister wurde zur Königin/zum König bestellt.
palace: ~ grounds *npl* Schloßgelände *nt*; **~ guard** *n* Schloßwache *f*; **~ revolution** *n* (*lit, fig*) Palastrevolution *f*; **~ wall** *n* Schloßmauer *f*.
paladin ['pælədɪn] *n* Paladin *m*.
palaeo- ['pælɪəʊ-] *pref see* **paleo-**.
palanquin [,pælən'kiːn] *n* Sänfte *f*.
palatability [,pælətə'bɪlɪtɪ] *n* **(a)** Schmackhaftigkeit *f*. **(b)** (*fig*) Attraktivität *f*.
palatable ['pælətəbl] *adj* genießbar; *food also* schmackhaft (*to* für); (*fig*) attraktiv ◆ **to some the truth is not always ~** manchen Leuten schmeckt die Wahrheit nicht immer.
palatably ['pælətəblɪ] *adv* schmackhaft; (*fig also*) attraktiv.
palatal ['pælətl] [1] *adj* Gaumen-; (*Phon*) palatal.
[2] *n* (*Phon*) Palatal(laut) *m*.
palatalize ['pælətəlaɪz] *vti* (*Phon*) den Palatallaut bilden ◆ **the "t" is ~d** das „t" wird im vorderen Gaumen gebildet.
palate ['pælɪt] *n* (*lit*) Gaumen *m* ◆ **hard ~** harter Gaumen, Vordergaumen *m*; **soft ~** weicher Gaumen, Gaumensegel *nt*; **to have a delicate ~** einen empfindlichen Gaumen haben; **to have no ~ for sth** (*fig*) keinen Sinn für etw haben.
palatial [pə'leɪʃəl] *adj* (*spacious*) palastartig; (*luxurious*) luxuriös, prunkvoll, feudal (*hum inf*).
palatially [pə'leɪʃəlɪ] *adv* luxuriös, prunkvoll, feudal (*hum inf*).
palatinate [pə'lætɪnɪt] *n* Pfalz *f*.
palatine ['pælətaɪn] *n* (*also* **count ~**) Pfalzgraf *m*.
palaver [pə'lɑːvəʳ] *n* (*inf*) **(a)** (*fuss and bother*) Umstand *m*, Theater *nt* (*inf*). **(b)** (*conference*) Palaver *nt*.
pale¹ [peɪl] [1] *adj* (*+er*) *colour, complexion, face* blaß; *light also, face* (*implying unhealthy etc*) bleich, fahl ◆ **she has ~ gold hair** sie hat rötlichblondes Haar; **~ green/orange** *etc* blaß- *or* zartgrün/blaß- *or* zartorange *etc*; **to go** *or* **turn ~ with fear/anger** vor Schreck/Wut bleich *or* blaß werden; **but a ~ imitation of the real thing** nur ein Abklatsch *m* des Originals.
[2] *vi* (*person*) erbleichen, blaß *or* bleich werden; (*paper etc*) verblassen ◆ **but X ~s beside Y** neben Y verblaßt X direkt; **to ~ into insignificance** zur Bedeutungslosigkeit herabsinken.
pale² *n* (*stake*) Pfahl *m* ◆ **those last few remarks were quite beyond the ~** diese letzten Bemerkungen haben eindeutig die Grenzen überschritten; **he is now regarded as beyond the ~** man betrachtet ihn jetzt als indiskutabel.
pale: ~ ale *n* (*Brit*) helleres Dunkelbier; **~face** *n* Bleichgesicht *nt*; **~-faced** *adj* bleich, blaß.
palely ['peɪllɪ] *adv shine, lit* schwach, matt.
paleness ['peɪlnɪs] *n* Blässe *f*.
paleo- [,pælɪəʊ-] *pref* paläo-, Paläo-.
paleography [,pælɪ'ɒgrəfɪ] *n* Paläographie *f*.
paleolithic [,pælɪəʊ'lɪθɪk] *adj* paläolithisch, altsteinzeitlich.
paleontology [,pælɪɒn'tɒlədʒɪ] *n* Paläontologie *f*.
paleozoic [,pælɪəʊ'zəʊɪk] *adj* paläozoisch.
Palestine ['pælɪstaɪn] *n* Palästina *nt*.
Palestinian [,pælə'stɪnɪən] [1] *adj* palästinensisch.
[2] *n* Palästinenser(in *f*) *m*.
palette ['pælɪt] *n* Palette *f* ◆ **~ knife** Palettenmesser *nt*.
palfrey ['pɔːlfrɪ] *n* Zelter *m*.
palimony ['pælɪmənɪ] *n* (*inf*) Unterhaltszahlung *f* (*bei der Auflösung einer Ehe ohne Trauschein*).
palimpsest ['pælɪmpsest] *n* Palimpsest *m*.
palindrome ['pælɪndrəʊm] *n* Palindrom *nt*.
paling ['peɪlɪŋ] *n* (*stake*) Zaunpfahl *m*; (*fence*) Lattenzaun *m*; (*bigger*) Palisadenzaun *m*.
palisade [,pælɪ'seɪd] [1] *n* **(a)** Palisade *f*. **(b) ~s** *pl* (*US*) Steilufer *nt*.
[2] *vt* einpfählen.
pall¹ [pɔːl] *n* **(a)** (*over coffin*) Bahrtuch, Sargtuch *nt* ◆ **a ~ of smoke** (*fig*) (*covering*) eine Dunstglocke; (*rising in air*) eine Rauchwolke. **(b)** (*Eccl*) Pallium *nt*.
pall² *vi* an Reiz verlieren (*on sb* für jdn).
palladium [pə'leɪdɪəm] *n* (*Chem*) Palladium *nt*.
pall-bearer ['pɔːl,bɛərəʳ] *n* Sargträger *m*.
pallet ['pælɪt] *n* (*bed*) Pritsche *f*; (*for storage*) Palette *f*.
palletization [,pælɪtaɪ'zeɪʃən] *n* Palettisierung *f*.
palliasse ['pælɪæs] *n* Strohsack *m*.
palliate ['pælɪeɪt] *vt* (*form*) **(a)** *disease* lindern. **(b)** *offence, seriousness of situation* (*make less serious*) mildern; (*make seem less serious*) beschönigen.
palliative ['pælɪətɪv] (*form*) [1] *adj drug, remedy* lindernd, Linderungs-; *explanation* beschönigend.
[2] *n* Linderungsmittel, Palliativ(um) *nt*.
pallid ['pælɪd] *adj* blaß, fahl; (*unhealthy looking*) bleich, fahl.

pallor ['pælə^r] *n* Blässe, Fahlheit *f.*

pally ['pælɪ] *adj* (+er) (*inf*) **he's a ~ sort** er ist ein freundlicher Bursche; **they're very ~** sie sind dicke Freunde (*inf*); **to be ~ with sb** mit jdm gut Freund sein; **to get ~ with sb** sich mit jdm anfreunden; **he immediately tried to get ~ with the boss** er versuchte sofort, sich beim Chef anzubiedern.

palm¹ [pɑːm] *n* (*Bot*) Palme *f*; (*as carried at Easter*) Palmzweig *m* ♦ **to carry off** *or* **bear the ~** die Siegespalme erringen, siegen.

palm² [1] *n* (*Anat*) Handteller *m*, Handfläche *f*; (*of glove*) Innenfläche *f* ♦ **the magician had concealed the ball in the ~ of his hand** der Zauberkünstler hielt den Ball in der hohlen Hand versteckt; **to grease sb's ~** jdn schmieren (*inf*); **to read sb's ~** jdm aus der Hand lesen; *see* **itching.**
[2] *vt* (a) *card* im Ärmel verstecken.
(b) **the goalie just managed to ~ the ball over the crossbar** der Torwart schaffte es gerade noch, den Ball mit der Handfläche über die Querlatte zu lenken.

♦**palm off** *vt sep* (*inf*) *rubbish, goods* andrehen (*on(to) sb* jdm) (*inf*); *sb* (*with explanation*) abspeisen (*inf*).

palmcorder ['pɑːmkɔːdə^r] *n* Palmcorder *m.*

palmetto [pæl'metəʊ] *n* Palmetto *f.*

palmist ['pɑːmɪst] *n* Handliniendeuter(in *f*), Handleser(in *f*) *m.*

palmistry ['pɑːmɪstrɪ] *n* Handliniendeutung, Handlesekunst *f.*

palm: ~ leaf *n* Palmwedel *m*; **~ oil** *n* Palmöl *nt*; **P~ Sunday** *n* Palmsonntag *m*; **~top** ['pɑːmtɒp] *n* (*Comput*) Palmtop *m*; **~ tree** *n* Palme *f*; **~ wine** *n* Palmwein *m.*

palmy ['pɑːmɪ] *adj* (+er) *days* glücklich, unbeschwert.

palomino [,pælə'miːnəʊ] *n* Palomino *nt.*

palpable ['pælpəbl] *adj* (a) greifbar; (*Med*) tastbar, palpabel (*spec*). (b) (*clear*) *lie, error* offensichtlich.

palpably ['pælpəblɪ] *adv* (*clearly*) eindeutig.

palpate [pæl'peɪt] *vt* (*Med*) palpieren.

palpitate ['pælpɪteɪt] *vi* (*heart*) heftig klopfen; (*tremble*) zittern.

palpitation [,pælpɪ'teɪʃən] *n* (*of heart*) Herzklopfen *nt*; (*trembling*) Zittern *nt* ♦ **to have ~s** Herzklopfen haben.

palsied ['pɔːlzɪd] *adj* gelähmt.

palsy ['pɔːlzɪ] *n* Lähmung *f* ♦ **cerebral ~** zerebrale Lähmung; **sick of the ~** (*hum inf*) krank; (*Bibl*) gelähmt.

palsy-walsy ['pælzɪ'wælzɪ] *adj* (*hum inf*) **they are all ~ again** sie sind wieder ein Herz und eine Seele; *see also* **pally.**

paltriness ['pɔːltrɪnɪs] *n* Armseligkeit, Schäbigkeit *f*; (*of reason*) Unbedeutendheit, Geringfügigkeit *f.*

paltry ['pɔːltrɪ] *adj* armselig, schäbig ♦ **for a few ~ pounds** für ein paar lumpige *or* armselige Pfund; **for some ~ reason** aus irgend einem unbedeutenden *or* geringfügigen Grund.

pampas ['pæmpəs] *npl* Pampas *pl* ♦ **~ grass** Pampasgras *nt.*

pamper ['pæmpə^r] *vt* verwöhnen; *child also* verhätscheln, verzärteln; *dog* verhätscheln ♦ **why don't you ~ yourself and buy the de-luxe edition?** warum gönnst du dir nicht mal etwas und kaufst die Luxusausgabe?

pamphlet ['pæmflɪt] *n* (*informative brochure*) Broschüre *f*; (*literary*) Druckschrift *f*; (*political, handed out in street*) Flugblatt *nt*, Flugschrift *f.*

pamphleteer [,pæmflɪ'tɪə^r] *n* Verfasser(in *f*) *m* von Druckschriften/Flugblättern.

pan¹ [pæn] [1] *n* (a) (*Cook*) Pfanne *f*; (*sauce~*) Topf *m.* (b) (*of scales*) Waagschale *f*; (*for gold etc*) Goldpfanne *f*; (*of lavatory*) Becken *nt.* (c) (*in ground*) Mulde *f.*
[2] *vt* (a) *gold* waschen. (b) (*US*) *fish* braten. (c) (*US inf: slate*) *new play etc* verreißen.
[3] *vi* **to ~ for gold** Gold waschen.

♦**pan out** *vi* (*inf*) sich entwickeln ♦ **to ~ ~ well** klappen (*inf*); **if it ~s ~ as we hope** wenn's so wird, wie wir es uns erhoffen.

pan² (*Film*) [1] *n* (Kamera)schwenk *m.*
[2] *vti* panoramieren ♦ **a ~ning shot** ein Schwenk *m*; **the shot ~ned along the wall** die Kamera fuhr langsam die Mauer ab; **they ~ned the camera across the whole width of the scene** sie fuhren mit der Kamera die ganze Szene ab; **the camera ~ned in to the group in the centre** die Kamera schwenkte auf die Gruppe in der Mitte ein; **as the shot ~s slowly away** während die Kamera langsam abschwenkt.

pan- *pref* pan-, Pan-.

panacea [,pænə'sɪə] *n* Allheilmittel *nt* ♦ **there's no universal ~ for ...** es gibt kein Allheilmittel für ...

panache [pə'næʃ] *n* Schwung, Elan *m* ♦ **she dresses with ~** sie kleidet sich sehr extravagant.

Pan-African ['pæn'æfrɪkən] *adj* panafrikanisch.

Pan-Africanism ['pæn'æfrɪkənɪzəm] *n* Panafrikanismus *m.*

Panama [,pænə'mɑː] *n* Panama *nt* ♦ **~ Canal** Panamakanal *m.*

panama (hat) *n* Panamahut *m.*

Panamanian [,pænə'meɪnɪən] [1] *adj* panamaisch.
[2] *n* Panamaer(in *f*) *m*, Panamese *m*, Panamesin *f.*

Pan-American ['pænə'merɪkən] *adj* panamerikanisch.

Pan-Americanism ['pænə'merɪkənɪzəm] *n* Panamerikanismus *m.*

Pan-Arabic ['pæn'ærəbɪk] *adj* panarabisch.

Pan-Arabism ['pæn'ærəbɪzəm] *n* Panarabismus *m.*

panatella [,pænə'telə] *n* (dünne, lange) Zigarre *f.*

pancake ['pænkeɪk] [1] *n* Pfannkuchen *m* ♦ **P~ Day** Fastnachtsdienstag *m*; **~ landing** Bauchlandung *f*; **pancake roll** Frühlingsrolle *f.*
[2] *vi* (*aeroplane*) eine Bauchlandung machen.

panchromatic ['pænkrəʊ'mætɪk] *adj* panchromatisch.

pancreas ['pæŋkrɪəs] *n* Bauchspeicheldrüse *f*, Pankreas *nt.*

pancreatic [,pæŋkrɪ'ætɪk] *adj* Bauchspeicheldrüsen-.

panda ['pændə] *n* Panda, Katzenbär *m.*

panda car *n* (*Brit*) (Funk)streifenwagen *m.*

pandemic [pæn'demɪk] *adj* **~ disease** Seuche *f.*

pandemonium [,pændɪ'məʊnɪəm] *n* Chaos *nt* ♦ **at this there was ~** daraufhin brach ein Chaos aus *or* die Hölle los; **judging by the ~ coming from the classroom** dem Höllenlärm in der Klasse nach zu urteilen.

pander ['pændə^r] [1] *n* (*rare*) Kuppler *m.*
[2] *vi* nachgeben (*to* dat) ♦ **to ~ to sb's desires** jds Bedürfnisse (*acc*) befriedigen wollen; **this is ~ing to the public's basest instincts** damit wird an die niedrigsten Instinkte der Öffentlichkeit appelliert; **to ~ to sb's ego** jdm um den Bart gehen.

Pandora's box [pæn'dɔːrəz'bɒks] *n* Büchse *f* der Pandora.

p and p *abbr of* **post(age) and packing.**

pane [peɪn] *n* Glasscheibe *f.*

panegyric [,pænɪ'dʒɪrɪk] *n* Lobrede *f*, Panegyrikus *m* (*Liter*).

panel ['pænl] [1] *n* (a) (*piece of wood*) Platte, Tafel *f*; (*in wainscoting, ceiling, door*) Feld *nt*; (*Sew*) Streifen, Einsatz *m*; (*Art*) Tafel *f*; (*painting*) Tafelbild *nt*; (*part of a plane's wing, fuselage*) Verschalungs(bau)teil *nt*; (*part of bodywork of a car*) Karosserieteil *nt* ♦ **door/wing ~** (*on car*) Tür-/Kotflügelblech *nt.*
(b) (*of instruments, switches*) Schalttafel *f* ♦ **instrument ~** Armaturenbrett *nt*; (*on machine*) Kontrolltafel *f.*
(c) (*Jur*) (*list of names*) Geschworenenliste *f*; (*Brit Med*) ≃ Liste *f* der Kassenärzte.
(d) (*of interviewers etc*) Gremium *nt*; (*in discussion*) Diskussionsrunde *f*; (*in quiz*) Rateteam *nt* ♦ **a ~ of experts** ein Sachverständigengremium *nt*; **on the ~ tonight we have ...** als Teilnehmer der Diskussionsrunde/des Rateteams begrüßen wir heute abend ...; **a ~ of judges** eine Jury.
[2] *vt wall, ceiling* täfeln, paneelieren.

panel: ~ beater *n* Autoschlosser *m*; **~-beating** *n* (*repair work*) Ausbeulen *nt*; **~ discussion** *n* Podiumsdiskussion *f*; **~ doctor** *n* Kassenarzt *m*, Kassenärztin *f*; **~ game** *n* Ratespiel *nt.*

panel lighting *n* indirekte Beleuchtung.

panelling, (*US*) **paneling** ['pænəlɪŋ] *n* Täfelung *f*, Paneel *nt*; (*to conceal radiator etc, of plane*) Verschalung *f.*

panellist, (*US*) **panelist** ['pænəlɪst] *n* Diskussionsteilnehmer(in *f*) *m.*

panel: ~-pin *n* Stift *m*; **~ truck** *n* (*US*) Lieferwagen *m.*

pang [pæŋ] *n* **~ of conscience** Gewissensbisse *pl*; **I felt a ~ of conscience** ich hatte Gewissensbisse; **~s of hunger** quälender Hunger; **~s of childbirth** (*old*) Geburtswehen *pl.*

pan: ~handle (*US*) [1] *n* Pfannenstiel *m*; (*shape of land*) Zipfel *m*; [2] *vi* (*US inf*) die Leute anhauen (*inf*); **~handler** *n* (*US inf*) Bettler, Schnorrer (*inf*) *m.*

panic ['pænɪk] (*vb: pret, ptp* **~ked**) [1] *n* Panik *f* ♦ **~ on the stock exchange** Börsenpanik *f*; **to flee in ~** panikartig die Flucht ergreifen; **a ~ reaction** eine Kurzschlußreaktion; **the country was thrown into a (state of) ~** das Land wurde von Panik erfaßt; **a feeling of ~ in the bowels** eine panische Angst; **~ buying/selling** Panikkäufe *pl*/-verkäufe *pl*; **to hit the ~ button** (*fig inf: panic*) in Panik geraten, durchdrehen (*inf*).
[2] *vi* in Panik geraten ♦ **don't ~** nur keine Panik!
[3] *vt* Panik auslösen unter (+*dat*) ♦ **to ~ sb into doing sth** jdn veranlassen, etw überstürzt zu tun.

panic attack *n* (*Psych*) Panikanfall *m* ♦ **to have a ~** einen Panikanfall bekommen.

panicky ['pænɪkɪ] *adj person* überängstlich; *act, measure etc* Kurzschluß- ♦ **I get this ~ feeling whenever ...** ich werde immer nervös *or* gerate immer in Panik, wenn ...; **to get ~** in Panik geraten; **don't get ~!** keine Panik!, dreh bloß nicht durch! (*inf*).

panic-stricken ['pænɪk,strɪkən] *adj* von panischem Schrecken ergriffen; *look* panisch.

pannier ['pænɪə^r] *n* Korb *m*; (*on motor-cycle etc*) Satteltasche *f*; (*for mule etc*) Tragkorb *m.*

panoplied ['pænəplɪd] *adj knight* in Rüstung ♦ **in its ~ splendour** in seinem vollen Glanz.

panoply ['pænəplɪ] *n* (*armour*) Rüstung *f*; (*covering*) Baldachin *m*; (*fig liter*) Dach *nt*; (*array*) Palette *f*, Spektrum *nt* ♦ **beneath the oak's ~ of leaves** unter dem Blätterdach der Eiche; **the ~ of the sky/of stars** das Himmels-/Sternenzelt (*liter*).

panorama [,pænə'rɑːmə] *n* (*view, also fig: of life etc*) Panorama *nt* (*of gen*); (*survey*) Übersicht *f* (*of* über +*acc*) ♦ **~ window** (*Aut, Rail*) Panoramafenster *nt.*

panoramic [,pænə'ræmɪk] *adj view* Panorama- ♦ **~ shot** (*Phot*) Panoramaaufnahme *f*; **a ~ view of the hills** ein Blick *m* auf das Bergpanorama; **a ~ view of social development** ein umfassender Überblick über die gesellschaftliche Entwicklung; **~ sight** (*Mil*) Rundblickzielfernrohr *nt.*

pan-pipes ['pænpaɪps] *npl* Panflöte *f.*

pansy ['pænzɪ] *n* (a) (*Bot*) Stiefmütterchen *nt.* (b) (*sl: homosexual*) Schwule(r) *m* (*inf*).

pant [pænt] [1] *n* Atemstoß *m* ♦ **he was breathing in short ~s** er atmete stoßartig.
[2] *vi* (a) keuchen; (*dog*) hecheln; (*train*) schnaufen ♦ **to be ~ing for a drink** nach etwas zu trinken lechzen; **he was ~ing for breath** er schnappte nach Luft (*inf*), er rang nach Atem.
(b) (*inf: desire*) lechzen (*for* nach) ♦ **to be ~ing to do sth** danach lechzen *or*

darauf brennen, etw zu tun.
[3] *vt* (*also* ~ **out**) *message* hervorstoßen.
pantaloon [ˌpæntəˈluːn] *n* (*Theat*) Hanswurst *m*.
pantaloons [ˌpæntəˈluːnz] *npl* (*Hist*) Pantalons *pl*.
pantechnicon [pænˈteknɪkən] *n* (*Brit*) Möbelwagen *m*.
pantheism [ˈpænθiːɪzəm] *n* Pantheismus *m*.
pantheist [ˈpænθiːɪst] *n* Pantheist(in *f*) *m*.
pantheistic [ˌpænθiːˈɪstɪk] *adj* pantheistisch.
pantheon [ˈpænθɪən] *n* Pantheon *nt*.
panther [ˈpænθəʳ] *n* Panther *m*.
panties [ˈpæntɪz] *npl* (*for children*) Höschen *nt*; (*for women also*) (Damen)slip *m* ◆ **a pair of** ~ ein Höschen *nt*/ein Slip *m*.
pantile [ˈpæntaɪl] *n* Dachpfanne *f*.
panto [ˈpæntəʊ] *n* (*Brit inf*) = **pantomime (a)**.
pantograph [ˈpæntəgrɑːf] *n* Pantograph *m*.
pantomime [ˈpæntəmaɪm] *n* **(a)** (*in GB*) Weihnachtsmärchen *nt* ◆ **what a ~!** (*inf*) was für ein Theater! (*inf*). **(b)** (*mime*) Pantomime *f*.
pantry [ˈpæntrɪ] *n* Speisekammer *f*.
pants [pænts] *npl* (*trousers*) Hose *f*; (*Brit: under*~) Unterhose *f* ◆ **a pair of** ~ eine Hose/Unterhose; **to wear the** ~ (*US fig*) die Hosen anhaben (*inf*).
pantsuit [ˈpæntsuːt] *n* (*US*) Hosenanzug *m*.
panty: ~-girdle *n* Miederhöschen *nt*; **~-hose** *n* Strumpfhose *f*; **~-liner** *n* Slipeinlage *f*; **~waist** *n* (*US sl*) Schwächling *m*, Memme *f* (*inf*).
pap [pæp] *n* (*food*) Brei *m*.
papa [pəˈpɑː] *n* (*dated inf*) Papa *m*.
papacy [ˈpeɪpəsɪ] *n* Papsttum *nt* ◆ **during the ~ of ...** während der Amtszeit des Papstes ..., unter Papst ...
papadum [ˈpæpədəm] *n großes, dünnes, rundes, knusprig gebratenes Teigstück als Beilage zu indischen Gerichten*.
papal [ˈpeɪpəl] *adj* päpstlich.
paparazzo [ˌpæpəˈrætsəʊ], *pl* **paparazzi** [ˌpæpəˈrætsɪ] *n* Fotojäger, Paparazzo *m*.
papaya [pəˈpaɪə] *n* Papaye *f*; (*fruit*) Papaya *f*.
paper [ˈpeɪpəʳ] [1] *n* **(a)** (*material*) Papier *nt* ◆ **a piece of** ~ ein Stück *nt* Papier; **a sheet of** ~ ein Blatt *nt* Papier; **a writer who finds it hard to commit himself to** ~ ein Schriftsteller, der nur zögernd etwas zu Papier bringt; **to get** *or* **put sth down on** ~ etw schriftlich festhalten; **can we get your acceptance down on ~?** können wir Ihre Einwilligung schriftlich haben?; **on ~ they're the best firm** auf dem Papier ist das die beste Firma; **it's not worth the ~ it's written on** das ist schade ums Papier, auf dem es steht; **the walls are like** ~ die Wände sind wie Pappe.
(b) (*newspaper*) Zeitung *f* ◆ **to write to the ~s about sth** Leserbriefe/einen Leserbrief schreiben; **a world-famous** ~ eine weltbekannte Zeitung, ein weltbekanntes Blatt; **he's/his name is always in the ~s** er/sein Name steht ständig in der Zeitung.
(c) **~s** *pl* (*identity* ~*s*) Papiere *pl*.
(d) **~s** *pl* (*writings, documents*) Papiere *pl* ◆ **private ~s** private Unterlagen *pl*.
(e) (*set of questions in exam*) Testbogen *m*; (*exam*) (*Univ*) Klausur *f*; (*Sch*) Arbeit *f* ◆ **to do a good ~ in maths** eine gute Mathematikklausur/-arbeit schreiben.
(f) (*academic*) Referat, Paper (*sl*) *nt* ◆ **he's going to read a ~ to the society** er wird vor der Gesellschaft ein Referat halten.
(g) (*wall*~) Tapete *f*.
(h) (*Parl*) **a white** ~ ein Weißbuch *nt*.
(i) (*packet*) **a ~ of pins** ein Päckchen *nt* Stecknadeln.
[2] *vt wall, room* tapezieren.
◆**paper over** *vt sep* überkleben; (*fig*) *cracks* übertünchen.
paper *in cpds* Papier-; **~back** *n* Taschenbuch, Paperback (*inf*) *nt*; **~backed** *adj* Taschenbuch-; **~ bag** *n* Tüte *f*; **~boy** *n* Zeitungsjunge *m*; **~ chain** *n* Girlande *f*; **~ chase** *n* Schnitzeljagd *f*; **~-clip** *n* Büroklammer *f*; **~ cup** *n* Pappbecher *m*; **~ feed** *n* (*Comput*) Papiervorschub *m*; **~ handkerchief** *n* Tempo(taschen)tuch ®, Papiertaschentuch *nt*; **~ handling** *n* (*Comput: of printer*) Papierführung *f*; **~-hanger** *n* Tapezierer *m*; **~-hanging** *n* Tapezieren *nt*; **~ knife** *n* Brieföffner *m*; **~ lantern** *n* Lampion *m*; **~less** *adj* papierlos; **~ mill** *n* Papierfabrik, Papiermühle *f*; **~ money** *n* Papiergeld *nt*; **~ plate** *n* Pappteller *m*; **~ profit** *n* rechnerischer Gewinn; **~ round** *n* **to do a ~ round** Zeitungen austragen; **~ shop** *n* Zeitungsladen *m*; **~ tape** *n* Lochstreifen *m*; **~-thin** *adj walls* hauchdünn; **~ tiger** *n* Papiertiger *m*; **~ tissue** *n* Papiertuch *nt*; **~ trail** *n* (*US*) belastende Unterlagen *pl*; **investigations found a ~ trail of documents** Nachforschungen brachten belastende Dokumente zutage; **~ tray** *n* (*Comput: for printer etc*) Papierschacht *m*; **~weight** *n* Briefbeschwerer *m*; **~work** *n* Schreibarbeit *f*.
papery [ˈpeɪpərɪ] *adj plaster, pastry* bröckelig, krümelig.
papier mâché [ˈpæpɪeɪˈmæʃeɪ] [1] *n* Papiermaché, Pappmaché *nt*.
[2] *adj* aus Papiermaché *or* Pappmaché.
papism [ˈpeɪpɪzəm] *n* (*pej*) Papismus *m*.
papist [ˈpeɪpɪst] *n* (*pej*) Papist(in *f*) *m*.
papistry [ˈpeɪpɪstrɪ] *n* (*pej*) Papismus *m*.
papoose [pəˈpuːs] *n* Indianerbaby *nt*; (*carrier for Indian baby*) Winkelbrettwiege *f*; (*carrier for baby*) Tragegestell *nt*.
pappy [ˈpæpɪ] *n* (*US inf*) Papi *m* (*inf*).
paprika [ˈpæprɪkə] *n* Paprika *m*.
Pap smear, Pap test [ˈpæp-] *n* (*esp US Med: cervical smear*) Pap-Test *m*.
Papua [ˈpæpjʊə] *n* Papua *nt*.
Papuan [ˈpæpjʊən] [1] *adj* papuanisch.
[2] *n* **(a)** Papua *mf*. **(b)** (*language*) Papuasprache *f*.
Papua New Guinea *n* Papua-Neuguinea *nt*.
papyrus [pəˈpaɪərəs] *n*, *pl* **papyri** [pəˈpaɪəraɪ] (*plant*) Papyrus(staude *f*) *m*; (*paper*) Papyrus *m*; (*scroll*) Papyrus(rolle *f*) *m*.
par [pɑːʳ] *n* **(a)** (*Fin*) Pari, Nennwert *m* ◆ **to be above/below** ~ über/unter pari *or* dem Nennwert stehen; **at** ~ zum Nennwert, al pari.
(b) **to be on a ~ with sb/sth** sich mit jdm/etw messen können; **this objection is on a ~ with Harry's** dieser Einwand liegt auf der gleichen Ebene wie Harrys; **he's nowhere near on a ~ with her** er kann ihr nicht das Wasser reichen; **culturally, the two countries are on** *or* **can be put on a** ~ in kultureller Hinsicht sind die beiden Länder miteinander vergleichbar; **an above-~ performance** eine überdurchschnittliche Leistung.
(c) **below** ~ (*fig*) unter Niveau; **I'm feeling physically/mentally below** ~ ich fühle mich körperlich/seelisch nicht auf der Höhe; **I'm not feeling quite up to ~ today** ich bin heute nicht ganz auf dem Damm (*inf*) *or* Posten (*inf*).
(d) (*Golf*) Par *nt* ◆ **to go round in six under/over** ~ sechs Schläge unter/über dem Par spielen; **that's ~ for the course for him** (*fig inf*) das kann man von ihm erwarten.
par, para [ˈpærə] *abbr of* **paragraph** Abschn.
parable [ˈpærəbl] *n* Parabel *f*, Gleichnis *nt*.
parabola [pəˈræbələ] *n* (*Math*) Parabel *f*.
parabolic [ˌpærəˈbɒlɪk] *adj* **(a)** Parabol-; *curve* parabelförmig. **(b)** (*Liter*) gleichnishaft.
paracetamol [ˌpærəˈsiːtəmɒl] *n* Schmerztablette *f*.
parachute [ˈpærəʃuːt] [1] *n* Fallschirm *m* ◆ **by** ~ mit dem Fallschirm.
[2] *vt troops* mit dem Fallschirm absetzen; *supplies* abwerfen ◆ **to ~ food to sb** für jdn Lebensmittel abwerfen.
[3] *vi* (*also* ~ **down**) (mit dem Fallschirm) abspringen ◆ **they ~d into the wrong zone** sie sprangen über dem falschen Gebiet ab; **to ~ to safety** sich mit dem Fallschirm retten.
◆**parachute in** [1] *vt sep troops* mit dem Fallschirm absetzen; *supplies* abwerfen.
[2] *vi* (mit dem Fallschirm) abspringen.
parachute: ~ brake *n* Bremsfallschirm *m*; **~ drop** *n* (*by person*) (Fallschirm)absprung *m*; (*of supplies*) (Fallschirm)abwurf *m*; **there was a ~ drop of ten men** zehn Leute sprangen (mit dem Fallschirm) ab; **they got a ~ drop of medical supplies** medizinische Versorgungsmittel wurden (mit dem Fallschirm) für sie abgeworfen; **~ jump** *n* Absprung *m* (mit dem Fallschirm); **~ regiment** *n* Fallschirmjägertruppe *f*; **~ training** *n* Übung *f* im Fallschirmspringen.
parachutist [ˈpærəʃuːtɪst] *n* Fallschirmspringer(in *f*) *m*.
parade [pəˈreɪd] [1] *n* **(a)** (*procession*) Umzug *m*; (*Mil, of boy scouts, circus*) Parade *f*; (*political*) Demonstration *f* ◆ **church** ~ Prozession *f*; **to be on** ~ (*Mil*) eine Parade abhalten; **the regiment on** ~ das Regiment bei der Parade; **in the school procession you'll be on ~ in front of the public** bei der Schulparade sieht dich alle Welt; **and all the new hats will be out on** ~ und dann werden alle neuen Hüte spazierengeführt.
(b) (*public walk*) Promenade *f*.
(c) (*fashion* ~) Modenschau *f*.
(d) (*display*) Parade *f*; (*of wealth etc*) Zurschaustellung *f*.
(e) (*US mil*) (*review*) Truppeninspektion *f*; (*ground*) Truppenübungsplatz, Exerzierplatz *m*.
(f) (*shopping* ~) *Reihe f von Geschäften*.
[2] *vt* **(a)** *troops* auf- *or* vorbeimarschieren lassen; *military might* demonstrieren; *placards* vor sich her tragen.
(b) (*show off*) zur Schau stellen; *new clothes, new camera etc also* spazierentragen.
[3] *vi* (*Mil*) auf- *or* vorbeimarschieren; (*political party*) eine Demonstration veranstalten ◆ **the strikers ~d through the town** die Streikenden zogen durch die Stadt; **she ~d up and down with the hat on** sie stolzierte mit ihrem Hut auf und ab.
parade ground *n* Truppenübungsplatz, Exerzierplatz *m*.
paradigm [ˈpærədaɪm] *n* Musterbeispiel *nt*; (*Gram*) Paradigma *nt*.
paradigmatic [ˌpærədɪgˈmætɪk] *adj* beispielhaft, paradigmatisch.
paradise [ˈpærədaɪs] *n* (*lit, fig*) Paradies *nt* ◆ **a shopper's** ~ ein Einkaufsparadies *nt*; **an architect's** ~ ein Paradies *nt* für Architekten; **living there must be ~ compared with this place** dort zu leben muß geradezu paradiesisch sein verglichen mit hier; **~, she sighed** himmlisch, seufzte sie; **an earthly** ~ ein Paradies auf Erden; **I'm in** ~ ich bin im Paradies; **~!** wie im Paradies!, paradiesisch!
paradisiac(al) [ˌpærəˈdɪzɪək(əl)] *adj* paradiesisch.
paradox [ˈpærədɒks] *n* Paradox, Paradoxon (*liter*) *nt* ◆ **life/he is full of ~es** das Leben/er steckt voller Widersprüche.
paradoxical [ˌpærəˈdɒksɪkəl] *adj* paradox; *person* widersprüchlich.
paradoxically [ˌpærəˈdɒksɪkəlɪ] *adv* paradoxerweise; *worded* paradox.
paraffin [ˈpærəfɪn] *n* (*Brit: oil, US: wax*) Paraffin *nt*.
paraffin: ~ lamp *n* Paraffinlampe *f*; **~ oil** *n* (*Brit*) Paraffinöl *nt*; **~ stove** *n* (*Brit*) Paraffinofen *m*; **~ wax** *n* Paraffin *nt*.
paragliding [ˈpærəglaɪdɪŋ] *n* Gleitschirmfliegen, Paragliding *nt*.
paragon [ˈpærəgən] *n* Muster *nt* ◆ **a ~ of virtue** ein Muster *nt* an Tugendhaftigkeit, ein Ausbund *m* an Tugend (*hum*).
paragraph [ˈpærəgrɑːf] [1] *n* **(a)** Absatz, Abschnitt *m* ◆ **"new ~"** „(neuer) Absatz". **(b)** (*brief article*) Notiz *f*.
[2] *vt* (in Abschnitte) gliedern, aufgliedern.
Paraguay [ˈpærəgwaɪ] *n* Paraguay *nt*.

Paraguayan [ˌpærəˈgwaɪən] 1 *adj* paraguayisch.
2 *n* Paraguayer(in *f*) *m*.
parakeet [ˈpærəkiːt] *n* Sittich *m*.
paraldehyde [pəˈrældɪhaɪd] *n* Paraldehyd *nt*.
paralegal [ˌpærəˈliːgəl] (*esp US*) 1 *n* Rechtsassistent(in) *m(f)*.
2 *adj attr* ~ **assistant** Rechtsassistent(in) *m(f)*; ~ **secretary** Sekretärin und Rechtsassistentin *f*.
parallax [ˈpærəlæks] *n* Parallaxe *f*.
parallel [ˈpærəlel] 1 *adj* **(a)** *lines, streets,* (*Comput*) parallel ◆ **at this point the road and river are ~** an dieser Stelle verlaufen Straße und Fluß parallel (zueinander); **~ bars** Barren *m*; **~ connection** (*Elec*) Parallelschaltung *f*; **in a ~ direction** parallel; **~ interface** Parallelschnittstelle *f*; **~ printer** Paralleldrucker *m*; **~ turn** (*Ski*) Parallelschwung *m*.
(b) (*fig*) *case, career, development* vergleichbar; *career, development also* parallel verlaufend ◆ **a ~ case** ein Parallelfall *m*; **the two systems developed along ~ lines** die Entwicklung der beiden Systeme verlief vergleichbar; **he argues along ~ lines to me** er argumentiert ähnlich wie ich.
2 *adv* **to run ~** (*roads, careers*) parallel verlaufen.
3 *n* **(a)** (*Geometry*) Parallele *f*.
(b) (*Geog*) Breitenkreis *m* ◆ **the 49th ~** der 49. Breitengrad.
(c) (*Elec*) **connected in ~** parallel geschaltet.
(d) (*fig*) Parallele *f* ◆ **without ~** ohne Parallele; **it has no ~** es gibt dazu keine Parallele; **to draw a ~ between X and Y** eine Parallele zwischen X und Y ziehen; **in ~ with** parallel mit.
4 *vt* (*fig*) gleichen (*+dat*) ◆ **a case ~led only by ...** ein Fall, zu dem es nur eine einzige Parallele gibt, nämlich ...; **it is ~led by ...** es ist vergleichbar mit ...
parallelism [ˈpærəlelɪzəm] *n* (*of lines*) Parallelität *f*; (*of cases also*) Ähnlichkeit *f* ◆ **don't try to exaggerate the ~** versuche nicht, zu viele Parallelen zu ziehen.
parallelogram [ˌpærəˈleləʊgræm] *n* Parallelogramm *nt*.
paralysis [pəˈræləsɪs] *n, pl* **paralyses** [pəˈrælɪsiːz] Lähmung, Paralyse *f*; (*of industry etc*) Lahmlegung *f* ◆ **creeping ~** progressive Paralyse; **infantile ~** Kinderlähmung *f*.
paralytic [ˌpærəˈlɪtɪk] 1 *adj* **(a)** paralytisch, Lähmungs-. **(b)** (*Brit sl: very drunk*) total blau (*inf*), stockvoll (*sl*).
2 *n* Paralytiker(in *f*) *m*, Gelähmte(r) *mf*.
paralyze [ˈpærəlaɪz] *vt* **(a)** lähmen, paralysieren (*spec*) ◆ **to be ~d in both legs** in beiden Beinen gelähmt sein; **to be ~d with fright** vor Schreck wie gelähmt sein. **(b)** *industry, economy* lahmlegen; *traffic also* zum Erliegen bringen.
paramedic [ˌpærəˈmedɪk] *n* Sanitäter(in *f*) *m*; (*in hospital*) medizinisch-technischer Assistent, medizinisch-technische Assistentin.
parameter [pəˈræmɪtəʳ] *n* **(a)** (*Math*) Parameter *m*. **(b) ~s** *pl* (*framework, limits*) Rahmen *m*.
paramilitary [ˌpærəˈmɪlɪtərɪ] *adj* paramilitärisch.
paramount [ˈpærəmaʊnt] *adj* Haupt- ◆ **of ~ importance** von größter *or* höchster Wichtigkeit; **solvency must be ~** der Zahlungsfähigkeit muß Priorität eingeräumt werden.
paramour [ˈpærəmʊəʳ] *n* (*old*) Liebhaber *m*, Buhle *mf* (*old*); (*hum*) (*man*) Hausfreund *m* (*hum*); (*woman*) Geliebte *f*.
paranoia [ˌpærəˈnɔɪə] *n* Paranoia *f*; (*inf*) Verfolgungswahn *m* ◆ **this ~ which stops nations trusting each other** dieses krankhafte Mißtrauen, das die Völker voneinander trennt.
paranoiac [ˌpærəˈnɔɪɪk] 1 *n* Paranoiker(in *f*) *m*.
2 *adj* paranoisch.
paranoid [ˈpærənɔɪd] *adj* paranoid ◆ **or am I just being ~?** oder bilde ich mir das nur ein?; **she's getting ~ about what other people think of her** die Angst vor dem, was andere von ihr denken, wird bei ihr langsam zur Manie; **aren't you being rather ~?** du scheinst unter Verfolgungswahn zu leiden.
paranormal [ˌpærəˈnɔːməl] *adj* paranormal.
parapet [ˈpærəpɪt] *n* (*on rampart*) (*of bridge*) Brüstung *f*; (*of well*) (Brunnen)wand *f*.
paraphernalia [ˈpærəfəˈneɪlɪə] *npl* Brimborium, Drum und Dran *nt*.
paraphrase [ˈpærəfreɪz] 1 *n* Umschreibung, Paraphrase (*geh*) *f*.
2 *vt* umschreiben, paraphrasieren (*geh*).
paraplegia [ˌpærəˈpliːdʒə] *n* doppelseitige Lähmung.
paraplegic [ˌpærəˈpliːdʒɪk] 1 *adj* doppelseitig gelähmt, paraplegisch (*spec*).
2 *n* Paraplegiker(in *f*) *m* (*spec*).
parapsychology [ˌpærəsaɪˈkɒlədʒɪ] *n* Parapsychologie *f*.
paras [ˈpærəz] *npl* (*inf*) Fallschirmjäger *pl*.
parascending [ˈpærəˌsendɪŋ] *n* Paragliding *nt* (*bei dem der Start mit Hilfe eines Schnellboots erfolgt*).
parasite [ˈpærəsaɪt] *n* (*lit, fig*) Parasit, Schmarotzer *m*.
parasitic(al) [ˌpærəˈsɪtɪk(əl)] *adj animal, plant* Schmarotzer-, parasitisch, parasitär (*also fig*) ◆ **a ~ worm** ein Schmarotzer *m*; **to be ~ (up)on sth** von etw schmarotzen.
parasitology [ˌpærəsɪˈtɒlədʒɪ] *n* Parasitologie *f*.
parasol [ˈpærəsɒl] *n* Sonnenschirm, Parasol (*dated*) *m*.
paratrooper [ˈpærətruːpəʳ] *n* Fallschirmjäger *m*.
paratroops [ˈpærətruːps] *npl* (*soldiers*) Fallschirmjäger *pl*; (*division also*) Fallschirmjägertruppe *f*.
paratyphoid [ˈpærəˈtaɪfɔɪd] *n* Paratyphus *m*.
parboil [ˈpɑːbɔɪl] *vt* vorkochen, halbgar kochen.
parcel [ˈpɑːsl] *n* **(a)** Paket *nt* ◆ **to do sth up in a ~** etw als Paket packen; **~ post** Paketpost *f*; **to send sth (by) ~ post** etw als Paket schicken. **(b) a ~ of land** ein Stück *nt* Land; *see* **part**.
◆**parcel out** *vt sep land, inheritance* aufteilen.
◆**parcel up** *vt sep* als Paket verpacken.
parcel(s) office *n* (*Rail*) Paketstelle *f*.
parch [pɑːtʃ] *vt* ausdörren, austrocknen.
parched [pɑːtʃt] *adj lips, throat* ausgetrocknet; *land also* verdorrt ◆ **to be ~ (with thirst)** (vor Durst) verschmachten; **I'm ~** ich habe furchtbaren Durst.
parchment [ˈpɑːtʃmənt] *n* Pergament *nt*.
pard [pɑːd] *n* (*obs: leopard*) Leopard *m*.
pardon [ˈpɑːdn] 1 *n* **(a)** (*Jur*) Begnadigung *f* ◆ **he got a ~** er ist begnadigt worden; **there will be no ~ for deserters** für Fahnenflüchtige gibt es keinen Pardon; **to grant sb a ~** jdn begnadigen; **general ~** Amnestie *f*.
(b) I beg your ~, but could you ...? verzeihen *or* entschuldigen Sie bitte, könnten Sie ...?; **I beg your ~!** erlauben Sie mal!, ich muß doch sehr bitten!; **(beg) ~?** (*Brit*), **I beg your ~?** (*Brit*) bitte?, wie bitte?; **to beg sb's ~** jdn um Verzeihung bitten; **I beg your ~, beg ~** (*apology*) verzeihen *or* entschuldigen Sie, Verzeihung, Entschuldigung; **a thousand ~s!** ich bitte tausendmal um Verzeihung *or* Entschuldigung!; **we beg the reader's ~ for ...** wir bitten den Leser für ... um Nachsicht.
2 *vt* **(a)** (*Jur*) begnadigen.
(b) (*forgive*) verzeihen, vergeben (*sb* jdm, *sth* etw) ◆ **to ~ sb sth** jdm etw verzeihen *or* vergeben; **~ me, but could you ...?** entschuldigen *or* verzeihen Sie bitte, könnten Sie ...?; **~ me!** Entschuldigung!, Verzeihung!; **~ me?** (*US*) bitte?, wie bitte?; **~ my mentioning it** entschuldigen *or* verzeihen Sie bitte, daß ich das erwähne; **~ me for asking!** (*iro*) entschuldige bitte, daß ich es gewagt habe zu fragen! (*iro*).
pardonable [ˈpɑːdnəbl] *adj offence* entschuldbar; *weakness, mistake also* verzeihlich.
pardonably [ˈpɑːdnəblɪ] *adv* **he was ~ angry** sein Ärger war verständlich; **and ~ so** und das war verständlich.
pare [pɛəʳ] *vt nails* schneiden; *fruit, stick* schälen ◆ **she ~d the skin off the apple** sie schälte den Apfel.
◆**pare down** *vt sep* (*fig*) *expenses* einschränken; *personnel* einsparen ◆ **to ~ sth ~ to the minimum** etw auf ein Minimum beschränken.
parent [ˈpɛərənt] 1 *n* **(a)** Elternteil *m* ◆ **~s** Eltern *pl*; **the duties of a ~** die elterlichen Pflichten; **his father was his favourite ~** von seinen Eltern hatte er seinen Vater am liebsten.
(b) (*fig*) Vorläufer *m* ◆ **the Copernican theory is the ~ of modern astronomy** die moderne Astronomie geht auf die Lehren des Kopernikus zurück.
2 *attr* **~ birds** Vogeleltern *pl*; **~ company** Muttergesellschaft *f*; **~ plant** Mutterpflanze *f*; **~ ship** (*Space*) Mutterschiff *nt*; **~-teacher association** (*Sch*) Lehrer- und Elternverband *m*.
parentage [ˈpɛərəntɪdʒ] *n* Herkunft *f* ◆ **of humble/unknown ~** (von) einfacher/unbekannter Herkunft.
parental [pəˈrentl] *adj care etc* elterlich *attr*.
parenthesis [pəˈrenθɪsɪs] *n, pl* **parentheses** [pəˈrenθɪsiːz] Klammer(zeichen *nt*) *f*, Parenthese *f*; (*words, statement*) Einschub *m*, Parenthese *f* ◆ **in ~** in Klammern; **could I just comment in ~ that ...** darf ich vielleicht einflechten, daß ...
parenthetic(al) [ˌpærənˈθetɪk(əl)] *adj* beiläufig ◆ **could I make one ~ comment?** darf ich eine Bemerkung einflechten?
parenthetically [ˌpærənˈθetɪkəlɪ] *adv* nebenbei, beiläufig.
parenthood [ˈpɛərənthʊd] *n* Elternschaft *f* ◆ **the joys of ~** die Vater-/Mutterfreuden *pl*; **the idea of ~ frightened her** sie schrak zurück vor dem Gedanken, Mutter zu sein.
parer [ˈpɛərəʳ] *n* (*apple-/fruit-~*) Schälmesser *nt*.
par excellence [ˌpɑːrˈeksəlɑ̃ːns] *adv* par excellence.
parhelion [pɑːˈhiːlɪən] *n* (*Astron*) Nebensonne *f*.
pariah [pəˈraɪə] *n* (*lit, fig*) Paria *m*; (*fig also*) Ausgestoßene(r) *mf*.
parietal [pəˈraɪɪtl] *adj* (*Anat*) parietal ◆ **~ bone** Scheitelbein *nt*.
pari mutuel [ˌpærɪˈmjuːtʊəl] *n Wettsystem nt, bei dem der gesamte Einsatz abzüglich der Verwaltungskosten prozentual an die Gewinner verteilt wird.*
paring knife [ˈpɛərɪŋˌnaɪf] *n* Schälmesser *nt*.
parings [ˈpɛərɪŋz] *npl* (*of nails*) abgeschnittene Fingernägel *pl*; (*of apple*) Schalen *pl*.
pari passu [ˈpærɪˈpæsuː] *adv* gleichlaufend, synchron.
Paris [ˈpærɪs] *n* Paris *nt*.
parish [ˈpærɪʃ] *n* Gemeinde *f*; (*district also*) Pfarrbezirk *m*, Pfarre, Pfarrei *f*.
parish: ~ church *n* Pfarrkirche *f*; **~ clerk** *n Verwaltungsangestellte(r) mf des Gemeinderates*; **~ council** *n* Gemeinderat *m*.
parishioner [pəˈrɪʃənəʳ] *n* Gemeinde(mit)glied *nt*.
parish: ~ priest *n* Pfarrer *m*; **~-pump politics** *n* Kirchturmpolitik *f*; **~ register** *n* Kirchenbuch, Kirchenregister *nt*.
Parisian [pəˈrɪzɪən] 1 *adj* Pariser *inv*.
2 *n* Pariser(in *f*) *m*.
parity [ˈpærɪtɪ] *n* **(a)** (*equality*) Gleichstellung *f*; (*as regards pay etc also, of opportunities*) Gleichheit *f* ◆ **~ of treatment** Gleichstellung *f*; **~ of pay** Lohngleichheit *f*.
(b) (*equivalence*) Übereinstimmung *f* ◆ **by ~ of reasoning** mit den gleichen Argumenten.
(c) (*Fin, Sci*) Parität *f* ◆ **the ~ of the dollar** die Dollarparität.
(d) (*US Agr*) Preisparität *f*.
(e) (*Comput*) Parität *f* ◆ **odd/even ~** ungerade/gerade Parität.
park [pɑːk] 1 *n* **(a)** Park *m* ◆ **national ~** Nationalpark *m*. **(b)** (*Sport*)

(Sport)platz *m*. **(c)** (*US: car ~*) Parkplatz *m*. **(d)** (*Mil*) Arsenal *nt*. **(e)** (*Aut*) **to put/leave a car in ~** das Getriebe in Parkstellung bringen/lassen.

[2] *vt* **(a)** *car* parken; (*for longer period also*) abstellen; *bicycle* abstellen ◆ **a ~ed car** ein parkendes Auto; **there's been a car ~ed outside for days** draußen parkt schon seit Tagen ein Auto; **he was very badly ~ed** er hatte miserabel geparkt.

(b) (*inf: put*) *luggage etc* abstellen ◆ **he ~ed himself right in front of the fire** er pflanzte sich direkt vor den Kamin (*inf*); **we ~ed the children with the neighbours** wir haben die Kinder bei den Nachbarn abgegeben *or* gelassen; **find somewhere to ~ your bum** (*hum*) such dir was, wo du dich platzen kannst (*hum*).

(c) (*Comput*) *hard disk* parken.

[3] *vi* parken ◆ **there was nowhere to ~** es gab nirgendwo einen Parkplatz; **to find a place to ~** einen Parkplatz finden; (*in line of cars*) eine Parklücke finden.

parka ['pɑːkə] *n* Parka *m*.

park-and-ride [,pɑːkən'raɪd] *n* Park-and-Ride-System *nt*.

parking ['pɑːkɪŋ] *n* Parken *nt* ◆ **women are usually good at ~** Frauen sind gewöhnlich gut im Einparken; **there's no ~ on this street** in dieser Straße ist Parken verboten *or* ist Parkverbot; **"no ~"** „Parken verboten"; **"good ~ facilities"** „gute Parkmöglichkeiten"; **"~ for 50 cars"** „50 (Park)plätze".

parking: ~ attendant *n* Parkplatzwächter *m*; **~ bay** *n* Parkbucht *f*; **~ disk** *n* Parkscheibe *f*; **~ fine** *n* Geldbuße *f* (für Parkvergehen); **~ level** *n* (*in multi-storey car park*) Parkdeck *nt*; **~ lights** *npl* Parklicht *nt*, Parkleuchte *f*; **~ lot** *n* (*US*) Parkplatz *m*; **~ meter** *n* Parkuhr *f*; **~ offender** *n* Parksünder *m*; **~ orbit** *n* (*Space*) Parkbahn *f*; **~ place** *n* Parkplatz *m*; **~ ticket** *n* Strafzettel *m*, Knöllchen *nt* (*dial inf*).

park: ~keeper *n* Parkwächter *m*; **~land** *n* Grünland *nt*; **~way** *n* (*US*) Allee *f*.

parky ['pɑːkɪ] *adj* (*+er*) (*Brit sl*) kühl, frisch ◆ **(it's a bit) ~ today** ganz schön kühl heute.

parlance ['pɑːləns] *n* **in common ~** im allgemeinen Sprachgebrauch; **in technical/legal ~** in der Fachsprache/Rechtssprache; **in modern ~** im modernen Sprachgebrauch.

parley ['pɑːlɪ] [1] *n* Verhandlungen *pl*.

[2] *vi* verhandeln.

parliament ['pɑːləmənt] *n* Parlament *nt* ◆ **to get into ~** ins Parlament kommen; **~ reconvenes in the early autumn** das Parlament tritt Anfang Herbst wieder zusammen; **the West German/East German ~** das west-/ostdeutsche Parlament, der Bundestag/die Volkskammer; **the Austrian/Swiss ~** die Bundesversammlung.

parliamentarian [,pɑːləmen'teərɪən] *n* Parlamentarier *m*.

parliamentarianism [,pɑːləmen'teərɪənɪzəm] *n* Parlamentarismus *m*.

parliamentary [,pɑːlə'mentərɪ] *adj* parlamentarisch ◆ **~ agent** Parlamentsbeauftragte(r) *mf*; **~ debates** Parlamentsdebatten *pl*; **the ~ Labour Party** die Parlamentsfraktion der Labour Party; **~ private secretary** (*Brit*) Abgeordnete(r), der/die einem Minister zuarbeitet; **~ privilege** parlamentarische Sonderrechte *pl*; (*immunity*) parlamentarische Immunität.

parlor car *n* (*US*) Salonwagen *m*.

parlour, (*US*) **parlor** ['pɑːləʳ] *n* **(a)** (*in house*) Salon *m*. **(b)** (*beauty ~, massage ~ etc*) Salon *m* ◆ **ice-cream ~** Eisdiele *f*.

parlour: ~ game *n* Gesellschaftsspiel *nt*; **~maid** *n* (*Brit*) Dienstmädchen *nt*.

parlous ['pɑːləs] *adj* (*old, liter*) **to be in a ~ state** sich in einem prekären Zustand befinden.

Parma ham ['pɑːmə'hæm] *n* Parmaschinken *m*.

Parmesan [,pɑːmɪ'zæn] *n* Parmesan *m*.

Parnassus [pɑː'næsəs] *n* **Mount ~** der Parnaß.

parochial [pə'rəʊkɪəl] *adj* **(a)** (*Eccl*) Pfarr-, Gemeinde- ◆ **the ~ duties of a priest** die Aufgaben eines Gemeindepfarrers; **the ~ boundaries** die Grenzen des Pfarrbezirks; **~ school** (*US*) Konfessionsschule *f*.

(b) (*fig*) *attitude, person* engstirnig; *mind, ideas* beschränkt ◆ **he's so ~ in his outlook** er hat einen sehr beschränkten Gesichtskreis.

parochialism [pə'rəʊkɪəlɪzəm] *n* (*fig*) Engstirnigkeit *f*.

parodist ['pærədɪst] *n* Parodist(in *f*) *m*.

parody ['pærədɪ] [1] *n* **(a)** Parodie *f* (*of* auf *+acc*). **(b)** (*travesty*) Abklatsch *m*. **a ~ of justice** eine Parodie auf die Gerechtigkeit.

[2] *vt* parodieren.

parole [pə'rəʊl] [1] *n* **(a)** (*Jur*) Bewährung *f*; (*temporary release*) Strafunterbrechung *f*, Kurzurlaub *m* ◆ **to put sb** *or* **let sb out on ~** jdn auf Bewährung entlassen; (*temporarily*) jdm Strafunterbrechung *or* Kurzurlaub gewähren; **to be on ~** unter Bewährung stehen; (*temporarily*) auf Kurzurlaub sein; **he's on six months' ~** er hat sechs Monate Bewährung(sfrist); **to break one's ~** den Kurzurlaub zur Flucht benutzen.

(b) (*Mil*) Parole *f*.

[2] *vt* *prisoner* auf Bewährung entlassen; (*temporarily*) Strafunterbrechung *or* Kurzurlaub gewähren (*+dat*).

paroxysm ['pærəksɪzəm] *n* Anfall *m* ◆ **~ of grief** Verzweiflungsanfall *m*; **to be seized by a ~ of rage** einen Wutanfall bekommen; **~s of laughter** ein Lachkrampf *m*.

parquet ['pɑːkeɪ] *n* **(a)** Parkett *nt*. **(b)** (*US Theat*) Parkett *nt* ◆ **~ circle** Parkett *nt*.

parquetry ['pɑːkɪtrɪ] *n* Mosaikparkett *nt*.

parricide ['pærɪsaɪd] *n* (*act*) Vater-/Muttermord *m*; (*person*) Vater-/Muttermörder(in *f*) *m*.

parrot ['pærət] [1] *n* Papagei *m* ◆ **he was** *or* **felt as sick as a ~** (*inf*) ihm war kotzübel (*sl*); **he was as sick as a ~** (*inf: vomited*) er kotzte wie ein Reiher (*sl*).

[2] *vt* (wie ein Papagei) nachplappern (*sb* jdm).

parrot: ~-fashion *adv* **to repeat sth ~-fashion** etw wie ein Papagei nachplappern; **he learnt the poem ~-fashion** er lernte das Gedicht stur auswendig; **~ fever** *n* Papageienkrankheit *f*; **~-fish** *n* Papageifisch *m*; **~-like** *adj* papageienhaft; **this ~-like way of learning** dies sture Auswendiglernen.

parry ['pærɪ] [1] *n* (*Fencing, fig*) Parade *f*; (*Boxing*) Abwehr *f*.

[2] *vti* (*Fencing, fig*) parieren; (*Boxing*) *blow* abwehren.

parse [pɑːz] [1] *vt* grammatisch analysieren.

[2] *vi* analysieren ◆ **this sentence doesn't ~ very easily** die Struktur dieses Satzes ist nicht leicht zu analysieren.

parser ['pɑːsəʳ] *n* (*Comput*) Parser *m*.

parsimonious [,pɑːsɪ'məʊnɪəs] *adj* geizig.

parsimoniously [,pɑːsɪ'məʊnɪəslɪ] *adv see adj* ◆ **he ~ refused to lend me any money at all** er war zu geizig, mir auch nur einen einzigen Pfennig zu leihen.

parsimony ['pɑːsɪmənɪ] *n* Geiz *m*.

parsing ['pɑːsɪŋ] *n* (*Gram*) Syntaxanalyse *f*; (*Comput*) Parsing *nt*.

parsley ['pɑːslɪ] *n* Petersilie *f*.

parsnip ['pɑːsnɪp] *n* Pastinak *m*, Pastinake *f*.

parson ['pɑːsn] *n* Pfarrer, Pastor, Pfaffe (*pej*) *m* ◆ **~'s nose** Bürzel, Sterz *m*.

parsonage ['pɑːsənɪdʒ] *n* Pfarrhaus *nt*.

part [pɑːt] [1] *n* **(a)** (*portion, fragment*) Teil *m* ◆ **the stupid ~ of it is that ...** das Dumme daran ist, daß ...; **you haven't heard the best ~ yet** ihr habt ja das Beste noch gar nicht gehört; **~ and parcel** fester Bestandteil; **it is ~ and parcel of the job** das gehört zu der Arbeit dazu; **are transport costs included? — yes, they're all ~ and parcel of the scheme** sind die Transportkosten enthalten? — ja, es ist alles inbegriffen; **the book is good in ~s** teilweise *or* streckenweise ist das Buch gut; **in ~** teilweise, zum Teil; **the greater ~ of it/of the work is done** der größte Teil davon/der Arbeit ist fertig; **it is in large ~ finished/true** das ist zum großen Teil erledigt/wahr; **a ~ of the country/city I don't know** eine Gegend, die ich nicht kenne; **this is in great ~ due to ...** das liegt größtenteils *or* vor allem an (*+dat*) ...; **the darkest ~ of the night is ...** es ist am dunkelsten ...; **during the darkest ~ of the night** in tiefster Nacht; **I kept ~ of it for myself** ich habe einen Teil davon für mich behalten; **I lost ~ of the manuscript** ich habe einen Teil des Manuskripts verloren; **that's ~ of the truth** das ist ein Teil der Wahrheit; **for the main** *or* **most ~** hauptsächlich, in erster Linie; **her performance was for the main** *or* **most ~ well controlled** ihre Darstellung war im großen und ganzen ausgewogen; **the house is built for the main** *or* **most ~ of wood** das Haus ist zum größten Teil aus Holz (gebaut); **in the latter ~ of the year** gegen Ende des Jahres; **the remaining ~ of our holidays** der Rest unseres Urlaubs; **she's become (a) ~ of me** sie ist ein Teil von mir geworden; **5 ~s of sand to 1 of cement** 5 Teile Sand auf ein(en) Teil Zement; **it's 3 ~s gone** drei Viertel sind schon weg.

(b) (*Mech, of kit etc*) Teil *nt* ◆ **spare ~** Ersatzteil *nt*.

(c) (*Gram*) **~ of speech** Wortart *f*; **principal ~s of a verb** Stammformen *pl*.

(d) (*of series*) Folge *f*; (*of serial*) Fortsetzung *f*; (*of encyclopaedia etc*) Lieferung *f* ◆ **end of ~ one** (*TV*) Ende des ersten Teils.

(e) (*share, role*) (An)teil *m*, Rolle *f*; (*Theat*) Rolle *f*, Part *m* (*geh*) ◆ **to play one's ~** (*fig*) seinen Beitrag leisten; **to take ~ in sth** an etw (*dat*) teilnehmen, bei etw (*dat*) mitmachen, sich an etw (*dat*) beteiligen; **who is taking ~?** wer macht mit?, wer ist dabei?; **he's taking ~ in the play** er spielt in dem Stück mit; **in the ~ of Lear** in der Rolle des Lear; **he looks the ~** (*Theat*) die Rolle paßt zu ihm; (*fig*) so sieht (d)er auch aus; **to play a ~** (*Theat, fig*) eine Rolle spielen; **to play no ~ in sth** (*person*) nicht an etw (*dat*) beteiligt sein; **he's just playing a ~** (*fig*) der tut nur so.

(f) (*Mus*) Stimme *f*, Part *m* ◆ **the soprano ~** der Sopranpart, die Sopranstimme; **the piano ~** der Klavierpart, die Klavierstimme; **to sing in ~s** mehrstimmig singen.

(g) **~s** *pl* (*region*) Gegend *f* ◆ **from all ~s** überallher, von überall her; **in** *or* **around these ~s** hier in der Gegend, in dieser Gegend; **in foreign ~s** in der Fremde, in fremden Ländern; **what ~s are you from?** aus welcher Gegend sind Sie?; **he's not from these ~s** er ist nicht aus dieser Gegend *or* von hier.

(h) (*side*) Seite *f* ◆ **to take sb's ~** sich auf jds Seite (*acc*) stellen, für jdn Partei ergreifen; **for my ~** was mich betrifft, meinerseits; **a miscalculation on my ~** eine Fehlkalkulation meinerseits; **on the ~ of** von seiten (*+gen*); seitens (*+gen*).

(i) **to take sth in good/bad ~** etw nicht übelnehmen/etw übelnehmen.

(j) **a man of ~s** ein vielseitiges Talent; **a man of many ~s** ein vielseitiger Mensch.

(k) (*US: in hair*) Scheitel *m*.

(l) **~s** *pl* (*male genitals*) Geschlechtsteile *pl*.

[2] *adv* teils, teilweise ◆ **is it X or Y? — ~ one and ~ the other** ist es X oder Y? — teils (das eine), teils (das andere); **it is ~ iron and ~ copper** es ist teils aus Eisen, teils aus Kupfer; **it was ~ eaten** es war halb aufgegessen; **he's ~ French, ~ Scottish and ~ Latvian** er ist teils Franzose, teils Schotte und teils Lette.

[3] *vt* **(a)** (*divide*) teilen; *hair* scheiteln; *curtain* zur Seite schieben ◆ **the police tried to ~ the crowd** (*make path through*) die Polizei versuchte, eine Gasse durch die Menge zu bahnen.

(b) (*separate*) trennen ◆ **to ~ sb from sb/sth** jdn von jdm/etw trennen; **till death us do ~** bis daß der Tod uns scheidet; **she's not easily ~ed from her money** sie trennt sich nicht gern von ihrem Geld; **to ~ company with sb/sth** sich von jdm/etw trennen; (*in opinion*) mit jdm nicht gleicher Meinung sein; **on that issue, I must ~ company with you** in dem Punkt gehen unsere

Meinungen auseinander; **to ~ company** sich trennen; **at this point the two theories ~ company** an diesem Punkt gehen die beiden Theorien auseinander; **the blouse had ~ed company with the skirt** (*hum*) die Bluse war aus dem Rock gerutscht.

[4] *vi* **(a)** (*divide*) sich teilen; (*curtains*) sich öffnen ◆ **her lips ~ed in a smile** ihre Lippen öffneten sich zu einem Lächeln.

(b) (*separate*) (*person*) sich trennen; (*temporarily also*) auseinandergehen, scheiden (*geh*); (*things*) sich lösen, abgehen ◆ **to ~ from** *or* **with sb** sich von jdm trennen; **we ~ed friends** wir gingen als Freunde auseinander, wir schieden als Freunde (*geh*); **to ~ with sth** sich von etw trennen; **to ~ with money** Geld ausgeben *or* locker machen (*inf*); **to ~ from this life** (*liter*) aus diesem Leben scheiden (*geh*).

partake [pɑːˈteɪk] *pret* **partook**, *ptp* **~n** [pɑːˈteɪkn] *vi* (*form*) **(a) to ~ of** *food, drink* zu sich (*dat*) nehmen; **will you ~ of a glass of sherry?** darf ich Ihnen ein Glas Sherry anbieten?; **will** *or* **do you ~?** (*form, hum*) darf *or* kann ich Ihnen etwas anbieten?; **no thank you, I don't ~** (*form, hum*) nein danke, für mich nicht.

(b) (*share in*) **to ~ of sb's triumph** *etc* an jds Triumph (*dat*) *etc* teilhaben, jds Triumph (*acc*) *etc* teilen.

(c) to ~ of a quality eine Eigenschaft an sich (*dat*) haben; **to a certain extent he ~s of his father's arrogance** er hat etwas von der Arroganz seines Vaters.

(d) to ~ in sth *in activity* an etw (*dat*) teilnehmen.

parterre [ˈpɑːtɛəʳ] *n* (*US*) Parterre *nt*.

part exchange *n* **to offer/take sth in ~** etw in Zahlung geben/nehmen.

parthenogenesis [ˈpɑːθɪnəʊˈdʒenɪsɪs] *n* Parthenogenese, Jungfernzeugung *f*.

Parthian shot [ˈpɑːθɪənˈʃɒt] *n* zum Abschied fallengelassene spitze Bemerkung.

partial [ˈpɑːʃəl] *adj* **(a)** (*not complete*) Teil-, partiell (*geh*), teilweise; *paralysis, eclipse* teilweise, partiell ◆ **to reach a ~ agreement** teilweise Übereinstimmung erzielen.

(b) (*biased*) voreingenommen; *judgement* parteiisch.

(c) to be ~ to sth eine Schwäche für etw haben; **after a while I became rather ~ to it** nach einiger Zeit hatte ich eine ziemliche Vorliebe dafür entwickelt.

partiality [ˌpɑːʃɪˈælɪtɪ] *n* **(a)** *see adj (b)* (*bias*) Voreingenommenheit *f*; Parteilichkeit *f* ◆ **without ~** unvoreingenommen; unparteiisch. **(b)** (*liking*) Vorliebe, Schwäche *f* (*for* für).

partially [ˈpɑːʃəlɪ] *adv* **(a)** (*partly*) zum Teil, teilweise. **(b)** (*with bias*) parteiisch.

participant [pɑːˈtɪsɪpənt] *n* Teilnehmer(in *f*) *m* (*in gen*, an +*dat*); (*in scuffle etc*) Beteiligte(r) *mf* (*in gen*, an +*dat*) ◆ **the bank will not be a ~ in this project** die Bank wird sich nicht an diesem Vorhaben beteiligen.

participate [pɑːˈtɪsɪpeɪt] *vi* **(a)** (*take part*) sich beteiligen, teilnehmen (*in* an +*dat*) ◆ **the council was accused of participating in a housing swindle** man beschuldigte die Stadtverwaltung der Beteiligung an einem Bauschwindel; **it's no good complaining of being lonely if you don't ~** es hat keinen Sinn, über deine Einsamkeit zu klagen, wenn du nirgends mitmachst; **he actively ~d in the success of the scheme** er hat aktiv zum Erfolg des Projekts beigetragen.

(b) (*share*) beteiligt sein (*in* an +*dat*) ◆ **to ~ in sb's sorrow** an jds Kummer (*dat*) Anteil nehmen.

participation [pɑːˌtɪsɪˈpeɪʃən] *n* Beteiligung *f*; (*in competition etc*) Teilnahme *f*; (*worker ~*) Mitbestimmung *f* ◆ **~ in the profits** Gewinnbeteiligung *f*.

participator [pɑːˈtɪsɪpeɪtəʳ] *n* Teilnehmer(in *f*) *m*.

participatory [ˌpɑːtɪsɪˈpeɪtərɪ] *adj* teilnehmend; (*Ind*) Mitbestimmungs-.

participial [ˌpɑːtɪˈsɪpɪəl] *adj* Partizipial-, partizipial.

participle [ˈpɑːtɪsɪpl] *n* Partizip *nt*; *see* **present, past**.

particle [ˈpɑːtɪkl] *n* **(a)** (*of sand etc*) Teilchen, Körnchen *nt*; (*Phys*) Teilchen *nt* ◆ **~ of dust** Stäubchen, Staubkörnchen *nt*; (*fig*) Körnchen *nt*; **there's not a ~ of truth in it** darin steckt kein Körnchen Wahrheit; **~ accelerator** Teilchenbeschleuniger *m*.

(b) (*Gram*) Partikel *f*.

parti-coloured, (*US*) **parti-colored** [ˈpɑːtɪˌkʌləd] *adj* bunt, vielfarbig.

▼ **particular** [pəˈtɪkjʊləʳ] [1] *adj* **(a)** (*as against others*) **this ~ house is very nice** dies (eine) Haus ist sehr hübsch; **it varies according to the ~ case** das ist von Fall zu Fall verschieden; **in this ~ instance** in diesem besonderen Fall; **in certain ~ cases** in einigen besonderen Fällen; **there's a ~ town in France where ...** in Frankreich gibt es eine Stadt, wo ...; **is there any one ~ colour you prefer?** bevorzugen Sie eine bestimmte Farbe?

▼ **(b)** (*special*) besondere(r, s) ◆ **in ~** besonders, vor allem; **the wine in ~ was excellent** vor allem der Wein war hervorragend; **nothing in ~** nichts Besonderes *or* Bestimmtes; **is there anything in ~ you'd like?** haben Sie einen besonderen Wunsch?; **he's a ~ friend of mine** er ist ein guter Freund von mir; **for no ~ reason** aus keinem besonderen *or* bestimmten Grund; **to take ~ care to ...** besonders darauf achten, daß ...

(c) (*fussy, fastidious*) eigen; (*choosy*) wählerisch ◆ **he is very ~ about cleanliness/his children's education** er nimmt es mit der Sauberkeit/der Erziehung seiner Kinder sehr genau; **he's ~ about his car** er ist sehr eigen *or* pingelig (*inf*) mit seinem Auto; **I'm ~ about my friends** ich suche mir meine Freunde genau aus; **you can't be too ~** man kann gar nicht wählerisch genug sein; **I'm not too ~ (about it)** es kommt mir nicht so darauf an, mir ist es gleich; **she was most ~ about it** (*was definite*) sie bestand darauf.

[2] *n* **~s** *pl* Einzelheiten *pl*; (*about person*) Personalien *pl* ◆ **in this ~** in diesem Punkt; **correct in every ~** in jedem Punkt richtig; **for further ~s apply to the personnel manager** weitere Auskünfte erteilt der Personalchef; **to give ~s** Angaben machen; **please give full ~s** bitte genaue Angaben machen; **the ~ and the general** das Besondere und das Allgemeine.

particularity [pəˌtɪkjʊˈlærɪtɪ] *n* **(a)** (*individuality*) Besonderheit *f*. **(b)** (*detailedness*) Ausführlichkeit *f*. **(c)** (*fastidiousness*) Eigenheit *f*.

particularize [pəˈtɪkjʊləraɪz] [1] *vt* spezifizieren, genau angeben.

[2] *vi* ins Detail *or* einzelne gehen ◆ **he did not ~** er nannte keine Einzelheiten.

particularly [pəˈtɪkjʊləlɪ] *adv* besonders, vor allem ◆ **everybody, but ~ Smith** alle, aber vor allem *or* ganz besonders Smith; **he said most ~ not to do it** er hat ausdrücklich gesagt, daß man das nicht tun soll; **do you want it ~ for tomorrow?** brauchen Sie es unbedingt morgen?; **we are ~ pleased to have with us today ...** wir freuen uns besonders, heute ... bei uns zu haben; **he was not ~ pleased** er war nicht besonders erfreut; **not ~** nicht besonders; **it's important, ~ since time is getting short** es ist wichtig, zumal die Zeit knapp wird.

parting [ˈpɑːtɪŋ] [1] *n* **(a)** Abschied *m* ◆ **~ is such sweet sorrow** (*prov*) o süßer Abschiedsschmerz!; **after the ~ of the ways** nachdem sich ihre Wege getrennt hatten; **is this the ~ of the ways then?** das ist also das Ende (unserer Beziehung)?; **this meeting was the ~ of the ways for the Leninists and the Trotskyites** seit dieser Tagung sind die Leninisten und Trotzkisten getrennte Wege gegangen.

(b) (*Brit: in hair*) Scheitel *m*.

[2] *adj* Abschieds-, abschließend ◆ **a ~ present** ein Abschiedsgeschenk *nt*; **Charles knows all about it already, was her ~ shot** Charles weiß schon alles, schleuderte sie ihm nach; **he made a ~ threat** zum Abschied stieß er eine Drohung aus; **his ~ words** seine Abschiedsworte *pl*.

partisan [ˌpɑːtɪˈzæn] [1] *adj* **(a)** parteiisch (*esp pej*), parteilich ◆ **~ spirit** Partei- *or* Vereinsgeist *m*. **(b)** (*Mil*) Partisanen- ◆ **~ warfare** Partisanenkrieg *m*.

[2] *n* **(a)** Parteigänger *m*. **(b)** (*Mil*) Partisan(in *f*) *m*, Freischärler *m*.

partisanship [ˌpɑːtɪˈzænʃɪp] *n* Parteilichkeit *f*.

partition [pɑːˈtɪʃən] [1] *n* **(a)** Teilung *f*. **(b)** (*wall*) Trennwand *f*. **(c)** (*section*) Abteilung *f*.

[2] *vt country* teilen, spalten; *room* aufteilen.

◆**partition off** *vt sep* abteilen, abtrennen.

partitive [ˈpɑːtɪtɪv] *adj* (*Gram*) partitiv.

part load *n* (*Comm*) Teilladung *f*.

partly [ˈpɑːtlɪ] *adv* zum Teil, teilweise, teils.

partner [ˈpɑːtnəʳ] [1] *n* Partner(in *f*) *m*; (*in limited company also*) Gesellschafter(in *f*) *m*; (*in crime*) Komplize *m*, Komplizin *f* ◆ **they were/became ~s in crime** sie waren/wurden Komplizen; **junior ~** Juniorpartner *m*; **senior ~** Seniorpartner *m*.

[2] *vt* **to ~ sb** jds Partner sein; **to be ~ed by sb** jdn zum Partner haben.

partnership [ˈpɑːtnəʃɪp] *n* **(a)** Partnerschaft, Gemeinschaft *f*; (*in sport, dancing etc*) Paar *nt* ◆ **we're** *or* **we make a pretty good ~** wir sind ein ziemlich gutes Paar; **a relationship based on ~** eine partnerschaftliche Beziehung; **to do sth in ~ with sb** etw mit jdm gemeinsam *or* in Zusammenarbeit machen.

(b) (*Comm*) Personengesellschaft *f* ◆ **to enter into a ~** in eine Gesellschaft eintreten; **to take sb into ~** jdn als Partner aufnehmen; **general ~** offene Handelsgesellschaft; **he left the ~** er ist aus der Gesellschaft ausgeschieden.

partook [pɑːˈtʊk] *pret of* **partake**.

part: ~ owner *n* Mitbesitzer(in *f*), Mitinhaber(in *f*) *m*; **~ payment** *n* Teilzahlung *f*.

partridge [ˈpɑːtrɪdʒ] *n* Rebhuhn *nt*.

part: ~ song *n* (*individual*) mehrstimmiges Lied; (*genre*) mehrstimmiger Gesang; **~-time** [1] *adj job, teacher, employee* Teilzeit-; **I'm just ~-time** ich arbeite nur Teilzeit; [2] *adv* **can I do the job ~-time?** kann ich (auf) Teilzeit arbeiten?; **she only teaches ~-time** sie unterrichtet nur stundenweise; **~-timer** *n* Teilzeitbeschäftigte(r) *mf*.

parturition [ˌpɑːtjʊəˈrɪʃən] *n* (*form*) Entbindung *f*.

▼ **party** [ˈpɑːtɪ] [1] *n* **(a)** (*Pol*) Partei *f* ◆ **to be a member of the ~** Parteimitglied sein, in der Partei sein (*inf*).

(b) (*group*) Gruppe, Gesellschaft *f*; (*Mil*) Kommando *nt*, Trupp *m* ◆ **a ~ of tourists** eine Reisegesellschaft; **we were a ~ of five** wir waren zu fünft; **I was one of the ~** ich war dabei; **to join sb's ~** sich jdm anschließen.

▼ **(c)** (*celebration*) Party, Fete (*inf*) *f*; (*more formal*) Gesellschaft *f* ◆ **to have** *or* **give** *or* **throw** (*inf*) **a ~** eine Party geben *or* machen *or* schmeißen (*inf*); eine Gesellschaft geben; **at the ~** auf der Party; bei der Gesellschaft; **let's keep the ~ clean** (*fig inf*) wir wollen doch lieber im Rahmen bleiben.

(d) (*Jur, fig*) Partei *f* ◆ **a/the third ~** ein Dritter *m*/der Dritte; **the parties to a dispute** die streitenden Parteien; **to be a ~ to an agreement** einer Übereinkunft (*dat*) zustimmen; **to be a ~ to a crime** an einem Verbrechen beteiligt sein; **were you a ~ to this?** waren Sie daran beteiligt?; **I will not be a ~ to any violence** ich will mit Gewaltanwendung nichts zu tun haben.

(e) (*inf: person*) **a ~ by the name of Johnson** ein gewisser Johnson.

[2] *vi* (*inf*) feiern.

party: ~ dress *n* Partykleid *nt*; **~goer** *n* Partygänger(in *f*), Fetengänger(in *f*) *m*; **~ line** *n* **(a)** (*Pol*) Parteilinie *f*; **(b)** (*Telec*) Gemeinschaftsanschluß *m*; **~ man** *n* Gefolgsmann *m*; **~ political** *adj* parteipolitisch; **~ political broadcast** *n* parteipolitische Sendung; **~ politics** *npl* Parteipolitik *f*; **~ pooper** *n* (*inf*) Partymuffel *m* (*inf*); **~ spirit** *n* (*Pol*) Parteigeist *m* *or* -gesinnung *f*; **~ spokesman** *n* Parteisprecher *m*.

parvenu [ˈpɑːvənuː] *n* Emporkömmling, Parvenü *m*.

PASCAL [ˈpæsˌkæl] *n* (*Comput*) PASCAL *nt*.

paschal [ˈpæskəl] *adj* Passah-, Oster-.

➤ LANGUAGE IN USE: **particular: 1b** → 6.3, 7.5, 26.2 **party: 1c** → 25.2

pas de deux ['pɑːdə'dɜː] *n* Pas de deux *m*.
pasha ['pæʃə] *n* Pascha *m*.
paso doble ['pæsəʊ'dəʊbleɪ] *n* Paso doble *m*.
pass [pɑːs] 1 *n* **(a)** *(permit)* Ausweis *m*; *(Mil etc)* Passierschein *m* ◆ **a free ~** eine Freikarte; *(permanent)* ein Sonderausweis *m*.
(b) *(Brit Univ)* Bestehen *nt* einer Prüfung ◆ **to get a ~ in German** seine Deutschprüfung bestehen; *(lowest level)* seine Deutschprüfung mit „ausreichend" bestehen; **I need a ~ in physics still** ich muß noch einen Abschluß in Physik machen.
(c) *(Geog, Sport)* Paß *m*; *(Ftbl: for shot at goal)* Vorlage *f*.
(d) *(Fencing)* Ausfall *m*.
(e) *(movement)* *(by conjurer, hypnotist)* Bewegung, Geste *f* ◆ **the conjurer made a few quick ~es with his hand over the top of the hat** der Zauberer fuhr mit der Hand ein paarmal schnell über dem Hut hin und her; **the paint-sprayer makes two ~es over the metal** der Lackierer spritzt das Metall zweimal; **the text had a special hyphenation ~** der Text wurde eigens in bezug auf Silbentrennung überprüft.
(f) things have come to a pretty ~ when ... so weit ist es schon gekommen, daß ...; **things had come to such a ~ that ...** die Lage hatte sich so zugespitzt, daß ...; **this is a fine ~ to be in, here's a pretty ~!** *(dated)* das ist ja eine schöne Bescherung!
(g) to make a ~ at sb bei jdm Annäherungsversuche machen.
(h) *(Aviat)* **the jet made three ~es over the ship** der Düsenjäger flog dreimal über das Schiff; **on its fourth ~ the plane was almost hit** beim vierten Vorbeifliegen wurde das Flugzeug fast getroffen; **the pilot made two ~es over the landing strip before deciding to come down** der Pilot passierte die Landebahn zweimal, ehe er sich zur Landung entschloß.
2 *vt* **(a)** *(move past)* vorbeigehen an (*+dat*); vorbeifahren an (*+dat*); vorbeifliegen an (*+dat*) ◆ **he ~ed me without even saying hello** er ging ohne zu grüßen an mir vorbei; **the ship ~ed the estuary** das Schiff passierte die Flußmündung.
(b) *(overtake) athlete, car* überholen ◆ **he's ~ed all the other candidates** er hat alle anderen Kandidaten überflügelt.
(c) *(cross) frontier etc* überschreiten, überqueren, passieren ◆ **not a word ~ed her lips** kein Wort kam über ihre Lippen.
(d) *(reach, hand)* reichen ◆ **they ~ed the photograph around** sie reichten *or* gaben das Foto herum; **~ (me) the salt, please** reich mir doch bitte das Salz!; **he ~ed the hammer up** er reichte den Hammer hinauf; **the characteristics which he ~ed to his son** die Eigenschaften, die er an seinen Sohn weitergab.
(e) it ~es belief es ist kaum zu fassen; **it ~es my comprehension that ...** es geht über meinen Verstand *or* meine Fassungskraft, daß ...; **love which ~es all understanding** Liebe, die jenseits allen Verstehens liegt.
(f) *(Univ etc) exam* bestehen; *candidate* bestehen lassen.
(g) this film will never ~ the censors dieser Film kommt nie und nimmer durch die Zensur; **the play won't ~ the critics easily** das Stück wird es mit den Kritikern nicht leicht haben.
(h) *(approve) motion* annehmen; *plan* gutheißen, genehmigen; *(Parl)* verabschieden ◆ **the censors will never ~ this film** die Zensur gibt diesen Film bestimmt nicht frei.
(i) *ball etc* **to ~ the ball to sb** jdm den Ball zuspielen; **you should learn to ~ the ball and not hang on to it** du solltest lernen abzuspielen, statt am Ball zu kleben.
(j) *forged bank notes* weitergeben.
(k) to ~ a cloth over sth mit einem Tuch über etw (*acc*) wischen; **he ~ed his hand across his forehead** er fuhr sich (*dat*) mit der Hand über die Stirn; **~ the thread through the hole** führen Sie den Faden durch die Öffnung; **he ~ed a chain around the front axle** er legte eine Kette um die Vorderachse.
(l) *(spend) time* verbringen ◆ **he did it just to ~ the time** er tat das nur, um sich (*dat*) die Zeit zu vertreiben.
(m) *remark* von sich geben; *opinion* abgeben; *(Jur) sentence* verhängen; *judgement* fällen.
(n) *(discharge) excrement, blood* absondern, ausscheiden ◆ **to ~ water** Wasser *or* Harn lassen.
(o) *(omit)* **I'll ~ this round** ich lasse diese Runde aus.
3 *vi* **(a)** *(move past)* vorbeigehen, vorbeifahren ◆ **the street was too narrow for the cars to ~** die Straße war so eng, daß die Wagen nicht aneinander vorbeikamen; **we ~ed in the corridor** wir gingen im Korridor aneinander vorbei; **there isn't room for him to ~** es ist so eng, daß er nicht vorbeikommt.
(b) *(overtake)* überholen.
(c) *(move, go)* **~ along the car please!** bitte weiter durchgehen!; **a stream of letters ~ed between them** sie tauschten eine Flut von Briefen aus; **words ~ed between them** es gab einige Meinungsverschiedenheiten; **the cars ~ down the assembly line** die Autos kommen das Fließband herunter; **as we ~ from feudalism to more open societies** beim Übergang vom Feudalismus zu offeneren Gesellschaftsformen; **as we ~ from youth to old age** mit zunehmendem Alter; **people were ~ing in and out of the building** die Leute gingen in dem Gebäude ein und aus; **to ~ into a tunnel** in einen Tunnel fahren; **to ~ into oblivion/a coma** in Vergessenheit geraten/in ein Koma fallen; **expressions which have ~ed into/out of the language** Redensarten, die in die Sprache eingegangen sind/aus der Sprache verschwunden sind; **to ~ out of sight** außer Sichtweite geraten; **the firm has ~ed out of existence** die Firma hat aufgehört zu bestehen; **he ~ed out of our lives** er ist aus unserem Leben verschwunden; **everything he said just ~ed over my head** was er sagte, war mir alles zu hoch; **when we ~ed over the frontier** als wir die Grenze passierten; **we're now ~ing over Paris** wir fliegen jetzt über Paris; **I'll just ~ quickly over the main points again** ich werde jetzt die Hauptpunkte noch einmal kurz durchgehen; **he's ~ing through a difficult period** er macht gerade eine schwere Zeit durch; **the manuscript has ~ed through a lot of hands** das Manuskript ist durch viele Hände gegangen; **the thread ~es through this hole** der Faden geht durch diese Öffnung; **shall we ~ to the second subject on the agenda**? wollen wir zum zweiten Punkt der Tagesordnung übergehen?; **the crown always ~es to the eldest son** die Krone geht immer auf den ältesten Sohn über; **the area then ~ed under Roman rule** das Gebiet geriet dann unter römische Herrschaft; **he ~ed under the archway** er ging/fuhr durch das Tor.
(d) *(time)* (*also* **~ by**) vergehen.
(e) *(disappear, end: anger, hope, era etc)* vorübergehen, vorbeigehen; *(storm)* *(go over)* vorüberziehen; *(abate)* sich legen; *(rain)* vorbeigehen ◆ **it'll ~** das geht vorüber!
(f) *(be acceptable)* gehen ◆ **to let sth ~** etw durchgehen lassen; **let it ~!** vergiß es!, vergessen wir's!; **it'll ~** das geht.
(g) *(be considered, be accepted)* angesehen werden (*for or as sth* als etw) ◆ **this little room has to ~ for an office** dieses kleine Zimmer dient als Büro; **in her day she ~ed for a great beauty** zu ihrer Zeit galt sie als große Schönheit; **she could easily ~ for 25** sie könnte leicht für 25 durchgehen; **or what ~es nowadays for a hat** oder was heute so als Hut betrachtet wird.
(h) *(in exam)* bestehen ◆ **I ~ed!** ich habe bestanden!; **did you ~ in chemistry**? hast du deine Chemieprüfung bestanden?
(i) *(Sport)* abspielen ◆ **to ~ to sb** jdm zuspielen, an jdn abgeben.
(j) *(Cards)* passen ◆ **(I) ~!** (ich) passe!; **~** *(in quiz etc)* passe!
(k) *(old: happen)* **to come to ~** sich begeben; **and it came to ~ in those days ...** und es begab sich zu jener Zeit ...; **to bring sth to ~** etw bewirken.
◆**pass away** 1 *vi* **(a)** *(end)* zu Ende gehen ◆ **the days of our youth have ~ed ~ for ever** die Tage unserer Jugend sind für immer dahin. **(b)** *(euph: die)* entschlafen, hinscheiden.
2 *vt sep hours* sich (*dat*) vertreiben.
◆**pass between** *vi +prep obj (words)* fallen zwischen ◆ **what has ~ed ~ us** was sich zwischen uns zugetragen hat.
◆**pass by** 1 *vi* *(go past)* vorbeigehen; *(car etc)* vorbeifahren; *(time, months etc)* vergehen ◆ **he just ~ed ~** er ging/fuhr einfach vorbei; **there was no room for the lorry to ~ ~** der Lastwagen kam nicht vorbei; **I can't let that ~ ~ without comment** ich kann das nicht kommentarlos durchgehen lassen; **to ~ ~ on the other side** *(fig)* achtlos vorbeigehen.
2 *vi +prep obj* **if you ~ ~ the grocer's ...** wenn du beim Kaufmann vorbeikommst, ...; **we ~ed ~ a line of hotels** wir kamen an einer Reihe Hotels vorbei.
3 *vt sep (ignore) problems* übergehen ◆ **life has ~ed her ~** das Leben ist an ihr vorübergegangen.
◆**pass down** *vt sep* **(a)** *traditions* weitergeben (*to* an *+acc*), überliefern (*to dat*); *characteristics* weitergeben (*to* an *+acc*) ◆ **~ed ~ by word of mouth** mündlich überliefert.
(b) *(transmit)* **the story was ~ed ~ through the ranks** die Sache sprach sich (bis) zu den Soldaten durch.
◆**pass off** 1 *vi* **(a)** *(take place)* ablaufen, vonstatten gehen.
(b) *(end)* vorüber- *or* vorbeigehen.
(c) *(be taken as)* durchgehen (*as* als) ◆ **she could ~ ~ as an Italian** sie würde als Italienerin durchgehen.
2 *vt sep* **to ~ oneself/sb/sth ~ as sth** sich/jdn/etw als *or* für etw ausgeben.
◆**pass on** 1 *vi* **(a)** *(euph: die)* entschlafen, verscheiden.
(b) *(proceed)* übergehen (*to* zu) ◆ **right gentlemen, shall we ~ ~?** gut, meine Herren, wollen wir nun zum nächsten Punkt übergehen?
2 *vt sep news, information* weitergeben; *disease* übertragen ◆ **~ it ~!** weitersagen!
◆**pass out** 1 *vi* **(a)** *(become unconscious)* in Ohnmacht fallen, umkippen *(inf)* ◆ **he drank till he ~ed ~** er trank bis zum Umfallen. **(b)** *(new officer)* ernannt werden, sein Patent bekommen *(dated)*.
2 *vt sep leaflets* austeilen, verteilen.
◆**pass over** 1 *vt sep* übergehen ◆ **he's been ~ed ~ again** er ist schon wieder übergangen worden.
2 *vi (euph: die)* entschlafen.
◆**pass through** *vi* **I'm only ~ing ~** ich bin nur auf der Durchreise; **you have to ~ ~ Berlin** du mußt über Berlin fahren.
◆**pass up** *vt sep chance* vorübergehen lassen.
passable ['pɑːsəbl] *adj* **(a)** passierbar; *road etc also* befahrbar. **(b)** *(tolerable)* leidlich, passabel.
passably ['pɑːsəblɪ] *adv* leidlich, einigermaßen.
passage ['pæsɪdʒ] *n* **(a)** *(transition: from youth to manhood etc)* Übergang *m* ◆ **the ~ of time** der Verlauf *or* Strom *(geh)* der Zeit; **in** *or* **with the ~ of time** mit der Zeit.
(b) *(through country)* Durchfahrt, Durchreise *f*; *(right of ~)* Durchreise *f*, Transit *m*, Durchreise- *or* Transitgenehmigung *f* ◆ **to grant sb ~ through an area** jdm die Durchreise durch ein Gebiet genehmigen.
(c) *(voyage)* Überfahrt, Schiffsreise *f*; *(fare)* Überfahrt, Passage *f*; *see* **work**.
(d) *(Parl: process)* parlamentarische Behandlung; *(final)* Annahme, Verabschiedung *f*.
(e) *(corridor)* Gang *m* ◆ **the narrow ~ between Denmark and Sweden** die schmale Durchfahrt zwischen Dänemark und Schweden; **secret ~** Geheimgang *m*; **he forced a ~ through the crowd** er bahnte sich (*dat*) einen

Weg durch die Menge.
(f) *(in book)* Passage *f*; *(Mus also)* Stück *nt* ◆ **a ~ from Shakespeare/the Bible** eine Shakespeare-/Bibelstelle.
passageway ['pæsɪdʒweɪ] *n* Durchgang *m*.
pass: ~ book *n* Sparbuch *nt*; **~ degree** *n niedrigster Grad an britischen Universitäten*, „Bestanden".
passé ['pæseɪ] *adj* überholt, passé *(inf)*.
passenger ['pæsɪndʒəʳ] *n* **(a)** *(on bus, in taxi)* Fahrgast *m*; *(on train)* Reisende(r) *mf*; *(on ship)* Passagier *m*; *(on plane)* Fluggast, Passagier *m*; *(in car)* Mitfahrer(in *f*), Beifahrer(in *f*) *m*; *(on motorcycle)* Beifahrer(in *f*) *m*.
(b) *(inf: ineffective member)* **we can't afford to carry any ~s** *(no incompetent people)* wir können es uns nicht leisten, Leute mit durchzuschleppen; *(no idle people)* wir können uns keine Drückeberger leisten; **he's just a ~ in the team** er wird von den anderen mit durchgeschleppt.
passenger: ~ aircraft *n* Passagierflugzeug *nt*; **~ liner** *n* Passagierschiff *nt*; **~ list** *n* Passagierliste *f*; **~ mile** *n (Aviat)* Flugkilometer *m* je Fluggast; *(Rail)* Bahnkilometer *m* je Reisender; **~ train** *n* Zug *m* im Personenverkehr.
passe-partout ['pæspɑːtuː] *n* Passepartout *nt*.
passer-by ['pɑːsə'baɪ] *n, pl* **passers-by** Passant(in *f*) *m*, Vorübergehende(r) *mf*.
passim ['pæsɪm] *adv* passim, verstreut.
passing ['pɑːsɪŋ] [1] *n* **(a)** Vorübergehen *nt* ◆ **with the ~ of time/the years** im Lauf(e) der Zeit/der Jahre; **I would like to mention in ~ that ...** ich möchte beiläufig noch erwähnen, daß ...
(b) *(disappearance)* Niedergang *m*; *(euph: death)* Heimgang *m* ◆ **the ~ of the old year** der Ausklang des alten Jahres.
(c) *(Parl: of bill) see* **passage (d)**.
[2] *adj car* vorbeifahrend; *clouds* vorüberziehend; *years* vergehend; *glance etc, thought* flüchtig; *comments, reference* beiläufig; *fancy* flüchtig, vorübergehend.
[3] *adv (old: very)* gar *(old)*, überaus *(liter)*.
passing: ~ note *n* Durchgangston *m*; **~-out (ceremony)** *n (Mil)* Abschlußfeier *f*; **~ place** *n (on narrow road)* Ausweichstelle *f*.
passion ['pæʃən] *n* **(a)** Leidenschaft *f*; *(fervour)* Leidenschaftlichkeit *f*; *(enthusiasm also)* Begeisterung *f* ◆ **to have a ~ for sth** eine Passion *or* Leidenschaft für etw haben; **with his ~ for accuracy/oysters/all things Greek** mit seinem Drang nach Genauigkeit/seiner Passion *or* ausgeprägten Vorliebe für Austern/alles Griechische; **~s were running high** die Erregung schlug hohe Wellen; **his ~ for the cause** sein leidenschaftliches Engagement für die Sache; **music is a ~ with him** die Musik ist bei ihm eine Leidenschaft; **his ~ is Mozart** Mozart ist seine Passion; **yes, my ~, what is it?** *(hum)* ja, du Traum meiner schlaflosen Nächte, was gibt's? *(hum)*; **to be in a ~** erregt sein; **to fly into a ~** in Erregung geraten, sich erregen.
(b) *(Rel, Art, Mus)* Passion *f*; *(Bibl: account of ~ also)* Leidensgeschichte *f* ◆ **The St Matthew P~** Die Matthäuspassion.
passionate ['pæʃənɪt] *adj* leidenschaftlich.
passionately ['pæʃənɪtlɪ] *adv* leidenschaftlich ◆ **oh yes, she said ~** o ja, sagte sie voller Leidenschaft; **she wept ~** sie weinte heiße Tränen.
passion: ~ flower *n* Passionsblume *f*; *(hum inf: as address)* Schatz *m*, Schätzchen *nt*; **~ fruit** *n* Passionsfrucht *f*; **~less** *adj* leidenschaftslos; **~ play** *n* Passionsspiel *nt*; **P~ Sunday** *n* Passionssonntag *m*; **P~ Week** *n* Karwoche *f*.
passive ['pæsɪv] [1] *adj* **(a)** passiv; *acceptance* widerspruchslos, widerstandslos ◆ **~ resistance** passiver Widerstand; **~ smoker** Passivraucher(in *f*) *m*, passiver Raucher, passive Raucherin; **~ smoking** passives Rauchen, Passivrauchen *nt*; **~ vocabulary** passiver Wortschatz.
(b) *(Gram)* passivisch, passiv *(rare)*, Passiv-.
[2] *n (Gram)* Passiv *nt*, Leideform *f* ◆ **in the ~** im Passiv.
passively ['pæsɪvlɪ] *adv* passiv; *accept* widerstandslos, widerspruchslos; *watch etc* tatenlos.
passiveness ['pæsɪvnɪs], **passivity** [pə'sɪvɪtɪ] *n* Passivität *f*.
pass key *n* Hauptschlüssel *m*.
Passover ['pɑːsəʊvəʳ] *n* Passah *nt*.
passport ['pɑːspɔːt] *n* Reisepaß, Paß *(inf) m*; *(fig)* Schlüssel *m (to* für, zu) ◆ **~ control** Paßkontrolle *f*.
password ['pɑːswɜːd] *n* Losungs- *or* Kennwort *nt*, Parole *f*; *(Comput)* Paßwort *nt*.
past [pɑːst] [1] *adj* **(a)** frühe(r, s) *attr*, vergangene(r, s) *attr* ◆ **for some time ~** seit einiger Zeit; **in times ~** in früheren *or* vergangenen Zeiten; **it's ~ history now** das gehört jetzt der Vergangenheit an; **all that is now ~** das ist jetzt alles vorüber *or* vorbei; **what's ~ is ~** was vorbei ist, ist vorbei; **in the ~ week** letzte *or* vorige *or* vergangene Woche, in der letzten *or* vergangenen Woche; **~ president** früherer Präsident.
(b) *(Gram)* **~ tense** Vergangenheit, Vergangenheitsform *f*; **~ participle** Partizip Perfekt, zweites Partizip; **~ perfect** Plusquamperfekt *nt*, Vorvergangenheit *f*.
[2] *n (also Gram)* Vergangenheit *f* ◆ **in the ~** in der Vergangenheit *(also Gram)*, früher; **to live in the ~** in der Vergangenheit leben; **the verb is in the ~** das Verb steht in der Vergangenheit; **to be a thing of the ~** der Vergangenheit *(dat)* angehören; **a town/woman with a ~** eine Stadt/Frau mit Vergangenheit; **he was believed to have a "~"** man nahm an, daß er kein unbeschriebenes Blatt sei.
[3] *prep* **(a)** *(motion)* an (+*dat*) ... vorbei *or* vorüber; *(position: beyond)* hinter (+*dat*), nach (+*dat*) ◆ **just ~ the library** kurz nach *or* hinter der Bücherei; **to run ~ sb** an jdm vorbeilaufen.
(b) *(time)* nach (+*dat*) ◆ **ten (minutes) ~ three** zehn (Minuten) nach drei; **half ~ four** halb fünf; **a quarter ~ nine** Viertel nach neun; **it's ~ 12** es ist schon nach 12 *or* 12 vorbei; **the trains run at a quarter ~ the hour** die Züge gehen jeweils um Viertel nach; **it's (well) ~ your bedtime** du solltest schon längst im Bett liegen.
(c) *(beyond)* über (+*acc*) ◆ **~ forty** über vierzig; **the patient is ~ saving** der Patient ist nicht mehr zu retten; **we're ~ caring** es kümmert uns nicht mehr; **to be ~ sth** für etw zu alt sein; **he's ~ heavy work** schwere Arbeit kann er nicht mehr leisten; **my car is getting ~ it** *(inf)* mein Auto tut's allmählich nicht mehr *or* bringt's nicht mehr *(inf)*; **he's ~ it** *(inf)* er ist zu alt, er ist ein bißchen alt (dafür), er bringt's nicht mehr *(sl)*; **she's getting a bit ~ it** *(inf)* sie wird allmählich alt; **I wouldn't put it ~ him** *(inf)* ich würde es ihm schon zutrauen.
[4] *adv* vorbei, vorüber ◆ **to walk/run ~** vorüber- *or* vorbeigehen/vorbeirennen.
pasta ['pæstə] *n* Teigwaren, Nudeln *pl*.
paste [peɪst] [1] *n* **(a)** *(for sticking)* Kleister *m*.
(b) mix to a smooth/firm ~ *(glue etc)* zu einem lockeren/festen Brei anrühren; *(cake mixture etc)* zu einem glatten/festen Teig anrühren.
(c) *(spread)* Brotaufstrich *m*; *(tomato ~)* Mark *nt*.
(d) *(jewellery)* Similistein, Straß *m*.
[2] *vt* **(a)** *(apply ~ to) wallpaper etc* einkleistern, mit Kleister bestreichen; *(affix)* kleben ◆ **to ~ pictures into a book** Bilder in ein Buch (ein)kleben; **to ~ sth to sth** etw an etw *(acc)* kleben.
(b) *(sl) opponent* eine Packung verabreichen (+*dat*) *(inf)*; *(Boxing)* die Hucke vollhauen (+*dat*) *(inf)*; *new play etc* verreißen ◆ **to ~ sb (one)** *(lit)* jdm eins vor den Latz knallen *(sl)*; **to ~ sb** *(defeat)* jdn in die Pfanne hauen *(inf)*; **to ~ sth** *(fig)* etw verhackstücken *(inf)*.
◆**paste up** *vt sep* aufkleben, ankleben; *(in publishing)* einen Klebeumbruch machen von.
pasteboard ['peɪstbɔːd] *n* Karton *m*, Pappe *f*.
pastel ['pæstl] [1] *n (crayon)* Pastellstift *m*, Pastellkreide *f*; *(drawing)* Pastellzeichnung *f*, Pastell *nt*; *(colour)* Pastellton *m*.
[2] *adj attr* Pastell-, pastellen, pastellfarben ◆ **~ colour** Pastellfarbe *f*, Pastellton *m*; **~ drawing** Pastellzeichnung *f*.
paste-up ['peɪstʌp] *n* Klebeumbruch *m* ◆ **to do a ~** einen Klebeumbruch herstellen *or* machen.
pasteurization [,pæstəraɪ'zeɪʃən] *n* Pasteurisierung, Pasteurisation *f*.
pasteurize ['pæstəraɪz] *vt* pasteurisieren, keimfrei machen.
pastiche [pæ'stiːʃ] *n* Pastiche *m*; *(satirical writing)* Persiflage *f*.
pastille ['pæstɪl] *n* Pastille *f*.
pastime ['pɑːstaɪm] *n* Zeitvertreib *m*.
pastiness ['peɪstɪnɪs] *n* **the ~ of her complexion** ihr bläßliches *or* käsiges *(inf) or* kränkliches Aussehen.
pasting ['peɪstɪŋ] *n (sl)* **to get a ~** *(from sb* von jdm) fertiggemacht werden *(inf)*; *(Sport, from critic also)* in die Pfanne gehauen werden *(inf)*; **to give sb a ~** jdn fertigmachen *(inf)*; *(Sport, as critic also)* jdn in die Pfanne hauen *(inf)*.
past master *n* erfahrener Könner; *(Art, Sport also)* Altmeister(in *f*) *m* ◆ **to be a ~ at doing sth** ein Experte *m* darin sein, etw zu tun.
pastor ['pɑːstəʳ] *n* Pfarrer *m*.
pastoral ['pɑːstərəl] [1] *adj* **(a)** *(Art, Liter, Mus)* pastoral ◆ **Beethoven's P~ Symphony** Beethovens Pastorale *f*; **~ poem** Schäfer- *or* Hirtengedicht *nt*; **~ picture** Pastorale *f or nt*.
(b) *(Eccl)* pastoral, pfarramtlich; *duties also* seelsorgerisch; *responsibility* seelsorgerlich ◆ **~ care** Seelsorge *f*; **~ staff** Bischofsstab *m*; **~ letter** Hirtenbrief *m*.
[2] *n* **(a)** *(Liter, Art, Mus)* Pastorale *f or nt*.
(b) *(Eccl)* Hirtenbrief *m*.
pastorale [,pæstə'rɑːl] *n (Mus)* Pastorale *f*.
pastrami [pə'strɑːmɪ] *geräuchertes, stark gewürztes Rindfleisch*.
pastry ['peɪstrɪ] *n* Teig *m*; *(cake etc)* Stückchen *nt* ◆ **pastries** *pl* Gebäck *nt*; **you've got a piece of ~ on your chin** du hast einen Krümel am Kinn; *see* **Danish**.
pastry: ~ brush *n* Backpinsel *m*; **~ case** *n* Törtchenform *f*; **~-cook** *n* Konditor(in *f*) *m*.
pasturage ['pɑːstjʊrɪdʒ] *n* **(a)** *(grass)* Weide *f*. **(b)** *(right of pasture)* Weiderecht *nt*.
pasture ['pɑːstʃəʳ] [1] *n* **(a)** *(field)* Weide *f* ◆ **to put out to ~** auf die Weide treiben; **to move on to ~s new** *(fig)* sich *(dat)* etwas Neues suchen, sich nach neuen Weidegründen *(geh)* umsehen.
(b) *no pl (also* **~ land***)* Weideland *nt*.
(c) *no pl (food)* Futter *nt*.
[2] *vt animals* weiden lassen.
[3] *vi* grasen.
pasty¹ ['peɪstɪ] *adj* **(a)** *consistency* zähflüssig; *material* klebrig. **(b)** *colour* bläßlich; *look also* käsig *(inf)*, kränklich.
pasty² ['pæstɪ] *n (esp Brit)* Pastete *f*.
pasty-faced ['peɪstɪ'feɪst] *adj* blaß- *or* bleichgesichtig.
Pat [pæt] *n (sl)* Ire *m*.
pat¹ [pæt] *n (of butter)* Portion *f* ◆ **cow ~** Kuhfladen *m*.
pat² [1] *adv* **to know** *or* **have sth off ~** etw wie am Schnürchen *(inf) or* wie aus dem Effeff *(inf)* können; **he knows the rules off ~** er kennt die Regeln in- und auswendig *or* aus dem Effeff *(inf)*; **to learn sth off ~** etw in- und auswendig lernen; **he's always got an answer ~** er hat immer eine Antwort parat; **to stand ~** keinen Zollbreit nachgeben.

[2] *adj answer, explanation* glatt ◆ **somehow his excuses seem a bit ~ to me** er ist mir immer ein bißchen zu schnell mit Ausreden bei der Hand.

pat³ [1] *n* Klaps *m* ◆ **he gave his nephew a ~ on the head** er tätschelte seinem Neffen den Kopf; **excellent work, said the teacher, giving her a ~ on the shoulder** hervorragende Arbeit, sagte der Lehrer und klopfte ihr auf die Schulter; **he gave her knee an affectionate ~** er tätschelte ihr liebevoll das Knie; **to give one's horse/the dog a ~** sein Pferd/seinen Hund tätscheln; (*once*) seinem Pferd *or* Hund einen Klaps geben; **to give sb/oneself a ~ on the back** (*fig*) jdm/sich selbst auf die Schulter klopfen; **that's a ~ on the back for you** das ist ein Kompliment für dich.

[2] *vt* (*touch lightly*) tätscheln; (*hit gently*) *ball* leicht schlagen; *sand* festklopfen; *face* abtupfen ◆ **to ~ sb/the dog on the head** jdm/dem Hund den Kopf tätscheln; **to ~ sth/one's face dry** etw/sein Gesicht trockentupfen; **she ~ted a few loose curls into place** sie drückte ein paar Locken an, die sich gelöst hatten; **the sculptor ~ted the plaster into shape** der Bildhauer klopfte den Gips in die richtige Form; **he ~ted aftershave onto his chin** er betupfte sein Kinn mit Rasierwasser; **to ~ sb on the back** (*lit*) jdm auf den Rücken klopfen; **to ~ sb/oneself on the back** (*fig*) jdm/sich selbst auf die Schulter klopfen.

◆**pat down** *vt sep* festklopfen; *hair* festdrücken, andrücken.

pat⁴ *abbr of* **patent**.

Patagonia [ˌpætəˈgəʊnɪə] *n* Patagonien *nt*.

Patagonian [ˌpætəˈgəʊnɪən] [1] *adj* patagonisch.
[2] *n* Patagonier(in *f*) *m*.

patch [pætʃ] [1] *n* **(a)** (*for mending*) Flicken *m*; (*on new garments*) Flecken *m*; (*eye ~*) Augenklappe *f*.
(b) it's/he's not a ~ on ... (*inf*) das/er ist gar nichts gegen ...
(c) (*small area, stain*) Fleck *m*; (*piece of land*) Stück *nt*; (*subdivision of garden*) Beet *nt*; (*part, section*) Stelle *f*; (*of time*) Phase *f*; (*inf: of policeman, prostitute*) Revier *nt* ◆ **a ~ of blue sky** ein Stückchen *nt* blauer Himmel; **purple ~es dotted the landscape** die Landschaft war übersät mit violetten Farbtupfern; **~es of colour** Farbtupfer *pl*; **a ~ of oil** ein Ölfleck *m*; **~es of sunlight dappled the floor of the forest** (die) Sonnenstrahlen tanzten auf dem Waldboden; **then we hit a bad ~ of road** dann kamen wir auf ein schlechtes Stück Straße; **the cabbage ~** das Kohlbeet; **we drove through a few ~es of rain on our way here** wir hatten auf dem Weg stellenweise Regen; **there were sunny ~es during the day** hin und wieder schien die Sonne; **~es of depression** depressive Phasen *pl*; **he's going through a bad ~ at the moment** ihm geht's im Augenblick nicht sonderlich gut.
(d) (*cosmetic beauty spot*) Schönheitspflästerchen *nt*.
(e) (*Comput*) Korrekturroutine *f*.
[2] *vt* flicken ◆ **this piece of cloth will just ~ that hole nicely** dieses Stück Stoff ist gerade richtig für das Loch.

◆**patch up** *vt sep* zusammenflicken; *quarrel* beilegen ◆ **to ~ things ~ temporarily** die Dinge notdürftig zusammenflicken; **they managed to ~ ~ their relationship** sie haben sich schließlich wieder ausgesöhnt; **I want to ~ things ~ between us** ich möchte unsere Beziehung wieder ins Lot bringen.

patchiness [ˈpætʃɪnɪs] *n* (*of work*) Unregelmäßigkeit *f*; (*of knowledge*) Lückenhaftigkeit *f*; (*of film, book, essay etc*) unterschiedliche Qualität.

patch: ~ pocket *n* aufgesetzte Tasche; **~-up** *n* (*inf*) Flickwerk *nt no art*; **~work** *n* Patchwork *nt*; **~work quilt** Patchwork- *or* Flickendecke *f*; (*fig*) a **~work of fields** ein Mosaik *nt* von Feldern; **a ~work of songs** eine bunte Folge von Liedern.

patchy [ˈpætʃɪ] *adj* (*+er*) **(a)** *work* ungleichmäßig, unterschiedlich; *knowledge, memory* lückenhaft ◆ **what was the performance like? — ~** wie war die Aufführung? — gemischt; **his second novel however was much patchier** sein zweiter Roman war wesentlicher unausgeglichener; **this is the patchiest production I've seen them do for a long time** eine derart ungleichmäßige Inszenierung habe ich von ihnen lange nicht mehr gesehen; **what's his work like? — ~** wie ist seine Arbeit? — unterschiedlich.
(b) (*lit*) *material* gefleckt; *pattern* Flecken- ◆ **the ~ appearance of the half rebuilt city** der Eindruck von Flickwerk, den die zur Hälfte neu aufgebaute Stadt vermittelt/vermittelte.

pate [peɪt] *n* Rübe (*inf*), Birne (*sl*) *f* ◆ **bald ~** Platte (*inf*), Glatze *f*.

pâté [ˈpæteɪ] *n* Pastete *f*.

-pated [-ˈpeɪtɪd] *adj suf* -köpfig.

patella [pəˈtelə] *n* (*Anat*) Patella (*spec*), Kniescheibe *f*.

paten [ˈpætən] *n* (*Eccl*) Patene *f*, Hostienteller *m*.

patent [ˈpeɪtənt] [1] *n* Patent *nt* ◆ **~ applied for** *or* **pending** Patent angemeldet; **to take out a ~ (on sth)** ein Patent (auf etw *acc*) erhalten; *see* **letter**.
[2] *vt* patentieren lassen ◆ **is it ~ed?** ist das patentrechtlich geschützt?
[3] *adj* **(a)** (*obvious*) offensichtlich. **(b)** (*~ed*) *invention* patentiert ◆ **he's got his own ~ method for doing that** (*fig*) dafür hat er seine Spezialmethode; **his ~ remedy for hangovers** (*fig*) sein Patent- *or* Spezialrezept gegen Kater.

patentable [ˈpeɪtəntəbl] *adj* patentierbar, patentfähig.

patent: ~ application *n* Patentanmeldung *f*; **~ attorney** *n* Patentanwalt *m*/-anwältin *f*.

patentee [ˌpeɪtənˈtiː] *n* Patentinhaber(in *f*) *m*.

patent leather *n* Lackleder *nt* ◆ **~ shoes** Lackschuhe *pl*.

patently [ˈpeɪtəntlɪ] *adv* offenkundig, offensichtlich ◆ **~ obvious/clear** ganz offensichtlich/klar; **I would have thought that was ~ obvious** ich würde meinen, das liegt doch auf der Hand.

patent: ~ medicine *n* patentrechtlich geschütztes Arzneimittel; **P~ Office** *n* Patentamt *nt*.

patentor [ˌpeɪtənˈtɔːʳ] *n* Patentgeber *m*.

pater [ˈpeɪtəʳ] *n* (*dated Brit inf*) Herr Vater (*dated*).

paterfamilias [ˈpɑːtəfəˈmiːlɪəs] *n* Familienvater, Paterfamilias (*geh*) *m*.

paternal [pəˈtɜːnl] *adj* väterlich ◆ **my ~ uncle/grandmother** *etc* mein Onkel *m*/meine Großmutter *etc* väterlicherseits.

paternalism [pəˈtɜːnəlɪzəm] *n* Bevormundung *f*.

paternalist [pəˈtɜːnəlɪst] *n* Patriarch *m*.

paternalist(ic) [pəˈtɜːnəlɪst, pəˌtɜːnəˈlɪstɪk] *adj*, **paternalistically** [pəˈtɜːnəˈlɪstɪkəlɪ] *adv* patriarchalisch.

paternally [pəˈtɜːnəlɪ] *adv see adj*.

paternity [pəˈtɜːnɪtɪ] *n* Vaterschaft *f* ◆ **~ suit** Vaterschaftsprozeß *m*; **~ leave** Vaterschaftsurlaub *m*; **he denied ~ of the child** er bestritt die Vaterschaft an dem Kind.

paternoster [ˈpætəˈnɒstəʳ] *n* (*prayer*) Vaterunser, Paternoster *nt*; (*~ bead*) Vaterunser-Perle *f*; (*lift*) Paternoster *m*.

path [pɑːθ] *n* **(a)** (*lit*) (*trodden*) Weg, Pfad *m*; (*surfaced*) Weg *m*; (*in field*) Feldweg *m* ◆ **we took a ~ across the fields** wir nahmen den Weg über das Feld.
(b) (*trajectory, route*) Bahn *f*; (*of hurricane*) Weg *m*.
(c) (*fig*) Weg *m* ◆ **the Christian ~** der Weg des Christentums; **the ~ of** *or* **to salvation** der Weg des Heils; **the ~ of virtue** der Pfad der Tugend.
(d) (*Comput*) Pfad *m*.

pathetic [pəˈθetɪk] *adj* **(a)** (*piteous*) mitleiderregend ◆ **the exhausted refugees made a ~ sight** die erschöpften Flüchtlinge boten ein Bild des Jammers; **it was ~ to see** es war ein Bild des Jammers.
(b) (*poor*) erbärmlich, jämmerlich ◆ **it's ~** es ist zum Weinen *or* Heulen (*inf*); **what a ~ bunch they are!** oh, was ist das für ein jämmerlicher Haufen!; **honestly you're ~, can't you even boil an egg?** ehrlich, dich kann man zu nichts brauchen, kannst du nicht einmal ein Ei kochen?
(c) the ~ fallacy die Vermenschlichung der Natur.

pathetically [pəˈθetɪkəlɪ] *adv* **(a)** (*piteously*) mitleiderregend ◆ **he limped along ~** es war ein mitleiderregender Anblick, wie er einherhumpelte; **~ thin/weak** erschreckend dünn/schwach.
(b) *slow, stupid, inefficient* erbärmlich ◆ **a ~ inadequate answer** eine äußerst dürftige Antwort; **a ~ weak attempt** ein kläglicher Versuch; **~ incapable** absolut unfähig; **the goalie dived ~ late** es war zum Weinen, wie spät sich der Torwart nach dem Ball warf; **the trains are ~ late** es ist zum Weinen *or* ein Jammer, wie unpünktlich die Züge sind; **it had become ~ obvious that she was ignoring him** es war schon peinlich zu sehen, wie sie ihn ignorierte.

path: ~finder *n* (*lit*) Führer *m*; (*fig: innovator*) Wegbereiter(in *f*) *m*; **~less** *adj* weglos; **~ name** *n* (*Comput*) Pfad *m*.

pathogen [ˈpæθədʒɪn] *n* (*Med*) Krankheitserreger *m*.

pathogenic [ˌpæθəˈdʒenɪk] *adj* pathogen, krankheitserregend.

pathological [ˌpæθəˈlɒdʒɪkəl] *adj* (*lit, fig*) pathologisch, krankhaft; *studies etc* pathologisch, Pathologie-.

pathologist [pəˈθɒlədʒɪst] *n* Pathologe *m*, Pathologin *f*.

pathology [pəˈθɒlədʒɪ] *n* (*science*) Pathologie *f* ◆ **the ~ of a disease** das Krankheitsbild.

pathos [ˈpeɪθɒs] *n* Pathos *nt*.

pathway [ˈpɑːθweɪ] *n see* **path (a)**.

patience [ˈpeɪʃəns] *n* **(a)** Geduld *f* ◆ **to have ~/no ~ (with sb/sth)** Geduld/keine Geduld (mit jdm/etw) haben; **to have no ~ with sb/sth** (*fig inf: dislike*) für jdn/etw nichts übrig haben; **to lose (one's) ~ (with sb/sth)** (mit jdm/etw) die Geduld verlieren; **~ is a virtue** (*prov*) Geduld ist eine Tugend; **~, ~!** nur Geduld!, immer mit der Ruhe!; *see* **possess**.
(b) (*Brit Cards*) Patience *f* ◆ **to play ~** eine Patience legen.

patient [ˈpeɪʃənt] [1] *adj* geduldig ◆ **a ~ piece of work** eine mit sehr viel Geduld angefertigte Arbeit; **~ endurance** zähe Geduld; **to be ~ with sb/sth** mit jdm/etw geduldig sein; **you must be very ~ about it** du mußt sehr viel Geduld haben *or* sehr geduldig sein; **we have been ~ long enough!** unsere Geduld ist erschöpft!
[2] *n* Patient(in *f*) *m*.

patiently [ˈpeɪʃəntlɪ] *adv see adj* ◆ **a very ~ reconstructed picture of Babylonian life** ein mit Akribie rekonstruiertes Bild babylonischer Lebensweise.

patina [ˈpætɪnə] *n* Patina *f*.

patio [ˈpætɪəʊ] *n* Veranda, Terrasse *f*; (*inner court*) Innenhof, Patio *m* ◆ **~ door** Terrassentür *f*.

patois [ˈpætwɑː] *n* Mundart *f*.

patriarch [ˈpeɪtrɪɑːk] *n* Patriarch *m*.

patriarchal [ˌpeɪtrɪˈɑːkəl] *adj* patriarchalisch.

patriarchy [ˌpeɪtrɪˈɑːkɪ] *n* Patriarchat *nt*.

patrician [pəˈtrɪʃən] [1] *adj* patrizisch ◆ **the ~ classes** das Patriziertum; **the old ~ houses** die alten Patrizierhäuser.
[2] *n* Patrizier(in *f*) *m*.

patricide [ˈpætrɪsaɪd] *n* Vatermord *m*; (*murderer*) Vatermörder(in *f*) *m*.

patrimony [ˈpætrɪmənɪ] *n* Patrimonium *nt*.

patriot [ˈpeɪtrɪət] *n* Patriot(in *f*) *m*.

patriotic *adj*, **~ally** *adv* [ˌpætrɪˈɒtɪk, -əlɪ] patriotisch.

patriotism [ˈpætrɪətɪzəm] *n* Patriotismus *m*, Vaterlandsliebe *f*.

patrol [pəˈtrəʊl] [1] *n* **(a)** (*patrolling*) (*by police*) Streife *f*; (*by aircraft, ship*) Patrouille *f*; (*by watchman etc*) Runde *f*, Rundgang *m* ◆ **the army/navy carry out** *or* **make weekly ~s of the area** das Heer/die Marine patrouilliert das Gebiet wöchentlich; **the army/navy maintain a constant ~** das Heer/die Marine

führt ständige Patrouillen durch; **on ~** (*Mil*) auf Patrouille; (*police*) auf Streife; (*guard dogs, squad car, detectives*) im Einsatz.
(b) (~ *unit*) (*Mil*) Patrouille *f*; (*police* ~) (Polizei)streife *f*; (*of boy scouts*) Fähnlein *nt*; (*of girl guides*) Gilde *f*.
[2] *vt* (*Mil*) *district, waters, sky, streets* patrouillieren, patrouillieren in (+*dat*); *frontier, coast* patrouillieren, patrouillieren vor (+*dat*); (*policeman, watchman*) seine Runden machen in (+*dat*); (*police car*) Streife fahren in (+*dat*); (*guard dogs, gamewarden*) einen Rund- *or* Streifengang *or* eine Runde machen in (+*dat*) ◆ **the frontier is not ~led** die Grenze wird nicht bewacht *or* ist unbewacht.
[3] *vi* (*soldiers, ships, planes*) patrouillieren; (*planes also*) Patrouille fliegen; (*policemen*) eine Streife/Streifen machen; (*watchman, store detective etc*) seine Runden machen ◆ **to ~ up and down** auf und ab gehen.

patrol: ~ boat *n* Patrouillenboot *nt*; **~ car** *n* Streifenwagen *m*; **~ leader** *n* (*of scouts*) Fähnleinführer *m*; (*of girl guides*) Gildenführerin *f*; **~man** *n* Wächter *m*; (*US: policeman*) Polizist *m*; **~ wagon** *n* (*US*) grüne Minna (*inf*), Gefangenenwagen *m*; **~woman** *n* (*US: policewoman*) Polizistin *f*.

patron ['peɪtrən] *n* (*customer of shop*) Kunde *m*, Kundin *f*; (*customer of restaurant, hotel*) Gast *m*; (*of society*) Schirmherr(in *f*) *m*; (*of artist*) Förderer, Gönner(in *f*) *m*; (~ *saint*) Schutzpatron(in *f*) *m* ◆ **~s only** nur für Kunden/Gäste; **a ~ of the arts** ein Kunstmäzen *m*; **our ~s** (*of shop*) unsere Kundschaft.

patronage ['pætrənɪdʒ] *n* **(a)** (*support*) Schirmherrschaft *f* ◆ **under the ~ of ...** unter der Schirmherrschaft des/der ...; **his lifelong ~ of the arts** seine lebenslange Förderung der Künste.
(b) (*form: of a shop etc*) **we enjoy the ~ of ...** zu unseren Kunden zählen ...; **we thank you for your ~** wir danken Ihnen für Ihr Vertrauen; **the attitude of the new sales assistant caused her to withdraw her ~** das Benehmen des neuen Verkäufers veranlaßte sie, dort nicht mehr einzukaufen.
(c) (*right to appoint to government jobs*) Patronat *nt* ◆ **under (the) ~ of** unter der Schirmherrschaft von.
(d) (*rare: condescension*) **an air of ~** eine gönnerhafte Miene.

patronize ['pætrənaɪz] *vt* **(a)** *pub, cinema etc* besuchen; *the railway* benutzen ◆ **I hope you will continue to ~ our store** ich hoffe, daß Sie uns weiterhin beehren; **it's not a shop I ~** in dem Geschäft kaufe ich nicht; **the shop is well ~d** das Geschäft hat viel Kundschaft.
(b) (*treat condescendingly*) gönnerhaft *or* herablassend behandeln, von oben herab behandeln.
(c) (*support*) *the arts etc* unterstützen, fördern.

patronizing ['pætrənaɪzɪŋ] *adj* gönnerhaft, herablassend ◆ **to be ~ to** *or* **towards sb** jdn herablassend *or* von oben herab behandeln; **there's no need to be so ~** du brauchst gar nicht so herablassend *or* von oben herab zu tun.

patronizingly ['pætrənaɪzɪŋlɪ] *adv see adj* ◆ **a ~ tolerant attitude** herablassende Nachsicht.

patronymic [,pætrə'nɪmɪk] [1] *adj* patronymisch.
[2] *n* Patronymikon *nt*, Vatersname *m*.

patsy ['pætsɪ] *n* (*US sl*) (*scapegoat*) Sündenbock *m*; (*easy victim*) Leichtgläubige(r) *mf*; (*weak man*) Schlappschwanz (*inf*), Schwächling *m*.

patten ['pætən] *n* Stelzenschuh *m*.

patter ['pætə^r] [1] *n* **(a)** (*of feet*) Getrippel *nt*; (*of rain*) Platschen *nt* ◆ **the ~ of tiny feet** (*fig*) Kindergetrappel *nt*.
(b) (*of salesman, comedian, conjurer, disc jockey*) Sprüche *pl* (*inf*) ◆ **to start one's ~** seine Sprüche loslassen; **you'll never pick up a girl unless you're good with the ~** du wirst nie eine Freundin aufreißen, wenn du nicht gut quatschen kannst (*inf*); **to have a good line in ~** (*of comedian, disc jockey etc*) gute Sprüche drauf *or* auf Lager haben (*inf*); **sales ~** Vertretersprüche *pl*.
(c) (*inf: jargon*) Fachjargon *m* (*inf*).
[2] *vi* (*person, feet*) trippeln; (*rain: also* **~ down**) platschen.

patter-merchant ['pætə,mɜːtʃənt] *n* (*inf*) Schönredner, Sprücheklopfer (*inf*) *m*.

pattern ['pætən] [1] *n* **(a)** Muster *nt* ◆ **to make a ~** ein Muster bilden.
(b) (*Sew*) Schnitt *m*, Schnittmuster *nt*; (*Knitting*) Strickanleitung *f*.
(c) (*fig: model*) Vorbild *nt* ◆ **according to a ~** nach einem (festen) Schema; **on the ~ of Albania, on the Albanian ~** nach albanischem Vorbild *or* Muster; **to set a** *or* **the ~ for sth** ein Muster *or* Vorbild für etw sein.
(d) (*fig: in events, behaviour etc*) Muster *nt*; (*set*) Schema *nt*; (*recurrent*) Regelmäßigkeit *f* ◆ **there's a distinct ~/no ~ to these crimes** in diesen Verbrechen steckt ein bestimmtes/kein Schema; **what ~ can we find in these events?** was verbindet diese Ereignisse?; **the ~ of events leading up to the war** der Ablauf der Ereignisse, die zum Krieg geführt haben; **a certain ~ emerged** es ließ sich ein gewisses Schema *or* Muster erkennen; **to follow the usual ~** nach dem üblichen Schema verlaufen; **behaviour ~s** Verhaltensmuster *pl*; **the natural ~ of life in the wild** die natürlichen Lebensvorgänge in der Wildnis; **the day-by-day ~ of his existence** die tägliche Routine seines Lebens; **the town's new buildings follow the usual ~ of concrete and glass** die Neubauten der Stadt entsprechen dem üblichen Baustil aus Beton und Glas; **it's the usual ~, the rich get richer and the poor get poorer** es läuft immer nach demselben Muster ab — die Reichen werden reicher und die Armen ärmer.
(e) (*verb ~, sentence ~ etc*) Struktur *f*.
[2] *vt* **(a)** (*model*) machen (*on* nach) ◆ **this design is ~ed on one I saw in a magazine** die Idee für dieses Muster habe ich aus einer Illustrierten; **many countries ~ their laws on the Roman system** viele Länder orientieren sich bei ihrer Gesetzgebung an dem römischen Vorbild; **to be ~ed on sth** einer Sache (*dat*) nachgebildet sein; (*music, poem, style etc*) einer Sache (*dat*) nachempfunden sein; **to ~ oneself on sb** sich (*dat*) jdn zum Vorbild nehmen; **he ~ed his lifestyle on that of a country squire** er ahmte den Lebensstil eines Landadligen nach.
(b) (*put ~s on*) mit einen Muster versehen; *see* **patterned**.

pattern book *n* Musterbuch *nt*.

patterned ['pætənd] *adj* gemustert.

patty ['pætɪ] *n* Pastetchen *nt*.

paucity ['pɔːsɪtɪ] *n* (*liter*) Mangel *m* (*of* an +*dat*).

Paul [pɔːl] *n* Paul *m*; (*Bibl*) Paulus *m*.

Pauline ['pɔːlaɪn] *adj* paulinisch.

paunch [pɔːntʃ] *n* Bauch, Wanst *m*; (*of cow etc*) Pansen *m*.

paunchy ['pɔːntʃɪ] *adj* (+*er*) dick ◆ **to be getting ~** einen (dicken) Bauch kriegen.

pauper ['pɔːpə^r] *n* Arme(r) *mf*; (*supported by charity*) Almosenempfänger(in *f*) *m* ◆ **~'s grave** Armengrab *nt*; **we are spiritual ~s** wir sind geistig verarmt.

pauperism ['pɔːpərɪzəm] *n* (*lit, fig*) Armut *f*.

pauperization [,pɔːpəraɪ'zeɪʃən] *n* Verarmung *f*; (*fig also*) Verkümmerung *f*.

pauperize ['pɔːpəraɪz] *vt* arm machen; (*fig*) verkümmern lassen.

pause [pɔːz] [1] *n* Pause *f* ◆ **a hesitant ~** ein kurzes Zögern; **an anxious/a pregnant ~** ein ängstliches/vielsagendes Schweigen; **there was a ~ while ...** es entstand eine Pause, während ...; **to have a ~** (eine) Pause machen; **without (a) ~** ohne Unterbrechung, pausenlos, ununterbrochen; **to give sb ~** (*esp liter*) jdm zu denken geben, jdn nachdenklich stimmen.
[2] *vi* **(a)** stehenbleiben, stoppen (*inf*); (*speaker*) innehalten ◆ **can't we ~ for a bit, I'm exhausted** können wir nicht eine kurze Pause machen, ich bin erschöpft; **the shooting ~d while they negotiated** das Feuer ruhte während der Verhandlungen; **he ~d dramatically** er legte eine Kunstpause ein; **~ before you act** überlege erst mal, bevor du etwas tust; **he ~d for breath/a drink** er machte eine Pause, um Luft zu holen/etwas zu trinken; **he spoke for thirty minutes without once pausing** er sprach eine halbe Stunde ohne eine einzige Pause; **let's ~ here** machen wir hier Pause; **it made him ~** das machte ihn nachdenklich.
(b) (*dwell on*) **to ~ (up)on sth** auf etw (*acc*) näher eingehen.

pave [peɪv] *vt* befestigen (*in, with* mit); *road, path* (*with stones also*) pflastern; *floor* (*with tiles*) fliesen, mit Fliesen auslegen; (*with slabs*) mit Platten auslegen ◆ **to ~ the way for sb/sth** (*fig*) jdm/einer Sache (*dat*) den Weg ebnen; **where the streets are ~d with gold** wo die Straßen mit Gold gepflastert sind, wo das Geld auf der Straße liegt; **the path to hell is ~d with good intentions** (*prov*) der Weg zur Hölle ist mit guten Vorsätzen gepflastert (*prov*); **the paths are ~d in** *or* **with purest marble** die Wege sind mit feinstem Marmor ausgelegt.

◆**pave over** *vt sep* betonieren; (*with slabs*) mit Platten auslegen.

pavement ['peɪvmənt] *n* (*Brit*) Gehsteig, Bürgersteig *m*, Trottoir *nt*; (*US: paved road*) Straße *f*; (*material*) Bodenbelag *m* ◆ **to leave the ~** (*US Aut*) von der Straße abkommen; **~ artist** Pflastermaler(in *f*) *m*.

pavilion [pə'vɪlɪən] *n* Pavillon *m*; (*old: tent*) Zelt *nt*; (*Sport*) (*changing* ~) Umkleideräume *pl*; (*clubhouse*) Klubhaus *nt*.

paving ['peɪvɪŋ] *n* Belag *m*; (*US: of road*) Decke *f*; (*material*) Belag *m*; (*action*) Pflastern *nt* ◆ **~ stone** Platte *f*.

Pavlovian [pæv'ləʊvɪən] *adj* Pawlowsch *attr*.

paw¹ [pɔː] [1] *n* (*of animal*) Pfote *f*; (*of lion, bear*) Pranke, Tatze *f*; (*pej inf: hand*) Pfote *f* (*inf*) ◆ **keep your ~s off!** Pfoten weg! (*inf*).
[2] *vt* **(a)** tätscheln; (*lion etc*) mit der Pfote *or* Tatze berühren ◆ **to ~ the ground** (*lit*) scharren; (*fig: be impatient*) ungeduldig *or* kribbelig (*inf*) werden.
(b) (*pej inf: handle*) betatschen (*inf*).
[3] *vi* **to ~ at sb/sth** jdn/etw betätscheln *or* betatschen (*inf*).

paw² *n* (*US dial inf*) Pa *m* (*inf*).

pawl [pɔːl] *n* Sperrklinke *f*.

pawn¹ [pɔːn] *n* (*Chess*) Bauer *m*; (*fig*) Schachfigur *f*.

pawn² [1] *n* (*security*) Pfand *nt* ◆ **in ~** verpfändet, versetzt; **to leave** *or* **put sth in ~** etw versetzen *or* auf die Pfandleihe *or* ins Leihhaus bringen; **the company is in ~ to foreigners** das Unternehmen ist an ausländische Kapitalgeber verpfändet.
[2] *vt* verpfänden, versetzen ◆ **he had ~ed his soul to the devil** er hatte seine Seele dem Teufel verpfändet.

pawn: ~broker *n* Pfandleiher *m*; **~broker's (shop), ~shop** *n* Pfandhaus, Leihhaus *nt*; **~ ticket** *n* Pfandschein, Leihschein *m*.

pawpaw ['pɔːpɔː] *n* Papaya *f*.

pax [pæks] *interj* (*Brit*) Friede.

pay [peɪ] (*vb: pret, ptp* **paid**) [1] *n* Lohn *m*; (*of salaried employee*) Gehalt *nt*; (*Mil*) Sold *m*; (*of civil servant*) Gehalt *nt*, Bezüge *pl*, Besoldung *f* ◆ **what's the ~ like?** wie ist die Bezahlung?; **it comes out of my ~** es wird mir vom Gehalt/Lohn abgezogen; **a low-~ country** ein Land mit niedrigen Löhnen, ein Niedriglohnland; **the discussions were about ~** in den Diskussionen ging es um die Löhne/Gehälter; **to be in sb's ~** für jdn arbeiten.
[2] *vt* **(a)** *money, a sum, person, bill, duty, debt, charge, account, fee* bezahlen; *interest, a sum, duty, charge also* zahlen; *dividend* ausschütten, zahlen ◆ **to ~ sb £10** jdm £ 10 zahlen; **to ~ shareholders** Dividenden ausschütten *or* zahlen; **how much is there to ~?** was macht das?; **to be** *or* **get paid** (*in regular job*) seinen Lohn/sein Gehalt bekommen; **when do I get paid for doing that?** wann bekomme ich mein Geld dafür?, wann werde ich dafür bezahlt?; **savings accounts that ~ 5%** Sparkonten, die 5% Zinsen bringen; **I ~ you to prevent such mistakes** Sie werden schließlich dafür bezahlt, daß solche Fehler nicht vorkommen; **"paid"** (*on bill*) „bezahlt"; *see* **paid**.
(b) (*lit, fig: be profitable to*) sich lohnen für; (*honesty*) sich auszahlen für ◆ **if it**

doesn't ~ them to work more wenn es sich für sie nicht lohnt, mehr zu arbeiten; **in future it would ~ you to ask** in Zukunft solltest du besser vorher fragen; **but it paid him in the long run** aber auf die Dauer hat es sich doch ausgezahlt.

(c) **to ~ (sb/a place) a visit** *or* **call, to ~ a visit to** *or* **a call on sb/a place** jdn/einen Ort besuchen; (*more formal*) jdm/einem Ort einen Besuch abstatten; **to ~ a visit to the doctor** den Arzt aufsuchen; *see* **attention, compliment, respect.**

[3] *vi* **(a)** zahlen ◆ **to ~ on account** auf Rechnung zahlen; **they ~ well for this sort of work** diese Arbeit wird gut bezahlt; **no, no, I'm ~ing** nein, nein, ich (be)zahle; **I'd like to know what I'm ~ing for** ich wüßte gern, für was ich eigentlich mein Geld ausgebe; **to ~ for sth** etw bezahlen; **it's already paid for** es ist schon bezahlt; **how much did you ~ for it?** wieviel hast du dafür bezahlt?; **to ~ for sb** für jdn zahlen; **I'll ~ for you this time** dieses Mal zahle ich; **they paid for her to go to America** sie zahlten ihr die Reise nach Amerika.

(b) (*be profitable*) sich lohnen ◆ **it's a business that ~s** es ist ein rentables Geschäft; **it's ~ing at last** es zahlt sich schließlich doch aus; **crime doesn't ~** (*prov*) Verbrechen lohnt sich nicht.

(c) (*fig: to suffer*) **to ~ for sth (with sth)** für etw (mit etw) bezahlen; **you'll ~ for that!** dafür wirst du (mir) büßen; **to make sb ~ (for sth)** jdn für etw büßen lassen; **I'll make you ~ for this!** das wirst du mir büßen, das werde ich dir heimzahlen!

◆**pay back** *vt sep* **(a)** *money* zurückzahlen ◆ **when do you want me to ~ you ~?** wann willst du das Geld wiederhaben?; **~ me ~ when you like** zahl's *or* gib's mir zurück, wenn du willst.

(b) *compliment, visit* erwidern; *insult, trick* sich revanchieren für ◆ **to ~ sb ~** es jdm heimzahlen.

◆**pay in** [1] *vt sep* einzahlen ◆ **to ~ money ~to an account** Geld auf ein Konto einzahlen.

[2] *vi* einzahlen.

◆**pay off** [1] *vt sep workmen* auszahlen; *seamen* abmustern; *debt* abbezahlen, tilgen; *HP* ab(be)zahlen; *mortgage* abtragen; *creditor* befriedigen ◆ **if this happens again we'll have to ~ him ~** wenn das noch einmal vorkommt, müssen wir ihn entlassen.

[2] *vi* sich auszahlen.

◆**pay out** [1] *vt sep* **(a)** *money* (*spend*) ausgeben; (*count out*) auszahlen. **(b)** *rope* ablaufen lassen.

[2] *vi* bezahlen.

◆**pay over** *vt sep* aushändigen.

◆**pay up** [1] *vt sep what one owes* zurückzahlen; *subscription* bezahlen ◆ **his account/he is paid ~** er hat alles bezahlt; *see* **paid-up.**

[2] *vi* zahlen.

payable ['peɪəbl] *adj* zahlbar; (*due*) fällig ◆ **~ to order** zahlbar an Order; **to make a cheque ~ to sb** einen Scheck auf jdn ausstellen.

pay: ~-as-you-earn *attr* **~-as-you-earn tax system** *Steuersystem nt, bei dem die Lohnsteuer direkt einbehalten wird*; **~ award** *n* Gehalts-/Lohnerhöhung *f*; **~-bed** *n* Privatbett *nt*; **~ cheque** *n* Lohn-/Gehaltsüberweisung *f*; **~-claim** *n* Lohn-/Gehaltsforderung *f*; **~-day** *n* Zahltag *m*; **~ dirt** *n* abbauwürdiges Erzlager.

PAYE (*Brit*) *abbr of* **pay-as-you-earn.**

payee [peɪ'iː] *n* Zahlungsempfänger *m*.

payer ['peɪəʳ] *n* Zahler *m* ◆ **slow ~** säumiger Zahler.

pay: ~ freeze *n* Lohnstopp *m*; **~ increase** *n* Lohn-/Gehaltserhöhung *f*.

paying ['peɪɪŋ] *adj* **(a)** (*profitable*) rentabel. **(b) ~ guest** zahlender Gast; **~ patient** Privatpatient(in *f*) *m*.

paying-in slip [ˌpeɪɪŋ'ɪnˌslɪp] *n* Einzahlungsschein *m*.

pay: ~load *n* Nutzlast *f*; (*of bomber*) Bombenlast *f*; **~master** *n* Zahlmeister *m*; **P~master General** *für Lohn- und Gehaltszahlungen im öffentlichen Dienst zuständiges Kabinettsmitglied.*

payment ['peɪmənt] *n* (*paying*) (*of person*) Bezahlung, Entlohnung *f*; (*of bill, instalment etc*) Bezahlung, Begleichung *f*; (*of debt, mortgage*) Abtragung, Rückzahlung *f*; (*of interest, bank charge etc*) Zahlung *f*; (*sum paid*) Zahlung *f*; (*fig: reward*) Belohnung *f* ◆ **three monthly ~s** drei Monatsraten; **as** *or* **in ~ of a debt/bill** in Begleichung einer Schuld/Rechnung; **as** *or* **in ~ for goods/his services** als Bezahlung für *or* von Waren/für seine Dienste; **to accept sth as** *or* **in ~ (for ...)** etw in Begleichung/als Bezahlung (für ...) annehmen; **on ~ of** bei Begleichung/Bezahlung von; **without ~** (*free*) umsonst; **to make a ~** eine Zahlung leisten; **to make a ~ on sth** eine Rate für etw zahlen; **to present sth for ~** etw zur Zahlung vorlegen; **to stop ~s** die Zahlungen *pl* einstellen; **to stop ~ of a cheque** einen Scheck sperren.

pay: ~ negotiations *npl see* **~ talks**; **~-off** *n* (*inf: bribe*) Bestechungsgeld *nt*; (*final outcome, climax*) Quittung *f*; (*of joke*) Pointe *f*.

payola [peɪ'əʊlə] *n* (*esp US*) (*bribery*) Bestechung *f*; (*bribe*) Schmiergeld *nt*.

pay: ~ packet *n* Lohntüte *f*; **~-per-view** *adj attr television, service* Pay-per-View; **~-per-view channel** Pay-per-View-Kanal *m*; **~ phone** *n* Münzfernsprecher *m*; **~ rise** *n* Lohn-/Gehaltserhöhung *f*; **~roll** *n* **they have 500 people on the ~roll** sie haben eine Belegschaft von 500, sie haben 500 Beschäftigte; **a monthly ~roll of £75,000** eine monatliche Lohn- und Gehaltssumme von £ 75.000; **~ round** *n* Tarifrunde *f*; **~slip** *n* Lohn-/Gehaltsstreifen *m*; **~ station** *n* (*US*) öffentlicher Fernsprecher; **~ talks** *npl* Lohnverhandlungen *pl*; (*for profession, area of industry*) Tarifverhandlungen *pl*; **~ tone** *n bei öffentlichen Fernsprechern: Ton, der anzeigt, daß Münzen eingeworfen werden müssen*; **~ TV** *n* Münzfernseher *m*.

PBX *abbr of* **private branch exchange** Nebenstellenanlage *f*.

PC (*Brit*) *abbr of* **(a) Police Constable. (b) Privy Council. (c) Privy Councillor. (d) personal computer** PC *m*. **(e) politically correct.**

pc *abbr of* **(a) post card. (b) per cent.**

PCB *abbr of* **printed circuit board.**

pcm *abbr of* **per calendar month** monatl ◆ **"Rent £230 ~"** „Miete £230 monatl."

pd *abbr of* **paid** bez.

PDQ (*inf*) *abbr of* **pretty damned quick** verdammt schnell (*inf*).

PDSA *abbr of* **People's Dispensary for Sick Animals** kostenloses Behandlungszentrum für Haustiere.

PDT (*US*) *abbr of* **Pacific Daylight Time** pazifische Sommerzeit.

PE *abbr of* **physical education.**

pea [piː] *n* Erbse *f* ◆ **they are as like as two ~s (in a pod)** sie gleichen sich (*dat*) wie ein Ei dem anderen.

peace [piːs] *n* **(a)** (*freedom from war*) Frieden, Friede (*geh*) *m* ◆ **the Versailles** *etc* **~** der Friede von Versailles *etc*; **a man of ~** ein friedfertiger *or* friedliebender Mensch; **to be at ~ with sb/sth** mit jdm/etw in Frieden leben; **the two countries are now at ~** zwischen den beiden Ländern herrscht jetzt Frieden; **to be at ~ with oneself** mit sich (*dat*) selbst in Frieden leben; **he is at ~** (*euph: dead*) er ruht in Frieden; **to hold one's ~** schweigen; **to make (one's) ~ (with sb)** sich (mit jdm) versöhnen *or* aussöhnen; **to make (one's) ~ with oneself** mit sich (*dat*) selbst ins reine kommen; **to make ~ between ...** Frieden stiften zwischen (*+dat*) ...; **to make one's ~ with the world** seinen Frieden mit der Welt schließen.

(b) (*Jur*) öffentliche (Ruhe und) Ordnung ◆ **the (King's/Queen's) ~** (*Jur*) die öffentliche Ordnung; **to keep the ~** (*Jur*) (*demonstrator, citizen*) die öffentliche Ordnung wahren; (*policeman*) die öffentliche Ordnung aufrechterhalten; (*fig*) Frieden bewahren.

(c) (*tranquillity, quiet*) Ruhe *f* ◆ **~ of mind** innere Ruhe, Seelenfrieden *m*; **the P~ of God** der Friede Gottes, Gottes Friede; **~ and quiet** Ruhe und Frieden; **to give sb some ~** jdn in Ruhe *or* Frieden lassen; **to give sb no ~** jdm keine Ruhe lassen; **to get some/no ~** zur Ruhe/nicht zur Ruhe kommen.

peaceable ['piːsəbl] *adj settlement, discussion* friedlich; *person, nature also* friedfertig, friedliebend.

peaceably ['piːsəblɪ] *adv see adj.*

peace: ~ campaign *n* Friedenskampagne *f*; **~ campaigner** *n* Friedenskämpfer(in *f*) *m*; **~ conference** *n* Friedenskonferenz *f*; **P~ Corps** *n* (*US*) Friedenskorps *nt*; **~ dividend** *n* Friedensdividende *f*.

peaceful ['piːsfʊl] *adj* friedlich; (*peaceable*) *nation, person etc* friedfertig, friedliebend; (*calm, undisturbed*) *holiday, sleep etc* ruhig; *death* sanft; *use of nuclear power* für friedliche Zwecke ◆ **a ~ transition to independence** die Erlangung der Unabhängigkeit auf friedlichem Wege; **he had a ~ reign** während seiner Regierungszeit herrschte Frieden; **I didn't get a ~ moment all day long** ich bin den ganzen Tag keine Sekunde zur Ruhe gekommen.

peacefully ['piːsfəlɪ] *adv* friedlich ◆ **to die ~ (in one's sleep)** sanft sterben *or* entschlafen (*liter*).

peacefulness ['piːsfʊlnɪs] *n see adj* Friedlichkeit *f*; Friedfertigkeit, Friedensliebe *f*; Ruhe *f*; Sanftheit *f* ◆ **the ~ of the takeover/the demonstration** der friedliche Charakter des Machtwechsels/der Demonstration; **the ~ of a summer's evening** die friedliche Atmosphäre eines Sommerabends.

peace: ~ initiative *n* Friedensinitiative *f*; **~keeper** *n* Friedenswächter *m*; **~keeping** [1] *n* Friedenssicherung *f*; [2] *adj* Friedens-; **UN troops have a purely ~keeping role** die UN-Truppen sind eine reine Friedenstruppe; **a ~keeping operation** Maßnahmen *pl* zur Sicherung des Friedens; **~-loving** *adj* friedliebend; **~maker** *n* Friedensstifter(in *f*) *m*; **~ movement** *n* Friedensbewegung *f*; **~ offensive** *n* Friedensoffensive *f*; **~-offering** *n* Friedensangebot *nt*; (*fig*) Versöhnungsgeschenk *nt*; **~-pipe** *n* Friedenspfeife *f*; **~ studies** *npl* Friedensforschung *f*; **~ talks** *npl* Friedensverhandlungen *pl*; **~time** [1] *n* Friedenszeiten *pl*; [2] *adj* in Friedenszeiten.

peach [piːtʃ] [1] *n* **(a)** (*fruit*) Pfirsich *m*; (*tree*) Pfirsichbaum *m* ◆ **~ Melba** Pfirsich Melba *m*; **her complexion is like ~es and cream, she has a ~es-and-cream complexion** sie hat eine Haut wie ein Pfirsich, sie hat eine Pfirsichhaut.

(b) (*inf*) **she's a ~** sie ist klasse (*inf*); **it's a ~** das ist prima *or* klasse *or* Spitze (*all inf*); **a ~ of a girl/dress/film** *etc* ein klasse Mädchen/Kleid/Film *etc* (*all inf*).

(c) (*colour*) Pfirsichton *m*.

[2] *adj* pfirsichfarben.

pea: ~cock *n* Pfau *m*; (*fig: man*) Geck *m*; **to strut like a ~cock** wie ein Pfau einherstolzieren; **~cock blue** *adj* pfauenblau; **~-green** *adj* erbsengrün; **~hen** *n* Pfauenhenne *f*; **~-jacket** *n* (*esp US*) Pijacke *f*.

peak [piːk] [1] *n* **(a)** (*of mountain*) Gipfel *m*; (*of roof*) First *m*; (*sharp point*) Spitze *f*.

(b) (*of cap*) Schirm *m*.

(c) (*maximum*) Höhepunkt *m*; (*on graph*) Scheitelpunkt *m* ◆ **he is at the ~ of fitness** er ist in Höchstform *or* Topform (*inf*); **when the empire was at its ~** als das Reich auf dem Höhepunkt seiner Macht stand; **when demand is at its ~** wenn die Nachfrage ihren Höhepunkt erreicht hat *or* am stärksten ist.

[2] *adj attr value, voltage* Spitzen-; *production, power, pressure* Höchst- ◆ **a ~ year for new car sales** ein Rekordjahr *nt* für den Neuwagenabsatz.

[3] *vi* den Höchststand erreichen; (*athlete: reach one's best*) seine Spitzenform erreichen ◆ **to have ~ed** (*be on the way down*) auf dem absteigenden Ast sein (*inf*).

◆**peak off** *vi* zurückgehen.

◆**peak out** *vi* den Höhepunkt erreichen.

peaked [piːkt] *adj* **(a)** *cap, helmet etc* spitz. **(b)** *person, complexion etc* verhärmt, abgehärmt.

peak: ~-hour *adj* **~-hour consumption** Verbrauch *m* in der Hauptbelastungszeit; **~-hour travel costs more** in der Hauptverkehrszeit sind die öffentlichen Verkehrsmittel teurer; **measures to reduce ~-hour traffic** Maßnahmen zur Reduzierung der Belastung in der Hauptverkehrszeit; **~ hours** *npl* (*of traffic*) Hauptverkehrszeit, Stoßzeit *f*; (*Telec, Elec*) Hauptbelastungszeit *f*; **~ season** *n* Hochsaison *f*; **~ times** *npl* Hauptbelastungszeit *f*.

peaky ['pi:kɪ] *adj* (+*er*) (*Brit inf*) *complexion* blaß; *face* verhärmt, abgehärmt; *look, child* kränklich ◆ **to look ~** nicht gut aussehen, angeschlagen aussehen (*inf*).

peal [pi:l] [1] *n* **~ of bells** (*sound*) Glockengeläut(e), Glockenläuten *nt*; (*set*) Glockenspiel *nt*; **~s of laughter** schallendes Gelächter; **~ of thunder** Donnerrollen *nt*, Donnerschlag *m*.
[2] *vt* läuten.
[3] *vi* (*bell*) läuten; (*thunder*) dröhnen.

◆**peal out** *vi* verhallen ◆ **the bells ~ed ~ over the fields** das Geläut der Glocken verhallte über den Feldern.

peanut ['pi:nʌt] *n* Erdnuß *f* ◆ **~s** (*inf: not much money*) Kleingeld *nt* (*to sb* für jdn); **the pay is ~s** die Bezahlung ist miserabel *or* lächerlich (*inf*); **£2,000? that's ~s these days** £ 2.000? das ist doch ein Klacks heutzutage (*inf*); **~ butter** Erdnußbutter *f*; **~ gallery** (*US inf*) Olymp *m* (*inf*).

peapod ['pi:pɒd] *n* Erbsenschote *f*.

pear [pɛəʳ] *n* Birne *f*; (*tree*) Birnbaum *m*.

pear: ~drop *n* (*pendant*) tropfenförmiger Anhänger *m*; (*sweet*) *hartes Bonbon in Birnenform*; **~-drop** *adj earring etc* tropfenförmig.

pearl[1] [pɜ:l] *n, vt, vi see* **purl**.

pearl[2] [1] *n* (*lit, fig*) Perle *f*; (*mother-of-~*) Perlmutt *nt*; (*of sweat etc*) Perle *f*, Tropfen *m*; (*colour*) Grauweiß *nt* ◆ **~ of wisdom** weiser Spruch; **to cast ~s before swine** (*prov*) Perlen *pl* vor die Säue werfen (*prov*).
[2] *adj* Perlen-; (*~-coloured*) grauweiß.

pearl: ~ barley *n* Perlgraupen *pl*; **~ blue** *adj* silberblau; **~ fisher** *n* Perlenfischer(in *f*) *m*; **~ fishing** *n* Perlenfischerei *f*; **~ grey** *adj* silbergrau; **~-handled** *adj* perlmuttbesetzt; **~ oyster** *n* Perlenauster *f*.

pearly ['pɜ:lɪ] *adj* (+*er*) (*in colour*) perlmuttfarben ◆ **~ white** perlweiß; **~ buttons** Perlmuttknöpfe *pl*; **a ~ costume** ein Kostüm *nt* mit Perlmuttknöpfen; **~ king/queen** *Straßenverkäufer(in) in London, der/die ein mit Perlmuttknöpfen und bunten Perlen besticktes Kostüm trägt*; **P~ Gates** Himmelstür *f*.

pear-shaped ['pɛəʃeɪpt] *adj* birnenförmig.

peasant ['pezənt] [1] *n* (*lit*) (armer) Bauer; (*pej inf*) (*ignoramus*) Banause *m*; (*lout*) Bauer *m*; (*pleb*) Prolet *m*.
[2] *adj attr* bäuerlich ◆ **~ farmer** (armer) Bauer; **~ labour** Landarbeiterschaft *f*, landwirtschaftliche Arbeitskräfte *pl*; **~ woman** (arme) Bäuerin.

peasantry ['pezəntrɪ] *n* Bauernschaft *f*; (*class, status*) Bauerntum *nt*.

pease-pudding ['pi:z'pʊdɪŋ] *n* Erbspüree *nt*.

pea: ~shooter *n* Pusterohr *nt*; **~ soup** *n* Erbsensuppe *f*; **~-souper** [pi:'su:pəʳ] *n* Waschküche (*inf*), Suppe (*inf*) *f*.

peat [pi:t] *n* Torf *m*; (*piece*) Stück *nt* Torf ◆ **~bog** Torfmoor *nt*.

peaty ['pi:tɪ] *adj* (+*er*) torfig; *taste* nach Torf.

pebble ['pebl] *n* Kiesel, Kieselstein *m*; (*rock crystal*) Bergkristall *m*; (*after polishing*) Kieselglas *nt* ◆ **he/she is not the only ~ on the beach** (*inf*) es gibt noch andere.

pebble: ~-dash *n* (*Brit*) (Kiesel)rauhputz *m*; **~ glasses** *npl Brille f mit Gläsern aus Kieselglas*.

pebbly ['peblɪ] *adj* steinig.

pecan [pɪ'kæn] *n* (*nut*) Pecannuß *f*; (*tree*) Hickory *m*.

peccadillo [,pekə'dɪləʊ] *n, pl* **-(e)s** kleine Sünde; (*of youth*) Jugendsünde *f*.

peccary ['pekərɪ] *n* Pekari, Nabelschwein *nt*.

peck[1] [pek] *n* (*dry measure*) Viertelscheffel *m*.

peck[2] [1] *n* (a) (*inf: kiss*) flüchtiger Kuß *m*, Küßchen *nt*. (b) **the hen gave him a ~** die Henne hackte nach ihm.
[2] *vt* (a) (*bird*) picken. (b) (*inf: kiss*) ein Küßchen *nt* geben (+*dat*).
[3] *vi* picken (*at* nach) ◆ **he just ~ed at his food** er stocherte nur in seinem Essen herum.

◆**peck out** *vt sep* aushacken.

pecker ['pekəʳ] *n* (a) (*Brit inf*) **keep your ~ up!** halt die Ohren steif! (*inf*). (b) (*US sl: penis*) Schwanz *m* (*sl*).

pecking order ['pekɪŋ,ɔ:dəʳ] *n* (*lit, fig*) Hackordnung *f*.

peckish ['pekɪʃ] *adj* (*Brit inf: hungry*) **I'm (feeling) a bit ~** ich könnte was zwischen die Zähne gebrauchen (*inf*).

pecs [peks] *npl* (*inf*) *abbr of* **pectorals** Muskeln *pl*.

pectic ['pektɪk] *adj* Pektin-.

pectin ['pektɪn] *n* Pektin *nt*.

pectoral ['pektərəl] *adj* pektoral; *fin, cross, ornament* Brust-.

peculiar [pɪ'kju:lɪəʳ] *adj* (a) (*strange*) seltsam, eigenartig. (b) (*exclusive, special*) eigentümlich (*to* für +*acc*) ◆ **an animal ~ to Africa** ein Tier, das nur in Afrika vorkommt; **his own ~ style** der ihm eigene Stil.

peculiarity [pɪ,kju:lɪ'ærɪtɪ] *n* (a) (*strangeness*) Seltsamkeit, Eigenartigkeit *f*. (b) (*unusual feature*) Eigentümlichkeit, Eigenheit, Besonderheit *f*.

peculiarly [pɪ'kju:lɪəlɪ] *adv* (a) (*strangely*) seltsam, eigenartig. (b) (*exceptionally*) besonders.

pecuniary [pɪ'kju:nɪərɪ] *adj* (*form*) *penalties, affairs* Geld-; *gain, advantage, problem, difficulties* finanziell.

pedagogic(al) [,pedə'gɒdʒɪk(əl)] *adj* (*form*) pädagogisch.

pedagogue ['pedəgɒg] *n* (*pedant*) Schulmeister *m*; (*form: teacher*) Pädagoge *m*, Pädagogin *f*.

pedagogy ['pedəgɒgɪ] *n* (*form*) Pädagogik *f*.

pedal ['pedl] [1] *n* Pedal *nt*; (*on waste bin etc*) Trethebel *m*.
[2] *vt* **he ~led the bicycle up the hill** er strampelte mit dem Fahrrad den Berg hinauf (*inf*); **he ~led the organ** er trat das Pedal der Orgel.
[3] *vi* (*on bicycle*) treten; (*on organ*) das Pedal treten ◆ **he ~led for all he was worth** er trat in die Pedale, er strampelte (*inf*), sosehr er konnte; **to ~ off** (mit dem Rad) wegfahren.

pedal: ~bin *n* Treteimer *m*; **~boat** *n* Tretboot *nt*; **~car** *n* Tretauto *nt*.

pedal(l)o ['pedələʊ] *n* Tretboot *nt*.

pedal-pushers ['pedəlpʊʃəz] *npl dreiviertellange Damen-/Mädchenhose*.

pedant ['pedənt] *n* Pedant(in *f*), Kleinigkeitskrämer(in *f*) *m*.

pedantic *adj*, **~ally** *adv* [pɪ'dæntɪk, -əlɪ] pedantisch.

pedantry ['pedəntrɪ] *n* Pedanterie *f*.

peddle ['pedl] *vt* feilbieten, verkaufen; (*fig*) *gossip etc* verbreiten ◆ **to ~ drugs** mit Drogen handeln.

peddler ['pedləʳ] *n* (*esp US*) *see* **pedlar**.

pederast ['pedəræst] *n* Päderast *m*.

pederasty ['pedəræstɪ] *n* Päderastie *f*.

pedestal ['pedɪstl] *n* Sockel *m* ◆ **to put** *or* **set sb (up) on a ~** (*fig*) jdn in den Himmel heben; **to knock sb off his ~** (*fig*) jdn von seinem Sockel stoßen.

pedestrian [pɪ'destrɪən] [1] *n* Fußgänger(in *f*) *m*.
[2] *adj* (a) *attr* (*of ~s*) Fußgänger- ◆ **~ controlled traffic lights** Fußgängerampel *f*; **~ crossing** (*Brit*) Fußgängerüberweg *m*; **~ precinct** Fußgängerzone *f*. (b) (*prosaic*) *style etc* schwunglos; *method etc* umständlich.

pedestrianize [pɪ'destrɪənaɪz] *vt street* in eine Fußgängerzone umwandeln.

pediatric [,pi:dɪ'ætrɪk] *etc* (*esp US*) *see* **paediatric** *etc*.

pedicure ['pedɪkjʊəʳ] *n* Pediküre *f*.

pedigree ['pedɪgri:] [1] *n* (*lit, fig*) Stammbaum *m*; (*document*) Ahnentafel *f*; (*fig*) Geschichte *f*.
[2] *attr* reinrassig.

pedigreed ['pedɪgri:d] *adj* reinrassig.

pediment ['pedɪmənt] *n* Giebeldreieck *nt*.

pedlar ['pedləʳ] *n* Hausierer(in *f*) *m*; (*of drugs*) Drogenhändler(in *f*), Pusher(in *f*) (*sl*) *m*.

pedology *etc* (*US*) *see* **paedology** *etc*.

pedometer [pɪ'dɒmɪtəʳ] *n* Pedometer *nt*, Schrittzähler *m*.

pedophile *etc* (*US*) *see* **paedophile** *etc*.

pee [pi:] (*inf*) [1] *n* (*urine*) Urin *m*, Pipi *nt* (*baby-talk*) ◆ **to need/have a ~** pinkeln müssen (*inf*)/pinkeln (*inf*); **I'm just off for a ~** ich geh' mal eben pinkeln (*inf*).
[2] *vi* (a) pinkeln (*inf*). (b) (*also* **~ down**) (*hum: rain*) pinkeln (*inf*).

peek [pi:k] [1] *n* kurzer Blick; (*furtive, from under blindfold etc*) verstohlener Blick ◆ **to take** *or* **have a ~** kurz/verstohlen gucken (*at* nach); **may I just have a ~?** darf ich mal eben *or* kurz sehen *or* gucken?; **to get a ~ at sb/sth** jdn/etw kurz zu sehen bekommen.
[2] *vi* gucken (*at* nach).

peekaboo ['pi:kəbu:] [1] *n* Guck-Guck-Spiel *nt* ◆ **to play ~** guck-guck spielen.
[2] *interj* kuckuck.

peel [pi:l] [1] *n* Schale *f*.
[2] *vt* schälen; *see* **eye**.
[3] *vi* (*wallpaper*) sich lösen; (*paint*) abblättern; (*skin, person*) sich schälen *or* pellen (*inf*) ◆ **the paper was ~ing off the wall** die Tapete löste sich *or* kam von der Wand.

◆**peel away** [1] *vt sep wallpaper, paint* abziehen, ablösen (*from* von); *wrapper* abstreifen (*from* von); *bark* abschälen (*from* von).
[2] *vi* (*lit, fig*) sich lösen (*from* von).

◆**peel back** *vt sep cover, wrapping* abziehen.

◆**peel off** [1] *vt sep* (+*prep obj* von) *sticky tape, wallpaper, paint* abziehen, ablösen; *tree bark* abschälen; *wrapper, dress, glove etc* abstreifen.
[2] *vi* (a) *see* **peel away 2**. (b) (*leave formation*) ausscheren; (*Aviat also*) abdrehen.

peeler[1] ['pi:ləʳ] *n* (*old Brit inf*) Gendarm *m* (*old*).

peeler[2] *n* (a) (*potato ~*) Schälmesser *nt*, Schäler *m*. (b) (*US sl: stripper*) Stripperin *f* (*inf*).

peeling ['pi:lɪŋ] *n* (a) Abschälen *nt*. (b) **~s** *pl* Schalen *pl*.

peep[1] [pi:p] [1] *n* (*sound*) (*of bird etc*) Piep *m*; (*of horn, whistle, inf: of person*) Ton *m* ◆ **to give a ~** (*bird*) einen Piep von sich geben; (*horn, whistle*) einen Ton von sich geben; **not to give a ~** keinen Pieps von sich geben (*inf*); **we haven't heard a ~ out of him** wir haben keinen Pieps von ihm gehört (*inf*); **one ~ out of you and ...** (*inf*) noch einen Mucks (*inf*) *or* Pieps (*inf*) und ...; **~! ~!** (*of horn*) tut! tut!; (*of whistle*) tüt! tüt!
[2] *vi* (*bird etc*) piepen; (*horn, car*) tuten; (*whistle*) pfeifen; (*person*) (*on horn*) tuten; (*on whistle*) pfeifen.
[3] *vt* **I ~ed my horn at him, I ~ed him** (*inf*) ich habe ihn angehupt (*inf*).

peep[2] [1] *n* (*look*) kurzer Blick; (*furtive, when forbidden etc*) verstohlener Blick ◆ **to get a ~ at sth** etw kurz zu sehen bekommen; **to take** *or* **have a ~ (at sth)** kurz/verstohlen (nach etw) gucken.
[2] *vt* **she ~ed her head out** sie streckte ihren Kopf hervor.
[3] *vi* gucken (*at* nach) ◆ **to ~ from behind sth** hinter etw (*dat*) hervorschauen; **to ~ over sth** über etw (*acc*) gucken; **to ~ through sth** durch etw gucken *or* lugen; **no ~ing!, don't ~!** (aber) nicht gucken!

◆**peep out** *vi* herausgucken ◆ **the sun ~ed ~ from behind the clouds** die

Sonne sah *or* kam hinter den Wolken hervor.

peepers ['pi:pəz] *npl (inf)* Gucker *pl (inf)*.

peephole ['pi:phəʊl] *n* Guckloch *nt*; *(in door also)* Spion *m*.

peeping Tom ['pi:pɪŋ'tɒm] *n* Spanner *(inf)*, Voyeur *m*.

peep: ~ show *n* Peepshow *f*; **~-toe** [1] *adj* offen; [2] *n (shoe)* offener Schuh.

peer[1] [pɪəʳ] *n* **(a)** *(noble)* Peer *m* ◆ **~ of the realm** Peer *m*.
(b) *(equal)* Gleichrangige(r) *mf*, Peer *m (spec)* ◆ **he was well-liked by his ~s** er war bei seinesgleichen beliebt; **to be tried by one's ~s** von seinesgleichen gerichtet werden; **as a musician he has** *or* **knows no ~** *or* **is without ~** als Musiker sucht er seinesgleichen; **~ pressure** Erwartungsdruck *m (von seiten Gleichaltriger)*.

peer[2] *vi* starren; *(short-sightedly, inquiringly)* schielen ◆ **to ~ (hard) at sb/sth** jdn/etw anstarren, jdn anschielen/auf etw *(acc)* schielen; **the driver ~ed through the fog** der Fahrer versuchte angestrengt, im Nebel etwas zu erkennen; **if you ~ through the mist you can just see ...** wenn es dir gelingt, im Nebel etwas zu erkennen, kannst du gerade noch ... sehen.

peerage ['pɪərɪdʒ] *n (peers)* Adelsstand *m*; *(in GB)* Peers *pl*; *(rank also)* Adelswürde *f*; *(in GB)* Peerage, Peerswürde *f*; *(book) das britische Adelsverzeichnis* ◆ **to raise** *or* **elevate sb to the ~** jdn in den Adelsstand erheben; **to give sb a ~** jdm einen Adelstitel verleihen, jdn adeln; **to get a ~** geadelt werden, einen Adelstitel verliehen bekommen.

peeress ['pɪərɪs] *n* Peeress *f*.

peer group *n* Peer Group, Alterskohorte *f*.

peerless *adj*, **~ly** *adv* ['pɪəlɪs, -lɪ] einzigartig, unvergleichlich.

peeve [pi:v] *vt (inf)* ärgern, reizen, fuchsen *(inf)*.

peeved [pi:vd] *adj (inf)* eingeschnappt, ärgerlich, verärgert; *look* ärgerlich, verärgert.

peevish ['pi:vɪʃ] *adj (irritated)* gereizt, mürrisch, brummig; *(irritable)* reizbar.

peevishly ['pi:vɪʃlɪ] *adv* gereizt.

peevishness ['pi:vɪʃnɪs] *n (irritation)* Gereiztheit, Brummigkeit *f*; *(irritability)* Reizbarkeit *f*.

peewit ['pi:wɪt] *n* Kiebitz *m*.

peg [peg] [1] *n (stake)* Pflock *m*; *(tent ~ also)* Hering *m*; *(for ~board, wood joints, in games)* Stift *m*; *(of musical instrument)* Wirbel *m*; *(Brit: clothes ~)* (Wäsche)klammer *f*; *(hook, for mountaineering)* Haken *m*; *(in barrel)* Zapfen, Spund *m* ◆ **off the ~** von der Stange; **a ~ of rum** *etc* ein Gläschen *nt* Rum *etc*; **to take** *or* **bring sb down a ~ or two** *(inf)* jdm einen Dämpfer geben; **a (convenient) ~ on which to hang one's prejudices** *etc* ein guter Aufhänger für seine Vorurteile *etc*.
[2] *vt* **(a)** *(fasten) (with stake)* anpflocken; *(with clothes ~)* anklammern; *(to ~board)* anheften; *(with tent ~)* festpflocken.
(b) *(mark out) area* abstecken.
(c) *(fig) prices, wages* festsetzen.

◆**peg away** *vi (inf)* nicht locker lassen *(at* mit*)*.

◆**peg down** *vt sep tent etc* festpflocken.

◆**peg out** [1] *vt sep* **(a)** *washing* aufhängen; *skins* ausspannen. **(b)** *(mark out) area* abstecken.
[2] *vi (sl) (die)* abkratzen *(sl)*, den Löffel abgeben *(sl)*; *(stop: machine)* verrecken *(sl)*.

◆**peg up** *vt sep washing* aufhängen; *notice* heften *(on* an *+acc)*.

Pegasus ['pegəsəs] *n* Pegasus *m*.

pegboard ['pegbɔ:d] *n* Lochbrett *nt*.

peg-leg ['pegleg] *n (inf) (person)* Stelzfuß *m*; *(leg also)* Holzbein *nt*.

peignoir ['peɪnwa:] *n* Négligé *nt*.

pejorative *adj*, **~ly** *adv* [pɪ'dʒɒrɪtɪv, -lɪ] pejorativ, abwertend, abschätzig.

peke [pi:k] *n (inf) see* **pekin(g)ese**.

Pekin(g) [pi:'kɪŋ] *n* Peking *nt* ◆ **~ man** Pekingmensch *m*.

pekin(g)ese [,pi:kɪ'ni:z] *n, pl* - *(dog)* Pekinese *m*.

pelerine ['peləri:n] *n (old)* Pelerine *f*, Umhang *m*.

pelican ['pelɪkən] *n* Pelikan *m* ◆ **~ crossing** Ampelübergang *m*.

pelisse [pə'li:s] *n (old)* pelzbesetztes Kleid.

pellet ['pelɪt] *n* Kügelchen *nt*; *(for gun)* Schrotkugel *m*; *(Biol: regurgitated ~)* Gewölle *nt*.

pellicle ['pelɪkəl] *n* Film *m*; *(Zool: membrane)* Pellicula *f*.

pell-mell ['pel'mel] *adv* durcheinander, wie Kraut und Rüben *(inf)*; *(with vbs of motion)* in heillosem Durcheinander.

pellucid [pe'lu:sɪd] *adj liquid, meaning* klar; *argument also* einleuchtend.

pelmet ['pelmɪt] *n* Blende *f*; *(of fabric)* Falbel *f*, Querbehang *m*.

Peloponnese [,peləpə'ni:z] *n* Peloponnes *m*.

Peloponnesian [,peləpə'ni:zɪən] *adj* peloponnesisch.

pelt[1] [pelt] *n* Pelz *m*, Fell *nt*.

pelt[2] [1] *vt* **(a)** *(throw)* schleudern *(at* nach*)* ◆ **to ~ sb/sth (with sth)** jdn/etw (mit etw) bewerfen.
(b) *(beat hard)* verprügeln.
[2] *vi (inf)* **(a)** *(go fast)* pesen *(inf)*.
(b) it ~ed (with rain) es hat nur so geschüttet *(inf)*; **the rain/hail ~ed against the windows** der Regen/Hagel prasselte an *or* schlug gegen die Fensterscheiben.
[3] *n (inf)* **(a)** *(speed)* **at full/a fair** *or* **quite a ~** volle Pulle *(inf)*.
(b) *(blow)* Schlag *m* ◆ **she gave her one good ~ round the ear** sie gab ihr eine kräftige Ohrfeige.

◆**pelt along** *vi (inf)* entlangrasen.

◆**pelt down** *vi* **it** *or* **the rain really ~ed ~** der Regen prasselte nur so herunter; **it's ~ing ~** es regnet in Strömen.

pelvic ['pelvɪk] *adj* Becken-; *complaint, pains* in der Beckengegend ◆ **~ girdle** Beckengürtel *m*; **~ fin** Bauchflosse *f*.

pelvis ['pelvɪs] *n* Becken *nt*.

pen[1] [pen] [1] *n (dip ~)* Feder *f*; *(fountain ~)* Füllfederhalter, Füller *m*; *(ball-point ~)* Kugelschreiber, Kuli *(inf)* *m* ◆ **to set** *or* **put ~ to paper** zur Feder greifen; **the ~ is mightier than the sword** *(prov)* die Feder ist mächtiger als das Schwert.
[2] *vt* niederschreiben; *poem etc also* verfassen.

pen[2] [1] *n* **(a)** *(for cattle etc)* Pferch *m*; *(for sheep)* Hürde *f*; *(for pigs)* Koben *m*; *(play~)* Laufstall *m*, Ställchen, Laufgitter *nt*. **(b)** *(US inf: prison)* Bau *(inf)*, Knast *(inf)* *m*. **(c)** *(for submarines)* Bunker *m*.
[2] *vt* einsperren.

◆**pen in** *vt sep* einsperren; *(fig) car etc* einklemmen, einkeilen.

◆**pen up** *vt sep* einsperren.

pen[3] *n (swan)* weiblicher Schwan.

penal ['pi:nl] *adj law, colony etc* Straf- ◆ **~ code** Strafgesetzbuch *nt*; **~ system** Strafrecht *nt*; **~ reform** Strafrechtsreform *f*; **~ offence** Straftat *f*; **~ servitude** Zwangsarbeit *f*.

penalization [,pi:nəlaɪ'zeɪʃən] *n* **(a)** *(punishment)* Bestrafung *f*; *(fig)* Benachteiligung *f*. **(b)** *(making punishable)* Unter-Strafe-Stellen *nt*.

penalize ['pi:nəlaɪz] *vt* **(a)** *(punish, Sport)* bestrafen. **(b)** *(fig)* benachteiligen ◆ **we are ~d by not having a car** wir sind im Nachteil *or* benachteiligt, weil wir kein Auto haben. **(c)** *(make punishable)* unter Strafe stellen.

penalty ['penəltɪ] *n* **(a)** *(punishment)* Strafe *f*; *(fig: disadvantage)* Nachteil *m* ◆ **the ~ (for this) is death** darauf steht die Todesstrafe; **you know the ~** Sie wissen, welche Strafe darauf steht; **"~ £5"** „bei Zuwiderhandlung wird eine Geldstrafe von £ 5 erhoben"; **on ~ of death/£5/imprisonment** bei Todesstrafe/bei einer Geldstrafe von £ 5/bei Gefängnisstrafe; **on ~ of excommunication** unter Androhung der Exkommunizierung; **to pay the ~** dafür büßen; **that's the ~ you pay for ...** das ist die Strafe dafür, daß ...
(b) *(Sport)* Strafstoß *m*; *(Soccer)* Elfmeter *m*; *(Golf, Bridge)* Strafpunkt *m*.

penalty: ~ area *n* Strafraum *m*; **~ box** *n (Ftbl)* Strafraum *m*; *(Ice Hockey)* Strafbank *f*; **~ clause** *n* Strafklausel *f*; **~ goal** *n (Rugby)* Straftor *nt*; **~ kick** *n* Strafstoß *m*; **~ line** *n* Strafraumgrenze *f*; **~ spot** *n* Elfmeterpunkt *m*.

penance ['penəns] *n (Rel)* Buße *f*; *(fig)* Strafe *f* ◆ **to do ~** Buße tun; *(fig)* büßen; **as a ~** *(Rel)* als Buße; *(fig)* zur *or* als Strafe.

pen-and-ink ['penənd'ɪŋk] *adj* Feder-.

pence [pens] *n* **(a)** Pence *m*. **(b)** *pl of* **penny**.

penchant ['pɑ̃:ŋʃɑ̃:ŋ] *n* Schwäche, Vorliebe *f (for* für*)*.

pencil ['pensl] [1] *n* Bleistift *m*; *(eyebrow ~)* Augenbrauenstift *m*; *(Math, Phys: of lines, rays etc)* Büschel *nt*.
[2] *vt* mit Bleistift schreiben/zeichnen *etc* ◆ **~led eyebrows** nachgezogene Augenbrauen *pl*.
[3] *attr drawing etc* Bleistift-; *line also* mit Bleistift gezogen.

◆**pencil in** *vt sep (make provisional arrangement with/for)* vorläufig vormerken ◆ **can I ~ you ~ for Tuesday?** kann ich Sie erst mal für Dienstag vormerken?

pencil: ~ box *n* Federkasten *m*; **~ case** *n* Federmäppchen *nt*; **~ sharpener** *n* (Bleistift)spitzer *m*.

pendant ['pendənt] *n* Anhänger *m*.

pendent ['pendənt] *adj* herabhängend; *lamps also* Hänge-.

pending ['pendɪŋ] [1] *adj* anstehend; *lawsuit* anhängig ◆ **"~"** „unerledigt"; **to be ~** *(decision etc)* noch anstehen; *(trial)* noch anhängig sein.
[2] *prep* **~ his arrival/return** bis zu seiner Ankunft/Rückkehr; **~ a decision** bis eine Entscheidung getroffen worden ist.

pendulous ['pendjʊləs] *adj* herabhängend ◆ **~ breasts** *or* **bosom** Hängebrüste *pl*, Hängebusen *m*.

pendulum ['pendjʊləm] *n* Pendel *nt* ◆ **the ~ has swung back in the opposite direction** *(lit, fig)* das Pendel ist in die entgegengesetzte Richtung ausgeschlagen; **the ~ has swung back in favour of** *or* **towards ...** *(fig)* die Tendenz geht wieder in Richtung *(+gen)* ...; **the swing of the ~** *(fig)* die Tendenzwende.

penetrable ['penɪtrəbl] *adj* zu durchdringen ◆ **the scarcely ~ jungle** der fast undurchdringliche Dschungel.

penetrate ['penɪtreɪt] [1] *vt* eindringen in *(+acc)*; *(go right through) walls etc* durchdringen; *(Mil) enemy lines* durchbrechen; *(Med) vein* durchstechen; *(infiltrate) party* infiltrieren ◆ **is there anything that will ~ that thick skull of yours?** geht denn auch überhaupt nichts in deinen Schädel rein!; **to ~ sb's disguise** hinter jds Maske *(acc)* schauen.
[2] *vi* eindringen; *(go right through)* durchdringen ◆ **the idea just didn't ~** *(fig)* das ist mir/ihm *etc* nicht klar geworden; **has that ~d?** hast du/habt ihr das endlich kapiert?

penetrating ['penɪtreɪtɪŋ] *adj* durchdringend; *mind also* scharf; *insight* scharfsinnig; *light* grell; *pain* stechend.

penetratingly ['penɪtreɪtɪŋlɪ] *adv* durchdringend; *comment, analyze* scharfsinnig; *shine* grell ◆ **a ~ accurate analysis** eine messerscharfe Analyse; **a ~ bright light** ein grelles Licht; **a ~ sharp pain** ein stechender Schmerz.

penetration [,penɪ'treɪʃən] *n see vt* Eindringen *nt (into* in *+acc)*; Durchdringen *nt (of gen)*; Durchbrechen *nt*, Durchbrechung *f*; Durchstechen *nt*; Infiltration *f* ◆ **the ~ of his gaze** sein durchdringender Blick; **the ~ of the needle was 3 mm** die Nadel war 3 mm tief eingedrungen; **the ~ of his mind/his powers of ~** sein Scharfsinn *m*.

penetrative ['penɪtrətɪv] *adj see* **penetrating**.

penfriend ['penfrend] *n* Brieffreund(in *f*) *m*.

penguin ['peŋgwɪn] *n* Pinguin *m* ◆ **~ suit** *(hum)* Frack, Schwalbenschwanz *(hum)* *m*.

penholder ['pen,həʊldəʳ] *n* Federhalter *m*.

penicillin [ˌpenɪˈsɪlɪn] *n* Penizillin *nt.*
peninsula [pɪˈnɪnsjʊlə] *n* Halbinsel *f.*
peninsular [pɪˈnɪnsjʊləʳ] *adj* Halbinsel- ◆ **the P~ War** der Krieg auf der Pyrenäenhalbinsel.
penis [ˈpiːnɪs] *n* Penis *m* ◆ **~ envy** Penisneid *m.*
penitence [ˈpenɪtəns] *n* Reue (*also Eccl*), Zerknirschtheit *f.*
penitent [ˈpenɪtənt] [1] *adj* reuig (*also Eccl*), zerknirscht.
[2] *n* Büßer(in *f*) *m;* (*Eccl*) reuiger Sünder, reuige Sünderin.
penitential [ˌpenɪˈtenʃəl] *adj* reuevoll, reumütig, reuig; (*Eccl*) Buß- ◆ **a ~ act** eine Bußtat.
penitentiary [ˌpenɪˈtenʃərɪ] *n* (*esp US: prison*) Strafanstalt *f*, Gefängnis *nt.*
pen: ~knife *n* Taschenmesser *nt;* **~ name** *n* Pseudonym *nt*, Schriftstellername *m.*
pennant [ˈpenənt] *n* Wimpel *m.*
pen nib *n* Feder *f.*
penniless [ˈpenɪlɪs] *adj* mittellos ◆ **to be ~** keinen Pfennig Geld haben; **her husband died, leaving her ~** ihr Mann starb, und sie stand völlig mittellos *or* ohne einen Pfennig Geld da.
Pennines [ˈpenaɪnz] *npl* Pennines *pl* (*Gebirgszug in Nordengland*).
pennon [ˈpenən] *n see* **pennant.**
penn'orth [ˈpenəθ] *n see* **pennyworth.**
Pennsylvania [ˌpensɪlˈveɪnɪə] *n* Pennsylvania *nt.*
Pennsylvania-Dutch [ˌpensɪlˈveɪnɪəˈdʌtʃ] [1] *n* **(a)** Pennsylvania-Deutsch *nt.* **(b)** *pl* (*people*) Pennsylvania-Deutsche *pl.*
[2] *adj* pennsylvania-deutsch.
Pennsylvanian [ˌpensɪlˈveɪnɪən] *adj* pennsylvanisch.
penny [ˈpenɪ] *n, pl* (*coins*) **pennies** *or* (*sum*) **pence** Penny *m;* (*US*) Centstück *nt* ◆ **in for a ~, in for a pound** (*prov*) wennschon, dennschon (*inf*); (*morally*) wer A sagt, muß auch B sagen (*prov*); **I'm not a ~ the wiser** ich bin genauso klug wie zuvor; **take care of the pennies and the pounds will take care of themselves** (*Prov*) spare im kleinen, dann hast du im großen; **a ~ for your thoughts** ich möchte deine Gedanken lesen können; **he keeps turning up like a bad ~** (*inf*) der taucht immer wieder auf (*inf*); **to spend a ~** (*inf*) austreten, mal eben verschwinden (*inf*); **the ~ dropped** (*inf*) der Groschen ist gefallen (*inf*); *see* **pretty, honest.**
penny: ~ arcade *n* Spielhalle *f;* **~ dreadful** *n* (*dated Brit*) Groschenroman *m;* **~-farthing** *n* Hochrad *nt;* **~-pinch** *vi* jeden Pfennig umdrehen; **~-pincher** *n* Pfennigfuchser *m;* **~-pinching** *adj* knauserig (*inf*); **~weight** *n* Pennygewicht *nt;* **~ whistle** *n* Kinderflöte *f;* **~ wise** *adj* **to be ~ wise and pound foolish** immer am falschen Ende sparen; **~worth** *n* (*dated*) **a ~worth of liquorice/common-sense** für einen Penny Lakritz/für fünf Pfennig gesunden Menschenverstand.
penologist [piːˈnɒlədʒɪst] *n* Kriminalpädagoge *m*, Kriminalpädagogin *f.*
penology [piːˈnɒlədʒɪ] *n* Kriminalpädagogik *f.*
pen: ~pal *n* (*inf*) Brieffreund(in *f*) *m;* **~pusher** *n* Schreiberling *m;* **~pushing** [1] *n* Schreiberei *f*, Schreibkram *m;* [2] *adj job* Schreib-; **~pushing clerk** Bürohengst *m* (*inf*).
pension [ˈpenʃən] *n* Rente *f;* (*for former salaried staff also*) Pension *f;* (*for civil servants also*) Ruhegehalt *nt* (*form*) ◆ **company ~** betriebliche Altersversorgung; **to be entitled to a ~** Anspruch auf eine Rente *etc* haben, rentenberechtigt/pensionsberechtigt sein; **to be living on a ~** von der Rente *etc* leben.
◆**pension off** *vt sep* (*inf*) vorzeitig pensionieren.
pensionable [ˈpenʃənəbl] *adj* **this position is ~** diese Stellung berechtigt zu einer Pension/einem Ruhegehalt; **of ~ age** im Renten-/Pensionsalter.
pension book *n* Rentenausweis *m.*
pensioner [ˈpenʃənəʳ] *n see* **pension** Rentner(in *f*) *m;* Pensionär(in *f*) *m;* Ruhegehaltsempfänger(in *f*) *m* (*form*).
pension: ~ fund *n* Rentenfonds *m;* **~ rights** *npl* Rentenanspruch *m;* **~ scheme** *n* Rentenversicherung *f.*
pensive *adj,* **~ly** *adv* [ˈpensɪv, -lɪ] nachdenklich; (*sadly serious*) schwermütig.
pensiveness [ˈpensɪvnɪs] *n see adj* Nachdenklichkeit *f;* Schwermütigkeit *f.*
pentagon [ˈpentəgən] *n* Fünfeck, Pentagon *nt* ◆ **the P~** das Pentagon.
pentagonal [penˈtægənl] *adj* fünfeckig.
pentagram [ˈpentəgræm] *n* Drudenfuß *m*, Pentagramm *nt.*
pentahedron [ˌpentəˈhiːdrən] *n* Fünfflächner *m*, Pentaeder *nt.*
pentameter [penˈtæmɪtəʳ] *n* Pentameter *m; see* **iambic.**
Pentateuch [ˈpentətjuːk] *n* die fünf Bücher *pl* Mose, Pentateuch *m.*
pentathlete [penˈtæθliːt] *n* Fünfkämpfer(in *f*) *m.*
pentathlon [penˈtæθlən] *n* Fünfkampf *m.*
pentatonic [ˌpentəˈtɒnɪk] *adj* pentatonisch ◆ **~ scale** fünfstufige Tonleiter.
Pentecost [ˈpentɪkɒst] *n* (*Jewish*) Erntefest *nt;* (*Christian*) Pfingsten *nt.*
pentecostal [ˌpentɪˈkɒstl] *adj* Pfingst-; *sect, service, revival* der Pfingstbewegung.
penthouse [ˈpenthaʊs] *n* (*apartment*) Penthouse *nt*, Dachterrassenwohnung *f;* (*roof*) Überdachung *f.*
Pentium processor ® [ˈpentɪəmˈprəʊsesəʳ] *n* Pentium-Prozessor *m.*
pent-up [ˈpentˈʌp] *adj person* (*with frustration, anger*) geladen *pred;* (*after traumatic experience*) aufgewühlt; (*nervous, excited*) innerlich angespannt; *emotions, passion, excitement* aufgestaut; *atmosphere* angespannt, geladen ◆ **to get ~ (about sth)** sich (über etw *acc*) erregen, sich (in etw *acc*) hineinsteigern; **she had been very ~ about it** es hatte sich alles in ihr gestaut; **~ feelings** ein Emotionsstau *m*, angestaute Gefühle *pl.*
penultimate [peˈnʌltɪmɪt] *adj* vorletzte(r, s).
penumbra [pɪˈnʌmbrə] *n, pl* **-e** [-briː] *or* **-s** Halbschatten *m.*
penurious [pɪˈnjʊərɪəs] *adj* (*liter*) (*poor*) arm, armselig; *existence also* karg, dürftig; (*mean*) geizig, knauserig.
penuriously [pɪˈnjʊərɪəslɪ] *adv see adj.*
penury [ˈpenjʊrɪ] *n* Armut, Not *f* ◆ **the company's present state of ~** die gegenwärtigen Finanzschwierigkeiten der Firma.
peony [ˈpiːənɪ] *n* Pfingstrose, Päonie (*spec*) *f.*
people [ˈpiːpl] [1] *npl* **(a)** Menschen *pl;* (*not in formal context*) Leute *pl* ◆ **we're concerned with ~** uns geht es um die Menschen; **French ~ are very fond of their food** die Franzosen lieben ihre gute Küche; **that's typical of Edinburgh ~** das ist typisch für (die) Leute aus Edinburgh; **a job where you meet ~** eine Arbeit, wo man mit Menschen *or* Leuten zusammenkommt; **~ who need ~** Menschen, die andere Menschen brauchen; **all the ~ in the world** alle Menschen auf der Welt; **all ~ with red hair** alle Rothaarigen; **some ~ don't like it** manche Leute mögen es nicht; **most ~ in show business** die meisten Leute im Showgeschäft; **aren't ~ funny?** was gibt es doch für seltsame Menschen *or* Leute!; **the ~ you meet!** Menschen *or* Leute gibt's!; **why me of all ~?** warum ausgerechnet ich/mich?; **I met Harry of all ~!** ausgerechnet Harry habe ich getroffen!; **of all ~ who do you think I should meet!** stell dir mal vor, wen ich getroffen habe?; **what do you ~ think?** was haltet ihr denn davon?; **poor/blind/disabled ~** arme Leute *or* Arme/Blinde/Behinderte; **middle-aged ~** Menschen mittleren Alters; **city ~** Stadtmenschen *pl;* **country ~** Menschen *pl* vom Land, Landleute *pl* (*dated*); **some ~!** Leute gibt's!; **some ~ have all the luck** manche Leute haben einfach Glück.
(b) (*inhabitants*) Bevölkerung *f* ◆ **the ~ of Rome/Egypt** *etc* die Bevölkerung von Rom/Ägypten *etc;* **Madrid has over 5 million ~** Madrid hat über 5 Millionen Einwohner.
(c) (*one, they*) man; (*~ in general, the neighbours*) die Leute ◆ **~ say that ...** man sagt, daß ...; **what will ~ think!** was sollen die Leute denken!; **~ in general tend to say ...** im allgemeinen neigt man zu der Behauptung ...
(d) (*nation, masses, subjects*) Volk *nt* ◆ **the common ~** das einfache Volk, die breite Masse; **a man of the ~** ein Mann *m* des Volkes; **government by the ~ (of the ~)** eine Regierung des Volkes; **the Belgian ~** die Belgier *pl*, das belgische Volk; **P~'s police/Republic** *etc* Volkspolizei *f*/-republik *f etc.*
[2] *vt* besiedeln ◆ **the world seems to be ~d with idiots** die Welt scheint von Idioten bevölkert zu sein.
people power *n* Basisdemokratie *f.*
pep [pep] *n* (*inf*) Schwung, Elan, Pep (*inf*) *m.*
◆**pep up** *vt sep* (*inf*) Schwung bringen in (+*acc*); *food, drink* pikanter machen; *person* munter machen ◆ **pills to ~ you ~** Aufputschmittel *pl.*
pepper [ˈpepəʳ] [1] *n* Pfeffer *m;* (*green, red ~*) Paprika *m;* (*plant*) Pfefferstrauch *m* ◆ **two ~s** zwei Paprikaschoten.
[2] *vt* **(a)** pfeffern. **(b)** (*fig*) **to ~ sth with quotations** etw mit Zitaten spicken; **to ~ sb with shot** jdn mit Kugeln durchlöchern.
pepper: ~-and-salt *adj* Pfeffer-und-Salz-; *hair* meliert; **~corn** *n* Pfefferkorn *nt;* **~corn rent** *n* (*US: nominal rent*) nominelle *or* symbolische Miete; **~mill** *n* Pfeffermühle *f;* **~mint** *n* Pfefferminz *nt;* (*Bot*) Pfefferminze *f;* **~ pot** *n* Pfefferstreuer *m;* **~ steak** *n* Pfeffersteak *m.*
peppery [ˈpepərɪ] *adj* gepfeffert; (*fig*) *old man etc* hitzig, hitzköpfig ◆ **it tastes rather ~** es schmeckt stark nach Pfeffer.
pep pill *n* Aufputschpille, Peppille *f.*
peppy [ˈpepɪ] *adj* (+*er*) (*sl*) peppig (*inf*), schwungvoll; *performance, music etc also* fetzig (*inf*).
pepsin [ˈpepsɪn] *n* Pepsin *nt.*
pep talk *n* (*inf*) aufmunternde Worte *pl* ◆ **to give sb a ~** jdm ein paar aufmunternde Worte sagen.
peptic [ˈpeptɪk] *adj* peptisch ◆ **~ ulcer** Magengeschwür *nt.*
per [pɜːʳ] *prep* pro ◆ **£20 ~ annum** £ 20 im *or* pro Jahr; **60 km ~ hour** 60 Stundenkilometer, 60 km pro Stunde *or* in der Stunde; **$2 ~ dozen** das Dutzend für $ 2, $ 2 das Dutzend; **£5 ~ copy** £ 5 pro *or* je Exemplar, £ 5 für jedes Exemplar; **as ~** gemäß (+*dat*); **~ se** an sich, per se (*geh*); *see* **usual.**
peradventure [ˌperədˈventʃəʳ] *adv* (*old: perhaps*) vielleicht ◆ **if/lest ~** falls.
perambulate [pəˈræmbjʊleɪt] (*form*) [1] *vt* sich ergehen in (+*dat*) (*geh*).
[2] *vi* sich ergehen (*liter*).
perambulation [pəˌræmbjʊˈleɪʃən] *n* (*form*) Spaziergang *m.*
perambulator [ˈpræmbjʊleɪtəʳ] *n* (*Brit form*) Kinderwagen *m.*
per capita [pəˈkæpɪtə] *adj income etc* Pro-Kopf-.
perceivable [pəˈsiːvəbl] *adj* erkennbar ◆ **scarcely ~** kaum auszumachen *or* zu erkennen.
perceive [pəˈsiːv] *vt* wahrnehmen; (*understand, realize, recognize*) erkennen ◆ **do you ~ anything strange?** fällt Ihnen irgend etwas Ungewöhnliches auf?; **..., which we ~ to be the case** (*form*) ..., was wir als zutreffend erkennen.
per cent, (*US*) **percent** [pəˈsent] *n* Prozent *nt* ◆ **what ~?** wieviel Prozent?; **20 ~** 20 Prozent; **a 10 ~ discount** 10 Prozent Rabatt.
percentage [pəˈsentɪdʒ] [1] *n* **(a)** Prozentsatz *m;* (*commission, payment*) Anteil *m;* (*proportion*) Teil *m* ◆ **a small ~ of the population** ein geringer Teil der Bevölkerung; **expressed as a ~** prozentual *or* in Prozenten ausgedrückt; **what ~?** wieviel Prozent?; **to get a ~ on all sales** prozentual am Umsatz beteiligt sein.
(b) (*inf: advantage*) **there's no ~ in it** das bringt nichts (*inf*).
[2] *attr* prozentual ◆ **on a ~ basis** prozentual, auf Prozentbasis; **the statistics are on a ~ basis** die Statistiken werden in Prozenten angegeben; **~ sign** Prozentzeichen *nt.*
perceptible [pəˈseptəbl] *adj* wahrnehmbar; *improvement, trend, increase etc*

spürbar, deutlich ◆ his unhappiness was ~ only to his close friends nur seine engsten Freunde spürten *or* merkten, daß er unglücklich war.

perceptibly [pə'septəblɪ] *adv* merklich, spürbar; *(to the eye)* wahrnehmbar, sichtbar ◆ he blanched ~ er wurde sichtbar blaß.

perception [pə'sepʃən] *n* **(a)** *no pl* Wahrnehmung *f* ◆ his colour ~ is impaired seine Farbwahrnehmung ist beeinträchtigt.
(b) *(mental image, conception)* Auffassung *f (of* von) ◆ he seems to have a clear ~ of the dilemma I face er scheint meine schwierige Lage vollauf zu erkennen; one's ~ of the situation die eigene Einschätzung der Lage.
(c) *(no pl: perceptiveness)* Einsicht *f*; *(perceptive remark, observation)* Beobachtung *f*.
(d) *no pl (act of perceiving) (of object, visible difference)* Wahrnehmung *f*; *(of difficulties, meaning, illogicality etc)* Erkennen *nt* ◆ his quick ~ of the danger saved us all from death weil er die Gefahr blitzschnell erkannte, rettete er uns allen das Leben.

perceptive [pə'septɪv] *adj* **(a)** *faculties* Wahrnehmungs-.
(b) *(sensitive) person* einfühlsam; *(penetrating) analysis, speech, study* erkenntnisreich, scharfsinnig; *book, remark* aufschlußreich ◆ he has the ~ mind of a true artist er hat das Einfühlungsvermögen eines wahren Künstlers; very ~ of you! *(iro)* du merkst auch alles! *(iro)*.

perceptively [pə'septɪvlɪ] *adv see adj.*

perceptiveness [pə'septɪvnɪs] *n see adj (b)* Einfühlsamkeit *f*; Erkenntnisreichtum *m*, Scharfsinnigkeit *f*; Einsichtigkeit *f*; Aufmerksamkeit *f*.

perch[1] [pɜːtʃ] *n (fish)* Flußbarsch *m*.

perch[2] [1] *n* **(a)** *(of bird)* Stange *f*; *(in tree)* Ast *m*; *(hen-roost)* Hühnerstange *f*; *(fig: for person etc)* Hochsitz *m*.
(b) *(Measure) Längenmaß (5.029 m)*.
[2] *vt* to ~ sth on sth etw auf etw *(acc)* setzen *or (upright)* stellen; to be ~ed on sth auf etw *(dat)* sitzen; *(birds also)* auf etw *(dat)* hocken; with his glasses ~ed on the end of his nose mit der Brille auf der Nasenspitze; Britain is ~ed on the edge of Europe Großbritannien liegt (ganz) am Rande Europas; a castle ~ed on the rock eine auf dem Felsen thronende Burg.
[3] *vi (bird, fig: person)* hocken; *(alight)* sich niederlassen.

perchance [pə'tʃɑːns] *adv (old)* vielleicht.

percipient [pə'sɪpɪənt] *adj see* **perceptive**.

percolate ['pɜːkəleɪt] [1] *vt* filtrieren; *coffee* (in einer Kaffeemaschine) zubereiten.
[2] *vi (lit, fig)* durchsickern ◆ the coffee is just percolating der Kaffee läuft gerade durch.

percolator ['pɜːkəleɪtəʳ] *n* Kaffeemaschine *f*.

percuss [pə'kʌs] *vt (Med)* perkutieren *(spec)*, abklopfen.

percussion [pə'kʌʃən] *n* **(a)** Perkussion *f (also Med)* ◆ ~ cap Zündhütchen *nt*; ~ drill Schlagbohrmaschine *f*. **(b)** *(Mus)* Schlagzeug *nt*. ~ instrument Schlaginstrument *nt*; ~ section Schlagzeug *nt*.

percussionist [pə'kʌʃənɪst] *n* Schlagzeuger(in *f*) *m*.

percussive [pə'kʌsɪv] *adj* perkussorisch *(spec)*.

perdition [pə'dɪʃən] *n* ewige Verdammnis.

peregrination [ˌperɪgrɪ'neɪʃən] *n (liter)* Fahrt *f* ◆ his literary ~s seine literarischen Exkurse.

peregrine (falcon) ['perɪgrɪn('fɔːlkən)] *n* Wanderfalke *m*.

peremptorily [pə'remptərɪlɪ] *adv see adj.*

peremptory [pə'remptərɪ] *adj command, instruction* kategorisch; *voice* gebieterisch; *person* herrisch.

perennial [pə'renɪəl] [1] *adj plant* mehrjährig, perennierend; *(perpetual, constant)* immerwährend, ewig; *(regularly recurring)* immer wiederkehrend ◆ buying Christmas presents is a ~ problem der Kauf von Weihnachtsgeschenken ist ein alljährlich wiederkehrendes *or* sich neu stellendes Problem.
[2] *n (Bot)* perennierende *or* mehrjährige Pflanze.

perennially [pə'renɪəlɪ] *adv (perpetually, constantly)* ständig; *(recurrently)* immer wieder.

perestroika [pere'strɔɪkə] *n* Perestroika *f*.

perfect ['pɜːfɪkt] [1] *adj* **(a)** perfekt; *wife, teacher, host, relationship also* vorbildlich; *harmony, balance, symmetry also* vollkommen; *meal, work of art, pronunciation, English also* vollendet; *weather, day, holiday also* ideal; *(Comm: not damaged)* einwandfrei ◆ it was the ~ moment es war genau der richtige Augenblick; that's the ~ hairstyle/woman for you das ist genau die richtige Frisur/Frau für dich; ~ number *(Math)* vollkommene Zahl; ~ rhyme rührender Reim; his Spanish is far from ~ sein Spanisch ist bei weitem nicht perfekt; with ~ self-confidence mit absolutem Selbstvertrauen; nobody is *or* can be ~ niemand ist perfekt *or* vollkommen.
(b) *(absolute, utter)* völlig; *fool, nonsense also* ausgemacht ◆ she's a ~ terror/bore sie ist einfach schrecklich/sie ist ausgesprochen langweilig; ~ strangers wildfremde Leute *pl*; a ~ stranger ein Wildfremder *m*, eine Wildfremde; he's a ~ stranger to me er ist mir völlig fremd; it's a ~ disgrace es ist wirklich eine Schande.
(c) *(Gram)* ~ tense Perfekt *nt*; ~ ending Endung *f* im Perfekt; ~ form Vergangenheitsform *f*.
(d) *(Mus) fourth* rein; *cadence* authentisch; *see* **pitch[2]**.
[2] *n (Gram)* Perfekt *nt* ◆ in the ~ im Perfekt.
[3] [pə'fekt] *vt* vervollkommnen; *technique, technology, process also* perfektionieren.

perfectibility [pəˌfektɪ'bɪlɪtɪ] *n see adj* Vervollkommnungsfähigkeit *f*; Perfektionierbarkeit *f*.

perfectible [pə'fektɪbl] *adj* vervollkommnungsfähig; *technique, technology, process* perfektionierbar.

perfection [pə'fekʃən] *n* Vollkommenheit, Perfektion *f* ◆ to do sth to ~ etw perfekt tun.

perfectionism [pə'fekʃənɪzəm] *n* Perfektionismus *m*.

perfectionist [pə'fekʃənɪst] [1] *n* Perfektionist *m*.
[2] *adj* perfektionistisch.

perfective [pə'fektɪv] *adj (also Gram)* perfektiv.

perfectly ['pɜːfɪktlɪ] *adv* **(a)** *(flawlessly, completely)* perfekt; *translated, drawn, cooked, matched also* vollendet ◆ he timed his entry ~ er hat seinen Eintritt genau abgepaßt; a ~ finished piece of work eine wirklich vollendete Arbeit; I understand you ~ ich weiß genau, was Sie meinen.
(b) *(absolutely, utterly)* absolut, vollkommen ◆ we're ~ happy about it wir sind damit völlig zufrieden; a ~ lovely day ein wirklich herrlicher Tag; you know ~ well that ... du weißt ganz genau, daß ...

perfidious *adj*, **~ly** *adv* [pɜː'fɪdɪəs, -lɪ] *(liter)* perfid(e) *(liter)*.

perfidiousness [pɜː'fɪdɪəsnɪs], **perfidy** ['pɜːfɪdɪ] *n (liter)* Perfidie *f (liter)*.

perforate ['pɜːfəreɪt] [1] *vt (with row of holes)* perforieren; *(pierce once)* durchstechen, lochen; *(Med)* perforieren.
[2] *vi (ulcer)* durchbrechen.

perforation [ˌpɜːfə'reɪʃən] *n (act)* Perforieren *nt*; *(row of holes, Med)* Perforation *f*.

perforce [pə'fɔːs] *adv (old, liter)* notgedrungen.

perform [pə'fɔːm] [1] *vt play, concerto* aufführen; *solo, duet* vortragen; *part* spielen; *trick* vorführen; *miracle* vollbringen; *task* verrichten, erfüllen; *duty, function* erfüllen; *operation* durchführen; *ritual, ceremony* vollziehen.
[2] *vi* **(a)** *(appear: orchestra, circus act etc)* auftreten ◆ to ~ on the violin Geige spielen.
(b) *(car, machine, football team etc)* leisten; *(examination candidate etc)* abschneiden ◆ the 2 litre version ~s better die Zweiliterversion leistet mehr; the car ~ed excellently in the speed trials in den Geschwindigkeitsversuchen brachte der Wagen ausgezeichnete Ergebnisse; the choir ~ed very well der Chor war sehr gut *or* hat sehr gut gesungen; this car ~s best between 50 and 60 kmph dieser Wagen bringt seine optimale Leistung zwischen 50 und 60 Stundenkilometern; how did he ~? *(actor, musician)* wie war er?; how did the car ~? wie ist der Wagen gelaufen?; he ~ed brilliantly as Hamlet er spielte die Rolle des Hamlet brillant; the car is not ~ing properly der Wagen läuft nicht richtig; how does the metal ~ under pressure? wie verhält sich das Metall unter Druck?; he couldn't ~ *(euph: sexually)* er konnte nicht.
(c) *(euph: excrete)* sein Geschäft verrichten.

performance [pə'fɔːməns] *n* **(a)** *(esp Theat: of play, opera etc)* Aufführung *f*; *(cinema)* Vorstellung *f*; *(by actor)* Leistung *f*; *(of a part)* Darstellung *f* ◆ the late ~ die Spätvorstellung; her ~ as Mother Courage was outstanding ihre Darstellung der Mutter Courage war hervorragend; he gave a splendid ~ er hat eine ausgezeichnete Leistung geboten, er hat ausgezeichnet gespielt/gesungen *etc*; it has not had a ~ since 1950 es ist seit 1950 nicht mehr aufgeführt worden; we are going to hear a ~ of Beethoven's 5th wir werden Beethovens 5. Sinfonie hören.
(b) *(carrying out) see vt* Aufführung *f*; Vortrag *m*; *(of part)* Darstellung *f*; Vorführung *f*; Vollbringung *f*; Erfüllung *f*; Durchführung *f*; Vollzug *m* ◆ in the ~ of his duties in Ausübung seiner Pflicht; he died in the ~ of his duty er starb in Erfüllung seiner Pflicht.
(c) *(effectiveness) (of machine, vehicle, sportsman etc)* Leistung *f*; *(of examination candidate etc)* Abschneiden *nt* ◆ he put up a good ~ er hat sich gut geschlagen *(inf)*; what was his ~ like in the test? wie hat er in der Prüfung abgeschnitten?; the team gave a poor ~ die Mannschaft hat eine schlechte Leistung gezeigt.
(d) *(inf) (to-do, palaver)* Umstand *m*; *(bad behaviour)* Benehmen *nt* ◆ what a ~! was für ein Umstand!; welch ein Benehmen!; what a ~ to put on in front of all the guests sich so vor den Gästen zu benehmen!

performative [pə'fɔːmətɪv] *(Ling)* [1] *n* performativer Ausdruck.
[2] *adj* performativ.

performer [pə'fɔːməʳ] *n* Künstler(in *f*) *m*.

performing [pə'fɔːmɪŋ] *adj animal* dressiert ◆ the ~ arts die darstellenden Künste; ~ rights Aufführungsrechte *pl*.

perfume ['pɜːfjuːm] [1] *n (substance)* Parfüm *nt*; *(smell)* Duft *m*.
[2] [pə'fjuːm] *vt* parfümieren ◆ the flowers ~d the air der Duft der Blumen erfüllte die Luft.

perfumer [pɜː'fjuːməʳ] *n (maker)* Parfümeur *m*; *(seller)* Parfümhändler(in *f*) *m*; *(device)* Parfümzerstäuber *m*.

perfumery [pɜː'fjuːmərɪ] *n (making perfume)* Parfümherstellung *f*; *(perfume factory)* Parfümerie *f*; *(perfumes)* Parfüm *nt*.

perfunctorily [pə'fʌŋktərɪlɪ] *adv see adj.*

perfunctory [pə'fʌŋktərɪ] *adj* flüchtig, der Form halber ◆ he said some ~ words of congratulation er gratulierte mit ein paar flüchtig hingeworfenen Worten.

pergola ['pɜːgələ] *n* Pergola, Laube *f*.

▼ **perhaps** [pə'hæps, præps] *adv* vielleicht ◆ ~ the greatest exponent of the art der möglicherweise bedeutendste Vertreter dieser Kunst; ~ so das kann *or* mag sein.

pericarp ['perɪkɑːp] *n* Perikarp *nt*.

perigee ['perɪdʒiː] *n (Astron)* Perigäum *nt*, Erdnähe *f*.

peril ['perɪl] *n* Gefahr *f* ◆ to be in ~ of one's life in Lebensgefahr sein; do it at your (own) ~ auf Ihre eigene Gefahr.

perilous ['perɪləs] *adj* gefährlich; *situation also* bedrohlich.

➤ LANGUAGE IN USE: **perhaps** → 1.1, 15.3, 26.3

perilously ['perɪləslɪ] *adv* gefährlich ♦ **he was clinging ~ to an outcrop of rock** er hing lebensgefährlich an einem Felsvorsprung; **we came ~ close to bankruptcy/the precipice** wir waren dem Bankrott/Abgrund gefährlich nahe; **she came ~ close to falling** sie wäre um ein Haar heruntergefallen.

perimeter [pə'rɪmɪtəʳ] *n* (*Math*) Umfang, Perimeter *m*; (*Med*) Perimeter *m*; (*of grounds*) Grenze *f* ♦ **~ fence** Umzäunung *f*; **to walk round the ~** um das Gelände herumgehen.

perinatal [perɪ'neɪtəl] *adj* (*Med*) perinatal.

perineum [perɪ'ni:əm] *n* (*Anat*) Damm *m*, Perineum *nt* (*spec*).

period ['pɪərɪəd] *n* **(a)** (*length of time*) Zeit *f*; (*age, epoch*) Zeitalter *nt*, Epoche *f*; (*Geol*) Periode *f* ♦ **Picasso's blue ~** Picassos blaue Periode; **for a ~ of eight weeks/two hours** für eine (Zeit)dauer *or* einen Zeitraum von acht Wochen/zwei Stunden; **within a three-month ~** innerhalb von drei Monaten; **for a three-month ~** drei Monate lang; **at that ~ (of my life)** zu diesem Zeitpunkt (in meinem Leben); **a ~ of cold weather** eine Kaltwetterperiode; **glacial ~** Eiszeit *f*; **the costume** *etc* **of the ~** die Kleidung *etc* der damaligen Zeit; **a writer of the ~** ein zeitgenössischer Schriftsteller.
(b) (*Sch*) (Schul)stunde *f* ♦ **double ~** Doppelstunde.
(c) (*form: sentence*) Periode *f*; (*esp US: full stop*) Punkt *m* ♦ **I don't know anything about American literature ~** (*esp US*) ich habe überhaupt keine Ahnung von amerikanischer Literatur; **I'm not going ~!** (*esp US*) ich gehe nicht, Schluß *or* und damit basta (*inf*)!
(d) (*menstruation*) Periode, Monatsblutung *f*, Tage *pl* (*inf*) ♦ **she missed a ~** sie bekam ihre Periode *etc* nicht.
(e) (*Chem*) Periode *f*.

period: ~ costume, ~ dress *n* zeitgenössische Kostüme *pl*; **~ furniture** *n* antike Möbel *pl*.

periodic [,pɪərɪ'ɒdɪk] *adj* (*intermittent*) periodisch; (*regular also*) regelmäßig ♦ **~ system/table** (*Chem*) Periodensystem *nt*.

periodical [,pɪərɪ'ɒdɪkəl] [1] *adj see* **periodic.**
[2] *n* Zeitschrift *f*; (*academic also*) Periodikum *nt*.

periodically [,pɪərɪ'ɒdɪkəlɪ] *adv see* **periodic.**

periodicity [,pɪərɪə'dɪsɪtɪ] *n* (*Chem*) Periodizität *f*.

periodontitis [,perɪəʊdɒn'taɪtɪs] *n* Wurzelhautentzündung *f*.

period: ~ pains *npl* Menstruationsbeschwerden *pl*; **~ piece** *n* **(a)** antikes Stück; (*painting, music etc*) Zeitdokument; **(b)** (*also* **~ play**) Zeitstück *nt*.

peripatetic [,perɪpə'tetɪk] *adj* umherreisend; *existence* rastlos; *teacher* an mehreren Schulen unterrichtend *attr*.

peripheral [pə'rɪfərəl] [1] *adj* Rand-; (*Anat*) peripher; (*fig*) nebensächlich, peripher; (*Comput*) Peripherie-.
[2] *n* (*Comput*) Peripheriegerät *nt*.

periphery [pə'rɪfərɪ] *n* Peripherie *f* ♦ **young people on the ~ of society** junge Menschen am Rande der Gesellschaft.

periphrastic [,perɪ'fræstɪk] *adj* periphrastisch.

periscope ['perɪskəʊp] *n* Periskop *nt*.

perish ['perɪʃ] [1] *vi* **(a)** (*liter*) (*die*) umkommen, sterben; (*be destroyed: cities, civilization*) untergehen ♦ **we shall do it or ~ in the attempt** wir werden es machen, koste es, was es wolle; **he ~ed at sea** er fand den Tod auf See.
(b) (*rubber, leather etc*) verschleißen, brüchig werden; (*food*) verderben, schlecht werden.
[2] *vt* **(a)** *rubber, leather* zerstören, brüchig werden lassen.
(b) (*inf*) **~ the thought!** Gott behüte *or* bewahre!

perishable ['perɪʃəbl] [1] *adj food* verderblich ♦ **"~"** „leicht verderblich".
[2] *npl* **~s** leicht verderbliche Ware(n).

perished ['perɪʃt] *adj* (*inf: with cold*) durchfroren.

perisher ['perɪʃəʳ] *n* (*Brit inf*) Teufelsbraten *m* (*inf*).

perishing ['perɪʃɪŋ] *adj* (*inf*) **(a)** (*very cold*) *room, weather* eisig kalt ♦ **I'm ~** ich geh' fast ein vor Kälte (*inf*). **(b)** (*Brit inf: objectionable*) verdammt (*inf*).

peristalsis [,perɪ'stælsɪs] *n* Peristaltik *f*.

peristyle ['perɪstaɪl] *n* Peristyl *nt*.

peritoneum [,perɪtəʊ'ni:əm] *n* Bauchfell, Peritoneum (*spec*) *nt*.

peritonitis [,perɪtəʊ'naɪtɪs] *n* Bauchfellentzündung *f*.

periwig ['perɪwɪg] *n* (*Hist*) Perücke *f*.

periwinkle ['perɪ,wɪŋkl] *n* (*Bot*) Immergrün *nt*; (*Zool*) Strandschnecke *f*.

perjure ['pɜ:dʒəʳ] *vr* einen Meineid leisten.

perjured ['pɜ:dʒəd] *adj evidence, witness* meineidig.

perjury ['pɜ:dʒərɪ] *n* Meineid *m* ♦ **to commit ~** einen Meineid leisten.

perk [pɜ:k] *n* (*esp Brit: benefit*) Vergünstigung *f*.

♦**perk up** [1] *vt sep* **(a)** (*lift*) *head* heben ♦ **he ~ed ~ his ears** (*dog, person*) er spitzte die Ohren.
(b) to ~ sb ~ (*make lively: coffee etc*) jdn aufmöbeln (*inf*) *or* munter machen; (*make cheerful: visit, idea etc*) jdn aufheitern.
[2] *vi* (*liven up: person, party*) munter werden; (*cheer up*) aufleben; (*become interested*) hellhörig werden ♦ **I hope this book ~s ~ soon** ich hoffe, das Buch wird bald interessanter.

perkily ['pɜ:kɪlɪ] *adv see adj*.

perky ['pɜ:kɪ] *adj* (*+er*) (*cheerful, bright*) munter; (*cheeky, pert*) keß, keck.

perm[1] [pɜ:m] *abbr of* **permanent wave** [1] *n* Dauerwelle *f* ♦ **to give sb a ~** jdm eine Dauerwelle machen.
[2] *vt* **to ~ sb's hair** jdm eine Dauerwelle machen; **she only had the ends ~ed** sie ließ sich (*dat*) nur an den Enden eine Dauerwelle machen.
[3] *vi* **my hair doesn't ~ very easily** Dauerwelle hält bei mir sehr schlecht.

perm[2] *n* (*for football pools*) *abbr of* **permutation.**

permafrost ['pɜ:məfrɒst] *n* Dauerfrostboden *m*.

permanence ['pɜ:mənəns], **permanency** ['pɜ:mənənsɪ] *n* Dauerhaftigkeit, Permanenz *f*; (*of relationship, marriage also*) Beständigkeit *f*; (*of arrangement also, of job*) Beständigkeit *f* ♦ **having bought a flat, she began to feel some degree of ~** nachdem sie sich (*dat*) eine Wohnung gekauft hatte, entwickelte sie ein gewisses Gefühl der Bodenständigkeit; **is there such a thing as ~?** ist überhaupt etwas beständig auf der Welt?

permanent ['pɜ:mənənt] [1] *adj* ständig, permanent; *arrangement, position, building* fest; *job, relationship, dye* dauerhaft; *agreement* unbefristet ♦ **the ~ revolution** die permanente Revolution; **I hope this is not going to become ~** ich hoffe, das wird kein Dauerzustand; **a ~ employee** ein Festangestellter *m*; **I'm not ~ here** ich bin hier nicht fest angestellt; **~ assets** Anlagevermögen *nt*; **~ capital** Anlagekapital *nt*; **~ fixture** (*lit*) festinstallierte Einrichtung; **he is a ~ fixture here** er gehört schon mit zum Inventar; **~ magnet** Permanentmagnet *m*; **~ memory** (*Comput*) Festspeicher *m*; **~ pleats** Dauerfalten *pl*; **~ residence/address** ständiger *or* fester Wohnsitz; **one's ~ teeth** die zweiten Zähne; **~ way** (*Brit*) Bahnkörper *m*; **~ wave** *see* **perm**[1] **1.**
[2] *n* (*US*) *see* **perm**[1] **1.**

permanently ['pɜ:mənəntlɪ] *adv* permanent, ständig; *fixed* fest ♦ **a ~ depressing effect** eine anhaltend deprimierende Wirkung; **~ employed** festangestellt *attr*, fest angestellt *pred*; **~ glued together** dauerhaft verbunden; **~ pleated skirt** Rock mit Dauerfalten; **are you living ~ in Frankfurt?** ist Frankfurt Ihr fester *or* ständiger Wohnsitz?

permanganate [pɜ:'mæŋgənɪt] *n* Permanganat *nt*.

permeability [,pɜ:mɪə'bɪlɪtɪ] *n* Durchlässigkeit, Permeabilität (*geh, Sci*) *f*.

permeable ['pɜ:mɪəbl] *adj* durchlässig, permeabel (*geh, Sci*).

permeate ['pɜ:mɪeɪt] [1] *vt* (*lit, fig*) durchdringen.
[2] *vi* dringen (*into* in *+acc*, *through* durch).

permissible [pə'mɪsɪbl] *adj* erlaubt (*for sb* jdm).

▼ **permission** [pə'mɪʃən] *n* Erlaubnis *f* ♦ **with your ~** mit Ihrer Erlaubnis, wenn Sie gestatten; **without ~ from sb** ohne jds Erlaubnis; **to do sth with/by sb's ~** etw mit jds Erlaubnis tun; **to get ~/sb's ~** eine/jds Erlaubnis erhalten; **to give ~ (for sth)** etw erlauben, die Erlaubnis (für etw) erteilen; **to give sb ~ (to do sth)** jdm die Erlaubnis geben *or* jdm erlauben(, etw zu tun); **no ~ is needed** eine Erlaubnis ist nicht erforderlich; **to ask sb's ~, to ask ~ of sb** jdn um Erlaubnis bitten; **"by (kind) ~ of ..."** „mit (freundlicher) Genehmigung (*+gen*) ...".

permissive [pə'mɪsɪv] *adj* nachgiebig, permissiv (*geh*); (*sexually*) freizügig ♦ **it encourages youngsters to be ~** es führt zu allzu großer Freizügigkeit unter Jugendlichen; **the ~ society** die permissive Gesellschaft.

permissiveness [pə'mɪsɪvnɪs] *n* Nachgiebigkeit, Permissivität (*geh*) *f*; (*sexually*) Freizügigkeit *f*.

▼ **permit** [pə'mɪt] [1] *vt sth* erlauben, gestatten ♦ **to ~ sb to do sth** jdm erlauben, etw zu tun; **is it/am I ~ted to smoke?** darf man/ich rauchen?; **visitors are not ~ted after 10** nach 10 Uhr sind keine Besucher mehr erlaubt; **~ me!** gestatten Sie bitte!
[2] *vi* **(a) if you (will) ~** wenn Sie gestatten *or* erlauben; **if the weather ~s, weather ~ting** wenn es das Wetter erlaubt *or* gestattet *or* zuläßt.
(b) (*form*) **to ~ of sth** etw zulassen.
[3] ['pɜ:mɪt] *n* Genehmigung *f* ♦ **~ holder** Inhaber(in *f*) *m* eines Berechtigungsscheins *or* (*for parking*) Parkausweises; **"~ holders only"** (*for parking*) „Parken nur mit Parkausweis".

permutation [,pɜ:mjʊ'teɪʃən] *n* Permutation *f*.

permute [pə'mju:t] *vt* permutieren.

pernicious [pɜ:'nɪʃəs] *adj* schädlich; (*Med*) perniziös, bösartig.

pernickety [pə'nɪkɪtɪ] *adj* (*inf*) pingelig (*inf*).

peroration [,perə'reɪʃən] *n* (*liter*) (*concluding part*) Resümee *nt*, Zusammenfassung *f*; (*lengthy speech*) endlose Rede.

peroxide [pə'rɒksaɪd] *n* Peroxyd *nt* ♦ **a ~ blonde** (*pej*) eine Wasserstoffblondine; **~ blonde hair** wasserstoffblonde Haare.

perpendicular [,pɜ:pən'dɪkjʊləʳ] [1] *adj* **(a)** senkrecht (*to* zu) ♦ **the wall is not quite ~ to the ceiling** die Mauer steht nicht ganz lotrecht zur Decke; **a ~ cliff** eine senkrecht abfallende Klippe.
(b) (*Archit*) perpendikular.
[2] *n* Senkrechte *f* ♦ **to drop a ~** ein Lot fällen; **to be out of ~** nicht im Lot sein.

perpendicularly [,pɜ:pən'dɪkjʊləlɪ] *adv* senkrecht.

perpetrate ['pɜ:pɪtreɪt] *vt* begehen; *crime also* verüben ♦ **this is the worst film he has ever ~d** (*hum*) das ist der schlimmste Film, den er je verbrochen hat (*hum inf*).

perpetration [,pɜ:pɪ'treɪʃən] *n* Begehen *nt*, Begehung *f*; (*of crime also*) Verübung *f*.

perpetrator ['pɜ:pɪtreɪtəʳ] *n* Täter *m* ♦ **the ~ of this crime** derjenige, der dieses Verbrechen begangen hat.

perpetual [pə'petjʊəl] *adj* ständig, fortwährend, immerwährend; *joy* stet; *ice, snow* ewig ♦ **you're a ~ source of amazement to me** ich muß mich immer wieder über dich wundern; **~ motion/motion machine** Perpetuum mobile *nt*.

perpetually [pə'petjʊəlɪ] *adv* ständig.

perpetuate [pə'petjʊeɪt] *vt* aufrechterhalten; *memory* bewahren ♦ **the old language of the area has been ~d in the place names** die alte Sprache der Gegend lebt in den Ortsnamen fort.

perpetuation [pə,petjʊ'eɪʃən] *n* Aufrechterhaltung *f*; (*of memory*) Bewahrung *f*; (*of old names etc*) Beibehaltung *f*.

perpetuity [,pɜ:pɪ'tju:ɪtɪ] *n* (*form*) Ewigkeit *f* ♦ **in ~** auf ewig; (*Jur*) lebenslänglich.

perplex [pə'pleks] *vt* verblüffen, verdutzen.

➤ LANGUAGE IN USE: **permission** → 9.1, 9.2 **permit** → 9.1, 9.2, 9.4

perplexed *adj*, **~ly** *adv* [pə'plekst, -sɪdlɪ] verblüfft, verdutzt, perplex.
perplexing [pə'pleksɪŋ] *adj* verblüffend.
perplexingly [pə'pleksɪŋlɪ] *adv* verwirrend ◆ **a ~ difficult problem** ein schwieriges und verwirrendes Problem.
perplexity [pə'pleksɪtɪ] *n* Verblüffung *f* ◆ **to be in some ~** etwas verblüfft *or* verdutzt *or* perplex sein.
perquisite ['pɜːkwɪzɪt] *n* (*form*) Vergünstigung *f*.
perry ['perɪ] *n* Birnenmost *m*.
per se ['pɜː'seɪ] *adv* an sich, per se (*geh*).
persecute ['pɜːsɪkjuːt] *vt* verfolgen.
persecution [ˌpɜːsɪ'kjuːʃən] *n* Verfolgung *f* (*of* von) ◆ **his ~ by the press** seine Verfolgung durch die Presse; **to have a ~ complex** an Verfolgungswahn leiden.
persecutor ['pɜːsɪkjuːtəʳ] *n* Verfolger(in *f*) *m*.
perseverance [ˌpɜːsɪ'vɪərəns] *n* Ausdauer (*with* mit), Beharrlichkeit (*with* bei) *f*.
persevere [ˌpɜːsɪ'vɪəʳ] *vi* durchhalten ◆ **to ~ in one's studies** mit seinem Studium weitermachen; **he ~d with German** er machte mit Deutsch weiter; **to ~ in** *or* **with one's attempts/efforts to do sth** unermüdlich weiter versuchen, etw zu tun.
persevering *adj*, **~ly** *adv* [ˌpɜːsɪ'vɪərɪŋ, -lɪ] ausdauernd, beharrlich.
Persia ['pɜːʃə] *n* Persien *nt*.
Persian ['pɜːʃən] 1 *adj* persisch ◆ **~ carpet** Perser(teppich) *m*; **~ cat** Perserkatze *f*; **the ~ Gulf** der Persische Golf; **~ lamb** (*animal*) Karakulschaf *nt*; (*skin, coat*) Persianer *m*.
2 *n* **(a)** Perser(in *f*) *m*. **(b)** (*language*) Persisch *nt*.
persiflage [ˌpɜːsɪ'flɑːʒ] *n* Persiflage *f*.
persimmon [pɜː'sɪmən] *n* Persimone *f*; (*wood*) Persimmon *nt*.
persist [pə'sɪst] *vi* (*persevere*) nicht lockerlassen, unbeirrt fortfahren (*with* mit); (*be tenacious: in belief, demand etc*) beharren, bestehen (*in* auf *+dat*); (*last, continue: fog, pain etc*) anhalten, fortdauern ◆ **if you ~ in misbehaving/coming late** wenn du dich weiterhin so schlecht benimmst/wenn du weiterhin zu spät kommst; **if the greenfly still ~** wenn das die Blattläuse nicht beseitigt; **we shall ~ in our efforts** wir werden in unseren Bemühungen nicht nachlassen.
persistence [pə'sɪstəns], **persistency** [pə'sɪstənsɪ] *n* (*tenacity*) Beharrlichkeit, Hartnäckigkeit *f*; (*perseverance*) Ausdauer *f*; (*of disease*) Hartnäckigkeit *f*; (*of fog, pain etc*) Anhalten, Fortdauern *nt* ◆ **the ~ of his questioning brought results** sein beharrliches Fragen hat schließlich doch zu etwas geführt; **the ~ of a high temperature** anhaltend hohes Fieber.
persistent [pə'sɪstənt] *adj* (*tenacious*) *demands, questions* beharrlich; *person* hartnäckig; *attempts, efforts* ausdauernd; (*repeated, constant*) *offender, drinking, drinker* gewohnheitsmäßig; *nagging, lateness, threats* ständig; *cheerfulness* gleichbleibend; (*continuing*) *rain, illness, pain, noise* anhaltend ◆ **despite our ~ warnings ...** obwohl wir sie/ihn *etc* immer wieder gewarnt haben ...; **~ vegetative state** (*Med*) waches Koma.
persistently [pə'sɪstəntlɪ] *adv see adj*.
person ['pɜːsn] *n* **(a)** *pl* **people** *or* (*form*) **-s** (*human being*) Mensch *m*; (*in official contexts*) Person *f* ◆ **no ~** kein Mensch, niemand; **I know no such ~** so jemanden kenne ich nicht; **any ~** jeder; **a certain ~** ein gewisser Jemand; **~ to ~ call** Gespräch *nt* mit Voranmeldung; **30 p per ~** 30 Pence pro Person; **the murder was committed by ~ or ~s unknown** der Mord wurde von einem oder mehreren unbekannten Tätern verübt.
(b) *pl* **-s** (*Gram, Jur: legal ~*) Person *f* ◆ **first ~ singular/plural** erste Person Singular/Plural.
(c) *pl* **-s** (*body, physical presence*) Körper *m*; (*appearance*) Äußere(s) *nt* ◆ **in ~** persönlich; **in the ~ of** in Gestalt (*+gen*); **crime against the ~** Vergehen gegen die Person; **on** *or* **about one's ~** bei sich.
-person *suf in Berufsbezeichnungen etc als neutralere Form anstelle von '-man'* ◆ **chair~** Vorsitzende(r) *mf*; **sales~** Verkäufer(in *f*) *m*.
persona [pɜː'səʊnə] *n, pl* **-e** (*Psych*) Persona *f* ◆ **~ grata** (*Jur*) Persona grata *f*; **~ non grata** (*Jur, fig*) Persona non grata *f*.
personable ['pɜːsnəbl] *adj* von angenehmer Erscheinung.
personae [pɜː'səʊniː] *pl of* **persona**.
personage ['pɜːsənɪdʒ] *n* Persönlichkeit *f*.
personal ['pɜːsənl] *adj* **(a)** persönlich ◆ **he gave several ~ performances to promote his new record** er trat mehrmals persönlich auf, um für seine neue Platte zu werben; **~ freshness** *or* **cleanliness/hygiene** Körperfrische *f*/-pflege *f*; **it's nothing ~, I just don't think you're the right person** nicht, daß ich etwas gegen Sie persönlich hätte, Sie sind nur nicht der/die Richtige; **don't be ~** nun werden Sie mal nicht persönlich; **I have no ~ knowledge of it** mir (persönlich) ist nichts davon bekannt; "~" (*on letter*) „privat"; **~ call** Privatgespräch *nt*; **~ column** Familienanzeigen *pl*; **~ computer** Personal-Computer, PC *m*; **~ effects** persönliches Eigentum; **~ loan** Personaldarlehen, Privatdarlehen *nt*; **~ organizer** Terminplaner, Zeitplaner *m*; (*electronic*) elektronisches Notizbuch, Datencenter *nt*; **~ property** persönliches Eigentum, Privateigentum *nt*; **~ stationery** Briefpapier *nt* mit persönlichem Briefkopf; **~ stereo** Walkman ® *m*.
(b) (*Gram*) **~ pronoun** Personalpronomen *nt*, persönliches Fürwort.
personality [ˌpɜːsə'nælɪtɪ] *n* **(a)** (*character, person*) Persönlichkeit *f* ◆ **~ cult** Personenkult *m*; **~ disorder** Persönlichkeitsstörung *f*; **~ development** Persönlichkeitsentfaltung *f*.
(b) (*personal remark*) **let's keep personalities out of this** lassen wir persönliche Dinge aus dem Spiel; **let's not descend to personalities** wir wollen nicht persönlich werden.

➤ LANGUAGE IN USE: **personally** → 6.1

personalize ['pɜːsənəlaɪz] *vt* **(a)** (*make more personal*) persönlicher gestalten; (*put initials etc on*) *diary, calculator, shirt* eine persönliche *or* individuelle Note geben (*+dat*) ◆ **~d letter paper** persönliches *or* individuelles Briefpapier. **(b)** (*treat as personal issue*) personalisieren.
personally ['pɜːsənəlɪ] *adv* persönlich ◆ **~, I think that ...** ich persönlich bin der Meinung, daß ...
personalty ['pɜːsənltɪ] *n* (*Jur*) bewegliches Vermögen.
personification [pɜːˌsɒnɪfɪ'keɪʃən] *n* Verkörperung, Personifizierung *f* ◆ **he is the ~ of good taste** er ist der personifizierte gute Geschmack.
personify [pɜː'sɒnɪfaɪ] *vt* personifizieren; (*be the personification of also*) verkörpern ◆ **he is greed personified** er ist der personifizierte Geiz *or* der Geiz in Person.
personnel [ˌpɜːsə'nel] 1 *n sing or pl* **(a)** Personal *nt*; (*on plane*) Besatzung *f*; (*on ship*) Besatzung, Mannschaft *f*; (*Mil*) Leute *pl* ◆ **this firm employs 800 ~** diese Firma beschäftigt 800 Leute; **with a larger ~** mit mehr Personal.
(b) (*~ department*) die Personalabteilung; (*~ work*) Personalarbeit *f*.
2 *attr* Personal- ◆ **~ agency** Personalagentur *f*; **~ carrier** (*Mil*) Mannschaftstransportwagen *m*/-transportflugzeug *nt*; **~ management** Personalführung *f*; **~ manager/officer** Personalchef *m*/-leiter *m*.
perspective [pə'spektɪv] *n* (*lit*) Perspektive *f*; (*fig also*) Blickwinkel *m* ◆ **to get a different ~ on a problem** ein Problem aus einer anderen Perspektive *or* aus einem anderen Blickwinkel sehen; **in ~** (*Art*) perspektivisch; **the foreground isn't in ~** der Vordergrund ist perspektivisch nicht richtig; **try to keep/get things in ~** versuchen Sie, nüchtern und sachlich zu bleiben/das nüchtern und sachlich zu sehen; **to get sth out of ~** (*lit: artist etc*) etw perspektivisch verzerren; (*fig*) etw verzerrt sehen; **in historical ~** aus historischer Sicht; **to see things in their proper** *or* **true ~** die Dinge so sehen, wie sie sind.
Perspex ® ['pɜːspeks] *n* Acrylglas *nt*.
perspicacious [ˌpɜːspɪ'keɪʃəs] *adj person, remark etc* scharfsinnig; *decision* weitsichtig.
perspicacity [ˌpɜːspɪ'kæsɪtɪ] *n* Scharfsinn, Scharfblick *m*; (*of decision*) Weitsicht *f*.
perspicuity [ˌpɜːspɪ'kjuːɪtɪ] *n* Klarheit *f*; (*clearness: of expression, statement also*) Verständlichkeit *f*.
perspicuous [ˌpə'spɪkjʊəs] *adj* einleuchtend; (*clear*) *expression, statement* klar, verständlich.
perspiration [ˌpɜːspə'reɪʃən] *n* (*perspiring*) Schwitzen *nt*, Transpiration *f* (*geh*); (*sweat*) Schweiß *m* ◆ **the ~ was dripping off him, he was dripping with ~** ihm lief der Schweiß in Strömen herunter; **beads of ~** Schweißperlen *pl*.
perspire [pə'spaɪəʳ] *vi* schwitzen, transpirieren (*geh*).
persuadable [pə'sweɪdəbl] *adj* **he may be ~** (*amenable*) vielleicht läßt er sich *or* ist er zu überreden; (*convincible*) vielleicht läßt er sich *or* ist er zu überzeugen.
persuade [pə'sweɪd] *vt* überreden; (*convince*) überzeugen ◆ **to ~ sb to do sth** jdn überreden, etw zu tun; **to ~ sb into doing sth** jdn dazu überreden, etw zu tun; **to ~ sb out of sth/doing sth** jdm etw ausreden/jdn dazu überreden, etw nicht zu tun; **to ~ sb of sth** jdn von etw überzeugen; **to ~ sb that ...** jdn davon überzeugen, daß ...; **I am ~d that ...** ich bin überzeugt, daß ...; **she is easily ~d** sie ist leicht zu überreden/überzeugen; **he doesn't take much persuading** ihn braucht man nicht lange zu überreden.
persuader [pə'sweɪdəʳ] *n* Überredungskünstler(in *f*) *m* ◆ **the hidden ~s** die heimlichen Verführer.
persuasible [pə'sweɪzəbl] *adj see* **persuadable**.
persuasion [pə'sweɪʒən] *n* **(a)** (*persuading*) Überredung *f* ◆ **advertising uses many subtle means of ~** die Werbung arbeitet mit vielen subtilen Überzeugungsmechanismen; **her powers of ~** ihre Überredungskünste; **she tried every possible means of ~ to get him to agree** sie setzte ihre ganze Überredungskunst ein, um seine Zustimmung zu erlangen; **I don't need much ~ to stop working** man braucht mich nicht lange zu überreden, damit ich aufhöre zu arbeiten.
(b) (*persuasiveness*) Überzeugungskraft *f*.
(c) (*belief*) Überzeugung *f*; (*sect, denomination*) Glaube(nsrichtung *f*) *m* ◆ **I am not of that ~** (*don't believe that*) davon bin ich nicht überzeugt; (*don't belong to that sect*) ich gehöre nicht diesem Glauben an; **and others of that ~** und andere, die dieser Überzeugung anhängen; **to be of left-wing ~, to have left-wing ~s** linke Ansichten haben.
persuasive [pə'sweɪsɪv] *adj salesman, voice* beredsam; *arguments etc* überzeugend ◆ **he can be very ~** er kann einen gut überreden; (*convincing*) er kann einen leicht überzeugen; **I had to be very ~** ich mußte meine ganze Überredungskunst aufwenden.
persuasively [pə'sweɪsɪvlɪ] *adv argue etc* überzeugend ◆ **..., he said ~** ..., versuchte er sie/ihn *etc* zu überreden.
persuasiveness [pə'sweɪsɪvnɪs] *n* (*of person, salesman etc*) Überredungskunst, Beredsamkeit *f*; (*of argument etc*) Überzeugungskraft *f*.
pert [pɜːt] *adj* (*+er*) keck, keß; (*impudent*) keck ◆ **a ~ little smile** ein kesses *or* freches Lächeln.
pertain [pɜː'teɪn] *vi* **to ~ to sth** etw betreffen; (*belong to: land etc*) zu etw gehören; **all documents ~ing to the case** alle den Fall betreffenden Dokumente; **and other matters ~ing to it** und andere damit verbundene Fragen; **of or ~ing to sth** etw betreffend.
pertinacious [ˌpɜːtɪ'neɪʃəs] *adj* (*persevering*) beharrlich, ausdauernd; (*tenacious, stubborn*) hartnäckig.
pertinacity [ˌpɜːtɪ'næsɪtɪ] *n see adj* Beharrlichkeit, Ausdauer *f*; Hartnäckigkeit *f*.
pertinence ['pɜːtɪnəns] *n* Relevanz *f* (*to* für); (*of information*) Sachdienlich-

keit *f*.
pertinent ['pɜːtɪnənt] *adj* relevant (*to* für); *information* sachdienlich.
pertinently ['pɜːtɪnəntlɪ] *adv* passend, völlig richtig ◆ **he asked very ~ whether ...** er stellte zu Recht die Frage, ob ...
pertly ['pɜːtlɪ] *adv see adj*.
pertness ['pɜːtnɪs] *n* Keckheit, Keßheit *f*; (*impudence*) Keckheit *f*.
perturb [pə'tɜːb] *vt* beunruhigen.
perturbation [,pɜːtɜː'beɪʃən] *n* (*state*) Unruhe *f*; (*act*) Beunruhigung *f* ◆ **to be in (a state of) some ~** ziemlich in Unruhe sein.
perturbing *adj*, **~ly** *adv* [pə'tɜːbɪŋ, -lɪ] beunruhigend.
Peru [pə'ruː] *n* Peru *nt*.
perusal [pə'ruːzəl] *n* Lektüre *f*; (*careful*) sorgfältige Durchsicht, Prüfung *f* ◆ **after a brief ~ of the newspaper he ...** nachdem er kurz einen Blick in die Zeitung geworfen hatte ...
peruse [pə'ruːz] *vt* (durch)lesen; (*carefully*) sorgfältig durchsehen, prüfen.
Peruvian [pə'ruːvɪən] 1 *adj* peruanisch.
2 *n* Peruaner(in *f*) *m*.
pervade [pɜː'veɪd] *vt* erfüllen; (*smell also*) durchziehen; (*light*) durchfluten ◆ **his writing is ~d with dialect expressions** seine Bücher sind voller Dialektausdrücke; **the universities are ~d with subversive elements/propaganda** die Universitäten sind mit subversiven Elementen durchsetzt/von subversiver Propaganda durchdrungen.
pervasive [pɜː'veɪsɪv] *adj smell etc* durchdringend; *influence, feeling, ideas* um sich greifend.
pervasively [pɜː'veɪsɪvlɪ] *adv* durchdringend ◆ **to spread ~** (*smell etc*) sich überall ausbreiten (*through* in +*dat*); (*ideas, mood etc also*) um sich greifen (*through* in +*dat*).
pervasiveness [pɜː'veɪsɪvnɪs] *n see adj* durchdringender Charakter; um sich greifender Charakter.
perverse [pə'vɜːs] *adj* (*contrary*) *idea* abwegig; (*perverted*) pervers, widernatürlich.
perversely [pə'vɜːslɪ] *adv see adj* ◆ **do you have to be so ~ different?** mußt du denn immer um jeden Preis anders sein?; **he is really ~ old-fashioned** er ist wirklich hoffnungslos altmodisch; **the translation still sounds ~ French** die Übersetzung klingt noch immer penetrant französisch.
perverseness [pə'vɜːsnɪs] *n see adj* Abwegigkeit *f*; Perversität, Widernatürlichkeit *f*.
perversion [pə'vɜːʃən] *n* (*esp sexual, Psych*) Perversion *f*; (*no pl: act of perverting*) Pervertierung *f*; (*Rel*) Fehlglaube *m*; (*no pl: act*) Irreleitung *f*; (*distortion: of truth etc*) Verzerrung *f*.
perversity [pə'vɜːsɪtɪ] *n see* **perverseness**.
pervert [pə'vɜːt] 1 *vt* (*deprave*) *person, mind* verderben, pervertieren; (*Rel*) *believer* irreleiten; (*change, distort*) *truth, sb's words* verzerren ◆ **to ~ the course of justice** (*Jur*) die Rechtsfindung behindern; (*by official*) das Recht beugen.
2 ['pɜːvɜːt] *n* Perverse(r) *mf*.
pervious ['pɜːvɪəs] *adj* (*lit*) durchlässig; (*fig*) zugänglich (*to* für) ◆ **chalk is ~ (to water)** Kalk ist wasserdurchlässig.
peseta [pə'seɪtə] *n* Peseta *f*.
pesky ['peskɪ] *adj* (+*er*) (*esp US inf*) nervtötend (*inf*).
pessary ['pesərɪ] *n* (*contraceptive*) Pessar *nt*; (*suppository*) Zäpfchen, Suppositorium (*spec*) *nt*.
pessimism ['pesɪmɪzəm] *n* Pessimismus *m*, Schwarzseherei *f*.
pessimist ['pesɪmɪst] *n* Pessimist(in *f*), Schwarzseher(in *f*) *m*.
pessimistic [,pesɪ'mɪstɪk] *adj* pessimistisch ◆ **I'm rather ~ about it** da bin ich ziemlich pessimistisch, da sehe ich ziemlich schwarz (*inf*); **I'm ~ about our chances of success** ich bin pessimistisch, was unsere Erfolgschancen angeht, ich sehe schwarz für unsere Erfolgschancen (*inf*).
pessimistically [,pesɪ'mɪstɪkəlɪ] *adv* pessimistisch.
pest [pest] *n* (**a**) (*Zool*) Schädling *m* ◆ **~ control** Schädlingsbekämpfung *f*. (**b**) (*fig*) (*person*) Nervensäge *f*; (*thing*) Plage *f*. (**c**) (*obs: plague*) Pest, Pestilenz (*old*) *f*.
pester ['pestəʳ] *vt* belästigen; (*keep on at: with requests etc*) plagen ◆ **to ~ the life out of sb** jdm keine Ruhe lassen; **she ~ed me for the book** sie ließ mir keine Ruhe wegen des Buches; **to ~ sb to do sth** jdn bedrängen, etw zu tun.
pesticide ['pestɪsaɪd] *n* Schädlingsbekämpfungsmittel, Pestizid (*spec*) *nt*.
pestiferous [pe'stɪfərəs] *adj* verpestet; (*inf: annoying*) lästig.
pestilence ['pestɪləns] *n* (*old, liter*) Pest, Pestilenz (*old*) *f*.
pestilent ['pestɪlənt], **pestilential** [,pestɪ'lenʃəl] *adj* pesterfüllt; (*fig: pernicious*) schädlich, verderblich; (*inf: loathsome*) ekelhaft ◆ **a ~ disease** eine Seuche.
pestle ['pesl] *n* Stößel *m*.
pet[1] [pet] 1 *adj attr animal* Haus-; (*favourite*) *pupil, idea etc* Lieblings- ◆ **a ~ lion** ein zahmer Löwe; **her two ~ dogs** ihre beiden Hunde; **a ~ name** ein Kosename *m*; **~ food** Tierfutter *nt*; *see* **hate**.
2 *n* (**a**) (*animal*) Haustier *nt*.
(**b**) (*favourite*) Liebling *m* ◆ **teacher's ~** Lehrers Liebling *m or* Schätzchen *nt* (*inf*); (*as derogatory name*) Streber *m*.
(**c**) (*inf: dear*) Schatz *m* ◆ **yes, (my) ~** ja, (mein) Schatz; **he's rather a ~** er ist wirklich lieb *or* ein Schatz.
(**d**) (*caress*) **he wants a ~** er möchte gestreichelt werden.
3 *vt animal* streicheln; *child also* liebkosen; (*fig: spoil*) (ver)- hätscheln.
4 *vi* (*sexually*) Petting machen.
pet[2] *n* (*dated inf: huff*) Verstimmung *f* ◆ **to be in/get into a ~** verstimmt *or* gekränkt sein/werden.
petal ['petl] *n* Blütenblatt *nt*.
petard [pe'tɑːd] *n* Petarde *f*; *see* **hoist**.
Pete [piːt] *n* **for ~'s** *or* **p~'s sake** (*inf*) um Himmels willen.
Peter ['piːtəʳ] *n* Peter *m*; (*apostle*) Petrus *m* ◆ **Saint ~** Sankt Peter, der Heilige Petrus; **to rob ~ to pay Paul** ein Loch mit dem anderen zustopfen; **he is a real ~ Pan** er will einfach nicht erwachsen werden; **~ Pan collar** Bubikragen *m*.
◆**peter out** *vi* langsam zu Ende gehen; (*mineral vein*) versiegen; (*river*) versickern; (*song, noise*) verhallen; (*interest*) sich verlieren, sich totlaufen; (*excitement*) sich legen; (*plan*) im Sande verlaufen.
peterman ['piːtəmən] *n, pl* **-men** [-mən] (*sl*) Schränker (*sl*), Panzerknacker (*inf*) *m*.
petersham ['piːtəʃəm] *n* (*ribbon*) Seidenripsband *nt*.
petiole ['petɪəʊl] *n* Stengel *m*.
petit bourgeois ['petɪ'bʊəʒwɑː] 1 *n* Kleinbürger(in *f*) *m*.
2 *adj* kleinbürgerlich.
petite [pə'tiːt] *adj woman, girl* zierlich.
petite bourgeoisie ['petɪ,bʊəʒwɑː'ziː] *n* Kleinbürgertum *nt*.
petit four ['petɪ'fɔːr] *n, pl* **-s -s** Petit four *nt*.
petition [pə'tɪʃən] 1 *n* (**a**) (*list of signatures*) Unterschriftenliste *f* ◆ **to get up a ~ for/against sth** Unterschriften für/gegen etw sammeln.
(**b**) (*request*) Gesuch *nt*, Bittschrift, Petition *f* ◆ **~ for mercy** Gnadengesuch *nt*.
(**c**) (*Jur*) **~ for divorce** Scheidungsantrag *m*.
2 *vt person, authorities* (*request, entreat*) ersuchen (*for* um); (*hand ~ to*) eine Unterschriftenliste vorlegen (+*dat*).
3 *vi* (**a**) (*hand in ~*) eine Unterschriftenliste einreichen.
(**b**) (*Jur*) **to ~ for divorce** die Scheidung einreichen.
petitioner [pə'tɪʃənəʳ] *n* Bittsteller(in *f*) *m*; (*Jur*) Kläger(in *f*) *m*.
petit ['petɪ]: **~ jury** *n see* **petty jury**; **~ point** *n* Petit point *nt*.
petits pois [,petɪ'pwɑː] *npl* (*form*) Petits pois *pl*.
Petrarch ['petrɑːk] *n* Petrarca.
petrel ['petrəl] *n* Sturmvogel *m*.
petri dish ['petrɪ,dɪʃ] *n* Petrischale *f*.
petrifaction [,petrɪ'fækʃən] *n* Versteinerung, Petrifikation *f*.
petrified ['petrɪfaɪd] *adj* (**a**) (*lit*) versteinert ◆ **as though ~** wie erstarrt. (**b**) (*fig*) **I was ~ (with fear)** ich war starr vor Schrecken; **she is ~ of spiders/of doing that** sie hat panische Angst vor Spinnen/davor, das zu tun.
petrify ['petrɪfaɪ] 1 *vt* (**a**) (*lit*) versteinern. (**b**) (*frighten*) **he really petrifies me** er jagt mir schreckliche Angst ein; **a ~ing experience** ein schreckliches Erlebnis; **to be petrified by sth** sich panisch vor etw fürchten.
2 *vi* versteinern.
petrochemical ['petrəʊ'kemɪkəl] 1 *n* petrochemisches Erzeugnis.
2 *adj* petrochemisch.
petrodollar ['petrəʊdɒləʳ] *n* Petrodollar *m*.
petrol ['petrəl] *n* (*esp Brit*) Benzin *nt*.
petrol *in cpds* Benzin-; **~ bomb** *n* Benzinbombe *f*, Molotowcocktail *m*; **~ can** *n* Reservekanister *m*; **~ cap** *n* Tankdeckel *m*.
petroleum [pɪ'trəʊlɪəm] *n* Petroleum *nt* ◆ **~ ether** Petroläther *m*; **~ jelly** Vaselin *nt*, Vaseline *f*.
petrol gauge *n* Benzinuhr *f*.
petrology [pɪ'trɒlədʒɪ] *n* Gesteinskunde, Petrologie *f*.
petrol: ~ pump *n* (*in engine*) Benzinpumpe *f*; (*at garage*) Zapfsäule *f*; **~ station** *n* Tankstelle *f*; **~ tank** *n* Benzintank *m*; **~ tanker** *n* (Benzin)tankwagen *m*.
petticoat ['petɪkəʊt] *n* Unterrock *m*; (*stiffened*) Petticoat *m* ◆ **~ government** Weiberherrschaft *f*, Weiberregiment *nt*.
pettifogging ['petɪfɒgɪŋ] *adj objections* kleinlich; *details* belanglos; *person* pedantisch.
pettiness ['petɪnɪs] *n see adj* (**a**) Unbedeutendheit, Belanglosigkeit, Unwichtigkeit *f*; Billigkeit *f*; Geringfügigkeit *f*. (**b**) Kleinlichkeit *f*; spitzer Charakter.
petting ['petɪŋ] *n* Petting *nt*.
pettish *adj*, **~ly** *adv* ['petɪʃ, -lɪ] bockig (*inf*).
pettishness ['petɪʃnɪs] *n* bockige Art (*inf*).
petty ['petɪ] *adj* (+*er*) (**a**) (*trivial*) unbedeutend, belanglos, unwichtig; *excuse* billig; *crime* geringfügig.
(**b**) (*small-minded*) kleinlich; (*spiteful*) *remark* spitz ◆ **you're being very ~ about it** du bist sehr kleinlich.
(**c**) (*minor*) *chieftain etc* untergeordnet; (*pej*) *official also* unbedeutend, unwichtig ◆ **the ~ wars of the time** die Kleinkriege jener Zeit.
petty: ~ bourgeois *n, adj see* **petit bourgeois**; **~ bourgeoisie** *n see* **petite bourgeoisie**; **~ cash** *n* Portokasse *f*; **~ jury** *n* ≃ Geschworene *pl*; **~ larceny** *n* einfacher Diebstahl; **~ officer** *n* Fähnrich *m* zur See; **~ sessions** *npl see* **magistrate's court**; **~ theft** *n* einfacher Diebstahl.
petulance ['petjʊləns], **petulancy** ['petjʊlənsɪ] *n* verdrießliche Art; (*of child*) bockige Art (*inf*).
petulant ['petjʊlənt] *adj* verdrießlich; *child* bockig (*inf*).
petulantly ['petjʊləntlɪ] *adv see adj*.
petunia [pɪ'tjuːnɪə] *n* Petunie *f*.
pew [pjuː] *n* (*Eccl*) (Kirchen)bank *f*; (*hum: chair*) Platz *m* ◆ **have** *or* **take a ~!** (*hum*) laß dich nieder! (*hum*).
pewit *n see* **peewit**.
pewter ['pjuːtəʳ] *n* (*alloy*) Zinn *nt*; (*vessel*) Zinnbecher *m*; (*articles also*) Zinngeschirr *nt*.
PG *abbr of* **parental guidance** *Klassifikation f für Kinofilme, welche Kinder nur in*

Begleitung Erwachsener sehen dürfen.
PGCE *(Brit) abbr of* **Postgraduate Certificate of Education.**
phalanx ['fælæŋks] *n, pl* **-es** *or* **phalanges** [fæ'lændʒi:z] **(a)** *(Anat)* Finger-/Zehenglied *nt,* Phalanx *f (spec).* **(b)** *(body of people, troops)* Phalanx *f.*
phalli ['fælaɪ] *pl of* **phallus.**
phallic ['fælɪk] *adj* Phallus-, phallisch; *symbol* Phallus-.
phallus ['fæləs] *n, pl* **-es** *or* **phalli** Phallus *m.*
phantasm ['fæntæzəm], **phantasma** [fæn'tæzmə] *n, pl* **phantasmata** Phantasma *nt.*
phantasmagoria [,fæntæzmə'gɔ:rɪə] *n* Phantasmagorie *f.*
phantasmagoric(al) [,fæntæzmə'gɒrɪk(əl)] *adj* phantasmagorisch.
phantasmal [fæn'tæzməl] *adj* imaginär.
phantasmata [fæn'tæzmətə] *pl of* **phantasm, phantasma.**
phantasy *n see* **fantasy.**
phantom ['fæntəm] [1] *n* Phantom *nt;* *(ghost: esp of particular person)* Geist *m* ◆ **~s of the mind** Phantasiegebilde *pl.*
[2] *adj attr* Geister-; *(mysterious)* Phantom- ◆ **a ~ child/knight** *etc* der Geist eines Kindes/Ritters *etc;* **~ limb pains** Phantomschmerzen *pl;* **~ pregnancy** eingebildete Schwangerschaft.
Pharaoh ['fɛərəʊ] *n* Pharao *m* ◆ **the tombs of the ~s** die Pharaonengräber *pl.*
Pharisaic(al) [,færɪ'seɪk(əl)] *adj* **(a)** pharisäisch. **(b) p~** *(fig)* pharisäerhaft.
Pharisee ['færɪsi:] *n (fig: also* **p~***)* Pharisäer *m.*
pharmaceutical [,fɑ:mə'sju:tɪkəl] [1] *adj* pharmazeutisch.
[2] *n usu pl* Arzneimittel *nt* ◆ **~s company** Pharmaunternehmen *nt.*
pharmaceutics [,fɑ:mə'sju:tɪks] *n sing see* **pharmacy (a).**
pharmacist ['fɑ:məsɪst] *n* Apotheker(in *f*) *m;* *(in research)* Pharmazeut(in *f*) *m.*
pharmacological [,fɑ:məkə'lɒdʒɪkəl] *adj* pharmakologisch.
pharmacologist [,fɑ:mə'kɒlədʒɪst] *n* Pharmakologe *m,* Pharmakologin *f.*
pharmacology [,fɑ:mə'kɒlədʒɪ] *n* Pharmakologie *f.*
pharmacopoeia [,fɑ:məkə'pi:ə] *n* Pharmakopöe *f (spec),* amtliches Arzneibuch.
pharmacy ['fɑ:məsɪ] *n* **(a)** *(science)* Pharmazie *f.* **(b)** *(shop)* Apotheke *f.*
pharyngeal [fə'rɪndʒɪəl], **pharyngal** [fə'rɪŋgəl] *adj* Rachen-.
pharyngitis [,færɪn'dʒaɪtɪs] *n* Rachenkatarrh *m,* Pharyngitis *f (spec).*
pharynx ['færɪŋks] *n* Rachen *m,* Pharynx *f (spec).*
phase [feɪz] [1] *n (all senses)* Phase *f;* *(of construction, project, history also)* Abschnitt *m;* *(of illness)* Stadium *nt* ◆ **out of/in ~** *(Tech, Elec)* phasenverschoben/phasengleich, in Phase; *(fig)* unkoordiniert/koordiniert; **~ modulation** *(Elec)* Phasenmodulation *f;* **he's just going through a ~** das ist nur so eine Phase bei ihm; **he's out of ~ with the times** er ist nicht im Gleichklang mit seiner Zeit.
[2] *vt (introduce gradually) plan, change-over, withdrawal* schrittweise durchführen; *(coordinate, fit to one another) starting times, production stages, traffic lights* aufeinander abstimmen; *machines etc* gleichschalten, synchronisieren ◆ **the traffic lights are not ~d here** hier gibt es keine grüne Welle; **a ~d withdrawal of troops** ein schrittweiser Truppenabzug.
◆**phase in** *vt sep* allmählich einführen.
◆**phase out** *vt sep* auslaufen lassen.
phasing ['feɪzɪŋ] *n* Synchronisierung, Gleichschaltung *f.*
phatic ['fætɪk] *adj (liter)* phatisch.
PhD *n* Doktor *m,* Dr ◆ **~ thesis** Doktorarbeit *f;* **to do/get one's ~** seinen Doktor machen *or* promovieren/den Doktor bekommen; **he has a ~ in English** er hat in Anglistik promoviert; **John Smith ~** Dr. John Smith.
pheasant ['feznt] *n* Fasan *m.*
phenix *n (US) see* **phoenix.**
phenobarbitone [,fi:nəʊ'bɑ:bɪtəʊn], **phenobarbital** [,fi:nəʊ'bɑ:bɪtəl] *n* Phenobarbital *nt.*
phenol ['fi:nɒl] *n* Phenol *nt.*
phenomena [fɪ'nɒmɪnə] *pl of* **phenomenon.**
phenomenal [fɪ'nɒmɪnl] *adj* phänomenal, sagenhaft *(inf);* *person, beauty, figure* fabelhaft; *boredom, heat* unglaublich.
phenomenalism [fɪ'nɒmɪnəlɪzəm] *n* Phänomenalismus *m.*
phenomenally [fɪ'nɒmɪnəlɪ] *adv* außerordentlich; *bad, boring etc* unglaublich.
phenomenology [fɪ,nɒmɪ'nɒlədʒɪ] *n* Phänomenologie *f.*
phenomenon [fɪ'nɒmɪnən] *n, pl* **phenomena** Phänomen *nt.*
phenotype ['fi:nəʊtaɪp] *n* Phänotyp(us) *m.*
phew [fju:] *interj* Mensch, puh.
phial ['faɪəl] *n* Fläschchen *nt;* *(for serum)* Ampulle *f.*
Phi Beta Kappa ['faɪ'bi:tə'kæpə] *n (US) Vereinigung f hervorragender Akademiker oder Mitglied dieser Vereinigung.*
philander [fɪ'lændə^r] *vi* tändeln *(liter).*
philanderer [fɪ'lændərə^r] *n* Schwerenöter *m.*
philandering [fɪ'lændərɪŋ] *n* Liebeleien *pl.*
philanthropic(al) [,fɪlən'θrɒpɪk(əl)] *adj* menschenfreundlich; *person also, organization* philanthropisch *(geh).*
philanthropically [,fɪlən'θrɒpɪkəlɪ] *adv* menschenfreundlich.
philanthropist [fɪ'lænθrəpɪst] *n* Menschenfreund, Philanthrop *(geh) m.*
philanthropy [fɪ'lænθrəpɪ] *n* Menschenfreundlichkeit, Philanthropie *(geh) f.*
philatelic [,fɪlə'telɪk] *adj* philatelistisch.
philatelist [fɪ'lætəlɪst] *n* Philatelist(in *f*), Briefmarkensammler(in *f*) *m.*
philately [fɪ'lætəlɪ] *n* Philatelie, Briefmarkenkunde *f.*
-phile [-faɪl] *suf* [1] *n* -phile(r), -freund *m* ◆ **Anglo~** Anglophile(r), Englandfreund *m.*
[2] *adj* -phil, -freundlich ◆ **Franco~** frankophil, frankreichfreundlich.
philharmonic [,fɪlɑ:'mɒnɪk] [1] *adj* philharmonisch ◆ **~ hall/society** Philharmonie *f.*
[2] *n* **P~** Philharmonie *f.*
Philip ['fɪlɪp] *n* Philipp *m;* *(Bibl)* Philippus *m.*
Philippians [fɪ'lɪpɪənz] *n sing (Bibl)* Philipper *pl.*
philippic [fɪ'lɪpɪk] *n (lit, fig)* Philippika *f.*
Philippine ['fɪlɪpi:n] *adj* philippinisch.
Philippines ['fɪlɪpi:nz] *npl* Philippinen *pl.*
Philistine ['fɪlɪstaɪn] [1] *adj* **(a)** *(lit)* Philister-. **(b)** *(fig)* **p~** kulturlos; **tell that p~ friend of yours ...** sag deinem Freund, diesem Banausen ...
[2] *n* **(a)** *(lit)* Philister *m.* **(b)** *(fig)* **p~** Banause *m.*
philistinism ['fɪlɪstɪnɪzəm] *n* Banausentum *nt.*
Phillips ® ['fɪlɪps]: **~ screw** *n* Kreuzschraube *f;* **~ screwdriver** *n* Kreuzschraubenzieher *m.*
philological [,fɪlə'lɒdʒɪkəl] *adj* philologisch.
philologist [fɪ'lɒlədʒɪst] *n* Philologe *m,* Philologin *f.*
philology [fɪ'lɒlədʒɪ] *n* Philologie *f.*
philosopher [fɪ'lɒsəfə^r] *n* Philosoph *m,* Philosophin *f* ◆ **~'s stone** Stein *m* der Weisen.
philosophic(al) [,fɪlə'sɒfɪk(əl)] *adj* philosophisch; *(fig also)* gelassen.
philosophically [,fɪlə'sɒfɪkəlɪ] *adv see adj* ◆ **his ideas are ~ naïve** philosophisch betrachtet sind seine Gedanken naiv.
philosophize [fɪ'lɒsəfaɪz] *vi* philosophieren *(about, on* über *+acc).*
philosophy [fɪ'lɒsəfɪ] *n* Philosophie *f* ◆ **~ of life** Lebensphilosophie *f;* **that's my ~** das ist meine Philosophie *or* Einstellung; **~ of education** Erziehungsphilosophie *f.*
philtre, *(US)* **philter** ['fɪltə^r] *n* Zaubertrank *m;* *(love ~)* Liebestrank *m.*
phiz [fɪz] *n (dated sl)* Visage *f (sl).*
phlebitis [flɪ'baɪtɪs] *n* Venenentzündung, Phlebitis *(spec) f.*
phlegm [flem] *n (mucus)* Schleim *m;* *(obs: humour)* Phlegma *nt;* *(fig) (coolness)* Gemütsruhe *f,* stoische Ruhe; *(stolidness)* Trägheit, Schwerfälligkeit *f,* Phlegma *nt.*
phlegmatic [fleg'mætɪk] *adj (cool)* seelenruhig, stoisch; *(stolid)* träge, schwerfällig, phlegmatisch.
phlox [flɒks] *n* Phlox *m.*
-phobe [-fəʊb] *n suf* -phobe(r), -feind *m* ◆ **Anglo~** Anglophobe(r), Englandfeind *m.*
phobia ['fəʊbɪə] *n* Phobie *f* ◆ **she has a ~ about it** sie hat krankhafte Angst davor.
-phobic [-'fəʊbɪk] *adj suf* -phob, -feindlich.
Phoenicia [fə'ni:ʃə] *n* Phönizien *nt.*
Phoenician [fə'ni:ʃən] [1] *adj* phönizisch.
[2] *n* Phönizier(in *f*) *m.*
phoenix, *(US)* **phenix** ['fi:nɪks] *n (Myth)* Phönix *m* ◆ **like a ~ from the ashes** wie ein Phönix aus der Asche.
▼ **phone^1** [fəʊn] [1] *n* Telefon *nt* ◆ **to pick up/put down the ~** (den Hörer) abnehmen/auflegen; **I'll give you a ~** *(inf)* ich ruf' dich an.
[2] *vt person* anrufen; *message* telefonisch übermitteln.
▼ [3] *vi* anrufen, telefonieren; *see also* **telephone.**
◆**phone back** *vti (vt: always separate)* zurückrufen.
◆**phone in** [1] *vi* anrufen.
[2] *vt sep* telefonisch übermitteln.
phone^2 *n (Ling)* Phon *nt.*
phone booth *n* **(a)** *(in station, hotel etc)* Fernsprechhaube *f.* **(b)** *(US: call box)* Telefonzelle *f.*
phonecard ['fəʊnkɑ:d] *n* Telefonkarte *f.*
phone-in ['fəʊnɪn] *n Rundfunkprogramm nt, an dem sich Hörer per Telefon beteiligen können,* Phone-in *nt.*
phoneme ['fəʊni:m] *n* Phonem *nt.*
phonemic [fəʊ'ni:mɪk] *adj* phonemisch.
phonetic *adj,* **~ally** *adv* [fəʊ'netɪk, -əlɪ] phonetisch.
phonetician [,fɒnɪ'tɪʃən] *n* Phonetiker(in *f*) *m.*
phonetics [fəʊ'netɪks] *n* **(a)** *sing (subject)* Phonetik *f.* **(b)** *pl (phonetic script)* Lautschrift *f,* phonetische Umschrift.
phon(e)y ['fəʊnɪ] *(inf)* [1] *adj (fake, pretentious)* unecht; *excuse, deal, peace* faul *(inf);* *name* falsch; *passport, money* gefälscht; *story, report* erfunden; *company* Schwindel- ◆ **a ~ doctor** ein Scharlatan *m;* **a ~ businessman** ein zwielichtiger Geschäftsmann; **he's so ~** der ist doch nicht echt *(inf);* **there's something ~ about it** da ist was faul dran *(inf).*
[2] *n (thing)* Fälschung *f;* *(banknote also)* Blüte *f (inf);* *(bogus policeman etc)* Schwindler(in *f*) *m;* *(doctor)* Scharlatan *m;* *(pretentious person)* Angeber(in *f*) *m.*
phonic ['fɒnɪk] *adj* phonisch.
phonograph ['fəʊnəgrɑ:f] *n (old, US)* Phonograph *m.*
phonological [,fəʊnə'lɒdʒɪkəl] *adj* phonologisch.
phonology [fəʊ'nɒlədʒɪ] *n (science)* Phonologie *f;* *(system)* Lautsystem *nt.*
phony *adj, n see* **phon(e)y.**
phooey ['fu:ɪ] *interj (scorn)* pah, bah; *(disgust)* pfui.
phosphate ['fɒsfeɪt] *n (Chem)* Phosphat *nt;* *(Agr: fertilizer)* Phosphatdünger *m.*
phosphide ['fɒsfaɪd] *n* Phosphid *nt.*
phosphor ['fɒsfə^r] *n* Phosphor *m.*
phosphoresce [,fɒsfə'res] *vi* phosphoreszieren.

➤ LANGUAGE IN USE: **phone^1: 3 → 27.4**

phosphorescence [ˌfɒsfəˈresns] *n* Phosphoreszenz *f*.
phosphorescent [ˌfɒsfəˈresnt] *adj* phosphoreszierend.
phosphoric [fɒsˈfɒrɪk] *adj* phosphorig.
phosphorous [ˈfɒsfərəs] *adj* phosphorsauer.
phosphorus [ˈfɒsfərəs] *n* Phosphor *m*.
photo [ˈfəʊtəʊ] *n* Foto, Photo *nt*, Aufnahme *f*; *see also* **photograph**.
photo: ~ call *n* Fototermin *m*; **~cell** *n* Photozelle *f*; **~compose** *vt* (*esp US Typ*) lichtsetzen, fotosetzen; **~composition** *n* (*Typ*) Lichtsatz, Filmsatz *m*; **~copier** *n* (Foto)kopierer *m*, (Foto)kopiergerät *nt*; **~copy** [1] *n* Fotokopie *f*; [2] *vt* fotokopieren; [3] *vi* **this won't ~copy** das läßt sich nicht fotokopieren; **~electric** *adj* photoelektrisch; **~electric cell** Photozelle *f*; **~electron** *n* Photoelektron *nt*; **~engraving** *n* (*process*) Klischieren *nt*; (*plate*) Klischee *nt*; **~ finish** *n* Fotofinish *nt*; **~flash** *n* Blitzlicht *nt*; **~flash lamp** Blitzgerät *nt*; **~flood (lamp)** *n* Jupiterlampe *f*.
photogenic [ˌfəʊtəʊˈdʒenɪk] *adj* fotogen.
photograph [ˈfəʊtəgræf] [1] *n* Fotografie, Aufnahme *f* ◆ **to take a ~ (of sb/sth)** (jdn/etw) fotografieren, eine Aufnahme *or* ein Bild (von jdm/etw) machen; **she takes a good ~** (*is photogenic*) sie ist fotogen; **this camera takes good ~s** diese Kamera macht gute Aufnahmen *or* Bilder *or* Fotos; **~ album** Fotoalbum *nt*.
[2] *vt* fotografieren, knipsen (*inf*) ◆ **"~ed by John Mayne"** „Foto/Fotos: John Mayne".
[3] *vi* **to ~ well/badly** sich gut/schlecht fotografieren lassen.
photographer [fəˈtɒgrəfəʳ] *n* Fotograf(in *f*) *m*.
photographic [ˌfəʊtəˈgræfɪk] *adj* fotografisch; *equipment, magazine, club* Foto-; *style of painting, art* naturgetreu ◆ **~ memory** fotografisches Gedächtnis.
photographically [ˌfəʊtəˈgræfɪkəlɪ] *adv* fotografisch ◆ **to record sth ~** etw im Bild festhalten.
photography [fəˈtɒgrəfɪ] *n* Fotografie *f*; (*in film, book etc*) Fotografien, Aufnahmen, Bilder *pl* ◆ **his ~ is marvellous** seine Fotografien *etc* sind hervorragend.
photogravure [ˈfəʊtəʊgrəˈvjʊəʳ] *n* Photogravüre, Heliogravüre *f*.
photo: ~ journalism *n* Fotojournalismus *m*; **~ journalist** *n* Fotojournalist(in *f*), Bildjournalist(in *f*) *m*; **~mechanical** *adj* fotomechanisch.
photometer [fəʊˈtɒmɪtəʳ] *n* Photometer *nt*.
photomontage [ˈfəʊtəʊmɒnˈtɑːʒ] *n* Fotomontage *f*.
photon [ˈfəʊtɒn] *n* Photon *nt*.
photo: ~sensitive *adj* lichtempfindlich; **~sensitize** *vt* lichtempfindlich machen; **~set** *vt* (*Typ*) im Lichtsatz herstellen; **~setting** *n* Lichtsatz *m*; **~stat** ® *n, vti see* **~copy**; **~synthesis** *n* Photosynthese *f*; **~telegraphy** *n* Bildtelegraphie *f*; **~tropic** *adj* phototrop(isch); **~tropism** *n* Phototropismus *m*; **~typesetting** *n* (*esp US Typ*) Lichtsatz *m*, Fotosatz *m*.
phrasal [ˈfreɪzəl] *adj* Satz- ◆ **~ verb** Verb *nt* mit Präposition.
phrase [freɪz] [1] *n* **(a)** (*Gram*) Phrase *f*, Satzglied *nt or* -teil *m*; (*in spoken language*) Phrase *f* ◆ **noun/verb ~** Nominal-/Verbalphrase *f*.
(b) (*mode of expression*) Ausdruck *m*; (*set expression*) Redewendung *f* ◆ **in a ~** kurz gesagt; *see* **set, turn**.
(c) (*Mus*) Phrase *f*.
[2] *vt* **(a)** formulieren; *criticism, suggestion also* ausdrücken.
(b) (*Mus*) phrasieren.
phrase: ~book *n* Sprachführer *m*; **~ marker** *n* (*Ling*) P-Marker, Formationsmarker *m*; **~monger** *n* (*pej*) Phrasendrescher *m*.
phraseology [ˌfreɪzɪˈɒlədʒɪ] *n* Ausdrucksweise *f*; (*of letter etc*) Diktion *f*; (*jargon*) Jargon *m*.
phrasing [ˈfreɪzɪŋ] *n* (*act*) Formulierung *f*; (*style*) Ausdrucksweise *f*, Stil *m*; (*Mus*) Phrasierung *f*.
phrenetic *adj see* **frenetic**.
phrenologist [frɪˈnɒlədʒɪst] *n* Phrenologe *m*, Phrenologin *f*.
phrenology [frɪˈnɒlədʒɪ] *n* Phrenologie *f*.
phthisis [ˈθaɪsɪs] *n* Schwindsucht, (Lungen)tuberkulose *f*.
phut [fʌt] (*inf*) [1] *n* Puff *m*.
[2] *adv*: **to go ~** (*make noise*) puff machen; (*break down*) kaputtgehen (*inf*); (*plans etc*) platzen (*inf*).
pH-value [piːˈeɪtʃvæljuː] *n* pH-Wert *m*.
phylum [ˈfaɪləm] *n, pl* **phyla** [ˈfaɪlə] (*Biol*) Stamm *m*.
physic [ˈfɪzɪk] *n* (*obs*) Arznei *f*; (*cathartic*) Purgativ *nt*.
physical [ˈfɪzɪkəl] [1] *adj* **(a)** (*of the body*) körperlich; (*not psychological also*) physisch; *check-up* ärztlich ◆ **you don't take/get enough ~ exercise** Sie bewegen sich nicht genug; **he's very ~** (*inf*) er ist sehr sinnlich; **play got too ~** (*Sport inf*) das Spiel wurde zu ruppig *or* rabiat (*inf*); **the ~ force of the impact** die Wucht des Aufpralls; **we don't actually need your ~ presence** Ihre persönliche Anwesenheit ist nicht unbedingt nötig.
(b) (*material*) physisch, körperlich; *world* faßbar.
(c) (*of physics*) *laws, properties* physikalisch ◆ **it's a ~ impossibility** es ist ein Ding der Unmöglichkeit.
[2] *n* ärztliche Untersuchung; (*Mil*) Musterung *f*.
physical: ~ chemistry *n* physikalische Chemie; **~ education** *n* (*abbr* **PE**) Sport *m*, Leibesübungen *pl* (*form*); **~ education college** *n* Sporthochschule, Sportakademie *f*; **~ education teacher** *n* Sportlehrer(in *f*) *m*; **~ geography** *n* physikalische Geographie, Physiogeographie *f*; **~ jerks** *npl* (*inf*) Gymnastik *f*.
physically [ˈfɪzɪkəlɪ] *adv* körperlich, physisch; (*Sci*) physikalisch ◆ **~ impossible** praktisch unmöglich; **the substance changed ~** die Substanz ging in einen anderen Zustand über; **the journey is ~ dangerous** die Reise ist gefährlich für Leib und Leben; **you don't have to be there ~** Ihre persönliche Anwesenheit ist nicht erforderlich; **they removed him ~ from the meeting** sie haben ihn mit Gewalt aus der Versammlung entfernt.
physical: ~ science *n* Naturwissenschaft *f*; **~ training** *n* (*abbr* **PT**) *see* **~ education**.
physician [fɪˈzɪʃən] *n* Arzt *m*, Ärztin *f*.
physicist [ˈfɪzɪsɪst] *n* Physiker(in *f*) *m*.
physics [ˈfɪzɪks] *n* (*sing: subject*) Physik *f* ◆ **the ~ of this are quite complex** die physikalischen Zusammenhänge sind hierbei ziemlich komplex.
physio [ˈfɪzɪəʊ] *n* (*inf*) Physiotherapeut(in *f*) *m*.
physiognomy [ˌfɪzɪˈɒnəmɪ] *n* (*face*) Physiognomie *f*; (*study*) Physiognomik *f*; (*fig*) äußere Erscheinung, Aussehen *nt* ◆ **the ~ of the Labour Party** das Gesicht der Labour Party.
physiological [ˌfɪzɪəˈlɒdʒɪkəl] *adj* physiologisch.
physiologist [ˌfɪzɪˈɒlədʒɪst] *n* Physiologe *m*, Physiologin *f*.
physiology [ˌfɪzɪˈɒlədʒɪ] *n* Physiologie *f*.
physiotherapist [ˌfɪzɪəˈθerəpɪst] *n* Physiotherapeut(in *f*) *m*.
physiotherapy [ˌfɪzɪəˈθerəpɪ] *n* Physiotherapie *f*, physikalische Therapie.
physique [fɪˈziːk] *n* Körperbau *m*, Statur *f*.
pi [paɪ] *n* (*Math*) Pi *nt*.
pianist [ˈpɪənɪst] *n* Klavierspieler(in *f*) *m*; (*concert ~*) Pianist(in *f*) *m*.
piano [ˈpjænəʊ] *n* (*upright*) Klavier, Piano (*geh, old*) *nt*; (*grand*) Flügel *m* ◆ **who was at *or* on the ~?** wer war am Klavier?
piano: ~-accordion *n* Pianoakkordeon *nt*; **~ concerto** *n* Klavierkonzert *nt*; **~forte** [ˈpjænəʊˈfɔːtɪ] *n* (*form*) Pianoforte *nt*.
pianola ® [pɪəˈnəʊlə] *n* Pianola *nt*.
piano: ~ lesson *n* Klavierstunde *f*; **~ music** *n* Klaviermusik *f*; **~-player** *n* Klavierspieler(in *f*) *m*; **~ stool** *n* Klavierhocker *m*; **~ tuner** *n* Klavierstimmer(in *f*) *m*.
piazza [pɪˈætsə] *n* Piazza *f*, (Markt)platz *m*; (*US: veranda*) (überdachte) Veranda.
pic [pɪk] *n* (*inf: photo*) Foto *nt*.
picaresque [ˌpɪkəˈresk] *adj* pikaresk; *novel also* Schelmen-.
picayune [ˌpɪkəˈjuːn] *adj* (*US*) (*paltry*) gering, minimal; (*petty*) kleinlich.
piccalilli [ˈpɪkəˌlɪlɪ] *n* Piccalilli *pl*.
piccaninny [ˌpɪkəˈnɪnɪ] *n* Negerkind *nt*.
piccolo [ˈpɪkələʊ] *n* Pikkoloflöte *f*.
pick [pɪk] [1] *n* **(a)** (*~axe*) Spitzhacke, Picke *f*, Pickel *m*; (*Mountaineering*) Eispickel *m*; (*tooth~*) Zahnstocher *m*.
(b) (*esp US: plectrum*) Plektron, Plektrum *nt*.
(c) (*choice*) **he was our ~** wir hatten ihn (aus)gewählt; **to have first ~** die erste Wahl haben; **take your ~!** such dir etwas/einen *etc* aus!
(d) (*best*) Beste(s) *nt*; *see* **bunch**.
[2] *vt* **(a)** (*choose*) (aus)wählen ◆ **to ~ a team** eine Mannschaft aufstellen; **he has been ~ed for England** er ist für England aufgestellt worden; **to ~ sides** wählen; **to ~ a winner** (*lit*) den Sieger erraten; (*fig*) das Große Los ziehen; **a handful of ~ed men** (*Mil*) ein paar ausgewählte Soldaten; **to ~ one's words** seine Worte mit Bedacht wählen; **to ~ one's time** den richtigen Zeitpunkt wählen; **you really ~ your times, don't you?** (*iro*) du suchst dir aber auch immer den günstigsten Augenblick aus! (*iro*); **to ~ one's way** seinen Weg suchen; **to ~ one's way through sth** seinen Weg durch etw finden; **he knows how to ~ 'em** (*inf*) er hat den richtigen Riecher (*inf*); **you do ~ 'em** (*iro*) du gerätst auch immer an den Falschen.
(b) (*pull bits off, make holes in*) *jumper, blanket etc* zupfen an (+*dat*); *spot, scab* kratzen an (+*dat*); *hole* (*with fingers, instrument*) bohren; (*with beak*) picken, hacken ◆ **to ~ one's nose** sich (*dat*) in der Nase bohren; **to ~ one's teeth** sich (*dat*) in den Zähnen herumstochern; **to ~ a lock** ein Schloß knacken *or* mit einem Dietrich öffnen; **to ~ a bone** (*with fingers*) einen Knochen abzupfen; (*with teeth, beak*) einen Knochen abnagen; **to ~ sth to pieces** (*lit*) etw zerzupfen; (*fig*) kein gutes Haar an etw (*dat*) lassen, etw verreißen; **to ~ holes in sth** (*fig*) etw bemäkeln; *in argument, theory* etw in ein paar Punkten widerlegen; **to ~ a fight *or* quarrel (with sb)** (mit jdm) einen Streit vom Zaun brechen; **to ~ pockets** sich als Taschendieb betätigen; **he's very good at ~ing pockets** er ist ein sehr geschickter Taschendieb; **to ~ sb's pocket** jdm die Geldbörse/Brieftasche stehlen; **to ~ sb's brains** sich von jdm inspirieren lassen; *see* **bone**.
(c) (*~ out and remove*) *fleas, splinter etc* entfernen (*from* von); (*pluck*) *flowers, fruit* pflücken.
(d) (*US: pluck*) *chicken etc* rupfen.
(e) (*esp US*) *strings* zupfen, anreißen; *banjo* zupfen.
(f) (*peck up*) *corn etc* picken.
[3] *vi* **(a)** (*choose*) wählen, aussuchen ◆ **to ~ and choose** wählerisch sein.
(b) (*esp US: on guitar etc*) zupfen.
◆**pick at** *vi +prep obj* **(a) to ~ ~ one's food** im Essen herumstochern, am Essen herumpicken. **(b)** (*inf: criticize*) **to ~ ~ sb/sth** auf jdm/etw herumhacken.
◆**pick off** *vt sep* **(a)** (*remove*) *fluff etc* wegzupfen; (*pluck*) *fruit* pflücken; *nail polish* abschälen ◆ **the crew were ~ed ~ by helicopter** die Mannschaft wurde von einem Hubschrauber aufgenommen. **(b)** (*shoot*) abschießen, abknallen (*inf*).
◆**pick on** *vi +prep obj* (*choose*) aussuchen; (*victimize*) herumhacken auf (+*dat*) ◆ **why ~ ~ me?** (*inf*) warum gerade ich?; **~ ~ somebody your own size!** (*inf*) leg dich doch mit einem Gleichstarken an! (*inf*); **stop ~ing ~ me!** hack nicht ständig auf mir herum!
◆**pick out** *vt sep* **(a)** (*choose*) aussuchen, auswählen ◆ **to ~ ~ a few examples**

um ein paar Beispiele herauszugreifen.
(b) (*remove*) *bad apples etc* heraussuchen, auslesen.
(c) (*see, distinguish*) *person, familiar face* ausmachen, entdecken ◆ **the spotlight ~ed ~ the leading dancer** der Scheinwerfer wurde auf den Haupttänzer gerichtet.
(d) (*highlight*) hervorheben (*in, with* durch).
(e) (*Mus*) **to ~ ~ a tune (on the piano)** eine Melodie (auf dem Klavier) improvisieren; **he ~ed ~ a few notes** er spielte ein paar Takte.
◆**pick over** *or* **through** *vi +prep obj* durchsehen, untersuchen.
◆**pick up** [1] *vt sep* **(a)** (*take up*) aufheben; (*lift momentarily*) hochheben; *stitch* aufnehmen ◆ **to ~ ~ a child in one's arms** ein Kind auf den Arm nehmen; **~ ~ your feet when you walk!** heb deine Füße (beim Gehen)!; **to ~ oneself ~** aufstehen; **as soon as he ~s ~ a book** sobald er ein Buch in die Hand nimmt; **it's the sort of book you can ~ ~ when you have a free minute** das ist so ein Buch, das man mal zwischendurch lesen kann; **to ~ ~ the phone** den Hörer abnehmen; **you just have to ~ ~ the phone** du brauchst nur anzurufen; **to ~ ~ the bill** (*pay*) die Rechnung bezahlen; **to ~ ~ a story** mit einer Geschichte fortfahren; **to ~ ~ the pieces** (*lit, fig*) die Scherben aufsammeln *or* zusammensuchen; **to ~ ~ the thread of a lecture** den Faden (eines Vortrags) wiederfinden; **the interviewer ~ed ~ this reference and ...** der Interviewer nahm diese Bemerkung auf *or* knüpfte an diese Bemerkung an und ...
(b) (*get*) holen; (*buy*) bekommen; (*acquire*) *habit* sich (*dat*) angewöhnen; *news, gossip* aufschnappen; *illness* sich (*dat*) holen *or* zuziehen; (*earn*) verdienen ◆ **to ~ sth ~ at a sale** etw im Ausverkauf erwischen; **to ~ ~ speed** schneller werden; **you never know what you'll ~ ~** (*what illness etc*) man weiß nie, was man sich (*dat*) da holen *or* zuziehen kann; **I must have ~ed ~ a flea** ich muß mir einen Floh geholt *or* gefangen haben; **he ~ed ~ a few extra points** er hat ein paar Extrapunkte gemacht.
(c) (*learn*) *skill etc* sich (*dat*) aneignen; *language also* lernen; *accent, word* aufschnappen; *information, tips etc* herausbekommen; *idea* aufgreifen ◆ **you'll soon ~ it ~** du wirst das schnell lernen; **where did you ~ ~ that idea?** wo hast du denn die Idee her?
(d) (*collect*) *person, goods* abholen ◆ **I'll come and ~ you ~** ich hole dich ab, ich komme dich abholen.
(e) (*bus etc*) *passengers* aufnehmen; (*in car*) mitnehmen.
(f) (*rescue: helicopter, lifeboat*) bergen.
(g) (*arrest, catch*) *wanted man, criminal* schnappen (*inf*) ◆ **they ~ed him ~ for questioning** sie haben ihn geholt, um ihn zu vernehmen.
(h) (*inf*) *girl* aufgabeln (*inf*) ◆ **she got ~ed ~ at a party** die ist auf einer Party (von einem) abgeschleppt *or* aufgegabelt worden (*inf*).
(i) (*find*) *road* finden ◆ **to ~ ~ the trail** (*Hunt, fig*) die Fährte *or* Spur aufnehmen.
(j) (*Rad*) *station* hereinbekommen, (rein)kriegen (*inf*); *message* empfangen, auffangen; (*see*) *beacon etc* ausmachen, sichten; (*on radar*) ausmachen; (*record stylus*) *sound* aufnehmen ◆ **the surface was clearly ~ed ~ by the satellite's cameras** das Bild der Oberfläche wurde von den Satellitenkameras deutlich übermittelt; **we ~ed ~ a rabbit in the car headlights** wir sahen ein Kaninchen im Scheinwerferlicht.
(k) (*correct, put right*) korrigieren ◆ **he ~ed me ~ for mispronouncing it** er hat meine falsche Aussprache korrigiert.
(l) (*restore to health*) wieder auf die Beine stellen.
(m) (*spot, identify*) *mistakes* finden.
(n) (*US inf: tidy*) *room* auf Vordermann bringen (*inf*).
[2] *vi* **(a)** (*improve*) besser werden; (*appetite also*) zunehmen; (*currency*) sich erholen; (*business: after slump*) sich erholen; (*engine*) rund laufen; (*accelerate*) schneller werden.
(b) (*continue*) weitermachen ◆ **to ~ ~ where one left off** da weitermachen, wo man aufgehört hat.
(c) (*inf*) **to ~ ~ with sb** (*get to know*) jds Bekanntschaft machen; **he has ~ed ~ with a rather strange crowd** er hat mit merkwürdigen Leuten Umgang.
pickaback ['pɪkəbæk] *n, adv see* **piggyback.**
pickaninny *n* (*US*) *see* **piccaninny.**
pickaxe, (*US*) **pickax** ['pɪkæks] *n* Spitzhacke, Pickel *m*.
picker ['pɪkəʳ] *n* (*of fruit etc*) Pflücker(in *f*) *m*.
picket ['pɪkɪt] [1] *n* **(a)** (*of strikers*) Streikposten *m* ◆ **to mount a ~ (at** *or* **on a gate)** (an *or* bei einem Tor) Streikposten aufstellen.
(b) (*Mil*) Feldposten, Vorposten *m*.
(c) (*stake*) Pfahl *m* ◆ **~ fence** Palisade *f*, Palisadenzaun *m*.
[2] *vt factory* Streikposten aufstellen vor (*+dat*); (*demonstrators etc*) demonstrieren vor (*+dat*).
[3] *vi* Streikposten aufstellen ◆ **he is ~ing at the front entrance** er ist Streikposten am Vordereingang.
picket duty *n* Streikpostendienst *m* ◆ **to be on ~** Streikposten sein.
picketing ['pɪkɪtɪŋ] *n* Aufstellen *nt* von Streikposten ◆ **there was no ~** es wurden keine Streikposten aufgestellt; **the ~ of the factory gates went on for six months** es standen sechs Monate lang Streikposten vor dem Betrieb.
picket line *n* Streikpostenkette *f* ◆ **to cross a ~** eine Streikpostenkette durchbrechen.
picking ['pɪkɪŋ] *n* **(a)** (*amount of fruit picked*) Ernte *f*.
(b) **~s** *pl* Ausbeute *f*; (*stolen goods*) Beute *f* ◆ **most office workers regard pens as legitimate ~s** die meisten Büroangestellten sehen es als ihr Recht an, Kulis mitgehen zu lassen (*inf*) *or* einzustecken; **she went along to see if there were any ~s** sie ging hin, um zu sehen, ob es für sie was zu holen gab; **the ~s are good** es lohnt sich, die Ausbeute ist gut.
pickle ['pɪkl] [1] *n* **(a)** (*food*) Pickles *pl*.
(b) (*solution*) (*brine*) Salzlake *f*, Pökel *m*; (*vinegar*) Essigsoße *f*; (*for leather, wood*) Beize *f*; (*Med, Sci*) Naßpräparat *nt*.
(c) (*inf: predicament*) Klemme *f* (*inf*) ◆ **he was in a bit of a ~/a sorry ~** er steckte in einer Klemme (*inf*), er saß in der Tinte (*inf*); **to get into a ~** in ein Kuddelmuddel geraten (*inf*); **what a ~!** so eine verzwickte Lage!
[2] *vt* einlegen; (*Med, Sci*) konservieren.
pickled ['pɪkld] *adj* **(a)** eingelegt. **(b)** *pred* (*inf: drunk*) besoffen (*inf*), alkoholisiert (*inf*).
pick: ~lock *n* (*tool*) Dietrich *m*; (*thief*) Einbrecher(in *f*) *m*; **~-me-up** *n* (*drink*) Muntermacher *m*, Stärkung *f*; (*holiday etc*) Erholung *f*; **we stopped off at the pub for a ~-me-up** wir sind auf ein Gläschen *or* einen Schluck in die Kneipe gegangen; **hearing that was a real ~-me-up** das hat mir richtig Auftrieb gegeben; **~pocket** *n* Taschendieb(in *f*) *m*.
pick-up ['pɪkʌp] *n* **(a)** Tonabnehmer *m* ◆ **~ arm** Tonarm *m*.
(b) (*also* **~ truck**) Kleinlieferwagen, Kleintransporter *m*.
(c) (*inf: acquaintance*) Bekanntschaft *f* ◆ **with his latest ~** mit seiner neusten Errungenschaft; **he's just looking for a ~** er will nur eine aufreißen (*inf*).
(d) (*collection*) Abholen *nt* ◆ **he was late for the ~** er kam zu spät zum Treffpunkt; **the mail van makes 3 ~s a day** der Postwagen kommt dreimal täglich(, um die Post abzuholen); **the bus makes four ~s** der Bus hält viermal(, um Leute aufzunehmen); **~ point** (*for excursion*) Sammelstelle *f*, Treffpunkt *m*; (*on regular basis*) Haltestelle *f*.
(e) (*improvement*) Verbesserung *f*; (*increase*) Ansteigen *nt*.
(f) (*acceleration*) Beschleunigung *f*.
picky ['pɪkɪ] *adj* (*+er*) (*inf*) pingelig (*inf*); *eater* wählerisch.
picnic ['pɪknɪk] (*vb: pret, ptp* **~ked**) [1] *n* Picknick *nt* ◆ **to have a ~** picknicken; **to go for** *or* **on a ~** ein Picknick veranstalten *or* machen; **a ~ lunch** ein Picknick *nt*; **it was no ~** (*fig inf*) es war kein Honiglecken.
[2] *vi* picknicken, ein Picknick machen ◆ **we went ~king every Sunday** wir machten jeden Sonntag ein Picknick.
picnic basket *or* **hamper** *n* Picknickkorb *m*.
picnicker ['pɪknɪkəʳ] *n* jd, der ein Picknick macht *or* der picknickt ◆ **the ~s left all their rubbish behind them** die Ausflügler ließen ihre Abfälle liegen.
picnic: ~ site *n* Rastplatz *m*; **~ table** *n* Campingtisch *m*.
pics [pɪks] *npl abbr of* **pictures** (*Brit inf*) *see* **picture 1 (c).**
Pict [pɪkt] *n* Pikte *m*, Piktin *f*.
Pictish ['pɪktɪʃ] [1] *adj* piktisch.
[2] *n* Piktisch *nt*.
pictogram ['pɪktəgræm], **pictograph** ['pɪktəgrɑːf] *n* Piktogramm *nt*.
pictorial [pɪk'tɔːrɪəl] [1] *adj calendar* bebildert; *magazine also* illustriert; *dictionary* Bild-; *impact* bildlich; *language, description* bildhaft ◆ **a ~ masterpiece** ein meisterliches Bild; **to keep a ~ record of sth** etw im Bild festhalten.
[2] *n* (*magazine*) Illustrierte *f*; (*stamp*) Sondermarke *f*.
pictorially [pɪk'tɔːrɪəlɪ] *adv* (*in pictures*) in Bildern, bildlich; *impressive* vom Bild her; *describe* bildhaft.
picture ['pɪktʃəʳ] [1] *n* **(a)** Bild *nt*; (*Art*) (*painting also*) Gemälde *nt*; (*drawing also*) Zeichnung *f* ◆ **~s in the fire** Phantasiegebilde *pl* im Kaminfeuer; **(as) pretty as a ~** bildschön.
(b) (*TV*) Bild *nt*.
(c) (*Film*) Film *m* ◆ **the ~s** (*Brit*) das Kino; **to go to the ~s** (*Brit*) ins Kino gehen; **what's on at the ~s?** (*Brit*) was gibt's im Kino?
(d) (*mental image*) Vorstellung *f*, Bild *nt* ◆ **these figures give the general ~** diese Zahlen geben ein allgemeines Bild; **have you got the general ~?** wissen Sie jetzt ungefähr Bescheid?; **to give you a ~ of what life is like here** damit Sie sich (*dat*) ein Bild vom Leben hier machen können; **the other side of the ~** die Kehrseite der Medaille; **to be in the ~** im Bilde sein; **to put sb in the ~** jdn ins Bild setzen; **I get the ~** (*inf*) ich hab's begriffen *or* kapiert (*inf*); **I'm beginning to get the ~** ich fange an zu begreifen *or* kapieren (*inf*); **he/that no longer comes into the ~** er/das spielt keine Rolle mehr.
(e) (*sight*) Bild *nt*; (*beautiful sight*) (*person also*) Traum *m*; (*thing also*) Gedicht *nt*, Traum *m* ◆ **his face was a ~** sein Gesicht war ein Bild für die Götter (*inf*); **she looked a ~** sie war bildschön; **the garden is a ~** der Garten ist eine Pracht.
(f) (*embodiment*) Bild *nt*, Verkörperung *f*; (*spitting image*) Abbild, Ebenbild *nt* ◆ **she looked** *or* **was the ~ of happiness/health** sie sah wie das Glück/die Gesundheit in Person aus; **she looked** *or* **was the ~ of misery** sie war ein Bild des Elends.
[2] *vt* **(a)** (*imagine*) sich (*dat*) vorstellen ◆ **to ~ sth to oneself** sich (*dat*) etw vorstellen.
(b) (*describe*) beschreiben, darstellen.
(c) (*by drawing, painting*) darstellen; (*in book*) abbilden.
picture: ~ book *n* Bildband *m*; (*for children*) Bilderbuch *nt*; **~ card** *n* Bild(karte *f*) *nt*; **~ frame** *n* Bilderrahmen *m*; **~ gallery** *n* Gemäldegalerie *f*; **~-goer** *n* (*Brit*) Kinogänger(in *f*) *or* -besucher(in *f*) *m*; **~ hat** *n* Florentiner(hut) *m*; **~ house** *n* (*dated Brit*) *see* **~ palace; ~-in-picture** *n* (*TV, Comput*) Bild-in-Bild *nt*; **~ library** *n* Bildarchiv *nt*; **~ palace** *n* (*dated Brit*) Lichtspielhaus (*old*), Lichtspieltheater *nt*; **~ paper** *n* (*Brit*) Illustrierte *f*; **~ postcard** *n* Ansichts(post)karte *f*; **~ rail** *n* Bilderleiste *f*; **~ researcher** *n* Bildbeschaffer(in *f*) *m*, Picture-researcher *m*; **~ search** *n* (*on video*) Bildsuchlauf *m*.
picturesque [,pɪktʃə'resk] *adj* malerisch, pittoresk (*geh*); (*fig*) *description* anschaulich, bildhaft.
picturesquely [,pɪktʃə'resklɪ] *adv see adj.*
picturesqueness [,pɪktʃə'resknɪs] *n* Malerische(s) *nt*; (*fig: of account, lan-*

guage) Bildhaftigkeit, Anschaulichkeit *f.*

picture: ~ tube *n* Bildröhre *f*; **~ window** *n* Aussichtsfenster *nt*; **~ writing** *n* Bilderschrift *f.*

piddle ['pɪdl] (*inf*) 1 *n* Pipi *nt* (*inf*).
2 *vi* (a) pinkeln (*inf*); (*esp child*) Pipi machen (*inf*). (b) **to ~ around** herummachen.

piddling ['pɪdlɪŋ] *adj* (*inf*) lächerlich.

pidgin ['pɪdʒɪn] *n* Mischsprache *f* ◆ **~ English** Pidgin-English *nt.*

pie [paɪ] *n* Pastete *f*; (*sweet*) Obstkuchen *m*; (*individual*) Tortelett *nt* ◆ **that's all ~ in the sky** (*inf*) das sind nur verrückte Ideen; **as nice/sweet as ~** (*inf*) superfreundlich (*inf*); **as easy as ~** (*inf*) kinderleicht.

piebald ['paɪbɔːld] 1 *adj* scheckig.
2 *n* Schecke *mf.*

piece [piːs] *n* (a) Stück *nt*; (*part, member of a set*) Teil *nt*; (*component part*) Einzelteil *nt*; (*fragment: of glass, pottery etc also*) Scherbe *f*; (*in draughts etc*) Stein *m*; (*in chess*) Figur *f*; (*Press: article*) Artikel *m*; (*Mil*) Geschütz *nt*; (*firearm*) Waffe *f*; (*coin*) Münze *f* ◆ **a 50p ~** ein 50-Pence-Stück, eine 50-Pence-Münze; **a ~ of cake/land/paper** ein Stück *nt* Kuchen/Land/Papier; **a ~ of furniture/luggage/clothing** ein Möbel-/Gepäck-/Kleidungsstück *nt*; **a ten-~ band/coffee set** eine zehnköpfige Band/ein zehnteiliges Kaffeeservice; **a ~ of news/information/luck** eine Nachricht/eine Information/ein Glücksfall *m*; **by a ~ of good luck** glücklicherweise; **a ~ of work** eine Arbeit; **~ by ~** Stück für Stück; **to take sth to ~s** etw in seine Einzelteile zerlegen; **to come to ~s** (*collapsible furniture etc*) sich auseinandernehmen *or* zerlegen lassen; **to come** *or* **fall to ~s** (*broken chair, old book etc*) auseinanderfallen; (*glass, pottery*) zerbrechen; **to be in ~s** (*taken apart*) (in Einzelteile) zerlegt sein; (*broken: vase etc*) in Scherben sein, zerbrochen sein; **to smash sth to ~s** etw kaputtschlagen; **he tore the letter (in)to ~s** er zerriß den Brief (in Stücke *or* Fetzen); **to put together the ~s of a mystery** die einzelnen Teile eines Rätsels zusammenfügen; **he said his ~ very nicely** (*poem etc*) er hat das sehr nett vorgetragen; **to recite a ~** etwas aufsagen; **down the road a ~** (*US inf*) ein Stückchen die Straße runter (*inf*).
(b) (*phrases*) **to go to ~s** (*crack up*) durchdrehen (*inf*); (*lose grip*) die Kontrolle verlieren; (*sportsman, team*) abbauen (*inf*); **he's going to ~s** mit ihm geht's bergab; **all in one ~** (*intact*) heil, unversehrt; **it's all of a ~ with his usual behaviour** so benimmt er sich immer; **his behaviour is all of a ~** sein Verhalten ist konsequent; **to give sb a ~ of one's mind** jdm gehörig *or* ordentlich die Meinung sagen; **he got a ~ of my mind** ich habe ihm meine Meinung gesagt, ich habe ihm Bescheid gestoßen (*inf*); **to say one's ~** seine Meinung sagen.
(c) (*sl: woman*) Weib *nt* (*sl*).

◆**piece together** *vt sep* (*lit*) zusammenstückeln; (*fig*) sich (*dat*) zusammenreimen; *evidence* zusammenfügen ◆ **to ~ ~ a mystery** die einzelnen Teile eines Rätsels zusammenfügen.

pièce de résistance [ˌpjeːsdəˈreɪzɪːˌstɑ̃ŋs] *n* Krönung *f* ◆ **and now the** *or* **my ~** und nun die Krönung!

piece: ~meal 1 *adv* Stück für Stück, stückweise; (*haphazardly*) kunterbunt durcheinander; 2 *adj* stückweise; (*haphazard*) wenig systematisch; **~ rate** *n* Akkordlohnsatz *m*; **~work** *n* Akkordarbeit *f*; **to be on ~work** im Akkord arbeiten; **~worker** *n* Akkordarbeiter(in *f*) *m.*

pie: ~ chart *n* Kreisdiagramm *nt*; **~crust** *n* Teigdecke *f.*

pied [paɪd] *adj* gescheckt, gefleckt ◆ **the P~ Piper of Hamelin** der Rattenfänger von Hameln.

pied-à-terre [ˌpɪeɪdɑːˈtɛəʳ] *n* Zweitwohnung *f.*

pie dish *n* Pastetenform *f.*

pied wagtail *n* Trauerbachstelze *f.*

pie-eyed ['paɪ'aɪd] *adj* (*sl*) blau (wie ein Veilchen) (*inf*).

pier [pɪəʳ] *n* (a) Pier *m or f*; (*landing-place also*) Anlegestelle *f*, Anleger *m.* (b) (*of bridge etc*) Pfeiler *m.*

pierce [pɪəs] *vt* durchstechen; (*knife, spear*) durchstoßen, durchbohren; (*bullet*) durchbohren; (*fig: sound, coldness etc*) durchdringen ◆ **to ~ a hole in sth** etw durchstechen; **to have one's ears ~d** sich (*dat*) die Ohrläppchen durchstechen lassen; **to ~ sth through and through** (*lit, fig*) etw durchbohren; **the news ~d him to the heart** die Nachricht traf ihn bis ins Herz.

piercing ['pɪəsɪŋ] *adj* durchdringend; *cold, wind also* schneidend; *sarcasm* beißend; *wit* scharf.

piercingly ['pɪəsɪŋlɪ] *adv see adj.*

pierrot ['pɪərəʊ] *n* Pierrot *m.*

pietà [ˌpɪeˈtɑː] *n* Pietà *f.*

pietism ['paɪətɪzəm] *n* (a) **P~** der Pietismus. (b) (*piety*) Pietät, Frömmigkeit *f*; (*pej*) Frömmelei *f.*

pietist ['paɪətɪst] *n see* **pietism** Pietist(in *f*) *m*; frommer Mensch; Frömmler(in *f*) *m.*

pietistic [ˌpaɪəˈtɪstɪk] *adj* (*pej*) frömmelnd.

piety ['paɪətɪ] *n* Pietät, Frömmigkeit *f* ◆ **filial ~** Respekt *m* gegenüber den Eltern.

piffle ['pɪfl] *n* (*inf*) Quatsch (*inf*), Schnickschnack (*inf*) *m.*

piffling ['pɪflɪŋ] *adj* (*inf*) lächerlich.

pig [pɪg] 1 *n* (a) Schwein *nt* ◆ **to buy a ~ in a poke** (*prov*) die Katze im Sack kaufen; **~ in the middle** Ball übern Kopf, einer in der Mitte; **~s might fly** (*prov*) wer's glaubt, wird selig; **they were living like ~s** sie haben wie die Schweine gehaust; **in a ~'s eye** (*US inf*) du spinnst wohl! (*inf*).
(b) (*inf: person*) (*dirty, nasty*) Schwein *nt*, Sau *f* (*inf*); (*greedy*) Vielfraß *m* (*inf*) ◆ **to make a ~ of oneself** sich (*dat*) den Bauch vollschlagen (*inf*), kräftig zulangen.
(c) (*inf: awkward thing*) fieses Ding (*inf*).
(d) (*sl: policeman*) Bulle *m* (*sl*).
(e) (*Metal*) (*ingot*) Massel *f*; (*mould*) Kokille *f.*
2 *vt* **to ~ it** (*inf*) hausen.

pigeon ['pɪdʒən] *n* (a) Taube *f.* (b) (*inf*) **that's not my ~** das ist nicht mein Bier (*inf*).

pigeon: ~ breast *n* (*Med*) Hühnerbrust *f*; **~-breasted** *adj* (*Med*) hühnerbrüstig; **~ fancier** *n* Taubenzüchter(in *f*) *m*; **~hole** 1 *n* (*in desk etc*) Fach *nt*; **to put people in ~holes** (*fig*) Menschen (in Kategorien) einordnen, Leute abstempeln; 2 *vt* (*lit*) (in Fächer) einordnen; (*fig: categorize*) einordnen, ein- *or* aufteilen; **~ house, ~ loft** *n* Taubenschlag *m*; **~ post** *n* Brieftaubenpost *f*; **~-toed** *adj, adv* mit einwärts gerichteten Fußspitzen; **he is/walks ~-toed** er geht über den großen Onkel (*inf*).

piggery ['pɪgərɪ] *n* (a) Schweinefarm, Schweinemästerei *f.* (b) (*inf: gluttony*) Völlerei *f.*

piggish ['pɪgɪʃ] *adj* (a) *eyes, face* Schweins-. (b) (*greedy*) gefräßig; *person also* verfressen (*inf*); *appetite* unmäßig, kannibalisch; (*dirty*) saumäßig (*inf*); (*nasty*) fies (*inf*), schweinisch (*inf*); (*stubborn*) fies (*inf*).

piggishly ['pɪgɪʃlɪ] *adv see adj (b).*

piggishness ['pɪgɪʃnɪs] *n see adj* (a) Schweineartigkeit *f.* (b) Gefräßigkeit *f*; Verfressenheit *f* (*inf*); Unmäßigkeit *f*; Saumäßigkeit *f* (*inf*); Fiesheit *f* (*inf*).

piggy ['pɪgɪ] 1 *n* (*baby-talk*) Schweinchen *nt.*
2 *adj* (*+er*) (a) *attr eyes, face* Schweins-. (b) (*inf: greedy*) verfressen (*inf*).

piggyback ['pɪgɪbæk] 1 *n* **to give sb a ~** jdn huckepack nehmen; **the little girl wanted a ~** das kleine Mädchen wollte huckepack getragen werden.
2 *adv* (*also Comput*) huckepack.

piggy bank *n* Sparschwein *nt.*

pigheaded ['pɪg'hedɪd] *adj* stur ◆ **that was a ~ thing to do** so was von stur (*inf*).

pigheadedly ['pɪg'hedɪdlɪ] *adv* stur.

pigheadedness ['pɪg'hedɪdnɪs] *n* Sturheit *f.*

pig: ~ in the middle *n Spiel nt, bei dem ein zwischen zwei anderen stehender Spieler einen Ball, den diese sich zuwerfen, zu fangen versucht* ◆ **I'm just ~ in the middle on this project** (*inf*) ich stehe bei diesem Projekt nur hilflos dabei *or* in der Mitte; **~ iron** *n* Roheisen *nt*; **~ Latin** *n kindliche Geheimsprache durch Anfügen von Silben.*

piglet ['pɪglɪt] *n* Ferkel *nt.*

pigman ['pɪgmən] *n, pl* **-men** [-mən] Schweinehirt(e) *m.*

pigment ['pɪgmənt] *n* Pigment *nt.*

pigmentation [ˌpɪgmənˈteɪʃən] *n* Pigmentierung *f.*

pigmy *n see* **pygmy.**

pig: ~pen *n* (*US*) *see* **~sty**; **~'s ear** *n* **to make a ~'s ear of sth** (*Brit sl*) etw vermasseln (*inf*); **~skin** *n* (a) Schweinsleder *nt*; (b) (*US inf: football*) Pille *f* (*inf*), Leder *nt* (*inf*); **~sty** *n* Schweinestall *m*; (*fig also*) Saustall *m* (*inf*); **~swill** *n* Schweinefutter *nt*; (*fig: coffee, soup etc*) Spülwasser *nt* (*inf*); (*porridge etc*) Schweinefraß *m* (*inf*); **~tail** *n* Zopf *m.*

pike¹ [paɪk] *n* (*weapon*) Pike *f*, Spieß *m.*

pike² *n* (*fish*) Hecht *m.*

pike³ *n* (*US inf*) (*toll-road*) Mautstraße *f*; (*barrier*) Mautschranke *f.*

pikestaff ['paɪkstɑːf] *n*: **as plain as a ~** sonnenklar.

pilaf ['piːlæf] *n* Pilaw *nt.*

pilaster [pɪ'læstəʳ] *n* Pilaster, Halbpfeiler *m.*

pilchard ['pɪltʃəd] *n* Sardine *f.*

pile¹ [paɪl] 1 *n* (a) (*heap*) Stapel, Stoß *m* ◆ **to put things in a ~** etw (auf)stapeln; **her things lay** *or* **were in a ~** ihre Sachen lagen auf einem Haufen; **he made a ~ of the books** er stapelte die Bücher aufeinander.
(b) (*inf: large amount*) Haufen *m*, Menge, Masse *f* ◆ **a great ~ of work** eine Menge *or* Masse (*inf*) Arbeit; **~s of money/trouble/food** eine *or* jede Menge (*inf*) Geld/Ärger/Essen; **a ~ of things to do** massenhaft zu tun (*inf*).
(c) (*inf: fortune*) Vermögen *nt* ◆ **to make a/one's ~** einen Haufen Geld/sein Vermögen verdienen.
(d) (*funeral ~*) Scheiterhaufen *m.*
(e) (*liter, hum: building*) ehrwürdiges Gebäude.
(f) (*atomic ~*) Atommeiler *m.*
2 *vt* stapeln ◆ **a table ~d high with books** ein Tisch mit Stapeln von Büchern; **the sideboard was ~d high with presents** auf der Anrichte stapelten sich die Geschenke.

◆**pile in** 1 *vi* (*inf*) (*-to* in *+acc*) hinein-/hereindrängen; (*get in*) einsteigen ◆ **~ ~!** immer herein!
2 *vt sep* einladen (*-to* in *+acc*).

◆**pile off** *vi* (*inf*) hinaus-/herausdrängen (*prep obj* aus).

◆**pile on** 1 *vi* (*inf*) hinein-/hereindrängen (*-to* in *+acc*).
2 *vt sep* (*lit*) aufhäufen (*-to* auf *+acc*) ◆ **she ~d rice ~(to) my plate** sie häufte Reis auf meinen Teller; **he's piling work ~(to) his staff** er überhäuft seine Leute mit Arbeit; **they are really piling ~ the pressure** sie setzen uns/euch *etc* ganz gehörig unter Druck; **to ~ ~ the agony** (*inf*) dick auftragen (*inf*); **to ~ it ~** (*inf*) dick auftragen (*inf*).

◆**pile out** *vi* (*inf*) hinaus-/herausdrängen (*of* aus).

◆**pile up** 1 *vi* (a) (*lit, fig*) sich (an)sammeln *or* anhäufen; (*traffic*) sich stauen; (*snow, work also*) sich (auf)türmen; (*reasons*) sich häufen; (*evidence*) sich verdichten ◆ **he let the work ~ ~** die Arbeit türmte sich auf.
(b) (*crash*) aufeinander auffahren.
2 *vt sep* (a) (auf)stapeln; *money* horten; (*fig*) *debts* anhäufen; *evidence* sammeln ◆ **her hair was ~d ~ on top of her head** sie trug ihre Haare hoch aufgetürmt; **to ~ ~ the fire ~ (with logs/coal)** (Holz/Kohle) nachlegen; **he's**

piling ~ trouble for himself er handelt sich (*dat*) Ärger ein.
(b) (*inf: crash*) *car* kaputtfahren.

pile[2] *n* Pfahl *m*.

pile[3] *n* (*of carpet, cloth*) Flor *m*.

pile: ~-driver *n* Ramme *f*; **~ dwelling** *n* Pfahlbau *m*.

piles [paɪlz] *npl* Hämorrhoiden *pl*.

pile-up ['paɪlʌp] *n* (*car crash*) (Massen)karambolage *f*, Massenzusammenstoß *m*.

pilfer ['pɪlfəʳ] *vti* stehlen, klauen (*inf*) ◆ **there's a lot of ~ing in the office** im Büro wird viel geklaut (*inf*).

pilferage ['pɪlfərɪdʒ] *n* Diebstähle *pl* (*in kleinem Rahmen*), Beraubung *f* (*Insur*).

pilferer ['pɪlfərəʳ] *n* Dieb(in *f*), Langfinger (*inf*) *m*.

pilgrim ['pɪlgrɪm] *n* Pilger(in *f*) *m* ◆ **the P~ Fathers** die Pilgerväter *pl*.

pilgrimage ['pɪlgrɪmɪdʒ] *n* Wallfahrt, Pilgerfahrt *f* ◆ **to go on** *or* **make a ~** pilgern, wallfahren, eine Pilger- *or* Wallfahrt machen; **in our ~ through this life** (*liter*) auf unserem langen Weg *or* unserer langen Reise durch dieses Leben.

pill [pɪl] *n* **(a)** Tablette *f* ◆ **the ~** die Pille; **to be/go on the ~** die Pille nehmen; *see* **bitter**. **(b)** (*sl: ball*) Pille *f* (*sl*).

pillage ['pɪlɪdʒ] [1] *n* (*act*) Plünderung *f*; (*booty*) Beute *f*.
[2] *vti* plündern.

pillar ['pɪləʳ] *n* Säule *f* ◆ **~ of salt** Salzsäule *f*; **~ of water** Wassersäule *f*; **the P~s of Hercules** die Säulen *pl* des Herkules; **a ~ of society** eine Säule *or* Stütze der Gesellschaft; **from ~ to post** von Pontius zu Pilatus.

pillar-box ['pɪləbɒks] *n* (*Brit*) Briefkasten *m* ◆ **~ red** knallrot.

pillbox ['pɪlbɒks] *n* **(a)** (*Med*) Pillenschachtel *f*. **(b)** (*Mil*) Bunker *m*. **(c)** (*also* **~ hat**) Pagenkäppi *nt*; (*for women*) Pillbox *f*.

pillion ['pɪljən] [1] *n* **(a)** (*on motor-bike*) Soziussitz *m* ◆ **~ passenger** Sozius, Beifahrer(in *f*) *m*. **(b)** (*Hist*) Damensattel *m*.
[2] *adv* **to ride ~** auf dem Sozius- *or* Beifahrersitz mitfahren.

pillory ['pɪlərɪ] [1] *n* (*Hist*) Pranger *m* ◆ **to be in the ~** am Pranger stehen.
[2] *vt* (*fig*) anprangern.

pillow ['pɪləʊ] [1] *n* (Kopf)kissen *nt*.
[2] *vt* betten.

pillow: ~case *n* (Kopf)kissenbezug *m*; **~ fight** *n* Kissenschlacht *f*; **~slip** *n* *see* **~case**; **~ talk** *n* Bettgeflüster *nt*.

pilot ['paɪlət] [1] *n* **(a)** (*Aviat*) Pilot(in *f*), Flugzeugführer(in *f*) *m* ◆ **~'s licence** Flugschein *m*, Flugzeugführererlaubnis *f* (*form*).
(b) (*Naut*) Lotse *m*.
(c) (**~** *light*) Zündflamme *f*.
(d) (*US: on train*) Schienenräumer *m*.
[2] *vt* *plane* führen, fliegen; *ship* lotsen; (*fig*) führen, leiten ◆ **to ~ a bill through the House** eine Gesetzesvorlage durch das Parlament bringen.

pilot: ~ boat *n* Lotsenboot *nt*; **~ fish** *n* Lotsen- *or* Piloten- *or* Leitfisch *m*; **~ flag** *n* Lotsenrufflagge *f*; **~ house** *n* Ruderhaus, Steuerhaus *nt*; **~ lamp** *n* Kontrollampe *f*; **~less** *adj* führerlos; **~ light** *n* Zündflamme *f*; **P~ Officer** *n* (*Brit Aviat*) Leutnant *m*; **~ scheme** *n* Pilotprojekt *nt*; **~ study** *n* Pilotstudie, Musterstudie *f*.

pimento [pɪ'mentəʊ] *n* **(a)** Paprikaschote *f*. **(b)** (*allspice*) Piment *m or nt*, Nelkenpfeffer *m*; (*tree*) Pimentbaum *m*.

pimp [pɪmp] [1] *n* Zuhälter *m*.
[2] *vi* Zuhälter sein ◆ **to ~ for sb** für jdn den Zuhälter machen.

pimpernel ['pɪmpənel] *n* (*Bot: also* **scarlet ~**) (Acker)gauchheil *m*.

pimple ['pɪmpl] *n* Pickel *m*, Pustel *f* ◆ **she/her face comes out in ~s** sie bekommt Pickel/sie bekommt Pickel im Gesicht.

pimply ['pɪmplɪ] *adj* (*+er*) pickelig.

pin [pɪn] [1] *n* **(a)** (*Sew*) Stecknadel *f*; (*tie ~, hat~, on brooch, hair~*) Nadel *f*; (*Mech*) Bolzen, Stift *m*; (*small nail*) Stift *m*; (*in grenade*) Sicherungsstift *m*; (*on guitar*) Wirbel *m*; (*Med*) Stift, Nagel *m*; (*Elec: of plug*) Pol *m*; (*Comput: on connector*) Pin *m*; (*on printhead*) Nadel *f* ◆ **a two-~ plug** ein zweipoliger Stecker; **~s and needles** *sing or pl* ein Kribbeln *nt*; **I've got ~s and needles in my foot** mir ist der Fuß eingeschlafen; **like a new ~** blitzsauber, funkelnagelneu; **neat as a (new) ~** wie aus dem Ei gepellt; **for two ~s I'd pack up and go** (*inf*) es fehlt nicht mehr viel, dann gehe ich; **I don't care a ~** (*dated inf*) es ist mir völlig egal *or* schnuppe (*inf*); **you could have heard a ~ drop** man hätte eine Stecknadel fallen hören können.
(b) (*esp US*) (*brooch*) Brosche, Schmucknadel *f*; (*badge: also lapel ~, fraternity ~*) Anstecknadel *f*, Abzeichen *nt*.
(c) (*Golf*) Flaggenstock *m*; (*Bowling*) Kegel *m*.
(d) **~s** *pl* (*inf: legs*) Gestell *nt* (*inf*) ◆ **he wasn't very steady on his ~s** er war etwas wackelig auf den Beinen; **to be quick on one's ~s** gut zu Fuß sein.
[2] *vt* **(a)** *dress* stecken ◆ **to ~ sth to sth** etw an etw (*acc*) heften; **to ~ papers together** Blätter zusammenheften; **the bone had to be ~ned in place** der Knochen mußte genagelt werden.
(b) (*fig*) **to ~ sb to the ground/against a wall** jdn an den Boden/an eine Wand pressen; **to ~ sb's arms to his side** jdm die Arme an den Körper pressen; **to ~ sb's arm behind his back** jdm den Arm auf den Rücken drehen; **to ~ one's hopes/faith on sb/sth** seine Hoffnungen/sein Vertrauen auf jdn/etw setzen; **you shouldn't ~ everything on one chance** Sie sollten nicht alles auf eine Karte setzen; **to ~ back one's ears** die Ohren spitzen (*inf*).
(c) (*inf: accuse of*) **to ~ sth on sb** jdm etw anhängen.
(d) (*US inf*) **to be/get ~ned** verlobt sein/sich verloben.

◆**pin down** *vt sep* **(a)** (*fix down*) (*with pins*) an- *or* festheften; (*hold, weight down*) beschweren, niederhalten; (*trap: rockfall etc*) einklemmen ◆ **he ~ned him ~ on the canvas** er drückte ihn auf die Matte; **two of the gang ~ned him ~** zwei aus der Bande drückten ihn zu Boden; **our troops were ~ned ~ by heavy artillery fire** unsere Truppen wurden durch heftiges Artilleriefeuer festgehalten.
(b) (*fig*) **to ~ sb ~** jdn festnageln *or* festlegen; **he wouldn't be ~ned ~ to any particular date** er ließ sich nicht auf ein bestimmtes Datum festnageln *or* festlegen; **he's a difficult man to ~ ~** man kann ihn nur schwer dazu bringen, sich festzulegen; **I've seen him/it somewhere before but I can't ~ him/it ~** ich habe ihn/es schon mal irgendwo gesehen, kann ihn/es aber nicht einordnen; **we can't ~ ~ the source of the rumours** wir können die Quelle der Gerüchte nicht lokalisieren; **it's difficult to ~ the meaning of this word ~** es ist schwierig, die Bedeutung dieses Wortes zu präzisieren *or* genau zu umreißen; **it's not easy to ~ ~ the precise cause of this** es ist nicht leicht, die genaue Ursache dafür festzustellen; **there's something odd here, but I can't ~ it ~** irgend etwas ist hier merkwürdig, aber ich kann nicht genau sagen, was.

◆**pin up** *vt sep notice* anheften; *hair* aufstecken, hochstecken; *hem, dress, sleeves* stecken.

pinafore ['pɪnəfɔːʳ] *n* (*overall: for children*) Kinderkittel *m*; (*apron*) Schürze *f*, Kittel *m* ◆ **~ dress** (*Brit*) Trägerkleid *nt*.

pinball ['pɪnbɔːl] *n* Flipper *m* ◆ **to have a game of ~** Flipper spielen, flippern; **~ machine** Flipper(automat) *m*.

pince-nez ['pɪnsneɪ] *n* Kneifer *m*, Pincenez *nt* (*old*).

pincer movement ['pɪnsə-] *n* (*Mil, fig*) Zangenbewegung *f*.

pincers ['pɪnsəz] *npl* **(a)** Kneifzange, Beißzange *f* ◆ **a pair of ~** eine Kneifzange, eine Beißzange. **(b)** (*Zool*) Schere, Zange *f*.

pinch [pɪntʃ] [1] *n* **(a)** (*with fingers*) Kneifen, Zwicken *nt no pl* ◆ **to give sb a ~ on the arm** jdn in den Arm kneifen *or* zwicken.
(b) (*small quantity*) Quentchen *nt*; (*Cook*) Prise *f* ◆ **a ~ of snuff** eine Prise Schnupftabak.
(c) (*pressure*) **I'm rather feeling the ~ at the moment** ich bin im Augenblick ziemlich knapp bei Kasse (*inf*); **to feel the ~** die schlechte Lage zu spüren bekommen; **if it comes to the ~** wenn es zum Schlimmsten *or* Äußersten kommt; **at a ~** zur Not.
[2] *vt* **(a)** (*with fingers*) kneifen, zwicken; (*with implement: squeeze*) *end of wire etc* zusammendrücken, zusammenklemmen; (*shoe*) drücken ◆ **to ~ sb's bottom** jdn in den Hintern kneifen; **to ~ oneself** sich kneifen; **to ~ one's finger in the door** sich (*dat*) den Finger in der Tür (ein)klemmen.
(b) (*inf: steal*) klauen, stibitzen, mopsen (*all inf*) ◆ **don't let anyone ~ my seat** paß auf, daß mir niemand den Platz wegnimmt; **he ~ed Johnny's girl** er hat Johnny (*dat*) die Freundin ausgespannt (*inf*); **he ~ed that idea from Shaw** die Idee hat er bei Shaw geklaut (*inf*); **I had my car ~ed** mein Auto ist geklaut worden (*inf*).
(c) (*inf: arrest*) schnappen (*inf*), erwischen.
[3] *vi* **(a)** (*shoe, also fig*) drücken.
(b) **to ~ and scrape** sich einschränken.

◆**pinch back** *or* **off** *vt sep bud* abknipsen.

pinchbeck ['pɪntʃbek] [1] *n* (*lit, fig*) Talmi *nt*.
[2] *adj jewels* aus Talmi.

pinched ['pɪntʃt] *adj* **(a)** verhärmt; (*from cold*) verfroren; (*from fatigue*) erschöpft. **(b)** (*inf: short*) **to be ~ for money/time** knapp bei Kasse sein (*inf*)/keine Zeit haben; **we're a bit ~ for space in here** wir sind hier ein wenig beengt.

pinch-hit ['pɪntʃhɪt] *vi* (*US*) Ersatzspieler sein; (*fig*) einspringen.

pinch-hitter ['pɪntʃˌhɪtəʳ] *n* (*US*) Ersatz(spieler) *m*; (*fig*) Ersatz *m*.

pinchpenny ['pɪntʃˌpenɪ] *adj* knauserig, pfennigfuchserisch.

pin: ~ curl *n* Löckchen *nt*; **~cushion** *n* Nadelkissen *nt*.

pine[1] [paɪn] *n* Kiefer *f*.

pine[2] *vi* **(a)** **to ~ for sb/sth** sich nach jdm/etw sehnen *or* verzehren. **(b)** (**~** *away, be sad*) sich vor Kummer verzehren.

◆**pine away** *vi* (*from grief*) sich (vor Kummer) verzehren, vor Gram vergehen; (*from disease*) (dahin)siechen; (*of animal, plant*) eingehen ◆ **she ~d ~ and died** sie starb an gebrochenem Herzen; **the dog just ~d ~ and died** der Hund ging langsam ein.

pineal gland ['pɪnɪəl-] *n* Zirbeldrüse, Epiphyse (*spec*) *f*.

pineapple ['paɪnˌæpl] *n* Ananas *f* ◆ **~ chunks** Ananasstücke *pl*; **~ juice** Ananassaft *m*.

pine: ~ cone *n* Kiefernzapfen *m*; **~ forest** *n* Kiefernwald *m*; **~ marten** *n* Baummarder *m*; **~ needle** *n* Kiefernnadel *f*; **~ tree** *n* Kiefer *f*; **~ wood** *n* Kiefernwald *m*; (*material*) Kiefernholz *nt*.

ping [pɪŋ] [1] *n* (*of bell*) Klingeln *nt*; (*of bullet*) Peng *nt* ◆ **to give** *or* **make a ~** (*sonar, lift bell etc*) klingeln; **the stone made a ~ as it hit the glass** der Stein machte klick, als er auf das Glas traf.
[2] *vi* (*bell*) klingeln; (*bullet*) peng machen.

ping-pong ['pɪŋpɒŋ] *n* Pingpong *nt* ◆ **~ ball** Pingpongball *m*.

pin: ~head *n* (Steck)nadelkopf *m*; (*inf: stupid person*) Holzkopf (*inf*), Strohkopf (*inf*) *m*; **~ holder** *n* Blumenigel *m*; **~hole** *n* Loch *nt*; **~hole camera** *n* Lochkamera, Camera obscura *f*.

pinion ['pɪnjən] [1] *n* **(a)** (*Mech*) Ritzel, Treibrad *nt*. **(b)** (*poet: wing*) Fittich *m* (*poet*), Schwinge *f* (*poet*). **(c)** (*Orn*) Flügelspitze *f*.
[2] *vt* **to ~ sb to the ground/against the wall** jdn zu Boden/gegen eine Wand drücken.

pink[1] [pɪŋk] [1] *n* **(a)** (*colour*) Rosa *nt*; (*hunting ~*) Rot *nt*.
(b) (*plant*) Gartennelke *f*.
(c) **to be in the ~** vor Gesundheit strotzen; **I'm in the ~** mir geht's prächtig;

to feel in the ~ sich bestens fühlen; **in the ~ of condition** in Top- *or* Hochform.
[2] *adj* **(a)** *(colour)* rosa *inv*, rosarot, rosafarben; *cheeks, face* rosig ◆ **~ gin** Pink Gin *m*; **to turn ~** erröten; **to see ~ elephants** *(inf) or* **mice** *(inf)* weiße Mäuse sehen *(inf)*.
(b) *(Pol inf)* rot angehaucht.
pink[2] *vt* **(a)** *(Sew)* mit der Zickzackschere schneiden. **(b)** *(nick)* streifen.
pink[3] *vi (Aut)* klopfen.
pink-eye ['pɪŋkaɪ] *n (inf)* Bindehautentzündung *f*.
pinkie ['pɪŋkɪ] *n (Scot inf, US inf)* kleiner Finger.
pinking shears ['pɪŋkɪŋ,ʃɪəz] *npl* Zickzackschere *f*.
pinkish ['pɪŋkɪʃ] *adj* rötlich ◆ **~ white** blaßrosa.
pinko ['pɪŋkəʊ] *n (Pol pej inf)* roter Bruder *(inf)*, rote Schwester *(inf)*.
pin money *n* Taschengeld, Nadelgeld *(old) nt*.
pinnace ['pɪnɪs] *n* Pinasse *f*.
pinnacle ['pɪnəkl] *n (Archit)* Fiale *f*; *(of rock, mountain)* Gipfel *m*, Spitze *f*; *(fig)* Gipfel, Höhepunkt *m*.
pinnate ['pɪneɪt] *adj (Bot)* gefiedert.
PIN number *n (for cash card)* Geheimnummer *f*.
pinny ['pɪnɪ] *n (inf)* Schürze *f*.
pinoc(h)le ['piːnʌkəl] *n (Cards)* Binokel *nt*.
pin: ~point [1] *n* Punkt *m*; **the buildings were mere ~points on the horizon** die Gebäude zeichneten sich wie Stecknadelköpfe am Horizont ab; **a ~point of light** ein Lichtpunkt *m*; **~point bombing** Punktzielbombardement *nt*; [2] *vt (locate)* genau an- *or* aufzeigen; *(define, identify)* genau feststellen *or* -legen; **~prick** *n* Nadelstich *m*; *(fig)* Kleinigkeit *f*; **~stripe** *n (stripe)* Nadelstreifen *m*; *(cloth)* Tuch *nt* mit Nadelstreifen; *(~stripe suit)* Nadelstreifenanzug *m*.
pint [paɪnt] *n* **(a)** *(measure)* Pint *nt*.
(b) *(esp Brit: quantity) (of milk)* Tüte *f*; *(bottle)* Flasche *f*; *(of beer)* Halbe *f*, Glas *nt* Bier ◆ **to have a ~** ein Bier trinken; **he likes his ~** er hebt ganz gern mal einen *(inf)*; **a good ~** ein gutes Bier.
pinta ['paɪntə] *n (Brit inf)* halber Liter Milch.
pin table *n* Flipper(automat) *m*.
pint-mug ['paɪnt'mʌg] *n* Humpen *m(, der ein Pint faßt)*.
pinto ['pɪntəʊ] *n (US)* Schecke *mf*.
pint-size(d) ['paɪntsaɪz(d)] *adj (inf)* stöpselig *(inf)*, knirpsig *(inf)* ◆ **a ~ boxer** ein Knirps von einem Boxer.
pin: ~ tuck *n* Biese *f*; **~-up** *n (picture)* Pin-up-Foto *nt*; *(person) (girl)* Pin-up-Girl *nt*; *(man)* Idol *nt*; **~-up girl** *n* Pin-up-Girl *nt*; **~wheel** *n (firework)* Feuerrad *nt*; *(US: toy)* Windrädchen *nt*.
Pinyin ['pɪn'jɪn] [1] *n* Pinyin(-Umschrift *f*) *nt*.
[2] *adj* Pinyin-.
pioneer [,paɪə'nɪəʳ] [1] *n (also Mil)* Pionier *m*; *(fig also)* Bahnbrecher, Wegbereiter *m*.
[2] *adj attr see* **pioneering**.
[3] *vt way* vorbereiten, bahnen; *(fig)* Pionierarbeit *f* leisten für ◆ **the firm which ~ed its technical development** die Firma, die die technische Pionierarbeit dafür geleistet hat.
[4] *vi* Pionierarbeit *or* Vorarbeit leisten, den Weg bahnen.
pioneering [,paɪə'nɪərɪŋ] *adj attr* Pionier- ◆ **the pride they take in their ~ ancestors** der Stolz auf ihre Vorfahren, die Pioniere.
pious ['paɪəs] *adj* fromm; *(pej also)* frömmlerisch ◆ **a ~ hope** ein frommer Wunsch.
piously ['paɪəslɪ] *adv* fromm.
piousness ['paɪəsnɪs] *n* Frömmigkeit *f*; *(pej also)* Frömmelei *f*.
pip[1] [pɪp] *n* **(a)** *(Bot)* Kern *m*.
(b) *(on card, dice)* Auge *nt*; *(Brit Mil inf)* Stern *m*; *(on radar screen)* Pip *m*, Echozeichen *nt*.
(c) *(Rad, Telec)* **the ~s** das Zeitzeichen; *(in public telephone)* das Tut-tut-tut; **at the third ~ it will be ...** beim dritten Ton des Zeitzeichens ist es ...; **put more money in when you hear the ~s** bitte Geld nachwerfen, sobald das Zeichen ertönt.
pip[2] *n (Vet)* Pips *m* ◆ **to give sb the ~** *(Brit inf)* jdn aufregen *(inf)*.
pip[3] *vt (Brit inf)* knapp besiegen *or* schlagen ◆ **to ~ sb at the post** *(in race)* jdn um Haaresbreite schlagen; *(fig)* jdm um Haaresbreite zuvorkommen; *(in getting orders etc)* jdm etw vor der Nase wegschnappen; **there I was, ~ped at the post again** da war mir wieder jemand zuvorgekommen.
pipe [paɪp] [1] *n* **(a)** *(tube) (for water, gas, sewage)* Rohr *nt*, Leitung *f*; *(fuel ~, for steam)* Leitung *f*; *(in body)* Röhre *f*.
(b) *(Mus)* Flöte *f*; *(fife, of organ, boatswain's)* Pfeife *f* ◆ **~s** *(bag~s)* Dudelsack *m*; **~s of Pan** Panflöte *f*.
(c) *(for smoking)* Pfeife *f* ◆ **~ of peace** Friedenspfeife; **to smoke a ~** Pfeife rauchen; **put that in your ~ and smoke it!** *(inf)* steck dir das hinter den Spiegel! *(inf)*.
[2] *vt* **(a)** *water, oil etc* in Rohren leiten; *music, broadcast* ausstrahlen ◆ **water has to be ~d in from the next state** Wasser muß in Rohrleitungen aus dem Nachbarstaat herangeschafft werden; **~d music** *(pej)* Musikberieselung *f* *(inf)*.
(b) *(Mus) tune* flöten, pfeifen; *(sing in high voice)* krähen; *(speak in high voice)* piepsen; *(Naut)* pfeifen ◆ **to ~ sb aboard** jdn mit Pfeifensignal an Bord begrüßen *or* empfangen; **he was even ~d to the gallows** selbst zum Galgen wurde er mit Dudelsackmusik geleitet.
(c) *(Cook)* spritzen; *cake* mit Spritzguß verzieren; *(Sew)* paspelieren, paspeln.
[3] *vi (Mus)* flöten, (die) Flöte spielen; *(bird)* pfeifen; *(young bird, anxiously)* piep(s)en.
◆**pipe down** *vi (inf) (be less noisy)* die Luft anhalten *(inf)*, ruhig sein; *(become less confident)* (ganz) klein werden *(inf)*.
◆**pipe up** *vi (inf) (person)* den Mund aufmachen, sich melden ◆ **suddenly a little voice ~d ~** plötzlich machte sich ein Stimmchen bemerkbar; **then he ~d ~ with another objection** dann kam er mit noch einem Einwand.
pipe: ~ band *n* Dudelsackkapelle *f*; **~ clay** *n (for making pipes)* Pfeifenton *m*; **~ cleaner** *n* Pfeifenreiniger *m*; **~ dream** *n* Hirngespinst *nt*; **that's just a ~ dream** das ist ja wohl nur ein frommer Wunsch; **~-layer** *n* Rohrleitungs(ver)leger(in *f*), Rohrleitungsmonteur(in *f*) *m*; **~-laying** *n* Verlegen *nt* von Rohrleitungen; **~line** *n* (Rohr)leitung *f*; *(for oil, gas also)* Pipeline *f*; **to be in the ~line** *(fig)* in Vorbereitung sein; **the pay rise hasn't come through yet but it's in the ~line** die Lohnerhöhung ist noch nicht durch, steht aber kurz bevor; **we've got a few changes in the ~line** wir müssen auf einige Änderungen gefaßt sein.
piper ['paɪpəʳ] *n* Flötenspieler(in *f*) *m*; *(on fife)* Pfeifer *m*; *(on bagpipes)* Dudelsackpfeifer *m* ◆ **to pay the ~** die Kosten tragen, für die Kosten aufkommen; **he who pays the ~ calls the tune** *(Prov)* wer bezahlt, darf auch bestimmen.
pipe: ~ rack *n* Pfeifenständer *m*; **~ smoker** *n* Pfeifenraucher(in *f*) *m*; **~ tobacco** *n* Pfeifentabak *m*.
pipette [pɪ'pet] *n* Pipette *f*, Saugröhrchen *nt*.
piping ['paɪpɪŋ] [1] *n* **(a)** *(pipework)* Rohrleitungssystem *nt*; *(pipe)* Rohrleitung *f*. **(b)** *(Sew)* Paspelierung *f*; *(on furniture)* Kordel *f*; *(Cook)* Spritzgußverzierung *f*. **(c)** *(Mus)* Flötenspiel *nt*; *(on bagpipes)* Dudelsackpfeifen *nt*.
[2] *adj voice* piepsend.
[3] *adv*: **~ hot** kochendheiß.
piping bag *n* Spritzbeutel *m*.
pipistrelle [,pɪpɪ'strel] *n* Zwergfledermaus *f*.
pipit ['pɪpɪt] *n* Pieper *m*.
pippin ['pɪpɪn] *n* Cox *m*.
pipsqueak ['pɪpskwiːk] *n (inf)* Winzling *m (inf)*.
piquancy ['piːkənsɪ] *n* Pikantheit, Würze *f*; *(fig)* Pikanterie *f*.
piquant ['piːkənt] *adj (lit, fig)* pikant.
pique [piːk] [1] *n* Groll *m*, Vergrämtheit *f* ◆ **he resigned in a fit of ~** er kündigte, weil er vergrämt war; **you don't have to go straight into a fit of ~ just because ...** du brauchst nicht gleich pikiert *or* beleidigt zu sein, nur weil ...; **to be in a ~ with sb** *(old)* gegen jdn einen Groll hegen.
[2] *vt (offend, wound)* kränken, verletzen ◆ **to be ~d at sb/sth** über jdn/etw *(acc)* ungehalten *or* pikiert sein.
[3] *vr* **to ~ oneself on sth** sich *(dat)* viel auf etw *(acc)* einbilden.
piqué ['piːkeɪ] *n* Pikee, Piqué *m*.
piracy ['paɪərəsɪ] *n* Seeräuberei, Piraterie *f*; *(of book etc)* Raubdruck *m*; *(of record)* Raubpressung *f* ◆ **an act of ~** Seeräuberei, Piraterie *f*.
piranha (fish) [pɪ'rɑːnjə(,fɪʃ)] *n* Piranha *m*.
pirate ['paɪərɪt] [1] *n* Seeräuber, Pirat *m*; *(~ ship)* Seeräuberschiff, Piratenschiff *nt*; *(also* **~ cab***)* nicht konzessioniertes Taxi ◆ **~ radio** Piratensender *m*.
[2] *vt book* einen Raubdruck herstellen von; *invention, idea* stehlen ◆ **a ~d version of the record** eine Raubpressung; **~d edition** Raubdruck *m*.
piratical [paɪ'rætɪkəl] *adj* seeräuberisch, piratenhaft.
pirouette [,pɪrʊ'et] [1] *n* Pirouette *f*.
[2] *vi* Pirouetten drehen, pirouettieren.
Pisces ['paɪsiːz] *npl (Astron)* Fische *pl*; *(Astrol)* Fisch *m* ◆ **I'm (a) ~** ich bin Fisch.
piss [pɪs] *(vulg)* [1] *n (act)* Piß *m (sl)*; *(urine)* Pisse *f (sl)* ◆ **to have a/go for a ~** pissen *(sl)*/pissen gehen *(sl)*; **to take the ~ out of sb** *(sl)* jdn verarschen *(sl)*.
[2] *vti* pissen *(sl)*.
◆**piss about** *or* **around** *vi (sl)* herummachen *(inf)*.
◆**piss off** *(esp Brit sl)* [1] *vi* abhauen *(inf)* ◆ **~ ~!** *(go away)* verpiß dich! *(sl)*; *(don't be stupid)* du kannst mich mal *(inf)*.
[2] *vt* ankotzen *(sl)* ◆ **to be ~ed ~ with sb/sth** von jdm/etw die Schnauze voll haben *(inf)*.
piss artist *n (sl) (drunk)* Säufer(in *f*) *m*; *(boaster)* Großmaul *nt (inf)*; *(incompetent)* Niete *f (inf)*; *(silly bastard)* Arschloch *nt (sl)*.
pissed [pɪst] *adj (sl) (Brit: drunk)* sturz- *or* stockbesoffen *(inf)*; *(US: angry)* stocksauer *(inf)*.
pistachio [pɪ'stɑːʃɪəʊ] [1] *n* Pistazie *f*.
[2] *adj (colour)* pistazienfarben.
piste [piːst] *n (Ski)* Piste *f*.
pistil ['pɪstɪl] *n* Stempel *m*, Pistill *nt (spec)*.
pistol ['pɪstl] *n* Pistole *f* ◆ **~ shot** Pistolenschuß *m*; *(person)* Pistolenschütze *m*/-schützin *f*; **to hold a ~ to sb's head** *(fig)* jdm die Pistole auf die Brust setzen; **~ grip camera** Kamera *f* mit Handgriff.
pistol-whip ['pɪstəlwɪp] *vt (US)* mit einer Pistole ein paar überziehen *(+dat)* *(inf)*.
piston ['pɪstən] *n* Kolben *m* ◆ **~ engine** Kolbenmotor *m*; **~ ring** Kolbenring *m*; **~ rod** Pleuel- *or* Kolbenstange *f*; **~ stroke** Kolbenhub *m*.
pit[1] [pɪt] [1] *n* **(a)** *(hole)* Grube *f*; *(coalmine also)* Zeche *f*; *(quarry also)* Steinbruch *m*; *(trap)* Fallgrube *f*; *(in zoo etc)* Grube *f*; *(for cock-fighting)* (Kampf)arena *f*; *(of stomach)* Magengrube *f* ◆ **to have a sinking feeling in the ~ of one's stomach** ein ungutes Gefühl in der Magengegend haben; **to go down the ~** Bergmann *or* Bergarbeiter werden; **he works down the ~(s)** er arbeitet unter Tage; **the ~** *(hell)* die Hölle; *see* **bottomless**.
(b) *(Aut) (in garage)* Grube *f*; *(motor-racing)* Box *f*; *(Sport) (for long jump)*

Sprunggrube *f*; (*for high jump*) Sprunghügel *m* ◆ **to make a ~ stop** einen Boxenstop machen.
(c) (*Theat*) (*usu pl Brit: for audience*) Parkett *nt*; (*orchestra ~*) Orchesterraum *m or* -versenkung *f or* -graben *m*.
(d) (*US St Ex*) Börsensaal *m*.
(e) (*scar, on ceramics*) Vertiefung *f*; (*on skin also*) Narbe *f*.
(f) **the ~s** (*sl: very bad*) das Allerletzte.
(g) (*sl: bed*) Falle *f* (*inf*).
[2] *vt* **(a)** **the surface of the moon is ~ted with small craters** die Mondoberfläche ist mit kleinen Kratern übersät; **where the meteorites have ~ted the surface** wo die Meteoriten Einschläge hinterlassen haben; **his face was ~ted with smallpox scars** sein Gesicht war voller Pockennarben; **the underside of the car was ~ted with rust-holes** die Unterseite des Wagens war mit Rostlöchern übersät.
(b) **to ~ one's strength/wits against sb/sth** seine Kraft/seinen Verstand an jdm/etw messen; **in the next round A is ~ted against B** in der nächsten Runde stehen sich A und B gegenüber; **they are clearly ~ting their new model against ours** mit ihrem neuen Modell nehmen sie offensichtlich den Kampf gegen uns auf; **to ~ oneself against the forces of nature** den Kampf gegen die Elemente aufnehmen.

pit² (*US*) [1] *n* Stein *m*.
[2] *vt* entsteinen.

pitapat ['pɪtə'pæt] [1] *adv* (*of heart*) poch poch, klopf klopf; (*of feet*) tapp tapp ◆ **to go ~** (*heart*) pochen, klopfen.
[2] *n* (*of rain, heart*) Klopfen *nt*; (*of feet*) Getrappel, Getrippel *nt*.

pit bull-terrier *n* Pit-Bull-Terrier *m*.

pitch¹ [pɪtʃ] *n* Pech *nt* ◆ **as black as ~** pechschwarz.

pitch² [1] *n* **(a)** (*throw*) Wurf *m* ◆ **he threw the ball back full ~** er schleuderte den Ball in hohem Bogen zurück.
(b) (*Naut*) Stampfen *nt*.
(c) (*esp Brit Sport*) Platz *m*, Feld *nt*.
(d) (*Brit*) (*for doing one's business: in market, outside theatre etc*) Stand *m*; (*fig: usual place: on beach etc*) Platz *m* ◆ **keep off my ~!** (*fig*) komm mir nicht ins Gehege!; *see* **queer**.
(e) (*inf: sales ~*) (*long talk*) Sermon *m* (*inf*); (*technique*) Verkaufstaktik, Masche (*inf*) *f* ◆ **he gave us his ~ about the need to change our policy** er hielt uns (wieder einmal) einen Vortrag über die Notwendigkeit, unsere Politik zu ändern.
(f) (*Phon, of note*) Tonhöhe *f*; (*of instrument*) Tonlage *f*; (*of voice*) Stimmlage *f* ◆ **to have perfect ~** das absolute Gehör haben; **their speaking voices are similar in ~** ihre Stimmlagen sind ähnlich; **a comedian has to find the right ~ for each audience** ein Komiker muß bei jedem Publikum aufs neue versuchen, den richtigen Ton zu treffen.
(g) (*angle, slope: of roof*) Schräge, Neigung *f*; (*of propeller*) Steigung *f* ◆ **the roofs have a high ~** die Dächer sind sehr steil; **the floor was sloping at a precarious ~** der Boden neigte sich gefährlich.
(h) (*fig: degree*) **he roused the mob to such a ~ that ...** er brachte die Massen so sehr auf, daß ...; **the crowd/music had reached such a frenzied ~ that ...** die Menge/Musik hatte einen solchen Grad rasender Erregung erreicht, daß ...; **at its highest ~** auf dem Höhepunkt *or* Gipfel; **we can't keep on working at this ~ much longer** wir können dieses Arbeitstempo nicht mehr lange durchhalten; **their frustration had reached such a ~ that ...** ihre Frustration hatte einen derartigen Grad erreicht, daß ...; **matters had reached such a ~ that ...** die Sache hatte sich derart zugespitzt, daß ...; *see* **fever**.
(i) (*US sl*) **what's the ~?** wie sieht's aus?, was liegt an? (*inf*).
[2] *vt* **(a)** (*throw*) *hay* gabeln; *ball* werfen ◆ **he was ~ed from** *or* **off his horse** er wurde vom Pferd geworfen; **he was ~ed through the windscreen** er wurde durch die Windschutzscheibe geschleudert; **as soon as he got the job he was ~ed into a departmental battle** kaum hatte er die Stelle, wurde er schon in einen Abteilungskrieg verwickelt.
(b) (*Mus*) *song* anstimmen; *note* (*give*) angeben; (*hit*) treffen; *instrument* stimmen ◆ **she ~ed her voice higher** sie sprach mit einer höheren Stimme.
(c) (*fig*) **to ~ one's aspirations too high** seine Erwartungen *or* Hoffnungen zu hoch stecken; **his speech was ~ed in rather high-flown terms** seine Rede war ziemlich hochgestochen; **the production must be ~ed at the right level for London audiences** das Stück muß auf das Niveau des Londoner Publikums abgestimmt werden; **that's ~ing it rather strong** *or* **a bit high** das ist ein bißchen übertrieben; **to ~ sb a story** *or* **line** (*inf*) jdm eine Geschichte *or* ein Märchen auftischen (*inf*).
(d) (*put up*) *camp* aufschlagen; *tent also, stand* aufstellen.
(e) (*Baseball*) **he ~ed the first two innings** er spielte *or* machte in den ersten beiden Runden den Werfer.
[3] *vi* **(a)** (*fall*) fallen, stürzen ◆ **to ~ forward** vornüberfallen; **he ~ed off his horse** er fiel kopfüber vom Pferd; **he ~ed forward as the bus braked** er fiel nach vorn, als der Bus bremste.
(b) (*Naut*) stampfen; (*Aviat*) absacken ◆ **the ship ~ed and tossed** das Schiff stampfte und rollte.
(c) (*Baseball*) werfen ◆ **he's in there ~ing** (*US fig inf*) er schuftet wie ein Ochse (*inf*).

◆**pitch in** [1] *vt sep* hineinwerfen *or* -schleudern.
[2] *vi* (*inf*) einspringen ◆ **if we all ~ ~ and help** wenn wir alle einspringen; **so we all ~ed ~ together** also packten wir alle mit an.

◆**pitch into** *vi +prep obj* (*attack*) herfallen über (*+acc*); *food also, work* sich hermachen über (*+acc*).

◆**pitch on** *vi +prep obj* (*inf: choose*) herauspicken (*inf*).

➤ LANGUAGE IN USE: **pity: 1b** → 26.3

◆**pitch out** *vt sep* (*lit, fig*) hinauswerfen; (*get rid of*) wegwerfen ◆ **he was ~ed ~ when the car crashed** beim Unfall wurde er aus dem Wagen geschleudert.

pitch: ~ black *adj* pechschwarz; **~blende** *n* Pechblende *f*; **~ dark** [1] *adj* pechschwarz; [2] *n* (tiefe) Finsternis.

pitched [pɪtʃt] *adj* **(a)** *roof* Sattel-, Giebel-. **(b)** *battle* offen.

pitcher¹ ['pɪtʃəʳ] *n* Krug *m*; (*two-handled*) Henkelkrug *m*.

pitcher² *n* (*Baseball*) Werfer *m*.

pitch: ~fork [1] *n* Heugabel *f*; (*for manure*) Mistgabel *f*; [2] *vt* gabeln; (*fig*) hineinwerfen; **~ invasion** *n* Sturm *m* auf das Spielfeld; **~ pine** *n* Pechkiefer *f*; **~ pipe** *n* (*Mus*) Stimmpfeife *f*.

piteous ['pɪtɪəs] *adj* mitleiderregend; *sounds* kläglich.

piteously ['pɪtɪəslɪ] *adv* mitleiderregend; *cry etc also* kläglich.

pitfall ['pɪtfɔːl] *n* (*fig*) Falle *f*, Fallstrick *m* ◆ **"P~s of English"** „Hauptschwierigkeiten der englischen Sprache".

pith [pɪθ] *n* (*Bot*) Mark *nt*; (*of orange, lemon etc*) weiße Haut; (*fig: core*) Kern *m*, Wesentliche(s) *nt* ◆ **remarks** *etc* **of great ~ (and moment)** bedeutungsschwere Äußerungen.

pithead ['pɪthed] *n* Übertageanlagen *pl* ◆ **at the ~** über Tage; **~ ballot** Abstimmung *f* der Bergarbeiter.

pith hat, pith helmet *n* Tropenhelm *m*.

pithily ['pɪθɪlɪ] *adv* prägnant, kernig, markig.

pithiness ['pɪθɪnɪs] *n* (*fig*) Prägnanz, Markigkeit *f*.

pithy ['pɪθɪ] *adj* (*+er*) (*Bot*) reich an Mark; *oranges etc* dickschalig; (*fig*) prägnant, markig ◆ **~ remarks** Kraftsprüche *pl*.

pitiable ['pɪtɪəbl] *adj* mitleiderregend, bemitleidenswert.

pitiful ['pɪtɪfʊl] *adj* **(a)** (*moving to pity*) *sight, story* mitleiderregend; *person* bemitleidenswert, bedauernswert; *cry, whimper also* jämmerlich.
(b) (*poor, wretched*) erbärmlich, jämmerlich, kläglich ◆ **what a ~ little wretch you are** was bist du doch für ein erbärmlicher kleiner Schuft; **he had only a few ~ hairs on his upper lip** er hatte nur ein paar kümmerliche Haare auf der Oberlippe.

pitifully ['pɪtɪfəlɪ] *adv see adj* ◆ **it was ~ obvious that ...** es war schon qualvoll offensichtlich, daß ...

pitiless ['pɪtɪlɪs] *adj* mitleidlos; *person also, sun, glare* unbarmherzig; *cruelty also* gnadenlos, erbarmungslos.

pitilessly ['pɪtɪlɪslɪ] *adv see adj*.

piton ['piːtɒn] *n* (*Mountaineering*) Felshaken *m*.

pit: ~ pony *n* Grubenpony *nt*; **~ prop** *n* Grubenstempel *m*.

pits [pɪts] *npl see* **pit¹ 1 (f)**.

pittance ['pɪtəns] *n* Hungerlohn *m*.

pitter-patter ['pɪtə'pætəʳ] [1] *n* (*of rain*) Klatschen *nt*; (*of feet*) Getrappel, Getrippel *nt*.
[2] *adv run* tapp tapp, tipp tapp ◆ **her heart went ~** ihr Herz klopfte *or* pochte.
[3] *vi* (*rain*) platschen, klatschen; (*run*) trappeln, trippeln.

pituitary (gland) [pɪ'tjuːɪtrɪ(ˌglænd)] *n* Hirnanhangdrüse *f*.

pit worker *n* Grubenarbeiter *m*.

▼ **pity** ['pɪtɪ] [1] *n* **(a)** Mitleid, Mitgefühl, Erbarmen *nt* ◆ **for ~'s sake!** Erbarmen!; (*less seriously*) um Himmels willen!; **to have** *or* **take ~ on sb, to feel ~ for sb** mit jdm Mitleid haben; **but the king took ~ on him and spared his life** aber der König hatte Erbarmen mit ihm und schonte sein Leben; **have you no ~?** hast du kein Mitleid?; **to do sth out of ~ (for sb)** etw aus Mitleid (mit jdm) tun; **to feel no ~** kein Mitgefühl *etc* haben, kein Mitleid fühlen; **to move sb to ~** jds Mitleid (*acc*) erregen.
▼ **(b)** (*cause of regret*) **(what a) ~!** (wie) schade!; **what a ~ he can't come** (wie) schade, daß er nicht kommen kann; **more's the ~!** leider; **and I won't be able to attend, more's the ~** und ich kann leider nicht teilnehmen; **it is a ~ that ...** es ist schade, daß ...; **the ~ of it was that ...** das Traurige daran war, daß ...; **it's a great ~** es ist sehr schade, es ist jammerschade; (*more formally*) es ist sehr bedauerlich.
[2] *vt* bemitleiden, bedauern; (*contemptuously*) bedauern ◆ **all I can say is that I ~ you** ich kann nur sagen, du tust mir leid.

pitying *adj*, **~ly** *adv* ['pɪtɪɪŋ, -lɪ] mitleidig; *glance also* bedauernd; (*with contempt*) verächtlich.

pivot ['pɪvət] (*vb: pret, ptp* **~ed**) [1] *n* Lagerzapfen, Drehzapfen *m*; (*Mil*) Flügelmann *m*; (*fig*) Dreh- und Angelpunkt *m* ◆ **~ bearing** Zapfenlager *nt*.
[2] *vt* drehbar lagern ◆ **he ~ed it on his hand** er ließ es auf seiner Hand kreiseln.
[3] *vi* sich drehen ◆ **to ~ on sth** (*fig*) sich um etw drehen.

pivotal ['pɪvətl] *adj* (*fig*) zentral.

pixel ['pɪksl] *n* (*Comput*) Pixel *nt*.

pixie, pixy ['pɪksɪ] *n* Kobold, Elf *m* ◆ **~ hat** *or* **hood** Rotkäppchenmütze *f*.

pixilated ['pɪksɪleɪtɪd] *adj* (*hum sl*) (*crazy, eccentric*) überspannt, überkandidelt (*inf*); (*drunk*) angeheitert (*inf*).

pizazz [pɪ'zæz] *n see* **pzazz**.

pizza ['piːtsə] *n* Pizza *f*.

pizzeria [ˌpiːtsə'riːə] *n* Pizzeria *f*.

pizzle ['pɪzl] *n* Ochsenziemer *m*.

Pl *abbr of* **Place** Pl.

placard ['plækɑːd] [1] *n* Plakat *nt*; (*at demonstrations also*) Transparent *nt*.
[2] *vt* plakatieren ◆ **to ~ a wall with posters** eine Wand mit Plakaten bekleben; **the new beer is ~ed all over town** für das neue Bier wird in der ganzen Stadt Plakatwerbung gemacht.

placate [plə'keɪt] *vt* besänftigen, beschwichtigen.

placatory [plə'keɪtərɪ] *adj* beschwichtigend, besänftigend; *gesture also* versöhnlich.

place [pleɪs] [1] *n* **(a)** (*in general*) Platz *m*, Stelle *f* ♦ **this is the ~ where he was ...** hier *or* an dieser Stelle wurde er ...; **from ~ to ~** von einem Ort zum anderen; **in another ~** woanders; **some/any ~** irgendwo; **a poor man with no ~ to go** ein armer Mann, der nicht weiß, wohin; **this is no ~ for you/children** das ist nichts *or* kein Platz für dich/für Kinder; **bed is the best ~ for him** im Bett ist er am besten aufgehoben; **we found a good ~ to watch the procession from** wir fanden einen Platz, von dem wir den Umzug gut sehen konnten; **there is no ~ for the unsuccessful in our society** für Erfolglose ist in unserer Gesellschaft kein Platz; **all over the ~** überall; **I can't be in two ~s at once!** ich kann doch nicht an zwei Stellen gleichzeitig sein; **it was the last ~ I expected to find him** da hätte ich ihn zuletzt *or* am wenigsten vermutet; **this isn't the ~ to discuss politics** dies ist nicht der Ort, um über Politik zu sprechen; **to laugh in the right ~s** an den richtigen Stellen lachen; **to go ~s** (*travel*) Ausflüge machen, herumreisen; **he's going ~s** (*fig inf*) er bringt's zu was (*inf*).
(b) (*specific ~*) Stätte *f*, Ort *m* ♦ **~ of amusement** Vergnügungsstätte *f*; **~ of birth/residence** Geburtsort *m*/Wohnort *m*; **~ of business** *or* **work** Arbeitsstelle *f*.
(c) (*on surface*) Stelle *f* ♦ **water is coming through in several ~s** an mehreren Stellen kommt Wasser durch.
(d) (*district etc*) Gegend *f*; (*country*) Land *nt*; (*building*) Gebäude *nt*; (*town*) Ort *m* ♦ **there's nothing to do in the evenings in this ~** hier kann man abends nichts unternehmen; **they're building a modern ~ out in the suburbs** sie bauen ein neues Gebäude am Stadtrand; **Sweden's a great ~** Schweden ist ein tolles Land.
(e) (*home*) Haus *nt*; Wohnung *f* ♦ **country ~** Gutshaus *nt*, Landsitz *m*; **a little ~ at the seaside** ein Häuschen *nt* am Meer; **come round to my ~ some time** besuch mich mal, komm doch mal vorbei; **let's go back to my ~** laß uns zu mir gehen; **I've never been to his ~** ich bin noch nie bei ihm gewesen; **where's your ~?** wo wohnst du?; **at Peter's ~** bei Peter; **your ~ or my ~?** (*hum inf*) gehen wir zu dir oder zu mir?
(f) (*in street names*) Platz *m*.
(g) (*proper or natural ~*) Platz *m* ♦ **do the spoons have a special ~?** haben die Löffel einen bestimmten Platz?; **make sure the wire/screw is properly in ~** achten Sie darauf, daß der Draht/die Schraube richtig sitzt; **to be out of ~** in Unordnung sein; (*one object*) nicht an der richtigen Stelle sein; (*fig*) (*remark*) unangebracht *or* deplaziert sein; (*person*) fehl am Platze *or* deplaziert sein; **to look out of ~** fehl am Platz *or* deplaziert wirken; **to feel out of ~** sich fehl am Platz *or* deplaziert fühlen; **not a hair out of ~** tipptopp frisiert (*inf*); **she likes to have a ~ for everything and everything in its ~** sie hält sehr auf Ordnung und achtet darauf, daß alles an seinem Platz liegt; **your ~ is by his side** dein Platz ist an seiner Seite; **everything was in ~** alles war an seiner Stelle; **in the right/wrong ~** an der richtigen/falschen Stelle.
(h) (*in book etc*) Stelle *f* ♦ **to find/keep one's ~** die richtige Stelle finden/sich (*dat*) die richtige Stelle markieren; **to lose one's ~** die Seite verblättern; (*on page*) die Zeile verlieren.
(i) (*seat, at table, in team, school, hospital etc*) Platz *m*; (*in hospital also*) Bettplatz *m*; (*university ~*) Studienplatz *m*; (*job*) Stelle *f* ♦ **to lay an extra ~ for sb** ein zusätzliches Gedeck für jdn auflegen; **to take one's ~ (at table)** Platz nehmen; **take your ~s for a square dance!** Aufstellung zur Quadrille, bitte!; **~s for 500 workers** 500 Arbeitsplätze; **to give up/lose one's ~** (*in a queue*) jdm den Vortritt lassen/sich wieder hinten anstellen müssen.
(j) (*social position etc*) Rang *m*, Stellung *f* ♦ **people in high ~s** Leute in hohen Positionen; **to know one's ~** wissen, was sich (für einen) gehört; **of course I'm not criticizing your work, I know my ~!** (*hum*) ich kritisiere dich selbstverständlich nicht, das steht mir gar nicht zu; **it's not my ~ to comment/tell him what to do** es steht mir nicht zu, einen Kommentar abzugeben/ihm zu sagen, was er tun soll; **to keep** *or* **put sb in his ~** jdn in seine Schranken weisen; **that put him in his ~!** das hat ihn erst mal zum Schweigen gebracht, da hab' ich's ihm gezeigt (*inf*).
(k) (*in exam, Sport etc*) Platz *m*, Stelle *f*; (*Math*) Stelle *f* ♦ **to work sth out to three decimal ~s** etw auf drei Stellen nach dem Komma berechnen; **P won, with Q in second ~** P hat gewonnen, an zweiter Stelle *or* auf dem zweiten Platz lag Q; **to win first ~** erste(r, s) sein.
(l) (*Horse-racing*) Plazierung *f* ♦ **to get a ~** eine Plazierung erreichen, einen der ersten drei Plätze belegen; **to back a horse for a ~** auf Platz wetten, eine Platzwette abschließen.
(m) **in ~ of** statt (*+gen*); **if I were in your ~** (wenn ich) an Ihrer Stelle (wäre); **put yourself in my ~** versetzen Sie sich in meine Lage; **to give ~ to sth** einer Sache (*dat*) Platz machen; **to take ~** stattfinden; **to take the ~ of sb/sth** jdn/etw ersetzen, jds Platz *or* den Platz von jdm/etw einnehmen.
(n) **in the first/second/third ~** erstens/zweitens/drittens; **in the next ~** weiterhin, auch.
[2] *vt* **(a)** (*put*) setzen, stellen, legen; *person at table etc* setzen; *guards* aufstellen; *shot* (*with gun*) anbringen; (*Ftbl, Tennis*) plazieren; *troops* in Stellung bringen; *announcement* (*in paper*) inserieren (*in* in *+dat*); *advertisement* setzen (*in* in *+acc*) ♦ **the magician ~d one hand over the other** der Zauberer legte eine Hand über die andere; **the dancer slowly ~d one foot forward** der Tänzer setzte langsam einen Fuß vor; **he ~d the cue-ball right behind the black** er setzte die Spielkugel direkt hinter die schwarze Kugel; **he ~d a knife at my throat** er setzte mir ein Messer an die Kehle; **she ~d a finger on her lips** sie legte den Finger auf die Lippen; **to ~ a matter before sb** jdm eine Angelegenheit vorlegen; **I shall ~ the matter in the hands of a lawyer** ich werde die Angelegenheit einem Rechtsanwalt übergeben; **to ~ a strain on sth** etw belasten; **that should be ~d first** das sollte an erster Stelle stehen; **where do you ~ love in your list of priorities?** an welcher Stelle steht die Liebe für dich?; **to ~ confidence/trust** *etc* **in sb/sth** Vertrauen in jdn/etw setzen; **historians ~ the book in the 5th century AD** Historiker datieren das Buch auf das 5. Jahrhundert; **in which school would you ~ this painting?** welcher Schule würden Sie dieses Gemälde zuordnen?; **I don't know, it's very difficult to ~** ich weiß es nicht, es ist sehr schwer einzuordnen.
(b) **to be ~d** (*shop, town, house etc*) liegen; **we are well ~d for the shops** was Einkaufsmöglichkeiten angeht, wohnen wir günstig; **the vase was dangerously ~d** die Vase stand an einer gefährlichen Stelle; **how are you ~d for time/money?** wie sieht es mit deiner Zeit/deinem Geld aus?; **Liverpool are well ~d in the league** Liverpool liegt gut in der Tabelle; **they were well ~d to observe the whole battle** sie hatten einen günstigen Platz, von dem sie die ganze Schlacht verfolgen konnten; **we are well ~d now to finish the job by next year** wir stehen jetzt so gut da, daß wir die Arbeit im nächsten Jahr fertigstellen können; **with the extra staff we are better ~d now than we were last month** mit dem zusätzlichen Personal stehen wir jetzt besser da als vor einem Monat; **he is well ~d** (*to get hold of things*) er sitzt an der Quelle; **he is well ~d to get information** er kommt leicht an Informationen, er sitzt an der Quelle.
(c) *order* erteilen (*with sb* jdm); *contract* abschließen (*with sb* mit jdm); *phone call* anmelden; *money* deponieren; (*Comm*) *goods* absetzen ♦ **who did you ~ the computer typesetting with?** wem haben Sie den Auftrag für den Computersatz erteilt?; **this is the last time we ~ any work with you** das ist das letzte Mal, daß wir Ihnen einen Auftrag erteilt haben; **to ~ money at sb's credit** jdm eine Geldsumme gutschreiben.
(d) (*in job etc*) unterbringen (*with* bei).
(e) (*in race, competition etc*) **the German runner was ~d third** der deutsche Läufer belegte den dritten Platz *or* wurde Dritter; **to be ~d** (*in horse-race*) (*Brit*) sich plazieren, unter den ersten drei sein; (*US*) Zweiter sein.
(f) (*remember, identify*) einordnen ♦ **I can't quite ~ him/his accent** ich kann ihn/seinen Akzent nicht einordnen.

placebo [plə'siːbəʊ] *n* (*Med*) Placebo *nt*.

place: **~ card** *n* Tischkarte *f*; **~ kick** *n* Platztritt *m*; **~ mat** *n* Set *nt*.

placement ['pleɪsmənt] *n* **(a)** (*act: of social worker, teacher etc*) Plazierung *f*; (*finding job for*) Vermittlung *f*. **(b)** (*period: of trainee*) Praktikum *nt* ♦ **I'm here on a six-month ~** (*for in-service training etc*) ich bin hier für sechs Monate zur Weiterbildung; (*on secondment*) ich bin für sechs Monate hierhin überwiesen worden.

place-name ['pleɪs,neɪm] *n* Ortsname *m*.

placenta [plə'sentə] *n* Plazenta *f*.

placid ['plæsɪd] *adj* ruhig; *person also* gelassen; *disposition* friedfertig; *smile* still; *scene* beschaulich, friedvoll.

placidity [plə'sɪdɪtɪ] *n see adj* Ruhe *f*; Gelassenheit *f*; Friedfertigkeit *f*; Stille *f*; Beschaulichkeit *f*.

placidly ['plæsɪdlɪ] *adv* ruhig, friedlich; *speak* bedächtig.

placket ['plækɪt] *n* Schlitz *m*.

plagiarism ['pleɪdʒjərɪzəm] *n* Plagiat *nt*.

plagiarist ['pleɪdʒjərɪst] *n* Plagiator(in *f*) *m*.

plagiarize ['pleɪdʒjəraɪz] *vt book, idea* plagiieren.

plague [pleɪg] [1] *n* (*Med*) Seuche *f*; (*Bibl, fig*) Plage *f* ♦ **the ~** die Pest; **to avoid sb/sth like the ~** jdn/etw wie die Pest meiden; **a ~ of reporters descended on the town** eine Horde von Reportern suchte die Stadt heim; **a ~ on him!** (*old*) die Pest möge über ihn kommen (*old*)!
[2] *vt* plagen ♦ **to ~ the life out of sb** jdn (bis aufs Blut) quälen, jdm das Leben schwermachen; **to be ~d by doubts** von Zweifeln geplagt werden; **to ~ sb with questions** jdn ständig mit Fragen belästigen.

plaice [pleɪs] *n, no pl* Scholle *f*.

plaid [plæd] *n* Plaid *nt* ♦ **~ skirt** karierter Rock.

plain [pleɪn] [1] *adj* (*+er*) **(a)** klar; (*obvious also*) offensichtlich; *tracks, differences* deutlich ♦ **~ to see** offensichtlich; **it's as ~ as the nose on your face** (*inf*) das sieht doch ein Blinder (mit Krückstock) (*inf*); **to make sth ~ to sb** jdm etw klarmachen *or* klar zu verstehen geben; **the reason is ~ to see** der Grund ist leicht einzusehen; **I'd like to make it quite ~ that ...** ich möchte gern klarstellen, daß ...; **do I/did I make myself** *or* **my meaning ~?** ist das klar/habe ich mich klar ausgedrückt?; **to make one's view** *etc* **~** seine Meinung klar zum Ausdruck bringen.
(b) (*frank, straightforward*) *question, answer* klar; *truth* schlicht ♦ **~ dealing** Redlichkeit *f*; **to be ~ with sb** jdm gegenüber offen *or* direkt sein; **in ~ language** *or* **English** unmißverständlich, auf gut Deutsch; **in ~ language** *or* **English, the answer is no** um es klar *or* auf gut Deutsch zu sagen: die Antwort ist nein; **it was ~ sailing** es ging glatt (über die Bühne) (*inf*); **it won't all be ~ sailing** es wird gar nicht so einfach sein; **from now on it'll be ~ sailing** von jetzt an geht es ganz einfach.
(c) (*simple, with nothing added*) einfach; *dress, design also* schlicht; *living also* schlicht, bescheiden; *cooking, food also* (gut)bürgerlich; *cook* gutbürgerlich; *water* klar; *chocolate* bitter; *paper* unliniert; *colour* einheitlich; *cigarette* filterlos, ohne Filter ♦ **in a ~ colour** einfarbig, uni *pred*; **under ~ cover** in neutraler Verpackung; (*in envelope*) in neutralem Umschlag; **he's a ~ Mr** er ist einfach Herr Sowieso; **he used to be ~ Mr** früher war er einfach *or* schlicht Herr X.
(d) (*sheer*) rein; *greed also* nackt; *nonsense etc also* völlig, blank (*inf*) ♦ **it's just ~ commonsense** das ist einfach gesunder Menschenverstand.
(e) (*not beautiful*) *person, appearance* nicht gerade ansprechend; *face also* alltäglich ♦ **she really is so ~** sie ist recht unansehnlich; **~ Jane** unansehn-

liches Mädchen; **she's a real ~ Jane** sie ist nicht gerade hübsch *or* eine Schönheit.
[2] *adv* **(a)** (*inf: simply, completely*) (ganz) einfach.
(b) I can't put it ~er than that deutlicher kann ich es nicht sagen.
[3] *n* **(a)** (*Geog*) Ebene *f*, Flachland *nt* ♦ **the ~s** das Flachland, die Ebene; (*in North America*) die Prärie.
(b) (*Knitting*) rechte Masche.
plain clothes *npl* **in ~** in Zivil.
plainclothesman ['pleɪn,kləʊðzmən] *n, pl* **-men** [-mən] Polizist *m* in Zivil, Zivile(r) *m* (*inf*).
plainly ['pleɪnlɪ] *adv* **(a)** (*clearly*) eindeutig; *explain, remember, visible* klar, deutlich. **(b)** (*frankly*) offen, direkt. **(c)** (*simply, unsophisticatedly*) einfach.
plainness ['pleɪnnɪs] *n* **(a)** (*frankness, straightforwardness*) Direktheit, Offenheit *f*. **(b)** (*simplicity*) Einfachheit *f*. **(c)** (*lack of beauty*) Unansehnlichkeit *f*.
plainsman ['pleɪnzmən] *n, pl* **-men** [-mən] Flachländer *m*.
plain: ~song *n* Cantus planus *m*, Gregorianischer Gesang; **~ speaking** *n* Offenheit *f*; **some/a bit of ~ speaking** ein paar offene Worte; **~-spoken** *adj* offen, direkt; *criticism also* unverhohlen; **to be ~-spoken** sagen, was man denkt.
plaint ['pleɪnt] *n* (*Poet*) (Weh)klage *f*.
plaintiff ['pleɪntɪf] *n* Kläger(in *f*) *m*.
plaintive ['pleɪntɪv] *adj* klagend; *voice etc also* wehleidig (*pej*); *song etc also* schwermütig, elegisch (*geh*); *look etc* leidend.
plaintively ['pleɪntɪvlɪ] *adv see adj*.
plait [plæt] [1] *n* Zopf *m* ♦ **she wears her hair in ~s** sie trägt Zöpfe.
[2] *vt* flechten.
➤ **plan** [plæn] [1] *n* **(a)** (*scheme*) Plan *m*; (*Pol, Econ also*) Programm *nt* ♦ **~ of action** (*Mil, fig*) Aktionsprogramm *nt*; **~ of campaign** (*Mil*) Strategie *f*; **the ~ is to meet at six** es ist geplant, sich um sechs zu treffen; **so, what's the ~?** was ist also geplant?; **the best ~ is to tell him first** am besten sagt man es ihm zuerst; **to make ~s (for sth)** Pläne (für etw) machen, (etw) planen; **to have great ~s for sb** mit jdm Großes vorhaben, große Pläne mit jdm haben; **have you any ~s for tonight?** hast du (für) heute abend (schon) etwas vor?; **according to ~** planmäßig, wie vorgesehen, programmgemäß.
(b) (*diagram*) Plan *m*; (*for novel etc also*) Entwurf *m*; (*for essay, speech*) Konzept *nt*; (*town ~*) Stadtplan *m*.
➤ [2] *vt* **(a)** (*arrange*) planen; *programme etc* erstellen.
➤ **(b)** (*intend*) vorhaben ♦ **we weren't ~ning to** wir hatten es nicht vor; **this development was not ~ned** diese Entwicklung war nicht eingeplant; **it wasn't ~ned to happen that way** so war das nicht geplant (gewesen).
(c) (*design*) planen; *buildings etc also* entwerfen.
[3] *vi* planen ♦ **to ~ for sth** sich einstellen auf (*+acc*), rechnen mit; **to ~ months ahead** (auf) Monate vorausplanen; **to ~ on sth** mit etw rechnen; **I'm not ~ning on staying** ich wollte nicht bleiben, ich habe nicht vor zu bleiben.
♦**plan out** *vt sep* in Einzelheiten planen.
plane¹ [pleɪn] *n* (*also* **~ tree**) Platane *f*.
plane² [1] *adj* eben (*also Math*); *surface also* plan.
[2] *n* **(a)** (*Math*) Ebene *f*.
(b) (*fig*) Ebene *f*; (*intellectual also*) Niveau *nt*; (*social ~*) Schicht *f* ♦ **he lives on a different ~** er lebt in anderen Sphären.
(c) (*tool*) Hobel *m*.
(d) (*aeroplane*) Flugzeug *nt* ♦ **to go by ~/take a ~** fliegen.
[3] *vt* hobeln ♦ **to ~ sth down** etw abhobeln, etw glatt hobeln.
[4] *vi* (*bird, glider, speedboat*) gleiten.
planeload ['pleɪnləʊd] *n* Flugzeugladung *f*.
planet ['plænɪt] *n* Planet *m*.
planetarium [,plænɪ'teərɪəm] *n* Planetarium *nt*.
planetary ['plænɪtərɪ] *adj* planetarisch, Planeten-; *travel* zu anderen Planeten.
plangent ['plændʒənt] *adj* (*liter*) getragen, klagend.
plank [plæŋk] [1] *n* **(a)** Brett *nt*; (*Naut*) Planke *f*; *see* **walk**. **(b)** (*Pol*) Schwerpunkt *m* ♦ **he stood for Parliament on a ~ of ...** bei seiner Kandidatur fürs Parlament war ... sein Schwerpunkt *or* profilierte er sich besonders als ...
[2] *vtr* (*inf*) *see* **plonk¹**.
planking ['plæŋkɪŋ] *n* Beplankung *f*, Planken *pl*.
plankton ['plæŋktən] *n* Plankton *nt*.
planned [plænd] *adj* geplant ♦ **~ economy** Planwirtschaft *f*; **~ obsolescence** geplanter Verschleiß.
planner ['plænəʳ] *n* Planer(in *f*) *m*.
planning ['plænɪŋ] *n* Planung *f*.
planning *in cpds* Planungs- ♦ **~ permission** Baugenehmigung *f*.
plant [plɑːnt] [1] *n* **(a)** (*Bot*) Pflanze *f* ♦ **rare/tropical ~s** seltene/tropische Gewächse *pl*.
(b) (*no pl: equipment*) Anlagen *pl*; (*equipment and buildings*) Produktionsanlage *f*; (*no pl: US: of school, bank etc*) Einrichtungen *pl*; (*factory*) Werk *nt* ♦ **~-hire** Baumaschinenvermietung *f*; **"heavy ~ crossing"** „Baustellenverkehr".
(c) (*inf*) *eingeschmuggelter Gegenstand etc, der jdn kompromittieren soll*; (*frame-up*) Komplott *nt*.
[2] *attr* Pflanzen- ♦ **~ life** Pflanzenwelt *f*.
[3] *vt* **(a)** *plants, trees* pflanzen, ein- *or* anpflanzen; *field* bepflanzen ♦ **to ~ a field with turnips/wheat** auf einem Feld Rüben anbauen *or* anpflanzen/Weizen anbauen *or* säen.
(b) (*place in position*) setzen; *bomb* legen; *kiss* drücken; *fist* pflanzen (*inf*); (*in the ground*) *stick* stecken; *flag* pflanzen ♦ **to ~ sth in sb's mind** jdm etw in den Kopf setzen, jdn auf etw (*acc*) bringen; **a policeman was ~ed at each entrance** an jedem Eingang wurde ein Polizist aufgestellt *or* postiert; **he ~ed himself right in the doorway** er pflanzte sich genau in den Eingang (*inf*); **he ~ed himself right in front of the fire** (*inf*) er pflanzte sich genau vor dem Kamin auf (*inf*); **she ~ed the children in the hall** sie stellte die Kinder im Flur ab (*inf*); **to ~ a punch on sb's chin** (*inf*) jdm einen Kinnhaken geben.
(c) (*inf*) *incriminating evidence, stolen goods etc* manipulieren, praktizieren; (*in sb's car, home*) schmuggeln; *informer, spy etc* (ein)schleusen ♦ **to ~ sth on sb** (*inf*) jdm etw unterjubeln (*inf*), jdm etw in die Tasche praktizieren.
♦**plant out** *vt sep* auspflanzen.
plantain ['plæntɪn] *n* (*Bot*) **(a)** Plantainbanane *f*. **(b)** (*weed*) Wegerich *m*.
plantation [plæn'teɪʃən] *n* Plantage, Pflanzung *f*; (*of trees*) Schonung, Anpflanzung *f*.
planter ['plɑːntəʳ] *n* Pflanzer(in *f*) *m*; (*plantation owner also*) Plantagenbesitzer(in *f*) *m*; (*machine*) Pflanzmaschine *f*; (*seed ~*) Sämaschine *f*; (*plantpot*) Übertopf *m*.
plaque [plæk] *n* **(a)** Plakette *f*; (*on building etc*) Tafel *f*. **(b)** (*Med*) Belag *m*; (*on teeth*) (Zahn)belag *m*.
plash [plæʃ] (*liter*) [1] *n* (*of water, rain*) Plätschern *nt*; (*of oars*) Platschen *nt*.
[2] *vi* (*water, rain*) plätschern; (*oars*) platschen.
plasm ['plæzəm], **plasma** ['plæzmə] *n* Plasma *nt*.
plaster ['plɑːstəʳ] [1] *n* **(a)** (*Build*) (Ver)putz *m*.
(b) (*Art, Med: also* **~ of Paris**) Gips *m*; (*Med: ~ cast*) Gipsverband *m* ♦ **to have one's leg in ~** das Bein in Gips haben.
(c) (*Brit: sticking ~*) Pflaster *nt*.
[2] *vt* **(a)** (*Build*) *wall* verputzen ♦ **to ~ over a hole** ein Loch zu- *or* vergipsen.
(b) (*inf: cover*) vollkleistern ♦ **to ~ a wall with posters** eine Wand mit Plakaten vollkleistern *or* bepflastern (*inf*); **~ed with mud** schlammbedeckt; **he ~ed down his wet hair with his hands** er klatschte sich das nasse Haar mit den Händen an.
plaster: ~board *n* Gipskarton(platten *pl*) *m*; **a sheet of ~board** eine Gipskartonplatte; **~ cast** *n* (*model, statue*) Gipsform *f*; (*of footprint etc*) Gipsabdruck *m*; (*Med*) Gipsverband *m*.
plastered ['plɑːstəd] *adj pred* (*sl*) voll (*sl*) ♦ **to get ~** sich vollaufen lassen (*sl*).
plasterer ['plɑːstərəʳ] *n* Gipser, Stukkateur *m*.
plastic ['plæstɪk] [1] *n* **(a)** Plastik *nt*, Plast *m* (*dial*), Plaste *f* (*dial inf*) ♦ **~s** Kunststoffe, Plaste (*dial*) *pl*. **(b)** (*inf: credit cards*) Kreditkarte(n *pl*) *f*.
[2] *adj* **(a)** (*made of ~*) Plastik-, aus Plastik, aus Plast (*dial*); (*pej inf*) *food* Plastik- (*inf*); *person* synthetisch; *pub* steril (*fig*), Plastik- (*inf*).
(b) (*flexible*) formbar (*also fig*), modellierbar (*also fig*), plastisch ♦ **the ~ arts** die gestaltenden Künste.
(c) (*Med*) plastisch.
plastic: ~ bag *n* Plastiktüte *f*; **~ bomb** *n* Plastikbombe *f*; **~ explosive** *n* Plastiksprengstoff *m*.
plasticine ® ['plæstɪsiːn] *n* Plastilin *nt*.
plasticity [plæ'stɪsɪtɪ] *n* Formbarkeit, Modellierbarkeit *f*.
plastic: ~ money *n* (*inf*) Plastikgeld *nt*; **~s industry** *n* Kunststoffindustrie *f*; **~ surgeon** *n* plastischer Chirurg; **~ surgery** *n* plastische Chirurgie; **he had to have ~ surgery** er mußte sich einer Gesichtsoperation unterziehen; **she decided to have ~ surgery on her nose** sie entschloß sich, eine Schönheitsoperation an ihrer Nase vornehmen zu lassen.
plate [pleɪt] [1] *n* **(a)** (*flat dish, ~ful, collection ~*) Teller *m*; (*warming ~*) Platte *f* ♦ **~ supper** (*US*) Tellergericht *nt*; **a dinner at $15.00 a ~** (*US*) ein Essen für *or* zu $ 15.00 pro Person; **cold ~** kalte Platte; **to have sth handed to one on a ~** (*fig inf*) etw auf einem Tablett serviert bekommen (*inf*); **to have a lot on one's ~** (*fig inf*) viel am Hals haben (*inf*).
(b) (*gold, silver*) Silber und Gold *nt*; Tafelsilber *nt*; Tafelgold *nt*; (*~d metal*) vergoldetes/versilbertes Metall; (*~d articles*) (*jewellery*) Doublé *nt*, plattierte Ware, Doublee *nt* ♦ **a piece of ~** ein Stück *or* Gegenstand aus Gold/Silber *etc*; (*~d article*) ein vergoldeter/versilberter *etc* Gegenstand; **it's only ~** es ist bloß *or* nur vergoldet/versilbert *etc*.
(c) (*Tech, Phot, Typ*) Platte *f*; (*name-~, number-~*) Schild *nt*.
(d) (*Racing*) Cup, Pokal *m*; (*race*) Cup- *or* Pokalrennen *nt*.
(e) (*illustration*) Tafel *f*.
(f) (*dental ~*) (Gaumen)platte *f*.
(g) (*Baseball: home ~*) Gummiplatte *f*.
[2] *vt ship* beplanken; (*with armour-plating*) panzern ♦ **to ~ (with gold/silver/nickel)** vergolden/-silbern/-nickeln.
plateau ['plætəʊ] *n, pl* **-s** *or* **-x** (*Geog*) Plateau *nt*, Hochebene *f* ♦ **the rising prices have reached a ~** die Preise steigen nicht mehr und haben sich eingependelt.
plateful ['pleɪtfʊl] *n* Teller *m* ♦ **two ~s of salad** zwei Teller (voll) Salat.
plate: ~ glass *n* Tafelglas *nt*; **~holder** *n* (*Phot*) Plattenkassette *f*; **~layer** *n* (*Brit Rail*) Streckenarbeiter *m*.
platelet ['pleɪtlɪt] *n* (*Physiol*) Plättchen *nt*.
platen ['plætən] *n* (*of typewriter, printer*) Walze *f*.
plate: ~ rack *n* (*Brit*) Geschirrständer *m*; **~ warmer** *n* Warmhalteplatte *f*.
platform ['plætfɔːm] *n* **(a)** Plattform *f*; (*stage*) Podium *nt*, Bühne *f*. **(b)** (*Rail*) Bahnsteig *m*. **(c)** (*Pol*) Plattform *f*.
platform: ~ party *n* Podiumsgäste *pl*; **~ shoe** *n* Plateauschuh *m*; **~ sole** *n* Plateausohle *f*; **~ ticket** *n* Bahnsteigkarte *f*.
plating ['pleɪtɪŋ] *n* (*act*) Vergolden *nt*, Vergoldung *f*; Versilbern *nt*, Versilberung *f*; (*material*) Auflage *f*; (*of copper also*) Verkupferung *f*; (*of nickel also*) Ver-

➤ LANGUAGE IN USE: **plan: 1a** → 8.1 **2a** → 8.2 **2b** → 25.2

nickelung *f*; (*on ship*) Beplankung, Außenhaut *f*; (*armour-~*) Panzerung *f*.

platinum ['plætɪnəm] *n* Platin *nt* ◆ **a ~ blonde** eine Platinblonde.

platitude ['plætɪtjuːd] *n* Platitüde, Plattheit *f*.

platitudinous [ˌplætɪ'tjuːdɪnəs] *adj* banal; *speech also* platt.

Platonic [plə'tɒnɪk] *adj philosophy* Platonisch ◆ **p~** *love, friendship* platonisch.

platoon [plə'tuːn] *n* (*Mil*) Zug *m*.

platter ['plætəʳ] *n* Teller *m*; (*wooden ~ also*) Brett *nt*; (*serving dish*) Platte *f*; (*sl: record*) Platte *f* ◆ **to have sth handed to one on a silver ~** etw auf einem Tablett serviert bekommen.

platypus ['plætɪpəs] *n* Schnabeltier *nt*.

plaudit ['plɔːdɪt] *n usu pl* (*liter*) Ovation (*usu pl*), Huldigung *f* (*geh*) ◆ **the headmaster's ~s made him blush** die Lobeshymnen des Direktors ließen ihn erröten.

plausibility [ˌplɔːzə'bɪlɪtɪ] *n see adj* Plausibilität *f*, Glaubwürdigkeit *f*, Geschicktheit *f*, überzeugende Art.

plausible ['plɔːzəbl] *adj* plausibel; *argument also* einleuchtend; *story, excuse also* glaubwürdig, glaubhaft; *liar* gut, geschickt; *manner, person* überzeugend.

plausibly ['plɔːzəblɪ] *adv* plausibel; *argue also* einleuchtend; *lie, present one's excuses* geschickt; *tell a story, act a part* auf überzeugende Art, überzeugend.

play [pleɪ] [1] *n* **(a)** (*amusement, gambling*) Spiel *nt* ◆ **to be at ~** beim Spielen sein; **to do/say sth in ~** etw aus Spaß tun/sagen; **~ on words** Wortspiel *nt*; **children at ~** spielende Kinder; **children learn through ~** Kinder lernen beim Spiel; **it's your ~** (*turn*) du bist dran; **he lost £800 in a few hours' ~** er hat beim Spiel innerhalb von ein paar Stunden £ 800 verloren.

(b) (*Sport*) Spiel *nt* ◆ **to abandon ~** das Spiel abbrechen; **because of bad weather ~ was impossible** es konnte wegen schlechten Wetters nicht gespielt werden; **in a clever piece of ~, in a clever ~** (*US*) in einem klugen Schachzug; **there was some exciting ~ towards the end** gegen Ende gab es einige spannende (Spiel)szenen; **to be in ~/out of ~** (*ball*) im Spiel/im Aus sein; **to kick the ball out of ~** den Ball aus *or* ins Aus schießen.

(c) (*Tech, Mech*) Spiel *nt* ◆ **1 mm (of) ~** 1 mm Spiel.

(d) (*Theat*) (Theater)stück *nt*; (*Rad*) Hörspiel *nt*; (*TV*) Fernsehspiel *nt* ◆ **the ~s of Shakespeare** Shakespeares Dramen.

(e) (*fig: moving patterns*) Spiel *nt*.

(f) (*fig phrases*) **to come into ~** ins Spiel kommen; **to give full ~ to one's imagination** seiner Phantasie (*dat*) freien Lauf lassen; **the game allows the child's imagination full ~** das Spiel gestattet die freie Entfaltung der kindlichen Phantasie; **to bring** *or* **call sth into ~** etw aufbieten *or* einsetzen; **the ~ of opposing forces** das Widerspiel der Kräfte; **to make great ~ of sth** viel Aufhebens von etw machen; **to make a ~ for sb/sth** sich um jdn bemühen/es auf etw (*acc*) abgesehen haben.

[2] *vt* **(a)** *game, card, ball, position* spielen; *player* aufstellen, einsetzen ◆ **to ~ sb (at a game)** gegen jdn (ein Spiel) spielen; **to ~ ball (with sb)** (mit jdm) mitspielen; **to ~ shop** (Kaufmanns)laden spielen, Kaufmann spielen; **to ~ a joke on sb** jdm einen Streich spielen; **to ~ a mean/dirty trick on sb** jdn auf gemeine/schmutzige Art hereinlegen; **to ~ the company game** sich in der Firma profilieren wollen; **they're all ~ing the game** die machen doch alle mit; see **card¹, game¹, market, hell** *etc*.

(b) (*Theat, fig*) *part, play* spielen; (*perform in*) *town* spielen in (*+dat*) ◆ **to ~ the fool** den Clown spielen, herumblödeln (*inf*).

(c) *instrument, record, tune* spielen ◆ **to ~ the piano** Klavier spielen; **to ~ sth through/over** etw durchspielen.

(d) (*direct*) *lights, jet of water* richten.

(e) (*Fishing*) drillen.

[3] *vi* **(a)** spielen ◆ **to go out to ~** rausgehen und spielen; **run away and ~!** geh spielen!; **can Johnny come out to ~?** darf Johnny zum Spielen rauskommen?; **to ~ with oneself** (*euph*) an sich (*dat*) herumspielen (*euph*); **to ~ with the idea of doing sth** mit dem Gedanken spielen, etw zu tun; **we don't have much time/money to ~ with** wir haben zeitlich/finanziell nicht viel Spielraum; **we don't have that many alternatives to ~ with** so viele Alternativen haben wir nicht zur Verfügung; **he wouldn't ~** (*fig inf*) er wollte nicht mitspielen (*inf*).

(b) (*Sport, at game, gamble*) spielen ◆ **to ~ at mothers and fathers/cowboys and Indians** Vater und Mutter/Cowboy und Indianer spielen; **to ~ at being a fireman** Feuerwehrmann spielen; **he was ~ing at being angry/the jealous lover** seine Wut war gespielt/er spielte den eifersüchtigen Liebhaber; **~!** Anspiel!; **he's just ~ing at it** er tut nur so; **what are you ~ing at?** (*inf*) was soll (denn) das? (*inf*); **to ~ for money** um Geld spielen; **to ~ for time** (*fig*) Zeit gewinnen wollen; **to ~ into sb's hands** (*fig*) jdm in die Hände spielen.

(c) (*Mus*) spielen ◆ **to ~ to sb** jdm vorspielen.

(d) (*move about, form patterns: sun, light, water*) spielen; (*fountain*) tanzen ◆ **a smile ~ed on his lips** ein Lächeln spielte um seine Lippen; **the firemen's hoses ~ed on the flames** die Schläuche der Feuerwehrmänner waren auf die Flammen gerichtet; **the searchlights ~ed over the roofs** die Suchscheinwerfer strichen über die Dächer.

(e) (*Theat*) (*act*) spielen; (*be performed*) gespielt werden.

(f) (*Sport: ground, pitch*) sich bespielen lassen ◆ **the pitch ~s well/badly** auf dem Platz spielt es sich gut/schlecht.

◆**play about** *or* **around** *vi* spielen ◆ **I wish he'd stop ~ing ~ and settle down to a steady job** ich wollte, er würde mit dem ständigen Hin und Her aufhören und sich eine feste Arbeit suchen; **to ~ ~ with sth/an idea** mit etw (herum)spielen/mit einer Idee spielen; **to ~ ~ with sb/sb's feelings** mit jdm/jds Gefühlen spielen.

◆**play along** [1] *vi* mitspielen ◆ **he ~ed ~ with the system** er arrangierte sich mit dem System; **to ~ ~ with a suggestion** auf einen Vorschlag eingehen/scheinbar eingehen.

[2] *vt always separate* hinters Licht führen, ein falsches Spiel spielen mit; (*in order to gain time*) hinhalten.

◆**play back** *vt sep tape recording* abspielen ◆ **the conversation was ~ed ~ to us** man spielte uns (*dat*) das Gespräch vor.

◆**play down** *vt sep* herunterspielen.

◆**play in** *vt sep* (*lead in with music*) musikalisch begrüßen.

◆**play off** [1] *vt sep* **to ~ X ~ against Y** X gegen Y ausspielen; **he was ~ing them ~ against each other** er spielte sie gegeneinander aus.

[2] *vi* (*Sport*) um die Entscheidung spielen.

◆**play on** [1] *vi* weiterspielen.

[2] *vi +prep obj* (*also* **~ upon**) (*exploit*) *sb's fears, feelings, good nature* geschickt ausnutzen; (*emphasize*) *difficulties, similarities* herausstreichen ◆ **the hours of waiting ~ed ~ my nerves** das stundenlange Warten zermürbte mich; **the author is ~ing ~ words** der Autor macht Wortspiele/ein Wortspiel.

◆**play out** *vt sep* **(a)** (*Theat*) *scene* (*enact*) darstellen; (*finish acting*) zu Ende spielen (*also fig*) ◆ **their romance was ~ed ~ against a background of civil war** ihre Romanze spielte sich vor dem Hintergrund des Bürgerkrieges ab.

(b) (*esp pass: use up*) *mine* ausbeuten ◆ **to ~ ~ (the) time** die Zeit herumbringen; (*Sport also*) auf Zeit spielen, Zeit schinden (*pej*); **a ~ed-~ joke** (*inf*) ein abgedroschener Witz; **a ~ed-~ theory** (*inf*) eine überstrapazierte Theorie; **his talent is pretty well ~ed ~** (*inf*) sein Talent ist einigermaßen *or* ganz schön (*inf*) verbraucht; **I was completely ~ed ~ after the game** (*inf*) nach dem Spiel war ich völlig geschafft (*inf*).

(c) (*Mus*) mit Musik hinausgeleiten ◆ **the organ ~ed them ~** das Spiel der Orgel geleitete sie hinaus.

◆**play through** *vi +prep obj a few bars etc* durchspielen.

◆**play up** [1] *vi* **(a)** (*play louder*) lauter spielen.

(b) (*Sport inf: play better*) aufdrehen (*inf*), (richtig) loslegen (*inf*) ◆ **~ ~!** vor!, ran!

(c) (*Brit inf: cause trouble: car, injury, child*) Schwierigkeiten machen, verrückt spielen (*inf*).

(d) (*inf: flatter*) **to ~ ~ to sb** jdn umschmeicheln.

[2] *vt sep* (*inf*) **(a)** (*cause trouble to*) **to ~ sb ~** jdm Schwierigkeiten machen; (*child, injury also*) jdn piesacken (*inf*).

(b) (*exaggerate*) hochspielen.

◆**play upon** *vi +prep obj see* **play on 2**.

playable ['pleɪəbl] *adj pitch* bespielbar; *ball* zu spielen *pred*.

play: ~-act *vi* (*dated Theat*) schauspielern; (*fig also*) Theater spielen; **~-acting** *n* (*dated Theat*) Schauspielerei *f*; (*fig also*) Theater(spiel) *nt*; **~-actor** *n* (*dated Theat*) Mime (*old, geh*), Schauspieler (*also fig*) *m*; **~back** *n* (*switch, recording*) Wiedergabe *f*; (*playing-back also*) Abspielen *nt*; **the producer asked for a ~back** der Produzent bat um eine Wiedergabe *or* ein Playback; **they listened to the ~back of their conversation** sie hörten sich (*dat*) die Aufnahme ihres Gespräches an; **~bill** *n* (*poster*) Theaterplakat *nt*; (*US: programme*) Theaterprogramm *nt*; **~boy** *n* Playboy *m*.

player ['pleɪəʳ] *n* (*Sport, Mus*) Spieler(in *f*) *m*; (*Theat*) Schauspieler(in *f*) *m*.

player-piano ['pleɪə'pjɑːnəʊ] *n* automatisches Klavier.

playfellow ['pleɪfeləʊ] *n* Spielkamerad(in *f*) *m*.

playful ['pleɪfʊl] *adj* neckisch; *remark, smile, look also* schelmisch; *child, animal* verspielt, munter ◆ **the dog is in a ~ mood/just being ~** der Hund will spielen/spielt nur; **the boss is in a ~ mood today** der Chef ist heute zu Späßen aufgelegt; **to do sth in a ~ way** etw zum Scherz *or* aus Spaß tun.

playfully ['pleɪfəlɪ] *adv* neckisch; *remark, smile, look also* schelmisch ◆ **to do/say sth ~** etw zum Scherz tun/sagen.

playfulness ['pleɪfʊlnɪs] *n* (*of child, animal*) Verspieltheit *f*; (*of adult*) Ausgelassenheit, Lustigkeit *f* ◆ **there was a touch of ~ in his manner as he replied** in der Art, wie er antwortete, lag etwas leicht Neckisches *or* Schelmisches.

play: ~goer *n* Theaterbesucher(in *f*) *m*; **~ ground** *n* Spielplatz *m*; (*Sch*) (Schul)hof *m*; (*fig*) Tummelplatz *m*, Spielwiese *f*; **~group** *n* Spielgruppe *f*; **~house** *n* **(a)** (*children's house*) Spielhaus *nt*; (*US: doll's house*) Puppenstube *f*; **(b)** (*Theat*) Schaubühne *f* (*dated*), Schauspielhaus *nt*.

playing ['pleɪɪŋ]: **~ card** *n* Spielkarte *f*; **~ field** *n* Sportplatz *m*; **the school ~ fields** der Schulsportplatz.

playlet ['pleɪlɪt] *n* Spiel, Stück *nt*.

play: ~list (*Rad*) *n Platten pl, die von einem Radiosender gespielt werden*; **artists who don't often make it on to the ~lists of radio stations** Künstler, die nicht oft im Radio gespielt werden; **~mate** *n see* **~fellow**; **~-off** *n* Entscheidungsspiel *nt*; (*extra time*) Verlängerung *f*; **~pen** *n* Laufstall *m*, Laufgitter *nt*; **~room** *n* Spielzimmer *nt*; **~ school** *n* Kindergarten *m*; **~thing** *n* (*lit, fig*) Spielzeug *nt*; **~things** *pl* Spielzeug *nt*, Spielsachen *pl*; **~time** *n* Zeit *f* zum Spielen; (*Sch*) große Pause.

playwright ['pleɪraɪt] *n* Dramatiker(in *f*) *m*; (*contemporary also*) Stückeschreiber(in *f*) *m*.

plaza ['plɑːzə] *n* Piazza *f*; (*US*) (*shopping complex*) Einkaufszentrum *or* -center *nt*; (*on motorway*) Raststätte *f*.

plc [piːel'siː] *n abbr of* **public limited company** AG *f*.

plea [pliː] *n* **(a)** Bitte *f*; (*general appeal*) Appell *m* ◆ **to make a ~ for sth** zu etw aufrufen; **to make a ~ for mercy/leniency** um Gnade/Milde bitten.

(b) (*excuse*) Begründung *f* ◆ **on the ~ of illness/ill health** aus Krankheitsgründen/aus gesundheitlichen Gründen.

(c) (*Jur*) Plädoyer *nt* ◆ **to enter a ~ of guilty/not guilty** ein Geständnis ablegen/seine Unschuld erklären; **to enter a ~ of insanity** Zurechnungsunfähigkeit geltend machen; **he put forward** *or* **made a ~ of self-defence** er machte Notwehr geltend, er berief sich auf Notwehr; ~ **bargaining** *Verhandlungen pl zwischen Richter und Verteidigung über die Möglichkeit, bestimmte Anklagepunkte fallenzulassen, wenn der Angeklagte sich in anderen Punkten schuldig bekennt.*

plead [pli:d] *pret, ptp* ~**ed** *or* (*Scot, US*) **pled** [1] *vt* **(a)** (*argue*) vertreten ◆ **to ~ sb's case, to ~ the case for sb** (*Jur*) jdn vertreten; **to ~ the case for the defence** (*Jur*) die Verteidigung vertreten; **to ~ the case for sth** (*fig*) sich für etw einsetzen; **to ~ sb's cause** (*fig*) jds Sache vertreten, für jds Sache eintreten.
(b) (*as excuse*) *ignorance, insanity* sich berufen auf (*+acc*).
[2] *vi* **(a)** (*beg*) bitten, nachsuchen (*for* um) ◆ **to ~ with sb to do sth** jdn bitten *or* ersuchen (*geh*), etw zu tun; **to ~ with sb for sth** (*beg*) jdn um etw bitten *or* ersuchen (*geh*).
(b) (*Jur*) (*counsel*) das Plädoyer halten ◆ **to ~ guilty/not guilty** sich schuldig/nicht schuldig bekennen; **how do you ~?** bekennen Sie sich schuldig?; **to ~ for sth** (*fig*) für etw plädieren.

pleading ['pli:dɪŋ] [1] *n* Bitten *nt*; (*Jur*) Plädoyer *nt*.
[2] *adj look, voice* flehend.

pleadingly ['pli:dɪŋlɪ] *adv* flehend.

pleasant ['pleznt] *adj* angenehm; *surprise also, news* erfreulich; *person also, face* nett; *manner also, smile* freundlich ◆ **to make oneself ~ to sb** jdn ein wenig unterhalten.

pleasantly ['plezntlɪ] *adv* angenehm; *smile, greet, speak etc* freundlich ◆ **~ decorated** nett *or* hübsch eingerichtet.

pleasantness ['plezntnɪs] *n* Freundlichkeit *f*; (*of news, surprise*) Erfreulichkeit *f* ◆ **the ~ of her manner/face** ihre freundliche Art/ihr nettes Gesicht.

pleasantry ['plezntrɪ] *n* (*joking remark*) Scherz *m*; (*polite remark*) Höflichkeit, Nettigkeit *f*.

pleasa(u)nce ['plezəns] *n* (*old*) Lustgarten *m* (*old*).

▼ **please** [pli:z] [1] *interj* bitte ◆ **(yes,) ~** (*acceptance*) (ja,) bitte; (*enthusiastic*) oh ja, gerne; **~ pass the salt, pass the salt, ~** würden Sie mir bitte das Salz reichen?; **may I? — ~ do!** darf ich? — aber bitte *or* bitte sehr!
[2] *vi* **(a) if you ~** (*form: in request*) wenn ich darum bitten darf; **do it now, if you ~** (*angrily*) aber sofort, wenn es recht ist *or* wenn ich bitten darf!; **and then, if you ~, he tried** ... und dann, stell dir vor, versuchte er ...; **(just) as you ~** ganz wie du willst, wie es Ihnen beliebt (*form*); **to do as one ~s** machen *or* tun, was man will, machen *or* tun, was einem gefällt.
(b) (*cause satisfaction*) gefallen ◆ **eager to ~** darum bemüht, alles richtig zu machen; (*girls*) darum bemüht, jeden Wunsch zu erfüllen; **a gift that is sure to ~** ein Geschenk, das sicher gefällt; **we aim to ~** wir wollen, daß Sie zufrieden sind.
[3] *vt* **(a)** (*give pleasure to*) eine Freude machen (*+dat*); (*satisfy*) zufriedenstellen; (*do as sb wants*) gefallen (*+dat*), gefällig sein (*+dat*) ◆ **just to ~ you** nur dir zuliebe; **it ~s me to see him so happy** es freut mich, daß er so glücklich ist; **well do it then if it ~s you** tu's doch, wenn es dir Spaß macht; **music that ~s the ear** Musik, die das Ohr erfreut; **you can't ~ everybody** man kann es nicht allen recht machen; **there's no pleasing him** er ist nie zufrieden; **he is easily ~d** *or* **easy to ~** er ist leicht zufriedenzustellen; (*iro*) er ist eben ein bescheidener Mensch; **to be hard to ~** schwer zufriedenzustellen sein; **the joke ~d him** der Witz hat ihm gefallen; **I was only too ~d to help** es war mir wirklich eine Freude zu helfen; *see* **~d**.
(b) (*iro, form: be the will of*) belieben (*+dat*) (*iro, form*) ◆ **it ~d him to order that** ... er beliebte anzuordnen, daß ... (*form*); **may it ~ Your Honour** (*Jur*) mit Erlaubnis des Herrn Vorsitzenden; **if it ~s God** wenn es Gott gefällt; **~ God he will recover** gebe Gott, daß er wieder gesund wird; **he will return safely, ~ God!** er wird wohlbehalten zurückkehren, das gebe Gott!
[4] *vr* **to ~ oneself** tun, was einem gefällt; **~ yourself!** wie Sie wollen!; **you can ~ yourself about where you sit** es ist Ihnen überlassen, wo Sie sitzen; **he has only himself to ~** er braucht auf keinen Menschen irgendwelche Rücksichten zu nehmen.
[5] *n* Bitte *nt* ◆ **without so much as a ~** ohne auch nur „bitte" zu sagen.

▼ **pleased** [pli:zd] *adj* (*happy*) erfreut; (*satisfied*) zufrieden ◆ **to be ~ (about sth)** sich (über etw *acc*) freuen; **I'm ~ to hear that** ... es freut mich zu hören, daß ...; **~ to meet you** angenehm (*form*), freut mich; **I'm ~ to be able to announce that** ... ich freue mich, mitteilen zu können, daß ...; **to be ~ at sth** über etw (*acc*) erfreut sein; **to be ~ with sb/sth** mit jdm/etw zufrieden sein; **~ with oneself** mit sich selbst zufrieden, selbstgefällig (*pej*); **that's nothing to be ~ about** das ist aber gar nicht gut.

pleasing ['pli:zɪŋ] *adj* angenehm ◆ **to be ~ to the eye/ear** ein recht netter Anblick sein/sich recht angenehm anhören.

pleasingly ['pli:zɪŋlɪ] *adv* angenehm ◆ **a ~ laid-out garden** ein hübsch angelegter Garten.

pleasurable ['pleʒərəbl] *adj* angenehm; *anticipation* freudig.

▼ **pleasure** ['pleʒə^r] *n* **(a)** (*satisfaction, happiness*) Freude *f* ◆ **it's a ~, (my) ~** gern (geschehen)!; **with ~** sehr gerne, mit Vergnügen (*form*); **the ~ is mine** (*form*) es war mir ein Vergnügen (*form*); **it gives me great ~ to be here** (*form*) es ist mir eine große Freude, hierzusein; **I have much ~ in informing you that** ... ich freue mich (sehr), Ihnen mitteilen zu können, daß ...; **it would give me great ~ to** ... es wäre mir ein Vergnügen, zu ...; **if it gives you ~** wenn es dir Vergnügen bereitet; **to have the ~ of doing sth** das Vergnügen haben, etw zu tun; **he finds ~ in books** er hat Freude an Büchern; **he gets a lot of ~ out of his hobby** er hat viel Freude *or* Spaß an seinem Hobby; **he seems to take ~ in annoying me** es scheint ihm Vergnügen zu bereiten, mich zu ärgern; **but don't think I'll take ~ in it** aber glaub nicht, daß mir das Spaß macht; **may I have the ~?** (*form*) darf ich (um den nächsten Tanz) bitten? (*form*); **will you do me the ~ of dining with me?** (*form*) machen Sie mir das Vergnügen, mit mir zu speisen? (*form*); **Mrs X requests the ~ of Mr Y's company** (*form*) Frau X gibt sich die Ehre, Herrn Y einzuladen (*form*); **Mr Y has great ~ in accepting** ... (*form*) Herr Y nimmt ... mit dem größten Vergnügen an (*form*).
(b) (*amusement*) Vergnügen *nt* ◆ **is it business or ~?** (ist es) geschäftlich oder zum Vergnügen?
(c) (*source of ~*) Vergnügen *nt* ◆ **he's a ~ to teach** es ist ein Vergnügen, ihn zu unterrichten; **the ~s of country life** die Freuden des Landlebens; **all the ~s of London** alle Vergnügungen Londons.
(d) (*iro, form: will*) Wunsch *m* ◆ **at (one's) ~** nach Belieben, nach Gutdünken; **to await sb's ~** abwarten, was jd zu tun geruht; **during Her Majesty's ~** (*Jur*) auf unbestimmte Zeit.

pleasure *in cpds* Vergnügungs-; ~ **boat** *n* **(a)** Vergnügungsdampfer *m or* -schiff *nt*, Ausflugsdampfer *m or* -schiff *nt*; **(b)** (*yacht etc*) Hobbyboot *nt*; ~ **craft** *n* Hobbyboot *nt*; **~-cruise** *n* Vergnügungsfahrt, Kreuzfahrt *f*; ~ **ground** *n* Parkanlage *f*; (*fairground*) Vergnügungspark *m*; **~-loving** *adj* lebenslustig, leichtlebig (*pej*); ~ **principle** *n* (*Psych*) Lustprinzip *nt*; **~-seeker** *n* Vergnügungshungrige(r) *mf*; **~-seeking** *adj* vergnügungshungrig; **~-trip** *n* Vergnügungsausflug *m or* -reise *f*.

pleat [pli:t] [1] *n* Falte *f*.
[2] *vt* fälteln.

pleated ['pli:tɪd] *adj* gefältelt, Falten- ◆ **~ skirt** Faltenrock *m*.

pleb [pleb] *n* (*pej inf*) Plebejer(in *f*) (*pej*), Prolet(in *f*) (*pej inf*) *m* ◆ **the ~s** die Proleten *pl* (*pej inf*), der Plebs (*pej*).

plebby ['plebɪ] *adj* (*pej inf*) primitiv.

plebeian [plɪ'bi:ən] [1] *adj* plebejisch.
[2] *n* Plebejer(in *f*) *m*.

plebiscite ['plebɪsɪt] *n* Plebiszit *nt*, Volksentscheid *m*.

plectrum ['plektrəm] *n* Plektron, Plektrum *nt*.

pled [pled] (*US, Scot*) *pret, ptp of* **plead**.

pledge [pledʒ] [1] *n* **(a)** (*in pawnshop, of love*) Pfand *nt*; (*promise*) Versprechen *nt*, Zusicherung *f* ◆ **I give you my ~** ich gebe dir mein Wort; **we have given them a ~ of aid** wir haben versprochen, ihnen zu helfen; **as a ~ of** als Zeichen (*+gen*); **under (the) ~ of secrecy** unter dem Siegel der Verschwiegenheit; **election ~s** Wahlversprechen *pl*; **to sign** *or* **take the ~** (*lit*) sich schriftlich zur Abstinenz verpflichten; (*hum inf*) dem Alkohol abschwören (*usu hum*).
(b) (*form: toast*) Toast (*form*), Trinkspruch *m* ◆ **to drink a ~ to sb/sth** einen Toast *etc* auf jdn/etw ausbringen.
[2] *vt* **(a)** (*give as security, pawn*) verpfänden.
(b) (*promise*) versprechen, zusichern ◆ **to ~ one's word** sein Wort geben *or* verpfänden; **to ~ support for sb/sth** jdm/einer Sache seine Unterstützung zusichern; **I am ~d to secrecy** ich bin zum Schweigen verpflichtet; **he ~d me to secrecy** er verpflichtete mich zum Schweigen; **to ~ (one's) allegiance to sb/sth** jdm/einer Sache Treue schwören *or* geloben.
(c) (*form: toast*) einen Trinkspruch ausbringen auf (*+acc*).
[3] *vr* **to ~ oneself to do sth** geloben *or* sich verpflichten, etw zu tun.

Pleiades ['plaɪədi:z] *npl* Plejaden *pl*.

Pleistocene ['plaɪstəʊsi:n] [1] *n* Pleistozän *nt*.
[2] *adj* pleistozän, Pleistozän-.

plenary ['pli:nərɪ] *adj* Plenar-, Voll- ◆ **~ session** Plenarsitzung, Vollversammlung *f*; **~ powers** unbeschränkte Vollmachten *pl*.

plenipotentiary [ˌplenɪpə'tenʃərɪ] [1] *n* (General)bevollmächtigte(r) *mf*.
[2] *adj ambassador* (general)bevollmächtigt ◆ **~ powers** Generalvollmachten *pl*.

plenitude ['plenɪtju:d] *n* (*liter*) Fülle *f*.

plenteous ['plentɪəs] *adj* (*liter*) *see* **plentiful**.

plentiful ['plentɪfʊl] *adj* reichlich; *commodities, gold, minerals etc* reichlich *or* im Überfluß vorhanden; *hair* voll ◆ **to be in ~ supply** reichlich *or* im Überfluß vorhanden sein.

plentifully ['plentɪfəlɪ] *adv* reichlich.

plenty ['plentɪ] [1] *n* **(a)** eine Menge ◆ **land of ~** Land des Überflusses; **times of ~** Zeiten des Überflusses, fette Jahre (*Bibl*) *pl*; **in ~** im Überfluß; **three kilos will be ~** drei Kilo sind reichlich; **there's ~ here for six** es gibt mehr als genug für sechs; **that's ~, thanks!** danke, das ist reichlich; **you've already had ~** du hast schon reichlich gehabt; **I met him once, and that was ~!** ich habe ihn nur einmal getroffen, und das hat mir gereicht!; **have I got problems? I've got ~** ob ich Probleme habe? mehr als genug!; **there's ~ more where that came from** davon gibt es genug; **take ~** nimm dir *or* bedien dich reichlich; **there are still ~ left** es sind immer noch eine ganze Menge da.
(b) ~ of viel, eine Menge; **~ of time/milk/eggs/reasons** viel *or* eine Menge Zeit/Milch/viele *or* eine Menge Eier/Gründe; **there is no longer ~ of oil** Öl ist nicht mehr im Überfluß vorhanden; **he's certainly got ~ of nerve** der hat vielleicht Nerven! (*inf*); **a country with ~ of natural resources** ein Land mit umfangreichen Bodenschätzen; **has everyone got ~ of potatoes?** hat jeder reichlich Kartoffeln?; **there will be ~ of things to drink** es gibt dort ausreichend zu trinken; **he had been given ~ of warning** er ist genügend oft gewarnt worden; **we arrived in ~ of time to get a good seat** wir kamen so rechtzeitig, daß wir einen guten Platz kriegten; **don't worry, there's ~ of time** keine Angst, es ist noch genug *or* viel Zeit; **take ~ of exercise** Sie müssen viel Sport treiben.
[2] *adj* (*US inf*) reichlich ◆ **~ bananas** reichlich Bananen.
[3] *adv* (*esp US inf*) **~ big (enough)** groß genug; **he's ~ mean** er ist ziemlich brutal; **he was ~ rude to her** er war ziemlich grob zu ihr; **it rained ~** es hat viel geregnet; **sure, I like it ~** sicher, ich mag das sehr.

➤ LANGUAGE IN USE: **please: 1 → 4** **pleased → 9.2, 19.3, 20.2, 25.2** **pleasure: a → 3.2**

plenum ['pliːnəm] *n* Plenum *nt*, Vollversammlung *f*.
pleonasm ['pliːənæzəm] *n* Pleonasmus *m*.
pleonastic [pliːə'næstɪk] *adj* pleonastisch.
plethora ['pleθərə] *n (form)* Fülle *f*.
pleurisy ['plʊərɪsɪ] *n* Brustfellentzündung, Pleuritis *(spec) f*.
plexus ['pleksəs] *n* Plexus *m*; *(of nerves also)* Nervengeflecht *nt*; *(of blood vessels also)* Gefäßgeflecht *nt*.
pliability [ˌplaɪə'bɪlɪtɪ] *n see adj* Biegsamkeit *f*; Geschmeidigkeit *f*; Formbarkeit *f*; Fügsamkeit *f*.
pliable ['plaɪəbl], **pliant** ['plaɪənt] *adj* biegsam; *leather* geschmeidig; *character, mind, person* formbar; *(docile)* fügsam.
plied [plaɪd] *pret, ptp of* **ply[2]**.
pliers ['plaɪəz] *npl (also* **pair of ~***)* (Kombi)zange *f*.
plight[1] [plaɪt] *vt (liter)* **to ~ one's word** sein (Ehren)wort geben; **to ~ one's troth (to sb)** *(old, hum)* (jdm) die Ehe versprechen.
plight[2] *n* Not *f*, Elend *nt*; *(of currency, economy etc)* Verfall *m* ◆ **to be in a sad** *or* **sorry ~** in einem traurigen Zustand sein; **the country's economic ~** die wirtschaftliche Misere des Landes.
plimsoll ['plɪmsəl] *n (Brit)* Turnschuh *m*.
Plimsoll line *or* **mark** *n* Höchstlademarke *f*.
plinth [plɪnθ] *n* Sockel *m*, Fußplatte, Plinthe *(spec) f*.
Pliocene ['plaɪəʊsiːn] [1] *n* Pliozän *nt*.
[2] *adj* pliozän.
PLO *abbr of* **Palestine Liberation Organization** PLO *f*.
plod [plɒd] [1] *n* Trott, Zockeltrab *(inf) m* ◆ **a steady ~** ein gleichmäßiger Trott.
[2] *vi* **(a)** trotten, zockeln *(inf)* ◆ **to ~ up a hill** einen Hügel hinaufstapfen; **to ~ along** *or* **on** weiterstapfen.
(b) *(fig: in work etc)* sich abmühen *or* abplagen *or* herumquälen ◆ **to ~ away at sth** sich mit etw abmühen *etc*; **to ~ on** sich weiterkämpfen, sich durchkämpfen.
plodder ['plɒdəʳ] *n* zäher Arbeiter, zähe Arbeiterin.
plodding ['plɒdɪŋ] *adj walk* schwerfällig, mühsam; *student, worker* hart arbeitend *attr*; *research* langwierig, mühsam.
plonk[1] [plɒŋk] [1] *n (noise)* Bums *m*.
[2] *adv fall, land* bums, peng ◆ **~ in the middle** genau in die/in der Mitte.
[3] *vt (inf: also* **~ down***)* *(drop, put down)* hinwerfen, hinschmeißen *(inf)*; *(bang down)* hinknallen *(inf)*, hinhauen *(inf)* ◆ **he ~ed a kiss on her cheek** er drückte ihr einen Kuß auf die Wange; **to ~ oneself (down)** sich hinwerfen, sich hinpflanzen *(inf)*; **he ~ed himself down in a chair** er warf sich in einen Sessel, er ließ sich in einen Sessel fallen; **just ~ yourself down somewhere** hau dich einfach irgendwo hin *(inf)*.
plonk[2] *n (Brit inf: wine)* (billiger) Wein, Gesöff *nt (hum, pej)*.
plonker ['plɒŋkəʳ] *n (sl)* **(a)** *(stupid person)* Niete *f*. **(b)** *(penis)* Pimmel *m (inf)*.
plook [pluːk] *n (Scot inf: pimple, zit)* Pickel *m*.
plop [plɒp] [1] *n* Plumps *m*; *(in water)* Platsch *m*.
[2] *adv* **it fell** *or* **went ~ into the water** es fiel mit einem Platsch ins Wasser.
[3] *vi* **(a)** *(make a plopping sound)* platschen.
(b) *(inf: fall)* plumpsen *(inf)*.
plosive ['pləʊsɪv] [1] *adj* Verschluß-, explosiv.
[2] *n* Verschlußlaut, Explosivlaut *m*, Explosivum *nt (spec)*.
plot [plɒt] [1] *n* **(a)** *(Agr)* Stück *nt* Land; *(bed: in garden)* Beet *nt*; *(building ~)* Grundstück *nt*; *(allotment)* Parzelle *f*; *(in graveyard)* Grabstelle *f* ◆ **a ~ of land** ein Stück *nt* Land; **a ~ of lettuces** ein Salatbeet *nt*; *(larger)* ein Salatfeld *nt*.
(b) *(US: diagram, chart) (of estate)* Plan *m*; *(of building)* Grundriß *m*.
(c) *(conspiracy)* Verschwörung *f*, Komplott *nt*; *see* **thicken**.
(d) *(Liter, Theat)* Handlung *f*, Plot *m (spec)*.
[2] *vt* **(a)** *(plan)* planen, aushecken *(inf)* ◆ **what are you ~ting now?** was heckst du nun schon wieder aus?; **they ~ted to kill him** sie planten gemeinsam, ihn zu töten.
(b) *position, course* feststellen; *(draw on map)* einzeichnen; *(Math, Med) curve* aufzeichnen.
[3] *vi* sich verschwören ◆ **to ~ against sb** sich gegen jdn verschwören, gegen jdn ein Komplott schmieden.
plotter[1] ['plɒtəʳ] *n* Verschwörer(in *f*) *m*.
plotter[2] *n (Comput)* Plotter *m*.
plotting ['plɒtɪŋ] *n* Verschwörertum *nt*.
plotting: ~ board, ~ table *n* Zeichentisch *m*.
plough, *(US)* **plow** [plaʊ] [1] *n* Pflug *m* ◆ **the P~** *(Astron)* der Wagen; **under the ~** unter dem Pflug; **to put one's hand to the ~** *(fig)* sich in die Riemen legen.
[2] *vt* **(a)** pflügen, umpflügen ◆ **to ~ a lonely furrow** *(fig)* allein auf weiter Flur stehen.
(b) *(Brit Univ dated sl)* reinreißen *(inf)*, durchfallen lassen.
[3] *vi* **(a)** pflügen.
(b) *(Brit Univ dated sl)* durchrasseln *(inf)*.
◆**plough back** *vt sep (Agr)* unterpflügen; *(Comm) profits* wieder (hinein)stecken, reinvestieren *(into* in *+acc)*.
◆**plough in** *vt sep manure, crop etc* unterpflügen.
◆**plough through** *vti +prep obj* **(a) the ship ~ed (its way) ~ the heavy seas** das Schiff pflügte sich durch die schwere See; **we had to ~ (our way) ~ the snow** wir mußten uns durch den Schnee kämpfen; **the car ~ed straight ~ our garden fence** der Wagen brach geradewegs durch unseren Gartenzaun.
(b) *(inf)* **to ~ (one's way) ~ a novel** *etc* sich durch einen Roman *etc* durchackern *(inf) or* hindurchquälen.
◆**plough up** *vt sep field* umpflügen; *(uncover)* beim Pflügen zutage bringen; *(uproot) tree* roden ◆ **the lorries had completely ~ed ~ the village green** die Lastwagen hatten den Dorfanger vollkommen zerpflügt; **the train ~ed ~ the track for 40 metres** der Zug riß 40 Meter Schienen aus ihrer Verankerung.
plough, *(US)* **plow: ~boy** *n* Pflüger *m*; **~ horse** *n* Ackergaul *m*.
ploughing, *(US)* **plowing** ['plaʊɪŋ] *n* Pflügen *nt* ◆ **the ~ back of profits into the company** die Reinvestierung von Gewinnen in die Firma.
plough, *(US)* **plow: ~land** *n* Ackerland *nt*; **~man** *n* Pflüger *m*; **~man's lunch** Käse und Brot als Imbiß; **~share** *n* Pflugschar *f*.
plover ['plʌvəʳ] *n* Regenpfeifer *m*; *(lapwing)* Kiebitz *m*.
plow *etc (US) see* **plough** *etc*.
ploy [plɔɪ] *n (stratagem)* Trick *m*.
pluck [plʌk] [1] *n* **(a)** *(courage)* Schneid *(inf)*, Mut *m*.
(b) *(of animal)* Innereien *pl*.
[2] *vt* **(a)** *fruit, flower* pflücken; *chicken* rupfen; *guitar, eyebrows* zupfen ◆ **to ~ (at) sb's sleeve** jdn am Ärmel zupfen; **he ~ed a stray hair off his coat** er zupfte sich *(dat)* ein Haar vom Mantel; **his rescuers had ~ed him from the jaws of death** seine Retter hatten ihn den Klauen des Todes entrissen; **to ~ up (one's) courage** all seinen Mut zusammennehmen.
(b) *(also* **~ out***) hair, feather* auszupfen ◆ **if thy right eye offend thee ~ it out** *(Bibl)* wenn dir dein rechtes Auge zum Ärgernis wird, so reiß es aus.
[3] *vi* **to ~ at sth** an etw *(dat)* (herum)zupfen.
pluckily ['plʌkɪlɪ] *adv* tapfer, mutig.
pluckiness ['plʌkɪnɪs] *n* Unerschrockenheit *f*, Schneid *m (inf)*.
plucky ['plʌkɪ] *adj (+er) person, smile* tapfer; *little pony, action, person* mutig.
plug [plʌg] [1] *n* **(a)** *(stopper)* Stöpsel *m*; *(for stopping a leak)* Propfen *m*; *(in barrel)* Spund *m* ◆ **a ~ of cotton wool** ein Wattebausch *m*; **to pull the ~** *(in lavatory)* die Spülung ziehen; **to pull the ~ on sb/sth** *(fig inf)* jdm/einer Sache den Boden unter den Füßen wegziehen.
(b) *(Elec)* Stecker *m*; *(incorrect: socket)* Steckdose *f*; *(Aut: spark ~)* (Zünd)kerze *f*.
(c) *(inf: piece of publicity)* Schleichwerbung *f no pl* ◆ **to give sb/sth a ~** für jdn/etw Schleichwerbung machen.
(d) *(of tobacco)* Scheibe *f*; *(for chewing)* Priem *m*.
(e) *(Geol)* Vulkanstotzen *m*.
(f) *(US: fire~)* Hydrant *m*.
(g) *(sl: punch)* **to take a ~ at sb** jdm eine verplätten *(sl)*.
[2] *vt* **(a)** *(stop) hole, gap, crevice, leak* verstopfen, zustopfen; *barrel* (ver)spunden; *tooth* plombieren ◆ **the doctor ~ged the wound with cotton wool** der Arzt stillte die Blutung mit Watte; **to ~ one's ears** sich *(dat)* die Ohren zuhalten; *(with cotton wool etc)* sich *(dat)* etwas in die Ohren stopfen; **to ~ the drain on the gold reserves** den Abfluß der Goldreserven stoppen; **to ~ the gaps in the tax laws** die Lücken im Steuergesetz schließen.
(b) *(insert)* stecken ◆ **~ the TV into the socket, please** steck bitte den Stecker vom Fernseher in die Steckdose; **an old rag had been ~ged into the hole** man hatte einen alten Lappen in das Loch gestopft.
(c) *(inf: publicize)* Schleichwerbung machen für.
(d) *(inf: push, put forward) idea* hausieren gehen mit.
(e) *(inf: shoot)* **to ~ sb in the head/stomach** *etc* jdm ein Loch in den Kopf/Bauch *etc* schießen; **they ~ged him full of lead** sie pumpten ihn mit Blei voll *(sl)*.
(f) *(sl: punch)* eine verplätten *(+dat) (sl)*.
◆**plug away** *vi (inf)* ackern *(inf)* ◆ **to ~ ~ at sth** sich mit etw abrackern *or* herumschlagen *(inf)*; **keep ~ging ~** (nur) nicht lockerlassen.
◆**plug in** [1] *vt sep TV, heater etc* hineinstecken, einstöpseln, anschließen ◆ **to be ~ged ~** angeschlossen sein.
[2] *vi* sich anschließen lassen ◆ **where does the TV ~ ~?** wo wird der Fernseher angeschlossen?; **~ ~, then switch on** schließen Sie das Gerät an und schalten Sie es dann ein.
◆**plug up** *vt sep gap, hole, leak etc* verstopfen, zustopfen; *crack* zuspachteln, verspachteln.
plug: ~ and play *adj attr (Comput) technology* Plug-and-Play-; **~ hat** *n (old US sl)* Angströhre *f (dated hum)*; **~hole** *n* Abfluß(loch *nt*) *m*; **to go down the ~hole** *(fig inf)* kaputtgehen *(inf)*; **~ tobacco** *n* Kautabak *m*; **~-ugly** *(inf)* [1] *n* Schlägertyp *(inf)*, Rabauke *(inf) m*; [2] *adj* potthäßlich *(inf)*.
plum [plʌm] [1] *n* **(a)** *(fruit, tree)* Pflaume *f*; *(Victoria ~, dark blue)* Zwetsch(g)e *f* ◆ **to speak with a ~ in one's mouth** *(fig inf)* sprechen, als hätte man eine heiße Kartoffel im Mund.
(b) *(colour)* Pflaumenblau *nt*.
(c) *(fig inf: good job)* **a real ~ (of a job)** ein Bombenjob *m (inf)*.
[2] *adj attr (inf) job, position* Bomben- *(inf)*, Mords- *(inf)*.
plumage ['pluːmɪdʒ] *n* Gefieder, Federkleid *(liter) nt*.
plumb [plʌm] [1] *n (~-line)* Lot, Senkblei *nt* ◆ **out of ~** nicht im Lot.
[2] *adv* **(a)** lotrecht, senkrecht.
(b) *(inf) (completely)* total *(inf)*, komplett *(inf)*; *(exactly)* genau ◆ **~ in the middle** (haar)genau in der Mitte; **it hit him ~ on the nose** es traf ihn genau *or* mitten auf die Nase.
[3] *vt* **(a)** *ocean, depth* (aus)loten.
(b) *(fig) mystery etc* ergründen ◆ **to ~ the depths of despair** die tiefste Verzweiflung erleben; **a look that ~ed his very soul** ein Blick, der in die Tiefen seiner Seele drang.
plumbago [plʌm'beɪgəʊ] *n* Graphit *m*.
plumb bob *n* Lot, Senkblei *nt*.
plumber ['plʌməʳ] *n* Installateur, Klempner *m*.

plumbic ['plʌmbɪk] *adj* Bleidi-, Blei(IV)- (*spec*).
plumbiferous [plʌm'bɪfərəs] *adj* bleihaltig, bleiführend.
plumbing ['plʌmɪŋ] *n* **(a)** (*work*) Installieren *nt* ◆ **he decided to learn ~** er beschloß, Installateur *or* Klempner zu werden; **he does all his own ~** er macht alle Installations- *or* Klempnerarbeiten selbst.
(b) (*fittings*) Rohre, Leitungen, Installationen *pl*; (*bathroom fittings*) sanitäre Anlagen *pl* ◆ **to inspect the ~** (*hum*) die Lokalitäten aufsuchen (*hum*).
plumb: ~-line *n* Lot, Senkblei *nt*; (*Naut also*) (Blei)lot *nt*; **~-rule** *n* Lotwaage *f*.
plumbous ['plʌmbəs] *adj* Blei-, Blei(II)- (*spec*).
plum duff ['plʌm'dʌf] *n* Plumpudding *m*.
plume [plu:m] [1] *n* Feder *f*; (*on helmet*) Federbusch *m* ◆ **~ of smoke** Rauchwolke, Rauchfahne *f*; **in borrowed ~s** mit fremden Federn geschmückt.
[2] *vr* **(a)** (*bird*) sich putzen. **(b) to ~ oneself on sth** auf etw (*acc*) stolz sein wie ein Pfau.
plumed [plu:md] *adj helmet etc* federgeschmückt, mit Federschmuck ◆ **the peacock with its magnificently ~ tail** der Pfau mit seinem prächtigen Schwanzgefieder.
plummet ['plʌmɪt] [1] *n* **(a)** (*weight*) Senkblei *nt*; (*Fishing*) Grundsucher *m*.
(b) (*falling*) (*Econ*) Sturz *m*; (*of bird, plane*) Sturzflug *m*.
[2] *vi* (*bird, plane etc*) hinunter-/herunterstürzen; (*Econ*) (*sales figures etc*) stark zurückgehen; (*currency, shares etc*) fallen, absacken ◆ **the £ has ~ted to DM 2.50** das £ ist auf DM 2,50 gefallen *or* abgesackt; **he has ~ted again to the depths of despair** er ist wieder in tiefster Verzweiflung.
plummy ['plʌmɪ] *adj* (*+er*) (*inf*) *job* Bomben- (*inf*), Mords- (*inf*); *voice* vornehm-sonor.
plump [plʌmp] [1] *adj* (*+er*) **(a)** rundlich, mollig, pummelig; *legs etc* stämmig; *face* rundlich, pausbäckig, voll; *chicken etc* gut genährt, fleischig.
(b) *phrasing, reply* direkt, unverblümt.
[2] *adv* **to fall ~ onto sth** mit einem Plumps auf etw (*acc*) fallen.
[3] *vt* (*drop*) fallen lassen; (*throw*) werfen; (*angrily, noisily*) knallen (*inf*) ◆ **to ~ sth down** etw hinfallen lassen/hinwerfen/hinknallen (*inf*); **she ~ed herself down in the armchair** sie ließ sich in den Sessel fallen; **he had ~ed himself in the best chair** er hatte sich im besten Sessel breitgemacht (*inf*).
[4] *vi* (*fall*) fallen ◆ **to ~ down onto a chair** auf einen Stuhl fallen *or* plumpsen (*inf*).
◆**plump for** *vi +prep obj* sich entscheiden für.
◆**plump out** *vi* (*person*) (Gewicht) ansetzen.
◆**plump up** *vt sep pillow* aufschütteln; *chicken* mästen.
plumpness ['plʌmpnɪs] *n see adj* Rundlichkeit *f*; Molligkeit, Pummeligkeit *f*; Stämmigkeit *f*; Pausbäckigkeit *f*; Wohlgenährtheit *f* ◆ **the ~ of her cheeks** ihre Pausbäckigkeit.
plum: ~ pudding *n* Plumpudding *m*; **~ tree** *n* Pflaumenbaum *m*; (*Victoria ~*) Zwetsch(g)enbaum *m*.
plunder ['plʌndə^r] [1] *n* **(a)** (*act*) (*of place*) Plünderung *f*; (*of things*) Raub *m*.
(b) (*loot*) Beute *f*.
[2] *vt place* plündern (*also hum*); (*completely*) ausplündern; *people* ausplündern; *thing* rauben.
[3] *vi* plündern.
plunderer ['plʌndərə^r] *n* Plünderer *m*.
plundering ['plʌndərɪŋ] *n* (*of place*) Plünderung *f*, Plündern *nt*; (*of things*) Raub *m*.
plunge [plʌndʒ] [1] *vt* **(a)** (*thrust*) stecken; (*into water etc*) tauchen ◆ **he ~d his knife into his victim's back** er jagte seinem Opfer das Messer in den Rücken; **he ~d his hand into the hole/his pocket** er steckte seine Hand tief in das Loch/in die Tasche; **he ~d his hands into his pockets** er vergrub seine Hände in den Taschen.
(b) (*fig*) **to ~ the country into war/debt** das Land in einen Krieg/in Schulden stürzen; **the room was/we were ~d into darkness** das Zimmer war in Dunkelheit getaucht/tiefe Dunkelheit umfing uns; **he was ~d into despair by the news** die Nachricht stürzte ihn in tiefe Verzweiflung.
[2] *vi* **(a)** (*dive*) tauchen; (*goalkeeper*) sich werfen, hechten.
(b) (*rush, esp downward*) stürzen ◆ **to ~ down the stairs** die Treppe hinunterstürzen; **to ~ to one's death** zu Tode stürzen; **the fireman ~d into the flames** der Feuerwehrmann stürzte sich in die Flammen; **the road ~d down the hill** die Straße fiel steil ab.
(c) (*share prices, currency etc*) stürzen, stark fallen.
(d) (*fig: into debate, studies, preparations etc*) sich stürzen (*into* in *+acc*).
(e) (*dip*) (*horse*) bocken; (*ship*) stampfen.
(f) (*neckline*) fallen ◆ **her deeply plunging neckline** der tiefe Ausschnitt ihres Kleides; **the dress ~s at the back** das Kleid ist hinten tief ausgeschnitten.
(g) (*speculate rashly*) sich verspekulieren.
[3] *vr* (*into studies, job etc*) sich stürzen (*into* in *+acc*).
[4] *n* **(a)** (*dive*) (Kopf)sprung, Köpper (*inf*) *m*; (*of goalkeeper*) Hechtsprung *m* ◆ **he takes/enjoys a quick ~ before breakfast** vor dem Frühstück schwimmt er/schwimmt er gern eine Runde; **to take the ~** (*fig inf*) den Sprung wagen.
(b) (*downward movement*) Sturz *m*.
(c) (*fig: into debt, despair etc, of shares, £ etc*) Sturz *m* ◆ **his ~ into debt began when his business collapsed** nach dem Bankrott seines Geschäftes stürzte er sich in Schulden; **shares took a ~ after the government's announcement** nach der Ankündigung der Regierung kam es zu einem Kurssturz.
(d) (*rash investment*) Fehlspekulation *f*.
◆**plunge in** [1] *vt sep knife* hineinjagen; *hand* hineinstecken; (*into water*) hineintauchen ◆ **he was ~d straight ~ (at the deep end)** (*fig*) er mußte gleich richtig ran (*inf*), er mußte gleich voll einsteigen (*inf*).
[2] *vi* (*dive*) hineinspringen.
plunger ['plʌndʒə^r] *n* **(a)** (*piston*) Tauchkolben *m*. **(b)** (*for clearing drain*) Sauger *m*. **(c)** (*speculator*) Spekulant(in *f*) *m*.
plunging ['plʌndʒɪŋ] *adj neckline, back* tief ausgeschnitten.
plunk[1] [plʌŋk] *vt banjo* zupfen.
plunk[2] *n, adv, vt see* **plonk**[1].
pluperfect ['plu:'pɜ:fɪkt] [1] *n* Vorvergangenheit *f*, Plusquamperfekt *nt*.
[2] *adj* in der Vorvergangenheit, im Plusquamperfekt ◆ **~ tense** Vorvergangenheit *f*, Plusquamperfekt *nt*.
plural ['plʊərəl] [1] *adj* **(a)** (*Gram*) Mehrzahl-, Plural-. **(b) ~ voting** Pluralwahlrecht, Mehrstimmenwahlrecht *nt*.
[2] *n* Mehrzahl *f*, Plural *m* ◆ **in the ~** im Plural, in der Mehrzahl.
pluralism ['plʊərəlɪzəm] *n* Pluralismus *m*.
pluralistic [,plʊərə'lɪstɪk] *adj* pluralistisch.
plurality [,plʊə'rælɪtɪ] *n* **(a)** Vielfalt, Mannigfaltigkeit *f*; (*Sociol*) Pluralität *f*. **(b)** (*US Pol*) (Stimmen)vorsprung *m*.
plus [plʌs] [1] *prep* (*added to, increased by*) plus (*+dat*); (*together with*) und (außerdem) ◆ **the day's takings were ~ £100** die Tageseinnahmen lagen um £ 100 höher; **~ or minus 10%** plus-minus 10%.
[2] *adj* **(a)** (*Math, Elec, fig*) **~ sign** Pluszeichen *nt*; **a ~ quantity** eine positive Menge; **the ~ terminal** der Pluspol; **a ~ factor/item** ein Pluspunkt *m*; **on the ~ side** auf der Habenseite.
(b) (*more than*) **he scored beta ~ in the exam** ≃ er hat in der Prüfung eine Zwei plus bekommen; **50 pages/hours ~ a week** mehr als *or* über 50 Seiten/Stunden pro Woche; **she has personality ~** sie hat ein gewinnendes Wesen.
[3] *n* (*sign*) Pluszeichen *nt*; (*positive factor*) Pluspunkt *m*; (*extra*) Plus *nt* ◆ **if after all the deductions you still finish up with a ~** wenn dir nach allen Abzügen noch etwas übrigbleibt.
plus fours ['plʌs'fɔ:z] *npl* Knickerbocker *pl*.
plush [plʌʃ] [1] *n* Plüsch *m*.
[2] *adj* (*+er*) **(a)** Plüsch-. **(b)** (*inf: luxurious*) feudal (*inf*); *hotel, restaurant also* Nobel-; *furnishing also* elegant, vornehm.
plushy ['plʌʃɪ] *adj* (*+er*) (*inf*) *see* **plush 2 (b)**.
Plutarch ['plu:tɑ:k] *n* Plutarch *m*.
Pluto ['plu:təʊ] *n* (*Myth*) Pluto, Pluton *m*; (*Astron*) Pluto *m*.
plutocracy [plu:'tɒkrəsɪ] *n* Plutokratie *f*.
plutocrat ['plu:təʊkræt] *n* Plutokrat(in *f*) *m*.
plutocratic [,plu:təʊ'krætɪk] *adj* plutokratisch.
plutonium [plu:'təʊnɪəm] *n* Plutonium *nt*.
pluvial ['plu:vɪəl] *adj* (*form*) Regen- ◆ **~ erosion** Erosion *f* durch Regen.
pluviometer [,plu:vɪ'ɒmɪtə^r] *n* Regen- *or* Niederschlagsmesser *m*, Pluviometer *nt*.
ply[1] [plaɪ] *n* **three-~** *wood* dreischichtig; *wool* Dreifach-, dreifädig; *tissues* dreilagig; **what ~ is this wool?** wievielfach ist diese Wolle?, wie viele Fäden hat diese Wolle?
ply[2] [1] *vt* **(a)** (*work with, use*) *tool, brush etc* gebrauchen, umgehen mit, führen; *needle* gebrauchen; *oars* einsetzen; (*work busily with*) *tool, brush etc* fleißig führen *or* umgehen mit; *needle* tanzen lassen (*geh*); *oars* kräftig einsetzen.
(b) (*work at*) *trade* ausüben, betreiben, nachgehen (*+dat*).
(c) (*ships*) *sea, river, route* befahren; *seas also* durchfahren.
(d) to ~ sb with questions jdn mit Fragen überhäufen; **to ~ sb with drink(s)** jdn immer wieder zum Trinken auffordern; **she kept her guests well plied with drinks** sie sorgte dafür, daß ihren Gästen die Getränke nicht ausgingen; **to ~ sb for information** jdn um Informationen angehen.
[2] *vi* (*ship*) **to ~ between** verkehren zwischen; **to ~ for hire** seine Dienste anbieten.
plywood ['plaɪwʊd] *n* Sperrholz *nt*.
PM *abbr of* **Prime Minister**.
pm *abbr of* **post meridiem** p.m.
PMT [pi:em'ti:] *n abbr of* **(a) pre-menstrual tension**. **(b) photomechanical transfer**.
pneumatic [nju:'mætɪk] *adj* **(a)** Luft-. **(b)** (*inf*) *young lady* vollbusig (*inf*); *breasts* prall.
pneumatically [nju:'mætɪkəlɪ] *adv* mit *or* durch Druck- *or* Preßluft ◆ **a ~ operated drill** ein preßluftbetriebener Bohrer.
pneumatic: ~ brake *n* Druckluftbremse *f*; **~ drill** *n* Preßluftbohrer *m*; **~ tyre** *n* Luftreifen *m*.
pneumonia [nju:'məʊnɪə] *n* Lungenentzündung *f*.
PO *abbr of* **post office** PA; **postal order**.
po [pəʊ] *n* (*inf*) (Nacht)topf, Pott (*inf*) *m*.
poach[1] [pəʊtʃ] *vt egg* pochieren; *fish* (blau) dünsten ◆ **~ed egg** pochiertes *or* verlorenes Ei; (*in poacher*) ≃ Ei *nt* im Glas.
poach[2] [1] *vt* unerlaubt *or* schwarz (*inf*) fangen.
[2] *vi* **(a)** wildern (*for* auf *+acc*) ◆ **to ~ for salmon** Lachs ohne Berechtigung *or* schwarz (*inf*) fangen.
(b) (*fig*) **to ~ (on sb's territory)** (*in sport*) jdm ins Gehege *or* in die Quere kommen; (*in work also*) jdm ins Handwerk pfuschen.
poacher[1] ['pəʊtʃə^r] *n* Wilderer *m*; (*of game also*) Wilddieb *m*.
poacher[2] *n* (*for eggs*) Pochierpfanne *f*.
poaching ['pəʊtʃɪŋ] *n* Wildern *nt*, Wilderei *f*.
pock [pɒk] *n* (*pustule*) Pocke, Blatter *f*; (*mark*) Pocken- *or* Blatternarbe *f*.
pocket ['pɒkɪt] [1] *n* **(a)** (*in garment*) Tasche *f* ◆ **to have sb/sth in one's ~** (*fig*) jdn/etw in der Tasche haben (*inf*); **take your hands out of your ~s!** nimm die Hände aus der Tasche!

(b) (*receptacle: in suitcase, file etc*) Fach *nt*; (*in book cover: for map etc*) Tasche *f*; (*Baseball*) Tasche *f*; (*Billiards*) Loch *nt*.
(c) (*resources*) Geldbeutel *m* ♦ **to be a drain on one's ~** jds Geldbeutel strapazieren (*inf*); **that hit his ~** das hat seinen Geldbeutel ganz schön strapaziert (*inf*); **to be in ~** auf sein Geld kommen (*inf*); **I was £100 in ~ after the sale** nach dem Verkauf war ich um £ 100 reicher; **to put one's hand in one's ~** tief in die Tasche greifen; *see* **out-of-~**.
(d) (*restricted area, space*) Gebiet *nt*; (*smaller*) Einsprengsel *nt* ♦ **~ of resistance** Widerstandsnest *nt*; **~ of unemployment** Gebiet *nt* mit hoher Arbeitslosigkeit; **~ of infection** Ansteckungsgebiet *nt*; **a ~ of ore** ein Einschluß *m* von Erz.
(e) (*Aviat: air ~*) Luftloch *nt*.
[2] *adj* (*for the pocket*) *comb, edition, dictionary* Taschen- ♦ **~ lens** Lupe *f* im Taschenformat.
[3] *vt* (a) (*put in one's pocket*) einstecken ♦ **to ~ one's pride** seinen Stolz überwinden.
(b) (*gain*) kassieren; (*misappropriate*) einstecken (*inf*), einsacken (*inf*) ♦ **the treasurer ~ed the club funds** der Schatzmeister hat die Vereinsgelder in die eigene Tasche gesteckt.
(c) (*Billiards*) ins Loch bringen, einlochen.
(d) (*US Pol*) *durch Veto aufschieben*.

pocket: ~ battleship *n* Westentaschenkreuzer *m*; **~ billiards** *n sing* (a) (*US*) Poolbillard *nt*; (b) (*hum sl*) Knickern (*sl*), Taschenbillard (*sl*) *nt*; **~-book** *n* (a) (*notebook*) Notizbuch *nt*; (b) (*wallet*) Brieftasche *f*; (c) (*US: handbag*) Handtasche *f*; **~ borough** *n* (*Brit Hist*) *vor 1832 ein Wahlbezirk, der sich praktisch in den Händen einer Person oder Familie befand*; **~ calculator** *n* Taschenrechner *m*.

pocketful ['pɒkɪtfʊl] *n* **a ~** eine Tasche voll.

pocket: ~ handkerchief *n* Taschentuch *nt*; **a ~ handkerchief(-sized) garden** ein Garten *m* im Westentaschenformat; **~-knife** *n* Taschenmesser *nt*; **~-money** *n* Taschengeld *nt*; **~-size(d)** *adj book* im Taschenformat; *camera* Miniatur-; *person* winzig; *garden, dictator* im Westentaschenformat; **~ veto** *n* (*US Pol*) *Verzögerung f der Gesetzesverabschiedung durch aufschiebendes Veto des Präsidenten*.

pock: ~mark *n* Pocken- *or* Blatternarbe *f*; **~-marked** *adj face* pockennarbig; *surface* narbig; **the ~-marked surface of the moon** die mit Kratern übersäte Oberfläche des Mondes; **~-marked with bullet holes** mit Einschüssen übersät.

pod [pɒd] [1] *n* (*Bot*) Hülse *f*; (*of peas also*) Schote *f*; (*Aviat*) (*for missiles etc*) Magazin *nt*; (*for jet engine*) Gehäuse *nt*.
[2] *vt peas* ent- *or* aushülsen, auslösen.

podgy ['pɒdʒɪ] *adj* (*+er*) rundlich, pummelig; *face* schwammig ♦ **~ fingers** Wurstfinger *pl*.

podiatrist [pɒ'di:ətrɪst] *n* (*US*) Fußspezialist(in *f*) *m*.

podiatry [pɒ'di:ətrɪ] *n* (*US*) Lehre *f* von den Fußkrankheiten; (*treatment*) Fußpflege *f*.

podium ['pəʊdɪəm] *n* Podest *nt*.

poem ['pəʊɪm] *n* Gedicht *nt* ♦ **epic ~** Epos *nt*.

poesy ['pəʊɪzɪ] *n* (*form: poetry*) Lyrik, Poesie (*old*) *f*.

poet ['pəʊɪt] *n* Dichter, Poet (*old*) *m*; *see* **laureate**.

poetaster [ˌpəʊɪ'tæstəʳ] *n* (*pej*) Poetaster, Dichterling *m*.

poetess ['pəʊɪtes] *n* Dichterin, Poetin (*old*) *f*.

poetic [pəʊ'etɪk] *adj* poetisch; *talent, ability also* dichterisch; *place, charm* stimmungsvoll, malerisch ♦ **~ beauty** (*visual*) malerische Schönheit; (*of thought, scene in play etc*) poetische Schönheit; **he's not at all ~** er hat überhaupt keinen Sinn für Poesie; **he grew** *or* **became ~** er wurde poetisch *or* lyrisch; **what's ~ about this sculpture?** was ist an dieser Skulptur künstlerisch?; **~ justice** poetische Gerechtigkeit; **~ licence** dichterische Freiheit.

poetical [pəʊ'etɪkəl] *adj see* **poetic**.

poetically [pəʊ'etɪkəlɪ] *adv see adj* ♦ **~ gifted** dichterisch begabt; **very ~ put** sehr poetisch ausgedrückt.

poetics [pəʊ'etɪks] *n sing* Poetik *f*.

poetry ['pəʊɪtrɪ] *n* (a) Dichtung *f*; (*not epic also*) Lyrik *f* ♦ **to write ~** Gedichte schreiben, dichten; **the rules of ~** die Regeln der Versdichtung; **~ reading** Dichterlesung *f*.
(b) (*fig*) Poesie *f* ♦ **there's no ~ in him** er ist völlig poesielos; **the dancing was ~ in motion** der Tanz war in Bewegung umgesetzte Poesie; **the sunset was sheer ~** der Sonnenuntergang war reinste Poesie; **her soufflés are/that dress is sheer ~** ihre Soufflés sind/dieses Kleid ist wirklich ein Gedicht.

po-faced ['pəʊfeɪst] *adj* (*sl*) (*disapproving*) grimmig, mürrisch ♦ **a ~ woman** (*ugly*) eine Schrulle (*inf*).

pogo stick ['pəʊgəʊˌstɪk] *n* Springstock *m*.

pogrom ['pɒgrəm] *n* Pogrom *nt*.

poignancy ['pɔɪnjənsɪ] *n see adj* Ergreifende(s) *nt*; Wehmut *f*; Schmerzlichkeit *f*; Schärfe *f* ♦ **the ~ of his words/look** die Wehmut, die in seinen Worten/seinem Blick lag; **he writes with great ~** er schreibt sehr ergreifend.

poignant ['pɔɪnjənt] *adj* ergreifend; *memories, look* wehmütig; *distress, regret* schmerzlich; *wit* scharf.

poignantly ['pɔɪnjəntlɪ] *adv see adj* ♦ **old memories stirred ~ within her** alte Erinnerungen rührten sich wehmütig in ihr.

poinsettia [pɔɪn'setɪə] *n* Weihnachtsstern *m*, Poinsettia *f* (*spec*).

▼ **point** [pɔɪnt] [1] *n* (a) (*dot, punctuation mark, Typ, Geometry*) Punkt *m*; (*in Hebrew texts*) Vokalzeichen *nt* ♦ **(nought) ~ seven (0.7)** null Komma sieben (0,7).
(b) (*unit on scale, on compass*) Punkt *m*; (*on thermometer*) Grad *m* ♦ **from all ~s (of the compass)** aus allen (Himmels)richtungen; **the bag is full to bursting ~** die Tüte ist zum Bersten voll; **up to a ~** bis zu einem gewissen Grad *or* Punkt.
(c) (*sharp end, of chin*) Spitze *f*; (*of a star*) Zacke *f*; (*of antler*) (Geweih)ende *nt*, (Geweih)spitze *f* ♦ **at the ~ of a gun/sword** mit vorgehaltener Pistole/vorgehaltenem Schwert; **things look different at the ~ of a gun** alles sieht ein bißchen anders aus, wenn einem jemand die Pistole auf die Brust setzt; **not to put too fine a ~ on it** (*fig*) um ganz offen zu sein, ehrlich gesagt.
▼ (d) (*place*) Punkt *m*, Stelle *f* ♦ **the train stops at Slough and all ~s east** der Zug hält in Slough und allen Orten östlich davon; **~ of departure** (*lit, fig*) Ausgangspunkt *m*; **~ of entry** (*over border*) Ort *m* der Einreise; (*of space capsule*) Ort *m* des Wiedereintritts; **here at the northernmost ~ of Scotland** hier, am nördlichsten Punkt Schottlands; **~ of view** Stand- *or* Gesichtspunkt *m*; **from my ~ of view** von meinem Standpunkt aus, aus meiner Perspektive *or* Sicht; **from the ~ of view of productivity** von der Produktivität her gesehen; **at this ~** (*spatially*) an dieser Stelle, an diesem Punkt; (*in time*) (*then*) in diesem Augenblick; (*now*) jetzt; **from that ~ on they were friends** von da an waren sie Freunde; **at what ~ ...?** an welcher Stelle ...?; **at no ~** nie; **at no ~ in the book** nirgends in dem Buch, an keiner Stelle des Buches; **to be (up)on the ~ of doing sth** im Begriff sein, etw zu tun; **he was on the ~ of telling me the story when** ... er wollte mir gerade die Geschichte erzählen, als ...; **he had reached the ~ of resigning** er war nahe daran zu resignieren; **to reach the ~ of no return** (*fig*) den Punkt erreichen, von dem an es kein Zurück gibt; **to be at the ~ of death** am Rande *or* an der Schwelle des Todes stehen; **they provoked him to the ~ where he lost his temper** sie reizten ihn so lange, bis er die Geduld verlor; **severe to the ~ of cruelty** streng bis an die Grenze der Grausamkeit; **she was indulgent to the ~ of spoiling the child** sie war nachgiebig in einem Maße, das schon in Verwöhnung des Kindes umschlug; **when it comes to the ~** wenn es darauf ankommt.
(e) (*Sport, in test, St Ex etc*) Punkt *m* ♦ **~s for/against** Pluspunkte *pl*/Minuspunkte *pl*; **~s decision** Entscheidung *f* nach Punkten; **~s win** Punktsieg *m*, Sieg *m* nach Punkten; **to win on ~s** nach Punkten gewinnen; **~s system** Punktesystem *nt*.
(f) (*purpose*) Zweck, Sinn *m* ♦ **there's no ~ in staying** es hat keinen Zweck *or* Sinn zu bleiben; **I don't see the ~ of carrying on/changing our system now** ich sehe keinen Sinn darin, weiterzumachen/unser System jetzt zu ändern; **what's the ~?** was soll's?; **I just don't see the ~ of it** *or* **any ~ in it** das sehe ich überhaupt nicht ein, ich sehe überhaupt keinen Sinn darin; **the ~ of this is ...** Sinn und Zweck ist ...; **what's the ~ of trying?** wozu versuchen?; **he doesn't understand the ~ of doing this** er versteht nicht, weswegen wir/sie *etc* das machen; **do you see the ~ of what I'm saying?** weißt du, worauf ich hinauswill?; **the ~ is that** ... es ist nämlich so ..., die Sache ist die, daß ...; **that's the whole ~ (of doing it this way)** gerade darum machen wir das so; **the ~ of the joke/story** die Pointe; **the news gave ~ to his arguments** die Nachrichten verliehen seinen Argumenten Nachdruck *or* Gewicht; **life has lost all ~** das Leben hat jeden *or* all seinen Sinn verloren.
▼ (g) (*detail, argument*) Punkt *m* ♦ **the ~ at issue** der strittige Punkt; **a 12-~ plan** ein Zwölfpunkteplan *m*; **a ~ of interest** ein interessanter Punkt; **on this ~ we are agreed** in diesem Punkt stimmen wir überein; **his arguments were off the ~** seine Argumente trafen den Kern der Sache nicht; **I'm afraid that's off the ~** das ist nicht relevant *or* gehört nicht hierher; **to come to the ~** zur Sache kommen; **to keep** *or* **stick to the ~** beim Thema bleiben; **beside the ~** unerheblich, irrelevant; **to the ~** zur Sache, zum Thema; **his remarks are very much to the ~** seine Bemerkungen sind sehr sachbezogen; **a useful ~** ein nützlicher Hinweis; **~ by ~** Punkt für Punkt; **a ~ by ~ answer** eine Antwort Punkt für Punkt; **my ~ was ...** was ich sagen wollte, war ...; **to make a ~** ein Argument *nt* anbringen; **he made the ~ that** ... er betonte, daß ...; **you've made your ~!** wissen wir ja schon!, das hast du ja schon gesagt!; **the chairman gave him just 30 seconds to make his ~** der Vorsitzende gab ihm nur 30 Sekunden, um sein Argument zu erläutern; **you have a ~ there** darin mögen Sie recht haben, da ist etwas dran (*inf*); **what ~ are you trying to make?** worauf wollen Sie hinaus?; **if I may make another ~** wenn ich noch auf einen weiteren Punkt aufmerksam machen darf; **he makes his ~s very clear** er bringt seine Argumente sehr klar; **I take your ~, ~ taken** ich akzeptiere, was Sie sagen; (*in exasperation*) ich habe schon begriffen; **do you take my ~?** verstehst du mich?; **he may have a ~ you know** da kann er recht haben, weißt du; **can I put that same ~ another way?** kann ich das noch einmal anders formulieren?; **would you put that ~ more succinctly?** können Sie das etwas knapper fassen?; **to gain** *or* **carry one's ~** sich durchsetzen; **to get** *or* **see the ~** verstehen, worum es geht; **to miss the ~** nicht verstehen, worum es geht; **he missed the ~ of what I was saying** er hat nicht begriffen, worauf ich hinauswollte; **that's not the ~** darum geht es nicht; **that's the whole ~** das ist es ja gerade; **but the pound has been devalued — that's the whole ~, your mark is worth more!** aber das Pfund wurde doch abgewertet — genau! deshalb ist die Mark jetzt mehr wert; **a case in ~** ein einschlägiger Fall; **the case in ~** der zur Debatte stehende Punkt; **to make a ~ of sth** auf etw (*dat*) bestehen, auf etw (*acc*) Wert legen; **he made a special ~ of being early** er legte besonderen Wert darauf, früh dazusein; **we make a ~ of stressing ordinary usage** wir legen besonderen Nachdruck auf den normalen Sprachgebrauch.
(h) (*matter*) **a ~ of principle** eine grundsätzliche Frage; **a ~ of law** eine Rechtsfrage; **a ~ of order** eine Frage der Geschäftsordnung; **a ~ of detail** eine Einzelfrage; *see* **honour**.
(i) (*characteristic*) **good/bad ~s** gute/schlechte Seiten *pl*; **he has his ~s** er hat

➤ LANGUAGE IN USE: **point: 1d** → 26.2 **1g** → 26.3

auch seine Vorzüge *or* guten Seiten; **the ~s to look for when buying a new car** die Punkte *or* Dinge, auf die man beim Kauf eines neuen Wagens achten muß.
(j) **~s** *pl (Brit Rail)* Weichen *pl.*
(k) *(Ballet: usu pl)* Spitze *f* ◆ **to dance on ~s** Spitzentanz machen, auf den Spitzen tanzen.
(l) *(Aut: usu pl)* Unterbrecherkontakte *pl.*
(m) *(Brit Elec)* Steckdose *f.*
[2] *vt* **(a)** *(aim, direct) gun, telescope etc* richten *(at* auf *+acc)* ◆ **he ~ed his stick in the direction of the house** er zeigte *or* wies mit dem Stock auf das Haus; **I asked him to ~ me on my way** ich bat ihn, mir den Weg zu zeigen; **he ~ed his boat upstream** er drehte sein Boot stromaufwärts; **he ~s his feet outwards when he walks** er dreht seine Fußspitzen beim Gehen nach außen; **they ~ed the drunk off in the right direction** sie schickten den Betrunkenen in die richtige Richtung.
(b) *(mark, show)* zeigen ◆ **to ~ the way** *(lit, fig)* den Weg weisen; **that really ~ed the moral** das bewies, wie recht wir/sie *etc* hatten; **he used the decline in the company's profits to ~ the moral that ...** er nahm das Absinken der Gewinne zum Anlaß zu betonen, daß ...
(c) *(sharpen) pencil, stick* (an)spitzen.
(d) *(Build) wall, brickwork* verfugen, ausfugen.
(e) *(punctuate) text* interpunktieren; *Hebrew* vokalisieren; *psalm* mit Deklarationszeichen versehen.
(f) *(Hunt) game* anzeigen.
[3] *vi* **(a)** *(with finger etc)* zeigen, deuten *(at, to* auf *+acc)* ◆ **it's rude to ~ (at strangers)** es ist unhöflich, mit dem Finger (auf Fremde) zu zeigen; **don't ~!** zeig nicht mit dem Finger!; **he ~ed in the direction of the house/towards the house/back towards the house** er zeigte *or* deutete in die Richtung des Hauses/zum Haus/zurück zum Haus; **the compass needle ~s (to the) north** die Kompaßnadel zeigt *or* weist nach Norden.
▼ **(b)** *(indicate) (facts, events)* hinweisen, hindeuten *(to* auf *+acc)*; *(person: point out)* hinweisen ◆ **everything ~s that way** alles weist in diese Richtung; **the problems which you have ~ed to in your paper** die Probleme, auf die du in deinem Aufsatz hingewiesen hast *or* die du in deinem Aufsatz aufgezeigt hast; **the poet doesn't state, he ~s in certain directions** der Dichter trifft keine Feststellungen, er deutet bestimmte Richtungen an; **all the signs ~ to success** alle Zeichen stehen auf Erfolg; **all the signs ~ to economic recovery** alles deutet *or* weist auf eine Erholung der Wirtschaft hin.
(c) *(face, be situated: building, valley etc)* liegen; *(be aimed: gun, vehicle etc)* gerichtet sein ◆ **with his gun ~ed** *or* **~ing right at me, he said ...** die Pistole direkt auf mich gerichtet, sagte er ...; **the wheels aren't ~ing in the same direction** die Räder zeigen nicht in dieselbe Richtung; **in which direction is it ~ing?** in welche Richtung zeigt es?
(d) *(Hunt)* (vor)stehen.
◆**point out** *vt sep* **(a)** zeigen auf *(+acc)* ◆ **to ~ sth ~ to sb** jdn auf etw hinweisen *or* aufmerksam machen; **could you ~ him ~ to me?** kannst du mir zeigen, wer er ist?; **I'll ~ him ~** ich zeige ihn dir; **the guide ~ed ~ the most interesting paintings** der Führer machte auf die interessantesten Gemälde aufmerksam.
▼ **(b)** *(mention)* **to ~ sth ~ (to sb)** (jdn) auf etw *(acc)* aufmerksam machen, (jdn) auf etw *(acc)* hinweisen; **may I ~ ~ that ...?** darf ich darauf aufmerksam machen *or* darauf hinweisen, daß ...?; **thank you for ~ing that ~ to me** vielen Dank, daß Sie mich darauf aufmerksam gemacht haben.
◆**point up** *vt sep (emphasize)* unterstreichen, betonen; *(make clear)* veranschaulichen, verdeutlichen.
point-blank ['pɔɪnt'blæŋk] [1] *adj* direkt; *refusal* glatt ◆ **at ~ range** aus kürzester Entfernung *or* Distanz; **a ~ shot** ein Schuß aus kürzester Distanz *or* Entfernung.
[2] *adv fire* aus kürzester Distanz *or* Entfernung; *ask* rundheraus ◆ **he refused ~ to help** er weigerte sich rundweg *or* lehnte es rundheraus *or* schlankweg ab zu helfen.
pointed ['pɔɪntɪd] *adj* **(a)** *(sharp) stick, roof, chin, nose* spitz; *window, arch* spitzbogig ◆ **a stick with a sharply ~ end** ein Stock mit sehr spitzem Ende; **the ~ windows in the old church** die Spitzbogenfenster in der alten Kirche.
(b) *(incisive) wit* scharf.
(c) *(obvious in intention) remark, comment* scharf, spitz; *reference* unverblümt; *absence, gesture, departure* ostentativ ◆ **her ~ lack of interest in my problems** ihr ostentatives *or* betontes Desinteresse an meinen Problemen; **that was rather ~** das war ziemlich deutlich.
pointedly ['pɔɪntɪdlɪ] *adv speak, comment* spitz; *refer* unverblümt; *leave, stay away etc* ostentativ.
pointer ['pɔɪntəʳ] *n* **(a)** *(indicator)* Zeiger *m.*
(b) *(stick)* Zeigestock *m.*
(c) *(dog)* Pointer, Vorstehhund *m.*
(d) *(fig: hint)* Hinweis, Fingerzeig, Tip *m* ◆ **he gave me some ~s on how to behave** er gab mir ein paar Hinweise, wie ich mich benehmen sollte.
(e) *(fig: indication)* Anzeichen *nt*, Hinweis *m* ◆ **a ~ to a possible solution** ein Hinweis auf eine mögliche Lösung.
pointillism ['pwæntɪlɪzəm] *n* Pointillismus *m.*
pointillist ['pwæntɪlɪst] [1] *n* Pointillist *m.*
[2] *adj* pointillistisch.
pointing ['pɔɪntɪŋ] *n (Build) (act)* Ausfugung *f*; *(material)* Fugenmörtel *m* ◆ **the ~ on these old buildings needs to be restored** das Mauerwerk dieser alten Gebäude muß neu ver- *or* ausgefugt werden.
pointless *adj*, **~ly** *adv* ['pɔɪntlɪs, -lɪ] sinnlos.
pointlessness ['pɔɪntlɪsnɪs] *n* Sinnlosigkeit *f.*
point of sale *n (Comm)* Verkaufsstelle *f.*
point-of-sale *adj attr advertising* an der Verkaufsstelle.
point(s) duty *n* Verkehrsdienst *m.*
pointsman ['pɔɪntsmən] *n, pl* **-men** [-mən] *(Brit Rail)* Weichensteller *m.*
point-to-point *n (also* **~ race***)* Geländejagdrennen *nt.*
poise [pɔɪz] [1] *n* **(a)** *(carriage of head, body)* Haltung *f*; *(grace)* Grazie *f* ◆ **the ~ of her head/body** ihre Kopfhaltung/Körperhaltung; **the graceful ~ of the dancer's body** die Grazie *or* graziöse Haltung der Tänzerin/des Tänzers.
(b) *(composure)* Gelassenheit *f*; *(self-possession)* Selbstsicherheit *f* ◆ **a woman of great ~ and charm** eine Frau voller Selbstsicherheit und Charme; **her ~ as a hostess** ihre Sicherheit als Gastgeberin; **he lacks ~** ihm fehlt die Gelassenheit.
[2] *vt* **(a)** *(balance, hold balanced)* balancieren ◆ **he ~d the knife ready to strike** er hielt das Messer so, daß er jederzeit zustechen konnte; **she ~d her pen over her notebook** sie hielt den Kugelschreiber schreibbereit über ihrem Notizblock; **the diver ~d himself for the leap** der Taucher machte sich sprungbereit *or* bereit zum Sprung; **the tiger ~d itself to spring** der Tiger machte sich sprungbereit.
(b) *(in passive)* **to be/hang ~d** *(bird, rock, sword)* schweben; **the diver was ~d on the edge of the pool** der Taucher stand sprungbereit auf dem Beckenrand; **the tiger was ~d ready to spring** der Tiger lauerte sprungbereit; **we sat ~d on the edge of our chairs** wir balancierten auf den Stuhlkanten; **women with water-jars ~d on their heads** Frauen, die Wasserkrüge auf dem Kopf balancierten/balancierten.
(c) *(fig)* **the enemy are ~d to attack** der Feind steht angriffsbereit; **they sat in the hall, ~d for departure** sie saßen abfahrtbereit in der Halle; **to be ~d on the brink/on the brink of sth** dicht davor/dicht vor etw *(dat) or* am Rande von etw stehen *or* sein; **a bright young man ~d on the brink of success** ein intelligenter junger Mann an der Schwelle zum Erfolg.
[3] *vi* (für einen Moment) unbeweglich bleiben; *(bird, helicopter)* schweben ◆ **he ~d for a second on the edge of the pool** er verharrte einen Augenblick am Beckenrand.
poised [pɔɪzd] *adj (self-possessed)* gelassen, selbstsicher.
poison ['pɔɪzn] [1] *n (lit, fig)* Gift *nt* ◆ **what's your ~?** *(inf)*, **name your ~** *(inf)* was willst du trinken?; **to hate sb like ~** jdn glühend *or* wie die Pest *(inf)* hassen; *see* **meat.**
[2] *vt* **(a)** vergiften; *atmosphere, rivers* verpesten ◆ **it won't ~ you** *(inf)* das wird dich nicht umbringen *(inf)*.
(b) *(fig)* vergiften; *marriage* zerrütten ◆ **to ~ sb's mind against sb/sth** jdn gegen jdn/etw aufstacheln.
poisoner ['pɔɪznəʳ] *n* Giftmörder(in *f*) *m.*
poison gas *n* Giftgas *nt.*
poisoning ['pɔɪznɪŋ] *n (lit, fig)* Vergiftung *f* ◆ **the gradual ~ of the atmosphere by ...** die zunehmende Luftverpestung durch ...; **to die of ~** an einer Vergiftung sterben.
poison ivy *n* kletternder Giftsumach, Gifteefeu *m.*
poisonous ['pɔɪznəs] *adj* **(a)** *snake, plants etc* giftig, Gift-; *substance, fumes etc* giftig ◆ **whisky on top of beer, that's absolutely ~** *(inf)* Whisky auf Bier, das ist tödlich *(inf)*.
(b) *(fig) literature, doctrine* zersetzend; *remark etc* giftig; *propaganda also* Hetz- ◆ **she has a ~ tongue** sie hat eine giftige Zunge; **he's a ~ individual** er ist ein richtiger Giftzwerg.
poison: ~-pen letter *n* anonymer Brief; **~ sumach** *n (US)* Giftsumach *m.*
poke¹ [pəʊk] *n (dial, Scot)* Beutel, Sack *(dial) m*; *(plastic, paper)* Tüte *f*; *see* **pig.**
poke² [1] *n* **(a)** *(jab)* Stoß, Schubs *(inf) m* ◆ **to give sb/sth a ~** *see vt (a)*; **I got a ~ in the eye from his umbrella** er stieß mir den Regenschirm ins Auge.
(b) *(US inf: punch)* Schlag *m* ◆ **~ on the nose** Nasenstüber *m.*
(c) *(Brit vulg: act of intercourse)* Vögeln *nt (sl)* ◆ **to have a ~** vögeln *(sl)*, ficken *(vulg)*, einen wegstecken *(sl)*.
[2] *vt* **(a)** *(jab with stick)* stoßen; *(with finger)* stupsen ◆ **to ~ the fire** das Feuer schüren, im Feuer stochern; **he ~d the ground with his stick** er stieß mit seinem Stock auf den Boden; **he accidentally ~d me in the eye** er hat mir aus Versehen ins Auge gestoßen.
(b) *(US inf: punch)* hauen *(inf)* ◆ **to ~ sb on the nose** jdn auf die Nase hauen *or* schlagen.
(c) *(thrust)* **to ~ one's head/finger/a stick** *etc* **into sth** seinen Kopf/Finger/einen Stock *etc* in etw *(acc)* stecken; **he ~d his head round the door/out of the window** er streckte seinen Kopf durch die Tür/aus dem Fenster.
(d) *(Brit vulg: have sex with)* vögeln *(sl)*, ficken *(vulg)*.
(e) *(make by poking) hole* bohren.
[3] *vi* **his elbows were poking through his sleeves** an seinen Ärmeln kamen schon die Ellenbogen durch; **to ~ at sth** *(testing)* etw prüfen; *(searching)* in etw *(dat)* stochern; **he ~d at me with his fist** er schlug mit der Faust nach mir; **he ~d at me with his finger** *(touching)* er stupste mich; *(not touching)* er stieß mit dem Finger nach mir; **the doctor ~d at his ribs** der Arzt tastete seine Rippen ab; **well, if you will go poking into things that don't concern you** ... na ja, wenn du deine Nase ständig in Dinge steckst, die dich nichts angehen ...
◆**poke about** *or* **around** *vi* **(a)** *(prod)* herumstochern. **(b)** *(inf: nose about)* stöbern, schnüffeln *(inf)*. **(c)** *+prep obj (inf: wander about)* (herum)bummeln ◆ **we spent a pleasant day poking ~ the shops** wir haben einen netten Tag mit Geschäftebummeln verbracht.
◆**poke in** *vt sep* hinein-/hereinstecken *or* -strecken ◆ **he ~d his head ~ through the window** er steckte *or* streckte seinen Kopf zum Fenster hinein/

➤ LANGUAGE IN USE: **point: 3b** → 15.2, 26.1 **point out: b** → 20.7, 26.1, 26.2

herein; **I'll just ~ my head ~ and say hello** (*inf*) ich will nur schnell vorbeischauen und guten Tag sagen.

◆**poke out** [1] *vi* vorstehen ◆ **he walked along with his stomach poking ~** er ging mit vorgestrecktem Bauch; **the tortoise had its head poking ~ of its shell** die Schildkröte hatte ihren Kopf aus dem Panzer gestreckt; **that dress ~s ~ a bit at the waist** dies Kleid bauscht sich etwas an der Taille; **a handkerchief was poking ~ of his top pocket** ein Taschentuch schaute *or* guckte aus seiner Brusttasche hervor.
[2] *vt sep* **(a)** (*extend*) heraus-/hinausstrecken.
(b) (*remove by poking*) **he ~d the dirt ~ with his fingers** er pulte (*inf*) *or* kratzte den Schmutz mit den Fingern heraus; **to ~ sb's eye ~** jdm ein Auge ausstechen.

◆**poke up** *vt sep fire* schüren ◆ **he ~d his finger ~ his nose** er bohrte mit dem Finger in der Nase.

poke bonnet *n* Kiepenhut *m*, Schute *f*.

poker[1] ['pəʊkə^r] *n* (*for fire*) Schürhaken, Feuerhaken *m*.

poker[2] *n* (*Cards*) Poker *nt*.

poker: ~ face *n* Pokergesicht, Pokerface *nt*; **~-faced** ['pəʊkə,feɪst] *adj* mit einem Pokergesicht *or* Pokerface; (*bored*) mit unbewegter Miene.

pokeweed ['pəʊkwiːd] *n* (*US*) Kermesbeere *f*.

poky ['pəʊkɪ] *adj* (*+er*) (*pej*) *room, house* winzig ◆ **it's so ~ in here** es ist so eng hier.

Polack ['pəʊlæk] *n* (*pej*) Polack(e) *m* (*pej*), Polackin *f* (*pej*).

Poland ['pəʊlənd] *n* Polen *nt*.

polar ['pəʊlə^r] *adj* **(a)** Polar-, polar ◆ **~ bear** Polar- *or* Eisbär *m*; **~ circle** Polarkreis *m*. **(b)** (*opposite*) polar.

polarity [pəʊ'lærɪtɪ] *n* (*Phys, fig*) Polarität *f*.

polarization [,pəʊləraɪ'zeɪʃən] *n* (*Phys*) Polarisation *f*; (*fig*) Polarisierung *f*.

polarize ['pəʊləraɪz] [1] *vt* polarisieren.
[2] *vi* sich polarisieren.

Polaroid ® ['pəʊlərɔɪd] *n* Polaroidkamera ®, Sofortbildkamera *f*.

polder ['pəʊldə^r] *n* Polder *m*.

Pole [pəʊl] *n* Pole *m*, Polin *f*.

pole[1] [pəʊl] [1] *n* **(a)** Stange *f*; (*flag~, telegraph ~ also*) Mast *m*; (*of cart*) Deichsel *f*; (*ski-~*) Stock *m*; (*for vaulting*) Stab *m*; (*for punting*) Stange, Stake (*spec*) *f* ◆ **to be up the ~** (*Brit inf*) eine Schraube locker haben (*inf*); **to drive sb up the ~** (*inf*) jdn die Wände hoch treiben (*inf*).
(b) (*Measure: old*) Rute *f* (*old*).
[2] *vt punt* staken.

pole[2] *n* (*Geog, Astron, Elec*) Pol *m* ◆ **they are ~s apart** sie (*acc*) trennen Welten, Welten liegen zwischen ihnen.

pole: ~-axe, (*US*) **~-ax** [1] *n* **(a)** (*Mil*) Streitaxt *f*; **(b)** (*for slaughtering*) Schlachtbeil *nt*; [2] *vt* **(a)** (mit der Streitaxt) niederschlagen *or* umhauen; **(b)** (mit dem Schlachtbeil) töten; **~cat** *n* Iltis *m*; (*US*) Skunk *m*, Stinktier *nt*.

polemic [pɒ'lemɪk] [1] *adj* polemisch.
[2] *n* Polemik *f*.

polemical [pɒ'lemɪkəl] *adj* polemisch.

polemicist [pɒ'lemɪsɪst] *n* Polemiker(in *f*) *m*.

polemics [pɒ'lemɪks] *n sing* Polemik *f*.

pole: ~ position *n* **(a)** (*Motor racing*) Pole Position *f*; **to start in ~ position** aus der Pole Position starten. **(b)** (*fig*) günstige Ausgangsposition; **to be in ~ position** in einer güngstigen Ausgangsposition sein; **~ star** *n* Polarstern *m*; **~ vault** [1] *n* Stabhochsprung *m*; (*one jump*) Sprung *m* mit dem Stab; **he did a ~ vault over the fence** er setzte *or* sprang mit einem Stab über dem Zaun; [2] *vi* stabhochspringen; **~ vaulter** *n* Stabhochspringer(in *f*) *m*; **~ vaulting** *n* Stabhochspringen *nt*, Stabhochsprung *m*.

police [pə'liːs] [1] *n* (*+sing vb: institution, +pl vb: policemen*) Polizei *f* ◆ **to join the ~** zur Polizei gehen; **he is in** *or* **a member of the ~** er ist bei der Polizei; **all ~ leave was cancelled** allen Polizisten wurde der Urlaub gesperrt; **hundreds of ~** hunderte von Polizisten; **extra ~ were called in** es wurden zusätzliche Polizeikräfte angefordert; **three ~ were injured** drei Polizeibeamte *or* Polizisten wurden verletzt.
[2] *vt road, frontier, territory, agreement* kontrollieren; *agreement, pop-concert also* überwachen ◆ **a heavily ~d area** ein Gebiet mit hoher Polizeidichte.

police: ~ car *n* Polizeiwagen *m*; **~ constable** *n* (*Brit*) Polizist, Wachtmeister (*form*) *m*; **~ court** *n* ≃ Polizeigericht *nt*; **~ dog** *n* Polizeihund *m*; **~ escort** *n* Polizei-Eskorte *f*; **~ force** *n* Polizei *f*; **one of the best-equipped ~ forces in the world** eine der bestausgestatteten Polizeitruppen der Welt; **~man** *n* Polizist *m*; **~ officer** *n* Polizeibeamte(r) *m*; **~ presence** *n* Polizeiaufgebot *nt*; **~ protection** *n* Polizeischutz *m*; **~ record** *n* Vorstrafen *pl*; **to have a ~ record** vorbestraft sein; **~ state** *n* Polizeistaat *m*; **~ station** *n* (Polizei)wache *f* *or* -revier *nt*; **~woman** *n* Polizistin *f*; **~ work** *n* Polizeiarbeit *f*; (*investigation*) polizeiliche Nachforschungen *pl*.

policing [pə'liːsɪŋ] *n see vt* Kontrolle *f*; Überwachung *f* ◆ **new ~ policies for sports events** neue polizeiliche Richtlinien bei Sportveranstaltungen.

policy[1] ['pɒlɪsɪ] *n* **(a)** Politik *f no pl*; (*of business also*) Geschäfts- *or* Firmenpolitik *f* (on bei), Praktiken *pl* (*pej*) (on in bezug auf *+acc*); (*of team, football manager: tactics*) Taktik *f*; (*principle*) Grundsatz *m* ◆ **social and economic ~** Wirtschafts- und Sozialpolitik *f*; **our ~ on immigration/recruitment** unsere Einwanderungs-/Einstellungspolitik; **what is company ~ on this matter?** wie sieht die Geschäfts- *or* Firmenpolitik in diesem Falle aus?; **the newspaper followed a ~ of attacking the church** die Zeitung verfolgte eine kirchenfeindliche Linie *or* Politik; **a ~ of restricting immigration** eine Politik zur Einschränkung der Einwanderung; **a matter of ~** eine Grundsatzfrage; **~ decision** Grundsatzentscheidung *f*; **~ statement** Grundsatzerklärung *f*; **~-maker** Parteiideologe *m*; **your ~ should always be to give people a second chance** du solltest es dir zum Grundsatz machen, Menschen eine zweite Chance zu geben; **my ~ is to wait and see** meine Devise heißt abwarten; **it's our ~ to cater for the mid-twenties** wir wenden uns mit unserer Firmenpolitik an die Mittzwanziger; **our ~ is one of expansion** wir verfolgen eine expansionsorientierte Geschäftspolitik.
(b) (*prudence, a prudent procedure*) Taktik *f* ◆ **~ demands that the government compromise** die Regierung muß aus taktischen Gründen Kompromisse eingehen; **it was good/bad ~** das war (taktisch) klug/unklug.

policy[2] *n* (*also* **insurance ~**) (Versicherungs)police *f*, Versicherungsschein *m* ◆ **to take out a ~** eine Versicherung abschließen; **~ holder** Versicherungsnehmer *m*.

polio ['pəʊlɪəʊ] *n* Polio, Kinderlähmung *f* ◆ **~ injection** (Spritz)impfung *f* gegen Kinderlähmung; **~ victim** Opfer *nt* der Kinderlähmung, Polioopfer *nt*.

poliomyelitis ['pəʊlɪəʊmaɪə'laɪtɪs] *n* (*form*) Poliomyelitis (*spec*), Kinderlähmung *f*.

Polish ['pəʊlɪʃ] [1] *adj* polnisch ◆ **~ corridor** Polnischer Korridor.
[2] *n* (*language*) Polnisch *nt*.

polish ['pɒlɪʃ] [1] *n* **(a)** (*material*) (*shoe ~*) Creme *f*; (*floor ~*) Bohnerwachs *nt*; (*furniture ~*) Politur *f*; (*metal ~*) Poliermittel *nt*; (*nail ~*) Lack *m*.
(b) (*act*) **to give sth a ~** etw polieren; *shoes, silver also* etw putzen; *floor* etw bohnern; **my shoes need a ~** meine Schuhe müssen geputzt werden.
(c) (*~ed state, shine*) Glanz *m*; (*of furniture*) Politur *f* ◆ **high ~** Hochglanz *m*, starker Glanz; **there was a high ~ on the floor** der Fußboden war stark gebohnert; **to put a ~ on sth** etw zum Glänzen bringen, Glanz auf etw (*acc*) bringen; **water will take the ~ off** Wasser nimmt den Glanz/greift die Politur an.
(d) (*fig: refinement*) (*of person, style, manners*) Schliff *m*; (*of performance*) Brillanz *f* ◆ **to acquire ~** Schliff bekommen; (*performance*) brillant werden; **he lacks ~** ihm fehlt der Schliff/die Brillanz; **his style lacks ~** an seinem Stil muß noch gearbeitet werden.
[2] *vt* **(a)** polieren; *silver, shoes also* putzen; *floor* bohnern.
(b) (*fig*) *person, performance* den letzten Schliff geben (*+dat*); *manner, style also* polieren (*inf*), verfeinern.

◆**polish off** *vt sep* (*inf*) *food* verdrücken (*inf*), verputzen (*inf*); *drink* wegputzen (*inf*); *work* wegschaffen (*inf*), erledigen; *opponent, competitor* abfertigen, abservieren (*inf*).

◆**polish up** [1] *vt sep* **(a)** *shoes, floor, silver etc* polieren, auf Hochglanz bringen. **(b)** (*fig: improve*) *style* aufpolieren, verfeinern; *work* überarbeiten; *one's French etc* aufpolieren (*inf*) ◆ **you'd better ~ ~ your ideas** (*inf*) du solltest dich besser auf den Hosenboden setzen (*inf*).
[2] *vi* sich polieren lassen.

polished ['pɒlɪʃt] *adj* **(a)** *surface, furniture* poliert, glänzend; *floor* gebohnert; *stone, glass* geschliffen ◆ **his highly ~ shoes** seine blankgeputzten Schuhe. **(b)** *style etc* verfeinert; *performance, performer* brillant. **(c)** *manners* geschliffen.

polisher ['pɒlɪʃə^r] *n* (*person*) Schleifer(in *f*) *m*; (*machine*) Schleif-/Polier-/Bohnermaschine *f*.

polite [pə'laɪt] *adj* (*+er*) **(a)** höflich ◆ **it wouldn't be ~** es wäre unhöflich; **be ~ about her cooking** mach ein paar höfliche Bemerkungen über ihre Kochkunst; **when I said it was good I was just being ~** als ich sagte, es sei gut, wollte ich nur höflich sein; **there's no need to be ~ about it if you don't like it** du kannst es ruhig sagen, wenn es dir nicht gefällt; **~ conversation** höfliche Konversation; **we sat around making ~ conversation** wir saßen zusammen und machten Konversation.
(b) *society* fein.

politely [pə'laɪtlɪ] *adv* höflich.

politeness [pə'laɪtnɪs] *n* Höflichkeit *f*.

politic ['pɒlɪtɪk] *adj* **(a)** klug ◆ **it would be ~ to apologize** es wäre (taktisch) klug, sich zu entschuldigen; **he tended to do what was ~ rather than that which was proper** er machte eher (das), was klug *or* günstig war, als das, was recht gewesen wäre.
(b) the body ~ das Staatswesen, das staatliche Gemeinwesen.

political [pə'lɪtɪkəl] *adj* politisch ◆ **~ asylum** politisches Asyl; **~ economy** Volkswirtschaft *f*; **~ correctness** (*usu pej*) politische Korrektheit *f*; **our society's obsession with ~ correctness** die Besessenheit unserer Gesellschaft, politisch korrekt zu sein; **~ prisoner** politischer Gefangener, politische Gefangene; **~ science** Politologie *f*.

politically [pə'lɪtɪkəlɪ] *adv* politisch ◆ **~ correct** politisch korrekt; **~ incorrect** politisch inkorrekt *or* nicht korrekt.

politician [,pɒlɪ'tɪʃən] *n* Politiker(in *f*) *m*.

politicization [pə,lɪtɪsaɪ'zeɪʃən] *n* Politisierung *f*.

politicize [pə'lɪtɪsaɪz] *vt* politisieren.

politicking [pə'lɪtɪkɪŋ] *n* (*pej*) politische Aktivitäten *pl*.

politico [pə'lɪtɪkəʊ] *n* (*US pej*) Politiker(in *f*) *m*.

politico- *pref* politisch-.

politics ['pɒlɪtɪks] *n* **(a)** (*+pl vb*) Politik *f*; (*views*) politische Ansichten *pl* ◆ **what are his ~?** welche politischen Ansichten hat er? **(b)** (*+sing or pl vb*) Politik *f* ◆ **to go into ~** in die Politik gehen; **to talk ~** über Politik (*acc*) reden; **interested in ~** politisch interessiert; **to play ~** (*pej*) große Politik spielen (*pej*).

polity ['pɒlɪtɪ] *n* (*form of government*) politische Ordnung, Staats- *or* Regierungsform *f*; (*politically organized society*) Staat(swesen *nt*) *m*, Gemeinwesen *nt*; (*management of public affairs*) Staatsverwaltung *f*.

polka ['pɒlkə] *n* Polka *f.*
polka dot [1] *n* Tupfen *m.*
[2] *adj* getupft, gepunktet.
poll [pəʊl] [1] *n* **(a)** (*Pol: voting*) Abstimmung *f;* (*election*) Wahl *f* ◆ **to take a ~** abstimmen lassen, eine Abstimmung durchführen; **a ~ was taken among the villagers** unter den Dorfbewohnern wurde abgestimmt; **to head the ~** bei der Wahl führen.
(b) (*total of votes cast*) Wahlbeteiligung *f;* (*for individual candidate*) Stimmenanteil *m* ◆ **there was an 84% ~** die Wahlbeteiligung betrug 84%; **they got 34% of the ~** sie bekamen 34% der Stimmen.
(c) ~s (*voting place*) Wahllokale *pl;* (*election*) Wahl *f* ◆ **to go to the ~s** wählen *or* zur Wahl gehen, an die Urnen gehen; **a crushing defeat at the ~s** eine vernichtende Niederlage bei den Wahlen, eine vernichtende Wahlniederlage; **a photograph of Trudeau at the ~s** ein Foto von Trudeau bei der Stimmabgabe.
(d) (*opinion ~*) Umfrage *f.*
(e) (*old: head, esp back of head*) Schädel *m.*
[2] *vt* **(a)** *votes* erhalten, auf sich (*acc*) vereinigen.
(b) (*in opinion ~*) befragen ◆ **40% of those ~ed supported the Government** 40% der Befragten waren für die Regierung.
(c) *horns* stutzen; *trees also* zurückschneiden ◆ **~ed cattle** Rinder mit gestutzten Hörnern.
[3] *vi* **he ~ed badly in the election** er erhielt bei der Wahl wenige Stimmen, er schnitt bei der Wahl schlecht ab.
pollard ['pɒləd] [1] *n* (*tree*) gekappter Baum.
[2] *vt* kappen.
pollen ['pɒlən] *n* Blütenstaub, Pollen *m* ◆ **~ basket** Höschen *nt,* Hose *f;* **~ count** Pollenzahl *f.*
pollinate ['pɒlɪneɪt] *vt* bestäuben.
pollination [ˌpɒlɪ'neɪʃən] *n* Bestäubung *f.*
polling ['pəʊlɪŋ] *n* **(a)** Stimmabgabe, Wahl *f* ◆ **~ will be on Thursday** die Wahl ist am Donnerstag; **~ has been heavy** die Wahlbeteiligung war (sehr) hoch *or* stark. **(b)** (*Comput*) Sendeaufruf *m.*
polling: ~ booth *n* Wahlkabine, Wahlzelle *f;* **~ card** *n* Wahlausweis *m;* **~ day** *n* Wahltag *m;* **~ station** *n* Wahllokal *nt.*
polliwog ['pɒlɪwɒg] *n* (*US*) Kaulquappe *f.*
pollster ['pəʊlstə^r] *n* Meinungsforscher(in *f*) *m.*
poll tax *n* Kopfsteuer *f.*
pollutant [pə'lu:tənt] *n* Schadstoff *m.*
pollute [pə'lu:t] *vt* *environment* verschmutzen; *river, atmosphere etc also* verunreinigen; *atmosphere also* verpesten (*pej*); (*fig*) *mind, morals* verderben, korrumpieren.
pollution [pə'lu:ʃən] *n* **(a)** Umweltverschmutzung *f* ◆ **the fight against ~** der Kampf gegen die Umweltverschmutzung. **(b)** *see vt* Verschmutzung *f;* Verunreinigung *f;* Verpestung (*pej*) *f;* (*fig*) Korrumpierung *f.*
pollywog *n see* **polliwog.**
polo ['pəʊləʊ] *n* Polo *nt.*
polonaise [ˌpɒlə'neɪz] *n* Polonaise, Polonäse *f.*
polo neck [1] *n* Rollkragen *m;* (*sweater*) Rollkragenpulli *or* -pullover *m.*
[2] *adj* Rollkragen-.
polonium [pə'ləʊnɪəm] *n* (*Chem*) Polonium *nt.*
poltergeist ['pɒltəgaɪst] *n* Poltergeist, Klopfgeist *m.*
poltroon [pɒl'tru:n] *n* (*liter*) feiger Wicht, Memme *f.*
poly (*Brit*) *abbr of* **polytechnic.**
polyandrous [ˌpɒlɪ'ændrəs] *adj* Vielmännerei betreibend, polyandrisch (*spec*); (*Bot*) polyadelphisch.
polyandry ['pɒlɪændrɪ] *n* Vielmännerei, Polyandrie (*form*) *f.*
polyanthus [ˌpɒlɪ'ænθəs] *n* (*primrose*) Gartenprimel *f;* (*narcissus*) Tazette *f.*
polychromatic [ˌpɒlɪkrəʊ'mætɪk] *adj* polychrom.
polyclinic ['pɒlɪklɪnɪk] *n* Poliklinik *f.*
polyester [ˌpɒlɪ'estə^r] *n* Polyester *m.*
polyethylene [ˌpɒlɪ'eθəli:n] *n* Polyäthylen *nt.*
polygamist [pɒ'lɪgəmɪst] *n* Polygamist *m.*
polygamous [pɒ'lɪgəməs] *adj* polygam.
polygamy [pɒ'lɪgəmɪ] *n* Polygamie, Vielehe, Vielweiberei *f.*
polyglot ['pɒlɪglɒt] [1] *adj* polyglott, vielsprachig.
[2] *n* (*person*) Polyglotte(r) *mf.*
polygon ['pɒlɪgən] *n* Polygon, Vieleck *nt.*
polygonal [pɒ'lɪgənl] *adj* polygonal, vieleckig.
polygraph ['pɒlɪgrɑ:f] *n* (*US: lie detector*) Lügendetektor *m.*
polyhedron [ˌpɒlɪ'hi:drən] *n* Polyeder *nt,* Vielflächner *m.*
polymath ['pɒlɪmæθ] *n* Mensch *m* mit vielseitigem Wissen.
polymer ['pɒlɪmə^r] *n* Polymer *nt.*
polymeric [ˌpɒlɪ'merɪk] *adj* polymer.
polymerization [ˌpɒlɪmərаɪ'zeɪʃən] *n* Polymerisation *f.*
polymorphic [ˌpɒlɪ'mɔ:fɪk] *adj* polymorph, vielgestaltig.
polymorphism [ˌpɒlɪ'mɔ:fɪzəm] *n* Polymorphismus *m.*
Polynesia [ˌpɒlɪ'ni:zɪə] *n* Polynesien *nt.*
Polynesian [ˌpɒlɪ'ni:zɪən] [1] *adj* polynesisch.
[2] *n* **(a)** Polynesier(in *f*) *m.* **(b)** (*language*) Polynesisch *nt.*
polynomial [ˌpɒlɪ'nəʊmɪəl] [1] *adj* polynomisch.
[2] *n* Polynom *nt.*
polyp ['pɒlɪp] *n* Polyp *m.*
polyphonic [ˌpɒlɪ'fɒnɪk] *adj* polyphon.
polyphony [pə'lɪfənɪ] *n* Polyphonie *f.*
polypropylene [ˌpɒlɪ'prɒpɪli:n] *n* Polypropylen *nt.*
polypus ['pɒlɪpəs] *n* Polyp *m.*
polysemous [pɒ'lɪsəməs] *adj* polysem.
polystyrene [ˌpɒlɪ'staɪri:n] [1] *n* Polystyrol *nt;* (*extended also*) Styropor ® *nt.*
[2] *adj* Polystyrol-; Styropor-.
polysyllabic [ˌpɒlɪsɪ'læbɪk] *adj* viel- *or* mehrsilbig.
polysyllable ['pɒlɪˌsɪləbl] *n* Polysyllabum *nt* (*spec*), vielsilbiges Wort.
polytechnic [ˌpɒlɪ'teknɪk] *n* (*Brit*) ≃ Polytechnikum *nt;* (*degree-awarding*) Technische Hochschule, TH *f.*
polytheism ['pɒlɪθi:ɪzəm] *n* Polytheismus *m.*
polytheistic [ˌpɒlɪθi:'ɪstɪk] *adj* polytheistisch.
polythene ['pɒlɪθi:n] *n* (*Brit*) Polyäthylen *nt;* (*in everyday language*) Plastik *nt* ◆ **~ bag** Plastiktüte *f.*
polyunsaturated fats [ˌpɒlɪʌn'sætjəreɪtɪd'fæts] *npl* mehrfach ungesättigte Fettsäuren *pl.*
polyunsaturates [ˌpɒlɪʌn'sætjərɪts] *npl* mehrfach ungesättigte Fettsäuren *pl.*
polyurethane [ˌpɒlɪ'jʊərɪθeɪn] *n* Polyurethan *nt.*
polyvalent [pə'lɪvələnt] *adj* mehrwertig, polyvalent.
pom[1] [pɒm] *n* (*Austral sl*) Engländer(in *f*), Tommy (*dated inf*) *m.*
pom[2] *n* (*inf*) *see* **Pomeranian 2.**
pomade [pə'mɑ:d] [1] *n* Pomade *f.*
[2] *vt* mit Pomade einreiben.
pomander [pəʊ'mændə^r] *n* Duftkugel *f.*
pomegranate ['pɒməˌgrænɪt] *n* Granatapfel *m;* (*tree*) Granatapfelbaum, Granatbaum *m.*
Pomerania [ˌpɒmə'reɪnɪə] *n* Pommern *nt.*
Pomeranian [ˌpɒmə'reɪnɪən] [1] *adj* pommer(i)sch.
[2] *n* Pommer(in *f*) *m;* (*dog*) Spitz *m.*
pommel ['pʌml] [1] *n* (*on sword*) Knauf *m;* (*on saddle*) Knopf *m.*
[2] *vt see* **pummel.**
pommy ['pɒmɪ] *n* (*Austral sl*) Engländer(in *f*), Tommy (*dated inf*) *m* ◆ **~ bastard** Scheißengländer *m* (*sl*).
pomp [pɒmp] *n* Pomp, Prunk *m,* Gepränge *nt* ◆ **~ and circumstance** Pomp und Prunk *m.*
pompadour ['pɒmpədʊə^r] *n* (*Hist*) Pompadourfrisur *f.*
Pompeian [pɒm'peɪən] [1] *adj* pompej(an)isch.
[2] *n* Pompej(an)er(in *f*) *m.*
Pompeii [pɒm'peɪi:] *n* Pompe(j)i *nt.*
Pompey ['pɒmpɪ] *n* Pompejus *m.*
pompom ['pɒmpɒm] *n* **(a)** (*gun*) automatische Flugzeugabwehrkanone *f.* **(b)** (*on hat etc*) Troddel, Bommel (*dial*) *f.*
pomposity [pɒm'pɒsɪtɪ] *n see adj* Aufgeblasenheit, Wichtigtuerei *f;* Gespreiztheit *f;* Schwülstigkeit *f,* Bombast *m.*
pompous ['pɒmpəs] *adj* *person* aufgeblasen, wichtigtuerisch; *attitude, behaviour also, phrase* gespreizt; *language, letter, remark* schwülstig, bombastisch ◆ **don't be so ~** tu nicht so aufgeblasen, sei nicht so wichtigtuerisch.
pompously ['pɒmpəslɪ] *adv* *write, speak* schwülstig, bombastisch; *behave* aufgeblasen, wichtigtuerisch.
'pon [pɒn] *prep* (*old, poet*) *contr of* **upon.**
ponce [pɒns] (*Brit sl*) [1] *n* (*pimp*) Zuhälter *m;* (*homosexual*) Schwule(r) (*inf*) *m.*
[2] *vi* **to ~ for sb** jds Zuhälter sein.
◆**ponce about** *or* **around** *vi* (*Brit sl*) herumtänzeln.
poncho ['pɒntʃəʊ] *n* Poncho *m.*
poncy ['pɒnsɪ] *adj* (*+er*) (*Brit sl*) (*homosexual*) warm (*sl*), schwul (*inf*); *pink sweater, walk, actor* tuntig (*sl*).
pond [pɒnd] *n* Teich *m* ◆ **the ~** (*inf: Atlantic*) der große Teich (*hum*); **~ life** Pflanzen- und Tierleben in Teichen.
ponder ['pɒndə^r] [1] *vt* nachdenken über (*+acc*); *possibilities, consequences etc* erwägen, bedenken.
[2] *vi* nachdenken (*on, over* über *+acc*).
ponderous ['pɒndərəs] *adj* schwerfällig: (*heavy*) massiv.
ponderously ['pɒndərəslɪ] *adv* schwerfällig.
ponderousness ['pɒndərəsnɪs] *n* Schwerfälligkeit *f;* (*heaviness*) Schwere, Gewichtigkeit *f.*
pondweed ['pɒndwi:d] *n* Laichkrautgewächs *nt.*
pone [pəʊn] *n* (*US*) Maisbrot *nt.*
pong [pɒŋ] (*Brit inf*) [1] *n* Gestank, Mief (*inf*) *m* ◆ **there's a bit of a ~ in here** hier stinkt's *or* mieft's (*inf*).
[2] *vi* stinken, miefen (*inf*).
poniard ['pɒnjəd] *n* (*liter, old*) Dolch *m.*
pontiff ['pɒntɪf] *n* Pontifex *m;* (*pope also*) Papst *m.*
pontifical [pɒn'tɪfɪkəl] *adj* **(a)** (*lit*) pontifikal; (*papal*) päpstlich ◆ **~ robes** Pontifikalien *pl*/päpstliche Gewänder *pl;* **~ duties** Pontifikalien *pl*/päpstliche Pflichten *pl;* **P~ Mass** Pontifikalamt *nt;* **~ office** Pontifikat *nt.* **(b)** (*fig*) päpstlich ◆ **his ~ pronouncements** seine feierlichen Verkündigungen.
pontifically [pɒn'tɪfɪkəlɪ] *adv* (*fig*) päpstlich.
pontificate [pɒn'tɪfɪkɪt] [1] *n* Pontifikat *nt.*
[2] [pɒn'tɪfɪkeɪt] *vi* (*fig*) dozieren ◆ **I wish you wouldn't ~ to me** ich wünschte, du würdest nicht in diesem belehrenden Ton mit mir reden.
Pontius Pilate ['pɒnʃəs'paɪlət] *n* Pontius Pilatus *m.*
pontoon[1] [pɒn'tu:n] *n* Ponton *m;* (*on flying boat*) Schwimmer *m* ◆ **~ bridge** Pontonbrücke *f.*
pontoon[2] *n* (*Brit Cards*) 17 und 4 *nt.*
pony ['pəʊnɪ] *n* **(a)** Pony *nt.* **(b)** (*Brit sl*) 25 Pfund. **(c)** (*US sl: crib*) Spickzettel

m. (d) (US inf: small glass) Gläschen nt.

pony: ~ express n Ponyexpreß m; ~tail n Pferdeschwanz m; she was wearing her hair in a ~tail sie trug einen Pferdeschwanz; ~ trekking n Ponyreiten nt; a ~ trekking holiday ein Ponyreiturlaub m.

pooch [pu:tʃ] n (inf) Hündchen nt.

poodle ['pu:dl] n Pudel m.

poof(ter) ['pʊf(təʳ)] n (Brit sl) Warme(r) (sl), Schwule(r) (inf) m.

poofy ['pʊfɪ] adj (+er) (Brit sl) warm (sl), schwul (inf); clothes, colour, actor tuntig (sl), tuntenhaft (inf).

pooh [pu:] interj (bad smell) puh, pfui; (disdain) pah, bah.

pooh-pooh ['pu:'pu:] vt verächtlich abtun.

pool[1] [pu:l] n (a) Teich, Tümpel m; (underground) See m.
(b) (of rain) Pfütze f; (of spilt liquid) Lache f ◆ a ~ of blood eine Blutlache; ~s of sunlight/shade sonnige/schattige Stellen.
(c) (in river) Loch nt.
(d) (artificial) Teich m; (swimming ~) (Schwimm)becken nt; (in private garden, hotel also) Swimmingpool m; (swimming baths) Schwimmbad nt ◆ to go to the (swimming) ~ ins Schwimmbad gehen; an olympic ~ should measure ... ein olympisches Wettkampfbecken muß ... groß sein; in the kiddies' ~ im Kinderbecken; we spent every afternoon down at the ~ wir verbrachten jeden Nachmittag im Schwimmbad; she was sitting at the edge of the ~ sie saß am Beckenrand.

pool[2] [1] n (a) (common fund) (gemeinsame) Kasse f ◆ each player put £10 in the ~ jeder Spieler gab £ 10 in die Kasse; the ~ was £40 es waren £ 40 in der Kasse.
(b) (supply, source) (typing ~) Schreibzentrale f; (car ~) Fahrbereitschaft f; (car-sharing) Fahrgemeinschaft f ◆ a ~ of labour ein Bestand m an Arbeitskräften; eine Arbeitskraftreserve; the Prime Minister's ~ of advisers der Beraterstab des Premierministers; among them they have a great ~ of experience/ideas zusammen verfügen sie über eine Menge Erfahrung/Ideen; there is a great ~ of untapped ability es gibt große, noch ungenutzte Begabungsreserven.
(c) the ~s pl (football ~s) Toto m or nt ◆ to do the ~s Toto spielen; to win the ~s im Toto gewinnen; he won £1000 on the ~s er hat £ 1000 im Toto gewonnen.
(d) (US: form of snooker) Poolbillard nt.
(e) (Comm) Interessengemeinschaft f; (US: monopoly, trust) Pool m, Kartell nt.
[2] vt resources, savings zusammenlegen; efforts vereinen (geh) ◆ if we ~ our efforts we'll get the work done sooner mit vereinten Kräften werden wir schneller mit der Arbeit fertig (werden); the two scientists ~ed their results die beiden Wissenschaftler kombinierten ihre Ergebnisse.

pool: ~ hall, ~ room n Billardzimmer nt; ~ table n Billardtisch m.

poop[1] [pu:p] n Hütte, Poop f ◆ ~ deck Hütten- or Poopdeck nt.

poop[2] vt (sl: exhaust) schlauchen (sl) ◆ to be ~ed (out) geschlaucht (sl) or fertig (inf) sein.

poo-poo ['pu:'pu:] n (baby-talk: excreta) Aa nt (baby-talk) ◆ has he done his ~s? hat er schon Aa gemacht?

poor [pʊəʳ] [1] adj (+er) (a) arm ◆ ~ whites arme weiße Bevölkerung im Süden der USA; a country ~ in natural resources ein an Bodenschätzen armes Land; it's the ~ man's Mercedes/Monte Carlo (inf) das ist der Mercedes/das Monte Carlo des kleinen Mannes (inf); ~ relation (fig) Sorgenkind nt.
(b) (not good) schlecht; (lacking quality also, meagre) mangelhaft; health, effort, performance, excuse also, sense of responsibility, leadership schwach; soil also mager, unergiebig; quality also minderwertig ◆ a ~ chance of success schlechte Erfolgsaussichten pl; we had a ~ time of it last night gestern Abend lief auch alles schief (inf); a ~ joke (weak) ein schwacher Witz; (in bad taste) ein geschmackloser Witz; only £55? that's pretty ~, isn't it? nur £ 55? das ist aber ziemlich wenig!; he is a ~ traveller/flier er verträgt Reisen/Flugreisen nicht gut; a ~ friend you are! du bist mir ein schöner Freund!; that's ~ consolation das ist ein schwacher Trost; it's a ~ thing for Britain if ... es ist schlecht für Großbritannien, wenn ...; it will be a ~ day for the world when ... es wird ein schwarzer Tag für die Welt sein, wenn ...; this is a pretty ~ state of affairs das sieht aber gar nicht gut aus; it's very ~ of them not to have replied es ist sehr unhöflich, daß sie uns etc (dat) nicht geantwortet haben; he has a very ~ grasp of the subject er beherrscht das Fach sehr schlecht; he showed a ~ grasp of the facts er zeigte wenig Verständnis für die Fakten; he is a ~ hand at public speaking in der Öffentlichkeit zu sprechen liegt ihm nicht; she was always ~ at languages sie war immer schlecht or schwach in Sprachen.
(c) (pitiful, pitiable) arm ◆ you ~ (old) chap (inf) or thing (inf) du armer Kerl (inf); ~ you! du Ärmste(r)!; she's all alone, ~ woman sie ist ganz allein, die arme Frau; ~ things, they look cold die Ärmsten, ihnen scheint kalt zu sein; ~ miserable creature that he is ... armseliger Kerl or Tropf (inf), der er ist ...; in my ~ opinion (iro) meiner bescheidenen or unmaßgeblichen Meinung nach (iro); it fell to my ~ self to ... es blieb meiner Wenigkeit (dat) überlassen, zu ... (iro).
[2] npl the ~ die Armen pl.

poor: ~ box n Armen- or Almosenbüchse f; ~house n (old) Armenhaus nt (old); ~ laws npl (Hist) Armengesetze pl.

poorly ['pʊəlɪ] [1] adv (a) arm; dressed, furnished ärmlich ◆ ~ off schlecht gestellt; her husband left her very ~ off ihr Mann ließ sie in sehr ärmlichen Verhältnissen zurück.
(b) (badly) schlecht ◆ ~ lit schlecht or schwach beleuchtet; to do ~ (at sth) (in etw dat) schwach or schlecht abschneiden; we're rather ~ off for staff/new ideas wir haben einen ziemlichen Mangel an Personal/neuen Ideen.
[2] adj pred (ill) schlecht, krank, elend ◆ to be ~ sich schlecht etc fühlen.

poorness ['pʊənɪs] n (a) (lack of money) Armut f.
(b) (lack of quality) Dürftigkeit, Mangelhaftigkeit f; (of soil) Magerkeit, Unergiebigkeit f; (of effort, excuse, harvest, performance) Dürftigkeit f; (of quality) Minderwertigkeit f; (of weather, memory, health, eyesight) Unzulänglichkeit f; (of leadership) Schwäche f.

poor-spirited ['pʊə'spɪrɪtɪd] adj person ängstlich.

poove [pu:v] n see **poof(ter)**.

pop[1] abbr of **population**.

pop[2] [pɒp] n (esp US inf) (father) Pa(pa) m (inf); (elderly man) Opa m (hum inf).

pop[3] n (~ music) Popmusik f, Pop m.

pop[4] [1] n (a) (sound) Knall m ◆ the toy gun went off with a ~ peng, ging die Spielzeugpistole los. (b) (inf: shot) Schuß m. to have or take a ~ at sth auf etw (acc) ballern (inf). (c) (fizzy drink) Brause, Limo (inf) f. (d) (dated inf: pawn) in ~ verpfändet, versetzt.
[2] adv to go ~ (cork) knallen, hochgehen (inf); (balloon) platzen; (ears) mit einem Knacken aufgehen or (when going down) zugehen; ~! peng!
[3] vt (a) balloon, corn zum Platzen bringen ◆ to ~ corn Popcorn machen.
(b) (inf: put) stecken ◆ to ~ a letter into the postbox einen Brief einwerfen or einschmeißen (inf); he ~ped his head round the door er streckte den Kopf durch die Tür; to ~ a jacket/hat on sich (dat) ein Jackett überziehen/sich (dat) einen Hut aufsetzen; to ~ the question einen (Heirats)antrag machen.
(c) (dated inf: pawn) versetzen.
(d) (inf) pills schlucken (inf).
[4] vi (a) (inf: go ~, burst) (cork) knallen; (balloon) platzen; (seed-pods, buttons, popcorn) aufplatzen; (ears) knacken ◆ his eyes were ~ping out of his head ihm gingen die Augen über, ihm fielen fast die Augen aus dem Kopf (inf); suddenly her blouse ~ped open plötzlich platzte or sprang ihre Bluse auf.
(b) (inf: go quickly or suddenly) to ~ along/down to the baker's schnell zum Bäcker laufen; I'll just ~ upstairs ich laufe mal eben nach oben; ~ across/over/round and see me sometime komm doch mal auf einen Sprung bei mir vorbei (inf); I thought I'd just ~ down to London for the weekend ich dachte, ich fahr mal eben übers Wochenende nach London; the rabbit ~ped into its burrow/through the hedge das Kaninchen sauste in seinen Bau/durch die Hecke.

◆**pop at** vi +prep obj (inf: shoot at) ballern auf (+acc) (inf).

◆**pop back** (inf) [1] vt sep (schnell) zurücktun (inf) ◆ ~ the lid ~ on the box klapp den Deckel wieder auf die Schachtel; ~ it ~ into the box tu es wieder in die Schachtel.
[2] vi schnell zurücklaufen ◆ she ~ped ~ for her book sie lief zurück, um ihr Buch zu holen.

◆**pop in** (inf) [1] vt sep hineintun ◆ to ~ sth ~to sth etw in etw (acc) stecken or werfen (inf).
[2] vi schnell hereinkommen/hereingehen; (visit) auf einen Sprung vorbeikommen (inf) ◆ to ~ ~ for a short chat auf einen kleinen Schwatz hereinschauen (inf); she kept ~ping ~ and out sie lief dauernd rein und raus; we just ~ped ~to the pub for a quickie wir gingen kurz in die Kneipe, um einen zu heben (inf); just ~ ~ any time you're passing komm doch mal vorbei, wenn du in der Gegend bist (inf).

◆**pop off** (inf) vi (a) (die suddenly) den Geist aufgeben (hum), den Löffel abgeben (sl). (b) (inf: go off) verschwinden (inf) (to nach) ◆ do you fancy ~ping ~ to Spain for a week? wie wär's, wollen wir für eine Woche nach Spanien verschwinden?

◆**pop out** (inf) vi (a) (go out) (schnell) rausgehen (inf)/rauskommen (inf); (spring, rabbit) herausspringen (of aus) ◆ he has just ~ped ~ for a beer er ist schnell auf ein Bierchen gegangen (inf); he has just ~ped ~ to buy a paper/to the shops er ist schnell eine Zeitung kaufen gegangen/er ist schnell zum Einkaufen gegangen.
(b) (eyes) vorquellen ◆ his eyes were ~ping ~ with amazement vor Staunen bekam er Stielaugen or fielen ihm fast die Augen aus dem Kopf (inf).

◆**pop up** (inf) [1] vt sep (a) (put up) head hochstrecken.
(b) (bring up) schnell raufbringen (inf).
(c) (sl: liven up) old film, musical etc aufmotzen (inf).
[2] vi (a) (appear suddenly) auftauchen; (head, toast) hochschießen (inf); (figures in illustrations) sich aufstellen.
(b) (come up) (mal eben) raufkommen (inf)/raufgehen (inf); (go up) (mal eben) raufgehen (inf) ◆ do you feel like ~ping ~ to my place? hast du Lust, mal eben zu mir raufzukommen? (inf).

pop: ~ art n Pop-art f; ~ concert n Popkonzert nt; ~corn n Popcorn nt.

Pope [pəʊp] n Papst m.

Popemobile ['pəʊpməʊ,bi:l] n (inf) Papamobil nt (inf).

popery ['pəʊpərɪ] n (pej) Pfaffentum nt ◆ no ~! Pfaffen raus!

pop: ~eyed adj person glotzäugig; (fig) mit Glotzaugen; ~ festival n Popfestival nt; ~ group n Popgruppe f; ~ gun n Spielzeugpistole f.

popinjay ['pɒpɪndʒeɪ] n (old) Geck, Laffe m.

popish ['pəʊpɪʃ] adj (pej) papistisch, ultramontan (geh).

poplar ['pɒpləʳ] n Pappel f.

poplin ['pɒplɪn] n Popeline f ◆ ~ dress Popelinekleid nt.

pop: ~ music n Popmusik f; ~over n (US) stark aufgehender hefiger Eierkuchen.

poppa ['pɒpə] n (US inf) Paps m (inf).

poppadom, poppadum ['pɒpədəm] n see **papadum**.

popper ['pɒpəʳ] n (Brit inf: press-stud) Druckknopf m.

poppet ['pɒpɪt] n (inf) Schatz m; (term of address also) Schätzchen nt.

poppy ['pɒpɪ] *n* Mohn *m*.
poppycock ['pɒpɪkɒk] *n* (*dated inf*) Unsinn, Blödsinn (*inf*) *m*.
poppy: P~ Day *n* (*Brit*) ≃ Volkstrauertag *m* (*BRD*); **~-seed** *n* Mohn *m*; **~-seed cake** Mohnkuchen *m*.
pops ['pɒps] *n* (*esp US inf*) Paps *m* (*inf*).
Popsicle ® ['pɒpsɪkl] *n* (*US*) Eis *nt* am Stiel.
pop: ~ shop *n* (*dated inf*) Pfandhaus *nt*; **~ singer** *n* Schlagersänger(in *f*) *m*; **~ song** *n* Popsong *m*; (*hit*) Schlager *m*; **~ star** *n* Popstar, Schlagerstar *m*.
popsy ['pɒpsɪ] *n* (*dated sl*) Biene (*inf*), Puppe (*inf*) *f*.
populace ['pɒpjʊlɪs] *n* Bevölkerung *f*; (*masses*) breite Öffentlichkeit ◆ **the ~ of Rome** das Volk von Rom, die Bürger von Rom.
popular ['pɒpjʊlə^r] *adj* **(a)** (*well-liked*) beliebt (*with* bei); (*with the public also*) populär (*with* bei); *decision, measure* populär ◆ **I know I won't be ~ if I decide that, but ...** ich weiß, daß ich mich nicht gerade beliebt mache, wenn ich so entscheide, aber ...; **he's not the most ~ of men at the moment** er ist im Augenblick nicht gerade einer der Beliebtesten *or* (*with the public also*) Populärsten; **he was a very ~ choice** seine Wahl fand großen Anklang.
(b) (*suitable for the general public*) populär; *music* leicht; *prices* erschwinglich; *science* Populär-; *edition* Volks-; *lectures, journal* populärwissenschaftlich ◆ **a series of ~ concerts** eine Reihe volkstümlicher Konzerte.
(c) (*widespread*) *belief, fallacy, conviction, discontent* weitverbreitet; (*of or for the people*) *government, approval, consent, support* des Volkes ◆ **~ front** Volksfront *f*; **~ remedy** Hausmittel *nt*; **it's ~ to despise politicians these days** es gehört heutzutage zum guten Ton, sich über Politiker abfällig zu äußern; **he isn't the ~ idea of a great leader** er entspricht nicht gerade der gängigen Vorstellung von einem großen Führer; **to rule by ~ consent** mit Zustimmung der Allgemeinheit regieren; **by ~ request** auf allgemeinen Wunsch.
popularity [,pɒpjʊ'lærɪtɪ] *n* Beliebtheit *f*; (*with the public also*) Popularität *f* (*with* bei) ◆ **he'd do anything to win ~** er würde alles tun, um sich beliebt zu machen; **he'd never win a ~ contest!** er ist nicht gerade beliebt; **the sport is growing/declining in ~** dieser Sport wird immer populärer/verliert immer mehr an Popularität; **~ rating** Beliebtheitsquote *f*; **to do well in the ~ ratings** bei Meinungsumfragen eine hohe Beliebtheitsquote erzielen.
popularization [,pɒpjʊləraɪ'zeɪʃən] *n* Popularisierung *f*; (*act also*) allgemeine Verbreitung ◆ **a ~ of Hamlet** eine Volksfassung des Hamlet.
popularize ['pɒpjʊləraɪz] *vt* **(a)** (*make well-liked*) populär machen, zum Durchbruch verhelfen (+*dat*). **(b)** (*make understandable*) *science* popularisieren, unter das Volk bringen (*inf*); *ideas also* zum Durchbruch verhelfen (+*dat*).
popularizer ['pɒpjʊləraɪzə^r] *n* **he is a great ~ of political/scientific ideas** er macht politische/wissenschaftliche Ideen auch der breiten Masse zugänglich.
popularly ['pɒpjʊləlɪ] *adv* allgemein ◆ **he is ~ believed to be a rich man** nach allgemeiner Ansicht ist er ein reicher Mann.
populate ['pɒpjʊleɪt] *vt* (*inhabit*) bevölkern; (*colonize*) besiedeln ◆ **this area is ~d mainly by immigrants** in diesem Stadtteil leben *or* wohnen hauptsächlich Einwanderer; **densely ~d areas/cities** dichtbesiedelte Gebiete *pl*/ dichtbevölkerte Städte *pl*.
population [,pɒpjʊ'leɪʃən] *n* (*of region, country*) Bevölkerung *f*; (*of village, town*) Bewohner, Einwohner *pl*; (*colonization*) Besiedlung *f*; (*number of inhabitants*) Bevölkerungszahl *f* ◆ **the ~ explosion** die Bevölkerungsexplosion; **the growing black ~ of London** die wachsende Zahl von Schwarzen in London.
populism ['pɒpjʊlɪzəm] *n* Populismus *m*.
populist ['pɒpjʊlɪst] [1] *n* Populist(in *f*) *m*.
[2] *adj* populistisch.
populous ['pɒpjʊləs] *adj country* dicht besiedelt; *town, area also* mit vielen Einwohnern, einwohnerstark.
pop-up ['pɒpʌp] *adj toaster* automatisch; *book, picture* Hochklapp- (*inf*) ◆ **~ menu** (*Comput*) Pop-up-Menü *nt*.
porage *n see* **porridge**.
porcelain ['pɔːsəlɪn] [1] *n* Porzellan *nt*.
[2] *adj* Porzellan-.
porch [pɔːtʃ] *n* (*of house*) Vorbau *m*, Vordach *nt*; (*US*) Veranda *f*; (*of church*) Vorhalle *f*, Portal *nt*.
porcine ['pɔːsaɪn] *adj* (*pig-like*) schweineartig; (*of pigs*) Schweine- ◆ **... are members of the ~ family** ... gehören zur Familie der Schweine *or* zu den Schweineartigen.
porcupine ['pɔːkjʊpaɪn] *n* Stachelschwein *nt* ◆ **~ fish** Igelfisch *m*.
pore [pɔː^r] *n* Pore *f*.
◆**pore over** *vi* +*prep obj* (*scrutinize*) genau studieren; (*meditate*) nachdenken *or* nachgrübeln über (+*acc*) ◆ **to ~ ~ one's books** über seinen Büchern hocken.
pork [pɔːk] *n* **(a)** Schweinefleisch *nt*. **(b)** (*US sl*) *von der Regierung aus politischen Gründen gewährte finanzielle Vergünstigungen oder Stellen.*
pork: ~ barrel *n* (*US inf*) *Geldzuwendungen pl der Regierung an örtliche Verwaltungsstellen, um deren Unterstützung zu gewinnen*; **~ butcher** *n* Schweinemetzger *m*; **~ chop** *n* Schweine- *or* Schweinskotelett *nt*.
porker ['pɔːkə^r] *n* Mastschwein *nt*.
pork: ~ pie *n* Schweinefleischpastete *f*; **~ pie hat** *n runder, niedriger Filzhut*; **~ sausage** *n* Schweinswurst *f*.
porky ['pɔːkɪ] *adj* (+*er*) **(a)** Schweinefleisch-. **(b)** (*inf: fat*) fett.
porn [pɔːn], (*esp US*) **porno** ['pɔːnəʊ] *n* (*inf*) Porno *m* (*inf*) ◆ **hard/soft ~** harter/weicher Porno; **~-shop** Pornoladen *m* (*inf*).
pornographic *adj*, **~ally** *adv* [,pɔːnə'græfɪk, -əlɪ] pornographisch.
pornography [pɔː'nɒgrəfɪ] *n* Pornographie *f*.
porosity [pɔː'rɒsɪtɪ] *n* (*of rocks, of substance*) Porosität *f*; (*of skin*) Porigkeit *f*.
porous ['pɔːrəs] *adj rock, substance* porös; *skin* porig.
porousness ['pɔːrəsnɪs] *n see* **porosity**.
porphyry ['pɔːfɪrɪ] *n* Porphyr *m*.
porpoise ['pɔːpəs] *n* Tümmler *m*.
porridge ['pɒrɪdʒ] *n* Porridge, Haferbrei *m* ◆ **~ oats** Haferflocken *pl*.
port¹ [pɔːt] *n* **(a)** (*harbour*) Hafen *m* ◆ **naval ~** Kriegshafen *m*; **to come/put into ~** in den Hafen einlaufen; **~ authority** Hafenamt *nt*, Hafenbehörde *f*; **~ dues** Hafengelder *pl*; **any ~ in a storm** (*prov*) in der Not frißt der Teufel Fliegen (*Prov*).
(b) (*city or town with a ~*) Hafen *m*, Hafenstadt *f*.
port² *n* **(a)** (*Naut, Aviat: ~hole*) Bullauge *nt*. **(b)** (*Naut: for cargo*) (Lade)luke *f*. **(c)** (*Tech*) Durchlaß(öffnung *f*) *m*. **(d)** (*Comput*) Anschluß, Port *m*.
port³ [1] *n* (*Naut, Aviat: left side*) Backbord *m* ◆ **land to ~**! Land an Backbord!
[2] *adj side* Backbord-; *cabin, deck also* auf der Backbordseite ◆ **on the ~ bow** Backbord voraus.
[3] *vt* (*Naut*): **to ~ the helm** nach Backbord drehen.
port⁴ *n* (*also* **~ wine**) Portwein *m*.
port⁵ (*Mil*) [1] *n* **to hold the rifle at ~** das Gewehr (schräg nach links) vor dem Körper halten.
[2] *vt arms* schräg nach links vor dem Körper halten ◆ **~ arms!** ≃ präsentiert das Gewehr!
portability [,pɔːtə'bɪlɪtɪ] *n* Tragbarkeit *f*.
portable ['pɔːtəbl] [1] *adj* **(a)** tragbar; *radio, typewriter also* Koffer- ◆ **easily ~** leicht zu tragen; **a ~ television** ein Portable *nt*, ein tragbarer Fernseher. **(b)** *pension* übertragbar.
[2] *n* (*computer, TV*) Portable *nt*.
portage ['pɔːtɪdʒ] *n* (*Comm*) (*act*) Transport *m*, Beförderung *f*; (*cost*) Rollgeld *nt*, Transportkosten *pl*, Beförderungsentgelt *nt*.
Portakabin ® ['pɔːtə,kæbɪn] *n* Container *m*; (*used as accommodation also*) Wohncontainer *m*; (*used as office also*) Bürocontainer *m*.
portal ['pɔːtl] *n* (*liter*) Portal *nt*, Pforte *f* (*geh*), Tor *nt* ◆ **the ~s of heaven** die Pforten *pl* des Himmels (*geh*).
portal vein *n* Pfortader *f*.
portcullis [pɔːt'kʌlɪs] *n* Fallgitter, Fallgatter *nt*.
porte-cochère [,pɔːtkɒ'ʃeə^r] *n* Wagenauffahrt *f*.
portend [pɔː'tend] *vt* (*form*) bedeuten, hindeuten auf (+*acc*) ◆ **what does this ~?** was hat das zu bedeuten?
portent ['pɔːtent] *n* Zeichen, Omen (*geh*) *nt* (*of* für) ◆ **a matter of great ~ for us all** eine Angelegenheit (von) großer Tragweite für uns alle; **a ~ of doom** ein böses Omen; **to be a ~ of sth** etw ahnen lassen.
portentous [pɔː'tentəs] *adj* (*ominous*) unheilschwanger; (*marvellous*) gewaltig; (*grave*) gewichtig; (*pompous*) bombastisch.
porter¹ ['pɔːtə^r] *n* (*of office etc*) Pförtner, Portier *m*; (*hospital ~*) Assistent *m*; (*at hotel*) Portier *m*; (*Rail, at airport*) Gepäckträger *m*; (*Sherpa etc*) (Lasten)träger *m*; (*US Rail*) Schlafwagenschaffner *m* ◆ **~'s lodge** Pförtnerloge *f*.
porter² *n* (*beer*) Porter *m or nt*.
porterage ['pɔːtərɪdʒ] *n* (*charge*) Trägerlohn *m*.
porterhouse steak ['pɔːtəhaʊs'steɪk] *n* Porterhouse Steak *nt*.
portfolio [pɔːt'fəʊlɪəʊ] *n* **(a)** (Akten)mappe *f*. **(b)** (*Pol: office*) Portefeuille (*form*) *nt*, Geschäftsbereich *m* ◆ **minister without ~** Minister ohne Portefeuille (*form*) *or* Geschäftsbereich. **(c)** (*Fin*) Portefeuille *nt*. **(d)** (*of artist, designer*) Kollektion *f*.
porthole ['pɔːthəʊl] *n* Bullauge *nt*.
portico ['pɔːtɪkəʊ] *n* Portikus *m*.
portion ['pɔːʃən] *n* **(a)** (*piece, part*) Teil *m*; (*of ticket*) Abschnitt *m* ◆ **your/my ~** dein/mein Anteil *m*. **(b)** (*of food*) Portion *f*. **(c)** (*old, form: marriage ~*) Mitgift *f*, Heiratsgut *nt* (*old*). **(d)** (*liter: fate*) Los, Schicksal *nt*.
◆**portion out** *vt sep* aufteilen, verteilen (*among* unter +*acc*).
portliness ['pɔːtlɪnɪs] *n* Beleibtheit, Korpulenz *f*.
portly ['pɔːtlɪ] *adj* (+*er*) beleibt, korpulent.
portmanteau [pɔːt'mæntəʊ] *n*, *pl* **-s** *or* **-x** Handkoffer *m* ◆ **~ word** Kombinationsform *f*.
Porto Rico ['pɔːtəʊ'riːkəʊ] *etc see* **Puerto Rico** *etc*.
portrait ['pɔːtrɪt] *n* (*also in words*) Porträt *nt* ◆ **to have one's ~ painted** sich malen lassen; **to sit for one's ~** für sein Porträt sitzen; **to paint a ~ of sb** jdn porträtieren.
portraitist ['pɔːtrɪtɪst] *n* Porträtist(in *f*) *m*.
portrait painter *n* Porträtmaler(in *f*) *m*.
portraiture ['pɔːtrɪtʃə^r] *n* (*portrait*) Porträt *nt*; (*portraits collectively*) Porträts *pl*; (*art of ~*) (*painting*) Porträtmalerei *f*; (*Phot*) Porträtfotografie *f*.
portray [pɔː'treɪ] *vt* darstellen; (*paint also*) malen.
portrayal [pɔː'treɪəl] *n* Darstellung *f*; (*description also*) Schilderung *f*.
Portugal ['pɔːtjʊgəl] *n* Portugal *nt*.
Portuguese [,pɔːtjʊ'giːz] [1] *adj* portugiesisch ◆ **~ man-of-war** Staats- *or* Röhrenqualle, Portugiesische Galeere *f*.
[2] *n* Portugiese *m*, Portugiesin *f*; (*language*) Portugiesisch *nt*.
pose [pəʊz] [1] *n* **(a)** (*position, attitude*) Haltung *f*; (*of model, pej also*) Pose *f* ◆ **to take up a ~** (*model*) eine Pose *or* Haltung einnehmen; **to hold a ~** eine Pose *or* Haltung beibehalten; **to strike a (dramatic) ~** sich (dramatisch) in Positur werfen; **she's always striking ~s** sie benimmt sich immer so theatralisch.
(b) (*affectation*) Pose *f* ◆ **it's only a ~** das ist nur Pose.
[2] *vt* **(a)** (*position*) *model* aufstellen.
(b) (*put forward*) *question, problem* vortragen ◆ **the question ~d by his speech**

➤ LANGUAGE IN USE: **position: 1e → 19.1 1f → 12.3**

die in seiner Rede aufgeworfene Frage.
(c) *(formulate) question, problem* formulieren.
(d) *(constitute, present) difficulties, problem* aufwerfen; *threat* darstellen.
3 *vi* **(a)** *(model)* posieren; *(sitting also)* (Modell) sitzen; *(standing also)* Modell stehen ♦ **to ~ in the nude** für einen Akt posieren *or* Modell sitzen/stehen.
(b) *(attitudinize)* posieren, sich in Pose werfen.
(c) *(present oneself as)* **to ~ as** sich ausgeben als.

Poseidon [pə'saɪdən] *n* Poseidon *m.*

poser ['pəʊzəʳ] *n* **(a)** *(person)* Angeber(in *f*) *m.* **(b)** *(inf: difficult problem or question)* harte Nuß *(inf).*

posh [pɒʃ] *(inf)* 1 *adj (+er)* piekfein *(inf)*, vornehm; *neighbourhood, hotel, wedding also* nobel; *friends* vornehm, fein.
2 *adv (+er)*: **to talk ~** mit vornehmem Akzent sprechen.
3 *vt* **to ~ sth up** *(inf)* etw verschönern *(inf).*

poshly ['pɒʃlɪ] *adj* piekfein *(inf)*, vornehm; *talk* vornehm.

poshness ['pɒʃnɪs] *n* Feinheit, Vornehmheit *f*; *(of accent)* Vornehmheit *f*, Distinguierte(s) *nt.*

posing pouch ['pəʊzɪŋ,paʊtʃ] *n knappe Herrenbadehose.*

posit ['pɒzɪt] 1 *n (claim)* Postulat *nt*, Grundannahme *f.*
2 *vt* **(a)** *(rare: put down)* absetzen. **(b)** *(claim)* postulieren; *hypothesis* aufstellen.

▼ **position** [pə'zɪʃən] 1 *n* **(a)** *(location, place where sb/sth is) (of person)* Platz *m*; *(of object also)* Stelle *f*; *(of microphone, statue, wardrobe, plant etc)* Standort *m*; *(of spotlight, table, in picture, painting)* Anordnung *f*; *(of town, house etc)* Lage *f*; *(of plane, ship, Sport: starting ~, Ftbl etc)* Position *f*; *(Mil: strategic site)* Stellung *f* ♦ **to be in/out of ~** an der richtigen/falschen Stelle sein; **the actors were in ~ on the stage** die Schauspieler hatten ihre Plätze auf der Bühne eingenommen; **to jockey** *or* **jostle for ~** *(lit)* um eine gute Ausgangsposition kämpfen; *(fig)* um eine gute Position rangeln; **the ~ of the picture/fireplace isn't very good** das Bild hängt nicht sehr günstig/der Kamin hat keinen sehr günstigen Platz; **what ~ do you play?** auf *or* in welcher Position spielst du?; **his ~ is full-back/goalkeeper** er spielt Außenverteidiger/Torwart.
(b) *(posture, way of standing, sitting etc)* Haltung *f*; *(in love-making, Art: of model)* Stellung *f*; *(Ballet)* Position *f* ♦ **in a reclining ~** zurückgelehnt.
(c) *(in class, league etc)* Platz *m* ♦ **after the third lap he was in fourth ~** nach der dritten Runde lag er auf dem vierten Platz *or* war er Vierter; **to finish in third ~** Dritter werden, auf dem dritten Platz landen *(inf).*
(d) *(social, professional standing)* Stellung, Position *f* ♦ **a man of ~** eine hochgestellte Persönlichkeit.
▼ **(e)** *(job)* Stelle *f* ♦ **he has a high ~ in the Ministry of Defence** er bekleidet eine hohe Stellung *or* Position im Verteidigungsministerium; **a ~ of trust** eine Vertrauensstellung.
▼ **(f)** *(fig: situation, circumstance)* Lage *f* ♦ **to be in a ~ to do sth** in der Lage sein, etw zu tun; **what is the ~ regarding ...?** wie sieht es mit ... aus?; **I'm not in a ~ to say anything about that** ich kann dazu nichts sagen; **my ~ is that I don't have the qualifications/money** mir geht es so, daß mir die Qualifikation/das Geld fehlt.
(g) *(fig: point of view, attitude)* Standpunkt *m*, Haltung, Einstellung *f* ♦ **what is the government's ~ on ...?** welchen Standpunkt vertritt die Regierung zu ...?; **to take up a ~ on sth** eine Haltung bei einer Sache einnehmen.
2 *vt* **(a)** *(place in ~) microphone, ladder, guards* aufstellen; *soldiers, policemen* postieren; *(artist, photographer etc)* plazieren; *(Comput) cursor* positionieren, plazieren ♦ **he ~ed himself where he could see her** er stellte *or (seated)* setzte sich so, daß er sie sehen konnte. **(b)** *(in marketing) product* positionieren.

positive ['pɒzɪtɪv] 1 *adj* **(a)** *(Math, Phot, Elec, Gram)* positiv; *pole* Plus- ♦ **the ~ degree** *(Gram)* der Positiv.
(b) *(affirmative, constructive) result, answer* positiv; *attitude also* bejahend; *criticism, suggestion* konstruktiv ♦ **he is a very ~ person** er hat eine sehr positive Einstellung zum Leben; **~ vetting** Sicherheitsüberprüfung *f.*
(c) *(definite) person, tone of voice* bestimmt; *instructions* streng; *evidence, answer* definitiv, eindeutig; *rule* fest ♦ **that is ~ proof** *or* **proof ~** das ist der sichere *or* eindeutige Beweis; **to be ~ that ...** sicher sein, daß ..., definitiv wissen, daß ...; **to be ~ about** *or* **of sth** sich *(dat)* einer Sache *(gen)* absolut sicher sein.
(d) *(real, downright)* **this is a ~ miracle/crime/disgrace** das ist wirklich ein Wunder/Verbrechen/eine Schande; **he's a ~ genius/menace** er ist wirklich ein Genie/Ärgernis, er ist ein wahres Genie/wirkliches Ärgernis.
2 *n (Phot)* Positiv *nt*; *(Gram)* Positiv *m*; *(Elec)* Pluspol *m.*

positively ['pɒzɪtɪvlɪ] *adv* **(a)** *(affirmatively, constructively, Sci)* positiv. **(b)** *(decisively)* bestimmt; *(definitely, indisputably) prove* definitiv, eindeutig. **(c)** *(really, absolutely)* wirklich, echt *(inf).*

positiveness ['pɒzɪtɪvnɪs] *n* **(a)** *(constructiveness)* Positive(s) *nt* ♦ **I was reassured by the ~ of his attitude** ich wurde durch seine positive Haltung bestärkt.
(b) *(certainty)* Überzeugung *f*; *(of voice also)* Bestimmtheit *f*; *(of evidence)* Überzeugungskraft *f* ♦ **her ~ about his innocence** die Überzeugung, mit der sie an seine Unschuld glaubte.

positivism ['pɒzɪtɪvɪzəm] *n* Positivismus *m.*

positivist ['pɒzɪtɪvɪst] 1 *adj* positivistisch.
2 *n* Positivist *m.*

positivistic *adj*, **~ally** *adv* [pɒzɪtɪ'vɪstɪk, -əlɪ] positivistisch.

positron ['pɒzɪtrɒn] *n* Positron *nt.*

poss [pɒs] *abbr of* **possible, possibly** mögl.

posse ['pɒsɪ] *n (US: sheriff's ~)* Aufgebot *nt*; *(fig)* Gruppe, Schar *f* ♦ **~ of searchers** Suchtrupp *m.*

possess [pə'zes] *vt* besitzen; *(form) foreign language, facts* verfügen über *(+acc)* ♦ **to ~ oneself of sth** *(form)* sich in den Besitz von etw bringen *(form)*, etw *(acc)* an sich nehmen; **to be ~ed of sth** *(form)* über etw *(acc)* verfügen; **it ~es many advantages** es hat viele Vorteile; **to be ~ed by demons/by an idea** von Dämonen/einer Idee besessen sein; **to be ~ed by** *or* **with rage** voll von *or* voller Wut sein; **to fight like one ~ed** wie ein Besessener kämpfen; **whatever ~ed you to do that?** was ist bloß in Sie gefahren, so etwas zu tun?; **to ~ one-self** *or* **one's soul in patience** *(form)* sich in Geduld fassen.

possession [pə'zeʃən] *n* **(a)** *(ownership)* Besitz *m*; *(Sport: of ball)* Ballbesitz *m*; *(fig: control: of feelings, oneself)* Kontrolle *f* ♦ **to have sth in one's ~** etw in seinem Besitz haben; **to have/take ~ of sth** etw in Besitz haben/nehmen; **to come into/get ~ of sth** in den Besitz von etw gelangen/kommen; **to get/have ~ of the ball** in Ballbesitz gelangen/sein; **to be in ~ of sth** im Besitz von etw sein; **I'm in full ~ of the facts** ich verfüge über alle Tatsachen; **he put me in ~ of the information I required** er lieferte *or* verschaffte mir die Informationen, die ich benötigte; **according to the information in my ~** nach den mir zur Verfügung stehenden Informationen; **to be in ~ of a house** ein Haus in Besitz haben; **to take ~ of a house** ein Haus in Besitz nehmen; **~ is nine points of the law** *(prov)* das Recht steht auf der Seite der Besitzenden.
(b) *(by demons)* Besessenheit *f.*
(c) *(thing possessed)* Besitz *m no pl*; *(territory)* Besitzung *f* ♦ **all his ~s** sein gesamter Besitz, seine gesamten Besitztümer.

possessive [pə'zesɪv] 1 *adj* **(a)** *(towards belongings)* eigen; *mother, boyfriend, love etc* besitzergreifend ♦ **to be ~ about sth** seine Besitzansprüche auf etw *(acc)* betonen; **to be ~ towards sb** an jdn Besitzansprüche stellen.
(b) *(Gram)* **~ pronoun/adjective** besitzanzeigendes Fürwort, Possessivpronomen *nt*; **~ case** Genitiv *m*, zweiter Fall.
2 *n (Gram: pronoun, adjective)* Possessiv(um) *nt.*

possessively [pə'zesɪvlɪ] *adv (about things)* eigen; *(towards people)* besitzergreifend.

possessiveness [pə'zesɪvnɪs] *n* eigene Art *(about* mit); *(towards people)* besitzergreifende Art *(towards* gegenüber).

possessor [pə'zesəʳ] *n* Besitzer(in *f*) *m* ♦ **to be the proud ~ of sth** der stolze Besitzer von etw sein.

posset ['pɒsɪt] *n heiße Milch mit Bier oder Wein und Gewürzen.*

▼ **possibility** [,pɒsə'bɪlɪtɪ] *n* Möglichkeit *f* ♦ **there's not much ~ of success/of his** *or* **him being successful** die Aussichten auf Erfolg/darauf, daß er Erfolg hat, sind nicht sehr groß; **within the bounds of ~** im Bereich des Möglichen; **do you by any ~ happen to know ...?** wissen Sie zufällig ...?; **the ~ of doing sth** die Möglichkeit *or* Chance, etw zu tun; **it's a distinct ~ that ...** es besteht eindeutig die Möglichkeit, daß ...; **he is a ~ for the job** er kommt für die Stelle in Frage *or* Betracht; **there is some** *or* **a ~ that ...** es besteht die Möglichkeit, daß ...; **a job with real possibilities** eine Stelle mit echten Möglichkeiten *or* Chancen; **he/that has possibilities** in ihm/darin stecken Möglichkeiten.

▼ **possible** ['pɒsəbl] 1 *adj* möglich ♦ **anything is ~** möglich ist alles; **to make sth ~** etw ermöglichen, etw möglich machen; **as soon/often/far as ~** so bald/oft/weit wie möglich; **the best/worst/quickest ~ ...** der/die/das bestmögliche/schlechtestmögliche/schnellstmögliche ...; **if (at all) ~** falls (irgend) möglich; **it's just ~ that I'll see you before then** eventuell sehe ich dich vorher noch; **it's just ~, I suppose** es ist unwahrscheinlich, aber möglich; **there is no ~ excuse for his behaviour** für sein Verhalten gibt es absolut keine Entschuldigung; **the only ~ choice, the only choice ~** die einzig mögliche Wahl; **it will be ~ for you to return the same day** es besteht *or* Sie haben die Möglichkeit, am selben Tag zurückzukommen.
2 *n* Möglichkeit *f* ♦ **a long list of ~s for the job** eine lange Liste möglicher Kandidaten für die Stelle; **the ~s played the probables** *(Sport)* die möglichen Kandidaten spielten gegen die wahrscheinlichen (Kandidaten); **he is a ~ for the English team** er kommt für die englische Mannschaft in Frage.

▼ **possibly** ['pɒsəblɪ] *adv* **(a)** **not ~** unmöglich; **that can't ~ be true** das kann unmöglich wahr sein; **can that ~ be true?** kann das (vielleicht doch) stimmen?; **how could I ~ have come?** wie hätte ich denn kommen können?; **how could he ~ have known that?** wie konnte er das nur wissen?; **he did all he ~ could** er tat, was er nur konnte; **if I ~ can** wenn ich irgend kann.
(b) *(perhaps)* vielleicht, möglicherweise.

possum ['pɒsəm] *n* Opossum *nt*, Beutelratte *f* ♦ **to play ~** *(sleeping)* sich schlafend stellen; *(dead)* sich tot stellen.

post¹ [pəʊst] 1 *n (pole, door~ etc)* Pfosten *m*; *(lamp~)* Pfahl *m*; *(telegraph ~)* Mast *m* ♦ **a wooden/metal ~** ein Holzpfosten *or* -pfahl *m*/ein Metallpfosten *m*; **starting/winning** *or* **finishing ~** Start-/Zielpfosten *m*; **the horses were at the ~** die Pferde standen am Start; **he was left at the ~** sie ließen ihn stehen; **to be beaten at the ~** im Ziel abgefangen werden; *see* **deaf.**
2 *vt* **(a)** *(display)* *(also* **~ up)** anschlagen ♦ **" ~ no bills"** „Plakate ankleben verboten"; **to ~ a wall with advertisements** eine Wand plakatieren *or* mit Werbeplakaten bekleben.
(b) *(announce) concert etc* durch Anschlag bekanntmachen ♦ **to ~ a reward** eine Belohnung ausschreiben; **to ~ (as) missing** als vermißt melden.

▼ **post²** 1 *n* **(a)** *(job)* Stelle *f*, Posten *m* ♦ **to look for/take up a ~** eine Stelle suchen/antreten.
(b) *(esp Mil: place of duty)* Posten *m* ♦ **at one's ~** auf seinem Posten; **to die at one's ~** im Dienst sterben.
(c) *(Mil: camp, station)* Posten *m* ♦ **a frontier ~** ein Grenzposten *m*; **a chain of ~s along the border** eine Postenkette entlang der Grenze; **~ exchange** *(abbr* **PX)** *(US) von der Regierung betriebener Vorzugsladen für Truppenangehörige*; **to**

➤ LANGUAGE IN USE: **possibility** → 15.2, 26.3 **possible: 1** → 9.1, 15.3, 19.4, 26.3 **possibly: a** → 12.3, 16.3, 26.3 **post²: 1a** → 19.1, 19.4

return to/leave the ~ zur Garnison zurückkehren/die Garnison verlassen; **most of the officers live on the ~** die meisten Offiziere leben in der Garnison; **the whole ~ fell sick** die ganze Garnison wurde krank.
(d) (*Brit Mil: bugle-call*) **first ~** Wecksignal *nt*; **last ~** Zapfenstreich *m*.
(e) (*trading ~*) Handelsniederlassung *f*.
[2] *vt* (a) (*position*) postieren; *sentry, guard also* aufstellen.
(b) (*send, assign*) versetzen; (*Mil also*) abkommandieren ◆ **to be ~ed to a battalion/an embassy/a ship** zu einem Bataillon/an eine Botschaft/auf ein Schiff versetzt *or* (*Mil*) abkommandiert werden; **he has been ~ed away** er ist versetzt *or* (*Mil*) abkommandiert worden.

post³ [1] *n* (a) (*esp Brit: mail*) Post *f* ◆ **by ~** mit der Post, auf dem Postweg (*form*); **it's in the ~** es ist unterwegs *or* in der Post; **to drop sth in the ~** etw (in den Briefkasten) einwerfen; (*in post office*) etw zur Post bringen; **to catch/miss the ~** (*letter*) noch/nicht mehr mit der Post mitkommen; (*person*) rechtzeitig zur Leerung kommen/die Leerung verpassen; **there is no ~ today** (*no delivery*) heute kommt keine Post, heute wird keine Post ausgetragen; (*no letters*) heute ist keine Post (für uns) gekommen; **has the ~ been?** war die Post schon da?
(b) (*Hist*) Post *f* ◆ **to travel ~** mit der Post(kutsche) reisen.
[2] *vt* (a) (*put in the ~*) aufgeben; (*in letter-box*) einwerfen, einstecken; (*send by ~ also*) mit der Post schicken ◆ **I ~ed it to you on Monday** ich habe es am Montag an Sie abgeschickt.
(b) (*inform*) **to keep sb ~ed** jdn auf dem laufenden halten.
(c) (*enter in ledger: also ~ up*) eintragen (*to* in *+acc*) ◆ **all transactions must be ~ed (up) weekly** alle Geschäftsvorgänge müssen wöchentlich verbucht werden.
[3] *vi* (*old: travel by ~*) mit der Post(kutsche) reisen.

◆**post off** *vt sep* abschicken.

post- [pəʊst-] *pref* nach-; (*esp with non-Germanic words*) post-.

postage ['pəʊstɪdʒ] *n* Porto *nt*, Postgebühr *f* (*form*) ◆ **~ and packing** (*abbr* **p&p**) Porto und Verpackung; **what is the ~ to Germany?** wie hoch ist das Porto nach Deutschland?

postage: ~ meter *n* (*US*) Frankiermaschine *f*; **~ paid** [1] *adj* portofrei; *envelope* frankiert, freigemacht, Frei-; [2] *adv* portofrei; **~ rate** *n* Porto *nt no pl*, Postgebühr *f*; **~ stamp** *n* Briefmarke *f*, Postwertzeichen *nt* (*form*).

postal ['pəʊstl] [1] *adj* Post-, postalisch (*form*).
[2] *n* (*US inf*) *see* **~ card**.

postal: ~ card *n* (*US*) (*letter card*) *Postkarte f mit aufgedruckter Briefmarke für offizielle Zwecke*; (*postcard*) Postkarte *f*; (*with picture*) Ansichtskarte *f*; **~ code** *n* (*Brit*) Postleitzahl *f*; **~ district** *n* (*of main sorting office*) ≃ Postort *m* (*form*); (*of local sorting office*) ≃ Postzustellbereich *m* (*form*); **~ order** *n* (*Brit*) *Geldgutschein, der bei der Post gekauft und eingelöst wird*; **~ tuition** *n* Fernunterricht *m*; **~ vote** *n* **to have a ~ vote** per Briefwahl wählen.

post: ~-bag *n* (*Brit*) Postsack *m*; **~box** *n* (*Brit*) Briefkasten *m*; **~card** *n* Postkarte *f*; **(picture) ~card** Ansichtskarte *f*; **~ chaise** *n* (*Hist*) Postkutsche *f*; **~-classical** *adj* nachklassisch; **~ code** *n* (*Brit*) Postleitzahl *f*; **~date** *vt* (a) *cheque etc* vordatieren; (b) (*be later than*) später datieren als (*+nom*); **~-doctoral** *adj* nach der *or* im Anschluß an die Promotion; **~edit** *vti* (*Comput: in machine translations*) redaktionell nachbearbeiten.

poster ['pəʊstəʳ] *n* (*advertising*) Plakat *nt*; (*for decoration also*) Poster *nt* ◆ **~ colour** *or* **paint** Plakatfarbe, Plakafarbe ® *f*.

poste restante ['pəʊst'restɑːnt] (*Brit*) [1] *n* Aufbewahrungsstelle *f* für postlagernde Sendungen.
[2] *adv* postlagernd.

posterior [pɒ'stɪərɪəʳ] [1] *adj* (*form*) hintere(r, s); (*in time*) spätere(r, s) ◆ **to be ~ to sth** hinter etw (*dat*) liegen; nach etw (*dat*) kommen, auf etw (*acc*) folgen.
[2] *n* (*hum*) Allerwerteste(r) *m* (*hum*).

posterity [pɒ'sterɪtɪ] *n* die Nachwelt.

postern ['pəʊstɜːn] *n* (*old*) Seitenpforte, Nebenpforte *f*.

post: ~-free *adj, adv* portofrei, gebührenfrei; **~glacial** *adj* postglazial, nacheiszeitlich; **~grad** (*inf*) [,pəʊst'græd], **~graduate** [1] *n jd, der seine Studien nach dem ersten akademischen Grad weiterführt*; [2] *adj* **~graduate course** Anschlußkurs *m*; **~haste** *adv* schnellstens, auf dem schnellsten Wege; **~-horn** *n* Posthorn *nt*; **~ house** *n* (*Hist*) Posthalterei *f*.

posthumous ['pɒstjʊməs] *adj* post(h)um; *child also* nachgeboren.

posthumously ['pɒstjʊməslɪ] *adv* post(h)um.

postil(l)ion [pə'stɪlɪən] *n* Reiter *m* des Sattelpferdes, Fahrer *m* vom Sattel (*form*).

post-impressionism ['pəʊstɪm'preʃənɪzəm] *n* Nachimpressionismus *m*.

post-impressionist ['pəʊstɪm'preʃənɪst] [1] *adj* nachimpressionistisch.
[2] *n* Nachimpressionist(in *f*) *m*.

post-industrial [,pəʊstɪn'dʌstrɪəl] *adj* postindustriell.

posting ['pəʊstɪŋ] *n* (*transfer, assignment*) Versetzung *f*; (*Mil also*) Abkommandierung *f* ◆ **he's got a new ~** er ist wieder versetzt/abkommandiert worden.

postlude ['pəʊstluːd] *n* Nachspiel *nt*.

post: ~man *n* Briefträger, Postbote *m*; **~man's knock** *n Kinderspiel, bei dem für einen Brief mit einem Kuß bezahlt wird*; **~mark** [1] *n* Poststempel *m*; **date as ~mark** Datum des Poststempels; [2] *vt* (ab)stempeln; **the letter is ~marked "Birmingham"** der Brief ist in Birmingham abgestempelt; **~master** *n* Postmeister *m*; **~master general** *n, pl* **~masters general** ≃ Postminister *m*; **~meridian** *adj* (*form*) nachmittäglich, Nachmittags-; **~ meridiem** ['pəʊstmə'rɪdɪəm] *adv* (*form*) nachmittags; **~mistress** *n* Postmeisterin *f*; **~modern** *adj* postmodern; **~modernism** *n* Postmodernismus *m*; **~modernist** [1] *n* Postmodernist(in *f*) *m*; [2] *adj* postmodernistisch. **~mortem** [,pəʊst'mɔːtəm] *n* (a) (*also* **~-mortem examination**) Obduktion, Autopsie, Leichenöffnung *f*; (b) (*fig*) nachträgliche Erörterung; **to hold** *or* **have a ~-mortem on sth** etw hinterher erörtern; **~-natal** *adj* nach der Geburt, postnatal (*spec*); **~ office** *n* Postamt *nt*; **the P~ Office** (*institution*) die Post; **~ office box** (*abbr* **PO Box**) Postfach *nt*; **~ office worker** Postarbeiter(in *f*) *m*; **he has £100 in ~ office savings** *or* **the P~ Office Savings Bank** (*Brit*) er hat £ 100 auf dem Postsparbuch; **~-operative** *adj* postoperativ; **~-paid** [1] *adj* portofrei; *envelope* frankiert, freigemacht, Frei-; [2] *adv* portofrei; **to reply ~-paid** mit freigemachter Postkarte/freigemachtem Briefumschlag antworten.

postpone [pəʊst'pəʊn] *vt* (a) aufschieben, hinausschieben; (*for specified period*) verschieben ◆ **it has been ~d till Tuesday** es ist auf Dienstag verschoben worden; **you mustn't ~ answering a day longer** Sie dürfen die Antwort keinen Tag länger hinausschieben. (b) (*Gram form*) nachstellen.

postponement [pəʊst'pəʊnmənt] *n* (*act*) Verschiebung *f*; (*result*) Aufschub *m*.

post: ~position *n* (*Gram*) Nachstellung *f*; (*part of speech*) Postposition *f*; **~positive** *adj* (*Gram*) nachgestellt; **~prandial** [,pəʊst'prændɪəl] *adj* (*hum*) nach dem Essen; *walk* Verdauungs-; **~ road** *n* (*Hist*) Poststraße *f*; **~script(um)** *n* (*abbr* **PS**: *to letter*) Postskriptum *nt*; (*to book, article etc*) Nachwort *nt*; (*fig: to affair*) Nachspiel *nt*; **he added a ~script** (*fig: in speech*) er fügte noch eine Bemerkung hinzu.

postulant ['pɒstjʊlənt] *n* (*Rel*) Postulant *m*.

postulate ['pɒstjʊlɪt] [1] *n* Postulat *nt*.
[2] ['pɒstʊleɪt] *vt* postulieren; *theory* aufstellen.

postulation [,pɒstjʊ'leɪʃən] *n* (*act*) Postulieren *nt*; (*theory*) Postulat *nt*.

posture ['pɒstʃəʳ] [1] *n* (*lit, fig*) Haltung *f*; (*pej*) Pose *f* ◆ **she has very poor ~** sie hat eine sehr schlechte Haltung.
[2] *vi* sich in Positur *or* Pose werfen ◆ **is he merely posturing (because of the election)?** ist das nur eine (Wahl)pose seinerseits?

postwar ['pəʊst'wɔːʳ] *adj* Nachkriegs- ◆ **~ London** das London der Nachkriegszeit.

posy ['pəʊzɪ] *n* Sträußchen *nt*.

pot [pɒt] [1] *n* (a) Topf *m*; (*tea~, coffee ~*) Kanne *f*; (*dated: tankard*) Krug *m*; (*lobster ~*) Korb *m*; (*chimney~*) Kaminaufsatz *m* ◆ **~s and pans** Töpfe und Pfannen; **a pint ~** ≃ ein Humpen *m*; **to keep the ~ boiling** (*earn living*) dafür sorgen, daß der Schornstein raucht (*inf*); (*keep sth going*) den Betrieb aufrechterhalten; **that's (a case of) the ~ calling the kettle black** (*prov*) ein Esel schimpft den anderen Langohr (*prov*); **to go to ~** (*inf*) (*person, business*) auf den Hund kommen (*inf*); (*plan, arrangement*) ins Wasser fallen (*inf*).
(b) (*inf: large amount*) **to have ~s of money/time** massenhaft (*inf*) *or* jede Menge (*inf*) Geld/Zeit haben.
(c) (*inf: important person*) **a big ~** ein hohes Tier (*inf*).
(d) (*sl: marijuana*) Pot *nt* (*sl*).
(e) (*Cards: pool*) Topf, Pott *m*.
(f) (*inf: prize, cup*) Topf *m* (*inf*).
(g) (*~shot*) Schuß *m* aufs Geratewohl.
(h) (*inf: ~belly*) Spitzbauch *m*.
[2] *vt* (a) *meat* einmachen, einkochen; *jam* einfüllen. (b) *plant* eintopfen. (c) (*shoot*) *game* schießen. (d) (*Billiards*) *ball* einlochen. (e) (*inf*) *baby* auf den Topf setzen.
[3] *vi* (a) **to ~ at** schießen auf (*+acc*); **to ~ away** wahllos schießen (*at* auf *+acc*). (b) (*inf: make pottery*) töpfern (*inf*).

potable ['pəʊtəbl] *adj* (*form*) trinkbar.

potash ['pɒtæʃ] *n* Pottasche *f*, Kaliumkarbonat *nt*.

potassium [pə'tæsɪəm] *n* Kalium *nt* ◆ **~ cyanide** Kaliumzyanid, Zyankali *nt*; **~ nitrate** Kaliumnitrat *nt*, Kalisalpeter *m*.

potations [pəʊ'teɪʃənz] *npl* (*liter*) Zecherei *f*.

potato [pə'teɪtəʊ] *n, pl* **-es** Kartoffel *f*; *see* **hot ~**.

potato: ~ beetle, ~ bug (*esp US*) *n* Kartoffelkäfer *m*; **~ chip** (*esp US*), **~ crisp** (*Brit*) *n* Kartoffelchip *m*; **~ masher** *n* Kartoffelstampfer *m*; **~ peeler** *n* Kartoffelschäler *m*; **~ salad** *n* Kartoffelsalat *m*.

pot: ~bellied ['pɒt'belɪd] *adj person* spitzbäuchig; (*through hunger*) blähbäuchig; *stove* Kanonen-; **~belly** *n* (*stomach*) (*from overeating*) Spitzbauch *m*; (*from malnutrition*) Blähbauch *m*; (*stove*) Kanonenofen *m*; **~boiler** *n* rein kommerzielles Werk; **~-bound** *adj plant* eingewachsen.

poteen [pɒ'tiːn, pɒ'tʃiːn] *n illegal destillierter irischer Whisky*.

potency ['pəʊtənsɪ] *n see adj* Stärke *f*; Durchschlagskraft *f*; Potenz *f*; Macht *f*.

potent ['pəʊtənt] *adj drink, drug, charm, motive etc* stark; *argument, reason etc* durchschlagend; *man* potent; *ruler* mächtig.

potentate ['pəʊtənteɪt] *n* Potentat *m*.

potential [pəʊ'tenʃəl] [1] *adj* potentiell.
[2] *n* Potential *nt* (*also Elec, Math, Phys*) ◆ **the ~ for growth** das Wachstumspotential; **to have ~** ausbaufähig sein (*inf*); **he shows quite a bit of ~** es steckt einiges in ihm.

potentiality [pəʊ,tenʃɪ'ælɪtɪ] *n* Möglichkeit *f*.

▼ **potentially** [pəʊ'tenʃəlɪ] *adv* potentiell.

potful ['pɒtfʊl] *n* Topf *m*; (*of coffee, tea*) Kanne *f*.

pothead ['pɒthed] *n* (*sl*) Kiffer(in *f*) *m* (*sl*).

pother ['pɒðəʳ] *n* (*old*) Aufruhr, Wirbel *m* ◆ **to make a ~ about sth** wegen etw (ein) Theater machen.

pot: ~herb *n* Küchenkraut *nt*; **~hole** *n* (a) (*in road*) Schlagloch *nt*; (b) (*Geol*) Höhle *f*; **~holer** *n* Höhlenforscher(in *f*) *m*; **~holing** *n* Höhlenforschung *f*; **~hook** *n* (a) (*for pot*) Kesselhaken *m*; (b) (*in writing*) Krakel *m*; **~hunter** *n*

➤ LANGUAGE IN USE: **potentially** → 15.3

(a) (*Sport*) unwaidmännischer Jäger; **(b)** (*for prizes*) Pokalsammler(in *f*) *m*.
potion ['pəʊʃən] *n* Trank *m*.
pot: ~luck *n*: **to take ~luck** nehmen, was es gerade gibt; **we took ~luck and went to the nearest pub** wir gingen aufs Geratewohl in die nächste Kneipe; **~pie** *n* (*US*) in einer Auflaufform gebackene Pastete; **~pourri** [,pəʊpʊ'ri:] *n* **(a)** (*lit*) Duftsträußchen *nt*; **(b)** (*fig: mixture, medley*) (kunter)bunte Mischung; (*of music*) Potpourri *nt*; **~ roast** [1] *n* Schmorbraten *m*; [2] *vt* schmoren; **~sherd** *n* (*Archeol*) Scherbe *f*; **~shot** *n* Schuß *m* aufs Geratewohl; **to take a ~shot at sth** aufs Geratewohl auf etw (*acc*) schießen.
potted ['pɒtɪd] *adj* **(a)** *meat* eingemacht; *fish* eingelegt. **(b)** *plant* Topf-. **(c)** (*shortened*) *history, biography* gekürzt, zusammengefaßt ◆ **he gave me a ~ version of the film** er erzählte mir in kurzen Worten, wovon der Film handelte.
potter[1] ['pɒtə^r] *n* Töpfer(in *f*) *m* ◆ **~'s clay** Töpferton *m*; **~'s wheel** Töpferscheibe *f*.
potter[2], (*US also*) **putter** ['pʌtə^r] *vi* (*do little jobs*) herumwerkeln; (*wander aimlessly*) herumschlendern ◆ **she ~s away in the kitchen for hours** sie hantiert stundenlang in der Küche herum; **to ~ round the house** im Haus herumwerkeln; **to ~ round the shops** einen Geschäftebummel machen; **to ~ along the road** (*car, driver*) dahinzuckeln; **we ~ along quite happily** wir leben recht zufrieden vor uns hin; **you'd be on time if you didn't ~ about** *or* **around so much in the morning** du könntest pünktlich sein, wenn du morgens nicht so lange trödeln würdest.
potterer ['pɒtərə^r] *n* Trödelheini *m*, Trödelsuse *f*.
pottery ['pɒtərɪ] *n* (*workshop, craft*) Töpferei *f*; (*pots*) Töpferwaren, Tonwaren *pl*; (*glazed*) Keramik *f*; (*archaeological remains*) Tonscherben *pl*.
potting: ~ compost *n* Pflanzerde *f*; **~ shed** *n* Schuppen *m*.
potty[1] ['pɒtɪ] *n* (*esp Brit*) Töpfchen *nt* ◆ **~-trained** sauber.
potty[2] *adj* (*+er*) (*Brit inf: mad*) verrückt ◆ **to drive sb ~** jdn zum Wahnsinn treiben; **he's ~ about her** er ist verrückt nach ihr.
pouch [paʊtʃ] *n* Beutel *m*; (*under eyes*) (Tränen)sack *m*; (*of pelican, hamster*) Tasche *f*; (*Mil*) (Patronen)tasche *f*; (*Hist: for gunpowder*) (Pulver)beutel *m*; (*esp US: mail ~*) Postsack *m*.
pouf(fe) [pu:f] *n* **(a)** (*seat*) Puff *m*. **(b)** (*Brit inf*) *see* **poof(ter)**.
poulterer ['pəʊltərə^r] *n* (*Brit*) Geflügelhändler(in *f*) *m* ◆ **~'s (shop)** Geflügelhandlung *f*.
poultice ['pəʊltɪs] [1] *n* Umschlag, Wickel *m*; (*for boil*) Zugpflaster *nt*.
[2] *vt* einen Umschlag *or* Wickel machen um; ein Zugpflaster kleben auf (*+acc*).
poultry ['pəʊltrɪ] *n* Geflügel *nt* ◆ **~ farm** Geflügelfarm *f*; **~ farmer** Geflügelzüchter *m*; **~ farming** Geflügelzucht *f*; **~ house** Hühnerhaus *nt*; **~man** (*esp US*) (*farmer*) Geflügelzüchter(in *f*) *m*; (*dealer*) Geflügelhändler(in *f*) *m*.
pounce [paʊns] [1] *n* Sprung, Satz *m*; (*swoop by bird*) Angriff *m*; (*by police*) Zugriff *m*.
[2] *vi* (*cat, lion etc*) einen Satz machen; (*bird*) niederstoßen; (*fig*) zuschlagen ◆ **to ~ on sb/sth** (*lit, fig*) sich auf jdn/etw stürzen; (*bird*) auf etw (*acc*) niederstoßen; (*police*) sich (*dat*) jdn greifen/in etw (*dat*) eine Razzia machen.
pound[1] [paʊnd] *n* **(a)** (*weight*) ≃ Pfund *nt* ◆ **two ~s of apples** zwei Pfund Äpfel; **by the ~** pfundweise; **he is making sure he gets his ~ of flesh** er sorgt dafür, daß er bekommt, was ihm zusteht.
(b) (*money*) Pfund *nt* ◆ **one ~ sterling** ein Pfund *nt* Sterling; **five ~s** fünf Pfund; **a five-~ note** eine Fünfpfundnote, ein Fünfpfundschein *m*; *see* **penny**.
pound[2] [1] *vt* **(a)** (*hammer, strike*) hämmern; *earth, paving slabs* feststampfen; *meat* klopfen; *dough* kneten, schlagen; *piano, typewriter* hämmern auf (*+dat*); *table* hämmern auf (*+acc*); *door, wall* hämmern gegen; (*waves, sea*) *ship* schlagen gegen; (*guns, shells, bombs*) ununterbrochen beschießen; (*troops, artillery*) unter Beschuß haben ◆ **the boxer ~ed his opponent with his fists** der Boxer hämmerte mit den Fäusten auf seinen Gegner ein; **the ship was ~ed by the waves** die Wellen schlugen gegen das Schiff; **the old-style policeman ~ing his beat** der Polizist alten Stils, der seine Runde abmarschiert.
(b) (*pulverize*) *corn etc* (zer)stampfen; *drugs, spices* zerstoßen ◆ **to ~ sth to pieces** etw kleinstampfen; **the guns ~ed the walls to pieces** die Kanonen zertrümmerten die Mauern; **the bombs ~ed the city to rubble** die Bomben verwandelten die Stadt in ein Trümmerfeld; **the waves ~ed the boat to pieces** die Wellen zertrümmerten das Boot.
[2] *vi* **(a)** (*beat*) hämmern; (*heart*) (wild) pochen; (*waves, sea*) schlagen (*on, against* gegen); (*drums*) dröhnen; (*engine, steamer, hooves*) stampfen ◆ **he ~ed at** *or* **on the door/on the table** er hämmerte an *or* gegen die Tür/auf den Tisch.
(b) (*run heavily*) stampfen; (*walk heavily, stamp*) stapfen ◆ **the sound of ~ing feet** das Geräusch stampfender Füße; **the messenger ~ed up and handed me a telegram** der Bote stampfte auf mich zu und übergab mir ein Telegramm.
◆**pound away** *vi* hämmern; (*music, drums, guns*) dröhnen ◆ **our guns were ~ing ~ at the enemy position** wir hatten die feindliche Stellung unter anhaltendem Beschuß; **he was ~ing ~ at the typewriter** er hämmerte auf der Schreibmaschine herum.
◆**pound down** *vt sep earth, rocks* feststampfen ◆ **to ~ sth ~ to a powder** etw pulverisieren.
◆**pound out** *vt sep* **to ~ ~ a tune/letter** eine Melodie/einen Brief herunterhämmern.
pound[3] *n* (*for stray dogs*) städtischer Hundezwinger; (*for cars*) Abstellplatz *m* (*für amtlich abgeschleppte Fahrzeuge*).
poundage ['paʊndɪdʒ] *n* **(a)** *auf Pfundbasis berechnete Gebühr oder Abgabe.*
(b) (*weight*) Gewicht *nt* (in Pfund).
pound-cake ['paʊndkeɪk] *n* (*US*) *reichhaltiger Früchtekuchen.*
-pounder [-'paʊndə^r] *n suf* -pfünder *m* (*also Mil*).
pound foolish *adj see* **penny wise.**
pounding ['paʊndɪŋ] *n* **(a)** Hämmern *nt*; (*of heart*) Pochen *nt*; (*of music, drums*) Dröhnen *nt*; (*of waves, sea*) Schlagen *nt*; (*of engine, steamer, pile-driver, hooves, feet etc*) Stampfen *nt*; (*of guns, shells, bombs*) Bombardement *nt* ◆ **the ship took a ~ from the waves** das Schiff wurde von den Wellen stark mitgenommen; **the city took a ~ last night** gestern Nacht wurde die Stadt schwer bombardiert; **his theory took a ~ from the critics** seine Theorie wurde von den Kritikern scharf angegriffen; **our team took quite a ~ on Saturday** unsere Mannschaft hat am Samstag eine ziemliche Schlappe einstecken müssen (*inf*).
(b) (*of corn etc*) Zerstampfen *nt*; (*of drugs*) Zerstoßen *nt*.
pour [pɔ:^r] [1] *vt liquid* gießen; *large amount also, sugar, rice etc* schütten; *drink* eingießen, einschenken ◆ **to ~ sth for sb** jdm etw eingießen *or* einschenken; **to ~ the water off the potatoes** die Kartoffeln abgießen; **she looks as if she's been ~ed into that dress!** (*inf*) das Kleid sitzt wie angegossen (*inf*); **to ~ money into a project/men into a war** Geld in ein Projekt/Männer in einen Krieg pumpen (*inf*); **he ~ed all his ideas into one book** alle seine Gedanken flossen in ein Buch.
[2] *vi* **(a)** (*lit, fig*) strömen; (*smoke also*) hervorquellen ◆ **the sweat ~ed off him** der Schweiß floß in Strömen an ihm herunter; **books are ~ing off the presses** Bücher werden in Massen ausgestoßen; **cars ~ed along the road** Autokolonnen rollten die Straße entlang.
(b) (*rain*) **it's ~ing (with rain)** es gießt (in Strömen), es schüttet (*inf*); **the rain ~ed down** es regnete *or* goß in Strömen; *see* **rain**.
(c) (*~ out tea, coffee etc*) eingießen, einschenken; (*US: act as hostess*) als Gastgeberin fungieren.
(d) this jug doesn't ~ well dieser Krug gießt nicht gut.
◆**pour away** *vt sep* weggießen.
◆**pour forth** *vt sep see* **pour out 1, 2 (b, c).**
◆**pour in** [1] *vi* hinein-/hereinströmen; (*donations, protests*) in Strömen eintreffen.
[2] *vt sep money, men* hineinpumpen (*inf*).
◆**pour out** [1] *vi* hinaus-/herausströmen (*of* aus); (*smoke also*) hervorquellen (*of* aus); (*words*) heraussprudeln (*of* aus).
[2] *vt sep* **(a)** *liquid* ausgießen; (*in large quantities*) *sugar, rice etc* ausschütten; *drink* eingießen, einschenken.
(b) (*factories, schools*) *car, students* ausstoßen.
(c) (*fig*) *feelings, troubles, story* sich (*dat*) von der Seele reden ◆ **to ~ ~ one's thanks** sich überströmend bedanken; **to ~ ~ one's heart to sb** jdm sein Herz ausschütten.
pouring ['pɔ:rɪŋ] *adj* **~ rain** strömender Regen; **a ~ wet day** ein völlig verregneter Tag; **~ custard** Vanillesoße *f*.
pout [paʊt] [1] *n* **(a)** (*facial expression*) Schmollmund *m*; (*because upset also*) Flunsch *m* (*inf*), Schnute *f* (*inf*).
(b) (*sulking fit*) Schmollen *nt* ◆ **to have a ~** schmollen.
[2] *vi* **(a)** (*with lips*) einen Schmollmund machen; einen Flunsch *or* eine Schnute ziehen (*inf*).
(b) (*sulk*) schmollen.
[3] *vt lips* schürzen; (*sulkingly*) zu einem Schmollmund *or* Schmollen verziehen.
poverty ['pɒvətɪ] *n* Armut *f* ◆ **~ of ideas** gedankliche Armut; **~-stricken** notleidend; *conditions* kümmerlich; **to be ~-stricken** Armut leiden; (*hum inf*) am Hungertuch nagen (*hum*); **to be above/below the ~ line** oberhalb/unterhalb der Armutsgrenze leben; **~ trap** *Situation f, wobei (vermehrte) Einkünfte zu einer Verringerung/zum Wegfall von Sozialleistungen führen*, Armutsfalle *f*.
PoW *abbr of* **prisoner of war.**
powder ['paʊdə^r] [1] *n* Pulver *nt*; (*face, talcum ~ etc*) Puder *m*; (*dust*) Staub *m* ◆ **to grind sth to ~** etw pulverig *or* zu Pulver mahlen; **to reduce sth to ~** etw zu Pulver machen.
[2] *vt* **(a)** *milk* pulverisieren; *sugar* stoßen; *chalk* zermahlen.
(b) (*apply ~ to*) *face, body, oneself* pudern ◆ **to ~ one's nose** (*lit*) sich (*dat*) die Nase pudern; (*euph*) kurz verschwinden (*euph*); **the trees were ~ed with snow** die Bäume waren mit Schnee überzuckert.
[3] *vi* (*crumble*) (zu Staub) zerfallen ◆ **it ~s easily** es zerfällt leicht; **the cement had ~ed away** der Mörtel war zu Staub zerfallen.
powder: ~ blue [1] *adj* taubenblau; [2] *n* Taubenblau *nt*; **~ compact** *n* Puderdose *f*.
powdered ['paʊdəd] *adj milk, eggs, chalk* -pulver *nt* ◆ **~ sugar** (*US*) Puderzucker, Staubzucker (*Aus*) *m*.
powder-horn ['paʊdə,hɔ:n] *n* Pulverhorn *nt*.
powdering ['paʊdərɪŋ] *n* (*liter*) **there was a light ~ of snow on the grass** das Gras war leicht mit Schnee überzuckert.
powder: ~ keg *n* (*lit, fig*) Pulverfaß *nt*; **~ magazine** *n* Pulvermagazin *nt*, Pulverkammer *f*; **~-monkey** *n* (*Mil Hist*) Pulverjunge *m*; (*explosives man*) Sprengmeister *m*; **~ puff** *n* Puderquaste *f*; **~ room** *n* Damentoilette *f*; **~ snow** *n* Pulverschnee *m*.
powdery ['paʊdərɪ] *adj* **(a)** (*like powder*) pulvrig. **(b)** (*crumbly*) bröckelig; *bones* morsch. **(c)** (*covered with powder*) gepudert.
power ['paʊə^r] [1] *n* **(a)** *no pl* (*physical strength*) Kraft *f*; (*force: of blow, explosion etc*) Stärke, Gewalt, Wucht *f*; (*fig: of argument etc*) Überzeugungskraft *f* ◆ **more ~ to your elbow!** (*inf*) setz dich/setzt euch durch!; **the ~ of love/log-**

ic/tradition die Macht der Liebe/Logik/Tradition.

(b) (*faculty, ability*) (*of hearing, imagination*) Vermögen *nt no pl* ◆ **his ~s of hearing** sein Hörvermögen *nt*; **mental/hypnotic ~s** geistige/hypnotische Kräfte *pl*; **to weaken their ~(s) of resistance** um ihre Widerstandskraft zu schwächen.

(c) (*capacity, ability to help etc*) Macht *f* ◆ **he did all in his ~ to help them** er tat (alles), was in seiner Macht *or* in seinen Kräften stand, um ihnen zu helfen; **it's beyond my** *or* **not within my ~ to ...** es steht nicht in meiner Macht, zu ...

(d) (*no pl: sphere or strength of influence, authority*) Macht *f*; (*Jur, parental*) Gewalt *f*; (*usu pl: thing one has authority to do*) Befugnis *f* ◆ **he has the ~ to act** er ist handlungsberechtigt; **the ~ of the police/of the law** die Macht der Polizei/des Gesetzes; **to be in sb's ~** in jds Gewalt (*dat*) sein; **that does not fall within my ~(s)/that is beyond** *or* **outside my ~(s)** das fällt nicht in meinen Machtbereich/das überschreitet meine Befugnisse; **~ of attorney** (*Jur*) (Handlungs)vollmacht *f*; **the party now in ~** die Partei, die im Augenblick an der Macht ist; **to fall from ~** abgesetzt werden; **to come into ~** an die Macht kommen; **they have no ~ over economic matters** in Wirtschaftsfragen haben sie keine Befugnisse; **I have no ~ over her** ich habe keine Gewalt über sie; **he has been given full ~(s) to make all decisions** man hat ihm volle Entscheidungsgewalt übertragen; **that man has no ~ over his destiny** daß der Mensch keine Gewalt über sein Schicksal hat; **"student/worker ~"** „Macht den Studenten/Arbeitern".

(e) (*person or institution having authority*) Autorität *f*, Machtfaktor *m* ◆ **to be the ~ behind the scenes/throne** die graue Eminenz sein; **the ~s that be** (*inf*) die da oben (*inf*); **the ~s of darkness/evil** die Mächte der Finsternis/des Bösen.

(f) (*nation*) Macht *f* ◆ **a four-~ conference** eine Viermächtekonferenz; **a naval ~** eine Seemacht.

(g) (*source of energy: nuclear, electric ~ etc*) Energie *f*; (*of water, steam also*) Kraft *f* ◆ **the ship made port under her own ~** das Schiff lief mit eigener Kraft in den Hafen ein; **they cut off the ~** (*electricity*) sie haben den Strom abgestellt.

(h) (*of engine, machine, loudspeakers, transmitter*) Leistung *f*; (*of microscope, lens, sun's rays, drug, chemical*) Stärke *f* ◆ **the ~ of suggestion** die Wirkung *or* Wirkkraft des Unterschwelligen; **a low-~ microscope** ein schwaches Mikroskop; **a 10-~ magnification** eine 10-fache Vergrößerung.

(i) (*Math*) Potenz *f* ◆ **to the ~ (of) 2** hoch 2, in der 2. Potenz.

(j) (*inf: a lot of*) **a ~ of help** eine wertvolle *or* große Hilfe; **that did me a ~ of good** das hat mir unheimlich gutgetan (*inf*).

[2] *vt* (*engine*) antreiben; (*fuel*) betreiben ◆ **~ed by electricity/by jet engines** mit Elektro-/Düsenantrieb; **as he ~s his way down the straight** wie er die Gerade entlangbraust; **he ~ed the ball into the net** er schoß den Ball mit Wucht ins Netz, er bombte den Ball ins Netz (*sl*).

[3] *vi* (*runner, racing car*) rasen ◆ **he ~ed away from the rest of the field** er raste dem übrigen Feld davon; **the swimmer ~ed through the water** der Schwimmer wuchtete durch das Wasser; **we're ~ing through the work now** unsere Arbeit geht jetzt mit Riesenschritten voran.

◆**power down** *vi* (*engine, turbine*) zum Stillstand kommen.

◆**power up** [1] *vt sep* starten.
[2] *vi* starten.

power: ~ base *n* Machtbasis *f*; **~boat** *n* Rennboot *nt*; **~ brakes** *npl* Servobremsen *pl*; **~ cable** *n* Stromkabel *nt*; **~ cut** *n* Stromsperre *f*; (*accidental*) Stromausfall *m*; **~ dive** (*Aviat*) [1] *n* (Vollgas)sturzflug *m*; [2] *vi* einen Sturzflug machen; **~ drill** *n* Bohrmaschine *f*; **~-driven** *adj tool* Motor-; **~ failure** *n* Stromausfall *m*.

powerful ['paʊəfʊl] *adj* **(a)** (*influential*) *government, person* mächtig, einflußreich.
(b) (*strong*) *boxer, engine, magnet, drug, emotions* stark; *stroke, punch, detergent* kraftvoll; *build, arm* kräftig.
(c) (*fig*) *speaker, actor* mitreißend; *music, film, performance also* ausdrucksvoll; *argument* durchschlagend, massiv (*inf*); *salesman* überzeugend.
(d) a ~ lot of (*dial*) ganz schön viel (*inf*), gehörig viel (*inf*).

powerfully ['paʊəfəlɪ] *adv* **(a)** kraftvoll ◆ **~ built** kräftig gebaut. **(b)** (*fig*) *speak* kraftvoll; *describe, act also* mitreißend; *argue* massiv (*inf*) ◆ **I was ~ affected by the book** das Buch hat mich mächtig (*inf*) *or* stark beeindruckt.

powerhouse ['paʊəhaʊs] *n* **(a)** (*lit*) *see* **power station**. **(b)** (*fig*) treibende Kraft (*behind u* hinter +*dat*) ◆ **he's a real ~/an intellectual ~** er ist ein äußerst dynamischer Mensch/er hat eine erstaunliche intellektuelle Kapazität; **he's a ~ of new ideas** er hat einen unerschöpflichen Vorrat an neuen Ideen.

power: ~less *adj* (*physically*) *punch, body* kraftlos; (*as regards ability to act*) *committee, person* machtlos; **to be ~less to resist** nicht die Kraft haben, zu widerstehen; **the government is ~less to deal with inflation** die Regierung steht der Inflation machtlos gegenüber; **we are ~less to help you** es steht nicht in unserer Macht, Ihnen zu helfen, wir sind machtlos; **~ loom** *n* Webmaschine *f*; **~ mower** *n* Motor-Rasenmäher *m*; (*electric*) Elektrorasenmäher *m*; **~ pack** *n* (*Elec*) Netzteil *nt*; (*inf: engine*) Motor *m*, Kraftpaket *nt* (*inf*); **~ plant** *n* **(a)** *see* **~ station**; **(b)** (*engine*) Motor *m*; **~ point** *n* (*Elec*) Steckdose *f*; **~ politics** *npl* Machtpolitik *f*; **~ saw** *n* Motorsäge *f*; (*electric*) Elektrosäge *f*; **~ station** *n* Kraftwerk *nt*; Elektrizitätswerk *nt*; **~ steering** *n* (*Aut*) Servolenkung *f*; **~ structure** *n* Machtstruktur *f*; **~ struggle** *n* Machtkampf *m*; **~ tool** *n* Elektrowerkzeug *nt*; **~-up** *n* Start *m*; **~ worker** *n* Elektrizitätsarbeiter *m*.

powwow ['paʊwaʊ] *n* (*of Red Indians*) Versammlung *f*; (*with Red Indians*) indianische Verhandlungen *pl*; (*inf*) Besprechung *f*; (*to solve problem*) Kriegsrat *m* (*hum*) ◆ **a family ~** ein Familienrat *m*.

pox [pɒks] *n* (*old*) (*small~*) Pocken, Blattern *pl*; (*syphilis*) Syphilis *f* ◆ **a ~ on ...!** (*old*) zur Hölle mit ...!

pp *abbr of* **(a) pages** S. **(b) per procurationem** (*on behalf of*) pp., ppa.

PPE *abbr of* **Philosophy, Politics and Economics.**

PPS *abbr of* **post-postscriptum** PPS.

PR [piːˈɑːʳ] *n abbr of* **(a) proportional representation. (b) public relations** PR *f* ◆ **~ agency** PR-Agentur *f*; **~ man** PR-Mann *m*; **~ work** PR-Arbeit, Öffentlichkeitsarbeit *f*.

pr *abbr of* **pair.**

practicability [ˌpræktɪkəˈbɪlɪtɪ] *n see adj* Durchführbarkeit, Praktikabilität (*rare*) *f*; Befahrbarkeit *f*.

practicable [ˈpræktɪkəbl] *adj* durchführbar, praktikabel; *road* befahrbar.

practicably [ˈpræktɪkəblɪ] *adv* **if it can ~ be done** falls (es) durchführbar (ist).

practical [ˈpræktɪkəl] *adj* praktisch; *person* praktisch (veranlagt) ◆ **to have a ~ mind** praktisch denken; **his ideas have no ~ application** seine Ideen sind nicht praxisnah *or* praktisch nicht anwendbar.

practicality [ˌpræktɪˈkælɪtɪ] *n* **(a)** *no pl* (*of person*) praktische Veranlagung ◆ **a person of great ~** ein sehr praktisch veranlagter Mensch. **(b)** *no pl* (*of scheme etc*) Durchführbarkeit *f* ◆ **your solution shows/lacks ~** Ihre Lösung ist praxisnah/-fremd. **(c)** (*practical detail*) praktische Einzelheit.

practical: ~ joke *n* Streich *m*; **~ joker** *n* Witzbold *m* (*inf*).

practically [ˈpræktɪkəlɪ] *adv* (*all senses*) praktisch.

practical nurse *n* (*US*) ≃ Hilfsschwester *f*.

practice [ˈpræktɪs] [1] *n* **(a)** (*habit, custom*) (*of individual*) Gewohnheit, Angewohnheit *f*; (*of group, in country*) Brauch *m*, Sitte *f*; (*bad habit*) Unsitte *f*; (*in business*) Verfahrensweise, Praktik *f* ◆ **he opposes the ~ of pubs being open on Sundays** er ist dagegen, daß Lokale am Sonntag geöffnet sind; **this is normal business ~** das ist im Geschäftsleben so üblich; **as is my (usual) ~** wie es meine Gewohnheit ist; **to make a ~ of doing sth, to make it a ~ to do sth** es sich (*dat*) zur Gewohnheit machen, etw zu tun; **Christian ~ dictates ...** das christliche Brauchtum verlangt ...; **it is the ~ of this Court to ...** es ist an diesem Gericht üblich, zu ...; **that's common ~** das ist allgemeine Praxis *or* allgemein üblich.

(b) (*exercise, training*) Übung *f*; (*rehearsal, trial run*) Probe *f*; (*Sport*) Training *nt*; (*~ game*) Trainingsspiel *nt* ◆ **~ makes perfect** (*Prov*) Übung macht den Meister (*Prov*); **Niki Lauda had the fastest time in ~** Niki Lauda fuhr im Training die schnellste Zeit; **this piece of music needs a lot of ~** für dieses (Musik)stück muß man viel üben; **you should do 10 minutes' ~ each day** du solltest täglich 10 Minuten (lang) üben; **to be out of/in ~** aus der/in Übung sein; **that was just a ~ run** das war nur mal zur Probe; **to have a ~ session** üben; Probe haben; trainieren; **the first ~ session** die erste Übung/Probe/das erste Training.

(c) (*doing, as opposed to theory*) Praxis *f* ◆ **in ~** in der Praxis; **that won't work in ~** das läßt sich praktisch nicht durchführen; **to put one's ideas into ~** seine Ideen in die Praxis umsetzen.

(d) (*of doctor, lawyer etc*) Praxis *f* ◆ **he took up the ~ of law/medicine** er praktizierte als Rechtsanwalt/Arzt; **to go into** *or* **set up in ~** eine Praxis aufmachen *or* eröffnen, sich als Arzt/Rechtsanwalt *etc* niederlassen; **not to be in ~ any more** nicht mehr praktizieren; **to retire from ~** sich aus der Praxis zurückziehen; **a large legal ~** eine große Rechtsanwaltspraxis.

[2] *vti* (*US*) *see* **practise.**

practise, (*US*) **practice** [ˈpræktɪs] [1] *vt* **(a)** *thrift, patience etc* üben; *self-denial, Christian charity* praktizieren ◆ **to ~ what one preaches** (*prov*) seine Lehren in die Tat umsetzen.

(b) (*in order to acquire skill*) üben; *song, chorus* proben ◆ **to ~ the violin** Geige üben; **to ~ the high jump/one's golf swing** Hochsprung/seinen Schlag im Golf üben *or* trainieren; **to ~ doing sth** etw üben; **I'm practising my German on him** ich probiere mein Deutsch an ihm aus.

(c) (*follow, exercise*) *profession, religion* ausüben, praktizieren ◆ **to ~ law/medicine** als Anwalt/Arzt praktizieren; **all a writer wants is peace to ~ his art** alles, was ein Schriftsteller braucht, ist Ruhe, um sich seiner Kunst widmen zu können.

[2] *vi* **(a)** (*in order to acquire skill*) üben.

(b) (*lawyer, doctor etc*) praktizieren ◆ **to ~ at the bar** als Anwalt bei Gericht praktizieren.

practised, (*US*) **practiced** [ˈpræktɪst] *adj* geübt; *marksman, liar also* erfahren ◆ **with a ~ eye/hand** mit geübtem Auge/geübter Hand; **he's ~ in getting his own way** er hat Übung darin, seinen Willen durchzusetzen; **with ~ skill** gekonnt.

practising, (*US*) **practicing** [ˈpræktɪsɪŋ] *adj lawyer, doctor, homosexual* praktizierend; *Christian also, socialist* aktiv.

practitioner [prækˈtɪʃənəʳ] *n* (*of method*) Benutzer, Anwender *m*; (*medical ~*) praktischer Arzt, praktische Ärztin; (*dental ~*) Zahnarzt *m*/-ärztin *f*; (*legal ~*) Rechtsanwalt *m*/-anwältin *f* ◆ **~s of this profession** diejenigen, die diesen Beruf ausüben; **a ~ of Zen Buddhism/Christianity** ein Anhänger *m* des Zen-Buddhismus/ein praktizierender Christ; *see* **general ~.**

praesidium [prɪˈsɪdɪəm] *n see* **presidium.**

praetor [ˈpriːtəʳ] *n* Prätor *m*.

Praetorian Guard [prɪˈtɔːrɪənˈgɑːd] *n* (*body*) Prätorianer *pl*.

pragmatic *adj*, **~ally** *adv* [prægˈmætɪk, -əlɪ] pragmatisch.

pragmatism [ˈprægmətɪzəm] *n* Pragmatismus *m*.

pragmatist [ˈprægmətɪst] *n* Pragmatiker(in *f*) *m*.

Prague [prɑːg] *n* Prag *nt*.

prairie [ˈprɛərɪ] *n* Grassteppe *f*; (*in North America*) Prärie *f*.

prairie: ~ chicken *n* (*US*) Präriehuhn *nt*; **~ dog** *n* Präriehund *m*; **~ oyster**

n Prärieauster *f*; ~ **schooner** *n* Planwagen *m*; ~ **wolf** *n* Präriewolf *m*.
praise [preɪz] [1] *vt* loben; (*to others, worshipfully also*) preisen (*geh*), rühmen (*geh*) ♦ **to ~ sb for having done sth** jdn dafür loben, etw getan zu haben.
[2] *n* Lob *nt no pl* ♦ **a hymn of ~** eine Lobeshymne; **a poem in ~ of beer** ein Loblied *nt* auf das Bier; **he spoke/held a speech in ~ of their efforts** er sprach lobend von ihren Bemühungen/hielt eine Lobrede auf ihre Bemühungen; **to win ~** (*person*) Lob ernten; (*efforts*) Lob einbringen; **to be loud** *or* **warm in one's ~ (of sth)** voll des Lobes (für etw) sein; **I have nothing but ~ for him** ich kann ihn nur loben; **he's beyond ~** er ist über jedes *or* alles Lob erhaben; **all ~ to him** alle Achtung!; **~ indeed!** (*also iro*) ein hohes Lob; **~ from him is ~ indeed** Lob aus seinem Mund will etwas heißen; **~ be to God!** (*in church*) gelobt sei der Herr!; **~(s) be!** Gott sei Dank!; *see* **sing**.
praiseworthiness ['preɪz,wɜːðɪnɪs] *n* (*of attempt, effort*) Löblichkeit *f* ♦ **I don't doubt his ~/the ~ of his motives** ich zweifle nicht an seinen lobenswerten Absichten/daran, daß seine Motive lobenswert sind.
praiseworthy ['preɪz,wɜːðɪ] *adj* lobenswert.
praline ['prɑːliːn] *n* Praline *f* mit Nuß-Karamelfüllung.
pram [præm] *n* (*Brit*) Kinderwagen *m*; (*dolls'*) Puppenwagen *m*.
prance [prɑːns] *vi* (*horse*) tänzeln; (*person*) (*jump around*) herumhüpfen *or* -tanzen; (*walk gaily, mince*) tänzeln ♦ **she was prancing about with nothing on** sie lief nackt durch die Gegend; **to ~ in/out** (*person*) herein-/hinausspazieren.
prang [præŋ] (*esp Brit inf*) [1] *n* (*crash*) Bums *m* (*inf*); (*of plane*) Bruchlandung *f*.
[2] *interj* krach.
[3] *vt* **(a)** (*crash*) *car* ramponieren (*inf*), lädieren; *plane* eine Bruchlandung machen. **(b)** (*bomb*) zerbomben, zusammenbomben (*inf*).
prank [præŋk] *n* Streich *m*; (*harmless also*) Ulk *m* ♦ **to play a ~ on sb** jdm einen Streich spielen; einen Ulk mit jdm machen.
prankish ['præŋkɪʃ] *adj person* zu Streichen aufgelegt *or* bereit; *behaviour, act* schelmisch.
prankster ['præŋkstə^r] *n* Schelm *m*.
praseodymium [,preɪzɪəʊ'dɪmɪəm] *n* (*Chem*) Praseodym *nt*.
prat [præt] *n* (*Brit sl: idiot*) Trottel *m* (*inf*).
prate [preɪt] *vi* faseln, schwafeln.
prating ['preɪtɪŋ] [1] *n* Gefasel, Geschwafel *nt*.
[2] *adj* faselnd, schwafelnd.
prattle ['prætl] [1] *n* Geplapper *nt*.
[2] *vi* plappern.
prawn [prɔːn] *n* Garnele *f* ♦ **~ cocktail** Krabbencocktail *m*.
pray [preɪ] [1] *vi* **(a)** (*say prayers*) beten ♦ **let us ~** lasset uns beten; **to ~ for sb/sth** für jdn/um etw beten; **to ~ for sth** (*want it badly*) stark auf etw (*acc*) hoffen; **he's past ~ing for!** (*inf*) bei ihm ist alles zu spät (*inf*), er ist nicht mehr zu retten (*inf*).
(b) (*old, liter*) **~ take a seat** bitte, nehmen Sie doch Platz, wollen Sie bitte Platz nehmen?; **what good is that, ~ (tell)?** was hilft das, wenn ich mir die Frage gestatten darf?
[2] *vt* (*old, liter*) inständig bitten, ersuchen (*geh*) ♦ **I ~ you tell me** (*old*) bitte, erzählen Sie mir doch; (*stronger*) ich bitte Sie inständig, erzählen Sie mir doch; **and what is that, I ~ you?** und was ist das, wenn ich mir die Frage gestatten darf?; **they ~ed the king for mercy** sie flehten den König um Gnade an (*geh*).
prayer [prɛə^r] *n* Gebet *nt*; (*service, ~ meeting*) Andacht *f* ♦ **to say one's ~s** beten, seine Gebete verrichten (*geh*); **to be at ~** beim Gebet sein; **a ~ for peace** ein Gebet für den Frieden; **a life of ~** ein Leben im Gebet; **Evening P~** Abendandacht *f*; **we attended Morning P~** wir besuchten die Morgenandacht; **we have ~s every morning** wir haben jeden Morgen eine Andacht; **family ~s** Hausandacht *f*; **the Book of Common P~** *das Gebetbuch der anglikanischen Kirche*.
prayer: ~ beads *npl* Gebetsperlen *pl*; **~ book** *n* Gebetbuch *nt*; **~ mat** *n* Gebetsteppich *m*; **~ meeting** *n* Gebetsstunde *f*; **~ rug** *n see* **~ mat**; **~ shawl** *n* Gebetsmantel *m*; **~ wheel** *n* Gebetsmühle *f*.
praying mantis ['preɪɪŋ'mæntɪs] *n* Gottesanbeterin *f*.
pre- [priː-] *pref* vor-; (*esp with Latinate words in German*) prä- ♦ **at ~-1980 prices** zu Preisen von vor 1980.
preach [priːtʃ] [1] *vt* predigen; (*fig*) *advantages etc* propagieren ♦ **to ~ a sermon** (*lit, fig*) eine Predigt halten; **to ~ the gospel** das Evangelium verkünden.
[2] *vi* (*give a sermon, be moralistic*) predigen ♦ **who is ~ing today?** wer predigt heute, wer hält heute die Predigt?; **to ~ to/at sb** jdm eine Predigt halten; **to ~ to the converted** (*prov*) offene Türen einrennen.
preacher ['priːtʃə^r] *n* Prediger *m*; (*fig: moraliser*) Moralprediger(in *f*) *m* ♦ **all these ~s of détente** alle diese Entspannungsprediger.
preachify ['priːtʃɪfaɪ] *vi* (*pej inf*) predigen, moralisieren.
preaching ['priːtʃɪŋ] *n* (*lit, fig*) (*act*) Predigen *nt*; (*sermon*) Predigt *f*.
preachy ['priːtʃɪ] *adj* (*inf*) moralisierend.
preadolescent [,priːædə'lesənt] *adj* vorpubertär.
preamble [priː'æmbl] *n* Einleitung *f*; (*of book*) Vorwort *nt*; (*Jur*) Präambel *f*.
preamplifier [priː'æmplɪ,faɪə^r], **preamp** (*inf*) [priː'æmp] *n* Vorverstärker *m*.
prearrange ['priːə'reɪndʒ] *vt* vorher vereinbaren.
prebend ['prebənd] *n* (*form*) (*stipend*) Pfründe, Präbende *f*; (*person*) Pfründner, Pfründeninhaber, Präbendar(ius) *m*.
prebendary ['prebəndərɪ] *n* Pfründner, Pfründeninhaber, Präbendar(ius) *m*.
Pre-Cambrian [priː'kæmbrɪən] *adj* präkambrisch.
precarious [prɪ'kɛərɪəs] *adj* unsicher; *situation also, relationship* prekär; *theory, assertion* anfechtbar ♦ **that cup/that shelf looks somewhat ~** die Tasse/das Regal sieht ziemlich gefährlich aus.
precariously [prɪ'kɛərɪəslɪ] *adv* **to be ~ balanced** (*lit, fig*) auf der Kippe stehen; **he lived rather ~ from his work as a photographer** er verdiente einen ziemlich unsicheren Lebensunterhalt als Photograph; **~ perched on the edge of the table** gefährlich nahe am Tischrand; **with a cup ~ balanced on the end of his nose** eine Tasse auf der Nase balancierend.
precast [priː'kɑːst] (*vb: pret, ptp* ~) [1] *vt* vorfertigen.
[2] *adj concrete* Fertigteil-, vorgefertigt.
precaution [prɪ'kɔːʃən] *n* Sicherheitsmaßnahme, (Sicherheits)vorkehrung, Vorsichtsmaßnahme *f* ♦ **to take ~s against sth** Vorsichtsmaßnahmen *pl* gegen etw treffen; **do you take ~s?** (*euph: use contraception*) nimmst *or* machst du (irgend) etwas?; **to take the ~ of doing sth** vorsichtshalber *or* sicherheitshalber etw tun.
precautionary [prɪ'kɔːʃənərɪ] *adj* Vorsichts-, Sicherheits-, vorbeugend ♦ **it's purely ~** es ist eine reine *or* nur eine Vorsichtsmaßnahme.
precede [prɪ'siːd] *vt* (*in order, time*) vorangehen (+*dat*); (*in importance*) gehen vor (+*dat*); (*in rank*) stehen über (+*dat*) ♦ **for a month preceding this** den (ganzen) Monat davor; **to ~ a lecture with a joke** einem Vortrag einen Witz vorausschicken.
precedence ['presɪdəns] *n* (*of person*) vorrangige Stellung (*over* gegenüber); (*of problem etc*) Vorrang *m* (*over* vor +*dat*) ♦ **to take/have ~ over sb/sth** jdm/einer Sache gegenüber eine Vorrangstellung einnehmen/vor jdm/etw Vorrang haben; **to give ~ to sb/sth** jdm/einer Sache Vorrang geben; **the guests entered the hall in order of ~** die Gäste betraten die Halle in der Reihenfolge ihres (gesellschaftlichen) Rangs; **dukes have ~ over barons** Herzöge stehen im Rang höher als Barone.
precedent ['presɪdənt] *n* Präzedenzfall *m*; (*Jur also*) Präjudiz *nt* ♦ **according to ~** nach den bisherigen Fällen; **against all the ~s** entgegen allen früheren Fällen; **without ~** noch nie dagewesen; **to establish** *or* **create** *or* **set a ~** einen Präzedenzfall schaffen; **is there any ~ for this?** ist der Fall schon einmal dagewesen?; **there is no ~ for this decision** diese Entscheidung kann sich nicht an einem vergleichbaren Fall ausrichten.
preceding [prɪ'siːdɪŋ] *adj time, month etc* vorangegangen; *page, example also* vorhergehend.
precentor [prɪ'sentə^r] *n* Vorsänger, Präzentor (*spec*) *m*.
precept ['priːsept] *n* Grundsatz *m*, Prinzip *nt*.
preceptor [prɪ'septə^r] *n* (*old, form*) Lehrer, Präzeptor (*old*) *m*.
pre-Christian [priː'krɪstɪən] *adj* vorchristlich.
precinct ['priːsɪŋkt] *n* (*pedestrian ~*) Fußgängerzone *f*; (*shopping ~*) Geschäfts- *or* Einkaufsviertel *nt*; (*US: police ~*) Revier *nt*; (*US: voting ~*) Bezirk *m* ♦ **~s** *pl* (*grounds, premises*) Gelände, Areal *nt*; (*environs*) Umgebung *f*; (*of cathedral*) Domfreiheit *f*.
preciosity [,presɪ'ɒsɪtɪ] *n* Preziosität *f*.
precious ['preʃəs] [1] *adj* **(a)** (*costly*) wertvoll, kostbar ♦ **~ stone/metal** Edelstein *m*/Edelmetall *nt*.
(b) (*treasured*) wertvoll; (*iro*) hochverehrt, heißgeliebt ♦ **my ~ (one)!** mein Schatz!; **I have very ~ memories of that time/of him** ich habe Erinnerungen an diese Zeit/an ihn, die mir sehr wertvoll *or* teuer (*geh*) sind.
(c) *language, humour etc* preziös.
[2] *adv* (*inf*) **~ little/few** herzlich wenig/wenige (*inf*); **I had ~ little choice** ich hatte keine große Wahl.
precipice ['presɪpɪs] *n* Steilabfall *m*; (*lit liter, fig*) Abgrund *m*.
precipitance [prɪ'sɪpɪtəns], **precipitancy** [prɪ'sɪpɪtənsɪ] *n* (*hastiness*) Hast, Eile *f*; (*overhastiness*) Voreiligkeit, Überstürztheit, Überstürzung *f*.
precipitant [prɪ'sɪpɪtənt] [1] *n* (Aus)fällungsmittel *nt*.
[2] *adj see* **precipitate 2**.
precipitate [prɪ'sɪpɪteɪt] [1] *n* (*Met*) Niederschlag *m*; (*Chem also*) Präzipitat *nt* (*spec*).
[2] [prə'sɪpɪtɪt] *adj* (*hasty*) hastig, eilig; (*overhasty*) übereilt, voreilig, überstürzt.
[3] *vt* **(a)** (*hurl*) schleudern; (*downwards*) hinunter- *or* hinabschleudern; (*fig*) stürzen. **(b)** (*hasten*) beschleunigen. **(c)** (*Chem*) (aus)fällen; (*Met*) niederschlagen.
[4] *vi* (*Chem*) ausfallen; (*Met*) sich niederschlagen.
precipitately [prɪ'sɪpɪtɪtlɪ] *adv see adj*.
precipitation [prɪ,sɪpɪ'teɪʃən] *n* **(a)** *see vt* Schleudern *nt*; Hinunter- *or* Hinabschleudern *nt*; Sturz *m*; Beschleunigung *f*; Ausfällen *nt*, (Aus)fällung *f*; Niederschlag *m*. **(b)** (*haste*) Hast, Eile *f*; (*over-hastiness*) Übereile, Übereiltheit, Überstürztheit *f*. **(c)** (*Met*) Niederschlag *m*.
precipitous [prɪ'sɪpɪtəs] *adj* steil; (*hasty*) überstürzt.
precipitously [prɪ'sɪpɪtəslɪ] *adv see adj* ♦ **to fall away ~** (*ground etc*) senkrecht *or* jäh abfallen.
précis ['preɪsiː] *n* Zusammenfassung *f*; (*Sch*) Inhaltsangabe *f*.
precise [prɪ'saɪs] *adj* genau; *answer, description etc, worker also* präzis ♦ **at that ~ moment** genau in dem Augenblick; **this was the ~ amount I needed** das war genau *or* exakt der Betrag, den ich brauchte; **please be more ~** drücken Sie sich bitte etwas genauer *or* deutlicher aus; **but was it this ~ colour?** aber war es genau diese Farbe?; **18, to be ~** 18, um genau zu sein; **or, to be more ~, ...** oder, um es genauer zu sagen, ...; **in that ~ voice of hers** präzise *or* exakt, wie sie nun einmal spricht; **these ~ British accents** die akzentuierte Aussprache der Briten.
precisely [prɪ'saɪslɪ] *adv* genau; *answer, describe, work also* präzis; *use instrument* exakt ♦ **at ~ 7 o'clock, at 7 o'clock ~** Punkt 7 Uhr, genau um 7 Uhr; **what ~ do you mean/want?** was meinen/wollen Sie eigentlich genau?; **but it is ~**

because the money supply is ... aber gerade deshalb, weil das Kapital ... ist; **that is ~ why I don't want it** genau deshalb will ich es nicht; **~ nothing** gar nichts.

preciseness [prɪ'saɪsnɪs] *n* Genauigkeit, Exaktheit *f*.

precision [prɪ'sɪʒən] *n* Genauigkeit *f*; (*of work, movement also*) Präzision *f*.

precision: ~ bombing *n* gezielter Bombenabwurf; **~-engineered** *adj* präzisionsgefertigt; **~ instrument** *n* Präzisionsinstrument *nt*; **~-made** *adj* präzisionsgefertigt; **~ tool** *n* Präzisionswerkzeug *nt*; **~ work** *n* Präzisionsarbeit *f*.

preclassical [priː'klæsɪkəl] *adj* vorklassisch.

preclude [prɪ'kluːd] *vt misunderstanding* ausschließen ◆ **to ~ sb from doing sth** jdn daran hindern, etw zu tun.

precocious [prɪ'kəʊʃəs] *adj interest, teenager, behaviour* frühreif; *statement, way of speaking* altklug.

precociously [prɪ'kəʊʃəslɪ] *adv* frühreif; *talk* altklug ◆ **~ dressed** auf „alt" angezogen (*inf*).

precociousness [prɪ'kəʊʃəsnɪs],

precocity [prɪ'kɒsɪtɪ] *n see adj* Frühreife *f*; Altklugheit *f*.

precognition [ˌpriːkɒg'nɪʃən] *n* (*Psych*) Präkognition *f*; (*knowledge*) vorherige Kenntnis, vorheriges Wissen.

preconceived [ˌpriːkən'siːvd] *adj opinion, idea* vorgefaßt.

preconception [ˌpriːkən'sepʃən] *n* vorgefaßte Meinung.

precondition [ˌpriːkən'dɪʃən] *n* (Vor)bedingung, Voraussetzung *f* ◆ **to make sth a ~** etw zur Voraussetzung *or* Bedingung machen.

precook [priː'kʊk] *vt* vorkochen.

precursor [priː'kɜːsəʳ] *n* Vorläufer *m*; (*herald: of event etc*) Vorbote *m*; (*in office*) (Amts)vorgänger(in *f*) *m*.

precursory [priː'kɜːsərɪ] *adj* einleitend.

predate [ˌpriː'deɪt] *vt* (*precede*) zeitlich vorangehen (+*dat*); *cheque, letter* zurückdatieren.

predator ['predətəʳ] *n* (*animal*) Raubtier *nt*; (*person*) Plünderer *m* ◆ **the main ~s of the gazelle** die Hauptfeinde der Gazelle.

predatory ['predətərɪ] *adj animal* Raub-; *attack also, tribe* räuberisch ◆ **he has a ~ attitude towards all the girls in the office** er betrachtet alle Mädchen im Büro als Freiwild.

predecease [ˌpriːdɪ'siːs] *vt* **to ~ sb** vor jdm sterben.

predecessor ['priːdɪsesəʳ] *n* (*person*) Vorgänger(in *f*) *m*; (*thing*) Vorläufer *m* ◆ **our ~s** (*ancestors*) unsere Ahnen *or* Vorfahren *pl*; **his latest book is certainly better than its ~s** sein neuestes Buch ist zweifellos besser als seine vorherigen.

predestination [priːˌdestɪ'neɪʃən] *n* Vorherbestimmung, Prädestination *f*.

predestine [priː'destɪn] *vt* vorherbestimmen, prädestinieren; *person* prädestinieren.

predetermination ['priːdɪˌtɜːmɪ'neɪʃən] *n see vt* Vorherbestimmung *f*; Prädetermination *f*; vorherige Festlegung *or* Festsetzung; vorherige Ermittlung.

predetermine [ˌpriːdɪ'tɜːmɪn] *vt course of events, sb's future etc* vorherbestimmen; (*Philos*) prädeterminieren; (*fix in advance*) *price, date etc* vorher *or* im voraus festlegen *or* festsetzen; (*ascertain in advance*) *costs* vorher ermitteln.

predicable ['predɪkəbl] *adj* **to be ~ of sth** von etw ausgesagt *or* behauptet werden können.

predicament [prɪ'dɪkəmənt] *n* Zwangslage *f*, Dilemma *nt* ◆ **to be in a ~** in einem Dilemma *or* in einer Zwangslage sein.

predicate ['predɪkɪt] [1] *n* (*Gram*) Prädikat *nt*, Satzaussage *f*; (*Logic*) Aussage *f* ◆ **~ noun** prädikatives Substantiv, Prädikativ(um) *nt*.

[2] ['predɪkeɪt] *vt* (*imply, connote*) aussagen; (*assert, state*) behaupten ◆ **to ~ sth on sth** (*base*) etw auf etw (*dat*) gründen; **to ~ sth of sth** (*assert as quality of*) etw von etw behaupten.

predicative *adj*, **~ly** *adv* [prɪ'dɪkətɪv, -lɪ] prädikativ.

predict [prɪ'dɪkt] *vt* vorher- *or* voraussagen, prophezeien.

predictability [prəˌdɪktə'bɪlɪtɪ] *n* Vorhersagbarkeit *f*.

predictable [prɪ'dɪktəbl] *adj* vorher- *or* voraussagbar ◆ **to be ~** vorher- *or* voraussagbar sein, vorher- *or* vorauszusagen sein; **that was ~!** das war vorherzusehen!; **you're so ~** man weiß doch genau, wie Sie reagieren.

predictably [prɪ'dɪktəblɪ] *adv react* vorher- *or* voraussagbar ◆ **~, he was late** wie vorauszusehen, kam er zu spät.

prediction [prɪ'dɪkʃən] *n* Prophezeiung, Voraussage *f*.

predigest [ˌpriːdaɪ'dʒest] *vt* vorverdauen; (*artificially, chemically*) aufschließen; (*fig*) vorkauen.

predilection [ˌpriːdɪ'lekʃən] *n* Vorliebe *f*, Faible *nt* (*for* für).

predispose [ˌpriːdɪ'spəʊz] *vt* geneigt machen; (*Med*) prädisponieren, anfällig machen ◆ **to ~ sb in favour of sb/sth** jdn für jdn/etw einnehmen; **that people are ~d to behave in certain ways** daß die Menschen so veranlagt sind, sich auf eine bestimmte Weise zu verhalten; **it ~s me to think that ...** das führt mich zu der Annahme, daß ...; **I'm not ~d to help him** ich bin nicht geneigt, ihm zu helfen.

predisposition [ˌpriːdɪspə'zɪʃən] *n* (*tendency, inclination*) Neigung *f* (*to* zu); (*Med*) Prädisposition, Anfälligkeit *f* (*to* für) ◆ **that children have a natural ~ to use language** daß Kinder eine natürliche Veranlagung haben, Sprache zu gebrauchen.

predominance [prɪ'dɒmɪnəns] *n* (*control*) Vorherrschaft, Vormachtstellung *f*; (*prevalence*) Überwiegen *nt* ◆ **the ~ of women in the office** die weibliche Überzahl im Büro.

predominant [prɪ'dɒmɪnənt] *adj* (*most prevalent*) *idea, theory* vorherrschend; (*dominating*) *person, animal* beherrschend ◆ **those things which are ~ in your life** die Dinge, die in Ihrem Leben von größter Bedeutung sind; **he was the ~ member of the group** er war in der Gruppe tonangebend.

predominantly [prɪ'dɒmɪnəntlɪ] *adv* überwiegend.

predominate [prɪ'dɒmɪneɪt] *vi* **(a)** vorherrschen. **(b)** (*in influence etc*) überwiegen ◆ **Good will always ~ over Evil** das Gute wird immer über das Böse siegen; **if you allow any one individual to ~ (over the others)** wenn man einem einzigen gestattet, die anderen zu beherrschen.

pre-eclampsia [ˌpriːɪ'klæmpsɪə] *n* (*Med*) Präeklampsie *f* (*spec*).

pre-election [ˌpriːɪ'lekʃən] *adj attr measure, atmosphere* Wahlkampf- ◆ **~ promise** Wahlversprechen *nt*.

pre-eminence [priː'emɪnəns] *n* überragende Bedeutung.

pre-eminent [priː'emɪnənt] *adj* herausragend, überragend.

pre-eminently [priː'emɪnəntlɪ] *adv* hauptsächlich, vor allem, in erster Linie; (*excellently*) hervorragend.

pre-empt [priː'empt] *vt* zuvorkommen (+*dat*); (*Bridge*) *seinen Gegenspielern durch eine schwer zu überbietende Ansage zuvorkommen* ◆ **his decision to leave was ~ed by his dismissal** die Entlassung kam seinem Entschluß wegzugehen zuvor.

pre-emption [priː'empʃən] *n* Zuvorkommen *nt*.

pre-emptive [priː'emptɪv] *adj* präventiv, Präventiv- ◆ **~ bid** (*Bridge*) *Ansage, die durch ihre Höhe weitere Ansagen erschwert*.

preen [priːn] [1] *vt feathers* putzen.

[2] *vr* **to ~ oneself** (*bird*) sich putzen; (*person*) (*be smug*) sich brüsten (*on* mit); (*dress up*) sich herausputzen, sich aufputzen.

pre-exist [ˌpriːɪg'zɪst] *vi* (*exist beforehand*) vorher existieren, vorher vorhanden sein; (*exist in previous life*) präexistieren.

pre-existence [ˌpriːɪg'zɪstəns] *n* (*no pl: existing before*) vorherige Existenz, vorheriges Vorhandensein; (*previous life*) früheres Leben *or* Dasein, Präexistenz *f*.

pre-existent [ˌpriːɪg'zɪstənt] *adj* (*existing before*) vorher vorhanden *or* existent; (*of an earlier life*) präexistent.

prefab ['priːfæb] *n* Fertig(teil)haus *nt*.

prefabricate [ˌpriː'fæbrɪkeɪt] *vt* vorfertigen.

prefabricated [ˌpriː'fæbrɪkeɪtɪd] *adj* vorgefertigt, Fertig-; *building* Fertig(teil)-.

prefabrication [priːˌfæbrɪ'keɪʃən] *n* Vorfertigung *f*.

preface ['prefɪs] [1] *n* Vorwort *nt*; (*of speech*) Vorrede *f*.

[2] *vt* einleiten; *book* mit einem Vorwort versehen.

prefaded ['priːfeɪdɪd] *adj denims* gebleicht, bleached *pred*.

prefatory ['prefətərɪ] *adj* einleitend.

prefect ['priːfekt] *n* Präfekt *m*; (*Brit Sch*) Aufsichtsschüler(in *f*) *m* ◆ **form ~** (*Sch*) ≃ Klassensprecher(in *f*) *m*.

prefecture ['priːfektjʊəʳ] *n* Präfektur *f*.

➤ **prefer** [prɪ'fɜːʳ] *vt* **(a)** (*like better*) vorziehen (*to dat*), lieber mögen (*to* als); *drink, food, music also* lieber trinken/essen/hören (*to* als); *applicant, solution* vorziehen, bevorzugen; (*be more fond of*) *person* lieber haben (*to* als) ◆ **he ~s coffee to tea** er trinkt lieber Kaffee als Tee. **he ~s blondes/hot countries** er bevorzugt Blondinen/warme Länder; **I ~ it that way** es ist mir lieber so; **which (of them) do you ~?** (*of people*) wen ziehen Sie vor?; (*emotionally*) wen mögen *or* haben Sie lieber?; (*of things*) welche(n, s) ziehen Sie vor *or* finden Sie besser?; (*find more pleasing*) welche(r, s) gefällt Ihnen besser?; **I'd ~ something less ornate** ich hätte lieber etwas Schlichteres; **to ~ to do sth** etw lieber tun, es vorziehen, etw zu tun; **I ~ to resign rather than ...** eher kündige ich, als daß ...; **I ~ walking/flying** ich gehe lieber zu Fuß/fliege lieber; **I ~ not to say** ich sage es lieber nicht; **I would ~ you to do it today** mir wäre es lieber, wenn Sie es heute täten.

(b) (*Jur*) **to ~ a charge/charges (against sb)** (gegen jdn) klagen, Klage (gegen jdn) einreichen *or* erheben.

(c) (*esp Eccl: promote*) befördern ◆ **the bishop was ~red to the archbishopric of York** dem Bischof wurde die Würde eines Erzbischofs von York verliehen.

preferable ['prefərəbl] *adj* **X is ~ to Y** X ist Y (*dat*) vorzuziehen; **death is ~ to dishonour** lieber tot als ehrlos; **it would be ~ to do it that way** es wäre besser, es so zu machen.

preferably ['prefərəblɪ] *adv* am liebsten ◆ **tea or coffee? — coffee, ~** Tee oder Kaffee? — lieber Kaffee; **but ~ not Tuesday** aber, wenn möglich, nicht Dienstag.

➤ **preference** ['prefərəns] *n* **(a)** (*greater liking*) Vorliebe *f* ◆ **for ~** lieber; **to have a ~ for sth** eine Vorliebe für etw haben, etw bevorzugen; **my ~ is for country life** ich ziehe das Leben auf dem Land vor; **I drink coffee in ~ to tea** ich trinke lieber Kaffee als Tee.

(b) (*thing preferred*) **what is your ~?** was wäre Ihnen am liebsten?; **just state your ~** nennen Sie einfach Ihre Wünsche; **I have no ~** mir ist das eigentlich gleich; **what are your ~s in the matter of food?** was essen Sie am liebsten?

(c) (*greater favour*) Vorzug *m* ◆ **to show ~ to sb** jdn bevorzugen; **to give ~ to sb/sth** jdn/etw bevorzugen, jdm/etw den Vorzug geben (*over* gegenüber); **to give certain imports ~** Vorzugs- *or* Präferenzzölle auf bestimmte Einfuhrartikel gewähren; **~ shares** *or* **stock** (*Brit Fin*) Vorzugsaktien *pl*.

preferential [prefə'renʃəl] *adj treatment* Vorzugs-; *terms* bevorzugt, Sonder- ◆ **to give sb ~ treatment** jdn bevorzugt behandeln; **~ trade** (*Comm*) Präferenz- *or* Vorzugshandel *m*; **~ tariff** (*Comm*) Präferenz- *or* Vorzugszoll *m*; **~ ballot** (*Pol*) Präferenzwahl *f*; **~ voting** (*Pol*) Präferenzwahlsystem *nt*.

preferentially [ˌprefə'renʃəlɪ] *adv treat etc* bevorzugt.

preferment [prɪ'fɜːmənt] *n* **(a)** (*esp Eccl: promotion*) Beförderung *f*. **(b)** (*Jur*) **~**

➤ LANGUAGE IN USE: **prefer: a** → 5.2, 7.1, 7.4, 26.3 **preference: a** → 7.4, 7.5

of charges Klageerhebung *f*.

preferred [prɪ'fɜːd] *adj creditor* bevorrechtigt ♦ **~ stock** (*US Fin*) Vorzugsaktien *pl*.

prefigure [priː'fɪgəʳ] *vt* (*indicate*) anzeigen, ankündigen; (*imagine beforehand*) sich (*dat*) ausmalen.

prefix ['priːfɪks] 1 *n* (*Gram*) Vorsilbe *f*, Präfix *nt*; (*title*) Namensvorsatz *m*; (*in code*) Vorsatz *m*; (*Telec*) Vorwahl *f*.
2 [priː'fɪks] *vt* (*Gram*) mit einer Vorsilbe *or* einem Präfix versehen; *name* mit einem Namensvorsatz versehen; *code* (*with acc*) voranstellen (*+dat*), voransetzen (*+dat*) ♦ **words ~ed by "un"** Wörter mit der Vorsilbe *or* dem Präfix „un".

preflight ['priː'flaɪt] *adj attr* **~ checks/instructions** Kontrollen *pl*/ Anweisungen *pl* vor dem Flug.

preform [priː'fɔːm] *vt* vorformen.

prefrontal [ˌpriː'frʌntl] *adj* des Stirnbeins, Stirnbein-.

preggers ['pregəz] *adj pred* (*esp Brit inf*) schwanger.

pregnancy ['pregnənsɪ] *n* Schwangerschaft *f*; (*of animal*) Trächtigkeit *f*; (*fig*) (*of remarks etc*) Bedeutungsgehalt *m*; (*of silence, pause*) Bedeutungsschwere, Bedeutungsgeladenheit *f* ♦ **~ test** Schwangerschaftsuntersuchung *f or* -test *m*.

pregnant ['pregnənt] *adj* **(a)** *woman* schwanger; *animal* trächtig, tragend ♦ **3 months ~** im dritten Monat schwanger. **(b)** (*fig*) *remark, silence, pause* bedeutungsvoll *or* -schwer *or* -geladen ♦ **~ with meaning/consequences** bedeutungsvoll *or* -geladen *or* -schwanger (*iro*)/folgenschwer.

preheat [priː'hiːt] *vt* vorheizen.

prehensile [prɪ'hensaɪl] *adj* Greif-.

prehistoric [ˌpriːhɪ'stɒrɪk] *adj* prähistorisch, vorgeschichtlich.

prehistory [ˌpriː'hɪstərɪ] *n* Vorgeschichte *f*.

pre-ignition [ˌpriːɪg'nɪʃən] *n* Frühzündung *f*.

pre-industrial [ˌpriːɪn'dʌstrɪəl] *adj* vorindustriell.

prejudge [priː'dʒʌdʒ] *vt case, issue, person* im voraus beurteilen; (*negatively*) *person* im voraus verurteilen.

prejudice ['predʒʊdɪs] 1 *n* **(a)** (*biased opinion*) Vorurteil *nt* ♦ **his ~ against ...** seine Voreingenommenheit gegen ...; **that's pure ~** das ist reine Voreingenommenheit; **the newspaper report was full of ~ against ...** der Zeitungsbericht steckte voller Vorurteile gegen ...; **to have a ~ against sb/ sth** ein Vorurteil *nt* gegen jdn/etw haben, gegen jdn/etw voreingenommen sein; **racial ~** Rassenvorurteile *pl*; **colour ~** Vorurteile *pl* gegen (Anders)farbige *or* aufgrund der Hautfarbe.
(b) (*esp Jur: detriment, injury*) Schaden *m* ♦ **to the ~ of sb/sth** (*form*) zu jds Schaden/unter Beeinträchtigung (*+gen*); **without ~ to one's own chances** ohne sich (*dat*) selbst zu schaden; **without ~** (*Jur*) ohne Verbindlichkeit *or* Obligo; **without ~ to any claim** (*Jur*) ohne Beeinträchtigung *or* unbeschadet irgendwelcher Ansprüche.
2 *vt* **(a)** (*bias*) einnehmen, beeinflussen; *see also* **prejudiced**.
(b) (*injure*) gefährden; *chances also* beeinträchtigen.

prejudiced ['predʒʊdɪst] *adj person* voreingenommen (*against* gegen); *opinion* vorgefaßt; *judge* befangen.

prejudicial [ˌpredʒʊ'dɪʃəl] *adj* abträglich (*to sth* einer Sache *dat*) ♦ **to be ~ to a cause/sb's chances** einer Sache (*dat*) schaden/jds Chancen gefährden.

prelacy ['preləsɪ] *n* (*office*) Prälatur *f*; (*bishops*) geistliche Würdenträger *pl*; (*system*) Kirchenhierarchie *f*.

prelate ['prelɪt] *n* Prälat *m*.

preliminary [prɪ'lɪmɪnərɪ] 1 *adj talks, negotiations, enquiry, investigation, stage* Vor-; *remarks also, chapter* einleitend; *steps, measures* vorbereitend ♦ **~ contacts** erste Kontakte.
2 *n* Einleitung *f* (*to* zu); (*preparatory measure*) Vorbereitung *f*, vorbereitende Maßnahme; (*Sport*) Vorspiel *nt* ♦ **preliminaries** Präliminarien *pl* (*geh, Jur*); (*for speech*) einführende *or* einleitende Worte; (*Sport*) Vorrunde *f*; **the preliminaries are complete, now the actual work can begin** die Vorarbeit ist getan, jetzt kann die eigentliche Arbeit anfangen; **all the preliminaries to sth** alles, was einer Sache (*dat*) vorausgeht; **as a necessary ~ to the actual application of the paint** als notwendige Maßnahme vor dem Auftragen der Farbe; **let's dispense with the preliminaries** kommen wir gleich zur Sache.

prelims ['priːlɪmz] *npl* **(a)** (*Univ*) Vorprüfung *f*. **(b)** (*in book*) Vorbemerkungen *pl*.

prelude ['preljuːd] 1 *n* Vorspiel *nt*; (*introduction to fugue*) Präludium *nt*; (*fig*) Auftakt *m*.
2 *vt* einleiten, den Auftakt (*+gen*) bilden.

premarital [priː'mærɪtl] *adj* vorehelich.

premature ['premətʃʊəʳ] *adj baldness, birth, arrival* vorzeitig; *decision, action* verfrüht ♦ **you were a little ~** da waren Sie ein wenig voreilig; **the baby was three weeks ~** das Baby wurde drei Wochen zu früh geboren; **~ baby** Frühgeburt *f*.

prematurely ['premətʃʊəlɪ] *adv bald* vorzeitig; *decide* verfrüht; *act* voreilig ♦ **he was born ~** er war eine Frühgeburt.

premed [priː'med] *n* (*inf*) **(a)** *see* **premedication**. **(b)** (*US*) *Medizinstudent, der einen auf das Medizinstudium vorbereitenden Einführungskurs besucht; dieser Kurs selbst*.

premedical [priː'medɪkl] *adj* (*US*) auf das Medizinstudium vorbereitend *attr*.

premedication [priːˌmedɪ'keɪʃən] *n* Beruhigungsspritze *f* (*vor Anästhesie*).

premeditate [priː'medɪteɪt] *vt* vorsätzlich planen.

premeditated [priː'medɪteɪtɪd] *adj* vorsätzlich.

premeditation [priːˌmedɪ'teɪʃən] *n* Vorsatz *m*.

premenstrual [priː'menstrʊəl] *adj* prämenstruell, vor der Menstruation auftretend ♦ **~ tension** prämenstruelles Syndrom, prämenstruelle Phase.

premier ['premɪəʳ] 1 *adj* führend ♦ **of ~ importance** von äußerster Wichtigkeit.
2 *n* Premier(minister) *m*.

première ['premɪɛəʳ] 1 *n* Premiere *f*; (*first ever also*) Uraufführung *f*; (*in particular place also*) Erstaufführung *f*.
2 *vt* uraufführen; erstaufführen.

premiership ['premɪəʃɪp] *n* (*period*) Amtsperiode *or* -zeit *f* als Premier(minister); (*office*) Amt *nt* des Premier(minister)s.

premise ['premɪs] *n* **(a)** (*esp Logic*) Prämisse (*spec*), Voraussetzung *f*.
(b) **~s** *pl* (*of school, factory*) Gelände *nt*; (*building*) Gebäude *nt*; (*shop*) Räumlichkeiten *pl*; (*form: house*) Besitz *m*, Anwesen *nt* ♦ **licensed ~s** Schankort *m*; **business ~s** Geschäftsräume *pl*; **to use as business ~s** geschäftlich nutzen; **drinking is not allowed in or on these ~s** es ist nicht erlaubt, hier Alkohol zu trinken; **will you escort him off the ~s?** würden Sie ihn bitte hinausbegleiten?; **he was asked to leave the ~s** man forderte ihn auf, das Gelände *etc* zu verlassen; **get off my ~s** verlassen Sie sofort mein Land *or* Grundstück!

premiss *n see* **premise (a)**.

premium ['priːmɪəm] *n* (*bonus, additional sum*) Bonus *m*, Prämie *f*; (*surcharge*) Zuschlag *m*; (*insurance ~*) Prämie *f*; (*St Ex*) Aufgeld, Agio *nt* ♦ **~ bond** (*Brit*) Prämien- *or* Lotterieaktie *f*; **to sell sth at a ~** etw über seinem Wert verkaufen; **to be at a ~** (*St Ex*) über Pari stehen; (*fig*) hoch im Kurs stehen; **to put a ~ on sth** (*fig*) etw hoch einschätzen *or* bewerten.

premolar [priː'məʊləʳ] *n* vorderer Backenzahn.

premonition [ˌpriːmə'nɪʃən] *n* (*presentiment*) (böse *or* schlechte) Vorahnung, (böses *or* schlechtes) Vorgefühl; (*forewarning*) Vorwarnung *f*.

premonitory [prɪ'mɒnɪtərɪ] *adj* warnend.

prenatal [priː'neɪtl] *adj* pränatal, vor der Geburt.

prenuptial [priː'nʌpʃəl] *adj* vor der Hochzeit.

preoccupation [priːˌɒkjʊ'peɪʃən] *n* **his face had a look of ~** seinem Gesicht sah man an, daß ihn etwas beschäftigte; **her ~ with her appearance** ihre ständige Sorge um ihr Äußeres; **her ~ with making money was such that ...** sie war so sehr mit dem Geldverdienen beschäftigt, daß ...; **that was his main ~** das war sein Hauptanliegen.

preoccupied [priː'ɒkjʊpaɪd] *adj look, tone of voice, smile* gedankenverloren ♦ **to be ~ with sth** nur an etw (*acc*) denken, sich ganz auf etw (*acc*) konzentrieren; **he has been (looking) rather ~ recently** er sieht in letzter Zeit so aus, als beschäftige ihn etwas; **he was too ~ to notice her** er war zu sehr mit anderen Dingen beschäftigt, um sie zu bemerken.

preoccupy [priː'ɒkjʊpaɪ] *vt* (stark) beschäftigen.

pre-op ['priːɒp] *adj* (*inf*) vor der Operation, präoperativ ♦ **~ medication** vor der Operation verabreichte Medikamente.

preordain ['priːɔː'deɪn] *vt* vorherbestimmen.

prep [prep] (*inf*) *n see* **preparation (d)**.

prepackaged [priː'pækɪdʒd], **prepacked** [priː'pækt] *adj* abgepackt.

prepaid [priː'peɪd] 1 *ptp of* **prepay**.
2 *adj postage, goods* vorausbezahlt; *envelope* vorfrankiert, freigemacht.

preparation [ˌprepə'reɪʃən] *n* **(a)** (*preparing*) Vorbereitung *f*; (*of meal, medicine etc*) Zubereitung *f* ♦ **in ~ for sth** als Vorbereitung für etw; **to be in ~** in Vorbereitung sein.
(b) (*preparatory measure*) Vorbereitung *f* ♦ **~s for war/a journey** Kriegs-/ Reisevorbereitungen *pl*; **to make ~s** Vorbereitungen treffen.
(c) (*Med, Sci*) Präparat *nt* ♦ **beauty ~s** Schönheitspräparate *pl*; **a ~ of herbs** (*Med*) ein Kräuterpräparat *nt*; (*Cook*) eine Kräutermischung.
(d) (*Brit Sch*) (*homework*) Hausaufgaben *pl*, Hausarbeit *f*; (*homework period*) Lernstunde *f*.

preparatory [prɪ'pærətərɪ] *adj* **(a)** *step, measure* vorbereitend; *plan, work also* Vorbereitungs- ♦ **the ~ arrangements** die Vorbereitungen *pl*.
(b) (*Sch*) **~ education** Erziehung *or* Ausbildung *f* in Vorbereitungsschulen; **~ school** (*Brit*) *private Vorbereitungsschule für die Public School*; (*US*) *private Vorbereitungsschule für die Hochschule*; **~ student** (*US*) *Schüler einer privaten Vorbereitungsschule für die Hochschule*.
(c) **talks were held ~ to the summit conference** es wurden Gespräche geführt, um die Gipfelkonferenz vorzubereiten.

prepare [prɪ'peəʳ] 1 *vt* vorbereiten (*sb for sth* jdn auf etw *acc*, *sth for sth* etw für etw); *meal, medicine* zubereiten; *guest-room* zurecht- *or* fertigmachen; (*Sci*) präparieren; *data* aufbereiten ♦ **~ yourself for a shock!** mach dich auf einen Schock gefaßt!; **we ~d ourselves for a long wait** wir machten uns auf eine lange Wartezeit gefaßt.
2 *vi* **to ~ for sth** sich auf etw (*acc*) vorbereiten; **the country is preparing for war** das Land trifft Kriegsvorbereitungen; **to ~ to do sth** Anstalten machen, etw zu tun.

prepared [prɪ'peəd] *adj* **(a)** (*also* **ready ~**) vorbereitet; *speech also* ausgearbeitet, abgefaßt; *food* Fertig-.
(b) (*in a state of readiness*) vorbereitet (*for* auf *+acc*) ♦ **I wasn't ~ for that!** darauf war ich nicht vorbereitet *or* gefaßt; **I wasn't ~ for him to do that** ich war nicht darauf vorbereitet, daß er das tut; **the country is ~ for war** das Land ist kriegsbereit *or* bereit zum Krieg; **are you ~ for your journey?** sind Sie reisefertig?; **"be ~"** „allzeit bereit".
(c) (*willing*) **to be ~ to do sth** bereit sein, etw zu tun.

preparedness [prɪ'peərdnɪs] *n* (*readiness*) Vorbereitetsein *nt* (*for* auf *+acc*); (*for untoward events*) Gefaßtsein *nt* (*for* auf *+acc*); (*willingness*) Bereitschaft *f* ♦ **lack of ~** mangelnde Vorbereitung (*for* auf *+acc*); **~ for war** Kriegsbereitschaft *f*; (*of army*) Einsatzbereitschaft *f*.

prepay [priː'peɪ] *pret, ptp* **prepaid** *vt* im voraus bezahlen.

prepayment [priː'peɪmənt] *n* Vorauszahlung *f*.

preponderance [prɪ'pɒndərəns] *n* Übergewicht *nt*; (*in number also*) Überwiegen *nt*.

preponderant [prɪ'pɒndərənt] *adj* überwiegend.

preponderate [prɪ'pɒndəreɪt] *vi* überwiegen.

preposition [ˌprepə'zɪʃən] *n* Präposition *f*, Verhältniswort *nt*.

prepositional [ˌprepə'zɪʃənl] *adj* präpositional; *phrase* Präpositional-, Verhältnis-.

prepossess [ˌpriːpə'zes] *vt* einnehmen (*in sb's favour* für jdn).

prepossessing [ˌpriːpə'zesɪŋ] *adj* einnehmend, anziehend.

preposterous [prɪ'pɒstərəs] *adj* grotesk, absurd ◆ **you're being ~** das ist ja grotesk.

preposterously [prɪ'pɒstərəslɪ] *adv* grotesk ◆ **he suggested, quite ~** ... er machte den grotesken *or* absurden Vorschlag ...; **it took a ~ long time** es dauerte absurd lange.

preposterousness [prɪ'pɒstərəsnɪs] *n* Absurdität *f*.

preppie, preppy ['prepɪ] *adj* adrett, popperhaft (*esp pej*).

preprinted ['priː'prɪntɪd] *adj* vorgedruckt.

preprogram ['priː'prəʊgræm] *vt* (*lit, fig*) vorprogrammieren ◆ **~med** vorprogrammiert.

prep school *n see* **preparatory (b)**.

prepublication [ˌpriːpʌblɪ'keɪʃən] *adj attr* vor der Veröffentlichung.

prepuce ['priːpjuːs] *n* Vorhaut *f*, Präputium *nt* (*spec*).

prequel ['priːkwəl] *n Film m, der die Vorgeschichte eines bereits erfolgreich gelaufenen Films erzählt.*

pre-Raphaelite [priː'ræfəlaɪt] [1] *adj* präraffaelitisch.
[2] *n* Präraffaelit *m*.

prerecord [ˌpriːrɪ'kɔːd] *vt* vorher aufzeichnen ◆ **~ed cassette** bespielte Kassette.

prerequisite [ˌpriː'rekwɪzɪt] [1] *n* (Grund)voraussetzung, Vorbedingung *f*.
[2] *adj* erforderlich, notwendig.

prerogative [prɪ'rɒgətɪv] *n* Vorrecht, Prärogativ (*geh*) *nt* ◆ **that's a woman's ~** das ist das Vorrecht einer Frau.

Pres *abbr of* **president** Präs.

presage ['presɪdʒ] [1] *n* (*omen*) Vorzeichen, Anzeichen *nt*, Vorbote *m*; (*feeling*) Vorahnung *f*.
[2] *vt* ankünd(ig)en, andeuten.

Presbyterian [ˌprezbɪ'tɪərɪən] [1] *adj* presbyterianisch.
[2] *n* Presbyterianer(in *f*) *m*.

presbytery ['prezbɪtərɪ] *n* (*priest's house*) (katholisches) Pfarrhaus; (*part of church*) Presbyterium *nt*.

preschool ['priː'skuːl] *adj attr* vorschulisch ◆ **a child of ~ age** ein Kind *nt* im Vorschulalter; **~ years** Vorschuljahre *pl*.

preschooling ['priː'skuːlɪŋ] *n* Vorschulerziehung *f*.

prescience ['presɪəns] *n* vorheriges Wissen, vorherige Kenntnis, Vorherwissen *nt*.

prescribe [prɪ'skraɪb] [1] *vt* (**a**) (*order, lay down*) vorschreiben ◆ **~d reading** Pflichtlektüre *f*. (**b**) (*Med, fig*) verschreiben, verordnen (*sth for sb* jdm etw).
[2] *vi* (*lay down rules*) Vorschriften machen.

prescription [prɪ'skrɪpʃən] *n* (**a**) (*Med*) Rezept *nt*; (*act of prescribing*) Verschreiben, Verordnen *nt* ◆ **to make up** *or* **fill** (*US*) **a ~** eine Medizin zubereiten; **~ charge** Rezeptgebühr *f*; **only available on ~** rezeptpflichtig, nur auf Rezept erhältlich.
(**b**) (*regulation*) Vorschrift *f*.

prescriptive [prɪ'skrɪptɪv] *adj* normativ ◆ **to be ~** Vorschriften machen.

prescriptivism [prɪ'skrɪptɪvɪzəm] *n* Präskriptivismus *m*.

presealed ['priː'siːld] *adj* versiegelt; *containers etc* plombiert.

preseason ['priː'siːzn] *adj* (*Sport*) *match, training* vor der Saison; (*in tourism*) *rates, weekend* Vorsaison-.

preselect [ˌpriːsɪ'lekt] *vt* vorher auswählen; *gear* vorwählen.

presence ['prezns] *n* (**a**) Gegenwart, Anwesenheit *f* ◆ **in sb's ~, in the ~ of sb** in jds (*dat*) Gegenwart *or* Anwesenheit, in Gegenwart *or* im Beisein von jdm; **he was admitted to the king's ~** er wurde zum König vorgelassen; **your ~ is requested/required** Sie sind eingeladen/Ihre Anwesenheit ist erforderlich; **to make one's ~ felt** sich bemerkbar machen; **in the ~ of danger** im Angesicht der Gefahr; **there is a strong German ~ in the 1500 metres** die Deutschen sind beim 1500-Meter-Lauf stark vertreten.
(**b**) **a military/police ~** Militär-/Polizeipräsenz *f*.
(**c**) (*bearing, dignity*) Auftreten *nt*, Haltung *f*; (*of actor: also* **stage ~**) Ausstrahlung *f*.
(**d**) **they felt a ghostly/an invisible ~** sie spürten, daß etwas Geisterhaftes/Unsichtbares anwesend war.

presence of mind *n* Geistesgegenwart *f*.

present[1] ['preznt] [1] *adj* (**a**) (*in attendance*) anwesend ◆ **to be ~** anwesend sein, da *or* dort/hier sein; **he was ever ~ in her thoughts** er war in ihren Gedanken immer gegenwärtig; **to be ~ at sth** bei etw (anwesend) sein; **~ company excepted** Anwesende ausgenommen; **all those ~** alle Anwesenden.
(**b**) (*existing in sth*) vorhanden ◆ **gases ~ in the atmosphere** in der Atmosphäre vorhandene Gase; **carbon is ~ in organic matter** Kohlenstoff ist in organischen Stoffen enthalten; **a quality ~ in all great men** eine Eigenschaft, die man bei allen großen Männern findet.
(**c**) (*at the ~ time*) *moment, state of affairs, world record etc* gegenwärtig, derzeitig, augenblicklich; *problems, manager, husband etc also* jetzig; *year, season etc* laufend ◆ **at the ~ moment** zum gegenwärtigen *or* derzeitigen *or* jetzigen Zeitpunkt; **in the ~ circumstances** unter den gegenwärtigen *or* gegebenen Umständen; **in the ~ case** im vorliegenden Fall; **the ~ writer** (*form*) der Autor des hier vorliegenden Werkes.
(**d**) (*Gram*) **in the ~ tense** in der Gegenwart, im Präsens; **~ participle** Partizip *nt* Präsens, Mittelwort *nt* der Gegenwart; **~ perfect (tense)** zweite Vergangenheit, Perfekt *nt*.
[2] *n* Gegenwart *f*; (*Gram also*) Präsens *nt* ◆ **at ~** zur Zeit, im Moment *or* Augenblick, derzeit; **up to the ~** bislang, bis jetzt; **there's no time like the ~** (*prov*) was du heute kannst besorgen, das verschiebe nicht auf morgen (*Prov*); **that will be all for the ~** das ist vorläufig *or* einstweilen alles.

present[2] [1] *n* (*gift*) Geschenk *nt* ◆ **to make sb a ~ of sth** jdm etw schenken (*also fig*), jdm etw zum Geschenk machen (*form*); **I got it** *or* **was given it as a ~** das habe ich geschenkt bekommen.
[2] [prɪ'zent] *vt* (**a**) (*hand over formally*) *medal, prize etc* übergeben, überreichen; (*give as a gift*) *art collection, book etc* schenken, zum Geschenk machen (*form*) ◆ **to ~ sb with sth, to ~ sth to sb** jdm etw übergeben *or* überreichen; (*as a gift*) jdm etw schenken *or* zum Geschenk machen (*form*); **they ~ed us with a hefty bill** sie präsentierten *or* überreichten uns (*dat*) eine gesalzene Rechnung; **she ~ed him with a son** sie schenkte ihm einen Sohn.
(**b**) (*put forward*) vorlegen; *cheque* (*for payment*) präsentieren; *proof also* erbringen (*of sth* für etw); *proposal also* unterbreiten ◆ **she asked me to ~ her apologies/compliments** (*form*) sie bat mich, ihre Entschuldigung/Komplimente weiterzuleiten; **please ~ my apologies to your mother** (*form*) bitte entschuldigen Sie mich bei Ihrer Mutter; **his report ~s the matter in another light** sein Bericht zeigt die Angelegenheit in anderem Licht *or* stellt die Angelegenheit in anderem Licht dar.
(**c**) (*offer, provide*) *target, view, opportunity* bieten ◆ **to ~ a brave face to the world** sich (*dat*) nichts anmerken lassen; **his action ~ed us with a problem** seine Tat stellte uns vor ein Problem; **he ~ed the appearance of normality** nach außen hin wirkte er ganz normal.
(**d**) (*Rad, TV*) präsentieren; (*Theat also*) zeigen, aufführen; (*commentator*) moderieren ◆ **~ing Nina Calcott as ...** (*Film*) und erstmals Nina Calcott als ...; **~ing, in the blue corner ...** in der blauen Ecke des Rings ...
(**e**) (*introduce*) vorstellen ◆ **to ~ Mr X to Miss Y** Herrn X Fräulein Y (*dat*) vorstellen; **may I ~ Mr X?** (*form*) erlauben Sie mir, Herrn X vorzustellen (*form*); **to be ~ed at Court** bei Hof eingeführt werden.
(**f**) (*point*) *gun etc* richten, zielen (*at* auf +*acc*) ◆ **~ arms!** (*Mil*) präsentiert das Gewehr!
[3] [prɪ'zent] *vr* (*opportunity, problem etc*) sich ergeben ◆ **to ~ oneself as a candidate** sich aufstellen lassen; **to ~ oneself for an exam** sich zu einer Prüfung anmelden; **he was asked to ~ himself for interview** er wurde gebeten, zu einem Gespräch zu erscheinen; **to ~ oneself at an ideal moment** im idealen Augenblick erscheinen.

presentable [prɪ'zentəbl] *adj* **to be ~** sich sehen lassen können, vorzeigbar sein; **it's not very ~** damit kann man sich nicht gut sehen lassen; **to make sth ~** etw so herrichten, daß man es zeigen kann; **to make oneself ~** sich zurechtmachen; **a ~ person** jemand, mit dem man sich sehen lassen kann; **you're not ~ enough to go** du siehst nicht akzeptabel genug aus, um dorthin zu gehen.

presentably [prɪ'zentəblɪ] *adv* annehmbar, akzeptabel ◆ **you have to be ~ dressed to get into that bar** man muß angemessen angezogen sein, wenn man in diese Bar will.

presentation [ˌprezən'teɪʃən] *n* (**a**) (*of gift etc*) Überreichung *f*; (*of prize, medal also*) Verleihung *f*; (*ceremony*) Ver leihung(szeremonie) *f*; (*gift*) Geschenk *nt* ◆ **to make the ~** die Preise/Auszeichnungen *etc* verleihen; **to make sb a ~** jdm ein Geschenk überreichen; **~ copy** Dedikationsexemplar *nt*.
(**b**) (*act of presenting*) (*of report, voucher, cheque etc*) Vorlage, Präsentation *f*; (*of petition*) Überreichung *f*; (*Jur: of case, evidence*) Darlegung *f* ◆ **on ~ of a certificate** gegen Vorlage einer Bescheinigung (*gen*).
(**c**) (*manner of presenting*) Darbietung, Präsentation *f* ◆ **the ~ is poor** die Darbietung *or* Präsentation ist schlecht.
(**d**) (*Theat*) Inszenierung *f*; (*TV also, Rad*) Produktion *f*; (*announcing, commentary*) Moderation *f*.
(**e**) (*Med: at birth*) Lage *f*.

present-day ['preznt'deɪ] *adj attr morality, problems, fashions* heutig ◆ **~ Britain** das heutige Großbritannien.

presenter [prɪ'zentə[r]] *n* (**a**) (*of cheque*) Überbringer(in *f*) *m* ◆ **the ~ of the petition was a child** die Petition wurde von einem Kind überreicht. (**b**) (*TV, Rad*) Moderator(in *f*) *m*.

presentiment [prɪ'zentɪmənt] *n* (Vor)ahnung *f*, Vorgefühl *nt* ◆ **to have a ~ about sth** ein ungutes Gefühl in bezug auf etw haben; **to have a ~ that ...** das Gefühl haben, daß ...

presently ['prezntlɪ] *adv* (**a**) (*soon*) bald. (**b**) (*at present*) zur Zeit, derzeit, gegenwärtig.

preservation [ˌprezə'veɪʃən] *n see vt* (**a**) Erhaltung *f*; Wahrung *f*; Aufrechterhaltung *f*; Bewahrung *f*. (**b**) Konservierung *f* (*also of leather, wood*); Präservierung *f* ◆ **to be in a good state of ~** gut erhalten sein. (**c**) Einmachen, Einkochen *nt*; Einwecken *nt*; Einlegen *nt*. (**d**) Bewahrung *f*.

preservative [prɪ'zɜːvətɪv] [1] *adj substance* Konservierungs-.
[2] *n* Konservierungsmittel *nt*.

preserve [prɪ'zɜːv] [1] *vt* (**a**) (*keep intact, maintain*) *customs, building, position, eyesight, manuscript* erhalten; *peace also, dignity, appearances* wahren; *memory,*

reputation aufrechterhalten, wahren; *sense of humour, silence* bewahren.
(b) *(keep from decay)* konservieren; *specimens etc* präservieren; *leather, wood* schützen ◆ **well ~d** gut erhalten.
(c) *(Cook)* einmachen, einkochen; *(bottle also)* einwecken; *(pickle)* einlegen ◆ **preserving jar** Weck- *or* Einmachglas *nt*.
(d) *(keep from harm, save)* bewahren ◆ **may God ~ you!** Gott steh dir bei!; **to ~ sb from sth** jdn vor etw *(dat)* schützen *or* bewahren; **heaven** *or* **the saints ~ me from that!** *(iro)* der Himmel möge mich damit verschonen *or* mir das ersparen!
(e) *(Hunt) game, fish* schützen, hegen ◆ **~d fishing/river/wood** unter Schutz stehende Fische/stehender Fluß/Wald.
[2] *n* **(a)** *(Cook)* **~s** *pl* Eingemachtes *nt*; *(bottled fruit also)* Eingewecktes *nt* ◆ **peach ~(s)** eingeweckte Pfirsiche *pl*; *(Brit: jam)* Pfirsichmarmelade *f*.
(b) *(special domain)* Ressort *nt* ◆ **to poach on sb's ~(s)** jdm ins Handwerk pfuschen; **game ~** *(Hunt)* Jagd *f*, Jagdrevier *nt*.

preserver [prɪ'zɜ:vəʳ] *n* Retter(in *f*) *m*.

preset [pri:'set] *pret, ptp ~ vt* vorher einstellen.

preshrink [pri:'ʃrɪŋk] *pret* **preshrank** [pri:'ʃræŋk], *ptp* **preshrunk** [pri:'ʃrʌŋk] *vt* vorwaschen.

preside [prɪ'zaɪd] *vi (at meeting etc)* den Vorsitz haben *or* führen *(at* bei); *(at meal)* den Vorsitz haben *(at* bei) ◆ **to ~ over an organization** *etc* eine Organisation *etc* leiten; **Mrs Jones ~d at the piano** am Klavier saß Frau Jones.

presidency ['prezɪdənsɪ] *n* Präsidentschaft *f*; *(esp US: of company)* Aufsichtsratsvorsitz *m*; *(US Univ)* Rektorat *nt*.

president ['prezɪdənt] *n* Präsident(in *f*) *m*; *(esp US: of company)* Aufsichtsratsvorsitzende(r) *mf*; *(US Univ)* Rektor(in *f*) *m*.

presidential [,prezɪ'denʃəl] *adj (Pol)* Präsidenten-; *election also* Präsidentschafts- ◆ **~ primary** Vorwahl *f* für die Präsidentschaft; **his ~ duties** seine Pflichten als Präsident.

presidium [prɪ'sɪdɪəm] *n* (Partei)präsidium *nt*.

press [pres] [1] *n* **(a)** *(machine, trouser ~, flower ~)* Presse *f*; *(racket ~)* Spanner *m*.
(b) *(Typ)* (Drucker)presse *f*; *(publishing firm)* Verlag *m* ◆ **to go to ~** in Druck gehen; **to be in the ~** im Druck sein.
(c) *(newspapers)* Presse *f* ◆ **the daily/sporting ~** die Tages-/Sportpresse; **the weekly ~** die Wochenzeitungen *pl*; **to get a good/bad ~** eine gute/schlechte Presse bekommen.
(d) *(squeeze, push)* Druck *m* ◆ **to give sth a ~** etw drücken; *dress etc* etw bügeln; **to take a suit for a ~** einen Anzug zum Bügeln bringen.
(e) *(dial, US: cupboard)* Wandschrank *m*.
(f) *(crush)* Gedränge *nt* ◆ **a ~ of people** eine Menschenmenge; **in the ~ of the battle** im Schlachtgetümmel.
(g) *(Weight-lifting)* Drücken *nt*.
[2] *vt* **(a)** *(push, squeeze)* drücken *(to an +acc)*; *button, doorbell, knob also, brake pedal* drücken auf *(+acc)*; *clutch, piano pedal* treten; *grapes, fruit* (aus)pressen; *flowers* pressen ◆ **to ~ the accelerator** Gas geben; **to ~ the trigger (of a gun)** abdrücken, den Abzug betätigen; **the shoe ~es my foot here** der Schuh drückt (mich) hier.
(b) *(iron) clothes* bügeln.
(c) *(urge, persuade)* drängen; *(harass, importune)* bedrängen, unter Druck setzen; *(insist on) claim, argument* bestehen auf *(+dat)* ◆ **to ~ sb hard** jdm (hart) zusetzen; **he didn't need much ~ing** man brauchte ihn nicht lange zu drängen; **to ~ sb for an answer** auf jds Antwort *(acc)* drängen; **to ~ the point** darauf beharren *or* herumreiten *(inf)*; **to ~ home an advantage** einen Vorteil ausnutzen, sich *(dat)* einen Vorteil zunutze machen; **to ~ home an attack** einen Angriff energisch vortragen; **to ~ money/one's views on sb** jdm Geld/seine Ansichten aufdrängen; **to be ~ed (for money/time)** knapp dran sein *(inf)*, in Geldnot sein/unter Zeitdruck stehen, in Zeitnot sein; **to ~ sb/sth into service** jdn/etw einspannen.
(d) *machine part, record etc* pressen ◆ **~ed steel** gepreßter Stahl, Preßstahl *m*; **~ed pork** gepreßtes Schweinefleisch.
[3] *vi* **(a)** *(lit, fig: bear down, exert pressure)* drücken ◆ **to ~ down on sb** *(debts, troubles)* schwer auf jdm lasten.
(b) *(urge, agitate)* drängen; *(be insistent also)* drängeln *(inf)* ◆ **to ~ for sth** auf etw *(acc)* drängen; **time ~es** die Zeit drängt.
(c) *(move, push)* sich drängen ◆ **to ~ ahead** *or* **forward (with sth)** *(fig)* (mit etw) weitermachen; *(with plans)* etw weiterführen.

◆**press on** *vi* weitermachen; *(with journey)* weiterfahren.

◆**press out** *vt sep juice* auspressen; *pop-out models etc* herausdrücken.

press: ~ agency *n* Presseagentur *f*; **~ agent** *n* Presseagent *m*; **~ attaché** *n* Presseattaché *m*; **~ baron** *n* Pressezar *m*; **~ box** *n* Pressetribüne *f*; **~ button** *n see* **push-button**; **~ campaign** *n* Pressekampagne *f or* -feldzug *m*; **~ card** *n* Presseausweis *m*; **~ clipping** *n* Zeitungsausschnitt *m*; **~ conference** *n* Pressekonferenz *f*; **~ cutting** *n (esp Brit)* Zeitungsausschnitt *m*; **~ gallery** *n (esp Jur, Parl)* Pressetribüne *f*; **~-gang** [1] *n (Hist) (for navy)* Preßpatrouille *f*; *(for army)* Werber *pl*; [2] *vt (inf)* dazu drängen; **to ~-gang sb into (doing) sth** jdn drängen, etw zu tun.

pressing ['presɪŋ] [1] *adj* **(a)** *(urgent)* dringend. **(b)** *(insistent) requests* nachdrücklich ◆ **he was very ~ in his invitation** er drängte mir *etc* seine Einladung richtig auf.
[2] *n (records issued at one time)* Auflage *f*; *(copy of record)* Pressung *f*.

press: ~ lord *n see* **~ baron**; **~man** *n* **(a)** *(esp Brit: reporter)* Zeitungsmann, Pressemann *m*; **(b)** *(Typ)* Drucker *m*; **~mark** *n* Signatur *f*; **~ office** *n* Pressestelle *f*; **~ officer** *n* Pressesprecher(in *f*) *m*; **~ photographer** *n* Pressefotograf(in *f*) *m*; **~ release** *n* Pressemitteilung *f or* -verlautbarung *f*; **~ report** *n* Pressebericht *m*; **~ room** *n* Druckerei *f*, (Druck)maschinensaal *m*; **~ stud** *n (Brit)* Druckknopf *m*; **~-up** *n* Liegestütz *m*.

pressure ['preʃəʳ] [1] *n* **(a)** Druck *m (also Phys, Met)* ◆ **at high/full ~** *(lit, fig)* unter Hochdruck.
(b) *(compulsion, influence)* Druck, Zwang *m* ◆ **parental ~** Druck von seiten der Eltern; **social ~s** gesellschaftliche Zwänge *pl*; **to do sth under ~** etw unter Druck *or* Zwang tun; **to be under ~ to do sth** unter Druck *(dat)* stehen, etw zu tun; **to be under ~ from sb (to do sth)** von jdm gedrängt werden(, etw zu tun); **to put ~ on sb** jdn unter Druck *(dat)* setzen; **to put the ~ on** *(inf)* Druck dahintermachen *(inf)*, Dampf machen *(inf)*.
(c) *(urgent demands, stress)* Druck, Streß *m no pl* ◆ **~ of work prevents me** Arbeitsüberlastung hindert mich daran; **the ~ of events** der Druck der Ereignisse; **business ~s** geschäftliche Belastungen *pl*; **the ~s of modern life** die Belastungen *pl or* der Streß des modernen Lebens; **he works better under ~** er arbeitet besser unter Druck; **to be subjected to ~, to be under ~** unter Druck *(dat)* stehen *or* sein.
[2] *vt see* **pressurize (b)**.

pressure: ~ cabin *n (Aviat)* Überdruckkabine *f*; **~-cook** *vt* mit Dampf kochen; **~ cooker** *n* Druck- *or* Dampf- *or* Schnellkochtopf *m*; **~ gauge** *n* Manometer *nt*, Druckmesser *m*; **~ group** *n* Pressure-group *f*; **~ point** *n (Anat)* Druckpunkt *m*; **~ suit** *n (Aviat)* Druckanzug *m*.

pressurization [,preʃəraɪ'zeɪʃən] *n (Aviat etc)* Druckausgleich *m*.

pressurize ['preʃəraɪz] *vt* **(a)** *cabin, spacesuit* auf Normaldruck halten ◆ **the cabin is only ~d when ...** der Druckausgleich in der Kabine wird erst hergestellt, wenn ...
(b) unter Druck setzen ◆ **to ~ sb into doing sth** jdn so unter Druck setzen, daß er schließlich etw tut; **I refuse to be ~d into agreeing/going** ich lasse mir meine Zustimmung nicht abpressen/ich lasse mich nicht zwingen zu gehen.

Prestel ® ['prestel] *n* ≃ Bildschirmtext *m*.

prestidigitation ['prestɪ,dɪdʒɪ'teɪʃən] *n (form)* Fingerfertigkeit, Geschicklichkeit *f*.

prestidigitator [,prestɪ'dɪdʒɪteɪtəʳ] *n (form)* Taschenspieler *m*.

prestige [pre'sti:ʒ] *n* Prestige *nt* ◆ **~ value** Prestigewert *m*.

prestigious [pre'stɪdʒəs] *adj* Prestige- ◆ **to be (very) ~** (einen hohen) Prestigewert haben.

presto ['prestəʊ] *adv see* **hey**.

prestressed ['pri:strest] *adj* vorgespannt; *concrete* Spann-.

presumable [prɪ'zju:məbl] *adj* vermutlich.

presumably [prɪ'zju:məblɪ] *adv see adj* ◆ **~ he is very rich, is he?** ich nehme an, er ist sehr reich, oder?; **~ he'll come later** er wird voraussichtlich später kommen.

presume [prɪ'zju:m] [1] *vt* **(a)** *(suppose)* annehmen, vermuten; *sb's death* unterstellen *(form)* ◆ **~d dead** mutmaßlich verstorben; **to be ~d innocent** als unschuldig gelten.
(b) *(venture)* **to ~ to do sth** sich *(dat)* erlauben *or* sich *(dat)* herausnehmen *or* sich erdreisten, etw zu tun.
[2] *vi* **(a)** *(suppose)* annehmen, vermuten ◆ **Dr Livingstone, I ~** Dr. Livingstone, wie ich annehme; **it was his decision, I ~** ich nehme an *or* vermute, das war seine Entscheidung.
(b) *(take liberties, be presumptuous)* **I didn't want to ~** ich wollte nicht aufdringlich sein; **I hope I'm not presuming** ich hoffe, man hält mich nicht für aufdringlich; **you ~ too much** Sie sind wirklich vermessen; **to ~ on** *or* **upon sth** etw überbeanspruchen.

presumption [prɪ'zʌmpʃən] *n* **(a)** *(assumption)* Annahme, Vermutung *f* ◆ **the ~ is that ...** es wird angenommen *or* man vermutet, daß ...; **~ of death/innocence** Todes-/Unschuldvermutung *f*. **(b)** *(boldness, arrogance)* Unverschämtheit, Dreistigkeit *f*; *(in connection with one's abilities)* Überheblichkeit, Anmaßung, Vermessenheit *(geh) f*.

presumptive [prɪ'zʌmptɪv] *adj* **(a)** *(Jur)* **~ evidence** Indizien(beweis *m*) *pl*; **~ case** Indizienprozeß *m*. **(b)** *(likely)* **~ heir, heir ~** mutmaßlicher Erbe.

presumptuous *adj*, **~ly** *adv* [prɪ'zʌmptjʊəs, -lɪ] unverschämt, dreist; *(in connection with one's abilities)* überheblich, anmaßend, vermessen *(geh)* ◆ **it would be ~ of me to ...** es wäre eine Anmaßung von mir, ... zu ...

presumptuousness [prɪ'zʌmptjʊəsnɪs] *n see adj* Unverschämtheit, Dreistigkeit *f*; Überheblichkeit, Anmaßung, Vermessenheit *(geh) f*.

presuppose [,pri:sə'pəʊz] *vt* voraussetzen; *(require also)* zur Voraussetzung haben.

presupposition [,pri:sʌpə'zɪʃən] *n* Voraussetzung *f*.

pre-tax [pri:'tæks] *adj* unversteuert, vor Besteuerung.

pre-teen ['pri:'ti:n] *adj* Kinder- *(bezogen auf die Zeit etwa zwischen dem zehnten und zwölften Lebensjahr)*.

pretence, *(US)* **pretense** [prɪ'tens] *n* **(a)** *(make-believe story)* erfundene Geschichte; *(make-believe person)* erfundene Gestalt ◆ **he didn't really shoot me, it was just ~** er hat nicht auf mich geschossen, er hat nur so getan; **the story of Red Riding Hood is only ~** Rotkäppchen ist nur eine erfundene Geschichte; **to make a ~ of being sth** so tun, als ob man etw sei *or* als sei man etw; **we soon saw through his ~ of being a foreigner** wir durchschauten bald, daß er nur vorspiegelte *or* vorgab, Ausländer zu sein; **he made not even the slightest ~ of being interested** er gab sich *(dat)* nicht einmal den Anschein des Interesses; **this constant ~ that all is well** die ständige Vorspiegelung, daß alles in Ordnung ist; **to maintain a ~ of democracy** den (An)schein einer Demokratie wahren; **it's all a ~** das ist alles nur gespielt *or* Mache *(inf)*.

(b) (*feigning, insincerity*) Heuchelei, Verstellung *f* ♦ **his coolness is just (a) ~** seine Kühle ist nur gespielt; **his ~ of innocence/friendship** seine gespielte Unschuld/Freundschaft; **he made a ~ of friendship** er heuchelte Freundschaft, er gab Freundschaft vor; **let's stop all this ~** hören wir mit der Heuchelei auf, hören wir auf, uns (*dat*) etwas vorzumachen; **he is incapable of ~** er kann sich nicht verstellen.
(c) (*affectation*) Unnatürlichkeit, Geziertheit *f* ♦ **there is not a scrap of ~ in** *or* **about her** sie ist durch und durch natürlich.
(d) **to make no ~ to sth** keinen Anspruch auf etw (*acc*) erheben.
(e) (*pretext, excuse*) Vorwand *m* ♦ **on** *or* **under the ~ of doing sth** unter dem Vorwand, etw zu tun.

pretend [prɪ'tend] [1] *vt* (a) (*make believe*) so tun, als ob; (*feign also*) vortäuschen, vorgeben ♦ **to ~ to be interested** so tun, als ob man interessiert wäre; **to ~ to be sick/have a cold** eine Krankheit/Erkältung vortäuschen *or* vorschützen; **to ~ to be asleep** sich schlafend stellen.
(b) (*claim*) **I don't ~ to ...** ich behaupte nicht, daß ich ...
[2] *vi* (a) so tun, als ob; (*keep up facade*) sich verstellen ♦ **he is only ~ing** er tut nur so (als ob); **let's stop ~ing** hören wir auf, uns (*dat*) etwas vorzumachen.
(b) (*lay claim*) **to ~ to sth** auf etw (*acc*) Anspruch erheben.
[3] *adj* (*inf: child language*) *jewellery, money, gun etc* Spiel- ♦ **it's just ~** (*story etc*) das ist nur Spaß (*inf*).

pretender [prɪ'tendəʳ] *n* (*to throne*) Prätendent *m* (*to* auf +*acc*).

pretense *n* (*US*) *see* **pretence**.

pretension [prɪ'tenʃən] *n* (a) (*claim*) Anspruch *m*; (*social, cultural*) Ambition *f* ♦ **he makes no ~(s) to originality** er beansprucht keineswegs, originell zu sein. (b) (*ostentation*) Prahlerei, Protzerei (*pej inf*) *f*; (*affectation*) Anmaßung *f*.

pretentious [prɪ'tenʃəs] *adj* (*pretending to be important*) anmaßend; *speech, style, book* hochtrabend, hochgestochen; (*ostentatious*) angeberisch, protzig (*inf*), großkotzig (*inf*); *house, restaurant, décor* pompös, bombastisch.

pretentiously [prɪ'tenʃəslɪ] *adv see adj*.

pretentiousness [prɪ'tenʃəsnɪs] *n see adj* Anmaßung *f*; Hochgestochenheit *f*; Angeberei, Protzigkeit (*inf*), Großkotzigkeit (*inf*) *f*; Pomp, Bombast *m*.

preter- ['priːtəʳ-] *pref* über-.

preterite ['pretərɪt] [1] *adj verb* im Imperfekt; (*in English*) im Präteritum; *form* Imperfekt-; Präteritums- ♦ **the ~ tense** das Präteritum, das Imperfekt.
[2] *n* Imperfekt *nt*; Präteritum *nt* ♦ **in the ~** im Imperfekt/Präteritum.

preternatural [,priːtə'nætʃrəl] *adj* (a) (*supernatural*) übernatürlich. (b) (*abnormal, exceptional*) außergewöhnlich.

pretext ['priːtekst] *n* Vorwand *m* ♦ **on** *or* **under the ~ of doing sth** unter dem Vorwand, etw zu tun.

prettify ['prɪtɪfaɪ] *vt* verschönern.

prettily ['prɪtɪlɪ] *adv* nett; *dress also* hübsch.

prettiness ['prɪtɪnɪs] *n* (*pretty appearance*) hübsches Aussehen; (*of manners, compliment etc*) Artigkeit *f* ♦ **the ~ of her hair/face** ihr hübsches Haar/Gesicht.

pretty ['prɪtɪ] [1] *adj* (+*er*) (a) hübsch, nett; *manners, compliment, speech* artig ♦ **to make oneself ~** sich hübsch machen; **I'm/she's not just a ~ face!** (*inf*) ich bin gar nicht so dumm (wie ich aussehe) (*inf*)/sie hat auch Köpfchen; **~ Polly!** (*to parrot*) Lora, Lora!; **it wasn't ~/a ~ sight** das war alles andere als schön/das war kein schöner Anblick; **~-pretty** (*inf*) niedlich.
(b) (*inf*) hübsch, schön (*inf*); *price, sum also* stolz ♦ **it'll cost a ~ penny** das wird eine schöne Stange Geld kosten (*inf*); **a ~ state of affairs/kettle of fish** eine schöne Geschichte/ein schöner Schlamassel; **a ~ mess we're in!** da sitzen wir ganz schön in der Tinte! (*inf*); **say ~ please** sag mal schön bitte.
[2] *adv* (*rather*) ziemlich; *good also* ganz; (*very also*) ganz schön (*inf*), ganz hübsch (*inf*) ♦ **~ nearly** *or* **well finished** so gut wie *or* so ziemlich fertig (*inf*); **how's your job/the patient? — ~ much the same** was macht die Arbeit/der Patient? — so ziemlich wie immer/immer noch so ziemlich gleich.
[3] *n* **my ~** mein Sternchen.
[4] *vt* (*inf*) **to ~ up** schönmachen, verschönern.

pretzel ['pretsl] *n* Brezel *f*.

prevail [prɪ'veɪl] *vi* (a) (*gain mastery*) sich durchsetzen (*over, against* gegenüber). (b) (*conditions, wind etc*) vorherrschen; (*be widespread: customs*) weit verbreitet sein. (c) (*persuade*) **to ~ (up)on sb to do sth** jdn dazu bewegen *or* bringen, etw zu tun.

prevailing [prɪ'veɪlɪŋ] *adj* (a) (*current*) *fashion, conditions* derzeitig, derzeit herrschend, aktuell; *opinion* aktuell; (vor)herrschend. (b) *wind* vorherrschend.

prevalence ['prevələns] *n* (*widespread occurrence*) Vorherrschen *nt*, weite Verbreitung; (*of crime, disease*) Häufigkeit *f*; (*of fashion, style*) Beliebtheit *f*.

prevalent ['prevələnt] *adj* (*widespread*) vorherrschend, weit verbreitet; *opinion, attitude* geläufig, weit verbreitet; *custom, disease* weit verbreitet; *conditions, situation* herrschend; *fashions, style* beliebt ♦ **that sort of thing is very ~ these days** das ist heutzutage sehr geläufig *or* häufig anzutreffen.

prevaricate [prɪ'værɪkeɪt] *vi* Ausflüchte machen.

prevarication [prɪ,værɪ'keɪʃən] *n* Ausflucht *f*; (*prevaricating*) Ausflüchte, Ausweichmanöver *pl*.

prevaricator [prɪ'værɪkeɪtəʳ] *n* Ausweichtaktiker(in *f*) *m*.

▼ **prevent** [prɪ'vent] *vt sth* verhindern, verhüten; (*through preventive measures*) vorbeugen (+*dat*) ♦ **to ~ sb (from) doing sth** jdn daran hindern *or* davon abhalten, etw zu tun; **the gate is there to ~ them from falling down the stairs** das Gitter ist dazu da, daß sie nicht die Treppe hinunterfallen; **to ~ sb from coming** jdn am Kommen hindern; **there is nothing to ~ me** nichts kann mich daran hindern *or* davon abhalten; **to ~ sth (from) happening** verhindern, daß etw geschieht.

➤ LANGUAGE IN USE: **prevent** → 26.3

preventable [prɪ'ventəbl] *adj* vermeidbar, verhütbar.

prevention [prɪ'venʃən] *n* Verhinderung, Verhütung *f*; (*through preventive measures*) Vorbeugung *f* (*of* gegen) ♦ **~ is better than cure** vorbeugen ist besser als heilen; **~ is better than crime** geben Sie dem Verbrechen keine Chance; **society for the ~ of cruelty to animals/children** Tierschutzverein *m*/Kinderschutzbund *m*; **fire ~** Feuerschutz *m*.

preventive [prɪ'ventɪv] [1] *adj* vorbeugend, präventiv, Präventiv- ♦ **to be ~** zur Vorbeugung dienen; **~ medicine** vorbeugende Medizin, Präventivmedizin *f*; **~ detention** (*Brit Jur*) Vorbeugehaft *f*; (*of habitual criminal*) Sicherungsverwahrung *f*; **~ war** Präventivkrieg *m*.
[2] *n* (*~ measure*) Präventivmaßnahme *f*; (*Med*) vorbeugendes Mittel, Präventiv *nt* ♦ **as a ~** als Vorbeugung.

preview ['priːvjuː] [1] *n* (a) (*of play, film*) Vorpremiere *f*; (*of exhibition*) Vorbesichtigung *f* ♦ **to give sb a ~ of sth** (*fig*) jdm eine Vorschau auf etw (*acc*) geben.
(b) (*Film: trailer, TV*) Vorschau *f* (*of* auf +*acc*).
[2] *vt* (*view beforehand*) vorher ansehen; (*show beforehand*) *film* vorher aufführen; *paintings, fashions* vorher zeigen.

previous ['priːvɪəs] *adj* (a) (*immediately preceding*) vorherig; *page, day* vorhergehend; *year* vorangegangen; (*with indef art*) früher ♦ **the ~ page/day/year** die Seite/der Tag/das Jahr davor; **the/a ~ holder of the title** der vorherige/ein früherer Titelträger; **in ~ years** in früheren Jahren, früher; **have you made any ~ applications?** haben Sie sich davor *or* früher schon einmal beworben?; **on a ~ occasion** zuvor, bei einer früheren Gelegenheit; **I have a ~ engagement** ich habe schon einen Termin; **no ~ experience necessary** Vorkenntnisse (sind) nicht erforderlich; **~ conviction** (*Jur*) Vorstrafe *f*; **to have a ~ conviction** vorbestraft sein; **~ owner** Vorbesitzer(in *f*) *m*.
(b) (*hasty*) voreilig.
(c) **~ to** vor (+*dat*); **~ to going out** bevor ich/er *etc* ausging.

previously ['priːvɪəslɪ] *adv* vorher, früher ♦ **he'd arrived three hours ~** er war drei Stunden zuvor angekommen.

pre-war ['priː'wɔːʳ] *adj* Vorkriegs-.

prewash ['priːwɒʃ] *n* (*on washing machine*) Vorwaschgang *m*.

prey [preɪ] [1] *n* (*lit, fig*) Beute *f*; (*animal also*) Beutetier *nt* ♦ **beast/bird of ~** Raubtier *nt*/Raubvogel *m*; **to be/fall ~ to sb/sth** (*lit*) eine Beute von jdm/etw werden; (*fig*) ein Opfer von jdm/etw werden; **she was a ~ to anxiety/depression/suspicion** sie verfiel in Angst/Depressionen/Argwohn.
[2] *vi* **to ~ (up)on** (*animals*) Beute machen auf (+*acc*); (*pirates, thieves*) (aus)plündern; (*swindler etc*) als Opfer aussuchen; (*doubts*) nagen an (+*dat*); (*anxiety*) quälen ♦ **it ~ed (up)on his mind** es ließ ihn nicht los, der Gedanke daran quälte ihn.

prezzie ['prezɪ] *n* (*inf: present*) Geschenk *nt*.

price [praɪs] [1] *n* (a) Preis *m* ♦ **the ~ of coffee/cars** die Kaffee-/Autopreise *pl*; **~s and incomes policy** Lohn-Preis-Politik *f*; **to go up** *or* **rise/to go down** *or* **fall in ~** teurer/billiger werden, im Preis steigen/fallen; **what is the ~ of that?** was kostet das?; **at a ~ of ...** zum Preis(e) von ...; **at a ~** zum entsprechenden Preis, wenn man genug dafür hinlegt (*inf*); **at a reduced ~** verbilligt, zu herabgesetztem *or* reduziertem Preis (*form*); **if the ~ is right** wenn der Preis stimmt; **ask him for a ~ for the job** frag ihn (mal), was das kostet.
(b) (*fig*) Preis *m* ♦ **everybody has his ~** jeder hat seinen Preis; **the ~ of victory/freedom/fame** der Preis für den Sieg/die Freiheit/den Ruhm; **but at what a ~!** aber zu welchem Preis!; **at any price** um jeden Preis; **not at any ~** um keinen Preis; **at the ~ of losing his health and his family** auf Kosten seiner Gesundheit und seiner Familie; **it's too big a ~ to pay** das ist ein zu hoher Preis; **but what ~ honour?** wie kann man Ehre bezahlen?
(c) (*value, valuation*) **a diamond of great ~** ein sehr wertvoller Diamant; **to put a ~ on sth** einen Preis für etw nennen; **but what ~ do you put on freedom?** aber wie ließe sich die Freiheit mit Gold aufwiegen?; **to be beyond/without ~** nicht mit Geld zu bezahlen *or* mit Gold aufzuwiegen sein.
(d) (*reward*) Preis *m* ♦ **to put a ~ on sb's head** eine Belohnung auf jds Kopf (*acc*) aussetzen; **to have a ~ on one's head** steckbrieflich gesucht werden.
(e) (*Betting: odds*) Quote *f* ♦ **what ~ are they giving on that horse?** wie stehen die Wetten für das Pferd?; **the horse had a starting ~ of 3 to 1** das Pferd wurde vor dem Start mit 3:1 gewettet; **what ~ our being able to ...?** (*inf*) wetten, daß wir ... können?; **what ~ freedom/workers' solidarity now?** (*inf*) wie steht es jetzt mit der Freiheit/der Solidarität der Arbeiter?
[2] *vt* (*fix ~ of*) den Preis festsetzen von; (*put ~ label on*) auszeichnen (*at* mit); (*ask ~ of*) nach dem Preis fragen von; (*fig: estimate value of*) schätzen ♦ **it was ~d at £5** (*marked £5*) es war mit £ 5 ausgezeichnet; (*cost £5*) es kostete £ 5; **reasonably ~d** angemessen im Preis; **~d too high/low** zu teuer/billig; **to ~ one's goods/oneself/sb out of the market** seine Waren/sich selbst durch zu hohe Preise konkurrenzunfähig machen/jdn durch niedrigere Preise vom Markt verdrängen.

♦**price down** *vt sep* heruntersetzen, herabsetzen.

♦**price up** *vt sep* heraufsetzen, teurer machen.

price: ~ bracket *n see* **~ range**; **~ control** *n* Preiskontrolle *f*; **~ cut** *n* Preissenkung *f*; **~ cutting** *n* Preissenkungen *pl*; **~ fixing** *n* Preisfestlegung *f*; **~ freeze** *n* Preisstopp *m*; **~ index** *n* Preisindex *m*.

priceless ['praɪslɪs] *adj* unschätzbar, von unschätzbarem Wert; (*inf: amusing*) *joke, film* köstlich; *person* unbezahlbar.

price: ~ limit *n* Preisgrenze *f*; **~ list** *n* Preisliste *f*; **~ range** *n* Preisklasse *f*; **~ rigging** *n* Preisabsprachen *pl*; **~ ring** *n* Preiskartell *nt*; **~ rise** *n* Preiserhöhung *f*; **~ support** *n* (*US*) Subvention, Preisstützung *f*; **~ tag, ~ ticket** *n* Preisschild *nt*; **~ war** *n* Preiskrieg *m*.

pricey ['praɪsɪ] *adj* (*Brit inf*) kostspielig ♦ **that's a bit ~!** das ist ein bißchen happig (*inf*).

pricing policy ['praɪsɪŋ,pɒlɪsɪ] *n* Preispolitik *f*.

prick [prɪk] 1 *n* **(a)** (*puncture, pricking sensation*) Stich *m* ◆ **to give sb/oneself a ~** jdn/sich stechen; **~s of conscience** Gewissensbisse *pl*; *see* **kick against.** **(b)** (*vulg: penis*) Schwanz *m* (*vulg*). **(c)** (*vulg: person*) Arsch(loch *nt*) *m* (*vulg*).
2 *vt* **(a)** (*puncture*) *oneself, sb* stechen; *balloon* durchstechen; *blister* aufstechen; *outline* (durch Löcher) markieren ◆ **to ~ one's finger (with/on sth)** sich (*dat*) (mit etw) in den Finger stechen/sich (*dat*) (an etw *dat*) den Finger stechen; **his conscience ~ed him** er bekam *or* hatte Gewissensbisse; **it/she ~ed his conscience** es/sie bereitete ihm Gewissensbisse.
(b) *see* **~ up 2.**
3 *vi* (*thorn, injection etc*) stechen; (*eyes*) brennen ◆ **the smoke makes my eyes ~** der Rauch brennt mir in den Augen.

◆**prick out** *vt sep* **(a)** *seedlings* pflanzen, setzen, pikieren (*spec*). **(b)** (*mark*) *pattern, shape, design* punktieren; (*with marking wheel*) ausrädeln.

◆**prick up** 1 *vi* **her/its ears ~ed ~** sie/es spitzte die Ohren.
2 *vt sep* **to ~ ~ its/one's ears** (*lit, fig*) die Ohren spitzen.

pricking ['prɪkɪŋ] *n* (*sensation*) Stechen *nt*.

prickle ['prɪkl] 1 *n* **(a)** (*sharp point*) Stachel *m*; (*on plants also*) Dorn *m*. **(b)** (*sensation*) Stechen *nt*; (*caused by wool, beard etc*) Kratzen *nt*; (*tingle, fig*) Prickeln *nt*.
2 *vi* stechen; (*wool, beard*) kratzen; (*tingle, fig*) prickeln.

prickly ['prɪklɪ] *adj* (*+er*) **(a)** *plant, fish, animal* stach(e)lig; *beard, material* kratzig; *sensation* stechend; (*tingling*) prickelnd (*also fig*). **(b)** (*fig*) *person* bissig; *girl also* kratzbürstig (*inf*) ◆ **as ~ as a hedgehog** stachelig wie ein Igel.

prickly: ~ heat *n* Hitzepocken *pl*; **~ pear** *n* (*plant*) Feigenkaktus *m*; (*fruit*) Kaktusfeige *f*.

prick-teaser ['prɪk,tiːzəʳ] *n* (*sl*) **she's just a ~** sie geilt die Männer nur auf (*sl*).

pride [praɪd] 1 *n* **(a)** Stolz *m*; (*arrogance*) Hochmut *m* ◆ **to have too much ~ to do sth** zu stolz sein, um etw zu tun; **to take (a) ~ in sth/in one's appearance** auf etw (*acc*) stolz sein/Wert auf sein Äußeres legen; **to be a (great) source of ~ to sb** jdn mit (großem) Stolz erfüllen; **her ~ and joy** ihr ganzer Stolz; **the ~ of the army/our young men** der Stolz der Armee/die Blüte unserer jungen Männer (*geh*); **to have** *or* **take ~ of place** den Ehrenplatz einnehmen; **~ comes before a fall** (*Prov*) Hochmut kommt vor dem Fall (*Prov*).
(b) (*of lions*) Rudel *nt*.
2 *vr* **to ~ oneself on sth** sich einer Sache (*gen*) rühmen können; **I ~ myself on being something of an expert in this field** ich darf wohl behaupten, mich auf diesem Gebiet auszukennen; **he ~s himself on the preciseness of his prose** er legt großen Wert auf präzise Formulierung.

prie-dieu ['priːdjɜː] *n* Betpult *nt*.

priest [priːst] *n* Priester, Geistliche(r) *m*.

priestess ['priːstɪs] *n* Priesterin *f*.

priest: ~ hole *n* verborgener Winkel (*in dem verfolgte Priester versteckt wurden*); **~hood** *n* Priestertum *nt*; (*priests collectively*) Priesterschaft *f*; **to enter the ~hood** Priester werden.

priestly ['priːstlɪ] *adj* priesterlich; *robes, office also* Priester-.

priest-ridden ['priːst,rɪdn] *adj* klerikalistisch.

prig [prɪg] *n* (*goody-goody*) Tugendlamm *nt* (*inf*); (*boy also*) Musterknabe *m*; (*snob*) Schnösel *m* (*inf*) ◆ **don't be such a ~** tu doch nicht so.

priggish ['prɪgɪʃ] *adj* tugendhaft; (*snobbish*) hochnäsig.

priggishness ['prɪgɪʃnɪs] *n see adj* tugendhaftes Getue, Tugendhaftigkeit *f*; Hochnäsigkeit *f*.

prim [prɪm] *adj* (*+er*) (*also* **~ and proper**) etepetete *pred* (*inf*); (*demure*) *person, dress* sittsam, züchtig; (*prudish*) prüde.

prima ballerina ['priːmə,bælə'riːnə] *n* Primaballerina *f*.

primacy ['praɪməsɪ] *n* **(a)** (*supremacy*) Vorrang *m*; (*position*) Vorrangstellung *f*. **(b)** (*Eccl*) Primat *nt or m*.

prima donna ['priːmə'dɒnə] *n* (*lit, fig*) Primadonna *f*.

primaeval *adj see* **primeval.**

prima facie ['praɪmə'feɪʃɪ] 1 *adv* allem Anschein nach.
2 *adj* **there are ~ reasons why ...** es gibt klar erkennbare Gründe, warum ...; **~ evidence** glaubhafter Beweis; **the police have a ~ case** die Polizei hat genügend Beweise; **a ~ case of ...** auf den ersten Blick ein Fall von ...

primal ['praɪməl] *adj* ursprünglich, Ur- ◆ **~ scream** Urschrei *m*.

primarily ['praɪmərɪlɪ] *adv* hauptsächlich, in erster Linie.

primary ['praɪmərɪ] 1 *adj* (*chief, main*) Haupt-, wesentlich, primär (*form*) ◆ **that is our ~ concern** das ist unser Hauptanliegen *or* unsere Hauptsorge; **of ~ importance** von größter Bedeutung, von äußerster Wichtigkeit; **the ~ meaning of a word** die Grundbedeutung eines Wortes.
2 *n* **(a)** (*colour*) Grundfarbe *f*.
(b) (*US: election*) (innerparteiliche) Vorwahl.

primary: ~ cell *n* Primärzelle *f*; **~ colour** *n* Grundfarbe *f*; **~ education** *n* Grundschul(aus)bildung *f*; **~ election** *n* (*US*) (innerparteiliche) Vorwahl; **~ feather** *n* Handschwinge *f*; **~ industry** *n* Grund(stoff)industrie *f*; (*agriculture etc*) Urindustrie *f*, primäre Industrie (*form*); (*main industry*) Hauptindustrie *f*; **~ institution** *n* Ureinrichtung *f*; **~ product** *n* Primärprodukt *nt*; (*main product*) Hauptprodukt *nt*; **~ rocks** *npl* Primärgestein *nt*; **~ school** *n* Grundschule *f*; **~ stress** *n* Hauptton *m*; **~ teacher** *n* Grundschullehrer(in *f*) *m*; **~ winding** *n* Primärwindung *f*.

primate ['praɪmɪt] *n* **(a)** (*Zool*) Primat *m*. **(b)** (*Eccl*) Primas *m* ◆ **P~ of England/all England** Erzbischof von York/Canterbury.

prime [praɪm] 1 *adj* **(a)** (*major, chief*) Haupt-, wesentlich ◆ **of ~ importance** von größter Bedeutung, von äußerster Wichtigkeit; **my ~ concern** mein Hauptanliegen *nt*; **she was a ~ favourite** sie war ein hoher Favorit.
(b) (*excellent*) erstklassig, beste(r, s); *example* erstklassig ◆ **in ~ condition** (*meat, fruit etc*) von hervorragender Qualität; (*athlete, car etc*) in erstklassiger *or* hervorragender Verfassung; **~ cut** Stück *nt* bester Qualität.
(c) (*Math*) *number, factor* Prim-.
2 *n* **(a)** (*full vigour*) **in the ~ of life/youth** in der Blüte seiner Jahre/der Jugend; **he is in/past his ~** er ist im besten Alter *or* in den besten Jahren/er ist über sein bestes Alter *or* seine besten Jahre hinaus; (*singer, artist*) er ist an seinem Höhepunkt angelangt/er hat seine beste Zeit hinter sich; **this chop/chair is past its ~** dieses Kotelett ist auch nicht mehr das jüngste/der Stuhl hat auch schon bessere Zeiten gesehen.
(b) (*Math*) Primzahl *f*.
(c) (*Eccl: also* **P~**) Prim *f*.
3 *vt* **(a)** *gun* schußfertig machen; *bomb* scharf machen; *pump* vorpumpen; *carburettor* Anlaßkraftstoff einspritzen in (*+acc*).
(b) *surface for painting* grundieren.
(c) (*with advice, information*) instruieren ◆ **to be well ~d for the interview/game** für das Interview/Spiel gut gerüstet sein.
(d) *person* (*with drink*) alkoholisieren, unter Alkohol setzen ◆ **well ~d** (*with drink*) gut gestärkt (*inf*).

prime: ~ costs *npl* (*Comm*) Selbstkosten, Gestehungskosten *pl*; **~ meridian** *n* Nullmeridian *m*; **~ minister** *n* Ministerpräsident(in *f*), Premierminister(in *f*) *m*; **~ ministerial** *adj* des Premierministers, der Premierministerin; **~ ministership** *n* Amt *nt* des Premierministers; **during her ~ ministership** während ihrer Amtszeit als Premierministerin; **~ mover** *n* (*Phys, Tech*) Zugmaschine *f*; (*Philos*) bewegende Kraft, Triebfeder *f*; (*fig: person*) treibende Kraft; **~ number** *n* Primzahl *f*.

primer ['praɪməʳ] *n* **(a)** (*paint*) Grundierfarbe, Grundierung *f*; (*coat*) Grundierung *f*, Grundieranstrich *m*. **(b)** (*book*) Fibel *f*. **(c)** (*explosive*) Zündhütchen *nt*, Treibladungszünder *m*.

prime: ~ ribs *npl* Hochrippen *pl*; **~ time** *n* (*US*) Haupteinschaltzeit *f*.

primeval [praɪ'miːvəl] *adj* urzeitlich; *forest* Ur- ◆ **~ soup** *or* **slime** Urschleim *m*.

primitive ['prɪmɪtɪv] 1 *adj* primitiv; (*Art*) naiv.
2 *n* (*Art*) (*artist*) Naive(r) *mf*; (*work*) naives Werk.

primitivism ['prɪmɪtɪvɪzəm] *n* (*Art*) naive Kunst.

primly ['prɪmlɪ] *adv* (*demurely*) sittsam, züchtig; überkorrekt; (*prudishly*) prüde ◆ **sitting ~ sipping tea** steif und vornehm an ihrem *etc* Tee nippend.

primness ['prɪmnɪs] *n* übertrieben sittsame Art (*inf*); (*demureness*) Sittsamkeit, Züchtigkeit *f*; (*prudishness*) Prüderie *f*.

primogenitor [,praɪməʊ'dʒenɪtəʳ] *n* (*ancestor*) Ahn(e), Vorfahr *m*; (*first ancestor*) Urahn(e), Stammvater *m*.

primogeniture [,praɪməʊ'dʒenɪtʃəʳ] *n* Erstgeburt *f* ◆ **right of ~** Erstgeburtsrecht *nt*.

primordial [praɪ'mɔːdɪəl] *adj* primordial (*spec*), ursprünglich; *matter* Ur-.

primp [prɪmp] 1 *vt* zurechtmachen; *hair also* richten ◆ **to ~ oneself (up)** sich feinmachen *or* schniegeln.
2 *vi* sich zurechtmachen.

primrose ['prɪmrəʊz] 1 *n* (*Bot*) Erd-Schlüsselblume *f*; (*colour*) Blaßgelb *nt*.
2 *adj* blaßgelb ◆ **the ~ path** (*fig*) der Rosenpfad.

primula ['prɪmjʊlə] *n* Primel *f*.

primus (stove) ® ['praɪməs(,stəʊv)] *n* Primuskocher *m*.

prince [prɪns] *n* (*king's son*) Prinz *m*; (*ruler*) Fürst *m* ◆ **P~ Charming** (*in fairy story*) der Königssohn; (*fig*) der Märchenprinz; **~ consort/regent** Prinzgemahl *m*/-regent *m*; **the P~ of Darkness/Peace** der Fürst der Finsternis/der Friedensfürst; **a ~ among men** eine herausragende Erscheinung.

princedom ['prɪnsdəm] *n* (*old*) Fürstentum *nt*.

princeling ['prɪnslɪŋ] *n* (*old, liter*) Prinzchen *nt*.

princely ['prɪnslɪ] *adj* (*lit, fig*) fürstlich.

princess [prɪn'ses] *n* Prinzessin *f*; (*wife of ruler*) Fürstin *f*.

principal ['prɪnsɪpəl] 1 *adj* Haupt-, hauptsächlich ◆ **the ~ cities of China** die wichtigsten Städte Chinas; **my ~ concern** mein Hauptanliegen *nt*; **~ teacher** Rektor *m*; **~ horn in the Philharmonic Orchestra** erster Hornist/erste Hornistin der Philharmoniker; **~ boy** (*Theat*) *jugendliche Hauptrolle in britischen Weihnachtsrevuen, die traditionsgemäß von einem Mädchen gespielt wird*; **~ parts** (*Gram: of verb*) Stammformen *pl*.
2 *n* **(a)** (*of school, college*) Rektor *m*; (*in play*) Hauptperson *f*; (*in duel*) Duellant *m*. **(b)** (*Fin*) (*of investment*) Kapital(summe *f*) *nt*; (*of debt*) Kreditsumme *f*. **(c)** (*esp Jur: client*) Klient(in *f*), Mandant(in *f*) *m*.

principality [,prɪnsɪ'pælɪtɪ] *n* Fürstentum *nt*.

principally ['prɪnsɪpəlɪ] *adv* vornehmlich, in erster Linie.

principle ['prɪnsɪpl] *n* **(a)** Prinzip *nt* ◆ **to go back to first ~s** zu den Grundlagen zurückgehen.
(b) (*moral precept*) Prinzip *nt*, Grundsatz *m*; (*no pl: integrity*) Prinzipien, Grundsätze *pl* ◆ **in/on ~** im/aus Prinzip, prinzipiell; **a man of ~(s)** ein Mensch mit *or* von Prinzipien *or* Grundsätzen; **it's against my ~s** es geht gegen meine Prinzipien; **it's a matter of ~, it's the ~ of the thing** es geht dabei ums Prinzip; **I'm doing it for reasons of ~** ich tue das aus Prinzip.
(c) (*basic element*) Element *nt*.

principled ['prɪnsɪpld] *adj man, statesman* mit Prinzipien *or* Grundsätzen, prinzipientreu ◆ **high-~** mit hohen Prinzipien *or* Grundsätzen; **low-~** ohne Prinzipien *or* Grundsätze.

prink [prɪŋk] *vti see* **primp.**

print [prɪnt] 1 *n* **(a)** (*typeface, characters*) Schrift *f*; (*~ed matter*) Gedruckte(s) *nt* ◆ **out of/in ~** vergriffen/gedruckt; **to be in ~ again** wieder erhältlich sein;

to see sth in cold ~ etw schwarz auf weiß sehen; **he'll never get into ~** er wird nie etwas veröffentlichen; **don't let that get into ~** das darf nicht erscheinen; **in big ~** groß gedruckt; *see* **small ~.**
(b) (*picture*) Druck *m.*
(c) (*Phot*) Abzug *m,* Kopie *f.*
(d) (*fabric*) bedruckter Stoff; (*cotton ~*) Kattun *m;* (*dress*) bedrucktes Kleid; (*of cotton*) Kattunkleid *nt.*
(e) (*impression: of foot, hand etc*) Abdruck *m* ◆ **to take sb's ~s** (*police*) von jdm Fingerabdrücke machen *or* nehmen.
2 *vt* **(a)** *book, design* drucken; (*Comput also*) ausdrucken; *fabric* bedrucken ◆ **it is ~ed on his memory** das hat sich in sein Gedächtnis eingegraben.
(b) (*publish*) *story* veröffentlichen.
(c) (*write in block letters*) in Druckschrift schreiben ◆ **to ~ sth in large letters** etw in Großbuchstaben schreiben.
(d) (*Phot*) abziehen.
(e) hoof marks ~ed in the sand Hufabdrücke *pl* im Sand.
3 *vi* **(a)** (*printer, printing machine*) drucken ◆ **ready to ~** (*book*) druckfertig; (*machine*) druckbereit; **the book is ~ing now** das Buch ist gerade im Druck; **the photos didn't ~ well** die Bilder kamen nicht gut heraus.
(b) (*write in block letters*) in Druckschrift schreiben.

◆**print off** *vt sep* (*Typ*) drucken; (*Phot*) abziehen.

◆**print out** *vt sep* (*Comput*) ausdrucken ◆ **~ ~ the results, please** würden Sie bitte die Ergebnisse ausdrucken lassen.

printable ['prɪntəbl] *adj* druckfähig; *photograph* abzugsfähig, reproduzierbar.

print drum *n* (*Comput*) Drucktrommel *f.*

printed ['prɪntɪd] *adj* Druck-, gedruckt; (*written in capitals*) in Großbuchstaben; *fabric* bedruckt ◆ **~ matter/papers** Drucksache *f;* **the ~ word** das gedruckte Wort; **~ circuit** gedruckte Schaltung; **~ circuit board** Leiterplatte *f.*

printer ['prɪntəʳ] *n* Drucker *m* ◆ **the text has gone to the ~** der Text ist in Druck gegangen; **~'s devil** Setzerjunge *m;* **~'s error** Druckfehler *m;* **~'s ink** Druckerschwärze *f.*

printer *in cpds see* **print; ~ driver** *n* (*Comput*) Druckertreiber *m.*

printery ['prɪntərɪ] *n* Druckerei *f.*

print head *n* (*Comput*) Druckkopf *m.*

printing ['prɪntɪŋ] *n* **(a)** (*process*) Drucken *nt.* **(b)** (*unjoined writing*) Druckschrift *f;* (*characters, print*) Schrift *f.* **(c)** (*quantity printed*) Auflage *f.*

printing: ~ frame *n* Kopierrahmen *m;* **~-ink** *n* Druckerschwärze *f;* **~ press** *n* Druckerpresse *f;* **~ works** *n sing or pl* Druckerei *f.*

print: ~ list *n* (*Comput*) Druckliste *f;* **~-maker** *n* (*artist*) Grafiker *m;* (*manufacturer*) Druckhersteller *m;* **~ menu** *n* (*Comput*) Druckmenü *nt;* **~-out** *n* (*Comput*) Ausdruck *m;* **~ queue** *n* (*Comput*) Druckerwarteschlange *f;* **~ run** *n* Auflage *f;* **~-seller** *n* Grafikhändler(in *f*) *m;* **~-shop** *n* Grafikhandlung *f;* (*in printing works*) Druckmaschinensaal *m;* **~ speed** *n* (*Comput*) Druckgeschwindigkeit *f;* **~-through paper** *n* (*Comput*) Durchschlagpapier *nt;* **~ wheel** *n* (*Comput*) Typenrad *nt.*

prior¹ ['praɪəʳ] *adj* **(a)** *knowledge, warning, agreement* vorherig; (*earlier*) früher ◆ **~ claim** Vorrecht *nt* (*to* auf *+acc*); **a ~ engagement** eine vorher getroffene Verabredung. **(b) ~ to sth** vor etw (*dat*); **~ to going out** bevor ich/er *etc* ausging.

prior² *n* (*Eccl*) Prior *m.*

prioress ['praɪərɪs] *n* Priorin *f.*

prioritization [praɪˌɒrɪtaɪ'zeɪʃən] *n* Ordnung *f* nach Priorität ◆ **~ of free market ideas was a mistake** es war ein Fehler, dem freien Markt eine Vorrangstellung einzuräumen.

prioritize [praɪ'ɒrɪtaɪz] *vt* (*arrange in order of priority*) der Priorität nach ordnen; (*make a priority*) Priorität einräumen (*+dat*).

priority [praɪ'ɒrɪtɪ] *n* Vorrang *m,* Priorität *f;* (*thing having precedence*) vorrangige Sache *or* Angelegenheit ◆ **a top ~** eine Sache *or* Angelegenheit (von) äußerster Dringlichkeit *or* höchster Priorität; **what is your top ~?** was steht bei Ihnen an erster Stelle?; **it must be given top ~** das muß vorrangig behandelt werden; **to have ~** Vorrang *or* Priorität haben; **to give ~ to sth** etw vorrangig behandeln, einer Sache (*dat*) Priorität geben; **in strict order of ~** ganz nach Dringlichkeit; **we must get our priorities right** wir müssen unsere Prioritäten richtig setzen; **you've got your priorities all wrong** du weißt ja nicht, was wirklich wichtig ist; **you should get your priorities right** du solltest deine Prioritäten finden; **high/low on the list of priorities** *or* **the ~ list** oben/unten auf der Prioritätenliste.

priority: ~ share *n* (*Fin*) Vorzugsaktie *f;* **~ treatment** *n* Vorzugsbehandlung *f;* **to get ~ treatment** bevorzugt behandelt werden.

priory ['praɪərɪ] *n* Priorat *nt;* (*in church names*) ≃ Münster *nt.*

prise, (*US*) **prize** [praɪz] *vt* **to ~ sth open** etw aufbrechen; **to ~ the lid up/off** den Deckel auf-/abbekommen; **to ~ sth out (of sth)** etw aus etw herausbekommen; **to ~ a secret out of sb** jdm ein Geheimnis entlocken.

prism ['prɪzəm] *n* Prisma *nt.*

prismatic [prɪz'mætɪk] *adj* prismatisch; *colour* Spektral-; (*multi-coloured*) in den Farben des Spektrums.

prison ['prɪzn] 1 *n* (*lit, fig*) Gefängnis *nt* ◆ **to be in ~** im Gefängnis sein *or* sitzen; **to go to ~ for 5 years** für *or* auf 5 Jahre ins Gefängnis gehen *or* wandern (*inf*); **to send sb to ~** jdn ins Gefängnis schicken, jdn zu einer Freiheitsstrafe verurteilen.
2 *attr* Gefängnis-; *system, facilities* Strafvollzugs- ◆ **~ camp** Gefangenenlager *nt;* **~ life** das Leben im Gefängnis; **~ visitor** Gefangenenbetreuer(in *f*) *m.*

prisoner ['prɪznəʳ] *n* Gefangene(r) *mf* (*also Mil, fig*); (*Jur*) (*under arrest*) Festgenommene(r) *mf;* (*facing charge, at the bar*) Angeklagte(r) *mf;* (*convicted also*) Häftling, Sträfling *m* ◆ **to hold** *or* **keep sb ~** jdn gefangenhalten; **to take sb ~** jdn gefangennehmen; **~ of war** Kriegsgefangene(r) *m;* **~ of war camp** (Kriegs)gefangenenlager *nt.*

prissy ['prɪsɪ] *adj* (*pej*) zimperlich; *dress, hairstyle* brav.

pristine ['prɪstaɪn] *adj* (*in unspoilt state*) *beauty* unberührt, ursprünglich; *condition* tadellos, makellos; (*original*) urtümlich, ursprünglich.

prithee ['prɪðiː] *interj* (*obs*) bitte.

privacy ['prɪvəsɪ, 'praɪvəsɪ] *n* Privatleben *nt* ◆ **there is no ~ in these flats** in diesen Mietwohnungen kann man kein Privatleben führen; **in the ~ of one's home** im eigenen Heim; **in an open-plan office one has no ~** in einem Großraumbüro hat man keinen privaten Bereich; **in the strictest ~** (*meeting, preparations*) unter äußerster Geheimhaltung.

private ['praɪvɪt] 1 *adj* **(a)** privat; (*personal also*) *letter, reasons* persönlich; (*confidential also*) *matter, affair* Privat-, vertraulich; (*secluded*) *place* abgelegen; *dining room* separat; (*not public*) *funeral, wedding* im engsten Kreis; *hearing, sitting* nichtöffentlich *attr* ◆ **they were sharing a ~ joke** sie fanden irgend etwas lustig; **it's just a ~ joke between us** das ist ein Privatwitz von uns; **no ~ jokes!** laß uns auch mitlachen!; **~ and confidential** streng vertraulich; **~ property** Privateigentum *nt;* **he acted in a ~ capacity** er handelte als Privatperson; **they wanted to be ~** sie wollten allein *or* für sich sein; **to keep sth ~** etw für sich behalten; **his ~ life** sein Privatleben *nt;* **in his ~ thoughts** in seinen ganz persönlichen Gedanken.
(b) ~ car Privatwagen *m;* **~ citizen** Privatperson *f;* **~ company** Privatgesellschaft *f;* **~ detective** Privatdetektiv *m;* **~ education** Ausbildung *f* in Privatschulen; **~ enterprise** Privatunternehmen *nt;* (*free enterprise*) freies Unternehmertum; **~ eye** (*inf*) Privatdetektiv, Schnüffler (*pej inf*) *m;* **~ individual** Einzelne(r) *mf;* **~ law** Privatrecht *nt;* **~ limited company** Aktiengesellschaft *f* (*die nicht an der Börse notiert ist*); **~ means** Privatvermögen *nt;* **~ member** Abgeordnete(r) *mf;* **~ member's bill** Gesetzesinitiative *f* eines Abgeordneten; **~ parts** (*genitals*) Geschlechtsteile *pl;* **~ (medical) practice** (*Brit*) Privatpraxis *f;* **he is in ~ practice** er hat Privatpatienten; **~ pupil** Privatschüler(in *f*) *m;* **~ secretary** Privatsekretär(in *f*) *m;* **~ school** Privatschule *f;* **~ sector** privater Sektor; **~-sector company** Unternehmen *nt* des privaten Sektors, privatwirtschaftliches Unternehmen; **~ soldier** (*Mil*) gemeiner *or* einfacher Soldat; **~ tuition** Privatunterricht *m;* **~ tutor** Privatlehrer(in *f*) *m;* **~ view** Vorabbesichtigung *f;* **~ ward** Privatabteilung *or* -station *f.*
2 *n* **(a)** (*Mil*) Gefreite(r) *mf* ◆ **P~ X** der Gefreite X; (*in address*) Gefreiter X; **~ first class** (*US*) Obergefreite(r) *mf.*
(b) ~s *pl* (*genitals*) Geschlechtsteile, Weichteile (*inf*) *pl.*
(c) in ~ privat; (*Jur*) unter Ausschluß der Öffentlichkeit; **we must talk in ~** wir müssen das unter uns besprechen.

privateer [ˌpraɪvə'tɪəʳ] *n* (*ship*) Freibeuter *m,* Kaperschiff *nt;* (*crew member*) Freibeuter, Kaperer *m.*

privately ['praɪvɪtlɪ] *adv* **(a)** (*not publicly*) privat ◆ **the meeting was held ~** das Treffen wurde in kleinem Kreis *or* Rahmen abgehalten; **a ~ owned company** eine Gesellschaft in Privatbesitz; **he is being ~ educated** er wird privat erzogen.
(b) (*secretly, personally, unofficially*) persönlich ◆ **I have been told ~ that ...** mir wurde vertraulich mitgeteilt, daß ...; **so he spoke ~ to me** deshalb sprach er mit mir unter vier Augen; **~ I think that ...** ich persönlich glaube, daß ...; **but ~ he was very upset** doch innerlich war er sehr aufgebracht.

privation [praɪ'veɪʃən] *n* **(a)** (*state*) Armut, Not *f* ◆ **a life of ~** ein Leben in Armut *or* Not. **(b)** (*hardship*) Entbehrung, Einschränkung *f* ◆ **to suffer many ~s** viele Entbehrungen erleiden; **war-time ~s** die Entbehrungen *pl* der Kriegszeit.

privatization [ˌpraɪvətaɪ'zeɪʃən] *n* Privatisierung *f.*

privatize ['praɪvətaɪz] *vt* privatisieren.

privet ['prɪvɪt] *n* (gemeiner) Liguster ◆ **~ hedge** Ligusterhecke *f.*

privilege ['prɪvɪlɪdʒ] 1 *n* (*prerogative*) Privileg, Sonderrecht *nt;* (*honour*) Ehre *f;* (*Parl*) Immunität *f* ◆ **it's a lady's ~** es ist das Vorrecht einer Dame.
2 *vt* privilegieren, bevorrechtigen ◆ **I was ~d to meet him** ich hatte das Privileg *or* die Ehre, ihm vorgestellt zu werden.

privileged ['prɪvɪlɪdʒd] *adj person, classes* privilegiert; (*Parl*) *speech* der Immunität unterliegend *attr; claim, debt* bevorrechtigt ◆ **for a ~ few** für wenige Privilegierte, für eine kleine Gruppe von Privilegierten; **~ communication** (*Jur*) vertrauliche Mitteilung; **~ stock** Vorzugsaktie *f.*

privily ['prɪvɪlɪ] *adv* (*old*) insgeheim, im geheimen.

privy ['prɪvɪ] 1 *adj* **(a) to be ~ to sth** in etw (*acc*) eingeweiht sein. **(b) P~** geheim; **P~ Council, P~ Councillor** Geheimer Rat; **P~ Purse** Privatschatulle *f.*
2 *n* Abort, Abtritt *m.*

prize¹ [praɪz] 1 *n* **(a)** Preis *m;* (*in lottery also*) Gewinn *m* ◆ **the glittering ~s of the pop world** der Flimmerglanz der Popwelt; **there are no ~s for guessing** (*inf*) dreimal darfst du raten.
(b) (*Naut: captured ship*) Prise *f* (*old*).
2 *adj* **(a)** (*awarded a ~*) *entry, essay, sheep* preisgekrönt ◆ **~ idiot** (*inf*) Vollidiot *m* (*inf*). **(b)** (*awarded as a ~*) *trophy* Sieges- ◆ **~ cup** (Sieger)pokal *m;* **~ medal** Medaille *f.* **(c)** (*offering a ~*) *competition* Preis- ◆ **~ draw** Lotterie, Tombola *f.*
3 *vt* (hoch)schätzen ◆ **to ~ sth highly** etw sehr *or* hoch schätzen; **to ~ sth above sth** etw über *or* vor etw (*acc*) stellen; **~d possession** wertvollster Besitz, wertvollstes Stück; (*of museum etc*) Glanzstück, Paradestück *nt.*

prize² *vt* (*US*) *see* **prise.**

prize: ~ day *n* (*Sch*) (Tag *m* der) Preisverleihung *f;* **~-fight** *n* Profi- *or* Berufsboxkampf *m;* **~-fighter** *n* Profi- *or* Berufsboxer *m;* **~-fighting** *n* Profi- *or* Berufsboxkampf *m;* **~-giving** *n* (*Sch*) Preisverleihung *or* -verteilung *f*; **~-list** *n* (*in lottery, competition*) Gewinnerliste *f*; **~ money** *n* **(a)** (*cash ~*) Geld- *or* Barpreis *m*; (*Boxing*) (Sieges)prämie *f*; (*in competition*) Gewinn *m*; **(b)** (*old Naut*) Prisengeld *nt*; **~-ring** *n* (*Boxing*) Ring *m*; **~winner** *n* (Preis)gewinner(in *f*) *m*; **~winning** *adj entry, novel* preisgekrönt; *ticket* Gewinn-.

PRO *abbr of* **public relations officer.**

pro¹ [prəʊ] *n* (*inf*) Profi *m*.

pro² *n* (*inf: prostitute*) Nutte *f* (*inf*).

pro³ [1] *prep* (*in favour of*) für.
[2] *n* **the ~s and cons** das Für und Wider, das Pro und Kontra.

pro- *pref* **(a)** (*in favour of*) pro- ◆ **~-Soviet** prosowjetisch. **(b)** (*acting for*) Pro-.

pro-am ['prəʊ'æm] *adj* **~ golf** *Golf nt, bei dem Profis gegen (prominente) Amateure spielen.*

▼ **probability** [,prɒbə'bɪlɪtɪ] *n* Wahrscheinlichkeit *f* ◆ **in all ~** aller Wahrscheinlichkeit nach, höchstwahrscheinlich; **what's the ~** *or* **what are the probabilities of that happening?** wie groß ist die Wahrscheinlichkeit, daß das geschieht?; **the ~ is that he will leave** wahrscheinlich wird er weggehen.

▼ **probable** ['prɒbəbl] *adj* wahrscheinlich.

▼ **probably** ['prɒbəblɪ] *adv see adj* ◆ **very ~, but ...** durchaus möglich, aber ...; **more ~ than not** höchstwahrscheinlich.

probate ['prəʊbɪt] *n* (*examination*) gerichtliche Testamentsbestätigung; (*will*) beglaubigte Testamentsabschrift ◆ **~ court** Nachlaßgericht *nt*; **to grant sb ~** jdm aufgrund der Testamentseröffnung einen Erbschein ausstellen.

probation [prə'beɪʃən] *n* **(a)** (*Jur*) Bewährung *f* ◆ **to put sb on ~ (for a year)** jdm (ein Jahr) Bewährung geben; **to be on ~** auf Bewährung sein, Bewährung haben; **~ officer** Bewährungshelfer(in *f*) *m*. **(b)** (*of employee*) Probe *f*; (*~ period*) Probezeit *f*; (*Rel*) Noviziat *nt*.

probationary [prə'beɪʃnərɪ] *adj* **(a)** Probe- ◆ **~ period** Probezeit *f*. **(b)** (*Jur*) Bewährungs-.

probationer [prə'beɪʃnəʳ] *n* (*Jur*) auf Bewährung Freigelassene(r) *mf*; (*Med*) Lernschwester *f*; (*Rel*) Novize *m*, Novizin *f*.

probe [prəʊb] [1] *n* **(a)** (*device*) Sonde *f*.
(b) (*investigation*) Untersuchung *f* (*into gen*) ◆ **a police ~ revealed ...** Nachforschungen der Polizei ergaben ...
[2] *vt* untersuchen, sondieren; *space, sb's past, subconscious, private life* erforschen; *mystery* ergründen, erforschen.
[3] *vi* suchen, forschen (*for* nach); (*Med*) untersuchen (*for* auf +*acc*); (*inquire*) forschen, bohren (*for* nach) ◆ **to ~ into a wound/sb's private life/sb's past** eine Wunde mit der Sonde untersuchen/in jds Privatleben (*dat*) herumschnüffeln/in jds Vergangenheit (*dat*) bohren.

probing ['prəʊbɪŋ] [1] *n* Untersuchung *f*; (*with device also*) Sondierung *f*, Sondieren *nt* ◆ **all this ~ into people's private affairs** dieses Herumschnüffeln in den privaten Angelegenheiten der Leute.
[2] *adj question, study, fingers* prüfend.

probity ['prəʊbɪtɪ] *n* (*form*) Redlichkeit, Integrität (*geh*) *f*.

▼ **problem** ['prɒbləm] *n* Problem *nt*; (*Math: as school exercise*) Aufgabe *f*; (*problematic area*) Problematik *f* ◆ **what's the ~?** wo fehlt's?; **he's got a drinking ~** er trinkt (zuviel); **I had no ~ in getting the money** ich habe das Geld ohne Schwierigkeiten bekommen; **no ~!** (*inf*) kein Problem!; **the whole ~ of modernization** die ganze Modernisierungsproblematik; **~ area** Problembereich *m*.

problematic(al) [,prɒblə'mætɪk(əl)] *adj* problematisch.

problem: ~ child *n* Problemkind *nt*; **~ family** *n* Problemfamilie *f*; **~-oriented** *adj* (*Comput*) problemorientiert; **~ page** *n* Problemseite *f*; **~ play** *n* Problemstück *nt*.

proboscis [prəʊ'bɒsɪs] *n* (*Zool, hum inf*) Rüssel *m*.

procedural [prə'siːdjʊrəl] *adj* verfahrenstechnisch; (*Jur*) verfahrensrechtlich.

procedure [prə'siːdʒəʳ] *n* Verfahren *nt* ◆ **parliamentary/legal ~(s)** parlamentarisches/gerichtliches Verfahren; **what would be the correct ~ in such a case?** wie geht man in einem solchen Falle vor?, wie verfährt man in einem solchen Falle?; **business ~** geschäftliche Verfahrensweise; **rules of ~** Vorschriften *pl*; **questions of ~** verfahrenstechnische *or* (*Jur*) verfahrensrechtliche Fragen *pl*; **~-oriented** (*Comput*) prozedurorientiert.

proceed [prə'siːd] [1] *vi* **(a)** (*form: go*) **vehicles must ~ with caution** vorsichtig fahren!; **I was ~ing along the High Street** ich ging die High Street entlang; **please ~ to gate 3** begeben Sie sich zum Flugsteig 3.
(b) (*form: go on*) (*person*) weitergehen; (*vehicle, by vehicle*) weiterfahren ◆ **we then ~ed to London** wir fuhren dann nach London weiter, wir begaben uns dann nach London (*geh*); **to ~ on one's way** seinen Weg fortsetzen.
(c) (*carry on, continue*) fortfahren; **can we now ~ to the next item on the agenda?** können wir jetzt zum nächsten Punkt der Tagesordnung übergehen?; **they ~ed with their plan** sie führten ihren Plan weiter; (*start*) sie gingen nach ihrem Plan vor; **to ~ about one's business** (*form*) seinen Geschäften (*dat*) nachgehen (*geh*); **~ with your work** fahren Sie mit Ihrer Arbeit fort; **the text ~s as follows** der Text lautet dann wie folgt; **everything/the plan is ~ing satisfactorily** alles läuft bestens/alles verläuft nach Plan; **negotiations are ~ing well** die Verhandlungen kommen gut voran; **you may ~** (*speak*) Sie haben das Wort; **I would like to make a statement — ~** ich möchte eine Aussage machen — bitte!
(d) (*set about sth*) vorgehen ◆ **how does one ~ in such cases?** wie verfährt man in solchen Fällen?, wie geht man in solchen Fällen vor?; **to ~ on the assumption that ...** von der Voraussetzung ausgehen, daß ...
(e) (*originate*) **to ~ from** kommen von; (*fig*) herrühren von; **all life ~s from the sea** alles Leben kommt aus dem Meer.
(f) (*Jur*) **to ~ against sb** gegen jdn gerichtlich vorgehen; **to ~ with a case** einen Prozeß anstrengen.
[2] *vt* **now, he ~ed** nun, fuhr er fort; **to ~ to do sth** (dann) etw tun.

proceeding [prə'siːdɪŋ] *n* **(a)** (*action, course of action*) Vorgehen *nt* ◆ **our best/safest way of ~ would be to ask him** am besten/sichersten wäre es, wenn wir ihn fragten; **there were some odd ~s** merkwürdige Dinge gingen vor.
(b) ~s *pl* (*function*) Veranstaltung *f*.
(c) ~s *pl* (*esp Jur*) Verfahren *nt* ◆ **court ~s** Gerichtsverhandlung *f*; **to take/start ~s against sb** gegen jdn gerichtlich vorgehen; **to take legal/divorce ~s** ein Gerichtsverfahren *or* einen Prozeß anstrengen/die Scheidung einreichen.
(d) ~s *pl* (*record*) (*written minutes etc*) Protokoll *nt*; (*published report*) Tätigkeitsbericht *m*.

proceeds ['prəʊsiːdz] *npl* (*yield*) Ertrag *m*; (*from sale, bazaar, raffle*) Erlös *m*; (*takings*) Einnahmen *pl*.

process¹ ['prəʊses] [1] *n* **(a)** Prozeß *m* ◆ **the ~es of the law** der Gesetzesweg; **the ~ of time will ...** die Zeit wird ...; **in the ~ of time** im Laufe der Zeit, mit der Zeit; **in the ~** dabei; **in the ~ of learning** beim Lernen; **to be in the ~ of doing sth/being made** dabei sein, etw zu tun/gerade gemacht werden; **in ~ of construction** im Bau.
(b) (*specific method, technique*) Verfahren *nt*; (*Ind also*) Prozeß *m* ◆ **~ engineering** Prozeß- *or* Verfahrenstechnik *f*; **~ printing** (*Typ*) Vierfarbendruck *m*.
(c) (*Jur*) Prozeß *m*, Verfahren *nt* ◆ **to serve a ~ on sb** jdn vorladen; **~-server** Zustellungsbeamte(r) *m*.
(d) (*Biol*) vorstehender Teil ◆ **a ~ of a bone/of the jaw** ein Knochen-/Kiefernvorsprung *m*.
[2] *vt* (*treat*) *raw materials, data, information, waste* verarbeiten; *food* konservieren; *milk* sterilisieren; *application, loan, wood* bearbeiten; *film* entwickeln; (*deal with*) *applicants, people* abfertigen ◆ **~ed cheese**, (*US*) **~ cheese** Schmelzkäse *m*.

process² [prə'ses] *vi* (*Brit: go in procession*) ziehen, schreiten.

processing ['prəʊsesɪŋ] *n see vt* Verarbeitung *f*; Konservierung *f*; Sterilisierung *f*; Bearbeitung *f*; Entwicklung *f*; Abfertigung *f*.

processing: ~ language *n* (*Comput*) Prozeßsprache *f*; **~ plant** *n* Aufbereitungsanlage *f*; **~ speed** *n* (*Comput*) Verarbeitungsgeschwindigkeit *f*; **~ unit** *n* (*Comput*) Prozessor *m*.

procession [prə'seʃən] *n* (*organized*) Umzug *m*; (*solemn*) Prozession *f*; (*line of people, cars etc*) Reihe, Schlange *f* ◆ **funeral/carnival ~** Trauer-/Karnevalszug *m*; **to go** *or* **walk in ~** einen Umzug/eine Prozession machen.

processional [prə'seʃənl] (*Eccl*) [1] *n* (*hymn*) Prozessionshymne *f*, Prozessionslied *nt*; (*book*) Prozessionsbuch *nt*.
[2] *adj* Prozessions-; *pace also* gemessen.

processor ['prəʊsesəʳ] *n* (*Comput*) Prozessor *m*; (*food ~*) Küchenmaschine *f*.

proclaim [prə'kleɪm] [1] *vt* **(a)** erklären; *revolution* ausrufen ◆ **to ~ sb king** jdn zum König erklären *or* ausrufen *or* proklamieren; **the day had been ~ed a holiday** der Tag war zum Feiertag erklärt worden. **(b)** (*reveal*) verraten, beweisen.
[2] *vr* **to ~ oneself king** sich zum König erklären.

proclamation [,prɒklə'meɪʃən] *n* **(a)** (*act*) (*of war*) Erklärung *f*; (*of laws, measures*) Verkündung *f*; (*of state of emergency*) Ausrufung *f* ◆ **after his ~ as Emperor** nach seiner Proklamation zum Kaiser. **(b)** (*that proclaimed*) Erklärung, Proklamation *f*.

proclivity [prə'klɪvɪtɪ] *n* Schwäche, Vorliebe *f* (*for* für).

proconsul [,prəʊ'kɒnsəl] *n* Prokonsul *m*.

procrastinate [prəʊ'kræstɪneɪt] *vi* zögern, zaudern ◆ **he always ~s** er schiebt die Dinge immer vor sich (*dat*) her.

procrastination [prəʊ,kræstɪ'neɪʃən] *n* Zögern, Zaudern *nt* ◆ **~ won't solve your problems** durch Aufschieben lösen sich Ihre Probleme nicht.

procrastinator [prəʊ'kræstɪneɪtəʳ] *n* Zögerer, Zauderer *m*.

procreate ['prəʊkrɪeɪt] [1] *vi* zeugen, sich fortpflanzen.
[2] *vt* zeugen, hervorbringen.

procreation [,prəʊkrɪ'eɪʃən] *n* Zeugung, Fortpflanzung *f*; (*of species*) Fortpflanzung *f*.

Procrustean [prəʊ'krʌstɪən] *adj* unnachgiebig, starr ◆ **~ bed** Prokrustesbett *nt*.

proctor ['prɒktəʳ] *n* (*Jur*) Prokurator *m*; (*Univ*) Proktor *m*; (*US: supervisor*) (Prüfungs)aufsicht *f*.

procurable [prə'kjʊərəbl] *adj* erhältlich, zu beschaffen *pred*.

procurator ['prɒkjʊreɪtəʳ] *n* (*Hist*) Prokurator *m*; (*Jur: agent also*) Bevollmächtigte(r) *m* ◆ **~ fiscal** (*Scot*) ≃ Staatsanwalt *m*.

procure [prə'kjʊəʳ] [1] *vt* **(a)** (*obtain*) beschaffen, sich (*dat*) ver- *or* beschaffen, besorgen; (*bring about*) bewirken, herbeiführen ◆ **to ~ sth for sb/oneself** jdm/sich etw beschaffen *or* besorgen, etw für jdn/sich beschaffen *or* besorgen ◆ **to ~ sb's release** jds Freilassung bewirken *or* erreichen.
(b) (*for prostitution*) *woman* beschaffen (*for sb* jdm).
[2] *vi* Kuppelei betreiben.

procurement [prə'kjʊəmənt] *n* Beschaffung *f*; (*of release*) Bewirkung *f*; (*of prostitutes*) Verkupplung *f*.

procurer [prə'kjʊərəʳ] *n* (*pimp*) Zuhälter, Kuppler *m*.

procuress [prə'kjʊərɪs] *n* Kupplerin *f*.

procuring [prə'kjʊərɪŋ] *n* (*for prostitution*) Zuhälterei *f*.

prod [prɒd] [1] *n* **(a)** Stoß, Knuff (*inf*), Puff (*inf*) *m* ◆ **to give sb a ~** jdm einen Stoß *etc* versetzen; **a ~ in the ribs** ein Rippenstoß *m*.
(b) (*fig*) Ansporn, Anstoß, Schubs (*inf*) *m* ◆ **to give sb a ~** jdn anstoßen.

➤ LANGUAGE IN USE: **probability** → 15.2 **probable** → 15.2 **probably** → 15.2, 16.2 **problem** → 26.1

[2] *vt* **(a)** stoßen, knuffen (*inf*), puffen (*inf*) ◆ **he ~ded the donkey (on) with his stick** er trieb den Esel mit seinem Stock vorwärts; **he ~ded the hay with his stick** er stach mit seinem Stock ins Heu; **..., he said, ~ding the map with his finger ...**, sagte er und stieß mit dem Finger auf die Karte.
(b) (*fig*) anspornen, anstacheln (*to do sth, into sth* zu etw) ◆ **to ~ sb into action** jdm einen Stoß geben.
[3] *vi* stoßen ◆ **he ~ded at the picture with his finger** er stieß mit dem Finger auf das Bild; **he ~ded at the cows with his stick** er trieb die Kühe mit seinem Stock an; **he doesn't need any ~ding** man braucht ihn nicht anzuspornen.

prodigal ['prɒdɪgəl] [1] *adj* verschwenderisch ◆ **to be ~ with** *or* **of sth** verschwenderisch mit etw umgehen; **the ~ son** (*Bibl, fig*) der verlorene Sohn.
[2] *n* Verschwender(in *f*) *m*.

prodigality [,prɒdɪ'gælɪtɪ] *n* (*liter*) Verschwendungssucht *f*; (*lavishness*) Fülle, Üppigkeit *f*.

prodigious [prə'dɪdʒəs] *adj* (*vast*) ungeheuer, außerordentlich; (*marvellous*) erstaunlich, wunderbar.

prodigiously [prə'dɪdʒəslɪ] *adv see adj*. •

prodigy ['prɒdɪdʒɪ] *n* Wunder *nt* ◆ **a ~ of nature** ein Naturwunder *nt*; **child** *or* **infant ~** Wunderkind *nt*.

produce ['prɒdju:s] [1] *n, no pl* (*Agr*) Produkt(e *pl*), Erzeugnis(se *pl*) *nt* ◆ **Italian ~, ~ of Italy** italienisches Erzeugnis; **the low level of ~ this year** der geringe diesjährige Ertrag; **the ~ of the soil** die Bodenprodukte *or* -erzeugnisse *pl*.
[2] [prə'dju:s] *vt* **(a)** (*manufacture*) produzieren; *cars, steel, paper etc also* herstellen; *agricultural products also, electricity, energy, heat* erzeugen; *crop* abwerfen; *coal also* fördern; (*create*) *book, article, essay* schreiben; *painting, sculpture* anfertigen; *ideas also, novel etc, masterpiece* hervorbringen; *interest, return on capital* bringen, abwerfen; *meal* machen, herstellen ◆ **the sort of environment that ~s criminal types** das Milieu, das Kriminelle hervorbringt; **to ~ offspring** Junge bekommen; (*hum: people*) Nachwuchs bekommen; **to be well ~d** gut gemacht sein; (*goods also*) gut gearbeitet sein.
(b) (*bring forward, show*) *gift, wallet etc* hervorholen (*from, out of* aus); *pistol* ziehen (*from, out of* aus); *proof, evidence* liefern, beibringen; *witness* beibringen; *ticket, documents* vorzeigen ◆ **she managed to ~ something special for dinner** es gelang ihr, zum Abendessen etwas Besonderes auf den Tisch zu bringen; **I can't ~ it out of thin air** ich kann es doch nicht aus dem Nichts hervorzaubern *or* aus dem Ärmel schütteln (*inf*); **where on earth does he ~ all these girlfriends from?** wo bekommt *or* kriegt (*inf*) er nur immer seine Freundinnen her?; **if we don't ~ results soon** wenn wir nicht bald Ergebnisse vorweisen können; **he ~d an incredible backhand** ihm gelang ein unglaublicher Rückhandschlag; **he ~d a sudden burst of energy** er hatte einen plötzlichen Energieausbruch.
(c) *play* inszenieren; *film* produzieren ◆ **who's producing you?** wer ist Ihr Regisseur?
(d) (*cause*) *famine, bitterness, impression* hervorrufen; *interest, feeling of pleasure also, spark* erzeugen ◆ **this news ~d a sensation** diese Nachricht hat Sensation gemacht.
(e) (*Math*) *line* verlängern.
[3] [prə'dju:s] *vi* **(a)** (*Theat*) das/ein Stück inszenieren; (*Film*) den/einen Film produzieren.
(b) (*factory, mine*) produzieren; (*land*) Ertrag bringen; (*tree*) tragen ◆ **this cow hasn't ~d for years** diese Kuh hat jahrelang nicht mehr gekalbt; diese Kuh hat jahrelang keine Milch mehr gegeben; **when is she going to ~?** (*hum*) wann ist es denn so weit?; **it's about time that you ~d** (*hum*) es wird bald Zeit, daß ihr mal an Nachwuchs denkt.

producer [prə'dju:sə^r] *n* Hersteller, Produzent *m*; (*Agr*) Produzent, Erzeuger *m*; (*Theat*) Regisseur *m*; (*Film, TV*) Produzent *m*; (*Rad*) Spielleiter *m* ◆ **~ goods** Produktionsgüter *pl*.

-producing [-prə'dju:sɪŋ] *adj suf* erzeugend, produzierend ◆ **coal-~ countries** Kohleförderländer *pl*.

product ['prɒdʌkt] *n* Produkt, Erzeugnis *nt*; (*fig: result, Math, Chem*) Produkt *nt* ◆ **food ~s** Nahrungsmittel *pl*; **~ placement** Produkt-Placement *nt*.

production [prə'dʌkʃən] *n* **(a)** *see vt (a)* Produktion *f*, Herstellung *f*, Erzeugung *f*, Förderung *f*, Schreiben *nt*; Anfertigung *f*, Hervorbringung *f* ◆ **to put sth into ~** die Herstellung *or* Produktion von etw aufnehmen; **when the new factory goes into ~** wenn die neue Fabrik ihre Produktion aufnimmt; **when the new car goes into ~** wenn der neue Wagen in die Produktion *or* Herstellung geht; **when we go into ~ (with this new model)** wenn wir (mit diesem neuen Modell) in die Produktion *or* Herstellung gehen; **is it still in ~?** wird das noch hergestellt?; **to take sth out of ~** etw aus der Produktion nehmen.
(b) (*output*) Produktion *f*.
(c) *see vt (b)* Hervorholen *nt*; Ziehen *nt*; Lieferung, Beibringung *f*, Vorzeigen *nt* ◆ **on ~ of this ticket** gegen Vorlage dieser Eintrittskarte.
(d) (*of play*) Inszenierung *f*; (*of film*) Produktion *f* ◆ **there's no need to make a ~ (number) out of it** (*inf*) es ist nicht notwendig, daraus eine Staatsaffäre zu machen (*inf*).

production: ~ capacity *n* Produktionskapazität *f*; **~ costs** *npl* Produktions- *or* Herstellungskosten *pl*; **~ engineer** *n* Betriebsingenieur *m*; **~ line** *n* Fließband *nt*, Fertigungsstraße *f*; **~ manager** *n* Produktionsleiter *m*; **~ method** *n* Produktions- *or* Herstellungsmethode *f*; **~ model** *n* (*car*) Serienmodell *nt*; **~ platform** *n* (*for oil*) Förderplattform *f*.

productive [prə'dʌktɪv] *adj* produktiv; *land* ertragreich, fruchtbar; *mind also* schöpferisch; *well, mine* ergiebig, ertragreich; *business, shop* rentabel ◆ **to be ~ of sth** etw einbringen; **I don't think it would be very ~ to argue with him** ich halte es nicht für sehr lohnenswert, mit ihm zu streiten (*inf*).

productively [prə'dʌktɪvlɪ] *adv* produktiv.

productivity [,prɒdʌk'tɪvɪtɪ] *n see adj* Produktivität *f*; Fruchtbarkeit *f*; schöpferische Kraft; Ergiebigkeit *f*; Rentabilität *f*.

productivity: ~ agreement *n* Produktivitätsvereinbarung *f*; **~ bonus** *n* Leistungszulage *f*; **~ incentive** *n* Leistungsanreiz *m*.

proem ['prəʊem] *n* Einleitung *f*.

prof [prɒf] *n* (*inf*) Prof *m* (*inf*).

profanation [,prɒfə'neɪʃən] *n* Entweihung, Profanierung *f*.

profane [prə'feɪn] [1] *adj* **(a)** (*secular*) weltlich, profan. **(b)** (*irreverent, sacrilegious*) (gottes)lästerlich ◆ **don't be ~** lästere nicht; **to use ~ language** gotteslästerlich fluchen, lästern; **a ~ expression** eine Gotteslästerung.
[2] *vt* entweihen, profanieren.

profanity [prə'fænɪtɪ] *n see adj* **(a)** Weltlichkeit, Profanität *f*. **(b)** Gotteslästerlichkeit *f*. **(c)** (*act, utterance*) (Gottes)lästerung *f*.

profess [prə'fes] [1] *vt* **(a)** *faith, belief etc* sich bekennen zu.
(b) (*claim to have*) *interest, enthusiasm, distaste* bekunden; *belief, disbelief* kundtun; *weakness, ignorance* zugeben ◆ **she ~es to be 25/a good driver** sie behauptet, 25/eine gute Fahrerin zu sein; **I don't ~ to ...** ich behaupte nicht, ...
[2] *vr* **to ~ oneself satisfied** seine Zufriedenheit bekunden (*with* über *+acc*); **the judge ~ed himself satisfied that this was so** der Richter fand den Sachverhalt als hinlänglich erwiesen; **to ~ oneself unable/willing to do sth** sich außerstande sehen/bereit erklären, etw zu tun.

professed [prə'fest] *adj* erklärt; (*pej: purported*) angeblich ◆ **a ~ nun/monk** (*Eccl*) eine Nonne, die/ein Mönch, der die Gelübde abgelegt hat; **to be a ~ Christian** sich zum christlichen Glauben bekennen; **he is a ~ coward** er gibt zu, ein Feigling zu sein.

professedly [prə'fesɪdlɪ] *adv* zugegebenermaßen; (*pej: purportedly*) angeblich.

profession [prə'feʃən] *n* **(a)** (*occupation*) Beruf *m* ◆ **the medical/teaching ~** der Arzt-/Lehrberuf; **the medical/architectural ~** (*members of the ~*) die Ärzteschaft/die Architekten *pl*; **the whole ~ was outraged** der gesamte Berufsstand war empört; **by ~** von Beruf; **the ~s** die gehobenen Berufe; **the oldest ~ in the world** das älteste Gewerbe der Welt.
(b) (*declaration*) (*Eccl*) Gelübde *nt* ◆ **~ of faith** Glaubensbekenntnis *nt*; **a ~ of love** eine Liebeserklärung; **a ~ of contempt** eine Mißfallensäußerung; **a ~ of loyalty** ein Treuegelöbnis *nt*; **the ~ of Christianity** das Bekenntnis zum Christentum; **he is, by his own ~, ...** nach eigenem Bekunden ist er ...

professional [prə'feʃənl] [1] *adj* **(a)** Berufs-, beruflich; *army, soldier, tennis player* Berufs-; *opinion* fachmännisch, fachlich ◆ **their ~ ability** ihre beruflichen Fähigkeiten; **his ~ life** sein Berufsleben; **our relationship is purely ~** unsere Beziehung ist rein geschäftlich(er Natur); **a ~ thief** ein professioneller Dieb; **we need your ~ help here** hier brauchen wir Ihre fachmännische Hilfe; **he's now doing it on a ~ basis** er macht das jetzt hauptberuflich; **in his ~ capacity as a doctor** in seiner Eigenschaft als Arzt; **to be a ~ singer/author** *etc* von Beruf Sänger/Schriftsteller *etc* sein; **"flat to let to quiet ~ gentleman"** „Wohnung zu vermieten an ruhigen gutsituierten Herrn"; **the pub is used mainly by ~ men** das Lokal wird hauptsächlich von Angehörigen der gehobenen Berufe besucht; **the ~ classes** die gehobenen Berufe, die höheren Berufsstände (*dated*); **to take ~ advice** fachmännischen Rat einholen; **it's not our ~ practice** es gehört nicht zu unseren geschäftlichen Gepflogenheiten; **to turn** *or* **go ~** Profi werden.
(b) (*skilled, competent*) *piece of work etc* fachmännisch, fachgemäß, fachgerecht; *worker, person* gewissenhaft; *company, approach* professionell ◆ **he didn't make a very ~ job of that** er hat das nicht sehr fachmännisch erledigt; **he handled the matter in a very ~ manner** er hat die Angelegenheit in sehr kompetenter Weise gehandhabt; **that's not a very ~ attitude to your work** das ist doch nicht die richtige Einstellung (zu Ihrem Beruf); **it's not up to ~ standards** es entspricht nicht fachlichen Normen; **a typed letter looks more ~** ein maschinengeschriebener Brief sieht professioneller aus.
(c) (*inf*) *worrier, moaner* notorisch, gewohnheitsmäßig.
[2] *n* Profi *m*.

professionalism [prə'feʃnəlɪzəm] *n* Professionalismus *m*; (*of job, piece of work*) Perfektion *f*; (*Sport*) Profitum *nt*.

professionally [prə'feʃnəlɪ] *adv* beruflich; (*in accomplished manner*) fachmännisch ◆ **now he plays ~** jetzt ist er Berufsspieler *or* Profi; **he is ~ recognized as the best ...** er ist in Fachkreisen als der beste ... bekannt; **X, ~ known as Y** (*of artist, musician etc*) X, unter dem Künstlernamen Y bekannt; (*of writer*) X, unter dem Pseudonym Y bekannt; **they acted most ~ in refusing to ...** daß sie ... ablehnten, zeugte von hohem Berufsethos.

professor [prə'fesə^r] *n* **(a)** Professor(in *f*) *m*; (*US also*) Dozent(in *f*) *m* ◆ **the ~s** die Professorenschaft. **(b)** (*of a faith*) Bekenner(in *f*) *m*.

professorial [,prɒfə'sɔ:rɪəl] *adj* (*of a professor*) eines Professors; (*professorlike*) wie ein Professor, professoral (*pej*).

professorship [prə'fesəʃɪp] *n* Professur *f*, Lehrstuhl *m*.

proffer ['prɒfə^r] *vt arm, gift, drink* anbieten; *apologies, thanks etc* aussprechen; *remark* machen; *suggestion* vorbringen.

proficiency [prə'fɪʃənsɪ] *n* **level** *or* **standard of ~** Leistungsstand *m*; **her ~ at teaching/as a secretary** ihre Tüchtigkeit als Lehrerin/Sekretärin; **his ~ in English/translating/accountancy** seine Englischkenntnisse/sein Können als Übersetzer/Buchhalter; **his ~ with figures** sein Können im Umgang mit Zahlen; **~ test** Leistungstest *m*.

proficient [prə'fɪʃənt] *adj* tüchtig, fähig ◆ **he is just about ~ in German** seine Deutschkenntnisse reichen gerade aus; **how long would it take to become ~**

in Japanese? wie lange würde es dauern, bis man Japanisch beherrscht?

profile ['prəʊfaɪl] [1] *n* Profil *nt*; (*picture, photograph*) Profilbild *nt*, Seitenansicht *f*; (*biographical* ~) Porträt *nt*; (*Tech: section*) (*vertical*) Längsschnitt *m*; (*horizontal*) Querschnitt *m* ◆ **in** ~ (*person, head*) im Profil; **to keep a low** ~ sich zurückhalten.

[2] *vt* (*draw a* ~ *of*) (*pictorially*) im Profil darstellen; (*biographically*) porträtieren; (*Tech*) im Längs- *or* Querschnitt zeichnen *or* darstellen.

profit ['prɒfɪt] [1] *n* (**a**) (*Comm*) Gewinn, Profit (*also pej*) *m* ◆ **there's not much (of a)** ~ **in this business** dieses Geschäft wirft kaum Gewinn *or* Profit ab; ~ **and loss account** Gewinn-und-Verlustrechnung *f*; **to make a** ~ **(out of** *or* **on sth)** (mit etw) einen Profit *or* Gewinn machen, (mit etw) ein Geschäft machen; **to show** *or* **yield a** ~ einen Gewinn *or* Profit verzeichnen; **to sell sth at a** ~ etw mit Gewinn verkaufen; **the business is now running at a** ~ das Geschäft wirft jetzt Gewinn *or* Profit ab, das Geschäft rentiert sich jetzt; **I'm not doing it for** ~ ich tue das nicht, um damit Geld zu verdienen; **a with-~s policy** (*Insur*) eine Police mit Gewinnbeteiligung.
(**b**) (*fig*) Nutzen, Vorteil *m* ◆ **to turn sth to** ~ Nutzen aus etw ziehen; **you might well learn something to your** ~ Sie können etwas lernen, was Ihnen von Nutzen *or* Vorteil ist.

[2] *vt* (*liter*) nutzen, nützen (*sb* jdm), von Nutzen sein (*sb* für jdn) ◆ **what does it** ~ **a man if** ... was nützt es dem Menschen, wenn ...

[3] *vi* (*gain*) profitieren (*by, from* von), Nutzen *or* Gewinn ziehen (*by, from* aus).

profitability [ˌprɒfɪtə'bɪlɪtɪ] *n* Rentabilität, Einträglichkeit *f* ◆ ~ **study** Rentabilitäts- *or* Wirtschaftlichkeitsstudie *f*.

profitable ['prɒfɪtəbl] *adj* (*Comm*) gewinn- *or* profitbringend, rentabel, profitabel; (*fig: beneficial*) nützlich, vorteilhaft ◆ **could you not find a more** ~ **way of spending your time?** kannst du nichts Besseres mit deiner Zeit anfangen?

profitably ['prɒfɪtəblɪ] *adv see adj* ◆ **you could** ~ **spend a couple of hours reading a book** es käme dir sehr zugute, wenn du ein paar Stunden mit Lesen verbringen würdest.

profit centre *n* Profit-center *nt*.

profiteer [ˌprɒfɪ'tɪəʳ] [1] *n* Profitmacher, Profitjäger, Profitgeier *m* ◆ **war** ~ Kriegsgewinnler *m*.

[2] *vi* sich bereichern.

profiteering [ˌprɒfɪ'tɪərɪŋ] *n* Wucherei *f*, Wucher *m*.

profitless ['prɒfɪtlɪs] *adj* (**a**) (*Comm*) unrentabel. (**b**) *discussion, exercise* zwecklos.

profitlessly ['prɒfɪtlɪslɪ] *adv* (**a**) (*Comm*) ohne Gewinn. (**b**) *argue* zwecklos.

profit: ~-making *adj organization* rentabel; (*~-orientated*) auf Gewinn gerichtet; ~ **margin** *n* Gewinnspanne *f*; ~ **motive** *n* Gewinnstreben *nt*; **~-seeking** *adj* gewinnorientiert; **~-sharing** [1] *adj scheme* Gewinnbeteiligungs-; [2] *n* Gewinnbeteiligung *f*.

profligacy ['prɒflɪgəsɪ] *n* (*dissoluteness*) Lasterhaftigkeit, Verworfenheit *f*; (*extravagance*) Verschwendungssucht *f*; (*an extravagance*) Verschwendung *f*.

profligate ['prɒflɪgɪt] [1] *adj* (*dissolute*) lasterhaft, verworfen; (*extravagant*) verschwenderisch.

[2] *n* (*roué*) Leichtfuß, Liederjan (*inf*) *m*; (*prodigal*) Verschwender(in *f*) *m*.

pro forma (invoice) [ˌprəʊ'fɔːmə(ɪnvɔɪs)] *n* Pro-forma-Rechnung *f*.

profound [prə'faʊnd] *adj sleep, sigh, sorrow, love* tief; *thought* tiefsinnig, tiefschürfend, tiefgründig; *book* gehaltvoll, profund (*geh*); *thinker, knowledge* profund (*geh*), tiefgehend *attr*; *regret* tiefgehend *attr*; *hatred, mistrust* tiefsitzend *attr*; *indifference* vollkommen, völlig; *interest* stark; *changes* tiefgreifend *attr* ◆ **you're very** ~ **today** (*also iro*) du bist heute sehr tiefsinnig; **that's very** ~ (*also iro*) das ist sehr tiefsinnig.

profoundly [prə'faʊndlɪ] *adv* zutiefst ◆ ~ **sad** tieftraurig; ~ **significant** äußerst bedeutsam; ~ **indifferent** völlig *or* vollkommen gleichgültig; ..., **he said** ~ ..., sagte er tiefsinnig; **to be** ~ **ignorant of sth** überhaupt keine Ahnung von etw haben.

profundity [prə'fʌndɪtɪ] *n* (**a**) *no pl* Tiefe *f*; (*of thought, thinker, book etc*) Tiefgründigkeit, Tiefsinnigkeit *f*; (*of knowledge*) Gründlichkeit *f*. (**b**) (*profound remark*) Tiefsinnigkeit *f*.

profuse [prə'fjuːs] *adj vegetation* üppig; *bleeding* stark; *thanks, praise* überschwenglich; *apologies* überreichlich ◆ **to be** ~ **in one's thanks/apologies** sich überschwenglich bedanken/sich vielmals entschuldigen; **he was** ~ **in his praise** er geizte nicht mit seinem Lob; **where flowers grow in** ~ **abundance** wo Blumen in üppiger *or* verschwenderischer Fülle wachsen.

profusely [prə'fjuːslɪ] *adv grow* üppig; *bleed* stark; *thank, praise* überschwenglich; *sweat* heftig, stark ◆ **he apologized** ~ er entschuldigte sich vielmals, er bat vielmals um Entschuldigung; ~ **illustrated** reich illustriert.

profusion [prə'fjuːʒən] *n* Überfülle *f*, verschwenderische Fülle ◆ **trees/ice-cream in** ~ Bäume/Eis in Hülle und Fülle; **his painting was a wild** ~ **of reds and blues** sein Gemälde war eine Orgie in Rot und Blau.

progenitor [prəʊ'dʒenɪtəʳ] *n* (*form*) Vorfahr, Ahn *m*; (*fig*) Vorläufer *m*.

progenitrix [prəʊ'dʒenɪtrɪks] *n* (*form*) Vorfahrin, Ahne *f*.

progeny ['prɒdʒɪnɪ] *n* Nachkommen *pl*, Nachkommenschaft *f*.

progesterone [prəʊ'dʒestəˌrəʊn] *n* Progesteron, Gelbkörperhormon *nt*.

prognosis [prɒg'nəʊsɪs] *n, pl* **prognoses** [prɒg'nəʊsiːz] Prognose, Vorhersage, Voraussage *f*.

prognostic [prɒg'nɒstɪk] *adj* (*form*) prognostisch.

prognosticate [prɒg'nɒstɪkeɪt] [1] *vi* (*often hum*) Prognosen stellen, Vorhersagen machen.

[2] *vt* prognostizieren.

prognostication [prɒgˌnɒstɪ'keɪʃən] *n* Prognose, Vorhersage, Voraussage *f*.

program ['prəʊgræm] [1] *n* (**a**) (*Comput*) Programm *nt*. (**b**) (*US*) *see* **programme 1**.

[2] *vt* (**a**) *computer* programmieren. (**b**) (*fig*) *person* vorprogrammieren ◆ **~d course/learning** programmierter Unterricht/programmiertes Lernen; **that's ~d for tomorrow** das steht für morgen auf dem Programm.

programmable ['prəʊgræməbl] *adj computer, device, oven etc* programmierbar.

programme, (*US*) **program** ['prəʊgræm] *n* (*all senses*) Programm *nt*; (*Rad, TV also*) Sendung *f* ◆ **we've got a very heavy** ~ **of meetings** wir haben sehr viele Besprechungen auf unserem Programm; **what's the** ~ **for tomorrow?** was steht für morgen auf dem Programm?; **what's on the other ~?** was gibt es *or* läuft im anderen Programm?; **our ~s for this evening** das Programm des heutigen Abends.

programme: ~ **music** *n* Programmusik *f*; ~ **notes** *npl* Programmhinweise *pl*; ~ **planner** *n* (*TV*) Programmplaner *m*.

programmer ['prəʊgræməʳ] *n* Programmierer(in *f*) *m*.

programme seller *n* (*in theatre etc*) Programmverkäufer(in *f*) *m*.

programming ['prəʊgræmɪŋ] *n* Programmieren *nt* ◆ ~ **language** Programmiersprache *f*.

progress ['prəʊgres] [1] *n* (**a**) *no pl* (*movement forwards*) Fortschreiten, Vorwärtskommen *nt*; (*Mil*) Vorrücken, Vordringen *nt* ◆ **we made slow** ~ **through the mud** wir kamen im Schlamm nur langsam vorwärts; **they made good** ~ **across the open country** sie kamen im offenen Gelände gut vorwärts.
(**b**) *no pl* (*advance*) Fortschritt *m* ◆ **the** ~ **of events** der Gang der Ereignisse; **to make (good/slow)** ~ (gute/langsame) Fortschritte machen; **I want to see some ~!** ich möchte Fortschritte sehen!; ~ **report** Fortschrittsbericht *m*.
(**c**) **in** ~ im Gange; **in full** ~ in vollem Gange; **"silence please, meeting in ~"** „Sitzung! Ruhe bitte"; **the work still in** ~ die noch zu erledigende Arbeit.
(**d**) (*obs: journey*) Reise *f*.

[2] [prə'gres] *vi* (**a**) (*move, go forward*) sich vorwärts bewegen, vorwärtsschreiten ◆ **we ~ed slowly across the ice** wir bewegten uns langsam über das Eis vorwärts; **by the third day the enemy/expedition had ~ed as far as** ... am dritten Tag war der Feind bis ... vorgerückt *or* vorgedrungen/die Expedition bis ... vorgedrungen *or* gekommen.
(**b**) (*in time*) **as the work ~es** mit dem Fortschreiten der Arbeit; **as the game ~ed** im Laufe des Spiels; **while negotiations were actually ~ing** während die Verhandlungen im Gange waren.
(**c**) (*improve, make* ~) (*student, patient*) Fortschritte machen ◆ **how far have you ~ed since our last meeting?** wie weit sind Sie seit unserer letzten Sitzung gekommen?; **investigations are ~ing well** die Untersuchungen kommen gut voran *or* machen gute Fortschritte; **we are, in fact, ~ing towards a solution** wir nähern uns jetzt einer Lösung; **that civilization is constantly ~ing (towards a state of perfection)** daß sich die Zivilisation ständig (auf einen Zustand der Perfektion hin) weiterentwickelt; **that mankind is ~ing towards some goal** daß sich die Menschheit auf ein Ziel zubewegt.
(**d**) (*through hierarchy etc*) **as you** ~ **through the orders of mammals** wenn man die Entwicklungsreihe der Säugetiere durchgeht; **the employee ~es upwards through the company hierarchy** der Angestellte macht seinen Weg durch die Firmenhierarchie.

[3] [prə'gres] *vt* (*esp Comm*) *matters etc* weiterverfolgen.

progression [prə'greʃən] *n* Folge *f*; (*Math*) Reihe, Progression *f*; (*Mus*) Sequenz *f*; (*development*) Entwicklung *f*; (*in taxation*) Progression *f*; (*discount rates etc*) Staffelung *f* ◆ **sales have shown a continuous** ~ im Absatz wurde eine stete Aufwärtsentwicklung verzeichnet; **his** ~ **from a junior clerk to managing director** sein Aufstieg vom kleinen Angestellten zum Direktor; **is there a natural** ~ **from marijuana to heroin?** ist das Umsteigen von Marihuana auf Heroin zwangsläufig?

progressive [prə'gresɪv] [1] *adj* (**a**) (*increasing*) zunehmend; *disease etc* fortschreitend; *paralysis, taxation* progressiv ◆ ~ **form/tense** (*Gram*) Verlaufsform *f*.
(**b**) (*favouring progress*) progressiv, fortschrittlich; (*Mus*) progressiv ◆ ~ **jazz** progressiver Jazz; ~ **party** (*Pol*) fortschrittliche Partei, Fortschrittspartei *f*.

[2] *n* (*person*) Progressive(r) *mf*.

progressively [prə'gresɪvlɪ] *adv* zunehmend ◆ **he is becoming** ~ **more addicted** er wird zunehmend *or* immer abhängiger.

progressiveness [prə'gresɪvnɪs] *n* Fortschrittlichkeit, Progressivität *f*.

prohibit [prə'hɪbɪt] *vt* (**a**) verbieten, untersagen ◆ **to** ~ **sb from doing sth** jdm etw verbieten *or* untersagen; **his health ~s him from swimming** sein Gesundheitszustand verbietet (es) ihm zu schwimmen; **"smoking ~ed"** „Rauchen verboten".
(**b**) (*prevent*) verhindern ◆ **to** ~ **sth being done** verhindern, daß etw geschieht; **to** ~ **sb from doing sth** jdn daran hindern, etw zu tun.

prohibition [ˌprəʊɪ'bɪʃən] [1] *n* Verbot *nt* ◆ **(the) P~** (*Hist*) die Prohibition; **the** ~ **of smoking** das Rauchverbot.

[2] *attr* (*in US*) *laws, party* Prohibitions-.

prohibitionism [ˌprəʊɪ'bɪʃənɪzəm] *n* Prohibition *f*.

prohibitionist [ˌprəʊɪ'bɪʃənɪst] [1] *adj* Prohibitions-.

[2] *n* Prohibitionist(in *f*) *m*.

prohibitive [prə'hɪbɪtɪv] *adj* (**a**) *tax* Prohibitiv-; *duty* Sperr- ◆ ~ **laws** Verbotsgesetze *pl*; ~ **signs** Verbotsschilder *pl*; ~ **rules** Verbote *pl*. (**b**) *price, cost* unerschwinglich. **the costs of producing this model have become** ~ die Kosten für die Herstellung dieses Modells sind untragbar geworden.

prohibitory [prə'hɪbɪtərɪ] *adj see* **prohibitive (a)**.

project[1] ['prɒdʒekt] *n* Projekt *nt*; (*scheme*) Unternehmen, Vorhaben *nt*; (*Sch,*

Univ) Referat *nt*; (*in primary school*) Arbeit *f* ◆ ~ **engineer** Projektingenieur *m*.

project[2] [prə'dʒekt] 1 *vt* (**a**) *film, map* projizieren ◆ **to ~ oneself/one's personality** sich selbst/seine eigene Person zur Geltung bringen; **to ~ one's neuroses/guilt onto somebody else** seine Neurosen/Schuldgefühle auf einen anderen projizieren; **to ~ one's voice** seine Stimme zum Tragen bringen; **to ~ one's voice to the back of the hall** seine Stimme so erheben, daß sie auch im hinteren Teil des Saals zu hören ist; **in order to ~ an adequate picture of our country** um ein angemessenes Bild unseres Landes zu vermitteln.
(**b**) (*plan*) (voraus)planen; *costs* überschlagen; *figures* projizieren; (*esp in elections*) hochrechnen.
(**c**) (*Math*) *line* verlängern; *solid* projizieren.
(**d**) (*propel*) abschießen ◆ **to ~ a missile into space** eine Rakete in den Weltraum schießen.
(**e**) (*cause to jut*) *part of building etc* vorspringen lassen.
2 *vi* (**a**) (*plan*) planen.
(**b**) (*jut out*) hervorragen (*from* aus) ◆ **the upper storey ~s over the road** das obere Stockwerk ragt über die Straße.
(**c**) (*Psych*) projizieren, von sich auf andere schließen.
(**d**) (*with one's voice: actor, singer*) **you'll have to ~ more than that, we can't hear you at the back** Sie müssen lauter singen/sprechen, wir können Sie hier hinten nicht hören.

projectile [prə'dʒektaɪl] *n* (Wurf)geschoß *nt*; (*Mil*) Geschoß, Projektil (*spec*) *nt*.

projection [prə'dʒekʃən] *n* (**a**) (*of films, guilt feelings, map*) Projektion *f* ◆ **~ booth** *or* **room** Vorführraum *m*. (**b**) (*protrusion, overhang, ledge etc*) Vorsprung, Überhang *m*. (**c**) (*extension: of line*) Verlängerung *f*. (**d**) (*prediction, estimate*) (Voraus)planung *f*; (*of cost*) Überschlagung *f*; (*of figures, esp in elections*) Hochrechnung *f*.

projectionist [prə'dʒekʃnɪst] *n* Filmvorführer *m*.

projective [prə'dʒektɪv] *adj geometry* Projektions-; (*Psych*) projizierend.

projector [prə'dʒektəʳ] *n* (*Film*) Projektor *m*, Vorführgerät *nt*.

prolapse ['prəʊlæps] *n* (*Med*) Vorfall, Prolaps (*spec*) *m*.

prole [prəʊl] *n* (*esp Brit pej inf*) Prolet(in *f*) *m* (*inf*).

proletarian [,prəʊlə'tɛərɪən] 1 *adj* proletarisch.
2 *n* Proletarier(in *f*) *m*.

proletariat [,prəʊlə'tɛərɪət] *n* Proletariat *nt*.

proliferate [prə'lɪfəreɪt] *vi* (*number*) sich stark erhöhen; (*ideas*) um sich greifen; (*insects, animals*) sich stark vermehren; (*weeds, cells*) wuchern, sich rasch ausbreiten.

proliferation [prə,lɪfə'reɪʃən] *n* (*in numbers*) starke Erhöhung; (*of animals*) zahlreiche Vermehrung; (*of nuclear weapons*) Weitergabe *f*; (*of ideas*) Ausbreitung *f*, Umsichgreifen *nt*; (*of sects*) Umsichgreifen, Wuchern *nt*; (*of weeds*) Wuchern *nt*.

prolific [prə'lɪfɪk] *adj* fruchtbar; *writer also* sehr produktiv.

prolix ['prəʊlɪks] *adj* weitschweifig.

prolixity [prəʊ'lɪksɪtɪ] *n* Weitschweifigkeit *f*.

prologue, (*US*) **prolog** ['prəʊlɒg] *n* Prolog *m*; (*of book*) Vorwort *nt*; (*fig*) Vorspiel *nt*.

prolong [prə'lɒŋ] *vt* verlängern; (*pej*) *process, pain* hinauszögern; (*Fin*) *draft* prolongieren.

prolongation [,prəʊlɒŋ'geɪʃən] *n see vt* Verlängerung *f*; Hinauszögern *nt*; Prolongation, Prolongierung *f*.

prom [prɒm] *n* (*inf*) (*Brit: promenade*) (Strand)promenade *f*; (*Brit: concert*) Konzert *nt* (*in gelockertem Rahmen*); (*US: ball*) Studenten-/Schülerball *m*.

promenade [,prɒmɪ'nɑːd] 1 *n* (*stroll, in dancing*) Promenade *f*; (*esp Brit: esplanade*) (Strand)promenade *f*; (*US: ball*) Studenten-/Schülerball *m* ◆ ~ **concert** Konzert *nt* (*in gelockertem Rahmen*); ~ **deck** Promenadendeck *nt*.
2 *vt* (*stroll through*) promenieren in (*+dat*); *avenue* entlangpromenieren; (*stroll with*) spazierenführen; (*in dance*) eine Promenade machen mit.
3 *vi* (*stroll*) promenieren; (*in dance*) eine Promenade machen.

Promethean [prə'miːθɪən] *adj* (*liter*) prometheisch (*liter*).

Prometheus [prə'miːθjuːs] *n* Prometheus *m*.

promethium [prəʊ'miːθɪəm] *n* (*Chem*) Promethium *nt*.

prominence ['prɒmɪnəns] *n* (**a**) *no pl* **the ~ of his forehead** seine ausgeprägte Stirn; **because of the ~ of the castle on a rock in the middle of the city** wegen der exponierten Lage des Schlosses auf einem Felsen inmitten der Stadt.
(**b**) (*of ideas, beliefs*) Beliebtheit *f*; (*of writer, politician etc*) Bekanntheit *f* ◆ **the undisputed ~ of his position as** ... seine unbestritten führende Position als ...; **if you give too much ~ to any one particular aspect** wenn Sie einen bestimmten Aspekt zu sehr in den Vordergrund stellen; **to bring sb/sth into ~** (*attract attention to*) jdn/etw herausstellen *or* in den Vordergrund rücken; (*make famous*) jdn/etw berühmt machen; **he came** *or* **rose to ~ in the Cuba affair** er wurde durch die Kuba-Affäre bekannt.
(**c**) (*prominent part*) Vorsprung *m*.

prominent ['prɒmɪnənt] *adj* (**a**) (*jutting out*) *cheek-bones, teeth* vorstehend *attr*; *crag* vorspringend *attr* ◆ **to be ~** vorstehen; vorspringen.
(**b**) (*conspicuous*) *markings* auffällig; *feature, characteristic* hervorstechend, auffallend ◆ **put it in a ~ position** stellen Sie es deutlich sichtbar hin; **the castle occupies a ~ position on the hill** das Schloß hat eine exponierte Lage auf dem Hügel.
(**c**) (*leading*) *role* führend; (*large, significant*) wichtig.
(**d**) (*well-known*) *personality, publisher* prominent ◆ **she is ~ in London society** sie ist ein bekanntes Mitglied der Londoner Gesellschaft.

prominently ['prɒmɪnəntlɪ] *adv display, place* deutlich sichtbar ◆ **he figured ~ in the case** er spielte in dem Fall eine bedeutende Rolle.

promiscuity [,prɒmɪ'skjuːɪtɪ] *n* (**a**) Promiskuität *f*, häufiger Partnerwechsel. (**b**) (*liter: confusion*) Wirrwarr *m*.

promiscuous [prə'mɪskjʊəs] *adj* (**a**) (*sexually*) promisk, promiskuitiv (*spec*) ◆ **to be ~** häufig den Partner wechseln; ~ **behaviour** häufiger Partnerwechsel. (**b**) (*liter*) wirr.

promiscuously [prə'mɪskjʊəslɪ] *adv see adj*.

promise ['prɒmɪs] 1 *n* (**a**) (*pledge*) Versprechen *nt* ◆ **their ~ of help** ihr Versprechen zu helfen; **~ of marriage** Eheversprechen *nt*; **under ~ of** (*form*) mit dem Versprechen (*+gen*); **under a ~ of secrecy** unter dem Siegel der Verschwiegenheit; **is that a ~?** ganz bestimmt?; **to make sb a ~** jdm ein Versprechen geben *or* machen; **make me one ~** versprich mir eins; **I'm not making any ~s** versprechen kann ich nichts; **to hold** *or* **keep sb to his ~** jdn an sein Versprechen binden; **~s, ~s!** Versprechen, nichts als Versprechen!
(**b**) (*hope, prospect*) Hoffnung, Aussicht *f* ◆ **a young man of ~** ein vielversprechender junger Mann; **to hold out a** *or* **the ~ of sth** jdm Hoffnungen auf etw (*acc*) machen; **to show ~** zu den besten Hoffnungen berechtigen; **she had a ~ of passion in her eyes** ihre Augen verrieten Leidenschaft.
2 *vt* (*pledge*) versprechen; (*forecast, augur*) hindeuten auf (*+acc*) ◆ **to ~ (sb) to do sth** (jdm) versprechen, etw zu tun; **to ~ sb sth, to ~ sth to sb** jdm etw versprechen; **to ~ sb the earth** jdm das Blaue vom Himmel herunter versprechen; **~ me one thing** versprich mir eins; **to be ~d to sb** (*dated*) jdm versprochen sein (*old*); **I'm not promising anything but** ... ich will nichts versprechen, aber ...; **I won't do it again, I ~ you** ich werde es nie wieder tun, das verspreche ich Ihnen; **you'll regret this, I ~ you** ich verspreche dir, das wirst du bereuen; **this ~s trouble** das sieht nach Ärger aus; **this ~s better things to come** das läßt auf Besseres hoffen; **the P~d Land** (*Bibl, fig*) das Gelobte Land.
3 *vi* (**a**) versprechen ◆ **(do you) ~?** versprichst du es?; **~!** (*will you ~*) versprich's mir, ehrlich?; (*I ~*) ehrlich!; **I'll try, but I'm not promising** ich werde es versuchen, aber ich kann nichts versprechen; **but you ~d!** aber du hast es doch versprochen!
(**b**) **to ~ well** vielversprechend sein.
4 *vr* **to ~ oneself sth** sich (*dat*) etw versprechen; **I've ~d myself never to do it again** ich habe mir geschworen, daß ich das nicht noch einmal mache.

promising *adj*, **~ly** *adv* ['prɒmɪsɪŋ, -lɪ] vielversprechend.

promissory note ['prɒmɪsərɪ'nəʊt] *n* Schuldschein *m*.

promo ['prəʊməʊ] *n* (*inf: promotional video*) Werbevideo *nt*.

promontory ['prɒməntrɪ] *n* Vorgebirge, Kap *nt*.

promote [prə'məʊt] *vt* (**a**) (*in rank*) befördern ◆ **he has been ~d (to) colonel** *or* **to the rank of colonel** er ist zum Obersten befördert worden; **our team was ~d** (*Ftbl*) unsere Mannschaft ist aufgestiegen.
(**b**) (*foster*) fördern; (*Parl*) *bill* sich einsetzen für.
(**c**) (*organize, put on*) *conference, race-meeting, boxing match etc* veranstalten.
(**d**) (*advertise*) werben für; (*put on the market*) auf den Markt bringen ◆ **the new model has been widely ~d in the media** für das neue Modell ist in den Medien intensiv geworben worden *or* Werbung gemacht worden.

promoter [prə'məʊtəʳ] *n* (*Sport, of beauty contest etc*) Promoter, Veranstalter *m*; (*of company*) Mitbegründer *m* ◆ **sales ~** Verkaufsleiter, Sales-promoter (*Comm*) *m*.

promotion [prə'məʊʃən] *n* (**a**) (*in rank*) Beförderung *f* ◆ **to get** *or* **win ~** befördert werden; (*football team*) aufsteigen.
(**b**) (*fostering*) Förderung *f*; (*Parl: of bill*) Einsatz *m* (*of* für).
(**c**) (*organization: of conference etc*) Veranstaltung *f*.
(**d**) (*advertising*) Werbung *f* (*of* für); (*advertising campaign*) Werbekampagne *f*; (*marketing*) Einführung *f* auf dem Markt ◆ **we've got a special ~ by the Rochas people in the store this week** wir haben diese Woche einen Rochas-Werbestand.

prompt [prɒmpt] 1 *adj* (*+er*) prompt; *action* unverzüglich, sofortig ◆ **he is always very ~ with** *or* **about such things** solche Dinge erledigt er immer prompt *or* sofort; **he is always very ~** (*on time*) er ist immer sehr pünktlich.
2 *adv* **at 6 o'clock ~** pünktlich um 6 Uhr, Punkt 6 Uhr.
3 *vt* (**a**) (*motivate*) veranlassen (*to* zu) ◆ **to ~ sb to do sth** jdn (dazu) veranlassen, etw zu tun; **what ~ed you to do it?** was hat Sie dazu veranlaßt?; **he was ~ed purely by a desire to help** sein Beweggrund war einzig und allein der Wunsch zu helfen; **in the hope that this might ~ a discussion** in der Hoffnung, daß das eine Diskussion in Gang setzen wird; **he didn't need any ~ing to ask her** man brauchte ihn nicht darum zu bitten, sie zu fragen; **he's a bit lazy, he needs a little ~ing** er ist ein bißchen faul, man muß ihm manchmal auf die Sprünge helfen; **I'll do it myself, I don't need you to ~ me** ich mache das schon selbst, du brauchst mich nicht erst zu ermahnen; **he doesn't need any ~ing, he's cheeky enough as it is** er braucht keine Ermunterung, er ist auch so schon frech genug.
(**b**) (*evoke*) *memories, feelings* wecken; *conclusion* nahelegen ◆ **it ~s the thought that** ... es drängt einem den Gedanken auf, daß ...
(**c**) (*help with speech*) vorsagen (*sb* jdm); (*Theat*) soufflieren (*sb* jdm) ◆ **he recited the whole poem without any ~ing** er sagte das ganze Gedicht auf, ohne daß ihm jemand (etwas) vorsagen mußte; **the teacher had to keep ~ing him** der Lehrer mußte ihm immer wieder Hilfestellung geben; **he forgot his speech and had to be ~ed** er hatte seine Rede vergessen, so daß man ihm mit Stichworten auf die Sprünge helfen mußte.
4 *vi* (*Theat*) soufflieren.
5 *n* (**a**) (*Theat*) **he needed a ~** ihm mußte souffliert werden; **he couldn't hear the ~** er hörte die Souffleuse nicht; **to give sb a ~** jdm weiterhelfen; (*Theat*) jdm soufflieren.

(b) *(reminder, encouragement)* **to give sb a ~** jdm einen Schubs geben *(inf)*, jdn anstoßen; **we have to give our debtors the occasional ~** wir müssen uns bei unseren Schuldnern hin und wieder in Erinnerung bringen.
(c) *(Comput)* Prompt *m*, Aufforderungsmeldung *f.*

prompt: ~ box *n* Souffleurkasten *m*; **~ copy** *n* Rollenheft *nt.*

prompter ['prɒmptəʳ] *n* Souffleur *m*, Souffleuse *f*; *(tele-~)* Teleprompter *m.*

prompting ['prɒmptɪŋ] *n* **(a)** *(Theat)* Soufflieren *nt.* **(b) the ~s of conscience/the heart** die Stimme des Gewissens/Herzens.

promptitude ['prɒmptɪtju:d] *n see* **promptness.**

promptly ['prɒmptlɪ] *adv* prompt ◆ **they left ~ at 6** sie gingen pünktlich um 6 Uhr *or* Punkt 6 Uhr; **of course he ~ forgot it all** er hat natürlich prompt alles vergessen.

promptness ['prɒmptnɪs] *n* Promptheit *f* ◆ **the fire brigade's ~** der prompte Einsatz der Feuerwehr.

prompt note *n (Comm)* Ermahnung *f.*

promulgate ['prɒməlgeɪt] *vt* verbreiten; *law* verkünden.

promulgation [,prɒməl'geɪʃən] *n see vt* Verbreitung *f*; Verkündung *f.*

prone [prəʊn] *adj* **(a)** *(lying)* **to be** *or* **lie ~** auf dem Bauch liegen; **in a ~ position** in Bauchlage. **(b)** *(liable)* **to be ~ to sth/to do sth** zu etw neigen/dazu neigen, etw zu tun.

proneness ['prəʊnnɪs] *n* Neigung *f (to* zu).

prong [prɒŋ] 1 *n* **(a)** *(of fork)* Zacke, Zinke *f*; *(of antler)* Sprosse *f*, Ende *nt.* **(b)** *(fig) (of argument)* Punkt *m*; *(of attack)* (Angriffs)spitze *f.*
2 *vt* aufspießen.

-pronged [-prɒŋd] *adj suf (of fork)* -zackig, -zinkig ◆ **a three-~ attack** ein Angriff mit drei Spitzen; **a three-~ argument** ein dreigleisiges Argument.

pronominal [prəʊ'nɒmɪnl] *adj* Pronominal-.

pronoun ['prəʊnaʊn] *n* Fürwort, Pronomen *nt.*

pronounce [prə'naʊns] 1 *vt* **(a)** *word etc* aussprechen ◆ **I find Russian hard to ~** ich finde die russische Aussprache schwierig; **the "p" isn't ~d** das „p" wird nicht ausgesprochen.
(b) *(declare)* erklären für ◆ **the doctors ~d him unfit for work** die Ärzte erklärten ihn für arbeitsunfähig; **to ~ oneself for/against sth** sich für/gegen etw aussprechen; **to ~ sentence** das Urteil verkünden.
2 *vi* **(a) to ~ in favour of/against sth** sich für/gegen etw aussprechen; **to ~ on sth** zu etw Stellung nehmen.
(b) he ~s badly er hat eine schlechte Aussprache.

pronounceable [prə'naʊnsəbl] *adj* aussprechbar.

pronounced [prə'naʊnst] *adj (marked)* ausgesprochen; *hip-bones* ausgeprägt; *improvement, deterioration* deutlich; *views* prononciert ◆ **he has a ~ limp** er hinkt sehr stark.

pronouncement [prə'naʊnsmənt] *n* Erklärung *f*; *(Jur: of sentence)* Verkündung *f* ◆ **to make a ~** eine Erklärung abgeben.

pronto ['prɒntəʊ] *adv (inf)* fix *(inf)* ◆ **do it ~** aber dalli! *(inf).*

pronunciation [prə,nʌnsɪ'eɪʃən] *n* Aussprache *f.*

proof [pru:f] 1 *n* **(a)** Beweis *m (of* für) ◆ **you'll need more ~ than that** die Beweise reichen nicht aus; **as** *or* **in ~ of** als *or* zum Beweis für; **to put sth to the ~** etw auf die Probe stellen; *(Tech)* etw erproben; **that is ~ that ...** das ist der Beweis dafür, daß ...; **to give** *or* **show ~ of sth** etw nachweisen, den Nachweis für etw liefern; **can you give us any ~ of that?** können Sie (uns) dafür Beweise liefern?; **show me your ~** beweisen Sie (mir) das; **what ~ is there that he meant it?** und was beweist, daß er es ernst gemeint hat?
(b) *(test, trial)* Probe *f* ◆ **withstanding these conditions is the ~ of a good paint** es ist der Beweis für die Qualität einer Farbe, wenn sie solchen Bedingungen standhält; **the ~ of the pudding is in the eating** *(Prov)* Probieren geht über Studieren *(Prov).*
(c) *(Typ)* (Korrektur)fahne *f*; *(Phot)* Probeabzug *m.*
(d) *(of alcohol)* Alkoholgehalt *m* ◆ **70 % ~** ≃ 40 Vol-%.
2 *adj (resistant)* **to be ~ against fire/water/moisture/bullets** feuersicher/wasserdicht/feuchtigkeitsundurchlässig/kugelsicher sein; **to be ~ against temptation** gegen Versuchungen gefeit *or* unempfindlich sein; **~ against inflation** inflationssicher.
3 *vt* **(a)** *(against water)* imprägnieren.
(b) *(Typ) (make ~)* einen Korrekturabzug herstellen; *(read ~)* Korrektur lesen.

proof: ~-read *vti* Korrektur lesen; **~-reader** *n* Korrektor(in *f*) *m*; **~-reading** *n* Korrekturlesen *nt*; **at the ~-reading stage** im Korrekturstadium.

prop¹ [prɒp] 1 *n (lit)* Stütze *f*; *(fig also)* Halt *m.*
2 *vt* **to ~ the door open** die Tür offenhalten; **to ~ oneself/sth against sth** sich/etw gegen etw lehnen; *see* **~ up.**

◆prop up *vt sep* **(a)** *(rest, lean)* **to ~ oneself/sth ~ against sth** sich/etw gegen etw lehnen. **(b)** *(support)* stützen; *tunnel, wall* abstützen; *engine* aufbocken; *(fig) régime, company, the pound* stützen; *organization* unterstützen ◆ **to ~ oneself ~ on sth** sich auf etw *(acc)* stützen; **he spends most of his time ~ping ~ the bar** *(inf)* er hängt die meiste Zeit an der Bar.

prop² *n (inf: propeller)* Propeller *m.*

prop³ *n (inf) see* **property (d).**

prop⁴ *abbr of* **proprietor.**

propaedeutic [,prəʊpi:'dju:tɪk] *n (form)* Propädeutik *f.*

propaganda [,prɒpə'gændə] *n* Propaganda *f* ◆ **~ machine** Propagandamaschinerie *f.*

propagandist [,prɒpə'gændɪst] 1 *n* Propagandist(in *f*) *m* ◆ **a tireless ~ for penal reform** ein unermüdlicher Verfechter der Strafrechtsreform.
2 *adj* propagandistisch.

propagate ['prɒpəgeɪt] 1 *vt* **(a)** fortpflanzen. **(b)** *(disseminate)* verbreiten; *views also* propagieren. **(c)** *(Phys) sound, waves* fortpflanzen. **(d)** *(Hort) plant* vermehren.
2 *vi* sich fortpflanzen *or* vermehren; *(views)* sich aus- *or* verbreiten.

propagation [,prɒpə'geɪʃən] *n (reproduction)* Fortpflanzung *f*; *(Hort: of plants)* Vermehrung *f*; *(dissemination)* Verbreitung *f*; *(of views)* Verbreitung, Propagierung *f.*

propane ['prəʊpeɪn] *n* Propan *nt.*

propel [prə'pel] *vt* antreiben; *(fuel)* betreiben ◆ **~led along by the wind** vom Wind getrieben; **~led by an unrelenting greed** von unersättlicher Habgier getrieben; **he was ~led through the window** er wurde aus dem Fenster geworfen.

propellant, propellent [prə'pelənt] 1 *n* Treibstoff *m*; *(in spray can)* Treibgas *nt.*
2 *adj* treibend.

propeller [prə'peləʳ] *n* Propeller *m* ◆ **~ shaft** Antriebswelle *f*; *(Aut)* Kardanwelle *f*; *(Naut)* Schraubenwelle *f.*

propelling: ~ force *n (lit, fig)* Triebkraft *f*; **~ pencil** *n (Brit)* Drehbleistift *m.*

propensity [prə'pensɪtɪ] *n* Hang *m*, Neigung *f (to* zu) ◆ **to have a ~ to do sth/for doing sth** dazu neigen, etw zu tun, die Neigung *or* den Hang haben, etw zu tun.

proper ['prɒpəʳ] 1 *adj* **(a)** *(peculiar, characteristic)* eigen ◆ **~ to the species** der Art eigen, arteigen.
(b) *(actual)* eigentlich ◆ **physics ~** die eigentliche Physik; **in the ~ sense of the word** in der eigentlichen Bedeutung des Wortes; **is that a ~ policeman's helmet?** ist das ein richtiger Polizeihelm?; **he's not a ~ electrician** er ist kein richtiger Elektriker; **not in Berlin ~** nicht in Berlin selbst.
(c) *(inf: real) fool etc* richtig; *(thorough) beating* gehörig, anständig *(inf)*, tüchtig *(inf)* ◆ **we got a ~ beating** *(team etc)* wir sind ganz schön geschlagen worden *(inf).*
(d) *(fitting, suitable)* richtig ◆ **in ~ condition** in ordnungsgemäßem Zustand; **in the ~ way** richtig; **as you think ~** wie Sie es für richtig halten; **to do the ~ thing by sb** das tun, was sich gehört; **the ~ thing to do would be to apologize** es gehört sich eigentlich, daß man sich entschuldigt; **don't touch the injured man unless you know the ~ thing to do** lassen Sie den Verletzten liegen, solange Sie nicht genau wissen, was man machen muß; **it wasn't really the ~ thing to say** es war ziemlich unpassend, das zu sagen; **we considered** *or* **thought it only ~ to ...** wir dachten, es gehört sich einfach zu ...
(e) *(seemly)* anständig ◆ **what is ~** was sich gehört; **it is not ~ for you to ...** es gehört sich nicht, daß Sie ...
(f) *(prim and ~)* korrekt.
2 *adv* **(a)** *(dial) cruel, poorly* richtig *(inf).*
(b) *(incorrect usage) behave* anständig; *talk* richtig.

proper fraction *n* echter Bruch.

properly ['prɒpəlɪ] *adv* **(a)** *(correctly)* richtig ◆ **~ speaking** genaugenommen, strenggenommen; **Holland, more ~ called the Netherlands** Holland, eigentlich *or* richtiger die Niederlande; **Yugoslav is ~ called Serbo-Croat** Jugoslawisch heißt korrekt Serbokroatisch.
(b) *(in seemly fashion)* anständig ◆ **to conduct oneself ~** sich korrekt verhalten; **she very ~ refused** sie hat sich zu Recht geweigert.
(c) *(justifiably)* zu Recht.
(d) *(inf: really, thoroughly)* ganz schön *(inf).*

proper name, proper noun *n* Eigenname *m.*

propertied ['prɒpətɪd] *adj* besitzend; *person* begütert ◆ **the ~ classes** die besitzenden Schichten, das Besitzbürgertum.

property ['prɒpətɪ] *n* **(a)** *(characteristic, Philos)* Eigenschaft *f* ◆ **it has healing properties** es besitzt heilende Kräfte.
(b) *(thing owned)* Eigentum *nt* ◆ **government/company ~** Eigentum *nt* der Regierung/Firma, Regierungs-/Firmeneigentum *nt*; **that's my ~** das gehört mir; **common ~** *(lit)* gemeinsames Eigentum; *(fig)* Gemeingut *nt*; **~ is theft** Eigentum ist Diebstahl; **to become the ~ of sb** in jds Eigentum *(acc)* übergehen; **a man of ~** ein begüterter Mann.
(c) *(building)* Haus *nt*; Wohnung *f*; *(office)* Gebäude *nt*; *(land)* Besitztum *nt*; *(estate)* Besitz *m* ◆ **this house is a very valuable ~** dieses Haus ist ein sehr wertvoller Besitz; **put your money in ~** legen Sie Ihr Geld in Immobilien an; **~ in London is dearer** die Preise auf dem Londoner Immobilienmarkt sind höher.
(d) *(Theat)* Requisit *nt.*

property: ~ developer *n* Häusermakler *m*; **~ man, ~ manager** *n (Theat)* Requisiteur *m*; **~ market** *n* Immobilienmarkt *m*; **~ mistress** *n (Theat)* Requisiteurin *f*; **~ owner** *n* Haus- und Grundbesitzer *m*; **~ speculation** *n* Immobilienspekulation *f*; **~ speculator** *n* Immobilienspekulant *m*; **~ tax** *n* Vermögenssteuer *f.*

prophecy ['prɒfɪsɪ] *n* Prophezeiung *f* ◆ **one skilled in the ~ of future events** jemand, der zukünftige Ereignisse vorhersagen kann *or* der die Gabe der Prophetie hat.

prophesy ['prɒfɪsaɪ] 1 *vt* prophezeien.
2 *vi* Prophezeiungen machen.

prophet ['prɒfɪt] *n* Prophet *m* ◆ **~ of doom** Unheilsverkünder(in *f*), Unheilsprophet(in *f*) *m.*

prophetess ['prɒfɪtɪs] *n* Prophetin *f.*

prophetic *adj*, **~ally** *adv* [prə'fetɪk, -əlɪ] prophetisch.

prophylactic [,prɒfɪ'læktɪk] 1 *adj* prophylaktisch, vorbeugend.
2 *n* Prophylaktikum *nt*; *(contraceptive)* Präservativ *nt.*

prophylaxis [,prɒfɪ'læksɪs] *n* Prophylaxe *f.*

propinquity [prə'pɪŋkwɪtɪ] *n (form)* Nähe *f (to* zu); *(in time)* zeitliche Nähe (*to* zu); (*of relationship*) nahe Verwandtschaft (*to* mit).

propitiate [prə'pɪʃɪeɪt] *vt* (*liter*) (*in favour of*) günstig *or* versöhnlich stimmen; (*appease*) besänftigen.

propitiation [prə,pɪʃɪ'eɪʃən] *n* (*liter*) *see vt* Versöhnung *f*; Besänftigung *f* ◆ **as ~ for, in ~ of** als Sühne für.

propitiatory [prə'pɪʃɪətərɪ] *adj see vt* versöhnend; besänftigend; *mood* versöhnlich.

propitious *adj*, **~ly** *adv* [prə'pɪʃəs, -lɪ] günstig (*to, for* für).

prop-jet ['prɒpdʒet] *n see* **turboprop**.

proponent [prə'pəʊnənt] *n* Befürworter(in *f*) *m*.

proportion [prə'pɔːʃən] [1] *n* **(a)** (*ratio, relationship in number*) Verhältnis *nt* (*of x to y* zwischen x und y); (*relationship in size, Art*) Proportionen *pl* ◆ **~s** (*size*) Ausmaß *nt*; (*of building*) Ausmaße *pl*; (*relative to one another: Art, of building etc*) Proportionen *pl*; **to be in/out of ~ (to one another)** (*in number*) im richtigen/nicht im richtigen Verhältnis zueinander stehen; (*in size, Art*) in den Proportionen stimmen/nicht stimmen; (*in time, effort etc*) im richtigen/in keinem Verhältnis zueinander stehen; **to be in/out of ~ to** *or* **with sth** im Verhältnis/in keinem Verhältnis zu etw stehen; (*in size, Art*) in den Proportionen zu etw passen/nicht zu etw passen; **in ~ to** *or* **with what she earns her contributions are very small** im Verhältnis zu dem, was sie verdient, ist ihr Beitrag äußerst bescheiden; **to get sth in ~** (*Art*) etw proportional richtig darstellen; (*fig*) etw objektiv betrachten; **he has got the arms out of ~** er hat die Arme proportional falsch dargestellt; **he has let it all get out of ~** (*fig*) er hat den Blick für die Proportionen verloren; **it's out of all ~!** das geht über jedes Maß hinaus!; **sense of ~** (*lit, fig*) Sinn *m* für Proportionen; **in ~ as** in dem Maße wie; **a man of huge ~s** ein Koloß von einem Mann; **he admired her ample ~s** er bewunderte ihre üppigen Formen; **a room of good ~s** ein Zimmer mit guter Raumaufteilung.
(b) (*part, amount*) Teil *m* ◆ **a certain ~ of the population** ein bestimmter Teil der Bevölkerung; **the ~ of drinkers in our society is rising constantly** der Anteil der Trinker in unserer Gesellschaft nimmt ständig zu; **what ~ of the industry is in private hands?** wie groß ist der Anteil der Industrie, der sich in Privathand befindet?; **a ~ of the industry is in private hands** ein Teil der Industrie befindet sich in Privathand.
[2] *vt* **you haven't ~ed the head properly** Sie haben den Kopf proportional falsch dargestellt; **he ~ed the building beautifully** er hat das Gebäude wunderbar ausgewogen gestaltet; **an accurately/roughly ~ed model** ein maßstabgetreues/ungefähres Modell; **a nicely ~ed woman/building** eine wohlproportionierte Frau/ein wohlausgewogenes Gebäude.

proportional [prə'pɔːʃənl] *adj* proportional (*to* zu); *share, distribution also* anteilmäßig (*to* zu) ◆ **~ representation/voting** Verhältniswahlrecht *nt*.

proportionally [prə'pɔːʃnəlɪ] *adv* proportional; *share, distribute also* anteilmäßig; *more, less* entsprechend; *elect* durch Verhältnis- *or* Proportionalwahl.

proportional (*Typ, Comput*): **~ printing** *n* Proportionaldruck *m*; **~ spacing** *n* Proportionalschrift *f*.

proportionate [prə'pɔːʃnɪt] *adj* proportional ◆ **to be/not to be ~ to sth** im Verhältnis/in keinem Verhältnis zu etw stehen.

proportionately [prə'pɔːʃnɪtlɪ] *adv see adj*.

proposal [prə'pəʊzl] *n* **(a)** Vorschlag *m* (*on, about* zu); (*~ of marriage*) (Heirats)antrag *m* ◆ **to make sb a ~** jdm einen Vorschlag/(Heirats)antrag machen.
(b) (*act of proposing*) (*of toast*) Ausbringen *nt*; (*of motion*) Einbringen *nt* ◆ **his ~ of this plan surprised his colleagues** daß er den Vorschlag zu diesem Plan machte, überraschte seine Kollegen; **his ~ of John as chairman was expected** daß er John zum Vorsitzenden vorschlägt, war erwartet worden.

➤ **propose** [prə'pəʊz] [1] *vt* **(a)** vorschlagen; *motion* stellen, einbringen ◆ **to ~ marriage to sb** jdm einen (Heirats)antrag machen; **I ~ leaving now** *or* **that we leave now** ich schlage vor, wir gehen jetzt *or* daß wir jetzt gehen; **to ~ sb's health** einen Toast auf jdn ausbringen; *see* **toast²**.
➤ **(b)** (*have in mind*) beabsichtigen, vorhaben ◆ **I don't ~ having any more to do with it/him** ich will nichts mehr damit/mit ihm zu tun haben; **but I don't ~ to** ich habe aber nicht die Absicht; **how do you ~ to pay for it**? wie wollen Sie das bezahlen?; **and just how do you ~ we pay for all that**? können Sie uns denn auch verraten, wie wir das alles bezahlen sollen?
[2] *vi* **(a)** (*marriage*) einen (Heirats)antrag machen (*to* dat).
(b) man ~s, God disposes (*Prov*) der Mensch denkt, Gott lenkt (*Prov*).

proposer [prə'pəʊzəʳ] *n* (*in debate*) Antragsteller(in *f*) *m* ◆ **if you want to stand for the committee you'll have to find a ~** wenn Sie sich in den Ausschuß wählen lassen wollen, müssen Sie jemanden finden, der Sie vorschlägt.

proposition [,prɒpə'zɪʃən] [1] *n* **(a)** (*statement*) Aussage *f*; (*Philos, Logic*) Satz *m*; (*Math*) (Lehr)satz *m*. **(b)** (*proposal*) Vorschlag *m*; (*argument*) These *f* ◆ **a paying ~** ein lohnendes Geschäft. **(c)** (*person or thing to be dealt with*) (*objective*) Unternehmen *nt*; (*opponent*) Fall *m*; (*prospect*) Aussicht *f*. **(d)** (*pej: improper ~*) unsittlicher Antrag.
[2] *vt* **he ~ed me** er hat mich gefragt, ob ich mit ihm schlafen würde.

propound [prə'paʊnd] *vt* darlegen.

proprietary [prə'praɪətərɪ] *adj class* besitzend; *rights* Besitz-; *attitude, manner* besitzergreifend; *medicine, article, brand* Marken- ◆ **the author has rather strong ~ feelings about his work** der Autor sieht sein Werk als persönlichen Besitz an.

proprietor [prə'praɪətəʳ] *n* (*of pub, hotel, patent*) Inhaber(in *f*) *m*; (*of house, newspaper*) Besitzer(in *f*) *m*.

proprietorship [prə'praɪətəʃɪp] *n see* **proprietor**. **under his ~** während er der Inhaber/Besitzer war.

proprietress [prə'praɪətrɪs] *n* (*of pub, hotel*) Inhaberin *f*; (*of newspaper*) Besitzerin *f*.

propriety [prə'praɪətɪ] *n* (*correctness*) Korrektheit, Richtigkeit *f*; (*decency*) Anstand *m*; (*of clothing*) Gesellschaftsfähigkeit, Züchtigkeit (*liter*) *f* ◆ **some countries still have doubts about the ~ of bikinis** in manchen Ländern werden Bikinis noch als anstößig betrachtet; **breach of ~** Verstoß *m* gegen die guten Sitten; **the proprieties** die Regeln *pl* des Anstands.

props [prɒps] *npl* (*Theat*) Requisiten *pl*.

propulsion [prə'pʌlʃən] *n* Antrieb *m*.

pro rata ['prəʊ'rɑːtə] *adj, adv* anteilmäßig.

prorate ['prəʊreɪt] *vt* (*US*) anteilmäßig aufteilen *or* verteilen.

prorogation [,prəʊrə'geɪʃən] *n* Vertagung *f*.

prorogue [prə'rəʊg] [1] *vt* vertagen.
[2] *vi* sich vertagen.

prosaic [prəʊ'zeɪɪk] *adj* prosaisch; (*down-to-earth*) nüchtern; *life, joke* alltäglich.

prosaically [prəʊ'zeɪɪkəlɪ] *adv see adj*.

proscenium [prəʊ'siːnɪəm] *n, pl* **proscenia** [prəʊ'siːnɪə] (*also* **~ arch**) Proszenium *nt* ◆ **~ stage** Bühne *f* mit Vorbühne.

proscribe [prəʊ'skraɪb] *vt* (*forbid*) verbieten; (*outlaw*) ächten; (*banish, exile*) verbannen.

proscription [prəʊ'skrɪpʃən] *n see vt* Verbot *nt*; Ächtung *f*; Verbannung *f*.

prose [prəʊz] *n* Prosa *f*; (*writing, style*) Stil *m*; (*Sch: translation text*) Übersetzung *f* in die Fremdsprache, Hinübersetzung *f*.

prose *in cpds* Prosa-; **~ composition** *n* Prosa *f*.

prosecutable ['prɒsɪkjuːtəbl] *adj* strafbar.

prosecute ['prɒsɪkjuːt] [1] *vt* **(a)** *person* strafrechtlich verfolgen *or* belangen (*for* wegen) ◆ **prosecuting counsel** Staatsanwalt *m*/-anwältin *f*; **"trespassers will be ~d"** „Betreten verboten". **(b)** (*form: carry on*) *inquiry, campaign etc* durchführen; *claim* weiterverfolgen.
[2] *vi* Anzeige erstatten, gerichtlich vorgehen ◆ **"shoplifting — we always ~"** „jeder Ladendiebstahl wird angezeigt *or* strafrechtlich verfolgt"; **Mr Jones, prosecuting, said ...** Herr Jones, der Vertreter der Anklage, sagte ...

prosecution [,prɒsɪ'kjuːʃən] *n* **(a)** (*Jur*) (*act of prosecuting*) strafrechtliche Verfolgung; (*in court: case, side*) Anklage *f* (*for* wegen) ◆ **(the) counsel for the ~** die Anklage(vertretung), der Vertreter/die Vertreterin der Anklage; **witness for the ~** Zeuge *m*/Zeugin *f* der Anklage, Belastungszeuge *m*/-zeugin *f*.
(b) (*form*) *see vt* (*b*) Durchführung *f*; Weiterverfolgung *f*.

prosecutor ['prɒsɪkjuːtəʳ] *n* Ankläger(in *f*) *m*.

proselyte ['prɒsɪlaɪt] *n* Neubekehrte(r) *mf*, Proselyt(in *f*) *m*.

proselytize ['prɒsɪlɪtaɪz] [1] *vt* bekehren.
[2] *vi* Leute bekehren.

prose: ~ poem *n* Prosagedicht *nt*; **~ style** *n* Stil *m*; **~ writer** *n* Prosaschriftsteller(in *f*) *m*; **~ writing** *n* Prosadichtung *f*.

prosodic [prə'sɒdɪk] *adj* prosodisch.

prosody ['prɒsədɪ] *n* Verslehre *f*.

prospect ['prɒspekt] [1] *n* **(a)** (*outlook, chance*) Aussicht *f* (*of* auf *+acc*) ◆ **what a ~!** (*iro*) das sind ja schöne Aussichten!; **he has no ~s** er hat keine Zukunft; **a job with no ~s** eine Stelle ohne Zukunft; **to hold out the ~ of sth** etw in Aussicht stellen; **to have sth in ~** etw in Aussicht haben.
(b) (*person, thing*) **he's not much of a ~ for her** er hat ihr nicht viel zu bieten; **I think this product would be a good ~** ich glaube, dieses Produkt ist sehr aussichtsreich; **Manchester is a good ~ for the cup** Manchester ist ein aussichtsreicher Kandidat für den Pokal; **a likely ~ as a customer/candidate/husband** ein aussichtsreicher Kunde/Kandidat/ein Mann, der als Ehemann in Frage kommt; **he's a good ~ for the team** (*could benefit it*) mit ihm hat die Mannschaft gute Aussichten.
(c) (*old, form*) (*view*) Aussicht *f* (*of* auf *+acc*); (*painting*) Ansicht *f* (*of* von).
(d) (*Min*) Schürfstelle *f*.
[2] [prə'spekt] *vt* (*Min*) nach Bodenschätzen suchen in (*+dat*).
[3] [prə'spekt] *vi* (*Min*) nach Bodenschätzen suchen ◆ **to ~ for gold** nach Gold suchen.

prospecting [prə'spektɪŋ] *n* (*Min*) Suche *f* nach Bodenschätzen.

prospective [prə'spektɪv] *adj attr* (*likely to happen*) *journey, return* voraussichtlich; (*future*) *son-in-law, owner* zukünftig; *buyer* interessiert ◆ **~ candidate** Kandidat *m*; **all the ~ cases** alle in Frage kommenden Fälle.

prospector [prə'spektəʳ] *n* Prospektor, Gold-/Erz-/Ölsucher *m*.

prospectus [prə'spektəs] *n* Verzeichnis *nt*; (*for holidays etc*) Prospekt *m*.

prosper ['prɒspəʳ] *vi* (*town, country, crime*) gedeihen, blühen; (*financially*) florieren, blühen; (*plan*) erfolgreich sein ◆ **how's he ~ing these days**? wie geht es ihm?

prosperity [prɒs'perɪtɪ] *n* Wohlstand, Reichtum *m*; (*of business*) Prosperität *f*.

prosperous ['prɒspərəs] *adj* wohlhabend, reich; *business* gutgehend, florierend; *economy* florierend, blühend ◆ **those were ~ times/years** das waren Zeiten/Jahre des Wohlstands; **he had a ~ look about him** er sah wohlhabend aus.

prosperously ['prɒspərəslɪ] *adv live* im Wohlstand.

prostaglandin [,prɒstə'glændɪn] *n* Prostaglandin *nt*.

prostate (gland) ['prɒsteɪt(,glænd)] *n* Prostata, Vorsteherdrüse *f*.

prosthesis [prɒs'θiːsɪs] *n* (*spec*) Prothese *f*.

prostitute ['prɒstɪtjuːt] [1] *n* Prostituierte *f* ◆ **male ~** männlicher Prostituierte (*form*), Strichjunge *m*.
[2] *vt* (*lit*) prostituieren; *one's talents, honour, ideals* verkaufen.

➤ LANGUAGE IN USE: **propose: 1b** → 8.1, 8.3

3 *vr* sich prostituieren; (*fig also*) sich verkaufen.
prostitution [ˌprɒstɪˈtjuːʃən] *n* (*lit, fig*) Prostitution *f*; (*of one's talents, honour, ideals*) Verkaufen *nt*.
prostrate [ˈprɒstreɪt] 1 *adj* ausgestreckt ◆ **he was found ~ on the floor** man fand ihn ausgestreckt am Boden liegend; **the servants lay ~ at their master's feet** die Diener lagen demütig *or* unterwürfig zu Füßen ihres Herrn; **she was ~ with grief/exhaustion** sie war vor Gram gebrochen/sie brach fast zusammen vor Erschöpfung.
2 [prɒˈstreɪt] *vt usu pass* (*lit*) zu Boden werfen; (*fig*) (*with fatigue*) erschöpfen, mitnehmen; (*with shock*) zusammenbrechen lassen, niederschmettern ◆ **to be ~d by an illness** einer Krankheit (*dat*) zum Opfer gefallen sein; **to be ~d by** *or* **with grief** vor Gram gebrochen sein; **he was almost ~d by the heat** die Hitze ließ ihn fast zusammenbrechen.
3 [prɒˈstreɪt] *vr* sich niederwerfen (*before* vor *+dat*).
prostration [prɒˈstreɪʃən] *n* (*lit*) Fußfall *m*; (*fig: exhaustion*) Erschöpfung *f*.
prosy [ˈprəʊzɪ] *adj* (*+er*) (*boring*) redselig; (*over-literary*) schwülstig.
Prot *abbr of* **Protestant** ev.
protactinium [ˌprəʊtækˈtɪnɪəm] *n* (*Chem*) Protaktinium *nt*.
protagonist [prəʊˈtægənɪst] *n* (*esp Liter*) Protagonist(in *f*) *m*; (*champion, supporter*) Verfechter(in *f*) *m*.
protean [ˈprəʊtɪən] *adj* (*liter*) proteisch (*liter*).
protect [prəˈtekt] 1 *vt* schützen (*against* gegen, *from* vor *+dat*); (*person, animal*) *sb, young* beschützen (*against* gegen, *from* vor *+dat*); *one's interests, rights also* wahren; (*Comput*) *cell etc* sichern ◆ **don't try to ~ the culprit** versuchen Sie nicht, den Schuldigen zu decken.
2 *vi* schützen (*against* vor *+dat*).
protection [prəˈtekʃən] *n* **(a)** Schutz *m* (*against* gegen, *from* vor *+dat*); (*of interests, rights*) Wahrung *f* ◆ **to be under sb's ~** unter jds Schutz (*dat*) stehen; **~ factor** (*of sun lotion*) Lichtschutzfaktor *m*. **(b)** (*also* **~ money**) Schutzgeld *nt* ◆ **~ racket** organisiertes Erpresserunwesen.
protectionism [prəˈtekʃənɪzəm] *n* Protektionismus *m*.
protectionist [prəˈtekʃənɪst] 1 *adj* protektionistisch.
2 *n* Protektionist *m*.
protective [prəˈtektɪv] *adj* Schutz-; *attitude, gesture* beschützend ◆ **~ custody** Schutzhaft *f*; **~ colouring** Tarnfarbe, Schutzfarbe *f*; **~ instinct** Beschützerinstinkt *m*; **the mother is very ~ towards her children** die Mutter ist sehr fürsorglich ihren Kindern gegenüber; **some parents can be too ~** manche Eltern sind übermäßig besorgt.
protectively [prəˈtektɪvlɪ] *adv* schützend; (*with regard to people*) beschützend ◆ **don't be frightened, he said ~** hab keine Angst, sagte er in beschützendem Ton.
protector [prəˈtektəʳ] *n* **(a)** (*defender*) Beschützer *m*. **(b)** (*protective wear*) Schutz *m*.
protectorate [prəˈtektərɪt] *n* Protektorat *nt*.
protectress [prəˈtektrɪs] *n* Beschützerin *f*.
protégé, protégée [ˈprɒtəʒeɪ] *n* Protegé, Schützling *m*.
protein [ˈprəʊtiːn] *n* Eiweiß, Protein *nt* ◆ **a high-~ diet** eine eiweißreiche *or* stark proteinhaltige Kost.
pro tem [ˈprəʊˈtem] *abbr of* **pro tempore** zur Zeit, z.Zt.
▼ **protest** [ˈprəʊtest] 1 *n* Protest *m*; (*demonstration*) Protestkundgebung *f* ◆ **under ~** unter Protest; **in ~** aus Protest; **to make a/one's ~** Protest *or* Widerspruch erheben; **letter of ~, ~ letter** Protestschreiben *nt*; **~ march** Protestmarsch *m*; **~ vote** Proteststimme *f*.
▼ 2 [prəʊˈtest] *vi* (*against, about* gegen) protestieren; (*demonstrate*) demonstrieren ◆ **the ~ing scream of the brakes** das gequälte Aufkreischen der Bremsen.
3 [prəʊˈtest] *vt* **(a)** *innocence* beteuern ◆ **it's mine, he ~ed** das gehört mir, protestierte er. **(b)** (*dispute*) *decision* protestieren gegen, Protest *or* Einspruch erheben gegen.
Protestant [ˈprɒtɪstənt] 1 *adj* protestantisch; (*esp in Germany*) evangelisch.
2 *n* Protestant(in *f*) *m*; Evangelische(r) *mf*.
Protestantism [ˈprɒtɪstəntɪzəm] *n* Protestantismus *m*.
protestation [ˌprɒteˈsteɪʃən] *n* **(a)** (*of love, loyalty etc*) Beteuerung *f*. **(b)** (*protest*) Protest *m*.
protester [prəˈtestəʳ] *n* Protestierende(r) *mf*; (*in demonstration*) Demonstrant(in *f*) *m*.
proto- [ˈprəʊtəʊ-] *pref* (*Chem*) proto-, Proto-; (*Ling*) ur-, Ur-.
protocol [ˈprəʊtəkɒl] *n* Protokoll *nt*.
proton [ˈprəʊtɒn] *n* Proton *nt*.
protoplasm [ˈprəʊtəʊplæzəm] *n* Protoplasma *nt*.
prototype [ˈprəʊtəʊtaɪp] *n* Prototyp *m*.
protozoan [ˈprəʊtəʊzəʊən] 1 *adj* einzellig.
2 *n* Protozoon (*spec*), Urtierchen *nt*.
protozoic [ˈprəʊtəʊzəʊɪk] *adj* einzellig.
protract [prəˈtrækt] *vt* hinausziehen, in die Länge ziehen; *illness* verlängern; *decision* hinauszögern.
protracted [prəˈtræktɪd] *adj illness* langwierig; *discussion, debate, negotiations also* sich hinziehend *attr*; *description* langgezogen; *absence, dispute* längere(r, s).
protraction [prəˈtrækʃən] *n* **that can only lead to the ~ of the discussion/illness** das kann nur dazu führen, daß sich die Diskussion/Krankheit hinzieht.
protractor [prəˈtræktəʳ] *n* (*Math*) Winkelmesser *m*.
protrude [prəˈtruːd] 1 *vi* (*out of, from* aus) vorstehen; (*ears*) abstehen; (*eyes*) vortreten.
2 *vt* hervorstrecken, herausstrecken ◆ **he ~d his gun slightly through the window** er schob sein Gewehr ein Stück durch die Fensteröffnung.
protruding [prəˈtruːdɪŋ] *adj* vorstehend; *rock, ledge also* herausragend; *ears* abstehend; *eyes* vortretend; *forehead, chin* vorspringend.
protrusion [prəˈtruːʒən] *n* **(a)** (*protruding object*) Vorsprung *m*. **(b)** (*protruding*) (*of rock, buttress, teeth etc*) Vorstehen *nt*; (*of forehead, chin*) Vorspringen *nt*; (*of eyes*) Vortreten *nt*.
protrusive [prəˈtruːsɪv] *adj see* **protruding**.
protuberance [prəˈtjuːbərəns] *n* (*bulge*) Beule *f*; (*of stomach*) Vorstehen *nt*; (*of eyes*) Vortreten *nt*.
protuberant [prəˈtjuːbərənt] *adj* vorstehend; *eyes* vortretend.
proud [praʊd] 1 *adj* **(a)** stolz (*of* auf *+acc*) ◆ **it made his parents feel very ~** das erfüllte seine Eltern mit Stolz; **to be ~ that ...** stolz (darauf) sein, daß ...; **to be ~ to do sth** stolz darauf sein, etw zu tun; **I hope you're ~ of yourself** (*iro*) ich hoffe, du bist stolz auf dich; **that's nothing to be ~ of** das ist nichts, worauf man stolz sein kann.
(b) (*projecting*) **to be ~** (*nail etc*) heraus- *or* hervorragen; (*Typ: character*) erhaben sein; **~ flesh** wildes Fleisch.
2 *adv* **to do sb/oneself ~** jdn/sich verwöhnen.
proudly [ˈpraʊdlɪ] *adv* stolz.
provable [ˈpruːvəbl] *adj hypothesis, story* beweisbar; *guilt, innocence also* nachweisbar.
▼ **prove** [pruːv] *pret* **~d**, *ptp* **~d** *or* **proven** 1 *vt* **(a)** (*verify*) beweisen; *will* beglaubigen ◆ **he ~d that she did it** er bewies *or* er wies nach, daß sie das getan hat; **to ~ sb innocent** *or* **sb's innocence** jds Unschuld beweisen *or* nachweisen; **to ~ something against sb** jdm etwas nachweisen; **whether his judgement was right remains to be ~d** es muß sich erst noch erweisen, ob seine Beurteilung zutrifft; **it all goes to ~ that ...** das beweist mal wieder, daß ...; **he was ~d right in the end** er hat schließlich doch recht behalten.
(b) (*test out, put to the proof*) *rifle, aircraft etc* erproben; *one's worth, courage* unter Beweis stellen, beweisen.
(c) (*Cook*) *dough* gehen lassen.
(d) *also vi* (*turn out*) **to ~ (to be) hot/useful** *etc* sich als heiß/nützlich *etc* erweisen; **if it ~s otherwise** wenn sich das Gegenteil herausstellt.
2 *vi* **(a)** (*Cook: dough*) gehen. **(b)** *see vt* (*d*).
3 *vr* **(a)** (*show one's value, courage etc*) sich bewähren.
(b) to ~ oneself innocent/indispensable *etc* sich als unschuldig/unentbehrlich *etc* erweisen.
proven [ˈpruːvən] 1 *ptp of* **prove**.
2 [ˈprəʊvən] *adj* bewährt ◆ **not ~** (*Scot Jur*) unbewiesen.
provenance [ˈprɒvɪnəns] *n* Herkunft *f*, Ursprung *m* ◆ **country of ~** Herkunfts- *or* Ursprungsland *nt*.
provender [ˈprɒvɪndəʳ] *n* Futter *nt*.
proverb [ˈprɒvɜːb] *n* Sprichwort *nt* ◆ **(the Book of) P~s** die Sprüche *pl*.
proverbial [prəˈvɜːbɪəl] *adj* (*lit, fig*) sprichwörtlich.
proverbially [prəˈvɜːbɪəlɪ] *adv* (*lit*) *express* in Form eines Sprichworts; (*fig*) sprichwörtlich.
provide [prəˈvaɪd] 1 *vt* **(a)** (*make available*) zur Verfügung stellen; *personnel* (*agency*) vermitteln; *money* bereitstellen; (*lay on, as part of service*) *chairs, materials, food etc* (zur Verfügung) stellen; (*see to, bring along*) *food, records etc* sorgen für; (*produce, give*) *ideas, specialist knowledge, electricity* liefern; *light, shade* spenden, geben; *privacy* sorgen für, schaffen; *topic of conversation* sorgen für, liefern ◆ **X ~d the money and Y (~d) the expertise** X stellte das Geld bereit und Y lieferte das Fachwissen; **a local band ~d the music** eine örtliche Kapelle sorgte für die Musik; **candidates must ~ their own pens** die Kandidaten müssen ihr Schreibgerät selbst stellen.
(b) to ~ sth for sb etw für jdn stellen; (*make available*) jdm etw zur Verfügung stellen; (*find, supply: agency etc*) jdm etw besorgen; **to ~ food and clothes for one's family** für Nahrung und Kleidung seiner Familie sorgen; **I can't ~ enough chairs/food for everyone** ich kann nicht genug Stühle/Nahrung für alle stellen; **it ~s a certain amount of privacy/shade for the inhabitants** es schafft für die Bewohner eine gewisse Abgeschlossenheit/es spendet den Bewohnern etwas Schatten; **they ~ a restroom/bus for the use of their workers** sie stellen einen Ruheraum/Bus für ihre Arbeiter.
(c) to ~ sb with sth (*with food, clothing etc*) jdn mit etw versorgen; (*equip*) jdn mit etw versehen *or* ausstatten; (*with excuse, idea, answer*) jdm etw geben *or* liefern; (*with opportunity, information*) jdm etw verschaffen *or* geben *or* liefern; **the house was ~d with a garden/with running water** das Haus hatte einen Garten/fließendes Wasser; **this job ~d him with enough money/with the necessary overseas experience** die Stelle verschaffte ihm genug Geld/die nötige Auslandserfahrung; **this ~d the school with enough money to build a gymnasium** dadurch hatte die Schule genügend Geld zur Verfügung, um eine Turnhalle zu bauen.
(d) (*stipulate: clause, agreement*) vorsehen ◆ **unless otherwise ~d** sofern nichts Gegenteiliges bestimmt ist; *see* **~d (that), providing (that)**.
2 *vi* **the Lord will ~** (*prov*) der Herr wird's schon geben; **a husband who ~s well** ein Ehemann, der gut für seine Familie/Frau sorgt.
3 *vr* **to ~ oneself with sth** sich mit etw ausstatten; **to ~ oneself with a good excuse** sich (*dat*) eine gute Entschuldigung zurechtlegen.
◆**provide against** *vi +prep obj* vorsorgen für, Vorsorge *or* Vorkehrungen treffen für ◆ **the law ~s ~ such abuses** das Gesetz schützt vor solchem Mißbrauch.
◆**provide for** *vi +prep obj* **(a)** *family etc* versorgen, sorgen für, Sorge tragen für ◆ **he made sure that his family would be well ~d ~** er stellte sicher, daß seine Familie gut versorgt war *or* daß für seine Familie gut gesorgt war.

➤ LANGUAGE IN USE: **protest: 2** → 12.2, 14 **prove: 1a** → 26.1

(b) the law/treaty ~s ~ penalties against abuses bei Mißbrauch sieht das Gesetz/der Vertrag Strafe vor; **as ~d ~ in the 1970 contract** wie in dem Vertrag von 1970 vorgesehen; **we ~d ~ all emergencies** wir haben für alle Notfälle vorgesorgt; **we have ~d ~ an increase in costs of 25%** wir haben eine Kostensteigerung von 25% einkalkuliert; **the design of the house ~s ~ the later addition of a garage** im Entwurf des Hauses ist der spätere Anbau einer Garage vorgesehen.

provided (that) [prəˈvaɪdɪd(ˈðæt)] *conj* vorausgesetzt, gesetzt den Fall(, daß).

providence [ˈprɒvɪdəns] *n* **(a)** *(fate)* die Vorsehung. **(b)** *(dated: prudent thriftiness)* Vorsorge *f* ◆ **his ~ in saving for his old age** sein vorsorgendes Sparen für das Alter.

provident [ˈprɒvɪdənt] *adj* vorsorglich, vorsorgend, vorausschauend ◆ **~ fund** Unterstützungskasse *f*; **~ society** *private Altersversicherung.*

providential [ˌprɒvɪˈdenʃəl] *adj* **(a) God's ~ care** die göttliche Vorsehung. **(b)** *(lucky)* glücklich ◆ **to be ~** (ein) Glück sein.

providentially [ˌprɒvɪˈdenʃəlɪ] *adv (luckily)* glücklicherweise ◆ **it happened almost ~** das war gleichsam eine Fügung (des Schicksals).

providently [ˈprɒvɪdəntlɪ] *adv see adj.*

provider [prəˈvaɪdə^r] *n (of family)* Ernährer(in *f*) *m*.

providing (that) [prəˈvaɪdɪŋ(ˈðæt)] *conj* vorausgesetzt(, daß), gesetzt den Fall(, daß).

province [ˈprɒvɪns] *n* **(a)** Provinz *f*.
(b) the ~s *pl* die Provinz.
(c) *(fig: area of knowledge, activity etc)* Gebiet *nt*, Bereich *m* ◆ **it's not within my ~** das fällt nicht in meinen Bereich *or* mein Gebiet; **it's outside the ~ of science** es liegt außerhalb des wissenschaftlichen Gebiets *or* Bereichs; **that is outside my ~** das ist nicht mein Gebiet.
(d) *(area of authority)* Kompetenzbereich *m* ◆ **that's not my ~** dafür bin ich nicht zuständig.

provincial [prəˈvɪnʃəl] **1** *adj* Provinz-; *custom, accent* ländlich; *(pej)* provinzlerisch ◆ **~ narrowness** Engstirnigkeit *f*.
2 *n* Provinzbewohner(in *f*) *m*; *(pej)* Provinzler(in *f*) *m*.

provincialism [prəˈvɪnʃəlɪzəm] *n* Provinzialismus *m*.

proving ground [ˈpruːvɪŋˌgraʊnd] *n (for theory)* Versuchsfeld *nt*; *(situation: for sb, sb's abilities)* Bewährungsprobe *f* ◆ **Belfast was his ~** Belfast war für ihn die Bewährungsprobe.

provision [prəˈvɪʒən] **1** *n* **(a)** *(act of supplying) (for others)* Bereitstellung *f*; *(for one's own team, expedition etc)* Beschaffung *f*; *(of food, gas, water etc)* Versorgung *f* (*of* mit, *to sb* jds).
(b) *(supply)* Vorrat *m* (*of* an *+dat*) ◆ **we had an ample ~ of reference books/houses** *etc* uns *(dat)* standen genügend Nachschlagewerke/Häuser *etc* zur Verfügung.
(c) ~s *(food)* Lebensmittel *pl*; *(Mil, for journey, expedition)* Verpflegung *f*, Proviant *m* ◆ **~s ship** Versorgungsschiff *nt*.
(d) *(allowance)* Berücksichtigung *f*; *(arrangement)* Vorkehrung *f*; *(stipulation)* Bestimmung *f* ◆ **with the ~ that** ... mit dem Vorbehalt *or* der Bedingung, daß ...; **is there no ~ for such cases in the legislation**? sind solche Fälle im Gesetz nicht berücksichtigt *or* vorgesehen?; **there's no ~ for later additions** spätere Erweiterungen sind nicht vorgesehen; **to make ~ for sb/one's family/the future** für jdn/für seine Familie/für die Zukunft Vorsorge *or* Vorkehrungen treffen; **to make ~ for sth** etw vorsehen; *(in legislation, rules also)* etw berücksichtigen; *for margin of error etc* etw einkalkulieren; **the council made ~ for recreation** die Stadt hat Freizeiteinrichtungen geschaffen; **to make ~ against sth** gegen etw Vorkehrungen treffen.
2 *vt* die Verpflegung liefern für; *expedition* verproviantieren; *troops* (mit Proviant) beliefern *or* versorgen.

provisional [prəˈvɪʒənl] **1** *adj* provisorisch; *measures, solution also, offer, acceptance, decision, legislation* vorläufig ◆ **~ driving licence** *(Brit)* vorläufige Fahrerlaubnis für Fahrschüler; **the ~ IRA** *see n.*
2 *n (Ir Pol)* **the P~s** *Mitglieder pl der provisorischen irisch-republikanischen Armee.*

provisionally [prəˈvɪʒnəlɪ] *adv* vorläufig; *appoint also* provisorisch.

proviso [prəˈvaɪzəʊ] *n (condition)* Vorbehalt *m*, Bedingung *f*; *(clause)* Vorbehaltsklausel *f* ◆ **he made several ~s** er hat mehrere Bedingungen gestellt.

provisory [prəˈvaɪzərɪ] *adj* **(a)** *(with a proviso)* vorbehaltlich ◆ **a ~ clause** eine Vorbehaltsklausel. **(b)** *see* **provisional 1**.

Provo [ˈprəʊvəʊ] *n (Ir Pol) see* **provisional 2**.

provocation [ˌprɒvəˈkeɪʃən] *n* Provokation, Herausforderung *f* ◆ **what ~ was there for you to hit him**? was hat dich dazu provoziert, ihn zu schlagen?; **he acted under ~** er wurde dazu provoziert *or* herausgefordert; **his deliberate ~ of a quarrel** seine bewußte Herbeiführung eines Streits; **to suffer great ~** sehr stark provoziert werden; **at the slightest ~** bei der geringsten Provokation *or* Herausforderung; **he hit me without any ~** er hat mich geschlagen, ohne daß ich ihn dazu provoziert hätte.

provocative [prəˈvɒkətɪv] *adj* provozierend, provokatorisch; *remark, behaviour also* herausfordernd; *dress* provozierend ◆ **he's just trying to be ~** er versucht nur zu provozieren.

provocatively [prəˈvɒkətɪvlɪ] *adv see adj.*

provoke [prəˈvəʊk] *vt sb* provozieren, reizen, herausfordern; *animal* reizen; *reaction, anger, criticism, dismay, smile* hervorrufen; *lust, pity* erwecken, erregen; *reply, dispute* provozieren; *discussion, revolt, showdown* herbeiführen, auslösen ◆ **to ~ a quarrel** *or* **an argument** *(person)* Streit suchen; *(action)* zu einem Streit führen; **to ~ sb into doing sth** *or* **to do sth** jdn dazu bringen, daß er etw tut; *(taunt)* jdn dazu treiben *or* so provozieren, daß er etw tut.

provoking [prəˈvəʊkɪŋ] *adj* provozierend; *(annoying) fact, circumstance* ärgerlich ◆ **a ~ child** ein Kind, das einen reizt; **how very ~!** wie ärgerlich!

provokingly [prəˈvəʊkɪŋlɪ] *adv* provozierend.

provost [ˈprɒvəst] *n* **(a)** *(Scot)* Bürgermeister *m*. **(b)** *(Univ)* ≃ Dekan *m*. **(c)** *(Eccl)* Propst *m*.

provost marshal [prəˈvəʊstˈmɑːʃəl] *n* Kommandeur *m* der Militärpolizei.

prow [praʊ] *n* Bug *m*.

prowess [ˈpraʊɪs] *n (skill)* Fähigkeiten *pl*, Können *nt*; *(courage)* Tapferkeit *f* ◆ **his (sexual) ~** seine Potenz, seine Manneskraft.

prowl [praʊl] **1** *n* Streifzug *m* ◆ **to be on the ~** *(cat, lion, burglar)* auf Streifzug sein; *(headmaster, boss)* herumschleichen; *(police car)* auf Streife sein; *(inf: for pick-up)* auf Frauen-/Männerjagd sein.
2 *vt* durchstreifen.
3 *vi (also ~* **about** *or* **around)** herumstreichen; *(of boss, headmaster)* herumschleichen ◆ **he's always ~ing round the clubs** er streicht immer um die Klubs herum.

prowl car *n (US)* Streifenwagen *m*.

prowler [ˈpraʊlə^r] *n* Herumtreiber(in *f*) *m*; *(peeping Tom)* Spanner *m (inf)* ◆ **he heard a ~ outside** er hörte, wie draußen jemand herumschlich.

prox [ˈprɒks] *abbr of* **proximo**.

proximity [prɒkˈsɪmɪtɪ] *n* Nähe *f* ◆ **in ~/in close ~ to** in der Nähe *(+gen)*/in unmittelbarer Nähe *(+gen)*; **~ in age** geringer Altersunterschied.

proximo [ˈprɒksɪməʊ] *adv (Comm)* (des) nächsten Monats.

proxy [ˈprɒksɪ] *n (power, document)* (Handlungs)vollmacht *f*; *(person)* Stellvertreter(in *f*) *m* ◆ **by ~** durch einen Stellvertreter; **to be married by ~** ferngetraut werden; **~ vote** stellvertretend abgegebene Stimme.

Prozac ® [ˈprəʊzæk] *n* Prozac ® *nt*.

prude [pruːd] *n* **to be a ~** prüde sein; **only ~s would object to that** nur prüde Leute würden sich daran stoßen.

prudence [ˈpruːdəns] *n see adj* Umsicht *f*; Klugheit *f*; Überlegtheit *f* ◆ **simple ~ should have made you stop** der gesunde Menschenverstand hätte Sie davon abbringen müssen.

prudent [ˈpruːdənt] *adj person* umsichtig; *measure, action, decision* klug; *answer* wohlüberlegt ◆ **I thought it ~ to change the subject** ich hielt es für klüger, das Thema zu wechseln; **how ~!** sehr klug *or* weise!

prudently [ˈpruːdəntlɪ] *adv* wohlweislich; *act* umsichtig; *answer* überlegt.

prudery [ˈpruːdərɪ] *n* Prüderie *f*.

prudish [ˈpruːdɪʃ] *adj* prüde; *clothes* sittsam, züchtig.

prudishly [ˈpruːdɪʃlɪ] *adv see adj* ◆ **they ~ cut out all the swearwords** prüde wie sie sind, haben sie alle Kraftausdrücke gestrichen.

prudishness [ˈpruːdɪʃnɪs] *n (prudish behaviour)* Prüderie *f*; *(prudish nature)* prüde Art; *(of clothes)* Sittsamkeit *f*.

prune[1] [pruːn] *n* Backpflaume *f*; *(inf: person)* Muffel *m (inf)*.

prune[2] *vt (also ~* **down)** beschneiden, stutzen; *hedge* schneiden, zurechtstutzen; *(fig) expenditure* kürzen; *workforce* reduzieren; *firm* schrumpfen lassen; *book, essay* zusammenstreichen, kürzen ◆ **to ~ away** ab- *or* wegschneiden; *unnecessary details, verbiage etc* wegstreichen; **to ~ an essay of superfluous matter** einen Aufsatz straffen.

pruners [ˈpruːnəz] *npl* Gartenschere, Rebschere *f*.

pruning [ˈpruːnɪŋ] *n see vt* Beschneiden, Stutzen *nt*; Schneiden, Zurechtstutzen *nt*; Kürzung *f*; Reduzierung *f*; Schrumpfung *f*; Zusammenstreichen *nt* ◆ **the tree needs ~** der Baum muß beschnitten *or* gestutzt werden.

pruning: ~ hook *n* Rebmesser *nt*; **~ knife** *n* Gartenmesser *nt*, Hippe *f*; **~ shears** *npl* Gartenschere, Rebschere *f*.

prurience [ˈprʊərɪəns] *n see adj* Anzüglichkeit *f*; Lüsternheit *f*.

prurient [ˈprʊərɪənt] *adj* anzüglich; *person* lüstern.

Prussia [ˈprʌʃə] *n* Preußen *nt*.

Prussian [ˈprʌʃən] **1** *adj* preußisch ◆ **~ blue** preußischblau.
2 *n* **(a)** Preuße *m*, Preußin *f*. **(b)** *(language)* Preußisch *nt* ◆ **Old ~** Altpreußisch *nt*.

prussic acid [ˈprʌsɪkˈæsɪd] *n* Blausäure *f*.

pry[1] [praɪ] *vi* neugierig sein; *(in drawers etc)* (herum)schnüffeln (*in* in *+dat*) ◆ **I don't mean to ~, but** ... es geht mich ja nichts an, aber ...; **to ~ into sb's affairs** seine Nase in jds Angelegenheiten *(acc)* stecken; **to ~ into sb's secrets** jds Geheimnisse ausspionieren wollen; **to ~ about** herumschnüffeln.

pry[2] *vt (US) see* **prise**.

prying [ˈpraɪɪŋ] *adj* neugierig.

PS *abbr of* **postscript** PS.

psalm [sɑːm] *n* Psalm *m* ◆ **(the Book of) P~s** der Psalter; **~ book** Psalmenbuch *nt*.

psalmist [ˈsɑːmɪst] *n* Psalmist *m*.

psalmody [ˈsælmədɪ] *n* Psalmodie *f*.

psalter [ˈsɔːltə^r] *n* Psalter *m*.

psaltery [ˈsɔːltərɪ] *n* Psalterium *nt*.

PSBR *abbr of* **public sector borrowing requirement**.

psephological [ˌsefəˈlɒdʒɪkəl] *adj* Wahlforschungs-.

psephologist [seˈfɒlədʒɪst] *n* Wahlforscher(in *f*) *m*.

psephology [seˈfɒlədʒɪ] *n* Wahlforschung *f*.

pseud [sjuːd] *(inf)* **1** *n* Möchtegern *m (inf)* ◆ **you ~!** du Angeber(in)!
2 *adj book, film* auf intellektuell gemacht *(inf)*, gewollt; *views, ideas* hochgestochen; *décor, pub etc* auf schick gemacht *(inf)*; *person* affektiert; pseudointellektuell ◆ **it's all so terribly ~** das ist alles so gewollt; **some of his friends are a bit ~** einige seiner Freunde machen wirklich nur auf Schau *(inf)*.

pseudo [ˈsjuːdəʊ] *(inf)* **1** *adj* **(a)** *(pretentious) see* **pseud 2**. **(b)** *(pretended)*

unecht; *affection, simplicity* aufgesetzt; *revolutionary, intellectual etc* Möchtegern- (*inf*), Pseudo-.
[2] *n see* **pseud 1**.
pseudo- *pref* Pseudo-, pseudo.
pseudonym ['sju:dənɪm] *n* Pseudonym *nt*.
pseudy ['sju:dɪ] *adj* (+*er*) (*inf*) *see* **pseud 2**.
pshaw [pʃɔ:] *interj* (*dated*) pah.
psittacosis [ˌpsɪtə'kəʊsɪs] *n* Papageienkrankheit, Psittakose (*spec*) *f*.
psoriasis [sɒ'raɪəsɪs] *n* Schuppenflechte, Psoriasis (*spec*) *f*.
PST (*US*) *abbr of* **Pacific Standard Time** pazifische Zeit.
psych(e) [saɪk] *vt* (*sl*) **(a)** (*psychoanalyst*) analysieren. **(b)** (*understand, get taped*) **to ~ sb (out), to get sb ~ed (out)** jdn durchschauen.
◆**psyche out** [1] *vt sep* (*inf*) psychologisch fertigmachen (*inf*).
[2] *vi* (*freak out*) ausflippen (*inf*).
◆**psyche up** *vt sep* (*inf*) hochputschen (*inf*) ◆ **to ~ oneself ~, to get oneself ~d ~** sich hochputschen (*inf*); **he was all ~d ~ for the match** er hatte sich für das Spiel so richtig hochgeputscht (*inf*).
Psyche ['saɪkɪ] *n* (*Myth*) Psyche *f*.
psyche ['saɪkɪ] *n* Psyche *f*.
psychedelic [ˌsaɪkɪ'delɪk] *adj* psychedelisch; *drugs also* bewußtseinserweiternd.
psychiatric [ˌsaɪkɪ'ætrɪk] *adj* psychiatrisch; *illness* psychisch.
psychiatrist [saɪ'kaɪətrɪst] *n* Psychiater(in *f*) *m*.
psychiatry [saɪ'kaɪətrɪ] *n* Psychiatrie *f*.
psychic ['saɪkɪk] [1] *adj* übersinnlich; *powers* übernatürlich ◆ **~ research** Parapsychologie *f*; **she is ~** sie besitzt übernatürliche Kräfte *or* übersinnliche Wahrnehmung; **you must be ~!** Sie müssen hellsehen können!
[2] *n* Mensch *m* mit übernatürlichen Kräften *or* übersinnlicher Wahrnehmung.
psychical ['saɪkɪkəl] *adj see* **psychic 1**.
psycho ['saɪkəʊ] *n* (*US inf*) Verrückte(r) *mf*.
psychoanalyse, (*US*) **psychoanalyze** [ˌsaɪkəʊ'ænəlaɪz] *vt* psychoanalytisch behandeln, psychoanalysieren.
psychoanalysis [ˌsaɪkəʊə'nælɪsɪs] *n* Psychoanalyse *f*.
psychoanalyst [ˌsaɪkəʊ'ænəlɪst] *n* Psychoanalytiker(in *f*) *m*.
psychobabble ['saɪkəʊˌbæbl] *n* (*inf*) Psychogeschwätz *nt*.
psycholinguistic [ˌsaɪkəʊlɪŋ'gwɪstɪk] *adj* psycholinguistisch.
psycholinguistics [ˌsaɪkəʊlɪŋ'gwɪstɪks] *n sing* Psycholinguistik *f*.
psychological [ˌsaɪkə'lɒdʒɪkəl] *adj* (*mental*) psychisch; (*concerning psychology*) psychologisch ◆ **~ make-up** Psyche *f*; **the ~ moment** der psychologisch günstige Augenblick; **~ terror** Psychoterror *m*; **~ profile** psychologisches Profil; **~ warfare** psychologische Kriegführung; **he's not really ill, it's all ~** er ist nicht wirklich krank, das ist alles psychisch bedingt; **it's all ~, you get further that way** das ist Psychologie, damit erreicht man mehr.
psychologically [ˌsaɪkə'lɒdʒɪkəlɪ] *adv see adj* ◆ **he is ~ unstable** er ist psychisch sehr unausgeglichen.
psychologist [saɪ'kɒlədʒɪst] *n* Psychologe *m*, Psychologin *f*.
psychology [saɪ'kɒlədʒɪ] *n* (*science*) Psychologie *f*; (*make-up*) Psyche *f* ◆ **it's all a matter of ~** (*inf*) das ist alles eine Frage der Psychologie.
psychometrics [ˌsaɪkəʊ'metrɪks] *n sing*, **psychometry** [saɪ'kɒmɪtrɪ] *n* Psychometrie *f*.
psychopath ['saɪkəʊpæθ] *n* Psychopath(in *f*) *m*.
psychopathic [ˌsaɪkəʊ'pæθɪk] *adj* psychopathisch.
psychosexual [ˌsaɪkəʊ'seksjʊəl] *adj* psychosexuell.
psychosis [saɪ'kəʊsɪs] *n, pl* **psychoses** [saɪ'kəʊsi:z] Psychose *f*.
psychosocial [ˌsaɪkəʊ'səʊʃəl] *adj* psychosozial.
psychosociological [ˌsaɪkəʊˌsəʊsɪə'lɒdʒɪkəl] *adj* psychosoziologisch.
psychosomatic [ˌsaɪkəʊsəʊ'mætɪk] *adj* psychosomatisch ◆ **~ medicine** Psychosomatik *f*, psychosomatische Medizin.
psychotherapist [ˌsaɪkəʊ'θerəpɪst] *n* Psychotherapeut(in *f*) *m*.
psychotherapy [ˌsaɪkəʊ'θerəpɪ] *n* Psychotherapie *f*.
psychotic [saɪ'kɒtɪk] [1] *adj* psychotisch ◆ **~ illness** Psychose *f*.
[2] *n* Psychotiker(in *f*) *m*.
PT *abbr of* **physical training**.
pt *abbr of* **part; pint; payment; point** Pkt.
PTA *abbr of* **parent-teacher association** Lehrer-Eltern-Ausschuß *m*.
ptarmigan ['tɑ:mɪgən] *n* Schneehuhn *nt*.
Pte (*Mil*) *abbr of* **Private**.
pterodactyl [ˌterəʊ'dæktɪl] *n* Pterodaktylus *m*.
pto *abbr of* **please turn over** bitte wenden, b.w.
Ptolemaic [ˌtɒlə'meɪɪk] *adj* ptolemäisch ◆ **~ system** ptolemäisches Weltbild *or* (Welt)system.
Ptolemy ['tɒləmɪ] *n* (*astronomer*) Ptolemäus *m*; (*king*) Ptolemaois *m*; (*dynasty*) Ptolemäer *pl*.
ptomaine ['təʊmeɪn] *n* Leichengift, Ptomain (*spec*) *nt* ◆ **~ poisoning** Leichenvergiftung *f*.
pub [pʌb] *n* (*Brit*) Kneipe (*inf*), Wirtschaft *f*, Lokal *nt*; (*in the country*) Gasthaus, Wirtshaus *nt* ◆ **let's go to the ~** komm, wir gehen einen trinken *or* wir gehen in die Kneipe (*inf*); **~ grub/lunch** *in Trinkgaststätten servierter Imbiß*.
pub-crawl ['pʌbkrɔ:l] *n* (*esp Brit inf*) Kneipenbummel *m* (*inf*) ◆ **to go on a ~** einen Kneipenbummel machen (*inf*), einen Zug durch die Gemeinde machen (*hum inf*).
puberty ['pju:bətɪ] *n* die Pubertät ◆ **to reach the age of ~** ins Pubertätsalter *or* in die Pubertät kommen.
pubes ['pju:bi:z] *pl of* **pubis**.
pubescence [pju:'besəns] *n* die Pubertät.
pubescent [pju:'besənt] *adj* pubertierend.
pubic ['pju:bɪk] *adj* Scham-.
pubis ['pju:bɪs] *n, pl* **pubes** Schambein *nt*.
public ['pʌblɪk] [1] *adj* öffentlich; *spending, debts* der öffentlichen Hand, Staats- ◆ **to be ~ knowledge** allgemein bekannt sein; **to become ~** publik werden; **at the ~ expense** aus öffentlichen Mitteln; **it's rather ~ here** es ist nicht gerade privat hier; **he is a ~ figure** *or* **person** er ist eine Persönlichkeit des öffentlichen Lebens; **in the ~ eye** im Blickpunkt der Öffentlichkeit; **to make sth ~** etw bekanntgeben, etw publik machen; (*officially*) etw öffentlich bekanntmachen; **in the ~ interest** im öffentlichen Interesse; **to create ~ awareness** öffentliches Interesse wecken; **to go ~** (*Comm*) in eine Aktiengesellschaft umgewandelt werden.
[2] *n sing or pl* Öffentlichkeit *f* ◆ **in ~** in der Öffentlichkeit; *speak also, agree, admit* öffentlich; **our/their** *etc* **~** unser/ihr *etc* Publikum; **the reading/sporting/theatre-going ~** die lesende/sportinteressierte/theaterinteressierte Öffentlichkeit; **the racing ~** die Freunde *pl* des Rennsports; **the great American/British ~** (*iro*) die breite amerikanische/britische Öffentlichkeit.
public address system *n* Lautsprecheranlage *f*.
publican ['pʌblɪkən] *n* **(a)** (*Brit*) Gastwirt(in *f*) *m*. **(b)** (*old: tax-collector*) Zöllner *m*.
public assistance *n* (*US*) staatliche Fürsorge.
publication [ˌpʌblɪ'keɪʃən] *n* Veröffentlichung, Publikation (*geh*) *f* ◆ **~ date** Erscheinungsdatum *nt*, Datum *nt* der Veröffentlichung; **when's ~?** wann erscheint das Buch?
public: ~ bar *n* ≃ Ausschank *m*, Schenke *f*; **~ building** *n* öffentliches Gebäude; **~ company** *n* Aktiengesellschaft *f*; **~ convenience** *n* öffentliche Toilette; **~ debt** *n* (*esp US*) Verschuldung *f* der öffentlichen Hand; (*national debt*) Staatsverschuldung *f*; **~ defender** *n* (*US*) Pflichtverteidiger(in *f*) *m*; **~ domain** *n* **(a)** (*land*) Domäne *f*; **(b)** (*unpatented status*) **this book/invention will soon become ~ domain** das Copyright für dieses Buch/das Patent für diese Erfindung läuft bald ab; **to be in the ~ domain** (*not private property*) allgemein zugänglich sein; (*generally known*) allgemein bekannt sein; **~ enemy** *n* Staatsfeind *m*; **~ enemy number one** Staatsfeind Nr. 1; **~ health** *n* (*community health care*) das (öffentliche) Gesundheitswesen; **a danger to ~ health** eine Gefahr für die Volksgesundheit; **~ holiday** *n* gesetzlicher Feiertag; **~ house** *n* (*Brit form*) Gaststätte *f*.
publicist ['pʌblɪsɪst] *n* Publizist(in *f*) *m*.
publicity [pʌb'lɪsɪtɪ] *n* **(a)** Publicity *f*. **(b)** (*Comm: advertising, advertisements*) Werbung, Reklame *f* ◆ **a whole sheaf of ~** ein ganzer Stoß Reklame; **we must get out some more ~ for this product** wir müssen mehr Werbung für dieses Produkt treiben.
publicity: ~ agent *n* Publicitymanager *m*; **~ campaign** *n* Publicitykampagne *f*; (*Comm*) Werbekampagne *f*; **~ material** *n* Publicitymaterial *nt*; (*Comm*) Werbematerial *nt*; **~-shy** *adj* öffentlichkeitsscheu.
publicize ['pʌblɪsaɪz] *vt* **(a)** (*make public*) bekanntmachen, an die Öffentlichkeit bringen ◆ **I don't want this ~d** ich möchte nicht, daß das publik wird; **I don't ~ the fact** ich will das nicht an die große Glocke hängen (*inf*).
(b) (*get publicity for*) *film, author* Publicity machen für; *new product also* Werbung treiben *or* Reklame machen für ◆ **it has been well ~d** es hat viel Publicity bekommen; dafür ist viel Werbung getrieben *or* Reklame gemacht worden.
public law *n* öffentliches Recht.
publicly ['pʌblɪklɪ] *adv* öffentlich ◆ **this factory is ~ owned** diese Fabrik ist Gemeineigentum.
public: ~ money *n* öffentliche Gelder *pl*; **~ opinion** *n* die öffentliche Meinung; **~ opinion poll** *n* Meinungsumfrage *f*; **~ ownership** *n* öffentlicher Besitz; **under ~ ownership** in öffentlichem Besitz; **~ property** *n* **(a)** (*land etc*) öffentliches Eigentum; **(b)** (*fig*) **to be ~ property** (*person*) im Rampenlicht der Öffentlichkeit stehen; (*private life*) Allgemeingut sein; **intimate aspects of her personal life had been made ~ property** intime Aspekte ihres Privatlebens waren allgemein bekannt geworden; **~ prosecutor** *n* Staatsanwalt *m*/-anwältin *f*; **~ purse** *n* Staatskasse *f*, Staatssäckel *m* (*inf*); **P~ Record(s) Office** *n* (*Brit*) Nationalarchiv *nt*; Bundeszentralarchiv *nt* (*BRD*); **~ relations** *n* **(a)** *pl* Public Relations *pl*; **(b)** *sing* (*area of work also*) Öffentlichkeitsarbeit *f*; **~ relations officer** *n* Pressesprecher(in *f*) *m*; **~ school** *n* (*Brit*) Privatschule, Public School *f*; (*US*) staatliche Schule; **~ schoolboy** *n* (*Brit*) Schüler *m* einer Privatschule; **~ schoolgirl** *n* (*Brit*) Schülerin *f* einer Privatschule; **~ sector** *n* öffentlicher Sektor; **~-sector** *adj attr* des öffentlichen Sektors; **~-sector borrowing requirement** Kreditaufnahme *f* durch die öffentliche Hand; **~ servant** *n* Arbeitnehmer(in *f*) *m* im öffentlichen Dienst; **~ service** *n* (*Civil Service*) öffentlicher Dienst; (*facility: water, transport etc*) öffentlicher Dienstleistungsbetrieb; (*benefit*) Dienst *m* an der Allgemeinheit; **~ service broadcasting** *n* ≃ öffentlich-rechtlicher Rundfunk; öffentlich-rechtliches Fernsehen; **~ service vehicle** *n* öffentliches Verkehrsmittel; **~ speaker** *n* Redner(in *f*) *m*; **~ speaking** *n* Redenhalten *nt*; **a course in ~ speaking** ein Rednerlehrgang *m*; **I'm no good at ~ speaking** ich kann nicht in der Öffentlichkeit reden; **~ spending** *n* Ausgaben *pl* der öffentlichen Hand; **~ spirit** *n* Gemeinsinn *m*; **~-spirited** *adj act, attitude* gemeinsinnig (*geh*), von Gemeinschaftssinn zeugend *attr*; **it's not very ~-spirited of them to ...** es spricht nicht gerade für ihren Gemeinschaftssinn, daß sie ...; **~ transport** *n* öffentliche Verkehrsmittel *pl*; **~ utility** *n* öffentlicher Versorgungsbetrieb; **~ works** *npl* staatliche Bauvorhaben *pl*.

publish [ˈpʌblɪʃ] 1 *vt* **(a)** *(issue)* veröffentlichen; *book, magazine etc also* herausbringen; *research, thesis also* publizieren ◆ **~ed by Collins** bei Collins *or* im Verlag Collins erschienen; **"~ed monthly"** „erscheint monatlich"; **"just ~ed"** „neu erschienen"; **"to be ~ed shortly"** „erscheint in Kürze"; **who ~es that book?** in welchem Verlag ist das Buch erschienen?; **they ~ novels** sie verlegen Romane.
(b) *(make public) news, banns* veröffentlichen, bekanntgeben; *decree* herausgeben; *will* eröffnen ◆ **to ~ sth abroad** etw überall herumerzählen.
2 *vi* **the magazine ~es on Tuesdays** das Magazin erscheint dienstags; **when are we going to ~?** *(book)* wann bringen wir das Buch heraus?; *(research)* wann veröffentlichen *or* publizieren wir die Arbeit?; **he used to ~ with Collins** er hat seine Bücher früher bei Collins herausgebracht *or* veröffentlicht.

publisher [ˈpʌblɪʃəʳ] *n (person)* Verleger(in *f*) *m*; *(firm: also* **~s***)* Verlag *m* ◆ **who are your ~s?** wer ist Ihr Verleger?

publishing [ˈpʌblɪʃɪŋ] *n (trade)* das Verlagswesen ◆ **~ company** Verlagshaus *nt*; **the decline of children's book ~** der Rückgang bei den Kinderbüchern.

puce [pjuːs] 1 *n* Braunrot *nt*.
2 *adj* braunrot; *(fig: with rage, shame)* rot.

puck¹ [pʌk] *n (goblin)* Kobold, Puck *m*.

puck² *n (Sport)* Puck *m*.

pucker [ˈpʌkəʳ] 1 *n (in cloth)* Fältchen *nt*.
2 *vt (also* **~ up***) one's lips, mouth* verziehen; *(for kissing)* spitzen; *one's brow* runzeln; *material* Falten machen in (+*acc*).
3 *vi (also* **~ up***) (lips)* sich verziehen; *(to be kissed)* sich spitzen; *(brow)* sich runzeln; *(material)* Falten werfen.

puckish *adj*, **~ly** *adv* [ˈpʌkɪʃ, -lɪ] koboldhaft.

pud [pʊd] *n (inf) see* **pudding**.

pudding [ˈpʊdɪŋ] *n* **(a)** *(dessert)* Nachspeise *f*; *(crème caramel, instant whip etc)* Pudding *m* ◆ **what's for ~?** was gibt es als Nachspeise *or* Nachtisch? **(b)** *(savoury: meat in suet)* ≃ (Fleisch)pastete *f* ◆ **black ~** ≃ Blutwurst *f*; **white ~** ≃ Preßsack *m*. **(c)** *(inf) (idiot)* Knallkopp *m (inf)*; *(fatty)* Dickerchen *nt*.

pudding: ~ basin *n* Puddingform *f*; **~-basin haircut** *n* (Koch)topfschnitt *m (inf)*; **~ club** *n* **to be in the ~ club** *(sl)* einen dicken Bauch haben *(inf)*; **~-face** *n (inf)* Vollmondgesicht *nt (inf)*; **~-head** *n (inf)* Knallkopp *m (inf)*; **~ stone** *n* Puddingstein *m*.

puddle [ˈpʌdl] *n* Pfütze *f (also euph)*.

pudendum [pjuːˈdendəm] *n, pl* **pudenda** [pjuːˈdendə] **(a)** *(of woman)* Vulva *f*. **(b) pudenda** *pl (of either sex)* primäre Geschlechtsmerkmale *pl*, Scham *f (geh)*.

pudgy [ˈpʌdʒɪ] *adj (+er) see* **podgy**.

puerile [ˈpjʊəraɪl] *adj* infantil.

puerility [pjʊəˈrɪlɪtɪ] *n* Infantilität *f*.

puerperal fever [pjuːˈɜːpərəlˈfiːvəʳ] *n* Kindbettfieber, Puerperalfieber *(spec) nt*.

Puerto Rican [ˈpwɜːtəʊˈriːkən] 1 *adj* puertoricanisch.
2 *n (person)* Puertoricaner(in *f*) *m*.

Puerto Rico [ˈpwɜːtəʊˈriːkəʊ] *n* Puerto Rico *nt*.

puff [pʌf] 1 *n* **(a)** *(of breathing, of engine)* Schnaufen *nt no pl*; *(of horse)* Schnauben *nt no pl*; *(inf: breath)* Puste *f (inf)*; *(on cigarette etc)* Zug *m (at, of an* +*dat)* ◆ **a ~ of air/wind** ein Luft-/Windstoß *m*; **a ~ of smoke** eine Rauchwolke; **our hopes vanished in a ~ of smoke** unsere Hoffnungen lösten sich in nichts auf; **he blew out the candles with** *or* **in one ~** er blies die Kerzen auf einmal aus; **to be out of ~** *(inf)* außer Puste sein *(inf)*.
(b) *(powder ~)* Quaste *f*.
(c) *(Cook)* **cream ~** Windbeutel *m*; **jam ~** Blätterteigteilchen *nt* mit Marmelade; **~ pastry**, *(US)* **~ paste** Blätterteig *m*.
2 *vt* **(a)** *smoke* ausstoßen; *(person)* blasen; *cigarette, cigar* paffen *(inf)* ◆ **to ~ sth away/down** etw wegblasen/umblasen; **stop ~ing smoke in my face** blas mir nicht dauernd den Rauch ins Gesicht.
(b) *(Sew)* bauschen ◆ **~ed sleeves** Puffärmel *pl*.
(c) *(Cook)* **to ~ rice** Puffreis herstellen.
3 *vi (person, train)* schnaufen; *(horse)* schnauben; *(wind)* blasen; *(chimney, smoke)* qualmen ◆ **he was ~ing and panting** er pustete und schnaufte; **the train ~ed into the station** der Zug fuhr schnaufend in den Bahnhof ein; **to ~ (away) at** *or* **on a cigar** an einer Zigarre paffen.

◆**puff out** *vt sep* **(a)** *(expand) chest* herausstrecken, herausdrücken; *cheeks* aufblasen; *feathers* (auf)plustern; *sail* blähen. **(b)** *(emit) air, smoke* ausstoßen; *words* hervorstoßen. **(c)** *(blow out)* auspusten. **(d)** *(inf) always separate (make out of breath)* außer Puste bringen *(inf)*.

◆**puff up** 1 *vt sep* **(a)** *feathers* (auf)plustern; *(blow up)* aufblasen. **(b)** *(fig)* **to get/be ~ed ~** sich aufblasen; **to be ~ed ~ with pride** ganz aufgeblasen sein.
2 *vi* **(a)** *(swell: eyes, face etc)* anschwellen. **(b) he came ~ing ~ to me** er kam angeschnauft.

puff: ~-adder *n* Puffotter *f*; **~-ball** *n (Bot)* Bovist *m*.

puffed [pʌft] *adj (inf)* außer Puste *(inf)*.

puffer [ˈpʌfəʳ] *n (baby-talk: train)* Puffpuff *f (baby-talk)*.

puffin [ˈpʌfɪn] *n* Papageientaucher, Lund *m*.

puffiness [ˈpʌfɪnɪs] *n* Verschwollenheit *f*.

puff: ~-puff *n (baby-talk) (train)* Puffpuff *f (baby-talk)*; *(sound)* Puffpuff *nt*; **~ sleeve** *n* Puffärmel *m*.

puffy [ˈpʌfɪ] *adj (+er) (swollen)* geschwollen; *face, eyes also* verschwollen; *(from crying)* verquollen.

pug [pʌg] *n (also* **~ dog***)* Mops *m*.

pugilism [ˈpjuːdʒɪlɪzəm] *n (form)* Faustkampf *m*.

pugilist [ˈpjuːdʒɪlɪst] *n (form)* Faustkämpfer *m*.

pugnacious [pʌgˈneɪʃəs] *adj* kampfeslustig; *(verbally)* streitsüchtig; *expression, remark* herausfordernd; *support, defence* hartnäckig; *dog, campaign* aggressiv.

pugnaciously [pʌgˈneɪʃəslɪ] *adv see adj*.

pugnacity [pʌgˈnæsɪtɪ] *n see adj* Kampfeslust *f*; Streitsüchtigkeit *f*; Herausforderung *f (of in* +*dat)*; Hartnäckigkeit *f*; Aggressivität *f* ◆ **the ~ of his remarks** die aus seinen Bemerkungen klingende Streitsucht.

pug: ~ nose *n* Knollennase *f*; **~-nosed** *adj* knollennasig.

puke [pjuːk] *vti (sl)* kotzen *(sl)*, spucken *(inf)* ◆ **to ~ all over sth** *(sl)* etw vollkotzen; **he makes me ~** er kotzt mich an *(sl)*.

pukey [ˈpjuːkɪ] *adj (sl) colour* Kack- *(sl)*, eklig *(inf)*.

pukka, pucka [ˈpʌkə] *adj (inf) (genuine)* echt; Original-; *(proper)* anständig *(inf)*; *(excellent)* eins a *(inf)*, erstklassig; *(posh, upper-class)* vornehm ◆ **~ sahib** Gentleman *m*.

pulchritude [ˈpʌlkrɪtjuːd] *n (liter)* Schönheit *f*.

pull [pʊl] 1 *n* **(a)** *(tug)* Ziehen *nt*; *(short)* Ruck *m*; *(lit, fig: attraction)* Anziehungskraft *f*; *(of current)* Sog *m* ◆ **he gave her/the rope a ~** er zog sie/am Seil; **he gave her hair a ~** er zog sie an den Haaren; **I felt a ~ at my sleeve** ich spürte, wie mich jemand am Ärmel zog; **the ~ of family ties brought him home again** familiäre Bande zogen ihn wieder nach Hause.
(b) *(uphill journey)* Anstieg *m*.
(c) *(inf: influence)* Beziehungen *pl (with* zu) ◆ **she has ~ with the manager** sie kann beim Chef was erreichen *(inf)*; **he has ~ in the right places** er hat an den richtigen Stellen seine Leute sitzen.
(d) *(at pipe, beer)* Zug *m* ◆ **he took a ~ at his pipe/glass** er zog an seiner Pfeife/nahm einen Schluck aus seinem Glas.
(e) bell ~ Klingelzug *m*; **beer ~** Bierpumpengriff *m*.
(f) *(Typ: proof)* Abzug *m*.
2 *vt* **(a)** *(draw, drag)* ziehen ◆ **he ~ed the dog behind him** er zog den Hund hinter sich *(dat)* her; **to ~ a door shut** eine Tür zuziehen; **he ~ed her towards him** er zog sie an sich *(acc)*.
(b) *(tug) handle, rope, bell* ziehen an (+*dat*); *boat* rudern ◆ **he ~ed her hair** er zog sie an den Haaren; **to ~ sth to pieces** *(lit)* etw zerreißen, etw in Stücke reißen; *(fig: criticize)* etw verreißen; **to ~ sb's leg** *(inf)* jdn auf den Arm nehmen *(inf)*; **~ the other one(, it's got bells on)** *(inf)* das glaubst du ja selber nicht!, das kannst du deiner Großmutter erzählen! *(inf)*; **she was the one ~ing the strings** *or* **wires** sie war es, die alle Fäden in der Hand hielt; **to ~ rank (on sb)** (jdm gegenüber) den Vorgesetzten herauskehren; **to ~ one's punches** *(Boxing)* verhalten schlagen; *(fig)* sich zurückhalten; **when it came to criticizing other people he didn't ~ his** *or* **any punches** wenn es darum ging, andere zu kritisieren, zog er ganz schön vom Leder *(inf)*.
(c) *(extract, draw out) tooth, cork* (heraus)ziehen; *gun, knife* ziehen; *weeds, lettuce* herausziehen; *beer* zapfen; *(Cook) chicken* ausnehmen ◆ **to ~ a gun on sb** jdn mit der Pistole bedrohen.
(d) *(strain) muscle* sich *(dat)* zerren; *(tear) thread* ziehen.
(e) *(attract) crowd* anziehen ◆ **a sports car always ~s the girls** *(inf)* mit einem Sportwagen kommt man leichter an die Mädchen ran *(inf)*.
(f) *(inf: carry out, do) deal* durchziehen *(inf)*; *(criminal) job* drehen *(inf)* ◆ **what are you trying to ~?** *(inf)* was heckst du wieder aus? *(inf)*.
(g) *(Typ)* **to ~ a proof** einen Abzug machen.
(h) *(Golf, Cricket, Baseball)* verziehen, *auf die der Schlaghand entgegengesetzte Seite schlagen*.
3 *vi* **(a)** ziehen *(on, at an* +*dat)* ◆ **to ~ to the left/right** *(car, brakes)* nach links/rechts ziehen; **the car/engine isn't ~ing very well** der Wagen/Motor zieht nicht richtig; **to ~ on** *or* **at one's cigarette** an seiner Zigarette ziehen; **to ~ for sb/sth** *(US inf)* jdn/etw unterstützen.
(b) *(move: train, car etc)* fahren ◆ **the car ~ed into the driveway** der Wagen fuhr in die Einfahrt; **he ~ed across to the left-hand lane** er wechselte auf die linke Spur über; **to ~ alongside** seitlich heranfahren; *(Naut)* längsseits kommen; **the oarsmen ~ed for** *or* **towards the shore** die Ruderer hielten auf das Ufer zu; **to ~ ahead (of sb)** *(car, runner)* (an jdm) vorbeiziehen; *(fig: rival etc)* jdn hinter sich *(dat)* lassen.

◆**pull about** *vt sep (handle roughly) toy etc* herumzerren; *person* herumzerren an (+*dat*).

◆**pull apart** 1 *vt sep* **(a)** *(separate)* auseinanderziehen; *sheets of paper also, fighting people* trennen; *radio etc* auseinandernehmen. **(b)** *(fig inf) (search thoroughly)* auseinandernehmen *(inf)*; *(criticize also)* verreißen.
2 *vi (through design)* sich auseinandernehmen lassen; *(break)* auseinandergehen.

◆**pull away** 1 *vt sep* wegziehen ◆ **she ~ed it ~ from him** sie zog es von ihm weg; *(from his hands)* sie zog es ihm aus den Händen.
2 *vi (move off)* wegfahren; *(ship)* ablegen ◆ **the car/runner ~ed ~ from the others** der Wagen/Läufer setzte sich (von den anderen) ab.

◆**pull back** 1 *vt sep* zurückziehen.
2 *vi (lit)* sich zurückziehen ◆ **to ~ ~ (from doing sth)** *(fig)* einen Rückzieher machen (und etw nicht tun) *(inf)*; **he ~ed ~ from his offer/promise** er zog sein Angebot/Versprechen zurück.

◆**pull down** 1 *vt sep* **(a)** herunterziehen ◆ **he ~ed his hat ~ over his eyes** er zog sich *(dat)* den Hut über die Augen.
(b) *(demolish) buildings* abreißen.
(c) *(weaken, make worse) (illness) person* mitnehmen; *(exam, question) marks* herunterdrücken; *(failure, adverse conditions) company etc* mitnehmen; *profits, results* herunterdrücken ◆ **this bad mark ~ed you ~** diese schlechte Zensur hat deinen Notenschnitt (herunter)gedrückt.

(d) (*US inf: earn*) reinholen (*inf*), machen (*inf*).
[2] *vi* (*blind etc*) sich herunterziehen lassen.

◆**pull in** [1] *vt sep* **(a)** *claws, rope, stomach etc* einziehen; (*into room, swimming-pool etc*) hineinziehen ◆ **to ~ sb/sth ~(to) sth** jdn/etw in etw (*acc*) ziehen.
(b) (*rein in*) *horse* zügeln.
(c) (*attract*) *crowds* anziehen.
(d) (*inf: earn*) kassieren (*inf*).
(e) (*inf: take into custody*) einkassieren (*inf*).
[2] *vi* **(a)** (*claws*) sich einziehen lassen.
(b) (*into station, harbour, pier*) einfahren, einlaufen (*into* in +*acc*); (*into garage, driveway*) hineinfahren (*into* in +*acc*); (*stop, park*) anhalten ◆ **he ~ed ~to the next lay-by** er fuhr auf den nächsten Halteplatz; **he ~ed ~ to the kerb/the side of the road** er fuhr an den Bordstein heran/an den Straßenrand.

◆**pull off** *vt sep* **(a)** *wrapping paper* abziehen; *cover also* abnehmen; (*violently*) abreißen; *clothes, pullover, shoes* ausziehen; *gloves, tights* ausziehen, abstreifen ◆ **he ~ed his clothes ~ and jumped into the water** er riß sich (*dat*) die Kleider vom Leib und sprang ins Wasser; **he quickly ~ed his/her coat ~** er zog sich/ihr schnell den Mantel aus.
(b) (*inf: succeed in*) schaffen (*inf*); *deal, coup also* zuwege bringen (*inf*); *order* an Land ziehen (*inf*); *bank job, burglary* drehen (*inf*).

◆**pull on** *vt sep coat etc* sich (*dat*) überziehen; *hat* aufsetzen.

◆**pull out** [1] *vt sep* **(a)** (*extract*) (*of* aus) herausziehen; *tooth* ziehen; *page* heraustrennen. **(b)** (*elongate*) *table, dough* ausziehen. **(c)** (*withdraw*) zurückziehen; *troops* abziehen.
[2] *vi* **(a)** (*come out*) sich herausziehen lassen; *pages* sich heraustrennen lassen.
(b) (*elongate*) sich ausziehen lassen.
(c) (*withdraw*) aussteigen (*of* aus) (*inf*); (*troops*) abziehen.
(d) (*leave: train etc*) herausfahren (*of* aus).
(e) (*move on*) herausfahren ◆ **the car/driver ~ed ~ from behind the lorry** der Wagen/Fahrer scherte hinter dem Lastwagen aus; **the boat ~ed ~ into mid-stream** das Boot fuhr in die Flußmitte hinaus.

◆**pull over** [1] *vt sep* **(a)** hinüber-/herüberziehen (*prep obj* über +*acc*). **(b)** (*topple*) umreißen ◆ **he ~ed the whole bookcase ~ on top of him** er hat das ganze Bücherregal mit sich gerissen.
[2] *vi* (*car, driver*) zur Seite fahren.

◆**pull round** [1] *vt sep* **(a)** (*turn round*) herumdrehen. **(b)** (*bring back to consciousness*) wieder zu sich bringen; (*help recover*) durchbringen.
[2] *vi* (*regain consciousness*) wieder zu sich kommen; (*recover*) durchkommen.

◆**pull through** [1] *vt sep* (*lit*) durchziehen; (*fig: help recover, help succeed*) durchbringen ◆ **to ~ sb/sth ~ sth** (*lit*) jdn/etw durch etw ziehen; **to ~ sb ~ a difficult period** jdm helfen, eine schwierige Zeit zu überstehen.
[2] *vi* (*fig: recover*) durchkommen ◆ **to ~ ~ sth** (*lit*) sich durch etw ziehen lassen; (*fig*) etw überstehen.

◆**pull together** [1] *vi* (*lit*) gemeinsam ziehen; (*row jointly*) im gleichen Takt rudern; (*fig: cooperate*) an einem *or* am gleichen Strang ziehen.
[2] *vt sep* (*fig*) *political party, members of family etc* zusammenschweißen; *novel etc* in einen Zusammenhang bringen.
[3] *vr* sich zusammenreißen.

◆**pull under** *vt sep swimmer* nach unten ziehen.

◆**pull up** [1] *vt sep* **(a)** (*raise by pulling*) hochziehen; *see* **sock**[1].
(b) (*uproot*) herausreißen ◆ **to ~ ~ one's roots, to ~ ~ stakes** (*esp US*) alles aufgeben.
(c) (*stop*) anhalten.
(d) (*reprimand*) (*for behaviour*) zurechtweisen; (*for pronunciation, grammar*) korrigieren ◆ **he ~ed me ~ about** *or* **on that** er hat mich deswegen zurechtgewiesen/korrigiert.
(e) (*improve*) *marks* verbessern ◆ **that good mark ~ed you ~ a bit** durch diese gute Note hast du ein wenig aufgeholt.
[2] *vi* **(a)** (*stop*) anhalten.
(b) (*improve one's position*) aufholen ◆ **to ~ ~ with sb/sth** jdn/etw einholen, mit jdm/etw gleichziehen (*inf*).

pull-down menu ['pʊldaʊn'menju:] *n* (*Comput*) Pull-down-Menü *nt*.
pullet ['pʊlɪt] *n* junges Huhn, Hühnchen *nt*.
pulley ['pʊlɪ] *n* (*wheel*) Rolle *f*; (*block*) Flaschenzug *m*; (*hospital apparatus*) Streckapparat *m*.
pull-in ['pʊlɪn] *n* (*Brit*) (*lay-by*) Halteplatz *m*; (*café*) Raststätte *f*.
Pullman ® ['pʊlmən] *n* (~ *car*) Pullmanwagen ® *m*; (~ *train*) Pullman ® *m*.
pull: ~-out [1] *n* **(a)** (*withdrawal*) Abzug *m*; **(b)** (*supplement*) heraustrennbarer Teil; [2] *attr supplement* heraustrennbar; *table leaf, seat* ausziehbar; **~over** *n* Pullover *m*; **~-up** *n* (*Sport*) Klimmzug *m*.
pulmonary ['pʌlmənərɪ] *adj* Lungen-.
pulp [pʌlp] [1] *n* **(a)** (*soft mass, paper ~, wood ~*) Brei *m* ◆ **to reduce sth to ~** etw in Brei auflösen; *wood etc* (*for paper*) etw zu einem Brei verarbeiten; **to beat sb to a ~** (*inf*) jdn zu Brei schlagen (*sl*); **crushed to (a) ~** zu Brei zerquetscht.
(b) (*of plant stem*) Mark *nt*; (*of fruit, vegetable*) Fruchtfleisch *nt*; (*of tooth*) Zahnmark *nt*, Pulpa *f* (*spec*).
(c) (*also* **~ magazine**) (*pej*) Schundmagazin *nt*.
[2] *vt fruit, vegetables* zerdrücken; *paper, book* einstampfen; *wood* zu Brei verarbeiten.
pulpit ['pʊlpɪt] *n* Kanzel *f*.
pulpy ['pʌlpɪ] *adj* (+*er*) breiig.
pulsar ['pʌlsaʳ] *n* Pulsar *m*.
pulsate [pʌl'seɪt] *vi* (*lit, fig*) pulsieren; (*head, heart*) klopfen, pochen; (*voice, building*) beben; (*music*) rhythmisch klingen ◆ **the whole school ~d with excitement** die ganze Schule fieberte vor Aufregung; **the whole town was pulsating with life** die ganze Stadt war von pulsierendem Leben erfüllt.
pulsation [pʌl'seɪʃən] *n* (*pulsating*) Pulsieren *nt*; (*of head, heart*) Klopfen, Pochen *nt*; (*one beat*) Schwingung *f*; (*of heart, in artery*) Schlag *m*.
pulse[1] [pʌls] [1] *n* (*Anat*) Puls *m*; (*Phys*) Impuls *m*; (*fig: of drums, music*) Rhythmus *m* ◆ **~ beat** Pulsschlag *m*; **~ rate** Puls(zahl *f*) *m*; **to feel** *or* **take sb's ~** jdm den Puls fühlen; **he felt the ~ of life in his veins** er spürte, wie das Leben in seinen Adern pulsierte; **he still keeps his finger on the ~ of economic affairs** er hat in Wirtschaftsfragen immer noch den Finger am Puls der Zeit.
[2] *vi* pulsieren; (*machines*) stampfen.
pulse[2] *n* (*Bot, Cook*) Hülsenfrucht *f*.
pulverization [,pʌlvəraɪ'zeɪʃən] *n* Pulverisierung *f*.
pulverize ['pʌlvəraɪz] *vt* pulverisieren; (*fig inf*) (*beat up*) Kleinholz machen aus (*inf*); (*defeat*) fertigmachen (*inf*).
puma ['pju:mə] *n* Puma *m*.
pumice (stone) ['pʌmɪs(,stəʊn)] *n* Bimsstein *m*.
pummel ['pʌml] *vt* eintrommeln auf (+*acc*).
pump[1] [pʌmp] [1] *n* Pumpe *f*.
[2] *vt* pumpen; *stomach* auspumpen; *pedal* mehrmals treten ◆ **to ~ sth dry** etw leerpumpen; **to ~ sb dry** (*fig*) jdn aussaugen; **to ~ bullets/ten bullets into sb** jdn mit Blei vollpumpen (*sl*)/jdm zehn Kugeln in den Körper jagen (*inf*); **he ~ed my arm up and down** er riß meinen Arm wie einen Pumpenschwengel auf und ab; **to ~ money into sth** Geld in etw (*acc*) hineinpumpen; **to ~ sb (for information)** jdn aushorchen *or* löchern (*inf*); **to ~ information out of sb** Informationen aus jdm herausholen.
[3] *vi* pumpen; (*water, blood*) herausschießen ◆ **the piston ~ed up and down** der Kolben ging auf und ab.

◆**pump in** *vt sep* (*lit, fig*) hineinpumpen.

◆**pump out** *vt sep liquid, air* herauspumpen; *boat, cellar* auspumpen, leerpumpen; *stomach* auspumpen.

◆**pump up** *vt sep* **(a)** (*inflate*) *tyre etc* aufpumpen. **(b)** *liquid* hochpumpen; (*from below ground also*) heraufpumpen.

pump[2] *n* (*dancing shoe*) Lackschuh *m*; (*ballet shoe*) Ballettschuh *m*; (*gym shoe*) Turnschuh *m*; (*US: court shoe*) Pumps *m*.
pumpernickel ['pʌmpənɪkl] *n* Pumpernickel *m*.
pumping station ['pʌmpɪŋ,steɪʃən] *n* Pumpwerk *nt*, Pumpstation *f*; (*on a pipeline*) Förderpumpe *f*.
pumpkin ['pʌmpkɪn] *n* Kürbis *m*.
pump-room ['pʌmpru:m] *n* Trinkhalle *f*, Brunnenhaus *nt*.
pun [pʌn] [1] *n* Wortspiel *nt*.
[2] *vi* Wortspiele machen.
Punch [pʌntʃ] *n* Kasper *m*, Kasperle *nt* ◆ **~-and-Judy show** Kasper(le)-theater *nt*; **to be (as) pleased as ~** (*inf*) sich wie ein Schneekönig freuen (*inf*).
punch[1] [pʌntʃ] [1] *n* **(a)** (*blow*) Schlag *m*. **(b)** *no pl* (*fig: vigour*) Schwung *m*.
[2] *vti* boxen ◆ **I wanted to ~ his face when he said that** als er das sagte, hätte ich ihn *or* ihm am liebsten ins Gesicht geschlagen; *see* **pack, pull**.
punch[2] [1] *n* (*for ~ing holes*) Locher *m*; (*in tickets*) Lochzange *f*; (*in leather*) Lochstanzer *m*; (*for stamping metal, leather etc*) Prägestempel *m*; (*for knocking out rivets etc*) Punze *f*.
[2] *vt ticket etc* lochen; *leather, metal* stanzen; *holes* stechen, stanzen; (*stamp*) *metal, pattern* prägen; (*US*) *cattle* hüten ◆ **to ~ the time clock/card** die Uhr stechen/Karte stempeln.

◆**punch in** *vt sep* **(a) I'll ~ your face ~** (*inf*) ich hau' dir auf die Schnauze (*sl*).
(b) (*Comput*) *data* tasten, tippen (*inf*).

◆**punch out** *vt sep* ausstechen, ausstanzen; *pattern etc* prägen.

punch[3] *n* (*drink*) Bowle *f*; (*hot*) Punsch *m*.
punch: ~ bag *n* Sandsack *m*; **~ ball** *n* Punchingball *m*; (*round*) Lederball *m*; **~ bowl** *n* Bowle *f*; **~ card** *n* Lochkarte *f*; **~-drunk** *adj* (*Boxing*) benommen; (*fig*) durcheinander *pred*.
Punchinello [pʌntʃɪ'neləʊ] *n* Pulcinella *f*; (*clown*) Hanswurst *m*.
punching bag ['pʌntʃɪŋ,bæg] *n* (*US*) *see* **punch bag**.
punch: ~-line *n* Pointe *f*; **~ operator** *n* Locher(in *f*) *m*; **~ tape** *n* Lochstreifen *m*; **~-up** *n* (*Brit inf*) Schlägerei *f*.
punchy ['pʌntʃɪ] *adj* (+*er*) (*inf*) flott (*inf*).
punctilious [pʌŋk'tɪlɪəs] *adj* (*regarding etiquette*) korrekt; (*scrupulous, fastidious*) sehr *or* peinlich genau ◆ **he is always ~ about arriving in time/writing to thank his host** er nimmt es mit der Pünktlichkeit sehr genau/er achtet immer darauf, daß er sich bei seinem Gastgeber schriftlich bedankt.
punctiliously [pʌŋk'tɪlɪəslɪ] *adv* korrekt; (*scrupulously, fastidiously*) (+*vb*) peinlich genau; (+*adj*) peinlich; *correct* höchst ◆ **he was ~ polite to his mother-in-law** er war äußerst korrekt gegenüber seiner Schwiegermutter.
punctual ['pʌŋktjʊəl] *adj* pünktlich ◆ **to be ~** pünktlich kommen.
punctuality [,pʌŋktjʊ'ælɪtɪ] *n* Pünktlichkeit *f*.
punctually ['pʌŋktjʊəlɪ] *adv* pünktlich.
punctuate ['pʌŋktjʊeɪt] [1] *vt* **(a)** (*Gram*) mit Satzzeichen versehen, interpunktieren.
(b) (*intersperse*) unterbrechen ◆ **he ~d his talk with jokes** er spickte seine Rede mit Witzen; **a long happy life, ~d with** *or* **by short spells of sadness** ein langes glückliches Leben, das zeitweise von traurigen Augenblicken überschattet war.
(c) (*emphasize*) betonen.
[2] *vi* Satzzeichen setzen.
punctuation [,pʌŋktjʊ'eɪʃən] *n* Zeichensetzung, Interpunktion *f* ◆ **~ mark**

Satzzeichen, Interpunktionszeichen *nt.*

puncture ['pʌŋktʃəʳ] 1 *n* (*in tyre, balloon etc*) Loch *nt;* (*in skin*) (Ein)stich *m;* (*flat tyre*) Reifenpanne *f,* Platte(r) *m* (*inf*) ◆ **lumbar ~** Lumbalpunktion *f.*
2 *vt* stechen in (*+acc*); *membrane* durchstechen; *blister* aufstechen; *tyre, balloon* Löcher/ein Loch machen in (*+acc*); *pride* einen Stich versetzen (*+dat*) ◆ **a ~d lung** eine perforierte Lunge.
3 *vi* (*tyre*) einen Platten haben (*inf*); (*balloon*) platzen ◆ **my front tyre ~d** ich hatte einen Platten am Vorderrad.

pundit ['pʌndɪt] *n* (*lit*) Pandit *m;* (*fig*) Experte *m,* Expertin *f.*

pungency ['pʌndʒənsɪ] *n* (*lit, fig*) Schärfe *f.*

pungent ['pʌndʒənt] *adj* (*lit, fig*) scharf; *smell also* stechend, durchdringend ◆ **to have a ~ style of writing** eine spitze *or* scharfe Feder führen.

pungently ['pʌndʒəntlɪ] *adv see adj.*

Punic ['pju:nɪk] *adj* punisch ◆ **the ~ Wars** die Punischen Kriege.

puniness ['pju:nɪnɪs] *n* Schwächlichkeit, Mickerigkeit (*pej*) *f.*

punish ['pʌnɪʃ] *vt* (**a**) *person* bestrafen, strafen (*geh*); *offence* bestrafen ◆ **he was ~ed by a fine** er wurde mit einer Geldstrafe belegt; **he has been ~ed enough** er ist genug bestraft worden; (*has suffered enough*) er ist gestraft genug; **our team was ~ed for making that mistake** unsere Mannschaft mußte für diesen Fehler büßen; **the other team ~ed us for that mistake** die andere Mannschaft ließ uns für diesen Fehler büßen.
(**b**) (*fig inf: drive hard, treat roughly*) strapazieren; *horses, oneself* schinden; *opponent* vorführen (*inf*), zusetzen (*+dat*).

punishable ['pʌnɪʃəbl] *adj* strafbar ◆ **this offence is ~ by 2 years' imprisonment** dieses Verbrechen wird mit 2 Jahren Gefängnis bestraft; **it is a ~ offence** es ist strafbar.

punishing ['pʌnɪʃɪŋ] 1 *adj blow* hart ◆ **to get *or* take some ~ treatment** (*cars, furniture*) strapaziert werden; (*Sport*) vorgeführt werden (*inf*), eins aufs Dach bekommen (*inf*).
2 *n* **to take a ~** (*inf*) (*car, furniture etc*) strapaziert werden; (*team, boxer etc*) vorgeführt werden (*inf*); **he got a real ~ from his opponent** (*inf*) er wurde von seinem Gegner regelrecht vorgeführt (*inf*); **his self-confidence took a ~** sein Selbstbewußtsein litt darunter *or* bekam einen Knacks (*inf*).

punishment ['pʌnɪʃmənt] *n* (**a**) (*penalty*) Strafe *f;* (*punishing*) Bestrafung *f* ◆ **you know the ~ for such offences** Sie wissen, welche Strafe darauf steht; **to take one's ~** seine Strafe akzeptieren. (**b**) (*fig inf*) **to take a lot of ~** (*car, furniture etc*) stark strapaziert werden; (*Sport*) vorgeführt werden (*inf*).

punitive ['pju:nɪtɪv] *adj* Straf-; *taxation, fines etc* extrem (hoch).

Punjab ['pʌndʒɑ:b] *n* **the ~** das Pandschab.

Punjabi [pʌn'dʒɑ:bɪ] 1 *adj* Pandschab-.
2 *n* (**a**) Pandschabi *mf.* (**b**) (*language*) Pandschabi *nt.*

punk [pʌŋk] 1 *n* (**a**) (*person: also* **~ rocker**) Punker, Punkrocker *m;* (*music: also* **~ rock**) Punk(rock) *m;* (*culture*) Punk *m.* (**b**) (*US sl: hoodlum*) Ganove *m* (*inf*). (**c**) (*dated inf: nonsense*) Stuß *m* (*inf*).
2 *adj* (*sl*) Punk- ◆ **~ rock** Punkrock *m.*

punnet ['pʌnɪt] *n* (*Brit*) Körbchen *nt.*

punster ['pʌnstəʳ] *n* **he is a brilliant ~** er versteht es hervorragend, Wortspiele zu machen.

punt¹ [pʌnt] 1 *n* (*boat*) Stechkahn, Stocherkahn *m.*
2 *vti* staken, stochern; (*go or take by ~*) im Stechkahn fahren ◆ **to go ~ing** Stechkahn fahren.

punt² 1 *n* Schuß *m* (aus der Hand) ◆ **he gave the ball a ~** er schoß den Ball aus der Hand.
2 *vti* **to ~ (the ball)** (den Ball) aus der Hand schießen; **he ~ed the ball back** er schoß den Ball zurück.

punt³ 1 *n* (*bet*) Wette *f;* (*gamble*) Spiel *nt.*
2 *vi* wetten; spielen.

punter¹ ['pʌntəʳ] *n* (*boater*) Stechkahnfahrer(in *f*) *m.*

punter² *n* (**a**) (*better*) Wetter *m;* (*gambler*) Spieler(in *f*) *m.* (**b**) (*sl*) (*customer etc*) Macker *m* (*sl*); (*of prostitute*) Freier *m* (*sl*) ◆ **the average ~** Otto Normalverbraucher.

puny ['pju:nɪ] *adj* (*+er*) (*weak*) *person* schwächlich, mick(e)rig (*pej*); *effort* kläglich.

pup [pʌp] 1 *n* (**a**) Junge(s) *nt* ◆ **in ~** (*bitch*) trächtig; **she's still a ~** sie ist noch jung *or* klein; **to be sold a ~** (*fig inf*) übers Ohr gehauen werden (*inf*). (**b**) (*pej: youth*) *see* **puppy** (**b**).
2 *vi* werfen.

pupa ['pju:pə] *n, pl* **-e** ['pju:pi:] Puppe *f.*

pupate ['pju:peɪt] *vi* sich verpuppen.

pupil¹ ['pju:pl] *n* (*Sch, fig*) Schüler(in *f*) *m.*

pupil² *n* (*Anat*) Pupille *f.*

puppet ['pʌpɪt] *n* Puppe *f;* (*glove ~*) Handpuppe *f;* (*string ~, fig*) Marionette *f.*

puppeteer [pʌpɪ'tɪəʳ] *n* Puppenspieler(in *f*) *m.*

puppet: ~ government *n* Marionettenregierung *f;* **~ régime** *n* Marionettenregime *nt.*

puppetry ['pʌpɪtrɪ] *n* das Puppenspiel.

puppet: ~-show *n* Puppenspiel *nt;* (*with string ~s also*) Marionettentheater *nt;* **~ state** *n* Marionettenstaat *m.*

puppy ['pʌpɪ] *n* (**a**) (*young dog*) junger *or* kleiner Hund, Hündchen *nt* ◆ **when he was still a ~** als er noch jung *or* klein war. (**b**) (*pej dated: youth*) Schnösel *m* (*inf*).

puppy: ~ dog *n* Hündchen *nt;* **~ fat** *n* Babyspeck *m;* **~ love** *n* Schwärmerei *f.*

purblind ['pɜ:blaɪnd] *adj* (*liter*) (*lit*) halbblind *attr,* halb blind *pred;* (*fig*) blind.

purchasable ['pɜ:tʃəsəbl] *adj* käuflich (zu erwerben *geh*).

purchase ['pɜ:tʃɪs] 1 *n* (**a**) Kauf *m;* (*of furniture, machine, flat, car also*) Anschaffung *f* ◆ **to make a ~** einen Kauf tätigen; eine Anschaffung machen.
(**b**) (*grip*) Halt *m* ◆ **he couldn't get a ~ on the wet rope** er konnte an dem nassen Seil keinen Halt finden.
2 *vt* (*buy*) kaufen, erwerben (*form*), erstehen (*form*); (*fig*) *success, victory* erkaufen ◆ **purchasing power** Kaufkraft *f.*

purchase: ~-money *n* Kaufgeld *nt;* **~ order** *n* Auftragsbestätigung *f;* **~ price** *n* Kaufpreis *m.*

purchaser ['pɜ:tʃɪsəʳ] *n* Käufer(in *f*) *m.*

purchase tax *n* (*Brit*) *nach dem Großhandelspreis berechnete Kaufsteuer.*

purdah ['pɜ:də] *n Vorhang m vor den Frauengemächern im Islam* ◆ **a woman in ~** (*lit*) eine Frau, die von (fremden) Männern ferngehalten wird; **he keeps his wife (like a woman) in ~** er hält seine Frau von allem fern.

pure [pjʊəʳ] *adj* (*+er*) rein; *motive* ehrlich, lauter (*geh*); (*utter*) *madness, nonsense etc also* reinste(r, s) ◆ **she stared at him in ~ disbelief** sie starrte ihn ganz ungläubig an; **malice ~ and simple** reine Bosheit; **a ~ wool dress** ein Kleid aus reiner Wolle, ein reinwollenes Kleid; **blessed are the ~ in heart** (*Bibl*) selig, die reinen Herzens sind.

purebred ['pjʊəbred] 1 *adj* reinrassig.
2 *n* reinrassiges Pferd *etc.*

purée ['pjʊəreɪ] 1 *n* Püree *nt,* Brei *m* ◆ **tomato ~** Tomatenmark *nt.*
2 *vt* pürieren.

purely ['pjʊəlɪ] *adv* rein.

pure-minded ['pjʊə'maɪndɪd] *adj* unverdorben.

pureness ['pjʊənɪs] *n see* **purity.**

purgation [pɜ:'geɪʃən] *n* (*liter*) Reinigung *f;* (*of sin, guilt*) Buße *f;* (*form: of bowels also*) Entleerung *f.*

purgative ['pɜ:gətɪv] 1 *adj* (*Med*) abführend, purgativ (*spec*); (*fig liter*) läuternd (*geh*).
2 *n* Abführmittel, Purgativ (*spec*) *nt.*

purgatorial [,pɜ:gə'tɔ:rɪəl] *adj* (*Rel*) Fegefeuer-; (*fig*) höllisch ◆ **~ fire** Fegefeuer *nt.*

purgatory ['pɜ:gətərɪ] *n* (*Rel*) das Fegefeuer; (*fig: state*) die Hölle.

purge [pɜ:dʒ] 1 *n* (**a**) (*Med*) (starkes) Abführmittel. (**b**) (*Pol etc*) Säuberung(saktion) *f* ◆ **a ~ of all radical elements in the party** eine Säuberung der Partei von allen radikalen Elementen.
2 *vt* reinigen; *body* entschlacken; *guilt, offence, sin* büßen; (*Pol etc*) *party, organization* säubern (of von); *traitor, member* eliminieren (*from* aus) ◆ **to ~ the bowels** den Darm entleeren.

purification [,pjʊərɪfɪ'keɪʃən] *n* Reinigung *f.*

purifier ['pjʊərɪfaɪəʳ] *n* Reinigungsanlage *f;* (*air-freshener*) Luftreiniger *m.*

purify ['pjʊərɪfaɪ] *vt* reinigen.

purism ['pjʊərɪzəm] *n* Purismus *m.*

purist ['pjʊərɪst] *n* Purist(in *f*) *m.*

puritan ['pjʊərɪtən] (*Rel:* **P~**) 1 *adj* puritanisch.
2 *n* Puritaner(in *f*) *m.*

puritanical [,pjʊərɪ'tænɪkəl] *adj* puritanisch.

puritanism ['pjʊərɪtənɪzəm] (*Rel:* **P~**) *n* Puritanismus *m.*

purity ['pjʊərɪtɪ] *n* Reinheit *f;* (*of motives*) Lauterkeit (*geh*), Ehrlichkeit *f.*

purl [pɜ:l] 1 *n* linke Masche ◆ **is the next row (in) ~?** ist die nächste Reihe links?
2 *vti* links stricken ◆ **~ two** zwei links.

purlieus ['pɜ:lju:z] *npl* (*liter*) Umgebung *f.*

purloin [pɜ:'lɔɪn] *vt* (*form, hum*) entwenden (*form, hum*).

purple ['pɜ:pl] 1 *adj* violett, lila; *face* dunkelrot, hochrot; (*pej*) *prose, passage* hochgestochen, hochtrabend ◆ **to go ~ (in the face)** hochrot *or* dunkelrot werden *or* anlaufen (*inf*).
2 *n* (**a**) (*colour*) Violett, Lila *nt.* (**b**) (*fig*) **the ~** (*nobility*) der Adel; (*bishops*) der Kardinalsstand; **to be born in the ~** von königlichem Geblüt sein; **to be raised to the ~** den Kardinalspurpur anlegen.

purple heart *n* (**a**) (*Brit*) Amphetamintablette *f.* (**b**) (*US*) **P~ H~** Purpurherz *nt,* Verwundetenabzeichen *nt.*

purplish ['pɜ:plɪʃ] *adj* leicht violett *or* lila.

purport ['pɜ:pət] 1 *n* Tenor *m.*
2 [pɜ:'pɔ:t] *vt* (**a**) (*convey, mean*) hindeuten auf (*+acc*).
(**b**) (*profess, claim*) **to ~ to be/do sth** (*person*) vorgeben, etw zu sein/tun; (*object*) etw sein/tun sollen; **he is ~ed to be a spy** es wird behauptet, er sei ein Spion; **the law is ~ed to be in the public interest** das Gesetz soll dem Interesse der Öffentlichkeit dienen.

purpose ['pɜ:pəs] 1 *n* (**a**) (*intention*) Absicht *f;* (*result aimed at, set goal*) Zweck *m* ◆ **on ~** mit Absicht, absichtlich; **what was your ~ in doing this?** was haben Sie damit beabsichtigt?, was war Ihre Absicht dabei?; **he did it for *or* with the ~ of improving his image** er tat es in der Absicht *or* mit dem Ziel, sein Image zu verbessern; **he's a man with a ~ in life** er ist ein Mensch mit einem Lebensziel; **a novel with a ~** ein Roman, der einen Zweck erfüllen soll; **to answer *or* serve sb's ~(s)** jds Zweck(en) entsprechen *or* dienen; **his activities seem to lack ~** seine Aktivitäten scheinen nicht zweckgerichtet zu sein; **for our ~s** für unsere Zwecke; **for the ~s of this meeting** zum Zweck dieser Konferenz; **for all practical ~s** in der Praxis; **to the ~** relevant; **to some/good/little ~** mit einigem/gutem/wenig Erfolg; **to no ~** ohne Erfolg.
(**b**) *no pl* (*resolution, determination*) Entschlossenheit *f* ◆ **weakness of ~** Mangel *m* an Entschlossenheit, Entschlußlosigkeit *f;* **strength of ~** Entschlußkraft, Entschlossenheit *f;* **sense of ~** Zielbewußtsein *nt;* (*of nation*) Ziel *nt,* Zielvorstellungen *pl;* **to have a/no sense of ~** zielbewußt sein/kein Zielbewußtsein haben, ein/kein Ziel haben.

[2] vt (*liter*) beabsichtigen ◆ **to ~ to do sth** etw zu tun gedenken.
purpose-built ['pɜːpəs'bɪlt] *adj* speziell angefertigt, Spezial-; *building* speziell gebaut, Spezial-.
purposeful *adj*, **~ly** *adv* ['pɜːpəsfʊl, -fəlɪ] entschlossen.
purposefulness ['pɜːpəsfʊlnɪs] *n* Entschlossenheit *f*.
purposeless ['pɜːpəslɪs] *adj* sinnlos; *person* ziellos.
purposely ['pɜːpəslɪ] *adv* bewußt, absichtlich.
purposive ['pɜːpəsɪv] *adj remark, statement, behaviour* gezielt ◆ **to be ~** einen Zweck verfolgen.
purr [pɜːʳ] [1] *vi* (*cat, fig: person*) schnurren; (*engine*) surren.
[2] *vt* (*say*) säuseln.
[3] *n* Schnurren *nt no pl*; Surren *nt no pl*.
purse [pɜːs] [1] *n* **(a)** (*for money*) Portemonnaie *nt*, Geldbeutel *m* (*dial*), Geldbörse *f* (*form*) ◆ **to hold the ~ strings** (*fig*) über die Finanzen bestimmen, die Finanzen in der Hand haben; **she decided to loosen/tighten the ~ strings** sie beschloß, ihm/ihr mehr Geld zu geben/sie beschloß, ihn/sie kurzzuhalten; **the government has tightened the ~ strings on public spending** die Regierung hat den Geldhahn zugedreht (*inf*).
(b) (*US: handbag*) Handtasche *f*.
(c) (*funds*) Gelder *pl* ◆ **that's beyond my ~** das übersteigt meine Finanzen (*inf*); *see* **public ~**.
(d) (*sum of money*) (*as prize*) Preisgeld *nt*; (*as gift*) (*to widow, refugee etc*) (Geld)spende *f*; (*on retirement*) Geldgeschenk *nt*.
[2] *vt* **to ~ one's lips/mouth (up)** einen Schmollmund machen.
purser ['pɜːsəʳ] *n* Zahlmeister *m*.
pursuance [pə'sjuːəns] *n* (*form*) (*of plan*) Verfolgung *f*; (*of instruction*) Ausführung *f*; (*of duties*) Erfüllung *f*.
pursuant [pə'sjuːənt] *adj* (*form*) **~ to** gemäß (+*dat*), entsprechend (+*dat*); **~ to our agreement** unserem Abkommen gemäß *or* entsprechend.
pursue [pə'sjuː] *vt* **(a)** verfolgen; *girl, film star etc also, success* nachlaufen (+*dat*); *pleasure, success* nachjagen (+*dat*), aussein auf (+*acc*); *happiness* streben nach ◆ **bad luck seems to ~ him** er scheint vom Pech verfolgt zu sein.
(b) (*carry on*) *train of thought, course of action, idea* verfolgen; *inquiry* durchführen; *profession also, studies* nachgehen (+*dat*); *subject* weiterführen.
pursuer [pə'sjuːəʳ] *n* Verfolger(in *f*) *m*.
pursuit [pə'sjuːt] *n* **(a)** (*act of pursuing*) (*of person*) Verfolgung (*of gen*), Jagd (*of* auf +*acc*) *f*; (*of knowledge*) Streben, Trachten *nt* (*of* nach); (*of pleasure*) Jagd *f* (*of* nach); (*of happiness*) Streben *nt* (*of* nach) ◆ **he set off in ~ (of her)** er rannte/fuhr (ihr) hinterher; **to go in ~ of sb/sth** sich auf die Jagd nach jdm/etw machen; **in hot ~ of sb** hart auf jds Fersen (*dat*); **in (the) ~ of his goal** in Verfolgung seines Ziels; **Kissinger's ~ of peace** Kissingers Friedensbemühungen *pl*.
(b) (*occupation*) Beschäftigung *f*; (*hobby, pastime*) Freizeitbeschäftigung *f*, Zeitvertreib *m* ◆ **his literary ~s** seine Beschäftigung mit der Literatur.
pursuit plane *n* Jagdflugzeug *nt*.
purulence ['pjʊərʊləns], **purulency** ['pjʊərʊlənsɪ] *n* Eitern *nt*; (*pus*) Eiter *m*.
purulent ['pjʊərʊlənt] *adj* eitrig ◆ **to become ~** eitern.
purvey [pɜː'veɪ] *vt* (*form*) (*sell*) verkaufen ◆ **to ~ sth to sb** (*supply*) jdm etw liefern; *food also* jdn mit etw beliefern; *information also* jdn mit etw versorgen.
purveyance [pɜː'veɪəns] *n* (*form: sale*) Verkauf *m* ◆ **the ~ of food to the Navy** die Lieferung von Lebensmitteln an die Marine.
purveyor [pɜː'veɪəʳ] *n* (*form*) (*seller*) Händler *m*; (*supplier*) Lieferant *m*.
purview ['pɜːvjuː] *n* (*form*) Rahmen *m*; (*of department*) Aufgabenbereich *m*, Ressort *nt* ◆ **to come within/lie outside the ~ of an inquiry** noch/nicht mehr im Rahmen einer Untersuchung liegen.
pus [pʌs] *n* Eiter *m*.
push [pʊʃ] [1] *n* **(a)** Schubs *m* (*inf*); (*short*) Stoß *m*; (*in childbirth*) Drücken *nt no pl* ◆ **to give sb/sth a ~** jdn/etw schieben; jdm/einer Sache einen Stoß versetzen; **to give a car a ~** einen Wagen anschieben; **he needs a little ~ now and then** (*fig*) den muß man mal ab und zu in die Rippen stoßen (*inf*); **to get the ~** (*Brit inf*) (*employee*) (raus)fliegen (*inf*) (*from* aus); (*boyfriend*) den Laufpaß kriegen (*inf*); **to give sb the ~** (*Brit inf*) *employee* jdn rausschmeißen (*inf*); *boyfriend* jdm den Laufpaß geben (*inf*).
(b) (*effort*) Anstrengung *f*; (*sales ~*) Kampagne, Aktion *f*; (*Mil: offensive*) Offensive *f* ◆ **to make a ~** sich ranhalten (*inf*), Dampf machen (*inf*); (*Mil*) eine Offensive starten; **let's make a ~ to get it finished** halten wir uns ran (*inf*), damit wir fertig werden; **to have a ~ on sales** eine Verkaufskampagne führen.
(c) (*drive, aggression*) Durchsetzungsvermögen *nt*.
(d) (*inf*) **at a ~** notfalls, im Notfall; **if/when it comes to the ~** wenn es darauf ankommt.
[2] *vt* **(a)** (*shove, move by ~ing*) schieben; (*quickly, violently*) stoßen, schubsen (*inf*); (*press*) *button, controls* drücken ◆ **to ~ a door open/shut** eine Tür auf-/zuschieben; (*quickly, violently*) eine Tür auf-/zustoßen; **he ~ed the book into my hand** er drückte mir das Buch in die Hand; **to ~ a car to get it started** einen Wagen anschieben; **he ~ed his way through the crowd** er drängte sich durch die Menge; **he ~ed the thought to the back of his mind** er schob den Gedanken beiseite; **he ~ed the ball over the bar** (*Sport*) er hat den Ball über die Latte gestoßen.
(b) (*fig*) *views, claims, interests* durchzusetzen versuchen; *candidate* die Werbetrommel rühren für; *export side* intensiv fördern; *product* propagieren, massiv Werbung machen für, pushen (*sl*); *drugs* schieben, pushen (*sl*) ◆ **to ~ home an attack/one's advantage** einen Angriff forcieren/seinen Vorteil ausnützen; **the speaker ~ed home his points** der Sprecher machte nachdrücklich seinen Standpunkt klar; **don't ~ your luck** treib's nicht zu weit!; **he's ~ing his luck trying to do that** er legt es wirklich darauf an, wenn er das versucht; **he must be ~ing 70** (*inf*) er muß auf die 70 zugehen.
(c) (*fig: put pressure on*) drängen, drängeln (*inf*); *athlete, pupil, employee* antreiben ◆ **to ~ sb into doing sth** jdn dazu treiben, etw zu tun; **to ~ sb to do sth** jdn dazu drängen, etw zu tun; **to ~ sb for payment** jdn zum Zahlen drängen; **don't ~ him so hard to make a decision** drängen *or* drängeln (*inf*) Sie ihn nicht zu sehr zu einer Entscheidung; **they ~ed him to the limits** sie trieben ihn bis an seine Grenzen; **that's ~ing it a bit** (*inf*) das ist ein bißchen übertrieben; **to be ~ed (for time/money)** (*inf*) mit der Zeit/mit Geld knapp dransein, unter Zeitdruck stehen/knapp bei Kasse sein (*inf*); **I was ~ed to find the money/an answer** ich hatte Probleme *or* Schwierigkeiten, das Geld zusammenzubringen/eine Antwort zu finden; **to ~ oneself hard** sich schinden.
[3] *vi* **(a)** (*shove*) schieben; (*quickly, violently*) stoßen; (*press, in childbirth*) drücken; (*in a crowd*) drängen, drängeln (*inf*); (*press onward*) sich (vorwärts)kämpfen; (*fig*) (*be ambitious, assert oneself*) kämpfen; (*apply pressure*) drängen, drängeln (*inf*) ◆ **"~"** (*on door*) „drücken"; (*on bell*) „klingeln"; **~ harder!** fester schieben/stoßen/drücken!; **he ~es too much** (*fig*) er ist zu aggressiv.
(b) this door ~es (open) bei dieser Tür muß man drücken.
◆**push about** *vt sep see* **push around**.
◆**push across** *vt sep see* **push over (a)**.
◆**push ahead** *vi* sich ranhalten (*inf*), voranmachen (*inf*) ◆ **to ~ ~ with one's plans** seine Pläne vorantreiben.
◆**push along** [1] *vt sep wheelbarrow etc* vor sich (*dat*) her schieben; (*fig: speed up*) *work etc* voranbringen, vorantreiben.
[2] *vi* (*inf*) sich auf den Weg *or* auf die Socken machen (*inf*).
◆**push around** *vt sep* **(a)** (*lit*) herumschieben; (*quickly, violently*) herumstoßen. **(b)** (*fig inf: bully*) *child* herumschubsen; *adult* herumkommandieren.
◆**push aside** *vt sep* zur Seite *or* beiseite schieben; (*quickly, violently*) zur Seite *or* beiseite stoßen; (*fig*) *problems, suggestions* einfach abtun; *rival* zur Seite drängen.
◆**push away** *vt sep* wegschieben; (*quickly*) wegstoßen.
◆**push back** *vt sep people* zurückdrängen; (*with one push*) zurückstoßen; *curtains, cover, lock of hair* zurückschieben.
◆**push by** *vi see* **push past**.
◆**push down** [1] *vt sep* **(a)** (*press down*) nach unten drücken. **(b)** (*knock over*) umstoßen; *fence* niederreißen.
[2] *vi* (*press down*) hinunterdrücken, nach unten drücken; (*in childbirth*) drücken.
◆**push for** *vi +prep obj* drängen auf (+*acc*).
◆**push forward** [1] *vi* **(a)** (*Mil*) vorwärts drängen. **(b)** *see* **push ahead**.
[2] *vt sep* (*lit*) nach vorn schieben; (*fig*) *claim* geltend machen; *ideas* hervorheben, herausstellen; *sb, oneself* in den Vordergrund schieben.
◆**push in** [1] *vt sep* **(a)** hineinschieben; (*quickly, violently*) hineinstoßen ◆ **to ~ sb/sth ~(to) sth** jdn/etw in etw (*acc*) schieben/stoßen; **to ~ one's way ~** sich hineindrängen.
(b) (*break*) *window, sides of box* eindrücken.
[2] *vi* (*lit: in queue, into room etc*) sich hineindrängen *or* -drängeln (*inf*); (*fig: interfere*) sich dazwischen drängen, sich reindrängen (*inf*) ◆ **he ~ed ~to the queue** er drängelte sich (in der Schlange) vor.
◆**push off** [1] *vt sep* **(a)** hinunterschieben; (*quickly, violently*) hinunterstoßen; *lid, cap* wegdrücken ◆ **to ~ sb ~ sth** jdn von etw schieben/stoßen; **to ~ sth ~ sth** etw von etw schieben/stoßen/drücken; **I was ~ed ~ the pavement** ich wurde vom Bürgersteig gedrängt. **(b)** *boat* abstoßen.
[2] *vi* **(a)** (*in boat*) abstoßen. **(b)** (*inf: leave*) abhauen (*inf*) ◆ **~ ~!** mach 'ne Fliege! (*sl*), hau *or* zieh ab! (*inf*). **(c) the top just ~es ~** der Deckel läßt sich einfach wegdrücken.
◆**push on** [1] *vi* (*with journey*) weiterfahren; (*walking*) weitergehen; (*with job*) weitermachen.
[2] *vt sep* **(a)** *top, lid* festdrücken ◆ **he ~ed the lid ~(to) the jar** er drückte den Deckel auf das Glas. **(b)** (*fig*) (*urge on*) antreiben; (*incite*) anstacheln.
◆**push out** [1] *vt sep* **(a)** hinausschieben; (*quickly, violently*) hinausstoßen ◆ **to ~ sb/sth ~ of sth** jdn/etw aus etw schieben/stoßen; **to ~ one's way ~ (of sth)** sich (aus etw) hinausdrängen.
(b) (*fig*) *employee, government, member of group* hinausdrängen ◆ **to ~ sb ~ of sth** jdn aus etw drängen.
(c) (*Bot*) *root, shoots* treiben.
[2] *vi* (*Bot: roots, shoots*) treiben.
◆**push over** *vt sep* **(a)** (*pass over, move over*) hinüber-/herüberschieben; (*quickly, violently*) hinüber-/herüberstoßen ◆ **to ~ sb/sth ~ sth** jdn/etw über etw (*acc*) schieben/stoßen. **(b)** (*knock over*) umwerfen.
◆**push past** *vi* sich vorbeischieben (*prep obj* an +*dat*); (*move violently*) sich vorbeidrängen (*prep obj* an +*dat*).
◆**push through** [1] *vt sep* **(a)** (*shove through*) durchschieben; (*quickly, violently*) durchstoßen ◆ **to ~ sb/sth ~ sth** jdn/etw durch etw schieben/stoßen; **to ~ one's way ~/~ the crowd** sich durchdrängen/sich durch die Menge drängen; **to ~ sb ~ an exam** jdn durch eine Prüfung bringen (*inf*).
(b) (*get done quickly*) *bill, decision* durchpeitschen (*inf*); *business* durchziehen (*inf*).
[2] *vi* (*through crowd*) sich durchschieben; (*more violently*) sich durchdrängen; (*new shoots*) sich herausschieben ◆ **he ~ed ~ the crowd** er schob/drängte

sich durch die Menge.

◆**push to** *vt always separate door* anlehnen.

◆**push up** *vt sep* **(a)** *(lit)* hinaufschieben; *(quickly, violently)* hinaufstoßen; *window* hochschieben/-stoßen; *see* **daisy. (b)** *(fig) (raise, increase)* hochtreiben, hochdrücken.

push: ~ball *n* Pushball *m*; **~bar** *n* Riegel *m*; **~-bike** *n (Brit)* Fahrrad *nt*; **~-button** *n* Drucktaste *f*, Druckknopf *m*; **~-button controls** Druckknopfsteuerung *f*; **~-button radio** Radio *nt* mit Drucktasten; **~-button telephone** Tastentelefon *nt*; **~-button warfare** Krieg *m* auf Knopfdruck; **~-cart** *n* (Hand)karren *m*; **~chair** *n (Brit)* Sportwagen *m*.

pusher ['pʊʃəʳ] *n (inf)* **(a)** *(of drugs)* Pusher(in *f*) *m (inf)*; *(small-time)* Dealer(in *f*) *m (inf)*. **(b)** *(ambitious person)* **he's a ~** er setzt sich durch.

pushiness ['pʊʃɪnɪs] *n (inf)* penetrante Art *(pej)*.

pushing ['pʊʃɪŋ], **pushy** *(inf) adj* penetrant *(pej)*.

push: ~-over *n (inf) (job etc)* Kinderspiel *nt*; *(match also)* Geschenk *nt (inf)*; *(person)* leichtes Opfer; **he's a ~-over for a pretty face** bei einem hübschen Gesicht wird er schwach; **~-pull** *adj circuit etc* Gegentakt-; **~rod** *n (Mech)* Stößelstange *f*; **~-start** [1] *vt car* anschieben; [2] *n* **to give sb a ~-start** jdn anschieben; **~-up** *n* Liegestütz *m*.

pushy ['pʊʃɪ] *adj (+er) (inf) see* **pushing.**

pusillanimity [,pju:sɪlə'nɪmɪtɪ] *n (liter)* Unbeherztheit, Feigheit *f*.

pusillanimous [,pju:sɪ'lænɪməs] *adj (liter)* unbeherzt, feige.

puss [pʊs] *n (inf)* Mieze *(inf)*, Muschi *(inf) f* ◆ **~, ~!** Miez, Miez!; **P~ in Boots** der Gestiefelte Kater; **she's a sly ~** *(inf)* sie ist ein schlaues Ding *(inf)*.

pussy ['pʊsɪ] *n* **(a)** *(cat)* Mieze *(inf)*, Muschi *(inf) f*. **(b)** *(sl: female genitals)* Kätzchen *nt (sl)*, Muschi *f (inf)*.

pussy: ~-cat *n (baby-talk)* Miezekatze *f (baby-talk)*; **~foot** *vi (inf)* **(a)** *(move cautiously)* auf Zehenspitzen tappen, auf Samtpfoten schleichen; **(b)** *(act cautiously)* **to ~foot (about** *or* **over sth)** (um etw) wie die Katze um den heißen Brei schleichen *(inf)*; **~footing** *(inf)* [1] *adj* überängstlich; [2] *n* **I'm fed up with his ~footing** ich habe es satt, wie er immer wie die Katze um den heißen Brei schleicht; **~ willow** *n* Salweide *f*.

pustule ['pʌstju:l] *n* Pustel *f*, Eiterpickel *m*.

put¹ [pʊt] *(vb: pret, ptp ~)* [1] *n (Sport)* Stoß *m*.

[2] *vt* **to ~ the shot** kugelstoßen; **~ting the shot** Kugelstoßen *nt*.

▼ **put²** *pret, ptp ~* [1] *vt* **(a)** *(place)* tun; *(~ down, position)* stellen, setzen; *(lay down)* legen; *(push in)* stecken ◆ **~ the lid on the box** tu *or* mach den Deckel auf die Schachtel; **to ~ sth in a drawer** etw in eine Schublade tun *or* legen; **he ~ his hand in his pocket** er steckte die Hand in die Tasche; **you've ~ the picture too high up** du hast das Bild zu hoch (auf)gehängt; **he ~ the corpse down the well** er warf die Leiche in den Brunnen; **they ~ a plank across the stream** sie legten ein Brett über den Bach; **he ~ his rucksack over the fence** er setzte seinen Rucksack über den Zaun; **he ~ some more coal on the fire** er legte Kohle nach; **~ the dog in the kitchen** tu *or* steck den Hund in die Küche; **to ~ milk/sugar in one's coffee** Milch/Zucker in den Kaffee tun *or* geben; **he ~ his hat on his head** er setzte sich *(dat)* den Hut auf; **to ~ the ball in the net** *(Ftbl)* den Ball ins Netz setzen; *(Tennis)* den Ball ins Netz schlagen; **he ~ the ball over the wall** er schoß den Ball über die Mauer; **her aunt ~ her on the train** ihre Tante setzte sie in den Zug; **to ~ sb across a river** jdn über einen Fluß setzen; **to ~ men on the moon** Menschen auf den Mond bringen; **to ~ a bullet through sb's head** jdm eine Kugel durch den Kopf schießen; **he ~ his toe in the water** er steckte seinen Zeh ins Wasser; **he ~ his hand/head on my shoulder** er legte seine Hand auf/seinen Kopf an meine Schulter; **he ~ his lips to my ear and whispered ...** er kam ganz dicht und flüsterte mir ins Ohr ...; **to ~ a glass to one's lips** ein Glas zum Mund(e) führen; **she ~ the shell to her ear** sie hielt (sich *dat*) die Muschel ans Ohr; **to ~ a heifer to a bull** die Kuh mit dem Stier zusammenbringen *or* -führen; **to ~ a horse to a fence** mit einem Pferd ein Hindernis angehen *or* anreiten; **to ~ one's hand over one's/sb's mouth** sich/jdm die Hand vor den Mund halten; **~ it there!** *(concluding deal)* abgemacht!; *(congratulatory)* gratuliere!; *(conciliatory)* schon gut; **I didn't know where to ~ myself** ich wußte gar nicht, wo ich hingucken sollte.

(b) *(thrust)* stecken ◆ **he ~ his head round the door** er steckte den Kopf zur Tür herein; **to ~ one's fist through a window** mit der Faust ein Fenster einschlagen.

(c) *(fit, fix)* machen *(on* an *+acc)*, anbringen *(on* an *+dat)* ◆ **to ~ a patch on sth** einen Flicken auf etw *(acc)* setzen.

(d) to stay ~ liegen-/stehen-/hängen- *etc* bleiben; *(hair)* halten; *(person) (not move)* bleiben; *(not stand up)* sitzen bleiben; **just stay ~!** bleib, wo du bist!

(e) to ~ a child in a home ein Kind in ein Heim stecken; **he was ~ under the care of a nurse** er wurde in die Obhut einer Krankenschwester gegeben; **to ~ money into sth** (sein) Geld in etw *(acc)* stecken; **he ~ £10/money on Red Rum** er setzte £ 10/setzte auf Red Rum; **I'm ~ting my money on him** ich setzte auf ihn; **I'm ~ting my money on him to get the job** ich gehe jede Wette ein, daß er die Stelle bekommt; **we'll each ~ £5 towards the cost of it** jeder von uns gibt £ 5 (zum Betrag) dazu; **to ~ a lot of time into sth** viel Zeit auf etw *(acc)* verwenden *or* in etw *(acc)* stecken; **to ~ a lot of effort into one's work** viel Mühe in seine Arbeit stecken; **she has ~ a lot into her marriage** sie hat eine Menge in ihre Ehe gesteckt *or* investiert; **I would ~ complete confidence in him** ich würde mein volles Vertrauen auf ihn *or* in ihn setzen; **to ~ sb in possession of the facts** jdn über den Stand der Dinge unterrichten; *see also nouns.*

(f) *(cause to be, do etc)* **to ~ sb in a good/bad mood** jdn fröhlich/mißmutig stimmen; **that ~s him in another category** das stuft ihn in eine andere Klasse ein; **I ~ the children on their best behaviour** ich habe den Kindern eingeschärft, sich ja gut zu benehmen; **to ~ sb to do** *or* **doing sth** jdn abordnen, etw zu tun; **he ~ four men on the job** er setzte (für diese Arbeit) vier Leute ein; **they ~ her to work on the new project** ihr wurde das neue Projekt als Arbeitsbereich zugewiesen; **they ~ someone over/under him in the office** sie haben jemanden über ihn gesetzt/ihm jemanden unterstellt; **he ~ his watch 5 minutes fast** er stellte seine Uhr 5 Minuten vor; **to ~ sb to great expense** jdm große Ausgaben verursachen; **I don't want to be ~ to a lot of expense** ich möchte nicht, daß mir damit große Ausgaben entstehen; **to be ~ to a lot of inconvenience over sth** mit etw viele Unannehmlichkeiten haben.

(g) *(write)* schreiben; *comma, line* machen; *(draw)* zeichnen, malen ◆ **to ~ one's signature to a document** seine Unterschrift unter ein Schriftstück setzen; **~ your name here** schreiben *or* setzen Sie Ihren Namen hierhin; **to ~ a cross/tick against sb's name** jds Namen ankreuzen/abhaken; **he ~ it in his next novel** er brachte das in seinem nächsten Roman.

(h) *(~ forward) case, question, proposal* vorbringen ◆ **to ~ a matter before a committee** eine Angelegenheit vor einen Ausschuß bringen; **to ~ the arguments for and against sth** das Für und Wider von etw *(dat)* aufzählen; **to ~ sth on the agenda** etw auf die Tagesordnung setzen; **you might ~ it to him that a contribution would be welcome** du könntest ihm nahelegen, daß ein Beitrag erwünscht wäre; **to ~ a question/suggestion to sb** jdm eine Frage stellen/einen Vorschlag unterbreiten; **I ~ it to you that ...** ich behaupte, daß ...; **it was ~ to me that ...** es wurde mir nahegelegt, daß ...; **I ~ it to him that this might not fit in with his theory** ich gab ihm zu bedenken, daß dies vielleicht nicht in seine Theorie passen würde.

(i) *(express)* ausdrücken, sagen ◆ **that's one way of ~ting it** so kann man's auch sagen; **as he would ~ it** wie er sich ausdrücken würde; **as Shakespeare ~s it** wie Shakespeare es ausdrückt; **~ it so as not to offend her** formulieren Sie es so, daß Sie sie nicht beleidigen; **how shall I ~ it?** wie soll ich (es) sagen?; **how will you ~ it to him?** wie wirst du es ihm beibringen?; **if I may ~ it so** wenn ich das so sagen darf, wenn ich mich (mal) so ausdrücken darf; **to ~ it bluntly** um es klipp und klar zu sagen; **the compliment was gracefully ~** das Kompliment war elegant formuliert.

(j) to ~ a text into Greek einen Text ins Griechische übersetzen; **to ~ a verb into the past tense** ein Verb in die Vergangenheit setzen; **to ~ a poem to music** ein Gedicht vertonen.

(k) *(rate)* schätzen *(at* auf *+acc)* ◆ **he ~s money before his family's happiness** er stellt Geld über das Glück seiner Familie; **I ~ him above Tennyson** ich schätze ihn höher ein als Tennyson; **I wouldn't ~ him amongst the greatest poets** ich würde ihn nicht zu den größten Dichtern zählen; **to ~ a value of £10 on sth** den Wert einer Sache *(gen)* auf £ 10 schätzen.

[2] *vi (Naut)* **to ~ to sea** in See stechen.

◆**put about** [1] *vt sep* **(a)** *(circulate) news, rumour* verbreiten, in Umlauf bringen ◆ **he ~ it ~ that ...** er verbreitete (das Gerücht), daß ... **(b)** *(Naut)* **to ~ a ship ~** den Kurs (eines Schiffes) ändern.

[2] *vi (Naut)* den Kurs ändern.

◆**put across** *vt sep* **(a)** *(communicate) ideas* verständlich machen *(to sb* jdm), klar zum Ausdruck bringen; *knowledge* vermitteln *(to sb* jdm); *(promote)* an den Mann bringen *(inf)* ◆ **to ~ a product ~ to the public** ein Produkt an den Mann bringen; **to ~ oneself ~** den richtigen Eindruck von sich geben.

(b) *(inf: play a trick)* **to ~ it** *or* **one ~ sb** jdn anführen; **he's just trying to ~ one ~ (you)** er will dich nur anführen.

◆**put aside** *vt sep* **(a)** *book, knitting etc* beiseite legen. **(b)** *(save for later use)* beiseite *or* auf die Seite legen, zurücklegen; *(in shop)* zurücklegen. **(c)** *(fig: forget, abandon)* ablegen, über Bord werfen *(inf)*; *anger, grief, animosity* begraben; *thought* aufgeben; *differences* vergessen.

◆**put away** *vt sep* **(a)** *(in usual place)* einräumen; *toys also* aufräumen; *(tidy away)* wegräumen ◆ **~ that money ~ in your bag** steck das Geld in deine Tasche; **~ that money ~!** steck das Geld weg!; **to ~ the car ~** das Auto einstellen.

(b) *(save)* zurücklegen.

(c) *(inf: consume)* schaffen *(inf)*; *food also* verdrücken *(inf)*, verputzen *(inf)*; *drink also* schlucken *(inf)* ◆ **he can certainly ~ it ~!** der kann was verdrücken/schlucken!

(d) *(lock up: in prison, mental home)* einsperren.

(e) *(put to sleep) pet* einschläfern.

◆**put back** [1] *vt sep* **(a)** *(replace) see* **put 1 (a)** zurücktun/-stellen *or* -setzen/-legen/-stecken. **(b)** *(postpone) meeting, date* verschieben; *(set back) plans, production* zurückwerfen; *(readjust) watch etc* zurückstellen ◆ **to be ~ ~ a class** *(Sch)* eine Klasse zurückgestuft werden; *see* **clock.**

[2] *vi (Naut: go back)* zurückkehren *(to* nach).

◆**put by** *vt sep* zurücklegen, auf die hohe Kante legen ◆ **I've got a few pounds ~ ~** ich habe ein paar Pfund auf der hohen Kante.

◆**put down** [1] *vt sep* **(a)** *(set down) object see* **put 1 (a)** wegtun/-setzen *or* -stellen/weglegen; *surface* verlegen ◆ **the punch ~ him ~ for (the count of) 8** der Schlag hat ihn bis 8 auf die Bretter geschickt *(inf)*; **~ it ~ on the floor** stellen *or* setzen Sie es auf den Boden; **I simply couldn't ~ that book ~** ich konnte das Buch einfach nicht aus der Hand legen; *see* **foot 1 (b).**

(b) *(lower) umbrella* zumachen, zuklappen; *aerial* einschieben; *car roof* zurückklappen; *lid* zuklappen.

(c) *passenger* absetzen.

(d) *(land)* landen.

(e) *(crush) rebellion* niederschlagen; *rebels* niederwerfen; *crime* besiegen; *prostitution, gambling, drinking* unterdrücken; *rumour* zum Verstummen bringen; *critic, heckler* zum Schweigen bringen; *(reject, humiliate)* demütigen.

(f) (*pay*) anzahlen; *deposit* machen.
(g) (*store*) einlagern.
(h) (*destroy*) *rats, vermin* vernichten; *pets* einschläfern; *injured horse etc* den Gnadenschuß geben (*+dat*).
(i) (*write down*) niederschreiben, aufschreiben; (*on form, in register*) angeben; (*Parl*) *motion, resolution* vorlegen, einbringen ◆ **to ~ one's name ~ for sth** sich *or* seinen Namen (in eine Liste) für etw eintragen; **to ~ one's son ~ for Eton** seinen Sohn für Eton anmelden; **you can ~ me ~ for £10** für mich können Sie £ 10 eintragen; **~ it ~ to** *or* **on my account/my husband's account** schreiben Sie es (mir)/meinem Mann an; **~ it ~ under sundries/on expenses** schreiben Sie es unter Verschiedenes auf/als Spesen an; *see* **paper 1 (a), name.**
(j) (*classify*) halten (*as* für) ◆ **I should ~ her ~ as about 30** ich würde sie auf etwa 30 schätzen.
▼(k) (*attribute*) zurückführen (*to* auf *+acc*), zuschreiben (*to dat*).
[2] *vi* (*Aviat*) landen, niedergehen.

◆**put forth** *vt insep* (*liter*) *buds, shoots* hervorbringen.

◆**put forward** *vt sep* (a) (*propose*) *idea, suggestion, plan* vorbringen; *person* (*for job etc*) vorschlagen; (*as candidate*) aufstellen; (*nominate*) vorschlagen ◆ **he ~ himself/his name ~ for the job** er hat sich für den Posten angeboten. (b) (*advance*) *date, meeting* vorverlegen (*to* auf *+acc*); *schedule* voranbringen, weiterbringen (*by* um); *watch etc* vorstellen.

◆**put in** [1] *vt sep* (a) (*place in*) *see* **put** hineintun/-setzen *or* -stellen/-legen/-stecken; (*pack*) einpacken ◆ **he opened the drawer and ~ his hand ~** er öffnete die Schublade und fuhr *or* griff mit der Hand hinein; **I'll just ~ the car ~** ich stelle eben den Wagen weg.
(b) (*insert in book, speech etc*) einsetzen, einfügen; (*add*) hinzufügen, dazusagen.
(c) (*interpose*) *remark* einfügen.
(d) (*enter*) *application, protest* einreichen; *claim also* stellen ◆ **to ~ ~ a plea of not guilty** (*Jur*) auf „nicht schuldig" plädieren; **to ~ one's name ~ for sth** sich um etw bewerben; *for evening classes, exam* sich für etw anmelden; **to ~ sb ~ for an exam/a race/an award** jdn für *or* zu einer Prüfung/für ein Rennen anmelden/für eine Ehrung vorschlagen; **to ~ the car ~ for a service** das Auto zur Wartung (in die Werkstatt) bringen.
(e) (*install*) *central heating, car radio* einbauen.
(f) (*employ*) *night-watchman* einsetzen; (*elect*) *political party* an die Regierung bringen, ranbringen (*inf*).
(g) (*Sport: send in*) *player* hereinnehmen; *team to bat* (als Innenmannschaft) hereinschicken.
(h) (*devote, expend*) *time* zubringen, verbringen (*with* mit), verwenden (*with* auf) ◆ **we have a couple of hours to ~ ~ at Heathrow** wir müssen uns in Heathrow ein paar Stunden die Zeit vertreiben; **to ~ ~ an hour at the piano/an hour's painting** eine Stunde Klavier spielen/eine Stunde lang malen; **could you ~ ~ a few hours' work at the weekend?** könnten Sie am Wochenende ein paar Stunden Arbeit einschieben?; **he ~ ~ a lot of hard work on the project** er hat eine Menge harter Arbeit in das Projekt gesteckt; **he always ~s ~ a good day's work** er schafft jeden Tag ein ordentliches Arbeitspensum.
[2] *vi* (a) **to ~ ~ for sth** *for job* sich um etw bewerben; *for leave, rise, house also* etw beantragen.
(b) (*Naut: enter port*) **to ~ ~ at a port** in einen Hafen einlaufen; (*call at*) einen Hafen anlaufen; **to ~ ~ to Bremen/harbour** in Bremen/in den Hafen einlaufen; **to ~ ~ for supplies** einen Hafen anlaufen, um die Vorräte aufzufüllen.

◆**put inside** *vt sep* (*inf: in prison*) einsperren (*inf*).

◆**put off** *vt sep* (a) (*set down*) *passengers* aussteigen lassen (*prep obj* aus); (*forcibly*) hinauswerfen (*prep obj* aus) ◆ **the conductor ~ us ~ at the theatre** der Schaffner sagte uns (*dat*) am Theater Bescheid, daß wir aussteigen müßten; **we asked to be ~ ~ at the theatre** wir baten darum, uns (*dat*) am Theater Bescheid zu sagen.
(b) (*lay aside*) *uniform* ablegen, ausziehen; *responsibilities, worries* ablegen.
(c) (*postpone, delay*) *match, appointment etc* verschieben; *decision* aufschieben; *sth unpleasant* hinauszögern ◆ **it's too late to ~ our visitors ~** es ist zu spät, die Besucher (wieder) auszuladen; **to ~ sth ~ till later** etw auf später verschieben; **to ~ sth ~ for 10 days/until January** etw um 10 Tage herausschieben *or* aufschieben/auf Januar verschieben.
(d) (*make excuses to, be evasive with*) *questioner, boyfriend, creditor* hinhalten ◆ **he's not easily ~ ~** er läßt sich nicht so leicht beirren; **I won't be ~ ~ any longer** ich lasse mich nicht länger hinhalten.
(e) (*discourage from doing sth*) **to ~ sb ~ doing sth** jdn davon abbringen *or* (*person also*) es jdm ausreden, etw zu tun.
▼(f) (*repel*) die Lust nehmen *or* verderben (*+dat*) ◆ **to ~ sb ~ sth** jdm etw verleiden, jdm die Lust an etw (*dat*) nehmen; **don't let his rudeness ~ you ~** störe dich nicht an seiner Flegelhaftigkeit; **are you trying to ~ me ~?** versuchst du, mir das mieszumachen (*inf*) *or* zu verleiden?; **I've been ~ ~ the idea** diese Idee ist mir verleidet worden.
(g) (*distract*) ablenken (*prep obj* von) ◆ **to ~ sb ~ the track** jdn von der Fährte abbringen; **he is easily ~ ~ his game** er läßt sich leicht vom Spiel ablenken; **I'd like to watch you if it won't ~ you ~** ich würde dir gern zusehen, wenn es dich nicht stört.
(h) (*switch off*) *light, TV, heater* ausmachen, ausschalten; *power, motor* abstellen.

◆**put on** *vt sep* (a) *coat, shoes etc* anziehen; *hat* (sich *dat*) aufsetzen; *make-up* auftragen, auflegen; (*fig: assume*) *accent, manners* annehmen; *facade, front* aufsetzen, vortäuschen ◆ **to ~ ~ one's make-up** sich schminken; **to ~ ~ an air of innocence** eine unschuldige Miene aufsetzen; **his sorrow is all ~ ~** sein Kummer ist bloß Schau (*inf*); **to ~ it ~** (*inf*) so tun(, als ob); **to ~ sb ~** (*inf*) jdn verkohlen (*inf*); **she's just ~ting it ~ when she talks about her aristocratic relations** sie will nur angeben, wenn sie von ihren adligen Verwandten spricht; *see* **front.**
(b) (*increase, add*) **to ~ ~ weight/a few pounds** zunehmen/ein paar Pfund zunehmen; **to ~ ~ speed** schneller fahren, beschleunigen; **he ~ ~ fifty runs** (*Cricket*) er erhöhte (das Gesamtergebnis) um fünfzig Punkte; **10p was ~ ~ the price of a gallon of petrol** der Benzinpreis wurde um 10 Pence pro Gallone erhöht; **he saw I wanted it and promptly ~ another £10 ~ (the price)** er sah, daß ich es haben wollte, und hat gleich noch einmal £ 10 aufgeschlagen; **he's been ~ting it ~ a bit** er hat ganz schön zugenommen.
(c) *play* aufführen; *party* geben; *exhibition* veranstalten; *film* vorführen; *train, bus* einsetzen; *food* (*on menu*) auf die Speisekarte setzen; (*fig*) *act, show* abziehen (*inf*) ◆ **Sobers was ~ ~ to bowl** Sobers wurde als Werfer eingesetzt; **he ~ ~ quite a show of being angry** er tat so, als wäre er wütend; **she ~ ~ a display of temper** sie inszenierte einen Wutanfall.
(d) (*on telephone*) **to ~ sb ~ to sb** jdn mit jdm verbinden; **would you ~ him ~?** könnten Sie ihn mir geben?
(e) (*switch on*) *light, TV* anmachen, einschalten ◆ **to ~ the kettle/dinner ~** das Wasser/das Essen aufsetzen *or* aufstellen.
(f) *watch etc* vorstellen; *see* **clock.**
(g) **to ~ sb ~ to sth** (*inform about*) jdm etw vermitteln; **to ~ sb ~ to a plumber/garage** *etc* jdm einen Installateur/eine Reparaturwerkstatt *etc* empfehlen; **he ~ me ~ to a first-rate dentist** durch ihn bin ich an einen erstklassigen Zahnarzt gekommen; **what ~ you ~ to it?** was hat dich darauf gebracht?; **to ~ the police ~ to sb** die Polizei auf jds Spur bringen; **to ~ sb ~ to a winner/good thing** *etc* jdm einen heißen (*inf*) *or* todsicheren Tip geben.

◆**put out** [1] *vt sep* (a) (*place outside*) *rubbish etc* hinausbringen; *cat, drunk* vor die Tür setzen ◆ **to ~ the washing ~ (to dry)** die Wäsche (zum Trocknen) raushängen; **to be ~ ~** (*asked to leave*) vor die Tür gesetzt werden; **to be ~ ~ of a restaurant** aus einem Restaurant herausgeworfen werden; **to ~ sb ~ of business** jdn aus dem Markt drängen; **she could not ~ him ~ of her thoughts** er ging ihr nicht aus dem Sinn; **to ~ sb's eyes ~** jdm die Augen ausstechen; *see* **grass.**
(b) (*stretch out, push out*) *hand, foot* ausstrecken; *tongue, head* herausstrecken ◆ **to ~ one's head ~ of the window** den Kopf zum Fenster hinausstrecken; *see* **feeler.**
(c) (*sprout*) *leaves, roots* hervorbringen, treiben.
(d) *cards, dishes, cutlery* auflegen; *chessmen etc* aufstellen.
(e) (*farm out*) *work* weggeben, vergeben (*to* an *+acc*).
(f) (*bring out, circulate*) *pamphlet, book* herausbringen; *propaganda* machen; *statement* abgeben; *message, appeal* durchgeben; *description* bekanntgeben; (*on TV, radio*) *programme* bringen, senden.
(g) (*generate*) *kilowatts etc* abgeben; *horsepower* leisten.
(h) (*extinguish*) *fire, light, candle* ausmachen, löschen.
(i) (*make unconscious*) bewußtlos machen, betäuben; (*boxer*) k.o. schlagen.
(j) (*discontent, vex*) **to be ~ ~ (by sth)** (über etw *acc*) verärgert *or* ungehalten sein; **nothing seems to ~ her ~** sie scheint sich über nichts zu ärgern.
(k) (*inconvenience*) **to ~ sb ~** jdm Umstände bereiten *or* machen; **to ~ oneself ~ (for sb)** sich (*dat*) (wegen jdm) Umstände machen.
(l) (*dislocate*) *knee, shoulder* ausrenken; (*more severely*) auskugeln; *back* verrenken; *see* **nose.**
(m) (*make inaccurate*) (*fig*) *calculations, figures* verfälschen; *instruments* ungenau machen.
(n) **to ~ money ~ at interest/at 12%** Geld für Zinsen/zu 12% (Zinsen) verleihen.
[2] *vi* (*Naut: set sail*) auslaufen ◆ **to ~ ~ to sea** in See stechen; **to ~ ~ of port/from Bremen** aus dem Hafen/von Bremen auslaufen.

◆**put over** *vt sep* (a) *see* **put across.** (b) (*esp US: postpone*) verschieben (*to, until* auf *+acc*).

◆**put through** *vt sep* (a) *plan, reform, proposal, bill* durchbringen; (*+prep obj*) bringen durch; *claim* weiterleiten; *job* durchführen, durchziehen (*inf*); *deal* tätigen.
(b) *+prep obj* (*cause to undergo*) durchmachen lassen ◆ **to ~ sb ~ a test/an exam** jdn einem Test/einer Prüfung unterziehen; **he has ~ his family ~ a lot of suffering** seine Familie hat seinetwegen viel durchgemacht; **his guilty conscience ~ him ~ hell** sein schlechtes Gewissen machte ihm das Leben zur Hölle; **to ~ sb ~ university** jdn durch die Universität bringen; **they really ~ him ~ it!** (*inf*) den haben sie vielleicht durch die Mangel gedreht! (*inf*); *see* **mill, pace² 1 (a).**
(c) (*connect by telephone*) *person* verbinden (*to* mit); *call* durchstellen (*to* zu) ◆ **to ~ a call ~ to Beirut** ein Gespräch nach Beirut vermitteln *or* (*caller*) anmelden.

◆**put together** *vt sep* (a) (*put in same room, cage etc*) zusammentun; (*seat together*) zusammensetzen ◆ **he's better than all the others ~ ~** er ist besser als alle anderen zusammen; *see* **head 1 (c).**
(b) (*assemble*) zusammensetzen; *furniture, machine also* zusammenbauen; *book, essay, menu* zusammenstellen; *meal* auf die Beine stellen (*inf*); (*Jur*) *case* zusammenstellen; *collection, evidence, facts* zusammentragen; *see* **two.**

◆**put under** *vt sep* (*doctor*) betäuben.

◆**put up** [1] *vt sep* (a) (*raise, lift up*) *hand* hochheben; *car window* zumachen; *sash window* hochschieben; *umbrella* aufklappen; *hair* hochstecken; *collar* hochschlagen, hochklappen ◆ **~ 'em ~!** (*inf*) (*hands in surrender*) Hände

➤ LANGUAGE IN USE: put down: 1k → 17.2 put off: f → 7.3

hoch!; (*fists to fight*) na, mach schon!; *see* **back 1 (a), foot 1 (a), wind[1] 1 (a).**
(b) (*hoist*) *flag, sail* hissen, aufziehen.
(c) (*fasten up*) *picture, decorations, curtains* aufhängen; *poster also* anmachen (*inf*); *notice also* anschlagen.
(d) (*erect*) *building, fence, barrier, memorial* errichten; *ladder, scaffolding* aufstellen; *tent* aufschlagen.
(e) (*send up*) *missile, flare, space probe* hochschießen.
(f) (*increase*) *numbers, sales, demands* erhöhen; *rent also* heraufsetzen; *prices* (*company*) erhöhen; (*rising costs*) hochtreiben; *sb's temperature, blood pressure* hochtreiben.
(g) *see* **put forward (a).**
(h) (*offer*) **to ~ sth ~ for sale/auction** etw zum Verkauf anbieten/zur Versteigerung geben; **to ~ ~ resistance (to sb)** (jdm) Widerstand leisten, sich (gegen jdn) wehren; *see* **fight 1 (a), struggle, performance.**
(i) (*feign*) *facade* vortäuschen.
(j) (*give accommodation to*) unterbringen.
(k) (*provide*) *capital* bereitstellen; *reward* aussetzen.
(l) to ~ sb ~ to sth jdn zu etw anstiften.
2 *vi* **(a)** (*stay*) wohnen; (*for one night*) übernachten.
(b) to ~ ~ for election sich zur Wahl stellen.
(c) ~ ~ or shut up! Geld her oder Maul halten! (*inf*).
◆**put upon** *vi +prep obj* (*impose on*) ausnutzen ◆ **I won't be ~ ~ any longer** ich lasse mich nicht länger ausnutzen.
◆**put up with** *vi +prep obj* sich abfinden mit ◆ **I won't ~ ~ ~ that** das lasse ich mir nicht gefallen.
putative ['pju:tətɪv] *adj* (*form*) vermutlich; *father, culprit* mutmaßlich.
put: ~-down *n* (*snub*) Abfuhr *f*; **~-off** *n* (*inf*) faule Ausrede (*inf*); **~-on** (*inf*) **1** *adj* unecht, vorgetäuscht, aufgesetzt; *smile also* falsch; **2** *n* Bluff *m*, Schau *f* (*inf*); **it's just a ~-on** das ist nur Schau *or* (ein) Bluff.
put-put ['pʌtpʌt] **1** *n* (*sound*) Tuckern *nt*.
2 *vi* tuckern.
putrefaction [ˌpju:trɪ'fækʃən] *n* Verwesung *f*.
putrefy ['pju:trɪfaɪ] *vi* verwesen.
putrescent [pju:'tresnt] *adj* (*form*) verwesend.
putrid ['pju:trɪd] *adj* verfault; *smell* faulig; (*fig: corrupt*) zersetzt; (*inf: horrible*) gräßlich, ekelhaft ◆ **the rubbish had become ~** der Abfall war verfault.
putsch [pʊtʃ] *n* Putsch *m*.
putt [pʌt] **1** *n* Schlag *m* (*mit dem man einlocht*) ◆ **he needed a long ~ at the 5th hole** am 5. Loch mußte er aus großem Abstand einlochen.
2 *vti* putten, einlochen.
puttee, putty ['pʌtɪ] *n* (Wickel)gamasche *f*.
putter[1] ['pʌtə^r] *n* (*golf-club*) Putter *m* ◆ **he's a good ~** er kann gut einlochen.
putter[2] (*US*) *vi see* **potter.**
putting ['pʌtɪŋ] *n* Putten, Einlochen *nt*; (*as game*) Putten *nt* ◆ **~ green** kleiner Rasenplatz zum Putten; (*green*) Grün *nt*.
putty[1] ['pʌtɪ] **1** *n* Kitt *m* ◆ **~ knife** Spachtel *m*; **he was ~ in her hands** er war Wachs in ihren Händen.
2 *vt* kitten.
putty[2] *n see* **puttee.**
put: ~-up *adj* (*inf*) **a ~-up job** ein abgekartetes Spiel; **~-upon** *adj* (*inf*) ausgenutzt; **she had a rather ~-upon air** sie guckte so, als fiele ihr ein Zacken aus der Krone; **~-you-up** *n* (*Brit inf*) Schlafcouch *f*.
puzzle ['pʌzl] **1** *n* **(a)** (*wordgame etc*) Rätsel *nt*; (*toy*) Geduldsspiel *nt*; (*jigsaw*) Puzzle(spiel) *nt* ◆ **books of ~s** *or* **~ books for children** Rätselbücher *pl* für Kinder.
(b) (*mystery*) Rätsel *nt* ◆ **it's a ~ to me** es ist mir ein Rätsel.
2 *vt* **(a)** verblüffen ◆ **to be ~d about sth** sich über etw (*acc*) im unklaren sein; **the authorities are ~d** die Behörden stehen vor einem Rätsel. **(b) to ~ sth out** etw (her)austüfteln.
3 *vi* **to ~ about** *or* **over sth** sich (*dat*) über etw (*acc*) den Kopf zerbrechen.
puzzled ['pʌzld] *adj look, frown* verdutzt, verblüfft.
puzzlement ['pʌzlmənt] *n* Verblüffung, Verwirrung *f* ◆ **the look of ~ on her face** die Verwirrung in ihrem Gesicht.
puzzler ['pʌzlə^r] *n* (*problem*) harter Brocken (*inf*).
puzzling ['pʌzlɪŋ] *adj* rätselhaft; *story, mechanism, attitude, question* verwirrend.
PVC *abbr of* **polyvinyl chloride** PVC *nt*.
PVS *abbr of* **(a) persistent vegetative state. (b) postviral syndrome.**
Pvt (*US Mil*) *abbr of* **Private.**
PX (*US*) *abbr of* **Post Exchange** *Laden/Kantine für Armeeangehörige*.
pygmy, pigmy ['pɪgmɪ] **1** *n* **(a) P~** Pygmäe *m*. **(b)** (*small person, fig*) Zwerg *m*.
2 *adj* **(a) P~** Pygmäen-. **(b)** Zwergen-.
pyjama, (*US*) **pajama** [pə'dʒɑ:mə] *adj attr jacket, trousers* Schlafanzug-, Pyjama-; *party* Pyjama-.
pyjamas, (*US*) **pajamas** [pə'dʒɑ:məz] *npl* Schlafanzug, Pyjama *m*.
pylon ['paɪlən] *n* Mast *m*.
pyramid ['pɪrəmɪd] *n* Pyramide *f* ◆ **~ selling** ≃ Schneeballsystem *nt*.
pyramidal [pɪ'ræmɪdl] *adj* pyramidenförmig, Pyramiden-.
pyre ['paɪə^r] *n* Scheiterhaufen *m* (*zum Verbrennen von Leichen*).
Pyrenean [pɪrə'ni:ən] *adj* pyrenäisch ◆ **~ mountain dog** Pyrenäenhund *m*.
Pyrenees [pɪrə'ni:z] *npl* Pyrenäen *pl*.
Pyrex ® ['paɪreks] *n* Hartglas, Jenaer Glas ® *nt*.
pyrite(s) ['paɪraɪt(s)] *n* Eisen- *or* Schwefelkies, Pyrit *m*.
pyromania [ˌpaɪrəʊ'meɪnɪə] *n* Pyromanie *f*.
pyromaniac [ˌpaɪərəʊ'meɪnɪæk] *n* Pyromane *m*, Pyromanin *f*.
pyrotechnic [ˌpaɪərəʊ'teknɪk] *adj* (*lit*) pyrotechnisch; (*fig*) brillant.
pyrotechnics [ˌpaɪrəʊ'teknɪks] *n* (*sing*) Pyrotechnik *f*; (*pl: display*) Feuerwerk *nt* ◆ **a display of ~** (*lit, fig*) ein Feuerwerk *nt*.
Pyrrhic ['pɪrɪk] *adj*: **~ victory** Pyrrhussieg *m*.
Pythagoras [paɪ'θægərəs] *n* Pythagoras *m* ◆ **~' theorem** der Satz des Pythagoras.
Pythagorean [paɪˌθægə'rɪən] *adj* pythagoräisch.
python ['paɪθən] *n* Python(schlange *f*) *m*.
pyx [pɪks] *n* Hostienkelch *m*; (*for sick communion*) Bursa *f*.
pzazz [pzæz] *n* Flair *nt*, Pfiff *m* (*inf*).

Q, q [kju:] *n* Q, q *nt*; *see* **P**.
Q *abbr of* **Queen**.
Qatar [kæ'tɑ:ʳ] *n* Katar *nt*.
QC *abbr of* **Queen's Counsel**.
QED *abbr of* **quod erat demonstrandum** q.e.d.
qt *abbr of* **quart**.
q.t. [ˌkju:'ti:] *n*: **on the ~** (*inf*) heimlich.
qtr *abbr of* **quarter**.
qua [kwɑ:] *adv* als.
quack¹ [kwæk] **1** *n* Schnattern, Quaken *nt no pl* ◆ **~-quack** (*baby-talk*) Entchen *nt*.
2 *vi* (*duck*) schnattern, quaken, quak machen (*inf*) ◆ **what? she ~ed** was?, quakte sie.
quack² **1** *n* (*also* **~ doctor**) Quacksalber, Kurpfuscher *m*; (*hum: doctor*) Doktor, Medizinmann (*hum*) *m*.
2 *adj attr methods* Kurpfuscher- ◆ **~ remedy/medicine** Mittelchen *nt*.
quackery ['kwækərɪ] *n* Quacksalberei, Kurpfuscherei *f*.
quad [kwɒd] *n abbr of* **(a) quadrangle** Hof *m*. **(b) quadruplet** Vierling *m*. **(c)** (*Typ*) **quadrat** Quadrat *nt*, Blockade *f* ◆ **em/en ~** Geviert/Halbgeviert *nt*. **(d)** (*Comput*) **quadruple** ◆ **~ density** Vierfachdichte *f*.
Quadragesima [ˌkwɒdrə'dʒesɪmə] *n* Quadragesima *f*.
quadrangle ['kwɒdræŋgl] *n* **(a)** (*Math*) Viereck *nt*. **(b)** (*Archit*) (viereckiger) (Innen)hof.
quadrangular [kwɒ'dræŋgjʊləʳ] *adj* viereckig.
quadrant ['kwɒdrənt] *n* (*all senses*) Quadrant *m*.
quadrat ['kwɒdrət] *n* (*Typ*) *see* **quad (c)**.
quadratic [kwɒ'drætɪk] *adj* (*Math*) quadratisch.
quadrature ['kwɒdrətʃəʳ] *n* (*Math, Astron*) Quadratur *f*.
quadrilateral [ˌkwɒdrɪ'lætərəl] **1** *adj* (*Math*) vierseitig.
2 *n* Viereck *nt*.
quadrille [kwə'drɪl] *n* Quadrille *f*.
quadrinomial [ˌkwɒdrɪ'nəʊmɪəl] *adj* viergliedrig, vierteilig.
quadripartite ['kwɒdrɪ'pɑ:taɪt] *adj* (*Pol form*) Vierer- ◆ **~ agreement** Viermächteabkommen *nt*; **the ~ division of Berlin** die Teilung Berlins in vier Sektoren.
quadriplegia [ˌkwɒdrɪ'pli:dʒə] *n* Tetraplegie *f*.
quadriplegic [ˌkwɒdrɪ'pli:dʒɪk] **1** *adj* tetraplegisch.
2 *n* Tetraplegiker(in *f*) *m*.
quadroon [kwɒ'dru:n] *n* Viertelneger(in *f*) *m*, Terzerone *m* (*spec*), Terzeronin *f* (*spec*).
quadrophonic [ˌkwɒdrə'fɒnɪk] *adj* quadrophonisch.
quadruped ['kwɒdrʊped] **1** *n* Vierfüß(l)er *m*.
2 *adj* vierfüßig.
quadruple ['kwɒdrʊpl] **1** *adj* vierfach; (*Mus, Pol*) Vierer- ◆ **~ time** (*Mus*) Viertertakt *m*.
2 *n* Vierfache(s) *nt*.
3 *vt* vervierfachen.
4 *vi* sich vervierfachen.
quadruplet [kwɒ'dru:plɪt] *n* (*child*) Vierling *m*.
quadruplicate [kwɒ'dru:plɪkɪt] **1** *adj* vierfach.
2 *n*: **in ~** in vierfacher Ausfertigung.
quaff [kwɒf] (*old, hum*) **1** *vt* trinken, schlürfen (*hum*).
2 *vi* zechen (*old, hum*); (*take a swig*) schlucken ◆ **he ~ed long and deep** er nahm einen langen, kräftigen Schluck.
quagmire ['kwægmaɪəʳ] *n* Sumpf, Morast *m*; (*fig*) (*of vice etc*) Morast *m*; (*difficult situation*) Schlamassel *m* (*inf*) ◆ **the paths were reduced to a ~** die Wege waren völlig aufgeweicht *or* matschig; **he was bogged down in a ~ of tiny details** er hatte sich in einem Wust von kleinen Einzelheiten festgebissen; **a ~ of sin** ein Sündenpfuhl *m*.
quail¹ [kweɪl] *vi* (vor Angst) zittern *or* beben (*before* vor +*dat*).
quail² *n* (*Orn*) Wachtel *f*.
quaint [kweɪnt] *adj* (+*er*) **(a)** (*picturesque*) *cottage, village, scene* malerisch, idyllisch; (*charmingly old-fashioned*) *pub, custom, expression* urig, reizend (*used esp by women*).
(b) (*pleasantly odd*) *idea* kurios, schnurrig, putzig (*used esp by women*); *nickname* originell; *old lady, way of speaking* drollig ◆ **a ~ little dog/dress** ein putziges Hündchen/Kleidchen; **how ~ to live in such an old house** das ist ja urig, in so einem alten Haus zu wohnen; **what a thought, my dear, how ~!** nein so was, meine Liebe, wie originell!
quaintly ['kweɪntlɪ] *adv* **(a)** (*picturesquely*) malerisch, idyllisch; *decorated, finished* malerisch, urig.
(b) *written* schnurrig; *dressed* putzig; *nicknamed* originell ◆ **their little daughter got up and danced so ~ that ...** ihr Töchterchen ist aufgestanden und hat so drollig getanzt, daß ...
quaintness ['kweɪntnɪs] *n see adj* **(a)** malerischer *or* idyllischer Anblick; Urigkeit *f*. **(b)** Kuriosität, Schnurrigkeit, Putzigkeit *f*; Originalität *f*; Drolligkeit *f*.
quake [kweɪk] **1** *vi* zittern, beben (*with* vor +*dat*); (*earth, rafters etc*) beben, erzittern.
2 *n* **(a)** (*inf: earth~*) (Erd)beben *nt*. **(b)** (*of rafters etc*) Beben *nt*.
Quaker ['kweɪkəʳ] *n* Quäker(in *f*) *m*.
Quakerism ['kweɪkərɪzəm] *n* Quäkertum *nt*.
qualification [ˌkwɒlɪfɪ'keɪʃən] *n* **(a)** (*on paper*) Qualifikation *f*; (*document itself*) Zeugnis *nt*; (*skill, ability, suitable quality*) Voraussetzung *f* ◆ **what ~s do you have for this job?** welche Qualifikationen haben Sie für diese Stelle?; **English ~s are not recognized by Scottish schools** englische Zeugnisse werden von schottischen Schulen nicht anerkannt; **the only ~ needed is patience/is a knowledge of French** die einzige Voraussetzung ist Geduld/sind Französischkenntnisse.
(b) (*act of qualifying*) Abschluß *m* von jds Ausbildung ◆ **after his ~ as a doctor/an insurance broker** nachdem er seine Ausbildung als Arzt/Versicherungsagent abgeschlossen hatte; **prior to his ~** vor Abschluß seines Studiums.
(c) (*Sport*) Qualifikation *f*.
(d) (*prerequisite*) Voraussetzung *f*.
(e) (*limitation*) Einschränkung *f*, Vorbehalt *m*; (*modification*) Modifikation *f* ◆ **to accept a plan with/without ~(s)** einen Plan unter Vorbehalt/vorbehaltlos billigen.
(f) (*Gram*) nähere Bestimmung.
qualified ['kwɒlɪfaɪd] *adj* **(a)** (*having training*) ausgebildet; *engineer* graduiert; (*with university degree*) Diplom- ◆ **highly ~** hochqualifiziert; **to be ~ to do sth** qualifiziert sein, etw zu tun; **~ to practice** *doctor, lawyer* zugelassen; **he is/is not ~ to teach** er besitzt die/keine Lehrbefähigung; **he was not ~ for the job** ihm fehlte die Qualifikation für die Stelle; **he is fully ~** er ist voll ausgebildet; **now that you are ~** nachdem Sie nun Ihre Ausbildung abgeschlossen haben.
(b) (*able, entitled*) berechtigt ◆ **to be ~ to vote** wahlberechtigt sein; **I'm not ~ to speak for her** ich bin nicht kompetent, in ihrem Namen zu sprechen; **what makes you think you're ~ to judge her?** mit welchem Recht meinen Sie, sie beurteilen zu können?
(c) (*limited*) *praise, approval* bedingt, nicht uneingeschränkt ◆ **we're only prepared to make a ~ statement about ...** wir können uns nur bedingt *or* mit Einschränkungen zu ... äußern; **his theory is so ~ as to be ...** seine Theorie hat so viele Einschränkungen, daß sie ...; **in a ~ sense** mit Einschränkungen; **a ~ success** kein voller Erfolg; **~ acceptance** (*Comm*) bedingte Annahme.
qualifier ['kwɒlɪfaɪəʳ] *n* (*Gram*) Ausdruck *m* des Grades.
qualify ['kwɒlɪfaɪ] **1** *vt* **(a)** (*make competent*) qualifizieren; (*make legally entitled*) berechtigen, das Recht geben (+*dat*) ◆ **to ~ sb to do sth** (*entitle*) jdn berechtigen, etw zu tun; **his experience qualifies him to make these decisions** aufgrund seiner Erfahrung ist er qualifiziert *or* kompetent, diese Entscheidungen zu treffen; **this qualifies him for promotion** dadurch kommt er für eine Beförderung in Betracht.
(b) (*limit*) *statement, criticism* einschränken; (*change slightly*) *opinion, remark* modifizieren, relativieren.
(c) (*Gram*) charakterisieren, näher bestimmen ◆ **the adjective qualifies the noun** das Adjektiv bestimmt das Substantiv näher *or* ist eine nähere Bestimmung zum Substantiv.
(d) (*describe*) bezeichnen, klassifizieren.
2 *vi* **(a)** (*acquire degree etc*) seine Ausbildung abschließen, sich qualifizieren ◆ **to ~ as a lawyer/doctor/teacher** sein juristisches/medizinisches Staatsexamen machen/die Lehrbefähigung erhalten; **to ~ as an officer** das

Offizierspatent erwerben; **your salary increases when you ~** Sie bekommen nach bestandener Prüfung ein höheres Gehalt.
(b) *(Sport, in competition)* sich qualifizieren *(for* für) ♦ **those who pass the first round of tests ~ for the final interviews** diejenigen, die die erste Testreihe erfolgreich bearbeiten, kommen in die engere und letzte Auswahl.
(c) *(fulfil required conditions)* in Frage kommen *(for* für) ♦ **does he ~ for admission to the club?** erfüllt er die Bedingungen für die Aufnahme in den Klub?; **he hardly qualifies as a poet** er kann kaum als Dichter angesehen werden.

qualifying ['kwɒlɪfaɪɪŋ] *adj adjective* erläuternd; *round, heat* Qualifikations- ♦ **~ examination** Auswahlprüfung *f.*

qualitative *adj,* **~ly** *adv* ['kwɒlɪtətɪv, -lɪ] qualitativ.

quality ['kwɒlɪtɪ] [1] *n* **(a)** *(degree of goodness)* Qualität *f*; *(Comm: categorized also)* Güteklasse *f*; *(of justice, education etc)* (hoher) Stand ♦ **of the best ~** von bester Qualität; **of good/poor ~** von guter/schlechter Qualität, qualitativ gut/schlecht; **~ matters more than quantity** Qualität geht vor Quantität; **they vary in ~** sie sind qualitativ verschieden; **this wine has ~** dieser Wein hat Qualität; **he's got ~** er hat Format; **the excellent ~ of her mind** ihr hervorragender Verstand; **~ of life** Lebensqualität *f.*
(b) *(characteristics) (of person, thing)* Eigenschaft *f*; *(desirable also)* Qualität *f* ♦ **the ~ of patience/selflessness** *etc* Geduld *f*/Selbstlosigkeit *f etc.*
(c) *(nature)* Art *f* ♦ **because of the special ~ of the relationship** da es eine Beziehung besonderer Art war; **the sad ~ of the song** die traurige Stimmung des Liedes.
(d) *(of voice, sound)* Klangfarbe *f*; *(Ling)* Qualität *f*; *(of colour)* Farbqualität *f.*
(e) *(old, hum: high rank)* vornehmer Stand ♦ **the ~** die Oberschicht, die vornehme Welt; **people of ~** Leute von Rang und Namen; **a lady of ~** eine vornehme Dame.
(f) **the qualities** *(newspapers)* die seriösen Zeitungen *pl.*
[2] *attr* **(a)** *goods etc* Qualitäts-; *rating also, mark* Güte-.
(b) *(inf: good)* erstklassig *(inf)*; *newspaper* angesehen, seriös.

quality control *n* Qualitätskontrolle *f.*

quality time *n* intensiv genutzte Zeit.

qualm [kwɑːm] *n* **(a)** *(doubt, scruple)* Skrupel *m*, Bedenken *nt* ♦ **I would feel no ~s about killing that dog** ich würde keine Bedenken *or* Skrupel haben, den Hund zu töten; **without the slightest ~** ohne die geringsten Skrupel *or* Bedenken; **without a ~** ohne jeden Skrupel; **~s of conscience** Gewissensbisse *pl*; **he suddenly had ~s about it** ihn überkamen plötzlich Skrupel *or* Bedenken.
(b) *(misgiving)* Bedenken *nt* ♦ **I had some ~s about his future** ich hatte mancherlei Bedenken wegen seiner Zukunft.
(c) *(old: nausea)* Übelkeit *f.*

quandary ['kwɒndərɪ] *n* Verlegenheit *f*, Dilemma *nt* ♦ **what a ~ he was in!** was für ein Dilemma!; **he was in a ~ as to** *or* **about what to do** er wußte nicht, was er tun sollte; **to put sb in a ~** jdn in Verlegenheit *or* eine mißliche Lage bringen.

quango ['kwæŋgəʊ] *n abbr of* **quasi-autonomous non-governmental organization** Kommission *f.*

quanta ['kwɒntə] *pl of* **quantum.**

quantification [ˌkwɒntɪfɪ'keɪʃən] *n* Quantifizierung *f.*

quantifier ['kwɒntɪfaɪəʳ] *n (Logic)* Quantor *m.*

quantify ['kwɒntɪfaɪ] *vt* quantifizieren *(form)*, in Zahlen ausdrücken.

quantitative *adj,* **~ly** *adv* ['kwɒntɪtətɪv, -lɪ] quantitativ.

quantity ['kwɒntɪtɪ] *n* **(a)** Quantität *f*; *(amount)* Menge *f*; *(proportion)* Anteil *m (of* an *+dat)*, Quantum *nt* ♦ **to prefer ~ to quality** Quantität der Qualität vorziehen; **in ~, in large quantities** in großen Mengen; **how big was the ~ you ordered?** welche Menge haben Sie bestellt?; **a tiny ~ of poison** eine kleine Menge/eine kleine Dosis Gift; **what ~ of yeast was used?** wieviel Hefe wurde benutzt?; **the ~ of meat in these sausages is very small** der Fleischanteil in diesen Würsten ist sehr klein; **in equal quantities** zu gleichen Mengen *or* Teilen.
(b) *often pl (large amount or number of)* Unmenge *f* ♦ **quantities of books/beer** Unmengen von Büchern/Bier.
(c) *(Math, Phys, fig)* Größe *f.*
(d) *(Poet, Phon)* Quantität *f.*

quantity: ~ mark *n* Quantitätszeichen *nt*; **~ surveyor** *n* Baukostenkalkulator *m.*

quantum ['kwɒntəm] *n, pl* **quanta** *(Phys)* Quant *nt* ♦ **the quality of life cannot be measured as a ~** Lebensqualität kann nicht in Zahlen ausgedrückt werden; **the ~ of satisfaction** das (Aus)maß an Zufriedenheit.

quantum: ~ leap *n (Phys)* Quantensprung *m*; *(fig)* Riesenschritt *m*; **~ mechanics** *n sing* Quantenmechanik *f*; **~ number** *n* Quantenzahl *f*; **~ physics** *n sing* Quantenphysik *f*; **~ theory** *n* Quantentheorie *f.*

quarantine ['kwɒrəntiːn] [1] *n* Quarantäne *f* ♦ **to be in ~** in Quarantäne sein; *(ship)* unter Quarantäne liegen; **to put sb in ~** jdn unter Quarantäne stellen.
[2] *attr* Quarantäne-.
[3] *vt person, ship* unter Quarantäne stellen.

quark¹ [kwɑːk] *n (Phys)* Quark *nt.*

quark² *n (cheese)* Quark *m.*

quarrel¹ ['kwɒrəl] *n (in window)* rautenförmiges Fensterglas.

quarrel² [1] *n* **(a)** Streit *m*; *(dispute)* Auseinandersetzung *f* ♦ **they have had a ~** sie haben Streit gehabt, sie haben sich gestritten; **let's not have a ~ about it** wir wollen uns nicht darüber streiten; **to start** *or* **pick a ~** einen Streit anfangen *(with* mit).
(b) *(cause for complaint)* Einwand *m (with* gegen) ♦ **I have no ~ with him** ich habe nichts gegen ihn.
[2] *vi* **(a)** *(have a dispute)* sich streiten *(with* mit, *about, over* über *+acc, over inheritance/girl* wegen *or* um Erbe/Mädchen); *(more trivially also)* sich zanken ♦ **you can't ~ with that** daran kann man doch nichts aussetzen.
(b) *(find fault)* etwas auszusetzen haben *(with* an *+dat)* ♦ **you can't ~ with that** daran kann man doch nichts aussetzen.

quarrelling, *(US)* **quarreling** ['kwɒrəlɪŋ] *n* Streiterei *f.*

quarrelsome ['kwɒrəlsəm] *adj* streitsüchtig; *woman also* zänkisch.

quarrelsomeness ['kwɒrəlsəmnɪs] *n* Streitsucht *f.*

quarrier ['kwɒrɪəʳ] *n see* **quarryman.**

quarry¹ ['kwɒrɪ] [1] *n* **(a)** Steinbruch *m* ♦ **sandstone/slate** *etc* **~** Sandstein-/Schieferbruch *etc.* **(b)** *(fig)* Fundgrube *f.*
[2] *vt* brechen, hauen.
[3] *vi* Steine brechen *or* hauen ♦ **to ~ for sth** etw hauen *or* brechen; *(fig)* nach etw suchen.

♦**quarry out** *vt sep block* heraushauen *or* -brechen.

quarry² *n* **(a)** Beute *f.* **(b)** *(fig) (thing)* Ziel *nt*; *(person)* Opfer *nt.*

quarryman ['kwɒrɪmən] *n, pl* **-men** [-mən] Steinbrucharbeiter, Steinhauer *m.*

quart¹ [kwɔːt] *n (Measure)* Quart *nt* ♦ **to try to put a ~ into a pint pot** *(prov)* Unmögliches versuchen.

quart² *n* **(a)** *(Fencing)* Quart *f.* **(b)** *(Cards)* Vierersequenz, Quart *f* ♦ **~ major** Quartmajor *f.*

quarter ['kwɔːtəʳ] [1] *n* **(a)** *(fourth part)* Viertel *nt* ♦ **to divide sth into ~s** etw in vier Teile teilen; **the bottle was a ~/three-~s full** die Flasche war zu einem Viertel/drei Vierteln gefüllt *or* viertel/dreiviertel voll; **a ~ (of a pound) of tea** ein Viertel(pfund) Tee; **a mile and a ~** eineinviertel Meilen; **a ~ of a mile** eine Viertelmeile; **it was a ~ as big as the other one** es war ein Viertel so groß wie das andere; **for a ~ (of) the price, for ~ the price** zu einem Viertel des Preises.
(b) *(in expressions of time)* Viertel *nt* ♦ **a ~ of an hour** eine Viertelstunde; **a ~ to seven** *(Brit)*, **a ~ of seven** *(US)* (ein) Viertel vor sieben, dreiviertel sieben *(dial)*; **a ~ past six** *(Brit)*, **a ~ after six** *(esp US)* (ein) Viertel nach sechs, viertel sieben *(dial)*; **it's just on the ~** es ist gerade Viertel; **the clock strikes the ~s** die Uhr schlägt alle Viertelstunde; **the clock has just struck the ~** die Uhr hat eben Viertel *or* die Viertelstunde geschlagen; **an hour and a ~** eineinviertel Stunden, fünf viertel Stunden.
(c) *(fourth of year)* Vierteljahr, Quartal *nt* ♦ **paid by the ~** vierteljährlich bezahlt; **a ~'s rent** die Miete für ein Quartal.
(d) *(US)* Vierteldollar *m*, 25-Cent-Stück *nt.*
(e) *(district in town)* Viertel *nt.*
(f) *(area)* **he has travelled in all ~s of the globe** er ist schon kreuz und quer durch die Welt gereist; **they came from all ~s of the earth** sie kamen aus allen Teilen der Welt; **in these ~s** in dieser Gegend.
(g) *(direction)* (Himmels)richtung *f* ♦ **they came from all ~s** sie kamen aus allen Himmelsrichtungen.
(h) *(Naut: direction of wind)* Richtung *f* ♦ **what ~ is the wind in?** aus welcher Richtung kommt der Wind?
(i) *(side)* Seite *f*; *(place)* Stelle *f* ♦ **he won't get help from that ~** von dieser Seite wird er keine Hilfe bekommen; **in high ~s** höheren Orts; **in various ~s** an verschiedenen Stellen; **at close ~s** in der Nähe; *(from nearby)* aus der Nähe; **they were unaccustomed to fighting at close ~s** sie waren nicht an den Nahkampf gewöhnt.
(j) **~s** *pl (lodgings)* Quartier *nt (also Mil)*, Unterkunft *f* ♦ **to take up one's ~s** *(Mil)* sein Quartier beziehen; **to be confined to ~s** *(Mil)* Stubenarrest haben.
(k) *(Naut: for battle)* Posten *m* ♦ **to take up one's ~s** Posten beziehen.
(l) *(Naut: part of ship)* Achterschiff *nt* ♦ **on the port/starboard ~** backbord/steuerbord.
(m) *(mercy in battle)* Schonung *f*, Pardon *m* ♦ **to give ~** Schonung *or* Pardon gewähren; **to ask** *or* **cry for ~** um Schonung bitten; **he showed no ~** er kannte kein Pardon; **no ~ was asked for and none given** es wurde auf beiden Seiten schonungslos gekämpft.
(n) *(Her)* Wappenfeld *nt.*
(o) *(of moon)* Viertel *nt.*
(p) *(Sport: of match)* (Spiel)viertel *nt.*
(q) *(Measure)* ≃ Viertelzentner *m.*
[2] *adj pound, mile* Viertel- ♦ **the/a ~ part** das/ein Viertel.
[3] *vt* **(a)** vierteln; *(divide into four also)* in vier Teile teilen; *beef, horse* (in vier Teile) zerlegen; *traitor's body* vierteilen.
(b) *(lodge)* unterbringen, einquartieren *(also Mil)* (on bei).

quarter: ~-back *n (US Ftbl)* Quarterback *m*; **~-day** *n* Quartalstag *m*; **~deck** *n (Naut)* Achterdeck, Quarterdeck *nt*; **~-final** *n* Viertelfinalspiel *nt*; **~-finalist** *n* Teilnehmer(in *f*) *m* am Viertelfinale; **~-finals** *npl* Viertelfinale *nt.*

quartering ['kwɔːtərɪŋ] *n* **(a)** *see vt (a)* Vierteln *nt*; Teilung *f* in vier Teile; Zerlegen *nt*; Vierteilen *nt.* **(b)** *(Mil)* Einquartierung *f.* **(c)** *(Her)* Einteilung *f* in vier Felder.

quarterlight ['kwɔːtəlaɪt] *n (Brit)* Dreieckfenster *nt*; *(openable)* Ausstellfenster *nt.*

quarterly ['kwɔːtəlɪ] [1] *adj* vierteljährlich.
[2] *n* Vierteljahresschrift *f.*
[3] *adv* vierteljährlich, alle Vierteljahre.

quartermaster ['kwɔːtəˌmɑːstəʳ] *n* **(a)** *(Mil)* Quartiermeister *m.* **(b)** *(Navy)* Steuermannsmaat *m* ♦ **~'s store** Versorgungslager *nt.*

Quartermaster General *n* Generalquartiermeister *m.*

quarter: ~-note *n (US Mus)* Viertel(note *f*) *nt*; **~-note rest** Viertelpause *f*; ~

sessions *npl* vierteljährliche Gerichtssitzungen *pl*; **~staff** *n* (*Hist*) Schlagstock *m*; **~-tone** *n* Vierteltonintervall *nt*.
quartet(te) [kwɔːˈtet] *n* (*Mus, foursome*) Quartett *nt*.
quarto [ˈkwɔːtəʊ] 1 *n* (*Typ*) Quart(format) *nt*.
2 *attr paper, volume* in Quart.
quartz [ˈkwɔːts] *n* Quarz *m* ◆ **~ clock/watch** Quarzuhr *f*; **~ crystal** Quarzkristall *m*; **~ (iodine) lamp** Quarzlampe *f*.
quartzite [ˈkwɔːtsaɪt] *n* Quarzfels *m*.
quasar [ˈkweɪzɑːʳ] *n* Quasar *m*.
quash [kwɒʃ] *vt* **(a)** (*Jur*) *verdict* aufheben, annullieren. **(b)** *rebellion* unterdrücken; *suggestion, objection* ablehnen.
quasi- [ˈkwɑːzɪ-] *pref* quasi-, quasi ◆ **acting in a ~-managerial function** quasi als Manager handelnd.
quatercentenary [ˌkwætəsenˈtiːnərɪ] *n* (*also* **~ celebrations**) Vierhundertjahrfeier *f*; (*anniversary*) vierhundertster Jahrestag.
quaternary [kwəˈtɜːnərɪ] 1 *adj* (*Geol*) quartär; (*Chem*) quaternär, aus vier Teilen bestehend.
2 *n* (*Geol*) Quartär *nt*.
quatrain [ˈkwɒtreɪn] *n* Vierzeiler *m*.
quaver [ˈkweɪvəʳ] 1 *n* **(a)** (*esp Brit Mus*) Achtel(note *f*) *nt* ◆ **~ rest** Achtelpause *f*. **(b)** (*in voice*) Beben, Zittern *nt* ◆ **with a ~ in her voice** mit bebender *or* zitternder Stimme.
2 *vi* (*voice*) beben, zittern; (*Mus*) tremolieren.
3 *vt* mit bebender *or* zitternder Stimme sagen.
quavering [ˈkweɪvərɪŋ], **quavery** [ˈkweɪvərɪ] *adj voice* bebend, zitternd; *notes* tremolierend.
quay [kiː] *n* Kai *m* ◆ **alongside the ~** am Kai.
quayside [ˈkiːsaɪd] *n* Kai *m* ◆ **the ~ bars** die Hafenkneipen *pl*.
queasiness [ˈkwiːzɪnɪs] *n* Übelkeit *f*.
queasy [ˈkwiːzɪ] *adj* (*+er*) **I feel ~** mir ist (leicht) übel; **it makes me ~** da wird mir übel; **a ~ feeling** ein Gefühl *nt* der Übelkeit, ein Übelkeitsgefühl *nt*; **don't do it if you feel ~ about it** wenn dir nicht wohl dabei ist, dann tu's doch nicht.
queen [kwiːn] 1 *n* **(a)** (*also fig*) Königin *f* ◆ **she was ~ to George V** sie war die Gemahlin von Georg V.; **~ of the May** Maikönigin *f*.
(b) (*bee, ant etc*) Königin *f*.
(c) (*Cards*) Dame *f* ◆ **~ of spades** Pikdame.
(d) (*Chess*) Dame *f* ◆ **~'s bishop/pawn** Damenläufer/-bauer *m*.
(e) (*sl: homosexual*) Schwule(r) *m* (*inf*), Tunte *f* (*sl*).
(f) (*sl: rocker ~*) Braut *f* (*sl*).
2 *vt* **(a)** (*Chess*) in eine Dame ver- *or* umwandeln.
(b) (*inf*) **to ~ it** die große Dame spielen *or* heraushängen (*inf*); **to ~ it over sb** jdn herumkommandieren (*inf*).
3 *vi* (*Chess*) sich in eine Dame verwandeln.
queen: ~ bee *n* Bienenkönigin *f*; **she's the ~ bee round here** (*fig inf*) sie ist hier die Nummer eins (*inf*); **~ consort** *n* Königin *f*, Gemahlin *f* des Königs; **~ dowager** *n* Königinwitwe *f*.
queenly [ˈkwiːnlɪ] *adj* königlich; *rule also* der Königin.
queen: ~ mother *n* Königinmutter *f*; **Q~'s Bench** *n* Oberster Gerichtshof.
Queensberry rules [ˈkwiːnzbərɪˈruːlz] *npl* Queensberry-Regeln *pl*.
queen's: Q~ Counsel *n* Kronanwalt *m*, Anwalt *m* der Krone, ≃ Staatsanwalt *m*; (*as title*) Justizrat *m*; **~ English** *n* englische Hochsprache; **don't you understand the ~ English?** verstehst du denn kein Englisch?; **~ evidence** *n*: **to turn ~ evidence** als Kronzeuge auftreten; **Q~ Guide** *n* Pfadfinderin *f* mit den höchsten Auszeichnungen; **~ peace** *n* **to keep the ~ peace** sich ordnungsgemäß verhalten; **a breach of the ~ peace** öffentliche Ruhestörung; **Q~ Scout** *n* Pfadfinder *m* mit den höchsten Auszeichnungen; **~ shilling** *n* **to take the ~ shilling** (*old*) des Königs Rock anziehen (*obs*); **Q~ Speech** *n* Thronrede *f*.
queer [kwɪəʳ] 1 *adj* (*+er*) **(a)** (*strange*) eigenartig, seltsam, komisch; (*eccentric*) komisch, kauzig ◆ **a ~-sounding name** ein komischer Name; **he's a bit ~ in the head** (*inf*) er ist nicht ganz richtig (im Kopf) (*inf*); **doesn't it feel ~ being the only woman?** kommst du dir nicht komisch vor als einzige Frau?
(b) (*causing suspicion*) verdächtig, nicht ganz hasenrein ◆ **there's something ~ about it** da ist etwas faul dran (*inf*).
(c) (*inf*) (*unwell*) unwohl; (*peculiar*) *feeling* komisch ◆ **I feel ~** mir ist nicht gut/mir ist ganz komisch (*inf*); **I came over all ~** mir wurde ganz anders (*inf*) *or* komisch (*inf*).
(d) (*inf: homosexual*) schwul (*inf*).
2 *n* (*inf: homosexual*) Schwule(r) *mf* (*inf*).
3 *vt* (*sl: spoil*) versauen (*sl*), vermasseln (*sl*) ◆ **to ~ sb's pitch** (*inf*) jdm einen Strich durch die Rechnung machen.
queer-bashing [ˈkwɪəˌbæʃɪŋ] *n* Verprügeln *nt* von Schwulen.
queerly [ˈkwɪəlɪ] *adv* eigenartig, seltsam, komisch.
queerness [ˈkwɪənɪs] *n* **(a)** Eigenartigkeit, Merkwürdigkeit, Seltsamkeit *f*. **(b)** (*inf: homosexuality*) Schwulheit *f* (*inf*).
Queer Street *n* (*Brit sl*) **to be in ~** pleite *or* blank sein (*inf*); **we'll really be in ~ if that happens** wenn das passiert, sind wir wirklich in Schwulitäten (*inf*); **I spent most of my life in ~** ich pfeife schon immer auf dem letzten Loch (*inf*).
quell [kwel] *vt fear* bezwingen; *passion* bändigen, zügeln; *riot* unterdrücken, niederschlagen; *anxieties* überwinden.
quench [kwentʃ] *vt flames, fire* löschen; *thirst also,* (*liter*) *desire* stillen; *enthusiasm* dämpfen.
quenchless [ˈkwentʃlɪs] *adj* (*liter*) *flames* unlöschbar.
quern [kwɜːn] *n* Hand- *or* Drehmühle *f*; (*Archeol*) Mahlstein *m*.
querulous [ˈkwerʊləs] *adj* nörglerisch, mißmutig ◆ **a ~ person** ein Querulant *m*.
querulously [ˈkwerʊləslɪ] *adv see adj*.
query [ˈkwɪərɪ] 1 *n* **(a)** (*question*) Frage *f* ◆ **there was a note of ~ in his voice** seine Stimme hatte einen fragenden Unterton; **that raises a ~ as to whether/about ...** das wirft die Frage auf, ob .../das wirft die Frage (*+gen*) ... auf.
(b) (*Typ*) Fragezeichen *nt*.
(c) (*Comput*) Abfrage *f* ◆ **~ language** Abfragesprache *f*.
2 *vt* **(a)** (*express doubt about*) bezweifeln; *statement, motives* in Frage stellen; *bill, item, invoice* reklamieren ◆ **I'm not ~ing your right to do that but ...** ich bezweifle ja nicht, daß Sie dazu berechtigt sind, aber ...; **£500! I'd ~ that if I were you** £ 500! da würde ich an Ihrer Stelle reklamieren; **I ~ whether ...** ich bezweifle, ob ...
(b) (*check*) **to ~ sth with sb** etw mit jdm abklären.
(c) (*with a question mark*) mit einem Fragezeichen versehen.
(d) (*Comput*) *database* abfragen.
quest [kwest] 1 *n* (*search*) Suche *f* (*for* nach); (*for knowledge, happiness etc*) Streben *nt* (*for* nach) ◆ **to go in ~ of sth** (*old, liter*) sich auf die Suche nach etw machen.
2 *vi* **(a)** (*old, liter: seek*) suchen (*for* nach) ◆ **to ~ for riches/truth** nach Reichtümern/der Wahrheit streben.
(b) (*Hunt*) die Beute aufspüren.
▼ **question** [ˈkwestʃən] 1 *n* **(a)** (*Gram etc*) Frage *f* (*to* an *+acc*); (*Parl also*) Anfrage *f* (*to* an *+acc*) ◆ **to ask sb a ~** jdm eine Frage stellen; **don't ask so many ~s** frag nicht so viel; **they'll buy anything, no ~s asked** sie kaufen alles und stellen keine dummen Fragen; **what a ~ (to ask)!** was für eine Frage!; **let me put the ~ another way** ich werde die Frage anders formulieren.
▼ **(b)** *no pl* (*doubt*) Zweifel *m*, Frage *f* ◆ **beyond (all)** *or* **without ~** ohne Frage, ohne (jeden) Zweifel; **his honesty is beyond ~** seine Ehrlichkeit steht außer Zweifel *or* Frage; **there is no ~ but that he has gone** (*form*) es besteht kein Zweifel darüber, er ist fort; **your sincerity is not in ~** niemand zweifelt an Ihrer Aufrichtigkeit; **to call sth into ~** etw in Frage stellen.
▼ **(c)** (*matter*) Frage *f* ◆ **that's another ~ altogether** das ist etwas völlig anderes; **that's not the ~** darum geht es nicht; **the German ~** die deutsche Frage; **success is a ~ of time** Erfolg ist eine Frage der Zeit; **it's not just a ~ of money** es ist nicht nur eine Geldfrage *or* Frage des Geldes; **if it's only a ~ of whether ...** wenn es nur darum geht (*inf*) *or* sich darum handelt, ob ...
▼ **(d)** *no pl* (*possibility, likelihood*) **there is some ~ of a reunion/of him resigning** es ist die Rede von einer Wiedervereinigung/davon, daß er zurücktreten will, eine Wiedervereinigung/sein Rücktritt ist im Gespräch; **there's no ~ of that happening/of a strike** es steht außer Diskussion *or* es kann keine Rede davon sein, daß das passiert/von einem Streik kann keine Rede sein; **that's out of the ~** das kommt nicht in Frage; **the person/matter in ~** die fragliche *or* in Frage *or* in Rede (*form*) stehende Person/Angelegenheit.
2 *vt* **(a)** (*ask ~s of*) fragen (*about* nach); (*police etc*) befragen, vernehmen, verhören (*about* zu); (*examiner*) prüfen (*on* über *+acc*) ◆ **my father started ~ing me about where I'd been** mein Vater fing an, mich auszufragen, wo ich gewesen war; **they were ~ed by the immigration authorities** ihnen wurden von der Einwanderungsbehörde viele Fragen gestellt; **I don't like being ~ed, she said** ich mag diese Verhöre nicht, sagte sie.
▼ **(b)** (*express doubt about*) bezweifeln, zweifeln an (*+dat*); (*dispute, challenge*) in Frage stellen ◆ **I ~ whether it's worth it** ich bezweifle, daß es der Mühe wert ist; **but I'm not ~ing that!** das bezweifle *or* bestreite ich ja nicht; **he ~ed her inclusion on the committee** er äußerte Bedenken gegen ihre Aufnahme in den Ausschuß.
▼ **questionable** [ˈkwestʃənəbl] *adj* **(a)** (*suspect*) fragwürdig ◆ **of ~ honesty** von zweifelhaftem Ruf; **in ~ taste** geschmacklos. **(b)** (*open to doubt*) *statement, figures* fraglich; *value, advantage also* zweifelhaft.
questioner [ˈkwestʃənəʳ] *n* Fragesteller(in *f*), Frager *m*.
questioning [ˈkwestʃənɪŋ] 1 *adj look* fragend.
2 *n* (*by parents, husband*) Verhör *nt*; (*by police also*) Vernehmung *f*; (*of candidate*) Befragung *f* ◆ **after hours of ~ by the immigration authorities** nach stundenlanger Befragung durch die Einwanderungsbehörde; **they brought him in for ~** sie holten ihn, um ihn zu vernehmen.
questioningly [ˈkwestʃənɪŋlɪ] *adv* fragend.
question: ~ mark *n* Fragezeichen *nt*; **to put a ~ mark over sth** etw in Frage stellen; **~-master** *n* Quizmaster *m*.
questionnaire [ˌkwestʃəˈneəʳ] *n* Fragebogen *m*.
question time *n* Zeit *f* für Fragen; (*Parl*) Fragestunde *f*.
queue [kjuː] 1 *n* **(a)** (*Brit: of people, cars*) Schlange *f* ◆ **to form a ~** eine Schlange bilden; **to stand in a ~** Schlange stehen, anstehen; **to join the ~** sich (hinten) anstellen; **a ~ of cars** eine Autoschlange; **a long ~ of people** eine lange Schlange.
(b) (*Hist: pigtail*) Zopf *m*.
2 *vi* (*Brit: also* **~ up**) Schlange stehen; (*people also*) anstehen; (*form a ~*) eine Schlange bilden; (*people*) sich anstellen ◆ **they were queuing outside the cinema** sie standen vor dem Kino Schlange; **we ~d for an hour** wir haben eine Stunde angestanden; **they were queuing for the bus** sie standen an der Bushaltestelle Schlange; **they were queuing for bread** sie standen nach Brot an.
queue: ~-jumper *n* (*Brit*) *jd, der sich vordräng(el)t*; **the ~-jumpers were booed** die, die sich vordräng(el)ten, wurden ausgebuht; **~-jumping** *n* (*Brit*) Vordränge(l)n *nt*; **hey you, no ~-jumping!** he, Vordränge(l)n gibt's nicht! (*inf*).

➤ LANGUAGE IN USE: **question: 1a** → 26.1 **1b** → 26.1 **1c** → 26.3 **1d** → 8.3, 12.3, 16.3 **2b** → 26.3 **questionable: a** → 26.3

quibble ['kwɪbl] [1] *vi* (*be petty-minded*) kleinlich sein (*over, about* wegen); (*argue with sb*) sich herumstreiten (*over, about* wegen) ◆ **to ~ over details** auf Einzelheiten herumreiten; **he ~d about the design** er krittelte am Design herum; **they weren't arguing, just quibbling** sie diskutierten nicht, sondern stritten sich nur über Spitzfindigkeiten.
[2] *n* **these aren't really serious criticisms at all, just ~s** das ist doch keine ernsthafte Kritik, das sind doch nur Spitzfindigkeiten *or* Haarspaltereien; **I've got a few ~s about her work/the design** ich habe ein paar Kleinigkeiten an ihrer Arbeit/am Design auszusetzen; **I hope you don't think this is a ~, but ...** ich hoffe, Sie halten mich nicht für kleinlich, aber ...

quibbler ['kwɪbləʳ] *n* (*petty critic*) Krittler, Kritikaster (*pej*) *m*; (*hair-splitter*) Wortklauber, Haarspalter *m*.

quibbling ['kwɪblɪŋ] [1] *adj* (*petty*) *person* kleinlich; (*hair-splitting*) *person, details, argument* spitzfindig.
[2] *n* kleinliches Getue (*inf*); (*petty criticism*) Krittelei *f*; (*hair-splitting*) Haarspalterei, Wortklauberei *f* ◆ **all this ~ about details** dieses Herumreiten auf Einzelheiten.

quiche [ki:ʃ] *n* Quiche *f*.

quick [kwɪk] [1] *adj* (*+er*) **(a)** (*rapid*) schnell; *answer also* prompt ◆ **be ~!** mach schnell!; (*on telephone etc*) faß dich kurz!; **come on, ~, ~!** komm, schnell, schnell *or* zack, zack (*inf*)!; **and be ~ about it** aber ein bißchen dalli (*inf*); **you were/he was ~** das ist ja schnell gegangen, das war ja schnell; **he was the ~est to be promoted** er wurde am schnellsten befördert; **he was too ~ for me** (*in speech*) das ging mir zu schnell; (*in escaping*) er war zu schnell für mich; **~ march!** (*Mil*) im Eilschritt, marsch!; **it's ~er by train** mit dem Zug geht es schneller; **to be ~ to do sth** etw ganz schnell tun; **he is ~ to criticize other people** er ist mit seiner Kritik schnell bei der Hand; **he is ~ to anger** er wird leicht zornig; **the ~est way to the station** der schnellste Weg zum Bahnhof; **what's the ~est way to the station?** wie komme ich am schnellsten zum Bahnhof?; **what's the ~est way to finish it?** wie werde ich am schnellsten damit fertig?
(b) (*short, ~ly done*) *kiss* flüchtig; *speech, synopsis* kurz; *rest* klein, kurz ◆ **let me have a ~ look** laß mich mal schnell *or* kurz sehen; **we had a ~ meal** wir haben schnell etwas gegessen; **let's go for a ~ drive** komm, wir machen eine kleine Spritztour; **he took a ~ swig of whisky** er trank schnell einen Schluck Whisky; **could I have a ~ word?** könnte ich Sie mal kurz sprechen?; **could I have a ~ try?** darf ich mal schnell *or* kurz versuchen?; **I'll just write him a ~ note** ich schreibe ihm schnell mal *or* mal kurz; **I grabbed a ~ sleep** ich legte mich kurz hin; **time for a ~ beer** genügend Zeit, um schnell ein Bierchen zu trinken; **a ~ one** eine(r, s) auf die Schnelle (*inf*); (*question*) eine kurze Frage.
(c) (*lively, ~ to understand*) *mind* wach; *person* schnell von Begriff (*inf*); *child* aufgeweckt; *temper* hitzig, heftig; *eye, ear* scharf ◆ **the ~er children soon get bored** die Kinder, die schneller begreifen *or* eine schnellere Auffassungsgabe haben, langweilen sich bald; **he is ~ at figures** er kann schnell rechnen; **he's very ~** er begreift *or* kapiert (*inf*) schnell; **he's too ~ for me** mit ihm komme ich nicht mit; **~, isn't he?** (*in repartee*) der ist aber schlagfertig.
[2] *n* **(a)** (*Anat*) empfindliches Fleisch (*besonders unter den Fingernägeln*) ◆ **to bite one's nails to the ~** die Nägel bis zum Fleisch abkauen; **to be cut to the ~** tief getroffen sein; **to cut sb to the ~** jdn zutiefst verletzen.
(b) *pl* (*liter*) **the ~ and the dead** die Lebenden und die Toten.
[3] *adv* (*+er*) schnell.

quick: ~-acting *adj medicine* schnell wirkend *attr*; **~-change artist** *n* (*Theat*) Verwandlungskünstler(in *f*) *m*.

quicken ['kwɪkən] [1] *vt* **(a)** (*also ~ up*) beschleunigen.
(b) (*liter: make more lively*) *feelings* erhöhen; *appetite* anregen; *imagination* beflügeln (*geh*), anregen.
[2] *vi* **(a)** (*also ~ up*) schneller werden, sich beschleunigen ◆ **the pace ~ed** das Tempo nahm zu.
(b) (*liter*) (*hope, interest*) wachsen; (*foetus*) sich bewegen.

quick: ~-fire questions *npl* Fragen *pl* wie aus der Maschinenpistole; **~-firing** *adj* (*Mil*) Schnellfeuer-; **~-freeze** *vt food* einfrieren, einfrosten; **~-frozen** *adj* Gefrier-, tiefgekühlt.

quickie ['kwɪkɪ] *n* (*inf*) eine(r, s) auf die Schnelle (*inf*); (*question*) kurze Frage ◆ **the meeting has to be a ~** mit der Besprechung müssen wir's kurz machen (*inf*).

quicklime ['kwɪklaɪm] *n* ungelöschter Kalk.

quickly ['kwɪklɪ] *adv* schnell.

quickness ['kwɪknɪs] *n* **(a)** (*speed*) Schnelligkeit *f* ◆ **his ~ to appreciate the problem** die Schnelligkeit, mit der er das Problem erfaßt hat. **(b)** (*intelligence*) schnelle Auffassungsgabe ◆ **~ of mind** Fähigkeit, schnell zu denken; **~ of temper** heftiges *or* aufbrausendes Temperament.

quick: ~sand *n* Treibsand *m*; **~set hedge** *n* Hecke *f*; (*hawthorn*) Weißdornhecke *f*; **~-setting** *adj glue etc* schnell trocknend *attr*; *cement* schnell bindend *attr*; **~silver** [1] *n* Quecksilber *nt*; [2] *adj attr* (*fig liter*) quecksilbrig, lebhaft; **~step** *n* Quickstep *m*; **~-tempered** *adj* hitzig, leicht erregbar; **to be ~-tempered** leicht aufbrausen; **~thorn** *n* Rotdorn *m*; **~-witted** *adj* geistesgegenwärtig; *answer* schlagfertig; **the more ~-witted candidates** die Kandidaten mit einer schnelleren Auffassungsgabe; **~-wittedness** *n* Geistesgegenwart *f*; Schlagfertigkeit *f*; schnelle Auffassungsgabe.

quid¹ [kwɪd] *n, pl* - (*inf*) Pfund *nt* ◆ **20 ~** 20 Eier (*sl*); **to be ~s in** auf sein Geld kommen (*inf*).

quid² *n* (*tobacco*) Priem *m*.

quiddity ['kwɪdɪtɪ] *n* **(a)** (*Philos*) Quiddität *f* (*spec*), Wesen *nt*. **(b)** (*liter: quibble*) Spitzfindigkeit *f*.

quid pro quo ['kwɪdprəʊ'kwəʊ] *n* Gegenleistung *f*.

quiescence [kwɪ'esns] *n* Ruhe, Stille *f*.

quiescent [kwɪ'esnt] *adj* ruhig, still.

quiet ['kwaɪət] [1] *adj* (*+er*) **(a)** (*silent*) still; *neighbours, person also, engine* ruhig; *footsteps, music, car, voice* leise ◆ **at night when the office is ~** nachts, wenn im Büro alles still ist; **double-glazing makes the house ~er** durch Doppelfenster wird das Haus ruhiger; **(be) ~!** Ruhe!, ruhig!; **to keep ~** (*not speak*) still sein; (*not make noise*) leise sein; **keep ~!** sei/seid still!; **can't you keep your dog ~!** können Sie nicht zusehen, daß Ihr Hund still ist?; **to keep ~ about sth** über etw (*acc*) nichts sagen; **you've kept very ~ about it** du hast ja nicht viel darüber verlauten lassen; **to go ~** still werden; (*music etc*) leise werden; **could you make the class ~ for a minute?** könnten Sie die Klasse für eine Minute zur Ruhe bringen?; **turn the volume down ~** dreh die Lautstärke zurück; **I can't make the radio any ~er** ich kann das Radio nicht (noch) leiser stellen.
(b) (*peaceful*) ruhig; *evening also* geruhsam; *conscience also* gut; *smile* leise ◆ **things are very ~ at the moment** im Augenblick ist nicht viel los; **business is ~** das Geschäft ist ruhig; **to have a ~ mind** beruhigt sein; **he had a ~ sleep** er hat ruhig geschlafen; **to lead a ~ life** ein ruhiges Leben führen; **yesterday everything was ~ on the Syrian border** gestern herrschte Ruhe *or* war alles ruhig an der syrischen Grenze; **I was just sitting there having a ~ drink** ich saß da und habe in aller Ruhe mein Bier *etc* getrunken.
(c) (*gentle*) *face, character* sanft; *child* ruhig; *horse* brav, gutwillig; *irony* leise.
(d) (*unpretentious, simple*) *dress, tie* dezent; *colour also* ruhig; *style* einfach, schlicht; *elegance* schlicht; *wedding, dinner, funeral* im kleinen Rahmen.
(e) (*not overt*) *hatred, envy* still; *resentment* heimlich ◆ **I'll have a ~ word with him** ich werde mal ein Wörtchen (im Vertrauen) mit ihm reden; **could we have a ~ word together some time?** könnten wir uns mal unter vier Augen unterhalten?; **I caught him having a ~ drink** ich habe ihn dabei erwischt, wie er heimlich getrunken hat; **they had a ~ laugh over it** sie haben im stillen darüber gelacht; **he kept the matter ~** er behielt die Sache für sich; **keep it ~** behalte es für dich.
[2] *n* Ruhe *f* ◆ **in the ~ of the night** in der Stille der Nacht; **on the ~** heimlich; **he left on the ~** er ist still und heimlich weggegangen; *see* **peace**.
[3] *vt see* **quieten**.

quieten ['kwaɪətn] *vt* **(a)** *sb* zum Schweigen bringen; *noisy class, dog* zur Ruhe bringen; *crying baby* beruhigen; *engine* ruhiger machen. **(b)** (*make calm*) *person, conscience* beruhigen; *suspicion, fear* zerstreuen; *pain* lindern.

◆**quieten down** [1] *vi* (*become silent*) leiser werden; (*become calm*) sich beruhigen; (*after wild youth*) ruhiger werden ◆ **~ ~, boys!** ein bißchen ruhiger, Jungens!; **things have ~ed ~ a lot** es ist viel ruhiger geworden.
[2] *vt sep person* beruhigen; *engine* ruhiger machen.

quietism ['kwaɪɪtɪzəm] *n* Quietismus *m*.

quietist ['kwaɪɪtɪst] [1] *n* Quietist(in *f*) *m*.
[2] *adj* quietistisch.

quietly ['kwaɪətlɪ] *adv* (*making little noise*) leise; (*peacefully, making little fuss*) ruhig; (*secretly*) still und heimlich; *dressed* dezent ◆ **he's very ~ spoken** er spricht sehr leise; **a very ~ spoken young man** ein sehr ruhiger junger Mann; **to be ~ confident** insgeheim sehr sicher sein; **I was sitting here ~ sipping my wine** ich saß da und trank in aller Ruhe meinen Wein; **he sat down and ~ died** er setzte sich hin und starb in aller Stille; **he slipped off ~** er machte sich in aller Stille davon (*inf*); **they got married very ~** sie haben im kleinen Rahmen geheiratet; **and all the time he was ~ writing a novel about all of us** und die ganze Zeit hat er still und heimlich einen Roman über uns geschrieben.

quietness ['kwaɪətnɪs] *n* **(a)** (*lack of noise*) Stille *f*; (*of engine, car*) Geräuscharmut *f*; (*of footsteps etc*) Geräuschlosigkeit, Lautlosigkeit *f*; (*of person*) stille Art ◆ **the ~ of her voice** ihre leise Stimme; **then with the sudden ~ of the music ...** und dann, als die Musik plötzlich leise wurde ...
(b) (*peacefulness*) Ruhe *f*.
(c) (*of tie, colour*) Dezentheit *f*; (*of style*) Schlichtheit *f*.

quietude ['kwaɪətju:d] *n* (*liter*) Ruhe *f*, Friede(n) *m*.

quietus [kwaɪ'i:təs] *n* (*old, liter*) Todesstoß *m* ◆ **to give sb his/sth its ~** jdm/einer Sache den Todesstoß versetzen; **he found his ~** er schied von hinnen (*liter*).

quiff [kwɪf] *n* (*esp Brit*) Stirnlocke, Tolle *f*.

quill [kwɪl] *n* **(a)** (*feather*) Feder *f*; (*feather stem*) Federkiel *m*. **(b)** (*also ~-pen*) Feder(kiel *m*) *f*. **(c)** (*of porcupine*) Stachel *m*.

quilt [kwɪlt] [1] *n* (*continental ~*) Steppdecke *f*; (*unstitched*) Federbett *nt*; (*bedspread*) Bettdecke *f*.
[2] *vt* absteppen; (*with padding*) wattieren ◆ **~ed jacket** Steppjacke *f*.

quilting ['kwɪltɪŋ] *n* **(a)** (*process*) (Ab)steppen *nt*; Wattieren *nt*. **(b)** (*material*) Steppstoff *m*.

quin [kwɪn] *n* (*Brit*) *abbr of* **quintuplet** Fünfling *m*.

quince [kwɪns] *n* (*fruit, tree*) Quitte *f* ◆ **~ jelly** Quittengelee *nt*.

quincentenary [ˌkwɪnsen'ti:nərɪ] *n* fünfhundertster Jahrestag; (*also ~ celebrations*) Fünfhundertjahrfeier *f*.

quinine [kwɪ'ni:n] *n* Chinin *nt*.

Quinquagesima [ˌkwɪŋkwə'dʒesɪmə] *n* Quinquagesima *f*.

quinquennia [kwɪŋ'kwenɪə] *pl of* **quinquennium.**

quinquennial [kwɪŋ'kwenɪəl] *adj* alle fünf Jahre (stattfindend); (*lasting five years*) fünfjährig.

quinquennium [kwɪŋ'kwenɪəm] *n, pl* **quinquennia** (*form*) Jahrfünft *nt*.

quinsy ['kwɪnzɪ] *n* (*old*) Mandelentzündung *f*.

quint [kwɪnt] *n (US) abbr of* **quintuplet** Fünfling *m.*
quintessence [kwɪn'tesns] *n (Philos, fig)* Quintessenz *f; (embodiment)* Inbegriff *m.*
quintessential [ˌkwɪntɪ'senʃəl] *adj (liter)* fundamental *(geh)* ◆ **the ~ English gentleman** der Inbegriff des englischen Gentleman; **an instance of his ~ bad taste** ein Beispiel für seinen von Grund auf schlechten Geschmack; **the ~ Catholicism of his whole attitude** seine fundamental *(geh) or* durch und durch katholische Haltung.
quintessentially [ˌkwɪntɪ'senʃəlɪ] *adv (liter)* durch und durch ◆ **they are ~ different** sie sind fundamental *(geh) or* von Grund auf verschieden; **this is ~ Bach** das ist Bach reinsten Wassers.
quintet(te) [kwɪn'tet] *n (Mus, group of five)* Quintett *nt.*
quintuple ['kwɪntjʊpl] [1] *adj* fünffach.
[2] *n* Fünffache(s) *nt.*
[3] *vt* verfünffachen.
[4] *vi* sich verfünffachen.
quintuplet [kwɪn'tjuːplɪt] *n* Fünfling *m.*
quip [kwɪp] [1] *n* witzige *or* geistreiche Bemerkung.
[2] *vti* witzeln.
quipster ['kwɪpstəʳ] *n* Spaßvogel *m.*
quire¹ ['kwaɪəʳ] *n* **(a)** *(24 sheets)* 24 Bogen Papier. **(b)** *(folded, unbound sheets)* Bogen *m.*
quire² *n (obs) see* **choir.**
quirk [kwɜːk] *n* Schrulle, Marotte *f; (of nature, fate)* Laune *f* ◆ **by a strange ~ of fate** durch eine Laune des Schicksals.
quirkiness ['kwɜːkɪnɪs] *n* Schrulligkeit *f.*
quirky ['kwɜːkɪ] *adj (+er) person, character* schrullig.
quirt [kwɜːt] *n (US)* geflochtene Reitpeitsche.
quisling ['kwɪzlɪŋ] *n* Quisling *m.*
quit [kwɪt] *(vb: pret, ptp* **~ted** *or* **~)** [1] *vt* **(a)** *(leave) town, army* verlassen; *this life* scheiden aus; *(give up) job* aufgeben, kündigen ◆ **I've given her/I've had notice to ~ the flat** *(form)* ich habe ihr die Wohnung gekündigt/mir ist (die Wohnung) gekündigt worden; **the dog would not ~ his prey** *(liter)* der Hund wollte nicht von seiner Beute ablassen *(liter).*
(b) *(inf: stop)* aufhören mit ◆ **to ~ doing sth** aufhören, etw zu tun; **~ it!** hör (damit) auf!; **to ~ work** mit der Arbeit aufhören.
(c) *(Comput) job, program* verlassen, aussteigen aus *(inf).*
[2] *vi* **(a)** *(leave one's job)* kündigen.
(b) *(go away)* weg- *or* fortgehen ◆ **notice to ~** Kündigung *f;* **they gave me notice to ~** sie haben mir gekündigt.
(c) *(accept defeat)* aufgeben.
(d) *(Comput)* das Programm/die Datei *etc* verlassen, aussteigen *(inf).*
[3] *adj* **~ of** los *or* frei von, ledig *(+gen) (geh);* **we are ~ of him** wir sind ihn los.
quite [kwaɪt] *adv* **(a)** *(entirely)* ganz; *(emph)* völlig ◆ **I am ~ happy where I am** ich fühle mich hier ganz wohl; **it's ~ impossible to do that** das ist völlig *or* gänzlich unmöglich; **you're being ~ impossible** du bist einfach unmöglich; **are you ~ finished!** bist du jetzt fertig?; **when you're ~ ready ...** *(iro)* wenn du dann fertig bist ...; **he's ~ grown up now** er ist jetzt schon richtig erwachsen; **I ~ agree with you** ich stimme völlig mit Ihnen überein; **he ~ understands that he must go** er sieht es durchaus *or* völlig ein, daß er gehen muß; **he has ~ recovered** er ist völlig *or* ganz wiederhergestellt; **that's ~ another matter** das ist doch etwas ganz anderes; **he said it in ~ another tone** er sagte es in einem ganz anderen Ton; **that's ~ enough for me** das reicht wirklich; **that's ~ enough of that** das reicht jetzt aber; **it was ~ four days ago** (es war) vor mindestens vier Tagen; **not ~** nicht ganz; **you weren't ~ early/tall enough** Sie waren ein bißchen zu spät dran/zu klein; **I don't ~ see what he means** ich verstehe nicht ganz, was er meint; **you don't ~ understand** Sie verstehen mich anscheinend nicht richtig; **that's not ~ your colour** das ist nicht ganz die richtige Farbe für Sie; **he's not ~ the James Bond type** er ist nicht gerade der James-Bond-Typ; **it was not ~ midnight** es war noch nicht ganz Mitternacht; **sorry! — that's ~ all right** entschuldige! — das macht nichts; **I'm ~ all right, thanks** danke, mir geht's gut; **thank you — that's ~ all right** danke — bitte schön; **that's ~ all right, thank you, I can manage alone** das geht schon, danke, ich komme alleine zurecht; **~ (so)!** genau!, sehr richtig!, ganz recht!; **~ the thing** *(inf)* ganz große Mode.
(b) *(to some degree)* ziemlich ◆ **~ likely/unlikely** sehr wahrscheinlich/unwahrscheinlich; **he's had ~ a lot to drink** er hat ziemlich viel *or* ganz schön viel *(inf)* getrunken; **~ a few people** ziemlich viele Leute; **he is ~ a good singer** er ist ein ziemlich guter Sänger; **I ~ like this painting** dieses Bild gefällt mir ganz gut; **yes, I'd ~ like to** ja, eigentlich ganz gern.
(c) *(really, truly)* wirklich ◆ **she was ~ a beauty** sie war wirklich eine Schönheit; **she's ~ a girl/cook** *etc* sie ist ein tolles Mädchen/eine tolle Köchin *etc;* **it's ~ delightful** es ist entzückend, es ist einfach wunderbar; **it was ~ a shock/disappointment/change** es war ein ziemlicher *or* ganz schöner *(inf)* Schock/eine ziemliche *or* ganz schöne *(inf)* Enttäuschung/Veränderung; **that's ~ some bruise/bill/car** *(inf)* das ist vielleicht ein blauer Fleck/eine Rechnung/ein Auto *(inf);* **it was ~ a party** das war vielleicht eine Party! *(inf);* **it was ~ an experience** das war schon ein Erlebnis; **he's ~ the gentleman now** er ist jetzt ganz der feine Herr; **he's ~ a hero now** jetzt ist er ein richtiger Held; **~ the little party-goer, aren't we?** *(inf)* du bist wohl so eine richtige kleine Partynudel, wie? *(inf);* **he's ~ a comedian, isn't he?** er ist ja sehr komisch.

quits [kwɪts] *adj* quitt ◆ **to be/get ~ with sb** mit jdm quitt sein/werden; **to cry ~** aufgeben, klein beigeben; **shall we call it ~?** lassen wir's?; *see* **double.**
quittance ['kwɪtəns] *n* Schuldenerlaß *m.*
quitter ['kwɪtəʳ] *n (inf)* **he's a ~** er gibt immer gleich auf.
quiver¹ ['kwɪvəʳ] [1] *vi* zittern; *(person also)* beben *(with* vor *+dat); (wings)* flattern; *(lips, eyelids, heart)* zucken; *(flesh)* wabbeln.
[2] *n* Zittern *nt;* Beben *nt;* Flattern *nt;* Zucken *nt;* Wabbeln *nt.*
quiver² *n* Köcher *m.*
quiverful ['kwɪvəfʊl] *n (of arrows)* Köchervoll *m.*
qui vive [ˌkiː'viːv] *n:* **on the ~** auf dem Quivive *(dated),* auf der Hut.
quixotic [kwɪk'sɒtɪk] *adj behaviour, gesture etc* edelmütig, ritterlich; *ideals* schwärmerisch, idealistisch ◆ **a foolish ~ act** eine Donquichotterie; **a strange ~ character** ein eigenartiger, an Don Quichotte erinnernder Mensch; **don't you find that a little ~?** finden Sie das nicht etwas versponnen?
quixotically [kwɪk'sɒtɪkəlɪ] *adv see adj.*
quiz [kwɪz] [1] *n* **(a)** Quiz *nt.* **(b)** *(US Sch inf)* Prüfung *f.*
[2] *vt* **(a)** *(question closely)* ausfragen *(about* über *+acc).* **(b)** *(US Sch inf)* abfragen, prüfen. **(c)** *(obs: stare at impudently)* mustern, beäugen. **(d)** *(obs: mock)* necken *(geh).*
quiz: ~master *n* Quizmaster *m;* **~ programme,** *(US)* **~ program** *n* Quizsendung *f;* **~ show** *n* Quiz *nt.*
quizzical ['kwɪzɪkəl] *adj* **(a)** *air, look* fragend; *smile* zweifelnd. **(b)** *(odd)* eigenartig, drollig.
quizzically ['kwɪzɪkəlɪ] *adv look* fragend, zweifelnd.
quoin [kwɔɪn] *n* **(a)** *(outer corner of wall)* Ecke *f; (cornerstone)* Eckstein *m.* **(b)** *(Typ)* Schließzeug *nt.*
quoit [kwɔɪt] *n* Wurfring *m.*
quoits [kwɔɪts] *n sing* Wurfringspiel *nt* ◆ **to play ~** Wurfring spielen.
quondam ['kwɒndæm] *adj (liter)* ehemalig, früher ◆ **his ~ wife** weiland seine Gattin *(obs).*
Quonset (hut) ® ['kwɒnsɪt('hʌt)] *n (US)* Nissenhütte *f.*
quorate ['kwɔːreɪt] *adj (form)* **to be ~** ein Quorum haben.
quorum ['kwɔːrəm] *n* Quorum *nt.*
quota ['kwəʊtə] *n* **(a)** *(of work)* Pensum *nt.* **(b)** *(permitted amount)* Quantum *nt; (share allotted)* Anteil *m; (of goods)* Kontingent *nt* ◆ **the ~ of immigrants allowed into the country** die zugelassene Einwanderungsquote; **import ~** Einfuhrkontingent *nt.*
quotability [ˌkwəʊtə'bɪlɪtɪ] *n* Zitierbarkeit *f* ◆ **something with a little more ~ for the headlines** ein Zitat, das sich besser als Schlagzeile eignet.
quotable ['kwəʊtəbl] *adj* zitierbar, zitierfähig ◆ **a highly ~ author** ein gern zitierter Autor; **~ quips from his speech** geistreiche Bemerkungen aus seiner Rede, die sich als Zitate eignen.
quotation [kwəʊ'teɪʃən] *n* **(a)** *(passage cited)* Zitat *nt; (act)* Zitieren *nt* ◆ **dictionary of ~s** Zitatenlexikon *nt;* **a ~ from the Bible/Shakespeare** ein Bibelzitat/Shakespeare-Zitat; **a two-bar ~ from Bach** zwei Takte, die von Bach übernommen sind.
(b) *(Fin: statement of price)* (Börsen- *or* Kurs)notierung *f.*
(c) *(Comm: estimate)* (Preis)angebot *nt; (for building work etc)* Kosten(vor)anschlag *m.*
quotation marks *npl* Anführungszeichen, Anführungsstriche *pl* ◆ **open/close ~** Anführungsstriche unten/oben; **to put a word in ~** ein Wort in Anführungszeichen *or* -striche setzen.
▼ **quote** [kwəʊt] [1] *vt* **(a)** *author, text* zitieren ◆ **you can ~ me (on that)** Sie können das ruhig wörtlich wiedergeben; **please don't ~ me on this, but ...** *(this isn't authoritative)* ich kann mich nicht hundertprozentig dafür verbürgen, aber ...; *(don't repeat it)* bitte wiederholen Sie nicht, was ich jetzt sage, aber ...; **he was ~d as saying that ...** er soll gesagt haben, daß ...; **~ ... end ~** *or* **un~** Zitat Anfang ... Zitat Ende; **and the ~ liberals** und die Liberalen in Anführungszeichen.
(b) *(cite)* anführen ◆ **to ~ sb/sth as an example** jdn/etw als Beispiel anführen.
(c) *(Comm) price* nennen; *reference number* angeben ◆ **how much did they ~ you for that?** wieviel haben sie dafür verlangt?, wieviel wollten sie dafür haben?
(d) *(St Ex)* notieren ◆ **the shares are ~d at £2** die Aktien werden mit £ 2 notiert.
▼[2] *vi* **(a)** zitieren ◆ **to ~ from an author** einen Schriftsteller zitieren, aus dem Werk eines Schriftstellers zitieren; **... and I ~ ...** und ich zitiere.
(b) *(Comm)* ein (Preis)angebot machen; *(building firm etc)* einen Kostenvoranschlag machen ◆ **we asked six companies to ~** wir baten sechs Firmen um Preisangaben.
▼[3] *n* **(a)** *(from author, politician)* Zitat *nt* ◆ **a two-bar ~ from Bach** zwei von Bach übernommene Takte.
(b) **~s** *pl* Anführungszeichen, Gänsefüßchen *(inf) pl* ◆ **in ~s** in Anführungszeichen.
(c) *(Comm)* Preis *m; (estimate)* Kostenvoranschlag *m.*
quoth [kwəʊθ] *defective vb (obs, hum)* sagte, sprach *(liter).*
quotidian [kwəʊ'tɪdɪən] *adj (form: daily)* alltäglich ◆ **the ~ lives of the people** der Alltag der Menschen.
quotient ['kwəʊʃənt] *n (Math)* Quotient *m.*
qv *abbr of* **quod vide** s.d.
qwerty keyboard ['kwɜːtɪ'kiːbɔːd] *n* Qwerty-Tastatur *f.*

➤ LANGUAGE IN USE: **quote: 2a** → 26.2 **3a** → 26.2

R

R, r [ɑːʳ] *n* R, r *nt* ◆ **the three Rs** Lesen, Schreiben und Rechnen (*with sing or pl vb*).
R *abbr of* **(a) Rex, Regina. (b) river** Fl. **(c)** (*US Film*) **restricted** für Jugendliche nicht geeignet.
r *abbr of* **right** r.
RA *abbr of* **Royal Academy**.
rabbet ['ræbɪt] *n* (*notch*) Nut *f*; (*joint*) Nutnaht *f*.
rabbi ['ræbaɪ] *n* Rabbiner *m*; (*as title*) Rabbi *m*.
rabbinical [rə'bɪnɪkəl] *adj* rabbinisch.
rabbit ['ræbɪt] 1 *n* Kaninchen *nt*; (*fur also*) Kanin *nt* (*spec*).
2 *vi* **(a) to go ~ing** Kaninchen jagen, auf Kaninchenjagd gehen. **(b)** (*Brit inf: also* **~ on**) quasseln, schwafeln, sülzen (*all inf*).
rabbit *in cpds* Kaninchen-; **~ burrow** *or* **hole** *n* Kaninchenbau *m*; **~ hutch** *n* Kaninchenstall *m*; **~ punch** *n* Nacken- *or* Genickschlag *m*; **~ warren** *n* **(a)** Gänge *pl* des Kaninchenbaus; **(b)** (*fig: maze*) Labyrinth *nt*.
rabble ['ræbl] *n* (*disorderly crowd*) lärmende Menge, lärmender Haufen (*inf*); (*pej: lower classes*) Pöbel *m*.
rabble: ~-rouser *n* Hetzer, Volksverhetzer *m*; **~-rousing** 1 *n* Hetze, Volksverhetzung *f*; 2 *adj* (auf)hetzerisch.
Rabelaisian [,ræbə'leɪzɪən] *adj* **(a)** (*of Rabelais*) des Rabelais. **(b)** (*like Rabelais*) im Stile Rabelais'.
rabid ['ræbɪd] *adj* **(a)** (*Vet*) tollwütig. **(b)** (*fanatical*) fanatisch; *reformer also* wild; *hatred also* rasend, wild.
rabidness ['ræbɪdnɪs] *n see adj (b)* Fanatismus *m*; Wildheit *f*.
rabies ['reɪbiːz] *n* Tollwut *f*.
RAC *abbr of* **Royal Automobile Club**.
raccoon *n see* **racoon**.
race[1] [reɪs] 1 *n* **(a)** Rennen *nt*; (*on foot also*) (Wett)lauf *m*; (*swimming*) Wettschwimmen *nt* ◆ **100 metres ~** 100-m-Lauf *m*; **to run a ~ (with** *or* **against sb)** (mit jdm um die Wette *or* gegen jdn) laufen; **to go to the ~s** zum Pferderennen gehen; **a day at the ~s** ein Tag auf der Pferderennbahn; **we were at the ~s yesterday** wir waren gestern beim Pferderennen; **the ~ for the Democratic nomination** das Rennen um die Nominierung des demokratischen Kandidaten; **it was a ~ to get the work finished** es war eine Hetze, die Arbeit fertigzumachen; **a ~ against time** ein Wettlauf *m* mit der Zeit; **his ~ is run** (*fig*) er ist erledigt (*inf*).
(b) (*swift current*) Strömung *f*; (*mill ~*) Gerinne *nt*.
(c) (*liter: of sun, moon*) Lauf *m*.
2 *vt* **(a)** (*compete with*) um die Wette laufen/reiten/fahren/schwimmen *etc* mit; (*Sport*) laufen/reiten/fahren/schwimmen *etc* gegen ◆ **I'll ~ you to school** ich mache mit dir ein Wettrennen bis zur Schule; **the car was racing the train** das Auto fuhr mit dem Zug um die Wette.
(b) *engine* hochjagen; *car* rasen *or* jagen mit ◆ **he ~d me off to the station** er raste *or* jagte mit mir zum Bahnhof.
(c) (*Sport*) *car* ins Rennen schicken; *horse also* laufen *or* rennen lassen.
3 *vi* **(a)** (*compete*) laufen/reiten/fahren/schwimmen *etc* ◆ **to ~ with** *or* **against sb** gegen jdn laufen *etc*, mit jdm um die Wette laufen *etc*; **we're racing against time (to get this finished)** wir arbeiten gegen die Uhr(, um fertigzuwerden); **he ~s at Newmarket** er läßt seine Pferde in Newmarket laufen.
(b) (*rush*) rasen, jagen; (*on foot also*) rennen, hetzen; (*with work*) hetzen ◆ **to ~ about** herumrasen/-rennen *etc*; **to ~ after sb/sth** hinter jdm/etw herhetzen *or* herjagen; **to ~ to get sth finished** Dampf machen, um etw fertigzubekommen (*inf*); **to ~ ahead with one's plans/work** *etc* seine Pläne/Arbeit *etc* vorantreiben; **the project is racing ahead** die Arbeit am Projekt geht mit Riesenschritten voran; **clouds ~d across the sky** Wolken jagten über den Himmel.
(c) (*engine*) durchdrehen; (*pulse*) jagen, fliegen.
race[2] *n* **(a)** (*ethnic group, species*) Rasse *f* ◆ **of mixed ~** gemischtrassig; **of noble ~** (*person*) edler Herkunft *or* Abstammung; (*horse*) (von) edler Rasse; **~ is causing a problem in this town** es gibt Rassenprobleme in dieser Stadt.
(b) (*fig: of authors, poets etc*) Kaste *f*.
race: ~ card *n* Rennprogramm *nt*; **~course** *n* Rennbahn *f*; **~-goer** *n* Rennbesucher(in *f*) *m*; **~ hatred** *n* Rassenhaß *m*; **~horse** *n* Rennpferd *nt*; **~ meeting** *n* Rennveranstaltung *f*.
racer ['reɪsəʳ] *n* Rennfahrer(in *f*) *m*; (*car*) Rennwagen *m*; (*bicycle*) Rennrad *nt*; (*yacht*) Rennjacht *f*; (*horse*) Rennpferd *nt*.
race: ~ relations *n* **(a)** *pl* Beziehungen *pl* zwischen den Rassen; **(b)** *sing* (*subject*) Rassenintegration *f*; **R~ Relations Board** *n* (*Brit*) Amt *nt* für Rassenfragen; **~ riot** *n* Rassenkrawall *m*; **~track** *n* Rennbahn *f*.
rachitic [ræ'kɪtɪk] *adj* rachitisch.
Rachmanism ['rækmænɪzəm] *n* (*Brit*) Mietwucher *m*.
racial ['reɪʃəl] *adj* rassisch, Rassen- ◆ **~ discrimination** Rassendiskriminierung *f*; **~ equality** Rassengleichheit *f*.
racialism ['reɪʃəlɪzəm] *n* Rassismus *m*.
racialist ['reɪʃəlɪst] 1 *n* Rassist(in *f*) *m*.
2 *adj* rassistisch.
racially ['reɪʃəlɪ] *adv* in bezug auf die Rasse ◆ **he is ~ biassed** er hat Rassenvorurteile; **to be of ~ mixed parentage** gemischtrassige Eltern haben; **~ superior** rassenmäßig überlegen; **to be ~ motivated** (*riots etc*) auf Rassenprobleme zurückzuführen sein.
racial: ~ minority *n* rassische Minderheit; **~ prejudice** *n* Rassenvorurteil *nt*.
racily ['reɪsɪlɪ] *adv see adj*.
raciness ['reɪsɪnɪs] *n see adj* **(a)** Schwung *m*, Feuer *nt*; Gewagtheit *f*. **(b)** Rassigkeit, Feurigkeit *f*. **(c)** Rasanz *f*.
racing ['reɪsɪŋ] *n* (*horse-~*) Pferderennsport *m*, Pferderennen *nt*; (*motor ~*) Motorrennen *nt* ◆ **he often goes ~** er geht oft zu Pferderennen/Motorrennen; (*participates*) er nimmt oft an Pferderennen/Motorrennen teil.
racing *in cpds* Renn-; **~ bicycle** *n* Rennrad *nt*; **~ car** *n* Rennwagen *m*; **~ colours** *npl* Rennfarben *pl*; **~ cyclist** *n* Radrennfahrer(in *f*) *m*; **~ driver** *n* Rennfahrer(in *f*) *m*; **~ man** *n* Anhänger *m* des Pferderennsports; **~ pigeon** *n* Brieftaube *f*; **~ stable** *n* Rennstall *m*; **~ tyres** *npl* Rennreifen *pl*; **~ world** *n* Welt *f* des Pferderennsports/Motorrennens; **~ yacht** *n* Rennjacht *f*.
racism ['reɪsɪzəm] *n* Rassismus *nt*.
racist ['reɪsɪst] 1 *n* Rassist(in *f*) *m*.
2 *adj* rassistisch.
rack[1] [ræk] 1 *n* **(a)** (*for hats, toast, pipes etc*) Ständer *m*; (*for bottles, plates also*) Gestell *nt*; (*shelves*) Regal *nt*; (*luggage ~*) Gepäcknetz *nt*; (*on car, bicycle*) Gepäckträger *m*; (*for bombs*) Bombenträger *m*; (*for fodder*) Raufe *f*; (*Tech*) Zahnstange *f*.
(b) (*US Billiards*) *see* **frame**.
(c) (*Hist*) Folter(bank) *f* ◆ **to put sb on the ~** (*lit, fig*) jdn auf die Folter spannen; **to be on the ~** (*lit*) auf der Folterbank sein; (*fig*) Folterqualen leiden.
2 *vt* **(a)** (*pain*) quälen, plagen ◆ **~ed by** *or* **with pain/remorse** von Schmerz/Gewissensbissen gequält *or* geplagt.
(b) to ~ one's brains sich (*dat*) den Kopf zerbrechen, sich (*dat*) den Kopf *or* das Hirn zermartern (*inf*).
(c) (*Hist*) auf die Folter spannen, auf der Folter strecken.
rack[2] *n*: **to go to ~ and ruin** (*person*) verkommen, vor die Hunde gehen (*inf*); (*country, economy*) herunterkommen, vor die Hunde gehen (*inf*); (*building*) verfallen, in Schutt und Asche zerfallen.
rack[3] *vt wine, beer* abfüllen.
rack-and-pinion steering ['rækən'pɪnjən,stiːrɪŋ] *n* (*Aut*) Zahnstangenlenkung *f*.
racket[1] ['rækɪt] *n* (*Sport*) Schläger *m* ◆ **~ press** Spanner *m*.
racket[2] *n* **(a)** (*uproar*) Krach, Lärm, Krawall (*inf*) *m* ◆ **to make a ~** Krach *etc* machen.
(b) (*inf*) (*dishonest business*) Schwindelgeschäft *nt* (*inf*), Gaunerei *f* (*inf*); (*making excessive profit*) Wucher *m* ◆ **the drugs ~** das Drogengeschäft; **to be in on a ~** bei einer Gaunerei mitmischen (*inf*).
(c) (*sl: business, job*) Job *m* (*inf*) ◆ **what's his ~?** was macht er? (*inf*); **what ~ are you in?** was ist Ihr Job? (*inf*).
racketeer [,rækɪ'tɪəʳ] *n* Gauner *m* (*inf*); (*in serious crime*) Gangster *m*; (*making excessive profit*) Halsabschneider *m* (*inf*).
racketeering [,rækɪ'tɪərɪŋ] *n* Gaunereien *pl* (*inf*); (*organized crime*) organisiertes Verbrechen; (*excessive profit-making*) Beutelschneiderei *f* (*inf*) ◆ **drugs ~** Drogenhandel *m*, Drogenschieberei *f* (*inf*).
racking ['rækɪŋ] *adj attr pain* rasend, entsetzlich; *cough* fürchterlich, quälend.

rack: ~ railway *n* Zahnradbahn *f*; **~ rent** *n* Wuchermiete *f*.
raclette [rəˈklet] *n* (*Cook*) Raclette *f or nt*.
raconteur [ˌrækɒnˈtɜːʳ] *n* Erzähler(in *f*) *m* von Anekdoten.
racoon, raccoon [rəˈkuːn] *n* Waschbär *m*.
racquet [ˈrækɪt] *n see* **racket¹**.
racy [ˈreɪsɪ] *adj* (+*er*) **(a)** *speech, style, play* schwungvoll, feurig; (*risqué*) gewagt. **(b)** *wine* feurig. **(c)** (*inf*) *car* rasant.
RADA [ˈrɑːdə] *abbr of* **Royal Academy of Dramatic Art**.
radar [ˈreɪdɑːʳ] *n* Radar *nt or m*.
radar *in cpds* Radar-; **~ beacon** *n* Radarbake *f*, Radarfunkfeuer *nt*; **~ operator** *n* Bediener(in *f*) *m* eines/des Radargerätes; **~ scanner** *n* Rundsuchradargerät *nt*; **~ station** *n* Radarstation *f*; **~ trap** *n* Radarfalle *f*.
raddle [ˈrædl] [1] *n* Rötel, Roteisenstein *m*.
[2] *vt sheep* (mit Rötel) zeichnen ◆ **her ~d face** ihr rouge-geschminktes Gesicht.
radial [ˈreɪdɪəl] [1] *adj* (*Tech*) radial; *beams, bars, lines also* strahlenförmig, strahlig; (*Anat*) Speichen- ◆ **~ engine** Sternmotor *m*; **~(-ply) tyre** Gürtelreifen *m*.
[2] *n* Gürtelreifen *m*.
radiance [ˈreɪdɪəns] *n see adj* Strahlen *nt*; Leuchten *nt*.
radiant [ˈreɪdɪənt] *adj* **(a)** *sun* strahlend; *colours also* leuchtend; (*fig*) *person, beauty, smile* strahlend (*with* vor +*dat*); *face* leuchtend, strahlend ◆ **to be ~ with health/joy** vor Gesundheit strotzen/vor Freude strahlen.
(b) (*Phys*) Strahlungs- ◆ **~ heat** Strahlungswärme *f*.
radiantly [ˈreɪdɪəntlɪ] *adv* strahlend.
radiate [ˈreɪdɪeɪt] [1] *vi* **(a)** Strahlen aussenden; (*emit heat*) Wärme ausstrahlen; (*heat*) ausgestrahlt werden.
(b) (*lines, roads*) strahlenförmig ausgehen (*from* von).
[2] *vt heat, light* ausstrahlen; *electric waves also* abstrahlen; (*fig*) *happiness, health, love* (förmlich) ausstrahlen.
radiation [ˌreɪdɪˈeɪʃən] *n* (*of heat etc*) (Aus)strahlung *f*; (*rays*) radioaktive Strahlung ◆ **contaminated with ~** strahlenverseucht; **exposure to ~** Strahlenbelastung *f*; **~ sickness** Strahlenkrankheit *f*; **~ therapy** *or* **treatment** Strahlenbehandlung *f*; **~ damage/injuries** Strahlenschäden *pl*.
radiator [ˈreɪdɪeɪtəʳ] *n* (*for heating*) Heizkörper, Radiator *m*; (*Aut*) Kühler *m* ◆ **~ cap** Kühlerverschlußdeckel *m*; **~ grill** Kühlergrill *m*.
radical [ˈrædɪkəl] [1] *adj* **(a)** (*basic*) fundamental, Grund-; (*extreme*) *change, reform* radikal, grundlegend; *rethinking, re-examination* total; (*Pol*) radikal ◆ **to effect a ~ cure** eine Radikalkur machen; **~ surgery** Radikalchirurgie *f*.
(b) (*Math*) *sign* Wurzel- ◆ **a ~ expression** eine Wurzel.
(c) (*Bot*) Wurzel-; *leaves* bodenständig.
[2] *n* (*Pol*) Radikale(r) *mf*; (*Math, Gram*) Wurzel *f*; (*in Chinese*) Radikal *m*; (*Chem*) Radikal *nt*.
radicalism [ˈrædɪkəlɪzəm] *n* (*Pol*) Radikalismus *m*.
radically [ˈrædɪkəlɪ] *adv see adj* ◆ **there's something ~ wrong with this** hier stimmt etwas ganz und gar nicht.
radices [ˈreɪdɪsiːz] *pl of* **radix**.
radicle [ˈrædɪkl] *n* (*Bot*) Keimwurzel *f*; (*small root*) Würzelchen *nt*; (*Chem*) Radikal *nt*.
radii [ˈreɪdɪaɪ] *pl of* **radius**.
radio [ˈreɪdɪəʊ] [1] *n* **(a)** Rundfunk *m*; (*also* **~ set**) Radio *nt* ◆ **to listen to the ~** Radio hören; **to hear sth on the ~** etw im Radio hören; **the programmes on the ~** die Radioprogramme *pl*; **he was on the ~ yesterday** er kam gestern im Radio.
(b) (*in taxi etc*) Funkgerät *nt* ◆ **over the/by ~** über *or* per Funk; **to talk over the ~** über Funk sprechen; **they don't have (a) ~** sie haben keinen Funk.
[2] *vt person* per *or* über Funk verständigen; *message, one's position* funken, durchgeben ◆ **to ~ that all is well** funken *or* über Funk durchgeben, daß alles in Ordnung ist.
[3] *vi* **to ~ for help** per Funk einen Hilferuf durchgeben.
radio: ~active *adj* radioaktiv; **~active waste** radioaktiver Müll; **~activity** *n* Radioaktivität *f*; **~ alarm (clock)** *n* Radiowecker *m*; **~ amateur** *n* Funkamateur *m*; **~ announcer** *n* Rundfunkansager(in *f*), Rundfunksprecher(in *f*) *m*; **~ astronomy** *n* Radioastronomie *f*; **~ beacon** *n* (*Aviat, Naut*) Funkfeuer *nt*, Funkbake *f*; **~ beam** *n* Funkleitstrahl *m*; **~ broadcast** *n* Radiosendung *f*; **~carbon dating** *n* Radiokarbonmethode, Kohlenstoffdatierung *f*; **~ cassette recorder** *n* Radiorecorder *m*; **~ communication** *n* Funkverbindung *f*; **~ compass** *n* Radiokompaß *m*; **~ contact** *n* Funkkontakt *m*; **~ control** *n* Funksteuerung *f*; **~-controlled** *adj* ferngesteuert, ferngelenkt; **~ direction finding** *n* Funkpeilung *f*; **~ engineer** *n* Rundfunktechniker(in *f*) *m*; **~ frequency** *n* Radiofrequenz *f*.
radiogram [ˈreɪdɪəʊɡræm] *n* **(a)** (*apparatus*) Musiktruhe *f*. **(b)** (*message*) Funkspruch *m*. **(c)** *see* **radiograph**.
radiograph [ˈreɪdɪəʊɡrɑːf] *n* Radiogramm *nt*; (*X-ray*) Röntgenogramm, Röntgenbild *nt*.
radiographer [ˌreɪdɪˈɒɡrəfəʳ] *n* Röntgenassistent(in *f*) *m*.
radiography [ˌreɪdɪˈɒɡrəfɪ] *n* Röntgenographie *f*.
radio: ~ ham *n* Funkamateur *m*; **~isotope** *n* Radioisotop *nt*; **~ link** *n* Funkverbindung *f*.
radiological [ˌreɪdɪəʊˈlɒdʒɪkəl] *adj* radiologisch.
radiologist [ˌreɪdɪˈɒlədʒɪst] *n* Röntgenologe *m*, Röntgenologin *f*.
radiology [ˌreɪdɪˈɒlədʒɪ] *n* Radiologie *f*; (*X-ray also*) Röntgenologie *f*.
radio: ~ mast *n* Funkmast *m*; **~-pager** *n* Funkrufempfänger, Piepser (*inf*) *m*; **~-paging** *n* Funkruf *m*; **~ programme** *n* Radio- *or* Rundfunkprogramm *nt*.
radioscopy [ˌreɪdɪˈɒskəpɪ] *n* Radioskopie *f*; (*Med*) Röntgenuntersuchung *f*.
radio: ~ set *n* Radioapparat *m*, Rundfunkgerät *nt*; **~ station** *n* Rundfunkstation *f*; **~ taxi** *n* Funktaxi *nt*; **~telephone** *n* Funksprechgerät *nt*; **~telephony** *n* Sprechfunk *m*; **~ telescope** *n* Radioteleskop *nt*; **~therapy** *n* Strahlen- *or* Röntgentherapie *f*; **~ van** *n* Funk- *or* Übertragungswagen *m*; **~ wave** *n* Radiowelle *f*.
radish [ˈrædɪʃ] *n* (*small red variety*) Radieschen *nt*; (*all other varieties*) Rettich *m*.
radium [ˈreɪdɪəm] *n* Radium *nt* ◆ **~ treatment** (*Med*) Radiumtherapie *f*.
radius [ˈreɪdɪəs] *n, pl* **radii (a)** (*Math*) Radius, Halbmesser *m*; (*of ship, aircraft*) Aktionsradius, Wirkungsbereich *m* ◆ **within a 6 km ~ (of Hamburg)** in einem Umkreis von 6 km (von Hamburg). **(b)** (*Anat*) Speiche *f*.
radix [ˈreɪdɪks] *n, pl* **radices** (*Math*) Grundzahl *f*.
radon [ˈreɪdɒn] *n* (*Chem*) Radon *nt*.
RAF *abbr of* **Royal Air Force** königliche (britische) Luftwaffe.
raffia [ˈræfɪə] *n* (*plant*) Raphia(palme) *f*; (*fibre*) Raphia(bast *m*), Raffia(bast *m*) *f*; (*for handicraft, garden*) Bast *m* ◆ **~ work** Bastarbeit *f*; **~ table-mat** Bastuntersetzer *m*.
raffish [ˈræfɪʃ] *adj appearance* flott, verwegen.
raffle [ˈræfl] [1] *n* Tombola, Verlosung *f* ◆ **~ ticket** Los *nt*.
[2] *vt* (*also* **~ off**) verlosen.
raft [rɑːft] *n* Floß *nt*.
rafter [ˈrɑːftəʳ] *n* (Dach)sparren *m*.
rag¹ [ræɡ] *n* **(a)** Lumpen, Fetzen *m*; (*for cleaning*) Lappen, Lumpen *m*; (*for paper*) Lumpen, Hadern *pl*; (*inf: shirt, dress*) Fetzen *m* (*inf*) ◆ **~s** Lumpen *pl*; (*inf: clothes*) Klamotten *pl* (*inf*); **in ~s** zerlumpt, abgerissen; **~s and tatters** abgerissene Lumpen *pl*; **in ~s and tatters** zerlumpt und abgerissen; **to go from ~s to riches** (*by luck*) vom armen Schlucker zum reichen Mann/zur reichen Frau werden; (*by work*) vom Tellerwäscher zum Millionär werden; **to feel like a wet ~** (*inf*) total ausgelaugt sein (*inf*); *see* **red ~**.
(b) (*pej inf: newspaper*) Käseblatt *nt*.
rag² [1] *n* (*Brit inf*) (*joke*) Jux *m* (*inf*); (*Univ*) *karnevalistische Veranstaltung der Studenten zu Wohltätigkeitszwecken* ◆ **for a ~** aus Jux (*inf*); **~ week** (*Univ*) *Woche, in der Studenten durch Aufführungen Geld für Wohltätigkeitszwecke sammeln.*
[2] *vt* **(a)** (*tease*) aufziehen, foppen.
(b) (*Brit: play a trick on*) **to ~ sb** jdm einen Streich spielen, einen Jux mit jdm machen (*inf*).
ragamuffin [ˈræɡəˌmʌfɪn] *n* Vogelscheuche *f* (*inf*); (*boy*) Bengel *m*; (*girl*) Göre *f* ◆ **you little ~** du kleiner Fratz.
rag: ~-and-bone man *n* Lumpenhändler, Lumpensammler *m*; **~bag** *n* Lumpensack *m*; (*woman*) Schlampe *f*; (*fig*) Sammelsurium *nt* (*inf*); **~ doll** *n* Flickenpuppe *f*.
rage [reɪdʒ] [1] *n* Wut *f*, Zorn *m*; (*liter*) (*of sea*) Toben *nt*; (*of storm*) Toben, Rasen *nt* ◆ **to be in a ~** wütend sein, toben; **to fly into a ~** einen Wutanfall bekommen; **fit of ~** Wutanfall *m*; **to put sb into a ~** jdn wütend *or* (*stronger*) rasend machen; **to be (all) the ~** (*inf*) der letzte Schrei sein (*inf*).
[2] *vi* toben, rasen; (*sea*) toben ◆ **to ~ against sb/sth** gegen jdn/etw wettern.
ragged [ˈræɡɪd] *adj person, clothes* zerlumpt, abgerissen; *beard, hair* zottig, strähnig; *coastline, rocks* zerklüftet; *wound* schartig, zerfetzt; *edge, cuff* ausgefranst; (*fig*) *performance, singing* stümperhaft ◆ **to run sb ~** (*inf: exhaust*) jdn fertigmachen (*inf*); **~ right** (*Typ*) Flattersatz *m*; **to set sth ~ left/right** rechts-/linksbündig setzen.
ragged robin *n* Kuckuck-Lichtnelke, Kuckucksnelke *f*.
raging [ˈreɪdʒɪŋ] [1] *adj person* wütend; *fever* heftig, sehr hoch; *thirst* brennend; *pain, toothache* rasend; *storm, sea, wind* tobend ◆ **he was ~** er tobte; **to be in a ~ temper** eine fürchterliche Laune haben; **to be ~ mad** (*inf*) eine Stinkwut haben (*inf*).
[2] *n* (*of person, storm*) Toben, Rasen *nt*; (*of sea*) Toben *nt*.
raglan [ˈræɡlən] [1] *adj* Raglan-.
[2] *n* (*coat*) Mantel *m* mit Raglanärmeln.
rag man *n see* **rag-and-bone man**.
ragout [ˈræɡuː] *n* (*Cook*) Ragout *nt*.
rag: ~ rug *n* Flickenteppich *m*; **~, tag and bobtail** *n* Hinz und Kunz (+*pl or sing vb*); **the ~, tag and bobtail of society** Krethi und Plethi (+*pl or sing vb*); **~time** *n* Ragtime *m*; **~ trade** *n* (*sl*) Kleiderbranche *f*; **~weed** *n* (*Bot*) beifußblättrige Ambrosia; **~wort** *n* (*Bot*) Jakobskraut *nt*.
raid [reɪd] [1] *n* Überfall *m*; (*Mil also*) Angriff *m*; (*air ~*) Luftangriff *m*; (*police ~*) Razzia *f*; (*by thieves*) Einbruch *m*.
[2] *vt* **(a)** überfallen; (*police*) eine Razzia durchführen in (+*dat*); (*thieves*) einbrechen in (+*acc*). **(b)** (*fig hum*) plündern.
raider [ˈreɪdəʳ] *n* (*bandit*) Gangster *m*; (*thief*) Einbrecher *m*; (*in bank*) Bankräuber *m*; (*ship*) Kaperschiff *nt*; (*plane*) Überfallflugzeug *nt*.
rail¹ [reɪl] [1] *n* **(a)** (*on bridge, stairs etc*) Geländer *nt*; (*Naut*) Reling *f*; (*curtain ~*) Schiene *f*; (*towel ~*) Handtuchhalter *m*; (*altar ~*) Kommunionbank *f* ◆ **~s** (*fence*) Umzäunung *f*.
(b) (*for train, tram*) Schiene *f*, Gleis *nt* ◆ **to go off the ~s** (*lit*) entgleisen; (*fig*) (*morally*) auf die schiefe Bahn geraten; (*mentally*) zu spinnen anfangen (*inf*).
(c) (*~ travel, ~way*) die (Eisen)bahn ◆ **to travel by ~** mit der Bahn fahren.
[2] *vt goods* per *or* mit der Bahn verschicken *or* senden.
◆**rail in** *vt sep* einzäunen.
◆**rail off** *vt sep* abzäunen ◆ **~ed ~ from the road** gegen die Straße abgezäunt.
rail² *vi* **to ~ at/against sb** jdn beschimpfen/über jdn schimpfen; **to ~ at fate** mit dem Schicksal hadern.
rail *in cpds* Bahn-; **~car** *n* Triebwagen *m*; **~card** *n* (*Rail*) ≈ Wochen-/Monats(fahr)karte *f*; (*for young people also*) ≈ Juniorenpaß *m*; (*for families also*)

≃ Familienpaß *m*; (*for senior citizens also*) ≃ Seniorenpaß *m*; **~head** *n* Endbahnhof *m*; (*end of track*) Gleisende *nt*.

railing ['reɪlɪŋ] *n* (*rail*) Geländer *nt*; (*Naut*) Reling *f*; (*fence: also* **~s**) Zaun *m*.

railroad ['reɪlrəʊd] [1] *n* (*US*) (Eisen)bahn *f*.

[2] *vt* **(a)** (*US*) *goods* per *or* mit der Bahn befördern. **(b)** (*esp US inf*) **to ~ a bill** eine Gesetzesvorlage durchpeitschen; **to ~ sb into doing sth** jdn dazu hetzen, etw zu tun.

rail: ~ strike *n* Bahnstreik *m*; **~ traffic** *n* Bahnverkehr *m*.

railway ['reɪlweɪ] *n* (*esp Brit*) (Eisen)bahn *f*; (*track*) Gleis *nt*.

railway: ~ carriage *n* (*Brit*) Eisenbahnwagen *m*; **~ crossing** *n* Bahnübergang *m*; **~ engine** *n* Lokomotive *f*; **~ engineering** *n* Bahntechnik, Bahnbautechnik *f*; **~ guide** *n* Kursbuch *nt*; **~ line** *n* (Eisen)bahnlinie *f*; (*track*) Gleis *nt*; **~man** *n* Eisenbahner *m*; **~ network** *n* Bahnnetz *nt*; **~ porter** *n* Gepäckträger *m*; **~ station** *n* Bahnhof *m*.

railworker ['reɪlwɜːkəʳ] *n* Bahnarbeiter(in *f*) *m*.

raiment ['reɪmənt] *n* (*liter*) Gewand *nt* (*liter*).

rain [reɪn] [1] *n* **(a)** Regen *m* ♦ **in the ~** im Regen; **~ or shine, come ~ or come shine** (*lit*) ob es regnet oder schneit; (*fig*) was auch geschieht; **the ~s** die Regenzeit; *see* **right**.

(b) (*fig: of arrows, bullets, blows*) Hagel *m*.

[2] *vti impers* (*lit, fig*) regnen ♦ **it is ~ing** es regnet; **it never ~s but it pours** (*prov*) ein Unglück kommt selten allein (*prov*); **it's ~ing buckets** (*inf*) *or* **cats and dogs** (*inf*) es gießt wie aus Kübeln, es schüttet nur so (*inf*).

[3] *vt* **to ~ blows on sb** einen Hagel von Schlägen auf jdn niedergehen lassen.

♦**rain down** *vi* (*blows etc*) niederprasseln (*upon* auf +*acc*).

♦**rain off,** (*US*) **rain out** *vt sep* **to be ~ed ~** wegen Regen nicht stattfinden; (*abandoned*) wegen Regen abgebrochen werden.

rain *in cpds* Regen-; **~ belt** *n* Regenzone *f*.

rainbow ['reɪnbəʊ] *n* Regenbogen *m* ♦ **a dress (in) all the colours of the ~** ein Kleid in allen Regenbogenfarben; **~ trout** Regenbogenforelle *f*.

rain: ~-check *n* (*US*) **to take a ~-check** (*fig inf*) die Sache auf ein andermal verschieben; **~ cloud** *n* Regenwolke *f*; **~coat** *n* Regenmantel *m*; **~drop** *n* Regentropfen *m*; **~fall** *n* Niederschlag *m*; **~ forest** *n* Regenwald *m*; **~ gauge** *n* Regenmesser *m*; **~ hood** *n* Regenhaube *f*; (*of anorak etc*) Kapuze *f*.

raininess ['reɪnɪnɪs] *n* regnerisches Wetter, Regenwetter *nt*; (*of season, area*) Neigung *f* zu regnerischem Wetter.

rain: ~less *adj* niederschlagsfrei (*Met*), ohne Regen, regenfrei; **~proof** [1] *adj* wasserfest, wasserdicht; [2] *vt* imprägnieren; **~storm** *n* schwere Regenfälle *pl*; **~water** *n* Regenwasser *nt*; **~wear** *n* Regenkleidung *f*.

rainy ['reɪnɪ] *adj* (+*er*) regnerisch, Regen-; *day also* verregnet; *area also* regenreich ♦ **~ season** Regenzeit *f*; **to keep sth for a ~ day** (*fig*) etw für schlechte Zeiten zurücklegen *or* aufheben.

➤ **raise** [reɪz] [1] *vt* **(a)** (*lift*) *object, arm, head* heben; *blinds, eyebrow,* (*Theat*) *curtain* hochziehen; (*Naut*) *anchor* lichten; *sunken ship* heben; (*Med*) *blister* bilden ♦ **to ~ one's hat to sb** (*lit, fig*) den Hut vor jdm ziehen *or* lüften; **to ~ one's glass to sb** jdm zutrinken; **to ~ one's fist to sb** jdm mit der Faust drohen; **to ~ one's hand against sb** die Hand gegen jdn erheben; **to ~ one's eyes to heaven** die Augen zum Himmel erheben; **to ~ the pitch** (*Mus*) eine höhere Tonlage wählen; **to ~ sb from the dead** jdn von den Toten erwecken; **to ~ one's voice** lauter sprechen; (*get angry*) laut werden; **not a voice was ~d in protest** nicht eine Stimme des Protests wurde laut; **to ~ sb's/one's hopes** jdm/sich Hoffnung machen; **to ~ the people to revolt** das Volk zur Revolution aufhetzen; **to ~ the roof** (*fig*) (*with noise*) das Haus zum Beben bringen; (*with approval*) in Begeisterungsstürme ausbrechen; (*with anger*) fürchterlich toben; **the Opposition ~d the roof at the Government's proposals** die Opposition buhte gewaltig, als sie die Vorschläge der Regierung hörte.

(b) (*in height*) (*by* um) *wall, ceiling* erhöhen; *level* anheben.

(c) (*increase*) (*to* auf +*acc*) erhöhen; *price also, limit, standard* anheben, heraufsetzen ♦ **to ~ the tone** das Niveau heben.

(d) (*promote*) (er)heben (*to* in +*acc*); *see* **peerage**.

(e) (*build, erect*) *statue, building* errichten.

➤ **(f)** (*create, evoke*) *problem, difficulty* schaffen, aufwerfen; *question* aufwerfen, vorbringen; *objection* erheben; *suspicion, hope* (er)wecken; *spirits, ghosts* (herauf)beschwören; *mutiny* anzetteln ♦ **to ~ a cheer/laugh/smile** (*in others*) Beifall ernten/Gelächter ernten/ein Lächeln hervorrufen; (*oneself*) Beifall spenden/lachen/lächeln; **to ~ a protest** protestieren; **to ~ hell** (*inf*) einen Höllenspektakel machen (*inf*).

(g) (*grow, breed*) *children* aufziehen, großziehen; *animals* aufziehen; *crops* anbauen ♦ **to ~ a family** Kinder großziehen.

(h) (*get together*) *army* auf die Beine stellen, aufstellen; *taxes* erheben; *funds, money* aufbringen, auftreiben; *loan, mortgage* aufnehmen.

(i) (*end*) *siege, embargo* aufheben, beenden.

(j) (*Cards*) erhöhen ♦ **I'll ~ you 6** (*Poker*) ich erhöhe um 6.

(k) (*Telec: contact*) Funkkontakt aufnehmen mit.

(l) (*Math*) **to ~ a number to the power of 2/3** *etc* eine Zahl in die zweite/dritte *etc* Potenz erheben.

[2] *n* **(a)** (*in salary*) Gehaltserhöhung *f*; (*in wages*) Lohnerhöhung *f*.

(b) (*Cards*) Erhöhung *f*.

♦**raise up** *vt sep* heben ♦ **he ~d himself ~ on his elbow** er stützte sich auf den Ellbogen.

raised [reɪzd] *adj arm* angehoben; *voice* erhoben, laut ♦ **~ type** (*Typ*) erhabener Druck; *see* **eyebrow**.

raisin ['reɪzən] *n* Rosine *f*.

➤ LANGUAGE IN USE: **raise: 1f** → 26.1, 26.3

raj [rɑːdʒ] *n* Herrschaft *f* eines Radscha ♦ **the British R~** die britische Oberherrschaft in Indien.

rajah ['rɑːdʒə] *n* Radscha *m*.

rake¹ [reɪk] [1] *n* (*garden ~, croupier's ~*) Harke *f*, Rechen *m* (*dial*); (*for grate*) Kaminrechen *m*; (*for furnace*) Ofenkrücke *f*.

[2] *vt* **(a)** *garden, hay, leaves* harken, rechen (*dial*); *grate* säubern; *fire* ausräumen.

(b) (*machine gun, searchlight*) bestreichen.

[3] *vi* (*search*) **to ~ around** *or* **about** (herum)wühlen *or* (herum)stöbern; **to ~ among** *or* **through old papers** in alten Papieren wühlen *or* stöbern.

♦**rake in** *vt sep* (*inf*) *money* kassieren (*inf*) ♦ **he's raking it ~** er scheffelt das Geld nur so.

♦**rake out** *vt sep fire* ausräumen; (*inf*) *information* auskundschaften, herausfinden.

♦**rake over** *vt sep earth, plot* harken; (*fig*) *past* begraben.

♦**rake up** *vt sep* **(a)** *leaves* zusammenharken. **(b)** (*fig*) *people, things* auftreiben (*inf*); *money also* zusammenkratzen (*inf*). **(c)** *fire* schüren; (*fig*) *quarrel* schüren; *memories, grievance* aufwärmen ♦ **to ~ ~ the past** in der Vergangenheit wühlen.

rake² *n* (*person*) Lebemann, Schwerenöter *m*.

rake³ [1] *n* (*Naut: of mast*) schiefe Stellung, Neigung *f*; (*of stage, seating*) Neigung *f*; (*Aviat: of wing*) Anstellwinkel *m*; (*Aut: of seat*) verstellbare Rückenlehne.

[2] *vi* (*Naut*) sich neigen; (*Theat*) ansteigen.

rake-off ['reɪkɒf] *n* (*inf*) (Gewinn)anteil *m*, Prozente *pl* (*inf*).

rakish¹ ['reɪkɪʃ] *adj person, appearance* flott, verwegen ♦ **to wear one's hat at a ~ angle** den Hut verwegen aufgesetzt haben.

rakish² *adj* (*Naut*) schnittig.

rakishly ['reɪkɪʃlɪ] *adv* flott, verwegen ♦ **..., he said ~** ..., sagte er verwegen.

rally¹ ['rælɪ] [1] *n* **(a)** (*gathering*) (Massen)versammlung *f*; (*with speaker*) Kundgebung *f*; (*of troops*) (Ver)sammlung *f*; (*Aut*) Rallye *f* ♦ **electoral ~** Wahlversammlung *f*; **peace ~** Friedenskundgebung *f*; **youth ~** Jugendtreffen *nt*. **(b)** (*in health, spirits*) Erholung *f*. **(c)** (*Tennis*) Ballwechsel *m*. **(d)** (*St Ex*) Erholung *f*.

[2] *vt troops, supporters* (ver)sammeln, zusammenrufen ♦ **to ~ one's strength** all seine Kräfte sammeln *or* zusammennehmen.

[3] *vi* **(a)** (*sick person*) Fortschritte machen; (*St Ex*) sich erholen.

(b) (*troops, people*) sich sammeln, sich versammeln ♦ **~ing point** Sammelplatz *m*; **to ~ to the support of sb** (*fig*) jdm in Scharen zu Hilfe eilen.

(c) (*Aut*) **to go ~ing** Rallyes/eine Rallye fahren *or* machen; **to enjoy ~ing** gern Rallyes fahren.

♦**rally round** [1] *vi +prep obj leader* sich scharen um; *person in distress* sich annehmen (+*gen*).

[2] *vi* sich seiner/ihrer *etc* annehmen.

rally² *vt* (*obs*) (*tease*) necken, hänseln.

RAM [ræm] *n* (*Comput*) *abbr of* **random access memory** RAM *m or nt* ♦ **~ chip** RAM-Chip *m*; **1 megabyte of ~** 1 Megabyte RAM.

ram [ræm] [1] *n* **(a)** (*animal*) Widder, Schafbock *m* ♦ **the R~** (*Astrol*) der Widder.

(b) (*Tech*) Ramme *f*, Rammbär, Rammbock *m*; (*of hydraulic press*) Stoßheber *m*, hydraulischer Widder.

(c) (*Mil*) *see* **battering ~**.

(d) (*sl: man*) Rammler *m* (*sl*).

[2] *vt* **(a)** (*push*) *stick, post, umbrella* stoßen; (*with great force*) rammen; (*pack*) zwängen; (*Tech*) *pile* rammen ♦ **to ~ cotton wool in(to) one's ears** sich (*dat*) Watte in die Ohren stopfen; **to ~ a charge home** (*Mil*) laden; (*Min*) eine Sprengladung anbringen; **to ~ home an argument** ein Argument durchsetzen; **to ~ sth down sb's throat** (*inf*) jdm etw eintrichtern (*inf*); **to ~ sth into sb's head** (*inf*) jdm etw einbleuen (*inf*).

(b) (*crash into*) *ship, car* rammen ♦ **the car ~med a lamppost** das Auto prallte gegen einen Laternenpfahl.

♦**ram down** *vt sep earth* feststampfen; (*Tech*) *pile* einrammen ♦ **his hat was ~med ~ over his ears** sein Hut war fest über beide Ohren gezogen.

♦**ram in** *vt sep* hineinstoßen; (*with great force*) hineinrammen.

Ramadan [ˌræmə'dæn] *n* der Ramadan.

ramble ['ræmbl] [1] *n* Streifzug *m*; (*hike*) Wanderung *f* ♦ **to go for** *or* **on a ~** einen Streifzug/eine Wanderung machen.

[2] *vi* **(a)** (*wander about*) Streifzüge/einen Streifzug machen; (*go on hike*) wandern.

(b) (*in speech*) (*old person*) unzusammenhängendes Zeug reden, faseln (*inf*); (*pej: also* **~ on**) schwafeln (*inf*), vom Hundertsten ins Tausendste kommen.

(c) (*Hort*) ranken, klettern.

rambler ['ræmbləʳ] *n* **(a)** (*person*) Spaziergänger(in *f*) *m*; (*member of club*) Wanderer *m*, Wanderin *f*, Wanderfreund *m*. **(b)** (*also* **~ rose**) Kletterrose *f*.

rambling ['ræmblɪŋ] [1] *adj* **(a)** *speech, writing* weitschweifig, umständlich; *old person* faselnd (*inf*), schwafelnd (*inf*); *building, town* weitläufig.

(b) *plant* rankend, kletternd ♦ **~ rose** Kletterrose *f*.

(c) ~ club/society Wanderklub *m*/-verein *m*.

[2] *n* **(a)** (*wandering about*) Streifzüge *pl*; (*hiking*) Wandern *nt*.

(b) (*in speech: also* **~s**) Gefasel (*inf*), Geschwafel (*inf*) *nt*.

Rambo ['ræmbəʊ] *n* (*inf*) Rambo *m* (*inf*).

ramekin ['ræmɪkɪn] *n* (*Cook*) **(a)** kleiner Käseauflauf. **(b)** (*also* **~ dish**) Auflaufförmchen *nt*.

ramification [ˌræmɪfɪ'keɪʃən] *n* (*lit*) Verzweigung *f*; (*smaller*) Verästelung *f*; (*of arteries*) Verästelung *f*, Geäst *nt* ♦ **the ~s of this matter are several** (*form*) dies ist eine sehr verzweigte Angelegenheit; **the race question and its many ~s** die Rassenfrage und die damit verbundenen Probleme.

ramified ['ræmɪfaɪd] *adj* (*lit, fig*) verzweigt; (*more intricate*) verästelt.

ramify ['ræmɪfaɪ] *vi* (*lit, fig*) sich verzweigen ◆ **the problem ramifies into several areas** das Problem greift in verschiedene Bereiche über.

ramjet (engine) ['ræmdʒet('endʒɪn)] *n* Staustrahltriebwerk, Ram-Jet *nt*.

rammer ['ræmə^r] *n* Ramme *f*.

ramp [ræmp] *n* Rampe *f*; (*hydraulic* ~) Hebebühne *f*; (*Aviat: also* **approach** *or* **boarding** ~) Gangway *f* ◆ **"(beware** *or* **caution) ~"** (*on road sign*) „Vorsicht Rampe *or* unebene Fahrbahn".

rampage [ræm'peɪdʒ] [1] *n* **to be/go on the ~** randalieren; (*be angry*) (herum)toben/einen Wutanfall bekommen; (*looting*) auf Raubzug sein/gehen.
[2] *vi* (*also* ~ **about** *or* **around**) herumwüten; (*angrily*) herumtoben.

rampancy ['ræmpənsɪ] *n see adj* (**a**) Üppigkeit *f*, Wuchern *nt*; wilde(s) Wuchern.

rampant ['ræmpənt] *adj* (**a**) (*unrestrained*) *plants, growth* üppig, wuchernd *attr*; *heresy, evil, social injustice etc* wild wuchernd *attr* ◆ **the ~ growth of** das Wuchern (*+gen*); **to be ~** (wild) wuchern. (**b**) (*Her*) (drohend) aufgerichtet ◆ **lion ~** aufgerichteter Löwe.

rampart ['ræmpɑːt] *n* Wall *m*; (*fig: defence*) Schutzwall *m*.

ramrod ['ræmrɒd] *n* Ladestock *m* ◆ **he's sitting there as stiff as a ~** er sitzt da, als hätte er einen Besenstiel verschluckt.

ramshackle ['ræm,ʃækl] *adj building* morsch, baufällig; *car* klapprig, altersschwach.

ran [ræn] *pret of* **run**.

ranch [rɑːntʃ] [1] *n* Ranch, Viehfarm *f* ◆ **~-hand** Farmhelfer *m*; **~-house** (*on* ~) Farmhaus *nt*; **~(-style) house** (*US*) Bungalow *m*.
[2] *vi* Viehwirtschaft treiben.

rancher ['rɑːntʃə^r] *n* Rancher, Viehzüchter *m*.

rancid ['rænsɪd] *adj* ranzig.

rancidity [ræn'sɪdɪtɪ], **rancidness** ['rænsɪdnɪs] *n* Ranzigkeit *f*.

rancor *n* (*US*) *see* **rancour**.

rancorous ['ræŋkərəs] *adj tone* bitter; *attack* bösartig.

rancour, (*US*) **rancor** ['ræŋkə^r] *n see adj* Bitterkeit, Verbitterung *f*; Boshaftigkeit *f*.

rand [rænd] *n* (*monetary unit*) Rand *m*.

randan ['ræn,dæn] *n* (*sl*) **to be out on the ~** eine Sause machen (*inf*); (*rowdy behaviour*) auf den Putz hauen (*inf*), Remmidemmi machen (*inf*).

R & B [ɑːrən'biː] *n* (*Mus*) *abbr of* **Rhythm and Blues** R & B *m*.

R & D [ɑːrən'diː] *n abbr of* **research and development** Forschung und Entwicklung *f*.

randiness ['rændɪnɪs] *n* (*Brit*) Geilheit *f*.

random ['rændəm] [1] *n* **at ~** *speak, walk, drive* aufs Geratewohl; *shoot, drop bombs* ziellos; *take* wahllos; **to hit out at ~** ziellos um sich schlagen; **to talk at ~** ins Blaue hineinreden; **a few examples chosen** *or* **taken at ~** ein paar willkürlich gewählte Beispiele; **he just said anything at ~** er hat einfach irgend etwas gesagt, er hat einfach drauflosgeredet; **I (just) chose one at ~** ich wählte einfach irgendeine (beliebige).
[2] *adj selection* willkürlich, Zufalls- ◆ **killed by a ~ bullet** von einer verirrten Kugel getötet; **to give a ~ shot** einen Schuß ins Blaue abgeben; **to make a ~ guess** auf gut Glück raten; **~ sample** Stichprobe *f*; **~ sampling** Stichproben *pl*; **~ access** (*Comput*) wahlfreier Zugriff; **~ access memory** (*Comput*) Schreib-/Lesespeicher, Direktzugriffsspeicher *m*.

R & R [,ɑːrən'ɑː^r] (*US Mil*) *abbr of* **rest and recreation**.

randy ['rændɪ] *adj* (*+er*) (*Brit*) scharf (*inf*), geil ◆ **you ~ old devil** du alter Lustmolch (*inf*).

rang [ræŋ] *pret of* **ring**[2].

range [reɪndʒ] [1] *n* (**a**) (*scope, distance covered*) Aktionsradius *m*; (*of missile, telescope also*) Reichweite *f*; (*of gun also*) Reichweite, Schußweite *f*; (*of vehicle also*) Fahrbereich *m*; (*of plane also*) Flugbereich *m* ◆ **at a ~ of** auf eine Entfernung von; **at close** *or* **short/long ~** auf kurze/große Entfernung; **to find the ~** (*Mil*) das Visier einstellen; **to be out of ~** außer Reichweite sein; (*of telescope*) außer Sichtweite sein; (*of gun*) außer Schußweite sein; **within shouting ~** in Hörweite; **within (firing) ~** in Schußweite; **~ of vision** Gesichtsfeld *nt*.
(**b**) (*spread, selection*) Reihe *f*; (*of goods also*) Sortiment *nt*; (*of colours also*) Skala *f*; (*of patterns, sizes, models*) Angebot *nt*, Auswahl *f* (*of an +dat*); (*of interest, abilities*) Palette *f* ◆ **a wide ~** eine große Auswahl; **in this price/temperature ~** in dieser Preisklasse *or* Preislage/in diesem Temperaturbereich; **out of/within my price ~** außerhalb/innerhalb meiner (finanziellen) Möglichkeiten *or* meiner Preisklasse; **what sort of price ~ were you thinking of?** an welche Preislage haben Sie gedacht?; **a ~ of prices/temperatures/clients** unterschiedliche Preise *pl*/Temperaturen *pl*/Klienten *pl*; **models available in a whole ~ of prices** Modelle in unterschiedlichen Preislagen erhältlich; **we have the whole ~ of models/prices** wir führen sämtliche Modelle/Waren in allen Preislagen; **we cater for the whole ~ of customers** wir sind auf alle Kundenkreise eingestellt; **his ~ of knowledge is very limited** sein Wissen ist sehr beschränkt.
(**c**) (*Mus*) (*of instruments*) (Ton)umfang *m*; (*of voice also*) (Stimm)umfang *m*.
(**d**) (*domain, sphere*) Kompetenz *f*; (*of influence*) (Einfluß)bereich *m* ◆ **this is outside the ~ of the department/committee/this official** dies liegt außerhalb der Kompetenz dieser Abteilung/dieses Komitees/dieses Beamten.
(**e**) (*also* **shooting** ~) (*Mil*) Schießplatz *m*; (*rifle* ~) Schießstand *m*; (*at fair*) Schießbude *f*.
(**f**) (*cooking stove*) Koch- *or* Küchenherd *m*.
(**g**) (*row*) Reihe *f*; (*mountain* ~) Kette *f*.
(**h**) (*US: grazing land*) Freiland, Weideland *nt* ◆ **~ cattle** Freilandvieh *nt*.
[2] *vt* (**a**) (*place in a row*) aufstellen; *objects also* anordnen ◆ **they ~d themselves along the pavement** sie stellten sich am Bürgersteig entlang auf; **to ~ oneself with sb** *or* **on sb's side** (*fig*) sich auf jds Seite (*acc*) stellen.
(**b**) (*classify*) *person* zählen (*among, with* zu).
(**c**) (*roam over*) durchstreifen, durchziehen ◆ **to ~ the seas** die Meere befahren; **he ~d the whole country looking for ...** er suchte das ganze Land nach ... ab.
(**d**) (*direct*) *gun, telescope* ausrichten (*on* auf *+acc*).
(**e**) (*US*) *cattle* grasen lassen.
(**f**) (*Comput*) **~d left/right** links-/rechtsbündig.
[3] *vi* (**a**) (*extend*) (*from ... to*) gehen (von ... bis); (*temperature, value*) liegen (zwischen ... und) ◆ **the discussion ~d from the president to the hot-water system** die Diskussion umfaßte alles, vom Präsidenten bis zum Heißwassersystem; **his interests ~ from skiing to chess** seine Interessen reichen vom Skifahren bis zum Schachspielen; **the conversation ~d over a number of subjects** die Unterhaltung kreiste um eine ganze Reihe von Themen; **his knowledge ~s over a wide field** er hat ein sehr umfangreiches Wissen; **the search ~d over the whole country** die Suche erstreckte sich auf das ganze Land.
(**b**) (*roam*) streifen ◆ **to ~ over the area** im Gebiet umherstreifen.

range-finder ['reɪndʒ'faɪndə^r] *n* Entfernungsmesser *m*.

ranger ['reɪndʒə^r] *n* (**a**) (*of forest etc*) Förster, Aufseher *m*. (**b**) (*US: mounted patrolman*) Ranger *m*; (*commando*) Überfallkommando *nt*. (**c**) (*Brit*) **~ (scout)/(guide)** Ranger *m*.

Rangoon [ræŋ'guːn] *n* Rangun *nt*.

rangy ['reɪndʒɪ] *adj* (*+er*) langglied(e)rig.

rani ['rɑːnɪ] *n* Rani *f*.

rank[1] [ræŋk] [1] *n* (**a**) (*Mil: grade*) Rang *m* ◆ **officer of high ~** hoher Offizier; **to reach the ~ of general** den Rang eines Generals erlangen; *see* **pull**.
(**b**) (*class, status*) Stand *m*, Schicht *f* ◆ **people of all ~s** Leute *pl* aller Stände; **a person of ~** eine hochgestellte Persönlichkeit; **a singer of the first ~** ein erstklassiger Sänger; **a second-~ painter** ein zweitklassiger Maler.
(**c**) (*row*) Reihe *f*; (*taxi* ~) Taxistand *m* ◆ **the taxi at the head of the ~** das erste Taxi in der Reihe.
(**d**) (*Mil: formation*) Glied *nt* ◆ **to break ~(s)** aus dem Glied treten; **to keep ~(s)** in Reih und Glied stehen; **to serve in the ~s** gemeiner Soldat sein; **the ~s, other ~s** (*Brit*) die Mannschaften und die Unteroffiziere; **the ~ and file** (*Mil*) die Mannschaft; **the ~ and file of the party/union** die Basis der Partei/Gewerkschaft, die einfachen Partei-/Gewerkschaftsmitglieder; **the ~ and file workers** die einfachen Arbeiter; **to rise from the ~s** aus dem Mannschaftsstand zum Offizier aufsteigen; (*fig*) sich hocharbeiten; **to reduce sb to the ~s** jdn degradieren; *see* **close**[2].
(**e**) (*Mus*) Register *nt*.
[2] *vt* (*class, consider*) **to ~ sb among the best/great** *etc* jdn zu den Besten/Großen *etc* zählen; **where would you ~ Napoleon among the world's statesmen?** wie würden Sie Napoleon als Weltpolitiker einordnen *or* einstufen?
[3] *vi* **to ~ among** zählen zu; **to ~ above/below sb** bedeutender/weniger bedeutend als jd sein; (*athlete*) leistungsmäßig über/unter jdm liegen; (*officer*) rangmäßig über/unter jdm stehen; **to ~ high among the world's statesmen** einer der großen Staatsmänner sein; **he ~s high among her friends** er hat eine Sonderstellung unter ihren Freunden; **he ~s as a great composer** er gilt als großer Komponist; **to ~ 6th** den 6. Rang *or* Platz belegen.

rank[2] *adj* (*+er*) (**a**) *plants* üppig; *grass* verwildert; *soil* überwuchert ◆ **~ with weeds** von Unkraut überwuchert; **to grow ~** wuchern.
(**b**) (*offensive*) *smell* übel; *dustbin, drain* stinkend *attr*; *fat* ranzig; *person* derb, vulgär.
(**c**) *attr* (*utter*) *disgrace* wahr; *injustice* schreiend; *nonsense, insolence* rein; *traitor, liar* übel; *stupidity* ausgesprochen.

ranker ['ræŋkə^r] *n* (*Mil*) (*soldier*) einfacher *or* gemeiner Soldat; (*officer*) *aus dem Mannschaftsstand aufgestiegener Offizier*.

ranking officer ['ræŋkɪŋ'ɒfɪsə^r] *n* ranghöchster/ranghöherer Offizier.

rankle ['ræŋkl] *vi* **to ~ (with sb)** jdn wurmen.

rankness ['ræŋknɪs] *n see adj* (**a**) Üppigkeit *f*; Verwildertheit *f*; Überwucherung *f*. (**b**) Übelkeit *f*; Gestank *m*, Stinken *nt*; Ranzigkeit *f*, Derbheit, Vulgarität *f*.

ransack ['rænsæk] *vt* (*search*) *room, cupboards* durchwühlen; (*pillage*) *house* plündern; *town, region* herfallen über (*+acc*).

ransom ['rænsəm] [1] *n* Lösegeld *nt*; (*rescue*) Auslösung *f*; (*release*) Freilassung *f*; (*Rel*) Erlösung *f* ◆ **to hold sb to ~** (*lit*) jdn als Geisel halten; (*fig*) jdn erpressen; *see* **king**.
[2] *vt* (*buy free*) auslösen, Lösegeld bezahlen für; (*set free*) gegen Lösegeld freilassen; (*Rel*) erlösen.

rant [rænt] *vi* (*emotionally, angrily*) eine Schimpfkanonade loslassen; (*talk nonsense*) irres Zeug reden (*inf*) ◆ **to ~ (and rave)** (*be angry*) herumschimpfen; **to ~ (and rave) at sb** mit jdm schimpfen; **what's he ~ing (on) about?** worüber läßt er sich denn da aus? (*inf*).

ranting ['ræntɪŋ] [1] *n see vi* Geschimpfe *nt*; irres Zeug.
[2] *adj* pathetisch.

ranunculus [rə'nʌŋkjʊləs] *n* (*garden flower*) Ranunkel *f*.

rap[1] [ræp] [1] *n* (*noise, blow*) Klopfen *nt no pl* ◆ **there was a ~ at the door** es hat geklopft; **to give sb a ~ on the knuckles** (*lit, fig*) jdm auf die Finger klopfen; **he got a ~ on the knuckles for that** (*lit, fig*) dafür hat er eins auf die Finger bekommen (*inf*); **to take the ~** (*inf*) die Schuld zugeschoben kriegen (*inf*); **to take the ~ for sb** (*inf*) für jdn den Kopf hinhalten (*inf*); **I don't care a ~** (*inf*) das ist mir piepe (*inf*); **to beat the ~** (*US inf*) (von der Anklage) freigesprochen werden.

[2] *vt table* klopfen auf (+*acc*); *window* klopfen an (+*acc*) ◆ **to ~ sb's knuckles, to ~ sb over the knuckles** (*lit, fig*) jdm auf die Finger klopfen.

[3] *vi* klopfen ◆ **to ~ at the door/window** kurz (an die Tür)/ans Fenster klopfen.

◆**rap out** *vt sep* **(a)** (*say curtly*) *oath, order* ausstoßen. **(b)** (*Spiritualism*) *message* klopfen.

rap² *n* (*Mus*) Rap *m*.

rapacious *adj*, **~ly** *adv* [rə'peɪʃəs, -lɪ] habgierig.

rapacity [rə'pæsɪtɪ] *n* Habgier *f*.

rape¹ [reɪp] [1] *n* Vergewaltigung, Notzucht (*Jur*) *f*; (*obs: abduction*) Raub *m* ◆ **~ crisis centre** Beratungszentrum *nt für Frauen, die Opfer einer Vergewaltigung geworden sind*.

[2] *vt* vergewaltigen, notzüchtigen (*Jur*).

rape² *n* (*plant*) Raps *m* ◆ **~ oil/seed** Rapsöl *nt*/Rapssamen *m*.

rape³ *n* (*grape pulp*) Trester *pl*.

rapid ['ræpɪd] [1] *adj* schnell; *action, movement also* rasch; *improvement, change, spread also* rapide; *decline, rise* rapide, steil; *smile also* kurz; *heartbeat, pulse also* flink; *loss of heat* plötzlich; *river, waterfall* reißend; *slope, descent* steil ◆ **~ fire/firing** (*Mil*) Schnellfeuer *nt*; **~ fire of questions** Feuerwerk *nt* von Fragen; **~ eye movement sleep** REM-Phase *f*.

[2] *n* **~s** *pl* (*Geog*) Stromschnellen *pl*.

rapidity [rə'pɪdɪtɪ] *n see adj* Schnelligkeit *f*; Raschheit *f*; Rapidheit *f*; Steilheit *f*; Plötzlichkeit *f*.

rapidly ['ræpɪdlɪ] *adv see adj*.

rapier ['reɪpɪəʳ] *n* Rapier *nt* ◆ **~ thrust** (*lit*) Stoß *m* mit dem Rapier; (*fig*) (*remark*) Hieb *m*; (*retort*) Parade *f*; **~ wit** Schlagfertigkeit *f*.

rapine ['ræpaɪn] *n* (*liter*) Plünderung *f*.

rapist ['reɪpɪst] *n* Vergewaltiger *m*.

rapping ['ræpɪŋ] *n* Klopfen *nt*.

rapport [ræ'pɔːʳ] *n* **the ~ I have with my father** das enge Verhältnis zwischen mir und meinem Vater; **I envied them the obvious ~ that they had** ich beneidete sie um ihr offensichtlich enges Verhältnis zueinander; **in ~ with** in Harmonie mit; **they are in ~ with each other** sie harmonieren gut (miteinander).

rapprochement [ræ'prɒʃmɑ̃ːŋ] *n* Annäherung *f*.

rapscallion [ræp'skæliən] *n* (*old, hum*) Halunke, Gauner *m*.

rapt [ræpt] *adj* **(a)** *interest* gespannt; *attention* atemlos, höchste(r, s) ◆ **~ in contemplation/in thought** in Betrachtungen/Gedanken versunken. **(b)** *look, smile* verzückt.

rapture ['ræptʃəʳ] *n* (*delight*) Entzücken *nt*; (*ecstasy*) Verzückung *f* ◆ **to be in ~s** entzückt sein (*over* über +*acc*, *about* von); **she was in ~s when she heard he was returning** sie war außer sich vor Freude, als sie hörte, daß er zurückkommt; **to go into ~s** ins Schwärmen geraten; **to send sb into ~s** jdn in Entzücken versetzen.

rapturous ['ræptʃərəs] *adj applause, reception* stürmisch, begeistert; *exclamation* entzückt; *look* verzückt, hingerissen.

rapturously ['ræptʃərəslɪ] *adv see adj*.

rare [rɛəʳ] *adj* (+*er*) **(a)** (*uncommon*) selten, rar; *occurrence* selten ◆ **with very ~ exceptions** mit sehr wenigen Ausnahmen; **it's ~ for her to come** sie kommt nur selten.

(b) *atmosphere* dünn; *gas* Edel-; *earths* selten.

(c) *meat* roh; *steak also* blutig, englisch.

(d) (*inf: great*) irrsinnig (*inf*) ◆ **a person of ~ kindness** ein selten freundlicher Mensch (*inf*); **kind to a ~ degree** selten freundlich.

rarebit ['rɛəbɪt] *n see* **Welsh ~**.

rarefaction [ˌrɛərɪ'fækʃən] *n* Dünne *f*; (*fig*) Exklusivität *f*.

rarefied ['rɛərɪfaɪd] *adj atmosphere, air* dünn; (*fig*) exklusiv.

rarefy ['rɛərɪfaɪ] [1] *vt air, atmosphere* verdünnen, dünn werden lassen; (*fig*) exklusiv machen.

[2] *vi* (*air*) dünn werden.

rarely ['rɛəlɪ] *adv* selten.

rareness ['rɛənɪs] *n see adj* **(a)** Seltenheit, Rarheit *f*; (*of occurrence*) Rarheit *f*. **(b)** Dünne *f*. **(c)** Roheit *f*.

raring ['rɛərɪŋ] *adj*: **to be ~ to go** (*inf*) in den Startlöchern sein.

rarity ['rɛərɪtɪ] *n* Seltenheit *f*; (*rare occurrence also*) Rarität *f*.

rascal ['rɑːskəl] *n* Gauner *m*; (*child*) Schlingel, Frechdachs *m*; (*old: scoundrel*) Schurke *m*.

rascally ['rɑːskəlɪ] *adj* (*old, liter*) *trick* schändlich, schimpflich (*old, liter*); *person* schurkisch ◆ **a ~ fellow** ein Schurke *m*.

rash¹ [ræʃ] *n* (*Med*) Ausschlag *m* ◆ **to come out** *or* **break out in a ~** einen Ausschlag bekommen.

rash² *adj* (+*er*) *person* unbesonnen; *act also* voreilig, überstürzt; *thoughts* voreilig; *promise, words, decision* voreilig, vorschnell ◆ **it was ~ of him to promise that** es war etwas voreilig von ihm, das zu versprechen.

rasher ['ræʃəʳ] *n* Streifen *m* ◆ **~ of bacon** Speckstreifen *m*.

rashly ['ræʃlɪ] *adv see adj*.

rashness ['ræʃnɪs] *n see adj* Unbesonnenheit *f*; Voreiligkeit, Überstürztheit *f*; Voreiligkeit *f*.

rasp [rɑːsp] [1] *n* (*tool*) Raspel *f*; (*noise*) Kratzen *nt no pl*; (*of cough, when breathing*) Keuchen *nt no pl*.

[2] *vt* **(a)** (*Tech*) raspeln, feilen ◆ **to ~ sth away** *or* **off** etw weg- *or* abraspeln *or* -feilen.

(b) (*say: also* **~ out**) *insults* krächzen; *orders* schnarren.

[3] *vi* kratzen; (*breath*) rasseln; *see also* **rasping**.

raspberry ['rɑːzbərɪ] [1] *n* Himbeere *f*; (*plant: also* **~ bush** *or* **cane**) Himbeerstrauch *m* ◆ **to blow a ~** (*inf*) verächtlich schnauben; **to get a ~ (from sb)** (*inf*) (von jdm) nur ein verächtliches Schnauben ernten; **"new proposals get ~ from electorate"** (*inf*) „Wähler erteilen neuen Vorschlägen eine Abfuhr".

[2] *adj ice-cream, jam, flavour* Himbeer-; *colour* himbeerrot.

rasping ['rɑːspɪŋ] [1] *adj sound* kratzend; *voice* kratzig (*inf*), krächzend; *cough* keuchend; *breath* rasselnd, keuchend.

[2] *n* (*sound*) Kratzen *nt*; (*of voice*) Krächzen, Gekrächze *nt*.

Rasta ['ræstə] *n* Rasta *m*.

Rastafarian [ræstə'fɛərɪən] [1] *n* Rastafarier *m*.

[2] *adj* der Rastafarier.

raster ['ræstəʳ] *n* Raster *m or nt*.

rat [ræt] [1] *n* (*Zool*) Ratte *f*; (*pej inf: person*) elender Verräter (*inf*) ◆ **he's a dirty ~** (*inf*) er ist ein dreckiges *or* gemeines Schwein (*inf*); **you ~!** du Hund! (*inf*); **~s!** (*inf*) (*annoyance*) Mist! (*inf*); (*rejection*) Quatsch! (*inf*); *see* **smell**.

[2] *vi* **(a) to ~ on sb** (*inf*) (*desert*) jdn sitzenlassen (*inf*); (*inform on*) jdn verpfeifen (*inf*).

(b) to go ~ting auf Rattenfang gehen.

ratable *adj see* **rateable**.

rat *in cpds* Ratten-; **~-arsed** *adj* (*sl: drunk*) sturzbesoffen (*sl*); **to get ~-arsed** sich sinnlos besaufen (*sl*); **~bag** *n* (*pej inf*) Schrulle *f* (*inf*); **~-catcher** *n* Rattenfänger *m*; **~-catching** *n* Rattenfang *m*.

ratchet ['rætʃɪt] *n* Ratsche *f* ◆ **~ wheel** Sperrad *nt*.

rate¹ [reɪt] [1] *n* **(a)** (*ratio, proportion, frequency*) Rate *f*; (*speed*) Tempo *nt* ◆ **the failure ~ on this course/for this exam** die Durchfallrate *or* -quote bei diesem Kurs/Examen; **at the** *or* **a ~ of 100 litres an hour/14 feet per minute** (in einem Tempo von) 100 Liter pro Stunde/14 Fuß pro Minute; **~ of climb** (*Aviat*) Steigleistung *f*; **~ of consumption** Verbrauch *m*; **~ of flow** (*of water, electricity*) Fluß *m*; **pulse ~** Puls *m*; **at a great** *or* **terrific** (*inf*) **~, at a ~ of knots** (*inf*) in irrsinnigem Tempo (*inf*); (*move also*) mit hundert Sachen (*inf*); **if you continue at this ~** (*lit, fig*) wenn du so *or* in diesem Tempo weitermachst; **at his ~ of working** bei seinem Arbeitstempo; **at the ~ you're going you'll be dead before long** wenn du so weitermachst, bist du bald unter der Erde; **at any ~** auf jeden Fall; **at that ~ I suppose I'll have to agree** wenn das so ist, muß ich wohl zustimmen.

(b) (*Comm, Fin*) Satz *m*; (*St Ex*) Kurs *m* ◆ **~ of exchange** Wechselkurs *m*; **what's the ~ at the moment?** wie steht der Kurs momentan?; **what's the ~ of pay?** wie hoch ist der Satz (für die Bezahlung)?; **~ of interest** Zinssatz *m*; **~ of taxation** Steuersatz *m*; **~ of pay for overtime** Satz *m* für Überstunden; **postage/advertising/insurance ~s** Post-/Werbe-/Versicherungsgebühren *pl*; **there is a reduced ~ for children** Kinderermäßigung wird gewährt; **basic salary ~** Grundgehaltssatz *m*; **to pay sb at the ~ of £10 per hour** jdm einen Stundenlohn von £ 10 bezahlen.

(c) ~s *pl* (*Brit: municipal tax*) Gemeindesteuern, Kommunalsteuern *pl* ◆ **~s and taxes** Kommunal- und Staatssteuern *pl*; **~(s) office** Gemeindesteueramt *nt*; *see* **water-~**.

[2] *vt* **(a)** (*estimate value or worth of*) (ein)schätzen ◆ **to ~ sb/sth among ...** jdn/etw zu ... zählen *or* rechnen; **how do you ~ this effort/these results?** was halten Sie von dieser Leistung/diesen Ergebnissen?; **to ~ sb/sth as sth** jdn/etw für etw halten; **he is generally ~d as a great statesman** er gilt allgemein als großer Staatsmann; **how does he ~ that film?** was hält er von dem Film?; **to ~ sb/sth highly** jdn/etw hoch einschätzen.

(b) (*Brit: Local Government*) veranlagen ◆ **a house ~d at £1,000 per annum** ein Haus, dessen steuerbarer Wert £ 1.000 pro Jahr ist.

(c) (*deserve*) verdienen ◆ **does this hotel ~ 3 stars?** verdient dieses Hotel 3 Sterne?; **I think he ~s a pass (mark)** ich finde, seine Leistung kann man mit „ausreichend" oder besser bewerten.

(d) (*sl: think highly of*) gut finden (*inf*).

[3] *vi* (*be classed*) **to ~ as/among ...** gelten als .../zählen zu ...

rate² *vt* (*liter*) *see* **berate**.

rateable, ratable ['reɪtəbl] *adj* (*Brit*) *property* steuerpflichtig, steuerbar ◆ **~ value** steuerbarer Wert.

rate-cap ['reɪtkæp] *vt* (*Brit*) **the council was ~ped** dem Stadtrat wurde eine Höchstsatz für die Kommunalsteuer auferlegt.

rate capping ['reɪtˌkæpɪŋ] *n* (*Brit*) *Festlegung f eines Kommunalsteuer-Höchstsatzes durch die Zentralregierung*.

ratepayer ['reɪtˌpeɪəʳ] *n* (*Brit*) Steuerzahler *m* (*von Kommunalsteuern*).

rate rebate *n* (*Brit*) Kommunalsteuer-Rückerstattung *f*.

ratfink ['rætfɪnk] *n* (*US sl*) Arschloch *nt* (*sl*); (*informer*) Spitzel *m*.

▼ **rather** ['rɑːðəʳ] *adv* **(a)** (*for preference*) lieber ◆ **~ than wait, he went away** er ging lieber, als daß er wartete; **I would ~ have the blue dress** ich hätte lieber das blaue Kleid; **I would ~ be happy than rich** ich wäre lieber glücklich als reich; **I would ~ you came yourself** mir wäre es lieber, Sie kämen selbst; **I'd ~ not** lieber nicht; **I'd ~ not go** ich würde lieber nicht gehen; **I'd ~ die!** eher sterbe ich!; **he expected me to phone ~ than (to) write** er erwartete eher einen Anruf als einen Brief von mir; **it would be better to phone ~ than (to) write** es wäre besser zu telefonieren, als zu schreiben.

▼ **(b)** (*more accurately*) vielmehr ◆ **he is, or ~ was, a soldier** er ist, beziehungsweise *or* vielmehr war, Soldat; **a car, or ~ an old banger** ein

➤ LANGUAGE IN USE: **rather: a** → 6.3, 7.4, 8.3 **b** → 26.1, 26.3

Auto, genauer gesagt eine alte Kiste.
(c) (*to a considerable degree*) ziemlich; (*somewhat, slightly*) etwas ◆ **he's a ~ clever person** *or* **~ a clever person** er ist ziemlich klug; **he felt ~ better** er fühlte sich bedeutend wohler; **it's ~ more difficult than you think** es ist um einiges schwieriger, als du denkst; **it's ~ too difficult for me** es ist etwas zu schwierig für mich; **she's ~ an idiot/a killjoy** sie ist reichlich doof/ein richtiger Spielverderber; **I ~ think he's wrong** ich glaube fast, er hat Unrecht; **I've ~ got the impression** ... ich habe ganz den Eindruck, ...; ~! (*inf*) und ob! (*inf*), klar! (*inf*).
ratification [ˌrætɪfɪ'keɪʃən] *n* Ratifizierung *f*.
ratify ['rætɪfaɪ] *vt* ratifizieren.
rating[1] ['reɪtɪŋ] *n* **(a)** (*assessment*) (Ein)schätzung *f*; (*Brit: of house*) Veranlagung *f* ◆ **what's your ~ of his abilities?** wie schätzen Sie seine Fähigkeiten ein?
(b) (*class, category*) (*Sport: of yacht, car*) Klasse *f*; (*Fin: also* **credit ~**) Kreditfähigkeit *f*; (*Elec*) Leistung *f*; (*of petrol: also* **octane ~**) Oktanzahl *f* ◆ **what's his ~?** wie wird er eingestuft?; **he has attained world-class ~** er hat Weltklasse(format) erreicht; **the popularity ~ of a TV programme** die Zuschauerzahlen eines Fernsehprogramms; **security ~** Sicherheitseinstufung *f*; **voltage ~** Grenzspannung *f*.
(c) (*Naut*) (*rank*) Rang *m*; (*sailor*) Matrose *m*.
rating[2] *n* (*scolding*) Schelte *f*.
ratio ['reɪʃɪəʊ] *n* Verhältnis *nt* ◆ **the ~ of men to women** das Verhältnis von Männern zu Frauen; **in the** *or* **a ~ of 100 to 1** (*written* **100:1**) im Verhältnis 100 zu 1; **in inverse ~** (*Math*) umgekehrt proportional; **inverse** *or* **indirect ~** umgekehrtes Verhältnis.
ratiocinate [ˌrætɪ'ɒsɪneɪt] *vi* (*form*) reflektieren.
ration ['ræʃən, (*US*) 'reɪʃən] 1 *n* Ration *f*; (*fig*) Quantum *nt* ◆ **~s** (*food*) Rationen *pl*; **to put sb on short ~s** jdn auf halbe Ration setzen; **~ book/card** Bezug(s)scheinbuch *nt*/Bezug(s)schein *m*; (*for food*) ≃ Lebensmittelkarte *f*/ Lebensmittelmarke *f*.
2 *vt goods, food* rationieren; (*state, government also*) bewirtschaften ◆ **he was ~ed to 1 kg** ihm wurde nur 1 kg erlaubt; **sugar is short, so housewives are being ~ed** Zucker ist knapp und wird daher für die Hausfrau rationiert; **I'm going to ~ you to one apple a day** ich werde dich kurzhalten, du bekommst nur einen Apfel pro Tag; **he ~ed himself to five cigarettes a day** er erlaubte sich (*dat*) nur fünf Zigaretten pro Tag.
◆**ration out** *vt sep* zuteilen.
rational ['ræʃənl] *adj* **(a)** (*having reason*) *creature, person* vernunftbegabt, rational.
(b) (*sensible, reasonable*) *person, action, thinking* vernünftig, rational; *activity, solution* vernünftig, sinnvoll; (*Med: lucid, sane*) *person* bei klarem Verstand ◆ **it was the only ~ thing to do** es war das einzig Vernünftige.
(c) (*Math*) rational.
rationale [ræʃə'nɑːl] *n* Gründe *pl* ◆ **there doesn't seem to be any ~** das scheint jeglicher Begründung zu entbehren.
rationalism ['ræʃnəlɪzəm] *n* Rationalismus *m*.
rationalist ['ræʃnəlɪst] *n* Rationalist *m*.
rationalistic [ˌræʃnə'lɪstɪk] *adj* rationalistisch.
rationality [ˌræʃə'nælɪtɪ] *n see adj (b)* Vernünftigkeit, Rationalität *f*; Vernünftigkeit *f*; (*Med*) klarer Verstand.
rationalization [ˌræʃnəlaɪ'zeɪʃən] *n* Rationalisierung *f*; (*of problem*) vernünftige Betrachtung.
rationalize ['ræʃnəlaɪz] 1 *vt* **(a)** *event, conduct etc* rationalisieren; *problem* vernünftig sehen *or* betrachten. **(b)** (*organize efficiently*) *industry, production, work* rationalisieren. **(c)** (*Math*) in eine rationale Gleichung umändern.
2 *vi* rationalisieren.
rationally ['ræʃnəlɪ] *adv act, behave, think* vernünftig, rational; (*Med*) bei klarem Verstand ◆ **~, it should be possible to do it** rational gesehen sollte es möglich sein.
rationing ['ræʃənɪŋ] *n see vt* Rationierung *f*; Bewirtschaftung *f*.
ratline, ratlin ['rætlɪn] *n* (*Naut*) Webeleine *f*.
rat: ~pack *n* (*Brit pej inf*) Journalistenmeute *f* (*pej inf*); **~ poison** *n* Rattengift *nt*; **~-race** *n* ständiger Konkurrenzkampf; **~ run** *n* (*Brit inf*) Ausweichroute *f*, Schleichweg *m* (*inf*); **drivers were using the area as a ~ run** die Gegend wurde von Autofahrern als Ausweichroute *or* Schleichweg (*inf*) genutzt.
rats' tails *npl* (*pej*) Zotteln *pl* (*pej*); (*inf: bunches*) Rattenschwänze *pl* (*inf*) ◆ **her hair was** *or* **hung in ~** ihr Haar war zottelig *or* hing zottelig herunter; sie hatte Rattenschwänze.
rattan [ræ'tæn] *n* (*plant*) Rotangpalme *f*; (*cane*) Rattan, Peddigrohr *nt*.
rattle ['rætl] 1 *vi* klappern; (*chains*) rasseln, klirren; (*bottles*) klirren; (*gunfire*) knattern; (*drums*) schlagen; (*hailstones*) prasseln; (*rattlesnake*) klappern ◆ **to ~ at the door** an der Tür rütteln; **there's something rattling** da klappert etwas; **to ~ along/away** (*vehicle*) entlang-/davonrattern; **they ~d through the village** sie ratterten durch das Dorf.
2 *vt* **(a)** *box, dice, keys* schütteln; *bottles, cans* zusammenschlagen; *chains* rasseln mit; *windows* rütteln an (*+dat*).
(b) (*inf: alarm*) *person* durcheinanderbringen ◆ **don't get ~d!** reg dich nicht auf!; **she was ~d at** *or* **by the news, the news ~d her** die Nachricht hat ihr einen Schock versetzt.
3 *n* **(a)** (*sound*) *see vi* Klappern *nt no pl*; Rasseln, Klirren *nt no pl*; Klirren *nt no pl*; Knattern *nt no pl*; Schlagen *nt no pl*; Prasseln *nt no pl*; Klappern *nt no pl*; (*Med: also* **death ~**) Röcheln *nt*.
(b) (*child's*) Rassel, Klapper *f*; (*sports fan's*) Schnarre *f*.
◆**rattle down** *vi* herunterprasseln, herunterhageln.
◆**rattle off** *vt sep poem, speech, list* herunterrasseln.
◆**rattle on** *vi* (*inf*) (unentwegt) quasseln (*inf*) (*about* über +*acc*).
◆**rattle through** *vi +prep obj speech etc* herunterrasseln; *work, music* rasen durch.
rattlebrain ['rætlbreɪn] *n* (*inf*) Spatzenhirn *nt* (*inf*).
rattler ['rætləʳ] *n* (*US inf*) Klapperschlange *f*.
rattle: ~snake *n* Klapperschlange *f*; **~trap** *n* (*hum inf*) Klapperkiste *f* (*hum inf*).
rattling ['rætlɪŋ] 1 *n see vi* Klappern *nt*; Rasseln, Klirren *nt*; Knattern *nt*; Schlagen *nt*; Prasseln *nt*.
2 *adj see vi* klappernd; rasselnd, klirrend; knatternd; schlagend; prasselnd ◆ **a ~ noise** ein Klappern *nt*/Rasseln *nt etc*; **at a ~ pace** (*inf*) in rasendem Tempo (*inf*).
3 *adv*: **~ good** (*dated inf*) verdammt gut (*inf*).
rattrap, rat trap ['rættræp] *n* Rattenfalle *f*.
ratty ['rætɪ] *adj* (*+er*) (*inf*) **(a)** (*irritable*) gereizt. **(b)** (*US: run-down*) verlottert (*inf*).
raucous ['rɔːkəs] *adj* rauh, heiser.
raucously ['rɔːkəslɪ] *adv shout* rauh, heiser; *sing* mit rauher *or* heiserer Stimme.
raucousness ['rɔːkəsnɪs] *n* Rauheit, Heiserkeit *f*.
raunchy ['rɔːntʃɪ] *adj* (*+er*) (*US inf*) geil; *novel* rasant.
ravage ['rævɪdʒ] 1 *n* (*of war*) verheerendes Wüten *no pl*; (*of disease*) Wüten *nt no pl*, Zerstörung *f* (*of* durch) ◆ **~s** (*of war*) Verheerung *f* (*of* durch); (*of disease*) Zerstörung *f* (*of* durch); **the ~s of time** die Spuren *pl* der Zeit; **a face marked by the ~s of time** ein von der Zeit schwer gezeichnetes Gesicht.
2 *vt* (*ruin*) verwüsten, verheeren; (*plunder*) plündern ◆ **~d by disease** von Krankheit schwer gezeichnet.
rave [reɪv] 1 *vi* (*be delirious*) phantasieren, delirieren (*spec*); (*talk wildly*) phantasieren, spinnen (*inf*); (*speak furiously*) toben; (*inf: speak, write enthusiastically*) schwärmen (*about, over* von); (*liter*) (*storm*) toben; (*wind*) brausen; (*sea*) toben ◆ **to ~ against sb/sth** gegen jdn/etw wettern; **he ~d at the children for breaking the window** er donnerte die Kinder wegen der eingeworfenen Fensterscheibe an; *see* **rant**.
2 *n* **(a)** (*Brit sl: also* **~-up**) Fete *f* (*inf*), tolle Party.
(b) (*sl: praise*) Schwärmerei *f* ◆ **to have a ~ about sth** von etw schwärmen *or* ganz weg sein (*inf*); **the play got a ~ review** (*inf*) das Stück bekam eine glänzende *or* begeisterte Kritik.
(c) (*Brit sl: fashion*) **it's all the ~** das ist große Mode.
ravel ['rævəl] 1 *vt* **(a)** (*disentangle*) *see* **ravel out 2**. **(b)** (*old: entangle*) verwirren.
2 *vi* (*become tangled*) sich verwirren; (*fray*) ausfransen.
◆**ravel out** 1 *vi* ausfransen; (*rope*) faserig werden.
2 *vt sep material* ausfransen; *threads* entwirren; *knitting* auftrennen, aufziehen; (*fig*) *difficulty* klären.
raven ['reɪvən] *n* Rabe *m* ◆ **~-black** rabenschwarz; **~-haired** mit rabenschwarzem Haar.
ravening ['rævənɪŋ] *adj* beutehungrig, räuberisch.
ravenous ['rævənəs] *adj animal* ausgehungert; *person also* heißhungrig; *appetite, hunger* gewaltig ◆ **I'm ~** ich habe einen Bärenhunger (*inf*).
ravenously ['rævənəslɪ] *adv* **to be ~ hungry** (*animal*) ausgehungert sein; (*person also*) einen Bärenhunger haben (*inf*).
raver ['reɪvəʳ] *n* (*Brit sl*) flotte Biene (*sl*) ◆ **she's a real little ~** sie führt ein flottes Leben.
rave-up ['reɪvʌp] *n* (*Brit sl*) *see* **rave 2 (a)**.
ravine [rə'viːn] *n* Schlucht, Klamm *f*.
raving ['reɪvɪŋ] 1 *adj* **(a)** (*frenzied*) wahnsinnig, verrückt; (*delirious*) im Delirium, phantasierend *attr* ◆ **his ~ fantasies** seine verrückten Phantastereien; **a ~ lunatic** (*inf*) ein kompletter Idiot (*inf*). **(b)** (*inf: remarkable*) *success* toll (*inf*); *beauty* hinreißend.
2 *adv* **~ mad** (*inf*) total verrückt (*inf*).
3 *n* **~(s)** Phantasien *pl*.
ravioli [ˌrævɪ'əʊlɪ] *n* Ravioli *pl*.
ravish ['rævɪʃ] *vt* **(a)** (*delight*) hinreißen. **(b)** (*old, liter: rape*) schänden (*geh*); (*obs: abduct*) rauben.
ravisher ['rævɪʃəʳ] *n* (*old, liter*) Schänder *m* (*geh*).
ravishing ['rævɪʃɪŋ] *adj woman, sight* atemberaubend; *beauty also, meal* hinreißend.
ravishingly ['rævɪʃɪŋlɪ] *adv beautiful* hinreißend, atemberaubend; *dressed, decorated* atemberaubend schön.
ravishment ['rævɪʃmənt] *n see vt* **(a)** atemloses Staunen, Hingerissenheit *f*. **(b)** Schändung *f* (*geh*); Raub *m*.
raw [rɔː] 1 *adj* (*+er*) **(a)** (*uncooked*) *meat, food* roh; (*unprocessed*) *ore, sugar, silk, brick also* Roh-; *spirit, alcohol* rein, unvermischt; *cloth* ungewalkt; *leather* ungegerbt; (*fig*) *statistics* nackt ◆ **it's a ~ deal** (*inf*) das ist eine Gemeinheit (*inf*); **to give sb a ~ deal** (*inf*) jdn benachteiligen, jdn unfair behandeln; **to get a ~ deal** schlecht wegkommen (*inf*); **the old get a ~ deal from the state** (*inf*) alte Leute werden vom Staat stiefmütterlich behandelt; **~ edge** (*of cloth etc*) ungesäumte Kante; **~ material** Rohstoff *m*; **~ spirits** reiner Alkohol; **~ data** (*Comput*) unaufbereitete Daten *pl*.
(b) (*inexperienced*) *troops, recruit* neu, unerfahren ◆ **~ recruit** (*fig*) blutiger Anfänger (*inf*).
(c) (*sore*) *wound* offen; *skin* wund; *nerves* empfindlich.
(d) *climate, wind, air* rauh.
(e) (*esp US: coarse*) *humour, story, person* derb; *colour* grell.
2 *n* **(a)** **to touch** *or* **get sb on the ~** (*Brit*) bei jdm einen wunden Punkt

berühren.
(b) **in the ~** (*inf: naked*) im Naturzustand; **life/nature in the ~** die rauhe Seite des Lebens/der Natur.

raw: ~boned *adj* mager, knochig; **~hide** *n* (*leather*) ungegerbtes Leder; (*whip*) Lederpeitsche *f*.

rawlplug ® ['rɔːlplʌg] *n* Dübel *m*.

rawness ['rɔːnɪs] *n* (a) (*of meat, food*) Roheit *f*. (b) (*lack of experience*) Unerfahrenheit *f*. (c) (*soreness*) Wundheit *f*. (d) (*of weather*) Rauheit *f*. (e) (*esp US: coarseness*) Derbheit *f*.

ray[1] [reɪ] *n* (a) Strahl *m* ♦ **a ~ of hope/solace** ein Hoffnungsschimmer *or* -strahl *m*/ein kleiner Trost; **~ gun** Strahlenpistole *f*. (b) (*of fish*) Flossenstrahl *m*; (*of starfish*) Arm *m*.

ray[2] *n* (*fish*) Rochen *m*.

rayon ['reɪɒn] [1] *n* Reyon *nt*.
[2] *adj* Reyon-, aus Reyon.

raze [reɪz] *vt* zerstören; (*Mil*) schleifen ♦ **to ~ to the ground** dem Erdboden gleichmachen.

razor ['reɪzəʳ] *n* Rasierapparat *m*; (*cutthroat*) Rasiermesser *nt* ♦ **electric ~** Elektrorasierer *m*; **~'s edge** (*fig*) *see* **~-edge (b)**.

razor: ~back *n* (*Zool*) Finnwal *m*; **~bill** *n* (*Zool*) Tordalk *m*; **~ blade** *n* Rasierklinge *f*; **~-cut** [1] *n* Messerschnitt *m*; [2] *vt* mit dem Messer schneiden; **~-edge** *n* (a) (*mountain ridge*) Grat *m*; (b) (*fig*) **our fate is poised/we stand poised on a ~-edge** unser Schicksal steht auf Messers Schneide/wir stehen vor einem Abgrund; **the decision rests on a ~-edge** die Entscheidung steht auf Messers Schneide; **the ~-edge that divides belief and unbelief** der schmale Grat zwischen Glaube und Unglaube; **~-sharp** *adj knife* scharf (wie ein Rasiermesser); (*fig*) *person* sehr scharfsinnig; *mind, wit* messerscharf; **~-wire** *n* Bandstacheldraht, Nato-Draht (*inf*) *m*.

razz [ræz] *vt* (*US inf*) aufziehen (*inf*), verhohnepiepeln (*inf*).

razzle ['ræzl] *n* (*dated sl*): **to go on the ~/be out on the ~** eine Sause machen (*inf*).

razzle-dazzle ['ræzl'dæzl], **razzmatazz** ['ræzmə'tæz] *n* (*inf*) Rummel, Trubel *m*.

RC *abbr of* **Roman Catholic** rk, r.-k.

Rd *abbr of* **Road** Str.

RDA *abbr of* **recommended daily allowance.**

RE *abbr of* **Religious Education.**

re[1] [reɪ] *n* (*Mus*) re *nt*.

re[2] [riː] *prep* (*Admin, Comm etc: referring to*) betreffs (+*gen*), bezüglich (+*gen*); (*Jur: also* **in ~**) in Sachen gegen ♦ **~ your letter of 16th** Betr(eff): Ihr Brief vom 16.

re- [riː-] *pref* wieder-.

reach [riːtʃ] [1] *n* (a) (*act of reaching*) **to make a ~ for sth** nach etw greifen.
(b) (*denoting accessibility*) **within/out of sb's ~** in/außer jds Reichweite (*dat*), in/außer Reichweite für jdn; **within arm's ~** in greifbarer Nähe; **put it out of the children's ~** *or* **out of the ~ of children** stellen Sie es so, daß Kinder es nicht erreichen können; **keep out of ~ of children** von Kindern fernhalten; **cars are within everyone's ~ nowadays** Autos sind heute für jeden erschwinglich; **mountains within easy ~** Berge, die leicht erreichbar sind; **within easy ~ of the sea** in unmittelbarer Nähe des Meers; **this town is within easy ~ of London for a day trip** man kann von dieser Stadt aus gut Tagesflüge nach London machen; **I keep it within easy ~** ich habe es in greifbarer Nähe; **she was beyond (the) ~ of human help** für sie kam jede menschliche Hilfe zu spät; **this subject is beyond his ~** dieses Thema geht über seinen Horizont (*inf*).
(c) (*distance one can ~*) Reichweite *f*; (*Boxing*) Aktionsradius *m* ♦ **a long ~** lange Arme *pl*; ein großer Aktionsradius.
(d) (*sphere of action, influence*) Einflußbereich *m* ♦ **beyond the ~ of the law** außerhalb des Gesetzes.
(e) (*stretch*) (*of beach, river*) Strecke *f*; (*of canal*) Wasserhaltung *f*; (*of woodland*) Gebiet *nt*.
[2] *vt* (a) (*arrive at*) erreichen; *place, goal also, point* ankommen an (+*dat*); *town, country* ankommen in (+*dat*); *perfection also* erlangen; *agreement, understanding* erzielen, kommen zu; *conclusion* kommen *or* gelangen zu ♦ **we ~ed London at 3pm** wir kamen um 15 Uhr in London an; **when we ~ed him he was dead** als wir zu ihm kamen, war er tot; **to ~ the terrace you have to cross the garden** um auf die Terrasse zu kommen, muß man durch den Garten gehen; **to ~ page 50** bis Seite 50 kommen; **this advertisement is geared to ~ the under 25's** diese Werbung soll Leute unter 25 ansprechen; **you can ~ me at my hotel** Sie erreichen mich in meinem Hotel.
(b) (*stretch to get or touch*) **to be able to ~ sth** an etw (*acc*) (heran)reichen können, bis zu etw langen können (*inf*); **can you ~ it?** kommen Sie dran?; **can you ~ the ceiling?** kannst du bis an die Decke reichen *or* langen? (*inf*).
(c) (*come up to, go down to*) reichen *or* gehen bis zu ♦ **he ~es her shoulder** er reicht *or* geht ihr bis zur Schulter.
(d) (*inf: get and give*) langen (*inf*), reichen ♦ **~ me (over) that book** reiche *or* lang (*inf*) mir das Buch (herüber).
(e) (*US Jur*) *witness* bestechen.
[3] *vi* (a) (*to, as far as* bis) (*territory etc*) sich erstrecken, gehen, reichen; (*voice, sound*) tragen.
(b) (*stretch out hand or arm*) greifen ♦ **to ~ for sth** nach etw greifen *or* langen (*inf*); **~ for the sky!** (*US*) Hände hoch!; **to ~ for the moon** (*fig*) nach den Sternen greifen.
(c) **can you ~?** kommen Sie dran?

♦**reach across** *vi* hinüber-/herübergreifen *or* -langen (*inf*).

♦**reach back** *vi* (*in time*) zurückreichen, zurückgehen (*to* bis).

♦**reach down** [1] *vi* (*clothes, curtains, hair etc*) hinunter-/herunterreichen (*to* bis); (*person*) hinunter-/heruntergreifen *or* -langen (*inf*) (*for* nach).
[2] *vt sep* hinunter-/herunterreichen.

♦**reach out** [1] *vt sep* **he ~ed ~ his hand to take the book** er streckte die Hand aus, um das Buch zu nehmen; **he ~ed ~ his hand for the cup** er griff nach der Tasse.
[2] *vi* die Hand/Hände ausstrecken ♦ **to ~ ~ for sth** nach etw greifen *or* langen (*inf*); **he ~ed ~ to grasp the door handle** er griff *or* langte (*inf*) nach dem Türgriff; **she ~ed ~ and slapped him** sie holte aus und haute ihm eine runter (*inf*).

♦**reach over** *vi see* **reach across.**

♦**reach up** [1] *vi* (a) (*water, level etc*) (hinauf-/herauf)reichen *or* -gehen (*to* bis). (b) (*person*) hinauf-/heraufgreifen (*for* nach).
[2] *vt sep* (*inf*) herauf-/hinaufreichen.

reachable ['riːtʃəbl] *adj* erreichbar.

reach-me-down ['riːtʃmɪˌdaʊn] *n* (*inf*) *see* **hand-me-down.**

react [riː'ækt] *vi* (a) (*respond, Chem, Phys*) reagieren (*to* auf +*acc*) ♦ **slow to ~** (*Chem*) reaktionsträge; **she was slow to ~ to my offer** sie reagierte nur langsam auf mein Angebot; **to ~ against** negativ reagieren auf (+*acc*).
(b) (*have an effect*) wirken (*on, upon* auf +*acc*) ♦ **to ~ upon sb's mood** sich auf jds Stimmung (*acc*) auswirken.

reaction [riː'ækʃən] *n* (a) (*response, Chem, Phys*) Reaktion *f* (*to* auf +*acc, against* gegen) ♦ **what was his ~ to your suggestion?** wie hat er auf Ihren Vorschlag reagiert?, wie war seine Reaktion auf Ihren Vorschlag?; **a ~ against violence** eine Absage an die Gewalt; **action and ~** Wirkung und Gegenwirkung (+*pl vb*).
(b) (*Pol*) Reaktion *f* ♦ **forces of ~** reaktionäre Kräfte *pl*.
(c) (*Mil*) Gegenschlag *m*.
(d) (*St Ex*) Umschwung, Rückgang *m*.

reactionary [riː'ækʃənrɪ] *adj* reaktionär.

reactivate [riː'æktɪveɪt] *vt* reaktivieren.

reactive [riː'æktɪv] *adj* (*Chem, Phys*) reaktiv.

reactor [riː'æktəʳ] *n* (*Phys*) Reaktor *m*; (*Chem also*) Reaktionsapparat *m*; (*Elec*) Blindwiderstand *m*.

read[1] [riːd] (*vb: pret, ptp* **read** [red]) [1] *vt* (a) (*also Comput*) lesen; (*to sb*) vorlesen (*to dat*) ♦ **do you ~ music?** können Sie Noten lesen?; **I read him to sleep** ich las ihm vor, bis er einschlief; **to take sth as read** (*fig*) (*as self-evident*) etw als selbstverständlich voraussetzen; (*as agreed*) etw für abgemacht halten; **they took the minutes as read** (*in meeting*) sie setzten das Protokoll als bekannt voraus; **for "meet" ~ "met"** anstelle von „meet" soll „met" stehen; *see* **paper.**
(b) (*interpret*) *thoughts, feelings* lesen; *dream* deuten; *words* verstehen ♦ **to ~ sb's thoughts/mind** jds Gedanken lesen; **to ~ sb's hand** jdm aus der Hand lesen; **to ~ the tea leaves** *or* **the teacups** ≃ aus dem Kaffeesatz lesen; **these words can be read in several ways** diese Wörter können unterschiedlich verstanden werden; **to ~ something into a text** etwas in einen Text (hinein)lesen.
(c) (*Univ: study*) studieren.
(d) *thermometer, barometer etc* sehen auf (+*acc*), ablesen ♦ **to ~ a meter** einen Zähler(stand) ablesen.
(e) (*meter*) (an)zeigen, stehen auf (+*dat*); (*flight etc instruments*) anzeigen ♦ **the thermometer ~s 37°** das Thermometer steht auf *or* zeigt 37°.
(f) (*Telec*) verstehen ♦ **do you ~ me?** (*Telec*) können Sie mich verstehen?; (*fig*) haben Sie mich verstanden?
[2] *vi* (a) lesen; (*to sb*) vorlesen (*to dat*) ♦ **she ~s well** sie liest gut; (*learner, beginner*) sie kann schon gut lesen; **to ~ aloud** *or* **out loud** laut lesen; **to ~ to oneself** für sich lesen; **he likes being read to** er läßt sich (*dat*) gern vorlesen; **will you ~ to me, mummy?** Mutti, liest du mir etwas vor?
(b) (*convey impression when read*) **this book ~s well/badly** das Buch liest sich gut/nicht gut; **this ~s like an official report/a translation** das klingt wie ein offizieller Bericht/eine Übersetzung; **that's how it ~s to me** so verstehe ich das.
(c) (*have wording*) lauten ♦ **the letter ~s as follows** der Brief geht so *or* lautet folgendermaßen *or* besagt folgendes.
(d) (*Univ: study*) **to ~ for an examination** sich auf eine Prüfung vorbereiten; *see* **bar[1]**.
[3] *n* **she enjoys a good ~** sie liest gern; **to have a quiet/little ~** ungestört *or* in Ruhe/ein wenig lesen; **this book is quite a good ~** das Buch liest sich gut.

♦**read back** *vt sep shorthand* lesen; *one's notes etc* noch einmal lesen; (*to sb*) noch einmal vorlesen.

♦**read in** *vt sep* (*Comput*) *text, data* einlesen.

♦**read off** *vt sep* ablesen; (*without pause*) herunterlesen.

♦**read on** *vi* weiterlesen.

♦**read out** *vt sep* vorlesen; *instrument readings* ablesen.

♦**read over** *or* **through** *vt sep* durchlesen.

♦**read up** [1] *vt sep* nachlesen über (+*acc*), sich informieren über (+*acc*).
[2] *vi* nachlesen, sich informieren (*on* über +*acc*).

read[2] [red] [1] *pret, ptp of* **read[1]**.
[2] *adj* **he is well/badly ~** er ist sehr/wenig belesen.

readable ['riːdəbl] *adj* (*legible*) *handwriting* lesbar; (*worth reading*) *book etc* lesenswert ♦ **not very ~** schlecht lesbar/nicht besonders lesenswert.

readdress [ˌriːə'dres] *vt letter, parcel* umadressieren.

reader ['riːdəʳ] *n* (a) Leser(in *f*) *m* ♦ **publisher's ~** Lektor(in *f*) *m*.
(b) (*Brit Univ*) ≃ Dozent(in *f*) *m*.

(c) *(schoolbook)* Lesebuch *nt;* *(to teach reading)* Fibel *f;* *(foreign language text)* Text *m,* Lektüre *f;* *(anthology)* Sammelband *m* ◆ **a ~ in the Classics** eine Klassikersammlung; **"first French ~"** „Französisches Lesebuch für Anfänger".

readership ['riːdəʃɪp] *n* **(a)** *(of newspaper, magazine)* Leserschaft *f,* Leser *pl* ◆ **a big** *or* **wide ~/a ~ of millions** eine große Leserschaft/Millionen Leser. **(b)** *(Brit Univ)* ≃ Dozentur *f.*

read head *n (Comput)* Lesekopf *m.*

readies ['rediːz] *npl (sl: ready cash)* Bare(s) *nt (inf)* ◆ **the ~** das Bare *(inf);* **that'll cost you 100 in ~** das kostet dich 100 bar auf die Hand *(inf) or* Kralle *(sl);* **I don't have the ~** ich hab nicht die Kohle *(sl).*

readily ['redɪlɪ] *adv* bereitwillig; *(easily)* leicht ◆ **~ to hand** griffbereit.

readiness ['redɪnɪs] *n* **(a)** Bereitschaft *f* ◆ **~ for war** Kriegsbereitschaft *f;* **to be (kept) in ~ (for sth)** (für etw) bereitgehalten werden; **his ~ to help** seine Hilfsbereitschaft. **(b)** *(ease)* Leichtigkeit *f.*

reading ['riːdɪŋ] *n* **(a)** *(action)* Lesen *nt.*
(b) *(~ matter)* Lektüre *f* ◆ **this book is** *or* **makes very interesting ~** dieses Buch ist sehr interessant zu lesen; **have you any light ~?** haben Sie eine leichte Lektüre?
(c) *(recital, excerpt)* Lesung *f* ◆ **play ~** Lesen *nt* mit verteilten Rollen.
(d) *(interpretation)* Interpretation *f,* Verständnis *nt* ◆ **my ~ of this sentence** mein Verständnis des Satzes.
(e) *(variant)* Version *f.*
(f) *(from meter)* Thermometer-/Barometer-/Zählerstand *etc m;* *(on flight etc instruments)* Anzeige *f;* *(in scientific experiment)* Meßwert *m* ◆ **to take a ~** den Thermometerstand *etc* ablesen; die Anzeige ablesen; den Meßwert ablesen; **the ~ is ...** das Thermometer *etc* steht auf ...; die Anzeige ist ...; der Meßwert ist ...
(g) *(Parl: of bill)* Lesung *f* ◆ **the Senate gave the bill its first/a second ~** der Senat beriet das Gesetz in erster/zweiter Lesung.
(h) *(knowledge)* Belesenheit *f* ◆ **a man of wide ~** ein sehr belesener Mann.

reading: ~ age *n* **when they reach ~ age** wenn sie das lesefähige Alter erreichen; **a ~ age of 7** die Lesefähigkeit eines 7jährigen; **~ book** *n* Lesebuch *nt;* **~ desk** *n* (Lese)tisch *m;* **~ glass** *n* Lupe *f;* **~ glasses** *npl* Lesebrille *f;* **~ knowledge** *n* **to have a ~ knowledge of Spanish** Spanisch lesen können; **~ lamp** *n* Leselampe *f;* **~ list** *n* Leseliste *f;* **~ matter** *n* Lesestoff *m;* **~ room** *n* Lesesaal *m;* **~ speed** *n (of child, Comput)* Lesegeschwindigkeit *f.*

readjust [ˌriːə'dʒʌst] **1** *vt instrument, mechanism* neu einstellen; *(correct)* nachstellen; *prices, salary* anpassen, neu regeln; *opinion* korrigieren.
2 *vi* sich neu *or* wieder anpassen *(to* an *+acc),* sich neu *or* wieder einstellen *(to* auf *+acc).*

readjustment [ˌriːə'dʒʌstmənt] *n see vb* Neueinstellung *f,* Nachstellung *f,* Anpassung, Neuregelung *f,* Korrektur *f,* Wiederanpassung *f.*

read: ~ only memory *n (Comput)* (Nur)lesespeicher, Festwertspeicher *m;* **~-out** *n* Anzeige *f;* **~-write head** *n (Comput)* Schreib-/Lesekopf *m;* **~-write memory** *n (Comput)* Schreib-/Lesespeicher *m.*

ready ['redɪ] **1** *adj* **(a)** *(prepared) person, thing* bereit, fertig; *(finished, cooked etc)* fertig ◆ **~ to leave** abmarschbereit; *(for journey)* abfahrtbereit, reisefertig; **~ to use** *or* **for use** gebrauchsfertig; **~ to serve** tischfertig; **~ for battle** kampfbereit; **~ for anything** zu allem bereit; **dinner is ~** das Essen ist fertig; **"dinner's ~"** „essen kommen", „zum Essen"; **are you ~ to go?** sind Sie soweit?, kann es losgehen? *(inf);* **are you ~ to push?** alles fertig zum Schieben?; **are you ~ to take the weight?** können Sie das Gewicht jetzt übernehmen?; **well, I think we're ~** ich glaube, wir sind soweit; **I'm not quite ~ yet** ich bin noch nicht ganz fertig; **I'm ~ for him!** ich warte nur auf ihn, er soll nur kommen; **to be ~ with an excuse** eine Entschuldigung bereit haben *or* bereithalten; **to get (oneself) ~** sich fertigmachen; **to get ~ to go out/play tennis** sich zum Ausgehen/Tennisspielen fertigmachen; **to get ~ for sth** sich auf etw *(acc)* vorbereiten; **get ~ for it!** *(before blow etc)* Achtung!, paß auf!; *(before momentous news)* mach dich auf was gefaßt *(inf);* **to get** *or* **make sth ~** etw fertigmachen, etw bereitmachen; *room, bed, breakfast etc* etw vorbereiten; **~ about!** *(Naut)* klar zum Wenden!; **~, steady, go!** Achtung *or* auf die Plätze, fertig, los!
(b) ~ to do sth *(willing)* bereit, etw zu tun; *(quick)* schnell dabei, etw zu tun; **he's always ~ to find fault** er ist immer schnell dabei, wenn es gilt, Fehler zu finden; **don't be so ~ to criticize** kritisieren Sie doch nicht so schnell; **I'm ~ to believe it** ich möchte das fast glauben; **he was ~ to cry** er war den Tränen nahe; **he's always ~ with an answer** er ist mit einer Antwort immer schnell bei der Hand.
(c) *(prompt) reply* prompt; *wit* schlagfertig ◆ **to have a ~ tongue** schlagfertig sein.
(d) *(available)* **~ money** jederzeit verfügbares Geld; **~ cash** Bargeld *nt;* **to pay in ~ cash** auf die Hand bezahlen; **~ to hand** zur Hand; **"now ~"** „jetzt zu haben".
(e) *(practical) solution* sauber; *(competent) speaker* gewandt ◆ **to have a ~ sale** *(Comm)* guten Absatz finden.
2 *n* **(a)** *(Mil)* **to come to the ~** das Gewehr in Anschlag nehmen; **at the ~** *(Mil)* mit dem Gewehr im Anschlag; *(fig)* marsch-/fahrbereit *etc;* **with his pen at the ~** mit gezücktem Federhalter.
(b) *(money)* **the ~** *(inf)* das nötige Kleingeld *(inf); see also* **readies.**

ready *in cpds* fertig-; **~-cooked** *adj* vorgekocht; **~-furnished** *adj* fertig eingerichtet; **~-made** *adj curtains* fertig; *clothes* Konfektions-; *solution* Patent-; *answer, ideas* vorgefertigt; **~-mix** *adj attr (Cook)* aus einer Packung; **~ reckoner** *n* Rechentabelle *f;* **~-to-serve** *adj* tischfertig; **~-to-wear** *adj, pred* **~ to wear** Konfektions-, von der Stange *(inf).*

reaffirm [ˌriːə'fɜːm] *vt* **(a)** *(assert again)* wieder *or* erneut versichern, beteuern. **(b)** *(strengthen, reconfirm) suspicion, doubts* bestätigen; *principles, wish* bestärken.

reafforest ['riːə'fɒrɪst] *vt* wiederaufforsten.

reafforestation ['riːəˌfɒrɪs'teɪʃən] *n* Wiederaufforstung *f.*

reagent [riː'eɪdʒənt] *n (Chem)* Reagens *nt.*

real [rɪəl] **1** *adj* **(a)** *(genuine) gold, flowers, silk etc, sympathy, joy, desire* echt; *need, improvement also* wirklich; *(as opposed to substitute)* richtig; *name* richtig; *(true, as opposed to apparent) owner, boss, reason, purpose, state of affairs* wirklich, tatsächlich, eigentlich; *(not imaginary) creature, object, life, world* wirklich, real *(esp Philos);* *(Phys, Math)* reell; *(Econ)* real ◆ **you can touch it, it's ~** das können Sie anfassen, es ist wirklich da; **was the unicorn ever a ~ creature?** gab es das Einhorn je wirklich *or* tatsächlich?; **~ coffee** Bohnenkaffee *m;* **~ ale** Real Ale *nt;* **in ~ life** im wirklichen Leben; **in ~ terms** effektiv; **he has no ~ power** er hat keine wirkliche Macht; **his grief was very ~** sein Schmerz war echt, er empfand seinen Schmerz zutiefst; **it's the ~ thing** *or* **McCoy, this whisky!** dieser Whisky ist der Echte; **it's not the ~ thing** das ist nicht das Wahre; *(not genuine)* das ist nicht echt; **climbing this hill isn't much when you've done the ~ thing** dieser Hügel ist gar nichts, wenn man schon einmal richtig geklettert hat; **in ~ terms** effektiv; **this increase is in ~ terms equivalent to ...** dieser Anstieg entspricht effektiv ...; **R~ Presence** *(Rel)* Realpräsenz *f.*
(b) *(proper, complete)* richtig; *sportsman, gentleman, coward also* echt; *champion, friend, friendship* wahr, echt; *threat* echt, wirklich; *idiot, disaster* komplett ◆ **it's a ~ miracle** das ist wirklich *or* echt *(inf)* ein Wunder, das ist ein wahres Wunder; **he doesn't know what ~ contentment/family life is** er weiß ja nicht, was Zufriedenheit/Familienleben wirklich ist; **that's what I call a ~ car** das nenne ich ein Auto; **that's a ~ racket** das ist wirklich ein Schwindel.
(c) ~ estate Immobilien *pl;* **~ estate developer** *(US)* Immobilienhändler(in *f) m;* **~ estate office** *(US)* Immobilienbüro *nt;* **~ estate register** *(US)* Grundbuch *nt;* **~ property** Grundbesitz *m.*
2 *adv (esp US inf)* echt *(inf),* wirklich ◆ **we had a ~ good laugh** wir haben so gelacht.
3 *n* **(a) for ~** wirklich, echt *(inf);* **is that invitation for ~?** ist die Einladung ernst gemeint?; **he's not for ~** *(not sincere)* er meint es nicht wirklich; *(not genuine)* er ist nicht echt; **is this for ~ or is it another practice?** ist das echt *(inf) or* ernst oder schon wieder eine Übung?
(b) *(Philos)* **the ~** das Reale, die Wirklichkeit.

realism ['rɪəlɪzəm] *n* Realismus *m.*

realist ['rɪəlɪst] *n* Realist *m.*

realistic [rɪə'lɪstɪk] *adj* realistisch; *painting also* naturgetreu.

realistically [rɪə'lɪstɪkəlɪ] *adv see adj.*

➤ **reality** [riː'ælɪtɪ] *n* **(a)** Wirklichkeit, Realität *f* ◆ **to become ~** sich verwirklichen; **(the) ~ is somewhat different** die Wirklichkeit *or* Realität sieht etwas anders aus; **in ~** *(in fact)* in Wirklichkeit; *(actually)* eigentlich; **to bring sb back to ~** jdn auf den Boden der Tatsachen zurückbringen; **the realities of the situation** der wirkliche Sachverhalt.
(b) *(trueness to life)* Naturtreue *f.*

realizable ['rɪəlaɪzəbl] *adj assets* realisierbar, zu verflüssigen *pred; hope, plan* realisierbar, zu verwirklichen *pred.*

realization [ˌrɪəlaɪ'zeɪʃən] *n* **(a)** *(of assets)* Realisation, Verflüssigung *f;* *(of hope, plan)* Realisierung, Verwirklichung *f.* **(b)** *(awareness)* Erkenntnis *f.*

realize ['rɪəlaɪz] **1** *vt* **(a)** *(become aware of)* erkennen, sich *(dat)* klarwerden *(+gen),* sich *(dat)* bewußt werden *(+gen);* *(be aware of)* sich *(dat)* klar sein über *(+acc),* sich *(dat)* bewußt sein *(+gen);* *(appreciate, understand)* begreifen; *(notice)* (be)merken; *(discover)* feststellen ◆ **does he ~ the problems?** sind ihm die Probleme bewußt *or* klar?; **he had not fully ~d that she was dead** es war ihm nicht voll bewußt, daß sie tot war; **I ~d what he meant** mir wurde klar *or* ich begriff, was er meinte; **I ~d how he had done it** ich erkannte *or* mir wurde klar, wie er es gemacht hatte; **I hadn't ~d you were going away** mir war nicht klar, daß Sie weggehen; **I've just ~d I won't be here** mir ist eben aufgegangen *or* klargeworden, daß ich dann nicht hier sein werde; **when will you ~ you can't ...?** wann werden Sie endlich begreifen, daß Sie nicht ... können?; **I hadn't ~d how late it was** ich habe gar nicht gemerkt, wie spät es war; **he didn't ~ she was cheating him** er merkte nicht, daß sie ihn betrog; **when the parents ~d their child was deaf** als die Eltern (be)merkten *or* feststellten, daß ihr Kind taub war; **I ~d I didn't have any money on me** ich stellte fest, daß ich kein Geld dabei hatte; **I made her ~ that I was right** ich machte ihr klar, daß ich recht hatte; **you couldn't be expected to ~ that** das konnten Sie nicht wissen; **yes, I ~ that** ja, das ist mir klar *or* bewußt; **yes, I ~ that I was wrong** ja, ich sehe ein, daß ich unrecht hatte.
(b) *hope, plan* verwirklichen, realisieren.
(c) *(Fin) assets* realisieren, verflüssigen; *price* bringen, erzielen; *interest* abwerfen, erbringen; *(goods)* einbringen ◆ **how much did you ~ on your Rembrandt?** wieviel hat Ihr Rembrandt (ein)gebracht?
2 *vi* **didn't you ~?** war Ihnen das nicht klar?; *(notice)* haben Sie das nicht gemerkt?; **I've just ~d** das ist mir eben klargeworden; *(noticed)* das habe ich eben gemerkt; **I should have ~d** das hätte ich wissen müssen; **I thought you'd never ~** ich dachte, Sie merken es nie; **he'll never ~** *(notice)* das wird er nie merken; *(understand)* das wird ihm nie klarwerden.

really ['rɪəlɪ] **1** *adv* **(a)** *(in reality)* wirklich, tatsächlich ◆ **I ~ don't know what to think** ich weiß wirklich *or* tatsächlich nicht, was ich davon halten soll; **I don't ~ know what I'm going to do** ich weiß eigentlich nicht, was ich ma-

➤ LANGUAGE IN USE: **reality: a → 26.3**

chen werde; **I don't ~ think so** das glaube ich eigentlich nicht; **well yes, I ~ think we should** ich finde eigentlich schon, daß wir das tun sollten; **before he ~ knew/understood** bevor er richtig *or* wirklich wußte/verstand; **~ and truly** wirklich.
(b) (*intensifier*) wirklich, echt (*inf*); *happy, glad, disappointed also* richtig ◆ **he ~ is an idiot** er ist wirklich *or* echt (*inf*) ein Idiot; **you ~ must visit Paris** Sie müssen wirklich Paris besuchen; **I ~ must say** ... ich muß schon sagen ...
[2] *interj* (*in doubt, disbelief, surprise*) wirklich, tatsächlich; (*in protest, indignation*) also wirklich! ◆ **not ~!** ach wirklich?

realm [relm] *n* (*liter: kingdom*) Königreich *nt*; (*fig*) Reich *nt* ◆ **within the ~s of possibility** im Bereich des Möglichen.

real: ~ number *n* reelle Zahl; **~ tennis** *n* Ballhaustennis *nt*; **~ time** *n* (*Comput*) Echtzeit *f*; **~-time clock** *n* (*Comput*) Echtzeituhr *f*.

realtor [ˈrɪəltɔːʳ] *n* (*US*) Grundstücksmakler *m*.

realty [ˈrɪəltɪ] *n, no pl* (*Jur*) Immobilien *pl*.

ream [riːm] *n* (*of paper*) (altes) Ries ◆ **he always writes ~s** (*inf*) er schreibt immer ganze Bände (*inf*).

reanimate [ˌriːˈænɪmeɪt] *vt* (*Med form*) *patient, person* wiederbeleben; (*fig*) *party, conversation also* neu beleben.

reap [riːp] [1] *vt* **(a)** *corn* (*cut*) schneiden, mähen; (*harvest*) ernten; *field* abernten. **(b)** (*fig*) *profit* ernten; *reward* bekommen ◆ **to ~ the fruit of one's labours** die Früchte seiner Arbeit ernten; **to ~ what one has sown** ernten, was man gesät hat; *see* **sow**[1].
[2] *vi* schneiden, mähen; (*person*) ernten.

reaper [ˈriːpəʳ] *n* (*person*) Schnitter(in *f*) *m*; (*machine*) Mähbinder *m* ◆ **the R~** (*fig: death*) der Schnitter.

reaping [ˈriːpɪŋ] *n see vt (a)* Schneiden, Mähen *nt*; Ernten *nt*; Abernten *nt*.

reaping: ~ hook *n* Sichel *f*; **~ machine** *n* Mähbinder *m*.

reappear [ˌriːəˈpɪəʳ] *vi* wiedererscheinen; (*person, sun also*) sich wieder zeigen; (*character in novel*) wiederauftauchen.

reappearance [ˌriːəˈpɪərəns] *n see vi* Wiedererscheinen *nt*; Wiederauftauchen *nt*.

reappoint [ˌriːəˈpɔɪnt] *vt* (*to a job*) wieder einstellen (*to* als); (*to a post*) wiederernennen (*to* zu).

reappointment [ˌriːəˈpɔɪntmənt] *n see vt* Wiedereinstellung *f*; Wiederernennung *f*.

reapportion [ˌriːəˈpɔːʃən] *vt money, food, land* neu aufteilen; *duties* neu zuteilen.

reappraisal [ˌriːəˈpreɪzəl] *n see vt* Neubeurteilung *f*; Neubewertung *f*.

reappraise [ˌriːəˈpreɪz] *vt situation, problem* von neuem beurteilen; *author, film etc also* neu bewerten.

rear[1] [rɪəʳ] [1] *n* **(a)** (*back part*) hinterer Teil; (*inf: buttocks*) Hintern *m* (*inf*) ◆ **in** *or* **at the ~** hinten (*of* in +*dat*); **to be situated at/to(wards) the ~ of the plane** hinten im Flugzeug/am hinteren Ende des Flugzeugs sein; **at** *or* **to the ~ of the building** (*outside*) hinter dem Haus; (*inside*) hinten im Haus; **go to the ~ of the house** (*behind the house*) geh hinter das Haus; (*inside the house*) geh nach hinten; **from the ~** von hinten.
(b) (*Mil*) Schwanz *m* (der Truppe) ◆ **to attack an army in the ~** eine Armee im Rücken angreifen; **to bring up the ~** (*lit, fig*) die Nachhut bilden.
[2] *adj* Hinter-, hintere(r, s); (*Aut*) *engine, window* Heck- ◆ **~ door** (*of car*) hintere Tür; **~ wheel/lights** (*Aut*) Hinterrad *nt*/Rücklichter *pl*.

rear[2] [1] *vt* **(a)** *animals, family* großziehen, aufziehen.
(b) to ~ its head (*animal*) den Kopf zurückwerfen; (*snake*) sich aufstellen; **violence/racialism ~ed its ugly head (again)** die Gewalt/der Rassismus kam (wieder) zum Vorschein; **sex ~s its ugly head** der Trieb meldet sich.
[2] *vi* (*also* **~ up**) (*horse*) sich aufbäumen.

rear: ~ admiral *n* Konteradmiral *m*; **~-engined** *adj* (*Aut*) mit Heckmotor, heckmotorig; **~guard** *n* (*Mil*) Nachhut *f*; **~guard action** *n* Nachhutgefecht *nt*; **~ gunner** *n* (*Mil*) Heckschütze *m*.

rearm [ˌriːˈɑːm] [1] *vt country* wiederbewaffnen; *forces, troops* neu ausrüsten *or* ausstatten.
[2] *vi* wieder aufrüsten; neue Ausrüstung anschaffen, sich neu ausrüsten.

rearmament [ˌriːˈɑːməmənt] *n see vb* Wiederbewaffnung, Wiederaufrüstung *f*; Neuausrüstung, Neuausstattung *f*.

rearmost [ˈrɪəməʊst] *adj* hinterste(r, s) ◆ **we were ~ in the queue** wir waren die letzten in der Schlange.

rear: ~ mounted engine *n* (*Aut*) Heckmotor *m*; **~ projection** *n* (*Film, Theat*) Rückprojektion *f*.

rearrange [ˌriːəˈreɪndʒ] *vt furniture, system* umstellen; *plans also, layout, formation, order, ideas* ändern; *appointment, meeting* neu abmachen.

rearrangement [ˌriːəˈreɪndʒmənt] *n see vt* Umstellung *f*; Änderung *f*; Neuabmachung *f*.

rear-view mirror [ˈrɪəˌvjuːˈmɪrəʳ] *n* Rückspiegel *m*.

rearward [ˈrɪəwəd] [1] *adj part* hintere(r, s); *position* am Ende; *movement* nach hinten, rückwärtig.
[2] *adv* (*also* **~s**) rückwärts.

rear-wheel drive [ˈrɪəˌwiːlˈdraɪv] *n* Heckantrieb *m*.

reason [ˈriːzn] [1] *n* **(a)** (*cause, justification*) Grund *m* (*for* für) ◆ **my ~ for going, the ~ for my going** (der Grund,) weshalb ich gehe/gegangen bin; **to give sb ~ for complaint** jdm Anlaß *or* Grund zu Klagen geben; **the police had no ~ to interfere** die Polizei hatte keinen Grund einzugreifen; (*but did*) die Polizei hat ohne Grund eingegriffen; **what's the ~ for this celebration**? aus welchem Anlaß wird hier gefeiert?; **I want to know the ~ why** ich möchte wissen, weshalb; **and that's the ~ why** ... und deshalb ...; **and that's the ~ why!** und das ist der Grund dafür!; **I have (good)/every ~ to believe that** ... ich habe (guten) Grund/allen Grund zu glauben, daß ...; **there is ~ to believe that** ... es gibt Gründe, zu glauben, daß ...; **there is every ~ to believe** ... es spricht alles dafür ...; **for that very ~ (that)** eben deswegen(, weil); **with (good) ~** mit gutem Grund, mit Recht; **without any ~** ohne jeden Grund *or* Anlaß, grundlos; **for no ~ at all** ohne ersichtlichen Grund; **for no particular ~** ohne einen bestimmten Grund; **why did you do that? — no particular ~** warum haben Sie das gemacht? — einfach nur so; **for no other ~ than that** ... aus keinem anderen Grund, als daß ...; **for some ~ or (an)other** aus irgendeinem Grund; **for ~s best known to himself/myself** aus unerfindlichen/bestimmten Gründen; **all the more ~ for doing it** *or* **to do it** um so mehr Grund, das zu tun; **by ~ of** wegen (+*gen*); **for ~s of State this was never disclosed** die Staatsräson machte die Geheimhaltung erforderlich.
(b) *no pl* (*mental faculty*) Verstand *m* ◆ **to lose one's ~** den Verstand verlieren; **to reach the age of ~** verständig werden; **the Age of R~** (*Hist*) das Zeitalter der Vernunft.
(c) *no pl* (*common sense*) Vernunft *f* ◆ **to listen to ~** auf die Stimme der Vernunft hören; **he won't listen to ~** er läßt sich (*dat*) nichts sagen; **he's beyond ~** ihm ist mit Vernunft nicht beizukommen; **that stands to ~** das ist logisch; **we'll do anything within ~ to** ... wir tun alles, was in unserer Macht steht, um zu ...; **you can have anything within ~** Sie können alles haben, solange es sich in Grenzen hält.
[2] *vi* **(a)** (*think logically*) vernünftig *or* logisch denken ◆ **the ability to ~** logisches Denkvermögen.
(b) (*argue*) **to ~ (with sb)** vernünftig mit jdm reden; **there's no ~ing with him** mit ihm kann man nicht vernünftig reden.
[3] *vt* **(a) to ~ sb out of/into sth** jdm etw ausreden/jdn zu etw überreden; **to ~ why/what** ... sich (*dat*) klarmachen, warum/was ...; **he ~ed that we could get there by 6 o'clock** er rechnete vor, daß wir bis 6 Uhr dort sein könnten.
(b) (*also* **~ out**) (*deduce*) schließen, folgern; (*verbally*) argumentieren; (*work out*) *problem* durchdenken.

reasonable [ˈriːznəbl] *adj* **(a)** vernünftig; *price also, chance* reell; *claim* berechtigt; *amount* angemessen; (*acceptable*) *excuse, offer* akzeptabel, angemessen ◆ **be ~!** sei vernünftig; **vegetables are ~ (in price) just now** Gemüse ist momentan preiswert; **~ doubt** berechtigter Zweifel; **beyond (all) ~ doubt** ohne (jeden) Zweifel; **guilty beyond (all) ~ doubt** (*Jur*) hinreichend schuldig; **it would be ~ to assume that** ... man könnte durchaus annehmen, daß ...
(b) (*quite good*) ordentlich, ganz gut ◆ **his work was only ~** seine Arbeit war nur einigermaßen (gut); **with a ~ amount of luck** mit einigem Glück.

reasonableness [ˈriːznəblnɪs] *n see adj (a)* Vernünftigkeit *f*; Berechtigung *f*; Angemessenheit *f*.

reasonably [ˈriːznəblɪ] *adv* **(a)** *behave, act, think* vernünftig ◆ **one could ~ think/argue that** ... man könnte durchaus annehmen/anführen, daß ...; **~ priced** preiswert. **(b)** (*quite, fairly*) ziemlich, ganz.

reasoned [ˈriːznd] *adj* durchdacht ◆ **~ thought** Vernunftdenken *nt*.

reasoning [ˈriːznɪŋ] *n* logisches Denken; (*arguing*) Argumentation *f* ◆ **I don't follow your ~** ich kann Ihrem Gedankengang *or* Ihrer Argumentation nicht folgen; **this (piece of) ~ is faulty** das Argument ist falsch; **his ~ is all wrong** er argumentiert ganz falsch, seine Argumente sind falsch.

reassemble [ˌriːəˈsembl] [1] *vt* **(a)** *people, troops* wieder versammeln. **(b)** *tool* wieder zusammenbauen; *car, machine also* wieder montieren.
[2] *vi* sich wieder versammeln; (*troops*) sich wieder sammeln.

reassert [ˌriːəˈsɜːt] *vt* mit Nachdruck behaupten ◆ **to ~ oneself** seine Autorität wieder geltend machen.

reassess [ˌriːəˈses] *vt* neu überdenken; *proposals, advantages* neu abwägen; (*for taxation*) neu veranlagen; *damages* neu schätzen.

reassume [ˌriːəˈsjuːm] *vt work* wiederaufnehmen; *office* wieder übernehmen.

reassurance [ˌriːəˈʃʊərəns] *n* **(a)** (*feeling of security*) Beruhigung *f* ◆ **to give sb ~** jdn beruhigen; **a mother's presence gives a child the ~ it needs** die Gegenwart der Mutter gibt dem Kind das nötige Gefühl der Sicherheit.
(b) (*renewed confirmation*) Bestätigung *f* ◆ **despite his ~(s)** trotz seiner Versicherungen; (*of lover etc*) trotz seiner Beteuerungen.
(c) *see* **reinsurance**.

reassure [ˌriːəˈʃʊəʳ] *vt* **(a)** (*relieve sb's mind*) beruhigen; (*give feeling of security to*) das Gefühl der Sicherheit geben (+*dat*).
(b) (*verbally*) versichern (+*dat*); (*lover*) beteuern (+*dat*) ◆ **to ~ sb of sth** jdm etw versichern/beteuern; **she needs to be constantly ~d that her work is adequate** man muß ihr ständig versichern *or* bestätigen, daß ihre Arbeit gut genug ist.
(c) *see* **reinsure**.

reassuring *adj*, **~ly** *adv* [ˌriːəˈʃʊərɪŋ, -lɪ] beruhigend.

reawaken [ˌriːəˈweɪkən] [1] *vt person* wiedererwecken; *love, passion, interest also* neu erwecken.
[2] *vi* wieder aufwachen; (*interest, love, passion*) wieder aufleben, wiedererwachen *nt*.

reawakening [ˌriːəˈweɪknɪŋ] *n* (*of person*) Wiedererwachen *nt*; (*of ideas, interest also*) Wiederaufleben *nt*.

rebarbative [rɪˈbɑːbətɪv] *adj* (*form*) abstoßend.

rebate [ˈriːbeɪt] *n* (*discount*) Rabatt, (Preis)nachlaß *m*; (*money back*) Rückvergütung, Rückzahlung *f*.

rebel [ˈrebl] [1] *n* Rebell(in *f*), Aufrührer(in *f*) *m*; (*by nature*) Rebell *m*.
[2] *adj attr* rebellisch; *forces, troops also* aufständisch.
[3] [rɪˈbel] *vi* rebellieren; (*troops, forces also*) sich erheben.

➤ LANGUAGE IN USE: **reason: 1a** → 16.1, 17.1, 17.2, 26.3

rebellion [rɪ'beljən] *n* Rebellion *f*, Aufstand *m* ◆ **to rise (up) in ~** einen Aufstand machen, sich erheben.

rebellious [rɪ'beljəs] *adj soldiers, peasants etc* rebellisch, aufrührerisch; *child, nature* rebellisch, widerspenstig.

rebelliousness [rɪ'beljəsnɪs] *n* (*of troops, subordinates etc*) Rebellion *f*; (*nature, of child etc*) Widerspenstigkeit *f*.

rebirth [,riː'bɜːθ] *n* Wiedergeburt *f*; (*of desire*) Wiederaufflackern *nt*.

reboot [,riː'buːt] *vti* (*Comput*) neu laden, rebooten.

rebore [,riː'bɔːʳ] 1 *vt* wieder bohren; *hole* noch einmal bohren; (*Aut*) *engine* ausbohren.
2 ['riː,bɔːʳ] *n* (*Aut*) **this engine needs a ~** der Motor muß ausgebohrt werden.

reborn [,riː'bɔːn] *adj* **to be ~** wiedergeboren werden; **to be ~ in** (*fig*) weiterleben in (+*dat*); **to feel ~** sich wie neugeboren fühlen.

rebound [rɪ'baʊnd] 1 *vi* (*ball, bullet*) zurückprallen, abprallen (*against, off* von) ◆ **your violent methods will ~ (on you)** Ihre rauhen Methoden werden auf Sie zurückfallen.
2 ['riːbaʊnd] *n* (*of ball, bullet*) Rückprall *m*; (*Baseball*) Rebound *m* ◆ **to hit a ball on the ~** den zurück- *or* abgeprallten Ball schlagen; **she married him on the ~** sie heiratete ihn, um sich über einen anderen hinwegzutrösten.

rebroadcast [,riː'brɔːdkɑːst] 1 *n* Wiederholung(ssendung) *f*.
2 *vt* wiederholen, noch einmal senden.

rebuff [rɪ'bʌf] 1 *n* Abfuhr *f*, kurze Zurückweisung ◆ **to meet with a ~** zurück- *or* abgewiesen werden, eine Abfuhr bekommen; (*from opposite sex*) einen Korb bekommen (*inf*).
2 *vt* zurückweisen *or* abweisen; einen Korb geben (+*dat*) (*inf*).

rebuild [,riː'bɪld] *vt* (**a**) (*restore*) *house, wall* wieder aufbauen; (*fig*) *society, relationship* wiederherstellen; *country* wiederaufbauen. (**b**) (*convert*) *house* umbauen; *society* umorganisieren.

rebuilding [,riː'bɪldɪŋ] *n see vt* Wiederaufbau *m*; Wiederherstellung *f*; Umbau *m*; Umorganisation *f*.

rebuke [rɪ'bjuːk] 1 *n* Verweis, Tadel *m*.
2 *vt* zurechtweisen (*for* wegen), tadeln (*for* für) ◆ **to ~ sb for having spoken unkindly** jdn dafür tadeln, daß er so unfreundlich gesprochen hat.

rebukingly [rɪ'bjuːkɪŋlɪ] *adv* tadelnd.

rebus ['riːbəs] *n* Bilderrätsel *nt*, Rebus *m or nt*.

rebut [rɪ'bʌt] *vt argument, contention* widerlegen.

rebuttal [rɪ'bʌtl] *n* Widerlegung *f*.

rec *abbr of* **recommended** empf.

recalcitrance [rɪ'kælsɪtrəns] *n* Aufsässigkeit *f*.

recalcitrant [rɪ'kælsɪtrənt] *adj* aufsässig.

recall [rɪ'kɔːl] 1 *vt* (**a**) (*summon back*) zurückrufen; *ambassador also* abberufen; *library book* zurückfordern; (*Fin*) *capital* zurückfordern, einziehen ◆ **this music ~s the past** diese Musik ruft die Vergangenheit zurück; **to ~ sb to life** jdn ins Leben zurückrufen; **her voice ~ed him to the present** ihre Stimme brachte ihn in die Wirklichkeit zurück.
(**b**) (*remember*) sich erinnern an (+*acc*), sich entsinnen (+*gen*) ◆ **I cannot ~ meeting him** ich kann mich nicht daran erinnern, daß ich ihn kennengelernt habe.
(**c**) (*Comput*) *file* wieder aufrufen.
2 *n* (**a**) *see vt* (*a*) Rückruf *m*; Abberufung *f*; Rückforderung, Einmahnung *f*; Einzug *m* ◆ **to sound the ~** (*Mil*) zum Rückzug blasen; **this book is on ~** das Buch wird zurückgefordert; **~ slip** Aufforderung *f* zur Rückgabe eines/des Buches; **beyond** *or* **past ~** für immer vorbei.
(**b**) (*remembrance*) **powers of ~** Erinnerungsvermögen *nt*.

recant [rɪ'kænt] 1 *vt religious belief* widerrufen; *statement also* zurücknehmen ◆ **to ~ one's opinion** seiner Meinung abschwören.
2 *vi* widerrufen.

recantation [,riːkæn'teɪʃən] *n see vt* Widerruf *m*; Zurücknahme *f*.

recap[1] ['riːkæp] (*inf*) 1 *n* kurze Zusammenfassung ◆ **can we have a quick ~?** können wir kurz rekapitulieren *or* zusammenfassen?
2 *vti* rekapitulieren, kurz zusammenfassen.

recap[2] [,riː'kæp] (*US Aut*) 1 *n* laufflächenerneuerter Reifen.
2 *vt* die Laufflächen erneuern (+*gen*).

recapitulate [,riːkə'pɪtjʊleɪt] 1 *vt* rekapitulieren, kurz zusammenfassen; (*Mus*) *theme* wiederaufnehmen.
2 *vi* rekapitulieren, kurz zusammenfassen; (*Mus*) eine Reprise bringen.

recapitulation ['riːkə,pɪtjʊ'leɪʃən] *n* Rekapitulation *f*, kurze Zusammenfassung; (*Mus*) Reprise *f*.

recapture [,riː'kæptʃəʳ] 1 *vt animal* wieder einfangen; *prisoner* wiederergreifen; *town, territory* wiedererobern; (*fig*) *atmosphere, emotion, period* wieder wachwerden lassen ◆ **they ~d the spark that had originally united them** sie entzündeten den Funken, der einst da war, noch einmal.
2 *n see vt* Wiedereinfangen *nt*; Wiederergreifung *f*; Wiedereroberung *f*; Heraufbeschwörung *f*.

recast [,riː'kɑːst] 1 *vt* (**a**) (*Metal*) neu gießen, umgießen. (**b**) *play, film* eine neue Besetzung wählen für; *parts, roles* umbesetzen, neu besetzen. (**c**) (*rewrite*) umformen.
2 *n* (*Metal*) Neuguß, Umguß *m*.

recce ['rekɪ] *n, vi* (*Brit Mil sl*) *abbr of* **reconnaissance, reconnoitre**.

recd *abbr of* **received** erh.

recede [rɪ'siːd] *vi* (**a**) (*tide*) zurückgehen; (*fig*) sich entfernen; (*hope*) schwinden ◆ **to ~ into the distance** in der Ferne verschwinden; **all hope is receding** jegliche Hoffnung schwindet.
(**b**) **his chin/forehead ~s a bit** er hat ein leicht fliehendes Kinn/eine leicht fliehende Stirn; **his hair is receding** er hat eine leichte Stirnglatze; *see also* **receding**.
(**c**) (*price*) zurückgehen.
(**d**) **to ~ from** *opinion, view etc* abgehen von, aufgeben.

receding [rɪ'siːdɪŋ] *adj chin, forehead* fliehend; *hairline* zurückweichend.

▼ **receipt** [rɪ'siːt] 1 *n* (**a**) *no pl* Empfang *m*; (*Comm also*) Erhalt, Eingang *m* ◆ **on ~ of your remittance/the goods, we shall be pleased to ...** nach Empfang *etc* Ihrer Zahlung/der Waren werden wir gerne ...; **to pay on ~ (of the goods)** bei Empfang *etc* (der Waren) bezahlen; **I am in ~ of** (*on letter*) ich bin im Besitz (+*gen*); **~ stamp** Empfangsstempel *m*.
(**b**) (*paper*) Quittung *f*, Beleg *m*; (*for parcel, letter also*) Empfangsschein *m*; (*~ of posting*) Einlieferungsschein *m* ◆ **~ book** Quittungsbuch *nt*.
(**c**) (*Comm, Fin: money taken*) **~s** Einnahmen, Einkünfte *pl*.
2 *vt bill* quittieren.

receivable [rɪ'siːvəbl] *adj* (*Jur*) zulässig ◆ **accounts/bills ~** (*Comm*) Außenstände *pl*/Wechselforderungen *pl*.

receive [rɪ'siːv] 1 *vt* (**a**) (*get*) bekommen, erhalten; (*take possession or delivery of*) *letter, present, salary, orders etc also* empfangen; *punch* (ab)bekommen; *refusal, setback* erfahren; *impression* gewinnen, bekommen; *recognition* finden; (*Jur*) *stolen goods* Hehlerei (be)treiben mit; (*Tennis*) *ball, service* zurückschlagen; *sacrament* empfangen ◆ **to ~ nothing but abuse** nichts als Beleidigungen hören; **he ~d nothing worse than a few bruises** er bekam nur ein paar blaue Flecke ab; **"~d with thanks"** (*Comm*) „dankend erhalten".
(**b**) *offer, proposal, news, new play etc, person* (*into group, the Church*) aufnehmen ◆ **to ~ a warm welcome** herzlich empfangen werden; **given the welcome we ~d ...** so, wie wir empfangen worden sind, ...; **to ~ sb into one's family** jdn in seine Familie aufnehmen; **the play was well ~d** das Stück wurde gut aufgenommen.
(**c**) (*Telec, Rad, TV*) empfangen ◆ **are you receiving me?** hören Sie mich?
2 *vi* (**a**) (*form*) (Besuch) empfangen ◆ **Mrs X ~s on Mondays** Frau X empfängt an Montagen.
(**b**) (*Jur*) Hehlerei treiben.
(**c**) (*Tennis*) rückschlagen ◆ **Borg to ~** Rückschläger Borg.
(**d**) (*Telec*) empfangen.

received [rɪ'siːvd]: **~ opinion** *n* die allgemeine Meinung; **~ pronunciation** *n* hochsprachliche Aussprache (*nach Daniel Jones*).

▼ **receiver** [rɪ'siːvəʳ] *n* (**a**) (*of letter, goods*) Empfänger(in *f*) *m*; (*Jur: of stolen property*) Hehler(in *f*) *m*. (**b**) (*Fin, Jur*) **official ~** Konkursverwalter *m*; **to call in** ▼ **the ~** Konkurs anmelden. (**c**) (*Telec*) Hörer *m* ◆ **~ rest** Gabel *f*. (**d**) (*Rad*) Empfänger *m*. (**e**) (*Tennis*) Rückschläger(in *f*) *m*.

receivership [rɪ'siːvəʃɪp] *n*: **to go into ~** in Konkurs gehen.

receiving [rɪ'siːvɪŋ] *n* (*Jur: of stolen goods*) Hehlerei *f*.

receiving: ~ end *n* (*inf*): **to be on the ~ end (of it)/of sth** derjenige sein, der es/etw abkriegt (*inf*); **~ set** *n* Empfangsgerät *nt*.

recency ['riːsənsɪ] *n* Neuheit *f*.

recension [rɪ'senʃən] *n* Rezension *f*.

recent ['riːsənt] *adj* kürzlich (*usu adv*); *event, development, closure* jüngste(r, s), neueste(r, s); *news* neueste(r, s), letzte(r, s); *acquaintance, invention, edition, addition* neu; *publication* Neu- ◆ **the ~ improvement** die vor kurzem eingetretene Verbesserung; **their ~ loss** ihr vor kurzem erlittener Verlust; **a ~ decision** eine Entscheidung, die erst vor kurzem gefallen ist; **most ~** neueste(r, s); **he is a ~ acquaintance of mine** ich kenne ihn erst seit kurzem; **his ~ arrival/holiday** seine Ankunft vor kurzem/sein erst kurz zurückliegender Urlaub; **he is a ~ arrival** er ist erst vor kurzem angekommen, er ist erst kurz hier; **in the ~ past** in jüngerer *or* jüngster Zeit (*geh*), erst vor kurzem; **in ~ years/times** in den letzten Jahren/in letzter *or* jüngster (*geh*) Zeit; **of ~ date** neueren Datums; **~ developments** jüngste Entwicklungen, Entwicklungen in jüngster Zeit.

recently ['riːsəntlɪ] *adv* (*a short while ago*) vor kurzem, kürzlich; (*the other day also*) neulich; (*during the last few days or weeks*) in letzter Zeit ◆ **~ he has been doing it differently** seit kurzem macht er das anders; **as ~ as** erst; **quite ~** erst vor kurzem, erst kürzlich; **until (quite) ~** (noch) bis vor kurzem; **he lived there until as ~ as last year** er hat bis letztes Jahr noch dort gelebt.

receptacle [rɪ'septəkl] *n* Behälter *m*.

▼ **reception** [rɪ'sepʃən] *n* (**a**) *no pl* (*receiving, welcome*) (*of person*) Empfang *m*; (*into group, of play, book etc*) Aufnahme *f* ◆ **the play met with** *or* **had a very favourable ~** das Stück fand gute Aufnahme, das Stück wurde gut aufgenommen; **what sort of ~ did you get?** wie sind Sie empfangen *or* aufgenommen worden?; **to give sb a warm/chilly ~** jdm einen herzlichen/kühlen Empfang bereiten, jdn herzlich/kühl empfangen; **~ area/camp/centre** Empfangsbereich *m*/Aufnahmelager *nt*/Durchgangslager *nt*; **~ desk** Empfang *m*, Rezeption *f*; **~ room** Wohnzimmer *nt*; (*in hotel*) Aufenthaltsraum *m*.
(**b**) (*party, ceremony*) Empfang *m*.
(**c**) (*in hotel etc*) der Empfang ◆ **at/to ~** am/zum Empfang.
(**d**) (*Rad, TV*) Empfang *m*.
(**e**) (*Brit Sch: also* **~ class**) Anfängerklasse *f*.

receptionist [rɪ'sepʃənɪst] *n* (*in hotel*) Empfangschef *m*, Empfangsdame *f*; (*with firm*) Herr *m*/Dame *f* am Empfang, Portier *m*, Empfangssekretärin *f*; (*at airport*) Bodenhostess *f*; (*at doctor's, dentist's etc*) Sprechstundenhilfe *f*.

receptive [rɪ'septɪv] *adj person, mind* aufnahmefähig; *audience* empfänglich ◆ **~ to** empfänglich für.

receptiveness [rɪ'septɪvnɪs] *n see adj* Aufnahmefähigkeit *f*, Empfänglichkeit *f* ◆ **~ to** Empfänglichkeit *f* für.

receptor [rɪ'septəʳ] *n* (*nerve*) Reizempfänger, Rezeptor *m*; (*Rad*) Empfänger

➤ LANGUAGE IN USE: **receipt: 1a** → 20.5 **receiver: c** → 27.3 **reception: a** → 13

m.

recess [rɪ'ses] [1] n (a) (cessation) (of Parliament) (Sitzungs)pause f; (of lawcourts) Ferien pl; (US Sch) Pause f.
(b) (alcove) Nische f.
(c) (secret place) Winkel m ♦ **in the (deepest) ~es of my heart** in den (tiefsten) Tiefen meines Herzens.
[2] vt (set back) in eine/die Nische stellen; cupboard, cooker einbauen; windows vertiefen; lighting versenken; (make a ~ in) wall etc eine Nische machen in (+acc), vertiefen.

recession [rɪ'seʃən] n (a) no pl (receding) Zurückweichen f, Rückgang m; (Eccl) Auszug m.
(b) (Econ) Rezession f, (wirtschaftlicher) Rückgang.

recessional [rɪ'seʃənl] (Eccl) [1] n während des Auszugs gesungene Schlußhymne.
[2] adj hymn Schluß-.

recessive [rɪ'sesɪv] adj zurückweichend; (Econ, Biol) rezessiv.

recharge [ˌriː'tʃɑːdʒ] [1] vt battery aufladen; gun neu or wieder laden, nachladen.
[2] vi sich wieder aufladen ♦ **it ~s automatically** es lädt sich automatisch (wieder) auf.

recheck [ˌriː'tʃek] vt nochmals prüfen or kontrollieren.

recherché [rə'ʃɛəʃeɪ] adj gewählt; book, subject ausgefallen; expression gesucht.

rechristen [ˌriː'krɪsən] vt umtaufen ♦ **it was ~ed Leningrad** es wurde in Leningrad umbenannt or umgetauft.

recidivism [rɪ'sɪdɪvɪzəm] n Rückfälligkeit f.

recidivist [rɪ'sɪdɪvɪst] [1] n Rückfällige(r) mf.
[2] adj rückfällig.

recipe ['resɪpɪ] n Rezept nt; (fig also) Geheimnis nt ♦ **an easy ~ for ...** (fig) ein Patentrezept für ...; **that's a ~ for disaster** das führt mit Sicherheit in die Katastrophe; **a ~ for success** ein Erfolgsrezept nt.

recipient [rɪ'sɪpɪənt] n Empfänger(in f) m ♦ **Susan, as the ~ of his attentions** Susan, der seine Aufmerksamkeiten galten.

reciprocal [rɪ'sɪprəkəl] [1] adj (mutual) gegenseitig; favour Gegen-; (Gram, Math) reziprok ♦ **the ~ relationship between these two phenomena** die Wechselbeziehung zwischen diesen zwei Phänomenen; **~ trade** Handel untereinander.
[2] n (Math) reziproker Wert.

reciprocally [rɪ'sɪprəkəlɪ] adv admire, help gegenseitig; trade, correspond untereinander, miteinander; (Gram) reziprok.

reciprocate [rɪ'sɪprəkeɪt] [1] vt (a) smiles, wishes erwidern; help, kindness also sich revanchieren für.
(b) (Tech) hin- und herbewegen; piston auf- und abbewegen.
[2] vi (a) sich revanchieren ♦ **she ~d by throwing the saucepan at him** sie wiederum warf ihm den Topf nach.
(b) (Tech) hin- und hergehen; (piston) auf- und abgehen ♦ **reciprocating engine** Kolbenmotor m.

reciprocation [rɪˌsɪprə'keɪʃən] n (a) (of help, kindness) Erwiderung f (of gen), Revanche f (of für). (b) (Tech) Hin und Her nt; (of pistons) Auf und Ab nt.

reciprocity [ˌresɪ'prɒsɪtɪ] n (of feelings, kindness etc) Gegenseitigkeit f; (of favours) Austausch m; (Pol) Gegenseitigkeit, Reziprozität (form) f.

recital [rɪ'saɪtl] n (a) (of music, poetry) Vortrag m; (piano ~ etc) Konzert nt ♦ **song ~** Matinee f, Liederabend m. (b) (account) Schilderung f; (of details) Aufführung, Aufzählung f.

recitation [ˌresɪ'teɪʃən] n Vortrag m.

recitative [ˌresɪtə'tiːv] n Rezitativ nt.

recite [rɪ'saɪt] [1] vt (a) poetry vortragen, rezitieren. (b) facts hersagen; details aufzählen.
[2] vi vortragen, rezitieren.

reckless ['reklɪs] adj leichtsinnig; driver, driving rücksichtslos; speed gefährlich; attempt gewagt ♦ **~ of the danger** (liter) ungeachtet der Gefahr (liter).

recklessly ['reklɪslɪ] adv see adj.

recklessness ['reklɪsnɪs] n see adj Leichtsinn m; Rücksichtslosigkeit f; Gefährlichkeit f; Gewagtheit f.

reckon ['rekən] [1] vt (a) (calculate) time, numbers, points, costs, area ausrechnen, berechnen ♦ **he ~ed the cost to be £40.51** er berechnete die Kosten auf £ 40,51.
(b) (judge) rechnen, zählen (among zu) ♦ **she is ~ed a beautiful woman** sie gilt als schöne Frau.
(c) (think, suppose) glauben; (estimate) schätzen ♦ **what do you ~?** was meinen Sie?; **I ~ we can start** ich glaube, wir können anfangen; **I ~ he must be about forty** ich schätze, er müßte so um die Vierzig sein; **he ~s himself to be one of the best ...** er hält sich für einen der besten ...
(d) (sl) (like) gutfinden (inf); (think likely to succeed) große Chancen geben (+dat).
[2] vi (calculate) rechnen ♦ **it's difficult to ~** (eg how far/long etc) das ist schwer zu schätzen; **~ing from tomorrow** ab morgen gerechnet.

♦**reckon on** vi +prep obj rechnen or zählen auf (+acc) ♦ **you can ~ ~ 30** Sie können mit 30 rechnen; **I was ~ing ~ doing that tomorrow** ich wollte das morgen machen; **I wasn't ~ing ~ having to do that** ich habe nicht damit gerechnet, daß ich das tun muß.

♦**reckon up** [1] vt sep zusammenrechnen.
[2] vi abrechnen (with mit).

♦**reckon with** vi +prep obj rechnen mit ♦ **if you insult him you'll have the whole family to ~ ~** wenn Sie ihn beleidigen, müssen Sie mit der ganzen Familie rechnen; **he's a person to be ~ed ~** er ist jemand, mit dem man rechnen muß.

♦**reckon without** vi +prep obj nicht rechnen mit ♦ **he ~ed ~ the fact that ...** er hatte nicht damit gerechnet, daß ...; **you must ~ ~ my being there to help you** du mußt damit rechnen, daß ich nicht da bin(, um dir zu helfen).

reckoner ['rekənəʳ] n see **ready ~**.

reckoning ['rekənɪŋ] n (a) (calculation) (Be)rechnung f; (old: bill, account) Rechnung f ♦ **to be out in one's ~** sich ziemlich verrechnet haben; **the day of ~** der Tag der Abrechnung; **to the best of my ~** nach meiner Schätzung; **in your ~** Ihrer Meinung or Schätzung nach. (b) (Naut) see **dead ~**.

reclaim [rɪ'kleɪm] [1] vt (a) land gewinnen; (by irrigation etc) kultivieren ♦ **to ~ land from the sea** dem Meer Land abringen.
(b) (liter) person abbringen (from von).
(c) (from waste) wiedergewinnen, regenerieren (from aus).
(d) (demand or ask back) rights, privileges zurückverlangen; lost item, baggage abholen.
[2] n (a) **past or beyond ~** rettungslos or für immer verloren.
(b) **baggage or luggage ~** Gepäckausgabe f.

reclaimable [rɪ'kleɪməbl] adj land nutzbar; by-products regenerierbar.

reclamation [ˌreklə'meɪʃən] n see vt (a) Gewinnung f; Kultivierung f. (b) Abbringung f. (c) Wiedergewinnung, Regeneration f. (d) Rückgewinnung f.

recline [rɪ'klaɪn] [1] vt arm zurücklegen (on auf +acc); head also zurücklehnen (on an +acc); seat zurückstellen.
[2] vi (person) zurückliegen; (seat) sich verstellen lassen ♦ **she was reclining on the sofa** sie ruhte auf dem Sofa; **reclining in his bath** im Bade liegend; **reclining chair** Ruhesessel m; **reclining seat** verstellbarer Sitz; (in car, on boat) Liegesitz m; **reclining figure** (Art) Liegende(r) mf.

recliner [rɪ'klaɪnəʳ] n Ruhesessel m.

recluse [rɪ'kluːs] n Einsiedler(in f) m.

recognition [ˌrekəg'nɪʃən] n (a) (acknowledgement, Pol) Anerkennung f ♦ **in ~ of** in Anerkennung (+gen); **his ~ of these facts** daß er diese Tatsachen akzeptierte; **by or on your own ~** wie Sie selbst zugeben; **to gain/receive ~** Anerkennung finden.
(b) (identification) Erkennen nt ♦ **the baby's ~ of its mother/mother's voice** daß das Baby seine Mutter/die Stimme seiner Mutter erkennt/erkannte; **he has changed beyond or out of all ~** er ist nicht wiederzuerkennen; **he has changed it beyond or out of all ~** er ist nicht wiederzuerkennen.

recognizable ['rekəgnaɪzəbl] adj erkennbar ♦ **you're scarcely ~ with that beard** Sie sind mit dem Bart kaum zu erkennen; **Poland is no longer ~ as the country I knew in 1940** Polen ist nicht mehr das Land, das ich 1940 kannte.

recognizance [rɪ'kɒgnɪzəns] n (Jur) Verpflichtung f; (for debt) Anerkenntnis f; (sum of money) Sicherheitsleistung f ♦ **to enter into ~ (for sb)** für jdn Kaution stellen.

recognize ['rekəgnaɪz] vt (a) (know again) person, town, face, voice etc wiedererkennen; (identify) erkennen (by an +dat) ♦ **you wouldn't ~ him/the house etc** Sie würden ihn/das Haus etc nicht wiedererkennen; **do you ~ this tune?** erkennen Sie die Melodie?; **I wouldn't have ~d him in his disguise** ich hätte ihn in der Verkleidung nicht erkannt.
(b) (acknowledge, Pol) anerkennen (as, to be als) ♦ **she doesn't ~ me any more when she goes past** sie kennt mich nicht mehr, wenn sie mich trifft; **he doesn't even ~ my existence** er nimmt mich nicht einmal zur Kenntnis.
(c) (be aware) erkennen; (be prepared to admit) zugeben, eingestehen ♦ **you must ~ what is necessary** Sie müssen erkennen, was notwendig ist; **I ~ that I am not particularly intelligent** ich gebe zu, daß ich nicht besonders intelligent bin.
(d) (US: let speak) das Wort erteilen (+dat, an +acc).

recognized ['rekəgnaɪzd] adj anerkannt.

recoil [rɪ'kɔɪl] [1] vi (a) (person) (from vor +dat) zurückweichen; (in fear) zurückschrecken; (in disgust) zurückschaudern ♦ **he ~ed from (the idea of) doing it** ihm graute davor, das zu tun.
(b) (gun) zurückstoßen; (spring) zurückschnellen ♦ **the gun will ~** das Gewehr hat einen Rückstoß.
(c) (fig: actions) **to ~ on sb** auf jdn zurückfallen, sich an jdm rächen.
[2] ['riːkɔɪl] n (of gun) Rückstoß m; (of spring) Zurückschnellen nt no pl.

recollect [ˌrekə'lekt] [1] vt sich erinnern an (+acc), sich entsinnen (+gen).
[2] vi sich erinnern, sich entsinnen ♦ **as far as I can ~** soweit ich mich erinnern kann.

recollection [ˌrekə'lekʃən] n (memory) Erinnerung f (of an +acc) ♦ **to the best of my ~** soweit ich mich erinnern kann; **his ~ of it is vague** er erinnert sich nur vage daran; **I have some/no ~ of it** ich kann mich schwach/nicht daran erinnern.

recommence [ˌriːkə'mens] vti wiederbeginnen.

▼ **recommend** [ˌrekə'mend] vt (a) empfehlen (as als) ♦ **what do you ~ for a cough?** was empfehlen or raten Sie gegen Husten?; **to ~ sb sth or sth to sb** jdm etw empfehlen; **it is not to be ~ed** es ist nicht zu empfehlen; **~ed price** unverbindlicher Richtpreis; **~ed speed** Richtgeschwindigkeit f.
(b) (make acceptable) sprechen für ♦ **she has much/little to ~ her** es spricht sehr viel/wenig für sie; **his manners do little to ~ him** seine Manieren sind nicht gerade eine Empfehlung für ihn; **this book has little/a great deal to ~ it** das Buch ist nicht gerade/sehr empfehlenswert.
(c) (old, liter: entrust) child, one's soul empfehlen (to sb jdm).

recommendable [ˌrekə'mendəbl] adj empfehlenswert; course of action, measures also ratsam ♦ **it is not ~ reading** das ist als Lesestoff nicht zu empfehlen.

➤ LANGUAGE IN USE: **recommend: a** → 2.1, 19.4

recommendation [ˌrekəmen'deɪʃən] *n* Empfehlung *f* ◆ **on the ~ of** auf Empfehlung von; **to make a ~** jemanden/etwas empfehlen; **letter of ~** Empfehlung(sschreiben *nt*) *f*.

recommendatory [ˌrekə'mendətərɪ] *adj* empfehlend.

recompense ['rekəmpens] [1] *n* **(a)** (*reward*) Belohnung *f* ◆ **as a ~** als *or* zur Belohnung; **in ~ for** als Belohnung für. **(b)** (*Jur, fig*) Entschädigung *f*; (*of loss*) Wiedergutmachung *f*.
[2] *vt* **(a)** (*reward*) belohnen.
(b) (*Jur, fig: repay*) *person* entschädigen; *damage, loss* wiedergutmachen.

recompose [ˌri:kəm'pəʊz] *vt* **(a)** (*rewrite*) umschreiben; (*Mus also*) umkomponieren. **(b)** (*calm*) **to ~ oneself** sich wieder beruhigen.

reconcilable ['rekənsaɪləbl] *adj people* versöhnbar; *ideas, opinions* miteinander vereinbar.

reconcile ['rekənsaɪl] *vt* **(a)** *people* versöhnen, aussöhnen; *differences* beilegen; *dispute* schlichten ◆ **they became** *or* **were ~d** sie versöhnten sich, sie söhnten sich aus.
(b) (*make compatible*) *facts, ideas, theories, principles* miteinander in Einklang bringen, miteinander vereinbaren ◆ **to ~ sth with sth** etw mit etw in Einklang bringen, etw mit etw vereinbaren; **these ideas cannot be ~d** diese Ideen sind unvereinbar; **how do you ~ that with the fact that you said no last week?** wie läßt sich das damit vereinbaren, daß Sie letzte Woche nein gesagt haben?
(c) (*make accept*) **to ~ sb to sth** jdn mit etw versöhnen; **to ~ oneself to sth, to become ~d to sth** sich mit etw abfinden; **what ~d him to it was ...** was ihn damit versöhnte, war ...

reconciliation [ˌrekənsɪlɪ'eɪʃən] *n* (*of persons*) Versöhnung, Aussöhnung *f*; (*of opinions, principles*) Vereinbarung, Versöhnung (*esp Philos*) *f*; (*of differences*) Beilegung *f*.

recondite [rɪ'kɒndaɪt] *adj* abstrus.

recondition [ˌri:kən'dɪʃən] *vt* generalüberholen ◆ **a ~ed engine** ein Austauschmotor *m*.

reconnaissance [rɪ'kɒnɪsəns] *n* (*Aviat, Mil*) Aufklärung *f* ◆ **~ plane** Aufklärer *m*, Aufklärungsflugzeug *nt*; **~ flight/patrol** Aufklärungsflug *m*/Spähtrupp *m*; **~ mission** Aufklärungseinsatz *m*; **to be on ~** bei einem Aufklärungseinsatz sein.

reconnoitre, (*US*) **reconnoiter** [ˌrekə'nɔɪtə^r] [1] *vt* (*Aviat, Mil*) *region* auskundschaften, erkunden, aufklären.
[2] *vi* das Gelände erkunden *or* aufklären.

reconquer [ˌri:'kɒŋkə^r] *vt town, territory* zurückerobern; *enemy* erneut *or* wieder besiegen.

reconquest [ˌri:'kɒŋkwest] *n see vt* Zurückeroberung *f*; erneuter Sieg (*of* über +*acc*).

reconsider [ˌri:kən'sɪdə^r] [1] *vt decision, judgement* noch einmal überdenken; (*change*) revidieren; *facts* neu erwägen; (*Jur*) *case* wiederaufnehmen ◆ **won't you ~ your decision and come?** wollen Sie es sich (*dat*) nicht überlegen und doch kommen?; **I have ~ed my decision, I'd rather not accept** ich habe es mir noch einmal überlegt, ich lehne lieber ab.
[2] *vi* **ask him to ~** sagen Sie ihm, er soll es sich (*dat*) noch einmal überlegen; **there's still time to ~** es ist noch nicht zu spät, seine Meinung zu ändern *or* es sich anders zu überlegen.

reconsideration ['ri:kənˌsɪdə'reɪʃən] *n see vt* Überdenken *nt*; Revision *f*; erneute Erwägung; Wiederaufnahme *f* ◆ **following his ~** da er es sich (*dat*) anders überlegt hat/hatte.

reconstitute [ˌri:'kɒnstɪtju:t] *vt* **(a)** *assembly, committee* neu einrichten, rekonstituieren (*form*); (*reconstruct*) wiederherstellen. **(b)** *food* aus einem Konzentrat zubereiten; *solution* in Wasser auflösen.

reconstitution ['ri:ˌkɒnstɪ'tju:ʃən] *n see vt* **(a)** Rekonstitution *f* (*form*); Wiederherstellung *f*. **(b)** Zubereitung *f* aus einem Konzentrat; Auflösen *nt* in Wasser.

reconstruct [ˌri:kən'strʌkt] *vt* rekonstruieren; *cities* wiederaufbauen; *building* wieder aufbauen ◆ **to ~ one's life** (im Leben) noch einmal von vorn anfangen.

reconstruction [ˌri:kən'strʌkʃən] *n see vt* Rekonstruktion *f*; Wiederaufbau *m*.

reconstructive [ˌri:kən'strʌktɪv] *adj attr* (*Med*) wiederherstellend ◆ **~ surgery** Wiederherstellungschirurgie *f*.

record [rɪ'kɔ:d] [1] *vt* **(a)** *facts, story, events* (*diarist, person*) aufzeichnen; (*documents, diary etc*) dokumentieren; (*in register*) eintragen; (*keep minutes of*) protokollieren; *one's thoughts, feelings etc* festhalten, niederschreiben; *protest, disapproval* zum Ausdruck bringen ◆ **these facts are not ~ed anywhere** diese Tatsachen sind nirgends festgehalten; **it's not ~ed anywhere** das ist nirgends dokumentiert *or* belegt; **to ~ sth photographically** etw im Bild festhalten; **to ~ one's vote** seine Stimme abgeben; **history/the author ~s that ...** es ist geschichtlich dokumentiert/der Verfasser berichtet, daß ...
(b) (*thermometer, meter etc*) verzeichnen, registrieren; (*needle*) aufzeichnen, registrieren; (*pen needle*) aufzeichnen.
(c) (*on tape, cassette etc*) *music, person* aufnehmen; *programme, speech also* aufzeichnen ◆ **a ~ed programme** eine Aufzeichnung; **~ing apparatus** Aufnahmegerät *nt*.
[2] *vi* (Tonband)aufnahmen machen ◆ **he is ~ing at 5 o'clock** er hat um 5 Uhr eine Aufnahme; **his voice does not ~ well** seine Stimme läßt sich nicht gut aufnehmen; **the tape-recorder won't ~** man kann mit dem Tonbandgerät nicht aufnehmen.
[3] ['rekɔ:d] *n* **(a)** (*account*) Aufzeichnung *f*; (*of attendance*) Liste *f*; (*of meeting*) Protokoll *nt*; (*official document*) Unterlage, Akte *f*; (*lit, fig: of the past, of civilization*) Dokument *nt* ◆ **(public) ~s** im Staatsarchiv gelagerte Urkunden; **a photographic ~** eine Bilddokumentation; **it's nice to have a photographic ~ of one's holidays** es ist nett, den Urlaub im Bild festgehalten zu haben; **to keep a ~ of sth** über etw (*acc*) Buch führen; (*official, registrar*) etw registrieren; (*historian, chronicler*) etw aufzeichnen; **to keep a personal ~ of sth** sich (*dat*) etw notieren; **it is on ~ that ...** es gibt Belege dafür, daß ...; (*in files*) es ist aktenkundig, daß ...; **there is no similar example on ~** es ist kein ähnliches Beispiel bekannt; **I'm prepared to go on ~ as saying that ...** ich stehe zu der Behauptung, daß ...; **he's on ~ as having said ...** es ist belegt, daß er gesagt hat, ...; **last night the PM went on ~ as saying ...** gestern abend hat sich der Premier dahin gehend geäußert, daß ...; **to put sth on ~** etw schriftlich festhalten; **there is no ~ of his having said it** es ist nirgends belegt, daß er es gesagt hat; **to put** *or* **set the ~ straight** für klare Verhältnisse sorgen; **just to set the ~ straight** nur damit Klarheit herrscht; **for the ~** der Ordnung halber; (*for the minutes*) zur Mitschrift; **this is strictly off the ~** dies ist nur inoffizell; **(strictly) off the ~ he did come** ganz im Vertrauen: er ist doch gekommen.
(b) (*police ~*) Vorstrafen *pl* ◆ **~s** (*files*) Strafregister *nt*; **he's got a ~** er ist vorbestraft; **~ of previous convictions** Vorstrafen *pl*; **he's got a clean ~, he hasn't got a ~** er ist nicht vorbestraft; **to keep one's ~ clean** sich (*dat*) nichts zuschulden kommen lassen.
(c) (*history*) Vorgeschichte *f*; (*achievements*) Leistungen *pl* ◆ **to have an excellent ~** ausgezeichnete Leistungen vorweisen können; **the applicant with the best ~** der Bewerber mit den besten Voraussetzungen; **with a ~ like yours you should be able to handle this job** mit den Leistungen, die Sie vorzuweisen haben, *or* mit Ihren Voraussetzungen müßten Sie sich in dieser Stelle leicht zurechtfinden; **he has a good ~ of service** er ist ein verdienter Mitarbeiter; **service ~** (*Mil*) militärisches Führungszeugnis; **his attendance ~ is bad** er fehlt oft; **his past ~** seine bisherigen Leistungen; **to have a good ~ at school** ein guter Schüler sein; **to have a good safety ~** in bezug auf Sicherheit einen guten Ruf haben; **to have a dubious ~ as far as sth is concerned** in bezug auf etw (*acc*) einen zweifelhaften Ruf haben; **he's got quite a ~** (*has done bad things*) er hat so einiges auf dem Kerbholz; **he left a splendid ~ of achievements behind him** er hat sehr viel geleistet; **to spoil one's ~** es sich (*dat*) verderben, sich (*dat*) ein Minus einhandeln (*inf*); **I've been looking at your ~, Jones** ich habe mir Ihre Akte angesehen, Jones.
(d) (*Mus*) (Schall)platte *f*; (*~ing*) (*of voice, music etc*) Aufnahme *f*; (*of programme, speech*) Aufzeichnung, Aufnahme *f* ◆ **to make** *or* **cut a ~** eine Schallplatte machen.
(e) (*Sport, fig*) Rekord *m* ◆ **to beat** *or* **break the ~** den Rekord brechen; **to hold the ~** den Rekord halten *or* innehaben; **long-jump ~** Weitsprungrekord, Rekord im Weitsprung; **a ~ amount/time/result** ein Rekordbetrag *m*/eine Rekordzeit/ein Rekordergebnis *nt*.
(f) (*on seismograph etc*) Aufzeichnung, Registrierung *f*.
(g) (*Comput: in database*) Datensatz *m*.

record ['rekɔ:d]: **~ album** *n* Plattenalbum *nt*; **~ breaker** *n* (*Sport*) Rekordbrecher(in *f*) *m*; **~-breaking** *adj* (*Sport, fig*) rekordbrechend, Rekord-; **~ cabinet** *n* Plattenschrank *m*; **~ card** *n* Karteikarte *f*; **~ changer** *n* Plattenwechsler *m*; **~ dealer** *n* Schallplattenhändler(in *f*) *m*.

recorded [rɪ'kɔ:dɪd] *adj* **(a)** *music, programme* aufgezeichnet ◆ **~ delivery** (*Brit*) eingeschriebene Sendung; **by ~ delivery** *or* **post** (*Brit*) per Einschreiben. **(b)** *fact, occurrence* schriftlich belegt ◆ **in all ~ history** seit unserer Geschichtsschreibung.

recorder [rɪ'kɔ:də^r] *n* **(a)** (*apparatus*) Registriergerät *nt* ◆ **cassette/tape ~** Kassettenrekorder *m*/Tonbandgerät *nt*. **(b)** (*Mus*) Blockflöte *f*. **(c)** (*of official facts*) Berichterstatter *m*; (*historian*) Chronist *m*. **(d)** (*Brit Jur*) *nebenher als Richter tätiger Rechtsanwalt.*

record holder *n* (*Sport*) Rekordhalter(in *f*) *or* -inhaber(in *f*) *m*.

recording [rɪ'kɔ:dɪŋ] *n* (*of sound*) Aufnahme *f*; (*of programme*) Aufzeichnung *f*.

recording: ~ angel *n Engel, der gute und böse Taten aufschreibt*; **~ artist** *n* Musiker(in *f*) *m*, der/die Schallplattenaufnahmen macht; Plattensänger(in *f*) *m*; **~ session** *n* Aufnahme *f*; **~ studio** *n* Aufnahmestudio *nt*; **~ tape** *n* Tonband *nt*; **~ van** *n* (*Rad, TV*) Aufnahmewagen *m*.

record ['rekɔ:d]: **~ library** *n* Plattenverleih *m*; (*collection*) Plattensammlung *f*; **~-player** *n* Plattenspieler *m*; **~ token** *n* Plattengutschein *m*.

recount [rɪ'kaʊnt] *vt* (*relate*) erzählen, wiedergeben.

re-count [ˌri:'kaʊnt] [1] *vt* nachzählen.
[2] ['ri:ˌkaʊnt] *n* (*of votes*) Nachzählung *f*.

recoup [rɪ'ku:p] *vt* **(a)** (*make good*) *money, amount* wieder einbringen *or* hereinbekommen; *losses* wiedergutmachen, wettmachen. **(b)** (*reimburse*) entschädigen ◆ **to ~ oneself** sich entschädigen. **(c)** (*Jur*) einbehalten.

recourse [rɪ'kɔ:s] *n* Zuflucht *f* ◆ **to have ~ to sb/sth** sich an jdn wenden/Zuflucht zu etw nehmen; **without ~ to his books** ohne seine Bücher zu konsultieren; **without ~** (*Fin*) ohne Regreß.

recover¹, re-cover [ˌri:'kʌvə^r] *vt chairs, pillow, umbrella* neu beziehen *or* überziehen; *book* neu einbinden.

recover² [rɪ'kʌvə^r] [1] *vt sth lost* wiederfinden; *one's appetite, balance also* wiedergewinnen; *sth lent* zurückbekommen; *health* wiedererlangen; *goods, property, lost territory* zurückgewinnen, zurückbekommen; (*police*) *stolen/missing goods* sicherstellen; *space capsule, wreck* bergen; (*Ind etc*) *materials* gewinnen; *debt* eintreiben, beitreiben; (*Jur*) *damages* Ersatz erhalten für; *losses* wiedergutmachen; *expenses* decken, wieder einholen; (*Comput*) *file* retten ◆ **to ~ one's breath/strength** wieder zu Atem/Kräften kommen; **to ~ consciousness** wieder zu Bewußtsein kommen *or* gelangen, das Bewußtsein

wiedererlangen (*geh*); **to ~ one's sight** wieder sehen können; **to ~ land from the sea** dem Meer Land abringen; **to ~ lost ground** (*fig*) aufholen; **to ~ oneself** *or* **one's composure** seine Fassung wiedererlangen; **to be quite ~ed** sich ganz erholt haben.
[2] *vi* **(a)** (*after shock, accident etc, St Ex, Fin*) sich erholen; (*from illness also*) genesen (*geh*); (*from falling*) sich fangen; (*regain consciousness*) wieder zu sich kommen.
(b) (*Jur*) (den Prozeß) gewinnen.
recoverable [rɪ'kʌvərəbl] *adj* (*Fin*) *debt* ein- *or* beitreibbar; *losses, damages* ersetzbar; *deposit* zurückzahlbar.
recovery [rɪ'kʌvərɪ] *n* **(a)** *see vt* Wiederfinden *nt*; Wiedergewinnung *f*; Zurückbekommen *nt*; Wiedererlangung *f*; Zurückgewinnung *f*; Bergung *f*; Gewinnung *f*; Ein- *or* Beitreibung *f*; Ersatz *m* (*of* für); Wiedergutmachung *f*; Deckung *f* ◆ **~ vehicle/service** Abschleppwagen *m*/-dienst *m*.
(b) *see vi* Erholung *f*; Genesung *f* (*geh*); Zusichkommen *nt*; Prozeßgewinn *m*; (*Golf*) Schlag *m* vom Rauh zum Fairway ◆ **to be on the road** *or* **way to ~** auf dem Weg der Besserung sein; **he is making a good ~** er erholt sich gut; **past ~** nicht mehr zu retten; **to make a ~** (*regain strength etc*) sich erholen.
recovery: ~ room *n* (*in hospital*) Wachstation *f*; **~ service** *n* Abschleppdienst *m*; **~ ship** *n* Bergungsschiff *nt*; **~ vehicle** *n* Abschleppwagen *m*.
recreant ['rekrɪənt] (*liter*) [1] *n* (*coward*) Memme *f*; (*traitor*) Verräter *m*.
[2] *adj see n* memmenhaft; verräterisch.
recreate [,riːkrɪ'eɪt] *vt* (*reproduce*) *atmosphere* wiederschaffen; *scene* nachschaffen; *love, friendship etc* wiederbeleben.
recreation [,rekrɪ'eɪʃən] *n* **(a)** (*leisure*) Erholung, Entspannung *f*; (*pastime*) Hobby *nt* ◆ **for ~ I go fishing** zur Erholung gehe ich Angeln; **~ centre** Freizeitzentrum *nt*; **~ facilities** Möglichkeiten *pl* zur Freizeitgestaltung; **~ period** Freistunde *f*; **~ room** Freizeitraum *m*; **~ ground** Freizeitgelände *nt*; **~ vehicle** (*US*) Caravan *m*.
(b) (*Sch*) Pause *f*.
recreational [,rekrɪ'eɪʃənəl] *adj facilities, activity* Freizeit-.
recreative ['rekrɪ,eɪtɪv] *adj* erholsam, entspannend.
recriminate [rɪ'krɪmɪneɪt] *vi* Gegenbeschuldigungen vorbringen.
recrimination [rɪ,krɪmɪ'neɪʃən] *n* Gegenbeschuldigung *f*; (*Jur*) Gegenklage *f* ◆ **(mutual) ~s** gegenseitige Beschuldigungen *pl*; **there's no point in all these ~s** es hat keinen Sinn, sich gegenseitig zu beschuldigen.
recrudesce [,riːkruː'des] *vi* (*form*) (*wound*) wieder aufbrechen; (*illness*) wieder ausbrechen; (*problems*) wieder beginnen.
recruit [rɪ'kruːt] [1] *n* (*Mil*) Rekrut *m* (*to gen*); (*to party, club*) neues Mitglied (*to* in +*dat*); (*to staff*) Neue(r) *mf* (*to* in +*dat*).
[2] *vt soldier* rekrutieren; *member* werben; *staff* einstellen, anstellen ◆ **to be ~ed from** (*member, staff*) sich rekrutieren aus; **he ~ed me to help** er hat mich dazu herangezogen.
[3] *vi see vt* Rekruten ausheben *or* anwerben; Mitglieder werben; neue Leute einstellen.
recruiting [rɪ'kruːtɪŋ] *n see vt* Rekrutierung *f*; Werben *nt*; Einstellung *f* ◆ **~ office** (*Mil*) Rekrutierungsbüro *nt*; **~ officer** Aushebungsoffizier, Werbeoffizier (*Hist*) *m*.
recruitment [rɪ'kruːtmənt] *n* (*of soldiers*) Rekrutierung, Aushebung *f*; (*of members*) (An)werbung *f*; (*of staff*) Einstellung *f* ◆ **a large ~** eine Menge Rekruten/neue Mitglieder *pl*/neue Leute *pl*; **~ agency** Personalagentur *f*; **~ drive** Anwerbungskampagne *f*.
recta ['rektə] *pl of* **rectum**.
rectal ['rektəl] *adj* rektal (*spec*), des Mastdarms ◆ **~ passage** Mastdarm *m*.
rectangle ['rek,tæŋgl] *n* Rechteck *nt*.
rectangular [rek'tæŋgjʊlə^r] *adj* rechteckig; *coordinates* rechtwinklig.
rectifiable ['rektɪfaɪəbl] *adj* **(a)** korrigierbar; *instrument* richtig einstellbar; *omission* nachholbar; *abuse* abstellbar. **(b)** (*Chem, Math*) rektifizierbar.
rectification [,rektɪfɪ'keɪʃən] *n see vt* **(a)** Korrektur, Verbesserung *f*; Richtigstellung, Berichtigung *f*; Korrektur *f*; richtige Einstellung; Nachholen *nt*, Wiedergutmachung *f*; Abhilfe *f* (*of* für). **(b)** Gleichrichtung *f*. **(c)** Rektifikation *f*.
rectifier ['rektɪ,faɪə^r] *n* (*Elec*) Gleichrichter *m*.
rectify ['rektɪfaɪ] *vt* **(a)** korrigieren, verbessern; *error, statement also* richtigstellen, berichtigen; *position, anomaly* korrigieren; *instrument* richtig einstellen, korrigieren; *omission* nachholen, wiedergutmachen; *abuse* abhelfen (+*dat*). **(b)** (*Elec*) gleichrichten. **(c)** (*Chem, Math*) rektifizieren.
rectilineal [,rektɪ'lɪnɪəl], **rectilinear** [,rektɪ'lɪnɪə^r] *adj* geradlinig ◆ **in a ~ direction** geradlinig.
rectitude ['rektɪtjuːd] *n* Rechtschaffenheit *f*.
rector ['rektə^r] *n* **(a)** (*Rel*) Pfarrer *m* (*der Anglikanischen Kirche*). **(b)** (*Scot*) (*Sch*) Direktor(in *f*) *m*; (*Univ*) Rektor(in *f*) *m*.
rectorship ['rektəʃɪp] *n see* **rector** Zeit *f* als Pfarrer; Direktorat *nt*; Rektorat *nt*.
rectory ['rektərɪ] *n* (*house*) Pfarrhaus *nt*.
rectum ['rektəm] *n, pl* **-s** *or* **recta** Rektum *nt* (*spec*), Mastdarm *m* ◆ **a kick up the ~** (*inf*) ein Tritt *m* in den Hintern (*inf*).
recumbent [rɪ'kʌmbənt] *adj* (*form*) ruhend *attr*, liegend *attr* ◆ **~ figure** (*Art*) liegende Figur, Liegende(r) *mf*; **to be ~** liegen.
recuperate [rɪ'kuːpəreɪt] [1] *vi* sich erholen; (*from illness also*) genesen (*geh*).
[2] *vt losses* wettmachen, wiedergutmachen.
recuperation [rɪ,kuːpə'reɪʃən] *n see vb* Erholung *f*; Genesung *f* (*geh*); Wiedergutmachung *f* ◆ **after my ~** nachdem ich mich erholt hatte/habe; **powers of ~** Heilkräfte *pl*.
recuperative [rɪ'kuːpərətɪv] *adj* erholsam; *treatment* Heil-.
recur [rɪ'kɜː^r] *vi* **(a)** (*happen again*) wiederkehren; (*error also, event*) sich wiederholen, wieder passieren; (*opportunity*) sich wieder bieten, sich noch einmal bieten; (*problem, symptoms also*) wieder auftreten; (*idea, theme also*) wieder auftauchen.
(b) (*Math*) sich periodisch wiederholen; *see* **recurring**.
(c) (*come to mind again*) wieder einfallen (*to sb* jdm); (*thought, idea*) wiederkommen (*to sb* jdm).
recurrence [rɪ'kʌrəns] *n see vi* Wiederkehr *f*; Wiederholung *f*; erneutes Auftreten; Wiederauftauchen *nt* ◆ **let there be no ~ of this** das darf nie wieder vorkommen.
recurrent [rɪ'kʌrənt] *adj* **(a)** *idea, theme, illness, symptom(s)* (ständig) wiederkehrend *attr*; *error, problem also* häufig (vorkommend); *event(s)* sich wiederholend *attr*; *expenses* regelmäßig wiederkehrend. **(b)** (*Anat*) sich zurückziehend.
recurring [rɪ'kɜːrɪŋ] *adj attr* **(a)** *see* **recurrent (a)**. **(b)** (*Math*) **~ decimal** periodische Dezimalzahl; **four point nine three ~** vier Komma neun Periode drei.
recusant ['rekjʊzənt] *adj* (*Rel Hist*) der/die sich weigert, dem anglikanischen Gottesdienst beizuwohnen; (*fig liter*) renitent.
recyclable [,riː'saɪkləbl] *adj* wiederverwertbar, recycelbar.
recycle [,riː'saɪkl] *vt waste, paper etc* wiederverwerten, wiederaufbereiten ◆ **~d paper** Recyclingpapier *nt*; **made from ~d paper** aus Altpapier (hergestellt).
recycling [,riː'saɪklɪŋ] *n* Wiederaufbereitung *f*, Recycling *nt*. **~ plant** Wiederaufbereitungsanlage *f*, Recyclingwerk *nt*.
red [red] [1] *adj* (+*er*) (*also Pol*) rot ◆ **~ meat** Rind-/Lammfleisch *nt*; **~ as a beetroot** rot wie eine Tomate; **was my face ~!** da habe ich vielleicht einen roten Kopf bekommen; **she turned ~ with embarrassment** sie wurde rot vor Verlegenheit; **there'll be some ~ faces in the town hall** das wird einigen Leuten im Rathaus sauer aufstoßen (*inf*).
[2] *n* (*colour*) Rot *nt*; (*Pol: person*) Rote(r) *mf*; (*Billiards*) Karambole *f*, roter Ball; (*Roulette*) Rot, Rouge *nt* ◆ **to underline mistakes in ~** Fehler rot unterstreichen; **to go through the lights on ~, to go through on ~** bei Rot über die Ampel fahren; **to be (£100) in the ~** (*inf*) (mit £ 100) in den roten Zahlen *or* in den Roten (*inf*) sein; **to get out of the ~** (*inf*) aus den roten Zahlen *or* aus den Roten (*inf*) herauskommen; **to see ~** (*fig*) rot sehen.
red *in cpds* Rot-, rot; **~ admiral** *n* Admiral *m*; **R~ Army** *n* Rote Armee; **R~ Army Faction** *n* Rote Armee Fraktion *f*; **~-blooded** *adj* heißblütig; **~breast** *n* Rotkehlchen *nt*; **~-brick university** *n* (*Brit*) *um die Jahrhundertwende erbaute britische Universität*; **~cap** *n* (*Brit Mil sl*) Militärpolizist *m*; (*US*) Gepäckträger *m*; (*Orn*) Stieglitz *m*; **~ carpet** *n* (*lit, fig*) roter Teppich; **a ~-carpet reception** ein Empfang *m* mit rotem Teppich; (*fig also*) ein großer Bahnhof; **to roll out the ~ carpet for sb, to give sb the ~-carpet treatment** (*inf*) den roten Teppich für jdn ausrollen, jdn mit großem Bahnhof empfangen; **~ cedar** *n* Bleistiftzeder *f*, Virginischer Wacholder; **~ cent** *n* (*US inf*) roter Heller (*inf*); **R~ China** *n* Rotchina *nt*; **~coat** *n* (*Brit Hist*) Rotrock *m* (*britischer Soldat im amerikanischen Unabhängigkeitskrieg*); **R~ Crescent** *n* Roter Halbmond; **R~ Cross** [1] *n* Rotes Kreuz; [2] *attr* Rotkreuz-, Rote-Kreuz-; **~currant** *n* (rote) Johannisbeere; **~ deer** *n* Rothirsch *m*; *pl* Rotwild *nt*.
redden ['redn] [1] *vt* röten; *sky, foliage* rot färben.
[2] *vi* (*face*) sich röten; (*person*) rot werden; (*sky, foliage*) sich rot färben.
reddish ['redɪʃ] *adj* rötlich.
red duster *n* (*Naut inf*) *see* **red ensign**.
redecorate [,riː'dekəreɪt] *vti* (*paper*) neu tapezieren; (*paint*) neu streichen ◆ **we'll have to ~** wir müssen das Haus/die Wohnung *etc* neu machen (*inf*).
redecoration [riː,dekə'reɪʃən] *n see vb* (*action*) Neutapezieren *nt*; Neustreichen *nt*; (*result*) neue Tapeten *pl*; neuer Anstrich.
redeem [rɪ'diːm] *vt pawned object, trading stamps, coupons, bill etc* einlösen (*for* gegen); *promise also, obligation* einhalten, erfüllen; (*Fin*) *debt* abzahlen, löschen; *mortgage* tilgen, abzahlen; *shares* verkaufen; (*US*) *banknote* wechseln (*for* in +*acc*); *one's honour, situation* retten; (*Rel*) *sinner* erlösen; (*compensate for*) *failing, fault* wettmachen, ausgleichen ◆ **to ~ oneself** sich reinwaschen.
redeemable [rɪ'diːməbl] *adj* **(a)** *debt* tilgbar; *pawned object, trading stamps, coupons, bill* einlösbar ◆ **~ for cash/goods** gegen Bargeld/Waren einzulösen.
(b) (*Rel*) erlösbar.
Redeemer [rɪ'diːmə^r] *n* (*Rel*) Erlöser, Retter, Heiland *m*.
redeeming [rɪ'diːmɪŋ] *adj quality* ausgleichend ◆ **~ feature** aussöhnendes Moment; **the only ~ feature of this novel is ...** das einzige, was einen mit diesem Roman aussöhnt, ist ...
redefine [,riːdɪ'faɪn] *vt* neu definieren.
redemption [rɪ'dempʃən] *n see vt* Einlösung *f*; Einhaltung, Erfüllung *f*; Abzahlung, Löschung *f*; Tilgung *f*; Verkauf *m*; Wechsel *m*; Rettung *f*; (*Rel*) Erlösung *f*; Ausgleich *m* ◆ **beyond** *or* **past ~** (*fig*) nicht mehr zu retten; **~ centre** (*Comm*) Einlösestelle *f*.
redemptive [rɪ'demptɪv] *adj* (*Rel*) erlösend, rettend.
red ensign *n* (*Naut*) *britische Handelsflagge*.
redeploy [,riːdɪ'plɔɪ] *vt troops* umverlegen; *workers* anders einsetzen; *staff* umsetzen.
redeployment [,riːdɪ'plɔɪmənt] *n see vt* Umverlegung *f*; Einsatz *m* an einem anderen Arbeitsplatz; Umsetzung *f*.
redevelop [,riːdɪ'veləp] *vt building, area* sanieren.
redevelopment [,riːdɪ'veləpmənt] *n* Sanierung *f* ◆ **~ area** Sanierungsgebiet *nt*.
red: ~ eye *n* (*Phot*) *Rotfärbung f der Augen auf Blitzlichtfotos*; **~-eye** *n* (*US sl*)

Fusel *m* (*inf*), schlechter Whisky; **~-eyed** *adj* mit geröteten *or* roten Augen; **~-faced** *adj* mit rotem Kopf; **R~ Flag** *n* Rote Fahne; **~-haired** *adj* rothaarig; **~-handed** *adv*: **to catch sb ~-handed** jdn auf frischer Tat ertappen; (*esp sexually*) jdn in flagranti erwischen (*inf*); **~head** *n* Rothaarige(r) *mf*, Rotschopf *m*; **~-headed** *adj* rothaarig; **~ heat** *n* Rotglut *f*; **to bring iron to ~ heat** Eisen auf Rotglut erhitzen; **~ herring** *n* (*lit*) Räucherhering *m*; (*fig*) Ablenkungsmanöver *nt*; (*in thrillers, historical research*) falsche Spur; **that's a ~ herring** (*irrelevant*) das führt vom Thema ab; **~-hot** *adj* **(a)** (*lit*) rotglühend; (*very hot*) glühend heiß; **(b)** (*fig inf*) (*enthusiastic*) Feuer und Flamme *pred* (*inf*); (*very recent*) *news* brandaktuell; **~hot poker** *n* (*Bot*) Fackellilie *f*.

redial [riːˈdaɪəl] (*Telec*) [1] *vti* nochmals wählen.
[2] *n* **automatic ~** automatische Wahlwiederholung.

Red Indian *n* Indianer(in *f*) *m*.

redirect [ˌriːdaɪˈrekt] *vt letter, parcel* umadressieren; (*forward*) nachsenden; *traffic* umleiten.

rediscounting [ˌriːdɪsˈkaʊntɪŋ] *n* Rediskontierung *f*.

rediscover [ˌriːdɪˈskʌvəʳ] *vt* wiederentdecken.

rediscovery [ˌriːdɪˈskʌvərɪ] *n* Wiederentdeckung *f*.

redistribute [ˌriːdɪˈstrɪbjuːt] *vt wealth* umverteilen, neu verteilen; (*reallocate*) *work* neu zuteilen.

redistribution [ˌriːdɪstrɪˈbjuːʃən] *n see vt* Umverteilung, Neuverteilung *f*; Neuzuteilung *f*.

red: ~ lead *n* Bleirot *nt*, Bleimennige *f*; **~-letter day** *n* besonderer Tag, Tag, den man im Kalender rot anstreichen muß; **~ light** *n* (*lit*) (*warning light*) rotes Licht; (*traffic light*) Rotlicht *nt*; **to go through the ~ light** (*Mot*) bei Rot über die Ampel fahren, die Ampel überfahren (*inf*); **to see the ~ light** (*fig*) die Gefahr erkennen; **the ~-light district** die Strichgegend, der Strich (*inf*); (*with night-clubs*) das Rotlichtviertel; **~ man** *n* (*at street crossing*) rotes Licht; (*as said to children*) rotes Männchen; **~ meat** *n Rind-, Lamm- und Rehfleisch nt*; **~neck** *n* (*US inf*) Prolet(in *f*) *m* (*inf*).

redness [ˈrednɪs] *n* Röte *f*.

redo [ˌriːˈduː] *vt* **(a)** noch einmal machen, neu machen; *hair* in Ordnung bringen. **(b)** *see* **redecorate**.

redolence [ˈredəʊləns] *n* (*liter*) Duft *m*.

redolent [ˈredəʊlənt] *adj* (*liter*) duftend ◆ **~ of** *or* **with lavender** nach Lavendel duftend; **to be ~ of the 19th century/my youth** stark an das 19. Jahrhundert/meine Jugend erinnern.

redouble [ˌriːˈdʌbl] [1] *vt* **(a)** *efforts, zeal etc* verdoppeln. **(b)** (*Bridge*) rekontrieren.
[2] *vi* (*zeal, efforts*) sich verdoppeln.
[3] *n* (*Bridge*) Rekontra *nt*.

redoubt [rɪˈdaʊt] *n* (*Mil*) Redoute *f*; (*inside a fort*) Kasematte *f*.

redoubtable [rɪˈdaʊtəbl] *adj* (*formidable*) *task* horrend; (*to be feared*) *person, teacher* respektgebietend *attr*.

redound [rɪˈdaʊnd] *vi* (*form*) **to ~ to sb's honour/advantage** jdm zur Ehre/zum Vorteil gereichen (*geh*); **to ~ to sb's credit** jdm hoch angerechnet werden; **to ~ upon** wieder treffen.

red: ~ pepper *n* roter Paprika, rote Paprikaschote; **~ pine** *n* Südkiefer *f*; (*wood*) Redpine *nt*.

redraft [ˌriːˈdrɑːft] [1] *n see vt* Neuentwurf *m*; Neufassung *f*; Umschrift *f*.
[2] *vt* nochmals *or* neu entwerfen; *speech also* nochmals *or* neu abfassen; *literary work* umschreiben.

red rag *n* rotes Tuch ◆ **it's like a ~ to a bull** das ist ein rotes Tuch für ihn/sie *etc*.

redress [rɪˈdres] [1] *vt one's errors, wrongs* wiedergutmachen, sühnen; *situation* bereinigen; *grievance* beseitigen; *abuse* abhelfen (+*dat*); *balance* wiederherstellen.
[2] *n see vt* Wiedergutmachung *f*; Bereinigung *f*; Beseitigung *f*; Abhilfe *f* ◆ **to seek ~ for** Wiedergutmachung verlangen für; **he set out to seek ~ for these grievances** er wollte zu seinem Recht kommen; **there is no ~** das steht unumstößlich fest; **legal ~** Rechtshilfe *f*; **to have no ~ in law** keinen Rechtsanspruch haben; **but what ~ does a manager have against an employee?** aber welche Wege stehen dem Manager offen, gegen den Arbeitnehmer zu klagen?; **to gain ~** zu seinem Recht kommen.

red: R~ Riding Hood *n*: **(Little) R~ Riding Hood** Rotkäppchen *nt*; **~ salmon** *n* Pazifiklachs *m*; **R~ Sea** *n* Rotes Meer; **~ setter** *n* (Roter) Setter; **~shank** *n* (*Orn*) Rotschenkel *m*; **~ shift** *n* Rotverschiebung *f*; **~skin** *n* Rothaut *f*; **~ spider mite** *n* Rote Spinne; **R~ Spot** *n* (*Astron*) roter Punkt; **~ squirrel** *n* Eichhörnchen *nt*; **~start** *n* (*Orn*) Rotschwanz *m*; **~ tape** *n* (*fig*) Papierkrieg *m* (*inf*); (*with authorities also*) Behördenkram *m* (*inf*).

reduce [rɪˈdjuːs] [1] *vt* **(a)** *pressure, weight, swelling* verringern, reduzieren; *speed also* verlangsamen; *authority also* schwächen; (*lower also*) *standards, temperatures* herabsetzen; *prices* ermäßigen, herabsetzen; *taxes* senken; (*shorten*) verkürzen; *expenses, wages* kürzen; (*in size*) *width, staff, drawing, photo* verkleinern, reduzieren; *scale of operations* einschränken; *temperature* senken; (*Cook*) *sauce* einkochen lassen; *output* drosseln, reduzieren; (*Mil etc: in rank*) degradieren ◆ **to ~ one's weight** abnehmen; **to ~ the strength of a solution** eine Lösung abschwächen; **to ~ speed** (*Mot*) langsamer fahren; **"~ speed now"** (*Mot*) ≃ langsam; **the facts may all be ~d to four main headings** die Tatsachen können alle auf vier Hauptpunkte reduziert werden.
(b) (*in price*) *goods, item* heruntersetzen, herabsetzen.
(c) (*change the form of*) (*Chem*) reduzieren; (*Math*) zerlegen (*to* in +*acc*) ◆ **to ~ sth to a powder/to its parts** etw pulverisieren/in seine Einzelteile zerlegen; **to ~ sth to a common denominator** (*Math, fig*) etw auf einen gemeinsamen Nenner bringen; **to ~ an argument to its simplest form** ein Argument auf die einfachste Form bringen; **it has been ~d to a mere ...** es ist jetzt nur noch ein ...; **it has been ~d to nothing** es ist zu nichts zusammengeschmolzen; **he's ~d to a skeleton** er ist zum Skelett abgemagert; **to ~ sb to silence/obedience/despair/tears** jdn zum Schweigen/Gehorsam/zur Verzweiflung/zum Weinen bringen; **to ~ sb to begging/to slavery** jdn zum Betteln/zur Sklaverei zwingen; **are we ~d to this!** so weit ist es also gekommen!; **to be ~d to submission** aufgeben müssen.
(d) (*Med*) *joint* wieder einrenken.
[2] *vi* (*esp US: slim*) abnehmen ◆ **to be reducing** eine Schlankheitskur machen.

reduced [rɪˈdjuːst] *adj price, fare* ermäßigt, *goods* herabgesetzt; *scale, version* kleiner; *circumstances* beschränkt.

reducer [rɪˈdjuːsəʳ] *n* (*Phot*) Abschwächer *m*.

reducible [rɪˈdjuːsəbl] *adj* (*to* auf +*acc*) (*Chem, fig*) reduzierbar; (*Math*) zerlegbar; *drawing, scale also* verkleinerbar; *time also* verkürzbar; *costs* herabsetzbar ◆ **to be ~ to sth** sich auf etw (*acc*) reduzieren lassen.

reduction [rɪˈdʌkʃən] *n* **(a)** *no pl* (*in sth gen*) Reduzierung, Reduktion, Verringerung *f*; (*in speed also*) Verlangsamung *f*; (*in authority*) Schwächung *f*; (*in standards, temperatures also*) Herabsetzung *f*; (*in prices also*) Ermäßigung, Herabsetzung *f*; (*in taxes also*) Senkung *f*; (*in expenses, wages*) Kürzung *f*; (*in size*) Verkleinerung *f*; (*shortening*) Verkürzung *f*; (*in output also*) Drosselung *f*; (*in scale of operations*) Einschränkung *f*; (*of goods, items*) Herabsetzung *f*; (*of fever*) Senkung *f*; (*of joint*) Wiedereinrenken *nt* ◆ **to make a ~ on an article** einen Artikel heruntersetzen; **~ for cash** Preisabschlag *m* bei Barzahlung; **~ of taxes** Steuersenkung *f*; **~ in rank** Degradierung *f*.
(b) (*to another state*) (*Chem*) Reduktion *f*; (*Math also*) Zerlegung *f* (*to* in +*acc*) ◆ **~ of sth to powder/to a pulp** Zermahlung *f* einer Sache (*gen*) zu Pulver/zu Brei.
(c) (*amount reduced*) (*in sth gen*) (*in pressure, temperature, output*) Abnahme *f*, Rückgang *m*; (*of speed also*) Verlangsamung *f*; (*in size*) Verkleinerung *f*; (*in length*) Verkürzung *f*; (*in taxes*) Nachlaß *m*; (*in prices*) Ermäßigung *f*; (*Jur: of sentence*) Kürzung *f*; (*of swelling*) Rückgang *m* ◆ **to sell (sth) at a ~** etw verbilligt *or* zu ermäßigtem Preis verkaufen; **what a ~!** wie billig!; **~ of strength** Nachlassen *nt* der Kräfte.
(d) (*copy*) Verkleinerung *f*.

reductionism [rɪˈdʌkʃənɪzəm] *n* Reduktionismus *m*.

reductive [rɪˈdʌktɪv] *adj* verkürzt, zu kurz gegriffen; (*Philos*) reduktiv.

redundancy [rɪˈdʌndənsɪ] *n* Überflüssigkeit *f*; (*of style*) Weitschweifigkeit, Redundanz *f* (*geh*); (*Ind*) Arbeitslosigkeit *f* ◆ **redundancies** Entlassungen *pl*; **the depression caused a lot of ~** *or* **many redundancies** der Konjunkturrückgang brachte viel Arbeitslosigkeit mit sich; **he feared ~** er hatte Angst, seinen Arbeitsplatz zu verlieren; **~ payment** Abfindung *f*.

redundant [rɪˈdʌndənt] *adj* überflüssig; *style* zu wortreich, redundant (*geh*); (*Ind: out of work*) arbeitslos ◆ **to become/to be made ~** (*Ind*) den Arbeitsplatz verlieren; **he found himself ~** er war plötzlich ohne Arbeitsplatz.

reduplicate [rɪˈdjuːplɪkeɪt] [1] *vt* wiederholen; (*Ling*) reduplizieren.
[2] *adj* (*Ling*) redupliziert.

reduplication [rɪˌdjuːplɪˈkeɪʃən] *n see vt* Wiederholung *f*; Reduplikation *f*.

reduplicative [rɪˈdjuːplɪkətɪv] *adj* (*Ling*) reduplizierend.

red: ~wing *n* Rotdrossel *f*; **~wood** *n* Redwood *nt*.

re-echo [ˌriːˈekəʊ] [1] *vi* widerhallen.
[2] *vt* echoen ◆ **he ~ed his wife's opinion** er war wie das Echo seiner Frau.

reed [riːd] *n* **(a)** (*Bot*) Schilf(rohr), Ried *nt* ◆ **in the ~s** im Schilf *or* Ried; **a broken ~** (*fig*) ein schwankendes Rohr. **(b)** (*of wind instrument*) Rohrblatt *nt*; (*of harmonium*) Durchschlagzunge *f*; (*of organ*) Zungenpfeife *f* ◆ **~s** Rohrblattinstrumente *pl*.

reed: ~ basket *n* Korb *m* aus Schilfrohr; **~ bunting** *n* Rohrammer *f*; **~ instrument** *n* Rohrblattinstrument *nt*.

re-edit [ˌriːˈedɪt] *vt* neu herausgeben; *book, text* noch einmal redigieren; *film, tape* neu schneiden.

reed: ~ organ *n* Harmonium *nt*; **~ pipe** *n* Schalmei *f*; **~ stop** *n* Zungenregister *nt*.

re-educate [ˌriːˈedjʊkeɪt] *vt* (um)erziehen ◆ **to ~ one's palate** sich in seinem Geschmack umstellen.

re-education [ˈriːˌedjʊˈkeɪʃən] *n* (Um)erziehung *f*.

reed-warbler [ˈriːdwɔːbləʳ] *n* Rohrsänger *m*.

reedy [ˈriːdɪ] *adj* (+*er*) schilfig; *instrument* Rohrblatt-; *sound* näselnd; *voice* durchdringend.

reef¹ [riːf] *n* **(a)** (*in sea*) Riff *nt*. **(b)** (*Min*) Ader *f*, Gang *m*.

reef² (*Naut*) [1] *n* Reff *nt* ◆ **~ knot** Kreuz- *or* Weberknoten *m*.
[2] *vt sail* reffen.

reefer [ˈriːfəʳ] *n* (*jacket*) Seemannsjacke *f*; (*sl*) Reefer *m* (*sl*).

reek [riːk] [1] *n* Gestank *m*.
[2] *vi* stinken (*of* nach).

reel [riːl] [1] *n* **(a)** (*of thread, wire etc*) Rolle, Spule *f*; (*of film, magnetic tape*) Spule *f*; (*Fishing*) (Angel)rolle *f* ◆ **~-to-~ (tape recorder)** Tonbandgerät *nt*, Tonbandmaschine *f*.
(b) (*dance*) Reel *m*.
[2] *vt* (*Tech*) *thread* aufspulen.
[3] *vi* (*person*) taumeln; (*drunk also*) torkeln, schwanken ◆ **he went ~ing down the street** er torkelte *or* schwankte die Straße hinunter; **the blow made him ~** *or* **sent him ~ing** er taumelte unter dem Schlag; **the street ~ed before her eyes** die Straße drehte sich ihr vor den Augen; **my head is ~ing** mir dreht sich der Kopf; **the news made him** *or* **his mind ~** bei der Nachricht drehte

sich ihm alles; **the whole country is still ~ing from the shock** das ganze Land ist noch tief erschüttert von diesem Schock.
◆**reel in** *vt sep* (*Fishing*) einrollen; *fish* einholen.
◆**reel off** *vt sep list* herunterrasseln (*inf*); (*monotonously*) herunterleiern (*inf*); *thread* abwickeln, abspulen.
◆**reel up** *vt sep* (*Fishing*) aufrollen, aufspulen.
re-elect [ˌriːɪ'lekt] *vt* wiederwählen.
re-election [ˌriːɪ'lekʃən] *n* Wiederwahl *f*.
reeling ['riːlɪŋ] [1] *n see vi* Taumeln *nt*; Torkeln, Schwanken *nt*.
[2] *adj head* brummend (*inf*).
re-embark [ˌriːɪm'bɑːk] [1] *vt* wieder einschiffen.
[2] *vi* sich wieder einschiffen ◆ **to ~ on an enterprise** ein Unternehmen von neuem beginnen.
re-embarkation ['riːˌembɑː'keɪʃən] *n* Wiedereinschiffung *f*.
re-emerge [ˌriːɪ'mɜːdʒ] *vi* (*object, swimmer*) wieder auftauchen; (*facts*) (wieder) herauskommen.
re-employ [ˌriːɪm'plɔɪ] *vt person* wiedereinstellen.
re-enact [ˌriːɪ'nækt] *vt* **(a)** (*Jur*) wieder in Kraft setzen. **(b)** (*repeat*) *scene* nachspielen; *crime, meeting* nachvollziehen; *crime* (*for police purposes*) einen Lokaltermin abhalten wegen.
re-enactment [ˌriːɪ'næktmənt] *n* (*of law etc*) Wiederinkraftsetzung *f*; (*of scene*) Nachspiel *nt*; (*repetition*) Nachvollzug *m*; (*of crime for police purposes*) Lokaltermin *m*.
re-engage [ˌriːɪn'geɪdʒ] *vt employee* wieder einstellen; (*Tech*) *gear wheels* wieder ineinandergreifen lassen; *gear* wieder einlegen; *clutch* wieder kommen lassen.
re-enlist [ˌriːɪn'lɪst] [1] *vi* (*Mil*) sich wieder melden *or* verpflichten.
[2] *vt* (*Mil*) neu verpflichten ◆ **to ~ sb's help** jds Hilfe erneut in Anspruch nehmen.
re-enter [ˌriː'entəʳ] [1] *vi* **(a)** wieder hereinkommen/hineingehen; (*walk in*) wieder eintreten; (*drive in*) wieder einfahren; (*penetrate: bullet etc*) wieder eindringen; (*climb in*) wieder einsteigen; (*cross border*) wieder einreisen; (*ship*) wieder einlaufen.
(b) (*Theat*) wieder auftreten.
(c) (*for race, exam etc*) sich wieder melden (*for* zu).
[2] *vt* **(a)** *room* wieder hereinkommen/hineingehen in (*+acc*), wieder betreten; (*Space*) *atmosphere* wieder eintreten in (*+acc*); *club etc* wieder beitreten (*+dat*).
(b) *name* (*on list etc*) wieder eintragen.
re-entrant [ˌriː'entrənt] *n* Wiederholungskandidat(in *f*) *m*.
re-entry [ˌriː'entrɪ] *n* **(a)** (*also Space*) Wiedereintritt *m*; (*for exam*) Wiederantritt *m* (*for* zu) ◆ **~ point, point of ~** (*Space*) Wiedereintrittsstelle *f*.
(b) (*Jur*) Wiederinbesitznahme *f*.
re-erect [ˌriːɪ'rekt] *vt building, bridge* wieder aufbauen; *scaffolding also* wieder aufstellen.
re-establish [ˌriːɪ'stæblɪʃ] *vt order* wiederherstellen; *custom* wieder einführen ◆ **to ~ sb as sth/in a position** jdn wieder als etw/in eine Stelle einsetzen.
re-establishment [ˌriːɪ'stæblɪʃmənt] *n see vt* Wiederherstellung *f*; Wiedereinführung *f*; (*in a position, office*) Wiedereinsetzung *f*.
reeve[1] [riːv] *n* **(a)** (*Hist*) Vogt *m*. **(b)** (*in Canada*) ≃ Gemeindevorsteher *m*.
reeve[2] *vt* (*Naut*) (*thread*) einscheren; (*fasten*) festmachen.
re-examination ['riːɪgˌzæmɪ'neɪʃən] *n* Überprüfung *f*, erneute *or* nochmalige Prüfung; (*Jur: of witness*) erneute *or* nochmalige Vernehmung.
re-examine [ˌriːɪg'zæmɪn] *vt* überprüfen, erneut *or* nochmals prüfen; (*Jur*) *witness* erneut *or* nochmals vernehmen.
re-export [1] [riːɪk'spɔːt] *vt* wieder ausführen.
[2] [riː'ekspɔːt] *n* **goods for ~** Waren *pl* zur Wiederausfuhr.
ref[1] [ref] *n* (*Sport inf*) *abbr of* **referee** Schiri *m* (*sl*).
ref[2] *abbr of* **reference (number)**.
refectory [rɪ'fektərɪ] *n* (*in college*) Mensa *f*; (*in monastery*) Refektorium *nt*.
refer [rɪ'fɜːʳ] [1] *vt* **(a)** (*pass*) *matter, problem* weiterleiten (*to* an *+acc*); *decision* übergeben (*to sb* jdm) ◆ **the dispute was ~red to arbitration** der Streit wurde einem Schiedsgericht übergeben; **it was ~red to us for (a) decision** es wurde uns (*dat*) zur Entscheidung übergeben; **I ~red him to the manager** ich verwies ihn an den Geschäftsführer; **to ~ sb to the article on ...** jdn auf den Artikel über (*+acc*) ... verweisen; **to ~ a cheque to drawer** (*Comm*) einen Scheck an den Aussteller zurücksenden.
(b) (*Brit Univ*) *thesis* zur Änderung zurückgeben.
[2] *vi* **(a) to ~ to** (*allude to*) sprechen von; (*mention also*) erwähnen; (*words*) sich beziehen auf (*+acc*); **I am not ~ring to you** ich meine nicht Sie; **what can he be ~ring to?** was meint er wohl?, wovon spricht er wohl?; **the letter ~s to you all** der Brief gilt euch allen; **~ring to your letter** (*Comm*) mit Bezug auf Ihren Brief.
(b) (*apply to*) **to ~ to** (*orders, rules*) gelten für; (*criticism, remark*) sich beziehen auf (*+acc*).
(c) (*consult*) **to ~ to** *to notes, book* nachschauen in (*+dat*), konsultieren (*geh*); *to person* sich wenden an (*+acc*); **you must ~ to the original** Sie müssen aufs Original zurückgreifen.
◆**refer back** [1] *vi* **(a)** (*person, remark*) sich beziehen (*to* auf *+acc*). **(b)** (*check back, consult again*) zurückgehen (*to* zu).
[2] *vt sep* (*pass back*) *decision etc* zurückgeben (*to* an *+acc*) ◆ **he ~red me ~ to you** er hat mich an Sie zurückverwiesen.
referee [ˌrefə'riː] [1] *n* **(a)** (*Ftbl, Rugby, fig*) Schiedsrichter *m*; (*Boxing*) Ringrichter *m*; (*Judo, Wrestling*) Kampfrichter *m*.
(b) (*Jur*) Schiedsrichter *m*.
(c) (*Brit: person giving a reference*) Referenz *f* ◆ **to be a ~ for sb** jdm als Referenz dienen.
[2] *vt* (*Sport, fig*) Schiedsrichter sein bei; *match also* (als Schieds-/Ring-/Kampfrichter) leiten; (*Ftbl also*) pfeifen (*inf*).
[3] *vi* (*Sport, fig*) Schiedsrichter sein, (den) Schiedsrichter machen *or* spielen (*inf*); (*Ftbl also*) pfeifen (*inf*).
▼ **reference** ['refrəns] *n* **(a)** (*act of mentioning*) Erwähnung *f* (*to sb/sth* jds/einer Sache); (*allusion*) (*direct*) Bemerkung *f* (*to* über *+acc*); (*indirect*) Anspielung *f* (*to* auf *+acc*) ◆ **to make (a) ~ to sth** etw erwähnen; **~ to any such delicate issue should be avoided** eine so delikate Sache sollte nicht erwähnt werden; **this was not said with ~ to you** diese Worte waren nicht auf dich gemünzt; **in** *or* **with ~ to** was ... anbetrifft; (*Comm*) bezüglich (*+gen*); **~ your letter ...** (*Comm*) mit Bezug auf Ihren Brief (*form*); **without ~ to age/to one's notes** ungeachtet des Alters/ohne seine Aufzeichnungen zu Hilfe zu nehmen.
(b) *no pl see vt (a)* (*to* an *+acc*) Weiterleitung *f*; Übergabe *f*.
▼ **(c)** (*testimonial: also ~s*) Referenz(en *pl*) *f*, Zeugnis *nt* ◆ **to give sb a good ~** *or* **good ~s** jdm gute Referenzen *or* ein gutes Zeugnis ausstellen; **a banker's ~** eine Bankauskunft *or* -referenz; **I've been asked to give a ~ for him** man hat mich gebeten, ihm eine Referenz zu geben.
(d) (*note redirecting reader*) (*in book, on map etc*) Verweis *m*; (*Comm*) Zeichen *nt*; *see* **cross-~**.
(e) (*connection*) **to have ~ to** in Beziehung stehen mit *or* zu; **this has no/little ~ to** das steht in keiner/kaum in Beziehung zu.
(f) (*authority, scope: of committee, tribunal*) Zuständigkeitsbereich *m*; *see* **term**.
(g) (*esp US*) *see* **referee 1 (c)**.
reference: ~ book *n* Nachschlagewerk *nt*; **~ library** *n* Präsenzbibliothek *f*; **~ number** *n* Aktenzeichen *nt*; (*of subscriber etc*) Nummer *f*.
referendum [ˌrefə'rendəm] *n, pl* **referenda** [ˌrefə'rendə] Volksentscheid *m*, Referendum *nt* ◆ **to hold a ~** einen Volksentscheid durchführen, ein Referendum abhalten.
refill [ˌriː'fɪl] [1] *vt* nachfüllen, wieder füllen.
[2] ['riːfɪl] *n* (*for fountain pen, lighter*) Nachfüllpatrone *f*; (*for ballpoint*) Nachfüll- *or* Ersatzmine *f*; (*lipstick*) Nachfüllstift *m*; (*for propelling pencil*) Ersatzmine *f*; (*for notebook*) Nachfüllblätter *pl* ◆ **would you like a ~?** (*inf: drink*) darf ich nachschenken?; **he wants another ~** er will noch einmal nachgeschenkt haben.
refinancing [riːfaɪ'nænsɪŋ] *n* Refinanzierung, Neufinanzierung *f*.
refine [rɪ'faɪn] *vt* **(a)** *metal, oil, sugar* raffinieren. **(b)** *language, manners* verfeinern, kultivieren; *taste(s) also* bilden. **(c)** *techniques, methods* verfeinern, verbessern.
◆**refine upon** *vi +prep obj point, detail* näher ausführen; *method* verbessern, verfeinern.
refined [rɪ'faɪnd] *adj* **(a)** *metal, oil* raffiniert, rein ◆ **~ sugar** Raffinade *f*. **(b)** *taste* fein; *person, style also* vornehm.
refinement [rɪ'faɪnmənt] *n* **(a)** *no pl* (*of metal, oil, sugar*) Raffination, Raffinierung, Reinigung *f*.
(b) *no pl* (*of person, language, style*) Vornehmheit, Feinheit *f* ◆ **a person of no ~** ein ganz unkultivierter Mensch.
(c) (*improvement: in technique, machine etc*) Verfeinerung, Verbesserung *f* (*in sth gen*) ◆ **a ~ of cruelty/torture** subtile Grausamkeit/Folterung.
refinery [rɪ'faɪnərɪ] *n* (*metal, oil, sugar ~*) Raffinerie *f*.
refit [ˌriː'fɪt] [1] *vt ship* neu ausrüsten; *factory* neu ausstatten.
[2] *vi* (*ship*) neu ausgerüstet werden.
[3] ['riːfɪt] *n* (*Naut*) Neuausrüstung *f*.
refitting [ˌriː'fɪtɪŋ], **refitment** [ˌriː'fɪtmənt] *n see* **refit 3**.
reflate [ˌriː'fleɪt] [1] *vt* (*Econ*) bewußt inflationieren, ankurbeln.
[2] *vi* (*economy*) sich beleben, angekurbelt werden ◆ **they decided to ~** man beschloß, die Konjunktur anzukurbeln.
reflation [riː'fleɪʃən] *n* (*Econ*) Reflation *f*, Ankurbelung *f* der Konjunktur.
reflationary [riː'fleɪʃnərɪ] *adj* (*Econ*) reflationär.
reflect [rɪ'flekt] [1] *vt* **(a)** (*cast back*) *light, image, heat, sound* zurückwerfen, reflektieren; (*surface of water, mirror also*) spiegeln; (*fig*) *views, reality etc* widerspiegeln ◆ **the moon was ~ed in the lake** der Mond spiegelte sich im See; **I saw him/myself ~ed in the mirror** ich sah ihn/mich im Spiegel; **~ing prism** Spiegelprisma *nt*; **to bask in ~ed glory** sich in jds Glanz (*dat*) sonnen; **the many difficulties ~ed in his report/attitude** die vielen Schwierigkeiten, die sich in seinem Bericht/seiner Haltung spiegeln; **to ~ credit (up)on sb** ein gutes Licht auf jdn werfen; **his music ~s his love for her** in seiner Musik spiegelt sich seine Liebe zu ihr wider.
(b) (*think*) **I ~ed that thus was the way of the world** ich dachte bei mir, daß das eben der Lauf der Welt sei; **do you ever ~ that ...?** denken Sie je darüber nach, daß ...?
[2] *vi* (*meditate*) nachdenken, reflektieren (*geh*) (*on, about* über *+acc*).
◆**reflect (up)on** *vi + prep obj* etwas aussagen über (*+acc*); *person also* ein gutes/schlechtes Licht werfen auf (*+acc*); *motives, reasons also* in gutem/schlechtem Licht erscheinen lassen; *reputation, sb's honour* sich auswirken auf (*+acc*); (*unfavourably*) schaden (*+dat*), ein schlechtes Licht werfen auf (*+acc*).
reflectingly [rɪ'flektɪŋlɪ] *adv see* **reflectively**.
reflecting telescope [rɪ'flektɪŋ'telɪskəʊp] *n* Spiegelteleskop *nt*.
reflection [rɪ'flekʃən] *n* **(a)** *no pl* (*reflecting*) Reflexion *f*, (*by surface of lake, mirror*) Spiegelung *f*; (*fig*) Widerspiegelung *f*.
(b) (*image*) Spiegelbild *nt*, Reflexion *f*; (*fig*) Widerspiegelung *f* ◆ **to see one's ~ in a mirror** sich im Spiegel sehen; **a pale ~ of ...** ein matter Abglanz (*+gen*).
(c) *no pl* (*consideration*) Überlegung *f*; (*contemplation*) Reflexion, Betrachtung

➤ LANGUAGE IN USE: **reference: c → 19.2, 19.4**

f ♦ **(up)on ~** wenn ich mir das recht überlege; **on serious ~** bei ernsthafter Überlegung.
(d) (*thoughts, comments*) **~s on language** Reflexionen *or* Betrachtungen *pl* über die Sprache.
(e) (*adverse criticism*) **a ~ on his honour** ein Schatten auf seiner Ehre; **this is a ~ on your motives** das zeigt Ihre Motive in schlechtem Licht; **this is no ~ on your motives** damit soll gar nichts über Ihre Motive gesagt sein.
(f) (*Anat*) Zurückbiegung *f*.
reflective [rɪ'flektɪv] *adj* **(a)** (*Phys etc*) *surface* reflektierend, spiegelnd; *light* reflektiert. **(b)** *faculty, powers* Denk-, der Reflexion; *person* nachdenklich. **(c)** (*Gram*) *see* **reflexive**.
reflectively [rɪ'flektɪvlɪ] *adv say, speak* überlegt.
reflectiveness [rɪ'flektɪvnɪs] *n* (*of person*) Nachdenklichkeit *f*.
reflectivity [rɪflek'tɪvɪtɪ] *n* (*Phys*) Reflexionsvermögen *nt*.
reflector [rɪ'flektə^r] *n* (*on car, cycle*) Rückstrahler *m*; (*telescope*) Reflektor *m*.
reflex ['riːfleks] 1 *adj* (*Physiol, Psych, Phys, fig*) Reflex-; (*Math*) *angle* überstumpf ♦ **~ action** Reflex *m*; **~ camera** (*Phot*) Spiegelreflexkamera *f*.
2 *n* (*Physiol, Psych, fig*) Reflex *m*; (*Phys: image*) Reflexion *f*; *see* **condition**.
reflexion [rɪ'flekʃən] *n see* **reflection**.
reflexive [rɪ'fleksɪv] (*Gram*) 1 *adj* reflexiv.
2 *n* Reflexiv *nt*.
reflexively [rɪ'fleksɪvlɪ] *adv see adj*.
reflexology [ˌriːflek'sɒlədʒɪ] *n* (*Med*) Reflexologie *f*; (*practice*) Reflexzonenmassage *f*.
refloat [ˌriː'fləʊt] *vt ship, business* wieder flottmachen.
reflux ['riːflʌks] *n* Rückfluß *m*.
reforest [riː'fɒrɪst] *vt* (*US*) *see* **reafforest**.
reforestation [ˌriːfɒrɪs'teɪʃən] *n* (*US*) *see* **reafforestation**.
reform¹ [rɪ'fɔːm] 1 *n* Reform *f* (*in sth gen*); (*of person*) Besserung *f* ♦ **~ measures** Reformmaßnahmen *pl*; **~ school** Besserungsanstalt *f*; *see* **land ~**.
2 *vt law, institutions, services, spelling system* reformieren; *society also* verbessern; *conduct, person* bessern.
3 *vi* (*person*) sich bessern.
reform², re-form [ˌriː'fɔːm] 1 *vt* **(a)** (*form again*) wieder bilden; (*Mil*) *ranks, troops* neu formieren.
(b) (*give new form to*) umformen, umgestalten (*into* zu).
2 *vi* sich wieder *or* erneut bilden; (*Mil*) sich neu formieren.
reformable [rɪ'fɔːməbl] *adj person, conduct* besserungsfähig.
reformat [riː'fɔːmæt] *vt* (*Comput*) *disk* neu formatieren.
reformation [ˌrefə'meɪʃən] *n* (*of person*) Reformierung, Besserung *f* ♦ **the R~** die Reformation.
reformative [rɪ'fɔːmətɪv] *adj effect* reformierend; *fervour* Reform-.
reformatory [rɪ'fɔːmətərɪ] *n* Besserungsanstalt *f*.
reformed [rɪ'fɔːmd] *adj* reformiert; *person also* gewandelt; *behaviour* gebessert ♦ **he's a ~ character** er hat sich gebessert.
reformer [rɪ'fɔːmə^r] *n* (*Pol*) Reformer *m*; (*Rel*) Reformator *m*.
reformism [rɪ'fɔːmɪzəm] *n* Reformismus *m*.
reformist [rɪ'fɔːmɪst] 1 *n* Reformist *m*.
2 *adj* reformistisch.
refract [rɪ'frækt] *vt* brechen.
refracting telescope [rɪ'fræktɪŋ'telɪskəʊp] *n* Refraktor *m*.
refraction [rɪ'frækʃən] *n* Brechung, Refraktion (*spec*) *f* ♦ **angle of ~** Brechungswinkel *m*.
refractive [rɪ'fræktɪv] *adj material, surface* brechend ♦ **~ index** Brechzahl *f*, Brechungsindex *m*.
refractor [rɪ'fræktə^r] *n* **(a)** (*Phys*) brechendes Medium. **(b)** (*telescope*) Refraktor *m*.
refractoriness [rɪ'fræktərɪnɪs] *n see adj* Eigensinn *m*, störrische Art; Hartnäckigkeit *f*; Hitzebeständigkeit *f*.
refractory [rɪ'fræktərɪ] *adj* **(a)** *person* eigensinnig, störrisch. **(b)** (*Med*) hartnäckig. **(c)** (*Chem, Miner*) hitzebeständig.
refrain¹ [rɪ'freɪn] *vi* **please ~!** bitte unterlassen Sie das!; **he ~ed from comment** er enthielt sich eines Kommentars; **they ~ed from such measures** sie sahen von solchen Maßnahmen ab; **I couldn't ~ from laughing** ich konnte mir das Lachen nicht verkneifen; **kindly ~ from saying that in front of the children** würden Sie das bitte nicht vor den Kindern sagen; **please ~ from smoking** bitte nicht rauchen!
refrain² *n* (*Mus, Poet, fig*) Refrain *m*.
refrangible [rɪ'frændʒəbl] *adj* brechbar.
refresh [rɪ'freʃ] *vt* (*drink, bath, sleep, rest*) erfrischen; (*meal*) stärken ♦ **to ~ oneself** (*with drink*) eine Erfrischung zu sich (*dat*) nehmen; (*with a bath*) sich erfrischen; (*with food*) sich stärken; (*with sleep, rest*) sich ausruhen; **to ~ oneself with a glass of beer** zur Erfrischung ein Glas Bier trinken; **to ~ one's memory** sein Gedächtnis auffrischen; **let me ~ your memory** ich will Ihrem Gedächtnis nachhelfen.
refresher [rɪ'freʃə^r] *n* **(a)** (*Brit Jur*) zusätzliches Anwaltshonorar. **(b) ~ course** (*Univ etc*) Auffrischungskurs *m*. **(c)** (*inf: drink*) Erfrischung *f* ♦ **to have a ~** etwas trinken.
refreshing *adj*, **~ly** *adv* [rɪ'freʃɪŋ, -lɪ] (*lit, fig*) erfrischend.
refreshment [rɪ'freʃmənt] *n* **(a)** (*of mind, body*) Erfrischung *f*; (*through food*) Stärkung *f*. **(b)** (*food, drink*) **(light) ~s** (kleine) Erfrischungen *pl*; **~ bar** *or* **stall** Büfett *nt*.
refrigerant [rɪ'frɪdʒərənt] 1 *n* Kühlmittel *nt*; (*Med*) kühlendes Mittel; (*fluid in fridge*) Kältemittel *nt*.
2 *adj* kühlend.
refrigerate [rɪ'frɪdʒəreɪt] *vt* (*chill*) kühlen; (*freeze*) tiefkühlen ♦ **"~ after opening"** „nach dem Öffnen kühl aufbewahren".
refrigeration [rɪˌfrɪdʒə'reɪʃən] *n see vt* Kühlung *f*, Tiefkühlung *f*.
refrigerator [rɪ'frɪdʒəreɪtə^r] *n* Kühlschrank, Eisschrank *m*; (*room*) Kühlraum *m*.
refuel [ˌriː'fjʊəl] *vti* auftanken.
refuelling [ˌriː'fjʊəlɪŋ] *n* Auftanken *nt* ♦ **~ stop** Zwischenstopp *m* zum Auftanken.
refuge ['refjuːdʒ] *n* **(a)** (*lit, fig*) Zuflucht *f* (*from* vor +*dat*) ♦ **place of ~** Zufluchtsort *m*; **to seek ~** Zuflucht suchen; **to take ~** Zuflucht nehmen (*in* in +*dat*), sich flüchten (*in* in +*acc*). **(b)** (*for climbers, pedestrians*) Unterstand *m*.
refugee [ˌrefjʊ'dʒiː] *n* Flüchtling *m* ♦ **~ camp** Flüchtlingslager *nt*.
refulgence [rɪ'fʌldʒəns] *n* (*liter*) Strahlen *nt*.
refund [rɪ'fʌnd] 1 *vt money* zurückzahlen, zurückerstatten; *expenses* erstatten; *postage* vergüten, zurückerstatten.
2 ['riːfʌnd] *n see vt* Rückzahlung, Rückerstattung *f*; Erstattung *f*; Vergütung *f* ♦ **they wouldn't give me a ~** man wollte mir das Geld nicht zurückgeben; **I'd like a ~ on this blouse, please** ich hätte gern mein Geld für diese Bluse zurück; **we will send (you) a ~** wir senden Ihnen das Geld zurück.
refundable [rɪ'fʌndəbl] *adj money, payment(s)* zurückzahlbar, zurückerstattbar ♦ **these expenses are/postage is ~** diese Ausgaben werden erstattet/das Porto wird vergütet.
refurbish [ˌriː'fɜːbɪʃ] *vt* aufpolieren; *hat, dress, furniture also* verschönern; *house* renovieren.
refurnish [ˌriː'fɜːnɪʃ] *vt* neu möblieren.
refusal [rɪ'fjuːzəl] *n* **(a)** Ablehnung *f*; (*of offer also*) Zurückweisung *f*; (*of food, permission, visa, permit*) Verweigerung *f*; (*to do sth*) Weigerung *f* ♦ **to meet with** *or* **get a ~** eine Absage erhalten; **to give (sb) a flat ~** jdm eine glatte Absage erteilen; **to give sb first ~ of sth** jdm etw als erstem *or* zuerst anbieten; **to have (the) first ~ of sth** etw als erster angeboten bekommen; **right of first ~** Vorkaufsrecht *nt*.
(b) (*Show-jumping*) Verweigerung *f*.
▼ **refuse¹** [rɪ'fjuːz] 1 *vt invitation, candidate, proposal* ablehnen; (*stronger*) abweisen, zurückweisen; *offer also* ausschlagen; *request also* abschlagen, nicht gewähren; *visa, permit, permission* verweigern ♦ **to ~ to do sth** sich weigern, etw zu tun, etw nicht tun wollen; **I ~ to believe it** ich weigere mich, das zu glauben, ich glaube das einfach nicht; **I ~/he ~d to be blackmailed** ich lasse mich nicht erpressen/er wollte sich nicht erpressen lassen; **he was ~d a visa** ihm wurde das Visum verweigert; **to be ~d sth** etw nicht bekommen; **they were ~d permission (to leave)** es wurde ihnen nicht gestattet (wegzugehen); **he ~d food** er verweigerte die Nahrungsaufnahme; **he/his request was ~d** seine Bitte wurde abgelehnt; **she ~d him** sie wies ihn ab *or* zurück; **the horse ~d the fence** das Pferd hat am Hindernis verweigert.
2 *vi* ablehnen; (*to do sth*) sich weigern; (*horse*) verweigern.
refuse² ['refjuːs] *n* Müll *m*; (*food waste*) Abfall *m* ♦ **household ~** Haus(halts)müll *m*; **garden ~** Gartenabfälle *pl*.
refuse ['refjuːs] *in cpds* Müll-; **~ bin** *n* Mülleimer *m*; **~ chute** *n* Müllschlucker *m*; **~ collection** *n* Müllabfuhr *f*; **~ collector** *n* Müllmann *m*; **~ destructor** *n* Müllvernichtungsanlage *f*; **~ disposal** *n* Müllbeseitigung *f*; **~ disposal service** *n* Müllabfuhr *f*; **~ disposal unit** *n* Müllzerkleinerer *m*; **~ dump** *n* Müllabladeplatz *m*; **~ lorry** *n* Müllwagen *m*.
refusenik [rɪ'fjuːznɪk] *n* (*inf*) Verweigerer(in *f*) *m*.
refutable [rɪ'fjuːtəbl] *adj* widerlegbar.
refutation [ˌrefjʊ'teɪʃən] *n* Widerlegung *f*.
refute [rɪ'fjuːt] *vt* widerlegen.
regain [rɪ'geɪn] *vt* **(a)** wiedererlangen; *lost time* aufholen; *control, one's sight also* wiedergewinnen; *territory* zurückbekommen ♦ **to ~ one's strength/health** wieder zu Kräften kommen/wieder gesund werden; **to ~ one's footing** wieder Stand finden; (*fig*) wieder auf die Beine kommen; **to ~ possession of sth** wieder in den Besitz einer Sache (*gen*) gelangen.
(b) (*reach again*) *main road/firm ground* wieder gelangen an (+*acc*)/auf (+*acc*).
regal ['riːgəl] *adj* königlich; (*fig*) hoheitsvoll.
regale [rɪ'geɪl] *vt* (*with food, drink*) verwöhnen; (*with stories*) ergötzen (*geh*).
regalia [rɪ'geɪlɪə] *npl* Insignien *pl* ♦ **she was in full ~** (*hum*) sie war in großer Gala *or* Aufmachung (*hum*).
regally ['riːgəlɪ] *adv* königlich; *say* hoheitsvoll.
▼ **regard** [rɪ'gɑːd] 1 *vt* **(a)** (*consider*) betrachten ♦ **to ~ sb/sth as sth** jdn/etw für etw halten, jdn/etw als etw betrachten; **to ~ sb/sth with favour** jdn/etw wohlwollend betrachten; **to ~ sth with horror** mit Schrecken an etw (*acc*) denken; **to be ~ed as ...** als ... angesehen werden; **he is ~ed as a great poet** er wird als großer Dichter angesehen, er gilt als großer Dichter; **it's not generally ~ed as worth doing** es wird im allgemeinen angenommen, daß sich das nicht lohnt; **we ~ it as worth doing** wir glauben, daß es sich lohnt(, das zu tun); **we don't ~ it as necessary/our responsibility** wir halten es nicht für notwendig/wir betrachten es nicht als unsere Verantwortung; **to ~ sb/sth highly** *or* **with great esteem** jdn/etw hochschätzen *or* sehr schätzen; **he is highly ~ed** er ist hoch angesehen; **his work is highly ~ed** seine Arbeit wird sehr geschätzt.
(b) (*concern*) **as ~s that/him/your application** was das/ihn/Ihren Antrag betrifft *or* anbelangt; *see also* **regarding**.
(c) (*liter: look at*) betrachten.
(d) (*heed*) berücksichtigen ♦ **without ~ing his wishes** ohne Rücksicht auf

➤ LANGUAGE IN USE: **refuse¹: 1** → 9.3, 12.2

seine Wünsche.

[2] *n* **(a)** (*attention, concern*) Rücksicht *f* (*for* auf *+acc*) ◆ **to have some ~ for sb/sth** auf jdn/etw Rücksicht nehmen; **to show little/no ~ for sb/sth** wenig/keine Rücksichtnahme für jdn/etw zeigen; **with no ~ for his safety** ohne Rücksicht auf seine Sicherheit (zu nehmen); **without ~ to** *or* **for her advice/what people might think** ohne sich um ihren Rat zu kümmern/ohne sich darum zu kümmern, was die Leute denken mochten.

▼ **(b) in this ~** diesbezüglich (*form*), in diesem Zusammenhang; **with** *or* **in ~ to** in bezug auf (*+acc*).

(c) (*respect*) Achtung *f* ◆ **to hold sb in high ~** jdn achten *or* sehr schätzen; **to have a great ~ for sb** jdn hochachten.

▼ **(d) ~s** *pl* (*in message*) Gruß *m* ◆ **to send sb one's ~s** jdn grüßen lassen; **give him my ~s** grüßen Sie ihn von mir; **(kindest) ~s, with kind ~s** mit freundlichen Grüßen.

(e) (*liter: look*) Blick *m*.

regardful [rɪ'gɑːdfʊl] *adj* (*form*) **~ of (one's) duty** sich (*dat*) seiner Pflicht (*gen*) bewußt, pflichtbewußt; **to be ~ of sb's feelings** jds Gefühle achten *or* respektieren.

regarding [rɪ'gɑːdɪŋ] *prep* in bezug auf (*+acc*), bezüglich (*+gen*).

regardless [rɪ'gɑːdlɪs] [1] *adj* **~ of** ohne Rücksicht auf (*+acc*), ungeachtet (*+gen*); **to do sth ~ of the consequences** etw ohne Rücksicht auf die Folgen tun; **~ of what it costs** egal, was es kostet; **~ of the fact that** ... ungeachtet dessen, daß ...

[2] *adv* trotzdem ◆ **he did it ~** er hat es trotzdem getan.

regatta [rɪ'gætə] *n* Regatta *f*.

regd *abbr of* **registered** reg.

regency ['riːdʒənsɪ] *n* Regentschaft *f* ◆ **the R~ (period)** (*Brit Art etc*) der Regency; **R~ furniture/style** Regencymöbel *pl*/-stil *m*.

regenerate [rɪ'dʒenəreɪt] [1] *vt* **(a)** (*renew, re-create*) erneuern; *tissue also* neu bilden, regenerieren ◆ **to be ~d** sich erneuern; sich neu bilden, sich regenerieren; (*fig: person*) (*by holiday etc*) sich erholen; (*esp Rel*) erneuert werden.

(b) (*Elec*) rückkoppeln.

[2] *vi* (*esp Sci*) sich regenerieren; (*tissue also*) sich neu bilden.

[3] [rɪ'dʒenərɪt] *adj* regeneriert.

regeneration [rɪˌdʒenə'reɪʃən] *n see vb* Erneuerung *f*; Neubildung, Regeneration *f*; Erholung *f*; Rückkoppelung *f*.

regenerative [rɪ'dʒenərətɪv] *adj* **(a)** *tissue* sich regenerierend; (*esp Rel*) erneuernd. **(b)** (*Elec*) positiv rückgekoppelt.

regent ['riːdʒənt] *n* Regent *m*; (*US Univ*) Mitglied *nt* des Universitäts- *or* Schulverwaltungsrats; *see* **prince**.

reggae ['regeɪ] *n* Reggae *m*.

regicide ['redʒɪsaɪd] *n* (*act*) Königsmord *m*; (*person*) Königsmörder(in *f*) *m*.

regime [reɪ'ʒiːm] *n* **(a)** (*Pol*) Regime *nt*; (*fig: management, social system etc*) System *nt*. **(b)** *see* **regimen**.

regimen ['redʒɪmen] *n* (*Med*) Kur *f*.

regiment ['redʒɪmənt] [1] *n* (*Mil*) Regiment *nt*; (*fig*) Kompanie *f*.

[2] *vt* (*fig*) reglementieren.

regimental [ˌredʒɪ'mentl] [1] *adj* (*Mil*) Regiments-.

[2] *n* **~s** *pl* (*Mil*) Uniform *f*; (*of particular regiment*) Regimentsuniform *f*.

regimentation [ˌredʒɪmen'teɪʃən] *n* (*fig*) Reglementierung *f*.

region ['riːdʒən] *n* (*of country*) Gebiet *nt*, Region *f* (*also Admin, TV*); (*of body*) Gegend, Region *f*; (*of atmosphere, fig*) Bereich *m* ◆ **the lower ~s** die Unterwelt; **in the ~ of 5 kg** um die 5 kg.

regional ['riːdʒənl] *adj* regional ◆ **~ council** (*Scot*) ≃ Gemeinderat *m*; **~ development** Gebietserschließung *f*; **~ television** Regionalfernsehen *nt*.

regionalism ['riːdʒənəlɪzəm] *n* Regionalismus *m*; (*division into regions*) Einteilung *f* in Regionen; (*loyalty*) Lokalpatriotismus *m*; (*word*) nur regional verwendeter Ausdruck.

regionalist ['riːdʒənəlɪst] [1] *adj* regionalistisch.

[2] *n* Regionalist(in *f*) *m*.

register ['redʒɪstəʳ] [1] *n* **(a)** (*book*) Register *nt*; (*at school*) Namensliste *f*; (*in hotel*) Gästebuch *nt*; (*of members etc*) Mitgliedsbuch *nt* ◆ **to take the ~** die Namen aufrufen; **electoral ~** Wählerverzeichnis *nt*; **~ of births, deaths and marriages** Personenstandsbuch *nt*; **~ of wills** (*US: person*) Testamentsbeamte(r) *m*.

(b) (*Tech*) (*recording device*) Registriergerät *nt*; (*for controlling airflow*) Klappe *f*; *see* **cash ~**.

(c) (*Mus*) Register *nt*; (*organ stop*) Registerzug *m*.

(d) (*Ling*) (Sprach)ebene *f*, Register *nt* (*geh*).

(e) (*Typ*) Register *nt*.

[2] *vt* **(a)** (*authorities: record formally*) registrieren; (*in book, files*) eintragen; *fact, figure also* erfassen ◆ **he is ~ed as disabled** er ist anerkannter Schwerbeschädigter; *see* **registered**.

(b) (*individual: have recorded*) *birth, marriage, death*, (*Comm*) *company, trademark* anmelden, eintragen lassen; *vehicle, child at school etc, candidate* anmelden; *student* einschreiben ◆ **to ~ a protest** Protest anmelden.

(c) (*indicate*) (*machines*) *speed, quantity, rainfall, temperature* registrieren; (*face, expression*) *happiness, disapproval* zum Ausdruck bringen ◆ **he ~ed surprise** er zeigte sich überrascht; **he ~ed no emotion** er zeigte keine Gefühlsbewegung.

(d) (*Post*) *letter* einschreiben; *see* **registered**.

(e) (*Typ*) in Register bringen.

(f) (*realize*) registrieren ◆ **I ~ed the fact that he had gone** ich registrierte, daß er gegangen war.

[3] *vi* **(a)** (*on electoral list etc*) sich eintragen; (*in hotel*) sich anmelden; (*student*) sich einschreiben, sich immatrikulieren ◆ **to ~ with a doctor/dentist** sich bei einem Arzt/Zahnarzt auf die Patientenliste setzen lassen; **to ~ with the police** sich polizeilich melden; **to ~ for a course/for maths** einen Kurs/Mathematik belegen.

(b) (*inf: be understood*) **it hasn't ~ed (with him)** er hat es noch nicht registriert.

registered ['redʒɪstəd] *adj* **(a)** *student* eingeschrieben; *voter, company, name* eingetragen; *vehicle* amtlich zugelassen ◆ **~ capital** Grundkapital, Nominalkapital *nt*; **~ nurse** (*US*) staatlich geprüfte Krankenschwester, staatlich geprüfter Pfleger; **~ office** eingetragener (Gesellschafts)sitz; **~ shareholder** Inhaber *m* von Namensaktien; **~ trademark** eingetragenes Warenzeichen.

(b) (*Post*) *letter* eingeschrieben, Einschreib- ◆ **by ~ post** per Einschreiben.

register ton *n* (*Naut*) Registertonne *f*.

registrar [ˌredʒɪ'strɑːʳ] *n* (*Admin*) Standesbeamte(r) *m*; (*Univ*) höchster Verwaltungsbeamter, Kanzler *m*; (*Med*) Krankenhausarzt *m*/-ärztin *f* ◆ **~'s office** (*Brit Admin*) Standesamt *nt*; **to be married by the ~** sich standesamtlich trauen lassen.

registration [ˌredʒɪ'streɪʃən] *n see vt* **(a)** Registrierung *f*; Eintragung *f*; Erfassung *f*.

(b) Anmeldung *f*; Einschreibung *f* ◆ **~ fee** Anmeldegebühr *f*; (*for evening class*) Kursgebühr *f*; (*Univ*) Einschreib(e)gebühr *f*; **~ number** (*Aut*) Kraftfahrzeugkennzeichen *nt*, polizeiliches Kennzeichen; **~ document** (*Aut*) Kraftfahrzeugbrief *m*.

(c) Registrierung *f*; Ausdruck *m*.

(d) Aufgabe *f* als Einschreiben ◆ **~ fee** Einschreibegebühr *f*.

registry ['redʒɪstrɪ] *n* Sekretariat *nt*; (*in church*) Sakristei *f*; (*Brit: also* **~ office**) Standesamt *nt* ◆ **to get married in a ~ office** standesamtlich heiraten; **port of ~** Heimathafen *m*.

regius ['riːdʒəs] *adj* (*Brit Univ*): **~ professor** *Inhaber m eines von einem Monarchen eingerichteten Lehrstuhls.*

regorge [rɪ'gɔːdʒ] [1] *vt* (*form*) erbrechen.

[2] *vi* sich ergießen.

regress [rɪ'gres] *vi* (*lit form: move backwards*) sich rückwärts bewegen; (*fig*) (*society*) sich rückläufig entwickeln; (*Biol, Psych, Med*) sich zurückentwickeln ◆ **he is ~ing into childhood** er fällt wieder ins Kindesalter zurück.

regression [rɪ'greʃən] *n* (*lit form*) *see vi* Rückwärtsbewegung *f*; rückläufige Entwicklung; Zurückentwicklung *f* ◆ **his ~ into his childhood** sein Rückfall *m* in die Kindheit.

regressive [rɪ'gresɪv] *adj* regressiv; *trend* rückläufig.

▼ **regret** [rɪ'gret] [1] *vt* bedauern; *one's youth, lost opportunity* nachtrauern (*+dat*) ◆ **I ~ that we will not be coming** ich bedauere, daß wir nicht kommen können; **I ~ to say that** ... ich muß Ihnen leider mitteilen, daß ...; **he is very ill, I ~ to say** er ist leider *or* bedauerlicherweise sehr krank; **we ~ to hear that** ... wir hören mit Bedauern, daß ...; **it is to be ~ted that** ... es ist bedauerlich, daß ...; **you won't ~ it!** Sie werden es nicht bereuen; **he is much ~ted** er wird sehr vermißt.

[2] *n* Bedauern *nt no pl* ◆ **to feel ~ for one's past youth** seiner vergangenen Jugend (*dat*) nachtrauern; **much to my ~** sehr zu meinem Bedauern; **I have no ~s** ich bereue nichts; **please give her my ~s that I cannot come** bitte, sagen Sie ihr, daß ich leider nicht kommen kann; **he sends his ~s** er läßt sich entschuldigen, er muß leider absagen.

regretful [rɪ'gretfʊl] *adj look, attitude* bedauernd *attr* ◆ **he was extremely ~** es tat ihm sehr leid, er bedauerte es sehr.

regretfully [rɪ'gretfəlɪ] *adv* mit Bedauern ◆ **very ~ I must announce** ... sehr zu meinem Bedauern muß ich bekanntgeben, ...

▼ **regrettable** [rɪ'gretəbl] *adj* bedauerlich.

regrettably [rɪ'gretəblɪ] *adv* bedauerlicherweise, leider ◆ **a ~ poor turnout** eine bedauerlich schwache Beteiligung.

regroup [ˌriː'gruːp] [1] *vt* um- *or* neugruppieren.

[2] *vi* sich umgruppieren, sich neu gruppieren.

regrouping [ˌriː'gruːpɪŋ] *n see vt* Um- *or* Neugruppierung *f*.

regt *abbr of* **regiment** Reg.

regular ['regjʊləʳ] [1] *adj* **(a)** (*symmetrical, Gram*) regelmäßig; *features also* ebenmäßig; *surface* gleichmäßig; (*Geometry*) gleichseitig.

(b) (*at even intervals*) *service, bus, reminders* regelmäßig; *footsteps also* gleichmäßig; *employment* fest, regulär; *way of life, bowel movements* geregelt ◆ **to be ~ in one's habits** ein geregeltes Leben führen; **to eat ~ meals** regelmäßig essen; **to keep ~ hours** feste Zeiten haben; **she is as ~ as clockwork** bei ihr geht alles auf die Minute genau; **his visits are as ~ as clockwork** nach seinen Besuchen kann man die Uhr stellen.

(c) (*habitual*) *size, price, time* normal; *staff, customer, pub, butcher* Stamm-; *listener, reader* regelmäßig ◆ **our ~ cleaning woman** unsere normale Reinemachefrau; **my ~ dentist** mein Hauszahnarzt *m*.

(d) (*permissible, accepted*) *action, procedure* richtig ◆ **~ procedure demands that** ... der Ordnung halber muß man ...; **it is quite ~ to apply in person** es ist ganz in Ordnung, sich persönlich zu bewerben.

(e) (*Mil*) *soldier, army, officer* Berufs-, regulär.

(f) (*Rel*) **~ clergy** Ordensgeistlichkeit *f*.

(g) (*inf*) echt (*inf*) ◆ **he's a ~ idiot** er ist ein regelrechter Idiot; **~ guy** (*US*) ein klasse *or* echter Kerl (*inf*).

[2] *n* **(a)** (*Mil*) Berufssoldat *m*, regulärer Soldat; (*habitual customer etc*) Stammkunde *m*, Stammkundin *f*; (*in pub, hotel*) Stammgast *m* ◆ **he's one of the ~s on that programme** er ist einer der Stammgäste dieser Sendung.

➤ LANGUAGE IN USE: **regard: 2b** → 20.5 **2d** → 21.2 **regret: 1** → 12.3, 18.1, 18.2, 20.6 **regrettable** → 14

(b) *(petrol)* Normalbenzin *nt.*

regularity [ˌregjʊˈlærɪtɪ] *n* **(a)** *see adj (a)* Regelmäßigkeit *f*; Ebenmäßigkeit *f*; Gleichmäßigkeit *f*; Gleichseitigkeit *f.* **(b)** *see adj (b)* Regelmäßigkeit *f*; Gleichmäßigkeit *f*; Festheit *f*; Geregeltheit *f.* **(c)** *see adj (d)* Richtigkeit *f.*

regularize [ˈregjʊləraɪz] *vt breathing, service* regulieren; *situation, relationship* normalisieren.

regularly [ˈregjʊləlɪ] *adv* regelmäßig; *breathe, beat also* gleichmäßig.

regulate [ˈregjʊleɪt] *vt (control)* regulieren; *flow, expenditure also, traffic, life-style* regeln.

regulation [ˌregjʊˈleɪʃən] [1] *n* **(a)** *(regulating) see vt* Regulierung *f*; Regelung *f.* **(b)** *(rule)* Vorschrift *f*; *(of government etc also)* Verordnung *f* ◆ **the ~s of the society** die Satzung der Gesellschaft; **according to (the) ~s** laut Vorschrift/Satzung; **to be contrary to** *or* **against (the) ~s** gegen die Vorschrift(en)/Satzung verstoßen.
[2] *attr boots, dress* vorgeschrieben ◆ **army ~ boots** vorgeschriebene Armeestiefel *pl.*

regulative [ˈregjʊlətɪv] *adj* regulativ, regulierend.

regulator [ˈregjʊleɪtəʳ] *n (instrument)* Regler *m*; *(in clock, watch)* Gangregler *m*; *(for manual adjustment)* Rücker *m.*

regulatory [ˈregjʊlətərɪ] *adj* Regulierungs- ◆ **~ authority** Regulierungsbehörde *f*; **~ body** Regulierungsorgan *nt*; **~ control** behördliche Kontrolle *f*; **~ approval** Genehmigung *f* durch die Regulierungsbehörde.

regulo ® [ˈregjʊləʊ] *n* **at ~ 4** auf Gasstufe 4.

regurgitate [rɪˈgɜːdʒɪteɪt] *vt* wieder hochbringen, wieder von sich geben; *(fig) information* wiederkäuen ◆ **the young feed on ~d insects** die Jungen leben von vorverdauten Insekten.

regurgitation [rɪˌgɜːdʒɪˈteɪʃən] *n see vt* Wiederhochbringen *nt*; Wiederkäuen *nt.*

rehab [ˈriːˌhæb] *abbr of* **rehabilitation.**

rehabilitate [ˌriːəˈbɪlɪteɪt] *vt* **(a)** *refugee, troops* (in die Gesellschaft) eingliedern; *ex-criminal, the disabled also* rehabilitieren. **(b)** *(restore position to)* rehabilitieren.

rehabilitation [ˈriːəˌbɪlɪˈteɪʃən] *n see vt* Eingliederung *f* in die Gesellschaft; Rehabilitation *f* ◆ **~ centre** *(Admin)* Rehabilitationszentrum *nt.*

rehash [ˌriːˈhæʃ] [1] *vt literary material etc* aufbereiten.
[2] [ˈriːhæʃ] *n (action)* Aufbereitung *f*; *(result)* Aufguß *m.*

rehearsal [rɪˈhɜːsəl] *n* **(a)** *(Theat, Mus)* Probe *f* ◆ **this play is in ~** das Stück wird geprobt. **(b)** *(recital: of facts)* Aufzählung *f.*

rehearse [rɪˈhɜːs] [1] *vt* **(a)** *(Theat, Mus) play, concert* proben; *person* proben lassen ◆ **to ~ what one is going to say** einüben, was man sagen will. **(b)** *(recite)* aufzählen.
[2] *vi* proben.

reheat [ˌriːˈhiːt] *vt* aufwärmen.

rehouse [ˌriːˈhaʊz] *vt* unterbringen.

reify [ˈreɪfaɪ] *vt* verdinglichen, reifizieren *(Philos).*

reign [reɪn] [1] *n (lit, fig)* Herrschaft *f*; *(of monarch also)* Regentschaft *f* ◆ **in the ~ of ...** während der Herrschaft ... *(+gen)*; **Queen Victoria had a long ~** Königin Viktoria übte eine lange Herrschaft aus; **the R~ of Terror** die Schreckensherrschaft.
[2] *vi (lit, fig)* herrschen *(over* über *+acc)* ◆ **silence ~s** es herrscht Ruhe; *see* **supreme.**

reigning [ˈreɪnɪŋ] *adj attr* regierend; *champion* amtierend ◆ **the ~ beauty** die Schönheitskönigin.

reimburse [ˌriːɪmˈbɜːs] *vt person* entschädigen; *loss* ersetzen; *expenses, costs* (zurück)erstatten, ersetzen ◆ **to ~ sb for his expenses** jdm die Auslagen zurückerstatten.

reimbursement [ˌriːɪmˈbɜːsmənt] *n see vt* Entschädigung *f*; Ersatz *m*; (Rück)erstattung *f*, Ersatz *m.*

reimport [ˌriːɪmˈpɔːt] *vt* wiedereinführen, reimportieren.

reimpose [ˌriːɪmˈpəʊz] *vt task, conditions* neu aufzwingen *or* auferlegen *(form)* *(on sb* jdm*)*; *sanctions, fine* erneut verhängen *(on* gegen*)*; *one's will, authority* erneut aufzwingen *(on sb* jdm*)* ◆ **to ~ a tax on sth** etw erneut besteuern.

rein [reɪn] *n (lit, fig)* Zügel *m* ◆ **~s** *(for child)* Laufgurt *m*; **to hold the ~s** *(lit, fig)* die Zügel *or* das Heft in der Hand haben; **he kept the horse on a long/short ~** er ließ die Zügel lang/hielt die Zügel kurz; **to keep a tight ~ on sb/sth** *(lit, fig)* bei jdm/etw die Zügel kurz halten; **to give free ~ to sb/sth, to allow sb/sth free ~** *(fig)* jdm/einer Sache freien Lauf lassen *(+dat).*

◆**rein back** *vti sep* zügeln.

◆**rein in** [1] *vt sep horse* zügeln; *(fig) passions also* im Zaum halten ◆ **to ~ the horse ~ to a trot/canter** das Pferd im Trab/leichten Galopp gehen lassen.
[2] *vi* zügeln.

reincarnate [ˌriːɪnˈkɑːneɪt] [1] *vt* reinkarnieren *(liter)* ◆ **to be ~d** wiedergeboren werden; **the belief that man is ~d (after death)** der Glaube an die Reinkarnation des Menschen *or* an die Wiedergeburt.
[2] [ˌriːɪnˈkɑːnɪt] *adj* wiedergeboren.

reincarnation [ˌriːɪnkɑːˈneɪʃən] *n* die Wiedergeburt, die Reinkarnation.

reindeer [ˈreɪndɪəʳ] *n, pl* - Ren(tier) *nt* ◆ **Rudolph the red-nosed ~** Rudolf Rotnase *m.*

reinforce [ˌriːɪnˈfɔːs] *vt (lit, fig, Psych)* verstärken; *concrete also* armieren *(spec)*; *sb's demands* stärken, stützen; *evidence, statement* stützen, bestätigen; *opinion* bestätigen ◆ **to ~ sb's decision/determination** jdn in seiner Entscheidung/Absicht bestärken; **~d concrete** Stahlbeton *m.*

reinforcement [ˌriːɪnˈfɔːsmənt] *n* **(a)** *no pl (act) see vt* Verstärkung *f*; Armierung *f*; Stärkung, Stützung *f*; Bestätigung *f* ◆ **~ troops** *(Mil)* Verstärkungstruppen *pl.* **(b)** *(thing)* Verstärkung *f* ◆ **~s** *(Mil, fig)* Verstärkung *f.*

reinsert [ˌriːɪnˈsɜːt] *vt* wieder einfügen; *thermometer* wieder einführen; *coin* wieder einwerfen; *filing card* zurückstecken; *needle* wieder einstecken; *zip* wieder einsetzen.

reinstate [ˌriːɪnˈsteɪt] *vt person* wieder einstellen *(in* in *+acc)*; *law and order* wiederherstellen *(in* in *+dat).*

reinstatement [ˌriːɪnˈsteɪtmənt] *n see vt* Wiedereinstellung *f*; Wiederherstellung *f.*

reinsurance [ˌriːɪnˈʃʊərəns] *n* Rückversicherung *f.*

reinsure [ˌriːɪnˈʃʊəʳ] *vt* rückversichern.

reintegrate [ˌriːˈɪntɪgreɪt] *vt* wiedereingliedern, wieder *or* erneut integrieren *(into* in *+acc).*

reintegration [ˈriːˌɪntɪˈgreɪʃən] *n* Wiedereingliederung, Reintegration *f.*

reinvest [ˌriːɪnˈvest] *vt* reinvestieren.

reissue [ˌriːˈɪʃjuː] [1] *vt book* neu auflegen; *stamps, recording, coins* neu herausgeben.
[2] *n see vt* Neuauflage *f*; Neuausgabe *f.*

reiterate [riːˈɪtəreɪt] *vt* wiederholen.

reiteration [riːˌɪtəˈreɪʃən] *n* Wiederholung *f.*

reiterative [riːˈɪtərətɪv] *adj comments* sich wiederholend *attr*; *style* repetitiv.

reject [rɪˈdʒekt] [1] *vt* **(a)** *damaged goods etc (customer)* ablehnen, zurückweisen; *(maker, producer)* aussortieren, ausscheiden.
(b) *(turn down) application, request etc* ablehnen; *(stronger)* abweisen, zurückweisen; *candidate (through vote)* durchfallen lassen; *suitor, advances* abweisen, zurückweisen; *offer also* ausschlagen; *plea also* abschlagen; *possibility* verwerfen.
(c) *(Med) drug* nicht vertragen, ablehnen; *transplant also* abstoßen; *(stomach) food* verweigern.
[2] [ˈriːdʒekt] *n (Comm)* Ausschuß *m no pl* ◆ **~ goods** Ausschußware *f*; **although this jacket's a ~ ...** obwohl dieses Jackett zweite Wahl ist, ...; **society's ~s** die Ausgestoßenen *pl*; **~ shop** *Geschäft nt für Ausschußware*, Ramschladen *m (inf).*

rejection [rɪˈdʒekʃən] *n see vt* **(a)** Ablehnung, Zurückweisung *f*; Aussortierung, Ausscheidung *f.*
(b) Ablehnung *f*; Abweisung, Zurückweisung *f*; Verwerfen *nt* ◆ **~ slip** Absage *f.*
(c) *(Med)* Ablehnung *f*; Abstoßung *f*; Verweigerung *f.*

rejig [riːˈdʒɪg] *vt (Brit: redo)* neu machen; *system, structures also* umkrempeln.

rejoice [rɪˈdʒɔɪs] [1] *vt (liter) person* erfreuen.
[2] *vi* sich freuen; *(jubilate)* jubeln; *(Rel)* jauchzen ◆ **~ in the Lord!** freut euch im Herrn!; **he ~s in the name of Marmaduke** *(hum)* er erfreut sich des Namens Marmaduke.

rejoicing [rɪˈdʒɔɪsɪŋ] *n* Jubel *m* ◆ **~s** Jubel *m.*

rejoin[1] [ˌriːˈdʒɔɪn] *vt person, regiment* sich wieder anschließen *(+dat)* ◆ **to ~ ship** *(Naut)* wieder aufs Schiff kommen; **then we ~ed the motorway** danach fuhren wir wieder auf die Autobahn.

rejoin[2] [rɪˈdʒɔɪn] *vt (reply)* erwidern; *(Jur)* duplizieren.

rejoinder [rɪˈdʒɔɪndəʳ] *n* Erwiderung *f*; *(Jur)* Duplik *f.*

rejuvenate [rɪˈdʒuːvɪneɪt] *vt* verjüngen; *(fig)* erfrischen.

rekindle [ˌriːˈkɪndl] [1] *vt (lit) fire, flame* wieder anzünden; *(fig) passions, love* wieder entzünden *or* entflammen; *hope* wiedererwecken.
[2] *vi (lit)* wieder aufflackern; *(fig) (passion, love also)* wieder entflammen; *(hope)* wiedererwachen.

relapse [rɪˈlæps] [1] *n (Med)* Rückfall, Rückschlag *m*; *(fig) (in economy)* Rückschlag *m*; *(into vice, crime)* Rückfall *m (into* in *+acc)* ◆ **to have a ~** einen Rückfall haben.
[2] *vi (Med)* einen Rückfall haben; *(economy)* einen Rückschlag erleiden ◆ **to ~ (into crime/vice)** rückfällig werden; **to ~ into unconsciousness** wieder bewußtlos werden.

relate [rɪˈleɪt] [1] *vt* **(a)** *(recount) story* erzählen; *details* aufzählen ◆ **strange to ~** so unglaublich es klingt.
(b) *(associate)* in Verbindung *or* Beziehung *or* Zusammenhang bringen *(to, with* mit*)* ◆ **to try to ~ events (to each other)** versuchen, die Dinge im Zusammenhang zu sehen; **it is often difficult to ~ the cause to the effect** der Zusammenhang zwischen Ursache und Wirkung ist oft schwer zu erkennen.
[2] *vi* **(a)** zusammenhängen *(to* mit*).*
(b) *(form relationship)* eine Beziehung finden *(to* zu*).*

related [rɪˈleɪtɪd] *adj* **(a)** *(in family)* verwandt *(to* mit*).* **(b)** *(connected)* zusammenhängend; *elements, languages etc* verwandt ◆ **to be ~ to sth** mit etw zusammenhängen/verwandt sein.

relating [rɪˈleɪtɪŋ] *adj* **~ to** in Zusammenhang mit.

relation [rɪˈleɪʃən] *n* **(a)** *(relative)* Verwandte(r) *mf* ◆ **he's a/no ~ (of mine)** er ist/ist nicht mit mir verwandt; **what ~ is she to you?** wie ist sie mit Ihnen verwandt?
(b) *(relationship)* Beziehung *f* ◆ **to bear a ~ to** in Beziehung stehen zu; **to bear no ~ to** in keinerlei Beziehung stehen zu, keinerlei Beziehung haben zu; **in ~ to** *(as regards)* in bezug auf *(+acc)*; *(compared with)* im Verhältnis zu.
(c) **~s** *pl (dealings, ties, sexual ~s)* Beziehungen *pl* ◆ **to have business ~s with sb** geschäftliche Beziehungen zu jdm haben; **~s are rather strained** die Beziehungen sind etwas gespannt.
(d) *no pl (of story)* Erzählung *f*; *(of details)* Aufzählung *f.*

relational [rɪˈleɪʃənəl] *adj* relational ◆ **~ database** *(Comput)* relationale Datenbank.

relationship [rɪˈleɪʃənʃɪp] *n* **(a)** Verwandtschaft *f (to* mit*)* ◆ **what is your ~**

(to him)? wie sind Sie (mit ihm) verwandt?
(b) *(connection: between events etc)* Beziehung, Verbindung *f*; *(relations)* Verhältnis *nt*, Beziehungen *pl*; *(in business)* Verbindung *f* ◆ **to have a (sexual) ~ with** ein Verhältnis haben mit; **what kind of a ~ do you have with him?** *(is it good or bad)* wie ist Ihr Verhältnis zu ihm?; *(on what footing)* in welchem Verhältnis stehen Sie zu ihm?; **to have a good ~ with sb** ein gutes Verhältnis *or* gute Beziehungen zu jdm haben; **they have a good ~** sie haben ein gutes Verhältnis (zueinander); **we have a business ~** wir haben geschäftlich miteinander zu tun; **it is a strictly business ~** es ist eine rein geschäftliche Beziehung.

relative ['relətɪv] [1] *adj* **(a)** *(comparative, not absolute, Sci)* relativ; *(respective)* jeweilig ◆ **happiness is ~** Glück ist relativ; **~ to him, she is in a very happy position** verglichen mit ihm ist sie gut dran; **fuel consumption is ~ to speed** der Benzinverbrauch hängt von der Geschwindigkeit ab; **to live in ~ luxury** verhältnismäßig *or* relativ luxuriös leben; **the ~ merits of A and B** die jeweiligen Verdienste von A und B.
(b) *(relevant)* **~ to** sich beziehend auf (+*acc*).
(c) *(Gram) pronoun, clause* Relativ-.
(d) *(Mus) minor, major* parallel.
[2] *n* **(a)** *(person) see* **relation (a)**.
(b) *(Gram) (clause)* Relativsatz *m*; *(pronoun)* Relativpronomen *nt*.

relatively ['relətɪvlɪ] *adv* relativ, verhältnismäßig ◆ **~ speaking** relativ gesehen *or* betrachtet.

relativism ['relətɪvɪzəm] *n* Relativismus *m*.

relativist ['relətɪvɪst] *n* Relativist(in *f*) *m*.

relativistic [ˌrelətɪ'vɪstɪk] *adj* relativistisch.

relativity [ˌrelə'tɪvɪtɪ] *n (Phys, Philos)* Relativität *f* ◆ **~ theory, the theory of ~** die Relativitätstheorie.

relax [rɪ'læks] [1] *vt* lockern; *muscles also, person, one's mind* entspannen; *attention, effort* nachlassen in (+*dat*) ◆ **to ~ the bowels** *(Med)* den Stuhlgang fördern.
[2] *vi* (sich) entspannen; *(rest)* (sich) ausruhen; *(calm down)* sich beruhigen ◆ **let's just ~!** ganz ruhig!; **~!** reg dich nicht auf!, immer mit der Ruhe!; **his face ~ed into a smile** sein Gesicht entspannte sich zu einem Lächeln.

relaxant [rɪ'læksənt] *n (Med)* Relaxans *nt*.

relaxation [ˌriːlæk'seɪʃən] *n* **(a)** *see vt* Lockerung *f*; Entspannung *f*; Nachlassen *nt*.
(b) *(rest)* Entspannung *f*; *(recreation also)* Erholung *f* ◆ **you need some ~ after work** Sie sollten sich nach der Arbeit entspannen; Sie brauchen ein wenig Erholung nach der Arbeit; **books are her ~** zur Entspannung *or* Erholung liest sie.

relaxed [rɪ'lækst] *adj* locker; *person, smile, voice* entspannt, ruhig; *atmosphere* zwanglos, gelockert; *throat (Med)* angegriffen ◆ **to feel ~** *(physically)* entspannt sein; *(mentally)* sich wohl fühlen; **to feel ~ about sth** etw ganz gelassen sehen.

relaxing [rɪ'læksɪŋ] *adj* entspannend; *climate* erholsam.

relay ['riːleɪ] [1] *n* **(a)** *(of workers etc)* Ablösung *f*; *(of horses)* frisches Gespann ◆ **to work in ~s** sich ablösen. **(b)** *(Sport: also* **~ race***)* Staffel(lauf *m*) *f*. **(c)** *(Rad, TV)* Relais *nt*.
[2] *vt* **(a)** *(Rad, TV etc) programme, signal* (weiter) übertragen. **(b)** *message* ausrichten (*to sb* jdm).

re-lay [ˌriː'leɪ] *vt carpet, cable* neu verlegen.

release [rɪ'liːs] [1] *vt* **(a)** *animal, person* freilassen; *(from prison also)* entlassen; *employee, football player etc* freigeben; *(rescue)* befreien; *(from obligation, vow)* entbinden, befreien; *(from pain)* erlösen ◆ **to ~ sb from a debt** jdm eine Schuld erlassen; **can you ~ him for a few hours each week?** können Sie ihn für ein paar Stunden pro Woche freistellen?
(b) *(let go of)* loslassen; *spring also* zurückspringen lassen; *handbrake* losmachen; *(Phot) shutter* auslösen; *bomb* abwerfen; *grip, clasp* lösen; *(police) confiscated articles* freigeben ◆ **to ~ the (foot)brake/clutch** den Fuß von der Bremse/Kupplung nehmen, die Kupplung kommen lassen; **to ~ one's hold** *or* **grip (on sth)** (etw) loslassen.
(c) *(Comm: issue) film, goods* herausbringen; *record also* veröffentlichen.
(d) *(make known) news, statement* veröffentlichen.
(e) *(emit) gas, energy* freisetzen; *smell* ausströmen; *(let off, into atmosphere) pressure, steam* ablassen.
(f) *(Jur) property, title* aufgeben, verzichten auf (+*acc*).
[2] *n see vt* **(a)** Freilassung *f*; Entlassung *f*; Freigabe *f*; Befreiung *f*; Entbindung *f*; Erlösung *f* ◆ **death was a happy ~ for him** der Tod war eine Erlösung für ihn.
(b) *(act)* Loslassen *nt*; Lösen *nt*; Auslösen *nt*; Abwurf *m*; Freigabe *f*; *(mechanism)* Auslöser *m*; *see* **shutter**.
(c) *(act)* Herausbringen *nt*; Veröffentlichung *f*; *(film)* Film *m*; *(record)* Platte *f* ◆ **this film is now on general ~** dieser Film ist nun überall zu sehen; **a new ~ from Michael Jackson/XYZ Films Inc.** eine Neuerscheinung von Michael Jackson/ein neuer Film der XYZ Filmgesellschaft.
(d) *(act)* Veröffentlichung *f*; *(statement)* Verlautbarung *f*.
(e) Freisetzung *f* ◆ **~ valve** Entlastungsventil *nt*.
(f) Aufgabe *f (of gen)*, Verzicht *m (of* auf +*acc)*.

release date *n* **(a)** *(of film)* Premieren- *or* Erstaufführungstag *m*; *(of record, book)* Erscheinungstag *m*. **(b)** *(of prisoner)* Entlassungsdatum *nt* ◆ **his first possible ~ is 1999** er kann frühestens 1999 entlassen werden.

relegate ['relɪgeɪt] *vt* **(a)** *(lit, fig: downgrade)* degradieren; *(Sport) team* absteigen lassen (*to* in +*acc*); *old toys, furniture* verbannen (*to* in +*acc*) ◆ **to be ~d** *(Sport)* absteigen; **~d to second place** *(fig)* an zweite Stelle abgeschoben *or* verbannt.
(b) *(hand over) matter, question* weiterleiten (*to* an +*acc*).

relegation [ˌrelɪ'geɪʃən] *n see vt* **(a)** Degradierung *f*; Abstieg *m*; Verbannung *f*. **(b)** Weiterleitung *f*.

relent [rɪ'lent] *vi (person)* nachgeben; *(pace, pain)* nachlassen; *(weather)* sich bessern.

relentless [rɪ'lentlɪs] *adj* erbarmungslos; *person also* unerbittlich; *attitude, opposition also* unnachgiebig; *pain, cold* nicht nachlassend.

relentlessly [rɪ'lentlɪslɪ] *adv* unerbittlich, erbarmungslos; *oppose, maintain* unnachgiebig; *hurt, rain* unaufhörlich.

relet [ˌriː'let] *vt* neu vermieten.

relevance ['reləvəns], **relevancy** ['relɪvənsɪ] *n* Relevanz *f* ◆ **what is the ~ of your question to the problem?** inwiefern ist Ihre Frage für das Problem relevant?

relevant ['reləvənt] *adj* relevant (*to* für); *information, document also* entsprechend *attr*; *course, study also* sachbezogen; *authority, person* zuständig ◆ **a course ~ to one's studies** ein studienbezogener *or* für sein Studium relevanter Kurs; **the police are looking for any ~ information** die Polizei bittet um sachdienliche Hinweise.

reliability [rɪˌlaɪə'bɪlɪtɪ] *n see adj* Zuverlässigkeit *f*; Verläßlichkeit *f*; Seriosität, Vertrauenswürdigkeit *f*.

reliable [rɪ'laɪəbl] *adj* zuverlässig; *person also* verläßlich; *firm, company* seriös, vertrauenswürdig.

reliably [rɪ'laɪəblɪ] *adv* zuverlässig ◆ **I am ~ informed that ...** ich weiß aus zuverlässiger Quelle, daß ...

reliance [rɪ'laɪəns] *n (trust, confidence)* Vertrauen *nt (on* auf +*acc)* ◆ **to place ~ on sth** sich auf etw (*acc*) verlassen; **his ~ on his memory rather than his notes always gets him into difficulties** er verläßt sich auf sein Gedächtnis statt auf seine Notizen und kommt dadurch immer in Schwierigkeiten.

reliant [rɪ'laɪənt] *adj (dependent)* angewiesen (*on, upon* auf +*acc*); *see* **self-reliant**.

relic ['relɪk] *n* Überbleibsel, Relikt *nt*; *(Rel)* Reliquie *f* ◆ **a ~ of** *or* **from a past age** ein Überbleibsel aus vergangener Zeit; **an old ~** *(pej inf) (person)* ein alter Knochen *(inf)*; *(car, wardrobe etc)* ein vorsintflutlicher Karren/Schrank *etc (pej inf)*.

relief [rɪ'liːf] [1] *n* **(a)** *(from anxiety, pain)* Erleichterung *f* ◆ **to bring sb ~** *(drug)* jdm Erleichterung verschaffen; *(news)* jdn erleichtern; **that brought him some ~ from his headache** das hat seine Kopfschmerzen etwas gelindert; **that's a ~!** mir fällt ein Stein vom Herzen; **it was a ~ to find it** ich/er *etc* war erleichtert, als ich/er *etc* es fand.
(b) *(from monotony, boredom)* Abwechslung *f* ◆ **to provide a little light/comic ~** eine kleine Abwechslung schaffen/für etwas Humor sorgen.
(c) *(assistance)* Hilfe *f* ◆ **to go/come to sb's ~** jdm zu Hilfe eilen/kommen; **~ was available in the form of blankets and cups of tea** für Decken und heißen Tee war gesorgt; **to send ~ in the form of food to sb** jdm mit Nahrungsmitteln zu Hilfe kommen; **~ of the poor** Armenfürsorge *f*; **to provide ~ for the poor** für die Armen sorgen; **to be on ~** *(US)* Fürsorge bekommen, von der Fürsorge leben.
(d) *(esp Mil: act of relieving, replacement forces)* Entsatz *m*; *(substitute)* Ablösung *f* ◆ **~ watchman/driver** *etc* Ablösung *f*; **~ train/bus** Entlastungszug *m* /-bus *m*.
(e) *(Art, Geog)* Relief *nt*; *(Typ also)* Hochdruck *m* ◆ **high/low ~** Hoch-/Flachrelief *nt*; **in ~** erhaben; **to stand out in ~ against sth** *(lit)* sich (deutlich) von etw abheben; *(fig)* im Gegensatz zu etw stehen; **to bring** *or* **throw sth into ~** *(lit)* etw (deutlich) hervortreten lassen; *(fig)* etw hervorheben.
(f) *(Jur)* Rechtshilfe *f (of* bei*)*.
[2] *attr* **(a)** *fund, organization* Hilfs- ◆ **~ supplies** Hilfsgüter *pl*.
(b) *watchman, driver* Ablöse-; *troops* Entsatz-; *bus, train, road* Entlastungs- ◆ **~ valve** Ausgleichsventil *nt*.
(c) *map* Relief-; *printing also* Hoch-.

relieve [rɪ'liːv] *vt* **(a)** *person* erleichtern; *(of pain)* helfen (+*dat*) ◆ **to feel ~d** erleichtert sein; **he was ~d to learn that** er war erleichtert, als er das hörte; **to ~ sb's mind** jdn beruhigen.
(b) **to ~ sb of sth** *of burden, pain* jdn von etw befreien; *of duty, post, command* jdn einer Sache (*gen*) entheben *(geh)*; *of coat, suitcase* jdm etw abnehmen; *(hum) of wallet, purse etc* jdn um etw erleichtern *(hum)*.
(c) *(mitigate) anxiety* mildern, schwächen; *pain* lindern; *(completely)* stillen; *tension* abbauen; *monotony (interrupt)* unterbrechen; *(liven things up)* beleben; *poverty* erleichtern; *(Med) congestion* abhelfen (+*dat*); *(completely)* beheben ◆ **to ~ one's feelings** seinen Gefühlen Luft machen; **the black of her dress was ~d by a white collar** das Schwarz ihres Kleides wurde durch einen weißen Kragen etwas aufgelockert; **the new road ~s peak-hour congestion** die neue Straße entlastet den Berufsverkehr; **to ~ oneself** *(euph)* sich erleichtern.
(d) *(help) stricken country, refugees etc* helfen (+*dat*).
(e) *(take over from, also Mil)* ablösen.
(f) *(Mil) town* entsetzen, befreien.

religion [rɪ'lɪdʒən] *n* Religion *f*; *(set of beliefs)* Glaube(n) *m* ◆ **the Christian ~** der christliche Glaube; **wars of ~** Glaubenskriege *pl*; **her name in ~** ihr Klostername *m*; **to get ~** *(pej inf)* fromm werden; **study of ~** Religionswissenschaft *f*; **to make a ~ of doing sth** *(fig)* sich (*dat*) ein Gewissen daraus machen, etw zu tun; **it's an absolute ~ with him, it's his ~** *(fig)* das ist ihm heilig.

religiosity [rɪˌlɪdʒɪ'ɒsɪtɪ] *n* Frömmlertum *nt*.

religious [rɪ'lɪdʒəs] [1] *adj* **(a)** religiös; *order* geistlich; *freedom also, wars* Glaubens-, Religions- ◆ **~ instruction** *(Sch)* Religionsunterricht *m*; **~ leader**

Religionsführer *m*.
(b) (*having ~ beliefs*) *person* gläubig; (*pious*) fromm.
(c) (*fig: conscientious*) gewissenhaft; *silence* ehrfürchtig.
2 *n* Ordensmann *m*, Ordensfrau *f* ♦ **the ~** *pl* die Ordensleute *pl*.

religiously [rɪ'lɪdʒəslɪ] *adv live* fromm, gottesfürchtig; (*fig: conscientiously*) gewissenhaft, treu und brav.

religiousness [rɪ'lɪdʒəsnɪs] *n* (*piety*) Frömmigkeit *f*; (*fig: conscientiousness*) Gewissenhaftigkeit *f*.

reline [ˌriː'laɪn] *vt coat, jacket* neu füttern; *brakes* neu belegen.

relinquish [rɪ'lɪŋkwɪʃ] *vt* **(a)** (*give up*) *hope, habit, plan* aufgeben; *right, possessions, power, post also* verzichten auf (+*acc*) ♦ **to ~ sth to sb** jdm etw abtreten *or* überlassen.
(b) (*let go*) **to ~ one's hold on sb/sth** (*lit, fig*) jdn/etw loslassen; **he ~ed his hold on life/reality** er gab seinen Willen zum Leben auf/er verlor jeden Bezug zur Realität.

relinquishment [rɪ'lɪŋkwɪʃmənt] *n* (*form: of claim, possessions etc*) Verzicht *m* (*of* auf +*acc*).

reliquary ['relɪkwərɪ] *n* Reliquiar *nt*, Reliquienschrein *m*.

relish ['relɪʃ] **1** *n* **(a)** (*enjoyment*) Geschmack, Gefallen *m* (*for* an +*dat*) ♦ **to do sth with (great) ~** etw mit (großem) Genuß tun; **he rubbed his hands with ~ at the prospect** er rieb sich (*dat*) beim Gedanken daran genüßlich die Hände; **he ate with (great) ~** er aß mit großem Genuß *or* Appetit; **he had no further ~ for such activities** er fand an solchen Dingen keinen Geschmack *or* Gefallen mehr.
(b) (*Cook*) Soße *f*; (*spiciness*) Würze *f*; (*fig: charm*) Reiz *m* ♦ **tomato/fruit ~** Tomaten-/Obstchutney *nt*; **hunger is the best ~** (*Prov*) Hunger ist der beste Koch (*Prov*); **it had lost all ~ (for me)** (*fig*) das hatte für mich jeglichen Reiz verloren.
2 *vt* genießen; *food, wine also* sich (*dat*) schmecken lassen ♦ **I don't ~ doing that** (*enjoy*) das ist gar nicht nach meinem Geschmack; (*look forward to*) darauf freue ich mich überhaupt nicht; **I don't ~ the thought of getting up at 5 a.m.** der Gedanke, um 5 Uhr aufzustehen, behagt *or* schmeckt (*inf*) mir gar nicht.

relive [ˌriː'lɪv] *vt life* noch einmal leben; *experience, one's childhood* noch einmal erleben *or* durchleben.

reload [ˌriː'ləud] *vt* neu beladen; *gun* nachladen, neu laden.

relocate [ˌriːləu'keɪt] **1** *vt* umsiedeln, verlegen.
2 *vi* (*individual*) umziehen; (*company*) den Standort wechseln ♦ **many companies are relocating out of London** viele Firmen verlegen ihren Standort nach außerhalb von London; **we will help you ~** wir helfen Ihnen beim Umzug *or* (*referring to company*) beim Standortwechsel.

relocation [ˌriːləu'keɪʃən] *n* Umzug *m*; (*of company*) Standortwechsel *m*; (*of refugees etc*) Umsiedlung *f* ♦ **~ allowance** Umzugsbeihilfe *f*.

reluctance [rɪ'lʌktəns] *n* **(a)** Widerwillen *m*, Abneigung *f* ♦ **to do sth with ~** etw widerwillig *or* ungern tun; **to make a show of ~** sich widerwillig geben.
(b) (*Phys*) magnetischer Widerstand.

reluctant [rɪ'lʌktənt] *adj* unwillig, widerwillig; *admission, consent, praise* widerwillig ♦ **he is ~ to do it** es widerstrebt ihm, es zu tun; **I'm ~ to go, as he may not even be there** ich gehe nur ungern, denn er ist vielleicht nicht einmal da; **he seems ~ to admit it** er scheint es nicht zugeben zu wollen; **he is a ~ soldier/student** er ist nur widerwillig Soldat/Student.

reluctantly [rɪ'lʌktəntlɪ] *adv* widerwillig.

rely [rɪ'laɪ] *vi* **to ~ (up)on sb/sth** sich auf jdn/etw verlassen; (*be dependent on*) auf jdn/etw angewiesen sein; **she relied on the trains being on time** sie verließ sich darauf, daß die Züge pünktlich waren; **I ~ on him for my income** ich bin finanziell auf ihn angewiesen; **you can ~ (up)on my help/on me to help you** du kannst dich darauf verlassen, daß ich dir helfe; **she is not to be relied upon** man kann sich nicht auf sie verlassen.

REM *abbr of* **rapid eye movement** ♦ **~ sleep** REM-Phase *f*.

remain [rɪ'meɪn] *vi* **(a)** bleiben; (*be left over*) übrigbleiben ♦ **much ~s to be done** es ist *or* bleibt noch viel zu tun; **nothing ~s to be said** es gibt *or* bleibt nichts mehr zu sagen; **nothing ~s but to accept** wir/sie *etc* brauchen nur noch anzunehmen; (*no alternative*) es bleibt uns nichts anderes übrig, als anzunehmen; **all that ~s is for me to wish you every success** ich möchte Ihnen nur noch viel Erfolg wünschen; **all that ~s (for me/us *etc* to do) is to lock up** ich brauche/wir brauchen jetzt nur noch abzuschließen; **that ~s to be seen** das wird sich zeigen, das bleibt abzuwarten; **the fact ~s that he is wrong** das ändert nichts an der Tatsache, daß er unrecht hat.
(b) (*stay*) bleiben ♦ **~ seated!** bleiben Sie sitzen, behalten Sie Platz (*geh*); **to ~ silent** weiterhin schweigen; **to ~ behind/up** zurück-/aufbleiben; **let the matter ~ as it is** lassen Sie die Sache so, wie sie ist; **it ~s the same** das bleibt sich gleich; **"I ~ yours faithfully John Smith"** „mit besten Grüßen verbleibe ich Ihr John Smith".

remainder [rɪ'meɪndəʳ] **1** *n* **(a)** Rest *m* (*also Math*) ♦ **the ~** (*remaining people*) der Rest, die übrigen (Leute); **for the ~ of the week** für den Rest der Woche, für die übrige Woche. **(b) ~s** *pl* (*Comm*) Restbestände *pl*; (*books also*) Remittenden *pl* (*spec*). **(c)** (*Jur*) Erbanwartschaft *f*.
2 *vt books* als Remittenden abgeben.

remaining [rɪ'meɪnɪŋ] *adj* übrig, restlich ♦ **the ~ four, the four ~** die übrigen vier, die vier übrigen; **I have only one ~** ich habe nur noch einen/eine/eins (übrig).

remains [rɪ'meɪnz] *npl* (*of meal*) Reste *pl*; (*of fortune, army*) Rest *m*; (*of building*) Überreste *pl*; (*archaeological ~*) Ruinen *pl* ♦ **literary ~** literarischer Nachlaß; **his (mortal) ~** seine sterblichen Überreste; **human ~** menschliche Überreste *pl*.

remake [ˌriː'meɪk] (*vb: pret, ptp* **remade** [ˌriː'meɪd]) **1** *vt* wieder *or* nochmals machen; (*in new form*) neu machen ♦ **to ~ a film** ein Thema neu verfilmen.
2 ['riːmeɪk] *n* (*Film*) Neuverfilmung *f*, Remake *nt* (*spec*).

remand [rɪ'mɑːnd] **1** *vt* (*Jur*) *case* vertagen ♦ **to ~ sb (in custody/on bail)** jdn weiterhin in Untersuchungshaft behalten/unter Kaution halten; **to ~ sb to a higher court** jdm an eine höhere Instanz verweisen; **he was ~ed in custody/on bail** er blieb in Untersuchungshaft/unter Kaution; **the man ~ed in custody** der Untersuchungsgefangene.
2 *n* (*of person*) Aufrechterhaltung *f* der Untersuchungshaft/der Erhebung von Kaution (*of* gegen); (*form: of case*) Vertagung *f* ♦ **to be on ~** in Untersuchungshaft sein; (*on bail*) auf Kaution freigelassen sein; **~ home** *or* **centre** (*Brit*) Untersuchungsgefängnis *nt* für Jugendliche; **~ wing** Flügel *m or* Trakt *m* für Untersuchungsgefangene.

remark [rɪ'mɑːk] **1** *n* **(a)** (*comment*) Bemerkung *f* ♦ **I have a few/no ~s to make on that subject** ich habe einiges zu diesem Thema zu bemerken/nichts zu diesem Thema zu sagen; **~s were passed about our absence** man redete über unsere Abwesenheit.
(b) *no pl* (*notice*) **worthy of ~** bemerkenswert; **without ~** unbemerkt.
2 *vt* **(a)** (*say*) bemerken.
(b) (*old, liter: notice*) bemerken, wahrnehmen.
3 *vi* **to ~ (up)on sth** über etw (*acc*) eine Bemerkung machen, sich zu etw äußern; **nobody/everybody ~ed on it** niemand hat etwas dazu gesagt/alle haben ihre Bemerkungen dazu gemacht.

remarkable [rɪ'mɑːkəbl] *adj* (*notable*) bemerkenswert; *intelligence, talent, wit also* beachtlich; (*extraordinary*) außergewöhnlich ♦ **to be ~ for sth** sich durch etw auszeichnen.

remarkably [rɪ'mɑːkəblɪ] *adv* außergewöhnlich.

remarriage [ˌriː'mærɪdʒ] *n* Wiederverheiratung *f* (*to* mit).

remarry [ˌriː'mærɪ] *vi* wieder heiraten.

remediable [rɪ'miːdɪəbl] *adj situation* rettbar; *fault, defect* behebbar.

remedial [rɪ'miːdɪəl] *adj attr action, measures* Hilfs-; (*Med*) Heil- ♦ **~ exercises** Heilgymnastik *f*; **to teach ~ English/reading** einen/den Förderkurs in Englisch/im Lesen leiten; **~ teaching/work** Förder- *or* Hilfsunterricht *m*/Förderaufgaben *pl*; **~ class** Förderklasse *f* (für Lernschwache).

remedy ['remədɪ] **1** *n* (*Med, fig*) Mittel *nt* (*for* gegen); (*medication*) Heilmittel *nt* (*for* gegen); (*Jur*) Rechtsmittel *nt* ♦ **the situation is past** *or* **beyond ~** die Lage ist hoffnungslos verloren *or* irreparabel; **unless we can find a ~** wenn wir keinen Ausweg *or* keine Lösung finden.
2 *vt* (*Med*) heilen; (*fig*) *defect, fault* beheben; *situation* bessern; *abuse, evil* abhelfen (+*dat*) ♦ **his faults cannot be remedied** man kann ihn nicht von seinen Fehlern heilen; **the situation cannot be remedied** die Lage ist hoffnungslos.

➤ **remember** [rɪ'membəʳ] **1** *vt* **(a)** (*recall*) sich erinnern an (+*acc*); *person, occasion also* sich entsinnen (+*gen*) (*geh*), sich besinnen auf (+*acc*) (*geh*); (*bear in mind*) denken an (+*acc*); (*learn*) *formula, facts, vocabulary* sich (*dat*) merken ♦ **I ~ that he was very tall** ich erinnere mich (daran), daß er sehr groß war; **I ~ her as a beautiful girl** ich habe sie als schönes Mädchen in Erinnerung; **I ~ her as a young girl** *or* **when she was young** ich erinnere mich noch, wie sie als kleines Mädchen war; **we must ~ that he's only a child** wir sollten bedenken *or* daran denken, daß er noch ein Kind ist; **to ~ to do sth** daran denken, etw zu tun; **I ~ doing it** ich erinnere mich daran, daß ich es getan habe; **I can't ~ the word at the moment** das Wort fällt mir im Moment nicht ein; **I've just ~ed his name** mir ist gerade sein Name wieder eingefallen; **don't you ~ me?** erinnern Sie sich nicht an mich?; **here's something to ~ me by** da hast du etwas, das dich (immer) an mich erinnern wird; **do you ~ when ...?** (*reminiscing*) weißt du noch, als ...?; (*asking facts*) weißt du (noch), wann ... ?; **I don't ~ a thing about it** ich kann mich überhaupt nicht daran erinnern; (*about lecture, book*) ich weiß nichts mehr davon; **I can never ~ phone numbers** ich kann mir Telefonnummern einfach nicht merken; **we can't always ~ everything** wir können nicht immer an alles denken; **~ where/who you are!** denken Sie daran *or* bedenken Sie, wo/wer Sie sind!; **to ~ sb in one's prayers/one's will** jdn in sein Gebet einschließen/jdn in seinem Testament bedenken.
(b) (*commemorate*) *the fallen, a battle* gedenken (+*gen*).
➤ **(c)** (*give good wishes to*) **~ me to your mother** grüßen Sie Ihre Mutter von mir; **he asks to be ~ed to you** er läßt Sie grüßen.
2 *vi* sich erinnern ♦ **I can't ~** ich weiß das nicht mehr, ich hab's vergessen; **not as far as I ~** soweit ich mich erinnere, nicht!; **if I ~ right(ly)** wenn ich mich recht erinnere *or* entsinne.

remembrance [rɪ'membrəns] *n* **(a)** Erinnerung *f* (*of* an +*acc*) ♦ **R~ Day** (*Brit*) ≃ Volkstrauertag *m*; **~ service** Gedenkgottesdienst *m*; **in ~ of** zur Erinnerung an (+*acc*); **to the best of my ~** soweit ich mich erinnern kann; **I have no ~ of that** ich habe keinerlei Erinnerung daran.
(b) (*keepsake*) Andenken *nt* (*of* an +*acc*).
(c) ~s *pl* (*old form: greetings*) Empfehlungen *pl*.

remind [rɪ'maɪnd] *vt* erinnern (*of* an +*acc*) ♦ **you are ~ed that ...** wir weisen darauf hin, daß ...; **to ~ sb to do sth** jdn daran erinnern, etw zu tun; **that ~s me!** da(bei) fällt mir was ein.

reminder [rɪ'maɪndəʳ] *n* (*note, knot etc*) Gedächtnisstütze *f* ♦ **(letter of) ~** (*Comm*) Mahnung *f*; **as a ~ that ...** um dich/ihn *etc* daran zu erinnern, daß ...; **to give sb a ~ to do sth** jdn daran erinnern, etw zu tun; **his presence was a ~ of ...** seine Gegenwart erinnerte mich/dich *etc* an (+*acc*) ...; **a gentle ~** ein zarter Wink; **give him a gentle ~** weis ihn sachte darauf hin.

reminisce [ˌremɪ'nɪs] *vi* sich in Erinnerungen ergehen (*about* über +*acc*).

➤ LANGUAGE IN USE: **remember: 1a** → 26.1, 26.2 **1c** → 21.2

reminiscence [ˌremɪ'nɪsəns] *n (action)* Zurückgehen *nt (of zu)*; *(thought)* Reminiszenz, Erinnerung *(of an +acc) f.*

reminiscent [ˌremɪ'nɪsənt] *adj* **(a) to be ~ of sth** an etw *(acc)* erinnern; **a style ~ of Shakespeare** ein an Shakespeare erinnernder Stil. **(b)** *(reminiscing) style, chapter* nostalgisch ◆ **to be feeling ~, to be in a ~ mood** in nostalgischer Stimmung sein.

reminiscently [ˌremɪ'nɪsəntlɪ] *adv smile, sigh etc* in der Erinnerung ◆ **to think ~ of sth** nostalgisch an etw *(acc)* zurückdenken; **he talked ~ of the war** er erzählte von seinen Kriegserinnerungen.

remiss [rɪ'mɪs] *adj* nachlässig ◆ **he has been ~ in not doing it** es war nachlässig von ihm, das zu unterlassen.

remission [rɪ'mɪʃən] *n (form) see* **remit[1] (a)** Erlassen *nt*; *(Jur)* (Straf)erlaß *m*; *(Rel)* Nachlaß *m* ◆ **he got 3 years' ~ for good behaviour** ihm wurden wegen guter Führung 3 Jahre erlassen.
(b) Überweisung *f.*
(c) Verschiebung, Vertagung *f.*
(d) Verweisung *f.*
(e) Nachlassen *nt*; *(Med)* Besserung, Remission *(spec) f.*

remissness [rɪ'mɪsnɪs] *n* Nachlässigkeit *f.*

remit[1] [rɪ'mɪt] *(form)* [1] *vt* **(a)** *(cancel, pardon) debt, sentence, sins* erlassen. **(b)** *(send) money* überweisen. **(c)** *(postpone)* verschieben, vertagen *(to* auf *+acc, till* bis). **(d)** *(Jur: transfer) case* verweisen *(to* an *+acc).*
[2] *vi (become less)* nachlassen.

remit[2] ['riːmɪt] *n (form)* Aufgabe *f*, Auftrag *m* ◆ **that is outside our ~** das liegt außerhalb unseres Aufgabenbereiches.

remittal [rɪ'mɪtl] *n see* **remission (b-d).**

remittance [rɪ'mɪtəns] *n* Überweisung *f (to* an *+acc)* ◆ **~ advice** Überweisungsbescheid *m.*

remittee [rɪmɪ'tiː] *n (Comm)* Empfänger *m* einer/der Überweisung.

remittent [rɪ'mɪtənt] *adj (Med) symptoms, fever* remittierend *(spec)* ◆ **~ fever** Wechselfieber *nt.*

remitter [rɪ'mɪtə^r] *n (sender)* Überweiser *m.*

remix ['riːmɪks] *n (record)* Remix *m.*

remnant ['remnənt] *n* Rest *m*; *(fig: of splendour, custom)* Überrest *m* ◆ **the ~ of his fortune/~s of his former glory** was von seinem Vermögen/Ruhm übriggeblieben war; **~ day** *(Comm)* Resteverkaufstag *m*; **~ sale** Resteausverkauf *m.*

remodel [ˌriː'mɒdl] *vt (also Art, Tech)* umformen; *nose* richten; *(fig) society, constitution also* umgestalten.

remonstrance [rɪ'mɒnstrəns] *n* Protest *m (with* bei).

remonstrant [rɪ'mɒnstrənt] *adj* protestierend.

remonstrate ['remənstreɪt] *vi* protestieren *(against* gegen) ◆ **to ~ with sb (about sth)** jdm Vorhaltungen (wegen etw) machen.

remorse [rɪ'mɔːs] *n* Reue *f (at, over* über *+acc)* ◆ **he is completely without ~** er zeigt überhaupt keine Reue; **without ~** *(merciless)* erbarmungslos.

remorseful [rɪ'mɔːsfʊl] *adj* reumütig, reuig ◆ **to feel ~** Reue spüren.

remorsefully [rɪ'mɔːsfəlɪ] *adv see adj.*

remorsefulness [rɪ'mɔːsfʊlnɪs] *n* Reue *f*; *(of person also)* Reumütigkeit *f.*

remorseless [rɪ'mɔːslɪs] *adj* reulos, ohne Reue; *(fig: merciless)* unbarmherzig.

remorselessly [rɪ'mɔːslɪslɪ] *adv see adj.*

remorselessness [rɪ'mɔːslɪsnɪs] *n see adj* Reuelosigkeit *f*; Unbarmherzigkeit *f.*

remote [rɪ'məʊt] *adj (+er)* **(a)** *(in place) (distant)* entfernt, fern *(geh) attr*; *(isolated)* entlegen, abgelegen; *(Comput)* rechnerfern ◆ **in the ~st parts of Africa** in den abgelegensten Teilen Afrikas; **in a ~ spot** an einer entlegenen *or* abgelegenen Stelle.
(b) *(in time) past, future* fern ◆ **~ antiquity** die früheste Antike; **a ~ ancestor** ein Urahn *m*/eine Urahne.
(c) *relative, (fig) connection, relevance etc* entfernt.
(d) *(aloof)* unnahbar, unzugänglich.
(e) *(slight) possibility, resemblance* entfernt; *chance* gering, winzig ◆ **I haven't the ~st idea** ich habe nicht die leiseste Idee.

remote: ~ control *n* Fernsteuerung, Fernlenkung *f*; *(Rad, TV)* Fernbedienung *f*; **~ control model** Modell *nt* mit Fernbedienung; **~-controlled** *adj model aeroplane etc* ferngesteuert, ferngelenkt; **~ data entry** *n (Comput)* Datenverarbeitung *f* mit Datenfernübertragung.

remotely [rɪ'məʊtlɪ] *adv situated, related* entfernt ◆ **it's just ~ possible** es ist gerade eben noch möglich; **if it's ~ possible** wenn es auch nur irgend möglich ist; **they're not even ~ similar** sie sind sich nicht im entferntesten ähnlich.

remoteness [rɪ'məʊtnɪs] *n see adj* **(a)** Ferne *f*, Abgelegenheit *f.* **(b)** (weite) Ferne. **(c)** Entferntheit *f* ◆ **his ~ from everyday life** seine Lebensfremdheit. **(d)** Unnahbarkeit, Unzugänglichkeit *f.* **(e)** Entferntheit *f*; Winzigkeit *f.*

remould [ˌriː'məʊld] [1] *vt (Tech) tyre* runderneuern.
[2] ['riːməʊld] *n (tyre)* runderneuerter Reifen.

remount [ˌriː'maʊnt] [1] *vt* **(a)** *horse, bicycle* wieder besteigen; *ladder* wieder hinaufsteigen *or* -klettern. **(b)** *picture, photo* wieder aufziehen.
[2] *vi* wieder aufsitzen.

removable [rɪ'muːvəbl] *adj cover, attachment* abnehmbar; *trimming* abtrennbar; *lining* abknöpfbar; *stain* zu entfernen *pred or* entfernend *attr*; *(from container)* herausnehmbar ◆ **the motor is easily ~** der Motor ist leicht auszubauen.

removal [rɪ'muːvəl] *n see vt* **(a)** Entfernung *f*; Abnahme *f*; Beseitigung *f*; Abtrennung *f*; Abknöpfen *nt* ◆ **his ~ to hospital** seine Einlieferung ins Krankenhaus.
(b) Herausnehmen *nt*; Entfernung *f*; Streichen *nt*; Ausbau *m.*
(c) Beseitigung *f*; Aufhebung *f*; Ausräumung *f*; Zerstreuung *f.*
(d) Entfernung *f.*
(e) *(move from house)* Umzug *m* ◆ **our ~ to this house/to York** unser Umzug in dieses Haus/nach York; **"Brown & Son, ~s"** „Spedition Brown & Sohn", „Brown & Sohn, Umzüge".

removal: ~ allowance *n* Umzugsbeihilfe *f*; **~ expenses** *npl* Umzugskosten *pl*; **~ firm** *n* Spedition *f*; **~ man** *n* Möbelpacker *m*; **~ van** *n* Möbelwagen *m.*

remove [rɪ'muːv] [1] *vt* **(a)** *(take off, take away etc)* entfernen; *cover, lid, attachments also, splint, bandage, tie* abnehmen; *stain also* beseitigen; *buttons, trimmings also* abtrennen; *lining* abknöpfen ◆ **to ~ sth from sb** jdm etw wegnehmen; **to ~ one's clothes** die Kleider ablegen; **to ~ sb to hospital/the cells** jdn ins Krankenhaus einliefern/jdn in die Zelle bringen; **to ~ a child from school** ein Kind von *or* aus der Schule nehmen; **he ~d himself to another room** er begab sich in ein anderes Zimmer.
(b) *(take out) (from container)* herausnehmen *(from* aus); *(Med) lung, kidney also* entfernen *(from* aus); *paragraph, word, item on list* streichen; *(Tech)* ausbauen *(from* aus).
(c) *(eradicate) threat* beseitigen *(usu pass)*, Schluß machen mit; *tax* aufheben; *objection, obstacle* aus dem Weg schaffen *or* räumen; *difficulty, problem* beseitigen, ein Ende machen *or* setzen *(+dat)*; *doubt, suspicion, fear* zerstreuen; *abuse, evil* abstellen, beseitigen; *(euph: kill)* beseitigen ◆ **to ~ all obstacles from one's path** *(fig)* alle Hindernisse aus dem Weg räumen.
(d) *(form: dismiss) official* entfernen.
(e) *(form: to another house)* transportieren.
(f) to be far ~d from ... weit entfernt sein von ...; **a cousin once/twice ~d** ein Cousin ersten/zweiten Grades; **but he's several times ~d** *(inf)* ich bin mit ihm verwandt, aber um ein paar Ecken herum *(inf).*
[2] *vi (form: move house)* **to ~ to London/to larger premises** nach London/in größere Geschäftsräume (um)ziehen.
[3] *n* **(a) to be only a few ~s from ...** nicht weit entfernt sein von ...; **this is but one ~ from disaster** das kommt einer Katastrophe nahe; **it's a far ~ from ...** es ist weit entfernt von ...
(b) *(Brit Sch)* Klasse *f* für lernschwache Schüler.

remover [rɪ'muːvə^r] *n* **(a)** *(for nail varnish, stains etc)* Entferner *m.* **(b)** *(removal man)* Möbelpacker *m.*

remunerate [rɪ'mjuːnəreɪt] *vt (pay)* bezahlen, vergüten; *(reward)* belohnen.

remuneration [rɪˌmjuːnə'reɪʃən] *n* Bezahlung, Vergütung *f*; *(reward)* Belohnung *f.*

remunerative [rɪ'mjuːnərətɪv] *adj* lohnend, einträglich.

renaissance [rɪ'neɪsɑ̃ːns] *n (liter)* Wiedergeburt *f*; *(of nature)* Wiedererwachen *nt* ◆ **the R~** *(Hist)* die Renaissance.

Renaissance man, *pl* **Renaissance men** *n (fig: all-rounder)* Allround-Talent *nt.*

renal ['riːnl] *adj* Nieren-, renal *(spec).*

rename [ˌriː'neɪm] *vt* umbenennen *(also Comput)*, umtaufen ◆ **Petrograd was ~d Leningrad** Petrograd wurde in Leningrad umbenannt.

renascence [rɪ'næsns] *n see* **renaissance.**

renascent [rɪ'næsnt] *adj (liter)* wiedererwachend.

rend [rend] *pret, ptp* **rent** *vt (liter) cloth* zerreißen; *armour* aufreißen ◆ **to ~ sth from sb/sth** jdm/einer Sache etw entreißen; **a country rent by civil war** ein vom Bürgerkrieg zerrissenes Land; **a cry rent the silence** ein Schrei zerriß die Stille; **to ~ sb's heart** jdm das Herz zerreißen.

render ['rendə^r] *vt* **(a)** *(form: give) service, help* leisten; *judgement, explanation* abgeben; *homage* erweisen ◆ **~ unto Caesar the things which are Caesar's** *(Bibl, prov)* gebet dem Kaiser, was des Kaisers ist *(Bibl)*; **to ~ thanks to sb/God** jdm/Gott Dank sagen *or* abstatten; **to ~ assistance** Hilfe leisten; **to ~ an account of one's expenditure** Rechenschaft über seine Ausgaben ablegen.
(b) *(Comm)* **to ~ account** Rechnung legen *or* vorlegen; **(to) account ~ed £10** £ 10 laut früherer Rechnung.
(c) *(interpret, translate)* wiedergeben; *(in writing)* übertragen; *music, poem also* vortragen.
(d) *(form: make)* machen ◆ **his accident ~ed him helpless** der Unfall hat ihn hilflos gemacht.
(e) *(also* **~ down)** *fat* auslassen.
(f) *(Build)* verputzen.

◆**render up** *vt sep fortress, prisoner* übergeben.

rendering ['rendərɪŋ] *n* **(a)** Wiedergabe *f*; *(in writing)* Übertragung *f*; *(of piece of music, poem also)* Vortrag *m.* **(b)** *(Build)* Putz *m.*

rendez-vous ['rɒndɪvuː] [1] *n (place)* Treffpunkt *m*; *(agreement to meet)* Rendezvous *nt.*
[2] *vi* sich treffen *(with* mit).

rendition [ren'dɪʃən] *n (form) see* **rendering (a).**

renegade ['renɪgeɪd] [1] *n* Renegat(in *f*) *m*, Abtrünnige(r) *mf.*
[2] *adj* abtrünnig.

renege [rɪ'niːg] *vi* nicht Wort halten; *(Cards)* nicht bedienen ◆ **to ~ on a promise/an agreement** ein Versprechen/eine Übereinkunft brechen.

renew [rɪ'njuː] *vt* erneuern; *contract, passport etc (authority also)* verlängern; *(holder)* erneuern *or* verlängern lassen; *negotiations, discussions, attack, attempts* wiederaufnehmen; *one's strength* wiederherstellen; *supplies* auffrischen ◆ **to ~ a library book** ein Buch verlängern lassen; **with ~ed enthusiasm** mit neuem Schwung; **~ed efforts/strength/courage** neue Anstrengungen/frische Kraft/frischer Mut; **~ed outbreaks of rioting** erneute Krawalle *pl*; **to feel spiritually ~ed** sich wie ein neuer Mensch fühlen.

➤ LANGUAGE IN USE: **reminiscent: a → 5.1**

renewable [rɪ'nju:əbl] *adj* erneuerbar; *contract also, passport, bill of exchange* verlängerbar; *(must be renewed)* zu erneuern; zu verlängern ◆ **some library books are not ~** einige Bibliotheksbücher können nicht verlängert werden.

renewal [rɪ'nju:əl] *n see vt* Erneuerung *f*; Verlängerung *f*; Wiederaufnahme *f*; Wiederherstellung *f*; Auffrischung *f* ◆ **spiritual ~** geistige Erneuerung.

rennet ['renɪt] *n (Cook)* Lab *nt*.

renounce [rɪ'naʊns] 1 *vt title, right* verzichten auf (+*acc*), aufgeben; *religion, devil* abschwören (+*dat*); *(Rel) world* entsagen (+*dat*); *opinions, cause, treaty* leugnen, abschwören (+*dat*); *friend* verleugnen.
2 *vi (Cards)* renoncieren.

renouncement [rɪ'naʊnsmənt] *n see* **renunciation**.

renovate ['renəʊveɪt] *vt building* renovieren; *painting, furniture* restaurieren.

renovation [,renəʊ'veɪʃən] *n see vt* Renovierung, Renovation *f*; Restaurierung *f*.

renown [rɪ'naʊn] *n* guter Ruf, Ansehen *nt* ◆ **of high ~** von hohem Ansehen, sehr berühmt.

renowned [rɪ'naʊnd] *adj* berühmt *(for* für).

rent[1] [rent] 1 *n (for house, room)* Miete *f*; *(for farm, factory)* Pacht *f* ◆ **for ~** *(US)* zu vermieten/verpachten/verleihen.
2 *vt* **(a)** *(also vi) house, room* mieten; *farm, factory* pachten; *TV, car etc* leihen ◆ **we don't own it, we only ~ it** es gehört uns *(dat)* nicht, wir haben es nur gemietet *etc*.
(b) *(also* **~ out)** vermieten; verpachten; verleihen.

rent[2] 1 *pret, ptp of* **rend**.
2 *n (lit, fig)* Riß *m*; *(in rock)* Spalte *f*.

rental ['rentl] *n (amount paid) (for house)* Miete *f*; *(for TV, car, boat etc also)* Leihgebühr *f*; *(for land)* Pacht *f*; *(income from rents)* Miet-/Pacht-/Leihgebühreinnahmen *pl* ◆ **~ car** Mietwagen *m*; **~ library** *(US)* Leihbücherei *f*.

rent: ~boy *n (inf)* Strichjunge *(inf)*, Stricher *(inf) m*; **~ collector** *n* Mietkassierer(in *f*) *m*; **~ control** *n* Mietkontrolle *f*, Mieterschutz *m*; **~-controlled** *adj* bewirtschaftet *(form)*, mit gebundener Miete; **~-free** *adj* mietfrei; **~-man** *n (inf) see* **~ collector**; **~ rebate** *n* Mietrückzahlung *f*; *(reduction)* Mietnachlaß *m or* -ermäßigung *f*; **~ review** *n* Neufestsetzung *f* der Miete; **~ tribunal** *n* Mieterschiedsgericht *nt*.

renumber [,ri:'nʌmbə^r] *vt* umnumerieren.

renunciation [rɪ,nʌnsɪ'eɪʃən] *n see* **renounce** Verzicht *m (of* auf +*acc)*, Aufgabe *f*; Abschwören *nt*; Entsagung *f*; Leugnung *f*; Verleugnung *f*.

reoccupy [,ri:'ɒkjʊpaɪ] *vt post, position* wieder innehaben *or* bekleiden; *house, hotel room etc* wieder belegen.

reopen [,ri:'əʊpən] 1 *vt* wieder öffnen, wieder aufmachen; *school, shop, theatre, fight, hostilities* wiedereröffnen; *debate, discussion, negotiations* wiederaufnehmen; *(Jur) case* wieder aufrollen, wiederaufnehmen.
2 *vi* wieder aufgehen; *(shop, theatre etc)* wieder eröffnen *or* aufmachen; *(school after holidays)* wieder beginnen; *(negotiations)* wiederbeginnen; *(case)* wieder aufgerollt werden; *(wound)* wieder aufgehen.

reopening [,ri:'əʊpnɪŋ] *n (of shop etc)* Wiedereröffnung *f*; *(of school after holiday)* Wiederbeginn *m*; *(of negotiations, debate, case)* Wiederaufnahme *f*.

reorder [,ri:'ɔ:də^r] *vt* **(a)** *(also vi) goods, supplies* nachbestellen; *(because first order is lost etc)* neu bestellen. **(b)** *(reorganize)* neu ordnen, umordnen; *books, names on a list also* umstellen; *people in a row* umstellen; *appointments* umlegen.

reorganization [ri:,ɔ:gənaɪ'zeɪʃən] *n see vt* Neu- *or* Umorganisation *f*; Neu- *or* Umordnung *f*; Neueinteilung *f*; Neuaufbau *m*.

reorganize [,ri:'ɔ:gənaɪz] 1 *vt* neu organisieren, umorganisieren; *furniture, books* umordnen; *work, time* neu einteilen; *essay* neu aufbauen.
2 *vi (Pol)* sich neu organisieren.

rep[1] [rep] 1 *n abbr of* **(a)** *(Theat)* **repertory** Repertoire-Theater *nt*. **(b)** *(Comm)* **representative** Vertreter(in *f*) *m*.
2 *vi* als Vertreter arbeiten.

rep[2] *n (Tex)* Rips *m*.

Rep *abbr of* **(a) Republic** Rep. **(b) Republican** Rep., rep.

repaid [,ri:'peɪd] *pret, ptp of* **repay**.

repaint [,ri:'peɪnt] *vt* neu streichen.

repair[1] [rɪ'peə^r] 1 *vt (lit, fig)* reparieren; *tyre also, clothes* flicken; *roof, wall also, road* ausbessern; *(fig) error, wrong, damage* wiedergutmachen.
2 *n* **(a)** *see vt* Reparatur *f*; Flicken *nt*; Ausbesserung *f*; Wiedergutmachung *f* ◆ **to be under ~** *(car, ship, machine)* in Reparatur sein; **to put sth in for ~** etw zur Reparatur bringen; **the road is under ~** an der Straße wird gerade gearbeitet; **beyond ~** nicht mehr zu reparieren/zu flicken/auszubessern/wiedergutzumachen; **damaged beyond ~** irreparabel, nicht mehr zu reparieren; **closed for ~s** wegen Reparaturarbeiten geschlossen; **"road ~s"** „Straßenbauarbeiten"; **"~s while you wait"** „Sofortdienst", „Soforteparaturen".
(b) *no pl (condition)* **to be in good/bad ~** in gutem Zustand *or* in Schuß *(inf)* sein/in schlechtem Zustand sein.

repair[2] *vi (liter: go)* sich begeben *(to* nach).

repairable [rɪ'peərəbl] *adj see vt* zu reparieren, reparabel; zu flicken, auszubessern *pred* ◆ **is that ~?** läßt sich das reparieren?

repairer [rɪ'peərə^r] *n* **(watch/boot) ~** Uhr-/Schuhmacher *m*.

repair: ~ kit *n* Flickzeug *nt*; **~-man** *n (in house)* Handwerker *m*; **she took her shoes to the ~-man** sie brachte ihre Schuhe zum Schuster; **~ shop** *n* Reparaturwerkstatt *m*.

repaper [,ri:'peɪpə^r] *vt* neu tapezieren.

reparable ['repərəbl] *adj damage* reparabel, wiedergutzumachen; *loss* ersetzbar.

reparation [,repə'reɪʃən] *n (for damage)* Entschädigung *f*; *(usu pl: after war)* Reparationen *pl*; *(for wrong, misdeed)* Wiedergutmachung *f* ◆ **to make ~ for sth** etw wiedergutmachen.

repartee [,repɑ:'ti:] *n* Schlagabtausch *m*; *(retort)* schlagfertige Antwort ◆ **to be good at ~** schlagfertig sein; **renowned for his ~** bekannt für seine Schlagfertigkeit.

repast [rɪ'pɑ:st] *n (liter)* Mahl *nt (geh)*.

repatriate [,ri:'pætrɪeɪt] 1 *vt* in das Heimatland zurücksenden, repatriieren.
2 *n* [,ri:'pætrɪɪt] Repatriierte(r) *mf*.

repatriation ['ri:,pætrɪ'eɪʃən] *n* Repatriierung *f*.

repay [,ri:'peɪ] *pret, ptp* **repaid** *vt money* zurückzahlen; *expenses* erstatten; *debt* abzahlen; *kindness* vergelten; *visit* erwidern ◆ **if you lend me £2 I'll ~ it** *or* **you on Saturday** leih mir doch mal 2 Pfund, ich zahle sie dir am Samstag zurück; **I shall ~ my obligation to you one day** ich werde es dir eines Tages vergelten *or* lohnen; **to ~ sb for his generosity** sich für jds Großzügigkeit revanchieren; **to be repaid for one's efforts** für seine Mühen belohnt werden; **how can I ever ~ you?** wie kann ich das jemals wiedergutmachen?

repayable [,ri:'peɪəbl] *adj* rückzahlbar.

repayment [,ri:'peɪmənt] *n (of money)* Rückzahlung *f*; *(of effort, kindness)* Lohn *m* ◆ **~s can be spread over 3 years** die Rückzahlung kann über 3 Jahre verteilt werden; **in ~** als Rückzahlung/Lohn; **~ mortgage** Tilgungshypothek *f*.

repeal [rɪ'pi:l] 1 *vt law* aufheben.
2 *n* Aufhebung *f*.

repeat [rɪ'pi:t] 1 *vt* wiederholen; *(tell to sb else)* weitersagen *(to sb* jdm) ◆ **to ~ oneself** sich wiederholen; **he wasn't keen to ~ the experience** er war nicht darauf aus, die Erfahrung noch einmal zu machen; **he ~ed his lesson to the teacher** er sagte seine Lektion vor dem Lehrer auf; **to ~ an order** *(Comm)* nachbestellen; **this offer will never be ~ed!** dies ist ein einmaliges Angebot!
2 *vi* **(a)** *(say again)* wiederholen ◆ **I ~, it is impossible** ich wiederhole, es ist unmöglich; **~ after me** sprecht mir nach.
(b) *(Mus)* wiederholen ◆ **~!** *(conductor)* noch einmal!
(c) radishes ~ on me Radieschen stoßen mir auf.
(d) *(gun, clock etc)* repetieren.
(e) *(Math)* periodisch sein.
3 *n* **(a)** *(Rad, TV)* Wiederholung *f*.
(b) *(Mus) (section repeated)* Wiederholung *f*; *(~ sign)* Wiederholungszeichen *nt*.

repeated *adj*, **~ly** *adv* [rɪ'pi:tɪd, -lɪ] wiederholt.

repeater [rɪ'pi:tə^r] *n (gun)* Repetier- *or* Mehrladegewehr *nt*; *(watch)* Repetieruhr *f*.

repeat function *n (Comput)* Wiederholungsfunktion *f*.

repeating [rɪ'pi:tɪŋ] *adj (Math) see* **recurring (b)**.

repeat: ~ mark *n (Mus)* Wiederholungszeichen *nt*; **~ order** *n (Comm)* Nachbestellung *f*; **~ performance** *n (Theat)* Wiederholungsvorstellung *f*; **he gave a ~ performance** *(fig)* er machte es noch einmal; *(pej)* er machte noch einmal das gleiche Theater *(inf)*; **~ sign** *n (Mus)* Wiederholungszeichen *nt*.

repel [rɪ'pel] *vt* **(a)** *enemy, attack* zurückschlagen; *sb's advance, insects, flies* abwehren; *water* abstoßen. **(b)** *(also vi) (disgust)* abstoßen.

repellent [rɪ'pelənt] 1 *adj* **(a) ~ to water** wasserabstoßend. **(b)** *(disgusting)* abstoßend.
2 *n (insect ~)* Insektenschutzmittel *nt*.

repelling [rɪ'pelɪŋ] *adj see* **repellent 1 (b)**.

repent [rɪ'pent] 1 *vi* Reue empfinden *(of* über +*acc)*.
2 *vt* bereuen.

repentance [rɪ'pentəns] *n* Reue *f*.

repentant [rɪ'pentənt] *adj look, expression* reuig, reuevoll ◆ **he was very ~** es reute ihn sehr; **to feel ~** Reue empfinden; **a ~ sinner** ein reuiger Sünder.

repercussion [,ri:pə'kʌʃən] *n* **(a)** *(consequence)* Auswirkung *f (on* auf +*acc)* ◆ **~s** *pl (of misbehaviour etc)* Nachspiel *nt*; **that is bound to have ~s** das wird Kreise ziehen; **to have ~s on sth** sich auf etw *(acc)* auswirken. **(b)** *(of shock)* Erschütterung *f*; *(of sounds)* Widerhall *m*.

repertoire ['repətwɑ:^r] *n (Theat, Mus)* Repertoire *nt*.

repertory ['repətərɪ] *n* **(a)** *(also* **~ theatre)** Repertoire-Theater *nt* ◆ **~ company** Repertoire-Ensemble *nt*; **to act in ~, to play ~** Repertoire-Stücke spielen; **he was in ~** er spielte an einem Repertoire-Theater. **(b)** *(songs, plays) see* **repertoire**.

repetition [,repɪ'tɪʃən] *n* Wiederholung *f* ◆ **there are six ~s of the pattern** das Muster wiederholt sich sechsmal.

repetitious [,repɪ'tɪʃəs] *adj* sich wiederholend.

repetitive [rɪ'petɪtɪv] *adj* sich dauernd wiederholend; *work also* monoton ◆ **to be ~** sich dauernd wiederholen; **standing in a production line is such ~ work** die Arbeit am Fließband ist äußerst eintönig.

repine [rɪ'paɪn] *vi (liter)* hadern *(geh) (at, against* mit).

replace [rɪ'pleɪs] *vt* **(a)** *(put back)* zurücksetzen; *(on end, standing up)* zurückstellen; *(on its side, flat)* zurücklegen ◆ **to ~ the receiver** *(Telec)* (den Hörer) auflegen.
(b) *(provide or be substitute for) person, thing, ingredient, goods, (Comput)* ersetzen; *employee (permanently also)* die Stelle einnehmen (+*gen*); *(temporarily)* vertreten ◆ **the boss has ~d Smith with Jones** der Chef hat Smith durch Jones ersetzt.
(c) *(renew) components, parts* austauschen, ersetzen.

➤ LANGUAGE IN USE: **repeat: 1 → 27.3**

replaceable [rɪ'pleɪsəbl] *adj person* ersetzbar, zu ersetzen; (*renewable*) *components, parts also* austauschbar.

replacement [rɪ'pleɪsmənt] *n* **(a)** *see vt (a)* Zurücksetzen *nt*; Zurückstellen *nt*; Zurücklegen *nt*; (*of receiver*) Auflegen *nt*.
(b) (*substituting*) Ersatz *m*; (*by deputy*) Vertretung *f* ◆ **~ cost** (*of equipment*) Wiederbeschaffungskosten *pl*; (*of personnel*) Wiederbesetzungskosten *pl*.
(c) (*person or thing*) Ersatz *m*; (*deputy*) Vertretung *f* ◆ **~ engine** Austauschmotor *m*; **~ part** Ersatzteil *nt*.

replant [ˌriː'plɑːnt] *vt cabbages, trees etc* umpflanzen; *garden, field* neu bepflanzen.

replay ['riːpleɪ] (*Sport*) [1] *n* (*recording*) Wiederholung *f*; (*match also*) Wiederholungsspiel *nt*; *see* **action ~**.
[2] [ˌriː'pleɪ] *vt match, game* wiederholen, nochmals austragen.

replenish [rɪ'plenɪʃ] *vt* ergänzen; (*when badly depleted*) wieder auffüllen; *glass* auffüllen.

replenishment [rɪ'plenɪʃmənt] *n see vt* Ergänzung *f*; Wiederauffüllen *nt*; Auffüllen *nt*.

replete [rɪ'pliːt] *adj* (*form*) reichlich versehen *or* ausgestattet (*with* mit); (*well-fed*) *person* gesättigt.

repletion [rɪ'pliːʃən] *n* (*form*) Sättigung *f* ◆ **to eat to ~** essen, bis man gesättigt ist.

replica ['replɪkə] *n* (*of painting, statue*) Reproduktion, Kopie *f*; (*of document*) Kopie *f*; (*of ship, building etc*) Nachbildung *f* ◆ **she is a ~ of her sister** sie ist das Ebenbild ihrer Schwester.

▼ **reply** [rɪ'plaɪ] [1] *n* (*letter*) Antwort *f*; (*spoken also*) Erwiderung *f* ◆ **in ~** (als Antwort) darauf; **in ~ to your letter/remarks** in Beantwortung Ihres Briefes (*form*), auf Ihren Brief/Ihre Bemerkungen; **~ coupon** Antwortschein *m*; **to send a letter ~ paid** einen Brief gebührenfrei senden; **~-paid envelope** freigemachter Briefumschlag, Freiumschlag *m*.
[2] *vt* **to ~ (to sb) that ...** (jdm) antworten, daß ...
[3] *vi* (*to sth* auf etw *+acc*) antworten; (*spoken also*) erwidern.

repoint [ˌriː'pɔɪnt] *vt* (*Build*) neu verfugen.

repointing [ˌriː'pɔɪntɪŋ] *n* (*Build*) Neuverfugung *f*.

repopulate [ˌriː'pɒpjʊleɪt] *vt area* neu besiedeln.

report [rɪ'pɔːt] [1] *n* **(a)** (*account, statement*) Bericht *m* (*on* über *+acc*); (*Press, Rad, TV also*) Reportage *f* (*on* über *+acc*) ◆ **to give a ~ on sth** Bericht über etw (*acc*) erstatten/eine Reportage über etw (*acc*) machen; **an official ~ on the motor industry** ein Gutachten *nt* über die Autoindustrie; **(school) ~** Zeugnis *nt*; **chairman's ~** Bericht *m* des Vorsitzenden; **~ card** (*Sch*) Zeugnis(blatt) *nt*; **the bill has reached the ~ stage** (*Brit Parl*) der Gesetzentwurf kommt nach seiner Beratung im Ausschuß zur Berichterstattung wieder vors Parlament; **~ generator** (*Comput*) Berichtgenerator *m*.
(b) (*rumour*) **to know sth only by ~** etw nur vom Hörensagen kennen; **there is a ~ that ...** es wird gesagt, daß ...
(c) (*reputation*) Ruf *m* ◆ **of good ~** von gutem Ruf.
(d) (*of gun*) Knall *m* ◆ **with a loud ~** mit lautem Knall.
[2] *vt* **(a)** *results, findings* berichten über (*+acc*); (*announce officially also*) melden; (*tell to particular person also*) melden (*to sb* jdm) ◆ **to ~ that ...** berichten, daß ...; **to ~ progress** einen Tätigkeitsbericht abgeben; **the papers ~ed the crime as solved** laut Presseberichten ist das Verbrechen aufgeklärt; **he is ~ed as having said ...** er soll gesagt haben ...; **it is ~ed that a prisoner has escaped, a prisoner is ~ed to have escaped** ein Gefangener wird als geflüchtet gemeldet *or* gilt als vermißt; **it is ~ed from the White House that ...** es wird vom Weißen Haus berichtet *or* gemeldet, daß ...
(b) (*to sb* jdm) (*notify authorities of*) *accident, crime, suspect, criminal, culprit* melden; (*to police also*) anzeigen; *one's position* angeben ◆ **to ~ sb for sth** jdn wegen etw melden; **to ~ sb sick** jdn krank melden; **~ed missing** als vermißt gemeldet; **nothing to ~** keine besonderen Vorkommnisse!
[3] *vi* **(a)** (*announce oneself*) sich melden ◆ **~ to the director on Monday** melden Sie sich am Montag beim Direktor; **to ~ for duty** sich zum Dienst melden; **to ~ sick** sich krank melden.
(b) (*give a ~*) berichten, Bericht erstatten (*on* über *+acc*); (*work as journalist*) Reporter(in *f*) *m* sein ◆ **the committee is ready to ~** der Ausschuß hat seinen Bericht fertig; **this is Michael Brown ~ing (from Rome)** (*Rad, TV*) Michael Brown (mit einem Bericht aus Rom).

◆**report back** *vi* **(a)** (*announce one's return*) sich zurückmelden. **(b)** (*give report*) Bericht erstatten (*to sb* jdm).

◆**report to** *vi + prep obj* (*in organization*) unterstellt sein (*+dat*), unterstehen (*+dat*) ◆ **who do you ~ ~?** wer ist Ihr Vorgesetzter?

reportage [ˌrepɔː'tɑːʒ] *n* Reportage *f*; (*style*) Reporterstil *m*.

reported [rɪ'pɔːtɪd] *adj* **(a)** gemeldet. **(b)** (*Gram*) **~ speech** indirekte Rede.

reportedly [rɪ'pɔːtɪdlɪ] *adv* wie verlautet.

reporter [rɪ'pɔːtə^r] *n* **(a)** (*Press, Rad, TV*) Reporter(in *f*), Berichterstatter(in *f*) *m*; (*on the spot*) Korrespondent(in *f*) *m* ◆ **special ~** Sonderberichterstatter *m*; **~s' gallery** (*Jur, Parl*) Pressetribüne *f*. **(b)** (*Jur, Parl: stenographer*) Stenograph(in *f*), Gerichtsschreiber(in *f*) (*old*) *m*.

reporting structure *n* Organisationsstruktur *f*.

repose [rɪ'pəʊz] [1] *n* (*liter*) (*rest, peace*) Ruhe *f*; (*composure*) Gelassenheit *f* ◆ **in ~** in Ruhe.
[2] *vt* (*form, liter*) **(a)** *trust* setzen (*in* in *or* auf *+acc*). **(b) to ~ oneself** (*rest*) sich ausruhen.
[3] *vi* (*form, liter*) **(a)** (*rest, be buried*) ruhen. **(b)** (*be based*) beruhen (*upon* auf *+dat*).

repository [rɪ'pɒzɪtərɪ] *n* (*warehouse*) Lager, Magazin *nt*; (*fig*) (*of facts etc*) Quelle *f* (*of* für); (*book, library*) Fundgrube *f* (*of* für); (*liter: of secret*) Hüter(in *f*) *m*.

repossess [ˌriːpə'zes] *vt* wieder in Besitz nehmen.

repossession [ˌriːpə'zeʃən] *n* Wiederinbesitznahme *f*.

repp *n see* **rep**[2].

reprehend [ˌreprɪ'hend] *vt* tadeln, rügen.

reprehensible [ˌreprɪ'hensɪbl] *adj* verwerflich, tadelnswert.

reprehensibly [ˌreprɪ'hensɪblɪ] *adv* verwerflich.

reprehension [ˌreprɪ'henʃən] *n* **(a)** *no pl* (*act*) Tadeln, Rügen *nt*. **(b)** (*rebuke*) Tadel *m*, Rüge *f*.

represent [ˌreprɪ'zent] *vt* **(a)** darstellen; (*stand for also*) stehen für; (*symbolize also*) symbolisieren ◆ **he ~s all that is best in ...** er verkörpert das Beste (*+gen*) ...
(b) (*act or speak for, Parl, Jur*) vertreten ◆ **he ~s their firm in London** er vertritt *or* repräsentiert die Firma in London; **many countries were ~ed at the ceremony** viele Länder waren bei der Feier vertreten; **the foreign tourist should never forget that he ~s his country** ein Tourist sollte im Ausland nie vergessen, daß er sein Land repräsentiert.
(c) (*declare to be*) (*as* als) *person, event, risk etc* darstellen; (*falsely*) hinstellen ◆ **he ~ed me as a fool/a saint** er stellte mich als Narren/Engel hin; **it is exactly as ~ed in the advertisement** es ist genau, wie in der Anzeige dargestellt.
(d) (*set forth, explain*) vor Augen führen (*to sb* jdm).
(e) (*Theat*) *character, part* darstellen.

re-present [ˌriːprɪ'zent] *vt* nochmals vorlegen.

representation [ˌreprɪzen'teɪʃən] *n* **(a)** *no pl* (*representing*) *see vt (a-c)* Darstellung *f*; Symbolisierung *f*; Vertretung *f*; Hinstellung *f*.
(b) (*drawing, description, Theat*) Darstellung *f*.
(c) ~s *pl* (*esp Pol: remonstrations*) Vorstellungen, Vorhaltungen *pl* ◆ **the ambassador made ~s to the government** der Botschafter wurde bei der Regierung vorstellig.

representational [ˌreprɪzen'teɪʃənəl] *adj art, picture* gegenständlich ◆ **in ~ form** symbolisch; **these matchsticks are a purely ~ device to show ...** diese Streichhölzer sind nur ein Mittel, um ... darzustellen; **a ~ party of** eine Vertretung (*+gen*).

representative [ˌreprɪ'zentətɪv] [1] *adj* **(a)** (*of* für) (*typical*) *cross-section, sample* repräsentativ; *attitude also* typisch; (*symbolic*) symbolisch.
(b) (*acting for*) repräsentativ; *delegation* Repräsentativ- ◆ **a ~ body** eine Vertretung.
(c) (*Parl*) *government* repräsentativ ◆ **~ assembly** Abgeordnetenversammlung *f*.
[2] *n* (*Comm*) Vertreter(in *f*) *m*; (*Jur*) Bevollmächtigte(r), Beauftragte(r) *mf*; (*US Pol*) Abgeordnete(r) *mf* ◆ **authorized ~** Bevollmächtigte(r) *mf*; *see* **house**.

repress [rɪ'pres] *vt revolt, rebellion, population* unterdrücken; *emotions, desires also* zurückdrängen; *laugh, sneeze also* zurückhalten; (*Psych*) verdrängen.

repressed [rɪ'prest] *adj* unterdrückt; (*Psych*) verdrängt.

repression [rɪ'preʃən] *n* Unterdrückung *f*; (*Psych*) Verdrängung *f*.

repressive [rɪ'presɪv] *adj* repressiv.

reprieve [rɪ'priːv] [1] *n* (*Jur*) Begnadigung *f*; (*postponement*) Strafaufschub *m*; (*fig*) Gnadenfrist *f*.
[2] *vt* **he was ~d** (*Jur*) er wurde begnadigt; (*sentence postponed*) seine Strafe wurde aufgeschoben; **the building/firm has been ~d for a while** das Gebäude/die Firma ist vorerst noch einmal verschont geblieben.

reprimand ['reprɪmɑːnd] [1] *n* Tadel *m*; (*official also*) Verweis *m*.
[2] *vt* tadeln; maßregeln (*geh*).

reprint [ˌriː'prɪnt] [1] *vt* neu auflegen, neu abdrucken, nachdrucken.
[2] ['riːprɪnt] *n* Neuauflage *f*, Nachdruck *m*.

reprisal [rɪ'praɪzəl] *n* (*for* gegen) Vergeltungsmaßnahme *f*; (*Mil, between companies, countries etc also*) Repressalie *f* ◆ **to take ~s** zu Repressalien greifen; **as a ~ for** als Vergeltung für.

repro ['reprəʊ] *n* (*inf*) *abbr of* **reproduction** Repro *f or nt*.

▼ **reproach** [rɪ'prəʊtʃ] [1] *n* **(a)** (*rebuke*) Vorwurf *m* ◆ **to heap ~es on sb** jdn mit Vorwürfen überhäufen; **a term/look of ~** ein Vorwurf *m*/ein vorwurfsvoller Blick; **above** *or* **beyond ~** über jeden Vorwurf erhaben.
(b) (*discredit*) **to be a ~ to sb/sth** eine Schande für jdn/etw sein; **to bring ~ (up)on sb/sth** jdn/etw in schlechten Ruf bringen; **to bring ~ (up)on oneself** in schlechten Ruf kommen.
▼ [2] *vt* Vorwürfe machen (*+dat*) ◆ **to ~ sb for his mistake** jdm einen Fehler vorwerfen; **to ~ sb for having done sth** jdm Vorwürfe dafür machen, daß er etw getan hat; **he has nothing to ~ himself for** *or* **with** er hat sich (*dat*) nichts vorzuwerfen.

reproachful *adj*, **~ly** *adv* [rɪ'prəʊtʃfʊl, -fəlɪ] vorwurfsvoll.

reprobate ['reprəʊbeɪt] [1] *adj action* ruchlos, verwerflich; *person* verkommen; (*Eccl*) verdammt.
[2] *n* verkommenes Subjekt, Gestrauchelte(r) *mf* (*geh*); (*Eccl*) Verdammte(r) *mf*.

reprobation [ˌreprəʊ'beɪʃən] *n* Verdammung *f*.

reprocess [ˌriː'prəʊses] *vt* wiederverwerten; *sewage, atomic waste* wiederaufbereiten ◆ **~ing plant** Wiederaufbereitungsanlage *f*.

reproduce [ˌriːprə'djuːs] [1] *vt* **(a)** wiedergeben; (*Art, mechanically, electronically also*) reproduzieren; (*Typ*) abdrucken.
(b) (*Biol*) **to ~ its kind** sich *or* seine Art fortpflanzen.
(c) (*Theat*) *play* neu inszenieren.
[2] *vi* **(a)** (*Biol*) sich fortpflanzen *or* vermehren.
(b) (*Typ*) **this picture won't ~ well** dieses Bild läßt sich nicht gut reproduzieren.

➤ LANGUAGE IN USE: **reply: 1** → 19.1, 19.4, 27.3, 27.5, 27.7 **reproach: 2** → 26.3

reproducible [ˌriːprəˈdjuːsɪbəl] *adj* reproduzierbar.
reproduction [ˌriːprəˈdʌkʃən] *n* **(a)** *(procreation)* Fortpflanzung *f*.
(b) *(copying)* Reproduktion *f*; *(of documents also)* Vervielfältigung *f* ♦ **sound ~** Klang- *or* Tonwiedergabe *f*; **this radio has good ~** das Radio gibt den Ton gut wieder.
(c) *(copy)* Reproduktion *f*; *(photo)* Kopie *f*; *(sound ~)* Wiedergabe *f* ♦ **~ furniture** (moderne) Stilmöbel *pl*.
reproductive [ˌriːprəˈdʌktɪv] *adj* Fortpflanzungs-.
reproof¹ [ˈrɪːˈpruːf] *vt garment* frisch *or* neu imprägnieren.
reproof² [rɪˈpruːf] *n* Tadel *m*, Rüge *f*.
reproval [rɪˈpruːvəl] *n* **(a)** *no pl (act)* Tadeln, Rügen *nt*. **(b)** *see* **reproof²**.
reprove [rɪˈpruːv] *vt person, action* tadeln, rügen.
reproving *adj*, **~ly** *adv* [rɪˈpruːvɪŋ, -lɪ] tadelnd.
reptile [ˈreptaɪl] **1** *n* Reptil, Kriechtier *nt*; *(fig pej)* Kriecher *m (pej)*.
2 *adj* Reptilien-, reptilartig.
reptilian [repˈtɪlɪən] **1** *adj* Reptilien-, reptilartig; *(fig pej)* kriecherisch *(pej)*.
2 *n* Reptil, Kriechtier *nt*.
republic [rɪˈpʌblɪk] *n* Republik *f*.
republican [rɪˈpʌblɪkən] **1** *adj* republikanisch.
2 *n* Republikaner(in *f*) *m*.
republicanism [rɪˈpʌblɪkənɪzəm] *n* Republikanismus *m*.
republication [ˈriːˌpʌblɪˈkeɪʃən] *n see* **republish** Wieder- *or* Neuveröffentlichung *f*; erneutes Aushängen.
republish [ˌriːˈpʌblɪʃ] *vt book* wieder *or* neu veröffentlichen *or* herausbringen; *banns* wieder aushängen.
repudiate [rɪˈpjuːdɪeɪt] *vt person* verstoßen; *authorship, debt, obligation* nicht anerkennen; *accusation* zurückweisen.
repudiation [rɪˌpjuːdɪˈeɪʃən] *n see vt* Verstoßung *f*; Nichtanerkennung *f*; Zurückweisung *f*.
repugnance [rɪˈpʌgnəns] *n* Widerwille *m*, Abneigung *f (towards, for* gegen).
repugnant [rɪˈpʌgnənt] *adj* widerlich, abstoßend.
repulse [rɪˈpʌls] **1** *vt (Mil) enemy, attack* zurückschlagen, abwehren; *(fig) person, help, offer* abweisen, zurückweisen.
2 *n (Mil)* Abwehr *f*, Zurückschlagen *nt*; *(fig)* Abweisung, Zurückweisung *f* ♦ **to meet with** *or* **suffer a ~** abgewiesen *or* zurückgewiesen werden.
repulsion [rɪˈpʌlʃən] *n* **(a)** *(distaste)* Widerwille *m (for* gegen). **(b)** *(Phys)* Abstoßung *f*.
repulsive [rɪˈpʌlsɪv] *adj* **(a)** *(loathsome)* abstoßend, widerwärtig. **(b)** *(Phys) forces* abstoßend, Repulsiv-.
repulsively [rɪˈpʌlsɪvlɪ] *adv* abstoßend, widerwärtig ♦ **~ ugly** abstoßend häßlich.
repulsiveness [rɪˈpʌlsɪvnɪs] *n see adj (a)* Abstoßende(s) *nt (of* an *+dat)*, Widerwärtigkeit *f*.
repurchase [ˌriːˈpɜːtʃɪs] **1** *n* Rückkauf *m*.
2 *vt* zurückkaufen.
reputable [ˈrepjʊtəbl] *adj* ehrenhaft; *occupation* ordentlich, anständig; *dealer, firm* seriös.
reputation [ˌrepjʊˈteɪʃən] *n* Ruf, Name *m*; *(bad ~)* schlechter Ruf ♦ **what sort of ~ does she have?** wie ist ihr Ruf?; **he has a ~ for being ...** er hat den Ruf, ... zu sein; **to have a ~ for honesty** als ehrlich gelten; **you don't want to get (yourself) a ~, you know** du willst dich doch sicherlich nicht in Verruf bringen.
repute [rɪˈpjuːt] **1** *n* Ruf *m*, Ansehen *nt* ♦ **to know sb by ~** von jdm schon viel gehört haben; **to be of good ~** einen guten Ruf genießen; **a restaurant of ~** ein angesehenes Restaurant; **a house of ill ~** ein Haus von zweifelhaftem Ruf; **to hold sb in high ~** eine hohe Meinung von jdm haben; **to be held in high ~** in hohem Ruf *or* Ansehen stehen.
2 *vt (pass only)* **he is ~d to be ...** man sagt, daß er ... ist; **to be ~d rich** als reich gelten; **he is ~d to be the best** er gilt als der Beste, er steht in dem Ruf, der Beste zu sein.
reputed [rɪˈpjuːtɪd] *adj* angenommen ♦ **the ~ father** *(Jur)* der vermutliche Vater.
reputedly [rɪˈpjuːtɪdlɪ] *adv* wie man annimmt ♦ **he is ~ the best player in the world** er gilt als der beste Spieler der Welt.
▼ **request** [rɪˈkwest] **1** *n* Bitte *f*, Wunsch *m*, Ersuchen *nt (geh)* ♦ **at sb's ~** auf jds Bitte *etc*; **on/by ~** auf Wunsch; **no parking by ~** bitte nicht parken; **to make a ~ for sth** um etw bitten; **I have a ~ to make of** *or* **to you** ich habe eine Bitte an Sie, ich muß eine Bitte an Sie richten; **record ~s** Plattenwünsche *pl*.
▼**2** *vt* bitten um, ersuchen *(geh)*; *(Rad) record* sich *(dat)* wünschen ♦ **to ~ silence** um Ruhe bitten *or* ersuchen *(geh)*; **to ~ sth of** *or* **from sb** jdn um etw bitten *or* ersuchen *(geh)*; **"you are ~ed not to smoke"** „bitte nicht rauchen"; *see* **presence, pleasure**.
request: ~ programme *n (Rad)* Wunschsendung *f*; **~ stop** *n (Brit)* Bedarfshaltestelle *f*.
requiem [ˈrekwɪem] *n* Requiem *nt* ♦ **~ mass** Totenmesse *f*.
▼ **require** [rɪˈkwaɪəʳ] *vt* **(a)** *(need)* brauchen, benötigen; *thing also* nötig haben; *work, action* erfordern; *(desire)* wünschen, mögen ♦ **I have all I ~** ich habe alles, was ich brauche; **the journey will ~ 3 hours** man braucht *or* benötigt 3 Stunden für die Reise; **it ~s great care** das erfordert große Sorgfalt; **it ~s repairing** es muß repariert werden; **what qualifications are ~d?** welche Qualifikationen werden verlangt *or* sind erforderlich?; **to be ~d to do sth** etw machen *or* tun müssen; **that is not ~d** das ist nicht nötig *or* erforderlich; **if you ~ me** wenn Sie mich benötigen; **if ~d** falls notwendig *or* erforderlich; **when (it is) ~d** auf Wunsch, wenn es gewünscht wird; **as and when ~d** nach Bedarf; **dilute as ~d** nach Bedarf verdünnen.
(b) *(order)* verlangen ♦ **to ~ sb to do sth** von jdm verlangen, daß er etw tut; **you are ~d to report to the boss immediately** Sie sollen sich sofort beim Chef melden; **to ~ sth of sb** etw von jdm verlangen; **as ~d by law** den gesetzlichen Bestimmungen gemäß *or* entsprechend.
required [rɪˈkwaɪəd] *adj* erforderlich, notwendig; *date* vorgeschrieben; *(desired)* gewünscht ♦ **the ~ amount** die benötigte Menge; **~ reading** *(Sch, Univ)* Pflichtlektüre *f*.
requirement [rɪˈkwaɪəmənt] *n* **(a)** *(need)* Bedürfnis *nt*, Bedarf *m no pl*; *(desire)* Wunsch, Anspruch *m* ♦ **to meet sb's ~s** jds Bedürfnisse erfüllen; jds Wünschen *(dat)* entsprechen, jds Ansprüchen *(dat)* gerecht werden; **there isn't enough bread to meet the ~** es ist nicht genügend Brot da, um den Bedarf zu decken.
(b) *(condition, thing required)* Erfordernis *nt* ♦ **to fit the ~s** den Erfordernissen entsprechen.
requisite [ˈrekwɪzɪt] **1** *n* Artikel *m*; *(necessary thing)* Erfordernis *nt* ♦ **bath/toilet/travel ~s** Bade-/Toiletten-/Reiseartikel *pl or* -utensilien *pl*.
2 *adj* erforderlich, notwendig ♦ **the ~ time** die dazu erforderliche Zeit.
requisition [ˌrekwɪˈzɪʃən] **1** *n* Anforderung *f*; *(act: of objects)* Requisition *f* ♦ **to make a ~ for sth** etw anfordern.
2 *vt sb's services* anfordern; *supplies, food* requirieren.
requital [rɪˈkwaɪtl] *n (repayment)* Vergeltung *f*; *(revenge also)* Rache *f*.
requite [rɪˈkwaɪt] *vt* **(a)** *(repay) person* es vergelten *(+dat)*; *action* vergelten ♦ **~d love** erwiderte Liebe. **(b)** *(avenge) action* vergelten; *person* rächen.
reran [ˌriːˈræn] *pret of* **rerun**.
reread [ˌriːˈriːd] *pret, pt*, **reread** [ˌriːˈred] *vt* wieder *or* nochmals lesen.
reredos [ˈrɪədɒs] *n* Retabel *nt*.
reroute [ˌriːˈruːt] *vt train, bus* umleiten.
rerun [ˌriːˈrʌn] *(vb: pret* **reran**, *ptp ~)* **1** *vt film* wieder *or* nochmals aufführen; *tape* wieder *or* nochmals abspielen; *race* wiederholen.
2 [ˈriːrʌn] *n see vt* Wiederaufführung *f*; Wiederabspielen *nt*; Wiederholung *f*.
resale [ˈriːseɪl] *n* Weiterverkauf *m* ♦ **"not for ~"** „nicht zum Weiterverkauf bestimmt"; *(on free sample)* „unverkäufliches Muster"; **~ price maintenance** Preisbindung *f*; **~ value** Wiederverkaufswert *m*.
resat [ˌriːˈsæt] *pret, ptp of* **resit**.
rescind [rɪˈsɪnd] *vt decision* rückgängig machen, widerrufen; *judgement, contract also* annullieren; *law, act* aufheben.
rescue [ˈreskjuː] **1** *n (saving)* Rettung *f*; *(freeing)* Errettung, Befreiung *f* ♦ **~ was difficult** die Rettung war schwierig; **to go/come to sb's ~** jdm zu Hilfe kommen; **to the ~!** zu Hilfe!; **it was Bob to the ~** Bob war unsere/seine *etc* Rettung; **~ attempt/operation/party** Rettungsversuch *m*/-aktion *f*/-mannschaft *f*; **~ services** Rettungsdienst *m*; *see* **air-sea ~**.
2 *vt (save)* retten; *(free)* erretten, befreien ♦ **you ~d me from a difficult situation** du hast mich aus einer schwierigen Lage gerettet; **the ~d were taken to hospital** die Geretteten wurden ins Krankenhaus gebracht.
rescuer [ˈreskjʊəʳ] *n see vt* Retter(in *f*) *m*; Befreier(in *f*) *m*.
research [rɪˈsɜːtʃ] **1** *n* Forschung *f (into, on* über *+acc)* ♦ **a piece of ~** eine Forschungsarbeit; **to do ~** forschen, Forschung betreiben; **to carry out ~ into the effects of sth** Forschungen über die Auswirkungen einer Sache *(gen)* anstellen.
2 *vi* forschen, Forschung betreiben ♦ **to ~ into** *or* **on sth** etw erforschen, über etw *(acc)* forschen *or* Forschung betreiben.
3 *vt* erforschen, untersuchen ♦ **a well-~ed book** ein Buch, das auf solider Forschungsarbeit beruht; *(journalistic investigation)* ein gutrecherchiertes Buch.
research *in cpds* Forschungs-; **~ assistant** *n* wissenschaftlicher Assistent, wissenschaftliche Assistentin.
researcher [rɪˈsɜːtʃəʳ] *n* Forscher(in *f*) *m*.
research: ~ establishment *n* Forschungsstätte *f*; **~ fellow** *n (Univ)* Forschungsstipendiat(in *f*) *m*; **~ fellowship** *n* Forschungsstipendium *nt*; **~ student** *n (Univ) Student, der Forschungen für einen höheren akademischen Grad betreibt*, ≃ Doktorand(in *f*) *m*; **~ worker** *n* Forscher *m*.
reseat [ˌriːˈsiːt] *vt* **(a)** *chair* einen neuen Sitz geben *(+dat)*; *trousers* einen neuen Hosenboden anfertigen für. **(b)** *(Tech) valve* neu einschleifen. **(c)** *person* umsetzen ♦ **when everyone was ~ed** *(had sat down again)* als sich alle wieder gesetzt hatten.
resection [riːˈsekʃən] *n* **(a)** *(Med)* Resektion *f*. **(b)** *(Surv)* Triangulation *f*.
resell [ˌriːˈsel] *vt* weiterverkaufen, wieder verkaufen.
▼ **resemblance** [rɪˈzembləns] *n* Ähnlichkeit *f* ♦ **to bear a strong/a faint/no ~ to sb/sth** starke/leichte/keine Ähnlichkeit mit jdm/etw haben; **there's not the slightest ~ between them** es besteht nicht die geringste Ähnlichkeit zwischen ihnen, sie sind sich *(dat)* nicht im geringsten ähnlich.
resemble [rɪˈzembl] *vt* ähneln, gleichen ♦ **they ~ each other** sie ähneln *or* gleichen sich *(dat) or* einander.
resent [rɪˈzent] *vt remarks, behaviour* übelnehmen, sich ärgern über *(+acc)*; *person* ein Ressentiment haben gegen ♦ **he ~ed her for the rest of his life** er nahm ihr das sein Leben lang übel; **he ~ed my having** *or* **me for having got the job** er nahm es mir übel, daß ich die Stelle bekommen hatte; **he ~ed the fact that ...** er ärgerte sich darüber, daß ...; **to ~ sb's success** jdm seinen Erfolg mißgönnen; **I ~ that** das gefällt mir nicht; **he may ~ my being here** es könnte ihn ärgern, daß ich hier bin.
resentful [rɪˈzentfʊl] *adj* ärgerlich *(of sb* auf jdn); *(of stepmother, younger brother etc)* voller Ressentiment *(of* gegen) ♦ **to be ~ of sb's success** jdm seinen Erfolg nicht gönnen; **~ of the criticisms levelled at him** die an ihm

➤ LANGUAGE IN USE: **request: 2** → 10.1, 25.1 **require: a** → 20.4 **resemblance** → 5.3

geübte Kritik übelnehmend; **he felt ~ about her promotion** er nahm es ihr übel, daß sie befördert worden war.

resentfully [rɪ'zentfəlɪ] *adv* ärgerlich.

resentment [rɪ'zentmənt] *n* Ärger, Groll *m no pl* (*of* über +*acc*).

reservation [ˌrezə'veɪʃən] *n* **(a)** (*qualification of opinion*) Vorbehalt *m*; (*Philos*) Mentalreservation *f* (*spec*) ◆ **without ~** ohne Vorbehalt, vorbehaltlos; **with ~s** unter Vorbehalt(en); **to have ~s about sb/sth** Bedenken in bezug auf jdn/etw haben.
(b) (*booking*) Reservierung *f* ◆ **to make a ~ at the hotel/on the boat** ein Zimmer im Hotel/einen Platz auf dem Schiff reservieren lassen *or* bestellen; **how many ~s did you make?** für wieviel Personen haben Sie reservieren lassen?; **to have a ~ (for a room)** ein Zimmer reserviert haben; **~(s) desk** Reservierungsschalter *m*.
(c) (*area of land*) Reservat *nt*, Reservation *f* ◆ **(central) ~** (*Brit: on motorway*) Mittelstreifen *m*.

▼ **reserve** [rɪ'zɜːv] [1] *vt* **(a)** (*keep*) aufsparen, aufheben ◆ **to ~ judgement/one's decision** mit einem Urteil/seiner Entscheidung zurückhalten; **to ~ the right to do sth** sich (*dat*) (das Recht) vorbehalten, etw zu tun; **to ~ a warm welcome for sb** einen herzlichen Empfang für jdn bereithalten; **to ~ oneself for sth** sich für etw schonen.
▼ **(b)** (*book in advance: client*) reservieren lassen ◆ **the box office lady ~d 4 seats for us** die Dame an der Kasse hat uns 4 Plätze reserviert; **are you reserving these seats for anyone?** haben Sie diese Plätze für jdn reserviert?
[2] *n* **(a)** (*store*) (*of* an +*dat*) Reserve *f*, Vorrat *m*; (*Fin*) Reserve *f* ◆ **to have great ~s of energy** große Kraftreserven haben; **cash ~** Barreserve *f*; **~ fund** Rücklage *f*, Reservefonds *m*; **world ~s of copper** die Weltkupferreserven *pl*, die Weltreserven *pl* an Kupfer; **to have/keep in ~** in Reserve haben/halten.
(b) without ~ ohne Vorbehalt, vorbehaltlos; **with certain ~s** unter *or* mit gewissen Vorbehalten.
(c) *see* **~ price**.
(d) (*piece of land*) Reservat *nt*, Reservation *f*.
(e) (*coolness, reticence*) Reserve, Zurückhaltung *f* ◆ **he treated me with some ~** er behandelte mich etwas reserviert.
(f) (*Mil*) (*force*) Reserve *f*; (*soldier*) Soldat *m* der Reserve ◆ **the ~s** die Reserveeinheiten.
(g) (*Sport*) Reservespieler(in *f*) *m*.

reserve *in cpds* Reserve-; **~ currency** *n* Leitwährung *f*.

reserved [rɪ'zɜːvd] *adj* **(a)** (*reticent*) zurückhaltend, reserviert (*about* in bezug auf +*acc*). **(b)** *room, seat* reserviert, belegt. **(c)** (*Publishing*) **all rights ~** alle Rechte vorbehalten.

reservedly [rɪ'zɜːvɪdlɪ] *adv* zurückhaltend, reserviert.

reserve: ~ list *n* (*Mil*) Reserveliste *f*; **~ player** *n* Reservespieler(in *f*) *m*; **~ price** *n* Mindest- *or* Ausrufpreis *m*; **~ tank** *n* Reservetank *m*; **~ team** *n* Reserve(mannschaft) *f*.

reservist [rɪ'zɜːvɪst] *n* (*Mil*) Reservist *m*.

reservoir ['rezəvwɑːʳ] *n* (*lit*) (*for water*) Reservoir *nt*; (*for gas*) Speicher *m*; (*fig: of knowledge, facts, talent etc*) Fundgrube *f*.

reset [ˌriː'set] *pret, ptp* **~** *vt precious stone* neu (ein)fassen; *watch* neu stellen (*to* auf +*acc*); *dial, gauge* zurückstellen (*to* auf +*acc*); (*Med*) *limb, bone* wieder einrichten; *dislocated shoulder* wieder einrenken; (*Typ*) *text* neu setzen; (*Comput*) rücksetzen ◆ **~ switch** *or* **button** (*Comput*) Reset-Taste *f*.

resettle [ˌriː'setl] *vt refugees* umsiedeln; *land* neu *or* wieder besiedeln.

resettlement [ˌriː'setlmənt] *n see vt* Umsiedlung *f*; Neubesied(e)lung *f*.

reshape [ˌriː'ʃeɪp] *vt dough, clay etc* umformen, neu formen; *text* umschreiben; *policy* umstellen.

reshuffle [ˌriː'ʃʌfl] [1] *vt cards* neu mischen; (*fig*) *Cabinet* umbilden; *board of directors* umbilden, umbesetzen.
[2] *n* (*of cards*) erneutes Mischen; (*fig: of board*) Umbesetzung, Umbildung *f* ◆ **cabinet ~** (*Pol*) Kabinettsumbildung *f*.

reside [rɪ'zaɪd] *vi* **(a)** (*form: live*) seinen Wohnsitz haben; *monarch, ambassador etc* residieren. **(b)** (*fig form*) **to ~ in sth** in etw (*dat*) liegen; **the power ~s in the President** die Macht liegt *or* ruht beim Präsidenten.

residence ['rezɪdəns] *n* **(a)** (*house*) Wohnhaus *nt*; (*hostel: for students, nurses*) Wohnheim *nt*; (*of monarch, ambassador etc*) Residenz *f* ◆ **the President's official ~** der Amtssitz des Präsidenten; *see* **hall**.
(b) *no pl* (*stay, living*) **country/place of ~** Aufenthaltsland *nt*/Wohnort *m*; **after 5 years' ~ in Britain** nach 5 Jahren Aufenthalt in Großbritannien; **to take up ~ in the capital** sich in der Hauptstadt niederlassen; **~ in the country is restricted to nationals** nur Staatsangehörige können im Land Wohnsitz nehmen (*form*); **to be in ~** (*monarch, governor etc*) anwesend sein; **poet** *etc* **in ~** (*Univ*) ansässiger Dichter *etc*; **the students are now in ~** das Semester hat angefangen; **there is always a doctor in ~** es ist immer ein Arzt am Ort; **~ permit** Aufenthaltsgenehmigung *f*.

residency ['rezɪdənsɪ] *n* **(a)** (*US*) *see* **residence (b)**. **(b)** (*Brit*) Residenz *f*. **(c)** (*of doctor*) Assistenzzeit *f* im Krankenhaus.

resident ['rezɪdənt] [1] *n* **(a)** Bewohner(in *f*) *m*; (*in town also*) Einwohner(in *f*) *m*; (*of institution also*) Insasse *m*, Insassin *f*; (*in hotel*) Gast *m* ◆ **"access restricted to ~s only"** „Anlieger frei"; **parking for ~s only** Parkplatz nur für Mieter; (*on road*) Parken nur für Anlieger gestattet; (*at hotel*) Parkplatz nur für Gäste; **~s' association** (*of area*) Bürgerinitiative *f*. **(b)** (*doctor*) Anstaltsarzt *m*/-ärztin *f*.
[2] *adj* **(a)** (*in country, town*) wohnhaft; (*attached to institution*) ansässig, Haus-; *chaplain, tutor, physician* Haus- ◆ **they are ~ in Germany** sie haben ihren Wohnsitz in Deutschland; **the ~ population** die ansässige Bevölkerung; **are you ~ in the hotel?** sind Sie Hotelgast/Hotelgäste? **(b) to be ~ in sb/sth** *see* **reside (b)**.

residential [ˌrezɪ'denʃəl] *adj area* Wohn-; *job* im Haus; *college* mit einem Wohnheim verbunden; *course* mit Wohnung im Heim ◆ **~ requirements for voting** Meldevoraussetzungen zur Ausübung des Wahlrechts.

residual [rɪ'zɪdjʊəl] [1] *adj* restlich, Rest-; (*Chem*) Rückstands-, rückständig ◆ **~ soil** (*Geol*) Alluvialboden *m*; (*by erosion*) Verwitterungsboden *m*.
[2] *n* (*Chem*) Rückstand *m*; (*Statistics, Math*) Abweichung *f* ◆ **~s** (*US: royalties*) Wiederholungsgage *f*.

residuary [rɪ'zɪdjʊərɪ] *adj* restlich, Rest-; (*Chem*) rückständig.

residue ['rezɪdjuː] *n* Rest *m*; (*Chem*) Rückstand *m*; (*Jur*) Nachlaß *m* nach Abzug sämtlicher Verbindlichkeiten.

residuum [rɪ'zɪdjʊəm] *n* (*Chem*) Rückstand *m*, Residuum *nt*; (*Jur*) *see* **residue**.

resign [rɪ'zaɪn] [1] *vt* **(a)** (*give up*) *office, post* zurücktreten von, abgeben; *claim, rights* aufgeben, verzichten auf (+*acc*) ◆ **to ~ power** abtreten; **he ~ed the leadership to his colleague** er übergab *or* überließ die Leitung seinem Kollegen; **to ~ one's commission** (*Mil*) seinen Abschied nehmen.
(b) to ~ oneself to sth/to doing sth sich mit etw abfinden/sich damit abfinden, etw zu tun; *see also* **resigned**.
[2] *vi* (*from public appointment, committee*) zurücktreten; (*employee*) kündigen; (*civil servant, clergyman*) sein Amt niederlegen; (*teacher*) aus dem Dienst ausscheiden ◆ **to ~ from office** sein Amt nied erlegen; **he ~ed from (his job with) "The Times"** er hat (seine Stelle) bei der „Times" gekündigt; **the Prime Minister was forced to ~** der Premierminister wurde zum Rücktritt gezwungen.

resignation [ˌrezɪg'neɪʃən] *n* **(a)** *see vi* Rücktritt *m*; Kündigung *f*; Amtsniederlegung *f*; Ausscheiden *nt* aus dem Dienst ◆ **to hand in** *or* **tender** (*form*) **one's ~** seinen Rücktritt/seine Kündigung einreichen/sein Amt niederlegen/aus dem Dienst ausscheiden.
(b) (*mental state*) Resignation (*to* gegenüber +*dat*), Ergebung (*to* in +*acc*) *f*.
(c) (*form: of right, claim etc*) Verzicht *m* (*of* auf +*acc*).

resigned [rɪ'zaɪnd] *adj person* resigniert ◆ **to become ~ to sth** sich mit etw abfinden; **I was ~ to walking, when ...** ich hatte mich schon damit abgefunden, zu Fuß gehen zu müssen, als ...; **to be ~ to one's fate** sich in sein Schicksal ergeben haben.

resignedly [rɪ'zaɪnɪdlɪ] *adv see adj*.

resilience [rɪ'zɪlɪəns] *n see adj* Federn *nt*; Unverwüstlichkeit *f*.

resilient [rɪ'zɪlɪənt] *adj* **(a)** *material* federnd *attr* ◆ **to be ~** federn. **(b)** (*fig*) *person, nature* unverwüstlich.

resin ['rezɪn] *n* Harz *nt*.

resinous ['rezɪnəs] *adj* harzig, Harz-.

resist [rɪ'zɪst] [1] *vt* **(a)** sich widersetzen (+*dat*); *arrest, sb's advances, enemy, attack also* Widerstand leisten gegen, sich wehren gegen; (*fig*) *proposal, change also* sich entgegenstellen (+*dat*), sich sträuben *or* wehren gegen.
(b) *temptation, sb, sb's charms* widerstehen (+*dat*) ◆ **I couldn't ~ (eating) another cake** ich konnte der Versuchung nicht widerstehen, noch ein Stück Kuchen zu essen.
(c) (*wall, door*) standhalten (+*dat*) ◆ **the lock ~ed my attempts at opening it** das Schloß widerstand meinen Versuchen, es zu öffnen; **to ~ corrosion** korrosionsbeständig sein.
[2] *vi see vt* **(a)** sich widersetzen; Widerstand leisten, sich wehren; sich sträuben *or* wehren. **(b)** widerstehen. **(c)** standhalten.

resistance [rɪ'zɪstəns] *n* (*to* gegen) Widerstand *m* (*also Elec, Phys, Mil*); (*Med*) Widerstandsfähigkeit, Resistenz (*geh*) *f* ◆ **~ to water/heat** Wasser-/Hitzebeständigkeit *f*; **his ~ of this temptation** daß er dieser Versuchung widerstanden hat; **to meet with ~** auf Widerstand stoßen; **to offer no ~ (to sb/sth)** (*to attacker, advances etc*) (jdm/gegen etw) keinen Widerstand leisten; (*to proposals*) sich (jdm/einer Sache) nicht entgegenstellen *or* widersetzen; **~ fighter** Widerstandskämpfer *m*; **the (French) R~** (*Hist*) die Résistance; **the R~ movement** (*Hist*) die französische Widerstandsbewegung; *see* **line**[1], **passive**.

resistant [rɪ'zɪstənt] *adj material, surface* strapazierfähig; (*Med*) immun (*to* gegen) ◆ **water-~** wasserbeständig.

resistor [rɪ'zɪstəʳ] *n* (*Elec*) Widerstand *m*.

resit [ˌriː'sɪt] (*vb: pret, ptp* **resat**) [1] *vt exam* wiederholen.
[2] *vi* die Prüfung wiederholen.
[3] ['riːsɪt] *n* Wiederholung(sprüfung) *f*.

resole [ˌriː'səʊl] *vt* neu besohlen.

resolute ['rezəluːt] *adj* energisch, entschlossen; *answer* entschieden, bestimmt.

resolutely ['rezəluːtlɪ] *adv see adj*.

resoluteness ['rezəluːtnɪs] *n see adj* Entschlossenheit *f*; Entschiedenheit, Bestimmtheit *f*.

▼ **resolution** [ˌrezə'luːʃən] *n* **(a)** (*decision*) Beschluß *m*; (*Pol, Admin etc also*) Resolution *f*; (*governing one's behaviour*) Vorsatz *m* ◆ **good ~s** gute Vorsätze *pl*.
(b) *no pl* (*resoluteness*) Entschlossenheit, Bestimmtheit *f*.
(c) *no pl* (*solving: of problem, puzzle*) Lösung *f*.
(d) (*Phys, Mus*) Auflösung *f* (*into* in +*acc*).
(e) (*Med: of swelling*) Rückgang *m*.

resolvable [rɪ'zɒlvəbl] *adj see vt (a, c)* lösbar; zerstreubar; zerlegbar; auflösbar.

resolve [rɪ'zɒlv] [1] *vt* **(a)** *problem* lösen; *doubt* zerstreuen.
(b) (*decide*) **to ~ that ...** beschließen, daß ...; **to ~ to do sth** beschließen, etw zu tun; **that ~d me to ...** das hat mich zu dem Entschluß veranlaßt zu ...
(c) (*break up: into elements*) zerlegen (*into* in +*acc*); (*convert*) auflösen (*also*

➤ LANGUAGE IN USE: **reserve: 1b** → 21.3 **resolution: a** → 8.1

Phys) (*into* in *+acc*).
(d) (*Mus*) *chord, harmony* auflösen (*into* in *+acc*).
(e) (*Med*) zum Rückgang bringen.
[2] *vi* **(a)** (*decide*) **to ~ (up)on sth** etw beschließen.
(b) (*into* in *+acc*) (*break up*) zerfallen; (*be converted*) sich auflösen.
[3] *vr* (*into* in *+acc*) sich zerlegen lassen; (*be converted*) sich auflösen.
[4] *n* **(a)** (*decision*) Beschluß *m* ◆ **to make a ~ to do sth** den Beschluß fassen, etw zu tun. **(b)** *no pl* (*resoluteness*) Entschlossenheit *f* ◆ **to do sth with ~** etw fest entschlossen tun.

resolved [rɪ'zɒlvd] *adj* (fest) entschlossen.

resonance ['rezənəns] *n* Resonanz *f*; (*of voice*) voller Klang.

resonant ['rezənənt] *adj sound* voll; *voice* klangvoll; *room* mit Resonanz ◆ **~ with the sound of singing/a thousand voices** von Gesang/vom Klang von tausend Stimmen erfüllt.

resonator ['rezəneɪtə^r] *n* Resonator *m*.

resort [rɪ'zɔːt] [1] *n* **(a)** (*recourse*) Ausweg *m*; (*thing, action resorted to also*) Rettung *f* ◆ **without ~ to violence** ohne Gewaltanwendung; **as a last ~** als letztes; **in the last ~** im schlimmsten Fall, wenn alle Stricke reißen (*inf*); **you were my last ~** du warst meine letzte Rettung.
(b) (*place*) Urlaubsort *m* ◆ **coastal ~** Seebad *nt*; **seaside/summer ~** Seebad *nt*/Sommerurlaubsort *m*; **winter sports ~** Wintersportort *m*; *see* **health ~, holiday ~**.
[2] *vi* **(a)** (*have recourse*) **to ~ to sth/sb** zu etw greifen/sich an jdn wenden; **to ~ to violence** Gewalt anwenden, gewalttätig werden; **to ~ to beggary/stealing/swearing** sich aufs Betteln/Stehlen/Fluchen verlegen.
(b) (*frequent*) **to ~ to a place** häufig an einem Ort verkehren.

resound [rɪ'zaʊnd] *vi* (wider)hallen (*with* von) ◆ **my ears were still ~ing with the noise** mir tönten noch die Ohren von dem Lärm; **his name ~ed throughout the land** (*fig*) sein Name war in aller Munde; **his speech will ~ throughout the country** (*fig*) seine Rede wird im ganzen Land widerhallen.

resounding [rɪ'zaʊndɪŋ] *adj noise, shout* widerhallend; *laugh, voice* schallend; (*fig*) *triumph, victory, failure* gewaltig; *success* durchschlagend; *defeat* haushoch ◆ **the response was a ~ "no"** die Antwort war ein überwältigendes „Nein".

resoundingly [rɪ'zaʊndɪŋlɪ] *adv* **the play was ~ successful** das Stück war ein durchschlagender Erfolg.

resource [rɪ'sɔːs] [1] *n* **(a) ~s** *pl* (*wealth, supplies, money etc*) Mittel, Ressourcen *pl* ◆ **financial/mineral/natural ~s** Geldmittel *pl*/Bodenschätze *pl*/Naturschätze *pl*; **~s in** *or* **of men and materials** Reserven *pl* an Menschen und Material; **he has no inner ~s** er weiß sich (*dat*) nie zu helfen; **he has no ~s against boredom** er weiß sich (*dat*) gegen Langeweile nicht zu helfen; **left to his own ~s** sich (*dat*) selbst überlassen; **a man of ~s** ein Mensch, der sich (*dat*) immer zu helfen weiß.
(b) (*expedient*) Ausweg *m*, Mittel *nt* ◆ **as a last ~** als letzter Ausweg; **you are my last ~** du bist meine letzte Rettung.
[2] *vt project* mit den nötigen Mitteln *or* Ressourcen versorgen, finanzieren; (*with personnel*) personell ausstatten.

resourceful [rɪ'sɔːsfʊl] *adv person* einfallsreich, findig; *scheme* genial.

resourcefully [rɪ'sɔːsfəlɪ] *adv see adj*.

resourcefulness [rɪ'sɔːsfʊlnɪs] *n see adj* Einfallsreichtum *m*, Findigkeit *f*; Genialität *f*.

▼ **respect** [rɪ'spekt] [1] *n* **(a)** (*esteem*) Respekt *m*, Achtung *f* (*for* vor *+dat*) ◆ **to have/show ~ for** Respekt *or* Achtung haben/zeigen vor (*+dat*); *for the law* achten; **I have the highest ~ for his ability** ich halte ihn für außerordentlich fähig; **to behave with ~** sich respektvoll verhalten; **to hold sb in (great) ~** jdn (sehr) achten; **he commands ~** er ist eine Respektsperson *or* (*public figure*) respektgebietende Persönlichkeit; **to command the ~ of the nation** dem Volk Respekt *or* Achtung abnötigen; **you should have a bit more ~ for his right hook** du solltest etwas mehr auf seinen rechten Haken achten.
(b) (*consideration*) Rücksicht *f* (*for* auf *+acc*) ◆ **to treat with ~** *person* rücksichtsvoll behandeln; *dangerous person etc* sich in acht nehmen vor (*+dat*); *toys, clothes etc* schonend behandeln; **nitroglycerine should be treated with ~** Nitroglyzerin muß mit äußerster Vorsicht behandelt werden; **she has** *or* **shows no ~ for other people's feelings** sie nimmt keine Rücksicht auf die Gefühle anderer; **out of ~ for** aus Rücksicht auf (*+acc*); **with (due) ~, I still think that ...** bei allem Respekt, meine ich dennoch, daß ...
(c) (*reference*) **with ~ to ...** was ... anbetrifft, in bezug auf ... (*+acc*); **good in ~ of content** inhaltlich gut.
(d) (*aspect*) Hinsicht, Beziehung *f* ◆ **in some/other ~s** in gewisser/anderer Hinsicht *or* Beziehung; **in many ~s** in vieler Hinsicht; **in this ~** in der *or* dieser Hinsicht *or* Beziehung; **in what ~ ...?** in welcher Hinsicht *or* Beziehung?
(e) ~s *pl* (*regards*) Empfehlungen (*geh*), Grüße *pl* ◆ **to pay one's ~s to sb** jdm seine Aufwartung machen; **give my ~s to** meine Empfehlung an (*+acc*) (*geh*); **to pay one's last ~s to sb** jdm die letzte Ehre erweisen.
▼[2] *vt* **(a)** respektieren; *person, customs, the law, privacy also* achten; *ability* anerkennen ◆ **a ~ed company** eine angesehene Firma. **(b) as ~s** was ... anbelangt *or* betrifft.

respectability [rɪ,spektə'bɪlɪtɪ] *n see adj (a)* Ehrbarkeit *f*; Ehrenhaftigkeit *f*; Anständigkeit *f*; Angesehenheit, Geachtetheit *f*; Korrektheit *f*.

respectable [rɪ'spektəbl] *adj* **(a)** (*estimable*) *person* ehrbar; *motives also* ehrenhaft; (*decent*) *life, district, club* anständig, bieder (*pej*); (*socially approved*) *person* angesehen, geachtet, bieder (*pej*); *clothes, behaviour* korrekt, anständig ◆ **they are very ~ people** sie sind sehr ehrbare Leute; **he was outwardly ~ but ...** er wirkte sehr ehrbar, aber ...; **in ~ society** in guter Gesellschaft; **that's not ~** das schickt *or* gehört sich nicht.
(b) (*large*) *size, income, sum* ansehnlich, beachtlich.
(c) (*fairly good*) *advantage* beträchtlich; *score, lead* beachtlich ◆ **a ~ writer** ein ganz ordentlicher Schriftsteller.

respectably [rɪ'spektəblɪ] *adv dress, behave* anständig.

respecter [rɪ'spektə^r] *n* **death/the law is no ~ of persons** vor dem Tod/dem Gesetz sind alle gleich; **death is no ~ of wealth** der Tod nimmt keine Rücksicht auf Reichtum; **he is no ~ of persons** er läßt sich von niemandem beeindrucken.

respectful [rɪ'spektfʊl] *adj* respektvoll (*towards* gegenüber).

respectfully [rɪ'spektfəlɪ] *adv* **(a)** *see adj*. **(b)** (*in letters*) **I remain ~ yours** *or* **yours ~** ich verbleibe mit vorzüglicher Hochachtung Ihr ... (*form*).

respectfulness [rɪ'spektfʊlnɪs] *n* Respekt *m* ◆ **~ of others** Rücksicht *f* auf andere.

respecting [rɪ'spektɪŋ] *prep* bezüglich (*+gen*).

respective [rɪ'spektɪv] *adj* jeweilig ◆ **we took our ~ partners/glasses** wir nahmen jeder unseren Partner/unser Glas, wir nahmen unsere jeweiligen Partner/Gläser; **they each have their ~ merits** jeder von ihnen hat seine eigenen Vorteile.

respectively [rɪ'spektɪvlɪ] *adv* beziehungsweise ◆ **the girls' dresses are green and blue ~** die Mädchen haben grüne beziehungsweise blaue Kleider; **and then allocate the funds ~** und die Mittel dann dementsprechend verteilen.

respiration [,respɪ'reɪʃən] *n* (*Bot, Med*) Atmung *f*.

respirator ['respɪreɪtə^r] *n* (*Med*) Respirator *m*; (*Mil*) Atemschutzmaske *f*.

respiratory [rɪ'spaɪərətərɪ] *adj* Atem-, respiratorisch (*spec*); *organs, problem* Atmungs-; *infection, disease* der Atemwege ◆ **~ system** Atmungssystem *nt*; **~ tract** Atemwege *pl*.

respire [rɪ'spaɪə^r] *vti* (*Med, form*) atmen, respirieren (*spec*).

respite ['respaɪt] *n* **(a)** (*rest*) Ruhepause *f* (*from* von); (*easing off*) Nachlassen *nt* ◆ **without (a) ~** ohne Unterbrechung *or* Pause. **(b)** (*reprieve*) Aufschub *m*.

resplendence [rɪ'splendəns] *n see adj* Glanz *m*, Strahlen *nt*; Pracht *f*; Funkeln *nt*.

resplendent [rɪ'splendənt] *adj person, face* glänzend, strahlend; *clothes* prächtig ◆ **the hills shone ~ in the evening sun** die Berge erglänzten *or* erstrahlten im Schein der Abendsonne; **there he was, ~ in his new uniform** da war er, in seiner funkelnden neuen Uniform; **the stage, ~ in blue and gold** die Bühne in einer Pracht von Gold- und Blautönen.

respond [rɪ'spɒnd] *vi* **(a)** (*reply*) antworten ◆ **to ~ to a question** eine Frage beantworten, auf eine Frage antworten *or* erwidern; **to ~ to a toast** einen Toast erwidern.
(b) (*show reaction*) (*to* auf *+acc*) reagieren; (*brakes, meter also*) ansprechen ◆ **to ~ to an appeal** einen Appell beantworten; **to ~ to an appeal for money** einem Spendenaufruf folgen; **they ~ed well to the appeal for money** der Spendenaufruf fand ein großes Echo; **to ~ to a call** einem Ruf folgen; **the patient did not ~ to the treatment/his mother's voice** der Patient sprach auf die Behandlung nicht an/reagierte nicht auf die Stimme seiner Mutter; **the illness ~ed to treatment** die Behandlung schlug an.

respondent [rɪ'spɒndənt] *n* (*Jur*) Scheidungsbeklagte(r) *mf*.

response [rɪ'spɒns] *n* **(a)** (*reply*) Antwort, Erwiderung *f*; (*Eccl*) Antwort *f* ◆ **in ~ (to)** als Antwort (auf *+acc*), in Erwiderung (*+gen*) (*geh*).
(b) (*reaction*) Reaktion *f* ◆ **£50,000 was raised in ~ to the radio appeal** auf den Aufruf im Rundfunk hin gingen Spenden in Höhe von 50.000 Pfund ein; **we had hoped for a bigger ~ from the public** wir hatten uns ein stärkeres Echo aus *or* größere Resonanz in der Öffentlichkeit erhofft; **my appeals met with no ~** meine Bitten fanden kein Echo *or* keine Resonanz; **~ time** (*Tech*) Ansprechzeit *f*.

▼ **responsibility** [rɪ,spɒnsə'bɪlɪtɪ] *n* **(a)** *no pl* Verantwortung *f* ◆ **to put** *or* **place the ~ for sth on sb** jdm die Verantwortung für etw übertragen; **to take** *or* **assume (full) ~ (for sth)** die (volle) Verantwortung (für etw) übernehmen; **the management takes no ~ for objects left here** die Firma haftet nicht für liegengelassene Gegenstände; **that's his ~** dafür ist er verantwortlich; **it's not my ~ to do that** ich bin nicht dafür verantwortlich, das zu tun; **on my own ~** auf eigene Verantwortung; **sense of ~** Verantwortungsgefühl *nt*; **~ payment** Verantwortlichkeitszuschlag *m*.
(b) (*duty, burden*) Verpflichtung *f* (*to* für) ◆ **the responsibilities of state/office** die Pflichten eines Staatsmanns/die Dienstpflichten *pl*.

responsible [rɪ'spɒnsəbl] *adj* **(a)** (*denoting cause*) verantwortlich; (*to blame also*) schuld (*for* an *+dat*) ◆ **bad workmanship/he was ~ for the failure** schlechte Arbeit/er war für das Versagen verantwortlich/an dem Versagen schuld; **what's ~ for the hold-up?** woran liegt die Verzögerung?
(b) (*liable, answerable*) verantwortlich ◆ **she is not ~ for her actions** sie ist für ihre Handlungen nicht voll verantwortlich; **to be ~ to sb for sth** jdm gegenüber für etw verantwortlich sein; **to be directly ~ to sb** jdm unmittelbar unterstellt sein; **to hold sb ~ for sth** jdn für etw verantwortlich machen.
(c) (*trustworthy*) *person, attitude* verantwortungsbewußt; *firm* seriös, zuverlässig.
(d) (*involving responsibility*) *job* verantwortungsvoll.

responsibly [rɪ'spɒnsəblɪ] *adv act, behave* verantwortungsbewußt; *carry out one's duties* zuverlässig.

responsive [rɪ'spɒnsɪv] *adj person, audience* interessiert, mitgehend; *class, pupil also* mitmachend; *steering, brakes, motor* leicht reagierend *or* ansprechend ◆ **to be ~ to sth** auf etw (*acc*) reagieren *or* ansprechen; **to be ~ to sb's pleas** jds Bitten (*dat*) nachkommen; **he wasn't very ~ when I suggested it to him** er war nicht sehr begeistert, als ich ihm das vorschlug; **the pupils wer-**

➤ LANGUAGE IN USE: **respect: 2a** → 11.3 **responsibility: a** → 18.3, 20.6

en't very ~ die Schüler machten nicht richtig mit; **he wasn't very ~** (*to my complaint*) er ging kaum darauf ein.

responsiveness [rɪ'spɒnsɪvnɪs] *n* **because of the tremendous ~ of the audiences** weil das Publikum so hervorragend mitging; **a class not noted for its ~** eine Klasse, die dafür bekannt ist, daß sie kaum mitmacht; **they have improved the ~ of the steering** es ist ein leichteres Ansprechen der Steuerung erzielt worden; **I was somewhat surprised at their ~ to my suggestion** ich war über ihre positive Reaktion auf meinen Vorschlag einigermaßen überrascht.

rest¹ [rest] 1 *n* **(a)** (*relaxation*) Ruhe *f*; (*pause*) Pause, Unterbrechung *f*; (*in ~ cure, on holiday etc*) Erholung *f* ◆ **a day of ~** ein Ruhetag *m*; **to need ~** Ruhe brauchen; **I need a ~** ich muß mich ausruhen; (*vacation*) ich brauche Urlaub; **to go to the mountains for a ~** zur Erholung in die Berge fahren; **to have** *or* **take a ~** (*relax*) (sich) ausruhen; (*pause*) (eine) Pause machen; **she took** *or* **had an hour's ~** (*relaxation*) sie ruhte sich eine Stunde aus; (*pause*) sie machte eine Stunde Pause; **take a ~!** mach mal Pause!; **to have a good night's ~** sich ordentlich ausschlafen; **to give one's eyes a ~** seine Augen ausruhen; **to give sb/the horses a ~** jdn/die Pferde ausruhen lassen; **give it a ~!** hör doch auf!

(b) to be at ~ (*peaceful*) ruhig sein; (*immobile*) sich in Ruhelage/-stellung befinden; (*euph: dead*) ruhen; **to lay to ~** (*euph*) zur letzten Ruhe betten; **to set at ~** *fears, doubts* beschwichtigen; **to put** *or* **set sb's mind at ~** jdn beruhigen; **you can set** *or* **put your mind at ~** Sie können sich beruhigen, Sie können beruhigt sein; **to come to ~** (*ball, car etc*) zum Stillstand kommen; (*bird, insect*) sich niederlassen; (*gaze, eyes*) hängenbleiben (*upon* an +*dat*).

(c) (*support*) Auflage *f*; (*of telephone*) Gabel *f*; (*Billiards*) Steg *m*; *see* **arm~, foot~**.

(d) (*Mus*) Pause *f*; (*Poet*) Zäsur *f*.

2 *vi* **(a)** (*lie down, take ~*) ruhen (*geh*); (*relax, be still*) sich ausruhen; (*pause*) Pause machen, eine Pause einlegen; (*on walk, in physical work*) rasten, Pause machen; (*euph: be buried*) ruhen ◆ **you must ~ for an hour** Sie sollten eine Stunde ausruhen; **she never ~s** sie arbeitet ununterbrochen; **he will not ~ until he discovers the truth** er wird nicht (rasten und) ruhen, bis er die Wahrheit gefunden hat; **to ~ easy (in one's bed)** ruhig schlafen; **to be ~ing** ruhen (*geh*); (*euph: out of work*) ohne Engagement sein; **to let a field ~** einen Acker brachliegen lassen; **(the case for) the prosecution ~s** das Plädoyer der Anklage ist abgeschlossen; **to let a matter ~** eine Sache auf sich beruhen lassen; **let the matter ~!** laß es dabei!; **may he ~ in peace** er ruhe in Frieden; **to ~ in the Lord** im Herrn ruhen.

(b) (*remain*) (*decision, authority, blame, responsibility etc*) liegen (*with* bei) ◆ **the matter must not ~ there** man kann die Sache so nicht belassen; **and there the matter ~s for the moment** und damit ist die Sache momentan erledigt; **(you may) ~ assured that ...** Sie können versichert sein, daß ...

(c) (*lean*) (*person, head, ladder*) lehnen (*on* an +*dat*, *against* gegen); (*be supported: roof etc*) ruhen (*on* auf +*dat*); (*fig: eyes, gaze*) ruhen (*on* auf +*dat*); (*fig: be based*) (*argument, case*) sich stützen (*on* auf +*acc*); (*reputation*) beruhen (*on* auf +*dat*); (*responsibility*) liegen, ruhen (*on* auf +*dat*) ◆ **her elbows were/ head was ~ing on the table** ihre Ellbogen waren auf den Tisch gestützt/ihr Kopf lag auf dem Tisch.

3 *vt* **(a)** *one's eyes* ausruhen; *voice* schonen; *horses* ausruhen lassen ◆ **to ~ oneself** sich ausruhen; **to be/feel ~ed** ausgeruht sein/sich ausgeruht fühlen; **(may) God ~ his soul** Gott hab ihn selig!; **to ~ one's case** (*Jur*) das Plädoyer abschließen.

(b) (*lean*) *ladder* lehnen (*against* gegen, *on* an +*acc*); *elbow, (fig) theory, suspicions* stützen (*on* auf +*acc*) ◆ **to ~ one's hand on sb's shoulder** jdm die Hand auf die Schulter legen; **to ~ one's head on the table** den Kopf auf den Tisch legen; **he ~ed his head against the wall** er lehnte den Kopf an die Wand.

◆**rest up** *vi* (*inf*) sich ausruhen.

rest² *n* (*remainder*) **the ~** der Rest, das übrige/die übrigen; **the ~ of the money/meal** der Rest des Geldes/Essens, das übrige Geld/Essen; **the ~ of the boys** der Rest der Jungen, die übrigen Jungen; **you go off and the ~ of us will wait here** ihr geht, und der Rest von uns wartet hier; **he was as drunk as the ~ of them** er war so betrunken wie der Rest *or* die übrigen; **she's no different from the ~** sie ist wie alle anderen; **all the ~ of the money** der ganze Rest des Geldes, das ganze übrige Geld; **all the ~ of the books** alle übrigen Bücher; **and all the ~ of it** (*inf*) und so weiter und so fort; **Mary, Jane and all the ~ of them** Mary, Jane und wie sie alle heißen; **for the ~** im übrigen.

restart [,riː'stɑːt] 1 *vt job, activity* wiederaufnehmen; *negotiations, career also* wieder beginnen *or* anfangen; *engine* wieder anlassen; *machine* wieder anschalten ◆ **to ~ work** wieder zu arbeiten anfangen.

2 *vi* wieder anfangen *or* beginnen; (*machine*) wieder starten; (*engine*) wieder anspringen.

restate [,riː'steɪt] *vt* **(a)** (*express again*) *reasons* wieder *or* erneut nennen; *problem, argument, theory* wieder *or* erneut vortragen; *case, one's position* wieder *or* erneut darstellen; (*Mus*) *theme* wiederaufnehmen. **(b)** (*express differently*) umformulieren; *case, one's position* neu darstellen.

restatement [,riː'steɪtmənt] *n see vt* **(a)** erneute Nennung; erneuter Vortrag; erneute Darstellung; Wiederaufnahme *f*. **(b)** Umformulierung *f*; Neudarstellung *f*.

restaurant ['restərɔ̃ːŋ] *n* Restaurant *nt*, Gaststätte *f* ◆ **~ food/prices** Gaststättenessen *nt*/-preise *pl*; **~ car** (*Brit Rail*) Speisewagen *m*.

restaurateur [,restərə'tɜːʳ] *n* Gastwirt, Gastronom *m*.

rest: ~ cure *n* Erholung *f*; (*in bed*) Liegekur *f*; **~ day** *n* Ruhetag *m*.

restful ['restfʊl] *adj occupation, pastime etc* erholsam; *colour* ruhig; *place* friedlich ◆ **she is very ~ to be with** es ist sehr gemütlich, mit ihr zusammen zu sein.

rest-home ['rest,həʊm] *n* Altersheim, Pflegeheim *nt*.

resting-place ['restɪŋ,pleɪs] *n* Rastplatz *m*; (*euph: grave*) Ruhestätte *f*.

restitution [,restɪ'tjuːʃən] *n* **(a)** (*giving back*) Rückgabe *f*; (*of objects, money also*) Rückerstattung *f* ◆ **to make ~ of sth** (*form*) etw zurückgeben/zurückerstatten; **~ of conjugal rights** (*Jur*) Wiederherstellung *f* der ehelichen Gemeinschaft. **(b)** (*reparation*) Schadenersatz *m*, Entschädigung *f*.

restive ['restɪv] *adj horse* (*stubborn*) störrisch; (*nervous*) unruhig; (*restless*) *person, manner* rastlos; *tribes* widerspenstig, aufsässig.

restiveness ['restɪvnɪs] *n see adj* störrische Art; Unruhe *f*; Rastlosigkeit *f*; Widerspenstigkeit, Aufsässigkeit *f*.

restless ['restlɪs] *adj person, manner, sea, night* unruhig; (*not wanting to stay in one place*) rastlos.

restlessly ['restlɪslɪ] *adv see adj*.

restlessness ['restlɪsnɪs] *n see adj* Unruhe *f*; Rastlosigkeit *f*.

restock [,riː'stɒk] *vt shop* wieder auffüllen; *pond* wieder (mit Fischen) besetzen; *farm* den Viehbestand (+*gen*) erneuern.

restoration [,restə'reɪʃən] *n* **(a)** (*return*) Rückgabe *f* (*to* an +*acc*); (*of property also*) Rückerstattung *f* (*to* an +*acc*); (*of confidence, order etc*) Wiederherstellung *f*; (*to office*) Wiedereinsetzung *f* (*to* in +*acc*). **(b) the R~** (*Hist*) die Restauration. **(c)** (*of monument, work of art*) Restaurierung *f*.

restorative [rɪ'stɔːrətɪv] 1 *adj* stärkend; *remedy also* Stärkungs-.

2 *n* Stärkungsmittel *nt*.

restore [rɪ'stɔːʳ] *vt* **(a)** *sth lost, borrowed, stolen* (*give back*) zurückgeben; (*bring back*) zurückbringen; *confidence, order, calm* wiederherstellen ◆ **to ~ sb's health, to ~ sb to health** jds Gesundheit *or* jdn wiederherstellen; **~d to health** wiederhergestellt; **to ~ sb to freedom** jdm die Freiheit wiedergeben; **to ~ sb to life** jdn ins Leben zurückrufen; **to ~ sth to its former condition** etw wiederherstellen; **the brandy ~d my strength** *or* **me** der Weinbrand hat mich wiederhergestellt.

(b) (*to former post*) wiedereinsetzen (*to* in +*acc*) ◆ **to ~ sb to the throne** jdn als König wiedereinsetzen; **to ~ to power** wieder an die Macht bringen.

(c) (*repair*) *building, painting, furniture, text* restaurieren.

restorer [rɪ'stɔːrəʳ] *n* (*Art*) Restaurator(in *f*) *m*; *see* **hair ~**.

restrain [rɪ'streɪn] *vt person* zurückhalten; *prisoner* mit Gewalt festhalten; *animal, unruly children, madman* bändigen; *radicals* in Schranken halten; *sb's activities, power* einschränken; *emotions, laughter* unterdrücken ◆ **to ~ sb from doing sth** jdn davon abhalten, etw zu tun; **to ~ oneself** sich beherrschen.

restrained [rɪ'streɪnd] *adj emotions* unterdrückt; *manner, words* beherrscht; *tone, voice, colour* verhalten; *criticism* maßvoll, gezügelt ◆ **he was very ~ when he heard the news** er war sehr beherrscht, als er die Nachricht hörte.

restraining order [rɪ'streɪnɪŋ,ɔːdəʳ] *n* (*Jur*) Verbotsverfügung *f* ◆ **to get a ~** eine gerichtliche (Verbots)verfügung erwirken.

restraint [rɪ'streɪnt] *n* **(a)** (*restriction*) Einschränkung, Beschränkung *f* ◆ **without ~** unbeschränkt; *develop* ungehemmt; **to place under ~** (*Jur*) in Haft nehmen.

(b) (*moderation*) Beherrschung *f* ◆ **to show a lack of ~** wenig Beherrschung zeigen; **he said with great ~ that ...** er sagte sehr beherrscht, daß ...; **to express oneself without ~** sich zwangslos ausdrücken; **wage ~** Zurückhaltung *f* bei Lohnforderungen.

(c) (*head ~*) Kopfstütze *f*.

restrict [rɪ'strɪkt] *vt* beschränken (*to* auf +*acc*); *freedom, authority also* einschränken; *time, number also* begrenzen (*to* auf +*acc*) ◆ **all speakers are ~ed to three hours** die Redezeit ist auf drei Stunden beschränkt; **~ing clothes** beengende Kleidungsstücke.

restricted [rɪ'strɪktɪd] *adj view* beschränkt, begrenzt; (*Admin, Mil*) *document, information* geheim; *locality* nur bestimmten Gruppen zugänglich; *admission* begrenzt ◆ **within a ~ area** auf begrenztem Gebiet; **~ area** (*Brit Mot*) Strecke *f* mit Geschwindigkeitsbeschränkung; (*US*) Sperrgebiet *nt*.

restriction [rɪ'strɪkʃən] *n see vt* (*on gen*) Beschränkung *f*, Einschränkung *f*; Begrenzung *f* ◆ **to place ~s on sth** etw beschränken *or* einschränken; **~s of space** räumliche Beschränktheit; **without ~s** uneingeschränkt; **speed ~** (*Mot*) Geschwindigkeitsbegrenzung *or* -beschränkung *f*; **price ~** Preisbeschränkung *f*.

restrictive [rɪ'strɪktɪv] *adj* restriktiv, einschränkend *attr* ◆ **~ practices** (*Jur, Ind*) wettbewerbsbeschränkende Geschäftspraktiken *pl*.

restring [,riː'strɪŋ] *pret, ptp* **restrung** [,riː'strʌŋ] *vt instrument* neu besaiten; *bow, racket* neu bespannen; *pearls* neu aufziehen.

rest-room ['rest,ruːm] *n* (*US*) Toilette *f*.

▼ **result** [rɪ'zʌlt] 1 *n* **(a)** Folge *f* ◆ **as a ~ he failed** folglich fiel er durch; **as a ~ of this** und folglich; **as a ~ of which he ...** was zur Folge hatte, daß er ...; **to be the ~ of** resultieren aus.

(b) (*of election, exam, race, Math etc*) Ergebnis, Resultat *nt*; (*good ~*) Resultat *nt* ◆ **~s** (*of test, experiment*) Werte *pl*; **I want to see ~s** ich möchte einen Erfolg *or* ein Resultat sehen; **to get ~s** (*person*) Erfolg *or* Resultate erzielen; **we had very good ~s with this** wir hatten damit großen Erfolg *or* sehr gute Resultate; **as a ~ of my inquiry** auf meine Anfrage (hin); **what was the ~?** (*Sport*) wie ist es ausgegangen?; **without ~** ergebnislos.

2 *vi* sich ergeben, resultieren (*from* aus) ◆ **from which it ~s that ...** woraus folgt, daß ...

◆**result in** *vi* +*prep obj* führen zu ◆ **this ~ed ~ his being late** das führte dazu, daß er zu spät kam.

resultant [rɪ'zʌltənt] 1 *adj* resultierend, sich daraus ergebend.

2 *n* (*Phys*) Resultierende *f*.

➤ LANGUAGE IN USE: **result: 1a → 17.1**

resume [rɪ'zjuːm] [1] *vt* **(a)** (*restart*) *activity* wiederaufnehmen, weitermachen mit; *tale, account also* fortfahren in (+*dat*); *journey* fortsetzen ♦ **to ~ work** die Arbeit wiederaufnehmen; **well?, he ~d** nun?, fuhr er fort.
(b) *command, possession* wieder übernehmen; *name* wieder annehmen ♦ **to ~ one's seat** seinen Platz wieder einnehmen; **to ~ possession of sth** etw wieder in Besitz nehmen.
(c) (*sum up*) zusammenfassen.
[2] *vi* (*classes, work etc*) wieder beginnen.

résumé ['reɪzjuːmeɪ] *n* Resümee *nt*, Zusammenfassung *f*; (*US: curriculum vitae*) Lebenslauf *m*.

resumption [rɪ'zʌmpʃən] *n* (*of activity*) Wiederaufnahme *f*; (*of command, possession*) erneute Übernahme; (*of journey*) Fortsetzung *f*; (*of classes*) Wiederbeginn *m*.

resurface [ˌriː'sɜːfɪs] [1] *vt road* neu belegen.
[2] *vi* (*diver, submarine, fig*) wieder auftauchen.

resurgence [rɪ'sɜːdʒəns] *n* Wiederaufleben *nt*.

resurgent [rɪ'sɜːdʒənt] *adj* wieder auflebend.

resurrect [ˌrezə'rekt] *vt* **(a)** (*lit*) *person* wiederbeleben; (*Rel*) auferstehen lassen ♦ **to be ~ed** auferstehen. **(b)** (*fig*) *law* wieder einführen; *ideology, institution* wieder ins Leben rufen; *custom, fashion, style* wiederbeleben; *ideas, memories* wieder aufleben lassen; (*inf*) *old dress etc* ausgraben (*inf*).

resurrection [ˌrezə'rekʃən] *n see vt* **(a)** Wiederbelebung *f* ♦ **the R~** (*Rel*) die Auferstehung. **(b)** Wiedereinführung *f*; Wiederbelebung *f*; Auflebenlassen *nt*.

resuscitate [rɪ'sʌsɪteɪt] *vt* (*Med*) wiederbeleben; (*fig*) beleben, neue Lebensgeister geben (+*dat*).

resuscitation [rɪˌsʌsɪ'teɪʃən] *n see vt* Wiederbelebung *f*; Belebung *f*.

resuscitator [rɪ'sʌsɪteɪtə^r] *n* (*Med*) Sauerstoffapparat *m*.

retail ['riːteɪl] [1] *n* Einzelhandel, Kleinhandel, Detailhandel (*dated*) *m* ♦ **~ and wholesale** Einzel- und Großhandel *m*.
[2] *vt* **(a)** im Einzel- *or* Kleinhandel *or* en detail (*dated*) verkaufen. **(b)** (*fig*) *gossip* weitererzählen.
[3] *vi* (*goods*) **to ~ at ...** im Einzelhandel ... kosten.
[4] *adv* im Einzelhandel ♦ **to sell ~** im Einzelhandel *or* en detail (*dated*) verkaufen.

retail *in cpds* Einzelhandels-; **~ business** *n* Einzel- *or* Kleinhandel *m*; (*shop*) Einzelhandelsgeschäft *nt*; **~ dealer** *n* Einzelhändler, Detailhändler (*dated*) *m*.

retailer ['riːteɪlə^r] *n* Einzelhändler, Kleinhändler *m*.

retailing ['riːteɪlɪŋ] *n* der Einzelhandel.

retail: ~ outlet *n* Einzelhandelsverkaufsstelle *f*; **~ park** *n* (*Brit*) großes Einkaufszentrum, Shopping-Center *nt*; **~ price** *n* Einzelhandelspreis *m*; **~ price index** *n* Einzelhandelspreisindex *m*.

retain [rɪ'teɪn] *vt* **(a)** (*keep*) behalten; *money, possession, person* zurück(be)halten; *custom* beibehalten, bewahren; *urine* zurückhalten; *colour* behalten; *flavour* beibehalten; (*battery*) *charge* halten; (*dam*) *water* stauen ♦ **to ~ water** (*soil, body*) Wasser speichern; (*sponge*) Wasser halten; **to ~ control (of sth)** etw weiterhin in der Gewalt haben; **to ~ the use of a limb/one's eyes** ein Glied/seine Augen noch gebrauchen können.
(b) (*remember*) sich (*dat*) merken; (*computer*) *information* speichern.
(c) (*engage*) *lawyer* beauftragen.

retainer [rɪ'teɪnə^r] *n* **(a)** (*old: servant*) Faktotum *nt*. **(b)** (*fee*) Vorschuß *m*.

retaining: ~ fee *n* Vorschuß *m*; **~ nut** *n* Befestigungsschraube *f*; **~ wall** *n* Stützmauer *f*.

retake [ˌriː'teɪk] (*vb: pret* **retook**, *ptp* **retaken** [ˌriː'teɪkən]) [1] *vt* **(a)** (*Mil*) *town* zurückerobern ♦ **he was ~n (prisoner)** er wurde wieder gefangengenommen. **(b)** (*Film*) nochmals aufnehmen. **(c)** (*Sport*) *penalty* wiederholen. **(d)** *exam* wiederholen.
[2] ['riːteɪk] *n* (*Film*) Neuaufnahme *f*; (*of exam*) Wiederholung(sprüfung) *f* ♦ **we need a ~ of that scene** wir müssen die Szene noch einmal filmen.

retaliate [rɪ'tælɪeɪt] *vi* Vergeltung üben; (*for bad treatment, insults etc*) sich revanchieren (*against sb* an jdm); (*in battle*) zurückschlagen; (*Sport, in fight, with measures in argument*) kontern ♦ **he ~d by pointing out that ...** er konterte, indem er darauf hinwies, daß ...; **he ~d by kicking him on the shins** er hat sich mit einem Tritt gegen das Schienbein revanchiert; **then she ~d by calling him a pig** sie revanchierte sich damit *or* zahlte es ihm damit heim, daß sie ihn ein Schwein nannte; **how will the unions ~?** wie werden die Gewerkschaften kontern?

retaliation [rɪˌtælɪ'eɪʃən] *n* Vergeltung *f*; (*in fight also*) Vergeltungsschlag *m*; (*in argument, diplomacy etc*) Konterschlag *m* ♦ **his ~ was vicious** er hat sich auf üble Weise revanchiert; **in ~** zur Vergeltung; **that's my ~ for what you did to me** das ist meine Revanche für das, was Sie mir angetan haben; **in ~ for your unkindness** um mich für Ihre Unfreundlichkeit zu revanchieren; **policy of ~** Vergeltungspolitik *f*.

retaliatory [rɪ'tælɪətərɪ] *adj* **~ measures** Vergeltungsmaßnahmen *pl*; **a ~ assassination** ein Vergeltungsmord *m*.

retard [rɪ'tɑːd] *vt development* verlangsamen, verzögern; *explosion*, (*Aut*) *ignition* verzögern; (*Biol, Phys*) retardieren.

retarded [rɪ'tɑːdɪd] *adj* zurückgeblieben ♦ **~ ignition** (*Aut*) Spätzündung *f*; **mentally ~** geistig zurückgeblieben.

retch [retʃ] [1] *vi* würgen.
[2] *n* Würgen *nt*.

retching ['retʃɪŋ] *n* Würgerei *f*, Gewürge *nt*.

ret(d) *abbr of* **retired** a.D.

retell [ˌriː'tel] *pret, ptp* **retold** *vt* wiederholen; (*novelist*) *old legend* nacherzählen.

retention [rɪ'tenʃən] *n* **(a)** Beibehaltung *f*; (*of possession*) Zurückhaltung *f*; (*of water*) Speicherung *f*; (*of facts*) Behalten *nt*; (*of information by computer*) Speicherung *f*; (*of lawyer*) Beauftragung *f*; (*Med: also* **~ of urine**) Harnverhaltung *f*.
(b) (*memory*) Gedächtnis *nt* ♦ **his powers of ~** sein Gedächtnis *nt*, seine Merkfähigkeit.

retentive [rɪ'tentɪv] *adj memory* aufnahmefähig ♦ **he is very ~** er hat ein gutes Gedächtnis.

retentiveness [rɪ'tentɪvnɪs] *n* (*of memory*) Aufnahmefähigkeit *f*; (*of person*) Merkfähigkeit *f*.

rethink [ˌriː'θɪŋk] (*vb: pret, ptp* **rethought** [ˌriː'θɔːt]) [1] *vt* überdenken.
[2] ['riːˌθɪŋk] *n* (*inf*) Überdenken *nt* ♦ **we'll have to have a ~** wir müssen das noch einmal überdenken.

reticence ['retɪsəns] *n* Zurückhaltung *f*.

reticent ['retɪsənt] *adj* zurückhaltend ♦ **to be ~ about sth** in bezug auf etw (*acc*) nicht sehr gesprächig sein.

reticently ['retɪsəntlɪ] *adv see adj*.

reticle ['retɪkl] *n* (*Opt*) Meßkreuz *nt*.

reticulate [rɪ'tɪkjʊlɪt], **reticulated** [rɪ'tɪkjʊleɪtɪd] *adj* netzartig, retikular.

retina ['retɪnə] *n, pl* **-e** ['retɪniː] *or* **-s** Netzhaut, Retina (*spec*) *f*.

retinue ['retɪnjuː] *n* Gefolge *nt*.

retire [rɪ'taɪə^r] [1] *vi* **(a)** (*give up work*) aufhören zu arbeiten; (*civil servant, military officer*) in Pension gehen, sich pensionieren lassen, in den Ruhestand treten; (*self-employed*) sich zur Ruhe setzen; (*soldier*) aus der Armee ausscheiden; (*singer, player etc*) (zu singen/spielen *etc*) aufhören ♦ **to ~ from business** sich zur Ruhe setzen, sich aus dem Geschäftsleben zurückziehen.
(b) (*withdraw, Mil*) sich zurückziehen; (*Sport*) aufgeben; (*Ftbl, Rugby etc*) vom Feld gehen ♦ **to ~ into oneself** sich in sich (*acc*) selbst zurückziehen; **to ~ from public life** sich aus dem öffentlichen Leben zurückziehen.
(c) (*old, form: go to bed*) sich zurückziehen.
[2] *vt* aus Altersgründen entlassen; *civil servant, military officer* pensionieren, in den Ruhestand versetzen; *soldier* verabschieden; (*Fin*) *bond* aus dem Verkehr ziehen.

retired [rɪ'taɪəd] *adj* **(a)** (*no longer working*) *worker, employee* aus dem Arbeitsleben ausgeschieden (*form*); *civil servant, military officer* pensioniert, im Ruhestand; *soldier* aus der Armee ausgeschieden ♦ **he is ~** er arbeitet nicht mehr, er ist Rentner/ist pensioniert *or* im Ruhestand/nicht mehr in der Armee; **a ~ worker/teacher/soldier** ein Rentner/pensionierter Lehrer/ehemaliger Soldat; **"occupation — ~"** „Beruf — Rentner/Pensionär/Veteran"; **~ list** (*Mil*) Liste *f* der aus dem aktiven Dienst Geschiedenen.
(b) (*secluded*) *life* zurückgezogen.

retiree [ˌrɪtaɪ'riː] *n* Ruheständler(in *f*) *m*.

retirement [rɪ'taɪəmənt] *n* **(a)** (*stopping work*) Ausscheiden *nt* aus dem Arbeitsleben (*form*); (*of civil servant, military officer*) Pensionierung *f*; (*of soldier*) Verabschiedung *f* ♦ **~ at 60/65** Altersgrenze bei 60/65; **to announce one's ~** sein Ausscheiden (aus seinem Beruf/seiner Stellung *etc*) ankündigen; sich pensionieren lassen wollen.
(b) (*period*) **how will you spend your ~?** was tun Sie, wenn Sie einmal nicht mehr arbeiten/wenn Sie pensioniert *or* im Ruhestand sind?; **to come out of ~** wieder zurückkommen.
(c) (*seclusion*) Zurückgezogenheit *f* ♦ **to live in ~** zurückgezogen leben.
(d) (*Mil*) Rückzug *m*; (*Sport*) Aufgabe *f*; (*Ftbl, Rugby etc*) Abgang *m* vom Spielfeld.

retirement: ~ age *n* Rentenalter *nt*; **to reach ~ age** das Rentenalter erreichen; (*of civil servant*) Pensionsalter *nt*; **~ benefit** *n* Altenhilfe *f*; **~ pay** *n* Altersrente *f*; **~ pension** *n* Altersruhegeld *nt* (*form*).

retiring [rɪ'taɪərɪŋ] *adj* **(a)** (*shy*) zurückhaltend. **(b)** **~ age** *see* **retirement age**.

retold [ˌriː'təʊld] *pret, ptp of* **retell**.

retook [ˌriː'tʊk] *pret of* **retake**.

retort [rɪ'tɔːt] [1] *n* **(a)** (*answer*) scharfe Erwiderung *or* Antwort. **(b)** (*Chem*) Retorte *f* ♦ **~ stand** Retortenhalter *m or* -stand *m*.
[2] *vt* scharf erwidern, zurückgeben.
[3] *vi* scharf erwidern.

retouch [ˌriː'tʌtʃ] *vt* (*Art, Phot*) retuschieren.

retrace [rɪ'treɪs] *vt past, argumentation* zurückverfolgen; *development also* nachgehen (+*dat*), nachvollziehen ♦ **to ~ one's path** *or* **steps** denselben Weg zurückgehen.

retract [rɪ'trækt] [1] *vt* **(a)** (*withdraw*) *offer* zurückziehen; *statement* zurücknehmen. **(b)** (*draw back*) *claws*, (*Aviat*) *undercarriage* einziehen.
[2] *vi* **(a)** (*withdraw*) einen Rückzieher machen. **(b)** (*claws, undercarriage*) eingezogen werden.

retractable [rɪ'træktəbl] *adj see vt* **(a)** zurückziehbar; zurücknehmbar. **(b)** einziehbar.

retraction [rɪ'trækʃən] *n see vt* **(a)** (*act*) Rückzug *m*; Rücknahme *f*; (*that retracted*) Rückzieher *m*. **(b)** Einziehen *nt*.

retrain [ˌriː'treɪn] [1] *vt* umschulen.
[2] *vi* umlernen, umgeschult werden, sich umschulen lassen.

retraining [ˌriː'treɪnɪŋ] *n see vb* Umschulung *f*; Umlernen *nt*.

retransmit [ˌriːtrænz'mɪt] *vt* weiterübertragen.

retread [ˌriː'tred] [1] *vt tyre* die Laufflächen erneuern von.
[2] ['riːˌtred] *n* (*tyre*) laufflächenerneuerter Reifen.

retreat [rɪ'triːt] [1] *n* **(a)** (*Mil*) Rückzug *m* ♦ **to sound the ~** zum Rückzug blasen; **the army is in ~** die Armee befindet sich *or* ist auf dem Rückzug; **to make** *or* **beat a (hasty** *or* **swift) ~** (*Mil*) (schnell) den Rückzug antreten; (*fig*)

(schleunigst) das Feld räumen; **his ~ into silence** seine Zuflucht zum Schweigen.
(b) (*place*) Zuflucht(sort *m*) *f*; (*hiding place*) Schlupfwinkel *m* ◆ **this is my ~** hierhin ziehe ich mich zurück; **he has gone to his country ~** er hat sich aufs Land zurückgezogen.
2 *vi* (*Mil*) den Rückzug antreten; (*in fear*) zurückweichen; (*flood, glacier*) zurückgehen, zurückweichen ◆ **to ~ within oneself** sich in sich (*acc*) selbst zurückziehen.
3 *vti* (*Chess*) zurückziehen.

retrench [rɪ'trentʃ] 1 *vt expenditure* einschränken, kürzen; *personnel* einsparen; *book* kürzen.
2 *vi* sich einschränken.

◆**retrench on** *vi +prep obj see* **retrench 1.**

retrenchment [rɪ'trentʃmənt] *n see vt* Einschränkung, Kürzung *f*; Einsparung *f*.

retrial [riː'traɪəl] *n* (*Jur*) Wiederaufnahmeverfahren *nt* ◆ **to subject a case to (a) ~** einen Fall wiederaufnehmen; **he requested a ~** er verlangte eine Wiederaufnahme des Verfahrens.

retribution [ˌretrɪ'bjuːʃən] *n* Vergeltung *f* ◆ **in ~** als Vergeltung.

retributive [rɪ'trɪbjʊtɪv] *adj action* Vergeltungs-, vergeltend; *justice* ausgleichend.

retrievable [rɪ'triːvəbl] *adj* **(a)** *see vt (a)* zurück-/hervor-/heraus-/herunterholbar; rettbar; zu bergen; rückgewinnbar; abrufbar; wiedererlangbar; wiedergutmachbar. **(b)** *error* wiedergutmachbar; *situation* zu retten.

retrieval [rɪ'triːvəl] *n see vt* **(a)** Zurück-/Hervor-/Heraus-/Herunterholen *nt*; Rettung *f*; Bergung *f*; Rückgewinnung *f*; Abfragen *nt*; Wiedererlangen *nt*; Wiedergutmachen *nt*. **(b)** Wiedergutmachung *f*; Rettung *f* ◆ **beyond** *or* **past ~** hoffnungslos. **(c)** Apportieren *nt*.

retrieve [rɪ'triːv] 1 *vt* **(a)** (*recover*) zurück-/hervor-/heraus-/herunterholen; (*rescue*) retten; (*from wreckage etc*) bergen; *material from waste* zurückgewinnen; (*Comput*) *information* abrufen; *honour, position, money, investment* wiedererlangen; *loss* wiedergutmachen ◆ **to ~ a writer's work from oblivion** das Werk eines Schriftstellers der Vergessenheit entreißen.
(b) (*set to rights*) *error* wiedergutmachen; *situation* retten.
(c) (*dog*) apportieren.
2 *vi* (*dog*) apportieren.

retriever [rɪ'triːvəʳ] *n* (*breed*) Retriever *m* ◆ **he is a good ~** er ist ein guter Apportierhund.

retro ['retrəʊ] 1 *pref* rück-, Rück-.
2 *n abbr of* **retrorocket.**
3 *adj fashion, music* Retro-.

retroactive [ˌretrəʊ'æktɪv] *adj* rückwirkend ◆ **a ~ effect** eine Rückwirkung.

retrograde ['retrəʊgreɪd] 1 *adj* rückläufig; *order* umgekehrt; *policy* rückschrittlich; (*Phys, Biol, Astron also*) retrograd (*spec*) ◆ **~ step** Rückschritt *m*.
2 *vi* (*Biol*) sich zurückentwickeln; (*Astron*) sich retrograd bewegen.

retrogress [ˌretrəʊ'gres] *vi* (*go backwards*) sich rückwärts bewegen; (*deteriorate*) sich zurückentwickeln.

retrogression [ˌretrəʊ'greʃən] *n see vi* rückläufige Bewegung; Rückentwicklung *f*.

retrogressive [ˌretrəʊ'gresɪv] *adj* (*moving backwards*) *motion etc* rückläufig, Rückwärts-; (*fig*) *plan, policy* rückschrittlich; (*Biol*) rückläufig ◆ **~ step** Rückschritt *m*.

retrorocket ['retrəʊ'rɒkɪt] *n* Bremsrakete *f*.

retrospect ['retrəʊspekt] *n* **in ~, what would you have done differently?** was hätten Sie rückblickend *or* im Rückblick anders gemacht?; **everything looks different in ~** im nachhinein *or* im Rückblick sieht alles anders aus.

retrospection [ˌretrəʊ'spekʃən] *n* Zurückblicken *nt*.

retrospective [ˌretrəʊ'spektɪv] 1 *adj thought* rückblickend; *wisdom* im nachhinein; (*Admin, Jur*) *pay rise* rückwirkend ◆ **~ effect** Rückwirkung *f*; **a ~ look (at)** ein Blick zurück (auf *+acc*).
2 *n* Retrospektive *f*.

retrospectively [ˌretrəʊ'spektɪvlɪ] *adv act* rückwirkend ◆ **to look ~ at sth** (*fig*) auf etw (*acc*) zurückblicken.

retrovirus ['retrəʊˌvaɪrəs] *n* Retrovirus *nt or m*.

retry [riː'traɪ] *vt* (*Jur*) *case* wiederaufnehmen, neu verhandeln; *person* neu verhandeln gegen, wieder vor Gericht bringen.

retsina [ret'siːnə] *n* Retsina *m*.

retune ['riː'tjuːn] 1 *vt* **(a)** (*Mus*) neu stimmen. **(b)** *engine* neu einstellen.
2 *n* **the engine needs a ~** der Motor muß neu eingestellt werden.

▼ **return** [rɪ'tɜːn] 1 *vi* (*come back: person, vehicle*) zurück- *or* wiederkommen, zurück- *or* wiederkehren (*geh*); (*go back*) (*person*) zurückgehen; (*vehicle*) zurückfahren; (*symptoms, doubts, fears*) wiederkommen, wieder auftreten; (*property: pass back to*) zurückfallen (*to* an *+acc*) ◆ **to ~ to London/the town/the group** nach London/in die Stadt/zur Gruppe zurückkehren; **to ~ to school** wieder in die Schule gehen; **to ~ to (one's) work** (*after short pause*) wieder an seine Arbeit gehen; (*after strike*) die Arbeit wiederaufnehmen; **to ~ to a subject** auf ein Thema zurückkommen; **to ~ to one's old ways** in seine alten Gewohnheiten zurückfallen; **to ~ home** nach Hause kommen/gehen, heimkehren (*geh*); **his good spirits ~ed** seine gute Laune kehrte wieder; **to ~ to health** wieder gesund werden; **to ~ to dust** wieder zu Staub werden.
2 *vt* **(a)** (*give back*) *sth borrowed, stolen, lost* zurückgeben (*to sb* jdm); (*bring or take back*) zurückbringen (*to sb* jdm); (*put back*) zurücksetzen/-stellen/-legen; (*send back*) (*to* an *+acc*) *letter etc* zurückschicken *or* -senden; (*refuse*) *cheque* zurückweisen; *ball* zurückschlagen/-werfen; *sound, light* zurückwerfen; *salute, visit, sb's love, compliment* erwidern ◆ **to ~ a/sb's blow** zurückschlagen; **to ~ a book to the shelf/box** ein Buch auf das Regal zurückstellen/in die Kiste zurücklegen; **to ~ goods to the shop** Waren in das Geschäft zurückbringen; **to ~ thanks** (*form*) danksagen; **to ~ thanks to sb** jdm Dank sagen; **I hope to ~ your kindness/favour** ich hoffe, daß ich mich einmal bei Ihnen revanchieren kann; **to ~ good for evil** Böses mit Gutem vergelten; **to ~ like for like** Gleiches mit Gleichem vergelten; **to ~ fire** (*Mil*) das Feuer erwidern; **to ~ hearts** (*Cards*) Herz nachspielen.
(b) (*reply*) erwidern, zurückgeben.
(c) (*declare*) *details of income* angeben ◆ **to ~ a verdict of guilty (on sb)** (*Jur*) (jdn) schuldig sprechen, einen Schuldspruch (gegen jdn) fällen; **to ~ a verdict of murder** (*Jur*) jdn des Mordes für schuldig erklären; **he was ~ed guilty** (*Jur*) er wurde schuldig gesprochen.
(d) (*Fin*) *income* einbringen; *profit, interest* abwerfen.
(e) (*Brit Parl*) *candidate* wählen.
▼ 3 *n* **(a)** (*coming/going back*) (*of person, vehicle, seasons*) Rückkehr, Wiederkehr *f* (*geh*); (*of illness*) Wiederauftreten *nt* ◆ **on my ~** bei meiner Rückkehr; **~ home** Heimkehr *f*; **~ to school** Schulbeginn *m*; **by ~ (of post)** postwendend; **~ to work** (*after strike*) Wiederaufnahme *f* der Arbeit; **~ to health** Genesung *f*; **a ~ to one's old habits** ein Rückfall *m* in seine alten Gewohnheiten; **many happy ~s (of the day)!** herzlichen Glückwunsch zum Geburtstag!; *see* **point.**
(b) (*giving/bringing/taking/sending back*) *see vt (a)* Rückgabe *f*; Zurückbringen *nt*; Zurücksetzen/-stellen/-legen *nt*; Zurückschicken *or* -senden *nt*; Zurückweisen *nt*; Zurückschlagen *nt*/-werfen *nt*; Zurückwerfen *nt*; Erwiderung *f*.
(c) (*Brit: also* **~ ticket**) Rückfahrkarte *f*; (*Aviat*) Flugschein *m* für Hin- und Rückreise.
(d) (*profit: from investments, shares*) (*on* aus) Einkommen *nt*; (*on capital also*) Ertrag, Gewinn *m*; (*product: from land, mine etc*) Ertrag *m* ◆ **~s** (*profits*) Gewinn *m*; (*receipts*) Einkünfte *pl*; **~ on capital** (*Fin*) Kapitalertrag *m*, Rendite *f*.
(e) (*fig: recompense*) **in ~** dafür; **in ~ for** für; **to do sb a kindness in ~** sich für einen Gefallen revanchieren.
(f) (*act of declaring*) (*of verdict, election results*) Verkündung *f*; (*report*) Bericht *m* ◆ **the population ~s show that ...** die Bevölkerungszahlen zeigen, daß ...; **the ~ of the jury** ≃ das Urteil der Schöffen; **the (election) ~s** das Wahlergebnis; **tax ~** Steuererklärung *f*.
(g) (*Brit Parl: of candidate*) Wahl *f* (*to* in *+acc*).
(h) (*Sport*) (*game, match*) Rückspiel *nt*; (*stroke*) Rückschlag *m*; (*Tennis*) Return *m*; (*throw*) Rückwurf *m*; (*~ pass*) Rückpaß *m* ◆ **to make a good ~** den Ball gut zurückschlagen/-werfen.
(i) (*Comm: ~ed item*) zurückgebrachte Ware; (*Theat*) zurückgebrachte Karte; (*book*) Remittende *f*.
(j) (*carriage ~*) (*Comput*) Return *nt*; (*on typewriter*) Rücklauftaste *f*.

returnable [rɪ'tɜːnəbl] *adj bottle* Mehrweg-; (*with deposit*) Pfand-.

returnee [rɪ'tɜːniː] *n* (*Pol*) Rückkehrer(in) *m(f)*.

returner [rɪ'tɜːnəʳ] *n* Wiedereinsteiger(in) *m(f)* (ins Berufsleben).

return: ~ fare *n* Preis *m* für eine Rückfahrkarte *or* (*Aviat*) einen Rückflugschein; **~ flight** *n* Rückflug *m*; (*both ways*) Hin- und Rückflug *m*; **~ half** *n* (*of ticket*) Abschnitt *m* für die Rückreise.

returning officer [rɪ'tɜːnɪŋ'ɒfɪsəʳ] *n* (*Brit Parl*) Wahlleiter *m*.

return: ~ journey *n* Rückreise *f*; (*both ways*) Hin- und Rückreise *f*; **~ match** *n* Rückspiel *nt*; **~ pass** *n* (*Sport*) Rückpaß *m*; **~ ticket** *n* (*Brit*) Rückfahrkarte *f*; (*Aviat*) Rückflugschein *m*.

reunification [riːˌjuːnɪfɪ'keɪʃən] *n* Wiedervereinigung *f*.

reunify [ˌriː'juːnɪfaɪ] *vt* wiedervereinigen.

reunion [rɪ'juːnjən] *n* **(a)** (*coming together*) Wiedervereinigung *f*. **(b)** (*gathering*) Treffen *nt*, Zusammenkunft *f* ◆ **a family/an office ~** ein Familien-/Belegschaftstreffen *nt*.

reunite [ˌriːjuː'naɪt] 1 *vt* wiedervereinigen ◆ **they were ~d at last** sie waren endlich wieder vereint.
2 *vi* (*countries, parties*) sich wiedervereinigen; (*people*) wieder zusammenkommen.

re-usable [ˌriː'juːzəbl] *adj* wiederverwendbar, wiederverwertbar.

Rev [rev] *abbr of* **Reverend.**

rev [rev] 1 *n abbr of* **revolution** (*Aut*) Umdrehung *f* ◆ **the number of ~s per minute** die Dreh- *or* Tourenzahl pro Minute; **4,000 ~s per minute** 4.000 Umdrehungen *or* Touren (*inf*) pro Minute; **~ counter** Drehzahlmesser, Tourenzähler *m*.
2 *vti* **to ~ (up)** (*driver*) den Motor auf Touren bringen; (*noisily*) den Motor aufheulen lassen; (*engine*) aufheulen.

revaluation [riːˌvæljʊ'eɪʃən] *n* (*Fin*) Aufwertung *f*.

revalue [ˌriː'væljuː] *vt* (*Fin*) aufwerten.

revamp [ˌriː'væmp] *vt* (*inf*) *book, play* aufpolieren (*inf*); *company* auf Vordermann bringen (*inf*); *house, room* aufmöbeln.

revanchist [rɪ'væntʃɪst] *adj* revanchistisch.

reveal [rɪ'viːl] *vt* **(a)** (*make visible*) zum Vorschein bringen; (*show*) zeigen ◆ **stripping off the plaster ~ed an old frieze** das Abschlagen des Putzes hatte einen alten Fries zum Vorschein gebracht; **a nightdress that ~ed her slender form** ein Nachthemd, das ihre schlanke Gestalt abzeichnete; **a neckline that ~ed her bosom** ein Ausschnitt, der ihren Busen freigab.
(b) (*make known*) *truth, facts* enthüllen, aufdecken; *one's identity* zu erkennen geben, enthüllen; *ignorance, knowledge* erkennen lassen ◆ **I cannot ~ to you what he said** ich kann Ihnen nicht verraten, was er gesagt hat; **he ~ed himself as being ...** er verriet sich als ...; (*deliberately*) er gab sich als ... zu

➤ LANGUAGE IN USE: **return: 3a** → 20.3, 21.3, 23.3

erkennen; **he could never ~ his feelings for her** er konnte seine Gefühle für sie nie zeigen; **what does this ~ about the motives of the hero?** was sagt das über die Motive des Helden aus?; **Nixon ~s all** Nixon packt aus (*inf*); **the doctor did not ~ to him how hopeless his situation was** der Arzt hat ihn nicht darüber aufgeklärt, wie hoffnungslos sein Zustand war.
(c) (*Rel*) offenbaren (*to sb* jdm) ◆ **~ed religion** Offenbarungsreligion *f*.

revealing [rɪ'vi:lɪŋ] *adj* (a) aufschlußreich. (b) *material, slit skirt etc* viel zeigend; *dress, neckline also* offenherzig (*hum*).

reveille [rɪ'vælɪ] *n* (*Mil*) Reveille *f*, Wecksignal *nt* ◆ **(the) ~ is at 6** um 6 Uhr ist Wecken.

revel ['revl] 1 *vi* (a) (*make merry*) feiern. (b) (*delight*) **to ~ in gossip/one's freedom** seine wahre Freude an Klatschgeschichten haben/seine Freiheit aus ganzem Herzen genießen; **to ~ in doing sth** seine wahre Freude daran haben, etw zu tun; **like it? I ~ in it** gefallen? es macht mir Riesenspaß!
2 *n* **~s** *pl* Feiern *nt*.

revelation [,revə'leɪʃən] *n* Enthüllung *f*; (*Rel*) Offenbarung *f* ◆ **(the book of) R~s** die Offenbarung (des Johannes); **it was a ~ to me** das hat mir die Augen geöffnet; **what a ~!** unglaublich!

reveller ['revləʳ] *n* Feiernde(r) *mf*.

revelry ['revlrɪ] *n usu pl* Festlichkeit *f*.

revenge [rɪ'vendʒ] 1 *n* Rache *f*; (*Sport*) Revanche *f* ◆ **to take ~ on sb (for sth)** sich an jdm (für etw) rächen; (*Mil etc*) an jdm (für etw) Vergeltung üben; **to get one's ~** sich rächen, seine Rache bekommen; (*Sport*) sich revanchieren; **out of ~** aus Rache; **in ~ for** als Rache für; **~ is sweet** Rache ist süß.
2 *vt insult, murder, sb* rächen ◆ **to ~ oneself** *or* **to be ~d (for sth)** sich (für etw) rächen; **to ~ oneself on sb (for sth)** sich (für etw) an jdm rächen.

revengeful [rɪ'vendʒfʊl] *adj* rachsüchtig ◆ **~ act** Racheakt *m*.

revengefully [rɪ'vendʒfəlɪ] *adv* rachsüchtig; *act* aus Rache.

revenger [rɪ'vendʒəʳ] *n* Rächer(in *f*) *m*.

revenue ['revənju:] *n* (*of state*) Staatseinkünfte, öffentliche Einnahmen *pl*; (*tax ~*) Steueraufkommen *nt*; (*of individual*) Einnahmen, Einkünfte *pl*; (*department*) Finanzbehörde *f*, Fiskus *m* ◆ **~ man** *or* **officer** Finanzbeamte(r) *m*; **~ stamp** (*US*) Steuermarke *or* -banderole *f*; *see* **inland, internal**.

reverberate [rɪ'vɜ:bəreɪt] 1 *vi* (*sound*) widerhallen, nachhallen; (*light, heat*) zurückstrahlen, reflektieren.
2 *vt sound, light, heat* zurückwerfen, reflektieren.

reverberation [rɪ,vɜ:bə'reɪʃən] *n* (*of sound*) Widerhall, Nachhall *m*; (*of light, heat*) Zurückstrahlen *nt*, Reflexion *f*.

revere [rɪ'vɪəʳ] *vt* verehren.

reverence ['revərəns] 1 *n* (a) Ehrfurcht, Reverenz (*geh*) *f*; (*veneration*) Verehrung *f* (*for* für) ◆ **to have ~ for sb, to hold sb in ~** jdn verehren; **to treat sth with ~** etw ehrfürchtig behandeln; **to show** *or* **pay ~ to** Ehrfurcht bezeigen (*+dat*).
(b) **your R~** (Euer) Hochwürden.
(c) (*obs: bow*) Reverenz *f*.
2 *vt* verehren.

reverend ['revərənd] 1 *adj* **the R~ Robert Martin** ≃ Pfarrer Robert Martin; **the Most R~ John Smith** Erzbischof John Smith; **the Very R~ John Smith** Dekan John Smith; **the Right R~ John Smith** Bischof John Smith; **the R~ Mother** die Mutter Oberin.
2 *n* (*inf*) ≃ Pfarrer *m*.

reverent ['revərənt] *adj* ehrfürchtig, ehrfurchtsvoll.

reverential [,revə'renʃəl] *adj awe, respect* ehrfürchtig; *bow, gesture etc* ehrerbietig.

reverently ['revərəntlɪ] *adv see adj*.

reverie ['revərɪ] *n* (*liter*) Träumereien *pl* ◆ **he fell into a ~** er kam ins Träumen.

revers [rɪ'vɪəʳ] *n, pl* - Revers *nt or m*.

reversal [rɪ'vɜ:səl] *n see vt* (a) Umkehren *nt*; Umstellen *nt*, Vertauschung *f*; Wenden *nt*; Umdrehen *nt*. (b) Rückwärtslaufenlassen *nt*; Zurückstellen *nt*. (c) Umstoßung *f*; Aufhebung *f*; Umkehrung *f*; völlige Umstellung. (d) **to suffer a ~** einen Rückschlag erleiden.

reverse [rɪ'vɜ:s] 1 *adj* (a) (*opposite*) umgekehrt; *direction* entgegengesetzt; (*Opt*) *image* seitenverkehrt ◆ **in ~ order** in umgekehrter Reihenfolge; **~ video** (*Comput*) invertierte Darstellung.
(b) **~ gear** (*Aut*) Rückwärtsgang *m*; **~ motion** *or* **action** (*Tech*) (*backwards*) Rückwärtsbewegung *f*; (*opposite direction*) entgegengesetzte Bewegung.
2 *n* (a) (*opposite*) Gegenteil *nt* ◆ **quite the ~!** ganz im Gegenteil!; **he is the ~ of polite** er ist alles andere als höflich.
(b) (*back*) Rückseite *f*; (*of cloth also*) Abseite *f*, linke Seite; (*of coin, medal also*) Kehrseite *f*.
(c) (*setback, loss*) Rückschlag *m*; (*defeat*) Niederlage *f* ◆ **the ~s of fortune** die Mißgeschicke *pl*.
(d) (*on typewriter*) Rückstelltaste *f*; (*on tape-recorder*) Rücklauftaste *f*; (*Aut*) Rückwärtsgang *m* ◆ **in ~** (*Aut*) im Rückwärtsgang; **to go into ~** (*Aut*) in den Rückwärtsgang schalten.
3 *vt* (a) (*turn the other way round*) *order, situation, procedure* umkehren; *objects, sentences, words also* umstellen, vertauschen; *garment* wenden; *result also* umdrehen; (*Phot*) *negative* umkehren ◆ **to ~ the order of sth** etw herumdrehen; **to ~ the charges** (*Brit Telec*) ein R-Gespräch führen; **~d charge call** R-Gespräch *nt*.
(b) (*cause to move backwards*) *moving belt* rückwärts laufen lassen ◆ **to ~ one's car into the garage/down the hill/into a tree** rückwärts in die Garage fahren *or* setzen/rückwärts den Berg hinunterfahren/rückwärts gegen einen Baum fahren.
(c) *verdict, judgement, decision* umstoßen; *decree* aufheben; *trend* umkehren; *policy* völlig umstellen.
4 *vi* (*move backwards*) (*car, driver*) zurücksetzen; (*dancer*) rückwärts tanzen; (*machine*) rückwärts laufen ◆ **to ~ into the garage** rückwärts in die Garage fahren; **reversing lights** Rückfahrscheinwerfer *pl*.

◆**reverse out** *vt sep* (*Typ*) invertieren.

reversibility [rɪ,vɜ:sɪ'bɪlɪtɪ] *n see adj* Umstoßbarkeit *f*, Umkehrbarkeit *f*.

reversible [rɪ'vɜ:səbl] *adj decision* umstoßbar; (*Phys, Chem*) umkehrbar; *garment* Wende- ◆ **~ cloth** Doubleface *m or nt*.

reversion [rɪ'vɜ:ʃən] *n* (a) (*return to former state: of person*) Umkehr *f* (*to* zu); (*to bad state*) Rückfall *m* (*to* in *+acc*) ◆ **the ~ of this country to a republic** die Rückverwandlung dieses Landes in eine Republik; **~ to type** (*Biol*) (Arten)rückschlag *m*; **his ~ to type** das erneute Durchbrechen seiner alten Natur.
(b) (*Jur: of property*) Zurückfallen *nt* (*to* an *+acc*).

reversionary [rɪ'vɜ:ʃnərɪ] *adj* (a) (*Jur*) Anwartschafts-. (b) (*Biol*) atavistisch (*spec*).

revert [rɪ'vɜ:t] *vi* (*return*) (*to former state*) zurückkehren (*to* zu); (*to bad state*) zurückfallen (*to* in *+acc*); (*to topic*) zurückkommen (*to* auf *+acc*); (*Jur: property*) zurückfallen (*to* an *+acc*) ◆ **he has ~ed to being a child** er ist wieder ins Kindheitsalter zurückgefallen; **but to ~ to the question** aber um auf die Frage zurückzukommen; **to ~ to type** (*Biol*) in der Art zurückschlagen; **he has ~ed to type** (*fig*) seine alte Natur ist wieder durchgebrochen; **fields ~ing to moorland/woodland** Felder, die wieder versumpfen/zu Wäldern werden.

review [rɪ'vju:] 1 *n* (a) (*look back*) Rückblick *m* (*of* auf *+acc*); (*report*) Überblick *m* (*of* über *+acc*) ◆ **I shall keep your case under ~** ich werde Ihren Fall genau verfolgen *or* im Auge behalten; **to pass one's life in ~** das Leben noch einmal an sich (*dat*) vorüberziehen lassen.
(b) (*re-examination*) nochmalige Prüfung ◆ **the agreement comes up for ~** *or* **comes under ~ next year** das Abkommen wird nächstes Jahr nochmals geprüft; **salary due for ~ in January** Gehaltsaufbesserung *f* im Januar geplant; **there will be a ~ of the situation in 3 months' time** in 3 Monaten wird die Lage noch einmal überprüft.
(c) (*Mil: inspection*) Inspektion *f* ◆ **to hold a ~** eine Inspektion vornehmen.
(d) (*of book, film, play etc*) Kritik, Besprechung, Rezension *f* ◆ **~ copy** (*of book*) Rezensionsexemplar *nt*.
(e) (*magazine*) Zeitschrift *f*.
2 *vt* (a) (*look back at*) *one's life, the past etc* zurückblicken auf (*+acc*), überdenken.
(b) (*re-examine*) *situation, case* erneut (über)prüfen.
(c) (*Mil*) *troops* inspizieren, mustern.
(d) *book, play, film* besprechen, rezensieren.
(e) (*US: before exam*) wiederholen.

review body *n* Untersuchungsausschuß *m*.

reviewer [rɪ'vju:əʳ] *n* Kritiker(in *f*), Rezensent(in *f*) *m*.

review panel *n see* **review body**.

revile [rɪ'vaɪl] 1 *vt* schmähen, verunglimpfen.
2 *vi* **to ~ against sb/sth** gegen jdn/etw schmähen.

revise [rɪ'vaɪz] 1 *vt* (a) (*change*) *opinion, estimate* überholen, revidieren.
(b) (*correct*) *proof, text* revidieren, überarbeiten ◆ **~d edition** überarbeitete Ausgabe; **the R~d Version** (*Brit*), **the R~d Standard Version** (*US*) *die revidierte Übersetzung der Bibel*.
(c) (*Brit: learn up*) wiederholen.
2 *vi* (*Brit*) (den Stoff) wiederholen.

reviser [rɪ'vaɪzəʳ] *n* Bearbeiter *m*; (*of translations etc*) Korrektor *m*.

revision [rɪ'vɪʒən] *n* (a) (*of opinion, estimate*) Überholen, Revidieren *nt*. (b) (*of proofs*) Revision, Überarbeitung *f*. (c) (*Brit: for exam*) Wiederholung *f* (des Stoffs). (d) (*revised version*) überarbeitete Ausgabe.

revisionism [rɪ'vɪʒənɪzəm] *n* Revisionismus *m*.

revisionist [rɪ'vɪʒənɪst] 1 *adj* revisionistisch.
2 *n* Revisionist(in *f*) *m*.

revisit [,ri:'vɪzɪt] *vt place, person* wieder *or* nochmals besuchen.

revitalize [,ri:'vaɪtəlaɪz] *vt* neu beleben.

revival [rɪ'vaɪvəl] *n* (a) (*bringing back*) (*of custom, usage*) Wiedererwecken, Wiederauflebenlassen *nt*; (*of old ideas, affair*) Wiederaufnehmen, Wiederaufgreifen *nt*; (*from faint, fatigue*) Wiederbeleben *nt*, Wiederbelebung *f*; (*of play*) Wiederaufnahme *f*; (*of law*) Wiederinkrafttreten *nt*.
(b) (*coming back, return: of old ideas etc*) Wiederaufleben *nt*; (*of custom, usage also*) Wiederaufblühen *nt*, Renaissance *f* (*geh*); (*from faint, fatigue*) Wiederbelebung *f* ◆ **there has been a ~ of interest in ...** das Interesse an ... ist wieder wach geworden *or* erwacht; **the dollar experienced a slight ~** der Dollar verzeichnete wieder einen leichten Aufschwung; **an economic ~** ein wirtschaftlicher Wiederaufschwung.
(c) (*Rel*) Erweckung *f* ◆ **~ meeting** Erweckungsversammlung *f*.

revivalism [rɪ'vaɪvəlɪzəm] *n* (*Rel*) Erweckungsbewegung *f*.

revivalist [rɪ'vaɪvəlɪst] (*Rel*) 1 *adj* erneuernd.
2 *n* Anhänger(in *f*) *m* der Erweckungsbewegung.

revive [rɪ'vaɪv] 1 *vt person* (*from fainting, from fatigue*) (wieder *or* neu) beleben; munter machen (*inf*); (*from near death*) wiederbeleben; *fashion, custom, usage, conversation, hatred* wiederaufleben lassen; *friendship, hobby, old usage, word* wiederaufgreifen, wiederaufnehmen; *old play* wiederaufnehmen ◆ **a glass of brandy will ~ you** ein Glas Weinbrand wird Sie wieder beleben *or* wieder auf die Beine bringen.
2 *vi* (*person*) (*from fainting*) wieder zu sich kommen; (*from fatigue*) wieder aufleben, wieder munter werden; (*hope, feelings*) wiederaufleben; (*business, trade*) wiederaufblühen.

revivify [riːˈvɪvɪfaɪ] *vt person* wieder beleben *or* munter machen; (*restore to life*) wiederbeleben.
revocation [ˌrevəˈkeɪʃən] *n see* **revoke** Aufhebung *f*; Zurückziehen *nt*; Widerruf *m*; Entzug *m*.
revoke [rɪˈvəʊk] 1 *vt law* aufheben; *order, promise* zurückziehen; *decision* widerrufen, rückgängig machen; *licence* entziehen.
2 *vi* (*Cards*) nicht Farbe bekennen.
3 *n* (*Cards*) Nichtfarbebekennen *nt*.
revolt [rɪˈvəʊlt] 1 *n* Empörung, Revolte *f*, Aufstand *m* ♦ **to rise (up) in ~, to break out in ~** einen Aufstand *or* eine Revolte machen, sich erheben; **to be in ~ (against)** rebellieren (gegen).
2 *vi* **(a)** (*rebel*) (*against* gegen) revoltieren, rebellieren.
(b) (*be disgusted*) (*at, against* bei, gegen) (*one's nature, sensibilities*) sich empören; (*stomach*) rebellieren.
3 *vt* abstoßen, anekeln (*inf*) ♦ **I was ~ed by it** es hat mich angeekelt *or* abgestoßen.
revolting [rɪˈvəʊltɪŋ] *adj* (*repulsive, disgusting*) abstoßend; *meal, story* ekelhaft; (*inf: unpleasant*) *weather, colour, dress* scheußlich, abscheulich; *person* widerlich.
revolution [ˌrevəˈluːʃən] *n* **(a)** (*Pol, fig*) Revolution *f*; (*radical change also*) Umwälzung *f*. **(b)** (*turn*) (*around own axis*) Umdrehung *f*; (*of planet around sun*) Umlauf *m* ♦ **4,000 ~s per minute** eine Drehzahl von 4.000 pro Minute.
revolutionary [ˌrevəˈluːʃnərɪ] 1 *adj* (*lit, fig*) revolutionär.
2 *n* Revolutionär, Revoluzzer (*pej*) *m*.
revolutionize [ˌrevəˈluːʃənaɪz] *vt* revolutionieren.
revolve [rɪˈvɒlv] 1 *vt* drehen.
2 *vi* sich drehen ♦ **to ~ on an axis/around the sun** sich um eine Achse/um die Sonne drehen; **he thinks everything ~s around him** (*fig*) er glaubt, alles drehe sich nur um ihn.
revolver [rɪˈvɒlvə^r] *n* Revolver *m*.
revolving [rɪˈvɒlvɪŋ] *in cpds* Dreh-; **~ chair** *n* Drehstuhl *m*; **~ credit** *n* revolvierender Kredit; **~ door** *n* Drehtür *f*; **~ light** *n* Drehleuchtfeuer *nt*; **~ stage** *n* Drehbühne *f*.
revue [rɪˈvjuː] *n* (*Theat*) Revue *f*; (*satirical*) Kabarett *nt* ♦ **~ artist** Revuestar *m*; Kabarettist(in *f*) *m*.
revulsion [rɪˈvʌlʃən] *n* **(a)** (*disgust*) Abscheu, Ekel *m* (*at* vor +*dat*). **(b)** (*sudden change*) Umschwung *m*; (*reaction*) Empörung *f*.
reward [rɪˈwɔːd] 1 *n* Belohnung *f*; (*money*) Entgelt *nt* (*form*) ♦ **as a ~ for helping me** als Belohnung für Ihre Hilfe; **DM 1,000 ~** 1.000 DM Belohnung; **~ offered for the return of ...** Finderlohn für ...; **the ~s of this job** die Vorzüge dieser Arbeit.
2 *vt* belohnen ♦ **"finder will be ~ed"** „Finderlohn (ist) ausgesetzt".
rewarding [rɪˈwɔːdɪŋ] *adj* (*financially*) lohnend, einträglich; (*mentally, morally*) *experience* lohnend; *task, work* dankbar ♦ **this is a very ~ book/film** es lohnt sich wirklich, dieses Buch zu lesen/diesen Film zu sehen; **bringing up a child is ~** ein Kind großzuziehen ist eine dankbare *or* lohnende Aufgabe.
rewind [ˌriːˈwaɪnd] *pret, ptp* **rewound** *vt thread* wieder aufwickeln; *watch* wieder aufziehen; *film, tape* zurückspulen ♦ **~ button** Rückspultaste *f*.
rewire [ˌriːˈwaɪə^r] *vt* neu verkabeln.
reword [ˌriːˈwɜːd] *vt explanation, question* umformulieren, anders ausdrücken; *paragraph, sentence also* neu abfassen.
rework [ˌriːˈwɜːk] *vt* (*use again*) *theme* wieder verarbeiten; (*revise*) neu fassen.
rewound [ˌriːˈwaʊnd] *pret, ptp of* **rewind.**
rewrite [ˌriːˈraɪt] (*vb: pret* **rewrote** [ˌriːˈrəʊt], *ptp* **rewritten** [ˌriːˈrɪtn]) 1 *vt* (*write out again*) neu schreiben; (*recast*) umschreiben.
2 [ˈriːˌraɪt] *n* **this is just a ~ of his first novel** dies ist nur ein Neuaufguß *m* seines ersten Romans; **it needs a complete ~** es muß vollständig neu geschrieben werden.
RGN (*Brit*) *abbr of* **Registered General Nurse.**
Rhaeto-Romanic [ˈriːtəʊrəʊˈmænɪk] *n* Rätoromanisch *nt*.
rhapsodic [ræpˈsɒdɪk] *adj* (*Mus*) rhapsodisch; (*fig*) ekstatisch.
rhapsodize [ˈræpsədaɪz] *vi* überschwenglich schwärmen (*over, about* von).
rhapsody [ˈræpsədɪ] *n* (*Mus*) Rhapsodie *f*; (*fig*) Schwärmerei *f*.
rhd *abbr of* **right hand drive.**
rhea [ˈriːə] *n* Nandu, Pampasstrauß *m*.
Rhenish [ˈrenɪʃ] *adj wine* Rhein-; *region also* rheinisch.
rhenium [ˈriːnɪəm] *n* (*Chem*) Rhenium *nt*.
rheostat [ˈriːəʊstæt] *n* Regelwiderstand, Rheostat (*spec*) *m*.
rhesus [ˈriːsəs] *n* Rhesus *m* ♦ **~ baby** Rhesus-geschädigtes Baby; **~ monkey** Rhesusaffe *m*; **~ factor** Rhesusfaktor *m*; **~-negative/-positive** Rhesus negativ/positiv; **~-negative baby** Baby *nt* mit Rhesus negativ.
rhetoric [ˈretərɪk] *n* Rhetorik *f*; (*pej*) Phrasendrescherei *f* (*pej*).
rhetorical [rɪˈtɒrɪkəl] *adj* rhetorisch; (*pej*) phrasenhaft, schwülstig (*pej*) ♦ **~ question** rhetorische Frage.
rhetorically [rɪˈtɒrɪkəlɪ] *adv* (*pej*) schwülstig; *ask* rhetorisch.
rhetorician [ˌretəˈrɪʃən] *n* Rhetoriker *m*; (*pej*) Phrasendrescher *m* (*pej*).
rheumatic [ruːˈmætɪk] 1 *n* **(a)** (*person*) Rheumatiker(in *f*) *m*. **(b) ~s** *sing* Rheumatismus *m*.
2 *adj pains* rheumatisch; *joint* rheumakrank ♦ **~ fever** rheumatisches Fieber, akuter Rheumatismus.
rheumatism [ˈruːmətɪzəm] *n* Rheuma(tismus *m*) *nt*.
rheumatoid [ˈruːmətɔɪd] *adj* **~ arthritis** chronischer Rheumatismus, Gelenkrheumatismus *m*.
rheumatologist [ˌruːməˈtɒlədʒɪst] *n* Rheumatologe *m*, Rheumatologin *f*.
rheumatology [ˌruːməˈtɒlədʒɪ] *n* Rheumatologie *f*.
rheumy [ˈruːmɪ] *adj eyes* wäßrig.
Rhine [raɪn] *n* Rhein *m* ♦ **~ wine** Rheinwein *m*.
Rhine: ~land *n* Rheinland *nt*; **r~stone** *n* Rheinkiesel *m*.
rhino [ˈraɪnəʊ] *n abbr of* **rhinoceros.**
rhinoceros [raɪˈnɒsərəs] *n* Nashorn, Rhinozeros *nt*.
rhizome [ˈraɪzəʊm] *n* Rhizom *nt*, Wurzelstock *m*.
Rhodes [rəʊdz] *n* Rhodos *nt* ♦ **in ~** auf Rhodos.
Rhodesia [rəʊˈdiːʒə] *n* (*Hist*) Rhodesien *nt*.
Rhodesian [rəʊˈdiːʒən] (*Hist*) 1 *adj* rhodesisch.
2 *n* Rhodesier(in *f*) *m*.
rhodium [ˈrəʊdɪəm] *n* (*Chem*) Rhodium *nt*.
rhododendron [ˌrəʊdəˈdendrən] *n* Rhododendron *m or nt*.
rhomb [rɒm] *n* Rhombus *m*.
rhombic [ˈrɒmbɪk] *adj* rhombisch.
rhomboid [ˈrɒmbɔɪd] 1 *n* Rhomboid *nt*.
2 *adj* rhomboid.
rhombus [ˈrɒmbəs] *n* Rhombus *m*.
Rhone [rəʊn] *n* Rhone *f*.
rhubarb [ˈruːbɑːb] *n* Rhabarber *m* ♦ "**~**, **~**, **~**" (*Theat hum*) „Rhabarbarhabarbarhabarba".
rhyme [raɪm] 1 *n* **(a)** Reim *m* ♦ **for (the sake of) the ~** damit es sich reimt, des Reimes willen; **~ scheme** Reimschema *nt*; **without ~ or reason** ohne Sinn und Verstand; **there seems to be neither ~ nor reason to it, that has neither ~ nor reason** das hat weder Sinn noch Verstand.
(b) (*poem*) Gedicht *nt* ♦ **in ~** in Reimen *or* Versen; **to put into ~** in Reime *or* Verse bringen *or* setzen.
2 *vt* reimen.
3 *vi* **(a)** sich reimen.
(b) (*pej: write verse*) reimen, Verse schmieden.
rhymester [ˈraɪmstə^r], **rhymer** [ˈraɪmə^r] *n* (*pej*) Verseschmied (*pej*), Dichterling (*pej*) *m*.
rhyming [ˈraɪmɪŋ] *adj* **~ couplets** Reimpaare *pl*; **~ dictionary** Reimwörterbuch *nt*; **~ slang** *Slang, bei dem ein Wort durch ein sich darauf reimendes Wort ersetzt wird.*
rhythm [ˈrɪðm] *n* Rhythmus *m* ♦ **the ~ method (of contraception)** die Knaus-Ogino-Methode; **~ section** (*of band*) Rhythmusgruppe *f*; **~ and blues** Rhythm-and-Blues *m*.
rhythmic(al) [ˈrɪðmɪk(əl)] *adj* rhythmisch; *breathing, pulse* gleichmäßig.
rhythmically [ˈrɪðmɪkəlɪ] *adv* rhythmisch; gleichmäßig.
RI *abbr of* **Religious Instruction.**
rib [rɪb] 1 *n* **(a)** (*Anat, Cook*) Rippe *f* ♦ **to dig** *or* **poke sb in the ~s** jdn in die Rippen stoßen. **(b)** (*of leaf, ceiling, ship, shell*) Rippe *f*; (*of umbrella*) Speiche *f*. **(c)** (*Knitting*) Rippen *pl* ♦ **in ~** in Rippen.
2 *vt* (*tease*) necken, foppen.
RIBA [ˈriːbə] *abbr of* **Royal Institute of British Architects.**
ribald [ˈrɪbəld, ˈraɪbəld] *adj* deftig, zotig (*pej*); *behaviour* derb; *company* liederlich ♦ **~ talk** Ferkeleien *pl*.
ribaldry [ˈrɪbəldrɪ] *n* Ferkeleien, Schweinereien *pl*.
riband [ˈrɪbənd] *n* (*obs*) *see* **ribbon.**
ribbed [rɪbd] *adj knitting* gerippt; *shell, ceiling* Rippen-, mit Rippen.
ribbon [ˈrɪbən] *n* **(a)** (*for hair, dress*) Band *nt*; (*for typewriter*) Farbband *nt*; (*on medal*) Ordensband *nt*; (*fig: narrow strip*) Streifen *m* ♦ **~ development** (*Brit*) Zeilenbauweise *f*.
(b) ~s *pl* (*tatters*) Fetzen *pl* ♦ **to tear sth to ~s** etw zerfetzen *or* zerreißen; (*fig*) *play etc* etw in der Luft zerreißen.
rib cage *n* Brustkorb *m*.
riboflavin [ˈraɪbəʊˈfleɪvɪn] *n* Riboflavin *nt*.
ribonucleic acid [ˈraɪbəʊnjuːˈkliːɪkˈæsɪd] *n* Ribonukleinsäure *f*.
rib tickler *n* (*hum inf*) **it's a real ~** das ist die reinste Zwerchfellmassage (*inf*).
ribwort [ˈrɪbwɜːt] *n* Spitzwegerich *m*.
rice [raɪs] *n* Reis *m*.
rice *in cpds* Reis-; **~field** *n* Reisfeld *nt*; **~ growing** *n* Reis(an)bau *m*; **~-growing** *adj* Reis anbauend; **~ paper** *n* Reispapier *nt*; **~ pudding** *n* Milchreis *m*; **~ wine** *n* Reiswein *m*.
rich [rɪtʃ] 1 *adj* (+*er*) **(a)** (*wealthy*) reich.
(b) (*splendid*) *furniture, decoration, style, clothes* prächtig; *gift* teuer; *banquet* großartig.
(c) *food* schwer ♦ **~ tea biscuit** ≃ Butterkeks *m*; **a ~ diet** reichhaltige Kost.
(d) (*fertile*) *soil* fett; *land* fruchtbar, reich.
(e) (*full*) *colour* satt; *sound also, voice* voll; *wine* schwer.
(f) (*inf: amusing*) köstlich ♦ **that's ~!** (*iro*) das ist ja großartig!
(g) (*Aut*) *mixture* fett.
(h) ~ in vitamins vitaminreich; **~ in corn/minerals** reich an Getreide/Bodenschätzen; **~ in detail/illustrations/examples** sehr detailliert/mit vielen Abbildungen/Beispielen; **to be ~ in spirit** ein gutes Herz haben.
2 *n* **(a) the ~** *pl* die Reichen *pl*. **(b) ~es** Reichtümer *pl*.
Richard [ˈrɪtʃəd] *n* Richard *m* ♦ **~ (the) Lionheart** Richard Löwenherz.
richly [ˈrɪtʃlɪ] *adv dress, decorate* prächtig ♦ **he ~ deserves it** er hat es mehr als verdient; **he was ~ rewarded** (*lit*) er wurde reich belohnt; (*fig*) er wurde reichlich belohnt.
richness [ˈrɪtʃnɪs] *n see adj* (*a-e, g, h*) **(a)** Reichtum *m*. **(b)** Pracht *f*; Großartigkeit *f*. **(c)** Schwere *f* ♦ **the ~ of the diet** die reichhaltige Kost. **(d)** Fruchtbarkeit *f*. **(e)** Sattheit *f*; Schwere *f* ♦ **the ~ of his voice** seine volle Stimme. **(f)** Fettheit *f*. **(g)** Reichtum *m* (*in* an +*dat*).
Richter scale [ˈrɪktəˈskeɪl] *n* Richterskala *f*.

rick[1] [rɪk] *n* Schober *m.*
rick[2] *n, vt see* **wrick.**
rickets ['rɪkɪts] *n sing* Rachitis *f,* die englische Krankheit.
rickety ['rɪkɪtɪ] *adj* **(a)** *furniture etc* wackelig. **(b)** *(Med)* rachitisch.
rickshaw ['rɪkʃɔː] *n* Rikscha *f.*
ricochet ['rɪkəʃeɪ] [1] *n see vi* Abprall *m;* Rikoschettieren *nt (spec).*
[2] *vi (off* von) abprallen; *(bullet also)* rikoschettieren *(spec)* ♦ **the stone ~ed off the water** der Stein hüpfte auf dem Wasser.
rictus ['rɪktəs] *n (Anat, Zool)* Sperrweite *f.*
rid [rɪd] *pret, ptp ~ or* **~ded** *vt* **to ~ of** *(of pests, disease)* befreien von; *(of bandits etc)* säubern von; **to ~ oneself of sb/sth** jdn/etw loswerden; *(of pests also)* sich von etw befreien; *(of ideas, prejudice etc)* sich von etw lösen; **to get ~ of sb/sth** jdn/etw loswerden; **to be ~ of sb/sth** jdn/etw los sein; **get ~ of it** sieh zu, daß du das loswirst; *(throw it away)* schmeiß es weg *(inf);* **you are well ~ of him** ein Glück, daß du den los bist.
riddance ['rɪdəns] *n* **good ~ (to bad rubbish)!** *(inf)* ein Glück, daß wir das/den *etc* los sind.
ridden ['rɪdn] [1] *ptp of* **ride.**
[2] *adj* **~ by fears, fear-~** angsterfüllt; **strike-~** streikgeschüttelt; **disease-~** von Krankheiten befallen; **doubt-~** von Zweifeln zernagt; **strife-~** zerstritten; **~ by prejudice** von Vorurteilen beherrscht.
riddle[1] ['rɪdl] [1] *n (sieve)* (Schüttel)sieb *nt.*
[2] *vt* **(a)** *soil etc* sieben; *coal also* schütteln.
(b) to ~ sb/sth with bullets jdn/etw mit Kugeln durchlöchern; **~d with holes** völlig durchlöchert; **~d with woodworm** wurmzerfressen; **~d with corruption** von der Korruption zerfressen; **~d with troublemakers** von Störenfrieden durchsetzt; **~d with mistakes** voller Fehler.
riddle[2] *n* Rätsel *nt* ♦ **I'll ask you a ~** ich werde Ihnen ein Rätsel aufgeben; **to speak in ~s** in Rätseln sprechen.
ride [raɪd] *(vb: pret* **rode,** *ptp* **ridden)** [1] *n* **(a)** *(in vehicle, on bicycle)* Fahrt *f; (on horse)* Ritt *m; (for pleasure)* Ausritt *m* ♦ **to go for a ~** eine Fahrt machen/reiten gehen; **after a hard ~ across country** nach einer langen Überlandfahrt/einem langen Ritt querfeldein; **he gave the child a ~ on his back** er ließ das Kind auf den Schultern reiten; **cycle/car/coach ~** Rad-/Auto-/Busfahrt *f;* **to go for a ~ in the car** mit dem Auto wegfahren, eine Fahrt (mit dem Auto) machen; **to take sb for a ~** *(in car etc)* mit jdm eine Fahrt machen; *(inf)* jdn anschmieren *(inf);* **he gave me a ~ into town in his car** er nahm mich im Auto in die Stadt mit; **it's my first ~ in a Rolls/in a train** ich fahre zum ersten Mal in einem Rolls Royce/Zug; **can I have a ~ on your bike?** kann ich mal mit deinem Rad fahren?; **3 ~s on the merry-go-round** 3 Karussellfahrten; **to have a ~ in a helicopter** in einem Hubschrauber fliegen; **we had a ~ in a taxi/train** wir sind in einem Taxi/Zug gefahren; **it's an 80p ~ from the station** ab Bahnhof kostet die Fahrt 80 Pence; **the R~ of the Valkyries** der Ritt der Walküren.
(b) *(quality of ~)* **this car gives a smooth/bumpy ~** mit diesem Auto fährt es sich sanft/unsanft.
(c) *(path for horses)* Reitweg *m.*
[2] *vi* **(a)** *(on a horse etc, Sport)* reiten *(on* auf *+dat)* ♦ **to go riding** reiten gehen; **the jockey was riding just under 65 kilos** der Jockey brachte knapp 65 kg auf die Waage; **Harold Wilson ~s again!** *(fig hum)* Harold Wilson ist wieder da!
(b) *(go in vehicle, by cycle etc)* fahren ♦ **he was riding on a bicycle** er fuhr mit einem Fahrrad; **to ~ on a bus/in a car/in a train/in a cart** in einem Bus/Wagen/Zug/Schubkarren fahren; **to ~ away** *or* **off/down** weg- *or* davon-/hinunterfahren.
(c) *(fig: float)* **the seagull ~s on the wind** die Möwe läßt sich vom Wind tragen; **the moon was riding high in the sky** der Mond zog hoch am Himmel dahin; **he's riding high** *(fig)* er schwimmt ganz oben; **to ~ at anchor** *(ship)* vor Anker liegen; **we'll just have to let the matter** *or* **to let things ~ for a while** wir müssen einfach für eine Weile den Dingen ihren Lauf lassen; **... but I'll let it ~** ich lasse es vorerst einmal.
(d) *(horse)* **to ~ well** gut laufen.
[3] *vt* **(a)** *horse, donkey etc* reiten mit *or* auf *(+dat),* reiten; *bicycle, motorbike* fahren mit, fahren ♦ **I have never ridden a bicycle/a motorbike** ich bin noch nie Rad/Motorrad gefahren; **may I ~ your bike?** darf ich mit deinem Fahrrad fahren?; **he rode his horse away/back** *etc* er ritt mit seinem Pferd weg/zurück *etc;* **he rode him hard** er ritt es scharf; **he rode the horse into the stable** er ritt das Pferd in den Stall; **Jason will be ridden by H. Martin** Jason wird unter H. Martin laufen; **to ~ a race** bei einem Rennen reiten; **to ~ a good race** (bei einem Rennen) gut reiten; **they had ridden 10 km** sie waren 10 km geritten/gefahren; **they had ridden all the way** sie waren den ganzen Weg geritten/gefahren; **he rode the country looking for ...** er durchritt/durchfuhr das ganze Land auf der Suche nach ...; **the birds riding the wind** die Vögel, die sich vom Wind tragen lassen; **the ship rode the waves** das Schiff trieb auf den Wellen; **witches ~ broomsticks** Hexen reiten auf einem Besen; **to ~ a horse to death** ein Pferd zu Tode reiten; **to ~ an argument to death** ein Argument totreden; *see also* **ridden.**
(b) *(US inf: torment)* piesacken *(inf),* schikanieren, zusetzen *(+dat)* ♦ **don't ~ him too hard** treibt's nicht so toll mit ihm.
◆**ride about** *or* **around** *vi (on horse etc)* herumreiten; *(in vehicle, on motorcycle)* herumfahren; *(on bicycle)* herumradeln *(inf),* herumfahren.
◆**ride behind** *vi (on same horse, bicycle)* hinten sitzen; *(on different horse/bicycle)* hinterherreiten; hinterherfahren.
◆**ride down** *vt sep* **(a)** *(trample)* umreiten. **(b)** *(catch up with)* einholen.
◆**ride out** [1] *vt sep* überstehen ♦ **to ~ ~ the storm** *(lit, fig)* den Sturm überstehen.
[2] *vi (on horse)* ausreiten, einen Ausritt machen.
◆**ride up** *vi* **(a)** *(horseman)* heranreiten; *(motorcyclist etc)* heranfahren. **(b)** *(skirt etc)* hochrutschen.
rider ['raɪdəʳ] *n* **(a)** *(person) (on horse)* Reiter(in *f*) *m; (on bicycle, motorcycle)* Fahrer(in *f*) *m.* **(b)** *(addition)* Zusatz *m; (to document, will etc)* Zusatzklausel *f; (to bill)* Allonge *f; (to jury's verdict)* zusätzliche Empfehlung ♦ **I'd just like to add one ~ to that** zusätzlich (dazu) möchte ich noch eins sagen.
ridge [rɪdʒ] [1] *n* **(a)** *(raised strip) (on fabric, cardboard etc)* Rippe *f; (on corrugated iron)* Welle *f; (on sand)* Rippelmarke *f; (on ploughed land)* Grat *m; (in sea: reef)* Riff *nt* ♦ **a ~ of hills/mountains** eine Hügelkette/ein Höhenzug *m;* **a ~ of high pressure** *(Met)* ein Hochdruckkeil *m.*
(b) *(of hills, mountains)* Rücken, Kamm *m; (pointed, steep)* Grat *m; (of roof)* First *m; (of nose)* Rücken *m.*
[2] *vt rocks, land, sand* zerfurchen.
ridge: ~ pole *n (of tent)* Firststange *f;* **~ tent** *n* Firstzelt *nt;* **~ tile** *n* Firstziegel *m;* **~way** *n* Gratweg *m.*
ridicule ['rɪdɪkjuːl] [1] *n* Spott *m* ♦ **to hold sb/sth up to ~** sich über jdn/etw lustig machen; **she's an object of ~** alles macht sich über sie lustig; **to become an object of ~** der Lächerlichkeit preisgegeben werden.
[2] *vt* verspotten, verlachen.
ridiculous [rɪ'dɪkjʊləs] *adj* lächerlich ♦ **don't be ~** red keinen Unsinn; **to make oneself (look) ~** sich lächerlich machen.
ridiculously [rɪ'dɪkjʊləslɪ] *adv see adj.*
ridiculousness [rɪ'dɪkjʊləsnɪs] *n* Lächerlichkeit *f.*
riding ['raɪdɪŋ] *n* Reiten *nt* ♦ **I enjoy ~** ich reite gern.
riding *in cpds* Reit-; **~ breeches** *npl* Reithosen, Breeches *pl;* **a pair of ~ breeches** eine Reithose; **~ crop** *n* Reitgerte *f;* **~ habit** *n* Reitkostüm, Reitkleid *nt;* **~ jacket** *n* Reitjacke *f;* **~-light** *n (Naut)* Ankerlicht *nt;* **~ master** *n* Reitlehrer *m;* **~ whip** *n* Reitpeitsche *f.*
rife [raɪf] *adj* **(a)** *(widespread) disease, corruption* weit verbreitet ♦ **to be ~** grassieren; *(rumour)* umgehen. **(b)** *(full of)* **~ with** voll von, voller *+gen;* **the garden was ~ with weeds** der Garten strotzte vor Unkraut.
riffle ['rɪfl] *vt (also* **~ through)** *pages* blättern durch; *cards* mischen.
riffraff ['rɪfræf] *n* Pöbel *m,* Gesindel *nt.*
rifle[1] ['raɪfl] *vt town* plündern; *(also* **~ through)** *sb's pockets, drawer, till, house* durchwühlen.
rifle[2] *n (gun) Gewehr nt mit gezogenem Lauf; (for hunting)* Büchse *f* ♦ **the R~s** *(Mil)* ≃ die Schützen *pl.*
rifle: ~ butt *n* Gewehrkolben *m;* **~man** *n* (Gewehr)schütze *m;* **~ range** *n* Schießstand *m;* **~ shot** *n* Gewehrschuß *m;* **within ~ range** *or* **shot** in Schußweite (eines Gewehrs).
rift [rɪft] *n* **(a)** Spalt *m* ♦ **~ valley** Grabenbruch *m.* **(b)** *(fig: in friendship)* Riß *m; (Pol also)* Spalt *m.*
rig [rɪg] [1] *n* **(a)** *(Naut)* Takelage, Takelung *f.* **(b)** *(oil ~)* (Öl)förderturm *m; (offshore)* Ölbohrinsel *f.* **(c)** *(inf: outfit: also* **~-out)** Ausrüstung *f* ♦ **in full ~** in großer Aufmachung, in voller Montur *(inf).* **(d)** *(US inf: articulated lorry)* Sattelschlepper *m.*
[2] *vt* **(a)** *(Naut)* auftakeln. **(b)** *(fig) election, market etc* manipulieren ♦ **it was ~ged!** das war Manipulation.
◆**rig out** *vt sep (inf) (equip)* ausstaffieren *(inf); (dress)* auftakeln *(inf).*
◆**rig up** *vt sep ship* auftakeln; *equipment* aufbauen; *(fig) (make)* improvisieren; *(arrange)* arrangieren.
rigger ['rɪgəʳ] *n (Naut)* Takler *m.*
rigging ['rɪgɪŋ] *n* **(a)** *(Naut) (action)* Auftakeln *nt; (ropes)* Tauwerk *nt.* **(b)** *(inf: dishonest interference)* Manipulation, Schiebung *(inf) f.*
▼ **right** [raɪt] [1] *adj* **(a)** *(just, fair, morally good)* richtig, recht *(S Ger)* ♦ **it isn't ~ to lie** es ist nicht richtig *or* recht zu lügen; **he thought it ~ to warn me** er hielt es für richtig, mich zu warnen; **it seemed only ~ to give him the money** es schien richtig, ihm das Geld zu geben; **it's only ~ (and proper)** es ist nur recht und billig; **it is only ~ to point out that ...** es ist nur recht und billig, wenn man darauf hinweist, daß ...; **to do the ~ thing by sb** sich jdm gegenüber anständig benehmen.
▼ **(b)** *(true, correct) answer, solution, time, train* richtig ♦ **to be ~** *(person)* recht haben; *(answer, solution)* richtig sein, stimmen; *(clock)* richtig gehen; **you're quite ~** Sie haben ganz recht; **how ~ you are!** *(inf)* da haben Sie ganz recht!; **you were ~ to refuse** *or* **in refusing** Sie hatten recht, als Sie ablehnten; **my guess was ~** ich habe richtig geraten; **let's get it ~ this time!** mach es dieses Mal richtig; *(in reporting facts etc)* sag es dieses Mal richtig; **to put** *or* **set ~** *error* korrigieren; *clock* richtig stellen; *situation* wieder in Ordnung bringen; **I tried to put things ~ after their quarrel** ich versuchte, nach ihrem Streit wieder einzulenken; **to put** *or* **set sb ~** jdn berichtigen; **put me ~ if I'm wrong** korrigieren *or* verbessern Sie mich, wenn ich unrecht habe; *see also category (d).*
(c) *(proper) clothes, document* richtig ♦ **what's the ~ thing to do in this case?** was tut man da am besten?; **to come at the ~ time** zur rechten Zeit kommen; **to do sth the ~ way** etw richtig machen; **that is the ~ way of looking at it** das ist die richtige Einstellung; **the ~ man for the job** der rechte *or* richtige Mann für die Stelle; **Mr/Miss R~** *(inf)* der/die Richtige *(inf);* **we will do what is ~ for the country** wir werden tun, was für das Land gut ist; **to know the ~ people** die richtigen Leute kennen; **more than is ~** mehr als recht ist.
(d) *(well)* **the medicine soon put** *or* **set him ~** die Medizin hat ihn schnell wiederhergestellt *or* wieder auf die Beine gebracht; **I don't feel quite ~ today** ich fühle mich heute nicht ganz wohl; **to be as ~ as rain** *(Brit)* kerngesund sein; *(after accident)* keine Schramme abbekommen haben *(inf);* **to put the**

➤ LANGUAGE IN USE: **right: 1b → 11.1, 13**

engine ~ den Motor reparieren; **the plumber put things ~** der Klempner brachte alles wieder in Ordnung; **to be in one's ~ mind** klar bei Verstand sein; **he's not ~ in the head** (*inf*) bei ihm stimmt's nicht im Oberstübchen (*inf*); *see* **all ~**.

(e) (*phrases*) **~!, ~-oh!** (*Brit inf*), **~ you are!** (*Brit inf*) gut, schön, okay (*inf*); **~ on!** (*esp US sl*) super! (*sl*); **that's ~!** (*correct, true*) das stimmt!; **that's ~, dear, put it on the table** schön, stell es bitte auf den Tisch; **so they came in the end — is that ~?** und so kamen sie schließlich — wirklich?; **~ enough!** (das) stimmt!; **it's a ~ mess in there** (*inf*) das ist vielleicht ein Durcheinander hier (*inf*); **he's a ~ fool!** (*inf*) er ist wirklich doof (*inf*); **you're a ~ one** (*inf*) du bist mir der Richtige (*inf*).

(f) (*opposite of left*) rechte(r, s) ◆ **~ hand** rechte Hand; **I'd give my ~ hand to know the answer** ich würde was drum geben, wenn ich die Antwort wüßte (*inf*); **on your ~ hand you see the bridge** rechter Hand *or* rechts sehen Sie die Brücke.

[2] *adv* **(a)** (*straight, directly*) direkt; (*exactly also*) genau ◆ **~ in front/ahead of you** direkt *or* genau vor Ihnen; **go ~ on** gehen/fahren Sie geradeaus weiter; **~ away, ~ off** (*immediately*) sofort, schnurstracks (*inf*); **~ off** (*at the first attempt*) auf Anhieb (*inf*); **~ now** (*at this very moment*) in diesem Augenblick; (*immediately*) sofort; **~ here** genau hier; **~ in the middle** genau *or* direkt in der/die Mitte; **~ at the beginning** gleich am Anfang; **I'll be ~ with you** ich bin gleich da; **it hit me ~ on the face** der Schlag traf mich genau *or* voll ins Gesicht.

(b) (*completely, all the way*) ganz ◆ **~ round the house** ganz um das Haus herum; (*inside*) durch das ganze Haus; **rotten ~ through** durch und durch verfault *or* (*fig*) verdorben; **pierced ~ through** mitten durchgestochen.

(c) (*correctly*) richtig ◆ **to guess/answer ~** richtig raten/antworten; **you did ~ to refuse** es war richtig (von Ihnen) abzulehnen; **if everything goes ~** wenn alles klappt (*inf*); **nothing goes ~ for them** nichts klappt bei ihnen (*inf*), bei ihnen läuft alles schief (*inf*); **if I get you ~** (*inf*) wenn ich Sie (da) richtig verstehe; **I'll see you ~** (*inf*) ich werde aufpassen, daß Sie nicht zu kurz kommen (*inf*); *see* **serve**.

(d) (*old, dial: very*) sehr ◆ **the R~ Honourable John Smith MP** (*not old, dial*) der Abgeordnete John Smith.

(e) (*opposite of left*) rechts ◆ **it is ~ of the bridge** es ist rechts von der Brücke; **turn ~** biegen Sie rechts ab; **~ of centre** (*Pol*) rechts von der Mitte; **~, left and centre** (*everywhere*) überall; **to be cheated ~, left and centre** (*inf*) *or* **~ and left** (*inf*) von vorne bis hinten betrogen werden (*inf*); **to owe money ~, left and centre** (*inf*) bei Gott und der Welt Schulden haben (*inf*).

[3] *n* **(a)** *no pl* (*moral, legal*) Recht *nt* ◆ **he doesn't know ~ from wrong** er kann Recht und Unrecht nicht auseinanderhalten; **I want to know the ~s and wrongs of it first** ich möchte erst beide Seiten kennenlernen; **to be in the ~** im Recht sein.

(b) (*entitlement*) Recht *nt*; (*to sth also*) Anrecht *nt*, Anspruch *m* ◆ **(to have) a ~ to sth** ein (An)recht *or* einen Anspruch auf etw (*acc*) (haben); **to have a** *or* **the ~ to do sth** ein *or* das Recht haben, etw zu tun; **what ~ have you to say that?** mit welchem Recht sagen Sie das?; **by what ~?** mit welchem Recht?; **he is within his ~s** das ist sein gutes Recht; **by ~s** rechtmäßig, von Rechts wegen; **in one's own ~** selber, selbst; **the divine ~ (of kings)** das Gottesgnadentum; *see* **civil ~s**.

(c) (*Comm*) **~s** *pl* Rechte *pl* ◆ **to have the (sole) ~s to sth** die (alleinigen) Rechte an etw (*dat*) haben; **~s issue** (*St Ex*) Aktienausgabe *f*.

(d) to put *or* **set sth to ~s** etw (wieder) in Ordnung bringen; **to put things** *or* **the world to ~s** die Welt verbessern.

(e) (*not left*) rechte Seite ◆ **to drive on the ~** rechts fahren; **to keep to the ~** sich rechts halten, rechts bleiben; **on my ~** rechts (von mir); **on** *or* **to the ~ of the church** rechts von der Kirche; **the R~** (*Pol*) die Rechte; **those to the ~ of him** (*Pol*) diejenigen, die weiter rechts stehen/standen als er.

[4] *vt* **(a)** (*return to upright position*) aufrichten.

(b) (*make amends for*) *wrong* wiedergutmachen.

(c) the problem should ~ itself (*fig*) das Problem müßte sich von selbst lösen.

right: ~ angle *n* rechter Winkel; **at ~ angles (to)** rechtwinklig (zu); **~-angled** ['raɪt,æŋgld] *adj* rechtwinklig.

righteous ['raɪtʃəs] *adj* **(a)** rechtschaffen; (*pej*) selbstgerecht (*pej*). **(b)** *indignation* gerecht; *anger also* heilig.

righteously ['raɪtʃəslɪ] *adv* rechtschaffen.

righteousness ['raɪtʃəsnɪs] *n* Rechtschaffenheit *f*.

rightful ['raɪtfʊl] *adj* **(a)** *heir, owner* rechtmäßig. **(b)** *punishment* gerecht.

rightfully ['raɪtfəlɪ] *adv see adj* rechtmäßig; gerechterweise.

right: ~-hand drive *adj* rechtsgesteuert; **~-handed** *adj person* rechtshändig; *punch, throw also* mit der rechten Hand; **~-hander** *n* (*punch*) Rechte *f*; (*person*) Rechtshänder(in *f*) *m*; **~-hand man** *n* rechte Hand; **~-hand side** *n* rechte Seite.

rightist ['raɪtɪst] [1] *n* (*Pol*) Rechte(r) *mf*.

[2] *adj* rechtsorientiert.

rightly ['raɪtlɪ] *adv* **(a)** (*correctly*) **he said, ~, that ...** er sagte sehr richtig, daß ...; **I don't ~ know** ich weiß nicht genau. **(b)** (*justifiably*) mit *or* zu Recht ◆ **~ or wrongly** ob das nun richtig ist/war oder nicht; **and ~ so** und zwar mit Recht.

right: ~-minded *adj* vernünftig; **~ of way** *n* (*across property*) Durchgangsrecht *nt*; (*Mot: priority*) Vorfahrt(srecht *nt*) *f*; **it's his ~ of way, he has the ~ of way** (*Mot*) er hat Vorfahrt; **~-thinking** *adj* vernünftig; **~ wing** *n* (*Sport, Pol*) rechter Flügel; **he's the ~ wing** (*Sport*) er ist (der) Rechtsaußen; **~-wing** *adj* (*Pol*) rechtsorientiert; **~-wing extremist** Rechtsextremist(in *f*) *m*; **~-wing extremism** Rechtsextremismus *m*; **~-winger** *n* (*Sport*) Rechtsaußen *m*; (*Pol*) Rechte(r) *mf*.

> ➤ LANGUAGE IN USE: **rightly: a → 11.1, 13, 26.3 b → 26.3**

rigid ['rɪdʒɪd] *adj* (*lit*) *board, material, frame* starr, steif; (*fig*) *person, character* strikt, streng, stur (*pej*); *discipline, principles* streng, strikt; (*inflexible*) unbeugsam; *interpretation* genau, stur (*pej*); *specifications* genau festgelegt, strikt; *system* starr, unbeugsam ◆ **~ with fear** starr *or* steif vor Angst.

rigidity [rɪ'dʒɪdɪtɪ] *n see adj* Starrheit, Steifheit *f*; Striktheit, Strenge, Sturheit (*pej*) *f*; Unbeugsamkeit *f*; Genauigkeit *f*.

rigidly ['rɪdʒɪdlɪ] *adv stand etc* starr, steif; (*fig*) *behave, treat* streng, strikt; *oppose* stur, strikt; (*inflexibly*) unbeugsam.

rigmarole ['rɪgmərəʊl] *n* Gelaber *nt*; (*process*) Gedöns *nt* (*inf*) ◆ **to go through the whole** *or* **same ~ again** nochmal mit demselben Gelaber/Gedöns anfangen.

rigor *n* (*US*) *see* **rigour**.

rigor mortis ['rɪgə'mɔːtɪs] *n* die Toten- *or* Leichenstarre.

rigorous ['rɪgərəs] *adj* (*strict*) *person, character, discipline, rule, structure, method* streng, strikt; *measures* rigoros; (*accurate*) *book-keeping, work* peinlich genau; *analysis, tests* gründlich; (*harsh*) *climate* streng ◆ **with ~ precision/accuracy** mit äußerster Präzision/peinlicher Genauigkeit.

rigour, (*US*) **rigor** ['rɪgə[r]] *n* **(a)** *no pl* (*strictness*) Strenge, Striktheit *f* ◆ **to punish with ~** hart *or* streng bestrafen; **the full ~ of the law** die ganze Strenge des Gesetzes. **(b) ~s** *pl* (*of climate, famine etc*) Unbilden *pl*.

rig-out ['rɪgaʊt] *n* (*inf*) *see* **rig 1 (c)**.

rile [raɪl] *vt* (*inf*) ärgern, reizen.

rill [rɪl] *n* (*poet*) Bächlein *nt*.

rim [rɪm] *n* (*of cup, bowl*) Rand *m*; (*of hat also*) Krempe *f*; (*of spectacles also*) Fassung *f*; (*of wheel*) Felge *f*, Radkranz *m*.

rime¹ [raɪm] *n see* **rhyme**.

rime² *n* (*liter*) (Rauh)reif *m*.

rimless ['rɪmlɪs] *adj spectacles* randlos.

rimmed [rɪmd] *adj* mit Rand; *wheel* Felgen- ◆ **gold-~ spectacles** Brille *f* mit Goldfassung *or* -rand.

rind [raɪnd] *n* (*of cheese*) Rinde *f*; (*of bacon*) Schwarte *f*; (*of fruit*) Schale *f*.

ring¹ [rɪŋ] [1] *n* **(a)** Ring *m*; (*for swimmer*) Schwimmring *or* -reifen *m*.

(b) (*circle*) Ring *m*; (*in tree trunk*) Jahresring *m* ◆ **the ~s of Saturn** die Saturnringe *pl*; **to have ~s round one's eyes** (dunkle) Ringe unter den Augen haben; **to stand in a ~** im Kreis stehen; **to run ~s round sb** (*inf*) jdn in die Tasche stecken (*inf*).

(c) (*group*) (*Pol*) Gruppe *f*; (*of dealers, spies*) Ring *m*.

(d) (*enclosure*) (*at circus*) Manege *f*; (*at exhibition*) Ring *m*; (*Horse-racing*) Buchmacherring *m*; (*boxing ~*) (Box)ring *m*.

[2] *vt* (*surround*) umringen; (*in game: with hoop*) einen/den Ring werfen über (*+acc*); (*put ~ on or round*) *item on list etc* einkreisen, einen Kreis machen um; *bird* beringen; *bear, bull* einen/den Nasenring verpassen (*+dat*); *tree* ringeln.

ring² (*vb: pret* **rang**, *ptp* **rung**) [1] *n* **(a)** (*sound*) Klang *m*; (*~ing: of bell, alarm bell*) Läuten *nt*; (*of electric bell, also alarm clock, phone*) Klingeln *nt*; (*metallic sound: of swords etc*) Klirren *nt*; (*of crystal*) Klang *m* ◆ **there was a ~ at the door** es hat geklingelt *or* geläutet; **to hear a ~ at the door** die Türklingel hören; **give two ~s for the maid** für das Zimmermädchen zweimal läuten; **the ~ of the hammers** der Schall der Hämmer.

(b) (*esp Brit Telec*) Anruf *m* ◆ **to give sb a ~** jdn anrufen.

(c) (*fig*) Klang *m* ◆ **his voice had an angry ~ (in** *or* **to it)** seine Stimme klang etwas böse; **that has the** *or* **a ~ of truth (to** *or* **about it)** das klingt sehr wahrscheinlich.

(d) (*set*) **~ of bells** Glockenspiel *nt*.

[2] *vi* **(a)** *see n (a)* klingen; läuten; klingeln; klirren; klingen; (*hammers*) schallen ◆ **the (door)bell rang** es hat geläutet *or* geklingelt; **the bell rang for dinner** es hat zum Essen geläutet; **when the bell ~s** wenn es klingelt *or* läutet; (*churchbell*) wenn die Glocke läutet; **to ~ for sb** (nach) jdm läuten; **to ~ for sth** für etw läuten; **you rang, sir?** (gnädiger Herr,) Sie haben geläutet?; **please ~ for attention** bitte läuten; **to ~ at the door** (an der Tür) klingeln *or* läuten.

(b) (*esp Brit Telec*) anrufen.

(c) (*sound, resound*) (*words, voice*) tönen, schallen; (*music, singing*) erklingen (*geh*), tönen ◆ **to ~ false/true** falsch/wahr klingen; **my ears are ~ing** mir klingen die Ohren; **the valley rang with their shouts** das Tal hallte von ihren Rufen wider (*geh*); **the town rang with his praises** (*liter*) die ganze Stadt sang sein Lob; **his voice rang with emotion** seine Rührung klang (bei seinen Worten) deutlich durch; **his words still ~ in my ears** seine Worte klingen mir noch im Ohr.

[3] *vt* **(a)** *bell* läuten ◆ **to ~ the doorbell** (an der Tür) läuten *or* klingeln; **that/his name ~s a bell** (*fig inf*) das/sein Name kommt mir bekannt vor; **to ~ the hours** die Stunden schlagen; **to ~ the changes (on sth)** (*lit: on bells*) (etw) im Wechsel läuten; (*fig*) etw in allen Variationen durchspielen.

(b) (*esp Brit: also* **~ up**) anrufen.

◆**ring back** *vti sep* (*esp Brit*) zurückrufen.

◆**ring down** *vt sep* **to ~ the curtain ~** (*Theat*) den Vorhang niedergehen lassen; **to ~ ~ the curtain on sth** (*fig*) *on project* einen Schlußstrich unter etw (*acc*) ziehen; *on era* den Vorhang über etw (*acc*) fallen lassen.

◆**ring in** [1] *vi* **(a)** (*esp Brit Telec*) sich telefonisch melden (*to* in *+dat*). **(b)** (*US: clock in*) (zu Beginn der Arbeit) stempeln *or* stechen.

[2] *vt sep* **to ~ ~ the New Year** das neue Jahr einläuten.

◆**ring off** *vi* (*esp Brit Telec*) aufhängen, (den Hörer) auflegen.

◆**ring out** [1] *vi* **(a)** ertönen; (*bell also*) laut erklingen; (*shot also*) krachen; (*sound above others*) herausklingen. **(b)** (*US: clock out*) (am Ende der Arbeit) stempeln *or* stechen.

2 *vt sep* **to ~ ~ the Old Year** das alte Jahr ausläuten.

◆**ring up** *vt sep* **(a)** (*esp Brit Telec*) anrufen. **(b) to ~ ~ the curtain** (*Theat*) den Vorhang hochgehen lassen; **to ~ ~ the curtain on sth** (*fig*) den Vorhang zu etw hochgehen lassen. **(c)** (*cashier*) eintippen.

ring: ~-a-~-o'-roses *n* Ringelreihen *m*; **~ binder** *n* Ringbuch *nt*; **~bolt** *n* Ringbolzen *m*; **~ circuit** *n* Ringverzweigung *f*; **~dove** *n* Ringeltaube *f*.

ringer [ˈrɪŋəʳ] *n* **(a)** (*bell-~*) Glöckner *m*. **(b) to be a dead ~ for sb** (*sl*) jdm aufs Haar gleichen.

ring exercise *n* (*Sport*) Übung *f* an den Ringen.

ring-finger [ˈrɪŋˈfɪŋgəʳ] *n* Ringfinger *m*.

ringing [ˈrɪŋɪŋ] 1 *adj bell* läutend; *voice, tone* schallend ◆ **~ tone** (*Brit Telec*) Rufzeichen *nt*.

2 *n* (*of bell*) Läuten *nt*; (*of electric bell also, of phone*) Klingeln *nt*; (*in ears*) Klingen *nt*.

ringleader [ˈrɪŋˌliːdəʳ] *n* Anführer(in *f*) *m*.

ringlet [ˈrɪŋlɪt] *n* Ringellocke, Korkenzieherlocke *f*.

ring: ~master *n* Zirkusdirektor *m*; **~-pull** *n* (*on can*) Dosenring, Ring-pull *m*; **~-pull can** *n* Aufreißdose, Ring-pull-Dose *f*; **~ road** *n* (*Brit*) Umgehung(sstraße) *f*; **~side** *n* **at the ~side** am Ring; **~side seat** *n* (*Boxing*) Ringplatz *m*; (*in circus*) Manegenplatz *m*; **to have a ~side seat** (*fig*) einen Logenplatz haben; **~ spanner** *n* Ringschlüssel *m*; **~-tailed** *adj* mit Ringelschwanz; **~worm** *n* Scherpilzflechte *f*.

rink [rɪŋk] *n* Eisbahn *f*; (*roller-skating ~*) Rollschuhbahn *f*.

rinse [rɪns] 1 *n* **(a)** (*act*) Spülung *f* ◆ **to give sth a ~** *see vt (a)*; **have a ~** (*dentist*) bitte spülen.

(b) (*for hair*) Spülung *f*; (*colorant*) Tönung *f*.

2 *vt* **(a)** *clothes, hair* spülen; *plates* abspülen; *cup, mouth, basin* ausspülen ◆ **to ~ one's hands** sich (*dat*) die Hände abspülen; **to ~ the soap off one's hands** sich (*dat*) die Seife von den Händen abspülen.

(b) (*colour with a ~*) *hair* tönen ◆ **she ~d her hair black** sie hat sich (*dat*) das Haar schwarz getönt.

◆**rinse down** *vt sep car, wall* abspülen ◆ **to ~ sth ~ the plughole** etw den Abfluß hinunterspülen.

◆**rinse out** *vt sep* **(a)** *hair, tint, colour, soap, cup* ausspülen, auswaschen ◆ **to ~ ~ one's mouth** sich (*dat*) den Mund ausspülen. **(b)** (*wash quickly*) *clothes* auswaschen.

Rio (de Janeiro) [ˈriːəʊ(dədʒəˈnɪərəʊ)] *n* Rio (de Janeiro) *nt*.

riot [ˈraɪət] 1 *n* **(a)** (*Pol*) Aufstand, Aufruhr *m no pl*; (*by mob, football fans etc*) Krawall *m*, Ausschreitungen *pl*; (*fig: wild occasion*) Orgie *f* ◆ **there'll be a ~ if you announce that** wenn Sie das verkünden, gibt es einen Aufstand; **to run ~** (*people*) randalieren; (*vegetation*) wuchern; **his imagination runs ~** seine Phantasie geht mit ihm durch; **ivy had run ~ all over the house** Efeu hatte das ganze Haus überwuchert; **the R~ Act** (*Hist*) die Aufruhrakte; **to read sb the ~ act** (*fig*) jdm die Leviten lesen; **the ~ police/squad** die Bereitschaftspolizei/das Überfallkommando; **~ gear** Schutzausrüstung *f*; **~ shield** Schutzschild *m*.

(b) a ~ of colour(s) eine Farbenexplosion, eine Farbenorgie; **a ~ of reds and blues** eine Explosion von Rot- und Blautönen; **a ~ of flowers** ein wildes Blumenmeer.

(c) to be a ~ (*inf*) zum Schießen *or* Schreien sein (*inf*).

2 *vi* randalieren; (*revolt*) einen Aufruhr machen.

rioter [ˈraɪətəʳ] *n* Randalierer *m*; (*rebel*) Aufrührer *m*.

rioting [ˈraɪətɪŋ] *n* Krawalle *pl*; (*Pol also*) Aufstände *pl* ◆ **~ in the streets** Straßenkrawalle *or* -schlachten *pl*.

riotous [ˈraɪətəs] *adj* **(a)** *person, crowd* randalierend; *living, behaviour, child* wild. **(b)** (*inf*) wild (*inf*); (*hilarious*) urkomisch (*inf*) ◆ **we had a ~ time** es ging hoch her (*inf*); **a ~ success** ein Riesen- *or* Bombenerfolg (*inf*) *m*.

riotously [ˈraɪətəslɪ] *adv behave, live* wild ◆ **it was ~ funny** (*inf*) es war zum Schreien (*inf*).

RIP *abbr of* **rest in peace** R.I.P.

rip [rɪp] 1 *n* Riß *m*; (*made by knife etc*) Schlitz *m*.

2 *vt material, clothes* einen Riß machen in (*+acc*); (*stronger*) zerreißen; (*vandalize*) *pictures etc* zerschlitzen ◆ **you've ~ped your jacket** du hast einen Riß in der Jacke; du hast dir die Jacke zerrissen; **to ~ sth down the middle** etw mitten durchreißen; **to ~ open** aufreißen; (*with knife*) aufschlitzen.

3 *vi* **(a)** (*cloth, garment*) reißen.

(b) (*inf*) **the car ~s along** der Wagen rast dahin; **let her ~!** volle Pulle! (*inf*); **to let ~** loslegen (*inf*); **he let ~ a stream of complaints** er hat einen Schwall Beschwerden vom Stapel gelassen (*inf*); **he let ~ at me** er ist auf mich losgegangen (*inf*).

◆**rip down** *vt sep* herunterreißen; *old buildings* abreißen.

◆**rip off** *vt sep* **(a)** (*lit*) abreißen (*prep obj* von); *clothing* herunterreißen ◆ **he ~ped ~ her dress** er riß ihr das Kleid vom Leib. **(b)** (*sl*) *object, goods* mitgehen lassen (*inf*); *bank, shop, house* ausrauben; *person* schröpfen (*inf*), ausnehmen (*sl*).

◆**rip out** *vt sep* herausreißen (*of* aus).

◆**rip up** *vt sep* zerreißen; *road* aufreißen.

riparian [raɪˈpeərɪən] *adj* (*form*) Ufer- ◆ **~ right** Uferanliegerrecht *nt*.

rip-cord [ˈrɪpˌkɔːd] *n* Reißleine *f*.

ripe [raɪp] *adj* (*+er*) **(a)** *fruit, cheese* reif; (*fig*) *lips* voll. **(b)** (*mature*) reif ◆ **to live to a ~ old age** ein hohes Alter erreichen; **to be ~ for sth** (*fig*) für etw reif sein; **when the time is ~** wenn die Zeit dafür reif ist.

ripen [ˈraɪpən] 1 *vt* (*lit, fig*) reifen lassen.

2 *vi* reifen.

ripeness [ˈraɪpnɪs] *n* Reife *f*.

rip-off [ˈrɪpɒf] *n* (*inf*) Wucher, Nepp (*inf*) *m*; (*cheat*) Schwindel *m* ◆ **it's a ~** das ist Wucher *or* Nepp (*inf*)/Schwindel; **he'd been the victim of a ~** er war ausgenommen worden (*inf*).

riposte [rɪˈpɒst] 1 *n* (*retort*) scharfe Antwort, Gegenschlag *m*; (*Fencing*) Riposte *f*.

2 *vi* (*retort*) scharf erwidern, parieren; (*Fencing*) parieren und eine Riposte bringen.

ripper [ˈrɪpəʳ] *n* (*murderer*) Frauenmörder *m*.

ripping [ˈrɪpɪŋ] *adj* (*dated Brit inf*) herrlich, wunderbar.

ripple [ˈrɪpl] 1 *n* **(a)** (*in water*) kleine Welle; (*of crops*) sanftes Wogen *no pl* ◆ **little ~s spread out in the water** das Wasser kräuselte sich; **the wind blew across the grass in ~s** das Gras wogte im Wind.

(b) (*noise*) Plätschern *nt*; (*of waves*) Klatschen *nt* ◆ **a ~ of laughter** ein kurzes Lachen; (*girls'*) ein perlendes Lachen.

2 *vi* **(a)** (*undulate*) (*water*) sich kräuseln; (*crops*) wogen.

(b) (*murmur: water*) plätschern; (*waves*) klatschen.

3 *vt water* kräuseln; *corn* wogen lassen.

ripple effect *n* (*knock-on effect*) Nachwirkungen *pl*.

rip: ~-rap *n* (*Build*) Steinbettung, Steinschüttung *f*; **~-roaring** *adj* (*inf*) sagenhaft (*inf*); **~tide** *n* Kabbelung *f*.

▼ **rise** [raɪz] (*vb: pret* **rose**, *ptp* **risen**) 1 *n* **(a)** (*increase*) (*in gen*) (*in temperature, pressure, of tide, river*) Anstieg *m*, Steigen *nt no pl*; (*in number*) Zunahme *f*; (*in prices, bank rate also*) Steigerung *f*; (*St Ex*) Aufschwung *m* ◆ **a (pay) ~** (*Brit*) eine Gehaltserhöhung; **prices are on the ~** die Preise steigen; **there has been a ~ in the number of participants** die Zahl der Teilnehmer ist gestiegen; **a ~ in the population** ein Bevölkerungszuwachs *m*.

(b) (*upward movement*) (*of theatre curtain*) Hochgehen, Heben *nt*; (*of sun*) Aufgehen *nt*; (*Mus: in pitch*) Erhöhung *f* (*in gen*); (*fig: to fame, power etc*) Aufstieg *m* (*to* zu) ◆ **the ~ of the working classes** der soziale Aufstieg der Arbeiterklasse; **the ~ and fall of an empire** der Aufstieg und Niedergang eines Weltreichs; **to get a ~ out of sb** (*inf*) jdn zur Reaktion bringen.

(c) (*small hill*) Erhebung *f*; (*slope*) Steigung *f*.

(d) (*origin*) (*of river*) Ursprung *m* ◆ **the river has its ~ in** der Fluß entspringt in (*+dat*); **to give ~ to sth** etw verursachen; *to questions* etw aufwerfen; *to complaints* Anlaß zu etw geben.

2 *vi* **(a)** (*get up*) (*from sitting, lying*) aufstehen, sich erheben (*geh*), um zu gehen ◆ **to ~ from the table** vom Tisch aufstehen, sich vom Tisch erheben (*geh*); **to ~ in the saddle** sich im Sattel heben; **he rose from his sickbed to go and see her** er verließ sein Krankenlager, um sie zu sehen; **~ and shine!** (*inf*) raus aus den Federn! (*inf*); **the horse rose on its hind legs** das Pferd stellte sich auf die Hinterbeine; (*rear up*) das Pferd bäumte sich auf; **to ~ from the dead** (*liter, Bibl*) von den Toten auferstehen.

(b) (*go up*) steigen; (*smoke, mist etc also*) aufsteigen, emporsteigen; (*prices, temperature, pressure etc also*) ansteigen (*to* auf *+acc*); (*balloon, aircraft, bird*) (auf)steigen, sich heben (*geh*); (*lift*) hochfahren, nach oben fahren; (*theatre curtain*) hochgehen, sich heben; (*sun, moon, bread, dough*) aufgehen; (*wind, storm*) aufkommen, sich erheben; (*voice*) (*in volume*) sich erheben; (*in pitch*) höher werden; (*swimmer, fish*) hochkommen; (*new buildings*) entstehen; (*fig*) (*hopes*) steigen; (*anger*) wachsen, zunehmen; (*stomach*) sich heben ◆ **to ~ to the surface** an die Oberfläche kommen; **the fish are rising well** die Fische beißen gut; **he won't ~ to any of your taunts** er läßt sich von dir nicht reizen; **the idea/image rose in his mind** ihm kam der Gedanke/das Bild tauchte vor ihm auf; **I can't ~ to £10** ich kann nicht bis £ 10 gehen; **her spirits rose** ihre Stimmung hob sich; **his voice rose to screaming pitch** seine Stimme wurde kreischend *or* schrill; **to ~ to a crescendo** zu einem Crescendo anschwellen; **the colour rose to her cheeks** die Röte stieg ihr ins Gesicht.

(c) (*ground*) ansteigen; (*mountains, hills, castle*) sich erheben ◆ **the mountain ~s to 3,000 metres** der Berg erhebt sich auf 3.000 m; **where the hills ~ against the sky** wo sich die Berge gegen den Himmel abheben.

(d) (*fig: in society, rank*) **to ~ in the world/in society** es zu etwas bringen; **to ~ from nothing** sich aus dem Nichts empor- *or* hocharbeiten; **he rose to be President/a captain** er stieg zum Präsidenten/Kapitän auf; *see* **rank¹**.

(e) (*adjourn*) (*assembly*) auseinandergehen; (*meeting*) beendet sein ◆ **the House rose at 2 a.m.** (*Parl*) das Haus beendete die Sitzung um 2 Uhr morgens; **Parliament will ~ on Thursday** das Parlament geht Donnerstag in Ferien.

(f) (*originate: river*) entspringen.

(g) (*also* **~ up**) (*revolt: people*) sich empören, sich erheben; (*rebel: one's soul etc*) sich empören ◆ **to ~ (up) in protest/anger (at sth)** (*people*) sich protestierend (gegen etw) erheben/sich (gegen etw) empören; (*soul, inner being etc*) sich (gegen etw) auflehnen/zornig empören.

◆**rise above** *vi +prep obj insults etc* erhaben sein über (*+acc*), stehen über (*+dat*).

◆**rise up** *vi* (*person*) aufstehen, sich erheben (*geh*); (*mountain etc*) sich erheben; *see also* **rise 2 (g)**.

risen [ˈrɪzn] 1 *ptp of* **rise**.

2 *adj* (*Rel*) **the ~ Lord** der Auferstandene; **Jesus Christ is ~!** Christ ist erstanden!

riser [ˈraɪzəʳ] *n* **(a)** (*person*) **to be an early ~** Frühaufsteher(in *f*) *m* sein, früh aufstehen; **to be a late ~** spät aufstehen, ein Langschläfer *m*/eine Langschläferin sein (*inf*). **(b)** (*of stair*) Setzstufe *f*. **(c)** (*for gas, water etc*) Steigrohr *nt*, Steigleitung *f*.

risibility [ˌrɪzɪˈbɪlɪtɪ] *n* (*liter: disposition*) Lachlust *f*.

➤ LANGUAGE IN USE: **rise: 1a** → 17.2

risible ['rɪzɪbl] *adj* (*liter: laughable*) lächerlich, lachhaft.

rising ['raɪzɪŋ] 1 *n* (**a**) (*rebellion*) Erhebung *f*, Aufstand *m*.
(**b**) (*of sun, star*) Aufgehen *nt*, Aufgang *m*; (*of barometer, prices, river*) (An)steigen *nt*; (*from dead*) Auferstehung *f*; (*of theatre curtain*) Hochgehen *nt*; (*of ground*) Steigung *f*, Anstieg *m* ◆ **the ~ and falling of ...** das Auf und Ab (+*gen*)...
(**c**) (*adjournment: of Parliament etc*) Auseinandergehen *nt*.
2 *adj* (**a**) *sun* aufgehend; *tide, barometer, prices, hopes* steigend; *wind* aufkommend; *anger, fury* wachsend ◆ **~ damp** Bodenfeuchtigkeit *f*; **the ~ sap** der aufsteigende Saft.
(**b**) (*fig*) **a ~ young doctor** ein aufstrebender junger Arzt; **a ~ politician** ein kommender Politiker; **the ~ generation** die kommende Generation.
3 *adv* (*inf*) **she's ~ sixteen** sie ist fast sechzehn.

▼ **risk** [rɪsk] 1 *n* (**a**) Risiko *nt*; (*in cpds*) -gefahr *f* ◆ **to take** *or* **run ~s/a ~** Risiken/ein Risiko eingehen; **to take** *or* **run the ~ of doing sth** das Risiko eingehen, etw zu tun; **you('ll) run the ~ of losing a lot of money** Sie laufen dabei Gefahr, eine Menge Geld zu verlieren; **there is no ~ of his coming** *or* **that he will come** es besteht keine Gefahr, daß er kommt; **at one's own ~** auf eigene Gefahr, auf eigenes Risiko; **goods sent at sender's ~** Warenversand auf Risiko des Senders; **at the ~ of seeming stupid** auf die Gefahr hin, dumm zu erscheinen; **at the ~ of his life** unter Einsatz seines Lebens; **children at ~** gefährdete Kinder; **some jobs are at ~** einige Stellen sind gefährdet; **to put sb/sth at ~** jdn gefährden/etw riskieren.
(**b**) (*Insur*) Risiko *nt* ◆ **fire ~** Feuerrisiko; **he's a bad accident ~** bei ihm besteht ein hohes Unfallrisiko; **to be a good/bad ~** (*Fin*) gute/schlechte Bonität haben; *see* **security ~**.
▼ 2 *vt* (**a**) *career, future, reputation, savings* riskieren, aufs Spiel setzen; *life also* wagen; *see* **neck**.
(**b**) *defeat, quarrel, accident* riskieren; (*venture*) *criticism, remark also* wagen ◆ **you'll ~ losing your job/falling** Sie riskieren dabei, Ihre Stelle zu verlieren/hinzufallen; **she won't ~ coming today** sie wird es heute nicht riskieren, zu kommen; **I'll ~ it** das riskiere ich, ich lasse es darauf ankommen.

risk capital *n* Risikokapital *nt*.

riskiness ['rɪskɪnɪs] *n* Riskantheit *f*.

risk: ~ management *n* Absicherung *f* von Risiken; **~ sharing** *n* Risikoteilung *f*.

risky ['rɪskɪ] *adj* (+*er*) (**a**) *enterprise, deed* riskant ◆ **it's ~, it's a ~ business** das ist riskant. (**b**) *joke, story* pikant, gewagt.

risotto [rɪ'zɒtəʊ] *n* Risotto *m*.

risqué ['ri:skeɪ] *adj* pikant, gewagt.

rissole ['rɪsəʊl] *n* ≃ Frikadelle *f*.

rite [raɪt] *n* Ritus *m* ◆ **burial ~s** Bestattungsriten *pl*.

ritual ['rɪtjʊəl] 1 *adj* rituell; *laws, objects* Ritual-.
2 *n* Ritual *nt*; (*pej also*) Zeremoniell *nt no pl* ◆ **he went through the same old ~** (*fig*) er durchlief dasselbe alte Ritual *or* Zeremoniell; **he went through the ~ of checking all the locks** er überprüfte nach dem üblichen Zeremoniell *or* Ritual, ob alles abgeschlossen war.

ritualism ['rɪtjʊəlɪzəm] *n* Ritualismus *m*.

ritualist ['rɪtjʊəlɪst] *n* Ritualist(in *f*) *m*; (*expert*) Ritualienforscher(in *f*) *m*.

ritualistic [,rɪtjʊə'lɪstɪk] *adj* rituell.

ritually ['rɪtjʊəlɪ] *adv slaughter* auf rituelle Art.

ritzy ['rɪtsɪ] *adj* (+*er*) (*sl*) nobel (*inf*), protzig (*pej inf*).

rival ['raɪvəl] 1 *n* Rivale *m*, Rivalin *f* (*for* um, *to* für); (*in love also*) Nebenbuhler(in *f*) *m* (*old*); (*Comm*) Konkurrent(in *f*) *m*.
2 *adj* (*to* für) *claims, attraction* konkurrierend; *firm, enterprise also* Konkurrenz-.
3 *vt* (*in love, for affections*) rivalisieren mit; (*Comm*) konkurrieren mit ◆ **he can't ~ her in intelligence** er kann sich mit ihr in bezug auf Intelligenz nicht messen; **his achievements ~ even yours** seine Leistungen können sich sogar mit deinen messen; **I can't ~ that** da kann ich nicht mithalten.

rivalry ['raɪvəlrɪ] *n* Rivalität *f*; (*Comm*) Konkurrenzkampf *m*.

rive [raɪv] *pret* **~d**, *ptp* **riven** ['rɪvn] *vt* (*old, liter*) spalten ◆ **riven by grief** (*fig*) von Schmerz zerrissen.

river ['rɪvəʳ] *n* Fluß *m*; (*major*) Strom *m* ◆ **down ~** fluß-/stromabwärts; **up ~** fluß-/stromaufwärts; **the ~ Rhine** (*Brit*), **the Rhine ~** (*US*) der Rhein; **~s of blood/lava** Blut-/Lavaströme *pl*; *see* **sell**.

river *in cpds* Fluß-; **~ basin** *n* Flußbecken *nt*; **~bed** *n* Flußbett *nt*; **~ fish** *n* Flußfisch *m*; **~ fishing** *n* Flußangeln *nt*; **~-head** *n* Flußquelle *f*.

riverine ['rɪvəraɪn] *adj* (*form*) (*of river*) Fluß-; (*like river*) flußartig; *people* am Fluß wohnend.

river: ~ mouth *n* Flußmündung *f*; **~ police** *n* Wasserschutzpolizei *f*; **~side** 1 *n* Flußufer *nt*; **on/by the ~side** am Fluß; 2 *adj* am Fluß(ufer); **~ traffic** *n* Flußschiffahrt *f*.

rivet ['rɪvɪt] 1 *n* Niete *f*.
2 *vt* (*lit*) nieten; *two things* vernieten; (*fig*) *audience, attention* fesseln ◆ **his eyes were ~ed to the screen** sein Blick war auf die Leinwand geheftet; **it ~ed our attention** das fesselte uns *or* unsere Aufmerksamkeit; **~ed (to the spot) with fear** vor Angst wie festgenagelt; **~ joint** Nietnaht, Nietung *f*.

riveter ['rɪvɪtəʳ] *n* Nieter(in *f*) *m*; (*tool*) Nietmaschine *f*.

rivet(t)ing ['rɪvɪtɪŋ] 1 *n* Nieten *nt*.
2 *adj* (*fig*) fesselnd.

Riviera [,rɪvɪ'ɛərə] *n* **the (French)/Italian ~** die französische/italienische Riviera.

rivulet ['rɪvjʊlɪt] *n* Flüßchen *nt*, Bach *m*.

rm *abbr of* **room** Zim.

➤ LANGUAGE IN USE: **risk: 1a** → 2.3, 16.2 **2** → 2.3

RM *abbr of* **Royal Marines**.

RN *abbr of* (**a**) **Royal Navy**. (**b**) (*US*) **registered nurse**.

RNA *abbr of* **ribonucleic acid** RNS *f*.

RNLI (*Brit*) *abbr of* **Royal National Lifeboat Institution** ≃ DLRG *f*.

RNR *abbr of* **Royal Navy Reserve**.

RNVR *abbr of* **Royal Navy Volunteer Reserve**.

roach [rəʊtʃ] *n* Plötze *f*; (*inf: cock~*) Schabe *f*.

road [rəʊd] *n* (**a**) Straße *f* ◆ **"~ up"** „Straßenbauarbeiten"; **"~ narrows"** „Straßenverengung"; **by ~** (*send sth*) per Spedition; (*travel*) mit dem Bus/Auto *etc*; **she lives across the ~ (from us)** sie wohnt gegenüber (von uns); **my car is off the ~ just now** ich kann mein Auto momentan nicht benutzen; **my car has never been/is never off the ~** mein Auto war noch nie/ist nie in der Werkstatt; **I hope to put the car back on the ~ soon** ich hoffe, das Auto bald wieder fahren zu können; **this vehicle shouldn't be on the ~** das Fahrzeug ist nicht verkehrstüchtig; **he is a danger on the ~** er ist eine Gefahr für den Straßenverkehr; **to take to the ~** sich auf den Weg machen, losfahren; (*as tramp*) Vagabund werden; **to be on the ~** (*travelling*) unterwegs sein; (*theatre company*) auf Tournee sein; (*car*) fahren; **is this the ~ to London**? geht es hier nach London?; **the London ~** die Straße nach London; **"Westlands/London ~"** „Westlandsstraße/Londoner Straße"; **to have one for the ~** (*inf*) zum Abschluß noch einen trinken; **gentleman of the ~** Vagabund *m*.
(**b**) (*fig*) Weg *m* ◆ **you're on the right ~** (*lit, fig*) Sie sind auf dem richtigen Weg; **on the ~ to ruin/success** auf dem Weg ins Verderben/zum Erfolg; **somewhere along the ~ he changed his mind** irgendwann hat er seine Meinung geändert; **you're in my ~** (*dial inf*) du bist mir im Weg; **(get) out of the ~!** (*dial inf*) geh weg!; **any ~** (*dial inf*) *see* **anyhow**.
(**c**) **~s** *pl* (*Naut*) Reede *f*.
(**d**) (*US*) *abbr of* **railroad**.

road *in cpds* Straßen-; **~ accident** *n* Verkehrsunfall *m*; **~block** *n* Straßensperre *f*; **~-book** *n* Straßenatlas *m*; **~ construction** *n* Straßenbau *m*; **~ fund licence** *n* (*Brit*) ≃ Verkehrssteuer *f*; **~ haulage** *n* Spedition *f*; **~ haulier** *n* Spediteur *m*; **~hog** *n* (*inf*) Verkehrsrowdy *m* (*inf*); **~holding (ability)** *n* Straßenlage *f*; (*of tyres*) Griffigkeit *f*; **~house** *n* Rasthaus *nt*.

roadie ['rəʊdi:] *n* (*inf*) Roadie *m* (*inf*).

road: ~making *n* Straßenbau *m*; **~man** *n* (*inf*) Straßenbauarbeiter *m*; **~mender** *n* Straßenbauarbeiter *m*; **~ metal** *n* Straßenschotter *m*; **~pricing** *n* (*Brit*) Straßenbenutzungsgebühren *pl*; **~ race** *n* Straßenrennen *nt*; **~ racer** *n* (*bicycle*) *Rennrad nt für Straßenrennen*; **~ rage** *n* Aggressivität *f* im Straßenverkehr; **~roller** *n* Straßenwalze *f*; **~ safety** *n* Verkehrssicherheit *f*, Sicherheit *f* im Straßenverkehr; **~ sense** *n* Verkehrssinn *m*; **~ show** *n* (*Theat*) Tournee *f*; **~side** 1 *n* Straßenrand *m*; **along** *or* **by the ~side** am Straßenrand; 2 *adj stall, toilet* an der Straße; *inn, pub also* Straßen-; **~side repairs** (*professional*) Sofortdienst *m*; (*done alone*) Reparatur *f* am Straßenrand; **~sign** *n* (Straßen)verkehrszeichen *nt*; **~stead** *n* (*Naut*) Reede *f*.

roadster ['rəʊdstəʳ] *n* (*old*) (*car*) Vehikel *nt* (*inf*); (*bicycle*) Drahtesel *m* (*inf*).

road: ~sweeper *n* (*person*) Straßenkehrer(in *f*) *m*; (*vehicle*) Straßenkehrmaschine *f*; **~-test** 1 *n* Straßentest *m*; 2 *vt* probefahren; **~ transport** *n* Straßengüterverkehr *m*; **~-trials** *npl* (**~-test**) Straßentest *m*; (*rally*) Straßenwettbewerb *m*; **~-user** *n* Verkehrsteilnehmer *m*; **~way** *n* Fahrbahn *f*; **~work** *n* (*Sport*) Straßentraining *nt*; **~works** *npl* Straßenbauarbeiten *pl*; **~worthy** *adj* verkehrstüchtig.

roam [rəʊm] 1 *vt streets, countryside* wandern *or* ziehen durch ◆ **to ~ the (seven) seas** die sieben Meere durchkreuzen; **to ~ the streets** (*child, dog*) (in den Straßen) herumstreunen.
2 *vi* (herum)wandern; (*hum: hands*) wandern, sich verirren ◆ **to ~ about the house/streets** durch das Haus/die Straßen wandern; **to ~ about the world** in der Welt herumziehen.

◆**roam about** *or* **around** *vi* herumwandern; (*dogs, looters*) herumstreunen.

roamer ['rəʊməʳ] *n* Vagabund *m*; (*dog*) Herumstreuner *m*; (*child*) Stromer *m* (*inf*).

roaming ['rəʊmɪŋ] 1 *adj* (*fig*) *thoughts* wandernd.
2 *n* Herumwandern *nt* ◆ **this life of ~** dieses Vagabundenleben.

roan [rəʊn] 1 *adj horse* rötlich-grau.
2 *n* Rotschimmel *m*.

roar [rɔːʳ] 1 *vi* (*person, crowd, lion, bull*) brüllen (*with* vor +*dat*); (*fire in hearth*) prasseln; (*wind, engine, plane*) heulen; (*sea, waterfall*) tosen; (*thunder, forest fire*) toben; (*gun*) donnern ◆ **to ~ at sb** jdn anbrüllen; **the trucks ~ed past** die Lastwagen donnerten vorbei; **the car ~ed up the street** der Wagen donnerte die Straße hinauf; **he had them ~ing (with laughter)** sie brüllten vor Lachen.
2 *vt* (**a**) (*also* **~ out**) *order, song etc* brüllen.
(**b**) *engine* aufheulen lassen.
3 *n* (**a**) *no pl see vi* Gebrüll *nt*; Prasseln *nt*; Heulen *nt*; Tosen *nt*; Toben *nt*; Donnern *nt*.
(**b**) **~s of laughter** brüllendes Gelächter; **the ~s of the crowd/lion** das Brüllen der Menge/des Löwen.

roaring ['rɔːrɪŋ] 1 *adj see vi* brüllend; prasselnd; heulend; tosend; tobend; donnernd ◆ **the R~ Forties, the ~ forties** (*Geog*) stürmischer Teil des Ozeans (zwischen dem 39. und 50. Breitengrad); **~ drunk** (*inf*) sternhagelvoll (*inf*); **the ~ Twenties** die wilden zwanziger Jahre; **a ~ success** ein voller Erfolg, ein Bombenerfolg *m* (*inf*); **to do a ~ trade (in sth)** ein Riesengeschäft *nt* (mit etw) machen.
2 *n see* **roar 3**.

roast [rəʊst] 1 *n* Braten *m* ◆ **pork ~** Schweinebraten *m*.

[2] *adj pork, veal* gebraten; *chicken* Brat-, gebraten; *potatoes* in Fett im Backofen gebraten ◆ **~ beef** Roastbeef *nt*; **we had ~ pork** es gab Schweinebraten.

[3] *vt* **(a)** *meat* braten; *chestnuts, coffee beans, ore* rösten ◆ **to ~ oneself by the fire/in the sun** sich am Feuer/in der Sonne braten lassen; **to be ~ed alive** *(fig)* sich totschwitzen *(inf)*; *(by sun)* gebraten werden *(inf)*; *see also* **~ing**.
(b) *(inf: criticize)* ins Gericht gehen mit *(inf)*.

[4] *vi (meat)* braten; *(inf: person)* irrsinnig schwitzen *(inf)*; *(in sun)* in der Sonne braten; *see also* **~ing**.

roaster ['rəʊstə[r]] *n (oven)* Bratofen *m*, Bratröhre *f*; *(dish)* Bräter *m*; *(coffee ~)* Röstapparat *m*; *(for ore)* Röstofen *m*; *(chicken)* Brathähnchen *nt*; *(pig)* Spanferkel *nt* ◆ **it's a real ~ today!** *(inf)* das ist heute eine richtige Affenhitze *(inf)*.

roasting ['rəʊstɪŋ] [1] *n* **(a)** *(lit)* Braten *nt* ◆ **~ spit** Bratspieß *m*.
(b) *(inf) (criticism)* Verriß *m*; *(telling-off)* Standpauke *f* ◆ **to give sb/sth a ~** jdn/etw verreißen; jdm eine Standpauke halten.
[2] *adj* **(a)** *(inf: hot) days, weather* knallheiß *(inf)*.
(b) *(Cook)* zum Braten; *chicken* Brat-; *meat* Braten-.

rob [rɒb] *vt person* bestehlen; *(more seriously)* berauben; *shop bank* ausrauben; *orchard* plündern ◆ **to ~ sb of sth** *(lit, fig)* jdn einer Sache *(gen)* berauben *(geh)*, jdm etw rauben; *(lit also)* jdm etw stehlen; **I've been ~bed!** ich bin bestohlen worden!; *(had to pay too much)* ich bin geneppt worden *(inf)*; **to ~ the till** die Ladenkasse ausräumen *or* plündern; **he was ~bed of the pleasure of seeing her** es war ihm nicht vergönnt, sie zu sehen; **the shock ~bed him of speech** er hat vor Schreck die Stimme verloren; *(briefly also)* der Schreck hat ihm die Sprache verschlagen; **our team was ~bed** *(sl)* das ist nicht fair(, wir hätten gewinnen müssen).

robber ['rɒbə[r]] *n* Räuber *m*.

robbery ['rɒbərɪ] *n* Raub *m no pl*; *(burglary)* Einbruch *m (of in +acc)* ◆ **~ with violence** *(Jur)* Raubüberfall *m*; **at that price it's sheer ~!** *(inf)* das ist der reinste Nepp *(inf)*, das ist reiner Wucher *(inf)*; **the bank ~** der Überfall auf die Bank.

robe [rəʊb] [1] *n* **(a)** *(garment) (of office)* Robe *f*, Talar *m*; *(for priest also)* Rock *m*; *(for baby)* langes Kleidchen; *(esp US: for house wear)* Morgenrock, Haus- *or* Bademantel *m*; *(obs: gown)* Kleid *nt* ◆ **he was wearing his ~ of office** er war im Ornat; **ceremonial ~s** Festgewänder *pl*; **christening ~** Taufkleid *nt*.
(b) *(US: wrap)* Decke *f*.
[2] *vt (lit)* ankleiden, die Amtsrobe *or* den Ornat anlegen *(+dat)* ◆ **to ~ sb/sth in sth** *(lit, fig)* jdn/etw in etw *(acc)* kleiden.
[3] *vi (judge etc)* die Amtsrobe *or* den Ornat anlegen.

robin ['rɒbɪn] *n* Rotkehlchen *nt*; *see* **round ~**.

robot ['rəʊbɒt] *n* Roboter *m*; *(fig also)* Automat *m* ◆ **~ guidance, ~ pilot** Selbststeuerung *f*.

robotics [rəʊ'bɒtɪks] *n sing or pl* Robotertechnik, Robotik *f*.

robust [rəʊ'bʌst] *adj person, material, toy, machine* robust, widerstandsfähig; *build* kräftig, robust; *exercise* hart; *defence* stark; *appetite, humour* gesund, unverwüstlich; *structure* massiv, stabil; *style* markig; *wine* kernig.

robustness [rəʊ'bʌstnɪs] *n see adj* Robustheit *f*; Widerstandsfähigkeit *f*; Kräftigkeit *f*; Härte *f*; Stärke *f*; Gesundheit, Unverwüstlichkeit *f*; Massivität, Stabilität *f*; Markigkeit *f*; Kernigkeit *f*.

rock[1] [rɒk] [1] *vt* **(a)** *(swing)* schaukeln; *(gently: lull)* wiegen ◆ **to ~ a child to sleep** ein Kind in den Schlaf wiegen; **~ed by the waves** von den Wellen hin und her geschaukelt.
(b) *(shake) town* erschüttern, zum Beben bringen; *building also* ins Wanken bringen; *ship* hin und her werfen; *(fig inf) person* erschüttern ◆ **to ~ the boat** *(fig)* für Unruhe sorgen.
[2] *vi* **(a)** *(gently)* schaukeln ◆ **he was ~ing back and forth (in his chair)** er schaukelte (auf seinem Stuhl) vor und zurück.
(b) *(violently) (building, tree, post)* schwanken; *(ship)* hin und her geworfen werden; *(ground)* beben ◆ **they ~ed with laughter** sie schüttelten sich *or* bebten vor Lachen.
(c) *(~ and roll)* rocken.
[3] *n (pop music)* Rock *m*; *(dance)* Rock 'n' Roll *m* ◆ **~-and-roll** Rock and Roll, Rock 'n' Roll *m*; **to do the ~-and-roll** Rock 'n' Roll tanzen, rocken.

rock[2] *n* **(a)** *(substance)* Stein *m*; *(~ face)* Fels(en) *m*; *(Geol)* Gestein *nt* ◆ **caves hewn out of the ~** aus dem Fels(en) gehauene Höhlen; **hewn out of solid ~** aus massivem Stein/Fels gehauen; **built on ~** *(lit, fig)* auf Fels gebaut; **porous/volcanic ~** poröses/vulkanisches Gestein; **the study of ~s** Gesteinskunde *f*.
(b) *(large mass)* Fels(en) *m*; *(boulder also)* Felsbrocken *m*; *(smaller)* (großer) Stein ◆ **the R~ (of Gibraltar)** der Felsen von Gibraltar; **on the R~** *(inf)* in Gibraltar; **as solid as a ~** *structure* massiv wie ein Fels; *firm, marriage* unerschütterlich wie ein Fels; **the ship went on the ~s** das Schiff lief (auf die Felsen) auf; **on the ~s** *(inf) (with ice)* mit Eis; *(marriage etc)* kaputt *(inf)*; *(broke)* bankrott; **"danger, falling ~s"** „Steinschlaggefahr".
(c) *(sl: diamond)* Diamant *m* ◆ **~s** *(jewels)* Klunker *pl (inf)*.
(d) *no pl (Brit: sweet)* Zuckerstange *f*.

rock: ~-bottom [1] *n* der Tiefpunkt; **to touch/reach ~-bottom** auf dem Nullpunkt *or* Tiefpunkt sein/den Nullpunkt *or* Tiefpunkt erreichen; **this is ~-bottom** *(inf)* schlimmer kann es nicht werden; [2] *adj (inf) prices* niedrigste(r, s), Niedrigst-; **~ bun, ~ cake** *n* ≃ Rosinenhäufchen *nt*; **~ carving** *n* Felszeichnung *f*; *(writing)* Felsschrift *f*; *(action)* Ritzen *nt* in Fels; **~-climber** *n* (Felsen)kletterer(in *f*) *m*; **~ climbing** *n* Klettern *nt* (im Fels); **~ club** *n* Rockclub, Rockschuppen *(sl) m*; **~ crystal** *n* Bergkristall *m*.

rocker ['rɒkə[r]] *n* **(a)** *(of cradle etc)* Kufe *f* ◆ **to be/go off one's ~** *(sl)* übergeschnappt sein *(inf)*/überschnappen *(inf)*. **(b)** *(sl: person)* Rocker *m*. **(c)** *(Aut: also* **~ arm***)* Kipphebel *m*.

rockery ['rɒkərɪ] *n* Steingarten *m*.

rocket ['rɒkɪt] [1] *n* **(a)** Rakete *f*.
(b) *(Brit inf: reprimand) (from boss)* Zigarre *f (inf)*; *(from parent)* Anschiß *m (sl)* ◆ **to get a ~** eine Zigarre *(inf)*/einen Anschiß *(sl)* bekommen; **to give sb a ~** jdm eine Zigarre verpassen *(inf)*/jdm einen Anschiß geben *(sl)*.
[2] *vi (prices)* hochschießen, hochschnellen ◆ **to ~ to fame** über Nacht berühmt werden; *(person also)* kometenhaft aufsteigen; **he went ~ing past my door** *(inf)* er zischte *or* schoß (wie ein geölter Blitz) an meiner Tür vorbei *(inf)*.

rocket *in cpds* Raketen-; **~ attack** *n* Raketenangriff *m*; **~ launcher** *n* Raketenabschußgerät *nt*; *(on plane)* Raketenwerfer *m*; *(multiple)* Stalinorgel *f*; **~ plane** *n* Raketenflugzeug *nt*; **~-propelled** *adj* mit Raketenantrieb; **~ propulsion** *n* Raketenantrieb *m*; **~ range** *n* Raketenversuchsgelände *nt*; **within ~-range** mit Raketen zu erreichen.

rocketry ['rɒkɪtrɪ] *n* Raketentechnik *f*; *(rockets)* Raketen *pl*.

rocket: ~ship *n* Raketenträger *m*; *(~-propelled)* Raketenschiff *nt*; **~ silo** *n* Raketensilo *nt*.

rock: ~ face *n* Felswand *f*; **~ fall** *n* Steinschlag *m*; **~ garden** *n* Steingarten *m*.

rocking ['rɒkɪŋ]: **~ chair** *n* Schaukelstuhl *m*; **~ horse** *n* Schaukelpferd *nt*.

rock: ~ plant *n* Steinpflanze *f*; **~ rose** *n* Sonnenröschen *nt*; **~ salmon** *n (Brit)* Dorsch *m*; **~ salt** *n* Steinsalz *nt*.

rocky[1] ['rɒkɪ] *adj (unsteady)* wackelig *(also fig inf)*.

rocky[2] *adj (+er) mountain, hill* felsig; *road, path* steinig ◆ **the R~ Mountains, the Rockies** die Rocky Mountains *pl*.

rococo [rəʊ'kəʊkəʊ] [1] *n* Rokoko *nt*.
[2] *adj* Rokoko- ◆ **~ period** Rokoko *nt*, Rokokozeit *f*.

rod [rɒd] *n* **(a)** Stab *m*, Stange *f*; *(switch)* Rute, Gerte *f*; *(in machinery)* Stange *f*; *(for punishment, fishing)* Rute *f*; *(symbol of authority)* Stab *m* ◆ **~ bacterium** Stäbchenbakterie *f*.
(b) *(measure)* ≃ Rute *f (5,5 Yards)*.
(c) *(US sl: gun)* Schießeisen *nt (sl)*.

rode [rəʊd] *pret of* **ride**.

rodent ['rəʊdənt] *n* Nagetier *nt*.

rodeo ['rəʊdɪəʊ] *n* Rodeo *nt*.

rodomontade [ˌrɒdəmɒn'teɪd] *n (liter)* Prahlerei *f*, Bramarbasieren *nt (geh)*.

roe[1] [rəʊ] *n, pl* **-(s)** *(species: also* **~ deer***)* Reh *nt* ◆ **~ buck** Rehbock *m*; **~ deer** *(female)* Reh *nt*, Ricke *f (spec)*.

roe[2] *n, pl* **-** *(of fish)* Rogen *m* ◆ **hard ~** Rogen *m*; **soft ~** Milch *f*; **herring ~** Heringsrogen *m*.

roentgen ['rɒntjən] [1] *n* Röntgen *nt*.
[2] *adj* Röntgen-.

rogation [rəʊ'geɪʃən] *n (Eccl) (litany)* Litanei *f*; *(period: also* **R~** *or* **R~-tide***)* Bittwoche *f* ◆ **R~ Days** Bittage, Rogationstage *pl*; **R~ Sunday** (Sonntag *m*) Rogate *no art*.

roger ['rɒdʒə[r]] *interj* "~" „verstanden".

rogue [rəʊg] *n* **(a)** *(scoundrel)* Gauner, Schurke *m*; *(scamp)* Schlingel, Spitzbube *m* ◆ **~s' gallery** *(Police inf)* Verbrecheralbum *nt*; **they look like a real ~s' gallery** sie sehen wie Gauner aus. **(b)** *(Zool)* Einzelgänger(in *f*) *m* ◆ **~ elephant** Einzelgänger(-Elefant) *m*.

roguery ['rəʊgərɪ] *n no pl (wickedness)* Gaunerei, Schurkerei *f*; *(mischief)* Spitzbüberei *f*.

roguish ['rəʊgɪʃ] *adj* spitzbübisch; *(old: wicked)* schurkisch.

roguishly ['rəʊgɪʃlɪ] *adv see adj*.

roister ['rɔɪstə[r]] *vi (revel)* herumtollen.

roisterer ['rɔɪstərə[r]] *n* Krawallmacher *m*.

role [rəʊl] *n (Theat, fig)* Rolle *f* ◆ **in the ~ of Ophelia** in der Rolle der Ophelia; **~ model** *(Psych)* Rollenbild *nt*; **~-playing** Rollenspiel *nt* ◆ **~ reversal** *(Psych)* Rollentausch *m*;

roll [rəʊl] [1] *n* **(a)** *(of paper, netting, film, hair etc)* Rolle *f*; *(of fabric)* Ballen *m*; *(of banknotes)* Bündel *nt*; *(of butter)* Röllchen *nt*; *(of flesh, fat)* Wulst *m*, Röllchen *nt* ◆ **a ~ of paper/banknotes** eine Rolle Papier/ein Bündel *nt* Banknoten.
(b) *(Cook) (also* **bread ~***)* Brötchen *nt* ◆ **ham/cheese ~** Schinken-/Käsebrötchen *nt*; *see* **sausage ~** *etc*.
(c) *(movement, of sea, waves)* Rollen *nt*; *(of ship also)* Schlingern *nt*; *(somersault, Aviat)* Rolle *f*; *(of person's gait)* Schaukeln, Wiegen *nt* ◆ **to walk with a ~** einen schaukelnden Gang haben; **to do a ~** eine Rolle machen; **the ship gave a sudden ~** das Schiff schlingerte plötzlich; **the dog was having a ~ on the grass** der Hund wälzte sich im Gras; **to have a ~ in the hay with sb** *(inf)* mit jdm ins Heu gehen *(inf)*.
(d) *(sound) (of thunder)* Rollen *nt*; *(of drums)* Wirbel *m*; *(of organ)* Brausen *nt*.
(e) *(list, register)* Liste *f*, Register *nt*; *(of solicitors)* Anwaltsliste *f* ◆ **we have 60 pupils on our ~(s)** bei uns sind 60 Schüler angemeldet; **to call the ~** die Namensliste verlesen, die Namen aufrufen; **~ of honour** Ehrenliste *f*; *(plaque)* Ehrentafel *f*; **to strike sb** *or* **sb's name off the ~s** jdn *or* jds Namen von der Liste streichen; *see* **electoral ~**.
[2] *vi* **(a)** rollen; *(from side to side: ship)* schlingern; *(presses)* laufen; *(Aviat)* eine Rolle machen ◆ **to ~ over and over** rollen und rollen, kullern und kullern *(inf)*; **the children/stones ~ed down the hill** die Kinder/Steine rollten *or* kugelten *(inf)* den Berg hinunter; **tears were ~ing down her cheeks** Tränen rollten *or* kullerten *(inf)* ihr über die Wangen; **the newspapers were ~ing off the presses** die Zeitungen rollten von den Druckerpressen; **heads will ~!** *(fig)* da werden die Köpfe rollen!; **to keep the show ~ing** *(Theat inf)* die Show in Gang halten; **can you keep the ball** *or* **things ~ing while I'm away?** *(inf)*

können Sie den Laden in Schwung halten, solange ich weg bin? (*inf*); **the dog ~ed in the mud** der Hund wälzte sich im Schlamm; **he's ~ing in money** *or* **in it** (*inf*) er schwimmt im Geld (*inf*); **the words just ~ed off his tongue** die Worte flossen ihm nur so von der Zunge; **he ~s from side to side as he walks** er hat einen schaukelnden Gang.
(b) (*sound*) (*thunder*) rollen, grollen; (*drum*) wirbeln; (*organ*) brausen; (*echo*) rollen.
[3] *vt barrel, hoop, ball, car* rollen; *umbrella* aufrollen; *cigarette* drehen; *pastry, dough* ausrollen; *metal, lawn, road* walzen ◆ **to ~ one's eyes** die Augen rollen *or* verdrehen; **to ~ one's r's** das R rollen; **to ~ sth between one's fingers** etw zwischen den Fingern drehen; **to ~ one's own** (*cigarettes*) sich (*dat*) seine eigenen drehen; **to ~ wool into a ball** Wolle zu einem Knäuel aufwickeln; **the hedgehog ~ed itself into a ball** der Igel rollte sich zu einer Kugel zusammen; **he ~ed himself in a blanket** er wickelte sich in eine Decke; *see also* **rolled**.

◆**roll about** *vi* (*balls*) herumrollen *or* -kugeln (*inf*); (*ship*) schlingern; (*person, dog*) sich herumwälzen, sich wälzen; (*inf: with laughter*) sich kugeln (vor Lachen) (*inf*).

◆**roll along** [1] *vi* **(a)** (*ball*) entlang- *or* dahinrollen ◆ **we were ~ing ~ enjoying the countryside** wir rollten dahin und genossen die Landschaft. **(b)** (*inf: arrive*) aufkreuzen (*inf*), eintrudeln (*inf*).
[2] *vt sep* rollen.

◆**roll away** [1] *vi* (*ball, vehicle*) wegrollen; (*clouds, mist*) abziehen.
[2] *vt sep trolley, table* wegrollen.

◆**roll back** [1] *vi* zurückrollen; (*eyes*) nach innen rollen.
[2] *vt sep object, carpet* zurückrollen; *sheet* zurückschlagen ◆ **if only we could ~ ~ the years** wenn wir nur die Uhr zurückdrehen könnten.

◆**roll by** *vi* (*vehicle, procession*) vorbeirollen; (*clouds*) vorbeiziehen; (*time, years*) dahinziehen.

◆**roll down** [1] *vi* (*ball, person, tears*) hinunter-/herunterrollen *or* -kugeln (*inf*).
[2] *vt sep cart* hinunter-/herunterrollen.

◆**roll in** [1] *vi* herein-/hineinrollen; (*letters, money, contributions, suggestions*) hereinströmen; (*inf: person*) eintrudeln (*inf*).
[2] *vt sep barrel, trolley* hinein-/hereinrollen.

◆**roll off** *vi* **(a)** (*vehicle, procession*) weg- *or* davonrollen. **(b)** (*fall off*) (*object, person*) herunter-/hinunterrollen.

◆**roll on** [1] *vi* weiterrollen; (*time*) verfliegen ◆ **~ ~ the holidays**! wenn doch nur schon Ferien wären!
[2] *vt sep stockings* (die Beine) hochrollen.

◆**roll out** [1] *vt sep* **(a)** *barrel* hinaus-/herausrollen. **(b)** *pastry, dough* ausrollen; *metal* auswalzen. **(c)** (*inf*) *sentence, verse* produzieren (*inf*).
[2] *vi* hinaus-/herausrollen.

◆**roll over** [1] *vi* herumrollen; (*vehicle*) umkippen; (*person*) sich umdrehen ◆ **the dog ~ed ~ onto his back** der Hund rollte sich auf den Rücken.
[2] *vt sep person, animal, object* umdrehen; *patient* auf die andere Seite legen.

◆**roll past** *vi see* **roll by**.

◆**roll up** [1] *vi* **(a)** (*animal*) sich zusammenrollen (*into* zu).
(b) (*inf: arrive*) antanzen (*inf*).
(c) (*at fairground etc*) **~ ~**! treten Sie näher!
[2] *vt sep cloth, paper, map, umbrella* auf- *or* zusammenrollen; *sleeves, trouser legs* hochkrempeln.

roll: ~-bar *n* Überrollbügel *m*; **~call** *n* (*Sch*) Namensaufruf *m*; (*Mil*) (Anwesenheits)appell *m*; **~ collar** *n* Rollkragen *m*.

rolled [rəʊld] *adj blanket, paper etc* zusammengerollt; *tobacco* gerollt, gedreht ◆ **~ gold** Dubleegold *nt*; **~ oats** Haferflocken *pl*.

roller [ˈrəʊləʳ] *n* **(a)** (*for pressing, smoothing*) Rolle *f*; (*pastry ~*) Nudelholz *nt*; (*for lawn, road, Ind*) Walze *f*; (*paint ~*) Rolle *f*.
(b) (*for winding sth round*) Rolle *f*; (*hair ~*) (Locken)wickler *m* ◆ **to put one's hair in ~s** sich (*dat*) die Haare aufdrehen *or* eindrehen; **with her ~s in** mit Lockenwicklern (im Haar).
(c) (*for moving things*) Rolle *f*; (*log-shaped*) Rollklotz *m*.
(d) (*wave*) Brecher *m*.

roller: ~ bandage *n* Rollbinde *f*; **~ bearing** *n* Rollenlager *nt*; **~ blind** *n* Springrollo *nt*; **~ coaster** *n* Achterbahn, Berg-und-Tal-Bahn *f*; **~ skate** *n* Rollschuh *m*; **~-skate** *vi* Rollschuh laufen; **he ~-skated down the street** er lief *or* fuhr mit seinen Rollschuhen die Straße entlang; **~-skating** *n* Rollschuhlaufen *nt*; **~ towel** *n* Rollhandtuch *nt*.

rollick [ˈrɒlɪk] *vi* (*also* **~ about**) herumtollen.

rollicking [ˈrɒlɪkɪŋ] [1] *adj person* ausgelassen; *play, farce* Klamauk-; *occasion, life* wild ◆ **~ (good) fun** Mordsspaß *m* (*inf*); **to have a ~ time** richtig auf die Pauke hauen (*inf*).
[2] *n* (*Brit inf: telling-off*) **to get a ~** runtergeputzt werden (*inf*); **to give sb a ~** jdn runterputzen (*inf*).

rolling [ˈrəʊlɪŋ] *adj ship* schlingernd; *sea* rollend, wogend; *countryside* wellig ◆ **to have a ~ gait** einen schaukelnden Gang haben; **a ~ stone gathers no moss** (*Prov*) wer rastet, der rostet (*Prov*); **he's a ~ stone** er ist ein unsteter Bursche.

rolling: ~ mill *n* (*factory*) Walzwerk *nt*; (*machine*) Walze *f*; **~ pin** *n* Nudelholz *nt*, Teigrolle *f*; **~ stock** *n* (*Rail*) rollendes Material, Fahrzeuge *pl*; **~ train** *n* Walzstraße *f*.

roll: ~over [1] *n* (*Fin: of loan etc*) Laufzeitverlängerung *f*; [2] *attr* (*Brit Lottery*) **~over week** *Woche f mit Lotto-Jackpot, da es in der vorhergehenden Woche keinen Hauptgewinner gab;* **~over jackpot** Jackpot *m*; **~mop (herring)** *n* Rollmops *m*; **~-neck** *n* Rollkragen *m*; **~-neck(ed)** *adj* Rollkragen-; **~-on** *n* **(a)** Elastikschlüpfer *m*; **(b)** (*deodorant*) (Deo-)Roller *m*; **~-on-~-off, ~-on/~-off** *adj* Roll-on-roll-off-; **~-top** *n* Rolladen *m*; **~-top desk** *n* Rollschreibtisch *m*; **~-up** *n* Selbstgedrehte *f*; **to have a ~-up** sich (*dat*) eine drehen.

roly-poly [ˈrəʊlɪˈpəʊlɪ] [1] *adj* (*inf*) kugelrund, mopsig (*inf*).
[2] *n* **(a)** (*Brit: also* **~ pudding**) *mit Nierentalg hergestellter Strudel, der gebacken oder im Wasserbad gekocht wird.* **(b)** (*inf: plump child*) Rollmops (*inf*), Pummel (*inf*) *m*. **(c)** (*inf: somersault*) Purzelbaum *m* (*inf*).

ROM [rɒm] *n* (*Comput*) *abbr of* **read only memory** ROM *m or nt*.

romaine [ˌrəʊˈmeɪn] *n* (*US*) Romagna-Salat *m*, römischer Salat.

Roman [ˈrəʊmən] [1] *n* **(a)** (*Hist*) Römer(in *f*) *m*. **(b)** (*Typ: also* **~ type**) Magerdruck *m*.
[2] *adj* römisch; (*~ Catholic*) römisch-katholisch ◆ **r~** (*Typ*) mager; **r~ letters** (*Typ*) Magerdruck *m*.

roman à clef [ˈrəʊmɑ̃ŋæˈkleɪ] *n* Schlüsselroman *m*.

Roman: ~ candle *n* Goldrausch *m*; **~ Catholic** [1] *adj* (römisch-) katholisch; **the ~ Catholic Church** die (römisch-)katholische Kirche; [2] *n* Katholik(in *f*) *m*, (Römisch-)Katholische(r) *mf*.

romance [rəʊˈmæns] [1] *n* **(a)** (*book*) Phantasieerzählung *f*, Roman *m*; (*love-story*) Liebesgeschichte *f or* -roman *m*; (*adventure story*) Abenteuerroman *m*; (*tale of chivalry*) Ritterroman(ze *f*) *m*; (*no pl: romantic fiction*) Liebesromane *pl*; (*fig: lies*) Märchen *nt* ◆ **it's pure ~** es ist das reinste Märchen.
(b) (*love affair*) Romanze *f* ◆ **it's quite a ~** das ist eine richtige Liebesgeschichte.
(c) *no pl* (*romanticism*) Romantik *f* ◆ **an air of ~ pervaded the village** ein romantischer Zauber umgab das Dorf; **the ~ of foreign lands** der Zauber ferner Länder.
(d) (*Mus*) Romanze *f*.
(e) **R~** (*R~ languages*) die romanischen Sprachen *pl*.
[2] *adj* **R~** *language etc* romanisch.
[3] *vi* phantasieren, fabulieren.

romancer [rəʊˈmænsəʳ] *n* (*fig*) Phantast *m*.

Romanesque [ˌrəʊməˈnesk] *adj* romanisch.

Roman holiday *n* Spaß *m* auf Kosten anderer.

Romania [rəʊˈmeɪnɪə] *n* Rumänien *nt*.

Romanian [rəʊˈmeɪnɪən] [1] *adj* rumänisch.
[2] *n* **(a)** Rumäne *m*, Rumänin *f*. **(b)** (*language*) Rumänisch *nt*.

Romanic [rəʊˈmænɪk] *adj language* romanisch.

romanize [ˈrəʊmənaɪz] *vt* (*Hist*) romanisieren; (*Rel*) nach dem Katholizismus ausrichten.

Roman: ~ law *n* Römisches Recht; **~ nose** *n* Römernase *f*; **~ numeral** *n* römische Ziffer.

Romansh [rəʊˈmænʃ] [1] *adj* romantsch.
[2] *n* Romantsch *nt*.

romantic [rəʊˈmæntɪk] [1] *adj* (*Art, Liter, Mus: also* **R~**) romantisch; *person also* romantisch veranlagt ◆ **~ novel** Liebes-/Abenteuerroman *m*; **he played the ~ lead in several plays** er spielte in mehreren Stücken den romantischen Liebhaber.
[2] *n* (*Art, Liter, Mus: also* **R~**) Romantiker(in *f*) *m*.

romantically [rəʊˈmæntɪkəlɪ] *adv* romantisch.

romanticism [rəʊˈmæntɪsɪzəm] *n* (*Art, Liter, Mus: also* **R~**) Romantik *f* ◆ **his ~** sein romantisches Wesen.

romanticist [rəʊˈmæntɪsɪst] *n* (*Art, Liter, Mus: also* **R~**) Romantiker(in *f*) *m*.

romanticize [rəʊˈmæntɪsaɪz] [1] *vt* romantisieren, zu romantisch sehen.
[2] *vi* phantasieren.

Romany [ˈrəʊmənɪ] [1] *n* **(a)** Roma *mf*. **(b)** (*language*) die Zigeunersprache, Romani *nt*.
[2] *adj* Roma-.

Rome [rəʊm] *n* Rom *nt* ◆ **when in ~ (do as the Romans do)** (*prov*) ≃ andere Länder, andere Sitten (*Prov*); **~ wasn't built in a day** (*Prov*) Rom ist auch nicht an einem Tag erbaut worden (*Prov*); **all roads lead to ~** (*Prov*) viele Wege führen nach Rom (*prov*); **the Church of ~** die römische Kirche.

Romeo [ˈrəʊmɪəʊ] *n* Romeo *m*; (*fig*) Herzensbrecher *m* ◆ **a Latin ~** ein Papagallo *m* (*inf*).

Romish [ˈrəʊmɪʃ] *adj* (*pej*) Katholen- (*pej*), papistisch (*pej*).

romp [rɒmp] [1] *n* Tollerei *f* ◆ **the play was just a ~** das Stück war reiner Klamauk; **to have a ~** herumtollen *or* -toben.
[2] *vi* **(a)** (*children, puppies*) herumtollen *or* -toben ◆ **to ~ away** weghopsen; **he came ~ing up to me** er kam auf mich zugetollt.
(b) **to ~ home** (*win*) spielend gewinnen.
(c) **to ~ through sth** mit etw spielend fertig werden, etw mit der linken Hand erledigen.

rompers [ˈrɒmpəz] *npl* (*also* **pair of ~**) einteiliger Spielanzug.

rondeau [ˈrɒndəʊ], **rondel** [ˈrɒndəl] *n* (*Mus*) Rondeau *nt*; (*Liter also*) Rondel *nt*.

rondo [ˈrɒndəʊ] *n* (*Mus*) Rondo *nt*.

Roneo ® [ˈrəʊnɪəʊ] [1] *vt* (mit Matrize) kopieren.
[2] *n* Kopie *f*.

rood [ruːd] *n* **(a)** (*Archit*) Kruzifix *nt* ◆ **~ screen** Lettner *m* (*spec*). **(b)** (*Brit: measure*) Rute *f*, ≃ Viertelmorgen *m*.

roof [ruːf] [1] *n* Dach *nt*; (*of car also*) Verdeck *nt*; (*of cave, tunnel*) Gewölbe *nt* ◆ **the ~ of the mouth** der Gaumen; **the ~ of the world** das Dach der Welt; **a ~ of branches** ein Blätterdach *nt*; **without a ~ over one's head** ohne Dach über dem Kopf; **a room in the ~** ein Zimmer unter dem Dach; **to live under the same ~ as sb** mit jdm unter demselben Dach wohnen; **as long as you live**

under my ~ solange du deine Beine unter meinen Tisch streckst; **to go through the ~** *(inf) (person)* an die Decke gehen *(inf)*; *(prices etc)* untragbar werden; *see* **hit, raise.**
[2] *vt house* mit einem Dach decken ◆ **red-~ed** mit rotem Dach.
◆**roof in** *or* **over** *vt sep* überdachen.
roof *in cpds* Dach-; **~-garden** *n* Dachgarten *m.*
roofing ['ru:fɪŋ] *n* Material *nt* zum Dachdecken; *(action)* Dachdecken *nt* ◆ **~ felt** Dachpappe *f.*
roof: ~ lining *n (in car)* Himmel *m*; **~-rack** *n* Dach(gepäck)träger *m*; **~-top** *n* Dach *nt*; **to shout** *or* **scream sth from the ~-tops** *(fig)* etw überall herumposaunen *(inf)*, etw an die große Glocke hängen *(inf)*.
rook [rʊk] [1] *n* **(a)** *(bird)* Saatkrähe *f.* **(b)** *(swindler)* Betrüger, Gauner *m.* **(c)** *(Chess)* Turm *m.*
[2] *vt (swindle)* übers Ohr hauen *(inf)*, betrügen ◆ **to ~ sb of £5** jdm £ 5 abgaunern.
[3] *vi (Chess)* mit dem Turm ziehen.
rookery ['rʊkərɪ] *n* Kolonie *f.*
rookie ['rʊkɪ] *n (esp Mil sl)* Grünschnabel *m (inf)*.
room [ru:m] [1] *n* **(a)** *(in house, building)* Zimmer *nt*, Raum *m (geh)*; *(public hall, ball~ etc)* Saal *m*; *(hotel bed~)* Zimmer *nt*; *(office)* Büro *nt* ◆ **the whole ~ laughed** alle im Zimmer lachten; der ganze Saal lachte; **"~s to let"** „Zimmer zu vermieten"; **~ and board** Unterkunft mit Verpflegung; *(in lodgings also)* Zimmer mit Pension; **they used to live in ~s** sie haben früher in möblierten Zimmern gewohnt; **I'll come to your ~s** ich komme in deine Wohnung *or* auf deine Bude *(esp Univ inf)*.
(b) *no pl (space)* Platz *m*; *(fig)* Spielraum *m* ◆ **is there (enough) ~?** ist da genügend Platz?; **there is ~ for two (people)** es ist genügend Platz für zwei (Leute); **there is no ~ (for you/that box)** es ist nicht genug Platz (für dich/die Kiste); **to make ~ for sb/sth** für jdn/etw Platz machen *or* schaffen; **there is still ~ for hope** es besteht immer noch Hoffnung; **there is little ~ for hope** es besteht wenig Hoffnung; **there is no ~ for doubt** es kann keinen Zweifel geben; **there is ~ for improvement in your work** Ihre Arbeit könnte um einiges besser sein.
[2] *vi* zur Untermiete wohnen ◆ **~ing house** *(esp US)* Mietshaus *nt (mit möblierten Wohnungen)*.
room: ~ clerk *n (US)* Empfangschef *m*, Empfangsdame *f*; **~ divider** *n* Raumteiler *m.*
-roomed [-ru:md] *adj suf* **a 6-~ house** ein Haus mit 6 Zimmern; **a two-~ flat** eine Zweizimmerwohnung.
roomer ['ru:mə^r] *n (US)* Untermieter(in *f*) *m.*
roomful ['ru:mfʊl] *n* **there was quite a ~** das Zimmer war ganz schön voll; **a ~ of people** ein Zimmer voll(er) Leute.
roominess ['ru:mɪnɪs] *n* Geräumigkeit *f*; *(of garment)* Weite *f.*
room: ~mate *n* Zimmergenosse *m*, Zimmergenossin *f*; **~ service** *n* Zimmerservice, Etagendienst *m*; **~ temperature** *n* Zimmertemperatur *f*; **wine at ~ temperature** Wein mit *or* auf Zimmertemperatur.
roomy ['ru:mɪ] *adj (+er)* geräumig; *garment* weit.
roost [ru:st] [1] *n (pole)* Stange *f*; *(henhouse)* Hühnerhaus *nt or* -stall *m* ◆ **at ~** auf der Stange; **to come home to ~** *(fig)* auf den Urheber zurückfallen; *see* **cock, rule.**
[2] *vi (settle)* sich niederlassen; *(sleep)* auf der Stange schlafen.
rooster ['ru:stə^r] *n* Hahn *m.*
root [ru:t] [1] *n* **(a)** *(of plant, hair, tooth)* Wurzel *f* ◆ **~s** *(fig: of person)* Wurzeln; **by the ~s** mit der Wurzel; **to take ~** *(lit, fig)* Wurzeln schlagen; **her ~s are in Scotland** sie ist in Schottland verwurzelt; **she has no ~s** sie ist nirgends zu Hause; **to put down ~s in a country** in einem Land Fuß fassen; **~ and branch** *(fig)* mit Stumpf und Stiel; *see* **grass-roots, pull up.**
(b) *(fig) (source: of evil, of trouble etc)* Wurzel *f* ◆ **the ~ of the matter** der Kern der Sache; **to get to the ~(s) of the problem** dem Problem auf den Grund gehen; **that is** *or* **lies at the ~ of his behaviour** das ist der eigentliche Grund für sein Benehmen.
(c) *(Math, Ling)* Wurzel *f*; *(of equation)* Lösung *f*; *(Ling: base form also)* Stamm *m*; *see* **cube, square ~.**
[2] *vt plant* Wurzeln schlagen lassen bei ◆ **deeply ~ed** *(fig)* tief verwurzelt; **to be** *or* **stand ~ed to the spot** *(fig)* wie angewurzelt dastehen.
[3] *vi (plants etc)* Wurzeln schlagen *or* fassen.
◆**root about** *or* **around** *vi* herumwühlen *(for* nach).
◆**root for** *vi +prep obj team* anfeuern ◆ **to ~ ~ sb** jdm die Daumen drücken; *(esp Sport: cheer on)* jdn anfeuern.
◆**root out** *vt sep* **(a)** *(lit) see* **root up. (b)** *(fig) (remove) evil* mit der Wurzel ausreißen; *(find)* aufspüren, ausgraben *(inf)*.
◆**root up** *vt sep plant* herausreißen; *(dig up)* ausgraben.
root *in cpds* Wurzel-; **~ beer** *n (US) Art f Limonade*; **~ cause** *n* eigentlicher Grund; **~ crop** *n* Wurzelgemüse *nt no pl*; **~less** *adj plant* wurzellos; *(fig) person* ohne Wurzeln; **~ sign** *n (Math)* Wurzelzeichen *nt*; **~stock** *n (Bot)* Wurzelstock *m*; **~ vegetable** *n* Wurzelgemüse *nt*; **~ word** *n (Ling)* Wortwurzel *f*; *(base form also)* Wortstamm *m.*
rope [rəʊp] [1] *n* **(a)** Seil *nt*; *(Naut)* Tau *nt*; *(of bell)* Glockenstrang *m*; *(hangman's ~)* Strang, Strick *m* ◆ **a ~ of pearls** eine Perlenschnur; **to give sb more/plenty of ~** *(fig)* jdm mehr/viel Freiheit lassen; **give him enough ~ and he'll hang himself** *(fig)* der dreht sich *(dat)* schon selbst seinen Strick.
(b) *(Mountaineering)* Seil *nt* ◆ **a ~ of climbers** eine Seilschaft; **to put on the ~s** anseilen; **to be on the ~** angeseilt sein; **there were three of them on the ~** sie waren zu dritt am Seil.
(c) the ~s *(Boxing etc)* die Seile *pl* ◆ **to be on the ~s** *(boxer)* in den Seilen hängen; *(inf)* in der Klemme sein; **to know the ~s** *(inf)* sich auskennen; **to show sb the ~s** *(inf)* jdn in alles einweihen; **to learn the ~s** *(inf)* sich einarbeiten.
[2] *vt* **(a)** *box, case* verschnüren ◆ **to ~ sb to a tree** jdn an einen Baum binden; **to ~ sb's feet together** jdm die Füße zusammenbinden; **to ~ climbers (together)** Bergsteiger anseilen.
(b) *(lasso)* mit dem Lasso fangen.
◆**rope in** *vt sep* **(a)** *area* (mit einem Seil) abgrenzen; *cattle* mit einem Seil einfrieden. **(b)** *(fig)* rankriegen *(inf)* ◆ **how did you get ~d ~to that?** wie bist du denn da reingeraten? *(inf)*; **I don't want to get ~d ~to helping** ich will nicht, daß die mich zum Helfen rankriegen *(inf)*.
◆**rope off** *vt sep area* mit einem Seil abgrenzen.
◆**rope together** *vt sep objects* zusammenbinden; *climbers* an(einander)seilen.
◆**rope up** [1] *vi (climbers)* sich anseilen.
[2] *vt sep* anseilen.
rope *in cpds* Seil-; **~ ladder** *n* Strickleiter *f*; **~maker** *n* Seiler *m*; **~ sole** *n* (aus Seil) geflochtene Sohle; **~-soled** *adj* mit (aus Seil) geflochtener Sohle; **~walker** *n* Seiltänzer(in *f*) *m.*
rop(e)y ['rəʊpɪ] *adj (+er) (inf) (bad)* miserabel *(inf)*; *(worn)* mitgenommen ◆ **the battery is a bit ~** die Batterie pfeift auf dem letzten Loch *(inf)*.
rosary ['rəʊzərɪ] *n (Rel)* Rosenkranz *m* ◆ **to say the ~** den Rosenkranz beten.
rose[1] [rəʊz] *pret of* **rise.**
rose[2] [1] *n* **(a)** Rose *f* ◆ **wild ~** Wildrose *f*; **~-bush/-tree** Rosenbusch *m*/-bäumchen *nt*; **my life isn't all ~s** *(inf)* ich bin auch nicht auf Rosen gebettet; **life/marriage isn't all ~s** *(inf)* das Leben/die Ehe hat auch seine/ihre Schattenseiten; **an English ~** *(fig)* eine englische Schöne; **that will put the ~s back in your cheeks** davon bekommst du wieder etwas Farbe im Gesicht; **under the ~** *(fig liter)* unter dem Siegel der Verschwiegenheit; **the Wars of the R~s** die Rosenkriege *pl.*
(b) *(nozzle)* Brause *f*; *(rosette, Archit)* Rosette *f.*
(c) *(colour)* Rosarot, Rosenrot *nt.*
[2] *adj* rosarot, rosenrot.
rosé ['rəʊzeɪ] [1] *adj* rosé.
[2] *n* Rosé *m.*
roseate ['rəʊzɪɪt] *adj (liter)* rosenfarben.
rose *in cpds* Rosen-; **~bay** *n* Oleander *m*; **~bowl** *n* Rosenpokal *m*; **~-bud** *n* Rosenknospe *f*; **~-bud mouth** Rosenmund *m*; **~-coloured** *adj* rosarot, rosenrot; **to see everything/life through ~-coloured spectacles** alles/das Leben durch die rosarote Brille sehen; **~-cut** *adj* mit Rosetteschliff; **~ garden** *n* Rosengarten *m*; **~hip** *n* Hagebutte *f*; **~hip syrup** *n* Hagenbuttensirup *m.*
rosemary ['rəʊzmərɪ] *n* Rosmarin *m.*
rose: ~ petal *n* Rosen(blüten)blatt *nt*; **~-pink** [1] *adj* rosarot; [2] *n* Rosarot *nt*; **~ quartz** *n* Rosenquarz *m*; **~-red** *adj* rosenrot; **~ tree** *n* Rosenstrauch *m.*
Rosetta stone [rəʊ'zetə'stəʊn] *n* Stein *m* von Rosette.
rosette [rəʊ'zet] *n* Rosette *f.*
rose: ~water *n* Rosenwasser *nt*; **~ window** *n* (Fenster)rosette *f*; **~wood** *n* Rosenholz *nt.*
Rosicrucian [rəʊzɪ'kru:ʃən] [1] *n* Rosenkreu(t)zer *m.*
[2] *adj* der Rosenkreu(t)zer.
rosin ['rɒzɪn] [1] *n* Harz, Kolophonium *(esp Mus) nt.*
[2] *vt* mit Harz/Kolophonium behandeln.
ROSPA ['rɒspə] *n (Brit) abbr of* **Royal Society for the Prevention of Accidents** Königliche Gesellschaft für Unfallverhütung.
roster ['rɒstə^r] *n* Dienstplan *m*; *see* **duty ~.**
rostrum ['rɒstrəm] *n, pl* **rostra** ['rɒstrə] Tribüne *f*, Rednerpult *nt*; *(for conductor)* Dirigentenpult *nt.*
rosy ['rəʊzɪ] *adj (+er) (pink)* rosarot; *complexion, cheeks* rosig; *(rose-covered) fabric* mit Rosenmuster; *design* Rosen-; *(fig: promising) future, situation* rosig ◆ **to paint a ~ picture of sth** etw in den rosigsten Farben ausmalen.
rot [rɒt] [1] *n* **(a)** *(in teeth, plants, wood)* Fäulnis *f no pl* ◆ **to stop the ~** *(lit, fig)* den Fäulnisprozeß aufhalten; **then the ~ set in** *(fig)* dann setzte der Fäulnisprozeß *or* Verfall ein; *see* **dry ~.**
(b) *(inf: rubbish)* Quatsch *(inf)*, Blödsinn *(inf) m.*
[2] *vi (wood, material, rope)* verrotten, faulen; *(teeth, plant)* verfaulen; *(fig)* verrotten ◆ **to ~ in jail** im Gefängnis verrotten; **let him ~!** *(inf)* soll er doch vor die Hunde gehen! *(inf)*.
[3] *vt* verfaulen lassen.
◆**rot away** *vi* verfaulen.
rota ['rəʊtə] *n* **(a)** Dienstplan *m.* **(b)** *(Eccl)* **R~** Rota *f.*
Rotarian [rəʊ'teərɪən] [1] *adj* Rotarier-.
[2] *n* Rotarier *m.*
rotary ['rəʊtərɪ] *adj* **(a)** *motion* rotierend, Dreh-; *wheel* Rotations- ◆ **~ iron** Heißmangel *f*; **~ (printing) press** Rotationsmaschine *f*; **~ printer** Rotationsdrucker *m*; **~ pump** Kreiselpumpe *f.* **(b) R~ Club** Rotary Club *m.*
rotate [rəʊ'teɪt] [1] *vt* **(a)** *(around axis)* drehen, rotieren lassen; *(Math)* rotieren lassen; *(Comput)* rotieren. **(b)** *crops* im Wechsel anbauen; *work, jobs* turnusmäßig erledigen.
[2] *vi* **(a)** sich drehen, rotieren; *(Math)* rotieren. **(b)** *(crops)* im Wechsel angebaut werden; *(people: take turns)* sich (turnusmäßig) abwechseln.
rotating [rəʊ'teɪtɪŋ] *adj (revolving)* rotierend, sich drehend; *crops* im Wechsel angebaut.
rotation [rəʊ'teɪʃən] *n* **(a)** *no pl* Drehung, Rotation *(also Math) f*; *(of crops)*

Wechsel *m*, Rotation *f*; (*taking turns*) turnusmäßiger Wechsel ◆ **in** *or* **by ~** abwechselnd im Turnus; **~ of crops, crop ~** Fruchtwechsel *m*. **(b)** (*turn*) (Um)drehung, Rotation *f*.

rotatory [rəʊ'teɪtərɪ] *adj* **(a)** *movement* Dreh-, rotierend. **(b)** *schedule* turnusmäßig; *cultivation* abwechselnd.

rote [rəʊt] *n*: **by ~** *learn* auswendig; *recite* mechanisch.

rotgut ['rɒt,gʌt] *n* (*pej inf*) Fusel *m* (*inf*).

rotisserie [rəʊ'tɪsərɪ] *n* (*spit*) Grillspieß *m*; (*restaurant*) Rotisserie *f*.

rotogravure [,rəʊtəʊgrə'vjʊə^r] *n* Kupferdruck *m*.

rotor ['rəʊtə^r] *n* (*Aviat, Elec, Aut*) Rotor *m* ◆ **~ arm** Verteilerfinger *m*; **~ blade** Flügelblatt *nt*.

rot-proof ['rɒt,pru:f] *adj* fäulnissicher.

rotten ['rɒtn] *adj* **(a)** *vegetation, egg, tooth* faul; *wood also* morsch; *fruit also* verdorben; (*fig: corrupt*) korrupt, verdorben ◆ **~ to the core** (*fig*) durch und durch verdorben.

(b) (*inf*) (*bad*) scheußlich (*inf*); *weather, book, film, piece of work also* mies (*inf*); (*mean*) gemein, eklig; (*unwell*) elend, mies (*inf*) ◆ **what ~ luck!** so ein Pech!; **it's a ~ business** das ist eine üble Sache; **that was a ~ trick/a ~ thing to do** das war ein übler Trick/eine Gemeinheit.

rottenness ['rɒtnnɪs] *n see adj (a)* Faulheit *f*; Morschheit *f*; Verdorbenheit *f*; Korruptheit *f*.

rotter ['rɒtə^r] *n* (*dated Brit inf*) Lump *m*.

rotting ['rɒtɪŋ] *adj meat* verfaulend; *wood also* modrig; *carcass, bones also* verwesend.

rotund [rəʊ'tʌnd] *adj person* rund(lich); *object* rund; *speech, literary style* bombastisch, hochtrabend; *voice* voll.

rotunda [rəʊ'tʌndə] *n* Rotunde *f*, Rundbau *m*.

rotundity [rəʊ'tʌndɪtɪ] *n see adj* Rundlichkeit *f*; Rundheit *f*.

rouble, (*US*) **ruble** ['ru:bl] *n* Rubel *m*.

roué ['ru:eɪ] *n* (*dated*) Lebemann *m*.

rouge [ru:ʒ] [1] *n* Rouge *nt*.

[2] *vt* **to ~ one's cheeks** Rouge auflegen.

rough [rʌf] [1] *adj* (*+er*) **(a)** (*uneven*) *ground* uneben; *path, road also* holprig; *surface, skin, hands, cloth* rauh ◆ **~ edges** (*fig*) Ecken und Kanten *pl*.

(b) (*harsh*) *sound* hart; *voice, tone* rauh; *taste, wine* sauer; *words* grob, hart ◆ **to have ~ luck** schweres Pech haben; **to have a ~ tongue** (*fig*) eine scharfe Zunge haben; **he got the ~ side of her tongue** er bekam (von ihr) den Marsch geblasen.

(c) (*coarse, unrefined*) *person* ungehobelt; *manners also, speech* grob, roh.

(d) (*violent*) *person, child* grob, roh; *treatment, handling* grob, hart; *life* wüst; *children's game* wild; *match, sport, work* hart; *neighbourhood, manners, pub* rauh; *sea, weather, wind* rauh, stürmisch; *sea crossing* stürmisch ◆ **to be ~ with sb** grob mit jdm umgehen, unsanft mit jdm umspringen (*inf*); **~ play** (*Sport*) Holzerei *f* (*inf*); **~ stuff** Schlägereien *pl*/eine Schlägerei; **he had a ~ time (of it)** (*fig inf*) es ging ihm ziemlich dreckig (*inf*); **to be in for a ~ time (of it)** (*inf*) harten Zeiten entgegensehen; **the examiners gave him a ~ time** (*inf*) die Prüfer haben ihn ganz schön rangenommen (*inf*); **to make things ~ for sb** (*inf*) jdm Schwierigkeiten machen; **to be ~ on sb** (*Brit inf*) grob mit jdm umspringen; **it's ~ on him** (*Brit inf*) das ist hart für ihn.

(e) (*approximate, rudimentary*) *plan, calculation, estimate, translation* grob, ungefähr; *draft also* Roh-; *workmanship* schludrig; *justice* grob ◆ **~ copy** Konzept *nt*; **~ sketch** Faustskizze *f*; **~ paper** Konzeptpapier *nt*; **in its ~ state** im Rohzustand; **do your ~ work on the paper provided** macht euer Konzept auf dem dafür bereitgestellten Papier.

(f) (*inf: unwell*) **to feel ~** sich mies fühlen (*inf*); **the engine sounds pretty ~** der Motor hört sich nicht gerade gut an.

[2] *adv live* wüst; *play* wild ◆ **to sleep ~** im Freien übernachten.

[3] *n* **(a)** unwegsames Gelände; (*Golf*) Rauh *nt* ◆ **~ or smooth?** (*Sport*) untere oder obere Seite? (*des Schlägers, die durch einen roten Faden gekennzeichnet ist; zum Bestimmen, wer anfängt*); **she likes a bit of ~** (*sl: sexually*) sie hat's gern auf die grobe Tour (*sl*).

(b) (*unpleasant aspect*) **to take the ~ with the smooth** das Leben nehmen, wie es kommt.

(c) (*draft, sketch*) Rohentwurf *m* ◆ **in the ~** im Rohzustand.

(d) (*person*) Rowdy, Schläger *m*.

[4] *vt* **to ~ it** (*inf*) primitiv leben.

◆**rough out** *vt sep plan, drawing* grob entwerfen.

◆**rough up** *vt sep hair* zersausen, verstrubbeln (*inf*); (*sl*) *person* zusammenschlagen.

roughage ['rʌfɪdʒ] *n* Ballaststoffe *pl*.

rough: ~-and-ready *adj method, equipment* provisorisch; *work* zusammengehauen (*inf*), zusammengepfuscht (*inf*); *person* rauh(beinig); **~-and-tumble** *n* (*play*) Balgerei *f*; (*fighting*) Keilerei *f*; **after the ~-and-tumble of life in the navy** nach seinem wilden Leben in der Marine; **~ book** *n* (*Sch*) Schmierheft *nt*; **~cast** (*vb: pret, ptp* **~cast**) [1] *n* Rauhputz *m*; [2] *vt* rauh verputzen; **~ diamond** *n* (*lit*) Rohdiamant *m*; **he's a ~ diamond** er ist rauh, aber herzlich; **~-dry** *vt* einfach trocknen.

roughen ['rʌfn] [1] *vt ground* uneben machen; *skin, cloth* rauh machen, rauh werden lassen; *surface* aufrauhen.

[2] *vi* **(a)** (*skin*) rauh werden.

(b) (*sound*) hart werden; (*voice*) rauh werden.

(c) (*treatment*) hart werden; (*neighbourhood*) verrohen; (*sea, wind, weather*) rauh *or* stürmisch werden.

rough: ~-hew *vt timber* grob behauen; **~-house** (*inf*) [1] *n* Schlägerei *f*; [2] *vt* herumstoßen.

roughly ['rʌflɪ] *adv* **(a)** (*not gently*) grob, roh; *play* rauh; *answer, order* grob, hart. **(b)** *make, sew, sketch* grob. **(c)** (*approximately*) ungefähr ◆ **~ (speaking)** grob gesagt.

roughneck ['rʌf,nek] *n* (*inf*) Grobian *m*; (*thug*) Schläger *m*.

roughness ['rʌfnɪs] *n see adj* **(a)** Unebenheit *f*; Holprigkeit *f*; Rauheit *f*. **(b)** Härte *f*; Rauheit *f*; saurer Geschmack; Grobheit *f*. **(c)** Ungehobeltheit *f*; Grobheit, Roheit *f*. **(d)** Grobheit *f*, Roheit *f*; Härte *f*; Wüstheit *f*; Wildheit *f*; Rauheit *f*. **(e)** Grobheit *f*.

rough: ~ note book *n* (*Sch*) Schmierheft *nt*; **~rider** *n* Zureiter *m*; **~shod** *adv*: **to ride ~shod over sb/sth** rücksichtslos über jdn/etw hinweggehen; **~-spoken** *adj* **to be ~-spoken** sich ungehobelt ausdrücken; **~ trade** *n* (*sl*) (*ohne feste Bindungsabsicht ausgewählter*) *homosexueller Geschlechtspartner mit grobem oder gewalttätigem Verhalten*.

roulette [ru:'let] *n* Roulett(e) *nt*; *see* **Russian**.

Roumania [ru:'meɪnɪə] *etc see* **Romania** *etc*.

round [raʊnd] [1] *adj* (*+er*) **(a)** rund; (*Ling*) *vowel* gerundet ◆ **in rich ~ tones** mit vollem, rundem Klang; **~ arch** (*Archit*) Rundbogen *m*; **a ~ dozen** ein rundes Dutzend; **~ figure, ~ number** runde Zahl; **in ~ figures, that will cost 20 million** es kostet rund (gerechnet) *or* runde 20 Millionen.

(b) (*dated*) (*unequivocal*) *oath* kräftig; (*considerable*) *sum* rund; *pace* flott ◆ **in ~ terms** klar und deutlich.

[2] *adv* **there was a wall right ~** *or* **all ~** rings- *or* rundherum war eine Mauer; **you can't get through here, you'll have to go ~** Sie können hier nicht durch, Sie müssen außen herum gehen; **the long way ~** der Umweg, der längere Weg; **that's a long way ~** (*detour*) das ist ein großer Umweg; (*round field, town*) das ist eine ganz schöne Strecke; **for 5 km ~** im Umkreis von 5 km; **~ and ~** (*in circles, round field etc*) rundherum; (*all over the place*) überall herum; **I asked him ~ for a drink** ich lud ihn auf ein Glas Wein/Bier *etc* bei mir ein; **I'll be ~ at 8 o'clock** ich werde um 8 Uhr da sein; **spring will soon be ~ again** der Frühling steht bald wieder vor der Tür; **for the second time ~** zum zweitenmal; **all (the) year ~** das ganze Jahr über *or* hindurch; **all ~** (*lit*) ringsherum; (*fig: for everyone*) für alle; **drinks all ~!** eine Runde!; **taking things all ~, taken all ~** insgesamt gesehen, wenn man alles zusammennimmt; **a pillar 2 m ~** eine Säule mit 2 m Umfang; *see also vbs*.

[3] *prep* **(a)** (*of place etc*) um (... herum) ◆ **~ the table/fire** um den Tisch/das Feuer (herum); **the ribbon ~ her hat** das Band um ihren Hut; **all ~ the house** (*inside*) im ganzen Haus; (*outside*) um das ganze Haus herum; **~ and ~ the field** rings um das Feld herum; **to go ~ a corner/bend** um eine Ecke/Kurve gehen/fahren *etc*; **if you're ~ this way** wenn Sie in der Gegend sind; **to look** *or* **see ~ a house** sich (*dat*) ein Haus ansehen; **to show sb ~ a town** jdm eine Stadt zeigen, jdn in einer Stadt herumführen; **they went ~ the cafés looking for him** sie gingen in alle Cafés, um nach ihm zu suchen; **to talk ~ a subject** um ein Thema herumreden; **she's 75 cm ~ the waist** um die Taille mißt *or* ist sie 75 cm.

(b) (*approximately*) ungefähr ◆ **~ (about) 7 o'clock** ungefähr um 7 Uhr; **~ (about) £800** um die £ 800.

[4] *n* **(a)** (*circle etc*) Kreis, Ring *m*; (*slice: of bread, meat*) Scheibe *f* ◆ **a ~ of toast** eine Scheibe Toast; **a ~ of beef sandwiches** ein belegtes Brot mit Braten, eine Bratenschnitte.

(b) (*delivery* ~) Runde *f* ◆ **~(s)** (*of policeman, watchman, doctor*) Runde *f*; **to do** *or* **make one's ~(s)** seine Runde machen; **to be (out) on one's ~(s)** auf seiner Runde sein; **to go** *or* **make** *or* **do the ~s** (*visiting relatives etc*) die Runde machen; **to do the ~s of the clubs** *etc* (*inf*) durch die Klubs *etc* ziehen; **he does a paper ~** er trägt Zeitungen aus; **the daily ~** (*fig*) die tägliche Arbeit, der tägliche Trott (*pej*); **her life was one long ~ of parties** ihr Leben war eine einzige Folge von Partys.

(c) **to go the ~s** (*story etc*) reihum gehen; **the story went the ~s of the club** die Geschichte ging im ganzen Verein reihum; **this coat has gone the ~s of the family** dieser Mantel ist durch die ganze Familie gegangen.

(d) (*Sport, of election, talks*) Runde *f*; (*Show-jumping*) Durchgang *m* ◆ **a ~ (of drinks)** eine Runde; **a new ~ of negotiations** eine neue Verhandlungsrunde; **~ of ammunition** Ladung *f*; **10 ~s of bullets** 10 Schuß; **a ~ of 5 shots** eine Folge von 5 Schüssen; **a ~ of applause** Applaus *m*.

(e) (*Mus*) Kanon *m*.

(f) **in the ~** (*as a whole*) insgesamt; **theatre/sculpture in the ~** Arenatheater *nt*/Rund- *or* Vollplastik *f*.

[5] *vt* **(a)** (*make* ~) runden.

(b) (*go* ~) *corner, bend* gehen/fahren um; *cape* umfahren, herumfahren um; *obstacle* herumgehen/-fahren *etc* um.

◆**round down** *vt sep price, number* abrunden.

◆**round off** *vt sep* **(a)** *edges etc* abrunden.

(b) (*complete, perfect*) *list, series* voll machen; *speech, sentence, meal* abrunden; *debate, meeting, one's career* beschließen, abschließen ◆ **and now, to ~ ~, I would like to say ...** und zum Abschluß möchte ich nun sagen ...

◆**round on** *vi +prep obj* (*verbally*) anfahren; (*in actions*) herumfahren zu.

◆**round out** [1] *vt sep story etc* runden.

[2] *vi* sich runden.

◆**round up** *vt sep* **(a)** (*bring together*) *people* zusammentrommeln (*inf*); *cattle* zusammentreiben; *criminals* hochnehmen (*inf*); *facts* zusammentragen. **(b)** *price, number* aufrunden.

◆**round upon** *vi +prep obj see* **round on.**

roundabout ['raʊndəbaʊt] [1] *adj* **~ route** Umweg *m*; **we came a ~ way** *or* **by a ~ route** wir sind auf Umwegen gekommen, wir haben einen Umweg gemacht; **he has a ~ way of going about things** er geht sehr umständlich an die Dinge heran; **what a ~ way of doing things!** wie kann man nur so um-

ständlich sein!; **by ~ means** auf Umwegen; **~ phrase** (umständliche) Umschreibung.
[2] *n* (*Brit*) (*at fair*) Karussell *nt*; (*Mot*) Kreisverkehr *m*.

round: ~-cheeked ['raʊnd'tʃi:kt] *adj* mit runden Backen; **~-dance** *n* Reigen *m*; (*ballroom dance*) Rundtanz *m*.

rounded ['raʊndɪd] *adj* rundlich; *edges* abgerundet; *vowel* gerundet ◆ **(well-)~** *sentences, style* (wohl) abgerundet; *bosom, figure* wohlgerundet.

roundelay ['raʊndɪleɪ] *n* (*Mus*) Lied *nt* mit Refrain.

rounder ['raʊndə^r] *n* (*Brit Sport*) **to score a ~** einen Lauf machen.

rounders ['raʊndəz] *n sing* (*Brit Sport*) ≃ Schlagball *m*.

round: ~-eyed *adj* großäugig; **~-faced** *adj* rundgesichtig, mit rundem Gesicht; **R~head** *n* (*Brit Hist*) Rundkopf *m*; **~house** *n* (*esp US Rail*) Lokomotivschuppen *m*.

roundly ['raʊndlɪ] *adv* (*fig*) (*bluntly*) ohne Umschweife; (*dated: conscientiously*) gründlich, gewissenhaft.

round-necked ['raʊnd'nekt] *adj* mit rundem Ausschnitt.

roundness ['raʊndnɪs] *n* Rundheit *f*; (*of sound also*) Vollheit *f*; (*of vowel*) Gerundetheit *f*.

round: ~ robin *n* **(a)** (*petition*) gemeinsamer Antrag(, *bei dem die Unterschriften (oft) im Kreis angeordnet sind*); **(b)** (*esp US Sport*) Wettkampf *m*, in dem jeder gegen jeden spielt; **~-shouldered** ['raʊnd'ʃəʊldəd] *adj* mit runden Schultern; **to be ~-shouldered** runde Schultern haben.

roundsman ['raʊndzmən] *n, pl* **-men** [-mən] (*Brit*) Austräger *m* ◆ **milk ~** Milchmann(, *der an die Tür kommt*).

round: R~ Table *n* (*Hist*) (König Artus') Tafelrunde *f*; **~-table discussion/conference** Diskussion *f*/Konferenz *f* am runden Tisch; **~-the-clock** *adj* rund um die Uhr *not attr*; **~ trip** *n* Rundreise *f*; **~-trip ticket** *n* (*US*) Rückfahrkarte *f*; (*Aviat*) Hin- und Rückflug-Ticket *nt*; **~-up** *n* **(a)** (*act*) (*of cattle*) Zusammentreiben *nt*; (*of people*) Zusammentrommeln *nt* (*inf*); (*of criminals*) Hochnehmen *nt* (*inf*); (*of facts*) Sammlung *f*, Zusammentragen *nt*; **(b)** (*group of cattle*) zusammengetriebene Herde; **a ~-up of today's news** eine Zusammenfassung der Nachrichten vom Tage; **(c)** (*US: rodeo*) Rodeo *nt*; **~worm** *n* Fadenwurm *m*.

rouse [raʊz] [1] *vt* **(a)** (*from sleep, daydream etc*) wecken.
(b) (*stimulate*) *person* bewegen; *feeling, admiration, interest* wecken, wachrufen; *hatred, indignation* erregen; *suspicions* erwecken, erregen ◆ **to ~ sb (to anger)** jdn reizen; **to ~ sb to enthusiasm/hatred** jds Begeisterung entfachen/jds Haß anstacheln; **to ~ sb to action** jdn zum Handeln bewegen; **to ~ sb out of his/her apathy** jdn aus seiner Apathie aufrütteln; **to ~ the masses** die Massen aufrütteln; **~ yourself!** raff dich auf!
[2] *vi* (*waken*) wach werden; (*become active*) lebendig werden.

rousing ['raʊzɪŋ] *adj speech, sermon* zündend, mitreißend; *cheers, applause* stürmisch; *music* schwungvoll.

roustabout ['raʊstəbaʊt] *n* **(a)** (*US Naut*) (*deckhand*) Deckhelfer *m*; (*in dock*) Werft- *or* Hafenarbeiter *m*. **(b)** (*US: unskilled labourer*) Hilfsarbeiter *m*. **(c)** (*Austral*) Helfer *m* beim Scheren.

rout¹ [raʊt] [1] *n* **(a)** (*defeat*) Schlappe *f* ◆ **to put to ~** in die Flucht schlagen. **(b)** (*Jur: mob*) Bande, Rotte *f*.
[2] *vt* (*defeat*) in die Flucht schlagen.

rout² *vi* (*pig: also* **~ about**) herumwühlen.

◆**rout out** *vt sep* (*find*) aufstöbern; (*force out*) (heraus)jagen (*of* aus).

route [ru:t], (*US*) [raʊt] [1] *n* **(a)** Strecke, Route *f*; (*bus service*) Linie *f*; (*fig: in planning etc*) Weg *m* ◆ **shipping/air ~s** Schifffahrtsstraßen *or* -wege/ Flugwege; **what ~ does the 39 bus take?** welche Strecke *or* Route fährt der 39er-Bus?; **we live on a bus ~** wir wohnen an einer Buslinie; **the ~ to the coast goes through Easthampton** der Weg zur Küste führt durch Easthampton; **"all ~s"** (*Mot*) „alle Richtungen"; **~ map** Straßenkarte *f*.
(b) (*Mil*) Marschbefehl *m* ◆ **~ march** Geländemarsch *m*.
(c) (*US: delivery round*) Runde *f* ◆ **he has a paper ~** er trägt Zeitungen aus.
(d) (*Med: of drug*) Weg *m*.
[2] *vt train, coach, bus* legen ◆ **my luggage was ~d through Amsterdam** mein Gepäck wurde über Amsterdam geschickt; **the train is ~d (to go) through Birmingham** der Zug wird durch Birmingham geführt *or* über Birmingham gelegt.

routine [ru:'ti:n] [1] *n* **(a)** Routine *f* (*also Comput*) ◆ **business** *or* **office ~** Büroroutine *f*; **as a matter of ~** routinemäßig.
(b) (*Dancing, Skating*) Figur *f*; (*Gymnastics*) Übung *f* ◆ **he gave me the old ~ about his wife not understanding him** er kam mit der alten Geschichte, daß seine Frau ihn nicht versteht.
[2] *adj* Routine-, routinemäßig ◆ **~ duties** tägliche Pflichten *pl*; **to be ~ procedure** Routine(sache) sein; **it was quite ~** es war eine reine Formsache.

roux [ru:] *n* Mehlschwitze, Einbrenne *f*.

rove [rəʊv] [1] *vi* (*person*) umherwandern *or* -ziehen; (*eyes*) umherwandern *or* -schweifen ◆ **to ~ over sth** (*eyes*) über etw (*acc*) schweifen *or* wandern.
[2] *vt countryside, streets* wandern *or* ziehen durch, durchwandern *or* -ziehen.

rover ['rəʊvə^r] *n* **(a)** (*wanderer*) Vagabund *m*. **(b)** (*also* **R~ Scout**) Rover *m*.

roving ['rəʊvɪŋ] [1] *adj* **he has a ~ eye** er riskiert gern ein Auge; **~ life** Vagabundenleben *nt*; **~ ambassador** Botschafter *m* für mehrere Vertretungen; **~ reporter** Reporter, der ständig unterwegs ist, rasender Reporter (*hum*); **~ commission** weitläufiges Mandat; (*travelling*) Reisemandat *nt*.
[2] *n* Vagabundieren *nt no pl*.

row¹ [rəʊ] *n* Reihe *f* ◆ **4 failures in a ~** 4 Mißerfolge hinter- *or* nacheinander; **arrange them in ~s** stell sie in Reihen auf.

row² [1] *vti* (*in boat*) rudern ◆ **to ~ sb across** jdn hinüber-/herüberrudern; **to ~ away/back** weg-/zurückrudern; **to ~ stroke** Schlagmann sein.
[2] *n* **I enjoy a ~** ich rudere gern; **to go for a ~** rudern gehen.

row³ [raʊ] [1] *n* **(a)** (*noise*) Lärm, Krach (*inf*) *m* ◆ **to make a** *or* **kick up** (*inf*) **a ~** Krach schlagen (*inf*). **(b)** (*quarrel*) Streit, Krach (*inf*) *m* ◆ **to have a ~ with sb** mit jdm Streit *or* Krach (*inf*) haben; **to start a ~** Streit anfangen. **(c)** (*scolding*) **to get into a ~** Krach bekommen (*inf*).
[2] *vi* (*quarrel*) (sich) streiten.

rowan ['raʊən] *n* (*tree*) Eberesche, Vogelbeere *f* ◆ **~ berry** Vogelbeere *f*.

rowboat ['rəʊ,bəʊt] *n* (*US*) Ruderboot *nt*.

rowdiness ['raʊdɪnɪs] *n see adj* Krawall *m*; Rüpel- *or* Flegelhaftigkeit *f*; Randalieren, Rowdytum *nt*.

rowdy ['raʊdɪ] [1] *adj* (*+er*) (*noisy*) laut; *football fans* randalierend ◆ **the party got a bit ~** die Party artete in Krawall aus.
[2] *n* Krawallmacher *m* ◆ **football rowdies** Fußballrowdys *pl*.

rowdyism ['raʊdɪɪzəm] *n* Rowdytum *nt*.

rower ['rəʊə^r] *n* Ruderer *m*.

row house ['rəʊ,haʊs] *n* (*US*) Reihenhaus *nt*.

rowing¹ ['rəʊɪŋ] *n* Rudern *nt*.

rowing² ['raʊɪŋ] *n* (*quarrelling*) Streiterei *f*, Streitereien *pl*.

rowing ['rəʊɪŋ]: **~ boat** *n* (*Brit*) Ruderboot *nt*; **~ club** *n* Ruderklub *or* -verein *m*.

rowlock ['rəʊ,lɒk] *n* (*esp Brit*) Dolle *f*.

royal ['rɔɪəl] [1] *adj* königlich; *family, palace also* Königs-; (*fig also*) fürstlich ◆ **the ~ road to freedom/success** *etc* (*fig*) der sichere Weg zur Freiheit/zum Erfolg *etc*.
[2] *n* **(a)** (*inf*) Angehörige(r) *mf* der königlichen Familie. **(b)** (*stag*) kapitaler Bock.

royal: R~ Academy *n* (*Brit*) Königliche Akademie; **R~ Air Force** *n* (*Brit*) Königliche Luftwaffe; **~ blue** [1] *adj* königsblau; [2] *n* Königsblau *nt*; **R~ Canadian Mounted Police** *n kanadische berittene Polizei*; **R~ Commission** *n* (*Brit*) königliche Untersuchungskommission; **R~ Engineers** *n* (*Brit Mil*) Königliches Pionierkorps; **~ flush** *n* (*Cards*) Royal Flush *m*; **R~ Highness** *n* **Your/His R~ Highness** Eure/Seine Königliche Hoheit; **~ household** *n* königlicher Haushalt.

royalism ['rɔɪəlɪzəm] *n* Royalismus *m*, Königstreue *f*.

royalist ['rɔɪəlɪst] [1] *adj* royalistisch, königstreu.
[2] *n* Royalist(in *f*) *m*, Königstreue(r) *mf*.

royally ['rɔɪəlɪ] *adv* königlich; (*fig also*) fürstlich.

Royal Navy (*Brit*) [1] *n* Königliche Marine.
[2] *attr* der Königlichen Marine.

royalty ['rɔɪəltɪ] *n* **(a)** (*dignity, rank*) das Königtum; (*collectively: royal persons*) das Königshaus, die königliche Familie ◆ **symbols of ~** Wahrzeichen *pl* der Königswürde; **he's ~** er gehört zur königlichen Familie.
(b) royalties *pl* (*on* auf *+acc*) (*from book, records*) Tantiemen *pl*; (*from patent*) Patent- *or* Lizenzgebühren *pl*.

rozzer ['rɒzə^r] *n* (*Brit sl*) Bulle, Polyp (*sl*) *m*.

RP *abbr of* **received pronunciation**.

RPM (*Brit*) *abbr of* **resale price maintenance** vertikale Preisbindung.

rpm *abbr of* **revolutions per minute** U/min.

RR (*US*) *abbr of* **Railroad**.

RSPCA *abbr of* **Royal Society for the Prevention of Cruelty to Animals** ≃ Tierschutzverein *m*.

RSVP *abbr of* **répondez s'il vous plaît** u.A.w.g.

Rt Hon *abbr of* **Right Honourable**.

rub [rʌb] [1] *n* **(a)** Reiben *nt*; (*with duster etc*) Polieren *nt* ◆ **to give sth a ~** etw reiben; *furniture, shoes, silver* etw polieren; **~-a-dub(-dub)!** (*inf*) rubbel-rubbel! (*inf*).
(b) (*fig*) **there's the ~!** da liegt der Hase im Pfeffer.
[2] *vt* reiben; (*with towel also*) frottieren; (*polish*) polieren; (*Art*) *brass, inscription* durchzeichnen ◆ **to ~ sth/oneself with a lotion** etw/sich mit einer Lotion einreiben; **to ~ sth with sandpaper** etw (mit Sandpapier) abschmirgeln; **to ~ one's hands (together)** sich (*dat*) die Hände reiben; **to ~ sth dry** etw trockenreiben *or* -rubbeln (*inf*); **to ~ noses** (*as greeting*) Nasen reiben; **to ~ sb's nose in sth** (*fig*) jdm etw dauernd unter die Nase reiben *or* halten; **to ~ shoulders with all sorts of people** (*fig*) mit allen möglichen Leuten in Berührung kommen.
[3] *vi* (*thing*) (*against* an *+dat*) reiben; (*shoes, collar*) scheuern ◆ **you must have ~bed against some wet paint** da mußt du an feuchte Farbe gekommen sein; **the cat ~bed against my legs/the tree** die Katze strich mir um die Beine/ scheuerte sich am Baum.

◆**rub along** *vi* (*inf*) (*manage*) sich durchschlagen (*inf*) ◆ **to ~ ~ (together)** recht und schlecht miteinander auskommen.

◆**rub away** *vt sep* wegreiben.

◆**rub down** *vt sep horse* (*dry*) abreiben; (*clean*) striegeln; *person* abrubbeln (*inf*), abfrottieren; *wall, paintwork* (*clean*) abwaschen; (*sandpaper*) abschmirgeln.

◆**rub in** *vt sep* **(a)** *oil, lotion* einreiben (*prep obj, -to* in *+acc*). **(b)** (*fig*) *sb's stupidity* herumreiten auf (*+dat*) ◆ **he's always ~bing (it) ~ how rich he is** (*inf*) er reibt es uns/ihnen *etc* immer unter die Nase, wie reich er ist (*inf*); **don't ~ it ~!** (*don't keep mentioning*) reite nicht so darauf herum!; (*don't keep alluding to*) mußt du auch noch Salz in die Wunde streuen?

◆**rub off** [1] *vt sep dirt* abreiben; *writing* ausradieren; *tape* löschen; (*from blackboard*) aus- *or* wegwischen; *paint, gold-plating* abreiben; (*through wear*) abwetzen.
[2] *vi* (*lit, fig*) abgehen; (*through wear also*) sich abwetzen ◆ **to ~ ~ on(to) sb**

(*fig*) auf jdn abfärben.

◆**rub out** [1] *vt sep stain etc* herausreiben; (*with eraser*) ausradieren; (*sl: kill*) auslöschen.

[2] *vi* herausgehen; (*with eraser*) sich ausradieren lassen.

◆**rub up** [1] *vt sep* **(a)** *vase, table* blank reiben, (auf)polieren.
(b) to ~ sb ~ the wrong way bei jdm anecken.

[2] *vi* **the cat ~bed ~ against my leg** die Katze strich mir um die Beine; **to ~ ~ against all sorts of people** (*fig*) mit allen möglichen Leuten in Berührung kommen.

rubber[1] ['rʌbəʳ] [1] *n* (*material*) Gummi *m*; (*unprocessed, synthetic also*) Kautschuk *m* (*spec*); (*Brit: eraser*) (Radier)gummi *m*; (*sl: contraceptive*) Gummi *m* (*inf*) ◆ **~s** (*shoes*) Turnschuhe *pl*; (*overshoes*) (Gummi)überschuhe *pl*; (*clothing*) Ölzeug *nt*.

[2] *adj* Gummi-; Kautschuk- (*spec*) ◆ **is that cheque ~?** (*sl*) platzt der Scheck?; **~ goods** Gummiwaren.

rubber[2] *n* (*Cards*) Rubber, Robber *m*.

rubber: ~ band *n* Gummiband *nt*; **~ bullet** *n* Gummi(wucht)geschoß *nt*.

rubberize ['rʌbəraɪz] *vt* (*cover*) mit Gummi überziehen; (*impregnate*) gummieren.

rubber: ~neck (*US inf*) [1] *n* Gaffer *m* (*inf*); [2] *vi* gaffen (*inf*); **~ plant** *n* Gummibaum *m*; **~ plantation** *n* Kautschukplantage *f*; **~ stamp** *n* Stempel *m*; **~-stamp** *vt* (*lit*) stempeln; (*fig inf*) genehmigen; **~ tree** *n* Kautschukbaum *m*; **~-tyred** ['rʌbə'taɪəd] *adj* mit Gummireifen.

rubbery ['rʌbərɪ] *adj material* gummiartig; *meat* zäh, wie Gummi *pred*; (*hum*) *lips* wulstig.

rubbing ['rʌbɪŋ] *n* **(a)** (*action*) Reiben *nt*; (*of shoes, collar also*) Scheuern *nt*; (*with towel*) Frottieren *nt*; (*polishing*) Polieren *nt*; (*with sandpaper*) Schmirgeln *nt*. **(b)** (*Art*) *see* **brass ~**.

rubbish ['rʌbɪʃ] [1] *n* (*waste material*) Abfall *m*, Abfälle *pl*; (*household ~, in factory also*) Müll *m*; (*on building site*) Schutt *m*; (*fig*) (*trashy goods, record etc*) Mist *m*; (*nonsense*) Quatsch (*inf*), Blödsinn *m* ◆ **household ~** Hausmüll *m*; **garden ~** Gartenabfälle *pl*; **most modern furniture is ~** die meisten modernen Möbel sind nichts wert; **don't talk ~!** red keinen Quatsch! (*inf*); **he talked a lot** *or* **a load of ~** er hat eine Menge Blödsinn verzapft (*inf*); **(what a lot of) ~!** (so ein) Quatsch! (*inf*); **this book is ~** das Buch ist Quatsch (*inf*).

[2] *attr* (*inf*) *see* **rubbishy**.

rubbish *in cpds* (*esp Brit*) Müll-; **~ bin** *n* Mülleimer *m*; **~ cart** *n* Müllwagen *m*; **~ chute** *n* Müllschlucker *m*; **~ collection** *n* Müllabfuhr *f*; **~ dump** *n* Müllabladeplatz *m*; (*in garden: also* **~ heap**) Abfallhaufen *m*; **~ tip** *n* Müllabladeplatz *m*.

rubbishy ['rʌbɪʃɪ] *adj* (*inf*) (*worthless*) *goods* wertlos; (*nonsensical*) *ideas* blödsinnig ◆ **~ shoes** Schuhe, die nichts taugen; **this is ~ stuff** (*article*) das taugt nichts *or* ist Mist; (*book, theory*) das ist Quatsch (*inf*).

rubble ['rʌbl] *n* Trümmer *pl*; (*smaller pieces*) Schutt *m*; (*Geol*) Geröll *nt*.

rub-down ['rʌb'daʊn] *n* **to give sb/sth a ~** *see* **rub down**.

rube [ru:b] *n* (*US sl*) (Bauern)tölpel *m* (*inf*).

rubella [ru:'belə] *n* Röteln *pl*.

Rubicon ['ru:bɪkən] *n*: **to cross the ~** den Rubikon überschreiten.

rubicund ['ru:bɪkənd] *adj* rot.

rubidium [ru:'bɪdɪəm] *n* (*Chem*) Rubidium *nt*.

Rubik's cube ['ru:bɪks'kju:b] *n* Zauberwürfel *m*.

ruble *n* (*US*) *see* **rouble**.

rubric ['ru:brɪk] *n* (*heading*) Überschrift; (*Eccl*) (liturgische) Anweisungen *pl*; (*on exam paper*) Prüfungsanweisungen *pl* ◆ **under the ~** ... in der Rubrik ...

ruby ['ru:bɪ] [1] *n* (*stone*) Rubin *m*; (*colour: also* **~ red**) Rubinrot *nt*.

[2] *adj* (*~-coloured*) *wine, lips* rubinrot; (*made of rubies*) *necklace, ring* Rubin- ◆ **~ red** rubinrot; **~ wedding (anniversary)** vierzigster Hochzeitstag.

RUC *abbr of* **Royal Ulster Constabulary** *nordirische Polizeibehörde*.

ruche [ru:ʃ] *n* Rüsche *f*.

ruched [ru:ʃt] *adj* Rüschen-, gerüscht.

ruching ['ru:ʃɪŋ] *n* Rüschen *pl*.

ruck[1] [rʌk] *n* (*Racing*) Pulk *m* ◆ **the (common) ~** (*fig*) die (breite) Masse; **to get out of the ~** (*fig*) sich von der breiten Masse absetzen.

ruck[2] *n* (*wrinkle*) Falte *f*.

◆**ruck up** [1] *vt sep seam* zusammenziehen; *rug* verschieben ◆ **his shirt is all ~ed ~** sein Hemd hat sich hochgeschoben.

[2] *vi* (*seam*) sich zusammenziehen; (*shirt etc*) sich hochschieben; (*rug*) Falten schlagen.

rucksack ['rʌksæk] *n* (*esp Brit*) Rucksack *m*.

ruckus ['rʌkəs] *n* (*inf*) Krawall *m*.

ruction ['rʌkʃən] *n* (*inf: usu pl*) (*dispute, scolding*) Krach *m no pl*; (*uproar also*) Krawall *m no pl* ◆ **there'll be ~s if you do that** es gibt Krach, wenn du das tust.

rudder ['rʌdəʳ] *n* (*Naut, Aviat*) Ruder *nt*.

rudderless ['rʌdəlɪs] *adj* ohne Ruder; (*fig*) führungslos.

ruddiness ['rʌdɪnɪs] *n* Röte *f* ◆ **the ~ of his complexion** seine gesunde Gesichtsfarbe.

ruddy ['rʌdɪ] *adj* (*+er*) **(a)** *complexion* gesund, rot; *sky, glow* rötlich. **(b)** (*Brit sl*) verdammt (*inf*).

rude [ru:d] *adj* (*+er*) **(a)** (*bad-mannered*) unhöflich; (*stronger*) unverschämt; (*rough, uncouth*) grob ◆ **it's ~ to stare** es gehört sich nicht, Leute anzustarren, man starrt andere Leute nicht an; **don't be so ~!** so was sagt man/tut man nicht!; **talk about ~!** der/die hat vielleicht einen Ton am Leib! (*inf*).
(b) (*obscene*) unanständig, unflätig (*geh*) ◆ **to make a ~ noise/smell** (*euph*) pup(s)en (*inf*).
(c) (*harsh*) *shock* bös, hart; *blast, weather* wüst, rauh; *reminder* unsanft; *see* **awakening**.
(d) (*liter: primitive*) primitiv; *fare* einfach, schlicht.
(e) (*liter: vigorous*) *strength* gewaltig ◆ **he is in ~ health/strength** er strotzt (nur so) vor Gesundheit/Kraft.

rudely ['ru:dlɪ] *adv see adj (a - d)*.

rudeness ['ru:dnɪs] *n see adj* **(a)** Unhöflichkeit *f*; Unverschämtheit *f*; Grobheit *f*. **(b)** Unanständigkeit, Unflätigkeit (*geh*) *f*. **(c)** Härte *f*; Wüstheit, Rauheit *f*. **(d)** Primitivität *f*; Einfachheit, Schlichtheit *f*. **(e)** gewaltige Größe.

rudiment ['ru:dɪmənt] *n* **(a) ~s** *pl* Anfangsgründe, Grundlagen *pl*. **(b)** (*Biol*) Rudiment *nt*.

rudimentary [ˌru:dɪ'mentərɪ] *adj* (*basic*) *knowledge, principles* elementar; *language, system*, (*Biol*) rudimentär ◆ **a ~ sort of building** ein primitives Gebäude.

rue[1] [ru:] *vt* (*liter*) bereuen ◆ **to ~ the day that** ... den Tag verwünschen, an dem ...

rue[2] *n* (*Bot*) Raute *f*.

rueful ['ru:fʊl] *adj look* reuig, reuevoll; *situation* beklagenswert.

ruefully ['ru:fəlɪ] *adv* reuevoll.

ruff[1] [rʌf] *n* **(a)** (*on dress etc, of bird, animal*) Halskrause *f*. **(b)** (*bird*) Kampfläufer *m*.

ruff[2] (*Cards*) [1] *n* Trumpfen *nt*.

[2] *vti* trumpfen, stechen.

ruffian ['rʌfɪən] *n* Rüpel, Grobian *m*; (*violent*) Schläger *m* ◆ **you little ~!** du kleiner Halbstarker!

ruffle ['rʌfl] [1] *n* (*on dress*) Rüsche *f*; (*on water*) Kräuseln *nt no pl*.

[2] *vt* **(a)** (*disturb*) *hair, feathers* zerzausen; *surface, water* kräuseln; *bedspread, clothes* verkrumpeln (*inf*) ◆ **the bird ~d (up) its feathers** der Vogel plusterte sich auf.
(b) (*fig*) (*upset, disturb*) aus der Ruhe bringen; (*annoy also*) verärgern, aufbringen ◆ **to ~ sb's calm/temper** jdn aus der Ruhe bringen/jdn aufregen; **to get ~d** aus der Ruhe kommen.

rug [rʌg] *n* **(a)** Teppich *m*; (*rectangular also*) Läufer *m*; (*valuable also*) Brücke *f*; (*bedside*) (Bett)vorleger *m* ◆ **fireside ~** Kaminvorleger *m*. **(b)** (*blanket*) (Woll)decke *f*.

rugby ['rʌgbɪ] *n* (*also* **~ football**) Rugby *nt* ◆ **R~ League** Rugby *nt* (*mit 13 (Profi)spielern pro Team)*; **~ footballer, ~ player** Rugbyspieler *m*; **R~ Union** Rugby *nt* (*mit 15 Amateurspielern pro Team)*.

rugged ['rʌgɪd] *adj* rauh; *country, landscape also* wild; *cliff, rocks, mountains* zerklüftet; *ground* felsig; *statue* grob; *face, features* markig; *determination* wild; *resistance* verbissen ◆ **a ~ test** eine harte Prüfung; **~ individualism** stolzer *or* unverwüstlicher Individualismus.

ruggedness ['rʌgɪdnɪs] *n see adj* Rauheit *f*; Wildheit *f*; Zerklüftetheit *f*; Felsigkeit *f*; Grobheit *f*; Markigkeit *f*; Verbissenheit *f*.

rugger ['rʌgəʳ] *n* (*Brit inf*) *see* **rugby**.

ruin ['ru:ɪn] [1] *n* **(a)** *no pl* (*of thing, person*) Untergang *m*; (*of event*) Ende *nt*; (*financial, social*) Ruin *m* ◆ **the palace was going to ~** *or* **falling into ~** der Palast verfiel (zur Ruine); **~ stared him in the face** er stand vor dem (finanziellen/gesellschaftlichen) Ruin.
(b) (*cause of ~*) Ende *nt*; (*of person also*) Ruin *m* ◆ **the ~ of my hopes** das Ende meiner Hoffnungen; **it will be the ~ of him** das wird ihn ruinieren; **you will be the ~ of me** du bist mein Ruin.
(c) (*ruined building*) Ruine *f*; (*fig: person*) Wrack *nt* ◆ **~s** (*of building*) Ruinen *pl*; (*of reputation, beauty*) Reste *pl*; (*of hopes, career*) Trümmer *pl*; **to be** *or* **lie in ~s** (*lit*) eine Ruine sein; (*fig*) zerstört sein; (*life: financially, socially*) ruiniert sein.

[2] *vt* (*destroy*) *building, hopes* zerstören; *reputation, health, sb's life also* ruinieren; (*financially, socially*) *person* ruinieren, zugrunde richten; (*spoil*) *clothes, event, enjoyment, child, horse* verderben ◆ **they ~ed my birthday party** sie haben (mir) die Geburtstagsfeier verdorben.

ruination [ˌru:ɪ'neɪʃən] *n see vt* Zerstörung *f*; Ruinierung *f*; Verderben *nt* ◆ **to be the ~ of sb** jds Ruin sein.

ruined ['ru:ɪnd] *adj building* in Ruinen *pred*, zerfallen; *person* ruiniert.

ruinous ['ru:ɪnəs] *adj* (*financially*) ruinös; *price* extrem.

ruinously ['ru:ɪnəslɪ] *adv* **~ expensive** wahnsinnig teuer (*inf*).

rule [ru:l] [1] *n* **(a)** Regel *f*; (*Sport, Cards also*) Spielregel *f*; (*Admin also*) Vorschrift, Bestimmung *f* ◆ **the ~s of the game** (*lit, fig*) die Spielregeln; **to play by the ~s** (*lit, fig*) die Spielregeln einhalten; **running is against the ~s, it's against the ~s to run** Rennen ist nicht erlaubt; **~s and regulations** Regeln und Bestimmungen; **it's a ~ that ...** es ist Vorschrift, daß ...; **that's the ~ of the road** (*Mot*) das ist im Straßenverkehr üblich; **the Franciscan ~** die Regeln des Franziskanerordens; **to do sth by ~** etw vorschriftsmäßig tun; **the ~ of three** (*Math*) der Dreisatz; **by ~ of thumb** über den Daumen gepeilt; **~ book** Regelheft *nt*; Vorschriftenbuch *nt*; **to throw the ~ book at sb** (*fig*) jdn wegen jeder Kleinigkeit drankriegen (*inf*).
(b) (*custom*) Regel *f* ◆ **I make it a ~ to get up early** ich habe es mir zur Regel gemacht, früh aufzustehen; **as a (general) ~** in der Regel; **ties are the ~ at the office** Krawatten sind im Büro die Regel; **violence is the ~ rather than the exception** Gewalt ist eher (die) Regel als (die) Ausnahme.
(c) (*authority, reign*) Herrschaft *f*; (*period also*) Regierungszeit *f* ◆ **the ~ of law** die Rechtsstaatlichkeit.
(d) (*for measuring*) Metermaß *nt*, Maßstab *m* ◆ **a foot ~** (*1 foot long*) ein (30 cm langes) Lineal; (*showing feet*) ein Maßstab *m* mit Fußeinteilung; **folding ~** Zollstock *m*; *see* **slide ~**.

[2] *vt* **(a)** beherrschen, regieren; (*individual also*) herrschen über (*+acc*); (*fig*) *passions, emotion* beherrschen, zügeln; *person* beherrschen ◆ **to ~ the roost**

(*fig*) Herr im Haus sein (*inf*); **to be ~d by jealousy/destiny** von Eifersucht/vom Schicksal beherrscht werden; **if you would only be ~d by what I say** wenn du nur auf mich hören würdest; **I won't be ~d by what he wants** ich richte mich nicht nach seinen Wünschen.
(b) (*Jur, Sport, Admin: give decision*) entscheiden ◆ **his question was ~d out of order** seine Frage wurde als unzulässig abgewiesen; **the judge ~d the defence out of order** (*Jur*) der Richter rügte die Verteidigung.
(c) (*draw lines on*) *paper* linieren; (*draw*) *line, margin* ziehen ◆ **~d paper** liniertes Papier.
3 *vi* **(a)** (*lit, fig: reign*) herrschen (*over* über +*acc*), regieren (*over acc*).
(b) (*Fin: prices*) notieren ◆ **the prices ruling in London** die in London notierten Preise.
(c) (*Jur*) entscheiden (*against* gegen, *in favour of* für, *on* in +*dat*).
◆**rule off** *vt sep* einen Schlußstrich ziehen unter (+*acc*).
◆**rule out** *vt sep word, sentence* einen Strich ziehen durch; (*fig: exclude, dismiss*) ausschließen.
ruler ['ru:lər] *n* **(a)** (*for measuring*) Lineal *nt*. **(b)** (*sovereign*) Herrscher *m*.
ruling ['ru:lıŋ] **1** *adj principle* leitend, Leit-; *factor* ausschlaggebend; *passion* vorherrschend; (*prevalent*) (vor)herrschend; (*Fin, St Ex*) *prices* notiert ◆ **the ~ class** die herrschende Klasse; **the ~ party** (*Pol*) die Regierungspartei.
2 *n* (*Admin, Jur*) Entscheid *m* ◆ **to receive/give a ~** einen Bescheid erhalten/einen Entscheid fällen.
rum¹ [rʌm] *n* Rum *m* ◆ **~ toddy** Grog *m*.
rum² *adj* (*dated Brit inf*) komisch (*inf*); *person also* kauzig.
Rumania [ru:'meınıə] *etc see* **Romania** *etc*.
rumba ['rʌmbə] *n* Rumba *m or f*.
rumble ['rʌmbl] **1** *n* **(a)** *see vi* Grollen *nt*; Donnern *nt*; Knacken *nt*; Knurren *nt*; Rumpeln *nt* (*all no pl*) ◆ **his stomach gave a ~** sein Magen knurrte.
(b) (*sl: fight*) Schlägerei *f*.
2 *vi* (*thunder*) grollen; (*cannon*) donnern; (*pipes*) knacken; (*stomach*) knurren; (*train, truck*) rumpeln ◆ **to ~ past/along/off** vorbei-/entlang-/davonrumpeln.
3 *vt* (*inf: see through*) *swindle, trick, person* durchschauen ◆ **I soon ~d him** *or* **his game** *or* **what he was up to** ich bin ihm bald auf die Schliche gekommen (*inf*).
rumble: ~ seat *n* Notsitz *m*; **~ strip** *n* (*Mot*) akustische Schwelle.
rumbling ['rʌmblıŋ] *n see vi* Grollen *nt*; Donnern *nt*; Knacken *nt*; Knurren *nt*; Rumpeln *nt* (*all no pl*).
rumbustious [rʌm'bʌstʃəs] *adj* derb.
ruminant ['ru:mınənt] **1** *n* Wiederkäuer *m*.
2 *adj* (*lit*) wiederkäuend, Wiederkäuer-; (*fig*) grübelnd.
ruminate ['ru:mıneıt] **1** *vi* (*lit*) wiederkäuen; (*fig*) grübeln (*over, about, on* über +*acc*).
2 *vt* wiederkäuen.
rumination [,ru:mı'neıʃən] *n* (*lit*) Wiederkäuen *nt no pl*; (*fig*) Grübeln *nt no pl*.
ruminative *adj*, **~ly** *adv* ['ru:mınətıv, -lı] (*fig*) grübelnd.
rummage ['rʌmıdʒ] **1** *n* **(a) to have a good ~ in sth/around** etw gründlich durchstöbern *or* durchwühlen/gründlich herumstöbern *or* herumwühlen.
(b) (*jumble*) Ramsch *m* ◆ **~ sale** (*US*) Ramschverkauf *m*.
2 *vi* (*also* **~ about, ~ around**) herumstöbern, herumwühlen (*among, in* in +*dat, for* nach).
rummy ['rʌmı] *n* (*Cards*) Rommé *nt*.
rumour, (US) rumor ['ru:mər] **1** *n* Gerücht *nt* ◆ **~ has it that** ... es geht das Gerücht, daß ...; **as ~ has it** wie es Gerüchten zufolge heißt; **there is a ~ of war** es gehen Kriegsgerüchte um.
2 *vt* **it is ~ed that** ... es geht das Gerücht, daß ...; (*through gossip*) man munkelt, daß ...; **he is ~ed to be in London** Gerüchten zufolge ist er in London; **he is ~ed to be rich** er soll angeblich reich sein; **his ~ed resignation/death** das Gerücht von seinem Rücktritt/Tod.
rump [rʌmp] *n* (*of animal*) Hinterbacken *pl*; (*of fowl*) Bürzel *m*; (*inf: of person*) Hinterteil *nt*, Allerwerteste(r) *m* (*hum*) ◆ **~ (steak)** Rumpsteak *nt*; **The R~** (*Brit Hist*) das Rumpfparlament (*im 17. Jahrhundert in England*).
Rumpelstiltskin ['rʌmpəl'stıltskın] *n* Rumpelstilzchen *nt*.
rumple ['rʌmpl] *vt* (*also* **~ up**) *clothes, paper* zerknittern; *hair* verwuscheln, zerzausen.
rumpus ['rʌmpəs] *n* (*inf*) (*noise*) Spektakel (*inf*), Krach *m*; (*quarrel*) Krach *m* (*inf*) ◆ **to make a ~, to kick up a ~** (*make noise*) einen Spektakel *or* Heidenlärm machen (*inf*); (*complain*) Krach schlagen (*inf*); **to have a ~ with sb** (*inf*) sich mit jdm in die Haare geraten; **~ room** (*US*) Spielzimmer *nt*.
run [rʌn] (*vb: pret* **ran**, *ptp* **~**) **1** *n* **(a)** (*act of running, Cricket, Baseball*) Lauf *m* ◆ **to go for a 2-km ~** einen 2 km-Lauf machen; **his ~ is slower than my walk** ich kann schneller gehen, als er laufen kann; **let the dog have a ~** laß den Hund laufen; **he came in at a ~** er kam hereingelaufen; **he took the fence at a ~** er nahm die Hürde im Lauf; **to break into a ~** zu laufen *or* rennen anfangen; **to take a ~ at a hurdle** auf eine Hürde loslaufen; **to make a ~ for it** weglaufen, wegrennen; **he made a ~ for the door** er lief *or* rannte zur Tür; **on the ~** (*from the police etc*) auf der Flucht; **we have the enemy on the ~** der Feind ist auf der Flucht; **to keep the enemy on the ~** den Feind weiter zur Flucht zwingen; **the house and family keep you on the ~** Haus und Familie halten einen ganz schön auf Trab; **we've given him a good ~ for his money,** **he has had a good ~ for his money** (*inf*) er hat was für sein Geld bekommen; (*competition*) er hat einen ordentlichen Kampf bekommen; (*pleasure*) er kann sich nicht beklagen; **my old car has given me a good ~ for my money** (*inf*) mein altes Auto hat mir gute Dienste geleistet; **the theory had a good ~ for its money** (*inf*) die Theorie hat sich lange gehalten.
(b) (*journey: in vehicle*) Fahrt *f*; (*outing also*) Ausflug *m* ◆ **to go for a ~ in the car** eine Fahrt/einen Ausflug im Auto machen; **I'll give you a ~ up to town** ich fahre Sie in die Stadt.
(c) (*distance travelled*) (*in bus, tram, boat, car*) Fahrt *f*; (*in plane*) Flug *m*; (*route*) Strecke *f* ◆ **it's a 30-minute ~** es ist eine Fahrt von 30 Minuten; **the boat no longer does that ~** das Schiff fährt die Strecke nicht mehr; **on the outward/inward ~** auf der Hinfahrt/Rückfahrt; auf dem Hinflug/Rückflug; **the ferries on the Dover-Calais ~** die Fähren der Linie Dover-Calais; **the ships on the China ~** die Schiffe der China-Linie.
(d) (*Aviat*) Flug *m* ◆ **approach ~** Anflug *m*; **bombing ~** Bombenzielanflug *m*; **the plane made a low ~ over the village** das Flugzeug flog im Tiefflug über das Dorf.
(e) to have the ~ of a place einen Ort zur freien Verfügung haben; **to give sb the ~ of one's house** jdm sein Haus überlassen.
(f) in the short/long ~ fürs nächste/auf die Dauer; *plan etc* auf kurze/lange Sicht, kurz-/langfristig.
(g) (*series*) Folge, Reihe, Serie *f*; (*Cards*) Sequenz *f*; (*Theat*) Spielzeit *f*; (*of film*) Laufzeit *f* ◆ **a ~ on the red** (*Roulette*) eine Serie von roten Zahlen; **the ~ of the cards** die Verteilung der Karten; **this fashion is having a long ~** diese Mode hat sich lange gehalten; **when the London ~ was over** (*Theat*) als das Stück in London abgelaufen war; **the play had a long ~** das Stück lief sehr lange; **a two-year ~ in office** eine zweijährige Amtszeit; **a ~ of luck/of bad luck** eine Glücks-/Pechsträhne; **a ~ of misfortunes** eine Serie von Mißgeschicken.
(h) (*rush, great demand*) **~ on** Ansturm *m* auf (+*acc*); (*St Ex, Fin also*) Run *m* auf (+*acc*); **there has been a ~ on sugar** (*Comm*) es gab einen Ansturm auf Zucker.
(i) (*average type*) **the common ~ of mankind** der Durchschnittsmensch; **the usual ~ of students** die gewöhnliche Sorte Studenten.
(j) (*trend: of market, opinion*) Tendenz *f*; (*course: of events*) Lauf *m* ◆ **the ordinary ~ of things** der normale Gang der Dinge.
(k) the ~ of the grain die Maserung; (*of paper*) die Faserrichtung.
(l) (*track for sledging, skiing etc*) Bahn *f* ◆ **ski ~** Abfahrt(sstrecke) *f*.
(m) (*animal enclosure*) Gehege *nt*; (*chicken*) Hühnerhof *m*.
(n) (*in stocking*) Laufmasche *f*.
(o) (*Mus*) Lauf *m*.
(p) the ~s (*inf: diarrhoea*) der flotte Otto (*inf*), die Renneritis (*hum inf*).
(q) (*Typ: printing* ~) Auflage *f*.
2 *vi* **(a)** laufen, rennen; (*in race*) laufen ◆ **to ~ past/off** vorbei-/davonlaufen *or* -rennen; **she came ~ning out** sie kam herausgelaufen *or* -gerannt; **to ~ down a slope** einen Abhang hinunterlaufen *or* -rennen; **he is always ~ning about the streets** er treibt sich immer auf der Straße herum; **~!** lauf!; **walk don't ~** du sollst gehen, nicht rennen!; **to ~ for the bus** zum Bus laufen *or* rennen; **she ran to meet him** sie lief *or* rannte ihm entgegen; **she ran to help him** sie kam ihm schnell zu Hilfe; **to ~ in the 100 metres** die 100 Meter laufen; **eleven ran** (*Horse-racing*) elf (Pferde) waren am Start; **X, Y, Z also ran** (*Horse-racing*) X, Y, Z waren ebenfalls am Start; **this horse will ~ in the National** das Pferd startet im National; *see* **also-ran**.
(b) (*flee*) davonlaufen, weglaufen, wegrennen ◆ **to ~ for one's life** um sein Leben laufen *or* rennen; **~ for it!** lauft *or* rennt, was ihr könnt!; **to ~ to earth** (*fox, criminal*) sich verkriechen; **go on then, ~ to mummy!** na, lauf doch schon zu deiner Mutti!
(c) (*fig*) (*news, rumour etc*) umgehen ◆ **the news ran like wildfire through the crowd** die Nachricht ging wie ein Lauffeuer durch die Menge; **the order ran down the column** der Befehl wurde von Mund zu Mund weitergegeben; **he ran down the list** er ging die Liste durch; **a shiver ran down her spine** ein Schauer lief ihr über den Rücken; **a ripple of fear ran through the town** ein Schaudern durchlief die Stadt; **his eyes/fingers ran over the sculpture** seine Augen/Finger glitten über die Plastik; **the idea ran through my head that ...** der Gedanke *or* es ging mir durch den Kopf, daß ...
(d) (*story, words*) gehen, lauten; (*tune*) gehen ◆ **how does the last sentence ~?** wie lautet der letzte Satz?; **so the story ~s** die Geschichte geht so; **the wording ran as follows** es hieß *or* lautete folgendermaßen; **the conversation ran on that very subject** das Gespräch drehte sich um eben das Thema; **my thoughts ran on my sister** ich dachte an meine Schwester.
(e) (*stand as candidate*) kandidieren; sich aufstellen lassen ◆ **to ~ for President** *or* **for the Presidency** für die Präsidentschaft kandidieren; **to ~ against sb** jds Gegenkandidat sein.
(f) (*become*) **to ~ dry** (*river*) austrocknen; (*pen*) leer werden; (*resources*) ausgehen; **he ran dry of ideas** ihm gingen die Ideen aus; **supplies are ~ning short** *or* **low** die Vorräte werden knapp; *see* **seed, short, wild**.
(g) (*roll, slide: things*) (*drawer, curtains, rope*) laufen, gleiten; (*vehicle*) rollen ◆ **it ~s on wheels** es läuft *or* fährt auf Rädern; **money just ~s through his fingers** das Geld rinnt ihm (nur so) durch die Finger.
(h) (*flow*) (*water, tears, tap, nose, butter, cheese*) laufen; (*river, electric current*) fließen; (*eyes*) tränen; (*sore, abscess*) eitern; (*paint, colour*) zerfließen, ineinanderfließen; (*colour, dye: in washing*) färben; (*ink*) fließen ◆ **my shirt has ~** mein Hemd hat gefärbt; **my ice cream is ~ning** mein Eis schmilzt; **this pen doesn't ~ very well** dieser Kuli schreibt nicht sehr gut; **where the river ~s into the sea** wo der Fluß ins Meer mündet; **the street ~s into the square** die Straße mündet auf den Platz; **interest rates are ~ning at record levels/15%** die Zinssätze sind auf Rekordhöhe/stehen auf 15%; **inflation is ~ning at 20%** die Inflationsrate beträgt 20%; **a heavy sea was ~ning** die See ging hoch; **where the tide is ~ning strongly** wo die Gezeiten sehr stark sind; **let**

➤ LANGUAGE IN USE: **rule out** → 16.3

the tap/water ~ hot laß das Wasser laufen, bis es heiß kommt; **your bath is ~ning** Ihr Badewasser läuft ein; **the walls were ~ning with moisture** die Wände tropften vor Feuchtigkeit; **~ning with sweat** schweißüberströmt; **his blood ran cold** das Blut gefror ihm in den Adern.

(i) *(extend in time)* *(play, film, contract, Jur: sentence)* laufen; *(Fin: interest rate)* gelten ◆ **the expenditure ~s into thousands of pounds** die Ausgaben gehen in die Tausende (von Pfund); **the book has ~ into three editions** das Buch hat schon drei Auflagen erreicht; **the poem ~s (in)to several hundred lines** das Gedicht geht über mehrere hundert Zeilen.

(j) to ~ to *(afford)* **I can't ~ to a new car** ich kann mir kein neues Auto leisten; **the funds won't ~ to a party** die Finanzen reichen nicht für eine Party.

(k) *(Naut)* **to ~ before the wind** vor dem Wind segeln; **to ~ onto the rocks** (auf die Felsen) auflaufen; **to ~ into port** in den Hafen einlaufen.

(l) *(drive)* fahren.

(m) *(provide service: bus, train etc)* fahren, verkehren ◆ **the train doesn't ~ on Sundays** der Zug fährt sonntags nicht; **no trains ~ there any more** dorthin gibt es keine Zugverbindung mehr.

(n) *(function)* *(machine, wheel)* laufen; *(factory)* arbeiten; *(fig: ceremony)* laufen ◆ **when the central heating is ~ning** wenn die Zentralheizung angeschaltet ist; **my sewing machine doesn't ~ very well** meine Nähmaschine funktioniert nicht besonders gut; **you mustn't leave the engine ~ning** Sie dürfen den Motor nicht laufen lassen; **this model ~s on diesel** dieses Auto fährt mit Diesel; **the radio ~s off the mains/off batteries** das Radio läuft auf Netz/Batterie; **things are ~ning smoothly/badly for them** bei ihnen läuft zur Zeit alles wunschgemäß/alles schief; **the principle on which democracy ~s** das Prinzip, auf dem die Demokratie basiert; **all planes/trains are ~ning late** alle Flugzeuge/Züge haben Verspätung; **the project is ~ning late/to schedule** das Projekt hat sich verzögert/geht ganz nach Plan voran.

(o) *(extend in space)* *(road)* gehen, führen; *(mountains)* sich ziehen, sich erstrecken; *(river)* fließen ◆ **he has a scar ~ning across his chest** eine Narbe zieht sich quer über seine Brust; **a wall ~s round the garden** um den Garten zieht sich *or* läuft eine Mauer; **the river ~s for 300 km** der Fluß ist 300 km lang; **this theme ~s right through his work** dieses Thema zieht sich durch sein ganzes Werk.

(p) to ~ in the family in der Familie liegen.

(q) *(stocking)* eine Laufmasche bekommen; *(stitch)* laufen.

(r) *(Comput: software, computer)* laufen ◆ **it can ~ on single-drive computers** es ist auf Computern mit nur einem Laufwerk lauffähig.

3 *vt* **(a)** *distance* laufen, rennen; *race* laufen ◆ **he ~s 3 km every day** er läuft jeden Tag 3 km; **the first race will be ~ at 2 o'clock** das erste Rennen findet um 2 Uhr statt; **to ~ errands/messages** Botengänge machen; **to ~ the streets** *(child, dog)* sich auf der Straße herumtreiben; **to ~ a blockade** eine Blockade brechen; **they ran the rapids** sie meisterten die Stromschnellen; **to ~ sb a close second** *(Sport)* nur knapp von jdm auf den zweiten Platz verwiesen werden; **to ~ sb close** *(Sport, fig)* nur knapp von jdm geschlagen werden.

(b) *(fig)* **to ~ its/their course** *(events, disease)* seinen/ihren Lauf nehmen; **to ~ a temperature** *or* **a fever** Fieber haben; **he was ~ning a high temperature** er hatte Fieber; *see* **gauntlet.**

(c) *(chase, hunt)* *fox, deer* treiben; *(make run)* *person, animal* jagen ◆ **they ran him out of the house** sie jagten ihn aus dem Haus; **to ~ sb off his feet** *(inf)* jdn ständig in Trab halten *(inf)*; **she is absolutely ~ off her feet** *(inf)* sie ist ständig in Trab *(inf)*; **to ~ oneself out of breath** außer Atem kommen; **that will ~ him into trouble** das wird ihn in Schwierigkeiten bringen; **that will ~ you into a lot of expense** das wird Sie eine ganze Menge *or* schöne Stange *(inf)* kosten; **to ~ sb into debt** jdn in Schulden stürzen; *see* **earth, ground[1].**

(d) *candidate* aufstellen; *(Sport)* *horse* laufen lassen.

(e) *(cause to flow)* **to ~ water into a bath** Wasser in die Badewanne einlaufen lassen; **I'll ~ you a bath** ich lasse Ihnen ein Bad einlaufen; **he ~s his words together** bei ihm fließen alle Wörter ineinander über.

(f) *(transport)* *person, thing* fahren, bringen; *(drive)* *vehicle* fahren ◆ **I'll ~ your luggage to the station** ich fahre Ihr Gepäck zum Bahnhof; **he ran the car into the garage/a tree** er fuhr das Auto in die Garage/gegen einen Baum.

(g) *buses, trains* unterhalten; *extra buses, trains* einsetzen ◆ **this company ~s a bus service** diese Firma unterhält einen Busdienst; **they ~ trains to London every hour** es besteht stündlicher Zugverkehr nach London; **how many machines does this factory ~?** wie viele Maschinen laufen in dieser Fabrik?

(h) *(operate, cause to function)* *machine, engine* betreiben *(on* mit); *(person)* bedienen ◆ **to ~ a radio off the mains** ein Radio auf Netz laufen lassen.

(i) I can't afford to ~ a car ich kann es mir nicht leisten, ein Auto zu unterhalten; **he ~s a Rolls** er fährt einen Rolls Royce; **this car is cheap to ~** dieses Auto ist billig im Unterhalt.

(j) *(conduct)* *experiment, test* durchführen; *(manage)* *business, hotel* führen, leiten; *shop* führen; *mine* betreiben; *school, organization, newspaper* leiten; *(organize)* *course of study, competition* veranstalten, durchführen; *(be in charge of)* *course, competition, department, project* leiten ◆ **a well-~ hotel** ein gutgeführtes Hotel; **he ~s a small hotel/shop in the village** er hat ein kleines Hotel/Geschäft im Dorf; **to ~ a house** einen Haushalt führen; **a house which is easy to ~** ein Haus, das leicht in Schuß gehalten werden kann; **I want to ~ my own life** ich möchte mein eigenes Leben leben; **she's the one who really ~s everything** sie ist diejenige, die den Laden schmeißt *(inf)*; **I'm ~ning this show!** *(inf)* ich bestimme, was gemacht wird.

(k) *(smuggle)* *guns etc* schmuggeln.

(l) *(move, put)* **to ~ one's fingers over the piano keys** die Finger über die (Klavier)tasten gleiten lassen; **to ~ one's finger down a list** mit dem Finger eine Liste durchgehen; **to ~ one's fingers/a comb through one's hair** sich *(dat)* mit den Fingern/einem Kamm durch die Haare fahren; **to ~ one's eye over a page** eine Seite überfliegen; **he ran the vacuum cleaner over the carpet** er ging mit dem Staubsauger über den Teppich.

(m) *(take, lead etc)* *rope, road* führen; *piece of elastic, line, ditch* ziehen; *pipe, wires* (ver)legen; *(above ground)* führen ◆ **to ~ a rope round a tree** ein Seil um einen Baum legen.

(n) *(thrust)* **he ran a sword into his side** er stieß ihm das Schwert in die Seite, er durchbohrte ihn mit dem Schwert.

(o) *(issue)* *(Press)* *article, series* bringen; *(Film also)* zeigen, spielen; *(Comm)* verkaufen.

(p) *(Comput)* *computer* laufen lassen; *software* benutzen; *(load)* *program* laden ◆ **can you ~ SuperText 3 on your computer?** läuft SuperText 3 auf deinem Computer?

◆**run about** *or* **around** *vi* *(lit, fig)* herumlaufen *or* -rennen ◆ **to ~ ~ with sb** sich mit jdm herumtreiben; **I'm not going to ~ ~ after you cleaning up** ich putze doch nicht dauernd hinter dir her.

◆**run across** **1** *vi* **(a)** *(lit)* hinüber-/herüberlaufen *or* -rennen. **(b)** *(go to see)* kurz rüberlaufen *or* -gehen *(to* zu).

2 *vi +prep obj* *(meet)* *person* zufällig treffen; *(find)* *object, reference* stoßen auf (+*acc*).

◆**run after** **1** *vi* **to come ~ning ~** hinterherlaufen *or* -rennen.

2 *vi +prep obj* nachlaufen *or* -rennen (+*dat*) ◆ **I'm not going to spend my days ~ning ~ you!** *(fig)* ich denke gar nicht daran, nur immer für dich dazusein!

◆**run along** *vi* laufen, rennen; *(go away)* gehen ◆ **~ ~!** nun geht mal schön!

◆**run around** *vi see* **run about.**

◆**run at** *vi +prep obj* zu- *or* loslaufen auf (+*acc*); *(attack)* losstürzen auf (+*acc*).

◆**run away** **1** *vi* **(a)** *(child, animal)* weglaufen, wegrennen; *(person)* weglaufen; *(horse)* durchgehen ◆ **to ~ ~ from home** von zu Hause weglaufen; **don't ~ ~, I need your advice** *(inf)* gehen Sie nicht weg, ich möchte Sie um Rat fragen; **~ ~ and play!** geht (mal schön) spielen!

(b) *(water)* auslaufen.

2 *vt sep* *water* auslaufen lassen.

◆**run away with** *vi +prep obj* *(use up)* *funds, money, resources* verschlucken *(inf)*, verbrauchen; *(steal)* *money, object* durchgehen *or* durchbrennen mit *(inf)*; *(Sport etc: win easily)* *race, prize* spielend gewinnen ◆ **don't ~ ~ ~ the idea that ...** *(fig)* kommen Sie nur nicht auf den Gedanken, daß ...; **he lets his imagination/enthusiasm ~ ~ ~ him** seine Phantasie/seine Begeisterung geht leicht mit ihm durch.

◆**run back** **1** *vi* *(lit)* zurücklaufen, zurückrennen ◆ **let's just ~ ~ over what we've agreed** gehen wir noch einmal durch, was wir vereinbart haben; **she'll come ~ning ~** sie wird reumütig zurückkommen.

2 *vt sep* **(a)** *person* zurückfahren *or* -bringen. **(b)** *(rewind)* *tape, film* zurückspulen.

◆**run down** **1** *vi* **(a)** *(lit: person)* hinunter-/herunterlaufen *or* -rennen.

(b) *(watch, clock)* ablaufen; *(battery)* leer werden ◆ **to let stocks ~ ~** das Lager leer werden lassen; *(deliberately)* die Vorräte abbauen.

2 *vt sep* **(a)** *(knock down)* umfahren; *(run over)* überfahren.

(b) *(Naut)* *ship* rammen; *(in battle)* versenken.

(c) *(limit, reduce)* *factory, shop* (allmählich) auflösen; *department, stocks, staff* abbauen; *battery* zu stark belasten.

(d) *(disparage)* schlechtmachen, runtermachen *(inf)*.

(e) *(pursue and capture)* *stag* zur Strecke bringen; *criminal also* zu fassen kriegen; *person* ausfindig machen.

◆**run in** **1** *vi* *(lit)* hinein-/hereinlaufen *or* -rennen.

2 *vt sep* **(a)** *car* einfahren ◆ **"~ning ~, please pass"** *(Brit Mot)* „bitte überholen, Wagen wird eingefahren". **(b)** *(inf: arrest)* sich *(dat)* schnappen.

◆**run into** *vi +prep obj* *(meet)* zufällig treffen; *(collide with)* rennen/fahren gegen ◆ **to ~ ~ difficulties/trouble/problems** Schwierigkeiten/Ärger bekommen/auf Probleme stoßen; **to ~ ~ danger/debt** in Gefahr/Schulden geraten; *see also* **run 2 (h).**

◆**run off** **1** *vi see* **run away 1 (a).**

2 *vt sep* **(a)** *water* ablassen.

(b) *poem, letter, article* herunterschreiben, hinhauen *(inf)*.

(c) *(reproduce)* *copy* abziehen.

(d) *(Sport)* **to ~ ~ the heats** die Ausscheidungskämpfe durchführen.

(e) *(excess weight)* sich *(dat)* ablaufen *or* abrennen.

(f) *(on machine)* *a few dresses, a sample* schnell machen.

◆**run on** **1** *vi* **(a)** *(lit)* weiterlaufen, weiterrennen ◆ **you ~ ~, I'll catch up** geh schon mal voraus, ich komme nach.

(b) *(fig: in speaking)* **he does ~ ~ so!** er redet wie ein Buch!; **it ran ~ for four hours** das zog sich über vier Stunden hin.

(c) *(letters)* verbunden sein; *(words)* fortlaufend geschrieben sein; *(line of type)* ohne Absatz gedruckt sein.

(d) *(time)* weitergehen.

2 *vt sep* *letters* verbinden; *words* fortlaufend schreiben; *line of type* ohne Absatz drucken.

◆**run out** **1** *vi* **(a)** *(person)* hinaus-/herauslaufen *or* -rennen; *(rope, chain)* ablaufen; *(liquid)* herauslaufen; *(through leak)* auslaufen.

(b) *(come to an end)* *(lease, contract, period of time)* ablaufen; *(money, supplies)* ausgehen, zu Ende gehen ◆ **my patience is ~ning ~** mir geht langsam die Geduld aus.

2 *vt sep* **(a)** *rope, chain* abwickeln. **(b)** *(Cricket)* ausschlagen *(während der Schlagmann seinen Lauf macht)*.

◆**run out of** *vi +prep obj* **he ran ~ ~ supplies/money/patience/time** ihm gingen die Vorräte/ging das Geld/die Geduld aus/er hatte keine Zeit mehr; **we're ~ning ~ ~ time** wir haben nicht mehr viel Zeit.

◆**run over** [1] *vi* **(a)** *(to neighbour etc)* kurz hinüberlaufen *or* hinübergehen *or* rübergehen *(inf)*.
(b) *(overflow: liquid, container)* überlaufen.
(c) *(Rad, TV etc)* **the play ran ~ by 10 minutes** das Stück hatte 10 Minuten Überlänge; **we're ~ning ~** wir überziehen.
[2] *vi +prep obj story, part in play, details* durchgehen; *text, notes* durchsehen ◆ **I'll ~ ~ your part with you** ich gehe Ihre Rolle kurz mit Ihnen durch.
[3] *vt sep (in vehicle)* überfahren.

◆**run round** *vi* kurz vorbeigehen ◆ **to ~ ~ and see sb** kurz bei jdm vorbeigehen; *see also* **run about.**

◆**run through** [1] *vi (lit)* durchlaufen.
[2] *vi +prep obj* **(a)** *(use up) money, fortune* durchbringen. **(b)** *(rehearse) piece of music, play* durchspielen; *ceremony also, part* durchgehen. **(c)** *see* **run over 2.**
[3] *vt sep* **to ~ sb ~ (with a sword)** jdn (mit einem Schwert) durchbohren.

◆**run up** [1] *vi (lit) (up mountain, upstairs)* hinauf-/herauflaufen; *(towards sb/sth)* hin-/herlaufen *or* -rennen (to zu) ◆ **to ~ ~ against difficulties** auf Schwierigkeiten stoßen.
[2] *vt sep* **(a)** *flag* hissen, hochziehen ◆ **they ran the flag ~ (the mast)** sie hißten die Fahne.
(b) *(incur)* machen ◆ **to ~ ~ one's account** sein Kreditkonto belasten; **to ~ ~ a debt** Schulden machen.
(c) *(sew quickly)* schnell zusammennähen.

run: ~about *n (car)* kleiner Flitzer *(inf)*; *(boat)* kleines Motorboot; **~around** *n (inf)*: **to give sb the ~around** jdn an der Nase herumführen *(inf)*; **to get the ~around (from sb)** (von jdm) an der Nase herumgeführt werden *(inf)*; **~away** [1] *n* Ausreißer(in *f*) *m*; [2] *adj slave* entlaufen; *person, couple, horse* durchgebrannt *(inf)*, ausgerissen; *car, railway truck* der/die/das sich selbständig gemacht hat; *inflation* unkontrollierbar; **the ~away child** der kleine Ausreißer; **they planned a ~away wedding** sie beschlossen, wegzulaufen und zu heiraten; **he had a ~away victory** er hatte einen sehr leichten Sieg; **~-down** [1] *n* **(a)** *(of factory, shop)* (allmähliche) Auflösung; *(of department, stock, personnel)* Abbau *m*; **(b)** *(inf: report)* Bericht *m*; **to give sb a ~-down on sth** jdn über etw *(acc)* informieren, jdm einen Bericht über etw *(acc)* geben; [2] *adj (dilapidated)* heruntergekommen; *(tired)* abgespannt; *battery* leer.

rune [ruːn] *n* Rune *f*.

rung[1] [rʌŋ] *ptp of* **ring**[2].

rung[2] *n (of ladder)* Sprosse *f*; *(of chair)* Querstab *m*.

runic [ˈruːnɪk] *adj* runisch, Runen-.

run-in [ˈrʌnɪn] *n (inf: argument)* Streit *m*.

runner [ˈrʌnəʳ] *n* **(a)** *(athlete)* Läufer(in *f*) *m*; *(horse)* Rennpferd *nt*; *(messenger)* Bote, Laufbursche *m*; *(smuggler)* Schmuggler *m* ◆ **(Bow Street) R~s** *(Brit Hist)* ≃ Büttel *pl*; **it's a good ~, this car** *(inf)* das Auto läuft wirklich einwandfrei.
(b) *(on sledge, skate)* Kufe *f*; *(for curtain)* Vorhangröllchen *nt*; *(for drawer, machine part)* Laufschiene *f*.
(c) *(carpet, for table)* Läufer *m*.
(d) *(Bot)* Ausläufer *m* ◆ **~ bean** *(Brit)* Stangenbohne *f*.
(e) **to do a ~** *(sl)* ('ne) Mücke machen *(sl)*.

runner-up [ˈrʌnərˈʌp] *n* Zweite(r), Zweitplazierte(r) *mf* ◆ **the runners-up** die weiteren Plätze; *(in competition)* die weiteren Gewinner.

running [ˈrʌnɪŋ] [1] *n* **(a)** Laufen, Rennen *nt* ◆ **~ style, style of ~** Laufstil *m*; **to make the ~** *(lit, fig)* das Rennen machen; **to be in the ~ (for sth)** im Rennen (für etw) liegen; **out of the ~** aus dem Rennen; **to take up the ~** *(lit, fig)* sich an die Spitze setzen.
(b) *(functioning: of machine, vehicle)* Laufen *nt*.
(c) *(management) see* **run 3 (j)** Führung *f*; Leitung *f*; Betrieb *m*; Veranstaltung, Durchführung *f*.
(d) *(smuggling)* Schmuggel *m*.
[2] *adj* **(a)** **~ jump** Sprung *m* mit Anlauf; **to take a ~ jump at sth** mit Anlauf über etw springen; **go and take a ~ jump** *(inf)* du kannst mich gern haben *(inf)*; **~ kick** Schuß *m* aus vollem Lauf; **~ commentary** *(Rad, TV)* fortlaufender Kommentar; **we don't need a ~ commentary** *(inf)* wir brauchen keinen Kommentar; **~ account** *(Fin)* laufendes Konto; *see also cpds*.
(b) *(after n)* **4 days ~** 4 Tage hintereinander *or* nacheinander.
(c) *(flowing) water, stream* fließend; *tap, nose* laufend; *eyes* tränend ◆ **~ sore** *(Med)* eiternde Wunde; *(fig)* Eiterbeule *f*; **~ cold** schwerer Schnupfen.
(d) *(current) prices* momentan; *costs* laufend.

running: ~ battle *n (Mil) Gefecht nt, bei dem eine Seite immer weiter zurückgedrängt wird*; *(fig)* Kleinkrieg *m*; **to fight a ~ battle** *(fig)* einen Kleinkrieg führen; **~-board** *n* Trittbrett *nt*; **~ costs** *npl* Betriebskosten *pl*; *(of car)* Unterhaltskosten *pl*; **~ head** *n (Typ)* Kolumnentitel *m*; **~ knot** *n* Schlaufenknoten *m*; **~ mate** *n (US Pol) Kandidat m für die Vizepräsidentschaft*; **~ order** *n*: **in ~ order** betriebsbereit; **~ shoe** *n* Rennschuh *m*; **~ stitch** *n (Sew)* Vorstich, Reihstich *m*; **~ text** *n* fortlaufender Text; **~ title** *n see* **~ head**; **~ track** *n* Aschenbahn *f*.

runny [ˈrʌnɪ] *adj (+er)* flüssig; *nose* laufend; *eyes* wässerig, tränend; *honey* dünnflüssig ◆ **I've got a ~ nose** mir läuft die Nase, meine Nase läuft.

run: ~-off *n (Sport)* Entscheidungslauf *m*, Stechen *nt*; **~-of-the-mill** *adj* durchschnittlich, gewöhnlich; *theme, novel* Feld-Wald-Wiesen- *(inf)*; **~-on (line)** *n* fortlaufende Zeile; **~-out** *n (Ski)* Auslauf *m*; **~-proof** *adj tights etc* laufmaschenfest.

runt [rʌnt] *n* kleinstes Ferkel (eines/des Wurfes); *(pej)* Wicht *m*; *(despicable)* Fiesling *m (inf)*.

run: ~-through *n* Durchgehen *nt*; **let's have a final ~-through** gehen wir das noch einmal durch; **to give sth a ~-through** etw durchgehen; **~-up** *n (Sport)* Anlauf *m*; *(fig)* Vorbereitungszeit *f*; **in the ~-up to the election** in der Zeit vor der Wahl; **~way** *n (Aviat)* Start- und Landebahn *f*, Runway *f or m*.

rupee [ruːˈpiː] *n* Rupie *f*.

rupture [ˈrʌptʃəʳ] [1] *n (lit, fig)* Bruch *m*; *(Pol: of relations)* Abbruch *m*.
[2] *vt* brechen ◆ **to ~ oneself** *(inf)* sich *(dat)* einen Bruch heben *(inf)*.
[3] *vi* brechen.

rural [ˈrʊərəl] *adj* ländlich; *population, life also* Land- ◆ **~ district** *(Brit Admin)* Landbezirk *m*; **~ depopulation** Abwanderung *f* der Landbevölkerung, Landflucht *f*; **~ deprivation** Strukturschwäche *f* in ländlichen Gebieten.

ruse [ruːz] *n* List *f*.

rush[1] [rʌʃ] [1] *n* **(a)** *(rapid movement) (of crowd)* Andrang *m*, Gedränge *nt*; *(of air)* Stoß *m*; *(Mil: attack)* Sturm *m* ◆ **he was caught in the ~ for the door** die zur Tür drängende Menge riß ihn mit; **they made a ~ for the door** sie drängten zur Tür; **to make a ~ at** losstürzen auf *(+acc)*; **there was a ~ for the empty seats** alles stürzte sich auf die leeren Sitze; **there's been a ~ on these goods** diese Waren sind rasend weggegangen; **we have a ~ on in the office just now** bei uns im Büro herrscht zur Zeit Hochbetrieb; **the Christmas ~** der Weihnachtsbetrieb; **we've had a ~ of orders** wir hatten eine Flut von Aufträgen; **there was a ~ of water** Wasser strömte *or* schoß herein/heraus *etc*; **water streamed out in a ~** das Wasser schoß in einem Schwall heraus; **a ~ of blood to the head** Blutandrang *m* im Kopf; *see* **gold ~**.
(b) *(hurry)* Eile *f*; *(stronger)* Hetze, Hast *f* ◆ **the ~ of city life** die Hetze des Stadtlebens; **to be in a ~** in Eile sein; **I had a ~ to get here on time** ich mußte ganz schön hetzen, um rechtzeitig hier zu sein; **I did it in a ~** ich habe es sehr schnell *or* hastig gemacht; **what's (all) the ~?** wozu die Eile/Hetzerei?; **is there any ~ for this?** eilt das?; **it all happened in such a ~** das ging alles so plötzlich.
(c) **~es** *pl (Film)* erste Kopie.
[2] *vi (hurry)* eilen; *(stronger)* hetzen, hasten; *(run)* stürzen; *(wind)* brausen; *(water)* schießen, stürzen; *(make ~ing noise)* rauschen ◆ **they ~ed to help her** sie eilten ihr zu Hilfe; **I ~ed to her side** ich eilte an ihre Seite; **I'm ~ing to finish it** ich beeile mich, es fertigzumachen; **don't ~, take your time** überstürzen Sie nichts, lassen Sie sich Zeit; **you shouldn't just go ~ing into things** Sie sollten die Dinge nicht so überstürzen; **to ~ through** *book* hastig lesen; *meal* hastig essen; *museum, town* hetzen durch; *work* hastig erledigen; **to ~ past** *(person)* vorbeistürzen; *(vehicle)* vorbeischießen; **to ~ in/out/back** *etc* hinein-/hinaus-/zurückstürzen *or* -stürmen; **the ambulance ~ed to the scene** der Krankenwagen raste zur Unfallstelle; **to ~ to the attack** auf ihn/sie *etc* losgehen; **to ~ into print** vorzeitig veröffentlichen; **the blood ~ed to his face** das Blut schoß ihm ins Gesicht; **memories ~ed into his mind** Erinnerungen schossen ihm durch den Kopf.
[3] *vt* **(a)** **to ~ sb to hospital** jdn schnellstens ins Krankenhaus bringen; **they ~ed more troops to the front** sie schickten eilends mehr Truppen an die Front; **they ~ed him out (of the room)** sie brachten ihn eilends aus dem Zimmer; **they ~ed the bill through Parliament** sie peitschten die Gesetzesvorlage durch das Parlament; **to ~ a book into print** ein Buch eilends in Druck geben.
(b) *(force to hurry)* hetzen, drängen ◆ **don't ~ me!** hetz mich nicht; **he won't be ~ed** er läßt sich nicht drängen *or* treiben; **to be ~ed off one's feet** dauernd auf Trab sein; **to ~ sb off his feet** jdn dauernd auf Trab halten; **to ~ sb into a decision** jdn zu einer hastigen Entscheidung treiben; **to ~ sb into doing sth** jdn dazu treiben, etw überstürzt zu tun.
(c) *(charge at)* stürmen; *fence* zustürmen auf *(+acc)* ◆ **the mob ~ed the line of policemen** der Mob stürmte auf den Polizeikordon zu; **to ~ one's fences** *(fig)* die Sache überstürzen.
(d) *(do hurriedly) job, task* hastig machen, schnell machen; *(do badly)* schludern bei *(pej)* ◆ **you can't ~ this sort of work** für solche Arbeit muß man sich *(dat)* Zeit lassen.
(e) *(sl: charge exorbitantly)* schröpfen *(inf)* ◆ **what were you ~ed for it?** wieviel haben sie dir dafür abgeknöpft? *(inf)*.

◆**rush about** *or* **around** *vi* herumhasten *or* -hetzen.

◆**rush at** *vi +prep obj* **(a)** losstürzen auf *(+acc)*, sich stürzen auf *(+acc)*. **(b)** **he tends to ~ ~ things** er neigt dazu, die Dinge überstürzt zu machen.

◆**rush down** *vi* hinunter-/heruntereilen; *(very fast)* hinunter-/herunterstürzen; *(stream)* hinunter-/herunterstürzen.

◆**rush out** [1] *vi* hinaus-/herauseilen; *(very fast)* hinaus-/herausstürzen ◆ **he ~ed ~ and bought one** er kaufte sofort eines.
[2] *vt sep order* eilends wegschicken; *troops, supplies* eilends hintransportieren.

◆**rush through** *vt sep order* durchjagen; *goods, supplies* eilends durchschleusen ◆ **they ~ed medical supplies ~ to him** sie schickten eilends Medikamente zu ihm.

◆**rush up** [1] *vi (lit)* hinauf-/heraufeilen; *(very fast)* hinauf-/heraufstürzen.
[2] *vt sep help, reinforcements* eilends schicken.

rush[2] *n (Bot)* Binse *f* ◆ **in the ~es** im Schilf.

rush: ~-hour(s *pl*) *n* Hauptverkehrszeit(en *pl*), Stoßzeit(en *pl*), Rush-hour *f*; **~-hour traffic** Stoßverkehr *m*; **~ job** *n* eiliger Auftrag; *(pej: bad work)* Schluderarbeit *f (inf)*; **can you do a ~ job for me?** können Sie das ganz schnell für mich machen?; **~light** *n* aus Binsen und Talg hergestellte Kerze; **~ mat, ~ matting** *n* Binsenmatte *f*; **~ order** *n (Comm)* Eilauftrag *m*.

rusk [rʌsk] *n* Zwieback *m*.

russet [ˈrʌsɪt] [1] *n* **(a)** *(colour)* gelbliches Rotbraun. **(b)** *(apple)* Boskop *m*.
[2] *adj* rostfarben.

Russia ['rʌʃə] *n* Rußland *nt.*
Russian ['rʌʃən] [1] *adj* russisch ◆ ~ **leather** Juchten *nt;* ~ **roulette** russisches Roulette; ~ **salad** russischer Salat.
[2] *n* **(a)** Russe *m,* Russin *f.* **(b)** (*language*) Russisch *nt.*
Russky ['rʌskɪ] *n* (*pej*) Iwan *m* ◆ **the Russkies** der Iwan.
rust [rʌst] [1] *n* Rost *m;* (*Bot*) Brand *m* ◆ **covered in** ~ völlig verrostet.
[2] *adj* (*also* ~**-coloured**) rostfarben.
[3] *vt* (*lit*) rosten lassen.
[4] *vi* rosten; (*talent*) verkümmern; (*brain, language*) (ein)rosten.
◆**rust in** *vi* (*screw*) einrosten.
◆**rust over** *vi* verrosten ◆ **to be ~ed** ~ verrostet sein.
◆**rust through** [1] *vi* durchrosten.
[2] *vt sep* durchrosten lassen.
◆**rust up** *vi* festrosten.
rust converter *n* Rostumwandler *m.*
rustic ['rʌstɪk] [1] *n* Bauer *m.*
[2] *adj* bäuerlich; *furniture, style* rustikal; *manners* bäurisch (*pej*).
rusticate ['rʌstɪkeɪt] *vt* **(a)** (*form, liter*) (*send to country*) aufs Land schicken; (*make rustic*) bäurisch machen. **(b)** (*Brit Univ*) vorübergehend von der Universität verweisen.
rustiness ['rʌstɪnɪs] *n* Rostigkeit *f;* (*fig*) eingerostete Kenntnisse (*of* in *+dat*).
rustle ['rʌsl] [1] *n* Rascheln *nt;* (*of foliage*) Rauschen *nt.*
[2] *vi* (*leaves, silk, papers*) rascheln; (*foliage, skirts*) rauschen ◆ **the wind ~d through the leaves** der Wind rauschte in den Blättern; (*on the ground*) der Wind raschelte mit den Blättern.
[3] *vt* **(a)** *paper, skirt, leaves on ground etc* rascheln mit; (*wind*) *leaves on tree* rauschen in (*+dat*).
(b) (*steal*) *cattle* klauen (*inf*).
◆**rustle up** *vt sep* (*inf*) *meal* improvisieren (*inf*) ◆ **can you ~ ~ a cup of coffee?** können Sie eine Tasse Kaffee auftreiben?
rustler ['rʌsləʳ] *n* (*cattle-thief*) Viehdieb *m.*
rustling ['rʌslɪŋ] *n* (*cattle theft*) Viehdiebstahl *m.*
rust: ~proof [1] *adj* rostfrei; [2] *vt* einem Rostschutzverfahren unterziehen; **~proofing** *n* (*substance*) Rostschutzmittel *nt;* (*applied to surface etc*) Rostschutz *m;* ~ **resistant** *adj* nichtrostend.
rusty ['rʌstɪ] *adj* (*+er*) (*lit*) rostig; (*fig*) *mind, maths* eingerostet; *talent* verkümmert ◆ **I'm a bit ~** ich bin etwas aus der Übung.
rut¹ [rʌt] (*Zool*) [1] *n* Brunft, Brunst *f.*
[2] *vi* brunften, brunsten ◆ **~ting call** Brunftschrei *m;* **~ting season** Brunftzeit *f.*
rut² [1] *n* (*in track, path*) Spur, Furche *f;* (*fig: routine*) Trott *m* (*inf*) ◆ **to be in a ~** (*fig*) im Trott sein (*inf*); **to get into/out of a ~** (*fig*) (*person*) in einen Trott geraten (*inf*)/aus dem Trott herauskommen (*inf*); (*mind*) sich in einem eingefahrenen Gleis bewegen/aus dem eingefahrenen Gleis herauskommen.
[2] *vt* furchen.
rutabaga [ˌruːtə'beɪgə] *n* (*US*) Steckrübe *f.*
ruthenium [ruː'θiːnɪəm] *n* (*Chem*) Ruthenium *nt.*
ruthless ['ruːθlɪs] *adj person* rücksichtslos; *cuts, treatment, self-analysis* schonungslos; *irony, sarcasm* unbarmherzig, schonungslos ◆ **you'll have to be ~** man muß hart sein.
ruthlessly ['ruːθlɪslɪ] *adv see adj.*
ruthlessness ['ruːθlɪsnɪs] *n see adj* Rücksichtslosigkeit *f;* Schonungslosigkeit *f;* Unbarmherzigkeit *f;* Härte *f.*
RV *abbr of* **Revised Version.**
Rwanda [rʊ'ændə] *n* Ruanda *nt.*
Rwandan [rʊ'ændən] [1] *n* Ruander(in) *m(f).*
[2] *adj* ruandisch.
rye [raɪ] *n* (*grain*) Roggen *m;* (*US inf*) Roggenwhisky, Rye(whisky) *m;* (*bread*) Roggenbrot *nt.*
rye: ~ bread *n* Roggenbrot *nt;* ~ **whisk(e)y** *n* Roggen- *or* Ryewhisky *m.*

S

S, s [es] *n* S, s *nt.*
S *abbr of* **(a) south** S. **(b) Saint** St. **(c) small.**
s *(Brit old) abbr of* **shilling.**
's (a) he's *etc* = **he is/has; what's** = **what is/has/does? (b)** *(genitive)* **John's book** Johns Buch; **my brother's car** das Auto meines Bruders; **at the Browns'/ butcher's** bei den Browns/beim Fleischer. **(c) let's** = **let us.**
SA *abbr of* **(a) South Africa. (b) South America. (c) South Australia. (d) Salvation Army.**
sab [sæb] *n (Brit inf)* Jagdsaboteur(in) *m(f) (bei Fuchsjagden).*
Sabbatarian [ˌsæbəˈtɛərɪən] *n* strenger Befürworter des Sonntagsgebots *or (Jewish)* Sabbatgebots.
Sabbath [ˈsæbəθ] *n* Sabbat *m; see* **witch.**
sabbatical [səˈbætɪkəl] 1 *adj* **(a)** *(Rel)* Sabbat-. **(b)** *(Univ) year, term* Forschungs- ◆ **he is on ~ leave** er hat akademischen Urlaub *or* Forschungsurlaub.
2 *n (Univ)* akademischer Urlaub, Forschungsurlaub *m* ◆ **to have a/be on ~** Forschungsurlaub *or* akademischen Urlaub haben.
saber *n (US) see* **sabre.**
Sabine [ˈsæbaɪn] 1 *adj* sabinisch.
2 *n* Sabiner(in *f*) *m.*
sable [ˈseɪbl] 1 *n* Zobel *m; (fur)* Zobelfell *nt or* -pelz *m; (liter: colour)* Schwarz *nt.*
2 *adj* Zobel-; *(liter: black)* schwarz.
sabot [ˈsæbəʊ] *n* Holzschuh *m.*
sabotage [ˈsæbətɑːʒ] 1 *n* Sabotage *f.*
2 *vt (lit, fig)* sabotieren.
saboteur [ˌsæbəˈtɜːʳ] *n* Saboteur *m.*
sabre, *(US)* **saber** [ˈseɪbəʳ] *n* Säbel *m.*
sabre: ~-rattler *n* Säbelraßler *m;* **~-rattling** *n* Säbelrasseln *nt;* **~-tooth, ~-toothed tiger** *n* Säbelzahntiger *m.*
sac [sæk] *n (Anat)* Sack *m; (pollen ~)* Staubbeutel *m.*
saccharin(e) [ˈsækərɪn] *n* Saccharin *nt.*
saccharine [ˈsækəriːn] *adj* Saccharin-; *(fig liter)* zuckersüß.
sacerdotal [ˌsæsəˈdəʊtl] *adj* Priester-.
sachet [ˈsæʃeɪ] *n* Beutel *m; (of powder)* Päckchen *nt; (of shampoo, cream)* Briefchen *nt; (lavender ~)* Kissen *nt.*
sack¹ [sæk] 1 *n* **(a)** Sack *m* ◆ **2 ~s of coal** 2 Säcke *or* Sack Kohlen; **to buy sth by the ~** etw sackweise *or* in Säcken kaufen.
(b) *(inf: dismissal)* Entlassung *f,* Rausschmiß *m (inf)* ◆ **to get the ~** rausgeschmissen werden *(inf),* rausfliegen *(inf);* **to give sb the ~** jdn rausschmeißen *(inf);* **it's the ~ for him** er wird rausgeschmissen *(inf),* er fliegt raus *(inf).*
(c) *(sl: bed)* **to hit the ~** sich in die Falle *or* Klappe hauen *(sl).*
2 *vt* **(a)** *(put in ~s)* einsacken.
(b) *(inf: dismiss)* rausschmeißen *(inf),* entlassen.
sack² 1 *n (pillage)* Plünderung *f.*
2 *vt* plündern.
sack³ *n (old)* Sherry *m.*
sackbut [ˈsækbʌt] *n (Hist)* Posaune *f.*
sackcloth [ˈsækklɒθ] *n* Sackleinen *nt* ◆ **in ~ and ashes** in Sack und Asche.
sackful [ˈsækfʊl] *n* Sack *m* ◆ **two ~s of potatoes** zwei Sack Kartoffeln.
sacking [ˈsækɪŋ] *n* **(a)** *(material)* Sackleinen *nt.* **(b)** *(inf: dismissal)* Entlassung *f.*
sack-race [ˈsækreɪs] *n* Sackhüpfen *nt.*
sacral [ˈseɪkrəl] *adj* **(a)** *(Rel)* sakral. **(b)** *(Anat)* Kreuzbein-.
sacrament [ˈsækrəmənt] *n* Sakrament *nt* ◆ **the (Blessed** *or* **Holy) S~** das heilige Sakrament; **to receive the Holy S~** die heilige Kommunion *or (Protestant)* das heilige Abendmahl empfangen; **the last ~s** die Sterbesakramente *pl.*
sacramental [ˌsækrəˈmentl] *adj vows, rites, significance* sakramental; *wine, bread, rites* Opfer-.
sacred [ˈseɪkrɪd] *adj* heilig; *music, poetry* geistlich; *building* sakral ◆ **~ to the memory of ...** zum Gedenken *or* Andenken an *(+acc)* ...; **a statue ~ to Venus** eine der Venus geweihte Statue; **these memories are ~ to me** diese Erinnerungen sind mir heilig; **is nothing ~?** *(inf)* ist denn nichts mehr heilig?; **~ cow** *(lit, fig)* heilige Kuh.
sacrifice [ˈsækrɪfaɪs] 1 *n (lit, fig)* Opfer *nt; (thing sacrificed also)* Opfergabe *f* ◆ **to make a ~ of sb/sth** jdn/etw opfern *or* zum Opfer bringen; **to make ~s** *(lit, fig)* Opfer bringen; **what a ~ (to make)!** welch ein Opfer!; **the ~ of quality to speed** wenn Qualität der Geschwindigkeit geopfert wird *or* zum Opfer fällt; **to sell sth at a ~** *(inf)* etw mit Verlust verkaufen.
2 *vt* opfern *(sth to sb* jdm etw).
sacrificial [ˌsækrɪˈfɪʃəl] *adj* Opfer-.
sacrilege [ˈsækrɪlɪdʒ] *n* Sakrileg *nt; (fig also)* Frevel *m* ◆ **that would be ~** das wäre ein Sakrileg *nt or* Frevel *m.*
sacrilegious [ˌsækrɪˈlɪdʒəs] *adj (lit)* gotteslästerlich, sakrilegisch *(geh); (fig)* frevelhaft, frevlerisch.
sacristan [ˈsækrɪstən] *n* Sakristan *m.*
sacristy [ˈsækrɪstɪ] *n* Sakristei *f.*
sacrosanct [ˈsækrəʊˌsæŋkt] *adj (lit, fig)* sakrosankt.
sacrum [ˈsækrəm] *n* Kreuzbein *nt.*
sad [sæd] *adj (+er)* traurig; *loss* schmerzlich; *colour* trist; *disappointment* schlimm; *result also, mistake, lack* bedauerlich ◆ **to feel ~** traurig sein; **to be ~ at heart** *(liter)* zutiefst betrübt sein *(geh);* **he left a ~der and wiser man** er ging betrübt und geläutert weg; **the ~ death of our father** der schmerzliche Verlust unseres Vaters; **how ~ for you!** wie schrecklich für Sie!, wie traurig!; **it's pretty ~ stuff for a writer of his ability** für einen Schriftsteller seines Formats ist das traurig; **a ~ state of affairs** eine traurige Sache.
sadden [ˈsædn] *vt* betrüben.
saddle [ˈsædl] 1 *n (also of hill)* Sattel *m; (of meat)* Rücken *m* ◆ **to be in the ~** *(lit)* im Sattel sein; *(fig)* im Sattel sitzen.
2 *vt* **(a)** *horse* satteln. **(b)** *(inf)* **to ~ sb/oneself with sb/sth** jdm/sich jdn/etw aufhalsen *(inf);* **to be/have been ~d with sb/sth** jdn/etw auf dem *or* am Hals haben *(inf).*
◆**saddle up** *vti sep* aufsatteln.
saddle: ~-backed *adj hill* sattelförmig; *pig, gull* mit sattelförmiger Markierung am Rücken; **~bag** *n* Satteltasche *f;* **~cloth** *n* Satteldecke *f;* **~-horse** *n* Reitpferd *nt.*
saddler [ˈsædləʳ] *n* Sattler *m.*
saddle roof *n* Satteldach *nt.*
saddlery [ˈsædlərɪ] *n* Sattlerei *f; (articles)* Sattelzeug *nt.*
saddle: ~ shoes *npl (US) Sportschuhe pl aus hellem Leder mit andersfarbigem Einsatz;* **~ soap** *n Seife f für die Behandlung von Sätteln;* **~ sore** *n* wundgescheuerte Stelle; **~-sore** *adj person* wundgeritten; *horse* wundgescheuert; **to get ~-sore** sich wund reiten/scheuern.
Sadducee [ˈsædjʊsiː] *n* Sadduzäer *m.*
sadism [ˈseɪdɪzəm] *n* Sadismus *m.*
sadist [ˈseɪdɪst] *n* Sadist(in *f*) *m.*
sadistic *adj,* **~ally** *adv* [səˈdɪstɪk, -əlɪ] sadistisch.
sadly [ˈsædlɪ] *adv* **(a)** traurig; *(unfortunately)* traurigerweise ◆ **she will be ~ missed** sie wird (uns/ihnen) allen sehr fehlen.
(b) *(regrettably)* bedauerlicherweise ◆ **~ enough he has ...** bedauerlicherweise hat er ...; **he is ~ lacking in any sense of humour** ihm fehlt absolut jeglicher Humor; **the house had been ~ neglected** es war traurig, wie vernachlässigt das Haus war.
sadness [ˈsædnɪs] *n* Traurigkeit *f* ◆ **our ~ at his death** unsere Trauer über seinen Tod.
sadomasochism [ˌseɪdəʊˈmæsəʊkɪzəm] *n* Sadomasochismus *m.*
sae *abbr of* **stamped addressed envelope.**
safari [səˈfɑːrɪ] *n* Safari *f* ◆ **to be/go on ~** eine Safari machen, auf Safari sein/ gehen; **to go on ~ to Kenya** nach Kenia auf Safari fahren; **~ jacket** Safarijacke *f;* **~ park** Safaripark *m.*
safe¹ [seɪf] *n (for valuables)* Safe *m or nt,* Panzerschrank, Tresor *m; (for meat)* Fliegenschrank *m.*
safe² 1 *adj (+er)* **(a)** *(not in danger)* sicher; *(out of danger)* in Sicherheit; *(not injured)* unverletzt ◆ **to be ~ from sb/sth** vor jdm/etw sicher sein; **no girl is ~ with him** bei ihm ist kein Mädchen sicher; **to keep sth ~** etw sicher aufbewahren; **all the passengers/climbers are ~** alle Passagiere/Bergsteiger sind in Sicherheit *or (not injured)* wohlbehalten *or* unverletzt; **you're not ~ without a seat-belt** es ist gefährlich *or* nicht sicher, ohne Gurt zu fahren; **~ journey!** gute Fahrt/Reise!; **~ journey home!** komm gut nach Hause!; **we've found him — is he ~?** wir haben ihn gefunden! — ist ihm etwas passiert?; **thank God you're ~** Gott sei Dank ist dir nichts passiert; **he was ~ at home**

all the time er saß die ganze Zeit wohlbehalten zu Hause; **~ and sound** gesund und wohlbehalten; **the patient is ~ now** der Patient ist jetzt außer Gefahr; **my life's not ~ here** ich bin hier meines Lebens nicht sicher; **your reputation is ~** Ihr Ruf ist nicht in Gefahr; **the secret is ~ with me** bei mir ist das Geheimnis gut aufgehoben; **the thieves are now ~ in prison** die Diebe sind jetzt in sicherem Gewahrsam.

(b) (*not likely to cause harm, not dangerous, not presenting risks*) ungefährlich; (*stable, secure*) *building, roof etc* sicher ◆ **not ~** gefährlich; **this car is not ~ to drive** das Auto ist nicht verkehrssicher; **she is not ~ on the roads** sie ist eine Gefahr im Straßenverkehr; **is this beach ~ for bathing?** kann man an diesem Strand gefahrlos *or* ohne Gefahr baden?; **it is ~ to leave it open/tell him** man kann es unbesorgt *or* ohne weiteres auflassen/es ihm unbesorgt *or* ohne weiteres erzählen; **is it ~ to touch that/drive so fast/light a fire?** ist es auch nicht gefährlich, das anzufassen/so schnell zu fahren/ein Feuer anzumachen?; **the dog is ~ with children** der Hund tut Kindern nichts.

(c) (*reliable*) *job, contraceptive, driver* sicher; *mountain guide, method also, player* zuverlässig, verläßlich ◆ **~ period** sichere *or* ungefährliche Zeit.

(d) (*not likely to be/go wrong*) *investment, theory* sicher; *policy* vorsichtig, risikolos; *estimate* realistisch ◆ **it's a ~ assumption that ...** man kann mit ziemlicher Sicherheit annehmen, daß ...; **it's a ~ guess** es ist so gut wie sicher; **they appointed a ~ man as headmaster** sie bestimmten einen gemäßigten Mann als Rektor; **he plays a ~ game (of tennis)** er spielt (Tennis) auf Sicherheit; **I think it's ~ to say ...** ich glaube, man kann wohl *or* ruhig sagen ...; **is it ~ to generalize/draw that conclusion?** kann man das ohne weiteres verallgemeinern/kann man diesen Schluß so ohne weiteres ziehen?; **do you feel ~ just taking on three extra staff?** haben Sie keine Bedenken, wenn Sie nur drei extra Leute einstellen?; **just to be ~** *or* **on the ~ side** um ganz sicher zu sein, um sicherzugehen; **better ~ than sorry** Vorsicht ist besser als Nachsicht (*Prov*).

(e) (*certain*) **a ~ seat** (*Pol*) ein sicherer Sitz; **he is ~ to win/get the job** er wird sicher gewinnen/die Stelle sicher bekommen.

[2] *adv* **to play (it) ~** (*inf*) auf Nummer Sicher gehen (*inf*).

safe: ~-blower, ~-breaker *n* Schränker (*sl*), Safeknacker (*inf*) *m*; **~-conduct** *n* freies *or* sicheres Geleit; (*document*) Geleitbrief *m*; **~-cracker** *n* (*inf*) Schränker (*sl*), Safeknacker (*inf*) *m*; **~-deposit** *n* Tresorraum *m*; **~-deposit box** *n* Banksafe *m or nt*; **~guard** [1] *n* Schutz *m*; **as a ~guard against** zum Schutz gegen; **double-check these figures as a ~guard** überprüfen Sie diese Zahlen zur Sicherheit noch einmal; [2] *vt* schützen (*against* vor +*dat*); *interests* wahrnehmen; [3] *vi* **to ~guard against sth** sich gegen etw absichern; **~ house** *n* Zufluchtsort *m*; (*police term for house used by terrorists*) konspirative Wohnung; **~-keeping** *n* sichere Verwahrung; **to give sb sth for ~-keeping** jdm etw zur (sicheren) Aufbewahrung geben; **~light** *n* (*Phot*) Dunkelkammerlicht *nt*.

safely ['seɪflɪ] *adv* (*unharmed*) *arrive, get home* wohlbehalten, heil; (*without problems also*) sicher, gut; (*without running risks*) unbesorgt, gefahrlos; *drive* vorsichtig; (*solidly, firmly*) sicher, fest; (*not dangerously*) ungefährlich ◆ **we can ~ estimate that ...** wir können mit einiger Sicherheit annehmen, daß ...; **I think I can ~ say/claim/assume ...** ich glaube, ich kann wohl *or* ruhig sagen/behaupten/annehmen ...; **I got ~ through the first interview** ich bin gut *or* heil durch das erste Interview gekommen; **money ~ deposited in the bank** sicher auf der Bank deponiertes Geld; **~ invested** sicher angelegt; **to put sth away ~** etw an einem sicheren Ort verwahren; **he put it ~ away in a drawer** er verwahrte es sicher in einer Schublade; **put it ~ out of the reach of the children** bringen Sie es vor den Kindern in Sicherheit; **he's ~ locked away in prison** er sitzt hinter Schloß und Riegel; **once the children are ~ tucked up in bed** wenn die Kinder erst mal im Bett sind; **he was ~ tucked up in bed** er lag wohlvermummt im Bett.

safeness ['seɪfnɪs] *n* Sicherheit *f*.

safety ['seɪftɪ] *n* Sicherheit *f* ◆ **in a place of ~** an einem sicheren Ort; **for ~'s sake** aus Sicherheitsgründen; **with complete ~** vollkommen sicher; **I can say with complete ~ that ...** ich kann mit Sicherheit behaupten, daß ...; **to play for ~** (*Sport*) auf Sicherheit spielen; (*fig*) sichergehen; **(there's) ~ in numbers** zu mehreren ist man sicherer; **to reach ~** in Sicherheit gelangen; **when we reached the ~ of the opposite bank** als wir sicher das andere Ufer erreicht hatten; **to leap to ~** sich in Sicherheit bringen; **to seek ~ in flight** sein Heil in der Flucht suchen; **"~ first"** (*as slogan*) „Sicherheit geht vor"; **to believe in ~ first** der Sicherheit den Vorrang geben.

safety: ~ belt *n* Sicherheitsgurt *m*; **~ bicycle** *n* (*old*) Sicherheitsrad (*old*), Niederrad (*old*) *nt*; **~ binding** *n* (*Ski*) Sicherheitsbindung *f*; **~ catch** *n* (*on gun*) (Abzugs)sicherung *f*, Sicherungsbügel *m*; **was the ~ catch on/off?** war das Gewehr gesichert/entsichert?; **~ chain** *n* Sicherheitskette *f*; **~ curtain** *n* (*Theat*) eiserner Vorhang; **~ first campaign** *n* Unfallverhütungskampagne *f*; **~ glass** *n* Sicherheitsglas *nt*; **~ harness** *n* Sicherheitsgurt *m*; **~ lamp** *n* Grubenlampe *f*; **~ margin** *n* Sicherheitsmarge *f*; **~ match** *n* Sicherheitsholz *nt or* -zünder *m*; **~ measure** *n* Sicherheitsmaßnahme *f*; **~ net** *n* Sprung- *or* Sicherheitsnetz *nt*; **~ pin** *n* Sicherheitsnadel *f*; **~ precaution** *n* Sicherheitsvorkehrung *f*; **~ razor** *n* Rasierapparat, Naßrasierer (*inf*) *m*; **~ valve** *n* Sicherheitsventil *nt*; (*fig*) Ventil *nt*.

saffron ['sæfrən] [1] *n* Safran *m*; (*colour*) Safrangelb *nt*.

[2] *adj* Safran-; (*in colour*) safrangelb.

sag [sæg] [1] *n* **there's a bit of a ~ in the bed/ceiling** das Bett/die Decke hängt etwas durch; **if the ~ in the roof gets any worse ...** wenn das Dach noch weiter durchhängt ...; **the ~ of her shoulders** ihre herabhängenden Schultern.

[2] *vi* absacken; (*in the middle*) durchhängen; (*shoulders*) herabhängen; (*breasts*) schlaff herunterhängen; (*production, rate*) zurückgehen; (*price, spirit*) sinken; (*conversation*) abflauen ◆ **don't ~, stand up straight** steh nicht so schlaff da (*inf*), stell dich gerade hin; **a drink will revive his ~ging spirits** ein Drink wird seine Stimmung wieder heben.

saga ['sɑːgə] *n* Saga *f*; (*novel also*) Generationsroman *m*; (*fig*) Geschichte, Story (*sl*) *f*.

sagacious *adj*, **~ly** *adv* [sə'geɪʃəs, -lɪ] weise, klug.

sagacity [sə'gæsɪtɪ] *n* Weisheit, Klugheit *f*.

sage[1] [seɪdʒ] [1] *n* Weise(r) *m*.

[2] *adj* (+*er*) weise.

sage[2] *n* (*Bot*) Salbei *m*.

sage-green ['seɪdʒ'griːn] [1] *n* Graugrün *nt*.

[2] *adj* graugrün.

sagely ['seɪdʒlɪ] *adv* weise.

sageness ['seɪdʒnɪs] *n* Weisheit *f*.

Sagittarian [ˌsædʒɪ'tɛərɪən] [1] *n* Schütze *m*.

[2] *adj* des Schützen.

Sagittarius [ˌsædʒɪ'tɛərɪəs] *n* Schütze *m*.

sago ['seɪgəʊ] *n* Sago *m*.

Sahara [sə'hɑːrə] *n* Sahara *f* ◆ **the ~ Desert** die (Wüste) Sahara.

sahib ['sɑːhɪb] *n* Sahib *m*.

said [sed] [1] *pret, ptp of* **say**.

[2] *adj* (*form*) besagt.

sail [seɪl] [1] *n* **(a)** Segel *nt*; (*of windmill*) Flügel *m* ◆ **under ~** mit aufgezogenen Segeln; **in** *or* **under full ~** mit vollen Segeln; **with all ~s set** mit gesetzten Segeln; **to make ~** (*hoist*) Segel setzen; **to set** *or* **make ~ (for ...)** los- *or* abfahren (nach ...); (*with sailing boat*) absegeln (nach ...).

(b) (*trip*) Fahrt *f* ◆ **it's (a) 3 days' ~ from here** von hier aus fährt *or* (*in yacht*) segelt man 3 Tage; **to go for a ~** segeln gehen; **to take sb for a ~** mit jdm segeln gehen; **have you ever had a ~ in his yacht?** sind Sie schon einmal auf seiner Jacht gefahren *or* gesegelt?

(c) (*boat*) (Segel)schiff *nt*; (*small*) (Segel)boot *nt* ◆ **20 ~** 20 Schiffe/Boote; **there was not a ~ in sight** kein einziges Schiff war zu sehen.

[2] *vt ship* segeln mit; *liner etc* steuern ◆ **they ~ed the ship to Cadiz** sie segelten nach Cadiz; **he ~s his own yacht** er hat eine eigene Jacht; **to ~ the seas** die Meere befahren.

[3] *vi* **(a)** (*Naut*) fahren; (*with yacht*) segeln ◆ **are you flying? — no, ~ing** fliegen Sie? — nein, ich fahre mit dem Schiff; **I went ~ing for a week** ich ging eine Woche segeln; **to ~ round the world** um die Welt segeln, die Erde umsegeln; **to ~ round a headland** eine Landzunge umfahren/umsegeln.

(b) (*leave*) (*for* nach) abfahren; (*yacht, in yacht*) absegeln ◆ **passengers ~ing for New York** Passagiere nach New York.

(c) (*fig: glider, swan etc*) gleiten; (*moon, clouds*) ziehen; (*ball, object*) fliegen ◆ **she ~ed past/out of the room/into the room** sie rauschte vorbei/aus dem Zimmer/sie kam ins Zimmer gerauscht (*all inf*); **she ~ed through all her exams** sie schaffte alle Prüfungen spielend *or* mit Leichtigkeit; **all the heat just ~s out of the window** (*inf*) die ganze Wärme verpufft (durchs Fenster) (*inf*); **the holidays just ~ed by** (*inf*) die Ferien vergingen wie im Flug.

◆**sail in** *vi* (*inf: enter argument*) sich einschalten.

◆**sail into** *vi +prep obj* (*inf*) *person* anfahren; *discussion* sich einschalten in (+*acc*).

sail: ~board [1] *n* Windsurfbrett *nt*; [2] *vi* windsurfen; **~boarder** *n* Windsurfer(in *f*) *m*; **~boarding** *n* Windsurfen *nt*; **~ boat** *n* (*US*) Segelboot *nt*; **~cloth** *n* Segeltuch *nt*; **~ fish** *n* Fächerfisch *m*.

sailing ['seɪlɪŋ] *n* **(a)** Segeln *nt*; (*as sport also*) Segelsport *m*. **(b)** (*departure*) **when is the next ~ for Arran?** wann fährt das nächste Schiff nach Arran?; *see* **plain**.

sailing: ~ boat *n* (*Brit*) Segelboot *nt*; **~ date** *n* Abfahrtstermin *m*; **~ school** *n* Segelschule *f*; **~ ship** *n* Segelschiff *nt*; **~ time** *n* Abfahrtszeit *f*; **~ vessel** *n* Segelschiff *nt*.

sail maker *n* Segelmacher *m*.

sailor ['seɪləʳ] *n* **(a)** Seemann *m*; (*in navy*) Matrose *m*; (*sportsman*) Segler(in *f*) *m* ◆ **~ suit** Matrosenanzug *m*; **hello ~** (*hum*) hallo Süßer. **(b) to be a bad/good ~** (*get seasick*) nicht seefest/seefest sein.

sailplane ['seɪlpleɪn] *n* Segelflugzeug *nt*.

➤ **saint** [seɪnt] *n* **(a)** Heilige(r) *mf*.

(b) (*before name abbr to* **St** [snt]) **St John** der heilige Johannes, Sankt Johannes, St. Johannes; **St Francis** der heilige Franziskus; **St Mark's (Church)** die Markuskirche.

(c) (*fig*) Heilige(r) *mf* ◆ **she is a ~ to put up with that** sie muß ja eine Engelsgeduld haben, daß sie sich das gefallen läßt.

sainted ['seɪntɪd] *adj* heiliggesprochen ◆ **my ~ aunt!** (*inf*) heiliger Strohsack! (*inf*), heiliger Bimbam! (*inf*).

sainthood ['seɪnthʊd] *n* Heiligkeit *f* ◆ **martyrs who were elevated to ~** Märtyrer, die in die Gemeinschaft der Heiligen aufgenommen wurden.

saintliness ['seɪntlɪnɪs] *n* Heiligmäßigkeit *f*; (*fig pej: of person*) frömmlerisches Wesen ◆ **the ~ of his smile** sein lammfrommes Lächeln.

saintly ['seɪntlɪ] *adj* (+*er*) heiligmäßig; (*fig pej*) *person* frömmlerisch; *smile* lammfromm ◆ **he stood there with a ~ look on his face** (*lit*) er hatte einen verklärten Gesichtsausdruck; (*iro*) er sah aus, als ob er kein Wässerchen trüben könnte.

saint's day ['seɪntsdeɪ] *n* Heiligenfest *nt*, Tag *m* des/der heiligen ... ◆ **when is your ~?** wann ist Ihr Namenstag?

saith [seθ] (*old*) = **says**.

➤ LANGUAGE IN USE: **saint: a** → 23.2

sake[1] [seɪk] *n* **for the ~ of ...** um (+*gen*) ... willen; **for my ~** meinetwegen; (*to please me*) mir zuliebe; **for your own ~** dir selbst zuliebe; **for your family's ~** um Ihrer Familie willen, Ihrer Familie wegen; **for heaven's** *or* **Christ's ~!** (*inf*) um Gottes willen!; **for heaven's** *or* **Christ's ~ shut up** (*inf*) nun halt doch endlich die Klappe (*inf*); **for old times' ~** in Erinnerung an alte Zeiten; **for the ~ of those who ...** für diejenigen, die ...; **for whose ~ is the writer writing, his own or the public's?** für wen schreibt der Schriftsteller, (für) sich selbst oder den Leser?; **I'd do anything for your ~** für dich tue ich alles; (*to keep you happy*) dir zuliebe tue ich alles; **I did it just for the ~ of having a new experience** ich habe es nur getan, um eine neue Erfahrung zu machen; **and all for the ~ of a few pounds** und alles wegen ein paar Pfund; **to talk for talking's ~** reden, nur damit etwas gesagt wird; **I do the job for its own ~** ich mache die Arbeit um ihrer selbst willen *or* ihrer selbst wegen.

sake[2], saki ['sɑːkɪ] *n* (*drink*) Sake *m*.

sal *abbr of* **salary** Geh.

salaam [sə'lɑːm] 1 *n, interj* Salem *m*.
2 *vi* sich mit Salem begrüßen.

salable *adj* (*US*) *see* **saleable**.

salacious [sə'leɪʃəs] *adj* schlüpfrig; *picture* aufreizend; *chuckle* anzüglich.

salaciousness [sə'leɪʃəsnɪs] *n see adj* Schlüpfrigkeit *f*; aufreizende Darstellung; Anzüglichkeit *f*.

salad ['sæləd] *n* Salat *m*.

salad: ~ bowl *n* Salatschüssel *f*; **~ cream** *n* ≃ Mayonnaise *f*; **~ days** *npl* unschuldige Jugendtage *pl*; **in the ~ days of his youth** als er noch jung und unschuldig war; **~ dressing** *n* Salatsoße *f*; **lettuce with ~ dressing** angemachter Salat; **~ oil** *n* Salatöl *nt*.

salamander ['sælə,mændəʳ] *n* Salamander *m*; (*Myth*) Feuergeist *m*.

salami [sə'lɑːmɪ] *n* Salami *f*.

sal ammoniac [,sælə'məʊnɪæk] *n* Ammoniumsalz *nt*, Salmiak *m*.

salaried ['sælərɪd] *adj* **~ post** Angestelltenposten *m*; **~ employee** Gehaltsempfänger(in *f*) *m*; **~ staff** Gehaltsempfänger *pl*.

➤ **salary** ['sælərɪ] *n* Gehalt *nt* ◆ **he earns a good ~** er hat ein gutes Gehalt; **what is his ~?** wie hoch ist sein Gehalt?

salary: ~ earner *n* Gehaltsempfänger(in *f*) *m*; **~ increase** *n* Gehaltserhöhung *f*; **~ package** *n* Gehalt *nt* (*einschließlich Sonderleistungen*), Gehaltspaket *nt*; **~ range** *n* Gehaltsrahmen *m*, Gehaltsspanne *f*; **~ scale** *n* Gehaltsskala *f*.

sale [seɪl] *n* **(a)** (*selling*) Verkauf *m* ◆ **for ~** zu verkaufen; **to put sth up for ~** etw zum Verkauf anbieten; **is it up for ~?** steht es zum Verkauf?; **not for ~** nicht verkäuflich; **going cheap for a quick ~** umständehalber billig abzugeben; **to be on ~** verkauft werden; **on ~ at all bookshops** in allen Buchhandlungen erhältlich; **there is a very slow ~ in these goods** diese Waren verkaufen sich schlecht; **on a ~ or return basis** auf Kommission(sbasis).
(b) (*instance*) Geschäft *nt*; (*of insurance, bulk order*) Abschluß *m* ◆ **~s** *pl* (*turnover*) der Absatz; **how many ~s have you made?** wieviel (Stück) haben Sie verkauft?/wie viele Abschlüsse haben Sie gemacht?; **we've made no ~ to China** mit China haben wir keine Geschäfte abgeschlossen; **"no ~"** (*on till*) ≃ Nullbon.
(c) **~s** *sing* (*department*) Verkaufsabteilung *f*.
(d) (*at reduced prices*) Ausverkauf *m*; (*at end of season also*) Schlußverkauf *m*; (*clearance ~*) Räumungsverkauf *m* ◆ **to go to the ~s** zum Ausverkauf gehen; **they've got a ~ on** da ist Ausverkauf; **in the ~, on ~** (*US*) im (Sonder)angebot; **to buy in** *or* **at the ~s** im Ausverkauf kaufen.
(e) (*auction, selling off*) Auktion *f* ◆ **~ of work** Basar *m*.

saleable, (*US*) salable ['seɪləbl] *adj* (*marketable*) absatzfähig; (*in ~ condition*) verkäuflich ◆ **not in a ~ condition** nicht zum Verkauf geeignet.

sale: ~ and leaseback *n* Verkauf *m* mit Rückmiete; **~ price** *n* Ausverkaufspreis *m*; **~room** *n* Auktionsraum *m*.

sales: ~ clerk *n* (*US*) Verkäufer(in *f*) *m*; **~ department** *n* Verkaufsabteilung *f*; **~ director** *n* Verkaufsdirektor *m*; **~ drive** *n* Verkaufskampagne *f*; **~ figures** *npl* Verkaufs- *or* Absatzziffern *pl*; **~ force** *n* Vertreterstab *m*; **~girl, ~lady** *n* Verkäuferin *f*; **~man** *n* Verkäufer *m*; (*representative*) Vertreter *m*; **~ manager** *n* Verkaufsleiter *m*.

salesmanship ['seɪlzmənʃɪp] *n* Verkaufstechnik *f*.

sales: ~person *n* Verkäufer(in *f*) *m*; **~ pitch** *n* Verkaufstechnik *or* -masche (*inf*) *f*; **he gave me a long ~ pitch** (*inf*) er hat mir einen langen Sermon (*inf*) *or* eine lange Story (*sl*) erzählt; **~ representative** *n* Vertreter(in *f*) *m*; **~ resistance** *n* Kaufunlust *f*; **to meet with ~ resistance** auf Absatzschwierigkeiten stoßen; **~room** *n see* **saleroom**; **~ slip** *n* Kassenzettel, Bon *m*; (*received prior to payment*) Kaufbeleg *m*; **~ talk** *n* Verkaufsgespräch *nt*; **his ~ talk won me over** die Art, wie er die Ware angepriesen hat, hat mich überzeugt; **that's just ~ talk** er/sie macht nur Reklame; **~ tax** *n* (*US*) Verkaufssteuer *f*; **~woman** *n* Verkäuferin *f*.

salient ['seɪlɪənt] *adj* (*lit*) hervorstehend; (*fig*) hervorstechend ◆ **the ~ points of his argument** die Hauptpunkte *pl* seiner Argumentation.

saline ['seɪlaɪn] *adj* salzig ◆ **~ drip** (*Med*) (*device*) Infusionsapparat *m or* Tropf *m* (*inf*) mit Kochsalzlösung; (*liquid*) Kochsalzlösung *f*; **~ solution** Salzlösung *f*.

salinity [sə'lɪnɪtɪ] *n* Salzigkeit *f*; (*content*) Salzgehalt *m*.

saliva [sə'laɪvə] *n* Speichel *m*.

salivary ['sælɪvərɪ] *adj* Speichel- ◆ **~ gland** Speicheldrüse *f*.

salivate ['sælɪveɪt] *vi* Speichel produzieren; (*animal*) geifern; (*old people, baby*) sabbern; (*with lust*) lüstern geifern.

salivation [,sælɪ'veɪʃən] *n* Speichelfluß *m*.

sallow ['sæləʊ] *adj* bleich, teigig; *colour* fahl.

sallowness ['sæləʊnɪs] *n* Blässe *f*, Fahlheit *f*.

sally ['sælɪ] 1 *n* Ausbruch *m*; (*of troops*) Ausfall *m* ◆ **to make a ~** (*troops*) einen Ausfall machen; (*fig: verbally*) eine Tirade loslassen; **I made a ~ into town** ich habe einen Trip in die Stadt gemacht.
2 *vi* (*old, hum*) **to ~ forth** (*Mil*) einen Ausfall machen; (*rush out*) hinaus-/herausstürmen; (*set out*) sich aufmachen.

Sally Army ['sælɪ'ɑːmɪ] *n* (*Brit inf*) *see* **Salvation Army**.

salmon ['sæmən] 1 *n, pl* - Lachs, Salm *m*; (*colour*) Lachs(rosa) *nt*.
2 *adj* (*in colour*) lachs(farben).

salmonella [,sælmə'nelə] *n* (*also* **~ poisoning**) Salmonellenvergiftung *f*.

salmon: ~ leap *n* Lachssprung *m*; (*man-made*) Lachsleiter *or* -treppe *f*; **~ pink** 1 *n* Lachsrosa *nt*; 2 *adj* lachsrosa; **~ river** *n Fluß m, in dem Lachse vorkommen*; **~ trout** *n* Lachsforelle *f*.

salon ['sælɒn] *n* (*all senses*) Salon *m*.

saloon [sə'luːn] *n* **(a)** Saal *m*; (*Naut*) Salon *m*. **(b)** (*Brit Aut*) Limousine *f*; (*in motor racing*) Tourenwagen *m*. **(c)** (*US: bar*) Wirtschaft *f*; (*in Westerns*) Saloon *m*.

saloon: ~ bar *n* (*Brit*) *vornehmerer Teil eines Lokals*; **~ car** *n* (*Brit*) Limousine *f*.

Salop ['sæləp] *abbr of* **Shropshire**.

salopettes [,sælə'pets] *npl* (*Ski*) Lifthose *f*.

salsify ['sælsɪfɪ] *n* Schwarzwurzel *f*.

salt [sɔːlt] 1 *n* **(a)** (*Cook, Chem*) Salz *nt*; (*for icy roads*) Streusalz *nt* ◆ **~ of the earth** (*fig*) Salz der Erde; **to be worth one's ~** (*fig*) etwas taugen; **to take sth with a pinch** *or* **grain of ~** (*fig*) etw nicht ganz für bare Münze *or* so wörtlich nehmen; *see* **old ~**.
(b) **~s** *pl* (*smelling ~s*) Riechsalz *nt*; (*for bowels*) salinisches Abführmittel ◆ **that drink went through me like a dose of ~s** (*inf*) das Getränk hat mich richtig durchgeputzt (*inf*); **the new director went through the board like a dose of ~s** (*inf*) der neue Direktor hat im Vorstand mit eisernem Besen ausgekehrt.
(c) (*fig: zest, flavour*) Würze *f*.
2 *adj meat, water etc* Salz-; *butter* gesalzen; *taste* Salz-, salzig ◆ **it's very ~** es ist sehr salzig.
3 *vt* (*cure*) einsalzen; (*flavour*) salzen ◆ **~ed herrings** Salzheringe *pl*.

◆**salt away** *vt sep* (*inf*) *money* auf die hohe Kante legen (*inf*).

SALT [sɔːlt] *abbr of* **Strategic Arms Limitation Treaty** SALT.

salt: ~ cellar *n* Salzfäßchen *nt*; (*shaker*) Salzstreuer *m*; **~ flats** *npl* Salztonebene *f*.

saltiness ['sɔːltɪnɪs] *n* Salzigkeit *f*.

salt: ~ lake *n* Salzsee *m*; **~-lick** *n* Salzlecke *f*; **~-marsh** *n* Salzsumpf *m*; **~-mine** *n* Salzbergwerk *nt*.

saltness ['sɔːltnɪs] *n* Salzigkeit *f*.

salt: ~-pan *n* Salzpfanne *f*; **~petre**, (*US*) **~peter** [,sɔːlt'piːtəʳ] *n* Salpeter *m*; **~ shaker** *n* Salzstreuer *m*; **~ water** *n* Salzwasser *nt*; **~-water** *adj fish etc* Meeres-; *lake* Salz-; **~ works** *n sing or pl* Saline *f*.

salty ['sɔːltɪ] *adj* (+*er*) salzig.

salubrious [sə'luːbrɪəs] *adj* **(a)** (*form*) *air, climate* gesund. **(b)** (*inf*) *district, friends* ersprießlich ◆ **not a very ~ pub** eine recht zweifelhafte Kneipe.

salutary ['sæljʊtərɪ] *adj* **(a)** (*healthy*) gesund. **(b)** (*beneficial*) *advice* nützlich; *experience* heilsam, lehrreich; *effect* günstig.

salutation [,sæljʊ'teɪʃən] *n* Begrüßung *f*; (*in letters*) Anrede *f* ◆ **he raised his hand in ~** er hob die Hand zum Gruß.

salutatorian [səluːtə'tɔːrɪən] *n* (*US*) *Student, der die Begrüßungsrede hält*.

salutatory [sə'luːtətərɪ] *adj oration, gesture* Begrüßungs-.

salute [sə'luːt] 1 *n* Gruß *m*; (*of guns*) Salut *m* ◆ **flags were raised in ~** zur Begrüßung wurden die Fahnen gehißt; **to stand at the ~** salutieren; **a 21-gun ~** 21 Salutschüsse; **to take the ~** die Parade abnehmen; **he gave a smart ~** er salutierte zackig.
2 *vt* (*Mil*) *flag etc* grüßen; *person also* salutieren vor (+*dat*); (*fig liter: welcome*) begrüßen; *courage* bewundern, den Hut ziehen vor (+*dat*) ◆ **to ~ the arrival of sb/sth** jdn/etw begrüßen; **we ~ the glorious dead** wir gedenken der gefallenen Helden.
3 *vi* (*Mil*) salutieren, grüßen.

salutories [sə'luːtərɪz] *npl* (*US*) Begrüßungsrede *f* (*bei Semesterabschluß und Zeugnisüberreichung*).

salvage ['sælvɪdʒ] 1 *n* (*act*) Bergung *f*; (*objects*) Bergungsgut *nt*; (*payment*) Bergelohn *m*; (*proceeds from ~d goods*) Wert *m* der geretteten Waren ◆ **to collect newspapers for ~** Zeitungen zur Wiederverwertung sammeln.
2 *vt* (*from wreck, building*) bergen (*from* aus); (*fig*) retten (*from* von) ◆ **to ~ sth from the fire** etw aus den Flammen retten; **~ what you can** (*lit, fig*) rettet, was ihr retten könnt; **a few happy memories can be ~d from the marriage** ein paar glückliche Erinnerungen können aus den Trümmern der Ehe geborgen werden.

salvage: ~ operation *n* Bergungsaktion *f*; (*fig*) Rettungsaktion *f*; **~ tug** *n* Bergungsschlepper *m*; **~ vessel** *n* Bergungsschiff *nt*.

salvation [sæl'veɪʃən] *n* (*act of saving*) Rettung *f*; (*state of being saved also, esp Rel*) Heil *nt* ◆ **he found ~ in the Church** er fand sein Heil in der Kirche; **he found a kind of emotional ~ in this poetry** er fand Erlösung in dieser Dichtung; **the path to ~** der Weg des Heils; **you were/that was my ~** du warst/das war meine Rettung; **everyone has to work out his own ~** jeder muß für sein eigenes Heil sorgen.

Salvation Army 1 *n* Heilsarmee *f*.
2 *attr hostel, band, meeting* der Heilsarmee.

➤ LANGUAGE IN USE: **salary** → 19.2

salvationist [sæl'veɪʃənɪst] *n* Heilsprediger(in *f*) *m*; (*usu* **S~**: *of Salvation Army*) Angehörige(r) *mf* der Heilsarmee.
salve[1] [sælv] *vt* (*liter*) *see* **salvage.**
salve[2] [1] *n* Salbe *f*; (*fig liter*) Balsam *m* ◆ **as a ~ for his conscience** um sein Gewissen zu beruhigen.
[2] *vt* (*rare lit*) (ein)salben; (*fig*) *conscience* beruhigen.
salver ['sælvə^r] *n* Tablett *nt.*
salvo ['sælvəʊ] *n* (*of guns, fig*) Salve *f* ◆ **a ~ of applause** ein Beifallssturm *m.*
sal volatile [ˌsælvə'lætəlɪ] *n* Riechsalz *nt.*
Samaritan [sə'mærɪtən] *n* Samariter *m* ◆ **good ~** (*lit, fig*) barmherziger Samariter.
samarium [sə'mɛərɪəm] *n* (*Chem*) Samarium *nt.*
samba ['sæmbə] [1] *n* Samba *f or m.*
[2] *vi* Samba tanzen.
sambo ['sæmbəʊ] *n* (*pej*) Kaffer *m.*
➤ **same** [seɪm] [1] *adj* **the ~** der/die/das gleiche; (*numerically identical also, one and the ~*) derselbe/dieselbe/dasselbe; **they were both wearing the ~ dress** sie hatten beide das gleiche Kleid an; **they both live in the ~ house** sie wohnen beide in demselben *or* im selben Haus; **they are all the ~** sie sind alle gleich; **that's the ~ tie as I've got** so eine Krawatte habe ich auch, ich habe die gleiche Krawatte; **she just wasn't the ~ person** sie war ein anderer Mensch; **it's the ~ thing** das ist das gleiche; **see you tomorrow, ~ time ~ place** bis morgen, gleicher Ort, gleiche Zeit *or* Ort und Zeit wie gehabt; **we sat at the ~ table as usual** wir saßen an unserem üblichen Tisch; **how are you? — ~ as usual** wie geht's? — wie immer; **I've made the ~ mistake myself** den Fehler habe ich auch gemacht, ich habe den gleichen Fehler gemacht; **this ~ person** eben dieser Mensch; (*Jur*) besagte Person; **she was killed with this ~ knife** sie wurde mit eben *or* genau diesem Messer erstochen; **he is the ~ age as his wife** er ist (genau) so alt wie seine Frau; **it happened the ~ day** es ist am gleichen *or* selben Tag passiert; **if you can do the two jobs in the ~ day** wenn sie die beiden Arbeiten an einem Tag erledigen können; **in the ~ way** (genau) gleich; (*by the ~ token*) ebenso; *see* **time.**
➤ [2] *pron* **(a) the ~** der/die/das gleiche; derselbe/dieselbe/dasselbe; **and I would do the ~ again** und ich würde es wieder tun; **he left and I did the ~** er ist gegangen, und ich auch *or* ebenfalls; **they are one and the ~** das ist doch dasselbe; (*people*) das ist doch ein und derselbe/dieselbe; **another drink? — thanks, (the) ~ again** noch etwas zu trinken? — ja bitte, das gleiche noch mal; **~ again, Joe** und noch einen, Joe; **she's much the ~** sie hat sich kaum geändert; (*in health*) es geht ihr kaum besser; **you're not the ~ any more** du bist nicht mehr derselbe/dieselbe; **I'm not the ~ as my brother** ich bin nicht so wie mein Bruder; **it's always the ~** es ist immer das gleiche; **it comes** *or* **amounts to the ~** das kommt *or* läuft aufs gleiche hinaus.
(b) *no art* (*Comm*) **for repairing chair: £10, for recovering ~: £25** Stuhlreparatur: £ 10, Beziehen: £ 25.
(c) (*in adverbial uses*) **the ~** gleich; **to pay/treat everybody the ~** alle gleich bezahlen/behandeln; **things go on just the ~ (as always)** es ändert sich nichts; **it's not the ~ as before** es ist nicht wie früher; **I don't feel the ~ about it** ich sehe das nicht so; **I used to love you but I don't feel the ~ any more** ich habe dich mal geliebt, aber das ist jetzt anders; **I still feel the ~ about you** an meinen Gefühlen dir gegenüber hat sich nichts geändert; **if it's all the ~ to you** wenn es Ihnen egal ist; **it's all the ~ to me (what you do)** es ist mir egal(, was du tust).
➤ **(d)** (*phrases*) **all** *or* **just the ~** (*nevertheless*) trotzdem; **~ here** ich/wir auch; **~ to you** (danke) gleichfalls; **I'd have hit him, ~** (*inf*) *or* **the ~ as you did** ich hätte ihn (an Ihrer Stelle) auch geschlagen; **we left our country the ~ as you did** wir haben unsere Heimat verlassen, wie Sie auch.
sameness ['seɪmnɪs] *n* Eintönigkeit *f.*
samey ['seɪmɪ] *adj* (*inf*) eintönig, dasselbe in Grün (*inf*).
Samoa [sə'məʊə] *n* Samoa *nt.*
Samoan [sə'məʊən] [1] *adj* samoanisch.
[2] *n* **(a)** Samoaner(in *f*) *m.* **(b)** (*language*) Samoanisch *nt.*
samovar [ˌsæməʊ'vɑː^r] *n* Samowar *m.*
sampan ['sæmpæn] *n* Sampan *m.*
sample ['sɑːmpl] [1] *n* (*example*) Beispiel *nt* (*of* für); (*for tasting, fig: of talent, behaviour*) Kostprobe *f*; (*Comm*) (*of cloth etc*) Muster *nt*; (*of commodities, urine, blood etc*) Probe *f*; (*Statistics*) (Zufalls)stichprobe *f*, Sample *nt* ◆ **that's a typical ~ of her cooking/the local dialect** genau so kocht sie immer/das ist ein typisches Beispiel für den örtlichen Dialekt; **give us a ~ of your playing/singing** spielen/singen Sie uns etwas vor; **up to ~** (*Comm*) mustergetreu; **a representative ~ of the population** eine repräsentative Auswahl aus der Bevölkerung; **to take ~s of public opinion/of goods produced** Stichproben zur öffentlichen Meinung/bei der gefertigten Ware machen.
[2] *adj attr pieces, books* Muster-; *pages, copy* Probe-; *bottle, sachet etc* Probier- ◆
◆**~survey** Stichprobenerhebung *f*; **a ~ section of the population** eine Auswahl aus der Bevölkerung.
[3] *vt wine, food* probieren, kosten; *pleasures* kosten ◆ **to ~ wines** eine Weinprobe machen.
sampler ['sɑːmplə^r] *n* **(a)** (*person*) Probierer(in *f*) *m.* **(b)** (*Sew*) Stickmustertuch *nt.* **(c)** (*record*) Auswahlplatte *f.*
sampling ['sɑːmplɪŋ] [1] *n* (*of food*) Kostprobe *f*; (*of wine*) Weinprobe *f*; (*Statistics*) Stichprobenverfahren *nt.*
[2] *attr methods, techniques* Stichproben-.
Samson ['sæmsn] *n* (*lit*) Samson *m*; (*fig*) Herkules *m.*
Samurai ['sæmjʊraɪ] [1] *n* Samurai *m.*
[2] *attr* Samurai-.

➤ LANGUAGE IN USE: **same: 2a** → 5.4, 26.2 **2d** → 26.3

sanatorium [ˌsænə'tɔːrɪəm] *n, pl* **sanatoria** [ˌsænə'tɔːrɪə] Sanatorium *nt*; (*in cpds*) -heilanstalt *f.*
sanctification [ˌsæŋktɪfɪ'keɪʃən] *n see vt* Heiligung *f*; Weihe *f*; Annahme *f.*
sanctify ['sæŋktɪfaɪ] *vt* (*make holy*) heiligen; (*give quasi-moral sanction to also*) sanktionieren; (*consecrate*) weihen; (*make binding*) *vows* annehmen ◆ **a custom sanctified by tradition** ein durch die Tradition geheiligter Brauch.
sanctimonious [ˌsæŋktɪ'məʊnɪəs] *adj* frömmlerisch ◆ **don't be so ~ about it** tu doch nicht so fromm.
sanctimoniously [ˌsæŋktɪ'məʊnɪəslɪ] *adv see adj.*
sanctimoniousness [ˌsæŋktɪ'məʊnɪəsnɪs] *n* frömmlerisches Wesen ◆ **the ~ of his comments** seine frömmlerischen Bemerkungen.
sanction ['sæŋkʃən] [1] *n* **(a)** (*permission, approval*) Zustimmung *f* ◆ **to give one's ~ to sth** etw sanktionieren, seine Zustimmung zu etw geben; **rituals which have received the ~ of tradition** Rituale, die durch die Tradition sanktioniert sind. **(b)** (*enforcing measure*) Sanktion *f.*
[2] *vt* sanktionieren.
sanctity ['sæŋktɪtɪ] *n* Heiligkeit *f*; (*of rights*) Unantastbarkeit *f* ◆ **a man of great ~** ein sehr heiliger Mann; **through time these customs have acquired an unquestionable ~** im Laufe der Zeit sind diese Sitten zur geheiligten Tradition geworden.
sanctuary ['sæŋktjʊərɪ] *n* **(a)** (*holy place*) Heiligtum *nt*; (*altar ~*) Altarraum *m.* **(b)** (*refuge*) Zuflucht *f* ◆ **to seek ~ with** Zuflucht suchen bei. **(c)** (*for animals*) Schutzgebiet *nt.*
sanctum ['sæŋktəm] *n* **(a)** (*holy place*) heiliger Ort. **(b)** (*fig: private place*) Allerheiligste(s) *nt.*
sand [sænd] [1] *n* Sand *m no pl* ◆ **~s** (*of desert*) Sand *m*; (*beach*) Sandstrand *m*; **the ~s are running out** (*fig*) die Zeit *or* Uhr läuft ab; **the ~s of time** (*fig*) die Zeit.
[2] *vt* (*smooth*) schmirgeln; (*sprinkle with ~*) streuen.
◆**sand down** *vt sep* (ab)schmirgeln.
sandal ['sændl] *n* Sandale *f.*
sandalled ['sændəld] *adj* **in her ~ feet** in *or* mit Sandalen.
sandalwood ['sændlwʊd] [1] *n* Sandelholz *nt.*
[2] *attr* Sandelholz-.
sand: ~bag [1] *n* Sandsack *m*; [2] *vt* mit Sandsäcken schützen; **~bank** *n* Sandbank *f*; **~bar** *n* Sandbank *f*; **~blast** *vt* sandstrahlen; **~blaster** *n* Sandstrahler *m*; **~blasting** *n* Sandstrahlen *nt*; **~-box** *n* (*Rail*) Sandstreuer *m*; (*Metal*) Sandform *f*; (*for playing*) Sandkasten *m*; **~boy** *n*: **as happy as a ~boy** quietschvergnügt (*inf*); **~castle** *n* Sandburg *f*; **~ dune** *n* Sanddüne *f.*
sander ['sændə^r] *n* (*tool*) Rutscher, Vibrationsschleifer *m.*
sand: ~-flea *n* Strandfloh *m*; (*harmful*) Sandfloh *m*; **~-fly** *n* Sandfliege *f*; **~-glass** *n* Sanduhr *f*; **~ hopper** *n* Sandhüpfer *m.*
sandiness ['sændɪnɪs] *n* Sandigkeit *f* ◆ **noted for the ~ of its beaches** berühmt für seine Sandstrände.
sand: ~lot *adj* (*US*) **~lot baseball** *auf einem nicht als Spielfeld markierten Gelände und zum Spaß gespielter Baseball*; **~man** *n* Sandmann *m*; **~-martin** *n* Uferschwalbe *f*; **~paper** [1] *n* Sand- *or* Schmirgelpapier *nt*; [2] *vt* schmirgeln; **~paper down** *vt sep* abschmirgeln; **~piper** *n* Strandläufer *m*; **~pit** *n* Sandkasten *m or* -kiste *f*; **~shoe** *n* Stoffschuh *m*; (*for beach*) Strandschuh *m*; **~stone** [1] *n* Sandstein *m*; [2] *adj* Sandstein-, aus Sandstein; **~storm** *n* Sandsturm *m*; **~-table** *n* (*Mil*) Sandkasten *m.*
sandwich ['sænwɪdʒ] [1] *n* Doppelschnitte *or* -stulle (*N Ger*) *f*, Sandwich *nt* ◆ **open ~** belegtes Brot; **he has ~es for lunch** er ißt Brote *or* Schnitten *or* Stullen (*N Ger*) zum Mittagessen.
[2] *vt* (*also* **~ in**) hineinzwängen; *car* einkeilen ◆ **to be ~ed between two things/people** (*car, house*) zwischen zwei Dingen/Menschen eingekeilt sein; (*person also, small object*) zwischen zwei Dingen/Menschen eingezwängt sein; **~ed between two slices of bread** zwischen zwei Brotscheiben.
sandwich: ~ bar *n* Snackbar *f*; **~board** *n* Reklametafel *f*, Sandwich *nt* (*hum*); **~ course** *n Ausbildungsgang m, bei dem sich Theorie und Praxis abwechseln*; **~man** *n* Plakatträger, Sandwichmann *m.*
sandy ['sændɪ] *adj* (*+er*) **(a)** sandig; *beach, soil* Sand-, sandig *pred.* **(b)** (*in colour*) rötlich; *hair* rotblond.
sand-yacht ['sændjɒt] *n* Segelwagen *m.*
sane [seɪn] *adj* (*+er*) *person* normal; (*Med, Psych etc*) geistig gesund; (*Jur*) zurechnungsfähig; *world, society etc* gesund; (*sensible*) *advice, policy, person* vernünftig ◆ **it's simply not ~ to ...** es ist doch verrückt, zu ...
sang [sæŋ] *pret of* **sing.**
sangfroid ['sɑ̃ːŋ'frwɑː] *n* Gelassenheit, Seelenruhe *f.*
sangria [sæŋ'griːə] *n* Sangria *f.*
sanguinary ['sæŋgwɪnərɪ] *adj* (*liter*) *battle* blutig; *person* blutrünstig; *expression etc* derb ◆ **~ language** (*hum*) ≃ Fäkalsprache *f.*
sanguine ['sæŋgwɪn] *adj* **(a)** (*optimistic*) optimistisch ◆ **to have a ~ nature** *or* **disposition** von Natur aus ein Optimist sein; **I remain ~ about his chances** was seine Chancen betrifft, bin ich noch immer zuversichtlich; **~ that we shall succeed** zuversichtlich, daß wir Erfolg haben werden.
(b) ~ complexion rote *or* gesunde (*euph*) Gesichtsfarbe.
sanguinely ['sæŋgwɪnlɪ] *adv* optimistisch; *say* zuversichtlich.
sanguinity [sæŋ'gwɪnɪtɪ] *n* Optimismus *m.*
sanies ['seɪnɪiːz] *n* (*Med*) Jauche *f.*
sanitariness ['sænɪtərɪnɪs] *n* Hygiene *f* ◆ **the ~ of conditions** die hygienischen Zustände; **the ~ of the toilets is not up to standard** bei den Toiletten läßt die Hygiene zu wünschen übrig.
sanitarium [ˌsænɪ'tɛərɪəm] *n* (*US*) *see* **sanatorium.**
sanitary ['sænɪtərɪ] *adj* hygienisch; *arrangements, installations* sanitär *attr*;

regulations Gesundheits-; *recommendations* in bezug auf die Hygiene; *questions* der Hygiene.

sanitary: ~ belt *n* Bindengürtel *m*; **~ inspector** *n* Gesundheitsaufseher *m*; **~ towel,** (*US*) **~ napkin** *n* Damenbinde *f*.

sanitation [ˌsænɪˈteɪʃən] *n* Hygiene *f*; (*toilets etc*) sanitäre Anlagen *pl*; (*sewage disposal*) Kanalisation *f* ◆ **the ~ department** das Amt für Stadtreinigung; **~ man** (*US*) Stadtreiniger *m*.

sanitize [ˈsænɪtaɪz] *vt* **(a)** (*esp US*) keimfrei machen. **(b)** *novel, film etc* von anstößigen Stellen reinigen *or* säubern.

sanity [ˈsænɪtɪ] *n* **(a)** (*mental balance*) geistige Gesundheit; (*of individual also*) gesunder Verstand; (*Jur*) Zurechnungsfähigkeit *f* ◆ **to lose one's ~** den Verstand verlieren; **to doubt sb's ~** an jds Verstand (*dat*) zweifeln; **the line between ~ and insanity** die Grenze zwischen gesundem und krankem Verstand.
(b) (*sensibleness*) Vernünftigkeit *f* ◆ **~ of judgement** ein gesundes Urteilsvermögen; **~ demands that it be done soon** die Vernunft gebietet, es bald zu tun; **to return to ~** Vernunft annehmen.

sank [sæŋk] *pret of* **sink**[1].

San Marino [ˌsænməˈriːnəʊ] *n* San Marino *nt*.

sanserif [ˌsɒnseˈriːf] [1] *n* serifenlose Schrift; (*character*) serifenloser Buchstabe.
[2] *adj* serifenlos.

Sanskrit [ˈsænskrɪt] [1] *adj* sanskritisch.
[2] *n* Sanskrit *nt*.

Santa (Claus) [ˈsæntə(ˈklɔːz)] *n* der Weihnachtsmann.

sap[1] [sæp] *n* (*Bot*) Saft *m*; (*fig*) Lebenskraft *f* ◆ **the ~ is rising** (*lit*) der Saft steigt; (*fig*) die Triebe erwachen.

sap[2] [1] *n* (*Mil*) Sappe *f*.
[2] *vt* **(a)** (*Mil*) unterminieren, untergraben; *fortification also* Sappen graben unter (*+dat*). **(b)** (*fig*) untergraben; *confidence also* schwächen ◆ **to ~ sb's strength** jdn entkräften, jds Kräfte angreifen; **to ~ sb's energy/enthusiasm** jdm die Energie/Begeisterung nehmen.

sap[3] *n* (*sl*) Trottel *m* (*inf*).

sapling [ˈsæplɪŋ] *n* junger Baum.

sapper [ˈsæpəʳ] *n* (*Mil*) Pionier *m*.

Sapphic [ˈsæfɪk] *adj* sapphisch.

sapphire [ˈsæfaɪəʳ] [1] *n* Saphir *m*; (*colour*) Saphirblau *nt*.
[2] *adj ring* Saphir-; (*liter*) *sky* strahlend blau.

saraband [ˈsærəbænd] *n* Sarabande *f*.

Saracen [ˈsærəsn] [1] *adj* Sarazenen-.
[2] *n* Sarazene *m*, Sarazenin *f*.

sarcasm [ˈsɑːkæzəm] *n* Sarkasmus *m* ◆ **~s** sarkastische Bemerkungen *pl*.

sarcastic [sɑːˈkæstɪk] *adj* sarkastisch ◆ **he has a ~ tongue** er hat eine sarkastische Art; **are you being ~?** sind Sie jetzt sarkastisch?, das soll wohl ein Witz sein (*inf*).

sarcastically [sɑːˈkæstɪkəlɪ] *adv* sarkastisch.

sarcoma [sɑːˈkəʊmə] *n, pl* **-s** *or* **-ta** [-tə] (*Med*) Sarkom *nt*.

sarcophagus [sɑːˈkɒfəgəs] *n, pl* **sarcophagi** [sɑːˈkɒfəgaɪ] Sarkophag *m*.

sardine [sɑːˈdiːn] *n* Sardine *f* ◆ **packed in like ~s** wie die Sardinen.

Sardinia [sɑːˈdɪnɪə] *n* Sardinien *nt*.

Sardinian [sɑːˈdɪnɪən] [1] *adj* sardisch, sardinisch.
[2] *n* Sarde *m*, Sardin *f*, Sardinier(in *f*) *m*.

sardonic *adj*, **~ally** *adv* [sɑːˈdɒnɪk, -əlɪ] süffisant; *grin, laugh also* sardonisch (*liter*).

sari [ˈsɑːrɪ] *n* Sari *m*.

sarky [ˈsɑːkɪ] *adj* (*+er*) (*Brit inf*) sarkastisch.

sarong [səˈrɒŋ] *n* Sarong *m*.

sarsaparilla [ˌsɑːsəpəˈrɪlə] *n* (*plant*) Sarsaparille *f*; (*drink*) *dunkelbraunes Limonadengetränk aus Sarsaparillenwurzeln*.

sartorial [sɑːˈtɔːrɪəl] *adj* **his ~ elegance** sein elegantes Aussehen, seine elegante Art, sich zu kleiden; **the very last word in ~ elegance** der letzte Schrei in der Herrenmode; **his unusual ~ preferences** seine Vorliebe für ungewöhnliche Kleidung; **~ styles** Herrenmoden *pl*.

sartorially [sɑːˈtɔːrɪəlɪ] *adv dressed* elegant, stilvoll.

SAS (*Brit*) *abbr of* **Special Air Service** *Spezialeinheit f der britischen Armee*.

sash[1] [sæʃ] *n* Schärpe *f*.

sash[2] *n* (*~ window*) Schiebefenster *nt*; (*cord*) Gewichtsschnur *f*.

sashay [ˈsæʃeɪ] *vi* (*esp US inf*) stolzieren ◆ **I'll just ~ down to the bar** ich latsche mal eben zur Bar (*inf*).

sash: ~-cord *n* Gewichtsschnur *f*; **~-window** *n* Schiebefenster *nt*.

sass [sæs] (*US inf*) [1] *n* Frechheit *f*.
[2] *vt* frech antworten (*+dat*).

sassafras [ˈsæsəfræs] *n* Sassafras *m*.

Sassenach [ˈsæsənæx] *n, adj* (*Scot pej, hum*) *Bezeichnung der Schotten für die Engländer/Englisches*.

sassy [ˈsæsɪ] *adj* (*+er*) (*US inf*) frech.

sat [sæt] *pret, ptp of* **sit**.

SAT ® (*US*) *abbr of* **Scholastic Aptitude Test** *Eignungstest m für Studenten*.

Sat *abbr of* **Saturday** Sa.

Satan [ˈseɪtən] *n* Satan *m*.

satanic [səˈtænɪk] *adj* satanisch.

Satanism [ˈseɪtənɪzəm] *n* Satanismus, Satanskult *m*.

satchel [ˈsætʃəl] *n* Schultasche *f*, Schulranzen *m*.

sate [seɪt] *vt* (*liter*) *appetite, desires* stillen (*geh*), befriedigen ◆ **now that he was ~d** nun, da seine Lüste gestillt waren (*geh*); **a nation ~d with every luxury** ein Volk, von jedem erdenklichen Luxus übersättigt; **to ~ oneself** (*with food*) sich sättigen (*on* an *+dat*) (*liter*); (*sexually*) seine Lust befriedigen.

sateen [sæˈtiːn] *n* Baumwollsatin *m*.

satellite [ˈsætəlaɪt] *n* Satellit *m*; (*natural also, fig*) Trabant *m*.

satellite: ~ broadcasting *n* Satellitenfunk *m*; **~ country** *n* Satellitenstaat *m*; **~ dish** *n* Parabolantenne, Satellitenantenne *f*; **~ state** *n* Satellitenstaat *m*; **~ television** *n* Satellitenfernsehen *nt*; **~ town** *n* Satelliten- *or* Trabantenstadt *f*.

satiate [ˈseɪʃɪeɪt] *vt appetite, desires, lust etc* stillen (*geh*); *person, animal* sättigen; (*to excess*) übersättigen ◆ **we were ~d with food and drink** wir hatten unseren Hunger und Durst zur Genüge gestillt; **I'm quite ~d** (*liter, hum*) mein Bedarf ist gedeckt (*hum inf*), ich bin gesättigt (*hum, geh*).

satiation [ˌseɪʃɪˈeɪʃən] *n* (*act*) Befriedigung *f* ◆ **a state of ~** ein Zustand der Sättigung *or* (*excessive*) Übersättigung.

satiety [səˈtaɪətɪ] *n* (*liter*) Sättigung *f* ◆ **they fed to ~** sie aßen sich satt; **to do sth to (the point of) ~** etw bis zum Überdruß tun.

satin [ˈsætɪn] [1] *n* Satin *m*.
[2] *adj* Satin-; *skin* samtig.

satin: ~ stitch *n* Plattstich *m*; **~wood** *n* Satinholz *nt*.

satiny [ˈsætɪnɪ] *adj* seidig; *skin* samtig.

satire [ˈsætaɪəʳ] *n* Satire *f* (*on* auf *+acc*) ◆ **the (tone of) ~ in his voice** die Ironie in seiner Stimme.

satirical [səˈtɪrɪkəl] *adj literature, film etc* satirisch; (*mocking, joking*) ironisch.

satirically [səˈtɪrɪkəlɪ] *adv see adj*.

satirist [ˈsætərɪst] *n* Satiriker(in *f*) *m*.

satirize [ˈsætəraɪz] *vt* satirisch darstellen *or* (*written also*) beschreiben ◆ **his novel ~s** *or* **in his novel he ~s contemporary American life** sein Roman ist eine Satire auf die zeitgenössische amerikanische Lebensart.

satisfaction [ˌsætɪsˈfækʃən] *n* **(a)** (*act: of person, needs, creditors, curiosity etc*) Befriedigung *f*; (*of debt*) Begleichung, Tilgung *f*; (*of employer etc*) Zufriedenstellung *f*; (*of ambition*) Verwirklichung *f*; (*of conditions, contract*) Erfüllung *f*.
(b) (*state*) Zufriedenheit *f* (*at* mit) ◆ **the ~ of having solved a difficult problem** die Genugtuung *or* das befriedigende Gefühl, ein schwieriges Problem gelöst zu haben; **to feel a sense of ~ at sth** Genugtuung über etw (*acc*) empfinden; **at least you have the ~ of seeing him pay** Sie haben wenigstens die Genugtuung, daß er zahlen muß; **he did it just for the ~ of seeing her suffer** er tat es nur, um sie leiden zu sehen; **we hope the meal was to your complete ~** wir hoffen, Sie waren mit dem Essen zufrieden *or* das Essen ist zu Ihrer vollen Zufriedenheit ausgefallen (*form*); **has it been done to your ~?** sind Sie damit zufrieden?, ist es zu Ihrer Zufriedenheit erledigt worden? (*form*); **if anything in the hotel is not to your ~** sollte irgend etwas im Hotel nicht zu Ihrer Zufriedenheit sein; **our aim, your ~** bei uns ist der Kunde König; **it gives every** *or* **full ~** es fällt zur vollständigen Zufriedenheit aus; **the machine is guaranteed to give complete ~** wir garantieren mit diesem Gerät vollste Zufriedenheit; **it gives me much ~ to introduce ...** es ist mir eine besondere Freude, ... vorstellen zu können; **to get ~ out of sth** Befriedigung in etw (*dat*) finden; (*find pleasure*) Freude an etw (*dat*) haben; **I can't get any ~** ich bin unbefriedigt; **he gets ~ out of his job** seine Arbeit befriedigt ihn; **I get a lot of ~ out of listening to music** Musik gibt mir viel; **what ~ do you get out of climbing mountains?** was gibt Ihnen das Bergsteigen?; **he proved to my ~ that ...** er hat überzeugend bewiesen, daß ...; **he has shown to the examiners'/court's ~ that ...** der Prüfungsausschuß hat befunden, daß er .../er hat dem Gericht überzeugend dargelegt, daß ...
(c) (*satisfying thing*) **your son's success must be a great ~ to you** der Erfolg Ihres Sohnes muß für Sie sehr befriedigend *or* eine große Freude sein; **it is no ~ to me to know that ...** es ist kein Trost (für mich) zu wissen, daß ...; **what ~ is that supposed to be!** das ist ein schwacher Trost.
(d) (*redress*) Genugtuung, Satisfaktion (*old*) *f* ◆ **to demand/obtain ~ from sb** Genugtuung *or* Satisfaktion (*old*) von jdm verlangen/erhalten; **to give sb ~** jdm Genugtuung *or* Satisfaktion (*old*) geben.

satisfactorily [ˌsætɪsˈfæktərɪlɪ] *adv* zufriedenstellend ◆ **does that answer your question ~?** ist damit Ihre Frage hinreichend beantwortet?; **was it done ~?** waren Sie damit zufrieden?; **he is progressing ~** er macht zufriedenstellende Fortschritte *pl*.

satisfactory [ˌsætɪsˈfæktərɪ] *adj* befriedigend, zufriedenstellend; *account, completion of contract* zufriedenstellend; (*only just good enough*) ausreichend, hinlänglich *attr*; *reason* triftig, einleuchtend; *excuse* angemessen, annehmbar; (*in exams*) ausreichend; befriedigend ◆ **work is proceeding at a ~ pace** die Arbeit geht zufriedenstellend voran; **how ~ do you find the new conditions?** wie sind Sie mit den neuen Verhältnissen zufrieden?; **his work is only just ~** seine Arbeit ist gerade noch annehmbar *or* geht gerade *or* (*Sch*) ist gerade noch befriedigend; **this is just not ~!** das geht so nicht!; (*not enough*) das reicht einfach nicht (aus)!; **it's hardly ~ being given only one hour's notice** das geht doch nicht, wenn einem nur eine Stunde vorher Bescheid gesagt wird; **an offer of 8% is simply not ~** ein Angebot von 8% reicht einfach nicht; **your attitude is not ~** Ihre Einstellung läßt zu wünschen übrig.

satisfy [ˈsætɪsfaɪ] [1] *vt* **(a)** (*make contented*) befriedigen; *employer, customers etc* zufriedenstellen; (*meal*) *person* sättigen ◆ **to be satisfied (with sth)** (mit etw) zufrieden sein; **you'll have to be satisfied with that** Sie werden sich damit zufriedengeben *or* begnügen *or* bescheiden (*geh*) müssen; **that won't ~ the boss** damit wird der Chef nicht zufrieden sein; **not satisfied with that he ...** damit noch immer nicht zufrieden, er ...; **nothing satisfies him** ihn kann nichts befriedigen; (*always wants more*) er ist mit nichts zufrieden; **with a satisfied look on his face** mit einem zufriedenen Gesichtsausdruck; **more**

pudding? — no thank you, I'm quite satisfied noch etwas Nachtisch? — nein danke, ich bin satt *or* gesättigt (*geh*); **this little drink didn't ~ him/his thirst** das bißchen hat ihm nicht gereicht/hat seinen Durst nicht gelöscht; **you've really upset her now, I hope you're satisfied** sie ist ganz außer sich, bist du jetzt zufrieden?
(b) *needs, wishes, lust, demand, sb* (*sexually*) befriedigen; *wants, curiosity also, hunger* stillen; *contract, conditions* erfüllen; *requirements* genügen (+*dat*); *ambitions* verwirklichen ◆ **to do sth to ~ one's pride** etw nur aus reinem Stolz tun.
(c) (*convince*) überzeugen ◆ **they were not satisfied with the answers** sie waren mit den Antworten nicht zufrieden; **if you can ~ him that ...** wenn Sie ihn davon überzeugen können, daß ...; **X has satisfied the examiners that ...** der Prüfungsausschuß hat befunden, daß X ...; **X has satisfied the examiners in the following subjects** X hat in den folgenden Fächern die Prüfung bestanden.
(d) (*Comm*) *debt* begleichen, tilgen; *claims* nachkommen (+*dat*); *creditors* befriedigen.
(e) (*Math*) *equation* erfüllen.
2 *vr* **to ~ oneself about sth** sich von etw überzeugen; **to ~ oneself that ...** sich davon überzeugen, daß ...
3 *vi* (*meal*) sättigen ◆ **we aim to ~** wir bemühen uns, allen Wünschen zu entsprechen; **pleasures which no longer ~** Genüsse, die einen nicht mehr befriedigen; **riches do not always ~** Reichtum macht nicht immer zufrieden.

satisfying ['sætɪsfaɪɪŋ] *adj* befriedigend; *food, meal* sättigend ◆ **a ~ experience** ein befriedigendes Erlebnis; **they had the ~ experience of seeing him fail** es tat ihnen gut, seinen Mißerfolg zu erleben; **sounds which are very ~ to the ear** angenehme Klänge *pl*; **a cool ~ lager** ein kühles, durststillendes Bier.

satsuma [,sæt'suːmə] *n* Satsuma *f*.

saturate ['sætʃəreɪt] *vt* **(a)** (*with liquid*) (durch)tränken; (*rain*) durchnässen ◆ **I'm ~d** (*inf*) ich bin klatschnaß (*inf*).
(b) (*Chem*) sättigen ◆ **a ~d solution/colour** eine gesättigte Lösung/Farbe.
(c) (*fig*) *market* sättigen ◆ **this area is ~d with a sense of history** dies ist eine geschichtsträchtige Gegend; **he ~d himself in French literature until the exam was over** er hat sich mit französischer Literatur vollgepfropft, bis die Prüfung vorbei war; **the government ~d the area with troops** die Regierung entsandte massenhaft *or* pumpte (*inf*) Truppen in das Gebiet; **the area is ~d with troops** die Gegend wimmelt von Soldaten.

saturation [,sætʃə'reɪʃən] *n* Sättigung *f* ◆ **after ~ in a red dye** nach Tränkung mit einem roten Farbstoff.

saturation: ~ bombing *n* völliges Zerbomben; **~ point** *n* Sättigungspunkt *m*; (*fig*) Sättigungsgrad *m*; **to have reached ~ point** seinen Sättigungsgrad erreicht haben.

Saturday ['sætədɪ] *n* Samstag, Sonnabend (*esp N Ger*) *m*; *see also* **Tuesday**.

Saturn ['sætən] *n* (*Astron, Myth*) Saturn *m*.

saturnalia [,sætə'neɪlɪə] *npl* **(a) S~** Saturnalien *pl*. **(b)** (*liter: wild revelry*) wilde Feste *pl*, Freudenfeste *pl*.

saturnine ['sætənaɪn] *adj* (*liter*) finster, düster.

satyr ['sætəʳ] *n* Satyr *m*.

sauce [sɔːs] *n* **(a)** Soße, Sauce *f* ◆ **white ~** Mehlsoße *f*; **what's ~ for the goose is ~ for the gander** (*Prov*) was dem einen recht ist, ist dem anderen billig (*prov*). **(b)** *no pl* (*inf: cheek*) Frechheit *f* ◆ **none of your ~!** werd bloß nicht frech! (*inf*). **(c)** (*US sl: alcohol*) Alkohol *m* ◆ **to be on the ~** saufen (*inf*).

sauce: ~-boat *n* Sauciere *f*; **~box** *n* (*inf*) Frechdachs *m*.

saucepan ['sɔːspən] *n* Kochtopf *m*.

saucer ['sɔːsəʳ] *n* Untertasse *f*.

saucily ['sɔːsɪlɪ] *adv see adj*.

sauciness ['sɔːsɪnɪs] *n, no pl* Frechheit *f*.

saucy ['sɔːsɪ] *adj* (+*er*) frech ◆ **don't be ~!** sei nicht so frech!; **with her hat at a ~ angle** mit frech *or* keck aufgesetztem Hut.

Saudi ['saʊdɪ] *n* (*inf*) *see* **Saudi Arabia**.

Saudi Arabia ['saʊdɪə'reɪbɪə] *n* Saudi-Arabien *nt*.

Saudi (Arabian) ['saʊdɪ(ə'reɪbɪən)] 1 *n* Saudi(araber) *m*, Saudiaraberin *f*.
2 *adj* saudisch, saudiarabisch.

Saul [sɔːl] *n* Saul(us) *m*.

sauna ['sɔːnə] *n* Sauna *f* ◆ **to have a ~** in die Sauna gehen.

saunter ['sɔːntəʳ] 1 *n* Bummel *m* ◆ **to have a ~ in the park** einen Parkbummel machen, durch den Park schlendern.
2 *vi* schlendern ◆ **he ~ed up to me** er schlenderte auf mich zu; **she came ~ing in four hours late** sie tanzte vier Stunden zu spät an (*inf*).

saurian ['sɔːrɪən] *n* Echse *f*; (*dinosaur etc*) Saurier *m*.

sausage ['sɒsɪdʒ] *n* **(a)** Wurst *f* ◆ **you can't judge a ~ by its skin** (*prov*) man kann nicht nach dem Äußeren urteilen; **not a ~** (*inf*) rein gar nichts (*inf*).
(b) (*Brit inf: silly person*) Dummerchen (*inf*), Schäfchen (*inf*) *nt*.

sausage: ~ dog *n* (*Brit hum*) Dackel *m*; **~ machine** *n* Wurstfüllmaschine *f*; (*fig hum: school*) Bildungsfabrik *f*; **~meat** *n* Wurstbrät *nt*; **~ roll** *n* ≃ Bratwurst *f* im Schlafrock.

sauté ['səʊteɪ] 1 *adj* **~ potatoes** Brat- *or* Röstkartoffeln *pl*.
2 *vt potatoes* rösten; (*sear*) (kurz) anbraten.

sauterne [səʊ'tɜːn] *n* Sauternes *m*.

savable ['seɪvəbl] *adj* zu retten *pred*; *goal* haltbar, zu halten *pred*.

savage ['sævɪdʒ] 1 *adj* wild; *sport, fighter, guard, punch, revenge* brutal; *custom* grausam; *animal* gefährlich; *competition* scharf, brutal (*inf*); (*drastic, severe*) *cuts, measures* rigoros, drastisch, brutal (*inf*); *changes* drastisch; *criticism* schonungslos, brutal (*inf*) ◆ **the ~ people of New Guinea** die Wilden Neuguineas; **to put up a ~ fight** sich wütend *or* grimmig (*geh*) *or* wild (*inf*) verteidigen, sich verbissen wehren; **with a ~ snap of its jaws the crocodile ...** wütend biß das Krokodil ...; **the dog became a ~ beast** der Hund wurde zur reißenden Bestie; **the guard dogs are ~** die Wachhunde sind scharf *or* gefährlich; **to make a ~ attack on sb** brutal über jdn herfallen; (*fig*) jdn scharf angreifen; **he has a ~ temper** er ist ein äußerst jähzorniger Mensch; **he is in a ~ temper** er ist fuchsteufelswild (*inf*); **the critics were really ~ with her new play** die Kritiker haben ihr neues Stück wirklich schonungslos verrissen.
2 *n* Wilde(r) *mf*.
3 *vt* (*animal*) anfallen; (*fatally*) zerfleischen.

savagely ['sævɪdʒlɪ] *adv attack, fight, punch* brutal; *bite* gefährlich; *reduce services* drastisch, rigoros; *criticize* schonungslos, brutal (*inf*) ◆ **he glared at her ~** er warf ihr einen wilden Blick zu.

savageness ['sævɪdʒnɪs] *n see adj* Wildheit *f*; Brutalität *f*; Grausamkeit *f*; Gefährlichkeit *f*; Schärfe *f*; drastische *or* brutale (*inf*) Härte; Schonungslosigkeit *f* ◆ **the ~ of these changes** diese drastischen Veränderungen.

savagery ['sævɪdʒərɪ] *n* **(a)** (*of tribe, people*) Wildheit *f*.
(b) (*cruelty*) Grausamkeit *f*; (*of attack*) Brutalität *f*; (*of treatment, prison life, cuts*) brutale Härte ◆ **the savageries committed ...** die Grausamkeiten *or* Greueltaten *pl* ...

savanna(h) [sə'vænə] *n* Savanne *f*.

save[1] [seɪv] 1 *n* (*Ftbl etc*) Ballabwehr *f* ◆ **what a ~!** eine tolle Parade!; **he made a fantastic ~** er hat den Ball prima abgewehrt *or* gehalten.
2 *vt* **(a)** (*rescue, Rel*) retten ◆ **to ~ sb from sth** jdn vor etw (*dat*) retten; **to ~ sb from disaster/ruin** jdn vor einer Katastrophe/dem Ruin bewahren *or* retten; **he ~d me from falling/making that mistake** er hat mich davor bewahrt, hinzufallen/den Fehler zu machen; **to ~ sth from sth** etw aus etw retten; **his goal ~d the match** sein Tor hat das Spiel gerettet *or* herausgerissen (*inf*); **to ~ the day (for sb)** jds Rettung sein; **God ~ the Queen** Gott schütze die Königin; **to ~ a building for posterity** ein Gebäude der Nachwelt erhalten.
(b) (*put by*) aufheben, aufbewahren, aufsparen; *money* sparen; (*collect*) *stamps etc* sammeln ◆ **~ some of the cake for me** laß mir etwas Kuchen übrig; **~ me a seat** halte mir einen Platz frei; **~ it for later, I'm busy now** (*inf*) spar dir's für später auf, ich habe jetzt zu tun (*inf*); **~ it!** (*inf*) spar dir das! (*inf*).
(c) (*avoid using up*) *fuel, time, space, money* sparen; (*spare*) *strength, eyes, battery* schonen; (*~ up*) *strength, fuel etc* aufsparen ◆ **that will ~ you £20 a week** dadurch sparen Sie £ 20 die Woche; **you don't ~ much by taking this short cut** Sie gewinnen nicht viel, wenn Sie diese Abkürzung nehmen; **he's saving himself for the big match** er schont sich für das große Spiel; **she's saving herself for the right man** sie spart sich für den Richtigen auf.
(d) (*prevent*) *bother, trouble* ersparen ◆ **at least it ~d the rain coming in** es hat wenigstens den Regen abgehalten; **it'll ~ a lot of hard work if we ...** es erspart uns (*dat*) sehr viel Mühe, wenn wir ...; **it ~d us having to do it again** das hat es uns (*dat*) erspart, es noch einmal machen zu müssen; **I've been ~d a lot of expense** mir blieben *or* wurden sehr viel Ausgaben erspart.
(e) *goal* verhindern; *shot, penalty* halten ◆ **well ~d!** gut gehalten!
(f) (*Comput*) sichern ◆ **to ~ sth to disk** etw auf Diskette sichern *or* abspeichern.
3 *vi* **(a)** (*with money*) sparen ◆ **to ~ for sth** für *or* auf etw (*acc*) sparen; **~ as you earn** (*Brit: savings scheme*) *Sparprogramm nt, bei dem der monatliche Beitrag unversteuert bleibt.*
(b) (*inf: keep*) (*food*) sich halten; (*news*) warten können.
(c) (*Comput*) **the file won't ~** die Datei läßt sich nicht sichern *or* abspeichern.

◆**save up** 1 *vi* sparen (*for* für, auf +*acc*).
2 *vt sep* (*not spend*) sparen; (*not use*) aufheben, aufbewahren ◆ **he's saving himself ~ for the big match** er schont sich für das große Spiel.

save[2] 1 *prep* außer +*dat*.
2 *conj* **(a)** (*old, liter*) es sei denn (*geh*). **(b) ~ that** nur daß.

saveable *adj see* **savable**.

saveloy ['sævəlɔɪ] *n* Zervelatwurst *f*.

saver ['seɪvəʳ] *n* **(a)** Retter(in *f*) *m* ◆ **a ~ of souls** ein Seelenretter *m*. **(b)** (*with money*) Sparer(in *f*) *m*.

-saver *n suf* **it is a time-/money-~** es spart Zeit/Geld.

saving ['seɪvɪŋ] 1 *adj* **(a)** (*redeeming*) **the one ~ feature of the scheme** das einzig Gute an dem Plan, das einzige, was für den Plan spricht; **his/the book's ~ sense of humour** sein Humor/der Humor in dem Buch, der manches wettmacht; **the ~ beauty of a pair of lovely eyes in an otherwise unattractive face** die Schönheit der Augen, durch die das sonst unscheinbare Gesicht gewinnt; **its/his ~ grace** was einen damit/mit ihm versöhnt.
(b) sparsam ◆ **she's not the ~ sort** sie ist nicht gerade sparsam.
(c) ~ clause Sicherheitsklausel *f*, einschränkende Klausel.
2 *n* **(a)** *no pl* (*act: rescue, Rel*) Rettung *f*.
(b) *no pl* (*of money*) Sparen *nt* ◆ **to encourage ~** zum Sparen ermutigen.
(c) (*of cost etc*) (*act*) Einsparung *f*; (*amount saved*) Ersparnis *f* ◆ **how much of a ~ is there?** wieviel wird eingespart?; **we must make ~s** wir müssen sparen.
(d) ~s *pl* Ersparnisse *pl*; (*in account*) Spareinlagen *pl* ◆ **post-office ~s** Postsparguthaben *nt*.
3 *prep, conj see* **save**[2].

-saving *adj suf* -sparend.

savings *in cpds* Spar-; **~ account** *n* Sparkonto *nt*; **~ bank** *n* Sparkasse *f*; **~ book** *n* Sparbuch *nt*; **~ stamp** *n* (*Brit*) Sparmarke *f*.

saviour, (*US also*) **savior** ['seɪvjəʳ] *n* Retter(in *f*) *m*; (*Rel also*) Erlöser, Heiland *m* ♦ **Our S~** unser Erlöser.

savoir-faire [ˌsævwɑːˈfɛəʳ] *n* Gewandtheit *f*; (*in social matters*) gute Umgangsformen *pl* ♦ **it's a question of ~** es ist nur eine Frage, wie man es anfaßt.

savor *etc* (*US*) *see* **savour** *etc.*

savory ['seɪvərɪ] *n* (*Bot*) Bohnenkraut *nt.*

savour, (*US*) **savor** ['seɪvəʳ] [1] *n* **(a)** Geschmack *m* ♦ **a ~ of garlic** ein Knoblauchgeschmack *m*.
(b) (*slight trace*) Spur *f* ♦ **there is a ~ of pride in everything he says** in allem, was er sagt, schwingt ein gewisser Stolz mit.
(c) (*enjoyable quality*) Reiz *m*.
[2] *vt* **(a)** (*form*) kosten (*geh*), verkosten (*form*); *aroma (of food)* riechen. **(b)** (*fig liter*) genießen, auskosten.
[3] *vi* **to ~ of sth** (*fig liter*) etw ahnen lassen.

savouriness, (*US*) **savoriness** ['seɪvərɪnɪs] *n* **(a)** (*tastiness*) Schmackhaftigkeit *f* ♦ **the ~ of the smells** die leckeren Gerüche. **(b)** (*spiciness*) Würzigkeit, Pikantheit *f* ♦ **the excessive ~ of all the food** das zu stark gewürzte Essen.

savourless, (*US*) **savorless** ['seɪvəlɪs] *adj* geschmacklos.

savoury, (*US*) **savory** ['seɪvərɪ] [1] *adj* **(a)** (*appetizing*) lecker; *meal also* schmackhaft.
(b) (*not sweet*) pikant ♦ **~ omelette** gefülltes Omelett; **~ biscuits** Salzgebäck *nt*.
(c) (*fig*) angenehm, ersprießlich; *sight also* einladend; *joke* fein ♦ **that was not the most ~ adjective to have chosen** das war ja nicht gerade das feinste Adjektiv.
[2] *n* Häppchen *nt* ♦ **would you like a sweet or a ~?** hätten Sie gern etwas Süßes oder etwas Pikantes *or* Salziges?

savoy (cabbage) [sə'vɔɪ('kæbɪdʒ)] *n* Wirsing(kohl) *m*.

savvy ['sævɪ] (*sl*) [1] *n* (*common sense*) Grips *m* (*inf*), Köpfchen *nt* (*inf*); (*know-how*) Können, Know-how *nt* ♦ **he hasn't got much ~** er hat keine Ahnung (*inf*) *or* keinen Dunst (*inf*); **show a bit of ~, use your ~!** streng mal dein Köpfchen *or* deinen Grips an (*inf*).
[2] *vt* kapieren (*inf*) ♦ **~?** kapiert? (*inf*), kapisko? (*sl*); **no ~** keine Ahnung (*inf*); (*don't understand*) kapier' ich nicht (*inf*).

saw¹ [sɔː] *pret of* **see¹**.

saw² *n* Spruch *m*, Weisheit *f*.

saw³ (*vb: pret* **~ed**, *ptp* **~ed** *or* **sawn**) [1] *n* Säge *f* ♦ **musical** *or* **singing ~** singende Säge.
[2] *vt* **(a)** sägen ♦ **to ~ sth through** etw durchsägen; **to ~ sth in two** etw entzweisägen; **~ the wood into smaller logs** zersägen Sie das Holz in kleinere Scheite; **~n timber** Schnittholz *nt*.
(b) the bird/the bird's wings ~ed the air der Vogel schlug wild mit den Flügeln; **he/his arms ~ed the air** er schlug wild um sich, er fuchtelte mit den Armen (durch die Luft).
[3] *vi* **(a)** (*person, saw*) sägen; (*wood*) sich sägen lassen.
(b) to ~ (away) at the violin auf der Geige herumsägen; **to ~ (away) at the meat** am Fleisch herumsäbeln (*inf*).

♦**saw down** *vt sep* um- *or* absägen.

♦**saw off** *vt sep* absägen ♦ **a ~n-~ shotgun** ein Gewehr mit abgesägtem Lauf.

♦**saw up** *vt sep* zersägen (*into* in +*acc*).

saw: ~bones *n* (*dated sl*) Medizinmann *m* (*inf*); **~buck** *n* (*US*) Sägebock *m*; (*sl*) Zehndollarschein *m*; **~dust** *n* Sägemehl *nt*; **~fish** *n* Sägefisch *m*; **~horse** *n* Sägebock *m*; **~mill** *n* Sägewerk *nt*.

sawn [sɔːn] *ptp of* **saw³**.

saw-toothed [ˌsɔː'tuːθt] *adj* gezähnt.

sawyer ['sɔːjəʳ] *n* Sägewerker *m*.

sax [sæks] *n* (*inf: saxophone*) Saxophon *nt*.

saxhorn ['sækshɔːn] *n* (*Mus*) Saxhorn *nt*.

saxifrage ['sæksɪfrɪdʒ] *n* Steinbrech *m*.

Saxon ['sæksn] [1] *n* **(a)** Sachse *m*, Sächsin *f*; (*Hist*) (Angel)sachse *m*/-sächsin *f*. **(b)** (*Ling*) Sächsisch *nt*.
[2] *adj* sächsisch; (*Hist*) (angel)sächsisch ♦ **~ genitive** sächsischer Genitiv.

Saxony ['sæksənɪ] *n* Sachsen *nt*.

saxophone ['sæksəfəʊn] *n* Saxophon *nt*.

saxophonist [ˌsæk'sɒfənɪst] *n* Saxophonist(in *f*) *m*.

▼ **say** [seɪ] (*vb: pret, ptp* **said**) [1] *n* **(a)** (*what a person has to ~*) **let him have his ~** laß ihn mal reden *or* seine Meinung äußern; **everyone should be allowed to have his ~** jeder sollte seine Meinung äußern dürfen, jeder sollte zu Wort kommen; **you've had your ~** Sie haben Ihre Meinung äußern können.
(b) (*right to decide etc*) Mitspracherecht *nt* (*in* bei) ♦ **to have no/a ~ in sth** bei etw nichts/etwas zu sagen haben, bei etw kein/ein Mitspracherecht haben; **I want more ~ in determining ...** ich möchte mehr Mitspracherecht bei der Entscheidung ... haben; **to have the last** *or* **final ~ (in sth)** (etw) letztlich entscheiden; (*person also*) das letzte Wort (bei etw) haben.
[2] *vti* **(a)** sagen; *poem* aufsagen; *prayer, text* sprechen; (*pronounce*) aussprechen ♦ **~ after me ...** sprechen Sie mir nach ...; **he didn't have much to ~ for himself** er sagte *or* redete nicht viel; (*in defence*) er konnte nicht viel (zu seiner Verteidigung) sagen; **what have you got to ~ for yourself?** was haben Sie zu Ihrer Verteidigung zu sagen?; **who shall I ~?** wen darf ich melden?; **you can ~ what you like ...** Sie können sagen, was Sie wollen, ...; **that's not for him to ~** es steht ihm nicht zu, sich darüber zu äußern; (*to decide*) das kann ich/er nicht entscheiden; **I never thought I'd hear him ~ that word** ich hätte nie gedacht, daß er das sagen würde; **if you see her, ~ I haven't changed my mind** wenn du sie siehst, sag ihr *or* richte ihr aus, daß ich es mir nicht anders überlegt habe; **he said to wait here** er hat gesagt, ich soll/wir sollen *etc* hier warten; **I'm not ~ing it's the best, but ...** ich sage *or* behaupte ja nicht, daß es das beste ist, aber ...; **never let it be said that I didn't try** es soll keiner sagen können *or* mir soll keiner nachsagen, ich hätte es nicht versucht; **well, all I can ~ is ...** na ja, da kann ich nur sagen ...; **do it this way — if you ~ so** machen Sie es so — wenn Sie meinen; **if you don't like it, ~ so** wenn Sie es nicht mögen, dann sagen Sie es doch; **why don't you ~ so?** warum sagen Sie es dann nicht?; **you'd better do it — who ~s?** tun Sie das lieber — wer sagt das?; **well, what can I ~?** na ja, was kann man da sagen?; **what does it mean? — I wouldn't like to ~** was bedeutet das? — das kann ich auch nicht sagen; **having said that, I must point out ...** ich muß allerdings darauf hinweisen ...; **so ~ing, he sat down** und mit den Worten setzte er sich.
(b) (*weather forecast, newspaper, dictionary, clock, horoscope*) sagen (*inf*); (*thermometer also*) anzeigen; (*law, church, Bible, computer*) sagen ♦ **it ~s in the papers that ...** in den Zeitungen steht, daß ...; **what does the paper/this book/your horoscope** *etc* **~?** was steht in der Zeitung/diesem Buch/deinem Horoskop *etc*?; **the rules ~ that ...** in den Regeln heißt es, daß ...; **what does the weather forecast ~?** wie ist *or* lautet (*form*) der Wetterbericht?; **the weather forecast said that ...** es hieß im Wetterbericht, daß ..., laut Wetterbericht ...; **what does your watch ~?** wie spät ist es auf Ihrer Uhr?, was sagt Ihre Uhr? (*hum*); **did the news ~ anything about the strike?** kam in den Nachrichten etwas über den Streik?; **they weren't allowed to ~ anything about it in the papers** sie durften in den Zeitungen nichts darüber schreiben.
▼ **(c)** (*tell*) sagen ♦ **it's hard to ~ what's wrong** es ist schwer zu sagen, was nicht stimmt; **what does that ~ about his intentions/the main character?** was sagt das über seine Absichten/die Hauptperson aus?; **that ~s a lot about his character/state of mind** das läßt tief auf seinen Charakter/Gemütszustand schließen; **these figures ~ a lot about recent trends** diese Zahlen sind in bezug auf neuere Tendenzen sehr aufschlußreich *or* sagen viel über neuere Tendenzen aus; **and that's ~ing a lot** und das will schon etwas heißen; **that's not ~ing much** das will nicht viel heißen; **that doesn't ~ much for him** das spricht nicht für ihn; **that ~s a lot for him** das spricht für ihn; **there's no ~ing** das weiß keiner; **she blushed? that ~s a lot** sie ist rot geworden? das läßt tief blicken.
▼ **(d) what would you ~ to a whisky/holiday/game of tennis?** wie wär's mit einem Whisky/mit Urlaub/, wenn wir Tennis spielen würden?; **I wouldn't ~ no to a cup of tea** ich hätte nichts gegen eine Tasse Tee; **he never ~s no to a drink** er schlägt einen Drink nie aus, er sagt nie nein zu einem Drink; **what did he ~ to your plan?** was hat er zu Ihrem Plan gesagt?; **I'll offer £500, what do you ~ to that?** ich biete £ 500, was meinen Sie dazu?; **what do you ~ we go now?** (*inf*) was hieltest du davon *or* wie wär's, wenn wir jetzt gingen?, was meinst du, sollen wir jetzt gehen?; **shall we ~ Tuesday/£50?** sagen wir Dienstag/£ 50?; **let's try again, what d'you ~?** (*inf*) was meinste (*inf*), versuchen wir's noch mal?; **what do you ~?** was meinen Sie?
(e) (*exclamatory*) **well, I must ~!** na, ich muß schon sagen!; **I ~!** (*dated*) na so was!; (*to attract attention*) hallo!; **I ~, are you serious?** (*dated*) das ist doch wohl nicht Ihr Ernst?; **I ~, thanks awfully, old stick!** (*dated*) na dann vielen Dank, altes Haus! (*dated*); **I ~, are you crazy?** (*dated*) sag mal, bist du denn wahnsinnig?; **~, what a great idea!** (*esp US*) Mensch, tolle Idee! (*inf*); **~, buddy!** (*esp US*) he, Mann! (*inf*); **I should ~ (so)!** das möchte ich doch meinen!; **you don't ~!** (*also iro*) nein wirklich?, was du nicht sagst!; **well said!** (ganz) richtig!; **you('ve) said it!** Sie sagen es!; **you can ~ that again!** das kann man wohl sagen!; **~ no more!** ich weiß Bescheid!; **~s you!** (*inf*) das meinst auch nur du! (*inf*); **~s who?** (*inf*) wer sagt das?; **and so ~ all of us** und wir stimmen alle zu; **though I ~ it myself** wenn ich das mal selbst sagen darf.
(f) (it's) easier said than done das ist leichter gesagt als getan; **no sooner said than done** gesagt, getan; **when all is said and done** letzten Endes; **he is said to be very rich** er soll sehr reich sein, es heißt, er sei sehr reich; **a building said to have been built by ...** ein Gebäude, das angeblich von ... gebaut wurde *or* das von ... gebaut worden sein soll; **it goes without ~ing that ...** es versteht sich von selbst *or* ist selbstverständlich, daß ...; **that goes without ~ing** das ist selbstverständlich; **that is to ~** das heißt; (*correcting also*) beziehungsweise; **to ~ nothing of the noise/costs** *etc* von dem Lärm/den Kosten *etc* ganz zu schweigen *or* mal ganz abgesehen; **to ~ nothing of being ...** davon, daß ich/er *etc* ..., ganz zu schweigen *or* mal ganz abgesehen; **that's not to ~ that ...** das soll nicht heißen, daß ...; **they ~ ..., it is said ...** es heißt ...; **enough said!** (na ja) genug!
(g) (*suppose*) **~ it takes three men to ...** angenommen, man braucht drei Leute, um zu ...; **if it happens on, ~, Wednesday** wenn es am, sagen wir mal Mittwoch, passiert?

sayest ['seɪəst] (*obs*) *2nd pers sing of* **say**.

saying ['seɪɪŋ] *n* Redensart *f*; (*proverb*) Sprichwort *nt* ♦ **as the ~ goes** wie man so sagt, wie es so schön heißt.

say-so ['seɪsəʊ] *n* (*inf*) (*assertion*) Wort *nt*; (*authority*) Plazet *nt* ♦ **on whose ~?** wer sagt das? (*inf*); mit welchem Recht?

s/c *abbr of* **self-contained**.

scab [skæb] [1] *n* **(a)** (*on cut*) Schorf, Grind *m*. **(b)** (*scabies*) Krätze *f*. **(c)** (*inf: strikebreaker*) Streikbrecher(in *f*) *m* ♦ **~ labour** Streikbrecher *pl*.
[2] *vi* **(a)** (*inf*) den Streik brechen. **(b)** (*wound*) **to ~ over** Schorf bilden.

scabbard ['skæbəd] *n* Scheide *f*.

scabby ['skæbɪ] *adj* (+*er*) **(a)** *skin, hands* schorfig, grindig. **(b)** (*having scabies*) räudig.

➤ LANGUAGE IN USE: **say: 2c** → 6.3, 13 **2d** → 1.1, 3.3

scabies ['skeɪbiːz] *n* Krätze, Skabies (*spec*) *f*; (*of animal also*) Räude, Schäbe *f*.
scabious ['skeɪbɪəs] *adj* (*having scabies*) räudig.
scabrous ['skeɪbrəs] *adj* (*indecent*) geschmacklos.
scaffold ['skæfəld] *n* (*on building*) Gerüst *nt*; (*for execution*) Schafott *nt*.
scaffolding ['skæfəldɪŋ] *n* Gerüst *nt* ◆ **to put up ~** ein Gerüst aufbauen.
scag [skæg] *n* (*US Drugs sl*) Schnee *m* (*sl*).
scalawag ['skæləwæg] *n* (*US*) *see* **scallywag**.
scald [skɔːld] [1] *n* Verbrühung *f*.
[2] *vt* **(a)** *oneself, skin etc* verbrühen ◆ **he was ~ed to death** er erlitt tödliche Verbrennungen *pl*. **(b)** *instruments, vegetables* abbrühen; *milk* abkochen.
scalding ['skɔːldɪŋ] *adj* siedend; (*inf: also* **~ hot**) siedend heiß.
scale[1] [skeɪl] [1] *n* (*of fish, snake, skin*) Schuppe *f*; (*of rust*) Flocke *f*; (*of paint*) Plättchen *nt*; (*kettle ~*) Kesselstein *m no pl* ◆ **to take the ~s from sb's eyes** jdm die Augen öffnen; **the ~s fell from his eyes** es fiel ihm wie Schuppen von den Augen.
[2] *vt* **(a)** *fish* (ab)schuppen. **(b) to ~ teeth** den Zahnstein entfernen.
[3] *vi* (*also* **~ off**) sich schuppen; (*paint, rust*) abblättern.
scale[2] [1] *n* **(pair of) ~s** *pl*, **~** (*form*) Waage *f*; **the S~s** (*Astron*) die Waage; **~-pan** Waagschale *f*; **he turns** *or* **tips the ~s at 80 kilos** er bringt 80 Kilo auf die Waage; **the extra votes have tipped** *or* **turned the ~s in favour of Labour** die zusätzlichen Stimmen gaben den Ausschlag für die Labour Party.
[2] *vi* wiegen.
scale[3] *n* **(a)** Skala *f*; (*on thermometer etc also*) Gradeinteilung *f*; (*on ruler*) (Maß)einteilung *f*; (*fig*) Leiter *f*; (*social ~*) Stufenleiter *f*; (*list, table*) Tabelle *f* ◆ **~ of charges** Gebührenordnung *f*, Tarife *pl*; **he ranks at the top of the ~ of contemporary violinists** er steht an der Spitze der zeitgenössischen Geiger.
(b) (*instrument*) Meßgerät *nt*.
(c) (*Mus*) Tonleiter *f* ◆ **the ~ of G** die G(-Dur)-Tonleiter.
(d) (*of map etc*) Maßstab *m* ◆ **on a ~ of 5 km to the cm** in einem Maßstab von 5 km zu 1 cm; **what is the ~?** welchen Maßstab hat es?, in welchem Maßstab ist es?; **to draw sth to ~** etw im Maßstab *or* maßstabgerecht zeichnen.
(e) (*fig: size, extent*) Umfang *m*, Ausmaß *nt* ◆ **to entertain on a large/small/different ~** Feste im größeren/im kleineren/in einem anderen Rahmen geben; **large stores buy on a different ~ from small shops** große Kaufhäuser kaufen in ganz anderen Mengen als kleine Geschäfte; **inflation on an unprecedented ~** Inflation von bisher nie gekanntem Ausmaß; **they differ enormously in ~** sie haben völlig verschiedene Größenordnungen; **a house designed on a magnificent ~** ein in großem Stil *or* großzügig angelegtes Haus; **it's similar but on a smaller ~** es ist ähnlich, nur kleiner; **on a national ~** auf nationaler Ebene.
◆**scale down** *vt sep* (*lit*) verkleinern; (*fig*) verringern ◆ **a sort of ~d-~ Parthenon** eine Art Parthenon im Kleinformat.
◆**scale up** *vt sep* (*lit*) vergrößern; (*fig*) erhöhen.
scale[4] *vt mountain, wall* erklettern.
scale: ~ drawing *n* maßstabgerechte *or* maßstabgetreue Zeichnung; **~ model** *n* maßstäbliches *or* maßstabgetreues Modell.
scalene ['skeɪliːn] *adj triangle* ungleichseitig; *cone* schief.
scaliness ['skeɪlɪnɪs] *n* Schuppigkeit *f*.
scaling ladder ['skeɪlɪŋ'lædəʳ] *n* Sturmleiter *f*.
scallop ['skɒləp] [1] *n* **(a)** (*Zool*) Kammuschel, Jakobsmuschel (*esp Cook*) *f* ◆ **~ shell** (*for cooking*) Muschelschale *f*.
(b) ['skæləp] (*loop*) Bogen *m*, bogenförmige Verzierung; (*on linenware*) Feston *m*.
[2] ['skæləp] *vt* (*decorate with loops*) mit Bögen *or* einem Bogenrand versehen; *linenware* festonieren.
scalloped ['skæləpt] *adj* **(a)** mit einem Bogenrand; *linenware* festoniert ◆ **~ edge** Bogen-/Festonrand *m*. **(b)** ['skɒləpt] (*Cook*) überbacken.
scallywag ['skælɪwæg] *n* (*inf*) Schlingel (*inf*), Strolch (*inf*) *m*.
scalp [skælp] [1] *n* Kopfhaut *f*; (*Indian trophy*) Skalp *m* ◆ **to be after sb's ~** (*fig*) jdn fertigmachen wollen (*inf*).
[2] *vt* skalpieren; (*hum: barber*) kahlscheren (*hum*) ◆ **you've really been ~ed** (*hum*) du bist wohl die Treppe runtergefallen (*inf*).
scalpel ['skælpəl] *n* Skalpell *nt*.
scaly ['skeɪlɪ] *adj* (*+er*) schuppig; *walls* abblätternd.
scam [skæm] *n* (*inf: deception*) Betrug, Beschiß (*sl*) *m*.
scamp[1] [skæmp] *n* Frechdachs, Lausebengel (*inf*) *m*.
scamp[2] *vt work* pfuschen *or* schludern (*inf*) bei.
scamper ['skæmpəʳ] [1] *n* **they can go for a ~ in the garden** sie können im Garten herumtollen.
[2] *vi* (*person, child, puppy*) trippeln, trappeln; (*squirrel, rabbit*) hoppeln; (*mice*) huschen ◆ **the rabbit ~ed down its hole** das Kaninchen verschwand blitzschnell in seinem Loch.
scampi ['skæmpɪ] *npl* Scampi *pl*.
scan [skæn] [1] *vt* **(a)** (*search with sweeping movement*) schwenken über (*+acc*); (*person*) seine Augen wandern lassen über (*+acc*); *newspaper, book* überfliegen; (*examine closely*) *horizon* absuchen; (*by radar*) absuchen, abtasten ◆ **he ~ned her face for a sign of emotion** er suchte in ihrem Gesicht nach Anzeichen einer Gefühlsregung.
(b) (*TV*) abtasten, rastern.
(c) *verse* in Versfüße zerlegen.
[2] *vi* (*verse*) das richtige Versmaß haben, sich reimen (*inf*) ◆ **he couldn't make it ~** er konnte es nicht ins richtige Versmaß bringen; **stressed differently so that the line ~s** anders betont, um das richtige Metrum in der Zeile zu bekommen.
[3] *n* (*Med*) Scan *m*; (*in pregnancy*) Ultraschalluntersuchung *f*; (*picture*) Ultraschallaufnahme *f*.
◆**scan in** *vt sep* (*Comput*) *graphics* einbinden, einfügen, scannen.
scandal ['skændl] *n* **(a)** Skandal *m* ◆ **the ~ of our overcrowded hospitals** unsere skandalös überfüllten Krankenhäuser; **to cause/create a ~** einen Skandal verursachen; (*amongst neighbours etc*) allgemeines Aufsehen erregen; **it's a ~!** (das ist) ein Skandal!; **it is a ~ that ...** es ist skandalös, daß ...
(b) *no pl* (*gossip*) Skandalgeschichten *pl*; (*piece of gossip*) Skandalgeschichte *f* ◆ **the latest ~** der neueste Klatsch.
scandalize ['skændəlaɪz] *vt* schockieren ◆ **she was ~d** sie war entrüstet *or* empört (*by* über *+acc*).
scandal: ~monger *n* Klatschmaul *nt* (*inf*), Lästerzunge *f*; **~mongering** *n* Klatschsucht *f*; (*by press*) Skandalsucht *f*.
scandalous ['skændələs] *adj* skandalös ◆ **~ talk** böswilliger Klatsch; **a ~ report/tale** eine Skandalgeschichte.
scandalously ['skændələslɪ] *adv* skandalös ◆ **to talk ~ about sb** böse *or* üble Gerüchte über jdn verbreiten; **she's ~ neglectful of her children** es ist skandalös *or* ein Skandal, wie sie ihre Kinder vernachlässigt.
scandal sheet *n* Skandalblatt, Revolverblatt (*inf*) *nt*.
Scandinavia [ˌskændɪ'neɪvɪə] *n* Skandinavien *nt*.
Scandinavian [ˌskændɪ'neɪvɪən] [1] *adj* skandinavisch.
[2] *n* Skandinavier(in *f*) *m*.
scanner ['skænəʳ] *n* (*Rad*) Richtantenne *f*; (*TV*) Bildabtaster *m*; (*Comput: OCR reader, Med*) Scanner *m*.
scansion ['skænʃən] *n* (*Poet*) metrische Gliederung; (*Sch*) Zerlegung *f* in Versfüße.
scant [skænt] *adj* (*+er*) wenig *inv*; *satisfaction, attention, respect also, chance* gering; *success* gering, mager; *supply, grazing, amount* dürftig, spärlich ◆ **to do ~ justice to sth** einer Sache (*dat*) wenig *or* kaum gerecht werden; **a ~ 3 hours** knappe *or* kaum 3 Stunden.
scantily ['skæntɪlɪ] *adv* spärlich ◆ **~ clad** spärlich bekleidet.
scantiness ['skæntɪnɪs] *n see* **scanty** Spärlichkeit, Dürftigkeit *f*; Kärglichkeit *f*; Schütterkeit *f*; Knappheit *f*.
scanty ['skæntɪ] *adj* (*+er*) *amount, supply* spärlich, dürftig; *vegetation, meal also* kärglich; *harvest also* mager; *hair* schütter; *piece of clothing, supply* knapp.
scapegoat ['skeɪpgəʊt] *n* Sündenbock *m* ◆ **to be a ~ for sth** für etw der Sündenbock sein; **to use sb/sth as a ~, to make sb/sth one's ~** jdm/einer Sache die Schuld zuschieben.
scapula ['skæpjʊlə] *n* (*Anat*) Schulterblatt *nt*.
scar [skɑːʳ] [1] *n* (*on skin, tree*) Narbe *f*; (*scratch*) Kratzer *m*; (*burn*) Brandfleck *m*, Brandloch *nt*; (*fig*) (*emotional*) Wunde *f*; (*on good name*) Makel *m* ◆ **~ tissue** vernarbtes Fleisch.
[2] *vt skin, tree* Narben/eine Narbe hinterlassen auf (*+dat*); *furniture* zerkratzen; Brandflecken hinterlassen auf (*+dat*); (*fig*) *person* zeichnen ◆ **he was ~red for life** (*lit*) er behielt bleibende Narben zurück; (*fig*) er war fürs Leben gezeichnet; **her ~red face** ihr narbiges Gesicht; **the table was ~red with cigarette burns** der Tisch war mit Brandlöchern *or* Brandflecken von Zigaretten übersät; **his mind was ~red forever by this tragic occurrence** dieses tragische Ereignis hatte bei ihm tiefe Wunden hinterlassen.
[3] *vi* Narben/eine Narbe hinterlassen.
scarab ['skærəb] *n* Skarabäus *m*.
scarce [skeəs] [1] *adj* (*+er*) (*in short supply*) knapp; (*rare*) selten ◆ **to make oneself ~** (*inf*) verschwinden (*inf*), abhauen (*inf*).
[2] *adv* (*old*) *see* **scarcely**.
scarcely ['skeəslɪ] *adv* **(a)** kaum ◆ **~ anybody** kaum einer *or* jemand; **~ anything** fast *or* beinahe nichts; **~ ever** kaum jemals, fast *or* beinahe nie; **I ~ know what to say** ich weiß nicht recht, was ich sagen soll.
(b) (*not really*) wohl kaum ◆ **you can ~ expect him to believe that** Sie erwarten doch wohl nicht *or* kaum, daß er das glaubt; **he's ~ the most polite of men** er ist nicht gerade *or* er ist wohl kaum der Höflichste.
scarceness ['skeəsnɪs], **scarcity** ['skeəsɪtɪ] *n* (*shortage*) Knappheit *f*; (*rarity*) Seltenheit *f* ◆ **because of the ~ of talent among the singers/pupils** weil so wenige Sänger/Schüler wirklich begabt sind; **his pictures are expensive because of their ~** seine Bilder sind teuer, weil es so wenige davon gibt; **a ~ of qualified people** ein Mangel *m* an qualifizierten Kräften; **in years of ~** in schlechten Jahren; **there are many scarcities in wartime** in Kriegszeiten ist vieles knapp; **scarcity value** Seltenheitswert *m*.
scare [skeəʳ] [1] *n* (*fright, shock*) Schreck(en) *m*; (*general alarm*) Panikstimmung, Hysterie *f* (*about* in bezug auf *+acc*, wegen) ◆ **to give sb a ~** jdm einen Schrecken einjagen; (*make sb jump also*) jdn erschrecken; **the devaluation ~** die Abwertungshysterie; **to create** *or* **cause a ~** eine Panik auslösen.
[2] *vt* einen Schrecken einjagen (*+dat*); (*worry also*) Angst machen (*+dat*); (*frighten physically*) *person, animal* erschrecken; *birds* aufschrecken ◆ **to be ~d** Angst haben (*of* vor *+dat*); **to be easily ~d** sehr schreckhaft sein; (*easily worried*) sich (*dat*) leicht Angst machen lassen; (*timid: deer etc*) sehr scheu sein; **to be ~d stiff** *or* **to death** *or* **out of one's wits** (*all inf*) Todesängste ausstehen, fürchterliche Angst haben; **she was too ~d to speak** sie konnte vor Angst nicht sprechen; **she was always too ~d to speak in public** sie getraute sich nie, in der Öffentlichkeit zu sprechen; **he's ~d of telling her the truth** er getraut sich nicht, ihr die Wahrheit zu sagen.
[3] *vi* **I don't ~ easily** ich bekomme nicht so schnell Angst.
◆**scare away** *vt sep* verscheuchen; *people* verjagen.
◆**scare off** *vt sep* **(a)** *see* **scare away**. **(b)** (*put off*) abschrecken (*prep obj* von).
scarecrow *n* (*lit, fig*) Vogelscheuche *f*.

scaredy-cat ['skɛədɪˌkæt] *n (inf)* Angsthase *m (inf)*.
scare: ~head *n (US)* Sensationsschlagzeile *f*; **~monger** *n* Panikmacher *m*; **~mongering** *n* Panikmache(rei) *f (inf)*; **~ story** *n* Schauergeschichte *f*; **~ tactics** *npl* Panikmache(rei) *(inf)*, Verängstigungstaktik *f*.
scarf [skɑːf] *n, pl* **scarves** Schal *m*; *(neck ~)* Halstuch *nt*; *(head~)* Kopftuch *nt*; *(round the shoulders)* Schultertuch *nt* ◆ **~ pin** Brosche, Busen- *or* Vorstecknadel *f*.
scarifying ['skɛərɪfaɪŋ] *adj (inf)* beängstigend; *film* grus(e)lig *(inf)* ◆ **that was really ~** da konnte man Angst kriegen *(inf)*.
scarlatina [ˌskɑːlə'tiːnə] *n* Scharlach *m*.
scarlet ['skɑːlɪt] [1] *n* Scharlach(rot) *nt* ◆ **~ fever** Scharlach *m*, Scharlachfieber *nt*.
[2] *adj* (scharlach)rot, hochrot ◆ **to turn ~** hochrot werden, rot anlaufen *(inf)*; **he was ~ with rage** er war rot *or* knallrot *(inf)* vor Wut; **a ~ woman** *(old, hum)* eine verrufene *or* liederliche Frau.
scarp [skɑːp] *n* Abhang *m*.
scarper ['skɑːpə^r] *vi (Brit sl)* abhauen *(inf)*, verduften *(sl)*.
scarves [skɑːvz] *pl of* **scarf**.
scary ['skɛərɪ] *adj (+er) (inf)* **(a)** unheimlich; *house also, film* grus(e)lig *(inf)* ◆ **it was pretty ~** da konnte man schon Angst kriegen *(inf)*. **(b)** *(nervous) horse, person* schreckhaft; *(easily worried)* ängstlich.
scat [skæt] *interj (inf)* verschwinde; verschwindet.
scathing ['skeɪðɪŋ] *adj* bissig; *remark also* schneidend; *attack* scharf, schonungslos; *look* vernichtend; *criticism* beißend, vernichtend ◆ **to be ~** bissige *or* schneidende Bemerkungen *pl* machen *(about* über *+acc)*.
scathingly ['skeɪðɪŋlɪ] *adv answer* mit schneidendem Hohn; *look* vernichtend; *criticize, attack* scharf, schonungslos.
scatology [skæ'tɒlədʒɪ] *n (Med)* Koprologie *f (spec)*; *(fig)* Fäkalsprache, Skatologie *(geh) f*.
scatter ['skætə^r] [1] *n see* **scattering**.
[2] *vt* **(a)** *(distribute at random)* verstreuen; *seeds, gravel, (Phys) light* streuen *(on, onto* auf *+acc)*; *money* verschleudern; *(not group together)* (unregelmäßig) verteilen; *votes* verteilen *(between* auf *+acc)* ◆ **to ~ sth around** *or* **about** etw überall umherstreuen *or* verstreuen; **to ~ sth with sth** etw mit etw bestreuen; **the books were ~ed (about) all over the room** die Bücher lagen im ganzen Zimmer herum *or* verstreut; **she knocked the table over, ~ing glasses all over the room** sie stieß den Tisch um, und die Gläser flogen durch das ganze Zimmer; **don't ~ your investments here and there** investieren Sie nicht so kleckerweise.
(b) *(disperse)* auseinandertreiben; *army etc also* zersprengen; *demonstrators, crowd also* zerstreuen ◆ **his friends were ~ed all over the country** seine Freunde waren über das ganze Land verstreut *or* zerstreut; *see also* **scattered**.
[3] *vi* sich zerstreuen *(to* in *+acc)*; *(in a hurry, in fear)* auseinanderlaufen.
scatter: ~brain *n (inf)* Schussel *m (inf)*; **~brained** ['skætəˌbreɪnd] *adj (inf)* schußlig *(inf)*, schusselig *(inf)*, zerfahren, flatterhaft; **~ cushion** *n* (Sofa)kissen *nt*.
scattered ['skætəd] *adj population* weit verstreut; *villages* verstreut; *clouds, showers* vereinzelt.
scattering ['skætərɪŋ] *n (of people)* vereinzeltes Häufchen; *(Phys: of light, waves)* Streuung *f* ◆ **a ~ of books/houses** vereinzelte Bücher *pl*/Häuser *pl*; **a thin ~ of snow on the hillside** dünner Schneefall auf dem Hügel.
scatty ['skætɪ] *adj (+er) (inf)* **(a)** *(scatterbrained)* schußlig *(inf)*, schusselig *(inf)*. **(b)** *(mad)* verrückt, närrisch *(inf)*.
scavenge ['skævɪndʒ] [1] *vt (lit, fig)* ergattern ◆ **the scraps are ~d by hungry gulls** hungrige Möwen ergattern *or* holen sich *(dat)* die Essensreste; **the tramp ~d food from the bins** der Landstreicher plünderte die Abfalleimer; **the car had been completely ~d** das Auto war völlig ausgeschlachtet worden.
[2] *vi (lit)* Nahrung suchen ◆ **jackals live by scavenging** Schakale leben von Aas; **to ~ in the bins** die Abfalleimer plündern; **he's always scavenging around in the scrapyards** er durchstöbert dauernd die Schrottplätze.
scavenger ['skævɪndʒə^r] *n (animal)* Aasfresser *m*; *(fig: person)* Aasgeier *m*.
scenario [sɪ'nɑːrɪəʊ] *n* Szenar(ium) *nt*; *(fig)* Szenario *nt*.
scene [siːn] *n* **(a)** *(place, setting)* Schauplatz *m*; *(of play, novel)* Ort *m* der Handlung ◆ **the ~ of the crime** der Tatort, der Schauplatz des Verbrechens; **the ~ of the battle was a small hill** die Schlacht fand auf einem kleinen Hügel statt; **to set the ~** *(lit, fig)* den Rahmen geben; **the ~ is set in Padua** Ort der Handlung ist Padua, das Stück/der Roman *etc* spielt in Padua; **a change of ~ does you good** ein Tapetenwechsel *m* tut dir gut; **to come** *or* **appear on the ~** auftauchen, auf der Bildfläche erscheinen; **after the accident the police were first on the ~** nach dem Unfall war die Polizei als erste zur Stelle.
(b) *(description, incident)* Szene *f* ◆ **to make a ~** eine Szene machen.
(c) *(Theat)* Szene *f* ◆ **Act II, ~ i** Akt II, 1. Auftritt *or* Szene.
(d) *(Theat: scenery)* Bühnenbild *nt*, Kulisse *f* ◆ **the stagehands move the ~s** die Bühnenarbeiter wechseln die Kulissen; **behind the ~s** *(lit, fig)* hinter den Kulissen.
(e) *(sight)* Anblick *m*; *(landscape)* Landschaft *f*; *(tableau)* Szene *f* ◆ **colourful ~s of Parisian life** bunte Szenen aus dem Pariser Leben; **favourite Glasgow ~s** die beliebtesten Ansichten von Glasgow; **they left behind a ~ of destruction** sie hinterließen eine Stätte der Verwüstung.
(f) *(fuss, argument)* Szene *f* ◆ **to make a ~** eine Szene machen.
(g) *(inf)* **the London drug/pop** *etc* **~** die Londoner Drogen-/Popszene *etc*; **on the fashion ~** in der Modewelt; **that's not my ~** da steh' ich nicht drauf *(sl)*; **to know the ~** *or* **what the ~ is** wissen, was läuft *(sl)*; **it's a whole different ~ here** hier sieht alles ganz anders aus, hier läuft alles ganz anders *(inf)*; **to make the ~** groß herauskommen *(inf)*; **he knew he'd made the ~ when ...** er wußte, daß er es geschafft hatte, als ... *(inf)*.
scene: ~ change *n* Szenenwechsel *m*; **~ painter** *n* Bühnen- *or* Kulissenmaler(in *f*) *m*.
scenery ['siːnərɪ] *n* **(a)** *(landscape)* Landschaft *f* ◆ **there was no ~ at all to look at** die Landschaft bot überhaupt nichts Sehenswertes; **do you like the ~?** gefällt Ihnen die Gegend?; **the new typist has improved the ~ in the office** *(hum)* seit wir die neue Schreibkraft haben, bietet unser Büro einen erfreulicheren Anblick; **I'm tired of all the city ~** ich bin stadtmüde.
(b) *(Theat)* Bühnendekoration *f*, Kulissen *pl*.
scene shifter *n* Kulissenschieber *m*.
scenic ['siːnɪk] *adj* **(a)** *(of landscape)* landschaftlich ◆ **~ shots** *(Phot)* Landschaftsaufnahmen *pl*.
(b) *(picturesque)* malerisch ◆ **~ railway** *Touristenbahnlinie f durch landschaftlich schönes Gebiet*, ≃ Berg- und Tal-Bahn *f*; *(roller coaster)* Achterbahn *f*.
(c) *(theatrical)* bühnentechnisch; filmtechnisch ◆ **~ effects** *(Theat)* Bühneneffekte *pl*; *(Film)* landschaftliche Effekte *pl*.
scent [sent] [1] *n* **(a)** *(smell)* Duft, Geruch *m* ◆ **there was the ~ of danger in the air** es roch nach Gefahr.
(b) *(perfume)* Parfüm *nt*.
(c) *(of animal)* Fährte *f* ◆ **to be on the ~** *(lit, fig)* auf der Fährte *or* Spur sein *(of sb/sth* jdm/einer Sache); **to lose the ~** *(lit, fig)* die Spur *or* Fährte verlieren; **to put** *or* **throw sb off the ~** *(lit, fig)* jdn von der Spur *or* Fährte abbringen *or* ablenken.
(d) *(sense of smell)* Geruchssinn *m*; *(fig)* (Spür)nase *f*.
[2] *vt* **(a)** *(smell, suspect)* wittern. **(b)** *(perfume)* parfümieren ◆ **roses ~ed the air** der Duft von Rosen erfüllte die Luft.
◆**scent out** *vt sep (lit, fig)* aufspüren; *story* ausfindig machen.
scent: ~ bottle *n* Parfümfläschchen *nt*; **~ gland** *n (pleasant smell)* Duftdrüse *f*; *(unpleasant smell)* Stinkdrüse *f*; **~less** *adj flower* duftlos, geruchlos; **~ spray** *n* Parfümzerstäuber *m*.
scepter *n (US) see* **sceptre**.
sceptic, *(US)* **skeptic** ['skeptɪk] *n* Skeptiker(in *f*) *m*.
sceptical, *(US)* **skeptical** ['skeptɪkəl] *adj* skeptisch ◆ **he was ~ about it** er stand der Sache skeptisch gegenüber, er war skeptisch; **I'm ~ about the necessity of this** ich bin skeptisch *or* ich bezweifle, ob das nötig ist.
sceptically, *(US)* **skeptically** ['skeptɪkəlɪ] *adv* skeptisch.
scepticism, *(US)* **skepticism** ['skeptɪsɪzəm] *n* Skepsis *f (about* gegenüber).
sceptre, *(US)* **scepter** ['septə^r] *n* Zepter *nt*.
sch *abbr of* **school** Sch.
schedule ['ʃedjuːl *(esp Brit)*, 'skedʒʊəl] [1] *n* **(a)** *(of events)* Programm *nt*; *(of work)* Zeitplan *m*; *(of lessons)* Stundenplan *m*; *(esp US: timetable)* Fahr-/Flugplan *m*; *(US: list)* Verzeichnis *nt* ◆ **what's on the ~ for today?** was steht für heute auf dem Programm?; **according to ~** planmäßig; *(work also)* nach Plan; **the train is behind ~** der Zug hat Verspätung; **the bus was on ~** der Bus war pünktlich *or* kam fahrplanmäßig an; **the building will be opened on ~** das Gebäude wird wie geplant eröffnet werden; **the work is up to ~** die Arbeit verläuft nach Zeitplan; **the work is ahead of/behind ~** wir/sie *etc* sind (mit der Arbeit) dem Zeitplan voraus/in Verzug *or* im Rückstand; **we are working to a very tight ~** wir arbeiten nach einem knapp bemessenen *or* sehr knappen Zeitplan.
(b) *(insurance, mortgage ~)* Urkunde *f*; *(US Jur: appendix)* Anhang *m*.
[2] *vt* planen; *(put on programme, timetable)* ansetzen; *(US: list)* aufführen ◆ **the work is ~d for completion in 3 months** die Arbeit soll (nach dem *or* laut Zeitplan) in 3 Monaten fertig(gestellt) sein; **this is not ~d for this year** das steht für dieses Jahr nicht auf dem Programm; **this building is ~d for demolition** es ist geplant, dieses Gebäude abzureißen; **you are ~d to speak for 20 minutes/tomorrow** für Sie sind 20 Minuten Sprechzeit vorgesehen/Ihre Rede ist für morgen geplant *or* angesetzt; **trains/buses to New York will be ~d differently** die Abfahrtszeiten der Züge/Busse nach New York werden geändert; **the plane is ~d for 2 o'clock** planmäßige Ankunft/planmäßiger Abflug ist 2 Uhr; **the journey is ~d to last 7 hours** die Fahrt soll 7 Stunden dauern; **this stop was not ~d** dieser Aufenthalt war nicht eingeplant.
scheduled ['ʃedjuːld *(esp Brit)*, 'skedʒʊəld] *adj* vorgesehen, geplant; *departure etc* planmäßig ◆ **~ flight** *(not charter)* Linienflug *m*; *(on timetable)* planmäßiger Flug; **S~ Territories** *(Fin)* Sterlingblock *m*.
schema ['skiːmə] *n, pl* **-ta** ['skiːmətə] Darstellung *f*; *(Philos)* Schema *nt*.
schematic *adj*, **~ally** *adv* [skɪ'mætɪk, -əlɪ] schematisch.
scheme [skiːm] [1] *n* **(a)** *(plan)* Plan *m*, Programm *nt*; *(project)* Projekt *nt*; *(insurance ~)* Programm *nt*; *(idea)* Idee *f* ◆ **the ~ for the new ring road** das neue Umgehungsstraßenprojekt; **a ~ of work** ein Arbeitsprogramm *nt or* -plan *m*; **savings/pension ~** Sparprogramm *nt*/Rentenschema *nt*.
(b) *(plot)* (raffinierter) Plan; *(political also)* Komplott *nt*; *(at court, in firm etc)* Intrige *f* ◆ **a ~ to overthrow the government** ein Komplott gegen die Regierung, Pläne *pl*, die Regierung zu stürzen; **the CIA's ~s to discredit Castro** die Machenschaften *pl* des CIA, um Castro zu diskreditieren.
(c) *(arrangement, layout) (of town centre etc)* Anlage *f*; *(of room etc)* Einrichtung *f* ◆ **the new road ~** das neue Straßensystem; **rhyme ~** Reimschema *nt*; **it doesn't fit into my ~ of things** es hat keinen Platz in meiner Betrachtungsweise.
(d) *(housing ~)* Siedlung *f*.
[2] *vi* Pläne schmieden *or* aushecken *(inf)*; *(at court, in firm etc)* intrigieren ◆ **to ~ for sth** auf etw *(acc)* hinarbeiten.

schemer ['ski:mə^r] *n* raffinierter Schlawiner; (*at court, in firm etc*) Intrigant(in *f*), Ränkeschmied (*liter*) *m* ◆ **my mother's a real ~** meine Mutter schmiedet immer ganz raffinierte Pläne.

scheming ['ski:mɪŋ] [1] *n* raffiniertes Vorgehen, Tricks *pl* (*inf*); (*of politicians, businessmen etc*) Machenschaften, Schliche *pl*; (*at court, in firm etc*) Intrigen, Ränke (*liter*) *pl*.
[2] *adj girl, methods, businessman* raffiniert, durchtrieben; *colleague, courtier* intrigant; *politician* gewieft (*inf*) ◆ **what's in your ~ little mind?** was führst du im Schild?; **her ~ mother-in-law** ihre hinterhältige Schwiegermutter.

scherzo ['skɜ:tsəʊ] *n* Scherzo *nt*.

schism ['sɪzəm] *n* (*Eccl*) Schisma *nt*; (*general also*) Spaltung *f*.

schismatic [sɪz'mætɪk] [1] *adj* schismatisch.
[2] *n* Schismatiker(in *f*) *m*.

schist [ʃɪst] *n* Schiefer *m*.

schizo ['skɪtsəʊ] (*inf*) [1] *n* (*schizophrenic*) Schizophrene(r) *mf*; (*crazy*) Verrückte(r) *mf* (*inf*).
[2] *adj* (*schizophrenic*) schizophren; (*crazy*) verrückt (*inf*).

schizoid ['skɪtsɔɪd] [1] *adj* schizoid.
[2] *n* Schizoide(r) *mf*.

schizophrenia [ˌskɪtsəʊ'fri:nɪə] *n* Schizophrenie *f*.

schizophrenic [ˌskɪtsəʊ'frenɪk] [1] *adj person, reaction* schizophren ◆ **his symptoms are ~** er zeigt die Symptome eines Schizophrenen; **a ~ illness** eine Art Schizophrenie.
[2] *n* Schizophrene(r) *mf*.

schizophrenically [ˌskɪtsəʊ'frenɪkəlɪ] *adv* schizophren ◆ **a ~ disturbed person** ein Mensch mit Bewußtseinsspaltung.

schmal(t)z [ʃmɔ:lts] *n* (*inf*) Schmalz *m* (*inf*).

schmo [ʃməʊ] *n* (*US sl: fool*) Bekloppte(r) (*sl*), Beknackte(r) (*sl*) *mf*.

schmuck [ʃmʌk] *n* (*US sl: fool*) Bekloppte(r) (*sl*), Beknackte(r) (*sl*) *mf*.

schnap(p)s [ʃnæps] *n* Schnaps *m*.

schnitzel ['ʃnɪtsəl] *n* (Wiener) Schnitzel *nt*.

schnorkel ['ʃnɔ:kl] *n see* **snorkel**.

schnozzle ['ʃnɒzəl] *n* (*esp US sl*) Zinken *m* (*sl*).

scholar ['skɒlə^r] *n* (**a**) (*learned person*) Gelehrte(r) *mf* ◆ **the foremost ~s of our time** die führenden Wissenschaftler unserer Zeit; **a famous Shakespeare ~** ein bekannter Shakespearekenner; **I'm no ~** ich bin ja kein Gelehrter.
(**b**) (*student*) Student(in *f*) *m*; Schüler(in *f*) *m*.
(**c**) (*scholarship holder*) Stipendiat(in *f*) *m*.

scholarliness ['skɒləlɪnɪs] *n* (*of person, work*) Gelehrtheit, Gelehrsamkeit *f* ◆ **the ~ of his interests** sein Interesse an hochgeistigen Dingen; **the ~ of his appearance** sein gelehrtes Aussehen.

scholarly ['skɒləlɪ] *adj* wissenschaftlich; (*learned*) gelehrt; *interests* hochgeistig ◆ **he's not at all ~** er hat keinen Hang zum Hochgeistigen; (*in his approach*) er geht überhaupt nicht wissenschaftlich vor; **his way of life was very ~** er führte ein sehr beschauliches Leben.

scholarship ['skɒləʃɪp] *n* (**a**) (*learning*) Gelehrsamkeit *f* ◆ **~ flourished during the Renaissance** die Gelehrsamkeit entfaltete sich in der Renaissance zur vollen Blüte.
(**b**) (*money award*) Stipendium *nt* ◆ **to win a ~ to Cambridge** ein Stipendium für Cambridge bekommen; **on a ~** mit einem Stipendium; **~ holder** Stipendiat(in *f*) *m*.

scholastic [skə'læstɪk] *adj* (**a**) (*relative to school*) schulisch, Schul-; (*Univ*) Studien- ◆ **the ~ profession** der Lehrberuf. (**b**) (*relative to scholasticism*) scholastisch.

scholasticism [skə'læstɪsɪzəm] *n* Scholastik *f*.

school[1] [sku:l] [1] *n* (**a**) Schule *f*; (*US: college, university*) College *nt*; Universität *f* ◆ **at ~** in der Schule/im College/an der Universität; **to go to ~** in die Schule/ins College/zur Universität gehen; **there's no ~ tomorrow** morgen ist schulfrei *or* keine Schule; **~ of art/dancing** Kunst-/Tanzschule *f*; **to learn in a tough ~** (*fig*) durch eine harte Schule gehen.
(**b**) (*Univ: department*) Fachbereich *m*; (*of medicine, law*) Fakultät *f* ◆ **S~ of Arabic Studies** Institut *nt* für Arabistik.
(**c**) (*group of artists, philosophers etc*) Schule *f* ◆ **Plato and his ~** Platon und seine Schüler(schaft); **I'm not one of that ~** ich gehöre nicht zu den Leuten, die das meinen; **he belongs to a different ~ of thought** er vertritt eine andere Lehrmeinung; **he's a diplomat of the old ~** er ist ein Diplomat der alten Schule.
[2] *vt* lehren; *animal* dressieren; *one's temper* zügeln ◆ **to ~ sb in a technique** jdn eine Technik lehren, jdn in einer Technik unterrichten *or* unterweisen; **he had been ~ed by poverty to ...** Armut hatte ihn gelehrt, ...; **he ~ed himself to control his temper** er hatte sich dazu erzogen, sich zu beherrschen.

school[2] *n* (*of fish*) Schule *f*; (*of herrings*) Schwarm *m*.

school *in cpds* Schul-; **~ age** *n* schulpflichtiges Alter, Schulalter *nt*; **is he of ~ age yet?** ist er schon schulpflichtig *or* im schulpflichtigen Alter?; **~ bag** *n* Schultasche *f*; **~ board** *n* (*US*) Schulbehörde *f*; (*Brit*) Schulaufsichtsrat *m*; **~boy** [1] *n* Schuljunge, Schüler *m*; [2] *adj attr* Pennäler-, Schulbuben-; **~children** *npl* Schulkinder, Schüler *pl*; **~days** *npl* Schulzeit *f*; **~ dinner** *n* Schulessen *nt*; **~ fees** *npl* Schulgeld *nt*; **~girl** *n* Schulmädchen *nt*, Schülerin *f*; **~house** *n* (*teacher's house*) Lehrerhaus *nt*; (*school*) Schulhaus *nt*.

schooling ['sku:lɪŋ] *n* (*education*) Ausbildung *f* ◆ **compulsory ~ was introduced in 1870** 1870 wurde die Schulpflicht eingeführt; **compulsory ~ lasts 11 years** die (gesetzlich) vorgeschriebene Schulzeit dauert 11 Jahre.

school: ~-leaver *n* Schulabgänger(in *f*) *m*; **~-leaving age** *n* Schulabgangsalter, Schulentlassungsalter *nt*; **~ma'am, ~marm** *n* (*pej*) Schulmeisterin *f* (*pej*); **~master** *n* Lehrer, Schulmeister (*dated*) *m*; **village ~master** Dorfschulleiter, Dorfschulmeister (*dated*) *m*; **~mate** *n* Schulkamerad(in *f*), Schulfreund(in *f*) *m*; **~ meals** *npl* Schulessen *nt*; **~mistress** *n* Lehrerin, Schulmeisterin (*dated*) *f*; **~room** *n* (*in school*) Klassenzimmer *nt*; (*in private house*) Schulzimmer *nt*; **~teacher** *n* Lehrer(in *f*) *m*; **~ uniform** *n* Schuluniform *f*; **~ yard** *n* Schulhof *m*; **~ year** *n* Schuljahr *nt*.

schooner ['sku:nə^r] *n* (**a**) (*boat*) Schoner *m*. (**b**) (*sherry glass*) großes Sherryglas; (*US, Austral: beer ~*) *hohes Bierglas*.

schuss [ʃʊs] (*Ski*) [1] *n* Schuß *m*.
[2] *vi* (im) Schuß fahren.

schwa [ʃwɑ:] *n* (*Phon*) Schwa *nt*.

sciatic [saɪ'ætɪk] *adj* Ischias-, ischiadisch (*spec*).

sciatica [saɪ'ætɪkə] *n* Ischias *m or nt*.

science ['saɪəns] *n* (**a**) Wissenschaft *f*; (*natural ~*) Naturwissenschaft *f* ◆ **to study ~** Naturwissenschaften studieren; **a man of ~** ein Wissenschaftler *m*; **things that ~ cannot explain** Dinge, die man nicht naturwissenschaftlich erklären kann; **on the ~ side of the school** im naturwissenschaftlichen Zweig der Schule; **the ~ of cooking** die Kochkunst; **the ~ of life/astrology** die Lehre vom Leben/von den Gestirnen.
(**b**) (*systematic knowledge or skill*) Technik *f* ◆ **it wasn't luck that helped me to do it, it was ~!** das war kein Zufall, daß mir das gelungen ist, das war Können; **there's a lot of ~ involved in that** dazu gehört großes Können.

science fiction *n* Science-fiction *f* ◆ **~ novel** Zukunftsroman, Science-fiction-Roman *m*.

science park *n* Forschungspark *m*.

scientific [ˌsaɪən'tɪfɪk] *adj* (**a**) (*of natural sciences*) naturwissenschaftlich; *apparatus, equipment* wissenschaftlich.
(**b**) (*systematic, exact*) *classification, methods etc* wissenschaftlich ◆ **a keen but not ~ football player** ein begeisterter, doch technisch schwacher Fußballspieler; **his ~ boxing technique** seine gekonnte Boxtechnik.

scientifically [ˌsaɪən'tɪfɪkəlɪ] *adv* wissenschaftlich; (*relating to natural sciences*) naturwissenschaftlich; *box, fence etc* technisch gekonnt ◆ **he approaches sport very ~** der Sport wird bei ihm zur Wissenschaft; **~, his work is ...** vom naturwissenschaftlichen Standpunkt aus ist seine Arbeit ...

scientist ['saɪəntɪst] *n* (Natur)wissenschaftler(in *f*) *m*.

scientology [ˌsaɪən'tɒlɪdʒɪ] *n* Scientology *f*.

sci-fi ['saɪfaɪ] *n* (*inf*) *see* **science fiction**.

Scillies ['sɪlɪz], **Scilly Isles** ['sɪlɪˌaɪlz] *npl* Scilly-Inseln *pl*.

scimitar ['sɪmɪtə^r] *n* Krummschwert *nt*.

scintillate ['sɪntɪleɪt] *vi* (*diamonds, stars*) funkeln; (*fig: person, conversation*) vor Geist sprühen.

scintillating ['sɪntɪleɪtɪŋ] *adj* funkelnd *attr*; (*fig*) (*witty, lively*) *wit, humour* sprühend *attr*; *person, speech* vor Geist sprühend *attr*; (*fascinating*) *information* faszinierend ◆ **to be ~** funkeln; sprühen; vor Geist sprühen; faszinierend sein.

scintillatingly ['sɪntɪleɪtɪŋlɪ] *adv* **~ witty** vor Geist sprühend.

scion ['saɪən] *n* (**a**) (*Bot*) Schößling *m*; (*for grafting*) (Pfropf)reis *nt*. (**b**) (*form*) Nachkomme, Nachfahr *m*.

scissors ['sɪzəz] *n* (**a**) *pl* Schere *f* ◆ **a pair of ~** eine Schere. (**b**) *sing* (*Sport*) (*also* **~ jump**) Schersprung *m*; (*also* **~ hold**) Schere *f* ◆ **~ kick** (*Swimming, Ftbl*) Scherenschlag *m*.

sclerosis [sklɪ'rəʊsɪs] *n* Sklerose *f*; *see* **multiple ~**.

scoff[1] [skɒf] [1] *n* verächtliche *or* abschätzige Bemerkung.
[2] *vi* spotten ◆ **to ~ at sb/sth** jdn/etw verachten; (*verbally*) sich verächtlich *or* abschätzig über jdn/etw äußern.

scoff[2] (*inf*) [1] *n* (*food*) Fressalien *pl* (*inf*); (*eating*) Fresserei *f* (*inf*).
[2] *vt* futtern (*inf*), in sich (*acc*) hineinstopfen (*inf*) ◆ **she ~ed (up) the lot** sie hat alles verputzt (*inf*) *or* verdrückt (*inf*).

scoffer ['skɒfə^r] *n* Spötter(in *f*) *m*.

scoffing ['skɒfɪŋ] [1] *n* Spötterei *f*, verächtliche Bemerkungen *pl*.
[2] *adj* spöttisch, verächtlich.

scoffingly ['skɒfɪŋlɪ] *adv see adj*.

scold [skəʊld] [1] *vt* (aus)schelten, ausschimpfen (*for* wegen) ◆ **she ~ed him for coming home late** sie schimpfte ihn aus, weil er so spät heimgekommen war.
[2] *vi* schimpfen.
[3] *n* (*person*) Beißzange *f* (*inf*); (*woman also*) Xanthippe *f* (*inf*) ◆ **don't be such a ~, mother!** schimpf doch nicht dauernd, Mutter!

scolding ['skəʊldɪŋ] *n* Schelte *f no pl*; (*act*) Schimpferei *f* ◆ **to give sb a ~** jdn ausschimpfen, jdn (aus)schelten.

scollop *n see* **scallop 1 (a)**.

sconce [skɒns] *n* Wandleuchter *m*.

scone [skɒn] *n brötchenartiges Buttergebäck*.

scoop [sku:p] [1] *n* (**a**) (*instrument*) Schaufel *f*; (*for ice cream, potatoes etc*) Portionierer *m*; (*ball of ice-cream, potato*) Kugel *f* ◆ **at one ~** (*lit, fig*) auf einmal. (**b**) (*inf: lucky gain*) Fang *m* (*inf*). (**c**) (*Press*) Knüller (*inf*), Scoop (*sl*) *m*.
[2] *vt* (**a**) schaufeln; *liquid* schöpfen. (**b**) **The Times ~ed the other papers** die Times ist den anderen Zeitungen zuvorgekommen.

◆**scoop out** *vt sep* (**a**) (*take out*) herausschaufeln; *liquid* herausschöpfen ◆ **the cat ~ed ~ the goldfish with its paw** die Katze hat den Goldfisch mit ihrer Pfote herausgefischt. (**b**) (*hollow out*) *melon, marrow etc* aushöhlen; *hole* graben.

◆**scoop up** *vt sep* aufschaufeln; *liquid* aufschöpfen ◆ **she ~ed the child/cards/money ~** sie raffte das Kind/die Karten/das Geld an sich (*acc*).

scoop: ~ neck *n* U-Ausschnitt *m*; **~-necked** ['sku:p'nekt] *adj* mit U-

Ausschnitt.

scoot [sku:t] *vi* (*inf*) (*scram*) abzischen (*sl*); (*walk quickly*) rennen ◆ **~ across and get it!** spritz mal rüber und hol's! (*inf*).

scooter ['sku:tə^r] *n* (Tret)roller *m*; (*motor ~*) (Motor)roller *m*.

scope [skəʊp] *n* **(a)** (*of topic, idea, investigation*) Umfang *m*; (*of law, measures*) Reichweite *f*; (*of sb's duties, department, tribunal*) Kompetenzbereich *m* ◆ **sth is within the ~ of sth** etw hält sich *or* bleibt im Rahmen einer Sache (*gen*); **sth is within the ~ of sb's duties/a department** *etc* etw fällt in jds Aufgabenbereich (*acc*)/in den Kompetenzbereich einer Abteilung *etc*; **sth is beyond** *or* **outside the ~ of sth** etw geht über etw (*acc*) hinaus; **that's beyond the ~ of his duties/this department** das geht über seinen Aufgabenbereich/den Kompetenzbereich dieser Abteilung hinaus; **it's not within the ~ of my power to authorize that** das überschreitet meine Kompetenzen.
(b) (*extent of one's perception, grasp*) Fassungsvermögen *nt*; (*of talents, knowledge*) Umfang *m* ◆ **that job would be beyond my ~** diese Arbeit würde meine Fähigkeiten übersteigen; **that is beyond my ~** *or* **the ~ of my understanding** das übersteigt mein Fassungsvermögen; **that job is within his ~** diese Arbeit liegt im Bereich seiner Fähigkeiten.
(c) (*opportunity*) Möglichkeit(en *pl*) *f*; (*to develop one's talents*) Entfaltungsmöglichkeit *f*; (*to use one's talents*) Spielraum *m* ◆ **there is ~ for improvement** es könnte noch verbessert werden; **there is ~ for further projects** es ist Spielraum für weitere Vorhaben; **to give sb ~ to do sth** jdm den nötigen Spielraum geben, etw zu tun; **that job gave his ability/imaginative powers full ~** in diesem Beruf konnten sich seine Fähigkeiten/konnte sich seine Phantasie frei entfalten.
(d) (*inf*) *see* **microscope, periscope** *etc*.

scorbutic [skɔ:'bju:tɪk] *adj* skorbutisch.

scorch [skɔ:tʃ] **1** *n* (*also* **~ mark**) verbrannte *or* versengte Stelle, Brandfleck *m*.
2 *vt* versengen ◆ **the sun ~ed our faces** die Sonne brannte auf unsere Gesichter; **~ed earth policy** (*Mil*) Politik *f* der verbrannten Erde.
3 *vi* **(a) the sun ~ed down** die Sonne brannte herunter. **(b)** (*become ~ed*) **that dress will ~ easily** das Kleid kann man leicht versengen. **(c)** (*inf: go fast*) rasen (*inf*).

scorcher ['skɔ:tʃə^r] *n* (*inf*) **yesterday/last summer was a real ~** gestern war eine Knallhitze (*inf*)/im letzten Sommer war es wirklich heiß; **his speech was quite a ~** das war eine gepfefferte Rede (*inf*).

scorching ['skɔ:tʃɪŋ] *adj* (*very hot*) *sun, iron* glühend heiß; *day, weather* brütend heiß, knallheiß (*inf*); (*inf: very fast*) *speed* rasend; *driver* rasant; (*fig: scathing*) gepfeffert (*inf*).

score [skɔ:^r] **1** *n* **(a)** (*number of points*) (Punkte)stand *m*; (*of game, Sport also*) Spielstand *m*; (*final ~*) Spielergebnis *nt* ◆ **what was your ~ in the test?** wie viele Punkte hast du bei dem Test erreicht *or* gemacht? (*inf*); **England didn't get a very good ~** England hat nicht sehr gut abgeschnitten; (*in game, test also*) England hat nicht sehr viele Punkte erzielt; (*Ftbl etc also*) England hat nicht sehr viele Tore erzielt *or* geschossen; **the ~ was Celtic 2, Rangers 1** es stand 2:1 für Celtic (gegen Rangers); (*final ~*) Celtic schlug Rangers (mit) 2:1; **there was no ~ at half-time** zur Halbzeit stand es 0:0; **to keep (the) ~** (mit)zählen; (*officially*) Punkte zählen; (*on scoreboard*) Punkte anschreiben; **what's the ~?** wie steht es?; (*fig also*) wie sieht es aus? (*on mit*) (*inf*); **he doesn't know the ~** (*fig*) er weiß nicht, was gespielt wird (*inf*); **to make a ~ with sb** (*fig*) jdn stark beeindrucken; **to make a ~ off sb** (*fig*) jdm eins auswischen (*inf*).
(b) (*reckoning, grudge*) Rechnung *f* ◆ **what's the ~?** was bin ich schuldig?, wieviel macht das?; **to pay off old ~s** alte Schulden begleichen; **to have a ~ to settle with sb** mit jdm eine alte Rechnung zu begleichen haben.
(c) (*Mus*) (*printed music*) Noten *pl*; (*of classical music also*) Partitur *f*; (*of film, musical*) Musik *f*.
(d) (*line, cut*) Rille, Kerbe *f*; (*on body*) Kratzer *m*; (*weal*) Striemen *m*.
(e) (*20*) zwanzig ◆ **~s of ...** (*many*) Hunderte von ..., jede Menge ... (*inf*); **a ~ of people** zwanzig Leute; **3 ~ years and 10** (*old*) 70 Jahre; **~s and ~s** Hunderte, jede Menge (*inf*); **~s of times** hundertmal, zigmal (*inf*); **by the ~** massenweise (*inf*).
(f) (*reason, ground*) Grund *m* ◆ **on the ~ of illness** wegen Krankheit; **on that ~** aus diesem Grund, deshalb.
2 *vt* **(a)** erzielen; *marks, points also* bekommen; *goals also* schießen; *runs also* schaffen ◆ **he ~d an advantage over his opponent** er war gegenüber seinem Gegner im Vorteil; **our last contestant ~d one hundred points** unser letzter Kandidat hat hundert Punkte; **each correct answer ~s five points** jede richtige Antwort zählt fünf Punkte; **to ~ a point off sb** (*fig*) auf jds Kosten (*acc*) glänzen, jdn ausstechen; **to ~ a hit with sb** jdn stark beeindrucken; **that remark ~d a hit** diese Bemerkung hat ins Schwarze getroffen.
(b) (*groove*) einkerben, Rillen/eine Rille machen in (+*acc*); (*mark*) Kratzer/einen Kratzer machen in (+*acc*); (*Cook*) *fat, meat etc* einschneiden ◆ **the wall is heavily ~d with lines** die Wand weist tiefe Rillen auf; **the mountainside had been ~d by glaciers** Gletscher hatten ihre Spuren am Berg hinterlassen.
(c) (*Mus*) schreiben.
3 *vi* **(a)** einen Punkt erzielen *or* machen (*inf*); (*Ftbl etc*) ein Tor schießen ◆ **to ~ well/badly** gut/schlecht abschneiden; (*in game, test etc also*) eine gute/keine gute Punktzahl erreichen; (*Ftbl etc also*) viele/wenig Tore schießen; **the batsman didn't ~ off the fast balls** der Schlagmann konnte die schnellen Bälle nicht verwandeln; **that's where he ~s** (*fig*) das ist sein großes Plus.
(b) (*keep ~*) (mit)zählen.
(c) (*sl: sexually*) **did you ~ with her?** hast du sie aufs Kreuz gelegt? (*sl*).
(d) (*sl: obtain drugs*) sich (*dat*) Stoff beschaffen.

◆**score off** **1** *vt sep* (*delete*) ausstreichen.
2 *vi +prep obj* **to ~ ~ sb** jdn als dumm hinstellen.

◆**score out** *or* **through** *vt sep* aus- *or* durch streichen.

◆**score up** *vt sep* anschreiben (*to sb* für jdn) ◆ **~ it ~ to me** (*fig*) eins zu null für mich (*inf*).

score: ~board *n* Anzeigetafel *f*; (*on TV*) Tabelle *f* der Spielergebnisse; **~card** *n* Spielprotokoll *nt*; (*Golf*) Zählkarte *f*; **~keeper** *n* (*official*) (*Sport*) Anschreiber *m*; (*in quiz etc*) Punktezähler *m*; **who's the ~keeper?** wer zählt (mit)?

scorer ['skɔ:rə^r] *n* **(a)** (*Ftbl etc: player*) Torschütze *m* ◆ **Chelsea were the highest ~s** Chelsea schoß die meisten Tore; **the leading ~ in the quiz** der, der die meisten Punkte im Quiz erzielt. **(b)** *see* **scorekeeper**.

score sheet *n* Spielbericht(sbogen) *m*, Protokoll *nt*.

scoring ['skɔ:rɪŋ] **1** *n* Erzielen *nt* eines Punktes; (*Ftbl etc*) Tor(schuß *m*) *nt*; (*scorekeeping*) Zählen *nt* ◆ **rules for ~** Regeln über die Zählweise; **X did most of the ~** X erzielte die meisten Punkte; (*Ftbl etc*) X schoß die meisten Tore.
2 *adj suf* **a low-/high-~ match** ein Spiel, in dem wenig/viele Punkte/Tore erzielt wurden.

scorn ['skɔ:n] **1** *n* (*disdain*) Verachtung *f*; (*verbal also*) Hohn *m* ◆ **to laugh sb/sth to ~** jdn höhnisch verlachen/etw mit Hohnlachen quittieren; **to pour ~ on sth** etw verächtlich abtun; **to be the ~ of sb** von jdm verachtet werden.
2 *vt* (*treat scornfully*) verachten; (*condescendingly*) verächtlich behandeln; (*turn down*) *gift, advice* verschmähen; *idea* mit Verachtung von sich weisen ◆ **to ~ to do sth** es für seiner (*gen*) unwürdig halten, etw zu tun; **to ~ sb as sth** jdn verächtlich als etw abtun.

scornful ['skɔ:nfʊl] *adj* verächtlich; *laughter also, person* spöttisch, höhnisch ◆ **to be ~ of sb/sth** jdn/etw verachten; (*verbally*) jdn/etw verhöhnen; **to be ~ about sb/sth** sich über jdn/etw verächtlich äußern.

scornfully ['skɔ:nfəlɪ] *adv see adj*.

scornfulness ['skɔ:nfʊlnɪs] *n* Verachtung *f* (*of* für) ◆ **her ~ at the mere mention of his name** ihre verächtliche *or* höhnische Reaktion bei der bloßen Erwähnung seines Namens.

Scorpio ['skɔ:pɪəʊ] *n* (*Astrol*) Skorpion *m*.

scorpion ['skɔ:pɪən] *n* Skorpion *m*.

Scot [skɒt] *n* Schotte *m*, Schottin *f*.

Scotch [skɒtʃ] **1** *adj* schottisch ◆ **~ broth** *Gemüsesuppe f mit Gerstengraupen und Hammelfleischbrühe*; **~ egg** *hartgekochtes Ei in Wurstbrät, paniert und ausgebacken*; **~ fir** Föhre *f*, (gemeine) Kiefer; **~ tape** ® Tesafilm ® *m*; **~ terrier** Scotchterrier *m*, schottischer Terrier.
2 *n* **(a)** (*~ whisky*) Scotch *m*. **(b) the ~** *pl* die Schotten *pl*.

scotch [skɒtʃ] *vt rumour* aus der Welt schaffen; *idea, plan* unterbinden, einen Riegel vorschieben (+*dat*) ◆ **the rain has ~ed that** der Regen hat uns (*dat*) einen Strich durch die Rechnung gemacht (*inf*).

Scotchman ['skɒtʃmən], **Scotchwoman** ['skɒtʃwʊmən] *n see* **Scotsman, Scotswoman**.

scot-free ['skɒt'fri:] *adv* ungeschoren ◆ **to get off ~** ungeschoren davonkommen.

Scotland ['skɒtlənd] *n* Schottland *nt*.

Scots [skɒts] **1** *adj* schottisch.
2 *n* (*dialect*) Schottisch *nt* ◆ **the ~** (*people*) die Schotten *pl*.

Scots: ~man *n* Schotte *m*; **~ pine** *n* Föhre *f*, (gemeine) Kiefer; **~woman** *n* Schottin *f*.

Scotticism ['skɒtɪsɪzəm] *n* schottischer Ausdruck.

scotticize ['skɒtɪsaɪz] *vt* schottifizieren, verschotten (*hum*).

Scottie ['skɒtɪ] *n* **(a)** (*also* **~ dog**) Scotchterrier *m*, schottischer Terrier. **(b)** (*inf: Scotsman*) Schotte *m*.

Scottish ['skɒtɪʃ] **1** *adj* schottisch.
2 *n* **(a)** (*dialect*) Schottisch *nt*. **(b) the ~** *pl* die Schotten *pl*.

scoundrel ['skaʊndrəl] *n* (*dated*) Schurke *m*; (*inf*) Bengel *m*.

scoundrelly ['skaʊndrəlɪ] *adj* (*dated*) schurkisch.

scour[1] ['skaʊə^r] **1** *vt* scheuern.
2 *n* Scheuern *nt* ◆ **give the pan a good ~** scheuern Sie den Topf gründlich.

◆**scour away** *or* **off** *vt sep* abscheuern; *rust* abreiben.

◆**scour out** *vt sep pan* ausscheuern.

scour[2] *vt area, town, shops* absuchen, abkämmen (*for* nach).

◆**scour about** *or* **around** *vi* herumsuchen (*for* nach).

scourer ['skaʊərə^r] *n* Topfkratzer *m*.

scourge [skɜ:dʒ] **1** *n* (*lit, fig*) Geißel *f*.
2 *vt* **(a)** geißeln. **(b)** (*fig*) (*punish*) (be)strafen; (*devastate*) heimsuchen; (*verbally*) geißeln (*geh*).

Scouse [skaʊs] **1** *adj* Liverpooler.
2 *n* **(a)** (*person: also* **~r** ['skaʊsə^r]) Liverpooler(in *f*) *m*. **(b)** (*dialect*) Liverpooler Dialekt *m*.

scout [skaʊt] **1** *n* **(a)** (*Mil*) (*person*) Kundschafter, Späher *m*; (*ship, plane*) Aufklärer *m*.
(b) (*reconnaissance*) Erkundung *f*; (*Mil*) Aufklärung *f*; (*search*) Suche *f* ◆ **to have** *or* **take a ~ about** *or* **(a)round for sth** sich nach etw umsehen.
(c) Pfadfinder *m*; (*US: girl ~*) Pfadfinderin *f*.
(d) (*football ~ etc*) Kundschafter, Spion *m*; (*talent ~*) Talentsucher *m*.
(e) (*employed by motoring organization*) Pannenhelfer *m*.
(f) (*Brit Univ*) *Diener m für die College-Studenten*.
2 *vi* erkunden, auskundschaften ◆ **they were ~ing inside enemy territory** sie waren auf Erkundung in feindlichem Gebiet; **to ~ for sth** nach etw Aus-

schau *or* Umschau halten; **he was ~ing for new talent** er war auf Talentsuche.

◆**scout about** *or* **around** *vi* sich umsehen (*for* nach).

◆**scout out** *vt sep* (*Mil*) auskundschaften; (*inf*) aufstöbern.

scout car *n* Aufklärungsfahrzeug *nt*; (*heavier*) Aufklärungs- *or* Spähpanzer *m*.

scouting ['skaʊtɪŋ] [1] *n* **(a)** Erkunden, Auskundschaften *nt*; (*Mil*) Aufklärung *f*; (*looking*) Suche *f* (*for* nach); (*for talent*) Talentsuche *f*. **(b)** (*scout movement*) Pfadfinderei *f* (*inf*), Pfadfindertum *nt*.
[2] *adj attr* Pfadfinder-.

scout: ~ master *n* Gruppenführer *m*; **~ movement** *n* Pfadfinderbewegung *f*; **~ troop** *n* Pfadfindergruppe *f*.

scow [skaʊ] *n* (*Naut*) Prahm *m*.

scowl [skaʊl] [1] *n* unmutiger Ausdruck, finsterer Blick, böses Gesicht ◆ **to give sb a ~** jdn böse ansehen.
[2] *vi* ein böses *or* finsteres Gesicht machen ◆ **to ~ at sb** jdn böse ansehen; **what are you ~ing about** *or* **at?** warum machst du so ein böses Gesicht?

scowling ['skaʊlɪŋ] *adj* mißmutig.

scrabble ['skræbl] [1] *vi* (*also* **~ about**) (herum)tasten; (*among movable objects*) (herum)wühlen ◆ **the hens ~d (about) in the earth** die Hühner wühlten im Boden herum.
[2] *n* **S~** ® Scrabble ® *nt*.

scrag [skræg] [1] *n* (*also* **~ end**) Hals *m*.
[2] *vt* (*sl: kill*) abmurksen (*inf*).

scragginess ['skrægɪnɪs] *n* Magerkeit *f*; (*of meat*) minderwertige Qualität, Sehnigkeit *f*.

scraggy ['skrægɪ] *adj* (+*er*) dürr; *meat* minderwertig, sehnig.

scram [skræm] *vi* (*inf*) abhauen (*sl*) ◆ **~!** ab!, verschwinde/ verschwindet!

scramble ['skræmbl] [1] *n* **(a)** (*climb*) Kletterei *f* ◆ **we went for a ~ in the hills** wir sind in den Bergen herumgeklettert.
(b) (*mad dash*) Gerangel, Gedrängel *nt* ◆ **a ~ for the better-paid jobs** die Jagd nach den besser bezahlten Stellen.
(c) (*Motor sport*) Querfeldeinrennen *nt*.
[2] *vt* **(a)** *pieces, letters* (untereinander- *or* ver)mischen.
(b) *eggs* verquirlen, verrühren ◆ **~d eggs** Rührei(er *pl*) *nt*.
(c) (*Telec*) *message* chiffrieren, verschlüsseln; *line* an das Verschlüsselungsgerät anschließen.
[3] *vi* **(a)** (*climb*) klettern ◆ **to ~ out** heraus-/hinausklettern; **he ~d to his feet** er rappelte sich auf (*inf*); **to ~ through the hedge** durch die Hecke kriechen *or* krabbeln (*inf*); **to ~ up sth** auf etw (*acc*) hinaufklettern *or* hinaufkraxeln (*inf*).
(b) (*struggle*) **to ~ for sth/to get sth** sich um etw balgen *or* raufen/sich balgen *or* raufen, um etw zu bekommen; *for ball etc* um etw kämpfen/darum kämpfen, etw zu bekommen; *for bargains, job, good site* sich um etw drängeln/sich drängeln, um etw zu bekommen.
(c) (*Aviat*) einen Soforteinsatz fliegen ◆ **~!** höchste Alarmstufe.

scrambler ['skræmblə^r] *n* **(a)** (*Telec*) Chiffriergerät *nt*. **(b)** (*motorcyclist*) Querfeldeinfahrer(in *f*) *m*.

scrap[1] [skræp] [1] *n* **(a)** (*small piece*) Stückchen *nt*; (*fig*) bißchen *no pl*; (*of papers also, of conversation, news*) Fetzen *m*; (*of truth*) Fünkchen *nt*, Spur *f*; (*of poetry*) Fragment *nt* ◆ **there isn't a ~ of food in the house** es ist überhaupt nichts *or* kein Bissen zu essen im Haus; **his few ~s of German** seine paar Brocken Deutsch; **his few ~s of knowledge** das bißchen Wissen, das er hat; **a few ~s of information** ein paar magere Auskünfte; **it's a ~ of comfort** es ist wenigstens ein kleiner Trost; **not a ~!** nicht die Spur!; **not a ~ of evidence** nicht der geringste Beweis; **he was not a ~ of help** er war überhaupt keine Hilfe, er war nicht die geringste Hilfe; **that won't help a ~** das hilft kein bißchen.
(b) (*usu pl: leftover*) Rest *m*.
(c) (*waste material*) Altmaterial *nt*, Altwaren *pl*; (*metal*) Schrott *m*; (*paper*) Altpapier *nt* ◆ **these bits are ~** diese Sachen werden nicht mehr gebraucht; **are these notes ~?** können die Notizen weggeworfen werden?; **to sell a ship for ~** ein Schiff als Schrott *or* zum Verschrotten verkaufen; **what is your car worth as ~?** wie hoch ist der Schrottwert Ihres Autos?
[2] *vt car, ship etc* verschrotten; *furniture, clothes* ausrangieren; *idea, plan etc* fallenlassen; *piece of work* wegwerfen ◆ **~ that** (*inf: forget it*) vergiß es!

scrap[2] (*inf*) [1] *n* Balgerei *f*; (*verbal*) Streiterei *f* ◆ **to get into** *or* **have a ~ with sb** mit jdm in die Wolle geraten (*inf*).
[2] *vi* sich balgen; (*verbal*) sich streiten.

scrap: ~book *n* Sammelalbum *nt*; **~ dealer** *n* Altwarenhändler *m*; (*in metal*) Schrott- *or* Altmetallhändler *m*.

scrape [skreɪp] [1] *n* **(a)** (*act*) **to give sth a ~** *see vt (a, b)*.
(b) (*mark, graze*) Schramme *f*.
(c) (*sound*) Kratzen *nt* ◆ **the ~ of his feet on the gravel** das Knirschen seiner Füße auf dem Kies.
(d) (*difficulty*) Schwulitäten *pl* (*inf*) ◆ **he goes from one ~ to another** er handelt sich (*dat*) dauernd Ärger ein (*inf*); **to get sb out of a ~** jdm aus der Patsche *or* Klemme helfen (*inf*).
[2] *vt* **(a)** (*make clean or smooth*) *potatoes, carrots etc* schaben; *plate, wall, shoes* abkratzen; *dish, saucepan* auskratzen ◆ **that's really scraping the (bottom of the) barrel** (*fig*) das ist wirklich das Letzte vom Letzten.
(b) *car* schrammen; *wall, gatepost* streifen; *arm, knee* auf- *or* abschürfen ◆ **the paint was ~d in the crash** der Lack bekam bei dem Unfall Kratzer.
(c) (*grate against*) kratzen an (+*dat*) ◆ **he ~d his bow across the violin** er kratzte mit dem Bogen auf der Geige; **he ~d his nail along the glass** er kratzte mit dem Nagel über das Glas.
(d) (*make by scraping*) *hole* scharren ◆ **to ~ a living** gerade so sein Auskommen haben; **he ~d a living as a freelance reporter** er hielt sich als freier Reporter gerade so über Wasser (*inf*); **he was trying to ~ (up) an acquaintance with him** er versuchte mit allen Mitteln, seine Bekanntschaft zu machen.
[3] *vi* **(a)** (*make clean*) kratzen ◆ **he ~d at the paint for hours** er kratzte stundenlang an der Farbe herum.
(b) (*rub*) streifen (*against acc*); (*grate*) kratzen (*against* an +*dat*) ◆ **the bird's broken wing ~d along the ground** der gebrochene Flügel des Vogels schleifte am Boden; **as he ~d past me** als er sich an mir vorbeizwängte; **the car just ~d past the gatepost** der Wagen fuhr um Haaresbreite am Torpfosten vorbei; *see* **bow**[2].
(c) (*be economical*) knapsen (*inf*), knausern ◆ **they ~d for years to pay the debt** sie mußten jahrelang daran knapsen, die Schulden zu bezahlen (*inf*).

◆**scrape along** *vi* sich schlecht und recht durchschlagen (*inf*) (*on* mit).

◆**scrape away** [1] *vi* herumkratzen (*at* an +*dat*).
[2] *vt sep* abkratzen.

◆**scrape by** *vi* (*lit*) sich vorbeizwängen; (*fig*) sich durchwursteln (*inf*) (*on* mit).

◆**scrape in** *vi* **he just managed to ~ ~** er ist gerade noch hineingerutscht (*inf*).

◆**scrape off** [1] *vi* sich abkratzen lassen.
[2] *vt sep* abkratzen (*prep obj* von).

◆**scrape out** *vt sep* auskratzen, ausschaben; *eyes of potato, bad parts* ausschneiden.

◆**scrape through** [1] *vi* (*lit*) (*object*) gerade so durchgehen; (*person*) sich durchzwängen; (*in exam*) durchrutschen (*inf*).
[2] *vi* +*prep obj narrow gap* sich durchzwängen durch; *exam* durchrutschen durch (*inf*).

◆**scrape together** *vt sep leaves* zusammenharken, zusammenrechen; *money* zusammenkratzen; *people* zusammenbringen, organisieren; *support* organisieren.

◆**scrape up** *vt sep* (*lit*) aufkratzen, zusammenkratzen; *money* auftreiben (*inf*); *support* organisieren.

scraper ['skreɪpə^r] *n* (*tool*) Spachtel *m*; (*at door*) Kratzeisen *nt*.

scrap heap *n* Schrotthaufen *m* ◆ **to be thrown on the ~** (*thing*) zum Schrott geworfen werden; (*person*) zum alten Eisen geworfen werden; (*idea*) über Bord geworfen werden; **at 55 you're on the ~** mit 55 gehört man zum alten Eisen.

scrapings ['skreɪpɪŋz] *npl* (*of food*) Reste *pl*; (*potato ~*) Schalen *pl*; (*carrot ~*) Schababfälle, Schabsel *pl*; (*metal ~*) Späne *pl* ◆ **~ of old paint/of rust** abgekratzte alte Farbe/abgekratzter Rost.

scrap: ~ iron *n* Alteisen *nt*; **~ merchant** *n* Schrotthändler(in *f*) *m*; **~ metal** *n* Schrott *m*, Altmetall *nt*.

scrappiness ['skræpɪnɪs] *n* (*of knowledge*) Lückenhaftigkeit *f* ◆ **she apologized for the ~ of the meal** sie entschuldigte sich für das zusammengestoppelte Essen.

scrappy ['skræpɪ] *adj* (+*er*) zusammengestückelt, zusammengestoppelt (*inf*); *knowledge* lückenhaft.

scrap yard *n* Schrottplatz *m*.

scratch [skrætʃ] [1] *n* **(a)** (*mark*) Kratzer *m*.
(b) (*act*) **to give sb a ~** jdn kratzen; **to have a ~** sich kratzen; **the dog enjoys a ~** der Hund kratzt sich gern; **a ~ of the pen** ein Federstrich *m*.
(c) (*sound*) Kratzen *nt no pl*.
(d) to start from ~ (ganz) von vorn(e) anfangen; (*Sport*) ohne Vorgabe anfangen; **to start sth from ~** etw ganz von vorne anfangen; *business* etw aus dem Nichts aufbauen; **to learn a language/a new trade from ~** eine Sprache ganz von Anfang an *or* von Grund auf erlernen/einen neuen Beruf von der Pike auf *or* von Grund auf erlernen; **to be** *or* **come up to ~** (*inf*) die Erwartungen erfüllen, den Anforderungen entsprechen; **he/it is not quite up to ~ yet** (*inf*) er/es läßt noch zu wünschen übrig; **to bring sb up to ~** jdn auf Vordermann bringen (*inf*).
[2] *adj attr* **(a)** *meal* improvisiert; *crew, team* zusammengewürfelt. **(b)** (*with no handicap*) ohne Vorgabe.
[3] *vt* **(a)** kratzen; *hole* scharren; (*leave ~es on*) zerkratzen ◆ **the spots will get worse if you ~ them** die Pickel werden nur schlimmer, wenn du (daran) kratzt; **she ~ed the dog's ear** sie kratzte den Hund am Ohr; **to ~ sth away** etw abkratzen; **we ~ed our names in the wood** wir ritzten unsere Namen ins Holz; **to ~ a living** sich (*dat*) einen kümmerlichen Lebensunterhalt verdienen; **he ~ed a living out of** *or* **from the soil** er konnte sich nur mühsam von den Erträgen des Bodens ernähren; **to ~ one's head** (*lit, fig*) sich am Kopf kratzen; **if you ~ my back, I'll ~ yours** (*fig*) eine Hand wäscht die andere; **to ~ the surface of sth** (*fig*) etw oberflächlich berühren.
(b) to ~ sth through etw durchstreichen; **to ~ sb/sb's name off a list** jdn/jds Namen von *or* aus einer Liste streichen.
(c) (*Sport etc*) (*withdraw*) streichen; *horse* zurückziehen.
[4] *vi* **(a)** (*make ~ing movement/noise*) kratzen; (*in soil etc*) scharren; (*~ oneself*) sich kratzen.
(b) (*become ~ed*) **the new paint will ~ easily/won't ~** die neue Farbe bekommt leicht Kratzer/bekommt keine Kratzer.
(c) (*Sport*) zurücktreten ◆ **to ~ from** nicht antreten zu.

◆**scratch about** *or* **around** *vi* (*lit*) herumscharren; (*fig inf*) sich umtun (*inf*) *or* umsehen (*for* nach).

◆**scratch out** *vt sep* auskratzen; (*cross out*) ausstreichen.

◆**scratch together** *see* **scratch up (b)**.

◆**scratch up** *vt sep* **(a)** (*lit*) ausscharren. **(b)** (*fig*) *money* zusammenkratzen; *team* zusammenbringen, auftreiben (*inf*).
scratch card *n* (*for lottery etc*) Rubbellos *nt*.
scratchily ['skrætʃɪlɪ] *adv* kratzend.
scratchiness ['skrætʃɪnɪs] *n* Kratzen *nt*.
scratching ['skrætʃɪŋ] *n* (*Mus: disc jockey technique*) Scratching *nt*.
scratch: ~ line *n* (*US*) (*in races*) Startlinie *f*; (*jumping*) Absprunglinie *f*; (*throwing*) Abwurflinie *f*; **~ method** *n* (*Med*) (*test*) Skarifikation *f* (*spec*); (*inoculation*) Ritzmethode *f*; **~ pad** *n* (*US, Comput*) Notizblock *m*; (*Comput also*) Notizblockspeicher *m*; **~ paper** *n* (*US*) Notizpapier *nt*; **~ test** *n* (*Med*) Kutanreaktionstest, Einreibungstest *m*.
scratchy ['skrætʃɪ] *adj* (+*er*) *sound, pen* kratzend *attr*; *record* zerkratzt; *feel, sweater* kratzig ◆ **does his beard feel ~?** kratzt sein Bart?; **my old record-player has a rather ~ tone** mein alter Plattenspieler kracht ziemlich.
scrawl [skrɔːl] [1] *n* Krakelei *f*, Gekrakel *nt* (*inf*); (*handwriting*) Klaue *f* (*inf*); (*inf: message*) gekritzelte Nachricht ◆ **the word finished in a ~** das Wort hörte mit einem Krakel auf (*inf*).
[2] *vt* hinschmieren (*inf*), hinkritzeln ◆ **it's been ~ed all over** es war ganz vollgeschmiert.
[3] *vi* krakeln (*inf*), schmieren.
scrawny ['skrɔːnɪ] *adj* (+*er*) dürr.
scream [skriːm] [1] *n* **(a)** Schrei *m*; (*of saw, tyres*) Kreischen *nt*; (*of engines, siren*) Heulen *nt* ◆ **there were ~s of laughter from the audience** das Publikum kreischte vor Lachen; **to give a ~** einen Schrei ausstoßen; **a ~ of pain/fear** ein Schmerzensschrei/ ein Aufschrei *m*; **the car stopped with a ~ of tyres** das Auto hielt mit quietschenden *or* kreischenden Reifen an.
(b) (*fig inf*) **to be a ~** zum Schreien sein (*inf*).
[2] *vt* schreien; *command* brüllen; (*fig: headlines*) ausschreien ◆ **to ~ sth at sb** jdm etw zuschreien; **you idiot, she ~ed at me** du Idiot, schrie sie mich an; **she ~ed insults at him** sie schrie ihm Beleidigungen ins Gesicht; **to ~ one's head off** (*inf*) sich (*dat*) die Lunge aus dem Leib *or* Hals schreien.
[3] *vi* schreien; (*saw, tyres*) kreischen; (*wind, engine, siren*) heulen ◆ **to ~ at sb** jdn anschreien; **to ~ for sth** nach etw schreien; **to ~ with pain** vor Schmerzen schreien; **to ~ with laughter** vor Lachen kreischen; **an ambulance ~ed past** ein Krankenwagen heulte vorbei; **newspaper headlines which ~ at you** (*fig*) Schlagzeilen, die einem entgegenschreien.
◆**scream out** [1] *vi* aufschreien ◆ **to ~ ~ for sth** (*lit, fig*) nach etw schreien.
[2] *vt sep* ausschreien; (*person*) hinausschreien; *name* schreien, rufen; *warning* ausstoßen.
screaming ['skriːmɪŋ] *adj* (*lit, fig*) schreiend; *saw, tyres* kreischend; *wind, engine, siren* heulend.
screamingly ['skriːmɪŋlɪ] *adv*: **~ funny** (*inf*) zum Schreien komisch (*inf*).
scree [skriː] *n* Geröll *nt* ◆ **~ slope** Geröllhalde *f*, Geröllfeld *nt*.
screech [skriːtʃ] [1] *n* Kreischen *nt no pl*; (*of women, tyres also, of brakes*) Quietschen *nt no pl*; (*of owl*) Schrei *m*; (*of whistle*) Schrillen *nt no pl* ◆ **the car stopped with a ~ of brakes** das Auto hielt mit quietschenden Bremsen; **to give a ~ of laughter/anger** vor Lachen/zornig kreischen; **~ owl** Schleiereule *f*.
[2] *vt* schreien; *high notes* quietschen.
[3] *vi* kreischen; (*women, brakes, tyres also*) quietschen ◆ **to ~ with pain** vor Schmerzen schreien; **to ~ with laughter/anger** vor Lachen/zornig kreischen; **to ~ with delight** vor Vergnügen quietschen; **jet planes ~ing over the housetops** Düsenflugzeuge, die heulend über die Hausdächer fliegen.
screed [skriːd] *n* Roman *m* (*inf*) ◆ **to write ~s (and ~s)** (*inf*) ganze Romane schreiben (*inf*).
screen [skriːn] [1] *n* **(a)** (*protective*) Schirm *m*; (*for privacy etc*) Wandschirm *m*; (*as partition*) Trennwand *f*; (*against insects*) Fliegenfenster *nt*; (*against light*) Verdunklungsschutz *m*; (*fig*) (*for protection*) Schutz *m*; (*of trees*) Wand *f*; (*of mist, secrecy*) Schleier *m*; (*of indifference*) Mauer *f* ◆ **~ of smoke** Rauchschleier *m*, Nebelwand *f*; **protected by a ~ of destroyers** durch eine Zerstörerflotte geschützt.
(b) (*Film*) Leinwand *f*; (*TV, radar ~*) (Bild) schirm *m* ◆ **stars of the ~** Filmstars *pl*; **to write for the ~** für den Film/das Fernsehen schreiben; **the big ~** die Leinwand; **the small ~** die Mattscheibe.
(c) (*Comput*) Bildschirm *m* ◆ **on ~** auf Bildschirm (*dat*); **to edit on ~** am Bildschirm editieren; **to move forward a ~** einen Bildschirm vorrücken.
(d) (*sieve*) (Gitter)sieb *nt*.
(e) (*in church*) Lettner *m*.
(f) (*Cricket*) *see* **sight ~**.
[2] *vt* **(a)** (*hide*) verdecken; (*protect*) abschirmen; (*fig*) schützen (*from* vor +*dat*), abschirmen (*from* gegen) ◆ **to ~ the windows/doors** (*with screen*) einen Schirm vor die Fenster/Türen stellen; (*with fabric*) die Fenster/Türen verhängen; (*against light*) die Fenster/Türen verdunkeln; (*against insects*) Fliegenfenster an den Fenstern/Türen anbringen; **to ~ sth from the enemy** etw vor dem Feind tarnen *or* verbergen; **he ~ed his eyes from the sun** er schützte die Augen vor der Sonne.
(b) *TV programme* senden; *film* vorführen ◆ **they gave permission for the conference to be ~ed** sie genehmigten die Vorführung der Filmaufzeichnungen von der Konferenz.
(c) (*sift*) sieben.
(d) (*investigate*) *applicants, security risks* überprüfen.
◆**screen off** *vt sep* (durch einen Schirm/Vorhang/eine Wand *etc*) abtrennen.
screen: ~ actor *n* Filmschauspieler *m*; **~ actress** *n* Filmschauspielerin *f*.
screening ['skriːnɪŋ] *n* **(a)** (*of applicants, security risks*) Überprüfung *f*. **(b)** (*of film*) Vorführung *f*; (*TV*) Sendung *f*.
screen: ~play *n* Drehbuch *nt*; **~-print** [1] *n* Siebdruck *m*; [2] *vt* im Siebdruckverfahren drucken; **~-printing** *n* Siebdruck(verfahren *nt*) *m*; **~ test** *n* Probeaufnahmen *pl*; **~ writer** *n* Drehbuchautor(in *f*) *m*.
screw [skruː] [1] *n* **(a)** (*Mech*) Schraube *f* ◆ **he's got a ~ loose** (*inf*) bei dem ist eine Schraube locker (*inf*); **to put the ~s on sb** (*inf*) jdm die Daumenschrauben anlegen (*inf*).
(b) (*Naut, Aviat*) Schraube *f*, Propeller *m*.
(c) (*action*) Drehung *f* ◆ **to give sth a ~** an etw (*dat*) drehen.
(d) (*sl: sexual intercourse*) Nummer *f* (*sl*) ◆ **he/she is a good ~** er/sie bumst gut (*inf*); **to have a ~** vögeln (*sl*), bumsen (*inf*).
(e) (*Brit sl: wage*) **he earns a good ~** er verdient einen schönen Zaster (*sl*) *or* ganz schön viel Kies (*sl*); **that's not a bad ~** bei dem Job stimmen die Piepen (*sl*).
(f) (*Brit sl: prison officer*) Schließer (*inf*), Kapo (*dial*) *m*.
[2] *vt* **(a)** schrauben (*to* an +*acc*, *onto* auf +*acc*) ◆ **he ~ed his head round** er drehte seinen Kopf herum; **she ~ed her handkerchief into a ball** sie knüllte ihr Taschentuch zu einem Knäuel zusammen; **he ~ed his face into a smile** er verzog das Gesicht zu einem Lächeln.
(b) (*inf: put pressure on*) in die Mangel nehmen (*inf*) ◆ **to ~ sb for sth** etw aus jdm herausquetschen (*inf*).
(c) (*sl: have intercourse with*) bumsen (*inf*), vögeln (*sl*).
(d) (*sl: rip off*) abzocken (*sl*); (*cheat also*) bescheißen (*sl*) ◆ **we're not out to ~ you for every penny you've got** wir wollen dir nicht jeden Pfennig abzocken (*sl*).
[3] *vi* **(a)** (*can be ~ed*) sich schrauben lassen; (*fasten with screw*) angeschraubt werden.
(b) (*sl: have intercourse*) bumsen (*inf*), vögeln (*sl*).
◆**screw down** *vt sep* an- *or* festschrauben.
◆**screw in** [1] *vt sep* (hin)einschrauben (*prep obj, -to* in +*acc*).
[2] *vi* (hin)eingeschraubt werden (*prep obj, -to* in +*acc*).
◆**screw off** [1] *vt sep* abschrauben (*prep obj* von).
[2] *vi* abgeschraubt werden (*prep obj* von).
◆**screw on** [1] *vt sep* anschrauben ◆ **to ~ sth ~(to) sth** etw an etw (*acc*) schrauben; *lid, top* etw auf etw (*acc*) schrauben; **it was ~ed ~ tightly** es war festgeschraubt; (*lid, top*) es war fest zugeschraubt; **to have one's head ~ed ~ (the right way)** (*inf*) ein vernünftiger Mensch sein.
[2] *vi* aufgeschraubt werden; (*be fastened with screws*) angeschraubt werden.
◆**screw out** [1] *vt sep* herausschrauben (*of* aus) ◆ **to ~ sth ~ of sb** (*inf*) *money* etw aus jdm herausquetschen (*inf*); *concessions* etw aus jdm herauspressen.
[2] *vi* herausgeschraubt werden.
◆**screw together** [1] *vt sep* zusammenschrauben.
[2] *vi* zusammengeschraubt werden.
◆**screw up** [1] *vt sep* **(a)** *screw, nut* anziehen.
(b) (*crush*) *paper, material* zusammenknüllen, zerknüllen.
(c) *eyes* zusammenkneifen; *face* verziehen ◆ **to ~ ~ one's courage** seinen ganzen Mut zusammennehmen; **to ~ oneself ~ to do sth** sich aufraffen, etw zu tun.
(d) (*sl: spoil*) vermasseln (*inf*).
(e) (*sl: make uptight*) *sb* neurotisch machen ◆ **he's so ~ed ~** er ist total verkorkst (*inf*), der hat einen Knacks weg (*sl*); **to be ~ed ~ about sth** sich wegen etw ganz verrückt machen; **to get ~ed ~ about sth** sich in etw (*acc*) hineinsteigern.
[2] *vi* (*sl: make a mess*) Scheiße bauen (*sl*) (*on sth* bei etw).
screw: ~ball (*esp US sl*) [1] *n* Spinner(in *f*) *m* (*inf*); [2] *adj* hirnverbrannt (*inf*); **~driver** *n* Schraubenzieher *m*.
screwed [skruːd] *adj* (*Brit sl: drunk*) voll (*sl*), fett (*sl*).
screw: ~ top *n* Schraubverschluß *m*; **~-topped** ['skruːˌtɒpt] *adj* mit Schraubverschluß; **~-up** *n* (*sl: muddle*) Chaos *nt* (*inf*); **it was one big ~-up** es war das totale Chaos (*inf*).
screwy ['skruːɪ] *adj* (+*er*) (*inf*) verrückt, bekloppt (*sl*); *person, humour* komisch, schrullig ◆ **you must be ~!** du bist wohl bekloppt (*sl*) *or* verrückt!
scribal ['skraɪbl] *adj* Schreib-; (*copying*) Abschreib-.
scribble ['skrɪbl] [1] *n* Gekritzel *nt no pl*; (*note*) schnell hingekritzelte Nachricht ◆ **covered in ~(s)** vollgekritzelt.
[2] *vt* hinkritzeln ◆ **to ~ sth on sth** etw auf etw (*acc*) kritzeln; **paper ~d (over) with notes** mit Notizen vollgekritzeltes Papier; **to ~ sth down** etw hinkritzeln.
[3] *vi* **(a)** kritzeln ◆ **the children ~d all over the wallpaper** die Kinder haben die ganze Tapete vollgekritzelt.
(b) (*inf: write novel etc*) schreiben ◆ **he ~s away all day at his novel** er schreibt den ganzen Tag an seinem Roman herum.
scribbler ['skrɪbləʳ] *n* (*inf*) Schreiberling *m*.
scribbling block ['skrɪblɪŋˌblɒk], **scribbling pad** ['skrɪblɪŋˌpæd] *n* (*Brit*) Schreibblock, Notizblock *m*.
scribe [skraɪb] *n* Schreiber *m*; (*Bibl*) Schriftgelehrte(r) *m*.
scrimmage ['skrɪmɪdʒ] [1] *n* (*US Ftbl*) Gedränge *nt*; (*inf: struggle also*) Rangelei *f* (*inf*); (*Rugby*) offenes Gedränge ◆ **~s with the police** Handgemenge *nt* mit der Polizei.
[2] *vi* sich drängen.
scrimp [skrɪmp] *vi* sparen, knausern ◆ **to ~ on sth** an etw (*dat*) sparen; **to ~ and save** geizen und sparen.
script [skrɪpt] [1] *n* **(a)** (*style of writing*) Schrift *f*; (*joined writing*) Schreibschrift *f*; (*handwriting*) Handschrift *f*; (*Typ: cursive*) Kursivdruck *m*. **(b)** (*Sch, Univ*) (schriftliche) Arbeit. **(c)** (*of play, documentary*) Text *m*; (*screenplay*) Drehbuch

nt; (*of talk etc*) (Manu)skript *nt.*
[2] *vt* den Text schreiben zu/das Drehbuch/(Manu)skript schreiben für ◆ **a ~ed discussion** eine vorbereitete Diskussion.

script girl *n* (*Film*) Scriptgirl *nt.*

scriptorium [skrɪp'tɔːrɪəm] *n, pl* **scriptoria** [skrɪp'tɔːrɪə] Schreibstube *f* (*eines Klosters*).

scriptural ['skrɪptʃərəl] *adj* Bibel-; *characters* biblisch ◆ **that isn't strictly ~** das entspricht nicht genau der Bibel.

scripture ['skrɪptʃəʳ] *n* **(a) S~, the S~s** die (Heilige) Schrift; **the Hindu ~s** die heiligen Schriften *or* Bücher der Hindus. **(b)** (*Sch*) Religion *f.*

scriptwriter ['skrɪpt,raɪtəʳ] *n* Textautor(in *f*) *m*/Drehbuchautor(in *f*) *m*/ Verfasser(in *f*) *m* des (Manu)skripts.

scrivener ['skrɪvənəʳ] *n* (*Hist*) Schreiber *m.*

scrofula ['skrɒfjʊlə] *n* (*dated Med*) Skrofulose, Skrofel *f.*

scrofulous ['skrɒfjʊləs] *adj* (*dated Med*) skrofulös; (*depraved*) verkommen.

scroll [skrəʊl] [1] *n* **(a)** Schriftrolle *f*; (*decorative*) Schnörkel *m*; (*volute, of violin*) Schnecke *f.*
(b) (*Comput*) Scrollen *nt.*
[2] *vi* (*Comput*) scrollen.

◆**scroll down** [1] *vt sep* vorrollen, vorscrollen.
[2] *vi* vorrollen, vorscrollen.

◆**scroll up** [1] *vt sep* zurückrollen, zurückscrollen.
[2] *vi* zurückrollen, zurückscrollen.

Scrooge [skruːdʒ] *n* Geizhals *m.*

scrotum ['skrəʊtəm] *n* (*Anat*) Hodensack *m*, Skrotum *nt* (*spec*).

scrounge [skraʊndʒ] (*inf*) [1] *vi* **(a)** (*sponge*) schnorren (*inf*) (*off, from* bei) ◆ **he ~d off his parents for years** er lag seinen Eltern jahrelang auf der Tasche (*inf*).
(b) (*hunt*) **to ~ around for sth** nach etw herumsuchen.
[2] *vt* schnorren (*inf*), abstauben (*inf*) (*from, off* bei).
[3] *n* (*inf*) **to be on the ~** am Schnorren *or* Abstauben sein (*inf*); **he's always on the ~ for cigarettes** er schnorrt dauernd Zigaretten (*inf*).

scrounger ['skraʊndʒəʳ] *n* (*inf*) Schnorrer *m* (*inf*).

scrounging ['skraʊndʒɪŋ] *n* (*inf*) Schnorrerei *f* (*inf*).

scrub¹ [skrʌb] *n* Gebüsch, Gestrüpp *nt*; (*also* **~land**) Gestrüpp *nt*; (*tropical*) Busch(land *nt*) *m.*

scrub² [1] *n* Schrubben *nt no pl* ◆ **to give sth a ~/a good ~** etw schrubben/ gründlich abschrubben; **~woman** (*US*) Scheuer- *or* Putzfrau *f.*
[2] *vt* schrubben; *vegetables* putzen; (*inf: cancel*) abblasen (*inf*); *idea* abschreiben (*inf*) ◆ **to ~ oneself down** sich abschrubben; **to ~ off a dirty mark** einen Schmutzfleck wegschrubben.

◆**scrub down** *vt sep walls, oneself* abschrubben.

◆**scrub out** *vt sep pans etc* ausscheuern.

◆**scrub up** *vi* sich (*dat*) die Hände waschen *or* schrubben (*inf*).

scrubber ['skrʌbəʳ] *n* (*Brit sl*) (billiges) Flittchen.

scrubbing brush ['skrʌbɪŋ,brʌʃ] *n* Scheuerbürste *f.*

scrubby ['skrʌbɪ] *adj* (*+er*) *bushes, beard* struppig; *countryside* Busch-, mit Buschwerk bewachsen; *chin* stoppelig.

scruff¹ [skrʌf] *n* **by the ~ of the neck** am Genick.

scruff² *n* (*inf: scruffy person*) (*woman*) Schlampe *f* (*inf*); (*man*) abgerissener Typ (*inf*).

scruffily ['skrʌfɪlɪ] *adv* (*inf*) vergammelt (*inf*).

scruffiness ['skrʌfɪnɪs] *n* (*inf*) vergammelter Zustand (*inf*), vergammeltes Aussehen (*inf*).

scruffy ['skrʌfɪ] *adj* (*+er*) (*inf*) vergammelt (*inf*); *house, park also* verlottert (*inf*), verwahrlost.

scrum [skrʌm] *n* (*Rugby*) Gedränge *nt* ◆ **loose ~** offenes Gedränge; **set ~** Gedränge *nt*; **~ half** Gedrängehalbspieler *m.*

scrummage ['skrʌmɪdʒ] *n* offenes Gedränge.

scrump [skrʌmp] [1] *vt apples* stehlen.
[2] *vi* Äpfel stehlen.

scrumptious ['skrʌmpʃəs] *adj* (*inf*) *meal etc* lecker; *girl* zum Anbeißen (*inf*).

scrumpy ['skrʌmpɪ] *n* ≃ Most *m* (*S Ger, Aus, Sw*), *starker Cider in Südwestengland.*

scrunch [skrʌntʃ] [1] *n* Knirschen *nt* ◆ **the car came up the snowy road with a ~ of tyres** die Reifen des Wagens knirschten auf der schneebedeckten Straße.
[2] *vt* **his feet ~ed the gravel/snow** der Kies/Schnee knirschte unter seinen Füßen.
[3] *vi* (*gravel, snow*) knirschen ◆ **he came ~ing up the garden path** er ging mit knirschenden Schritten den Gartenweg hinauf; **they ~ed through the fallen leaves** das Laub raschelte unter ihren Schritten.

scruple ['skruːpl] [1] *n* Skrupel *m* ◆ **~s** (*doubts*) (moralische) Bedenken *pl*; **to be without ~, to have no ~s** keine Skrupel haben.
[2] *vi* **not to ~ to do sth** keine Skrupel haben, etw zu tun.

scrupulous ['skruːpjʊləs] *adj* (*person*) gewissenhaft; *honesty, fairness* unbedingt, kompromißlos; *cleanliness* peinlich; *account* (peinlich) genau ◆ **he can't afford to be too ~** er kann sich keine allzu großen Skrupel leisten; **he is not too ~ in his business dealings/in matters of cleanliness** er hat keine allzu großen Skrupel bei seinen Geschäften/er nimmt es mit der Sauberkeit nicht so genau.

scrupulously ['skruːpjʊləslɪ] *adv* (*honestly, conscientiously*) gewissenhaft; (*meticulously*) *exact, clean* peinlich; *fair, careful* äußerst ◆ **he's ~ careful about telling the truth** er nimmt es mit der Wahrheit äußerst *or* peinlichst genau.

scrupulousness ['skruːpjʊləsnɪs] *n* (*honesty, fairness*) Gewissenhaftigkeit *f*; (*meticulousness*) (peinliche) Genauigkeit.

scrutineer [,skruːtɪ'nɪəʳ] *n* (*Brit Pol*) Wahlprüfer(in *f*) *m.*

scrutinize ['skruːtɪnaɪz] *vt* (*examine*) (genau) untersuchen; (*check*) genau prüfen; *votes* prüfen; (*stare at*) prüfend ansehen, mustern ◆ **to ~ sth for sth** etw auf etw (*acc*) untersuchen *or* prüfen.

scrutiny ['skruːtɪnɪ] *n* **(a)** (*examination*) Untersuchung *f*; (*checking*) (Über)prüfung *f*; (*of person*) Musterung *f*; (*stare*) prüfender *or* musternder Blick ◆ **everyone was subject to police ~** jeder wurde einer Überprüfung durch die Polizei unterzogen; **it does not stand up to ~** es hält keiner genauen Untersuchung *or* Prüfung stand. **(b)** (*Pol*) Wahlprüfung *f.*

scuba ['skuːbə] *n* (Schwimm)tauchgerät *nt* ◆ **~ diver** Sport-taucher(in *f*) *m*; **~ diving** Sporttauchen *nt.*

scud [skʌd] *vi* flitzen; (*clouds*) jagen.

scuff [skʌf] [1] *vt* abwetzen ◆ **don't ~ your feet like that!** schlurf nicht so!
[2] *vi* schlurfen ◆ **the children ~ed through the pile of leaves** die Kinder raschelten *or* wateten durch den Laubhaufen.
[3] *n* **(a)** (*~ mark*) abgewetzte Stelle. **(b)** (*US: slipper*) Pantolette *f.*

scuffle ['skʌfl] [1] *n* (*skirmish*) Rauferei *f* (*inf*), Handgemenge *nt.*
[2] *vi* (*have skirmish*) sich raufen; (*make noise*) poltern ◆ **to ~ with the police** ein Handgemenge mit der Polizei haben.

scull [skʌl] [1] *n* (*oar*) Skull *nt*; (*boat*) Skullboot *nt.*
[2] *vt* rudern.
[3] *vi* rudern, skullen (*spec*).

scullery ['skʌlərɪ] *n* Spülküche *f* ◆ **~-maid** Küchenmagd *f.*

sculpt [skʌlpt] [1] *vt see* **sculpture 2.**
[2] *vi* bildhauern (*inf*) ◆ **he ~s for a living** er verdient sich (*dat*) seinen Lebensunterhalt als Bildhauer, er lebt vom Bildhauern (*inf*).

sculptor ['skʌlptəʳ] *n* Bildhauer(in *f*) *m.*

sculptress ['skʌlptrɪs] *n* Bildhauerin *f.*

sculptural ['skʌlptʃərəl] *adj* plastisch; (*of statues*) bildhauerisch ◆ **the ~ work on the cathedral** die Skulpturenarbeit der Kathedrale; **~ details** plastisch gearbeitete Details *pl*; **the ~ triumphs of Ancient Greece** die Meisterwerke der altgriechischen Bildhauerkunst.

sculpture ['skʌlptʃəʳ] [1] *n* (*art*) Bildhauerkunst, Skulptur *f*; (*work*) Bildhauerei *f*; (*object*) Skulptur, Plastik *f.*
[2] *vt* formen, arbeiten; (*in stone*) hauen, meißeln; (*in clay etc*) modellieren ◆ **decorated with ~d flowers** mit plastisch gearbeiteten Blumen verziert; **he ~d the tombstone out of marble** er haute den Grabstein in Marmor.

scum [skʌm] *n* **(a)** (*on liquid*) Schaum *m*; (*residue*) Rand *m* ◆ **a pond covered in green ~** ein mit einer grünen Schleimschicht bedeckter Teich; **a greasy ~ floated on the soup** auf der Suppe schwamm eine Fettschicht.
(b) (*pej inf*) Abschaum *m*; (*one individual*) Dreck(s)kerl *m* (*inf*) ◆ **the ~ of the earth** der Abschaum der Menschheit.

scupper ['skʌpəʳ] [1] *n* Speigatt *nt.*
[2] *vt* **(a)** (*Naut*) versenken. **(b)** (*Brit inf: ruin*) zerschlagen ◆ **if he finds out, we'll be ~ed** wenn er das erfährt, sind wir erledigt (*inf*).

scurf [skɜːf] *n* Schuppen *pl.*

scurrility [skʌ'rɪlɪtɪ] *n* (*abusiveness*) Ehrenrührigkeit *f*; (*of person*) verleumderische Art; (*abusive remark*) Verleumdung, Verunglimpfung *f*; (*indecency*) Zotigkeit, Unflätigkeit *f*; (*indecent remark*) zotige *or* unflätige Bemerkung.

scurrilous ['skʌrɪləs] *adj* (*abusive*) verleumderisch; *remark, attack, story also* ehrenrührig; (*indecent*) unflätig, zotig.

scurrilously ['skʌrɪləslɪ] *adv see adj.*

scurry ['skʌrɪ] [1] *n* (*hurry*) Hasten *nt*; (*sound*) Trippeln *nt* ◆ **there was a ~ to leave the room** alle hatten es eilig, das Zimmer zu verlassen.
[2] *vi* (*person*) hasten; (*with small steps*) eilig trippeln; (*animals*) huschen ◆ **to ~ along** entlanghasten/entlangtrippeln/entlanghuschen; **they scurried out of the classroom** sie hatten es alle eilig, aus dem Klassenzimmer zu kommen; **to ~ for shelter** sich (*dat*) eilig einen Unterschlupf suchen; **she scurried through her work** hastig erledigte sie ihre Arbeit.

scurvy ['skɜːvɪ] [1] *n* Skorbut *m.*
[2] *adj* (*obs*) *knave* schändlich.

'scuse [skjuːz] *vt* (*inf*) = **excuse 1.**

scut [skʌt] *n* Stummelschwanz *m*; (*of rabbit also*) Blume *f* (*Hunt*); (*of deer also*) Wedel *m* (*Hunt*).

scutcheon ['skʌtʃən] *n see* **escutcheon.**

scuttle¹ ['skʌtl] *n* Kohleneimer *m.*

scuttle² *vi* (*person*) trippeln; (*animals*) hoppeln; (*spiders, crabs etc*) krabbeln ◆ **she/it ~d off in a hurry** sie/es flitzte davon.

scuttle³ (*Naut*) [1] *n* Luke *f.*
[2] *vt* versenken.

scythe [saɪð] [1] *n* Sense *f.*
[2] *vt* (mit der Sense) mähen.

Scythia ['sɪθɪə] *n* Skythien *nt.*

SDI *abbr of* **strategic defence initiative** SDI *f.*

SDP (*Brit*) *abbr of* **Social Democratic Party.**

SE *abbr of* **south-east** SO.

sea [siː] *n* **(a)** Meer *nt*, See *f* ◆ **by ~** auf dem Seeweg; **to travel by ~** mit dem Schiff fahren; **a town by** *or* **on the ~** eine Stadt am Meer *or* an der See; **(out) at ~** auf See; **as I looked out to ~** als ich aufs Meer hinausblickte; **to be all at ~** (*fig*) nicht durchblicken (*with* bei) (*inf*); **I'm all at ~ about how to answer this question** ich habe keine Ahnung, wie ich die Frage beantworten soll; **that left him all at ~** er hatte überhaupt keinen Durchblick (*inf*); **to go to ~** zur See gehen; **to put to ~** in See stechen; **beyond/from beyond the ~s** (*dated*) überm großen Meer (*old*), in Übersee/übers große Meer (*old*), von *or*

aus Übersee.
(b) *(state of the ~)* See *f no pl*, Seegang *m* ◆ **heavy/strong ~s** schwere/rauhe See.
(c) *(fig)* Meer *nt* ◆ **a ~ of faces** ein Meer von Gesichtern; **a ~ of flame** ein Flammenmeer.

sea: ~ air *n* Seeluft *f*; **~ anemone** *n* Seeanemone *f*; **~ animal** *n* Meerestier *nt*; **~-based** *adj missiles* seegestützt; **~ bathing** *n* Baden *nt* im Meer; **~ battle** *n* Seeschlacht *f*; **~bed** *n* Meeresboden, Meeresgrund *(geh) m*; **~ bird** *n* Seevogel *m*; **~board** *n (US)* Küste *f*; **~borne** *adj trade* See-; *fruit, articles etc* auf dem Seeweg befördert; **~borne goods** Seefrachtgüter *pl*; **~ breeze** *n* Seewind *m*; **~ calf** *n* Meerkalb *nt*, Seehund *m*; **~ change** *n* totale Veränderung; **~ coast** *n* Meeresküste *f*; **~ cow** *n* Seekuh *f*; **~ cucumber** *n* Seegurke, Seewalze *f*; **~ dog** *n (inf: sailor)* Seebär *m*; *(seal)* Seehund *m*; **~ elephant** *n* Elefantenrobbe *f*, See-Elefant *m*; **~farer** *n* Seefahrer *m*; **~faring** [1] *adj nation, people* seefahrend; *boat* hochseetüchtig; **~faring man** Seefahrer *m*; [2] *n* Seefahrt *f*; **~ fight** *n* Seegefecht *nt*; **~fish** *n* See- *or* Meeresfisch *m*; **~fog** *n* Küstennebel, Seenebel *m*; **~food** *n* Meeresfrüchte *pl*; **~food restaurant** Fischrestaurant *nt*; **~ front** *n (beach)* Strand *m*; *(promenade)* Strandpromenade *f*; **~ god** *n* Meer(es)gott *m*; **~going** *adj boat etc* hochseetüchtig; *nation, family* Seefahrer-; **~-green** *adj* meergrün; **~gull** *n* Möwe *f*; **~horse** *n* Seepferdchen *nt*; **~kale** *n* See- *or* Strandkohl *m*.

seal[1] [siːl] [1] *n (Zool)* Seehund *m*; *(~skin)* Seal *m*.
[2] *vi* Seehunde jagen ◆ **to go ~ing** auf Seehundfang *or* -jagd gehen; **to go on a ~ing expedition** an einer Seehundjagd teilnehmen.

seal[2] [1] *n* **(a)** *(impression in wax etc)* Siegel *nt*; *(against unauthorized opening)* Versiegelung *f*; *(of metal)* Plombe *f*; *(die)* Stempel *m*; *(ring)* Siegelring *m*; *(decorative label)* Aufkleber *m* ◆ **under the ~ of secrecy** unter dem Siegel der Verschwiegenheit; **the ~ of the confessional** das Beichtgeheimnis; **~ of quality** Gütesiegel *nt*; **to put one's *or* the ~ of approval on sth** einer Sache *(dat)* seine offizielle Zustimmung geben; **to set one's ~ to sth** *(lit, fig)* unter etw *(acc)* sein Siegel setzen; **this set the ~ on their friendship** das besiegelte ihre Freundschaft; **as a ~ of friendship** zum Zeichen der Freundschaft.
(b) *(airtight closure)* Verschluß *m*; *(washer)* Dichtung *f*.
[2] *vt* versiegeln; *envelope, parcel also* zukleben; *(with wax)* siegeln; *(make air- or watertight) joint, container* abdichten; *porous surface* versiegeln; *(fig: settle, finalize)* besiegeln ◆ **~ed envelope** verschlossener Briefumschlag; **~ed orders** versiegelte Order; **~ the meat before adding the stock** Poren (durch rasches Anbraten) schließen und dann Fleischbrühe hinzufügen; **my lips are ~ed** meine Lippen sind versiegelt; **this ~ed his fate** dadurch war sein Schicksal besiegelt.

◆**seal in** *vt sep* einschließen ◆ **this process ~s all the flavour ~** dieses Verfahren erhält das volle Aroma.

◆**seal off** *vt sep* absperren, abriegeln.

◆**seal up** *vt sep* versiegeln; *parcel, letter* zukleben; *crack, windows* abdichten.

sea-launched ['siː,lɔːnʃt] *adj missiles* seegestützt.

sea legs *npl*: **to get *or* find one's ~** *(inf)* standfest werden.

sealer[1] ['siːləʳ] *n (boat, person)* Robbenfänger *m*.

sealer[2] *n (varnish)* (Ver)siegeler *m*.

sea level *n* Meeresspiegel *m* ◆ **above/below ~** über/unter dem Meeresspiegel.

sealing wax ['siːlɪŋ,wæks] *n* Siegelwachs *nt*.

sea lion *n* Seelöwe *m*.

seal: ~ ring *n* Siegelring *m*; **~skin** *n* Seehundfell *nt*, Seal *m*.

Sealyham ['siːlɪəm] *n* Sealyham-Terrier *m*.

seam [siːm] [1] *n* **(a)** Naht *f*; *(scar)* Narbe *f*; *(Naut)* Fuge *f* ◆ **are my ~s straight?** sitzen meine Nähte gerade?; **to come apart at the ~s** aus den Nähten gehen; **to be bursting at the ~s** *(lit, fig)* aus allen Nähten platzen *(inf)*. **(b)** *(Geol)* Flöz *nt*.
[2] *vt (sew, join)* nähen; *(fig: mark with lines)* durchziehen ◆ **a face ~ed by suffering** ein von Kummer zerfurchtes Gesicht.

seaman ['siːmən] *n, pl* **-men** [-mən] Seemann *m*.

seaman-: ~like *adj* seemännisch; **~ship** *n* Seemannschaft *f*.

sea mile *n* Seemeile *f*.

seamless ['siːmlɪs] *adj stockings* nahtlos; *cardigan* ohne Nähte.

seamstress ['semstrɪs] *n* Näherin *f*.

seam-welding ['siːm,weldɪŋ] *n* Nahtverschweißung *f*.

seamy ['siːmɪ] *adj (+er) club, bar, person* heruntergekommen; *story, area, past* zwielichtig ◆ **the ~ side of life** die Schattenseite des Lebens.

séance ['seɪɑ̃ːns] *n* spiritistische Sitzung, Séance *f*.

sea: ~ pink *n* (gemeine) Grasnelke; **~ plane** *n* Wasserflugzeug *nt*; **~ port** *n* Seehafen *m*; **~ power** *n* Seemacht *f*.

sear [sɪəʳ] *vt* **(a)** *(burn: hot metal, water etc)* verbrennen; *(pain)* durchzucken; *(Med: cauterize)* ausbrennen; *(Cook: brown quickly)* rasch anbraten; *(fig)* zutiefst treffen.
(b) *(scorch, wither: sun, wind)* ausdörren, austrocknen.

search [sɜːtʃ] [1] *n (hunt: for lost object, missing person etc)* Suche *f (for* nach); *(examination: of cupboard, luggage, suspect etc)* Durchsuchung *f (of gen)*; *(esp Jur: of documents)* Nachforschungen *pl (of* über *+acc)*; *(Comput)* Suchlauf *m* ◆ **right of ~** Durchsuchungsrecht *nt*; **to go in ~ of sb/sth** auf die Suche nach jdm/etw gehen; **to make a ~ in *or* of a house** eine Haus(durch)suchung machen; **I found an interesting book in my ~** bei meiner Suche *or* beim Suchen habe ich ein interessantes Buch gefunden; **to make a ~ for sb/sth** nach jdm/etw suchen; **they arranged a ~ for the missing child** sie veranlaßten eine Suchaktion nach dem vermißten Kind; **to do a ~ (and replace) for sth** *(Comput)* etw suchen (und ersetzen).
[2] *vt (for* nach) durchsuchen; *archives, records* suchen in *(+dat)*, durchforschen; *conscience* erforschen; *memory, sb's face* durchforschen ◆ **to ~ a place for sb/sth** einen Ort nach jdm absuchen/nach etw durch- *or* absuchen; **~ me!** *(inf)* was weiß ich? *(inf)*; **if you ~ your heart ...** wenn Sie Ihr Herz fragen, ...
[3] *vi (also Comput)* suchen *(for* nach).

◆**search about *or* around** *vi* herumstöbern *(in* in *+dat)*; *(in country etc)* (herum)suchen *(in* in *+dat)*.

◆**search out** *vt sep* heraussuchen; *person* ausfindig machen, aufspüren; *cause* herausfinden.

◆**search through** *vi +prep obj* durchsuchen; *papers, books* durchsehen.

searcher ['sɜːtʃəʳ] *n (customs etc)* Durchsuchungsbeamte(r) *m*, Durchsuchungsbeamtin *f* ◆ **the ~s** *(search party)* die Suchmannschaft *f*.

searching *adj*, **~ly** *adv* ['sɜːtʃɪŋ, -lɪ] *look* prüfend, forschend; *question* durchdringend, bohrend ◆ **his questions became more ~** er stellte tiefergehende Fragen.

search: ~light *n* Suchscheinwerfer *m*; **~ party** *n* Suchmannschaft *f*; **~ tuning** *n (Rad)* Sendersuchlauf *m*; **~ warrant** *n* Durchsuchungsbefehl *m*.

searing ['sɪərɪŋ] *adj heat* glühend; *pain also* scharf; *wind* glühend heiß; *(fig) grief, sense of loss* quälend.

sea: ~scape *n* Seestück *nt*; **~ serpent** *n* Seeschlange *f*; **~ shanty** *n* Seemannslied *nt*; **~ shell** *n* Muschel(schale) *f*; **~shore** *n* Strand *m*; **on the ~shore** am Strand; **the life of the ~shore** die Strandflora und -fauna; **~sick** *adj* seekrank; **~sickness** *n* Seekrankheit *f*; **~side** [1] *n* **at the ~side** am Meer; **to go to the ~side** ans Meer fahren; [2] *attr resort, town* See-; *concert* Strand-; **~side holidays/activities** Ferien/Vergnügungsmöglichkeiten am Meer; **~ snake** *n (Zool)* Seeschlange *f*.

season ['siːzn] [1] *n* **(a)** *(of the year)* Jahreszeit *f* ◆ **rainy/monsoon ~** Regen-/Monsunzeit *f*.
(b) *(social ~, sporting ~ etc)* Saison *f* ◆ **holiday ~** Urlaubszeit *f*; **nesting/hunting ~** Brut-/Jagdzeit *f*; **the football ~** die Fußballsaison; **the strawberry ~** die Erdbeerzeit; **strawberries are in ~/out of ~ now** für Erdbeeren ist jetzt die richtige/nicht die richtige Zeit; **their bitch is in ~** ihre Hündin ist läufig; **in and out of ~** andauernd, jahrein (und) jahraus; **at the height of the ~/London ~** in der *or* zur Hochsaison/auf dem Höhepunkt der Londoner Saison; **the ~ of good will** *(Christmas)* die Zeit der Nächstenliebe; **"S~'s greetings"** „fröhliche Weihnachten und ein glückliches neues Jahr".
(c) *(Theat)* Spielzeit *f* ◆ **they did a ~ at La Scala** sie spielten eine Saison lang an der Scala; **for a ~** eine Spielzeit lang.
(d) *(fig liter)* **in due ~** zu gegebener Zeit; **in good ~** rechtzeitig; **if I might offer a word in ~** wenn ich dazu meinen Rat anbieten darf.
[2] *vt* **(a)** *food* würzen; *(fig: temper)* durchsetzen.
(b) *wood* ablagern; *(fig: inure) troops* stählen.

seasonable ['siːzənəbl] *adj* **(a)** *dress, weather etc* der Jahreszeit entsprechend *attr* ◆ **to be ~** der Jahreszeit entsprechen. **(b)** *(form: timely) advice, rebuke* zur rechten Zeit.

seasonal ['siːzənl] *adj employment, workers, rates etc* Saison-; *disease* jahreszeitlich bedingt.

seasonally ['siːzənəlɪ] *adv* **~ adjusted** *figures* saisonbereinigt.

seasoned ['siːznd] *adj* **(a)** *food* gewürzt. **(b)** *timber* abgelagert. **(c)** *(fig: experienced)* erfahren; *troops also* kampfgestählt.

seasoning ['siːznɪŋ] *n (Cook)* Gewürz *nt*; *(fig)* Würze *f*.

season ticket *n (Rail)* Zeitkarte *f*; *(Theat)* Abonnement *nt* ◆ **~ holder** Inhaber(in *f*) *m* einer Zeitkarte; Abonnent(in *f*) *m*.

seat [siːt] [1] *n* **(a)** *(place to sit)* (Sitz)platz *m*; *(actual piece of furniture)* Sitz *m*; *(usu pl: ~ing)* Sitzgelegenheit *f* ◆ **to have a front ~ at the opera** in der Oper in den vorderen Reihen sitzen; **an aircraft with 250 ~s** ein Flugzeug mit 250 Plätzen *or* Sitzen; **we'll have to borrow some ~s** wir werden uns wohl ein paar Stühle borgen müssen; **we haven't enough ~s** wir haben nicht genügend Sitzgelegenheiten; **to lose one's ~** seinen Platz verlieren *or* loswerden *(inf)*; **will you keep my ~ for me?** würden Sie mir meinen Platz freihalten?; **I've booked two ~s** ich habe zwei Plätze reservieren lassen; *see* **take**.
(b) *(of chair etc)* Sitz *m*, Sitzfläche *f*; *(of trousers)* Hosenboden *m*; *(buttocks)* Hinterteil *nt* ◆ **he picked him up by the ~ of his pants** er packte ihn beim Hosenboden; **to fly by the ~ of one's pants** *(Aviat sl)* mit dem Hintern fliegen *(inf)*; **it's a ~-of-the-pants operation** *(inf)* es kommt dabei auf den richtigen Riecher an *(inf)*.
(c) *(on committee)* Sitz *m* ◆ **a ~ in Parliament** ein Sitz im Parlament, ein Mandat *nt*; **to win a ~** ein Mandat gewinnen; **his ~ is in Devon** sein Wahlkreis *m* ist in Devon.
(d) *(centre) (of government, commerce etc)* Sitz *m*; *(of fire, trouble)* Herd *m* ◆ **~ of emotions** Sitz der Gefühle; **~ of learning** Lehrstätte *f*.
(e) *(country ~, bishop's ~ etc)* Sitz *m*.
(f) *(of rider)* Sitz *m* ◆ **to keep/lose one's ~** im Sattel bleiben/aus dem Sattel fallen.
[2] *vt* **(a)** *person etc* setzen ◆ **to ~ oneself** sich setzen; **to be ~ed** sitzen; **please be ~ed** bitte, setzen Sie sich; **to remain ~ed** sitzen bleiben.
(b) *(have sitting room for)* **the car/table/sofa ~s 4** im Auto/am Tisch/auf dem Sofa ist Platz für 4 Personen; **the theatre ~s 900** das Theater hat 900 Sitzplätze.
(c) *(Tech: fix in place)* einpassen.
[3] *vi (skirt etc: go baggy)* ausbeulen, sich durchsitzen.

seat belt *n* Sicherheits- *or* Sitzgurt *m* ◆ **to fasten one's ~, to put one's ~ on** sich anschnallen, seinen Sicherheitsgurt anlegen; **"fasten ~s"** „bitte anschnallen".

-seater [-siːtəʳ] *suf* [1] *n* -sitzer *m.*
[2] *attr car, plane* -sitzig.

seating ['siːtɪŋ] *n* Sitzgelegenheiten, Sitzplätze *pl* ◆ **~ arrangements** Sitzordnung *f;* **~ plan** (*Theat etc*) Sitzplan, Bestuhlungsplan *m;* **~ room** Platz *m* zum Sitzen.

SEATO ['siːtəʊ] *abbr of* **South-East Asia Treaty Organization** SEATO *f.*

sea: ~ transport *n* Seetransport *m;* **~ trip** *n* Seereise *f;* **~ trout** *n* Meerforelle *f;* **~ urchin** *n* Seeigel *m;* **~ wall** *n* Deich *m;* **~ward** [1] *adj direction, course* aufs Meer hinaus; **~ward wind** Seewind *m;* [2] *adv* (*also* **~wards**) see- *or* meerwärts; **~ water** *n* Meer- *or* Seewasser *nt;* **~way** *n* (*route*) Seestraße *f;* (*waterway*) Wasserweg *m or* -straße *f;* **~weed** *n* (Meeres)alge *f,* (See)tang *m,* Seegras *nt;* **~worthy** *adj* seetüchtig.

sebaceous [sɪ'beɪʃəs] *adj* Talg- ◆ **~ glands** Talgdrüsen *pl.*

seborrhoea, (*US*) **seborrhea** [sebə'rɪə] *n* Seborrhö(e) *f.*

sebum ['siːbəm] *n* Talg *m.*

sec [sek] *abbr of* **second(s)** Sek ◆ **wait a ~** (*inf*) Augenblick *or* Moment mal.

secant ['siːkənt] *n* **(a)** Sekans *m.* **(b)** (*line*) Sekante *f.*

secateurs [ˌsekə'tɜːz] *npl* Gartenschere *f.*

secede [sɪ'siːd] *vi* sich abspalten.

secession [sɪ'seʃən] *n* Abspaltung *f;* (*US Hist*) Sezession *f.*

secessionist [sɪ'seʃənɪst] [1] *adj* Sezessions-, sezessionistisch.
[2] *n* Sezessionist(in *f*) *m.*

seclude [sɪ'kluːd] *vt* absondern.

secluded [sɪ'kluːdɪd] *adj spot, house* abgelegen; *life* zurückgezogen, abgeschieden.

seclusion [sɪ'kluːʒən] *n* (*act of secluding*) Absondern *nt,* Absonderung *f;* (*being secluded*) Abgeschlossenheit, Abgeschiedenheit *f;* (*of house, spot*) Abgelegenheit *f* ◆ **in ~ from the world** in Weltabgeschiedenheit.

second[1] ['sekənd] [1] *adj* zweite(r, s) ◆ **the ~ floor** (*Brit*) der zweite Stock; (*US*) der erste Stock; **a ~ Goethe** ein zweiter Goethe; **every ~ house** jedes zweite Haus; **to be ~** Zweite(r, s) sein; **to be ~ to none** unübertroffen *or* unerreicht sein; **in ~ place** (*Sport etc*) an zweiter Stelle; **in the ~ place** (*secondly*) zweitens; **to be ~ in command** (*Mil*) stellvertretender Kommandeur sein; (*fig*) der zweite Mann sein; **~ violin/tenor** zweite Geige/zweiter Tenor; **~ language** Zweitsprache *f;* **will you have a ~ cup?** möchten Sie noch eine Tasse?; **I won't tell you a ~ time** ich sage dir das kein zweites Mal; **you won't get a ~ chance** die Möglichkeit kriegst du so schnell nicht wieder (*inf*); **the ~ thing he did was (to) get himself a drink** als zweites holte er sich etwas zu trinken; *see* **fiddle, string, wind**[1].
[2] *adv* (*+adj*) zweit-; (*+vb*) an zweiter Stelle ◆ **the speaker against a motion always speaks ~** der Gegenredner spricht immer als zweiter; **to come/lie ~** (*in race, competition*) Zweite(r) werden/an zweiter Stelle liegen, Zweite(r) sein; **to go** *or* **travel ~** (*by rail, bus etc*) zweiter Klasse fahren *or* reisen; **the ~ largest house** das zweitgrößte Haus.
[3] *vt motion, proposal* unterstützen ◆ **I'll ~ that!** (*at meeting*) ich unterstütze das; (*in general*) (genau) meine Meinung.
[4] *n* **(a)** (*of time, Math, Sci*) Sekunde *f;* (*inf: short time*) Augenblick *m* ◆ **just a ~!** (einen) Augenblick!; **it won't take a ~** es dauert nicht lange, es geht ganz schnell; **I'll only be a ~ (or two)** ich komme gleich; (*back soon*) ich bin gleich wieder da; **at that very ~** genau in dem Augenblick.
(b) the ~ (*in order*) der/die/das zweite; (*in race, class etc*) der/die/das Zweite; **to come a poor/good ~** einen schlechten/guten zweiten Platz belegen; **Elizabeth the S~** Elizabeth die Zweite.
(c) (*Aut*) der zweite Gang ◆ **to drive in ~** im zweiten Gang *or* im Zweiten fahren.
(d) (*Mus: interval*) Sekunde *f.*
(e) (*Brit Univ: degree*) *mittlere Noten bei Abschlußprüfungen* ◆ **he got an upper/a lower ~** ≃ er hat mit Eins bis Zwei/Zwei bis Drei abgeschnitten.
(f) (*Sport, in duel*) Sekundant *m* ◆ **~s out!** Ring frei!
(g) ~s *pl* (*inf: ~ helping*) Nachschlag *m* (*inf*) ◆ **there aren't any ~s** es ist nichts mehr da; **can I have ~s?** kann ich noch etwas nachbekommen?
(h) (*Comm*) **this is a ~** das ist zweite Wahl; **~s are much cheaper** Waren zweiter Wahl sind viel billiger.

second[2] [sɪ'kɒnd] *vt* (*Brit*) abordnen, abstellen.

secondarily ['sekəndərɪlɪ] *adv* in zweiter Linie.

secondary ['sekəndərɪ] *adj* **(a)** sekundär, Sekundär- (*also Sci*); *road, route, effect, stress* Neben-; *industry* verarbeitend; *reason* weniger bedeutend ◆ **of ~ importance** von untergeordneter *or* sekundärer Bedeutung; **that was only ~ to our need to save money** das kam erst an zweiter Stelle nach der Notwendigkeit, Geld zu sparen; **~ picketing** *Aufstellung f von Streikposten vor nur indirekt beteiligten Firmen;* **~ smoking** Passivrauchen *nt;* **~ feather** Armschwinge *f.*
(b) (*higher*) *education, school* höher ◆ **~ modern (school)** (*Brit*) ≃ Realschule *f.*

second: ~-best [1] *n* Zweitbeste(r, s); **(the) ~-best isn't good enough for him** das Beste ist gerade gut genug für ihn; [2] *adj* zweitbeste(r, s); **she always felt she was ~-best** sie hatte immer das Gefühl, zweite Wahl zu sein; **he was always ~-best to his older brother** er stand immer im Schatten seines älteren Bruders; **that job was ~-best for him** diese Stelle war eine Ausweichlösung für ihn; [3] *adv* **to come off ~-best** es nicht so gut haben; (*come off badly*) den kürzeren ziehen; **~ chamber** *n* zweite Kammer; **~ childhood** *n* zweite Kindheit; **~ class** *n* (*Rail etc, mail*) zweite Klasse; **~-class** [1] *adj* **(a)** *travel, mail, citizen* zweiter Klasse (*after noun*); **~-class degree** (*Brit Univ*) *see* **second**[1] **(e)**; **(b)** *see* **~-rate**; [2] *adv* zweiter Klasse; **S~ Coming** *n* Wiederkunft *f;* **~ cousin** *n* Cousin *m*/Cousine *f* zweiten Grades; **~-degree burn** *n* Verbrennung *f* zweiten Grades.

seconder ['sekəndəʳ] *n* Befürworter(in *f*) *m.*

second: ~-guess (*esp US*) *vt* (*criticize*) nachträglich *or* im nachhinein kritisieren; (*predict*) vorhersagen, prophezieren; **to ~-guess sb** vorhersagen, was jd machen/sagen wird; **~ hand** *n* (*of watch*) Sekundenzeiger *m;* **~-hand** [1] *adj* gebraucht; *car* Gebraucht-; *dealer* Gebrauchtwaren-; (*for cars*) Gebrauchtwagen-; *bookshop* Antiquariats-; *clothes* getragen, second hand (*esp Comm*); (*fig*) *information* indirekt, aus zweiter Hand; *knowledge* aus zweiter Hand; [2] *adv* gebraucht, aus zweiter Hand; **I only heard it ~-hand** ich habe es nur aus zweiter Hand; **~ lieutenant** *n* Leutnant *m.*

➤ **secondly** ['sekəndlɪ] *adv* zweitens; (*secondarily*) an zweiter Stelle, in zweiter Linie.

secondment [sɪ'kɒndmənt] *n* (*Brit*) Abordnung *f* ◆ **to be on ~** abgeordnet sein.

second: ~ nature *n* zweite Natur; **to become ~ nature (to sb)** (jdm) in Fleisch und Blut übergehen; **~ person** *n* (*Gram*) zweite Person; **~-rate** *adj* (*pej*) zweitklassig, zweitrangig; **~ sight** *n* das Zweite Gesicht; **you must have ~ sight** du mußt hellsehen können; **~ thoughts** *npl* **to have ~ thoughts about sth** sich (*dat*) etw anders überlegen; **on ~ thoughts I decided not to** dann habe ich mich doch dagegen entschieden; **on ~ thoughts maybe I'd better do it myself** vielleicht mache ich es, genau besehen, doch lieber selbst.

secrecy ['siːkrəsɪ] *n* (*of person*) (*ability to keep secrets*) Verschwiegenheit *f;* (*secretiveness*) Geheimnistuerei, Heimlichtuerei *f;* (*of event, talks*) Heimlichkeit *f* ◆ **in ~** im geheimen; **in strict ~** ganz im geheimen; **there is no ~ about it** das ist kein Geheimnis; *see* **swear.**

secret ['siːkrɪt] [1] *adj* geheim; *negotiations, treaty, code also* Geheim-; *door, drawer also* Geheim-, verborgen; *pocket* versteckt; *drinker, admirer* heimlich ◆ **the ~ ingredient** die geheimnisvolle Zutat; (*fig: of success etc*) die Zauberformel; **to keep sth ~ (from sb)** etw (vor jdm) geheimhalten; **it's all highly ~** es ist alles streng geheim.
[2] *n* Geheimnis *nt* ◆ **to keep sb/sth a ~ from sb** jdn/etw vor jdm geheimhalten; **in ~** im geheimen; **I told you that in ~** *or* **as a ~** ich habe Ihnen das im Vertrauen erzählt; **they always met in ~** sie trafen sich immer heimlich; (*society etc*) sie hatten immer geheime Versammlungen; **she pretended to hate London, but in ~ she loved the place** sie gab vor, London zu hassen, aber insgeheim liebte sie die Stadt; **to be in on the ~** (in das Geheimnis) eingeweiht sein; **there's no ~ about it** das ist kein Geheimnis; **to keep a ~** ein Geheimnis bewahren; **can you keep a ~?** kannst du schweigen?; **to make no ~ of sth** kein Geheimnis *or* keinen Hehl aus etw machen; **the ~ of being a good teacher** das Geheimnis eines guten Lehrers; **I have no ~s from you** ich habe keine Geheimnisse vor dir.

secret agent *n* Geheimagent(in *f*) *m.*

secretaire [ˌsekrə'tɛəʳ] *n* Sekretär *m.*

secretarial [ˌsekrə'tɛərɪəl] *adj* Sekretärinnen-; *job, qualifications* als Sekretärin/Sekretär; *work, job* Sekretariats- ◆ **~ staff** Sekretärinnen und Schreibkräfte *pl;* (*of politician*) Stab *m;* **she joined his ~ staff** sie wurde Sekretärin bei ihm; **basic ~ skills** grundlegende Fertigkeiten *pl* einer Sekretärin.

secretariat [ˌsekrə'tɛərɪət] *n* Sekretariat *nt.*

secretary ['sekrətrɪ] *n* **(a)** Sekretär(in *f*) *m;* (*of society*) Schriftführer(in *f*) *m;* (*esp US Pol: minister*) Minister(in *f*) *m* ◆ **~ to the board** Schriftführer(in *f*) *m.*
(b) (*desk*) *see* **secretaire.**

secretary: ~ bird *n* Sekretär *m;* **S~-General** *n, pl* **Secretaries-General, S~-Generals** Generalsekretär *m;* **S~ of State** *n* (*Brit*) Minister(in *f*) *m;* (*US*) Außenminister(in *f*) *m;* **~ship** *n* (*office*) Amt *nt* des Schriftführers; (*period*) Zeit *f* als Schriftführer.

secrete [sɪ'kriːt] [1] *vt* **(a)** (*hide*) verbergen. **(b)** (*Med*) absondern.
[2] *vi* (*Med*) absondern.

secretion [sɪ'kriːʃən] *n* **(a)** (*hiding*) Verbergen *nt.* **(b)** (*Med*) (*act*) Absonderung, Sekretion *f;* (*substance*) Sekret *nt.*

secretive[1] [sɪ'kriːtɪv] *adj* (*Med*) sekretorisch.

secretive[2] ['siːkrətɪv] *adj person* (*by nature*) verschlossen; (*in action*) geheimnistuerisch; *smile, behaviour* geheimnisvoll ◆ **to be ~ about sth** mit etw geheimnisvoll tun.

secretively ['siːkrətɪvlɪ] *adv* geheimnisvoll ◆ **to behave ~** geheimnistuerisch sein.

secretiveness ['siːkrətɪvnɪs] *n* (*character trait*) Verschlossenheit *f;* (*secretive behaviour*) Geheimnistuerei *f* ◆ **the ~ of his smile/behaviour** sein geheimnisvolles Lächeln/Benehmen.

secretly ['siːkrətlɪ] *adv* (*in secrecy*) im geheimen; *meet* heimlich; (*privately*) insgeheim, im stillen ◆ **he was ~ concerned** insgeheim war er beunruhigt.

secretory [sɪ'kriːtərɪ] *adj gland etc* sekretorisch.

secret: ~ police *n* Geheimpolizei *f;* **~ service** *n* Geheimdienst *m;* **~ society** *n* Geheimgesellschaft *f.*

sect [sekt] *n* Sekte *f.*

sectarian [sek'tɛərɪən] [1] *adj policy, politics, views* religiös beeinflußt; *school, education also* konfessionell; *war, troubles, differences* Konfessions-, zwischen den Konfessionen; *groups* sektiererisch ◆ **it was a ~ killing/bombing** der Mord/der Bombenanschlag hing mit den Konfessionsstreitigkeiten zusammen; **~ loyalties** konfessionelles Zugehörigkeitsgefühl.
[2] *n* Konfessionalist(in *f*) *m.*

sectarianism [sek'tɛərɪənɪzəm] *n* Konfessionalismus *m.*

section ['sekʃən] [1] *n* **(a)** (*part*) Teil *m;* (*wing of building also*) Trakt *m;* (*of book*) Abschnitt *m;* (*of document, law*) Absatz *m;* (*of motorway etc*) Abschnitt *m;*

➤ LANGUAGE IN USE: **secondly** → 26.2

(*under construction*) Trakt *m*; (*of railway*) Streckenabschnitt *m*; (*of orange*) Stück *nt* ◆ **the brass/string ~ of the orchestra** die Blechbläser *pl*/Streicher *pl* des Orchesters; **the sports ~** (*Press*) der Sportteil; **all ~s of the public** alle Teile der Öffentlichkeit; **the Indian ~ of the community** die Gruppe der Inder in der Gesellschaft.
(b) (*department, Mil*) Abteilung *f*; (*esp of academy etc*) Sektion *f* ◆ **passports ~** Paßabteilung *f*.
(c) (*diagram*) Schnitt *m* ◆ **in ~** im Schnitt; **vertical/longitudinal ~** Quer-/Längsschnitt *m*.
(d) (*cutting: of rock, tissue*) Schnitt *m*; (*Med: operation*) Sektion *f* ◆ **he took a horizontal ~ of the tissue** er machte einen Horizontalschnitt von dem Gewebe.
[2] *vt* **(a)** (*cut to show a ~*) einen Schnitt machen durch.
(b) (*divide into ~s*) teilen.
◆**section off** *vt sep* abteilen; (*cordon off*) absperren.
sectional ['sekʃənl] *adj* **(a)** (*in sections*) *road-building* abschnittsweise; *furniture, pipe, fishing rod* zerlegbar ◆ **~ drawing** Darstellung *f* im Schnitt. **(b)** *differences, rivalries* zwischen den Gruppen; *interests* partikularistisch.
sectionalism ['sekʃənəlɪzəm] *n* Partikularismus *m*.
sector ['sektəʳ] *n* (*also Comput*) Sektor *m*.
secular ['sekjʊləʳ] *adj* weltlich, säkular; *music, art* profan; *court, education* weltlich ◆ **~ priest** Weltgeistliche(r) *m*.
secularism ['sekjʊlərɪzəm] *n* Säkularismus *m*; (*of attitude*) Weltlichkeit *f*.
secularization [ˌsekjʊləraɪ'zeɪʃən] *n* Säkularisation *f*; (*of education, court, Sunday also*) Säkularisierung *f*.
secularize ['sekjʊləraɪz] *vt* säkularisieren.
secure [sɪ'kjʊəʳ] [1] *adj* (*+er*) sicher; (*emotionally*) geborgen; *existence, income* gesichert; (*firm, well-fastened*) *grip, knot, tile* fest ◆ **~ in the knowledge that ...** ruhig in dem Bewußtsein, daß ...; **to be ~ against** *or* **from sth** vor etw (*dat*) sicher sein; **to feel ~** sich sicher fühlen; (*emotionally*) sich geborgen fühlen; **to feel ~ about one's future** der Zukunft sicher entgegensehen; **is the window/lid ~?** ist das Fenster fest zu/ist der Deckel fest drauf?; **to make a door/window/rope ~** eine Tür/ein Fenster/ein Seil sichern; **to make a tile ~** einen Ziegel befestigen.
[2] *vt* **(a)** (*fasten, make firm*) festmachen; (*tie up also*) befestigen; *window, door* fest zumachen; (*with chain, bolt etc*) sichern; *tile* befestigen; (*make safe*) sichern (*from, against* gegen), schützen (*from, against* vor *+dat*).
(b) (*obtain*) sich (*dat*) sichern; *majority of votes, order* erhalten; *profits, higher prices* erzielen; *share, interest in business* erwerben; (*buy*) erstehen; *cook, employee* verpflichten ◆ **to ~ sb's services** jdn verpflichten.
(c) (*guarantee*) sichern, garantieren; *loan* (ab)sichern.
securely [sɪ'kjʊəlɪ] *adv* (*firmly*) fest; (*safely*) sicher ◆ **the prisoner was kept ~ in his cell** der Gefangene wurde streng gesichert in seiner Zelle gehalten.
secureness [sɪ'kjʊənɪs] *n see adj* Sicherheit *f*; (*emotional*) Geborgenheit *f*.
security [sɪ'kjʊərɪtɪ] *n* **(a)** Sicherheit *f*; (*emotional*) Geborgenheit *f*; (*~ measures*) Sicherheitsvorkehrungen *or* -maßnahmen *pl* ◆ **for ~** zur Sicherheit; **~ of tenure** Kündigungsschutz *m*; **airports have tightened their ~** die Flughäfen haben ihre Sicherheitsvorkehrungen verschärft; **in the ~ of one's own home** sicher im eigenen Heim; (*from emotional point of view*) in der Geborgenheit des eigenen Heims.
(b) (*~ department*) Sicherheitsdienst *m*.
(c) (*Fin*) (*guarantee*) Sicherheit *f*; (*guarantor*) Bürge *m* ◆ **up to £500 without ~** bis zu £ 500 ohne Sicherheit; **to lend money on ~** Geld gegen Sicherheit leihen; **to stand ~ for sb** für jdn Bürge sein *or* Bürgschaft leisten.
(d) (*Fin*) **securities** *pl* Effekten, (Wert)papiere *pl*; **securities market** Wertpapiermarkt *m*.
security *in cpds* Sicherheits-; (*Fin*) Effekten-, Wertpapier-; **~ blanket** *n* **(a)** (*around politicians etc*) Sicherheitsnetz *nt*; **to throw a ~ blanket around sb/sth** jdm/etw mit einem Sicherheitsnetz umgeben; **(b)** (*of child*) Kuscheldecke *f*; **~ check** *n* Sicherheitskontrolle *f*; **S~ Council** *n* Sicherheitsrat *m*; **~ firm** *n* Wach- und Sicherheitsdienst *m*; **~ force** *n* Sicherheitstruppe *f*; (*UN*) Friedenstruppe *f*; **~ forces** *npl* Sicherheitskräfte *pl*; (*UN*) Friedensstreitmacht *f*; **~ guard, ~ man** *n* Wache *f*, Wächter *m*; (*for ~ checks*) Sicherheitsbeamte(r) *m*; **one of the ~ men** einer der Sicherheitsleute; **~ police** *n* Sicherheitspolizei *m*; **~ risk** *n* Sicherheitsrisiko *nt*.
sec(y) *abbr of* **secretary**.
sedan [sɪ'dæn] *n* **(a)** (*also* **~ chair**) Sänfte *f*. **(b)** (*US Aut*) Limousine *f*.
sedate [sɪ'deɪt] [1] *adj* (*+er*) gesetzt; *little girl, colour* ruhig; *furnishings, décor* gediegen; *life* geruhsam; *speed* gemächlich; *prose* bedächtig.
[2] *vt* Beruhigungsmittel geben (*+dat*), sedieren (*spec*) ◆ **he was heavily ~d** er stand stark unter dem Einfluß von Beruhigungsmitteln.
sedately [sɪ'deɪtlɪ] *adv see adj*.
sedateness [sɪ'deɪtnɪs] *n see adj* Gesetztheit *f*; ruhige Art; (*of colour*) ruhiger Ton; Gediegenheit *f*; Geruhsamkeit *f*; Gemächlichkeit *f*; Bedächtigkeit *f*.
sedation [sɪ'deɪʃən] *n* Beruhigungsmittel *pl* ◆ **to put sb under ~** jdm Beruhigungsmittel geben; **drugs used for ~** Drogen zur Beruhigung.
sedative ['sedətɪv] [1] *n* Beruhigungsmittel, Sedativum (*spec*) *nt*.
[2] *adj* beruhigend, sedativ (*spec*).
sedentariness ['sedntərɪnɪs] *n* **(a)** **as a result of the ~ of the job** durch das dauernde Sitzen bei der Arbeit; **the excessive ~ of his daily life** das übermäßige tägliche Sitzen. **(b)** (*of tribe*) Seßhaftigkeit *f*; (*of bird*) Verbleiben *nt* am Nistort.
sedentary ['sedntərɪ] *adj* **(a)** *job, occupation* sitzend *attr*; *worker* Sitz- ◆ **to lead a ~ life** sehr viel sitzen; **any job of a ~ nature** jede im Sitzen ausgeübte Tätigkeit. **(b)** *tribe* seßhaft; *bird* Stand-.
sedge [sedʒ] *n* Riedgras *nt*, Segge *f* ◆ **~-warbler** Seggenrohrsänger *m*.
sediment ['sedɪmənt] *n* (Boden)satz *m*; (*in river*) Ablagerung *f*; (*in chemical solution*) Niederschlag *m*, Sediment *nt*.
sedimentary [ˌsedɪ'mentərɪ] *adj* sedimentär ◆ **~ rocks** Sedimentgestein *nt*.
sedimentation [ˌsedɪmen'teɪʃən] *n* Ablagerung, Sedimentation *f*.
sedition [sə'dɪʃən] *n* Aufwiegelung, Verhetzung *f*.
seditious [sə'dɪʃəs] *adj* aufrührerisch, aufwieglerisch.
seduce [sɪ'djuːs] *vt* verführen ◆ **to ~ sb into doing sth** jdn zu etw verleiten, jdn dazu verleiten, etw zu tun; **to ~ sb (away) from his duty/a party/his wife/a place** jdn seine Pflichten vergessen lassen/jdn einer Partei/seiner Frau abspenstig machen/jdn von einem Ort weglocken.
seducer [sɪ'djuːsəʳ] *n* Verführer *m*.
seducible [sɪ'djuːsɪbl] *adj* verführbar.
seduction [sɪ'dʌkʃən] *n* Verführung *f*.
seductive [sɪ'dʌktɪv] *adj* verführerisch; *salary, offer, suggestion* verlockend.
seductively [sɪ'dʌktɪvlɪ] *adv see adj*.
seductiveness [sɪ'dʌktɪvnɪs] *n* verführerische Art ◆ **the ~ of the offer** *etc* das verlockende Angebot *etc*.
seductress [sɪ'dʌktrɪs] *n* Verführerin *f*.
sedulous *adj*, **~ly** *adv* ['sedjʊləs, -lɪ] unermüdlich, unentwegt.
see[1] [siː] *pret* **saw**, *ptp* **seen** [1] *vt* **(a)** sehen; (*in newspaper etc also*) lesen; (*check also*) nachsehen, gucken (*inf*); (*go and ~*) *film, show, sights* sich (*dat*) ansehen ◆ **worth ~ing** sehenswert; **to ~ sb do sth** sehen, wie jd etw macht; **I've never ~n him swim(ming)** ich habe ihn noch nie schwimmen sehen; **he was ~n to enter the building** man hat ihn gesehen *or* er wurde gesehen, wie er das Gebäude betrat; **I saw it happen** ich habe gesehen, wie es passiert ist; **I've ~n it done three times** das habe ich schon dreimal gesehen; **I wouldn't ~ you starve** ich würde doch nicht zusehen, wie du verhungerst; **I don't like to ~ people mistreated** ich kann es nicht sehen, wenn Menschen schlecht behandelt werden; **I wouldn't like to ~ you unhappy** ich möchte doch nicht, daß du unglücklich bist; **I'll go and ~ who it is** ich gehe mal nachsehen *or* ich gucke mal(, wer das ist); **~ page 8** siehe Seite 8; **there was nothing to be ~n** es war nichts zu sehen; **I don't know what she ~s in him** ich weiß nicht, was sie an ihm findet; **we don't ~ much of them nowadays** wir sehen sie zur Zeit nur selten; **I shall be ~ing them for dinner** ich treffe sie beim Abendessen; **~ you (soon)!** bis bald!; **be ~ing you!, ~ you later!** bis später!, bis nachher!; **~ you on Sunday!** bis Sonntag!; **she doesn't want to ~ me any more** sie will mich nicht mehr sehen; **I want to ~ (a bit of) the world** ich möchte etwas von der Welt sehen *or* kennenlernen; **I'll ~ him damned** *or* **in hell first** (*inf*) ich denke nicht (im Schlaf) daran; **she won't ~ 40 again** sie ist gut und gern 40; **I/you must be ~ing things** ich sehe/du siehst wohl Gespenster!; **I must be ~ing things, if it isn't Peter!** ich glaub', ich seh' nicht richtig, das ist doch der Peter!; **am I ~ing things or is ...?** seh' ich richtig, ist das nicht ...?; **I can't ~ my way to doing that** ich sehe mich nicht in der Lage, das zu tun; **I saw myself obliged to/faced with the need to ...** ich sah mich gezwungen, zu ...; **I suddenly saw myself being cheated** ich sah *or* erkannte plötzlich, daß man mich betrog/betrügen wollte.
(b) (*visit*) besuchen; (*on business*) aufsuchen ◆ **to call** *or* **go and ~ sb** jdn besuchen (gehen); **to ~ the doctor** zum Arzt gehen, einen Arzt aufsuchen; **he is the man you ought to ~ about this** Sie sollten sich damit an ihn wenden.
(c) (*meet with*) sehen; (*have a word with, talk to*) sprechen; (*receive visit of*) empfangen ◆ **the boss can't ~ you now, you can't ~ the boss now** Sie können den Chef jetzt nicht sprechen, Sie können jetzt nicht zum Chef (*inf*); **the boss/doctor will ~ you now** der Chef/Herr Doktor ist jetzt frei; **what did he want to ~ you about?** weswegen wollte er Sie sprechen?; **I'll have to ~ my wife about that** das muß ich mit meiner Frau besprechen; **have you ~n Personnel yet?** waren Sie schon bei der Personalabteilung?; **the minister saw the Queen yesterday** der Minister war gestern bei der Königin; **the Queen will ~ the minister tomorrow** die Königin wird den Minister morgen empfangen; **she refused to ~ us** sie wollte uns nicht empfangen *or* sehen; **there was only one applicant worth ~ing** es war nur ein Bewerber dabei, den es sich anzusehen lohnte.
(d) (*accompany*) begleiten, bringen ◆ **to ~ sb to the door** jdn zur Tür bringen; *see also phrasal vbs.*
(e) **we'll/he'll ~ if we can help** mal sehen/er wird mal sehen, ob wir helfen können; **we'll soon ~ who is right** wir werden ja bald sehen, wer recht hat; **that remains to be ~n** das wird sich zeigen; **let's just ~ what happens** wollen wir mal sehen *or* abwarten, was passiert; **I don't ~ any way I can help** ich sehe nicht, wie ich da helfen kann; **let me ~ if I can fix up something** ich werde mal sehen, ob sich etwas arrangieren läßt; **let me ~ if I can't find a better way** mal sehen, ob ich nicht etwas Besseres finden kann.
(f) (*visualize*) sich (*dat*) vorstellen ◆ **I can't** *or* **don't ~ that working/him winning/myself living there** ich kann mir kaum vorstellen, daß das klappt/daß er gewinnt/daß ich da leben möchte; **I can't ~ myself in that job** ich glaube nicht, daß das eine Stelle für mich wäre; **he saw himself as the saviour** er sah sich als Retter; **I can ~ it happening** ich sehe es kommen; **I can't ~ any chance of that happening** das halte ich für unwahrscheinlich *or* kaum möglich.
(g) (*experience*) erleben ◆ **he lived to ~ the beginning of a new age** er hat den Anfang eines neuen Zeitalters miterlebt; **now I've ~n everything!** ist das denn zu fassen *or* die Möglichkeit?; **what a cheek, I've never ~n anything like it!** so eine Frechheit, so etwas habe ich ja noch nie gesehen *or* erlebt!; **it's ~n a lot of hard wear** das ist schon sehr strapaziert worden.
(h) (*hear, notice*) sehen ◆ **I ~ you still haven't done that/he's got married again** wie ich sehe, hast du das immer noch nicht gemacht/hat er wieder

geheiratet.
(i) (*understand*) verstehen; (*understand the reason for*) einsehen; (*realize*) erkennen ◆ **I don't ~ the importance of doing it/the need for the change** ich sehe nicht ein, warum das unbedingt gemacht werden muß/warum das geändert werden muß; **I can ~ that it might be a good thing** ich sehe ja ein, daß das eine gute Idee wäre; **I can ~ I'm going to be busy** ich sehe schon, ich werde viel zu tun haben; **I fail to** *or* **don't ~ how anyone could** ... ich begreife einfach nicht, wie jemand nur ... kann; **I don't ~ where the problem is** ich sehe das Problem nicht; **I ~ from this report that** ... ich ersehe aus diesem Bericht, daß ...; **(do you) ~ what I mean?** verstehst du(, was ich meine)?; (*didn't I tell you!*) siehst du's jetzt!; **I ~ what you mean** ich weiß *or* verstehe, was du meinst; (*you're quite right*) ja, du hast recht; **to make sb ~ sth** jdm etw klarmachen; **I saw only too clearly that** ... ich sah *or* erkannte nur zu deutlich, daß ...
(j) (*look at*) *problem* sehen ◆ **as I ~ it** so, wie ich das sehe; **this is how I ~ it** ich sehe das so; **that's how I ~ it** so sehe ich das jedenfalls; **try to ~ it my way** versuchen Sie doch einmal, es aus meiner Sicht zu sehen; **I don't ~ it that way** ich sehe das anders.
(k) (*ensure*) **~ that it is done by tomorrow** sieh zu, daß es bis morgen fertig ist; (*done by sb else also*) sorge dafür, daß es bis morgen fertig ist; **~ that it doesn't happen again** sieh zu *or* paß auf, daß das nicht noch mal passiert.
(l) (*Cards*) **I'll ~ you** ich halte.
[2] *vi* **(a)** (*have sight*) sehen.
(b) (*look*) sehen ◆ **let me ~, let's ~** lassen Sie mich mal sehen; **can you ~ if I sit here?** können Sie (etwas) sehen, wenn ich hier sitze?; **it was so dark I couldn't ~** es war so dunkel, ich konnte nichts sehen; **who was it? — I couldn't/didn't ~** wer war das? — ich konnte es nicht sehen; **can you ~ to read?** ist es Ihnen hell genug zum Lesen?; **as far as the eye can ~** so weit das Auge reicht; **~ for yourself!** sieh doch selbst!; **now ~ here!** nun hören Sie mal her!
(c) (*check, find out*) nachsehen, gucken (*inf*) ◆ **is he there? — I'll ~** ist er da? — ich sehe mal nach *or* ich guck mal (*inf*); **I'll go and ~** ich gehe mal nachsehen; **~ for yourself!** sieh doch selbst (nach)!; **let me ~** lassen Sie mich mal nachsehen.
(d) (*discover*) sehen ◆ **will he come? — we'll soon ~** kommt er? — das werden wir bald sehen *or* rausfinden (*inf*); **what kind of person is she? — you'll soon ~ for yourself** was für ein Mensch ist sie? — das werden Sie bald selbst sehen *or* feststellen.
(e) (*understand*) verstehen ◆ **as far as I can ~** ... so wie ich das sehe ...; **it's all over, ~?** es ist vorbei, verstehst du?; **it's logical, do you ~?** es ist logisch, nicht wahr?; **he's dead, don't you ~?** er ist tot, begreifst du das denn nicht?; **as I ~ from your report** wie ich in Ihrem Bericht lese, wie ich aus Ihrem Bericht ersehe; **it's too late, (you) ~** (*explaining*) weißt du, es ist zu spät; (*I told you so*) siehst du, es ist zu spät!; **(you) ~, it's like this** es ist nämlich so; **(you) ~, we can't do that** weißt du, das können wir nicht machen; **that's the way he is, (you) ~** das ist eben seine Art(, weißt du); **but this still has to be improved, you ~** das muß natürlich noch verbessert werden; **and we went out, ~, and saw this film, ~, and** ... (*dial*) und wir sind weggegangen, weißte (*inf*) *or* nich (*N Ger*), und haben uns den Film angesehen, weißte *etc*, und ...; **I ~!** aha!; (*after explanation*) ach so!; (*to keep conversation going, I'm with you*) ja; **yes, I ~** ja, aha.
(f) (*consider*) **we'll ~** (wir werden *or* wollen) mal sehen; **I don't know, I'll have to ~** ich weiß nicht, ich muß mal sehen; **will you be there? — I'll ~** bist du da? — mal sehen; **he said he'll ~** er sagt, er will mal sehen; **let me ~, let's ~** warten Sie mal, lassen Sie mich mal überlegen.

◆**see about** *vi +prep obj* **(a)** (*attend to*) sich kümmern um ◆ **I'll have to ~ ~ getting the roof mended** ich muß mich darum kümmern, daß das Dach repariert wird; **he came to ~ ~ the TV** er kam, um sich (*dat*) den Fernseher anzusehen; **I've still a few things to ~ ~** ich muß noch ein paar Dinge erledigen; **he came to ~ ~ the rent** er ist wegen der Miete gekommen; **we'd better ~ ~ going now** wir sehen besser zu, daß wir jetzt gehen.
(b) (*consider*) **I'll ~ ~ it** ich will mal sehen *or* schauen (*esp S Ger*); **we'll ~ ~ that!** (*iro*) das wollen wir mal sehen.

◆**see across** *vt always separate* hinüberbegleiten *or* -bringen (*prep obj* über +*acc*).

◆**see in** [1] *vi* (*look in*) herein-/hineinsehen.
[2] *vt sep* (*show in*) herein-/hineinbringen ◆ **to ~ the New Year ~** das neue Jahr begrüßen.

◆**see into** *vi +prep obj* **(a)** *house, room* hineinsehen in (+*acc*). **(b)** (*investigate*) untersuchen, prüfen, nachgehen (+*dat*) ◆ **this needs ~ing ~** das muß geprüft *or* untersucht werden.

◆**see off** *vt sep* **(a)** (*bid farewell to*) verabschieden ◆ **are you coming to ~ me ~?** kommt ihr mit mir (zum Flughafen *etc*)? **(b)** (*chase off*) Beine machen (+*dat*) (*inf*) ◆ **~ him ~, boy!** verjag ihn! **(c)** (*sl: be better than*) in die Tasche stecken (*inf*).

◆**see out** [1] *vi* (*look out*) heraus-/hinaussehen ◆ **I can't ~ ~ of the window** ich kann nicht zum Fenster hinaussehen.
[2] *vt sep* **(a)** (*show out*) hinausbringen *or* -begleiten (*of* aus) ◆ **I'll ~ myself ~** ich finde (schon) alleine hinaus.
(b) (*last to the end of*) (*coat, car*) *winter etc* überdauern; (*old man, invalid*) *wife, year etc* überleben ◆ **to ~ the old year ~** das alte Jahr verabschieden.

◆**see over** *or* **round** *vi +prep obj house etc* sich (*dat*) ansehen.

◆**see through** [1] *vi* **(a)** (*lit*) (hin)durchsehen (*prep obj* durch).
(b) *+prep obj* (*fig: not be deceived by*) durchschauen ◆ **I can ~ right ~ you** ich habe dich durchschaut *or* erkannt.
[2] *vt always separate* **(a)** (*help through difficult time*) beistehen (+*dat*) ◆ **to ~ sb ~ a bad time** jdm über eine schwierige Zeit hinweghelfen; **he had £100 to ~ him ~ the term** er hatte £ 100 für das ganze Semester; **I hope £10 will ~ you ~** die £ 10 reichen dir hoffentlich.
(b) *job* zu Ende bringen; (*Parl*) *bill* durchbringen.

◆**see to** *vi +prep obj* sich kümmern um ◆ **these shoes need/that cough needs ~ing ~** mit den Schuhen muß etwas gemacht werden/um den Husten muß man sich kümmern; **~ ~ it that you don't/he doesn't forget** sieh zu, daß du/er das nicht vergißt; **there's no chance now, the rain has ~n ~ that** es ist aussichtslos, dafür hat der Regen schon gesorgt.

◆**see up** [1] *vi* (*look up*) herauf-/hinaufsehen (*prep obj acc*) ◆ **I could ~ ~ her skirt** ich konnte ihr unter den Rock sehen.
[2] *vt sep* (*show up*) herauf-/hinaufbringen.

see² *n* Bistum *nt*; (*Catholic also*) Diözese *f*; (*Protestant in Germany*) Landeskirche *f* ◆ **Holy S~, S~ of Rome** Heiliger Stuhl.

seed [si:d] [1] *n* **(a)** (*Bot*) (*one single*) Same(n) *m*; (*of grain, poppy, sesame etc*) Korn *nt*; (*within fruit*) (Samen)kern *m*; (*collective*) Samen *pl*; (*for birds*) Körner *pl*; (*grain*) Saat *f*, Saatgut *nt*; (*liter: sperm*) Samen *pl*; (*liter: offspring*) Nachkommen *pl*; (*fig: of unrest, idea etc*) Keim *m* (*of* zu) ◆ **to go** *or* **run to ~** (*vegetables*) schießen; (*flowers*) einen Samenstand bilden; (*fig: person*) herunterkommen; **to sow the ~s of doubt (in sb's mind)** (bei jdm) Zweifel säen *or* den Keim des Zweifels legen; **he sowed the ~ from which ... developed** er hat den Keim gelegt, aus dem sich ... entwickelte; **I don't want to make a direct proposal, just to sow the ~s** ich möchte keinen direkten Vorschlag machen, ich möchte nur den Boden dafür bereiten.
(b) (*Sport*) **to be the third ~** als dritter plaziert *or* gesetzt sein; **the number one ~** der/die als Nummer eins Gesetzte.
[2] *vt* **(a)** (*sow with ~*) besäen. **(b)** (*extract ~s from*) entkernen. **(c)** (*Sport*) setzen, plazieren ◆ **~ed number one** als Nummer eins gesetzt; **~ed players** gesetzte *or* plazierte Spieler.
[3] *vi* (*vegetables*) schießen; (*flowers*) Samen entwickeln.
[4] *vr* **to ~ itself** (*plant*) sich aussäen.

seed: ~bed *n* Saatbeet, Saatbett *nt*; **~ box** *n* Setzkasten *m*; **~cake** *n* Kümmelkuchen *m*; **~case** *n* Samenkapsel *f*; **~ corn** *n* Samenkorn *nt*; **~ drill** *n* Sämaschine *f*.

seediness ['si:dɪnɪs] *n see adj (a)* Zwielichtigkeit *f*; Schäbigkeit *f*.

seed: ~ leaf *n* Keimblatt *nt*; **~less** *adj* kernlos.

seedling ['si:dlɪŋ] *n* Sämling *m*.

seed: ~ pearl *n* Staubperle *f*; **~ plant** *n* Samenpflanze *f*; **~ potato** *n* Saatkartoffel *f*.

seedsman ['si:dzmən] *n, pl* **-men** [-mən] Samenhändler *m*.

seedtime ['si:dtaɪm] *n* Saatzeit *f*.

seedy ['si:dɪ] *adj* (+*er*) **(a)** (*disreputable*) *person, character* zweifelhaft, zwielichtig; *area, place* zwielichtig; *clothes* schäbig, abgerissen. **(b)** (*inf: unwell*) **I feel ~** mir ist flau (*inf*) *or* nicht gut; **to look ~** angeschlagen (*inf*) *or* nicht gut aussehen.

seeing ['si:ɪŋ] [1] *n* Sehen *nt* ◆ **I'd never have thought it possible but ~ is believing** (*prov*) ich hätte es nie für möglich gehalten, aber ich habe es mit eigenen Augen gesehen; **look, ~ is believing, you can't deny it now** da haben Sie den Beweis vor Augen, jetzt können Sie es nicht mehr abstreiten.
[2] *conj* **~ (that)** da.

seek [si:k] *pret, ptp* **sought** *vt* **(a)** suchen; *fame, wealth* erlangen wollen, streben nach ◆ **to ~ sb's advice** jdn um Rat fragen; **the reason is not far to ~** der Grund liegt auf der Hand; **the quarrel is not of my ~ing** ich habe den Streit nicht gesucht; **~ time** (*Comput*) Zugriffszeit *f*.
(b) (*liter: attempt*) suchen (*geh*) ◆ **those who sought his downfall** die(jenigen), die ihn zu Fall bringen wollten.

◆**seek after** *vi +prep obj* **(a)** suchen. **(b)** *see* **sought-after**.

◆**seek for** *vi +prep obj* suchen nach; *reforms, changes* anstreben ◆ **long-sought-~ reforms/changes** langerstrebte Reformen *pl*/Veränderungen *pl*.

◆**seek out** *vt sep* ausfindig machen; *opinion* herausfinden ◆ **~ him ~, discover what he thinks** (*liter*) erforschen Sie ihn, finden Sie heraus, was er denkt (*geh*).

seeker ['si:kəʳ] *n* Suchende(r) *mf*; (*pursuer*) Verfolger *m* ◆ **~ of justice** nach Gerechtigkeit Suchende(r) *mf*; **~ of** *or* **after truth** Wahrheitssucher(in *f*) *m*.

seem [si:m] *vi* **(a)** scheinen ◆ **he ~s (to be) honest/a nice young man** er scheint ehrlich/ein netter junger Mann zu sein; **he may ~ poor but** ... er mag arm scheinen *or* wirken, aber ...; **he ~s younger than he is** er wirkt jünger, als er ist; **that makes it ~ longer** dadurch wirkt es länger *or* kommt es einem länger vor; **he doesn't ~ (to be) able to concentrate** er scheint sich nicht konzentrieren zu können; **he is not what he ~s to be** er ist nicht (das), was er zu sein scheint; **things aren't always what they ~** vieles ist anders, als es aussieht; **I ~ to have heard that before** das habe ich doch schon mal gehört; **what ~s to be the trouble?** worum geht es denn?; (*doctor*) was kann ich für Sie tun?; **there ~s to be no need/solution** das scheint nicht nötig zu sein/da scheint es keine Lösung zu geben; **it ~s to me that I'll have to do that again** mir scheint, ich muß das noch einmal machen; **he has left, it ~s** er ist anscheinend weggegangen, es scheint, er ist weggegangen; **we are not welcome, it ~s** wir sind anscheinend *or* scheinbar (*inf*) nicht willkommen; **so it ~s** es sieht (ganz) so aus; **he is, so it ~s,** ... er scheint ... zu sein; **it ~s** *or* **would ~ that he is coming after all** es sieht so aus, als ob er doch noch kommt, es scheint, er kommt doch noch; **it doesn't ~ that he'll be coming** es sieht nicht so aus, als ob er kommt; **if it ~s right to you** wenn Sie es für richtig halten; **it ~s** *or* **would ~ (to be) advisable** das scheint ratsam (zu sein); **how does it ~ to you?** was meinen *Sie*?; **it ~s a shame to leave it un-**

➤ LANGUAGE IN USE: **seem: a** → 6.2, 26.2, 26.3

finished es ist doch irgendwie *or* eigentlich schade, das nicht fertig zu machen; **it just doesn't ~ right somehow** das ist doch irgendwie nicht richtig; **it would ~ that ...** es scheint fast so, als ob ...; **I can't ~ to do it** ich kann das anscheinend *or* scheinbar (*inf*) *or* irgendwie nicht.
(b) it only ~s like it das kommt einem nur so vor; **I ~ to be floating in space** es kommt mir so vor, als ob ich schweben würde; **it all ~s so unreal to him/me** es kommt ihm/mir alles so unwirklich vor; **I ~ to remember that you had that problem before** es kommt mir so vor, als hätten Sie das Problem schon einmal gehabt.

seeming ['si:mɪŋ] *adj attr* scheinbar.

seemingly ['si:mɪŋlɪ] *adv* scheinbar (*inf*), anscheinend.

seemliness ['si:mlɪnɪs] *n* Schicklichkeit *f*.

seemly ['si:mlɪ] *adj* (+*er*) schicklich ◆ **it isn't ~ (for sb to do sth)** es schickt sich nicht (für jdn, etw zu tun).

seen [si:n] *ptp of* **see**1.

seep [si:p] *vi* sickern ◆ **to ~ through/into sth** durch etw durchsickern/in etw (*acc*) hineinsickern.

◆**seep away** *vi* (*water*) versickern; (*strength*) schwinden.

seepage ['si:pɪdʒ] *n* (*out of sth*) Aussickern *nt*; (*through sth*) Durchsickern *nt*; (*into sth*) Hineinsickern *nt* ◆ **there is an excessive amount of ~** es läuft zuviel aus/es dringt zuviel ein; (*Comm*) die Leckage ist zu groß.

seer [sɪəʳ] *n* Seher *m*.

seeress ['sɪəres] *n* Seherin *f*.

seersucker ['sɪə,sʌkəʳ] *n* Krepp, Seersucker *m*.

seesaw ['si:sɔ:] [1] *n* Wippe *f*; (*fig*) (*back and forth*) Hin und Her *nt*; (*up and down*) Auf und Ab *nt*.
[2] *adj* schaukelnd ◆ **~ changes** ständiges Hin und Her.
[3] *vi* wippen; (*fig*) (*emotional states*) auf und ab gehen; (*prices, public opinion*) schwanken.

seethe [si:ð] *vi* (*boil*) sieden; (*surge*) schäumen; (*fig*) (*be crowded*) wimmeln (*with* von); (*be angry*) kochen (*inf*) ◆ **to ~ with anger** vor Wut schäumen *or* kochen; **the crowd ~d forward** die Menge drängte sich vor.

see-through ['si:θru:] *adj* durchsichtig ◆ **~ pack** Klarsichtpackung *f*.

segment ['segmənt] [1] *n* Teil *m*; (*of worm*) Glied, Segment *nt*; (*of orange*) Stück *nt*, Rippe *f*, Schnitz *m* (*dial*); (*of circle*) Abschnitt *m*, Segment *nt*.
[2] [seg'ment] *vt* zerlegen, segmentieren.
[3] [seg'ment] *vi* sich teilen.

segmental [,seg'mentl] *adj* (*Ling*) Segment-.

segmentation [,segmən'teɪʃən] *n* Zerlegung, Segmentierung *f*; (*Biol*) Zellteilung *f*.

segregate ['segrɪgeɪt] *vt individuals* absondern; *group of population* nach Rassen/Geschlechtern/Konfessionen trennen ◆ **to be ~d from sb/sth** von jdm/etw abgesondert sein; **~d** (*racially*) *school, church* nur für Weiße/Schwarze; *schools* mit Rassentrennung; *society* nach Rassen getrennt.

segregation [,segrɪ'geɪʃən] *n* Trennung *f* ◆ **racial/sexual ~** Rassentrennung *f*/Geschlechtertrennung *f*.

segregationist [,segrɪ'geɪʃənɪst] *n* Befürworter(in *f*) *m* der Rassentrennung.

segue ['segweɪ](*Mus, fig*) [1] *vi* **to ~ from/into** übergehen von/in (+*acc*); **the washing machine ~d into its spin cycle** die Waschmaschine begann zu schleudern.
[2] *n* Übergang *m*.

seine [seɪn] *n* Wade *f*.

seismic ['saɪzmɪk] *adj* seismisch ◆ **~ focus** Erdbebenherd *m*.

seismograph ['saɪzməgrɑ:f] *n* Seismograph *m*.

seismography [saɪz'mɒgrəfɪ] *n* Seismologie *f*.

seismologist [saɪz'mɒlədʒɪst] *n* Seismologe *m*, Seismologin *f*.

seismology [saɪz'mɒlədʒɪ] *n* Seismologie, Erdbebenkunde *f*.

seize [si:z] [1] *vt* **(a)** (*grasp*) packen, ergreifen; (*as hostage*) nehmen; (*confiscate*) beschlagnahmen; *passport* einziehen; *ship* (*authorities*) beschlagnahmen; (*pirates*) kapern; (*capture*) *town* einnehmen; *train, building* besetzen; *criminal* fassen ◆ **to ~ sb's arm, to ~ sb by the arm** jdn am Arm packen.
(b) (*fig*) (*lay hold of: panic, fear, desire*) packen, ergreifen; *power, leadership* an sich (*acc*) reißen; (*leap upon*) *idea, suggestion* aufgreifen; *opportunity* ergreifen.
[2] *vi see* **seize up**.

◆**seize on** *or* **upon** *vi +prep obj* **(a)** (*clutch at*) *idea, offer* sich stürzen auf (+*acc*); *excuse* beim Schopf packen. **(b)** (*pick out for criticism*) herausgreifen.

◆**seize up** *vi* **(a)** (*engine, brakes*) sich verklemmen. **(b)** (*inf*) **my back ~d ~** es ist mir in den Rücken gefahren (*inf*); **she talks so much it's a miracle her jaw doesn't ~ ~** sie redet so viel, es ist ein Wunder, daß ihr Mundwerk nicht ausleiert (*inf*).

seizure ['si:ʒəʳ] *n* **(a)** (*confiscation*) Beschlagnahmung *f*; (*of passport*) Einzug *m*; (*of ship*) Beschlagnahme *f*; (*by pirates*) Kapern *nt*; (*capture*) Einnahme *f*; (*of train, building*) Besetzung *f*. **(b)** (*Med*) Anfall *m*; (*apoplexy*) Schlaganfall *m*.

seldom ['seldəm] *adv* selten ◆ **I ~ go there** ich gehe (nur) selten dorthin; **~ have I ...** ich habe selten ...; **~, if ever, does he do that** er tut das nur äußerst selten.

select [sɪ'lekt] [1] *vti* (aus)wählen; (*in buying also*) aussuchen; (*Sport*) auswählen; (*for football match etc*) aufstellen ◆ **~ed poems** ausgewählte Gedichte *pl*.
[2] *adj* (*exclusive*) exklusiv; (*carefully chosen*) auserwählt, auserlesen; *tobacco* auserlesen; *fruit* ausgesucht ◆ **~ committee** Sonderausschuß *m*.

selection [sɪ'lekʃən] *n* **(a)** (*choosing*) (Aus)wahl *f*; (*Biol*) Auslese, Selektion *f*.
(b) (*person, thing selected*) Wahl *f*; (*likely winner*) Tip *m* ◆ **to make one's ~** seine Wahl treffen; **~s from Rossini/Goethe** ausgewählte Stücke *pl* von Rossini/eine Auswahl aus Goethe; **~ committee** Auswahlkomitee *nt*.
(c) (*range, assortment*) Auswahl *f* (*of* an +*dat*).

selective [sɪ'lektɪv] *adj* **(a)** wählerisch; *reader* kritisch, anspruchsvoll; *examination, processes* Auslese-; *school* Elite- ◆ **we can't treat everything, we have to be ~** wir können nicht alles abhandeln, wir müssen eine Auswahl treffen *or* selektiv vorgehen *or* (*choose carefully*) wählerisch sein; **a more ~ approach to the available material ...** wenn Sie aus dem vorhandenen Material etwas kritischer auswählen würden ...; **a very ~ admission procedure** ein stark aussiebendes Aufnahmeverfahren; **the computer program has to be made more ~** man sollte mehr Wahlmöglichkeiten in das Computerprogramm einbauen; **~ service** (*US*) Wehrdienst *m*.
(b) *radio* trennscharf, selektiv.

selectively [sɪ'lektɪvlɪ] *adv* wählerisch; *read also, operate* selektiv ◆ **to read/buy ~** beim Lesen wählerisch/beim Einkaufen kritisch sein; **if you approach the material more ~** wenn Sie das Material besser auswählen *or* selektiver behandeln (*geh*); **he built up his collection very ~** er wählte bei der Zusammenstellung seiner Sammlung sorgfältig aus.

selectivity [,sɪlek'tɪvɪtɪ] *n* **(a)** Selektivität *f*; (*of reader, buyer*) kritisches Auswählen ◆ **his collection shows great ~** seine Sammlung ist mit viel Sorgfalt ausgewählt; **to develop ~** kritisches Bewußtsein entwickeln; **to show ~** anspruchsvoll *or* wählerisch sein; **to show ~ in one's taste** einen anspruchsvollen Geschmack haben; **it diminishes the level of ~** es verringert die (Aus)wahlmöglichkeiten *pl*.
(b) (*of radio*) Trennschärfe, Selektivität *f*.

selectman [sɪ'lektmən] *n, pl* **-men** [-mən] (*US*) Stadtrat *m*.

selector [sɪ'lektəʳ] *n* **(a)** (*Tech*) Wählschalter *m*; (*lever*) Schaltgriff *m*; (*knob*) Schaltknopf *m*; (*TV*) Programmtaste *f*; (*Rad*) Stationstaste *f*; (*on record-player*) Geschwindigkeitsregler *m*; (*Aut*) Schalthebel *m*.
(b) (*Sport*) *jd, der die Mannschaftsaufstellung vornimmt*.

selenium [sɪ'li:nɪəm] *n* Selen *nt*.

self [self] [1] *n, pl* **selves** Ich, Selbst (*esp Psych*) *no pl nt*; (*side of character*) Seite *f* ◆ **he showed his worst ~** er zeigte sich von der schlechtesten Seite; **one's other/better ~** sein anderes/besseres Ich; **my whole ~ revolted at the idea** alles in mir lehnte sich gegen diese Idee auf; **he's quite his old ~ again, he's back to his usual ~** er ist wieder ganz der alte (*inf*); **back to her usual cheerful ~** wieder fröhlich wie immer; **to be all ~** (*inf*), **to think of nothing but ~** nur an sich (*acc*) selbst denken; **with no thought of ~** ohne an sich (*acc*) selbst zu denken; **my humble ~** meine Wenigkeit; **how is your good ~?** wie geht es Ihnen?
[2] *pron* (*Comm*) **pay ~** zahlbar an selbst; **a room for wife and ~** ein Zimmer für meine Frau und mich.
[3] *adj attr lining* aus gleichem Material ◆ **in a ~ colour** in uni.

self: ~-abasement *n* Selbsterniedrigung *f*; **~-absorbed** *adj* mit sich selbst beschäftigt; **~-abuse** *n* (*euph*) Selbstbefleckung *f* (*euph*); **~-accusation** *n* Selbstanklage *f*; **~-accusing** *adj* selbstanklagend; **~-acting** *adj* selbsttätig; **~-activating** *adj bomb* selbstzündend; **~-addressed** *adj envelope* adressiert; **~-adhesive** *adj* selbstklebend; **~-adjusting** *adj* selbstregulierend *attr*; *brakes* selbst-nachstellend *attr*; **to be ~-adjusting** sich selbst regulieren/nachstellen; **~-admiration** *n* Selbstbewunderung *f*; **~-advertisement** *n* Eigenreklame *f*; **~-aggrandizement** *n* Selbstverherrlichung *f*; **~-appointed** *adj* selbsternannt; **he is the ~-appointed spokesman of the group** er hat sich selbst zum Sprecher der Gruppe gemacht; **~-approval** *n* Selbstgefälligkeit *f*; **~-assertion** *n* Durchsetzungsvermögen *nt*; (*pej*) Überheblichkeit *f*, Eingenommenheit *f* von sich selbst; **~-assertive** *adj* selbstbewußt; (*pej*) von sich selbst eingenommen; **~-assessment** *n* (*for tax*) Selbstveranlagung *f*; **~-assurance** *n* Selbstsicherheit *f*; **~-assured** *adj* selbstsicher; **~-aware** *adj* sich (*dat*) seiner selbst bewußt, selbstbewußt; **~-awareness** *n* Selbsterkenntnis *f*, Selbstbewußtsein *nt*.

self: ~-cancelling *adj indicator* sich automatisch abschaltend *attr*; **~-catering** [1] *n* Selbstversorgung *f*; **to go ~-catering** (*holidaymaker*) Urlaub *m* für Selbstversorger machen; (*hotel owner*) auf Selbstversorger umstellen; [2] *adj* für Selbstversorger; **~-centred,** (*US*) **~-centered** *adj* egozentrisch, ichbezogen; **~-centredness,** (*US*) **~-centeredness** *n* Egozentrik, Ichbezogenheit *f*; **~-cleaning** *adj* selbstreinigend; **~-closing** *adj* automatisch *or* von selbst schließend *attr*; **~-coloured,** (*US*) **~-colored** *adj* einfarbig, uni; **~-composed** *adj* ruhig, gelassen; **~-conceit** *n* Eingebildetheit *f*; **~-confessed** *adj* erklärt *attr*; **~-confidence** *n* Selbstvertrauen, Selbstbewußtsein *nt*; **~-confident** *adj* selbstbewußt, selbstsicher; **~-conscious** *adj* befangen, gehemmt; *piece of writing, style etc* bewußt; (*Philos: ~-aware*) selbstbewußt; **~-consciousness** *n see adj* Befangenheit, Gehemmtheit *f*; Bewußtheit *f*; Selbstbewußtsein *nt*; **~-contained** *adj person* distanziert; (*~-sufficient*) selbstgenügsam; *flat* separat; *community* unabhängig; **~-contradictory** *adj* sich (*dat*) selbst widersprechend *attr*, *alibi* widersprüchlich; **his argument is ~-contradictory** seine Argumente widersprechen sich (*dat*); **~-control** *n* Selbstbeherrschung *f*; **~-controlled** *adj* selbstbeherrscht; **~-correcting** *adj* selbstregulierend *attr*, *computer* sich selbst korrigierend *attr*; **to be ~-correcting** sich selbst regulieren/korrigieren; **~-critical** *adj* selbstkritisch; **~-criticism** *n* Selbstkritik *f*.

self: ~-deception *n* Selbsttäuschung *f*, Selbstbetrug *m*; **~-defeating** *adj* sinnlos, unsinnig; *argument* sich selbst widerlegend *attr*; **the government's plan was ~-defeating** dieser Plan der Regierung hat das Gegenteil erzielt; **a ~-defeating move** ein Eigentor *nt*; **~-defence,** (*US*) **~-defense** *n* Selbstverteidigung *f*; (*Jur*) Notwehr *f*; **to act in ~-defence** in Notwehr handeln; **the noble art of ~-defence** Boxen *nt*; **~-denial** *n* Selbstzucht *f*; (*Rel*) Selbstverleugnung *f*; **~-denying** *adj* sich selbst einschränkend *attr*; (*Rel*) sich selbst verleugnend *attr*; **to be ~-denying** sich einschränken/verleugnen; **~-deprecating** *adj* bescheiden; **~-destruct** *vi* sich selbst zerstören; **~-destruction** *n* Selbstzerstörung *f*; (*of person, race*) Selbstmord *m*; **~-determination** *n* Selbstbestimmung *f* (*also Pol*); **~-discipline** *n* Selbstdisziplin *f*; **~-doubt** *n* Zweifel *m* an sich (*dat*) selbst; **~-dramatization** *n* **his tendency towards ~-dramatization** seine Neigung, sich in Szene zu setzen; **~-drive** *adj car* für Selbstfahrer.

self: ~-educated *adj* autodidaktisch; **~-educated person** Autodidakt(in *f*) *m*; **he is ~-educated** er ist Autodidakt; **~-effacement** *n* Zurückhaltung *f*; **~-effacing** *adj* zurückhaltend; **~-employed** *adj* selbständig; *artist* freischaffend; *journalist* freiberuflich; **~-esteem** *n* (*~-respect*) Selbstachtung *f*; (*conceit*) Selbstüberschätzung *f*; **~-evident** *adj* offensichtlich; (*not needing proof*) selbstverständlich; **we'll need more money — that's ~-evident** wir brauchen mehr Geld — das versteht sich von selbst; **~-examination** *n* Selbstprüfung *f*; **~-explanatory** *adj* unmittelbar verständlich; **this word is ~-explanatory** das Wort erklärt sich selbst; **~-expression** *n* Selbstdarstellung *f*.

self: ~-fertilization *n* Selbstbefruchtung *f*; **~-financing** *adj* selbstfinanzierend; **~-flagellation** *n* Selbstgeißelung *f*; **~-fulfilling** *adj* **a ~-fulfilling prophecy** eine sich selbst bewahrheitende Voraussage, eine self-fulfilling prophecy (*Sociol*); **the ~-fulfilling prophecy of war** der herbeigeredete Krieg; **to be ~-fulfilling** sich selbst bewahrheiten; **~-fulfilment** *n* Erfüllung *f*.

self: ~-governed, ~-governing *adj* selbstverwaltet, sich selbst verwaltend *attr*; **to become ~-governing** eine eigene Regierung bekommen; **~-government** *n* Selbstverwaltung *f*.

self-help [ˌself'help] *n* Selbsthilfe *f* ◆ **she never was one for ~** sie konnte sich noch nie selbst behelfen.

self: ~-image *n* Selbstbild *nt*; **~-importance** *n* Aufgeblasenheit *f*; **~-important** *adj* aufgeblasen; **~-imposed** *adj* selbstauferlegt *attr*; **his exile is ~-imposed** er hat sich (*dat*) sein Exil selbst auferlegt; **~-improvement** *n* Weiterbildung *f*; **~-induced** *adj* selbstverursacht *attr*; **her miscarriage was ~-induced** sie hat die Fehlgeburt selbst verursacht; **~-induction** *n* (*Elec*) Selbstinduktion *f*; **~-indulgence** *n see adj* genießerische Art; Hemmungslosigkeit *f*; Maßlosigkeit *f*; **go on, take one, a little ~-indulgence never hurt anyone** nehmen Sie doch einen, jeder darf sich doch einmal verwöhnen *or* gehenlassen; **the distinction between humorous style and pure ~-indulgence** der Unterschied zwischen humorvollem Stil und reiner Selbstbefriedigung; **~-indulgent** *adj* genießerisch; (*sexually*) hemmungslos; (*in eating, drinking also*) maßlos; **his columns grew ever more ~-indulgent** er schrieb seine Spalten immer mehr zum eigenen Vergnügen; **be ~-indulgent, have another slice** verwöhnen Sie sich, nehmen Sie noch ein Stück; **~-inflicted** *adj wounds* sich (*dat*) selbst zugefügt *or* beigebracht *attr*; *task, punishment* sich (*dat*) freiwillig auferlegt; **his wounds are ~-inflicted** er hat sich (*dat*) die Wunden selbst beigebracht; **~-interest** *n* (*selfishness*) Eigennutz *m*; (*personal advantage*) eigenes Interesse; **in our own ~-interest** in unserem eigenen Interesse; **~-invited** *adj* selbsteingeladen *attr*; **he is a ~-invited guest** er hat sich selbst eingeladen.

selfish *adj*, **~ly** *adv* ['selfɪʃ, -lɪ] egoistisch, selbstsüchtig.

selfishness ['selfɪʃnɪs] *n* Egoismus *m*, Selbstsüchtigkeit *f*.

self: ~-justification *n* Rechtfertigung *f*; **he felt no need for ~-justification** er sah keinen Grund, sich zu rechtfertigen; **..., he said in ~-justification ...**, sagte er zu seiner eigenen Rechtfertigung; **~-justifying** *adj* sachlich gerechtfertigt; **..., he added in a ~-justifying way ...**, fügte er zur eigenen Rechtfertigung an; **~-knowledge** *n* Selbsterkenntnis *f*.

selfless ['selflɪs] *adj* selbstlos.

selflessly ['selflɪslɪ] *adv* selbstlos, in selbstloser Weise.

selflessness ['selflɪsnɪs] *n* Selbstlosigkeit *f*.

self: ~-loading *adj* **~-loading gun** Selbstlader *m*; **~-locking** *adj* von selbst schließend *attr*; *attachment* von selbst einrastend *attr*; **~-locking door** Tür mit Schnappschloß; **~-love** *n* Eigenliebe, Selbstliebe (*also Philos*) *f*.

self: ~-made *adj* **~-made man** Selfmademan *m*; **~ -mutilation** *n* Selbstverstümmelung *f*.

self-neglect [ˌselfnɪ'glekt] *n* Vernachlässigung *f* seiner (*gen*) selbst ◆ **as a result of his ~** weil er sich selbst vernachlässigt hat.

self: ~-opinionated *adj* rechthaberisch; *nonsense, drivel* selbstherrlich; **he's too ~-opinionated to change his mind** er ist viel zu sehr von sich selbst überzeugt, um seine Meinung zu ändern; **~-opinionatedness** *n* rechthaberisches und selbstherrliches Wesen; **this stream of ~-opinionatedness** dieses selbstherrliche Gerede.

self: ~-perpetuating *adj* sich selbst erneuernd *or* erhaltend *attr*; **~-perpetuating poverty/dictatorship** sich ständig fortsetzende Armut/Diktatur; **the system is ~-perpetuating** das System erhält sich selbst; **~-perpetuation** *n* Selbstperpetuierung *f*; **~-pity** *n* Selbstmitleid *nt*; **~-pitying** *adj* selbstbemitleidend; **~-pollination** *n* Selbstbestäubung *f*; **~-portrait** *n* Selbstporträt *or* -bildnis *nt*; **~-possessed** *adj* selbstbeherrscht; **~-possession** *n* Selbstbeherrschung *f*; **~-praise** *n* Eigenlob *nt*; **~-preservation** *n* Selbsterhaltung *f*; **the instinct for ~-preservation** der Selbsterhaltungstrieb; **~-propagating** *adj flower* sich selbst aussäend *attr*; *poverty, bad state of affairs* sich aus sich selbst weiterentwickelnd *attr*; **~-propelled** *adj* selbstangetrieben *attr*, mit Selbstantrieb.

self: ~-raising, (*US*) **~-rising** *adj flour* selbsttreibend, *mit bereits beigemischtem Backpulver*; **~-realization** *n* Selbstverwirklichung *f*; **~-regulating** *adj* selbstregulierend *attr*; **this mechanism is ~-regulating** dieser Mechanismus reguliert sich selbst; **~-reliance** *n* Selbständigkeit *f*; **~-reliant** *adj* selbständig; **~-reproach** *n* Selbstvorwurf *m*; **all this ~-reproach** diese Selbstvorwürfe *pl*; **~-respect** *n* Selbstachtung *f*; **have you no ~-respect?** schämen Sie sich gar nicht?; **~-respecting** *adj* anständig; **no ~-respecting person would ...** niemand, der etwas auf sich hält, würde ...; **~-restraint** *n* Selbstbeherrschung *f*; **~-righteous** *adj* selbstgerecht; **~-righteousness** *n* Selbstgerechtigkeit *f*; **~-righting** *adj boat* sich (von) selbst aufrichtend *attr*; **~-rising** *adj* (*US*) *see* **~-raising**; **~-rule** *n* Selbstbestimmung, Selbstverwaltung *f*.

self: ~-sacrifice *n* Selbstaufopferung *f*; **it should not be too much of a ~-sacrifice** das sollte kein zu großes Opfer sein; **~-sacrificing** *adj* aufopfernd; **~same** *adj*: **the ~same** genau der/die/das gleiche, der-/die-/ dasselbe; **on the ~same day** noch am selben Tag; **~-satisfaction** *n* Selbstzufriedenheit *f*; (*smugness*) Selbstgefälligkeit *f*; **~-satisfied** *adj* (*smug*) selbstgefällig, selbstzufrieden; **~-sealing** *adj envelope* selbstklebend; *tyre* selbstdichtend; **~-seeking** [1] *adj* selbstsüchtig; [2] *n* Selbstsucht *f*; **~-serve** (*esp US*), **~-service** [1] *adj* Selbstbedienungs-; **the petrol station has gone ~-service** die Tankstelle hat jetzt auf Selbstbedienung umgestellt; [2] *n* Selbstbedienung *f*; **~-starter** *n* Selbstanlasser *m*; **~-styled** *adj* selbsternannt; **~-sufficiency** *n* (*of person*) Selbständigkeit *f*; (*emotional*) Selbstgenügsamkeit *f*; (*of country*) Autarkie *f*; (*of community*) Selbstversorgung *f*; **~-sufficient** *adj person* selbständig; (*emotionally*) selbstgenügsam; *country* autark; **they are ~-sufficient in oil** sie können ihren Ölbedarf selbst decken; **a ~-sufficient community** eine Gemeinde, die sich selbst versorgen kann; **~-supporting** *adj person* finanziell unabhängig; *structure* freitragend; *chimney* freistehend; **the club is ~-supporting** der Club trägt sich selbst; **our commune is ~-supporting** wir sind in unserer Kommune Selbstversorger.

self: ~-tapping screw *n* selbstschneidende Schraube, Treibschraube *f*; **~-taught** *adj skills* selbsterlernt; **he is ~-taught** er hat sich (*dat*) das selbst beigebracht; (*intellectually*) er hat sich durch Selbstunterricht gebildet; **he's a ~-taught guitarist** er hat sich (*dat*) das Gitarrespielen selbst beigebracht; **~-test** [1] *n* (*of machine*) Selbsttest *m*; **to do a ~-test** einen Selbsttest durchführen; **~-test program/routine** Selbsttestprogramm *nt*/-routine *f*; [2] *vi* (*machine*) einen Selbsttest durchführen.

self: ~-will *n* Eigenwilligkeit *f*, Eigensinn *m* (*pej*); **~-willed** *adj* eigenwillig, eigensinnig (*pej*); **~-winding** *adj watch* Automatik-.

sell [sel] (*vb: pret, ptp* **sold**) [1] *vt* **(a)** verkaufen (*sb sth, sth to sb* jdm etw, etw an jdn); *insurance policy* abschließen (*to* mit); (*business*) *goods also* absetzen ◆ **I was sold this in Valencia** man hat mir das in Valencia verkauft; **the book sold 3,000 copies** von dem Buch wurden 3.000 Exemplare verkauft; **he could ~ a fridge to an Eskimo** er könnte einem Eskimo einen Eisschrank andrehen (*inf*) *or* aufschwatzen (*inf*); **to ~ insurance (for a living)** Versicherungsvertreter sein; **to ~ one's life dearly** sein Leben teuer verkaufen; **he sold himself to the enemy** er hat sich an den Feind verkauft; **to ~ one's soul to sb/sth** jdm/einer Sache seine Seele verschreiben; **modern man has sold his soul** der moderne Mensch hat seine Seele verloren; **what are you ~ing it for?** wieviel verlangen Sie dafür?, wieviel wollen Sie dafür haben?; **I can't remember what I sold it for** ich weiß nicht mehr, für wieviel ich es verkauft habe.

(b) (*stock*) führen, haben (*inf*); (*deal in*) vertreiben.

(c) (*promote the sale of*) zugkräftig machen, einen guten Absatz verschaffen (+*dat*) ◆ **you need advertising to ~ your product** Sie müssen werben, um Ihr Produkt zu verkaufen *or* abzusetzen; **nothing will ~ this product, it's so bad** das Produkt ist so schlecht, daß es sich nicht verkaufen *or* an den Mann bringen (*inf*) läßt; **she finished up ~ing toothpaste on television** sie warb schließlich im Fernsehen für Zahnpasta.

(d) (*inf: gain acceptance for*) schmackhaft machen (*to sb* jdm), gewinnen für (*to sb* jdn); *religion* aufschwatzen (*inf*), verkaufen (*inf*) (*to sb* jdm) ◆ **you'll never ~ them that idea** dafür sind sie nicht zu haben; **I know I'll never be able to ~ it to him** ich weiß, daß ich ihn dafür nicht erwärmen kann *or* daß er dafür nicht zu haben ist; **to ~ oneself** (*put oneself across*) sich profilieren (*to* bei), sich verkaufen (*to* an +*acc*).

(e) (*inf: convince of the worth of*) **to ~ sb on sth** jdn von etw überzeugen; **to be sold on sb/sth** von jdm/etw begeistert sein; **how sold is he on the idea?** wie sehr hat es ihm diese Idee angetan? (*inf*).

(f) (*fig: betray*) verraten ◆ **to ~ sb down the river** (*inf*) jdn ganz schön verschaukeln (*inf*).

[2] *vi* (*person*) verkaufen (*to sb* an jdn); (*article*) sich verkaufen (lassen) ◆ **his book is ~ing well/won't ~** sein Buch verkauft sich gut/läßt sich nicht verkaufen; **the house sold for £85,000** das Haus wurde für £ 85.000 verkauft; **what are they ~ing at *or* for?** wieviel kosten sie?; **the idea didn't ~** (*fig*) die Idee kam nicht an *or* fand keinen Anklang.

[3] *n* **(a)** (*Comm inf: sales appeal*) Zugkraft, Attraktivität *f*. **(b)** (*selling technique*) Verkaufstaktik *or* -methode *f*; *see* **hard ~, soft ~**. **(c)** (*dated inf: disappointment*) Reinfall *m*, Pleite *f* (*inf*).

◆**sell off** *vt sep* verkaufen; (*get rid of quickly, cheaply*) abstoßen; (*at auction*) versteigern.

◆**sell out** [1] *vt sep* **(a)** (*sell entire stock of*) ausverkaufen ◆ **sorry, sold ~** wir sind leider ausverkauft; **we're sold ~ of ice-cream/size 10** wir haben kein Eis/keine Größe 10 mehr, das Eis/Größe 10 ist ausverkauft. **(b)** *share, interest* verkaufen, abgeben. **(c)** (*inf: betray*) verraten (*to* an +*acc*).

[2] *vi* **(a)** (*sell entire stock*) alles verkaufen *or* absetzen ◆ **this book/we sold ~ in two days** das Buch war/wir waren in zwei Tagen ausverkauft.

(b) (*in business*) sein Geschäft/seine Firma/seinen Anteil *etc* verkaufen *or*

abstoßen.
(c) (*inf: betray*) **the union leader sold ~ to the bosses** der Gewerkschaftsführer verkaufte die Arbeiter an die Bosse (*inf*); **he sold ~ to the right wing/the enemy** er hat sich an den rechten Flügel/den Feind verkauft.

◆**sell up** [1] *vt sep* zu Geld machen (*inf*); (*Brit Fin*) zwangsverkaufen ◆ **he was sold ~ by his creditors** die Gläubiger ließen seinen Besitz zwangsverkaufen.
[2] *vi* sein Haus/seinen Besitz/seine Firma *etc* verkaufen *or* zu Geld machen (*inf*).

sell-by date ['selbaɪ,deɪt] *n* ≃ Haltbarkeitsdatum *nt* ◆ **to be past one's ~** (*hum inf*) seine besten Tage hinter sich (*dat*) haben.

seller ['selə^r] *n* **(a)** Verkäufer(in *f*) *m* ◆ **you should take faulty goods back to the ~** du solltest fehlerhafte Ware (zum Händler) zurückbringen; **it's a ~s' market in housing just now** zur Zeit bestimmen die Verkäufer die Hauspreise.
(b) (*thing sold*) **big ~** Verkaufsschlager *m*; **bad ~** schlecht gehender *or* verkäuflicher Artikel; (*in shop also*) Ladenhüter *m*; **this book is a good/slow ~** das Buch verkauft sich gut/schlecht; **it's the best/worst ~ we've had** das ist der bestgehende/am schlechtesten gehende Artikel, den wir je hatten.

selling ['selɪŋ] [1] *n* Verkauf *m*, Verkaufen *nt* ◆ **they get a special training in ~** sie werden besonders im Verkaufen ausgebildet.
[2] *adj* Verkaufs- ◆ **~ price** Verkaufspreis *m*; **~ point** Verkaufsanreiz *m*.

sellotape ® ['seləʊteɪp] (*Brit*) [1] *n* Tesafilm ® *m*.
[2] *vt* (*also*: **~ down/up**) mit Tesafilm ® festkleben.

sell-out ['selaʊt] *n* **(a)** (*inf: betrayal*) fauler Kompromiß *or* Handel (*to* mit); (*of one's ideals etc*) Ausverkauf *m* (*to* an *+acc*). **(b)** (*Theat, Sport*) ausverkauftes Haus ◆ **to be a ~** ausverkauft sein. **(c)** (*Comm*) Verkaufsschlager *m*.

seltzer (water) ['seltsə('wɔːtə^r)] *n* Selterswasser *nt*.

selvage, selvedge ['selvɪdʒ] *n* Web(e)kante *f*.

selves [selvz] *pl of* **self**.

semantic *adj*, **~ally** *adv* [sɪ'mæntɪk, -əlɪ] semantisch.

semanticist [sɪ'mæntɪsɪst] *n* Semantiker(in *f*) *m*.

semantics [sɪ'mæntɪks] *n sing* Semantik *f* ◆ **the discussion got bogged down in ~** die Diskussion blieb in Wortklaubereien stecken; **it's just a question of ~** es ist nur eine Frage der Formulierung *or* (*interpretation*) Auslegung.

semaphore ['seməfɔː^r] [1] *n* **(a)** (*Rail*) Semaphor *nt*, Signalmast *m*. **(b)** (*system*) Signalsprache *f*, Winken *nt* ◆ **transmitted by ~** durch optische Signale übermittelt; **to learn ~** das Winkeralphabet lernen.
[2] *vti* durch Winkzeichen signalisieren.

semblance ['sembləns] *n* (*with def art*) Anschein *m* (*of* von); (*with indef art*) Anflug *m* (*of* von) ◆ **without a ~ of regret/fear/a smile** ohne den leisesten Anflug von Bedauern/Angst/eines Lächelns; **he had the ~ of an experienced lawyer** er erweckte den Anschein eines erfahrenen Anwalts; **I saw in him the ~ of his father** (*liter*) ich konnte in ihm die Ähnlichkeit mit seinem Vater erkennen; **it possessed more the ~ of a dream than reality** (*liter*) es war von eher traumhaftem als wirklichem Charakter (*liter*); **to put on a ~ of gaiety** (*liter*) eine fröhliche Miene zur Schau tragen (*geh*).

semen ['siːmən] *n* Samenflüssigkeit *f*, Sperma *nt*.

semester [sɪ'mestə^r] *n* Semester *nt*.

semi[1] ['semɪ] *n* (*Brit inf*) *see* **semidetached**.

semi[2] *n* (*US inf*) *see* **semitrailer**.

semi- *pref* halb-, Halb-.

semi: ~-automatic [1] *adj* halbautomatisch; [2] *n* (*weapon*) halbautomatische Waffe; **~breve** *n* (*esp Brit*) ganze Note; **~circle** *n* Halbkreis *m*; **~circular** *adj* halbkreisförmig; **~circular canal** (*Anat*) Bogengang *m*; **~colon** *n* Strichpunkt *m*, Semikolon *nt*; **~conductor** *n* Halbleiter *m*; **~conscious** *adj* halb bewußtlos; **he's ~conscious now, you can talk to him** er ist zwar noch nicht ganz bei Bewußtsein, Sie können aber jetzt mit ihm reden; **~darkness** *n* Halbdunkel *nt*; **~detached** [1] *adj* **~detached house** Doppelhaushälfte *f*; [2] *n* Doppelhaushälfte *f*; **~final** *n* Halb- *or* Semifinalspiel *nt*; **~finals** Halb- *or* Semifinale *nt*; **~finalist** *n* Teilnehmer(in *f*) *m* am Halbfinale.

seminal ['semɪnl] *adj* **(a)** **~ fluid** Samenflüssigkeit *f*. **(b)** (*embryonic*) keimhaft (*geh*) ◆ **to be present in a ~ state** im Keim vorhanden sein. **(c)** (*generative*) *ideas* ertragreich.

seminar ['semɪnɑː^r] *n* Seminar *nt*.

seminarian [,semɪ'neərɪən], **seminarist** ['semɪnərɪst] *n* Seminarist *m*.

seminary ['semɪnərɪ] *n* Priesterseminar *nt*.

semiofficial ['semɪə'fɪʃəl] *adj* halbamtlich, offiziös; *rule* halboffiziell.

semiotic [semɪ'ɒtɪk] *adj* semiotisch.

semiotics [semɪ'ɒtɪks] *n sing* Semiotik *f*.

semi: ~precious *adj* **~precious stone** Halbedelstein *m*; **~quaver** *n* (*esp Brit*) Sechzehntel(note *f*) *nt*; **~skilled** *adj worker* angelernt; *job* Anlern-; **~skilled labour** (*workforce*) Angelernte *pl*; (*work*) Arbeit *f* für Angelernte; **~-skimmed milk** *n* Halbfettmilch *f*, teilentrahmte Milch; **~solid** [1] *adj* halbfest; [2] *n* halbfeste Substanz; **~submersible** *n* (*oil rig*) schwimmende Bohrinsel, Halbtaucher *m*.

Semite ['siːmaɪt] *n* Semit *m*, Semitin *f*.

Semitic [sɪ'mɪtɪk] *adj* semitisch.

semi: ~tone *n* Halbton *m*; **~trailer** *n* (*US*) Sattelschlepper *m*; (*part*) Sattelauflieger *m*; **~vowel** *n* Halbvokal *m*.

semolina [,semə'liːnə] *n* Grieß *m*.

sempiternal [,sempɪ'tɜːnl] *adj* (*liter*) immerwährend (*liter*).

sempstress ['sempstrɪs] *n* Näherin *f*.

Sen (*US*) *abbr of* **Senator**.

SEN (*Brit*) *abbr of* **State Enrolled Nurse** *staatlich geprüfte Krankenschwester; staatlich geprüfter Krankenpfleger.*

senate ['senɪt] *n* Senat *m*.

senator ['senɪtə^r] *n* Senator *m*; (*as address*) Herr Senator.

senatorial [,senə'tɔːrɪəl] *adj* des/eines Senators ◆ **a family with a long ~ tradition** eine Familie, aus der schon viele Senatoren hervorgegangen sind.

➤ **send** [send] *pret, ptp* **sent** [1] *vt* **(a)** schicken; *letter, messenger also* senden (*geh*); (*~ off*) *letter* abschicken; (*Rad*) *radio wave* ausstrahlen; *signal, SOS* senden; (*through wires*) übermitteln ◆ **the satellite ~s signals (to us)** der Satellit sendet Signale aus/sendet uns Signale; **to ~ sb to prison/to his death** jdn ins Gefängnis/in den Tod schicken; **to ~ sb on a course/tour** jdn auf einen *or* zu einem Kurs/auf eine Tour schicken; **to ~ sb to university** jdn studieren lassen; **to ~ sb for sth** jdn nach etw schicken.
(b) **she ~s her love/congratulations/apologies** *etc* sie läßt grüßen/Ihnen ihre Glückwünsche ausrichten/sich entschuldigen *etc*; **~ him my love/best wishes** grüßen Sie ihn von mir.
(c) (*propel, make go*) *arrow, ball* schießen; (*hurl*) schleudern; (*conveyor belt*) leiten, befördern ◆ **he/the explosion sent everything crashing to the ground** er/die Explosion ließ alles krachend zu Boden fallen; **the blow sent him sprawling** der Schlag schleuderte ihn zu Boden; **the fire sent everyone running out of the building** das Feuer ließ alle das Gebäude fluchtartig verlassen; **the blue ball sent the red across the table** die blaue Kugel ließ die rote über den Tisch rollen; **the particle is sent off at an angle** das Teilchen fliegt schräg zur Seite weg; **this ~s a spark into the engine** das leitet einen Funken zum Motor; **his speech sent a wave of excitement through the audience** seine Rede ließ eine Woge der Aufregung durch die Zuschauer gehen; **the explosion had sent the spaceship off course** die Explosion hatte das Raumschiff vom Kurs abgebracht.
(d) (*cause to become, cause to go*) **this sent him into such a temper** das machte ihn fürchterlich wütend; **this sent him off into one of his diatribes/into fits of laughter** das ließ ihn eine seiner Schimpfkanonaden vom Stapel lassen/in einen Lachkrampf ausbrechen.
(e) (*sl*) hinreißen ◆ **that tune/he ~s me** ich bin ganz weg von der Melodie/von ihm (*inf*); *see also* **sent**.
(f) (*old*) geben ◆ **~ her victorious** möge sie siegreich sein (*liter*).
[2] *vi* **she sent to say that ...** sie ließ sagen *or* ausrichten *or* bestellen, daß ...; **the mail-order firm suddenly stopped ~ing** die Versandfirma lieferte plötzlich nicht mehr.

◆**send across** *vt sep* herüber-/hinüberschicken; (*+prep obj*) schicken über (*+acc*).

◆**send after** [1] *vt sep* **to ~ sb ~ sb** jdn jdm nachschicken.
[2] *vi +prep obj* **they sent ~ him** sie schickten ihm jemanden nach.

◆**send along** *vt sep* her-/hinschicken.

◆**send away** [1] *vt sep* **(a)** wegschicken, fortschicken; *letter etc also* abschicken ◆ **his parents sent him ~ to Europe/to school** seine Eltern schickten ihn nach Europa/ins Internat.
(b) **I had to ~ him ~ without an explanation** ich mußte ihn ohne Erklärung weggehen lassen *or* wegschicken.
[2] *vi* schreiben ◆ **the number of people who sent ~ when they saw the TV advert** die Anzahl von Leuten, die auf die Fernsehreklame hin schrieben; **to ~ ~ for sth** etw anfordern.

◆**send back** [1] *vt sep* zurückschicken; *food in restaurant* zurückgehen lassen.
[2] *vi* **to ~ ~ for reinforcements** nach Verstärkung schicken, Verstärkung holen lassen.

◆**send down** *vt sep* **(a)** *temperature, prices* fallen lassen; (*gradually*) senken. **(b)** (*Brit Univ: expel*) relegieren. **(c)** *prisoner* verurteilen (*for* zu).

◆**send for** *vi +prep obj* **(a)** *person* kommen lassen; *doctor, police, priest also* rufen; *help* herbeirufen; *reinforcements* herbeibeordern; *food* bringen lassen; (*person in authority*) *pupil, secretary, minister* zu sich bestellen ◆ **I'll ~ ~ you/these books when I want you/them** ich lasse Sie rufen/ich schicke nach den Büchern, wenn ich Sie/sie brauche; **to ~ ~ sb to do sth** jdn herbeiholen *or* nach jdm schicken, um etw zu tun; **has the doctor been sent ~ yet?** ist der Arzt schon gerufen worden?
(b) *copy, catalogue* anfordern, sich (*dat*) kommen lassen.

◆**send forth** *vt sep* (*liter*) aussenden (*geh*); *blossom* hervorbringen; *smell* verströmen (*geh*); *heat, light* ausstrahlen.

◆**send in** [1] *vt sep* einschicken, einsenden; *person* herein-/hineinschicken; *troops* einsetzen.
[2] *vi see* **send away 2**.

◆**send off** [1] *vt sep* **(a)** *letter, parcel* abschicken.
(b) *children to school* wegschicken ◆ **he sent his son ~ to Paris** er schickte seinen Sohn nach Paris.
(c) *see* **send away 1 (b)**.
(d) (*Sport*) vom Platz verweisen (*for* wegen); (*Ice hockey*) auf die Strafbank schicken ◆ **he was sent ~ the pitch** er wurde vom Platz verwiesen; **~ him ~, ref!** Platzverweis!
(e) (*see off*) verabschieden.
[2] *vi see* **send away 2**.

◆**send on** *vt sep* **(a)** (*forward*) *letter* nachschicken; (*pass on*) *memo* weiterleiten. **(b)** (*in advance*) *troops, luggage etc* vorausschicken. **(c)** *substitute* aufs Feld schicken, einsetzen; *actor* auf die Bühne schicken.

◆**send out** *vt sep* **(a)** (*out of house, room*) hinaus-/herausschicken (*of* aus) ◆ **he sent me ~ to the shop/to buy a paper** er hat mich zum Geschäft geschickt/losgeschickt, um eine Zeitung zu kaufen; **the company started ~ing work ~** die Firma hat angefangen, Arbeit außer Haus zu geben.
(b) (*emit*) *rays, radio signals* aussenden; *light, heat, radiation* ausstrahlen,

➤ LANGUAGE IN USE: **send: 1a** → 20.1, 20.3, 21.1, 21.3

abgeben; *smoke* ausstoßen, abgeben.
(c) *leaflets, invitations, application forms* verschicken.

◆**send out for** [1] *vi +prep obj* holen lassen.
[2] *vt sep* **to ~ sb ~ ~ sth** jdn nach etw schicken.

◆**send up** *vt sep* **(a)** *rocket* hochschießen; *balloon* steigen lassen; *flare* in die Luft schießen. **(b)** *prices, temperature* hochtreiben, in die Höhe treiben; *pressure* steigen lassen. **(c)** *(destroy)* in die Luft gehen lassen ◆ **to ~ sth ~ in flames** etw in Flammen aufgehen lassen. **(d)** *(Brit inf: satirize)* verulken *(inf)*.
(e) *(US inf: send to prison)* hinter Gitter bringen *(inf)*.

sender ['sendəʳ] *n* Absender(in *f*) *m* ◆ **return to ~** zurück an Absender.

send: ~-off *n* Abschied *m*, Verabschiedung *f*; **to give sb a good ~-off** jdn ganz groß verabschieden *(inf)*; **~-up** *n (Brit inf)* Verulkung *f (inf)*; **to do a ~-up of sb/sth** jdn/etw verulken *(inf)*.

Senegal [ˌsenɪ'gɔːl] *n* Senegal *nt*.

Senegalese [ˌsenɪgə'liːz] [1] *adj* senegalesisch.
[2] *n* Senegalese *m*, Senegalesin *f*.

senescence [sɪ'nesəns] *n (form)* Alterungsprozeß *m*, Seneszenz *f (spec)*.

senescent [sɪ'nesənt] *adj (form)* alternd.

senile ['siːnaɪl] *adj person* senil; *(physically)* altersschwach ◆ **~ decay** Altersabbau *m*; **he must be getting ~** er wird langsam senil *or (physically)* ein richtiger Tattergreis *(inf)*.

senility [sɪ'nɪlɪtɪ] *n* Senilität *f*; *(physical)* Altersschwäche *f*.

senior ['siːnɪəʳ] [1] *adj (in age)* älter; *(in rank)* vorgesetzt, übergeordnet; *(with longer service)* dienstälter; *rank, civil servant* höher; *officer* ranghöher; *position* höher, leitend; *designer, editor, executive, accountant etc* leitend; *doctor, nurse etc* Ober- ◆ **he is ~ to me** *(in age)* er ist älter als ich; *(in rank)* er ist mir übergeordnet; *(in length of service)* er ist *or* arbeitet schon länger hier als ich; **~ section** ältere *or* höhere Altersgruppe; **the ~ management** die Geschäftsleitung; **~ partner** Seniorpartner *m*; **~ consultant** Chefarzt *m*/-ärztin *f*; **~ citizen** älterer (Mit)bürger, ältere (Mit)bürgerin; **~ citizen rail pass** Seniorenpaß *m*; **~ service** *(Brit)* Kriegsmarine *f*; **~ school, ~ high school** *(US)* Oberstufe *f*; **~ pupil** Oberstufenschüler(in *f*) *m*; **my ~ officer** mein Vorgesetzter; **a very ~ officer** ein sehr hoher Offizier; **he's very/not very ~** er hat eine ziemlich hohe/keine sehr hohe Stellung; **can I speak to somebody more ~?** könnte ich bitte jemanden sprechen, der verantwortlich ist?; **J. B. Schwartz, S~** J. B. Schwartz senior.
[2] *n (Sch)* Oberstufenschüler(in *f*) *m*; *(US Univ)* Student(in *f*) *m* im 4./letzten Studienjahr; *(in club etc)* Senior *m* ◆ **he is my ~** *(in age)* er ist älter als ich; *(in rank)* er ist mir übergeordnet; *(in length of service)* er ist *or* arbeitet schon länger hier als ich; **he is two years my ~, he is my ~ by two years** er ist zwei Jahre älter als ich.

seniority [ˌsiːnɪ'ɒrɪtɪ] *n (in age)* (höheres) Alter; *(in rank)* (höhere) Position; *(Mil)* (höherer) Rang; *(in civil service etc)* (höherer) Dienstgrad; *(in service)* (längere) Betriebszugehörigkeit; *(in civil service etc)* (höheres) Dienstalter ◆ **promotion on the basis of ~** Beförderung *f* nach Länge der Dienstjahre/Betriebszugehörigkeit.

senna ['senə] *n (drug)* Sennesblätter *pl*; *(plant)* Sennespflanze *f*.

sennight ['senɪt] *n (obs)* Woche *f*.

sen(r) *abbr of* **senior** sen.

sensation [sen'seɪʃən] *n* **(a)** *(feeling)* Gefühl *nt*; *(of heat, cold etc)* Empfindung *f*; *(of the external world)* Sinneseindruck *m* ◆ **a/the ~ of falling** das Gefühl zu fallen; **a ~ of fear/hunger** ein Gefühl *nt* der Angst, ein Angst-/Hungergefühl *nt*; **how can one describe the ~ of touching silk?** wie kann man beschreiben, was man beim Berühren von Seide empfindet?
(b) *(great success)* Sensation *f* ◆ **to cause** *or* **create a ~** (großes) Aufsehen erregen.

sensational [sen'seɪʃənl] *adj* **(a)** sensationell, aufsehenerregend; *newspaper, film, book* reißerisch aufgemacht, auf Sensation bedacht; *news item* Sensations-; *style, writing* reißerisch; *journalist* sensationsgierig *or* -lüstern *(inf)*. **(b)** *(inf: very good etc)* sagenhaft *(inf)*.

sensationalism [sen'seɪʃnəlɪzəm] *n (of paper, reporter etc)* Sensationsmache *f (inf)*; *(of reader)* Sensationsgier *f* ◆ **the cheap ~ of his style** die billige Effekthascherei in seinem Stil; **to edit out the ~** die zu reißerisch aufgemachten Stellen herausstreichen.

sensationalist [sen'seɪʃnəlɪst] *adj style, journalism* Sensations-, sensationslüstern.

sensationally [sen'seɪʃnəlɪ] *adv* **(a)** *write, report* in einem reißerischen Stil.
(b) *(inf: amazingly)* sagenhaft *(inf)*.

sense [sens] [1] *n* **(a)** *(bodily)* Sinn *m* ◆ **~ of hearing** Gehör(sinn *m*) *nt*; **~ of sight** Sehvermögen *nt*; **~ of smell** Geruchssinn *m*; **~ of taste** Geschmack(sinn) *m*; **~ of touch** Tastsinn *m*.
(b) ~s *pl (right mind)* Verstand *m* ◆ **no man in his ~s ...** kein einigermaßen vernünftiger Mensch ...; **to be out of one's ~s** nicht ganz bei Trost sein, von Sinnen sein *(geh)*; **to frighten sb out of his ~s** jdn zu Tode erschrecken; **his ~s were deranged by ...** er war durch ... völlig verstört; **to bring sb to his ~s** jdn zur Vernunft *or* Besinnung bringen; **to come to one's ~s** zur Vernunft *or* Besinnung kommen, Vernunft annehmen.
(c) *(feeling)* Gefühl *nt* ◆ **~ of duty** Pflichtbewußtsein *or* -gefühl *nt*; **a ~ of pleasure** *etc* ein Gefühl der Freude *etc*; **he has an exaggerated ~ of his own importance** er nimmt sich selbst übertrieben wichtig; **imbued with a ~ of history** von Geschichte durchtränkt *(liter)*; **there's a ~ of impermanence in these buildings** diese Gebäude haben etwas Unbeständiges an sich; **these buildings create a ~ of space** diese Gebäude vermitteln den Eindruck von Weite.
(d) *(instinct, appreciation)* Sinn *m* ◆ **his ~ for what is appropriate** sein Gefühl *nt or* Gespür *nt* dafür, was angebracht ist; **~ of colour/justice** Farben-/Gerechtigkeitssinn.
(e) *(good ~)* **(common) ~** gesunder Menschenverstand; **haven't you ~ enough** *or* **enough ~ to stop when you're tired?** bist du nicht vernünftig genug aufzuhören, wenn du müde bist?; **he had the (good) ~ to ...** er war so vernünftig *or* klug *or* gescheit und ...; **you should have had more ~ than to ...** du hättest vernünftiger sein sollen und nicht ...; **there is no ~/a lot of ~ in that** das hat keinen Sinn, es ist zwecklos/das hat Hand und Fuß, das ist ganz vernünftig; **what's the ~ of** *or* **in doing this?** welchen Sinn hat es denn, das zu tun?; **there is no ~ in doing that** es ist zwecklos *or* sinnlos, das zu tun; **there is no ~ in crying** es hat keinen Sinn zu heulen; **there's some ~ in what he says/in doing that** was er sagt, ist ganz vernünftig/es wäre ganz vernünftig, das zu tun; **a man of good ~** ein (ganz) vernünftiger Mann; **to talk ~** vernünftig sein; **you're just not talking ~** du bist doch völlig unvernünftig; **now you're talking ~** das läßt sich schon eher hören; **he hasn't the ~ he was born with** er hat nicht für fünf Pfennig Verstand *(inf)*; **to make sb see ~** jdn zur Vernunft bringen.
(f) to make ~ *(sentence etc)* (einen) Sinn ergeben; *(be sensible, rational etc)* sinnvoll *or* vernünftig sein, Sinn machen *(inf)*; **it doesn't make ~ doing it that way/to spend all that money** es ist doch Unsinn *or* unvernünftig, es so zu machen/soviel Geld auszugeben; **why did he decide that? — I don't know, it doesn't make ~** warum hat er das beschlossen? — ich weiß es nicht, das ist mir unverständlich *or* ich verstehe das nicht; **the whole scheme fails to make ~ to me** die ganze Sache leuchtet mir nicht ein; **it makes good** *or* **sound ~** das scheint sehr vernünftig; **it makes good financial/political ~ to ...** aus finanzieller/politischer Sicht gesehen ist es sehr vernünftig, zu ...; **sometimes life just doesn't make ~** manchmal ergibt das Leben einfach keinen Sinn; **her behaviour doesn't make ~ (to me)** man wird/ich werde aus ihrem Verhalten nicht schlau *(inf)*; **he/his theory doesn't make ~** er/seine Theorie ist völlig unverständlich; **it all makes ~ now** jetzt wird einem alles klar; **it doesn't make ~, the jewels were there a minute ago** das ist ganz unverständlich, die Juwelen waren doch eben noch da; **to make ~ of sth** etw verstehen, aus etw schlau werden *(inf)*; **you're not making ~** *(in explaining sth, in plans, intentions etc)* das ist doch Unsinn; *(in behaviour, attitude)* ich werde aus Ihnen nicht schlau *(inf)*; **now you're making ~** *(in explaining sth)* jetzt verstehe ich, was Sie meinen; *(in plans, intentions etc)* das ist endlich eine vernünftige Idee.
(g) *(meaning)* Sinn *m no pl* ◆ **in the full ~ of the word** im wahrsten Sinn des Wortes; **it has three distinct ~s** es hat drei verschiedene Bedeutungen; **in what ~ are you using the word?** in welchem Sinn *or* welcher Bedeutung gebrauchen Sie das Wort?; **he is an amateur in the best ~** er ist Amateur im eigentlichen Sinn des Wortes; **in every ~ of the word** in der vollen Bedeutung des Wortes.
(h) *(way, respect)* **in a ~** in gewisser Hinsicht, gewissermaßen; **in every ~** in jeder Hinsicht; **in what ~?** inwiefern?; **there is a ~ in which what he claims is true** in einer Hinsicht hat er mit seiner Behauptung recht.
[2] *vt* fühlen, spüren ◆ **I could ~ someone there in the dark** ich fühlte *or* spürte, daß da jemand in der Dunkelheit war.

sense datum *n* Sinnesdatum *nt*.

senseless ['senslɪs] *adj* **(a)** *(unconscious)* besinnungslos, bewußtlos ◆ **to knock sb ~** jdn bewußtlos schlagen. **(b)** *(stupid)* unvernünftig, unsinnig; *(futile) waste, discussion* sinnlos ◆ **what a ~ thing to do/say** *etc* welch ein Unsinn.

senselessly ['senslɪslɪ] *adv see adj (b)*.

senselessness ['senslɪsnɪs] *n see adj (b)* Unvernunft, Unsinnigkeit *f*; Sinnlosigkeit *f*.

sense organ *n* Sinnesorgan *nt*.

sensibility [ˌsensɪ'bɪlɪtɪ] *n (to beauty etc)* Empfindsamkeit *f*; *(artistic ~ also)* Sensibilität *f*; *(emotional ~, susceptibility to insult)* Empfindlichkeit, Sensibilität *f* ◆ **sensibilities** Zartgefühl *nt*; **the body's ~ to touch/cold** die Empfindlichkeit des Körpers für Berührungen/gegen(über) Kälte.

sensible ['sensəbl] *adj* **(a)** vernünftig ◆ **be ~ about it** seien Sie vernünftig; **that's the ~ thing to do** das ist vernünftig.
(b) *(liter: aware)* **to be ~ of sth** sich *(dat)* einer Sache *(gen)* bewußt sein; **he seems not to be ~ of the cold** er scheint gegen Kälte unempfindlich zu sein.
(c) *(rare: appreciable)* spürbar, merklich.

sensibleness ['sensəblnɪs] *n* Vernünftigkeit *f*.

sensibly ['sensəblɪ] *adv* vernünftig ◆ **he very ~ ignored the question** er hat die Frage vernünftigerweise ignoriert.

sensitive ['sensɪtɪv] *adj* **(a)** *(emotionally) person* sensibel, empfindsam; *(easily hurt)* empfindlich; *(understanding)* einfühlsam; *novel, film, remark* einfühlend ◆ **to be ~ about sth** in bezug auf etw *(acc)* empfindlich sein; **she is very ~ to criticism/the mention of that** sie reagiert sehr empfindlich auf Kritik/darauf, wenn das erwähnt wird.
(b) *(physically) instruments, part of body, leaves, plants* empfindlich; *(Phot) emulsion, film* lichtempfindlich; *(delicate) balance, adjustment* fein; *(fig) topic, issue* heikel, prekär ◆ **~ to heat/light** wärme-/lichtempfindlich; **he has access to some highly ~ information** er hat Zugang zu streng vertraulichen Informationen; **just how ~ are these figures?** inwiefern sind diese Zahlen als vertraulich zu behandeln?

sensitiveness ['sensɪtɪvnɪs], **sensitivity** [ˌsensɪ'tɪvɪtɪ] *n see adj* **(a)** Sensibilität, Empfindsamkeit *f*; Empfindlichkeit *f*; Einfühlsamkeit *f*; Einfühlungsvermögen *nt*. **(b)** Empfindlichkeit *f*; Lichtempfindlichkeit *f*; Feinheit *f*; heikle Natur ◆ **~ to heat/light** Wärme-/Lichtempfindlichkeit *f*.

sensitize ['sensɪtaɪz] *vt (Phot)* sensibilisieren.

sensor ['sensəʳ] *n* Sensor *m*; *(non-electronic also)* Fühler *m*.

sensorimotor ['sensərɪ'məʊtəʳ] *adj* sensomotorisch.

sensory ['sensərɪ] *adj* sensorisch; *data, organs* Sinnes-.

sensual ['sensjʊəl] *adj* sinnlich, wollüstig (*pej*); *person, life also* sinnesfreudig, lustbetont ◆ **~ moments** Augenblicke *pl* der Lust.

sensualism ['sensjʊəlɪzəm] *n* Sinnlichkeit, Wollüstigkeit (*pej*) *f*; (*Philos*) Sensualismus *m*.

sensualist ['sensjʊəlɪst] *n* Genußmensch, sinnlicher Mensch, Lüstling (*pej*) *m*; (*Philos*) Sensualist *m*.

sensuality [ˌsensjʊ'ælɪtɪ] *n* Sinnlichkeit, Wollüstigkeit (*pej*) *f*; (*of person also*) Sinnesfreudigkeit *f*.

sensually ['sensjʊəlɪ] *adv* sinnlich, wollüstig (*pej*).

sensuous *adj*, **~ly** *adv* ['sensjʊəs, -lɪ] sinnlich, sinnenhaft.

sensuousness ['sensjʊəsnɪs] *n* Sinnlichkeit, Sinnenhaftigkeit *f*.

sent [sent] [1] *pret, ptp of* **send**.
[2] *adj* (*inf*) *look* hingerissen (*inf*) ◆ **he's ~** er ist ganz weg (*inf*).

sentence ['sentəns] [1] *n* **(a)** (*Gram*) Satz *m* ◆ **~ structure** Satzbau *m*; (*of particular* ~) Satzaufbau *m*, Satzstruktur *f*.
(b) (*Jur*) Strafe *f* ◆ **to be under ~ of death** zum Tode verurteilt sein; **the judge gave him a 6-month ~** der Richter verurteilte ihn zu 6 Monaten Haft *or* Freiheitsentzug; **to pass ~ (on sb)** (über jdn) das Urteil verkünden; (*fig*) jdn verurteilen.
[2] *vt* (*Jur*) verurteilen ◆ **he was ~d to life imprisonment** er wurde zu lebenslänglichem Freiheitsentzug verurteilt.

sententious *adj*, **~ly** *adv* [sen'tenʃəs, -lɪ] salbungsvoll.

sententiousness [sen'tenʃəsnɪs] *n* **the ~ of the lecture/speaker** der salbungsvolle Vortrag/Redner; **..., he said with great ~** ..., sagte er salbungsvoll.

sentience ['sentɪəns] *n* Empfindungsvermögen *nt* ◆ **the ~ of approaching death** das Vorgefühl des nahenden Todes.

sentient ['sentɪənt] *adj* empfindungsfähig.

sentiment ['sentɪmənt] *n* **(a)** (*feeling, emotion*) Gefühl *nt*. **(b)** (*sentimentality*) Sentimentalität, Rührseligkeit *f*. **(c)** (*opinion*) Ansicht, Meinung *f* ◆ **my ~s exactly!** genau meine Ansicht *or* Meinung! **(d)** (*thought behind words or deeds*) Gedanke *m*.

sentimental [ˌsentɪ'mentl] *adj* sentimental; *person, mood also* gefühlvoll; *novel, song, music also* gefühlsselig, kitschig (*pej*), schmalzig (*pej*); *value* Gefühls- ◆ **for ~ reasons** aus Sentimentalität; **to make a ~ visit to a place** einem Ort aus Sentimentalität einen Besuch abstatten; **a certain ~ attachment** eine gewisse gefühlsmäßige Bindung.

sentimentalism [ˌsentɪ'mentəlɪzəm] *n* Sentimentalität *f*.

sentimentalist [ˌsentɪ'mentəlɪst] *n* Gefühlsmensch *m*, sentimentaler Mensch.

sentimentality [ˌsentɪmen'tælɪtɪ] *n* Sentimentalität *f*.

sentimentalize [ˌsentɪ'mentəlaɪz] [1] *vt* sentimental *or* gefühlvoll darstellen.
[2] *vi* sentimental sein.

sentimentally [ˌsentɪ'mentəlɪ] *adv important, attached etc* gefühlsmäßig; *say, reminisce* sentimental; *sing, play music* gefühlvoll; (*pej*) sentimental, kitschig, schmalzig.

sentinel ['sentɪnl] *n* Wache *f* ◆ **to stand ~ over sth** (*liter*) über etw (*acc*) wachen *or* Wacht halten.

sentry ['sentrɪ] *n* Wache *f*, Wachtposten *m* ◆ **to be on ~ duty** auf Wache sein; **~ box** Wachhäuschen *nt*.

sep *abbr of* **separate**.

sepal ['sepəl] *n* Kelchblatt *nt*.

separability [ˌseprə'bɪlɪtɪ] *n* Trennbarkeit *f*.

separable ['sepərəbl] *adj* trennbar.

separate ['seprət] [1] *adj* **(a)** getrennt, gesondert (*from* von); *section, piece also* extra *attr inv*; *organization, unit also* eigen *attr*; *two organizations, issues, parts* gesondert *attr*, voneinander getrennt, verschieden *attr*; *provisions, regulations* besondere(r, s) *attr*, separat, gesondert; *beds, rooms, accounts* getrennt; *account, bill, agreement, department* gesondert, extra *attr inv*; *entrance, toilet, flat* separat; *treaty, peace* Separat-, Sonder-; *existence* eigen *attr* ◆ **that is a ~ question/issue** das ist eine andere Frage, das ist eine Frage für sich; **on two ~ occasions** bei zwei verschiedenen Gelegenheiten; **on a ~ occasion** bei einer anderen Gelegenheit; **there will be ~ discussions on this question** diese Frage wird extra *or* separat *or* gesondert diskutiert; **they live ~ lives** sie gehen getrennte Wege; **a ~ sheet of paper** ein anderes Blatt Papier; (*additional*) ein gesondertes *or* extra Blatt Papier; **this is quite ~ from his job** das hat mit seinem Beruf nichts zu tun; **to keep two things ~** zwei Dinge nicht zusammentun; *questions, issues* zwei Dinge auseinanderhalten; **always keep your cheque book ~ from your banker's card** bewahren Sie Scheckbuch und Scheckkarte immer getrennt auf; **keep this book ~ from the others** halten Sie dieses Buch von den anderen getrennt.
(b) (*individual*) einzeln ◆ **all the ~ sections/pieces/units/questions** alle einzelnen Abschnitte/Teile/Einheiten/Fragen; **everybody has a ~ cup/task** jeder hat eine Tasse/Aufgabe für sich *or* seine eigene Tasse/Aufgabe.
[2] *n* **~s** *pl* Röcke, Blusen, Hosen *etc*.
[3] ['sepəreɪt] *vt* trennen; (*Chem also*) scheiden; (*milk*) entrahmen; (*divide up*) aufteilen (*into* in *+acc*) ◆ **to ~ the good from the bad** die Guten von den Schlechten trennen *or* scheiden; **he can't ~ his private life from his work** er kann Privatleben und Arbeit nicht (voneinander) trennen, er kann das Privatleben nicht von der Arbeit trennen; **he is ~d from his wife** er lebt von seiner Frau getrennt.
[4] ['sepəreɪt] *vi* sich trennen; (*Chem also*) sich scheiden ◆ **it ~s into four parts** es läßt sich in vier Teile auseinandernehmen; (*fig: problem etc*) es zerfällt in vier Teile.

◆**separate out** [1] *vt sep* trennen (*from* von), absondern (*from* von), aussondern.
[2] *vi* getrennt werden.

separated ['sepəreɪtɪd] *adj* getrennt; *couple* getrennt lebend *attr* ◆ **the couple are ~** das Paar lebt getrennt.

separately ['seprətlɪ] *adv* getrennt, gesondert, separat; *live* getrennt; (*singly*) einzeln.

separateness ['seprətnɪs] *n* Getrenntheit, Gesondertheit *f*.

separation [ˌsepə'reɪʃən] *n* Trennung *f*; (*Chem also*) Scheidung *f*; (*of rocket etc*) Abtrennung *f* (*from* von).

separation allowance *n* Trennungsentschädigung *f*.

separatism ['sepərətɪzəm] *n* Separatismus *m*.

separatist ['sepərətɪst] [1] *adj* separatistisch.
[2] *n* Separatist(in *f*) *m*.

separator ['sepəreɪtəʳ] *n* Separator *m*.

sepia ['si:pjə] [1] *n* Sepia *f*.
[2] *adj paint, pigment, drawing* Sepia-; (*also* **~-coloured**) sepia(farben).

sepoy ['si:pɔɪ] *n* Sepoy *m*.

sepsis ['sepsɪs] *n* Vereiterung, Sepsis (*spec*) *f*.

Sept *abbr of* **September** Sept.

September [sep'tembəʳ] [1] *n* September *m* ◆ **the first/tenth of ~** der erste/zehnte September; **on ~ 1st/19th** (*written*), **on 1st/19th ~** (*written*), **on the 1st/19th of ~** (*spoken*) am 1./19. September; **~ 3rd, 1990, 3rd ~ 1990** (*on letter*) 3. September 1990; **in ~** im September; **during ~** im September; **every** *or* **each ~** jeden September; **at the beginning/end of ~** Anfang/Ende September; **~ is a pleasant month** der September ist ein angenehmer Monat; **there are 30 days in ~** der September hat 30 Tage.
[2] *adj attr* September-; *weather, mists etc also* septemberlich.

septennial [sep'tenɪəl] *adj* siebenjährig; (*every seven years*) alle sieben Jahre stattfindend, siebenjährlich.

septet [sep'tet] *n* Septett *nt*.

septic ['septɪk] *adj* vereitert, septisch ◆ **the wound turned ~** die Wunde eiterte; **~ tank** Faulbehälter, Klärbehälter *m*.

septicaemia, (*US*) **septicemia** [ˌseptɪ'si:mɪə] *n* Vergiftung *f* des Blutes, Septikämie *f* (*spec*).

septuagenarian [ˌseptjʊədʒɪ'nɛərɪən] [1] *adj* siebzigjährig.
[2] *n* Siebzigjährige(r) *mf* ◆ **to be a ~** ein(e) Siebziger(in) sein.

Septuagesima [ˌseptjʊə'dʒesɪmə] *n* Sonntag *m* Septuagesima.

septuplet [sep'tju:plɪt] *n* (*baby*) Siebenling *m*; (*Mus*) Septimole *f*.

sepulcher *n* (*US*) *see* **sepulchre**.

sepulchral [sɪ'pʌlkrəl] *adj* (*liter*) sepulkral (*liter*); (*fig*) düster; *voice* Grabes-; *atmosphere* Friedhofs-.

sepulchre, (*US*) **sepulcher** ['sepəlkəʳ] *n* Grabstätte *f* ◆ **the Holy S~** das Heilige Grab; *see* **whited ~**.

sequel ['si:kwəl] *n* Folge *f* (*to* von); (*of book, film*) Fortsetzung *f* (*to* von) ◆ **it had a tragic ~** es hatte ein tragisches Nachspiel.

sequence ['si:kwəns] *n* **(a)** (*order*) Folge, Reihenfolge *f* ◆ **~ of tenses/words** Zeiten-/Wortfolge *f*; **in ~** der Reihe nach; **to do sth in logical ~** etw in der logisch richtigen Reihenfolge tun. **(b)** (*things following*) Reihe, Folge *f*; (*Mus, Cards, Eccl*) Sequenz *f*; (*Math*) Reihe *f*. **(c)** (*Film, dance* ~) Sequenz *f*.

sequencer ['si:kwənsəʳ] *n* (*Comput*) Ablaufsteuerung *f*.

sequential [sɪ'kwenʃəl] *adj* (*form*) der Reihe nach, in regelmäßiger Folge; (*following*) folgend; (*Comput*) sequentiell ◆ **to be ~ to** *or* **upon sth** auf etw (*acc*) folgen.

sequester [sɪ'kwestəʳ] *vt* **(a)** (*liter: isolate*) abkapseln. **(b)** (*Jur*) *see* **sequestrate**.

sequestered [sɪ'kwestəd] *adj* (*liter*) *village* abgeschieden; *spot* abgelegen; *life* zurückgezogen.

sequestrate [sɪ'kwestreɪt] *vt* (*Jur*) sequestrieren.

sequestration [ˌsi:kwe'streɪʃən] *n* (*Jur*) Sequestration *f*; (*in bankruptcy case also*) Zwangsverwaltung *f*.

sequin ['si:kwɪn] *n* Paillette *f*.

sequined ['si:kwɪnd] *adj* mit Pailletten besetzt.

sequoia [sɪ'kwɔɪə] *n* Mammutbaum *m*, Sequoie *f*.

seraglio [se'rɑ:lɪəʊ] *n* Serail *nt*.

seraph ['serəf] *n, pl* **-s** *or* **-im** Seraph *m*.

seraphic [sə'ræfɪk] *adj* verklärt, verzückt.

seraphim ['serəfɪm] *pl of* **seraph**.

Serb [sɜ:b] *n* Serbe *m*, Serbin *f*.

Serbia ['sɜ:bɪə] *n* Serbien *nt*.

Serbian ['sɜ:bɪən] [1] *adj* serbisch.
[2] *n* **(a)** Serbe *m*, Serbin *f*. **(b)** (*language*) Serbisch *nt*.

Serbo-Croat ['sɜ:bəʊ'krəʊæt] *n* (*language*) Serbokroatisch *nt* ◆ **the ~s** *pl* (*people*) die Serben und Kroaten.

Serbo-Croatian ['sɜ:bəʊkrəʊ'eɪʃən] [1] *adj* serbokroatisch.
[2] *n* **the ~s** *pl* die Serben und Kroaten.

serenade [ˌserə'neɪd] [1] *n* Serenade *f*.
[2] *vt* ein Ständchen *nt* bringen (*+dat*).

serendipity [ˌserən'dɪpɪtɪ] *n* Spürsinn *m* (*fig*), mehr Glück als Verstand.

serene [sə'ri:n] *adj* gelassen; *sea* ruhig; *sky* heiter, klar ◆ **His S~ Highness** seine Durchlaucht, Serenissimus.

serenely [sə'ri:nlɪ] *adv* gelassen ◆ **~ indifferent to the noise** gleichmütig dem Lärm gegenüber.

serenity [sɪ'renɪtɪ] *n* Gelassenheit *f*; (*as title: also* **S~**) Durchlaucht *f*.

serf [sɜːf] *n* Leibeigene(r) *mf.*
serfdom ['sɜːfdəm] *n* Leibeigenschaft *f*; (*fig*) Knechtschaft *f.*
serge [sɜːdʒ] *n* Serge, Sersche *f.*
sergeant ['sɑːdʒənt] *n* (*Mil*) Feldwebel *m*; (*police*) Polizeimeister *m* ◆ **~ at arms** (*Hist*) Waffenmeister *m*; (*Brit Parl*) Exekutivbeamte(r) *m* des Parlaments; **~ first class** (*US*) Oberfeldwebel *m*; **~ major** Oberfeldwebel *m.*
serg(t) *abbr of* **sergeant.**
serial ['sɪərɪəl] 1 *adj* Serien-; *novel* Fortsetzungs-; *story, radio etc programme etc* in Fortsetzungen; *writer* von Fortsetzungsromanen; *music* seriell; (*Comput*) *printer, interface, port* seriell ◆ **published in ~ form** in Fortsetzungen veröffentlicht; **~ number** fortlaufende Nummer; (*on manufactured goods*) Fabrikationsnummer *f*; **~ rights** Rechte *pl* für die Veröffentlichung in Fortsetzungen.
2 *n* (*novel*) Fortsetzungsroman *m*; (*Rad*) Sendereihe *f* (in Fortsetzungen); (*TV*) Serie *f*; (*spec: magazine*) (periodisch erscheinende) Zeitschrift ◆ **it was published/broadcast as a ~** es wurde in Fortsetzungen veröffentlicht/gesendet.
serialization [ˌsɪərɪəlaɪ'zeɪʃən] *n* (*Rad, TV*), Sendung *f* in Fortsetzungen; (*in magazines etc*) Fortsetzung(sreihe) *f*; (*serializing*) Umarbeitung *f* in Fortsetzungen.
serialize ['sɪərɪəlaɪz] *vt* in Fortsetzungen veröffentlichen; (*Rad, TV*) in Fortsetzungen senden; (*put into serial form*) in Fortsetzungen umarbeiten.
serially ['sɪərɪəlɪ] *adv publish, broadcast* in Fortsetzungen; (*in order*) *number* fortlaufend; (*Mus, Comput*) seriell.
serial port *n* (*Comput*) serielle Schnittstelle.
seriatim [ˌsɪərɪ'eɪtɪm] *adv* (*form*) der Reihe nach.
sericulture [ˌserɪ'kʌltʃə^r] *n* Seidenraupenzucht *f.*
series ['sɪərɪz] *n, pl* - Serie *f*; (*Rad*) Sendereihe *f*; (*TV*) Serie *f*; (*of books, lectures etc also, of films, talks, Math, Mus, Elec*) Reihe *f*; (*of events also, succession of things*) Reihe, Folge *f* ◆ **a ~ of articles** eine Artikelserie *or* -reihe; **a ~ of visitors** eine Besucherserie; **in ~** der Reihe nach; (*Elec*) in Reihe; (*Comm*) serienmäßig; *publish* als Serie.
series-wound ['sɪəriːzˌwaʊnd] *adj* (*Elec*) in Serie *or* Reihe geschaltet.
serif ['serɪf] 1 *n* Serife *f.*
2 *adj* Serifen-.
serio-comic(al) ['sɪərɪəʊ'kɒmɪk(l)] *adj* halb ernst, halb heiter.
serious ['sɪərɪəs] *adj* **(a)** ernst; *person, manner* (*not frivolous*) ernsthaft; (*subdued*) ernst; *consideration, discussion, conversation also* ernsthaft; *newspaper, publication, interest* ernsthaft, seriös; *offer, suggestion* ernstgemeint *attr*, ernst gemeint *pred*, seriös; *doubts also* ernstlich, ernsthaft ◆ **to be ~ about doing sth** etw im Ernst tun wollen; **I'm ~ (about it)** ich meine das ernst, das ist mein Ernst; **he is ~ about her** er meint es ernst mit ihr; **be ~ about your studies** du mußt dein Studium ernst nehmen; **you can't be ~!** das meinst du doch nicht ernst!, das kann nicht dein Ernst sein!; **to give ~ thought to sth** sich (*dat*) etw ernsthaft *or* ernstlich überlegen; **the ~ student of jazz will** ... wer sich ernsthaft mit Jazz beschäftigt, wird ...
(b) (*critical*) *accident, flooding, deficiencies, loss* schwer; *mistake, injury, damage also* schlimm; *problem also* ernst, ernstzunehmend *attr*; *illness also, situation* ernst, schlimm; *patient's condition* ernst, bedenklich; *threat, shortage, lack* ernst, ernstlich; *situation, deterioration* bedenklich ◆ **it's ~** das ist schlimm; **it's getting ~** es wird ernst; **inflation is getting ~** die Inflation nimmt ernste Ausmaße an.
➤ **seriously** ['sɪərɪəslɪ] *adv* **(a)** ernst; *talk, interested, work* ernsthaft; (*not jokingly*) im Ernst ◆ **to take sb/sth ~** jdn/etw ernst nehmen; **do you ~ want to do that?** wollen Sie das wirklich *or* im Ernst tun?; **~ now/though** ... jetzt/aber mal ganz im Ernst ...; **do you mean that ~?** meinen Sie das ernst?, ist das Ihr Ernst?; **he offered it quite ~** er hat das ernstlich angeboten.
(b) *wounded, flooded* schwer; *ill also, worried* ernstlich; *damaged, injured also* schlimm; *deteriorate* bedenklich ◆ **he/the take-off went ~ wrong** er hat einen schweren Fehler gemacht/beim Start ist etwas schlimm daneben gegangen; **we are ~ short of water** bei uns herrscht schwerer *or* schlimmer Wassermangel.
seriousness ['sɪərɪəsnɪs] *n see adj* **(a)** Ernst *m*; Ernsthaftigkeit *f*; Seriosität *f*; Ernstlichkeit *f* ◆ **in all ~** ganz im Ernst. **(b)** Schwere *f*; Ernst *m*; Bedenklichkeit *f.*
serjeant ['sɑːdʒənt] *n see* **sergeant.**
sermon ['sɜːmən] *n* (*Eccl*) Predigt *f*; (*homily*) Moralpredigt *f*; (*scolding*) Strafpredigt *f* ◆ **the S~ on the Mount** die Bergpredigt.
sermonize ['sɜːmənaɪz] *vi* Vorträge halten; (*reproving*) Moralpredigten halten.
serous ['sɪərəs] *adj* serös; *fluid* Serum-.
serpent ['sɜːpənt] *n* **(a)** (*liter*) Schlange *f* (*also fig*). **(b)** (*Mus*) Serpent *nt.*
serpentine ['sɜːpəntaɪn] *adj lane, river* gewunden, mit vielen Windungen; *road also* kurvenreich.
Serps [sɜːps] *n* (*Brit*) *abbr of* **state earnings-related pension scheme** *staatliche Rentenversicherung.*
serrated [se'reɪtɪd] *adj* gezackt; *leaves also* gesägt ◆ **~ knife** Sägemesser *nt.*
serration [se'reɪʃən] *n* Zacke *f*; (*edge*) gezackter Rand; (*on knife*) Sägerand *m*; (*of leaves*) gesägter Rand.
serried ['serɪd] *adj*: **~ ranks** enggeschlossene Reihen *pl.*
serum ['sɪərəm] *n* Serum *nt.*
servant ['sɜːvənt] *n* (*lit, fig*) Diener(in *f*) *m*; (*also* **~ girl**) Dienstmädchen *nt*; (*domestic*) Bedienstete(r) *mf*, Dienstbote *m* ◆ **to keep** *or* **have ~s** Bedienstete *or* Diener haben; **~s' quarters** Gesinderäume (*Hist*), Dienstbotenräume *pl*; **your devoted** *or* **humble** *or* **obedient ~** (*old*) Ihr ergebenster *or* untertänigster Diener (*old*); *see* **public ~, civil ~.**
serve [sɜːv] 1 *vt* **(a)** dienen (+*dat*); (*be of use*) dienlich sein (+*dat*), nützen (+*dat*) ◆ **he ~d his country/the firm well** er hat sich um sein Land/die Firma verdient gemacht; **he has ~d our cause faithfully** er hat sich um unsere Sache verdient gemacht, er hat unserer Sache treue Dienste geleistet; **if my memory ~s me right** wenn ich mich recht erinnere; **to ~ its/sb's purpose** seinen Zweck erfüllen/jds Zwecken (*dat*) dienen; **it ~s a variety of purposes** es hat viele verschiedene Verwendungsmöglichkeiten; **it ~s no useful purpose** es hat keinen praktischen Wert; **that will ~ my needs** das ist genau (das), was ich brauche; **this box has ~d us as a table** diese Kiste hat uns (*dat*) als Tisch gedient; **it has ~d us well** es hat uns gute Dienste geleistet; **his knowledge of history ~d him well** seine Geschichtskenntnisse kamen ihm sehr zugute.
(b) (*work out*) abdienen, ableisten; *term of office* durchlaufen; *apprenticeship* durchmachen; *sentence* verbüßen, absitzen (*inf*) ◆ **when he ~d his term as Prime Minister** während seiner Amtszeit als Premierminister.
(c) (*supply: transport, gas etc*) versorgen.
(d) (*in shop*) bedienen ◆ **to ~ sb with 5 kilos of potatoes** jdm 5 kg Kartoffeln bringen *or* geben; **I'm being ~d, thank you** danke, ich werde schon bedient *or* ich bekomme schon (*inf*).
(e) (*esp in restaurant*) *food, drink* servieren; (*bring to table also*) auftragen; (*put on plate*) aufgeben; *guests* bedienen; (*waiter*) bedienen, servieren (+*dat*); (*pour drink for*) einschenken (+*dat*); *wine etc* einschenken; *rations* verteilen (*to* an +*acc*) ◆ **dinner is ~d** (*butler*) das Essen *or* es ist aufgetragen; (*hostess*) darf ich zu Tisch bitten?; **"~s three"** (*on packet etc*) „(ergibt) drei Portionen".
(f) *Mass, Communion* ministrieren bei.
(g) (*Tennis etc*) *ball* aufschlagen ◆ **he ~d a double fault** er hat einen Doppelfehler gemacht.
(h) (*Jur*) zustellen (*on sb* jdm) ◆ **to ~ a summons on sb, to ~ sb with a summons** jdn vor Gericht laden; **the landlord ~d notice (to quit) on his tenants** der Vermieter kündigte den Mietern.
(i) (*old: treat*) behandeln ◆ **to ~ sb ill** jdm einen schlechten Dienst erweisen, jdm übel mitspielen; **(it) ~s you right!** (*inf*) das geschieht dir (ganz) recht!; **it ~s him right for being so greedy** (*inf*) das geschieht ihm ganz recht, was muß er auch so gierig sein!; **it would have ~d you right if** ... (*inf*) es wäre dir ganz recht geschehen, wenn ...
(j) (*stallion etc*) decken.
2 *vi* **(a)** dienen ◆ **to ~ on the jury** Geschworene(r) *mf* sein; **to ~ on a committee/the council** einem Ausschuß angehören/im Stadt- *or* Gemeinderat sein; **to ~ as chairman** das Amt des Vorsitzenden innehaben *or* bekleiden (*form*).
(b) (*Mil*) dienen.
(c) (*at table*) aufgeben; (*waiter, butler etc*) servieren (*at table* bei Tisch) ◆ **is there anyone serving at this table?** bedient hier jemand?
(d) to ~ as, to ~ for dienen als; **it will ~** das tut's; **it ~s to show/explain** ... das zeigt/erklärt ...; **these facts merely ~ to prove my point** diese Fakten dienen lediglich dazu, mein Argument zu beweisen; **when the occasion ~s** wenn es gerade paßt.
(e) (*Eccl*) ministrieren.
(f) (*Tennis etc*) aufschlagen.
3 *n* (*Tennis etc*) Aufschlag *m* ◆ **whose ~ is it?** wer hat Aufschlag?
◆**serve out** *vt sep* **(a)** *food* ausgeben; *rations etc* vergeben, verteilen. **(b)** (*work out*) *time in army* ableisten; *apprenticeship* beenden, abschließen; *sentence* absitzen.
◆**serve up** *vt sep* **(a)** *food* servieren; *rations* verteilen ◆ **you can't ~ this muck ~** (*inf*) so etwas kann man doch niemandem vorsetzen! **(b)** (*inf: present*) servieren (*inf*); *excuse* auftischen.
server ['sɜːvə^r] *n* **(a)** (*tray*) Servierbrett *nt.* **(b)** (*spoon, fork*) Servierlöffel, Vorlegelöffel *m*/-gabel *f*; (*pie ~*) Tortenheber *m*; (*fish ~*) Fischvorlegelöffel *m* ◆ **a pair of ~s** ein Vorlegebesteck *nt*; **salad ~s** Salatbesteck *nt.* **(c)** (*Tennis*) Aufschläger(in *f*) *m* ◆ **he's a strong ~** er hat einen guten Aufschlag. **(d)** (*Eccl*) Ministrant, Meßdiener *m.*
service ['sɜːvɪs] 1 *n* **(a)** Dienst *m* ◆ **his faithful ~** seine treuen Dienste; **~s to God** Dienst an Gott; **~s to one's country/the Queen** (*soldier etc*) Dienst an seinem Vaterland/für die Königin; **his ~s to industry/the country** (*politician, industrialist*) seine Verdienste in der Industrie/um das Land; **he died in the ~ of his country** er starb in Pflichterfüllung für sein Vaterland; **he has ten years' ~ behind him** er hat zehn Jahre Dienstzeit hinter sich (*dat*); **to do sb a ~** jdm einen Dienst erweisen; **to do** *or* **see good ~** gute Dienste leisten; **this box did ~ as a table** diese Kiste hat schon als Tisch gedient; **to be of ~** nützlich sein; **to be of ~ to sb** jdm nützen; **it's of no ~ in an emergency** im Notfall nützt es nichts; **to be at sb's ~** jdm zur Verfügung stehen; (*person also*) jdm zu Diensten stehen; **can I be of ~ to you?** kann ich Ihnen behilflich sein?; **out of ~** außer Betrieb; **to need the ~s of a doctor/lawyer** einen Arzt/Anwalt brauchen, einen Arzt/Anwalt zuziehen müssen; **on Her/His Majesty's S~** (*abbr* **OHMS**) *Aufdruck auf Dienstsachen, Umschlägen von Behörden etc*; ≃ Dienstsache *f.*
(b) (*operation*) Betrieb *m* ◆ **to be out of ~** außer Betrieb sein; **to bring sth into ~** etw in Betrieb nehmen; **to come into ~** in Betrieb genommen werden.
(c) (*Mil*) Militärdienst *m* ◆ **to see ~ as a soldier/sailor** beim Militär/in der Marine dienen; **when I was in the ~s** als ich beim Militär war; **the three ~s** die drei Waffengattungen.
(d) (*with adj attr: branch, department etc*) -dienst *m* ◆ **telephone ~** Telefondienst *m*; **postal ~** Postwesen *nt*, Postdienst *m*; **medical ~(s)** ärztliche Versorgung.

➤ LANGUAGE IN USE: **seriously: a** → 12.2, 26.1

(e) (*to customers*) Service *m*; (*in shop, restaurant etc*) Bedienung *f*.
(f) (*bus, train, plane etc*) Bus-/Zug-/Flugverbindung *f* ♦ **to increase ~s in rural areas** den Verkehr *or* die Verkehrslage in ländlichen Gebieten verbessern; **there's no ~ to Oban on Sundays** sonntags besteht kein Zug-/Busverkehr nach Oban; **the number 12 (bus)** ~ die Linie 12.
(g) (*domestic* ~) Dienst *m*, Stellung *f* ♦ **to be in ~ (with sb)** (bei jdm) in Stellung sein, in jds Dienst (*dat*) stehen; **to go into ~ (with sb)** (bei jdm) in Stellung gehen, in jds Dienst (*acc*) treten.
(h) (*Eccl*) Gottesdienst *m*.
(i) (*of machines*) Wartung *f*; (*Aut: major* ~) Inspektion *f* ♦ **my car is in for/has had a ~** mein Auto wird/wurde gewartet; mein Auto ist/war zur *or* bei der Inspektion.
(j) (*tea or coffee set*) Service *nt*.
(k) (*Tennis*) Aufschlag *m* ♦ **to lose one's ~** seinen Aufschlag abgeben; **whose ~ is it?** wer hat Aufschlag?
(l) (*Jur*) Zustellung *f*.
(m) **~s** *pl* (*commercial*) Dienstleistungen *pl*; (*gas, electricity, water*) Versorgungsnetz *nt* ♦ **all the ~s have been cut off** Gas, Wasser und Strom sind abgestellt worden; **the house is close to all ~s** das Haus ist in günstiger Lage.
(n) (*Mot*) **~s** *pl* Tankstelle und Raststätte (+*pl vb*).
[2] *vt* **(a)** *car, machine* warten ♦ **to send a car to be ~d** ein Auto warten lassen; (*major* ~) ein Auto zur Inspektion geben.
(b) *area* bedienen; *committee etc* zuarbeiten (+*dat*).
(c) *cow, mare* decken.
(d) (*Fin*) *loan, debt* bedienen.

serviceability [ˌsɜːvɪsəˈbɪlɪtɪ] *n see adj* Strapazierfähigkeit *f*; Zweckmäßigkeit *f*; Brauchbarkeit *f*.

serviceable [ˈsɜːvɪsəbl] *adj* (*durable*) strapazierfähig; (*practical*) praktisch, zweckmäßig; (*usable*) brauchbar.

service: **~ area** *n* Tankstelle und Raststätte (+*pl vb*); **~ bus** *n* Linienbus *m*; **~ charge** *n* Bedienung(sgeld *nt*) *f*; (*of bank*) Bearbeitungsgebühr *f*; **~ court** *n* (*Tennis etc*) Aufschlagfeld *nt*; **~ department** *n* Kundendienst(abteilung *f*) *m*; **~ dress** *n* Dienstkleidung *f*; **~ elevator** *n* (*esp US*) Lasten- *or* Warenaufzug *m*; **~ engineer** *n* Servicemechaniker *m*; **~ entrance** *n* Dienstboteneingang *m*; **~ family** *n* Familie *f* von Militärpersonal; **~ flat** *n* (*Brit*) Appartement *nt* mit vollem Service (*Portier, Hausmeister etc*); **~ game** *n* Aufschlagspiel *nt*; **~ hatch** *n* Durchreiche *f*; **~ industry** *n* Dienstleistungsbranche *f*; **~ lift** *n* (*Brit*) Lasten- *or* Warenaufzug *m*; **~ line** *n* (*Tennis etc*) Aufschlaglinie *f*; **~man** *n* Militärangehörige(r) *m*; **~ module** *n* (*Space*) Versorgungsteil *nt*; **~ road** *n* (*for access*) Zufahrtsstraße *f*; (*for works traffic*) Versorgungsstraße *f*; (*for delivery*) Andienungsstraße *f*; **~ sector** *n* (*of economy*) Dienstleistungssektor *m*; **~ station** *n* Tankstelle *f* (mit Reparaturwerkstatt); **~woman** *n* Militärangehörige *f*.

serviette [ˌsɜːvɪˈet] *n* Serviette *f* ♦ **~ ring** Serviettenring *m*.

servile [ˈsɜːvaɪl] *adj* unterwürfig; *obedience* sklavisch.

servility [sɜːˈvɪlɪtɪ] *n* Unterwürfigkeit *f*.

serving [ˈsɜːvɪŋ] *n* (*helping of food*) Portion *f* ♦ **~ dish** Servierplatte *f*; **~ hatch** Durchreiche *f*; **~ spoon** Vorlegelöffel *m*.

servitude [ˈsɜːvɪtjuːd] *n* Knechtschaft *f*.

servo [ˈsɜːvəʊ] [1] *n* (*inf*) Servomechanismus *m*.
[2] *adj attr* Servo- ♦ **~-assisted brakes** Servobremsen *pl*; **~mechanism** Servomechanismus *m*.

sesame [ˈsesəmɪ] *n* **(a)** (*Bot*) Sesam *m* ♦ **~ oil** Sesamöl *nt*; **~ seeds** Sesamkörner *pl*; **~ seed roll** Sesambrötchen *nt*. **(b)** **open ~!** Sesam, öffne dich!; **an open ~** (*fig*) ein Sesam-öffne-dich *nt*.

sessile [ˈsesaɪl] *adj* (*Bot*) festgewachsen, sessil (*spec*).

session [ˈseʃən] *n* **(a)** (*meeting*) Sitzung *f*; (*Jur, Parl: period*) Sitzungsperiode *f*; (*Parl: term of office*) Legislaturperiode *f* ♦ **to be in ~** eine Sitzung abhalten; (*Jur, Pol*) tagen; **to go into secret ~** eine Geheimsitzung abhalten; **a ~ of talks/negotiations** Gespräche *pl*/Verhandlungen *pl*; *see* **quarter ~s, court.**
(b) (*with psychiatrist etc, period devoted to activity*) Sitzung *f*; (*at doctor's, dentist's*) Behandlung *f*; (*discussion, meeting*) Besprechung *f* ♦ **recording ~** Aufnahme *f*; **we're in for a long ~** das wird lange dauern; **I'll have a cleaning ~ tomorrow** (*inf*) morgen werde ich mal ausgiebig putzen (*inf*); **to have a ~ with one's girlfriend** (*inf*) mit seiner Freundin zusammensein.
(c) (*academic year*) (*Univ*) Studienjahr *nt*; (*Sch*) Schuljahr *nt*; (*term*) Semester/Trimester *nt*; (*esp Sch*) Halbjahr *nt*; (*division of course*) Stunde, Sitzung (*esp Univ*) *f* ♦ **the afternoon ~s begin ...** der Nachmittagsunterricht fängt ... an.

sestet [sesˈtet] *n* (*Mus*) Sextett *nt*; (*Poet*) Sestine *f*.

▼ **set** [set] (*vb: pret, ptp* ~) [1] *n* **(a)** Satz *m*; (*of two*) Paar *nt*; (*of underwear, cutlery, furniture, hairbrushes etc*) Garnitur *f*; (*tea-~ etc*) Service *nt*; (*of tablemats etc*) Set *nt*; (*chess or draughts ~ etc, of knitting needles*) Spiel *nt*; (*chemistry ~ etc*) Bastelkasten *m*; (*painting* ~) Malkasten *m*; (*Meccano* ®, *construction* ~) Baukasten *m*; (*of books*) (*on one subject*) Reihe, Serie *f*; (*by one author*) gesammelte Ausgabe; (*gift or presentation* ~) Kassette *f*; (*of rooms*) Zimmerflucht *f* ♦ **a ~ of tools** Werkzeug *nt*; **a ~ of teeth** ein Gebiß *nt*; **a complete ~ of Dickens' novels/the "Times" for 1972** eine Gesamtausgabe von Dickens/eine vollständige Sammlung der „Times" von 1972.
(b) (*batch, large number*) Reihe *f* ♦ **he had a whole ~ of questions** er hatte eine ganze Menge *or* Reihe Fragen; **a strange ~ of morals/ideas** eigenartige Moralanschauungen/Ideen.
(c) (*group of people*) Kreis *m*; (*pej*) Bande *f*; (*Brit Sch: stream*) Kurs *m* ♦ **the literary ~** die Literaten *pl*; **the golfing ~** die Golffreunde *pl*; **that ~ of people** dieser Personenkreis; **a nice ~ of people** nette Leute *pl*.
(d) (*Tennis*) Satz *m*; (*Table-tennis*) Spiel *nt* ♦ **~ point** Set- *or* Satzpunkt *m*.
(e) (*Math*) Reihe *f*; (*in set theory*) Menge *f*.
▼ **(f)** (*performance of songs, poems*) Programmnummer *f*.
(g) (*Telec, Rad, TV*) Gerät *nt*, Apparat *m*; (*head*~) Paar *nt* ♦ **~ of headphones** Kopfhörer *m*.
(h) (*Dancing*) Gruppe *f* ♦ **to make up a ~** eine Gruppe bilden; **they then move up the ~** sie rücken (in der Gruppe) auf.
(i) (*Hunt*) Vorstehen *nt* ♦ **to make a dead ~ at sb** (*dated: try to attract*) sich an jdn ranmachen (*inf*); **to make a dead ~ for sb** (*head for*) sich auf jdn stürzen, auf jdn losstürzen.
▼ **(j)** (*fit of garment*) Sitz *m*; (*position of head, shoulders etc*) Haltung *f*; (*of wind*) Richtung *f* ♦ **the ~ of sb's mouth** jds Mundstellung *f*.
(k) (*hair*~) Frisur, Form *f* ♦ **to have a (shampoo and) ~** sich (*dat*) die Haare (waschen und) legen lassen.
(l) (*Theat*) Bühnenbild *nt*; (*Film*) Szenenaufbau *m* ♦ **to be on the ~** bei den Dreharbeiten sein.
(m) (*US*) *see* **sett**.
[2] *adj* **(a)** *pred* (*ready*) fertig, bereit ♦ **all ~?** alles klar?; **are we all ~?** sind wir alle startklar?; **to be all ~ for sth** für etw gerüstet *or* auf etw (*acc*) vorbereitet sein; (*mentally prepared*) auf etw (*acc*) eingestellt sein; **to be all ~ to do sth** (*have made all the arrangements*) sich darauf eingerichtet haben, etw zu tun; (*mentally prepared*) fest entschlossen *or* drauf und dran sein, etw zu tun; **we're all ~ to go** wir sind soweit *or* startklar; **with their cameras all ~** mit schußbereiter Kamera.
(b) (*rigid*) starr; *face also* unbeweglich; *expression* feststehend; *forms also* fest; *habit, custom* fest; (*prescribed*) festgesetzt, fest; *task* bestimmt; *essay topic* vorgegeben, bestimmt; (*pre-arranged*) *time, place* festgesetzt, bestimmt, ausgemacht (*inf*) ♦ **~ book(s)** Pflichtlektüre *f*; **~ menu** Tageskarte *f*; **~ lunch/meal** Tagesgericht *nt*; **~ speech** Standardrede *f*; **~ phrase** feststehender Ausdruck; **~ piece** Standardstück *nt*; (*for exam etc*) Pflichtstück *nt*; (*fireworks*) Feuerwerksstück *nt*; (*attached to frame*) (Feuerwerks)bild *nt*; **one of my ~ tasks is ...** eine der mir übertragenen Aufgaben ist es, ...; **~ hours for studying** feste Zeiten zum Lernen; **his ~ purpose was to ...** er war fest entschlossen, zu ...; **to be ~ in one's ways** in seinen Gewohnheiten festgefahren sein.
(c) (*resolved*) entschlossen ♦ **to be (dead) ~ on sth/doing sth** etw auf Biegen oder Brechen haben/tun wollen; **to be (dead) ~ against sth/doing sth/sb doing sth** (absolut) gegen etw sein/etw (absolut) nicht tun wollen/(absolut) dagegen sein, daß jd etw tut; **she is far too ~ on getting her own way** sie will immer nur ihren eigenen Kopf durchsetzen.
[3] *vt* **(a)** (*put, place*) stellen; (*on its side, flat*) legen; (*deliberately, carefully*) setzen ♦ **to ~ the chairs by the window** die Stühle ans Fenster setzen *or* stellen; **he ~ the stones carefully on top of each other** er setzte *or* legte die Steine vorsichtig aufeinander; **to ~ the child in his chair/on his feet** das Kind in sein Stühlchen setzen/auf die Beine stellen; **to ~ a plan before a committee** einem Ausschuß einen Plan vorlegen; **I ~ him on his way** (*lit*) ich schickte ihn los; (*fig*) ich habe ihm zu einem guten Anfang verholfen; **I ~ him/his books above all others** ich schätze ihn/seine Bücher höher ein als alle anderen.
(b) (*regulate, adjust*) einstellen (*at* auf +*acc*); *clock* stellen (*by* nach, *to* auf +*acc*); (*fix*) *trap, snare* aufstellen; (*fig*) stellen (*for sb* jdm) ♦ **to be ~ fair** (*barometer*) auf „schön" stehen; (*weather*) beständig *or* freundlich sein; **everything is ~ fair for sth** nichts steht einer Sache (*dat*) im Wege.
(c) (*prescribe, impose*) *target, limit etc* festsetzen, festlegen; *task, question* stellen (*sb* jdm); *homework* aufgeben; *exam, exam questions* zusammenstellen; *book for exam* vorschreiben; (*arrange*) *time, date* festsetzen, ausmachen (*inf*), anberaumen (*form*); *place* bestimmen, ausmachen (*inf*); (*establish*) *record* aufstellen; *fashion* bestimmen ♦ **Hamlet is not ~ this year** Hamlet steht dieses Jahr nicht auf dem Lehrplan; **he was ~ a target** ihm wurde ein Soll vorgeschrieben; **England was ~ then 75 to win** (*Sport*) England brauchte 75 (Punkte), um zu gewinnen; **to ~ the date (of the wedding)** die Hochzeit festsetzen; **to ~ a value/price on sth** einen Wert/Preis für etw festsetzen; **to ~ a high value on sth** einer Sache (*dat*) großen Wert beimessen, etw hoch bewerten; **to ~ sb a problem** (*lit*) jdm ein Problem aufgeben; (*fig*) jdn vor ein Problem stellen; **the attack was ~ for midnight** der Angriff war für Mitternacht geplant.
(d) (*mount*) *gem* fassen (*in* in +*dat*); *piece of jewellery* besetzen (*with* mit); *windowpane* einsetzen (*in* in +*acc*); (*embed firmly*) einlegen (*in* in +*acc*); (*in ground*) einlassen (*in* in +*acc*) ♦ **to ~ stones in concrete** Steine einzementieren.
▼ **(e)** *usu pass* **to be ~ in the valley** im Tal liegen; **a house ~ on a hillside** ein am Berghang gelegenes Haus.
(f) (*Liter*) **the book** *etc* **is ~ in Rome** das Buch *etc* spielt in Rom; **he ~ the book in 19th century France/in Rome** er wählte das Frankreich des 19. Jahrhunderts/Rom als Schauplatz für sein Buch; **she ~ the action in the 16th century/in Vienna** sie verlegte die Handlung ins 16. Jahrhundert/nach Wien.
(g) (*Med*) *bone* einrichten; *dislocated joint* einrenken.
(h) (*lay with cutlery*) *table* decken ♦ **to ~ places for 14** für 14 decken, 14 Gedecke auflegen.
(i) (*station*) *guard* aufstellen ♦ **to ~ a guard on sth** etw bewachen lassen.
(j) (*Typ*) setzen, absetzen (*spec*).
(k) *hair* legen, eindrehen.
(l) *jam* fest werden *or* gelieren lassen; *dye* fixieren.
(m) **to ~ a dog/the police after sb** einen Hund/die Polizei auf jdn ansetzen

➤ LANGUAGE IN USE: **set: 1f** → 15.2 **1j** → 6.1, 6.2, 12.1 **3e** → 26.3

or hetzen.
(n) (*Mus*) **to ~ sth to music** etw vertonen.
(o) to ~ sth going/in motion etw in Gang/Bewegung bringen; **to ~ sb doing sth** jdn dazu veranlassen, etw zu tun; **to ~ sb laughing** jdn zum Lachen bringen; **that ~ me thinking** das gab mir zu denken; **that ~ me thinking that** ... das ließ mich denken, daß ...; **to ~ people talking** Anlaß zu Gerede geben; **what ~ the dog barking?** warum bellt der Hund?; **to ~ sb/oneself to doing** *or* **do sth** jdn etw tun lassen/sich daranmachen, etw zu tun.
(p) (*phrases*) *see also other elements* **to ~ a match to sth** ein (brennendes) Streichholz an etw (*acc*) halten, etw anzünden; **to ~ sb free** jdn freilassen; **to ~ sb ashore** jdn an Land setzen; **to ~ sth/things right** etw/die Dinge in Ordnung bringen; **to ~ sb right (about sth)** jdn (in bezug auf etw *acc*) berichtigen.
[4] *vi* **(a)** (*sun etc*) untergehen ♦ **his star is ~ting** (*fig*) sein Stern ist im Sinken. **(b)** (*jelly, cement*) hart *or* fest werden; (*jam also*) gelieren; (*dye*) farbbeständig werden; (*bone*) zusammenwachsen. **(c)** (*Dancing*) **to ~ to one's partner** sich dem Partner zuwenden. **(d)** (*Hunt*) vorstehen.

♦**set about** *vi +prep obj* **(a)** (*begin*) sich machen an (*+acc*), anfangen; (*tackle*) anfassen, anpacken (*inf*), anstellen (*inf*) ♦ **to ~ ~ doing sth** (*begin*) sich daranmachen, etw zu tun; **how do I ~ ~ getting a loan?** wie fasse *or* packe (*inf*) ich es an, um ein Darlehen zu bekommen? **(b)** (*attack*) herfallen über (*+acc*).

♦**set against** *vt sep +prep obj* **(a)** (*influence against*) einnehmen gegen; (*cause trouble between*) Zwietracht säen zwischen (*+dat*) ♦ **to ~ oneself ~ sth** sich einer Sache (*dat*) entgegenstellen; **the civil war ~ friend ~ friend/father ~ son** der Bürgerkrieg ließ Freunde/Väter und Söhne zu Feinden werden; *see also* **set 2 (c)**.
(b) (*balance against*) gegenüberstellen (*+dat*) ♦ **his story must be ~ ~ the evidence of the police** man muß seine Darstellung den Aussagen der Polizei gegenüberhalten.

♦**set apart** *vt sep* **(a)** (*distinguish*) abheben, unterscheiden ♦ **he felt ~ ~ from the other boys** er fühlte, daß er nicht so war wie die anderen Jungen. **(b)** (*save*) *money* beiseite legen, auf die Seite legen; *time* einplanen.

♦**set aside** *vt sep* **(a)** *work, money* beiseite legen; *time* einplanen; *plans* aufschieben; *differences, quarrels, hostilities* beiseite schieben, begraben; *dislike* vergessen; *mistrust, bitterness* sich freimachen von; *formality* verzichten auf (*+acc*); *rules, protest* übergehen, außer acht lassen.
(b) (*Jur*) aufheben; *will* für nichtig *or* ungültig erklären.

♦**set back** *vt sep* **(a)** (*place at a distance*) zurücksetzen ♦ **the house is ~ ~ from the road** das Haus liegt etwas von der Straße ab *or* liegt nicht direkt an der Straße.
(b) (*retard*) verzögern, behindern; (*by a certain length of time*) zurückwerfen ♦ **the programme has been ~ ~ (by) 2 years** das Programm ist um 2 Jahre zurückgeworfen.
(c) (*inf: cost*) kosten ♦ **the dinner ~ me ~ £35** das Essen hat mich 35 Pfund gekostet *or* ärmer gemacht (*inf*).

♦**set down** *vt sep* **(a)** (*put down*) *suitcase* absetzen; *passenger also* aussteigen lassen. **(b)** (*in writing*) (schriftlich) niederlegen. **(c)** (*attribute*) zuschreiben (*to dat*). **(d)** (*classify as*) **to ~ sb/sth ~ as sth** jdn/etw für etw halten.

♦**set forth** [1] *vt sep* (*expound*) *theory, plan* darlegen.
[2] *vi* (*liter*) ausziehen (*old*).

♦**set in** [1] *vi* (*start*) einsetzen; (*panic*) ausbrechen; (*night*) anbrechen; (*Med: gangrene, complications*) sich einstellen ♦ **the rain has ~ ~** es hat sich eingeregnet.
[2] *vt sep* **(a)** (*Typ: indent*) einrücken. **(b)** (*Sew*) *sleeve* einsetzen; *pocket* einarbeiten (*into* in *+acc*).

♦**set off** [1] *vt sep* **(a)** (*ignite*) *bomb, firework* losgehen lassen.
(b) (*start*) führen zu; *speculation, quarrel* auslösen ♦ **that ~ us all ~ laughing** das brachte uns (*acc*) alle zum Lachen; **to ~ sb ~ on a new line of thought** jdn auf einen neuen Gedanken bringen; **her remark ~ him ~ on a story** auf ihre Bemerkung hin erzählte er eine Geschichte; **don't ~ him ~!** laß ihn nur nicht damit anfangen!; **that really ~ him ~** daraufhin legte er richtig los *or* war er nicht mehr zu halten *or* bremsen (*inf*).
(c) (*offset*) **to ~ sth ~ against sth** etw einer Sache (*dat*) gegenüberstellen.
(d) (*enhance*) hervorheben ♦ **to ~ sth ~ from sth** etw von etw abheben.
[2] *vi* (*depart*) sich auf den Weg machen, aufbrechen; (*car, in car etc*) losfahren ♦ **to ~ ~ on a journey** eine Reise antreten; **to ~ ~ for Spain** nach Spanien abfahren; **the police ~ ~ in pursuit** die Polizei nahm die Verfolgung auf.

♦**set on** [1] *vt sep +prep obj dogs* hetzen *or* ansetzen auf (*+acc*); *see* **eye**.
[2] *vi +prep obj see* **set upon**.

♦**set out** [1] *vt sep* (*display*) ausbreiten; (*arrange*) *chess pieces* aufstellen; *printed matter, essay* anordnen, anlegen; (*state*) darlegen, darstellen.
[2] *vi* **(a)** (*depart*) *see* **set off 2**. **(b)** (*intend*) beabsichtigen; (*start*) sich daranmachen.

♦**set to** [1] *vi* (*start working, fighting*) loslegen (*inf*); (*start eating also*) reinhauen (*inf*) ♦ **they ~ ~ and repaired it** sie machten sich an die Arbeit *or* daran (*inf*) und reparierten es.
[2] *vi +prep obj* **to ~ ~ work** sich an die Arbeit machen.

♦**set up** [1] *vi* (*establish oneself*) **to ~ ~ as a doctor** sich als Arzt niederlassen; **to ~ ~ in business** sein eigenes Geschäft aufmachen; **to ~ ~ for oneself** sich selbständig machen.
[2] *vt sep* **(a)** (*place in position*) *statue, post* aufstellen; (*assemble, get ready to work*) *tent, stall, apparatus* aufbauen; (*Typ*) einrichten; (*fig: arrange*) *meeting* arrangieren, vereinbaren; *robbery* planen, vorbereiten ♦ **to ~ sth ~ for sb** etw für jdn vorbereiten; **one comic ~s ~ the joke, the other ...** ein Komiker liefert das Stichwort (für den Witz), der andere ...
(b) (*establish*) gründen; *school, office, system* einrichten; *inquiry* veranlassen, anordnen; *record* aufstellen ♦ **to ~ sb ~ in business/a flat** jdm zu einem Geschäft verhelfen/jdm eine Wohnung einrichten; **to ~ sb ~ as sth** (es) jdm ermöglichen, etw zu werden; **to ~ oneself ~ as sth** sich als jd/etw aufspielen; **to be ~ ~ for life** für sein ganzes Leben ausgesorgt haben; **to be well ~ ~** sich gut stehen; *see* **house, shop**.
(c) (*restore to health*) guttun (*+dat*) ♦ **a holiday will ~ you ~ again** ein Urlaub wird dich schon wieder auf die Beine bringen.
(d) (*raise*) *cry, protest, cheer* anstimmen ♦ **to ~ ~ a commotion** allgemeinen Aufruhr auslösen *or* hervorrufen; (*make noise*) Krach machen.
(e) (*cause*) *infection, reaction* auslösen, verursachen.
(f) (*inf: frame*) **to ~ sb ~** jdm etw anhängen; **I've been ~ ~** das will mir einer anhängen (*inf*) *or* in die Schuhe schieben.
(g) (*inf: rig*) **the fight had been ~ ~** der Kampf war von vornherein eine abgekartete Sache.

♦**set upon** *vi +prep obj* überfallen; (*animal*) anfallen.

set: **~-back** *n* Rückschlag *m*; **~-down** *n* (*dated*) Rüffel *m*; **to give sb a ~-down** jdm den Kopf zurechtsetzen, jdm einen Rüffel erteilen; **~-in** *adj sleeve* eingesetzt; *pocket* eingearbeitet; **~ square** *n* Zeichendreieck *nt*.

sett, (US) set [set] *n* (*badger's den*) Bau *m*.

settee [se'tiː] *n* Couch *f*, Sofa *nt*.

setter ['setəʳ] *n* **(a)** (*type-~*) Setzer(in *f*) *m*. **(b)** (*dog*) Setter *m*.

set theory *n* Mengenlehre *f*.

setting ['setɪŋ] *n* **(a)** (*of sun, moon*) Untergang *m*.
(b) (*background, atmosphere*) Rahmen *m*; (*environment, surroundings*) Umgebung *f*; (*of novel etc*) Schauplatz *m* ♦ **a film with a medieval ~** ein Film, der im Mittelalter spielt.
(c) (*of jewel*) Fassung *f*.
(d) (*place ~*) Gedeck *nt*.
(e) (*position on dial etc*) Einstellung *f*.
(f) (*musical arrangement*) Vertonung *f*.
(g) (*hair*) Legen *nt* ♦ **~ lotion** (Haar)festiger *m*.

settle¹ ['setl] *n* (Wand)bank *f*.

settle² [1] *vt* **(a)** (*decide*) entscheiden; (*sort out*) regeln, erledigen; *problem, question, points* klären; *dispute, differences, quarrel* beilegen, schlichten; *doubts* ausräumen, beseitigen; *date, place* vereinbaren, ausmachen (*inf*); *venue* festlegen *or* -setzen; *deal* abschließen; *price* sich einigen auf (*+acc*), aushandeln; *terms* aushandeln ♦ **that should ~ the winner** damit müßte es sich entscheiden, wer gewinnt; **the result of the game was ~d in the first half** das Ergebnis des Spiels stand schon in der ersten Halbzeit fest; **when my future is ~d** wenn sich meine Zukunft entschieden hat; **to ~ one's affairs** seine Angelegenheiten in Ordnung bringen; **to ~ an estate** (*Jur*) die Verteilung des Nachlasses regeln; **to ~ a case out of court** einen Fall außergerichtlich klären; **that's ~d then** das ist also klar *or* geregelt; **that ~s it** damit wäre der Fall (ja wohl) erledigt; (*angry*) jetzt reicht's.
(b) (*pay*) *bill* begleichen, bezahlen; *account* ausgleichen.
(c) (*calm*) *nerves, stomach* beruhigen ♦ **we need rain to ~ the dust** wir brauchen Regen, damit sich der Staub setzt.
(d) (*place carefully*) legen; (*in upright position*) stellen; (*make comfortable for sleep etc*) *child, invalid* versorgen; *pillow* zurechtlegen ♦ **to ~ oneself comfortably in an armchair** es sich (*dat*) in einem Sessel bequem machen; **to ~ oneself to doing sth** sich daranmachen, etw zu tun.
(e) (*establish*) (*in house*) unterbringen; (*in business also*) etablieren ♦ **to get one's daughter ~d with a husband** seine Tochter verheiraten *or* unter die Haube bringen (*inf*).
(f) to ~ sb into a house/job jdm helfen, sich häuslich einzurichten/sich in eine Stellung einzugewöhnen; **we'd just ~d the children into a new school** wir hatten die Kinder gerade in einer neuen Schule gut untergebracht; *see* **~ in 2**.
(g) (*colonize*) *land* besiedeln; (*set up*) *people* ansiedeln.
(h) (*form*) **to ~ money/property on sb** jdm Geld/Besitz überschreiben *or* übertragen; (*in will*) jdm Geld/Besitz vermachen; **to ~ an annuity on sb** für jdn eine Rente aussetzen.
(i) (*inf: put an end to*) **I'll soon ~ his nonsense** ich werde ihm schon die Flausen austreiben; **I'll soon ~ him** dem werd' ich's geben (*inf*); (*verbally also*) dem werd' ich was erzählen (*inf*); **that ~d him!** da hatte er sein Fett weg (*inf*).
[2] *vi* **(a)** (*put down roots*) seßhaft werden; (*in country, town, profession*) sich niederlassen; (*as settler*) sich ansiedeln; (*in house*) sich häuslich niederlassen, sich einrichten; (*feel at home in house, town, country*) sich einleben (*into* in *+dat*); (*in job, surroundings*) sich eingewöhnen (*into* in *+dat*) ♦ **to ~ into a way of life** sich an einen Lebensstil gewöhnen; **to ~ into a habit** sich (*dat*) etw angewöhnen; **as he ~d into middle age** als er älter und reifer wurde.
(b) (*become less variable: weather*) beständig werden ♦ **the wind ~d in the east** der Wind kam schließlich aus Osten.
(c) (*become calm*) (*child, matters, stomach*) sich beruhigen; (*panic, excitement*) sich legen; (*become less excitable or restless*) zur Ruhe kommen, ruhiger werden ♦ **he couldn't ~ to anything** er konnte sich auf nichts konzentrieren.
(d) (*come to rest, sit down*) (*person, bird, insect*) sich niederlassen *or* setzen; (*dust*) sich setzen *or* legen; (*sink slowly, subside*) (*building, walls*) sich senken; (*ground, liquid, sediment, coffee grounds*) sich setzen; (*wine*) sich beruhigen ♦ **to**

~ comfortably in an armchair es sich (*dat*) in einem Sessel gemütlich *or* bequem machen; **the boat ~d in the water** das Boot hörte auf zu schaukeln; **fog/silence ~d over the city** Nebel/Stille legte sich über die Stadt *or* breitete sich über der Stadt aus; **gloom ~d over the meeting** eine bedrückte Stimmung breitete sich in der Versammlung aus.
(e) (*Jur*) **to ~ (out of court)** sich vergleichen.
(f) (*pay*) bezahlen; *see also* **~ with.**

◆**settle back** *vi* sich (gemütlich) zurücklehnen.

◆**settle down** [1] *vi* **(a)** *see* **settle 2 (a). it's time he ~d ~** es ist Zeit, daß er ein geregeltes Leben anfängt *or* zur Ruhe kommt; **to marry and ~ ~** heiraten und seßhaft *or* häuslich werden; **to ~ ~ at school/in a new house/job** sich an einer Schule/in einem Haus einleben/sich in einer Stellung eingewöhnen; **he ought to ~ ~ in a steady job** er sollte sich (*dat*) endlich eine feste Stellung suchen; **~ ~, children!** ruhig, Kinder!
(b) *see* **settle 2 (c).**
(c) to ~ ~ to work sich an die Arbeit machen *or* setzen; **to ~ ~ for a chat/for the night** sich zu einem Schwatz (gemütlich) zusammensetzen/sich schlafen legen; **to ~ ~ to watch TV** es sich (*dat*) vor dem Fernseher gemütlich machen.
[2] *vt sep* **(a)** (*calm down*) beruhigen.
(b) *baby* hinlegen; *patient* versorgen ◆ **to ~ oneself ~ to work/to finish the job** sich an die Arbeit machen *or* setzen/sich daranmachen, die Arbeit fertigzumachen; **the cat ~d itself ~ for the night** die Katze kuschelte sich zum Schlafen zurecht; **the campers ~d themselves ~ for the night** die Zeltenden richteten alles für die Nacht her.

◆**settle for** *vi +prep obj* sich zufriedengeben mit ◆ **I'd ~ ~ a diamond necklace** ich wäre schon mit einem Diamanthalsband zufrieden; **I think I'll ~ ~ this one** ich glaube, ich nehme doch das da; **she won't ~ ~ anything less** mit weniger gibt sie sich nicht zufrieden; **he was glad to ~ ~ a bronze medal** er war schon mit einer Bronzemedaille zufrieden.

◆**settle in** [1] *vi* (*in house, town*) sich einleben; (*in job, school*) sich eingewöhnen ◆ **how are you settling ~?** haben Sie sich schon eingelebt/eingewöhnt?
[2] *vt sep* **to ~ sb ~** jdm helfen, sich einzuleben/sich einzugewöhnen.

◆**settle on** *or* **upon** *vi +prep obj* sich entscheiden für *or* entschließen zu; (*agree on*) sich einigen auf (*+acc*).

◆**settle up** [1] *vi* (be)zahlen ◆ **to ~ ~ with sb** (*lit, fig*) mit jdm abrechnen.
[2] *vt sep bill* bezahlen.

◆**settle with** [1] *vi +prep obj* (*lit, fig*) abrechnen mit.
[2] *vt sep +prep obj* **(a)** *debt etc* abrechnen mit ◆ **to ~ one's account ~ sb** (*lit, fig*) mit jdm abrechnen. **(b)** (*come to agreement with*) **to ~ sth ~ sb** sich mit jdm auf etw (*acc*) einigen.

settled ['setld] *adj weather* beständig; *way of life* geregelt; *opinions* fest; *procedure* feststehend, festgelegt ◆ **to be ~** in geregelten Verhältnissen leben, etabliert sein; (*in place*) seßhaft sein; (*have permanent job etc*) festen Fuß gefaßt haben; (*in a house*) sich häuslich niedergelassen haben; (*be less restless*) ruhiger *or* gesetzter sein; **to feel ~** sich wohl fühlen; **I don't feel very ~ at the moment** ich hänge zur Zeit in der Luft (*inf*), ich fühle mich zur Zeit verunsichert.

settlement ['setlmənt] *n* **(a)** (*act*) (*deciding*) Entscheidung *f*; (*sorting out*) Regelung, Erledigung *f*; (*of problem, question etc*) Klärung *f*; (*of dispute, differences etc*) Beilegung, Schlichtung *f*; (*of estate*) Regelung *f*; (*of bill, claim*) Bezahlung *f*; (*of account*) Ausgleich *m*; (*contract, agreement etc*) Übereinkunft *f*, Übereinkommen *nt* ◆ **a ~ out of court** (*Jur*) ein außergerichtlicher Vergleich; **to reach a ~** sich einigen, einen Vergleich treffen; **the terms of the** (*Jur*) **~** die Bedingungen des Übereinkommens; **this payment is made in ~ of all claims** mit dieser Zahlung werden alle Forderungen beglichen; **in ~ of our account** zum Ausgleich unseres Kontos; **~ discount** Skonto *nt or m*.
(b) (*settling of money*) Übertragung, Überschreibung *f* (*on* auf *+acc*); (*in will also*) Vermächtnis *nt*; (*of annuity, income*) Aussetzung *f*; (*document, agreement*) Schenkungsvertrag *m* ◆ **he receives £10,000 by the ~** auf ihn wurden £ 10.000 übertragen *or* überschrieben; ihm wurden £ 10.000 vermacht.
(c) (*of building*) Senkung *f*; (*of sediment*) Absetzen *nt*.
(d) (*colony, village*) Siedlung, Niederlassung *f*; (*act of settling persons*) Ansiedlung *f*; (*colonization*) Besiedlung *f*.
(e) (*US: also* **~ house**) (*institution*) Wohlfahrtseinrichtung *f*; (*building*) Gemeindezentrum *nt*.

settler ['setləʳ] *n* Siedler(in *f*) *m*.

set: ~-to *n* (*inf*) Krach *m*, Streiterei *f* (*inf*); **to have a ~-to with sb** sich mit jdm in die Wolle kriegen (*inf*); **~-up** *n* **(a)** (*inf*) (*situation*) Umstände *pl*; (*way of organizing things*) Organisation *f*, Drum und Dran *nt* (*inf*); **it's a funny ~-up** das sind (vielleicht) komische Zustände!; **what's the ~-up here?** wie verhält sich *or* läuft (*inf*) das hier (alles)?; **she didn't quite understand the ~-up** sie verstand die Sachlage nicht ganz; **(b)** (*equipment*) Geräte, Instrumente *pl*; **(c)** (*US: for drinks*) Zubehör *nt* für Cocktails *etc*; **(d)** (*inf: rigged contest*) abgekartete Sache.

seven ['sevn] [1] *adj* sieben ◆ **to sail the ~ seas** die sieben Meere befahren; **he's got the ~-year itch** (*inf*) er ist im verflixten siebenten Jahr.
[2] *n* Sieben *f*; *see also* **six.**

sevenfold ['sevnfəʊld] [1] *adj* siebenfach.
[2] *adv* um das Siebenfache.

seventeen ['sevn'tiːn] [1] *adj* siebzehn.
[2] *n* Siebzehn *f*; *see also* **sixteen.**

seventeenth ['sevn'tiːnθ] [1] *adj* siebzehnte(r, s) ◆ **a ~ part** ein Siebzehntel *nt*.
[2] *n* (*fraction*) Siebzehntel *nt*; (*of series*) Siebzehnte(r, s).

seventh ['sevnθ] [1] *adj* siebte(r, s) ◆ **a ~ part** ein Siebtel *nt*; **S~-day Adventist** Adventist(in *f*) *m* vom Siebenten Tag.
[2] *n* (*fraction*) Siebtel *nt*; (*in series*) Siebte(r, s); (*Mus*) (*interval*) Septime *f*; (*chord*) Septimenakkord *m*; *see also* **sixth.**

seventhly ['sevnθlɪ] *adv* siebtens.

seventieth ['sevntɪɪθ] [1] *adj* siebzigste(r, s).
[2] *n* (*fraction*) Siebzigstel *nt*; (*in series*) Siebzigste(r, s).

seventy ['sevntɪ] [1] *adj* siebzig.
[2] *n* Siebzig *f* ◆ **~-eight** Achtundsiebzig *f*; (*record*) Achtundsiebziger(platte *f*), 78er-Platte *f*.

sever ['sevəʳ] [1] *vt* (*cut through*) durchtrennen; (*violently*) durchschlagen; (*cut off*) abtrennen; (*violently*) abschlagen; (*fig*) (*break off*) *ties* lösen; *relations, links, friendship* abbrechen; *communications* unterbrechen; (*divide*) *nation* teilen ◆ **the wires were ~ed in the storm** beim Sturm sind die Leitungen (durch)gerissen; **to ~ sb from sb/sth** jdn von jdm/etw trennen; **to ~ sth from sth** etw von etw abtrennen.
[2] *vi* (durch)reißen.

several ['sevrəl] [1] *adj* **(a)** (*some*) einige, mehrere; (*different, diverse, various*) verschiedene ◆ **I went with ~ others** ich ging mit einigen *or* ein paar anderen zusammen; **I've seen him ~ times/~ times already** ich habe ihn einige Male gesehen/schon mehrmals *or* mehrere Male gesehen; **there are ~ ways of doing it** das kann man auf mehrere *or* verschiedene Arten machen; **I'll need ~ more** ich brauche noch einige.
(b) (*dated: respective*) jeweilig ◆ **they went their ~ ways** jeder ging seinen Weg, sie gingen ihrer Wege (*old*).
[2] *pron* einige ◆ **~ of the houses** einige (der) Häuser; **~ of us** einige von uns.

severally ['sevrəlɪ] *adv* einzeln.

severance ['sevərəns] *n see vt* (*a*) Durchtrennen *nt*; Durchschlagen *nt*; Abtrennen *nt*; Abschlagen *nt*; Lösen *nt*; Abbruch *m*; Unterbrechung *f*; Teilung *f*; Abschneiden *nt*, Absonderung *f* ◆ **~ pay** eine Abfindung.

severe [sɪ'vɪəʳ] *adj* (*+er*) (*strict*) *person, appearance, style* streng; (*harsh*) *critic, law, winter also, punishment, competition, test* hart; *criticism* scharf; *reprimand* ernst, scharf; *test* hart, schwer; (*serious*) *expression, crime, warning* ernst; *illness, injury, blow, frost, drought, storm, loss* schwer, schlimm; *pain, storm* stark, heftig; *weather* rauh ◆ **to be ~ with sb** streng mit jdm sein; **to be ~ on sb** hart über jdn urteilen.

severely [sɪ'vɪəlɪ] *adv see adj* ◆ **to be ~ critical of sth** sich äußerst kritisch über etw (*acc*) äußern; **to leave sb/sth ~ alone** sich sehr *or* schwer vor jdm/etw hüten.

severeness [sɪ'vɪənɪs], **severity** [sɪ'verɪtɪ] *n see adj* Strenge *f*; Härte *f*; Schärfe *f*; Ernst *m*; Schwere *f*; Stärke, Heftigkeit *f*; Rauheit *f* ◆ **the ~ of the cold/drought/frost** die große *or* schwere Kälte/Dürre/der starke *or* schwere Frost; **severities** Härte *f*.

Seville [sə'vɪl] *n* Sevilla *nt* ◆ **~ orange** Bitterorange, Pomeranze *f*.

sew [səʊ] *pret* **~ed**, *ptp* **~n** *vti* nähen ◆ **to ~ sth on/down/together** etw an-/auf-/zusammennähen; **she's been ~ing that seam all evening** an dem Saum hat sie den ganzen Abend genäht.

◆**sew up** *vt sep* **(a)** nähen (*also Med*); *opening* zunähen ◆ **to ~ sth ~ in sth** etw in etw (*acc*) einnähen. **(b)** (*fig*) unter Dach und Fach bringen ◆ **it's all ~n ~** es ist unter Dach und Fach; **we've got the game all ~n ~** das Spiel ist gelaufen (*inf*).

sewage ['sjuːɪdʒ] *n* Abwasser *nt* ◆ **~ disposal** Abwasserbeseitigung *f*; **~ farm/works** Rieselfeld *nt*/Kläranlage *f*; **~ sludge** Klärschlamm *m*.

sewer¹ ['səʊəʳ] *n* Näher(in *f*) *m*.

sewer² ['sjʊəʳ] *n* (*pipe*) Abwasserleitung *f or* -rohr *nt*; (*main ~*) Abwasserkanal *m*; (*fig*) (*smelly place*) Kloake *f*; (*evil place*) Sündenpfuhl *m*, Kloake *f* (*liter*) ◆ **~ gas** Faulschlammgas *nt*; **~ rat** Wanderratte *f*; **he has a mind like a ~** (*inf*) er hat eine schmutzige *or* dreckige (*inf*) Phantasie.

sewerage ['sjʊərɪdʒ] *n* Kanalisation *f*; (*service*) Abwasserbeseitigung *f*; (*sewage*) Abwässer *pl*.

sewing ['səʊɪŋ] *n* (*activity*) Nähen *nt*; (*piece of work*) Näharbeit *f* ◆ **~ basket** Nähkorb *m*; **~ machine** Nähmaschine *f*.

sewn [səʊn] *ptp of* **sew.**

sex [seks] [1] *n* **(a)** (*Biol*) Geschlecht *nt* ◆ **what ~ is the baby?** welches Geschlecht hat das Baby? **(b)** (*sexuality*) Sexualität *f*, Sex *m*; (*sexual intercourse*) Sex (*inf*), Geschlechtsverkehr (*form*) *m* ◆ **to teach pupils (about) ~** Schüler aufklären; **to have ~** (Geschlechts)verkehr haben.
[2] *adj attr* Geschlechts-; *hormone, organs, drive also, hygiene* Sexual-; *crime* Trieb-, Sexual-; *aids, film, scandal* Sex-.
[3] *vt* das Geschlecht (*+gen*) bestimmen.

sexagenarian [,seksədʒɪ'neərɪən] [1] *adj* sechzigjährig ◆ **~ members of the club** Clubmitglieder, die in den Sechzigern sind.
[2] *n* Sechzigjährige(r) *mf* ◆ **to be a ~** in den Sechzigern sein.

Sexagesima [,seksə'dʒesɪmə] *n* Sonntag *m* Sexagesima.

sex: ~ appeal *n* Sex-Appeal *m*; **~ change** [1] *n* Geschlechtsumwandlung *f*; **to have a ~ change** sich einer Geschlechtsumwandlung unterziehen; [2] *attr* **~ change operation** (Operation *f* zur) Geschlechtsumwandlung; **~ discrimination** *n* Diskriminierung *f* auf Grund des Geschlechts.

sexed [sekst] *adj* **to be highly ~** einen starken Geschlechtstrieb haben; *see* **oversexed, undersexed.**

sex: ~ education *n* Sexualerziehung *f*; **~ hormone** *n* Geschlechts- *or* Sexualhormon *nt*.

sexily ['seksɪlɪ] *adv* aufreizend, sexy (*inf*).

sexism ['seksɪzəm] *n* Sexismus *m*.

➤ LANGUAGE IN USE: **settlement: a → 20.7**

sexist ['seksɪst] [1] *n* Sexist(in *f*) *m*.
[2] *adj* sexistisch.
sex: ~ **killing** *n* Sexualmord *m*; ~ **kitten** *n* (*inf*) Sexkätzchen *nt* (*inf*), Sexmieze *f* (*inf*); ~**less** *adj* geschlechtslos; ~ **life** *n* Geschlechtsleben *nt*; (*of people also*) Liebesleben *nt*; ~**-linked** *adj* geschlechtsgebunden; ~ **maniac** *n* (*criminal*) Triebverbrecher *or* -täter *m*; **he/she is a** ~ **maniac** (*inf*) er/sie ist ganz verrückt nach *or* wild auf Sex (*inf*); **you're a** ~ **maniac** (*inf*) du denkst aber auch nur an Sex; ~ **object** *n* Sex(ual)objekt, Lustobjekt *nt*; ~ **offender** *n* Sexualtäter(in *f*) *m*; ~ **organ** Geschlechts- *or* Sexualorgan *nt*.
sexpert ['sekspɜːt] *n* (*hum*) Experte *m* in Sachen Sex (*inf*), Sexperte *m* (*hum*).
sexploit ['seksplɔɪt] *n* (*hum*) Liebesabenteuer *nt*.
sex: ~**pot** *n* (*inf*) (*woman*) Sexbombe *f* (*inf*); **to be a real little** ~**pot** unheimlich sexy sein (*inf*); ~ **shop** *n* Sexshop, Sexladen *m*; ~ **symbol** *n* Sexsymbol *nt*.
sextant ['sekstənt] *n* Sextant *m*.
sextet(te) [seks'tet] *n* Sextett *nt*.
sexton ['sekstən] *n* Küster *m*.
sextuplet [seks'tjuːplɪt] *n* Sechsling *m*.
sexual ['seksjʊəl] *adj* geschlechtlich; *behaviour, attraction, excitement* sexuell; *intercourse, maturity* Geschlechts-; *crime* Sexual-, Trieb- ♦ **his** ~ **exploits** seine Liebesabenteuer *pl*; ~ **characteristics** Geschlechtsmerkmale *pl*; ~ **harrassment** sexuelle Belästigung; ~ **partner** Sexual- *or* Intimpartner(in *f*) *m*.
sexuality [ˌseksjʊ'ælɪtɪ] *n* Sexualität *f*.
sexually ['seksjʊəlɪ] *adv* sexuell ♦ ~ **mature** geschlechtsreif; ~ **transmitted diseases** durch Geschlechtsverkehr übertragene Krankheiten.
sexy ['seksɪ] *adj* (+*er*) (*inf*) sexy *pred*; *smile, pose also* aufreizend; *joke, film* erotisch ♦ **the sexiest girl in the class** das Mädchen in der Klasse, das am meisten Sex-Appeal hat.
SF *abbr of* **science fiction**.
s.g. *abbr of* **specific gravity**.
sgraffito [sgræ'fiːtəʊ] *n* Sgraffito *nt*.
sgt *abbr of* **sergeant**.
sh [ʃ] *interj* sch(t).
shabbily ['ʃæbɪlɪ] *adv* (*lit, fig*) schäbig.
shabbiness ['ʃæbɪnɪs] *n* (*lit, fig*) Schäbigkeit *f*.
shabby ['ʃæbɪ] *adj* (+*er*) (*lit, fig*) schäbig ♦ **they were** ~**-genteel** sie gehörten zur verarmten Oberschicht.
shack [ʃæk] [1] *n* Hütte *f*, Schuppen *m*.
[2] *vi* (*inf*) **to** ~ **up with sb** mit jdm zusammenziehen; **to** ~ **up together** zusammenziehen.
shackle ['ʃækl] [1] *n* (a) *usu pl* Kette, Fessel (*also fig*) *f*.
(b) (*Tech*) Schäkel *m*.
[2] *vt* in Ketten legen ♦ **they were** ~**d together/to the wall** sie waren aneinandergekettet/an die Wand (an)gekettet; **to** ~ **oneself with sth** sich mit etw belasten; **to be** ~**d by sth** (*fig*) an etw (*acc*) gebunden sein; **to be** ~**d with sth** die Belastung einer Sache (*gen*) haben.
shad [ʃæd] *n* Alse *f*.
shade [ʃeɪd] [1] *n* (a) Schatten *m* ♦ **30° in the** ~ 30 Grad im Schatten; **to give** ~ Schatten spenden; **the** ~**s of night were falling fast** (*liter*) der Schatten der Nacht senkte sich hernieder (*liter*); **to put** *or* **cast sb/sth in the** ~ (*fig*) jdn/etw in den Schatten stellen.
(b) (*lamp*~) (Lampen)schirm *m*; (*eye* ~) Schild *nt*, Schirm *m*; (*esp US: blind*) Jalousie *f*; (*roller blind*) Springrollo *nt*; (*outside house*) Markise *f* ♦ ~**s** (*esp US: sunglasses*) Sonnenbrille *f*.
(c) (*of colour*) (Farb)ton *m*; (*fig*) (*of opinion*) Schattierung *f*; (*of meaning*) Nuance *f* ♦ **turquoise is a** ~ **of blue** Türkis ist ein blauer Farbton; **a brighter** ~ **of red** ein leuchtenderer Rotton; **a new** ~ **of lipstick** ein neuer Farbton für Lippenstifte; ~**-card** Farb(en)probe *f*; **of all** ~**s and hues** (*lit*) in den verschiedensten Farben, in allen Schattierungen; (*fig*) aller Schattierungen.
(d) (*small quantity*) Spur *f* ♦ **it's a** ~ **long/too long** es ist etwas lang/etwas *or* eine Spur zu lang.
(e) (*liter: ghost*) Schatten *m* ♦ **the** ~**s** (*Myth*) die Bewohner *pl* des Schattenreiches; (*Hades*) das Reich der Schatten, das Schattenreich; ~**s of Professor Jones!** (*inf*) wie mich das an Professor Jones erinnert!
[2] *vt* (a) (*cast shadow on*) Schatten werfen auf (+*acc*), beschatten (*geh*); (*protect from light, sun*) abschirmen; *lamp, window* abdunkeln ♦ **that part is** ~**d by a tree** der Teil liegt im Schatten eines Baumes; **to be** ~**d from the sun** im Schatten liegen *or* sein; (*protected against sun*) vor der Sonne geschützt sein; **he** ~**d his eyes with his hand** er hielt die Hand vor die Augen(, um nicht geblendet zu werden).
(b) (*darken with lines*) schraffieren; (*for artistic effect*) schattieren ♦ **to** ~ **sth in** etw ausschraffieren; (*colour in*) etw ausmalen; **to** ~ **one colour into another** eine Farbe langsam in die andere übergehen lassen.
[3] *vi* (*lit, fig*) übergehen ♦ **to** ~ **off** allmählich blasser werden; **blue that** ~**s (off) into black** Blau, das in Schwarz übergeht.
shadeless ['ʃeɪdlɪs] *adj* schattenlos.
shadiness ['ʃeɪdɪnɪs] *n* Schattigkeit *f*; (*fig*) Zwielichtigkeit *f*.
shading ['ʃeɪdɪŋ] *n* (*shaded area*) Schraffierung, Schraffur *f*; (*Art*) Schattierung *f*.
shadow ['ʃædəʊ] [1] *n* (a) (*lit, fig*) Schatten *m* (*also Med, Art*); (*growth of beard*) Anflug *m* von Bartstoppeln; (*fig: threat*) (Be)drohung *f* ♦ **in the** ~ im Schatten; **in the** ~**s** im Dunkel; **the valley of the** ~ **of death** das finstere Tal des Todes; **sb lives under the** ~ **of sth** etw liegt *or* lastet wie ein Schatten auf jdm; **to be in sb's** ~ (*fig*) in jds Schatten (*dat*) stehen; **to be afraid of one's own** ~ sich vor seinem eigenen Schatten fürchten; **to wear oneself to a** ~ sich aufreiben, sich zugrunde richten; **to be just a** ~ **of one's former self** nur noch ein Schatten seiner selbst sein; **to catch at** *or* **chase** ~**s** (*fig*) einem Phantom *or* Schatten nachjagen.
(b) (*trace*) Spur *f* ♦ **a** ~ **of hope** ein Hoffnungsschimmer *m*; **without a** ~ **of a doubt** ohne den geringsten Zweifel.
(c) (*person following sb*) Schatten *m* ♦ **to put a** ~ **on sb** jdn beschatten lassen (*inf*).
[2] *attr* (*Brit Pol*) Schatten- ♦ **the** ~ **Foreign Secretary** der Außenminister des Schattenkabinetts.
[3] *vt* (a) (*darken*) Schatten werfen auf (+*acc*); (*fig*) überschatten ♦ **the room is** ~**ed by a high wall** das Zimmer bekommt den Schatten *or* liegt im Schatten einer hohen Mauer.
(b) (*follow*) beschatten (*inf*).
shadow: ~**-boxing** *n* (*lit, fig*) Schattenboxen *nt*; ~ **cabinet** *n* (*Brit*) Schattenkabinett *nt*; ~ **printing** *n* (*Comput*) Schattendruck *m*.
shadowy ['ʃædəʊɪ] *adj* schattig; (*blurred*) *outline, form* schattenhaft, verschwommen; (*vague*) *thought, fear* unbestimmt, vage ♦ **the** ~ **world beyond the grave** die dunkle Welt nach dem Tode; **a** ~ **existence** ein undurchsichtiges Dasein.
shady ['ʃeɪdɪ] *adj* (+*er*) (a) *place* schattig; *tree, hat* schattenspendend. (b) (*inf: of dubious honesty*) zwielichtig, zweifelhaft ♦ **to be on the** ~ **side of the law** dunkle Geschäfte treiben; **on the** ~ **side of forty** (*US inf*) vierzig vorbei (*inf*); **there's something** ~ **about it** da ist etwas faul dran (*inf*).
shaft [ʃɑːft] [1] *n* (a) Schaft *m*; (*of tool, golf club etc*) Stiel *m*; (*of cart, carriage*) Deichsel *f*; (*of light*) Strahl *m*; (*Mech*) Welle *f*; (*liter: arrow*) Pfeil *m*; (*liter: spear*) Speer *m*; (*fig: remark*) Spitze *f* ♦ ~**s of wit/malice** geistreiche/boshafte Spitzen *pl*; **the** ~**s of Cupid** Amors Pfeile *pl*. (b) (*of lift, mine etc*) Schacht *m*.
[2] *vt* (*sl: have sex with*) stoßen (*sl*), pimpern (*sl*).
shag[1] [ʃæg] *n* (a) (*tobacco*) Shag *m*. (b) (*of carpet etc*) Flor *m* ♦ ~**-pile carpet** langfloriger Teppich.
shag[2] *n* (*Orn*) Krähenscharbe *f*.
shag[3] (*sl*) [1] *n* (*intercourse, partner*) Nummer *f* (*sl*) ♦ **to have a** ~ eine Nummer machen (*sl*).
[2] *vti* (a) (*have sex*) bumsen (*inf*). (b) **to be** ~**ged out** ausgebufft sein (*sl*).
shaggy ['ʃægɪ] *adj* (+*er*) (*long-haired*) zottig; (*unkempt*) zottelig ♦ ~ **carpet** zotteliger Teppich; ~ **dog story** *breitgewalzte Geschichte mit schwacher Pointe*.
shagreen [ʃæ'griːn] *n* Chagrin(leder) *nt*.
Shah [ʃɑː] *n* Schah *m*.
shake [ʃeɪk] (*vb: pret* **shook**, *ptp* **shaken**) [1] *n* (a) (*act of shaking*) Schütteln *nt* ♦ **to give a rug a** ~ einen Läufer ausschütteln; **give the paint a** ~ die Farbe (gut) durchschütteln; **to give sb/oneself a good** ~ jdn/sich kräftig schütteln; **with a** ~ **of her head** mit einem Kopfschütteln; **with a** ~ **in his voice** mit zitternder Stimme; **to be all of a** ~ (*inf*) am ganzen Körper zittern.
(b) (*milk*~) Shake *m*, Mixgetränk *nt*.
(c) (*inf: moment*) Minütchen *nt* (*inf*) ♦ **in two** ~**s (of a lamb's tail)** in zwei Sekunden; **in half a** ~ sofort.
(d) **to be no great** ~**s** (*inf*) nicht umwerfend sein (*at* in +*dat*).
(e) **the** ~**s** (*inf*) der Tatterich (*inf*); (*esp with fear*) das Zittern; **he's got the** ~**s** er hat einen Tatterich (*inf*); (*due to alcoholism also*) ihm zittern die Hände, er hat einen Flattermann (*sl*); (*esp with fear*) er hat das große Zittern (*inf*); (*esp with cold, emotion*) er zittert am ganzen Körper.
[2] *vt* (a) schütteln; *building* erschüttern; *cocktail* durchschütteln ♦ **"**~ **well before using"** „vor Gebrauch gut schütteln"; **to be** ~**n to pieces** total durchgeschüttelt werden; **she shook the door-handle which seemed to have stuck** sie rüttelte an der Türklinke, die zu klemmen schien; **to** ~ **pepper on a steak** Pfeffer auf ein Steak streuen; **to** ~ **one's fist at sb** jdm mit der Faust drohen; **to** ~ **oneself/itself free** sich losmachen; **to** ~ **hands** sich (*dat*) die Hand geben; (*for longer time, in congratulations etc*) sich (*dat*) die Hand schütteln; **to** ~ **hands with sb** jdm die Hand geben/schütteln; **I'd like to** ~ **him by the hand** ihm würde ich gern die Hand schütteln *or* drücken; **English people don't often** ~ **hands** Engländer geben sich (*dat*) selten die Hand; ~ **hands** (*to dog*) (gib) Pfötchen; (*to child*) gib mal die Hand; **to** ~ **a leg** (*inf*) (*hurry*) Dampf machen (*inf*); (*dated: dance*) das Tanzbein schwingen (*dated*).
(b) (*weaken*) *faith, foundation of society* erschüttern; *evidence, reputation, courage, resolve* ins Wanken bringen ♦ **society was** ~**n to its very core** die Gesellschaft wurde bis in ihre Grundfesten erschüttert.
(c) (*shock, amaze*) erschüttern ♦ **that shook him!** da war er platt (*inf*); **it shook me rigid** (*inf*) da war ich schwer geschockt (*inf*); **it was a nasty accident, he's still rather badly** ~**n** es war ein schlimmer Unfall, der Schreck sitzt ihm noch in den Knochen; **she was badly** ~**n by the news** die Nachricht hatte sie sehr mitgenommen *or* erschüttert; **her nerves are badly** ~**n** sie ist mit den Nerven am Ende.
(d) (*inf*) *see* ~ **off**.
[3] *vi* wackeln; (*hand, voice*) zittern; (*earth, voice*) beben ♦ **the whole boat shook as the waves hit** das ganze Boot wurde vom Aufprall der Wellen erschüttert; **the trees shook in the wind** die Bäume schwankten im Wind; **to** ~ **like a leaf** zittern wie Espenlaub; **to** ~ **with fear/cold** vor Angst/Kälte zittern; **he was shaking all over** er zitterte am ganzen Körper; **to** ~ **with laughter** sich vor Lachen schütteln; **to** ~ **in one's shoes** (*inf*) das große Zittern kriegen (*inf*); ~**!,** ~ **on it!** (*inf*) Hand drauf; ~**!** (*me too*) da können wir uns ja die Hand reichen!; **they shook on the deal** sie bekräftigten das Geschäft mit Handschlag.
♦**shake down** [1] *vt sep* (a) *fruit* herunterschütteln.
(b) (*US sl: extort money from*) ausnehmen (*inf*) ♦ **to** ~ **sb** ~ **for $500** jdn um

500 Dollar erleichtern (*inf*).
(**c**) (*US sl: search*) absuchen, durchsuchen (*for* nach).
[2] *vi* (*inf*) (**a**) (*sleep*) kampieren, sein Lager aufschlagen.
(**b**) (*settle*) (*people*) sich eingewöhnen; (*machinery*) sich einlaufen; (*situation*) sich einspielen.

◆**shake off** *vt sep dust, snow, pursuer* abschütteln; *visitor, cold* loswerden ◆ **to ~ the dust (of a place) ~ one's feet** (*fig*) den Staub (eines Ortes) von seinen Schuhen schütteln.

◆**shake out** [1] *vt sep* (**a**) herausschütteln; *tablecloth, rug* ausschütteln ◆ **she took off her hat and shook ~ her long hair** sie nahm den Hut ab und schüttelte sich (*dat*) die langen Haare zurecht.
(**b**) (*fig: out of complacency etc*) aufrütteln (*of* aus).
[2] *vi* (*Mil: spread out*) ausschwärmen.

◆**shake up** *vt sep* (**a**) *bottle, liquid* schütteln; *pillow* aufschütteln ◆ **they were really ~n ~ by the rough crossing** sie wurden bei der stürmischen Überfahrt durchgeschüttelt.
(**b**) (*upset*) erschüttern ◆ **he was badly ~n ~ by the accident** der Unfall hat ihm einen schweren Schock versetzt; **she's still a bit ~n ~** sie ist immer noch ziemlich mitgenommen.
(**c**) *management, recruits* auf Zack bringen (*inf*); *ideas* revidieren ◆ **your ideas could do with a bit of shaking ~** deine Ansichten müßten auch mal wieder revidiert werden.

shakedown ['ʃeɪkdaʊn] [1] *n* (*bed*) Lager, Notbett *nt*; (*US sl: extortion*) Gaunerei *f*; (*US sl: search*) Razzia (*inf*), Durchsuchung *f* ◆ **he slept on a ~ in the living room** er hatte sein Lager im Wohnzimmer aufgeschlagen, er kampierte im Wohnzimmer; **to give a room a ~** ein Zimmer auf den Kopf stellen.
[2] *adj trial, cruise* Probe-.

shaken ['ʃeɪkən] *ptp of* **shake**.

shake-out ['ʃeɪkaʊt] *n* (*inf*) Gesundschrumpfung *f* (*inf*).

shaker ['ʃeɪkəʳ] *n* (*cocktail ~*) Mix- *or* Schüttelbecher, Shaker *m*; (*flour/salt ~*) Mehl-/Salzstreuer *m*.

Shakespearean, Shakespearian [ʃeɪk'spɪərɪən] [1] *adj* Shakespearesch, Shakespearisch; *style* shakespearesch, shakespearisch; *actor* Shakespeare-.
[2] *n* Shakespeareforscher(in *f*) *m*.

shake-up ['ʃeɪkʌp] *n* (*inf*) (*reorganization*) Umbesetzung *f* ◆ **to give a department** *etc* **a good ~** (*revitalization*) eine Abteilung *etc* auf Zack bringen (*inf*); (*reorganization*) eine Abteilung *etc* umbesetzen *or* umorganisieren.

shakily ['ʃeɪkɪlɪ] *adv* wackelig; *talk, say* mit zitteriger Stimme; *walk* mit wackeligen Schritten; *pour etc* zitterig.

shakiness ['ʃeɪkɪnɪs] *n see adj* Wackeligkeit *f*; Fragwürdigkeit, Unsicherheit *f*; Zittern, Beben *nt*; Zitterigkeit *f*; Unsicherheit *f*; Holprigkeit *f* ◆ **the ~ of their position** ihre wackelige Position.

shaking ['ʃeɪkɪŋ] *n* Zittern *nt* ◆ **to give sb/sth a good ~** jdn/etw kräftig schütteln; (*fig*) jdn kräftig treten; **a nasty experience, it gave me a bit of a ~** ein unangenehmes Erlebnis, das sitzt mir immer noch in den Knochen.

shako ['ʃækəʊ] *n* Tschako *m*.

shaky ['ʃeɪkɪ] *adj* (*+er*) *chair, position* wackelig; *evidence* fragwürdig, unsicher; *voice, hands, writing* zitterig; *knowledge* unsicher, wackelig ◆ **in rather ~ French** in ziemlich holprigem Französisch; **to be ~ on one's legs** wackelig auf den Beinen sein; **to feel ~** (*physically*) sich ganz schwach fühlen; **I still feel a bit ~ about this theory** diese Theorie sitzt bei mir noch nicht.

shale [ʃeɪl] *n* Schiefer *m* ◆ **~ oil** Schieferöl *nt*.

▼ **shall** [ʃæl] *pret* **should** *modal aux vb* (**a**) (*future*) **I/we ~** *or* **I'll/we'll go to France this year** ich werde/wir werden dieses Jahr nach Frankreich fahren, ich fahre/wir fahren dieses Jahr nach Frankreich; **~ do** (*inf*) wird gemacht (*inf*); **no, I ~ not** *or* **I shan't/yes, I ~** nein, das werde ich nicht tun *or* das tue ich nicht/jawohl, das werde ich tun *or* das tue ich!
(**b**) (*determination, obligation*) **you ~ pay for this!** dafür sollst *or* wirst du büßen!; **but I say you *shall* do it!** aber ich sage dir, du wirst das machen!; **the directors ~ not be disturbed** (*form*) die Direktoren dürfen nicht gestört werden; **the court ~ rise** das Gericht muß sich erheben; (*command*) erheben Sie sich!; **thou shalt not kill** (*Bibl*) du sollst nicht töten; **the manufacturer ~ deliver ...** (*in contracts etc*) der Hersteller liefert ...; **I want to go too — and so you ~** ich will auch mitkommen — aber gewiß doch *or* (*in fairy stories*) es sei!
▼ (**c**) (*in questions, suggestions*) **what ~ we do?** was sollen wir machen?, was machen wir?; **let's go in, ~ we?** komm, gehen wir hinein!; **~ I go now?** soll ich jetzt gehen?; **I'll buy 3, ~ I?** soll ich 3 kaufen?, ich kaufe 3, oder?

shallot [ʃə'lɒt] *n* Schalotte *f*.

shallow ['ʃæləʊ] [1] *adj* flach; *water also* seicht; (*fig*) oberflächlich; *talk, person, novel* seicht, oberflächlich ◆ **in the ~ end of the pool** am flachen *or* niedrigen Ende des Beckens.
[2] *n* **~s** *pl* seichte *or* flache Stelle (im Wasser), Untiefe *f*.

shallowness ['ʃæləʊnɪs] *n see adj* Flachheit *f*; Seichtheit *f*; Oberflächlichkeit *f*.

shalt [ʃælt] (*obs*) *2nd pers sing of* **shall**.

sham [ʃæm] [1] *n* (**a**) (*pretence*) Heuchelei *f* ◆ **he's not really sorry, it's all a big ~** es tut ihm nicht wirklich leid, er heuchelt nur *or* das ist geheuchelt; **this so-called emotion is all ~** dieses sogenannte Gefühl ist reine Heuchelei; **their marriage had become a ~** ihre Ehe war zur Farce geworden *or* bestand nur noch zum Schein; **his life seemed a ~** sein Leben erschien ihm als Lug und Trug; **this lighthouse is just a ~, built to deceive enemy bombers** dieser Leuchtturm ist nur eine Attrappe, die die feindlichen Bomber täuschen soll.
(**b**) (*person*) Scharlatan *m* ◆ **you don't really feel anything, you big ~!** du empfindest überhaupt nichts, du Heuchler!
[2] *adj diamonds, oak etc* unecht, imitiert; *politeness etc* vorgetäuscht, geheuchelt ◆ **~ battle** Scheingefecht *nt*.
[3] *vt* vortäuschen, vorgeben; *illness also* simulieren; *emotions, sympathy* heucheln.
[4] *vi* so tun; (*esp with illness*) simulieren; (*with feelings*) heucheln ◆ **he's just ~ming** er tut nur so.

shamble ['ʃæmbl] *vi* trotten; (*people also*) latschen (*inf*) ◆ **every morning he ~s in half an hour late** er kommt jeden Morgen eine halbe Stunde zu spät angelatscht (*inf*).

shambles ['ʃæmblz] *n sing* heilloses Durcheinander; (*esp of room etc*) Tohuwabohu *nt* ◆ **the room was a ~** im Zimmer herrschte das reinste Tohuwabohu *or* ein heilloses Durcheinander; **the economy/country is in a ~** die Wirtschaft/das Land befindet sich in einem Chaos; **they left the house in a ~** sie hinterließen das Haus wie ein Schlachtfeld; **the game was a ~** das Spiel war das reinste Kuddelmuddel (*inf*); **he made a ~ of that job** da hat er vielleicht einen Mist gebaut! (*inf*).

shambolic [ʃæm'bɒlɪk] *adj* (*inf*) chaotisch (*inf*).

▼ **shame** [ʃeɪm] [1] *n* (**a**) (*feeling of ~*) Scham *f*; (*cause of ~*) Schande *f* ◆ **to feel ~ at sth** sich für etw schämen; **he hung his head in ~** er senkte beschämt den Kopf; (*fig*) er schämte sich; **to bring ~ upon sb/oneself** jdm/sich Schande machen; **he is without ~, he is lost to all sense of ~** er hat keinerlei Schamgefühl, ihm fehlt jegliches Schamgefühl; **she is past all (sense of) ~** sie hat jegliches Schamgefühl verloren; **she has no ~, dancing around like that** daß sie sich nicht schämt, so herumzutanzen; **to put sb/sth to ~** (*lit*) jdm/etw Schande machen; (*fig*) jdn/etw in den Schatten stellen; **by working so hard he puts us to ~** er arbeitet so schwer, daß er uns alle beschämt; **to my (eternal) ~** zu meiner (ewigen) Schande; **I'll never forget the ~ of it** ich werde nie vergessen, wie ich mich schämte; **to cry ~ on sb** sich über jdn entrüsten; **the ~ of it all** die Schande *or* Schmach; **the ~ of it!** was für eine Schande!, diese Schande!; **the street is the ~ of the town** die Straße ist der Schandfleck *or* die Schande dieser Stadt; **have you no ~?** schämst du dich (gar) nicht?; **for ~!** schäm dich!/schämt euch!; **she didn't! for ~!** nein! sie sollte sich schämen!; **~ on you!** du solltest dich/ihr solltet euch schämen!
▼ (**b**) (*pity*) **it's a ~ you couldn't come** schade, daß du nicht kommen konntest; **it's a (great) ~ we have to leave so early** es ist (so) schade *or* ein Jammer, daß wir schon so früh gehen müssen; **what a ~!** (das ist aber) schade!, wie schade!; **what a ~ he ...** schade, daß er ...; *see* **crying**.
[2] *vt* Schande machen (*+dat*); (*fig: by excelling*) in den Schatten stellen ◆ **he ~d us by working so hard** er hat uns alle durch sein hartes Arbeiten beschämt; **by giving so much he ~d me into making a bigger contribution** dadurch, daß er soviel gab, fühlte ich mich moralisch gezwungen, mehr zu spenden; **see if you can ~ him into changing his mind** appelliere an sein besseres Ich, dann überlegt er es sich vielleicht anders.

shamefaced ['ʃeɪm'feɪst] *adj*, **~ly** ['ʃeɪm'feɪsɪdlɪ] *adv* betreten.

shamefacedness ['ʃeɪm'feɪstnɪs] *n* Betretenheit *f*.

shameful ['ʃeɪmfʊl] *adj* schändlich ◆ **another ~ day for the pound** noch ein schmachvoller Tag für das Pfund Sterling; **how ~!** was für eine Schande!; **what ~ prices/behaviour!** diese Preise sind/dieses Benehmen ist eine Schande.

shamefully ['ʃeɪmfəlɪ] *adv* schändlich ◆ **he is ~ ignorant** es ist eine Schande, wie wenig er weiß.

shamefulness ['ʃeɪmfʊlnɪs] *n* Ungeheuerlichkeit *f*.

shameless ['ʃeɪmlɪs] *adj* schamlos ◆ **are you completely ~?** hast du gar kein Schamgefühl?; **he was quite ~ about it** er schämte sich überhaupt nicht; **he was quite ~ about lying to his parents** er belog seine Eltern schamlos.

shamelessly ['ʃeɪmlɪslɪ] *adv see adj*.

shamelessness ['ʃeɪmlɪsnɪs] *n* Schamlosigkeit *f*.

shaming ['ʃeɪmɪŋ] *adj* beschämend.

shammy (leather) ['ʃæmɪ('leðəʳ)] *n* Fenster-/Autoleder *nt*.

shampoo [ʃæm'puː] [1] *n* (*liquid*) Shampoo, Schampon *nt*; (*for hair also*) Haarwaschmittel *nt*; (*act of washing*) Reinigung *f*; (*of hair*) Waschen *nt* ◆ **to give the carpet a ~** den Teppich reinigen *or* shamponieren; **~ and set** Waschen und Legen; **to have a ~ and set** sich (*dat*) die Haare waschen und legen lassen.
[2] *vt person* die Haare waschen (*+dat*); *hair* waschen; *carpet, upholstery* reinigen, shamponieren ◆ **to have one's hair ~ed** sich (*dat*) die Haare waschen lassen.

shamrock ['ʃæmrɒk] *n* Klee *m*; (*leaf*) Kleeblatt *nt*.

shandy ['ʃændɪ] *n* Bier *nt* mit Limonade ◆ **lemonade ~** Alsterwasser *nt* (*N Ger*), Radlermaß *nt* (*S Ger*).

shanghai [ʃæŋ'haɪ] *vt* (*Naut*) schanghaien ◆ **to ~ sb into doing sth** (*fig inf*) jdn zwingen, etw zu tun.

shank [ʃæŋk] *n* (**a**) (*part of leg*) (*of person*) Unterschenkel *m*; (*of horse*) Unterarm *m*; (*of beef*) Hachse *f* ◆ **~s** (*inf: legs*) Hachsen *pl* (*inf*); **(to go) on S~s' pony** auf Schusters Rappen (reiten). (**b**) (*of anchor, key etc*) Schaft *m*; (*of spoon*) Stiel *m*.

shan't [ʃɑːnt] *contr of* **shall not** ◆ **~!** (*inf*) will nicht! (*inf*).

shantung [ʃæn'tʌŋ] *n* Schantungseide *f*.

shanty[1] ['ʃæntɪ] *n* (*hut*) Baracke, Hütte *f* ◆ **~ town** Slum(vor)stadt, Bidonville *f*.

shanty[2] *n* (*Mus*) Seemannslied, Shanty *nt*.

SHAPE [ʃeɪp] *abbr of* **Supreme Headquarters Allied Powers Europe**

➤ LANGUAGE IN USE: **shall: c** → 3.3 **shame: 1b** → 14, 18.2

Hauptquartier nt der alliierten Streitkräfte in Europa während des 2. Weltkriegs.

shape [ʃeɪp] 1 n (a) (*geometrical form, outline*) Form f ◆ **what ~ is it?** welche Form hat es?; **it's rectangular** *etc* **in ~** es ist rechteckig *etc*; **that dress hasn't much/has lost its ~** das Kleid hat keine richtige Form/hat seine Form verloren; **she's the right ~ for a model** sie hat die richtige Figur für ein Mannequin; **to hammer metal into ~** Metall zurechthämmern *or* -schlagen; **to knock sth out of ~** etw zerbeulen; **to take ~** (*lit*) Form bekommen; (*fig*) Gestalt *or* Konturen annehmen; **a flowerbed in the ~ of a circle** ein Blumenbeet in der Form eines Kreises; **government action took the ~ of a ban** die Regierung griff mit einem Verbot ein; **help in the ~ of a cheque** Hilfe in Form eines Schecks; **of all ~s and sizes, of every ~ and size** aller Art, jeder Art, in allen Variationen; **I don't accept gifts in any ~ or form** ich nehme überhaupt keine Geschenke an; **we do not know the ~ of things to come** wir wissen nicht, wie sich die Zukunft gestalten wird; **this may be the ~ of things to come** so könnte das vielleicht in Zukunft sein.
(b) (*unidentified figure*) Gestalt f; (*object*) Form f.
(c) (*guise*) Gestalt f ◆ **in human ~** in Menschengestalt, in menschlicher Gestalt.
(d) (*fig: order, condition*) **in good/bad ~** (*sportsman*) in Form/nicht in Form; (*mentally, healthwise*) in guter/schlechter Verfassung; (*things*) in gutem/schlechtem Zustand; (*business*) gut/schlecht in Schuß (*inf*), in gutem/schlechtem Zustand; **what sort of ~ is your boxer in?** wie fit ist Ihr Boxer?; **what sort of ~ was the business in?** in welchem Zustand war das Unternehmen?; **to get sb/a business into ~** jdn/ein Geschäft *or* Unternehmen auf Vordermann bringen (*inf*); **to get a house into ~** ein Haus in Ordnung bringen; **to get one's affairs into ~** seine Angelegenheiten ordnen.
(e) (*mould*) (*for hats*) Hutform f; (*for dressmaking*) Schneiderpuppe f; (*Cook*) Form f; (*for cutting*) Ausstecher m.
2 vt (*lit*) *stone, wood etc* bearbeiten; *clay etc* formen (*into* zu); (*fig*) *character, ideas* formen, prägen; *one's life* gestalten ◆ **he ~d the wood/stone into the desired form** er verlieh dem Holz/Stein die gewünschte Form; **the factors which ~ one's life** die Faktoren, die das Leben prägen *or* bestimmen; **those who ~ the course of history** die(jenigen), die den Lauf der Geschichte bestimmen; **those who have helped ~ our society** die(jenigen), die unsere Gesellschaft mitgeformt haben; **we must ~ our strategy according to our funds** wir müssen unsere Strategie nach den zur Verfügung stehenden Mitteln ausrichten.
3 vi (*also* **~ up**) sich entwickeln ◆ **to ~ up well** sich gut entwickeln, vielversprechend sein; **he is shaping (up) nicely as a goalkeeper** er ist ein vielversprechender Torwart; **things are shaping up well** es sieht sehr gut aus.

shaped [ʃeɪpt] *adj* geformt ◆ **an oddly ~ hat** ein Hut mit einer komischen Form; **~ like a ...** in der Form einer/eines ...

-shaped [-ʃeɪpt] *adj suf* -förmig.

shapeless ['ʃeɪplɪs] *adj* formlos; (*ugly*) unförmig.

shapelessly ['ʃeɪplɪslɪ] *adv* unförmig.

shapelessness ['ʃeɪplɪsnɪs] *n see adj* Formlosigkeit f; Unförmigkeit f.

shapeliness ['ʃeɪplɪnɪs] *n* (*of figure*) Wohlproportioniertheit f; (*of legs, bust*) Wohlgeformtheit f.

shapely ['ʃeɪplɪ] *adj* (+*er*) *figure, woman* wohlproportioniert; *legs, bust* wohlgeformt.

shard [ʃɑːd] *n* (Ton)scherbe f.

▼ **share¹** [ʃɛəʳ] 1 n (a) (*portion*) Anteil m (*in or of an* +*dat*) ◆ **we want fair ~s for all** wir wollen, daß gerecht geteilt wird; **I want my fair ~** ich will meinen (An)teil, ich will, was mir zusteht; **he didn't get his fair ~** er ist zu kurz gekommen; **I've had more than my fair ~ of bad luck** ich habe mehr (als mein Teil an) Pech gehabt; **I'll give you a ~ in the profit** ich beteilige Sie am Gewinn; **in equal ~s** zu gleichen Teilen; **your ~ is £5** du bekommst £ 5; du mußt £ 5 bezahlen; **how much is my ~?** wie groß ist mein Anteil?; **to come in for one's full ~** seinen vollen Anteil bekommen; **he came in for his full ~ of criticism** er hat sein Teil an Kritik abbekommen; **to fall to sb's ~** (*liter*) jdm zufallen (*liter*); **to go ~s** (*inf*) teilen; **to bear one's ~ of the cost** seinen Anteil an den Kosten tragen; **to take one's ~ of the proceeds/blame** sich (*dat*) seinen Anteil am Gewinn nehmen/sich mitschuldig erklären; **to pay one's ~** seinen (An)teil bezahlen; **to do one's ~** sein(en) Teil *or* das Seine tun *or* beitragen; **to have a ~ in sth** an etw (*dat*) beteiligt sein; **I had no ~ in that** damit hatte ich nichts zu tun.
(b) (*Fin*) (*general*) (Geschäfts)anteil m; (*in a public limited company*) Aktie f ◆ **to hold ~s in a company** (Geschäfts)anteile *pl* an einem Unternehmen besitzen/Aktien eines Unternehmens besitzen.
▼ 2 vt (*divide*) teilen; (*have in common also*) gemeinsam haben; *responsibility* gemeinsam tragen ◆ **we ~ the same birthday** wir haben am gleichen Tag Geburtstag; **they ~ a room** sie teilen ein Zimmer, sie haben ein gemeinsames Zimmer; **I do not ~ that view** diese Ansicht teile ich nicht.
3 vi (a) teilen ◆ **there were no rooms free so I had to ~** es gab keine freien Zimmer mehr, also mußte ich (ein Zimmer) mit jemandem teilen; **children have to learn to ~** Kinder müssen lernen, mit anderen zu teilen; **to ~ and ~ alike** (brüderlich) mit (den) anderen teilen.
(b) **to ~ in sth** sich an etw (*dat*) beteiligen; (*in profit*) an etw (*dat*) beteiligt werden; (*in enthusiasm*) etw teilen; (*in success, sorrow*) an etw (*dat*) Anteil nehmen.

◆**share out** *vt sep* verteilen.

share² *n* (*Agr*) (Pflug)schar f.

share: ~ certificate *n* Aktienzertifikat *nt*; **~cropper** *n* (*US etc Agr*) (Farm)pächter *m* (*der Pacht in Form eines Ernteanteils zahlt*); **~holder** *n* Aktionär(in *f*) *m*; **~ index** *n* Aktienindex *m*; **~ option** *n* Aktienoption *f*; **~-out** *n* Verteilung *f*; (*St Ex*) (Dividenden)ausschüttung *f*.

shark [ʃɑːk] *n* (a) Hai(fisch) *m*. (b) (*inf: swindler*) Schlitzohr *nt* (*inf*) ◆ **loan/property ~** Kredit-/Grundstückshai *m* (*inf*).

sharp [ʃɑːp] 1 *adj* (+*er*) (a) *knife, blade etc* scharf; *needle, point etc* spitz.
(b) (*clear-cut, not blurred*) *outline, photo, contrast* scharf.
(c) (*observant, keen*) *eyes, wits, glance, mind* scharf; *nose* gut, empfindlich; *observation, remark* scharfsinnig, schlau; (*intelligent*) *person* schlau, gewieft, auf Draht (*inf*); *child* schlau, aufgeweckt ◆ **that was pretty ~ of you** das war ganz schön schlau *or* clever (*inf*) von dir; **to keep a ~ watch for mistakes** gut *or* scharf auf Fehler aufpassen; **keep a ~ watch for him/the train** paß gut auf, ob du ihn/den Zug siehst.
(d) (*sudden, intense*) *whistle, cry* durchdringend, schrill; *drop in prices* steil; *frost* scharf; *shower, desire, pain* heftig; *hunger* nagend (*geh*), groß ◆ **after a short, ~ struggle** nach kurzem, heftigem Kampf; **be ~ about it!** (*inf*) (ein bißchen) dalli! (*inf*), zack, zack! (*inf*).
(e) (*acute*) *angle* spitz; *bend, turn by car* scharf.
(f) (*pej: cunning*) *person* gerissen, raffiniert, clever (*inf*); *trick etc* raffiniert ◆ **~ practice** unsaubere Geschäfte *pl*; **there's some ~ practice going on there** da sind Gaunereien im Gange; **that was a pretty ~ move** das war ein raffinierter Schachzug.
(g) (*harsh, fierce*) *tongue, retort, tone of voice* scharf; *person* schroff; *temper* hitzig ◆ **he has a ~ temper** er ist jähzornig.
(h) (*acidic, pungent*) *taste* scharf; *apple* sauer; *wine* herb, sauer (*pej*); (*fig: biting*) *air* schneidend kalt; *wind also* beißend.
(i) (*Mus*) *note* (*too high*) zu hoch; (*raised a semitone*) (um einen Halbton) erhöht ◆ **her voice goes ~ on the higher notes** sie singt die höheren Töne zu hoch.
(j) (*inf: stylish*) *person, clothes* toll (*inf*), todschick (*inf*); *piece of driving* clever (*inf*).
2 *adv* (+*er*) (a) (*Mus*) zu hoch.
(b) (*punctually*) pünktlich, genau ◆ **at 5 o'clock ~** Punkt 5 Uhr.
(c) **look ~!** dalli! (*inf*), zack, zack! (*inf*); **if you don't look ~ ...** wenn du nicht schnell machst ...; **to pull up ~** plötzlich anhalten; **to turn ~ left** scharf nach links abbiegen.
3 *n* (*Mus*) Kreuz *nt* ◆ **you played F natural instead of a ~** du hast f statt fis gespielt.

sharp-edged [ʃɑːp'edʒd] *adj knife, outline etc* scharf; *piece of furniture etc* scharfkantig.

sharpen ['ʃɑːpən] 1 *vt* (a) *knife* schleifen, schärfen, wetzen; *razor* wetzen; *pencil* spitzen; (*fig*) *appetite* anregen; *wits* schärfen; *sensation* erhöhen. (b) (*Mus*) (*by a semitone*) (um einen Halbton) erhöhen; (*raise pitch*) höher singen/spielen/stimmen.
2 *vi* **her voice ~s** sie singt zu hoch.

sharp end *n* **at the ~** (*fig*) in vorderster Front.

sharpener ['ʃɑːpnəʳ] *n* Schleifgerät *nt*; (*in rod shape*) Wetzstahl *m*; (*pencil ~*) (Bleistift)spitzer *m*.

sharper ['ʃɑːpəʳ] *n* Gauner *m*; (*card ~*) Falschspieler *m*.

sharp: ~-eyed *adj* scharfsichtig; **to be ~-eyed** scharfe *or* gute Augen haben; **it was ~-eyed of you to see that** du hast ja Augen wie ein Luchs; **~-featured** *adj* mit scharfen (Gesichts)zügen.

sharpness ['ʃɑːpnɪs] *n see adj* (a) Schärfe *f*; Spitzheit *f*.
(b) Schärfe *f*.
(c) Schärfe *f*; Empfindlichkeit *f*; Scharfsinnigkeit *f*; Schläue, Gewieftheit (*inf*) *f*; Aufgewecktheit *f*.
(d) Schrillheit *f*; Schärfe *f*; Heftigkeit *f*; Größe *f* ◆ **because of the unexpected ~ of the drop in prices** wegen des unerwartet steilen Preissturzes.
(e) Spitzheit *f*; Schärfe *f*.
(f) Gerissenheit, Raffiniertheit, Cleverneß (*inf*) *f*.
(g) Schärfe *f*; Schroffheit *f*; Hitzigkeit *f*.
(h) Schärfe *f*; Säure *f*; Herbheit *f*; schneidende Kälte ◆ **there is a ~ in the air** es ist sehr frisch.

sharp: ~shooter *n* Scharfschütze *m*; **~-sighted** *adj see* **~-eyed**; **~-tempered** *adj* hitzig; **~-tongued** *adj* scharfzüngig; **~-witted** *adj* scharfsinnig.

shat [ʃæt] *pret, ptp of* **shit¹**.

shatter ['ʃætəʳ] 1 *vt* (a) (*lit*) zertrümmern, zerschmettern; *hopes, dreams* zunichte machen; *nerves* zerrütten ◆ **he hurled a brick at the window, ~ing it into a thousand pieces** er schleuderte einen Ziegel gegen das Fenster, das in tausend Stücke zersplitterte *or* zersprang; **the blast ~ed all the windows** durch die Explosion zersplitterten alle Fensterscheiben; **to ~ sth against a wall** etw gegen eine Wand schmettern; **his hopes were ~ed** seine Hoffnungen hatten sich zerschlagen.
(b) (*fig inf: exhaust*) erledigen, fertigmachen (*inf*); (*mentally*) mitnehmen ◆ **she was absolutely ~ed by the divorce** die Scheidung hatte sie schwer mitgenommen.
(c) (*inf: flabbergast*) erschüttern ◆ **I've won the pools? I'm ~ed!** ich habe im Toto gewonnen? ich bin platt! (*inf*).
2 *vi* zerbrechen, zerspringen; (*windscreen*) (zer)splittern.

shattering ['ʃætərɪŋ] *adj* (a) *blow* wuchtig, gewaltig; *explosion* gewaltig; *defeat* vernichtend ◆ **it had a ~ effect on the state of the pound** es wirkte sich verheerend auf das Pfund aus.
(b) (*fig inf: exhausting*) erschöpfend, anstrengend; (*psychologically*) niederschmetternd ◆ **a ~ blow to his ego** ein schwerer Schlag für sein Ich; **I had a ~ day at the office** der Tag im Büro hat mich wahnsinnig geschlaucht (*inf*), ich bin total erledigt vom Büro (*inf*); **the divorce was a ~ experience for**

➤ LANGUAGE IN USE: **share¹: 2** → 12.1, 26.3

her die Scheidung hat sie unheimlich mitgenommen (*inf*).
(c) (*inf: flabbergasting*) *news, realization, ignorance* erschütternd; *effect* umwerfend (*inf*) ◆ **this new film is a ~ experience** dieser neue Film ist ein umwerfendes Erlebnis (*inf*); **it must have been absolutely ~ for you to have found out that ...** das war bestimmt entsetzlich für Sie, als Sie erfuhren, daß ...

shatterproof ['ʃætəpruːf] *adj* splitterfest *or* -frei.

shave [ʃeɪv] (*vb: pret* **~d**, *ptp* **~d** *or* **shaven**) 1 *n* Rasur *f* ◆ **to have a ~** sich rasieren; (*at a barber's*) sich rasieren lassen; **this new razor gives you a good ~** dieser neue Rasierapparat rasiert gut; **a close ~** (*lit*) eine glatte Rasur; **to have a close** *or* **narrow ~** (*fig*) gerade noch *or* mit knapper Not davonkommen, gerade noch Glück haben; **he got a place at university, but it was a close ~** er bekam einen Studienplatz, aber nur mit knapper Not; **that was a close ~** das war knapp.
2 *vt face, legs* rasieren; *leather* (ab)falzen; *wood* hobeln; (*graze*) streifen.
3 *vi* (*person*) sich rasieren; (*razor*) rasieren, schneiden.

◆**shave off** *vt sep beard* sich (*dat*) abrasieren; *sb's beard* abrasieren; *wood* abhobeln.

shaven ['ʃeɪvn] *adj head etc* kahlgeschoren ◆ **~-headed** kahlgeschoren.

shaver ['ʃeɪvəʳ] *n* (a) (*razor*) Rasierapparat *m*. (b) (*inf*) **young ~** junger Bengel (*inf*); (*as address*) junger Freund.

Shavian ['ʃeɪvɪən] *adj* Shawsch.

shaving ['ʃeɪvɪŋ] *n* (a) Rasieren *nt*. (b) **~s** *pl* Späne *pl*.

shaving *in cpds* Rasier-; **~ brush** *n* Rasierpinsel *m*; **~ cream** *n* Rasiercreme *f*; **~ foam** *n* Rasierschaum *m*; **~ mug** *n* Rasierschale *f*; **~ point** *n* Steckdose *f* für Rasierapparate; **~ soap, ~ stick** *n* Rasierseife *f*; **~ tackle** *n* Rasierzeug *nt*.

shawl [ʃɔːl] *n* (*round shoulders*) (Umhänge)tuch *nt*; (*tailored*) Umhang *m*; (*covering head*) (Kopf)tuch *nt*.

s/he *pron* (*he or she*) er/sie.

she [ʃiː] 1 *pron* sie; (*of boats, cars etc*) es ◆ **~ who ...** (*liter*) diejenige, die ...; **it is ~** (*form*) sie ist es.
2 *n* Sie *f*.

she- *pref* weiblich ◆ **~-bear** weiblicher Bär, Bärin *f*.

sheaf [ʃiːf] *n, pl* **sheaves** (*of wheat, corn*) Garbe *f*; (*of arrows etc, papers, notes*) Bündel *nt*.

shear [ʃɪəʳ] *pret* **~ed**, *ptp* **shorn** 1 *vt sheep* scheren; *wool* (ab)scheren; *see* **shorn**.
2 *vi* (a) **the knife ~s through the metal** das Messer zerschneidet das Metall; **the bird ~ed through the air** der Vogel segelte durch die Luft; **the motorboat ~ed through the water** das Motorboot durchpflügte das Wasser. (b) (*Mech: fracture*) **the metal plate had ~ed** in der Metallplatte hatte sich ein Riß gebildet.

◆**shear off** 1 *vt sep sheep's wool* abscheren ◆ **the ship had its bows shorn ~ in the collision** beim Zusammenstoß wurde dem Schiff der Bug abrasiert.
2 *vi* (*break off*) abbrechen.

shearer ['ʃɪərəʳ] *n* (Schaf)scherer *m*.

shearing ['ʃɪərɪŋ] *n* (Schaf)schur *f* ◆ **~s** Schur- *or* Scherwolle *f*.

shearing: ~ machine *n* Schermaschine *f*; **~ time** *n* Schurzeit *f*, Zeit *f* der Schafschur.

shears [ʃɪəz] *npl* (große) Schere; (*for hedges*) Heckenschere *f*; (*for metal*) Metallschere *f*.

shearwater ['ʃɪəwɔːtəʳ] *n* Sturmtaucher *m*.

sheath [ʃiːθ] *n* (*for sword etc*) Scheide *f*; (*Bot*) (Blatt)scheide *f*; (*on cable*) Mantel *m*, Armierung *f*; (*contraceptive*) Gummischutz *m*, Kondom *m or nt*; (*dress*) Futteralkleid *nt* ◆ **the cat withdrew its claws into their ~s** die Katze zog die Krallen ein; **the wing-~ of an insect** die Flügeldecke eines Insekts.

sheathe [ʃiːð] *vt sword* in die Scheide stecken; *claws* einziehen; *cables* armieren ◆ **to ~ sth in metal** etw mit Metall verkleiden.

sheathing ['ʃiːðɪŋ] *n* (*on roof, house*) Verkleidung *f*; (*on ship also*) Beschlag *m*; (*with wood*) Verschalung *f*; (*on cables*) Armierung, Bewehrung *f*.

sheath knife *n* Fahrtenmesser *nt*.

sheaves [ʃiːvz] *pl of* **sheaf**.

shebang [ʃə'bæŋ] *n* (*sl*) **the whole ~** die ganze Chose (*inf*), der ganze Kram (*inf*) *or* Laden (*inf*).

shebeen [ʃɪ'biːn] *n* (*Ir*) Kaschemme, Spelunke *f*.

shed[1] [ʃed] *pret, ptp* **~** 1 *vt* (a) *leaves, hair etc* verlieren; *horns* abwerfen; *clothes* ausziehen, ablegen ◆ **the dancer slowly ~ another layer** die Tänzerin schälte sich langsam aus einer weiteren Hülle; **to ~ its skin** sich häuten; **you should ~ a few pounds** Sie sollten ein paar Pfund abnehmen *or* loswerden.
(b) *tears, blood* vergießen ◆ **he ~ his blood** sein Blut floß; (*die also*) sein Blut wurde vergossen; **why should I ~ my blood?** warum sollte ich Leib und Leben einsetzen?; **I won't ~ any tears over him** ich weine ihm keine Träne nach.
(c) *burden, leader* loswerden; *cares, ideas* ablegen; *friend* fallenlassen; *jobs* abbauen ◆ **an actress who ~s husbands like a snake ~s skins** eine Schauspielerin, die die Ehemänner wechselt wie andere das Hemd.
(d) *light, perfume* verbreiten ◆ **to ~ light on sth** (*fig*) etw erhellen, Licht auf etw (*acc*) werfen.
2 *vi* (*dog, cat etc*) sich haaren.

shed[2] *n* Schuppen *m*; (*industrial also*) Halle *f*; (*cattle ~*) Stall *m*; (*night shelter etc*) Unterstand *m*; *see* **watershed**.

she'd [ʃiːd] *contr of* **she would; she had**.

sheen [ʃiːn] *n* Glanz *m*.

sheep [ʃiːp] *n, pl* - (*lit, fig*) Schaf *nt* ◆ **the vicar and his ~** der Pfarrer und seine Schäfchen; **to count ~** Schäfchen zählen; **to separate the ~ from the goats** (*fig*) die Schafe von den Böcken trennen; **to make ~'s eyes at sb** jdn anhimmeln; **you might as well be hanged for a ~ as a lamb** (*prov*) wennschon, dennschon.

sheep: ~-dip *n* Desinfektionsbad *nt* für Schafe; (*for mange*) Räudebad *nt*; **~dog** *nt* Hütehund *m*; **~dog trials** *npl* Gehorsamkeits- und Geschicklichkeitsprüfungen *pl* für Hütehunde; **~ farm** *n* Schaffarm *f*; **~fold** *n* Schafhürde *f*.

sheepish ['ʃiːpɪʃ] *adj* verlegen ◆ **I felt a bit ~ about it** das war mir ein bißchen peinlich.

sheepishly ['ʃiːpɪʃlɪ] *adv* verlegen.

sheep: ~-run *n* Schafweide *f*; **~-shearer** *n* (*person*) Schafscherer(in *f*) *m*; **~shearing** *n* Schafschur *f*; **~skin** *n* (a) Schaffell *nt*; **~skin (jacket)** Schaffelljacke *f*; (b) (*US inf: diploma*) Pergament *nt*.

sheer [ʃɪəʳ] 1 *adj* (**+er**) (a) (*absolute*) rein; *nonsense also* bar, glatt; *stupidity also* schier; *madness also* glatt ◆ **by the ~ force of his own muscles** durch bloße Muskelkraft; **by ~ chance** rein zufällig; **by ~ hard work** durch nichts als harte Arbeit; **the ~ impossibility of doing that** die schiere Unmöglichkeit, das zu tun; **that's ~ robbery!** das ist der reinste Nepp! (*inf*).
(b) (*steep*) *cliff, drop* steil, jäh (*geh*) ◆ **there is a ~ drop of 200 metres** es fällt 200 Meter steil *or* senkrecht ab.
(c) (*of cloth etc*) (hauch)dünn, (hauch)zart ◆ **~ nylon stockings** hauchdünne Nylonstrümpfe *pl*.
2 *adv* steil, jäh (*geh*); (*vertically*) senkrecht.
3 *vi* (*Naut*) ausscheren.

◆**sheer away** *vi* (a) (*ship, plane*) ausweichen. (b) (*avoid*) **to ~ ~ from sb/sth** jdm/einer Sache ausweichen.

◆**sheer off** *vi* (a) (*ship*) ausscheren. (b) (*person: make off*) sich davonmachen.

sheerness ['ʃɪənɪs] *n* (*of cliffs*) Steilheit *f*.

sheet[1] [ʃiːt] *n* (a) (*for bed*) (Bett)laken, Lein- *or* Bettuch *nt*; (*waterproof ~*) Gummidecke *f*; (*for covering furniture*) Tuch *nt* ◆ **between the ~s** (*inf*) im Bett (*inf*); **the furniture was covered with (dust)~s** die Möbel waren verhängt.
(b) (*of paper, inf: a newspaper*) Blatt *nt*; (*big, as of wrapping paper, stamps etc, Typ*) Bogen *m* ◆ **~ of music** Notenblatt *nt*.
(c) (*of plywood, metal*) Platte *f*; (*of glass also*) Scheibe *f*; (*baking ~*) (Back)blech *nt*; (*Geol*) Schicht *f*; (*of water, ice etc*) Fläche *f*; (*of flame*) Flammenmeer *nt* ◆ **a ~ of ice covered the lake** eine Eisschicht bedeckte den See; **the ~ of water covering the lawn** das Wasser, das auf dem Rasen stand; **the lake, a glasslike ~ of water** der See, eine spiegelblanke Wasserfläche; **a huge ~ of flame engulfed the building** das Gebäude ging in einem Flammenmeer unter; **the rain was coming down in ~s** es regnete in Strömen.

sheet[2] *n* (*Naut: rope*) Schot, (Segel)leine *f* ◆ **~s** (*space*) Vorder-/Achterteil *nt*.

sheet: ~ anchor *n* Notanker *m*; (*fig*) Rettungsanker *m*; **~ anchor man** *n* Eckpfeiler *m*; **~bend** *n* Schotstek *m*; **~ feed** *n* (*Comput*) Einzelblatteinzug *m*; **~ glass** *n* Flach- *or* Scheibenglas *nt*.

sheeting ['ʃiːtɪŋ] *n* (*cloth*) Leinen *nt*; (*metal etc*) Verkleidung *f*; (*wood*) Verschalung *f* ◆ **plastic ~** Plastiküberzug *m*/-überzüge *pl*.

sheet: ~ lightning *n* Wetterleuchten *nt*; **~ metal** *n* Walzblech *nt*; **~ music** *n* Notenblätter *pl*.

sheik(h) [ʃeɪk] *n* Scheich *m*.

sheik(h)dom ['ʃeɪkdəm] *n* Scheichtum *nt*.

sheila ['ʃiːlə] *n* (*Austral inf*) Biene (*inf*), Puppe (*inf*) *f*.

shekel ['ʃekl] *n* Sekel, Schekel *m* ◆ **~s** (*sl*) Moneten *pl* (*sl*).

sheldrake ['ʃeldreɪk] *n* Brandente *f*.

shelf [ʃelf] *n, pl* **shelves** (a) Brett, Bord *nt*; (*for books*) Bücherbrett *or* -bord *nt* ◆ **shelves** (*unit of furniture*) Regal *nt*; **book~** *or* **-shelves** Bücherregal *or* -bord; **to be on the ~** (*girl*) eine alte Jungfer sein, sitzengeblieben sein; (*worker*) zum alten Eisen gehören; **she was left on the ~** sie ist eine alte Jungfer geworden, sie ist sitzengeblieben.
(b) (*ledge of rock etc*) (*on rock face*) Gesims *nt*, (Fels-)vorsprung *m*; (*under water*) (Felsen)riff *nt*, Felsbank *f*; (*sandbank*) Sandbank, Untiefe *f*.

shelf: ~ life *n* Lagerfähigkeit *f*; **~ mark** *n* Standortzeichen *nt*; **~ room** *n* Platz *m* in den Regalen.

shell [ʃel] 1 *n* (a) (*of egg, nut, mollusc*) Schale *f*; (*on beach*) Muschel *f*; (*of pea etc*) Hülse *f*; (*of snail*) (Schnecken)haus *nt*; (*of tortoise, turtle, insect*) Panzer *m*; (*pastry ~*) Form *f* ◆ **to come out of one's ~** (*fig*) aus seinem Schneckenhaus kommen, aus sich (*dat*) herausgehen; **to retire into one's ~** (*fig*) sich in sein Schneckenhaus verkriechen; **I'm just an empty ~** (*fig*) ich bin nur noch eine leere Hülse.
(b) (*frame*) (*of building*) Mauerwerk *nt*, Mauern *pl*; (*gutted also*) (leere) Schale; (*unfinished*) Rohbau *m*; (*ruin*) Gemäuer *nt*, Ruine *f*; (*of car*) (*unfinished*) Karosserie *f*; (*gutted*) Wrack *nt*; (*of ship*) Gerippe *nt*, Rumpf *m*; (*gutted*) Wrack *nt*.
(c) (*Mil*) Granate *f*; (*esp US: cartridge*) Patrone *f*.
(d) (*boat*) Rennruderboot *nt*.
2 *vt* (a) *peas etc* enthülsen; *eggs, nuts* schälen; *egg* abschälen. (b) (*Mil*) (mit Granaten) beschießen ◆ **the town is still being ~ed** die Stadt steht immer noch unter Beschuß.

◆**shell out** (*inf*) 1 *vt sep* blechen (*inf*).
2 *vi* **to ~ ~ for sth** für etw blechen (*inf*).

she'll [ʃiːl] *contr of* **she will; she shall**.

shellac [ʃə'læk] (*vb: pret, ptp* **~ked**) 1 *n* Schellack *m*.
2 *vt* (a) (*varnish*) mit Schellack behandeln. (b) (*US sl: defeat utterly*) in die Pfanne hauen (*sl*); (*beat*) vermöbeln (*inf*), verwichsen (*inf*) ◆ **to get a ~king** eins auf die Schnauze kriegen (*sl*)/eine Tracht Prügel kriegen.

shell: ~fire *n* Granatfeuer *nt*; **~fish** *n* Schaltier(e *pl*) *nt*; (*Cook*) Meeresfrüchte *pl*; **~-hole** *n* Granattrichter *m*.

shelling [ˈʃelɪŋ] *n* Granatfeuer *nt* (*of* auf *+acc*).

shell: ~ program *n* (*Comput*) Shell-Programm *nt*; **~proof** *adj* bombensicher; **~ shock** *n* Kriegsneurose *f*; **~-shocked** *adj* **to be ~-shocked** (*lit*) unter einer Kriegsneurose leiden; (*fig*) verstört sein.

shelter [ˈʃeltəʳ] [1] *n* (*protection*) Schutz *m*; (*place*) Unterstand *m*; (*air-raid ~*) (Luftschutz)keller *or* -bunker *m*; (*bus ~*) Wartehäuschen *nt*; (*mountain ~*) (Berg- *or* Schutz)hütte *f*; (*for the night*) Obdach *nt* (*liter*), Unterkunft *f* ◆ **a night ~ for homeless people** ein Obdachlosenheim *or* -asyl *nt*; **in the ~ of one's home** in der Geborgenheit des Hauses; **under the ~ of the rock** im Schutze des Felsens; **under ~ of night** im Schutze der Nacht; **when the ship reached ~** als das Schiff den sicheren *or* schützenden Hafen erreichte; **to get under ~, to take ~** sich in Sicherheit bringen; (*from rain, hail etc*) sich unterstellen; **to seek ~/to run for ~** Schutz *or* Zuflucht suchen; **to give sb ~** jdn beherbergen; **to provide ~ for sb** jdm Schutz bieten; (*accommodation*) jdn beherbergen; **the peasants offered the guerrillas ~** die Bauern boten den Partisanen Zuflucht.

[2] *vt* schützen (*from* vor *+dat*); *criminal* verstecken ◆ **to ~ sb from blame** jdn gegen Vorwürfe in Schutz nehmen; **to ~ sb from harm** jdn vor Schaden bewahren; **the police think he's trying to ~ someone** die Polizei glaubt, daß er jemanden deckt; **parents ~ing their children from harsh reality** Eltern, die ihre Kinder vor der rauhen Wirklichkeit behüten.

[3] *vi* **there was nowhere to ~** man konnte nirgends Schutz finden; (*from rain etc*) man konnte sich nirgends unterstellen; **a good place to ~** eine Stelle, wo man gut geschützt ist; **we ~ed in a shop doorway** wir stellten uns in einem Ladeneingang unter; **we ~ed behind the rocks** wir stellten uns zum Schutz hinter die Felsen; **to ~ behind a friend/one's reputation** (*fig*) sich hinter einem Freund/seinem Ansehen verstecken.

sheltered [ˈʃeltəd] *adj place* geschützt; *life* behütet ◆ **~ from the wind** windgeschützt; **~ housing** Wohnungen *pl* für Behinderte/Senioren; **~ workshop** beschützende Werkstätte, Behindertenwerkstatt *f*.

shelve [ʃelv] [1] *vi* (*slope*) abfallen.

[2] *vt* **(a)** *room* mit Regalen versehen, Regale einbauen in (*+acc*). **(b)** *problem* aufschieben; *plan, project* ad acta legen.

shelves [ʃelvz] *pl of* **shelf**.

shelving [ˈʃelvɪŋ] *n* Regale *pl*; (*material also*) Bretter *pl*.

shenanigans [ʃəˈnænɪgən(z)] *n pl* (*inf*) (*tomfoolery*) Faxen *pl* (*inf*), Mumpitz *m* (*inf*); (*goings-on*) Dinger (*inf*), Sachen (*inf*) *pl*; (*trickery*) üble Tricks (*inf*) *or* Dinger (*inf*) *pl*.

shepherd [ˈʃepəd] [1] *n* **(a)** Schäfer, (Schaf)hirt *m* ◆ **~ boy** Hütejunge *m*; **the Good S~** der Gute Hirte; **~'s pie** *Auflauf m aus Hackfleisch und Kartoffelbrei*; **~'s plaid** *schwarz-weiß karierter Wollstoff*; **~'s purse** Hirtentäschel(kraut) *nt*. **(b)** (*US*) *see* **German ~**.

[2] *vt* führen.

shepherdess [ˈʃepədɪs] *n* Schäferin *f*.

sherbet [ˈʃɜːbət] *n* (*powder*) Brausepulver *nt*; (*drink*) Brause *f*, Sorbet(t) *m or nt*; (*US: water ~ ice*) Fruchteis *nt*.

sherd [ʃɜːd] *n see* **shard**.

sheriff [ˈʃerɪf] *n* Sheriff *m*; (*Scot*) Friedensrichter *m*.

Sherpa [ˈʃɜːpə] *n* Sherpa *m*.

sherry [ˈʃerɪ] *n* Sherry *m*.

she's [ʃiːz] *contr of* **she is; she has**.

Shetland Islands [ˈʃetləndˈaɪləndz] *npl* Shetlandinseln *pl*.

Shetland pony [ˈʃetləndˈpəʊnɪ] *n* Shetlandpony *nt*.

Shetlands [ˈʃetləndz] *npl* Shetlandinseln *pl*.

shew [ʃəʊ] *vti* (*old*) *ptp* **shewn** [ʃəʊn] *see* **show**.

shibboleth [ˈʃɪbəleθ] *n* (*custom*) Gepflogenheit, Konvention *f*; (*catchword*) Losung, Parole *f*, Schibboleth *nt* (*rare, liter*).

shield [ʃiːld] [1] *n* (*Mil, Her*) Schild *m*; (*Zool also*) Panzer *m*; (*sporting trophy also*) Trophäe *f*; (*on machine*) Schutzschirm *or* -schild *m*; (*eye~, radiation ~*) Schirm *m*; (*fig*) Schutz *m* ◆ **riot ~** Schutzschild *m*; **God is our ~** Gott ist unser Schild.

[2] *vt* schützen (*sb from sth* jdn vor etw *dat*); *industry* absichern, abschirmen ◆ **she tried to ~ him from the truth** sie versuchte, ihm die Wahrheit zu ersparen.

shift [ʃɪft] [1] *n* **(a)** (*change*) Änderung *f*; (*in policy, opinion also*) Wandel *m*; (*Ling*) Verschiebung *f*; (*Mus*) Lagenwechsel *m*; (*from one place to another*) Verlegung *f* ◆ **a ~ of scene** ein Szenenwechsel *m*; **a ~ in direction** eine Richtungsänderung; **a ~ in public opinion** ein Meinungsumschwung *m* in der Bevölkerung; **a ~ of emphasis** eine Gewichtsverlagerung; **a population ~** eine Bevölkerungsverschiebung; **this shows a ~ away from the government** dies läßt eine für die Regierung ungünstige Tendenz erkennen; **a new ~ towards liberalism** ein neuer Trend zum Liberalismus.

(b) (*Aut: gear~*) Schaltung *f* ◆ **~ key** (*on typewriter*) Umschalttaste *f*; (*Comput*) Shift-Taste *f*; **~ lock** Umschaltfeststeller *m*.

(c) (*period at work, group of workers*) Schicht *f* ◆ **to work in ~s** in Schichten arbeiten.

(d) (*stratagem*) List *f*, Kniff *m*; (*expedient*) Ausweg *m* ◆ **to make ~ with/without sth** sich mit/ohne etw behelfen.

(e) (*dress*) Hemdkleid *nt*; (*old: undergarment*) Hemd *nt*.

[2] *vt* **(a)** (*move*) (von der Stelle) bewegen; *screw, nail* loskriegen, rauskriegen; *lid* abkriegen; *cork* rauskriegen; *furniture also* verrücken; *head, arm* wegnehmen; (*from one place to another*) verlagern, verschieben; *offices etc* verlegen; *rubble, boulder also* wegräumen ◆ **to ~ scenery** Kulissen schieben; **to ~ one's ground** seinen Standpunkt ändern; **to ~ sb from an opinion** jdn von einer Meinung abbringen; **he stood ~ing his weight from foot to foot** er trat von einem Fuß auf den anderen; **to ~ the blame onto somebody else** die Verantwortung auf jemand anders schieben; **to ~ sth to another room** etw in ein anderes Zimmer schaffen; **~ the table over to the wall** rück den Tisch an die Wand (rüber)!; **can you ~ your car back a bit?** können Sie ein Stück zurücksetzen?; **they ~ed him to Munich** sie haben ihn nach München versetzt; **we'll ~ all this junk out of the cupboard** wir räumen das ganze Gerümpel aus dem Schrank.

(b) (*inf: get rid of*) loswerden.

(c) (*US Aut*) **to ~ gears** schalten.

(d) (*inf*) *food* verputzen (*inf*); *drink* schlucken (*sl*).

[3] *vi* **(a)** (*move*) sich bewegen; (*ballast, cargo, scene*) sich verlagern; (*scene*) wechseln; (*wind*) umspringen; (*from one's opinion*) abgehen ◆ **he ~ed out of the way** er ging aus dem Weg; **he was ~ing about in his chair** er rutschte auf seinem Stuhl hin und her; **~ over, you're taking up too much room** rück mal rüber, du nimmst zuviel Platz weg!; **he ~ed onto his back** er drehte sich auf den Rücken; **he refused to ~** (*fig*) er war nicht umzustimmen; **~ing sands** (*Geol*) Flugsand *m*.

(b) (*Aut*) schalten.

(c) (*inf: move quickly*) (*cars, runners*) flitzen (*inf*), rasen ◆ **that's really ~ing!** das nenne ich Tempo!

(d) (*manage*) **to ~ for oneself** sich (*dat*) (selbst) behelfen.

shiftily [ˈʃɪftɪlɪ] *adv see adj* zwielichtig, nicht ganz sauber (*inf*); verstohlen; ausweichend; *behave* verdächtig.

shiftiness [ˈʃɪftɪnɪs] *n see adj* Zwielichtigkeit *f*, Fragwürdigkeit *f*, Verstohlenheit *f*, Ausweichen *nt* ◆ **there was a certain ~ in his manner** sein Verhalten hatte etwas Verdächtiges.

shiftless [ˈʃɪftlɪs] *adj* träge, energielos.

shiftlessness [ˈʃɪftlɪsnɪs] *n* Trägheit, Energielosigkeit *f*.

shift: ~work *n* Schichtarbeit *f*; **to do ~work** Schicht arbeiten, Schichtarbeit machen; **~worker** *n* Schichtarbeiter(in *f*) *m*.

shifty [ˈʃɪftɪ] *adj* (*+er*) zwielichtig, nicht ganz sauber (*inf*); *person, character also* fragwürdig; *glance* verstohlen; *reply* ausweichend ◆ **there was something ~ about ...** mit ... war etwas faul (*inf*); **he has a ~ look in his eyes** er hat so einen unsicheren Blick; **a ~ expression came over his face** sein Gesicht nahm einen gerissenen Ausdruck an; **a ~ little man** ein verdächtiger kleiner Kerl.

Shiite [ˈʃiːaɪt] [1] *n* Schiit(in *f*) *m*.

[2] *adj* schiitisch.

shillelagh [ʃəˈleɪlə] *n* (*Ir*) (Schlehdorn- *or* Eichen)knüppel *m*.

shilling [ˈʃɪlɪŋ] *n* (*Brit old, Africa etc*) Shilling *m*.

shilly-shally [ˈʃɪlɪˌʃælɪ] *vi* (*inf*) unschlüssig sein ◆ **stop ~ing** laß das Fackeln; **you've shilly-shallied long enough** du hast lange genug gezögert.

shimmer [ˈʃɪməʳ] [1] *n* Schimmer *m*.

[2] *vi* schimmern.

shin [ʃɪn] [1] *n* Schienbein *nt*; (*of meat*) Hachse *f* ◆ **to kick sb on the ~** jdm *or* jdn vors Schienbein treten.

[2] *vi* **to ~ up/down** (geschickt) hinauf-/hinunterklettern.

shinbone [ˈʃɪnbəʊn] *n* Schienbein *nt*.

shindig [ˈʃɪndɪg] *n* (*inf*) Remmidemmi *nt* (*inf*).

shindy [ˈʃɪndɪ] *n* (*inf*) Radau *m* (*inf*); (*noise also, dispute*) Krach *m* (*inf*).

shine [ʃaɪn] (*vb: pret, ptp* **shone**) [1] *n* Glanz *m* ◆ **to give one's shoes a ~** seine Schuhe polieren *or* blank putzen; **~, sir?** Schuhe putzen, der Herr?; **to have a ~** glänzen; **to put a ~ on sth** etw blank polieren; **to take the ~ off sth** (*lit, fig*) einer Sache (*dat*) den Glanz nehmen; **she's taken a real ~ to Oxford/my brother** (*inf*) Oxford/mein Bruder hat es ihr wirklich angetan; *see* **rain**.

[2] *vt* **(a)** *pret, ptp usu* **~d** (*polish: also* **~ up**) blank putzen; *shoes also* polieren.

(b) (*direct a light*) **to ~ a light on sth** etw beleuchten; **~ the torch this way!** leuchte einmal hierher!; **don't ~ it in my eyes!** blende mich nicht!

[3] *vi* **(a)** leuchten; (*stars, eyes, face also, metal, nose, paint*) glänzen; (*moon, sun, lamp*) scheinen; (*glass*) blitzblank sein ◆ **to ~ like a beacon** (*fig*) wie ein Licht in der Dunkelheit sein *or* leuchten; (*hum: face, nose*) wie ein Lampion leuchten.

(b) (*fig: excel*) glänzen ◆ **to ~ at/in sth** bei/in etw (*dat*) glänzen; **he doesn't exactly ~ at sports/his work** er ist keine *or* nicht gerade eine Leuchte im Sport/bei der Arbeit.

◆**shine down** *vi* herabscheinen (*on* auf *+acc*).

◆**shine out** *vi* **(a)** (*light*) **the light shining ~ from the windows across the lawn** das durch die Fenster auf den Rasen fallende Licht; **a light (suddenly) shone ~ from the darkness** in der Dunkelheit blitzte (plötzlich) ein Licht auf; **the sun shone ~ from behind a cloud** die Sonne schien hinter einer Wolke hervor.

(b) (*fig: qualities*) **his courage ~s ~** sein Mut ragt heraus.

shiner [ˈʃaɪnəʳ] *n* (*sl: black eye*) Veilchen *nt* (*sl*).

shingle[1] [ˈʃɪŋgl] [1] *n* **(a)** (*tile*) Schindel *f*; (*US inf: signboard*) Schild *nt* ◆ **to put up one's ~** (*US*) ein Geschäft eröffnen; (*doctor, lawyer*) sich niederlassen.

(b) (*hairstyle*) Herrenschnitt, Bubikopf *m*.

[2] *vt* **(a)** *roof etc* mit Schindeln decken.

(b) *hair* einen Herrenschnitt *or* Bubikopf machen (*+dat*).

shingle[2] *n, no pl* (*pebbles*) Kiesel *m*, Kieselsteine *pl*; (*~ beach*) Kiesel(strand) *m*.

shingles [ˈʃɪŋglz] *n sing* (*Med*) Gürtelrose *f*.

shingly [ˈʃɪŋglɪ] *adj beach* steinig, voller Kieselsteine.

shin-guard [ˈʃɪngɑːd] *n* Schienbeinschützer *m*.

shininess [ˈʃaɪnɪnɪs] *n* Glanz *m*.

shining ['ʃaɪnɪŋ] *adj (lit, fig)* leuchtend; *light* strahlend; *eyes also, nose, metal, paint* glänzend; *car* blitzend, blitzblank ◆ **a ~ light** *(fig)* eine Leuchte; **~ white** leuchtend *or* strahlend weiß.

Shinto ['ʃɪntəʊ] *(Rel)* 1 *n* Schintoismus *m.*
2 *adj* schintoistisch, Schinto-.

Shintoism ['ʃɪntəʊɪzəm] *n (Rel)* Schintoismus *m.*

shinty ['ʃɪntɪ] *n dem Hockey ähnliches Spiel.*

shiny ['ʃaɪnɪ] *adj (+er)* glänzend; *elbows, trousers also* blank.

ship [ʃɪp] 1 *n* (a) Schiff *nt* ◆ **the good ~ Venus** die gute Venus; **on board ~** an Bord; **to take ~ (for)** *(liter)* sich einschiffen (nach); **when my ~ comes home** *or* **in** *(fig)* wenn ich das große Los ziehe; **~ of the line** Kriegsschiff *nt;* **~ of the desert** Wüstenschiff *nt;* **the great ~ of state** das Staatsschiff.
(b) **~'s articles** Heuervertrag *m,* Schiffsartikel *pl;* **~'s biscuit,** *(US)* **~ biscuit** Schiffszwieback *m;* **~'s company** (Schiffs)besatzung *f;* **~'s doctor** Schiffsarzt *m;* **~'s manifest** *(for goods)* Ladeverzeichnis *nt; (for passengers)* Passagierliste *f;* **~'s papers** Schiffspapiere *pl.*
(c) *(US inf: plane)* Maschine *f; (space~)* (Raum)schiff *nt.*
2 *vt* (a) *(take on board)* an Bord nehmen; *mast* setzen ◆ **to ~ oars** die Riemen einlegen; **to ~ water** leck sein; **we're ~ping water** unser Boot leckt *or* ist leck. (b) *(transport)* versenden; *coal, grain etc* verfrachten; *(by sea also)* verschiffen.
3 *vi (take employment)* anheuern.

◆**ship off** *vt sep* versenden; *coal, grain etc* verfrachten; *(by ship also)* verschiffen ◆ **they ~ped their sons ~ to boarding school** sie steckten ihre Söhne ins Internat *(inf).*

◆**ship out** *vt sep* versenden; *coal, grain etc* verfrachten ◆ **to ~ supplies ~ to sb** jdn (per Schiff) mit Vorräten versorgen.

ship: ~board *n:* **on ~board** an Bord; **a ~board romance** eine Romanze auf See; **~breaker** *n* Schiffsverschrotter *m;* **~builder** *n* Schiffbauer *m;* **a firm of ~builders** eine Schiffbaufirma; **~building** *n* Schiffbau *m;* **~ canal** *n* (See)kanal *m;* **~load** *n* Schiffsladung *f;* **the tourists were arriving by the ~load** *or* **in ~loads** *(inf)* ganze Schiffsladungen von Touristen kamen an; **~mate** *n* Schiffskamerad *m.*

shipment ['ʃɪpmənt] *n* Sendung *f; (of coal, grain, tractors)* Transport *m; (transporting by sea)* Verschiffung *f; (taking on board)* Verladen *nt.*

shipowner ['ʃɪpəʊnəʳ] *n* Schiffseigner *m; (of many ships)* Reeder *m.*

shipper ['ʃɪpəʳ] *n (company)* Speditionsfirma *f,* Spediteure *pl; (sender)* Absender *m.*

shipping ['ʃɪpɪŋ] 1 *n, no pl* (a) Schiffahrt *f; (ships)* Schiffe *pl* ◆ **the Suez Canal has been reopened to ~** der Suezkanal ist wieder für die Schiffahrt *or* den Schiffsverkehr geöffnet. (b) *(transportation)* Verschiffung *f; (by rail etc)* Versand *m.*
2 *adj attr* **~ agent** Reeder(in *f*) *m;* **~ business** Reederei- *or* Schiffahrtsgeschäft *nt;* **~ clerk** Expedient(in *f*) *m,* Angestellte(r) *mf* in der Versandabteilung; **~ costs** Frachtkosten *pl;* **~ company, ~ line** Schiffahrtsgesellschaft *or* -linie, Reederei *f;* **~ documents** Versanddokumente, Warenbegleitpapiere *pl;* **~ lane** Schiffahrtsstraße *f;* **~ losses** Verluste *pl* von *or* an Schiffen; **~ office** *(agent's office)* Büro *nt* einer Reedereivertretung; *(place where seamen get jobs)* Heuerbüro *nt;* **~ route** Schiffahrtslinie *f.*

ship: ~shape *adj, adv* tipptopp *(inf);* **to get everything ~shape** alles tipptopp machen *(inf);* **we'll soon have you ~shape again, said the doctor** Sie werden bald wieder auf dem Damm *(inf)* sein, sagte der Arzt; **~shape and Bristol fashion** in bester Ordnung; **~-to-shore radio** *n* Seefunk *m;* **~way** *n (support)* Stapel *m; (ship canal)* (See)kanal, Schiffahrtsweg *m;* **~wreck** 1 *n (lit, fig)* Schiffbruch *m; (fig also)* Scheitern *nt;* **in the ~wreck** bei dem Schiffbruch; 2 *vt (lit)* schiffbrüchig werden lassen; *(fig)* zum Scheitern bringen, scheitern lassen; **to be ~wrecked** *(lit)* schiffbrüchig sein; *(fig)* Schiffbruch erleiden, scheitern; **~wright** *n* Schiffbauer *m;* **~yard** *n* (Schiffs)werft *f.*

shire ['ʃaɪəʳ] *n (Brit old)* Grafschaft *f* ◆ **~ horse** Zugpferd *nt.*

shirk [ʃɜːk] 1 *vt* sich drücken vor (+*dat*), ausweichen (+*dat*).
2 *vi* sich drücken ◆ **you're ~ing!** du willst dich drücken!

shirker ['ʃɜːkəʳ] *n* Drückeberger(in *f*) *m.*

shirking ['ʃɜːkɪŋ] *n* Drückebergerei *f.*

shirr [ʃɜːʳ] *vt* kräuseln.

shirring ['ʃɜːrɪŋ] *n* Kräuselarbeit *f* ◆ **~ elastic** Gummizug *m.*

shirt [ʃɜːt] *n (men's)* (Ober)hemd *nt; (Ftbl)* Hemd, Trikot *nt; (women's: also US* **~waist)** Hemdbluse *f* ◆ **keep your ~ on** *(inf)* reg dich nicht auf!; **to put one's ~ on a horse** *(inf)* den letzten Pfennig auf ein Pferd setzen; **I'm putting my ~ on him to get the job** *(inf)* ich gehe jede Wette ein, daß er die Stelle bekommt; **he'd give you the ~ off his back** *(inf)* er würde einem sein letztes Hemd geben; **he'll have the ~ off your back!** *(inf)* er zieht dich aus bis aufs letzte Hemd! *(inf).*

shirt: ~ collar *n* Hemdkragen *m;* **~-front** *n* Hemdbrust *f.*

shirting ['ʃɜːtɪŋ] *n* Hemdenstoff *m.*

shirt-sleeve ['ʃɜːtsliːv] 1 *adj* hemdsärmelig ◆ **it's real ~ weather now** jetzt kann man wirklich in Hemdsärmeln gehen.
2 *n* **~s** *pl* Hemdsärmel *pl* ◆ **in his/their ~s** in Hemdsärmeln.

shirttail ['ʃɜːtteɪl] *n* Hemd(en)schoß *m.*

shirtwaister ['ʃɜːtˌweɪstəʳ], *(US)* **shirtwaist** ['ʃɜːtˌweɪst] *n* Hemdblusenkleid *nt.*

shirty ['ʃɜːtɪ] *adj (+er) (esp Brit inf)* sauer *(inf),* verärgert; *(as characteristic)* griesgrämig *(inf)* ◆ **he got pretty ~ about it** er wurde ganz schön sauer *(inf);* **now don't get ~ with me!** nun werd nicht gleich sauer! *(inf).*

shit¹ [ʃɪt] *(vb: pret, ptp* **shat**) *(vulg)* 1 *n* (a) *(excrement)* Scheiße *f (sl)* ◆ **to have a ~** scheißen *(sl).*
(b) *(person)* Arschloch *nt (vulg).*
(c) *(nonsense)* Scheiße *f (sl),* Scheiß *m (sl)* ◆ **don't give me that ~!** erzähl mir nicht solche Scheiße *(sl) or* solchen Scheiß *(sl)!*
(d) **~s** *pl (state of fear)* Schiß *m (sl),* Muffensausen *nt (sl)* ◆ **to have/get the ~s** Schiß *or* Muffensausen haben/kriegen *(sl);* **it gives me the ~s** da krieg' ich Schiß *(sl).*
(e) **to be up ~ creek (without a paddle)** bis zum Hals in der Scheiße sitzen *(vulg);* **to be in the ~** in der Scheiße sitzen *(vulg).*
2 *vi* scheißen *(sl)* ◆ **to ~ on sb** *(inform)* jdn verpfeifen *(inf);* **all offenders will be shat on from a great height** *(vulg hum)* wer nicht spurt, wird unheimlich zur Sau gemacht *(sl) or* zusammengeschissen *(sl).*
3 *vr* **to ~ oneself** sich vollscheißen *(vulg); (with fear)* sich *(dat)* vor Angst in die Hose scheißen *(sl).*
4 *interj* Scheiße *(sl).*

shit² *n (sl: drugs)* Shit *m (sl).*

shite [ʃaɪt] *n vir, interj (vulg) see* **shit**¹.

shitless ['ʃɪtlɪs] *adj:* **to be scared ~** *(vulg)* sich *(dat)* vor Angst in die Hosen scheißen *(sl).*

shitty ['ʃɪtɪ] *adj (+er) (sl)* beschissen *(sl),* Scheiß- *(sl).*

shiver¹ ['ʃɪvəʳ] 1 *n* (a) *(of cold)* Schauer *m; (of horror also)* Schauder *m* ◆ **a ~ of cold** ein kalter Schauer; **a ~ ran down my spine** es lief mir kalt den Rücken hinunter; **a little ~ of fear ran down my spine** ein Angstschauer überlief mich; **the sight sent ~s down my back** bei dem Anblick überlief es mich kalt *or* lief es mir kalt den Rücken hinunter; **his touch sent ~s down her spine** es durchzuckte sie bei seiner Berührung.
(b) *(fig)* **to get/have the ~s** eine Gänsehaut kriegen/haben; **it gives me the ~s** ich kriege davon eine Gänsehaut.
2 *vi* zittern *(with* vor +*dat); (with fear also)* schaudern.

shiver² 1 *n* Splitter *m,* Scherbe *f.*
2 *vti* zersplittern, zerbrechen.

shivery ['ʃɪvərɪ] *adj* **to feel ~** frösteln; **the 'flu made him a bit ~** wegen seiner Grippe fröstelte er leicht; **she's a ~ person** sie friert leicht.

shmo [ʃməʊ] *n (US sl) see* **schmo.**

shmuck [ʃmʌk] *n (US sl) see* **schmuck.**

shoal¹ [ʃəʊl] *n (shallow place)* Untiefe *f; (sandbank)* Sandbank *f.*

shoal² *n (of fish)* Schwarm *m* ◆ **in ~s** *(letters, applications etc)* massenweise, in Massen; *(people)* in hellen Scharen; **~s of applications** Unmengen *pl* von Bewerbungen.

shock¹ [ʃɒk] 1 *n* (a) *(of explosion, impact)* Wucht *f; (of earthquake)* (Erd)stoß *m.*
(b) *(Elec)* Schlag *m; (Med)* (Elektro)schock *m* ◆ **to get a ~** einen Schlag bekommen.
(c) *(emotional disturbance)* Schock, Schlag *m; (state)* Schock(zustand) *m* ◆ **to suffer from ~** einen Schock (erlitten) haben; **to be in (a state of) ~** unter Schock stehen; **the ~ killed him** den Schock hat er nicht überlebt; **rabbits can die of ~** für ein *or* bei einem Kaninchen kann ein Schock tödlich sein; **a feeling of ~ spread through the town** Entsetzen verbreitete sich in der Stadt; **our feeling is one of ~** wir sind zutiefst bestürzt; **a ~ to one's system** ein Kreislaufschock; **it comes as a ~ to hear that ...** mit Bestürzung höre ich/hören wir, daß ...; **to give sb a ~** jdn erschrecken; **it gave me a nasty ~** es hat mir einen bösen Schreck(en) eingejagt; **to get the ~ of one's life** den Schock seines Lebens kriegen; **I got the ~ of my life when I heard ...** ich dachte, mich trifft der Schlag *(inf),* als ich hörte ...; **he is in for a ~!** *(inf)* der wird sich wundern *(inf);* **~ horror story** *(Press, hum)* Horrorgeschichte *f.*
2 *vt (affect emotionally)* erschüttern, bestürzen; *(make indignant)* schockieren, schocken *(inf)* ◆ **to be ~ed by sth** über etw *(acc)* erschüttert *or* bestürzt sein; *(morally)* über etw *(acc)* schockiert *or* geschockt *(inf)* sein; **she is easily ~ed** sie ist leicht *or* schnell schockiert; **he was ~ed when they took his passport away** es hat ihn geschockt, daß man ihm den Paß abgenommen hat *(inf);* **to ~ sb into doing sth** jdm eine solche Angst einjagen, daß er etw tut/unternimmt *etc;* **to ~ sb into acting/out of his lethargy** jdn zum Handeln/aus seiner Lethargie aufrütteln.
3 *vi (film, writer etc)* schockieren, schocken *(inf).*

shock² *n (Agr)* Garbenbündel *nt,* Hocke *f.*

shock³ *n (also* **~ of hair)** (Haar)schopf *m.*

shock absorber ['ʃɒkæbˌzɔːbəʳ] *n* Stoßdämpfer *m.*

shocked [ʃɒkt] *adj* erschüttert, bestürzt; *(indignant, outraged)* schockiert, empört; *(amazed)* geschockt *(inf)* ◆ **to be ~** *(Med)* unter Schock stehen, in einem Schockzustand sein; **the patient is badly ~** der Patient hat einen schweren Schock (erlitten).

shocker ['ʃɒkəʳ] *n (inf)* Reißer *(inf),* Schocker *(inf) m* ◆ **he told me a ~ about conditions in jail** er erzählte mir eine Schauergeschichte über die Zustände im Gefängnis; **it's a ~** das haut einen um *(inf);* **I have a ~ of a cold** ich habe eine grausige *(inf) or* entsetzliche Erkältung; **he's a ~** er ist ein ganz Schlimmer *(hum);* **he's a ~ for drink/women** er ist vielleicht ein Schluckspecht *(inf)*/Weiberheld *(inf).*

shockheaded ['ʃɒkˌhedɪd] *adj:* **to be ~** strubbeliges *or* zotteliges Haar haben, ein Struwwelpeter sein *(inf).*

shocking ['ʃɒkɪŋ] *adj* (a) *news, report* erschütternd, schockierend ◆ **~ pink** knallrosa *(inf),* pink *(Fashion).*
(b) *(very bad)* entsetzlich, furchtbar ◆ **what a ~ thing to say/way to behave!** wie kann man bloß so etwas Schreckliches sagen/wie kann man sich bloß so schrecklich benehmen!; **isn't it ~!** es ist doch furchtbar!

shockingly ['ʃɒkɪŋlɪ] *adv* (a) *(badly)* schrecklich, furchtbar ◆ **to behave ~ (towards sb)** sich (jdm gegenüber) haarsträubend *or* miserabel benehmen.
(b) *(extremely)* entsetzlich, schrecklich.

shock: ~ jock *n (esp US inf) Radio-Diskjockey m, der seine kontroversen (meist rechtsradikalen) Ansichten provokativ vertritt;* **~proof** *adj* stoßfest *or* -sicher; **~ tactics** *npl (Mil)* Stoß- *or* Durchbruchstaktik *f; (fig)* Schocktherapie *f;* **~ therapy** *or* **treatment** *n* Schocktherapie *or* -behandlung *f;* **~ troops** *npl* Stoßtruppen *pl;* **~ wave** *n (lit)* Druckwelle *f; (fig)* Erschütterung *f,* Schock *m no pl.*

shod [ʃɒd] *pret, ptp of* **shoe.**

shoddily [ˈʃɒdɪlɪ] *adv* schäbig.

shoddiness [ˈʃɒdɪnɪs] *n* Schäbigkeit *f; (of work)* Schludrigkeit *f; (of goods also)* Minderwertigkeit *f.*

shoddy [ˈʃɒdɪ] [1] *adj (+er)* schäbig; *work* schludrig; *goods also* minderwertig.
[2] *n (cloth)* Shoddy *nt or m.*

shoe [ʃuː] *(vb: pret, ptp* **shod)** [1] *n* **(a)** Schuh *m* ◆ **I wouldn't like to be in his ~s** ich möchte nicht in seiner Haut stecken; **to put oneself in sb's ~s** sich in jds Lage *(acc)* versetzen; **to step into** *or* **fill sb's ~s** an jds Stelle *(acc)* treten *or* rücken; **where the ~ pinches** *(fig)* wo mich/uns der Schuh drückt.
(b) *(horse~)* (Huf)eisen *nt.*
(c) *(brake ~)* Bremsschuh *m.*
(d) *(for electric power cable)* (Gleit)schuh *m; (for mast)* Schuh *m; (on sledge)* Beschlag *m.*
[2] *vt horse* beschlagen ◆ **to be well-shod** *(of person)* gut beschuht sein *(hum, geh).*

shoe: ~black *n* Schuhputzer *m;* **~brush** *n* Schuhbürste *f;* **~horn** *n* Schuhanzieher *or* -löffel *m;* **~lace** *n* Schnürsenkel *m;* **~ leather** *n* Schuhleder *nt;* **to wear out one's ~ leather** seine Schuhe auftragen; **save ~ leather by taking the bus** fahr mit dem Bus und schone deine Schuhsohlen; **~less** *adj* ohne Schuhe; **~maker** *n* Schuhmacher, Schuster *m;* **~mender** *n* (Flick)schuster *m;* **~ polish** *n* Schuhcreme *f;* **~ repairer** *n (person)* Schuster *m; (shop)* Schuh-Reparaturdienst *m;* **~shine** *n (US)* Schuh(e)putzen *nt;* **to have a ~shine** sich *(dat)* die Schuhe putzen lassen; **~shine boy** *n* Schuhputzer *m;* **~shop** *n* Schuhgeschäft *nt;* **~string** *n* **(a)** *(US: ~lace)* Schnürsenkel *m,* Schnürband *nt;* **(b)** *(fig)* **to live on a ~string** von der Hand in den Mund leben; **the project is run on a ~string** das Projekt wird mit ganz wenig Geld finanziert; **~string budget** *n* Minibudget *nt (inf);* **~tree** *n* (Schuh)spanner *m.*

shone [ʃɒn] *pret, ptp of* **shine.**

shoo [ʃuː] [1] *interj* sch; *(to dog etc)* pfui; *(to child)* husch.
[2] *vt* **to ~ sb away** jdn ver- *or* wegscheuchen; **I ~ed the children into the garden** ich scheuchte die Kinder in den Garten.

shook[1] [ʃʊk] *pret of* **shake.**

shook[2] *n (of corn)* Garbenbündel *nt,* Hocke *f.*

shoot [ʃuːt] *(vb: pret, ptp* **shot)** [1] *n* **(a)** *(Bot)* Trieb *m; (sprouting from seed, potato etc also)* Keim *m; (out of ground: of bushes, trees)* Schößling, Schoß *m; (young branch)* Reis *nt.*
(b) *(hunting expedition)* Jagd *f; (~ing party)* Jagdgesellschaft *f; (competition)* (Wett)schießen *nt; (land)* (Jagd)revier *nt,* Jagd *f.*
[2] *vt* **(a)** *(Mil etc)* schießen; *bullet, gun* abfeuern.
(b) *person, animal (hit)* anschießen; *(wound seriously)* niederschießen; *(kill)* erschießen ◆ **to ~ sb dead** jdn erschießen; **he shot himself** er hat sich erschossen; **he shot himself in the foot** er schoß sich *(dat)* in den Fuß; *(fig inf)* er hat ein Eigentor geschossen *(inf);* **he was shot in the leg** er wurde ins Bein getroffen; **the bird had been shot through the wing** dem Vogel war ein Flügel durchschossen worden; **he was fatally shot in the neck** ihn traf ein tödlicher Genickschuß; **you'll get me shot** *(fig inf)* du bringst mich um Kopf und Kragen *(inf);* **you'll get shot for doing that!** *(fig inf)* das kann dich Kopf und Kragen kosten! *(inf);* **people have been shot for less!** *(hum inf)* es sind schon Leute für weniger an den Galgen gekommen! *(inf).*
(c) *(throw, propel)* schleudern ◆ **to ~ a question at sb** eine Frage auf jdn abfeuern; **to ~ a glance at sb, to ~ sb a glance** jdm einen (schnellen) Blick zuwerfen; **to ~ a line** *(inf)* aufschneiden, sich wichtig tun *(to sb* bei jdm).
(d) to ~ the bolt den Riegel vorlegen; **to ~ one's bolt** *(fig)* sein Pulver verschießen; **to ~ the rapids** über die Stromschnellen jagen; **to ~ the lights** eine Ampel (bei Rot) überfahren.
(e) *(Sport)* schießen; *ball also (with foot)* schlagen; *(US sl: play) craps, pool* spielen ◆ **to ~ dice** würfeln, Würfel spielen.
(f) *(Phot) film, scene* drehen; *snapshot* schießen; *subject* aufnehmen.
(g) *(sl: inject) drug* schießen *(sl),* drücken *(sl).*
[3] *vi* **(a)** schießen; *(as hunter)* jagen ◆ **to ~ to kill** gezielt schießen; *(police)* einen gezielten Todesschuß/gezielte Todesschüsse abgeben; **don't ~!** nicht schießen!; **stop or I'll ~!** stehenbleiben oder ich schieße!; **to ~ at sb/sth** auf jdn/etw schießen; **to ~ straight/wide** genau/daneben schießen; **to ~ from the hip** aus der Hüfte schießen; **~!** *(fig inf: ask away etc)* schieß los!
(b) *(move rapidly)* schießen *(inf)* ◆ **to ~ ahead/into the lead** an die Spitze vorpreschen; **he shot ahead of the other boys in maths** er ließ die anderen Jungen in Mathe weit hinter sich *(dat);* **the car shot along the track** der Wagen schoß *or* jagte die Piste entlang; **he shot down the stairs** er schoß *or* jagte die Treppe hinunter; **to ~ by** *or* **past** vorbeischießen *or* -jagen; **to ~ in** (he)reingeschossen kommen.
(c) *(Sport)* schießen ◆ **to ~ at goal** aufs Tor schießen.
(d) *(pain)* **the pain shot up his leg** der Schmerz durchzuckte sein Bein; **~ing pains** stechende Schmerzen *pl.*
(e) *(Bot)* treiben.
(f) *(Phot)* knipsen *(inf); (Film)* drehen.

◆**shoot away** [1] *vi* **(a)** *(move rapidly)* davonschießen, losjagen. **(b)** *(shoot continuously)* schießen ◆ **we shot ~ at them for two hours** wir beschossen sie zwei Stunden lang; **~ ~!** *(fig inf)* schieß los!
[2] *vt sep* wegschießen.

◆**shoot down** *vt sep plane* abschießen; *(fig inf) person* fertigmachen *(inf); suggestion* abschmettern *(inf); argument* in der Luft zerreißen ◆ **the plane was shot ~ in flames** die Maschine wurde in Brand geschossen und stürzte ab.

◆**shoot off** [1] *vi* **(a)** davonschießen, losjagen *(inf).*
(b) *(sl: ejaculate)* abspritzen *(vulg).*
[2] *vt sep* abschießen; *gun etc also* abfeuern ◆ **to ~ one's mouth ~** *(sl) (indiscreetly)* tratschen *(inf); (boastfully)* das Maul aufreißen *(sl);* **he'll start ~ing his mouth ~ to the police** er wird bei der Polizei anfangen zu quatschen *(inf).*

◆**shoot out** [1] *vi (emerge swiftly)* herausschießen *(of* aus).
[2] *vt sep* **(a)** *(put out swiftly) hand etc* blitzschnell ausstrecken; *tongue etc* hervor- *or* herausschnellen (lassen); *(inf: eject)* an die Luft setzen *(inf),* raussetzen *(inf)* ◆ **they were shot ~ of the car** sie wurden aus dem Auto geschleudert.
(b) to ~ it ~ sich *(dat)* ein (Feuer)gefecht liefern; **the cowboys shot it ~** die Cowboys machten die Sache mit ihren Colts aus *(inf);* **nobody dared to ~ it ~ with Bad Jake** keiner wagte es, sich mit Bad Jake zu schießen *(inf).*

◆**shoot up** [1] *vi (hand, prices, temperature)* in die Höhe schnellen; *(grow rapidly) (children, plant)* in die Höhe schießen; *(new towns, buildings etc)* aus dem Boden schießen.
[2] *vt sep* **(a) to ~ ~ a town** *(inf)* in einer Stadt herumballern *(inf) or* -knallen *(inf);* **the aerodrome was shot ~** das Flugfeld wurde heftig beschossen; **he was badly shot ~ in the war** er ist im Krieg übel zusammengeschossen worden.
(b) *drug* schießen *(sl).*

shooter [ˈʃuːtəʳ] *n (sl: gun)* Ballermann *m (sl).*

shooting [ˈʃuːtɪŋ] *n* **(a)** *(shots)* Schießen *nt; (by artillery)* Feuer *nt* ◆ **was there any ~?** gab es Schießereien?
(b) *(murder, execution)* Erschießung *f* ◆ **there was a ~ last night** gestern nacht ist jemand erschossen worden; **"new outbreak of ~s in Belfast"** „Schießereien in Belfast wieder aufgeflammt"; **the police are investigating the ~** die Polizei untersucht den Mord.
(c) *(Sport: Ftbl etc, with guns)* Schießen *nt.*
(d) *(Hunt)* Jagen *nt,* Jagd *f; (~ rights)* Jagdrecht(e *pl) nt; (land)* Jagd *f,* Jagdrevier *nt* ◆ **there is good ~ in Scotland** in Schottland kann man gut jagen; **to go ~** auf die Jagd gehen; **good ~!** Weidmannsheil!
(e) *(Film)* Drehen *nt* ◆ **~ script** Drehplan *m;* **~ was interrupted** die Dreharbeiten wurden unterbrochen.

shooting: ~ box *n* Jagdhütte *f;* **~ brake** *n (Aut)* Kombiwagen *m;* **~ club** *n* Schießklub *m;* **~ gallery** *n* Schießstand *m,* Schießbude *f;* **~ iron** *n (US sl)* Schießeisen *nt (sl),* Schießprügel *m (sl);* **~ jacket** *n* Jagdrock *m;* **~ lodge** *n see* **~ box; ~ match** *n* Wett- *or* Preisschießen *nt;* **the whole ~ match** *(inf)* der ganze Laden *(inf);* **~ party** *n* Jagdgesellschaft *f;* **~ range** *n* Schießplatz *m;* **~ rights** *npl* Jagdrecht(e *pl) nt;* **~ star** *n* Sternschnuppe *f;* **~ stick** *n* Jagdstuhl *m;* **~ war** *n* offener *or* heißer Krieg.

shootout [ˈʃuːtaʊt] *n* Schießerei *f.*

shop [ʃɒp] [1] *n* **(a)** Geschäft *nt,* Laden *m; (esp Brit: large store)* Kaufhaus *nt* ◆ **I have to go to the ~s** ich muß einkaufen gehen; **~!** Bedienung!; **to set up ~** ein Geschäft *or* einen Laden eröffnen; **you've come to the wrong ~** *(fig inf)* da sind Sie an der falschen Adresse; **all over the ~** *(inf)* in der ganzen Gegend herum *(inf);* **to talk ~** über die *or* von der Arbeit reden; *(of professional people also)* fachsimpeln; **no ~, please!** wir wollen nicht von der Arbeit reden/keine Fachsimpelei, bitte!
(b) *(work~)* Werkstatt *f; (workers)* Arbeiter *pl,* Arbeiterschaft *f.*
[2] *vi* einkaufen, Einkäufe machen ◆ **to go ~ping** einkaufen gehen; **we spend Saturday mornings ~ping** samstags vormittags gehen wir einkaufen; **~ at Macfarlane's!** kaufen Sie bei Macfarlane!; **to ~ for fish** Fisch kaufen gehen.
[3] *vt (Brit sl)* **to ~ sb (to sb)** jdn (bei jdm) verpfeifen *(inf).*

◆**shop around** *vi (lit, fig)* sich umsehen *(for* nach).

shop: ~ assistant *n (Brit)* Verkäufer(in *f) m;* **~breaker** *n* Einbrecher *m;* **~breaking** *n* Ladeneinbruch *m;* **~fitter** *n* Geschäftsausstatter *m;* **~fittings** *npl* Ladeneinrichtungen *pl;* **~ floor** *n* **(a)** *(place)* Produktionsstätte *f; (for heavier work)* Werkstatt *f;* **the manager's son started off working on the ~ floor** der Sohn des Direktors hat (ganz unten) in der Fabrik *or* Produktion angefangen; **on the ~ floor** in der Werkstatt *etc;* bei *or* unter den Arbeitern; **(b)** *(workers)* Arbeiter *pl,* Leute *pl* in der Produktion; **~-floor opinion** die Meinung der Arbeiter; **~ front** *n* Ladenfassade *f;* **~girl** *n (Brit)* Ladenmädchen *nt;* **~ hours** *npl* Öffnungszeiten *pl;* **~-in-~** *n* Shop-in-Shop *m;* **~keeper** *n* Ladenbesitzer(in *f) m,* Geschäftsinhaber(in *f) m;* **a nation of ~keepers** ein Krämervolk *nt;* **~lifter** *n* Ladendieb(in *f) m;* **~lifting** *n* Ladendiebstahl *m.*

shopper [ˈʃɒpəʳ] *n* Käufer(in *f) m* ◆ **she's a good ~** sie kann gut einkaufen; **the streets were thronged with ~s** in den Straßen drängten sich die Kauflustigen.

shopping [ˈʃɒpɪŋ] *n (act)* Einkaufen *nt; (goods bought)* Einkäufe *pl* ◆ **she had her ~ in a plastic bag** sie hatte ihre Einkäufe in einer Plastiktüte; **to do one's ~** einkaufen, Einkäufe machen.

shopping: ~ bag *n* Einkaufstasche *f;* **~ basket** *n* Einkaufskorb *m;* **~ cart** *n* Einkaufswagen *m;* **~ centre,** *(US)* **~ center** *n* Einkaufszentrum *nt;* **~ list** *n* Einkaufszettel *m;* **~ mall** *n* Shopping-Center *nt;* **~ precinct** *n* Ladengegend *f,* Ladenbereich *m;* **~ spree** *n* Einkaufsbummel *m;* **~ street** *n* Einkaufsstraße *f.*

shop: ~-soiled *adj clothes, furniture, wallpaper* angestaubt, angeschmutzt; *goods, material* leicht beschädigt; **~ steward** *n* (gewerkschaftlicher) Vertrauensmann (*im Betrieb*); **~ talk** *n* Reden *nt* über die Arbeit; (*of professional people also*) Fachsimpelei *f*; **~walker** *n* (*Brit*) Aufsichtsperson (*form*), Aufsicht *f*; **~ window** *n* (*lit, fig*) Schaufenster *nt*; **~worn** *adj goods, furniture etc* leicht beschädigt.

shore[1] [ʃɔːʳ] *n* **(a)** (*sea~, lake ~*) Ufer, Gestade (*liter*) *nt*; (*beach*) Strand *m* ◆ **these ~s** (*fig*) dieses Land, diese Gestade *pl* (*liter*); **he returned to his native ~s** er kehrte zurück zu heimatlichen Gefilden; **a house on the ~s of the lake** ein Haus am Seeufer; **no invader has since set foot on these ~s** seitdem hat kein Eroberer mehr diesen Boden betreten.
(b) (*land*) Land *nt* ◆ **on ~** an Land.

shore[2] [1] *n* (*Min, Naut*) Stützbalken *m*, Strebe(balken *m*) *f*.
[2] *vt* (*also* **~ up**) (ab)stützen; (*fig*) stützen.

shore: ~ dinner *n* (*US*) Meeresfrüchte *pl*; **~ leave** *n* (*Naut*) Landurlaub *m*; **~line** *n* Wasserlinie, Uferlinie *f*; **~ pass** *n* (*Naut*) Landurlaubsschein *m*; **~ patrol** *n* (*US*) Küstenstreife, Küstenpatrouille *f* (*der US-Marine*); **~ward(s)** [1] *adj wind* See-; **in a ~ward(s) direction** in Richtung Küste *or* Land, landwärts; [2] *adv* landwärts, zum Land (hin).

shorn [ʃɔːn] [1] *ptp of* **shear**.
[2] *adj* **(a) to be ~ of sth** einer Sache (*gen*) entkleidet sein. **(b)** *sheep* geschoren; *head also* kahlgeschoren ◆ **her ~ locks** ihr kurzgeschorenes Haar.

short [ʃɔːt] [1] *adj* (*+er*) **(a)** kurz; *steps also, person* klein; *waist* (*of dress*) hoch ◆ **a ~ way off** nicht weit entfernt; **to be ~ in the leg** (*person*) kurze Beine haben; (*trousers*) zu kurz sein; **to be in ~ trousers** in kurzen Hosen herumlaufen; (*fig*) ein kleiner Junge sein; **a ~ time ago** vor kurzer Zeit, vor kurzem; **in a ~ time** *or* **while** in Kürze, in kurzer Zeit; **time is getting/is ~** die Zeit wird/ist knapp; **to take the ~ view** die Sache auf kurze Sicht betrachten; **in ~ order** (*US inf*) sofort; **~ drink** Kurze(r) (*inf*), Schnaps *m*.
(b) (*Ling*) *vowel, syllable* kurz; (*unstressed*) unbetont.
(c) (*brief*) kurz ◆ **~ and sweet** schön kurz, kurz und ergreifend (*iro*); **the ~ answer is that he refused** kurz gesagt, er lehnte ab; **in ~** kurz gesagt; **she's called Pat for ~** sie wird kurz *or* einfach Pat genannt; **Pat is ~ for Patricia** Pat steht für *or* ist die Kurzform von Patricia.
(d) (*curt*) *reply* knapp; (*rude*) barsch, schroff; *manner, person* schroff, kurz angebunden (*inf*) ◆ **to have a ~ temper** unbeherrscht sein; **his ~ temper** seine Unbeherrschtheit; **to be ~ with sb** jdn schroff behandeln, jdm gegenüber kurz angebunden sein (*inf*).
(e) (*insufficient*) zuwenig *inv*; *rations* knapp ◆ **to be in ~ supply** knapp sein; (*Comm*) beschränkt lieferbar sein; **to be ~** (*in ~ supply*) knapp sein; (*shot, throw*) zu kurz sein, nicht weit genug sein; **we are (five/£3) ~, we are ~ (of five/£3)** wir haben (fünf/£ 3) zuwenig, uns (*dat*) fehlen fünf/£ 3; **it's five/£3 ~** es fehlen fünf/£ 3; **we are ~ of books/staff** wir haben zuwenig Bücher/Personal; **we are not ~ of volunteers** wir haben genug Freiwillige, uns fehlt es nicht an Freiwilligen; **to be ~ of time** wenig Zeit haben; **I'm a bit ~ (of cash)** (*inf*) ich bin etwas knapp bei Kasse (*inf*); **we are £2,000 ~ of our target** wir liegen £ 2.000 unter unserem Ziel; **we are not far ~ of our destination now** wir sind nicht mehr weit von unserem Ziel entfernt; **not far/much ~ of £100** nicht viel weniger als £ 100, beinahe £ 100, knapp unter £ 100; **to be ~ on experience/examples** wenig Erfahrung/Beispiele haben; **to give sb ~ change** jdm zuwenig herausgeben *or* zu wenig Wechselgeld geben; *see* **measure**.
(f) (*Fin*) *sale* ohne Deckung, ungedeckt, Blanko-; *loan, bill* kurzfristig ◆ **~ stock** auf Baisse gekaufte Aktien.
(g) *pastry* mürbe.
[2] *adv* **(a)** (*below the expected amount*) **to fall ~** (*arrow etc*) zu kurz landen; (*shot*) zu kurz sein; (*supplies etc*) nicht ausreichen; **that's where the book falls ~** daran fehlt es dem Buch; **to fall ~ of sth** etw nicht erreichen; *of expectations* etw nicht erfüllen; **it fell 10 metres ~ of the target** es fehlten 10 Meter zum Ziel, es war 10 Meter zu kurz; **it falls far ~ of what we require** das bleibt weit hinter unseren Bedürfnissen zurück; (*in quantity*) das bleibt weit unter unseren Bedürfnissen; **production has fallen ~ by 100 tons** die Produktion ist um 100 Tonnen zu niedrig; **to go ~ (of money/food** *etc*) zuwenig (Geld/zu essen *etc*) haben; **the parents went ~ of food so that the children could eat** die Eltern haben an sich (*dat*) selbst gespart, damit die Kinder zu essen hatten; **they never let the children go ~** sie ließen es den Kindern an nichts fehlen; **we are running ~ (of petrol/time)** wir haben nicht mehr viel (Benzin/Zeit); **I'm running ~ of ideas** mir gehen die Ideen aus; **my patience is running ~** meine Geduld ist bald zu Ende; **sugar/petrol is running ~** Zucker/Benzin ist knapp; **to sell sb ~** (*in shop*) jdm zuwenig geben; (*betray, cheat*) jdn betrügen; **to sell ~** (*Fin*) ungedeckt *or* ohne Deckung verkaufen.
(b) (*abruptly, suddenly*) plötzlich, abrupt ◆ **to pull up** *or* **stop ~** (*while driving*) plötzlich *or* abrupt anhalten; (*while walking also*) plötzlich *or* abrupt stehenbleiben; **to stop ~** (*while talking*) plötzlich *or* unvermittelt innehalten; **to stop a conversation ~** eine Unterhaltung plötzlich *or* unvermittelt abbrechen; **to stop sb ~** jdn unterbrechen; **I'd stop ~ of** *or* **at murder** vor Mord würde ich haltmachen; **he stopped ~ of actually calling me a liar** er ging nicht soweit, mich tatsächlich einen Lügner zu nennen; **to be caught ~** (*inf*) (*unprepared*) überrascht werden; (*without money, supplies*) zu knapp (dran) sein; (*need the toilet*) dringend mal müssen (*inf*); **to catch sb ~** (*inf*) jdn in einer Verlegenheit antreffen; **to be caught ~ by sth** auf etw (*acc*) nicht vorbereitet sein.
(c) ~ of (*except*) außer (*+dat*); **it is nothing ~ of robbery** das ist glatter Diebstahl; **nothing ~ of a revolution can ...** nur eine Revolution kann ...; **it's little ~ of madness** das grenzt an Wahnsinn; **it's little ~ of suicide** das kommt ja Selbstmord gleich; **I don't see what you can do ~ of asking him yourself** ich sehe keine andere Möglichkeit, außer daß *or* als daß Sie ihn selbst fragen; **~ of telling him a lie ...** außer ihn zu belügen ...
[3] *n* (*~ circuit*) Kurzschluß, Kurze(r) (*inf*) *m*; (*inf: ~ drink*) Kurze(r) *m* (*inf*); (*inf: ~ film*) Kurzfilm *m* ◆ **to have/get sb by the ~ and curlies** (*inf*) jdn am Wickel haben/kriegen (*inf*); *see* **long[2]**.
[4] *vt* (*Elec*) kurzschließen.
[5] *vi* (*Elec*) einen Kurzschluß haben.

shortage [ˈʃɔːtɪdʒ] *n* (*of goods, objects*) Knappheit *f no pl* (*of an +dat*); (*of people*) Mangel *m no pl* (*of an +dat*) ◆ **the housing ~** die Wohnungsknappheit; **a ~ of staff** ein Mangel *m* an Arbeitskräften, Personalmangel *m*; **in times of ~** in Zeiten der Knappheit; **there are always ~s** irgend etwas ist immer knapp; **there's no ~ of advice** es fehlt nicht an guten Ratschlägen.

short: ~ arse *n* (*sl*) (kleiner) Pimpf (*inf*), Knirps (*inf*), Murkel (*dial inf*) *m*; **~bread** *n* Shortbread *nt*, ≃ Butterkeks *m*; **~cake** *n* (*Brit: ~bread*) Butterkeks *m*; (*US: sponge*) Biskuittörtchen *nt*; **strawberry ~cake** Erdbeertörtchen *nt*; **~-change** *vt* **to ~-change sb** (*lit*) jdm zuwenig Wechselgeld geben, jdm zuwenig herausgeben; (*fig inf*) jdn übers Ohr hauen (*inf*); **~-circuit** [1] *n* Kurzschluß *m*; [2] *vt* kurzschließen; (*fig: bypass*) umgehen; [3] *vi* einen Kurzschluß haben; **~coming** *n* (*esp pl*) Mangel *m*; (*of person*) Fehler *m*; **~crust** *n* (*also* **~crust pastry**) Mürbeteig *m*; **~ cut** *n* Abkürzung *f*; (*fig*) Schnellverfahren *nt*; (*easy solution*) Patentlösung *f*; **there's no ~ cut to success** der Erfolg fällt einem nicht in den Schoß; **~-dated** *adj* (*Fin*) *stock* kurzfristig.

shorten [ˈʃɔːtn] [1] *vt* **(a)** verkürzen; *dress, rope* kürzer machen, kürzen; *book, programme, letter, syllabus etc* kürzen; *odds* verringern; *sail* reffen. **(b)** *pastry* Fett beigeben (*+dat*).
[2] *vi* (*evenings, days*) kürzer werden; (*odds*) sich verringern.

shortening [ˈʃɔːtnɪŋ] *n* (*Cook*) (Back)fett *nt*.

short: ~fall *n* Defizit *nt*; **~-haired** *adj* kurzhaarig; **~hand** *n* Kurzschrift, Stenographie *f*; **in ~hand** in Kurzschrift; **to write ~hand** stenographieren; **to take sth down in ~hand** etw stenographieren; **~-handed** *adj* **to be ~-handed** zuwenig Personal haben; **~hand notebook** *n* Stenoblock *m*; **~hand notes** *npl* stenographische Notizen *pl*; **~hand typist** *n* Stenotypist(in *f*) *m*; **~hand writer** *n* Stenograph(in *f*) *m*; **~ haul** *n* Nahtransport *m*; **~-haul jet** *n* Kurzstreckenflugzeug *nt*; **~horn** *n* Kurzhornrind, Shorthorn *nt*; **~horn cattle** Kurzhornrinder *pl*.

shortie [ˈʃɔːtɪ] *n* **(a)** (*inf: also* **~ nightie**) Shorty *nt*, kurzes Nachthemd. **(b)** *see* **shorty**.

shortish [ˈʃɔːtɪʃ] *adj* ziemlich kurz; (*scarce*) ziemlich knapp.

short: ~ list *n* (*esp Brit*) Auswahlliste *f*; **to be on the ~ list** in der engeren Wahl sein; **~-list** *vt* (*esp Brit*) **to ~-list sb** jdn in die engere Wahl nehmen *or* ziehen; **he has not been ~-listed** er ist nicht in die engere Wahl gekommen; **~-lived** *adj* (*lit, fig*) kurzlebig; *protests, attempts* nicht lange andauernd; **to be ~-lived** (*success, happiness*) von kurzer Dauer sein.

shortly [ˈʃɔːtlɪ] *adv* **(a)** (*soon*) bald, in Kürze; *after, before, afterwards* kurz. **(b)** (*briefly*) kurz. **(c)** (*curtly*) barsch.

shortness [ˈʃɔːtnɪs] *n* **(a)** Kürze *f*; (*of person*) Kleinheit *f* ◆ **~ of sight/breath** Kurzsichtigkeit/Kurzatmigkeit *f*. **(b)** (*curtness*) Schroffheit, Barschheit *f*. **(c)** (*of supplies, money*) Knappheit *f*.

short: ~-order *adj* (*US*) *dishes* Schnell-; *cook* im Schnellimbiß; **~ pastry** *n* Mürbeteig *m*; **~-range** *adj gun* Nahkampf-; *missile, aircraft* Kurzstrecken-; (*fig*) *plans* kurzfristig; **~-range weather forecast** Wetterbericht *m* für die nächsten Tage.

shorts [ʃɔːts] *npl* **(a)** (*short trousers*) Shorts *pl*, kurze Hose(n *pl*). **(b)** (*esp US: underpants*) Unterhose *f*.

short: ~-sighted *adj*, **~-sightedly** *adv* (*lit, fig*) kurzsichtig; **~-sightedness** *n* (*lit, fig*) Kurzsichtigkeit *f*; **~-sleeved** *adj* kurzärmelig; **~-staffed** *adj* **to be ~-staffed** zuwenig Personal haben; **~-stay** *adj* **~-stay parking** Kurzparken *nt*; **~ story** *n* Kurzgeschichte, Short story, Erzählung *f*; **a ~-story writer** ein Kurzgeschichtenautor *m*; **~-tempered** *adj* (*in general*) unbeherrscht; (*in a bad temper*) gereizt; **to be ~-tempered with sb** mit jdm ungeduldig sein; **~-temperedly** *adv* unbeherrscht; *reply* unwirsch, ungeduldig; **~ term** *n* **for the ~ term** auf kurze Frist gesehen, vorläufig; **plans for the ~ term** kurzfristige Pläne; **in the ~ term** auf kurze Sicht; **~-term** *adj* kurzfristig; **~-term memory** Kurzzeitgedächtnis *nt*; **~ time** *n* Kurzarbeit *f*; **to be on ~ time, to work ~ time** kurzarbeiten, Kurzarbeit haben; **~ ton** *n Tonne von 2000 Pounds = 907,18 kg*; **~-waisted** *adj person* mit kurzer Taille; *coat* hochtailliert; **to be ~-waisted** eine kurze/hohe Taille haben; **~wave** [1] *n* (*also* **~wave radio**) Kurzwelle *f*; [2] *adj transmission* auf Kurzwelle; **a ~wave radio** ein Kurzwellenempfänger *m*; **~-winded** *adj* (*breathless*) kurzatmig.

shorty [ˈʃɔːtɪ] *n* (*inf*) Kleine(r) *mf*, Knirps *m* (*inf*).

shot[1] [ʃɒt] [1] *pret, ptp of* **shoot**.
[2] *n* **(a)** (*from gun, bow etc*) Schuß *m* ◆ **to fire** *or* **take a ~ at sb/sth** einen Schuß auf jdn/etw abfeuern *or* abgeben; **a ~ across the bows** (*lit, fig*) ein Schuß vor den Bug; **to exchange ~s** sich (*dat*) einen Schußwechsel liefern; **the first ~s in the election campaign** (*fig*) die ersten scharfen Schüsse im Wahlkampf; **to call the ~s** (*fig sl*) das Sagen haben (*inf*); *see* **long ~, parting**.
(b) (*projectile*) Kugel *f*; (*no pl: lead ~*) Schrot(kugeln *pl*) *m*.
(c) (*person*) Schütze *m*; *see* **big ~**.
(d) (*attempt*) Versuch *m* ◆ **at the first ~** beim ersten Versuch, auf Anhieb; **to make** *or* **take** *or* **have a ~ (at it)** (*try*) es (mal) versuchen; (*guess*) (auf gut Glück) raten; **I had a ~ at water-skiing** ich habe auch mal versucht, Wasserski zu laufen; **it's your ~** du bist dran; *see* **dark**.
(e) (*space-~*) (Raum)flug *m*; (*launch*) Start *m*.

(f) (*inf: quickly*) **like a ~** *run away, be off* wie der Blitz (*inf*); *do sth* sofort; *agree* sofort, ohne zu überlegen.

(g) (*injection*) Spritze *f*; (*immunization*) Impfung *f*; (*of alcohol*) Schuß *m* ◆ **he gave him a ~ of morphine** er gab ihm eine Morphiumspritze; **a ~ of rum** ein Schuß *m* Rum; **to give a company a ~ in the arm** (*fig*) einer Firma eine Finanzspritze geben.

(h) (*Phot*) Aufnahme *f* ◆ **out of ~** nicht im Bild.

(i) (*Sport*) (*Ftbl, Hockey etc*) Schuß *m*; (*throw*) Wurf *m*; (*Tennis, Golf*) Schlag *m* ◆ **to take a ~ at goal** aufs Tor schießen.

(j) (*~-putting*) **the ~** (*discipline*) Kugelstoßen *nt*; (*weight*) die Kugel; **to put the ~** kugelstoßen.

shot² *adj* **(a)** (*variegated*) durchzogen, durchschossen (*with* mit); *silk* eingeschossen, changierend. **(b)** (*inf: rid*) **to be/get ~ of sb/sth** jdn/etw los sein/loswerden.

shot: ~gun *n* Schrotflinte *f*; **~gun wedding** *n* Mußheirat *f*; **~-put** *n* (*event*) Kugelstoßen *nt*; (*throw*) Wurf, Stoß *m*; **~-putter** *n* Kugelstoßer(in *f*) *m*; **~ tower** *n* Schrotturm *m*.

▼ **should** [ʃʊd] *pret of* **shall**, *modal aux vb* **(a)** (*expressing duty, advisability, command*) **I/you/he/we/you/they ~ do that** ich sollte/du solltest/er sollte/wir sollten/ihr solltet/sie sollten das tun; **you ~n't do that** Sie sollten das nicht tun; **I ~ have done it** ich hätte es tun sollen *or* müssen; **I ~n't have done it** ich hätte es nicht tun sollen *or* dürfen; **all is as it ~ be** alles ist so, wie es sein sollte *or* muß; **which is as it ~ be** und so soll(te) es auch sein; **he ~ know that it's wrong to lie** er sollte *or* müßte wissen, daß man nicht lügen darf; **you really ~ see that film** den Film sollten *or* müssen Sie wirklich sehen; **~ I go too? — yes you ~** sollte ich auch gehen? — ja, das sollten Sie schon; **was it a good film? — I ~ think it was** war der Film gut? — und ob; **he's coming to apologize — I ~ think so** er will sich entschuldigen — das möchte ich auch meinen *or* hoffen; **... and I ~ know ...** und ich müßte es ja wissen; **how ~ I know?** woher soll ich das wissen?

▼ **(b)** (*expressing probability*) **he ~ be there by now** er müßte eigentlich schon da sein; **they ~ arrive tomorrow** sie müßten morgen ankommen; **this ~ be enough** das müßte eigentlich reichen; **why ~ he suspect me?** warum sollte er mich verdächtigen?; **this book ~ help you** dieses Buch wird Ihnen bestimmt helfen; **this ~ be good!** (*inf*) das wird bestimmt gut!

▼ **(c)** (*in tentative statements*) **I ~n't like to say** das möchte ich nicht gern sagen; **I ~ hardly have called him an idiot** ich hätte ihn wohl kaum einen Idioten genannt; **I ~ think there were about 40** ich würde schätzen, daß etwa 40 dort waren; **~ I open the window?** soll ich das Fenster aufmachen?; **I ~ like to disagree** da möchte ich widersprechen; **I ~ like to know** ich wüßte gern, ich möchte gern wissen; **I ~ like to apply for the job** ich würde mich gern um die Stelle bewerben; **thanks, I ~ like to** danke, gern.

(d) (*expressing surprise*) **who ~ I see/~ it be but Anne!** und wen sehe ich/und wer war's? Anne!; **why ~ he want to know/do that?** warum will er das wohl wissen/machen?; **why ~ he have done it, if ...?** warum hat er es dann gemacht, wenn ...?

(e) (*subjunc, cond*) **I/you/he/we/you/they ~ go if ...** ich würde/du würdest/er würde/wir würden/ihr würdet/sie würden gehen, wenn ...; **we ~ have come if ...** wir wären gekommen, wenn ...; **it seems unbelievable that he ~ have failed/be so young** es scheint unglaublich, daß er versagt hat/so jung ist; **I don't see why he ~n't have paid by now** ich verstehe nicht, warum er bis jetzt noch nicht bezahlt hat; **if they ~ send for me** wenn *or* falls sie nach mir schicken sollten; **if he ~ come, ~ he come** falls er kommen sollte, sollte er kommen; **~ it not be true** sollte das nicht wahr sein; **I ~n't be surprised if he comes** *or* **came** *or* **were to come** ich wäre nicht *or* keineswegs überrascht, wenn er kommen würde *or* käme; **I ~n't (do it) if I were you** ich würde das an Ihrer Stelle nicht tun; **I ~n't worry about it** ich würde mir darüber keine Gedanken machen; **it is necessary that he ~ be told** es ist nötig, daß man es ihm sagt; **unless he ~ change his mind** falls er es sich (*dat*) nicht anders überlegt.

shoulder [ˈʃəʊldəʳ] 1 *n* **(a)** (*of person, animal*) Schulter *f*; (*of bird*) Schultergürtel *m*; (*of meat*) Bug *m*; (*of pork*) Schulter *f*, Schulterstück *nt*; (*of garment*) Schulter(partie) *f* ◆ **to shrug one's ~s** mit den Schultern *or* Achseln zucken; **to have broad ~s** (*lit*) breite Schultern haben; (*fig also*) einen breiten Rücken *or* Buckel (*inf*) haben; **to put one's ~ to the wheel** (*fig*) sich ins Zeug legen; **to cry** *or* **weep on sb's ~** sich an jds Brust (*dat*) ausweinen; **a ~ to cry on** jemand, bei dem man sich ausweinen kann; **~ to ~** Schulter an Schulter; *see* **cold, rub, straight.**

(b) (*of mountain*) Schulter *f*; (*of road*) Seitenstreifen *m*, Bankett *nt*; (*of vase, bottle*) Ausbuchtung *f*.

2 *vt* **(a)** schultern, auf die Schulter nehmen; (*fig*) *responsibilities, blame, task* auf sich (*acc*) nehmen; *expense* tragen ◆ **~ arms!** (*Mil*) das Gewehr über!; **the fans ~ed him off the pitch** die Fans trugen ihn auf den Schultern vom Platz.

(b) (*push*) (mit der Schulter) stoßen ◆ **to ~ sb aside** (*lit*) jdn zur Seite stoßen; (*fig*) jdn beiseite drängen; **to ~ one's way through (the crowd)** sich durch die Menge drängen *or* boxen.

shoulder: ~ bag *n* Umhängetasche *f*; **~ blade** *n* Schulterblatt *nt*; **~ flash** *n* (*Mil*) Dienstgradabzeichen, Schulterstück *nt*; **~-high** *adv* **to carry sb ~-high** jdn auf den Schultern tragen; **to stand ~-high to sb** jdm bis an die Schultern reichen; **~ holster** *n* Schulterholster *nt*; **~-length** *adj hair* schulterlang; **~ loop** *n* Dienstgradabzeichen *nt*; **~ pad** *n* Schulterpolster *nt*; **~ strap** *n* (*Mil*) Schulterklappe *f*; (*of dress*) Träger *m*; (*of satchel, bag etc*) (Schulter)riemen *m*.

shouldn't [ˈʃʊdnt] *contr of* **should not.**

shout [ʃaʊt] 1 *n* Ruf, Schrei *m* ◆ **a ~ of protest/joy/pain** ein Protestruf *m*/Freuden-/Schmerzensschrei *m*; **a ~ of excitement** ein aufgeregter Schrei; **~s of applause/laughter** Beifallsrufe *pl*/Lachsalven *pl*, brüllendes Gelächter; **to give a ~** einen Schrei ausstoßen; **to give sb a ~** jdn rufen; **give me a ~ when you're ready** (*inf*) sag Bescheid, wenn du fertig bist; **his voice rose to a ~** seine Stimme steigerte sich bis zum Brüllen; **it's my ~** (*inf: turn*) ich bin dran.

2 *vt* schreien; (*call*) rufen; *order* brüllen; *protest, disapproval etc* laut(stark) kundtun ◆ **to ~ abuse at sb** jdn (laut) beschimpfen; **to ~ a warning to sb** jdm eine Warnung zurufen.

3 *vi* (*call out*) rufen; (*very loudly*) schreien; (*angrily, commanding*) brüllen ◆ **to ~ for sb/sth** nach jdm/etw rufen; **she ~ed for Jane to come** sie rief, Jane solle kommen; **to ~ at sb** (mit jdm) schreien; (*abusively*) jdn anschreien; **don't ~!** schrei nicht (so)!; **to ~ to sb** jdm zurufen; **he ~ed to me to open the door** er rief mir zu, ich sollte die Tür öffnen; **to ~ for help** um Hilfe rufen; **to ~ for joy** einen Freudenschrei/Freudenschreie ausstoßen; **to ~ with laughter** vor Lachen brüllen; **it was nothing to ~ about** (*inf*) es war nicht umwerfend.

4 *vr* **to ~ oneself hoarse/silly** sich heiser/krumm und dusselig (*inf*) schreien.

◆**shout down** *vt sep person* niederbrüllen; *play* ausbuhen.

◆**shout out** 1 *vi* einen Schrei ausstoßen; (*in pain, rage, protest*) aufschreien ◆ **to ~ ~ in delight** Freudenrufe/einen Freudenruf ausstoßen; **~ ~ when you're ready** ruf, wenn du fertig bist.

2 *vt sep* ausrufen; *order* brüllen.

shouting [ˈʃaʊtɪŋ] *n* (*act*) Schreien *nt*; (*sound*) Geschrei *nt* ◆ **it's all over bar the ~** (*inf*) es ist so gut wie gelaufen (*inf*).

shove [ʃʌv] 1 *n* Schubs(er) (*inf*), Stoß *m* ◆ **to give sb a ~** jdn schubsen (*inf*) *or* stoßen; **to give sth a ~** etw rücken; *door* gegen etw stoßen; *ball* etw anstoßen; *car* etw anschieben; **one more ~** noch einmal schieben, noch einen Ruck.

2 *vt* **(a)** (*push*) schieben; (*with one short push*) stoßen, schubsen (*inf*); (*jostle*) drängen ◆ **stop shoving me** hör auf zu drängeln *or* mich zu schubsen (*inf*); **to ~ sb against a wall** jdn gegen die Wand drücken; **to ~ sb off the pavement** jdn vom Bürgersteig herunterschubsen (*inf*); jdn vom Bürgersteig herunterdrängen; **to ~ one's way forward** sich nach vorn durchdrängen; **to ~ a door open** eine Tür aufstoßen.

(b) (*inf: put*) **to ~ sth on(to) sth** etw auf etw (*acc*) werfen (*inf*); **to ~ sth in(to) sth/between sth** etw in etw (*acc*)/zwischen etw (*acc*) stecken; **he ~d his head through the window** er steckte den Kopf durchs Fenster; **he ~d a book into my hand** er drückte mir ein Buch in die Hand.

3 *vi* stoßen; (*to move sth*) schieben; (*jostle*) drängeln.

◆**shove about** *or* **around** *vt sep* (*inf*) herumstoßen.

◆**shove away** *vt sep* (*inf*) wegstoßen, wegschubsen (*inf*).

◆**shove back** *vt sep* (*inf*) *chair etc* zurückschieben; *sb, plate* zurückstoßen, zurückschubsen (*inf*); (*replace*) zurücktun; (*into pocket etc*) wieder hineinstecken.

◆**shove down** *vt sep* (*inf*) (*put*) hinlegen, hinwerfen (*inf*); (*write*) hinschmieren (*inf*), aufschreiben.

◆**shove off** 1 *vt sep* (*Naut*) vom Ufer abstoßen.

2 *vi* **(a)** (*in boat*) ablegen. **(b)** (*inf: leave*) abschieben (*inf*).

◆**shove on** *vt sep* (*inf*) *coat* anziehen; *hat* aufsetzen; *record* auflegen.

◆**shove out** *vt sep boat* abstoßen; *person* rausschmeißen (*inf*).

◆**shove over** (*inf*) 1 *vt sep* rüberwerfen (*inf*), rüberschmeißen (*inf*).

2 *vi* (*also* **shove up**) rutschen.

shove-halfpenny [ʃʌvˈheɪpnɪ] *n Spiel, bei dem Münzen in auf einer Platte vorgezeichnete Felder gestoßen werden.*

shovel [ˈʃʌvl] 1 *n* Schaufel *f*; (*with long handle also*) Schippe *f*; (*on power-~*) Löffel *m*; (*power-~*) Löffelbagger *m* ◆ **a ~ of coal** eine Schaufel Kohle.

2 *vt* schaufeln; *coal, snow also* schippen; *path* schaufeln ◆ **to ~ food into one's mouth** (*inf*) Essen in sich (*acc*) hineinschaufeln; **to ~ a path clear of snow** einen Pfad vom Schnee freischaufeln.

shoveler [ˈʃʌvələʳ] *n* (*Orn*) Löffelente *f*.

shovelful [ˈʃʌvlfʊl] *n* Schaufel *f* ◆ **a ~ of coal** eine Schaufel Kohle; **they dug up ~s of potatoes** sie gruben schaufelweise *or* haufenweise Kartoffeln aus.

▼ **show** [ʃəʊ] (*vb: pret* **~ed**, *ptp* **shown**) 1 *n* **(a)** (*display*) **a fine ~ of roses** eine Rosenpracht; **the dahlias make a fine ~** die Dahlien sind eine Pracht; **~ of force** Machtdemonstration *f*; **~ of hands** Handzeichen, Hand(er)heben *nt*.

(b) (*outward appearance*) Schau *f*; (*trace*) Spur *f*; (*of hatred, affection*) Kundgebung *f* ◆ **it's just for ~** das ist nur zur Schau da; (*pretence*) das ist nur Schau (*inf*); **to do sth for ~** etw tun, um Eindruck zu schinden (*inf*) *or* zu machen; **it's all done for ~** das ist alles nur dazu da, um Eindruck zu machen; **to make a great ~ of being impressed/overworked/pleased** sich (*dat*) ganz den Anschein geben, beeindruckt/überarbeitet/erfreut zu sein; **to make a great ~ of resistance/sympathy** ganz Ablehnung/Mitleid sein; **they made a great ~ of their wealth** sie protzten mit ihrem Reichtum (*inf*); **without any ~ of emotion** ohne irgendwelche Gefühle zu zeigen; **it was all ~** es war alles nur Schau (*inf*); **to be fond of ~** gerne prunken.

(c) (*exhibition*) Ausstellung *f* ◆ **dog/fashion ~** Hunde-/Modenschau *f*; **to be on ~** ausgestellt *or* zu sehen sein.

(d) (*Theat*) Aufführung *f*; (*TV, variety or pop ~*) Show *f*; (*Rad*) Sendung *f*; (*Film*) Vorstellung *f* ◆ **to go to a ~** ins Theater gehen; **the ~ must go on** es muß trotz allem weitergehen; **on with the ~!** anfangen!; (*continue*) weitermachen!; **to stop the ~** (*lit*) die Aufführung unterbrechen; (*fig*) alle plötzlich innehalten lassen; *see* **steal.**

(e) (*esp Brit inf*) **(jolly) good ~!** (*dated*) ausgezeichnet!, bravo!; **bad ~!** (*dated*) schwaches Bild (*inf*); (*what a pity*) so ein Pech!; **to put up a good/poor ~** eine

➤ LANGUAGE IN USE: **should: a** → 1.1, 2.1, 14, 26.1 **b** → 15.2 **c** → 26.1

gute/schwache Leistung zeigen; **to make a poor ~** eine traurige Gestalt abgeben; **it's a pretty poor ~ when ...** das ist vielleicht traurig *or* ein schwaches Bild (*inf*), wenn ...

(f) (*inf: undertaking, organization*) Laden *m* (*inf*) ◆ **he runs the ~** er schmeißt hier den Laden (*inf*); **to give the (whole) ~ away** alles verraten.

▼**2** *vt* **(a)** zeigen; (*at exhibition also*) ausstellen; (*demonstrate*) *dog also* vorführen; *slides, film also* vorführen; *passport, ticket* vorzeigen ◆ **to ~ sb sth, to ~ sth to sb** jdm etw zeigen; **~ me how to do it** zeigen Sie mir, wie man das macht; **it's been ~n on television** das kam im Fernsehen; **the film was first ~n in 1988** der Film wurde 1988 uraufgeführt; **to ~ one's face** sich zeigen; **he had nothing to ~ for it** er hatte am Ende nichts vorzuweisen; **he has nothing to ~ for all his effort** seine ganze Mühe hat nichts gebracht; **I'll ~ him!** (*inf*) dem werd' ich's zeigen! (*inf*); **that ~ed him!** (*inf*) dem habe ich's aber gezeigt! (*inf*); *see* **hand, heel[1]**.

(b) (*register*) (an)zeigen; *loss, profit* haben, verzeichnen; *rise in numbers* aufzeigen; (*thermometer, speedometer*) stehen auf (+*dat*); (*calendar*) zeigen ◆ **it ~s that ...** es zeigt, daß ...; **as ~n in the illustration** wie in der Illustration dargestellt; **the roads are ~n in red** die Straßen sind rot (eingezeichnet); **what time does your watch ~?** wie spät ist es nach Ihrer Uhr?; **the dial will ~ red if ...** der Zeiger zeigt auf Rot, wenn ...

(c) (*indicate*) zeigen; (*prove*) beweisen; *kindness, favour* erweisen; *courage also, loyalty, taste, tact, intelligence* beweisen; *respect* bezeigen; *proof* erbringen ◆ **to ~ one's gratitude** sich dankbar zeigen; **this ~s him to be a thief** das zeigt/beweist, daß er ein Dieb ist; **I hope I have ~n how silly it is** ich habe hoffentlich (auf)gezeigt, wie dumm das ist; **it all** *or* **just goes to ~ that ...** das zeigt doch nur, daß ...

(d) (*reveal*) zeigen ◆ **that dress ~s her bra** bei dem Kleid sieht man ihren BH; **it was ~ing signs of rain** es sah nach Regen aus; **it ~ed signs of having been used** man sah, daß es gebraucht worden war; **to ~ signs of wear/tiredness** Abnutzungserscheinungen *pl* aufweisen/Ermüdungserscheinungen *pl* zeigen; **~ a leg!** (*inf*) raus aus den Federn! (*inf*); **she's beginning to ~ her age** man sieht ihr allmählich das Alter an; **the carpet ~s the dirt** auf dem Teppich sieht man den Schmutz.

(e) (*direct*) zeigen ◆ **to ~ sb the way** jdm den Weg zeigen; **to ~ sb in/out** jdn hereinbringen/hinausbringen *or* -begleiten; **to ~ sb out of/into a room** jdn hinausbegleiten, jdn aus dem Zimmer begleiten/jdn hereinbringen, jdn ins Zimmer bringen; **to ~ sb to his seat/to the door** jdn an seinen Platz/an die *or* zur Tür bringen; **to ~ sb over** *or* **round the house** jdm das (ganze) Haus zeigen; **they were ~n over** *or* **round the factory** ihnen wurde die Fabrik gezeigt, sie wurden in der Fabrik herumgeführt.

3 *vi* **(a)** (*be visible*) zu sehen sein, sichtbar sein; (*petticoat etc*) vorsehen, rausgucken (*inf*); (*film*) gezeigt werden, laufen; (*exhibit: artist*) ausstellen ◆ **the dirt doesn't ~** man sieht den Schmutz nicht; **his anger ~ed in his eyes** man konnte ihm seinen Ärger von den Augen ablesen; **don't let your anger ~** lassen Sie sich (*dat*) den Ärger nicht anmerken!; **the tulips are beginning to ~** die Tulpen kommen langsam heraus; **his bad leg ~s when he walks** beim Gehen merkt man, daß er ein schlimmes Bein hat; **it only ~s when ...** (*be visible*) man sieht es nur, wenn ...; (*be noticed*) man merkt es nur, wenn ...; **to ~ through** durchkommen; **the house ~s through the gap** durch den Spalt kann man das Haus sehen; **he didn't ~** (*inf*) er hat sich nicht blicken lassen (*inf*).

(b) (*prove*) **it just goes to ~!** da sieht man's mal wieder!

(c) (*Horse-racing*) sich plazieren.

4 *vr* **to ~ oneself** sich blicken lassen (*inf*); **to ~ oneself (to be) incompetent** sich (als) unfähig erweisen; **he ~ed himself to be a coward** es zeigte sich, daß er ein Feigling war; **it ~s itself in his speech** das merkt man an seiner Sprache.

◆**show off** **1** *vi* angeben (*to, in front of* vor +*dat*).

2 *vt sep* **(a)** (*flaunt*) *knowledge, medal* angeben mit; *new car, son* vorführen (*to sb* jdm); *wealth* protzen mit (*inf*). **(b)** (*enhance*) *beauty, picture* hervorheben; *figure also* betonen ◆ **to ~ sth ~ to advantage** etw vorteilhaft wirken lassen; **the dress ~s her ~ to advantage** das Kleid ist sehr vorteilhaft für sie.

◆**show up** **1** *vi* **(a)** (*be seen*) zu sehen *or* zu erkennen sein; (*stand out*) hervorstechen ◆ **the stain ~s ~** man sieht den Fleck; **the tower ~ed ~ clearly against the sky** der Turm zeichnete sich deutlich gegen den Himmel ab; **to ~ ~ well/badly** (*fig*) eine gute/schlechte Figur machen.

(b) (*inf: turn up*) auftauchen, sich blicken lassen (*inf*).

2 *vt sep* **(a)** (*highlight*) (deutlich) erkennen lassen ◆ **the bright light ~ed ~ the faded wallpaper** in dem hellen Licht konnte man sehen, wie verblichen die Tapete war.

(b) (*reveal*) *flaws, bad condition, errors* zum Vorschein bringen; *sb's character, intentions* deutlich zeigen; *impostor* entlarven; *fraud* aufdecken; *person* bloßstellen ◆ **my question ~ed him ~ to be a liar** meine Frage entlarvte ihn als Lügner.

(c) (*shame*) blamieren ◆ **his bad manners ~ his parents ~** mit seinen schlechten Manieren blamiert er seine Eltern; **he always gets drunk and ~s her ~** er betrinkt sich immer und bringt sie dadurch in eine peinliche Situation; **to ~ oneself ~** sich blamieren.

(d) (*direct*) heraufbringen.

show: **~ biz** *n* (*inf*) *see* **~ business**; **~ boat** *n* (*esp US*) *Dampfer m, auf dem eine Schauspieltruppe etc Vorstellungen gibt*; **~ business** *n* Showbusineß, Showgeschäft *nt*; **to be in ~ business** im Showgeschäft (tätig) sein; **~ business personalities** Persönlichkeiten *pl* aus dem Showgeschäft; **~case** *n* **1** Schaukasten *m*, Vitrine *f*; (*fig*) Schaufenster *nt*. **2** *vt* präsentieren, vorstellen; **~down** *n* (*inf*) Kraftprobe, Machtprobe *f*, Showdown *m* (*sl*); **there was a ~down between the two rivals** zwischen den Rivalen kam es zur Kraftprobe; **to have a ~down with sb** sich mit jdm auseinandersetzen.

shower ['ʃaʊəʳ] **1** *n* **(a)** (*of rain etc*) Schauer *m*; (*of arrows, stones, blows, bullets etc*) Hagel *m*; (*of curses, questions*) Schwall *m* ◆ **a ~ of sparks** ein Funkenregen *m*; **~ of water** Dusche *f*, Wasserstrahl *m*.

(b) (*~ bath*) Dusche *f*; (*device also*) Brause *f* ◆ **to take** *or* **have a ~** duschen.

(c) (*Brit fig inf*) Blödmänner *pl* (*inf*) ◆ **what a ~!** so ein lausiges Volk! (*inf*).

(d) (*US inf: party*) *Party, auf der jeder ein Geschenk für den Ehrengast mitbringt*; (*for bride-to-be*) ≃ Polterabend *m*.

2 *vt* **to ~ sb with sth, to ~ sth on sb** *curses* etw auf jdn niederregnen lassen; *blows* etw auf jdn niederprasseln *or* niederhageln lassen; *honours, presents* jdn mit etw überschütten *or* überhäufen; **the broken pipe ~ed water on the passers-by** das Wasser aus dem kaputten Rohr bespritzte die Passanten; **to ~ abuse on sb, to ~ sb with abuse** einen Schwall von Beschimpfungen gegen jdn loslassen.

3 *vi* **(a)** (*wash*) duschen, brausen (*dated*).

(b) (*descend: also* **~ down**) niedergehen auf (+*acc*).

shower: **~ base** *n* Duschwanne *f*; **~ bath** *n* Dusche *f*; **~ cabinet** *n* Duschkabine *f*; **~ cap** *n* Duschhaube *f*; **~ curtain** *n* Duschvorhang *m*; **~ gel** *n* Duschgel *nt*; **~proof** *adj* regenfest.

showery ['ʃaʊərɪ] *adj* regnerisch.

show: **~girl** *n* Revuegirl *nt*; **~ground** *n* Ausstellungsgelände *nt*; (*for circus*) Zirkusgelände *nt*; **~ house** *n* Musterhaus *nt*.

showily ['ʃəʊɪlɪ] *adv* protzig; *furnished also, produced* bombastisch; *behave* theatralisch ◆ **~ dressed** aufgeputzt.

showiness ['ʃəʊɪnɪs] *n see adj* Protzigkeit *f* (*inf*); auffallende Art; Aufgeputztheit *f*; theatralische Art; bombastische Art; Auffälligkeit *f*; Effekthascherei *f*.

showing ['ʃəʊɪŋ] *n* **(a)** (*exhibition*) Ausstellung *f*.

(b) (*performance*) Aufführung *f*; (*of film*) Vorstellung *f*; (*of programme*) Ausstrahlung *f*.

(c) (*standard of performance*) Leistung *f* ◆ **to make a good/poor ~** eine gute/schwache Leistung zeigen; **on his present ~** mit seinen jetzigen Leistungen; **on the present ~** so, wie die Dinge zur Zeit stehen.

(d) **on his own ~** nach eigenen Angaben.

showing-off ['ʃəʊɪŋ'ɒf] *n* Angeberei *f*.

show: **~-jumper** *n* Springreiter(in *f*) *m*; **~-jumping** *n* Springen, Springreiten *nt*.

showman ['ʃəʊmən] *n, pl* **-men** [-mən] Showman *m*; (*fig*) Schauspieler *m*.

showmanship ['ʃəʊmənʃɪp] *n* (*of person*) Talent *nt* für effektvolle Darbietung; (*of act*) effektvolle Darbietung; (*fig*) Talent *nt*, sich in Szene zu setzen ◆ **he knows nothing about ~** er hat keine Ahnung, wie man etwas effektvoll darbietet *or* in Szene setzt; **it's just ~** das ist reine Schau *or* Effekthascherei.

shown [ʃəʊn] *ptp of* **show**.

show: **~-off** *n* (*inf*) Angeber(in *f*) *m*; **~piece** *n* Schaustück *nt*; (*fine example*) Paradestück *nt*; **~place** *n* (*tourist attraction*) Sehenswürdigkeit *f*; **~room** *n* Ausstellungsraum *m*; **in ~room condition** in makellosem Zustand; **~-stopper** *n* (*inf*) Publikumshit *m* (*inf*); (*fig*) Clou *m* des Abends/der Party *etc*; **~ trial** *n* Schauprozeß *m*.

showy ['ʃəʊɪ] *adj* (+*er*) protzig; *person* auffallend; (*as regards clothes*) protzig angezogen; *manner* theatralisch; *ceremony also, decor* bombastisch; *colour* grell, auffällig; *production* bombastisch, auf Schau (*inf*) *or* Effekte gemacht.

shrank [ʃræŋk] *pret of* **shrink**.

shrapnel ['ʃræpnl] *n* Schrapnell *nt*.

shred [ʃred] **1** *n* (*scrap*) Fetzen *m*; (*of paper also*) Schnipsel, Schnippel (*inf*) *m*; (*of vegetable, meat*) Stückchen *nt*; (*fig*) Spur *f*; (*of truth*) Fünkchen *nt* ◆ **~ of cloth** Stoffetzen *m*; **not a ~ of evidence** keinerlei Beweis; **without a ~ of clothing on** splitter(faser)nackt; **to be** *or* **hang in ~s** zerfetzt sein; **her dress hung in ~s** ihr Kleid hing ihr in Fetzen vom Leib; **his reputation was in ~s** sein (guter) Ruf war ruiniert; **to tear sth to ~s** etw total zerreißen, etw in Stücke reißen; (*fig*) etw verreißen; *argument* etw total zerpflücken; **to tear sb to ~s** keinen guten Faden an jdm lassen.

2 *vt* **(a)** *food* zerkleinern, schnitzeln; (*grate*) *carrots* raspeln; *cabbage* hobeln; *paper* zerstückeln, schnitzeln; (*in shredder*) in den Papierwolf geben.

(b) (*tear*) in kleine Stücke reißen; (*with claws*) zerfetzen.

shredder ['ʃredəʳ] *n* Zerkleinerungsmaschine *f*; (*grater*) Reibe *f*; (*in electric mixer*) Gemüseschneider *m*; (*for waste paper*) Papierwolf, Reißwolf *m*.

shredding machine ['ʃredɪŋmə'ʃi:n] *n* Zerkleinerungsmaschine *f*; (*for waste paper*) Papierwolf, Reißwolf *m*.

shrew [ʃru:] *n* Spitzmaus *f*; (*fig*) Xanthippe *f*.

shrewd [ʃru:d] *adj* (+*er*) *person* gewitzt, klug, clever (*inf*); *businessman also, plan, move* clever (*inf*), raffiniert, geschickt; *investment, argument* taktisch geschickt, klug; *assessment, observer* scharf, genau; *smile* verschmitzt, wissend; *eyes* schlau; *mind* scharf; *glance* durchdringend, prüfend ◆ **I can make a ~ guess** ich kann ja mal raten; **that was a ~ guess** das war gut geraten; **I have a ~ idea that ...** ich habe so das bestimmte Gefühl, daß ...; **I have a ~ idea of what he'll say** ich kann mir gut denken, was er sagen wird; **to have a ~ understanding of sth** in bezug auf etw (*acc*) Durchblick haben.

shrewdly ['ʃru:dlɪ] *adv* geschickt, clever (*inf*) ◆ **he ~ guessed that/what ...** er hat gut geraten, daß/was ...; **~, he decided ...** gewitzt *or* clever (*inf*) wie er ist, hat er beschlossen ...; **... he said ~ ...** sagte er schlau *or* clever (*inf*).

shrewdness ['ʃru:dnɪs] *n see adj* Gewitztheit *f*; Klugheit *f*; Cleverneß (*inf*), Raffiniertheit, Geschicktheit *f*; Schärfe *f*; Genauigkeit *f*; Verschmitztheit *f*; Schläue *f*; durchdringende Art; (*of guess*) Treffsicherheit *f*.

shrewish ['ʃru:ɪʃ] *adj* zänkisch, boshaft, giftig.

➤ LANGUAGE IN USE: **show: 2a** → 26.2

shrewishly ['ʃruːɪʃlɪ] *adv* giftig.
shrewishness ['ʃruːɪʃnɪs] *n* Boshaftigkeit, Giftigkeit *f.*
shriek [ʃriːk] [1] *n* (schriller) Schrei; (*of whistle*) schriller Ton; (*of brakes, hinges*) Quietschen *nt no pl* ◆ **a ~ of pain/horror** ein Schmerzens-/Schreckensschrei *m*; **~s of laughter** kreischendes Lachen; **to give a ~** einen schrillen Schrei ausstoßen.
[2] *vt* kreischen, schreien ◆ **to ~ abuse at sb** jdn ankeifen.
[3] *vi* aufschreien ◆ **to ~ at sb** jdn ankreischen; **to ~ with pain** vor Schmerz aufschreien; **to ~ with laughter** vor Lachen quietschen; **to ~ out** aufschreien, einen Schrei ausstoßen.
shrift [ʃrɪft] *n* **to give sb/sth short ~** jdn/etw kurz abfertigen.
shrike [ʃraɪk] *n* Würger *m.*
shrill [ʃrɪl] [1] *adj* (*+er*) schrill; *criticism, speech* scharf.
[2] *vi* schrillen.
[3] *vt* kreischen, schrill schreien.
shrillness ['ʃrɪlnɪs] *n* Schrillheit *f.*
shrilly ['ʃrɪlɪ] *adv* schrill.
shrimp [ʃrɪmp] [1] *n* Garnele, Krevette *f* ◆ **that ~ of a child** der kleine Steppke (*inf*).
[2] *vi* **to go ~ing** auf Krevetten- *or* Garnelenfang gehen; **~ing net** Reuse *f* (*für den Garnelenfang*).
shrine [ʃraɪn] *n* Schrein *m*; (*sacred place also*) Heiligtum *nt*; (*tomb*) Grabstätte *f*; (*chapel*) Grabkapelle *f*; (*altar*) Grabaltar *m* ◆ **to worship at sb's ~** (*fig inf*) jdm zu Füßen liegen.
shrink [ʃrɪŋk] (*vb: pret* **shrank**, *ptp* **shrunk**) [1] *vt* eingehen *or* einlaufen lassen ◆ **the fabric is shrunk before it is used** der Stoff wird vor Gebrauch gewaschen, damit er danach nicht mehr einläuft; **to ~ a part on** (*Tech*) ein Teil aufschrumpfen.
[2] *vi* **(a)** (*get smaller*) kleiner werden, schrumpfen; (*clothes etc*) eingehen, einlaufen; (*metal etc*) sich zusammenziehen, schrumpfen; (*wood*) schwinden; (*fig*) (*popularity*) abnehmen, schwinden; (*trade*) zurückgehen ◆ **to ~ away to nothing** auf ein Nichts zusammenschrumpfen; **a ~ing violet** (*fig*) ein schüchternes Pflänzchen; **~-proof/-resistant** nicht einlaufend.
(b) (*fig: recoil*) zurückschrecken ◆ **to ~ from doing/saying sth** davor zurückschrecken, etw zu tun/sich davor scheuen, etw zu sagen; **to ~ from the truth** vor der Wahrheit die Augen verschließen; **to ~ back** zurückweichen; **to ~ away from sb** vor jdm zurückweichen.
[3] *n* (*sl*) Klapsdoktor *m* (*inf*).
shrinkage ['ʃrɪŋkɪdʒ] *n* (*of material, clothes*) Einlaufen, Eingehen *nt*; (*of wood*) Schwund *m*; (*of metal*) Schrumpfung *f*; (*fig: of tourism, economic growth etc*) Schrumpfung *f*, Rückgang *m*; (*Comm*) Schwund *m*, Einbußen *pl* ◆ **there will be ~ with this material** dieser Stoff geht *or* läuft noch ein.
shrink-wrap ['ʃrɪŋkræp] *vt* einschweißen.
shrink-wrapping ['ʃrɪŋkræpɪŋ] *n* (*process*) Einschweißen *nt*; (*material*) Klarsichtfolie *f.*
shrive [ʃraɪv] *pret* **shrove**, *ptp* **shriven** *vt* (*old*) die Beichte abnehmen (*+dat*).
shrivel ['ʃrɪvl] [1] *vt plants* (*frost, dryness*) welk werden lassen; (*heat*) austrocknen; *skin, fruit* runzlig werden lassen; *nylon* zusammenschrumpfen lassen.
[2] *vi* kleiner werden, schrumpfen; (*balloon, nylon*) zusammenschrumpfen; (*plants*) welk werden; (*through heat*) austrocknen; (*fruit, skin*) runzlig werden ◆ **a ~(l)ed old lady** eine kleine, vertrocknete alte Dame.
◆**shrivel away** *vi* zusammenschrumpfen; (*leaves*) verwelken, vertrocknen; (*nylon*) zusammenschmelzen; (*worries, problems*) sich in Luft auflösen.
◆**shrivel up** [1] *vt sep see* **shrivel 1**.
[2] *vi* **(a)** *see* **shrivel 2**.
(b) (*fig: become timid*) **I just want to ~ ~ when he looks at me like that** wenn er mich so ansieht, möchte ich am liebsten in den Boden versinken; **he just ~led ~ when the boss questioned him** bei den Fragen des Chefs wurde er ganz klein.
shriven ['ʃrɪvn] *ptp of* **shrive**.
shroud [ʃraʊd] [1] *n* **(a)** Leichentuch, Totenhemd *nt.* **(b)** (*fig*) Schleier *m* ◆ **a ~ of mist** ein Nebelschleier *m*; **a ~ of mystery** der Schleier eines Geheimnisses. **(c)** **~s** *pl* (*Naut*) Wanten *pl.*
[2] *vt* **(a)** (*lit*) in ein Leichentuch hüllen.
(b) (*fig*) hüllen ◆ **the whole thing is ~ed in mystery** die ganze Angelegenheit ist von einem Geheimnis umgeben.
shrove [ʃrəʊv] *pret of* **shrive**.
Shrovetide ['ʃrəʊvtaɪd] *n* Fastnacht *f* (*die drei Tage vor Aschermittwoch*).
Shrove Tuesday *n* Fastnachtsdienstag *m.*
shrub [ʃrʌb] *n* Busch, Strauch *m.*
shrubbery ['ʃrʌbərɪ] *n* (*shrub bed*) Strauchrabatte *f*; (*shrubs*) Büsche, Sträucher *pl*, Buschwerk *nt* ◆ **the ball got lost in the ~** der Ball ging im Gebüsch verloren.
shrug [ʃrʌg] [1] *n* Achselzucken *nt no pl* ◆ **to give a ~** die *or* mit den Schultern *or* Achseln zucken; **a ~ of despair** ein verzweifeltes Achselzucken.
[2] *vt shoulders* zucken (mit) ◆ **she ~ged herself out of the coat** sie schüttelte den Mantel ab.
◆**shrug off** *vt sep* mit einem Achselzucken abtun; *coat* abschütteln ◆ **he simply ~ged the whole affair ~** er hat die ganze Sache einfach von sich abgeschüttelt.
shrunk [ʃrʌŋk] *ptp of* **shrink**.
shrunken ['ʃrʌŋkən] *adj* (ein)geschrumpft; *old person* geschrumpft; *profits, savings* zusammengeschrumpft ◆ **~ head** Schrumpfkopf *m.*
shtoom [ʃtʊm] *adj* (*sl: quiet*) **to keep ~ about sth** über etw (*acc*) die Klappe halten (*inf*).
shuck [ʃʌk] (*US*) [1] *n* Schale *f*; (*of corn, peas*) Hülse *f.*
[2] *vt* **(a)** schälen; *peas* enthülsen. **(b)** (*inf*) **he ~ed his jacket** er warf seine Jacke ab.
shucks [ʃʌks] *interj* (*US*) verflixt, Mist (*inf*); (*rubbish*) Unsinn, Quatsch (*inf*) ◆ **~, I'm sorry** Mist!, tut mir leid (*inf*); **~ to you** (*inf*) bätsch! (*inf*).
shudder ['ʃʌdəʳ] [1] *n* Schauer, Schauder *m* ◆ **to give a ~** (*person*) sich schütteln, erschaudern (*geh*); (*ground*) beben; **she gave a ~ of revulsion** sie schüttelte sich vor Ekel; **the dying man gave a last great ~** ein letztes Zucken lief durch den Körper des Sterbenden; **a ~ ran through her/her body** ein Schauer überlief sie; **she realized with a ~ that ...** schaudernd erkannte sie, daß ...; **a ~ of fear/cold** ein Angst-/Kälteschauer; **with a ~ of anticipation/pleasure** zitternd *or* bebend vor Erwartung/Freude; **a ~ went through the building as the heavy lorry passed by** das Gebäude bebte, als der schwere Lastwagen vorbeifuhr; **with a ~ the old car moved into second gear** der alte Wagen vibrierte, als der zweite Gang eingelegt wurde; **that gives me the ~s** (*inf*) da läuft's mir kalt den Buckel runter (*inf*); **he gives me the ~s** (*inf*) er ist mir unheimlich.
[2] *vi* (*person*) schaudern, schauern; (*house, ground*) beben, zittern; (*car, train*) rütteln, geschüttelt werden ◆ **her whole body was ~ing** sie zitterte am ganzen Körper; **the train ~ed to a halt** der Zug kam rüttelnd zum Stehen; **I ~ to think** mir graut, wenn ich nur daran denke.
shudderingly ['ʃʌdərɪŋlɪ] *adv* (*with fear etc*) schaudernd; (*with cold*) zitternd ◆ **the rocket climbed ~ into the sky** die Rakete stieg zitternd zum Himmel auf.
shuffle ['ʃʌfl] [1] *n* **(a)** Schlurfen *nt no pl* ◆ **to walk with a ~** schlurfen.
(b) (*dance*) Shuffle *m.*
(c) (*Cards*) **to give the cards a ~** die Karten mischen.
(d) (*change round*) Umstellung *f*; (*of jobs*) Umbesetzung *f* ◆ **the latest ~ in the cabinet** die letzte Kabinettsumbildung.
[2] *vt* **(a)** **he ~d his feet as he walked** er schlurfte beim Gehen; **he sat there shuffling his feet** er saß da und scharrte mit den Füßen.
(b) *cards* mischen ◆ **he ~d the papers on his desk** er durchwühlte die Papiere auf seinem Schreibtisch.
(c) (*fig: change round*) *cabinet* umbilden; *jobs* umbesetzen ◆ **top men are ~d around quite often** die Männer an der Spitze werden oft von einem Ressort ins andere versetzt.
[3] *vi* **(a)** (*walk*) schlurfen ◆ **the dancers ~d round on the floor** die Tänzer schoben sich über die Tanzfläche; **he ~d into his slippers** er schlüpfte umständlich in seine Pantoffeln; **he just ~s through life** er läßt sich einfach treiben.
(b) (*Cards*) mischen.
◆**shuffle off** *vt sep skin, dress* abstreifen; *worries, fear* ablegen; *responsibility* abwälzen, abschieben (*onto* auf *+acc*).
shuffling ['ʃʌflɪŋ] *adj walk, steps* schlurfend ◆ **the ~ movement of a badger** das Watscheln eines Dachses.
shun [ʃʌn] *vt* meiden; *publicity, light* scheuen ◆ **to feel ~ned by the world** sich ausgestoßen fühlen.
'shun [ʃʌn] *interj* (*Mil*) Achtung.
shunt [ʃʌnt] [1] *n* Stoß *m*; (*sl: car crash*) Bums *m* (*inf*) ◆ **they gave the waggon a ~ into the siding** sie schoben *or* rangierten den Waggon auf das Abstellgleis; **to give sth a ~** etw anstoßen, einer Sache (*dat*) einen Stoß geben.
[2] *vt* **(a)** (*Rail*) rangieren, verschieben ◆ **they ~ed the train off the main line** sie schoben den Zug auf ein Nebengleis.
(b) (*inf*) *person* schieben; (*out of the way*) abschieben ◆ **to ~ sb to and fro** jdn herumschubsen (*inf*); **our department then has to ~ the papers back for signing** unsere Abteilung muß die Papiere dann zur Unterschrift zurückverfrachten (*inf*).
(c) (*sl: crash*) *car* einen Unfall bauen mit (*sl*).
[3] *vi* (*Rail*) (*train*) rangiert *or* verschoben werden; (*person*) rangieren ◆ **a line of trucks ~ed past** eine Reihe Güterwagen schob sich vorbei.
shunter ['ʃʌntəʳ] *n* (*Rail*) Rangierer *m.*
shunting ['ʃʌntɪŋ] *n* (*Rail*) Rangieren *nt* ◆ **~ engine** Rangierlokomotive *f*; **~ yard** Rangier- *or* Verschiebebahnhof *m.*
shush [ʃʊʃ] [1] *interj* pst, sch.
[2] *vt* beruhigen, zum Schweigen bringen ◆ **the teacher ~ed the excited children** der Lehrer brachte die aufgeregten Kinder mit einem „Pst!“ zum Schweigen.
[3] *vi* still sein ◆ **oh ~, will you!** sei doch still!, pst!
shut [ʃʌt] (*vb: pret, ptp ~*) [1] *vt* **(a)** zumachen; *box, door, book, shop, office also, sportsground* schließen; *penknife, book, wallet also* zuklappen ◆ **they ~ the office at 6.00** das Büro wird um 18^{00} geschlossen; **the strike ~ the factory for a week** der Streik legte die Fabrik für eine Woche still; **~ your eyes** mach die Augen zu; **to ~ one's ears to sth** vor etw (*dat*) die Ohren verschließen; **to ~ one's mind to sth** sich einer Sache (*dat*) verschließen; **he ~ his mind to thoughts of the past** Gedanken an die Vergangenheit schob er weit von sich; **~ your mouth** (*sl*) *or* **face** (*sl*), **~ it** (*sl*) halt's Maul! (*sl*).
(b) **to ~ sb/sth in(to) sth** jdn/etw in etw (*dat*) einschließen; **she was ~ in the cellar as a punishment** sie wurde zur Strafe im Keller eingesperrt; **to ~ one's fingers in the door** sich (*dat*) die Finger in der Tür einklemmen.
[2] *vi* (*door, window, box*) schließen, zugehen; (*shop, factory*) schließen, geschlossen werden, zumachen (*inf*); (*sportsground*) geschlossen werden ◆ **the suitcase just won't ~** der Koffer will einfach nicht zugehen; **it ~s very easily** es läßt sich ganz leicht schließen *or* zumachen; **it ~s with a zip** es hat einen Reißverschluß; **when do the shops ~?** wann schließen die Geschäfte?,

wann machen die Geschäfte zu? (*inf*); **the door ~ in the wind** der Wind schlug die Tür zu.

[3] *adj* geschlossen, zu *pred* (*inf*) ◆ **sorry sir, we're ~** wir haben leider geschlossen; **the door swung ~** die Tür schlug zu; **to find the door ~** vor verschlossener Tür stehen; **~ in his dungeon** in seinem Kerker eingeschlossen; **~ in his own little world** abgekapselt in seiner eigenen kleinen Welt; **the ~ mind of a reactionary** die Verbohrtheit eines Reaktionärs; **his mind is ~ to anything new** er verschließt sich allem Neuen.

◆**shut away** *vt sep* (*put away*) wegschließen; (*in sth*) einschließen (*in* in +*dat*); (*keep locked away*) *books, papers etc* aufbewahren; (*safely*) verwahren; *persons* verborgen halten ◆ **to keep sb ~ ~ from sth** jdn von etw fernhalten; **he was ~ ~ in a mental hospital** er wurde in eine Nervenklinik gesteckt.

◆**shut down** [1] *vt sep shop, factory* zumachen (*inf*), schließen ◆ **Heathrow is completely ~ ~** Heathrow ist zu.

[2] *vi* (*shop, factory etc*) zumachen (*inf*), schließen ◆ **the television service ~s ~ at midnight** um Mitternacht ist Sendeschluß im Fernsehen.

◆**shut in** *vt sep* einschließen (*also fig*), einsperren (*inf*) (*prep obj, -to* in +*dat*) ◆ **close the door and ~ the heat ~** schließe die Tür, damit die Wärme drinnen bleibt.

◆**shut off** [1] *vt sep* **(a)** *gas, water, electricity* abstellen; *light, engine* ab- *or* ausschalten; *street* (ab)sperren ◆ **the kettle ~s itself ~** der Wasserkessel schaltet von selbst ab.

(b) (*isolate*) (ab)trennen ◆ **I feel very ~ ~ on this island** ich fühle mich auf dieser Insel sehr abgeschlossen; **I feel ~ ~ from my friends/civilization** ich komme mir von meinen Freunden/der Zivilisation abgeschnitten vor; **they tried to ~ their daughter ~ from the evil things in life** sie versuchten, ihre Tochter von allem Bösen fernzuhalten.

[2] *vi* abschalten ◆ **the heater ~s ~ automatically** das Heizgerät schaltet (sich) automatisch ab.

◆**shut out** *vt sep* **(a)** *person, oneself* aussperren (*of* aus); *view* versperren; *light* nicht hereinlassen (*of* in +*acc*) ◆ **the child was ~ ~ of the house** das Kind war ausgesperrt; **don't ~ the sun ~** laß doch die Sonne herein; **draw the curtains to ~ ~ the light** zieh die Vorhänge zu, damit das Licht nicht hereinfällt; **she closed the door to ~ ~ the noise/draught** sie schloß die Tür, damit kein Lärm hereinkam/damit es nicht zog.

(b) (*fig*) *foreign competition* ausschalten; *memory* loswerden, unterdrücken; (*censor*) *foreign news etc* unterdrücken ◆ **I can't ~ her ~ of my life** ich kann sie nicht von meinem Leben ausschließen.

(c) (*US Sport*) *opponent* nicht zum Zuge kommen lassen ◆ **they ~ the opponents ~ with two hits** sie schalteten ihre Gegner mit zwei Treffern aus; **they ~ them ~ 1-0** sie warfen sie mit 1:0 aus dem Rennen.

◆**shut to** *vt sep* ganz *or* richtig zumachen; (*not quite closed*) anlehnen ◆ **the door wasn't ~ ~** die Tür war nicht ganz zu.

◆**shut up** [1] *vt sep* **(a)** *house* verschließen ◆ **to ~ ~ shop** (*lit*) das Geschäft schließen; (*fig*) Feierabend machen (*inf*).

(b) (*imprison*) einsperren ◆ **you can't spend your whole life ~ ~ in libraries** Sie können sich doch nicht Ihr ganzes Leben in Bibliotheken vergraben.

(c) (*inf: silence*) zum Schweigen bringen ◆ **that'll soon ~ him ~** das wird ihm schon den Mund stopfen (*inf*); **every time I try to say something she always tries to ~ me ~** jedes Mal, wenn ich etwas sagen will, fährt sie mir über den Mund.

[2] *vi* (*inf*) den Mund (*inf*) *or* die Klappe (*sl*) halten ◆ **~ ~!** halt die Klappe! (*inf*).

shut: ~down *n* Stillegung *f*; (*TV, Rad*) Sendeschluß *m*; **~-eye** *n* (*inf*) Schlaf *m*; **I need some ~-eye** ich brauche etwas *or* ein paar Stunden Schlaf; **~-in** [1] *adj* **(a)** (*US*) ans Haus/ans Bett gefesselt; **(b) a ~-in feeling** ein Gefühl des Eingeschlossenseins; [2] *n* (*US*) **he is a ~-in** er ist ans Haus/ans Bett gefesselt; **~-off** [1] *n* (*of gas, water*) Abstellen *nt*; **we regret the temporary water ~-off yesterday** wir bedauern, daß wir gestern vorübergehend das Wasser abstellen mußten; [2] *adj* **(a) a ~-off feeling** ein Gefühl des Abgeschlossenseins *or* Abgeschnittenseins; **(b) ~-off switch** (*of electricity, engine*) Hauptschalter *m*.

shutter ['ʃʌtəʳ] [1] *n* (Fenster)laden *m*; (*Phot*) Verschluß *m* ◆ **to put up the ~s** (*lit*) die (Fenster)läden zumachen; (*fig*) den Laden dichtmachen (*inf*); **~ release** (*Phot*) Auslöser *m*.

[2] *vt* **the ~ed windows of the old mansion** die geschlossenen (Fenster)läden der alten Villa; **~ the windows** mach die (Fenster)läden zu; **a ~ed look** ein verschlossener Blick.

shuttle ['ʃʌtl] [1] *n* **(a)** (*of loom, sewing machine*) Schiffchen *nt*.

(b) (*~ service*) Pendelverkehr *m*; (*plane, train etc*) Pendelflugzeug *nt*/-zug *m etc*; (*space ~*) Raumtransporter *m*.

[2] *vt passengers, goods* hin- und hertransportieren ◆ **to ~ sb about** jdn herumschieben; **the form was ~d about between different departments** das Formular wurde in den verschiedenen Abteilungen herumgereicht.

[3] *vi* (*people*) pendeln; (*goods*) hin- und hertransportiert werden; (*forms*) herumgereicht werden.

shuttle: ~cock *n* Federball *m*; **~ diplomacy** *n* Pendeldiplomatie *f*; **~ service** *n* Pendelverkehr *m*.

shy[1] [ʃaɪ] [1] *adj* (*+er*) **(a)** schüchtern; *smile also, animal* scheu ◆ **don't be ~** nur keine Hemmungen! (*inf*); **to be ~ of/with sb** Hemmungen vor/gegenüber jdm haben; **to be ~ of doing sth** Hemmungen haben, etw zu tun; **to feel ~** schüchtern sein; **don't be ~ of telling me if there's anything you need** sagen Sie mir ruhig, wenn Sie etwas brauchen; **to make sb ~** jdn verschüchtern; *see* **fight**.

(b) (*esp US inf: short*) **we're $ 3 ~** wir haben 3 Dollar zuwenig.

[2] *vi* (*horse*) scheuen (*at* vor +*dat*).

◆**shy away** *vi* (*horse*) zurückscheuen; (*person*) zurückweichen ◆ **to ~ ~ from sb/sth** vor jdm zurückweichen/vor etw (*dat*) zurückschrecken; **he shies ~ from accepting responsibilities** er scheut sich, Verantwortung zu übernehmen.

shy[2] [1] *n* (*throw*) Wurf *m* ◆ **to have** *or* **take a ~ at sth** nach etw werfen; **to have a ~ at sth** (*fig*) sich an etw (*dat*) versuchen; **I'll have a ~ at it** ich kann's ja mal versuchen; **to have a ~ at doing sth** etw zu tun versuchen.

[2] *vt* werfen.

Shylock ['ʃaɪlɒk] *n* (*fig*) (*mean person*) Geizhals *m*; (*dated: moneylender*) Wucherer *m*.

shyly ['ʃaɪlɪ] *adv see adj*.

shyness ['ʃaɪnɪs] *n* Schüchternheit *f*; (*esp of animals*) Scheu *f* ◆ **his ~ of meeting people/of strangers** seine Scheu, andere Leute kennenzulernen/vor Fremden.

shyster ['ʃaɪstəʳ] *n* (*US sl*) Gauner *m*; (*lawyer*) Rechtsverdreher *m* (*inf*).

Siam [saɪ'æm] *n* Siam *nt*.

Siamese [,saɪə'mi:z] [1] *adj* siamesisch ◆ **~ cat** Siamkatze *f*, siamesische Katze; **~ twins** siamesische Zwillinge *pl*.

[2] *n* **(a)** Siamese *m*, Siamesin *f*. **(b)** (*language*) Siamesisch *nt*. **(c)** (*cat*) Siamkatze *f*, siamesische Katze.

Siberia [saɪ'bɪərɪə] *n* Sibirien *nt*.

Siberian [saɪ'bɪərɪən] [1] *adj* sibirisch.

[2] *n* Sibirier(in *f*) *m*.

sibilant ['sɪbɪlənt] [1] *adj* zischend; *hiss* scharf; (*Phon*) Zisch-, gezischt.

[2] *n* (*Phon*) Zischlaut *m*.

sibling ['sɪblɪŋ] *n* Geschwister *nt* (*form*).

sibyl ['sɪbɪl] *n* (*lit*) Sibylle *f*; (*fig*) Prophetin *f*, Weissagerin *f*.

sibylline ['sɪbɪlaɪn] *adj* (*lit*) sibyllinisch; (*fig*) prophetisch.

sic [sɪk] *adv* sic.

Sicilian [sɪ'sɪlɪən] [1] *adj* sizilianisch.

[2] *n* **(a)** Sizilianer(in *f*) *m*. **(b)** (*dialect*) Sizilianisch *nt*.

Sicily ['sɪsɪlɪ] *n* Sizilien *nt*.

▼ **sick** [sɪk] [1] *n* (*vomit*) Erbrochene(s) *nt*.

▼[2] *adj* (*+er*) **(a)** (*ill*) krank (*also fig*) ◆ **the ~** die Kranken *pl*; **to be (off) ~** (wegen Krankheit) fehlen; **to fall** *or* **take** *or* **be taken ~** krank werden; **to go ~** krank werden; **he was ~ at heart** (*liter*) er war von Kummer verzehrt (*liter*).

(b) (*vomiting or about to vomit*) **to be ~** brechen, sich übergeben, kotzen (*sl*); (*esp cat, baby, patient*) spucken; **he was ~ all over the carpet** er hat den ganzen Teppich vollgespuckt *or* vollgekotzt (*sl*); **I think I'm going to be ~** ich glaube, ich muß brechen *or* mich übergeben (*form*) *or* kotzen (*sl*); **I felt ~** mir war schlecht *or* übel; **I get ~ in aeroplanes** im Flugzeug wird mir immer schlecht *or* übel; **that smell/that food makes me ~** bei dem Geruch/von dem Essen wird mir übel *or* schlecht; **to make sb ~** (*fig inf*) jdn (ganz) krank machen (*inf*); **it makes you ~ the way he's always right** es ist zum Weinen *or* zum Kotzen (*sl*), daß er immer recht hat; **to be ~ at sth** (*fig*) (*disgusted*) von etw angewidert sein; (*upset*) wegen etw geknickt sein; **~ with envy** grün vor Neid.

(c) (*inf: fed up*) **to be ~ of doing sth** es satt haben, etw zu tun; **I'm ~ and tired of it** ich habe davon die Nase (gestrichen) voll (*inf*), ich habe es gründlich satt; **I get ~ of listening to her complaining** ich habe es langsam satt, immer ihr Gejammer hören zu müssen.

(d) (*inf*) geschmacklos; *joke also* übel, makaber; *person* abartig, pervers ◆ **~ humour** schwarzer Humor; **he has a ~ mind** er ist abartig; **a comedy about life in Dachau, how ~ can you get!** eine Komödie über das Leben in Dachau, das ist ja schon pervers!

◆**sick up** *vt sep* erbrechen.

sick: ~ bag *n* Spucktüte *f*; **~ bay** *n* Krankenrevier *nt*; **~-bed** *n* Krankenlager *nt*.

sicken ['sɪkn] [1] *vt* (*turn sb's stomach*) anekeln, anwidern; (*upset greatly*) erschüttern, krank machen (*inf*); (*disgust*) anwidern ◆ **what they saw in the camp ~ed them** sie waren entsetzt über das, was sie im Lager sahen; **it ~s me the way he treats her** es macht mich krank, wie er sie behandelt (*inf*); **doesn't it ~ you?** das ist doch unerträglich *or* zum Kotzen (*sl*).

[2] *vi* **(a)** (*feel ill*) **to ~ at sth** sich vor etw (*dat*) ekeln.

(b) (*become ill*) krank werden ◆ **he's definitely ~ing for something** er wird bestimmt krank; **you must be ~ing for something** (*lit, iro*) ist mit dir was nicht in Ordnung?; **he's ~ing for measles** bei ihm sind die Masern im Anzug.

(c) to ~ of sth einer Sache (*gen*) müde (*geh*) werden *or* sein, etw satt haben; **to ~ of doing sth** es müde werden, etw zu tun.

sickening ['sɪknɪŋ] *adj* (*lit*) ekelerregend; *smell, sight also* widerlich; (*upsetting*) erschütternd; (*disgusting, annoying*) ekelhaft, zum Kotzen (*sl*); *treatment* abscheulich; *delays, price increase* unerträglich ◆ **his ~ habit of always being right** seine unerträgliche Angewohnheit, immer recht zu haben.

sickeningly ['sɪknɪŋlɪ] *adv* (*lit*) ekelerregend; (*fig*) unerträglich ◆ **his English is ~ good** es ist schon unerträglich, wie gut sein Englisch ist; **we had all that ~ good weather during the exams** es war richtig gemein, daß wir ausgerechnet während des Examens so schönes Wetter hatten; **now it's all ~ obvious** das schreit ja schon zum Himmel (*inf*).

sick headache *n* ≃ Migräne(anfall *m*) *f*.

sickle ['sɪkl] *n* Sichel *f* ◆ **~-cell anaemia** Sichelzellenanämie *f*.

sick-leave ['sɪkli:v] *n* **to be on ~** krank geschrieben sein; **employees are allowed six weeks' ~ per year** Angestellte dürfen insgesamt sechs Wochen pro Jahr wegen Krankheit fehlen; **he has three months' ~ because of his accident** aufgrund seines Unfalls hat er drei Monate Genesungsurlaub; **he**

➤ LANGUAGE IN USE: **sick: 2a** → 7.3

only gets two weeks' paid ~ im Krankheitsfall wird sein Gehalt nur zwei Wochen weitergezahlt.

sickliness ['sɪklɪnɪs] *n see adj* Kränklichkeit *f*; Blässe *f*; Widerlichkeit, Ekelhaftigkeit *f*; Mattheit *f*; Schwachheit *f*.

sick-list ['sɪklɪst] *n* (*because of illness*) Krankenliste *f*; (*because of injury*) Verletztenliste *f* ◆ **to be on/off the ~** (*Mil, Sport*) auf der/nicht mehr auf der Kranken-/Verletztenliste stehen; (*inf*) (wegen Krankheit) fehlen/wieder im Einsatz sein (*inf*).

sickly ['sɪklɪ] *adj* (*+er*) *person, appearance* kränklich; *complexion, light* blaß; *smell, taste, food, sentimentality, colour* widerlich, ekelhaft; *smile* matt; *grin* schwach; *climate* ungesund ◆ **~ sweet smell** unangenehm süßer Geruch; **~ sweet smile** übersüßes *or* zuckersüßes Lächeln.

sick-making ['sɪkmeɪkɪŋ] *adj* (*inf*) gräßlich (*inf*).

sickness ['sɪknɪs] *n* (*Med*) Krankheit *f* (*also fig*); (*nausea*) Übelkeit *f*; (*vomiting*) Erbrechen *nt*; (*of joke, book, film*) Geschmacklosigkeit *f* ◆ **there is ~ on board** an Bord geht eine Krankheit um; **the ~ of his mind** seine Abartigkeit; **~ benefit** Krankengeld *nt*.

sick: ~-pay *n* Bezahlung *f* im Krankheitsfall; **~-room** *n* Krankenzimmer *nt*.

side [saɪd] [1] *n* **(a)** (*wall, vertical surface*) (*of car, box, hole, ditch*) Seite *f*; (*of cave, artillery trench, mining shaft, boat, caravan*) Wand *f*; (*of cliff, mountain*) Hang *m* ◆ **the ~s of the hill** die Berghänge *pl*.

(b) (*flat surface, line*) (*of triangle, cube, coin, paper, material, record*) Seite *f* ◆ **this ~ up!** (*on parcel etc*) oben!; **right/wrong ~** (*of cloth*) rechte/linke Seite; **this sock is right/wrong ~ out** dieser Strumpf ist rechts/links (herum).

(c) (*edge*) Rand *m* ◆ **at the ~ of the road** am Straßenrand; **the body was found in the ~ of the wood nearest to the road** die Leiche wurde am Waldrand neben der Straße gefunden; **at** *or* **on the ~ of his plate** auf dem Tellerrand.

(d) (*not back or front, area to one ~*) Seite *f* ◆ **by/at the ~ of sth** seitlich von etw; **the destroyer rammed the ~ of the boat** der Zerstörer rammte das Boot seitlich; **to drive on the left ~ of the road** auf der linken Straßenseite fahren; **the path goes down the ~ of the house** der Weg führt seitlich am Haus entlang; **it's this/the other ~ of London** (*out of town*) es ist auf dieser/auf der anderen Seite Londons; (*in town*) es ist in diesem Teil/am anderen Ende von London; **the south/respectable ~ of Glasgow** der Süden/der vornehme Teil Glasgows; **the debit/credit ~ of an account** die Soll-/Habenseite eines Kontos; **the enemy attacked them on** *or* **from all ~s** der Feind griff sie von allen Seiten an; **this statement was attacked on** *or* **from all ~s** diese Behauptung wurde von allen angegriffen; **he stood** *or* **moved to one ~** er trat zur Seite; **the car moved to one ~ of the road and stopped** der Wagen fuhr seitlich heran und hielt; **he stood to one ~ and did nothing** (*lit*) er stand daneben und tat nichts; (*fig*) er hielt sich raus; **to put sth on one ~** etw beiseite *or* auf die Seite legen; (*shopkeeper*) etw zurücklegen; **I'll put that question on one ~** ich werde diese Frage vorerst zurückstellen; **to take sb to** *or* **on one ~** jdn beiseite nehmen; **just this ~ of the boundary** (*lit*) (noch) diesseits der Grenze; (*fig*) gerade an der Grenze; **just this ~ of respectability** gerade noch annehmbar; **just this ~ of the line between sanity and madness** gerade an der Grenze zum Wahnsinn; **on the other ~ of death/the boundary** nach dem Tod/jenseits der Grenze; **with one's head on one ~** mit zur Seite geneigtem Kopf.

(e) to be on the safe ~ sichergehen; **we'll take an extra £50 just to be on the safe ~** wir werden vorsichtshalber *or* für alle Fälle 50 Pfund mehr mitnehmen; **to get/stay on the right ~ of sb** jdn für sich einnehmen/es (sich *dat*) mit jdm nicht verderben; **to get on the wrong ~ of sb** es (sich *dat*) mit jdm verderben; **to be on the right/wrong ~ of 40** noch nicht/über 40 sein; **on the right ~ of the law** auf dem Boden des Gesetzes; **only just on the right ~ of the law** an der Grenze der Legalität; **to make a bit (of money) on the ~** (*inf*) sich (*dat*) etwas nebenher *or* nebenbei verdienen (*inf*); **to have a bit on the ~** (*inf*) einen Seitensprung machen; (*for longer*) noch nebenher etwas laufen haben (*inf*); **I'm not going to be your bit on the ~** (*inf*) ich will nicht deine Nebenfrau/dein Nebenmann sein (*inf*).

(f) (*of person, Anat*) Seite *f* ◆ **~ of bacon** Speckseite *f*; **by sb's ~** neben jdm; **~ by ~** nebeneinander, Seite an Seite; **to stand/sit ~ by ~ with sb** direkt neben jdm stehen/sitzen; **to fight ~ by ~ with sb** Seite an Seite mit jdm kämpfen; **I'll be by your ~** (*fig*) ich werde Ihnen zur Seite stehen; *see* **split**.

(g) (*branch*) (*of family*) Seite *f*; (*of business, school*) Zweig *m* ◆ **the Catholic/intellectual ~ of the family** der katholische Teil/die Intelligenz der Familie; **on one's father's/mother's ~** väterlicherseits/mütterlicherseits; **there's French blood on the paternal/maternal ~** von väterlicher/mütterlicher Seite ist französisches Blut da.

(h) (*aspect*) Seite *f* ◆ **a problem with many ~s to it** ein vielschichtiges Problem; **there are always two ~s to every story** alles hat seine zwei Seiten; **let's hear your ~ of the story** erzählen Sie mal Ihre Version (der Geschichte); **the management's ~ of the story was quite different** die Geschichte hörte sich von seiten des Managements ganz anders an; **to hear both ~s of the question** bei einer Frage beide Seiten (an)hören; **the bright/seamy ~ of life** die Sonnen-/Schattenseite des Lebens; **to look on the bright ~** (*be optimistic*) zuversichtlich sein; (*look on the positive ~*) etw von der positiven Seite betrachten; **you don't know his cruel ~** Sie kennen ihn nicht von seiner grausamen Seite.

(i) (a bit) on the large/high/formal *etc* **~** etwas groß/hoch/förmlich *etc*; (*for somebody*) etwas zu groß/hoch/förmlich *etc*; **he errs on the ~ of overgenerosity** er ist eher etwas zu großzügig.

(j) (*opposing team*) (*Sport, in quiz*) Mannschaft *f*; (*fig*) Seite *f* ◆ **there are two ~s in the dispute** in dem Streit stehen sich zwei Parteien gegenüber; **the management ~ refused to give in** die Managementseite weigerte sich nachzugeben; **with a few concessions on the government ~** mit einigen Zugeständnissen von seiten der Regierung; **to change ~s** sich auf die andere Seite schlagen; (*Sport*) die Seiten wechseln; **to take ~s** parteiisch sein; **to take ~s with sb** für jdn Partei ergreifen; **he's on our ~** er steht auf unserer Seite; **whose ~ are you on?** (*supporting team*) für wen sind Sie?; (*playing for team*) bei wem spielen Sie mit?; (*in argument*) zu wem halten Sie eigentlich?

(k) (*dated inf: superiority*) **there's no ~ about** *or* **to him** er sitzt nicht auf dem hohen Roß; **to put on ~** sich aufplustern.

[2] *adj attr* (*on one ~*) *window, door, entrance, road, street* Seiten-; (*not main*) *entrance, room, door, road, street, job* Neben-; (*to one ~*) *punch* seitlich, Seiten-.

[3] *vi* **to ~ with/against sb** jds Partei (*acc*)/Partei gegen jdn ergreifen.

side: ~ arm *n* an der Seite getragene Waffe; (*sword etc*) Seitenwaffe *f*; **~board** *n* Anrichte *f*, Sideboard *nt*; **~boards, ~burns** *npl* Koteletten *pl*; (*longer*) Backenbart *m*; **~car** *n* Beiwagen *m*; (*esp Sport*) Seitenwagen *m*.

-sided [-saɪdɪd] *adj suf* -seitig.

side: ~-dish *n* Beilage *f*; **~ drum** *n* kleine Trommel; **~ effect** *n* Nebenwirkung *f*; **~ elevation** *n* Seitenansicht *f*, Seitenriß *m*; **~-impact protection** *n* (*Aut*) Seitenaufprallschutz *m*; **~ issue** *n* Randproblem *nt*; **that's just a ~ issue** das ist Nebensache; **~kick** *n* (*esp US inf*) Kumpan (*inf*), Kumpel (*inf*) *m*; (*assistant*) Handlanger *m* (*pej*); **the rancher and his ~kicks** der Farmer und seine Leute; **~light** *n* (*Aut*) Parklicht *nt*, Parkleuchte *f*; (*incorporated in headlight*) Standlicht *nt*; **that was an interesting ~light on his character** das warf ein neues Licht auf seinen Charakter; **~line** *n* (*extra business*) Nebenerwerb *m*; **it's just a ~line** das läuft so nebenher (*inf*); **to do sth as a ~line** etw nebenher *or* nebenbei tun; **~lines** *npl* Seitenlinien *pl*; **the trainer sat at the ~lines** der Trainer saß am Spielfeldrand; **to keep to the ~lines** (*fig*) im Hintergrund bleiben; **to be** *or* **stand** *or* **sit on the ~lines** (*fig*) unbeteiligter Außenstehender *or* Zuschauer sein; **~long** *adj, adv glance* Seiten-; (*surreptitious*) verstohlen, versteckt; **to give sb a ~long glance, to glance ~long at sb** jdn kurz aus den Augenwinkeln anblicken.

sidereal [saɪ'dɪərɪəl] *adj* (*spec*) siderisch.

side: ~-saddle [1] *n* Damensattel *m*; [2] *adv* im Damensattel *or* Damensitz; **~ salad** *n* Salat *m* (als Beilage); **~ show** *n* Nebenvorstellung *f*; (*exhibition*) Sonderausstellung *f*; **~ slip** *n* (*Aviat*) Slippen *nt*, Seitenrutsch *m*.

sidesman ['saɪdzmən] *n, pl* **-men** [-mən] ≃ Kirchendiener *m*.

side: ~-splitting *adj* urkomisch, zum Totlachen (*inf*); **~-step** [1] *n* Schritt *m* zur Seite; (*dancing*) Seitenschritt *m*; (*Sport*) Ausfallschritt *m*; (*fig: dodge*) Ausweichmanöver *nt*; **a master of the dribble and ~-step** ein Meister im Dribbeln und Ausweichen; [2] *vt tackle, punch* (seitwärts) ausweichen (*+dat*); *person* ausweichen (*+dat*); (*fig*) ausweichen (*+dat*), umgehen; [3] *vi* (seitwärts *or* zur Seite) ausweichen; (*fig*) ausweichen, ausweichende Antworten geben; **~ street** *n* Seitenstraße *f*; **~stroke** *n* Seitenschwimmen *nt*; **to do the ~stroke** seitenschwimmen; **~swipe** *n* Puff *m* (*inf*); (*fig*) Seitenhieb *m* (*at* gegen); **to take a ~swipe at sb** (*lit*) jdm einen Puff geben; (*verbally*) jdm einen Seitenhieb versetzen; **~ table** *n* Beistelltisch *m*; **~track** [1] *n* (*esp US*) *see* **siding**; [2] *vt* ablenken; **I got ~tracked onto something else** ich wurde durch irgend etwas abgelenkt; (*from topic*) ich wurde irgendwie vom Thema abgebracht *or* auf ein anderes Thema gebracht; **she's easily ~tracked** sie läßt sich leicht ablenken; **~ view** *n* Seitenansicht *f*; **to have a ~ view of sth** etw von der Seite sehen; **I just caught a ~ view of her head** ich konnte sie nur kurz im Profil sehen; **~walk** *n* (*US*) Bürgersteig, Gehsteig *m*, Trottoir (*S Ger*) *nt*; **~ wall** *n* Seitenwand *f*; **~ward** *adj see* **~wards 1**; **~wards, ~ways** [1] *adj movement* zur Seite; *glance* von der Seite; **to give sb/sth a ~wards** *or* **~ways glance** jdn/etw von der Seite ansehen; [2] *adv move* zur Seite, seitwärts; *look at sb* von der Seite; **it goes in ~ways** *or* **~wards** es geht seitwärts hinein; **~ways on** seitlich (*to sth* zu etw); **~ whiskers** *npl* Backenbart *m*; **~ wind** *n* Seitenwind *m*; **~winder** *n* (*US: blow*) Haken *m*.

siding ['saɪdɪŋ] *n* Rangiergleis *nt*; (*dead end*) Abstellgleis *nt*.

sidle ['saɪdl] *vi* (sich) schleichen ◆ **to ~ away** (sich) wegschleichen; **he must have ~d off** er muß sich verdrückt haben (*inf*); **to ~ up to sb** sich an jdn heranschleichen.

siege [si:dʒ] *n* (*of town*) Belagerung *f*; (*by police*) Umstellung *f* ◆ **to lay ~ to a town/a house** eine Stadt/ein Haus belagern/umstellen; **he attempted to lay ~ to her emotions** er versuchte, ihr Herz zu erobern.

sienna [sɪ'enə] [1] *n* (*earth*) Sienaerde *f*; (*colour*) Ockergelb *nt* ◆ **raw ~** Ockergelb *nt*; **burnt ~** gebrannte Siena.

[2] *adj* ockergelb ◆ **raw ~** ockergelb; **burnt ~** siena(braun), rotbraun.

sierra [sɪ'erə] *n* Sierra *f*.

Sierra Leone [sɪ'erəlɪ'əʊn] *n* Sierra Leone *f*.

siesta [sɪ'estə] *n* Siesta *f* ◆ **to have** *or* **take a ~** Siesta halten *or* machen.

sieve [sɪv] [1] *n* Sieb *nt* ◆ **to have a memory like a ~** (*inf*) ein Gedächtnis wie ein Sieb haben (*inf*).

[2] *vt see* **sift 1 (a)**.

sift [sɪft] [1] *vt* **(a)** sieben; *coal* schütteln ◆ **~ the sugar onto the cake** den Kuchen mit Zucker besieben. **(b)** (*fig*) (*search*) sichten, durchgehen; (*separate*) trennen.

[2] *vi* (*fig*) sieben ◆ **to ~ through the evidence** das Beweismaterial durchgehen; **a ~ing process** ein Siebeverfahren *nt*.

◆**sift out** *vt sep* **(a)** *stones, seed, wheat* aussieben. **(b)** (*fig*) herausfinden, herauskristallisieren; (*eliminate*) absondern; *applicants* aussieben.

sifter ['sɪftə^r] *n* Mehl-/Zuckerstreuer *m*.

sigh [saɪ] [1] *n* (*of person*) Seufzer *m*; (*of wind*) (*murmur*) Säuseln *nt no pl*; (*moan*) Seufzen *nt no pl* (*liter*) ◆ **a ~ of relief** ein Seufzer der Erleichterung; *see* **breathe**.

[2] *vti* seufzen; (*wind*) (*murmur*) säuseln; (*moan*) seufzen (*liter*) ◆ to ~ with relief erleichtert aufatmen; to ~ with contentment zufrieden seufzen; to ~ for sb/sth sich nach jdm/etw sehnen.

sighing ['saɪɪŋ] *n see vti* Seufzen *nt*; Säuseln *nt*; Seufzen *nt* (*liter*).

sight [saɪt] [1] *n* (a) (*faculty*) Sehvermögen *nt* ◆ the gift of ~ die Gabe des Sehens; long/short ~ Weit-/Kurzsichtigkeit *f*; to have long/short ~ weit-/kurzsichtig sein; to lose/regain one's ~ sein Augenlicht verlieren/wiedergewinnen; he has very good ~ er sieht sehr gut; ~ is the most valuable sense das Auge ist das wertvollste Sinnesorgan.
(b) (*glimpse, seeing*) it was my first ~ of Paris das war das erste, was ich von Paris gesehen habe; to hate sb at first ~ *or* on ~ jdn vom ersten Augenblick an nicht leiden können; at first ~ I hated him, but then ... als ich ihn zum erstenmal sah, *or* zuerst konnte ich ihn gar nicht leiden, aber dann ...; at first ~ it seemed easy auf den ersten Blick erschien es einfach; to shoot at *or* on ~ sofort schießen; to translate at *or* on ~ vom Blatt übersetzen; he played the music by *or* at ~ er hat vom Blatt gespielt; love at first ~ Liebe auf den ersten Blick; at the ~ of the police they ran away als sie die Polizei sahen, rannten sie weg; to know sb by ~ jdn vom Sehen kennen; to catch ~ of sb/sth jdn/etw entdecken *or* erblicken; if I catch ~ of you round here again ... wenn du mir hier noch einmal unter die Augen kommst, ...; don't let me catch ~ of you with her again ich möchte dich nicht noch einmal mit ihr erwischen; to get *or* have a ~ of sb/sth jdn/etw zu sehen *or* zu Gesicht bekommen; we had a glorious ~ of the mountains wir hatten einen herrlichen Blick auf die Berge; to lose ~ of sb/sth (*lit, fig*) jdn/etw aus den Augen verlieren; don't lose ~ of the fact that ... Sie dürfen nicht außer acht lassen, daß ...; *see* second ~.
(c) (*sth seen*) Anblick *m* ◆ the ~ of blood/her makes me sick wenn ich Blut/sie sehe, wird mir übel; that is the most beautiful ~ I've ever seen das ist das Schönste, was ich je gesehen habe; I hate *or* can't bear the ~ of him/his greasy hair ich kann ihn (einfach) nicht ausstehen/ich finde seine fettigen Haare widerlich; to be a ~ to see *or* behold ein herrlicher Anblick sein; (*funny*) ein Bild *or* Anblick für die Götter sein (*inf*); what a horrible ~! das sieht ja furchtbar aus!; it was a ~ for sore eyes es war eine wahre Augenweide; you're a ~ for sore eyes es ist schön, dich zu sehen.
(d) (*inf*) to be *or* look a ~ (*funny*) zum Schreien aussehen (*inf*); (*horrible*) fürchterlich aussehen; he looks a ~ der sieht vielleicht aus (*inf*); what a ~ you are! wie siehst du denn aus!
(e) (*range of vision*) Sicht *f* ◆ to be in *or* within ~ in Sicht *or* in Sichtweite sein; land in ~! Land in Sicht!; our goal is in ~ unser Ziel ist in greifbare Nähe gerückt; we are in ~ of victory unser Sieg liegt in greifbarer Nähe; we came in ~ of the coast die Küste kam in Sicht; at last we were in ~ of land endlich war Land in Sicht; to keep sb in ~ jdn im Auge behalten; to keep out of ~ sich verborgen halten; to keep sb/sth out of ~ jdn/etw nicht sehen lassen; keep out of my ~! laß dich bloß bei mir nicht mehr sehen *or* blicken; to be out of *or* lost to ~ nicht mehr zu sehen sein, außer Sicht sein; the minute I was out of ~ of the school/the headmaster sobald ich von der Schule aus nicht mehr zu sehen war/sobald mich der Rektor nicht mehr sehen konnte; when he's out of our ~ wenn wir ihn nicht sehen; somewhere out of ~ a cat was mewing irgendwo miaute eine (unsichtbare) Katze; don't let the children out of your ~ laß die Kinder nicht aus den Augen; darling, I'll never let you out of my ~ again Schatz, ich lasse dich nie mehr fort; to drop out of (sb's) ~ langsam verschwinden, (jds Blick *dat*) entschwinden (*geh*); to be lost to ~ nicht mehr zu sehen sein; out of ~, out of mind (*Prov*) aus den Augen, aus dem Sinn (*Prov*).
(f) (*Comm*) payable at ~ zahlbar bei Sicht; 30 days' ~ 30 Tage nach Sicht; ~ unseen unbesehen, ohne Besicht (*form*); we need to have ~ of the document first das Dokument muß uns (*dat*) zuerst vorliegen.
(g) (*fig: opinion*) in sb's ~ in jds Augen (*dat*); in the ~ of God vor Gott.
(h) *usu pl* (*of city etc*) Sehenswürdigkeit *f* ◆ to see the ~s of a town *etc* eine Stadt *etc* besichtigen.
(i) (*on gun, telescope etc*) Visiereinrichtung *f*; (*on gun also*) Visier *nt* ◆ to set one's ~s too high (*fig*) seine Ziele zu hoch stecken; to lower one's ~s (*fig*) seine Ansprüche herabsetzen *or* herunterschrauben; to set one's ~s on sth (*fig*) ein Auge auf etw (*acc*) werfen; to have sb/sth in one's ~s (*fig*) jdn/etw im Fadenkreuz haben.
(j) (*aim, observation*) to take a ~ with a gun *etc* at sth etw mit einem Gewehr *etc* anvisieren.
(k) (*inf*) not by a long ~ bei weitem nicht; we're not finished yet, not by a long ~ wir sind noch lange nicht fertig; a ~ better/cheaper einiges besser/billiger; he's a damn ~ cleverer than you think er ist ein ganzes Ende gescheiter als du meinst (*inf*).
(l) (*sl*) out of ~ sagenhaft (*sl*), 'ne Wucht (*sl*).
[2] *vt* (a) (*see*) sichten (*also Mil*); *person* ausmachen. (b) *gun* (*provide with ~s*) mit Visier versehen; (*adjust ~s*) richten.

sight bill *n* Sichtwechsel *m*.

sighted ['saɪtɪd] *adj* sehend.

-sighted *adj suf* -sichtig.

sighting ['saɪtɪŋ] *n* Sichten *nt* ◆ at the first ~ of land als zum ersten Mal Land gesichtet wurde; another ~ of the monster was reported das Ungeheuer soll erneut gesehen *or* gesichtet worden sein.

sightless ['saɪtlɪs] *adj* blind ◆ worms are completely ~ Würmer haben kein Sehvermögen (*form*), Würmer können überhaupt nicht sehen; with ~ eyes mit blicklosen (*geh*) *or* toten Augen.

sightlessness ['saɪtlɪsnɪs] *n* Blindheit *f*.

sightly ['saɪtlɪ] *adj* ansehnlich.

sight: ~-read *vti* vom Blatt spielen/lesen/singen; ~ **screen** *n* (*Cricket*) Sichtblende *f* hinter dem Tor; ~**seeing** [1] *n* Besichtigungen *pl*; I hate ~seeing ich hasse Sightseeing; ~seeing in Ruritania eine Rundreise durch Ruritanien; (*list of sights*) Sehenswürdigkeiten *pl* von Ruritanien; to go ~seeing auf Besichtigungstour gehen; [2] *adj* ~seeing tour Rundreise *f*; (*in town*) (Stadt)rundfahrt *f*; ~seeing tourists Touristen *pl* (*auf Besichtigungstour*); ~**seer** *n* Tourist(in *f*) *m*.

sign [saɪn] [1] *n* (a) (*with hand etc*) Zeichen *nt* ◆ he nodded as a ~ of recognition er nickte zum Zeichen, daß er mich/ihn *etc* erkannt hatte; to give sb a ~ jdm ein Zeichen geben; to make a ~ to sb jdm ein Zeichen machen *or* geben; he gave *or* made me a ~ to stay er gab mir durch ein Zeichen zu verstehen, ich solle bleiben; he made a rude ~ er machte eine unverschämte Geste.
(b) (*indication, Med*) Anzeichen *nt* (*of* für, *gen*); (*evidence*) Zeichen *nt* (*of* von, *gen*); (*trace*) Spur *f* ◆ a sure/good/bad ~ ein sicheres/gutes/schlechtes Zeichen; it's a ~ of the times es ist ein Zeichen unserer Zeit; it's a ~ of the true expert daran erkennt man den wahren Experten; at the slightest/first ~ of disagreement beim geringsten/ersten Anzeichen von Uneinigkeit; there is no ~ of their agreeing nichts deutet darauf hin, daß sie zustimmen werden; to show ~s of sth Anzeichen von etw erkennen lassen; he shows ~s of doing it es sieht so aus, als ob er es tun würde; our guest showed no ~s of leaving unser Gast machte keine Anstalten zu gehen; the rain showed no ~s of stopping nichts deutete darauf hin, daß der Regen aufhören würde; there was no ~ of life in the village es gab keine Spur *or* kein Anzeichen von Leben im Dorf; there was no ~ of him/the book anywhere von ihm/von dem Buch war keine Spur zu sehen; is there any ~ of him yet? ist er schon zu sehen?
(c) (*road~, inn ~, shop ~*) Schild *nt*.
(d) (*written symbol*) Zeichen *nt*; (*Astron*) (Stern- *or* Tierkreis)zeichen *nt*.
[2] *vt* (a) to ~ one's name unterschreiben; to ~ one's name in a book sich in ein Buch eintragen; he ~s himself J.G. Jones er unterschreibt mit J.G. Jones.
(b) *letter, contract, cheque* unterschreiben, unterzeichnen (*form*); *picture, book* signieren ◆ to ~ the guest book sich ins Gästebuch eintragen; to ~ the register sich eintragen; ~ed and sealed (unterschrieben und) besiegelt; ~ed, sealed and delivered unter Dach und Fach, fix und fertig (*inf*); ~ed copy handsigniertes Exemplar.
[3] *vi* (a) (*signal*) to ~ to sb to do sth jdm Zeichen/ein Zeichen geben, etw zu tun. (b) (*with signature*) unterschreiben.

◆**sign away** *vt sep* verzichten auf (+*acc*) ◆ she felt she was ~ing ~ her life sie hatte den Eindruck, ihr Leben abzuschreiben; I'm not going to ~ ~ my life ~ with a mortgage ich werde mich nicht ein Leben lang mit einer Hypothek belasten.

◆**sign for** *vi +prep obj* den Empfang (+*gen*) bestätigen.

◆**sign in** [1] *vt sep person* eintragen ◆ to ~ sb ~ at a club jdn als Gast in einen Klub mitnehmen.
[2] *vi* sich eintragen.

◆**sign off** *vi* (*Rad, TV*) sich verabschieden; (*in letter*) Schluß machen.

◆**sign on** [1] *vt sep see* sign up 1.
[2] *vi* (a) *see* sign up 2. (b) (*for unemployment benefit etc*) to ~ ~ (for unemployment benefit) (*apply*) sich arbeitslos melden; he's still ~ing ~ er ist immer noch arbeitslos; er bezieht immer noch Arbeitslosenunterstützung. (c) (*disc jockey etc*) sich melden.

◆**sign out** [1] *vi* sich austragen ◆ to ~ ~ of a hotel (aus einem Hotel) abreisen.
[2] *vt sep* austragen.

◆**sign over** *vt sep* überschreiben (*to sb* jdm).

◆**sign up** [1] *vt sep* (*employ, enlist*) verpflichten; *workers, employees* anstellen; *mercenaries* anwerben; *sailors* anheuern.
[2] *vi* sich verpflichten; (*mercenaries*) sich melden (*with* zu); (*employees, players also*) unterschreiben; (*sailors*) anheuern; (*for evening class etc*) sich einschreiben.

signal[1] ['sɪgnl] [1] *n* (a) (*sign*) Zeichen *nt*; (*as part of code*) Signal *nt*; (*message*) Nachricht *f* ◆ to give the ~ for sth das Zeichen/Signal zu etw geben; to make a ~ to sb jdm ein Zeichen geben.
(b) (*apparatus, Rail*) Signal *nt* ◆ the ~ is at red das Signal steht auf Rot.
(c) (*Telec*) Signal *nt*.
(d) (*Brit Mil*) S~s ≃ Fernmelder *pl*, *Angehörige pl der britischen Fernmeldetruppe Royal Corps of Signals*.
[2] *vt* (a) (*indicate*) anzeigen; *arrival*, (*fig*) *future event, spring etc* ankündigen ◆ to ~ sb to do sth jdm ein/das Zeichen geben, etw zu tun; the policeman ~led the cars on der Polizist gab den Autos das Zeichen weiterzufahren; he ~led that he was going to turn left er zeigte an, daß er (nach) links abbiegen wollte; the train was ~led onto another line der Zug wurde durch Signale auf ein anderes Gleis gewiesen *or* geleitet; the green light ~led the train on das grüne Licht gab dem Zug freie Fahrt.
(b) *message* signalisieren.
[3] *vi* Zeichen/ein Zeichen geben ◆ he ~led to the waiter er winkte dem Ober; he ~led for his bill er winkte zum Zeichen, daß er zahlen wollte; the driver didn't ~ der Fahrer hat kein Zeichen gegeben *or* hat nicht angezeigt; the general ~led for reinforcements der General forderte Verstärkung an.

signal[2] *adj attr* (*liter*) *victory, courage* beachtlich, bemerkenswert; *failure, stupidity* eklatant (*geh*).

signal: ~ box *n* Stellwerk *nt*; ~ **flag** *n* Signalflagge *f*.

signalize ['sɪgnəlaɪz] *vt* kennzeichnen.

signal lamp *n* Signallampe *f*.

signaller ['sɪgnələʳ] *n* (*Mil*) Fernmelder, Funker *m*.
signalling ['sɪgnəlɪŋ] *n* (*Mil*) Nachrichtenübermittlung *f*.
signally ['sɪgnəlɪ] *adv* (*liter*) *see adj* bemerkenswert; eklatant ◆ **he has ~ failed** er hat eindeutig versagt.
signal: ~man *n* (*Rail*) Stellwerkswärter *m*; (*Mil*) Fernmelder, Funker *m*; **~ red** *adj* signalrot.
signatory ['sɪgnətərɪ] [1] *adj* Signatar- ◆ **the ~ powers to an agreement** die Signatarmächte eines Abkommens.
[2] *n* Unterzeichner, Signatar (*form*) *m* ◆ **the signatories of** *or* **to the EC treaty** die Signatarstaaten des EG-Abkommens.
signature ['sɪgnətʃəʳ] *n* **(a)** Unterschrift *f*; (*of artist*) Signatur *f*. **(b)** (*Mus*) Vorzeichnung *f* ◆ **~ tune** (*Brit*) Erkennungsmelodie *f*. **(c)** (*Typ*) Signatur *f*.
signboard ['saɪnbɔːd] *n* Schild *nt*; (*hoarding*) Anschlagtafel *f*.
signer ['saɪnəʳ] *n* Unterzeichner *m*.
signet ring ['sɪgnɪtˌrɪŋ] *n* Siegelring *m*.
significance [sɪg'nɪfɪkəns] *n* Bedeutung *f*; (*of action also*) Tragweite *f*; (*of one special event also*) Wichtigkeit *f* ◆ **what is the ~ of this?** was bedeutet das?, welche Bedeutung hat das?; **of no ~** belanglos, bedeutungslos; **to attach great ~ to sth** einer Sache (*dat*) große Bedeutung beimessen; **he attaches great ~ to us arriving on time** er legt großen Wert darauf, daß wir pünktlich sind.
significant [sɪg'nɪfɪkənt] *adj* (*considerable, having consequence*) bedeutend; (*important*) wichtig; (*meaningful*) bedeutungsvoll; *look* vielsagend, bedeutsam ◆ **is it of any ~ interest?** ist das von wesentlichem Interesse?; **it is ~ that ...** es ist bezeichnend, daß ...; **to be ~ to** *or* **for sth** eine bedeutende *or* wichtige Rolle in etw (*dat*) spielen; **he wondered whether her glance was ~** er fragte sich, ob ihr Blick etwas zu bedeuten habe; **to be ~ of sth** (*liter*) ein (An)zeichen für etw sein.
significantly [sɪg'nɪfɪkəntlɪ] *adv* (*considerably*) bedeutend; (*meaningfully*) bedeutungsvoll; *look* vielsagend, bedeutsam ◆ **it is not ~ different** das ist kaum anders, da besteht kein wesentlicher Unterschied; **~ enough, they both had the same name** bezeichnenderweise trugen sie beide denselben Namen.
signification [ˌsɪgnɪfɪ'keɪʃən] *n* **(a)** (*meaning*) Sinn *m*, Bedeutung *f*. **(b)** (*indication*) Bezeichnung *f* ◆ **a ~ of one's intentions** eine Absichtsbekundung *or* -erklärung.
signify ['sɪgnɪfaɪ] [1] *vt* **(a)** (*mean*) bedeuten. **(b)** (*indicate*) andeuten, erkennen lassen; (*person also*) zu erkennen geben.
[2] *vi* (*dated*) **it/he doesn't ~** das/er spielt keine Rolle.
sign: ~ language *n* Zeichensprache *f*; **~ painter** *n* Plakat- *or* Schildermaler *m*; **~post** [1] *n* Wegweiser *m*; [2] *vt way* beschildern; *diversion, special route* ausschildern; **~posting** *n* Beschilderung *f*; (*of special route, diversion*) Ausschilderung *f*; **~writer** *n* Schriften- *or* Schildermaler *m*.
Sikh [siːk] *n* Sikh *mf*.
silage ['saɪlɪdʒ] *n* Silage *f*, Silofutter *nt*.
silence ['saɪləns] [1] *n* Stille *f*; (*quietness also*) Ruhe *f*; (*absence of talk also, of letters etc*) Schweigen *nt*; (*on a particular subject*) (Still)schweigen *nt* ◆ **~!** Ruhe!; **in ~** still; (*not talking also*) schweigend; **there was ~** alles war still; **there was a short ~** es herrschte für kurze Zeit Stille; **the conversation was full of awkward ~s** die Unterhaltung kam immer wieder ins Stocken; **radio ~** (*Mil*) Funkstille *f*; **to break the/one's ~** die Stille durchbrechen/sein Schweigen brechen.
[2] *vt* (*lit, fig*) zum Schweigen bringen ◆ **to ~ sb's tongue** jdn zum Schweigen bringen.
silencer ['saɪlənsəʳ] *n* (*on gun, Brit: on car*) Schalldämpfer *m*; (*whole fitting on car*) Auspufftopf *m*.
silent ['saɪlənt] *adj* still; (*not talking also*) schweigsam; *engine, machine etc* (*running quietly*) ruhig; *agreement, disapproval* (still)schweigend *attr* ◆ **~ movie/letter** Stummfilm *m*/stummer Buchstabe; **~ partner** (*US*) stiller Teilhaber *or* Gesellschafter; **the ~ majority** die schweigende Mehrheit; **to be ~ (about sth)** (über etw *acc*) schweigen; **to keep** *or* **remain ~** still sein *or* bleiben, sich still verhalten; (*about sth*) nichts sagen, sich nicht äußern; **he kept completely ~ when questioned** er sagte kein einziges Wort *or* überhaupt nichts, als man ihn verhörte; **everyone kept ~** keiner sagte etwas; **be ~!** sei/seid still!; **to become ~** still werden; (*people also, guns*) verstummen.
silently ['saɪləntlɪ] *adv* lautlos; (*without talking*) schweigend; (*with little noise*) leise.
Silesia [saɪ'liːzɪə] *n* Schlesien *nt*.
Silesian [saɪ'liːzɪən] [1] *adj* schlesisch.
[2] *n* Schlesier(in *f*) *m*.
silhouette [ˌsɪluː'et] [1] *n* Silhouette *f*; (*picture*) Schattenriß, Scherenschnitt *m*.
[2] *vt* **to be ~d against sth** sich (als Silhouette) gegen *or* von etw abzeichnen.
silica ['sɪlɪkə] *n* Kieselerde *f* ◆ **~ gel** Kieselgel *nt*.
silicate ['sɪlɪkɪt] *n* Silikat, Silicat *nt*.
siliceous [sɪ'lɪʃəs] *adj* kiesig, Kies-.
silicon ['sɪlɪkən] *n* Silizium *nt* ◆ **~ chip** Siliziumchip *nt*; **~ valley** Silicon Valley *nt*.
silicone ['sɪlɪkəʊn] *n* Silikon *nt* ◆ **~ treatment** Silikonbehandlung *f*.
silicosis [ˌsɪlɪ'kəʊsɪs] *n* (*Med*) Staublunge, Silikose (*spec*) *f*.
silk [sɪlk] [1] *n* **(a)** Seide *f*; (**~** *dress*) Seidene(s), Seidenkleid *nt* ◆ **dressed in beautiful ~s** in herrliche Seidengewänder gekleidet; **dressed in ~s and satins** in Samt und Seide (gekleidet).
(b) (*Brit Jur*) (*barrister*) Kronanwalt *m*; (*gown*) Seidengewand *nt* ◆ **to take ~** Kronanwalt werden.
(c) ~s *pl* (*racing colours*) (Renn)farben *pl*.
[2] *adj* Seiden-, seiden ◆ **the dress is ~** das Kleid ist aus Seide.
silken ['sɪlkən] *adj* (*old: of silk*) seiden; (*like silk also*) seidig; *manner* glatt; *voice* (bedrohlich) sanft.
silk hat *n* Zylinder *m*.
silkiness ['sɪlkɪnɪs] *n* (*appearance*) seidiger Glanz; (*feeling*) seidige Weichheit; (*of voice*) Sanftheit *f*; (*of manner*) Glätte *f*.
silk: ~ moth *n* Seidenspinner *m*; **~ screen** *n* Seidensieb *nt*; (*also* **~-screen printing**) Seidensiebdruck *m*; **~ stocking** *n* Seidenstrumpf *m*; **~-stocking** *adj* (*US*) vornehm; **~worm** *n* Seidenraupe *f*.
silky ['sɪlkɪ] *adj* (*+er*) seidig; *voice* samtig; *manner* glatt.
sill [sɪl] *n* Sims *m or nt*; (*window~*) (Fenster)sims *m or nt*; (*esp of wood*) Fensterbrett *nt*; (*door~*) Schwelle *f*; (*on car*) Türleiste *f*.
sillabub *n see* **syllabub**.
silliness ['sɪlɪnɪs] *n* Albernheit *f* ◆ **no ~ while we're out, children!** macht keine Dummheiten, wenn wir nicht da sind!
silly ['sɪlɪ] [1] *adj* (*+er*) albern, dumm, doof (*inf*) ◆ **~ season** närrische Zeit; (*Press*) Sauregurkenzeit *f*; **don't be ~** (*do ~ things*) mach keinen Quatsch (*inf*); (*say ~ things*) red keinen Unsinn; (*ask ~ questions*) frag nicht so dumm; **that was ~ of you, that was a ~ thing to do** das war dumm (von dir); **I've done a ~ thing and come without the key** ich war so dumm, ohne Schlüssel zu kommen, ich Dussel bin ohne Schlüssel gekommen (*inf*); **I've done a ~ thing and told you a pointless lie** ich habe dich ohne Grund angelogen, das war dumm von mir; **I feel ~ in this hat** mit diesem Hut komme ich mir albern *or* lächerlich vor; **to make sb look ~** jdn lächerlich machen; **that remark of yours made him look/left him looking a bit ~** nach dieser Bemerkung von dir stand er ziemlich dumm da; **to knock sb ~** jdn windelweich schlagen (*inf*); **to laugh oneself ~** sich dumm und dämlich lachen (*inf*); **to worry sb ~** jdn vor Sorge (ganz) krank machen.
[2] *n* (*Brit: also* **~-billy**) Dussel *m* (*inf*) ◆ **you big ~** du Dummerchen (*inf*); **don't be such a ~** sei nicht albern.
silo ['saɪləʊ] *n* Silo *nt*; (*for missile*) unterirdische Startrampe.
silt [sɪlt] [1] *n* Schwemmsand *m*; (*river mud*) Schlick *m*.
[2] *vt* (*also* **~ up**) mit Schlick /Schwemmsand füllen.
[3] *vi* (*also* **~ up**) verschlammen.
Silurian [saɪ'ljuːrɪən] *adj* (*Geol*) silurisch, Silur-.
silver ['sɪlvəʳ] [1] *n* **(a)** (*metal*) Silber *nt*. **(b)** (*coins*) Silber(geld) *nt*, Silbermünzen *pl* ◆ **£10 in ~** £ 10 in Silber. **(c)** (*tableware, articles*) Silber *nt*.
[2] *adj* Silber-, silbern ◆ **to be born with a ~ spoon in one's mouth** (*prov*) mit einem silbernen Löffel im Mund geboren sein (*prov*).
[3] *vt metal, mirror* versilbern ◆ **old age had ~ed his hair** das Alter hatte sein Haar silbergrau werden lassen.
silver: ~ birch *n* Weißbirke *f*; **~ fir** *n* Weiß- *or* Silbertanne *f*; **~fish** *n* Silberfischchen *nt*; **~ foil** *n* (*kitchen foil*) Alu(minium)folie *f*; (**~** *paper*) Silberpapier *nt*; **~ fox** *n* Silberfuchs *m*; **~-grey** *adj* silbergrau; *hair* silberweiß; **~-haired** *adj* silberhaarig; **he is ~-haired** er hat silberweißes Haar.
silveriness ['sɪlvərɪnɪs] *n* silbriger Schimmer; (*of sound, voice*) silberheller Klang.
silver: ~ jubilee *n* 25jähriges Jubiläum; **~ nitrate** *n* Silbernitrat *nt*; **~ oxide** *n* Silberoxid *nt*; **~ oxide battery** *n* Silberoxidbatterie *f*; **~ paper** *n* Silberpapier *nt*; **~ plate** *n* (*plating*) Silberauflage, Versilberung *f*; (*articles*) versilberte Sachen *pl*; **is that ~ plate?** ist das versilbert?; **~-plate** *vt* versilbern; **~plating** *n* Versilberung *f*; (*layer also*) Silberauflage *f*; **~ screen** *n* Leinwand *f*; **~ service** *n* (*in restaurant*) *Servieren nt/Vorlegen nt nach allen Regeln der Kunst*; **~side** *n* (*Cook*) *quergeschnittenes Stück aus der Rindskeule*; **~smith** *n* Silberschmied *m*; **~smith's (shop)** *n* Silberschmiede *f*; **~ standard** *n* Silberstandard *m*; **~-tongued** *adj* (*liter*) wort- *or* redegewandt; **~ware** *n* Silber(zeug *inf*) *nt*; (*in shop also*) Silberwaren *pl*; **~ wedding** *n* Silberhochzeit *f*.
silvery ['sɪlvərɪ] *adj* silbern, silbrig; *sound, voice* silberhell.
simian ['sɪmɪən] [1] *adj* (*form*) der Affen; *appearance* affenartig.
[2] *n* Affe *m*.
similar ['sɪmɪləʳ] *adj* ähnlich (*also Math*); *amount, size* fast *or* ungefähr gleich ◆ **this is ~ to what happened before** etwas Ähnliches ist schon einmal geschehen; **she and her sister are very ~, she is very ~ to her sister** ihre Schwester und sie sind sich sehr ähnlich, sie ähnelt ihrer Schwester sehr; **they are very ~ in appearance/character** sie ähneln sich äußerlich/charakterlich sehr; **~ in size** ungefähr *or* fast gleich groß; **in a ~ way** ähnlich; (*likewise*) genauso, ebenso.
similarity [ˌsɪmɪ'lærɪtɪ] *n* Ähnlichkeit *f* (*to* mit).
similarly ['sɪmɪləlɪ] *adv* ähnlich; (*equally*) genauso, ebenso ◆ **a ~ abstruse expression** ein genauso wirrer Ausdruck; **~, you could maintain ...** genausogut könnten Sie behaupten ...
simile ['sɪmɪlɪ] *n* Gleichnis *nt* ◆ **his use of ~** sein Gebrauch von Gleichnissen.
similitude [sɪ'mɪlɪtjuːd] *n* (*liter*) Ähnlichkeit *f*.
simmer ['sɪməʳ] [1] *n* **to be on the ~** (*Cook*) auf kleiner Flamme kochen; **to keep sb/sth on the ~** (*lit*) etw auf kleiner Flamme kochen lassen; (*fig*) jdn/etw nicht zur Ruhe kommen lassen.
[2] *vt* auf kleiner Flamme kochen lassen.
[3] *vi* auf kleiner Flamme kochen; (*fig*) (*with rage*) kochen (*inf*); (*with excitement*) fiebern.
◆**simmer down** *vi* sich beruhigen, sich abregen (*inf*).
simnel cake ['sɪmnlkeɪk] *n* (*Brit*) marzipanüberzogener Früchtekuchen.
simonize ® ['saɪmənaɪz] *vt* polieren.

simony ['saɪmənɪ] *n* (*old, Eccl*) Simonie *f*.

simper ['sɪmpəʳ] [1] *n* **her ~s and poses** ihr Gehabe und Getue; ... **she said with a ~** sagte sie affektiert.
[2] *vi* (*smile*) geziert *or* albern lächeln; (*talk*) säuseln.
[3] *vt* säuseln.

simpering ['sɪmpərɪŋ] *adj* geziert, albern.

simperingly ['sɪmpərɪŋlɪ] *adv* geziert, albern; *talk* säuselnd.

simple ['sɪmpl] *adj* (+*er*) **(a)** (*easy, not complicated, Math, Med, Gram*) einfach; (*Fin*) *interest also* gewöhnlich ◆ **~ time** (*Mus*) gerader Takt; **"chemistry made ~"** „Chemie leichtgemacht".
(b) (*plain, not elaborate*) einfach; *decor, dress also* schlicht ◆ **the ~ fact** *or* **truth is ...** es ist einfach so, daß ...
(c) (*unsophisticated, unworldly*) einfach, schlicht ◆ **I'm a ~ soul** ich bin (nur) ein einfacher Mensch.
(d) (*foolish, mentally deficient*) einfältig.

simple: ~-minded *adj* einfältig; **~-mindedness** *n* Einfältigkeit, Einfalt *f*.

simpleton ['sɪmpltən] *n* Einfaltspinsel *m*.

simplex ['sɪmpleks] *n* (*Ling*) Simplex *nt*.

simplicity [sɪm'plɪsɪtɪ] *n* **(a)** Einfachheit *f*; (*unworldliness, lack of sophistication, of decor, dress also*) Schlichtheit *f* ◆ **it's ~ itself** das ist das Einfachste, das ist die einfachste Sache der Welt. **(b)** (*foolishness*) Einfalt, Einfältigkeit *f*.

simplifiable ['sɪmplɪfaɪəbl] *adj* zu vereinfachend *attr*, zu vereinfachen *pred*, simplifizierbar.

simplification [,sɪmplɪfɪ'keɪʃən] *n* Vereinfachung, Simplifizierung *f*.

simplify ['sɪmplɪfaɪ] *vt* vereinfachen, simplifizieren.

simplistic [sɪm'plɪstɪk] *adj* simpel, simplistisch (*geh*) ◆ **or am I being ~?** oder sehe ich das zu einfach?

simply ['sɪmplɪ] *adv* einfach; (*merely*) nur, bloß ◆ **but you ~ must!** aber du mußt einfach!; **to put it ~** ... um es einfach auszudrücken ...

simulate ['sɪmjʊleɪt] *vt* **(a)** (*feign*) *emotions* vortäuschen; *enthusiasm also* spielen; *illness* simulieren ◆ **to ~ (the appearance of) sth** (*material*) etw imitieren; (*animal, person*) sich als etw tarnen; **~d leather/sheepskin** Lederimitation *f*/falsches Schafsfell. **(b)** (*reproduce*) *conditions* simulieren.

simulation [,sɪmjʊ'leɪʃən] *n* **(a)** Vortäuschung *f*; (*simulated appearance*) Imitation *f*; (*of animals*) Tarnung *f* ◆ **his ~ of epilepsy** seine simulierte Epilepsie. **(b)** (*reproduction*) Simulation *f*.

simulator ['sɪmjʊleɪtəʳ] *n* Simulator *m*.

simultaneity [,sɪməltə'nɪətɪ] *n* Gleichzeitigkeit, Simultan(e)ität (*geh*) *f*.

simultaneous [,sɪməl'teɪnɪəs] *adj* gleichzeitig, simultan (*geh*) ◆ **~ equations** (*Math*) Simultangleichungen *pl*; **~ translation/interpreting** Simultanübersetzung *f*/-dolmetschen *nt*.

simultaneously [,sɪməl'teɪnɪəslɪ] *adv* gleichzeitig, zur gleichen Zeit, simultan (*geh*).

sin [sɪn] [1] *n* (*Rel, fig*) Sünde *f* ◆ **to live in ~** (*inf*) in wilder Ehe leben; (*Rel*) in Sünde leben; **I've been chosen to organize the office party, for my ~s** (*hum*) man hat mich drangekriegt (*inf*), ich darf die Büroparty organisieren; **is that your work/family? — yes for my ~s** (*hum*) haben Sie das gemacht/ist das Ihre Familie? — ja, leider; **to cover a multitude of ~s** (*hum*) viele Schandtaten verdecken; **this hat is covering a multitude of ~s, she said** (*hum*) aber fragen Sie bloß nicht, wie es unter dem Hut aussieht!, sagte sie; **isn't it a ~!** ist das nicht unerhört *or* eine (Sünde und) Schande?
[2] *vi* sündigen (*against* gegen, an +*dat*), sich versündigen (*against* an +*dat*); (*against principles, standards etc*) verstoßen (gegen) ◆ **he was more ~ned against than ~ning** er hat mehr Unrecht erlitten als begangen.

Sinai ['saɪneɪaɪ] *n* Sinai *m* ◆ **~ Peninsula** Sinaihalbinsel *f*; **Mount ~** der Berg Sinai.

▼ **since** [sɪns] [1] *adv* (*in the meantime*) inzwischen; (*up to now*) seitdem ◆ **ever ~** seither; **a long time ~, long ~** schon lange; **he died long ~** er ist schon lange tot; **not long ~** erst vor kurzem.
▼ [2] *prep* seit ◆ **ever ~ 1900** (schon) seit 1900; **he had been living there ~ 1900** er lebte da schon seit 1900; **I've been coming here ~ 1982** ich komme schon seit 1982 hierher; **it's a long time ~ then** das ist schon lange her; **how long is it ~ the accident?** wie lange ist der Unfall schon her?
[3] *conj* **(a)** (*time*) seit(dem) ◆ **ever ~ I've known him** seit(dem) ich ihn kenne. **(b)** (*because*) da.

sincere [sɪn'sɪəʳ] *adj* aufrichtig, lauter (*liter*); *person also* offen; *intention also* ernst, ehrlich ◆ **a ~ friend** ein wahrer Freund; **it is our ~ hope that ...** wir hoffen aufrichtig, daß ...

sincerely [sɪn'sɪəlɪ] *adv see adj* aufrichtig; offen; ernsthaft ◆ **yours ~** mit freundlichen Grüßen, hochachtungsvoll (*form*).

sincerity [sɪn'serɪtɪ] *n see adj* Aufrichtigkeit *f*, Offenheit *f*, Ernsthaftigkeit *f* ◆ **in all ~** in aller Offenheit; **I was acting in all ~ when ...** ich habe es ganz aufrichtig *or* ehrlich gemeint, als ...

sine [saɪn] *n* (*Math*) Sinus *m*.

sinecure ['saɪnɪkjʊəʳ] *n* Pfründe, Sinekure (*geh*) *f* ◆ **this job is no ~!** diese Arbeit ist kein Ruheposten.

sine die [,saɪnɪ'daɪiː, 'siːneɪ'diːeɪ] *adv* **to adjourn ~** auf unbestimmte Zeit vertagen.

sine qua non [,sɪnɪkwɑː'nəʊn] *n* unerläßliche Voraussetzung, Conditio sine qua non *f* (*to, for* für).

sinew ['sɪnjuː] *n* Sehne *f* ◆ **~s** *pl* (*fig*) Kräfte *pl*, Stärke *f*.

sinewy ['sɪnjʊɪ] *adj* sehnig; (*fig*) *plant, tree* knorrig; *prose style* kraftvoll, kernig.

sinfonia [sɪn'fəʊnɪə] *n* (*symphony*) Sinfonie, Symphonie *f*; (*overture*) Opernsinfonia *f*; (*orchestra*) Sinfonie- *or* Symphonieorchester *nt*, Sinfoniker, Symphoniker *pl*.

sinfonietta [,sɪnfəʊnɪ'etə] *n* (*music*) Sinfonietta *f*; (*orchestra*) kleines Sinfonie- *or* Symphonieorchester.

sinful ['sɪnfʊl] *adj* sündig; *person, act, thought also* sündhaft (*geh*) ◆ **it is ~ to ...** es ist eine Sünde, zu ...

sinfully ['sɪnfəlɪ] *adv* sündig, sündhaft (*geh*).

sinfulness ['sɪnfʊlnɪs] *n* Sündigkeit, Sündhaftigkeit (*geh*) *f*.

sing [sɪŋ] (*vb: pret* **sang**, *ptp* **sung**) [1] *n* **to have a (good) ~** (tüchtig) singen; **I used to go there for a ~** ich ging immer zum Singen hin.
[2] *vt* **(a)** singen ◆ **to ~ a child to sleep** ein Kind in den Schlaf singen; **to ~ the praises of sb/sth** ein Loblied auf jdn/etw singen. **(b)** (*poet*) besingen, singen von.
[3] *vi* singen; (*ears*) dröhnen; (*kettle*) summen.

◆**sing along** *vi* mitsingen.

◆**sing away** [1] *vi* (*person, bird*) (ununterbrochen) singen; (*kettle*) summen; (*to oneself*) vor sich (*acc*) hin trällern.
[2] *vt sep troubles* fortsingen.

◆**sing of** *vi* +*prep obj* singen von (*poet*), besingen.

◆**sing out** [1] *vi* **(a)** (*sing loudly*) (*person, bird*) laut *or* aus voller Kehle singen; (*voice*) erklingen, tönen; (*kettle*) summen ◆ **come on, ~ ~, let's hear you** na los, singt mal tüchtig, wir wollen was hören (*inf*); **their voices sang ~ through the church** ihr Singen tönte durch die Kirche. **(b)** (*inf: shout*) schreien (*inf*).
[2] *vt sep words, tune* singen, hervorbringen; (*shout out*) (mit singender Stimme) ausrufen.

◆**sing up** *vi* lauter singen.

singable ['sɪŋəbl] *adj* sangbar (*geh*) ◆ **that tune is (not/very) ~** diese Melodie läßt sich (nicht/sehr) gut singen.

Singapore [,sɪŋgə'pɔːʳ] *n* Singapur *nt*.

singe [sɪndʒ] [1] *vt* sengen; *clothes also* versengen; (*slightly*) ansengen; *hair-ends, poultry also* absengen.
[2] *vi* versengt/angesengt werden, sengen.
[3] *n* (*on clothes etc*) versengte/angesengte Stelle ◆ **there's a slight ~ on the sleeve** der Ärmel ist leicht angesengt.

singer ['sɪŋəʳ] *n* Sänger(in *f*) *m* ◆ **~-songwriter** Liedermacher(in *f*) *m*.

Singhalese [,sɪŋgə'liːz] [1] *adj* singhalesisch.
[2] *n* **(a)** Singhalese *m*, Singhalesin *f*. **(b)** (*language*) Singhalesisch *nt*.

singing ['sɪŋɪŋ] *n* Singen *nt*; (*of person, bird also*) Gesang *m*; (*in the ears*) Dröhnen *nt*; (*of kettle*) Summen *nt* ◆ **he teaches ~** er gibt Sing- *or* Gesangstunden, er gibt Singen (*inf*); **do you like my ~?** gefällt dir, wie ich singe?, gefällt dir mein Gesang?

singing: ~ lesson *n* Gesangstunde *f*; **~ telegram** *n durch eine Agentur persönlich übermittelter, in Gesangsform vorgetragener Geburtstagsgruß etc*; **~ voice** *n* Singstimme *f*.

single ['sɪŋgl] [1] *adj* **(a)** (*one only*) einzige(r, s) ◆ **not a ~ one spoke up** nicht ein einziger äußerte sich dazu; **every ~ day was precious** jeder (einzelne) Tag war kostbar; **I've missed the bus every ~ day this week** diese Woche habe ich jeden Tag den Bus verpaßt; **every ~ book I looked at** (aber auch) jedes Buch, das ich mir ansah; **with a ~ voice they cried out for reform** wie mit einer Stimme riefen sie nach Reformen; **not a ~ thing** überhaupt nichts; **the ~ most expensive product** das teuerste Produkt.
(b) (*not double etc*) einzeln; *bed, room* Einzel-; (*Typ*), *carburettor*, (*Brit*) *ticket* einfach ◆ **a ~-tank aqualung** ein Preßluftatmer mit nur einer Sauerstoffflasche.
(c) (*not married*) unverheiratet, ledig ◆ **he was tired of the ~ life** er hatte das Junggesellendasein satt; **~ people** Ledige, Unverheiratete *pl*; **I'm a ~ man/girl** ich bin ledig.
[2] *n* **(a)** (*Cricket*) Schlag *m* für einen Lauf; (*Baseball*) Lauf *m* zum ersten Mal; (*Golf*) Zweier *m*.
(b) (*ticket*) Einzelfahrschein *m*; (*Rail also*) Einzelfahrkarte *f*; (*room*) Einzelzimmer *nt*; (*record*) Single *f*; (*bank note*) Ein-pfund-/-dollarschein *m* ◆ **a ~/two ~s to Xanadu** einmal/zweimal einfach nach Xanadu.
(c) (*unmarried person*) Single *m* ◆ **~s holiday/apartment** Urlaub *m*/Wohnung *f* für Singles; **~s bar** Singles-Bar *f*.

◆**single out** *vt sep* (*choose*) auswählen; *victim, prey* sich (*dat*) herausgreifen; (*distinguish, set apart*) herausheben (*from* über +*acc*) ◆ **to ~ sb ~ for special attention** jdm besondere Aufmerksamkeit zuteil werden lassen; **you couldn't ~ any one pupil ~ as the best** es wäre unmöglich, einen einzelnen Schüler als den besten hinzustellen.

single: ~-action *adj rifle* Einzelfeuer-; **~-barrelled** [,sɪŋgl'bærld] *adj gun* mit einem Lauf; **~-breasted** *adj jacket* einreihig; **~-breasted suit** Einreiher *m*; **~-cell(ed)** *adj* (*Biol*) einzellig; **~-chamber** *adj* (*Pol*) Einkammer-; **~ combat** *n* Nah- *or* Einzelkampf *m*; (*esp of knights etc*) Kampf *m* Mann gegen Mann, Zweikampf *m*; **~ cream** *n* Sahne *f* (*mit geringem Fettgehalt*); **~-decker** *n* einstöckiger Omnibus/einstöckige Straßenbahn, Eindecker *m*; **~-density** *adj* (*Comput*) *disk* mit einfacher Dichte; **~-drive** *adj computer* mit Einzellaufwerk; **~-engined** *adj plane* einmotorig; **~-entry book-keeping** *n* einfache Buchführung; **~ file** *n* **in ~ file** im Gänsemarsch; **~-handed** [1] *adj* (ganz) allein (*after noun*); *achievement* allein *or* ohne (fremde) Hilfe vollbracht; *arrest* allein *or* ohne (fremde) Hilfe durchgeführt; *struggle* einsam; [2] *adv* (*also* **~-handedly**) ohne Hilfe, im Alleingang; **to sail ~-handed round the world** ganz allein *or* als Einhandsegler um die Welt fahren; **~-lens-reflex (camera)** *n* (einäugige) Spiegelreflexkamera; **~-line** *adj* eingleisig; *railway also, traffic* einspurig; **there was ~-line traffic only on the main road** die Hauptstraße konnte nur einspurig befahren werden;

➤ LANGUAGE IN USE: since: 2 → 21.1

~-masted *adj ship* einmastig; **~-masted ship** Einmaster *m*; **~-minded** *adj* zielbewußt, zielstrebig, beharrlich; *devotion* unbeirrbar; **his ~-minded pursuit of money** sein ausschließlich auf Geld gerichtetes Streben; **~-mindedness** *n* Zielstrebigkeit, Beharrlichkeit *f*; *see adj* Unbeirrbarkeit *f*.

singleness ['sɪŋglnɪs] *n* **~ of purpose** Zielstrebigkeit *f*; **his ~ of purpose caused him to neglect his family** er ging so vollkommen in der Sache auf, daß er seine Familie vernachlässigte.

single: ~ parent *n* Alleinerziehende(r) *mf*; **I as a ~ parent ...** ich als alleinerziehende Mutter/alleinerziehender Vater ...; **~-parent** *adj* **a ~-parent family** eine Familie mit nur einem Elternteil, eine Einelternfamilie; **~-party** *adj* Einparteien-; **~-phase** *adj* einphasig, Einphasen-.

singles ['sɪŋglz] *n sing or pl* (*Sport*) Einzel *nt* ◆ **the ~ finals** das Finale im Einzel; **~ is more tiring** Einzel sind anstrengender.

single: ~-seater *n* Einsitzer *m*; **~-sex** *adj education* nach Geschlechtern getrennt; **a ~-sex school** eine reine Jungen-/Mädchenschule; **~-sided** *adj* (*Comput*) *disk* einseitig.

singlet ['sɪŋglɪt] *n* (*Brit*) (*Sport*) ärmelloses Trikot; (*underclothing*) (ärmelloses) Unterhemd, Trikothemd *nt*.

singleton ['sɪŋgltən] *n* (*Cards*) Single *nt* (*einzige Karte einer Farbe*).

single: ~-tongue *vti* mit einfachem Zungenschlag spielen; **~-tonguing** *n* der einzelne Zungenschlag; **~-track** *adj* einspurig; (*Rail also*) eingleisig.

singly ['sɪŋglɪ] *adv* einzeln; (*solely*) einzig, nur.

singsong ['sɪŋsɒŋ] [1] *adj* **the ~ Welsh accent** der walisische Singsang; **in his ~ voice** mit *or* in seinem Singsang.
[2] *n* Liedersingen *nt no indef art, no pl* ◆ **we often have a ~ down the pub** in der Wirtschaft singen wir oft zusammen.

singular ['sɪŋgjʊlər] [1] *adj* **(a)** (*Gram*) im Singular, singularisch (*form*) ◆ **a ~ noun** ein Substantiv im Singular. **(b)** (*odd*) sonderbar, eigenartig ◆ **how very ~!** das ist aber sehr sonderbar *or* eigenartig! **(c)** (*outstanding*) einzigartig, einmalig.
[2] *n* Singular *m* ◆ **in the ~** im Singular.

singularity [ˌsɪŋgjʊ'lærɪtɪ] *n* (*oddity*) Sonderbarkeit, Eigenartigkeit *f*.

singularly ['sɪŋgjʊləlɪ] *adv* **(a)** außerordentlich. **(b)** (*dated: strangely*) sonderbar, eigenartig.

Sinhalese [sɪnhə'li:z] *see* **Singhalese**.

sinister ['sɪnɪstər] *adj* **(a)** unheimlich; *person, night, scheme also* finster; *music, look also* düster; *atmosphere, meaning also* unheilverkündend; *fate* böse. **(b)** (*Her*) linke(r, s).

sink[1] [sɪŋk] *pret* **sank**, *ptp* **sunk** [1] *vt* **(a)** *ship* versenken.
(b) (*fig: ruin*) *theory* zerstören; *hopes also* zunichte machen ◆ **now we're sunk!** (*inf*) jetzt sind wir geliefert (*inf*).
(c) *shaft* senken, teufen (*spec*); *hole* ausheben ◆ **to ~ a post in the ground** einen Pfosten in den Boden einlassen; **they sank a pipe under the riverbed** sie versenkten ein Rohr unter dem Flußbett; *see* **well**[1].
(d) (*inf*) *drink* hinunterschütten (*inf*), hinunterspülen (*inf*).
(e) *teeth, claws* schlagen ◆ **I'd like to ~ my teeth into a juicy steak** ich möchte in ein saftiges Steak reinbeißen (*inf*).
(f) *differences* begraben ◆ **to ~ one's identity in that of a group** vollkommen in der Anonymität einer Gruppe aufgehen.
(g) **to ~ money in sth** Geld in etw (*acc*) stecken.
(h) *golf ball* einlochen; *billiard ball* in das Loch treiben.
(i) (*lower*) *eyes, voice, value of currency* senken ◆ **he sank his hands deep in his pockets** er vergrub die Hände in der Tasche; **he sank his head in his hands** er stützte den Kopf auf die Hände.
(j) **to be sunk in thought** in Gedanken versunken sein; **to be sunk in a book** in ein Buch vertieft sein; **sunk in depression** völlig deprimiert; **to be sunk in debt** tief in Schulden stecken.
[2] *vi* **(a)** untergehen; (*ship also*) sinken ◆ **to ~ to the bottom** auf den Grund sinken; **he was left to ~ or swim** (*fig*) er war ganz auf sich allein angewiesen; **if I go down I'll make sure you all ~ with me** wenn es mich erwischt, werde ich euch alle mitreißen.
(b) (*go down, subside*) sinken; (*sun also*) versinken; (*voice*) sich senken; (*building, land etc*) sich senken, absinken ◆ **the building is gradually ~ing into the mud** das Gebäude versinkt allmählich im Schlamm; **he sank up to his knees in the mud** er sank bis zu den Knien im Schlamm ein; **to ~ (down) into a chair/back into the cushions** in einen Sessel (nieder)sinken/in die Kissen versinken; **the flames sank lower and lower** das Feuer fiel immer mehr in sich zusammen; **the sun sank beneath the horizon** die Sonne versank am Horizont; **the record has sunk to the bottom of the charts** die Platte ist ans Ende der Liste gerutscht; **to ~ to one's knees** auf die Knie sinken; **to ~ out of sight** vor jds Augen (*dat*) versinken; **to ~ into a deep sleep/a depression** in tiefen Schlaf/in Schwermut versinken; **my spirits** *or* **my heart sank at the sight of the work** beim Anblick der Arbeit verließ mich der Mut; **with ~ing heart** mutlos; **the sick man is ~ing fast** der Kranke verfällt zusehends.
(c) (*deteriorate, lessen: output, shares, standards*) sinken ◆ **to ~ into insignificance** zur Bedeutungslosigkeit herabsinken; **to ~ deeper into degradation** immer tiefer sinken; **she has sunk in my estimation** sie ist in meiner Achtung gesunken.

◆**sink away** *vi* (*seabed, ground*) abfallen.

◆**sink in** [1] *vi* **(a)** (*into mud etc*) einsinken (*prep obj, -to* in +*acc*).
(b) (*inf: be understood*) kapiert werden (*inf*) ◆ **it's only just sunk ~ that it really did happen** ich kapiere/er kapiert *etc* erst jetzt, daß das tatsächlich passiert ist (*inf*); **can't you get this to ~ ~(to your thick head)!** kannst du das denn nicht in deinen dicken Schädel bekommen? (*inf*); **repeat each line so that the words ~ ~** wiederhole jede Zeile, damit du's dir merkst (*inf*).
[2] *vt sep stakes, pylons etc* einlassen (*prep obj, -to* in +*acc*).

sink[2] *n* Ausguß *m*; (*in kitchen also*) Spülbecken *nt* ◆ **~ unit** Spültisch *m*, Spüle *f*; **~ of iniquity** Sündenpfuhl *m*, Stätte *f* des Lasters; *see* **kitchen ~**.

sinker ['sɪŋkər] *n* (*Fishing*) Senker *m*, Senkgewicht *nt*.

sinking ['sɪŋkɪŋ] [1] *n* (*of ship*) Untergang *m*; (*deliberately*) Versenkung *f*; (*of shaft*) Senken, Abteufen (*spec*) *nt*; (*of well*) Bohren *nt*.
[2] *adj* **~ feeling** flaues Gefühl (im Magen) (*inf*); **I got that horrible ~ feeling when I realized ...** mir wurde ganz anders, als ich erkannte ...; **~ fund** Tilgungsfonds *m*.

sinless ['sɪnlɪs] *adj person* ohne Sünde, frei von Sünde; *life also* sündenlos, sündenfrei.

sinner ['sɪnər] *n* Sünder(in *f*) *m*.

Sino- ['saɪnəʊ-] *pref* chinesisch-, Sino- (*form*).

sinologist [ˌsaɪ'nɒlədʒɪst] *n* Sinologe *m*, Sinologin *f*.

sinology [ˌsaɪ'nɒlədʒɪ] *n* Sinologie *f*.

sinuosity [ˌsɪnjʊ'ɒsɪtɪ] *n* (*liter*) Schlangenbewegungen *pl*; (*of river*) Windungen *pl*; (*fig*) Gewundenheit *f*.

sinuous ['sɪnjʊəs] *adj* (*lit, fig*) gewunden; *motion of snake* schlängelnd *attr*; *dancing etc* geschmeidig, schlangenartig ◆ **the lane follows a ~ course between ...** der Pfad schlängelt sich zwischen (+*dat*) ... durch.

sinuously ['sɪnjʊəslɪ] *adv see adj*.

sinus ['saɪnəs] *n* (*Anat*) Sinus *m* (*spec*); (*in head*) (Nasen)-nebenhöhle, Stirnhöhle *f*.

sinusitis [ˌsaɪnə'saɪtɪs] *n* Stirnhöhlenkatarrh *m*, Sinusitis *f*.

Sioux [su:] [1] *n* Sioux *mf*.
[2] *adj* Sioux-, der Sioux.

sip [sɪp] [1] *n* Schluck *m*; (*very small*) Schlückchen *nt*.
[2] *vt* in kleinen Schlucken trinken; (*suspiciously, daintily*) nippen an (+*dat*); (*savour*) schlürfen.
[3] *vi* **to ~ at sth** an etw (*dat*) nippen.

siphon ['saɪfən] [1] *n* Heber *m*; (*soda ~*) Siphon *m*.
[2] *vt* absaugen; (*into tank*) (mit einem Heber) umfüllen.

◆**siphon off** *vt sep* **(a)** (*lit*) abziehen, absaugen; *petrol* abzapfen; (*into container*) (mit einem Heber) umfüllen *or* abfüllen. **(b)** (*fig*) *staff, money* abziehen; *profits* abschöpfen.

◆**siphon out** *vt sep liquid* mit einem Heber herausleiten.

SIPS *abbr of* **side-impact protection system.**

sir [sɜ:r] *n* **(a)** (*in direct address*) mein Herr (*form*), Herr X ◆ **no, ~** nein(, Herr X); (*Mil*) nein, Herr Leutnant/General *etc*; **you will apologize, ~!** (*dated*) dafür werden Sie sich entschuldigen (müssen); **S~** (*to editor of paper*) *not translated*; **Dear S~ (or Madam), ...** sehr geehrte (Damen und) Herren!; **my dear** *or* **good ~!** (*dated*) mein (lieber) Herr! (*dated*).
(b) (*knight etc*) **S~** Sir *m*.
(c) (*Sch sl: teacher*) er (*Sch sl*) ◆ **please ~!** Herr X!; **I'll tell ~** ich sag's ihm.

sire ['saɪər] [1] *n* **(a)** (*Zool*) Vater(tier *nt*) *m*; (*stallion also*) Deck- *or* Zuchthengst, Beschäler (*form*) *m*.
(b) (*old: to monarch etc*) **S~** Majestät *f*, Sire *m*.
(c) (*old, poet: father, forebear*) Erzeuger, Ahn *m* ◆ **~ of a great nation** Vater *m* einer großen Nation.
[2] *vt* zeugen ◆ **the horse A, ~d by B** Pferd A, Vater B; **he ~d 49 children** (*hum*) er hat 49 Kinder in die Welt gesetzt.

siren ['saɪərən] *n* (*all senses*) Sirene *f*.

sirloin ['sɜ:lɔɪn] *n* (*Cook*) Lendenfilet *nt*.

sirocco [sɪ'rɒkəʊ] *n* Schirokko *m*.

sirrah ['sɪrə] *n* (*obs*) Bube *m* (*obs*).

sirup *n* (*US*) *see* **syrup**.

sis [sɪs] *n* (*inf*) Schwesterherz *nt* (*inf*).

sisal ['saɪsəl] *n* Sisal *m*.

sissified ['sɪsɪfaɪd] *adj* weibisch, wie ein Weib.

sissy ['sɪsɪ] [1] *n* Waschlappen *m* (*inf*), Memme *f*.
[2] *adj* weibisch.

sister ['sɪstər] *n* **(a)** Schwester *f*; (*in trade union*) Kollegin *f*; (*ship*) Schwesterschiff *nt* ◆ **to be ~ to** (*form*) *or* **the ~ of sb** jds Schwester sein. **(b)** (*nun*) (Ordens)schwester *f*; (*before name*) Schwester *f*. **(c)** (*Brit: senior nurse*) Oberschwester *f*.

sisterhood ['sɪstəhʊd] *n* **(a)** Schwesterschaft *f* ◆ **she emphasized the ~ of women all over the world** sie betonte, daß alle Frauen der ganzen Welt Schwestern seien. **(b)** (*Eccl*) Schwesternorden *m*. **(c)** (*association of women*) Frauenvereinigung *f*.

sister *in cpds* Schwester-; **~-in-law**, *pl* **~s-in-law** Schwägerin *f*.

sisterly ['sɪstəlɪ] *adj* schwesterlich.

Sistine ['sɪsti:n] *adj* Sixtinisch.

Sisyphus ['sɪsɪfəs] *n* Sisyphus *m*.

sit [sɪt] (*vb: pret, ptp* **sat**) [1] *vi* **(a)** (*be ~ting*) sitzen (*in/on* in/auf +*dat*); (*~ down*) sich setzen (*in/on* in/auf +*acc*) ◆ **~!** (*to dog*) sitz!; **a place to ~** ein Sitzplatz *m*; **~ by/with me** setz dich zu mir/neben mich; **to ~ for a painter** für einen Maler Modell sitzen; **to ~ for an exam** eine Prüfung ablegen (*form*) *or* machen; **to be ~ting pretty** (*fig inf*) gut dastehen (*inf*); **he's ~ting pretty for the directorship** der Direktorsposten ist ihm so gut wie sicher; **don't just ~ there, do something**! sitz nicht nur tatenlos da (herum), tu (endlich) was!; *see* **still**[1].
(b) (*assembly*) tagen; (*have a seat*) einen Sitz haben ◆ **he ~s for Liverpool** (*Brit Parl*) er ist der Abgeordnete für Liverpool; **to ~ in parliament/on a committee** einen Sitz im Parlament haben/in einem Ausschuß sitzen.
(c) (*object: be placed, rest*) stehen ◆ **the car sat in the garage** das Auto stand

in der Garage; **the parcel is ~ting in the hall** das Päckchen liegt im Flur; **this food ~s heavy on the stomach** dieses Essen liegt schwer im Magen; **the cares ~ heavy on his brow** (*liter*) die Sorgen lasten schwer auf ihm.
(**d**) (*bird: hatch*) sitzen, brüten ♦ **the hen is ~ting on two eggs** das Huhn brütet zwei Eier aus, das Huhn sitzt auf zwei Eiern.
(**e**) (*fig: clothes*) sitzen (*on sb* bei jdm).
(**f**) **how ~s the wind?** (*liter*) wie steht der Wind?
(**g**) (*inf*) *see* **babysit**.
[2] *vt* (**a**) setzen (*in* in *+acc, on* auf *+acc*); (*place*) *object also* stellen ♦ **to ~ a child on one's knees** sich (*dat*) ein Kind auf die Knie setzen; **the table/car ~s 5 people** an dem Tisch/in dem Auto haben 5 Leute Platz. (**b**) *horse* sitzen auf (*+dat*) ♦ **to ~ a horse well** gut zu Pferde sitzen. (**c**) *examination* ablegen (*form*), machen.
[3] *vr* **to ~ oneself down** sich gemütlich niederlassen *or* hinsetzen; **~ you down** (*dial*) setz dich hin.
[4] *n* **to have a ~** sitzen.
♦**sit about** *or* **around** *vi* herumsitzen.
♦**sit back** *vi* (*lit, fig*) sich zurücklehnen; (*fig: do nothing, not take action*) die Hände in den Schoß legen.
♦**sit down** *vi* (**a**) sich (hin)setzen ♦ **to ~ ~ in a chair** sich auf einen Stuhl setzen. (**b**) (*fig*) **to take sth/an insult ~ting ~** etw einfach hinnehmen/eine Beleidigung einfach schlucken.
♦**sit in** *vi* (**a**) (*demonstrators*) ein Sit-in machen *or* veranstalten. (**b**) (*take place of*) **to ~ ~ (for sb)** jdn vertreten. (**c**) (*attend as visitor*) dabeisein, dabeisitzen (*on sth* bei etw). (**d**) (*stay in*) zu Hause *or* im Haus sitzen.
♦**sit on** [1] *vi* (*continue sitting*) sitzen bleiben.
[2] *vi +prep obj* (**a**) *committee, panel, jury* sitzen in (*+dat*) ♦ **I was asked to ~ ~ the committee** man bat mich, Mitglied des Ausschusses zu werden.
(**b**) (*not deal with*) sitzen auf (*+dat*).
(**c**) (*inf: suppress*) *idea, invention, product* unterdrücken, nicht hochkommen lassen; *person* einen Dämpfer aufsetzen (*+dat*) (*inf*) ♦ **to get sat ~** (*suppressed*) unterdrückt werden; (*rebuked*) eins draufkriegen (*inf*).
♦**sit out** [1] *vi* draußen sitzen.
[2] *vt sep* (**a**) (*stay to end*) *play, film, meeting* bis zum Schluß *or* Ende (sitzen)bleiben bei, bis zum Schluß *or* Ende durch- *or* aushalten (*pej*); *storm* auf das Ende (*+gen*) warten ♦ **we'd better ~ it ~** wir bleiben besser bis zum Ende (hier). (**b**) *dance* auslassen. **I'll ~ this one ~** ich setze diesmal aus; **to ~ ~ a round** (*in game*) eine Runde aussetzen.
♦**sit through** *vi +prep obj* durchhalten, aushalten (*pej*).
♦**sit up** [1] *vi* (**a**) (*be sitting upright*) aufrecht sitzen; (*action*) sich aufrichten, sich aufsetzen ♦ **to ~ ~ (and beg)** (*dog etc*) Männchen machen (*inf*).
(**b**) (*sit straight*) aufrecht *or* gerade sitzen ♦ **~ ~!** setz dich gerade hin!, sitz gerade!; **to make sb ~ ~ (and take notice)** (*fig inf*) jdn aufhorchen lassen.
(**c**) (*not go to bed*) aufbleiben, aufsitzen (*dated*) ♦ **she sat ~ with the sick child** sie wachte bei dem kranken Kind; **to ~ ~ for sb** aufbleiben und auf jdn warten.
(**d**) **to ~ ~ to table** sich an den Tisch setzen.
[2] *vt sep* aufrichten, aufsetzen; *doll also, baby* hinsetzen.
♦**sit upon** *vi +prep obj see* **sit on 2**.
sitar [sɪ'tɑːʳ] *n* Sitar *m*.
sitcom ['sɪtkɒm] *n* (*inf*) Situationskomödie *f*.
sit-down ['sɪtdaʊn] [1] *n* (*inf: rest*) Verschnaufpause *f* (*inf*).
[2] *attr* **to have a ~ strike** einen Sitzstreik machen; **a ~ meal** eine richtige Mahlzeit.
site [saɪt] [1] *n* (**a**) Stelle *f*, Platz *m*; (*Med: of infection*) Stelle *f*. (**b**) (*Archeol*) Stätte *f*. (**c**) (*building ~*) (Bau)gelände *nt*, Baustelle *f* ♦ **missile ~** Raketenbasis *f*; **~ foreman** Polier *m*; **~ office** (Büro *nt* der) Bauleitung *f*. (**d**) (*camping ~*) Campingplatz *m*.
[2] *vt* legen, anlegen ♦ **to be ~d** liegen, (gelegen) sein; **a badly ~d building** ein ungünstig gelegenes Gebäude.
sit-in ['sɪtɪn] *n* Sit-in *nt* ♦ **to hold** *or* **stage a ~** ein Sit-in veranstalten.
siting ['saɪtɪŋ] *n* Legen *nt* ♦ **the ~ of new industries away from London is being encouraged** man fördert die Errichtung neuer Betriebe außerhalb Londons; **the ~ of the town here was a mistake** es war ein Fehler, die Stadt hierher zu legen.
sitter ['sɪtəʳ] *n* (*Art*) Modell *nt*; (*baby-~*) Babysitter *m*; (*bird*) brütender Vogel; (*Sport sl*) todsicherer Ball (*inf*).
sitting ['sɪtɪŋ] [1] *adj* sitzend; *bird* brütend; *conference* tagend, in Sitzung ♦ **~ and standing room** Sitz- und Stehplätze *pl*.
[2] *n* (*of committee, parliament, for portrait*) Sitzung *f* ♦ **they have two ~s for lunch** sie servieren das Mittagessen in zwei Schüben; **the first ~ for lunch is at 12 o'clock** die erste Mittagessenzeit ist um 12 Uhr; **at one ~** (*fig*) auf einmal.
sitting: ~ duck *n* (*fig*) leichte Beute; **~ member** *n* (*Brit Parl*) (derzeitiger) Abgeordneter, (derzeitige) Abgeordnete; **~ room** *n* (*lounge*) Wohnzimmer *nt*; (*in guest house etc*) Aufenthaltsraum *m*; **~ target** *n* (*lit, fig*) leichte Beute; **~ tenant** *n* (derzeitiger) Mieter.
situate ['sɪtjʊeɪt] *vt* legen.
situated ['sɪtjʊeɪtɪd] *adj* gelegen; *person* (*financially*) gestellt, situiert (*geh*) ♦ **it is ~ in the High Street** es liegt an der Hauptstraße; **a pleasantly ~ house** ein Haus in angenehmer Lage; **how are you ~ (for money)?** wie ist Ihre finanzielle Lage?; **he is well ~ to appreciate the risks** er ist sehr wohl (dazu) in der Lage, die Risiken abzuschätzen.
situation [ˌsɪtjʊ'eɪʃən] *n* (**a**) (*state of affairs*) Lage, Situation *f*; (*financial, marital etc*) Lage *f*, Verhältnisse *pl*; (*in play, novel*) Situation *f* ♦ **to save the ~** die Lage *or* Situation retten; **a 2-0 ~** eine 2:0-Situation; **~ comedy** Situationskomödie *f*. (**b**) (*of house etc*) Lage *f*. (**c**) (*job*) Stelle *f* ♦ **"~s vacant/wanted"** „Stellenangebote/Stellengesuche".
sit-up ['sɪtʌp] *n* (*Sport*) **to do a ~** sich aus der Rückenlage aufsetzen.
sitz bath ['zɪtsbɑːθ] *n* Sitzbadewanne *f*.
six [sɪks] [1] *adj* sechs ♦ **she is ~ (years old)** sie ist sechs (Jahre alt); **at (the age of) ~** im Alter von sechs Jahren, mit sechs Jahren; **it's ~ (o'clock)** es ist sechs (Uhr); **there are ~ of us** wir sind sechs; **it cost ~ pounds** es kostete sechs Pfund; **~ and a half/quarter** sechseinhalb/sechseinviertel; **in ~-eight time** (*Mus*) im Sechsachteltakt; **to be ~ foot under** (*hum*) sich (*dat*) die Radieschen von unten besehen (*hum*); **it's ~ of one and half a dozen of the other** (*inf*) das ist Jacke wie Hose (*inf*), das ist gehupft wie gesprungen (*inf*).
[2] *n* (**a**) (*Math, figure, mark, tram*) Sechs *f*; (*bus*) Sechser *m* ♦ **~ and a half/quarter** Sechseinhalb/-einviertel *f*.
(**b**) (*Cards, on dice, Golf*) Sechs *f*; (*Cricket also*) Sechserschlag *m*; (*team of ~ also*) Sechsermannschaft *f* ♦ **to divide sth into ~** etw in sechs Teile teilen; **we divided up into ~es** wir teilten uns in Sechsergruppen auf; **they are sold in ~es** sie werden in Sechserpackungen verkauft; **to be at ~es and sevens** (*things*) wie Kraut und Rüben durcheinanderliegen (*inf*); (*person*) völlig durcheinander sein; **to knock sb for ~** (*inf*) jdn umhauen.
six: ~fold [1] *adj* sechsfach; [2] *adv* um das Sechsfache; **~-footer** *n* **to be a ~-footer** über 1,80 (*gesprochen:* einsachtzig) sein; **~ hundred** [1] *adj* sechshundert; [2] *n* Sechshundert *f*.
sixish ['sɪksɪʃ] *adj* um sechs herum.
six: ~ million *adj, n* sechs Millionen; **~pack** *n* Sechserpackung *f*; **~pence** *n* (*old: coin*) Sixpencestück *nt*; **~penny** [1] *adj* für Sixpence; [2] *n* (*stamp*) Sixpence-Marke *f*; **~-shooter** *n* (*inf*) sechsschüssiger Revolver.
sixteen ['sɪks'tiːn] [1] *adj* sechzehn.
[2] *n* Sechzehn *f*.
sixteenth ['sɪks'tiːnθ] [1] *adj* sechzehnte(r, s) ♦ **a ~ part** ein Sechzehntel *nt*; **a ~ note** (*esp US Mus*) eine Sechzehntelnote, ein Sechzehntel *nt*.
[2] *n* (**a**) (*fraction*) Sechzehntel *nt*; (*in series*) Sechzehnte(r, s). (**b**) (*date*) **the ~** der Sechzehnte.
sixth [sɪksθ] [1] *adj* sechste(r, s) ♦ **a ~ part** ein Sechstel *nt*; **he was** *or* **came ~** er wurde Sechster; **he/it was ~ from the end/left** er/es war der/das Sechste von hinten/von links.
[2] *n* (**a**) (*fraction*) Sechstel *nt*; (*in series*) Sechste(r, s).
(**b**) (*date*) **the ~** der Sechste; **on the ~** am Sechsten; **the ~ of September** der sechste September.
(**c**) (*Mus*) (*interval*) Sexte *f*; (*chord*) Sextakkord *m*.
(**d**) (*Brit*) *see* **~ form**.
[3] *adv* **he did it ~** (*the ~ person to do it*) er hat es als Sechster gemacht; (*the ~ thing he did*) er hat es als sechstes *or* an sechster Stelle gemacht.
sixth: ~ form *n* (*Brit*) Abschlußklasse, ≃ Prima *f*; **~-former** *n* (*Brit*) Schüler(in *f*) *m* der Abschlußklasse, ≃ Primaner(in *f*) *m*.
sixthly ['sɪksθlɪ] *adv* sechstens, als sechstes.
six thousand [1] *adj* sechstausend.
[2] *n* Sechstausend *f*.
sixth sense *n* sechster Sinn.
sixtieth ['sɪkstɪɪθ] [1] *adj* sechzigste(r, s) ♦ **a ~ part** ein Sechzigstel *nt*.
[2] *n* (*fraction*) Sechzigstel *nt*; (*in series*) Sechzigste(r, s).
sixty ['sɪkstɪ] [1] *adj* sechzig.
[2] *n* Sechzig *f* ♦ **the sixties** die sechziger Jahre; **to be in one's sixties** in den Sechzigern sein; **to be in one's late/early sixties** Ende/Anfang sechzig sein; *see also* **six**.
sixty: ~-fourth note *n* (*esp US Mus*) Vierundsechzigstel(note *f*) *nt*; **~-four thousand dollar question** *n* (*hum*) Zehntausendmarkfrage *f* (*hum*).
sixtyish ['sɪkstɪɪʃ] *adj* um die Sechzig (*inf*), ungefähr sechzig.
sixty-one ['sɪkstɪ'wʌn] [1] *adj* einundsechzig.
[2] *n* Einundsechzig *f*.
six-year-old ['sɪksjɪəˌəʊld] [1] *adj* sechsjährig *attr*, sechs Jahre alt *pred*; *war* schon sechs Jahre dauernd.
[2] *n* Sechsjährige(r) *mf*.
sizable *adj see* **sizeable**.
size[1] [saɪz] [1] *n* (*all senses*) Größe *f*; (*of problem, operation also*) Ausmaß *nt* ♦ **collar/hip/waist ~** Kragen-/Hüft-/Taillenweite *f*; **it's the ~ of a brick** es ist so groß wie ein Ziegelstein; **he's about your ~** er ist ungefähr so groß wie du; **what ~ is it?** wie groß ist es?; (*clothes, shoes, gloves etc*) welche Größe ist es?; **it's quite a ~** es ist ziemlich groß; **it's two ~s too big** es ist zwei Nummern zu groß; **to cut sth to ~** etw auf die richtige Größe zurechtschneiden; **do you want to try it for ~?** möchten Sie es anprobieren, ob es Ihnen paßt?; **try this one for ~** (*fig inf*) wie wär's denn damit?; **that's about the ~ of it** (*inf*) ja, so ungefähr kann man es sagen.
[2] *vt* größenmäßig ordnen.
♦**size up** *vt sep* abschätzen ♦ **I can't quite ~ him ~** ich werde aus ihm nicht schlau.
size[2] [1] *n* (Grundier)leim *m*.
[2] *vt* grundieren.
sizeable ['saɪzəbl] *adj* ziemlich groß, größer; *car, estate, jewel also* ansehnlich; *sum, problem, difference also* beträchtlich.
sizeably ['saɪzəblɪ] *adv* beträchtlich.
-size(d) [-saɪz(d)] *adj suf* -groß ♦ **medium-~** mittelgroß, von mittlerer Größe.
sizzle ['sɪzl] [1] *vi* brutzeln.
[2] *n* Brutzeln *nt*, Brutzelei *f*.
sizzling ['sɪzlɪŋ] [1] *adj fat, bacon* brutzelnd.

[2] *adv*: ~ **hot** kochend heiß; **it was a ~ hot day** (*inf*) es war knallheiß (*inf*).

skate¹ [skeɪt] *n* (*fish*) Rochen *m*.

skate² [1] *n* (*shoe*) Schlittschuh *m*; (*blade*) Kufe *f* ◆ **put** *or* **get your ~s on** (*fig inf*) mach/macht mal ein bißchen dalli! (*inf*); *see* **iceskate, roller ~**.
[2] *vi* eislaufen, Schlittschuh laufen; (*figure-~*) eiskunstlaufen; (*roller-~*) Rollschuh laufen ◆ **he ~d across the pond** er lief (auf Schlittschuhen) über den Teich; **she ~d up to him** sie lief auf ihn zu; **the next couple to ~** das nächste Paar auf dem Eis; **it went skating across the room** (*fig*) es rutschte durch das Zimmer.

◆**skate over** *or* **round** *vi +prep obj* links liegenlassen; *difficulty, problem* einfach übergehen.

skateboard ['skeɪtbɔːd] *n* Skateboard, Rollbrett *nt* ◆ ~ **park** Skateboard-Anlage *f*.

skateboarder ['skeɪtbɔːdə^r] *n* Skateboardfahrer(in *f*) *m*.

skateboarding ['skeɪtbɔːdɪŋ] *n* Skateboardfahren *nt*.

skatepark ['skeɪtpɑːk] *n* Skateboardanlage *f*.

skater ['skeɪtə^r] *n* (*ice~*) Eisläufer(in *f*), Schlittschuhläufer(in *f*) *m*; (*figure-~*) Eiskunstläufer(in *f*) *m*; (*roller-~*) Rollschuhläufer(in *f*) *m*.

skating ['skeɪtɪŋ] *n* (*ice~*) Eislauf, Schlittschuhlauf *m*; (*figure-~*) Eiskunstlauf *m*; (*roller-~*) Rollschuhlauf *m*.

skating *in cpds* Eislauf-; Rollschuh-; ~ **rink** *n* Eisbahn/Rollschuhbahn *f*.

skedaddle [skɪ'dædl] *vi* (*Brit inf*) Reißaus nehmen (*inf*), türmen (*inf*) ◆ ~! weg mit dir/euch!, verzieh dich/verzieht euch!

skein [skeɪn] *n* (*of wool etc*) Strang *m*; (*of geese*) Schwarm *m*; (*of evidence, lies etc*) Geflecht *nt*.

skeletal ['skelɪtl] *adj* Skelett-; *person* bis aufs Skelett abgemagert; *appearance* wie ein Skelett; *shapes of trees etc* skelettartig.

skeleton ['skelɪtn] [1] *n* (*lit, fig*) Skelett *nt*; (*esp of ship*) Gerippe *nt* ◆ **a ~ in one's cupboard** ein dunkler Punkt (in der Familiengeschichte); (*of public figure*) eine Leiche im Keller.
[2] *adj plan, outline etc* provisorisch; *staff, service etc* Not- ◆ ~ **key** Dietrich, Nachschlüssel *m*.

skep [skep] *n* (*old*) (*basket*) Korb *m*; (*bee ~*) Bienenkorb *m*.

skeptic *etc* (*US*) *see* **sceptic** *etc*.

sketch [sketʃ] [1] *n* (*Art, Liter*) Skizze *f*; (*Mus*) Impression *f*; (*Theat*) Sketch *m*; (*draft, design also*) Entwurf *m*.
[2] *vt* (*lit, fig*) skizzieren.
[3] *vi* Skizzen machen.

◆**sketch in** *vt sep* (*draw*) (grob) einzeichnen; (*verbally*) umreißen.

◆**sketch out** *vt sep* (*draw*) grob skizzieren; (*outline also*) umreißen.

sketch-book ['sketʃbʊk] *n* Skizzenbuch *nt*.

sketchily ['sketʃɪlɪ] *adv* flüchtig, oberflächlich.

sketchiness ['sketʃɪnɪs] *n* Flüchtigkeit, Oberflächlichkeit *f*; (*insufficiency*) Unzulänglichkeit *f*.

sketching ['sketʃɪŋ] *n* (*Art*) Skizzenzeichnen *nt*.

sketch: ~-map *n* Kartenskizze *f*; **~-pad** *n* Skizzenblock *m*.

sketchy ['sketʃɪ] *adj* (*+er*) (*inadequate*) *knowledge, account* flüchtig, oberflächlich; (*incomplete*) *record* bruchstückhaft.

skew [skjuː] [1] *n* **on the ~** schief; (*on the diagonal*) schräg.
[2] *adj* (*lit, fig*) schief; (*diagonal*) schräg ◆ **~-whiff** (*lit, fig*) (wind)schief.
[3] *vt* (*turn round*) umdrehen; (*make crooked*) krümmen; (*fig: distort*) verzerren.
[4] *vi* **the car ~ed off the road** der Wagen kam von der Straße ab; **the road ~s to the right** die Straße biegt nach rechts ab; **he ~ed round** er drehte sich um.

skewbald ['skjuːbɔːld] [1] *n* Schecke *mf*.
[2] *adj* scheckig.

skewer ['skjʊə^r] [1] *n* Spieß *m*.
[2] *vt* aufspießen.

ski [skiː] [1] *n* Ski, Schi *m*; (*Aviat*) Kufe *f*.
[2] *vi* Ski laufen *or* fahren ◆ **they ~ed down the slope/over the hill** sie fuhren (auf ihren Skiern) den Hang hinunter/sie liefen (mit ihren Skiern) über den Hügel.

ski *in cpds* Ski-, Schi-; **~-bob** *n* Skibob *m*; ~ **boot** *n* Skistiefel *or* -schuh *m*.

skid [skɪd] [1] *n* **(a)** (*sliding movement*) (*Aut etc*) Schleudern *nt* ◆ **to steer into/against a ~** mitsteuern/gegensteuern; **to go into a ~** ins Schleudern geraten *or* kommen; **to correct** *or* **get out of a ~** das Fahrzeug abfangen *or* wieder in seine Gewalt bekommen; **to stop with a ~** schleudernd zum Stehen kommen.
(b) (*on wheel*) Rolle *f*.
(c) (*runner*) Gleiter *m*; (*of plane, sledge etc*) Gleitkufe *f*.
(d) ~s *pl* (*fig*) **he was on** *or* **hit the ~s** (*US inf*) es ging abwärts mit ihm; **to put the ~s under sb/sb's plans** (*inf*) jdn/jds Pläne zu Fall bringen, jdm die Suppe versalzen (*inf*).
[2] *vi* (*car, objects*) schleudern; (*person*) ausrutschen ◆ **to ~ across the floor** über den Boden rutschen *or* schlittern; **the car ~ded into a tree** der Wagen schleuderte gegen einen Baum.

skid: ~ lid *n* (*sl*) Sturzhelm *m*; **~mark** *n* Reifenspur *f*; (*from braking*) Bremsspur *f*; **~pan** *n* Schleuderstrecke *f*; ~ **row** *n* (*esp US inf*) (Kaschemmen- und) Pennergegend *f* (*inf*); **to be on** *or* **in ~ row** heruntergekommen *or* verpennert (*sl*) sein; **he ended up in ~ row** er ist als Penner geendet (*inf*).

skier ['skiːə^r] *n* Skiläufer(in *f*), Skifahrer(in *f*) *m*.

skiff [skɪf] *n* Skiff *nt*; (*Sport*) Einer *m*.

skiffle ['skɪfl] *n* Skiffle *m* ◆ ~ **group** Skiffle Group *f*.

ski-flying ['skiːˌflaɪɪŋ] *n* Skifliegen *nt*.

skiing ['skiːɪŋ] *n* Skilaufen, Skifahren *nt* ◆ **to go ~** Skilaufen *or* Skifahren gehen.

ski: ~-jump *n* (*action*) Skisprung *m*; (*place*) Sprungschanze *f*; **~-jumping** *n* Skispringen *nt*.

skilful, (*US*) **skillful** ['skɪlfʊl] *adj* geschickt; *piano-playing etc also* gewandt; *sculpture, painting etc* kunstvoll.

skilfully, (*US*) **skillfully** ['skɪlfəlɪ] *adv see adj*.

skilfulness, (*US*) **skillfulness** ['skɪlfʊlnɪs] *n see* **skill (a)**.

ski-lift ['skiːlɪft] *n* Skilift *m*.

skill [skɪl] *n* **(a)** *no pl* (*skilfulness*) Geschick *nt*, Geschicklichkeit *f*; (*of sculptor etc*) Kunst(fertigkeit) *f* ◆ **his ~ at billiards/in persuading people** sein Geschick beim Billard/sein Geschick *or* seine Fähigkeit, andere zu überreden.
(b) (*acquired technique*) Fertigkeit *f*; (*ability*) Fähigkeit *f* ◆ **to learn new ~s** etwas Neues lernen; **it's a ~ that has to be acquired** so etwas muß gelernt sein.

skilled [skɪld] *adj* (*skilful*) geschickt, gewandt (*at* in *+dat*); (*trained*) ausgebildet, Fach-; (*requiring skill*) Fach-, fachmännisch ◆ **he's ~ in persuading people** er versteht es, andere zu überreden; **a man ~ in diplomacy** ein geschickter Diplomat.

skillet ['skɪlɪt] *n* Bratpfanne *f*.

skillful *etc* (*US*) *see* **skilful** *etc*.

skim [skɪm] [1] *vt* **(a)** (*remove floating matter*) abschöpfen; *milk* entrahmen ◆ **~med** *or* (*US*) ~ **milk** Magermilch *f*.
(b) (*pass low over*) streifen *or* streichen über (*+acc*); (*fig: touch on*) berühren ◆ **he ~med stones across the surface of the water** er ließ Steine übers Wasser hüpfen *or* springen; **he ~med his hat across the room** er schleuderte seinen Hut quer durchs Zimmer; **the book merely ~s the surface of the problem** das Buch berührt das Problem nur an der Oberfläche.
(c) (*read quickly*) überfliegen.
[2] *vi* (*across, over* über *+acc*) (*move quickly*) fliegen; (*aircraft also*) rasch gleiten; (*stones*) springen, hüpfen.

◆**skim off** *vt sep* abschöpfen; (*fig*) absahnen ◆ **to ~ the cream ~ the milk** die Milch entrahmen.

◆**skim through** *vi +prep obj book etc* überfliegen.

skimmer ['skɪmə^r] *n* **(a)** Schaumlöffel *m*. **(b)** (*Orn*) Scherenschnabel *m*.

skimp [skɪmp] [1] *vt food, material* sparen an (*+dat*), knausern mit; *work* hudeln bei (*inf*), nachlässig erledigen; *details* zu kurz kommen lassen.
[2] *vi* sparen (*on* an *+dat*), knausern (*on* mit).

skimpily ['skɪmpɪlɪ] *adv* dürftig; *live, eat also* kärglich; *dressed* spärlich.

skimpy ['skɪmpɪ] *adj* (*+er*) dürftig; *meal also* kärglich; *clothes* knapp ◆ **to be ~ with sth** mit etw sparsam *or* geizig sein.

skin [skɪn] [1] *n* **(a)** Haut *f* ◆ **to be soaked to the ~** bis auf die Haut naß sein; **he's nothing but ~ and bone(s) nowadays** er ist nur noch Haut und Knochen; **that's no ~ off his nose** (*inf*) das braucht ihn nicht zu stören; **that's no ~ off my nose** (*inf*) das juckt mich nicht (*inf*); **to get inside the ~ of a part** (*Theat*) in einer Rolle aufgehen; **all men/women are brothers/sisters under the ~** im Grunde sind alle Menschen gleich; **to save one's own ~** die eigene Haut retten; **to jump** *or* **leap out of one's ~** (*inf*) erschreckt hochfahren; **to get under sb's ~** (*inf*) (*irritate*) jdm auf die Nerven gehen (*inf*); (*fascinate*) (*music, voice*) jdm unter die Haut gehen; (*person*) jdn faszinieren; **I've got you under my ~** du hast mir's angetan; **to have a thick/thin ~** (*fig*) ein dickes Fell (*inf*)/eine dünne Haut haben; **by the ~ of one's teeth** (*inf*) mit knapper Not, mit Ach und Krach (*inf*).
(b) (*hide*) Haut *f*; (*fur*) Fell *nt*; (*of small animals also*) Balg *m*.
(c) (*oilskins*) Ölhaut *f*, Ölzeug *nt*.
(d) (*for wine etc*) Schlauch *m*.
(e) (*of fruit etc*) Schale *f*; (*of grape, tomato also*) Haut *f*.
(f) (*on sausage etc*) Haut *f*, Darm *m*.
(g) (*on milk etc*) Haut *f*.
(h) (*for duplicating*) Matrize *f*.
(i) (*~head*) Skinhead, Skin *m*.
[2] *vt animal* häuten; *fruit* schälen; *grapes, tomatoes* enthäuten ◆ **to ~ sb alive** (*inf*) jdm den Kopf abreißen (*hum inf*); *see* **eye**.

skin: ~-deep *adj see* **beauty**; ~ **disease** *n* Hautkrankheit *f*; **~-diver** *n* Sporttaucher(in *f*) *m*; **~-diving** *n* Sporttauchen *nt*; **~-flick** *n* (*inf*) Porno(film) *m*; **~flint** *n* (*inf*) Geizkragen *m* (*inf*); ~ **food** *n* Nahrung *f* für die Haut.

skinful ['skɪnfʊl] *n* (*inf*) **to have had a ~** einen über den Durst getrunken haben, einen sitzen haben (*inf*).

skin: ~ game *n* (*US inf*) Schwindel *m*; ~ **graft** *n* Hauttransplantation *or* -verpflanzung *f*; **~head** [1] *n* Skinhead *m*; [2] *adj attr style, gang* Skinhead-; **~less** *adj sausage* ohne Haut *or* Darm.

-skinned [-skɪnd] *adj suf* -häutig.

skinner ['skɪnə^r] *n* (*removing skins*) Abdecker *m*; (*preparing skins*) Gerber *m*.

skinny ['skɪnɪ] *adj* (*+er*) (*inf*) *person, legs, arms* dünn; *sweater* eng anliegend *attr*, hauteng.

skinny: ~-dip *vi* (*inf*) im Adams-/Evaskostüm baden (*hum*); **~-rib** *adj sweater* Rippen-.

skint [skɪnt] *adj* (*Brit inf*) **to be ~** pleite *or* blank sein (*inf*).

skin: ~ test *n* Hauttest *m*; **~-tight** *adj* hauteng.

skip¹ [skɪp] [1] *n* (kleiner) Sprung, Hüpfer *m*; (*in dancing*) Hüpfschritt *m* ◆ **she gave a little ~ of pleasure** sie machte einen Freudensprung.
[2] *vi* **(a)** hüpfen; (*jump, gambol*) springen; (*with rope*) seilhüpfen, seilspringen ◆ **she came ~ping up to us** sie kam auf uns zugesprungen; **she was ~ping** (*with rope*) sie sprang Seil.

(b) *(move from subject to subject)* springen.
(c) *(inf: abscond, flee)* abhauen *(inf)*, türmen *(inf)*.
[3] *vt* **(a)** *(omit, miss) school, church etc* schwänzen *(inf)*; *passage, chapter etc* überspringen, auslassen; *(Comput: printer)* überspringen ◆ **my heart ~ped a beat** mein Herzschlag setzte für eine Sekunde aus; **to ~ lunch** das Mittagessen ausfallen lassen; **~ it!** ist ja auch egal!
(b) *(US)* **to ~ rope** seilhüpfen, seilspringen.
(c) *(US inf)* **to ~ town** aus der Stadt verschwinden *(inf)*.
◆**skip about** *vi (lit)* herumhüpfen; *(fig: author, speaker)* springen.
◆**skip across** *vi (inf)* rüberspritzen *(inf)*, rüberspringen *(inf* ◆ **~ ~ to the other office** spritz *or* spring doch mal rüber ins andere Büro! *(inf)*; **we ~ped ~ to Paris** wir machten eine Spritztour nach Paris *(inf)*.
◆**skip off** *vi (inf)* abhauen *(inf)*.
◆**skip over** [1] *vi (inf) see* **skip across**.
[2] *vi +prep obj (pass over)* überspringen.
◆**skip through** *vi +prep obj book* durchblättern.
skip² *n* **(a)** *(Build)* Container *m*, Bauschuttmulde *f (form)*; *(Min)* Förderkorb *m*. **(b)** *see* **skep**.
skip³ *n (Sport)* Kapitän *m*.
ski: ~ pants *npl* Skihose(n *pl*) *f*; **~ pass** *n* Skipaß *m*; **~plane** *n* Flugzeug *nt* mit Schneekufen; **~ pole** *n see* **~ stick**.
skipper ['skɪpəʳ] [1] *n* Kapitän *m* ◆ **aye, aye ~!** jawohl, Käpt'n!
[2] *vt* anführen ◆ **the team was ~ed by X** Kapitän der Mannschaft war X.
skipping ['skɪpɪŋ] *n* Seilhüpfen, Seilspringen *nt* ◆ **~ rope** Hüpf- *or* Sprungseil *nt*.
ski-rack ['skiːræk] *n* Skiträger *m*.
skirl [skɜːl] *n* **the ~ of the bagpipes** das Pfeifen der Dudelsäcke.
skirmish ['skɜːmɪʃ] [1] *n (Mil)* Gefecht *nt*, Plänkelei *f*; *(scrap, fig)* Zusammenstoß *m*.
[2] *vi (Mil)* kämpfen; *(scrap, fig)* zusammenstoßen.
skirmisher ['skɜːmɪʃəʳ] *n* Kämpfende(r) *m*.
skirt [skɜːt] [1] *n* **(a)** Rock *m*; *(of jacket, coat)* Schoß *m*. **(b)** *(sl: woman)* Weibse *f (sl)* ◆ **a bit** *or* **piece of ~** ein Weibsstück *nt (sl)*.
[2] *vt (also* **~ (a)round)** umgehen; *(encircle)* umgeben.
skirting (board) ['skɜːtɪŋ(ˌbɔːd)] *n (Brit)* Fußleiste *f*.
ski: ~-run *n* Skipiste *f*; **~ school** *n* Skischule *f*; **~ stick** *n* Skistock *m*; **~ suit** *n* Skianzug *m*.
skit [skɪt] *n* (satirischer) Sketch (*on* über *+acc*), Parodie *f* (*on gen*).
ski: ~-touring *n* Skitouren *nt*; **~ tow** *n* Schlepplift *m*.
skitter ['skɪtəʳ] *vi* rutschen.
skittish ['skɪtɪʃ] *adj (playful)* übermütig, schelmisch; *(flirtatious) woman* neckisch, kokett; *(nervous) horse* unruhig.
skittishly ['skɪtɪʃlɪ] *adv see adj*.
skittishness ['skɪtɪʃnɪs] *n see adj* Übermütigkeit *f*, Übermut *m*; Neckereien *pl*; Unruhe, Nervosität *f*.
skittle ['skɪtl] *n (Brit)* Kegel *m* ◆ **to play ~s** kegeln; **~ alley** Kegelbahn *f*.
skive [skaɪv] *(Brit sl)* [1] *n* **to be on the ~** blaumachen *(inf)*; *(from school etc)* schwänzen *(inf)*; **to have a good ~** sich *(dat)* einen schönen Tag machen *(inf)*, sich vor der Arbeit drücken.
[2] *vi* blaumachen *(inf)*; *(from school etc)* schwänzen *(inf)*.
◆**skive off** *vi (Brit sl)* sich abseilen *(sl)*, sich drücken *(inf)*.
skiver ['skaɪvəʳ] *n (Brit sl)* fauler Bruder *(inf)*, faule Schwester *(inf)*.
skivvy ['skɪvɪ] *n (Brit inf)* Dienstmagd *f*.
skua ['skjuːə] *n* Skua *f*, Große Raubmöwe.
skulduggery [skʌl'dʌgərɪ] *n (inf)* üble Tricks *pl (inf)* ◆ **a piece of ~** ein übler Trick *(inf)*; **what ~ are you planning?** *(hum)* na, was für Schandtaten hast du denn vor? *(inf)*.
skulk [skʌlk] *vi (move)* schleichen, sich stehlen; *(lurk)* sich herumdrücken.
◆**skulk off** *vi* sich davonschleichen, sich davonstehlen.
skull [skʌl] *n* Schädel *m* ◆ **I couldn't get it into his thick ~** *(inf)* das wollte einfach nicht in seinen Schädel *(inf)*; **~ and crossbones** Totenkopf *m*; **~cap** Scheitelkäppchen *nt*.
-skulled [-skʌld] *adj suf* -schädelig.
skunk [skʌŋk] *n* Skunk *m*, Stinktier *nt*; *(inf: person)* Schweinehund *m*.
sky [skaɪ] *n* Himmel *m* ◆ **under the open ~** unter freiem Himmel; **in the ~** am Himmel; **the ~'s the limit!** nach oben sind keine Grenzen gesetzt; **out of a clear (blue) ~** aus heiterem Himmel; **to praise** *or* **extol sb to the skies** jdn in den Himmel heben, jdn über den grünen Klee loben *(inf)*.
sky: ~ blue *n* Himmelblau *nt*; **~-blue** *adj* himmelblau; **~-diver** *n* Fallschirmspringer(in *f*) *m*; **~-diving** *n* Fallschirmspringen *nt*.
Skye terrier ['skaɪ'terɪəʳ] *n* Skye-Terrier *m*.
sky: ~-high [1] *adj prices* schwindelnd hoch; [2] *adv* zum Himmel; **to blow a bridge ~-high** *(inf)* eine Brücke in die Luft sprengen *(inf)*; **to blow a theory ~-high** *(inf)* eine Theorie zum Einsturz bringen; **~jack** [1] *vt* entführen; [2] *n* Flugzeugentführung *f*; **~jacker** *n* Luftpirat(in *f*), Flugzeugentführer(in *f*) *m*; **~lark** [1] *n* Feldlerche *f*; [2] *vi (inf) (frolic)* tollen; *(fool around)* blödeln *(inf)*; **~larking** *n (inf)* Tollen *nt*; *(fooling around)* Blödelei *f (inf)*; **~light** *n* Oberlicht *nt*; *(in roof also)* Dachfenster *nt*; **~line** *n (horizon)* Horizont *m*; *(of building, hills etc)* Silhouette *f*; *(of city)* Skyline, Silhouette *f*; **~ pilot** *n (sl)* Schwarzrock *m (inf)*; **~rocket** [1] *n* (Feuerwerks)rakete *f*; [2] *vi (prices, expenses)* in die Höhe schießen; **he ~rocketed to fame** er wurde mit einem Schlag berühmt; [3] *vt* in die Höhe schießen lassen; **the novel ~rocketed its author to fame** der Roman machte den Autor mit einem Schlag berühmt; **~scraper** *n* Wolkenkratzer *m*.
skyward(s) ['skaɪwəd(z)] [1] *adj* zum *or* gen *(geh)* Himmel gerichtet ◆ **in a ~ direction** zum *or* gen *(geh)* Himmel.
[2] *adv* zum *or* gen *(geh)* Himmel.
sky: ~way *n* Luftweg *m*; **~-writing** *n* Himmelsschrift *f*.
slab [slæb] *n (of wood etc)* Tafel *f*; *(of stone, concrete etc)* Platte *f*; *(in mortuary)* Tisch *m*; *(slice)* dicke Scheibe; *(of cake, bread)* großes Stück; *(of chocolate)* Tafel *f*.
slack [slæk] [1] *adj (+er)* **(a)** *(not tight)* locker.
(b) *(lazy)* bequem, träge; *student* verbummelt; *(negligent)* nachlässig, schlampig *(inf)* ◆ **they are very ~ about renewing contracts** das Erneuern der Verträge wird sehr nachlässig gehandhabt; **to be ~ about one's work** in bezug auf seine Arbeit nachlässig sein.
(c) *(not busy) (Comm) market* flau; *period, season also* ruhig ◆ **business is ~** das Geschäft geht schlecht.
(d) *(slow) water* träge; *wind* flau.
[2] *n* **(a)** *(of rope etc)* durchhängendes Teil (des Seils/Segels *etc*), Lose(s) *nt (spec)* ◆ **to take up the ~ (on a rope/sail)** ein Seil/Segel straffen *or* spannen; **there is too much ~** das Seil/Segel hängt zu sehr durch; **to take up the ~ in the economy** die brachliegenden Kräfte (der Wirtschaft) nutzen.
(b) *(coal)* Grus *m*.
[3] *vi* bummeln.
◆**slack off** *vi see* **slacken off (b)**.
slacken ['slækn] [1] *vt* **(a)** *(loosen)* lockern.
(b) *(reduce)* vermindern, verringern.
[2] *vi* **(a)** *(become loose)* sich lockern. **(b)** *(speed)* sich verringern; *(rate of development)* sich verlangsamen; *(wind, demand, market)* abflauen, nachlassen.
◆**slacken off** *vi* **(a)** *(diminish)* nachlassen; *(wind, trade also)* abflauen; *(work, trade)* abnehmen. **(b)** *(person: relax)* nachlassen; *(for health reasons)* sich schonen.
◆**slacken up** *vi see* **slacken off (b)**.
slackening ['slæknɪŋ] *n (loosening)* Lockern *nt*; *(reduction)* Abnahme *f*; *(of rate of development, speed)* Verlangsamung *f*; *(of wind, efforts, market)* Abflauen *nt* ◆ **there is no ~ off in the demand** die Nachfrage ist nicht zurückgegangen.
slacker ['slækəʳ] *n* Bummelant *m*.
slackly ['slæklɪ] *adv hold* locker; *hang* lose.
slackness ['slæknɪs] *n* **(a)** *(of rope, reins)* Schlaffheit *f*, Durchhängen *nt*. **(b)** *(laziness)* Bummelei *f*; *(negligence)* Nachlässigkeit, Schlampigkeit *(inf) f*. **(c)** *(of business, market etc)* Flaute *f*.
slacks [slæks] *npl* Hose *f*.
slag [slæg] [1] *n* **(a)** Schlacke *f* ◆ **~ heap** Schlackenhalde *f*. **(b)** *(sl: woman)* Schlampe *f (inf)*.
[2] *vt (inf: run down)* miesmachen *(inf)*, runtermachen *(inf)*.
◆**slag off** *vt sep (inf: run down)* miesmachen *(inf)*, runtermachen *(inf)*.
slain [sleɪn] *ptp of* **slay**.
slake [sleɪk] *vt* **(a)** *(liter: quench)* stillen. **(b)** *lime* löschen ◆ **~d lime** gelöschter Kalk, Löschkalk *m*.
slalom ['slɑːləm] *n* Slalom *m*.
slam [slæm] [1] *n* **(a)** *(of door etc)* Zuschlagen, Zuknallen *nt no pl*; *(of fist etc)* Aufschlagen *nt no pl* ◆ **with a ~** mit voller Wucht.
(b) *(Cards)* Schlemm *m* ◆ **little** *or* **small ~** Kleinschlemm *m*; *see* **grand ~**.
[2] *vt* **(a)** *(close violently)* zuschlagen, zuknallen ◆ **to ~ the door** *(lit, fig)* die Tür zuschlagen; **to ~ sth shut** etw zuknallen; **to ~ the door in sb's face** jdm die Tür vor der Nase zumachen; **to ~ home a bolt** einen Riegel vorwerfen.
(b) *(inf: put, throw etc with force)* knallen *(inf)* ◆ **he ~med his fist into my face/on the table** er knallte mir die Faust ins Gesicht *(inf)*/er knallte mit der Faust auf den Tisch *(inf)*; **to ~ the brakes on** *(inf)* auf die Bremse latschen *(inf)*.
(c) *(inf: defeat)* vernichtend schlagen, am Boden zerstören.
(d) *(inf: criticize harshly)* verreißen; *person* herunterputzen *(inf)*, miesmachen *(inf)*.
[3] *vi (door, window)* zuschlagen, zuknallen.
◆**slam down** *vt sep (put down violently)* hinknallen *(inf)*; *phone* aufknallen *(inf)*; *window* zuknallen ◆ **to ~ sth ~ on the table** etw auf den Tisch knallen.
slammer ['slæməʳ] *n (sl: prison)* Knast *(inf)*, Bau *(sl) m*.
slander ['slɑːndəʳ] [1] *n* Verleumdung *f*.
[2] *vt* verleumden.
slanderer ['slɑːndərəʳ] *n* Verleumder(in *f*) *m*.
slanderous ['slɑːndərəs] *adj* verleumderisch.
slang [slæŋ] [1] *n* Slang *m*; *(army ~, schoolboy ~ etc)* Jargon *m* ◆ **thieves' ~** Gaunersprache *f*, Rotwelsch *nt*; **gipsy ~** Zigeunersprache *f*.
[2] *adj* Slang-.
[3] *vt (inf: esp Brit)* **to ~ sb/sth** jdn beschimpfen/über etw *(acc)* schimpfen; **~ing match** Wettschimpfen *nt*; **they were having a ~ing match** sie beschimpften sich um die Wette *(inf)*.
slangy *adj (+er)*, **slangily** *adv* ['slæŋɪ, -lɪ] salopp.
slant [slɑːnt] [1] *n* **(a)** Neigung, Schräge *f* ◆ **to be on the ~** sich neigen, schräg sein; **his handwriting has a definite ~ to the right/left** er schreibt stark nach rechts/links.
(b) *(fig) (bias, leaning)* Tendenz, Neigung *f*; *(of newspaper article)* Anstrich *m* ◆ **these newspapers have a right-wing ~** diese Zeitungen sind rechtsgerichtet *or* haben einen Rechtsdrall; **to get a ~ on sth** sich *(dat)* einen Eindruck von etw verschaffen; **~-eyed** mit schräggestellte Augen; **she is ~-eyed** sie hat schräggestellte Augen.
[2] *vt* verschieben; *report* färben ◆ **the book is ~ed towards women** das Buch ist auf Frauen ausgerichtet.

[3] *vi* (*road*) sich neigen ◆ **the light ~ed in at the window** das Licht fiel durch das Fenster herein; **her eyes ~ up at the corners** ihre Augen sind schräggestellt.
slanted ['slɑ:ntɪd] *adj* (*fig*) gefärbt.
slanting ['slɑ:ntɪŋ] *adj* schräg.
slap [slæp] [1] *n* Schlag, Klaps *m* ◆ **to give sb a ~** jdm einen Klaps geben; **a ~ in the face** (*lit, fig*) ein Schlag ins Gesicht; (*lit also*) eine Ohrfeige; **to give sb a ~ on the back** jdm (anerkennend) auf den Rücken klopfen; (*fig*) jdn loben; **~ and tickle** (*hum inf*) Balgerei (*inf*), Kalberei (*inf*) *f*; **to give sb a ~ on the wrist** (*fig inf*) jdn zurechtweisen, jdm einem Anpfiff geben (*inf*); **a £1,000 fine to him is just a ~ on the wrist** eine Geldstrafe von £ 1.000 ist für ihn allenfalls ein kleiner Denkzettel.
[2] *adv* (*inf*) direkt.
[3] *vt* **(a)** schlagen ◆ **to ~ sb's face, to ~ sb on** *or* **round the face** jdn ohrfeigen, jdm ins Gesicht schlagen, jdm eine runterhauen (*inf*); **to ~ sb on the back** jdm auf den Rücken klopfen; **to ~ one's knee(s)** sich (*dat*) auf die Schenkel schlagen.
(b) (*put noisily*) knallen (*on(to)* auf +*acc*).
(c) (*inf: put carelessly*) **a piece of cheese ~ped between two slices of bread** ein Stück Käse zwischen zwei Scheiben Brot geklatscht (*inf*).
◆**slap down** *vt sep* (*inf*) **(a)** (*put down*) hinknallen. **(b)** (*fig*) **to ~ sb ~** jdm eins aufs Dach *or* auf den Deckel geben (*inf*); **to be ~ped ~** eins aufs Dach *or* auf den Deckel bekommen (*inf*).
◆**slap on** *vt sep* (*inf*) **(a)** (*apply carelessly*) *paint, make-up* draufklatschen (*inf*). **(b)** (*put on top*) draufklatschen (*inf*); (*fig*) *tax, money* draufhauen (*inf*).
slap: ~-bang *adv* (*inf*) mit Karacho (*inf*); **it was ~-bang in the middle** es war genau in der Mitte; **~dash** *adj* flüchtig, schludrig (*pej*); **~-happy** *adj* unbekümmert; **~head** *n* (*sl*) Glatzkopf *m* (*inf*); **~jack** *n* (*US*) ≃ Pfannkuchen *m*.
slapper ['slæpəʳ] *n* (*sl*) Flittchen *nt* (*inf*).
slap: ~stick *n* Klamauk *m* (*inf*); **~stick comedy** Slapstick *m*; **~-up** *adj* (*inf*) super *pred*, Super- (*inf*); *meal* mit allem Drum und Dran (*inf*).
slash [slæʃ] [1] *n* **(a)** (*action*) Streich *m*; (*wound*) Schnitt *m*; (*made with sword etc also*) Schmiß *m*.
(b) (*Sew*) Schlitz *m* ◆ **a velvet dress with ~es of silk** ein Samtkleid mit seidenunterlegten Schlitzen.
(c) (*sl*) **to go for/have a ~** schiffen gehen (*sl*)/schiffen (*sl*).
[2] *vt* **(a)** (*cut*) zerfetzen; *face also* aufschlitzen; *undergrowth* abhauen, wegschlagen; (*with sword*) hauen auf (+*acc*), schlagen ◆ **to ~ sb with a knife** jdn durch Messerstiche verletzen; **to ~ sth to ribbons** etw zerfetzen; **he ~ed the air with his sword** er ließ das Schwert durch die Luft sausen; *see* **wrist**.
(b) (*inf: reduce drastically*) *price* radikal herabsetzen; *estimate, budget* zusammenstreichen (*inf*).
(c) (*Sew*) mit Schlitzen versehen ◆ **~ed sleeves** Schlitzärmel *pl*; **~ed doublet** Schlitzwams *nt*.
[3] *vi* **to ~ at sb/sth** nach jdm/etw schlagen.
◆**slash off** *vt sep* abschlagen ◆ **to ~ £500 ~ the budget** £ 500 aus dem Etat streichen.
slasher movie, slasher film ['slæʃəʳ-] *n* (*inf*) *Horrorfilm m mit Szenen, in denen Menschen mit Messern, Rasierklingen etc verletzt werden.*
slashing ['slæʃɪŋ] *adj blow* zerschmetternd; *attack also* scharf; *criticism* vernichtend.
slat [slæt] *n* Leiste *f*; (*wooden also*) Latte *f*; (*in grid etc*) Stab *m*.
slate [sleɪt] [1] *n* **(a)** (*rock*) Schiefer *m*; (*roof ~*) Schieferplatte *f*; (*writing ~*) (Schiefer)tafel *f* ◆ **~ quarry** Schieferbruch *m*; **he has a ~ loose** (*inf*) bei ihm ist eine Schraube locker (*inf*); **put it on the ~** (*inf*) schreiben Sie es mir an; **to have a clean ~** (*fig*) eine reine Weste haben, nichts auf dem Kerbholz haben (*inf*); **to wipe the ~ clean** (*fig*) reinen Tisch machen.
(b) (*US Pol*) (Kandidaten)liste *f*.
[2] *adj* Schiefer-, schief(e)rig ◆ **the roof is ~** das Dach ist aus Schiefer.
[3] *vt* **(a)** *roof* (mit Schiefer) decken. **(b)** (*US*) (*propose*) vorschlagen; (*schedule*) ansetzen ◆ **it is ~d to start at nine** es ist für neun Uhr angesetzt. **(c)** (*inf: criticize harshly*) *play, performance* verreißen; *person* zusammenstauchen (*inf*).
slate: ~-blue *adj* blaugrau; **~-coloured** *adj* schiefergrau, schieferfarben; **~-grey** *adj* schiefergrau; **~ pencil** *n* Griffel *m*.
slater ['sleɪtəʳ] *n* Dachdecker, Schieferdecker (*rare*) *m*.
slating ['sleɪtɪŋ] *n* (*inf*) Verriß *m* ◆ **to give sb a ~** jdn zusammenstauchen (*inf*); **to get a ~** zusammengestaucht werden (*inf*); (*play, performance etc*) verrissen werden.
slatted ['slætɪd] *adj see* **slat** aus Leisten/Latten/Stäben bestehend ◆ **a ~ fence** ein Lattenzaun *m*.
slattern ['slætən] *n* Schlampe *f*.
slatternly ['slætənlɪ] *adj* liederlich, schlampig.
slaty ['sleɪtɪ] *adj material* schief(e)rig; (*in colour*) schieferfarben ◆ **~ blue eyes** graublaue Augen *pl*.
slaughter ['slɔ:təʳ] [1] *n* (*of animals*) Schlachten *nt no pl*; (*of persons*) Gemetzel, Abschlachten (*liter*) *nt no pl* ◆ **the S~ of the Innocents** (*Bibl*) der Mord der Unschuldigen Kinder; **the ~ on the roads** das Massensterben auf den Straßen.
[2] *vt* schlachten; *persons* (*lit*) abschlachten; (*fig*) fertigmachen (*inf*).
slaughterer ['slɔ:tərəʳ] *n* (*lit*) Schlachter *m*; (*fig*) Schlächter *m*.
slaughterhouse ['slɔ:təhaʊs] *n* Schlachthof *m or* -haus *nt*.
Slav [slɑ:v] [1] *adj* slawisch.
[2] *n* Slawe *m*, Slawin *f*.
slave [sleɪv] [1] *n* Sklave *m*, Sklavin *f* ◆ **to be a ~ to sb/sth** jds Sklave sein/ Sklave von etw sein.
[2] *vi* sich abplagen, schuften (*inf*) ◆ **to ~ (away) at sth** sich mit etw herumschlagen; **to ~ over a hot stove** (den ganzen Tag) am Herd stehen.
slave: ~ driver *n* (*lit, fig*) Sklaventreiber *m*; **~ labour** *n* **(a)** (*work*) Sklavenarbeit *f*; **(b)** (*work force*) Sklaven *pl*; **he uses ~ labour** seine Leute müssen wie die Sklaven arbeiten.
slaver¹ ['sleɪvəʳ] *n* (*ship*) Sklavenschiff *nt*; (*person*) Sklavenhändler *m*.
slaver² ['slævəʳ] [1] *vi* speicheln (*geh*), geifern ◆ **the dog ~ed at the mouth** der Hund hatte Schaum vor dem Maul; **he began to ~ at the thought of food** bei dem Gedanken ans Essen lief ihm das Wasser im Munde zusammen.
[2] *n* Speichel, Geifer *m*.
slavery ['sleɪvərɪ] *n* Sklaverei *f*; (*condition*) Sklavenleben *nt*; (*fig: addiction*) sklavische Abhängigkeit (*to* von) ◆ **she was tired of domestic ~** sie hatte es satt, sich immer im Haushalt abrackern zu müssen.
slave: ~-ship *n* Sklavenschiff *nt*; **~-trade** *n* Sklavenhandel *m*; **~-trader** *n see* **slaver¹**.
slavey ['sleɪvɪ] *n* (*dated Brit inf*) (Dienst)mädchen *nt*.
Slavic ['slɑ:vɪk] [1] *adj* slawisch.
[2] *n* das Slawische.
slavish *adj*, **~ly** *adv* ['sleɪvɪʃ, -lɪ] sklavisch.
slavishness ['sleɪvɪʃnɪs] *n* sklavische Abhängigkeit; (*submissiveness*) Unterwürfigkeit *f* ◆ **the ~ with which she imitated him** die sklavische Art, in der sie ihn nachahmte.
Slavonic [slə'vɒnɪk] [1] *adj* slawisch.
[2] *n* das Slawische.
slaw [slɔ:] *n* (*US*) Krautsalat *m*.
slay [sleɪ] *pret* **slew**, *ptp* **slain** *vt* erschlagen; (*with gun etc, esp US: kill*) ermorden ◆ **this will ~ you** (*inf*) da lachst du dich tot! (*inf*); **he really ~s me** (*inf*) ich könnte mich über ihn totlachen (*inf*).
slayer ['sleɪəʳ] *n* (*liter*) Mörder, Töter (*old liter*) *m*.
slaying ['sleɪɪŋ] *n* (*esp US: murder*) Mord *m* ◆ **an increasing number of ~s** eine Zunahme von Mordfällen.
SLD (*Brit Pol*) *abbr of* **Social and Liberal Democrats**.
sleaze [sli:z] *n* (*inf*) Skandalgeschichten *pl*.
sleazo ['sli:zəʊ] *n* (*sl: sleazy person*) schmierige Type (*inf*).
sleazy ['sli:zɪ] *adj* (+*er*) (*inf*) schäbig.
sled [sled], **sledge** [sledʒ] [1] *n* Schlitten *m*.
[2] *vi* Schlitten fahren.
sledge(hammer) ['sledʒ(ˌhæməʳ)] *n* Vorschlaghammer *m*.
sleek [sli:k] [1] *adj* (+*er*) *hair, fur, animal* geschmeidig, glatt; (*of general appearance*) gepflegt; *car also* schnittig, elegant; *behaviour* aalglatt (*pej*), glatt.
[2] *vt* glätten; (*cat*) lecken ◆ **to ~ one's hair down/back** sich (*dat*) die Haare glätten *or* zurechtstreichen/zurückstreichen.
sleekness ['sli:knɪs] *n see adj* Geschmeidigkeit *f*, Gepflegtheit *f*, Schnittigkeit, Eleganz *f*, aalglatte Art (*pej*), Glätte *f*.
sleep [sli:p] (*vb: pret, ptp* **slept**) [1] *n* Schlaf *m* ◆ **to go to ~** (*person, limb*), **to drop off to ~** (*person*) einschlafen; **I couldn't get to ~ last night** ich konnte letzte Nacht nicht einschlafen; **try and get some ~** versuche, etwas zu schlafen; **to have a ~** (etwas) schlafen; **to have a good night's ~** sich richtig ausschlafen, richtig schlafen; **to put sb to ~** (*person, cocoa etc*) jdn zum Schlafen bringen; (*drug*) jdn einschläfern; **to put an animal to ~** (*euph*) ein Tier einschläfern; **that film sent me to ~** bei dem Film bin ich eingeschlafen; **to walk/talk in one's ~** schlafwandeln/im Schlaf sprechen.
[2] *vt* **(a) to ~ the hours away** vor sich hin dösen (*inf*); (*all day*) den ganzen Tag verschlafen; **to ~ the sleep of the just/the sleep of the dead** *or* **the last sleep** den Schlaf des Gerechten/den ewigen (*liter*) *or* letzten Schlaf (*liter*) schlafen.
(b) unterbringen ◆ **the house ~s 10** in dem Haus können 10 Leute schlafen *or* übernachten.
[3] *vi* schlafen ◆ **to ~ like a log** *or* **top** *or* **baby** wie ein Klotz *or* wie ein Murmeltier *or* unschuldig wie ein Kind schlafen; **to ~ late** lange schlafen; **to ~ right round the clock** rund um die Uhr schlafen; **the village slept** (*liter*) das Dorf schlief (*geh*); **you must have been ~ing** (*fig*) da mußt du geschlafen haben.
◆**sleep around** *vi* (*inf*) mit jedem schlafen (*inf*).
◆**sleep in** *vi* **(a)** ausschlafen; (*inf: oversleep*) verschlafen. **(b)** (*live in*) im Hause wohnen.
◆**sleep off** *vt sep* (*inf*) *hangover etc* ausschlafen ◆ **to ~ it ~** seinen Rausch ausschlafen; *cold etc* sich gesund schlafen; **to ~ ~ one's lunch** ein Verdauungsschläfchen *nt* halten.
◆**sleep on** [1] *vi* (*continue sleeping*) weiterschlafen.
[2] *vi* +*prep obj problem etc* überschlafen ◆ **let's ~ ~ it** schlafen wir erst einmal darüber, überschlafen wir die Sache erst einmal.
◆**sleep out** *vi* **(a)** (*in open air*) draußen *or* im Freien schlafen. **(b)** (*hotel staff: live out*) außer Haus wohnen.
◆**sleep through** [1] *vi* durchschlafen.
[2] *vi* +*prep obj* weiterschlafen bei ◆ **to ~ ~ the alarm (clock)** den Wecker verschlafen.
◆**sleep together** *vi* zusammen schlafen.
◆**sleep with** *vi* +*prep obj* schlafen mit.
sleeper ['sli:pəʳ] *n* **(a)** (*person*) Schlafende(r) *mf*, Schläfer(in *f*) *m* ◆ **to be a heavy/light ~** einen festen/leichten Schlaf haben.
(b) (*Brit Rail: on track*) Schwelle *f*.
(c) (*Rail*) (*train*) Schlafwagenzug *m*; (*coach*) Schlafwagen *m*; (*berth*) Platz *m* im Schlafwagen ◆ **I've booked a ~** ich habe Schlafwagen gebucht.

(d) *(earring) einfacher Ohrring, der das Zuwachsen des Loches im Ohrläppchen verhindern soll.*

sleepily ['sli:pılı] *adv see adj (a)* schläfrig, müde; verschlafen.

sleepiness ['sli:pınıs] *n see adj* **(a)** Müdigkeit, Schläfrigkeit *f;* Verschlafenheit *f.* **(b)** Lahmheit *(inf),* Müdigkeit *f;* Verschlafenheit *f;* Einschläfernde(s) *nt;* Schläfrigkeit *f.*

sleeping ['sli:pıŋ] 1 *adj* schlafend ◆ **S~ Beauty** Dornröschen *nt;* **let ~ dogs lie** *(Prov)* schlafende Hunde soll man nicht wecken *(Prov).*
2 *n* Schlafen *nt* ◆ **between ~ and waking** zwischen Schlaf und Wachen.

sleeping: ~ accommodation *n* Schlafgelegenheit *f;* **~ bag** *n* Schlafsack *m;* **~ car** *n* Schlafwagen *m;* **~ draught** *n* Schlaftrunk *m;* **~ partner** *n (Brit)* stiller Teilhaber *or* Gesellschafter; **~ pill** *n* Schlaftablette *f;* **~ policeman** *n (traffic bump)* (fahrdynamische) Schwelle, Bodenschwelle *f;* **~ quarters** *npl* Schlafräume *pl;* Schlafsaal *m;* **~ sickness** *n* Schlafkrankheit *f.*

sleepless ['sli:plıs] *adj* schlaflos.

sleeplessness ['sli:plısnıs] *n* Schlaflosigkeit *f.*

sleep: ~walk *vi* schlafwandeln; **he was ~walking** er hat *or* ist geschlafwandelt; **~walker** *n* Schlafwandler(in *f*) *m;* **~walking** 1 *n* Schlafwandeln *nt;* 2 *attr* schlafwandlerisch.

sleepy ['sli:pı] *adj (+er)* **(a)** *(drowsy) person, voice etc* müde, schläfrig; *(not yet awake)* verschlafen ◆ **to be/look ~** müde sein/aussehen; **I feel very ~ at midnight** um 12 Uhr werde ich immer sehr müde.
(b) *(inactive) person* lahm *(inf),* müde; *place, atmosphere* verschlafen; *climate* schläfrig machend; *afternoons* schläfrig.

sleepyhead ['sli:pıhed] *n (inf)* Schlafmütze *f.*

sleet [sli:t] 1 *n* Schneeregen *m.*
2 *vi* **it was ~ing** es gab Schneeregen.

sleeve [sli:v] *n* **(a)** *(on garment)* Ärmel *m* ◆ **to roll up one's ~s** *(lit)* sich *(dat)* die Ärmel hochkrempeln; *(fig)* die Ärmel aufkrempeln *(inf);* **to have sth/a card up one's ~** *(fig inf)* etw/etwas in petto haben *or* auf Lager haben; *see* **laugh.**
(b) *(for record, on book)* Hülle *f.* **(c)** *(Tech)* Muffe, Manschette *f.*

-sleeved [-sli:vd] *adj suf* -ärmelig.

sleeveless ['sli:vlıs] *adj* ärmellos.

sleigh [sleı] *n* (Pferde)schlitten *m* ◆ **~-bell** Schlittenglocke *or* -schelle *f;* **~ ride** Schlittenfahrt *f.*

sleighing ['sleıŋ] *n* Schlittenfahren *nt.*

sleight [slaıt] *n:* **~ of hand** Fingerfertigkeit *f;* **by ~ of hand** durch Taschenspielertricks.

slender ['slendəʳ] *adj* schlank; *hand, waist also* schmal; *resources, income* knapp, mager; *chance, hope* schwach, gering; *excuse* dürftig, schwach.

slenderize ['slendəraız] *vt (US)* schlank machen.

slenderly ['slendəlı] *adv:* **~ built** *or* **made** schlank.

slenderness ['slendənıs] *n see adj* Schlankheit *f;* Schmalheit *f;* Schwäche *f;* Dürftigkeit *f* ◆ **the ~ of his income/of the margin** sein geringes Einkommen/der knappe Abstand.

slept [slept] *pret, ptp of* **sleep.**

sleuth [slu:θ] *(inf)* 1 *n* Spürhund *m (inf).*
2 *vi* Detektiv spielen.

slew[1], *(US)* **slue** [slu:] *(also* **~ round)** 1 *vt crane, lorry* (herum)schwenken; *head* drehen ◆ **to ~ sth to the left** etw nach links schwenken.
2 *vi* (herum)schwenken.

slew[2] *(US inf: also* **slue)** *n* Haufen *m (inf).*

slew[3] *pret of* **slay.**

slewed [slu:d] *adj pred (sl)* voll *(inf),* besoffen *(sl)* ◆ **to get ~** sich vollaufen lassen *(sl).*

slice [slaıs] 1 *n* **(a)** Scheibe *f;* *(of bread also)* Schnitte *f.*
(b) *(fig: portion) (of population, profits)* Teil *m;* *(of land)* Stück *nt* ◆ **a ~ of life in contemporary Paris** ein Ausschnitt aus dem Leben im heutigen Paris; **a ~ of luck** eine Portion Glück; **that was a ~ of luck!** das war ein glücklicher Zufall.
(c) *(esp Brit: food server)* Wender *m* ◆ **cake ~** Tortenheber *m.*
(d) *(Sport)* angeschnittener Ball ◆ **to put a bit of ~ on the ball** den Ball etwas anschneiden.
2 *vt* **(a)** durchschneiden; *bread, meat etc* (in Scheiben) schneiden ◆ **to ~ sth in two** etw durchschneiden, etw in zwei Teile schneiden. **(b)** *ball* (an)schneiden.
3 *vi* **(a)** schneiden ◆ **to ~ through sth** etw durchschneiden. **(b)** *(Sport)* schneiden.

◆**slice off** *vt sep* abschneiden ◆ **he ~d ~ the top of his egg** er köpfte sein Ei *(inf).*

◆**slice up** *vt sep* (ganz) in Scheiben schneiden; *bread, meat, sausage also* aufschneiden; *(divide)* aufteilen.

sliced [slaıst] *adj* (in Scheiben) geschnitten; *loaf, bread, sausage* (auf)geschnitten.

slicer ['slaısəʳ] *n (cheese-~, cucumber-~ etc)* Hobel *m;* *(machine) (bread-~)* Brot(schneide)maschine *f,* Brotschneider *m;* *(bacon-~)* ≃ Wurstschneidemaschine *f.*

slick [slık] 1 *adj (+er) (inf)* **(a)** *(often pej: clever)* gewieft *(inf),* clever *(inf);* *answer, solution* glatt; *show, performance, translation, style* glatt, professionell ◆ **a ~ novel** ein glatt *or* professionell geschriebener Roman; **a ~ customer** ein ganz gewiefter Kerl *(inf);* **he's a ~ operator** er geht raffiniert vor.
(b) *hair* geschniegelt.
(c) *(US: slippery)* glatt, schlüpfrig.
2 *n* **(a)** *(oil~)* (Öl)teppich *m,* Schlick *nt.* **(b)** *(US inf: glossy)* Hochglanzmagazin *nt.* **(c)** *(racing tyre)* Slick *m (inf).*

◆**slick back** *vt sep* **to ~ one's hair ~** sich *(dat)* die Haare anklatschen *(inf);* **the ~ed-~ hairstyles of the 50s** die geschniegelten Frisuren der 50er Jahre.

slicker ['slıkəʳ] *n (US)* **(a)** *(coat)* Regenjacke *f.* **(b)** *(inf: swindler)* Gauner *(inf),* Ganove *(inf) m.* **(c)** *see* **city ~.**

slickly ['slıklı] *adv (inf) see adj (a).*

slickness ['slıknıs] *n (inf) see adj* **(a)** Gewieftheit *(inf),* Cleverneß *(inf) f* ◆ **we were impressed by the ~ with which he answered** wir waren davon beeindruckt, wie glatt er antwortete. **(b)** *(appearance)* geschniegeltes Aussehen.

slide [slaıd] *(vb: pret, ptp* **slid** [slıd]) 1 *n* **(a)** *(place for sliding, chute)* Rutschbahn *f;* *(in playground, for logs etc)* Rutsche *f.*
(b) *(fig: fall, drop)* Abfall *m* ◆ **the ~ in share prices** der Preisrutsch bei den Aktien; **his slow ~ into alcoholism** sein langsamer Abstieg zum Alkoholiker.
(c) *(land~)* Rutsch *m,* Rutschung *f (spec).*
(d) *(of trombone)* Zug *m;* *(sequence of notes)* Schleifer *m.*
(e) *(Tech: part)* gleitendes Teil, Schlitten *m.*
(f) *(esp Brit: for hair)* Spange *f.*
(g) *(Phot)* Dia, Diapositiv *(form) nt;* *(microscope ~)* Objektträger *m* ◆ **a lecture with ~s** ein Diavortrag, ein Lichtbildervortrag *m.*
2 *vt (push)* schieben; *(slip)* gleiten lassen ◆ **he slid the gun into the holster** er ließ den Revolver ins Halfter gleiten; **to ~ the drawer (back) into place** die Schublade (wieder) zurückschieben.
3 *vi* **(a)** rutschen; *(deliberately also)* schlittern ◆ **to ~ down the banisters** das Treppengeländer hinunterrutschen; **suddenly it all slid into place** plötzlich paßte alles zusammen.
(b) *(move smoothly: machine part etc)* sich schieben lassen ◆ **it slid into its place** es glitt *or* rutschte an die richtige Stelle.
(c) *(person)* schleichen ◆ **he slid into the room** er kam ins Zimmer geschlichen; **he slid off into the dark** er verschwand in der Dunkelheit.
(d) *(fig)* **the days slid by** *or* **past** die Tage schwanden dahin *(geh);* **to ~ into bad habits** (allmählich) in schlechte Gewohnheiten verfallen; **to let sth ~** etw schleifen lassen, etw vernachlässigen; **to let things/everything ~** die Dinge laufen *or* schleifen lassen/sich um nichts mehr kümmern.

slide: ~ control *n* Schieberegler *m;* **~ fastener** *n (US)* Reißverschluß *m;* **~ film** *n* Diafilm *m;* **~ projector** *n* Diaprojektor *m;* **~ rule** *n* Rechenschieber, Rechenstab *(form) m.*

sliding ['slaıdıŋ] *adj part* gleitend; *door, roof, seat* Schiebe-; *seat (in rowing boat)* Roll- ◆ **~ scale** gleitende Skala.

slight [slaıt] 1 *adj (+er)* **(a)** *person, build* zierlich.
(b) *(small, trivial)* leicht; *improvement also, change, possibility* geringfügig; *importance, intelligence* gering; *error also* klein; *pain also* schwach; *acquaintance* flüchtig ◆ **the wound is only ~** es ist nur eine leichte Verwundung; **to a ~ extent** in geringem Maße; **he showed some ~ optimism** er zeigte gewisse Ansätze von Optimismus; **just the ~est bit short** ein ganz kleines bißchen zu kurz; **the ~est optimism/criticism/possibility** das gering(fügig)ste Zeichen von Optimismus/die geringste Kritik/die allergeringste Möglichkeit; **he takes offence at the ~est thing** er ist wegen jeder kleinsten Kleinigkeit gleich beleidigt; **I haven't the ~est idea** ich habe nicht die geringste *or* leiseste *(inf)* Ahnung; **not in the ~est** nicht im geringsten *or* mindesten *(geh);* **without the ~est difficulty** ohne die kleinste *or* mindeste Schwierigkeit.
2 *n (affront)* Affront *m* (on gegen) ◆ **a ~ on one's/sb's character** eine persönliche Kränkung *or* Beleidigung.
3 *vt (offend)* kränken, beleidigen; *(ignore)* ignorieren ◆ **to feel ~ed** gekränkt *or* beleidigt sein.

slighting ['slaıtıŋ] *adj (offensive)* kränkend; *(disparaging) behaviour* geringschätzig; *remark* abschätzig, abfällig.

slightingly ['slaıtıŋlı] *adv speak* abschätzig, abfällig; *treat* geringschätzig.

slightly ['slaıtlı] *adv* **(a) ~ built** *or* **made** *person* zierlich. **(b)** *(to a slight extent)* etwas, ein klein(es) bißchen; *know* flüchtig; *smell* leicht, etwas.

slightness ['slaıtnıs] *n* **(a)** *(of person, build)* Zierlichkeit *f.* **(b)** *(triviality)* Geringfügigkeit *f;* *(of acquaintance)* Flüchtigkeit *f.*

slim [slım] 1 *adj (+er)* **(a)** schlank; *ankle, waist etc* schmal; *volume* schmal, dünn. **(b)** *resources, profits* mager; *excuse, hope also* schwach; *chances* gering.
2 *vi* eine Schlankheitskur machen.
3 *vt (also* **~ down)** schlank(er) machen; *(fig) demands etc* schrumpfen.

◆**slim down** 1 *vt sep* **(a)** *person* abnehmen lassen, dünner machen. **(b)** *(fig) business etc* verschlanken.
2 *vi* **(a)** *(person)* abnehmen, abspecken *(inf).* **(b)** *(fig: business etc)* verschlanken, abspecken *(inf).*

slime [slaım] *n* Schleim *m* ◆ **trail of ~** Schleimspur *f.*

sliminess ['slaımınıs] *n see adj* Schleimigkeit *f;* Glitschigkeit *f;* Schmierigkeit *f;* Öligkeit *f.*

slimmer ['slıməʳ] *n* Kalorienzähler(in *f*) *m (hum)* ◆ **special meals for ~s** spezielle Gerichte für Leute, die abnehmen wollen.

slimming ['slımıŋ] 1 *adj* schlankmachend *attr* ◆ **crispbread is ~** Knäckebrot macht schlank; **to be on a ~ diet** eine Schlankheitskur machen; **~ club** Diätklub, Schlankheitsklub *m;* **~ foods** kalorienarme Nahrungsmittel *pl.*
2 *n* Abnehmen *nt* ◆ **is ~ really worth it?** lohnt es sich wirklich abzunehmen?

slimness ['slımnıs] *n see adj* **(a)** Schlankheit *f;* Schmalheit, Dünne *f.* **(b)** Magerkeit *f* ◆ **because of the ~ of their chances** weil ihre Chancen so gering waren.

slimy ['slaımı] *adj (+er) liquid, secretion* schleimig; *stone, wall* glitschig; *hands* schmierig; *(fig)* schleimig; *smile, person also* ölig.

sling [slıŋ] *(vb: pret, ptp* **slung)** 1 *n* **(a)** *(Med)* Schlinge *f* ◆ **to have one's arm in a ~** den Arm in der Schlinge tragen.
(b) *(for hoisting)* Schlinge, Schlaufe *f;* *(for rifle)* (Trag)riemen *m;* *(for baby)*

(Baby)tragetuch *nt*, (Baby)trageschlinge *f* ◆ **to carry a rifle/baby in a ~** ein Gewehr am Riemen/ein Baby in einer *or* der Schlinge tragen.
(c) (*weapon*) Schleuder *f*.
[2] *vt* **(a)** (*throw*) schleudern; (*inf*) schmeißen (*inf*) ◆ **to ~ sth away** etw wegschleudern/wegschmeißen (*inf*); **to ~ sth over to sb** (*inf*) jdm etw zuschmeißen (*inf*); **he slung the box onto his back** er warf sich (*dat*) die Kiste auf den Rücken; **to ~ one's hook** (*fig inf*) Leine ziehen (*inf*).
(b) (*hoist with a ~*) in einer Schlinge hochziehen.
(c) (*hang*) aufhängen.
◆**sling out** *vt sep* (*inf*) rausschmeißen (*inf*).
sling: ~back [1] *adj* **~back shoes** Slingpumps *pl*; (*sandals*) Sandaletten *pl*; [2] *n* **~backs** Slings, Slingpumps *pl*; **~ bag** *n* (*US*) Schultertasche *f*; **~shot** *n* (*US*) (Stein)schleuder *f*.
slink [slɪŋk] *pret, ptp* **slunk** *vi* schleichen ◆ **to ~ away** *or* **off** sich davonschleichen; **to ~ along the wall** sich an der Wand entlangdrücken; **to ~ off with one's tail between one's legs** (*fig inf*) mit eingezogenem Schwanz abziehen (*inf*).
slinky *adj* (*+er*), **slinkily** *adv* ['slɪŋkɪ, -lɪ] (*inf*) aufreizend; *walk etc also* katzenhaft.
slip [slɪp] [1] *n* **(a)** (*slide*) **she had a nasty ~** sie ist ausgerutscht und bös gefallen.
(b) (*mistake*) Ausrutscher, Patzer *m* ◆ **to make a (bad) ~** sich (übel) vertun (*inf*), einen (ganz schönen) Bock schießen (*inf*); **a ~ of the pen/tongue** ein Flüchtigkeitsfehler *m*/Versprecher *m*; **it was just a ~ of the pen** da habe ich mich nur verschrieben; **there's many a ~ ('twixt cup and lip)** (*Prov*) man soll den Tag nicht vor dem Abend loben (*Prov*), zwischen Lipp' und Kelchesrand (schwebt der finster'n Mächte Hand) (*liter*).
(c) to give sb the ~ jdm entwischen.
(d) (*pillow~*) Kissenbezug *m*.
(e) (*undergarment*) Unterrock *m* ◆ **waist ~** Halbunterrock *m*; **full-length ~** Unterkleid *nt*.
(f) (*of paper*) Zettel *m* ◆ **~s of paper** Zettel *pl*; **withdrawal ~** Auszahlungsschein *m*; **sales ~** Kassenzettel *m*.
(g) (*person*) **a (mere) ~ of a girl** (*slightly built*) ein zierliches Persönchen; (*young*) eine halbe Portion (*inf*).
(h) (*Hort*) (*for planting*) Steckling *m*; (*for grafting*) Reis *nt*.
(i) (*Cricket*) (*position/area*) *Position f/Gebiet nt neben dem Torwächter*; (*fielder*) Eckmann *m*.
(j) ~s *pl* (*Theat*) Bühnenloge *f*.
(k) (*Pottery*) geschlämmter Ton.
(l) (*Aviat: side-~*) Schlipp *m*.
[2] *vt* **(a)** schieben; (*slide*) gleiten *or* rutschen lassen ◆ **to ~ sth across to sb** jdm etw zuschieben; (*unobtrusively*) jdm etw zuschmuggeln; **she ~ped the dress over her head** sie streifte sich (*dat*) das Kleid über den Kopf; **to ~ one's arm round sb's waist** jdm den Arm um die Taille legen; **to ~ one over on sb** (*inf*) jdn reinlegen (*inf*); **to ~ sb a fiver** jdm einen Fünfer zustecken.
(b) (*escape from*) sich losreißen von ◆ **the dog ~ped its chain** der Hund hat sich (von der Kette) losgerissen; **the boat had ~ped its moorings** das Boot hatte sich losgerissen; **to ~ anchor** (*Naut*) den Anker kappen (*form*); **it/his birthday ~ped my mind** *or* **memory** ich habe es/seinen Geburtstag vergessen *or* verschwitzt (*inf*); **it ~ped my notice** es ist mir entgangen.
(c) (*loose*) losmachen ◆ **he ~ped the dog from its chain** er machte den Hund (von der Kette) los.
(d) (*Med*) **to ~ a disc** sich (*dat*) einen Bandscheibenschaden zuziehen; **a ~ped disc** ein Bandscheibenschaden.
(e) (*Aut*) *clutch* schleifen lassen.
(f) to ~ a stitch eine Masche (ungestrickt) abheben.
[3] *vi* **(a)** (*person*) (aus)rutschen; (*feet, tyres*) (weg)rutschen; (*become loose: knot, nut*) sich lösen; (*Aut: clutch*) schleifen ◆ **the knife ~ped** das Messer rutschte ab; **it ~ped from her hand** es rutschte ihr aus der Hand; **the beads ~ped through my fingers** die Perlen glitten durch meine Finger; **money ~s through her fingers** das Geld rinnt ihr (nur so) durch die Finger; **suddenly everything ~ped into place** plötzlich paßte alles zusammen.
(b) (*move quickly*) schlüpfen; (*move smoothly*) rutschen ◆ **I'll ~ round to the shop** ich spring' schnell zum Laden; **the motorcycle ~s through the traffic** das Motorrad schlängelt sich durch den Verkehr.
(c) to let (it) ~ that ... fallenlassen, daß ...; **he let ~ an oath** ihm entfuhr ein Fluch; **to let a secret/chance ~** ein Geheimnis ausplaudern/eine Gelegenheit vorübergehen lassen; **the police let the thief ~ through their fingers** die Polizei ließ sich (*dat*) den Dieb in letzter Minute durch die Finger schlüpfen.
(d) (*decline: standards, morals etc*) fallen ◆ **you're ~ping!** (*inf*) du läßt nach (*inf*).
◆**slip away** *vi* sich wegschleichen, sich wegstehlen; (*time*) verstreichen, vergehen; (*chances*) (allmählich) schwinden; (*opportunity*) dahinschwinden ◆ **her life was ~ping ~ from her** ihr Leben schwand dahin.
◆**slip back** *vi* **(a)** (*return unobtrusively*) unbemerkt zurückgehen; (*quickly*) schnell zurückgehen. **(b)** (*deteriorate*) (*production*) zurückgehen; (*patient*) einen Rückfall haben.
◆**slip by** *vi* (*pass unobtrusively*) (*person*) sich vorbeischleichen *or* vorbeischmuggeln (*prep obj* an *+dat*); (*mistake*) durchgehen; (*years*) verfliegen, nur so dahinschwinden.
◆**slip down** *vi* (*fall*) ausrutschen, ausgleiten; (*go down*) hinunterlaufen ◆ **this wine ~s ~ easily** dieser Wein rutscht *or* kullert so schön (die Kehle hinunter) (*inf*).
◆**slip in** [1] *vi* (*enter unobtrusively*) (sich) hineinschleichen; (*burglar also, mistake*) sich einschleichen.
[2] *vt sep* (*mention casually*) einfließen lassen ◆ **to ~ the clutch ~** die Kupplung schleifen lassen; **to ~ sth ~to sb's pocket** jdm etw in die Tasche gleiten lassen; **to ~ a coin ~to a slot** eine Münze einwerfen; **she ~ped the car ~to first gear** sie legte den ersten Gang ein.
◆**slip off** [1] *vi* sich wegschleichen, sich wegstehlen.
[2] *vt sep clothes* ausziehen, abstreifen.
◆**slip on** *vt sep* schlüpfen in (*+acc*); *dress, gloves also* überstreifen, überziehen; *ring* aufziehen; *lid* drauftun (*prep obj* auf *+acc*) ◆ **he ~ped the ring ~to her finger** er steckte ihr den Ring an den Finger.
◆**slip out** *vi* **(a)** (*leave unobtrusively*) kurz weggehen *or* rausgehen. **(b)** (*be revealed*) herauskommen ◆ **the secret ~ped ~** das Geheimnis ist ihm/ihr *etc* herausgerutscht.
◆**slip past** *vi see* **slip by**.
◆**slip up** *vi* (*inf: err*) sich vertun (*inf*), (einen) Schnitzer machen (*over, in* bei) ◆ **you really ~ped ~ there!** da hast du aber wirklich Murks gemacht (*inf*); **he usually ~s ~ on spelling** meistens stolpert er über die Rechtschreibung (*inf*).
slip: ~ case *n* Schuber *m*; **~cover** *n* (*esp US*) Schonbezug *m*; **~knot** *n* Schlippstek *m* (*spec*); **~-ons** *npl* (*also* **~-on shoes**) Slipper *pl*; (*for women also*) Trotteurs *pl*; **~over** *n* Pullunder *m*.
slippage ['slɪpɪdʒ] *n* **(a)** (*Mech*) Schlupf *m*, Spiel *nt*. **(b)** (*fig*) Rückstand *m*. **to prevent ~** um Rückstände zu vermeiden.
slipper ['slɪpə^r] *n* (*bedroom ~*) Pantoffel, Hausschuh *m*; (*dancing ~*) Pumps, Slipper *m*.
slipperiness ['slɪpərɪnɪs] *n see adj* **(a)** Schlüpfrigkeit *f*; Glätte *f*; Glitschigkeit *f*. **(b)** Glätte *f*, aalglatte Art.
slippery ['slɪpərɪ] *adj* **(a)** schlüpfrig; *rope, road, ground* glatt, rutschig; *fish also* glitschig ◆ **to be on ~ ground** (*fig*) sich auf unsicherem Boden bewegen.
(b) (*pej inf*) *person* glatt, windig (*inf*) ◆ **a ~ customer** ein aalglatter Kerl (*inf*); **he's as ~ as they come** *or* **as an eel** er ist aalglatt; **he's on the ~ slope** er ist auf der schiefen Bahn; **it's a ~ slope** das ist ein gefährlicher Weg.
slippy ['slɪpɪ] *adj* (*inf*) **(a)** (*slippery*) glatt. **(b)** (*esp Brit*) **to be** *or* **look ~** einen Zahn zulegen (*inf*) (*about sth* bei etw); **... and look ~ (about it)!** ... und zwar flott *or* ein bißchen dalli! (*inf*).
slip-road ['slɪprəʊd] *n* (*Brit*) Zufahrtsstraße *f*; (*for entering motorway*) (Autobahn)auffahrt *f*; (*for leaving motorway*) (Autobahn)ausfahrt *f*.
slipshod ['slɪpʃɒd] *adj* schludrig.
slip: ~stream *n* (*Aviat*) Sog *m*; (*Aut*) Windschatten *m*; **~-up** *n* Schnitzer *m*; (*more serious*) Patzer *m*; **there's been a ~-up somewhere** da muß irgend etwas schiefgelaufen sein; **~way** *n* (*Aut*) Ablaufbahn, Gleitbahn *f*.
slit [slɪt] (*vb: pret, ptp ~*) [1] *n* Schlitz *m*; (*in castle wall also*) Schießscharte *f*.
[2] *vt* (auf)schlitzen ◆ **to ~ a sack open** einen Sack aufschlitzen; **to ~ sb's throat** jdm die Kehle aufschlitzen.
slit-eyed ['slɪt'aɪd] *adj* (*pej*) schlitzäugig.
slither ['slɪðə^r] *vi* rutschen; (*snake*) gleiten ◆ **to ~ about on the ice** auf dem Eis herumschlittern *or* -rutschen.
slit trench *n* Splittergraben *m*.
sliver ['slɪvə^r] *n* (*of wood, glass etc*) Splitter *m*; (*thin slice*) Scheibchen *nt*.
Sloane (Ranger) ['sləʊn('reɪndʒə^r)] *n* (*Brit inf*) *wohlhabendes (weibliches) Mitglied der gehobenen Mittelklasse.*
slob [slɒb] *n* (*inf*) Drecksau *f* (*inf*).
slobber ['slɒbə^r] [1] *n* Sabber *m* (*inf*).
[2] *vi* sabbern, sabbeln (*also fig*); (*dog*) geifern ◆ **to ~ over sb** (*fig inf*) von jdm schwärmen; (*kiss*) jdn abküssen; **to ~ over sth** (*fig inf*) etw anschmachten; (*dirty old man etc*) sich an etw (*dat*) aufgeilen (*sl*).
slobbery ['slɒbərɪ] *adj* (*inf*) naß ◆ **the newspaper is all ~** die Zeitung ist ganz vollgesabbert (*inf*).
sloe [sləʊ] *n* (*fruit*) Schlehe *f*; (*tree*) Schlehdorn *m* ◆ **~-gin** Schlehdornschnaps *m*; **~-eyed** *person* dunkeläugig.
slog [slɒg] (*inf*) [1] *n* **(a)** (*effort*) Schinderei, Plackerei *f* (*inf*) ◆ **it's a long ~ to the top of the hill** es ist eine ganz schöne Schinderei *or* Plackerei (*inf*), bis man oben ist.
(b) (*stroke*) wuchtiger Schlag ◆ **to give sb/sth a ~** jdm/etw einen (ordentlichen) Schlag versetzen; **to take a ~ at sb/sth** auf jdn/etw (ein)dreschen.
[2] *vt ball* dreschen (*inf*); *opponent* hart schlagen *or* treffen.
[3] *vi* **(a) to ~ at sth** (*hit*) auf etw (*acc*) (ein)dreschen (*inf*); (*work*) an etw (*dat*) schuften (*inf*); **to ~ away (at sth)** sich (mit etw) abrackern.
(b) (*walk*) **to ~ on/along** sich weiter-/dahinschleppen.
slogan ['sləʊgən] *n* Slogan *m*; (*motto*) Motto *nt*, Wahlspruch *m*; (*political also*) Schlagwort *nt*, Parole *f* ◆ **advertising ~** Werbeslogan, Werbespruch *m*.
slogger ['slɒgə^r] *n* (*inf*) Arbeitstier *nt*.
sloop [sluːp] *n* Slup, Schlup *f*.
slop [slɒp] [1] *vi* **(a)** (*spill*) (über)schwappen ◆ **to ~ over (into sth)** überschwappen (in *+acc*). **(b) to ~ about** (*splash*) herumschwappen (*inf*); (*fig inf: in slippers etc*) herumschlurfen.
[2] *vt* (*spill*) verschütten; (*pour out*) schütten.
[3] *n* **(a)** (*inf: sentimental*) rührseliges Zeug, Schmalz *m*.
(b) (*tasteless food: also* **~s**) Schlabber *m* (*inf*).
(c) *usu pl* (*waste*) Schmutzwasser, Abwasser *nt*; (*swill*) Schweinetrank *m* ◆ **~ pail** Eimer *m* für Schmutzwasser.
◆**slop out** *vi* (*in prison etc*) den/die Toiletteneimer (aus)leeren.
slop basin, slop bowl *n* Abgußschale *f* (*Teil des Teeservice, in das Teereste gegossen werden*).

slope [sləʊp] 1 *n* **(a)** (*angle*) Neigung *f*; (*downwards also*) Gefälle *nt*; (*of roof also*) Schräge *f*.
(b) (*sloping ground*) (Ab)hang *m* ◆ **on a ~** am Hang; **halfway up the ~** auf halber Höhe; **there is a ~ down to the town** es fällt zur Stadt hin ab; **he broke his leg on the (ski) ~s** er hat sich das Bein auf der Piste gebrochen.
(c) (*Mil*) **with his rifle at the ~** mit geschultertem Gewehr.
2 *vt* neigen, schräg (an)legen ◆ **~ arms!** (*Mil*) schultert Gewehr!
3 *vi* **(a)** geneigt sein; (*road, garden, floor*) sich neigen ◆ **the picture is sloping to the left/right** das Bild hängt schief; **his handwriting ~s to the left/backwards** seine Handschrift ist nach links/nach hinten geneigt.
(b) (*inf: move casually*) schlendern (*inf*).
◆**slope away** *vi* **(a)** abfallen. **(b)** (*slip away*) abziehen (*inf*).
◆**slope down** *vi* sich neigen, abfallen.
◆**slope off** *vi* abziehen (*inf*).
◆**slope up** *vi* **(a)** (*road etc*) ansteigen. **(b)** (*person*) herschlendern ◆ **to ~ ~ to sb** auf jdn zuschlendern.
sloping ['sləʊpɪŋ] *adj hill, road* (*upwards*) ansteigend; (*downwards*) abfallend; *roof, floor* schräg, geneigt; *shoulders* abfallend; *garden, field etc* am Hang; (*not aligned*) schief.
sloppily ['slɒpɪlɪ] *adv see adj (a)* **to write/talk English ~** nachlässig *or* schlampig (*inf*) Englisch schreiben/sprechen.
sloppiness ['slɒpɪnɪs] *n see adj* **(a)** Schlampigkeit *f* (*inf*); Nachlässigkeit, Schlud(e)rigkeit (*inf*) *f*. **(b)** Rührseligkeit *f*.
sloppy ['slɒpɪ] *adj* (*+er*) **(a)** (*inf: careless*) schlampig (*inf*); *work also* nachlässig, schlud(e)rig (*inf*) ◆ **~ joe** (*pullover*) Schlabberpullover *m* (*inf*).
(b) (*inf: sentimental*) rührselig; *film, novel also* schmalzig.
slosh [slɒʃ] (*inf*) 1 *vt* **(a)** (*Brit: hit*) *person* eine schmieren (*+dat*) (*inf*); *ball* dreschen. **(b)** (*splash*) klatschen ◆ **don't ~ the milk about** schwapp nicht so mit der Milch herum.
2 *vi* **to ~ (about)** (*children*) (herum)planschen; (*water*) (herum)schwappen.
sloshed [slɒʃt] *adj pred* (*esp Brit sl*) blau (*inf*), voll (*sl*) ◆ **to get ~** sich besaufen (*inf*).
slot [slɒt] *n* (*opening*) Schlitz *m*; (*groove*) Rille *f*; (*Comput*) Slot, Steckplatz *m*; (*for aircraft to land etc*) Slot *m*; (*inf: place*) Plätzchen *nt* (*inf*); (*TV inf*) (gewohnte) Sendezeit ◆ **~ machine** Münzautomat *m*; (*for gambling*) Spielautomat *m*; **~ meter** Münzzähler *m*; **do we have a ~ for this in our range?** können wir das in unser Programm einbauen?
◆**slot in** 1 *vt sep* hineinstecken ◆ **to ~ sth ~to sth** etw in etw (*acc*) stecken; **to ~ sb ~to the firm/a stereotype** jdn in der Firma unterbringen/in einen bestimmten Typ einordnen; **to ~ ~ commercials** Werbespots einbauen; **to ~ people/jobs ~to a scale** Leute/Arbeiten in eine Skala einordnen.
2 *vi* sich einfügen lassen ◆ **suddenly everything ~ted ~to place** plötzlich paßte alles zusammen.
◆**slot together** 1 *vi* (*parts, object*) sich zusammenfügen lassen; (*fig: pieces of mystery etc*) sich zusammenfügen, zusammenpassen.
2 *vt sep parts, object* zusammenfügen.
sloth [sləʊθ] *n* **(a)** (*laziness*) Trägheit, Faulheit *f*. **(b)** (*Zool*) Faultier *nt*.
slothful ['sləʊθfʊl] *adj* faul; *person, life also* träge.
slothfully ['sləʊθfəlɪ] *adv see adj*.
slothfulness ['sləʊθfʊlnɪs] *n* Trägheit, Faulheit *f*.
slouch [slaʊtʃ] 1 *n* **(a)** (*posture*) krumme Haltung; (*of shoulders*) Hängen *nt*; (*gait*) latschiger Gang (*inf*) ◆ **to walk with a ~** latschen, latschig gehen (*inf*); **~ hat** Schlapphut *m*.
(b) (*inf: incompetent or lazy person*) Niete *f* (*inf*) ◆ **to be no ~ at sth** etw ganz schön gut können (*inf*).
2 *vi* (*stand, sit*) herumhängen, sich lümmeln (*inf*); (*move*) latschen ◆ **to ~ off** davonzockeln (*inf*); **he was ~ed over his desk** er hing über seinem Schreibtisch, er war über seinen Schreibtisch gebeugt; **he sat ~ed on a chair** er hing auf einem Stuhl.
slough[1] [slaʊ] *n* (*liter*) Morast *m*; (*swamp also*) Sumpf *m* (*also fig liter*) ◆ **the news cast him into the S~ of Despond** die Nachricht stürzte ihn in tiefe Verzweiflung (*liter*).
slough[2] [slʌf] 1 *n* (*Zool*) abgestreifte Haut; (*Med*) Schorf *m*.
2 *vt* (*snake*) *skin* abstreifen ◆ **it ~s (off) its skin** sie häutet sich.
◆**slough off** *vt sep habits, cares* abwerfen, abschütteln; (*hum*) *husband* den Laufpaß geben (*+dat*).
Slovak ['sləʊvæk] 1 *adj* slowakisch.
2 *n* **(a)** Slowake *m*, Slowakin *f*. **(b)** (*language*) Slowakisch *nt*.
Slovakia [sləʊ'vækɪə] *n* die Slowakei.
Slovak Republic *n* Slowakische Republik, Slowakei *f*.
sloven ['slʌvn] *n* Schlampe *f* (*pej inf*); (*man*) Schlamper *m* (*inf*).
Slovene ['sləʊviːn], **Slovenian** [sləʊ'viːnɪən] 1 *adj* slowenisch.
2 *n* **(a)** Slowene *m*, Slowenin *f*, Slowenier(in *f*) *m*. **(b)** (*language*) Slowenisch *nt*.
slovenliness ['slʌvnlɪnɪs] *n* Schlampigkeit *f*; (*of person, work also*) Schlud(e)rigkeit *f* (*inf*).
slovenly ['slʌvnlɪ] *adj* schlud(e)rig (*inf*), schlampig (*inf*); *appearance, person also* verlottert (*inf*).
slow [sləʊ] 1 *adj* (*+er*) **(a)** langsam ◆ **it's ~ work** das braucht seine Zeit; **he's a ~ learner/reader** er lernt/liest langsam; **it was ~ going** es ging nur langsam voran; **to get off to a ~ start** (*race*) schlecht vom Start kommen; (*project*) nur langsam in Gang kommen; **to be ~/not to be ~ to do sth** sich (*dat*) mit etw Zeit lassen/etw prompt erledigen; **he is ~ to make up his mind/~ to anger** er braucht lange, um sich zu entscheiden/er wird nicht so leicht wütend; **they were ~ to act** sie ließen sich (*dat*) Zeit; **to be (20 minutes) ~** (*clock*) (20 Minuten) nachgehen.
(b) (*stupid*) *person* langsam, begriffsstutzig; *see* **uptake**.
(c) (*dull*) *person, place, event* langweilig; (*Comm*) flau.
(d) (*~ing down movement*) *surface, track, pitch* langsam; (*because of rain etc*) schwer; (*~-burning*) *fire* langsam brennend ◆ **bake in a ~ oven** bei schwacher Hitze backen.
2 *adv* (*+er*) langsam ◆ **to go ~** (*driver*) langsam fahren; (*workers*) einen Bummelstreik machen; **~-spoken** langsam sprechend; **~** (*on sign*) langsam fahren.
3 *vi* **to ~ (to a stop/standstill)** langsam zum Halten/zum Stillstand kommen.
4 *vt* verlangsamen ◆ **he ~ed his horse to a walk** er ließ sein Pferd langsamer gehen.
◆**slow down** *or* **up** 1 *vi* sich verlangsamen; (*drive/walk*) langsamer fahren/gehen; (*worker*) langsamer arbeiten; (*inflation*) abnehmen ◆ **if you don't ~ ~ you'll make yourself ill** Sie müssen zurückstecken, sonst werden Sie krank; **my mind has ~ed ~** ich werde immer langsamer im Denken.
2 *vt sep* (*lit*) verlangsamen; *engine* drosseln; *machine* herunterschalten; (*fig*) *project* verzögern, verlangsamen ◆ **to ~ ~ the car** langsamer fahren; **you just ~ me ~** du hältst mich nur auf.
slow: ~-burning *adj candle* langsam herunterbrennend; *fire also* langsam brennend; *stove* Dauerbrand-; **~coach** *n* (*Brit inf*) Langweiler *m*; (*mentally*) Transuse *f* (*inf*); **~down** *n* **(a)** (*slowing*) Verlangsamung *f* (*in, of gen*); **(b)** (*US: go-slow*) Bummelstreik *m*; **~ film** *n* unempfindlicher Film; **~ fuse** *n* Zündschnur *f*; **~ handclap** *n* rhythmisches Klatschen (*zum Zeichen des Protests*); **to give sb the/a ~ handclap** durch Klatschen gegen jdn protestieren.
slowly ['sləʊlɪ] *adv* langsam.
slow: ~ march *n* Trauermarsch *m*; **~ motion** *n* Zeitlupe *f*; **in ~ motion** in Zeitlupe; **a ~-motion shot** eine Einstellung in Zeitlupe; **~-moving** *adj* sich (nur) langsam bewegend; *traffic* kriechend; *plot* langatmig.
slowness ['sləʊnɪs] *n see adj* **(a)** Langsamkeit *f* ◆ **their ~ to act** ihr Zaudern.
(b) Begriffsstutzigkeit *f* ◆ **~ of mind** Begriffsstutzigkeit *f*. **(c)** Lahmheit, Langweiligkeit *f*; Flaute *f*. **(d)** Langsamkeit *f*; Schwere *f*.
slow: ~ poison *n* schleichendes Gift; **~poke** *n* (*US inf*) *see* **~coach**; **~ train** *n* (*Brit*) Personenzug, Bummelzug (*inf*) *m*; **~-witted** *adj* begriffsstutzig, schwer von Begriff; **~worm** *n* Blindschleiche *f*.
sludge [slʌdʒ] *n* Schlamm, Matsch (*inf*) *m*; (*sediment*) schmieriger Satz.
slue *n, vti* (*US*) *see* **slew**[1], **slew**[2].
slug[1] [slʌg] *n* Nacktschnecke *f* ◆ **~s and snails** Schnecken *pl* (mit und ohne Gehäuse).
slug[2] *n* **(a)** (*bullet*) Kugel *f*. **(b)** (*Typ*) (*piece of metal*) Reglette *f*; (*line*) (Setzmaschinen)zeile *f*. **(c)** (*inf*) **a ~ of whisky** ein Schluck *m* Whisky.
slug[3] (*inf: hit*) 1 *vt* (eine) knallen (*+dat*) (*inf*).
2 *n* gehöriger *or* tüchtiger Schlag (*inf*) ◆ **to give sb a ~** jdm eine knallen (*inf*).
sluggard ['slʌgəd] *n* Faulpelz *m*.
sluggardly ['slʌgədlɪ] *adj* faul, träge.
slugger ['slʌgə^r] *n* (*inf*) Schläger *m* (*inf*).
sluggish ['slʌgɪʃ] *adj* (*indolent, Med*) träge; *engine, car* lahm, langsam; *temperament* phlegmatisch; *steps also* schwerfällig; *business* flau; *market, stock exchange* flau, lustlos.
sluggishly ['slʌgɪʃlɪ] *adv move, flow* träge; *walk also* schwerfällig; (*Comm*) flau, lustlos.
sluggishness ['slʌgɪʃnɪs] *n see adj* Trägheit *f*; Lahmheit *f*; Phlegma *nt*; Schwerfälligkeit *f* ◆ **the ~ of the market/business** die Flaute am Markt/die geschäftliche Flaute.
sluice [sluːs] 1 *n* Schleuse *f*; (*Min*) (Wasch)rinne *f* ◆ **to give the car/wall a ~ down** Wasser über das Auto/gegen die Wand schütten; (*with hose*) das Auto/die Wand abspritzen.
2 *vt ore* waschen ◆ **to ~ sth (down)** etw abspritzen.
3 *vi* **to ~ out** herausschießen.
sluice: ~ gate *n* Schleusentor *nt*; **~way** *n* (Schleusen)kanal *m*.
slum [slʌm] 1 *n* (*usu pl: area*) Slum *m*, Elendsviertel *nt*; (*house*) Elendsquartier *nt* ◆ **to live in the ~s** im Slum *or* in den Slums leben; **~ schools/streets/children** Schulen *pl*/Straßen *pl* in den Slums/Slumkinder *pl*; **~ clearance** ≃ (Stadt)sanierung *f*, Beseitigung *f* der Slums; **~ dweller** Slumbewohner(in *f*) *m*.
2 *vi* (*also* **go ~ming**) sich unters gemeine Volk mischen.
3 *vti* (*inf: also* **~ it**) primitiv leben ◆ **we don't often see you round here — I'm ~ming it** du läßt dich doch sonst kaum hier sehen! — ich will mich eben mal unters gemeine Volk mischen.
slumber ['slʌmbə^r] (*liter*) 1 *n* Schlummer (*geh*), Schlaf *m* ◆ **~s** Schlummer *m*, Träume *pl*; (*fig: intellectual etc*) Dornröschenschlaf *m*; **to disturb sb's ~s** jds Schlummer stören.
2 *vi* schlummern (*geh*); (*fig also*) im Dornröschenschlaf liegen.
slumb(e)rous ['slʌmb(ə)rəs] *adj* (*liter*) (*sleepy*) schläfrig; (*inducing sleep*) einschläfernd, einlullend.
slummy ['slʌmɪ] *adj* (*+er*) (*inf*) verwahrlost; *district also* Slum-.
slump [slʌmp] 1 *n* (*in gen*) (*in numbers, popularity, morale etc*) (plötzliche) Abnahme; (*in production, sales*) Rückgang *m*; (*state*) Tiefstand *m*; (*Fin*) Sturz *m*, Baisse *f* (*spec*); (*of prices*) plötzliches Absinken ◆ **~ in prices** Preissturz *m* (*of* bei); **the 1929 S~** die Weltwirtschaftskrise von 1929.
2 *vi* **(a)** (*also* **~ off**) (*Fin, Comm*) (*prices*) stürzen, fallen; (*sales, production*) plötzlich zurückgehen; (*fig: morale etc*) sinken, fallen.
(b) (*sink*) fallen, sinken ◆ **to ~ into a chair** sich in einen Sessel fallen *or*

plumpsen (*inf*) lassen; **he was ~ed over the wheel/on the floor** er war über dem Steuer zusammengesackt/er lag in sich (*dat*) zusammengesunken auf dem Fußboden.

slung [slʌŋ] *pret, ptp of* **sling.**

slunk [slʌŋk] *pret, ptp of* **slink.**

slur [slɜːʳ] 1 *n* **(a)** Makel, Schandfleck *m*; (*insult*) Beleidigung *f* ◆ **to cast a ~ on sb/sth** jdn/etw in schlechtem Licht erscheinen lassen; (*person*) jdn/etw verunglimpfen; **it is no ~ on him to say that** ... es geht nicht gegen ihn, wenn man sagt, daß ...
(b) (*Mus*) (*mark*) Bindebogen *m*; (*notes*) Bindung *f*.
(c) to speak with a ~ unartikuliert sprechen.
2 *vt* **(a)** (*pronounce indistinctly*) undeutlich artikulieren; *words, syllable* (halb) verschlucken, verschleifen.
(b) (*Mus*) binden, gebunden spielen/singen.

◆**slur over** *vi +prep obj* hinweggehen über (*+acc*).

slurp [slɜːp] 1 *vti* (*inf*) schlürfen.
2 *n* Schlürfen *nt* ◆ **to drink sth with a ~** etw schlürfen.

slurred [slɜːd] *adj* undeutlich; (*Mus*) *note* gebunden.

slush [slʌʃ] *n* (*watery snow*) (Schnee)matsch *m*; (*mud*) Matsch, Morast *m*; (*inf: sentimental nonsense*) Kitsch *m* ◆ **~ fund** Schmiergelder *pl*, Schmiergeldfonds *m*.

slushy ['slʌʃɪ] *adj* (*+er*) *snow, mud, path* matschig; *mud, path also* morastig; (*inf: sentimental*) kitschig.

slut [slʌt] *n* (liederliche) Schlampe.

sluttish ['slʌtɪʃ] *adj* liederlich.

sly [slaɪ] 1 *adj* (*+er*) schlau, gerissen; *person, look also* verschlagen; (*artful*) *look, wink* verschmitzt; *humour* versteckt ◆ **to be (very) ~ about sth** etw schlau anstellen.
2 *n* **on the ~** heimlich, still und leise (*hum*), ganz heimlich.

slyly ['slaɪlɪ] *adv see adj*.

slyness ['slaɪnɪs] *n see adj* Schlauheit, Gerissenheit *f*; Verschlagenheit *f*; Verschmitztheit *f*; Versteckheit *f*.

smack¹ [smæk] 1 *n* (*taste*) (leichter) Geschmack (*of* nach), Spur *f* (*of* von); (*smell*) (leichter) Geruch (*of* nach), Hauch *m* (*of* von); (*fig*) Spur *f* (*of* von).
2 *vi* **to ~ of** (*taste*) leicht schmecken nach; (*smell*) leicht riechen nach; (*fig*) riechen nach.

smack² 1 *n* (klatschender) Schlag; (*slap also*) fester Klaps; (*sound*) Klatschen *nt* ◆ **to give a child/the ball a (hard) ~** einem Kind eine knallen (*inf*)/(fest) auf den Ball dreschen (*inf*); **you'll get a ~** du fängst gleich eine (*inf*); **a ~ in the eye** (*fig*) ein Schlag ins Gesicht; **to have a ~ at sth** (*esp Brit fig inf*) an etw (*acc*) rangehen (*inf*), etw mal probieren (*inf*); **to have a ~ at the title/record** einen Anlauf auf den Titel/Rekord machen.
2 *vt* (*slap*) knallen (*inf*) ◆ **to ~ a child/one's thigh** einem Kind eine runterhauen (*inf*)/sich (*dat*) auf den Schenkel klatschen; **I'll ~ your bottom, you'll get a ~ed bottom** ich versohl' dir gleich den Hintern! (*inf*); *see* **lip.**
3 *adv* (*inf*) direkt ◆ **he kissed her ~ on the lips** er gab ihr einen Schmatzer (*inf*), er küßte sie mit Schmackes (*dial*); **she ran ~ into the door** sie rannte rums! gegen die Tür (*inf*).

smack³ *n* (*Naut*) Schmack(e) *f*.

smacker ['smækəʳ] *n* (*inf*) **(a)** (*kiss*) Schmatzer *m* (*inf*). **(b)** (*blow*) Klaps *m*. **(c)** (*money*) Pfund *nt*; Dollar *m*.

smacking ['smækɪŋ] *n* Tracht *f* Prügel ◆ **to give sb a good ~** jdn tüchtig verdreschen (*inf*).

small [smɔːl] 1 *adj* (*+er*) **(a)** klein; *supply, stock also* gering; *waist* schmal; (*not much*) *reason, desire* wenig, gering; *letter* Klein-; (*humble*) *voice* kleinlaut ◆ **the ~est possible number of books** so wenig Bücher wie möglich; **to have a ~ appetite/be a ~ eater** wenig Appetit *or* keinen großen Appetit haben/kein großer Esser sein; **~ capitals** Kapitälchen *pl*; **no ~ success** ein beachtlicher Erfolg; **to feel/look ~** (*fig*) sich (ganz) klein (und häßlich) vorkommen/schlecht aussehen *or* dastehen; **he/it made me feel/look pretty ~** da kam ich mir ziemlich klein vor/da sah ich ziemlich schlecht aus.
(b) (*unimportant, minor*) klein; *present, sum also* bescheiden; *importance, consequence* gering ◆ **a few ~ matters/problems** ein paar Kleinigkeiten; **to help/contribute in a ~ way** bescheidene Hilfe/einen bescheidenen Beitrag leisten; **to start in a ~ way** bescheiden *or* klein anfangen.
(c) (*fig: mean, petty*) *person* kleinlich.
2 *n* **(a) the ~ of the back** das Kreuz.
(b) ~s *pl* (*Brit inf*) Unterwäsche *f*.
3 *adv* **to chop sth up ~** etw kleinhacken.

small: ~ ad *n* (*Brit*) Kleinanzeige *f*; **~ arms** *npl* Handfeuerwaffen *pl*; **~ beer** *n* (*old*) Dünnbier *nt*; **he's very ~ beer** (*inf*) er ist ein kleiner Fisch (*inf*); **~ business** *n* Kleinunternehmen *nt*; **~ businessman** *n* Kleinunternehmer *m*; **~ change** *n* Kleingeld *nt*; **~ claims court** *n Zivilgericht nt für Bagatellfälle*; **~ fry** *npl see* **fry¹**; **~holder** *n* Kleinbauer *m*; **~holding** *n* kleiner Landbesitz; **~ hours** *npl* früher Morgen; **in the ~ hours** in den frühen Morgenstunden; **~ intestine** *n* Dünndarm *m*.

smallish ['smɔːlɪʃ] *adj* (eher) kleiner ◆ **he is ~** er ist eher klein.

small: ~-minded *adj person, attitude* engstirnig; **~-mindedness** *n* Engstirnigkeit *f*.

smallness ['smɔːlnɪs] *n* Kleinheit *f*; (*of sum, present*) Bescheidenheit *f*; (*pettiness*) Kleinlichkeit *f*.

small: ~pox *n* Pocken, Blattern (*old*) *pl*; **~pox vaccination** *n* Pockenimpfung *f*; **~ print** *n* **the ~ print** das Kleingedruckte; **~-scale** *adj map, model* in verkleinertem Maßstab; *project* kleinangelegt; *war* begrenzt; **~-scale integration** (*Comput*) niedriger Integrationsgrad; **~ screen** *n* (*TV*) **on the ~ screen** auf dem Bildschirm; **~talk** *n* oberflächliche Konversation, Smalltalk *m*; **she has no ~talk** oberflächliche *or* höfliche Konversation liegt ihr nicht; **to engage in ~talk with sb** höflich mit jdm Konversation machen; **~-time** *adj* (*inf*) mickerig (*inf*), armselig; *crook* klein; *politician* Schmalspur-; **~-town** *adj* Kleinstadt-, kleinstädtisch.

smarm [smɑːm] (*Brit inf*) 1 *vt* **to ~ one's hair down** sich (*dat*) das Haar anklatschen (*inf*) *or* an den Kopf kleben.
2 *vi* **to ~ all over sb** sich an jdn heranschmeißen (*inf*); **to ~ one's way into sb's confidence** sich in jds Vertrauen (*acc*) einschleichen.

smarmy ['smɑːmɪ] *adj* (*+er*) (*Brit inf*) (*greasy*) schmierig; (*ingratiating*) kriecherisch (*pej*); *voice* einschmeichelnd.

smart [smɑːt] 1 *adj* (*+er*) **(a)** schick; *person, clothes, car also* flott; *society* fein; (*not shabby also*) *appearance* gepflegt ◆ **a ~-looking girl/garden** ein flott aussehendes Mädchen/ein gepflegter Garten; **the ~ set** die Schickeria (*inf*).
(b) (*bright, clever*) clever (*inf*), schlau, gewitzt; *thief, trick also* raffiniert; *young people also* hell (*inf*); (*pej*) *person, answer* superklug, neunmalklug (*pej inf*); (*Comput*) intelligent ◆ **to get ~** (*US inf*) sich am Riemen reißen (*inf*); (*get cheeky*) frech kommen (*with dat*); **he thinks it's ~ to run down his parents** er kommt sich toll vor, wenn er seine Eltern schlechtmacht.
(c) (*quick*) (blitz)schnell; *pace, work* rasch, flott (*inf*); *work also* flink, fix (*inf*) ◆ **and look ~ (about it)!** und zwar ein bißchen fix *or* plötzlich! (*inf*).
2 *n* Schmerz *m* (*also fig*); (*of ointment, from wound also*) Brennen *nt*.
3 *vi* brennen ◆ **it will make your mouth/cut ~** es wird (dir) im Mund/in der Wunde brennen; **to ~ under sth** (*fig*) unter etw (*dat*) leiden; **his injured vanity still ~ed** er spürte immer noch den Schmerz gekränkter Eitelkeit; **to ~ from sth** (*from blow etc*) von etw brennen; (*fig*) unter etw (*dat*) leiden.

smart: ~-aleck (*inf*) 1 *n* Schlauberger (*inf*), Besserwisser *m*; 2 *adj remarks* besserwisserisch, superschlau (*inf*); **~ ass** 1 *n* (*sl*) Klugscheißer *m* (*sl*); 2 *adj* klugscheißerisch (*sl*).

smarten ['smɑːtn] (*also* **~ up**) 1 *vt house, room* herausputzen; *appearance* (her)richten, aufmöbeln (*inf*) ◆ **to ~ oneself up** (*dress up*) sich in Schale werfen (*inf*); (*generally improve appearance*) mehr Wert auf sein Äußeres legen; **you'd better ~ up your ideas** (*inf*) du solltest dich am Riemen reißen (*inf*).
2 *vi* (*dress up*) sich in Schale werfen (*inf*); (*improve appearance*) sich herausmachen; (*pace*) schneller *or* flotter (*inf*) werden ◆ **he's ~ed up in his ideas/appearance** seine Ansichten haben/sein Aussehen hat sich gemacht.

smartly ['smɑːtlɪ] *adv see adj* **(a)** schick; *dress also* flott. **(b)** clever, schlau, gewitzt; (*pej*) superschlau (*inf*), neunmalklug (*inf*). **(c)** (blitz)schnell, fix (*inf*); *walk* rasch.

smartness ['smɑːtnɪs] *n* **(a)** *see adj (a)* Schick *m*; Feinheit *f*; Gepflegtheit *f*.
(b) (*brightness, cleverness*) Cleverneß (*inf*), Schlauheit, Gewitztheit *f*; (*of thief, trick*) Raffiniertheit *f*; (*pej*) (*of person*) Besserwisserei *f* (*pej*); (*of answer*) Vorwitzigkeit *f*.
(c) *see adj (c)* Schnelligkeit, Fixheit (*inf*) *f*; Raschheit *f*.

smarty ['smɑːtɪ] *n* (*inf*) Schlaumeier, Schlauberger (*inf*) *m*.

smash [smæʃ] 1 *vt* **(a)** (*break into pieces*) zerschlagen; *window also* einschlagen ◆ **I ~ed my glasses** mir ist die Brille kaputtgegangen.
(b) (*defeat or destroy*) zerschlagen; *rebellion, revolution also* niederschlagen; *fascism, the enemy also, opponent* zerschmettern; *record* haushoch schlagen; *business* ruinieren.
(c) (*strike, also Tennis*) schmettern ◆ **he ~ed his fist into his face** er schlug ihm mit der Faust ins Gesicht; **he ~ed him on the nose** er schlug ihm auf die Nase; **he ~ed his way through the mob** er mußte sich (*dat*) gewaltsam einen Weg durch den Mob bahnen; **to ~ one's way into a building** gewaltsam in ein Gebäude eindringen.
2 *vi* **(a)** (*break*) zerschlagen, zerbrechen ◆ **it ~ed into a thousand pieces** es (zer)sprang in tausend Stücke.
(b) (*crash*) prallen ◆ **the car ~ed into the wall** das Auto krachte gegen die Mauer; **the terrified animal ~ed through the fence** das verängstigte Tier durchbrach das Gatter; **the plane ~ed into the houses** das Flugzeug raste in eine Häusergruppe; **the ship ~ed onto the rocks** das Schiff prallte gegen die Felsen; **the sound of the waves ~ing against the rocks** das Geräusch der gegen die Felsen klatschenden Wellen.
3 *n* **(a)** (*noise*) Krachen *nt*; (*of waves*) Klatschen *nt* ◆ **there was a ~** es hat gekracht *or* (*of broken glass*) gescheppert.
(b) (*collision*) Unfall *m*; (*with another vehicle also*) Zusammenstoß *m* ◆ **rail ~** Zugunglück *nt*.
(c) (*blow*) Schlag *m*; (*Tennis*) Smash, Schmetterball *m* ◆ **to give sb a ~ on the nose** jdm auf die Nase schlagen; **he hit his head an awful ~ against the wall** er ist mit dem Kopf ganz fürchterlich gegen die Wand geschlagen.
4 *adv* (*inf*) mit Karacho (*inf*) ◆ **to go** *or* **run ~ into sth** mit Karacho gegen etw (*acc*) fahren/stoßen *etc* (*inf*).

◆**smash in** *vt sep* einschlagen ◆ **the firemen had to ~ their way ~** die Feuerwehrleute mußten sich gewaltsam eindringen; **to ~ sb's face ~** (*sl*) jdm die Schnauze einschlagen (*sl*).

◆**smash up** 1 *vt sep* zertrümmern; *face* übel zurichten; *car* kaputtfahren.
2 *vi* kaputtgehen ◆ **the capsule completely ~ed ~ on landing** die Kapsel zerschellte bei der Landung.

smash-and-grab (raid) [ˌsmæʃən'græb(reɪd)] *n* Schaufenstereinbruch *m*.

smashed [smæʃt] *adj pred* (*sl*) (*drunk*) stockvoll (*sl*); (*on drugs*) high (*sl*).

smasher ['smæʃəʳ] *n* (*esp Brit inf*) toller Typ (*inf*); (*woman also*) Klassefrau *f* (*inf*) ◆ **to be a ~** eine Wucht (*inf*) *or* (ganz große) Klasse sein (*inf*).

smash hit *n* (*inf*) Superhit *m* (*inf*) ◆ **her new boyfriend was a ~ with her family** ihr neuer Freund kam bei ihrer Familie unwahrscheinlich gut an (*inf*).

smashing ['smæʃɪŋ] *adj (esp Brit inf)* klasse *inv*, Klasse *pred*, dufte *(all inf)* ◆ **isn't it ~!** unheimlich dufte!
smash-up ['smæʃʌp] *n (Aut, Rail)* übler Unfall; *(with another vehicle also)* Karambolage *f*.
smattering ['smætərɪŋ] *n* **a ~ of French** ein paar Brocken Französisch.
smear [smɪəʳ] 1 *n* verschmierter Fleck; *(fig)* Beschmutzung, Verleumdung *f*; *(Med)* Abstrich *m* ◆ **he had ~s of blood/grease on his hands** er hatte blut-/fettbeschmierte Hände; **this left a ~ on his name** das hinterließ einen Fleck auf seinem Namen; **he angrily repudiated their ~s** empört wies er ihre Verleumdungen zurück; **~ campaign** Verleumdungskampagne *f*; **~-word** Schimpfwort *nt*; **~-test** *(Med)* Abstrich *m*.
2 *vt* **(a)** *grease, ointment* schmieren; *(spread)* verschmieren; *(mark, make dirty)* beschmieren; *face, body* einschmieren ◆ **don't ~ the paint** verschmiere die Farbe nicht!
(b) *(fig) person* verunglimpfen; *sb's reputation* beschmutzen, besudeln.
3 *vi (glass)* verschmieren; *(print)* verschmiert, verwischt werden; *(biro)* schmieren; *(paint, ink)* verlaufen.
smeary ['smɪərɪ] *adj (+er) glass* verschmiert; *clothes* schmierig; *(likely to smear) paint, ink* schmierend.
smell [smel] *(vb: pret, ptp* **~ed** *or* **smelt)** 1 *n (sense of ~, odour)* Geruch *m*; *(unpleasant also)* Gestank *m*; *(fragrant also)* Duft *m* ◆ **it has a nice ~** es riecht gut *or* angenehm; **there's a funny ~ in here** hier riecht es komisch; **to have** *or* **take a ~ at sth** an etw *(acc)* riechen *or (dog etc)* schnuppern.
2 *vt* **(a)** riechen ◆ **can** *or* **do you ~ burning?** riechst du, daß etwas brennt *or (Cook)* anbrennt?; **first he ~s the wine** zunächst einmal riecht er an dem Wein.
(b) *(fig) danger, treason* wittern ◆ **to ~ trouble** Ärger *or* Stunk *(inf)* kommen sehen; **to ~ a rat** *(inf)* Lunte *or* den Braten riechen, etw spitzkriegen; **aha, I can ~ a rat** *(inf)* da scheint mir doch etwas faul zu sein!
3 *vi* riechen; *(unpleasantly also)* stinken; *(fragrantly also)* duften ◆ **that ~s!** *(lit, fig)* das stinkt!; **to ~ of sth** *(lit, fig)* nach etw riechen; **to ~ at sth** an etw *(dat)* riechen *or (dog etc)* schnuppern; **his breath ~s** er riecht aus dem Mund, er hat Mundgeruch; **can fish ~?** können Fische riechen?
◆**smell out** *vt sep* **(a)** *rabbit, traitor etc* aufspüren; *plot* aufdecken. **(b) these onions are ~ing the house ~!** die Zwiebeln verpesten das ganze Haus!
smelling bottle ['smelɪŋ,bɒtl] *n* Riechfläschchen *nt*.
smelling salts ['smelɪŋ,sɔːlts] *npl* Riechsalz *nt*.
smelly ['smelɪ] *adj (+er)* übelriechend, stinkend ◆ **it's ~ in here** hier drin stinkt es; **you've got ~ feet** deine Füße stinken; **come here, ~!** komm her, du kleines Stinktier! *(inf)*.
smelt¹ [smelt] *pret, ptp of* **smell**.
smelt² *vt ore* schmelzen; *(refine)* verhütten.
smelt³ *n, pl* **-(s)** *(fish)* Stint *m*.
smelter ['smeltəʳ] *n (furnace)* Schmelzhütte, Schmelzerei *f*; *(person)* Schmelzer *m*.
smidgen, smidgin ['smɪdʒən] *n (inf)* **just a ~ for me** für mich nur ein (klitzekleines *inf*) bißchen.
smile [smaɪl] 1 *n* Lächeln *nt* ◆ **there was a sarcastic ~ on his face** ein sarkastisches Lächeln ging über sein Gesicht; **to be all ~s** übers ganze Gesicht strahlen; **to give sb a ~** jdm zulächeln; **come on, give me a ~** lach doch mal!; **take that ~ off your face!** hör auf, so zu grinsen!
2 *vi* lächeln ◆ **we tried to make the baby ~** wir versuchten, das Baby zum Lachen zu bringen; **come on, ~** lach mal!; **~ for the camera!** bitte recht freundlich!; **he's always smiling** er lacht immer; **keep smiling!** keep smiling!; **he kept smiling through all his troubles** trotz aller Schwierigkeiten ließ er den Kopf nicht hängen; **to ~ at sb** jdn anlächeln; *(cheerful person)* jdn anlachen; **to ~ at sth** über etw *(acc)* lächeln; **to ~ at danger** der Gefahr *(dat)* ins Gesicht lachen; **to ~ with joy/happiness** *etc* vor Freude/Glück *etc* strahlen; **fortune ~d on him** *(liter)* ihm lachte das Glück.
3 *vt* **she ~d her thanks** sie lächelte dankbar; **he ~d a bitter smile** er lächelte bitter.
smiling *adj*, **~ly** *adv* ['smaɪlɪŋ, -lɪ] lächelnd.
smirch [smɜːtʃ] *(liter)* 1 *n* Schmutz- *or* Schandfleck, Makel *(geh) m*.
2 *vt* beflecken *(liter)*, besudeln *(geh)*.
smirk [smɜːk] 1 *n* Grinsen *nt*.
2 *vi* grinsen, süffisant lächeln.
smite [smaɪt] *pret* **smote**, *ptp* **smitten** *vt (old, liter)* schlagen ◆ **he smote off his head** er schlug *or* hieb *(old, liter)* ihm den Kopf ab; **whosoever shall ~ thee on thy right cheek, ...** *(Bibl)* wenn dir jemand einen Streich gibt auf deine rechte Backe, ...; **the sound of gun-fire smote our ears** der Lärm von Schüssen schlug an unsere Ohren; **and the Lord shall ~ them down** und der Herr wird sie zerschmettern.
smith [smɪθ] *n* Schmied *m*.
smithereens [,smɪðə'riːnz] *npl* **to smash sth to ~** etw in tausend Stücke schlagen; **in ~** in tausend Stücken.
smithy ['smɪðɪ] *n* Schmiede *f*.
smitten ['smɪtn] 1 *ptp of* **smite**.
2 *adj* **to be ~ with the plague/remorse/fear** von der Pest heimgesucht/von Reue/Angst geplagt werden; **he's really ~ with her** *(inf)* er ist wirklich vernarrt in sie; **he's really ~ this time** *(inf)* diesmal hat's ihn erwischt *(inf)*; **I've never seen him so ~** *(inf)* ich habe ihn noch nie so vernarrt gesehen; **do you like it? — I'm not ~ with it** gefällt es dir? — ich bin nicht erpicht darauf.
smock [smɒk] 1 *n* Kittel *m*; *(as top)* Hänger *m*.
2 *vt* smoken.
smocking ['smɒkɪŋ] *n* Smokarbeit *f*.
smog [smɒg] *n* Smog *m*.
smoke [sməʊk] 1 *n* **(a)** Rauch *m* ◆ **there's no ~ without fire** *(prov)* kein Rauch ohne Flamme *(prov)*; **to go up in ~** in Rauch (und Flammen) aufgehen; *(fig)* sich in Wohlgefallen auflösen; *(inf: get angry)* in die Luft gehen *(inf)*.
(b) *(cigarette etc)* was zu rauchen *(inf)* ◆ **have you got a ~?** hast du was zu rauchen? *(inf)*; **it's a nice ~, this tobacco** dieser Tabak raucht sich gut; **~s** *(inf)* Glimmstengel *pl (dated inf)*.
(c) *(act)* **to have a ~** eine rauchen; **I'm dying for a ~** ich muß unbedingt eine rauchen; **the condemned were allowed a final ~** die Verurteilten durften eine letzte Zigarette rauchen.
2 *vt* **(a)** *tobacco* rauchen. **(b)** *bacon, fish etc* räuchern.
3 *vi* rauchen; *(oil-lamp etc)* qualmen ◆ **to ~ like a chimney** wie ein Schlot rauchen.
◆**smoke out** *vt sep* ausräuchern; *(fill with smoke)* einräuchern, einnebeln *(inf)*.
smoke-bomb ['sməʊkbɒm] *n* Rauchbombe *f*.
smoked [sməʊkt] *adj bacon, fish* geräuchert, Räucher- ◆ **~ glass** Rauchglas *nt*; **~ glasses** Gläser *pl* aus Rauchglas.
smoke: ~-dried *adj* geräuchert; **~-free** *adj zone* rauchfrei; **~less** *adj zone* rauchfrei; *fuel* rauchlos.
smoker ['sməʊkəʳ] *n* **(a)** *(person)* Raucher(in *f*) *m* ◆ **to be a heavy ~** stark rauchen, starker Raucher sein; **~'s cough** Raucherhusten *m*. **(b)** *(Rail)* Raucher(abteil *nt*) *m*. **(c)** *(entertainment)* Herrenabend *m*.
smoke: ~-ring *n* (Rauch)ring *m*; **~room** *n* Rauchsalon *m*, Rauchzimmer *nt*; **~screen** *n* Nebelwand *f*, Rauchvorhang *m*; *(fig)* Deckmantel, Vorwand *m*; **a ~screen of words** ein Schwall von Worten; **his answer was just a ~screen** seine Antwort war nur ein Ablenkungsmanöver; **~ signal** *n* Rauchzeichen *nt*; **~stack** *n* Schornstein *m*; **~stack industries** Schornsteinindustrien *pl*.
smoking ['sməʊkɪŋ] 1 *adj* rauchend.
2 *n* Rauchen *nt* ◆ **"no ~"** „Rauchen verboten".
smoking: ~ compartment, *(US)* **~ car** *n* Raucherabteil *nt*; **~ jacket** *n* Rauchjacke, Hausjacke *f*; **~ room** *n* Rauchzimmer *nt*.
smoky ['sməʊkɪ] *adj (+er) chimney, fire* rauchend; *room, atmosphere* verraucht; *(stained by smoke)* verräuchert; *(like smoke) flavour* rauchig; *colour* rauchfarben ◆ **~ blue** rauchblau.
smolder *vi (US) see* **smoulder**.
smooch [smuːtʃ] *(inf)* 1 *vi* knutschen *(inf)*.
2 *n* **to have a ~** rumknutschen *(inf)*.
smoochy ['smuːtʃɪ] *adj (+er) (inf) music, record* schmusig *(inf)*, Knutsch- *(inf)*, zum Knutschen *(inf)*; romantisch.
smooth [smuːð] 1 *adj (+er)* **(a)** *(in texture, surface etc)* glatt; *sea also* ruhig; *road, surface also* eben; *outline* sanft; *skin also, hair* weich ◆ **as ~ as silk** weich wie Seide, seidenweich; **as ~ as glass** spiegelglatt; **worn ~** *steps* glattgetreten; *knife* abgeschliffen; *tyre* abgefahren; **this razor gives you a really ~ shave** dieser Apparat rasiert wirklich sanft.
(b) *(in consistency) paste* sämig; *sauce* glatt ◆ **whisk sauce until ~** Soße glattrühren.
(c) *motion, flight, crossing* ruhig; *gear-change* weich, leicht; *take-off, landing* glatt; *breathing* gleichmäßig ◆ **the car came to a ~ stop** der Wagen kam glatt *or* ruhig zum Stehen; **he is a very ~ driver** er ist ein sehr angenehmer, ruhiger Fahrer; **to ensure a ~ fit** damit es genau paßt.
(d) *(trouble-free) transition, functioning* reibungslos, glatt ◆ **the bill had a ~ passage through Parliament** der Gesetzentwurf kam glatt durchs Parlament; **we want the move to the new offices to be as ~ as possible** wir wollen, daß der Umzug in die neuen Büroräume so reibungslos wie möglich verläuft.
(e) *(not harsh in taste) whisky, Guinness* weich.
(f) *style of writing* glatt, flüssig; *tones* sanft; *diction* flüssig, geschliffen ◆ **the ~, relaxing voice of the hypnotist** die sanft beruhigende Stimme des Hypnotiseurs.
(g) *(polite, often pej) manners, diplomat, salesman* glatt; *person also* aalglatt *(pej)*; *manners also* geschliffen; *(unruffled)* kühl, cool *(inf)* ◆ **to be a ~ talker** schönreden können; **he's too ~ to be sincere** er ist bestimmt nicht ehrlich, er redet zu schön; **a ~ operator** ein Schlawiner *m (inf)*.
(h) *(inf) restaurant, furniture, car, person* gepflegt.
(i) *(Tennis)* glatt.
2 *n* **to give sth a ~** etw glattstreichen; *see* **rough 3**.
3 *vt surface* glätten, glatt machen; *dress, hair* glätten, glattstreichen; *wood* glatthobeln; *(fig) feelings* besänftigen, beruhigen ◆ **to ~ the way for sb** jdm den Weg ebnen.
◆**smooth away** *vt sep* glätten; *(fig) fears* besänftigen.
◆**smooth back** *vt sep hair* zurückstreichen.
◆**smooth down** 1 *vt sep* glatt machen; *feathers, hair, dress* glattstreichen; *(fig) person, feelings* besänftigen ◆ **to ~ things ~** die Wogen glätten.
2 *vi (fig)* sich beruhigen.
◆**smooth out** *vt sep (make smooth) crease, surface* glätten; *(fig) difficulty* ausräumen, aus dem Weg räumen.
◆**smooth over** *vt sep (fig) quarrel* in Ordnung bringen, geradebiegen *(inf)* ◆ **to ~ things ~** die Sache geradebiegen *(inf)*.
smooth: ~-bore 1 *adj* glatt; 2 *n* Gewehr *nt* mit glattem Lauf; **~-faced** zarthäutig; *(fig)* scheinheilig.
smoothly ['smuːðlɪ] *adv* **(a)** *shave* sanft.
(b) *land, change gear* weich; *drive* ruhig; *fit* genau.
(c) *(without problems)* **to go ~** glatt über die Bühne gehen; **~**

organization reibungslos laufende Organisation.
(d) **~ flowing prose** flüssige Prosa; **the music passes ~ from one mood to another** die Musik fließt unmerklich von einer Stimmung in die andere über.
(e) *talk* schön; *behave* aalglatt (*pej*) ◆ **he handled the situation very ~** er hat die Lage sehr kühl gemeistert.

smoothness ['smu:ðnɪs] *n see adj* **(a)** Glätte *f*; Ruhe *f*; Ebenheit *f*; Sanftheit *f*; Weichheit *f* ◆ **it has the ~ of silk** es ist seidenweich. **(b)** Sämigkeit *f*; Glätte *f*. **(c)** Ruhe *f*; Weichheit *f*; Glätte *f*; Gleichmäßigkeit *f*; (*of fit*) Genauigkeit *f*. **(d)** Reibungslosigkeit *f*. **(e)** Weichheit *f*. **(f)** Flüssigkeit *f*; Sanftheit *f*. **(g)** Glätte *f*; (aal)glatte Art (*pej*).

smooth: ~-running *adj engine, car* ruhig laufend; **~-spoken, ~-tongued** *adj* (*pej*) schönredend (*pej*), schönrednerisch (*pej*).

smoothy ['smu:ðɪ] *n* (*inf*) Lackaffe *m* (*pej inf*).

smote [sməʊt] *pret of* **smite**.

smother ['smʌðəʳ] [1] *vt* **(a)** (*stifle*) *person, fire, criticism* ersticken; (*fig*) *criticism also, yawn, laughter* unterdrücken ◆ **to ~ sb with affection** jdn mit seiner Liebe erdrücken.
(b) (*cover*) bedecken, überschütten ◆ **fruit ~ed in cream** Obst, das in Sahne schwimmt; **~ed in dirt** schmutzstarrend; **~ed in dust** völlig eingestaubt; **she ~ed his face in kisses** sie bedeckte *or* übersäte sein Gesicht mit Küssen.
[2] *vi* ersticken.

smother-love ['smʌðə,lʌv] *n* (*inf*) übertriebene Mutterliebe.

smoulder, (*US*) smolder ['sməʊldəʳ] *vi* (*lit, fig*) glimmen, schwelen ◆ **his eyes were ~ing with anger/passion** seine Augen glühten vor Zorn/Leidenschaft; **a ~ing look** ein glühender Blick; **~ing hatred** glimmender *or* schwelender Haß.

smudge [smʌdʒ] [1] *n* **(a)** Fleck *m*; (*of ink*) Klecks *m*.
(b) (*US: fire*) (qualmendes) Feuer (*gegen Insekten*).
[2] *vt ink, lipstick, paint* verwischen ◆ **he had chocolate ~d all over his face** er hatte sich (*dat*) das ganze Gesicht mit Schokolade vollgeschmiert.
[3] *vi* verlaufen, verschmieren.

smudgy ['smʌdʒɪ] *adj* (*+er*) verschmiert; *outline* verwischt, verschwommen.

smug [smʌg] *adj* (*+er*) selbstgefällig; *grin, remark also* süffisant ◆ **~ self-confidence** eitle Selbstzufriedenheit.

smuggle ['smʌgl] *vti* (*lit, fig*) schmuggeln ◆ **to ~ sb/sth in** jdn/etw einschmuggeln, jdn einschleusen; **to ~ sb/sth out** jdn/etw herausschmuggeln, jdn herausschleusen.

smuggler ['smʌgləʳ] *n* Schmuggler(in *f*) *m*.

smuggling ['smʌglɪŋ] *n* Schmuggel *m* ◆ **~ ring** Schmugglerring *m*.

smugly ['smʌglɪ] *adv* selbstgefällig; *grin, say also* süffisant.

smugness ['smʌgnɪs] *n* Selbstgefälligkeit *f*.

smut [smʌt] *n* **(a)** (*piece of dirt*) Rußflocke *f* ◆ **there's a ~ on your nose/in your eye** du hast da was an der Nase/im Auge; **~s from the stove** Ruß *m* aus dem Ofen. **(b)** (*fig*) Schmutz *m* ◆ **to talk ~** Schweinereien erzählen. **(c)** (*Bot*) Brand *m*.

smuttiness ['smʌtɪnɪs] *n* (*fig*) Schmutz *m*; (*of joke, language*) Anstößigkeit, Unflätigkeit *f*.

smutty ['smʌtɪ] *adj* (*+er*) (*lit, fig*) schmutzig.

snack [snæk] *n* Kleinigkeit *f* (zu essen), Imbiß *m* ◆ **to have a ~** eine Kleinigkeit essen, einen Imbiß zu sich (*dat*) nehmen; **~ bar** Imbißstube *f*; **for us lunch is just a ~** mittags essen wir nicht viel *or* groß (*inf*); **too many ~s between meals ...** wenn man zwischen den Mahlzeiten zuviel ißt ...

snaffle[1] ['snæfl] *n* (*also* **~-bit**) Trense *f*.

snaffle[2] *vt* (*Brit inf*) sich (*dat*) unter den Nagel reißen (*inf*).

◆**snaffle up** *vt sep* (*Brit inf*) *bargain* wegschnappen (*inf*).

snafu [snæ'fu:] (*US sl*) [1] *n* Schlamassel *m* (*inf*).
[2] *vt* total durcheinanderbringen.

snag [snæg] [1] *n* **(a)** (*hidden difficulty*) Haken *m*, Schwierigkeit *f* ◆ **there's a ~** die Sache hat einen Haken; **what's the ~?** woran liegt es?, was ist das Problem?; **to run into** *or* **hit a ~** in Schwierigkeiten (*acc*) kommen. **(b)** (*flaw in clothes etc*) gezogener Faden. **(c)** (*in water*) Baumstumpf *m* (im Wasser).
[2] *vt* sich (*dat*) einen Faden ziehen ◆ **I ~ged my tights** ich habe mir an den Strumpfhosen einen Faden gezogen.
[3] *vi* Fäden ziehen.

snail [sneɪl] *n* Schnecke *f* ◆ **edible ~** Weinbergschnecke *f*; **at a ~'s pace** im Schneckentempo.

snail mail *n* (*hum*) Schneckenpost *f* (*inf*) (*im Gegensatz zur elektronischen Post*).

snake [sneɪk] [1] *n* Schlange *f* ◆ **a ~ in the grass** (*fig*) (*woman*) eine listige Schlange; (*man*) ein heimtückischer Kerl.
[2] *vi* sich schlängeln.

snake: ~bite *n* Schlangenbiß *m*; **~ charmer** *n* Schlangenbeschwörer *m*; **~pit** *n* Schlangengrube *f*; **~skin** [1] *n* Schlangenhaut *f*; (*leather*) Schlangenleder *nt*; [2] *adj* Schlangenleder-, aus Schlangenleder.

snaky ['sneɪkɪ] *adj windings* schläng(e)lig; *movements* schlangenartig.

nap [snæp] [1] *n* **(a)** (*sound*) Schnappen *nt*; (*with fingers*) Schnippen, ͡chnalzen *nt*; (*of sth breaking*) Knacken *nt*; (*click*) Klicken *nt*; (*of whip*) Knall *m* **the dog made a ~ at the biscuit** der Hund schnappte nach dem Keks.
(*fastener*) Druckknopf *m*.
'*Phot*) Schnappschuß *m*.
'*ards*) ≃ Schnippschnapp *nt*.
vigour) Schwung *m* ◆ **put a bit of ~ into it** mach ein bißchen zackig!
(‹) Plätzchen *nt*.
'älteeinbruch *m*.

(h) (*US inf: cinch*) **it's a ~** das ist ein Kinderspiel *or* ein Klacks (*inf*).
[2] *adj attr* plötzlich, spontan, Blitz- ◆ **~ vote** Blitzabstimmung *f*; **~ decision** plötzlicher Entschluß.
[3] *adv* **to go ~** schnapp/knack(s)/klick machen.
[4] *interj* **I bought a green one — ~!** (*inf*) ich hab' mir ein grünes gekauft — (ätsch,) ich auch!
[5] *vt* **(a)** *fingers* schnipsen *or* schnalzen mit; *whip* knallen mit ◆ **to ~ a book shut** ein Buch zuklappen; **he ~ped the lid down** er ließ den Deckel runterklappen; **to ~ sth into place** etw einschnappen lassen; **to ~ one's fingers at sb/sth** (*fig*) auf jdn/etw pfeifen (*inf*).
(b) (*break*) zerbrechen, entzweibrechen; *bone* brechen.
(c) (*also* **~ out**) **to ~ an order** bellend etwas befehlen; **she ~ped a few words at the children** sie pfiff die Kinder an.
(d) (*Phot*) knipsen.
[6] *vi* **(a)** (*click*) (zu)schnappen, einschnappen; (*crack, break*) entzweibrechen, zerbrechen; (*of whip*) knallen ◆ **to ~ shut** zuschnappen; **my patience finally ~ped** dann ist mir aber der Geduldsfaden gerissen.
(b) (*speak sharply*) bellen (*inf*), schnappen (*inf*) ◆ **to ~ at sb** jdn anpfeifen *or* anschnauzen (*inf*); **there's no need to ~** du brauchst nicht gleich so zu schnauzen!
(c) (*of dog, fish etc, fig*) schnappen (*at* nach) ◆ **to ~ at the opportunity** die Gelegenheit beim Schopf packen.
(d) to ~ to attention zackig Haltung annehmen; **~ to it!** mach 'n bißchen zackig! (*inf*).
(e) (*inf: crack up*) durchdrehen (*inf*) ◆ **something ~ped (in him)** da hat (bei ihm) etwas ausgehakt (*inf*).

◆**snap off** [1] *vt sep* (*break off*) abbrechen; (*bite off*) abbeißen ◆ **to ~ sb's head ~** (*fig inf*) jdm ins Gesicht springen (*inf*).
[2] *vi* (*break off*) abbrechen.

◆**snap out** [1] *vt sep order* brüllen, bellen.
[2] *vi* **to ~ ~ of sth** sich aus etw (*dat*) herausreißen, mit etw Schluß machen; **it's time he ~ped ~ of this depression** es wird höchste Zeit, daß er aus dieser Depression rauskommt; **~ ~ of it!** reiß dich zusammen *or* am Riemen! (*inf*); (*cheer up*) Kopf hoch!

◆**snap up** *vt sep* (*lit, fig*) wegschnappen.

snap: ~dragon *n* Löwenmaul *nt*; **~-fastener** *n* Druckknopf *m*.

snappish ['snæpɪʃ] *adj* (*lit, fig*) bissig.

snappishness ['snæpɪʃnɪs] *n* (*lit, fig*) Bissigkeit *f*.

snappy ['snæpɪ] *adj* (*+er*) **(a)** (*inf: quick*) flott (*inf*), zackig (*inf*) ◆ **and be ~ about it!, and make it ~!** und zwar ein bißchen flott *or* zackig! (*inf*). **(b)** (*lit, fig*) *dog, person* bissig. **(c)** (*inf*) *translation* kurz und treffend; *phrase* zündend.

snap: ~ ring *n* Karabinerhaken *m*; **~shot** *n* Schnappschuß *m*.

snare[1] [snɛəʳ] [1] *n* (*lit, fig: trap*) Falle *f*; (*fig also*) Fallstrick *m*.
[2] *vt* (*lit, fig*) (ein)fangen.

snare[2] *n* **(a)** (*of drum*) Schnarrsaite *f*. **(b)** (*also* **~ drum**) kleine Trommel.

snarl[1] [snɑ:l] [1] *n* Knurren *nt no pl* ◆ **..., he said with a ~** ..., sagte er knurrend.
[2] *vi* knurren ◆ **to ~ at sb** jdn anknurren.

snarl[2] [1] *n* (*in wool*) Knoten *m*, verhedderte Stelle.
[2] *vt wool* verheddern.

◆**snarl up** (*inf*) [1] *vt sep traffic, system* durcheinanderbringen; *plan also* vermasseln (*sl*) ◆ **traffic always gets ~ed ~ at the bridge** an der Brücke ist der Verkehr immer chaotisch; **I got ~ed ~ in a traffic jam** ich bin im Verkehr steckengeblieben.
[2] *vi* (*traffic*) chaotische Formen annehmen.

snarl-up ['snɑ:lʌp] *n* (*inf*) (*in traffic*) (Verkehrs)chaos *nt*; (*in system, on switchboard etc*) Kuddelmuddel *nt* (*inf*) ◆ **~s** ein großes Kuddelmuddel (*inf*); **the ~s at rush-hour periods** das Chaos in den Stoßverkehrszeiten.

snatch [snætʃ] [1] *n* **(a)** (*act*) Griff *m* ◆ **to make a ~ at sth** nach etw greifen; (*animal*) nach etw schnappen.
(b) (*Brit inf*) (*robbery*) Raub *m*; (*kidnapping*) Entführung *f*.
(c) (*snippet*) Stück *nt*, Brocken *m*; (*of conversation also*) Fetzen *m*; (*of music*) ein paar Takte ◆ **to do sth in ~es** etw in Etappen tun.
(d) (*Weightlifting*) Reißen *nt*.
(e) (*US sl: female genitals*) Möse (*vulg*), Pflaume (*vulg*) *f*.
[2] *vt* **(a)** (*grab*) greifen ◆ **to ~ sth from sb** jdm etw entreißen; **to ~ hold of sth** nach etw greifen, etw packen; **to ~ sth out of sb's hand** jdm etw aus der Hand reißen.
(b) *some sleep etc* ergattern ◆ **to ~ a quick meal** schnell etwas essen; **the Ferrari ~ed the lead on the last lap** der Ferrari riß in der letzten Runde die Führung an sich; **to ~ an opportunity** eine Gelegenheit ergreifen *or* beim Schopf packen; **they ~ed a quick kiss** sie gaben sich (*dat*) schnell einen Kuß; **he ~ed a kiss while she wasn't looking** als sie gerade wegsah, stahl er ihr schnell einen Kuß.
(c) (*Brit inf*) (*steal*) *money* klauen (*inf*); *handbag* aus der Hand reißen; (*kidnap*) entführen.
[3] *vi* greifen (*at* nach) ◆ **don't ~!** nicht grapschen! (*inf*); **to ~ at an opportunity** nach einer Gelegenheit greifen.

◆**snatch away** *vt sep* wegreißen (*sth from sb* jdm etw) ◆ **death ~ed him ~ from us** der Tod hat ihn uns (*dat*) entrissen.

◆**snatch up** *vt sep* schnappen ◆ **he ~ed ~ his camera** er schnappte sich (*dat*) seine Kamera; **the mother ~ed her child ~** die Mutter riß ihr Kind an sich (*acc*).

snatch squad *n* Greifertrupp *m* (*inf*).

snazzy *adj* (*+er*), **snazzily** *adv* ['snæzɪ, -lɪ] (*sl*) flott.

sneak [sni:k] [1] *n* Schleicher *m*; (*Sch sl*) Petze(r) *mf* (*Sch sl*) ◆ **~ preview** (*of film* *etc)* Vorschau *f;* *(of new car etc)* Vorbesichtigung *f;* **~ thief** Langfinger *(inf)*, Einschleichdieb *m.*

[2] *vt* **he ~ed a cake off the counter** er klaute *or* klemmte einen Kuchen vom Tresen *(inf);* **to ~ sth into a room** etw in ein Zimmer schmuggeln; **to ~ a look at sb/sth** auf jdn/etw schielen.

[3] *vi* **(a) to ~ about** herumschleichen; **to ~ away** *or* **off** sich wegschleichen *or* -stehlen; **to ~ in** sich einschleichen; **to ~ past sb** (sich) an jdm vorbeischleichen. **(b)** *(Sch sl: tell tales)* petzen *(inf)* ◆ **to ~ on sb** jdn verpetzen *(inf).*

sneakers ['sni:kəz] *npl (esp US)* Freizeitschuhe, Leisetreter *(hum)*, Schleicher *(hum) pl.*

sneaking ['sni:kɪŋ] *adj attr* geheim *attr; suspicion also* leise.

sneaky ['sni:kɪ] *adj (+er) (inf)* raffiniert, schlau.

sneer [snɪəʳ] [1] *n (expression)* spöttisches *or* höhnisches Lächeln; *(remark)* spöttische *or* höhnische Bemerkung.

[2] *vi* spotten; *(look sneering)* spöttisch *or* höhnisch grinsen ◆ **adolescents often ~ at what they cannot understand** Jugendliche spotten oft über das, was sie nicht verstehen können; **to ~ at sb** jdn verhöhnen; *(facially also)* jdn auslachen.

sneerer ['snɪərəʳ] *n* Spötter *m.*

sneering *adj,* **~ly** *adv* ['snɪərɪŋ, -lɪ] höhnisch, spöttisch.

sneeze [sni:z] [1] *n* Nieser *m* ◆ **~s** Niesen *nt.*

[2] *vi* niesen ◆ **not to be ~d at** nicht zu verachten.

snick [snɪk] [1] *n (small cut)* Kerbe *f.*

[2] *vt (with razor)* schneiden; *(with knife)* schnitzen; *(with tweezers)* zupfen; *(Cricket) ball* auf Kante schlagen.

snicker ['snɪkəʳ] *n, vi see* **snigger**.

snide [snaɪd] *adj (inf)* abfällig.

sniff [snɪf] [1] *n* Schniefen *nt no pl (inf); (disdainful)* Naserümpfen *nt no pl; (of dog)* Schnüffeln *nt no pl* ◆ **we never got a ~ of the vodka** wir durften noch nicht einmal an dem Wodka riechen; **have a ~ at this** riech mal hieran; **he had a good ~ to try to clear his nose** er zog kräftig hoch, um die Nase frei zu kriegen.

[2] *vt (test by smelling)* riechen, schnuppern an *(+dat) (inf); smelling salts* einziehen; *glue* einatmen, schnüffeln *(inf); snuff* schnupfen; *(fig: detect)* wittern, riechen ◆ **the dogs ~ed each other** die Hunde beschnupperten sich; **~ these flowers** riech mal an den Blumen.

[3] *vi (person)* schniefen *(inf); (dog)* schnüffeln, schnuppern ◆ **to ~ at sth** *(lit)* an etw *(dat)* schnuppern; *(fig)* die Nase über etw *(acc)* rümpfen; **not to be ~ed at** nicht zu verachten.

◆**sniff out** *vt sep (lit, fig)* aufspüren; *crime, plot* aufdecken.

sniffer dog ['snɪfəˌdɒg] *n* Spürhund *m.*

sniffle ['snɪfl] *n, vi see* **snuffle**.

sniffy ['snɪfɪ] *adj (+er) (inf) (disdainful)* naserümpfend; *(put out)* verschnupft, eingeschnappt *(inf)* ◆ **she was rather ~ about the plan** sie hat über den Plan nur die Nase gerümpft.

snifter ['snɪftəʳ] *n (dated inf)* Kurze(r) *m (inf)* ◆ **to have a ~** einen Kurzen trinken *or* nehmen *(inf).*

snigger ['snɪgəʳ] [1] *n* Kichern, Gekicher *nt* ◆ **to give a ~** loskichern.

[2] *vi* kichern *(at, about* wegen).

snip [snɪp] [1] *n* **(a)** *(cut, cutting action)* Schnitt *m; (sound)* Schnipsen, Klappern *nt no pl.*

(b) *(of cloth)* Stück *nt; (of paper)* Schnipsel, Schnippel *(inf) m or nt; (from newspaper)* Ausschnitt *m.*

(c) *(esp Brit inf: bargain)* Geschäft *nt*, günstiger Kauf ◆ **at only £2 it's a real ~** für nur £ 2 ist es unheimlich günstig.

(d) *(US inf: insignificant person)* Würstchen *nt (pej inf).*

[2] *vt* schnippeln *(inf)* ◆ **to ~ sth off** etw abschnippeln *(inf).*

[3] *vi* **to ~ at** schnippeln an *(+dat) (inf).*

snipe [snaɪp] [1] *n, pl - (Orn)* Schnepfe *f.*

[2] *vi* **to ~ at sb** *(lit, fig)* aus dem Hinterhalt auf jdn schießen.

sniper ['snaɪpəʳ] *n* Heckenschütze *m* ◆ **~-fire** Heckenschützenfeuer *nt.*

snippet ['snɪpɪt] *n* Stückchen *nt; (of paper also)* Schnipsel *m or nt; (of information)* (Bruch)stück *nt* ◆ **~s of a conversation** Gesprächsfetzen *pl.*

snitch [snɪtʃ] *(sl)* [1] *vt* klauen *(inf)*, klemmen *(inf).*

[2] *vi* **to ~ on sb** über jdn plaudern *(inf) or* klatschen.

snivel ['snɪvl] *vi* heulen, flennen *(inf).*

sniveller ['snɪvləʳ] *n* Jammerer *m.*

snivelling ['snɪvlɪŋ] [1] *adj* heulend, flennend *(inf).*

[2] *n* Geheul(e), Geflenne *(inf) nt.*

snob [snɒb] *n* Snob *m* ◆ **~ appeal** *or* **value** Snobappeal *m.*

snobbery ['snɒbərɪ] *n* Snobismus *m.*

snobbish *adj* ['snɒbɪʃ] snobistisch, versnobt *(inf); place* für Snobs.

snobbishly ['snɒbɪʃlɪ] *adv* snobistisch, versnobt *(inf).*

snobbishness ['snɒbɪʃnɪs] *n* Snobismus *m*, Versnobtheit *f (inf).*

snog [snɒg] *(Brit sl)* [1] *n* Knutscherei *f (inf)* ◆ **to have a ~ with sb** mit jdm rumknutschen *(inf).*

[2] *vi* rumknutschen *(inf).*

snood [snu:d] *n* Haarnetz *nt.*

snook [snu:k] *n see* **cock 2 (b)**.

snooker ['snu:kəʳ] [1] *n* Snooker *nt.*

[2] *vt* **to ~ sb** jdn sperren; **to be ~ed** *(fig inf)* festsitzen *(inf);* **I've ~ed myself** *(fig inf)* ich habe mich festgefahren.

snoop [snu:p] [1] *n* **(a)** *see* **snooper**. **(b)** *(act)* **I'll have a ~ around** ich gucke mich mal (ein bißchen) um.

[2] *vi* schnüffeln ◆ **to ~ about** *or* **around** herumschnüffeln.

snooper ['snu:pəʳ] *n* Schnüffler(in *f*) *m.*

snootily ['snu:tɪlɪ] *adv (inf)* hochnäsig, von oben herab.

snooty ['snu:tɪ] *adj (+er) (inf)* hochnäsig.

snooze [snu:z] [1] *n* Schläfchen, Nickerchen *nt* ◆ **to have a ~** ein Schläfchen machen; **~ button** *(on alarm clock)* Schlummertaste *f.*

[2] *vi* dösen, ein Nickerchen machen.

snore [snɔ:ʳ] [1] *n* Schnarchen *nt no pl.*

[2] *vi* schnarchen.

snorer ['snɔ:rəʳ] *n* Schnarcher(in *f*) *m.*

snoring ['snɔ:rɪŋ] *n* Schnarchen *nt.*

snorkel ['snɔ:kl] [1] *n* Schnorchel *m.*

[2] *vi* schnorcheln ◆ **to go ~ling** schnorcheln gehen.

snort [snɔ:t] [1] *n* Schnauben *nt no pl; (of boar)* Grunzen *nt no pl; (of person also)* Prusten *nt no pl* ◆ **with a ~ of rage** wutschnaubend; **he gave a ~ of contempt/rage/laughter** er schnaubte verächtlich/vor Wut/er prustete los.

[2] *vti* schnauben; *(boar)* grunzen; *(person also)* prusten.

snorter ['snɔ:təʳ] *n* **(a)** *(Brit sl: difficult thing)* schwierige Kiste *(sl)*, hartes Ding *(sl)*. **(b)** *(dated inf: drink)* Kurze(r) *m (inf).*

snot [snɒt] *n (inf)* Rotz *m (inf).*

snotty ['snɒtɪ] *adj (+er) (inf)* **(a)** *handkerchief, nose* Rotz- *(inf); child* rotznäsig *(inf)* ◆ **~-nose** Rotznase *f (inf);* **~-nosed** rotznäsig *(inf)*. **(b)** *(fig: snooty)* rotzig *(sl)*, pampig *(inf).*

snout [snaʊt] *n* **(a)** *(of animal)* Schnauze *f; (of pig also, of insect)* Rüssel *m; (inf: of person)* Rüssel *(inf)*, Zinken *(inf) m.* **(b)** *(sl: informer)* Spitzel *m.* **(c)** *(Brit sl: tobacco)* Knaster *m (inf).*

snow [snəʊ] [1] *n* **(a)** *(also sl: cocaine or heroin)* Schnee *m; (~fall)* Schneefall *m* ◆ **the ~s that lie on the plains** der Schnee in der Ebene; **the heavy ~s last winter** die heftigen Schneefälle im letzten Winter; **a ~ of confetti** ein Konfettiregen *m;* **as white as ~** schneeweiß, blütenweiß; **as pure as the driven ~** engelrein.

(b) *(TV)* Geflimmer *nt*, Schnee *m.*

[2] *vi* schneien.

◆**snow in** *vt sep (usu pass)* **to be** *or* **get ~ed ~** einschneien; **we are ~ed ~** wir sind eingeschneit.

◆**snow off** *vt sep (usu pass)* **to be ~ed ~** wegen Schnee abgesagt werden *or* ausfallen.

◆**snow under** *vt sep (inf: usu pass)* **to be ~ed ~** *(with work)* reichlich eingedeckt sein; *(with requests)* überhäuft werden.

◆**snow up** *vt sep (usu pass) see* **snow in**.

snow: ~ball [1] *n* Schneeball *m; (drink)* Snowball *m;* **he doesn't stand a ~ball's chance in hell** *(sl)* seine Chancen sind gleich Null; [2] *vt* Schneebälle werfen auf *(+acc);* [3] *vi* eskalieren; **we must take action now otherwise things will ~ball and get out of control** wir müssen jetzt etwas unternehmen, sonst wachsen uns die Dinge über den Kopf; **opposition to the referendum just ~balled** die Opposition gegen die Volksabstimmung wuchs lawinenartig an; **~ball effect** *n* Schneeballeffekt *m;* **~-blind** *adj* schneeblind; **~ blindness** *n* Schneeblindheit *f;* **~bound** *adj* eingeschneit; **~-capped** *adj* schneebedeckt; **~cat** *n (Ski)* Pistenwalze *f;* **~ chains** *npl* Schneeketten *pl;* **~-clad** *(poet)*, **~-covered** *adj* verschneit; **~-cuffs** *npl* Schneegamaschen *pl;* **~drift** *n* Schneewehe *f;* **~drop** *n* Schneeglöckchen *nt;* **~fall** *n* Schneefall *m;* **~field** *n* Schneefeld *nt;* **~flake** *n* Schneeflocke *f;* **~ goose** *n* Schneegans *f;* **~-in-summer** *n (Bot)* Hornkraut *nt;* **~ leopard** *n* Schneeleopard *m;* **~ line** *n* Schneegrenze *f;* **~man** *n* Schneemann *m; see* **abominable**; **~mobile** *n (US)* Schneemobil *nt;* **~plough**, *(US)* **~plow** *n (also Ski)* Schneepflug *m;* **~shed** *n (US)* Schneedach *nt;* **~shoe** *n* Schneeschuh *m;* **~slide** *n (US)* Schneerutsch *m;* **~storm** *n* Schneesturm *m;* **~suit** *n (US)* gefütterter Overall; **S~ White** *n* Schneewittchen *nt;* **~-white** *adj* schneeweiß; *hair also* schlohweiß.

snowy ['snəʊɪ] *adj (+er)* **(a)** *weather, region* schneereich; *hills* verschneit ◆ **it was very ~ yesterday** gestern hat es viel geschneit. **(b)** *(white as snow)* schneeweiß.

SNP *abbr of* **Scottish National Party**.

snub [snʌb] [1] *n* Brüskierung *f* ◆ **to give sb a ~** jdn brüskieren, jdn vor den Kopf stoßen; *subordinate, pupil etc (verbally)* jdm über den Mund fahren; **to get a ~ from sb** von jdm brüskiert *or* vor den Kopf gestoßen werden.

[2] *vt* **(a)** *person* brüskieren, vor den Kopf stoßen; *subordinate, pupil (verbally)* über den Mund fahren *(+dat); suggestion, proposal* kurz abtun. **(b)** *(ignore, not greet)* schneiden.

snub: ~ nose *n* Stupsnase *f;* **~-nosed** *adj* stumpfnasig; *person also* stupsnasig.

snuff [snʌf] [1] *n* Schnupftabak *m* ◆ **to take ~** schnupfen.

[2] *vt candle (extinguish: also* **~ out**) auslöschen; *(trim wick)* putzen, schneuzen *(old); (fig) revolt* ersticken; *hopes* zunichte machen, zerschlagen ◆ **to ~ it** *(Brit sl: die)* abkratzen *(sl).*

snuff box *n* Schnupftabakdose, Tabatiere *(geh) f.*

snuffer ['snʌfəʳ] *n* Kerzenlöscher *m* ◆ **~s, a pair of ~s** Lichtputzschere *f.*

snuffle ['snʌfl] [1] *n* Schniefen *nt no pl* ◆ **to have a touch of the ~s** *(inf)* einen leichten Schnupfen haben.

[2] *vi (person, animal)* schnüffeln; *(with cold, from crying also)* schniefen *(inf).*

snuff movie *n brutaler (Porno)film, in dem tatsächlich gestorben wird.*

snug [snʌg] [1] *adj (+er) (cosy, comfortable)* behaglich, gemütlich; *(cosy and warm) bed, garment, room etc* mollig warm, behaglich warm; *(sheltered) spot, harbour* geschützt; *(close-fitting)* gutsitzend *attr; (tight)* eng ◆ **to be ~ in bed/in one's sleeping bag** es im Bett/Schlafsack mollig *or* behaglich warm haben; **I was as ~ as a bug in a rug** *(inf)* es war urgemütlich; **it is a good ~ fit** es paßt gut; **it was a ~ fit with 6 of us in the car** wir paßten zu sechst noch gerade in den Wagen.

2 *n* (*Brit: in pub*) kleines Nebenzimmer.

snuggle ['snʌgl] 1 *vi* sich schmiegen, sich kuscheln ◆ **to ~ down in bed** sich ins Bett kuscheln; **to ~ up (to sb)** sich (an jdn) anschmiegen *or* ankuscheln; **I like to ~ up with a book** ich mache es mir gern mit einem Buch gemütlich; **to ~ into sth** sich in etw (*acc*) einkuscheln; **the cottages ~d in the valley** die Häuschen schmiegten sich ins Tal.

2 *vt* an sich (*acc*) schmiegen.

snugly ['snʌglɪ] *adv* (*cosily*) gemütlich, behaglich ◆ **~ tucked in, ~ tucked up (in bed)** mollig warm eingepackt (im Bett); **it fits ~** es paßt wie angegossen.

snugness ['snʌgnɪs] *n see adj* Behaglichkeit, Gemütlichkeit *f*; mollige *or* behagliche Wärme; Geschütztheit *f*; guter Sitz.

So *abbr of* **south** S.

so [səʊ] 1 *adv* **(a)** so ◆ **~ much tea/~ many flies** so viel Tee/so viele Fliegen; **he was ~ stupid (that)** er war so *or* dermaßen *or* derart dumm(, daß); **he's ~ quick I can't keep up with him** er ist so schnell, daß ich nicht mithalten kann; **not ~ ... as** nicht so ... wie; **he is not ~ fast a runner as you** er ist kein so schneller Läufer wie Sie, er kann nicht so schnell laufen wie Sie; **I am not ~ stupid as to believe that** so dumm bin ich nicht, daß ich das glaube(n würde); **he was ~ stupid as to tell her** er war so dumm und hat es ihr gesagt; **would you be ~ kind as to open the door**? wären Sie bitte so freundlich und würden die Tür öffnen?; **~ great a writer as Shakespeare** ein so großer Dichter wie Shakespeare; **he's not been ~ well recently** in letzter Zeit geht es ihm nicht so sonderlich; **how are things? — not ~ bad**! wie geht's? — nicht schlecht!; **not ~ as you'd notice** aber das fällt kaum auf.

(b) (*emphatic*) *glad, sorry, sure, rich, hurt* so; *pleased, relieved, hope, wish* sehr; *love* so sehr; *hate* so sehr, derart ◆ **that's ~ true** das ist ja so wahr, das ist wirklich wahr; **I'm ~ very tired** ich bin ja so müde; **it's not ~ very difficult** es ist gar nicht so schwer; **it would be ~ much better/nicer** *etc* es wäre soviel besser/netter *etc*; **~ much the better/worse (for sb)** um so besser/schlechter (für jdn); **that's ~ kind of you** das ist wirklich sehr nett von Ihnen; **I ~ hope you're right**! ich hoffe (wirklich) sehr, daß Sie recht haben!

(c) (*replacing longer sentence*) da, es ◆ **I hope ~** hoffentlich; (*emphatic*) das hoffe ich doch sehr; **I think ~** ich glaube schon; **I never said ~** das habe ich nie gesagt; **I told you ~** ich habe es dir doch *or* ja gesagt; **I told you ~ yesterday** das habe ich dir gestern gesagt; **why should I do it? — because I say ~** warum muß ich das tun? — weil ich es sage, darum; **I didn't say ~** das habe ich nicht gesagt; **can I go/will you do it? — I suppose ~** darf ich gehen/machen Sie es? — na ja, meinetwegen; **is that right/can I do it like that? — I suppose ~** stimmt das/kann ich es so machen? — ich glaube schon; **~ I believe** ja, ich glaube schon; **~ I see** ja, das sehe ich; **please, do ~** bitte(, tun Sie es ruhig); **perhaps ~** vielleicht; **it may be ~** es kann schon sein; **~ be it** nun gut; **if ~** wenn ja; **he said he would finish it this week, and ~ he did** er hat gesagt, er würde es diese Woche fertigmachen, und das hat er auch (gemacht); **how** *or* **why ~**? wieso *or* warum das?; **or ~ they say** oder so heißt es jedenfalls; **he's a millionaire, or ~ he says** er ist Millionär, zumindest *or* jedenfalls behauptet er das; **it is ~**! (*contradiction*) doch!; **I can ~**! (*contradiction*) und ob (ich das kann)!, doch!; **I didn't say that — you did ~** das habe ich nicht gesagt — doch, das hast du (sehr wohl gesagt)!; **you've got the papers? — yes, that's ~** haben Sie die Papiere? — jawohl; **that is ~** das stimmt; **if that's ~** wenn das stimmt; **he's coming by plane — is that ~**? er kommt mit dem Flugzeug — ach so, ja?, tatsächlich?; **you're a fool — is that ~**? du bist ein Idiot — ach, wirklich?; ... — **~ it is/I have/he did** *etc* ... — (ja) tatsächlich; **he's a nice chap — ~ he is** er ist ein netter Kerl — ja, wirklich *or* ja, das ist er auch.

(d) (*thus, in this way*) so ◆ **perhaps it was better ~** vielleicht war es auch besser so; **~ it was that** ... so kam es, daß ...; **and ~ it was** und so war es auch; **by ~ doing he has** ... dadurch hat er ..., indem er das tat, hat er ...; **bother them! he exclaimed, and ~ saying walked out** zum Kuckuck! rief er, und damit ging er hinaus; ... **and ~ to bed** ... und dann ins Bett.

(e) (*unspecified amount*) **how high is it? — oh, about ~ high** (*accompanied by gesture*) wie hoch ist das? — oh, ungefähr so; **~ much per head** soviel pro Kopf; **they looked like ~ many gypsies** sie sahen wie so viele andere Zigeuner auch aus; **how long will it take? — a week or ~** wie lange dauert das? — ungefähr eine Woche *or* so eine Woche; **50 or ~** etwa 50.

(f) (*likewise*) auch ◆ **~ am/would/do/could** *etc* **I** ich auch; **he's wrong and ~ are you** ihr irrt euch beide; **as A is to B, ~ D is to E** A verhält sich zu B wie D zu E.

(g) he walked past and didn't ~ much as look at me er ging vorbei, ohne mich auch nur anzusehen; **he didn't say ~ much as thank you** er hat nicht einmal danke gesagt; **I haven't ~ much as a penny** ich habe keinen Pfennig; **~ much for that**! (*inf*) das wär's ja wohl gewesen! (*inf*); **~ much for him/his help** (*inf*) das war ja wohl nichts mit ihm! (*inf*)/schöne Hilfe! (*inf*); **~ much for his ambition to be a doctor/for our holidays** aus der Traum vom Arztwerden/von den Ferien; **~ much for his promises** und er hat solche Versprechungen gemacht; *see* **ever, far 1 (d), just[1], long[2] 2 (a, c), more 1 (b), quite (a)**.

2 *conj* **(a)** (*expressing purpose*) damit ◆ **~ (that) you don't have to do it again** damit Sie es nicht noch einmal machen müssen; **we hurried ~ as not to be late** wir haben uns beeilt, um nicht zu spät zu kommen.

(b) (*expressing result, therefore*) also ◆ **it rained (and) ~ we couldn't go out** es regnete, also konnten wir nicht weggehen *or* und deshalb konnten wir nicht weggehen; **he refused to move ~ (that) finally the police had to carry him away** er weigerte sich wegzugehen, so daß ihn die Polizei schließlich wegtragen mußte; **he was standing in the doorway ~ (that) no-one could get past** er stand in der Tür, so daß niemand vorbeikonnte; **I told him to leave and ~ he did** ich habe ihm gesagt, er solle gehen, und das hat er auch getan; **~ I told him he could get lost** da habe ich ihm gesagt, er kann *or* könnte mir den Buckel runterrutschen; **~, far from helping us, he** ... nicht nur, daß er uns nicht geholfen hat, sondern ...; **~ you see** ... wie du siehst, ...

(c) (*in questions, exclamations*) also ◆ **~ you're Spanish/leaving?** Sie sind also Spanier(in)/Sie gehen also?; **~ you lost it, did you?** du hast es also verloren, wie?; **~ you *did* do it!** du hast es also doch gemacht!; **~ there you are!** hier steckst du also!; **~ what did you do?** und was haben Sie (da) gemacht?; **~ (what)?** (*inf*) (na) und?; **~ what if you don't do it?** (*inf*) (na) und wenn du's nicht machst?; **I'm not going, ~ there!** (*inf*) ich geh' nicht, fertig, aus!

soak [səʊk] 1 *vt* **(a)** (*wet*) durchnässen ◆ **to be/get ~ed** patschnaß *or* völlig durchnäßt sein/werden; **to be ~ed to the skin, to be ~ed through** bis auf die Haut *or* völlig durchnäßt sein.

(b) (*steep*) einweichen (*in* in *+dat*) ◆ **to ~ oneself in sth** (*fig*) sich in etw (*acc*) vertiefen.

(c) (*inf*) *the rich etc* schröpfen ◆ **to ~ sb for sth** jdn um etw angehen.

2 *vi* **(a)** (*steep*) **leave it to ~** weichen Sie es ein; (*in dye*) lassen Sie die Farbe einziehen; **to ~ in a bath** sich einweichen (*inf*).

(b) (*penetrate*) **rain has ~ed through the ceiling** der Regen ist durch die Decke gesickert; **the coffee was ~ing into the carpet** der Kaffee saugte sich in den Teppich; **blood was ~ing out of the wound** aus der Wunde sickerte Blut.

3 *n* **(a)** (*act of soaking*) **give the washing a good ~** lassen Sie die Wäsche gut einweichen; **the sheets are in ~** die Laken sind eingeweicht; **the garden needs a ~** der Garten muß gründlich bewässert werden.

(b) (*inf: drunkard*) Schluckbruder (*inf*), Säufer(in *f*) *m*.

◆**soak in** *vi* (*stain, dye etc*) einziehen ◆ **to leave sth to ~ ~** etw einziehen lassen; **I just hope that it has ~ed ~** (*fig*) ich hoffe nur, daß er/sie *etc* das kapiert hat (*inf*).

◆**soak off** 1 *vt sep* ablösen.

2 *vi* sich (ab)lösen (*prep obj* von).

◆**soak out** 1 *vt sep mark, stain* durch Einweichen entfernen.

2 *vi* beim Einweichen herausgehen.

◆**soak up** *vt sep liquid* aufsaugen; *sunshine* genießen; *alcohol* in sich (*acc*) hineinkippen; *sound* schlucken; (*fig*) in sich (*acc*) hineinsaugen; *information* aufsaugen.

soaking ['səʊkɪŋ] 1 *adj person* klitschnaß, patschnaß; *object also* triefend.

2 *adv* **~ wet** triefend naß, klitschnaß; **a ~ wet day** ein völlig verregneter Tag.

3 *n* (*steeping*) Einweichen *nt no indef art* ◆ **to get a ~** patschnaß werden; **to give sth a ~** etw einweichen.

so-and-so ['səʊənsəʊ] *n* (*inf*) **(a)** (*unspecified person*) Soundso *no art* ◆ **~ up at the shop** Herr/Frau Soundso im Laden. **(b)** (*pej*) **he's a real/an old ~** das ist ein gemeiner Kerl; **you old ~** du bist vielleicht eine/einer.

soap [səʊp] 1 *n* **(a)** (*substance*) Seife *f*. **(b)** (*~ opera*) Seifenoper *f* (*inf*).

2 *vt* einseifen, abseifen.

soap: ~box *n* (*lit: packing case*) Seifenkiste *f*; (*fig: platform*) Apfelsinenkiste *f*; (*as cart*) Seifenkiste *f*; **to get up on one's ~box** (*fig*) Volksreden halten; **~box derby** *n* Seifenkistenrennen *nt*; **~box evangelist** *n* Wanderprediger *m*; **~box orator** *n* Volksredner *m*; **~-bubble** *n* Seifenblase *f*; **~dish** *n* Seifenschale *f*; **~ dispenser** *n* Seifenspender *m*; **~flakes** *npl* Seifenflocken *pl*; **~ opera** *n* (*TV, Rad inf*) Fernseh-/Hörspielserie, Seifenoper (*inf*) *f*; **~ powder** *n* Seifenpulver *nt*; **~stone** *n* Speckstein *m*; **~suds** *npl* Seifenschaum *m*.

soapy ['səʊpɪ] *adj* (*+er*) seifig.

soar [sɔːʳ] *vi* **(a)** (*rise: also* **~ up**) aufsteigen ◆ **to ~ (up) into the sky** zum Himmel steigen.

(b) (*fig*) (*building, tower*) hochragen; (*price, cost, profit*) hochschnellen; (*ambition, popularity, reputation, hopes*) einen Aufschwung nehmen; (*morale, spirits*) einen Aufschwung bekommen ◆ **the tower/hill ~ed above the town** der Turm/Hügel ragte über die Stadt hinaus.

soaring ['sɔːrɪŋ] *adj bird, plane* aufsteigend, in die Luft steigend; *tower* hoch aufragend; *imagination, ideas, ambition* hochfliegend; *popularity, reputation* schnell zunehmend; *prices* in die Höhe schnellend; *inflation* unaufhaltsam; *pride, hopes* wachsend ◆ **I watched the lark's ~ flight** ich sah, wie sich die Lerche in die Lüfte schwang.

sob [sɒb] 1 *n* Schluchzer *m*, Schluchzen *nt no pl* ◆ **to give a ~** (auf)schluchzen; ..., **he said with a ~** ..., sagte er schluchzend.

2 *vi* schluchzen (*with* vor *+dat*) ◆ **~, ~** (*inf*) schluchz-schluchz.

3 *vt* schluchzen ◆ **to ~ oneself to sleep** sich in den Schlaf weinen.

◆**sob out** *vt sep information* schluchzend hervorstoßen; *story* schluchzend erzählen ◆ **to ~ one's heart** ~ sich (*dat*) die Seele aus dem Leib weinen.

s.o.b. (*US sl*) *abbr of* **son of a bitch.**

sobbing ['sɒbɪŋ] 1 *n* Schluchzen *nt*.

2 *adj* schluchzend.

sober ['səʊbəʳ] *adj* **(a)** (*not drunk*) nüchtern ◆ **to be as ~ as a judge** stocknüchtern sein (*inf*).

(b) (*sedate, serious*) *life, expression, mood, occasion* ernst; *person also* solide; (*sensible, moderate*) *opinion* vernünftig; *assessment, statement, advice, facts* nüchtern.

(c) (*not bright or showy*) schlicht, dezent; *colour* gedeckt.

◆**sober down** *vi* ruhiger werden.

◆**sober up** 1 *vt sep* (*lit*) nüchtern machen; (*fig*) zur Vernunft bringen.

[2] *vi* (*lit*) nüchtern werden; (*fig*) ruhiger werden; (*after laughing, joking etc*) sich beruhigen.
sober-headed ['səʊbə'hedɪd] nüchtern, vernünftig.
soberly ['səʊbəlɪ] *adv* nüchtern; *behave* vernünftig; *dress, furnish* schlicht, dezent.
sober-minded ['səʊbə'maɪndɪd] *adj* nüchtern, vernünftig.
soberness ['səʊbənɪs] *n see* **sobriety**.
sobersides ['səʊbəsaɪdz] *n* (*dated inf*) Fadian *m* (*inf*).
sobriety [sə'braɪɪtɪ] *n* **(a)** (*not being drunk*) Nüchternheit *f*. **(b)** (*seriousness, sedateness*) Solidität *f*; (*of dress etc*) Schlichtheit, Dezentheit *f*; (*of colour*) Gedecktheit *f*.
sobriquet ['səʊbrɪkeɪ], **soubriquet** *n* Spitzname *m*.
sob: **~-sister** *n* (*esp US inf*) Briefkastentante *f* (*inf*); **~-story** *n* (*inf*) rührselige Geschichte (*inf*); **~-stuff** *n* (*inf*) Schmalz *m* (*inf*); (*book, film*) Tränendrüsendrücker *m* (*inf*); (*heart-rending tale*) todtraurige Geschichte (*inf*).
soc *abbr of* **society** Ges.
Soc *abbr of* **Socialist** Soz.
so-called ['səʊ'kɔːld] *adj* sogenannt; (*supposed*) angeblich.
soccer ['sɒkəʳ] *n* Fußball *m* ◆ **~ player** Fußballer, Fußballspieler(in *f*) *m*.
sociability [,səʊʃə'bɪlɪtɪ] *n* Geselligkeit *f*.
sociable ['səʊʃəbl] *adj* (*gregarious*) gesellig; (*friendly*) freundlich ◆ **... just to be ~** ..., man möchte sich ja nicht ausschließen; **I'm not feeling very ~ today** mir ist heute nicht nach Geselligkeit (zumute).
sociably ['səʊʃəblɪ] *adv invite, say* freundlich ◆ **he didn't behave very ~** er war nicht gerade umgänglich; **to be ~ inclined** ein geselliger Mensch sein.
social ['səʊʃəl] [1] *adj* **(a)** (*relating to community, Admin, Pol*) sozial; *history, reform, legislation, policy* Sozial-; *evils* der Gesellschaft; *order, system, realism* Gesellschafts-, Sozial-; *structure, development, conditions also* gesellschaftlich ◆ **the ~ services** die Sozialeinrichtungen *pl*; **the ~ contract** (*Hist*) der Gesellschaftsvertrag; **to suffer from ~ deprivation** sozial benachteiligt sein.
(b) *engagements, pleasures, ambitions, life, equal, superior* gesellschaftlich; *behaviour* in Gesellschaft; *distinctions, advancement, rank, status also* sozial ◆ **~ class** gesellschaftliche Klasse, Gesellschaftsklasse *f*; **~ climber** Emporkömmling *m* (*pej*), sozialer Aufsteiger; **~ snobbery** Standesdünkel *m*; **to be sb's ~ inferior/superior** gesellschaftlich unter/über jdm stehen; **a room for ~ functions** ein Gesellschaftsraum *m*; (*larger*) ein Saal *m* für Gesellschaften; **there isn't much ~ life around here** hier in der Gegend wird gesellschaftlich nicht viel geboten; **how's your ~ life these days?** (*inf*) und was treibst du so privat? (*inf*); **a job which leaves no time for one's/a ~ life** ein Beruf, bei dem man keine Freizeit *or* kein Privatleben hat.
(c) (*gregarious*) *evening, person* gesellig; (*living in groups*) *animals, bees, ants etc* gesellig lebend, sozial ◆ **man is a ~ animal** der Mensch ist ein Gesellschaftswesen.
[2] *n* geselliger Abend.
social: **~ anthropology** *n* Sozialanthropologie *f*; **S~ Chapter** *n* (*Pol*) Sozialcharta *f*; **~ club** *n* Verein *m*, Klub *m* für geselliges Beisammensein; **~ column** *n* Gesellschaftsspalte *f*; **~ democrat** *n* Sozialdemokrat(in *f*) *m*; **~ democratic** *adj* sozialdemokratisch; **~ disease** *n* **(a)** (*euph: VD*) Geschlechtskrankheit *f*; **(b)** (*caused by ~ conditions*) Volksseuche *f*; **~ insurance** *n* Sozialversicherung *f*.
socialism ['səʊʃəlɪzəm] *n* Sozialismus *m*.
socialist ['səʊʃəlɪst] [1] *adj* sozialistisch.
[2] *n* Sozialist(in *f*) *m*.
socialistic [,səʊʃə'lɪstɪk] *adj* (*esp pej*) sozialistisch angehaucht.
socialite ['səʊʃəlaɪt] *n* (*inf*) Angehörige(r) *mf* der Schickeria *or* der feinen Gesellschaft; (*man also*) Salonlöwe *m* (*inf*) ◆ **a London ~** eine Figur der Londoner Schickeria.
socialization [,səʊʃəlaɪ'zeɪʃən] *n* (*Pol*) Vergesellschaftung, Sozialisierung *f*; (*Sociol, Psych*) Sozialisation *f*.
socialize ['səʊʃəlaɪz] [1] *vt* sozialisieren; *means of production* vergesellschaften.
[2] *vi* **to ~ with sb** (*meet socially*) mit jdm gesellschaftlich verkehren; (*chat to*) sich mit jdm unterhalten; **I don't ~ much these days** ich komme zur Zeit nicht viel unter die Leute; **she ~s a lot** sie hat ein reges gesellschaftliches Leben.
socially ['səʊʃəlɪ] *adv see adj* **(a)** gesellschaftlich; *deprived, structured etc* sozial. **(b)** gesellschaftlich; *meet* privat.
social: **~ science** *n* Sozialwissenschaft *f*; **~ scientist** *n* Sozialwissenschaftler(in *f*) *m*; **~ secretary** *n* persönlicher Sekretär, persönliche Sekretärin; (*of club*) Veranstaltungsklubwart *m*; **~ security** *n* Sozialhilfe *f*; (*scheme*) Sozialversicherung *f*; (*~ security office*) Sozialamt *nt*; **to be on ~ security** Sozialhilfeempfänger sein; **~ services** *npl* Sozialdienste *pl*, soziale Einrichtungen *pl*; **~ studies** *n sing or pl* Sozialwissenschaften *pl*; **~ welfare** *n* soziales Wohl; **~ work** *n* Sozialarbeit *f*; **~ worker** *n* Sozialarbeiter(in *f*) *m*.
societal [sə'saɪətl] *adj* gesellschaftlich.
society [sə'saɪətɪ] *n* **(a)** (*social community*) die Gesellschaft ◆ **modern industrial ~** die moderne Industriegesellschaft.
(b) (*company*) Gesellschaft *f* ◆ **I enjoy her ~** (*esp Liter*) ich bin gerne in ihrer Gesellschaft; **everyone needs human ~** jeder braucht die Gesellschaft anderer Menschen.
(c) (*high ~*) die Gesellschaft ◆ **London ~** die Londoner Gesellschaft, die gesellschaftlichen Kreise Londons; **to go into ~** in die Gesellschaft eingeführt werden; **the years she spent in ~** die Jahre, die sie in gesellschaftlichen *or* feinen Kreisen verbracht hat.
(d) (*club, organization*) Verein *m*; (*learned, Comm*) Gesellschaft *f*; (*debating, history, dramatic etc*) (*Sch*) Arbeitsgemeinschaft *f*; (*Univ*) Klub *m* ◆ **S~ for the Prevention of Cruelty to Animals/Children** Tierschutzverein *m*/ Kinderschutzbund *m*; **cooperative ~** Genossenschaft *f*; **S~ of Jesus** Gesellschaft Jesu.
society *in cpds* Gesellschafts-; **~ column** *n* Gesellschaftsspalte *f*; **~ gossip** *n* Gesellschaftsklatsch *m*; **~ man** *n* Mann *m* der Gesellschaft; **~ wedding** *n* Hochzeit *f* in den besseren Kreisen.
socio- [,səʊsɪəʊ-] *pref* sozio- ◆ **~economic** sozioökonomisch; **~economic grouping** sozioökonomische Gruppe; **~linguistic** soziolinguistisch; **~linguistics** Soziolinguistik *f*.
sociological *adj*, **~ly** *adv* [,səʊsɪə'lɒdʒɪkəl, -ɪ] soziologisch.
sociologist [,səʊsɪ'ɒlədʒɪst] *n* Soziologe *m*, Soziologin *f*.
sociology [,səʊsɪ'ɒlədʒɪ] *n* Soziologie *f*.
sociopolitical [,səʊsɪəʊpə'lɪtɪkəl] *adj* sozialpolitisch.
sock¹ [sɒk] *n* Socke *f*, Socken *m* (*inf*); (*knee-length*) Kniestrumpf *m*; (*insole*) Einlegesohle *f*; (*wind ~*) Wind- *or* Luftsack *m* ◆ **to pull one's ~s up** (*inf*) sich am Riemen reißen (*inf*); **put a ~ in it!** (*Brit inf*) hör auf!
sock² [1] *n* (*inf*) Schlag *m* (mit der Faust) ◆ **to give sb a ~ on the jaw/in the eye** jdm eine aufs Kinn/aufs Auge verpassen (*inf*).
[2] *vt* **(a)** (*inf: hit*) hauen (*inf*) ◆ **~ him one!** knall ihm eine! (*inf*), hau ihm eine rein! (*sl*); **he ~ed her right in the eye** er verpaßte ihr eine aufs Auge (*inf*).
(b) (*sl*) **~ it to me** dreh/dreht auf (*sl*).
socket ['sɒkɪt] *n* **(a)** (*of eye*) Augenhöhle *f*; (*of joint*) Gelenkpfanne *f*; (*of tooth*) Zahnhöhle *f* ◆ **to pull sb's arm out of its ~** jdm den Arm auskugeln. **(b)** (*Elec*) Steckdose *f*; (*for lightbulb*) Fassung *f*; (*Mech*) Sockel *m*, Fassung *f*.
socko ['sɒkəʊ] (*US inf*) [1] *n* (*great success*) Bombenerfolg *m* (*inf*).
[2] *adj* (*great*) bombig (*inf*).
Socrates ['sɒkrətiːz] *n* Sokrates *m*.
Socratic [sɒ'krætɪk] *adj* sokratisch.
sod¹ [sɒd] *n* (*turf*) Grassode *f* ◆ **beneath the ~** (*liter*) unter dem grünen Rasen (*liter*).
sod² (*Brit sl*) [1] *n* (*mean, nasty*) Sau *f* (*sl*) ◆ **the poor ~s** die armen Schweine (*inf*); **you stupid ~** blöde Sau! (*sl*).
[2] *vt* **~ it!** verdammte Scheiße! (*sl*); **~ him/you** der kann/du kannst mich mal (am Arsch lecken *vulg*)! (*sl*).
◆**sod off** *vi* (*Brit sl*) Leine ziehen (*sl*) ◆ **~ ~!** zieh Leine, du Arsch! (*sl*).
soda ['səʊdə] *n* **(a)** (*Chem*) Soda *nt*; (*sodium oxide*) Natriumoxyd *nt*; (*caustic ~*) Ätznatron *nt*. **(b)** (*drink*) Soda(wasser) *nt*.
soda: **~ biscuit**, (*US*) **~ cracker** *n* Cracker *m*; **~ bread** *n mit Backpulver gebackenes Brot*; **~ crystals** *npl* (Wasch)soda *nt*; **~-fountain** *n* (*US: café*) Erfrischungshalle *f*.
sod-all [,sɒd'ɔːl] [1] *n* (*sl: nothing*) rein gar nichts ◆ **how much did he give you? — ~** wieviel hat er dir gegeben? — Null Komma nichts (*inf*).
soda: **~ siphon** *n* Siphon *m*; **~-water** *n* Sodawasser *nt*.
sodden ['sɒdn] *adj* durchnäßt, triefnaß; *ground* durchnäßt, durchweicht ◆ **to be ~ with drink** sinnlos betrunken sein.
sodding ['sɒdɪŋ] *adj* (*Brit sl*) verflucht (*inf*), Scheiß- (*sl*) ◆ **what a ~ nuisance** verdammte Scheiße (*sl*).
sodium ['səʊdɪəm] *n* Natrium *nt*.
sodium: **~ bicarbonate** *n* Natron *nt*, doppeltkohlensaures Natrium; **~ carbonate** *n* Natriumkarbonat, Soda *nt*; **~ chloride** *n* Natriumchlorid, Kochsalz *nt*; **~ hydroxide** *n* Natriumhydroxid, Ätznatron *nt*; **~ nitrate** *n* Natriumnitrat *nt*.
Sodom ['sɒdəm] *n* Sodom *nt* ◆ **~ and Gomorrha** Sodom und Gomorr(h)a.
sodomite ['sɒdəmaɪt] *n jd, der Analverkehr betreibt*.
sodomy ['sɒdəmɪ] *n* Analverkehr *m*.
Sod's law ['sɒdz,lɔː] *n* (*inf*) „Gesetz" *nt, demzufolge eine Sache, die schiefgehen kann, auch bestimmt schiefgehen wird* ◆ **after all that it didn't work — that's ~, isn't it?** am Ende hat es noch nicht mal funktioniert — das mußte ja so kommen.
sofa ['səʊfə] *n* Sofa *nt*, Couch *f* ◆ **~ bed** Sofabett *nt*, Schlafcouch *f*.
soft [sɒft] *adj* (*+er*) **(a)** weich; *meat* zart; (*pej: flabby*) *muscle* schlaff ◆ **a photo taken in ~ focus** ein Foto mit weichen Kontrasten; **~-focus lens** Weichzeichner *m*; **a book in ~ covers** ein kartoniertes Buch; **~ cheese** Weichkäse *m*; **~ ice-cream** Softeis *nt*.
(b) (*smooth*) *skin* zart; *surface* glatt; *material, velvet* weich; *hair* seidig ◆ **as ~ as silk** seidenweich.
(c) (*gentle, not harsh*) sanft; (*subdued*) *light, sound also, music* gedämpft; (*not loud*) leise; *rain, breeze, tap, pressure also* leicht; *steps* leicht, leise; *heart* weich.
(d) (*Ling*) *consonant* weich.
(e) (*weak*) *character, government* schwach; *treatment* nachsichtig; (*lenient*) *teacher, parent* nachsichtig, gutmütig; *judge, punishment* mild(e) ◆ **to be ~ with** *or* **on sb** jdm gegenüber nachgiebig sein; *with children also* jdm alles durchgehen lassen.
(f) (*not tough*) verweichlicht ◆ **he thinks it's ~ for a boy to play the violin** er hält es für unmännlich, wenn ein Junge Geige spielt; **to make sb ~** jdn verweichlichen.
(g) (*easy*) *job, life* bequem ◆ **he has a ~ time of it** er hat's leicht *or* bequem; **that's a ~ option** das ist der Weg des geringsten Widerstandes.
(h) *currency* weich.
(i) *drink* alkoholfrei; *drug, pornography* weich.
(j) (*Typ, Comput*) *return, hyphen* weich.
(k) (*inf: foolish*) doof (*inf*), nicht ganz richtig im Kopf (*inf*) ◆ **he's ~ (in the head)** er ist nicht ganz richtig im Kopf (*inf*); **you must be ~!** du spinnst wohl! (*inf*); **I must be going ~** ich fange wohl an zu spinnen (*inf*).
(l) (*inf: feeling affection*) **to be ~ on sb** für jdn schwärmen; **to have a ~ spot**

for sb eine Schwäche für jdn haben.

soft: ~ball *n (US)* Softball *m*; **~-boiled** *adj egg* weich(gekocht); **~-centred** *adj* mit Cremefüllung; **~-core** *adj pornography* weich.

soften ['sɒfn] 1 *vt* weich machen; *water also* enthärten; *light, sound, colour* dämpfen; *effect, sb's anger, reaction, impression* mildern; *outline* weicher machen; *resistance* schwächen; *person* verweichlichen ◆ **to ~ the blow** *(fig)* den Schock mildern.
2 *vi (material, person, heart)* weich werden; *(voice, look)* sanft werden; *(anger, resistance)* nachlassen; *(outlines)* weicher werden.

◆**soften up** 1 *vt sep* **(a)** weich machen.
(b) *(fig) person, opposition* milde stimmen; *(by flattery etc)* schmeicheln (+*dat*); *customer* kaufwillig stimmen; *(by bullying)* einschüchtern, weichmachen; *enemy, resistance* zermürben; *enemy position* schwächen; *prisoner* weichmachen.
2 *vi (material)* weich werden; *(person, attitude)* nachgiebiger werden ◆ **to ~ ~ on sb** jdm gegenüber nachgiebig *or* schwach werden.

softener ['sɒfnəʳ] *n* Weichmacher *m*; *(for water also)* Enthärtungsmittel *nt*; *(fabric ~)* Weichspüler *m*, Weichspülmittel *nt*.

softening ['sɒfnɪŋ] *n* **(a)** *see vt* Weichmachen *nt*; Enthärten *nt*; Dämpfen *nt*; Mildern *nt*; Weichermachen *nt*; Schwächung *f*; Verweichlichung *f*.
(b) *see vi* Erweichen *nt*; Nachlassen *nt*; Weicherwerden *nt* ◆ **~ of the brain** *(Med)* Gehirnerweichung *f*; **there has been a ~ of his attitude** er ist nachgiebiger geworden.

soft: ~-footed *adj tiger, person* auf leisen Sohlen schleichend *attr*; *tread* leise, lautlos; **to be ~-footed** leise gehen; **~ fruit** *n* Beerenobst *nt*; **~ furnishings** *npl (Brit) Vorhänge, Teppiche, Kissen etc*; **~-headed** *adj (inf)* doof *(inf)*; **~-hearted** *adj* weichherzig; **~-heartedness** *n* Weichherzigkeit *f*.

softie ['sɒftɪ] *n (inf) (too tender-hearted)* gutmütiger Trottel *(inf)*; *(sentimental)* sentimentaler Typ *(inf)*; *(effeminate, cowardly)* Schlappschwanz *(inf)*, Weichling *(inf) m* ◆ **I know I'm an old ~ but ...** ich bin ja ein gutmütiger Typ *or* Mensch, aber ...

softkey ['sɒftki:] *n (Comput)* Softkey *m*.

softly ['sɒftlɪ] *adv* **(a)** *(gently, tenderly)* sanft; *(not loud)* leise; *rain, blow* leicht, sacht ◆ **her hair falls ~ round her shoulders** ihr Haar fällt weich auf die Schultern; **a ~ blowing breeze** ein sanfter *or* schwacher Wind. **(b)** *(leniently)* nachsichtig.

softness ['sɒftnɪs] *n see adj* **(a)** Weichheit *f*; Zartheit *f*; Schlaffheit *f*. **(b)** Zartheit *f*; Glätte *f*; Weichheit *f*; Seidigkeit *f*. **(c)** Sanftheit *f*; Gedämpftheit *f*; leiser Klang; Leichtheit *f*; Weichheit *f*. **(d)** Weichheit *f*. **(e)** Schwäche *f*; Nachsichtigkeit *f*; Gutmütigkeit *f*; Milde *f*. **(f)** Verweichlichung *f*. **(g)** Bequemlichkeit *f*. **(h)** Weichheit *f*.

soft: ~ palate *n* weicher Gaumen; **~-pedal** 1 *vt (Mus) note, passage* mit Dämpfer spielen; *(fig inf) demands etc* herunterschrauben; 2 *vi* zurückstecken; **~-sectored** *adj (Comput)* softsektoriert; **~ sell** *n* Softsell *m*, weiche Verkaufstaktik; **he's a master of the ~ sell** er kann die Leute auf sanfte Art *or* auf die sanfte Tour *(inf)* überreden; **~-shelled** *adj* weichschalig; **~-soap** *(fig)* 1 *n* Schmeichelei *f*; 2 *vt* einseifen *(inf)*, um den Bart gehen (+*dat*); **they ~-soaped him into doing it** sie sind ihm so lange um den Bart gegangen, bis er es getan hat *(inf)*; **~-spoken** *adj person* leise sprechend *attr*; **to be ~-spoken** leise sprechen; **~ target** *n* leicht verwundbares Ziel; **~ toy** *n* Stofftier *nt*; **~ verges** *npl* nicht befahrbare Bankette; *(on sign)* Seitenstreifen nicht befahrbar; **~ware** *n* Software *f*; **~ware company** *n* Softwarehaus *nt*; **~ware-controlled** *adj* softwaregesteuert; **~ware package** *n* Softwarepaket *nt*; **~ wood** *n* Weichholz *nt*.

softy *n (inf) see* **softie**.

SOGAT ['səʊgæt] *(Brit) abbr of* **Society of Graphical and Allied Trades** *britische Grafikergewerkschaft*.

sogginess ['sɒgɪnɪs] *n see adj* triefende Nässe; Aufgeweichtheit *f*; Matschigkeit *f (inf)*; Klitschigkeit *f*.

soggy ['sɒgɪ] *adj* (+*er*) durchnäßt, triefnaß; *soil* durchweicht; *food* matschig *(inf)*; *cake, bread* klitschig, matschig *(inf)*.

soi-disant [ˌswɑ:'di:zɑ:ŋ] *adj* sogenannt, angeblich.

soigné ['swɑ:njeɪ] *adj* gepflegt, soigniert *(geh)*.

soil¹ [sɔɪl] *n (earth, ground)* Erde *f*, Erdreich *nt*, Boden *m* ◆ **cover it with ~** bedecken Sie es mit Erde; **native/foreign/British ~** heimatlicher/fremder/britischer Boden, heimatliche/fremde britische Erde; **the ~** *(fig: farmland)* die Scholle; **a man of the ~** ein mit der Scholle verwachsener Mensch.

soil² 1 *vt (lit)* beschmutzen, schmutzig machen; *(fig) reputation* beschmutzen, beflecken; *honour* beflecken; *oneself* besudeln; *minds* verderben ◆ **the baby has ~ed its nappy** das Baby hat eine schmutzige Windel *or* hat in die Windel gemacht.
2 *vi* schmutzig werden, verschmutzen.

soiled [sɔɪld] *adj* schmutzig, verschmutzt; *sanitary towel* gebraucht ◆ **~ linen** Schmutzwäsche *f*.

soil-pipe ['sɔɪlpaɪp] *n* Abflußrohr *nt*.

soirée ['swɑ:reɪ] *n (form)* Soirée *f (geh)*.

soixante-neuf ['swæsɑ:nt'nɜ:f] *n* Neunundsechzig, Soixante-neuf *no art*.

sojourn ['sɒdʒɜ:n] 1 *n (liter)* Aufenthalt *m*; *(place)* Aufenthaltsort *m*.
2 *vi* (ver)weilen *(liter)* (*in* in +*dat*).

solace ['sɒlɪs] 1 *n* Trost *m*.
2 *vt* trösten.

solar ['səʊləʳ] *adj* Sonnen-, Solar- ◆ **~ battery** Sonnen- *or* Solarbatterie *f*; **~ cell** Solarzelle *f*; **~ constant** Solarkonstante *f*; **~ eclipse** Sonnenfinsternis *f*; **~ energy** Sonnenenergie *f*; **~ heat** Sonnenwärme *f*; **~ heating** Solarheizung *f*; **~ panel** Sonnenkollektor *m*; **~ plexus** Solarplexus *m (spec)*, Magengrube *f*; **~ power** Sonnenkraft *f*; **~ system** Sonnensystem *nt*.

solarium [səʊ'lɛərɪəm] *n, pl* **solaria** [səʊ'lɛərɪə] Solarium *nt*.

sold [səʊld] *pret, ptp of* **sell**.

solder ['səʊldəʳ] 1 *n* Lötmittel, Lötzinn *nt*.
2 *vt* löten; (*~ together*) verlöten ◆ **~ed joint** Lötstelle *f*.

soldering-iron ['səʊldərɪŋ'aɪən] *n* Lötkolben *m*.

soldier ['səʊldʒəʳ] 1 *n* **(a)** Soldat *m* ◆ **~ of fortune** Söldner *m*; **to play (at) ~s** Soldaten *or* Krieg spielen; **old ~** altgedienter Soldat; *(fig)* alter Kämpe; **old ~s never die(, they only fade away)** *(prov)* manche Leute sind nicht totzukriegen *(inf)*.
(b) *(Zool)* Soldat *m*.
2 *vi* Soldat sein, (in der Armee) dienen ◆ **after 6 years' ~ing** nach 6 Jahren Dienst in der Armee; **tired of ~ing** des Soldatenlebens müde.

◆**soldier on** *vi* unermüdlich weitermachen ◆ **two of them ~ed ~ to the top** zwei kämpften sich bis zum Gipfel vor.

soldierly ['səʊldʒəlɪ] *adj* soldatisch.

soldiery ['səʊldʒərɪ] *n* Soldaten *pl*, Soldateska *f (pej geh)*.

sole¹ [səʊl] 1 *n* Sohle *f*.
2 *vt* besohlen.

sole² *n (fish)* Seezunge *f*.

sole³ *adj* einzig; *heir also* Allein-.

sole: ~ agency *n* Alleinvertretung *f*; **~ agent** *n* Alleinvertreter(in *f*) *m*.

solecism ['sɒləsɪzəm] *n (linguistic)* Solözismus *(geh)*, Fehler *m*; *(in behaviour etc)* Fauxpas *m*.

-soled [-səʊld] *adj suf* mit ... Sohlen.

solely ['səʊllɪ] *adv* (einzig und) allein, nur ◆ **he is ~ responsible** er allein trägt die Verantwortung, er ist allein verantwortlich; **~ because of this ...** nur *or* allein deswegen ...

solemn ['sɒləm] *adj* feierlich; *face, mood, music also, person, plea, warning* ernst; *prose also, architecture* ehrwürdig, erhaben; *promise, duty, oath* heilig; *(drab) colour* trist ◆ **I give you my ~ assurance** ich verspreche es hoch und heilig.

solemnity [sə'lemnɪtɪ] *n see adj* Feierlichkeit *f*; Ernst *m*; Ehrwürdigkeit, Erhabenheit *f*; heiliger Ernst; Tristheit *f* ◆ **with all ~** feierlich (und würdig).

solemnization [ˌsɒləmnaɪ'zeɪʃən] *n* feierlicher Vollzug.

solemnize ['sɒləmnaɪz] *vt* feierlich begehen; *marriage* (feierlich) vollziehen.

solemnly ['sɒləmlɪ] *adv* feierlich; *walk* gemessenen Schrittes, würdevoll; *look, warn, plead* ernst; *promise* hoch und heilig; *swear* bei allem, was einem heilig ist.

solenoid ['səʊlənɔɪd] *n* Magnetspule *f* ◆ **~ switch** Magnetschalter *m*.

sole: ~ rights *npl* Alleinrechte *pl*; **~ trader** *n* Einzelunternehmer, Einzelkaufmann *m*.

solfa ['sɒl'fɑ:] *n* Solmisation *f*.

solicit [sə'lɪsɪt] 1 *vt support etc* erbitten, bitten um; *person* anflehen, inständig bitten; *votes* werben; *(prostitute)* ansprechen ◆ **to ~ sb for sth, to ~ sth of sb** jdn um etw bitten, etw von jdm erbitten; **to ~ custom/trade** um Kunden werben.
2 *vi (prostitute)* Kunden anwerben, zur Unzucht auffordern *(form)* ◆ **~ing** Aufforderung *f* zur Unzucht.

solicitation [səˌlɪsɪ'teɪʃən] *n (form)* Flehen *nt no pl (geh)*.

solicitor [sə'lɪsɪtəʳ] *n (Jur) (Brit)* Rechtsanwalt *m*/-anwältin *f (der/die normalerweise nicht vor Gericht plädiert)*; *(US)* Justizbeamte(r) *m*/-beamtin *f* ◆ **S~ General** *(Brit)* zweiter Kronanwalt; *(US)* ≃ Generalstaatsanwalt *m*.

solicitous [sə'lɪsɪtəs] *adj (form) (concerned)* besorgt (*about* um); *(eager)* dienstbeflissen ◆ **to be ~ to do sth** eifrig darauf bedacht sein, etw zu tun.

solicitude [sə'lɪsɪtju:d] *n see adj (form)* Besorgtheit *f*; Dienstbeflissenheit *f*.

solid ['sɒlɪd] 1 *adj* **(a)** *(firm, not liquid) fuel, food, substance* fest ◆ **~ body** Festkörper *m*; **to be frozen ~** hartgefroren sein; **to be stuck ~** festsitzen; **the soup/pudding is rather ~** die Suppe ist ziemlich dick/der Nachtisch ist ziemlich schwer; **~ figure** *(Geometry)* Körper *m*; **~ geometry** Raumlehre *f*.
(b) *(pure, not hollow, not broken) block, gold, oak, rock* massiv; *matter* fest; *crowd etc* dicht; *stretch, row, line* ununterbrochen; *queue, line of people etc* geschlossen; *week* ganz ◆ **~ ball/tyre** Vollgummiball *m*/-reifen *m*; **the square was packed ~ with cars** die Autos standen dicht an dicht auf dem Platz; **the garden was a ~ mass of colour** der Garten war ein einziges Farbenmeer; **they worked for two ~ days** *or* **for two days ~** sie haben zwei Tage ununterbrochen gearbeitet, sie haben zwei volle Tage gearbeitet; **he was 6 ft of ~ muscle** er war 2 Meter groß und bestand nur aus Muskeln; **a man of ~ build** ein kräftig *or* massiv gebauter Mann.
(c) *(stable, secure) bridge, house, car* stabil; *furniture also, piece of work, character* solide; *foundations also, (lit, fig) ground* fest; *business, firm* gesund, solide, reell ◆ **he's a good ~ worker** er ist ein solider *or* guter Arbeiter; **he's a good ~ bloke** er ist ein verläßlicher Kerl.
(d) *reason, argument* handfest, stichhaltig; *grounds* gut, fundiert ◆ **it makes ~ good sense** das leuchtet durchaus ein; **~ common sense** gesunder Menschenverstand.
(e) *(unanimous) vote* einstimmig; *support* voll, geschlossen ◆ **to be ~ on sth** *(accept/reject)* etw einstimmig *or* geschlossen annehmen/ablehnen; **we are ~ behind you/that proposal** wir stehen voll und ganz hinter Ihnen/diesem Vorschlag; **we are ~ for peace** wir sind hundertprozentig für den Frieden; **Newtown/he is ~ for Labour** Newtown wählt fast ausschließlich Labour/er ist überzeugter Labour-Anhänger.
(f) *(valuable, substantial) education, knowledge, grounding* solide; *relationship* stabil; *meal* kräftig, nahrhaft.
(g) *(not hyphenated)* **to be written ~** zusammengeschrieben werden.
2 *n* **(a)** fester Stoff ◆ **~s and liquids** feste und flüssige Stoffe *pl*; *(Sci)* Fest-

körper und Flüssigkeiten *pl.* **(b)** (*Geometry*) Körper *m.* **(c)** (*usu pl: food*) feste Nahrung *no pl.*

solidarity [ˌsɒlɪˈdærɪtɪ] *n* Solidarität *f.*

solid fuel *n* fester Brennstoff; (*for rockets*) Feststoff *m.*

solidification [səˌlɪdɪfɪˈkeɪʃən] *n see vi* Festwerden *nt,* Verfestigung *f;* Erstarrung *f;* Erhärtung *f;* Gerinnung *f;* Festigung *f.*

solidify [səˈlɪdɪfaɪ] **1** *vi* fest werden; (*planet, lava etc*) erstarren; (*metal also*) hart werden; (*blood*) gerinnen; (*fig: support*) sich festigen.
2 *vt see vi* fest werden lassen; erstarren lassen; hart werden lassen; gerinnen lassen; festigen.

solidity [səˈlɪdɪtɪ] *n see adj* **(a)** Festigkeit *f.*
(b) Massivität *f;* Festigkeit *f;* Dichtheit *f.*
(c) Stabilität *f;* solide Art; Festigkeit *f;* Solidität *f.*
(d) Handfestigkeit, Stichhaltigkeit *f;* Fundiertheit *f.*
(e) Einstimmigkeit *f;* Geschlossenheit *f.*
(f) Solidität *f;* Stabilität *f;* Kräftigkeit *f.*

solidly [ˈsɒlɪdlɪ] *adv* **(a)** (*firmly*) *stuck, secured* fest ◆ **~ built** *house* fest *or* solide gebaut; *person* kräftig *or* massiv gebaut.
(b) *reasoned, argued* stichhaltig.
(c) (*uninterruptedly*) *work* ununterbrochen.
(d) (*unanimous*) *vote* einstimmig; *support* geschlossen ◆ **to be ~ behind sb** geschlossen hinter jdm stehen.

solid-state [ˈsɒlɪdˈsteɪt] *adj* Festkörper-; (*Elec*) Halbleiter-.

soliloquize [səˈlɪləkwaɪz] **1** *vi* monologisieren; (*talk to oneself*) Selbstgespräche führen.
2 *vt* zu sich selbst sagen.

soliloquy [səˈlɪləkwɪ] *n* Monolog *m* (*also Theat*), Zwiegespräch *nt* mit sich selbst.

solipsism [ˈsɒlɪpsɪzəm] *n* Solipsismus *m.*

solipsist [ˈsɒlɪpsɪst] *n* Solipsist(in *f*) *m.*

solipsistic [ˌsɒlɪpˈsɪstɪk] *adj* solipsistisch.

solitaire [ˌsɒlɪˈtɛəʳ] *n* (*game*) Patience *f;* (*gem*) Solitär *m.*

solitary [ˈsɒlɪtərɪ] **1** *adj* **(a)** (*alone, secluded*) *life, person* einsam; *place also* abgelegen, abgeschieden ◆ **a few ~ houses** ein paar einzelne *or* vereinzelte Häuser; **to take a ~ walk** allein einen Spaziergang machen; **do you enjoy this ~ life?** gefällt Ihnen das Leben so allein?; **a ~ person** ein Einzelgänger *m;* **in ~ confinement** in Einzelhaft.
(b) (*sole*) *case, example* einzig ◆ **not a ~ one** kein einziger.
2 *n* (*~ confinement*) Einzelhaft *f.*

solitude [ˈsɒlɪtjuːd] *n* Einsamkeit *f;* (*of place also*) Abgelegenheit, Abgeschiedenheit *f.*

solo [ˈsəʊləʊ] **1** *n* Solo *nt.*
2 *adj flight* Allein-; *violinist, violin* Solo-.
3 *adv* allein; (*Mus*) solo ◆ **to fly ~** einen Alleinflug machen.

soloist [ˈsəʊləʊɪst] *n* Solist(in *f*) *m.*

Solomon [ˈsɒləmən] *n* Salomo(n) *m* ◆ **the ~ Islands** die Salomonen *pl.*

solstice [ˈsɒlstɪs] *n* Sonnenwende *f,* Solstitium *nt* (*spec*).

solubility [ˌsɒljʊˈbɪlɪtɪ] *n see adj* **(a)** Löslichkeit *f.* **(b)** Lösbarkeit *f.*

soluble [ˈsɒljʊbl] *adj* **(a)** löslich, auflösbar ◆ **~ in water** wasserlöslich. **(b)** *problem* lösbar.

▼ **solution** [səˈluːʃən] *n* **(a)** Lösung *f* (*to gen*); (*of crime*) Aufklärung *f* ◆ **a problem incapable of ~** ein unlösbares Problem. **(b)** (*Chem*) (*liquid*) Lösung *f;* (*act*) Auflösen *nt.*

solvable [ˈsɒlvəbl] *adj see* **soluble**.

solve [sɒlv] *vt problem, equation* lösen; *mystery* enträtseln; *crime, murder* aufklären ◆ **that question remains to be ~d** diese Frage muß noch geklärt werden.

solvency [ˈsɒlvənsɪ] *n* (*Fin*) Zahlungsfähigkeit, Solvenz *f.*

solvent [ˈsɒlvənt] **1** *adj* **(a)** (*Chem*) lösend; *agent* Lösungs-. **(b)** (*Fin*) zahlungsfähig, solvent.
2 *n* (*Chem*) Lösungsmittel *nt* ◆ **~ abuse** Lösungsmittelmißbrauch *m;* **~ abuser** Schnüffler(in *f*) *m* (*inf*).

Somali [səʊˈmɑːlɪ] **1** *adj* somali.
2 *n* Somali *mf,* Somalier(in *f*) *m.*

Somalia [səʊˈmɑːlɪə] *n* Somalia *nt.*

Somaliland [səʊˈmɑːlɪlænd] *n* Somaliland *nt.*

somatic [səʊˈmætɪk] *adj* somatisch.

sombre, (*US*) **somber** [ˈsɒmbəʳ] *adj* **(a)** (*dark*) dunkel; (*gloomy*) düster. **(b)** *mood, prospect* trüb, düster; *face* düster; *person* düster, finster; *music* trist, trauervoll.

sombrely, (*US*) **somberly** [ˈsɒmbəlɪ] *adv see adj.*

sombreness, (*US*) **somberness** [ˈsɒmbənɪs] *n see adj* **(a)** Dunkelheit *f;* Düsterkeit *f.* **(b)** Trübheit *f;* Düsterkeit *f;* finsteres *or* düsteres Wesen; trauervoller *or* trister Klang.

sombrero [sɒmˈbrɛərəʊ] *n* Sombrero *m.*

some [sʌm] **1** *adj* **(a)** (*with plural nouns*) einige; (*a few, emphatic*) ein paar; (*any: in "if" clauses, questions*) *meist nicht übersetzt* ◆ **if you have ~ questions** wenn Sie Fragen haben; **did you bring ~ records?** hast du Schallplatten mitgebracht?; **~ records of mine** einige meiner Platten; **would you like ~ more biscuits?** möchten Sie noch (ein paar) Kekse?; **take ~ nuts** nehmen Sie sich (*dat*) doch (ein paar) Nüsse; **~ few people** einige wenige Leute; **~ suggestions, please!** Vorschläge bitte!
(b) (*with singular nouns*) etwas, *meist nicht übersetzt;* (*a little, emph*) etwas, ein bißchen ◆ **there's ~ ink on your shirt** Sie haben Tinte auf dem Hemd; **would you like ~ cheese?** möchten Sie (etwas) Käse?; **~ more (tea)?** noch etwas (Tee)?; **leave ~ cake for me** laß mir ein bißchen *or* etwas Kuchen übrig; **did she give you ~ money/sugar?** hat sie Ihnen Geld/Zucker gegeben?; **have you got ~ money?** haben Sie Geld?; **well yes, it was ~ help** es war eine gewisse Hilfe; **we played ~ golf** wir haben ein bißchen Golf gespielt.
(c) (*certain, in contrast*) manche(r, s) ◆ **~ people say ...** manche Leute sagen ...; **~ people just don't care** es gibt Leute, denen ist das einfach egal; **there are ~ things you just don't say** es gibt (gewisse *or* manche) Dinge, die man einfach nicht sagt; **~ questions were really difficult** manche (der) Fragen waren wirklich schwierig; **~ work can be rewarding** manche Arbeit ist sehr lohnend; **~ butter is salty** manche Buttersorten sind salzig; **in ~ ways** in gewisser Weise.
(d) (*vague, indeterminate*) irgendein ◆ **~ book/man or other** irgendein Buch/Mann; **~ woman rang up** da hat eine Frau angerufen; **~ woman, whose name I forget** ... eine Frau, ich habe ihren Namen vergessen, ...; **~ idiot of a driver** irgend so ein Idiot von (einem) Autofahrer; **at ~ place in Africa** irgendwo in Afrika; **in ~ way or another** irgendwie; **or ~ such** oder so etwas ähnliches; **or ~ such name** oder so ein ähnlicher Name; **(at) ~ time before midnight/last week** irgendwann vor Mitternacht/letzte Woche; **~ time or other** irgendwann einmal; **~ other time** ein andermal; **~ day** eines Tages; **~ day next week** irgendwann nächste Woche.
(e) (*intensifier*) ziemlich; (*in exclamations*) vielleicht ein (*inf*) ◆ **it took ~ courage** dazu brauchte man schon (einigen) *or* ziemlichen Mut; **(that was) ~ argument/party!** das war vielleicht ein Streit/eine Party! (*inf*); **that's ~ whisky** das ist vielleicht ein Whisky! (*inf*); **it's ~ size!** das ist vielleicht ein Ding!; **this might take ~ time** das könnte einige Zeit dauern; **quite ~ time** ganz schön lange (*inf*), ziemlich lange; **to speak at ~ length** ziemlich lange sprechen; **it's ~ distance from the house** es ist ziemlich weit vom Haus entfernt.
(f) (*iro*) vielleicht ein (*inf*) ◆ **~ experts!** das sind vielleicht Experten! (*inf*); **~ help you are/this is** du bist/das ist mir vielleicht eine Hilfe (*inf*); **~ people!** Leute gibt's!
2 *pron* **(a)** (*~ people*) einige; (*certain people*) manche; (*in "if" clauses, questions*) welche ◆ **~ ..., others ...** manche ..., andere ...; **~ of my friends** einige *or* manche meiner Freunde; **there are still ~ who will never understand** es gibt immer noch Leute *or* welche, die das nicht begreifen werden; **~ of them were late** einige kamen zu spät.
(b) (*referring to plural nouns*) (*a few*) einige; (*certain ones*) manche; (*in "if" clauses, questions*) welche ◆ **~ of these books** einige dieser Bücher; **~ of them have been sold** einige sind verkauft worden; **I've only seen ~ of the mountains** ich habe nur ein paar von den Bergen gesehen; **they're lovely, try ~** die schmecken gut, probieren Sie mal; **I've still got ~** ich habe noch welche; **he took ~** er hat welche genommen; **tell me if you see ~** sagen Sie mir Bescheid, wenn Sie welche sehen; **would you like ~?** möchten Sie welche?
(c) (*referring to singular nouns*) (*a little*) etwas; (*a certain amount, in contrast*) manches; (*in "if" clauses, questions*) welche(r, s) ◆ **here is the milk, if you feel thirsty drink ~** hier ist die Milch, wenn du Durst hast, trinke etwas; **I drank ~ of the milk** ich habe (etwas) von der Milch getrunken; **I drank ~ of the milk but not all** ich habe etwas von der Milch getrunken, aber nicht alles; **have ~!** nehmen Sie sich (*dat*), bedienen Sie sich; **it's good cake, would you like ~?** das ist ein guter Kuchen, möchten Sie welchen?; **try ~ of this cake** probieren Sie doch mal diesen Kuchen; **would you like ~ money/tea? — no, I've got ~** möchten Sie Geld/Tee? — nein, ich habe Geld/ich habe noch; **have you got money? — no, but he has ~** haben Sie Geld? — nein, aber er hat welches; **~ of it had been eaten** einiges (davon) war gegessen worden; **he only believed/read ~ of it** er hat es nur teilweise geglaubt/gelesen; **~ of his speech was excellent** manches *or* einiges in seiner Rede war ausgezeichnet; **~ of his work is good** manches, was er macht, ist gut.
(d) this is ~ of the oldest rock in the world dies gehört zum ältesten Gestein der Welt; **~ of the finest poetry in the English language** einige der schönsten Gedichte in der englischen Sprache; **this is ~ of the finest scenery in Scotland** dies ist eine der schönsten Landschaften Schottlands.
3 *adv* **(a)** ungefähr, etwa, zirka ◆ **~ 20 people** ungefähr 20 Leute; **~ few difficulties** einige Schwierigkeiten.
(b) (*US inf*) (*a little*) etwas, ein bißchen; (*a lot*) viel ◆ **it sure bothered us ~** das hat uns ziemlich zu schaffen gemacht; **he's travelling ~** er fährt schnell; **I really drank ~ last night** ich habe gestern abend ganz schön was getrunken (*inf*); **that's going ~** das ist ganz schön schnell (*inf*).

somebody [ˈsʌmbədɪ] **1** *pron* jemand; (*dir obj*) jemand(en); (*indir obj*) jemandem ◆ **~ else** jemand anders; **~ or other** irgend jemand; **~ knocked at the door** es klopfte jemand an die Tür; **we need ~ German** wir brauchen einen Deutschen; **everybody needs ~ to talk to** jeder braucht einen, mit dem er sprechen kann; **~ or other** irgend jemand; **you must have seen somebody** Sie müssen doch irgend jemand(en) gesehen haben.
2 *n* **to be (a) ~** etwas vorstellen, wer (*inf*) *or* jemand sein; **he thinks he's ~ now** er bildet sich (*dat*) ein, er wäre jetzt jemand *or* wer (*inf*).

somehow [ˈsʌmhaʊ] *adv* irgendwie ◆ **it must be done ~ or other** es muß irgendwie gemacht werden; **~ (or other) I never liked him** irgendwie habe ich ihn nie gemocht *or* leiden können.

someone [ˈsʌmwʌn] *pron see* **somebody 1**.

someplace [ˈsʌmpleɪs] *adv* (*US inf*) *be* irgendwo; *go* irgendwohin.

somersault [ˈsʌməsɔːlt] **1** *n* Purzelbaum *m;* (*Sport, fig*) Salto *m* ◆ **to do** *or* **turn a ~** einen Purzelbaum schlagen/einen Salto machen; (*car*) sich überschlagen, einen Salto machen (*inf*).
2 *vi* (*person*) einen Purzelbaum schlagen; (*Sport*) einen Salto machen; (*car*)

➤ LANGUAGE IN USE: **solution: a → 26.3**

sich überschlagen, einen Salto machen (*inf*) ◆ **the car ~ed into a lamppost** das Auto hat sich überschlagen und ist gegen einen Laternenpfahl geprallt.

something ['sʌmθɪŋ] 1 *pron* **(a)** etwas ◆ **~ nice/unpleasant/serious** *etc* etwas Nettes/Unangenehmes/Ernstes; **~ or other** irgend etwas, irgendwas; **did you say ~?** hast du (et)was gesagt?; **~ of the kind** so (et)was (Ähnliches); **that's ~ I don't know** *das* weiß ich nicht; **there's ~ I don't like about him** irgend etwas *or* irgendwas gefällt mir an ihm nicht; **do you want to make ~ of it?** willst du dich mit mir anlegen? (*inf*); **there's ~ in what you say** an dem, was du sagst, ist (schon) was dran; **well, that's ~** (das ist) immerhin etwas; **he's ~ to do with the Foreign Office** er ist irgendwie beim Außenministerium; **she's called Rachel ~** sie heißt Rachel Soundso *or* Sowieso; **there were thirty ~** es waren etwas über dreißig; **three hundred and ~** dreihundert und ein paar (Zerquetschte *inf*); **we left at five ~** wir sind etwas nach fünf gegangen.
(b) (*inf: ~ special or unusual*) **it was ~ else** (*US*) *or* **quite ~** das war schon toll (*inf*); **it's ~ to be Prime Minister at 35** es will schon was heißen, mit 35 Premierminister zu sein; **what a beautiful dress! that's really ~** so ein schönes Kleid! ganz große Klasse! (*inf*).
(c) or ~ (*inf*) oder so (was); **are you drunk or ~?** (*inf*) bist du betrunken oder was? (*inf*).
2 *n* **a little ~** (*present etc*) eine kleine Aufmerksamkeit, eine Kleinigkeit; **a/the certain ~** ein gewisses/das gewisse Etwas; **that certain ~ that makes all the difference** das gewisse Etwas, auf das es ankommt.
3 *adv* **(a) ~ over 200** etwas über 200, etwas mehr als 200; **~ like 200** ungefähr 200, um die 200 herum; **you look ~ like him** du siehst ihm irgendwie ähnlich; **this is ~ like the one I wanted** so (et)was Ähnliches wollte ich haben; **now that's ~ like a rose!** das nenne ich eine Rose!; **another £500, now that's ~ like it** noch £ 500, und wir kommen der Sache schon näher.
(b) it's ~ of a problem das ist schon ein Problem; **I feel ~ of a stranger here** ich fühle mich hier irgendwie fremd; **he's ~ of a musician** er ist ein recht guter Musiker; **~ of a surprise/drunkard** eine ziemliche Überraschung/ein ziemlicher Säufer.
(c) (*dial*) **it's ~ chronic** das ist schon krankhaft (*inf*); **the weather was ~ shocking** das Wetter war einfach schrecklich.

-something *suf* **he's twenty-~** er ist zwischen zwanzig und dreißig; **thirty-~ professional men** berufstätige Männer zwischen dreißig und vierzig; **thirty-~s** Leute *pl* zwischen dreißig und vierzig; **most American twenty-~s** die meisten Amerikaner zwischen zwanzig und dreißig.

sometime ['sʌmtaɪm] 1 *adv* irgendwann ◆ **~ or other it will have to be done** irgendwann muß es gemacht werden; **write to me ~ soon** schreib mir (doch) bald (ein)mal; **~ before tomorrow** bis morgen, heute noch; **~ next year** irgendwann nächstes *or* im nächsten Jahr.
2 *adj attr* (*form*) ehemalig, früher, einstig.

sometimes ['sʌmtaɪmz] *adv* manchmal.

someway ['sʌmweɪ] *adv* (*US*) irgendwie.

somewhat ['sʌmwɒt] *adv* ein wenig ◆ **more than ~!** mehr als das!, und ob! (*inf*); **more than ~ disappointed/late** *etc* ganz schön enttäuscht/verspätet *etc*; **~ of a surprise/disappointment/drunkard** eine ziemliche *or* arge Überraschung/eine arge Enttäuschung/ein arger Trinker.

somewhere ['sʌmweəʳ] *adv* **(a)** *be* irgendwo; *go* irgendwohin ◆ **~ else** irgendwo anders, anderswo; irgendwo anders hin, anderswohin; **from ~/~ else** von irgendwo, irgendwoher/von irgendwo anders, anderswoher; **I left it ~ or other** ich habe es irgendwo liegen-/stehenlassen; **I know ~ where ...** ich weiß, wo ...
(b) (*fig*) **the temperature was ~ about 40°C** die Temperatur betrug ungefähr 40°C *or* war um die 40° (*inf*); **~ about £50** *or* **in the region of £50** um (die) £ 50 herum; **she is ~ in her fifties** sie muß in den Fünfzigern sein; **~ between midnight and one o'clock** irgendwann zwischen Mitternacht und ein Uhr.

somnambulism [sɒm'næmbjʊlɪzəm] *n* Nacht- *or* Schlafwandeln *nt*, Mondsüchtigkeit *f*, Somnambulismus *m* (*spec*).

somnambulist [sɒm'næmbjʊlɪst] *n* Nacht- *or* Schlafwandler(in *f*) *m*, Mondsüchtige(r), Somnambule (*spec*) *mf*.

somnolence ['sɒmnələns] *n* Schläfrigkeit *f* ◆ **the heavy ~ of this summer's day** die bleierne Schwere dieses Sommertages.

somnolent ['sɒmnələnt] *adj* **(a)** (*sleepy*) schläfrig. **(b)** (*causing sleep*) einschläfernd.

son [sʌn] *n* (*lit, fig*) Sohn *m*; (*as address*) mein Junge ◆ **S~ of God/Man** Gottes-/Menschensohn *m*; **the ~s of men** (*liter*) die Menschen; **he's his father's ~** er ist ganz der Vater; **~ of a bitch** (*esp US sl*) Scheißkerl (*sl*), Hurensohn (*sl*) *m*; (*thing*) Scheißding *nt* (*sl*); **~ of a gun** (*esp US sl*) Schlawiner *m* (*inf*).

sonar ['səʊnɑːʳ] *n* Sonar(gerät), Echolot *nt*.

sonata [sə'nɑːtə] *n* Sonate *f* ◆ **in ~ form** in Sonatenform.

son et lumière ['sɒneɪ'luːmɪeəʳ] *n* Son et Lumière *nt*.

song [sɒŋ] *n* **(a)** Lied *nt*; (*modern ballad also*) Chanson *nt*; (*folk~ also, blues-~*) Song *m* ◆ **give us a ~!** sing uns etwas vor!; **one of Brecht's ~s** ein Brechtsong *m*; **to burst into ~** ein Lied anstimmen; **~-and-dance act** Gesangs- und Tanznummer *f*; **S~ of S~s, S~ of Solomon** Lied der Lieder, Hohelied Salomos *nt*.
(b) (*singing, bird~*) Gesang *m*.
(c) (*fig inf*) **to make a ~ and dance about sth** eine Haupt- und Staatsaktion aus etw machen (*inf*); **to sell/buy sth for a ~** etw für einen Apfel und ein Ei *or* ein Butterbrot verkaufen/kaufen.

song: ~bird *n* Singvogel *m*; **~book** *n* Liederbuch *nt*; **~ cycle** *n* Liederzyklus *m*; **~less** *adj bird* nicht singend *attr*.

songster ['sɒŋstəʳ] *n* Sänger *m*.

songstress ['sɒŋstrɪs] *n* Sängerin *f*.

song: ~ thrush *n* Singdrossel *f*; **~writer** *n* Texter(in *f*) und Komponist(in *f*) *m*; (*of modern ballads*) Liedermacher(in *f*) *m*.

sonic ['sɒnɪk] *adj* Schall- ◆ **~ barrier** Schallmauer *f*; **~ boom** Überschallknall *m*; **was that a ~ boom?** hat da jemand die Schallmauer durchbrochen?; **~ depth finder** Echolot *nt*.

son-in-law ['sʌnɪnlɔː] *n, pl* **sons-in-law** Schwiegersohn *m*.

sonnet ['sɒnɪt] *n* Sonett *nt* ◆ **~ form** Sonettform *f*.

sonny ['sʌnɪ] *n* (*inf*) Junge *m* ◆ **~ Jim** (*inf*) mein Junge *m*.

sonority [sə'nɒrɪtɪ] *n* Klangfülle *f*.

sonorous ['sɒnərəs] *adj* volltönend, sonor (*geh*); *language, poem* klangvoll.

sonorously ['sɒnərəslɪ] *adv* volltönend, sonor (*geh*) ◆ **the French horns echoing ~ in the background** das volle Echo der Hörner im Hintergrund.

sonorousness ['sɒnərəsnɪs] *n* Klangfülle *f*.

sons-in-law *pl of* **son-in-law**.

soon [suːn] *adv* **(a)** (*in a short time from now*) bald; (*early*) früh; (*quickly*) schnell ◆ **it will ~ be Christmas** bald ist Weihnachten; **~ after his death** kurz nach seinem Tode; **~ afterwards** kurz *or* bald danach; **how ~ can you be ready?** wann kannst du fertig sein?; **how ~ would you like it back?** wann *or* bis wann möchtest du es wiederhaben?; **we got there too ~** wir kamen zu früh an; **Friday is too ~** Freitag ist zu früh; **all too ~** viel zu schnell; **we were none too ~** wir kamen gerade rechtzeitig; **as ~ as** sobald; **as ~ as possible** so schnell wie möglich; **when can I have it? — as ~ as you like** wann kann ich's kriegen? — wann du willst!
(b) I would as ~ not go (*prefer not to*) ich würde lieber nicht gehen; (*don't mind*) es ist mir egal, wenn ich nicht gehe; **I would as ~ you didn't tell him** es wäre mir lieber, wenn du es ihm nicht erzählen würdest.

sooner ['suːnəʳ] *adv* **(a)** (*time*) früher, eher ◆ **~ or later** früher oder später; **the ~ the better** je eher *or* früher, desto besser; **no ~ had we arrived than ...** wir waren gerade *or* kaum angekommen, da ...; **in 5 years or at his death, whichever is the ~** in 5 Jahren bzw. bei seinem Tode, je nachdem, was früher eintrifft; **no ~ said than done** gesagt, getan.
(b) (*preference*) lieber ◆ **I would ~ not do it** ich würde es lieber nicht tun; **which would you ~?** was möchtest du lieber?

soot [sʊt] *n* Ruß *m* ◆ **black as ~** rußschwarz.

sooth [suːθ] *n*: **in ~** (*obs, liter*) wahrlich (*obs*).

soothe [suːð] 1 *vt* beruhigen; *pain* lindern, mildern.
2 *vi* beruhigen; (*relieve pain*) lindern ◆ **an ointment which ~s** eine schmerzlindernde Salbe.

soothing ['suːðɪŋ] *adj* beruhigend, besänftigend; (*pain-relieving*) schmerzlindernd; *massage* wohltuend; *bath* entspannend.

soothingly ['suːðɪŋlɪ] *adv see adj* beruhigend, besänftigend; schmerzlindernd; wohltuend ◆ **she rubbed his bruised arm ~** sie rieb ihm den Arm, um den Schmerz zu lindern.

soothsayer ['suːθseɪəʳ] *n* (*old*) Wahrsager(in *f*) *m*.

soothsaying ['suːθseɪɪŋ] *n* (*old*) Wahrsagerei *f*.

sooty ['sʊtɪ] *adj* (*+er*) rußig, Ruß- ◆ **buildings covered with a ~ deposit** mit einer Rußschicht bedeckte Gebäude; **a dull ~ black** ein trübes, rußfarbenes Schwarz.

sop [sɒp] *n* **(a)** (*food*) eingetunktes Brotstück.
(b) (*to pacify*) Beschwichtigungsmittel *nt* ◆ **they're just offering you that as a ~ to keep you quiet** die bieten euch das nur an, damit ihr ruhig bleibt; **as a ~ to his pride** als Trost(, um seinen Stolz nicht zu verletzen).

◆**sop up** *vt sep gravy etc* aufnehmen.

sophism ['sɒfɪzəm] *n* Sophismus *m*.

sophist ['sɒfɪst] *n* Sophist(in *f*) *m*.

sophistic(al) [sə'fɪstɪk(əl)] *adj* sophistisch.

sophisticate [sə'fɪstɪkɪt] *n* **the ~s who haunt the fashionable restaurants** die Schickeria, die sich in den richtigen Restaurants zeigt.

sophisticated [sə'fɪstɪkeɪtɪd] *adj* **(a)** (*worldly, cultivated*) kultiviert; *manners, taste also* verfeinert; *cabaret act, audience also* anspruchsvoll, niveauvoll; *person, restaurant also, hairdo* gepflegt, elegant; *dress* raffiniert, schick ◆ **she's a very ~ young lady considering she's only twelve** für eine Zwölfjährige ist sie schon sehr weit; **she thinks she looks more ~ with a cigarette-holder** sie glaubt, mit einer Zigarettenspitze mehr darzustellen.
(b) (*complex, advanced*) hochentwickelt; *electronics, techniques also* raffiniert; *method also* durchdacht; *device also* ausgeklügelt.
(c) (*subtle, refined*) subtil; *mind also* differenziert; *prose, style also* anspruchsvoll; *discussion* von *or* auf hohem Niveau, anspruchsvoll; *plan* ausgeklügelt, raffiniert; *system, approach* differenziert, komplex ◆ **the conversation was too ~ for me** mir war die Unterhaltung zu hochgestochen.

sophistication [səˌfɪstɪ'keɪʃən] *n see adj* **(a)** Kultiviertheit *f*; Verfeinerung *f*; hohes Niveau; Gepflegtheit, Eleganz *f*; Raffiniertheit *f*, Schick *m*.
(b) hoher Entwicklungsstand *or* -grad; Raffiniertheit *f*; Durchdachtheit *f*; Ausgeklügeltheit *f*.
(c) Subtilität *f*; Differenziertheit *f*; hohe Ansprüche; hohes Niveau; Ausgeklügeltheit, Raffiniertheit *f*; Komplexheit *f*.

sophistry ['sɒfɪstrɪ] *n* Sophisterei *f*.

Sophocles ['sɒfəkliːz] *n* Sophokles *m*.

sophomore ['sɒfəmɔːʳ] *n* (*US*) *Student(in f) m im 2. Jahr*.

soporific [ˌsɒpə'rɪfɪk] 1 *adj* einschläfernd.
2 *n* (*drug*) Schlafmittel *nt*.

sopping ['sɒpɪŋ] *adj* (*also* **~ wet**) durchnäßt, triefend; *person* klitschnaß.

soppy ['sɒpɪ] *adj* (*inf*) (*sentimental*) *book, song* schmalzig (*inf*); *person* sentimental; *look* schmachtend; *(effeminate)* weibisch ◆ **she dresses her little boy in really ~ clothes** sie zieht ihren kleinen Jungen immer so püppchenhaft an.

soprano [sə'prɑːnəʊ] [1] *n* Sopran *m*; *(person also)* Sopranist(in *f*) *m*; *(voice also)* Sopranstimme *f*; *(part)* Sopran(partie *f*) *m*.
[2] *adj* Sopran- ◆ **~ saxophone** Sopransaxophon *nt*.
[3] *adv* im Sopran.

Sorb [sɔːb] *n* Sorbe *m*, Sorbin *f*.

sorbet ['sɔːbeɪ] *n* Sorbet *nt or m*, Fruchteis *nt* ◆ **lemon ~** Zitronensorbet *nt or m*.

sorcerer ['sɔːsərəʳ] *n* Hexenmeister, Hexer *m*.

sorceress ['sɔːsəres] *n* Hexe *f*.

sorcery ['sɔːsərɪ] *n* Hexerei *f*.

sordid ['sɔːdɪd] *adj* eklig; *place, room also* verkommen, heruntergekommen; *motive* schmutzig, niedrig, gemein; *conditions, life, story* elend, erbärmlich; *crime* gemein ◆ **he considers it ~ to discuss money** er hält es für unfein, über Geld zu sprechen.

sordidness ['sɔːdɪdnɪs] *n see adj* Ekligkeit *f*; Verkommenheit *f*; Schmutzigkeit, Niedrigkeit *f*; Gemeinheit *f*; Elend *nt*, Erbärmlichkeit *f*.

sore [sɔːʳ] [1] *adj (+er)* **(a)** *(hurting)* weh, schlimm *(inf)*; *(inflamed)* wund, entzündet ◆ **to have a ~ throat** Halsschmerzen haben; **my eyes are ~** mir tun die Augen weh; **my wrist feels ~** mein Handgelenk schmerzt *(geh) or* tut weh; **I'm ~ all over** mir tut alles weh; **where are you ~?** wo tut es (dir/Ihnen) weh?, was tut (dir/Ihnen) weh?; **to be ~ at heart** *(liter)* betrübt sein *(geh)*; **her heart was ~** *(liter)* ihr war weh ums Herz *(liter)*.
(b) *(fig)* **a ~ point** ein wunder Punkt; **a ~ subject** ein heikles Thema.
(c) *(inf: angry, upset)* verärgert, sauer *(inf) (about sth* über etw *(acc), at sb* über jdn) ◆ **now don't get ~ at me** werd doch nicht gleich sauer! *(inf)*.
(d) *(great)* **to be in ~ need of sth** etw unbedingt *or* dringend brauchen; **in ~ distress** *(liter)* in arger Not *(liter)*.
[2] *adv (obs: greatly)* arg *(old)*, gar sehr *(obs)* ◆ **and when they saw the angel they were ~ afraid** *(Bibl)* und als sie den Engel sahen, fürchteten sie sich sehr.
[3] *n (Med)* wunde Stelle; *(caused by friction)* wund(gescheuert)e Stelle ◆ **to open old ~s** *(fig)* alte Wunden aufreißen.

sorehead ['sɔːhed] *n (US sl)* Brummbär *m (inf)*.

sorely ['sɔːlɪ] *adv tempted* sehr, arg *(S Ger, Aus, Sw)*; *needed* dringend; *missed* schmerzlich; *(liter) afflicted, troubled, offended* zutiefst; *wounded* schwer ◆ **he has been ~ tried** seine Geduld wurde auf eine sehr harte Probe gestellt.

soreness ['sɔːnɪs] *n* **(a)** *(ache)* Schmerz *m*; *(rawness)* Wundsein *nt*. **(b)** *(inf: anger)* Verärgerung *f (at* über *+acc)*.

sorghum ['sɔːgəm] *n* Sorghum *nt*.

sororicide [sə'rɒrɪsaɪd] *n* Schwestermord *m*; *(person)* Schwestermörder(in *f*) *m*.

sorority [sə'rɒrɪtɪ] *n (US Univ)* Studentinnenvereinigung *f*.

sorrel ['sɒrəl] [1] *n* **(a)** *(Bot)* großer Sauerampfer; *(wood-~)* Sauerklee *m*. **(b)** *(horse)* Fuchs *m*.
[2] *adj horse* rotbraun.

▼ **sorrow** ['sɒrəʊ] [1] *n (no pl: sadness)* Traurigkeit *f*; *(no pl: grief)* Trauer *f*, Kummer *m*; *(trouble, care)* Sorge, Kümmernis *f*; *(affliction, suffering)* Leiden *nt* ◆ **more in ~ than in anger** eher aus Betrübnis als aus Zorn; **to my (great) ~** zu meinem größten Kummer; **this was a great ~ to me** das hat mir großen Kummer bereitet; **a feeling of ~** ein Gefühl von Traurigkeit, ein wehes Gefühl *(liter)*; **teenage ~s** Sorgen und Nöte *pl* der Teenager; **to drown one's ~s** seine Sorgen ertränken; **the ~s of their race** die Leiden ihres Volkes.
[2] *vi* sich grämen *(geh) (at, for, over* über *+acc)*.

sorrowful *adj*, **~ly** *adv* ['sɒrəʊfʊl, -fəlɪ] traurig.

▼ **sorry** ['sɒrɪ] *adj (+er)* **(a)** *pred (sad)* traurig ◆ **I was ~ to hear that** es tat mir leid, das zu hören *or* hören zu müssen; **we were ~ to hear about your mother's death** es tat uns leid, daß deine Mutter gestorben ist; **he wasn't in the least bit ~ to hear the news** das machte ihm überhaupt nichts aus, das kümmerte ihn überhaupt nicht; **I can't say I'm ~ he lost** es tut mir wirklich nicht leid, daß er verloren hat; **I'm not ~ I did it** es tut mir nicht leid, es getan zu haben; **this work is no good, I'm ~ to say** diese Arbeit taugt nichts, das muß ich leider sagen; **to be *or* feel ~ for sb/oneself** jdn/sich selbst bemitleiden; **I feel ~ for the child** das Kind tut mir leid; **I feel ~ for him having to ...** es tut mir leid, daß er ... muß; **I'm only ~ I didn't do it sooner** es tut mir nur leid, daß ich es nicht eher getan habe; **don't feel ~ for me, I don't need your pity!** du brauchst mich nicht zu bedauern, kein Mitleid, bitte!; **you'll be ~ for this!** das wird dir noch leid tun!
▼ **(b)** *(in apologizing, repentant)* **~!** Entschuldigung!, Verzeihung!; **I'm/he's ~** es tut mir/ihm leid; **I'm so ~!** entschuldige(n Sie) bitte!; **can you lend me £5?** — **~** kannst du mir £ 5 leihen? — bedaure, leider nicht; **~?** *(pardon)* wie bitte?; **to say ~ (to sb for sth)** sich (bei jdm für etw) entschuldigen; **I'm ~ to hurt you** es tut mir leid, daß ich dir weh tun muß; **I'm ~ but ...** (es) tut mir leid, aber ...; **I'm ~ about that vase/your dog** es tut mir leid um die Vase/um Ihren Hund; **I'm ~ about Thursday, but I can't make it** es tut mir leid mit Donnerstag, aber ich kann nicht; **I'm ~ about (what happened on) Thursday** es tut mir leid wegen Donnerstag.
(c) *(pitiful) condition, plight* traurig; *sight, figure also* jämmerlich; *excuse* faul.

sort [sɔːt] [1] *n* **(a)** *(kind)* Art *f*; *(species, type, model also)* Sorte *f* ◆ **a ~ of** eine Art *(+nom)*, so ein/so eine, so 'n/so 'ne *(inf)*; **this ~ of house** diese Art Haus, so ein Haus; **an odd ~ of novel** ein komischer Roman; **I felt a ~ of shame** ich schämte mich irgendwie; **a ~ of silly smile** so ein *or* so 'n *(inf)* albernes Grinsen; **I have a ~ of idea that ...** ich habe das *or* so ein Gefühl, daß ...; **what ~ of** was für ein; **what ~ of man is he?** was für ein Mensch ist er?; **he's not the ~ of man to do that** er ist nicht der Mensch, der das täte; **this ~ of thing** so etwas; **all ~s of things** alles mögliche; **people of all ~s** alle möglichen Leute; **he's a painter of a ~ *or* of ~s** er ist Maler, sozusagen; **it's coffee of a ~ *or* of ~s** das ist Kaffee oder so etwas ähnliches; **something of the ~** (irgend) so (et)was; **he's some ~ of administrator** er hat irgendwie in der Verwaltung zu tun; **he's got some ~ of job with ...** er hat irgendeinen Job bei ...; **nothing of the ~!** von wegen!; **you'll do nothing of the ~!** von wegen!, das wirst du schön bleiben lassen!; **that's the ~ of person I am** ich bin nun mal so!; **I'm not that ~ of girl** ich bin nicht so eine.
(b) *(person)* **he's a good ~** er ist ein prima Kerl; **she sounds a good ~** sie scheint in Ordnung zu sein; **he's not my ~** er ist nicht mein Typ; **I don't trust his ~** solchen Leuten traue ich nicht; **I know your ~** euch Brüder kenn' ich! *(inf)*; **your ~ never did any good** du und deinesgleichen, ihr habt noch nie etwas zustande gebracht; **it takes all ~s (to make a world)** es gibt so 'ne und solche.
(c) **to be out of ~s** nicht ganz auf der Höhe *or* dem Posten *(inf) or* dem Damm *(inf)* sein.
(d) *(Comput)* Sortieren *nt*, Sortiervorgang *m* ◆ **to do a ~** sortieren.
[2] *adv* **~ of** *(inf)* irgendwie; **it's ~ of heavy** es ist irgendwie schwer *(inf)*; **is it tiring? — ~ of** ist das anstrengend? — irgendwie schon; **it's ~ of finished** es ist so ziemlich *or* eigentlich schon fertig; **aren't you pleased? — ~ of** freust du dich nicht? — doch, eigentlich schon; **is this how he did it? — well, ~ of** hat er das so gemacht? — ja, so ungefähr.
[3] *vt (also Comput)* sortieren ◆ **to ~ the ripe tomatoes from the unripe ones** die reifen und die unreifen Tomaten aussortieren; **to ~ sth on sth** *(Comput)* etw nach etw sortieren.
[4] *vi* **(a)** **to ~ through sth** etw durchsehen. **(b)** **to ~ well/ill with** passen zu/nicht passen zu. **(c)** *(Comput)* sortieren.

◆**sort out** *vt sep* **(a)** *(arrange)* sortieren, ordnen; *(select)* aussortieren, aussuchen ◆ **to ~ sth ~ from sth** etw von etw trennen; **to ~ red apples ~ from green ones** rote und grüne Äpfel aussortieren.
(b) *(straighten out) muddle* in Ordnung bringen; *problem* lösen; *situation* klären ◆ **the problem will ~ itself ~** das Problem wird sich von selbst lösen *or* erledigen; **to ~ oneself ~** zur Ruhe kommen, sich *(dat)* über sich *(acc)* selbst klar werden; **you must come and visit us once we've ~ed ourselves ~** wenn wir uns erst mal richtig eingerichtet haben, mußt du uns unbedingt besuchen.
(c) *(inf)* **to ~ sb ~** sich *(dat)* jdn vorknöpfen *(inf)*.

sorta ['sɔːtə] *adv (sl)* = **sort of**; *see* **sort 2**.

sort code *n (Banking)* Bankleitzahl *f*.

sorter ['sɔːtəʳ] *n (person)* Sortierer(in *f*) *m*; *(machine)* Sortiermaschine *f*; *(Post: person)* Briefverteiler(in *f*) *m*.

sortie ['sɔːtɪ] *n (Mil)* Ausfall *m*; *(Aviat)* (Einzel)einsatz, Feindflug *m* ◆ **a ~ into town/literary criticism** ein Ausflug *or* Abstecher *m* in die Stadt/Literaturkritik.

sorting office ['sɔːtɪŋ'ɒfɪs] *n* Sortierstelle *f*.

SOS *n* SOS *nt*.

so-so ['səʊ'səʊ] *adj pred, adv (inf)* soso, so la la.

sot [sɒt] *n (pej)* Säufer, Trunkenbold *(dated) m*.

sottish ['sɒtɪʃ] *adj* dem Trunk ergeben; *grin* benebelt.

sotto voce ['sɒtəʊ'vəʊtʃɪ] *adv* leise; *(conspiratorial)* mit unterdrückter Stimme; *(Mus)* sotto voce.

sou [suː] *n (inf)* **I haven't a ~** ich habe keinen Pfennig.

sou' [saʊ] *(Naut) abbr of* **south**.

soubrette [suː'bret] *n (dated)* Soubrette *f (dated)*.

soubriquet ['suːbrɪkeɪ] *n see* **sobriquet**.

Soudanese *adj, n see* **Sudanese**.

sou'easter [saʊ'iːstəʳ] *n (Naut: wind)* Nordost(wind) *m*.

soufflé ['suːfleɪ] *n* Soufflé *nt*.

sough [saʊ] *(liter)* [1] *n* Rauschen *nt*.
[2] *vi (wind)* rauschen.

sought [sɔːt] *pret, ptp of* **seek**.

sought-after ['sɔːtɑːftəʳ] *adj* begehrt ◆ **much ~** vielbegehrt; *rare object* gesucht.

soul [səʊl] *n* **(a)** Seele *f* ◆ **upon my ~!** *(dated)*, **(God) bless my ~!** meiner Treu *(dated)*, na so was!; **All S~s' Day** Allerheiligen *nt*; **God rest his ~!** Gott hab ihn selig!; *see* **body (a)**.
(b) *(inner being)* Innerste(s), Wesen *nt* ◆ **he may not be a brilliant intellect, but he has a great ~** er ist vielleicht kein großer Geist, aber er hat innere Werte; **he loved her with all his ~** er liebte sie von ganzem Herzen *or* heiß und innig; **he loved her with all his heart and with all his ~** er liebte sie mit jeder Faser seines Herzens; **the priest urged them to search their ~s** der Priester drängte sie, ihr Gewissen zu erforschen; **a little humility is good for the ~** ein bißchen Bescheidenheit tut der Seele gut; **the ~ of the city has been destroyed by modernization** durch die Modernisierung ist die Stadt in ihrem innersten Wesen zerstört worden; **at least the old slum had ~** der alte Slum hatte wenigstens (noch) Herz; **to have a ~ above sth** über etw *(acc)* hoch erhaben sein; **the music lacks ~** der Musik fehlt echter Ausdruck; **freedom is the ~ of democracy** Freiheit ist das Wesen der Demokratie.
(c) *(finer feelings)* Herz, Gefühl *nt* ◆ **complete lack of ~** vollkommene Gefühllosigkeit; **a musician of considerable technical skill, but lacking ~** ein Musiker von beachtlichem technischem Können, aber ohne echtes Gefühl; **you've got to have ~** *(US sl)* du mußt Feeling haben *(sl)*; **~ brother/sister** Bruder/Schwester; **he's a ~ brother** er ist einer von uns.

➤ LANGUAGE IN USE: **sorrow: 1** → 24.4 **sorry: a** → 18.2 **b** → 18.1

(d) *(person)* Seele *f* ◆ **3,000 ~s** 3.000 Seelen *(geh)*; **poor ~!** *(inf)* Ärmste(r)!; **how is she, the wee ~?** wie geht's denn unsrer Kleinen?; **he's a good ~** er ist ein guter Mensch; **she's a simple ~** sie hat ein schlichtes Gemüt; **not a ~** keine Menschenseele; **every living ~ was indoors** keine Menschenseele war auf der Straße; **the ship was lost with all ~s** das Schiff ging mit (der ganzen Besatzung und) allen Passagieren unter.
(e) **he's the ~ of generosity/discretion** er ist die Großzügigkeit/Diskretion in Person.
(f) *(Mus)* Soul *m*.

soul-destroying ['səʊldɪˌstrɔɪɪŋ] *adj* geisttötend; *factory work etc* nervtötend.

soulful ['səʊlfʊl] *adj look* seelenvoll; *person* gefühlvoll; *song also* inbrünstig.

soulfully ['səʊlfəlɪ] *adv see adj.*

soulless ['səʊllɪs] *adj person* seelenlos; *work also* eintönig.

soul: ~ mate *n* Seelenfreund *m*; **~ music** *n* Soul *m*; **~-searching** *n* Gewissensprüfung *f*; **~-stirring** *adj speech, music* bewegend.

sound¹ [saʊnd] [1] *adj (+er)* **(a)** *(in good condition) person, animal, tree* gesund; *constitution, lungs also* kräftig; *condition also, building, chassis* einwandfrei ◆ **to be as ~ as a bell** kerngesund sein; **to be ~ in wind and limb** gesund und munter sein; **to be of ~ mind** *(esp Jur)* bei klarem Verstand sein, im Vollbesitz seiner geistigen Kräfte sein *(Jur)*; **the windows were broken, but the frames were ~** die Fensterscheiben waren zerbrochen, aber die Rahmen waren heil.
(b) *(valid, good, dependable)* solide; *business also* gesund; *argument, analysis also* vernünftig, fundiert; *scholarship also* gründlich; *economy, currency also* stabil; *person, goal-keeper* verläßlich; *idea* gesund, vernünftig; *move* vernünftig; *advice* wertvoll, vernünftig ◆ **he's ~ on financial policy** er hat gründliche Kenntnisse in der Finanzpolitik; **a ~ scholar** ein ernstzunehmender Gelehrter; **that's ~ sense** das ist vernünftig.
(c) *(thorough)* gründlich, solide; *beating* gehörig; *defeat* vernichtend.
(d) *(Jur) decision* rechtmäßig; *claim also* berechtigt.
(e) *(deep) sleep* tief, fest ◆ **I'm a very ~ sleeper** ich schlafe sehr tief *or* fest, ich habe einen gesunden Schlaf.
[2] *adv (+er)* **to be ~ asleep** fest schlafen; **I shall sleep the ~er for it** ich werde nur um so besser schlafen.

sound² [1] *n* **(a)** *(noise)* Geräusch *nt*; *(Ling)* Laut *m*; *(Phys)* Schall *m*; *(Mus, of instruments)* Klang *m*; *(verbal, TV, Rad, Film)* Ton *m* ◆ **don't make a ~** still!; **the speed of ~** (die) Schallgeschwindigkeit; **within ~ of** in Hörweite *(+gen)*; **to the ~(s) of the national anthem** zu den Klängen der Nationalhymne; **French has a soft ~** die französische Sprache hat einen weichen Klang; **would you still recognize the ~ of Karin's voice?** würdest du Karins Stimme immer noch erkennen?; **not a ~ was to be heard** man hörte keinen Ton; **~s/the ~ of laughter** Gelächter *nt*; **we heard the ~ of voices on the terrace** wir hörten Stimmen auf der Terrasse; **vowel ~** Vokallaut *m*; **~ and fury** leerer Schall.
(b) *(impression)* **I don't like the ~ of it** das klingt gar nicht gut; **from the ~ of it he had a hard time** es hört sich so an *or* klingt, als sei es ihm schlecht gegangen; **his remarks had a familiar ~** seine Bemerkungen klangen vertraut.
[2] *vt* **(a)** *(produce ~ from)* **~ your horn** hupen!; **the trumpeter ~ed a high note** der Trompeter spielte einen hohen Ton; **to ~ the alarm** Alarm schlagen; *(mechanism)* die Alarmanlage auslösen; **to ~ the retreat** zum Rückzug blasen; **to ~ the "r" in "cover"** das „r" in „cover" aussprechen; **his speech ~ed a note of warning** in seiner Rede klang eine Warnung an; **I think we need to ~ a note of warning** ich finde, wir sollten eine vorsichtige Warnung aussprechen.
(b) *(test by tapping, Med)* abklopfen.
[3] *vi* **(a)** *(emit ~)* erklingen, ertönen ◆ **feet ~ed in the corridor** im Flur waren Schritte zu hören; **a gun ~ed a long way off** in der Ferne hörte man einen Schuß.
(b) *(give aural impression)* klingen, sich anhören ◆ **it ~s hollow** es klingt hohl; **the children ~ happy** es hört sich so an, als ob die Kinder ganz lustig sind; **he ~s angry** es hört sich so an, als wäre er wütend; **he ~ed depressed on the phone** am Telefon klang er deprimiert; **he ~s French (to me)** er hört sich (für mich) wie ein Franzose an.
(c) *(seem)* sich anhören ◆ **that ~s very odd** das hört sich sehr seltsam an; **he ~s like a nice man** er scheint ein netter Mensch zu sein; **it ~s like a sensible idea** das klingt ganz vernünftig; **how does it ~ to you?** wie findest du das?

◆**sound off** *vi (inf)* sich verbreiten *or* auslassen *(about* über *+acc)* ◆ **don't listen to him, he's just ~ing ~** hör nicht auf ihn, er spielt sich nur auf!

sound³ *vt (Naut)* loten, ausloten; *(Met)* messen ◆ **~ing line** Lot, Senkblei *nt*; **~ing balloon** Versuchs- *or* Registrierballon *m*.

◆**sound out** *vt sep person* aushorchen, ausfragen; *intentions, opinions* herausfinden, herausbekommen ◆ **to sound sb ~ about** *or* **on sth** bei jdm in bezug auf etw *(acc)* vorfühlen.

sound⁴ *n (Geog)* Meerenge *f*, Sund *m*.

sound: ~ archives *npl* Tonarchiv *nt*; **~ barrier** *n* Schallmauer *f*; **~-board** *n see* **sounding-board (a)**; **~-box** *n (Mus)* Schallkörper, Schallkasten *m*; **~ card** *n (Comput)* Soundkarte *f*; **~ effects** *npl* Toneffekte *pl*; **~ engineer** *n* Toningenieur(in *f*) *m*; **~-hole** *n* Schalloch *nt*.

sounding ['saʊndɪŋ] *n (Naut)* Loten *nt*, Peilung *f* ◆ **to take ~s** *(lit)* Lotungen vornehmen; *(fig)* sondieren.

sounding-board ['saʊndɪŋˌbɔːd] *n* **(a)** *(on instrument)* Resonanzboden *m*; *(over platform etc)* Schalldeckel *m*. **(b)** *(fig)* Resonanzboden *m* ◆ **he used the committee as a ~ for his ideas** er benutzte den Ausschuß, um die Wirkung seiner Vorschläge zu sondieren.

soundless ['saʊndlɪs] *adj* lautlos.

soundly ['saʊndlɪ] *adv built, made* solide; *argue, reason, invest also* vernünftig; *thrash* tüchtig, gehörig; *train* gründlich ◆ **our team was ~ beaten** unsere Mannschaft wurde eindeutig *or* klar geschlagen; **to sleep ~** tief und fest schlafen.

soundness ['saʊndnɪs] *n* **(a)** *(good condition)* gesunder Zustand; *(of building, chassis)* guter Zustand.
(b) *(validity, dependability)* Solidität *f*; *(of argument, analysis also)* Vernünftigkeit, Fundiertheit *f*; *(of scholarship)* Gründlichkeit *f*; *(of economy, currency also)* Stabilität *f*; *(of idea, advice, move, policy)* Vernünftigkeit *f*; *(of person, goalkeeper)* Verläßlichkeit *f*.
(c) *(thoroughness)* Gründlichkeit, Solidität *f*.
(d) *(Jur: of decision, claim)* Rechtmäßigkeit *f*.
(e) *(of sleep)* Tiefe *f*.

sound: ~-proof [1] *adj* schalldicht; [2] *vt* schalldicht machen, schalldämmen; **~-proofing** *n* Schallisolierung *f*; **~ recording** *n* Tonaufnahme, Tonaufzeichnung *f*; **~ shift** *n* Lautverschiebung *f*; **~-track** *n* Tonspur *f*; *(sound, recording)* Ton *m*; Filmmusik *f*; **~-wave** *n* Schallwelle *f*.

soup [suːp] *n* Suppe *f* ◆ **to be in the ~** *(inf)* in der Tinte *or* Patsche sitzen *(inf)*.

◆**soup up** *vt sep (inf) car, engine* (hoch)frisieren *(inf)*.

soupçon ['suːpsɔ̃ːŋ] *n (of spice etc)* Spur *f*; *(of irony etc)* Anflug *m*; *(of melancholy also)* Hauch *m* ◆ **sauce? — just a ~** Soße? — (ja bitte, nur) eine Idee!

soup: ~-kitchen *n* Volksküche *f*; *(for disaster area etc)* Feldküche *f*; **~-plate** *n* Suppenteller *m*, tiefer Teller; **~ spoon** *n* Suppenlöffel *m*; **~ tureen** *n* Suppenterrine *f*.

sour ['saʊə^r] [1] *adj (+er)* **(a)** *fruit, soil* sauer; *wine, vinegar* säuerlich ◆ **whisky ~** *(esp US)* Whisky mit Zitrone.
(b) *(bad) milk* sauer; *smell also* streng, säuerlich ◆ **to go** *or* **turn ~** *(lit)* sauer werden; **to go** *or* **turn ~ (on sb)** *(fig) (relationship, marriage)* jdn anöden; *(plan, investment)* sich als Fehlschlag erweisen.
(c) *(fig) person* verdrießlich, griesgrämig; *expression also* sauer; *remark* bissig ◆ **he's feeling ~ about being demoted** er ist über seine Absetzung verbittert; **it's just ~ grapes** die Trauben sind sauer *or* hängen zu hoch; **it sounds like ~ grapes to me** das kennt man: der Fuchs und die sauren Trauben.
[2] *vt milk* sauer *or* dick werden lassen; *person* verdrießlich *or* griesgrämig machen; *soil* sauer *or* kalkarm machen.
[3] *vi (milk)* sauer *or* dick werden; *(person)* verbittern, griesgrämig werden; *(soil)* sauer *or* kalkarm werden.

source [sɔːs] *n (of river, light information)* Quelle *f*; *(of troubles, problems etc)* Ursache *f*, Ursprung *m* ◆ **a ~ of vitamin C** ein Vitamin-C-Spender *m*; **they tried to trace the ~ of the gas leak** sie versuchten, das Leck in der Gasleitung ausfindig zu machen; **he is a ~ of embarrassment to us** er bringt uns ständig in Verlegenheit; **~ of supply** Bezugsquelle *f*; **to have its ~ in sth** seine Ursache *or* seinen Ursprung in etw *(dat)* haben; **I have it from a good ~ that** ... ich habe es aus sicherer Quelle, daß ...; **at ~** *(tax)* unmittelbar, direkt; **these rumours must be stopped at ~** diese Gerüchte darf man gar nicht erst aufkommen lassen; **~s** *(in book etc)* Quellen, Literaturangaben *pl*; **from reliable ~s** aus zuverlässiger Quelle.

source: ~-book *n* Quellenwerk *nt*, Quellensammlung *f*; **~ language** *n* Ausgangssprache *f*; **~ material** *n* Quellenmaterial *nt*.

sourdough ['saʊədəʊ] *n* Sauerteig *m*.

sour(ed) cream ['saʊə(d)'kriːm] *n* saure Sahne, Sauerrahm *m*.

sour-faced ['saʊəfeɪst] *adj (inf)* vergrätzt *(inf)*.

sourly ['saʊəlɪ] *adv (fig)* verdrießlich, griesgrämig.

sourness ['saʊənɪs] *n (of lemon, milk)* saurer Geschmack; *(of wine, vinegar also, of smell)* Säuerlichkeit *f*; *(of soil)* saure Beschaffenheit; *(fig) (of person, expression)* Verdrießlichkeit, Griesgrämigkeit, Verbitterung *f*; *(of remark)* Bissigkeit *f*.

sourpuss ['saʊəpʊs] *n (inf)* Miesepeter *(inf)*, Sauertopf *(old) m*; *(woman)* miesepetrige Frau/miesepetriges Mädchen *(inf)*.

sousaphone ['suːzəfəʊn] *n* Sousaphon *nt*.

souse [saʊs] *vt* **(a)** *(cover with water etc)* naß machen; *fire* löschen ◆ **he ~d himself with water** er übergoß sich mit Wasser. **(b)** *(pickle) fish* einlegen, marinieren. **(c)** **to be/get ~d** *(sl)* sternhagelvoll sein *(inf)*/sich vollaufen lassen *(sl)*.

soutane [suː'tæn] *n (Eccl)* Soutane *f*.

south [saʊθ] [1] *n* Süden *m* ◆ **in the ~ of** im Süden *+gen*; **to the ~ of** im Süden *or* südlich von; **from the ~** aus dem Süden; *(wind)* aus Süden; **to veer to the ~** in südliche Richtung *or* nach Süden drehen; **the wind is in the ~** es ist Südwind; **the S~ of France** Südfrankreich *nt*.
[2] *adj* südlich, Süd-; *(in names)* Süd-.
[3] *adv* im Süden; *(towards the ~)* nach Süden, gen Süden *(liter)*, südwärts *(Liter, Naut)*; *(Met)* in südliche Richtung ◆ **to be further ~** weiter südlich sein; **~ of** südlich *or* im Süden von.

south *in cpds* Süd-; **S~ Africa** *n* Südafrika *nt*; **S~ African** [1] *adj* südafrikanisch; [2] *n* Südafrikaner(in *f*) *m*; **S~ America** *n* Südamerika *nt*; **S~ American** [1] *adj* südamerikanisch; [2] *n* Südamerikaner(in *f*) *m*; **~bound** *adj* (in) Richtung Süden; **~-east** [1] *n* Südosten, Südost *(esp Naut) m*; [2] *adj* südöstlich; *(in names)* Südost-; **~-east wind** Südost(wind) *m*, Wind *m* aus Südost *or* südöstlicher Richtung; [3] *adv* nach Südosten; **~-east of** südöstlich von; **~-easter** *n (esp Naut)* Südostwind, Südost *m*; **~-easterly** [1] *adj direction* südöstlich; *wind also* aus Südost; [2] *n (wind)* Südostwind *m*; **~-eastern** *adj* südöstlich, im Südosten; **the ~-eastern States** die Südoststaaten *pl*; **~-eastward(s)** *adv* nach Südosten.

southerly ['sʌðəlɪ] [1] *adj* südlich; *course also* nach Süden; *wind* aus Süden *or*

südlicher Richtung.
[2] *adv* nach Süden, südwärts (*esp Naut*).
[3] *n* Südwind *m*.
southern ['sʌðən] *adj* südlich; (*in names*) Süd-; (*Mediterranean*) südländisch ◆ **~ people** Südländer *pl*; **a ~ belle** eine Schönheit aus dem Süden; **S~ Cross** Kreuz des Südens *nt*; **~ lights** Südlicht *nt*; **S~ Africa** das südliche Afrika; **S~ Europe** Südeuropa *nt*; **S~ Ireland** (Süd)irland *nt*; **S~ States** (*US*) Südstaaten *pl*.
southerner ['sʌðənəʳ] *n* Bewohner(in *f*) *m* des Südens; Südengländer(in *f*) *m*/-deutsche(r) *mf etc*; (*from the Mediterranean*) Südländer(in *f*) *m*; (*US*) Südstaatler(in *f*) *m*.
southernmost ['sʌðənməʊst] *adj* südlichste(r, s).
south: S~ Korea *n* Südkorea *nt*; **S~ Korean** [1] *adj* südkoreanisch; [2] *n* Südkoreaner(in *f*) *m*; **~paw** *n* (*Boxing*) Linkshänder, Rechtsausleger *m*; **S~ Pole** *n* Südpol *m*; **S~ Sea Islands** *npl* Südseeinseln *pl*; **~-south-east** [1] *n* Südsüdosten, Südsüdost (*esp Naut*) *m*; [2] *adj* Südsüdost-, südsüdöstlich; [3] *adv* nach Südsüdost(en); **~-south-west** [1] *n* Südsüdwesten, Südsüdwest (*esp Naut*) *m*; [2] *adj* Südsüdwest-, südsüdwestlich; [3] *adv* nach Südsüdwest(en); **~-south-west of** südsüdwestlich von; **S~ Vietnam** *n* Südvietnam *nt*; **~ward(s)** [1] *adj* südlich; [2] *adv* nach Süden, südwärts; **~-west** [1] *n* Südwesten, Südwest (*esp Naut*) *m*; [2] *adj* Südwest-, südwestlich; *wind* aus südwestlicher Richtung, Südwest-; [3] *adv* nach Südwest(en); **~-west of** südwestlich von; **~-wester** *n* (*esp Naut*) Südwest(wind) *m*; **~-westerly** *adj* südwestlich, Südwest-; *wind* aus südwestlicher Richtung; **~-western** *adj* südwestlich, Südwest-; **~-westward(s)** *adv* nach Südwesten.
souvenir [ˌsuːvəˈnɪəʳ] *n* Andenken, Souvenir *nt* (*of* an *+acc*).
sou'wester [saʊ'westəʳ] *n* **(a)** (*hat*) Südwester *m*. **(b)** (*Naut: wind*) Südwest(wind) *m*.
sovereign ['sɒvrɪn] [1] *n* (*monarch*) Souverän *m*, Herrscher(in *f*) *m*; (*Brit old: coin*) 20-Shilling-Münze *f*.
[2] *adj* **(a)** (*supreme*) höchste(r, s), oberste(r, s); *state, power* souverän; *contempt* tiefste(r, s), äußerste(r, s) ◆ **the ~ power of the Pope** die Oberhoheit *or* Suprematie des Papstes; **our ~ Lord the King** (*old*) unser gnädiger Herr, der König.
(b) ~ cure (*lit, fig*) Allheilmittel *nt* (*for* gegen).
sovereignty ['sɒvrəntɪ] *n* Oberhoheit, Oberherrschaft *f*; (*right of self-determination*) Souveränität *f* ◆ **the ~ of papal decrees** die unumschränkte Gültigkeit der päpstlichen Erlasse.
soviet ['səʊvɪət] [1] *n* Sowjet *m* ◆ **the S~s** (*people*) die Sowjets.
[2] *adj attr* sowjetisch, Sowjet- ◆ **~ power** Sowjetmacht *f*; **~ citizen** Sowjetbürger(in *f*) *m*.
sovietize ['səʊvɪətaɪz] *vt* sowjetisieren.
sovietologist [ˌsəʊvɪəˈtɒlədʒɪst] *n* Sowjetologe *m*, Sowjetologin *f*.
Soviet: ~ Russia *n* Sowjetrußland *nt*; **~ Union** *n* Sowjetunion *f*.
sow¹ [səʊ] *pret* **~ed**, *ptp* **~n** *or* **~ed** *vt* **(a)** *corn, plants* säen; *seed* aussäen; (*Mil*) *mine* legen ◆ **to ~ the garden with grass** im Garten Gras (aus)säen; **to ~ a field with seed** auf einem Feld säen; **this field has been ~n with barley** auf diesem Feld ist Gerste gesät; **to ~ mines in a strait** eine Meerenge verminen.
(b) (*fig*) **to ~ (the seeds of) hatred/discord/rebellion** Haß/Zwietracht säen/Aufruhr stiften, die Saat des Hasses/Aufruhrs/der Zwietracht säen (*liter*); **to ~ the wind and reap the whirlwind** (*Prov*) wer Wind sät, wird Sturm ernten (*Prov*); **as you ~ so shall you reap** (*Prov*) was der Mensch säet, das wird er ernten (*Prov*); *see* **seed**.
sow² [saʊ] *n* **(a)** (*pig*) Sau *f*; (*of wild boar*) (Wild)sau *f*; (*of badger*) Dächsin *f*. **(b)** (*Tech*) (*block of iron*) Massel *f*; (*channel*) Masselgraben *m*.
sower ['səʊəʳ] *n* (*person*) Säer(in *f*), Sämann *m*; (*machine*) Sämaschine *f* ◆ **a ~ of discord/rebellion** ein Mensch, der Zwietracht sät/Aufruhr stiftet.
sowing ['səʊɪŋ] *n* (*action*) (Aus)säen *nt*, Aussaat *f*; (*quantity sown*) Saat *f* ◆ **the ~ of a field** die Aussaat auf einem Feld.
sown [səʊn] *ptp of* **sow¹**.
sox [sɒks] *npl* (*US Comm sl*) = **socks**.
soya ['sɔɪə], **soy** [sɔɪ] *n* Soja *f* ◆ **~ bean** Sojabohne *f*; **~ flour** Sojamehl *nt*; **~ sauce** Sojasoße *f*.
sozzled ['sɒzld] *adj* (*Brit inf*) **to be ~** einen sitzen haben (*inf*); **to get ~** beschwipst werden.
spa [spɑː] *n* (*town*) (Heil- *or* Mineral)bad *nt*, (Bade)kurort *m*; (*spring*) (Heil- *or* Mineral)quelle *f*.
space [speɪs] [1] *n* **(a)** Raum *m* (*also Phys*); (*outer ~ also*) der Weltraum, das Weltall ◆ **time and ~** Zeit und Raum; **to stare** *or* **gaze into ~** ins Leere starren; *see* **outer**.
(b) *no pl* (*room*) Platz, Raum *m*; (*Typ*) (*between letters*) Spatien *pl*; (*between lines*) Durchschuß *m* ◆ **to take up a lot of ~** viel Platz wegnehmen *or* einnehmen; **to clear/leave some ~ for sb/sth** für jdn/etw Platz schaffen/lassen; **to buy/sell ~** (*Press*) Platz für Anzeigen kaufen/verkaufen; (*TV*) Sendezeit kaufen/verkaufen; **parking ~** Platz *m* zum Parken.
(c) (*gap, empty area*) Platz *m no art*; (*between objects, words, lines*) Zwischenraum *m*; (*Mus: on stave*) Zwischenraum *m*; (*parking ~*) Lücke *f* ◆ **to leave a ~ for sb/sth** für jdn Platz lassen/für etw Platz (frei)lassen; **there was a (blank) ~ at the end of the document** am Ende des Dokuments war Platz gelassen; **please answer in the ~ provided** bitte an der dafür vorgesehenen Stelle beantworten; **to leave an empty ~ in a room/sb's heart** eine Lücke in einem Zimmer/jds Herz hinterlassen; **indent the line a few ~s** rücken Sie die Zeile ein paar Stellen ein; **the wide open ~s** das weite, offene Land.
(d) (*Typ: piece of metal*) (*between words*) Spatienkeil *m*; (*between lines*) Reglette *f*.
(e) (*of time*) Zeitraum *m* ◆ **in a short ~ of time** in kurzer Zeit; **in the ~ of one hour/three generations** innerhalb einer Stunde/in drei Generationen; **for a ~** eine Weile *or* Zeitlang.
[2] *vt* (*also* **~ out**) in Abständen verteilen; *chairs also* in Abständen aufstellen; *seedlings also* in Abständen setzen; *visits* verteilen; *words* Zwischenraum *or* Abstand lassen zwischen (*+dat*); (*Typ*) spatiieren (*spec*) ◆ **~ them out more, ~ them further out** *or* **further apart** lassen Sie etwas mehr Zwischenraum *or* Abstand (dazwischen); **houses ~d (out) along the road** Häuser, die sich entlang der Straße verteilen; **well ~d-out houses** genügend weit auseinander gebaute Häuser; **to ~ payments** nach und nach zahlen; **to ~ the family/children (out)** in vernünftigen (Zeit)abständen Kinder bekommen; *see* **spaced-out**.
space *in cpds* (Welt)raum-; **~ age** *n* (Welt)raumzeitalter *nt*; **~-age** *adj attr* des Raumzeitalters; **~-bar** *n* (*Typ*) Leertaste *f*; **~ blanket** *n* Rettungsdecke, (Alu-)Isoliermatte *f*; **~ capsule** *n* (Welt)raumkapsel *f*; **~craft** *n* Raumfahrzeug *nt*; (*unmanned*) Raumkörper *m*.
spaced-out ['speɪst'aʊt] *adj* (*sl*) (*confused etc*) geistig weggetreten (*inf*); (*on drugs*) high (*sl*).
space: ~ fiction *n* Zukunftsromane *pl* über den Weltraum; **~ flight** *n* Weltraumflug *m*; **~ heater** *n* (*esp US*) Heizgerät *nt*; **~ helmet** *n* Astronautenhelm *m*; **~ invaders** *n sing* (*game*) Space Invaders *nt*; **~ lab(oratory)** *n* Weltraumlabor *nt*; **~man** *n* (Welt)raumfahrer *m*; **~ platform** *n* Raumstation *f*; **~port** *n* Raumflugzentrum *nt*; **~ probe** *n* Raumsonde *f*; **~ programme** *n* Raumfahrtprogramm *nt*.
spacer ['speɪsəʳ] *n see* **space-bar**.
space: ~ rocket *n* Weltraumrakete *f*; **~-saving** *adj equipment, gadget* platzsparend; *furniture also* raumsparend; **a ~-saving kitchen** eine Küche, in der der Platz voll ausgenutzt wird; **~-seller** *n* (*Press*) Anzeigenakquisiteur(in *f*) *m*; (*TV*) Werbungspromoter(in *f*) *m*; **~ship** *n* Raumschiff *nt*; **~ shot** *n* (*launching*) Abschuß *m* eines Raumfahrzeugs/-körpers; (*flight*) Raumflug *m*; **~ shuttle** *n* Raumfähre *f*; **~ sickness** *n* Weltraumkrankheit *f*; **~ station** *n* (Welt)raumstation *f*; **~ suit** *n* Raumanzug *m*; **~-time (continuum)** *n* Raum-Zeit-Kontinuum *nt*; **~ travel** *n* die Raumfahrt; **~ vehicle** *n* Raumfahrzeug *nt*; **~ walk** [1] *n* Weltraumspaziergang *m*; [2] *vi* im Weltraum spazierengehen; **~woman** *n* (Welt)raumfahrerin *f*; **~ writer** *n* (*Press*) *Korrespondent(in f) m, der/die nach der Länge seiner/ihrer Artikel bezahlt wird*.
spacey ['speɪsɪ] *adj* (*inf*) *music* trancehaft, sphärisch; *person* ausgeflippt (*inf*).
spacing ['speɪsɪŋ] *n* Abstände *pl*; (*between two objects*) Abstand *m*; (*also* **~ out**) Verteilung *f*; (*of payments*) Verteilung *f* über längere Zeit ◆ **single/double ~** (*Typ*) einzeiliger/zweizeiliger Abstand.
spacious ['speɪʃəs] *adj* geräumig; *garden, park* weitläufig.
spaciousness ['speɪʃəsnɪs] *n see adj* Geräumigkeit *f*, Weitläufigkeit *f*.
spade [speɪd] *n* **(a)** (*tool*) Spaten *m*; (*children's ~*) Schaufel *f* ◆ **to call a ~ a ~** (*prov*) das Kind beim Namen nennen (*prov*). **(b)** (*Cards*) Pik *nt* ◆ **the Queen/two of S~s** die Pikdame/Pik-Zwei; **to play in ~s** Pik spielen; **~s are trumps** Pik ist Trumpf. **(c)** (*pej sl*) Nigger *m* (*pej sl*).
spadeful ['speɪdfʊl] *n* **a ~ of earth** ein Spaten *m or* eine Schaufel (voll) Erde; **by the ~** spaten- *or* schaufelweise.
spadework ['speɪdwɜːk] *n* (*fig*) Vorarbeit *f*.
spaghetti [spəˈgetɪ] *n* Spaghetti *pl*; (*fig inf: cabling*) Kabelgewirr *nt*, Kabelsalat *m* (*inf*) ◆ **~ junction** (*inf*) Autobahnknoten(punkt) *m*; **~ western** (*inf*) Italowestern *m*.
Spain [speɪn] *n* Spanien *nt*.
spake [speɪk] (*obs*) *pret of* **speak**.
spam ® [spæm] *n* Frühstücksfleisch *nt*.
span¹ [spæn] [1] *n* **(a)** (*of hand*) Spanne *f*; (*wing~, of bridge etc*) Spannweite *f*; (*arch of bridge*) (Brücken)bogen *m* ◆ **a single-~ bridge** eine eingespannte Bogenbrücke.
(b) (*time ~*) Zeitspanne *f*, Zeitraum *m*; (*of memory*) Gedächtnisspanne *f*; (*of attention*) Konzentrationsspanne *f*; (*range*) Umfang *m* ◆ **for a brief ~** eine kurze Zeit lang; **the whole ~ of world affairs** die Weltpolitik in ihrer ganzen Spannweite.
(c) (*of oxen*) Gespann *nt*.
(d) (*old: measurement*) Spanne *f*.
[2] *vt* (*rope, rainbow*) sich spannen über (*+acc*); (*bridge also*) überspannen; (*plank*) führen über (*+acc*); (*Mus*) *octave etc* greifen; (*encircle*) umfassen; (*in time*) sich erstrecken über (*+acc*), umfassen ◆ **to ~ a river/valley with a bridge** eine Brücke über einen Fluß/ein Tal führen *or* bauen.
span² (*old*) *pret of* **spin**.
spangle ['spæŋgl] [1] *n* Paillette *f*.
[2] *vt* mit Pailletten besetzen ◆ **~d with stars/flowers** mit Sternen/Blumen übersät.
Spaniard ['spænjəd] *n* Spanier(in *f*) *m*.
spaniel ['spænjəl] *n* Spaniel *m*.
Spanish ['spænɪʃ] [1] *adj* spanisch ◆ **the ~** die Spanier *pl*.
[2] *n* (*language*) Spanisch *nt*.
Spanish: ~ America *n die spanischsprachigen Länder Mittel- und Südamerikas*; **~-American** [1] *n* spanischsprachiger Lateinamerikaner, spanischsprachige Lateinamerikanerin; (*in US*) spanischstämmiger Amerikaner, spanischstämmige Amerikanerin; [2] *adj* spanisch-amerikanisch; **~ chestnut** *n* Edelkastanie *f*; **~ Main** *n* Karibik *f*; **~ moss** *n* (*US*) Spanisches Moos, Greisenbart *m*; **~ omelette** *n* Omelett *nt* mit Piment, Paprika und Tomaten; **~ onion** *n* Gemüsezwiebel *f*.
spank [spæŋk] [1] *n* Klaps *m* ◆ **to give sb a ~** jdm einen Klaps geben;

(*spanking*) jdm den Hintern versohlen.
[2] *vt* versohlen ◆ **to ~ sb's bottom** jdm den Hintern versohlen.
[3] *vi* **to ~ along** dahinjagen, dahinrasen.
spanker ['spæŋkəʳ] *n* **(a)** (*Naut: sail*) Besan *m*. **(b)** (*dated inf*) (*horse*) Renner *m* ◆ **a real ~** (*blow*) ein Schlag, der nicht von Pappe war (*inf*).
spanking ['spæŋkɪŋ] [1] *n* Tracht *f* Prügel ◆ **to give sb a ~** jdm eine Tracht Prügel verpassen, jdm den Hintern versohlen.
[2] *adj pace* scharf, schnell.
[3] *adv* (*dated inf: exceedingly*) **~ new** funkelnagelneu; **~ clean** blitzsauber.
spanner ['spænəʳ] *n* (*Brit*) Schraubenschlüssel *m* ◆ **to put** *or* **throw a ~ in the works** (*fig*) jdm Knüppel *or* einen Knüppel zwischen die Beine werfen; **that's a real ~ in the works** das ist wirklich ein Hemmschuh.
span roof *n* Satteldach *nt*.
spar¹ [spɑːʳ] *n* (*Naut*) Rundholz *nt*.
spar² *vi* (*Boxing*) sparren, ein Sparring *nt* machen; (*fig*) sich kabbeln (*inf*) (*about* um).
spar³ *n* (*Miner*) Spat *m*.
spare [spɛəʳ] [1] *adj* **(a)** den/die/das man nicht braucht, übrig *pred*; (*surplus*) überzählig, übrig *pred*; *bed, room* Gäste-; (*replacement*) *part etc* Ersatz- ◆ **have you any ~ string?, have you any string ~?** kannst du mir (einen) Bindfaden geben?, hast du (einen) Bindfaden für mich?; **I can give you a racket/pencil, I have a ~ one** ich kann dir einen Schläger/Bleistift geben, ich habe noch einen *or* ich habe einen übrig; **take a ~ pen in case that one doesn't work** nehmen Sie noch einen Füller mit, falls dieser nicht funktioniert; **take some ~ clothes** nehmen Sie Kleider zum Wechseln mit; **it's all the ~ cash I have** mehr Bargeld habe ich nicht übrig; **if you have any ~ cash** wenn Sie Geld übrig haben; **should you have any ~ time** *or* **a ~ minute** sollten Sie Zeit (übrig) haben; **when you have a few ~ minutes** *or* **a few minutes ~** wenn Sie mal ein paar freie Minuten haben *or* ein paar Minuten übrig haben; **we have two ~ seats** wir haben zwei Plätze übrig; **I still have one ~ place in the car** ich habe noch einen Platz im Auto (frei); **there are two seats (going) ~** es sind noch zwei Plätze frei; *see also cpds*.
(b) (*thin*) hager; (*meagre*) dürftig.
(c) to drive sb ~ (*inf*) jdn wahnsinnig machen (*inf*); **to go ~** durchdrehen (*inf*), wild werden (*inf*).
[2] *n* Ersatzteil *nt*.
[3] *vt* **(a)** *usu neg* (*grudge, use sparingly*) sparen mit; *expense, pains, effort* scheuen ◆ **don't ~ the horses** schone die Pferde nicht; **we must ~ no effort in trying to finish this job** wir dürfen keine Mühe scheuen, um diese Arbeit zu erledigen; **there was no expense ~d in building this hotel** beim Bau dieses Hotels ist an nichts gespart worden *or* hat man keine Kosten gescheut; **no expense ~d** es wurden keine Kosten gescheut; **she doesn't ~ herself** sie schont sich nicht; **~ the rod and spoil the child** (*Prov*) wer mit der Rute spart, verzieht das Kind (*Prov*).
(b) (*give*) *money etc* übrig haben; *space, room also* frei haben; *time* (übrig) haben ◆ **to ~ sb sth** jdm etw überlassen *or* geben; *money* jdm etw geben; **can you ~ the time to do it?** haben Sie Zeit, das zu machen?; **I can ~ you five minutes** ich habe fünf Minuten Zeit für Sie (übrig); **can you ~ a penny for a poor old man?** haben Sie einen Groschen für einen armen alten Mann?; **there is none to ~** es ist keine(r, s) übrig; **to have sth to ~** etw übrig haben; **there's enough and to ~** es ist mehr als genug da; **to have a few minutes/hours to ~** ein paar Minuten/Stunden Zeit haben; **I got to the theatre/airport with two minutes to ~** ich war zwei Minuten vor Beginn der Vorstellung im Theater/vor Abflug am Flughafen.
(c) (*do without*) *person, object* entbehren, verzichten auf (*+acc*) ◆ **I can't ~ him/it** ich kann ihn/es nicht entbehren, ich kann auf ihn/es nicht verzichten, ich brauche ihn/es unbedingt; **can you ~ this for a moment?** brauchst du das gerade?, kannst du das im Moment entbehren?; **if you can ~ it** wenn Sie es nicht brauchen; **to ~ a thought for sb/sth** an jdn/etw denken.
(d) (*show mercy to*) verschonen; (*refrain from upsetting*) *sb, sb's feelings* schonen ◆ **the fire ~d nothing** nichts blieb vom Feuer verschont; **the soldiers ~d no-one** die Soldaten verschonten keinen; **if we're ~d** wenn wir (dann) noch leben.
(e) (*save*) **to ~ sb/oneself sth** jdm/sich etw ersparen; **~ me the details** verschone mich mit den Einzelheiten; **to ~ him embarrassment** um ihn nicht in Verlegenheit zu bringen.
sparely ['spɛəlɪ] *adv* **~ built** schlank gebaut.
spare: ~ part *n* Ersatzteil *nt*; **~-part surgery** *n* (*inf*) Ersatzteilchirurgie *f* (*inf*); **~rib** *n* Rippchen *nt*, Spare Rib *no art*; **~ room** *n* Gästezimmer *nt*; **~ time** [1] *n* (*leisure time*) Freizeit *f*; [2] *adj attr* Freizeit-; **~ tyre** *n* Ersatzreifen *m*; (*fig inf*) Rettungsring *m* (*hum inf*); **~ wheel** *n* Ersatzrad *nt*.
sparing ['spɛərɪŋ] *adj* sparsam ◆ **to be ~ of (one's) praise/one's time** mit Lob/seiner Zeit geizen, mit seiner Zeit knausern; **to be ~ of words** nicht viel sagen, wortkarg sein.
sparingly ['spɛərɪŋlɪ] *adv* sparsam; *spend, drink, eat* in Maßen ◆ **to use sth ~** mit etw sparsam umgehen.
spark [spɑːk] [1] *n* **(a)** (*from fire, Elec*) Funke *m*; (*fig: glimmer*) Fünkchen *nt*, Funke(n) *m* ◆ **not a ~ of life** kein Fünkchen Leben, kein Lebensfunke; **a ~ of interest** ein Fünkchen *or* Funke(n) Interesse; **a few ~s of wit towards the end of the speech** ein paar geistreiche Bemerkungen am Ende der Rede; **when the ~s start to fly** (*fig*) wenn die Funken anfangen zu fliegen.
(b) (*dated inf: person*) Stutzer *m* (*dated*) ◆ **a bright ~** (*iro*) ein Intelligenzbolzen *m* (*iro*); (*clumsy*) ein Tolpatsch *m*.
[2] *vt* (*also* **~ off**) entzünden; *explosion* verursachen; (*fig*) auslösen; *quarrel also* entfachen; *interest, enthusiasm* wecken.
[3] *vi* Funken sprühen; (*Elec*) zünden.
spark: ~ coil *n* Zündspule *f*; **~ gap** *n* Funkenstrecke *f*.
spark(ing) plug ['spɑːk(ɪŋ)'plʌg] *n* Zündkerze *f*.
sparkle ['spɑːkl] [1] *n* Funkeln, Glitzern *nt*; (*of eyes*) Funkeln *nt* ◆ **he has no** *or* **lacks ~** ihm fehlt der (rechte) Schwung.
[2] *vi* funkeln, glitzern; (*eyes*) blitzen, funkeln (*with* vor *+dat*); (*fig: person*) vor Leben(sfreude) sprühen; (*with intelligence, wit etc*) brillieren ◆ **her eyes ~d with intelligence** ihre Augen blitzten vor Gescheitheit; **she was so happy she really ~d** sie sprühte geradezu vor Glück; **his conversation ~d (with wit)** seine Unterhaltung sprühte vor Geist.
sparkler ['spɑːkləʳ] *n* **(a)** (*firework*) Wunderkerze *f*. **(b)** (*inf: diamond*) Klunker *m* (*inf*).
sparkling ['spɑːklɪŋ] *adj lights* glänzend, funkelnd; *eyes* funkelnd; *wit* sprühend; (*lively*) *person* vor Leben sprühend; (*witty*) *person, speech, conversation* vor Geist sprühend; (*bubbling*) *lemonade etc* perlend; *wine* perlend, moussierend ◆ **~ wine** (*as type*) Schaumwein *m*; (*slightly ~*) Perlwein *m*; **the car was ~ (clean)** das Auto blitzte vor Sauberkeit.
spark plug *n see* **spark(ing) plug**.
sparring ['spɑːrɪŋ]: **~ match** *n* (*lit*) Sparringkampf *m*; (*fig*) (Wort)geplänkel, Wortgefecht *nt*; **~ partner** *n* (*lit*) Sparringpartner *m*; (*fig also*) Kontrahent(in *f*) *m*.
sparrow ['spærəʊ] *n* Sperling, Spatz *m* ◆ **house ~** Haussperling.
sparrowhawk ['spærəʊhɔːk] *n* (*European*) Sperber *m*; (*N American*) amerikanischer Falke.
sparse [spɑːs] *adj* (*+er*) spärlich; *covering, vegetation also, population* dünn; *furnishings also* dürftig; (*infrequent*) *references also* rar.
sparsely ['spɑːslɪ] *adv* spärlich; *wooded also, populated* dünn; *furnished also* dürftig ◆ **a hillside ~ covered with trees** ein Hang mit spärlichem Baumwuchs.
sparseness ['spɑːsnɪs] *n* Spärlichkeit *f*; (*of furnishings also*) Dürftigkeit *f*; (*of population*) geringe Dichte.
Sparta ['spɑːtə] *n* Sparta *nt*.
Spartan ['spɑːtən] [1] *adj* (*fig:* **s~**) spartanisch.
[2] *n* Spartaner(in *f*) *m*.
spasm ['spæzəm] *n* (*Med*) Krampf, Spasmus (*spec*) *m*; (*of asthma, coughing, fig*) Anfall *m* ◆ **~s of coughing** krampfartige Hustenanfälle *pl*; **there was a ~ of activity** es entwickelte sich fieberhafte Aktivität; **to work in ~s** sporadisch arbeiten.
spasmodic [spæz'mɒdɪk] *adj* (*Med*) krampfartig, spasmisch, spasmodisch (*spec*); (*fig: occasional*) sporadisch; *growth* schubweise ◆ **his generosity was ~** er hatte Phasen *or* Anfälle von Großzügigkeit.
spasmodically [spæz'mɒdɪkəlɪ] *adv* (*Med*) krampfartig; (*fig*) sporadisch, hin und wieder; *grow* in Schüben, schubweise.
spastic ['spæstɪk] [1] *adj* spastisch; (*fig sl*) schwach (*inf*).
[2] *n* Spastiker(in *f*) *m*.
spasticity [spæ'stɪsɪtɪ] *n* spastische Lähmung.
spat¹ [spæt] [1] *n* (*of oyster etc*) Muschellaich *m*.
[2] *vi* (*oyster etc*) laichen.
spat² *n* Halbgamasche *f*.
spat³ (*US inf*) [1] *n* (*quarrel*) Knatsch (*inf*), Krach (*inf*) *m*.
[2] *vi* (*quarrel*) zanken, streiten.
spat⁴ *pret, ptp of* **spit¹**.
spate [speɪt] *n* (*of river*) Hochwasser *nt*; (*fig*) (*of letters, orders etc*) Flut *f*; (*of burglaries, accidents*) Serie *f*; (*of words, abuse*) Schwall *m* ◆ **the river is in (full) ~** der Fluß führt Hochwasser; **a ~ of words** ein Wortschwall *m*; **a ~ of excited talk** aufgeregtes Stimmengewirr; **a ~ of work** ein Arbeitsandrang *m*.
spatial *adj*, **~ly** *adv* ['speɪʃəl, -ɪ] räumlich.
spatio-temporal ['speɪʃɪəʊ'tempərəl] *adj* räumlich-zeitlich, Raum-Zeit-.
spatter ['spætəʳ] [1] *vt* bespritzen ◆ **to ~ water over sb, to ~ sb with water** jdn naß spritzen; **a wall ~ed with blood** eine blutbespritzte Wand.
[2] *vi* **to ~ over sth** etw vollspritzen; **it ~ed all over the room** es verspritzte im ganzen Zimmer; **the rain ~ed (down) on the roof** der Regen klatschte aufs Dach.
[3] *n* (*mark*) Spritzer *pl*; (*sound: of rain*) Klatschen *nt* ◆ **a ~ of rain** ein paar Tropfen Regen; **a ~ of applause** kurzer Beifall.
spatula ['spætjʊlə] *n* Spachtel *m*; (*Med*) Spatel *m*.
spavin ['spævɪn] *n* Spat *m*.
spavined [spə'viːnd] *adj horse* spatkrank.
spawn [spɔːn] [1] *n* **(a)** (*of fish, shellfish, frogs*) Laich *m*. **(b)** (*of mushrooms*) Fadengeflecht *nt*.
[2] *vi* laichen.
[3] *vt* (*fig*) hervorbringen, erzeugen ◆ **bad living conditions ~ crime** schlechte Wohnverhältnisse sind Brutstätten des Verbrechens.
spay [speɪ] *vt cat* sterilisieren.
SPCA *abbr of* **Society for the Prevention of Cruelty to Animals** ≃ Tierschutzverein *m*.
speak [spiːk] *pret* **spoke** *or* (*obs*) **spake**, *ptp* **spoken** *or* (*obs*) **spoke** [1] *vt* **(a)** (*utter*) sagen; *one's thoughts* aussprechen, äußern; *one's lines* aufsagen ◆ **to ~ one's mind** seine Meinung sagen; **nobody spoke a word** niemand sagte ein Wort, keiner sagte etwas; **his eyes spoke his love** sein Blick verriet seine Liebe; *see* **volume**.
(b) *language* sprechen ◆ **English spoken here** man spricht Englisch.
[2] *vi* **(a)** (*talk, be on ~ing terms*) sprechen, reden (*about* über *+acc*, von); (*converse*) reden, sich unterhalten (*with* mit); (*fig: guns, drums*) sprechen,

ertönen ♦ **to ~ to** *or* **with sb** mit jdm sprechen *or* reden; **did you ~?** haben Sie etwas gesagt?; **to ~ in a whisper** flüstern; **~, don't shout** nun schreien Sie doch nicht (so)!; **we don't ~ (to one another)** wir reden *or* sprechen nicht miteinander; **I'm not ~ing to you** mit dir rede *or* spreche ich nicht mehr; **she never spoke to me again** seitdem hat sie nie wieder mit mir geredet *or* gesprochen; **to ~ to oneself** Selbstgespräche führen; **I'll ~ to him about it** (*euph: admonish*) ich werde ein Wörtchen mit ihm reden; **I'll have to ~ to my lawyer about it** das muß ich mit meinem Anwalt besprechen; **~ when you're spoken to** antworte, wenn man mit dir redet *or* spricht; **servants should only ~ when spoken to** Diener sollten nur dann etwas sagen, wenn man sie anspricht; **I don't know him to ~ to** ich kenne ihn nicht näher *or* nur vom Sehen; **music ~s directly to the soul** Musik spricht die Seele an; **this novel ~s to the rebel in all of us** dieser Roman spricht den Rebellen in uns an; **~ing of dictionaries ...** da *or* wo wir gerade von Wörterbüchern sprechen ..., apropos Wörterbücher ...; **not to ~ of ...** ganz zu schweigen von ...; **it's nothing to ~ of** es ist nicht weiter erwähnenswert, es ist nichts weiter; **no money/trees** *etc* **to ~ of** so gut wie kein Geld/keine Bäume *etc*; **to ~ well of sb/sth** jdn/etw loben, (nur) Gutes über jdn/etw sagen; **he is well spoken of** er genießt große Achtung; **so to ~** sozusagen, eigentlich; **roughly ~ing** grob gesagt; **strictly ~ing** genau genommen; **legally/biologically ~ing** rechtlich/biologisch gesehen; **generally ~ing** im allgemeinen; **~ing personally ...** wenn Sie mich fragen ..., was mich betrifft ...; **~ing as a member of the club I have ...** als Mitglied des Vereins habe ich ...; **to ~ down to sb** jdn von oben herab behandeln.

(b) (*make a speech*) reden (*on* zu), sprechen (*on* zu); (*give one's opinion*) sich äußern (*on, to* zu) ♦ **to ~ in public** in der Öffentlichkeit reden; **to ~ in the debate** in der Debatte das Wort ergreifen; **to ask sb to ~** jdm das Wort erteilen; **Mr X will ~ next** als nächster hat Herr X das Wort; **then Geoffrey rose to ~** dann stand Geoffrey auf, um das Wort zu ergreifen.

(c) (*Telec*) **~ing!** am Apparat!; **Jones ~ing!** (hier) Jones!; **who is that ~ing?** wer ist da, bitte?; (*on extension phone, in office*) wer ist am Apparat?

(d) (*fig: suggest*) zeugen (*of* von) ♦ **their appearance ~s of poverty** ihre Erscheinung verrät Armut *or* zeugt von Armut.

[3] *n suf* **EC-~** EG-Jargon *m*.

♦**speak against** *vi + prep obj* (*in debate*) sprechen gegen, sich aussprechen gegen; (*criticize*) etwas sagen gegen, kritisieren.

♦**speak for** *vi + prep obj* **(a)** (*in debate*) unterstützen.

(b) to ~ ~ sb (*on behalf of*) in jds Namen (*dat*) sprechen; (*in favour of*) ein gutes Wort für jdn einlegen; **he ~s ~ the miners/delegation** er ist der Sprecher der Bergleute/Abordnung; **I know I ~ ~ all of us** ich bin sicher, daß ich im Namen aller spreche; **~ing ~ myself ...** was mich angeht ...; **let her ~ ~ herself** laß sie selbst reden; **~ ~ yourself!** (*I don't agree*) das meinst auch nur du!; (*don't include me*) du vielleicht!; **I can ~ ~ his honesty** ich kann mich für seine Ehrlichkeit verbürgen; **that ~s well ~ him** das spricht für ihn; **to ~ well/badly ~ sth** ein Beweis *m*/nicht gerade ein Beweis *m* für etw sein.

(c) to ~ ~ itself (*be obvious*) für sich sprechen, alles sagen.

(d) to be spoken ~ (*dated: girl*) versprochen sein (*old*), vergeben sein (*hum*); **the chair had already been spoken ~** (*hum*) der Stuhl war schon reserviert; **that's already spoken ~** (*hum*) das ist schon vergeben.

♦**speak out** *vi* (*audibly*) deutlich sprechen; (*give one's opinion*) seine Meinung deutlich vertreten ♦ **to ~ ~ in favour of sth** für etw eintreten; **to ~ ~ against sth** sich gegen etw aussprechen.

♦**speak up** *vi* **(a)** (*raise one's voice*) lauter sprechen *or* reden; (*talk loudly*) laut (und verständlich) sprechen *or* reden ♦ **~ ~!** sprich lauter!; **if you want anything ~ ~** mach den Mund auf *or* sag, wenn du etwas willst.

(b) (*fig*) seine Meinung sagen *or* äußern ♦ **don't be afraid to ~ ~** sagen Sie ruhig Ihre Meinung, äußern Sie sich ruhig; **to ~ ~ for sb/sth** für jdn/etw eintreten; **what's wrong? ~ ~!** was ist los? heraus mit der Sprache!

speakeasy ['spi:ki:zɪ] *n* (*US*) Mondscheinkneipe *f* (*inf*) (*Lokal, in dem während der Prohibition Alkohol ausgeschenkt wurde*).

speaker ['spi:kəʳ] *n* **(a)** (*of language*) Sprecher *m* ♦ **all ~s of German** alle, die Deutsch sprechen, alle Deutschsprechenden; (*native ~s also*) alle Deutschsprachigen.

(b) Sprecher(in *f*) *m*; (*in discussion also, in lecture, public ~*) Redner(in *f*) *m* ♦ **the last** *or* **previous ~** der Vorredner; **our ~ today is ...** der heutige Referent ist ...; **he's a good/poor ~** er ist ein guter/schlechter Redner.

(c) (*loud~, in record-player*) Lautsprecher *m*; (*on hi-fi etc*) Box *f*.

(d) (*Parl*) **S~** Sprecher *m*; **Mr S~** ≃ Herr Präsident.

speaking ['spi:kɪŋ] [1] *n* (*act of ~*) Sprechen *nt*; (*speeches*) Reden *pl* ♦ **the art of ~** die Redekunst.

[2] *adj attr doll* sprechend, Mama- (*inf*); (*fig*) *likeness* verblüffend ♦ **~ voice** Sprechstimme *f*; **to be within ~ distance** nahe genug sein, daß man sich verständigen kann.

-speaking *adj suf* -sprechend; (*with native language also*) -sprachig.

speaking: ~ clock *n* (*Brit*) telefonische Zeitansage; **~ terms** *npl* **to be on ~ terms with sb** mit jdm sprechen *or* reden; **~ trumpet** *n* (*old*) Hörrohr *nt*; **~ tube** *n* Sprachrohr *nt*.

spear [spɪəʳ] [1] *n* Speer *m*; (*leaf*) Lanzettenblatt *nt*; (*of grass*) Halm *m*; (*of grain*) Keim *m* ♦ **~s of broccoli/asparagus** Brokkoliköpfe *pl*/Stangen *pl* Spargel.

[2] *vt* aufspießen; (*wound, kill*) durchbohren; (*catch with ~*) mit Speeren fangen ♦ **he ~ed him through the arm** er durchbohrte ihm den Arm; **he ~ed the meat with** *or* **onto his fork** er spießte das Fleisch auf die Gabel.

spear: ~head [1] *n* (*of spear*) Speerspitze *f*; (*Mil*) Angriffsspitze *f*; (*fig: person, thing*) Bahnbrecher *m* (*of* für); [2] *vt* (*lit, fig*) anführen; **~man** *n* Speerträger *m*; **~mint** *n* (*plant, flavour*) Grüne Minze; **~mint chewing gum** Spearmint-Kaugummi *m*.

spec [spek] *n* (*inf*) **on ~** auf Verdacht, auf gut Glück.

special ['speʃəl] [1] *adj* **(a)** besondere(r, s); (*specific*) *purpose, use, person, date also* bestimmt, speziell; (*exceptional*) *friend, favour, occasion also* speziell ♦ **I have no ~ person in mind** ich habe eigentlich an niemanden Bestimmtes gedacht; **in this one ~ instance** in diesem einen Fall; **take ~ care of it** passen Sie besonders gut darauf auf; **nothing ~** nichts Besonderes; **he expects ~ treatment** er will besonders behandelt werden, er will eine Extrawurst gebraten haben (*inf*); **this is rather a ~ day for me** heute ist ein ganz besonderer Tag für mich; **he uses the word in a ~ sense** er gebraucht das Wort in einer speziellen Bedeutung; **he's a very ~ person to her** er bedeutet ihr sehr viel; **you're extra ~!** (*inf*) du bist was ganz Besonderes! (*inf*); **what's so ~ about her/the house?** was ist denn an ihr/an dem Haus so besonders?; **what's so ~ about that?** na und? (*inf*), das ist doch nichts Besonderes!; **I do that my own ~ way** ich mache das ganz auf meine (eigene) Weise; **it's my ~ chair** das ist *mein* Stuhl; **everyone has his ~ place** jeder hat seinen eigenen Platz; **to feel ~** sich als etwas ganz Besonderes vorkommen; **make him feel ~** seien Sie besonders nett zu ihm.

(b) (*out of the ordinary*) *permission, fund, supplement, edition, (Pol) powers, legislation* Sonder-; *arrangement, wish, order also* besondere(r, s) ♦ **~ feature** (*Press*) Sonderartikel *m*.

(c) (*specialized*) *subject, dictionary, tool* Spezial-.

(d) (*inf: separate*) *place, book etc* gesondert.

[2] *n* (*constable*) Hilfspolizist(in *f*) *m*; (*TV, Rad*) Sonderprogramm *nt*; (*train*) Sonderzug *m*; (*Cook*) Tagesgericht *nt*; (*edition*) Sonder- *or* Extraausgabe *f* ♦ **chef's ~** Spezialität *f* des Küchenchefs.

special: ~ agent *n* (*spy*) Agent(in *f*) *m*; **S~ Branch** *n* (*Brit*) Sicherheitspolizei *f*, Sicherheitsdienst *m*; **~ case** *n* (*also Jur*) Sonderfall *m*; **~ character** *n* (*Comput*) Sonderzeichen *nt*; **~ constable** *n* Hilfspolizist *m*; **~ correspondent** *n* (*Press*) Sonderberichterstatter(in *f*) *m*; **~ delivery** *n* Eilzustellung *f*; **a ~-delivery letter** ein Eilbrief *m*; **by ~ delivery** durch Eilzustellung, per Eilboten (*inf*); **~ drawing rights** *npl* Sonderziehungsrechte *pl*; **~ edition** *n* Sonderausgabe *f*; **~ effects** *npl* Spezialeffekte, Tricks *pl*; **~ investigator** *n* Sonderbeauftragte(r) *mf*, Untersuchungsbeamte(r) *m*.

specialism ['speʃəlɪzəm] *n* (*specializing*) Spezialisierung *f*; (*special subject*) Spezialgebiet *nt*.

specialist ['speʃəlɪst] [1] *n* Spezialist(in *f*), Fachmann *m* (*in* für); (*Med*) Facharzt *m*/-ärztin *f* ♦ **a ~ in tropical diseases** ein Facharzt *or* Spezialist für Tropenkrankheiten.

[2] *adj attr knowledge, dictionary* Fach- ♦ **it's ~ work** dazu braucht man einen Fachmann.

speciality [,speʃɪ'ælɪtɪ], (*US*) **specialty** ['speʃəltɪ] *n* Spezialität *f*; (*subject also*) Spezialgebiet *nt* ♦ **to make a ~ of sth** sich auf etw (*acc*) spezialisieren; **a ~ of the house** eine Spezialität des Hauses.

specialization [,speʃəlaɪ'zeɪʃən] *n* Spezialisierung *f* (*in* auf *+acc*); (*special subject*) Spezialgebiet *nt*.

specialize ['speʃəlaɪz] [1] *vi* sich spezialisieren (*in* auf *+acc*) ♦ **we ~ in ...** wir haben uns auf ... (*acc*) spezialisiert.

[2] *vt* **the species/tail has been ~d** die Art/der Schwanz hat sich gesondert entwickelt.

specialized ['speʃəlaɪzd] *adj* spezialisiert ♦ **a ~ knowledge of biology** Fachkenntnisse *pl* in Biologie.

special licence *n* (*Brit*) (Ehe)dispens *f* (*des Bischofs von Canterbury*).

specially ['speʃəlɪ] *adv* besonders; (*specifically*) extra; (*for a particular purpose*) speziell, extra ♦ **a ~ difficult task** eine besonders schwierige Aufgabe; **I had it ~ made** ich habe es extra machen lassen; **we asked for it ~** wir haben extra darum gebeten; **he brought it ~ for me** er hat es extra *or* eigens für mich gebracht; **don't go to the post office ~/~ for me** gehen Sie deswegen/meinetwegen nicht extra zur Post.

special: ~ messenger *n* Expreßbote *m*; (*Mil*) Kurier *m*; **~ needs** *npl* **children with ~ needs, ~ needs children** behinderte Kinder, Kinder mit Behinderungen; **~ needs teacher** Behindertenlehrer(in) *m(f)*, Sonderschullehrer(in) *m(f)*; **~ offer** *n* Sonderangebot *nt*; **~ pleading** *n* (*Jur*) Beibringung *f* neuen Beweismaterials; (*fig*) Berufung *f* auf einen Sonderfall; **~ prosecutor** *n* (*US*) Sonderstaatsanwalt *m*; **~ school** *n* Sonderschule *f*; (*for physically handicapped*) Behindertenschule *f*.

specialty ['speʃəltɪ] *n* (*US*) *see* **speciality**.

specie ['spi:ʃi:] *n, no pl* Hartgeld, Münzgeld *nt* ♦ **payment in ~** Zahlung *f* in Hartgeld.

species ['spi:ʃi:z] *n, pl* - Art *f*; (*Biol also*) Spezies *f* ♦ **the human ~** der Mensch.

specific [spə'sɪfɪk] [1] *adj* **(a)** (*definite*) bestimmt, speziell; (*precise*) *statement, instructions* genau; *example* ganz bestimmt ♦ **9.3, to be ~** 9,3, um genau zu sein; **can you be a bit more ~?** können Sie sich etwas genauer äußern? **(b)** (*Biol, Chem, Phys, Med*) spezifisch ♦ **~ gravity** spezifisches Gewicht, Wichte *f*.

[2] *n* **(a)** (*old Med*) Spezifikum *nt*.

(b) ~s *pl* nähere *or* genauere Einzelheiten *pl*.

specifically [spə'sɪfɪkəlɪ] *adv warn, order, state, mention* ausdrücklich; (*specially*) *designed, request* speziell; (*precisely*) genau ♦ **~, we need three** wir brauchen genau drei.

specification [,spesɪfɪ'keɪʃən] *n* **(a)** (*specifying*) Angabe *f* ♦ **his ideas need more ~** seine Ideen müssen noch genauer ausgeführt werden.

(b) (*detailed statement*) (*of requirements*) genaue Angabe, Aufstellung *f*; (*for patent*) (genaue) Beschreibung; (*design*) (*for car, machine*) (detaillierter) Entwurf; (*for building*) Bauplan *m* ♦ **~s** *pl* genaue Angaben *pl*; (*of car, machine*)

technische Daten *or* Angaben *pl*; (*of new building*) Raum- und Materialangaben *pl*, Baubeschreibung *f*, Baubeschrieb *m*; **the new ~ includes ...** (*model*) die neue Ausführung hat auch ...
(c) (*stipulation*) Bedingung *f*; (*for building*) Vorschrift *f*.

specify ['spesɪfaɪ] [1] *vt* angeben; (*list individually or in detail*) spezifizieren, (einzeln) aufführen; (*stipulate*) vorschreiben; (*blueprint, contract etc*) vorsehen ◆ **in the order specified** in der angegebenen *or* vorgeschriebenen Reihenfolge; **to ~ how to do it** genauer *or* näher ausführen, wie es gemacht werden soll.
[2] *vi* genaue Angaben machen ◆ **unless otherwise specified** wenn nicht anders angegeben.

specimen ['spesɪmɪn] [1] *n* Exemplar *nt*; (*of urine, blood etc*) Probe *f*; (*sample*) Muster *nt* ◆ **a beautiful** *or* **fine ~** ein Prachtexemplar *nt*; **if that's a ~ of your work/intelligence** wenn das eine Probe deines Könnens/deiner Intelligenz ist; **he's an odd ~** (*inf*) er ist ein komischer Kauz (*inf*); **you're a pretty poor ~** (*inf*) du hast ja nicht viel zu bieten (*inf*).
[2] *adj attr page* Probe- ◆ **a ~ copy** ein Beleg- *or* Probeexemplar *nt*; **a ~ signature** eine Unterschriftenprobe.

specious ['spiːʃəs] *adj argument, proposal* vordergründig bestechend, Schein-; *excuse* vordergründig, fadenscheinig; *claim* unfundiert, fadenscheinig; *charm, phrases* leer.

speciousness ['spiːʃəsnɪs] *n see adj* Vordergründigkeit *f*, Fadenscheinigkeit *f*, Unfundiertheit *f*, Hohlheit *f*.

speck [spek] [1] *n* Fleck *m*; (*of blood, paint, mud also*) Spritzer *m*; (*of dust*) Körnchen *nt*; (*of soot*) Flocke *f*, Flöckchen *nt*; (*of gold, colour etc*) Sprenkel *m*; (*small portion*) (*of drink etc*) Tropfen *m*, Tröpfchen *nt*; (*of sugar, butter*) kleines bißchen; (*fig: of truth, confidence*) Fünkchen, Quentchen *nt* ◆ **a ~ on the horizon** ein Punkt *m or* Pünktchen *nt* am Horizont.
[2] *vt* **to be ~ed with black** schwarze Fleckchen haben; (*bird, eyes etc*) schwarz gesprenkelt sein; **his face was ~ed with dust/dirt** er hatte Staub-/Schmutzflecken im Gesicht; **to be ~ed with blood** blutbespritzt sein.

speckle ['spekl] [1] *n* Sprenkel, Tupfer, Tupfen *m*.
[2] *vt* sprenkeln ◆ **to be ~d with sth** mit etw gesprenkelt sein; **to be ~d with brown** braun gesprenkelt sein.

specs [speks] *npl* (a) (*inf*) Brille *f*. (b) *abbr of* **specifications.**

spectacle ['spektəkl] *n* (a) (*show*) Schauspiel *nt* ◆ **a sad ~** ein trauriger Anblick; **to make a ~ of oneself** unangenehm auffallen. (b) **~s** *pl* (*also* **pair of ~s**) Brille *f*.

spectacle case *n* Brillenetui *or* -futteral *nt*.

spectacled ['spektəkld] *adj* bebrillt; (*Zool*) Brillen-, brillenähnlich gezeichnet.

spectacular [spek'tækjʊlə^r] [1] *adj* sensationell; *improvement, success also* spektakulär.
[2] *n* (*Theat*) Show *f*.

spectacularly [spek'tækjʊləlɪ] *adv* sensationell; *improve, fail also* spektakulär ◆ **he was ~ wrong** er hat einen Riesenfehler gemacht.

spectate [spek'teɪt] *vi* (*inf: esp Sport*) zuschauen (*at* bei).

spectator [spek'teɪtə^r] *n* Zuschauer(in *f*) *m* ◆ **~ sport** Publikumssport *m*.

specter *n* (*US*) *see* **spectre.**

spectogram ['spektəʊgræm] *n* Spektogramm *nt*.

spectra ['spektrə] *pl of* **spectrum.**

spectral ['spektrəl] *adj* (a) (*of ghosts*) geisterhaft, gespenstisch. (b) (*of the spectrum*) spektral, Spektral-.

spectre, (*US*) **specter** ['spektə^r] *n* Gespenst *nt*; (*fig*) (Schreck)gespenst *nt* ◆ **the ~ of a woman in white** die Erscheinung einer Frau in Weiß.

spectroscope ['spektrəʊskəʊp] *n* Spektroskop *nt*.

spectroscopic [ˌspektrəʊ'skɒpɪk] *adj* spektroskopisch; *analysis* Spektral-.

spectrum ['spektrəm] *n, pl* **spectra** Spektrum *nt*; (*fig: range also*) Palette, Skala *f* ◆ **~ analysis** Spektralanalyse *f*.

specula ['spekjʊlə] *pl of* **speculum.**

speculate ['spekjʊleɪt] *vi* (a) (*meditate, ponder*) (nach)grübeln, nachdenken (*on* über +*acc*); (*conjecture*) Vermutungen anstellen, spekulieren (*about, on* über +*acc*) ◆ **I ~ that ...** ich vermute, daß ... (b) (*Fin*) spekulieren (*in* mit, *on* an +*dat*).

speculation [ˌspekjʊ'leɪʃən] *n* (*all senses*) Spekulation *f* (*on* über +*acc*); (*guesswork also*) Vermutung *f* ◆ **it is the subject of much ~** darüber sind viele Spekulationen *or* Vermutungen angestellt worden; **it's pure ~** das ist reine Vermutung.

speculative ['spekjʊlətɪv] *adj* (a) spekulativ (*esp Philos*); *approach, suggestions, ideas* rein theoretisch; *mind also, expression, look* grüblerisch. (b) (*Fin*) Spekulations- ◆ **~ builder** Bauspekulant *m*; **~ building** Bauspekulation *f*.

speculatively ['spekjʊlətɪvlɪ] *adv* spekulativ, theoretisch; *look, say* grüblerisch ◆ **to invest ~ in sth** mit etw spekulieren.

speculator ['spekjʊleɪtə^r] *n* (*also Fin*) Spekulant(in *f*) *m*.

speculum ['spekjʊləm] *n, pl* **specula** (*Med*) Spekulum *nt*; (*in telescope*) Metallspiegel *m*.

sped [sped] *pret, ptp of* **speed.**

speech [spiːtʃ] *n* (a) *no pl* (*faculty of ~*) Sprache *f*; (*act of speaking*) Sprechen *nt*; (*manner of speaking*) Sprechweise *f* ◆ **to be slow of ~** langsam sprechen; **his ~ was very indistinct** er sprach sehr undeutlich; **he expresses himself better in ~ than in writing** er drückt sich mündlich besser aus als schriftlich; **to burst into ~** in einen Redeschwall ausbrechen; **to lose/recover the power of ~** die Sprache verlieren/zurückgewinnen; **~ is silver, silence is golden** (*Prov*) Reden ist Silber, Schweigen ist Gold (*Prov*); **freedom of ~** Redefreiheit *f*.
(b) (*language*) Sprache *f* ◆ **in dockers' ~** in der Sprache der Werftarbeiter.
(c) (*oration, Theat*) Rede *f* (*on, about* über +*acc*); (*address also*) Ansprache *f*; (*in court*) Plädoyer *nt* ◆ **to give** *or* **make a ~** eine Rede *etc* halten; **the actor had three ~es** der Schauspieler hat dreimal gesprochen; **the chairman invited ~es from the floor** der Vorsitzende forderte das Publikum zu Meinungsäußerungen auf; **the ~ from the throne** die Thronrede.
(d) (*Brit Gram*) **direct/indirect** *or* **reported ~** direkte/indirekte Rede; *see* **figure, part.**
(e) (*US Sch, Univ: study of ~*) Sprechkunde *f*.

speech: ~ act *n* Sprechakt *m*; **~ community** *n* Sprachgemeinschaft *f*; **~ day** *n* (*Brit*) Schulfeier *f*; **~ defect** *n* Sprachfehler *m*.

speechify ['spiːtʃɪfaɪ] *vi* salbadern, Volksreden halten.

speechifying ['spiːtʃɪfaɪɪŋ] *n* Volksreden *pl*, Schwätzerei *f*.

speechless ['spiːtʃlɪs] *adj* (a) (*at a loss for words*) sprachlos (*with* vor); *anger* stumm ◆ **everybody was ~ at this** darüber waren alle völlig sprachlos; **his remark left me ~** seine Bemerkung machte mich sprachlos *or* verschlug mir die Sprache.
(b) (*lit: dumb*) stumm ◆ **to be ~** nicht sprechen können.

speechlessly ['spiːtʃlɪslɪ] *adv* wortlos; (*from surprise, shock etc*) sprachlos.

speechlessness ['spiːtʃlɪsnɪs] *n* (a) Sprachlosigkeit *f*. (b) (*lit*) Stummheit *f*; (*loss of speech*) Sprachverlust *m*.

speech: ~making *n* (*making speeches*) Redenhalten *nt*; (*pej: speechifying*) Schwätzerei *f*, Gelabere *nt* (*inf*); **~ organ** *n* Sprechwerkzeug *nt*; **~ recognition** *n* Spracherkennung *f*; **~ sound** *n* Sprachlaut *m*; **~ synthesizer** *n* Sprachsynthesizer *m*; **~ therapist** *n* Sprachtherapeut(in *f*), Logopäde *m*, Logopädin *f*; **~ therapy** *n* Sprachtherapie, Logopädie *f*; (*treatment*) logopädische Behandlung; **~ writer** *n* Ghostwriter(in *f*) (*inf*), Redenschreiber(in *f*) *m*.

speed [spiːd] (*vb: pret, ptp* **sped** *or* **~ed**) [1] *n* (a) Geschwindigkeit *f*; (*fast ~ also*) Schnelligkeit *f*; (*of moving object or person also*) Tempo *nt* ◆ **at ~** äußerst schnell; **at a high/low ~** mit hoher/niedriger Geschwindigkeit; **at full** *or* **top ~** mit Höchstgeschwindigkeit; **at a ~ of 50 mph** mit einer Geschwindigkeit *or* einem Tempo von 50 Meilen pro Stunde; **the ~ of light/sound** die Lichtgeschwindigkeit/Schallgeschwindigkeit; **at the ~ of light** mit Lichtgeschwindigkeit; **walking/reading ~** Schrittempo *nt*/Lesegeschwindigkeit *f*; **to pick up** *or* **gather ~** beschleunigen, schneller werden; (*fig*) (*development*) sich beschleunigen; (*person*) schneller werden; **to lose ~** (an) Geschwindigkeit verlieren; **what ~ were you doing?** wie schnell sind Sie gefahren?; **her typing/shorthand ~ is good** sie kann schnell maschineschreiben/stenographieren; **what is her typing/shorthand ~?** wieviele Anschläge/Silben (pro Minute) schreibt sie?; **with all possible ~** so schnell wie möglich; **with such ~** so schnell; **full ~ ahead!** (*Naut*) volle Kraft voraus!
(b) (*Aut, Tech: gear*) Gang *m* ◆ **three-~ bicycle** Fahrrad mit Dreigangschaltung; **a three-~ gear** ein Dreiganggetriebe *nt*.
(c) (*Phot*) (*film ~*) Lichtempfindlichkeit *f*; (*shutter ~*) Belichtungszeit *f*.
(d) (*sl: drug*) Speed *nt* (*sl*), Schnellmacher *m* (*sl*).
[2] *vt* **to ~ sb on his way** (*person*) jdn verabschieden; (*iro*) jdn hinauskomplimentieren; (*good wishes etc*) jdn auf seinem Weg begleiten; **if you fetch the visitors' coats it may ~ them on their way** wenn du die Mäntel der Gäste holst, machen sie sich vielleicht auf den Weg; **to ~ an arrow** (*old*) einen Pfeil abschießen; **God ~ you!** (*old*) Gott (sei) mit dir! (*old*).
[3] *vi* (a) *pret, ptp* **sped** (*move quickly*) jagen, flitzen; (*arrow*) sausen, flitzen ◆ **the years sped by** die Jahre verflogen *or* vergingen wie im Fluge; **God ~** (*old*) Gott mit dir (*old*).
(b) *pret, ptp* **~ed** (*Aut: exceed ~ limit*) zu schnell fahren, die Geschwindigkeitsbegrenzung überschreiten.

◆**speed along** *pret, ptp* **~ed** *or* **sped ~** [1] *vt sep work etc* beschleunigen.
[2] *vi* entlangjagen *or* -flitzen (*+prep obj acc*); (*work*) vorangehen.

◆**speed off** *pret, ptp* **~ed** *or* **sped ~** *vi* davonjagen; (*car also*) davonbrausen; (*person also*) davonflitzen.

◆**speed up** *pret, ptp* **~ed ~** [1] *vi* (*car, driver etc*) beschleunigen; (*person*) Tempo zulegen, schneller machen; (*work, production etc*) schneller werden ◆ **their pace ~ed ~** ihr Tempo wurde schneller; **with practice you'll ~ ~** wenn du erst mehr Übung hast, wirst du schneller.
[2] *vt sep* beschleunigen; *person* antreiben, auf Trab bringen (*inf*); *research also* vorantreiben ◆ **that ~ed me ~** das hat mir Antrieb gegeben; **tell her to ~ ~ that coffee** (*inf*) sag ihr, sie soll sich mit dem Kaffee beeilen.

speed: ~boat *n* Renn- *or* Schnellboot *nt*; **~ bump** *n* Bodenschwelle *f*; **~ cop** *n* (*inf*) weiße Maus (*inf*), Verkehrsbulle *m* (*inf*).

speeder ['spiːdə^r] *n* Temposünder(in *f*) *m* (*inf*), Raser *m* (*inf*).

speedily ['spiːdɪlɪ] *adv* schnell; *reply, return* prompt.

speediness ['spiːdɪnɪs] *n* Schnelligkeit *f*.

speeding ['spiːdɪŋ] *n* Geschwindigkeitsüberschreitung *f* ◆ **to get a ~ fine** eine Geldstrafe wegen Geschwindigkeitsüberschreitung bekommen.

speed: ~ limit *n* Geschwindigkeitsbegrenzung *f*; **a 30 mph ~ limit** eine Geschwindigkeitsbegrenzung von 50 km/h; (*inf: area*) eine Strecke mit einer Geschwindigkeitsbegrenzung von 50 km/h; **~ merchant** *n* (*inf*) Raser *m* (*inf*); **Nicholas is a real ~ merchant** Nicholas fährt wie der Henker (*inf*).

speedo ['spiːdəʊ] *n* (*Brit inf*) Tacho *m* (*inf*).

speedometer [spɪ'dɒmɪtə^r] *n* Geschwindigkeitsmesser, Tachometer *m*.

speed: ~ skater *n* Eisschnelläufer(in *f*) *m*; **~ skating** *n* Eisschnellauf *m*.

speedster ['spiːdstə^r] *n* (*inf*) (*car*) Flitzer *m*; (*person*) rasanter Fahrer, rasante Fahrerin, Raser *m* (*inf*).

speed: ~ trap *n* Radarfalle *f* (*inf*); **~-up** *n* (*inf*) schnelleres Tempo (*inf*) (*in* bei), Beschleunigung *f* (*in gen*); (*in research*) Vorantreiben *nt* (*in gen*); (*in rate of inflation*) Steigerung *f* (*in gen*); **~way** *n* (a) (*Sport*) Speedwayrennen *nt*;

(*track*) Speedway- *or* Aschenrennbahn *f*; **(b)** (*US*) (*race-track*) Rennstrecke *f*; (*expressway*) Schnellstraße *f*; **~well** *n* (*Bot*) Ehrenpreis *m or nt*, Veronika *f*; **~-writing** *n* Schnellschreiben *nt*.

speedy ['spiːdɪ] *adj* (+*er*) schnell; *answer, service also* prompt; *remedy* schnell wirkend.

speleologist [ˌspiːlɪ'ɒlədʒɪst] *n* Höhlenkundler(in *f*) *m*.

speleology [ˌspiːlɪ'ɒlədʒɪ] *n* Höhlenkunde, Speläologie (*spec*) *f*.

spell[1] [spel] *n* (*lit, fig*) Zauber *m*; (*incantation*) Zauberspruch *m* ◆ **to be under a ~** (*lit*) unter einem Zauber stehen, verzaubert *or* verhext sein; (*fig*) wie verzaubert sein; **to put a ~ on sb, to cast a ~ over sb, to put sb under a ~** (*lit*) jdn verzaubern *or* verhexen; (*fig*) jdn in seinen Bann ziehen, jdn verzaubern; **to be under sb's ~** (*fig*) in jds Bann (*dat*) stehen; **to break the ~** (*lit, fig*) den Bann brechen, den Zauber lösen.

spell[2] *n* (*period*) Weile *f*, Weilchen *nt* ◆ **for a ~** eine Weile, eine Zeitlang; **cold/hot ~** Kälte-/Hitzewelle *f*; **dizzy ~** Schwächeanfall *m*; **a short ~ of sunny weather** eine kurze Schönwetterperiode; **we had** *or* **spent a ~ in Chile** wir hielten uns eine Zeitlang in Chile auf; **to do a ~ on the assembly line/as a waitress** sich kurzzeitig am Fließband/als Serviererin betätigen; **he did** *or* **had a ~ in prison** er hat eine Zeitlang (im Gefängnis) gesessen; **to take a ~ at the wheel** eine Zeitlang *or* ein Weilchen das Steuer übernehmen; **they're going through a bad ~** sie machen eine schwierige Zeit durch.

spell[3] *pret, ptp* **~ed** *or* **spelt** [1] *vi* (*in writing*) (orthographisch) richtig schreiben; (*aloud*) buchstabieren ◆ **she can't ~** sie kann keine Rechtschreibung; **children should learn to ~** Kinder sollten richtig schreiben lernen.

[2] *vt* **(a)** schreiben; (*aloud*) buchstabieren ◆ **how do you ~ "onyx"?** wie schreibt man „Onyx"?; **how do you ~ your name?** wie schreibt sich Ihr Name?, wie schreiben Sie sich?; **what do these letters ~?** welches Wort ergeben diese Buchstaben?

(b) (*denote*) bedeuten ◆ **it ~s disaster (for us)** das bedeutet Unglück (für uns).

◆**spell out** *vt sep* (*spell aloud*) buchstabieren; (*read slowly*) entziffern; (*explain*) verdeutlichen, klarmachen ◆ **to ~ sth ~ for sb** jdm etw klarmachen; **he needs everything ~ed ~ to him** man muß ihm alles überdeutlich machen; **do I have to ~ it ~ for you?** (*inf*) muß ich noch deutlicher werden?

spellbinder ['spelbaɪndə[r]] *n* fesselnder Redner/Schauspieler/Sänger; (*film*) fesselnder Film, Knüller *m* (*inf*) ◆ **to be a ~** das Publikum fesseln.

spellbinding ['spelbaɪndɪŋ] *adj* fesselnd.

spellbound ['spelbaʊnd] *adj, adv* (*fig*) wie verzaubert, gebannt; (*lit*) *princess, castle* verzaubert ◆ **to hold sb ~** jdn fesseln; (*person also*) jdn in seinen Bann schlagen.

spell-checker ['spelˌtʃekə[r]] *n* (*Comput*) Rechtschreibprüfung *f*.

speller ['spelə[r]] *n* **to be a good/bad ~** in Rechtschreibung gut/schlecht sein.

spelling ['spelɪŋ] *n* Rechtschreibung, Orthographie *f*; (*of a word*) Schreibweise *f*; (*activity*) Rechtschreiben *nt*; (*Sch: lesson*) Rechtschreibeunterricht *m* ◆ **the correct ~ is ...** die richtige Schreibweise ist ...

spelling: ~ bee *n* (*Sch*) Buchstabierwettbewerb *m*; **~ book** *n* Fibel *f*; **~ check** *n* (*Comput*) Rechtschreibprüfung *f*; **~ mistake** *n* (Recht)schreibfehler *m*, orthographischer Fehler; **~ pronunciation** *n* buchstabengetreue Aussprache.

spelt[1] [spelt] *n* (*Bot*) Spelz(weizen), Dinkel *m*.

spelt[2] *pret, ptp of* **spell[3]**.

spelunker [spɪ'lʌŋkə[r]] *n* Hobby-Höhlenforscher(in *f*) *m*.

spend [spend] *pret, ptp* **spent** [1] *vt* **(a)** (*use*) *money* ausgeben (*on* für); *energy, strength* verbrauchen; *time* brauchen ◆ **I've spent all my strength** ich habe meine ganze Kraft aufgebraucht; **we spent a lot of time in useless discussion** wir haben sehr viel Zeit mit nutzlosen Diskussionen vertan; **I've spent three hours on this job** ich habe drei Stunden für diese Arbeit gebraucht; **time well spent** sinnvoll genutzte Zeit.

(b) (*pass*) *time, holiday, evening etc* verbringen ◆ **he ~s all his spare time on his car/with his friends** er verbringt jede freie Minute an seinem Auto/mit seinen Freunden; **I ~ my weekends sleeping** ich verschlafe meine Wochenenden; **he ~s his time reading** er verbringt seine Zeit mit Lesen.

(c) to ~ money/time/effort on sth (*devote to*) Geld/Zeit/Mühe für etw aufbringen *or* in etw (*acc*) investieren; **I spent a lot of effort on that** das hat mich viel Mühe gekostet.

(d) (*exhaust*) **to have spent itself** (*anger, fury*) sich erschöpft *or* gelegt haben; **the storm had spent itself** *or* **its fury** der Sturm hatte sich ausgetobt *or* gelegt; *see also* **spent**.

[2] *vi* Geld ausgeben ◆ **he was ~ing somewhat too freely** er gab das Geld mit vollen Händen aus.

spender ['spendə[r]] *n* **he is a big/free ~** bei ihm sitzt das Geld locker; **the Arabs are the big ~s nowadays** heutzutage haben die Araber das große Geld; **the last of the big ~s** (*iro*) ein echter Großkapitalist (*hum*).

spending ['spendɪŋ] *n, no pl* Ausgaben *pl* ◆ **government ~ cuts** Kürzungen im Etat.

spending: ~ money *n* Taschengeld *nt*; **~ power** *n* Kaufkraft *f*; **~ spree** *n* Großeinkauf *m*; **to go on a ~ spree** groß einkaufen gehen.

spendthrift ['spendθrɪft] [1] *adj* verschwenderisch.

[2] *n* Verschwender(in *f*) *m*.

spent [spent] [1] *pret, ptp of* **spend**.

[2] *adj ammunition, cartridge, match* verbraucht; *bullets also* verschossen; *person* erschöpft ◆ **to be/look ~** erschöpft sein/aussehen; (*prematurely aged*) müde und verbraucht sein/aussehen; **as a poet he was ~ at 25** mit 25 war seine dichterische Schaffenskraft verbraucht; **to be a ~ force** nichts mehr zu sagen haben; (*movement*) sich totgelaufen haben; (*ideology*) keine Zugkraft mehr haben.

sperm [spɜːm] *n* Samenfaden *m*, Spermatozoon, Spermium *nt*; (*fluid*) Samenflüssigkeit *f*, Sperma *nt*.

spermaceti [ˌspɜːmə'setɪ] *n* Spermazet, Walrat *nt*.

spermatic [spɜː'mætɪk] *adj* Samen-.

spermatozoon [ˌspɜːmætəʊ'zəʊɒn] *n, pl* **spermatozoa** [ˌspɜːmætə'zəʊə] Spermatozoon, Spermium *nt*.

sperm count *n* Spermienzahl *f*.

spermicidal [ˌspɜːmɪ'saɪdəl] *adj* spermizid.

spermicide ['spɜːmɪsaɪd] *n* Spermizid *nt*.

sperm: ~ oil *n* Walratöl *nt*; **~ whale** *n* Pottwal *m*.

spew [spjuː] [1] *vi* **(a)** (*sl: vomit*) brechen, spucken ◆ **it makes me ~** (*fig*) es kotzt mich an (*sl*).

(b) (*flow: also* **~ forth** (*form*) *or* **out**) sich ergießen (*geh*); (*liquid also*) hervorsprudeln ◆ **flames/water ~ed out of** *or* **from the cave** Flammen schlugen *or* züngelten aus der Höhle hervor/Wasser sprudelte aus der Höhle hervor.

[2] *vt* **(a)** (*also* **~ up**) (*sl: vomit*) erbrechen, ausspucken; *blood* spucken, speien.

(b) (*fig: also* **~ out**) *flames* spucken, speien; *lava also* auswerfen; *waste water etc* ablassen ◆ **the popular press ~s out lies** die Boulevardpresse überschüttet ihre Leser mit Lügen.

sphagnum ['sfægnəm] *n* Torf- *or* Bleichmoos *nt*.

sphere [sfɪə[r]] *n* **(a)** Kugel *f*; (*heavenly* **~**) Gestirn *nt* (*geh*); (*old Astron*) Sphäre *f* (*old*) ◆ **the celestial ~** (*poet*) das Himmelszelt (*poet*); **to be a ~** kugelförmig sein; *see* **music**.

(b) (*fig*) Sphäre, Welt *f*; (*of person, personal experience*) Bereich *m*; (*of knowledge etc*) Gebiet, Feld *nt*; (*social etc circle*) Kreis *m* ◆ **in the ~ of politics/poetry** in der Sphäre *or* Welt der Politik/Welt der Dichtung; **his ~ of interest/influence** sein Interessen-/Einflußbereich; **~ of activity** (*job, specialism*) Wirkungskreis *m*; **that's outside my ~** das geht über meinen Horizont; (*not my responsibility*) das ist nicht mein Gebiet.

spherical ['sferɪkəl] *adj* (*in shape*) kugelförmig, (kugel)rund; (*Math, Astron*) sphärisch.

spheroid ['sfɪərɔɪd] *n* (*Geometry*) Rotationsellipsoid *nt*.

sphincter ['sfɪŋktə[r]] *n* (*Anat*) Schließmuskel, Sphinkter (*spec*) *m*.

sphinx [sfɪŋks] *n* Sphinx *f*.

sphinx-like ['sfɪŋkslaɪk] *adj* sphinxhaft.

spice [spaɪs] [1] *n* **(a)** Gewürz *nt* ◆ **~ rack** Gewürzbord *or* -regal *nt*; **~ trade** Gewürzhandel *m*; **mixed ~** Gewürzmischung *f*.

(b) (*fig*) Würze *f*; (*trace: of irony, humour*) Anflug, Hauch *m* ◆ **the ~ of life** die Würze des Lebens; **stories with some ~** pikante Geschichten *pl*.

[2] *vt* (*lit, fig*) würzen ◆ **a highly ~d account** (*fig*) ein reichlich ausgeschmückter Bericht.

spiciness ['spaɪsɪnɪs] *n* (*quality*) Würzigkeit, Würze *f*; (*taste*) Würze *f*; (*fig*) Pikanterie *f* ◆ **because of its ~** weil das so stark gewürzt ist.

spick-and-span ['spɪkən'spæn] *adj house etc* blitzsauber, tipptopp in Ordnung *pred* ◆ **to look ~** (*person*) wie aus dem Ei gepellt aussehen; (*house*) blitzsauber sein.

spicy ['spaɪsɪ] *adj* (+*er*) würzig; *sauce, food also* stark gewürzt; (*fig*) *story etc* pikant.

spider ['spaɪdə[r]] *n* **(a)** Spinne *f* ◆ **~'s web** Spinnwebe *f*, Spinnengewebe, Spinnennetz *nt*. **(b)** (*inf: wheelbrace*) Kreuzschlüssel *m*.

spider: ~ crab *n* Spinnenkrabbe *f or* -krebs *m*; **~man** *n* (*inf*) **(a)** (*building worker*) Gerüstbauer *m*; **(b)** (*steeplejack*) Schornsteinarbeiter *m*; **~ monkey** *n* Klammeraffe *m*; **~ plant** *n* Grünlilie *f*; **~web** *n* (*US*) Spinnwebe *f*, Spinnengewebe, Spinnennetz *nt*.

spidery ['spaɪdərɪ] *adj writing* krakelig; *outline, drawing, pattern* fein, spinnwebartig; *limbs etc* spinnenhaft.

spiel [ʃpiːl] *n* (*inf*) Sermon *m* (*inf*), Blabla *nt* (*inf*); (*tall story, excuse*) Geschichte *f* (*inf*).

spiffing ['spɪfɪŋ] *adj* (*dated inf*) famos (*dated inf*).

spigot ['spɪgət] *n* (*on cask*) Spund, Zapfen *m*; (*in tap*) Abschlußkörper *m*; (*US: faucet*) Hahn *m*.

spike [spaɪk] [1] *n* **(a)** (*on wall, railing, helmet etc*) Spitze *f*; (*nail*) Nagel *m*; (*on plant*) Stachel *m*; (*on shoe, tyre etc*) Spike *m*; (*for receipts, wastepaper etc*) Dorn *m* ◆ **~ heel** Pfennigabsatz *m*; *see also* **spikes**. **(b)** (*Bot*) Ähre *f*. **(c)** (*Elec*) Spannungsspitze *f*.

[2] *vt* **(a)** aufspießen; (*with weapon also*) durchbohren ◆ **the editor ~d the story** (*Press*) der Redakteur ließ die Story in einer Schublade verschwinden.

(b) (*fig: frustrate*) *rumours* den Boden entziehen (+*dat*) ◆ **to ~ sb's guns** (*inf*) jdm den Wind aus den Segeln nehmen.

(c) (*US: lace*) *drink* einen Schuß zusetzen (+*dat*) ◆ **~d with rum** mit einem Schuß Rum.

spiked [spaɪkt] *adj shoe* mit Spikes; *drink* mit Schuß.

spikes [spaɪks] *npl* (*inf: running shoes*) Spikes *pl*.

spiky ['spaɪkɪ] *adj* (+*er*) **(a)** (*having spikes*) *railings, top of wall* mit Metallspitzen; *bush, animal* stach(e)lig; *branch* dornig.

(b) (*like spikes*) *grass* spitz, stach(e)lig; *flower* mit spitzen Blütenblättern; *plant* spitzblättrig; *leaf* spitz; *hair* hochstehend; *writing* steil.

(c) (*fig*) *person* empfindlich, leicht eingeschnappt (*inf*).

spill[1] [spɪl] (*vb: pret, ptp* **~ed** *or* **spilt**) [1] *n* (*fall*) Sturz *m* ◆ **to have a ~** stürzen.

[2] *vt* **(a)** verschütten; *liquid also, blood* vergießen ◆ **to ~ the beans (to sb)** (*inf*) (jdm gegenüber) nicht dichthalten (*inf*); **to ~ the beans about sth** etw ausplaudern.

(b) (*horse*) abwerfen ◆ **the lorry ~ed its load onto the road** die Ladung fiel

vom Lastwagen herunter auf die Straße.
[3] *vi* verschüttet werden; (*large quantity*) sich ergießen; (*tears*) strömen, laufen; (*fig: people*) strömen ♦ **the milk ~ed all over the carpet** die Milch war auf dem ganzen Teppich verschüttet; **the blood ~ed onto the floor** das Blut floß auf den Boden.

◆**spill out** [1] *vi* (*of* aus) (*liquid*) herausschwappen; (*grain*) herausrieseln; (*money, jewels*) herausfallen; (*fig: people*) (heraus)strömen ♦ **clothes were ~ing ~ of the drawer** Kleidungsstücke quollen aus der Schublade hervor.
[2] *vt sep* ausschütten; (*by accident also*) verschütten; *liquid also* vergießen.

◆**spill over** *vi* (*liquid*) überlaufen; (*grain etc, assembly*) überquellen; (*fig*) (*population*) sich ausbreiten (*into* auf *+acc*); (*meeting*) sich hinziehen (*into* bis in *+acc*).

spill² *n* (*of wood*) (Kien)span *m*; (*of paper*) Fidibus *m*.

spillage ['spɪlɪdʒ] *n* (*act*) Verschütten *nt*; (*of liquid also*) Vergießen *nt*; (*quantity*) verschüttete Menge, Spillage *f* (*Comm*) ♦ **the ~ amounted to ...** es waren ... verschüttet worden.

spillikin ['spɪlɪkɪn] *n* **(a)** (*old: spill*) Kienspan *m*. **(b)** **~s** *pl* (*game*) Mikado *nt*.

spill-over ['spɪləʊvə^r] *n* Überschuß *m* ♦ **~ population** überquellende Bevölkerung.

spillway ['spɪlweɪ] *n* Überlaufrinne *f*.

spilt [spɪlt] *pret, ptp of* **spill¹**.

spin [spɪn] (*vb: pret* **spun** *or* (*old*) **span**, *ptp* **spun**) [1] *n* **(a)** (*revolution*) Drehung *f*; (*washing machine programme*) Schleudern *nt no pl* ♦ **to give sth a ~** etw (schnell) drehen; *spinning top* etw treiben; (*in washing machine etc*) etw schleudern; **to be in a (flat) ~** (*fig inf*) am Rotieren *or* Durchdrehen sein (*inf*) (*about* wegen); **to send sb into a (flat) ~** (*fig inf*) jdn zum Rotieren bringen (*inf*).
(b) (*on ball*) Dreh, Drall *m*; (*Billiards*) Effet *m* ♦ **to put a ~ on the ball** dem Ball einen Drall/Effet geben; (*with racquet*) den Ball anschneiden.
(c) (*Aviat*) Trudeln *nt no pl* ♦ **to go into a ~** zu trudeln anfangen.
(d) (*dated: trip*) Spritztour *f* ♦ **to go for a ~** eine Spritztour machen.
[2] *vt* **(a)** spinnen; *see* **yarn**. **(b)** (*turn*) *wheel* drehen; (*fast*) herumwirbeln; *top* tanzen lassen, treiben; (*in washing machine*) schleudern; (*toss*) *ball, coin* (hoch)werfen; (*Sport*) *ball* einen Drall/Effet geben (*+dat*); (*with racquet*) (an)schneiden.
[3] *vi* **(a)** spinnen.
(b) (*revolve*) sich drehen; (*fast*) (herum)wirbeln; (*plane etc*) trudeln; (*in washing machine*) schleudern ♦ **to ~ round and round** sich im Kreis drehen; (*dancer*) im Kreis herumwirbeln; **the ball spun into the air/past him** der Ball flog wirbelnd in die Luft/an ihm vorbei; **the car spun out of control** der Wagen begann, sich unkontrollierbar zu drehen; **to send sb/sth ~ning** jdn/etw umwerfen; **my head is ~ning** mir dreht sich alles; **the wine/noise makes my head ~** von dem Wein dreht sich mir alles/mir schwirrt der Kopf von dem Lärm.

◆**spin along** *vi* (*move quickly*) (dahin)rasen, (dahin)sausen.

◆**spin out** *vt sep* (*inf*) *money, food* strecken (*inf*); *holiday, meeting* in die Länge ziehen; *story* ausspinnen.

◆**spin round** [1] *vi* (*revolve*) sich drehen; (*very fast*) (herum)wirbeln; (*in surprise*) herumwirbeln, herumfahren.
[2] *vt sep* (schnell) drehen; (*very fast*) herumwirbeln.

spina bifida ['spaɪnə'bɪfɪdə] [1] *n* offene Wirbelsäule, Spina bifida *f* (*spec*).
[2] *adj attr baby* mit einer offenen Wirbelsäule.

spinach ['spɪnɪtʃ] *n* Spinat *m*.

spinal ['spaɪnl] *adj vertebrae* Rücken-; *injury, muscle* Rückgrat-, spinal (*spec*); *nerves, anaesthesia* Rückenmark(s)- ♦ **~ column** Wirbelsäule *f*; **~ cord** Rückenmark *nt*.

spin bowler *n* (*Cricket*) *Werfer, der dem Ball einen Drall gibt.*

spindle ['spɪndl] *n* (*for spinning, Mech*) Spindel *f*.

spindleshanks ['spɪndlʃæŋks] *n* (*inf*) **(a)** *pl* (*legs*) Streichholzbeine (*inf*), Stelzen (*inf*) *pl*. **(b)** *sing* (*person*) Langbein *nt* (*inf*).

spindly ['spɪndlɪ] *adj* (*+er*) *legs, arms, plant* spindeldürr (*inf*); *chairs* zierlich.

spin: ~-drier, ~-dryer *n* (*Brit*) (Wäsche)schleuder *f*; **~drift** *n* Gischt *f*; **~-dry** *vti* schleudern; **~-dryer** *n see* **~-drier**.

spine [spaɪn] *n* **(a)** (*Anat*) Rückgrat *nt*; (*of book*) (Buch)rücken *m*; (*of mountain range*) (Gebirgs)grat *m*. **(b)** (*spike*) Stachel *m*; (*of plant also*) Dorn *m*.

spine: ~-chiller *n* (*inf*) Gruselgeschichte *f*; Gruselfilm *m*; **~-chilling** *adj* (*inf*) schaurig, gruselig; *noise also* unheimlich.

spineless ['spaɪnlɪs] *adj* **(a)** (*Anat*) wirbellos; (*fig*) *person* ohne Rückgrat; *compromise, refusal* feige ♦ **don't be so ~** beweisen Sie mal, daß Sie Rückgrat haben! **(b)** (*Zool*) ohne Stacheln, stachellos; (*Bot also*) ohne Dornen, dornenlos.

spinelessly ['spaɪnlɪslɪ] *adv* (*fig*) feige.

spinet [spɪ'net] *n* **(a)** Spinett *nt*. **(b)** (*US*) Kleinklavier *nt*.

spinnaker ['spɪnəkə^r] *n* (*Naut*) Spinnaker *m*.

spinner ['spɪnə^r] *n* **(a)** (*of cloth*) Spinner(in *f*) *m*. **(b)** (*inf*) *see* **spin-drier**. **(c)** (*Fishing*) Spinnköder *m*. **(d)** (*Cricket*) *Werfer, der den Bällen einen Drall gibt.*

spinney ['spɪnɪ] *n* (*esp Brit*) Dickicht *nt*.

spinning ['spɪnɪŋ] *n* Spinnen *nt*.

spinning *in cpds* Spinn-; **~ jenny** *n* Jenny-Maschine *f*; **~ top** *n* Kreisel *m*; **~ wheel** *n* Spinnrad *nt*; **~ works** *n sing or pl* Spinnerei, Spinnstoffabrik *f*.

spin-off ['spɪnɒf] *n* (*side-product*) Nebenprodukt *nt* ♦ **~ effect** Folgewirkung *f*.

spinster ['spɪnstə^r] *n* Unverheiratete, Ledige *f*; (*pej*) alte Jungfer (*pej*) ♦ **Mary Jones, ~** die ledige Mary Jones; **to be a ~** unverheiratet *or* ledig *or* eine alte Jungfer (*pej*) sein.

spinsterhood ['spɪnstəhʊd] *n* Ehelosigkeit *f*, Jungfernstand *m* (*old*) ♦ **she preferred ~** sie wollte lieber unverheiratet bleiben.

spinsterish ['spɪnstərɪʃ] *adj* (*pej*) altjüngferlich (*pej*).

spiny ['spaɪnɪ] *adj* (*+er*) stach(e)lig, Stachel-; *plant also* dornig ♦ **~ lobster** (*Zool*) Languste *f*, Stachelhummer *m*.

spiracle ['spɪrəkl] *n* (*of shark, ray etc*) Atemloch *nt*; (*of insect also*) Stigma *nt* (*spec*); (*of whale, dolphin*) Spritzloch *nt*.

spiral ['spaɪərəl] [1] *adj* spiralförmig, spiralig; *shell also* gewunden; *nebula, spring* Spiral-; *movement, descent* in Spiralen ♦ **a ~ curve** eine Spirale; **~ staircase** Wendeltreppe *f*.
[2] *n* (*lit, fig*) Spirale *f* ♦ **price/inflationary ~** Preis-/Inflationsspirale *f*.
[3] *vi* (*also* **~ up**) sich (hoch)winden; (*smoke also, missile etc*) spiralförmig *or* in einer Spirale aufsteigen; (*plane, bird also*) sich in die Höhe schrauben; (*prices*) (nach oben) klettern.

◆**spiral down** *vi* spiralförmig *or* in einer Spirale herunterkommen; (*staircase also*) sich abwärts winden; (*plane also*) sich herunterschrauben, sich nach unten schrauben.

spirally ['spaɪərəlɪ] *adv* in einer Spirale, spiralförmig.

spire [spaɪə^r] *n* (*of church*) Turmspitze *f*, Turm *m*.

spirit ['spɪrɪt] [1] *n* **(a)** (*soul*) Geist *m* ♦ **the life of the ~** das Seelenleben; **he was troubled in ~** (*liter*) etwas lastete auf seiner Seele (*geh*); **I'll be with you in ~** im Geiste werde ich bei euch sein; **the ~ is willing (but the flesh is weak)** der Geist ist willig(, aber das Fleisch ist schwach).
(b) (*supernatural being, ghost*) Geist *m*.
(c) (*leading person*) (*of age, movement etc*) Geist *m*; (*of party, enterprise also*) Kopf *m*.
(d) *no pl* (*courage*) Mut, Schneid *m*; (*vitality, enthusiasm*) Elan, Schwung *m* ♦ **a man of ~** (*courageous*) ein mutiger Mensch; **a horse with plenty of ~** ein feuriges Pferd; **to break sb's ~** jdn *or* jds Mut brechen; **to sing/reply with ~** mit Inbrunst singen/mutig antworten; **to put ~ into sb** jdm Mut machen.
(e) (*mental attitude: of country, group of people, doctrine, reform etc*) Geist *m*; (*mood*) Stimmung *f* ♦ **pioneering/team/community ~** Pionier-/Mannschaftsgeist *m*/Gemeinschaftssinn *m*; **Christmas ~** (*Rel*) weihnachtlicher Geist; (*mood*) weihnachtliche Stimmung; **party ~** Partystimmung *f*; **fighting ~** Kampfgeist; **a ~ of optimism/despair/rebellion** eine optimistische/verzweifelte/rebellische Stimmung; **to do sth in a ~ of optimism/humility** etw voll Optimismus/voller Demut tun; **in a ~ of forgiveness/revenge** aus einer vergebenden/rachsüchtigen Stimmung heraus; **Christian ~** Christlichkeit; **the ~ of the age** der Zeitgeist; **he has the right ~** er hat die richtige Einstellung; **to enter into the ~ of sth** bei etw mitmachen *or* dabeisein; **when the ~ moves him** wenn es ihn überkommt; **that's the ~!** (*inf*) so ist's recht! (*inf*).
(f) *no pl* (*intention*) Geist *m* ♦ **the ~ of the law** der Geist *or* Sinn des Gesetzes; **to take sth in the right/wrong ~** etw richtig/falsch auffassen; **to take sth in the ~ in which it was meant/given** etw so nehmen, wie es gemeint war; **the ~ in which it is done** wie es getan wird.
(g) **~s** *pl* (*state of mind*) Stimmung, Laune *f*; (*courage*) Mut *m* ♦ **to be in good/bad/out of ~s** guter/schlechter Laune/niedergeschlagen sein; **to keep up one's ~s** den Mut nicht verlieren; **my ~s rose/fell** ich bekam (neuen) Mut/mir sank der Mut; **to raise sb's ~s** jdn aufmuntern; **to revive sb's ~s** jds Lebensgeister wiedererwecken.
(h) **~s** *pl* (*alcohol*) Branntwein *m*, Spirituosen, geistige Getränke *pl* ♦ **raw ~s** reiner Alkohol.
(i) (*Chem*) Spiritus *m* ♦ **~s of ammonia** Salmiakgeist *m*; **~(s) of turpentine** Terpentinöl *nt*.
[2] *vt* **to ~ sb/sth away** *or* **off** jdn/etw verschwinden lassen *or* wegzaubern; **to ~ sb out of a room** *etc* jdn aus einem Zimmer *etc* wegzaubern.

spirited ['spɪrɪtɪd] *adj* temperamentvoll; *horse also* feurig; *book, performance* lebendig; (*courageous*) *person, reply, attack, attempt etc* beherzt, mutig.

spiritedly ['spɪrɪtɪdlɪ] *adv see adj*.

spiritedness ['spɪrɪtɪdnɪs] *n see adj* Temperament *nt*; Feurigkeit *f*; Lebendigkeit *f*; Beherztheit *f*, Mut *m*.

spirit: ~ gum *n* Mastix(gummi) *m*; **~ lamp** *n* Petroleumlampe *f*; **~less** *adj person, performance, book* saft- und kraftlos; *agreement, acceptance, reply* lustlos; *animal* brav, lahm (*inf*); **~ level** *n* Wasserwaage *f*; **~ stove** *n* Spirituskocher *m*.

spiritual ['spɪrɪtjʊəl] [1] *adj* geistig; *expression* vergeistigt; (*Eccl*) geistlich ♦ **~ life** Seelenleben *nt*; **my ~ home** meine geistige Heimat; **Lords ~** geistliche Lords (im Oberhaus).
[2] *n* (*Mus*) Spiritual *nt*.

spiritualism ['spɪrɪtjʊəlɪzəm] *n* Spiritismus *m*.

spiritualist ['spɪrɪtjʊəlɪst] *n* Spiritist(in *f*) *m*.

spirituality [,spɪrɪtjʊ'ælɪtɪ] *n see adj* Geistigkeit *f*; Vergeistigung *f*.

spiritually ['spɪrɪtjʊəlɪ] *adv* geistig ♦ **~, he is ...** in geistiger Hinsicht ist er ...

spirituous ['spɪrɪtjʊəs] *adj* (*form*) alkoholisch, spirituos (*rare*).

spit¹ [spɪt] (*vb: pret, ptp* **spat**) [1] *n* **(a)** (*action*) (Aus)spucken *nt*; (*saliva*) Spucke *f* ♦ **to have a ~** ausspucken; **there was just a ~ of rain** es tröpfelte nur; **to give sth a bit of ~ and polish** (*inf*) etw wienern (*inf*); **it needs a bit of ~ and polish** (*inf*) es müßte einmal tüchtig gewienert werden (*inf*).
(b) (*inf: image*) *see* **spitting image**.
[2] *vt* spucken, speien (*geh*); *curses* ausstoßen (*at* gegen).
[3] *vi* spucken, speien (*geh*); (*fat*) spritzen; (*fire*) zischen; (*person: verbally, cat*) fauchen, zischen ♦ **to ~ at sb** jdn anspucken, jdn anspeien (*geh*); jdn anfauchen, jdn anzischen; **to ~ in sb's face/eye** jdm ins Gesicht spucken; (*fig*) auf jdn pfeifen (*inf*); **it is ~ting (with rain)** es tröpfelt.

◆**spit out** *vt sep* ausspucken, ausspeien (*geh*); *words* ausstoßen ♦ **~ it ~!** (*fig* *inf*) spuck's aus! (*inf*), heraus mit der Sprache!

spit[2] [1] *n* (a) (*Cook*) (Brat)spieß *m* ♦ on the ~ am Spieß. (b) (*of land*) Landzunge *f*.
[2] *vt meat* (auf)spießen.

▼ **spite** [spaɪt] [1] *n* (a) (*ill will*) Boshaftigkeit, Gehässigkeit *f* ♦ to do sth out of *or* from ~ etw aus reiner Boshaftigkeit tun.
▼ (b) in ~ of (*despite*) trotz (+*gen*); it was a success/we went in ~ of him es war dennoch ein Erfolg/wir gingen dennoch; he did it in ~ of himself er konnte nicht anders; in ~ of the fact that he ... obwohl er ...; in ~ of that I'll still go ich gehe trotzdem.
[2] *vt* ärgern ♦ she just does it to ~ me sie tut es nur mir zum Trotz, sie tut es nur, um mich zu ärgern.

spiteful ['spaɪtfʊl] *adj* boshaft, gemein; (*gloating also*) schadenfroh, gehässig.

spitefully ['spaɪtfəlɪ] *adv see adj* ♦ ~, she told him voll Bosheit/voll Schadenfreude erzählte sie es ihm.

spitefulness ['spaɪtfʊlnɪs] *n* Boshaftigkeit, Gemeinheit *f*; (*gloating*) Schadenfreude, Gehässigkeit *f*.

spitfire ['spɪtfaɪəʳ] *n* feuerspeiender Drache; (*woman also*) Giftnudel *f* (*inf*).

spitroast ['spɪtrəʊst] *vt* am Spieß braten ♦ with ~ pieces of lamb mit Lammstücken vom Spieß.

spitting image ['spɪtɪŋ'ɪmɪdʒ] *n* (*inf*) Ebenbild *nt* ♦ to be the ~ of sb jdm wie aus dem Gesicht geschnitten sein, jdm zum Verwechseln ähnlich sehen.

spittle ['spɪtl] *n* Speichel *m*, Spucke *f*.

spittoon [spɪ'tu:n] *n* Spucknapf *m*.

spiv [spɪv] *n* (*Brit sl*) schmieriger Typ (*sl*).

spivvy ['spɪvɪ] *adj* (*Brit sl*) *person* schmierig (*inf*); *tie, suit etc* ordinär.

splash [splæʃ] [1] *n* (a) (*spray*) Spritzen *nt no pl*; (*noise*) Platschen *nt no pl*, Platscher *m* (*inf*) ♦ he dived in with a ~ es spritzte/platschte, als er hineinsprang; it made a ~ as it hit the water das Wasser spritzte nach allen Seiten, als es hineinfiel; (*noise*) es fiel platschend ins Wasser; to make a ~ (*fig*) Furore machen; (*news*) wie eine Bombe einschlagen; (*book*) einschlagen; a great ~ of publicity großes Tamtam (*inf*).
(b) (*sth ~ed*) Spritzer *m*; (*in drink etc also*) Schuß *m*; (*of colour, light*) Tupfen *m*; (*patch*) Fleck *m* ♦ ~es of paint Farbspritzer *pl*.
[2] *vt* (a) *water etc* spritzen; (*pour*) gießen; *person, object* bespritzen ♦ to ~ sb with water, to ~ water over sb jdn mit Wasser bespritzen; to ~ paint on sth etw mit Farbe bespritzen; (*with brush*) Farbe auf etw (*acc*) klatschen (*inf*); to ~ one's way through a stream platschend einen Bach durchqueren.
(b) (*Press inf*) *story* groß rausbringen (*inf*) ♦ the story was ~ed all over the papers die Geschichte wurde in allen Zeitungen groß rausgebracht (*inf*).
[3] *vi* (*liquid*) spritzen; (*rain, waves*) klatschen; (*tears*) tropfen; (*when diving, walking etc*) platschen; (*when playing*) planschen.

◆**splash about** [1] *vi* herumspritzen; (*in water*) herumplanschen; (*while walking*) herumplatschen.
[2] *vt sep water* herumspritzen mit; (*fig inf*) *money* um sich werfen mit (*inf*); *story* groß aufziehen *or* rausbringen (*inf*).

◆**splash down** *vi* (a) (*Space*) wassern. (b) (*rain*) herunterrinnen (*prep obj* an +*dat*).

◆**splash out** *vi* (*inf*) tüchtig in die Tasche greifen (*inf*); (*on reception, giving presents etc*) sich nicht lumpen lassen (*inf* ♦ to ~ ~ on sth sich (*dat*) etw spendieren (*inf*).

◆**splash up** [1] *vt sep* spritzen.
[2] *vi* (*water, mud*) aufspritzen.

splash: ~back, ~board *n* Spritzschutz *m*; **~down** *n* (*Space*) Wasserung *f*; **~ guard** *n* (*US Aut*) Schmutzfänger *m*.

splat [splæt] [1] *n* Platschen *nt*.
[2] *adv* to go ~ into sth gegen etw platschen.

splatter ['splætəʳ] [1] *n* Spritzen *nt no pl*; (*of rain*) Prasseln *nt no pl*; (*sth ~ed*) Fleck *m*; (*of ink, paint etc*) Klecks *m*; (*Art:* ~ *technique*) Spritztechnik *f*.
[2] *vi* spritzen; (*rain also*) prasseln; (*ink, paint also*) klecksen.
[3] *vt* bespritzen; (*with ink, paint etc*) beklecksen ♦ to ~ mud over sb jdn mit Schlamm bespritzen.

splay [spleɪ] [1] *vt* (a) (*spread out*) *legs, fingers, toes* spreizen; *feet* nach außen stellen ♦ the wheels are ~ed die Räder stehen nach außen, die Räder haben negativen Sturz.
(b) (*Tech*) *pipe* weiten; *window frame* ausschrägen.
[2] *vi* nach außen gehen; (*pillars also*) sich nach außen biegen; (*window frame*) ausgeschrägt sein ♦ he lay ~ed out on the ground er lag auf der Erde und hatte alle viere von sich gestreckt.
[3] *n* (*Archit*) Ausschrägung *f*.

splay: ~foot *n* nach außen gestellter Fuß; **~ footed** *adj* mit nach außen gestellten Füßen; to be ~footed nach außen gehen.

spleen [spli:n] *n* (*Anat*) Milz *f*; (*fig*) Zorn *m*, Rage *f* ♦ a fit of ~ ein Zornesausbruch *m*; to vent one's ~ seinem Ärger Luft machen; to vent one's ~ on sb seine Wut an jdm auslassen.

splendid ['splendɪd] *adj* (a) (*magnificent*) *clothes, sunset, music* herrlich; *occasion, scale, villain* großartig. (b) (*excellent*) hervorragend; *rider etc, chance, idea, amusement* glänzend, ausgezeichnet; *joke also* herrlich ♦ that's (simply) ~! (das ist ja) ausgezeichnet!

splendidly ['splendɪdlɪ] *adv* (a) (*magnificently*) herrlich. (b) (*excellently*) hervorragend, glänzend, ausgezeichnet.

splendiferous [splen'dɪfərəs] *adj* (*dated inf*) fabelhaft.

splendour, (*US*) **splendor** ['splendəʳ] *n* Pracht *f no pl*; (*of music, achievement*) Großartigkeit *f* ♦ the ~s of the Roman Empire der Glanz *or* die Pracht des Römischen Reiches.

splenetic [splɪ'netɪk] *adj* (a) (*Anat*) Milz-. (b) (*liter: peevish*) unwirsch ♦ his ~ anger seine Galligkeit.

splice [splaɪs] [1] *n* Verbindung *f*; (*of ropes also*) Spleiß *m* (*spec*); (*of tapes, film also*) Klebung *f*; (*of wood also*) Fuge *f*.
[2] *vt ropes* spleißen (*spec*); *tapes, film* (zusammen)kleben; *pieces of wood etc* verfugen ♦ to get ~d (*inf*) sich verehelichen (*hum*).

splicer ['splaɪsəʳ] *n* (*for films*) Klebepresse *f*.

splint [splɪnt] [1] *n* Schiene *f* ♦ to put a ~ on sb/sth jdn/etw schienen; to be in ~s geschient sein.
[2] *vt* schienen.

splinter ['splɪntəʳ] [1] *n* Splitter *m*; (*wooden ~ in finger etc also*) Spleiß, Spreißel (*S Ger*) *m*.
[2] *vt* (zer)splittern; (*with axe*) *wood* zerhacken; (*fig*) *party* spalten.
[3] *vi* (zer)splittern; (*fig: party*) sich spalten ♦ to ~ off absplittern; (*fig*) sich abspalten.

splinter: ~ group *n* Splittergruppe *f*; **~proof** *adj* splitterfrei.

splintery ['splɪntərɪ] *adj* splitt(e)rig.

split [splɪt] (*vb: pret, ptp* ~) [1] *n* (a) Riß *m* (*in* in +*dat*); (*in wall, rock, wood also*) Spalt *m* (*in* in +*dat*).
(b) (*fig: division*) Bruch *m* (*in* in +*dat*), Entzweiung *f* (+*gen*); (*Pol, Eccl*) Spaltung *f* (*in gen*) ♦ there is a ~ in the party over ... die Partei ist in der Frage (+*gen*) ... gespalten; there is a three-way ~ in the party over ... die Partei zerfällt in der Frage (+*gen*) ... in drei Lager, die Partei ist in der Frage (+*gen*) ... dreigeteilt; a three-way ~ of the profits eine Dreiteilung des Gewinns; I want my ~ (*inf*) ich will meinen Schnitt (*inf*).
(c) (*distinction: in meaning*) Aufteilung *f*.
(d) *pl* the ~s Spagat *m* ♦ to do the ~s (einen) Spagat machen.
(e) (*inf: sweet*) (*also* banana ~) (Bananen-)Split *m* ♦ jam/cream ~ *mit Marmelade/Sahne gefülltes Gebäckstück*.
(f) (*esp US: bottle*) kleine Flasche.
[2] *adj* gespalten (*on, over* in +*dat*).
[3] *vt* (a) (*cleave*) (zer)teilen; *wood also, atom* spalten; *stone* zerbrechen; *fabric, garment* zerreißen, zerschlitzen; *seam* aufplatzen lassen ♦ the sea had ~ the ship in two in dem Sturm zerbrach das Schiff in zwei Teile; I ~ the seam die Naht ist (auf)geplatzt; to ~ hairs (*inf*) Haarspalterei treiben (*inf*); to ~ one's sides (laughing) (*inf*) vor Lachen fast platzen (*inf*); to ~ sth open etw aufbrechen; his lip had been ~ open seine Lippe war aufgeplatzt; his head was ~ open when he fell er hatte sich (*dat*) beim Fallen den Kopf aufgeschlagen.
(b) (*divide*) spalten; (*share*) *work, costs etc* (sich *dat*) teilen ♦ to ~ sth into three parts etw in drei Teile aufteilen; to ~ the vote die Abstimmung zum Scheitern bringen; a party ~ three ways eine in drei Lager gespaltene Partei; to ~ one's vote *or* (*US*) ticket panaschieren; they ~ the profit three ways sie haben den Gewinn gedrittelt *or* in drei Teile geteilt; to ~ the difference (*fig: in argument etc*) sich auf halbem Wege einigen; (*lit: with money etc*) sich (*dat*) die Differenz teilen.
[4] *vi* (a) (*wood, stone*) (entzwei)brechen; (*hair*) sich spalten; (*trousers, seam etc*) platzen; (*fabric*) zerreißen; (*ship*) auseinanderbrechen ♦ to ~ open aufplatzen, aufbrechen; to ~ at the seams (*lit*) an den Nähten aufplatzen; (*fig*) aus allen *or* den Nähten platzen; my head is ~ting (*fig*) mir platzt der Kopf.
(b) (*divide*) sich teilen; (*people*) sich aufteilen; (*Pol, church*) sich spalten (*on, over* wegen).
(c) (*sl: leave*) abhauen (*inf*).
(d) (*inf: tell tales*) to ~ on sb jdn verpfeifen (*inf*).

◆**split off** [1] *vt sep* abtrennen (*prep obj* von); (*with axe also*) abspalten (*prep obj* von); (*break*) abbrechen (*prep obj* von).
[2] *vi* abbrechen; (*rock also*) sich lösen; (*fig*) sich trennen (*from* von).

◆**split up** [1] *vt sep money, work* (auf)teilen; *meanings* aufteilen; *party, organization* spalten; *meeting* ein Ende machen (+*dat*); *two people* trennen; *crowd* zerstreuen.
[2] *vi* zerbrechen; (*divide*) sich teilen; (*meeting, crowd*) sich spalten; (*partners*) sich voneinander trennen.

split: ~ decision *n* (*Boxing*) nicht einstimmige Entscheidung; **~ ends** *npl* gespaltene Haarspitzen *pl*, Spliß *m*; **~ infinitive** *n* (*Gram*) getrennter Infinitiv; **~-level** *adj* (*Archit*) mit versetzten Geschossen; **~-level cooker** *Herdkombination, bei der Koch- und Backteil getrennt und in Sichthöhe sind*; **~ peas** *npl* getrocknete (halbe) Erbsen *pl*; **~-pea soup** *n* Erbsensuppe *f*; **~ personality** *n* (*Psych*) gespaltene Persönlichkeit; **~ pin** *n* (*cotter pin*) Splint *m*; (*on envelope*) Musterklammer *f*; **~ screen** *n* (*Comput*) geteilter Bildschirm; **~ second** [1] *n* Bruchteil *m* einer Sekunde; in a ~ second in Sekundenschnelle; [2] *adj* ~-second timing Abstimmung *f* auf die Sekunde; (*of actor*) Gefühl *nt* für den richtigen Moment.

splitting ['splɪtɪŋ] [1] *n* Zerteilung *f*; (*of wood*) Spalten *nt* ♦ the ~ of the atom die Kernspaltung.
[2] *adj headache* rasend, heftig ♦ there was a ~ sound (*of wood*) es klang, als ob etwas zerbräche; (*of cloth*) es klang, als ob etwas zerrisse.

split-up ['splɪtʌp] *n* (*of friends*) Bruch *m* (*of* zwischen +*dat*); (*of partners*) Trennung *f* (*of gen*); (*of party*) Spaltung *f* (*of gen*).

splodge [splɒdʒ], **splotch** [splɒtʃ] [1] *n* Fleck, Klecks *m*; (*of cream etc*) Klacks *m*.
[2] *vt clothes* bespritzen; (*with paint, ink also*) beklecksen; *mud* spritzen; *paint* klecksen.

splurge [splɜ:dʒ] *n* (*inf*) (*shopping spree*) Kauforgie *f* (*pej inf*) ♦ I felt like a ~ ich wollte mir was leisten; to go on a ~ groß einkaufen gehen; a big publicity ~ eine groß aufgemachte Werbekampagne; we had a big ~ on the reception

➤ LANGUAGE IN USE: spite: 1b → 26.2

unser Empfang war ein Riesentamtam (*inf*).

◆**splurge out on** *vi +prep obj (inf)* sich in Unkosten stürzen mit.

splutter ['splʌtəʳ] 1 *n (of engine)* Stottern *nt*; *(of fire)* Zischen *nt*; *(of sausages)* Zischen *nt*; *(while talking)* Prusten *nt no pl*.
2 *vi (person) (spit)* prusten, spucken; *(stutter)* stottern; *(engine)* stottern; *(fire, lamp, fat)* zischen; *(sausages)* brutzeln, zischen ◆ **to ~ with indignation** vor Entrüstung prusten.
3 *vt* (hervor)stoßen ◆ **that's not true, he ~ed** das ist nicht wahr, platzte er los.

spoil [spɔɪl] *(vb: pret, ptp* **~ed** *or* **spoilt)** 1 *n usu pl* Beute *f no pl*; *(fig: profits also)* Gewinn *m* ◆ **the ~s of war/office** die Kriegsbeute/Amtsausbeute; **~s system** *(US Pol)* Ämterpatronage, Filzokratie *(inf) f*.
2 *vt* **(a)** *(ruin, detract from)* verderben; *view also, town, looks etc* verschandeln; *peace of mind* zerstören; *life* ruinieren; *ballot papers* ungültig machen ◆ **to ~ sb's fun** jdm den Spaß verderben; **it ~ed our evening** das hat uns *(dat)* den Abend verdorben; **if you eat now you'll ~ your lunch** wenn du jetzt etwas ißt, verdirbst du dir den Appetit fürs Mittagessen; **~ed ballot papers** ungültige Stimmzettel.
(b) *person* verwöhnen; *children also* verziehen ◆ **to ~ sb for sth** *(inf)* jdn für etw verderben; **to be ~t for choice** eine übergroße Auswahl haben, die Qual der Wahl haben.
3 *vi (food)* verderben ◆ **to be ~ing for trouble/a fight** Ärger/Streit suchen.

spoiler ['spɔɪləʳ] *n (Aut)* Spoiler *m*.

spoilsport ['spɔɪlspɔːt] *n (inf)* Spielverderber *m (inf)*.

spoilt [spɔɪlt] 1 *pret, ptp of* **spoil**.
2 *adj child* verwöhnt, verzogen; *meal* verdorben.

spoke¹ [spəʊk] *n* Speiche *f* ◆ **to put a ~ in sb's wheel** *(inf)* jdm Knüppel zwischen die Beine werfen *(inf)*.

spoke² *pret of* **speak**.

spoken ['spəʊkən] 1 *ptp of* **speak**.
2 *adj language* gesprochen ◆ **his ~ English is better than** ... er spricht Englisch besser als ...; **~-voice record** Sprechplatte *f*.

spokeshave ['spəʊkʃeɪv] *n* Schabhobel, Speichenhobel *m*.

spokesman ['spəʊksmən] *n, pl* **-men** [-mən] Sprecher *m* ◆ **to act as (a) ~ for a group** als Sprecher einer Gruppe auftreten.

spokesperson ['spəʊkspɜːsən] *n* Sprecher(in *f*) *m*.

spokeswoman ['spəʊkswʊmən] *n, pl* **-women** [-wɪmɪn] Sprecherin *f*.

spoliation [ˌspəʊlɪ'eɪʃən] *n (liter)* Plünderung *f*.

spondee ['spɒndiː] *n* Spondeus *m*.

sponge [spʌndʒ] 1 *n* **(a)** Schwamm *m*; *see* **throw in**.
(b) *(sponging)* **to give sth a ~** *floor* etw aufwischen; *car* etw waschen; *walls* etw abwaschen; *table* etw abwischen.
(c) *(Cook) (also* **~ cake**) Rührkuchen *m*; *(fatless)* Biskuit(kuchen) *m*; *(~ mixture)* Rührteig *m*; Biskuitmasse *f* ◆ **jam ~** Biskuit(kuchen) mit Marmeladenfüllung.
2 *vt* **(a)** *(clean)* abwischen; *wound* abtupfen.
(b) *(inf: scrounge)* schnorren *(inf) (from* bei).

◆**sponge down** *vt sep person* (schnell) waschen; *walls also* abwaschen; *horse* abreiben.

◆**sponge off** *vt sep stain, liquid* abwischen.

◆**sponge off** *or* **on** *vi +prep obj (inf)* **to ~ ~ sb** jdm auf der Tasche liegen *(inf)*.

◆**sponge out** *vt sep (remove) stain* herausreiben, herausmachen; *(clean out) drawer* auswaschen; *wound* austupfen.

◆**sponge up** *vt sep* aufwischen.

sponge: ~ bag *n (Brit)* Waschbeutel, Kulturbeutel *m*; **~ bath** *n (esp US)* **to give sb a ~ bath** jdn (gründlich) waschen; **~ cake** *n* Rührkuchen *m*; *(fatless)* Biskuit(kuchen) *m*; **~-down** *n* kurze Wäsche; **to give sb/sth a ~-down** jdn/etw kurz abwaschen; **~ pudding** *n* Mehlpudding *m*.

sponger ['spʌndʒəʳ] *n (inf)* Schmarotzer, Schnorrer *(inf) m*.

sponginess ['spʌndʒɪnɪs] *n see adj* Nachgiebigkeit, Weichheit *f*; Lockerheit *f*; Schwammigkeit *f*.

spongy ['spʌndʒɪ] *adj (+er)* nachgiebig, weich; *(light) pudding* locker; *skin etc* schwammig.

sponsor ['spɒnsəʳ] 1 *n* **(a)** Förderer *m*, Förderin *f*; *(for membership)* Bürge *m*, Bürgin *f*; *(for event)* Schirmherr(in *f*) *m*; *(Rad, TV, Sport etc)* Geldgeber(in *f*), Sponsor(in *f*) *m*; *(for fund-raising)* Spender(in *f*) *m*; *(Parl: of bill)* Befürworter(in *f*) *m* ◆ **to stand ~ for sb** jdn fördern; für jdn bürgen.
(b) *(godparent)* Pate *m*, Patin *f* ◆ **to stand ~ for a child** Pate/Patin eines Kindes sein.
2 *vt* **(a)** unterstützen; *(financially also)* fördern, sponsern; *event also* sponsern, die Schirmherrschaft übernehmen *(+gen)*; *future member* bürgen für; *membership, bill* befürworten, empfehlen; *(Rad, TV, Sport etc) programme* sponsern ◆ **he ~ed him at 5p a mile** er verpflichtete sich, ihm 5 Pence pro Meile zu geben.
(b) *(as godparent)* die Patenschaft *(+gen)* übernehmen.

sponsored ['spɒnsəd] *adj (for charity etc) walk, silence etc: zur Geldbeschaffung abgehalten, wobei die Leistung pro Einheit vom Spender mit einem abgemachten Einsatz honoriert wird.*

sponsorship ['spɒnsəʃɪp] *n see vt* **(a)** Unterstützung *f*, Förderung *f*, Sponsern *nt*; Schirmherrschaft *f*; Bürgschaft *f*; Befürwortung, Empfehlung *f*; Finanzierung *f* ◆ **he got into the club under my ~** durch *or* auf meine Empfehlung kam er in den Klub. **(b)** Patenschaft *f*.

spontaneity [ˌspɒntə'neɪətɪ] *n see adj* Spontaneität *f*; Ungezwungenheit *f*.

spontaneous [spɒn'teɪnɪəs] *adj* spontan; *style* ungezwungen ◆ **~ combustion** Selbstentzündung *f*.

spontaneously [spɒn'teɪnɪəslɪ] *adv* spontan; *(voluntarily also)* von sich aus, von selbst.

spoof [spuːf] *(inf)* 1 *n* **(a)** *(parody)* Parodie *f (of* auf *+acc)*. **(b)** *(hoax)* Ulk *(inf)*, (April)scherz *(inf) m*.
2 *adj attr poem, programme etc* parodiert; *version* verballhornt.
3 *vt (parody) novel* parodieren; *poem also* verballhornen.

spook [spuːk] *(inf)* 1 *n* Gespenst *nt*.
2 *vt (US: frighten)* einen Schrecken einjagen *(+dat)*.

spooky ['spuːkɪ] *adj (+er) (inf)* **(a)** gespenstisch, gruselig *(inf)*. **(b)** *(esp US: strange)* sonderbar ◆ **it was really ~** das war wirklich ein sonderbares *or* eigenartiges Gefühl.

spool [spuːl] 1 *n (Phot, on sewing machine)* Spule *f*; *(on fishing line)* Rolle *f*; *(for thread)* (Garn)rolle *f*; *(of thread)* Rolle *f*.
2 *vt (Comput)* spulen.

spooler ['spuːləʳ] *n (Comput)* (Drucker)spooler *m*.

spoon [spuːn] 1 *n* Löffel *m*; *see* **silver**.
2 *vt* löffeln.
3 *vi (dated inf)* schmusen, poussieren *(dated inf)*.

◆**spoon out** *vt sep* (löffelweise) ausschöpfen.

◆**spoon up** *vt sep* löffeln; *(eat up)* auslöffeln; *spillage* auflöffeln.

spoonbill ['spuːnbɪl] *n* Löffler, Löffelreiher *m*.

spoonerism ['spuːnərɪzəm] *n* lustiger Versprecher.

spoon-feed ['spuːnfiːd] *pret, ptp* **spoon-fed** ['spuːnfed] *vt baby, invalid* füttern; *(fig) (do thinking for)* gängeln; *(supply with)* füttern *(inf)*.

spoonful ['spuːnfʊl] *n* Löffel *m* ◆ **a ~ of soup** ein Löffel Suppe.

sporadic [spə'rædɪk] *adj* sporadisch; *(occasional also)* gelegentlich ◆ **we heard ~ gun-fire** wir hörten gelegentlich Schüsse.

sporadically [spə'rædɪkəlɪ] *adv* sporadisch; *(occasionally also)* gelegentlich ◆ **snow fell ~** es fiel vereinzelt Schnee.

spore [spɔːʳ] *n* Spore *f*.

sporran ['spɒrən] *n (über dem Schottenrock getragene)* Felltasche.

sport [spɔːt] 1 *n* **(a)** *(games collectively)* Sport *m no pl*; *(type of ~)* Sportart *f* ◆ **to be good at ~(s)** gut im Sport sein, sportlich sein; **tennis is my ~** Tennis ist mein Lieblingssport; **the ~ of kings** der königliche Sport, der Pferderennsport; **to offer good ~** gute Jagd-/Angelmöglichkeiten *pl* bieten; **outdoor/indoor ~s** Sport *m* im Freien/Hallensport *m*.
(b) **~s** *pl (also* **~s meeting**) Sportveranstaltung *f*.
(c) *(amusement)* Spaß *m* ◆ **to do sth for/in ~** etw zum Spaß tun; **it was great ~** es hat großen Spaß gemacht; **to say sth in ~** etw aus *or* im *or* zum Spaß sagen; **to make ~ of sb/sth** *(old)* sich über jdn/etw lustig machen.
(d) *(inf: person)* feiner *or* anständiger Kerl *(inf)*; *(Austral)* Junge *m* ◆ **to be a (good) ~** alles mitmachen; **they are such good ~s** mit ihnen kann man Pferde stehlen *(inf)*; **he's a good ~, he doesn't mind losing** er ist kein Spielverderber, er macht sich nichts daraus, wenn er verliert; **be a ~!** sei kein Spielverderber!, sei nicht so! *(inf)*.
(e) *(Biol, Zool)* Spielart, Abart *f*.
2 *vt tie, dress* anhaben; *(show off) ring etc* protzen mit; *black eye* herumlaufen mit *(inf)*.
3 *vi (frolic)* (herum)tollen; *(kitten)* (herum)spielen.
4 *adj attr (US) see* **sports**.

sporting ['spɔːtɪŋ] *adj* **(a)** *person, interests* sportlich; *equipment also* Sports-; *dog, gun* Jagd- ◆ **~ events** Wettkämpfe *pl*; **a great ~ man** ein großer Sportsmann.
(b) *(sportsmanlike)* sportlich; *spirit also* Sports-; *(fig) offer, solution* fair; *(decent)* anständig ◆ **it's ~ of you to** ... es ist anständig von dir, zu ...; **to give sb a ~ chance** jdm eine faire Chance geben; **there is a ~ chance that** ... die Chancen stehen nicht schlecht, daß ...

sporting editor *n (US)* Sportredakteur(in *f*) *m*.

sportingly ['spɔːtɪŋlɪ] *adv* fair; *(decently)* anständig ◆ **he ~ gave him a start** er gab ihm fairerweise einen Vorsprung.

sportive *adj*, **~ly** *adv* ['spɔːtɪv, -lɪ] *(liter)* fidel, launig *(liter)*.

sports, *(US also)* **sport** *in cpds* Sport-; **~ car** *n* Sportwagen *m*; **~cast** *n* Sportübertragung *or* -sendung *f*; **~caster, ~ commentator** *n* Sportreporter(in *f*), (Sport)kommentator(in *f*) *m*; **~ coat** *n see* **~ jacket**; **~ day** *n (Brit)* (Schul)sportfest *nt*; **~ department** *n* Sportabteilung *f*; **~ field, ~ ground** *n* Sportplatz *m*; **~ jacket** *n* Sportjackett *nt*, Sakko *m or nt*; **~man** [-mən] *n (player)* Sportler *m*; *(good ~man)* anständiger *or* feiner Kerl *(inf)*; *(hunter)* Jäger *m*; **~man of the year** Sportler *m* des Jahres; **~manlike** [-mənlaɪk] *adj* sportlich; *(fig) behaviour, act etc* fair; **~manship** [-mənʃɪp] *n (skill)* Sportlichkeit *f*; *(fairness also)* sportliches Verhalten, Fairneß *f*; **~ page** *n* Sportseite *f*; **~ programme** *n* Sportprogramm *nt*; **~wear** *n (for sport)* Sportkleidung *f*; *(leisure wear)* Freizeitkleidung *f*; **~woman** *n* Sportlerin *f*; **~ writer** *n* Sportjournalist(in *f*) *m*.

sporty ['spɔːtɪ] *adj (+er) (inf)* **(a)** *person* sportbegeistert, sportlich; *clothes* sportlich. **(b)** *(jaunty)* flott.

spot [spɒt] 1 *n* **(a)** *(dot)* Tupfen, Punkt *m*; *(on dice)* Punkt *m*; *(Zool, Bot also, stain, on fruit)* Fleck *m*; *(fig: on reputation, good name)* Makel *m (on an +dat)* ◆ **a dress with ~s** ein getupftes *or* gepunktetes Kleid; **~s of blood/grease** Blutflecken *pl*/Fettflecken *pl*; **~s of ink** Tintenkleckse *or* -flecke *pl*; **to knock ~s off sb/sth** *(fig inf)* jdn/etw in den Schatten stellen, jdn in die Tasche stecken *(inf)*; **to have ~s before one's eyes** Sternchen sehen; **without a ~ or stain** *(fig liter)* makellos.
(b) *(Med etc)* Fleck *m*; *(pimple)* Pickel *m*; *(place)* Stelle *f* ◆ **to break** *or* **come out in ~s** Flecken/Pickel bekommen.
(c) *(place)* Stelle *f*; *(point)* Punkt *m* ◆ **this is the ~ where Rizzio was murdered**

an dieser Stelle *or* hier ist Rizzio ermordet worden; **a pleasant ~** ein schönes Fleckchen (*inf*); **on the ~** (*at the scene*) an Ort und Stelle; (*at once*) auf der Stelle, sofort; **our man on the ~** unser Mann am Ort (des Geschehens) *or* vor Ort; **on-the-~ inquiry/investigation** (*at the scene*) Untersuchung *f* an Ort und Stelle; (*immediate*) sofortige Untersuchung; **an on-the-~ report/broadcast** ein Bericht vom Ort des Geschehens; **an on-the-~ fine** eine sofort *or* auf der Stelle zu bezahlende Geldstrafe.
(d) (*Brit inf: small quantity*) **a/the ~ of** ein/das bißchen; **we had a ~ of rain/a few ~s of rain** wir hatten ein paar Tropfen Regen; **there was a ~ of trouble/bother** es gab etwas Ärger; **we're in a ~ of bother** wir haben Schwierigkeiten; **why don't you do a ~ of work?** warum arbeiten Sie nicht mal ein bißchen?; **after a ~ of difficulty** nach einigen Schwierigkeiten; **would you like to do a ~ of driving?** möchten Sie ein bißchen fahren?
(e) (*fig: characteristic*) Punkt *m*, Stelle *f* ◆ **weak ~** schwache Stelle.
(f) (*difficulty*) Klemme *f* ◆ **to be in a (tight)** *or* **on the ~** in der Klemme sitzen (*inf*), in Schwulitäten sein (*inf*); **to put sb in a** *or* **on the ~** jdn in Verlegenheit *or* Schwulitäten (*inf*) bringen.
(g) (*in show*) Nummer *f*; (*Rad, TV*) (ein paar Minuten) Sendezeit *f*; (*for advertisement*) Werbespot *m*; (*announcement*) Kurzmeldung *f* ◆ **he's got a ~ in that show** er tritt in dieser Show auf; **a three-minute TV ~** drei Minuten Sendezeit im Fernsehen; ein dreiminütiger Werbespot im Fernsehen.
(h) ~s *pl* (*Comm*) Lokowaren (*spec*), sofort lieferbare Waren *pl*.
(i) (*Billiards*) (*on table*) Marke *f*; (*also* **~ ball**) Spielball *m*.
(j) (*esp Theat, inf: spotlight*) Scheinwerfer *m*.
[2] *vt* **(a)** (*notice, see*) entdecken, sehen; (*pick out*) erkennen; (*find*) *mistake, bargain* finden; (*Mil: pinpoint*) ausmachen ◆ **to ~ a winner** (*lit, fig*) richtig tippen (*inf*); **train/plane ~ting** *Hobby, das darin besteht, möglichst viele verschiedene Zug-/Flugzeugtypen zu sehen und zu notieren.*
(b) (*stain*) bespritzen ◆ **blue material ~ted with white** blauer Stoff mit weißen Tupfen.
(c) (*Billiards*) *ball* auf die Marke(n) setzen.
[3] *vi* **(a) it's ~ting (with rain)** es tröpfelt.
(b) (*stain*) Flecken bekommen, schmutzen.

spot: ~ cash *n* sofortige Bezahlung; **for ~ cash** gegen sofortige Bezahlung; **~ check** *n* Stichprobe *f*; **~-check** *vt* stichprobenweise untersuchen (*for* auf +*acc*); *motorists* Stichproben machen bei (*for* in bezug auf +*acc*); **~ goods** *npl* sofort lieferbare Waren, Lokowaren (*spec*) *pl*; **~ height** *n* Höhenangabe *f*.

spotless ['spɒtlɪs] *adj person, house, clothes* tadellos *or* makellos sauber, pikobello (*inf*); (*fig*) *reputation* makellos, untadelig ◆ **~ white** strahlend weiß.

spotlessly ['spɒtlɪslɪ] *adv*: **~ clean** blitzsauber.

spotlessness ['spɒtlɪsnɪs] *n* (*of person, house etc*) tadellose *or* makellose Sauberkeit; (*fig: of reputation*) Makellosigkeit, Untadeligkeit *f*.

spot: ~light (*vb: pret, ptp* **~lighted**) [1] *n* (*lamp*) (*in TV studio etc*) Scheinwerfer *m*; (*small, in room etc*) Spot, Strahler *m*; (*light*) Scheinwerferlicht, Rampenlicht (*also fig*) *nt*; (*on car etc*) Suchscheinwerfer *m*; **to be in the ~light** (*lit*) im Scheinwerferlicht *or* Rampenlicht stehen; (*fig*) im Rampenlicht der Öffentlichkeit stehen; **to turn the ~light on sb/sth** (*lit*) die Scheinwerfer auf jdn/etw richten; (*fig*) die Aufmerksamkeit auf jdn/etw lenken; [2] *vt* anstrahlen; (*fig*) aufmerksam machen auf (+*acc*); **~ market** *n* Spotmarkt, Kassamarkt *m*; **~-on** *adj* (*Brit inf*) *answer, analysis* exakt, haarscharf richtig (*inf*); **~-on!** richtig!, genau!; **his guess was ~-on** er hat es haarscharf getroffen; **~ price** *n* (*St Ex*) Kassapreis *m*; **~ remover** *n* Fleck(en)entferner *m*; **~ survey** *n* Stichprobenuntersuchung *f*.

spotted ['spɒtɪd] *adj* gefleckt; (*with dots*) getüpfelt; *material* getüpfelt, getupft; (*marked, stained*) fleckig.

spotted: ~ dick *n* (*Brit*) ≃ Kochpudding *m* mit Rosinen; **~ hyena** *n* Tüpfelhyäne *f*.

spotter ['spɒtə^r^] *n* **(a)** (*Aviat: also* **~ plane**) Aufklärer *m*; *see* **trainspotter**. **(b)** (*US inf: detective*) Detektiv *m*.

spottiness ['spɒtɪnɪs] *n* (*Med*) Fleckigkeit *f*, Flecken *pl*, fleckige Haut; (*pimples*) Pickeligkeit *f* (*inf*), Pickel *pl*, pickelige Haut.

spotty ['spɒtɪ] *adj* (+*er*) (*stained*) fleckig; (*Med*) fleckig, voller Flecken; (*pimply*) pick(e)lig, voller Pickel.

spot-weld ['spɒtweld] *vti* punktschweißen.

spouse [spaʊs] *n* (*form*) Gatte *m* (*form*), Gattin *f* (*form*).

spout [spaʊt] [1] *n* **(a)** Ausguß *m*, Tülle *f*; (*on teapot, cup also*) Schnabel *m*; (*of jug, kettle also*) Schnauze *f*; (*on gargoyle, guttering*) Speirohr *nt*; (*on pump, tap*) Ausflußrohr *nt*; (*on pipe*) Ausfluß *m*; (*on watering can*) Rohr *nt* ◆ **up the ~** (*sl*) (*plans, building, schedule etc*) im Eimer (*sl*); **she is up the ~** (*sl: pregnant*) sie hat's erwischt (*inf*).
(b) (*of whale: also* **~-hole**) Spritzloch, Atemloch *nt*.
(c) (*jet of water etc*) Fontäne *f*; (*Met: water-~*) Wasserhose *f*.
[2] *vt* **(a)** (*gush*) (*fountain etc*) (heraus)spritzen; (*whale also*) ausstoßen; (*volcano, gargoyle*) speien.
(b) (*inf: declaim*) *poetry, speeches* vom Stapel lassen (*inf*), loslassen (*at sb* auf jdn) (*inf*); *words* hervorsprudeln; *figures* herunterrasseln (*inf*); *nonsense* von sich geben.
[3] *vi* **(a)** (*water, fountain etc, whale*) spritzen (*from* aus); (*gargoyle*) speien ◆ **to ~ out (of sth)** (aus etw) hervorspritzen; (*lava*) (aus etw) ausgespien werden; **to ~ up (from sth)** (aus etw) hochspritzen *or* herausschießen.
(b) (*fig inf: declaim*) palavern (*inf*), salbadern (*pej*) ◆ **to ~ about sth** über etw (*acc*) salbadern.

sprain [spreɪn] [1] *n* Verstauchung *f*.
[2] *vt* verstauchen ◆ **to ~ one's wrist/ankle** sich (*dat*) das Handgelenk/den Fuß verstauchen.

sprang [spræŋ] *pret of* **spring**.

sprat [spræt] *n* Sprotte *f* ◆ **to set** *or* **use a ~ to catch a mackerel** *or* **whale** (*prov*) mit der Wurst nach der Speckseite werfen (*prov*).

sprawl [sprɔːl] [1] *n* (*posture*) Lümmeln (*inf*), Flegeln (*inf*) *nt no pl*; (*mass: of buildings, town etc*) Ausbreitung *f* ◆ **urban ~** wildwuchernde Ausbreitung des Stadtgebietes; **in the urban ~** in der riesigen Stadtlandschaft.
[2] *vi* (*person*) (*fall*) der Länge nach hinfallen; (*lounge*) (herum)lümmeln (*inf*), sich hinflegeln; (*plant, town*) (wild) wuchern ◆ **he was ~ing (out) on the floor/in a chair** er lag ausgestreckt auf dem Fußboden/er hatte sich in einem Sessel breitgemacht, er hatte sich in einen Sessel geflegelt; **to send sb ~ing** jdn zu Boden werfen, jdn der Länge nach umwerfen.
[3] *vt* **to be ~ed over sth/on sth** (*body*) ausgestreckt auf etw (*dat*) liegen; **his legs were ~ed over the arm of the chair** seine Beine hingen zwanglos über der Sessellehne.

sprawling ['sprɔːlɪŋ] *adj city, suburbs* wildwuchernd; *figure* hingeflegelt; *body* ausgestreckt; *handwriting* riesig.

spray[1] [spreɪ] *n* (*bouquet*) Strauß *m*; (*buttonhole*) Ansteckblume *f*; (*shoot, twig*) Zweig *m*; (*brooch*) Brosche *f* (*in Form eines Sträußchens*).

spray[2] [1] *n* **(a)** Sprühnebel, Sprühregen *m*; (*of sea*) Gischt *m* ◆ **the ~ from the lorries makes it difficult to see** die Lastwagen spritzen so, daß man kaum etwas sehen kann.
(b) (*implement*) Sprühdose, Sprühflasche *f*; (*insecticide ~, for irrigation*) Spritze *f*, Sprühgerät *nt*; (*scent ~*) Zerstäuber *m*; (*on shower*) Brause(kopf *m*) *f*.
(c) (*preparation, Med, hair-~ etc*) Spray *m or nt*.
(d) (*act of ~ing*) (Be)sprühen *nt* ◆ **to give sth a ~** etw besprühen; (*with paint, insecticide*) etw spritzen; (*with hair-~ etc*) etw sprayen.
[2] *vt plants, insects etc* besprühen; *garden, crops* (*with paint, insecticide*) spritzen; *hair* sprayen; *room* aussprühen; *water, paint, foam* sprühen, spritzen; *perfume* zerstäuben, (ver)sprühen ◆ **to ~ insecticide on plants** Pflanzen (mit Insektenmittel) spritzen; **to ~ sth with water/bullets** etw mit Wasser besprühen/mit Kugeln übersäen.
[3] *vi* sprühen; (*water, mud*) spritzen ◆ **to ~ out** heraussprühen/-spritzen.

spray-can ['spreɪkæn] *n* Sprühdose *f*.

sprayer ['spreɪə^r^] *n see* **spray**[2] **1 (b)**.

spray-gun ['spreɪgʌn] *n* Spritzpistole *f*.

spread [spred] (*vb: pret, ptp* ~) [1] *n* **(a)** (*of wings*) Spannweite, Flügelspanne *f*; (*range*) (*of marks*) Verteilung, Streuung *f*; (*of prices*) Spanne *f*; (*of ideas, interests*) Spektrum *nt*; (*distribution of wealth*) Verteilung *f*; (*scope: of theory, ideas*) Umfang *m* ◆ **middle-age ~** Fülligkeit *f*, Altersspeck *m* (*inf*); **Gerry's beginning to get a middle-age ~** Gerry setzt Speck an (*inf*).
(b) (*growth*) Ausbreitung, Verbreitung *f*; (*spatial*) Ausdehnung *f* ◆ **the ~ of nuclear weapons** die zunehmende Verbreitung von Atomwaffen.
(c) (*inf: of food etc*) Festessen *nt*, Festschmaus *m* ◆ **that was an excellent ~** das war prima, was du *etc* da aufgetischt hast.
(d) (*cover*) Decke *f*.
(e) (*for bread*) (Brot)aufstrich *m* ◆ **anchovy ~** Sardellenpaste *f*; **cheese ~** Streichkäse *m*.
(f) (*Press, Typ: two pages*) Doppelseite *f* ◆ **a full-page/double ~** ein ganz-/zweiseitiger Bericht; (*advertisement*) eine ganz-/zweiseitige Anzeige; **a picture ~** ein ganzseitiger Bildbericht; **the centre ~ of a paper** die Mittelseite einer Zeitung.
[2] *vt* **(a)** (*open or lay out: also* **~ out**) *rug, nets, hay, wings* ausbreiten; *fan* öffnen; *arms also* ausstrecken; *goods also* auslegen; *hands, legs* spreizen ◆ **the peacock ~ its tail** der Pfau schlug ein Rad; **he was lying with his arms and legs ~ out** er lag mit ausgestreckten Armen und Beinen da; **the fields were ~ (out) below us** die Felder breiteten sich unter uns aus; **the view which was ~ before us** die Sicht, die sich uns bot; **the yacht ~ its sails** die Segel des Bootes blähten sich.
(b) *bread, canvas, surface* bestreichen; *butter, paint etc* (ver- *or* auf)streichen; *table* decken ◆ **~ the paint evenly** verteilen Sie die Farbe gleichmäßig; **he ~ the plaster over the wall** er verstrich den Gips auf der Wand; **to ~ a cloth/blanket on sth, to ~ sth with a cloth/blanket** ein Tuch/eine Decke über etw (*acc*) breiten *or* auf etw (*dat*) ausbreiten; **the table was ~ with food** der Tisch war reichlich *or* üppig gedeckt.
(c) (*distribute: also* **~ out**) *forces, writing, objects, payments* verteilen; *sand, fertilizer also, muck* streuen; (*in time*) verteilen (*over* über +*acc*) ◆ **our resources are ~ very thin** unsere Mittel sind maximal beansprucht.
(d) (*disseminate*) *news, knowledge, panic, disease, smell* verbreiten; *rumour also* ausstreuen ◆ **I'll ~ the news to everyone in the office** ich werde es allen im Büro mitteilen.
[3] *vi* **(a)** (*extend*) (*spatially*) sich erstrecken, sich ausdehnen (*over, across* über +*acc*); (*with movement*) (*weeds, liquid, fire, smile, industry*) sich ausbreiten (*over, across* über +*acc*); (*towns, settlements*) sich ausdehnen; (*knowledge, fear etc, smell*) sich verbreiten; (*disease, trouble, fire*) sich verbreiten, um sich greifen ◆ **the course ~s over four months** der Kurs erstreckt sich über vier Monate; **to ~ to sth** etw erreichen; (*disease etc*) auf etw (*acc*) übergreifen; **to ~ into sth** sich in etw (*acc*) erstrecken; (*in time*) sich bis in etw (*acc*) erstrecken; **under the ~ing trees** unter den ausladenden Bäumen; **he's worried about his ~ing waistline** (*inf*) er macht sich Sorgen, weil er in die Breite geht (*inf*); *see* **wildfire**.
(b) (*butter etc*) sich streichen *or* schmieren (*inf*) lassen.
[4] *vr* **to ~ oneself** (*physically*) sich ausstrecken; (*~ one's things*) sich ausbreiten; (*in speech, writing*) sich verbreiten.

◆**spread about** *or* **around** *vt sep news, rumours, disease* verbreiten, unters

Volk bringen (*inf*); *toys, seeds etc* verstreuen.

◆**spread out** [1] *vt sep see* **spread 2 (a, c).**
[2] *vi* **(a)** (*countryside etc*) sich ausdehnen.
(b) (*troops, runners*) sich verteilen.

spread-eagle ['spred,iːgl] *vt* **he ~d his opponent against the wall** er drückte seinen Gegner, Arme und Beine gespreizt, an die Wand; **to be** *or* **lie ~d** mit ausgestreckten Armen und Beinen daliegen, alle viere von sich (*dat*) strecken (*inf*); **the policeman outlined the ~d body** der Polizist zeichnete die Umrisse des ausgestreckt daliegenden Toten.

spreader ['spredəʳ] *n* **(a)** Spachtel *m*; (*for butter etc*) Messer *nt*. **(b)** (*Agr: muck ~*) (Stall)miststreuer *m*.

spreadsheet ['spredʃiːt] *n* (*Comput*) Tabellenkalkulation *f*; (*software also*) Tabellenkalkulationsprogramm *nt*.

spree [spriː] *n* **spending** *or* **shopping** *or* **buying ~** Großeinkauf *m*; **drinking/gambling ~** Zech-/Spieltour *f* (*inf*); **to be/go (out) on a ~** (*drinking*) eine Zechtour machen; (*spending*) groß einkaufen/groß einkaufen gehen.

sprig [sprɪg] *n* Zweig *m* ◆ **embroidered with ~s of flowers** mit Blütenzweigen bestickt.

sprightliness ['spraɪtlɪnɪs] *n see adj* Munterkeit *f*; Lebhaftigkeit *f*; Schwung *m*; Rüstigkeit *f*; Leichtigkeit *f*.

sprightly ['spraɪtlɪ] *adj* (*+er*) *person, tune* munter, lebhaft; *old person* rüstig; *walk, dance* schwungvoll.

spring [sprɪŋ] (*vb: pret* **sprang** *or* (*US*) **sprung**, *ptp* **sprung**) [1] *n* **(a)** (*lit, fig liter: source*) Quelle *f* ◆ **~s** (*fig liter: origins*) Ursprung *m*; **the inner ~s of his being** sein Innerstes.
(b) (*season*) Frühling *m*, Frühjahr *nt*, Lenz *m* (*poet*) ◆ **in (the) ~** im Frühling, im Frühjahr; **~ is in the air** der Frühling liegt in der Luft, der Lenz hält seinen Einzug (*poet*); **in the ~ of his life** im Frühling seines Lebens, im Lenz des Lebens (*poet*).
(c) (*leap*) Sprung, Satz *m* ◆ **in one ~** mit einem Sprung *or* Satz; **to make a ~ at sb/sth** sich auf jdn/etw stürzen.
(d) (*Mech*) Feder *f*; (*in mattress, seat etc also*) Sprungfeder *f* ◆ **~s** (*Aut*) Federung *f*.
(e) *no pl* (*bounciness*) (*of chair*) Federung *f*; (*of wood, grass etc*) Nachgiebigkeit, Elastizität *f* ◆ **the floor has no/a good ~** der Boden federt nicht/federt gut; **to walk with a ~ in one's step** mit federnden Schritten gehen; **the news put a new ~ into his step** die Nachricht beflügelte seine Schritte.
[2] *adj attr* **(a)** (*seasonal*) Frühlings-.
(b) (*with springs*) gefedert; *mattress* Federkern-.
[3] *vt* **(a)** (*leap over*) überspringen, springen über (*+acc*).
(b) (*put springs in*) federn.
(c) (*cause to operate*) auslösen; *mine also* explodieren lassen; *lock, mousetrap etc* zuschnappen lassen ◆ **to ~ a leak** (*pipe*) (plötzlich) undicht werden; (*ship*) (plötzlich) ein Leck bekommen; **to ~ sth on sb** (*fig*) *idea, decision* jdn mit etw konfrontieren; **to ~ a piece of news on sb** jdn mit einer Neuigkeit überraschen; **to ~ a surprise on sb** jdn völlig überraschen.
(d) (*sl: free*) rausholen (*inf*).
[4] *vi* **(a)** (*leap*) springen; (*be activated*) ausgelöst werden; (*mousetrap*) zuschnappen ◆ **to ~ at sb** jdn anspringen; **to ~ out at sb** auf jdn losspringen; **to ~ open** aufspringen; **to be poised to ~** (*lit, fig*) sprungbereit sein; **to ~ into the saddle** sich in den Sattel schwingen; **to ~ to one's feet** aufspringen; **to ~ out of bed** aus dem Bett hüpfen; **a blush sprang to her cheeks** das Blut schoß ihr in die Wangen; **tears sprang to her eyes** ihr schossen die Tränen in die Augen; **his hand sprang to his gun** er griff (schnell) zur Waffe; **an oath sprang to his lips** ein Fluch drängte sich auf seine Lippen (*geh*); **to ~ into action** aktiv werden; (*police, fire brigade etc*) in Aktion treten; **to ~ to attention** (*Mil*) Haltung annehmen; **to ~ to arms** zu den Waffen eilen; **to ~ into view** plötzlich in Sicht kommen; **to ~ to mind** einem einfallen; **to ~ to sb's aid/defence** jdm zu Hilfe eilen; **he sprang to fame** er wurde plötzlich berühmt; **to ~ (in)to life** (plötzlich) lebendig werden; **the debate sprang (in)to life** es kam plötzlich Leben in die Debatte; **they sprang into the public eye** die Augen der Öffentlichkeit waren plötzlich auf sie gerichtet.
(b) (*issue: also* **~ forth**) (*liter*) (*water, blood*) (hervor)quellen (*from* aus); (*fire, sparks*) sprühen (*from* aus); (*shoot*) (hervor)sprießen (*from* aus); (*from family etc*) abstammen (*from* von); (*fig*) (*idea*) entstehen (*from* aus); (*interest, irritability etc*) herrühren (*from* von) ◆ **a man sprung from the people** ein Mann aus dem Volk; **where did you ~ from?** (*inf*) wo kommst du denn her?; **to ~ into existence** (plötzlich *or* rasch) entstehen.

◆**spring back** *vi* (*person*) zurückspringen; (*in fear*) zurückschrecken; (*object*) zurückschnellen.

◆**spring up** *vi* (*plant*) hervorsprießen; (*weeds*) aus dem Boden schießen; (*person*) hoch- *or* aufspringen; (*wind*) aufkommen; (*building, settlement*) aus dem Boden schießen; (*fig*) (*suspicion, friendship*) erwachen, (plötzlich) entstehen; (*firm, magazine*) entstehen; (*problem, rumour*) auftauchen ◆ **doubts sprang ~ in his mind** ihm kamen (plötzlich) Zweifel.

spring: ~-back file *n* (*Brit*) Klemmhefter *m*; **~ balance** *n* Federwaage *f*; **~ binder** *n* Klemmhefter *m*; **~board** *n* (*lit, fig*) Sprungbrett *nt*.

springbok ['sprɪŋbɒk] *n* Springbock *m*.

spring: ~ chicken *n* Stubenküken *nt*; **he's no ~ chicken** (*fig inf*) er ist nicht mehr feucht hinter den Ohren (*inf*); **~-clean** [1] *vt* gründlich putzen; **to ~-clean a house** (in einem Haus) Frühjahrsputz machen; [2] *vi* Frühjahrsputz machen; **~-cleaning** *n* Frühjahrsputz *m*.

springer (spaniel) ['sprɪŋəʳ-] *n* Springerspaniel *m*.

spring fever *n* **(a)** (*energetic feeling*) Frühlingsgefühle *pl* ◆ **it must be ~!** das muß der Frühling sein!, es muß am Frühling liegen! **(b)** (*lassitude*) Frühjahrsmüdigkeit *f*.

springiness ['sprɪŋɪnɪs] *n* Elastizität *f*; (*of turf, wood, grass, track also*) Nachgiebigkeit *f*; (*of springboard also*) Sprungkraft *f*; (*of bed*) Federung *f* ◆ **the ~ of his step** sein federnder Gang.

spring: ~less *adj* ungefedert; **~-like** *adj* frühlingshaft; **~-loaded** *adj* mit einer Sprungfeder; **to be ~-loaded** eine Sprungfeder haben; **~ onion** *n* Frühlingszwiebel *f*; **~ roll** *n* Frühlingsrolle *f*; **~ tide** *n* **(a)** Springflut *f*; **(b)** (*poet: ~time*) Lenz *m* (*poet*); **~time** *n* Frühling(szeit *f*) *m*, Frühjahr *nt*; (*fig*) Frühling, Lenz (*poet*) *m*; **~ water** *n* Quellwasser *nt*; **~ wheat** *n* Sommerweizen *m*.

springy ['sprɪŋɪ] *adj* (*+er*) *step* federnd; *plank, turf, grass also* nachgiebig, elastisch; *rubber, wood, plastic etc, hair* elastisch; *bed* weich gefedert.

sprinkle ['sprɪŋkl] [1] *vt water* sprenkeln, sprengen; *lawn, plant,* (*with holy water*) besprengen; *salt, dust, sugar etc* streuen; *dish, cake* bestreuen ◆ **a rose ~d with dew** eine taubenetzte Rose; **a lawn ~d with daisies** ein mit Gänseblümchen durchzogener Rasen; **his hair was ~d with grey** sein Haar war grau meliert; **churches/pubs are ~d about over the town** man findet Kirchen/Gasthäuser über die ganze Stadt verstreut; **~d with quotations** mit Zitaten durchsetzt.
[2] *n* (*of liquid, vinegar*) ein paar Spritzer; (*of salt etc*) Prise *f*.

sprinkler ['sprɪŋkləʳ] *n* **(a)** (*Hort, Agr*) Berieselungsapparat, Sprinkler *m*; (*in garden also*) (Rasen)sprenger *m*; (*for fire-fighting*) Sprinkler *m*; (*on watering can etc*) Sprenger, Gießkannenkopf *m*; (*on shower*) Brause *f*; (*sugar ~*) Streudose *f*, Streuer *m*. **(b)** (*Eccl*) Weihwasserwedel *m*.

sprinkler: ~ head *n* Sprinkler *m*; (*on watering can*) Sprenger, Gießkannenkopf *m*; (*on shower*) Brause *f*; **~ system** *n* Berieselungsanlage *f*; (*for fire-fighting also*) Sprinkleranlage *f*.

sprinkling ['sprɪŋklɪŋ] *n* (*of rain, dew etc*) ein paar Tropfen; (*of sugar etc*) Prise *f*; (*fig*) (*of humour, comedy etc*) Anflug *m*; (*of common sense*) Spur *f* ◆ **there was a ~ of grey in his hair** ein paar graue Fäden durchzogen sein Haar; **there was a ~ of young people** es waren ein paar vereinzelte junge Leute da; **a ~ of freckles** ein paar Sommersprossen; **to give sth a ~** (*with water*) etw besprengen *or* besprenkeln.

sprint [sprɪnt] [1] *n* Lauf *m*; (*race*) Sprint *m*; (*burst of speed*) Spurt, Sprint *m* ◆ **the 100-m ~** der 100-m-Lauf; **to put on a ~** einen Sprint *or* Spurt vorlegen, sprinten, spurten; **he made a ~ for safety/for the bus** er rannte in Sicherheit/er sprintete *or* spurtete zum Bus; **a ~ finish** ein Endspurt *m*; **he has a good ~ finish** er legt einen guten Endspurt vor.
[2] *vi* (*in race*) sprinten; (*dash*) rennen; (*for train etc also*) spurten.

sprinter ['sprɪntəʳ] *n* Kurzstreckenläufer(in *f*), Sprinter(in *f*) *m*.

sprit [sprɪt] *n* Spriet *nt*.

sprite [spraɪt] *n* Kobold *m* ◆ **water/wood ~** Wasser-/Waldgeist *m*.

spritsail ['sprɪtsəl] *n* Sprietsegel *nt*.

spritzer ['sprɪtsəʳ] *n* (Wein)schorle *f*, Gespritzte(r) *m*.

sprocket ['sprɒkɪt] *n* **(a)** (*tooth*) Zahn *m*. **(b)** (*~ wheel*) Kettenrad *nt*; (*on bicycle*) Kettenzahnrad *nt*, Zahnkranz *m*; (*Film*) Greifer *m*; (*on printer etc*) Stachelrad *nt*.

sprog(let) ['sprɒg(lɪt)] *n* (*sl: baby, child*) Kind, Kleine(s) *nt* ◆ **how are the ~s?** was macht der Nachwuchs? (*inf*).

sprout [spraʊt] [1] *n* **(a)** (*shoot*) (*of plant*) Trieb *m*; (*of tree also*) Schoß, Schößling, Sproß *m*; (*from seed*) Keim *m*.
(b) (*Brussels ~*) (Rosenkohl)röschen *nt* ◆ **~s** *pl* Rosenkohl *m*.
[2] *vt leaves, buds, shoots etc* treiben; *horns etc* entwickeln; *seeds, wheat etc* keimen lassen; (*inf*) *beard* sich (*dat*) wachsen lassen ◆ **the town is ~ing new buildings** in der Stadt sprießen neue Gebäude hervor; **he suddenly started ~ing hairs on his chest** er bekam plötzlich Haare auf der Brust.
[3] *vi* **(a)** (*grow*) wachsen, sprießen; (*seed, wheat etc*) keimen; (*potatoes, trees etc*) Triebe bekommen. **(b)** (*lit, fig: also* **~ up**) (*plants*) emporschießen, sprießen; (*new sects, new buildings*) wie die Pilze aus dem Boden schießen.

spruce[1] [spruːs] *n* (*also* **~ fir**) Fichte *f*.

spruce[2] *adj* (*+er*) *person, appearance* proper, gepflegt; *men's clothes* flott, schmuck (*dated*); *women, children, women's clothes, appearance* adrett; *building* schmuck; *lawn, flower beds* gepflegt ◆ **he was looking very ~** er sah geschniegelt und gebügelt *or* geschniegelt und gestriegelt aus.

◆**spruce up** *vt sep child* herausputzen; *house, garden* auf Vordermann bringen (*inf*) ◆ **to ~ oneself ~** (*in general*) sein Äußeres pflegen; (*get dressed up*) sich in Schale werfen; (*woman*) sich schönmachen; **he looks much better now that he has ~d himself ~** so gepflegt sieht er wesentlich besser aus; **all ~d ~** *children, men* geschniegelt und gestriegelt; *women* schön zurechtgemacht; *house* auf Hochglanz.

sprucely ['spruːslɪ] *adv dressed* (*man*) flott, schmuck (*dated*); (*woman, child*) adrett; *painted, decorated etc* schmuck; *laid out* sauber und ordentlich ◆ **~ kept gardens** gepflegte Gärten.

spruceness ['spruːsnɪs] *n see adj* Gepflegtheit *f*; Schmuckheit *f* (*dated*); Flottheit *f*; Adrettheit *f*.

sprung [sprʌŋ] [1] *ptp of* **spring.**
[2] *adj* gefedert.

spry [spraɪ] *adj* rüstig.

spud [spʌd] *n* (*inf: potato*) Kartoffel *f* ◆ **~-bashing** (*Brit Mil sl*) Küchendienst *m*.

spume [spjuːm] *n* (*liter*) Gischt *m*.

spun [spʌn] [1] *pret, ptp of* **spin.**
[2] *adj gold, silver, silk* gesponnen ◆ **~ sugar** (*candy floss*) Zuckerwatte *f*.

spunk [spʌŋk] *n* **(a)** (*inf*) Mumm *m* (*inf*), Courage *f*. **(b)** (*Brit sl: semen*) Soße *f* (*sl*).

spunky ['spʌŋkɪ] *adj* (*+er*) (*inf*) couragiert.

spur [spɜːʳ] [1] *n* **(a)** Sporn *m*; *(fig)* Ansporn, Antrieb *m* *(to* für) ◆ **he urged the horse on with his ~s** er gab dem Pferd die Sporen; **to win** *or* **gain one's ~s** *(fig)* sich *(dat)* die Sporen verdienen; **this might act as a ~ to his memory** das könnte seinem Gedächtnis einen Stoß geben; **this was a new ~ to his ambition** das gab seinem Ehrgeiz neuen Antrieb *or* Ansporn.
(b) on the ~ of the moment ganz spontan; **a ~-of-the-moment decision** ein spontaner Entschluß.
(c) *(Geog)* Vorsprung *m*.
(d) *(Zool)* Sporn *m*.
(e) *(Rail)* Nebengleis, Rangiergleis *nt*.
[2] *vt* **(a)** *horse* die Sporen geben (+*dat*). **(b)** *(urge on: also* **~ on)** (vorwärts) treiben, vorantreiben; *(fig)* anspornen ◆ **~red (on) by greed/ambition** von Habgier/vom Ehrgeiz getrieben.
[3] *vi (also* **~ on)** galoppieren, sprengen *(dated)*.

spurge [spɜːdʒ] *n (Bot)* Wolfsmilch *f* ◆ **~ laurel** Lorbeer-Seidelbast *m*.

spurious ['spjʊərɪəs] *adj claim, claimant* unberechtigt; *document, account* falsch; *anger, interest, affection* nicht echt.

spuriousness ['spjʊərɪəsnɪs] *n see adj* mangelnde Berechtigung; mangelnde Echtheit.

spurn [spɜːn] *vt* verschmähen.

spurred [spɜːd] *adj* gespornt.

spurt [spɜːt] [1] *n* **(a)** *(flow)* Strahl *m* ◆ **~s of flame** Stichflammen.
(b) *(burst of speed)* Spurt *m* ◆ **a final ~** *(lit, fig)* ein Endspurt *m*; **to put a ~ on** *(lit, fig)* einen Spurt vorlegen; **there was a ~ of activity** es brach plötzliche Aktivität aus; **in a sudden ~ of energy** in einer plötzlichen Energieanwandlung.
[2] *vi* **(a)** *(gush: also* **~ out)** (heraus)spritzen *(from* aus).
(b) *(run)* spurten.
[3] *vt* **the wound ~ed blood** aus der Wunde spritzte Blut; **the pipe ~ed water** aus dem Rohr spritzte das Wasser.

spur wheel *n* Stirnrad *nt*.

sputnik ['spʊtnɪk] *n* Sputnik *m*.

sputter ['spʌtəʳ] *vi* zischen; *(in frying pan)* brutzeln; *(fat)* spritzen; *(engine)* stottern; *(in speech)* sich ereifern *(about* über +*acc)* ◆ **he was ~ing with rage** er geiferte (vor Zorn); **the candle ~ed out** die Kerze ging flackernd aus.

sputum ['spjuːtəm] *n (Med)* Auswurf *m*, Sputum *nt (spec)*.

spy [spaɪ] [1] *n* Spion(in *f*) *m*; *(police ~)* Spitzel *m* ◆ **~ in the cab** *(inf: tachograph)* Fahrtenschreiber *m*.
[2] *vt* sehen, erspähen *(geh)* ◆ **finally I spied him coming** endlich sah ich ihn kommen; **I ~ with my little eye something ...** ≃ ich sehe was, was du nicht siehst, und ...
[3] *vi* spionieren, Spionage treiben ◆ **to ~ into sth** in etw *(dat)* herumspionieren; **to ~ on sb** jdn bespitzeln; *on neighbours* jdm nachspionieren; **I S~** *(game)* ich sehe was, was du nicht siehst.

◆**spy out** *vt sep* ausfindig machen ◆ **to ~ ~ the land** *(Mil)* die Gegend auskundschaften; *(fig)* die Lage peilen.

spy: ~ glass *n* Fernglas *nt*; **~ hole** *n* Guckloch *nt*, Spion *m*; **~ master** *n* Chefagent, Agentenführer *m*; **~ plane** *n* Spionageflugzeug *nt*; **~ ring** *n* Spionagering, Agentenring *m*; **~ satellite** *n* Spionagesatellit *m*; **~ story** *n* Spionagegeschichte *f*.

Sq *abbr of* **Square**.

sq *abbr of* **square** ◆ **~ m** qm, m^2.

squab [skwɒb] *n* **(a)** *(Orn)* Jungtaube *f*. **(b)** *(Aut)* Bank *f*.

squabble ['skwɒbl] [1] *n* Zank, Streit *m* ◆ **~s** Zankereien, Streitigkeiten *pl*.
[2] *vi* (sich) zanken, (sich) streiten *(about, over* um).

squabbling ['skwɒblɪŋ] *n* Zankerei, Streiterei *f*.

squad [skwɒd] *n (Mil)* Korporalschaft *f*; *(special unit of police etc)* Kommando *nt*; *(police department)* Dezernat *nt*; *(of workmen)* Trupp *m*; *(Sport, fig)* Mannschaft *f*.

squad car *n* Streifenwagen *m*.

squaddie ['skwɒdɪ] *n (Brit sl: private soldier)* Gefreite(r) *m* ◆ **20 years of being a bloody ~** 20 Jahre als Schütze Arsch *(sl)*; **the pub was full of ~s** die Kneipe war voller Soldaten.

squadron ['skwɒdrən] *n (of cavalry)* Schwadron *f*; *(Aviat)* Staffel *f*; *(Naut)* Geschwader *nt*.

squadron leader *n (Brit Aviat)* Luftwaffenmajor *m*.

squalid ['skwɒlɪd] *adj room, house* schmutzig und verwahrlost; *existence, conditions* elend, erbärmlich; *motive, manoeuvres, deed, idea etc* gemein, niederträchtig; *dispute, gossip* entwürdigend; *affair* schmutzig.

squalidly ['skwɒlɪdlɪ] *adv live* in elenden *or* erbärmlichen Verhältnissen; *behave, treat sb* gemein, niederträchtig.

squall [skwɔːl] [1] *n* **(a)** *(storm)* Bö(e) *f*; *(fig)* Gewitter *nt*, Sturm *m* ◆ **there are ~s ahead** *(fig)* wir gehen stürmischen Zeiten entgegen. **(b)** *(cry)* Schrei *m*.
[2] *vi* schreien.

squally ['skwɔːlɪ] *adj (+er)* stürmisch; *wind also* böig.

squalor ['skwɒləʳ] *n* Schmutz *m*; *(moral ~)* Verkommenheit *f* ◆ **the ~ of the conditions** die elenden *or* erbärmlichen Verhältnisse; **to live in ~** in unbeschreiblichen Zuständen leben.

squander ['skwɒndəʳ] *vt* verschwenden, vergeuden *(on* an +*acc)*; *opportunity* vertun.

square [skweəʳ] [1] *n* **(a)** *(shape, Geometry, on graph paper)* Quadrat *nt* ◆ **a 6 metre ~** 6 Meter im Quadrat.
(b) *(piece of material, paper etc)* Quadrat, Viereck *nt*; *(on chessboard etc)* Feld *nt*; *(on paper)* Kästchen, Karo *nt*; *(in crossword)* Kästchen *nt*; *(check on material etc)* Karo *nt*; *(head ~)* Kopftuch *nt* ◆ **form yourselves into a ~** stellen Sie sich im Viereck auf; **cut it in ~s** schneiden Sie es quadratisch *or* in Quadrate zu; **to go back to ~ one, to start (again) from ~ one** *(fig)* noch einmal von vorne anfangen; **we're back to ~ one** jetzt sind wir wieder da, wo wir angefangen haben.
(c) *(in town)* Platz *m*; *(US: of houses)* Block *m*; *(Mil: barrack ~)* (Kasernen)platz *m*.
(d) *(Math)* Quadrat(zahl *f*) *nt* ◆ **the ~ of 3 is 9** 3 hoch 2 *or* 3 (im) Quadrat ist 9.
(e) *(Tech)* Winkel(maß *nt*) *m*; *(set ~)* Zeichendreieck *nt*; *(T-~)* Reißschiene *f* ◆ **to cut sth on the ~** etw rechtwinklig schneiden; **to be on the ~** *(fig inf: above board)* in Ordnung sein.
(f) *(Mil: battle formation)* Karree *nt*.
(g) *(inf: old-fashioned person)* Spießer *m (inf)* ◆ **to be a ~** von (vor)gestern sein.
[2] *adj (+er)* **(a)** *(in shape)* quadratisch; *picture, lawn etc also, nib* viereckig; *file* Vierkant-; *block of wood etc* vierkantig ◆ **to be a ~ peg in a round hole** am falschen Platz sein.
(b) *(forming right angle) angle* recht; *corner* rechtwinklig; *bracket, shoulder* eckig; *chin, jaw* kantig, eckig; *build* vierschrötig.
(c) *(Math)* Quadrat- ◆ **3 ~ kilometres** 3 Quadratkilometer; **3 metres ~** 3 Meter im Quadrat; **there wasn't a ~ inch of space left** es war kein Zentimeter Platz mehr.
(d) *attr (complete) meal* anständig, ordentlich.
(e) *(fair) deal* gerecht, fair; *dealings, game, person* ehrlich ◆ **to give sb a ~ deal** jdn gerecht *or* fair behandeln; **I'll be ~ with you** ich will ehrlich *or* offen mit dir sein.
(f) *(fig: even)* **to be ~** *(accounts etc)* in Ordnung sein; **to get ~ with sb** mit jdm abrechnen; **we are (all) ~** *(Sport)* wir stehen beide/alle gleich; *(fig)* jetzt sind wir quitt; **he wanted to be ~ with his creditors** er wollte mit seinen Gläubigern im reinen sein; **we can start again all ~** wir sind wieder quitt.
(g) *(inf: old-fashioned)* überholt, verstaubt; *person, ideas* spießig *(inf)*; *fashion also* passé ◆ **he's ~** er ist von (vor)gestern.
[3] *adv (+er)* **(a)** *(at right angles)* rechtwinklig ◆ **~ with sth** im rechten Winkel *or* senkrecht zu etw. **(b)** *(directly)* direkt, genau. **(c)** *(honestly)* ehrlich, fair; *see* **fair**[1].
[4] *vt* **(a)** *(make ~)* quadratisch machen; *(make a right angle)* rechtwinklig machen ◆ **to ~ one's shoulders** die Schultern straffen; **to ~ a block of wood/stone** *(cut ~)* einen Holzklotz vierkantig zuschneiden/einen Steinblock vierkantig behauen; **to try to ~ the circle** die Quadratur des Kreises versuchen.
(b) *(Math) number* quadrieren ◆ **3 ~d is 9** 3 hoch 2 *or* 3 (im) Quadrat ist 9.
(c) *(adjust) debts* begleichen; *creditors* abrechnen mit; *(reconcile)* in Einklang bringen ◆ **to ~ one's accounts** abrechnen *(with* mit); **to ~ one's accounts with God/the world** mit Gott/der Welt ins reine kommen; **to ~ sth with one's conscience** etw mit seinem Gewissen vereinbaren *or* in Einklang bringen; **I'll ~ it with the porter** *(inf)* ich mache das mit dem Portier ab *(inf)*.
(d) *(inf: bribe)* schmieren *(inf)*.
[5] *vi* übereinstimmen.

◆**square off** [1] *vt sep* **(a)** *(make square) corner* rechtwinklig machen. **(b)** *(draw squares on)* in Quadrate einteilen.
[2] *vi (esp US)* in Kampfstellung gehen, Kampfstellung annehmen.

◆**square up** *vi* **(a)** in Kampfstellung gehen, Kampfstellung annehmen ◆ **to ~ ~ to sb** sich vor jdm aufpflanzen *(inf)*; *(boxer)* vor jdm in Kampfstellung gehen; *(fig)* jdm die Stirn bieten ◆ **to ~ ~ to sth** sich einer Sache *(dat)* stellen.
(b) *(lit, fig: settle)* abrechnen.

square: ~-bashing *n (Brit Mil sl)* Drill *m*; **~-built** *adj* stämmig *or* breit gebaut; *man* vierschrötig; *house* quadratisch gebaut.

squared [skweəd] *adj paper* kariert.

square: ~ dance *n* Squaredance *m*; **~ knot** *n (US)* Kreuzknoten *m*.

squarely ['skweəlɪ] *adv* **(a)** *(directly)* direkt, genau; *(fig: firmly)* fest ◆ **we must face this ~** wir müssen dieser Sache (dat) (fest) ins Auge sehen. **(b)** *(honestly)* ehrlich; *(fairly)* gerecht, fair ◆ **to deal ~ with sb** jdn gerecht *or* fair behandeln. **(c) ~ built** stämmig *or* breit gebaut.

square: ~ measure *n* Flächenmaß *nt*; **~ number** *n* Quadratzahl *f*; **~-rigged** *adj* vollgetakelt; **~ root** *n* Quadratwurzel *f*, zweite Wurzel; **to work out the ~ root of sth** die zweite Wurzel *or* Quadratwurzel aus etw ziehen; **~ sail** *n* Rahsegel *nt*; **~ shooter** *n (US inf)* ehrlicher Kerl *(inf)*; **~-shouldered** *adj* mit eckigen Schultern; **~-toed** *adj shoes* mit breiter Kappe.

squash[1] [skwɒʃ] [1] *n* **(a)** *(Brit) (fruit concentrate)* Fruchtsaftkonzentrat, Squash *nt*; *(drink)* Fruchtsaft *m* ◆ **a glass of orange ~** ein Glas Orangensaft.
(b) *(crowd)* (Menschen)menge *f*; *(crush)* Gedränge *nt* ◆ **it's a bit of a ~** es ist ziemlich eng.
[2] *vt* **(a)** *(also* **~ up)** zerdrücken, zerquetschen; *box etc* zusammendrücken ◆ **to be ~ed to a pulp** zu Brei gequetscht *or* zerquetscht werden; **my hat was ~ed flat** *or* **in** mein Hut war völlig zerdrückt.
(b) *(fig inf) (silence) person* über den Mund fahren (+*dat*); *(quash) protest, argument* vom Tisch fegen *(inf)* ◆ **~ed again!** schon wieder kein Erfolg; **I felt completely ~ed** ich kam mir ganz klein und häßlich vor *(inf)*.
(c) *(squeeze)* quetschen ◆ **to ~ sb/sth in** jdn einquetschen/etw hineinquetschen; **to be ~ed up against sb** gegen jdn gequetscht *or* gepreßt werden; **to be ~ed together** eng zusammengepreßt *or* -gequetscht sein.
[3] *vi* **(a)** *(get ~ed)* zerdrückt *or* zerquetscht werden.
(b) *(squeeze)* sich quetschen ◆ **to ~ in** sich hinein-/hereinquetschen; **could you ~ up?** könnt ihr etwas zusammenrücken?; *(one person)* kannst du dich

etwas kleiner machen?

squash² *n (Sport: also* ~ **racquets** *or (US)* **rackets**) Squash *nt* ◆ ~ **court** Squashplatz *m;* ~ **courts** *pl* Squashhalle *f.*

squash³ *n, no pl (US)* (Pâtisson-)Kürbis *m.*

squashy ['skwɒʃı] *adj (+er)* matschig; *cushion* weich.

squat [skwɒt] [1] *adj (+er)* gedrungen, kompakt; *chair* niedrig; *figure, person* gedrungen.
[2] *vi* **(a)** *(person)* hocken, kauern; *(animal)* hocken.
(b) *(also* ~ **down**) sich (hin)hocken *or* (hin)kauern.
(c) *(on land)* sich (illegal) ansiedeln ◆ **to ~ (in a house)** ein Haus besetzt haben, sich in einem Haus eingenistet haben *(inf);* **they are not tenants, they're just ~ting** das sind keine Mieter, das sind Hausbesetzer.
[3] *n (inf: place)* Unterschlupf *m (für Hausbesetzer)* ◆ **after their ~ in that house** ... nachdem sie sich in dem Haus eingenistet hatten ... *(inf),* nachdem sie das Haus als Unterschlupf benutzt hatten ...

squatter ['skwɒtəʳ] *n (on land)* Squatter *m,* illegaler Siedler; *(in house)* Hausbesetzer *m.*

squaw [skwɔː] *n* Squaw *f.*

squawk [skwɔːk] [1] *n* heiserer Schrei; *(fig inf: complaint)* Protest *m* ◆ **he let out a ~** er kreischte auf; **the ~s of the hens** das aufgeregte Gackern der Hühner.
[2] *vi (bird, person)* schreien, kreischen; *(fig inf: complain)* protestieren.

squeak [skwiːk] [1] *n (of hinge, wheel etc, shoe, pen)* Quietschen *nt no pl; (of person)* Quiekser *m; (of small animal)* Quieken *nt no pl; (of mouse, bird)* Piepsen *nt no pl; (fig inf: sound)* Pieps *(inf),* Mucks *(inf) m* ◆ **she gave a ~ of surprise/delight** sie quiekste überrascht/entzückt; **the door opened with a ~** die Tür ging quietschend auf; *see* **narrow**.
[2] *vi (door, hinge, shoes etc)* quietschen; *(person)* quieksen; *(small animal)* quieken, quieksen; *(mouse, bird)* piepsen.
[3] *vt* quieksen.

squeaky ['skwiːkı] *adj (+er)* quietschend; *voice* piepsig.

squeaky-clean [ˌskwiːkı'kliːn] *adj (inf)* absolut sauber *(inf),* blitzsauber *(inf)* ◆ **the ~ brigade** die Saubermänner *pl (inf).*

squeal ['skwiːl] [1] *n* Schrei *m; (of person, tyre, brakes)* Kreischen *nt no pl; (of protest)* (Auf)schrei *m; (of pig)* Quieken *nt no pl* ◆ **with a ~ of brakes/tyres** mit kreischenden Bremsen/Reifen; **a ~ of pain** ein Schmerzensschrei *m;* **~s of protest** Protestgeschrei *nt;* **~s/a ~ of laughter** schrilles Gelächter.
[2] *vi* **(a)** schreien, kreischen; *(brakes, tyres)* kreischen, quietschen; *(pig, puppy)* quieksen; *(fig inf)* jammern ◆ **to ~ with pain/pleasure/laughter** vor Schmerz aufheulen *or* kreischen/vor Vergnügen quietschen/laut auflachen; **to ~ for sb** nach jdm schreien; **to ~ for help** um Hilfe schreien.
(b) *(inf: confess, inform) (criminal)* singen *(sl) (to* bei); *(schoolboy etc)* petzen *(inf) (to* bei).
[3] *vt* schreien, kreischen.

squeamish ['skwiːmıʃ] *adj person (easily nauseated)* empfindlich, heikel *(dial); (easily shocked)* zartbesaitet, empfindlich ◆ **I felt a bit ~** *(sick)* mir war leicht übel; **it gave me a ~ feeling in my stomach** mein Magen revoltierte; **I felt a bit ~ about telling him the bad news** mir war gar nicht wohl dabei, daß ich ihm die schlechte Nachricht mitteilen mußte; **I'm not ~** *(not easily nauseated)* mir wird nicht so schnell schlecht *or* übel; *(not easily shocked)* ich bin nicht so zartbesaitet *or* empfindlich; *(not nervous about unpleasant things)* ich bin ja nicht zimperlich; **don't be so ~** sei nicht so zimperlich; **this book is not for the ~** das Buch ist nichts für zarte Gemüter.

squeamishness ['skwiːmıʃnıs] *n (nausea)* Übelkeit *f; (disgust)* Ekel *m; (prudishness)* Zimperlichkeit *f* ◆ **a feeling of ~** leichte Übelkeit; **his ~ when he sees blood** die Übelkeit, die ihn beim Anblick von Blut überkommt; **you have to overcome your ~** *(prudishness, reluctance)* Sie dürfen nicht so zimperlich sein; *(disgust)* Sie müssen Ihren Ekel überwinden.

squeegee [ˌskwiː'dʒiː] *n* (Gummi)wischer *m; (Phot)* Rollenquetscher *m.*

squeeze [skwiːz] [1] *n* **(a)** *(act of squeezing)* Drücken, Pressen *nt no pl; (hug)* Umarmung *f; (of hand)* Händedruck *m; (in bus etc)* Gedränge *nt* ◆ **to give sth a ~** etw drücken, etw pressen; *lemon, sponge* etw ausdrücken; **to give sb/sb's hand a ~** jdn an sich *(acc)* drücken/jdm die Hand drücken; **it was a terrible** *or* **tight ~** es war fürchterlich eng; **getting into that dress was a bit of a ~** es war nicht so leicht, mich in das Kleid zu zwängen.
(b) *(amount)* Spritzer *m* ◆ **put a ~ of toothpaste on the brush** drücken Sie etwas Zahnpasta auf die Bürste.
(c) *(credit ~)* Kreditbeschränkung *f.*
(d) to put the ~ on sb *(inf)* jdm die Daumenschrauben ansetzen *(inf).*
[2] *vt* drücken; *sponge, tube* ausdrücken; *orange* auspressen, ausquetschen; *(squash) person, hand* einquetschen ◆ **to ~ clothes into a case** Kleider in einen Koffer zwängen; **to ~ liquid out of** *or* **from sth** Flüssigkeit aus etw (heraus)pressen; **to ~ out water/juice** Wasser/Saft herauspressen *(from* aus); **he ~d the trigger** er drückte ab; **to ~ out a tear** eine Träne zerdrücken; **to ~ sth dry** *(lit)* etw auswringen; *(fig)* das Letzte aus etw herausholen; **to ~ sb dry** *(fig)* jdn ausbluten; **to ~ money/information** *etc* **out of sb** Geld/Informationen *etc* aus jdm herausquetschen; **to ~ the rich** die Reichen schröpfen; **to be ~d to death** erdrückt werden; **I'll see if we can ~ you in** vielleicht können wir Sie noch unterbringen.
[3] *vi* **you'll get through if you ~** wenn du dich klein machst, kommst du durch; **to ~ in/out** sich hinein-/hinausdrängen; **to ~ past sb** sich an jdm vorbeidrücken; **to ~ into the bus** sich in den Bus hineinzwängen; **to ~ through a crowd/hole/underneath a fence** sich durch eine Menge/ein Loch zwängen/sich unter einem Zaun durchzwängen; **you'll have to ~ up a bit** Sie müssen ein bißchen zusammenrücken.

squeeze-box ['skwiːzbɒks] *n (inf)* Quetschkommode *f (inf).*

squeezer ['skwiːzəʳ] *n* Presse *f.*

squeezy ['skwiːzı] *adj (+er) (inf)* nachgiebig.

squelch [skweltʃ] [1] *n* glucksendes *or* quatschendes *(inf)* Geräusch ◆ **I heard the ~ of his footsteps in the mud** ich hörte, wie er quatschend *(inf) or* platschend durch den Schlamm lief; **the tomato hit the floor with a ~** die Tomate schlug mit einem satten Platsch auf den Boden auf.
[2] *vt* **to ~ one's way through sth** durch etw p(l)atschen.
[3] *vi* patschen, platschen; *(shoes, mud)* quatschen ◆ **water ~ed in his boots** das Wasser gluckste *or* quatschte in seinen Stiefeln.

squib [skwıb] *n (firework)* Knallfrosch *m; see* **damp**.

squid [skwıd] *n* Tintenfisch *m.*

squiffy ['skwıfı] *adj (+er) (Brit inf)* angesäuselt *(inf).*

squiggle ['skwıgl] [1] *n* Schnörkel *m.*
[2] *vt* **to ~ a line under sth** eine Wellenlinie unter etw *(acc)* machen.

squiggly ['skwıglı] *adj (+er)* schnörkelig ◆ **~ tail** Ringelschwanz *m.*

squint [skwınt] [1] *n* **(a)** *(Med)* Schielen *nt no pl* ◆ **to have a ~** leicht schielen; **he has a terrible ~ in his left eye** er schielt furchtbar auf dem linken Auge.
(b) *(inf) (look)* Blick *m; (sidelong glance)* Seitenblick *m* ◆ **to have** *or* **take a ~ at sb/sth** einen Blick auf jdn/etw werfen; *(obliquely)* jdn/etw von der Seite ansehen, nach jdm/etw schielen.
[2] *vi* schielen; *(in strong light etc)* blinzeln; *(inf: look also)* linsen *(inf)* ◆ **to ~ at sb/sth** nach jdm/etw schielen; *(quickly)* einen kurzen Blick auf jdn/etw werfen.
[3] *adj (crooked)* schief.

squint-eyed ['skwınt'aıd] *adj person* schielend *attr; look* schräg, schief ◆ **to be ~** schielen.

squire ['skwaıəʳ] [1] *n* **(a)** *(esp Brit: landowner)* Gutsherr, ≃ Junker *(Hist) m* ◆ **right, ~** *(Brit sl)* jawohl, der Herr *(dated),* in Ordnung, Chef *(inf);* **the ~ of the manor** der Herr des Gutes.
(b) *(Hist: knight's attendant)* Knappe *m.*
(c) *(dated: escort)* Kavalier *m (dated).*
[2] *vt (dated)* begleiten, eskortieren *(dated).*

squirearchy ['skwaıərɑːkı] *n* Gutsbesitzer *pl,* ≃ Landjunkertum *nt (Hist).*

squirm [skwɜːm] [1] *n* Winden *nt* ◆ **to give a ~** sich winden.
[2] *vi* sich winden; *(in distaste)* schaudern; *(with embarrassment)* sich (drehen und) winden; *(from discomfort)* hin und her rutschen ◆ **blood/her poetry makes me ~** wenn ich Blut sehe,/bei ihren Gedichten dreht sich in mir alles herum; **spiders make me ~** vor Spinnen graust es mir.

squirrel ['skwırəl] [1] *n* Eichhörnchen *nt.*
[2] *adj attr coat, fur* Eichhörnchen-.

squirt [skwɜːt] [1] *n* **(a)** Spritzer *m.* **(b)** *(implement)* Spritze *f.* **(c)** *(pej inf: person)* Fatzke *m (inf); (small)* Pimpf *m (inf).*
[2] *vt liquid* spritzen; *object, person* bespritzen ◆ **to ~ water at sb, to ~ sb with water** jdn mit Wasser bespritzen.
[3] *vi* spritzen.

squish [skwıʃ] *vt (inf)* zermatschen *(inf).*

squishy ['skwıʃı] *adj (+er) (inf)* matschig *(inf).*

Sr *abbr of* **senior** sen., Sr.

SRC *(Brit) abbr of* **Student's Representative Council**.

Sri Lanka [ˌsriː'læŋkə] *n* Sri Lanka *nt.*

Sri Lankan [ˌsriː'læŋkən] [1] *adj* srilankisch.
[2] *n* Srilanker(in *f) m.*

SRN *(Brit) abbr of* **State Registered Nurse**.

SS *abbr of* **steamship**.

SSE *abbr of* **south-south-east** SSO.

SST *n (US) abbr of* **supersonic transport** Überschallflugzeug *nt.*

SSW *abbr of* **south-south-west** SSW.

St. *abbr of* **(a) Street** Str. **(b) Saint** hl., St. **(c) Strait**.

st *abbr of* **stone(s)**.

stab [stæb] [1] *n* **(a)** *(with knife etc, wound, of pain)* Stich *m* ◆ **~ wound** Stichwunde *f;* **a ~ of rheumatism** ein rheumatischer Schmerz; **to feel a ~ of pain** einen stechenden Schmerz empfinden; **to feel a ~ of conscience/guilt/remorse** ein schlechtes Gewissen haben, Gewissensbisse haben; **he felt a ~ of grief/pity** der Kummer/das Mitleid schnitt ihm in die Seele; **a ~ in the back** *(fig)* ein Dolchstoß *m.*
(b) *(inf: try)* Versuch *m* ◆ **to have a ~ at sth** etw probieren.
[2] *vt person* einen Stich versetzen *(+dat); (several times)* einstechen auf *(+acc); (wound seriously)* niederstechen; *food* durchstechen ◆ **to ~ sb (to death)** jdn erstechen; *(with dagger also)* jdn erdolchen; **to ~ sb with a knife, to ~ a knife into sb** jdn mit einem Messerstich/mit Messerstichen verletzen; **he ~bed his penknife into the desk** er stach sein Taschenmesser in den Tisch; **the knife ~bed her arm** das Messer drang ihr in den Arm; **he was ~bed through the arm/heart** er hatte eine Stichwunde am Arm/der Stich traf ihn ins Herz; **to ~ a knife/fork into sth** ein Messer in etw *(acc)* hineinstoßen/mit einer Gabel in etw *(acc)* hineinstechen; **to ~ sb in the back** *(lit)* jdm in den Rücken stechen; *(fig)* jdm in den Rücken fallen; **he ~bed the air with his fork** er fuchtelte mit der Gabel in der Luft herum *(inf).*
[3] *vi* **to ~ at sb/sth** *(with knife etc)* nach jdm/etw stechen; *(with finger)* auf jdn/etw zeigen.

stabbing ['stæbıŋ] [1] *n* Messerstecherei *f.*
[2] *adj pain* stechend.

stability [stə'bılıtı] *n* Stabilität *f; (of relationship also, of job)* Beständigkeit *f* ◆ **(mental) ~** (seelische) Ausgeglichenheit.

stabilization [ˌsteıbəlaı'zeıʃən] *n* Stabilisierung *f.*

stabilize ['steıbəlaız] [1] *vt (Fin, Naut, Aviat)* stabilisieren.

[2] *vi* sich stabilisieren.
stabilizer ['steɪbəlaɪzəʳ] *n* (*Naut, Chem*) Stabilisator *m*; (*Aviat*) Stabilisierungsfläche *f*; (*US Aviat*) Höhenflosse *f*; (*on bicycle*) Stützrad *nt*.
stable[1] ['steɪbl] *adj* (*+er*) stabil; *ladder, structure also* sicher; *relationship also, job* beständig, dauerhaft; *character* gefestigt ♦ **mentally ~** ausgeglichen, innerlich gefestigt.
stable[2] [1] *n* (*building*) Stall *m*; (*group of racehorses*) (Renn)stall *m* ♦ **riding ~s** Reitstall *m*; **to be out of the same ~** (*fig*) aus dem gleichen Stall stammen; **to lock the ~ door after the horse has bolted** (*prov*) den Brunnen erst zudecken, wenn das Kind hineingefallen ist (*prov*).
[2] *vt* (*put in ~*) in den Stall bringen; (*keep in ~*) im Stall halten ♦ **he ~s his horses with the trainer** seine Pferde stehen im Stall des Trainers.
stable: ~boy, ~-lad, ~man *n* Stallbursche *m*; **~mate** *n* (*horse*) Pferd *nt* aus demselben Stall.
stabling ['steɪblɪŋ] *n* Stallungen, Ställe *pl*.
staccato [stə'kɑːtəʊ] *adj, adv* (*Mus*) staccato, stakkato; (*fig*) abgehackt.
stack [stæk] [1] *n* **(a)** (*pile*) Haufen *m*; (*neatly piled*) Stoß, Stapel *m*; (*of hay also*) Schober *m* (*esp S Ger, Aus*); (*of rifles*) Pyramide *f* ♦ **to be in the ~** (*Aviat*) kreisen, Warteschleifen ziehen (*over* über *+dat*).
(b) (*inf: lots*) Haufen *m* (*inf*) ♦ **~s** jede Menge (*inf*); **~s of time/helpers** jede Menge (*inf*) Zeit/Hilfskräfte.
(c) (*in library: also* **~s**) Magazin *nt*.
(d) *see* **chimneystack, smokestack**.
(e) (*Geol*) Felssäule *f*.
[2] *vt* **(a)** stapeln ♦ **to ~ up** aufstapeln.
(b) (*Aviat*) **incoming planes had to be ~ed** ankommende Maschinen mußten kreisen *or* Warteschleifen ziehen.
(c) (*US Cards*) packen, *beim Mischen betrügen* ♦ **the cards** *or* **odds are ~ed against us** (*fig*) wir haben keine großen Chancen.
[3] *vi* sich stapeln lassen ♦ **~ing chairs** Stühle, die sich (gut) stapeln lassen.
stacked [stækt] *adj* (*sl*) **to be (well) ~** einen großen *or* üppigen Vorbau haben (*inf*), Holz vor der Hütte haben (*inf*).
stacker ['stækəʳ] *n* (*for printer*) Ablage *f*.
stadium ['steɪdɪəm] *n, pl* **stadia** ['steɪdɪə] *or* **-s** Stadion *nt*.
staff [stɑːf] [1] *n* **(a)** (*personnel*) Personal *nt*; (*Sch, Univ*) Lehrpersonal *nt*, Lehrkörper *m* (*form*); (*of one department, on one project*) Mitarbeiterstab *m* ♦ **all the ~ are behind this idea** die ganze Belegschaft *or* (*Sch, Univ*) das ganze Kollegium steht hinter diesem Vorschlag; **a large ~** viel Personal/ein großes Kollegium/ein großer Mitarbeiterstab; **we don't have enough ~ to complete the project** wir haben nicht genügend Mitarbeiter, um das Projekt zu beenden; **editorial ~** Redaktion *f*, Redaktionsstab *m*; **administrative ~** Verwaltungsstab *m*, Verwaltungspersonal *nt*; **a member of ~** ein Mitarbeiter *m*; (*Sch*) ein Kollege *m*; **my fellow members of ~** meine Kollegen; **we have 30 ... on the ~** bei uns sind 30 ... angestellt; **to be on the ~** zum Personal/Kollegium/Mitarbeiterstab gehören; **are you ~?** (*inf*) arbeiten Sie hier?; **he joined the** *or* **our ~ in 1976** er arbeitet seit 1976 bei uns; **he has left our ~** er arbeitet nicht mehr hier.
(b) *pl* **-s** *or* (*old*) **staves** (*stick, symbol of authority*) Stab *m*; (*flag~*) Stock *m*; (*fig liter: support*) Stütze *f* ♦ **~ of office** Amtsstab *m*; **the ~ of life** das wichtigste Nahrungsmittel.
(c) (*Mil: general ~*) Stab *m*.
(d) *pl* **staves** (*Mus*) Notenlinien *pl*, Notensystem *nt*.
[2] *vt department* Mitarbeiter finden für; *hospital, shop, hotel* mit Personal besetzen, Personal finden für; *school* mit Lehrpersonal besetzen ♦ **to be well ~ed** gut besetzt sein, ausreichend Personal haben; **the kitchens are ~ed by foreigners** das Küchenpersonal besteht aus Ausländern.
staff: ~ canteen *n* (Betriebs)kantine *f*; **~ college** *n* Generalstabsakademie *f*.
staffer ['stɑːfəʳ] *n* (*Press inf*) ständiger Mitarbeiter, ständige Mitarbeiterin.
staffing ['stɑːfɪŋ] *n* Stellenbesetzung *f*.
staffing: ~ costs *npl* Personalkosten *pl*; **~ problem** *n* Problem *nt* mit der Stellenbesetzung.
staff: ~ notation *n* Notenschrift *f*; **~ nurse** *n* (*Brit*) (voll)ausgebildete Krankenschwester, Vollschwester *f* (*inf*); **~ officer** *n* Stabsoffizier *m*; **~ problem** *n* Personalproblem *nt*; **~room** *n* Lehrerzimmer *nt*; **~ training** *n* betriebliche Ausbildung.
stag [stæg] [1] *n* **(a)** (*Zool*) (*deer*) Hirsch *m*; (*male animal*) Bock, Bulle *m*. **(b)** (*Brit Fin*) Spekulant *m* (*der junge Aktien aufkauft*). **(c)** (*inf*) Mann, der solo ist (*inf*).
[2] *adj* Herren-, nur für Männer.
[3] *adv* **to go ~** solo ausgehen (*inf*).
stag beetle *n* Hirschkäfer *m*.
stage [steɪdʒ] [1] *n* **(a)** (*Theat, fig*) Bühne *f* ♦ **the ~** (*profession*) das Theater, die Bühne; **to be on/go on/leave the ~** (*as career*) beim Theater sein/zum Theater gehen/das Theater verlassen; **to go on ~** (*actor*) die Bühne betreten; (*play*) anfangen; **to come off ~, to leave the ~** von der Bühne abtreten; **to put a play on the ~** ein Stück aufführen *or* auf die Bühne bringen; **to write for the ~** Theater- *or* Bühnenstücke schreiben; **to adapt a novel for the ~** einen Roman fürs Theater bearbeiten; **to hold** *or* **dominate the ~** (*lit, fig*) die Szene beherrschen; **the ~ was set** (*lit*) das Bühnenbild war aufgebaut; (*fig*) alles war vorbereitet; **the ~ was set for a confrontation** die Situation war reif für eine Auseinandersetzung.
(b) (*platform in hall*) Podium *nt*.
(c) (*period*) Stadium *nt*; (*of disease, process also, of operation, development*) Phase *f* ♦ **at this ~ such a thing is/was impossible** zum gegenwärtigen Zeitpunkt ist das/zum damaligen Zeitpunkt war das unmöglich; **at this ~ in the negotiations** an diesem Punkt der Verhandlungen; **at this ~ in the game** (*fig*) zu diesem Zeitpunkt; **in the early/final ~(s)** im Anfangs-/Endstadium; **at an early ~ in its history** ganz zu Anfang seiner Geschichte; **what ~ is your thesis at?** wie weit sind Sie mit Ihrer Dissertation?; **we have reached a ~ where ...** wir sind an einem Punkt angelangt, wo ...; **the child has reached the talking ~** das Kind ist jetzt im Alter, wo es zu reden anfängt; **to go through a difficult ~** eine schwierige Phase durchmachen; **to be at the experimental ~** im Versuchsstadium sein.
(d) (*part of journey, race etc*) Abschnitt *m*, Etappe *f*; (*fare~*) Teilstrecke, Fahrzone *f*; (*actual bus stop*) Zahlgrenze *f* ♦ **in** *or* **by (easy) ~s** (*lit*) etappenweise; (*fig also*) Schritt für Schritt.
(e) (*section of rocket*) Stufe *f* ♦ **a three-~ rocket** eine dreistufige Rakete.
(f) (*old inf: ~coach*) Postkutsche *f*.
[2] *vt play* aufführen, auf die Bühne bringen; (*fig*) *accident, scene etc* inszenieren; *welcome* arrangieren; *demonstration, strike etc* inszenieren, veranstalten ♦ **to ~ a recovery/comeback** sich erholen/sein Comeback machen; **the play is ~d in the 19th century** das Stück spielt im 19. Jahrhundert.
stage: ~ box *n* Bühnen- *or* Proszeniumsloge *f*; **~coach** *n* Postkutsche *f*; **~craft** *n* dramaturgisches Können; (*of actor*) schauspielerisches Können; **~ direction** *n* Bühnen- *or* Regieanweisung *f*; **~ door** *n* Bühneneingang *m*; **~ effect** *n* Bühneneffekt *m*; **~ fright** *n* Lampenfieber *nt*; **to have an attack of ~ fright** Lampenfieber haben; **~ hand** *n* Bühnenarbeiter(in *f*) *m*; **~manage** *vt* (*lit*) Inspizient sein bei; (*fig*) *demonstration, argument* inszenieren; **~ manager** *n* Inspizient *m*; **~ name** *n* Künstlername *m*.
stager ['steɪdʒəʳ] *n*: **old ~** alter Hase (*inf*).
stage: ~-struck *adj* theaterbesessen; **to be ~-struck** unbedingt zum Theater wollen; **~ whisper** *n* Bühnenflüstern *nt*; **to say sth in a ~ whisper** etw hörbar flüstern.
stagey *adj see* **stagy**.
stagflation [stæg'fleɪʃən] *n* (*Econ*) Stagflation *f*.
stagger ['stægəʳ] [1] *vi* schwanken, taumeln; (*because of illness, weakness*) wanken; (*drunkenly*) torkeln ♦ **he was ~ing along the street** er taumelte die Straße entlang.
[2] *vt* **(a)** (*fig: amaze*) (*news etc*) den Atem verschlagen (*+dat*), umhauen (*inf*) ♦ **he was ~ed to hear of his promotion** die Nachricht von seiner Beförderung verschlug ihm die Sprache *or* haute ihn um (*inf*); **you ~ me!** da bin ich aber platt! (*inf*).
(b) *hours, holidays* staffeln, stufen; *seats, spokes* versetzt anordnen, versetzen.
[3] *n* Taumeln *nt* ♦ **to give a ~** taumeln, schwanken; **with a ~** taumelnd, schwankend; **~s** (*Vet: of horses*) (Dumm)koller *m*.
staggered ['stægəd] *adj* **(a)** (*amazed*) verblüfft, platt (*inf*). **(b)** *working hours etc* gestaffelt, gestuft ♦ **they work ~ hours** ihre Arbeitszeit ist gestaffelt; **a ~ junction** eine Kreuzung mit versetzt angeordneten Straßen.
staggering ['stægərɪŋ] *adj* **(a) to give sb a ~ blow** (*lit*) jdm einen Schlag versetzen, der ihn taumeln läßt; (*fig*) jdm einen harten *or* schweren Schlag versetzen. **(b)** (*amazing*) atemberaubend; *news, beauty also* umwerfend.
staggeringly ['stægərɪŋlɪ] *adv* (*amazingly*) umwerfend (*inf*), erstaunlich.
stag: ~hound *n* (*für die Hirschjagd bestimmter*) Jagdhund; **~ hunt, ~ hunting** *n* Hirschjagd *f*.
stagily ['steɪdʒɪlɪ] *adv dressed, made up* auffallend.
staginess ['steɪdʒɪnɪs] *n* auffällige Art.
staging ['steɪdʒɪŋ] *n* **(a)** (*production*) Inszenieren *nt*; (*scenery etc*) Inszenierung *f*. **(b)** (*stage*) Bühne *f*.
stagnancy ['stægnənsɪ] *n* Stagnieren *nt*; (*of trade also*) Stagnation *f*, Stocken *nt*.
stagnant ['stægnənt] *adj* (*still, not moving*) *air, water* (still)stehend *attr*, gestaut; (*foul, stale*) *water* abgestanden; *air* verbraucht; *trade* stagnierend, stockend; *mind* träge.
stagnate [stæg'neɪt] *vi* (*not circulate*) stagnieren; (*become foul*) (*water*) abstehen; (*air*) verbraucht werden; (*trade*) stagnieren, stocken; (*person*) verdummen; (*mind*) einrosten.
stagnation [stæg'neɪʃən] *n* (*of water*) Stagnieren *nt*; (*of air*) Stau *m*; (*of trade also*) Stagnation *f*, Stocken *nt*; (*of person*) Verdummung *f*; (*of mind*) Verlangsamung *f*.
stag: ~ night *n* Saufabend *m* (*inf*) des Bräutigams mit seinen Kumpeln (*am Vorabend der Hochzeit*); **~ party** *n* **(a)** Herrenabend *m*; **(b)** *see* **~ night**.
stagy ['steɪdʒɪ] *adj* (*+er*) theatralisch; *appearance* auffallend.
staid [steɪd] *adj* (*+er*) seriös, gesetzt; *colour* gedeckt.
staidly ['steɪdlɪ] *adv* gesetzt; *dressed* gedeckt.
staidness ['steɪdnɪs] *n* Gesetztheit *f*.
stain [steɪn] [1] *n* **(a)** (*lit*) Fleck *m*; (*fig also*) Makel *m* ♦ **a blood/grease/mud ~** ein Blutfleck *m*/Fettfleck *m*/Schlammspritzer *m*; **~ remover** Fleckenentferner *m*; **without a ~ on his character** ohne (einen) Makel.
(b) (*colorant*) (Ein)färbemittel *nt*; (*wood~*) Beize *f*.
[2] *vt* beflecken; (*colour*) einfärben; (*with wood~*) beizen.
[3] *vi* **(a)** (*leave a ~*) Flecken hinterlassen *or* geben (*inf*).
(b) (*become ~ed*) fleckig werden, Flecken bekommen.
stained [steɪnd] *adj dress, floor* fleckig, befleckt (*geh*); *glass* bunt, bemalt; *reputation* befleckt ♦ **~-glass window** Buntglasfenster *nt*, farbiges Glasfenster; **~ with blood** blutbefleckt.
stainless ['steɪnlɪs] *adj* **(a)** (*character*) tadellos.
(b) (*rust-resistant*) rostfrei ♦ **~ steel** rostfreier (Edel)stahl; **"~ steel"** „rostfrei"; **~ steel cutlery** rostfreies Besteck.

stair [stɛəʳ] *n* **(a)** (*step*) Stufe *f*. **(b)** *usu pl* (*~way*) Treppe *f* ◆ **at the top of the ~s** oben an der Treppe; **below ~s** (*Brit dated*) beim (Haus)personal; *see* **flight**[1].

stair: ~ carpet *n* Treppenläufer *m*; **~case** *n* Treppe *f*; **~ rod** *n* Teppichstab *m*; **~way** *n* Treppe *f*; **~well** *n* Treppenhaus *nt*.

stake [steɪk] 1 *n* **(a)** (*post*) Pfosten, Pfahl *m*; (*for vampires*) Pfahl *m*; (*for plant*) Stange *f*; (*for animal*) Pflock *m*; *see* **pull up**.
(b) (*place of execution*) Scheiterhaufen *m* ◆ **to go to** *or* **to die at the ~** auf dem Scheiterhaufen sterben, verbrannt werden; **he was ready to be burnt at the ~ for his principles** er war bereit, sich für seine Prinzipien ans Kreuz nageln zu lassen.
(c) (*bet*) Einsatz *m*; (*financial interest*) Anteil *m* ◆ **to be at ~** auf dem Spiel stehen; **he has a lot at ~** er hat viel zu verlieren; **to have a ~ in sth** *in business* einen Anteil an etw (*dat*) haben; *in the future* von etw betroffen werden; **he has a big ~ in the success of the plan** für ihn hängt viel vom Erfolg des Planes ab; **that's precisely the issue at ~** genau darum geht es; **the issue at ~ is not ...** es steht nicht zur Debatte, ob ...
(d) **~s** *pl* (*prize*) Gewinn *m* ◆ **the Newmarket ~s** der Große Preis von Newmarket.
2 *vt* **(a)** *animal* anpflocken. **(b)** (*also* **~ up**) *plant* hochbinden; *fence* abstützen. **(c)** (*bet, risk*) setzen (*on* auf *+acc*); (*esp US: back financially*) finanziell unterstützen ◆ **to ~ one's life/reputation on sth** seine Hand für etw ins Feuer legen/sein Wort für etw verpfänden; **to ~ a/one's claim to sth** sich (*dat*) ein Anrecht auf etw (*acc*) sichern.

◆**stake off** *or* **out** *vt sep land* abstecken.

◆**stake out** *vt sep place* umstellen; *person* überwachen.

stakeout ['steɪkaʊt] *n* Überwachung *f*.

stalactite ['stæləktaɪt] *n* Stalaktit *m*.

stalagmite ['stæləgmaɪt] *n* Stalagmit *m*.

stale [steɪl] *adj* (*+er*) **(a)** (*old, musty*) alt; *cake also* trocken; *bread, biscuit also* altbacken; (*in taste, smell also*) muffig; *water, beer, wine* abgestanden, schal; *air* verbraucht.
(b) (*fig*) *news* veraltet; *joke* abgedroschen; *athlete, pianist etc* ausgepumpt, verbraucht ◆ **to be ~** (*person*) alles nur noch routinemäßig machen; **I'm getting ~** ich mache langsam alles nur noch routinemäßig; **don't let yourself get ~** paß auf, daß du nicht in Routine verfällst.

stalemate ['steɪlmeɪt] 1 *n* (*Chess*) Patt *nt*; (*fig*) Patt(situation *f*) *nt*, Sackgasse *f* ◆ **to reach ~** (*lit*) ein Patt erreichen; (*fig*) in eine Sackgasse geraten; **to end in (a) ~** (*lit*) mit (einem) Patt enden, patt enden; (*fig*) in einer Sackgasse enden.
2 *vt* (*Chess*) patt setzen; (*fig*) matt setzen; *negotiations* zum Stillstand bringen.

staleness ['steɪlnɪs] *n* **(a)** (*lit*) (*of beer, water etc*) Schalheit, Abgestandenheit *f*; (*of bread, biscuit*) Altbackenheit *f*; (*of taste, smell*) Muffigkeit *f* ◆ **the ~ of the air made them sleepy** die verbrauchte Luft machte sie schläfrig.
(b) (*fig*) (*of joke*) Abgedroschenheit *f* ◆ **the ~ of the news** die veraltete Nachricht; **he practised to the point of ~** er übte, bis er langsam alles nur noch routinemäßig machte.

stalk[1] [stɔːk] 1 *vt game* sich anpirschen an (*+acc*); *person* sich anschleichen an (*+acc*); (*animal*) beschleichen, sich heranschleichen an (*+acc*) ◆ **evil ~ed the streets** (*liter*) das Böse ging in den Straßen um.
2 *vi* **(a)** (*walk haughtily*) stolzieren. **(b)** (*Hunt*) pirschen ◆ **to go ~ing** auf die Pirsch gehen.

stalk[2] *n* (*of plant, leaf*) Stiel *m*; (*cabbage ~*) Strunk *m* ◆ **his eyes came out on ~s** (*inf*) er bekam Stielaugen (*inf*).

stalker ['stɔːkəʳ] *n* **(a)** Pirschjäger(in *f*) *m*. **(b)** *jd, der die ständige Nähe zu einer von ihm verehrten (prominenten) Person sucht oder sie mit Anrufen, Briefen etc belästigt.*

stalking-horse ['stɔːkɪŋ,hɔːs] *n* (*fig*) (*person*) Strohmann *m*; (*pretext*) Vorwand *m*.

stall [stɔːl] 1 *n* **(a)** (*in stable*) Box, Bucht *f*; (*old: stable*) Stall *m*.
(b) (*at market etc*) Stand *m*.
(c) **~s** *pl* (*Brit Theat, Film*) Parkett *nt* ◆ **in the ~s** im Parkett.
(d) (*Eccl*) Kirchenstuhl *m* ◆ **~s** Chorgestühl *nt*.
(e) (*Aviat*) überzogener Flug ◆ **to do a ~ turn** (*Aviat*) ein Flugzeug auffangen und neu starten.
2 *vt* **(a)** *horse, cow* einstellen.
(b) (*Aut*) abwürgen; (*Aviat*) überziehen.
(c) (*also* **~ off**) *person* hinhalten; *decision* hinauszögern.
3 *vi* **(a)** (*engine*) absterben; (*Aviat*) überziehen.
(b) (*delay*) Zeit schinden (*inf*) ◆ **stop ~ing!** hören Sie auf auszuweichen *or* drum herumzureden (*inf*)!; **to ~ on a decision** eine Entscheidung hinauszögern; **to ~ for time** versuchen, Zeit zu gewinnen *or* zu schinden (*inf*).

stallion ['stæljən] *n* Hengst *m*; (*for breeding*) Zuchthengst *m*.

stalwart ['stɔːlwət] 1 *adj* **(a)** (*in spirit*) treu, unentwegt; *supporter also* getreu; *belief* unerschütterlich. **(b)** (*in build*) kräftig, robust.
2 *n* (*supporter*) (getreuer) Anhänger ◆ **the party leader and his ~s** der Parteichef und seine Getreuen.

stalwartly ['stɔːlwətlɪ] *adv fight, oppose* tapfer, unentwegt, *support* treu; *believe* unerschütterlich; *built* kräftig.

stamen ['steɪmən] *n* Staubgefäß *nt*.

stamina ['stæmɪnə] *n* Stehvermögen, Durchhaltevermögen *nt*.

stammer ['stæməʳ] 1 *n* Stottern *nt* ◆ **to speak with a ~** stottern; **he has a bad ~** er stottert stark.
2 *vt* (*also* **~ out**) stammeln.
3 *vi* stottern ◆ **to start ~ing** ins Stottern geraten.

stammerer ['stæmərəʳ] *n* Stotterer *m*, Stotterin *f*.

stammering ['stæmərɪŋ] *n* (*act*) Stottern, Stammeln *nt*; (*stammered speech*) Gestotter(e), Gestammel(e) *nt*.

stammeringly ['stæmərɪŋlɪ] *adv* stammelnd, stotternd.

stamp [stæmp] 1 *n* **(a)** (*postage ~*) (Brief)marke *f*, (Post)wertzeichen *nt* (*form*); (*insurance ~, revenue ~ etc*) Marke *f*; (*trading ~*) (Rabatt)marke *f*; (*charity ~, airmail ~, sticker*) Aufkleber *m* ◆ **to collect (postage) ~s** Briefmarken sammeln; **to save (trading) ~s** Rabattmarken sammeln.
(b) (*rubber ~, die, impression*) Stempel *m*.
(c) (*fig*) **a man of his ~** ein Mann seines Schlags; **to bear the ~ of the expert/of authenticity** den Stempel des Experten/die Züge der Echtheit tragen.
2 *vt* **(a)** **to ~ one's foot** (mit dem Fuß) (auf)stampfen; **to ~ the ground** (mit dem Fuß/den Füßen) auf den Boden stampfen; **he ~ed the turf back into place** er stampfte die Sode wieder an ihrem Platz fest.
(b) (*put postage ~ on*) freimachen, frankieren ◆ **a ~ed addressed envelope** ein frankierter Rückumschlag.
(c) *paper, document etc* (*with rubber ~*) stempeln; (*with embossing machine*) prägen; *name, pattern* aufstempeln; aufprägen (*on* auf *+acc*); (*fig*) ausweisen (*as* als) ◆ **the new leader has ~ed his personality on the party** der neue Vorsitzende hat der Partei seine Persönlichkeit aufgeprägt *or* seinen Stempel aufgedrückt.
3 *vi* (*walk*) sta(m)pfen, trampeln; (*disapprovingly, in dancing*) (mit dem Fuß) (auf)stampfen; (*horse*) aufstampfen ◆ **he was ~ing about the house** er trampelte im Haus herum; **to ~ in/out** hinein-/hinausstapfen; **you ~ed on my foot** Sie haben mir auf den Fuß getreten.

◆**stamp on** 1 *vt sep pattern, design* aufprägen ◆ **to ~ a pattern ~ sth** auf etw (*acc*) ein Muster (auf)prägen; **to be ~ed ~ sb's memory** sich jdm eingeprägt haben.
2 *vi +prep obj* (*put one's foot on*) treten auf (*+acc*).

◆**stamp out** 1 *vt sep* **(a)** *fire* austreten; (*fig: eradicate*) *epidemic, crime* ausrotten; *opposition* unterdrücken, zunichte machen; *trouble* niederschlagen; *rebels* unschädlich machen. **(b)** (*punch or cut out*) *pattern, shape* ausstanzen. **(c)** *rhythm* (mit)stampfen.
2 *vi* heraustrampeln, heraussta(m)pfen.

stamp: ~ album *n* Briefmarkenalbum *nt*; **~ collecting** *n* Briefmarkensammeln *nt*; **~ collection** *n* Briefmarkensammlung *f*; **~ collector** *n* Briefmarkensammler(in *f*) *m*; **~ dealer** *n* Briefmarkenhändler(in *f*) *m*; **~ duty** *n* (Stempel)gebühr *f*.

stampede [stæm'piːd] 1 *n* (*of horses, cattle*) wilde Flucht; (*of people*) Massenandrang, Massenansturm *m* (*on* auf *+acc*); (*to escape*) wilde *or* panikartige Flucht ◆ **the exodus turned into a ~** der Exodus geriet zur Panik.
2 *vt cattle, horses, crowd* in (wilde *or* helle) Panik versetzen ◆ **to ~ sb into doing sth** (*fig*) jdn dazu drängen, etw zu tun; **let's not be ~d** (*fig*) wir wollen uns nicht kopfscheu machen lassen.
3 *vi* durchgehen; (*crowd*) losstürmen (*for* auf *+acc*).

stamping ground ['stæmpɪŋ,graʊnd] *n* **his old ~s** seine alten Jagdgründe; **it's the ~ of a lot of students** es ist der Treff(punkt) vieler Studenten.

stamp machine *n* Briefmarkenautomat *m*.

stance [stæns] *n* (*posture, Sport*) Haltung *f*; (*mental attitude also*) Einstellung *f*; (*Cricket, Golf etc also*) Stand *m* ◆ **to take up a ~** (*lit*) in Stellung gehen; (*fig*) eine Haltung einnehmen.

▼ **stand** [stænd] (*vb: pret, ptp* **stood**) 1 *n* **(a)** (*position*) Platz, Standort *m*; (*fig*) Standpunkt *m*, Einstellung *f* (*on* zu) ◆ **my ~ is that ...** ich stehe auf dem Standpunkt, daß ..., ich vertrete die Einstellung, daß ...; **to take a ~ (on a matter)** (zu einer Angelegenheit) eine Einstellung vertreten; **to take a firm ~** einen festen Standpunkt vertreten (*on* zu).
(b) (*Mil*) (*resistance*) Widerstand *m*; (*battle*) Gefecht *nt* ◆ **to make a ~** (*lit, fig*) sich widersetzen, Widerstand leisten.
(c) (*taxi ~*) Stand *m*.
(d) (*Theat*) Gastspiel *nt*; (*of pop group etc*) Konzert *nt*.
(e) (*furniture, lamp ~, music ~*) Ständer *m*.
(f) (*market stall etc*) Stand *m*.
(g) (*band~*) Podium *nt*.
(h) (*Sport*) Tribüne *f*; (*US Jur*) Zeugenstand *m* ◆ **(we sat) in the ~** (wir saßen) auf der Tribüne; **to take the ~** (*Jur*) in den Zeugenstand treten.
(i) (*esp US Forest*) (Baum)bestand *m*.
2 *vt* **(a)** (*place*) stellen; *see* **stead, head**.
(b) (*withstand*) *pressure, close examination etc* (*object*) standhalten (*+dat*); (*person*) gewachsen sein (*+dat*); *test* bestehen; *climate* vertragen; *heat, noise* ertragen, aushalten; *loss, cost* verkraften ◆ **the wall could ~ another coat of paint** (*inf*) die Wand könnte noch einen Anstrich vertragen.
▼ **(c)** (*inf: put up with*) *person, noise, interruptions etc* aushalten ◆ **I can't ~ him/it** (*don't like*) ich kann ihn nicht leiden *or* ausstehen/ich kann das nicht ausstehen *or* vertragen; **I can't ~ being kept waiting** ich kann es nicht leiden *or* ausstehen, wenn man mich warten läßt; **I can't ~ it any longer** ich halte das nicht mehr (länger) aus.
(d) (*inf: treat*) **to ~ sb a drink/a meal** jdm einen Drink/ein Essen spendieren.
3 *vi* **(a)** (*be upright*) stehen; (*get up*) aufstehen ◆ **all ~!** alles aufstehen!; **don't just ~ there!** stehen Sie nicht nur (dumm) rum! (*inf*); **to ~ still** stillstehen; **we stood talking** wir standen da und unterhielten uns; **~ and deliver!** (*old, hum*) anhalten, her mit dem Zeug! (*inf*); *see* **attention, ease**.
(b) (*measure*) (*person*) groß sein; (*tree etc*) hoch sein.
(c) (*be situated*) stehen ◆ **it has stood there for 600 years** es steht da schon seit 600 Jahren.

➤ LANGUAGE IN USE: **stand: 2c** → 7.3

(d) *(remain unchanged)* stehen; *(fig)* bestehen (bleiben).
(e) **to ~ as a candidate** kandidieren; *see also* **~ for (a).**
(f) *(continue to be valid) (offer, promise)* gelten; *(argument, objection, contract also)* gültig bleiben; *(decision, record, account)* stehen ◆ **the theory ~s or falls by this** damit steht und fällt die Theorie.
(g) *(be at a level of) (thermometer, record)* stehen *(at* auf *+dat)*; *(sales)* liegen *(at* bei).
(h) *(fig: be in a position)* **we ~ to lose/gain a lot** wir laufen Gefahr, eine Menge zu verlieren/wir können sehr viel gewinnen; **he ~s to earn a lot of money** er wird wohl eine Menge Geld (dabei) verdienen; **what do we ~ to gain by it?** was springt für uns dabei heraus? *(inf)*, was bringt uns *(dat)* das ein?
(i) *(fig: be placed)* **how do we ~?** wie stehen wir?; **I'd like to know where I ~ (with him)** ich möchte wissen, woran ich (bei ihm) bin; **where do you ~ with him?** wie stehen Sie sich mit ihm?; **where do you ~ on this issue?** welchen Standpunkt vertreten Sie in dieser Frage?; **as things ~** nach Lage der Dinge; **as it ~s** so wie die Sache aussieht; **to ~ alone** *(be best)* unerreicht sein; **to ~ accused of sth** einer Sache *(gen)* angeklagt sein.
(j) *(fig: be, continue to be)* **to ~ firm** *or* **fast** festbleiben; **to ~ ready** sich bereithalten; **to ~ in need of help** Hilfe brauchen; **to ~ together** zusammenhalten; **to ~ (as) security for sb** für jdn bürgen *or* Bürge sein; **nothing now ~s between us** es steht nichts mehr zwischen uns; *see also other elements.*

◆**stand about** *or* **around** *vi* herumstehen.

◆**stand apart** *vi (lit)* abseits stehen; *(fig)* sich fernhalten ◆ **to ~ ~ from the others** abseits stehen.

◆**stand aside** *vi (lit)* zur Seite treten; *(fig) (withdraw)* zurücktreten; *(play no part)* (tatenlos) danebenstehen.

◆**stand back** *vi (move back)* zurücktreten; *(be situated at a distance)* zurückstehen, abliegen, zurückliegen; *(fig) (distance oneself)* Abstand nehmen; *(play no part)* (tatenlos) danebenstehen ◆ **to ~ ~ and do nothing** tatenlos zusehen.

◆**stand by** [1] *vi* **(a)** *(remain uninvolved)* (unbeteiligt) danebenstehen ◆ **to ~ ~ and do nothing** tatenlos zusehen. **(b)** *(be on alert)* sich bereithalten ◆ **to ~ ~ for further news** auf weitere Nachrichten warten.
[2] *vi +prep obj* **to ~ ~ a promise/sb** ein Versprechen/zu jdm halten.

◆**stand down** *vi* **(a)** *(retire, withdraw)* zurücktreten. **(b)** *(Jur)* den Zeugenstand verlassen. **(c)** *(Mil)* aufgelöst werden.

◆**stand for** *vi +prep obj* **(a)** *(be candidate for)* kandidieren für, sich zur Wahl stellen für ◆ **to ~ ~ Labour** für Labour *or* für die Labour-Partei kandidieren; **to ~ ~ (the post of) chairman** für den Posten des Vorsitzenden kandidieren; **to ~ ~ election** (in einer Wahl) kandidieren, sich zur Wahl stellen; **to ~ ~ re-election** sich zur Wiederwahl stellen; **to ~ ~ election to sth** für etw kandidieren; **she is ~ing ~ election to Parliament** sie kandidiert in den Parlamentswahlen.
(b) *(be abbreviation for, represent)* stehen für, bedeuten.
(c) *(put up with)* hinnehmen, sich *(dat)* gefallen lassen.

◆**stand in** *vi* einspringen.

◆**stand off** *vi (Naut)* seewärts anliegen.

◆**stand out** *vi* **(a)** *(project)* hervorstehen; *(land, balcony)* herausragen. **(b)** *(contrast, be noticeable)* hervorstechen, auffallen ◆ **to ~ ~ against sth** sich gegen etw *or* von etw abheben; **to ~ ~ from the others** hervorstechen, auffallen. **(c)** *(hold out)* **to ~ ~ against sth** weiterhin gegen etw Widerstand leisten; **to ~ ~ for sth** auf etw *(acc)* bestehen.

◆**stand over** [1] *vi (work, project)* liegenbleiben ◆ **to let sth ~ ~** etw liegenlassen.
[2] *vi +prep obj (supervise)* auf die Finger sehen *(+dat)* ◆ **I can't work with you ~ing ~ me** ich kann nicht arbeiten, wenn du mir (dauernd) über die Schulter siehst.

◆**stand to** *vi (Mil)* in Bereitschaft *or* in Waffen stehen.

◆**stand up** [1] *vi* **(a)** *(get up)* aufstehen; *(be standing)* stehen ◆ **~ ~ straight!** stell dich gerade hin; **to ~ ~ and be counted** sich zu seiner Meinung *or* seinen Überzeugungen bekennen.
(b) *(be valid) (argument)* überzeugen; *(Jur)* bestehen.
(c) **to ~ ~ for sb/sth** für jdn/etw eintreten; **to ~ ~ to sth** *to test, pressure (object)* einer Sache *(dat)* standhalten; *(person)* einer Sache *(dat)* gewachsen sein; *to hard wear* etw vertragen *or* aushalten; **to ~ ~ to sb** sich jdm gegenüber behaupten.
[2] *vt sep* **(a)** *(put upright)* hinstellen.
(b) *(inf) boyfriend, sb* versetzen.

stand-alone ['stændə'ləʊn] *n (Comput)* eigenständiges Gerät, Stand-alone-Gerät *nt.*

standard ['stændəd] [1] *n* **(a)** *(average, established norm)* Norm *f*; *(criterion)* Maßstab *m*; *(usu pl: moral ~s)* (sittliche) Maßstäbe *pl* ◆ **to set a good ~** Maßstäbe setzen; **to be above/below ~** über/unter der Norm sein *or* liegen; **to be up to ~** den Anforderungen genügen; **his (moral) ~s are abysmally low** er hat eine erschreckend niedere Moral; **to conform to society's ~s** den Wertvorstellungen der Gesellschaft entsprechen; **he sets himself very high ~s** er stellt hohe Anforderungen an sich *(acc)* selbst; **by any ~(s)** egal, welche Maßstäbe man anlegt; **by today's ~(s)** aus heutiger Sicht.
(b) *(degree, level)* Niveau *nt* ◆ **~ of living** Lebensstandard *m*; **~ of culture** kulturelles Niveau; **first-year university ~** Wissensstand *m* des ersten Studienjahrs; **of high/low ~** von hohem/niedrigem Niveau.
(c) *(Measurement)* (Maß)einheit *f*, Standard *m*; *(monetary ~)* (Währungs)standard *m* ◆ **these coins don't contain enough silver to conform to the monetary ~** diese Münzen enthalten weniger Silber, als dem Münzfuß entspräche.
(d) *(flag)* Flagge, Fahne *f*; *(on car)* Stander *m*; *(royal ~)* (königliche) Standarte.
(e) *(pole)* Mast *m.*
(f) *(Hort)* (Hoch)stamm *m* ◆ **~ rose** Stammrose *f.*
[2] *adj* **(a)** *(usual, customary)* üblich; *(Comm also)* handelsüblich; *model, price, practice, reply* Standard-; *size, measure* Normal-; *(average) performance, work* Durchschnitts-, durchschnittlich; *(widely referred to) author, reference book* Standard-; *(generally established as a measure) weight, size* Norm-; *conditions, pressure, temperature, time* Normal-; *gauge* Regel-, Normal- ◆ **such requirements are not ~** solche Forderungen sind nicht die Norm *or* Regel.
(b) *(Ling)* (allgemein) gebräuchlich ◆ **~ English** korrektes Englisch; **~ German** Hochdeutsch *nt*; **that word is hardly ~** dieses Wort ist ziemlich ungebräuchlich.

standard-bearer ['stændəd,beərə^r] *n* Fahnenträger(in *f*), Bannerträger *(old, fig) m.*

standardization [,stændədaɪ'zeɪʃən] *n see vt* Vereinheitlichung *f*, Normung, Standardisierung *f.*

standardize ['stændədaɪz] [1] *vt education, style, approach* vereinheitlichen; *format, sizes etc* normen, standardisieren.
[2] *vi* **to ~ on sth** etw standardmäßig verwenden.

standard-lamp ['stændəd'læmp] *n* Stehlampe *f.*

stand-by ['stændbaɪ] [1] *n* **(a)** *(person)* Ersatz, Ersatzmann *m*; *(Sport also)* Ersatz- *or* Auswechselspieler(in *f*) *m*; *(thing)* Reserve *f*; *(Aviat) (plane)* Entlastungsflugzeug *nt*; *(ticket)* Standby-Ticket *nt*; *(passenger)* Passagier, der mit einem Standby-Ticket reist.
(b) *(state of readiness)* **on ~** in Bereitschaft; *(ready for action)* in Einsatzbereitschaft; **to be on 24-hour ~** 24 Stunden Bereitschaftsdienst haben.
[2] *adj attr troops, player, generator* Reserve-, Ersatz-; *(Aviat) plane* Entlastungs-; *passenger, ticket* Standby-.

standee [stæn'diː] *n (esp US) jd, der steht or einen Stehplatz hat.*

stand-in ['stændɪn] *n (Film, Theat)* Ersatz *m.*

standing ['stændɪŋ] [1] *n* **(a)** *(social)* Rang *m*, (gesellschaftliche) Stellung; *(professional)* Position *f*; *(financial)* (finanzielle) Verhältnisse *pl*; *(repute)* Ruf *m*, Ansehen *nt* ◆ **of high ~** von hohem Rang; *(repute)* von hohem Ansehen; **a man of some ~** ein angesehener Mann; **what is his ~ locally?** was hält man in der Gegend von ihm?; **to be in good ~ with sb** gute Beziehungen zu jdm haben.
(b) *(duration)* Dauer *f* ◆ **a treaty/her husband of only six months' ~** ein Vertrag, der erst seit sechs Monaten besteht/ihr Mann, mit dem sie erst seit sechs Monaten verheiratet ist; **of long ~** alt, langjährig; *relationship, agreement etc also* von langer Dauer.
[2] *adj attr* **(a)** *(established, permanent)* ständig; *rule, custom* bestehend; *army also* stehend ◆ **it's a ~ joke** das ist schon zu einem Witz geworden; **to pay sth by ~ order** etw per Dauerauftrag bezahlen; **~ committee** ständiger Ausschuß; **the ~ orders of an association** die Geschäftsordnung einer Gesellschaft.
(b) *(from a standstill)* aus dem Stand; *(not sitting) ticket* Stehplatz-; *(erect) corn* auf dem Halm (stehend); *stone* (aufrecht) stehend ◆ **~ room only** nur Stehplätze; **to give sb a ~ ovation** jdm eine stehende Ovation darbringen; **to receive a ~ ovation** eine stehende Ovation erhalten, stürmischen Beifall ernten.

stand: ~-offish [,stænd'ɒfɪʃ] *adj*, **~-offishly** [-lɪ] *adv (inf)* distanziert; **~-offishness** [-nɪs] *n (inf)* Distanziertheit *f*; **~ pipe** *n* Steigrohr *nt*; **~point** *n* Standpunkt *m*; **from the ~point of the teacher** vom Standpunkt des Lehrers (aus) gesehen; **~still** *n* Stillstand *m*; **to be at a ~still** *(plane, train)* stehen; *(machines, traffic)* stillstehen; *(trade, factory, production)* ruhen; **to bring production to a ~still** die Produktion lahmlegen *or* zum Erliegen bringen; **to come to a ~still** *(person)* stehenbleiben, anhalten; *(vehicle)* zum Stehen kommen, anhalten; *(traffic, machines)* zum Stillstand kommen; *(industry etc)* zum Erliegen kommen; **~-up** *adj attr buffet, collar* Steh-; *meal* im Stehen; **~-up fight** Schlägerei *f*; **~-up comedian** *n* Bühnenkomiker(in *f*), Alleinunterhalter(in *f*) *m.*

stank [stæŋk] *pret of* **stink.**

stannic ['stænɪk] *adj* Zinn-.

stanza ['stænzə] *n* Strophe *f.*

staple¹ ['steɪpl] [1] *n* Klammer *f*; *(for paper)* Heftklammer *f*; *(for wires, cables etc)* Krampe *f.*
[2] *vt* heften; *wire* mit Krampen befestigen ◆ **to ~ sth together** etw zusammenheften.

staple² [1] *adj diet, food* Grund-, Haupt-; *product, topic* Haupt-.
[2] *n* **(a)** *(main product)* Hauptartikel *m*; *(main element)* Ausgangsmaterial *nt*; *(main food)* Hauptnahrungsmittel *nt.* **(b)** *(of cotton)* Rohbaumwolle *f*; *(of wool)* Rohwolle *f.*

stapler ['steɪplə^r] *n* Hefter, Tacker *(inf) m.*

star [stɑː^r] [1] *n* **(a)** Stern *m*; *(asterisk also, Sch)* Sternchen *nt* ◆ **the S~s and Stripes** das Sternenbanner; **to be born under a lucky ~** unter einem glücklichen Stern geboren sein; **you can thank your lucky ~s that ...** Sie können von Glück sagen, daß ...; **it's all in the ~s** es steht (alles) in den Sternen; **to see ~s** Sterne sehen; **a three-~ general** *(US Mil)* ein Drei-Sterne-General *m.*
(b) *(person)* Star *m.*
[2] *adj attr attraction* Haupt-; *performer, pupil, player* Star-.
[3] *vt* **(a)** *(mark with ~s)* mit einem Stern/mit Sternen versehen; *(fig: scatter)*

besäen *or* übersäen.
(b) (*Film etc*) **to ~ sb** (*film*) jdn in der Hauptrolle zeigen; **a film ~ring Greta Garbo** ein Film mit Greta Garbo (in der Hauptrolle); **~ring** ... in der Hauptrolle/den Hauptrollen ...
[4] *vi* (*Film etc*) die Hauptrolle spielen *or* haben.

star: ~ billing *n* **to get ~ billing** auf Plakaten groß herausgestellt werden; **~board** [1] *n* Steuerbord *nt*; **to ~board** (*direction*) (nach) Steuerbord; (*place*) (in) Steuerbord; [2] *adj* Steuerbord-; [3] *adv* (nach) Steuerbord.

starch [stɑːtʃ] [1] *n* Stärke *f* ◆ **~-reduced** stärkearm.
[2] *vt* stärken.

starchily ['stɑːtʃɪlɪ] *adv* (*fig*) steif.

starchy ['stɑːtʃɪ] *adj* (+*er*) stärkehaltig; (*fig*) steif.

star-crossed ['stɑːkrɒst] *adj* **they were ~ lovers** ihre Liebe stand unter einem Unstern.

stardom ['stɑːdəm] *n* Berühmtheit *f*, Ruhm *m* ◆ **where he hoped to find ~** wo er hoffte, ein Star zu werden.

stare [steəʳ] [1] *n* (starrer) Blick ◆ **the village idiot looked at me with a vacant ~** der Dorftrottel sah mich mit stierem Blick an; **to give sb a ~** jdn anstarren.
[2] *vt* **the answer/his guilt was staring us in the face** die Antwort/seine Schuld lag klar auf der Hand.
[3] *vi* (*vacantly etc*) (vor sich hin) starren; (*cow, madman*) stieren, glotzen (*inf*); (*in surprise*) große Augen machen; (*eyes*) weit aufgerissen sein ◆ **he ~d in disbelief** er starrte ungläubig; **it's rude to ~** es ist unhöflich, andere Leute anzustarren; **to ~ at sb/sth** jdn/etw anstarren; (*cow, madman also*) jdn/etw anstieren *or* anglotzen (*inf*); **don't ~ (at me)!** starr (mich) nicht so (an)!; **to ~ at sb in horror/amusement/disbelief** *etc* jdn entsetzt/verblüfft/ungläubig *etc* anstarren; **to ~ after sb** jdm nachstarren *or* hinterherstarren.

◆**stare out** *or* **down** *vt sep* **they were trying to ~ each other ~** sie versuchten, sich so lange gegenseitig anzustarren, bis einer aufgab; **I bet I can ~ you ~** wetten, daß du zuerst wegguckst (*inf*); **the teacher just sat there and ~d him ~** der Lehrer saß da und fixierte ihn.

star: ~fish *n* Seestern *m*; **~gazer** *n* (*hum inf*) Sterngucker *m* (*hum inf*).

staring ['steərɪŋ] *adj* starrend *attr* ◆ **~ eyes** starrer Blick.

stark [stɑːk] [1] *adj* (+*er*) *realism, contrast, ignorance, poverty* kraß; *reality, poverty also, white, truth, terror* nackt; *clothing, simplicity* schlicht; *madness* schier, rein, hell; *landscape, cliffs, branches* nackt, kahl; *light, bulb* grell; *colour* eintönig; (*glaring*) grell; *black* trist; *silhouette* hart.
[2] *adv* **~ raving** *or* **staring mad** (*inf*) total verrückt (*inf*); **~ naked** splitternackt.

starkers ['stɑːkəz] *adj pred* (*inf*) im Adamskostüm/Evaskostüm (*hum*); *children* nackig (*inf*).

starkly ['stɑːklɪ] *adv lit* grell; *described* kraß, schonungslos ◆ **~ dressed in black** in tristes Schwarz gekleidet; **trees ~ silhouetted against the winter sky** Bäume, die sich hart gegen den Winterhimmel abhoben.

starkness ['stɑːknɪs] *n* (*of clothing*) Schlichtheit *f*; (*of colour*) Eintönigkeit *f*; (*glaring*) Grellheit *f*; (*of truth, contrast*) Härte, Kraßheit *f*; (*of landscape*) Nacktheit, Kahlheit *f*.

starless ['stɑːlɪs] *adj* sternenlos.

starlet ['stɑːlɪt] *n* (Film)sternchen, Starlet *nt*.

starlight ['stɑːlaɪt] *n* Sternenlicht *nt*.

starling ['stɑːlɪŋ] *n* Star *m*.

star: ~lit *adj sky, night* stern(en)klar; *woods, hills* von Sternen beschienen; **~ part** *n* Hauptrolle *f*.

starred [stɑːd] *adj* mit (einem) Sternchen bezeichnet.

starriness ['stɑːrɪnɪs] *n* (*of night, sky*) Stern(en)klarheit *f*; (*of eyes*) Leuchten, Strahlen *nt*.

star role *n see* **star part**.

starry ['stɑːrɪ] *adj* (+*er*) *night* stern(en)klar; *sky* Sternen-; *eyes* strahlend, leuchtend.

starry-eyed ['stɑːrɪ'aɪd] *adj idealist* romantisch, blauäugig; (*naively trusting*) arglos, blauäugig ◆ **to go all ~** glänzende Augen kriegen.

star: ~ shell *n* Leuchtkugel *f*, Leuchtgeschoß *nt*; **~-spangled** *adj* **(a)** (*liter*) *sky* stern(en)übersät (*liter*); **(b) The S~-spangled Banner** das Sternenbanner; **~-studded** *adj* **(a)** (*liter*) *night* stern(en)klar, voller Sterne; *sky also* stern(en)übersät (*liter*); **(b)** (*fig*) **~-studded cast** Starbesetzung *f*.

START [stɑːt] *n abbr of* **Strategic Arms Reduction Treaty** START(-Vertrag) *m*.

start[1] [stɑːt] [1] *n* **to give a ~** zusammenfahren; (*~ up*) aufschrecken; (*horse*) scheuen; **to give sb a ~** jdn erschrecken, jdm einen Schreck(en) einjagen; **to wake with a ~** aus dem Schlaf hochschrecken; **he looked up with a ~** er blickte erschreckt hoch; *see* **fit[2]**.
[2] *vi* **(a)** zusammenfahren; (*~ up*) aufschrecken ◆ **to ~ from one's chair/out of one's sleep** aus dem Stuhl hochfahren/aus dem Schlaf hochschrecken.
(b) tears ~ed to his eyes Tränen traten ihm in die Augen; **his eyes were ~ing out of his head** die Augen traten ihm fast aus dem Kopf.
[3] *vt pheasant etc* aufscheuchen (*from* aus).

▼ **start[2]** [1] *n* **(a)** (*beginning*) Beginn, Anfang *m*; (*departure*) Aufbruch *m*; (*of race*) Start *m*; (*of rumour, trouble, journey*) Ausgangspunkt *m* ◆ **at the ~** am Anfang, zu Beginn; (*Sport*) am Start; **for a ~** (*to begin with*) fürs erste; (*firstly*) zunächst einmal; **from the ~** von Anfang an; **from ~ to finish** von Anfang bis Ende, von vorn bis hinten (*inf*); **to get off to a good** *or* **flying ~** gut vom Start wegkommen; (*fig*) einen glänzenden Start haben; **to get sb/sth off to a good ~** jdm einen guten Start verschaffen/etw gut anlaufen lassen; **to give sb a (good) ~ in life** jdm eine (gute) Starthilfe geben; **the review gave the book a good ~** die Rezension war eine gute Starthilfe für das Buch; **to make a ~ (on sth)** (mit etw) anfangen; **to make an early ~/a ~ for home** frühzeitig aufbrechen/sich auf den Heimweg machen; **to make a new ~ (in life)** (noch einmal) von vorn anfangen.
(b) (*advantage, Sport*) Vorsprung *m* (*over* vor +*dat*).
▼[2] *vt* **(a)** (*begin*) anfangen mit; *argument, career, new life, negotiations* beginnen, anfangen; *new job, journey* antreten ◆ **to ~ work** anfangen zu arbeiten; **he ~ed life as a miner** er hat/hatte als Bergmann angefangen; **don't ~ that again!** fang nicht schon wieder (damit) an!; **to ~ smoking** das *or* mit dem Rauchen anfangen; **he ~ed coming late** er fing an, zu spät zu kommen; **you ~ed it!** du hast angefangen!
(b) (*runners*) starten zu; (*cause to begin*) *runners, race* starten; *rumour* in Umlauf setzen; *conversation* anfangen, anknüpfen; *fight* anfangen; *blaze, collapse, chain reaction* auslösen; *coal fire etc* anzünden; (*arsonist*) legen; (*found*) *enterprise, newspaper* gründen, starten (*inf*) ◆ **to ~ sb thinking/on a subject** jdn nachdenklich machen/jdn auf ein Thema bringen; **to ~ sb in business/on a career** jdm zu einem Start im Geschäftsleben/zu einer Karriere verhelfen; **the discovery ~ed a new line of research** mit der Entdeckung kam eine neue Forschungsrichtung in Gang; **I don't want to ~ anything but ...** ich will keinen Streit anfangen, aber ...; **just to ~ you getting used to it** nur damit Sie sich erst mal daran gewöhnen; **as soon as she ~ed the baby** (*inf*) sobald sich das Baby angekündigt hatte; **when she wore the first mini-skirt she didn't realize what she was ~ing** als sie den ersten Minirock trug, war ihr nicht bewußt, was sie damit auslösen würde; **look what you've ~ed now!** da hast du was Schönes angefangen! (*inf*).
(c) *car* starten; *engine also* anlassen; *clock* in Gang setzen; *machine, motor also* anwerfen.
(d) to ~ a horse in a race eine Nennung für ein Pferd abgeben.
▼[3] *vi* (*begin*) anfangen, beginnen; (*car, engine*) anspringen, starten; (*plane*) starten; (*move off*) anfahren; (*bus, train*) abfahren; (*boat*) ablegen; (*rumour*) in Umlauf kommen; (*violins, cellos etc*) einsetzen ◆ **~ing from Tuesday** ab Dienstag; **to ~ for home** (nach Hause) aufbrechen, sich auf den Heimweg machen; **to ~ for work** zur Arbeit gehen/fahren; **to ~ for London** nach London losfahren; **to ~ (off) with** (*adv*) (*firstly*) erstens, erst einmal; (*at the beginning*) zunächst; **what shall we have to ~ (off) with?** was nehmen wir als Vorspeise?; **I'd like soup to ~ (off) with** ich möchte erst mal eine Suppe; **to ~ after sb** jdn verfolgen; **to get ~ed** anfangen; (*on journey*) aufbrechen; **he finds it difficult to get ~ed in the morning** er kommt morgens nur schwer in Schwung *or* Gang; **to ~ on a task/journey/the food** sich an eine Aufgabe/auf eine Reise/ans Essen machen; **to ~ talking** *or* **to talk** zu sprechen beginnen *or* anfangen; **he ~ed by saying ...** er sagte zunächst ...; **don't you ~!** fang du nicht auch noch an!

◆**start back** *vi* sich auf den Rückweg machen ◆ **we ~ed ~ for home** wir machten uns auf den Heimweg; **the rocket ~ed ~ to earth** die Rakete trat die Rückreise zur Erde an.

◆**start in** *vi* (*inf*) **(a)** (*begin to scold*) loslegen (*inf*), vom Leder ziehen (*inf*) (*on sb* gegen jdn). **(b) to ~ ~ on sth** sich an etw (*acc*) machen.

◆**start off** [1] *vi* (*begin*) anfangen; (*begin moving: person*) losgehen; (*on journey*) aufbrechen; (*run*) loslaufen; (*drive*) losfahren; (*esp Sport*) starten; (*begin talking etc*) anfangen, loslegen (*inf*) (*on* mit) ◆ **to ~ ~ with** (*adv*) *see* **start[2] 3**.
[2] *vt sep sth* anfangen ◆ **to ~ sb ~ (talking)** jdm das Stichwort geben; **to ~ the baby ~ (crying)** das Baby zum Schreien bringen; **whatever you do, don't ~ her ~** sieh bloß zu, daß sie nicht damit anfängt; **that ~ed the dog ~** da fing der Hund an zu bellen; **to ~ sb ~ on sth/doing sth** jdn auf etw (*acc*) bringen/jdn dazu bringen, etw zu tun; **a few stamps to ~ you ~** ein paar Briefmarken für den Anfang; **I'll play a few bars to ~ you ~** ich spiele ein paar Takte, um Sie einzustimmen.

◆**start out** *vi* (*begin*) (zunächst) beginnen *or* anfangen; (*begin a journey*) aufbrechen (*for* nach) ◆ **we ~ed ~ on a long journey/new enterprise** wir machten uns auf eine lange Reise/an ein neues Unternehmen; **we ~ed ~ with great hopes for the future** wir hatten mit großen Zukunftshoffnungen begonnen.

◆**start over** *vi* (*US*) noch (ein)mal von vorn anfangen.

◆**start up** [1] *vi* **(a)** (*move suddenly*) **a rabbit ~ed ~ out of the undergrowth** ein Kaninchen schoß aus dem Unterholz hervor; **he ~ed ~ in bed at the noise** bei dem Geräusch schreckte *or* fuhr er im Bett hoch.
(b) (*begin: music etc*) anfangen; (*machine*) angehen (*inf*), in Gang kommen; (*motor*) anspringen; (*siren*) losheulen ◆ **when I ~ed ~ in business** als ich als Geschäftsmann anfing; **he ~ed ~ by himself when he was 21** er machte sich mit 21 selbständig.
[2] *vt sep* **(a)** (*cause to function*) anmachen (*inf*), in Gang bringen; *engine also* anlassen, starten; *machine also* anwerfen.
(b) (*begin*) eröffnen; *business also* anfangen; *conversation* anfangen, anknüpfen; (*amongst other people*) in Gang bringen.

starter ['stɑːtəʳ] *n* **(a)** (*Sport*) Starter(in *f*) *m* (*also horse*); (*competitor*) Teilnehmer(in *f*) *m*; (*runner also*) Läufer(in *f*) *m* am Start ◆ **to be under ~'s orders** auf das Startkommando warten.
(b) (*Aut etc: self-~*) Starter, Anlasser *m*.
(c) (*inf: person*) **to be a late ~** Spätzünder sein (*inf*); (*child*) Spätentwickler sein; **to be a late ~ in the presidential race/with girls** sich erst spät an den Präsidentschaftswahlen beteiligen/ein Spätzünder sein, was Mädchen betrifft (*inf*); **she is a slow ~ in the morning** sie kommt morgens nur langsam in Schwung; **~ flat** erste (eigene) Wohnung.
(d) (*inf: first course*) Vorspeise *f*.
(e) for ~s (*sl*) für den Anfang (*inf*).

starting ['stɑːtɪŋ] *in cpds* (*Sport*) *line, post* Start-; **~ block** *n* Startblock *m*; **~ gate** *n* Startmaschine *f*; **~ grid** *n* Start(platz) *m*; **~ gun** *n* Startpistole *f*; **~ handle** *n* Anlasserkurbel *f*; **~ point** *n* (*lit, fig*) Ausgangspunkt *m*; **~ post** *n*

➤ LANGUAGE IN USE: **start[2]: 2a** → 20.4 **3** → 26.1

Startpflock *m*; ~ **price** *n* (*Horse-racing*) letzter Kurs vor dem Start.

startle ['stɑːtl] [1] *vt* erschrecken; *animal also* aufschrecken ◆ **I was ~d to see how old he looked** ich stellte entsetzt fest, wie alt er aussah.
[2] *vi* **she ~s easily** sie ist sehr schreckhaft.

startling ['stɑːtlɪŋ] *adj news* überraschend; (*bad*) alarmierend, bestürzend; *coincidence, resemblance* erstaunlich, überraschend; *colour, originality* aufregend, erregend; *dress* aufregend; *discovery* aufregend, sensationell.

startlingly ['stɑːtlɪŋlɪ] *adv simple, alike* überraschend; *dressed* aufregend ◆ **nothing ~ new/original** nichts besonders *or* allzu Neues/Originelles.

start-up ['stɑːtʌp] *n* (*of machine, new business*) Start *m* ◆ **100 new ~s a week** (*new businesses*) 100 Neugründungen pro Woche; ~ **costs** (*of business, project*) Startkosten *pl*.

star turn *n* Sensation, Hauptattraktion *f*.

starvation [stɑː'veɪʃən] *n* (*act*) Hungern *nt*; (*of besieged people*) Aushungern *nt*; (*condition*) Hunger *m* ◆ **to die of ~** verhungern, Hungers *or* den Hungertod sterben (*geh*); **to live on a ~ diet** Hunger leiden; **the prisoners were kept on a ~ diet for months** man ließ die Gefangenen monatelang fast verhungern; **the ~ diet we get at this school** die erbärmlichen Portionen, die es in dieser Schule gibt; **to go on a ~ diet** (*hum*) eine Hungerkur machen; ~ **wages** Hungerlohn *m*, Hungerlöhne *pl*.

starve [stɑːv] [1] *vt* **(a)** (*deprive of food*) hungern lassen; (*also* ~ **out**) aushungern; (*kill: also* ~ **to death**) verhungern lassen, Hungers sterben lassen (*geh*) ◆ **to ~ oneself** hungern; **to ~ a town into surrender** eine Stadt durch Aushungern zur Kapitulation zwingen; **he ~d his way through college** er hat sich (*dat*) das Studium vom Mund abgespart.
(b) (*fig*) **to ~ sb of sth** jdm etw vorenthalten *or* verweigern; **to be ~d of capital/graduates** an akutem Kapital-/Akademikermangel leiden; **to be ~d of affection** zuwenig Zuneigung erfahren, an Liebesentzug leiden.
[2] *vi* hungern; (*die: also* ~ **to death**) verhungern ◆ **I'm simply starving!** (*inf*) ich sterbe vor Hunger! (*inf*); **you must be starving!** du mußt doch halb verhungert sein! (*inf*); **to ~ for sth** (*fig*) nach etw hungern.

◆**starve out** *vt sep garrison etc* aushungern.

starveling ['stɑːvlɪŋ] *n* (*dated*) Hungerleider *m*.

starving ['stɑːvɪŋ] *adj* (*lit*) hungernd *attr*; (*fig*) hungrig.

star wars *n sing* Sternenkrieg *m*, Krieg *m* der Sterne.

stash [stæʃ] *vt* (*also* ~ **away**) (*sl*) *loot* verschwinden lassen (*inf*), bunkern (*sl*); *money* beiseite schaffen.

stasis ['steɪsɪs] *n* Stauung, Stase (*spec*) *f*; (*Liter*) Stillstand *m*.

state [steɪt] [1] *n* **(a)** (*condition*) Zustand *m* ◆ ~ **of health/mind/war/siege** Gesundheits-/Geistes-/Kriegs-/Belagerungszustand *m*; **widowed/married/single ~** Witwer- *or* Witwen-/Ehe-/Ledigenstand *m*; **to be in a ~ of weightlessness** sich im Zustand der Schwerelosigkeit befinden; **the ~ of the nation** die Lage der Nation; **the present ~ of the economy** die gegenwärtige Wirtschaftslage; **in a liquid/solid ~** im flüssigen/festen Zustand, in flüssigem/festem Zustand; **where animals live in their natural ~** wo Tiere im Naturzustand leben; **in a good/bad ~** in gutem/schlechtem Zustand; **he's in no (fit) ~/~ of mind to do that** er ist nicht in dem (richtigen) Zustand dafür *or* dazu; **what a ~ of affairs!** was sind das für Zustände!; **look at the ~ of your hands!** guck dir bloß mal deine Hände an!; **my papers are in such a ~!** meine Papiere sind in einem furchtbaren Durcheinander!; **the room was in a terrible ~** im Zimmer herrschte ein fürchterliches Durcheinander.
(b) (*inf: anxiety*) **to get into a ~ (about sth)** (*inf*) wegen etw durchdrehen (*inf*); **to be in a great ~** (*inf*) in heller Aufregung *or* ganz durchgedreht (*inf*) sein.
(c) (*rank*) Stand, Rang *m* ◆ ~ **of bishop** Bischofswürde *f*; **men in all ~s of life** Menschen *or* Angehörige aller Stände.
(d) (*pomp*) Aufwand, Pomp *m* ◆ **to be received in great ~** mit großem Staat empfangen werden; **to travel in ~** aufwendig *or* pompös reisen; **to lie in ~** (feierlich) aufgebahrt sein.
(e) (*Pol*) Staat *m*; (*federal ~*) (Bundes)staat *m*; (*in BRD, Austria*) (Bundes)land *nt* ◆ **the S~s** die (Vereinigten) Staaten; **the S~ of Florida** der Staat Florida; **a ~ within a ~** ein Staat im Staate; **affairs of ~** Staatsangelegenheiten *pl*.
[2] *vt* darlegen, vortragen; *name, price, amount* nennen, angeben; *purpose* angeben ◆ **to ~ that ...** feststellen *or* erklären, daß ...; **to ~ one's case** seine Sache vortragen; **it must be clearly ~d in the records ...** es muß aus den Akten einwandfrei hervorgehen, ...; **to ~ the case for the prosecution** (*Jur*) die Anklage vortragen; **the theme is ~d in the first few bars** das Thema wird in den ersten paar Takten vorgestellt; **unless otherwise ~d** wenn nicht anders angegeben; **as ~d in my letter I ...** wie in meinem Brief erwähnt, ... ich ...

state *in cpds* Staats-; *control also, industry* staatlich; (*US etc*) des Bundes- *or* Einzelstaates, bundesstaatlich; (*ceremonial*) Staats-; **~-aided** *adj* staatlich gefördert; ~ **apartment** *n* Prunksaal *m*; ~ **bank** *n* Staatsbank *f*; **~craft** *n* die Staatskunst.

stated ['steɪtɪd] *adj* **(a)** (*declared*) *sum, date* angegeben, genannt; *limits* bestimmt. **(b)** (*fixed, regular*) *times, amount* fest(gesetzt) ◆ **at the ~ intervals** in den festgelegten Abständen; **on the ~ date** *or* **the date ~** zum festgesetzten Termin.

state: S~ Department *n* (*US*) Außenministerium *nt*; ~ **education** *n* staatliche Erziehung; (*system*) staatliches Erziehungs- *or* Bildungswesen.

statehood ['steɪthʊd] *n* Eigenstaatlichkeit *f* ◆ **to achieve ~** ein eigener *or* selbständiger Staat werden; **when was Alaska granted ~?** wann wurde Alaska zum Bundesstaat erklärt?

state: ~house *n* (*US*) Parlamentsgebäude, Kapitol *nt*; **~less** *adj* staatenlos; **~less person** Staatenlose(r) *mf*; **~lessness** *n* Staatenlosigkeit *f*.

stateliness ['steɪtlɪnɪs] *n see adj* Würde *f*; Gemessenheit *f*; Pracht *f*.

stately ['steɪtlɪ] *adj* (+*er*) *person, bearing* würdevoll; *pace, walk* gemessen; *palace, tree* prächtig ◆ ~ **home** herrschaftliches Anwesen, Schloß *nt*.

statement ['steɪtmənt] *n* **(a)** (*putting forward: of thesis etc*) Darstellung *f*; (*of problem also*) Darlegung *f* ◆ **a clear ~ of the facts** eine klare Feststellung der Tatsachen.
(b) (*that said*) Feststellung *f*; (*claim*) Behauptung *f*; (*Mus: of theme*) Vorstellen *nt*; (*official, Government ~*) Erklärung, Stellungnahme *f*; (*in court, to police*) Aussage *f*; (*written*) Protokoll *nt*, Aussage *f* ◆ **to make a ~ to the press** eine Presseerklärung abgeben.
(c) (*Philos*) Behauptung, These *f*; (*Logic*) Satz *m*; (*Gram*) Feststellung *f*.
(d) (*Fin*) Rechnung *f*; (*also* **bank ~**) Kontoauszug *m*.

state: ~ occasion *n* Staatsanlaß *m*, Staatsfeierlichkeit *f*; **~-of-the-art** *adj* hochmodern, dem neuesten Stand der Technik entsprechend *attr*; **to be ~-of-the-art** dem neuesten Stand der Technik entsprechen; **~-of-the-art technology** Spitzentechnologie *f*; **~-owned** *adj* staatseigen; ~ **registered nurse** *n* staatlich anerkannte Krankenschwester; **~room** *n* (*Naut*) Kabine *f*; (*US Rail*) Privat(schlafwagen)abteil *nt*; ~ **school** *n* öffentliche Schule; ~ **secret** *n* Staatsgeheimnis *nt*; **S~'s evidence** *n* (*US*) Aussage *f* eines Kronzeugen; **to turn S~'s evidence** als Kronzeuge auftreten; **~side** (*US inf*) [1] *adj* in den Staaten (*inf*); *newspaper* aus den Staaten (*inf*); [2] *adv* heim, nach Hause; **when I'm back ~side** ... wenn ich wieder zu Hause in den Staaten bin, ...

statesman ['steɪtsmən] *n, pl* **-men** [-mən] Staatsmann *m*.

statesmanlike ['steɪtsmənlaɪk] *adj* staatsmännisch.

statesmanship ['steɪtsmənʃɪp] *n* Staatskunst *f* ◆ **skills of ~** staatsmännische Fähigkeiten *pl*.

stateswoman ['steɪtswʊmən] *n, pl* **-women** Staatsmännin *f*.

state: ~ trooper *n* (*US*) Soldat *m* der amerikanischen Nationalgarde; ~ **visit** *n* Staatsbesuch *m*; **~wide** *adj* (*US*) im ganzen Bundesstaat, landesweit.

static ['stætɪk] [1] *adj* **(a)** (*Phys*) statisch.
(b) (*not moving or changing*) konstant; (*stationary*) feststehend *attr*; *condition, society* statisch ◆ **if the development of a civilization remains ~** ... wenn eine Kultur sich nicht mehr weiterentwickelt, ...; **their relationship became ~** ihre Beziehung stagnierte *or* trat auf der Stelle.
[2] *n* (*Phys*) Reibungselektrizität *f*; (*Rad also*) atmosphärische Störungen *pl*.

statics ['stætɪks] *n sing* Statik *f*.

station ['steɪʃən] [1] *n* **(a)** Station *f*; (*police ~, fire ~*) Wache *f*; (*space ~*) (Raum)station *f*; (*US: gas ~*) Tankstelle *f*; *see* **work ~**.
(b) (*railway ~, bus ~*) Bahnhof *m*; (*stop*) Station *f*.
(c) (*Mil: post*) Stellung *f*, Posten *m* ◆ **frontier/naval ~** Grenzstellung *f*/Flottenstützpunkt *m*.
(d) (*esp Austral: ranch*) Farm *f* ◆ **sheep/cattle ~** Schafs-/Rinderzuchtfarm *f*; **~-hand** Farmgehilfe *m*.
(e) (*Rad, TV*) Sender *m*, Sendestation *f*; (*channel*) Sender *m*.
(f) (*position*) Platz *m* ◆ **to take up one's ~** sich (auf)stellen, seinen Platz einnehmen; **the S~s of the Cross** die Stationen *pl* des Kreuzwegs.
(g) (*rank*) Stand, Rang *m* ◆ ~ **in life** Stellung *f* (im Leben), Rang *m*; **to marry below/above one's ~** nicht standesgemäß/über seinem Stand heiraten; **he has got ideas above his ~** er hat Ideen, die jemandem aus seinem Stand gar nicht zukommen.
[2] *vt* (auf)stellen, postieren; (*Mil*) stationieren.

station agent *n* (*US*) *see* **station-master**.

stationary ['steɪʃənərɪ] *adj* (*not moving*) *car* parkend *attr*; haltend *attr*; (*not movable*) fest(stehend *attr*) ◆ **to be ~** (*vehicles*) stehen; (*traffic, fig*) stillstehen; **to remain ~** sich nicht bewegen; (*traffic*) stillstehen; **he never remains ~ for long** er bleibt nirgendwo lange.

stationer ['steɪʃənə^r] *n* Schreibwarenhändler *m* ◆ **~'s (shop)** Schreibwarenhandlung *f*.

stationery ['steɪʃənərɪ] *n* (*notepaper*) Briefpapier *nt*; (*writing materials*) Schreibwaren *pl* ◆ **office ~** Büromaterial *nt*.

station: ~ house *n* (*US: police*) (Polizei)wache *f*, (Polizei)revier *nt*; **~-master** *n* Bahnhofsvorsteher, Stationsvorsteher (*dated*) *m*; ~ **police** *n* Bahnpolizei *f*; ~ **selector** *n* (*Rad*) Sendereinstellung *f*; ~ **wagon** *n* Kombi(wagen) *m*.

statistic [stə'tɪstɪk] *n* Statistik *f*.

statistical *adj*, **~ly** *adv* [stə'tɪstɪkəl, -ɪ] statistisch.

statistician [ˌstætɪ'stɪʃən] *n* Statistiker(in *f*) *m*.

statistics [stə'tɪstɪks] *n* **(a)** *sing* Statistik *f*. **(b)** *pl* (*data*) Statistiken *pl*; *see* **vital**.

stator ['steɪtə^r] *n* (*Elec*) Stator *m*.

statuary ['stætjʊərɪ] (*form*) [1] *adj* statuarisch (*geh*) ◆ ~ **art** Plastik *f*.
[2] *n* (*Art*) Plastik, Bildhauerei *f*; (*statues*) Plastiken, Statuen *pl*.

statue ['stætjuː] *n* Statue *f*, Standbild *nt* ◆ **S~ of Liberty** Freiheitsstatue *f*.

statuesque [ˌstætjʊ'esk] *adj* standbildhaft, statuesk (*liter*) ◆ **a woman of ~ beauty** eine Frau von klassischer Schönheit.

statuette [ˌstætjʊ'et] *n* Statuette *f*.

stature ['stætʃə^r] *n* **(a)** Wuchs *m*; (*esp of man*) Statur *f* ◆ **of short ~** von kleinem Wuchs. **(b)** (*fig*) Format *nt*.

status ['steɪtəs] *n* Stellung *f*; (*legal ~, social ~ also*) Status *m* ◆ **equal ~** Gleichstellung *f*; **marital ~** Familienstand *m*; **many people who merely desire ~** viele Menschen, die bloß nach Prestige streben; **unsupported statements have no ~ in law** unbewiesene Behauptungen sind rechtlich irrelevant; **the idea that possession brings ~** die Vorstellung, daß Besitz das Prestige erhöht.

status: ~-conscious *adj* statusbewußt; ~ **line** *n* (*Comput*) Statuszeile *f*.

status quo ['steɪtəs'kwəʊ] *n* Status quo *m*.

status: ~ report *n* Zwischenbericht *m*; ~ **symbol** *n* Statussymbol *nt*.

statute ['stætju:t] *n* Gesetz *nt*; (*of organization*) Satzung *f*, Statut *nt* ◆ **by ~** gesetzlich; statutarisch, satzungsgemäß.

statute: ~ book *n* Gesetzbuch *nt*; **to put sth in the ~ book** etw zum Gesetz machen *or* erheben; **to be on the ~ book** geltendes Recht sein; **~ law** *n* Gesetzesrecht, Statute Law *nt*; **~ mile** *n* britische Meile.

statutory ['stætjʊtərɪ] *adj* gesetzlich; *holiday also, quarantine* gesetzlich vorgeschrieben; (*in organization*) satzungsgemäß, statutarisch; *right also* verbrieft; *punishment* (vom Gesetz) vorgesehen ◆ **~ rape** Vergewaltigung *f*; **this is ~** das ist Gesetz.

staunch¹ [stɔ:ntʃ] *adj* (*+er*) *Catholic, loyalist* überzeugt; *Republican also* loyal; *member, supporter* ergeben, getreu; *support* standhaft, zuverlässig ◆ **to be ~ in one's belief** fest *or* unerschütterlich im Glauben sein.

staunch² *vt flow* stauen; *bleeding* stillen ◆ **to ~ a wound** die Blutung einer Wunde stillen.

staunchly ['stɔ:ntʃlɪ] *adv* treu, standhaft.

staunchness ['stɔ:ntʃnɪs] *n see adj* Überzeugung *f*; Loyalität *f*; Treue *f*; Standhaftigkeit *f*.

stave [steɪv] *n* **(a)** (*of barrel*) (Faß)daube *f*; (*rung*) (Leiter)sprosse *f*; (*stick*) Knüppel, Knüttel (*old*) *m*. **(b)** (*Mus: staff*) Notenlinien *pl*. **(c)** (*Liter: stanza*) Strophe *f*, Vers *m*.

◆**stave in** *pret, ptp* **~d** *or* **stove in** [1] *vt sep* eindrücken; *head* einschlagen. [2] *vi* eingedrückt werden.

◆**stave off** *vt sep* **(a)** *attack* zurückschlagen; *crisis, cold* abwehren; *hunger* lindern. **(b)** (*delay*) *person* hinhalten; *crisis* hinausschieben.

staves [steɪvz] *pl of* **staff 1 (b, d)**.

stay¹ [steɪ] [1] *n* **(a)** Aufenthalt *m* ◆ **come for a longer ~ next year** komm nächstes Jahr für länger; **a short ~ in hospital** ein kurzer Krankenhausaufenthalt.
(b) (*Jur*) Aussetzung *f* ◆ **~ of execution** Aussetzung *f*, Vollstreckungsaufschub *m*; (*fig*) Galgenfrist *f*; (*of death penalty*) Hinrichtungsaufschub *m*.
[2] *vt* **(a)** (*old, liter: stop*) Einhalt gebieten (*+dat*) (*geh*); *hunger* stillen ◆ **to ~ one's/sb's hand** sich/jdn zurückhalten. **(b)** (*Jur*) *order, sentence* aussetzen. **(c)** **to ~ the course** (*lit, fig*) durchhalten.
[3] *vi* **(a)** (*remain*) bleiben ◆ **to ~ for** *or* **to supper** zum Abendessen bleiben; **to have come to ~** (*fashion etc*) sich halten; **has unemployment come to ~?** ist die Arbeitslosigkeit nun ein Dauerzustand?; **if it ~s fine** wenn es schön bleibt; **if he can ~ with the others** wenn er mit den anderen mithalten kann; **~ with it!** nicht aufgeben!; *see* **put²**.
(b) (*reside*) wohnen; (*at youth-hostel etc*) übernachten ◆ **to ~ at a hotel** im Hotel wohnen *or* übernachten; **I ~ed in Italy for a few weeks** ich habe mich ein paar Wochen in Italien aufgehalten; **when I/Goethe was ~ing in Italy** als ich/Goethe in Italien war *or* weilte (*liter*); **where are you ~ing?** wo wohnen Sie?; **he is ~ing at Chequers for the weekend** er verbringt das Wochenende in Chequers; **he went to ~ in the country for a while** er ist für einige Zeit aufs Land gefahren; **we would ~ at a different resort each year** wir waren jedes Jahr an einem anderen Urlaubsort; **it was a nice place to ~ in the summer** dort konnte man gut den Sommer verbringen; **my brother came to ~ for a week** mein Bruder ist für eine Woche gekommen; **my brother came to ~** mein Bruder ist zu Besuch gekommen.
(c) (*old: wait*) ~! stehenbleiben!; **~, wanderer!** halt inne, Wanderer! (*old, liter*).

◆**stay away** *vi* (*from* von) wegbleiben; (*from person*) sich fernhalten ◆ **to ~ ~ from a girl** von einem Mädchen die Finger lassen; **he can't ~ ~ from the pub** ihn zieht es immer wieder in die Wirtschaft.

◆**stay behind** *vi* zurückbleiben; (*Sch: as punishment*) nachsitzen ◆ **I ~ed ~ after the party** ich blieb nach der Party noch da.

◆**stay down** *vi* (*keep down*) unten bleiben; (*Sch*) wiederholen ◆ **nothing I eat ~s ~** alles, was ich esse, kommt wieder hoch.

◆**stay in** *vi* (*at home*) zu Hause bleiben; (*in position, in book etc*) drinbleiben; (*Sch*) nachsitzen ◆ **he had to ~ ~ as a punishment** (*at home*) er kriegte zur Strafe Stubenarrest *or* Hausarrest.

◆**stay off** [1] *vi* **(a)** (*rain*) ausbleiben. **(b)** (*from work etc*) zu Hause bleiben.
[2] *vi +prep obj* **(a)** (*not go on*) nicht betreten ◆ **~ ~ my patch!** komm mir nicht ins Gehege! **(b) to ~ ~ work/school** nicht zur Arbeit/Schule gehen; **to ~ ~ the bottle** (*inf*) die Flasche nicht anrühren (*inf*).

◆**stay on** *vi* (*lid etc*) draufbleiben; (*light*) anbleiben; (*people*) (noch) bleiben ◆ **he ~ed ~ for another year** er blieb noch ein Jahr; **to ~ ~ at school/as manager** (in der Schule) weitermachen/(weiterhin) Geschäftsführer bleiben.

◆**stay out** *vi* draußen bleiben; (*on strike*) weiterstreiken; (*not come home*) wegbleiben ◆ **to ~ ~ of sth** sich aus etw heraushalten; **he never managed to ~ ~ of trouble** er war dauernd in Schwierigkeiten; **you ~ ~ of this!** halt du dich da raus!

◆**stay up** *vi* **(a)** (*person*) aufbleiben ◆ **don't ~ ~ for me!** bleib nicht meinetwegen auf!
(b) (*tent, fence, pole*) stehen bleiben; (*picture, decorations*) hängen bleiben; (*swimmer*) oben bleiben; (*roof*) draufbleiben ◆ **his trousers won't ~ ~** seine Hosen rutschen immer.
(c) (*at university*) (an der Uni) bleiben.
(d) he's still ~ing ~ with the front runners er liegt immer noch auf gleicher Höhe mit den Läufern an der Spitze.

stay² *n* (*guy-rope*) Stütztau, Halteseil *nt*; (*Naut*) Stag *nt* ◆ **the ~ of one's old age** (*fig*) die Stütze seines Alters; **~s** *pl* (*old: corsets*) Korsett *nt*.

stay-at-home ['steɪət,həʊm] [1] *n* Stubenhocker *m*.
[2] *adj attr* stubenhockerisch.

stayer ['steɪəʳ] *n* (*horse*) Steher *m*; (*person*) beständiger *or* ausdauernder Mensch ◆ **it's the ~s rather than the geniuses ...** es sind die Ausdauernden, nicht die Genies ...

staying power ['steɪɪŋ,paʊəʳ] *n* Stehvermögen, Durchhaltevermögen *nt*, Ausdauer *f*.

St Bernard [sənt'bɜ:nəd] *n* Bernhardiner *m*.

STD (*Brit Telec*) *abbr of* **subscriber trunk dialling** der Selbstwählferndienst ◆ **~ number/code** Vorwahl(nummer) *f*.

stead [sted] *n* **in his ~** an seiner Stelle *or* Statt (*liter, form*); **to stand sb in good ~** jdm zugute *or* zustatten kommen.

steadfast ['stedfəst] *adj* fest; *look also* unverwandt; *person, refusal also* standhaft; *person also, belief* unerschütterlich ◆ **to remain ~ in adversity/in one's faith** allen Unbillen zum Trotz (*liter*)/in seinem Glauben nicht schwanken.

steadfastly ['stedfəstlɪ] *adv* fest; *look* unverwandt; *adhere, refuse* standhaft, unerschütterlich.

steadfastness ['stedfəstnɪs] *n see adj* Festigkeit *f*; Unverwandtheit *f*; Standhaftigkeit *f*; Unerschütterlichkeit *f*.

steadily ['stedɪlɪ] *adv* **(a)** (*firmly*) ruhig; *balanced* fest; *gaze* fest, unverwandt. **(b)** (*constantly*) ständig; *rain* ununterbrochen. **(c)** (*reliably*) zuverlässig, solide.

steadiness ['stedɪnɪs] *n* (*stability*) Festigkeit *f*; (*of hand, eye*) Ruhe *f*; (*regularity*) Stetigkeit *f*; (*of gaze also*) Unverwandtheit *f*; (*of character*) Zuverlässigkeit, Solidität *f*.

steady ['stedɪ] [1] *adj* (*+er*) **(a)** (*firm, not wobbling*) *hand, nerves, eye* ruhig; *gaze* fest, unverwandt ◆ **with a ~ hand** mit ruhiger Hand; **~ on one's legs/feet** fest *or* sicher auf den Beinen; **to hold sth ~** etw ruhig halten; *ladder* etw festhalten; **the chair is not very ~** der Stuhl ist wacklig.
(b) (*constant*) *wind, progress, demand etc* ständig, stet (*geh*); *drizzle* ununterbrochen; *temperature* beständig ◆ **at a ~ pace/70** in gleichmäßigem Tempo/ständig mit 70.
(c) (*reliable, regular*) *worker* zuverlässig, solide ◆ **he plays a ~ game** er ist ein zuverlässiger Spieler.
(d) *job, boyfriend* fest.
[2] *adv* ~! (*carefully, gently*) vorsichtig!; (*Naut*) Kurs halten!; **~ (on)!, ~ the buffs!** immer mit der Ruhe! (*inf*), sachte! (*inf*); **to go ~ (with sb)** (*inf*) mit jdm (fest) gehen (*inf*); **they're going ~** (*inf*) sie gehen fest miteinander, sie sind fest zusammen.
[3] *n* (*inf*) fester Freund (*inf*), feste Freundin (*inf*).
[4] *vt plane, boat* wieder ins Gleichgewicht bringen; (*stabilize*) *nerves, person* beruhigen; (*in character*) ausgleichen ◆ **to ~ oneself** festen Halt finden; **she had a ~ing influence on him** durch ihren Einfluß wurde er ausgeglichener.
[5] *vi* sich beruhigen; (*person: also* **~ up**) ruhig(er) werden.

steady state theory *n* Theorie *f* des stationären Kosmos.

steak [steɪk] *n* Steak *nt*; (*of fish*) Filet *nt* ◆ **a ham/bacon ~** eine Scheibe gebackener Schinken/Speck; **~ and kidney pie** Fleischpastete *f* mit Nieren; **~ dinner** Steak-Menü *nt*; **~house** Steakhouse *nt*; **~ knife** Steakmesser *nt*; **~ tartare** Tatarbeefsteak *nt*.

steal [sti:l] (*vb: pret* **stole**, *ptp* **stolen**) [1] *vt object, idea, kiss, heart* stehlen ◆ **to ~ sth from sb** jdm etw stehlen; **to ~ sb's girlfriend** jdm die Freundin ausspannen (*inf*); **to ~ the show/sb's thunder/a march on sb** die Schau stehlen/jdm den Wind aus den Segeln nehmen/jdm zuvorkommen; **the baby stole all the attention** das Kind zog die ganze Aufmerksamkeit auf sich; **to ~ a glance at sb** verstohlen zu jdm hinschauen.
[2] *vi* **(a)** stehlen.
(b) (*move quietly etc*) sich stehlen, (sich) schleichen ◆ **to ~ away** *or* **off/into a room** sich weg- *or* davonstehlen/sich in ein Zimmer stehlen; **to ~ about/up on sb** herumschleichen/sich an jdn heranschleichen; **old age was ~ing up on her** das Alter machte sich allmählich bei ihr bemerkbar; **the mood/feeling which was ~ing over the country** die Stimmung, die sich allmählich im Land verbreitete; **he could feel the depression ~ing over him** er fühlte, wie ihn ein Gefühl der Niedergeschlagenheit beschlich; **to ~ home** (*Baseball*) ungehindert zur Ausgangsbase vorrücken.
[3] *n* (*US inf: bargain*) Geschenk *nt* (*inf*) ◆ **it's a ~!** das ist (ja) geschenkt! (*inf*).

stealth [stelθ] *n* List *f*; (*of fox also*) Schläue *f* ◆ **by ~** durch List.

stealth bomber *n* (*Aviat*) Tarn(kappen)bomber *m*, Stealth-Bomber *m*.

stealthily ['stelθɪlɪ] *adv* verstohlen.

stealthiness ['stelθɪnɪs] *n* Verstohlenheit *f*.

stealthy ['stelθɪ] *adj* (*+er*) verstohlen; *footsteps* verhalten.

steam [sti:m] [1] *n* Dampf *m*; (*from swamp also*) Dunst *m* ◆ **the windows were covered with ~** die Fensterscheiben waren beschlagen; **driven by ~** dampfgetrieben; **full ~ ahead!** (*Naut*) volle Kraft voraus!; **to get up ~** (*lit*) feuern, Dampf aufmachen (*dated*); (*fig*) in Schwung kommen; **to let off ~** (*lit, fig*) Dampf ablassen; **to run out of ~** (*lit*) Dampf verlieren; (*fig*) Schwung verlieren; **he ran out of ~** ihm ist die Puste ausgegangen (*inf*); **the ship went on under its own ~** das Schiff fuhr mit eigener Kraft weiter; **under one's own ~** (*fig*) allein, ohne Hilfe.
[2] *vt* dämpfen; *food also* dünsten ◆ **to ~ open an envelope** einen Briefumschlag über Dampf öffnen; **~ed pudding** Kochpudding *m*.
[3] *vi* **(a)** (*give off ~*) dampfen.
(b) (*move*) dampfen ◆ **we were ~ing along at 12 knots** wir fuhren mit 12 Knoten; **the ship ~ed into the harbour** das Schiff kam in den Hafen gefahren; **the train ~ed out** der Zug dampfte ab; **the runner came ~ing round the last bend** (*inf*) der Läufer kam mit Volldampf um die letzte Kurve (*inf*).

◆**steam ahead** *vi (inf: project, work)* gut vorankommen.
◆**steam off** [1] *vt sep stamp* über Dampf ablösen; *dirt* über Dampf entfernen; *excess flab* sich *(dat)* abschwitzen.
[2] *vi* abfahren; *(train also)* losdampfen.
◆**steam over** *vi (window)* beschlagen.
◆**steam up** [1] *vt sep window* beschlagen lassen ◆ **to be/get (all) ~ed ~** (ganz) beschlagen sein/(ganz) beschlagen; *(fig inf)* sich aufregen, hochgehen *(inf)*; **look at you, all ~ed ~ about nothing** deine ganze Aufregung war umsonst.
[2] *vi* beschlagen.
steam: ~boat *n* Dampfschiff *nt*, Dampfer *m*; **~-driven** *adj* mit Dampfantrieb, dampfgetrieben; **~ engine** *n* Dampflok *f*; *(stationary)* Dampfmaschine *f*.
steamer ['sti:məʳ] *n (ship)* Dampfer *m*; *(Cook)* Dampf(koch)topf *m*.
steam: ~hammer *n* Dampfhammer *m*; **~ iron** *n* Dampfbügeleisen *nt*; **~ radio** *n (hum)* Dampfradio *nt (hum)*; **~roller** [1] *n* Dampfwalze *f*; [2] *vt road* glattwalzen; **to ~roller a bill through parliament** *(fig)* ein Gesetz im Parlament durchpeitschen; [3] *adj* **~roller tactics** Holzhammermethode *f (inf)*; **~ room** *n* Saunaraum *m*; *(in Turkish bath)* Dampfraum *m*; **~ship** *n* Dampfschiff *nt*, Dampfer *m*; **~ship company** *n* Dampfschiffahrtsgesellschaft *f*; **~ship line** *n* Schiffahrtslinie, Dampferlinie *f*; **~ shovel** *n* Löffelbagger *m*; **~ turbine** *n* Dampfturbine *f*.
steamy ['sti:mɪ] *adj (+er)* dampfig, dunstig; *jungle, swamp* dunstig; *room, atmosphere* dampfig, voll Dampf; *window, mirror* beschlagen ◆ **it is so ~ in here** hier ist vielleicht ein Dampf!
steed [sti:d] *n (liter)* Roß *nt*.
steel [sti:l] [1] *n* Stahl *m*; *(sharpener)* Wetzstahl *m*; *(for striking spark)* Feuerstahl *m* ◆ **to fight with cold ~** mit dem blanken Messer kämpfen; **he felt cold ~ between his ribs** er spürte den kalten Stahl zwischen den Rippen; **a man of ~** ein stahlharter Mann; **as hard as ~** stahlhart, so hart wie Stahl; *see* **nerve**.
[2] *adj attr* Stahl-.
[3] *vt* **to ~ oneself** sich wappnen *(for* gegen); *(physically)* sich stählen *(for* für); **to ~ oneself to do sth** allen Mut zusammennehmen, um etw zu tun; **he had ~ed himself/his heart against her/their suffering** er hatte sich gegen sie/ihre Not innerlich hart gemacht; **he ~ed his troops for the battle** er machte seiner Truppe Mut für den Kampf; *(physically)* er stählte seine Truppe für den Kampf.
steel *in cpds* Stahl-, stahl-; **~ band** *n* Steelband *f*; **~-clad** *adj* stahlgepanzert; **~ grey** [1] *n* Stahlgrau *nt*; [2] *adj* stahlgrau; **~ guitar** *n* Hawaiigitarre *f*; **~ mill** *n* Stahlwalzwerk *nt*; **~-plated** *adj* mit Stahlüberzug; *(for protection)* stahlgepanzert; **~ wool** *n* Stahlwolle *f*; **~ worker** *n* (Eisen- und) Stahlarbeiter *m*; **~works** *n sing or pl* Stahlwerk *nt*.
steely ['sti:lɪ] *adj (+er) grip* stahlhart; *smile, expression* hart; *gaze* hart, stählern; *determination* eisern, ehern; *blue* Stahl- ◆ **~-eyed** mit hartem *or* stählernem Blick.
steel yard *n* Handwaage *f*.
steep[1] [sti:p] *adj (+er)* **(a)** steil ◆ **it's a ~ climb** es geht steil hinauf; **there's been a ~ drop in the value of the pound** das Pfund ist stark gefallen.
(b) *(fig inf) demand* unverschämt; *price also, bill* gepfeffert *(inf)*, gesalzen *(inf)* ◆ **that's pretty ~!** das ist allerhand!; **it seems a bit ~ that ...** es ist ein starkes Stück, daß ...
steep[2] [1] *vt* **(a)** *(in liquid)* eintauchen; *(in marinade, dye)* ziehen lassen; *dried food, washing* einweichen.
(b) *(fig)* **to be ~ed in sth** von etw durchdrungen sein; **~ed in history** geschichtsträchtig; **~ed in ignorance/vice/prejudice** durch und durch unwissend/verdorben/voreingenommen; **he is so ~ed in his own methods** er ist so auf seine eigenen Methoden geeicht; **a scholar ~ed in the classics** ein Gelehrter, der sich in die Klassiker versenkt hat.
[2] *vi* **to leave sth to ~** etw einweichen; *(in marinade, dye)* etw ziehen lassen.
steepen ['sti:pən] [1] *vt* steiler machen.
[2] *vi* steiler werden.
steeple ['sti:pl] *n* Kirchturm *m*.
steeple: ~chase *n (for horses)* Jagdrennen, Hindernisrennen *nt*; *(for runners)* Hindernislauf *m*; **~chaser** *n (horse)* Steepler *m*; *(jockey)* Reiter(in *f*) *m* in einem Jagdrennen; *(runner)* Hindernisläufer(in *f*) *m*; **~jack** *n* Turmarbeiter *m*.
steeply ['sti:plɪ] *adv* steil.
steepness ['sti:pnɪs] *n* **(a)** Steile, Steilheit *f*. **(b)** *(fig inf)* Unverschämtheit *f*.
steer[1] [stɪəʳ] [1] *vt (lit, fig)* lenken; *car also, ship* steuern; *person also* lotsen ◆ **to ~ an erratic course** *(lit, fig)* einen Zickzackkurs steuern; **to ~ a course for sth** *(Naut)* auf etw *(acc)* Kurs halten; *(fig)* auf etw *(acc)* zusteuern; **this car is easy to ~** der Wagen läßt sich leicht lenken.
[2] *vi (in car)* lenken; *(in ship)* steuern ◆ **to ~ due north** Kurs nach Norden halten; **~ left a bit** lenken *or (in ship)* steuern Sie etwas nach links; **to ~ for sth** auf etw *(acc)* zuhalten; *(Naut)* etw ansteuern, auf etw *(acc)* Kurs halten; *(fig)* auf etw *(acc)* zusteuern; *see* **clear**.
steer[2] *n* junger Ochse.
steerage ['stɪərɪdʒ] *n* Zwischendeck *nt*.
steerageway ['stɪərɪdʒweɪ] *n* Steuerkraft *f*.
steering ['stɪərɪŋ] *n (in car etc)* Lenkung *f*; *(Naut)* Steuerung *f*.
steering: ~ column *n* Lenksäule *f*; **~ committee** *n* Lenkungsausschuß *m*; **~ gear** *n (of plane)* Leitwerk *nt*; *(of boat)* Ruderanlage *f*; **~ lock** *n* Lenkradschloß *nt*; **~ wheel** *n* Steuer(rad) *nt*; *(of car also)* Lenkrad *nt*.
steersman ['stɪəzmən] *n*, *pl* **-men** [-mən] Steuermann *m*.
stein [ʃtaɪn] *n* Maßkrug *m*.
stele ['sti:lɪ] *n (Archeol)* Stele *f*.
stellar ['steləʳ] *adj* stellar.

▼ **stem** [stem] [1] *n* **(a)** *(of plant)* Stiel *m*; *(of woody plant, shrub)* Stamm *m*; *(of grain)* Halm *m*; *(fig: of family tree)* Hauptlinie *f*, Hauptzweig *m*.
(b) *(of glass)* Stiel *m*; *(of pipe)* Hals *m*; *(Mus: of note)* (Noten)hals *m*; *(in watch)* Welle *f*; *(of thermometer)* Röhre *f*.
(c) *(of word)* Stamm *m*.
(d) *(Naut)* Vordersteven *m* ◆ **from ~ to stern** von vorne bis achtern.
[2] *vt (check, stop)* aufhalten; *flood, tide* eindämmen; *bleeding* zum Stillstand bringen; *flow of words* Einhalt gebieten *(+dat)*.
▼ [3] *vi* **to ~ from sth** *(result from)* von etw kommen, von etw herrühren; *(have as origin)* aus etw (her)stammen, auf etw *(acc)* zurückgehen; **what does this increase in inflation ~ from?** welche Ursachen hat diese Zunahme der Inflation?
stem christie [stem'krɪstɪ] *n (Ski)* Kristianiaschwung *m*.
stemmed [stemd] *adj* Stiel-.
stem parallel *n (Ski)* (ausgestemmter) Parallelschwung.
stem-turn ['stemtɜ:n] *n* Stemmbogen *m*.
stench [stentʃ] *n* Gestank *m* ◆ **~ trap** Geruchsverschluß *m*.
stencil ['stensl] [1] *n* Schablone *f*; *(Printing: for duplicating)* Matrize *f*.
[2] *vt* mit Schablonen zeichnen; auf Matrize schreiben.
sten gun ['stengʌn] *n (Mil)* leichtes Maschinengewehr.
stenographer [ste'nɒgrəfəʳ] *n (form)* Stenograph(in *f*) *m*.
stenography [ste'nɒgrəfɪ] *n (form)* Stenographie *f*.
stentorian [sten'tɔ:rɪən] *adj* schallend; *voice* Stentor- *(geh)*.
step [step] [1] *n* **(a)** *(pace, in dancing)* Schritt *m*; *(sound of ~ also)* Tritt *m* ◆ **to take a ~** einen Schritt machen; **~ by ~** *(lit, fig)* Schritt für Schritt; **we followed his ~s in the snow** wir folgten seinen Fußstapfen im Schnee; **I recognized you from your ~** ich habe Sie am Schritt erkannt; **he watched my every ~** *(fig)* er beobachtete mich auf Schritt und Tritt; **to watch one's ~** achtgeben; *(fig also)* sich vorsehen.
(b) to be in ~ *(lit)* im Gleichschritt *or* Tritt sein *(with* mit); *(in dancing)* im Takt sein *(with* mit); *(fig)* im Gleichklang sein *(with* mit); **to be out of ~** *(lit)* nicht im Tritt *or* im gleichen Schritt sein *(with* mit); *(in dancing)* nicht im gleichen Takt sein *(with* wie); *(fig)* nicht im Gleichklang sein *(with* mit); **to get out of ~** *(lit)* aus dem Schritt *or* Tritt kommen; *(in dancing)* aus dem Takt kommen; *(fig)* von der gemeinsamen Linie abkommen; **to keep in/break ~** *(lit)* Tritt halten/aus dem Tritt kommen; *(fig)* Schritt halten/aus dem Schritt kommen; **to fall into ~** *(lit)* in Gleichschritt fallen *(with* mit); *(fig)* in den gleichen Takt kommen *(with* wie).
(c) *(distance)* **it's (quite) a good ~ (to the village)** es ist ein ziemlich weiter Weg (bis zum Dorf), es ist ziemlich weit (bis zum Dorf); **it's only a few ~s** es sind nur ein paar Schritte.
(d) *(move)* Schritt *m*; *(measure also)* Maßnahme *f* ◆ **the first ~ is to form a committee** als erstes muß ein Ausschuß gebildet werden; **it's a great ~ forward** es ist ein großer Schritt nach vorn; **that would be a ~ back/in the right direction for him** das wäre für ihn ein Rückschritt/ein Schritt in die richtige Richtung; **one can't take a single ~ without having to consult somebody** man kann (rein) gar nichts unternehmen, ohne fragen zu müssen; **to take ~s to do sth** Maßnahmen ergreifen, (um) etw zu tun; **to take legal ~s** gerichtlich vorgehen.
(e) *(in process, experiment)* Abschnitt *m*, Stufe *f*; *(in learning, course also)* Lernschritt *m*.
(f) *(stair, fig: in scale, hierarchy)* Stufe *f* ◆ **~s** *(outdoors)* Treppe *f*; **mind the ~** Vorsicht Stufe.
(g) ~s *pl (~-ladder: also* **pair of ~s)** Tritt- *or* Stufenleiter *f*.
[2] *vt* **(a)** *(old) dance* tanzen.
(b) *(arrange in ~s)* terrassenförmig anlegen, abstufen.
(c) ~ two paces to the left treten Sie zwei Schritte nach links.
[3] *vi* gehen ◆ **to ~ into/out of sth** *house, room, puddle* in etw *(acc)*/aus etw treten; *train, dress* in etw *(acc)*/aus etw steigen; **to ~ on(to) sth** *plane, train* in etw *(acc)* steigen; *platform, ladder* auf etw *(acc)* steigen; **to ~ on sth** *object, toy* auf etw *(acc)* treten; **he ~ped on my foot** er ist mir auf den Fuß getreten; **to ~ over sb/sth** über jdn/etw steigen; **please mind where you ~** geben Sie acht, wo Sie hintreten; **~ this way, please** hier entlang, bitte!; **he ~ped into the road** er trat auf die Straße; **he ~ped into his father's job/shoes** er übernahm die Stelle seines Vaters; **to ~ on board** an Bord gehen; **to ~ inside** herein-/hineintreten; **to ~ outside** heraus-/hinaustreten; *(for fight)* (mal eben) vor die Tür gehen; **just ~ outside a moment** kommen/gehen Sie einen Moment hinaus; **~ on it!** mach mal ein bißchen (schneller)! *(inf)*; *(in car)* gib Gas!
◆**step aside** *vi* **(a)** *(lit)* zur Seite treten. **(b)** *(fig)* Platz machen ◆ **to ~ ~ to make way for sb** jdm Platz machen.
◆**step back** *vi* **(a)** *(lit)* zurücktreten. **(b)** *(fig)* **to ~ ~ from sth** von etw Abstand gewinnen; **let us ~ ~ into the 18th century** versetzen wir uns einmal ins 18. Jahrhundert zurück.
◆**step down** *vi* **(a)** *(lit)* herab-/hinabsteigen. **(b)** *(fig)* **to ~ ~ in favour of sb** *or* **for sb** jdm Platz machen, zu jds Gunsten zurücktreten; **he decided to ~ ~ and not stand for the presidency** er beschloß, seine Kandidatur für das Amt des Präsidenten zurückzuziehen. **(c)** *(resign)* zurücktreten.
◆**step forward** *vi* vortreten; *(fig)* sich melden.
◆**step in** *vi* **(a)** *(lit)* eintreten *(-to, +prep obj* in *+acc)* ◆ **she suddenly ~ped ~to a totally new world** sie fand sich plötzlich in einer ganz neuen Welt wieder.
(b) *(fig)* eingreifen, einschreiten; *(interferingly)* dazwischenkommen.
◆**step off** *vi +prep obj (off bus, plane, boat)* aussteigen *(prep obj* aus) ◆ **to ~ ~ the pavement** vom Bürgersteig treten.
◆**step out** [1] *vt sep (measure)* abschreiten.

➤ LANGUAGE IN USE: **stem: 3 → 17.2**

2 *vi* **(a)** (*go out*) hinausgehen. **(b)** (*walk briskly*) zügig *or* schnell gehen, forsch ausschreiten (*liter*); (*speed up*) schneller gehen. **(c) to be ~ping ~ with sb** (*dated*) mit jdm gehen.

◆**step up** 1 *vt sep* steigern; *efforts also, security arrangements, campaign* verstärken; *volume, number* erhöhen.

2 *vi* **(a)** (*come forward*) vortreten ◆ **to ~ ~ to sb** auf jdn zugehen/zukommen; **~ ~, ladies and gentlemen** treten Sie näher, meine Damen und Herren; **he ~ped ~ onto the stage** er trat auf die Bühne; **he ~ped ~ another rung** er stieg eine Sprosse höher.

(b) (*increase*) zunehmen; (*rate, pressure*) ansteigen.

step- *pref brother, mother etc* Stief-.

step-down ['step'daʊn] *adj* (*Elec*) heruntertransformierend.

Stephen ['sti:vn] *n* Stephan *m.*

step-ladder ['step,lædəʳ] *n* Stufenleiter, Trittleiter *f.*

steppe [step] *n* Steppe *f.*

stepper motor ['stepə,məʊtəʳ] *n* Schrittmotor *m.*

stepping stone ['stepɪŋ,stəʊn] *n* (Tritt)stein *m*; (*fig*) Sprungbrett *nt.*

step-up ['step'ʌp] 1 *n* (*inf: increase*) Anstieg *m*, Zunahme *f* (*in gen*).

2 *adj* (*Elec*) herauftransformierend.

stereo ['sterɪəʊ] 1 *n* Stereo *nt*; (*record-player*) Stereoanlage *f* ◆ **in/on ~** in Stereo/auf einem Stereogerät.

2 *adj* Stereo-.

stereophonic [,sterɪəʊ'fɒnɪk] *adj* stereophon.

stereophony [sterɪ'ɒfənɪ] *n* Stereophonie *f*, Raumklang *m.*

stereoscope ['sterɪəʊ,skəʊp] *n* Stereoskop *nt.*

stereoscopic [,sterɪəʊ'skɒpɪk] *adj* stereoskop(isch); *film, screen also* 3-D-.

stereotype ['sterɪə,taɪp] 1 *n* **(a)** (*fig*) Klischee(vorstellung *f*), Stereotyp *nt*; (*~ character*) stereotype Figur ◆ **the ~ of the Englishman** der typische Engländer.

(b) (*Typ*) (*plate*) Stereotypplatte *f*; (*process*) Plattendruck *m.*

2 *attr* stereotyp; *ideas, thinking also* klischeehaft.

3 *vt* **(a)** (*fig: character*) klischeehaft *or* als Typ zeichnen *or* darstellen ◆ **the plot of the Western has become ~d** die Handlung des Western ist zu einem Klischee geworden; **I don't like being ~d** ich lasse mich nicht gern in ein Klischee zwängen.

(b) (*Typ*) stereotypieren.

stereotyped ['sterɪə,taɪpt] *adj see* **stereotype 2.**

sterile ['steraɪl] *adj* **(a)** *animal, soil* unfruchtbar; *person also* steril; (*fig: fruitless also*) ergebnislos, nutzlos. **(b)** (*germ-free*) steril, keimfrei; (*fig*) steril.

sterility [ste'rɪlɪtɪ] *n see adj* **(a)** Unfruchtbarkeit *f*; Sterilität *f*; Ergebnislosigkeit, Nutzlosigkeit *f.* **(b)** Sterilität *f.*

sterilization [,sterɪlaɪ'zeɪʃən] *n* Sterilisierung, Sterilisation *f.*

sterilize ['sterɪlaɪz] *vt person, instruments* sterilisieren.

sterilizer ['sterɪlaɪzəʳ] *n* (*for instruments*) Sterilisator *m.*

sterling ['stɜ:lɪŋ] 1 *adj* **(a)** (*Fin*) Sterling- ◆ **in pounds ~** in Pfund Sterling; **~ area** Sterlingländer *pl.*

(b) (*fig*) gediegen; *character* lauter.

(c) ~ silver Sterlingsilber *nt*; **~ cutlery** Silberbesteck *nt.*

2 *n* **(a)** *no art* (*money*) das Pfund Sterling, das englische Pfund ◆ **in ~** in Pfund Sterling. **(b)** (*silver*) (Sterling)silber *nt.*

3 *adj attr* aus (Sterling)silber.

stern¹ [stɜ:n] *n* (*Naut*) Heck *nt*; (*fig hum: of person*) Hinterteil *nt* ◆ **the ~ of the ship** das Achterschiff.

stern² *adj* (*+er*) (*strict*) streng; *words also, character, warning* ernst ◆ **with a ~ face** mit strenger Miene; **made of ~er stuff** aus härterem Holz geschnitzt.

sternly ['stɜ:nlɪ] *adv see adj.*

sternmost ['stɜ:nməʊst] *adj* achterste(r, s).

sternness ['stɜ:nnɪs] *n see adj* Strenge *f*; Ernst *m.*

sternum ['stɜ:nəm] *n* Brustbein, Sternum (*spec*) *nt.*

steroid ['stɪərɔɪd] *n* Steroid *nt.*

stertorous ['stɜ:tərəs] *adj* (*liter*) *breathing* röchelnd, rasselnd.

stet [stet] (*Typ*) 1 *interj* stehenlassen (*Punkte unter falscher Korrektur*).

2 *vt* die Korrektur (*+gen*) rückgängig machen.

stethoscope ['steθəskəʊp] *n* Stethoskop *nt.*

stetson ['stetsən] *n* Stetson, Texashut *m.*

stevedore ['sti:vɪdɔ:ʳ] *n* Stauer, Schauermann *m.*

Steven ['sti:vn] *n* Stefan *m.*

stew [stju:] 1 *n* **(a)** Eintopf(gericht *nt*) *m*; *see* **Irish. (b)** (*inf*) **to be in a ~ (about sth)** (über etw (*acc*) *or* wegen etw) (ganz) aufgeregt sein. **(c)** (*obs: brothel*) Bordell *nt.*

2 *vt* **(a)** *meat* schmoren; *fruit* dünsten ◆ **~ed apples** Apfelkompott *nt*; **the tea was ~ed** der Tee war bitter geworden. **(b) to be/get ~ed** (*sl: drunk*) voll sein (*inf*)/sich vollaufen lassen (*inf*).

3 *vi* (*meat*) schmoren; (*fruit*) dünsten; (*inf: tea*) bitter werden ◆ **to let sb ~ (in his/her own juice)** jdn (im eigenen Saft) schmoren lassen.

steward ['stju:əd] *n* Steward *m*; (*on estate etc*) Verwalter *m*; (*at dance, meeting*) Ordner *m*; (*shop ~*) (gewerkschaftlicher) Vertrauensmann (im Betrieb).

stewardess [,stju:ə'des] *n* Stewardeß *f.*

stewardship ['stju:ədʃɪp] *n* Verwaltung *f*; (*rank, duties*) Verwalteramt *nt.*

stewing ['stju:ɪŋ]: **~ pan** *n* Kasserolle *f*, Bratentopf *m*; **~ steak** *n* Rindfleisch *nt* für Eintopf.

stick¹ [stɪk] 1 *n* **(a)** Stock *m*; (*twig*) Zweig *m*; (*conductor's baton*) Taktstock *m*; (*hockey ~*) Schläger *m*; (*drum~*) Schlegel *m* ◆ **to give sb the ~, to take the ~ to sb** jdm eine Tracht Prügel geben; **to give sb/sth (a lot of) ~** (*inf: criticize*) jdn/etw heruntermachen (*inf*) *or* -putzen (*inf*); **to take (a lot of) ~** (*inf*) viel einstecken (müssen); **just a few ~s of furniture** nur ein paar Möbelstücke; **they adopted the policy of the big ~** sie holten den großen Knüppel raus (*inf*); **to get hold of the wrong end of the ~** (*fig inf*) etw falsch verstehen.

(b) (*of sealing wax, celery, rhubarb, dynamite*) Stange *f*; (*of chalk, shaving soap*) Stück *nt*; (*Aviat: joy~*) Steuerknüppel *m*; (*of bombs*) Bombenladung *f* für Reihenabwurf; (*Typ*) Winkelhaken *m* ◆ **a ~ deodorant** ein Deodorant-Stift *m*; **a ~ of rock** eine Zuckerstange.

(c) (*inf: person*) Kerl *m* (*inf*) ◆ **he's/she's a funny old ~** er/sie ist ein komischer Kauz; **he's/she's such a dry old ~** er/sie ist ein solcher Stockfisch.

(d) the ~s (*Horse-racing inf*) die Hürden *pl.*

(e) in the ~s (*esp US: backwoods*) in der hintersten *or* finsteren Provinz.

2 *vt plants* stützen.

stick² *pret, ptp* **stuck** 1 *vt* **(a)** (*with glue etc*) kleben ◆ **to ~ a stamp on sth** eine Briefmarke auf etw (*acc*) kleben; **please ~ the posters to the walls with pins not sellotape** bitte die Poster mit Stecknadeln und nicht mit Tesafilm an den Wänden befestigen; **is this glue strong enough to ~ it?** wird dieser Klebstoff das halten?; **to ~ the blame on sb** jdm die Schuld zuschieben.

(b) (*pin*) stecken ◆ **he stuck a badge on his lapel** er steckte sich (*dat*) ein Abzeichen ans Revers; **he stuck a badge on her** er steckte ihr ein Abzeichen an.

(c) (*jab*) *knife, sword etc* stoßen ◆ **he stuck a knife through her arm** er stieß ihr ein Messer in den Arm; **he stuck a pin into his finger** (*accidentally*) er hat sich (*dat*) mit einer Nadel in den Finger gestochen; *see also* **~ in.**

(d) *pig* (ab)stechen ◆ **he stuck him with his bayonet** er spießte ihn mit dem Bajonett auf.

(e) (*inf: place, put*) tun (*inf*); (*in sth also*) stecken (*inf*) ◆ **~ it on the shelf** tu's ins *or* aufs Regal; **he stuck his head round the corner** er steckte seinen Kopf um die Ecke; **to ~ one's hat on** sich (*dat*) den Hut aufsetzen; **he stuck a drink in my hand and a record on the turntable** er drückte mir ein Glas in die Hand und legte eine Platte auf; **you know where you can ~ that** (*sl*) du kannst mich am Arsch lecken! (*vulg*); **I'll tell him where he can ~ his complaint in a minute!** (*sl*) die Beschwerde kann er sich (*dat*) sonstwohin stecken (*inf*).

(f) (*decorate: with pearls*) besetzen.

(g) (*esp Brit inf: tolerate*) aushalten; *pace, pressure of work* durchhalten ◆ **I can't ~ him/that** ich kann ihn/das nicht ausstehen (*inf*); **I can't ~ it any longer!** ich halte das nicht mehr (länger) aus!

(h) to ~ sb with sth (*inf: lumber*) jdm etw aufladen *or* aufhalsen (*inf*); (*with bill*) jdm etw andrehen.

2 *vi* **(a)** (*glue, burr etc*) kleben (*to* an *+dat*) ◆ **to make a charge ~** genügend Beweismaterial haben; **you'll never make it ~!** damit kommen Sie nie durch!; **how do they hope to make the charge ~?** wie wollen sie das (je) beweisen?; **the name seems to have stuck** der Name scheint ihm/ihr geblieben zu sein.

(b) (*become caught, wedged etc*) steckenbleiben; (*drawer, window*) klemmen; *see* **stuck.**

(c) (*sth pointed*) stecken (*in* in *+dat*) ◆ **it stuck in my foot** das ist mir im Fuß steckengeblieben.

(d) (*Cards*) halten.

(e) (*project*) **his toes are ~ing through his socks** seine Zehen kommen durch die Socken; **we could see Manfred's head ~ing over the wall** wir sahen Manfreds Kopf über die Mauer gucken (*inf*).

(f) (*stay*) bleiben; (*slander*) haftenbleiben ◆ **to ~ in sb's mind** jdm im Gedächtnis bleiben; **to make sth ~ in one's mind** sich (*dat*) etw einprägen; **a teacher must be able to make things ~** der Lehrer muß den Stoff so bringen, daß er haftenbleibt.

◆**stick around** *vi* (*inf*) hier/dableiben ◆ **~ ~!** wart's ab!; **he decided to ~ ~ Bonn** er beschloß, noch in Bonn zu bleiben.

◆**stick at** *vi +prep obj* **(a)** (*persist*) bleiben an (*+dat*) (*inf*) ◆ **to ~ ~ it** dranbleiben (*inf*). **(b)** (*stop at*) zurückschrecken vor (*+dat*). **he will ~ ~ nothing** er macht vor nichts halt.

◆**stick by** *vi +prep obj sb* halten zu; *promise* stehen zu.

◆**stick down** *vt sep* **(a)** (*glue*) ankleben; *envelope* zukleben. **(b)** (*inf*) (*put down*) abstellen; (*write down*) aufschreiben.

◆**stick in** 1 *vt sep* **(a)** *stamps etc* einkleben ◆ **to ~ stamps ~(to) an album** Briefmarken in ein Album kleben.

(b) hineinstecken; *knife etc* einstechen ◆ **to ~ sth ~(to) sth** etw in etw (*acc*) stecken; (*prick*) *knife, pin etc* mit etw in etw (*acc*) stechen; **he stuck his knife ~(to) the table** er stieß das Messer in den Tisch; **she stuck a knife ~(to) him** sie stieß ihm ein Messer in den Leib.

2 *vi* (*knife, arrow*) stecken(bleiben).

◆**stick on** 1 *vt sep* **(a)** *label, cover* aufkleben (*prep obj* auf *+acc*). **(b)** (*add*) *money* draufschlagen; (*+prep obj*) aufschlagen auf (*+acc*).

2 *vi* **(a)** (*label etc*) kleben, haften (*prep obj* an *+dat*). **(b)** (*inf: on horse*) oben bleiben ◆ **to ~ ~ the horse** auf dem Pferd bleiben.

◆**stick out** 1 *vi* vorstehen (*of* aus); (*ears, hair*) abstehen; (*fig: be noticeable*) auffallen ◆ **his head was ~ing ~ of the turret** sein Kopf sah aus dem Turm vor.

2 *vt sep* hinaus-/herausstrecken.

◆**stick out for** *vi +prep obj* sich stark machen für.

◆**stick to** *vi +prep obj* **(a)** bleiben bei; (*remain faithful to*) *principles etc* treu bleiben (*+dat*).

(b) the photographers stuck ~ her wherever she went die Fotografen hefteten sich ihr überall an die Fersen.

(c) (*persist with*) *task* bleiben an (*+dat*).

◆**stick together** *vi* zusammenkleben; (*fig: partners etc*) zusammenhalten.
◆**stick up** [1] *vt sep* **(a)** (*with tape etc*) zukleben.
(b) (*inf: raise*) **~ 'em ~!** Hände hoch!; **~ ~ your hand if you want to go** Hand hoch, wer gehen will; **three pupils stuck ~ their hands** drei Schüler meldeten sich.
(c) (*inf: rob*) *bank* überfallen.
(d) (*inf*) **she just stuck ~ her nose and marched off** sie stolzierte erhobenen Hauptes weg; **don't ~ your nose ~ at my cooking** rümpf bloß nicht die Nase über meine Kochkünste.
[2] *vi* (*nail etc*) vorstehen; (*hair*) abstehen; (*collar*) hochstehen.
◆**stick up for** *vi +prep obj sb, one's principles* eintreten für ◆ **to ~ ~ ~ oneself** sich behaupten.
◆**stick with** *vi +prep obj* bleiben bei; (*remain loyal to*) halten zu; *the leaders* mithalten mit.
sticker ['stɪkəʳ] *n* **(a)** (*label*) Aufkleber *m*; (*price ~*) Klebeschildchen *nt*. **(b)** (*inf: determined person*) **he's a ~** er ist zäh.
stickiness ['stɪkɪnɪs] *n* (*lit*) Klebrigkeit *f*; (*of atmosphere, weather*) Schwüle *f*; (*of air*) Stickigkeit *f* ◆ **the ~ of the situation** die heikle Situation.
sticking ['stɪkɪŋ]: **~ plaster** *n* (*Brit*) Heftpflaster *nt*; **~ point** *n* **you can push her so far, then she reaches her ~ point** man kann sie bis zu einem gewissen Punkt überreden, dann macht sie einfach nicht mehr mit.
stick insect *n* Gespenstheuschrecke *f*.
stick-in-the-mud ['stɪkɪnðə,mʌd] (*inf*) [1] *n* Muffel *m* (*inf*).
[2] *adj* rückständig; *parents etc also* muffelig (*inf*).
stickleback ['stɪklbæk] *n* Stichling *m*.
stickler ['stɪkləʳ] *n* **to be a ~ for sth** es mit etw peinlich genau nehmen.
stick: ~-on *adj label* (Auf)klebe-; **~ pin** *n* (*US*) Krawattennadel *f*; **~-up** *n* (*inf*) Überfall *m*.
sticky ['stɪkɪ] *adj* (*+er*) **(a)** klebrig; *label* Klebe-; *paint* feucht; *atmosphere, weather* schwül; *air* stickig; (*sweaty*) *hands* feucht, verschwitzt ◆ **I'm all hot and ~** ich bin total verschwitzt; **~ tape** Klebeband *nt*.
(b) (*fig inf*) *problem, person* schwierig; *situation, moment* heikel ◆ **he was a bit ~ about it** er hat dabei Schwierigkeiten gemacht; **we had a ~ time in the discussion** wir hatten in der Diskussion ein paar heikle Augenblicke; **to come to a ~ end** ein böses Ende nehmen; **to be on a ~ wicket** in der Klemme sein; **he's got ~ fingers** (*fig*) er hat lange Finger (*inf*).
stiff [stɪf] [1] *adj* (*+er*) **(a)** steif; *corpse also* starr; *brush* hart; *dough, paste* fest.
(b) *resistance, drink, dose* stark; *fight* zäh, hart; *competition* hart; *breeze* steif; *climb, test* schwierig; *examination, task* schwer, schwierig; *penalty, punishment* schwer; *price, demand* hoch ◆ **that's a bit ~** das ist ganz schön happig (*inf*).
[2] *adv* steif.
[3] *n* (*sl*) Leiche *f*.
stiffen ['stɪfn] (*also* **~ up**) [1] *vt* steif machen; *shirt etc* stärken, steifen; (*disease*) *limb* steif werden lassen; *resistance etc* verstärken.
[2] *vi* steif werden; (*fig: resistance*) sich verhärten; (*breeze*) auffrischen ◆ **when I said this she ~ed (up)** als ich das sagte, wurde sie ganz starr.
stiffener ['stɪfnəʳ] *n* (*for collar*) Kragenstäbchen *nt*; (*starch etc*) Stärke *f*.
stiffening ['stɪfnɪŋ] *n* Einlage *f*.
stiffly ['stɪflɪ] *adv* steif.
stiff-necked ['stɪf'nekt] *adj* (*fig*) halsstarrig.
stiffness ['stɪfnɪs] *n see adj* **(a)** Steifheit *f*; Starre *f*; Härte *f*; Festigkeit *f*. **(b)** Stärke *f*; Zähigkeit *f*; Härte *f*; Steifheit *f*; Schwierigkeit *f*; Schwere *f*; Höhe *f*.
stifle ['staɪfl] [1] *vt* (*suffocate*) ersticken; (*fig*) *laugh, cough also, rage, opposition* unterdrücken ◆ **the heat nearly ~d them** sie sind fast umgekommen vor Hitze.
[2] *vi* ersticken.
stifling ['staɪflɪŋ] *adj* **(a)** *fumes, smoke* erstickend; *heat* drückend ◆ **it's ~ in here** es ist ja zum Ersticken hier drin (*inf*). **(b)** (*fig*) beengend.
stigma ['stɪgmə] *n* **(a)** *pl* **-s** (*mark of shame*) Brandmal, Stigma *nt*. **(b)** *pl* **-ta** [stɪg'mɑːtə] Wundmal *nt*; (*Rel*) Stigmatisierung *f*. **(c)** *pl* **-s** (*Bot*) Narbe *f*, Stigma *nt*.
stigmatize ['stɪgmətaɪz] *vt* **(a)** (*Rel*) stigmatisieren. **(b) to ~ sb as sth** jdn als etw brandmarken.
stile [staɪl] *n* (Zaun)übertritt *m*.
stiletto [stɪ'letəʊ] *n* **(a)** (*knife*) Stilett *nt*. **(b)** (*also* **~ heel**) Bleistift- *or* Pfennigabsatz, Stiletto-Absatz *m*. **(c)** (*also* **~-heeled shoe**) Schuh *m* mit Bleistift- *or* Pfennigabsatz.
still[1] [stɪl] [1] *adj, adv* (*+er*) **(a)** (*motionless*) bewegungslos; *person also* reglos; *sea, waters* ruhig ◆ **to keep ~** stillhalten, sich nicht bewegen; **to hold sth ~** etw ruhig *or* still halten; **to be ~** (*vehicle, measuring needle etc*) stillstehen; **to lie ~** still *or* reglos daliegen; **to stand/sit ~** still stehen/sitzen; **my heart stood ~** mir stockte das Herz; **~ waters run deep** (*Prov*) stille Wasser sind tief (*Prov*).
(b) (*quiet, calm*) still ◆ **be ~!** (*US*) sei still!; **a ~ small voice** ein leises Stimmchen.
[2] *adj wine* nicht moussierend; *drink* ohne Kohlensäure ◆ **a ~ photograph** ein Standfoto *nt*.
[3] *n* **(a)** Stille *f* ◆ **in the ~ of the night** in der nächtlichen Stille, in der Stille der Nacht. **(b)** (*Film*) Standfoto *nt*.
[4] *vt* (*liter*) (*calm*) beruhigen; *anger* besänftigen; *sounds* zum Verstummen bringen; *passion, pain* abklingen lassen, stillen ◆ **to ~ sb's fear** jdm die Furcht nehmen.
still[2] [1] *adv* **(a)** (*temporal*) noch; (*for emphasis, in exasperation, used on its own*) immer noch; (*in negative sentences*) noch immer, immer noch; (*now as in the past*) nach wie vor ◆ **is he ~ coming?** kommt er noch?; **she is ~ in the office** sie ist noch im Büro; (*with emphasis*) sie ist immer noch im Büro; **do you mean you ~ don't believe me?** willst du damit sagen, daß du mir immer noch nicht *or* noch immer nicht glaubst?; **it ~ hasn't come** es ist immer noch nicht gekommen; **I will ~ be here** ich werde noch da sein; **will you ~ be here at 6?** bist du um 6 noch da?; **there will ~ be objections, no matter ...** es wird nach wie vor *or* auch weiterhin Einwände geben, egal ...
(b) (*also* (*US inf*) **~ and all**) (*nevertheless, all the same*) trotzdem ◆ **~, it was worth it** es hat sich trotzdem gelohnt; **~, he's not a bad person** na ja, er ist eigentlich kein schlechter Mensch; **~, he is my brother** er ist trotz allem mein Bruder; **rich but ~ not happy** reich und doch nicht glücklich; **~, at least we didn't lose anything** na ja, wir haben wenigstens nichts dabei verloren; **~, what can you expect?** was kann man auch anderes erwarten?
(c) (*with comp*) noch ◆ **~ better** noch besser; **better ~, do it this way** oder noch besser, mach es so; **~ more (so) because ...** und um so mehr, als ..., und um so mehr, weil ...
[2] *conj* (und) dennoch.
still[3] *n* Destillierapparat *m*; (*small distillery*) Brennerei *f*.
still: ~birth *n* Totgeburt *f*; **~born** *adj* (*lit, fig*) totgeboren *attr*; **the child was ~born** das Kind war eine Totgeburt, das Kind kam tot zur Welt; **~ life** *n*, *pl* **~ lifes** Stilleben *nt*; **~-life** *adj attr* **a ~-life picture/composition** ein Stilleben *nt*.
stillness ['stɪlnɪs] *n* **(a)** (*motionlessness*) Unbewegtheit *f*; (*of person*) Reglosigkeit *f*. **(b)** (*quietness*) Stille, Ruhe *f*.
stillroom ['stɪlruːm] *n* (*pantry*) Vorratskammer *f*.
stilt [stɪlt] *n* Stelze *f*; (*Archit*) Pfahl *m* ◆ **a house built on ~s** ein Pfahlbau *m*.
stilted *adj*, **~ly** *adv* ['stɪltɪd, -lɪ] gestelzt, gespreizt.
stiltedness ['stɪltɪdnɪs] *n* Gestelztheit, Gespreiztheit *f*.
stimulant ['stɪmjʊlənt] [1] *n* Stimulans, Anregungsmittel *nt*; (*fig*) Ansporn *m*.
[2] *adj* anregend, belebend.
stimulate ['stɪmjʊleɪt] *vt* **(a)** (*excite*) *body, circulation, mind* anregen; (*cold shower, coffee etc*) *sb* beleben; (*Med also*) stimulieren; *nerve* reizen; (*sexually*) erregen, stimulieren; (*fig*) *person* animieren, anspornen; (*mentally, intellectually*) stimulieren; *sb's interest* erregen ◆ **to ~ sb to do sth** jdn anspornen *or* dazu animieren, etw zu tun; **to ~ sb into activity** jdn aktiv werden lassen.
(b) (*increase*) *economy, sales etc* ankurbeln; (*incite*) *response* hervorrufen; *criticism* anregen zu.
stimulating ['stɪmjʊleɪtɪŋ] *adj* anregend; *drug also* stimulierend; *bath, shower, walk, music* belebend; *prospect* ermunternd, animierend, beflügelnd; *experience* (*physically*) erfrischend, ermunternd; (*mentally*) stimulierend.
stimulation [,stɪmjʊ'leɪʃən] *n* **(a)** (*act*) (*physical, mental*) Anregung *f*; (*from shower, walk etc*) belebende Wirkung; (*Med also*) Stimulation *f*; (*sexual*) Stimulieren, Erregen *nt*; (*state*) Angeregtheit, Erregung *f*; (*sexual*) Erregung *f*; (*fig: incentive*) Anreiz, Ansporn *m*; (*intellectual*) Stimulation *f*.
(b) (*of economy, sales etc*) Ankurbelung *f* (*to gen*); (*of criticism*) Anregung *f* (*of zu*); (*of response*) Hervorrufen *nt*.
stimulative ['stɪmjʊlətɪv] *adj* anregend, belebend; (*esp Physiol*) stimulierend.
stimulus ['stɪmjʊləs] *n*, *pl* **stimuli** ['stɪmjʊlaɪ] Anreiz, Ansporn *m*; (*inspiration*) Anregung *f*, Stimulus *m*; (*Physiol*) Reiz *m*; (*Psych*) Stimulus *m* ◆ **it gave the trade new ~** das hat dem Handel neuen Aufschwung gegeben.
stimy *vt see* **stymie**.
sting [stɪŋ] (*vb: pret, ptp* **stung**) [1] *n* **(a)** (*Zool, Bot: organ*) (*of insect*) Stachel *m*; (*of jellyfish*) Brennfaden *m*; (*of nettle*) Brennhaar *nt*.
(b) (*of insect*) (*act, wound*) Stich *m*; (*of nettle, jellyfish*) (*act*) Brennen *nt*; (*wound*) Quaddel *f*.
(c) (*pain*) (*from needle etc*) Stechen *nt*, stechender Schmerz; (*of antiseptic, ointment, from nettle etc*) Brennen *nt*; (*of whip*) brennender Schmerz ◆ **there might be a bit of a ~** das brennt jetzt vielleicht ein bißchen; **we felt the ~ of the hail on our faces** wir spürten den Hagel wie Nadeln im Gesicht.
(d) (*fig*) (*of remark, irony*) Stachel *m*; (*of attack, criticism etc*) Schärfe *f* ◆ **a ~ of remorse** Gewissensbisse *pl*; **a ~ of regret** schmerzliches Bedauern; **to take the ~ out of sth** etw entschärfen; (*out of remark, criticism also*) einer Sache (*dat*) den Stachel nehmen; **to have a ~ in its tail** (*story, film*) ein unerwartet fatales Ende nehmen; (*remark*) gesalzen sein; **death, where now thy ~?** Tod, wo ist dein Stachel?
[2] *vt* **(a)** (*insect*) stechen; (*jellyfish*) verbrennen ◆ **she was stung by the nettles** sie hat sich an den Nesseln verbrannt.
(b) the hail stung our faces der Hagel stach uns wie mit Nadeln im Gesicht.
(c) (*comments, sarcasm etc*) treffen, schmerzen; (*remorse, conscience*) quälen ◆ **he was stung by their insults** ihre Beleidigungen haben ihn sehr getroffen *or* geschmerzt; **to ~ sb into doing sth** jdn antreiben, etw zu tun; **he was stung into replying** er ließ sich dazu hinreißen zu antworten; **to ~ sb into action** jdn aktiv werden lassen.
(d) (*inf*) **to ~ sb for sth** jdn bei etw ausnehmen (*inf*) *or* schröpfen (*inf*); **could I ~ you for a fiver?** kann ich dir einen Fünfer abknöpfen? (*inf*).
[3] *vi* **(a)** (*insect*) stechen; (*nettle, jellyfish etc*) brennen; (*burn: eyes, cut, ointment etc*) brennen ◆ **smoke makes your eyes ~** Rauch brennt in den Augen. **(b)** (*hail etc*) wie mit Nadeln stechen. **(c)** (*comments, sarcasm etc*) schmerzen.
stingaree ['stɪŋəriː] *n* (*US, Austral*) Stachelrochen *m*.
stingily ['stɪndʒɪlɪ] *adv* (*inf*) knauserig (*inf*), knickerig (*inf*) ◆ **he ~ donated a mere 20p** knauserig *or* knickerig, wie er ist, hat er nur 20 Pence gespendet.
stinginess ['stɪndʒɪnɪs] *n* (*inf*) *see adj* Geiz *m*, Knauserigkeit (*inf*), Knickerigkeit (*inf*) *f*, Schäbigkeit, Popeligkeit (*inf*) *f*.
stinging ['stɪŋɪŋ] *adj pain* stechend; *cut, ointment* brennend.

stinging nettle *n* Brennessel *f.*

stingray ['stɪŋreɪ] *n* Stachelrochen *m.*

stingy ['stɪndʒɪ] *adj* (+*er*) (*inf*) *person* geizig, knauserig (*inf*), knickerig (*inf*); *sum, portion, donation* schäbig, popelig (*inf*) ◆ **to be ~ with sth** mit etw knausern.

stink [stɪŋk] (*vb: pret* **stank**, *ptp* **stunk**) [1] *n* **(a)** Gestank *m* (*of* nach); (*fig: of corruption etc*) (Ge)ruch *m.* **(b)** (*inf: fuss, scandal*) Knatsch (*inf*), Stunk (*inf*) *m* ◆ **to kick up** *or* **make** *or* **create a ~** Stunk machen (*inf*). **(c) ~s** *sing* (*Brit Sch inf*) Chemie *f* ◆ **S~s** (*teacher*) der Chemielehrer.
[2] *vi* **(a)** stinken ◆ **it ~s in here** hier (drin) stinkt's; **it ~s to high heaven** das stinkt zum Himmel (*inf*).
(b) (*fig inf: be bad*) sauschlecht *or* miserabel sein (*inf*) ◆ **the idea ~s** das ist eine sauschlechte *or* miserable Idee (*inf*); **the whole business ~s** die ganze Sache stinkt (*inf*).

◆**stink out** *vt sep* **(a)** (*inf*) *room* verstänkern (*inf*). **(b)** *fox etc* ausräuchern.

◆**stink up** *vt sep* (*inf*) *room* verstänkern (*inf*).

stink bomb *n* Stinkbombe *f.*

stinker ['stɪŋkəʳ] *n* (*inf*) (*person*) Ekel *nt*, Fiesling *m* (*sl*); (*problem, question*) harter Brocken, harte Nuß; (*letter*) gesalzener *or* geharnischter Brief ◆ **that problem/meeting was a ~** das war ein ganz verzwicktes (*inf*) Problem/eine äußerst schwierige Besprechung.

stinking ['stɪŋkɪŋ] [1] *adj* **(a)** (*lit*) stinkend. **(b)** (*inf*) beschissen (*sl*) ◆ **you can keep your ~ money!** du kannst dein Scheißgeld behalten! (*sl*).
[2] *adv* (*inf*) **~ rich** stinkreich (*inf*); **~ awful** sauschlecht (*inf*).

stint [stɪnt] [1] *n* **(a)** (*allotted amount of work*) Arbeit, Aufgabe *f*; (*share*) Anteil *m*, Teil *nt or m* (*of an +dat*) ◆ **to do one's ~** (*daily work*) seine Arbeit leisten *or* tun; (*one's share*) sein(en) Teil beitragen *or* tun; **my ~ was from 3 to 6/lasted two hours** ich war von 3 bis 6/zwei Stunden lang dran; **he has done his ~ of washing up/at the wheel** er hat seinen (An)teil am Abwaschen geleistet/er ist lange genug gefahren; **would you like to do a ~ at the wheel?** wie wär's, wenn du auch mal fahren würdest?; **that was a long ~** das hat vielleicht lange gedauert!; **I've finished my ~ for today** für heute habe ich genug getan; **he does a ~ in the gym/at the typewriter every day** er betätigt sich jeden Tag eine Weile in der Turnhalle/an der Schreibmaschine.
(b) without ~ ohne Einschränkung.
[2] *vt* sparen mit, knausern mit ◆ **to ~ sb of sth** jdm gegenüber mit etw knausern; *of praise, reward* jdm etw vorenthalten; **to ~ oneself (of sth)** sich (mit etw) einschränken, an sich (*dat*) sparen; **it's silly to ~ yourself of the little extra luxuries** es ist dumm, sich (*dat*) das bißchen Extraluxus nicht zu gönnen.
[3] *vi* **to ~ on sth** mit etw sparen *or* knausern.

stipend ['staɪpend] *n* (*for official, clergyman*) Gehalt *nt*; (*liter: for scholar etc*) Stipendium *nt.*

stipendiary [staɪ'pendɪərɪ] *adj official, magistrate, duty* nicht ehrenamtlich ◆ **~ allowance** Gehalt *nt*, Bezüge *pl.*

stipple ['stɪpl] [1] *vt picture* in der Tupfentechnik malen; *paint* tupfen, in Tupfen auftragen.
[2] *vi* die Tupfentechnik anwenden.
[3] *n* Tupfen *pl*; (*technique*) Tupfentechnik *f.*

stipulate ['stɪpjʊleɪt] *vt* **(a)** (*make a condition*) zur Auflage machen, verlangen. **(b)** *delivery date, amount, price* festsetzen, sich (*dat*) ausbedingen; *size, quantity* vorschreiben, festsetzen; *conditions* stellen, fordern, stipulieren (*geh*).

stipulation [ˌstɪpjʊ'leɪʃən] *n* **(a)** (*condition*) Auflage *f* ◆ **with** *or* **on the ~ that ...** unter der Bedingung *or* mit der Auflage, daß ... **(b)** *see vt (b)* Festsetzung *f*; Ausbedingung *f*; Stellen, Fordern *nt*, Stipulation *f* (*geh*).

stir [stɜːʳ] [1] *n* **(a)** Rühren *nt* ◆ **to give sth a ~** etw rühren; *tea etc* etw umrühren. **(b)** (*fig: excitement*) Aufruhr *m* ◆ **to cause** *or* **create** *or* **make a ~** Aufsehen erregen.
[2] *vt* **(a)** *tea, paint, soup* umrühren; *cake mixture* rühren ◆ **~ sugar into the mixture** den Zucker darunterrühren; **he sat there thoughtfully ~ring his tea** er saß da und rührte gedankenverloren in seinem Tee.
(b) (*move*) bewegen; *limbs* rühren; *water, waves* kräuseln ◆ **come on, ~ yourself** *or* **your stumps, we're late** (*inf*) komm, beweg dich, wir sind ohnehin schon spät dran; **if you want to pass the exam you'd better ~ yourself** wenn du die Prüfung bestehen willst, solltest du dich besser ranhalten (*inf*).
(c) (*fig*) *emotions* aufwühlen; *passion* wachrufen; *imagination* anregen; *curiosity* anstacheln, erregen; *blood* in Wallung versetzen; (*incite*) *person* anstacheln; (*move*) *person, heart* rühren, bewegen ◆ **to ~ sb to do sth** jdn bewegen, etw zu tun; (*incite*) jdn dazu anstacheln, etw zu tun; **to ~ sb into action** jdn zum Handeln bewegen; **to ~ sb to pity** an jds Herz (*acc*) rühren, jds Mitleid erregen; **we were all ~red by the speech** wir waren alle von der Rede tief bewegt.
[3] *vi* **(a)** sich regen; (*person also*) sich rühren; (*leaves, curtains, animal etc*) sich bewegen; (*emotion, anger etc*) wachwerden; (*pity, love*) sich rühren, wachwerden. **(b)** (*inf: through gossip etc*) stänkern (*inf*) ◆ **he's always ~ring** er muß immer stänkern (*inf*).

◆**stir up** *vt sep* **(a)** *liquid, mixture* umrühren; *cream* rühren, schlagen; *mud* aufwühlen.
(b) (*fig*) *curiosity, attention, anger* erregen; *memories, the past* wachrufen; *opposition, discord* entfachen, erzeugen; *hatred* schüren; *revolution, revolt* anzetteln; *mob* aufstacheln; *lazy person* aufrütteln ◆ **to ~ ~ trouble** Unruhe stiften; **to ~ sb ~ to do sth** jdn dazu anstacheln, etw zu tun; **that'll ~ things ~** das kann heiter werden!; **he's always trying to ~ things ~ among the workers** er versucht immer, die Arbeiter aufzuhetzen.

stir-fry ['stɜːˌfraɪ] *vt* (unter Rühren) kurz anbraten.

stirrer ['stɜːrəʳ] *n* (*inf*) (*gossipmonger etc*) Stänkerer *m* (*inf*); (*trouble-maker*) Scharfmacher(in *f*) (*inf*), Agitator(in *f*) *m.*

stirring ['stɜːrɪŋ] *adj speech, music, scene, poetry* bewegend; (*stronger*) aufwühlend; *days, times* bewegt.

stirrup ['stɪrəp] *n* Steigbügel *m* (*also Anat*).

stirrup: ~ cup *n* Abschiedstrunk *m*; **~ pump** *n* Handspritze *f.*

stitch [stɪtʃ] [1] *n* **(a)** Stich *m*; (*in knitting etc*) Masche *f*; (*kind of ~*) (*in knitting etc*) Muster *nt*; (*in embroidery*) Stichart *f* ◆ **to put a few ~es in sth** etw mit ein paar Stichen nähen; **to put ~es in a wound** eine Wunde nähen; **he had to have ~es** er mußte genäht werden; **he needed ~es in his arm** sein Arm mußte genäht werden; **to have the ~es taken out** die Fäden gezogen bekommen; **a ~ in time saves nine** (*Prov*) was du heute kannst besorgen, das verschiebe nicht auf morgen (*Prov*).
(b) (*inf: piece of clothing*) **she hadn't a ~ on** sie war splitter(faser)nackt (*inf*); **I haven't a ~ to wear** ich habe überhaupt nichts anzuziehen.
(c) (*pain*) Seitenstiche *pl.*
(d) to be in ~es (*inf: from laughing*) sich schieflachen (*inf*); **the story had us all in ~es** wir haben uns alle darüber schiefgelacht (*inf*); **he had us all in ~es** er brachte uns alle furchtbar zum Lachen (*inf*).
[2] *vt* (*Sew, Med*) nähen; *book* (zusammen)heften, broschieren; (*mend*) *hole, tear* zunähen, stopfen; (*embroider*) sticken.
[3] *vi* nähen (*at* an +*dat*); (*embroider*) sticken (*at* an +*dat*).

◆**stitch down** *vt sep* festnähen.

◆**stitch on** *vt sep* aufnähen; *button* annähen.

◆**stitch up** *vt sep* **(a)** *seam, wound, patient* nähen; (*mend*) *hole etc* zunähen, stopfen; (*sew up*) *hem* hochnähen. **(b)** (*sl: frame*) **I've been ~ed up** man hat mich reingelegt (*inf*); (*something has been foisted on me*) man hat mir das untergejubelt (*inf*).

stitching ['stɪtʃɪŋ] *n* (*seam*) Naht *f*; (*ornamental*) Zierstiche *pl*, Ziernaht *f*; (*embroidery*) Stickerei *f*; (*of book*) Broschur *f.*

stoat [stəʊt] *n* Wiesel *nt.*

stock [stɒk] [1] *n* **(a)** (*supply*) Vorrat *m* (*of* an +*dat*); (*Comm*) Bestand *m* (*of* an +*dat*) ◆ **~ of knowledge/information** Wissensschatz *m*/Informationsmaterial *nt*; **to get** *or* **lay in a ~ of wood/candles** *etc* sich (*dat*) einen Holzvorrat/Kerzenvorrat *etc* anlegen; **to have sth in ~** etw vorrätig haben; **to be in ~/out of ~** vorrätig/nicht vorrätig sein; **to keep sth in ~** etw auf Vorrat haben; **to get sth from ~** etw vom Lager holen; **to take ~** (*Comm*) Inventur machen; **to take ~ of sb** jdn abschätzen; **to take ~** (*fig*) Bilanz ziehen; **to take ~ of sth** *of situation, prospects* sich (*dat*) klarwerden über etw (*acc*); *of one's life* Bilanz aus etw ziehen; **surplus ~** Überschuß *m*; **the ~ was auctioned** die Bestände wurden versteigert.
(b) (*live~*) Viehbestand *m* ◆ **some good ~** schönes Vieh.
(c) (*Cook*) Brühe *f.*
(d) (*Fin*) (*capital raised by company*) Aktienkapital *nt*; (*shares held by investor*) Anteil *m*; (*government ~*) Staatsanleihe *f* ◆ **to have** *or* **hold ~ in oil companies** Ölaktien haben; **~s and shares** (Aktien und) Wertpapiere *pl*, Effekten *pl.*
(e) (*Hort*) (*of tree, plant*) Stamm *m*; (*of vine, rose*) Stock *m*; (*for grafting onto*) Wildling *m*, Unterlage *f*; (*for supplying grafts*) das Edelreis liefernde Pflanze.
(f) (*Bot*) Levkoje *f.*
(g) (*tribe, race etc*) Stamm *m*; (*descent*) Abstammung, Herkunft *f*; (*Ling*) (Sprach)familie, (Sprach)gruppe *f* ◆ **to be** *or* **come of good ~** guter Herkunft sein; **to be from good farming ~** aus einer alten Bauernfamilie stammen.
(h) (*handle*) Griff *m*; (*of rifle*) Schaft *m.*
(i) to be on the ~s (*ship*) im Bau sein; (*book etc*) in Arbeit sein.
(j) ~s *pl* (*Hist: for punishment*) Stock *m.*
(k) (*neckcloth*) Halsbinde *f.*
(l) (*Rail*) rollendes Material.
(m) (*esp US Theat*) **to play in summer ~** bei den Sommeraufführungen mitwirken; **this play is in their ~** dieses Stück gehört zu ihrem Repertoire.
[2] *adj attr* (*Comm*) *size etc* Standard-; *model* Serien-; (*fig*) *phrase, remark, response etc* Standard-, stereotyp.
[3] *vt* **(a)** (*shop etc*) *goods* führen.
(b) (*provide with ~*) *cupboard* füllen; *shop also, library* ausstatten; *pond, river* (mit Fischen) besetzen; *farm* mit einem Viehbestand versehen.

◆**stock up** [1] *vi* sich eindecken (*on* mit); (*squirrel etc*) einen Vorrat anlegen ◆ **I must ~ ~ on rice, I've almost run out** mein Reis ist fast alle, ich muß meinen Vorrat auffüllen.
[2] *vt sep shop, larder etc* auffüllen; *library* anreichern; *farm* den Viehbestand (+*gen*) vergrößern; *lake, river* den Fischbestand vergrößern in (+*dat*).

stockade [stɒ'keɪd] *n* (*fence*) Palisade(nzaun *m*) *f*; (*area*) Einfriedung, Umzäunung *f.*

stock: ~breeder *n* Viehzüchter *m*; **~breeding** *n* Viehzucht *f*; **~broker** *n* Börsenmakler *m*; **the ~broker belt** ≃ die reichen Villenvororte *pl*; **~broking** *n* Effektenhandel, Wertpapierhandel *m*; **~ car** *n* **(a)** (*for racing*) Stock Car *nt* (*frisierter, verstärkter Serienwagen*); **(b)** (*US Rail: cattle truck*) Viehwaggon, Viehwagen *m*; **~-car racing** *n* Stock-Car-Rennen *nt*; **~ character** *n* (*Theat*) Typ *m* (im Rollenfach); **~ company** *n* **(a)** (*Fin*) Aktiengesellschaft *f*; **(b)** (*US Theat*) Repertoiretheater *nt*; **~ cube** *n* Brüh- *or* Suppenwürfel *m*; **~ exchange** *n* Börse *f*; **~ farmer** *n* Viehhalter *m*; **~ fish** *n* Stockfisch *m*; **~holder** *n* Aktionär(in *f*) *m.*

stockily ['stɒkɪlɪ] *adv* **~ built** stämmig.

stockiness ['stɒkɪnɪs] *n* Stämmigkeit *f.*

stockinet(te) [ˌstɒkɪ'net] *n* (Baumwoll)trikot *m.*

stocking ['stɒkɪŋ] *n* Strumpf *m*; (*knee-length*) Kniestrumpf *m*; (*of horse*) Fessel *f* ◆ **in one's ~(ed) feet** in Strümpfen.

stocking: ~ filler *n* kleines Geschenk (*für den Weihnachtsstrumpf*); **~ mask** *n* Strumpfmaske *f*; **~ stitch** *n* glatt rechts gestricktes Muster; **in ~ stitch** glatt rechts gestrickt.

stock-in-trade [ˌstɒkɪn'treɪd] *n* (*tools, materials, fig*) Handwerkszeug *nt* ◆ **that joke is part of his ~** den Witz hat er ständig auf Lager.

stockist ['stɒkɪst] *n* (*Brit*) (Fach)händler *m*.

stock: ~jobber *n* (*Brit*) Börsenhändler *m*; (*US pej*) Börsenjobber, Börsenspekulant *m*; **~ list** *n* **(a)** (*Comm*) Warenliste *f*; **(b)** (*Fin*) Börsenzettel *m*; **~man** *n* **(a)** (*US, Austral*) Viehzüchter *m*; (*farmhand*) Farmarbeiter *m*; **(b)** (*US: in shop etc*) Lagerist, Lagerverwalter *m*; **~ market** *n* Börse(nmarkt *m*) *f*; **~pile** [1] *n* Vorrat *m* (*of* an *+dat*); (*of weapons*) Lager *nt*; **the nuclear ~pile** das Atomwaffenlager, das Kernwaffenarsenal; [2] *vt* Vorräte an (*+dat*) ... anlegen; (*pej*) horten; **to ~pile weapons** Waffenlager *or* Waffenarsenale anlegen; **~ play** *n* (*Theat*) gängiges Repertoirestück; **~ room** *n* Lager(raum *m*) *nt*; **~-still** *adj, adv* **to be/stand ~-still** stockstill sein/stehen; **~taking** *n* Inventur *f*; (*fig*) Bestandsaufnahme *f*; **~taking sale** *n* Ausverkauf *m* wegen Inventur, ≃ Jahresschlußverkauf *m*.

stocky ['stɒkɪ] *adj* (*+er*) stämmig.

stockyard ['stɒkjɑːd] *n* Viehhof, Schlachthof *m*.

stodge [stɒdʒ] *n* (*inf*) Pampe *f* (*inf*).

stodgy ['stɒdʒɪ] *adj* (*+er*) *food* pampig (*inf*), schwer; *style* schwerfällig; *subject* trocken; *book* schwer verdaulich; *person* langweilig, fad.

stog(e)y, stogie ['stəʊgɪ] *n* (*US inf: cigar*) Zigarillo *nt*.

stoic ['stəʊɪk] (*Philos:* **S~**) [1] *n* Stoiker *m*.
[2] *adj* stoisch.

stoical *adj*, **~ly** *adv* ['stəʊɪkəl, -ɪ] stoisch.

stoicism ['stəʊɪsɪzəm] *n* (*Philos:* **S~**) Stoizismus *m*; (*fig*) stoische Ruhe, Gelassenheit *f*, Gleichmut *m*.

stoke [stəʊk] *vt furnace* (be)heizen, beschicken (*spec*); *fire*, (*fig*) schüren.

◆**stoke up** [1] *vt sep furnace* (be)heizen, beschicken (*spec*); *fire* schüren.
[2] *vi* (*eat*) sich satt essen (*on* an *+dat*); (*drink*) tanken (*inf*).

stoke: ~hold *n* (*Naut*) Heizraum *m*; **~hole** *n* **(a)** (*Naut*) Heizraum *m*; **(b)** (*in furnace*) Schürloch *nt*.

stoker ['stəʊkə^r] *n* Heizer *m*; (*device*) Beschickungsanlage *f*.

stole[1] [stəʊl] *n* Stola *f*.

stole[2] *pret of* **steal**.

stolen ['stəʊlən] [1] *ptp of* **steal**.
[2] *adj* gestohlen; *pleasures* heimlich ◆ **~ goods** Diebesgut *nt*; **to receive ~ goods** Hehler sein; **receiving ~ goods** Hehlerei *f*.

stolid ['stɒlɪd] *adj person* phlegmatisch, stur (*pej*); *indifference* stumpf; *determination, silence* beharrlich, stur (*pej*).

stolidly ['stɒlɪdlɪ] *adv* phlegmatisch, stur (*pej*); *remain silent, work* beharrlich, stur (*pej*).

stolidness ['stɒlɪdnɪs] *n see adj* Phlegma *nt*; Sturheit *f* (*pej*); Stumpfheit *f*; Beharrlichkeit *f* ◆ **the ~ of his manner** sein Phlegma *nt*, seine sture Art (*pej*).

stoma ['stəʊmə] *n, pl* **-ta** (*Bot*) Stoma *nt* (*spec*).

stomach ['stʌmək] [1] *n* (*abdomen*) Magen *m*; (*belly, paunch*) Bauch *m*; (*fig: appetite*) Lust *f* (*for* auf *+acc*), Interesse *nt* (*for* an *+dat*) ◆ **to lie on one's ~** auf dem Bauch liegen; **hold your ~ in** zieh den Bauch ein!; **to have a pain in one's ~** Magen-/Bauchschmerzen haben; **to hit sb in the ~** jdn in die Magengrube/Bauchgegend schlagen *or* (*bullet etc*) treffen; **on an empty ~** *drink, take medicine etc* auf leeren *or* nüchternen Magen; **on an empty/full ~** *swim, drive etc* mit leerem *or* nüchternem/vollem Magen; **an army marches on its ~** (*prov*) mit leerem Magen kann man nichts Ordentliches zustande bringen; **I have no ~ for that** das ist mir zuwider; *for party, journey etc* mir ist nicht danach (zumute); **he doesn't have the ~ for it** (*guts*) dazu hat er nicht den Mumm (*inf*).
[2] *vt* (*inf*) *behaviour, rudeness, cruelty* vertragen; *person, film, music etc* ausstehen.

stomach *in cpds* Magen-; **~-ache** *n* Magenschmerzen *pl*; **~-pump** *n* Magenpumpe *f*; **~ trouble** *n* Magenbeschwerden *pl*; **~ upset** *n* Magenverstimmung *f*.

stomata [stəʊ'mɑːtə] *pl of* **stoma**.

stomp [stɒmp] *vi* stapfen.

stone [stəʊn] [1] *n* **(a)** Stein *m* ◆ **a heart of ~** ein Herz aus Stein; **a ~'s throw from the station** nur einen Steinwurf *or* Katzensprung vom Bahnhof entfernt; **within a ~'s throw of success** kurz vor dem Erfolg, den Erfolg in greifbarer Nähe; **to leave no ~ unturned** nichts unversucht lassen; **to have a ~ in one's kidney/gall-bladder** einen Nieren-/Gallenstein haben.
(b) (*Brit: weight*) *britische Gewichtseinheit = 6,35 kg.*
[2] *adj* Stein-, aus Stein.
[3] *vt* **(a)** (*throw ~s at*) mit Steinen bewerfen; (*kill*) steinigen ◆ **~ the crows!** (*Brit sl*) jetzt brat mir einer einen Storch! (*inf*). **(b)** *fruit* entsteinen. **(c)** (*sl*) **to be ~d (out of one's mind)** (*on drugs*) (total) weg (*inf*) *or* stoned (*sl*) sein; (*drunk*) mächtig unter Strom stehen (*sl*).

stone: S~ Age *n* Steinzeit *f*; **~-blind** *adj* stockblind (*inf*); **~-broke** *adj* (*US inf*) *see* **stony-broke**; **~-cold** [1] *adj* eiskalt; [2] *adv* **~-cold sober** stocknüchtern (*inf*); **~-dead** *adj* mausetot (*inf*); **to kill sb/sth ~-dead** jdm/einer Sache den Garaus machen (*inf*); **~-deaf** *adj* stocktaub (*inf*); **~mason** *n* Steinmetz *m*; **~ pit, ~ quarry** *n* Steinbruch *m*; **~wall** *vi* (*fig: esp Parl*) obstruieren; (*in answering questions*) ausweichen; (*Sport*) mauern (*sl*); **~ware** [1] *n* Steingut *nt*; [2] *adj attr* Steingut-; **~washed** *adj jeans* stone-washed; **~work** *n* Mauerwerk *nt*.

stonily ['stəʊnɪlɪ] *adv* (*fig*) mit steinerner Miene, starr.

stoniness ['stəʊnɪnɪs] *n* (*of ground etc*) Steinigkeit *f*; (*fig: of look etc*) Versteinertheit *f*.

stony ['stəʊnɪ] *adj* (*+er*) *ground, beach* steinig; *texture* steinartig; (*fig*) *glance, silence* steinern; *person, welcome* kalt.

stony: ~-broke *adj* (*Brit inf*) völlig abgebrannt (*inf*), total blank *or* pleite (*inf*); **~-faced** ['stəʊnɪ'feɪst] *adj* (*solemn*) ernst; (*impassive*) mit steinerner Miene; **~-hearted** *adj* kaltherzig.

stood [stʊd] *pret, ptp of* **stand**.

stooge [stuːdʒ] *n* (*inf*) Handlanger *m*; (*comedian's ~*) Stichwortgeber *m*.

stook [stuːk] *n* Hocke *f*.

stool [stuːl] *n* **(a)** (*seat*) Hocker *m*; (*foot ~, kitchen ~, milking ~ also*) Schemel *m*; (*folding*) Stuhl *m* ◆ **to fall between two ~s** sich zwischen zwei Stühle setzen; (*be neither one thing nor the other*) weder dem einen noch dem anderen gerecht werden. **(b)** (*esp Med: faeces*) Stuhl *m*.

stool pigeon *n* **(a)** (*lit, fig: decoy*) Lockvogel *m*. **(b)** (*inf: informer*) Spitzel *m* (*inf*).

stoop[1] [stuːp] [1] *n* Gebeugtheit *f*; (*deformity*) krummer Rücken, Buckel *m* ◆ **to walk with a ~** gebeugt gehen; **to have a ~** einen Buckel *or* einen krummen Rücken haben.
[2] *vt* beugen; *head* (*to avoid sth*) einziehen.
[3] *vi* sich beugen *or* neigen (*over* über *+acc*); (*also* **~ down**) sich bücken; (*have a ~, walk with a ~*) gebeugt gehen ◆ **~ing shoulders** krumme Schultern *pl*; **to ~ to sth/to doing sth** (*fig*) sich zu etw herablassen *or* hergeben/sich dazu herablassen *or* hergeben, etw zu tun.

stoop[2] *n* (*US*) Treppe *f*.

stop [stɒp] [1] *n* **(a)** (*act of ~ping*) Halt *m*, Stoppen *nt* ◆ **the signal is at ~** das Signal steht auf Halt *or* Stop; **to be at a ~** stillstehen; **to bring sth to a ~** (*lit*) etw anhalten *or* stoppen, etw zum Stehen bringen; *traffic* etw zum Erliegen bringen; (*fig*) *project, meeting, development* einer Sache (*dat*) ein Ende machen; *conversation* etw verstummen lassen; **to come to a ~** (*car, machine*) anhalten, stoppen; (*traffic*) stocken; (*fig*) (*meeting, rain*) aufhören; (*research, project*) eingestellt werden; (*conversation*) verstummen; **to come to a dead/sudden ~** (*vehicle*) abrupt anhalten *or* stoppen; (*traffic*) völlig/plötzlich zum Erliegen kommen; (*rain*) ganz plötzlich aufhören; (*research, project, meeting*) ein Ende *nt*/ein abruptes Ende finden; (*conversation*) völlig/abrupt verstummen; **when the aircraft has come to a complete ~** wenn die Maschine völlig zum Stillstand gekommen ist; **to make a ~** (*bus, train, tram*) (an)halten; (*plane, ship*) (Zwischen)station machen; **to put a ~ to sth** einer Sache (*dat*) einen Riegel vorschieben.
(b) (*stay*) Aufenthalt *m*; (*break*) Pause *f*; (*Aviat: for refuelling etc*) Zwischenlandung *f* ◆ **to have a ~ for coffee** eine Kaffeepause machen; **to have a ~** haltmachen; **we had** *or* **made three ~s** wir haben dreimal haltgemacht; **to work for eight hours without a ~** acht Stunden ohne Unterbrechung arbeiten.
(c) (*~ping place*) Station *f*; (*for bus, tram, train*) Haltestelle *f*; (*for ship*) Anlegestelle *f*; (*for plane*) Landeplatz *m*.
(d) (*esp Brit: punctuation mark*) Punkt *m*.
(e) (*Mus*) (*of wind instruments*) (Griff)loch *nt*; (*on organ: also* **~knob**) Registerzug *m*; (*organ pipe*) Register *nt* ◆ **to pull out all the ~s** (*fig*) alle Register ziehen.
(f) (*stopper*) (*for door, window*) Sperre *f*; (*on typewriter*) Feststelltaste *f*.
(g) (*Phot: f number*) Blende *f*.
(h) (*Phon*) Verschlußlaut *m*; (*glottal ~*) Knacklaut *m*.
[2] *vt* **(a)** (*~ when moving*) *person* anhalten; *vehicle, clock also, ball* stoppen; *engine, machine etc* abstellen; *blow* abblocken, auffangen; (*~ from going away, from moving on*) *runaway, thief etc* aufhalten; *attack, enemy, progress* aufhalten, hemmen; *traffic* (*hold up*) aufhalten; (*bring to complete standstill*) zum Stehen *or* Erliegen bringen; (*policeman*) anhalten; (*keep out*) *noise, light* abfangen, auffangen ◆ **~ thief!** haltet den Dieb!; **to ~ a bullet** (*be shot*) eine Kugel verpaßt kriegen (*inf*); **to ~ sb dead** *or* **in his tracks** jdn urplötzlich anhalten lassen; (*in conversation*) jdn plötzlich verstummen lassen.
(b) (*~ from continuing*) *activity, rumour, threat, crime* ein Ende machen *or* setzen (*+dat*); *nonsense, noise* unterbinden; *match, conversation, work* beenden; *development* aufhalten; (*temporarily*) unterbrechen; *flow of blood* stillen, unterbinden; *progress, inflation* aufhalten, hemmen; *speaker, speech* unterbrechen; *production* zum Stillstand bringen; (*temporarily*) unterbrechen ◆ **he was talking and talking, we just couldn't ~ him** er redete und redete, und wir konnten ihn nicht dazu bringen, endlich aufzuhören; **the referee ~ped play** der Schiedsrichter hat das Spiel abgebrochen; (*temporarily*) der Schiedsrichter hat das Spiel unterbrechen lassen; **this will ~ the pain** das hilft gegen die Schmerzen.
(c) (*cease*) aufhören mit; *noise, nonsense also* unterlassen ◆ **to ~ doing sth** aufhören, etw zu tun; etw nicht mehr tun; **she never ~s talking** sie redet ununterbrochen *or* in einer Tour (*inf*); **to ~ smoking** mit dem Rauchen aufhören; (*temporarily*) das Rauchen einstellen; **I'm trying to ~ smoking** ich versuche, das Rauchen aufzugeben *or* nicht mehr zu rauchen; **~ saying that** nun sag das doch nicht immer; **~ it!** laß das!, hör auf!; **I just can't ~ it** ich kann es nicht lassen.
(d) (*suspend*) stoppen; *payments, delivery also, production, fighting* einstellen; *leave, cheque, water supply, wages* sperren; *privileges* unterbinden; *subsidy, allowances, grant etc* jdm streichen; *battle, negotiations, proceedings* abbrechen; (*cancel*) *subscription* kündigen; (*temporarily*) *delivery, newspaper* abbestellen ◆ **the money was ~ped out of his wages** das Geld wurde von seinem Lohn einbehalten.

(e) *(prevent from happening)* *sth* verhindern; *trouble also* unterbinden; *(prevent from doing)* *sb* abhalten ♦ **to ~ oneself** sich beherrschen, sich bremsen *(inf)*; **can't you ~ him?** können Sie ihn nicht davon abhalten?; **there's no ~ping him** *(inf)* er ist nicht zu bremsen *(inf)*; **there's nothing ~ping you** *or* **to ~ you** es hindert Sie nichts, es hält Sie nichts zurück.
(f) *(in participial construction)* **to ~ sb (from) doing sth** jdn davon abhalten *or* *(physically)* daran hindern, etw zu tun; *(put a ~ to)* dafür sorgen, daß jd etw nicht mehr tut *or* daß jd aufhört, etw zu tun; **to ~ sth (from) happening** *(prevent, put a ~ to)* (es) verhindern, daß etw geschieht; **that will ~ it (from) hurting** *(prevent)* dann wird es nicht weh tun; *(put a ~ to)* dann wird es nicht mehr weh tun; **how can we ~ the baby (from) crying?** *(prevent)* was können wir tun, damit das Baby nicht schreit?; **that'll ~ the gas (from) escaping/the pipe (from) leaking** das wird verhindern, daß Gas entweicht/das Rohr leckt; **to ~ the thief (from) escaping** den Dieb an der Flucht hindern; **it will ~ you from worrying/getting wet** dann brauchen Sie sich *(dat)* keine Sorgen zu machen/dann werden Sie nicht naß; **to ~ oneself from doing sth** sich zurückhalten und etw nicht tun.
(g) *(block)* verstopfen; *(with cork, bung, cement etc also)* zustopfen *(with* mit); *(fill)* *tooth* plombieren, füllen; *(fig)* *gap* füllen, stopfen; *leak of information* stopfen; *(Mus)* *string* greifen; *finger hole* zuhalten ♦ **to ~ one's ears with one's fingers/cotton wool** sich *(dat)* die Finger in die Ohren stecken/sich *(dat)* die Ohren mit Watte zustopfen.
[3] *vi* **(a)** *(halt)* anhalten; *(train, car also)* halten, stoppen; *(traveller, driver, hiker)* haltmachen; *(pedestrian, clock, watch)* stehenbleiben; *(engine, machine)* nicht mehr laufen ♦ **~!** halt!, stopp!; **~ right there!** halt!, stopp!; **we ~ped for a drink at the pub** wir machten in der Kneipe Station, um etwas zu trinken; **to ~ at nothing (to do sth)** *(fig)* vor nichts haltmachen(, um etw zu tun); **to ~ dead** *or* **in one's tracks** plötzlich *or* abrupt *or* auf der Stelle stehenbleiben; *see* **short**.
(b) *(finish, cease)* aufhören; *(pain, headache also)* weggehen; *(heart)* aufhören zu schlagen, stehenbleiben; *(production, payments, delivery)* eingestellt werden; *(programme, show, match, film)* zu Ende sein; *(music, speaker also)* verstummen ♦ **to ~ doing sth** aufhören, etw zu tun, mit etw aufhören; **ask him to ~** sag ihm, er soll aufhören; **he ~ped in mid sentence** er brach mitten im Satz ab; **I will not ~ until I find him/convince you** ich gebe keine Ruhe, bis ich ihn gefunden habe/dich überzeugt habe; **if you had ~ped to think** wenn du nur einen Augenblick nachgedacht hättest; **~ to think before you speak** erst denken, dann reden; **he never knows when** *or* **where to ~** er weiß nicht, wann er aufhören muß *or* Schluß machen muß; **my enjoyment/worry has ~ped** ich genieße das/sorge mich nicht mehr.
(c) *(inf: stay)* bleiben *(at* in *+dat, with* bei) ♦ **to ~ for** *or* **to supper** zum Abendessen bleiben.
♦**stop behind** *vi (inf)* (noch) dableiben, länger bleiben; *(Sch: as punishment)* nachsitzen.
♦**stop by** *vi* kurz vorbeikommen *or* vorbeischauen ♦ **to ~ ~ (at) sb's house** bei jdm hereinschauen *(inf)*.
♦**stop down** *vi (Phot)* abblenden, eine niedrigere Blende einstellen.
♦**stop in** *vi (inf)* drinbleiben *(inf)*; *(Sch: as punishment)* nachsitzen, dableiben.
♦**stop off** *vi* (kurz) haltmachen *(at sb's place* bei jdm); *(on travels also)* Zwischenstation machen *(at* in *+dat)*.
♦**stop on** *vi (inf)* (noch) dableiben, länger bleiben ♦ **to ~ ~ at school** in der Schule weitermachen.
♦**stop out** *vi (inf)* wegbleiben, streiken.
♦**stop over** *vi* kurz haltmachen; *(on travels)* Zwischenstation machen *(in* in *+dat)*; *(Aviat)* zwischenlanden.
♦**stop up** [1] *vt sep* verstopfen; *crack, hole also* zustopfen.
[2] *vi* **(a)** *(inf: stay up)* aufbleiben. **(b)** *(Phot)* eine größere Blende einstellen.
stop: ~ bit *n (Comput)* Stopbit *nt*; **~ button** *n* Halteknopf *m*; **~cock** *n* Absperrhahn *m*; **~gap** *n (thing)* Notbehelf *m*; *(scheme)* Notlösung *f*; *(person)* Lückenbüßer *m*; **~gap measure** *n* Überbrückungsmaßnahme *f*; **~-go** *adj attr* **~-go policies** Politik *f* des ewigen Hin und Her; **~-go traffic** Stop-and-go-Verkehr *m*; **~light** *n (brakelight)* Bremslicht, Stopplicht *nt*; *(esp US: traffic light)* rotes Licht; **~over** *n* Zwischenstation *f*; *(Aviat)* Zwischenlandung *f*; **to have a ~over** Zwischenstation/Zwischenlandung machen; **~over ticket** *n (Aviat)* Rundreiseticket *nt*.
stoppage ['stɒpɪdʒ] *n* **(a)** *(in work, game)* Unterbrechung *f*; *(in traffic)* Stokkung *f*; *(in production etc)* *(temporary, because of mechanical problems)* Unterbrechung *f*; *(for longer time, because of strike etc)* Stopp *m*; *(strike)* Streik *m*.
(b) *(of pay, leave, cheque)* Sperrung *f*; *(of delivery, supplies etc)* Stopp *m*; *(deduction)* Abzug *m*.
(c) *(blockage)* Verstopfung *f*, Stau *m*.
stopper ['stɒpə^r] [1] *n (plug)* Stöpsel *m*; *(cork also)* Pfropfen *m*.
[2] *vt* verstöpseln.
stopping ['stɒpɪŋ] *n* **~ and starting** *(in driving)* stückchenweises Vorwärtskommen, Stop-and-go-Verkehr *m*; *(in work)* ständige Unterbrechungen *pl*.
stopping: ~ place *n (of bus, train etc)* Haltestelle *f*; **this is an ideal ~ place** das ist ein idealer Platz zum Haltmachen; **~ train** *n* Personenzug *m*.
stop: ~-press *n (esp Brit)* *(space)* Spalte *f* für letzte Meldungen; *(news)* letzte Meldungen *pl*; **~ sign** *n* Stoppschild *nt*; **~watch** *n* Stoppuhr *f*.
storage ['stɔːrɪdʒ] *n (of goods, food)* Lagerung *f*; *(of books, documents, in household)* Aufbewahrung *f*; *(of water, electricity, data)* Speicherung *f*, Speichern *nt*; *(cost)* Lagergeld *nt* ♦ **to put sth into ~** etw unterstellen, etw (ein)lagern; *see* **cold ~**.
storage: ~ battery *n* Akkumulator *m*; **~ capacity** *n (of computer)* Speicherkapazität *f*; **~ charge** *n* Lagergeld *nt*; **~ device** *n (Comput)* Speichereinheit *f*; **~ heater** *n* (Nachtstrom)speicherofen *m*; **~ problems** *npl* Lagerungsprobleme *pl*; *(in house)* Probleme *pl* mit der Aufbewahrung, Platzmangel *m*; **~ space** *n* Lagerraum *m*; *(in house)* Schränke und Abstellräume *pl*; **~ tank** *n* Vorratstank *m*.
store [stɔː^r] [1] *n* **(a)** *(stock)* Vorrat *m (of* an *+dat)*; *(fig)* Fülle *f*, Schatz, Reichtum *m (of* an *+dat)* ♦ **~s** *pl (supplies)* Vorräte, Bestände *pl*; **to lay** *or* **get in a ~ of food/coal** einen Lebensmittel-/Kohlenvorrat anlegen; **to have** *or* **keep sth in ~** etw lagern, einen Vorrat von etw haben; *(in shop)* etw auf Lager *or* etw vorrätig haben; **to be in ~ for sb** jdm bevorstehen, auf jdn warten; **to have a surprise in ~ for sb** für jdn eine Überraschung auf Lager haben; **that's a treat in ~ (for you)** da habt ihr noch was Schönes vor euch, das ist etwas, worauf ihr euch freuen könnt; **what has the future in ~ for us?** was wird uns *(dat)* die Zukunft bringen?; **to set great/little ~ by sth** viel/wenig von etw halten, einer Sache *(dat)* viel/wenig Bedeutung beimessen; **a fine ~ of knowledge** ein großer Wissensschatz.
(b) *(place)* Lager *nt*; *(~house also)* Lagerhaus *nt*, Lagerhalle *f*; *(~room also)* Lagerraum *m* ♦ **he is** *or* **works in the ~s** er ist im Lager tätig; **to put one's furniture in ~** seine Möbel unterstellen *or* (ein)lagern.
(c) *(Comput)* (Daten)speicher *m*.
(d) *(large shop, book ~)* Geschäft *nt*; *(department ~)* Kaufhaus, Warenhaus *nt*; *(esp US: shop)* Laden *m*.
[2] *adj attr (US)* *clothes* von der Stange; *bread* aus der Fabrik.
[3] *vt* lagern; *documents* aufbewahren; *furniture* unterstellen; *(in depository)* einlagern; *information, electricity, heat* speichern; *(in one's memory)* sich *(dat)* merken; *(keep in reserve, collect: also* **~ up**) Vorräte an *(+dat)* ... anschaffen; *(equip, supply)* *larder etc* auffüllen ♦ **the cellar can ~ enough coal for the winter** der Keller hat genügend Platz für die Winterkohle; **to ~ sth away** etw verwahren; **squirrels ~ away nuts for the winter** Eichhörnchen legen einen Vorrat von Nüssen für den Winter an; **to ~ sth up** einen Vorrat von etw anlegen; *(fig)* etw anstauen; *surprise* etw auf Lager haben; **hatred ~d up over years** jahrelang angestauter Haß.
[4] *vi (fruit, vegetables)* sich lagern *or* aufbewahren lassen.
store: ~ detective *n* Kaufhausdetektiv(in *f*) *m*; **~house** *n* Lager(haus) *nt*; *(fig)* Fundgrube, Schatzkammer *f*; **~ keeper** *n (in ~house)* Lagerverwalter, Lagerist *m*; *(esp US: shopkeeper)* Ladenbesitzer(in *f*), Geschäftsinhaber(in *f*) *m*; **~man** *n* Lagerverwalter, Lagerist *m*; *(esp US: shopkeeper)* Ladenbesitzer *m*; **~room** *n* Lagerraum *m*; *(for food)* Vorratskammer *f*.
storey, (*esp US***) story** ['stɔːrɪ] *n, pl* **-s** *or (US)* **stories** Stock(werk *nt*) *m*, Etage *f* ♦ **a nine-~ building** ein neunstöckiges Gebäude, ein Gebäude mit neun Stockwerken *or* Etagen; **on the second ~** im zweiten Stock(werk), auf der zweiten Etage; *(US)* im ersten Stock(werk), auf der ersten Etage; **he fell from the third-~ window** er fiel aus dem Fenster des dritten *or (US)* zweiten Stock(werk)s *or* der dritten *or (US)* zweiten Etage.
-storeyed, (*esp US***) -storied** [-'stɔːrɪd] *adj suf* -stöckig ♦ **an eight-~ building** ein achtstöckiges Gebäude.
stork [stɔːk] *n* Storch *m*.
storm [stɔːm] [1] *n* **(a)** Unwetter *nt*; *(thunder~)* Gewitter *nt*; *(strong wind)* Sturm *m* ♦ **there is a ~ blowing** es stürmt; **come in out of the ~** kommen Sie herein ins Trockene; **to brave the ~** dem Unwetter/Gewitter/Sturm trotzen; *(fig)* das Gewitter über sich *(acc)* ergehen lassen; **a ~ in a teacup** *(fig)* ein Sturm im Wasserglas.
(b) *(fig)* *(of abuse, insults)* Flut *f (of* von); *(of applause, indignation, criticism)* Sturm *m (of gen)*; *(of blows, arrows, missiles)* Hagel *m (of* von); *(outcry)* Aufruhr *m* ♦ **~ of protest** Proteststurm *m*; **~ and stress** Sturm und Drang *m*.
(c) to take sth/sb by ~ *(Mil, fig)* etw/jdn im Sturm erobern.
[2] *vt* stürmen.
[3] *vi* **(a)** *(talk angrily)* toben, wüten *(at* gegen) ♦ **he ~ed on for an hour about the government** er schimpfte eine Stunde lang wütend über die Regierung.
(b) *(move violently)* stürmen ♦ **to ~ out of/into a room** aus einem/in ein Zimmer stürmen. **(c)** *(esp US: Met)* stürmen.
storm: ~bound *adj* vom Sturm aufgehalten; **~ centre** *or (US)* **center** *n* Sturmzentrum *nt*; *(fig)* (Unruhe)herd *m*; **~ cloud** *n (lit, fig)* Gewitterwolke *f*; **~ cone** *n* Sturmkegel *m*; **~ door** *n* äußere Windfangtür; **~ force** *n* Windstärke *f*.
stormily ['stɔːmɪlɪ] *adv (lit, fig)* stürmisch; *weep* heftig; *protest, reply, answer, react* hitzig, heftig.
storminess ['stɔːmɪnɪs] *n (of reaction, temper)* Heftigkeit *f* ♦ **the ~ of the weather** das stürmische Wetter; **the ~ of his reception** sein stürmischer Empfang.
storm: ~ lantern *n* Sturmlaterne *f*; **~ petrel** *n* Sturmschwalbe *f*; **~proof** *adj* sturmsicher; **~ signal** *n* Sturmsignal *nt*; **~-tossed** *adj (liter)* sturmgepeitscht *(liter)*; **~ trooper** *n (NS)* SA-Mann *m*; **~troopers** *npl (fig)* (Sonder)einsatzkommando *nt*; **~ troops** *npl* Sturmtruppe *f*; **~ warning** *n* Sturmwarnung *f*; **~ window** *n* äußeres Doppelfenster.
stormy ['stɔːmɪ] *adj (+er) (lit, fig)* stürmisch; *discussion also, temper* hitzig; *protests* heftig ♦ **he has a ~ temper** er ist jähzornig.
stormy petrel *n* Sturmschwalbe *f*; *(fig)* Unglücksbote *m*.
story[1] ['stɔːrɪ] *n* **(a)** *(tale)* Geschichte *f*; *(Liter also)* Erzählung *f*; *(joke)* Witz(geschichte *f*) *m* ♦ **it's a long ~** das ist eine lange Geschichte; **the ~ of her life** ihre Lebensgeschichte; **that's the ~ of my life** *(inf)* das plagt mich mein ganzes Leben lang! *(inf)*; *(said as a response)* wem sagen Sie das! *(inf)*; **that's another ~** das ist eine andere Geschichte; **the ~ goes that ...** man erzählt sich, daß ...; **his ~ is that ...** er behauptet, daß ...; **according to your ~** dir zufolge; **I've heard his ~** ich habe seine Version gehört; **the full ~ still has**

to be told die ganze Wahrheit muß noch ans Licht kommen; **that's not the whole ~** das ist nicht die ganze Wahrheit; **the marks tell their own ~** die Flecke sprechen für sich; **to cut a long ~ short** um es kurz zu machen, kurz und gut; **it's the (same) old ~** es ist das alte Lied;**but it's another ~ now** aber jetzt sieht die Sache anders aus.
(b) (*Press*) (*event*) Geschichte *f*; (*newspaper ~*) Artikel *m* ◆ **it'll make a good ~** das gibt einen guten Artikel.
(c) (*plot*) Handlung *f*.
(d) (*inf: lie*) Märchen *nt* ◆ **to tell stories** Märchen erzählen.

story² *n* (*US*) *see* **storey**.

story: ~board *n* (*TV, Film*) Storyboard *nt*; **~-book** [1] *n* Geschichtenbuch *nt*; [2] *adj attr castles, sights etc* märchenhaft; *romance* Märchen-; **~-book ending** Ende *nt* wie im Märchen, Happy-End *nt*; **~line** *n* Handlung *f*; **~teller** *n* **(a)** (*narrator*) Geschichtenerzähler(in *f*) *m*; **(b)** (*inf: liar*) Lügenbold *m*.

stoup [stu:p] *n* (*Eccl*) Weihwasserbecken *nt*.

stout [staʊt] [1] *adj* (*+er*) **(a)** (*corpulent*) korpulent; *woman also* füllig; *man also* untersetzt.
(b) (*strong*) *stick, horse etc* kräftig; *door, rope also, wall, gate* stark; *shoes* fest; *coat* dick.
(c) (*brave*) *heart* tapfer; *fellow, resistance also* beherzt, unerschrocken, mannhaft (*liter*); *refusal, denial* entschieden; *belief* fest ◆ **~ fellow!** (*dated inf*) tapferer Kerl! (*dated inf*); **with ~ heart** tapferen Herzens.
[2] *n* Starkbier *nt*; (*sweet ~*) Malzbier *nt*.

stout-hearted *adj*, **~ly** *adv* ['staʊt'hɑ:tɪd, -lɪ] tapfer, unerschrocken, mannhaft (*liter*).

stoutly ['staʊtlɪ] *adv* (*strongly*) *made* solide; (*resolutely*) *resist, defend, fight* tapfer, beherzt, mannhaft (*liter*); *believe, maintain* fest, steif und fest (*pej*); *resist, refuse, deny* entschieden ◆ **~ built** *person* stämmig, kräftig (gebaut); *wall, door* stark, kräftig; *house* solide gebaut.

stoutness ['staʊtnɪs] *n see adj* **(a)** Korpulenz *f*; Fülligkeit *f*; Untersetztheit *f*. **(b)** Kräftigkeit *f*; Stärke *f*; Festigkeit *f*; Dicke *f*. **(c)** Tapferkeit *f*; Beherztheit, Mannhaftigkeit (*liter*) *f*; Entschiedenheit *f*; Festigkeit *f*.

stove [stəʊv] *n* Ofen *m*; (*for cooking*) Herd *m* ◆ **electric/gas ~** Elektro-/Gasherd *m*.

stove: ~pipe *n* Ofenrohr *nt*; **~pipe hat** *n* (*esp US inf*) Angströhre *f* (*inf*), Zylinder *m*.

stow [stəʊ] *vt* **(a)** (*Naut*) *cargo* verladen, (ver)stauen; *ship* (be)laden. **(b)** (*put away: also ~* **away**) verstauen (*in* in *+dat*) ◆ **he ~ed the money (away) behind the clock** er versteckte das Geld hinter der Uhr. **(c)** (*sl: desist*) **~ it!** hör auf!

◆**stow away** *vi* als blinder Passagier fahren.

stowage ['stəʊɪdʒ] *n* (*stowing*) (Be)laden, Stauen *nt*; (*space*) Stauraum *m*; (*charge*) Staugeld *nt*, Staugebühr *f*.

stowaway ['stəʊəweɪ] *n* blinder Passagier.

strabismus [strə'bɪzməs] *n* (*Med*) Schielen *nt*.

straddle ['strædl] [1] *vt* (*standing*) breitbeinig *or* mit gespreizten Beinen stehen über (*+dat*); (*sitting*) rittlings sitzen auf (*+dat*); (*jumping*) grätschen über (*+acc*); (*fig*) *differences* überbrücken; *two continents* überspannen ◆ **he/his legs ~d the fence/horse** *etc* er saß rittlings auf dem Zaun/Pferd *etc*; **to ~ the border/river** sich über beide Seiten der Grenze/beide Ufer des Flusses erstrecken; **to ~ an issue** (*US inf*) in einer Frage zwischen zwei Lagern schwanken.
[2] *n* (*Sport*) Grätsche *f*; (*in high jump*) Schersprung *m*.

strafe [streɪf] *vt* unter Beschuß nehmen; (*with shells also*) mit Granaten bewerfen; (*with bombs*) bombardieren.

straggle ['strægl] *vi* **(a)** (*spread untidily*) (*houses, trees*) verstreut liegen; (*hair*) (unordentlich) hängen; (*plant*) (in die Länge) wuchern, in die Höhe schießen ◆ **the town ~s on for miles** die Stadt zieht sich über Meilen hin.
(b) to ~ behind zurückbleiben, hinterherzockeln (*inf*); **to ~ behind the leader** in weitem Abstand hinter dem Führer zurückbleiben *or* hinterherzockeln (*inf*); **to ~ along the road** die Straße entlangbummeln *or* -zockeln (*inf*); **to ~ in/out** vereinzelt kommen/gehen; **stop straggling** bleibt beieinander.

straggler ['stræglə^r] *n* Nachzügler *m*.

straggling ['stræglɪŋ] *adj* **(a)** *children, cattle etc* weit verteilt; (*~ behind*) zurückgeblieben, hinterherzottelnd (*inf*); *village* sich lang hinziehend; *houses* zerstreut liegend; *group, row of houses* auseinandergezogen. **(b)** (*inf: also* **straggly**) *hair* unordentlich, zottig; *plant* hochgeschossen.

straight [streɪt] [1] *adj* (*+er*) **(a)** gerade; *shot, pass* direkt; *stance, posture also* aufrecht; *hair* glatt; *skirt, trousers* gerade geschnitten ◆ **your tie isn't ~** deine Krawatte sitzt schief; **the picture isn't ~** das Bild hängt schief; **your hem isn't ~** dein Saum ist nicht gerade; **to pull sth ~** etw geradeziehen; **is my hat on ~?** sitzt mein Hut gerade?; **please put the picture ~** bitte hängen Sie das Bild gerade hin; **hold yourself ~** gerade!; **as ~ as a die** kerzengerade; *road* schnurgerade; (*honest*) grundehrlich; **to keep a ~ face, to keep one's face ~** ernst bleiben, das Gesicht nicht verziehen; **~ left/right** (*Boxing*) gerade Linke/Rechte.
(b) (*clear*) *thinking* klar.
(c) (*frank*) *answer, talking, question* offen, direkt; *piece of advice* offen, ehrlich; *denial, refusal* direkt, ohne Umschweife; (*honest*) *person, dealings* ehrlich ◆ **to be ~ with sb** offen und ehrlich zu jdm sein; **to keep sb ~** dafür sorgen, daß jd ehrlich bleibt *or* nicht auf die schiefe Bahn gerät (*inf*).
(d) (*plain, ~forward*) *drink* pur; (*Pol*) *fight* direkt; *yes or no, choice, exam pass* einfach ◆ **~ A's** glatte Einsen; **to vote the ~ ticket** (*US Pol*) seine Stimme einer einzigen Partei (*dat*) geben; **he's a ~ Democrat** er ist ein hundertprozentiger Demokrat; **to have a ~ choice between ...** nur die Wahl zwischen ... haben.
(e) (*continuous*) ununterbrochen ◆ **~ run** (*Cards*) Sequenz *f*; **for the third ~ day** (*US*) drei Tage ohne Unterbrechung; **the ~ line of succession to the throne** die Thronfolge in der direkten Linie; **our team had ten ~ wins** unsere Mannschaft gewann zehnmal hintereinander *or* in ununterbrochener Folge.
(f) (*Theat*) *production* konventionell; *actor* ernsthaft ◆ **a ~ play** ein reines Drama.
(g) *pred (in order)* **to be (all) ~** in Ordnung sein; (*fig: clarified also*) (völlig) geklärt sein; **now we're ~** jetzt haben wir die Sache geklärt; (*tidy*) jetzt ist alles in Ordnung; **to put things ~** (*tidy*) alles in Ordnung bringen; (*clarify*) alles klären; **let's get this ~** das wollen wir mal klarstellen; **and get this ~** und damit wir uns richtig verstehen; **to put** *or* **set sb ~ about sth** jdm etw klarmachen.
(h) (*inf*) (*heterosexual*) normal, hetero (*inf*); (*conventional*) etabliert, spießig (*pej*).
[2] *adv* **(a)** *hold, walk, fly, shoot, grow* gerade; *sit up, stand up also* aufrecht; *hit* genau; *leap at, aim for* direkt; *above* genau, direkt; *across* direkt ◆ **~ through sth** glatt durch etw; **he came ~ at me** er kam direkt *or* geradewegs auf mich zu; **it went ~ up in the air** es flog senkrecht in die Luft; **to look ~ ahead** geradeaus sehen; **the town lay ~ ahead of us** die Stadt lag direkt *or* genau vor uns; **the airport is ~ ahead** der Flughafen ist geradeaus; **go ~ ahead with your plan** führen Sie Ihren Plan wie vorgesehen durch; **to drive ~ on** geradeaus weiterfahren; **he drove ~ into a tree** er fuhr direkt *or* voll (*inf*) gegen einen Baum; **the arrow went ~ to the target** der Pfeil traf genau ins Ziel; **to go ~** (*criminal*) keine krummen Sachen (mehr) machen (*inf*).
(b) (*directly*) direkt ◆ **I went ~ home** ich ging direkt *or* sofort nach Hause; **to look sb ~ in the eye** jdm direkt *or* genau in die Augen sehen.
(c) (*immediately*) sofort ◆ **~ after this** sofort *or* unmittelbar danach; **~ away** *or* **off** sofort, gleich, auf der Stelle; **he said ~ off that ...** er sagte ohne Umschweife *or* sofort, daß ...; **to come ~ to the point** sofort *or* gleich zur Sache kommen.
(d) (*clearly*) *think, see* klar.
(e) (*frankly*) offen, rundheraus, ohne Umschweife ◆ **I'll give it to you ~, you're fired** ich sage es Ihnen rundheraus *or* ohne Umschweife, Sie sind entlassen; **~ out** (*inf*) unverblümt (*inf*), rundheraus; **to give** *or* **tell sb sth/it ~ from the shoulder** jdm etw/es jdm unverblümt *or* ohne Umschweife sagen.
(f) (*Theat*) *play, produce* konventionell.
(g) *drink* pur.
[3] *n* **(a)** (*~ part, on race track*) Gerade *f*; (*road, rail*) gerade Strecke ◆ **the final ~** die Zielgerade; **the ~ and narrow** der Pfad der Tugend; **to keep sb on the ~ and narrow** dafür sorgen, daß jd ehrlich bleibt *or* nicht auf die schiefe Bahn kommt.
(b) (*~ line*) Gerade *f* ◆ **to cut sth on the ~** etw gerade (ab)schneiden; (*cloth*) am Faden(lauf) entlang schneiden.
(c) (*inf: heterosexual*) Hetero *m* (*inf*).

straight: ~ angle *n* gestreckter Winkel, Winkel *m* von 180°; **~away** (*US*) [1] *n* Gerade *f*; (*road, rail*) gerade Strecke; [2] *adv see* **straight 2 (c)**; **~ edge** *n* Lineal *nt*.

straighten ['streɪtn] [1] *vt* **(a)** (*make straight*) gerade machen; *picture* gerade hinhängen; *road, river* begradigen; *hat* gerade aufsetzen; *tablecloth, sheet, rope, clothes, tie* geradeziehen; *wire* geradebiegen; *one's shoulders* straffen; *hair* glätten. **(b)** (*tidy*) in Ordnung bringen.
[2] *vi* (*road, plant etc*) gerade werden; (*hair*) glatt werden; (*person*) sich aufrichten.
[3] *vr* **to ~ oneself** sich aufrichten.

◆**straighten out** [1] *vt sep* **(a)** (*make straight*) gerade machen; *road* begradigen; *wire* geradebiegen; *rope* geradeziehen; *hair* glätten.
(b) (*put right*) *problem, situation* klären; *one's ideas* ordnen; *one's affairs* in Ordnung bringen; *misunderstanding* (auf)klären; *person* (*by discipline*) auf die richtige Bahn bringen ◆ **to ~ oneself ~** ins richtige Gleis kommen; **the problem will soon ~ itself ~** das Problem wird sich bald von selbst erledigen; **to ~ things ~** die Sache in Ordnung bringen *or* geradebiegen; (*clarify*) Klarheit in die Sache bringen.
[2] *vi* (*road etc*) gerade werden; (*hair*) glatt werden.

◆**straighten up** [1] *vi* sich aufrichten.
[2] *vt sep* **(a)** (*make straight*) gerade machen; *papers* ordentlich hinlegen; *picture* gerade hinhängen; *hat* gerade aufsetzen; *lines also* begradigen. **(b)** (*tidy*) in Ordnung bringen, aufräumen.

straight: ~faced ['streɪt'feɪst] [1] *adv* ohne die Miene zu verziehen; [2] *adj* **to be ~faced** keine Miene verziehen; **~forward** *adj* (*honest*) *person* aufrichtig; *explanation, look also* offen, freimütig; (*simple*) *question, problem* einfach; **I'm a ~ forward soldier** ich bin ein einfacher Soldat; **~forwardly** *adv see adj*; **~forwardness** *n see adj* Aufrichtigkeit *f*; Offenheit, Freimütigkeit *f*; Einfachheit, Klarheit *f*; **~ man** *n* (*Theat*) *Stichwortgeber m für einen Komiker*; **~-out** [1] *adj* (*esp US inf*) *resentment, threat* unverblümt (*inf*), offen; *opposition also* kompromißlos; *refusal* glatt (*inf*); **he's a ~-out Democrat** er ist durch und durch Demokrat; [2] *adv see* **straight 2 (e)**; **~way** *adv* (*liter*) sogleich (*liter*).

strain¹ [streɪn] [1] *n* **(a)** (*Mech*) Belastung, Beanspruchung *f*; (*on rope, arch also*) Spannung *f*; (*on beams, floor also*) Druck *m* ◆ **the ~ on a rope** die Seilspannung; **can you take some of the ~?** können Sie mal mit festhalten/mit ziehen?; **to put a (great) ~ on sth** etw (stark) belasten; **to show signs of ~** Zeichen von Überlastung *or* Überbeanspruchung zeigen; **to take the ~ off sth** etw entlasten.
(b) (*fig: mental, economic etc*) Belastung *f* (*on* für); (*effort*) Anstrengung *f*;

(*pressure*) (*of job etc also*) Beanspruchung *f* (*of* durch); (*of responsibility*) Last *f* ◆ **to be under a lot of ~** stark beansprucht sein; **to suffer from (nervous) ~** (nervlich) überlastet sein, im Streß sein; **I find her/that a bit of a ~** ich finde sie/das ziemlich anstrengend; **to put a (great) ~ on sb/sth** jdn/etw stark belasten; **to put too great a ~ on sb/sth** jdn/etw überlasten; **to show signs of ~** Zeichen von Überlastung *or* Überanstrengung zeigen; **to take the ~ off sb/sth** jdn/etw entlasten; **to be under ~** großen Belastungen ausgesetzt sein; **the ~ of six hours at the wheel** die Anstrengung, sechs Stunden am Steuer zu sitzen.

(c) (*muscle-~*) (Muskel)zerrung *f*; (*on eyes, heart etc*) Überanstrengung *f* (*on gen*) ◆ **back-/eye-~** überanstrengter Rücken/überanstrengte Augen *pl*; **new glasses will relieve the ~** eine neue Brille wird die Augen entlasten.

(d) **~s** *pl* (*of instrument, tune*) Klänge *pl* ◆ **to the ~s of** zu den Klängen (*+gen*).

[2] *vt* (a) (*stretch*) spannen.

(b) (*put ~ on*) *rope, beams, relationship, faith, budget* belasten; *nerves, patience also* strapazieren; (*put too much ~ on*) überlasten; *meaning, word* dehnen ◆ **it ~s my nerves** das zerrt an meinen Nerven; **to ~ one's ears/eyes to ...** angestrengt lauschen/gucken, um zu ...; **to ~ every nerve** jeden Nerv anspannen; **to ~ oneself** sich anstrengen; (*excessively*) sich überanstrengen; **don't ~ yourself!** (*iro inf*) überanstrenge dich bloß nicht!, reiß dir bloß kein Bein aus! (*inf*).

(c) (*Med*) *muscle* zerren; *ankle, arm* verrenken; *back, eyes, voice* anstrengen, strapazieren; (*excessively*) überanstrengen; *heart* belasten; (*excessively*) überlasten.

(d) (*filter*) (durch)sieben, (durch)seihen; (*pour water off*) *vegetables* abgießen ◆ **to ~ off water** Wasser abgießen; **to ~ out solids** feste Stoffe aussieben.

[3] *vi* (*exert effort*) sich anstrengen, sich abmühen; (*pull*) zerren, ziehen; (*fig: strive*) sich bemühen, streben ◆ **to ~ to do sth** sich anstrengen *or* abmühen, etw zu tun; **to ~ at sth** sich mit etw abmühen; (*pull*) an etw (*dat*) zerren *or* ziehen; **to ~ at the leash** (*dog*) an der Leine zerren; (*fig*) aufmucken, aufmüpfig werden (*inf*); **to ~ after sth** nach etw streben, sich um etw bemühen; **to ~ against sb** sich an jdn drücken; **to ~ against sth** sich gegen etw stemmen; **to ~ at a gnat and swallow a camel** (*prov*) Mücken seihen und Kamele verschlucken.

strain² *n* (a) (*streak*) Hang, Zug *m*; (*hereditary*) Veranlagung *f* ◆ **a ~ of madness** eine Veranlagung zum Wahnsinn; **a ~ of weakness** ein Hang *m* zur Schwäche.

(b) (*style*) Anflug *m* ◆ **there is a humorous ~ in his writing** seine Schriften haben einen humorvollen Anflug *or* Zug.

(c) (*breed*) (*animals*) Rasse *f*; (*of plants*) Sorte *f*; (*of virus etc*) Art *f*; (*old: race*) Geschlecht *nt* (*old*).

strained [streɪnd] *adj* (a) *liquids* durchgesiebt, durchgeseiht; *solids* ausgesiebt; *vegetables* abgegossen.

(b) *muscle* gezerrt; *back, eyes* überanstrengt, strapaziert ◆ **to have a ~ ankle** sich (*dat*) den Knöchel verrenkt haben.

(c) (*unnatural*) *expression, performance, style* unnatürlich, gekünstelt; *laugh, smile, conversation* gezwungen; *meeting* steif; *voice, relations, atmosphere, nerves* (an)gespannt ◆ **he looked rather ~** er sah ziemlich abgespannt aus.

strainer ['streɪnəʳ] *n* (a) (*Cook*) Sieb *nt*. (b) (*Tech*) Filter *m*.

strait [streɪt] *n* (a) (*Geog*) Meerenge, Straße *f* ◆ **the ~s of Dover/Gibraltar** die Straße von Dover/Gibraltar.

(b) **~s** *pl* (*fig*) Nöte, Schwierigkeiten *pl* ◆ **to be in dire *or* desperate ~s** in großen Nöten sein, in einer ernsten Notlage sein.

straitened ['streɪtnd] *adj means* beschränkt; *circumstances also* bescheiden, dürftig.

strait: ~jacket *n* (*lit, fig*) Zwangsjacke *f*; **~-laced** [streɪt'leɪst] *adj* prüde, puritanisch, spießig (*inf*).

strand¹ [strænd] [1] *n* (*liter: beach*) Gestade *nt* (*liter*).

[2] *vt ship, fish* stranden lassen; *person* (*in place*) verschlagen, geraten lassen; (*without money, help etc*) seinem Schicksal überlassen ◆ **to be ~ed** (*ship, fish, shipwrecked person*) gestrandet sein; **to be (left) ~ed** (*person*) festsitzen; (*without money also*) auf dem trockenen sitzen (*inf*); **to leave sb ~ed** jdn seinem Schicksal überlassen.

strand² *n* Strang *m*; (*of hair*) Strähne *f*; (*of thread, wool*) Faden *m*; (*of wire*) Litze *f*; (*of vine etc*) Ranke *f*; (*of beads*) Schnur *f*; (*fig*) (*in melody etc*) Melodienfolge *f*; (*in story*) Handlungsfaden *m* ◆ **a three-~ necklace** eine dreireihige Halskette.

strange [streɪndʒ] *adj* (*+er*) (a) seltsam, sonderbar, merkwürdig ◆ **he told me the ~st story** er erzählte mir eine sehr seltsame *etc* Geschichte; **by a ~ chance** eigenartigerweise, komischerweise; **~ to say** so seltsam es klingen mag.

(b) (*unfamiliar*) *country, surroundings, bed* fremd; (*unusual, unaccustomed*) *work, activity* nicht vertraut, ungewohnt ◆ **I felt rather ~ at first** zuerst fühlte ich mich ziemlich fremd; **I feel ~ in a skirt** ich komme mir in einem Rock komisch vor (*inf*); **the boys are ~ to the school** die Schule ist den Jungen noch nicht vertraut *or* noch fremd.

strangely ['streɪndʒlɪ] *adv* (*oddly*) seltsam, sonderbar, merkwürdig; *act, behave also* komisch (*inf*) ◆ **~ enough** seltsamerweise, sonderbarerweise, merkwürdigerweise.

strangeness ['streɪndʒnɪs] *n* (a) (*oddness*) Seltsamkeit, Merkwürdigkeit *f*. (b) (*unfamiliarity*) Fremdheit *f*; (*of surroundings also, of work, activity*) Ungewohntheit *f*.

stranger ['streɪndʒəʳ] *n* Fremde(r) *mf* ◆ **he's a perfect ~ to me** ich kenne ihn überhaupt nicht; **I'm a ~ here myself** ich bin selbst fremd hier; **he is no ~ to London** er kennt sich in London aus; **he is no ~ to misfortune** Leid ist ihm nicht fremd; **to be a ~ to this kind of work** mit dieser Art von Arbeit nicht vertraut sein; **hullo, ~!** (*inf*) hallo, lange nicht gesehen; **you're quite a ~ here** (*inf*) man kennt dich ja gar nicht mehr; **the little ~** (*hum*) der kleine Neuankömmling; **S~s' Gallery** (*Brit Parl*) Besuchergalerie *f*.

strangle ['stræŋgl] *vt* (*murder*) erwürgen, erdrosseln, strangulieren (*form*); (*fig*) *cry, freedom, originality* ersticken; *impulse, protests* abwürgen, ersticken ◆ **a ~d cry** ein erstickter Schrei; **this collar is strangling me** (*inf*) dieser Kragen schnürt mir den Hals zu *or* ein.

stranglehold ['stræŋgl,həʊld] *n* (*lit*) Würgegriff *m*, Manschette *f*; (*fig*) absolute Machtposition (*on* gegenüber) ◆ **they have a ~ on us** (*fig*) sie haben uns in der Zange.

strangler ['stræŋgləʳ] *n* Würger(in *f*) *m*.

strangling ['stræŋglɪŋ] *n* (a) (*murder*) Mord *m* durch Erwürgen. (b) (*act of ~*) Erwürgen, Erdrosseln *nt*; (*fig*) Ersticken *nt*.

strangulate ['stræŋgjʊleɪt] *vt* (*Med*) abschnüren, abbinden.

strangulation [,stræŋgjʊ'leɪʃən] *n* (a) (*being strangled*) Ersticken *nt*; (*act of strangling*) Erwürgen, Erdrosseln *nt* ◆ **death was due to ~** der Tod trat durch Ersticken ein. (b) (*Med*) Abschnürung, Abbindung *f*.

strap [stræp] [1] *n* Riemen *m*; (*for safety also*) Gurt *m*; (*in bus etc also*) Schlaufe, Lasche *f*; (*shoe ~ also*) Riemchen *nt*; (*on ski-pants etc*) Steg *m*; (*watch ~*) Band *nt*; (*shoulder ~*) Träger *m* ◆ **to give sb the ~** jdn verprügeln, jdn züchtigen.

[2] *vt* (a) (*fasten with ~*) festschnallen (*to* an *+dat*) ◆ **to ~ sth onto sth** etw auf etw (*acc*) schnallen; **he ~ped on his rucksack** er schnallte (sich *dat*) den Rucksack auf; **to ~ sb/sth down** jdn/etw festschnallen; **to ~ on one's watch/belt** sich (*dat*) die Uhr umbinden/sich (*dat*) den Gürtel umschnallen; **to ~ sb/oneself in** (*in car, plane*) jdn/sich anschnallen.

(b) (*Med: also ~ up*) bandagieren; *dressing* festkleben.

(c) (*punish*) *person* verprügeln, züchtigen.

(d) (*US inf*) **to be ~ped** (*broke*) pleite *or* blank sein (*inf*).

strap: ~-hang *vi* (*inf*) **I had to ~-hang** ich mußte stehen; **~-hanger** *n* (*inf*) Pendler(in *f*) *m*; **~-hanging** *n* (*inf*) Pendeln *nt*; **~less** *adj* trägerlos, schulterfrei; **~line** *n* (*Press*) Schlagzeile *f*.

strapping ['stræpɪŋ] *adj* (*inf*) stramm; *woman also* drall.

Strasbourg ['stræzbɜːg] *n* Straßburg *nt*.

strata ['strɑːtə] *pl of* **stratum**.

stratagem ['strætɪdʒəm] *n* (*Mil*) Kriegslist *f*; (*artifice*) List *f*.

strategic [strə'tiːdʒɪk] *adj* strategisch; (*strategically important*) strategisch wichtig; (*fig also*) taktisch.

strategically [strə'tiːdʒɪkəlɪ] *adv* strategisch; (*fig also*) taktisch ◆ **to be ~ placed** eine strategisch günstige Stellung haben; **~, his move was a mistake** strategisch gesehen war das falsch.

strategist ['strætɪdʒɪst] *n* Stratege *m*; (*fig also*) Taktiker *m*.

strategy ['strætɪdʒɪ] *n* (a) (*Mil*) Strategie *f*; (*Sport, fig also*) Taktik *f*. (b) (*art of ~*) (*Mil*) Kriegskunst *f*; (*fig*) Taktieren *nt*.

stratification [,strætɪfɪ'keɪʃən] *n* (*lit, fig*) Schichtung *f*; (*stratifying also*) Schichtenbildung *f*; (*Geol*) Stratifikation *f*.

stratify ['strætɪfaɪ] [1] *vt* schichten; (*Geol also*) stratifizieren ◆ **a highly stratified society** eine vielschichtige Gesellschaft.

[2] *vi* (*Geol*) Schichten bilden, sich aufschichten; (*fig*) Schichten herausbilden, in Schichten zerfallen.

stratosphere ['strætəʊsfɪəʳ] *n* Stratosphäre *f*.

stratospheric [,strætəʊ'sferɪk] *adj* stratosphärisch.

stratum ['strɑːtəm] *n, pl* **strata** (*Geol, fig*) Schicht *f*.

stratus ['strɑːtəs] *n* (*Met*) Stratus(wolke *f*) *m*, Schichtwolke *f*.

straw [strɔː] [1] *n* (a) (*stalk*) Strohhalm *m*; (*collectively*) Stroh *nt no pl* ◆ **it's the last ~ that breaks the camel's back** (*prov*) der letzte Tropfen bringt das Faß zum Überlaufen; **it's the last *or* final ~!** (*inf*) das ist der Gipfel! (*inf*); **it's a ~ in the wind** das ist ein Vorzeichen; **to clutch *or* grasp at ~s** sich an einen Strohhalm klammern; **man of ~** Strohmann *m*; (*in politics*) Marionette *f*; (*set-up opponent*) Scheingegner *m*; **not worth a ~** (*inf*) keinen Pfifferling wert; *see* **drowning**.

(b) (*drinking ~*) Trink- *or* Strohhalm *m*.

[2] *adj attr* Stroh-; *basket* aus Stroh.

strawberry ['strɔːbərɪ] *n* (*plant, fruit*) Erdbeere *f*.

strawberry *in cpds* Erdbeer-; **~ blonde** [1] *n* Rotblonde(r) *mf*; **she's a ~ blonde** sie hat rotblondes Haar; [2] *adj* rotblond; **~ mark** *n* (rotes) Muttermal.

straw: ~ boss *n* (*US inf*) Pro-forma-Vorgesetzte(r) *m*; **~-coloured** *adj* strohfarben, strohfarbig; *hair* strohblond; **~ hat** *n* Strohhut *m*; **~ man** *n* Strohmann *m*; (*in politics*) Marionette *f*; (*set-up opponent*) Scheingegner *m*; **~ mattress** *n* Strohsack *m*; **~ poll, ~ vote** *n* Probeabstimmung *f*; (*in election*) Wählerbefragung *f*.

stray [streɪ] [1] *vi* (*also ~ away*) sich verirren, abirren; (*also ~ about*) (umher)streunen; (*fig: thoughts, speaker*) abschweifen ◆ **to ~ (away) from sth** (*lit, fig*) von etw abkommen; **to ~ from *or* off a path** von einem Weg abkommen; **to ~ from the path of virtue** vom rechten Weg *or* vom Pfad der Tugend abkommen; **the cattle ~ed into the road** die Rinder haben sich auf die Straße verirrt; **they ~ed into the enemy camp** sie verirrten sich ins feindliche Lager.

[2] *adj child, bullet, cattle* verirrt; *cat, dog etc* streunend *attr*; (*ownerless*) herrenlos; (*isolated*) *remarks, houses, cases* vereinzelt; (*single*) *remark, success* einzeln; (*occasional*) gelegentlich; *thoughts* flüchtig.

[3] *n* (a) (*dog, cat*) streunendes Tier; (*ownerless*) herrenloses Tier ◆ **that cat's a ~** das ist eine herrenlose Katze; *see* **waif**.

(b) **~s** *pl* (*Rad*) (atmosphärische) Störungen *pl*.

streak [striːk] [1] *n* Streifen *m*; (*of light*) Strahl *m*; (*in hair*) Strähne *f*; (*of fat also*)

Schicht *f*; (*fig*) (*trace*) Spur *f*; (*of jealousy, meanness etc*) Zug *m*; (*of madness, humour*) Anflug *m* ◆ ~ **of lightning** Blitz(strahl) *m*; **there was a ~ of blood on his arm** eine Blutspur zog sich über seinen Arm; **there is a ~ of Spanish blood in her** sie hat spanisches Blut in den Adern; **his ~ of luck, his lucky ~** seine Glückssträhne; **a winning/losing ~** eine Glücks-/Pechsträhne; **he went past like a ~ (of lightning)** er sauste vorbei wie der Blitz.

[2] *vt* streifen ◆ **to be ~ed** gestreift sein; **the sky was ~ed with red** der Himmel hatte rote Streifen; **to have one's hair ~ed** sich (*dat*) Streifen ins Haar färben lassen; **hair ~ed with blonde/grey** Haar mit blonden/grauen Strähnen, graumeliertes Haar; **~ed with dirt/paint** schmutzverschmiert/mit Farbe beschmiert; **~ed with tears** tränenverschmiert; **rock ~ed with quartz** von Quarzadern durchzogener Stein.

[3] *vi* **(a)** (*lightning*) zucken; (*inf: move quickly*) flitzen (*inf*) ◆ **to ~ along/past** entlang-/vorbeiflitzen (*inf*).
(b) (*run naked*) blitzen, flitzen.

streaker ['striːkəʳ] *n* Blitzer(in *f*), Flitzer(in *f*) *m*.

streaky ['striːkɪ] *adj* (*+er*) *bacon* durchwachsen; *face* verschmiert; *window, mirror* streifig, verschmiert.

stream [striːm] [1] *n* **(a)** (*small river*) Bach *m*, Flüßchen *nt*; (*current*) Strömung *f* ◆ **to go with/against the ~** (*lit, fig*) mit dem/gegen den Strom schwimmen.
(b) (*flow*) (*of liquid, air, people, cars*) Strom *m*; (*of light, tears*) Flut *f*; (*of words, excuses, abuse*) Schwall *m*, Flut *f* ◆ **people were coming out in ~s** Menschen strömten heraus; **~ of consciousness** (*Liter*) Bewußtseinsstrom *m*.
(c) (*Brit Sch*) Leistungsgruppe *f*.
(d) (*Tech*) **to be/come on ~** (*oil well*) in Betrieb sein/genommen werden; (*oil*) fließen/zu fließen anfangen.

[2] *vt* **(a)** (*liter*) **the walls ~ed water** von den Wänden rann das Wasser; **his face ~ed blood** Blut rann *or* strömte ihm übers Gesicht. **(b)** (*Brit Sch*) in (Leistungs)gruppen einteilen.

[3] *vi* **(a)** (*flow*) (*liquid*) strömen, fließen, rinnen; (*eyes: because of cold, gas etc*) tränen; (*air, sunlight*) strömen, fluten; (*people, cars etc*) strömen ◆ **the wound was ~ing with blood** Blut strömte *or* rann aus der Wunde; **the walls were ~ing with water** die Wände trieften vor Nässe; **her eyes/cheeks were ~ing with tears** Tränen strömten ihr aus den Augen/ihre Wangen waren tränenüberströmt.
(b) (*wave: flag, hair*) wehen.

◆**stream down** *vi* (*liquid*) in Strömen fließen; (*+prep obj*) herunterströmen; (*cars*) in Strömen herunterfahren; (*hair*) wallend herunterfallen (*prep obj* über *+acc*) ◆ **the rain was ~ing ~** es regnete in Strömen; **tears ~ed ~ her face** Tränen rannen *or* strömten *or* liefen über ihr Gesicht.

◆**stream in** *vi* herein-/hineinströmen.

◆**stream out** *vi* heraus-/hinausströmen (*of* aus); (*liquid also*) herausfließen (*of* aus) ◆ **her hair ~ed ~ behind her** ihre Haare wehten nach hinten.

◆**stream past** *vi* vorbeiströmen (*prep obj* an *+dat*); (*cars*) in Strömen vorbeifahren (*prep obj* an *+dat*) ◆ **the cars kept ~ing ~** der Strom der Autos brach nicht ab.

streamer ['striːməʳ] *n* (*flag*) Banner *nt*; (*made of paper*) Papier- *or* Luftschlange *f*; (*made of cloth, as decoration*) Band *nt* ◆ ~ **headline** (*US*) Balkenüberschrift *f*.

stream feed *n* (*on photocopier*) automatischer Papiereinzug.

streaming ['striːmɪŋ] [1] *n* (*Brit Sch*) Einteilung *f* in Leistungsgruppen.
[2] *adj nose, windows* triefend; *eyes also* tränend ◆ **I have a ~ cold** ich habe einen fürchterlichen Schnupfen.

streamlet ['striːmlət] *n* (*poet*) Bächlein, Rinnsal (*liter*) *nt*.

streamline ['striːmlaɪn] *vt racing car, aeroplane* windschlüpfig machen, Stromlinienform geben (*+dat*); (*fig*) rationalisieren.

streamlined ['striːmlaɪnd] *adj wing* windschlüpfig; *car, plane also* stromlinienförmig; (*fig*) rationalisiert.

street [striːt] [1] *n* **(a)** Straße *f* ◆ **in** *or* **on the ~** auf der Straße; **to live in** *or* **on a ~** in einer Straße wohnen; **it's right up my ~** (*fig inf*) das ist genau mein Fall (*inf*); **to be ~s ahead of** *or* **better than sb** (*fig inf*) jdm haushoch überlegen sein (*inf*); **~s apart** (*fig*) grundverschieden; **he's not in the same ~ as her** (*fig inf*) zwischen ihm und ihr ist ein himmelweiter Unterschied (*inf*); **to take to the ~s** (*demonstrators*) auf die Straße gehen; **to be/go on the ~s** (*inf*) auf den Strich gehen (*inf*); **a woman of the ~s** ein Mädchen von der Straße, ein Straßenmädchen *nt*; *see* **man**.
(b) (*inf: residents*) Straße *f*.
[2] *adj attr* Straßen-.

street: ~ arab *n* (*dated*) Gassenkind *nt*; **~ battle** *n* Straßenschlacht *f*; **~car** *n* (*US*) Straßenbahn *f*; **~ cleaner** *n* (*esp US*) Straßenkehrer(in *f*) *or* -feger(in *f*) *m*; **~ cred** (*inf*), **~ credibility** *n* Glaubwürdigkeit *f*; **as an undercover agent in the Bronx you need ~ cred** als Geheimagent in der Bronx muß man sich dem Milieu anpassen können; **this jacket does nothing for my ~ cred** dieses Jackett versaut mein ganzes Image (*inf*); **~ door** *n* Tür *f* zur Straße hin; **~ fighter** *n* Straßenkämpfer(in *f*) *m*; **~ fighting** *n* Straßenkämpfe *pl*; **~ lamp** *n* Straßenlaterne *f*; **~ level** *n* **at ~ level** zu ebener Erde; **~ life** *n* (*inf*) Leben *nt* auf der Straße; **~ light** *n* Straßenlaterne *f*; **~ lighting** *n* Straßenbeleuchtung *f*; **~ map** *n* Stadtplan, Straßenplan *m*; **~ market** *n* Straßenmarkt *m*; **~ musician** *n* Straßenmusikant(in *f*) *m*; **~ party** *n* Straßenfest *nt*; **~ plan** *n* Straßen- *or* Stadtplan *m*; **~ sweeper** *n* (*person*) Straßenkehrer(in *f*) *or* -feger(in *f*) *m*; (*machine*) Kehrmaschine *f*; **~ theatre** *or* (*US*) **theater** *n* Straßentheater *nt*; **~ urchin** *n* Straßen- *or* Gassenjunge *m*; **~walker** *n* Prostituierte *f*, Straßenmädchen *nt*; **~wise** *adj* clever (*inf*).

strength [streŋθ] *n* **(a)** (*lit, fig*) Stärke *f*; (*of person, feelings*) Kraft *f*; (*of table, bolt, nail, wall*) Stabilität *f*; (*of material, character also, of conviction, shoes*) Festigkeit *f*; (*of views*) Überzeugtheit *f*; (*of imagination*) Lebhaftigkeit *f*; (*of reason, argument, evidence*) Überzeugungskraft *f*; (*of plea, protest*) Eindringlichkeit *f*; (*of letter*) geharnischte *or* starke Ausdrucksweise; (*of measure*) Drastik *f* ◆ ~ **of character/will** *or* **mind** Charakter-/Willensstärke *f*; **to increase in** *or* **gain ~** stärker werden; **on the ~ of sth** auf Grund einer Sache (*gen*); **he decided to be a writer on the ~ of selling one short story** er beschloß, Schriftsteller zu werden, nachdem er eine einzige Kurzgeschichte verkauft hatte; **his ~ failed him** seine Kräfte versagten, ihn verließen die Kräfte; **to be beyond sb's ~** über jds Kräfte (*acc*) gehen; **to save one's ~** mit seinen Kräften haushalten; **you don't know your own ~!** du weißt gar nicht, wie stark du bist!; **to argue from a position of ~** von einer starken Position aus argumentieren; **to go from ~ to ~** einen Erfolg nach dem anderen erzielen *or* haben; **he was a great ~ to me** er war mir eine große Stütze.
(b) (*health*) (*of constitution*) Robustheit, Kräftigkeit *f*; (*of eyes, heart*) Stärke *f* ◆ **the patient is recovering his** *or* **gaining ~** der Patient kommt wieder zu Kräften; **when she has her ~ back** wenn sie wieder bei Kräften ist.
(c) (*of colour*) Kräftigkeit, Intensität *f*; (*of acid, bleach*) Stärke *f*; (*of diluted solution*) Konzentration *f*.
(d) (*numbers*) (An)zahl *f*; (*Mil*) Stärke *f* ◆ **to be at full/bring up to ~** vollzählig sein/machen; **to be up to/below ~** (die) volle Stärke/nicht die volle Stärke haben; **to come in ~** in großer Zahl kommen, zahlreich erscheinen; **the police were there in ~** ein starkes Polizeiaufgebot war da.
(e) (*of currency*) Stärke *f*; (*of market prices*) Stabilität *f*; (*of economy*) Gesundheit *f*.

strengthen ['streŋθən] [1] *vt* stärken; *material, shoes, building, protest* verstärken; *eyesight* verbessern; *muscles, patient also* kräftigen; *person* (*lit*) Kraft geben (*+dat*); (*fig*) bestärken; *currency, market* festigen; *affection also, effect* vergrößern ◆ **to ~ sb's hand** (*fig*) jdn bestärken *or* ermutigen; **this only ~ed her determination** das bestärkte sie nur in ihrem Entschluß.
[2] *vi* stärker werden; (*wind, desire also*) sich verstärken.

strenuous ['strenjʊəs] *adj* **(a)** (*exhausting*) anstrengend; *march, game also* ermüdend. **(b)** (*energetic*) *attempt, supporter, support* unermüdlich, energisch; *attack, effort, denial* hartnäckig; *opposition, conflict, protest* heftig.

strenuously ['strenjʊəslɪ] *adv see adj (b)*.

strep throat ['strep'θrəʊt] *n* (*esp US inf*) Halsentzündung *f*.

streptococcus [ˌstreptəʊ'kɒkəs] *n, pl* **streptococci** [ˌstreptəʊ'kɒksaɪ] Streptokokkus *m*.

▼ **stress** [stres] [1] *n* **(a)** (*strain*) Belastung *f*, Streß *m*; (*Med*) Überlastung *f*, Streß *m* ◆ **the ~es and strains of modern life** die Belastungen *or* der Streß des heutigen Lebens; **times of ~** Krisenzeiten *pl*, Zeiten *pl* großer Belastung; **to be under ~** großen Belastungen ausgesetzt sein; (*as regards work*) unter Streß stehen, im Streß sein; **to put sb under great ~** jdn großen Belastungen aussetzen; **to break down under ~/the ~** unter Streß *or* bei Belastung/unter dem Streß *or* unter der Belastung zusammenbrechen.
(b) (*accent*) Betonung *f*, Ton *m*; (*fig: emphasis*) Akzent *m*, (Haupt)gewicht *nt* ◆ **to put** *or* **lay (great) ~ on sth** großen Wert auf etw (*acc*) legen, einer Sache (*dat*) großes Gewicht beimessen; *fact, detail* etw (besonders) betonen.
(c) (*Mech*) Belastung *f*; (*pressure also*) Druck *m*; (*tension also*) Spannung *f* ◆ **the ~ acting on the metal** die Belastung, der das Metall ausgesetzt ist.

▼[2] *vt* **(a)** (*lit, fig: emphasize*) betonen; *innocence also* beteuern; *good manners, subject* großen Wert legen auf (*+acc*); *fact, detail also* hervorheben.
(b) (*Mech*) belasten, beanspruchen.

stress disease *n* Streßkrankheit, Managerkrankheit (*inf*) *f*.

stressed [strest] *adj* **(a)** *syllable, word* betont. **(b)** (*under stress*) *person* gestreßt, über(be)lastet.

stress fracture *n* Spannungsriß *m*.

stressful ['stresfʊl] *adj* anstrengend, stressig ◆ **a ~ situation** eine angespannte Lage.

stress mark *n* Akzent *m*, Betonungszeichen *nt*.

stretch [stretʃ] [1] *n* **(a)** (*act of ~ing*) Strecken, Dehnen *nt* ◆ **to have a ~, to give oneself a ~** sich strecken *or* dehnen; (*person also*) sich recken; **to be at full ~** (*lit: material*) bis zum äußersten gedehnt sein; (*fig*) (*person*) mit aller Kraft arbeiten; (*factory etc*) auf Hochtouren arbeiten (*inf*); (*engine, production, work*) auf Hochtouren laufen; **by no ~ of the imagination** beim besten Willen nicht; **only by some ~ of the imagination** nur mit viel Phantasie; **not by a long ~** bei weitem nicht.
(b) (*elasticity*) Elastizität, Dehnbarkeit *f* ◆ **a fabric with plenty of ~** ein stark dehnbares *or* sehr elastisches Material; **there's not much ~ left in this elastic** das Gummi ist ziemlich ausgeleiert.
(c) (*expanse*) (*of road etc*) Strecke *f*, Stück *nt*; (*on racecourse*) Gerade *f*; (*of wood, river, countryside etc*) Stück *nt*; (*of journey*) Abschnitt, Teil *m* ◆ **a straight ~ of road** eine gerade Strecke; **that ~ of water is called ...** dieser Gewässerlauf heißt ...; **in that ~ of the river** in dem Teil des Flusses; **for a long ~** über eine weite Strecke.
(d) (*~ of time*) Zeit(raum *m* *or* -spanne *f*) *f* ◆ **for a long ~ of time** für (eine) lange Zeit, lange Zeit; **for hours at a ~** stundenlang; **three days at a ~** drei Tage an einem Stück *or* ohne Unterbrechung; **to do a ~** (*sl: in prison*) im Knast sein (*sl*).
[2] *adj attr* dehnbar, Stretch-; *socks, trousers, track suit etc* Stretch-, ≃ Helanca-®; *esp ski pants* Lastex-.
[3] *vt* **(a)** (*extend, lengthen*) strecken; (*widen*) *jumper, gloves also, elastic, shoes* dehnen; (*spread*) *wings, blanket etc* ausbreiten; (*tighten*) *rope, canvas* spannen ◆ **to become ~ed** ausleiern; **a curtain was ~ed across the room** ein Vorhang war quer durchs Zimmer gezogen; **she ~ed the bedspread over the bed** sie breitete die Tagesdecke übers Bett; **to ~ sth tight** etw straffen, etw

➤ LANGUAGE IN USE: **stress: 2a** → 26.3

straffziehen; *cover* etw strammziehen; **to ~ one's legs** (*go for a walk*) sich (*dat*) die Beine vertreten (*inf*); **to ~ one's neck** den Hals recken.
(b) (*make go further*) *meal, money* strecken; (*use fully*) *resources* voll (aus)nutzen; *credit* voll beanspruchen; *athlete, student etc* fordern; *one's abilities* bis zum äußersten fordern ◆ **to be fully ~ed** (*person*) voll ausgelastet sein.
(c) (*strain*) *meaning, word* äußerst weit fassen; *truth, law, rules* es nicht so genau nehmen mit, großzügig auslegen ◆ **this clause/law could be ~ed to allow ...** diese Klausel/dieses Gesetz könnte so weit gedehnt werden, daß sie/es ... zuläßt; **to ~ a point** ein Auge zudrücken, großzügig sein; **that's ~ing it too far/a bit (far)** das geht zu weit/fast zu weit.
[4] *vi* (*after sleep etc*) sich strecken; (*person also*) sich recken; (*be elastic*) sich dehnen, dehnbar sein; (*extend: time, area, authority, influence*) sich erstrecken (*to* bis, *over* über +*acc*); (*be enough: food, money, material*) reichen (*to* für); (*become looser*) weiter werden; (*become longer*) länger werden ◆ **the rope won't ~ to that post** das Seil reicht nicht bis zu dem Pfosten (hinüber); **to ~ to reach sth** sich recken, um etw zu erreichen; **he ~ed down and touched his toes** er beugte sich nieder und berührte seine Zehen; **he ~ed across and touched her cheek** er reichte herüber und berührte ihre Wange; **to ~ back to** zurückreichen bis; **the fields ~ed away into the distance** die Felder dehnten sich bis in die Ferne aus; **the years ~ed (out) ahead of him** die Jahre dehnten sich vor ihm aus; **a life of misery ~ed (out) before her** vor ihr breitete sich ein Leben voll Kummer und Leid aus; **I can't/my purse won't ~ to that** so viel kann ich mir nicht erlauben/das läßt mein Geldbeutel nicht zu.
[5] *vr* **(a)** (*after sleep etc*) sich strecken; (*person also*) sich recken.
(b) (*strain oneself*) sich verausgaben ◆ **if only he'd ~ himself a little** wenn er sich nur etwas anstrengen würde.

◆**stretch out** [1] *vt sep arms, wings, blanket* ausbreiten; *leg, hand* ausstrecken; *foot* vorstrecken; *rope* spannen; *meeting, discussion, essay, story* ausdehnen ◆ **to ~ oneself ~ (on the ground)** sich auf den Boden legen.
[2] *vi* sich strecken; (*inf: lie down*) sich hinlegen; (*countryside*) sich ausbreiten; (*in time*) sich erstrecken, sich hinziehen (*over* über +*acc*) ◆ **her arm ~ed ~** sie streckte den Arm aus; **he ~ed ~/lay ~ed ~ on the bed** er legte sich (ausgestreckt) aufs Bett/er lag ausgestreckt auf dem Bett.

stretcher ['stretʃəʳ] *n* **(a)** (*Med*) (Trag)bahre *f*. **(b)** (*for shoes, gloves*) Spanner *m*; (*Art: for canvas*) Rahmen *m*.

◆**stretcher off** *vt sep* auf einer (Trag)bahre wegtragen *or* abtransportieren.

stretcher: ~-bearer *n* Krankenträger *m*; **~ case** *n* Kranke(r) *mf*/Verletzte(r) *mf*, der/die nicht gehen kann; (*Mil*) Schwerverwundete(r) *mf*; **by the time I've finished this work I'll be a ~ case** (*hum*) bis ich diese Arbeit fertig habe, bin ich krankenhausreif (*inf*); **~ party** *n* Team *nt* von Krankenträgern.

stretch: ~ limo *n* (*inf*) Großraumlimousine *f*; **~ mark** *n* Dehnungsstreifen *m*; (*through pregnancy*) Schwangerschaftsstreifen *m or* -narbe *f*; **~ nylon** *n* Stretchnylon, Helanca ® *nt*; (*esp for ski pants*) Lastex *nt*.

stretchy ['stretʃɪ] *adj* (+*er*) elastisch, dehnbar.

strew [struː] *pret* **~ed**, *ptp* **~ed** *or* **strewn** [struːn] *vt* (*scatter*) verstreuen; *flowers, gravel, sand* streuen; (*cover with*) *floor etc* bestreuen ◆ **to ~ one's clothes around (the room)** seine Kleider im Zimmer verstreuen; **dresses were ~n about the room** Kleider lagen im ganzen Zimmer verstreut herum; **the floor was ~n with ...** ... lagen überall auf dem Boden verstreut.

strewth *interj* (*sl*) *see* **struth**.

striated [straɪ'eɪtɪd] *adj* (*form*) (*striped*) gestreift; (*furrowed*) gefurcht; (*Geol*) mit Schliffen *or* Schrammen.

striation [straɪ'eɪʃən] *n* (*form*) (*stripes*) Streifen *pl*; (*furrows*) Furchen *pl*, Furchung *f*; (*Geol*) Schliffe, Schrammen *pl*.

stricken ['strɪkən] [1] (*old*) *ptp of* **strike**.
[2] *adj* (*liter: wounded*) verwundet; (*afflicted*) leidgeprüft, schwergeprüft *attr*, schwer geprüft *pred*; (*with grief*) schmerzerfüllt, gramgebeugt (*liter*); (*ill*) leidend (*geh*); *ship, plane* in Not ◆ **~ with guilt/fear** *etc* von Schuld/Angst *etc* erfüllt, von Angst ergriffen; **~ in years** hochbetagt (*geh*); **to be ~ with illness** leidend sein (*geh*); **to be ~ with blindness** mit Blindheit geschlagen sein (*geh*).

-stricken *adj suf* (*with emotion*) -erfüllt; (*by catastrophe*) von ... heimgesucht ◆ **panic-~** von Panik ergriffen.

strict [strɪkt] *adj* (+*er*) **(a)** (*stern, severe*) *law, parent, principles, judge etc* streng; *order, ban, discipline also* strikt; *obedience* absolut, strikt; *Catholic* strenggläubig ◆ **they're very ~ about time-keeping** es wird streng auf Pünktlichkeit geachtet.
(b) (*precise*) streng; *accuracy, neutrality, secrecy also* absolut; *translation, meaning* genau ◆ **in the ~ sense of the word** genau genommen; **in ~ confidence** streng vertraulich; **there is a ~ time limit on that** das ist zeitlich genau begrenzt.

strictly ['strɪktlɪ] *adv* **(a)** streng ◆ **smoking is ~ forbidden** Rauchen ist streng *or* strengstens verboten.
(b) (*precisely*) genau; (*absolutely*) absolut, streng ◆ **to be ~ accurate** um ganz genau zu sein; **~ in confidence** ganz im Vertrauen; **~ personal/confidential** privat/streng vertraulich; **~ speaking** genau genommen; **not ~ true** nicht ganz richtig; **~ between ourselves** ganz unter uns.

strictness ['strɪktnɪs] *n* **(a)** Strenge *f*; (*of order, discipline also*) Striktheit *f*. **(b)** (*preciseness*) Genauigkeit *f*.

stricture ['strɪktʃəʳ] *n* **(a)** *usu pl* (*criticism*) (scharfe) Kritik *no pl* ◆ **to make** *or* **pass ~s upon sb** jdn (scharf) kritisieren. **(b)** (*Med*) Verengung, Striktur (*spec*) *f*.

stride [straɪd] (*vb: pret* **strode**, *ptp* **stridden** ['strɪdn]) [1] *n* (*step*) Schritt *m*; (*gait also*) Gang *m*; (*fig*) Fortschritt *m* ◆ **to get into one's/its ~** (*fig*) in Schwung *or* in Fahrt kommen; **to take sth in one's ~** mit etw spielend fertigwerden; *exam, interview* etw spielend schaffen; **to put sb off his ~** jdn aus dem Konzept bringen; **he took the disasters in his ~** die Katastrophen schienen spurlos an ihm vorübergegangen zu sein.
[2] *vi* schreiten (*geh*), mit großen Schritten gehen ◆ **to ~ along** ausschreiten (*geh*); **to ~ away** *or* **off** sich mit schnellen Schritten entfernen, davonschreiten (*geh*); **to ~ up to sb** (mit großen Schritten) auf jdn zugehen, auf jdn zuschreiten (*geh*); **to ~ up and down** auf- und abgehen *or* -schreiten (*geh*).

stridency ['straɪdənsɪ] *n see adj* Schrillheit, Durchdringlichkeit *f*; Grellheit *f*; Streitbarkeit *f*; Schärfe *f*; Stärke *f*.

strident ['straɪdənt] *adj sound, voice* schrill, durchdringend; *colour* grell; *person* streitbar; *protest, criticism, tone* scharf; *demand, protest* lautstark.

stridently ['straɪdəntlɪ] *adv talk etc* schrill, durchdringend; *object, protest* scharf, lautstark; *demand, behave* lautstark.

strife [straɪf] *n* Unmut (*geh*), Unfriede *m*; (*in family, between friends*) Zwietracht *f* (*geh*) ◆ **armed ~** bewaffneter Konflikt; **party ~** Zwietracht *f* (*geh*) *or* Zwistigkeiten *pl* in der Partei; **internal ~** innere Kämpfe *pl*; **civil/industrial ~** Auseinandersetzungen *pl* in der Bevölkerung/Industrie; **to cease from ~** (*liter*) allen Zwist begraben (*geh*).

strike [straɪk] (*vb: pret* **struck**, *ptp* **struck** *or* (*old*) **stricken**) [1] *n* **(a)** Streik, Ausstand *m* ◆ **official/unofficial ~** offizieller/wilder Streik; **to be on ~** streiken, im Ausstand sein; **to be on official/unofficial ~** offiziell/wild streiken; **to come out** *or* **go on ~** in den Streik *or* Ausstand treten; **to bring sb out on ~** jdn zum Streik veranlassen; *see* **hunger**.
(b) (*discovery of oil, gold etc*) Fund *m* ◆ **a big oil ~** ein großer Ölfund; **to make a ~** fündig werden; **a lucky ~** ein Treffer, ein Glücksfall *m*; **to make a lucky ~** Glück haben, einen Treffer landen (*inf*).
(c) (*Baseball*) verfehlter Schlag; (*Ten-pin bowling*) Strike *m*, alle zehne ◆ **to get a ~** alle zehne werfen, abräumen (*inf*); **to have the ~** (*Cricket*) schlagen.
(d) (*Fishing*) **he got three ~s** drei haben angebissen.
(e) (*Mil: attack*) Angriff *m*.
(f) (*act of striking*) Schlag *m*.
[2] *vt* **(a)** (*hit*) schlagen; *door* schlagen an *or* gegen (+*acc*); *nail, table* schlagen auf (+*acc*); *metal, hot iron etc* hämmern; (*stone, blow, bullet etc*) treffen; (*snake*) beißen; (*pain*) durchzucken, durchfahren; (*misfortune, disaster*) treffen; (*disease*) befallen ◆ **to ~ one's fist on the table, to ~ the table with one's fist** mit der Faust auf den Tisch schlagen; **to ~ sb/sth a blow** jdm/einer Sache einen Schlag versetzen; **who struck the first blow?** wer hat zuerst (zu)geschlagen?; **to ~ a blow for sth** (*fig*) eine Lanze für etw brechen; **to ~ a blow (at sth)** (*fig*) einen Schlag (gegen etw) führen; **to be struck by lightning** vom Blitz getroffen werden; **he struck his forehead in surprise** er schlug sich (*dat*) überrascht an die Stirn; **to ~ 38 (per minute)** 38 Ruderschläge (pro Minute) machen.
(b) (*collide with, meet*) (*person*) stoßen gegen; (*spade*) stoßen auf (+*acc*); (*car*) fahren gegen; *ground* aufschlagen *or* auftreffen auf (+*acc*); (*ship*) auflaufen auf (+*acc*); (*sound, light*) *ears, eyes* treffen; (*lightning*) *person* treffen; *tree* einschlagen in (+*acc*), treffen ◆ **to ~ one's head against sth** mit dem Kopf gegen etw *or* sich (*dat*) den Kopf an etw (*acc*) stoßen; **to ~ difficulties/obstacles** (*fig*) in Schwierigkeiten geraten/auf Hindernisse stoßen; **a terrible sight struck my eyes** plötzlich sah ich etwas Schreckliches.
(c) (*sound*) *instrument* zu spielen anfangen; *string, chord, note* anschlagen; (*clock*) schlagen ◆ **to ~ the piano/guitar** in die Tasten/Saiten greifen; **to ~ the hour** die volle Stunde schlagen; **to ~ 4** 4 schlagen; **that struck a familiar note** das kam mir/ihm *etc* bekannt vor; *see* **note**.
(d) (*Hort*) *cutting* schneiden; (*plant*) *roots* schlagen.
(e) (*occur to*) in den Sinn kommen (+*dat*) ◆ **to ~ sb as cold/unlikely** *etc* jdm kalt/unwahrscheinlich *etc* vorkommen; **that ~s me as a good idea** das kommt mir sehr vernünftig vor; **has it ever struck you that ...?** (*occurred to you*) haben Sie je daran gedacht, daß ...?; (*have you noticed*) ist Ihnen je aufgefallen, daß ...?; **it ~s me that ...** (*I have the impression*) ich habe den Eindruck, daß ...; (*I am noticing*) mir fällt auf, daß ...; **it struck me how ...** (*occurred to me*) mir ging plötzlich auf, wie ...; (*I noticed*) mir fiel auf, wie ...; **the funny side of it struck me later** erst später ging mir auf, wie lustig das war; **a thought struck me** mir kam plötzlich ein Gedanke.
(f) (*impress*) beeindrucken ◆ **to be struck by sth** von etw beeindruckt sein; **how does it ~ you?** wie finden Sie das?, was halten Sie davon?; **how does she ~ you?** welchen Eindruck haben Sie von ihr?; **she struck me as being very competent** sie machte auf mich einen sehr fähigen Eindruck; *see also* **struck**.
(g) (*produce, make*) *coin, medal* prägen; (*fig*) *agreement, truce* sich einigen auf (+*acc*), aushandeln ◆ **to ~ a light/match** Feuer machen/ein Streichholz anzünden; **to ~ sparks from sth** Funken aus etw schlagen; **to be struck blind/deaf/dumb** blind/taub/stumm werden, mit Blindheit/Taubheit/Stummheit geschlagen werden (*geh*); **to ~ fear** *or* **terror into sb/sb's heart** jdn mit Angst *or* Schrecken erfüllen; **~ a light!** (*sl*) ach du grüne Neune! (*inf*), hast du da noch Töne! (*inf*).
(h) (*find*) *gold, oil, correct path* finden, stoßen auf (+*acc*) ◆ **to ~ it rich** das große Geld machen; *see* **oil**.
(i) (*make*) *path* hauen.
(j) (*take down*) *camp, tent* abbrechen; (*Naut*) *flag, sail* einholen, streichen; *mast* kappen, umlegen; (*Theat*) *set* abbauen.
(k) (*remove*) streichen ◆ **to be struck** *or* (*US*) **stricken from a list/the record** von einer Liste/aus dem Protokoll gestrichen werden.

[3] *vi* (a) (*hit*) treffen; (*lightning*) einschlagen; (*snake*) zubeißen; (*tiger*) die Beute schlagen; (*attack, Mil etc*) zuschlagen, angreifen; (*disease*) zuschlagen; (*panic*) ausbrechen ◆ **to ~ against sth** gegen etw stoßen; **to ~ at sb/sth** (*lit*) nach jdm/etw schlagen; (*fig: at democracy, existence*) an etw (*dat*) rütteln; **they struck at his weakest point** sie trafen ihn an seinem wundesten Punkt; **to ~ at the roots of sth** etw an der Wurzel treffen; **they were within striking distance of the enemy camp/success** das feindliche Lager/der Erfolg war in greifbarer Nähe; **the snake struck at me** die Schlange fuhr auf mich los; **we're waiting for the blow to ~** wir warten darauf, daß es uns trifft; *see* **home, iron.**
(b) (*clock*) schlagen ◆ **when midnight ~s** wenn es Mitternacht schlägt.
(c) (*workers*) streiken.
(d) (*match*) zünden, angehen.
(e) (*Naut: run aground*) auflaufen (*on* auf +*acc*).
(f) (*Fishing*) anbeißen.
(g) **inspiration struck** er/sie *etc* hatte eine Eingebung; **to ~ on a new idea** eine neue Idee haben, auf eine neue Idee kommen.
(h) (*take root*) Wurzeln schlagen.
(i) (*go in a certain direction*) **to ~ across country** querfeldein gehen; **to ~ into the woods** sich in die Wälder schlagen; **to ~ right/left** sich nach rechts/links wenden; (*road*) nach rechts/links abbiegen; **the sun struck through the mist** die Sonne brach durch den Dunst.

◆**strike back** [1] *vi* zurückschlagen; (*fig also*) sich wehren, sich zur Wehr setzen ◆ **to ~ ~ at sb** jds Angriff (*acc*) erwidern; (*fig*) sich gegen jdn wehren *or* zur Wehr setzen.
[2] *vt sep* zurückschlagen.

◆**strike down** *vt sep* niederschlagen; (*God*) *enemies* vernichten; (*fig*) zu Fall bringen ◆ **to be struck ~** niedergeschlagen werden; (*by illness*) getroffen werden; (*by blow*) zu Boden gestreckt werden; **he was struck ~ in his prime** er wurde in seiner Blüte dahingerafft.

◆**strike off** [1] *vt sep* (a) (*cut off*) abschlagen.
(b) (*remove*) (*from list*) (aus)streichen; *solicitor* die Lizenz entziehen (+*dat*); *doctor* die Zulassung entziehen (+*dat*); (*from price*) abziehen (*prep obj* von) ◆ **to be struck ~** (*Med, Jur*) die Zulassung verlieren.
(c) (*print*) drucken ◆ **to ~ ~ a proof** einen Bürstenabzug machen.
[2] *vi* (*set off*) sich auf den Weg machen; (*road etc also*) abbiegen.

◆**strike out** [1] *vi* (a) (*hit out*) schlagen ◆ **to ~ ~ wildly** wild um sich schlagen; **to ~ ~ at sb** (*lit, fig*) jdn angreifen.
(b) (*change direction*) zuhalten (*for, towards* auf +*acc*); (*set out*) sich aufmachen, losziehen (*inf*) (*for* zu) ◆ **to ~ ~ for home** sich auf den Heimweg machen; **to ~ ~ on one's own** (*lit*) allein losziehen; (*fig*) eigene Wege gehen; **to ~ ~ in a new direction** (*fig*) neue Wege gehen.
(c) (*Baseball*) „aus" sein.
[2] *vt sep* (aus)streichen ◆ **to ~ sth ~ of the record** etw aus dem Protokoll streichen.

◆**strike through** *vt sep* durchstreichen.

◆**strike up** [1] *vi* (*band etc*) einsetzen, anfangen (zu spielen).
[2] *vt insep* (a) (*band*) *tune* anstimmen ◆ **~ ~ the band!** Musik! (b) *friendship* schließen, anknüpfen; *conversation* anfangen.

strike: **~ action** *n* Streikmaßnahmen *pl*; **~ ballot** *n* Urabstimmung *f*; **~-bound** *adj* bestreikt, vom Streik betroffen; **~breaker** *n* Streikbrecher *m*; **~breaking** *n* Streikbruch *m*; **~ call** *n* Aufruf *m* zum Streik; **~ force** *n* (*Mil*) Kampftruppe *f*; **~ fund** *n* Streikkasse *f*; **~-leader** *n* Streikführer *m*; **~ pay** *n* Streikgeld(er *pl*) *nt*.

striker ['straɪkəʳ] *n* (a) (*worker*) Streikende(r), Ausständige(r) *mf*. (b) (*Ftbl*) Stürmer *m*.

striking ['straɪkɪŋ] *adj* (a) (*arresting*) *contrast, colour, resemblance etc* auffallend, bemerkenswert; *difference* verblüffend, erstaunlich; *appearance, beauty* eindrucksvoll ◆ **a ~ example of sth** ein hervorragendes Beispiel für etw.
(b) *attr worker* streikend.
(c) *attr clock* mit Schlagwerk ◆ **the ~ clock keeps me awake** das Schlagen der Uhr läßt mich nicht schlafen; **~ mechanism** Schlagwerk *nt*.

strikingly ['straɪkɪŋlɪ] *adv see adj (a)*.

Strimmer ['strɪməʳ] ® *n* Rasentrimmer *m*.

strine [straɪn] *n* (*hum inf*) *australisches Englisch.*

string [strɪŋ] (*vb: pret, ptp* **strung**) [1] *n* (a) (*pl rare: cord*) Schnur, Kordel *f*, Bindfaden *m*; (*on apron etc*) Band *nt*; (*on anorak, belt*) Kordel *f*; (*of puppet*) Faden *m*, Schnur *f*, Draht *m* ◆ **to have sb on a ~** (*fig inf*) jdn am Gängelband haben (*inf*); **to pull ~s** (*fig inf*) Fäden ziehen, Beziehungen spielen lassen; **without ~s, with no ~s attached** ohne Bedingungen; **a relationship with no ~s attached** eine völlig lockere Beziehung; **he wants a girlfriend but no ~s attached** er möchte eine Freundin, will sich aber in keiner Weise gebunden fühlen.
(b) (*row*) (*of beads, onions etc*) Schnur *f*; (*of racehorses etc*) Reihe *f*; (*of people*) Schlange *f*; (*of vehicles*) Kette, Schlange *f*; (*fig: series*) Reihe *f*; (*of lies, curses*) Haufen *m*, Serie *f*.
(c) (*of musical instrument, tennis racquet etc*) Saite *f*; (*of bow*) Sehne *f* ◆ **the ~s** *pl* (*instruments*) die Streichinstrumente *pl*; (*players*) die Streicher *pl*; **he plays in the ~s** er ist Streicher, er gehört zu den Streichern; **a twelve-~ guitar** eine zwölfsaitige Gitarre; **to have two ~s** *or* **a second ~** *or* **more than one ~ to one's bow** zwei Eisen im Feuer haben; **history/translating is my second ~** ich kann jederzeit auf Geschichte/Übersetzungen als zweite Möglichkeit zurückgreifen.
(d) (*Bot*) Faden *m*.
(e) (*Comput: of characters*) Zeichenfolge *f*.
[2] *vt* (a) (*put on ~*) aufreihen, auffädeln, aufziehen ◆ **to ~ objects/sentences** *etc* **together** Gegenstände zusammenbinden *or* -schnüren/Sätze *etc* aneinanderreihen; **she can't even ~ two sentences together** sie bringt keinen vernünftigen Satz zusammen; **she can't ~ her thoughts together coherently** sie ist unfähig, zusammenhängend zu denken.
(b) *violin etc, tennis racquet* (mit Saiten) bespannen, besaiten; *bow* spannen; *see* **highly-strung.**
(c) *beans* abfasern, (die) Fäden (+*gen*) abziehen.
(d) (*space out*) aufreihen ◆ **they strung lights in the trees** sie haben Lampen in die Bäume gehängt.

◆**string along** (*inf*) [1] *vt sep* **to ~ sb ~** jdn hinhalten.
[2] *vi* (*go along, play along with*) sich anschließen (*with dat*).

◆**string out** [1] *vi* sich verteilen ◆ **the children strung ~ behind the teacher** die Kinder gingen in weiten Abständen hinter dem Lehrer her.
[2] *vt sep lanterns, washing* aufhängen; *guards, posts* verteilen.

◆**string up** *vt sep* (a) (*suspend with string*) aufhängen; (*inf: hang*) aufknüpfen (*inf*). (b) *see* **strung-up.**

string: **~ bag** *n* (*esp Brit*) Einkaufsnetz *nt*; **~ band** *n* Streichorchester *nt*; **~ bass** *n* Kontrabaß *m*; **~ bean** *n* (*esp US*) (*bean*) grüne Bohne; (*fig: person*) Bohnenstange *f* (*hum inf*).

stringed [strɪŋd] *adj instrument* Saiten-; (*played with bow also*) Streich-.

stringency ['strɪndʒənsɪ] *n see adj* Strenge *f*; Härte *f*; Schärfe *f* ◆ **economic ~** strenge Sparmaßnahmen *pl*.

stringent ['strɪndʒənt] *adj standards, laws, discipline* streng; *rules, testing, training etc also* hart; *measures also* schärfste(r, s), energisch; *market* gedrückt ◆ **~ economies** schärfste Sparmaßnahmen *pl*; **they have to practise ~ economy** sie müssen eisern sparen.

stringently ['strɪndʒəntlɪ] *adv control* streng; *enforce, train also* hart; *deal with* schärfstens, energisch; *economize* eisern.

stringer ['strɪŋəʳ] *n* (*Press sl*) Lokalreporter(in *f*) *m*.

string: **~ instrument** *n* Saiteninstrument *nt*; (*played with bow also*) Streichinstrument *nt*; **~ player** *n* Streicher(in *f*) *m*; **~-puller** *n* Drahtzieher *m*; **~-pulling** *n* Spielenlassen *nt* von Beziehungen; **~ quartet** *n* Streichquartett *nt*; **~ vest** *n* Netzhemd *nt*.

stringy ['strɪŋɪ] *adj* (+*er*) *meat* sehnig, zäh, faserig; *vegetable* faserig, voller Fäden; *person* sehnig; *plant, seaweed, root* lang und dünn.

strip [strɪp] [1] *n* (a) (*narrow piece*) Streifen *m*; (*of land also*) (schmales) Stück; (*of metal*) Band *nt*; *see* **comic, tear off.**
(b) (*Brit Sport*) Trikot *nt*, Dreß *m*.
(c) (*inf: air~*) Start- und Lande-Bahn, Piste (*inf*) *f*.
(d) (*inf: ~tease*) **to do a ~** strippen (*inf*).
[2] *vt* (a) (*remove clothes etc from*) *person* ausziehen; *bed* abziehen; *wall* (*remove paint from*) abkratzen; (*remove paper from*) die Tapeten abziehen von; *wallpaper* abziehen; (*remove contents from*) ausräumen ◆ **to ~ sb naked** *or* **to the skin** jdn bis auf die Haut *or* nackt ausziehen; **to ~ a house of its contents** ein Haus ausräumen; **to ~ a room of all its pictures** alle Bilder aus einem Zimmer entfernen; **to ~ sth from** *or* **off sth** etw von etw entfernen; **to ~ a tree of fruit, to ~ the fruit off** *or* **from a tree** einen Baum abernten; **the wind ~ped the leaves from** *or* **off the trees** der Wind wehte die Blätter von den Bäumen; **to ~ the bark from the trees** Bäume schälen *or* entrinden; **to ~ sth away** (*lit, fig*) etw wegnehmen, etw entfernen; **~ped of sth** ohne etw; **~ped of official language, this means ...** in einfachen Worten heißt das ...
(b) (*fig: deprive of*) berauben (*of gen*); *honours, title also* entkleiden (*geh*) (*of gen*) ◆ **he was ~ped of his titles** seine Titel wurden ihm aberkannt.
(c) (*Tech*) (*damage*) *gear* kaputtmachen (*inf*), beschädigen; *screw* überdrehen; (*dismantle*) *engine, car, gun* auseinandernehmen, zerlegen ◆ **to ~ the thread (off a screw)** eine Schraube überdrehen.
[3] *vi* (*remove clothes*) sich ausziehen; (*at doctor's*) sich freimachen; (*perform ~tease*) strippen (*inf*) ◆ **to ~ naked** sich bis auf die Haut *or* ganz ausziehen; **to ~ to the waist** den Oberkörper freimachen; **~ped to the waist** mit nacktem Oberkörper.

◆**strip down** *vt sep engine* auseinandernehmen, zerlegen.

◆**strip off** [1] *vt sep clothes* ausziehen; *berries, leaves* abmachen (*prep obj* von); (*wind*) herunterwehen (*prep obj* von); *paper* abziehen (*prep obj* von); *buttons, ornaments* entfernen, abmachen (*prep obj* von); *fruit skin, bark* abschälen, ablösen (*prep obj* von) ◆ **to ~ ~ the branches** die Blätter vom Zweig entfernen; die Äste entfernen.
[2] *vi* (a) (*take one's clothes off*) sich ausziehen; (*at doctor's*) sich freimachen; (*in striptease*) strippen (*inf*). (b) (*bark*) sich abschälen lassen; (*paper*) sich abziehen lassen.

strip: **~ cartoon** *n* Comic(strip) *m*; **~ club** *n* Striptease-Club *m*; **~ cropping** *n* Streifenpflanzung *f*.

stripe [straɪp] *n* (a) Streifen *m*.
(b) (*Mil*) (Ärmel)streifen, Winkel *m* ◆ **to gain** *or* **get/lose one's ~s** befördert/degradiert werden.
(c) (*old: stroke*) Schlag, Hieb *m*.
(d) (*US: kind*) (*of politics*) Färbung, Richtung *f*; (*of character, opinion*) Art *f*, Schlag *m*.
(e) **~s** *pl* (*US inf: prison uniform*) Sträflingsanzug *m* (*inf*).

striped [straɪpt] *adj* gestreift, Streifen- ◆ **~ with ...** mit ... Streifen; **to be ~ with grey** graue Streifen haben, grau gestreift sein.

strip: **~ light** *n* (*esp Brit*) Neonröhre *f*; **~ lighting** *n* (*esp Brit*) Neonlicht *nt or* -beleuchtung *f*.

stripling ['strɪplɪŋ] *n* (*liter*) Bürschchen *nt*; (*pej also*) Grünschnabel *m*.

strip: **~ mill** *n* Walzwerk *nt*; **~ mining** *n* (*esp US*) Abbau *m* über Tage.

strippagram ['strɪpəgræm] *n durch eine Angestellte einer Agentur persönlich übermittelter Geburtstagsgruß etc mit Striptease.*

stripper ['strɪpəʳ] *n* **(a)** *(performer)* Stripperin, Stripteasetänzerin *f* ◆ **male ~** Stripper, Stripteasetänzer *m.* **(b)** *(paint-~)* Farbentferner *m;* *(wallpaper ~)* Tapetenlöser *m.*

strip: ~ poker *n* Strip-Poker *nt;* **~-search** [1] *n* Leibesvisitation *f;* [2] *vt* einer Leibesvisitation *(dat)* unterziehen; **he was ~-searched** er mußte sich einer Leibesvisitation unterziehen; **~ show** *n* Striptease(schau *or* -show *f*) *m or nt;* **~tease** [1] *n* Striptease *m or nt;* **to do a ~tease** strippen *(inf)*, einen Striptease machen; [2] *adj attr* Striptease-.

stripy ['straɪpɪ] *adj (+er) (inf)* gestreift.

strive [straɪv] *pret* **strove,** *ptp* **striven** ['strɪvn] *vi (exert oneself)* sich bemühen; *(fight)* kämpfen ◆ **to ~ to do sth** bestrebt *or* bemüht sein, etw zu tun; **to ~ for** *or (old)* **after sth** etw anstreben, nach etw streben; **to ~ against sth** gegen etw (an)kämpfen; **to ~ with sb/sth** mit jdm/etw ringen *or* kämpfen.

strobe [strəʊb] [1] *adj* stroboskopisch.
[2] *n* stroboskopische Beleuchtung.

stroboscope ['strəʊbəskəʊp] *n* Stroboskop *nt.*

stroboscopic [ˌstrəʊbəʊ'skɒpɪk] *adj* stroboskopisch.

strode [strəʊd] *pret of* **stride.**

stroke [strəʊk] [1] *n* **(a)** *(blow)* Schlag, Hieb *m;* *(of sword also)* Streich *m (old)* ◆ **a ~ of lightning** ein Blitz(schlag) *m.*
(b) *(Cricket, Golf, Rowing, Tennis)* Schlag *m;* *(Billiards)* Stoß *m;* *(Swimming)* *(movement)* Zug *m;* *(type of ~)* Stil *m* ◆ **they are rowing (at) a fast ~** sie rudern mit hoher Schlagzahl; **to put sb off his ~** *(fig)* jdn aus dem Takt *or* Konzept bringen.
(c) *(Rowing: person)* Schlagmann *m.*
(d) *(of pen, brush etc)* Strich *m;* *(fig) (of work)* Schlag *m;* *(in diplomacy, business)* Schachzug *m* ◆ **he doesn't do a ~ (of work)** er tut keinen Schlag *(inf)*, er rührt keinen Finger *(inf);* **a ~ of genius** ein genialer Einfall; **a ~ of luck** ein Glücksfall *m;* **we had a ~ of luck** wir hatten Glück; **with one ~ of the pen** *(lit, fig)* mit einem Federstrich; **at a** *or* **one ~** mit einem Schlag.
(e) *(of clock)* Schlag *m* ◆ **on the ~ of twelve** Punkt zwölf (Uhr).
(f) *(of piston)* Hub *m* ◆ **two-~ engine** Zweitaktmotor *m.*
(g) *(Med)* Schlag *m* ◆ **to have a ~** einen Schlag(anfall) bekommen.
(h) *(caress)* Streicheln *nt no pl* ◆ **to give sb/sth a ~** jdn/etw streicheln; **with gentle ~s** mit sanftem Streicheln.
[2] *vt* **(a)** streicheln ◆ **he ~d his chin** er strich sich *(dat)* übers Kinn; **to ~ one's hair down** sich *(dat)* das Haar glattstreichen.
(b) to ~ a boat (to victory) als Schlagmann (ein Boot zum Sieg) rudern.

stroke play *n (Golf)* Zählspiel *nt.*

stroll [strəʊl] [1] *n* Spaziergang, Bummel *m* ◆ **to go for** *or* **have** *or* **take a ~** einen Spaziergang *or* Bummel machen.
[2] *vi* spazieren, bummeln ◆ **to ~ along/around** herumspazieren *or* -bummeln *or* -schlendern; **to ~ along the road** die Straße entlangspazieren *or* -bummeln *or* -schlendern; **to ~ around the house/town** um das Haus herumspazieren/durch die Stadt bummeln; **to ~ up to sb** auf jdn zuschlendern; **to ~ in(to the room)** (ins Zimmer) herein-/hineinspazieren *or* -schlendern; **to ~ out (of the room)** (aus dem Zimmer) hinaus-/herausspazieren *or* -schlendern; **to ~ up and down (the road)** die Straße auf und ab spazieren *or* bummeln *or* schlendern.

stroller ['strəʊləʳ] *n* **(a)** *(walker)* Spaziergänger(in *f*) *m.* **(b)** *(esp US: push-chair)* Sportwagen *m.*

strolling ['strəʊlɪŋ] *adj attr actor, minstrel* fahrend.

strong [strɒŋ] [1] *adj (+er)* **(a)** stark; *(physically) person, material, kick, hands, grip also, voice* kräftig; *table, bolt, nail, wall* stabil, solide; *shoes* fest; *(strongly marked) features* ausgeprägt ◆ **you need a ~ stomach to be a nurse** als Krankenschwester muß man allerhand verkraften können.
(b) *(healthy)* kräftig; *person, constitution also* robust; *teeth also, eyes, eyesight, heart, nerves* gut ◆ **when you're ~ again** wenn Sie wieder bei Kräften sind; **he's getting ~er every day** er wird mit jedem Tag wieder kräftiger.
(c) *(powerful, effective)* stark; *character, conviction, views* fest; *country* mächtig; *candidate, case* aussichtsreich; *influence, temptation* groß, stark; *reason, argument, evidence* überzeugend; *protest, plea* energisch; *measure* drastisch; *letter* geharnischt, in starken Worten abgefaßt; *(Liter) plot, sequence, passage* gut, stark *(sl)* ◆ **to have ~ feelings/views about sth** in bezug auf etw *(acc)* stark engagiert sein; **I didn't know you had such ~ feelings about it** ich habe nicht gewußt, daß Ihnen so viel daran liegt *or* daß Ihnen das so viel bedeutet; *(against it)* ich habe nicht gewußt, daß Sie so dagegen sind; **she has very ~ feelings about him** sie hat sehr viel für ihn übrig; *(as candidate etc)* sie hält sehr viel von ihm; *(against him)* sie ist vollkommen gegen ihn; **to have ~ feelings for** *or* **about sth** eine starke Bindung an etw *(acc)* haben; **he rules with a ~ hand** er regiert mit starker Hand; **his ~ point** seine Stärke; **to protest in ~ terms** energisch protestieren; **I had a ~ sense of déjà-vu** ich hatte ganz den Eindruck, das schon einmal gesehen zu haben.
(d) *(in numbers)* stark ◆ **a group 20 ~** eine 20 Mann starke Gruppe.
(e) *(capable)* gut, stark *(inf)* ◆ **he is ~ in/on sth** etw ist seine Stärke *or* starke Seite.
(f) *(enthusiastic, committed)* begeistert; *supporter, Catholic, socialist* überzeugt; *belief, faith* unerschütterlich, stark ◆ **he's very ~ for Smith** *(inf)* er ist (ein) Smith-Fan *(inf)*.
(g) *food* deftig; *smell, perfume etc* stark; *(pungent, unpleasant) smell, taste* streng; *(of butter)* ranzig; *colour, light* kräftig; *acid, bleach* stark; *solution* konzentriert ◆ **~ breath** *(euph)* schlechter Atem, Mundgeruch *m;* **a ~ drink/whisky** ein harter Drink/ein starker Whisky; **~ meat** *(fig)* starker Tobak *(inf)*.
(h) *accent, verb, rhyme* stark; *syllable etc* betont.
(i) *(Fin) market, economy* gesund; *price* stabil; *currency also* stark.
[2] *adv (+er)* **(a)** *(inf)* **to be going ~** *(old person, thing)* gut in Schuß sein *(inf)*; *(runner)* gut in Form sein; *(party, rehearsals)* in Schwung sein *(inf)*; **that's coming** *or* **going it a bit ~!** das ist ein starkes Stück!; **he pitched it pretty ~** *(inf)* er drückte sich ziemlich drastisch aus.
(b) *(Fin)* in einer starken Position.

strong: ~-arm *(inf)* [1] *adj tactics etc* brutal, Gewalt-; **~-arm man** Schläger *m;* [2] *vt (esp US) (beat up)* zusammenschlagen; *(intimidate)* unter Druck setzen; **they were ~-armed into paying** sie wurden so unter Druck gesetzt, daß sie zahlten; **~-box** *n* (Geld)kassette *f;* **~ breeze** *n (Met)* starke Winde *pl,* Windstärke 6; **~ gale** *n (Met)* Windstärke 9; **~hold** *n (castle, fortress)* Festung *f;* *(town etc)* Stützpunkt *m;* *(fig)* Hochburg *f.*

strongly ['strɒŋlɪ] *adv* **(a)** *(physically)* stark; *kick, grip, shine* kräftig; *fight, attack* heftig, energisch; *built, made* solide, stabil; *built (person)* kräftig; *marked* stark.
(b) *(mentally) influence, suspect, tempt* stark; *desire also* heftig; *interest also* brennend; *believe* fest ◆ **to feel ~ about sb/sth** *see* **strong 1 (c).**
(c) *(powerfully)* stark; *protest, defend* heftig, energisch; *plead* inständig; *support* kräftig; *sense* zutiefst; *answer, worded* in starken Worten ◆ **he spoke ~ against it** er sprach sich entschieden dagegen aus; **I ~ advise you ...** ich möchte Ihnen dringend(st) raten ...

strongman ['strɒŋmæn] *n, pl* **-men** [-men] *(lit, fig)* starker Mann.

strong-minded *adj,* **~ly** *adv* ['strɒŋ'maɪndɪd, -lɪ] willensstark.

strong-mindedness ['strɒŋ'maɪndɪdnɪs] *n* Willensstärke *f.*

strong: ~ point *n* Stärke *f;* **~room** *n* Tresorraum *m,* Stahlkammer *f;* **~-willed** ['strɒŋ'wɪld] *adj* willensstark, entschlossen; *(pej)* eigensinnig, trotzig.

strontium ['strɒntɪəm] *n* Strontium *nt.*

strop [strɒp] [1] *n* Streichriemen *m.*
[2] *vt* abziehen.

strophe ['strəʊfɪ] *n* Strophe *f.*

stroppiness ['strɒpɪnɪs] *n (Brit inf) see adj* Fuchtigkeit *f (inf);* Pampigkeit *f (inf);* Aggressivität *f;* Sturheit *f.*

stroppy ['strɒpɪ] *adj (+er) (Brit inf)* fuchtig *(inf); answer, children* pampig *(inf);* *bouncer etc* aggressiv; *(obstinate) official* stur ◆ **to be ~ about doing sth** fuchtig/pampig sein, weil man etw tun soll *(inf);* **don't get ~ with me** *(aggressive)* werd jetzt nicht pampig *(inf);* *(obstinate, uncooperative)* mach nicht so auf stur *(inf)*.

strove [strəʊv] *pret of* **strive.**

struck [strʌk] [1] *pret, ptp of* **strike.**
[2] *adj* **(a)** *pred* **to be ~ with sb/sth** *(impressed)* von jdm/etw begeistert *or* angetan sein; **I wasn't very ~ with him** er hat keinen großen Eindruck auf mich gemacht; **to be ~ on sb/sth** *(keen)* auf jdn/etw stehen *(inf)*, auf jdn/etw versessen sein.
(b) *(US attr) (striking) workers* streikend; *factory, employers* vom Streik betroffen, bestreikt.

structural ['strʌktʃərəl] *adj* **(a)** *(relating to structure)* strukturell; *(of building) alterations, damage, requirements* baulich; *fault, defect* Konstruktions-; *material, element, part* Bau-; *weight* Konstruktions-; *(fig)* Struktur- ◆ **the bridge suffered ~ damage** die Struktur der Brücke wurde beschädigt.
(b) *(weight-bearing) wall, beam* tragend; *(fig: essential)* essentiell, notwendig.

structural: ~ engineering *n* Bautechnik *f;* **~ formula** *n (Chem)* Strukturformel *f.*

structuralism ['strʌktʃərəlɪzəm] *n* der Strukturalismus.

structuralist ['strʌktʃərəlɪst] [1] *n* Strukturalist(in *f*) *m.*
[2] *adj attr* strukturalistisch.

structurally ['strʌktʃərəlɪ] *adv* strukturell ◆ **~ the novel is excellent** vom Aufbau her ist der Roman ausgezeichnet; **~ sound** sicher; **~ the building is in good condition** was das rein Bauliche betrifft, ist das Haus in gutem Zustand.

structure ['strʌktʃəʳ] [1] *n* **(a)** *(organization)* Struktur *f;* *(Sociol also)* Aufbau *m;* *(Ling also)* Bau *m;* *(Liter)* Aufbau *m;* *(Tech: of bridge, car etc)* Konstruktion *f* ◆ **bone ~** Knochenbau *m.* **(b)** *(thing constructed)* Konstruktion *f;* *(building also)* Gebäude *nt.*
[2] *vt* strukturieren; *essay, argument* aufbauen, gliedern; *layout, life* gestalten ◆ **highly ~d** *society* stark gegliedert; *novel etc* sorgfältig (auf)gebaut *or* gegliedert.

strudel ['ʃtru:dl] *n (esp US)* Strudel *m.*

struggle ['strʌgl] [1] *n (lit, fig)* Kampf *m (for* um); *(fig: effort)* Anstrengung *f* ◆ **without a ~** kampflos; **to put up a ~** sich wehren; **the ~ for survival/existence/to feed her seven children** der Überlebenskampf/der Daseinskampf/der Kampf, ihre sieben Kinder zu ernähren; **the ~ to find somewhere to live** der Kampf *or* die Schwierigkeiten, bis man eine Wohnung gefunden hat; **it is/was a ~** es ist/war mühsam; **she finds life a ~** sie findet das Leben mühsam; **I had a ~ to persuade him** es war gar nicht einfach, ihn zu überreden.
[2] *vi* **(a)** *(contend)* kämpfen; *(in self-defence)* sich wehren; *(writhe)* sich winden; *(financially)* in Schwierigkeiten sein, krebsen *(inf); (fig: strive)* sich sehr bemühen *or* anstrengen, sich abmühen ◆ **the police were struggling with the burglar** zwischen der Polizei und dem Einbrecher gab es ein Handgemenge; **to ~ to do sth** sich sehr anstrengen, etw zu tun; **to ~ for sth** um etw kämpfen, sich um etw bemühen; **to ~ against sb/sth** gegen jdn/etw kämpfen; **to ~ with sb** mit jdm kämpfen; **to ~ with sth** *with problem, difficulty* sich mit etw herumschlagen; *with language, subject, homework* sich

mit etw abmühen; *with doubts, one's conscience* mit etw ringen; **are you struggling?** hast du Schwierigkeiten?; **can you manage? — I'm struggling** schaffst du's? — mit Müh und Not; **he was struggling to make ends meet** er hatte seine liebe Not durchzukommen.
(b) (*move with difficulty*) sich quälen ◆ **to ~ to one's feet** mühsam aufstehen *or* auf die Beine kommen, sich aufrappeln (*inf*); **to ~ to get up** sich hochquälen; **he ~d through the tiny window** er zwängte sich durch das kleine Fenster; **to ~ on** (*lit*) sich weiterkämpfen; (*fig*) weiterkämpfen; **to ~ along/through** (*lit, fig*) sich durchschlagen *or* -kämpfen.

struggling ['strʌglɪŋ] *adj artist etc* am Hungertuch nagend.

strum [strʌm] 1 *vt tune* klimpern; *guitar* klimpern auf (+*dat*) ◆ **to ~ out a song** ein Liedchen klimpern.
2 *vi* klimpern (*on* auf +*dat*).

strumpet ['strʌmpɪt] *n* (*old*) Hure, Dirne *f*.

strung [strʌŋ] *pret, ptp of* **string**.

strung-up [ˌstrʌŋ'ʌp] *adj* **to be ~** nervös *or* gespannt sein (*about sth* wegen etw).

strut¹ [strʌt] 1 *vi* stolzieren ◆ **to ~ about (the yard)** (auf dem Hof) herumstolzieren; **to ~ past** vorbeistolzieren.
2 *n* angeberischer Gang, Stolzieren *nt* ◆ **to walk with a ~** stolzieren.

strut² *n* (*horizontal*) Strebe *f*; (*sloping also*) Stütze *f*; (*vertical*) Pfeiler *m*.

struth [stru:θ] *interj* (*sl*) heiliger Strohsack (*inf*).

strychnine ['strɪkni:n] *n* Strychnin *nt*.

stub [stʌb] 1 *n* (*of candle, pencil, tail*) Stummel *m*; (*of cigarette also*) Kippe *f*; (*of cheque, ticket*) Abschnitt *m*; (*of tree*) Stumpf *m* ◆ **~-axle** Achsschenkel *m*.
2 *vt* **to ~ one's toe (on** *or* **against sth)** sich (*dat*) den Zeh (an etw *dat*) stoßen, mit dem Zeh an *or* gegen etw (*acc*) stoßen; **to ~ out a cigarette** eine Zigarette ausdrücken.

stubble ['stʌbl] *n, no pl* Stoppeln *pl* ◆ **a field of ~** ein Stoppelfeld *nt*.

stubbly ['stʌblɪ] *adj* (+*er*) *field* Stoppel-; *chin, beard also* stoppelig.

stubborn ['stʌbən] *adj* (**a**) (*obstinate*) *person, insistence* stur; *animal also, child* störrisch ◆ **to be ~ about sth** stur auf etw (*dat*) beharren. (**b**) *refusal, resistance, campaign etc* hartnäckig. (**c**) *lock, material* widerspenstig; *weeds, cough* hartnäckig.

stubbornly ['stʌbənlɪ] *adv see adj*.

stubbornness ['stʌbənnɪs] *n see adj* (**a**) Sturheit *f*; störrische Art. (**b**) Hartnäckigkeit *f*. (**c**) Widerspenstigkeit *f*; Hartnäckigkeit *f*.

stubby ['stʌbɪ] *adj* (+*er*) *revolver etc* kurz; *tail* stummelig; *pencil, vase* kurz und dick; *person* gedrungen, stämmig, untersetzt; *legs* kurz und stämmig ◆ **~ fingers** Wurstfinger *pl* (*inf*).

stucco ['stʌkəʊ] 1 *n, pl* **-(e)s** Stuck *m*; (*also* **~ work**) Stuckarbeit, Stukkatur *f*.
2 *adj attr* Stuck-.
3 *vt* mit Stuck verzieren.

stuck [stʌk] 1 *pret, ptp of* **stick²**.
2 *adj* (**a**) (*baffled*) (*on, over* mit) **to be ~** nicht klarkommen, nicht zurechtkommen; **to get ~** nicht weiterkommen.
(**b**) (*inf*) **he/she is ~ for sth** es fehlt ihm/ihr an etw (*dat*), ihm/ihr fehlt etw; **I'm a bit ~ for cash** ich bin ein bißchen knapp bei Kasse; **he wasn't exactly ~ for something to say** man kann nicht gerade sagen, daß ihm der Gesprächsstoff fehlte.
(**c**) (*inf*) **to get ~ into sb/sth** jdn richtig in die Mangel nehmen (*inf*)/sich in etw (*acc*) richtig reinknien (*inf*); **Stephen got ~ into his steak** Stephen nahm sein Steak in Angriff; **get ~ in!** schlagt zu! (*inf*).
(**d**) (*inf: infatuated*) **to be ~ on sb** in jdn verknallt sein (*inf*).
(**e**) (*inf*) **to be ~ with sb/sth** mit jdm/etw dasitzen, jdn/etw am Hals haben (*inf*).

stuck-up ['stʌk'ʌp] *adj* (*inf*) *person, attitude, voice* hochnäsig ◆ **to be ~ about sth** sich (*dat*) viel auf etw (*acc*) einbilden.

stud¹ [stʌd] 1 *n* (**a**) (*nail*) Beschlagnagel *m*; (*decorative*) Ziernagel *m*; (*on boots*) Stollen *m* ◆ **reflector ~** Katzenauge *nt*. (**b**) (*collar* **~**) Kragenknopf *m*. (**c**) (*earring*) Ohrstecker *m*.
2 *vt* (*usu pass*) übersäen; (*with jewels*) (dicht) besetzen ◆ **their family tree is ~ded with generals** in ihrem Stammbaum wimmelt es von Generälen.

stud² *n* (*group of horses*) (*for breeding*) Gestüt *nt*, Zucht *f*; (*for racing etc*) Stall *m*; (*stallion*) (Zucht)hengst *m*; (*sl: man*) Sexprotz *m* (*inf*) ◆ **the stallion is at ~** der Hengst wird zur Zucht benutzt; **to put to ~** zu Zuchtzwecken verwenden.

stud-book ['stʌdbʊk] *n* Gestüt- *or* Zuchtbuch *nt*.

student ['stju:dənt] 1 *n* (*Univ*) Student(in *f*) *m*, Studierende(r) *mf*; (*esp US: at school, night school*) Schüler(in *f*) *m* ◆ **he is a ~ of French life/human nature** er studiert die französische Lebensart/die menschliche Natur; **he is a ~ of French** *or* **a French ~** (*Univ*) er studiert Französisch; (*Sch*) er lernt Französisch; **medical/law ~s** Medizin-/Jurastudenten *pl*.
2 *adj attr* Studenten-; *activities also, protest movement* studentisch ◆ **~ driver** (*US*) Fahrschüler(in *f*) *m*; **~ nurse** Krankenpflegeschüler(in *f*) *m*.

student: ~ship *n* (*Brit: grant*) Stipendium *nt*; **~ teacher** *n* Referendar(in *f*) *m*; **~ union** *n* (**a**) (*organization*) Studentenvereinigung *f*; (*political also*) Studentenbund *m*; (**b**) (*building*) Gebäude *nt* der Studentenvereinigung/des Studentenbundes.

stud: ~ farm *n* Gestüt *nt*; **~ horse** *n* Zuchthengst *m*.

studied ['stʌdɪd] 1 *pret, ptp of* **study**.
2 *adj* (*carefully considered*) *reply* (gut) durchdacht, wohlüberlegt; *simplicity* bewußt, ausgesucht; *prose, style* kunstvoll; (*deliberate*) berechnet; *calm, politeness* gewollt; *insult* beabsichtigt, bewußt; *avoidance* sorgfältig; *pose* einstudiert.

studio ['stju:dɪəʊ] *n* (*all senses*) Studio *nt*; (*of painter, photographer also*) Atelier *nt*; (*broadcasting* **~** *also*) Senderaum *m*.

studio: ~ apartment *n* Studiowohnung *f*; **~ audience** *n* Publikum *nt* im Studio; **~ couch** *n* Schlafcouch *f*; **~ flat** *n* (*Brit*) *see* **~ apartment**.

studious ['stju:dɪəs] *adj person* fleißig, eifrig; *life, habits* gelehrsam; *pupil also, turn of mind* lernbegierig; *attention, piece of work, research* gewissenhaft, sorgfältig; *avoidance* gezielt, sorgsam; *politeness* bewußt; *effort* eifrig, beflissen (*geh*) ◆ **a ~ atmosphere** eine eifrige Lernatmosphäre.

studiously ['stju:dɪəslɪ] *adv* fleißig, eifrig; (*painstakingly*) sorgsam, sorgfältig; *polite* bewußt; *avoid* gezielt, sorgsam; (*deliberate*) absichtlich, bewußt ◆ **he is not ~ inclined** er hat keinen Hang zum Studieren.

studiousness ['stju:dɪəsnɪs] *n see adj* Lerneifer, Fleiß *m*; Gelehrsamkeit *f*; Lernbegierde *f*; Gewissenhaftigkeit, Sorgfältigkeit *f*; Gezieltheit *f*; Bewußtheit *f*; Eifer *m*.

▼ **study** ['stʌdɪ] 1 *n* (**a**) (*studying, branch of* **~**) (*esp Univ*) Studium *nt*; (*at school*) Lernen *nt*; (*of situation, evidence, case*) Untersuchung *f*; (*of nature*) Beobachtung *f* ◆ **the ~ of cancer** die Krebsforschung; **the ~ of Chinese** das Chinesischstudium; **African studies** (*Univ*) afrikanische Sprache und Kultur, Afrikanistik *f*; **to make a ~ of sth** etw untersuchen; (*academic*) etw studieren; **to spend one's time in ~** seine Zeit mit Studieren/Lernen verbringen; **fond of ~** lernbegierig; **during my studies** während meines Studiums; **his face was a ~** (*inf*) sein Gesicht war sehenswert; *see* **brown ~**.
▼ (**b**) (*piece of work*) Studie *f* (*of* über +*acc*); (*Art, Phot*) Studie *f* (*of gen*); (*Liter, Sociol also*) Untersuchung *f* (*of* über +*acc*); (*Mus*) Etüde *f*.
(**c**) (*room*) Arbeits- *or* Studierzimmer *nt*.
2 *vt* studieren; (*Sch*) lernen; *nature also, stars* beobachten; *author, particular tune, text etc* sich befassen mit; (*research into*) erforschen; (*examine also*) untersuchen; *clue, evidence* prüfen, untersuchen.
3 *vi* studieren; (*esp Sch*) lernen ◆ **to ~ to be a teacher/doctor** ein Lehrerstudium/Medizinstudium machen; **to ~ for an exam** sich auf eine Prüfung vorbereiten, für eine Prüfung lernen; **to ~ under sb** bei jdm studieren.

study: ~ group *n* Arbeitsgruppe *or* -gemeinschaft *f*; **~ tour** *n* Informationsreise *f*; **~ visit** *n* Studienreise *f*.

stuff [stʌf] 1 *n* (**a**) Zeug *nt* ◆ **green/sweet** *etc* **~** Grünzeug *nt*/süßes *etc* Zeug; **the ~ that heroes/dreams are made of** der Stoff, aus dem Helden gemacht sind/die Träume sind; **the ~ of tragedy** echte Tragik; **show him what kind of ~ you're made of** zeig ihm, aus welchem Holz du geschnitzt bist; **there was a lot of rough ~** es ging ziemlich rauh zu; **there is some good ~ in that book** in dem Buch stecken ein paar gute Sachen; **it's poor/good ~** das ist schlecht/gut; **this tea/book is strong ~** der Tee ist ziemlich stark/das Buch ist starker Tobak; **I can't read his ~** ich kann sein Zeug nicht lesen; **his later ~ is less original** seine späteren Sachen sind weniger originell; **he brought me some ~ to read/to pass the time with** er hat mir etwas zum Lesen/zur Unterhaltung mitgebracht; **books and ~** Bücher und so (*inf*); **and ~ like that** und so was (*inf*); **all that ~ about how he wants to help us** all das Gerede, daß er uns helfen will; **~ and nonsense** Quatsch (*inf*), Blödsinn *m*; **all this ~ about Father Christmas** (*inf*) all der Quatsch vom Weihnachtsmann (*inf*).
(**b**) (*inf*) **she's a nice bit of ~** die ist nicht ohne (*inf*); **a drop of the hard ~** ein Schluck von dem scharfen Zeug; **that's the ~!** so ist's richtig!, weiter so!; **to do one's ~** seine Nummer abziehen (*inf*); **go on, do your ~!** nun mach mal *or* doch! (*inf*); **he did his ~ well** er hat seine Sache gut gemacht; **to know one's ~** wissen, wovon man redet, sich auskennen; *see* **hot ~**.
(**c**) (*possessions*) Zeug *nt*, Sachen *pl*.
(**d**) (*inf: drugs*) Stoff *m* (*inf*).
(**e**) (*old: cloth*) Material *nt*, Stoff *m*.
2 *vt* (**a**) (*fill*) *container, room, person* vollstopfen; *hole* zustopfen, verstopfen; *contents, object, books* (hinein)stopfen (*into* in +*acc*); (*into envelope*) stecken (*into* in +*acc*) ◆ **to ~ a person with food** jdn mit Essen vollstopfen, jdn mästen (*inf*); **to ~ sth away** etw wegstecken; **he ~ed it away in his pocket** er stopfte es in seine Tasche; **he ~ed some money into my hand** er drückte mir Geld in die Hand; **to ~ one's fingers into one's ears** sich (*dat*) die Finger in die Ohren stecken; **to be ~ed up (with a cold)** verschnupft sein, eine verstopfte Nase haben; **my nose is ~ed up** ich habe eine verstopfte Nase.
(**b**) (*Cook*) füllen.
(**c**) *cushion etc* füllen; *toy also* (aus)stopfen; (*in taxidermy*) ausstopfen ◆ **a ~ed toy** ein Stofftier *nt*.
(**d**) (*sl*) **~ it** (*be quiet*) halt's Maul!, Schnauze! (*sl*); **get ~ed!** du kannst mich mal (*sl*)!; **I told him to ~ it** *or* **to get ~ed** ich habe ihm gesagt, er kann mich mal (*sl*); **you can ~ your money/advice** *etc* du kannst dein blödes Geld *etc* behalten (*inf*)/du kannst dir deinen Rat schenken *or* an den Hut stecken (*inf*); **~ him!** der kann mich mal! (*sl*).
3 *vi* (*inf: eat*) sich vollstopfen (*inf*).
4 *vr* **to ~ oneself (with food/on cakes)** sich (mit Essen/Kuchen) vollstopfen (*inf*).

stuffed shirt ['stʌft'ʃɜ:t] *n* (*inf*) Stockfisch *m* (*inf*).

stuffily ['stʌfɪlɪ] *adv* (*narrow-mindedly*) spießig; (*prudishly*) prüde; (*stiffly*) steif, gezwungen; (*dully*) langweilig.

stuffiness ['stʌfɪnɪs] *n see adj* (**a**) Stickigkeit, Dumpfheit *f*. (**b**) Spießigkeit *f*; Prüderie, Zimperlichkeit *f*. (**c**) Steifheit *f*; Gezwungenheit *f*; Langweiligkeit, Fadheit *f*.

stuffing ['stʌfɪŋ] *n* (*of pillow, quilt, Cook*) Füllung *f*; (*of furniture*) Polstermaterial *nt*; (*in taxidermy, toys*) Füllmaterial, Stopfmaterial *nt* ◆ **to knock the ~ out of sb** (*inf*) jdn fertigmachen (*inf*), jdn schaffen (*inf*).

stuffy ['stʌfɪ] *adj* (+*er*) (**a**) *room, atmosphere* stickig, dumpf. (**b**) (*narrow-minded*) spießig; (*prudish*) prüde, zimperlich. (**c**) (*stiff*) steif; *atmosphere also*

➤ LANGUAGE IN USE: **study: 1b → 26.2**

gezwungen; (*dull*) langweilig, öde, fad.

stultify ['stʌltɪfaɪ] [1] *vt* lähmen; *mind, person* verkümmern *or* verdummen lassen ◆ **to become stultified** verkümmern, verdummen.
[2] *vi* verkümmern, verdummen.

stultifying ['stʌltɪfaɪɪŋ] *adj* lähmend; *boredom, inactivity also* abstumpfend ◆ **to have a ~ effect on sb/sb's mind** jdn verkümmern lassen.

stumble ['stʌmbl] [1] *n* Stolpern *nt no pl, no indef art*; (*in speech etc*) Stocken *nt no pl, no indef art*.
[2] *vi* (*lit, fig*) stolpern; (*in speech*) stocken ◆ **to ~ against sth** gegen etw stoßen; **to ~ on sth** (*lit*) über etw (*acc*) stolpern; (*fig*) auf etw (*acc*) stoßen; **he ~d through a waltz/his speech** stockend *or* holperig spielte er einen Walzer/hielt er seine Rede.

stumbling-block ['stʌmblɪŋ'blɒk] *n* (*fig*) Hürde *f*, Hindernis, Problem *nt* ◆ **to be a ~ to sth** einer Sache (*dat*) im Weg stehen.

stump [stʌmp] [1] *n* **(a)** (*of tree, limb*) Stumpf *m*; (*of tooth, candle also, of pencil, tail, cigar*) Stummel *m*; (*Cricket*) Stab *m* ◆ **to stir one's ~s** (*inf*) sich rühren, sich regen. **(b)** (*US Pol: platform*) Rednertribüne *f* ◆ **~ speaker** Wahlredner(in *f*) *m*; **to go out on the ~s** (öffentlich *or* vor Ort) als Redner auftreten.
[2] *vt* **(a)** (*Cricket*) (*durch Umwerfen der Stäbe*) ausschalten.
(b) (*fig inf*) **you've got me ~ed** da bin ich überfragt; **I'm ~ed, that problem's got me ~ed** ich bin mit meiner Weisheit *or* meinem Latein am Ende (*inf*); **to be ~ed for an answer** um eine Antwort verlegen sein.
(c) (*US Pol*) **to ~ the country** Wahl(kampf)reisen durch das Land machen.
[3] *vi* (*inf*) stapfen ◆ **to ~ along/about** entlang-/herumstapfen; **to ~ up to sb** auf jdn zustapfen.

◆**stump up** (*Brit inf*) [1] *vt insep* springen lassen (*inf*), locker machen (*inf*).
[2] *vi* blechen (*inf*).

stumpy ['stʌmpɪ] *adj* (+*er*) *pencil, candle* stummelig (*inf*), kurz; *person* stämmig, untersetzt; *tree* klein und gedrungen; *legs* kurz ◆ **a ~ tail** ein Stummelschwanz *m*.

stun [stʌn] *vt* (*make unconscious*) betäuben; (*noise also, daze*) benommen machen; (*fig*) (*shock*) fassungslos machen; (*amaze*) erstaunen, verblüffen ◆ **he was ~ned by the news** (*bad news*) er war über die Nachricht fassungslos *or* wie gelähmt; (*good news*) die Nachricht hat ihn überwältigt; **he was ~ned by his good fortune** er war sprachlos über sein Glück.

stun bullet *n* Wuchtgeschoß *nt*.

stung [stʌŋ] *pret, ptp of* **sting**.

stun grenade *n* Blendgranate *f*.

stunk [stʌŋk] *ptp of* **stink**.

stunned [stʌnd] *adj* (*unconscious*) betäubt; (*dazed*) benommen; (*fig*) (*shocked*) fassungslos; (*amazed*) sprachlos.

stunner ['stʌnəʳ] *n* (*inf*) (*thing*) Wucht *f* (*inf*); (*woman*) tolle Frau, tolles Weib (*inf*); (*man*) toller Mann *or* Kerl (*inf*).

stunning ['stʌnɪŋ] *adj* (*lit*) *blow* wuchtig, betäubend; (*fig*) *news, dress, girl etc* phantastisch, toll (*inf*); *shock* überwältigend.

stunningly ['stʌnɪŋlɪ] *adv* atemberaubend, phantastisch.

stunt¹ [stʌnt] *n* Kunststück *nt*, Nummer *f*; (*publicity ~, trick*) Gag *m*; (*Aviat*) Kunststück *nt* ◆ **to do ~s** (*be ~man*) ein Stuntman sein, doubeln; **he does most of his own ~s** gefährliche Szenen spielt er meist selbst.

stunt² *vt* (*lit, fig*) *growth, development* hemmen; *trees, mind etc* verkümmern lassen.

stunted ['stʌntɪd] *adj plant, mind* verkümmert; *child* unterentwickelt ◆ **the ~ growth of these trees** die verkümmerten Bäume; **his ~ growth** seine Verwachsenheit.

stunt: ~ flying *n* Kunstflug *m*; **~man** *n* Stuntman *m*, Double *nt*.

stupefaction [,stju:pɪ'fækʃən] *n* Verblüffung *f* ◆ **he looked at me in ~** er sah mich verblüfft *or* voller Verblüffung an.

stupefy ['stju:pɪfaɪ] *vt* benommen machen; (*fig: amaze, surprise*) verblüffen ◆ **to be stupefied by drink** vom Alkohol benommen sein.

stupefying ['stju:pɪfaɪɪŋ] *adj* betäubend; (*fig: amazing*) verblüffend.

stupendous [stju:'pendəs] *adj* phantastisch; *effort* enorm.

stupendously [stju:'pendəslɪ] *adv* phantastisch; *hard* enorm.

stupid ['stju:pɪd] [1] *adj* **(a)** dumm; (*foolish also, boring*) blöd(e) (*inf*) ◆ **don't be ~** sei nicht so blöd (*inf*); **I've done a ~ thing** ich habe etwas ganz Dummes *or* Blödes (*inf*) gemacht; **you ~ idiot!** du blöder Idiot!; **take that ~ look off your face** guck nicht so dumm *or* blöd (*inf*)!; **that was ~ of you, that was a ~ thing to do** das war dumm (von dir).
(b) (*stupefied*) benommen, benebelt ◆ **to drink oneself ~** sich sinnlos betrinken; **the blow knocked him ~** der Schlag hat ihn völlig benebelt.
[2] *adv* (*inf*) **to talk ~** Quatsch reden (*inf*); **to act ~** sich dumm stellen.
[3] *n* (*inf: person*) Blödmann (*inf*), Dummkopf (*inf*) *m*.

stupidity [stju:'pɪdɪtɪ] *n* Dummheit *f*; (*silliness also*) Blödheit *f* (*inf*) ◆ **of all the ~!** so was Dummes!

stupidly ['stju:pɪdlɪ] *adv* (*unintelligently*) dumm; (*foolishly also*) blöd (*inf*) ◆ **~ I'd forgotten my keys** dummerweise hatte ich meine Schlüssel vergessen; **he ~ refused** er war so dumm *or* blöd (*inf*) abzulehnen.

stupor ['stju:pəʳ] *n* Benommenheit *f* ◆ **he lay/sat there in a ~** er lag/saß benommen *or* apathisch *or* teilnahmslos da; **to be in a drunken ~** sinnlos betrunken *or* im Vollrausch sein.

sturdily ['stɜ:dɪlɪ] *adv* **(a)** stabil ◆ **~ built** *person* kräftig *or* stämmig gebaut; *chair, ship etc* stabil gebaut. **(b)** (*fig*) unerschütterlich, standhaft.

sturdiness ['stɜ:dɪnɪs] *n see adj* **(a)** Kräftigkeit, Stämmigkeit *f*; Robustheit *f*; Stabilität *f*. **(b)** Unerschütterlichkeit, Standhaftigkeit *f*.

sturdy ['stɜ:dɪ] *adj* (+*er*) **(a)** *person, body, plant* kräftig, stämmig; *material* kräftig, robust; *building, ship, car* stabil. **(b)** (*fig*) *opposition* unerschütterlich, standhaft.

sturgeon ['stɜ:dʒən] *n* Stör *m*.

stutter ['stʌtəʳ] [1] *n* (*of person, engine*) Stottern *nt no pl*; (*of guns*) Trommeln *nt* ◆ **he has a bad ~** er stottert sehr; **to say sth with a ~** etw stotternd sagen, etw stottern.
[2] *vti* stottern ◆ **he was ~ing with rage** er stotterte vor Wut; **she ~ed (out) an apology** sie entschuldigte sich stotternd.

stutterer ['stʌtərəʳ] *n* Stotterer *m*, Stottrerin *f*.

stuttering ['stʌtərɪŋ] *n* Stottern *nt*.

sty [staɪ] *n* (*lit, fig*) Schweinestall *m*.

sty(e) [staɪ] *n* (*Med*) Gerstenkorn *nt*.

stygian ['stɪdʒɪən] *adj* (*liter*) *gloom, darkness* stygisch (*liter*).

style [staɪl] [1] *n* **(a)** (*Art, Mus, Liter, personal etc*) Stil *m* ◆ **~ of painting** Malstil *m*; **the ~ of his writing** sein Stil *m*; **~ of life** Lebensstil *m*; **~ of management** Führungsstil *m*; **a poem in the Romantic ~** ein Gedicht im Stil der Romantik; **he won in fine ~** er gewann souverän *or* überlegen; **in his own inimitable ~** (*iro*) in seiner unnachahmlichen Art *or* Manier, auf die ihm typische Art; **that house is not my ~** so ein Haus ist nicht mein Stil; **hillwalking/flattering people is not his ~** Bergwanderungen liegen ihm nicht/es ist nicht seine Art zu schmeicheln; **that's the ~** (*inf*) so ist's richtig.
(b) (*elegance*) Stil *m* ◆ **the man has (real) ~** der Mann hat Klasse *or* Format; **in ~** stilvoll; **to do things in ~** alles im großen Stil tun; **to celebrate in ~** groß feiern; **to get married in ~** eine Hochzeit großen Stils *or* im großen Stil feiern.
(c) (*sort, type*) Art *f* ◆ **a new ~ of house/car** *etc* ein neuer Haus-/Autotyp *etc*; **just the ~ of car I like** ein Auto, wie es mir gefällt.
(d) (*Fashion*) Stil *m no pl*, Mode *f*; (*cut*) Schnitt *m*; (*hair~*) Frisur *f* ◆ **these coats are available in two ~s** diese Mäntel gibt es in zwei verschiedenen Schnittarten *or* Macharten; **I want something in that ~** ich hätte gern etwas in der Art *or* in dem Stil; **all the latest ~s** die neue(ste) Mode, Mode im neue(ste)n Stil; **the latest ~s in shoes** die neue(ste)n Schuhmoden.
(e) (*~ of address*) Anrede *f*; (*title*) Titel *m*.
(f) (*Bot*) Griffel *m*.
[2] *vt* **(a)** (*designate*) nennen.
(b) (*design*) entwerfen; *clothes, interior etc also* gestalten; *hair* stylen ◆ **a smartly ~d dress** ein elegant geschnittenes Kleid; **it is ~d for comfort not elegance** es ist auf Bequemlichkeit und nicht Eleganz zugeschnitten.

-style *adj suf* nach ... Art, auf (+*acc*) ... Art ◆ **American-~ fried chicken** Brathähnchen nach amerikanischer Art; **cowboy-~** auf Cowboyart, nach Art der Cowboys; **Swedish-~ furniture/design** Möbel/Design im schwedischen Stil; **the old-~ cricketer** der Cricketspieler der alten Schule.

stylebook ['staɪlbʊk] *n* (*Typ*) Stilvorschriften *pl*; (*Fashion*) Modeheft *nt*; (*for hairstyles*) Frisurenheft *nt*.

styli ['staɪlaɪ] *pl of* **stylus**.

styling ['staɪlɪŋ] *n* (*of car etc*) Design *nt*; (*of dress*) Machart *f*, Schnitt *m*; (*of hair*) Schnitt *m* ◆ **~ mousse** Schaumfestiger *m*.

stylish ['staɪlɪʃ] *adj person* elegant; *car, hotel, district also* vornehm; *furnishings* stilvoll; (*fashionable*) modisch; *wedding* großen Stils; *way of life* großartig, im großen Stil.

stylishly ['staɪlɪʃlɪ] *adv* elegant; *furnished* stilvoll; (*fashionably*) modisch; *live* im großen Stil; *travel* mit allem Komfort.

stylishness ['staɪlɪʃnɪs] *n see adj* Eleganz *f*; Vornehmheit *f*; stilvolle Art; modische Finesse; großangelegter Stil ◆ **the ~ of his way of life** sein großartiger Lebensstil.

stylist ['staɪlɪst] *n* **(a)** (*Fashion*) Modeschöpfer(in *f*), Modestylist(in *f*) *m*; (*hair~*) Friseur *m*, Friseuse *f*, Coiffeur *m* (*geh*), Coiffeuse *f* (*geh*). **(b)** (*Liter, Sport*) Stilist(in *f*) *m*.

stylistic [staɪ'lɪstɪk] *adj* stilistisch ◆ **~ device** Stilmittel *nt*.

stylistically [staɪ'lɪstɪkəlɪ] *adv see adj* ◆ **~ it lacks polish** stilistisch gesehen *or* vom Stil her fehlt es am letzten Schliff.

stylistics [staɪ'lɪstɪks] *n sing* Stilistik *f*.

stylite ['staɪlaɪt] *n* Säulenheilige(r), Stylit (*spec*) *m*.

stylize ['staɪlaɪz] *vt* stilisieren.

stylus ['staɪləs] *n, pl* **styli (a)** (*on record-player*) Nadel *f*. **(b)** (*writing instrument*) Griffel, Stilus (*Hist*) *m*.

stymie ['staɪmɪ] *vt* (*fig inf*) matt setzen (*inf*) ◆ **to be ~d** aufgeschmissen sein (*inf*).

styptic ['stɪptɪk] [1] *n* blutstillendes Mittel.
[2] *adj* **pencil** Blutstill-.

suave *adj*, **~ly** *adv* ['swɑ:v, -lɪ] weltmännisch, aalglatt (*pej*).

suaveness ['swɑ:vnɪs], **suavity** ['swɑ:vɪtɪ] *n* Gewandtheit *f*, aalglatte Art (*pej*).

sub [sʌb] *abbr of* **(a) sub-edit, sub-editor. (b) submarine. (c) subscription. (d) substitute.**

sub- *pref* (*under, subordinate, inferior*) Unter-, unter-; (*esp with foreign words*) Sub-, sub- ◆ **~alpine** subalpin.

subaltern ['sʌbltən] *n* (*Brit Mil*) Subalternoffizier *m*.

sub: ~aqua [sʌb'ækwə] *adj attr* Unterwasser-; *equipment, club* Taucher-; **~arctic** *adj* subarktisch; **~atomic** *adj particle* subatomar; **~-basement** *n* Kellergeschoß *nt*; **~class** *n* Unterabteilung *f*, **~classify** *vti* unterteilen; **~committee** *n* Unterausschuß *m*; **~conscious** [1] *adj* unterbewußt; [2] *n* **the ~conscious** das Unterbewußtsein; **in his ~conscious** im Unterbewußtsein; **~consciously** *adv* im Unterbewußtsein; **~continent** *n* Subkontinent *m*; **~contract** [1] *vt* (vertraglich) weitervergeben (*to* an +*acc*); [2] *n* Nebenvertrag, Untervertrag *m*; **~contractor** *n* Unterkontrahent, Subunternehmer *m*; **~culture** *n* Subkultur *f*; **~cutaneous** *adj* subkutan; **~divide** [1] *vt* unterteilen; [2] *vi* sich aufteilen; **~division** *n* (*act*) Unterteilung *f*; (*~group*) Unterabteilung *f*; **~dominant** [1] *n* Subdominante *f*; [2] *attr chord* Subdominant-.

subdue [səb'djuː] *vt rebels, country* unterwerfen; *rioters* überwältigen; *wilderness* besiegen; (*make submissive*) gehorsam *or* fügsam *or* gefügig machen; (*fig*) *anger, desire* unterdrücken, zähmen; *noise, light, high spirits* dämpfen; *animals, children* bändigen; *pain* lindern.

subdued [səb'djuːd] *adj* (*quiet*) *colour, lighting, voice* gedämpft; *manner, person* ruhig, still; *mood, atmosphere* gedrückt; (*submissive*) *voice, manner, person* fügsam, gehorsam, gefügig; (*repressed*) *feelings, excitement* unterdrückt.

sub: ~-edit *vti* (*esp Brit*) redigieren; **~-editor** *n* (*esp Brit*) Redakteur(in *f*) *m*; **~-entry** *n* (*Book-keeping*) Nebenposten *m*; **~-frame** *n* (*of car*) Zwischenrahmen, Nebenrahmen *m*; **~group** *n* Unterabteilung *f*; **~head** (*inf*), **~heading** *n* Untertitel *m*; **~human** *adj treatment etc* unmenschlich; **they were treated as if they were ~human** sie wurden behandelt, als seien sie Untermenschen.

▼ **subject** ['sʌbdʒɪkt] [1] *n* **(a)** (*Pol*) Staatsbürger(in *f*) *m*; (*of king etc*) Untertan *m*, Untertanin *f*.

(b) (*Gram*) Subjekt *nt*, Satzgegenstand *m*.

▼ **(c)** (*topic, Mus*) Thema *nt* ◆ **the ~ of the picture is ...** das Thema *or* Sujet (*geh*) des Bildes ist ...; **he paints urban ~s** er malt städtische Motive; **to change the ~** das Thema wechseln; **on the ~ of ...** zum Thema (*+gen*) ...; **while we're on the ~** da wir gerade beim Thema sind; **while we're on the ~ of mushrooms** wo wir gerade von Pilzen reden, apropos Pilze; **that's off the ~** das gehört nicht zum Thema.

(d) (*discipline*) (*Sch, Univ*) Fach *nt*; (*specialist ~*) (Spezial)gebiet *nt*.

(e) (*reason*) Grund, Anlaß *m* (*for* zu).

(f) (*object*) Gegenstand *m* (*of gen*); (*in experiment*) (*person*) Versuchsperson *f*, Versuchsobjekt *nt*; (*animal*) Versuchstier, Versuchsobjekt *nt*; (*esp Med: for treatment*) Typ *m* ◆ **he is the ~ of much criticism** er wird stark kritisiert, er ist Gegenstand häufiger Kritik; **he's a good ~ for treatment by hypnosis** er läßt sich gut hypnotisch behandeln; **the survey team asked 100 ~s** die Meinungsforscher befragten 100 Personen.

(g) (*Philos: ego*) Subjekt, Ich *nt*.

(h) (*Phot*) Objekt *nt*.

[2] *adj* **(a)** (*conquered*) unterworfen.

(b) ~ to (*under the control of*) unterworfen (*+dat*); **provinces ~ to foreign rule** Provinzen unter Fremdherrschaft; **to be ~ to sth** *to law, constant change, sb's will* einer Sache (*dat*) unterworfen sein; *to illness* für etw anfällig sein; *to consent, approval* von etw abhängig sein; **northbound trains are ~ to delays** bei Zügen in Richtung Norden muß mit Verspätung gerechnet werden; **prices/opening times are ~ to change** *or* **alteration without notice** Preisänderungen sind vorbehalten/bezüglich Öffnungszeiten sind Änderungen vorbehalten; **all these plans are ~ to last minute changes** all diese Pläne können in letzter Minute noch geändert werden; **~ to flooding** überschwemmungsgefährdet; **to be ~ to taxation** besteuert werden; **~ to correction** vorbehaltlich Änderungen; **~ to confirmation in writing** vorausgesetzt, es wird schriftlich bestätigt.

[3] [səb'dʒekt] *vt* **(a)** (*subjugate*) unterwerfen; *terrorists, guerrillas* zerschlagen.

(b) to ~ sb to sth *to questioning, analysis, treatment* jdn einer Sache (*dat*) unterziehen; *to test also* jdn einer Sache (*dat*) unterwerfen; *to torture, suffering, heat, ridicule, criticism* jdn einer Sache (*dat*) aussetzen; **to ~ sb to insults** jdn beschimpfen; **to ~ sb/a book to criticism** jdn/ein Buch unter Kritik nehmen, jdn/ein Buch kritisieren.

[4] [səb'dʒekt] *vr* **to ~ oneself to sth** *to insults, suffering* etw hinnehmen; *to criticism, ridicule* sich einer Sache (*dat*) aussetzen; *to examination, test, questioning* sich einer Sache (*dat*) unterziehen.

subject: ~ catalogue *n* Schlagwortkatalog *m*; **~ heading** *n* Überschrift *f*; (*in index*) Rubrik *f*; **~ index** *n* Sachregister *nt*.

subjection [səb'dʒekʃən] *n* **(a)** (*state*) Abhängigkeit *f* ◆ **to hold** *or* **keep a people in ~** ein Volk unterdrücken. **(b)** (*act*) Unterwerfung *f*; (*of terrorists, guerrillas etc*) Zerschlagung *f*. **(c) the ~ of sb to sth** *see* **subject 3 (b)**.

subjective [səb'dʒektɪv] *adj* **(a)** subjektiv. **(b)** (*Gram*) **~ case** Nominativ *m*.

subjectively [səb'dʒektɪvlɪ] *adv* subjektiv.

subjectivism [səb'dʒektɪvɪzəm] *n* Subjektivismus *m*.

subjectivity [ˌsʌbdʒek'tɪvɪtɪ] *n* Subjektivität *f*.

subject-matter ['sʌbdʒɪkt'mætəʳ] *n* (*theme*) Stoff *m*; (*content*) Inhalt *m*.

sub judice [ˌsʌb'dʒuːdɪsɪ] *adj* **to be ~** verhandelt werden.

subjugate ['sʌbdʒʊgeɪt] *vt* unterwerfen.

subjugation [ˌsʌbdʒʊ'geɪʃən] *n* Unterwerfung *f*.

subjunctive [səb'dʒʌŋktɪv] [1] *adj* konjunktivisch ◆ **a/the ~ verb/the ~ mood** der Konjunktiv; **~ form** Konjunktiv(form *f*) *m*.

[2] *n* (*mood, verb*) Konjunktiv *m*.

sub: ~lease [1] *n* (*contract*) (*on farm etc*) Unterpachtvertrag *m* (*on* für); (*on house etc*) Untermietvertrag *m* (*on* für); **they have a ~lease on that house/farm** das Haus ist an sie untervermietet worden/sie haben den Hof als Unterpächter; [2] *vt land* unter- *or* weiterverpachten (*to* an *+acc*); *house* unter- *or* weitervermieten (*to* an *+acc*); **she has ~leased the flat from the tenants** sie hat die Wohnung in Untermiete; **~let** *pret, ptp* **~let** [1] *vt house, room* unter- *or* weitervermieten (*to* an *+acc*); [2] *vi* untervermieten; **~letting** *n* Untervermietung *f*; **~-lieutenant** *n* (*esp Brit*) Leutnant *m* zur See.

sublimate ['sʌblɪmeɪt] [1] *n* (*Chem*) Sublimat *nt*.

[2] *vt* (*Chem, Psych*) sublimieren.

sublimation [ˌsʌblɪ'meɪʃən] *n* Sublimierung *f*.

sublime [sə'blaɪm] *adj* **(a)** *poetry, beauty, scenery* erhaben; *thoughts, feelings also* sublim; *achievement, courage, genius also* überragend ◆ **that's going from the ~ to the ridiculous** (*inf*) *or* **the gorblimey** (*hum sl*) das nenne ich tief sinken (*inf*).

(b) (*iro: extreme*) *ignorance* vollendet; *impertinence, confidence also* unglaublich, hanebüchen; *indifference also, contempt* herablassend.

sublimely [sə'blaɪmlɪ] *adv* erhaben; *unaware, ignorant* ergreifend (*iro*), vollkommen; *foolish, drunk* unglaublich ◆ **~ beautiful** von erhabener Schönheit; **a ~ contented expression on his face** ein überglücklicher Gesichtsausdruck; **~ contemptuous/indifferent he ...** mit souveräner Verachtung/Gleichgültigkeit ... er ...

subliminal [ˌsʌb'lɪmɪnl] *adj* (*Psych*) unterschwellig.

sublimity [sə'blɪmɪtɪ] *n* (*liter*) Erhabenheit *f*.

submachine gun [ˌsʌbmə'ʃiːn'gʌn] *n* Maschinenpistole *f*.

submarine ['sʌbməˌriːn] [1] *n* **(a)** Unterseeboot, U-Boot *nt*. **(b)** (*US inf: sandwich*) Jumbo-Sandwich *nt* (*inf*).

[2] *adj life, equipment, cable* unterseeisch, submarin.

submariner [sʌb'mærɪnəʳ] *n* U-Boot-Mann *m*.

submenu ['sʌbˌmenjuː] *n* (*Comput*) Untermenü *nt*.

submerge [səb'mɜːdʒ] [1] *vt* untertauchen; (*flood*) überschwemmen ◆ **to ~ sth in water** etw in Wasser (ein)tauchen; **the house was completely ~d** das Haus stand völlig unter Wasser.

[2] *vi* (*diver, submarine*) tauchen.

submerged [səb'mɜːdʒd] *adj rocks* unter Wasser; *wreck* gesunken; *city* versunken ◆ **she is ~ in work** sie erstickt in Arbeit.

submersible [səb'mɜːsəbl] [1] *adj* versenkbar; *submarine* tauchfähig.

[2] *n* Tauchboot *nt*.

submersion [səb'mɜːʃən] *n* Untertauchen *nt*; (*of submarine*) Tauchen *nt*; (*by flood*) Überschwemmung *f* ◆ **~ in liquid** Eintauchen *nt* in Flüssigkeit; **prolonged ~ in water** langes Liegen im Wasser.

submission [səb'mɪʃən] *n* **(a)** (*yielding*) Unterwerfung *f* (*to* unter *+acc*); (*submissiveness*) Gehorsam *m*; (*Sport*) Aufgabe *f* ◆ **to force sb into ~** jdn zwingen, sich zu ergeben; **to starve sb into ~** jdn aushungern.

(b) (*presentation*) Eingabe *f*; (*documents submitted*) Vorlage *f* ◆ **to make a ~ to sb** jdm eine Vorlage machen *or* unterbreiten; **his ~ to the appeals tribunal** seine Berufung.

(c) (*contention*) Einwurf *m* (*to* gegenüber) ◆ **it is our ~ that ...** wir behaupten, daß ...

submissive [səb'mɪsɪv] *adj* demütig, gehorsam, unterwürfig (*pej*) (*to* gegenüber) ◆ **~ to authority** autoritätsgläubig.

submissively [səb'mɪsɪvlɪ] *adv see adj*.

submissiveness [səb'mɪsɪvnɪs] *n* Demut *f*, Gehorsam *m*, Unterwürfigkeit *f* (*pej*) (*to* gegenüber).

submit [səb'mɪt] [1] *vt* **(a)** (*put forward*) vorlegen (*to dat*); *application, claim etc* einreichen (*to* bei) ◆ **to ~ that ...** (*esp Jur*) behaupten, daß ...; **to ~ an entry to a competition** (*participate*) an einem Wettbewerb teilnehmen.

(b) (*refer*) verweisen (*to* an *+acc*) ◆ **to ~ sth to scrutiny/investigation/tests** *etc* etw einer Prüfung/einer Untersuchung/Tests (*dat*) *etc* unterziehen; **to ~ sth to heat/cold** *etc* etw der Hitze/Kälte (*dat*) *etc* aussetzen.

[2] *vi* (*yield*) sich beugen, nachgeben; (*Mil*) sich ergeben (*to dat*); (*Sport*) aufgeben ◆ **to ~ to sth** *to sb's orders, judgement, God's will* sich einer Sache (*dat*) beugen *or* unterwerfen; *to indignity* sich (*dat*) etw gefallen lassen, etw erdulden; *to demands, pressure* einer Sache (*dat*) nachgeben; **to ~ to blackmail/questioning** sich erpressen/verhören lassen.

[3] *vr* **to ~ oneself to sth** *to examination, operation, questioning etc* sich einer Sache (*dat*) unterziehen.

subnormal [ˌsʌb'nɔːməl] *adj intelligence, temperature* unterdurchschnittlich; *person* minderbegabt; (*inf*) schwachsinnig ◆ **educationally ~** lernbehindert; **mentally ~** minderbemittelt.

subordinate [sə'bɔːdnɪt] [1] *adj officer* rangniedriger; *rank, position, (secondary) importance* untergeordnet ◆ **~ clause** (*Gram*) Nebensatz *m*; **to be ~ to sb/sth** jdm/einer Sache untergeordnet sein; **to be ~ in importance to** weniger wichtig sein als; **~ in rank** rangniedriger (*to* als).

[2] *n* Untergebene(r) *mf*.

[3] [sə'bɔːdɪneɪt] *vt* unterordnen (*to dat*) ◆ **subordinating conjunction** unterordnende Konjunktion.

subordination [səˌbɔːdɪ'neɪʃən] *n* (*subjection*) Unterordnung *f* (*to* unter *+acc*).

suborn [sʌ'bɔːn] *vt* (*Jur*) *witness* beeinflussen.

sub-plot ['sʌbˌplɒt] *n* Nebenhandlung *f*.

subpoena [sə'piːnə] (*Jur*) [1] *n* Vorladung *f* ◆ **to serve a ~ on sb** jdn vorladen.

[2] *vt witness* vorladen ◆ **he was ~ed to give evidence** er wurde als Zeuge vorgeladen.

sub: ~polar *adj* subpolar; **~-postmaster/-postmistress** *n* (*Brit*) Vorstand *m* einer Zweigstelle der Post; **~-post office** *n* (*Brit*) Poststelle *f*; **~ rosa** [ˌsʌb'rəʊzə] (*form*) [1] *adj* geheim, sub rosa (*geh*); [2] *adv* im geheimen, sub rosa (*geh*); **~routine** *n* (*Comput*) Unterroutine *f*, Unterprogramm *nt*.

▼ **subscribe** [səb'skraɪb] [1] *vt money* zeichnen (*form*); (*to appeal*) spenden (*to* für) ◆ **to ~ one's signature** *or* **name to a document** (*form*) ein Dokument (unter)zeichnen.

[2] *vi* **(a)** (*contribute, promise to contribute*) spenden, geben (*to dat*) ◆ **to ~ to an appeal** sich an einer Spendenaktion beteiligen; **to ~ for a book** ein Buch vorbestellen; **to ~ for shares in a company** Aktien einer Gesellschaft zeichnen.

(b) to ~ to a magazine *etc* eine Zeitschrift *etc* abonnieren.

▼ **(c)** (*support*) **to ~ to sth** *to proposal* etw gutheißen, etw billigen; *to opinion, theory* sich einer Sache (*dat*) anschließen.

➤ LANGUAGE IN USE: **subject: 1c** → 26.2 **subscribe: 2c** → 12.1

subscriber [səbˈskraɪbəʳ] *n* (*to paper*) Abonnent(in *f*) *m*; (*to fund*) Spender(in *f*), Zeichner(in *f*) (*form*) *m*; (*Telec*) Teilnehmer(in *f*) *m*; (*to opinion*) Befürworter(in *f*) *m*; (*of shares*) Zeichner *m* ◆ **~ trunk dialling** (*Brit*) der Selbstwählferndienst.
subscript [ˈsʌbskrɪpt] *adj character* tiefgestellt.
subscription [səbˈskrɪpʃən] *n* Subskription (*form*), Zeichnung (*form*) *f*; (*money subscribed*) Beitrag *m*; (*to newspaper, concert etc*) Abonnement *nt* (*to* gen) ◆ **to take out a ~ to sth** etw abonnieren; **to pay one's ~ (to a club)** seinen (Vereins)beitrag bezahlen; **by public ~** mit Hilfe von *or* durch Spenden; **by ~** durch Subskription(en *pl*) *f*.
subscription rate *n* Abonnements- *or* Bezugspreis *m*.
subsection [ˈsʌbˌsekʃən] *n* Unterabteilung *f*; (*Jur*) Paragraph *m*.
subsequent [ˈsʌbsɪkwənt] *adj* (nach)folgend, anschließend; (*in time*) später, anschließend ◆ **~ to** (*form*) im Anschluß an (+*acc*).
subsequently [ˈsʌbsɪkwəntlɪ] *adv* (*afterwards*) später, anschließend; *alter, add etc also* nachträglich; (*from that time*) von da an.
subserve [səbˈsɜːv] *vt* (*form*) dienen (+*dat*), dienlich *or* förderlich sein (+*dat*) (*form*).
subservience [səbˈsɜːvɪəns] *n* (*pej*) Unterwürfigkeit *f* (*to* gegenüber); (*form*) Unterworfenheit *f* (*to* unter +*acc*).
subservient [səbˈsɜːvɪənt] *adj* (*pej*) unterwürfig (*to* gegenüber); (*form*) unterworfen (*to dat*).
subserviently [ˌsʌbˈsɜːvɪəntlɪ] *adv* unterwürfig.
subset [ˈsʌbˌset] *n* (*Math*) Teilmenge *f*.
subside [səbˈsaɪd] *vi* **(a)** (*flood, river*) sinken; (*land, building, road*) sich senken, absacken (*inf*) ◆ **the lorry ~d into the mud** der Lastwagen sank im Schlamm ein; **to ~ into a chair** auf einen Stuhl sinken.
(b) (*storm, wind*) abflauen, nachlassen, sich legen; (*anger, excitement, laughter, noise also*) abklingen; (*fever*) sinken.
subsidence [səbˈsaɪdəns] *n* Senkung *f*, Absacken *nt* (*inf*) ◆ **there's a lot of ~ in the area** in der Gegend senkt sich das Erdreich; **"danger: ~"** „Achtung: Bodensenkung"; **we can't get a mortgage because of the ~** wir bekommen keine Hypothek, weil sich das Gelände senkt.
subsidiary [səbˈsɪdɪərɪ] **1** *adj role, interest, subject* Neben-; *company* Tochter- ◆ **to be ~ to sth** einer Sache (*dat*) untergeordnet sein.
2 *n* Tochtergesellschaft *f*.
subsidize [ˈsʌbsɪdaɪz] *vt company etc*, (*inf*) *sb's habits* subventionieren; (*inf*) *person* unterstützen.
subsidy [ˈsʌbsɪdɪ] *n* Subvention *f*, Zuschuß *m* ◆ **there is a ~ on butter** Butter wird subventioniert *or* bezuschußt; **rent ~** Wohnungsbeihilfe *f*; **housing subsidies** (*for building, renovation etc*) Wohnungsbaubeihilfen *pl*.
subsist [səbˈsɪst] *vi* (*form*) sich ernähren, leben (*on* von).
subsistence [səbˈsɪstəns] *n* (*living*) Leben *nt* (*on* von); (*means of ~*) Existenz *f*, (Lebens)unterhalt *m* ◆ **enough for ~** genug zum (Über)leben; **~ on £11 is impossible** es ist unmöglich, von £ 11 zu leben; **rice is their chief means of ~** sie ernähren sich hauptsächlich von Reis.
subsistence: ~ allowance *n* Unterhaltszuschuß *m*; **~ farmer** *n* Bauer, der nur für den Eigenbedarf anbaut; **~ farming** *n* Ackerbau *m* für den Eigenbedarf, Subsistenzwirtschaft *f*; **~ level** *n* Existenzminimum *nt*; **at ~ level** auf dem Existenzminimum; **~ wage** *n* Minimallohn *m*.
sub: ~soil *n* Untergrund *m*; **~sonic** *adj* Unterschall-; **~species** *n* Unterart, Subspezies *f*.
substance [ˈsʌbstəns] *n* **(a)** Substanz, Materie *f*, Stoff *m* ◆ **what is this ~?** was ist das für eine Substanz?; **he rubbed a yellow ~ on the wound** er strich eine gelbe Masse auf die Wunde.
(b) *no pl* (*subject matter*) Substanz *f*, Gehalt *m*; (*essence*) Kern *m* ◆ **in ~** im wesentlichen; **I agree with the ~ of his proposals** im wesentlichen stimme ich seinen Vorschlägen zu.
(c) *no pl* (*weight, importance*) Gewicht *nt* ◆ **the book/argument lacks ~** das Buch hat keine Substanz/das Argument hat keine Durchschlagskraft; **there is some ~ in his claim** seine Behauptung ist nicht unfundiert; **the meal lacked ~** das Essen war nicht sehr gehaltvoll.
(d) *no pl* **a man of ~** ein vermögender Mann.
substandard [ˌsʌbˈstændəd] *adj work, goods* minderwertig; *quality also, housing* unzulänglich; (*Ling*) nicht korrekt.
substantial [səbˈstænʃəl] *adj* **(a)** *meal, person, cloth* kräftig; *furniture also, building, firm* solide; *rope also* stark; *book* umfangreich.
(b) (*considerable*) *income, loss, gain, amount* beträchtlich, erheblich; *sum also* namhaft; *part, majority, contribution, improvement also* wesentlich, bedeutend; (*rich*) *landowner, businessman* vermögend, kapitalkräftig.
(c) (*weighty, important*) bedeutend; *proof, argument* überzeugend, stichhaltig; *difference* wesentlich, bedeutend ◆ **to be in ~ agreement** im wesentlichen übereinstimmen.
(d) (*real, material*) körperlich, wesenhaft.
substantially [səbˈstænʃəlɪ] *adv* **(a)** (*solidly*) solide; (*considerably*) erheblich, beträchtlich, wesentlich ◆ **~ built** *house* solide gebaut; *person* kräftig gebaut.
(b) (*essentially, basically*) im wesentlichen.
substantiate [səbˈstænʃɪeɪt] *vt* erhärten, untermauern.
substantiation [səbˌstænʃɪˈeɪʃən] *n* Erhärtung, Untermauerung *f* ◆ **as yet this theory lacks ~** diese Theorie ist bisher noch nicht erhärtet; **in ~ of** zur Erhärtung (+*gen*).
substantival [ˌsʌbstənˈtaɪvəl] *adj* (*Gram*) substantivisch, Substantiv-.
substantive [ˈsʌbstəntɪv] **1** *adj* **(a)** *evidence, argument* überzeugend, stichhaltig. **(b)** (*considerable*) *contribution, improvement* beträchtlich, wesentlich, bedeutend. **(c)** **~ motion** endgültige Formulierung des Antrags. **(d)** (*Gram*) *see* **substantival**.
2 *n* (*Gram*) Substantiv, Hauptwort *nt*.
substantivize [ˈsʌbstəntɪˌvaɪz] *vt* substantivieren.
substation [ˈsʌbˌsteɪʃən] *n* (*Elec*) Umspann(ungs)werk *nt*.
substitute [ˈsʌbstɪtjuːt] **1** *n* Ersatz *m no pl*; (*representative also*) Vertretung *f*; (*male person also*) Ersatzmann *m*; (*Sport*) Ersatzspieler(in *f*), Auswechselspieler(in *f*) *m* ◆ **to find a ~ for sb** für jdn Ersatz finden; **to use sth as a ~** etw als Ersatz benutzen; **coffee ~** Kaffee-Ersatz *m*; **various coffee ~s** verschiedene Sorten Kaffee-Ersatz; **there's no ~ for ...** es gibt keinen Ersatz für ..., ... kann man durch nichts ersetzen.
2 *adj attr* Ersatz-.
3 *vt* **to ~ A for B** B durch A ersetzen; (*Sport also*) B gegen A austauschen *or* auswechseln; **~ 3 for X** setze für X 3 ein, substituiere 3 für X.
4 *vi* **to ~ for sb/sth** jdn vertreten, für jdn einspringen/etw ersetzen.
substitution [ˌsʌbstɪˈtjuːʃən] *n* Ersetzen *nt* (*of X for Y* von Y durch X); (*Sport*) Austausch *m* (*of X for Y* von Y gegen X); (*Math*) Substitution *f*, Einsetzen *nt* (*of X for Y* von X für Y) ◆ **the ~ of margarine for butter** der Gebrauch von Margarine statt Butter.
substratum [ˈsʌbˌstrɑːtəm] *n*, *pl* **substrata** [ˈsʌbˌstrɑːtə] Substrat *nt*; (*Geol*) Untergrund *m*; (*Sociol*) Substratum *nt*.
substructure [ˈsʌbˌstrʌktʃəʳ] *n* Unterbau *m*; (*fig also*) Grundlage *f*; (*Build*) Fundament *nt*; (*of bridge*) Widerlager *nt*.
subsume [səbˈsjuːm] *vt* **to ~ sth under sth** etw unter etw (*dat*) zusammenfassen *or* subsumieren (*geh*).
subsystem [ˈsʌbˌsɪstəm] *n* Untersystem *nt*.
sub-teen [ˈsʌbˈtiːn] *n* (*esp US*) Schulkind *nt*.
sub-teenage [ˈsʌbˈtiːneɪdʒ] *adj attr* (*esp US*) Schulkinder- ◆ **~ drinking** der Alkoholkonsum von (Schul)kindern.
subtenancy [ˌsʌbˈtenənsɪ] *n* **during his ~ of the flat/farm** während er Untermieter in der Wohnung/Unterpächter des Bauernhofes war.
subtenant [ˌsʌbˈtenənt] *n* (*of flat etc*) Untermieter(in *f*) *m*; (*of land*) Unterpächter(in *f*) *m*.
subtend [səbˈtend] *vt* gegenüberliegen (+*dat*).
subterfuge [ˈsʌbtəfjuːdʒ] *n* (*trickery*) Täuschung, List *f*; (*trick*) Trick *m*, List *f* ◆ **to resort to ~** zu einer List greifen; **to be incapable of ~** (zu) keiner Falschheit *or* List fähig sein.
subterranean [ˌsʌbtəˈreɪnɪən] *adj* unterirdisch.
subtitle [ˈsʌbˌtaɪtl] **1** *n* Untertitel *m* (*also Film*).
2 *vt film* mit Untertiteln versehen; *book etc* einen Untertitel geben (+*dat*) ◆ **the film is ~d in English** der Film hat englische Untertitel; **the book is ~d ...** das Buch hat den Untertitel ...
subtle [ˈsʌtl] *adj* **(a)** (*delicate, gentle*) fein; *irony, distinction also* subtil (*geh*); *perfume, flavour also* zart; *hint, allusion* zart, leise; *charm* leise, unaufdringlich.
(b) (*ingenious, not obvious*) *remark, argument, point* scharfsinnig, spitzfindig; *design, construction, proof* raffiniert, fein ausgedacht *or* ausgetüftelt (*inf*) ◆ **he has a very ~ mind** er ist ein sehr subtiler Denker (*geh*); **be ~ about it** gehen Sie mit Zartgefühl vor.
(c) (*quick at seeing fine distinctions*) fein; *observer also* aufmerksam; *critic also* subtil (*geh*).
subtlety [ˈsʌtltɪ] *n see adj* **(a)** Feinheit *f*; Subtilität *f* (*geh*); Zartheit *f*; Unaufdringlichkeit *f*.
(b) Scharfsinn(igkeit *f*) *m*, Spitzfindigkeit *f*; Raffiniertheit *f* ◆ **his methods lack ~** seinen Methoden fehlt (die) Finesse *or* Subtilität (*geh*); **the subtleties of the novel** die Feinheiten *pl* des Romans; **~ is wasted on him** feine Andeutungen nützen bei ihm nichts.
(c) Feinheit *f*; Aufmerksamkeit *f*; Subtilität *f* (*geh*).
subtly [ˈsʌtlɪ] *adv* fein; *flavoured also* delikat; *argue, reply* scharfsinnig, subtil (*geh*); *analyse, think* scharfsinnig; *achieve one's ends* auf raffinierte Weise ◆ **~ different** auf subtile Weise verschieden *or* unterschiedlich; **he ~ suggested** er schlug geschickt vor; **it's just very ~ wrong** es ist schwer zu fassen, was falsch daran ist.
subtotal [ˈsʌbˌtəʊtl] *n* Zwischen- *or* Teilsumme *f*.
subtract [səbˈtrækt] *vti* abziehen, subtrahieren (*from* von).
subtraction [səbˈtrækʃən] *n* Subtraktion *f*; (*act also*) Abziehen *nt*.
subtrahend [ˈsʌbtrəˌhend] *n* (*Math form*) Subtrahend *m*.
subtropical [ˌsʌbˈtrɒpɪkəl] *adj* subtropisch.
subtype [ˈsʌbˌtaɪp] *n* Unterart *f*.
suburb [ˈsʌbɜːb] *n* Vorort *m* ◆ **in the ~s** am Stadtrand.
suburban [səˈbɜːbən] *adj* Vorort-; *area also* vorstädtisch; (*pej*) spießig, kleinbürgerlich ◆ **the area is becoming increasingly ~** die Gegend nimmt immer mehr vorstädtischen Charakter an; **~ line** (*Rail*) Vorortbahn *f*.
suburbia [səˈbɜːbɪə] *n* (*usu pej*) die Vororte *pl* ◆ **to live in ~** am Stadtrand wohnen; **that's typical of ~!** typisch Spießbürger!
subvention [səbˈvenʃən] *n* Subvention *f*.
subversion [səbˈvɜːʃən] *n*, *no pl* Subversion *f*; (*of rights, freedom etc*) Untergrabung, Unterminierung *f* ◆ **the US was accused of ~ in Chile** die USA wurden subversiver *or* umstürzlerischer Tätigkeiten in Chile beschuldigt; **~ is rife in the army** die Armee ist voll(er) subversiver Elemente.
subversive [səbˈvɜːsɪv] **1** *adj* subversiv, umstürzlerisch ◆ **~ elements** subversive Elemente *or* Kräfte *pl*.
2 *n* Umstürzler(in *f*) *m*, Subversive(r) *mf*.
subvert [səbˈvɜːt] *vt government* zu stürzen versuchen; *faith, morals etc* untergraben, unterminieren; *person* zum Umsturz anstacheln.
subway [ˈsʌbweɪ] *n* Unterführung *f*; (*for cars also*) Tunnel *m*; (*US Rail*) U-Bahn *f*.

subzero ['sʌb'zɪərəʊ] *adj temperature* unter Null, unter dem Nullpunkt.

succeed [sək'si:d] [1] *vi* **(a)** *(be successful) (person)* erfolgreich sein, Erfolg haben; *(plan etc also)* gelingen ◆ **to ~ in business/in a plan** geschäftlich/mit einem Plan erfolgreich sein; **I ~ed in doing it** es gelang mir, es zu tun; **you'll only ~ in making things worse** damit erreichst du nur, daß alles noch schlimmer wird; **nothing ~s like success** *(prov)* nichts ist so erfolgreich wie der Erfolg; **if at first you don't ~(, try, try, try again)** *(Prov)* wirf die Flinte nicht gleich ins Korn *(prov)*.
(b) *(come next)* **to ~ to an office** in einem Amt nachfolgen; **he ~ed to his father's position** er wurde (der) Nachfolger seines Vaters, er trat die Nachfolge seines Vaters an *(geh)*; **to ~ to the throne** die Thronfolge antreten; **to ~ to an estate** einen Besitz erben; **there ~ed a period of peace** *(form)* es folgte eine Zeit des Friedens.
[2] *vt (come after, take the place of)* folgen (+*dat*), folgen auf (+*acc*); *(person also)* Nachfolger(in *f*) *m* werden (+*gen*) ◆ **to ~ sb in a post/in office** jds Nachfolger werden, jds Stelle *(acc)* übernehmen/jdm im Amt nachfolgen; **who ~ed James I?** wer kam nach *or* folgte auf Jakob I.?

succeeding [sək'si:dɪŋ] *adj* folgend ◆ **~ generations** spätere *or* nachfolgende Generationen *pl*.

▼ **success** [sək'ses] *n* Erfolg *m* ◆ **without ~** ohne Erfolg, erfolglos; **wishing you every ~ in your exams/new career** mit besten Wünschen für eine erfolgreiche Prüfung/viel Erfolg im neuen Beruf; **to make a ~ of sth** mit *or* bei etw Erfolg haben, mit *or* bei etw erfolgreich sein; **they made a ~ of their marriage** ihre Ehe war ein Erfolg; **to be a ~ with sb** bei jdm ankommen; **the new car is not a ~** das neue Auto ist nicht gerade ein (durchschlagender) Erfolg; **the plan was a ~** der Plan war erfolgreich *or* ein voller Erfolg; **to meet with ~** Erfolg haben, erfolgreich sein; **~ story** Erfolgsstory *f*; *(person)* Erfolg *m*.

successful [sək'sesfʊl] *adj* erfolgreich ◆ **to be ~** erfolgreich sein, Erfolg haben *(in* mit, bei); **to be entirely ~** ein voller Erfolg sein; **I was ~ in doing it** es gelang mir, es zu tun.

successfully [sək'sesfəlɪ] *adv* erfolgreich, mit Erfolg.

succession [sək'seʃən] *n* **(a)** Folge, Serie *f*; *(with no intervening period)* (Aufeinander)folge, Kette *f* ◆ **a ~ of visitors** eine Kette *or* Serie von Besuchern; **life is a ~ of joys and sorrows** das Leben ist ein steter Wechsel von Kummer und Freude; **in ~** nacheinander, hintereinander; **in quick** *or* **rapid ~** in rascher Folge, schnell hintereinander.
(b) *(to post)* Nachfolge *f*; *(to throne)* Thronfolge *f*; *(to title, estate)* Erbfolge *f* ◆ **his ~ to the office/title/throne** seine Amtsübernahme/seine Übernahme des Titels/seine Thronbesteigung; **in ~ to sb** als jds Nachfolger(in *f*) *m*, in jds Nachfolge *(dat) (geh)*; **fourth in ~ to the throne** an vierter Stelle in der Thronfolge; *see* **apostolic.**

succession state *n* Nachfolgestaat *m*.

successive [sək'sesɪv] *adj* aufeinanderfolgend *attr* ◆ **4 ~ days** 4 Tage nacheinander *or* hintereinander, 4 aufeinanderfolgende Tage; **he was sacked from 3 ~ jobs** er wurde nacheinander *or* hintereinander aus 3 verschiedenen Stellen hinausgeworfen.

successively [sək'sesɪvlɪ] *adv* nacheinander, hintereinander.

successor [sək'sesəʳ] *n* Nachfolger(in *f*) *m (to gen)*; *(to throne)* Thronfolger(in *f*) *m*.

succinct [sək'sɪŋkt] *adj* knapp, kurz und bündig *pred*.

succinctly [sək'sɪŋktlɪ] *adv* kurz und bündig, in kurzen *or* knappen Worten *or* Zügen; *write* in knappem *or* gedrängtem Stil ◆ **as he very ~ put it** wie er so treffend bemerkte.

succinctness [sək'sɪŋktnɪs] *n* Knappheit, Kürze *f* ◆ **with great ~** kurz und bündig, in kurzen Worten; *(write)* in knappem Stil.

succour, (*US***) succor** ['sʌkəʳ] *(liter)* [1] *n* Beistand *m* ◆ **she was his ~** sie war ihm ein Beistand.
[2] *vt* beistehen (+*dat*).

succubus ['sʌkjʊbʌs] *n, pl* **succubi** ['sʌkjʊbaɪ] Sukkubus *m*.

succulence ['sʌkjʊləns] *n* Saftigkeit *f*.

succulent ['sʌkjʊlənt] [1] *adj peach, steak* saftig; *(Bot) plant, stem* fleischig, sukkulent *(spec)*.
[2] *n (Bot)* Fettpflanze, Sukkulente *(spec) f*.

succumb [sə'kʌm] *vi* erliegen *(to dat)*; *(to threats)* sich beugen *(to dat)*.

such [sʌtʃ] [1] *adj* **(a)** *(of that kind)* solche(r, s) ◆ **~ a person** so *or* solch ein Mensch, ein solcher Mensch; **~ a book** so ein Buch, ein solches Buch; **~ people/books** solche Leute/Bücher; **many/few/all ~ people/books** viele/wenige/all solche Leute/Bücher; **all ~ books are very expensive** solche Bücher sind sehr teuer; **do you have ~ a book?** haben Sie so ein Buch?; **~ a thing** so etwas, so was *(inf)*; **have you got ~ a thing as ...?** haben Sie so etwas wie ...?; **there's ~ a thing as divorce** es gibt so etwas wie eine Scheidung; **I said no ~ thing** das habe ich nie gesagt; **no ~ thing** nichts dergleichen; **I'll/you'll do no ~ thing** ich werde mich/du wirst dich hüten; **there's no ~ thing as a unicorn** so etwas wie ein Einhorn gibt es nicht; **... or some ~ idea ...** oder so etwas, ... oder so was in der Richtung *(inf)*, ... oder so ähnlich; **... or some ~ name/place ...** oder so (ähnlich); **he was ~ a one/just ~ another** er war einer von ihnen/auch (so) einer; **in ~ a case** in einem solchen Fall; **men/books ~ as these, ~ men/books as these** Männer/Bücher wie diese, solche Männer/Bücher; **writers ~ as Agatha Christie, ~ writers as Agatha Christie** (solche) Schriftsteller wie Agatha Christie; **he's not ~ a fool as you think** er ist nicht so dumm, wie Sie denken; **I'm not ~ a fool as to believe that** *or* **that I'd believe that** ich bin nicht so dumm *or* kein solcher Dummkopf, daß ich das glaube; **~ people as attended** die(jenigen), die anwesend waren; **I'll give you ~ books/money as I have** was ich an Büchern/Geld habe, gebe ich Ihnen.
(b) *(so much, so great etc) (with uncountable nouns)* solche(r, s); *(with countable nouns also)* so, solch, derartige(r, s) ◆ **he's ~ a liar** er ist so *or* solch ein Lügner, er ist ein derartiger *or* solcher Lügner; **he did it in ~ a way that ...** er machte es so, daß ...; **~ wealth/beauty!** welch (ein) Reichtum/welche Schönheit!; **he's always in ~ a hurry** er hat es immer so eilig.
(c) *pred* **his surprise was ~ that ..., ~ was his surprise that ...** seine Überraschung war so groß, daß ..., er war so überrascht, daß ...; **his manner was ~ that ...** er benahm sich so, daß ...; **her speech was ~ that ...** ihre Rede war so gehalten, daß ...
(d) *see* **such-and-such.**
[2] *adv* so, solch *(geh)* ◆ **nobody else makes ~ a good cup of tea as you** niemand kocht so guten Tee wie du; **it's ~ a long time ago** es ist so lange her.
[3] *pron* **rabbits and hares and ~** Kaninchen, Hasen und dergleichen; **~ being the case ...** in diesem Fall ...; **~ was not my intention** dies war nicht meine Absicht; **~ is not the case** dies ist nicht der Fall; **~ is life!** so ist das Leben!; **those and ~ as those** *(hum inf)* die oberen Zehntausend *(hum)*; **may all ~ perish!** mögen sie alle verderben!; **as ~** an sich; **~ as?** (wie) zum Beispiel?; **~ as it is** so, wie es nun mal ist; **the food, ~ as there was of it ...** das Essen, soweit vorhanden ..., was an Essen da war, ...; **I'll give you ~ as I have** ich gebe Ihnen, was ich habe.

such-and-such ['sʌtʃən'sʌtʃ] *(inf)* [1] *adj* **~ a time/town** die und die Zeit/Stadt.
[2] *n* Soundso *nt*.

suchlike ['sʌtʃ,laɪk] *(inf)* [1] *adj* solche.
[2] *pron* dergleichen.

suck [sʌk] [1] *n* **to have** *or* **take a ~** *(at straw)* saugen, ziehen *(at* an +*dat)*; *(at lemonade etc)* nuckeln *(inf)*, ziehen *(at* an +*dat)*; *(at lollipop)* lutschen *(at* an +*dat)*; **to give ~ (to a baby)** *(old)* (ein Baby) stillen.
[2] *vt* saugen; *breast, straw* saugen an (+*dat*); *sweet, pastille* lutschen; *lollipop* lutschen an (+*dat*); *thumb* lutschen *or* nuckeln *(inf)* an (+*dat*) ◆ **to ~ one's teeth** an den Zähnen saugen; **to ~ the juice out of** *or* **from sth** den Saft aus etw heraussaugen; **to ~ sb dry** *(fig)* jdn bis aufs Blut aussaugen; **don't teach your grandmother to ~ eggs** *(prov)* da will das Ei wieder klüger sein als die Henne *(prov)*.
[3] *vi* **(a)** *(at* an +*dat)* saugen; *(at bottle also, at dummy)* nuckeln *(inf)*; *(at lollipop)* lutschen; *(at thumb)* lutschen, nuckeln *(inf)*; *(at pipe, through straw)* ziehen ◆ **he always makes a ~ing noise with his soup** er schlürft seine Suppe immer. **(b)** *(US sl: be very bad)* **this city ~s** diese Stadt ist echt Scheiße *(sl)*.

◆**suck down** *vt sep* hinunterziehen.

◆**suck in** *vt sep liquid, dust* aufsaugen; *air (ventilator)* ansaugen; *(person)* in tiefen Zügen einatmen; *cheeks* einziehen; *(fig) knowledge, facts* (in sich *acc*) aufsaugen.

◆**suck off** *vt sep (vulg)* **to ~ sb ~** jdm einen (ab)lutschen *(vulg)*.

◆**suck under** *vt sep* hinunterziehen; *(completely)* verschlingen.

◆**suck up** [1] *vt sep liquid, dust* aufsaugen ◆ **the child ~ed ~ his milk** das Kind trank seine Milch (mit einem Strohhalm) aus.
[2] *vi (inf)* **to ~ ~ to sb** vor jdm kriechen.

sucker ['sʌkəʳ] *n* **(a)** *(rubber ~, Zool)* Saugnapf *m*; *(Bot)* unterirdischer Ausläufer; *(on creeper)* Häkchen *nt*.
(b) *(US inf: lollipop)* Lutscher *m* ◆ **all-day ~** Dauerlutscher *m*.
(c) *(sl: fool)* Simpel *(S Ger)*, Trottel *(inf) m* ◆ **to be a ~ for sth** (immer) auf etw *(acc)* hereinfallen; *(be partial to)* eine Schwäche für etw haben; **to be had for a ~** zum Narren gehalten werden, für dumm verkauft werden; **he's looking for some ~ who'll lend him £200** er sucht einen Dummen, der ihm £ 200 leiht.

sucking-pig ['sʌkɪŋ,pɪg] *n* Spanferkel *nt*.

suckle ['sʌkl] [1] *vt child* stillen; *animal* säugen.
[2] *vi* saugen, trinken.

suckling ['sʌklɪŋ] *n (old)* Säugling *m*; *(animal)* Jungtier *nt* ◆ **out of the mouths of babes and ~s** *(Bibl)* aus dem Mund von Kindern und Säuglingen; *(fig)* Kindermund tut Wahrheit kund *(Prov)*.

sucrose ['su:krəʊz] *n* Saccharose *f*, pflanzlicher Zucker.

suction ['sʌkʃən] *n* Saugwirkung *f*; *(caused by air or water currents)* Sog *m* ◆ **~-pump** Saugpumpe *f*.

Sudan [sʊ'dɑ:n] *n* **(the) ~** der Sudan.

Sudanese [,su:də'ni:z] [1] *adj* sudanesisch, sudanisch.
[2] *n* Sudanese *m*, Sudanesin *f*, Sudaner(in *f*) *m*.

sudden ['sʌdn] [1] *adj* plötzlich; *movement also* jäh, abrupt; *drop, silence also* jäh; *(unexpected) bend, change of direction* unerwartet ◆ **there was a ~ bend** da war plötzlich eine Kurve, da war eine unerwartete Kurve; **~ death (play-off)** Stich- *or* Entscheidungskampf *m*; *(Ftbl)* Elfmeterschießen *nt*.
[2] *n* **all of a ~** (ganz) plötzlich, urplötzlich *(inf)*.

suddenly ['sʌdnlɪ] *adv* plötzlich, auf einmal; *move also* jäh, abrupt.

suddenness ['sʌdnnɪs] *n* Plötzlichkeit *f*; *(of movement also)* Jäheit, Abruptheit *f*.

Sudetenland [su:'deɪtən,lænd] *n* Sudetenland *nt*.

suds [sʌdz] *npl* Seifenwasser *nt or* -lauge *f*; *(lather)* (Seifen)schaum *m*; *(US sl: beer)* Bier *nt*.

sue [su:] [1] *vt* **(a)** *(Jur)* verklagen, (gerichtlich) belangen ◆ **to ~ sb for sth** jdn auf etw *(acc) or* wegen etw verklagen; **to ~ sb for divorce** gegen jdn die Scheidung einreichen; **to ~ sb for damages** jdn auf Schadenersatz verklagen; **I'll ~ you for every penny you've got** ich werde (vor Gericht) den letzten Pfennig aus dir herausholen.

➤ LANGUAGE IN USE: **success** → 23.5

(b) (*liter: ask*) bitten, anflehen (*for* um).

2 *vi* (a) (*Jur*) klagen, einen Prozeß anstrengen, Klage erheben ◆ **to ~ for divorce** die Scheidung einreichen. (b) (*liter*) **to ~ for peace/mercy** um Frieden/Gnade bitten.

suede [sweɪd] 1 *n* Wildleder *nt*; (*soft, fine also*) Veloursleder *nt*.

2 *adj shoes, boots* Wildleder-, aus Wildleder; (*of finer quality*) *gloves, coat etc also* Veloursleder-, aus Veloursleder.

suet ['sʊɪt] *n* Nierenfett *nt*, Nierentalg *m* ◆ **~ pudding** (*sweet*) *im Wasserbad gekochte Süßspeise, zu der Nierenfett verwendet wird*; (*savoury*) *Pastetenteig mit Nierenfett*.

Suetonius [swiː'təʊnɪəs] *n* Sueton(ius) *m*.

suety ['suːɪtɪ] *adj* talgig.

Suez ['suːɪz] *n* Sues, Suez *nt* ◆ **~ Canal** Sueskanal, Suezkanal *m*.

suffer ['sʌfəʳ] 1 *vt* (a) (*undergo, be subjected to*) *pain, loss, setback* erleiden; *hardship also, hunger* leiden; *headache, stress, effects etc* leiden unter *or* an (*+dat*); *shock* haben ◆ **to ~ defeat/death** eine Niederlage/den Tod (*geh*) erleiden; **the pound ~ed further losses** das Pfund mußte weitere Einbußen hinnehmen; **her popularity ~ed a decline** ihre Beliebtheit hat gelitten.

(b) (*tolerate*) dulden, ertragen ◆ **he doesn't ~ fools gladly** Dummheit ist ihm ein Greuel.

(c) (*liter: allow*) zulassen, dulden ◆ **to ~ sth to be done** zulassen *or* dulden, daß etw geschieht; **~ the little children to come unto me** (*Bibl*) lasset die Kindlein zu mir kommen (*Bibl*).

2 *vi* (*physically, mentally, fig*) leiden (*from* unter *+dat, from illness* an *+dat*); (*as punishment, in hell etc*) büßen ◆ **he was ~ing from shock** er hatte einen Schock (erlitten); **your health/work will ~** deine Gesundheit/Arbeit wird darunter leiden; **the runners are clearly ~ing in this heat** die Hitze macht den Läufern sichtlich zu schaffen; **the regiment ~ed badly** das Regiment erlitt schwere Verluste; **the town ~ed badly in the raids** die Stadt wurde bei den Luftangriffen schwer in Mitleidenschaft gezogen; **how I ~ed!** was ich alles durchgemacht habe!; **to ~ for one's sins** für seine Sünden büßen; **you'll ~ for this!** das wirst du büßen!; **we will see that you don't ~ by the changes** wir werden zusehen, daß Ihnen aus den Umstellungen keine Nachteile entstehen.

sufferance ['sʌfərəns] *n* Duldung *f* ◆ **on ~** (nur *or* stillschweigend) geduldet; **he's allowed to sleep here on ~ only** es wird nur geduldet, daß er hier schläft.

sufferer ['sʌfərəʳ] *n* (*Med*) Leidende(r) *mf* (*from* an *+dat*) ◆ **diabetes ~s, ~s from diabetes** Diabeteskranke, an Diabetes Leidende *pl*; **he's been a ~ from arthritis for several years** er leidet seit mehreren Jahren an Arthritis; **the ~s from the earthquake** die Erdbebenopfer *pl*; **my fellow ~s at the concert** meine Leidensgenossen bei dem Konzert.

suffering ['sʌfərɪŋ] *n* Leiden *nt*; (*hardship, deprivation*) Leid *nt no pl*.

suffice [sə'faɪs] (*form*) 1 *vi* genügen, (aus)reichen.

2 *vt* genügen (*+dat*) (*geh*); *sb also* zufriedenstellen ◆ **~ it to say ...** es reicht wohl, wenn ich sage, ...

sufficiency [sə'fɪʃənsɪ] *n* (*adequacy*) Hinlänglichkeit *f* ◆ **to have a ~** genügend haben; **to have (an) ample ~** mehr als genug haben.

sufficient [sə'fɪʃənt] *adj* genügend, ausreichend, genug *inv*; *maturity, temperature* genügend *attr*, ausreichend; *reason, condition, explanation, translation* hinreichend ◆ **is that ~ reason for his dismissal?** ist das Grund genug *or* ein ausreichender Grund, ihn zu entlassen?; **to be ~** genügen, ausreichen, genug sein; **thank you, that's ~** danke, das genügt *or* reicht; **I think you have drunk quite ~** ich glaube, Sie haben genug getrunken; **we haven't got ~ to live on** wir haben nicht genug zum Leben.

sufficiently [sə'fɪʃəntlɪ] *adv* genug ◆ **~ good/warm** *etc* gut/warm *etc* genug *pred*, genügend *or* ausreichend gut/warm *etc*; **a ~ large number** eine ausreichend große Anzahl; **it's not ~ cooked** es ist nicht gar.

suffix ['sʌfɪks] 1 *n* (*Ling*) Suffix *nt*, Nachsilbe *f*; (*in code etc*) Zusatz *m*.

2 *vt* anfügen, anhängen (*to* an *+acc*).

suffocate ['sʌfəkeɪt] *vti* (*lit, fig*) ersticken ◆ **this existence/he is suffocating me** dieses Leben/er erdrückt mich; **he felt ~d in that environment** er hatte das Gefühl, in dieser Umgebung zu ersticken; **he was ~d by the smoke** er erstickte am Rauch.

suffocating ['sʌfəkeɪtɪŋ] *adj* (*lit*) erstickend *attr*; (*fig also*) erdrückend *attr*; *heat* drückend *attr*, brütend *attr* ◆ **intellectually ~** geisttötend.

suffocation [,sʌfə'keɪʃən] *n* (*lit, fig*) Ersticken *nt*.

suffragan ['sʌfrəgən] 1 *adj* Suffragan-.

2 *n* Suffragan(bischof) *m*.

suffrage ['sʌfrɪdʒ] *n* Wahl- *or* Stimmrecht *nt*; (*form: vote*) Stimme *f* ◆ **universal ~** das allgemeine Wahlrecht; **female ~** das Frauenstimmrecht.

suffragette [,sʌfrə'dʒet] *n* Suffragette *f*.

suffuse [sə'fjuːz] *vt* erfüllen; (*light*) durchfluten ◆ **~d with light** in Licht getaucht, lichtdurchflutet (*geh*); **eyes ~d with tears** Augen voller Tränen, tränenerfüllte Augen; **a blush ~d her face** Schamröte *or* (eine) Röte überzog ihr Gesicht.

sugar ['ʃʊgəʳ] 1 *n* (a) Zucker *m*. (b) (*inf: term of affection*) (meine) Süße, (mein) Süßer *m*, Schätzchen *nt* (*all inf*).

2 *vt* zuckern, süßen; (*fig*) *criticism etc* versüßen, mildern ◆ **to ~ the pill** die bittere Pille versüßen.

sugar *in cpds* Zucker-; **~ basin** *n* Zuckerdose *f*; **~ beet** *n* Zuckerrübe *f*; **~ bowl** *n* Zuckerdose *f*; **~ candy** *n* Kandis(zucker) *m*; (*US: sweet*) Bonbon *nt or m*; **~ cane** *n* Zuckerrohr *nt*; **~-coated** *adj* mit Zucker überzogen; **~-daddy** *n* (*inf*) **she's looking for a ~-daddy** sie sucht einen alten Knacker, der sie aushält (*inf*); **~ diabetes** *n* Zuckerkrankheit *f*, Diabetes (*spec*), Zucker (*inf*) *m*.

sugared ['ʃʊgəd] *adj* gezuckert; *almonds* Zucker-; *words* (honig)süß.

sugar: ~-free *adj* ohne Zucker; **~ loaf** *n* Zuckerhut *m*; **S~ Loaf Mountain** der Zuckerhut; **~ maple** *n* Zuckerahorn *m*; **~plum** *n* Bonbon *nt or m*, Süßigkeit *f*; **~plum fairy** Zuckerfee *f*; **~ tongs** *npl* Zuckerzange *f*.

sugary ['ʃʊgərɪ] *adj taste* süß; (*full of sugar*) zuckerig; (*fig*) *style, music etc* süßlich.

suggest [sə'dʒest] 1 *vt* (a) (*propose*) *candidate, place etc* vorschlagen; *plan, idea also* anregen ◆ **I ~ that we go, I ~ going** ich schlage vor, zu gehen *or* (daß) wir gehen; **what do you ~ we do?** was schlagen Sie vor?; **are you ~ing I should tell a deliberate lie?** soll das heißen, daß ich bewußt lügen soll?; **I am ~ing nothing of the kind** das habe ich nicht gesagt.

(b) (*put forward for consideration*) *explanation, theory* nahelegen, vorbringen ◆ **I ~ (to you) that ...** (*esp Jur*) ich möchte (Ihnen) nahelegen, daß ...

(c) (*insinuate, hint at*) andeuten; (*unpleasantly*) unterstellen ◆ **what are you trying to ~?** worauf wollen Sie hinaus?, was wollen Sie damit sagen?; **I'm not trying to ~ that he's lying** ich will damit nicht unterstellen *or* sagen, daß er lügt.

(d) (*indicate: facts, data, sb's action*) andeuten, hindeuten auf (*+acc*); (*evoke*) (*music, poem*) denken lassen an (*+acc*); (*symbolism, colours*) andeuten ◆ **it certainly ~s complicity** das deutet zweifellos auf Mittäterschaft hin; **the symptoms would ~ an operation** die Symptome lassen eine Operation angeraten erscheinen.

(e) (*Psych*) **to ~ sth to sb** jdm etw suggerieren.

2 *vr* (*idea, thought, plan*) sich aufdrängen, sich anbieten.

suggestibility [sə,dʒestɪ'bɪlɪtɪ] *n* Beeinflußbarkeit *f*.

suggestible [sə'dʒestɪbl] *adj person* beeinflußbar.

suggestion [sə'dʒestʃən] *n* (a) (*proposal, recommendation*) Vorschlag *m*, Anregung *f* ◆ **my ~ is that ...** mein Vorschlag lautet ..., ich schlage vor, daß ...; **following your ~** auf Ihren Vorschlag *or* Ihre Anregung hin; **Rome was your ~** Rom war deine Idee; **John was his ~ as candidate** er schlug John als Kandidaten vor; **I'm open to ~s** Vorschläge sind *or* jeder Vorschlag ist willkommen.

(b) (*theory, explanation*) Vermutung *f* ◆ **he made the ~ that ...** er äußerte die Vermutung, daß ...; **that theory was Professor Higgins' ~** die Theorie stammt von Professor Higgins.

(c) (*insinuation, hint*) Andeutung, Anspielung *f*; (*unpleasant*) Unterstellung *f* ◆ **I resent that ~** ich weise diese Unterstellung zurück; **I intended no ~ that ...** ich wollte damit nicht andeuten *or* unterstellen, daß ...; **there is no ~ that he was involved** (*nobody is suggesting it*) niemand deutet an *or* unterstellt, daß er beteiligt war; (*no indication*) es gibt keinen Hinweis darauf *or* Anhaltspunkt dafür, daß er beteiligt war.

(d) (*trace*) Spur *f* ◆ **with a ~ of irony in his voice** mit einer Spur *or* einem Anflug von Ironie in der Stimme.

(e) (*impression*) Eindruck *m*, Vorstellung *f* ◆ **to create a ~ of depth** um den Eindruck von Tiefe zu erwecken.

(f) (*also* **indecent ~**) unsittlicher Antrag.

(g) (*Psych*) Suggestion *f*.

suggestions-box [sə'dʒestʃənz,bɒks] *n* Kasten *m* für Verbesserungsvorschläge, Kummerkasten (*inf*) *m*.

suggestive [sə'dʒestɪv] *adj* (a) **to be ~ of sth** an etw (*acc*) denken lassen; (*create impression of*) den Eindruck von etw erwecken *or* vermitteln; (*be indicative of*) auf etw (*acc*) hindeuten. (b) (*Psych*) suggestiv, Suggestiv-. (c) (*indecent*) *joke, remark etc* zweideutig, anzüglich; *movements, gesture* aufreizend.

suggestively [sə'dʒestɪvlɪ] *adv* vielsagend, anzüglich; *move, dance* aufreizend.

suggestiveness [sə'dʒestɪvnɪs] *n* Zweideutigkeit, Anzüglichkeit *f* ◆ **the ~ of her dancing** ihr aufreizendes Tanzen.

suicidal [,sʊɪ'saɪdl] *adj* selbstmörderisch ◆ **that would be ~** das wäre glatter Selbstmord; **to have ~ tendencies** zum Selbstmord neigen; **I feel ~ this morning** ich möchte heute morgen am liebsten sterben.

suicide ['sʊɪsaɪd] *n* Selbstmord, Freitod (*euph*), Suizid (*spec*) *m*; (*person*) Selbstmörder(in *f*), Suizidär(in *f*) (*spec*) *m* ◆ **to commit ~** Selbstmord begehen; **to contemplate ~** sich mit Selbstmordgedanken tragen; **~ attempt** *or* **bid** Selbstmord- *or* Suizidversuch *m*; **~ pact** Selbstmordabkommen *nt*; **~ squad** Selbstmordkommando *nt*.

sui generis [,suːaɪ'dʒenərɪs] *adj* sui generis (*geh*), einzig(artig).

suit [suːt] 1 *n* (a) Anzug *m*; (*woman's*) Kostüm *nt* ◆ **~ of clothes** Garnitur *f* (Kleider); **they bought him a new ~ of clothes** sie kleideten ihn von Kopf bis Fuß neu ein; **~ of armour** Rüstung *f*.

(b) (*Jur*) Prozeß *m*, Verfahren *nt* ◆ **to bring a ~ (against sb for sth)** (wegen etw gegen jdn) Klage erheben *or* einen Prozeß anstrengen; **he lost his ~** er hat seinen Prozeß verloren.

(c) (*Cards*) Farbe *f* ◆ **short ~** kurze Farbe; **long/strong ~** lange/starke Farbe; (*fig*) starke Seite, Stärke *f*; **to follow ~** (*lit*) Farbe bedienen; (*fig*) jds Beispiel (*dat*) folgen.

(d) (*old, liter: in marriage*) Werbung *f* ◆ **to press one's ~** seiner Werbung (*dat*) Nachdruck verleihen; **he failed in his ~** seine Werbung wurde zurückgewiesen.

(e) (*form: request*) Anliegen *nt* (*form*), Bitte *f* ◆ **to press one's ~** seinem Anliegen *or* seiner Bitte Nachdruck verleihen.

2 *vt* (a) (*be convenient, pleasing to*) (*arrangement, date, price*) passen (*+dat*); (*climate, food*) bekommen (*+dat*); (*occupation, job*) gefallen (*+dat*) ◆ **~s me!** (*inf*) ist mir recht (*inf*), mir soll's recht sein (*inf*); **that ~s me fine!** (*inf*) das ist mir recht; **that would ~ me nicely** (*time, arrangement*) das würde mir gut (in den

➤ LANGUAGE IN USE: **suggest: 1a** → 1.1, 1.2 **suggestion: a** → 1.1, 1.2 **suit: 2a** → 7.4, 11.3

Kram *inf*) passen; (*house, job etc*) das wäre genau das richtige für mich; **when would it ~ you to come?** wann würde es Ihnen passen?, wann wäre es Ihnen recht?; **I know what ~s me best** ich weiß, was für mich das beste ist.
(b) to be ~ed for/to (*be suitable, right for*) geeignet sein für; **he is very well ~ed to the job** er eignet sich sehr gut für die Stelle; **he is not ~ed to be** *or* **for a doctor** er eignet sich nicht zum Arzt; **they are well ~ed (to each other)** sie passen gut zusammen.
(c) (*clothes, hairstyle*) (gut) stehen (+*dat*), passen zu ♦ **you ~ a beard/fringe** ein Bart/Pony steht dir gut; **such behaviour hardly ~s you** so ein Benehmen steht dir nicht an.
(d) (*adapt*) anpassen (*to dat*) ♦ **to ~ one's style to the audience** sich dem Publikumsgeschmack anpassen, sich nach dem Publikum richten; **~ing the action to the word he ...** er setzte seine Worte in die Tat um und ...
(e) (*please*) gefallen (+*dat*), zufriedenstellen ♦ **you can't ~ everybody** man kann es nicht jedem recht machen; **we try to ~ every taste** wir versuchen, etwas für jeden Geschmack zu finden *or* jedem Geschmack gerecht zu werden.
[3] *vr* **he ~s himself** er tut, was er will *or* was ihm paßt; **you can ~ yourself whether you come or not** du kannst kommen oder nicht, ganz wie du willst; **~ yourself!** wie du willst!, mach, was du willst!; **I like to be able to ~ myself** ich möchte gern tun und lassen können, was ich will.
[4] *vi* (*be suitable*) passen.

suitability [ˌsuːtəˈbɪlɪtɪ] *n* Angemessenheit *f*; (*of person for job*) Eignung *f* ♦ **they discussed his ~ as a husband for their daughter** sie diskutierten darüber, ob er sich als Ehemann für ihre Tochter eignete; **the ~ of a film for children** ob ein Film für Kinder geeignet ist.

suitable [ˈsuːtəbl] *adj* (*convenient, practical, right for the purpose*) geeignet, passend; (*socially, culturally appropriate to the occasion*) angemessen ♦ **to be ~ for sb** (*date, place*) jdm passen; (*film, job*) für jdn geeignet sein; (*hairstyle, clothes*) das richtige für jdn sein; **to be ~ for sth** für etw geeignet sein, sich für etw eignen; (*socially*) einer Sache (*dat*) angemessen sein; **the most ~ man for the job** der am besten geeignete Mann für den Posten; **would 8 o'clock be a ~ time?** würde Ihnen *etc* 8 Uhr passen?; **Tuesday is the most ~ day** Dienstag ist der günstigste *or* beste Tag, Dienstag paßt am besten; **she's not ~ for him** sie paßt nicht zu ihm.

suitably [ˈsuːtəblɪ] *adv* angemessen; *behave also, apologize* geziemend (*geh*), wie es sich gehört ♦ **he was ~ impressed** er war gehörig beeindruckt; **I'm ~ impressed** ich bin ja auch beeindruckt; **a ~ elegant room** ein Raum von angemessener Eleganz; **we camped ~ close to the hills** wir zelteten in günstiger Nähe der Berge.

suitcase *n* Koffer *m* ♦ **to live out of a ~** aus dem Koffer leben.

suite [swiːt] *n* (*of retainers*) Gefolge *nt*; (*of furniture*) Garnitur *f*; (*chairs and sofa*) Sitzgarnitur *f*; (*of rooms*) Suite, Zimmerflucht *f*; (*Mus*) Suite *f* ♦ **bedroom ~** Schlafzimmergarnitur *or* -einrichtung *f*; **3-piece ~** dreiteilige Sitzgarnitur.

suiting [ˈsuːtɪŋ] *n* (*fabric*) Anzugstoff *m*.

suitor [ˈsuːtəʳ] *n* **(a)** (*old: of woman*) Freier *m* (*old*). **(b)** (*Jur*) Kläger(in *f*) *m*.

sulfa *etc* (*US*) *see* **sulpha** *etc*.

sulk [sʌlk] [1] *vi* schmollen, eingeschnappt sein, beleidigt sein; (*photo model*) einen Schmollmund machen.
[2] *n* Schmollen *nt* ♦ **to have a ~/the ~s** schmollen, den Eingeschnappten/die Eingeschnappte spielen; **to go into a ~** sich in den Schmollwinkel zurückziehen, einschnappen.

sulkily [ˈsʌlkɪlɪ] *adv see adj*.

sulkiness [ˈsʌlkɪnɪs] *n* Schmollen *nt* ♦ **the ~ of his expression** sein eingeschnappter *or* schmollender Gesichtsausdruck.

sulky[1] [ˈsʌlkɪ] *adj* (*+er*) *answer* eingeschnappt, beleidigt; *person, expression also* schmollend ♦ **~ mouth** Schmollmund *m*.

sulky[2] *n* (*Sport*) Sulky *nt*.

sullen [ˈsʌlən] *adj* **(a)** (*morose*) mürrisch, mißmutig, verdrießlich. **(b)** (*liter*) *landscape, sky etc* düster, finster.

sullenly [ˈsʌlənlɪ] *adv see adj (a)*.

sullenness [ˈsʌlənnɪs] *n see adj* **(a)** Mißmutigkeit, Verdrießlichkeit *f*. **(b)** (*liter*) Düsterkeit *f*.

sully [ˈsʌlɪ] *vt reputation* besudeln.

sulpha, (*US*) **sulfa** [ˈsʌlfə] *adj* **~ drug** Sulfonamid *nt*.

sulphate, (*US*) **sulfate** [ˈsʌlfeɪt] *n* Sulfat *nt*, schwefelsaures Salz ♦ **copper ~** Kupfersulfat *or* -vitriol *nt*.

sulphide, (*US*) **sulfide** [ˈsʌlfaɪd] *n* Sulfid *nt*.

sulphite, (*US*) **sulfite** [ˈsʌlfaɪt] *n* Sulfit *nt*.

sulphonamide, (*US*) **sulfonamide** [sʌlˈfɒnəmaɪd] *n* Sulfonamid *nt*.

sulphur, (*US*) **sulfur** [ˈsʌlfəʳ] *n* Schwefel *m* ♦ **~ dioxide** Schwefeldioxid *nt*.

sulphuretted, (*US*) **sulfuretted** [ˈsʌlfjʊˌretɪd] *adj* geschwefelt ♦ **~ hydrogen** Schwefelwasserstoff *m*.

sulphuric, (*US*) **sulfuric** [sʌlˈfjʊərɪk] *adj* Schwefel- ♦ **~ acid** Schwefelsäure *f*.

sulphurize, (*US*) **sulfurize** [ˈsʌlfjʊˌraɪz] *vt* schwefeln.

sulphurous, (*US*) **sulfurous** [ˈsʌlfərəs] *adj* schwefelig, Schwefel-, schwefelhaltig ♦ **~ acid** schwefelige Säure.

sultan [ˈsʌltən] *n* Sultan *m*.

sultana [sʌlˈtɑːnə] *n* **(a)** (*person*) Sultanin *f*. **(b)** (*fruit*) Sultanine *f*.

sultanate [ˈsʌltənɪt] *n* Sultanat *nt*.

sultriness [ˈsʌltrɪnɪs] *n* (*lit*) Schwüle *f*; (*fig*) Heißblütigkeit *f*; (*of look*) Glut *f*.

sultry [ˈsʌltrɪ] *adj weather, atmosphere* schwül; *woman* heißblütig, temperamentvoll; *beauty, look* glutvoll, schwül (*liter*).

▼ **sum** [sʌm] *n* **(a)** (*total*) Summe *f* ♦ **that was the ~ (total) of his achievements** das war alles, was er geschafft hatte; **the ~ total of my ambitions** das Ziel meiner Wünsche.
▼ **(b)** (*of money*) Betrag *m*, Summe *f*.
(c) (*esp Brit: calculation*) Rechenaufgabe *f* ♦ **to do ~s (in one's head)** (im Kopf) rechnen; **I was bad at ~s** ich war schlecht im Rechnen.
(d) (*form: essence*) **in ~** mit einem Wort, zusammengefaßt.

♦**sum up** [1] *vt sep* **(a)** (*review, summarize*) zusammenfassen. **(b)** (*evaluate rapidly*) ab- *or* einschätzen, taxieren ♦ **she ~med me ~ at a glance** sie taxierte mich mit einem Blick.
[2] *vi* (*also Jur*) zusammenfassen, resümieren ♦ **to ~ ~, we can say that ...** zusammenfassend *or* als Resümee können wir feststellen, daß ...; **the judge hasn't ~med ~ yet** der Richter hat sein Resümee noch nicht gegeben.

sumac(h) [ˈsuːmæk] *n* (*plant*) Sumach, Gerberstrauch *m*; (*preparation*) Schmack *m*.

Sumatra [suːˈmɑːtrə] *n* Sumatra *nt*.

Sumatran [suːˈmɑːtrən] [1] *adj* von/aus Sumatra.
[2] *n* Bewohner(in *f*) *m* von Sumatra.

Sumerian [suːˈmɪərɪən] [1] *adj* sumerisch.
[2] *n* Sumerer(in *f*) *m*; (*language*) Sumerisch *nt*.

summa cum laude [ˈsʊmɑːkʊmˈlaʊdeɪ] *adv* (*US*) summa cum laude.

summarily [ˈsʌmərɪlɪ] *adv* (*briefly*) knapp, kurzgefaßt; (*fast, without ceremony*) kurz und bündig, ohne viel Federlesen(s); (*Jur*) *punish, try* summarisch; *read* flüchtig, kursorisch (*geh*).

summarize [ˈsʌməraɪz] *vt* zusammenfassen.

summary [ˈsʌmərɪ] [1] *n* Zusammenfassung *f*; (*Sci also*) Abriß *m* ♦ **here is a ~ of the main points of the news** hier eine Zusammenfassung der *or* ein Überblick *m* über die wichtigsten Meldungen; **he gave us a short ~ of the film** er gab uns eine kurze Inhaltsangabe des Films; **~ of contents** Inhaltsangabe *f*.
[2] *adj* **(a)** (*brief*) *account* knapp, gedrängt, kurzgefaßt.
(b) (*fast, without ceremony*) *treatment* kurz, knapp; *perusal* flüchtig; (*Jur*) *trial, punishment* summarisch; *dismissal* fristlos ♦ **the court dealt out ~ justice** das Gericht sprach Recht im Schnellverfahren; **~ offence** (*Jur*) ≃ Übertretung *f*.

summation [sʌˈmeɪʃən] *n* (*act*) Addition *f*; (*total*) Summe *f*; (*summary*) Zusammenfassung *f*; (*US Jur*) Plädoyers *pl* ♦ **in ~** zusammenfassend.

summer [ˈsʌməʳ] [1] *n* Sommer *m* ♦ **in (the) ~** im Sommer; **two ~s ago** im Sommer vor zwei Jahren; **a girl of seventeen ~s** (*liter*) ein Mädchen von siebzehn Lenzen (*liter*); **a ~'s day** ein Sommertag *m*.
[2] *adj attr* Sommer- ♦ **~ resort** Ferien- *or* Urlaubsort *m* (für die Sommersaison).
[3] *vi* den Sommer verbringen; (*birds also*) übersommern.

summer: ~house *n* Gartenhaus *nt*, (Garten)laube *f*; **~ lightning** *n* Wetterleuchten *nt*.

summersault *n, vi see* **somersault**.

summer: ~time *n* Sommer(szeit *f*) *m*; (*daylight-saving time*) Sommerzeit *f*; **~weight** *adj suit* sommerlich, Sommer-.

summery [ˈsʌmərɪ] *adj* sommerlich.

summing-up [ˈsʌmɪŋˈʌp] *n* (*Jur*) Resümee *nt*.

summit [ˈsʌmɪt] [1] *n* (*lit*) Gipfel *m*; (*fig also*) Höhepunkt *m*; (*~ conference*) Gipfel(konferenz *f*) *m*.
[2] *adj attr* (*Pol*) Gipfel- ♦ **at ~ level** auf Gipfelebene; **~ talks** Gipfelgespräche *pl*.

summiteer [ˌsʌmɪˈtiːəʳ] *n* Gipfelteilnehmer(in *f*) *m*, Teilnehmer(in *f*) *m* an der Gipfelkonferenz.

summon [ˈsʌmən] *vt* **(a)** *servant etc* (herbei)rufen, kommen lassen, herbeizitieren; *police, fire brigade etc* (herbei)rufen; *help* holen; *meeting, Parliament* einberufen ♦ **to ~ sb to do sth** (*order*) jdn auffordern, etw zu tun; **the King ~ed his ministers** der König rief seine Minister zusammen; **he was ~ed back** er wurde zurückgerufen; **to be ~ed into sb's presence** zu jdm befohlen *or* zitiert (*iro*) werden; **a bell ~ed them to their work** eine Glocke rief sie zur Arbeit.
(b) (*Jur*) vorladen ♦ **~ the next witness!** rufen Sie den nächsten Zeugen (auf)!

♦**summon up** *vt sep courage* zusammennehmen, zusammenraffen; *strength* aufbieten; *enthusiasm, energy* aufbieten, aufbringen ♦ **~ing ~ all his strength he lifted it up** unter Aufbietung aller Kräfte hob er es hoch.

summons [ˈsʌmənz] [1] *n* **(a)** (*Jur*) Vorladung *f* ♦ **to take out a ~ against sb** jdn vorladen lassen, jdn vor Gericht laden.
(b) (*order to appear etc*) Aufruf *m*, Aufforderung *f* ♦ **he received a ~ from the boss** er wurde zum Chef gerufen, er wurde aufgefordert, zum Chef zu kommen.
[2] *vt* (*Jur*) vorladen.

sump [sʌmp] *n* (*Brit Aut*) Ölwanne *f*; (*Min*) Sumpf *m*.

sumptuary [ˈsʌmptjʊərɪ] *adj law* Aufwands-, Luxus-.

sumptuous [ˈsʌmptjʊəs] *adj* (*splendid*) luxuriös; (*costly*) aufwendig, kostspielig; *food etc* üppig, verschwenderisch.

sumptuously [ˈsʌmptjʊəslɪ] *adv see adj*.

sumptuousness [ˈsʌmptjʊəsnɪs] *n see adj* Luxus *m*; Aufwand *m*, Kostspieligkeit *f*; Üppigkeit *f*.

Sun *abbr of* **Sunday** So.

sun [sʌn] [1] *n* Sonne *f* ♦ **I've got the ~ in my eyes** die Sonne scheint mir in die Augen *or* blendet mich; **he was up with the ~** er stand in aller Frühe auf; **to have a touch of the ~** einen Sonnenstich haben (*also fig*); **you've caught the ~** dich hat die Sonne erwischt; **there is no reason under the ~ why ...** es gibt keinen Grund auf Erden, warum ...; **he's tried everything under the ~** er hat alles Menschenmögliche versucht; **a place in the ~** (*fig*) ein Platz an der Sonne; **there's nothing new under the ~** (*Prov*) es ist alles schon einmal

➤ LANGUAGE IN USE: **sum: b → 20.7**

dagewesen (*prov*).
[2] *vt* der Sonne aussetzen.
[3] *vr* sich sonnen.

sun: ~-baked *adj* ausgedörrt; ~ **bath** *n* Sonnenbad *nt*; **~bathe** *vi* in der Sonne liegen, sonnenbaden; **~bather** *n* Sonnenanbeter(in *f*) *m* (*hum*); **all the ~bathers in the park** all die Leute, die sich im Park sonnen *or* die im Park in der Sonne liegen; **~bathing** *n* Sonnenbaden *nt*; **~beam** *n* Sonnenstrahl *m*; **~bed** *n* Sonnenbank *f*; ~ **blind** *n* (*awning*) Markise *f*; (*venetian blind*) Jalousie *f*; **~block** *n* Sonnenschutzcreme, Sun-Block-Creme *f*; ~ **bonnet** *n* Sonnenhut *m*; **~burn** *n* Bräune *f*; (*painful*) Sonnenbrand *m*; **~burnt** *adj* sonnengebräunt, sonnenverbrannt; (*painfully*) von der Sonne verbrannt; **to get ~burnt** braun werden; (einen) Sonnenbrand bekommen; **~burst** *n* **(a)** (*US*) plötzlicher Sonnenschein; **(b)** (*pattern*) Sonnenrad *nt*.

sundae ['sʌndeɪ] *n* Eisbecher *m*.

sun dance *n* Sonnenanbetungstanz *m*.

Sunday ['sʌndɪ] [1] *n* Sonntag *m* ◆ **a month of ~s** (*inf*) ewig (lange), eine Ewigkeit; **never in a month of ~s** (*inf*) nie im Leben; *see also* **Tuesday.**
[2] *adj attr* Sonntags- ◆ ~ **best** Sonntagskleider *pl*, Sonntagsstaat *m* (*old, hum*); ~ **school** Sonntagsschule *f*; ~ **driver** Sonntagsfahrer(in *f*) *m*; ~ **painter** Sonntagsmaler(in *f*) *m*.

sun deck *n* Sonnendeck *nt*.

sunder ['sʌndəʳ] (*liter*) [1] *vt* brechen; *chains* sprengen; (*fig*) *connection* abbrechen.
[2] *vi* brechen; (*fig*) sich trennen.

sun: ~dew *n* (*Bot*) Sonnentau *m*; **~dial** *n* Sonnenuhr *f*; **~down** *n* Sonnenuntergang *m*; **at/before ~down** bei/vor Sonnenuntergang; **~downer** *n* **(a)** (*Austral inf: tramp*) Penner (*inf*), Vagabund *m*; **(b)** (*drink*) Abendtrunk *m*; **~-drenched** *adj beaches* sonnenüberflutet, in Sonne getaucht; **~dress** *n* leichtes Sonnenkleid; **~-dried** *adj fruit* an *or* in der Sonne getrocknet.

sundry ['sʌndrɪ] [1] *adj* verschiedene.
[2] *pron* **all and ~** jedermann.
[3] *n* **sundries** *pl* Verschiedenes (+*sing vb*).

sun: ~fast *adj* (*esp US*) lichtecht; **~flower** *n* Sonnenblume *f*.

sung [sʌŋ] *ptp of* **sing.**

sun: ~glasses *npl* Sonnenbrille *f*; **~-god** *n* Sonnengott *m*; ~ **hat** *n* Sonnenhut *m*; ~ **helmet** *n* Tropenhelm *m*.

sunk [sʌŋk] *ptp of* **sink¹.**

sunken ['sʌŋkən] *adj wreck, ship* gesunken, versunken; *treasure* versunken; *garden* tiefliegend *attr*; *bath* eingelassen; *cheeks* eingefallen, hohl; *eyes* eingesunken.

sun: S~ King *n* Sonnenkönig *m*; ~ **lamp** *n* Höhensonne *f*; **~less** *adj garden* ohne Sonne; *room also* dunkel; *day also* trübe; **~light** *n* Sonnenlicht *nt*; **in the ~light** in der Sonne, im Sonnenlicht; **~lit** *adj room* sonnig; *fields etc also* sonnenbeschienen; ~ **lounge** *n* Wintergarten *m*, Glasveranda *f*; ~ **lounger** *n* Sonnenliege *f*.

sunnily ['sʌnɪlɪ] *adv* heiter; *smile also* sonnig.

sunny ['sʌnɪ] *adj* (+*er*) *place, room, day etc* sonnig; (*fig*) *smile, disposition also, answer, face* heiter ◆ ~ **intervals** (*Met*) Aufheiterungen *pl*; **on the ~ side of the house** auf der Sonnenseite (des Hauses); **~-side up** (*egg*) nur auf einer Seite gebraten; **the outlook is ~** (*Met*) die Wetteraussichten sind gut; (*fig*) die Aussichten sind rosig; **to look on the ~ side (of things)** die Dinge von der angenehmen Seite nehmen; **to be on the ~ side of forty** noch nicht vierzig sein, unter vierzig sein.

sun: ~ parlor *n* (*US*) Wintergarten *m*, Glasveranda *f*; ~ **porch** *n* Veranda *f*; **~ray** [1] *n* Sonnenstrahl *m*; [2] *adj attr* **~ray lamp** Höhensonne *f*; **~ray treatment** Ultraviolett-/Infrarot(strahlen) behandlung *f*; **~rise** *n* Sonnenaufgang *m*; **at ~rise** bei Sonnenaufgang; **~rise industry** *n* Zukunftsindustrie *f*; **~roof** *n* (*of car*) Schiebedach *nt*; (*of hotel etc*) Sonnenterrasse *f*; **~set** *n* Sonnenuntergang *m*; **at ~set** bei Sonnenuntergang; **~shade** *n* (*lady's, over table*) Sonnenschirm *m*; (*awning*) Markise, Sonnenblende *f*; **~shine** *n* **(a)** Sonnenschein *m*; **hours of ~shine** Sonnenstunden *pl*; **a daily average of 5 hours' ~shine** durchschnittlich 5 Stunden Sonne täglich; **(b)** (*inf: person*) mein Lieber, meine Liebe; **~shine roof** *n* Schiebedach *nt*; **~spot** *n* **(a)** Sonnenfleck *m*; **(b)** (*inf: for holiday*) Ferienparadies *nt*; **~stroke** *n* Sonnenstich *m*; **to get ~stroke** einen Sonnenstich bekommen; **~suit** *n* Spiel- *or* Sonnenanzug *m*; **~tan** *n* Sonnenbräune *f*; **to get a ~tan** braun werden; **~tan lotion/oil** *n* Sonnenöl *nt*; **~tanned** *adj* braungebrannt; **~trap** *n* sonniges Eckchen; **~-up** *n* Sonnenaufgang *m*; **at ~-up** bei Sonnenaufgang; **~-worship** *n* (*lit, fig*) Sonnenanbetung *f*; **~-worshipper** *n* (*lit, fig*) Sonnenanbeter(in *f*) *m*.

sup [sʌp] [1] *vt* (*esp N Engl, Scot*) trinken.
[2] *vi* (*old: dine*) zu Abend essen ◆ **to ~ off** *or* **on sth** etw zu Abend essen; **he that ~s with the devil must have a long spoon** (*Prov*) wer den Teufel zum Freund hat, kommt leicht in die Hölle (*Prov*).
[3] *n* (*drink*) Schluck *m*.

◆**sup up** *vti sep* (*esp N Engl, Scot*) austrinken.

super¹ ['suːpəʳ] *adj* (*inf*) phantastisch, sagenhaft, klasse *inv* (*inf*) ◆ **~!** Klasse! (*inf*); **we had a ~ time** es war große Klasse (*inf*) *or* phantastisch *or* sagenhaft.

super² *n abbr of* **(a)** (*inf*) **superintendent** Aufseher(in *f*) *m*; (*of police*) ≃ Kommissar(in *f*) *m*. **(b)** (*Theat, Film*) **supernumerary** Statist(in *f*) *m*.

super- *pref* super-, Super-.

superable ['suːpərəbl] *adj* überwindbar, überwindlich.

superabundance [ˌsuːpərə'bʌndəns] *n* (*of an* +*dat*) großer Reichtum; (*excessive amount*) Überfluß, Überschuß *m*; (*of enthusiasm*) Überschuß *m*.

superabundant [ˌsuːpərə'bʌndənt] *adj* überreichlich.

superannuate [ˌsuːpə'rænjʊeɪt] *vt* pensionieren, in den Ruhestand versetzen.

superannuated [ˌsuːpə'rænjʊeɪtɪd] *adj* pensioniert, im Ruhestand; (*fig inf*) veraltet, überholt.

superannuation [ˌsuːpəˌrænjʊ'eɪʃən] *n* (*act*) Pensionierung *f*, Versetzung *f* in den Ruhestand; (*state*) Pension *f*, Ruhestand *m*; (*pension*) Rente *f*; (*for civil servants, teachers*) Ruhegehalt *nt* (*form*) ◆ ~ **contribution** Beitrag *m* zur Altersversicherung.

superb [suː'pɜːb] *adj* großartig; *design, painting also* meisterhaft; *quality, food also* vorzüglich, superb (*dated, geh*).

superbly [suː'pɜːblɪ] *adv see adj* ◆ ~ **fit/self-confident** ungemein fit/selbstbewußt.

superbness [suː'pɜːbnɪs] *n see adj* Großartigkeit *f*, Vorzüglichkeit *f*.

Superbowl ['suːpəˌbəʊl] *n* (*US*) Superbowl *m*, *jährlich ausgetragenes American-Football-Turnier zwischen den Spitzenreitern der Nationalligen.*

supercargo ['suːpəˌkɑːgəʊ] *n, pl* **-es** Frachtaufseher *m*.

supercharged ['suːpəˌtʃɑːdʒd] *adj gas* vorverdichtet; *engine* aufgeladen; (*fig*) *atmosphere* gereizt.

supercharger ['suːpəˌtʃɑːdʒəʳ] *n* Lader *m*.

supercilious *adj*, **~ly** *adv* [ˌsuːpə'sɪlɪəs, -lɪ] hochnäsig.

superciliousness [ˌsuːpə'sɪlɪəsnɪs] *n* Hochnäsigkeit *f*.

supercomputer ['suːpəkəmˌpjuːtəʳ] *n* Supercomputer *m*.

supercool [ˌsuːpə'kuːl] *vt* unterkühlen.

super-duper ['suːpə'duːpəʳ] *adj* (*hum inf*) ganz toll (*inf*).

superego [ˌsuːpər'iːgəʊ] *n* Über-Ich *nt*.

supererogation ['suːpərˌerə'geɪʃən] *n* (*form*) Mehrleistung, Supererogation (*form*) *f*; (*Eccl*) freiwillige Gebete *pl*; gute Werke *pl* ◆ **an act of ~** eine Mehrleistung *or* Supererogation (*form*).

superficial [ˌsuːpə'fɪʃəl] *adj person, behaviour, injury, treatment* oberflächlich; *characteristics, resemblance* äußerlich.

superficiality ['suːpəˌfɪʃɪ'ælɪtɪ] *n see adj* Oberflächlichkeit *f*; Äußerlichkeit *f*.

superficially [ˌsuːpə'fɪʃəlɪ] *adv see adj* oberflächlich; äußerlich ◆ **~ this may be true** oberflächlich gesehen mag das stimmen.

superfine ['suːpəfaɪn] *adj distinction* übertrieben fein.

superfluity [ˌsuːpə'flʊɪtɪ] *n* Überfluß *m* ◆ **his ~ of style, the ~ of his style** sein verschwenderischer Stil.

superfluous [sʊ'pɜːflʊəs] *adj* überflüssig; *style* verschwenderisch ◆ **it is ~ to say ...** es ist überflüssig, zu sagen ...

superfluously [sʊ'pɜːflʊəslɪ] *adv see adj* ◆ **he added ~** er fügte überflüssigerweise hinzu.

super: ~glue *n* Sekundenkleber *m*; **~grass** *n* (*inf: informant*) Kronzeuge *m* (*inf*), Kronzeugin *f* (*inf*), Topinformant(in *f*) *m*; **~group** *n* (*Mus*) Supergruppe *f*; **~heat** *vt* überhitzen; **~hero** *n* Superheld *m*; **~highway** *n* (*US*) ≃ Autobahn *f*; **~human** *adj* übermenschlich.

superimpose [ˌsuːpərɪm'pəʊz] *vt* **to ~ sth on sth** etw auf etw (*acc*) legen; (*Phot*) etw über etw (*acc*) fotografieren; (*Film*) etw über etw (*acc*) filmen; (*Geol*) etw über etw (*acc*) lagern; (*fig*) etw mit etw überlagern; **by superimposing one image on another** indem man zwei Bilder aufeinanderlegt; **the images became ~d** die Bilder hatten sich überlagert.

superintend [ˌsuːpərɪn'tend] *vt* beaufsichtigen, überwachen.

superintendence [ˌsuːpərɪn'tendəns] *n* (Ober)aufsicht *f*.

superintendent [ˌsuːpərɪn'tendənt] *n* Aufsicht *f*; (*in swimming-pool*) Bademeister *m*; (*in park also*) Parkwächter *m*; (*of hostel, Sunday school etc*) Leiter(in *f*) *m*; (*of police*) (*Brit*) ≃ Kommissar(in *f*) *m*; (*US*) ≃ Polizeipräsident *m*.

➤ **superior** [sʊ'pɪərɪəʳ] [1] *adj* **(a)** (*better*) *quality, equipment* besser (*to* als); *intellect, ability, skill, technique* überlegen (*to sb/sth* jdm/einer Sache) ◆ **he thinks he's so ~** er hält sich für so überlegen *or* für soviel besser.
(b) (*excellent*) *work(manship), technique* großartig, hervorragend; *craftsman* ausgezeichnet; *intellect* überragend ◆ **goods of ~ quality, ~ quality goods** Waren *pl* bester Qualität.
(c) (*higher in rank etc*) höher ◆ ~ **officer** Vorgesetzte(r) *mf*; ~ **court** höheres Gericht; **to be ~ to sb/sth** jdm/einer Sache übergeordnet sein, höher stehen als jd/etw.
(d) (*greater*) überlegen (*to sb/sth* jdm/einer Sache); *forces also* stärker (*to* als); *strength also* größer (*to* als) ◆ **they were ~ to us in number(s)** sie waren uns zahlenmäßig überlegen.
(e) (*snobbish*) *person, manner* überheblich; *tone, smile also* überlegen; (*smart*) *restaurant, clientele* fein, vornehm.
(f) (*Typ*) *figure, letter* hochgestellt ◆ ~ **number** Hochzahl *f*.
[2] *n* **(a)** (*in rank*) Vorgesetzte(r) *mf*. **(b)** (*in ability*) Überlegene(r) *mf* ◆ **to be sb's ~** jdm überlegen sein; **he has few ~s when it comes to that** was das anbelangt, sind ihm wenige überlegen. **(c)** (*Eccl*) **Father/Mother S~** Vater Superior/Mutter Superiorin *or* Oberin.

superiority [sʊˌpɪərɪ'ɒrɪtɪ] *n* **(a)** (*of cloth etc*) bessere Qualität; (*of technique, ability etc*) Überlegenheit *f* ◆ **its ~ as a holiday resort** seine bessere Klasse als Ferienort.
(b) (*excellence*) Großartigkeit *f*; (*of intellect*) überragende Eigenschaft.
(c) (*in rank*) höhere Stellung, höherer Rang.
(d) (*in numbers etc*) Überlegenheit *f*.
(e) (*conceitedness*) Überheblichkeit *f*; (*of tone, smile also*) Überlegenheit *f* ◆ ~ **complex** Superioritätskomplex *m*.

superlative [sʊ'pɜːlətɪv] [1] *adj* (*excellent*) überragend, unübertrefflich;

➤ LANGUAGE IN USE: **superior: 1a → 5.2**

happiness größte(r, s), höchste(r, s); *indifference* höchste(r, s); (*Gram*) superlativisch, im Superlativ; (*exaggerated*) *style* überschwenglich.
[2] *n* Superlativ *m*.
superlatively [sʊˈpɜːlətɪvlɪ] *adv* (*excellently*) überragend, unübertrefflich; *happy, fit* höchst.
superman [ˈsuːpəmæn] *n, pl* **-men** [-men] Übermensch *m* ◆ **S~** (*in comics*) Supermann *m*.
supermarket [ˈsuːpəˌmɑːkɪt] *n* Supermarkt *m*.
supernatural [ˌsuːpəˈnætʃərəl] *adj* übernatürlich ◆ **the ~** das Übernatürliche.
supernormal [ˌsuːpəˈnɔːməl] *adj* übermenschlich.
supernova [ˌsuːpəˈnəʊvə] *n, pl* **-e** [-ˈnəʊviː] *or* **-s** Supernova *f*.
supernumerary [ˌsuːpəˈnjuːmərərɪ] [1] *adj* zusätzlich; (*superfluous*) überzählig.
[2] *n* Zusatzperson *f*, Supernumerar *m* (*form*); (*Theat, Film*) Statist(in *f*) *m*.
superpower [ˈsuːpəˌpaʊəʳ] *n* (*Pol*) Supermacht *f*.
superscript [ˈsuːpəˌskrɪpt] *adj character* hochgestellt.
supersede [ˌsuːpəˈsiːd] *vt* ablösen; *person, belief also* an die Stelle treten von ◆ **old, ~d ideas** alte, überholte Ideen.
supersonic [ˌsuːpəˈsɒnɪk] *adj* Überschall- ◆ **~ travel** Reisen *nt* mit Überschallgeschwindigkeit.
superstar [ˈsuːpəˌstɑːʳ] *n* (Super)star *m*.
superstition [ˌsuːpəˈstɪʃən] *n* Aberglaube *m no pl* ◆ **this is a ~** das ist Aberglaube.
superstitious *adj*, **~ly** *adv* [ˌsuːpəˈstɪʃəs, -lɪ] abergläubisch.
superstitiousness [ˌsuːpəˈstɪʃəsnɪs] *n* Aberglaube *m*, Abergläubigkeit *f*.
superstratum [ˌsuːpəˈstrɑːtəm] *n, pl* **-strata** [-ˈstrɑːtə] (*Geol*) obere Schicht; (*Ling*) Superstrat *nt*.
superstructure [ˈsuːpəˌstrʌktʃəʳ] *n* Überbau *m* (*also Sociol*); (*of ship*) Aufbauten *pl*.
supertanker [ˈsuːpəˌtæŋkəʳ] *n* Super- *or* Riesentanker *m*.
supertax [ˈsuːpəˌtæks] *n* Höchststeuer *f*.
supervene [ˌsuːpəˈviːn] *vi* dazwischenkommen, hinzukommen.
supervise [ˈsuːpəvaɪz] [1] *vt* beaufsichtigen; *work also* überwachen.
[2] *vi* Aufsicht führen, die Aufsicht haben.
supervision [ˌsuːpəˈvɪʒən] *n* Aufsicht *f*; (*action*) Beaufsichtigung *f*; (*of work*) Überwachung, Beaufsichtigung *f* ◆ **under the ~ of** unter der Aufsicht von.
supervisor [ˈsuːpəvaɪzəʳ] *n* (*of work*) Aufseher(in *f*) *m*, Aufsicht *f*; (*of research*) Leiter(in *f*) *m*; (*Brit Univ*) ≃ Tutor(in *f*) *m*; (*for PhD*) Doktorvater *m*.
supervisory [ˈsuːpəvaɪzərɪ] *adj role* beaufsichtigend, überwachend ◆ **in a ~ post** in einer Aufsichtsposition; **in his ~ capacity** in seiner Eigenschaft als Aufsichtsperson.
supine [ˈsuːpaɪn] [1] *adj* zurückliegend *attr*; (*fig liter*) *lethargy* träge, gleichgültig ◆ **in a ~ position** auf dem Rücken liegend; **to be/lie ~** auf dem Rücken liegen.
[2] *n* (*Gram*) Supinum *nt*.
supper [ˈsʌpəʳ] *n* (*evening meal*) Abendessen, Abendbrot, Abendmahl (*liter*) *nt*; (*late evening snack*) (später) Imbiß ◆ **they were at ~** sie waren beim Abendessen; **to have ~** zu Abend essen, Abendbrot essen.
supper: ~ club *n* (*US*) Luxusnachtklub *m*; **~time** *n* Abendessenszeit, Abendbrotzeit *f*; **at ~time** zur Abendbrotzeit; **when is ~time?** wann wird zu Abend gegessen?
supplant [səˈplɑːnt] *vt* ablösen, ersetzen; (*forcibly*) verdrängen; (*by ruse*) *rival* ausstechen.
supple [ˈsʌpl] *adj* (*+er*) *body, material etc* geschmeidig, elastisch; *shoes* weich; *mind, intellect* beweglich, flexibel.
supplement [ˈsʌplɪmənt] [1] *n* **(a)** Ergänzung *f* (*to gen*); (*of book*) Ergänzungsband *m* (*to zu*); (*food ~*) Zusatz *m*; (*at end of book*) Anhang, Nachtrag *m* ◆ **a ~ to his income** eine Aufbesserung seines Einkommens; **family income ~s** Kindergeld *nt*.
(b) (*colour ~ etc*) Beilage *f*, Magazin *nt*.
[2] *vt* ergänzen; *income also* aufbessern.
supplementary [ˌsʌplɪˈmentərɪ] *adj* zusätzlich, ergänzend; *volume, report also* Zusatz-, Ergänzungs- ◆ **~ question** (*Parl*) Zusatzfrage *f*; **~ angle** Supplement- *or* Ergänzungswinkel *m*; **~ benefit** (*Brit*) ≃ Arbeitslosenhilfe *f*.
suppleness [ˈsʌplnɪs] *n see adj* Geschmeidigkeit, Elastizität *f*; Weichheit *f*; Beweglichkeit, Flexibilität *f*.
suppliant [ˈsʌplɪənt], **supplicant** [ˈsʌplɪkənt] [1] *adj* flehend *attr*.
[2] *n* Flehende(r) *mf*, Bittsteller(in *f*) *m*.
supplicate [ˈsʌplɪkeɪt] *vt* (*form*) flehen.
supplication [ˌsʌplɪˈkeɪʃən] *n* Flehen *nt no pl*.
supplier [səˈplaɪəʳ] *n* (*Comm*) Lieferant(in *f*) *m*.
supply [səˈplaɪ] [1] *n* **(a)** (*supplying*) Versorgung *f*; (*Comm: delivery*) Lieferung *f* (*to an +acc*); (*Econ*) Angebot *nt* ◆ **electricity ~** Stromversorgung *f*; **the ~ of blood to the brain** die Versorgung des Gehirns mit Blut; **~ and demand** Angebot und Nachfrage (*+pl vb*).
(b) (*what is supplied*) Lieferung *f* ◆ **to cut off the ~** (*of gas, water etc*) das Gas/Wasser abstellen; **our wholesaler has cut off our ~** unser Großhändler hat die Lieferungen eingestellt; **where does the badger get its food ~?** woher bekommt der Dachs seine Nahrung?
(c) (*stock*) Vorrat *m* ◆ **supplies** *pl* (*food*) Vorräte *pl*; (*for expedition also, for journey*) Proviant *m*; **a good ~ of coal** ein guter Kohlenvorrat; **to get** *or* **lay in supplies** *or* **a ~ of** sich (*dat*) einen Vorrat an (*+dat*) anlegen *or* zulegen; **a month's ~** ein Monatsbedarf *m*; **to be in short ~** knapp sein; **to be in good ~** reichlich vorhanden sein; **our ~ is running out** unser Vorrat geht *or* unsere Vorräte gehen zu Ende; **fresh supplies** (*Mil*) Nachschub *m*; **office supplies** Bürobedarf *m*, Büromaterial *nt*; **medical supplies** Arzneimittel *pl*; (*including bandages*) Ärztebedarf *m*; **electrical supplies** Elektrowaren *or* -artikel *pl*.
(d) (*~ teacher*) Aushilfslehrer(in *f*) *m* ◆ **to be on ~** aushilfsweise *or* vertretungsweise unterrichten.
(e) (*Parl*) (Militär- und Verwaltungs)etat *m*.
[2] *vt* **(a)** *material, food, tools etc* sorgen für; (*deliver*) *goods* liefern; *clue, evidence, gas, electricity* liefern; (*put at sb's disposal*) stellen ◆ **pens and paper are supplied by the firm** Schreibmaterial wird von der Firma gestellt.
(b) (*with* mit) *person, army, city* versorgen; (*Comm*) beliefern ◆ **she supplies the humour in the office** sie sorgt für (den) Humor im Büro; **this supplied me with the chance ...** das gab mir die Chance ...; **we were not supplied with a radio** wir hatten/bekamen kein Radio.
(c) (*satisfy, make good*) *need* befriedigen; *want, deficiency* abhelfen (*+dat*); (*Comm*) *demand* decken.
supply: ~ base *n* Vorratslager *nt*; **~ day** *n* (*Parl*) *Tag m, an dem der Haushaltsplan vorgelegt wird*; **~ depot** *n* Versorgungslager *nt*; **~ industry** *n* Zulieferungsindustrie *f*; **~ lines, ~ routes** *npl* (*Mil, fig*) Versorgungslinien *pl*; **~ ship** *n* Versorgungsschiff *nt*; **~-side economics** *n sing or pl* Angebotswirtschaft *f*; **~ teacher** *n* Aushilfslehrer(in *f*) *m*; **~ train** *n* Versorgungszug *m*.
▼ **support** [səˈpɔːt] [1] *n* **(a)** (*lit*) Stütze *f* ◆ **to give ~ to sb/sth** jdn/etw stützen; **the ceiling will need some kind of ~** die Decke muß irgendwie abgestützt werden; **the bridge ~s** die Stützpfeiler *pl* der Brücke; **~ corset** Stützkorsett *nt*; **to lean on sb for ~** sich auf jdn stützen.
▼ **(b)** (*fig*) (*no pl: moral, financial backing*) Unterstützung *f*; (*person*) Stütze *f* ◆ **in ~ of** zur Unterstützung (*+gen*); **in ~ of an allegation** zur Untermauerung *or* Stützung einer Behauptung; **to speak in ~ of a candidate** einen Kandidaten unterstützen; **to depend on sb for financial ~** auf jds finanzielle Unterstützung angewiesen sein; **our ~ comes from the workers** wir stützen uns auf die Arbeiterschaft.
[2] *attr* (*Mil*) *troops, vessel etc* Hilfs-.
[3] *vt* **(a)** (*lit*) stützen; (*Tech also*) abstützen; (*bear the weight of*) tragen ◆ **it is ~ed on 4 columns** es wird von 4 Säulen getragen *or* gestützt.
▼ **(b)** (*fig*) unterstützen (*also Comput*); *plan, motion, sb's application also* befürworten; *party, cause also* eintreten für; (*give moral ~ to also*) beistehen (*+dat*), Rückhalt geben (*+dat*); (*corroborate*) *claim, theory* erhärten, untermauern; (*financially*) *family* unterhalten; *party, orchestra* finanziell unterstützen ◆ **he ~s Arsenal** er ist Arsenal-Anhänger *m*; **which team do you ~?** für welche Mannschaft bist du?; **without his family to ~ him** ohne die Unterstützung seiner Familie; **Burton and Taylor, ~ed by X and Y** Burton und Taylor, mit X und Y in den Nebenrollen; **his parents ~ed him through university** seine Eltern haben ihn während seines Studiums finanziell unterstützt.
(c) (*endure*) *bad behaviour, tantrums* dulden, ertragen.
[4] *vr* (*physically*) sich stützen (*on* auf *+acc*); (*financially*) seinen Unterhalt (selbst) bestreiten.
supportable [səˈpɔːtəbl] *adj* erträglich.
supporter [səˈpɔːtəʳ] *n* Anhänger(in *f*) *m*; (*of theory, cause, opinion also*) Befürworter(in *f*) *m*; (*Sport also*) Fan *m* ◆ **~s' club** Fanclub *m*.
supporting [səˈpɔːtɪŋ] *adj film* Vor-; *part, role* Neben- ◆ **with full ~ cast/programme** mit vielen anderen (bedeutenden) Darstellern/mit vollem Nebenprogramm.
supportive [səˈpɔːtɪv] *adj* stützend *attr* ◆ **if his parents had been more ~** wenn seine Eltern ihn mehr unterstützt hätten; **try to be more ~** du solltest versuchen, sie/mich *etc* mehr zu unterstützen.
supportiveness [səˈpɔːtɪvnɪs] *n* Unterstützung *f*.
▼ **suppose** [səˈpəʊz] *vt* **(a)** (*imagine*) sich (*dat*) vorstellen; (*assume, postulate also*) annehmen ◆ **let us ~ we are living in the 8th century** stellen wir uns einmal vor, wir lebten im 8. Jahrhundert; **let us ~ that X equals 3** angenommen, X sei gleich 3; **even supposing it were** *or* **was true** (sogar) angenommen, daß es wahr ist, angenommen, es sei wahr; **always supposing he comes** immer vorausgesetzt, (daß) er kommt; **~ they could see us now!** wenn sie uns jetzt sehen könnten!
▼ **(b)** (*believe, think*) annehmen, denken ◆ **I ~ he'll come** ich nehme an, (daß) er kommt, er wird wohl *or* vermutlich kommen; **I don't ~ he'll come** ich glaube kaum, daß er kommt; **I ~ he won't come** ich denke, er wird nicht kommen, er wird wohl nicht kommen; **I ~ that's the best thing, that's the best thing, I ~** das ist *or* wäre vermutlich das Beste; **he's rich, I ~** er muß wohl reich sein; **you're coming, I ~?** ich nehme an, du kommst?; **I don't ~ you could lend me a pound?** Sie könnten mir nicht zufällig ein Pfund leihen?; **will he be coming? — I ~ so** kommt er? — ich denke *or* glaube schon; **you ought to be leaving — I ~ so** du solltest jetzt gehen — stimmt wohl; **don't you agree with me? — I ~ so** bist du da nicht meiner Meinung? — na ja, schon; **I don't ~ so** ich glaube kaum; **isn't he coming? — I ~ not** kommt er nicht? — ich glaube kaum, wohl kaum; **so you see, it can't be true — I ~ not** da siehst du selbst, es kann nicht stimmen — du wirst wohl recht haben; **he can't very well refuse, can he? — I ~ not** er kann wohl kaum ablehnen, oder? — eigentlich nicht *or* kaum; **I never ~d him (to be) a hero** ich habe ihn nie für einen Helden gehalten; **he is generally ~d to be rich** er gilt als reich; **he's ~d to be coming** er soll (angeblich) kommen; **and he's ~d to be an expert!** und der soll (angeblich) (ein) Experte sein!
(c) (*modal use in pass: ought*) **to be ~d to do sth** etw tun sollen; **he's the one who's ~d to do it** er müßte es eigentlich tun; **you're ~d to be in bed** du solltest eigentlich im Bett sein, du gehörst eigentlich ins Bett; **he isn't ~d**

➤ LANGUAGE IN USE: **support: 1b** → 11.2, 12.2, 13 **3b** → 26.3 **suppose: a** → 1.1 **b** → 26.3

to find out er darf es nicht erfahren; **you're not ~d to (do that)** das darfst du nicht tun; **I am ~d to start work here today** ich soll hier heute anfangen; **you're ~d to report to the police** Sie müssen sich bei der Polizei melden.
(d) (*in imper: I suggest*) **~ we have a go?** warum versuchen wir es nicht einmal?; **~ we buy it?** wie wäre es, wenn wir es kauften?; **~ you have a wash?** wie wär's, wenn du dich mal wäschst?
(e) (*presuppose*) voraussetzen ◆ **that ~s unlimited resources** das setzt unbegrenzte Vorräte voraus.

supposed [sə'pəʊzd] *adj* vermutet; *date of birth, site of temple, author also* mutmaßlich.

supposedly [sə'pəʊzɪdlɪ] *adv* angeblich ◆ **the atom was ~ indivisible** das Atom galt als unteilbar.

supposing [sə'pəʊzɪŋ] *conj* angenommen ◆ **but ~ ...** aber wenn ...; **~ he can't do it?** und wenn er es nicht schafft?; **even ~ that ...** sogar wenn ...; **always ~ ...** immer unter der Annahme, daß ...

supposition [,sʌpə'zɪʃən] *n* (*no pl: hypothesizing*) Mutmaßung, Spekulation *f*; (*thing supposed*) Annahme *f* ◆ **based on (a) pure ~** auf reiner Spekulation beruhend; **acting on the ~ that you are right** vorausgesetzt, daß Sie recht haben; **to maintain the ~ of innocence until guilt is proved** so lange davon ausgehen, daß jemand unschuldig ist, bis seine Schuld bewiesen ist.

suppository [sə'pɒzɪtərɪ] *n* Zäpfchen, Suppositorium (*spec*) *nt*.

suppress [sə'pres] *vt* **(a)** unterdrücken. **(b)** (*Elec*) entstören.

suppressant [sə'presənt] *n* (*Med*) *Medikament nt zur Unterdrückung bestimmter Körperfunktionen* ◆ **appetite ~** Appetitzügler *m*.

suppression [sə'preʃən] *n* **(a)** Unterdrückung *f*. **(b)** (*Elec*) Entstörung *f*.

suppressive [sə'presɪv] *adj* Unterdrückungs-, repressiv.

suppressor [sə'presəʳ] *n* (*Elec*) Entstörungselement *nt*.

suppurate ['sʌpjʊəreɪt] *vi* eitern.

suppuration [,sʌpjʊə'reɪʃən] *n* Eiterung *f*.

supra- ['su:prə-] *pref* über-; (*esp with foreign words*) supra- ◆ **~national** überstaatlich, supra- *or* übernational.

supremacy [sʊ'preməsɪ] *n* Vormachtstellung *f*; (*Pol, Eccl, fig*) Supremat *nt or m* ◆ **air/naval ~** Luft-/Seeherrschaft *f*.

supreme [sʊ'pri:m] **1** *adj* **(a)** (*highest in authority*) höchste(r, s); *court, Soviet* oberste(r, s) ◆ **S~ Being** Höchstes Wesen; **S~ Commander** Oberbefehlshaber *m*.
(b) (*ultimate*) **to make the ~ sacrifice** das höchste Opfer bringen; **the ~ moment of the opera** der Höhepunkt der Oper.
(c) (*very great*) *courage, indifference etc* äußerste(r, s), größte(r, s) ◆ **with ~ indifference** äußerst *or* völlig unbeteiligt.
2 *adv* **to rule** *or* **reign ~** (*monarch*) absolut herrschen; (*champion, justice*) unangefochten herrschen; (*silence*) überall herrschen.

supremely [sʊ'pri:mlɪ] *adv confident, self-satisfied, indifferent* zutiefst.

supremo [sʊ'pri:məʊ] *n* (*Brit inf*) Oberboß *m* (*inf*).

Supt *abbr of* **Superintendent.**

surcharge ['sɜ:tʃɑ:dʒ] **1** *n* Zuschlag *m*; (*postal*) Nachporto, Strafporto (*inf*) *nt* ◆ **for a small ~** gegen einen geringen Aufschlag.
2 *vt* Zuschlag erheben auf (*+acc*) ◆ **parcels sent airmail are ~d** Luftpostpakete kosten Zuschlag.

surd [sɜ:d] *n* (*Math*) irrationaler Ausdruck.

▼ **sure** [ʃʊəʳ] **1** *adj* (*+er*) **(a)** (*reliable, steady, safe*) *hand, touch, marksman, footing* sicher; *criterion, proof, facts also* eindeutig; *method also, remedy, friend* zuverlässig, verläßlich ◆ **his aim was ~** er traf sicher ins Ziel.
(b) (*definite*) sicher ◆ **it is ~ that he will come** es ist sicher, daß er kommt, er kommt ganz bestimmt; **it's ~ to rain** es regnet ganz bestimmt; **be ~ to tell me/to turn the gas off** sag mir auf jeden Fall Bescheid/vergiß nicht, das Gas abzudrehen; **be ~ to go and see her** du mußt sie unbedingt besuchen; **you're ~ of a good meal/of success** ein gutes Essen/der Erfolg ist Ihnen sicher; **I want to be ~ of seeing him** ich möchte ihn auf jeden Fall sehen; **to make ~** (*check*) nachsehen, kontrollieren; **make ~ you get the leads the right way round** achten Sie darauf, daß die Kabel richtig herum sind; **make ~ you take your keys** denk daran, deine Schlüssel mitzunehmen; **it's best to make ~** sicher ist sicher; **to make ~ of one's facts** sich der Fakten (*gen*) versichern; **to make ~ of a seat** sich (*dat*) einen Platz sichern; **I've made ~ of having enough coffee for everyone** ich habe dafür gesorgt, daß genug Kaffee für alle da ist; **~ thing!** (*esp US inf*) klare Sache! (*inf*); **he's a ~ thing for president** (*esp US inf*) er ist ein todsicherer Tip für die Präsidentschaft; **he'll quit for ~** er kündigt ganz bestimmt; **I'll find out for ~** ich werde das genau herausfinden; **do you know for ~?** wissen Sie das ganz sicher?; **to be ~!** Mensch!, tatsächlich!; **and there he was, to be ~** (*esp Ir*) und da war er doch tatsächlich!
▼ **(c)** (*positive, convinced*) sicher ◆ **I'm perfectly ~** ich bin (mir da) ganz sicher; **to be ~ about sth** sich (*dat*) einer Sache (*gen*) sicher sein; **I'm not so ~ about that** da bin ich nicht so sicher; **to be ~ of one's facts** seiner *or* der Fakten sicher sein; **to be ~ of oneself** sich (*dat*) seiner Sache sicher sein; (*generally self-confident*) selbstsicher sein; **I'm ~ I don't know, I don't know, I'm ~** ich habe keine Ahnung; **I'm not ~ how/why ...** ich bin (mir) nicht sicher *or* ich weiß nicht genau, wie/warum ...
2 *adv* **(a) will you do it? — ~!** machst du das? — klar! (*inf*); **that meat was ~ tough** *or* **~ was tough** das Fleisch war vielleicht zäh!; **that's ~ pretty** (*US*) das ist doch schön, nicht?
(b) and ~ enough he did come und er ist tatsächlich gekommen; **he'll come ~ enough** er kommt ganz bestimmt, er kommt schon; **it's petrol ~ enough** es ist tatsächlich Benzin.
(c) as ~ as sure can be (*inf*), **as ~ as I'm standing here** (*inf*) garantiert, todsicher.

sure: ~-fire *adj* (*inf*) todsicher (*inf*), bombensicher (*inf*); **~-footed** *adj* (tritt)sicher.

surely ['ʃʊəlɪ] *adv* **(a)** bestimmt, sicher ◆ **~ you don't mean it?** das meinen Sie doch bestimmt *or* sicher nicht (so)?; **~ he's come(, hasn't he?)** er ist doch bestimmt gekommen(, oder?); **~ he hasn't come(, has he)?** er ist doch bestimmt *or* sicher nicht gekommen(, oder?); **~ not!** das kann doch nicht stimmen!; **~ someone must know the answer** irgend jemand muß doch die Antwort wissen; **there must ~ be something we can do** irgend etwas müssen wir doch (sicher) tun können; **I can't — oh, ~ you can** ich kann (es) nicht — aber sicher kannst du das!; **but ~ you can't expect us to believe that** Sie können doch wohl nicht erwarten, daß wir das glauben!; **~ if a = b, then c must ...** also, wenn a = b ist, dann muß c doch sicherlich ...
(b) (*esp US: gladly*) gern, mit Vergnügen.
(c) (*inevitably, with certainty*) zweifellos.

sureness ['ʃʊənɪs] *n* **(a)** (*positiveness, conviction*) Überzeugung, Sicherheit *f*. **(b)** (*reliability, steadiness, sure-footedness*) Sicherheit *f*; (*of method, cure*) Verläßlichkeit, Zuverlässigkeit *f*; (*of sb's judgement also*) Untrüglichkeit *f*.

surety ['ʃʊərətɪ] *n* **(a)** (*sum*) Bürgschaft, Sicherheit *f*; (*person*) Bürge *m* ◆ **to go** *or* **stand ~ for sb** für jdn bürgen; **he was granted bail in his own ~ of £5,000** er wurde gegen Hinterlegung einer Kaution von £ 5.000 auf freien Fuß gesetzt. **(b)** (*obs: certainty*) Sicherheit, Gewißheit *f* ◆ **of a ~** gewiß, sicherlich.

surf [sɜ:f] **1** *n* Brandung *f*.
2 *vi* surfen.

surface ['sɜ:fɪs] **1** *n* **(a)** (*lit, fig*) Oberfläche *f*; (*of road*) Decke *f*, Belag *m* ◆ **on the ~ it seems that ...** oberflächlich sieht es so aus, als ob ...; **on the ~ he is friendly enough** nach außen hin ist er sehr freundlich; **we never got beneath the ~ of the subject** wir haben immer nur die Oberfläche des Themas berührt.
(b) (*Math: of cube etc*) Fläche *f*; (*area also*) Flächeninhalt *m*.
(c) (*Min*) **at/on/up to the ~** über Tage.
(d) (*Aviat*) Tragfläche *f*.
2 *adj attr* **(a)** oberflächlich; *measurements, hardening* Oberflächen-. **(b)** (*not by air*) *travel* auf dem Land-/Seeweg. **(c)** (*Min*) *worker, job* über Tage.
3 *vt* **(a)** *road* mit einem Belag versehen; *wall* verblenden. **(b)** *submarine* auftauchen lassen.
4 *vi* (*lit, fig*) auftauchen.

surface: ~ area *n* Fläche *f*; (*Math*) Flächeninhalt *m*; **~ dressing** *n* (*on roads*) (*method*) Straßenreparatur *f* mit Rollsplitt; (*material*) Rollsplitt *m*; **~ grammar** *n* Oberflächengrammatik *f*; **~ mail** *n* Post *f* auf dem Land-/Seeweg; **by ~ mail** auf dem Land-/Seeweg; **~-mounted** *adj* oberflächenmontiert; **~ noise** *n* Rauschen *nt*; **~ structure** *n* (*Ling*) Oberflächenstruktur *f*; **~ tension** *n* Oberflächenspannung *f*; **~-to-air** *adj attr missile* Boden-Luft-; **~-to-surface** *adj attr missile* Boden-Boden-; **~ vessel** *n* Schiff *nt* (*im Gegensatz zu Unterseeboot*).

surfacing ['sɜ:fɪsɪŋ] *n* **what did they use as ~ for the roads/walls?** was für ein Material wurde für den Straßenbelag/als Wandbelag verwendet?

surfboard ['sɜ:f,bɔ:d] *n* Surfbrett *nt*.

surfeit ['sɜ:fɪt] **1** *n* Übermaß, Zuviel *nt* (*of* an *+dat*).
2 *vt sb, oneself* übersättigen, überfüttern (*on, with* mit).

surfer ['sɜ:fəʳ] *n* Surfer(in *f*), Wellenreiter(in *f*) *m*.

surfing ['sɜ:fɪŋ], **surfriding** ['sɜ:f,raɪdɪŋ] *n* Surfen, Surfing, Wellenreiten *nt* ◆ **a good ~ beach** ein guter Strand zum Surfen *or* Wellenreiten.

surge [sɜ:dʒ] **1** *n* (*of sea*) Wogen *nt*; (*of floodwater*) Schwall *m*; (*Elec*) Spannungsstoß *m* ◆ **a ~ of people** eine wogende Menschenmenge; **there was a ~ of sympathy for him** es gab eine Sympathiewelle für ihn; **he felt a sudden ~ of rage** er fühlte, wie die Wut in ihm aufstieg.
2 *vi* (*sea*) branden; (*floods, river*) anschwellen ◆ **blood ~d into her face** ihr schoß das Blut ins Gesicht; **they ~d towards/(a)round him** sie drängten auf ihn zu, sie umdrängten ihn/sie wogten um ihn (*liter*); **people ~d in/out** eine Menschenmenge flutete herein/heraus; **to ~ ahead** vorpreschen.

surgeon ['sɜ:dʒən] *n* Chirurg(in *f*) *m*; (*Mil*) Stabsarzt *m*/-ärztin *f*; (*Naut*) Marinearzt *m*/-ärztin *f* ◆ **S~ General** (*Mil*) Sanitätsinspekteur *m*; (*US*) ≃ Gesundheitsminister(in *f*) *m*; *see* **dental, veterinary.**

surgery ['sɜ:dʒərɪ] *n* **(a)** Chirurgie *f* ◆ **to have ~** operiert werden; **to need (heart) ~** (am Herzen) operiert werden müssen; **to undergo major heart ~** sich einer größeren Herzoperation unterziehen; **~ is the only solution** Operieren ist die einzige Lösung; **a fine piece of ~** eine großartige chirurgische Leistung.
(b) (*Brit*) (*room*) Sprechzimmer *nt* ; (*consultation*) Sprechstunde *f* ◆ **~ hours** Sprechstunden *pl*; **when is his ~?** wann hat er Sprechstunde?

surgical ['sɜ:dʒɪkəl] *adj treatment* operativ; *procedures, technique, instrument* chirurgisch; *training, skill* Chirurgen-, eines Chirurgen ◆ **~ appliance** Stützapparat *m*; (*false limb*) Prothese *f*; **~ boot** orthopädischer Schuh; **~ goods shop** orthopädisches Fachgeschäft; **~ spirit** Wundbenzin *nt*; **~ ward** chirurgische Station, Chirurgie *f* (*inf*).

surgically ['sɜ:dʒɪkəlɪ] *adv treat, remove* operativ ◆ **~, we have advanced a long way** wir haben in der Chirurgie große Fortschritte gemacht.

surging ['sɜ:dʒɪŋ] *adj water, corn, crowd* wogend ◆ **a ~ flood of emotion** eine Woge des Gefühls.

surliness ['sɜ:lɪnɪs] *n* Verdrießlichkeit, Mißmutigkeit *f*.

surly ['sɜ:lɪ] *adj* (*+er*) verdrießlich, mürrisch, mißmutig.

surmise ['sɜ:maɪz] **1** *n* Vermutung, Mutmaßung *f*.
2 [sɜ:'maɪz] *vt* vermuten, mutmaßen ◆ **I ~d as much** das hatte ich (schon) vermutet; **as one could ~ from his book** wie man nach seinem Buch ver-

➤ LANGUAGE IN USE: **sure: 1c** → 15.1, 16.1

muten *or* mutmaßen konnte.

surmount [sɜːˈmaʊnt] *vt* **(a)** *difficulty, obstacle* überwinden. **(b)** *(esp Archit, Her etc)* **~ed by sth** von *or* mit etw gekrönt.

surmountable [sɜːˈmaʊntəbl] *adj* überwindlich, zu überwinden.

surname [ˈsɜːneɪm] *n* Nachname, Familienname *m* ◆ **what is his ~?** wie heißt er mit Nachnamen?

surpass [sɜːˈpɑːs] **1** *vt* **(a)** *(be better than)* übertreffen. **(b)** *(exceed) comprehension* hinausgehen über *(+acc)*.

2 *vr* sich selbst übertreffen.

surpassing [sɜːˈpɑːsɪŋ] *adj (liter) beauty* unvergleichlich.

surplice [ˈsɜːpləs] *n* Chorrock *m*, Chorhemd *nt*.

surplus [ˈsɜːpləs] **1** *n* Überschuß *m (of* an *+dat)* ◆ **a balance of trade ~** ein Überschuß *m* in der Handelsbilanz.

2 *adj* überschüssig; *(of countable objects)* überzählig ◆ **~ value** Mehrwert *m*; **Army ~ goods** Stegwaren *pl*; **Army ~ anoraks** Anoraks *pl* aus Armeerestbeständen; **sale of ~ stock** Verkauf *m* von Lagerbeständen; **have you any ~ sheets I could borrow?** hast du Laken übrig, die ich mir borgen könnte?; **it is ~ to my requirements** das benötige ich nicht; **~ store** *Geschäft, das billig Lagerbestände verkauft*.

▼ **surprise** [səˈpraɪz] **1** *n* Überraschung *f* ◆ **in ~** voller Überraschung, überrascht; **much to my ~, to my great ~** zu meiner großen Überraschung; **with a look of ~** mit überraschtem Gesicht; **it was a ~ (for *or* to me) to find that ...** ich war überrascht, als ich entdeckte, daß ...; **it came as a ~ to us** wir waren überrascht, es hat uns überrascht; **what a ~!** was für eine Überraschung!; **to give sb a ~** jdn überraschen; **to take sb by ~** jdn überraschen; **~, ~, it's me!** rate mal, wer hier ist?; **~, ~!** *(iro)* was du nicht sagst!

2 *attr attack, defeat, visit, decision* Überraschungs-; *parcel, gift, phone call* überraschend.

▼ **3** *vt* überraschen; *(catch unawares also) army, sentry* überrumpeln; *thief* (auf frischer Tat) ertappen ◆ **you ~ me!** *(also iro)* das überrascht mich!; **I was ~d to hear it** ich war überrascht, das zu hören; **I wouldn't be ~d if ...** es würde mich nicht wundern, wenn ...; **don't be ~d if he refuses** wundern Sie sich nicht, wenn er ablehnt; **it's nothing to be ~d at** das ist nicht weiter verwunderlich; **I'm ~d at *or* by his ignorance** ich bin überrascht über seine Unkenntnis; **I'm ~d you didn't think of that** es wundert mich, daß du nicht daran gedacht hast; **go on, ~ me!** ich lass' mich überraschen!; **he ~d me into agreeing** er hat mich so verblüfft, daß ich zugestimmt habe.

surprising [səˈpraɪzɪŋ] *adj* überraschend, erstaunlich ◆ **there's nothing ~ about that** das ist nicht weiter verwunderlich; **it's hardly ~ he said no** es ist kaum verwunderlich, daß er nein gesagt hat.

surprisingly [səˈpraɪzɪŋlɪ] *adv see adj* ◆ **~ (enough), he was right** er hatte erstaunlicherweise recht; **and then ~ he left** und dann ist er zu unserer/ihrer *etc* Überraschung gegangen.

surreal [səˈrɪəl] *adj* unwirklich.

surrealism [səˈrɪəlɪzəm] *n* Surrealismus *m*.

surrealist [səˈrɪəlɪst] **1** *adj* surrealistisch.

2 *n* Surrealist(in *f*) *m*.

surrealistic [səˌrɪəˈlɪstɪk] *adj* surrealistisch.

surrender [səˈrendəʳ] **1** *vi* sich ergeben *(to dat)*; *(to police)* sich stellen *(to dat)* ◆ **I ~!** ich ergebe mich!

2 *vt (Mil)* übergeben; *goods, firearms also* ausliefern, herausgeben; *insurance policy* einlösen; *lease* kündigen; *claim, right, hope* aufgeben.

3 *vr* **to ~ oneself to sth** sich einer Sache *(dat)* hingeben; *to fate* sich in etw *(acc)* ergeben.

4 *n* **(a)** Kapitulation *f (to* vor *+dat)* ◆ **because of the gunman's quick ~** weil der Schütze sich so schnell ergab.

(b) *see vt* Übergabe *f (to* an *+acc)*; Auslieferung, Aushändigung *f (to* an *+acc)*; Einlösen *nt*; Kündigung *f*; Aufgabe, Preisgabe *f* ◆ **~ value** *(Insur)* Rückgabe- *or* Rückkaufswert *m*.

surreptitious [ˌsʌrəpˈtɪʃəs] *adj* heimlich; *whisper, glance, kiss also* verstohlen ◆ **he made a few ~ changes** er machte heimlich ein paar Änderungen.

surreptitiously [ˌsʌrəpˈtɪʃəslɪ] *adv see adj*.

surrey [ˈsʌrɪ] *n (US)* zweisitzige Kutsche.

surrogate [ˈsʌrəgɪt] **1** *n (substitute)* Ersatz *m*, Surrogat *nt (geh)*; *(Brit Eccl)* ≃ Weihbischof *m*.

2 *attr* Ersatz-; *(Eccl) bishop* ≃ Weih- ◆ **~ mother** Leihmutter *f*; **~ motherhood** Leihmutterschaft *f*.

surround [səˈraʊnd] **1** *n* Umrandung *f*; *(floor round carpet)* Ränder *pl*.

2 *vt* umgeben; *(Mil)* umstellen, umzingeln ◆ **she was ~ed by children/suitors** sie war von Kindern umgeben/von Verehrern umgeben *or* umschwärmt.

surrounding [səˈraʊndɪŋ] *adj* umliegend ◆ **in the ~ countryside** in der Umgebung *or* Umgegend; **in the ~ darkness** in der Dunkelheit, die mich/ihn *etc* umgab.

surroundings [səˈraʊndɪŋz] *npl* Umgebung *f*.

surtax [ˈsɜːtæks] *n* Steuerzuschlag *m*.

surveillance [sɜːˈveɪləns] *n* Überwachung, Observation *(form) f* ◆ **to be under ~** überwacht *or* observiert *(form)* werden; **to keep sb under ~** jdn überwachen *or* observieren *(form)*.

survey [ˈsɜːveɪ] **1** *n* **(a)** *(Surv) (of land, coast)* Vermessung *f*; *(report)* (Vermessungs)gutachten *nt*; *(of house)* Begutachtung *f*; *(report)* Gutachten *nt* ◆ **they are doing a ~ for a new motorway** sie machen die Vermessungsarbeiten für eine neue Autobahn; **to have a ~ done on a house** ein Gutachten über ein Haus erstellen lassen.

(b) *(comprehensive look, review) (of surroundings, countryside)* Musterung *f (of gen)*, Überblick *m (of* über *+acc)*; *(of subject, recent development)* Überblick *m*.

(c) *(inquiry)* Untersuchung *f (of, on* über *+acc)*; *(by opinion poll, market research etc)* Umfrage *f (of, on* über *+acc)*.

2 [sɜːˈveɪ] *vt* **(a)** *(look at) countryside, person, prospects, plans* betrachten, sich *(dat)* ansehen; *(appraisingly also)* begutachten; *person, goods* mustern ◆ **he is monarch of all he ~s** er beherrscht das Land, soweit er blicken kann.

(b) *(study) prospects, developments* untersuchen; *institutions* einer Prüfung *(gen)* unterziehen; *(take general view of) events, trends* einen Überblick geben über *(+acc)*.

(c) *(Surv) site, land* vermessen; *building* inspizieren.

surveying [sɜːˈveɪɪŋ] *n* **(a)** *see vt (c)* Vermessung *f*; Inspektion *f*. **(b)** *(profession)* Landvermessung *f*; *(of buildings)* Inspektion *f* von Gebäuden.

surveyor [səˈveɪəʳ] *n (land ~)* Landvermesser(in *f*) *m*; *(building ~)* Bauinspektor(in *f*), Baugutachter(in *f*) *m*.

survival [səˈvaɪvəl] *n* **(a)** Überleben *nt*; *(of species also)* Fortbestand *m*; *(of customs, usages)* Weiterleben *nt* ◆ **the ~ of the fittest** das Überleben der Stärkeren; **his ~ as prime minister seems unlikely** es ist unwahrscheinlich, daß er sich als Premierminister halten kann; **~ bag** Expeditionsschlafsack *m*; **~ kit** Überlebensausrüstung *f*.

(b) *(relic)* Überbleibsel *nt (of, from* aus).

survivalist [səˈvaɪvəlɪst] **1** *n* Überlebenskünstler(in *f*) *m*.

2 *adj attr* Überlebens-.

survive [səˈvaɪv] **1** *vi (person, animal etc)* überleben, am Leben bleiben; *(in job)* sich halten (können); *(house, treasures, book, play)* erhalten bleiben; *(custom, religion)* weiterleben, fortbestehen ◆ **only five copies ~ *or* have ~d** nur fünf Exemplare sind erhalten; **will this play ~ despite the critics?** wird sich das Stück trotz der Kritiken halten?; **you'll ~** *(iro)* das wirst du schon überleben!; **he ~d to tell the tale** er hat als Zeuge überlebt; *(hum)* er hat es überlebt *(hum)*.

2 *vt* überleben; *experience, accident also* (lebend) überstehen; *(house, objects) fire, flood* überstehen; *(inf) heat, boredom etc* aushalten ◆ **to ~ the ages** die Jahrhunderte überdauern; **he was ~d by his wife** seine Frau überlebte ihn.

survivor [səˈvaɪvəʳ] *n* Überlebende(r) *mf*; *(Jur)* Hinterbliebene(r) *mf* ◆ **he's a ~** *(fig: in politics etc)* er ist ein Überlebenskünstler.

Susan [ˈsuːzn] *n* Susanne *f*.

susceptibility [səˌseptəˈbɪlɪtɪ] *n* **(a)** *no pl see adj (a)* Beeindruckbarkeit *f* ◆ **~ to sth** Empfänglichkeit *f* für etw; Ausgesetztsein *nt* gegenüber etw; Anfälligkeit *f* für etw; **their ~ to trickery** ihre Gutgläubigkeit; **~ to pain/treatment** Schmerzempfindlichkeit *f*/Behandelbarkeit *f*; **~ to unkind remarks** Empfindlichkeit *f* in bezug auf unfreundliche Bemerkungen; **his ~ to her tears/pleas** daß er sich durch ihre Tränen/Bitten erweichen läßt/ließ.

(b) susceptibilities *pl (sensibilities)* Feingefühl *nt*.

susceptible [səˈseptəbl] *adj* **(a)** *(impressionable)* beeindruckbar, leicht zu beeindrucken *pred* ◆ **~ to sth** *to charms, flattery etc* für etw empfänglich; *to kindness, suggestion, influence etc* einer Sache *(dat)* zugänglich; *to attack* einer Sache *(dat)* ausgesetzt; *to rheumatism, colds* für etw anfällig; **to be ~ to trickery** sich leicht täuschen lassen, gutgläubig sein; **~ to pain/treatment** schmerzempfindlich/behandelbar; **he's very ~ to remarks about his big nose** er reagiert sehr empfindlich auf Anspielungen auf seine große Nase; **he was ~ to her tears/pleas** er ließ sich von ihren Tränen/Bitten erweichen.

(b) *(form)* **to be ~ of proof/corroboration/change** *etc* beweisbar/untermauerbar/änderbar *etc* sein.

suspect [ˈsʌspekt] **1** *adj* verdächtig, suspekt.

2 *n* Verdächtige(r) *mf*.

3 [səˈspekt] *vt* **(a)** *person* verdächtigen *(of sth* einer Sache *gen)*, in Verdacht haben; *plot, swindle* vermuten, ahnen, argwöhnen *(geh)* ◆ **I ~ her of having stolen it/written it** ich habe sie im Verdacht *or* ich verdächtige sie, es gestohlen/geschrieben zu haben; **he is ~ed of being a member of this sect, he is a ~ed member of this sect** er steht im Verdacht *or* man verdächtigt ihn, Mitglied dieser Sekte zu sein; **the ~ed bank robber/terrorist** *etc* der mutmaßliche Bankräuber/Terrorist *etc*; **he ~s nothing** er ahnt nichts; **does he ~ anything?** hat er Verdacht geschöpft?

(b) *(doubt) truth* bezweifeln, anzweifeln; *motive* argwöhnisch sein gegenüber.

(c) *(think likely)* vermuten ◆ **I ~ed as much** das habe ich doch vermutet *or* geahnt, das habe ich mir doch gedacht; **a ~ed case of measles, a case of ~ed measles** ein Fall, bei dem Verdacht auf Masern besteht.

4 [səˈspekt] *vi* einen Verdacht haben.

suspend [səˈspend] *vt* **(a)** *(hang)* (auf)hängen *(from* an *+dat)*; *(Chem)* suspendieren ◆ **to be ~ed in sth** in etw *(dat)* hängen; in etw *(dat)* suspendiert sein; **to hang ~ed from sth/in sth** von/in etw *(dat)* hängen.

(b) *(stop, defer) publication, payment* (zeitweilig) einstellen; *judgement* aufschieben, aussetzen; *sentence* zur Bewährung aussetzen ◆ **he was given a ~ed sentence** seine Strafe wurde zur Bewährung ausgesetzt; **to be in a state of ~ed animation** im Zustand vorübergehender Leblosigkeit sein.

(c) *person* suspendieren; *member, pupil, student* zeitweilig ausschließen; *(Sport)* sperren; *licence* zeitweilig einziehen; *law, privileges* aussetzen ◆ **to ~ from duty** suspendieren.

suspender [səˈspendəʳ] *n usu pl* **(a)** *(Brit) (for stockings)* Strumpfhalter, Straps *m*; *(for socks)* Sockenhalter *m* ◆ **~ belt** Strumpf(halter)gürtel *m*. **(b)** *(US)* **~s** *pl* Hosenträger *pl*.

suspense [səˈspens] *n (in book, film etc)* Spannung *f* ◆ **the ~ is killing me** ich bin gespannt wie ein Regenschirm *(hum inf)*; **to keep sb in ~** jdn in Spannung halten, jdn auf die Folter spannen *(inf)*; **to wait in ~** gespannt *or* voller Spannung warten.

➤ LANGUAGE IN USE: **surprise: 3** → 15.2, 16.1, 16.2

suspense account *n* Interimskonto *nt.*
suspension [sə'spenʃən] *n* **(a)** *see* **suspend (b)** zeitweilige Einstellung; Aufschub *m*, Aussetzung *f*; Aussetzung *f* (zur Bewährung).
(b) *see* **suspend (c)** Suspendierung *f*; zeitweiliger Ausschluß; Sperrung *f*; zeitweiliger Einzug; Aussetzen *nt.*
(c) (*Aut*) Federung *f*; (*of wheels*) Aufhängung *f.*
(d) (*Chem*) Suspension *f.*
(e) (*Mus*) **to be in ~** suspendiert sein, gehalten werden.
suspension: ~ bridge *n* Hängebrücke *f*; **~ file** *n* Hängemappe *f*; **~ point** *n* (*Typ*) Auslassungspunkt *m.*
suspensory [sə'spensərɪ] *adj ligament, muscle* Aufhänge-; *bandage* Schlingen-.
suspicion [sə'spɪʃən] *n* **(a)** Verdacht, Argwohn (*geh*) *m no pl* ◆ **to arouse sb's ~s** jds Verdacht *or* Argwohn (*geh*) erregen; **I have a ~ that ...** ich habe den Verdacht *or* das Gefühl, daß ...; **to have one's ~s about sth** seine Zweifel bezüglich einer Sache (*gen*) haben; **I was right in my ~s** mein Verdacht hat sich bestätigt; **to be above (all)/under ~** über jeden Verdacht erhaben sein/ unter Verdacht stehen; **to arrest sb on ~/on ~ of murder** jdn wegen Tatverdachts/Mordverdachts festnehmen; **to lay oneself open to ~** sich verdächtig machen; **~ fell on him** der Verdacht fiel auf ihn; **to view sb/sth with ~** jdn/etw argwöhnisch *or* mißtrauisch betrachten.
(b) (*trace, touch*) Hauch *m*, Spur *f.*
suspicious [sə'spɪʃəs] *adj* **(a)** (*feeling suspicion*) argwöhnisch, mißtrauisch (*of* gegenüber) ◆ **you have a ~ mind** Sie sind aber mißtrauisch; **to be ~ about sth** etw mit Mißtrauen *or* Argwohn (*geh*) betrachten. **(b)** (*causing suspicion*) verdächtig; *actions also* verdachterregend *attr.*
suspiciously [sə'spɪʃəslɪ] *adv see adj* **(a)** argwöhnisch, mißtrauisch. **(b)** verdächtig ◆ **it looks ~ like measles to me** das sieht mir verdächtig nach Masern aus.
suspiciousness [sə'spɪʃəsnɪs] *n see adj* **(a)** Verdacht, Argwohn (*geh*) *m.* **(b)** Verdächtigkeit *f.*
suss [sʌs] *vt* (*Brit inf*) **(a)** (*suspect*) *plan* kommen hinter (*+acc*) (*inf*) ◆ **to ~ it** dahinterkommen (*inf*); **as soon as he ~ed what was going on** sobald er dahinterkam, was da gespielt wurde (*inf*).
(b) to ~ sb out jdm auf den Zahn fühlen (*inf*); **I can't ~ him out** bei ihm blicke ich nicht durch (*inf*); **I've got him ~ed (out)** ich habe ihn durchschaut; **to ~ sth out** etw herausbekommen; **to ~ things out** die Lage peilen (*inf*).
sussed [sʌst] *adj* (*Brit inf: knowledgeable*) bewandert; (*clever*) clever.
sustain [sə'steɪn] *vt* **(a)** (*support*) *load, weight* aushalten, tragen; *life* erhalten; *family* unterhalten; *charity* unterstützen; (*nourish*) *body* bei Kräften halten ◆ **not enough to ~ life** nicht genug zum Leben; **that isn't enough food to ~ you** das wird Ihnen nicht reichen; **his support ~ed her in her hour of need** seine Hilfe gab ihr Kraft in der Stunde der Not (*liter*).
(b) (*keep going, maintain*) *pretence, argument, theory* aufrechterhalten; *effort also* nicht nachlassen in (*+dat*); (*Mus*) *note* (aus)halten; (*Theat*) *accent, characterization* durchhalten; (*Jur*) *objection* stattgeben (*+dat*) ◆ **objection ~ed** Einspruch stattgegeben; *see also* **sustained.**
(c) (*receive*) *injury, damage, loss* erleiden ◆ **to ~ an attack** angegriffen werden.
sustainable [sə'steɪnəbl] *adj* aufrechtzuerhalten(d *attr*) *pred* ◆ **to be ~** aufrechtzuerhalten sein.
sustained [sə'steɪnd] *adj effort etc* ausdauernd; *applause also* anhaltend; (*Mus*) *note* (aus)gehalten.
sustaining [sə'steɪnɪŋ] *adj food* nahrhaft, kräftig ◆ **~ pedal** (*Mus*) Fortepedal *nt*; **~ program** (*US Rad, TV*) nichtkommerzielle Sendung.
sustenance ['sʌstɪnəns] *n* (*food and drink*) Nahrung *f*; (*nutritive quality*) Nährwert *m* ◆ **to get one's ~ from sth** sich von etw ernähren.
susurration [,sju:sə'reɪʃən] *n* (*liter*) Säuseln *nt* (*liter*).
suture ['su:tʃə^r] (*Med*) [1] *n* Naht *f.*
[2] *vt* (ver)nähen.
suzerainty ['su:zəreɪntɪ] *n* Suzeränität *f.*
svelte [svelt] *adj* (*slender*) grazil; (*sophisticated*) vornehm, elegant.
SW *abbr of* **(a) South-West** SW. **(b) short wave** KW.
swab [swɒb] [1] *n* **(a)** (*Med*) Tupfer *m*; (*specimen*) Abstrich *m* ◆ **to take a ~** einen Abstrich machen. **(b)** (*Naut*) Mop *m.*
[2] *vt* **(a)** (*Med*) *wound etc* (ab)tupfen. **(b)** (*Naut: also* **~ down**) wischen.
Swabia ['sweɪbɪə] *n* Schwaben *nt.*
Swabian ['sweɪbɪən] [1] *adj* schwäbisch.
[2] *n* Schwabe *m*, Schwäbin *f*; (*dialect*) Schwäbisch *nt.*
swaddle ['swɒdl] *vt baby* wickeln (*in* in *+acc*) ◆ **swaddling clothes** (*esp Bibl*) Windeln *pl.*
swag [swæg] *n* (*inf*) Beute *f.*
swagger ['swægə^r] [1] *n* (*gait*) Stolzieren *nt*; (*behaviour*) Angeberei, Großtuerei *f* ◆ **to walk with a ~** stolzieren.
[2] *vi* **(a)** stolzieren ◆ **he ~ed down the street/over to our table** er stolzierte die Straße hinunter/zu unserem Tisch herüber. **(b)** (*boast, act boastfully*) angeben.
swaggering ['swægərɪŋ] [1] *adj* **(a)** *gait, manner* forsch. **(b)** (*boastful*) großtuerisch, angeberisch.
[2] *n* Großtuerei, Angeberei *f* ◆ **his ~ about** sein Herumstolzieren *nt.*
swagger-stick ['swægə'stɪk] *n* Offiziersstöckchen *nt.*
swain [sweɪn] *n* (*old*) (*suitor*) Freier *m*; (*lad*) Bursch(e) *m.*
swallow[1] ['swɒləʊ] [1] *n* Schluck *m* ◆ **after several ~s** nachdem er *etc* ein paarmal geschluckt hatte.
[2] *vt food, drink* (hinunter)schlucken; (*fig*) *story, evidence, insult* schlucken ◆ **to ~ one's pride** seinen Stolz schlucken; **to ~ sth whole** (*lit*) etw ganz schlucken; (*fig*) etw ohne weiteres schlucken; **that's a bit hard to ~** das glaubt ja kein Mensch (*inf*); **to ~ one's words** (*speak indistinctly*) seine Worte verschlucken; (*remain silent*) hinunterschlucken, was er/sie *etc* sagen wollte; (*retract*) seine Worte zurücknehmen; *see* **bait.**
[3] *vi* schlucken ◆ **to ~ hard** (*fig*) kräftig schlucken.
◆**swallow down** *vt sep* hinunterschlucken.
◆**swallow up** *vt sep* (*fig*) verschlingen ◆ **the mist/darkness seemed to ~ them ~** der Nebel/die Dunkelheit schien sie zu verschlucken; **I wished the ground would open and ~ me ~** ich könnte vor Scham in den Boden versinken.
swallow[2] *n* (*bird*) Schwalbe *f* ◆ **one ~ doesn't make a summer** (*Prov*) eine Schwalbe macht noch keinen Sommer (*Prov*).
swallow: ~-dive *n* Schwalbensprung *m*; **~-tail** *n* (*butterfly*) Schwalbenschwanz *m*; **~-tailed coat** *n* Schwalbenschwanz *m.*
swam [swæm] *pret of* **swim.**
swamp [swɒmp] [1] *n* Sumpf *m.*
[2] *vt* unter Wasser setzen, überschwemmen; (*fig: overwhelm*) überschwemmen ◆ **to be ~ed with sth** mit etw überschwemmt werden.
swamp: ~ buggy *n* Sumpffahrzeug *nt*; **~ fever** *n* Sumpffieber *nt*; **~land** *n* Sumpf(land *nt*) *m.*
swampy ['swɒmpɪ] *adj* (*+er*) sumpfig ◆ **to become ~** versumpfen.
swan [swɒn] [1] *n* Schwan *m* ◆ **~-dive** (*US*) Schwalbensprung *m.*
[2] *vi* (*inf*) **to ~ off** abziehen (*inf*); **to ~ around New York** in New York herumziehen (*inf*); **to ~ around (the house)** zu Hause herumschweben (*inf*); **a ~ning job** ein gemütlicher Posten.
swank [swæŋk] (*inf*) [1] *n* **(a)** (*boastfulness*) Angabe, Protzerei (*inf*) *f*; (*ostentation also*) Schau *f* (*inf*) ◆ **it's just a lot of ~** das ist doch nur Angabe/Schau. **(b)** (*person*) Angeber(in *f*) *m.*
[2] *vi* angeben (*about* mit).
swanky ['swæŋkɪ] *adj* (*+er*) (*inf*) *manner, words* großspurig; *car etc* protzig (*inf*), Angeber-.
swannery ['swɒnərɪ] *n* Schwanenteich *m.*
swansdown ['swɒnz,daʊn] *n* (*feathers*) Schwanendaunen *pl*; (*fabric*) *wolliges Material.*
swan: ~song *n* (*fig*) Schwanengesang *m*; **~-upping** [,swɒn'ʌpɪŋ] *n* feierliche Zeichnung der jungen Schwäne.
swap [swɒp] [1] *n* Tausch, Tauschhandel *m* ◆ **~s** (*stamps*) Tauschmarken *pl*; **it's a fair ~** das ist ein fairer Tausch; **to do a ~ (with sb)** (mit jdm) tauschen.
[2] *vt stamps, cars, houses etc* tauschen; *stories, reminiscences* austauschen ◆ **to ~ sth for sth** etw für etw eintauschen; **to ~ places with sb** mit jdm tauschen; **I'll ~ you!** (*inf*) ich tausch' mit dir (*inf*).
[3] *vi* tauschen.
SWAPO ['swɑ:pəʊ] *n abbr of* **South-West Africa People's Organization** SWAPO *f.*
sward [swɔ:d] *n* (*obs, poet*) Rasen *m.*
swarm [swɔ:m] [1] *n* (*of insects, birds*) Schwarm *m*; (*of people also*) Schar *f* ◆ **they came in (their) ~s** sie kamen scharenweise *or* in Scharen.
[2] *vi* (*bees, flies, people*) schwärmen ◆ **the place was ~ing with insects/people** es wimmelte von Insekten/Leuten; **the main street was ~ing** (*inf*) auf der Hauptstraße herrschte Hochbetrieb (*inf*); **tourists were ~ing everywhere** es wimmelte überall von Touristen; **children ~ed all round the car** Kinder schwärmten um das Auto herum.
◆**swarm up** *vi +prep obj* hinauf- *or* hochklettern.
swarthiness ['swɔ:ðɪnɪs] *n* (*of skin*) Dunkelheit *f*; (*of person also*) Dunkelhäutigkeit *f*, dunkle Farbe.
swarthy ['swɔ:ðɪ] *adj* (*+er*) *skin* dunkel; *person also* dunkelhäutig.
swash [swɒʃ] *vti* schwappen.
swashbuckler ['swɒʃ,bʌklə^r] *n* verwegener Kerl.
swashbuckling ['swɒʃ,bʌklɪŋ] *adj person, manner* verwegen.
swastika ['swɒstɪkə] *n* Hakenkreuz *nt*; (*religious symbol also*) Swastika *f.*
swat [swɒt] [1] *vt fly* totschlagen; *table* schlagen auf (*+acc*).
[2] *vi* **to ~ at a fly** nach einer Fliege schlagen.
[3] *n* **(a)** (*blow*) Schlag *m.* **(b)** (*fly ~*) Fliegenklatsche *f.*
swatch [swɒtʃ] *n* (Textil)muster *nt*; (*collection of samples*) Musterbuch *nt.*
swath [swɔ:θ], **swathe** [sweɪð] *n* Schwade *f* ◆ **to cut a ~ through sth** eine Bahn durch etw schneiden.
swathe [sweɪð] *vt* wickeln (*in* in *+acc*); (*in bandages also*) umwickeln (*in* mit) ◆ **to ~ oneself in sth** sich in etw (*acc*) einwickeln *or* einhüllen, etw um sich wickeln.
swatter ['swɒtə^r] *n* (*fly ~*) Fliegenklatsche *f.*
sway [sweɪ] [1] *n* **(a)** (*movement*) *see vi* Sich-Wiegen *nt*; Schwingen *nt*; Schwanken *nt*;Schaukeln *nt*; Wackeln *nt*; Schwenken *nt* ◆ **the graceful ~ of the dancer's body** das anmutige Wiegen der Tänzerin.
(b) (*influence, rule*) Macht *f* (*over* über *+acc*) ◆ **to bring sb/a people under one's ~** jdn seinem Willen/ein Volk seiner Macht unterwerfen; **to hold ~ over sb/a nation** jdn/ein Volk beherrschen *or* in seiner Macht haben.
[2] *vi* (*trees*) sich wiegen; (*hanging object*) schwingen; (*building, mast, bridge etc, unsteady person*) schwanken; (*train, boat*) schaukeln; (*hips*) wackeln; (*fig*) schwenken ◆ **the ladder ~ed away from the wall** die Leiter bewegte sich von der Mauer weg; **she ~s as she walks** sie wiegt beim Gehen die Hüften; **the drunk ~ed up the road** der Betrunkene schwankte die Straße entlang; **to ~ between two alternatives** zwischen zwei Alternativen schwanken.
[3] *vt* **(a)** schwenken; (*wind*) hin und her bewegen. **(b)** (*influence*) beeinflussen; (*change sb's mind*) umstimmen.
swear [swɛə^r] (*vb: pret* **swore**, *ptp* **sworn**) [1] *vt* **(a)** *allegiance, love, revenge*

schwören; *oath also* leisten, ablegen ♦ **I ~ it!** ich kann das beschwören!
(b) (*Jur*) *witness, jury* vereidigen ♦ **to ~ sb to secrecy** jdn schwören lassen, daß er nichts verrät; **I've been sworn to secrecy** ich habe schwören müssen, daß ich nichts sage.
[2] *vi* **(a)** (*use solemn oath*) schwören ♦ **to ~ on the Bible** auf die Bibel schwören; **to ~ by all one holds dear** schwören bei allem, was einem lieb ist; **to ~ to sth** etw beschwören; **to ~ blind that ...** (*inf*) Stein und Bein schwören, daß ... (*inf*).
(b) (*use swearwords*) fluchen (*about* über +*acc*) ♦ **to ~ at sb/sth** jdn/etw beschimpfen.
[3] *n* **to have a (good) ~** (tüchtig) fluchen.
♦**swear by** *vi +prep obj* (*inf*) schwören auf (+*acc*).
♦**swear in** *vt sep witness, jury, president* vereidigen.
♦**swear off** *vi +prep obj* (*inf*) abschwören (+*dat*).
swearing ['swɛərɪŋ] *n* Fluchen *nt*.
swearing-in [,swɛərɪŋ'ɪn] *n* Vereidigung *f*.
swearword ['swɛə,wɜːd] *n* Fluch, Kraftausdruck *m*.
sweat [swet] [1] *n* **(a)** Schweiß *m no pl*; (*on walls*) (Kondens)wasser *nt* ♦ **drops/beads of ~** Schweißtropfen *pl*/-perlen *pl*; **his face was running with ~** der Schweiß rann ihm von der Stirn; **all of a ~** schweißgebadet; **by the ~ of one's brow** (*fig*) im Schweiße seines Angesichts (*liter*); **to be in a ~** (*lit, fig*) schwitzen; **to get into a ~ about sth** (*fig*) wegen etw ins Schwitzen geraten *or* kommen; **no ~** (*inf*) kein Problem.
(b) (*inf: work*) **what a ~ that was!** das war eine Heidenarbeit! (*inf*); **we had a real ~ to do it** wir haben dabei wirklich geschuftet (*inf*); **that's too much ~ for me** das ist mir zu anstrengend.
[2] *vi* (*person, animal, wall*) schwitzen (*with* vor +*dat*); (*fig inf*) (*work hard*) sich abrackern (*inf*) (*over* mit); (*worry*) zittern, schwitzen (*inf*) (*with* vor +*dat*) ♦ **to ~ like a pig** (*inf*) wie ein Affe schwitzen (*inf*).
[3] *vt horse, athlete* schwitzen lassen; (*pej*) *worker* für einen Hungerlohn arbeiten lassen; *recruit* schleifen (*inf*) ♦ **to ~ blood** (*with worry*) Blut und Wasser schwitzen; (*with effort, work*) sich abrackern (*inf*).
♦**sweat out** *vt sep* **(a)** *illness, fever* herausschwitzen. **(b) to ~ it ~** (*fig inf*) durchhalten; (*sit and wait*) abwarten.
sweatband ['swet,bænd] *n* Schweißband *nt*.
sweated ['swetɪd] *adj worker* völlig unterbezahlt, ausgebeutet; *goods* für einen Hungerlohn hergestellt ♦ **~ labour** billige Arbeitskräfte *pl*; **it was ~ labour!** (*inf*) das war Ausbeutung.
sweater ['swetəʳ] *n* Pullover *m*.
sweat: ~ gland *n* Schweißdrüse *f*; **~shirt** *n* Sweatshirt *nt*; (*Sport*) Trainingspullover *m*; **~ pants** *npl* Jogginghose *f*; **~shop** *n* (*pej, hum inf*) Ausbeuterbetrieb *m* (*pej*).
sweaty ['swetɪ] *adj* (+*er*) *hands* schweißig; *feet, smell also* Schweiß-; *brow* schweißbedeckt; *body, person, socks* verschwitzt; *weather, day, work* zum Schwitzen ♦ **digging is ~ work** beim Graben kommt man leicht ins Schwitzen; **to have a ~ smell** nach Schweiß riechen.
swede [swiːd] *n* (*Brit*) Kohlrübe, Steckrübe *f*.
Swede [swiːd] *n* Schwede *m*, Schwedin *f*.
Sweden ['swiːdn] *n* Schweden *nt*.
Swedish ['swiːdɪʃ] [1] *adj* schwedisch.
[2] *n* Schwedisch *nt*.
sweep [swiːp] (*vb: pret, ptp* **swept**) [1] *n* **(a) to give the floor a ~** den Boden kehren *or* fegen; **the chimney needs a ~** der Schornstein muß gekehrt *or* gefegt werden.
(b) (*chimney ~*) Schornsteinfeger, Kaminkehrer *m*.
(c) (*of arm, pendulum*) Schwung *m*; (*of sword also*) Streich *m*; (*of dress*) Rauschen *nt no pl*; (*of oars*) Durchziehen *nt no pl*; (*of light, radar*) Strahl *m* ♦ **at** *or* **in one ~** (*fig*) auf einen Schwung; **with a ~ of her skirts** mit rauschenden Gewändern; **to make a ~ for mines** nach Minen suchen; **the police made a ~ of the district** die Polizei hat die Gegend abgesucht; **to make a clean ~** (*fig*) gründlich aufräumen *or* Ordnung schaffen; **the Russians made a clean ~ of the athletic events** die Russen haben beim Leichtathletikkampf tüchtig abgeräumt (*inf*) *or* alle Preise eingesteckt.
(d) (*range*) Bereich *m*; (*of gun also*) Schußbereich *m*.
(e) (*curve, line*) (*of road, river*) Bogen *m*; (*of facade, contour, hair*) Schwung *m* ♦ **the ~ of the plains** die Weite der Ebene; **a wide ~ of country** eine sich weit ausdehnende Landschaft; **a beautiful ~ of hills** herrliche Berge *pl*.
(f) *see* **sweepstake**.
[2] *vt* **(a)** *floor, street, chimney* kehren, fegen; *room also* auskehren, ausfegen; *dust, snow* wegfegen ♦ **to ~ a passage through the snow** einen Weg durch den Schnee bahnen; **to ~ sth under the carpet** (*fig*) etw unter den Teppich kehren.
(b) (*scan, move searchingly over*) absuchen (*for* nach); (*lights also, bullets*) streichen über (+*acc*); *minefield, sea* durchkämmen; *mines* räumen ♦ **to ~ a channel clear of mines** einen Kanal von Minen säubern.
(c) (*move quickly over*) (*wind, skirt*) fegen über (+*acc*); (*waves*) *deck, sand etc* überrollen, überschwemmen; (*glance*) gleiten über (+*acc*); (*fig*) (*wave of protest, violence, fashion*) überrollen; (*disease*) um sich greifen in (+*dat*).
(d) (*remove with ~ing movement*) (*wave*) spülen, schwemmen; (*current*) reißen; (*wind*) fegen; *person* reißen ♦ **to ~ sth off the table/onto the floor/into a bag** etw vom Tisch/zu Boden fegen/etw in eine Tasche raffen; **the crowd swept him into the square** er wurde von der Menge zum Platz hin mitgerissen; **he swept the obstacles from his path** er stieß die Hindernisse aus dem Weg; **the army swept the enemy before them** die Armee jagte die feindlichen Truppen vor sich her.
(e) (*triumph*) große Triumphe feiern in (+*dat*) ♦ **to ~ the polls** (*Pol*) die Wahlen haushoch gewinnen; **to ~ all before one** (*fig*) alle in die Tasche stecken (*inf*); **to ~ the board** (*fig*) alle Preise/Medaillen gewinnen, abräumen (*inf*).
[3] *vi* **(a)** (*with broom*) kehren, fegen; *see* **broom**.
(b) (*move*) (*person*) rauschen; (*vehicle, plane*) (*quickly*) schießen; (*majestically*) gleiten; (*skier*) fegen; (*road, river*) in weitem Bogen führen ♦ **panic/the disease swept through Europe** Panik/die Krankheit griff in Europa um sich *or* breitete sich in Europa aus; **the tornado swept across the fields** der Wirbelsturm fegte über die Felder.
♦**sweep along** [1] *vi* dahin- *or* entlangrauschen; (*majestically*) dahin- *or* entlanggleiten.
[2] *vt sep* (*lit, fig*) mitreißen.
♦**sweep aside** *vt sep* (*lit, fig*) wegfegen, beiseite fegen.
♦**sweep away** [1] *vi see* **sweep off**.
[2] *vt sep dust, leaves etc* wegfegen; (*storm also, avalanche*) wegreißen; (*flood etc*) wegspülen, wegschwemmen; (*fig*) *old laws* aufräumen mit; *work, accomplishments* zunichte machen.
♦**sweep down** [1] *vi* hinunter-/herunterrauschen; (*car, plane*) hinunter-/herunterschießen; (*majestically*) hinunter-/heruntergleiten; (*road, hill*) in sanftem Bogen abfallen ♦ **to ~ ~ on sb** sich auf jdn stürzen, über jdn herfallen.
[2] *vt sep* abkehren, abfegen.
♦**sweep off** [1] *vi* davonrauschen; (*car, plane*) davonschießen; (*majestically*) davongleiten; (*skier*) davonfegen.
[2] *vt sep vase, clock* hinunter-/herunterfegen ♦ **to ~ sb ~ somewhere** jdn irgendwohin entführen; **the children were swept ~ to bed** die Kinder wurden schleunigst ins Bett gesteckt (*inf*) *or* geschickt; **to ~ sb ~ his/her feet** (*lit*) jdn umreißen; (*fig*) *audience* jdn begeistern; **he swept her ~ her feet** sie hat sich Hals über Kopf in ihn verliebt (*inf*).
♦**sweep out** [1] *vi* hinaus-/herausrauschen; (*car*) hinaus-/herausschießen; (*majestically*) hinaus-/herausgleiten ♦ **to ~ ~ of a room** aus einem Zimmer rauschen.
[2] *vt sep room* auskehren, ausfegen; *dust* hinaus-/herauskehren *or* -fegen.
♦**sweep up** [1] *vi* **(a)** (*with broom*) zusammenkehren *or* -fegen ♦ **to ~ ~ after sb** hinter jdm herfegen.
(b) (*move*) **he swept ~ to me** er rauschte auf mich zu; **the car swept ~ to the house** der Wagen rollte aufs Haus zu; **she swept ~ in a Rolls Royce** sie rollte in einem Rolls Royce vor; **a broad driveway ~s ~ to the manor** ein breiter Zufahrtsweg schwingt sich zum Herrenhaus hinauf.
[2] *vt sep* zusammenkehren *or* -fegen; (*collect up*) *objects* zusammenraffen; *person* hochreißen; *hair* hochbinden.
sweepback ['swiːp,bæk] *n* (*Aviat*) Pfeilform *f*.
sweeper ['swiːpəʳ] *n* **(a)** (*road ~*) Straßenkehrer(in *f*) *or* -feger(in *f*) *m*; (*machine*) Kehrmaschine *f*; (*carpet ~*) Teppichkehrer *m*. **(b)** (*Ftbl*) Ausputzer *m*.
sweep hand *n* Sekundenzeiger *m*.
sweeping ['swiːpɪŋ] *adj* **(a)** *gesture* weit ausholend; *stroke also* mächtig; *bow, curtsey, lines* schwungvoll; *glance* streifend.
(b) (*fig*) *change, reduction* radikal, drastisch; *statement* pauschal; *victory* überragend, glänzend ♦ **to make a ~ condemnation of sth** etw in Bausch und Bogen verdammen.
sweepingly ['swiːpɪŋlɪ] *adv gesture* schwungvoll; *speak* verallgemeinernd; *condemn* in Bausch und Bogen.
sweepings ['swiːpɪŋz] *npl* Kehricht, Dreck *m*; (*fig: of society etc*) Abschaum *m*.
sweepstake ['swiːp,steɪk] *n* (*race*) *Rennen nt, in dem die Pferdebesitzer alle Einsätze machen*; (*prize*) *aus allen Einsätzen gebildeter Preis*; (*lottery*) *Wette, bei der die Preise aus den Einsätzen gebildet werden*.
sweet [swiːt] [1] *adj* (+*er*) **(a)** süß ♦ **to like ~ things** gern Süßes essen; **to have a ~ tooth** gern Süßes essen, naschhaft sein.
(b) (*fresh*) *food, water* frisch; *air, breath also* rein; *soil* nicht sauer; (*fragrant*) *smell* süß ♦ **the air was ~ with the scent of roses** die Luft war erfüllt vom Duft der Rosen.
(c) (*fig*) süß; (*kind also*) lieb ♦ **that's very ~ of you** das ist sehr lieb von dir; **that car/horse is a ~ little runner** das Auto/Pferd läuft prächtig; **to be ~ on sb** (*dated inf*) in jdn vernarrt sein; **to keep sb ~** (*inf*) jdn bei Laune halten; **the water tasted ~ to him** (*liter*) das Wasser schmeckte (ihm) so gut; **success was doubly ~ to him** er genoß den Erfolg doppelt; **once he caught the ~ smell of success** als erst der Erfolg lockte; **the words were ~ to his ear** die Worte klangen lieblich in seinen Ohren; **at his own ~ will** (*iro*) wie es ihm gerade paßt *or* einfällt; **in his own ~ way** (*iro*) auf seine unübertroffene Art; **~ Fanny Adams** *or* **FA** (*sl*) nix (*inf*), nicht die Bohne (*sl*); *see* **dream, nothing**.
[2] *n* **(a)** (*Brit: candy*) Bonbon *nt*.
(b) (*Brit: dessert*) Nachtisch *m*, Dessert *nt* ♦ **for ~** zum *or* als Nachtisch *or* Dessert.
(c) yes, (my) ~ (*inf*) ja, (mein) Schätzchen *or* Liebling.
(d) ~s *pl* (*fig: pleasures*) Freuden *pl* ♦ **once he had tasted the ~s of success** nachdem er einmal erfahren hatte, wie süß der Erfolg sein kann.
sweet: ~-and-sour *adj* süßsauer; **~bread** *n* Bries *nt*; **~-brier** *n* Weinrose *f*; **~ chestnut** *n* Edelkastanie *f*; **~corn** *n* Mais *m*.
sweeten ['swiːtn] [1] *vt coffee, sauce* süßen; *air, breath* reinigen; (*fig*) *temper* bessern; *task* versüßen ♦ **to ~ sb** (*inf*) jdn gnädig stimmen; (*sl: bribe*) jdn schmieren (*inf*).
[2] *vi* (*temper*) sich bessern; (*person*) gute Laune bekommen.
sweetener ['swiːtnəʳ] *n* (*Cook*) Süßungsmittel *nt*; (*artificial*) Süßstoff *m*; (*inf:

to make sth more acceptable) Anreiz *m*; (*sl: bribe*) Schmiergeld *nt* (*inf*).

sweetening ['swi:tnɪŋ] *n* (*Cook*) Süßungsmittel *nt*; (*artificial*) Süßstoff *m*.

sweetheart ['swi:t,hɑ:t] *n* Schatz *m*, Liebste(r) *mf* ◆ **soon they were ~s** (*dated*) bald waren sie ein Pärchen; **Vera Lynn, the Forces' ~** Vera Lynn, der Liebling der Armee.

sweetie ['swi:tɪ] *n* **(a)** (*inf: also* **~-pie**) **yes, ~** ja, Schatzi (*inf*) *or* Süße(r); **she's/he's a ~** sie/er ist ein Engel *or* ist süß (*inf*). **(b)** (*baby-talk, Scot: candy*) Bonbon *m*.

sweetish ['swi:tɪʃ] *adj taste, smell* süßlich.

sweetly ['swi:tlɪ] *adv sing, play* süß; *smile also, answer* lieb ◆ **the engine was running ~** der Motor ist prächtig gelaufen; **rather ~, he offered to drive me there** er bot an, mich hinzufahren, was wirklich süß *or* lieb von ihm war.

sweet: ~meat *n* (*old*) Leckerei *f*; **~-natured** *adj* lieb.

sweetness ['swi:tnɪs] *n* (*lit*) Süßigkeit, Süße *f*; (*fig*) Süße *f*; (*of smile, nature*) Liebenswürdigkeit *f*; (*of person*) liebe Art; (*freshness*) (*of food, water*) Frische *f*; (*of air, breath*) Reinheit, Frische *f* ◆ **now all is ~ and light** (*usu iro*) nun herrscht eitel Freude und Sonnenschein; **to go around spreading ~ and light** Freundlichkeit ausstrahlen.

sweet: ~ pea *n* Gartenwicke *f*; **~ potato** *n* Süßkartoffel, Batate *f*; **~-scented** *adj* süß duftend; **~-shop** *n* (*Brit*) Süßwarenladen *m or* -geschäft *nt*; **~-smelling** *adj* süß riechend; **~-talk** (*inf*) [1] *n* süße Worte *pl*; [2] *vt* **to ~-talk sb into doing sth** jdn mit süßen Worten dazu bringen, etw zu tun; **~-tempered** *adj* verträglich; **~ william** *n* Bartnelke *f*.

swell [swel] (*vb: pret* **~ed**, *ptp* **swollen** *or* **~ed**) [1] *n* **(a)** (*of sea*) Wogen *nt no pl*; (*wave*) Woge *f* ◆ **there was a heavy ~** es herrschte hoher Seegang *or* schwere See.

(b) (*dated inf*) (*stylish person*) feine Dame, feiner Herr; (*important person*) hohes Tier; (*of high society*) Größe *f* ◆ **the ~s** *pl* die feinen Leute.

(c) (*Mus*) (*sound*) Crescendo *nt* mit gleich anschließendem Decrescendo; (*control, knob*) Schweller *m*; (*mechanism*) Schwellwerk *nt*.

[2] *adj* (*inf*) **(a)** (*dated: stylish*) fein, vornehm; *house, restaurant also* nobel (*inf*).

(b) (*esp US: excellent*) klasse (*inf*), prima (*inf*).

[3] *vt ankle, river, sound etc* anschwellen lassen; *stomach* (auf)blähen; *wood* (auf)quellen; *sail* blähen; *numbers, population* anwachsen lassen; *sales* steigern ◆ **to be swollen with pride/rage** stolzgeschwellt sein/vor Wut (beinahe) platzen; **your praise will only ~ her head** dein Lob wird ihr nur zu Kopf steigen.

[4] *vi* **(a)** (*ankle, arm, eye etc: also* **~ up**) (an)schwellen; (*balloon, air bed, tyre*) sich füllen ◆ **to ~ (up) with rage/pride** vor Wut rot anlaufen/vor Stolz anschwellen; **the children's bellies had swollen with hunger** die Bäuche der Kinder waren vom Hunger (auf)gebläht.

(b) (*river, lake, sound etc*) anschwellen; (*cheers also*) anwachsen; (*sails: also* **~ out**) sich blähen; (*wood*) quellen; (*in size, number: population, debt etc*) anwachsen ◆ **to ~ into a crowd** sich zu einer Menschenmenge auswachsen; **the cheers ~ed to a roar** der Jubel schwoll zu einem Begeisterungssturm an; **the debt had swollen to a massive sum** die Schuld war zu einer riesigen Summe angewachsen; *see also* **swollen**.

swell-box ['swel,bɒks] *n* (*Mus*) Schwellwerk *nt*.

swellhead ['swel,hed] *n* (*esp US inf*) aufgeblasener Typ (*inf*).

swell-headed ['swel,hedɪd] *adj* (*inf*) aufgeblasen (*inf*).

swelling ['swelɪŋ] [1] *n* **(a)** Verdickung *f*; (*Med*) Schwellung *f*.

(b) (*act*) *see vi* Anschwellen *nt*; Anwachsen *nt*; Blähen *nt*; Quellen *nt*.

[2] *adj attr ankle etc* (an)schwellend; *sails* gebläht; *sound* anschwellend; *numbers* steigend, anwachsend, zunehmend; *line, curve* geschwungen ◆ **the ~ curve of her bosom** die Wölbung ihrer Brüste.

swelter ['sweltəʳ] *vi* (vor Hitze) vergehen, verschmachten (*inf*).

sweltering ['sweltərɪŋ] *adj day, weather* glühend heiß; *heat* glühend ◆ **it's ~ in here** (*inf*) hier verschmachtet man ja! (*inf*).

swept [swept] *pret, ptp of* **sweep**.

swept: ~back *adj wing* Delta-, Dreieck-; **~wing** *adj aircraft* mit Delta- *or* Dreieckflügeln.

swerve [swɜ:v] [1] *n* Bogen *m*; (*of road, coastline also*) Schwenkung *f*; (*of car etc also*) Schlenker *m* (*inf*); (*spin on ball*) Effet *m* ◆ **with a ~ he avoided his opponent** er wich seinem Gegner mit einer geschickten Bewegung aus; **to put a ~ on the ball** einen Ball anschneiden; **to make a ~** (*lit*) *see vi*.

[2] *vi* einen Bogen machen; (*car, driver*) ausschwenken; (*boxer*) ausweichen; (*horse*) ausbrechen; (*ball also*) im Bogen fliegen; (*fig*) (*from truth*) abweichen; (*from chosen path*) abschwenken ◆ **to ~ round sth** einen Bogen um etw machen; **the road ~s (round) to the right** die Straße schwenkt nach rechts; **he ~d in in front of me** er schwenkte plötzlich vor mir ein; **the car ~d in and out of the traffic** der Wagen schoß im Slalom durch den Verkehrsstrom.

[3] *vt car etc* herumreißen; *ball* anschneiden.

swift [swɪft] [1] *adj* (*+er*) schnell; *movement, steps also* flink; *reaction, reply also, revenge* prompt; *runner also* flink, flott; *pace* flott, rasch ◆ **~ of foot** (*liter*) schnellfüßig; **to be ~ to anger** jähzornig sein; **to be ~ to do sth** etw schnell tun.

[2] *n* (*bird*) Mauersegler *m*.

swift: ~-flowing *adj* schnellfließend *attr*; **~-footed** *adj* (*liter*) schnellfüßig.

swiftly ['swɪftlɪ] *adv see adj* ◆ **time passes ~** die Zeit vergeht wie im Flug.

swiftness ['swɪftnɪs] *n see adj* Schnelligkeit *f*; Flinkheit *f*; Promptheit *f*; Flottheit *f*; Raschheit *f* ◆ **the ~ of the current** die reißende Strömung.

swig [swɪg] (*inf*) [1] *n* Schluck *m* ◆ **to have** *or* **take a ~ of beer/at** *or* **from a bottle** einen Schluck Bier/aus einer Flasche nehmen; **have a ~ of this** trinken Sie mal einen Schluck (davon) (*inf*); **to down a drink in one ~** das Glas in einem Zug leeren.

[2] *vt* (*also* **~ down**) herunterkippen (*inf*).

swill [swɪl] [1] *n* **(a)** (*animal food*) (Schweine)futter *nt*; (*garbage, slops*) (*solid*) Abfälle *pl*; (*liquid*) Schmutzwasser *nt*; (*fig pej*) (Schweine)fraß *m* (*inf*); (*liquid*) Abwaschwasser *nt*.

(b) (*cleaning*) **to give sth a ~ (out/down)** *see vt* (*a*).

[2] *vt* **(a)** (*also* **~ out**) auswaschen; *cup, dish* ausschwenken ◆ **to ~ sth down** etw abspülen; *floor* etw waschen.

(b) (*inf*) *beer etc* kippen (*inf*) ◆ **he ~ed it down with beer** er hat es mit Bier runtergespült (*inf*).

swim [swɪm] (*vb: pret* **swam**, *ptp* **swum**) [1] *n* **(a) after a 2 km ~** nach 2 km Schwimmen, nachdem ich *etc* 2 km geschwommen bin/war; **it's a long ~** es ist weit (zu schwimmen); **that was a nice ~** das (Schwimmen) hat Spaß gemacht!; **I like** *or* **enjoy a ~** ich gehe gern (mal) schwimmen, ich schwimme gern (mal); **to have a ~** schwimmen.

(b) (*inf*) **to be in the/out of the ~** up to date/nicht mehr up to date sein; (*socially active*) mitmischen (*inf*)/den Anschluß verloren haben.

[2] *vt* schwimmen; *river, Channel* durchschwimmen.

[3] *vi* (*all senses*) schwimmen ◆ **to ~ back** zurückschwimmen; **we shall have to ~ for it** wir werden schwimmen müssen; **the room swam before my eyes** das Zimmer verschwamm vor meinen Augen; **my head is ~ming** mir dreht sich alles, mir ist ganz schwummrig (*inf*).

swim-bladder ['swɪm,blædəʳ] *n* Schwimmblase *f*.

swimmer ['swɪməʳ] *n* Schwimmer(in *f*) *m*.

swimming ['swɪmɪŋ] [1] *n* Schwimmen *nt* ◆ **do you like ~?** schwimmen Sie gern?

[2] *adj* (*for* ~) Schwimm-; (*dizzy*) *feeling* schwummrig (*inf*).

swimming: ~ bath *n usu pl see* **~ pool**; **~ cap** *n* Badekappe, Bademütze *f*; **~ costume** *n* Badeanzug *m*; **~ gala** *n* Schwimmfest *nt*.

swimmingly ['swɪmɪŋlɪ] *adv* (*inf*) glänzend.

swimming: ~ pool *n* Schwimmbad *nt*; (*outdoor also*) Freibad *nt*; (*indoor also*) Hallenbad *nt*; **~ ring** *n* Schwimmring *m*; **~ trunks** *npl* Badehose *f*.

swimsuit ['swɪmsu:t] *n* Badeanzug *m*.

swindle ['swɪndl] [1] *n* Schwindel, Betrug *m* ◆ **it's a ~!** das ist (der reinste) Schwindel!

[2] *vt person* beschwindeln, betrügen ◆ **to ~ sb out of sth** (*take from*) jdm etw abschwindeln *or* abgaunern (*inf*); (*withhold from*) jdn um etw beschwindeln *or* betrügen.

swindler ['swɪndləʳ] *n* Schwindler(in *f*), Gauner(in *f*) (*inf*) *m*.

swine [swaɪn] *n* **(a)** *pl* - (*old, form*) Schwein *nt*. **(b)** *pl* **-s** (*pej inf*) (*man*) (gemeiner) Hund (*inf*); (*woman*) gemeine Sau (*sl*) ◆ **this translation is a ~** diese Übersetzung ist wirklich gemein (*inf*).

swine: ~ fever *n* Schweinepest *f*; **~herd** *n* (*old*) Schweinehirt *m*.

swing [swɪŋ] (*vb: pret, ptp* **swung**) [1] *n* **(a)** (*movement*) Schwung *m*; (*to and fro*) Schwingen *nt*; (*of needle*) Ausschlag *m*; (*distance*) Ausschlag, Schwung(weite *f*) *m*; (*Boxing etc: blow*) Schwinger *m*; (*Golf, Skiing etc*) Schwung *m*; (*fig, Pol*) (Meinungs)umschwung *m* ◆ **to take a ~ at sb** nach jdm schlagen; **the golfer took a big ~ at the ball** der Golfer holte weit aus und schlug den Ball; **my ~ is too short** ich hole nicht weit genug aus; **a ~ in opinion** ein Meinungsumschwung.

(b) (*rhythm*) Schwung *m*; (*kind of music, dance*) Swing *m* ◆ **a tune with a ~** eine Melodie mit Schwung; **to walk with a ~** schwungvoll gehen; **to go with a ~** (*fig*) ein voller Erfolg sein (*inf*); **to be in full ~** voll im Gang sein; **to get into the ~ of things** (*inf*) reinkommen (*inf*).

(c) (*seat for* ~*ing*) Schaukel *f* ◆ **to give sb a ~** jdn anstoßen *or* anschubsen (*inf*); **to have a ~** schaukeln; **what you gain on the ~s (you lose on the roundabouts)** (*prov*) was man auf der einen Seite gewinnt, verliert man auf der anderen; **it's a ~s and roundabouts situation** (*inf*) es ist gehupft wie gesprungen.

(d) (*esp US: scope, freedom*) **he gave his imagination full ~** er ließ seiner Phantasie (*dat*) freien Lauf; **he was given full ~ to make decisions** man hat ihm bei allen Entscheidungen freie Hand gelassen.

[2] *vt* **(a)** schwingen; (*to and fro*) hin und her schwingen; (*on swing, hammock*) schaukeln; *arms, legs* (*vigorously*) schwingen (mit); (*dangle*) baumeln mit; *propeller* einen Schwung geben (*+dat*) ◆ **to ~ a child** ein Kind schaukeln; **to ~ one's hips** sich in den Hüften wiegen; **to ~ the lead** (*Brit inf*) sich drücken (*inf*); *see* **cat**.

(b) (*move*) **he swung his axe at the tree/at me** er schwang die Axt gegen den Baum/gegen mich; **he swung his racket at the ball** er holte mit dem Schläger aus; **to ~ a door open/shut** eine Tür aufstoßen/zustoßen; **he swung the case (up) onto his shoulder** er schwang sich (*dat*) die Kiste auf die Schulter; **he swung himself over the stream/wall/up into the saddle** er schwang sich über den Bach/über die Mauer/in den Sattel.

(c) (*influence*) *election, decision, voters* beeinflussen; *opinion* umschlagen lassen; *person* umstimmen, herumkriegen (*inf*) ◆ **his speech swung the decision in our favour** seine Rede ließ die Entscheidung zu unseren Gunsten ausfallen; **what swung it for me was the fact that ...** (*inf*) was dann letzten Endes den Ausschlag gegeben hat, war, daß ...; **to ~ it (so that ...)** (*inf*) es so drehen *or* deichseln (*inf*) (, daß ...); **he managed to ~ it in our favour** es gelang ihm, es zu unseren Gunsten zu drehen; **he managed to ~ the deal** (*inf*) er hat das Geschäft gemacht (*inf*).

(d) (*turn: also* **~ round**) *plane, car* herumschwenken.

[3] *vi* **(a)** schwingen; (*to and fro*) (hin und her) schwingen; (*hanging object also*) pendeln; (*pivot*) sich drehen; (*on swing*) schaukeln; (*arms, legs: dangle*) baumeln ◆ **he was left ~ing by his hands** er hing *or* (*dangerously*) baumelte nur noch an den Händen; **the boat was ~ing at anchor** das Boot lag

schaukelnd vor Anker; **he swung at me with his axe** er schwang die Axt gegen mich; **the golfer swung at the ball** der Golfer holte aus.
(b) (*move: into saddle, along rope etc*) sich schwingen ◆ **to ~ from tree to tree** sich von Baum zu Baum schwingen; **to ~ open/shut** aufschwingen/zuschlagen; **to ~ into action** in Aktion treten; **the car swung into the square** der Wagen schwenkte auf den Platz ein; **opinion/the party has swung to the right** die Meinung/die Partei hat einen Rechtsschwenk gemacht.
(c) (*music, tune*) Schwung haben ◆ **the town/club began to ~** in der Stadt/im Klub kam Stimmung auf (*inf*); **London really swung in the sixties** in den sechziger Jahren war in London schwer was los (*inf*).
(d) (*inf: be hanged*) **he'll ~ for it** dafür wird er baumeln (*inf*); **I'll ~ for him (yet)** ich bring ihn noch um (*inf*); **he's not worth ~ing for** es lohnt sich nicht, sich an ihm die Hände schmutzig zu machen (*inf*).

◆**swing across** *vi* hinüber-/herüberschwingen; (*hand-over-hand*) sich hinüber-/herüberhangeln; (*+prep obj*) schwingen über (*+acc*); (*person, animal*) sich schwingen über (*+acc*); (*hand-over-hand*) sich hangeln über (*+acc*).

◆**swing back** [1] *vi* zurückschwingen; (*opinion*) zurückschlagen.
[2] *vt sep* zurückschwingen; *opinion* zurückschlagen lassen.

◆**swing round** [1] *vi* (*person*) sich umdrehen, herumfahren (*inf*); (*car, ship, plane, crane*) herumschwenken; (*needle*) ausschlagen; (*fig: voters, opinion*) umschwenken ◆ **he has swung ~ in favour of the idea** er hat sich doch noch für diese Idee entschieden.
[2] *vt sep* herumschwenken; *voters* umstimmen; *opinion* umschlagen lassen.

◆**swing to** *vi* (*door*) zuschlagen.

swing: ~ band *n* (*Mus*) Swingband *f*; **~-boat** *n* Schiffsschaukel *f*; **~ bridge** *n* Drehbrücke *f*; **~-door** *n* (*Brit*) Pendeltür *f*.

swingeing ['swɪndʒɪŋ] *adj* (*Brit*) *blow* hart; *attack* scharf; *defeat* vernichtend; *taxation, price increases* extrem hoch; *cuts* extrem.

swinger ['swɪŋəʳ] *n* (*inf*) lockerer Typ (*sl*).

swinging ['swɪŋɪŋ] *adj step* schwungvoll; *movement* schaukelnd; *music* schwungvoll, swingend; (*fig inf*) *person* locker (*sl*) ◆ **~ door** (*US*) Pendeltür *f*; **London was a ~ place then** in London war damals wirklich was los (*inf*); **the ~ sixties** die flotten sechziger Jahre, die „swinging sixties" (*sl*).

swing-wing ['swɪŋ'wɪŋ] *adj aircraft* mit ausfahrbaren Tragflächenteilen.

swinish ['swaɪnɪʃ] *adj* (*fig*) gemein.

swipe [swaɪp] [1] *n* (*blow*) Schlag *m* ◆ **to take** *or* **make a ~ at sb/sth** nach jdm/etw schlagen.
[2] *vt* **(a)** *person, ball etc* schlagen ◆ **he ~d the wasp with the towel** er schlug mit dem Handtuch auf die Wespe. **(b)** (*inf: to steal*) mopsen (*inf*), klauen (*inf*).
[3] *vi* **to ~ at sb/sth** nach jdm/etw schlagen.

swirl [swɜːl] [1] *n* Wirbel *m*; (*whorl in pattern also*) Spirale *f* ◆ **the ~ of the dancers' skirts** die wirbelnden Röcke der Tänzerinnen; **she put a ~ of cream on the cake** sie spritzte ein Sahnehäufchen auf den Kuchen.
[2] *vt water, dust etc* wirbeln ◆ **to ~ sth along/away** *etc* (*river*) etw wirbelnd mitreißen/etw wegwirbeln; **he ~ed his partner round the room** er wirbelte seine Partnerin durchs Zimmer.
[3] *vi* wirbeln ◆ **to ~ around** herumwirbeln.

swish [swɪʃ] [1] *n see vi* Zischen *nt*; Sausen *nt*; Rascheln *nt*; Rauschen *nt*; Pfeifen *nt*; Wischen *nt*.
[2] *adj* (*+er*) (*esp Brit inf: smart*) (tod)schick.
[3] *vt cane* zischen *or* sausen lassen; *tail* schlagen mit; *skirt* rauschen mit; *water* schwenken ◆ **she ~ed water round the bowl** sie schwenkte die Schüssel mit Wasser aus.
[4] *vi* (*whip, cane*) zischen, sausen; (*grass*) rascheln; (*skirts*) rauschen, rascheln; (*water*) rauschen; (*tyres*) zischen, pfeifen; (*windscreen wipers*) wischen.

Swiss [swɪs] [1] *adj* Schweizer, schweizerisch ◆ **the ~-German part of Switzerland** die deutsch(sprachig)e Schweiz; **~ cheese** Schweizer Käse *m*; **~ cheese plant** Fensterblatt *nt*, Philodendron *m or nt*; **~ roll** Biskuitrolle *f*; **the/a ~ Guard** die Schweizergarde/ein Schweizer *m*.
[2] *n* Schweizer(in *f*) *m* ◆ **the ~** *pl* die Schweizer *pl*; **~ French/German** (*person*) Welsch-/Deutschschweizer(in *f*) *m*; (*language*) Schweizer Französisch *nt*/Schweizerdeutsch *or* Schwyzerdütsch *nt*.

switch [swɪtʃ] [1] *n* **(a)** (*Elec etc*) Schalter *m*.
(b) (*US Rail*) Weiche *f*.
(c) (*change*) Wechsel *m*; (*in plans, policies*) Änderung, Umstellung *f* (*in gen*); (*in opinion*) Änderung *f* (*in gen*); (*exchange*) Tausch *m* ◆ **a rapid ~ of plan** eine schnelle Änderung der Pläne; **to do** *or* **make a ~** tauschen.
(d) (*stick, cane*) Rute, Gerte *f*; (*riding-whip*) Gerte *f*.
(e) (*of hair*) falscher Zopf.
[2] *vt* **(a)** (*change, alter*) wechseln; *direction, plans* ändern; *allegiance* übertragen (*to* auf *+acc*); *attention, conversation* lenken (*to* auf *+acc*) ◆ **to ~ schools** die Schule wechseln.
(b) (*move*) *production* verlegen; *object* umstellen.
(c) (*exchange*) tauschen; (*transpose: also* **~ over, ~ round**) *objects, letters in word, figures in column* vertauschen ◆ **I ~ed hats with him** ich tauschte meinen Hut mit ihm; **we ~ed hats** wir tauschten die Hüte; **to ~ A for B** A für *or* gegen B (ein)tauschen; **to ~ A and B (over)** A und B vertauschen.
(d) (*Elec*) (um)schalten ◆ **~ the radio to another programme** schalten Sie auf ein anderes Radioprogramm um.
(e) *tail, cane* schlagen mit.
(f) (*esp US Rail*) rangieren.
[3] *vi* **(a)** (*change: also* **~ over**) (über)wechseln (*to* zu); (*Elec, TV, Rad*) umschalten (*to* auf *+acc*); (*exchange: also* **~ round, ~ over**) tauschen ◆ **to ~ (over) from Y to Z** von Y auf Z (*acc*) (über)wechseln; **we've ~ed (over) to gas** wir haben auf Gas umgestellt; **the wind ~ed to the east** der Wind hat (sich) nach Osten gedreht; **he ~ed to another line of attack** er wechselte seine Angriffstaktik; **she ~ed to being in favour of it** sie änderte ihre Meinung und war auf einmal dafür.
(b) (*Rail*) rangieren.

◆**switch back** [1] *vi* (*to original plan, product, allegiance etc*) zum Alten zurückkehren, auf das Alte zurückgreifen; (*Elec, Rad, TV*) zurückschalten (*to* zu).
[2] *vt sep heater, cooker* zurückschalten (*to* auf *+acc*) ◆ **to ~ the light ~ on** das Licht wieder anschalten.

◆**switch off** [1] *vt sep* **(a)** *light* ausschalten; *radio, TV, machine also, engine* abschalten; *gas, water supply* abstellen ◆ **the oven ~es itself ~** der Backofen schaltet sich selbsttätig ab *or* aus.
(b) (*inf*) **~ him ~ for goodness' sake!** (*inf*) kann den denn niemand abstellen, um Himmels willen.
[2] *vi* **(a)** *see vt* (*a*) ausschalten; abschalten; abstellen ◆ **the TV won't ~ ~** der Fernseher läßt sich nicht aus- *or* abschalten. **(b)** (*inf: person*) abschalten.

◆**switch on** [1] *vt sep* **(a)** *gas, water* anstellen; *machine, radio, TV also, light* einschalten, anschalten; *engine also* anlassen ◆ **please leave the TV ~ed ~** laß den Fernseher bitte an.
(b) (*sl*) *person* (*interest*) munter machen, begeistern; (*emotionally, by drugs*) anturnen (*sl*), high machen (*sl*); (*sexually*) auf Touren bringen (*inf*) ◆ **~ed ~** begeistert; (*emotionally, on drugs*) high (*sl*); (*sexually*) auf Touren (*inf*); (*up-to-date*) in (*sl*); **to be ~ed ~ to jazz** auf Jazz stehen (*inf*).
[2] *vi see vt* (*a*) anstellen; einschalten, anschalten; anlassen ◆ **the cooker will ~ ~ at 10** der Herd schaltet sich um 10 Uhr ein *or* an.

◆**switch over** [1] *vi see* **switch 3 (a)**.
[2] *vt sep* **(a)** *see* **switch 2 (b)**. **(b)** (*TV, Rad*) **to ~ the programme ~** auf ein anderes Programm umschalten.

◆**switch round** [1] *vt sep* (*swap round*) vertauschen; (*rearrange*) umstellen.
[2] *vi see* **switch 3 (a)**.

◆**switch through** *vt sep* (*Telec*) durchstellen (*to* zu), verbinden (*to* mit).

switch: ~back *n* Berg- und Talbahn *f*; (*Brit: roller-coaster also*) Achterbahn *f*; **~blade** *n* (*US*) Schnappmesser *nt*; **~board** *n* (*Telec*) (*exchange*) Vermittlung *f*; (*in office etc*) Zentrale *f*; (*actual panel, Elec*) Schalttafel *f*; **~board operator** *n* (*in office*) Telefonist(in *f*) *m*; **~-hit** *vi* (*Baseball*) beidhändig schlagen; **~-hitter** *n* (*Baseball*) beidhändiger Hitter; **~-man** *n* (*US Rail*) Weichensteller *m*; **~-over** *n* Wechsel *m* (*to* auf *+acc*, zu); (*exchange*) Tausch *m*; (*of letters, figures etc*) Vertauschung *f*; **~-round** *n* Tausch *m*; (*of letters, figures etc*) Vertauschung *f*; (*rearrangement*) Umstellen *nt*; **~-yard** *n* (*US Rail*) Rangierbahnhof *m*.

Switzerland ['swɪtsələnd] *n* die Schweiz ◆ **to ~** in die Schweiz; **French-/German-/Italian-speaking ~** die französische Schweiz/die deutsch-/italienischsprachige Schweiz.

swivel ['swɪvl] [1] *n* Drehgelenk *nt*.
[2] *attr* Dreh- ◆ **~ base** (*of monitor etc*) Schwenksockel *m*.
[3] *vt* (*also* **~ round**) (herum)drehen.
[4] *vi* (*also* **~ round**) sich drehen; (*person*) sich herumdrehen.

swivelling ['swɪvəlɪŋ] *adj* schwenkbar.

swizz [swɪz], **swizzle** ['swɪzl] *n* (*Brit inf*) (*swindle*) Bauernfängerei *f* (*inf*); (*disappointment*) Gemeinheit *f* (*inf*).

swizzle-stick ['swɪzl'stɪk] *n* Sektquirl *m*.

swollen ['swəʊlən] [1] *ptp of* **swell**.
[2] *adj ankle, face, glands etc* (an)geschwollen; *stomach* aufgedunsen, aufgebläht; *wood* verquollen, gequollen; *sails* gebläht; *river* angeschwollen, angestiegen; *numbers* (an)gestiegen, angewachsen ◆ **her eyes were ~ with tears** ihre Augen waren verweint; **he has a ~ head** (*fig*) er ist so aufgeblasen.

swollen-headed ['swəʊlən'hedɪd] *adj* aufgeblasen (*inf*).

swollen-headedness ['swəʊlən'hedɪdnɪs] *n* Aufgeblasenheit *f* (*inf*).

swoon [swuːn] [1] *n* (*old*) Ohnmacht *f* ◆ **to fall in(to)/be in a ~** in Ohnmacht fallen *or* sinken (*geh*)/ohnmächtig sein.
[2] *vi* (*old: faint*) in Ohnmacht fallen, ohnmächtig werden; (*fig: over pop star etc*) beinahe ohnmächtig werden (*over sb/sth* wegen jdm/einer Sache).

swoop [swuːp] [1] *vi* (*lit: also* **~ down**) (*bird*) herabstoßen, niederstoßen (*on* auf *+acc*); (*plane*) einen Sturzflug machen; (*fig*) (*police*) einen Überraschungsangriff machen (*on* auf *+acc*) *or* landen (*inf*) (*on* bei); (*person*) sich stürzen (*on* auf *+acc*) ◆ **the plane ~ed (down) low over the village** das Flugzeug flog im Tiefflug über das Dorf hinweg; **the police ~ed on 8 suspects** die Polizei schlug überraschend bei 8 Verdächtigen zu; **they're just waiting to ~** die lauern nur darauf zuzuschlagen.
[2] *n* (*of bird, plane*) Sturzflug *m*; (*by police*) Razzia *f* (*on* in *+dat*, *on sb* bei jdm) ◆ **to make a ~** (*bird*) herabstoßen (*on* auf *+acc*); **at one (fell) ~** auf einen Schlag.

swoosh [swuːʃ] [1] *vi* rauschen; (*air*) brausen; (*tyres in rain etc*) pfeifen, sirren; (*skirts, curtains*) rauschen.
[2] *n see vi* Rauschen *nt*; Brausen *nt*; Pfeifen, Sirren *nt*.

swop *n, vti see* **swap**.

sword [sɔːd] *n* Schwert *nt* ◆ **to cross ~s with sb** (*lit, fig*) mit jdm die Klinge(n) kreuzen; **by fire and (the) ~** mit Feuer und Schwert; **to put people to the ~** (*old*) Menschen mit dem Schwert töten; **those that live by the ~ die by the ~** (*prov*) wer das Schwert ergreift, der soll durchs Schwert umkommen.

sword *in cpds* Schwert-; **~ and sorcery** *n* (*Liter*) *Science-fiction f mit mittelalterlichen Themen*; **~bearer** *n* Schwertträger *m*; **~-cane** *n* Stockdegen *m*; **~-dance** *n* Schwert(er)tanz *m*; **~fish** *n* Schwertfisch *m*;

~play *n* (Schwert)fechten *nt*; **~-point** *n* **at ~-point** mit vorgehaltener Klinge.
swordsman ['sɔːdzmən] *n, pl* **-men** [-mən] Schwertkämpfer *m*; *(fencer)* Fechter *m*.
swordsmanship ['sɔːdzmənʃɪp] *n* Fechtkunst *f*.
sword: ~stick *n* Stockdegen *m*; **~-swallower** *n* Schwertschlucker *m*.
swore [swɔːʳ] *pret of* **swear.**
sworn [swɔːn] [1] *ptp of* **swear.**
[2] *adj enemy* eingeschworen; *(Jur) statement* beschworen, eidlich, unter Eid.
swot [swɒt] *(Brit inf)* [1] *vti* büffeln *(inf)*, pauken *(inf)* ◆ **to ~ up (on) one's maths** Mathe pauken *(inf)*; **to ~ at sth** etw pauken *(inf) or* büffeln *(inf)*.
[2] *n (pej) person* Streber(in *f*) *m*.
swotting ['swɒtɪŋ] *n (Brit inf)* Büffeln *(inf)*, Pauken *(inf) nt* ◆ **to do some ~** büffeln *(inf)*, pauken *(inf)*.
swum [swʌm] *ptp of* **swim.**
swung [swʌŋ] [1] *pret, ptp of* **swing.**
[2] *adj (Typ)* **~ dash** Tilde *f*.
sybarite ['sɪbəraɪt] *n (form)* Genußmensch *m*.
sybaritic [ˌsɪbə'rɪtɪk] *adj (form) person* genußsüchtig; *way of life* schwelgerisch.
sycamore ['sɪkəmɔːʳ] *n* Bergahorn *m*; *(US: plane tree)* nordamerikanische Platane; *(wood)* Ahorn *m*.
sycophancy ['sɪkəfənsɪ] *n* Kriecherei, Speichelleckerei *f (inf)*.
sycophant ['sɪkəfənt] *n* Kriecher, Speichellecker *m (inf)*.
sycophantic [ˌsɪkə'fæntɪk] *adj* kriecherisch, unterwürfig.
syllabary ['sɪləbərɪ] *n* Syllabar *nt*, Silbentabelle *f*.
syllabic [sɪ'læbɪk] *adj* silbisch, Silben-.
syllabification [sɪˌlæbɪfɪ'keɪʃən] *n* Silbentrennung *f*.
syllable ['sɪləbl] *n* Silbe *f* ◆ **a two-~(d) word** ein zweisilbiges Wort; **don't breathe a ~ of it** sag keinen Ton darüber; **in words of one ~** *(hum)* in einfachen Worten.
syllabub ['sɪləbʌb] *n (dessert) Obstspeise f mit Sahne*.
syllabus ['sɪləbəs] *n, pl* **-es** *or* **syllabi** ['sɪləbaɪ] *(Sch, Univ)* Lehrplan *m*; *(of club etc)* Programm *nt* ◆ **the S~ (of Errors)** *(Eccl)* der Syllabus (von Zeitirrtümern).
syllogism ['sɪlədʒɪzəm] *n* Syllogismus *m*.
syllogistic [ˌsɪlə'dʒɪstɪk] *adj* syllogistisch.
syllogize ['sɪlədʒaɪz] *vi* syllogistisch folgern.
sylph [sɪlf] *n (Myth)* Sylphe *mf*; *(fig: girl)* Sylphide, Nymphe *f*.
sylphid ['sɪlfɪd] *n* Sylphide *f*.
sylphlike ['sɪlfˌlaɪk] *adj figure etc* grazil, sylphidenhaft.
sylvan, silvan ['sɪlvən] *adj (liter)* Wald-; *shade, goddess also* des Waldes; *surroundings* waldig.
symbiosis [ˌsɪmbɪ'əʊsɪs] *n* Symbiose *f*.
symbiotic [ˌsɪmbɪ'ɒtɪk] *adj* symbiotisch.
symbol ['sɪmbəl] *n* Symbol, Zeichen *nt (of* für).
symbolic(al) [sɪm'bɒlɪk(əl)] *adj* symbolisch *(of* für) ◆ **to be ~ of sth** etw symbolisieren, ein Symbol für etw sein; **~ logic** mathematische Logik.
symbolically [sɪm'bɒlɪkəlɪ] *adv see adj*.
symbolism ['sɪmbəlɪzəm] *n* Symbolik *f*; *(Art, Liter: movement)* Symbolismus *m*.
symbolist ['sɪmbəlɪst] [1] *n* Symbolist(in *f*) *m*.
[2] *adj* symbolistisch.
symbolization [ˌsɪmbəlaɪ'zeɪʃən] *n* Symbolisierung *f*.
symbolize ['sɪmbəlaɪz] *vt* symbolisieren.
symmetrical *adj*, **~ly** *adv* [sɪ'metrɪkəl, -ɪ] symmetrisch.
symmetry ['sɪmɪtrɪ] *n* Symmetrie *f*.
sympathetic [ˌsɪmpə'θetɪk] *adj* **(a)** *(showing pity)* mitfühlend, teilnahmsvoll; *(understanding)* verständnisvoll; *(well-disposed)* wohlwollend, wohlgesonnen *(geh)*; *look, smile* verbindlich, freundlich ◆ **to be** *or* **feel ~ to(wards) sb** *(showing pity)* mit jdm mitfühlen; *(understanding)* jdm Verständnis entgegenbringen, für jdn Verständnis haben; *(being well-disposed)* mit jdm sympathisieren; **he was most ~ when I told him all my troubles** er zeigte sehr viel Mitgefühl für all meine Sorgen; **a ~ ear** ein offenes Ohr.
(b) *(likeable)* sympathisch.
(c) *(Physiol, Phys)* sympathisch ◆ **~ vibration** Mitschwingung *f*; **~ string** mitschwingende Saite, Bordunsaite *f*; **~ magic** Sympathiezauber *m*.
sympathetically [ˌsɪmpə'θetɪkəlɪ] *adv (showing pity)* mitfühlend; *(with understanding)* verständnisvoll; *(well-disposed)* wohlwollend ◆ **to be ~ inclined towards sb/sth** jdm/einer Sache wohlwollend gegenüberstehen; **to respond/vibrate ~** *(Phys etc)* mitreagieren/mitschwingen.
sympathize ['sɪmpəθaɪz] *vi (feel compassion)* mitfühlen, Mitleid haben *(with* mit); *(understand)* Verständnis haben *(with* für); *(agree)* sympathisieren *(with* mit) *(esp Pol)*; *(express sympathy)* sein Mitgefühl aussprechen; *(on bereavement)* sein Beileid aussprechen ◆ **to ~ with sb over sth** *(feel sorry)* mit jdm in einer Sache mitfühlen können; **to ~ with sb's views** jds Ansichten teilen; **to ~ with sb's troubles** mit jdm mitfühlen; **I really do ~** *(have pity)* das tut mir wirklich leid; *(understand your feelings)* ich habe wirklich vollstes Verständnis; **I ~ with you** *or* **with what you say/feel, but ...** ich teile Ihre Ansichten/Gefühle, aber ..., ich kann Ihnen das nachfühlen, aber ...; **to ~ with sb in his bereavement/grief** jds Verlust/Schmerz teilen; *(express sympathy)* jdm sein Beileid/Mitgefühl aussprechen.
sympathizer ['sɪmpəθaɪzəʳ] *n* Mitfühlende(r) *mf*; *(at death also)* Kondolierende(r) *mf*; *(with cause)* Sympathisant(in *f*) *m*.
▼ **sympathy** ['sɪmpəθɪ] *n* **(a)** *(pity, compassion)* Mitgefühl, Mitleid *nt (for* mit); *(at death)* Beileid *nt* ◆ **to feel** *or* **have ~ for sb** Mitgefühl *or* Mitleid mit jdm haben; **a letter of ~** ein mitfühlender Brief, ein Beileidsbrief *m*; **you have our deepest** *or* **heartfelt ~** *or* **sympathies** wir fühlen mit Ihnen; (unser) aufrichtiges *or* herzliches Beileid; **you have my ~!** *(hum)* herzliches Beileid *(hum)*; **my sympathies are with her family** mir tut ihre Familie leid; **to express one's ~** sein Mitgefühl aussprechen; sein Beileid aussprechen; **you won't get any ~ from me** erwarte kein Mitleid von mir.
(b) *(understanding)* Verständnis *nt*; *(fellow-feeling, agreement)* Sympathie *f* ◆ **to be in/out of ~ with sb/sth** mit jdm/etw einhergehen/nicht einhergehen; **the sympathies of the crowd were with him** *(in match, discussion)* die Zuschauer waren auf seiner Seite; **he has Democratic sympathies** er sympathisiert mit *or* seine Sympathien gehören den Demokraten; **politically there wasn't much ~ between them** sie verstanden sich politisch nicht gut; **to come out** *or* **strike in ~** *(Ind)* in Sympathiestreik treten; **the dollar fell and the pound fell in ~** der Dollar fiel und das Pfund fiel mit; **to resonate/vibrate in ~** mitklingen/mitschwingen; **~ strike** Sympathiestreik *m*.
symphonic [sɪm'fɒnɪk] *adj* symphonisch, sinfonisch ◆ **~ poem** symphonische Dichtung.
symphony ['sɪmfənɪ] *n* Symphonie, Sinfonie *f* ◆ **~ orchestra** Symphonie- *or* Sinfonieorchester *nt*; **the London S~** *(inf) or* **S~ Orchestra** die Londoner Symphoniker *pl*; **a ~ of colours** *(liter)* eine Sinfonie von Farben, eine Farbensinfonie.
symposium [sɪm'pəʊzɪəm] *n, pl* **-s** *or* **symposia** [sɪm'pəʊzɪə] Symposium, Symposion *nt*.
symptom ['sɪmptəm] *n (lit, fig)* Symptom *nt*.
symptomatic [ˌsɪmptə'mætɪk] *adj* symptomatisch *(of* für).
symptomize ['sɪmptəˌmaɪz] *vt* symptomatisch sein für.
synagogue ['sɪnəgɒg] *n* Synagoge *f*.
synapse ['saɪnæps] *n (Physiol)* Synapse *f*.
sync [sɪŋk] *n (Film, TV inf) abbr of* **synchronization** ◆ **in/out of ~** synchron/nicht synchron.
synchromesh ['sɪŋkrəʊˌmeʃ] *n* Synchrongetriebe *nt*.
synchronic [sɪŋ'krɒnɪk] *adj (Ling)* synchronisch.
synchronization [ˌsɪŋkrənaɪ'zeɪʃən] *n* **(a)** *see vt* Abstimmung *f*; Synchronisation *f*; Gleichstellung *f*. **(b)** *see vi* Synchronisation *f*; Gleichgehen *nt*; Zusammenfall *m*, gleichzeitiger Ablauf; Übereinstimmung *f*.
synchronize ['sɪŋkrənaɪz] [1] *vt* abstimmen *(with* auf *+acc)*; *two actions, movements* aufeinander abstimmen; *(Film)* synchronisieren *(with* mit); *clocks* gleichstellen *(with* mit) ◆ **~ your watches!** Uhrenvergleich!; **~d swimming** Synchronschwimmen *nt*.
[2] *vi (Film)* synchron sein *(with* mit); *(clocks)* gleichgehen; *(actions)* zusammenfallen, gleichzeitig ablaufen *(with* mit); *(movements)* in Übereinstimmung sein *(with* mit).
synchronous ['sɪŋkrənəs] *adj* gleichzeitig; *(Comput)* synchron.
syncopate ['sɪŋkəpeɪt] *vt (Mus)* synkopieren; *(Ling also)* zusammenziehen.
syncopation [ˌsɪŋkə'peɪʃən] *n* Synkope *f*; *(act)* Synkopierung *f*.
syncope ['sɪŋkəpɪ] *n (Ling, Med)* Synkope *f*.
syncretism ['sɪŋkrɪtɪzəm] *n (Ling)* Synkretismus *m*.
syndicalism ['sɪndɪkəlɪzəm] *n* Syndikalismus *m*.
syndicate ['sɪndɪkɪt] [1] *n* Interessengemeinschaft *f*; *(for gambling)* Wettgemeinschaft *f*; *(Comm)* Syndikat *nt*, Verband *m*; *(Press)* (Presse)zentrale *f*; *(crime ~)* Ring *m*.
[2] ['sɪndɪkeɪt] *vt (Press)* an mehrere Zeitungen verkaufen ◆ **there are several ~d articles in this newspaper** mehrere Artikel dieser Zeitung stammen aus einer Pressezentrale.
syndrome ['sɪndrəʊm] *n (Med)* Syndrom *nt*; *(fig, Sociol)* Phänomen *nt*.
synecdoche [sɪ'nekdəkɪ] *n* Synekdoche *f*.
synergy ['sɪnədʒɪ] *n* Synergie *f*.
synod ['sɪnəd] *n* Synode *f*.
synonym ['sɪnənɪm] *n* Synonym *nt*.
synonymous [sɪ'nɒnɪməs] *adj* synonym, synonymisch ◆ **her name was ~ with sex** ihr Name war gleichbedeutend mit Sex.
synonymy [sɪ'nɒnəmɪ] *n* Synonymik *f*.
synopsis [sɪ'nɒpsɪs] *n, pl* **synopses** [sɪ'nɒpsiːz] Abriß *m* der Handlung; *(of article, book)* Zusammenfassung *f*.
synoptic [sɪ'nɒptɪk] *adj* zusammenfassend ◆ **~ view** Überblick *m*, Übersicht *f*; **S~ Gospels** die Evangelien des Markus, Matthäus und Lukas; **~ chart** *(Met)* synoptische Karte.
syntactic(al) [sɪn'tæktɪk(əl)] *adj* syntaktisch.
syntax ['sɪntæks] *n* Syntax *f*; *(of sentence also)* Satzbau *m* ◆ **~ error** *(Comput)* Syntaxfehler *m*.
synthesis ['sɪnθəsɪs] *n, pl* **syntheses** ['sɪnθəsiːz] Synthese *f*; *(artificial production also)* Synthetisieren *nt*.
synthesize ['sɪnθəsaɪz] *vt* synthetisieren; *speech* synthetisch bilden; *theories etc* zusammenfassen.
synthesizer ['sɪnθəˌsaɪzəʳ] *n (Mus)* Synthesizer *m*.
synthetic [sɪn'θetɪk] [1] *adj* **(a)** synthetisch; *fibre, silk* Kunst- ◆ **~ smile** künstliches *or* gekünsteltes Lächeln. **(b)** *(Ling, Philos)* synthetisch.
[2] *n* Kunststoff *m*, synthetischer Stoff ◆ **~s** Synthetik *f*.
synthetically [sɪn'θetɪkəlɪ] *adv* synthetisch, künstlich; *(fig) smile* gekünstelt.
syphilis ['sɪfɪlɪs] *n* Syphilis *f*.
syphilitic [ˌsɪfɪ'lɪtɪk] [1] *adj* syphilitisch.
[2] *n* Syphilitiker(in *f*) *m*.
syphon *n see* **siphon.**
Syria ['sɪrɪə] *n* Syrien *nt*.
Syrian ['sɪrɪən] [1] *adj* syrisch.

➤ LANGUAGE IN USE: **sympathy: a → 24.4**

2 *n* Syr(i)er(in *f*) *m*.
syringa [sɪ'rɪŋgə] *n* (*Bot*) Falscher Jasmin, Pfeifenstrauch *m*; (*lilac*) Flieder *m*, Syringe *f*.
syringe [sɪ'rɪndʒ] (*Med*) **1** *n* Spritze *f*.
2 *vt* (aus)spülen.
syrup, (*US also*) **sirup** ['sɪrəp] *n* Sirup *m*; (*preservative also*) Saft *m* ◆ **~ of figs** Feigensaft *m*; **fruit ~** Fruchtsirup *m*; **cough ~** (*Med*) Hustensaft *or* -sirup *m*.
syrupy, (*US also*) **sirupy** ['sɪrəpɪ] *adj* sirupartig, sirupähnlich; (*pej*) *smile, voice* zucker- *or* honigsüß; (*sentimental*) *voice, song* schmalzig.
system ['sɪstəm] *n* **(a)** System *nt* ◆ **new teaching ~s** neue Lehrmethoden *pl*; **the democratic ~ of government** das demokratische (Regierungs)system; **the Pitman ~ of shorthand** die Kurzschriftmethode nach Pitman; **there's no ~ in his work** er hat kein System bei seiner Arbeit.
(b) (*working whole*) System *nt* ◆ **digestive ~** Verdauungsapparat *m*; **respiratory ~** Atmungsapparat *m*; **it's bad for the ~** das ist ungesund; **to pass through the ~** den Körper auf natürlichem Wege verlassen; **to be absorbed into the ~** aufgenommen werden; **it was a shock to his ~** er hatte schwer damit zu schaffen; **to get sth out of one's ~** (*fig inf*) sich (*dat*) etw von der Seele schaffen, etw loswerden (*inf*); **it's all ~s go!** (*inf*) jetzt heißt es: volle Kraft voraus!
(c) (*established authority*) **the ~** das System; **you can't beat** *or* **buck the ~** gegen das System kommst du *or* kommt man einfach nicht an.
(d) (*Comput: machine, operating ~*) System *nt* ◆ **~ disk** Systemdiskette *f*; **~ software** Systemsoftware *f*.
systematic [ˌsɪstə'mætɪk] *adj* systematisch; *liar, cruelty* ständig ◆ **he works in a ~ way** er arbeitet mit System.
systematically [ˌsɪstə'mætɪkəlɪ] *adv see adj*.
systematization [ˌsɪstəmətaɪ'zeɪʃən] *n* Systematisierung *f*.
systematize ['sɪstəmətaɪz] *vt* systematisieren.
systemic *adj* [sɪ'sti:mɪk] systemisch.
systems: ~ analysis *n* Systemanalyse *f*; **~ analyst** *n* Systemanalytiker(in *f*) *m*; **~ disk** *n* (*Comput*) Systemdiskette *f*; **~ software** *n* Systemsoftware *f*.
systole ['sɪstəlɪ] *n* (*Physiol*) Systole *f*.

T, t [tiː] *n* T, t *nt* ◆ **it suits him to a T** es ist genau das richtige für ihn; **that's him/it to a T** das ist er, wie er leibt und lebt/genau so ist es; **he got him to a T** er hat ihn haargenau getroffen.

TA *abbr of* **(a)** *(Brit)* **Territorial Army. (b)** *(US)* **teaching assistant.**

ta [tɑː] *interj (Brit inf)* danke.

tab¹ [tæb] *n* **(a)** *(loop on coat etc)* Aufhänger *m*; *(on back of boot, book)* Schlaufe *f*; *(fastener on coat etc)* Riegel *m*; *(name ~) (of owner)* Namensschild *nt*; *(of maker)* Etikett *nt*; *(on collar)* Verschluß(riegel) *m*; *(Mil)* Spiegel *m*; *(on shoulder, pocket)* Klappe, Patte *f*; *(on filing cards)* Reiter *m* ◆ **to keep ~s on sb/sth** *(inf)* jdn/etw genau im Auge behalten.
(b) *(Aviat)* Klappe *f*.
(c) *(US inf: bill)* Rechnung *f*.

tab² *(Comput, on typewriter)* [1] *n* Tabulator *m* ◆ **to set the ~s** tabulieren; **~ key** Tabulatortaste *f*.
[2] *vt columns* tabulieren.

tabard ['tæbəd] *n (of knight, herald)* Heroldsrock, Wappenrock, Tappert *m*; *(Fashion) ärmelloser, an den Seiten offener Kasak.*

tabasco [tə'bæskəʊ] *n* Tabasco(soße *f*) *m*.

tabby ['tæbɪ] *n* **(a)** *(also* **~ cat**) getigerte Katze; *(female cat)* (weibliche) Katze.
(b) *(inf: old maid)* Tantchen *nt (inf)*.

tabernacle ['tæbənækl] *n (church)* Gotteshaus *nt*; *(receptacle)* Tabernakel *m or nt* ◆ **the T~** *(Bibl)* die Stiftshütte.

table ['teɪbl] [1] *n* **(a)** Tisch *m*; *(banquet ~)* Tafel *f* ◆ **at the ~** am Tisch; **at ~** bei Tisch; **to sit down to** *or* **at ~** sich zu Tisch setzen; **he was sitting at the Mayor's ~** er saß am Bürgermeisterstisch; **who was on your ~?** wer saß an Ihrem Tisch *or* bei Ihnen am Tisch?; **to eat at sb's ~** seine Beine *or* Füße unter jds Tisch strecken *(inf)*; **to be under the ~** *(drunk)* unter dem Tisch liegen; **to drink sb under the ~** jdn unter den Tisch trinken; **the motion is on the ~** *(Brit Parl)* der Antrag liegt vor *or* ist eingebracht; **on the ~** *(US: postponed)* zurückgestellt, aufgeschoben; **to turn the ~s (on sb)** (gegenüber jdm) den Spieß umdrehen *or* umkehren.
(b) *(people at a ~)* Tisch *m*, Tischrunde *f* ◆ **the whole ~ laughed** der ganze Tisch *or* die ganze Runde lachte.
(c) *(of figures, prices etc, Sport)* Tabelle *f*; *(log ~)* Logarithmentafel *f* ◆ **(multiplication) ~s** Einmaleins *nt*; *(up to 10)* kleines Einmaleins; *(from 11 to 20)* großes Einmaleins; **to say one's three/five times ~** das Einmal-Drei/Einmal-Fünf aufsagen; **~ of contents** Inhaltsverzeichnis *nt*.
(d) *(Bibl: tablet)* Tafel *f*.
(e) *(Geog)* **water ~** Grundwasserspiegel *m*.
(f) *(~land)* Tafelland, Plateau *nt*, Hochebene *f*.
[2] *vt* **(a)** *motion* einbringen. **(b)** *(US: postpone) bill* zurückstellen. **(c)** *(put in tabular form)* tabellarisieren *(form)*, in einer Tabelle zusammenstellen.

tableau ['tæbləʊ] *n, pl* **-s** *or* **-x** ['tæbləʊ(z)] *(Art, Theat)* Tableau *nt*; *(fig)* Bild *nt*, Szene *f*.

table: ~cloth *n* Tischdecke *f or* -tuch *nt*; **~ d'hôte** ['tɑːbl'dəʊt] *n* Tagesmenü *or* -gedeck *nt*; **to eat ~ d'hôte** das Tagesgedeck *or* -menü nehmen, Menü essen; **~ d'hôte menu** *n* Tageskarte *f*; **~ lamp** *n* Tischlampe *f*; **~land** *n* Tafelland, Plateau *nt*, Hochebene *f*; **~ licence** *n* Schankerlaubnis *f* bei Abgabe von Speisen; **~-lifting** *n* Anheben *nt* von Tischen; **~ linen** *n, no pl* Tischwäsche *f*; **~ manners** *npl* Tischmanieren *pl*; **~ mat** *n* Untersetzer *m*; *(of cloth)* Set *nt*; **T~ Mountain** *n* Tafelberg *m*; **~ napkin** *n* Serviette *f*; **~-rapping** *n* Tischrücken *nt*; **~ salt** *n* Tafelsalz *nt*; **~spoon** *n* Eßlöffel *m*; **~spoonful** *n* Eßlöffel(voll) *m*.

tablet ['tæblɪt] *n* **(a)** *(Pharm)* Tablette *f*. **(b)** *(of paper)* Block *m*; *(of wax, clay)* Täfelchen *nt*; *(of soap)* Stückchen *nt*. **(c)** *(on wall etc)* Tafel, Platte *f*.

table: ~ talk *n, no pl* Tischgespräch *nt*; **~ tennis** *n* Tischtennis *nt*; **~ top** *n* Tischplatte *f*; **~-turning** *n* Drehen *nt* von Tischen; **~ware** *n, no pl* Tafelgeschirr *nt* und -besteck *nt*; **~ water** *n* Tafelwasser *nt*; **~ wine** *n* Tafelwein *m*.

tabloid ['tæblɔɪd] *n (also* **~ newspaper**) *bebilderte, kleinformatige Zeitung*; *(pej)* Boulevardzeitung *f*, Revolverblatt *nt (inf)* ◆ **~ journalism** Sensations- *or* Boulevardpresse *f*.

taboo, tabu [tə'buː] [1] *n* Tabu *nt* ◆ **to be under a ~** tabu sein, unter einem Tabu stehen.
[2] *adj* tabu ◆ **~ words** Tabuwörter *pl*.
[3] *vt* für tabu erklären, tabui(sier)eren.

tabo(u)ret ['tæbuːreɪ] *n (Sew)* Stickrahmen *m*.

tabu *n, adj, vt see* **taboo**.

tabular ['tæbjʊlə^r] *adj* tabellenförmig, Tabellen-, tabellarisch ◆ **in ~ form** in Tabellenform, tabellarisch.

tabulate ['tæbjʊleɪt] *vt* tabellarisch aufzeichnen *or* darstellen, tabellarisieren.

tabulation [ˌtæbjʊ'leɪʃən] *n* tabellarische Aufstellung, Tabellarisierung *f*.

tabulator ['tæbjʊleɪtə^r] *n (on typewriter)* Tabulator *m*.

tachograph ['tækəʊgrɑːf] *n* Fahrtenschreiber, Tachograph *m*.

tachometer [tæ'kɒmɪtə^r] *n* Drehzahlmesser *m*.

tachycardia [ˌtækɪ'kɑːdɪə] *n* Herzjagen *nt*, Tachykardie *f (spec)*.

tacit *adj*, **~ly** *adv* ['tæsɪt, -lɪ] stillschweigend.

taciturn ['tæsɪtɜːn] *adj* schweigsam, wortkarg.

taciturnity [ˌtæsɪ'tɜːnɪtɪ] *n* Schweigsamkeit, Wortkargheit *f*.

tack¹ [tæk] [1] *n* **(a)** *(nail)* kleiner Nagel; *(with small head also)* Stift *m*; *(for shoes)* Täcks *m*; *(esp US: drawing pin)* Reiß- *or* Heftzwecke *f*, Reißnagel *m*.
(b) *(Brit Sew)* Heftstich *m*.
(c) *(Naut: course)* Schlag *m*; *(fig)* Richtung *f*, Weg *m* ◆ **to be on the port/starboard ~** auf Backbord-/Steuerbordbug segeln; **they are on a new/different ~** *(fig)* sie haben eine neue/andere Richtung eingeschlagen; **to be on the right/wrong ~** *(fig)* auf der richtigen/falschen Spur sein, richtig/falsch liegen *(inf)*; **to try another ~** *(fig)* es anders versuchen.
(d) *(Naut: zigzag)* Aufkreuzen *nt* ◆ **to make a ~ towards land** landwärts kreuzen.
(e) *(for horse)* Sattel- und Zaumzeug *nt*.
[2] *vt* **(a)** *(with nail)* annageln *(to* an *+dat or acc)*; *(with clip, pin)* feststecken *(to* an *+dat)*. **(b)** *(Brit Sew)* heften.
[3] *vi* **(a)** *(Naut)* aufkreuzen ◆ **to ~ to port** mit Backbordbug kreuzen. **(b)** *(Brit Sew)* heften.

◆**tack about** *vi (Naut)* wenden.

◆**tack down** *vt sep* festnageln; *(Brit Sew)* festheften.

◆**tack on** *vt sep* annageln *(-to* an *+acc or dat)*; *(with drawing pin)* anstecken *(-to* an *+acc or dat)*; *(with clips)* anheften, anstecken *(-to* an *+acc or dat)*; *(Sew)* anheften; *(fig)* anhängen *(-to dat)*.

◆**tack together** *vt sep (with nails)* zusammennageln; *(with clips)* zusammenstecken *or* -heften; *(Sew)* zusammenheften.

◆**tack up** *vt sep (Brit) hem* heften.

tack² *n (Naut: biscuits)* Schiffszwieback *m*.

tackiness¹ ['tækɪnɪs] *n (of paint)* Klebrigkeit *f*.

tackiness² *n see* **tacky²** Billigkeit *f*; heruntergekommener Zustand; Geschmacklosigkeit *f*.

tacking ['tækɪŋ] *n* **(a)** *(Brit Sew)* Heften *nt* ◆ **~ stitches** Heftstiche *pl*; **~ thread** Heftfaden *m*. **(b)** *(Naut)* Aufkreuzen *nt*.

tackle ['tækl] [1] *n* **(a)** *(lifting gear)* Flaschenzug *m*; *(Naut)* Talje *f*, Takel *nt*, Zugwinde *f*. **(b)** *(Naut: rigging)* Tauwerk *nt*. **(c)** *(equipment)* Ausrüstung *f*, Zeug *nt (inf)* ◆ **fishing ~** Angelausrüstung *f or* -zeug *nt (inf)*; **shaving ~** Rasierzeug *nt*. **(d)** *(Sport)* Angriff *m*, Tackling *nt*.
[2] *vt* **(a)** *(physically, Sport)* angreifen, angehen *(geh)*; *(Rugby)* fassen; *thief also* sich stürzen auf *(+acc)*; *(verbally)* zur Rede stellen *(about* wegen).
(b) *(undertake) job* in Angriff nehmen; *new challenge* sich versuchen an *(+dat)*; *problem* angehen, anpacken *(inf)*; *(manage to cope with)* bewältigen, fertig werden mit ◆ **could you ~ another ice cream?** *(inf)* schaffst du noch ein Eis? *(inf)*; **I don't know how to ~ it** ich weiß nicht, wie ich es anfangen soll.
[3] *vi* angreifen.

tacky¹ ['tækɪ] *adj (+er)* klebrig ◆ **the paint is still ~** die Farbe klebt noch.

tacky² *adj (+er) (inf)* billig; *area, bar* heruntergekommen; *clothes also, food, colour scheme* geschmacklos.

tact [tækt] *n, no pl* Takt *m*.

tactful *adj*, **~ly** *adv* ['tæktfʊl, -fəlɪ] taktvoll.

tactfulness ['tæktfʊlnɪs] *n* Takt *m*; *(of person)* Feingefühl *nt*.

tactic ['tæktɪk] *n* Taktik *f*.

tactical *adj*, **~ly** *adv* ['tæktɪkəl, -ɪ] *(Mil, fig)* taktisch.

tactician [tæk'tɪʃən] *n (Mil, fig)* Taktiker(in *f*) *m*.

tactics ['tæktɪks] *n sing (art, science) (Mil)* Taktik *f*; *(fig also)* Taktiken *pl*.

tactile ['tæktaɪl] *adj* Tast-, taktil *(spec)*; *(tangible)* greifbar, fühlbar ◆ **a more ~ society** eine Gesellschaft, in der Körperkontakte eine größere Rolle spielen.

tactless *adj*, **~ly** *adv* ['tæktlɪs, -lɪ] taktlos.
tactlessness ['tæktlɪsnɪs] *n* Taktlosigkeit *f*.
tactual ['tæktjʊəl] *adj* taktil (*spec*) ◆ **~ pleasure** Berührungslust *f*.
tactually ['tæktjʊəlɪ] *adv* (*by touch*) durch Berühren *or* Fühlen ◆ **to be ~ pleasing** sich angenehm anfühlen; **~ oriented** berührungsorientiert.
tad [tæd] *n, no pl* (*inf*) **a ~** ein bißchen, etwas; **a ~ big/small** etwas *or* ein bißchen (zu) groß/klein.
Tadjikistan [tɑːˌdʒɪkɪ'stɑːn] *n see* **Tajikistan**.
tadpole ['tædpəʊl] *n* Kaulquappe *f*.
Tadzhikistan [tɑːˌdʒɪkɪ'stɑːn] *n see* **Tajikistan**.
taffeta ['tæfɪtə] *n* Taft *m*.
taffrail ['tæfreɪl] *n* (*Naut*) Heckreling *f*.
Taffy ['tæfɪ] *n* (*inf*) Waliser *m*.
taffy ['tæfɪ] *n* (*US*) Toffee *nt*.
tag [tæg] [1] *n* **(a)** (*label*) Schild(chen) *nt*; (*on clothes*) (*maker's name*) Etikett *nt*; (*owner's name*) Namensschild(chen) *nt*; (*loop*) Aufhänger *m* ◆ **the cattle had metal ~s in their ears** die Rinder hatten Blechmarken in den Ohren.
(b) (*hackneyed phrase*) stehende Redensart.
(c) (*Gram: question ~*) Bestätigungsfrage *f*.
(d) (*game*) Fangen *nt*.
(e) *see* **~ wrestling**.
[2] *vt* **(a)** *specimen* mit Schildchen versehen; *cattle* (mit Blechmarke) zeichnen; *garment, goods* etikettieren; (*with price*) auszeichnen; (*with owner's name*) (mit Namensschildchen) zeichnen; *suitcase* mit einem Anhänger versehen.
(b) (*US Mot inf*) einen Strafzettel verpassen (+*dat*).
[3] *vi* **to ~ behind** *or* **after sb** hinter jdm hertrotten *or* -zockeln (*inf*); **with her husband ~ging after her** mit ihrem Mann im Schlepptau (*inf*).
◆**tag along** *vi* (*unwillingly, unwanted*) mittrotten (*inf*) *or* -zockeln (*inf*) ◆ **to ~ ~ behind sb** hinter jdm herzockeln (*inf*) *or* -trotten (*inf*); **why don't you ~ ~?** (*inf*) warum kommst *or* gehst du nicht mit?
◆**tag on** [1] *vi* sich anhängen (*to* an +*acc*).
[2] *vt sep* (*attach*) anhängen (*to* an +*acc*), befestigen (*to* an +*dat*); (*add as afterthought*) anhängen (*to* an +*acc*).
◆**tag together** *vt sep* (*fasten*) zusammenheften.
tag: ~ end *n see* **fag end**; **~ question** *n* Bestätigungsfrage *f*.
tagmeme ['tægmiːm] *n* (*Ling*) Tagmem *nt*.
tagmemics ['tægmemɪks] *n* (*Ling*) Tagmemik *f*.
tag: ~rope *n* (*Sport*) Seil *nt* (*beim Tagwrestling*); **~ wrestler** *n* Ringer *m* (*beim Tagwrestling*); **~ wrestling** *n Ringkampf m zwischen 2 Ringerpaaren, wobei immer 2 auf der Matte sind, während die 2 Auswechselkämpfer an den Seilen warten.*
Tahiti [tɑː'hiːtɪ] *n* Tahiti *nt*.
Tahitian [tɑː'hiːʃən] [1] *adj* tahitisch.
[2] *n* **(a)** Tahitianer(in *f*) *m*. **(b)** (*language*) Tahitisch *nt*.
tail [teɪl] [1] *n* **(a)** (*of animal*) Schwanz *m*; (*of horse also*) Schweif *m* (*liter*); (*hum inf: of person*) Hinterteil *nt* (*inf*), Allerwerteste(r) *m* (*hum inf*) ◆ **with his ~ between his legs** (*fig*) wie ein geprügelter Hund, mit eingezogenem Schwanz (*inf*); **to turn ~** ausreißen, die Flucht ergreifen; **he was right on my ~** er saß mir direkt im Nacken.
(b) (*of aeroplane, kite, procession, list*) Schwanz *m*; (*of comet*) Schweif *m*; (*of shirt*) Zipfel *m*; (*of jacket, coat*) Schoß *m*; (*of letter*) Schleife *f*; (*Mus: of note*) Notenhals *m*.
(c) (*inf: person following sb*) Schatten (*inf*), Beschatter(in *f*) *m* (*inf*) ◆ **to put a ~ on sb** jdn beschatten lassen.
(d) (*sl*) **they were out looking for ~** sie hielten nach Weibern Ausschau (*sl*); **a nice piece of ~** ein dufter Arsch (*sl*).
(e) **~s** (*on coin*) Rück- *or* Zahlseite *f*; **~s I win!** bei Zahl gewinne ich; **it came down ~s** die Zahl kam nach oben.
(f) **~s** *pl* (*jacket*) Frack, Schwalbenschwanz (*inf*) *m* ◆ **"~s (will be worn)"** „Frackzwang" *m*.
[2] *vt* **(a)** *person, suspect* beschatten (*inf*); *car etc* folgen (+*dat*). **(b)** *see* **top**[1].
◆**tail after** *vi* +*prep obj* hinterherzockeln (+*dat*) (*inf*).
◆**tail away** *vi see* **tail off (a)**.
◆**tail back** *vi* (*traffic*) sich gestaut haben.
◆**tail off** *vi* **(a)** (*diminish*) abnehmen, schrumpfen; (*interest*) abflauen, abnehmen, schwinden; (*sounds*) sich verlieren, schwächer werden; (*sentence*) mittendrin abbrechen ◆ **his voice ~ed ~ into silence** seine Stimme wurde immer schwächer, bis sie schließlich verstummte.
(b) (*deteriorate*) sich verschlechtern, nachlassen ◆ **the article ~ed ~ into a jumble of figures** der Artikel war zum Schluß nur noch ein Gewirr von Zahlen.
tail: ~back *n* Rückstau *m*; **~board** *n* Ladeklappe *f*; **~ coat** *n* Frack *m*.
-tailed [-teɪld] *adj suf* -schwänzig.
tail: ~ end *n* Ende *nt*; (*of procession also*) Schwanz *m* (*inf*); **to come in at the ~ end** (*of discussion etc*) erst am Ende dazukommen; (*of race*) den Schwanz bilden; **~fin** *n* (*Aut*) Heckflosse *f*; **~gate** [1] *n* (*of car*) Hecktür *f*; (*of lorry*) Ladeklappe *f*; [2] *vi* (*inf*) zu dicht auffahren, schieben (*inf*); [3] *vt* (*inf*) **to ~gate sb** dicht hinter jdm herfahren; **~ gun** *n* Heckkanone *f*; **~ gunner** *n* Heckschütze *m*; **~-hopping** *n* (*Ski*) Sprungwedeln *nt*; **~less** *adj* schwanzlos; **~-light** *n* (*Aut*) Rücklicht *nt*.
tailor ['teɪlə^r] [1] *n* Schneider *m* ◆ **~'s chalk** Schneiderkreide *f*; **~'s dummy** (*lit*) Schneiderpuppe *f*; (*fig inf*) Ölgötze *m* (*inf*); **~('s) tack** Schlinge *f* beim Durchschlagen eines Musters.
[2] *vt* **(a)** *dress etc* schneidern ◆ **the dress was ~ed to reveal her figure** das Kleid war so geschnitten, daß es ihre Figur betonte.
(b) (*fig*) *plans, insurance, holiday* zuschneiden (*to* auf +*acc*); *products, salary structure* abstimmen (*to* auf +*acc*) ◆ **~ed to meet his needs** auf seine Bedürfnisse abgestimmt.
tailored ['teɪləd] *adj* (*classically styled*) klassisch; (*made by tailor*) vom Schneider gemacht ◆ **a well-~ suit** ein gut gearbeiteter Anzug; **his personally ~ clothes** seine für ihn persönlich gefertigten Kleider.
tailoring ['teɪlərɪŋ] *n* Verarbeitung *f*; (*profession*) Schneiderei *f* ◆ **this is a nice bit of ~** das ist sehr gut gearbeitet.
tailor-made ['teɪlə'meɪd] *adj* **(a)** maßgeschneidert, nach Maß gearbeitet ◆ **~ suit/costume** Maßanzug *m*/Schneiderkostüm *nt*.
(b) (*fig*) *role* maßgeschneidert (*for* für), zugeschnitten (*for* auf +*acc*) ◆ **the job was ~ for him** die Stelle war ihm wie auf den Leib geschnitten; **she seemed ~ for the part** sie schien für die Rolle wie geschaffen.
tail: ~ piece *n* **(a)** Anhang *m*, Anhängsel *nt* (*inf*); **(b)** (*Aviat*) Heck *nt*; **(c)** (*on violin*) Saitenhalter *m*; **(d)** (*Typ*) Schlußvignette *f*; **~pipe** *n* (*US*) Auspuffrohr *nt*; **~-plane** *n* (*Aviat*) Höhenleitwerk *nt*; **~ side** *n* (*of coin*) Zahlseite *f*; **~ skid** *n* **(a)** (*Aviat*) Schwanzsporn *m*; **(b)** (*Aut*) Schleudern *nt no pl* der Hinterräder; **to go into a ~ skid** mit den Hinterrädern herumrutschen *or* schleudern; **~spin** *n* (*Aviat*) Trudeln *nt*; **~ wheel** *n* (*Aviat*) Spornrad *nt*; **~wind** *n* Rückenwind *m*.
taint [teɪnt] [1] *n* **(a)** (*lit: of food etc*) Stich *m* ◆ **meat free from ~** einwandfreies Fleisch.
(b) (*fig*) (*blemish*) Makel *m*; (*trace*) Spur *f* ◆ **a ~ of madness** eine Anlage zum Irrsinn; **the hereditary ~** die krankhafte Erbanlage; **the ~ of sin** der Makel der Sünde; **a nasty ~ of fascism** ein übler faschistischer Beigeschmack.
[2] *vt* **(a)** *food* verderben ◆ **to become ~ed** schlecht werden, verderben. **(b)** *air, atmosphere* verderben, verpesten. **(c)** (*fig*) *reputation* beflecken, beschmutzen ◆ **not ~ed by prejudice** von Vorurteilen unbelastet; **to be ~ed with sth** mit etw belastet *or* behaftet sein.
Taiwan [taɪ'wɑːn] *n* Taiwan *nt*.
Taiwanese [ˌtaɪwɑː'niːz] [1] *adj* taiwanisch.
[2] *n* Taiwaner(in *f*) *m*.
Tajikistan [tɑːˌdʒɪkɪ'stɑːn] *n* Tadschikistan *nt*.
take [teɪk] (*vb*: *pret* **took**, *ptp* **taken**) [1] *vt* **(a)** (*remove, steal*) nehmen; (*~ away with one*) mitnehmen; (*remove from its place*) wegnehmen ◆ **to ~ sth from a drawer** etw aus einer Schublade nehmen; **to ~ sth from sb** jdm etw wegnehmen; **I took it by mistake** ich habe es aus Versehen mitgenommen; **the thieves took everything** die Einbrecher haben alles mitgenommen; **that man has ~n my wallet** der Mann hat mir meine Brieftasche weggenommen *or* gestohlen; **how much did he ~ off you for that?** wieviel hat er dir dafür abverlangt *or* abgenommen?
(b) (*carry, transport, accompany*) bringen; (*~ along with one*) *person, things* mitnehmen ◆ **I'll ~ you to the station** ich bringe Sie zum Bahnhof; **I'll ~ you (with me) to the party** ich nehme dich zur Party mit; **let me ~ your case** komm, ich nehme *or* trage deinen Koffer; **you can't ~ it with you when you're dead** wenn du tot bist, nützt es dir auch nichts mehr; **he took me a new way to the coast** er ist mit mir eine neue Strecke zur Küste gefahren; **to ~ sb to the cinema** (*treat*) jdn ins Kino einladen; (*~ along with one*) mit jdm ins Kino gehen; **I'll ~ you for a meal** ich lade Sie zum Essen ein; **to ~ sb on holiday** mit jdm Urlaub machen; **this bus will ~ you to the town hall** der Bus fährt zum Rathaus; **this road will ~ you to Paris** diese Straße führt *or* geht nach Paris; **if it won't ~ you out of your way** wenn es kein Umweg für Sie ist; **what ~s you to London this time?** was führt Sie diesmal nach London?; **his ability took him to the top of his profession** seine Begabung brachte ihn in seinem Beruf bis an die Spitze.
(c) (*get hold of, seize*) nehmen ◆ **to ~ sb's arm/hand** jds Arm/Hand nehmen; **to ~ sb by the throat** jdn am Kragen (*inf*) *or* an der Kehle packen; **to ~ a knife by the handle** ein Messer am Griff (an)fassen *or* beim Griff nehmen; **~ three eggs** (*Cook*) man nehme drei Eier; **how does that ~ you?** (*inf*) wie finden Sie das?; *see* **bait**.
(d) (*capture*) *person* fassen, fangen, festnehmen; *animal* fangen; *town, country etc* einnehmen, erobern; *ship* kapern; (*Chess etc*) schlagen, nehmen; (*Cards*) *trick* machen ◆ **to ~ sb prisoner** jdn gefangennehmen; **they took 200 prisoners** sie machten 200 Gefangene; **to be ~n alive** lebend gefaßt werden.
(e) (*accept, receive*) nehmen; *job, dye, perm* annehmen; *command, lead, second position, role* übernehmen ◆ **~ that!** da!; (*hold that*) halt mal; **I won't ~ less than £200** ich verkaufe es nicht unter £ 200; **would you ~ an offer?** kann ich Ihnen ein Angebot machen?; **she took paying guests** sie vermietete Zimmer an Gäste; **to ~ things as they come** die Dinge nehmen, wie sie kommen; **to ~ a bet** eine Wette annehmen; **I wouldn't ~ a bet on it** darauf würde ich keine Wette eingehen; **~ it from me!** das können Sie mir glauben; **~ it from me, he'll never ...** eines können Sie mir glauben, er wird nie ...; **(you can) ~ it or leave it** ja oder nein(, ganz wie Sie wollen); **I can ~ it or leave it** ich mache mir nicht besonders viel daraus; **he took the blow on his left arm** der Schlag traf ihn am linken Arm; (*in defence*) er wehrte den Schlag mit dem linken Arm ab; **to ~ sb into partnership/the business** jdn zu seinem Partner machen/jdn ins Geschäft aufnehmen; **will it ~ a British plug?** paßt da ein englischer Stecker (rein)?; **do you ~ me/my meaning?** verstehen Sie mich?/verstehen Sie, was ich meine?; **the school only ~s boys/private pupils** die Schule nimmt nur Jungen/Privatschüler (auf); **he ~s (private) pupils** er gibt (Privat)stunden.
(f) (*get for oneself*) sich (*dat*) nehmen; (*purchase, rent*) nehmen ◆ **~ a seat/chair!** nehmen Sie Platz!, setzen Sie sich doch!; **~ your seats!** nehmen Sie Ihre Plätze ein!; **this seat is ~n** dieser Platz ist besetzt; **I'll ~ a pound of apples**

ich nehme ein Pfund Äpfel; **I think I'll ~ the steak** ich glaube, ich nehme das Steak; **to ~ a wife** (*old*) sich (*dat*) eine Frau nehmen (*old*); **he took her** (*sexually*) er nahm sie; **~ your partners for a waltz** führen Sie Ihre Partnerinnen zum Walzer.
(g) (*buy regularly*) *newspaper etc* immer nehmen *or* kaufen, bekommen; (*on subscription*) beziehen, bekommen.
(h) (*gain, obtain*) *prize, honours etc* bekommen; *game, match* gewinnen; (*Comm*) *£500* einnehmen.
(i) *exam* machen, ablegen; *driving test* machen ◆ **to ~ a PhD** promovieren, den Doktor machen (*inf*); **he took his degree in 1985** er hat 1985 Examen gemacht *or* sein Examen abgelegt.
(j) (*teach*) *lesson* halten, geben; *subject* unterrichten, geben; *class* unterrichten, nehmen ◆ **he ~s 25 classes a week** er hat *or* gibt 25 Wochenstunden; **who ~s you for Latin?** bei wem habt ihr Latein?, wer unterrichtet *or* gibt bei euch Latein?
(k) (*study, learn*) *course, French* machen; (*as optional subject*) wählen; *lessons, private tuition* nehmen.
(l) (*conduct, run*) *census, poll* durchführen; *church service* (ab)halten ◆ **to ~ (the chair at) a meeting** den Vorsitz bei einer Versammlung führen; **he ~s a scout troop in the evenings** abends hat er eine Pfadfindergruppe.
(m) (*go on*) *walk, stroll* machen; *trip also* unternehmen.
(n) (*consume*) *drink, food* zu sich (*dat*) nehmen; *drugs, pill, medicine* nehmen; (*on directions for use*) einnehmen ◆ **to ~ sugar in one's tea** den Tee mit Zucker trinken; **to ~ a sip** *or* **nip/a drink** ein Schlückchen/einen Schluck trinken; **do you ~ sugar?** nehmen Sie Zucker?; **to ~ a meal** (*old*) (etwas) essen, speisen (*geh*); **I took tea with her** (*dated form*) ich war bei ihr zum Tee; **they took tea together once a week** (*old*) sie trafen sich einmal wöchentlich zum Tee; **they took coffee on the veranda** sie tranken den Kaffee auf der Veranda; **will you ~ coffee or tea?** möchten Sie Kaffee oder Tee?; **I always ~ coffee in the morning** morgens trinke ich immer Kaffee; **not to be ~n (internally)** (*Med*) nur zur äußerlichen Anwendung.
(o) (*Film*) *scene* drehen; (*Phot*) *photo* machen ◆ **he took the whole group** er nahm die ganze Gruppe auf.
(p) (*write down, record*) *letter, dictation* aufnehmen; *address, details, particulars* (sich *dat*) aufschreiben, (sich *dat*) notieren ◆ **to ~ notes** sich (*dat*) Notizen machen.
(q) (*measure*) *temperature, pulse* messen ◆ **to ~ sb's measurements** bei jdm Maß nehmen; **to ~ the measurements of a room** ein Zimmer ausmessen; **to ~ sb's temperature/pulse** jds Temperatur *or* bei jdm Fieber/den Puls messen.
(r) (*put up with*) sich (*dat*) gefallen lassen; (*endure, stand up to*) (*person*) *alcohol, climate* vertragen; *long journey* aushalten; *emotional experience, shock* fertig werden mit, verkraften; (*thing*) aushalten ◆ **I can ~ it** ich kann's verkraften, ich werde damit fertig; **I just can't ~ any more/it any more** ich bin am Ende/das halte ich nicht mehr aus; **I won't ~ any nonsense!** ich dulde keinen Unsinn!
(s) (*respond to, regard*) *news, blow* aufnehmen, reagieren auf (*+acc*); *person* nehmen ◆ **she knows how to ~ him** sie versteht es, ihn von der richtigen Seite zu nehmen; **she took his death very badly** sein Tod hat sie sehr mitgenommen.
(t) (*understand, interpret*) auffassen, verstehen ◆ **I would ~ that to mean ...** ich würde das so auffassen *or* verstehen ...; **how am I meant to ~ that?** wie soll ich das auffassen *or* verstehen?; **she took what he said as a compliment** sie hat das, was er sagte, als Kompliment aufgefaßt.
(u) (*assume*) annehmen ◆ **to ~ sb/sth for** *or* **to be ...** jdn/etw für ... halten; **how old do you ~ him to be?** für wie alt halten Sie ihn?, wie alt schätzen Sie ihn?; **what do you ~ me for?** wofür hältst du mich eigentlich?; **may I ~ it that ...?** darf ich annehmen, daß ...?; **I ~ it you don't want to come** ich nehme an, du willst nicht mitkommen, du willst wohl nicht mitkommen.
(v) (*consider*) *case, example* nehmen ◆ **~ (the case of) England in the 17th century** nehmen Sie zum Beispiel England im 17. Jahrhundert; **taking all things together, it's been a very successful day** alles in allem (genommen,) war es ein sehr erfolgreicher Tag; **taking one year with another** wenn man die Jahre zusammen betrachtet.
(w) (*extract*) entnehmen (*from dat*) ◆ **he ~s his examples from real life** seine Beispiele sind aus dem Leben gegriffen; **to ~ a quotation from a text** eine Stelle aus einem Text zitieren.
(x) (*require*) brauchen; *clothes size* haben ◆ **it ~s five hours/men ...** man braucht *or* benötigt fünf Stunden/Leute ...; **it ~s me five hours ...** ich brauche fünf Stunden ...; **it took ten men to complete the job** zehn Leute waren nötig *or* es wurden zehn Leute benötigt, um diese Arbeit zu erledigen; **it took him** *or* **he took two hours to write a page, it took two hours for him to write a page** er brauchte zwei Stunden, um eine Seite zu schreiben; **the journey ~s 3 hours** die Fahrt dauert 3 Stunden; **the wound took five weeks to heal** es dauerte fünf Wochen, bis die Wunde verheilt war; **it took a lot of courage/intelligence** dazu gehörte viel Mut/Intelligenz; **it ~s two to quarrel** (*prov*) zu einem Streit gehören immer zwei; **it ~s more than that to make me angry** deswegen werde ich noch lange nicht wütend; **it ~s time** es braucht (seine) Zeit, es dauert (eine Weile); **it took a long time** es hat lange gedauert; **it took me a long time** ich habe lange gebraucht; **I took a long time over it** ich habe lange dazu gebraucht; **it won't ~ long** das dauert nicht lange; **it won't ~ long to convince him** er ist schnell *or* leicht überzeugt; **that'll ~ some explaining** das wird schwer zu erklären sein; **it ~s some believing** das kann man kaum glauben; **she's got what it ~s** (*inf*) sie ist nicht ohne (*inf*), die bringt's (*sl*); (*is capable also*) sie kann was (*inf*); **it's a difficult job but he's got what it ~s** (*inf*) es ist eine schwierige Arbeit, aber er hat das Zeug dazu.
(y) (*support*) *weight* aushalten; (*have capacity or room for*) *people, books* Platz haben für; *gallons* fassen ◆ **the road can ~ 3,500 cars an hour** die Straße bewältigt eine Verkehrsdichte von 3.500 Autos pro Stunde; **the bridge can ~ 5 tons** die Brücke hat eine Höchstbelastung von 5 Tonnen.
(z) *taxi, train* nehmen, fahren mit; *motorway, country roads* nehmen, fahren auf (*+dat*) ◆ **to ~ the plane/next plane** fliegen/das nächste Flugzeug nehmen; **we took a wrong turning** wir sind falsch abgebogen.
(aa) (*negotiate*) *obstacle* nehmen; *hurdle, fence also* überspringen; *bend, corner* (*person*) nehmen; (*car*) fahren um; (*Ski also*) fahren; *hill* hinauffahren.
(bb) (*sing, dance, play etc*) **let's ~ it from the beginning of Act 2** fangen wir mit dem Anfang vom zweiten Akt an; **let's ~ that scene again** die Szene machen wir noch einmal; **the orchestra took that passage too quickly** das Orchester hat die Stelle zu schnell gespielt; **the director took her through her lines** der Regisseur ging die Rolle mit ihr durch.
(cc) (*Math: subtract*) abziehen (*from* von).
(dd) (*Gram*) stehen mit; (*preposition*) *case* gebraucht werden mit, haben (*inf*) ◆ **verbs that ~ "haben"** Verben, die mit „haben" konjugiert werden; **this word ~s the accent on the first syllable** dieses Wort wird auf der ersten Silbe betont.
(ee) (*old, dial*) *illness* bekommen ◆ **to ~ a cold** sich erkälten.
(ff) to be ~n sick *or* **ill** krank werden; **she has been ~n ill with pneumonia** sie hat eine Lungenentzündung bekommen.
(gg) to be ~n with sb/sth (*attracted by*) von jdm/etw angetan sein.
(hh) *in phrases see other element* **to ~ sb by surprise** jdn überraschen; **to ~ one's time** sich (*dat*) Zeit lassen (*over* mit); **to ~ a bath** baden, ein Bad nehmen (*form*); **to ~ a holiday** Urlaub machen; **to ~ one's holidays** seinen Urlaub nehmen; **to ~ a pitch** (*Baseball*) einen Ball durchlassen.
[2] *vi* **(a)** (*fire*) angehen; (*dye, perm, graft*) angenommen werden; (*vaccination*) anschlagen; (*plant*) anwachsen; (*seeds*) kommen; (*fish: bite*) anbeißen ◆ **the ink won't ~ on this paper** dieses Papier nimmt die Druckfarbe nicht an.
(b) (*fig*) (*gimmick*) ankommen (*inf*); (*novel, idea also*) Anklang finden.
(c) she took ill (*inf*) sie wurde krank.
(d) (*detract*) **that doesn't ~ from his merit** das tut seinen Verdiensten keinen Abbruch, das schmälert seine Verdienste nicht; **that ~s from its usefulness/attraction** das vermindert den Gebrauchswert/die Anziehungskraft.
[3] *n* **(a)** (*Film*) Aufnahme *f* ◆ **after several ~s they ...** nachdem sie die Szene mehrmals gedreht hatten, ... sie ... **(b)** (*Hunt*) Beute *f*; (*Fishing*) Fang *m*. **(c)** (*US inf: takings*) Einnahmen *pl*.
◆**take aback** *vt sep* überraschen ◆ **I was completely ~n ~** mir hatte es völlig den Atem verschlagen, ich war völlig perplex.
◆**take after** *vi +prep obj* nachschlagen (*+dat*); (*in looks*) ähneln (*+dat*), ähnlich sein (*+dat*).
◆**take along** *vt sep* mitnehmen.
◆**take apart** *vt sep* auseinandernehmen; (*dismantle also*) zerlegen; (*fig inf*) *person, team etc* auseinandernehmen (*sl*).
◆**take around** *vt sep* mitnehmen; (*show around*) herumführen.
◆**take aside** *vt sep* beiseite nehmen.
◆**take away** **[1]** *vi* **to ~ ~ from sth** etw schmälern; *merit, reputation also* Abbruch tun (*+dat*); *worth* mindern, verringern; *pleasure, fun etc also* beeinträchtigen.
[2] *vt sep* **(a)** (*subtract*) abziehen ◆ **6 ~ ~ 2** 6 weniger 2.
(b) (*remove*) *child, thing, privilege* wegnehmen (*from sb* jdm); (*from school etc*) nehmen (*from* aus); (*lead, transport, carry away*) weg- *or* fortbringen (*from* von); *prisoner* abführen (*to* in *+acc*) ◆ **to ~ sb/sth ~ (with one)** jdn/etw mitnehmen; **to ~ ~ sb's pain/freedom** *etc* jdm die Schmerzen/Freiheit *etc* nehmen; **they've come to ~ him ~** sie sind da, um ihn abzuholen; **"not to be ~n ~"** (*on library book*) „nicht für die Ausleihe"; **what ~s you ~ so early?** warum müssen Sie denn schon so früh gehen?
(c) *food* mitnehmen ◆ **pizza to ~ ~** Pizza zum Mitnehmen.
(d) from the 15th bar, ~ it ~! noch mal von Takt 15, los!
◆**take back** *vt sep* **(a)** (*reclaim, get back*) sich (*dat*) zurückgeben lassen; *toy etc* wieder wegnehmen; (*fig: retract*) *threat, statement* zurücknehmen.
(b) (*return*) zurückbringen ◆ **he took us ~ (home)** er brachte uns (nach Hause) zurück, er brachte uns wieder heim.
(c) (*agree to receive again*) *thing* zurücknehmen; *employee* wieder einstellen; *husband* wieder aufnehmen; *boyfriend* wieder gehen mit; *tenant* wieder vermieten an (*+acc*).
(d) (*remind*) **to ~ sb ~ to his childhood** jdn in seine Kindheit zurückversetzen; **this photograph/that ~s me ~** dieses Foto/das ruft Erinnerungen wach; **that ~s me ~ fifteen years** das erinnert mich an die Zeit vor fünfzehn Jahren.
◆**take down** *vt sep* **(a)** (*lit*) (*off high shelf etc*) herunternehmen; *curtains, decorations* abnehmen; *Christmas cards* wegräumen; *picture* abhängen; *flag* einholen ◆ **to ~ one's/sb's trousers** seine/jdm die Hose herunterlassen.
(b) (*dismantle*) *scaffolding etc* abbauen; *tent also* abbrechen; *railing, gate* entfernen.
(c) (*write down*) (sich *dat*) notieren *or* aufschreiben; *notes* (sich *dat*) machen; *letter* aufnehmen; *speech, lecture* mitschreiben ◆ **anything you say will be ~n ~ and ...** alles, was Sie sagen, wird festgehalten und ...; **~ this ~ please** notieren Sie bitte, bitte schreiben Sie.
(d) (*humble*) einen Dämpfer geben (*+dat*); *see* **peg**.
◆**take home** *vt sep £200 per week* netto verdienen *or* bekommen.
◆**take in** *vt sep* **(a)** (*bring in*) *thing, person* hinein-/hereinbringen *or* -nehmen;

harvest einbringen ◆ **I'll ~ the car ~(to work) on Monday** ich fahre am Montag mit dem Auto (zur Arbeit); **when are you taking the car ~ (to the garage)?** wann bringen Sie das Auto in die Werkstatt?; **to ~ a lady ~ to dinner** eine Dame zu Tisch führen.
(b) (*receive in one's home*) *refugee* (bei sich) aufnehmen, beherbergen; *child, stray dog* zu sich nehmen, ins Haus nehmen; (*for payment*) *student* (Zimmer) vermieten an (*+acc*) ◆ **she ~s ~ lodgers** sie vermietet (Zimmer).
(c) (*receive*) *money* einnehmen ◆ **to ~ ~ laundry/sewing** Wasch-/Näharbeiten übernehmen.
(d) (*make narrower*) *dress* enger machen ◆ **to ~ ~ sail** die Segel reffen.
(e) (*usu insep: include, cover*) einschließen ◆ **the lecture took ~ all the more recent developments** der Vortrag berücksichtigte auch alle neueren Entwicklungen.
(f) (*note visually*) *surroundings, contents* wahrnehmen, registrieren (*inf*); *area, room* überblicken; (*grasp, understand*) *meaning, lecture* begreifen; *impressions, sights* aufnehmen; *situation* erfassen ◆ **the children were taking it all ~** die Kinder haben alles mitbekommen *or* mitgekriegt (*inf*); **his death was so sudden that she couldn't ~ it ~** sein Tod kam so plötzlich, daß sie es gar nicht fassen konnte.
(g) (*deceive*) hereinlegen ◆ **to be ~n ~** hereingelegt werden; **to be ~n ~ by sb/sth** auf jdn/etw hereinfallen; **to be ~n ~ by appearances** sich vom äußeren Schein täuschen lassen.
(h) (*go to*) *film, party, town* (noch) mitnehmen (*inf*).

◆**take off** [1] *vi* **(a)** (*plane, passengers*) starten, abfliegen; (*plane: leave the ground*) abheben; (*Sport*) abspringen; (*fig*) (*project, sales*) anlaufen; (*film, product*) ankommen.
(b) (*inf: leave*) sich absetzen, sich davonmachen (*inf*).
[2] *vt sep* **(a)** (*remove, cut off: person*) abmachen (*prep obj* von); *beard, hat, lid* abnehmen (*prep obj* von); *tablecloth, bedspread* herunternehmen, entfernen (*prep obj* von); *pillowcases etc* abziehen (*prep obj* von); *coat, gloves etc* (sich *dat*) ausziehen; *leg, limb* abnehmen, amputieren; *play* absetzen; *food from menu, train, bus* streichen (*prep obj* von); *service, tax* abschaffen; (*remove from duty, job*) *detective, journalist etc* abziehen (*prep obj* von); *waitress, driver* ablösen ◆ **to ~ sth ~ sb** jdm etw abnehmen; **the sun will ~ the paint ~ the wood** durch die Sonne geht *or* blättert die Farbe ab; **double deckers have been ~n ~ this route** Doppeldecker werden auf dieser Strecke nicht mehr eingesetzt; **to ~ the receiver ~ (the hook)** den Hörer abnehmen, den Hörer von der Gabel nehmen; **he/she took her dress ~** er zog ihr das Kleid aus/sie zog ihr Kleid *or* (sich *dat*) das Kleid aus; **he took his/her clothes off** er zog sich/sie aus; **would you like to ~ your coat ~?** möchten Sie ablegen?; **he had two inches ~n ~ (his hair)** er hat sich (*dat*) die Haare 5 cm kürzer schneiden lassen; **please ~ a little ~ the top** bitte oben etwas kürzer; **the barber took too much ~** der Friseur hat zu viel abgeschnitten; **the 5 o'clock train has been ~n ~ today/for the summer** der 5-Uhr-Zug ist heute ausgefallen/wurde den Sommer über (vom Fahrplan) gestrichen.
(b) (*deduct*) abziehen (*prep obj* von); (*from price*) *5%, 50p* nachlassen ◆ **he took 50p ~ (the price)** er hat 50 Pence nachgelassen, er hat es 50 Pence billiger gemacht.
(c) (*lead away, go away with*) mitnehmen; (*under arrest etc*) abführen ◆ **he was ~n ~ to hospital** er wurde ins Krankenhaus gebracht; **to ~ oneself ~** (*inf*) sich auf den Weg machen.
(d) (*from ship, wreck*) von Bord holen; (*+prep obj*) holen von; (*from island, mountain*) herunterholen (*prep obj* von).
(e) (*have free*) *week, Monday* frei nehmen ◆ **to ~ time/a day ~ work** sich (*dat*) frei nehmen/einen Tag freimachen.
(f) (*imitate*) nachmachen, nachahmen.
(g) *+prep obj* (*in phrases*) **to ~ sb's mind** *or* **thoughts ~ sth** jdn von etw ablenken; **to ~ the weight ~ one's feet** seine Beine ausruhen; **to ~ sb/sth ~ sb's hands** jdm jdn/etw abnehmen; **to ~ years/ten years ~ sb** jdn um Jahre/zehn Jahre verjüngen.

◆**take on** [1] *vi* **(a)** (*inf: become upset*) sich aufregen.
(b) (*become popular: song, fashion etc*) sich durchsetzen.
[2] *vt sep* **(a)** (*undertake*) *job, work* an- *or* übernehmen; *responsibility* auf sich (*acc*) nehmen *or* laden, übernehmen; *sick person, backward child* sich annehmen (*+gen*); *bet* annehmen ◆ **when he married her he took ~ more than he bargained for** als er sie heiratete, hat er sich (*dat*) mehr aufgeladen *or* aufgebürdet, als er gedacht hatte; **he took ~ the fund-raising** er hat es übernommen, das Geld aufzutreiben.
(b) (*Sport etc: accept as opponent*) antreten gegen; *union, shop steward* sich anlegen mit ◆ **I could ~ ~ someone twice your size** ich könnte es mit einem aufnehmen, der zweimal so groß ist wie Sie; **I'll ~ you ~ at tennis** ich werde gegen Sie im Tennis antreten; **I bet you £50 — OK, I'll ~ you ~** ich wette mit Ihnen um 50 Pfund — gut, die Wette gilt.
(c) (*employ*) einstellen, anstellen; *apprentice* annehmen.
(d) (*take aboard*) (*coach, train etc*) *passengers* aufnehmen; (*plane, ship*) an Bord nehmen, übernehmen; *cargo, stores* (über)nehmen, laden; *fuel* tanken.
(e) (*assume*) *colour, aspect, expression* bekommen, annehmen ◆ **her face/eyes took ~ a doleful expression** ihr Gesicht nahm/ihre Augen nahmen einen traurigen Ausdruck an; **his face took ~ a greenish tinge** sein Gesicht verfärbte sich grün *or* bekam einen grünen Schimmer; **he took ~ an air of importance** er gab sich (*dat*) eine gewichtige Miene.

◆**take out** *vt sep* **(a)** (*bring or carry out*) (hinaus)bringen (of aus); (*out of house etc also*) nach draußen bringen; (*out of garage*) *car* hinaus-/herausfahren (of aus); (*for drive etc*) *car, boat* wegfahren mit ◆ **the current took the boat ~ to sea** die Strömung trieb das Boot aufs Meer hinaus.
(b) (*to theatre etc*) ausgehen mit, ausführen ◆ **to ~ the children/dog ~ (for a walk)** mit den Kindern/dem Hund spazierengehen *or* einen Spaziergang machen, den Hund ausführen; **to ~ sb ~ for a drive** mit jdm eine Autofahrt machen; **to ~ sb ~ to** *or* **for dinner/to the cinema** jdn zum Essen/ins Kino einladen *or* ausführen; **he has been taking her ~ for several months** er geht schon seit einigen Monaten mit ihr.
(c) (*pull out, extract*) herausnehmen; (*out of pocket, bag, cupboard etc also*) herausholen; *tooth also* ziehen; *appendix etc* herausnehmen, entfernen; *nail, screw* herausziehen (of aus) ◆ **to ~ sth ~ of** *or* **from sth** etw aus etw (heraus)nehmen/-holen; **~ your hands ~ of your pockets** nimm die Hände aus der Tasche.
(d) (*cause to disappear*) *stain* entfernen (*from* aus) ◆ **cold water will ~ the stain ~ of the tablecloth** mit kaltem Wasser geht der Fleck aus dem Tischtuch heraus.
(e) (*withdraw from bank etc*) abheben.
(f) (*deduct*) **~ it ~ of the housekeeping** nimm es vom Haushaltsgeld.
(g) (*procure*) *insurance* abschließen ◆ **to ~ ~ a subscription for sth** etw abonnieren; **to ~ ~ a patent on sth** etw patentieren lassen; **to ~ ~ a summons against sb** jdn gerichtlich vorladen lassen; **to ~ ~ a licence for sth** eine Lizenz für etw erwerben, sich (*dat*) eine Lizenz für etw geben lassen.
(h) **to ~ sb ~ of himself** jdn auf andere Gedanken bringen.
(i) (*inf*) **to ~ sth ~ on sb** etw an jdm auslassen (*inf*) *or* abreagieren (*inf*); **to ~ it ~ on sb** sich an jdm abreagieren.
(j) (*tire*) **to ~ it/a lot ~ of sb** jdn ziemlich/sehr schlauchen (*inf*).
(k) (*Mil, fig: Sport*) außer Gefecht setzen; *village* angreifen.
(l) (*US*) *see* **take away 2 (c)**.

◆**take over** [1] *vi* (*assume government*) an die Macht kommen; (*military junta etc*) die Macht ergreifen; (*party*) an die Regierung kommen; (*new boss etc*) die Leitung übernehmen; (*in a place: tourists, guests etc*) sich breitmachen (*inf*) ◆ **to ~ ~ (from sb)** jdn ablösen; **can you ~ ~?** können Sie mich/ihn *etc* ablösen?; **he's ill so I have to ~ ~** da er krank ist, muß ich (für ihn) einspringen; **his wife has ~n ~ completely** seine Frau führt das Regiment; **the next shift ~s ~ at 6 o'clock** die nächste Schicht übernimmt um 6 Uhr; **the Martians have ~n ~** die Marsmenschen haben die Erde/Stadt *etc* besetzt.
[2] *vt sep* **(a)** (*take control or possession of*) übernehmen ◆ **tourists ~ Edinburgh ~ in the summer** im Sommer machen sich die Touristen in Edinburgh breit (*inf*); **she took ~ the whole show** (*inf*) sie riß das Regiment an sich.
(b) (*escort or carry across*) *person* hinüberbringen; (*+prep obj*) bringen über (*+acc*); (*in boat also*) übersetzen; (*to visit town, people etc*) mitnehmen (*to* nach, *to sb* zu jdm).
(c) **to ~ sb ~ sth** (*show round*) jdn durch etw führen, jdm etw zeigen; (*tell about*) *facts* etw mit jdm durchgehen.

◆**take round** *vt sep* **(a)** **I'll ~ it ~ (to her place** *or* **to her)** ich bringe es zu ihr.
(b) (*show round*) führen (*prep obj* durch).

◆**take to** *vi +prep obj* **(a)** (*form liking for*) *person* mögen, sympathisch finden ◆ **sb ~s ~ a game/subject/place** ein Spiel/Fach/Ort sagt jdm zu; **the children soon took ~ their new surroundings** den Kindern gefiel es bald in der neuen Umgebung; **I'll never ~ ~ it** dafür werde ich mich nie erwärmen *or* begeistern können; **I don't know how she'll ~ ~ him/it** ich weiß nicht, wie sie auf ihn/darauf reagieren wird; **I don't ~ kindly ~ that/you doing that** ich kann das nicht leiden/es nicht leiden, wenn Sie das tun.
(b) (*form habit of*) **to ~ ~ doing sth** anfangen, etw zu tun; **to ~ ~ drink** zu trinken anfangen, sich (*dat*) das Trinken angewöhnen; **to ~ ~ drugs** anfangen, Drogen zu nehmen; **she took ~ telling everyone that ...** sie erzählte allen Leuten, daß ...
(c) (*escape to*) *woods, hills* sich flüchten *or* zurückziehen in (*+acc*), Zuflucht suchen in (*+dat*) ◆ **to ~ ~ the boats** sich in die Boote retten; **to ~ ~ one's bed** sich ins Bett legen; *see* **heel[1]**.

◆**take up** [1] *vi* (*continue*) (*person*) weitermachen ◆ **chapter 3 ~s ~ where chapter 1 left off** das dritte Kapitel schließt thematisch ans erste an.
[2] *vt sep* **(a)** (*raise, lift*) aufnehmen; *carpet, floorboards* hochnehmen; *road* aufreißen; *dress* kürzer machen, kürzen; *pen* zur Hand nehmen, greifen zu ◆ **~ ~ your bed and walk** (*Bibl*) nimm dein Bett und wandle.
(b) (*lead or carry upstairs etc*) *invalid, child* hinauf-/heraufbringen; *visitor* (mit) hinauf-/heraufnehmen; *thing also* hinauf-/herauftragen.
(c) (*vehicles*) *passengers* mitnehmen, einsteigen lassen.
(d) (*occupy*) *time, attention* in Anspruch nehmen, beanspruchen; *space* einnehmen.
(e) (*absorb*) (in sich *acc*) aufnehmen; *liquids also* aufsaugen.
(f) *matter, point* (*raise*) besprechen, zur Sprache bringen; (*go into*) eingehen auf (*+acc*) ◆ **I'll ~ that ~ with the headmaster** das werde ich beim Rektor zur Sprache bringen *or* mit dem Rektor besprechen; **I'd like to ~ ~ the point you made earlier on** ich möchte auf das eingehen, was Sie vorhin sagten.
(g) (*start doing as hobby*) *photography, archaeology* zu seinem Hobby machen; *a hobby* sich (*dat*) zulegen; *a language* (anfangen zu) lernen ◆ **to ~ ~ painting/pottery/the guitar** anfangen zu malen/zu töpfern/Gitarre zu spielen.
(h) (*adopt*) *cause* sich einsetzen für, verfechten; *idea* aufgreifen; *case* sich annehmen (*+gen*) ◆ **to ~ ~ an attitude** eine Haltung einnehmen; **to ~ ~ a person** (*as protégé*) sich eines Menschen annehmen; **to ~ ~ a position** (*lit*) eine Stellung einnehmen; (*fig*) eine Haltung einnehmen.
(i) (*accept*) *challenge, invitation* annehmen; *suggestion also* aufgreifen.
(j) (*start*) *job, employment* annehmen; *new job, post* antreten; *one's duties* übernehmen; *career* einschlagen ◆ **he left to ~ ~ a job as a headmaster** er ist gegangen, um eine Stelle als Schulleiter zu übernehmen; **to ~ ~ residence**

sich niederlassen (*at, in* in +*dat*); (*in house*) einziehen (*in* in +*acc*); (*sovereign etc*) Residenz beziehen (*in* in +*dat*).

(k) (*continue*) *story* aufnehmen; *conversation* fortfahren mit, weiterführen; (*join in*) *chorus, chant* einstimmen in (+*acc*) ◆ **the crowd took ~ the cry** die Menge nahm den Schrei auf.

(l) to ~ sb ~ on an invitation/offer von jds Einladung/Angebot Gebrauch machen; **to ~ sb ~ on a promise/boast** jdn beim Wort nehmen; **I'll ~ you ~ on that** ich werde davon Gebrauch machen; (*on promise etc*) ich nehme Sie beim Wort.

(m) (*question, argue with*) **I would like to ~ you ~ there** *or* **on that** ich möchte gern etwas dazu sagen; **he took me ~ on that point** dagegen hatte er etwas einzuwenden; **I would like to ~ you ~ on what you said about strikes** zu ihrer Bemerkung über Streiks hätte ich noch etwas zu sagen.

(n) (*Fin*) **to ~ ~ an option** Bezugsrecht ausüben; **to ~ ~ a bill** einen Wechsel einlösen; **to ~ ~ shares** Aktien beziehen.

(o) *collection* durchführen.

(p) to be ~n ~ with sb/sth mit jdm/etw sehr beschäftigt sein.

◆**take upon** *vt +prep obj* **he took that job ~ himself** er hat das völlig ungebeten getan; **he took it ~ himself to answer for me** er meinte, er müsse für mich antworten.

◆**take up with** *vi +prep obj person* sich anfreunden mit ◆ **to ~ ~ ~ bad company** in schlechte Gesellschaft geraten.

take: ~-away (*esp Brit*) [1] *n* **(a)** (*meal*) Speisen *pl* zum Mitnehmen; **let's get a ~-away** wir können uns ja etwas (zu essen) holen *or* mitnehmen; **(b)** (*restaurant*) Imbißstube *f*/Restaurant *nt* für Außer-Haus-Verkauf; [2] *adj attr* Außer-Haus-; **the ~-away menu is quite different** für Gerichte zum Mitnehmen gibt es eine ganz andere Speisekarte; **~-home pay** *n* Nettolohn *m*; **~-in** *n* (*inf*) Schwindel *m*.

taken ['teɪkən] *ptp of* **take**.

take: ~-off *n* **(a)** (*Aviat*) Start, Abflug *m*; (*moment of leaving ground also*) Abheben *nt*; (*Sport*) Absprung *m*; (*place*) Absprungstelle *f or* -brett *nt*; **the plane was ready for ~-off** das Flugzeug war startbereit *or* flugklar; **at ~-off** beim Start *or* Abheben; **to be cleared for ~-off** Starterlaubnis haben/bekommen; **(b)** (*imitation*) Parodie, Nachahmung *f*; **to do a ~-off of sb** jdn nachahmen *or* nachmachen (*inf*); **~-over** *n* (*Comm*) Übernahme *f*; **~-over bid** *n* Übernahmeangebot *nt*.

taker ['teɪkə[r]] *n* (*Betting*) Wettende(r) *mf*; (*at auction: fig*) Interessent(in *f*) *m* ◆ **any ~s?** wer wettet?; (*at auction*) wer bietet?; (*fig*) wer ist daran interessiert?; **there were no ~s** (*Betting*) niemand wettete *or* schloß eine Wette ab; (*at auction*) es wurden keine Angebote gemacht, niemand bot; (*fig*) niemand war daran interessiert.

take-up ['teɪkʌp] *n* **(a)** Inanspruchnahme *f* ◆ **there is a very low ~ of rent allowances** nur wenige nehmen Mietzuschüsse in Anspruch. **(b)** (*Tech: of tape etc*) Aufwickeln, Aufspulen *nt* ◆ **the rate of ~** die Aufwickel- *or* Aufspulgeschwindigkeit; **~ spool** Aufwickelspule *f*.

taking ['teɪkɪŋ] [1] *n* **(a) it's yours for the ~** das können Sie (umsonst) haben. **(b) ~s** *pl* (*Comm*) Einnahmen *pl*. **(c)** (*Mil: of town*) Einnahme, Eroberung *f*. **(d)** (*old: distress*) Aufregung, Erregung *f* ◆ **to be in a ~** aufgeregt *or* erregt sein.

[2] *adj manners, ways* einnehmend, gewinnend; *person* sympathisch, anziehend.

talc [tælk] [1] *n* (*also* **talcum** ['tælkəm]) **(a)** Talk *m*. **(b)** (*also* **talcum powder**) Talkumpuder *m*; (*perfumed also*) (Körper)puder *m*.

[2] *vt* pudern.

tale [teɪl] *n* **(a)** Geschichte *f*; (*Liter*) Erzählung *f* ◆ **fairy ~** Märchen *nt*; **T~s of King Arthur** Artussagen *pl*; **he had quite a ~ to tell** er hatte einiges zu erzählen, der hatte vielleicht was zu erzählen (*inf*); **I bet he/that bed could tell a ~ or two** (*inf*) er/das Bett könnte bestimmt so einiges erzählen; **it tells its own ~** das spricht für sich; **thereby hangs a ~** das ist eine lange/hübsche/pikante *etc* Geschichte; **I've heard a fine ~ about you** (*iro*) von dir hört man ja schöne Geschichten!

(b) to tell ~s petzen (*inf*) (*to dat*); (*dated: fib*) flunkern; **to tell ~s out of school** (*inf*) aus der Schule plaudern; **to tell ~s about sb** jdn verpetzen (*inf*) (*to* bei).

tale-bearing ['teɪlbɛərɪŋ] *n see* **taletelling**.

talent ['tælənt] *n* **(a)** Begabung *f*, Talent *nt* ◆ **to have a ~ for drawing/mathematics** Begabung zum Zeichnen/für Mathematik haben; **a painter of great ~** ein hochbegabter *or* sehr talentierter Maler.

(b) (*talented people*) Talente *pl*.

(c) (*inf*) (*girls*) Miezen (*inf*), Bräute (*sl*) *pl*; (*boys*) Typen (*sl*), Jungs (*inf*) *pl* ◆ **they went to inspect the local ~** sie zogen los, um zu sehen, wie die Miezen *etc* dort waren.

(d) (*Hist*) Talent *nt*.

talented ['tæləntɪd] *adj person* begabt, talentiert ◆ **a ~ book/painting** ein Buch/Gemälde, das von großer Begabung zeugt.

talent scout, talent spotter *n* Talentsucher *m*.

tale: ~teller *n* (*Sch*) Petzer(in *f*) *m* (*inf*); **~telling** *n* (*Sch*) Petzerei *f* (*inf*).

talisman ['tælɪzmən] *n, pl* **-s** Talisman *m*.

talk [tɔːk] [1] *n* **(a)** Gespräch *nt* (*also Pol*); (*conversation also*) Unterhaltung *f*; (*private also*) Unterredung *f*; (*heart-to-heart also*) Aussprache *f* ◆ **to have a ~** ein Gespräch führen/sich unterhalten/eine Unterredung haben/sich aussprechen (*with sb about sth* mit jdm über etw *acc*); **could I have a ~ with you?** könnte ich Sie mal sprechen?; **to hold** *or* **have ~s** Gespräche führen; **to have a friendly ~ with sb** sich mit jdm nett unterhalten, mit jdm plaudern; (*giving advice, warning*) mit jdm (mal) in aller Freundschaft reden; **I have enjoyed our ~** ich habe mich gern mit Ihnen unterhalten; **to meet for ~s** sich zu Gesprächen treffen.

(b) *no pl* (*~ing*) Reden *nt*, Rederei *f*; (*rumour*) Gerede *nt* ◆ **he's all ~** er ist ein fürchterlicher Schwätzer; (*and no action*) der führt bloß große Reden; **there is some ~ of his returning** es heißt, er kommt zurück; **there is too much ~ of going on strike in this factory** in dieser Fabrik wird zu viel vom Streiken geredet; **it's the ~ of the town** es ist Stadtgespräch; **she's the ~ of the town** sie ist zum Stadtgespräch geworden.

(c) (*lecture*) Vortrag *m* ◆ **to give a ~** einen Vortrag halten (*on* über +*acc*); **a series of ~s** eine Vortragsreihe; **her ~ on the dangers ...** ihre (kurze) Rede über die Gefahren ...

[2] *vi* **(a)** sprechen, reden (*of* von, *about* über +*acc*); (*have conversation also*) sich unterhalten (*of, about* über +*acc*); (*bird, doll, child*) sprechen ◆ **to ~ to** *or* **with** (*esp US*) **sb** mit jdm sprechen *or* reden (*about* über +*acc*); (*converse also*) sich mit jdm unterhalten (*about* über +*acc*); (*reprimand also*) mit jdm ein ernstes Wort reden; **could I ~ to Mr Smith please?** kann ich bitte Herrn Smith sprechen?; **don't ~ silly!** (*inf*) red keinen Stuß! (*inf*), red nicht so blöd (daher) (*inf*); **it's easy** *or* **all right for you to ~** (*inf*) du hast gut reden (*inf*); **don't (you) ~ to me like that!** wie redest du denn mit mir?; **who do you think you're ~ing to?** was meinst du denn, wen du vor dir hast?; **that's no way to ~ to your parents** so redet man doch nicht mit seinen Eltern!; **hey, that's no way to ~** hör mal, sag doch so was nicht!; **he sat there without ~ing** er saß da und sagte kein Wort; **~ to me!** erzähl mir was!; **to get/be ~ing to sb** mit jdm ins Gespräch kommen/im Gespräch sein; **I'm not ~ing to you** (*we're on bad terms*) mit dir spreche *or* rede ich nicht mehr; (*I mean somebody else*) ich spreche nicht mit dir; **he ~s very highly of you** er spricht sehr lobend von Ihnen; **he knows/doesn't know what he's ~ing about** er weiß (schon)/weiß (doch) nicht, wovon er spricht, er hat (davon) ziemlich Ahnung (*inf*)/(doch) überhaupt keine Ahnung; **you can** *or* **should ~!** (*inf*) du kannst gerade reden!; **to keep sb ~ing** jdn (mit einem Gespräch) hinhalten; **to ~ to oneself** Selbstgespräche führen; **now you're ~ing!** das läßt sich schon eher hören!

(b) (*mention*) sprechen, reden ◆ **he's been ~ing of going abroad** er hat davon gesprochen *or* geredet, daß er ins Ausland fahren will; **~ing of salaries/films ...** da *or* wo (*inf*) wir gerade von Gehältern/Filmen sprechen ...; **~ about impertinence/rude/hot!** so was von Frechheit/unverschämt/heiß! (*inf*).

(c) (*chatter*) reden, schwatzen ◆ **stop ~ing!** sei/seid ruhig!

(d) (*gossip*) reden, klatschen ◆ **everyone was ~ing about them** sie waren in aller Munde; (*because of scandal also*) alle haben über sie geredet *or* geklatscht; **to get oneself ~ed about** von sich reden machen; (*because of scandal*) ins Gerede kommen.

(e) (*reveal secret*) reden ◆ **the spy refused to ~** der Spion schwieg beharrlich *or* weigerte sich zu reden; **to make sb ~** jdn zum Reden bringen; **OK, Kowalski, ~!** OK!, Kowalski, raus mit der Sprache! (*inf*).

(f) we're ~ing about at least £2,000/3 months es geht um mindestens £ 2.000/3 Monate, wir müssen mit mindestens £ 2.000/3 Monaten rechnen; **what sort of sum are we ~ing about?** um welche Summe geht es?

[3] *vt* **(a)** (*speak*) *a language, slang* sprechen; *nonsense* reden ◆ **~ sense!** red keinen solchen Unsinn!; **he simply wasn't ~ing sense** er hat bloß Unsinn geredet *or* verzapft (*inf*).

(b) (*discuss*) *politics, cricket, business* reden über (+*acc*) *or* von, sich unterhalten über (+*acc*) ◆ **we have to ~ business for a while** wir müssen mal kurz etwas Geschäftliches besprechen; **then they got down to ~ing business** dann sind sie zum geschäftlichen Teil übergegangen; **let's ~ business** kommen wir zur Sache; **now you're ~ing business** das läßt sich schon eher hören; *see* **shop**.

(c) (*persuade*) **to ~ sb/oneself into doing sth** jdn überreden *or* jdn/sich dazu bringen, etw zu tun; (*against better judgement*) jdm/sich einreden, daß man etw tut; **he ~ed himself into believing she was unfaithful** er hat sich eingeredet, sie sei ihm nicht treu; **to ~ sb out of sth/doing sth** jdn von etw abbringen/davon abbringen, etw zu tun, jdm etw ausreden/jdm ausreden, etw zu tun.

(d) (*achieve by ~ing*) **he ~ed himself out of that job** durch sein Reden hat er sich (*dat*) diese Stelle verscherzt; **you won't be able to ~ your way out of this** jetzt können Sie sich nicht mehr herausreden; **he ~ed himself out of trouble** er redete sich (geschickt) heraus; **he ~ed himself into this situation** er hat sich selbst durch sein Reden in diese Lage gebracht; **to ~ sb into a better humour/out of his bad temper** jdn in eine bessere Laune bringen/jdm die schlechte Laune vertreiben.

(e) to ~ oneself hoarse sich heiser reden; *see* **head**.

◆**talk at** *vi +prep obj person* einreden auf (+*acc*).

◆**talk away** [1] *vi* ununterbrochen reden, schwatzen ◆ **we ~ed ~ for hours** wir haben stundenlang geschwatzt *or* uns stundenlang unterhalten.

[2] *vt sep* **(a)** (*spend talking*) im Gespräch verbringen ◆ **we ~ed the evening ~** wir haben den ganzen Abend lang geredet, wir haben den Abend im Gespräch verbracht. **(b)** *debts, problems etc* wegdiskutieren.

◆**talk back** *vi* (*be cheeky*) frech antworten (*to sb* jdm).

◆**talk down** [1] *vi* **to ~ ~ to sb** mit jdm herablassend *or* von oben herab reden *or* sprechen.

[2] *vt sep* **(a)** (*reduce to silence*) über den Haufen reden (*inf*), niederreden. **(b)** (*Aviat*) *pilot, plane* zur Landung einweisen.

◆**talk on** *vi* weiterreden ◆ **they ~ed ~ and on** sie redeten und redeten.

◆**talk out** *vt sep* **(a)** (*discuss*) *problems, differences* ausdiskutieren. **(b)** (*Parl*) **to ~ ~ a bill** die rechtzeitige Verabschiedung eines Gesetzes verschleppen.

◆**talk over** *vt sep* **(a)** *question, problem* bereden (*inf*), besprechen ◆ **let's ~ it ~**

quietly wir wollen jetzt einmal in aller Ruhe darüber reden. (b) *(persuade) see* talk round 1.

◆**talk round** [1] *vt always separate* umstimmen ◆ I ~ed her ~ to my way of thinking ich habe sie zu meiner Anschauung bekehrt.
[2] *vi +prep obj problem, subject* herumreden um.

talkative ['tɔːkətɪv] *adj person* gesprächig, redselig.

talkativeness ['tɔːkətɪvnɪs] *n* Gesprächigkeit, Redseligkeit *f*.

talkback ['tɔːkbæk] *n (device)* Gegensprechanlage *f*; *(talking)* Anweisungen *pl* im Hintergrund.

talked-of ['tɔːktɒv] *adj*: much ~ berühmt; *plans also* vielbesprochen; his much ~ brilliance was apparent seine vielgerühmte Brillanz wurde offensichtlich.

talker ['tɔːkəʳ] *n* Redner *m* ◆ the parrot was a good ~ der Papagei konnte gut sprechen; he's just a ~ er ist ein Schwätzer *m*.

talkie ['tɔːkɪ] *n (dated inf)* Tonfilm *m*.

talking ['tɔːkɪŋ] *n* Reden, Sprechen *nt* ◆ no ~ please! bitte Ruhe!, Sprechen verboten!; I'll let you do the ~ ich überlasse das Reden Ihnen; he did all the ~ er übernahm das Reden; his constant ~ will drive me mad sein dauerndes Gerede *or* Geschwätz macht mich noch verrückt; that's enough ~! Ruhe jetzt!, Schluß mit dem Reden!

talking: ~ **bird** *n* sprechender Vogel; ~ **doll** *n* sprechende Puppe, Sprechpuppe *f*; ~ **head** *n (TV)* Kopfaufnahme *f*, Brustbild *nt*; ~ **picture** *n (old)* Tonfilm *m*; ~ **point** *n* Gesprächsthema *nt*; ~ **shop** *n (pej inf)* Quasselbude *f (inf)*; ~**-to** *n (inf)* Standpauke *f (inf)*; to give sb a good ~-to jdm eine Standpauke halten *(inf)*.

talk radio *n* Talk-Radio *nt*.

talk show *n* Talkshow *f*.

tall [tɔːl] *adj (+er)* (a) *person* groß, lang *(inf)* ◆ how ~ are you? wie groß sind Sie?; he is 1 m 80 ~ er ist 1,80 m groß; to feel ten foot *or* feet ~ *(inf)* riesig stolz sein *(inf)*; *(after compliment also)* um einen halben Meter wachsen *(inf)*.
(b) *building, tree, grass* hoch; *mast also* lang ◆ ~ ship Klipper *m*.
(c) *(inf)* that's a ~ order das ist ganz schön viel verlangt; *(indignant also)* das ist eine Zumutung; a ~ story ein Märchen *nt (inf)*.

tallboy ['tɔːlbɔɪ] *n (Brit)* hohe Schlafzimmerkommode.

tallish ['tɔːlɪʃ] *adj person* ziemlich groß; *building* ziemlich hoch.

tallness ['tɔːlnɪs] *n see adj* (a) Größe, Länge *(inf) f*. (b) Höhe *f*; Länge *f*.

tallow ['tæləʊ] *n* Talg, Unschlitt *(old) m* ◆ ~ candle Talglicht *nt*.

tallowy ['tæləʊɪ] *adj* talgig.

tally ['tælɪ] [1] *n* (a) *(Hist: stick)* Kerbholz *nt*. (b) *(count, account)* to keep a ~ of Buch führen über *(+acc)*. (c) *(result of counting, number)* (An)zahl *f* ◆ what's the ~? wieviel ist/sind es?
[2] *vi* übereinstimmen; *(reports etc also)* sich decken ◆ they don't ~ sie stimmen nicht (miteinander) überein.
[3] *vt (also ~ up)* zusammenrechnen *or* -zählen.

tally clerk *n* Kontrolleur *m*.

tally-ho ['tælɪ'həʊ] [1] *interj* halali.
[2] *n* Halali *nt*.

Talmud ['tælmuːd] *n* Talmud *m*.

talon ['tælən] *n* Kralle, Klaue *f*; *(fig: of person)* Kralle *f*.

tamable *adj see* **tameable**.

tamarind ['tæmərɪnd] *n (tree, fruit)* Tamarinde *f*.

tamarisk ['tæmərɪsk] *n* Tamariske *f*.

tambour ['tæmˌbʊəʳ] *n* (a) *(old Mus)* Trommel *f*. (b) *(on desk etc)* Rouleau, Rollo *nt*.

tambourine [ˌtæmbə'riːn] *n* Tamburin *nt*.

tame [teɪm] [1] *adj (+er)* (a) *animal, person* zahm ◆ the village has its own ~ novelist *(hum)* der Ort hat seinen dorfeigenen Schriftsteller *(inf)*; I'll get my ~ lawyer to do that *(hum)* ich beauftrage meinen treuen Rechtsanwalt damit.
(b) *(dull) person, life, adventure etc* lahm *(inf)*; *story, film, answer, criticism, joke, shot, tennis service etc also* zahm.
[2] *vt animal, person* zähmen, bändigen; *passion* (be)zähmen, zügeln; *garden* unter Kontrolle bringen.

tameable ['teɪməbl] *adj* zähmbar.

tamely ['teɪmlɪ] *adv see adj* (a) zahm. (b) lahm *(inf)*; zahm.

tameness ['teɪmnɪs] *n see adj* (a) Zahmheit *f*. (b) Lahmheit *f (inf)*; Zahmheit *f*.

tamer ['teɪməʳ] *n (of animals)* Bändiger, Dompteur *m*.

taming ['teɪmɪŋ] *n* Zähmung, Bändigung *f* ◆ "The T~ of the Shrew" „Der Widerspenstigen Zähmung".

tam o'shanter [ˌtæmə'ʃæntəʳ], **tammy** ['tæmɪ] *n* (schottische) Baskenmütze.

tamp [tæmp] *vt* (a) *(block up) drill hole etc* (ver)stopfen. (b) *(ram down) earth* (fest)stampfen ◆ to ~ (down) tobacco in a pipe die Pfeife (fest) stopfen.

tampax ® ['tæmpæks] *n* Tampon *m*.

tamper ['tæmpəʳ] *n (for soil etc)* Stampfer *m*; *(for tobacco)* Stopfer *m*.

◆**tamper with** *vi +prep obj* herumhantieren an *(+dat)*; *(with evil intent)* sich *(dat)* zu schaffen machen an *(+dat)*; *(plan, schedule)* herumpfuschen an *(+dat) (inf)*; *document* verfälschen; *(Jur) witness* beeinflussen; *(bribe)* bestechen ◆ the car had been ~ed ~ jemand hatte sich am Auto zu schaffen gemacht.

tampon ['tæmpən] *n* Tampon *m*.

tan [tæn] [1] *n* (a) *(suntan)* Bräune *f* ◆ to get a ~ braun werden; she's got a lovely ~ sie ist schön braun; what a ~! du bist/er ist *etc* aber schön braun!
(b) *(colour)* Hellbraun *nt*.
[2] *adj* hellbraun.
[3] *vt* (a) *skins* gerben ◆ to ~ sb's hide *(fig inf)* jdm das Fell gerben. (b) *(sun) face, body etc* bräunen, braun werden lassen.
[4] *vi* braun werden ◆ she ~s easily sie wird schnell braun.

tandem ['tændəm] [1] *n (cycle)* Tandem *nt* ◆ the horses were in ~ die Pferde liefen hintereinander im Gespann; in ~ *(fig)* zusammen.
[2] *adv* hintereinander im Gespann.

tang [tæŋ] *n (smell)* scharfer Geruch; *(taste)* starker Geschmack ◆ the fish has a salty ~ der Fisch schmeckt salzig.

tangent ['tændʒənt] *n (Math)* Tangente *f* ◆ to go *or* fly off at a ~ *(fig)* (plötzlich) vom Thema abkommen *or* abschweifen; he went off at a ~ about flowers er schweifte plötzlich ab und fing an, über Blumen zu reden.

tangential [tæn'dʒənʃəl] *adj (Math)* tangential ◆ this is merely ~ to the problem dies berührt das Problem nur am Rande.

tangerine [ˌtændʒə'riːn] [1] *n (also ~ orange)* Mandarine *f*.
[2] *adj (in colour)* stark orange, rötlich orange.

tangibility [ˌtændʒɪ'bɪlɪtɪ] *n* Greifbarkeit *f*.

tangible ['tændʒəbl] *adj* (a) *(lit)* greifbar, berührbar. (b) *(fig) result* greifbar; *proof also* handfest; *assets* handfest, real.

tangibly ['tændʒəblɪ] *adv* greifbar ◆ he would prefer to be rewarded more ~ ihm wäre etwas Handfesteres als Belohnung lieber.

Tangier(s) [tæn'dʒɪə(z)] *n* Tanger *nt*.

tangle ['tæŋgl] [1] *n* (a) *(lit)* Gewirr *nt* ◆ the string was in a ~ die Schnur hatte sich verheddert; the ~s in her hair ihr verheddertes Haar; to get into a ~ sich verheddern.
(b) *(fig: muddle)* Wirrwarr *m*, Durcheinander *nt* ◆ to get into a ~ sich verheddern; I'm in such a ~ with my tax forms ich komme bei meinen Steuerformularen überhaupt nicht klar; an emotional ~ eine Verstrickung der Gefühle; she has got herself into an emotional ~ sie hat sich gefühlsmäßig verstrickt.
(c) *(fig: trouble)* Ärger *m*, Schwierigkeiten *pl* ◆ she's in a real ~ this time diesmal hat sie sich aber böse hineingeritten; he got into a ~ with the police er ist mit der Polizei aneinandergeraten, er hat Schwierigkeiten mit der Polizei gehabt.
[2] *vt (lit, fig)* verwirren, durcheinanderbringen; *wool, string also* verheddern; *hair* durcheinanderbringen ◆ to get ~d *(lit, fig)* sich verheddern; *(ropes)* sich verknoten; a ~d web ein Gespinst *nt*.

◆**tangle up** *vt sep (lit, fig)* verwirren, durcheinanderbringen; *wool, string also* verheddern ◆ to get ~d ~ durcheinandergeraten; *(wool etc also)* sich verheddern; *(ropes)* sich verknoten; *(person) (in talking, explaining etc)* sich verstricken *or* verheddern; *(become involved)* verwickelt *or* verstrickt werden; the paper got all ~d ~ in the machine das Papier hat sich in der Maschine verheddert; she got ~d ~ with a married man sie hat sich mit einem verheirateten Mann eingelassen.

◆**tangle with** *vi +prep obj (inf)* aneinandergeraten mit ◆ I'm not tangling ~ him mit ihm laß ich mich (doch) nicht ein.

tango ['tæŋgəʊ] [1] *n* Tango *m*.
[2] *vi* Tango tanzen ◆ they ~ed across the room sie tanzten im Tangoschritt durch das Zimmer; it takes two to ~ *(fig inf)* es gehören immer zwei dazu.

tangy ['tæŋɪ] *adj (+er) taste* scharf, streng; *smell also* durchdringend.

tank [tæŋk] *n* (a) *(container)* Tank *m*; *(for water also)* Wasserspeicher *m*; *(of boiler also)* Kessel *m*; *(Naut: for water supply)* Kessel *m*; *(in submarines)* Tauchtank *m*; *(Rail: in engine)* Kessel *m*; *(for diver: oxygen ~)* Flasche *f*; *(Phot)* Wanne *f* ◆ fill up the ~, please *(Aut)* volltanken, bitte.
(b) *(Mil)* Panzer, Tank *m*.
(c) *(US sl)* Kittchen *nt (inf)*, Knast *m (sl)*.

◆**tank along** *vi (inf: move fast) (car)* dahinbrettern *(inf)*; *(runner)* dahinsausen *(inf)*.

◆**tank up** [1] *vi* (a) *(ship, plane)* auftanken; *(car, driver also)* volltanken. (b) *(Brit sl: get drunk)* sich vollaufen lassen *(sl)*.
[2] *vt sep* (a) *ship, plane* auftanken; *car also* volltanken. (b) *(Brit sl)* to get/be ~ed ~ sich vollaufen lassen *(sl)* (on mit)/voll sein.

tankard ['tæŋkəd] *n* Humpen *m*; *(for beer also)* Seidel *nt*.

tank car *n (Rail)* Kesselwagen *m*.

tanker ['tæŋkəʳ] *n* (a) *(boat)* Tanker *m*, Tankschiff *nt*. (b) *(vehicle)* Tankwagen *m*.

tank farm *n (US)* Tanklager *nt*.

tankful ['tæŋkfʊl] *n* (a) Tank(voll) *m*. (b) *(Brit sl: drink)* he's had a ~ der ist total voll *(inf)*.

tank: ~**top** *n* Pullunder *m*; ~ **town** *n (US)* Wasser(auffüll)station *f*; *(fig)* Kuhnest *nt (inf)*; ~ **trap** *n* Panzersperre *f*; ~ **wagon** *n (Rail)* Kesselwagen *m*.

tanned [tænd] *adj* (a) *person* braun(gebrannt). (b) *skins* gegerbt.

tanner[1] ['tænəʳ] *n* Gerber *m*.

tanner[2] *n (old Brit inf)* Sixpence *m*.

tannery ['tænərɪ] *n* Gerberei *f*.

tannic ['tænɪk] *adj* Gerb-.

tannin ['tænɪn] *n* Tannin *nt*.

tanning ['tænɪŋ] *n* (a) *(of hides)* Gerben *nt*; *(craft)* Gerberei *f*. (b) *(punishment)* Tracht *f* Prügel ◆ to give sb a ~ jdm das Fell gerben.

Tannoy ® ['tænɔɪ] *n* Lautsprecheranlage *f* ◆ over *or* on the ~ über den Lautsprecher.

tansy ['tænzɪ] *n* Rainfarn *m*.

tantalize ['tæntəlaɪz] *vt* reizen; *(torment also)* quälen ◆ to be ~d Tantalusqualen ausstehen.

tantalizing ['tæntəlaɪzɪŋ] *adj smell, promise, blouse* verlockend, verführerisch;

behaviour also aufreizend ◆ **he spoke with ~ slowness** er sprach aufreizend langsam; **it is ~ to think that** ... es ist zum Verrücktwerden, zu denken, daß ... (*inf*).

tantalizingly ['tæntəlaɪzɪŋlɪ] *adv* verlockend, verführerisch ◆ **success was ~ near** der Erfolg schien zum Greifen nahe.

tantamount ['tæntəmaʊnt] *adj*: **to be ~ to sth** einer Sache (*dat*) gleichkommen, auf etw (*acc*) hinauslaufen.

tantrum ['tæntrəm] *n* Wutanfall, Koller (*inf*) *m* ◆ **to be in/have** *or* **throw a ~** einen Koller *or* Wutanfall haben/bekommen.

Tanzania [,tænzə'nɪə] *n* Tansania *nt*.

Tanzanian [,tænzə'nɪən] [1] *adj* tansanisch.
[2] *n* Tansanier(in *f*) *m*.

Taoism ['taʊɪzəm] *n* Taoismus *m*.

tap¹ [tæp] [1] *n* (**a**) (*esp Brit*) Hahn *m* ◆ **don't leave the ~s running** laß das Wasser nicht laufen!, dreh die Hähne zu!; **on ~** (*lit: beer etc*) vom Faß; (*fig*) zur Hand; **he has plenty of ideas on ~** er hat immer Ideen auf Lager (*inf*). (**b**) (*of phones*) Abhören *nt*, Abhöraktion *f*.
[2] *vt* (**a**) *cask, barrel* anzapfen, anstechen; *tree* anzapfen ◆ **to ~ a pine for resin** einer Kiefer (*dat*) Harz abzapfen.
(**b**) (*fig*) *resources* erschließen ◆ **to ~ an electric current** eine Stromleitung anzapfen; **to ~ telephone wires** Telephonleitungen anzapfen; **the wires are ~ped here** die Leitung hier wird abgehört; **to ~ sb for money/a loan** (*inf*) jdn anzapfen (*inf*), jdn anpumpen (*inf*); **he tried to ~ me for information** er wollte mich aushorchen.

tap² [1] *n* (**a**) (*light knock*) Klopfen *nt*.
(**b**) (*light touch*) Klaps *m*, leichter Schlag ◆ **to give sb a ~ on the shoulder** jdn *or* jdm auf die Schulter klopfen.
(**c**) **~s** *sing or pl* (*Mil*) Zapfenstreich *m*.
[2] *vt* klopfen ◆ **he ~ped me on the shoulder** er klopfte mir auf die Schulter; **to ~ in/out a nail** einen Nagel ein-/ausschlagen; **he ~ped his foot impatiently** er klopfte ungeduldig mit dem Fuß auf den Boden.
[3] *vi* klopfen ◆ **to ~ on** *or* **at the door** sachte an die Tür klopfen *or* pochen (*geh*), leise anklopfen; **she sat ~ping away at the typewriter** sie klapperte auf der Schreibmaschine herum; **he ~ped with his fingers on the table** er trommelte mit den Fingern auf den Tisch.

◆**tap out** *vt sep* (**a**) *pipe* ausklopfen. (**b**) *rhythm* klopfen ◆ **to ~ ~ a message (in Morse)** eine Nachricht morsen.

tap: ~-dance [1] *n* Steptanz *m*; [2] *vi* steppen; **~-dancer** *n* Steptänzer(in *f*), Stepper(in *f*) *m*; **~-dancing** *n* Steppen *nt*.

tape [teɪp] [1] *n* (**a**) Band *nt*; (*sticky paper*) Klebeband *nt*; (*Sellotape* ® *etc*) Kleb(e)streifen, Tesafilm ® *m*; (*ticker-~, computer ~ etc*) Lochstreifen *m*; (*Sport*) Zielband *nt* ◆ **to break** *or* **breast the ~** (*Sport*) durchs Ziel gehen.
(**b**) (*magnetic*) (Ton)band, Magnetband *nt* ◆ **on ~** auf Band; **to put** *or* **get sth on ~** etw auf Band aufnehmen.
[2] *vt* (**a**) *parcel* (mit Kleb(e)streifen/-band) verkleben *or* zukleben ◆ **to ~ together two documents** zwei Dokumente mit Kleb(e)streifen/-band zusammenkleben.
(**b**) (*~-record*) *song, message* (auf Band) aufnehmen.
(**c**) (*inf*) **I've got the situation ~d** ich habe die Sache im Griff (*inf*); **I've got him ~d** ich kenne mich mit ihm aus.

◆**tape back** *vt sep* (mit Kleb(e)streifen/-band) zurückkleben.

◆**tape down** *vt sep* (mit Kleb(e)streifen/-band) festkleben.

◆**tape on** *vt sep* (mit Kleb(e)streifen/-band) ankleben *or* -heften ◆ **to ~ sth ~(to) sth** etw auf etw (*acc*) kleben.

◆**tape up** *vt sep sth broken* mit Kleb(e)streifen/-band zusammenkleben; *parcel* mit Kleb(e)streifen/-band verkleben; *gap, windows, mouth* zukleben.

tape: ~ cassette *n* Tonbandkassette *f*; **~ deck** *n* Tapedeck *nt*; **~ measure** *n* Maßband, Bandmaß *nt*.

taper ['teɪpəʳ] [1] *n* (*candle*) (dünne) Kerze.
[2] *vt end of plank, stick etc* zuspitzen; *edge* abschrägen; *hair* spitz zuschneiden; *pair of trousers* (nach unten) verengen.
[3] *vi* sich zuspitzen; (*tower, vase also*) sich verjüngen; (*trousers*) nach unten enger werden; (*hair*) (im Nacken) spitz zulaufen ◆ **to ~ to a point** spitz zulaufen.

◆**taper off** [1] *vi* (**a**) spitz zulaufen, sich zuspitzen; (*tower also, vase*) sich verjüngen; (*road, trousers*) sich verengen.
(**b**) (*fig: decrease gradually*) langsam aufhören; (*numbers*) langsam zurückgehen; (*production*) langsam auslaufen.
[2] *vt sep edge* abschrägen; *end of plank, stick etc* zuspitzen; (*fig*) *production* zurückschrauben; (*bring to an end*) langsam auslaufen lassen.

tape: ~ reader *n* (*Comput*) Lochstreifenleser *m*; **~-record** *vt* auf Band aufnehmen; **~-recorder** *n* Tonbandgerät *nt*; **~-recording** *n* Bandaufnahme *f*.

tapered ['teɪpəd] *adj* spitz zulaufend ◆ **~ trousers** Hosen, die unten enger werden.

tapering ['teɪpərɪŋ] *adj* spitz zulaufend.

tape streamer *n* (*Comput*) Streamer *m*.

tapestry ['tæpɪstrɪ] *n* Wand- *or* Bildteppich *m*; (*fabric*) Gobelin *m* ◆ **~-making, ~-weaving** Tapisserie *f*.

tapeworm ['teɪpwɜːm] *n* Bandwurm *m*.

tapioca [,tæpɪ'əʊkə] *n* Tapioka *f*.

tapir ['teɪpəʳ] *n* Tapir *m*.

tappet ['tæpɪt] *n* (*Aut*) Stößel *m*.

tap: ~room *n* Schankstube, Schenke (*old*) *f*; **~root** *n* (*Bot*) Pfahlwurzel *f*.

tapster ['tæpstəʳ] *n* (*old*) Schankkellner(in *f*), Zapfer(in *f*) *m*.

tap water *n* Leitungswasser *nt*.

tar¹ [tɑːʳ] [1] *n* Teer *m*.
[2] *vt road, fence* teeren ◆ **they are all ~red with the same brush** (*fig*) sie sind alle vom gleichen Schlag; **to ~ and feather sb** jdn teeren und federn.

tar² *n* (*old Naut sl*) Teerjacke *f* (*hum*), Seemann *m*.

tarantella [,tærən'telə] *n* Tarantella *f*.

tarantula [tə'ræntjʊlə] *n* Tarantel *f*.

tarbrush ['tɑːbrʌʃ] *n*: **a touch of the ~** (*hum inf*) schwarzes Blut.

tardily ['tɑːdɪlɪ] *adv see adj* (**a**) (reichlich) spät. (**b**) zu spät.

tardiness ['tɑːdɪnɪs] *n* (**a**) (*of person*) Säumigkeit *f* (*geh*) ◆ **the ~ of his reply/offer** *etc* seine reichlich späte Antwort/sein reichlich spätes Angebot *etc*. (**b**) (*US: lateness*) Zuspätkommen *nt*; (*of train etc*) Verspätung *f*.

tardy ['tɑːdɪ] *adj* (*+er*) (**a**) (*belated*) *reply, arrival, offer to help* (reichlich) spät; *person* säumig (*geh*) ◆ **to be ~ in doing sth** etw erst reichlich spät tun.
(**b**) (*US: late*) **to be ~** (*person*) zu spät kommen; (*train etc*) Verspätung haben; **the train was ~ (in arriving at New York)** der Zug kam mit Verspätung (in New York) an.

tare¹ [tɛəʳ] *n* (*Bot*) Wicke *f*.

tare² *n* (*Comm*) Tara *f*; (*of vehicle*) Leergewicht *nt*.

target ['tɑːgɪt] [1] *n* (**a**) (*person, object, Mil*) Ziel *nt*; (*Sport: board*) Ziel- *or* Schießscheibe *f*; (*fig: of joke, criticism etc*) Zielscheibe *f* ◆ **he was a ~ for their mockery** er war Zielscheibe ihres Spotts; **his shot was off/on ~** (*Mil*) sein Schuß ist daneben gegangen/hat getroffen; (*Ftbl etc*) sein Schuß war ungenau/sehr genau; **the bombs landed on/off ~** die Bomben haben getroffen/sind daneben niedergegangen; **Apollo III is on ~ for the moon** Apollo III ist auf direktem Kurs zum Mond.
(**b**) (*objective, goal*) Ziel *nt*; (*in production*) (Plan)soll *nt* ◆ **industrial production ~** Produktionssoll *nt no pl*; **production is above/on/below ~** das Produktionssoll ist überschritten/erfüllt/nicht erfüllt; **we set ourselves the ~ of £10,000** wir haben uns £ 10.000 zum Ziel gesetzt; **to be on ~** auf Kurs sein; **we're on ~ for £10,000** alles läuft nach Plan, um auf £ 10.000 zu kommen; **to stay on ~** den Kurs halten; **to be behind ~** hinter dem Soll zurückliegen.
[2] *vt* sich (*dat*) zum Ziel setzen; *group, audience* als Zielgruppe haben, abzielen auf (*+acc*) ◆ **to ~ 500 t per day** das Produktionsziel mit 500 t pro Tag ansetzen.

target: ~ area *n* Zielbereich *m*, Zielgebiet *nt*; **~ cost** *n* Richtkosten, Plankosten *pl*; **~ date** *n* angestrebter Termin; **~ figure** *n* Richtsumme, Plansumme *f*; **we have a ~ figure of 100,000 visitors** wir haben uns (*dat*) 100.000 Besucher zum Ziel gesetzt; **~ group** *n* Zielgruppe *f*; **~ language** *n* Zielsprache *f*; **~ market** *n* Zielmarkt *m*; **~ practice** *n* (*Mil*) Zielschießen *nt*.

targetting ['tɑːgɪtɪŋ] *n* (*setting targets*) Zielsetzung *f* ◆ **the ~ of teenagers as customers** das Ansteuern von Teenagern *or* das Abzielen auf Teenager als Kunden; **we had agreed on the ~ of £10,000** wir hatten £ 10.000 als Ziel vereinbart.

tariff ['tærɪf] [1] *n* (**a**) (Gebühren)tarif *m*; (*in hotels*) Preisverzeichnis *nt*, Preisliste *f*. (**b**) (*Econ: tax*) Zoll *m*; (*table*) Zolltarif *m*.
[2] *attr* (*Econ*) **~ reform** Zolltarifreform *f*; (*Hist*) Einführung *f* von Schutzzöllen; **~ walls** Zollschranken *pl*.

tarmac ['tɑːmæk] [1] *n* (**a**) Makadam *m*; (*generally*) Asphalt, Makadam (*spec*) *m*. (**b**) (*esp Brit Aviat*) Rollfeld *nt*.
[2] *vt road* (*generally*) asphaltieren, makadamisieren (*spec*).

tarmacadam [,tɑːmə'kædəm] *n* Makadam *m*.

tarn [tɑːn] *n* kleiner Berg- *or* Gebirgssee.

tarnish ['tɑːnɪʃ] [1] *vt* (**a**) *metal* stumpf werden lassen ◆ **the silver was ~ed by exposure to air** das Silber war an der Luft angelaufen. (**b**) (*fig*) *reputation, glory* beflecken; *ideals* trüben, den Glanz nehmen (*+dat*).
[2] *vi* (*metal*) anlaufen.
[3] *n* Beschlag *m* ◆ **to prevent ~** das Anlaufen verhindern.

taro ['tɑːrəʊ] *n* Taro *m*.

tarot card ['tɑːrəʊkɑːd] *n* Tarockkarte *f*.

tarp [tɑːp] *n* (*US inf*) *see* **tarpaulin**.

tar paper *n* (*US*) Dachpappe, Teerpappe *f*.

tarpaulin [tɑː'pɔːlɪn] *n* (**a**) (*waterproof sheet*) Plane *f*; (*Naut*) Persenning *f*. (**b**) **~s** *pl* (*clothes*) Ölzeug *nt*.

tarpon ['tɑːpɒn] *n* Atlantischer Tarpon, Silberkönig *m*.

tarragon ['tærəgən] *n* Estragon *m*.

tarry¹ ['tɑːrɪ] *adj* teerig.

tarry² [tærɪ] *vi* (*old, liter*) (**a**) (*remain*) verweilen (*old, liter*). (**b**) (*delay*) säumen (*old, liter*), zögern.

tarsus ['tɑːsəs] *n* Tarsus *m*.

tart¹ [tɑːt] *adj* (*+er*) (**a**) *flavour, wine* herb, sauer (*pej*); *fruit* sauer. (**b**) (*fig*) *remark, manner* scharf; *humour* beißend; *person* schroff.

tart² *n* (*Cook*) Obstkuchen *m*, Obsttorte *f*; (*individual*) Obsttörtchen *nt* ◆ **apple/jam ~** Apfelkuchen *m*/Marmeladenkuchen *m*; Apfeltörtchen *nt*/Marmeladentörtchen *nt*.

tart³ *n* (*inf*) (*prostitute*) Nutte *f* (*sl*); (*loose woman*) Flittchen *nt* (*pej*); (*pej: woman*) Schachtel *f* (*inf*).

◆**tart up** *vt sep* (*esp Brit inf*) aufmachen (*inf*); *oneself* auftakeln (*inf*), aufdonnern (*inf*) ◆ **there she was, all ~ed ~** da stand sie, aufgetakelt wie eine Fregatte (*inf*).

tartan ['tɑːtən] [1] *n* (*pattern*) Schottenkaro *nt*; (*material*) Schottenstoff *m* ◆ **what ~ are you?** welches Clan-Muster tragen Sie?
[2] *adj skirt* im Schottenkaro *or* -muster.

tartar ['tɑːtəʳ] *n* (*of wine*) Weinstein *m*; (*in kettle*) Kesselstein *m*; (*on teeth*) Zahnstein *m*.

Tartar ['tɑːtəʳ] *n* Tatar *m* ◆ **t~** (*fig*) Tyrann *m*; **to catch a ~** (*fig*) sich (*dat*) etwas Übles einhandeln.

tartare [tɑː'tɑːʳ] *adj see* **steak**.

tartaric [tɑː'tærɪk] *adj* **~ acid** Weinsäure *f*.

tartar sauce *n* ≃ Remouladensoße *f*.

Tartary ['tɑːtərɪ] *n* Tatarei *f*.

tartly ['tɑːtlɪ] *adv speak* scharf.

tartness ['tɑːtnɪs] *n see adj* **(a)** Herbheit, Säure (*pej*) *f*; Säure *f*. **(b)** Schärfe *f*; Beißende(s) *nt*; Schroffheit *f*.

task [tɑːsk] [1] *n* Aufgabe *f* ◆ **to set** *or* **give sb a ~** jdm eine Aufgabe stellen *or* geben; **it is the ~ of the politician to ...** es ist Aufgabe des Politikers zu ...; **to take sb to ~** jdn ins Gebet nehmen, sich (*dat*) jdn vornehmen (*inf*) (*for, about* wegen).
[2] *vt see* **tax 2 (b)**.

task: ~ force *n* Sondereinheit, Spezialeinheit *f*; **~master** *n* (strenger) Arbeitgeber; **he's a hard ~master** er ist ein strenger Meister.

Tasmania [tæz'meɪnɪə] *n* Tasmanien *nt*.

Tasmanian [tæz'meɪnɪən] [1] *adj* tasmanisch.
[2] *n* Tasmanier(in *f*) *m*.

Tasman Sea ['tæzmən'siː] *n* Tasmansee *f*.

tassel ['tæsəl] *n* Quaste, Troddel *f*.

taste [teɪst] [1] *n* **(a)** (*sense*) Geschmack(sinn) *m* ◆ **to be sweet to the ~** süß schmecken, einen süßen Geschmack haben.
(b) (*flavour*) Geschmack *m* ◆ **I don't like the ~** das schmeckt mir nicht; **her cooking has no ~** ihr Essen schmeckt nach nichts; **a ~ of onions** ein Zwiebelgeschmack; **to leave a bad ~ in the mouth** (*lit, fig*) einen üblen Nachgeschmack hinterlassen.
(c) (*small amount*) Kostprobe *f*, Versucherchen *nt* (*inf*); (*fig: as an example*) Kostprobe *f*; (*of sth in the future*) Vorgeschmack *m* ◆ **would you like some? — just a ~** möchten Sie etwas? — nur eine Idee; **to have a ~ (of sth)** (*lit*) (etw) probieren *or* kosten; (*fig*) eine Kostprobe (von etw) bekommen; (*of sth to come*) einen Vorgeschmack (von etw) haben; **two years in the army will give him a ~ of discipline** zwei Jahre bei der Armee werden ihm zeigen *or* ihn spüren lassen, was Disziplin ist; **to give sb a ~ of the whip** jdn die Peitsche *or* Knute spüren lassen; **he gave them a ~ of his bad temper** er gab ihnen eine (Kost)probe seiner schlechten Laune; **a ~ of what was to come** ein Vorgeschmack dessen, was noch kommen sollte.
(d) (*liking*) Geschmack *m no pl* ◆ **to have a ~ for sth** eine Vorliebe für etw haben; **to acquire** *or* **develop a ~ for sth** Geschmack an etw (*dat*) finden; **it's an acquired ~** das ist etwas für Kenner; **she has expensive ~s in hats** was Hüte anbelangt, hat sie einen teuren Geschmack; **my ~ in music has changed over the years** mein musikalischer Geschmack hat sich mit der Zeit geändert; **to be to sb's ~** nach jds Geschmack sein; **it is a matter of ~** das ist Geschmack(s)sache; **there is no accounting for ~s** über Geschmack läßt sich (nicht) streiten; **~s differ** die Geschmäcker sind verschieden; **sweeten to ~** (*Cook*) nach Geschmack *or* Bedarf süßen.
(e) (*discernment*) Geschmack *m* ◆ **she has very good ~ in furniture** was Möbel anbelangt, hat sie einen sehr guten Geschmack; **she has no ~ at all when it comes to choosing friends** sie ist nicht sehr wählerisch in der Auswahl ihrer Freunde; **a man of ~** ein Mann mit Geschmack; **in good/bad ~** geschmackvoll/geschmacklos; **to be in doubtful ~** von zweifelhaftem Geschmack zeugen; **that joke shows very poor ~** dieser Witz ist geschmacklos.
[2] *vt* **(a)** (*perceive flavour of*) schmecken; *blood* lecken ◆ **I can't ~ anything** ich schmecke überhaupt nichts; **I can't ~ anything wrong** ich kann nichts Besonderes schmecken; **once you've ~d real champagne** wenn Sie einmal echten Sekt getrunken haben; **I've never ~d caviar** ich habe noch nie Kaviar gekostet (*geh*) *or* gegessen; **wait till you ~ this** warten Sie mal, bis Sie das probiert haben; **he hadn't ~d food for a week** er hatte seit einer Woche nichts zu sich genommen.
(b) (*take a little*) versuchen, probieren, kosten.
(c) (*test*) *wine* verkosten; *food products* probieren; (*official*) prüfen ◆ **~ the sauce before adding salt** schmecken Sie die Soße ab, bevor Sie Salz beigeben.
(d) (*fig*) *power, freedom* erfahren, erleben ◆ **once the canary had ~d freedom ...** als der Kanarienvogel erst einmal Geschmack an der Freiheit gefunden hatte ...
[3] *vi* **(a)** schmecken ◆ **to ~ good** *or* **nice** (gut) schmecken; **it ~s all right to me** ich schmecke nichts; (*I like it*) ich finde, das schmeckt nicht schlecht; **to ~ of sth** nach etw schmecken.
(b) to ~ of (*liter*) erfahren; **those who have ~d of the knowledge of Zen** diejenigen, denen die Weisheit des Zen zuteil geworden ist (*geh*).

taste bud *n* Geschmacksknospe *f*.

tasteful *adj*, **~ly** *adv* ['teɪstfʊl, -fəlɪ] geschmackvoll.

tastefulness ['teɪstfʊlnɪs] *n* guter Geschmack.

tasteless ['teɪstlɪs] *adj* (*lit, fig*) geschmacklos; *food also* fade.

tastelessly ['teɪstlɪslɪ] *adv see adj*.

tastelessness ['teɪstlɪsnɪs] *n* (*lit, fig*) *see adj* Geschmacklosigkeit *f*; Fadheit *f*.

taster ['teɪstəʳ] *n* **(a)** (*of wine, tobacco*) Prüfer, Probierer *m*; (*of tea*) Schmecker *m*; (*as bodyguard*) Vorkoster *m*. **(b)** (*fig*) Vorgeschmack *m* ◆ **this is just a ~ of what's to come** dies ist nur ein kleiner Vorgeschmack von dem, was noch kommt.

tastily ['teɪstɪlɪ] *adv see adj*.

tastiness ['teɪstɪnɪs] *n* Schmackhaftigkeit *f*.

tasty ['teɪstɪ] *adj* (+*er*) *dish* schmackhaft ◆ **a ~ morsel** (*lit*) ein Leckerbissen *m*; **his new girlfriend is a ~ morsel** (*inf*) seine neue Freundin ist zum Anbeißen (*inf*).

tat[1] [tæt] [1] *vi* Okkispitze *or* Schiffchenspitze machen.
[2] *vt* in Okkispitze *or* Schiffchenspitze arbeiten ◆ **she ~ted a strip of lace** sie stellte eine Spitze in Okkiarbeit her.

tat[2] *n see* **tit**[2].

ta-ta ['tæ'tɑː] *interj* (*Brit inf*) tschüs (*inf*), ada-ada (*baby-talk*).

tattered ['tætəd] *adj clothes, person* zerlumpt; *book, sheet* zerfleddert, zerfetzt; (*fig*) *pride, reputation* angeschlagen.

tatters ['tætəz] *npl* Lumpen, Fetzen *pl* ◆ **to be in ~** in Fetzen sein *or* hängen; **his jacket hung in ~** sein Jackett war zerrissen *or* hing ihm in Fetzen vom Leib; **his reputation/pride was in ~** sein Ruf/Stolz war sehr angeschlagen *or* hatte sehr gelitten.

tattily ['tætɪlɪ] *adv* (*inf*) *see adj*.

tattiness ['tætɪnɪs] *n* (*inf*) *see adj* Schmuddeligkeit *f*; Schäbigkeit *f*.

tatting ['tætɪŋ] *n* Okki- *or* Schiffchenspitze, Frivolitätenarbeit *f*.

tattle ['tætl] [1] *vi* tratschen (*inf*), klatschen.
[2] *n* Geschwätz, Gerede *nt* ◆ **office ~** Büroklatsch *or* -tratsch (*inf*) *m*.

tattler ['tætləʳ] *n* Klatschmaul *nt* (*pej sl*), Klatschbase *f* (*inf*).

tattoo[1] [tə'tuː] [1] *vt* tätowieren.
[2] *n* Tätowierung *f*.

tattoo[2] *n* **(a)** (*military pageant*) Musikparade *f*. **(b)** (*Mil: on drum or bugle*) Zapfenstreich *m* ◆ **to beat** *or* **sound the ~** den Zapfenstreich blasen; **to beat a ~ on the table** (*with one's fingers*) auf den Tisch trommeln.

tatty ['tætɪ] *adj* (+*er*) (*inf*) schmuddelig; *clothes* schäbig.

taught [tɔːt] *pret, ptp of* **teach**.

taunt [tɔːnt] [1] *n* Spöttelei *f*, höhnische Bemerkung ◆ **he paid no attention to their ~s of "traitor"** er kümmerte sich nicht darum, daß sie ihn als Verräter verhöhnten.
[2] *vt person* verspotten, aufziehen (*inf*) (*about* wegen) ◆ **to ~ sb with cowardice** jdm höhnisch *or* spöttisch Feigheit vorwerfen.

taunting *adj*, **~ly** *adv* ['tɔːntɪŋ, -lɪ] höhnisch, spöttisch.

Taurean [tɔː'rɪən] [1] *adj* Stier-.
[2] *n* Stier *m*.

Taurus ['tɔːrəs] *n* (*Astron, Astrol*) Stier *m*.

taut [tɔːt] *adj* (+*er*) **(a)** *rope* straff (gespannt); *muscles* stramm, gestrafft ◆ **~ round thighs** pralle Oberschenkel *pl*. **(b)** (*fig: tense*) *nerves, situation* (an)gespannt. **(c)** (*fig: precise, economical*) *style, prose* knapp.

tauten ['tɔːtn] [1] *vt rope* spannen, straff anziehen, straffen; *sail* straffen.
[2] *vi* sich spannen *or* straffen, straff werden.

tautly ['tɔːtlɪ] *adv see adj*.

tautness ['tɔːtnɪs] *n* (*of skin, rope*) Straffheit *f*; (*of muscles*) Strammheit *f*; (*fig*) (*of atmosphere*) Gespanntheit *f*; (*of nerves*) Anspannung *f*; (*of style*) Knappheit *f*.

tautological [ˌtɔːtə'lɒdʒɪkəl], **tautologous** [tɔː'tɒləgəs] *adj* tautologisch, doppelt gemoppelt (*inf*).

tautology [tɔː'tɒlədʒɪ] *n* Tautologie *f*, weißer Schimmel (*inf*).

tavern ['tævən] *n* (*old*) Taverne, Schenke (*old*) *f*.

tawdrily ['tɔːdrɪlɪ] *adv* billig und geschmacklos ◆ **~ dressed** aufgedonnert.

tawdriness ['tɔːdrɪnɪs] *n* (*of jewellery, decorations etc*) ordinäre Protzigkeit ◆ **the ~ of her appearance** ihre billige und geschmacklose Aufmachung.

tawdry ['tɔːdrɪ] *adj* (+*er*) *clothes* billig und geschmacklos; *hat, splendour, decorations* ordinär; *person, appearance* aufgedonnert ◆ **all this cheap and ~ jewellery** all dieser billige Flitterkram.

tawny ['tɔːnɪ] *adj* (+*er*) gelbbraun, goldbraun ◆ **~ port** bräunlicher Portwein, Tawny-Portwein *m*; **~ owl** Waldkauz *m*; (*in Brownies*) Helferin *f* der Wichtelmutter.

tax [tæks] [1] *n* **(a)** (*Fin, Econ*) Steuer *f*; (*on a company's profit*) Abgabe *f*; (*import ~*) Gebühr *f* ◆ **before/after ~** brutto/netto, vor/nach Abzug der Steuern; **profits before/after ~** Brutto-/Nettoverdienst *m*; **that's done for ~ purposes** das wird aus steuerlichen Gründen getan; **free of ~** steuer-/abgaben-/gebührenfrei; **to put a ~ on sb/sth** jdn/etw besteuern, jdn/etw mit einer Steuer belegen; **the heavy ~ on the rich** die hohe Besteuerung der Reichen; **the ~ on alcohol/cars** *etc* die Getränke-/Kraftfahrzeugsteuer *etc*.
(b) (*fig*) Belastung *f* (*on sth gen, on sb* für jdn).
[2] *vt* **(a)** (*Fin, Econ*) besteuern; *goods also* mit einer Steuer belegen; *country* mit Steuern belegen ◆ **this government is going to ~ us all out of existence** diese Regierung zieht uns den letzten Pfennig aus der Tasche (*inf*).
(b) (*fig*) *brain, imagination* strapazieren; *one's patience, nerves also* auf eine harte Probe stellen; *strength* stark beanspruchen; *savings, resources* angreifen, schmälern.
(c) (*liter: accuse*) **to ~ sb with sth** jdn einer Sache (*gen*) beschuldigen *or* bezichtigen *or* zeihen (*liter*); **to ~ sb with having lied** jdn einer Lüge (*gen*) zeihen (*liter*).

taxable ['tæksəbl] *adj person* steuerpflichtig; *income also* (be)steuerbar (*form*); *goods* besteuert, abgabenpflichtig.

tax *in cpds* Steuer-; **~ allowance** *n* Steuervergünstigung *f*; (*tax-free income*) Steuerfreibetrag *m*.

taxation [tæk'seɪʃən] *n* Besteuerung *f*; (*taxes also*) Steuern *pl* ◆ **money acquired from ~** Steuereinnahmen *or* -einkünfte *pl*; **exempt from ~** nicht besteuert; *goods, income also* steuerfrei; **subject to ~** steuerpflichtig.

tax: ~ avoidance *n* Steuerumgehung *f*; **~ bracket** *n* Steuergruppe *or* -klasse *f*; **~ burden** *n* Steuerlast *f*; **~ code, ~ coding** *n* Steuerkennziffer *f*; ~ **collecting** *n* Steuereinziehung *f*; ~ **collector** *n* Finanz- *or* Steuerbeamte(r) *m*; (*Bibl, Hist*) Zöllner *m*; ~**-deductible** *adj* (von der Steuer) absetzbar; *mortgage* steuerbegünstigt; ~ **disc** *n* (*on vehicle*) Steuermarke *f*; ~ **dodge** *n* Trick *m*, um Steuern zu umgehen; ~**-dodger** *n* Steuerhinterzieher *m*; (*who goes abroad*) Steuerflüchtling *m*; ~ **evasion** *n* Steuerhinterziehung *f*; (*by going abroad*) Steuerflucht *f*; ~**-exempt** *adj* (*US*) *person* steuerbefreit; *business* abgabenfrei; *income* steuerfrei; ~ **exile** *n* Steuerexil *nt*; (*person*) Steuerflüchtling *m*; ~ **form** *n* Steuerformular *nt*; ~**-free** *adj, adv* steuer-/abgabenfrei; ~ **haven** *n* Steuerparadies *nt*.

taxi ['tæksɪ] [1] *n* Taxi *nt*, Taxe *f* ◆ **to go by ~** mit dem Taxi *or* der Taxe fahren.
[2] *vi* (*Aviat*) rollen ◆ **the plane ~ed to a halt** das Flugzeug rollte aus.

taxi: ~cab *n* Taxi *nt*; ~ **dancer** *n* (*US*) Tanzdame *f*.

taxidermist ['tæksɪdɜːmɪst] *n* Präparator, Tierausstopfer *m*.

taxidermy ['tæksɪdɜːmɪ] *n* Taxidermie *f*.

taxi: ~-driver *n* Taxifahrer(in *f*), Taxichauffeur *m*; ~ **meter** *n* Fahrpreisanzeiger, Taxameter (*form*) *m*.

tax incentive *n* Steueranreiz *m*.

taxi: ~ plane *n* (*US*) Lufttaxi *nt*; ~ **rank, ~ stand** *n* Taxistand *m*.

taxman ['tæksmæn] *n* Steuer- *or* Finanzbeamte(r) *m* ◆ **the ~ gets 35%** das Finanzamt bekommt 35%.

taxonomy [tæk'sɒnəmɪ] *n* Taxonomie *f*.

tax: ~payer *n* Steuerzahler *m*; ~ **rebate** *n* Steuervergütung *or* -rückzahlung *f*; ~ **relief** *n* Steuervergünstigung *f*; ~ **relief of 5%** ein Steuernachlaß *m* von 5%; **it qualifies for ~ relief** das ist steuerbegünstigt; ~ **return** *n* Steuererklärung *f*; ~ **revenue** *n* Steueraufkommen *nt*; ~ **structure** *n* Steuersystem *nt*; ~ **system** *n* Steuerwesen, Steuer- *or* Besteuerungssystem *nt*; ~ **year** *n* Steuerjahr *nt*.

TB *abbr of* **tuberculosis** Tb, Tbc *f*.

T-bar ['tiːbɑːʳ] *n* Bügel *m*; (*lift*) Schlepplift *m*.

T-bone steak ['tiːbəʊn'steɪk] *n* T-bone-Steak *nt*.

tbs(p) *abbr of* **tablespoonful(s), tablespoon(s)** Eßl.

TD *abbr of* **touchdown**.

T.D. (*US*) *abbr of* **Treasury Department**.

➤ **tea** [tiː] *n* **(a)** (*substance, drink*) Tee *m* ◆ **to make (the) ~** (den) Tee machen; **a cup of ~** eine Tasse Tee; **not for all the ~ in China** nicht um alles Gold der Welt. **(b)** (*also* ~ **plant**) Tee(strauch) *m*. **(c)** ≃ Kaffee und Kuchen; (*meal*) Abendbrot *nt* ◆ **we have ~ at five** wir essen um 5 Uhr Abendbrot *or* zu Abend.

tea: ~ bag *n* Teebeutel *m*; ~ **ball** *n* (*esp US*) Tee-Ei *nt*; ~ **biscuit** *n* Butterkeks *m*; ~ **biscuits** *npl* Teegebäck *nt*; ~**boy** *n* Stift *m*; ~ **break** *n* Pause *f*; ~ **caddy** *n* Teebüchse *or* -dose *f*; (*dispenser*) Teespender *m*; ~**cake** *n* Rosinenbrötchen *nt*; ~ **cart** *n* (*US*) Tee- *or* Servierwagen *m*.

teach [tiːtʃ] (*vb: pret, ptp* **taught**) [1] *vt subject, person* unterrichten, lehren (*geh*); *animal* abrichten ◆ **to ~ sth to sb** jdm etw beibringen; (*teacher*) jdn in etw (*dat*) unterrichten, jdm Unterricht in etw (*dat*) geben; **to ~ sb to do sth** jdm beibringen, etw zu tun; **this accident taught me to be careful** durch diesen Unfall habe ich gelernt, vorsichtiger zu sein; **you can't ~ somebody how to be happy** man kann niemanden lehren, glücklich zu sein; **to ~ sb how to do sth** jdm zeigen, wie man etw macht, jdm etw beibringen; **he ~es French** er unterrichtet *or* gibt (*inf*) *or* lehrt (*geh*) Französisch; **who taught you to drive?** bei wem haben Sie Fahren gelernt?; **to ~ school** (*US*) Lehrer(in) sein/werden; **to ~ oneself sth** sich (*dat*) etw beibringen; **let that ~ you not to ...** laß dir das eine Lehre sein, nicht zu ...; **that'll ~ him a thing or two!** da werden ihm die Augen aufgehen, da wird er erst mal sehen (*inf*); **it taught me a thing or two** es war sehr lehrreich, da habe ich einiges gelernt; **that'll ~ him!** das hat er nun davon!; **make her pay, that'll ~ her** laß sie bezahlen, das wird ihr eine Lehre sein; **that'll ~ you to break the speed limit/not to pay your insurance** das hast du (nun) davon, daß du die Geschwindigkeitsbegrenzung überschritten/die Versicherung nicht bezahlt hast; **I'll ~ you to speak to me like that!** ich werde dir schon austreiben (*inf*) *or* werde dich lehren, so mit mir zu sprechen!; **you can't ~ him anything about that** darüber können Sie ihm nichts Neues mehr erzählen.
[2] *vi* unterrichten, Unterricht geben ◆ **he wants to ~** er möchte Lehrer werden; **he can't ~** (*not allowed*) er darf nicht unterrichten; (*no ability*) er gibt keinen guten Unterricht.
[3] *n* (*sl: teacher: as address*) Herr/Frau X.

teachability [ˌtiːtʃə'bɪlɪtɪ] *n* (*of pupil*) Lernfähigkeit *f*; (*of subject*) Lehrbarkeit *f*.

teachable ['tiːtʃəbl] *adj animal, child* lernfähig ◆ **music is a very ~ subject** Musik ist ein Fach, das sich gut unterrichten *or* lehren (*geh*) läßt; **things in life which are not ~** Dinge, die man niemandem beibringen kann.

teacher ['tiːtʃəʳ] *n* Lehrer(in *f*) *m* ◆ **university ~s** Hochschullehrer *pl*, Lehrkräfte *pl* an (den) Universitäten (*form*); **~s of English, English ~s** Englischlehrer *pl*; **she is a German ~** sie ist Deutschlehrerin.

teacher-training ['tiːtʃə'treɪnɪŋ] *n* Lehrer(aus)bildung *f*; (*for primary teachers*) Studium *nt or* Ausbildung *f* an einer/der pädagogischen Hochschule; (*for secondary teachers*) Referendarausbildung *f* ◆ ~ **certificate** *or* **qualification** (*document*) Zeugnis *nt* über die Prüfung für das Lehramt; **to do a ~ certificate** *or* **qualification** die Lehrerausbildung machen; **to get a ~ certificate** die Lehrbefähigung erhalten; ~ **college** (*for primary teachers*) pädagogische Hochschule; (*for secondary teachers*) Studienseminar *nt*.

tea-chest ['tiːtʃest] *n* Kiste *f*.

teach-in ['tiːtʃɪn] *n* Teach-in *nt*.

teaching ['tiːtʃɪŋ] *n* **(a)** das Unterrichten *or* Lehren (*geh*); (*as profession*) der Lehrberuf ◆ **to take up ~** den Lehrberuf ergreifen (*form*), Lehrer werden; **she enjoys ~** sie unterrichtet gern; **he is no good at ~** er ist kein guter Lehrer. **(b)** (*doctrine: also* ~**s**) Lehre *f* ◆ **his ~ on this subject was somewhat vague** seine Ausführungen zu diesem Thema waren ziemlich vage.

teaching: ~ aid *n* Lehr- *or* Unterrichtsmittel *nt*; ~ **hospital** *n* Ausbildungskrankenhaus *nt*; ~ **machine** *n* Lernmaschine *f*, Lehrmittel *nt* für den programmierten Unterricht; ~ **profession** *n* Lehrberuf *m*; (*all teachers*) Lehrer *pl*; ~ **staff** *n* Lehrerkollegium *nt*, Lehrkörper *m* (*form*).

tea: ~ cloth *n* Geschirrtuch *nt*; ~ **cosy** *n* Teewärmer *m*; ~**cup** *n* **(a)** Teetasse *f*; *see* **storm 1 (a)**; **(b)** (*also* ~**cupful**) Tasse *f* (voll); ~ **dance** *n* Tanztee *m*; ~ **garden** *n* Gartencafé *nt*; ~**house** *n* Teehaus *nt*.

teak [tiːk] *n* (*wood*) Teak(holz) *nt*; (*tree*) Teakbaum *m*.

tea-kettle ['tiːketl] *n* Wasserkessel *m*.

teal [tiːl] *n, pl* - Krickente *f*.

tea: ~ lady *n Frau, die in Büros etc für die Angestellten Tee zubereitet*; ~**-leaf** *n* **(a)** Teeblatt *nt*; *see* **read¹ 1 (b)**; **(b)** (*Brit sl: thief*) Langfinger *m* (*inf*).

team [tiːm] [1] *n* **(a)** Team *nt*; (*Sport also*) Mannschaft *f* ◆ **football ~** Fußballmannschaft *or* -elf *f*; **they work as a ~** sie arbeiten im *or* als Team; **they make a good ~** sie sind ein gutes Team *or* (*two also*) Gespann, sie arbeiten gut zusammen; **research ~** Forschungsgruppe *or* -gemeinschaft *f or* -team *nt*; **a ~ of scientists** eine Gruppe *or* ein Team *nt* von Wissenschaftlern. **(b)** (*of horses, oxen etc*) Gespann *nt*.
[2] *vt horses, oxen* zusammenspannen; (*fig*) zusammentun.

◆**team up** [1] *vi* (*people*) sich zusammentun (*with* mit); (*join group*) sich anschließen (*with sb* jdm, an jdn) ◆ **I see that John and Mary have ~ed ~** John und Mary gehen jetzt (anscheinend) miteinander (*inf*).
[2] *vt sep* zusammenschließen.

team: ~ effort *n* Teamarbeit *f*; ~ **game** *n* Mannschaftsspiel *nt*; ~**-mate** *n* Mannschaftskamerad *m*; ~ **member** *n* Teammitglied *nt*; (*Sport also*) Mannschaftsmitglied *nt*; ~ **spirit** *n* Gemeinschaftsgeist *m*; (*Sport*) Mannschaftsgeist *m*.

teamster ['tiːmstəʳ] *n* **(a)** (*US: truck driver*) Lastwagenfahrer, LKW-Fahrer *m*. **(b)** (*old Agr*) Fuhrmann *m*.

teamwork ['tiːmwɜːk] *n* Gemeinschaftsarbeit, Teamarbeit *f*, Teamwork *nt*.

tea: ~ party *n* Teegesellschaft *f*; ~**pot** *n* Teekanne *f*.

tear¹ [tεəʳ] (*vb: pret* **tore**, *ptp* **torn**) [1] *vt* **(a)** *material, paper, dress* zerreißen; *flesh* verletzen, aufreißen; *hole* reißen ◆ **I've torn a muscle** ich habe mir einen Muskel gezerrt; **the nail tore a gash in his arm** er hat sich (*dat*) an dem Nagel eine tiefe Wunde am Arm beigebracht; **to ~ sth in two** etw (in zwei Stücke *or* Hälften) zerreißen, etw in der Mitte durchreißen; **to ~ sth to pieces** etw in Stücke reißen; **the critics tore the play to pieces** die Kritiker haben das Stück total verrissen; **his reputation was torn to shreds by his critics** die Kritiker ließen keinen guten Faden an ihm; **to ~ sth open** etw aufreißen; **that's torn it!** (*fig inf*) das hat alles verdorben!
(b) (*pull away*) reißen ◆ **the wind tore the tent from the pole** der Wind riß das Zelt von der Stange; **her child was torn from her/from her arms** das Kind wurde ihr entrissen/ihr aus den Armen gerissen; **he tore it out of my hand** er riß es mir aus der Hand; **to ~ one's hair (out)** sich (*dat*) die Haare raufen.
(c) (*fig: usu pass*) **a country torn by war** ein vom Krieg zerrissenes Land; **a heart torn with remorse** ein von Reue gequältes Herz; **to be torn between two things/people** zwischen zwei Dingen/Menschen hin und her gerissen sein; **she was completely torn** sie war innerlich zerrissen.
[2] *vi* **(a)** (*material etc*) (zer)reißen ◆ **her coat tore on a nail** sie zerriß sich (*dat*) den Mantel an einem Nagel; ~ **along the dotted line** an der gestrichelten Linie abtrennen.
(b) (*move quickly*) rasen ◆ **to ~ past** vorbeirasen.
[3] *n* (*in material etc*) Riß *m*.

◆**tear along** *vi* entlangrasen ◆ **he tore ~ the street** er raste die Straße entlang *or* hinunter.

◆**tear apart** *vt sep place, house* völlig durcheinanderbringen; *meat, flesh, zebra, country* zerreißen.

◆**tear at** *vi +prep obj* zerren an (*+dat*) ◆ **he tore ~ the walls of his cell** er verkrallte sich in die Wände seiner Zelle; **the thorns tore ~ her hands** die Dornen zerkratzten ihr die Hände; **the waves tore ~ the cliffs** die Wellen peitschten gegen die Klippen.

◆**tear away** [1] *vi* davonrasen.
[2] *vt sep wrapping* abreißen, wegreißen (*from* von) ◆ **to ~ ~ sb's mask** jdm die Maske vom Gesicht reißen; **to ~ sth ~ from sb** jdm etw wegreißen *or* entreißen (*geh*); **if you can ~ yourself ~ from the paper** wenn du dich von der Zeitung losreißen kannst; **if you can ~ him ~ from the party** wenn du ihn von der Party wegkriegen *or* loseisen kannst (*inf*).

◆**tear down** [1] *vi* hinunter-/herunterrasen (*prep obj acc*).
[2] *vt sep poster* herunterreißen; *house* abreißen, abbrechen.

◆**tear into** *vi +prep obj* **(a)** (*shell, rocket*) ein Loch reißen in (*+acc*); (*animals*) *deer etc* zerfleischen; *food* sich hermachen über (*+acc*); (*saw*) *wood* sich fressen durch. **(b)** (*attack physically*) herfallen über (*+acc*). **(c)** (*attack verbally*) abkanzeln, zur Schnecke machen (*inf*); (*critic*) keinen guten Faden lassen an (*+dat*).

◆**tear off** [1] *vi* **(a)** wegrasen ◆ **he tore ~ down the street** er raste die Straße hinunter. **(b) the carbon ~s ~** die Durchschrift läßt sich abtrennen.
[2] *vt sep label, wrapping, calendar leaf* abreißen; *cover* wegreißen; *clothes* herunterreißen ◆ **please ~ ~ this part and complete** bitte hier abtrennen und ausfüllen; **he tore a strip ~ me** (*inf*), **he tore me ~ a strip** (*inf*) er hat mich zur Minna *or* Schnecke gemacht (*inf*).

◆**tear out** [1] *vi* heraus-/hinausrasen, wegrasen ◆ **he tore ~ through the front door** er raste *or* rannte zur Vordertür hinaus.

➤ LANGUAGE IN USE: **tea: a** → 7.3

[2] *vt sep* (her)ausreißen (*of* aus) ♦ **the tree was torn ~ by the roots** der Baum wurde entwurzelt.

◆**tear up** [1] *vi* angerast kommen ♦ **he tore ~ the hill/road** er raste den Berg hinauf/die Straße entlang.
[2] *vt sep* **(a)** *paper etc* zerreißen.
(b) (*fig: cancel*) *contract, agreement* zerreißen.
(c) (*pull from ground*) *post, stake, plant* (her)ausreißen.
(d) (*break surface of*) *ground* aufwühlen; *road* aufreißen.

tear[2] [tɪəʳ] *n* Träne *f* ♦ **in ~s** in Tränen aufgelöst; **wet with ~s** tränenfeucht; **there were ~s in her eyes** ihr standen Tränen in den Augen; **the news brought ~s to her eyes** als sie das hörte, stiegen ihr die Tränen in die Augen; **you are bringing ~s to my eyes** (*iro*) mir kommen die Tränen (*iro*); **the ~s were running down her cheeks** ihr Gesicht war tränenüberströmt; **smiling bravely through her ~s** unter Tränen tapfer lächelnd; **to laugh till the ~s come** Tränen lachen; **to weep ~s of joy** Freudentränen weinen *or* vergießen; *see* **shed**[1], **burst.**

tearaway ['tɛərəweɪ] *n* (*inf*) Rabauke *m* (*inf*) ♦ **I used to be a bit of a ~** ich war ein ziemlicher Rabauke.

tear drop *n* Träne *f*.

tearful ['tɪəfʊl] *adj look* tränenfeucht; *face* tränenüberströmt ♦ **there were a few ~ moments** es gab ein paar tränenvolle Augenblicke; **..., she said in a ~ voice** ..., sagte sie unter Tränen.

tearfully ['tɪəfəlɪ] *adv look* mit Tränen in den Augen; *say* unter Tränen.

teargas ['tɪəgæs] *n* Tränengas *nt*.

tearing ['tɛərɪŋ] *adj* (*inf*): **to be in a ~ hurry** es fürchterlich *or* schrecklich eilig haben.

tear: ~-jerker *n* (*inf*) Schmachtfetzen *m* (*inf*); **to be a ~-jerker** ein Schmachtfetzen sein (*inf*), auf die Tränendrüsen drücken (*inf*); **~-jerking** *adj* (*inf*) der/die/das auf die Tränendrüsen drückt (*inf*).

tearoff ['tɛərɒf] *adj sheet, form* zum Abtrennen *or* Abreißen ♦ **~ calendar** Abreißkalender *m*.

tea: ~room *n* Teestube *f*, Café *nt*; **~-rose** *n* Teerose *f*.

tear-stained ['tɪəsteɪnd] *adj face* verweint, verheult (*pej inf*), tränenverschmiert; *pillow, handkerchief* naßgeweint.

tease [ti:z] [1] *vt* **(a)** *person* necken; *animal* reizen; (*torment*) quälen; (*make fun of, because of stutter etc*) aufziehen, hänseln (*about* wegen); (*pull leg, have on*) auf den Arm nehmen (*inf*), veralbern (*inf*) ♦ **a problem to ~ your brain** ein Problem, an dem Sie sich die Zähne ausbeißen können.
(b) *see* **~ out (a).**
(c) (*raise nap on*) *cloth* kämmen.
(d) (*backcomb*) *hair* toupieren.
(e) (*ease gently*) **he ~d the red into the pocket/the rope through the crack** er manipulierte die rote Kugel ins Loch/schob das Seil geschickt durch den Spalt.
[2] *vi* **(a) give it back to her, don't ~** gib es ihr zurück und neck sie nicht. **(b)** (*joke*) Spaß machen.
[3] *n* (*inf: person*) Scherzbold *m* (*inf*) ♦ **don't be a ~, give it back to her** neck sie nicht, gib's ihr zurück; **he's a real ~** ihm sitzt der Schalk im Nacken (*hum*), er ist ein kleiner Schäker (*inf*); **she's just a ~** sie foppt einen nur.

◆**tease out** *vt sep* **(a)** *fibres* kardieren, karden; *wool* krempeln, kämmen; *flax* hecheln; *tangles* auskämmen.
(b) (*fig*) *significant factors etc* herausdestillieren ♦ **to ~ sth ~ of sth** etw aus etw herauspusseln (*inf*); **he managed to ~ the information ~ of her** er hat ihr die Auskunft abgelockt.

teasel ['ti:zl] *n* **(a)** (*Bot*) Karde *f*. **(b)** (*Tech*) Karde, Krempel *f*.

teaser ['ti:zəʳ] *n* **(a)** (*difficult question*) harte Nuß (*inf*); (*riddle*) Denksportaufgabe *f*. **(b)** (*person*) Schelm, Schäker(in *f*) (*inf*) *m* ♦ **don't be such a ~, tell me** neck mich nicht so, sag's schon; **he's a real ~** ihm sitzt der Schalk im Nacken; **she's just a ~** sie foppt einen nur.

tea: ~ service, ~ set *n* Teeservice *nt*; **~ shop** *n* Teestube *f*.

teasing ['ti:zɪŋ] [1] *adj voice, manner* neckend; (*making fun*) hänselnd.
[2] *n see vt (a)* Neckerei *f*; Reizen *nt*, Quälerei *f*; Hänselei *f*; Veralbern *nt*.

teasingly ['ti:zɪŋlɪ] *adv see adj.*

tea: ~spoon *n* **(a)** Teelöffel *m*; **(b)** (*also* **~spoonful**) Teelöffel *m* (voll); **~ strainer** *n* Teesieb *nt*.

teat [ti:t] *n* (*of animal*) Zitze *f*; (*of woman*) Brustwarze *f*; (*Brit: on baby's bottle*) (Gummi)sauger *m*.

tea: ~ table *n* **to lay the ~ table** den Tisch zum Tee/fürs Abendessen decken; **at the ~ table** beim Tee/Abendessen; **~time** *n* (*for afternoon ~*) Teestunde *f*; (*mealtime*) Abendessen *nt*; **when is ~time in your family?** wann trinkt Ihr Tee/eßt Ihr zu Abend?; **we'll talk about it at ~time** wir werden uns beim Tee/Abendessen darüber unterhalten; **I'll meet you at ~time** ich treffe Sie am späten Nachmittag; **~ towel** *n* Geschirrtuch *nt*; **~ tray** *n* Tablett, Teebrett *nt*; **~ trolley** *n* Tee- *or* Servierwagen *m*; **~ urn** *n* Teemaschine *f*; **~-wagon** *n* (*US*) Tee- *or* Servierwagen *m*.

teazel *n see* **teasel.**

tech [tek] (*Brit*) *abbr of* **technical college.**

technical ['teknɪkəl] *adj* **(a)** (*concerning technology and technique*) technisch ♦ **~ hitch** technische Schwierigkeit, technisches Problem; **~ school** Gewerbeschule, Fachschule *f*.
(b) (*of particular branch*) fachlich, Fach-; *adviser, journal, dictionary* Fach-; *problems, vocabulary* fachspezifisch; *details* formal ♦ **~ term** Fachausdruck, Terminus technicus (*geh*) *m*; **~ terminology** Fachsprache *f*; **~ question** (*Jur*) Verfahrensfrage *f*; **for ~ reasons** (*Jur*) aus verfahrenstechnischen Gründen; **the book is a bit too ~ for me** in dem Buch sind mir zu viele Fachausdrücke; **he uses very ~ language** er benutzt sehr viele Fachausdrücke; **am I getting too ~ for you?** benutze ich zu viele Fachausdrücke?; **a 2L 54, if you want to be ~** ein 2L 54, um den Fachausdruck zu gebrauchen; **that's true, if you want to be ~** das stimmt schon, wenn man's genau nimmt.

technical: ~ college *n* (*Brit*) Technische Fachschule; **~ defeat** *n* (*Mil*) rein formale Niederlage.

technicality [,teknɪ'kælɪtɪ] *n* **(a)** *no pl* **the ~ of the language/terms** die Fülle von Fachausdrücken; **avoid ~** vermeiden Sie Fachjargon; **the ~ of his style** (*complex style*) die formale Komplexität seines Stils; (*technical terms*) sein Fachjargon *m* (*pej*), seine Fachterminologie.
(b) (*technical detail, difficulty*) technische Einzelheit; (*fig, Jur*) Formsache *f* ♦ **because of a ~** auf Grund einer Formsache; **that's just a ~** das ist bloß ein Detail.

technical knockout *n* (*Boxing*) technischer K.o.

technically ['teknɪkəlɪ] *adv* **(a)** technisch. **(b)** (*concerned with specialist field*) vom Fachlichen her gesehen ♦ **he spoke very ~** er benutzte sehr viele Fachausdrücke. **(c)** (*strictly speaking*) **~ you're right** genau genommen haben Sie recht.

technical: ~ offence *n* Verstoß *m*; **~ sergeant** *n* (*US*) Oberfeldwebel *m*.

technician [tek'nɪʃən] *n* Techniker(in *f*) *m*; (*skilled worker*) Facharbeiter(in *f*) *m*.

Technicolor ® ['teknɪ,kʌləʳ] *n* Technicolor ® *nt*.

technique [tek'ni:k] *n* Technik *f*; (*method*) Methode *f*.

technocracy [tek'nɒkrəsɪ] *n* Technokratie *f*.

technocrat ['teknəʊkræt] *n* Technokrat(in *f*) *m*.

technocratic [,teknəʊ'krætɪk] *adj* technokratisch.

technological [,teknə'lɒdʒɪkəl] *adj* technologisch; *details, information* technisch.

technologist [tek'nɒlədʒɪst] *n* Technologe *m*, Technologin *f*.

technology [tek'nɒlədʒɪ] *n* Technologie *f* ♦ **the ~ of printing** die Technik des Druckens, die Drucktechnik; **University/College of T~** Technische Universität/Fachschule; **the age of ~** das technische Zeitalter, das Zeitalter der Technik; **~ transfer** Technologietransfer *m*.

technophobe ['teknəfəʊb] *n* Technikfeind *m*.

technophobic [,teknə'fəʊbɪk] *adj* technikfeindlich.

techy *adj see* **tetchy.**

tectonics [tek'tɒnɪks] *n sing* (*Geol*) Tektonik *f*.

Ted [ted] *n dim of* **Edward.**

ted [ted] *n* (*dated Brit sl*) Halbstarke(r) *m*.

tedder ['tedəʳ] *n* Heuwender *m*.

Teddy ['tedɪ] *n dim of* **Edward.**

teddy (bear) ['tedɪ(,beəʳ)] *n* Teddy(bär) *m*.

teddy boy *n* Halbstarke(r) *m*; (*referring to style of dress*) Teddy-Boy *m*.

tedious ['ti:dɪəs] *adj* langweilig, öde.

tediously ['ti:dɪəslɪ] *adv* langweilig ♦ **a ~ long journey** eine lange und langweilige Reise.

tediousness ['ti:dɪəsnɪs] *n* Lang(e)weile *f* ♦ **his ~** seine Langweiligkeit.

tedium ['ti:dɪəm] *n* Lang(e)weile *f*.

tee[1] [ti:] (*Golf*) [1] *n* Tee *nt*.
[2] *vt ball* auf das Tee legen.

◆**tee off** *vi* einen Ball vom (ersten) Abschlag spielen.

◆**tee up** [1] *vi* den Ball auf das Tee legen, aufteen (*spec*).
[2] *vt sep* auf das Tee legen.

tee[2] *n see* **T.**

tee-hee ['ti:'hi:] *interj* (*giggle*) hihi; (*snigger*) ätsch.

teem [ti:m] *vi* **(a)** (*with people, insects etc*) wimmeln (*with* von); (*with mistakes, information etc*) strotzen (*with* vor) ♦ **his mind was ~ing with ideas** in seinem Kopf wimmelte es nur so von Ideen.
(b) (*of rain: pour*) **it's ~ing (with rain)** es regnet *or* gießt (*inf*) in Strömen; **he watched the rain ~ing down** er sah zu, wie der Regen vom Himmel strömte.

teeming ['ti:mɪŋ] *adj* **(a)** *streets* von Menschen wimmelnd; *crowd* wuselnd ♦ **the world's ~ millions** die Millionen und Abermillionen von Menschen (auf der Erde). **(b)** (*pouring*) *rain* strömend.

teenage ['ti:n,eɪdʒ] *adj* Jugend-, Teenager-; *child, son* halbwüchsig.

teenaged ['ti:neɪdʒd] *adj* im Teenageralter ♦ **she is the mother of two ~ daughters** sie ist Mutter zweier Töchter im Teenageralter; **~ boy/girl** Teenager *m*.

teenager ['ti:n,eɪdʒəʳ] *n* Junge *m*/Mädchen *nt* im Teenageralter; (*esp girl*) Teenager *m* ♦ **~s** Teenager *pl*; **now that you're a ~ ...** jetzt, wo du 13 (Jahre alt) bist ...

teens [ti:nz] *npl* **(a)** Teenageralter *nt* ♦ **to be in/reach one's ~** im Teenageralter sein/ins Teenageralter kommen; **he is barely out of/still in his ~** er ist knapp über/noch keine zwanzig (Jahre alt). **(b)** (*inf: teenagers*) Teenager *pl*.

teeny-bopper ['ti:nɪ,bɒpəʳ] *n* Teenager *m*; (*girl also*) Pipimädchen *nt* (*pej inf*).

teeny(weeny) ['ti:nɪ('wi:nɪ)] *adj* (*inf*) winzig (klein), klitzeklein (*inf*) ♦ **just a ~ drop** nur ein ganz klein wenig.

tee-shirt *n see* **T-shirt.**

teeter ['ti:təʳ] *vi* **(a)** taumeln, schwanken ♦ **to ~ on the brink** *or* **edge of sth** (*lit*) am Rand von etw taumeln; (*fig*) am Rand von etw sein. **(b)** (*US: seesaw*) wippen, schaukeln.

teeterboard ['ti:tə,bɔ:d], **teeter-totter** ['ti:tə,tɒtəʳ] *n* (*US*) Wippe *f*.

teeth [ti:θ] *pl of* **tooth.**

teethe [ti:ð] *vi* zahnen.

teething ['ti:ðɪŋ] *n* Zahnen *nt*.
teething: ~ ring *n* Beißring *m*; **~ troubles** *npl (fig)* Kinderkrankheiten *pl*.
teetotal ['ti:'taʊtl] *adj person* abstinent; *party etc* ohne Alkohol ◆ **to be ~** abstinent sein, Antialkoholiker(in *f*) *m* sein.
teetotaler *n (US) see* **teetotaller**.
teetotalism ['ti:'taʊtəlɪzəm] *n* Abstinenz *f*.
teetotaller, *(US)* **teetotaler** ['ti:'taʊtlə^r] *n* Abstinenzler(in *f*), Nichttrinker(in *f*), Antialkoholiker(in *f*) *m*.
TEFL *abbr of* **Teaching (of) English as a Foreign Language**.
Teflon ® ['teflɒn] *n* Teflon ® *nt*.
tel *abbr of* **telephone (number)** Tel.
telebanking ['telɪ,bæŋkɪŋ] *n* Homebanking *nt*, Telebanking *nt*.
telecast ['telɪkɑ:st] [1] *n* Fernsehsendung *f*.
[2] *vt* im Fernsehen übertragen *or* senden.
telecaster ['telɪkɑ:stə^r] *n* Fernsehjournalist(in *f*) *m*.
telecommunications [,telɪkə,mju:nɪ'keɪʃənz] *n* **(a)** *pl* Fernmeldewesen *nt*. **(b)** *sing (science)* Fernmeldetechnik *f*.
telecommute ['telɪkəm,ju:t] *vi* Telearbeit machen.
telecommuter ['telɪkəm,ju:tə^r] *n* jd, der Telearbeit macht.
telecommuting ['telɪkəm,ju:tɪŋ] *n* Telearbeit *f*.
teleconferencing ['telɪ,kɒnfərənsɪŋ] *n* Telekonferenzschaltung *f*.
Telecopier ® ['telɪ,kɒpɪə^r] *n* Fernkopierer *m*, Telekopierer *m*.
telecopy ['telɪ,kɒpɪ] *n* Fernkopie *f*, Telekopie *f*.
telegram ['telɪgræm] [1] *n* Telegramm *nt*.
[2] *vti* telegraphieren.
telegrammatic [,telɪgrə'mætɪk] *adj* im Telegrammstil.
telegraph ['telɪgrɑ:f] [1] *n* **(a)** *(apparatus)* Telegraf *m*.
(b) *(message)* Telegramm *nt*.
[2] *vt* telegraphisch übermitteln; *message also* telegrafieren; *person* telegrafieren (+*dat*).
[3] *vi* telegrafieren.
telegraphese [,telɪgrə'fi:z] *n* Telegrammstil *m*.
telegraphic [,telɪ'græfɪk] *adj* telegrafisch; *address, style* Telegramm-.
telegraphist [tɪ'legrəfɪst] *n* Telegrafist(in *f*) *m*.
telegraph: ~ pole *n* Telegrafenmast *m or* -stange *f*; **~ wire** *n* Telegrafendraht *m or* -leitung *f*; *(under ground)* Telegrafenkabel *nt*.
telegraphy [tɪ'legrəfɪ] *n* Telegrafie *f*.
telekinesis [,telɪkɪ'ni:sɪs] *n* Telekinese *f*.
telemarketing ['telɪ'mɑ:kətɪŋ] *n* Telemarketing *nt*, Telefonverkauf *m*.
telemessage ['telɪmesɪdʒ] *n (Brit)* Telegramm *nt*.
telemeter ['telɪmi:tə^r] *n* Entfernungsmesser *m*, Telemeter *nt*.
telemetry [te'lemɪtrɪ] *n* Telemetrie, Fernmessung *f*.
teleological [telɪə'lɒdʒɪkl] *adj* teleologisch.
teleology [,telɪ'ɒlədʒɪ] *n* Teleologie *f*.
teleordering ['telɪ,ɔ:dərɪŋ] *n* Teleordern *nt*.
telepathic [,telɪ'pæθɪk] *adj* telepathisch ◆ **you must be ~!** du mußt ja ein Hellseher sein!
telepathically [,telɪ'pæθɪkəlɪ] *adv see adj*.
telepathist [tɪ'lepəθɪst] *n* Telepath(in *f*) *m*; *(believer in telepathy)* Telepathiegläubige(r) *mf*.
telepathy [tɪ'lepəθɪ] *n* Telepathie *f*.
telephone ['telɪfəʊn] [1] *n* Telefon *nt*, Fernsprecher *(form) m*; *(apparatus also)* Telefonapparat, Fernsprechapparat *(form) m* ◆ **there's somebody on the ~ for you, you're wanted on the ~** Sie werden am Telefon verlangt; **are you on the ~?, have you got a ~?** haben Sie Telefon?; *(can you be reached by ~)* sind Sie telefonisch zu erreichen?; **he's on the ~** *(is using the ~)* er telefoniert gerade; *(wants to speak to you)* er ist am Telefon; **by ~** telefonisch; **I've just been/I'll get on the ~ to him** ich habe eben mit ihm telefoniert/ich werde ihn anrufen; **we arranged it by ~** *or* **over the ~** wir haben es telefonisch vereinbart; **I heard a strange noise down the ~** ich hörte ein merkwürdiges Geräusch im Telefon.
[2] *vt* anrufen; *message, reply* telefonisch mitteilen *or* übermitteln ◆ **he ~d the news (through) to his mother/the newspaper** er rief seine Mutter an, um ihr die Nachricht mitzuteilen/er gab die Nachricht telefonisch an die Zeitung durch; **would you ~ the office to say ...** würden Sie im Büro *or* das Büro anrufen und sagen ...
[3] *vi* anrufen, telefonieren; *(make ~ call)* telefonieren ◆ **to ~ for an ambulance/a taxi** einen Krankenwagen/ein Taxi rufen.
◆**telephone back** *vti (vt: always separate) see* **phone back**.
◆**telephone in** *vti see* **phone in**.
telephone *in cpds* Telefon-, Fernsprech- *(form)*; **~-book** *n see* **~ directory**; **~ booth** *or* **box** *n* Telefonzelle, Fernsprechzelle *f*; **~ call** *n* Telefongespräch *nt*, Telefonanruf *m*; **~ directory** *n* Telefonbuch, Fernsprechbuch *nt*; **~ exchange** *n* Fernsprechamt *nt*, Vermittlungsstelle *f (form)*; **~ kiosk** *n* Telefonzelle, Sprechzelle *(form) f*; **~ line** *n* Fernsprechleitung, (Telefon)leitung *f*; **~ message** *n* telefonische Nachricht; **~ number** *n* Telefonnummer, Rufnummer *(form)*, Fernsprechnummer *(form) f*; **~ operator** *n (esp US)* Telefonist(in *f*) *m*; **~ sex** *n* Telefonsex *m*; **~ sex line** Telefonsexdienst *m*.
telephonic [,telɪ'fɒnɪk] *adj* telefonisch, Telefon-.
telephonically [telɪ'fɒnɪkəlɪ] *adv* fernsprechtechnisch; *(by telephone)* telefonisch.
telephonist [tɪ'lefənɪst] *n* Telefonist(in *f*) *m*.
telephony [tɪ'lefənɪ] *n* Fernsprechwesen *nt*.
telephotograph [,telɪ'fəʊtəgrɑ:f] *n (Telec)* durch Bildtelegrafie übertragenes Foto.
telephoto (lens) ['telɪ,fəʊtəʊ('lenz)] *n* Teleobjektiv *nt*.
teleport ['telɪpɔ:t] *vt (Sci-Fi)* teleportieren.
teleprinter ['telɪ,prɪntə^r] *n* Fernschreiber *m*.
teleprompter ® ['telɪ,prɒmptə^r] *n* Teleprompter *m*.
telerecord [,telɪrɪ'kɔ:d] *vt* fürs Fernsehen aufzeichnen.
telerecording [,telɪrɪ'kɔ:dɪŋ] *n* Fernsehaufzeichnung *f*.
telesales ['telɪseɪlz] *n sing or pl* Telefonverkauf *m*, Verkauf *m* per Telefon.
telescope ['telɪskəʊp] [1] *n* Teleskop, Fernrohr *nt*.
[2] *vi (also* **~ together***)* *(train carriages)* sich ineinanderschieben; *(aerial, umbrella)* sich ineinanderschieben lassen.
[3] *vt (also* **~ together***)* ineinanderschieben; *umbrella, aerial* zusammenschieben; *(fig)* komprimieren.
telescopic [,telɪ'skɒpɪk] *adj aerial etc* ausziehbar, zusammenschiebbar; *view* teleskopisch ◆ **~ lens** Fernrohrlinse *f*; **~ sight** Zielfernrohr *nt*; **~ umbrella** Taschenschirm, Knirps ® *m*.
teletext ['telɪtekst] *n* Videotext *m*.
telethon ['telɪ,θɒn] *n sehr lange Fernsehsendung, in deren Verlauf Spenden für wohltätige Zwecke gesammelt werden*, Fernseh-Spendenaktion *f*.
teletype ® ['telɪtaɪp] *n (US) (apparatus)* Fernschreiber *m*; *(message)* Fernschreiben, Telex *nt*.
teletypewriter [,telɪ'taɪpraɪtə^r] *n (US)* Fernschreiber *m*.
televise ['telɪvaɪz] *vt* (im Fernsehen) senden *or* übertragen ◆ **~d debate** Fernsehdebatte *f*.
television ['telɪ,vɪʒən] *n* Fernsehen *nt*; *(set)* Fernseher, Fernsehapparat *m* ◆ **to watch ~** fernsehen; **to be on ~** im Fernsehen kommen; **have you ever been on ~?** bist du schon einmal im Fernsehen gewesen?; **what's on ~ tonight?** was gibt es heute abend im Fernsehen?; **jobs in ~** Stellen *pl* beim Fernsehen.
television *in cpds* Fernseh-; **~ camera** *n* Fernsehkamera *f*; **~ personality** *n* bekannte Fernsehpersönlichkeit; **~ rights** *npl* Übertragungsrechte, Fernsehrechte *pl*; **~ screen** *n* Bildschirm *m*, Mattscheibe *f (inf)*; **~ set** *n* Fernsehapparat *m*, Fernsehgerät *nt*, Fernseher *m*; **~ studio** *n* Fernsehstudio *nt*; **~ viewer** *n* Fernsehzuschauer(in *f*) *m*.
televisual [,telɪ'vɪʒjʊəl] *adj* Fernseh-, TV-.
telework ['telɪwɜ:k] *vi* Telearbeit machen.
teleworker ['telɪ,wɜ:kə^r] *n* Telearbeiter(in) *m(f)*.
telex ['teleks] [1] *n* Telex *nt*; *(message also)* Fernschreiben *nt*; *(machine also)* Fernschreiber *m*.
[2] *vt message* telexen, per Fernschreiben *or* Telex mitteilen; *person* ein Fernschreiben *or* Telex schicken (+*dat*).
tell [tel] *pret, ptp* **told** [1] *vt* **(a)** *(relate) story, experiences, adventures* erzählen *(sb sth, sth to sb* jdm etw *acc)*; *(inform, say, announce)* sagen *(sb sth* jdm etw *acc)* ◆ **to ~ lies/tales/fortunes** lügen/petzen *(inf)*/wahrsagen; **to ~ sb's fortune** jdm wahrsagen *or* die Zukunft deuten; **to ~ the future** wahrsagen, die Zukunft deuten; **to ~ sb a secret** jdm ein Geheimnis anvertrauen *or (give away)* verraten; **to ~ sb about** *or* **of sth** jdm von etw erzählen; **I told my friend/boss about what had happened** ich erzählte meinem Freund/berichtete meinem Chef, was geschehen war; **... or so I've been told** ... so hat man es mir jedenfalls gesagt *or* erzählt; **I can't ~ you how pleased I am** ich kann Ihnen gar nicht sagen, wie sehr ich mich freue; **you can't ~ her anything** *(she can't keep a secret)* man kann ihr (aber auch) nichts sagen *or* anvertrauen; *(she's a know-all)* sie läßt sich *(dat)* nichts sagen; **to ~ sb the way** jdm den Weg sagen; **could you ~ me the way to the station, please?** könn(t)en Sir mir bitte sagen, wie ich zum Bahnhof komme?; **don't let me have to ~ you that again** ich will dir das nicht noch einmal sagen müssen; **(I'll) ~ you what, let's go to the cinema** weißt du was, gehen wir doch ins Kino!; **don't~ me you can't come!** sagen Sie bloß nicht, daß Sie nicht kommen können!; **I won't do it, I ~ you!** und ich sage dir, das mache ich nicht!; **let me ~ you that ...** ich kann Ihnen sagen, daß ..., lassen Sie sich von mir sagen, daß ...; **it was cold, I can ~ you** ich kann dir sagen, das war vielleicht kalt!; **I told you so** ich habe es (dir) ja gesagt; **~ me another!** nicht möglich!, wer's glaubt! *(inf)*; **that ~s me all I need to know** das sagt mir alles; **that ~s me a lot** das sagt mir allerlei; **no words could ~ how sad she was** es läßt sich nicht mit Worten sagen, wie traurig sie war.
(b) *(distinguish, discern)* erkennen ◆ **to ~ the time** die Uhr kennen; **to ~ the time by the sun** die Zeit an der Sonne ablesen; **to ~ the difference** den Unterschied sehen/fühlen/schmecken *etc*; **you can ~ that he's clever/getting worried** man sieht *or* merkt, daß er intelligent ist/sich Sorgen macht; **we couldn't ~ much from his letter** wir konnten aus seinem Brief nicht viel entnehmen; **you can't ~ whether it's moving** man kann nicht sagen *or* sehen, ob es sich bewegt; **to ~ sb/sth by sth** jdn/etw an etw *(dat)* erkennen; **I can't ~ butter from margarine** ich kann Butter nicht von Margarine unterscheiden; **to ~ right from wrong** wissen, was Recht und Unrecht ist, Recht von Unrecht unterscheiden; *see* **apart**.
(c) *(know, be sure)* wissen ◆ **how can/could I ~ that?** wie soll ich das wissen?/wie hätte ich das wissen können?; **how can I ~ that/whether he will do it?** wie kann ich sicher sein, daß er es tut?/wie kann ich sagen *or* wissen, ob er es tut?
(d) *(order)* sagen *(sb* jdm*)* ◆ **we were told to bring sandwiches with us** es wurde uns gesagt, daß wir belegte Brote mitbringen sollten; **~ him to stop singing** sagen Sie ihm, er soll aufhören zu singen; **don't you ~ me what to do!** Sie haben mir nicht zu sagen, was ich tun soll!; **I told you not to do that** ich habe dir doch gesagt, du sollst das nicht tun!; **do as** *or* **what you are told!** tu, was man dir sagt!

(e) (*old: count*) to ~ **one's beads** den Rosenkranz beten.

2 *vi +indir obj* es sagen (*+dat*) ◆ **I won't ~ you again** ich sage es dir nicht noch einmal; **you know what? — don't ~ me, let me guess** weißt du was? — sag's mir nicht, laß mich raten; **she wouldn't be told** sie hat sich (ja) nichts sagen lassen; **you're ~ing me!** das kann man wohl sagen!, wem sagen Sie das!

3 *vi* (a) (*discern, be sure*) wissen ◆ **who can ~?** wer weiß?; **how can I ~?** (*how should I know*) woher soll ich das wissen?; **how will I be able to ~?** wie kann ich das erkennen *or* wissen?; **no-one can/could ~** niemand kann/konnte das sagen, das weiß/wußte keiner; **you never can ~, you can never ~** man kann nie wissen.

(b) (*talk, ~ tales of*) sprechen ◆ **his face told of his sorrow** aus seinem Gesicht sprach Kummer; **that would be ~ing!** das kann ich nicht verraten; **promise you won't ~** du mußt versprechen, daß du nichts sagst; **more than words can ~** mehr als man mit Worten ausdrücken kann.

(c) (*have effect*) sich bemerkbar machen ◆ **his age told against him** (*in applying for job*) sein Alter war ein Nachteil für ihn; (*in competition*) sein Alter machte sich bemerkbar; **character always ~s in the end** zum Schluß schlägt doch die Veranlagung durch; **a boxer who makes every punch ~** ein Boxer, bei dem jeder Schlag sitzt.

◆**tell off** *vt sep* (a) (*inf: scold*) ausschimpfen, schelten (*for* wegen) ◆ **he told me ~ for being late** er schimpfte (mich aus), weil ich zu spät kam. (b) (*Mil etc*) abkommandieren (*for* zu).

◆**tell on** *vi +prep obj* (a) (*inf: inform on*) verpetzen (*inf*). (b) (*have a bad effect on*) sich bemerkbar machen bei.

teller ['teləʳ] *n* (a) (*in bank*) Kassierer(in *f*) *m*. (b) (*vote counter*) Stimmenauszähler(in *f*) *m*. (c) (*of story*) Erzähler(in *f*) *m*.

telling ['telɪŋ] 1 *adj* (*effective*) wirkungsvoll; *argument also* schlagend; *blow* (*lit, fig*) empfindlich; (*revealing*) aufschlußreich; *blush* verräterisch.

2 *n* (a) (*narration*) Erzählen *nt* ◆ **it loses in the ~** das kann man gar nicht so schön erzählen.

(b) **there is no ~ what he may do** man kann nicht sagen *or* wissen, was er tut; **there's no ~** das läßt sich nicht sagen; **there's never any ~ with him** bei ihm läßt sich das nie sagen.

telling-off ['telɪŋ'ɒf] *n* (*inf*) Standpauke *f* (*inf*) ◆ **to give sb a good ~** jdn kräftig ausschimpfen, jdm eine (kräftige) Standpauke halten (*inf*); **to get a good ~** kräftig ausgeschimpft werden, eine Standpauke bekommen (*inf*).

telltale ['telteɪl] 1 *n* (a) Petzer *m*, Petze *f*. (b) (*Tech*) Kontrollicht *nt*, Kontrollampe *f*.

2 *adj attr* verräterisch.

tellurium [te'lʊərɪəm] *n* (*Chem*) Tellur *nt*.

telly ['telɪ] *n* (*Brit inf*) Fernseher *m*, Glotze *f* (*inf*) ◆ **on ~** im Fernsehen; **to watch ~** fernsehen; *see also* **television**.

temerity [tɪ'merɪtɪ] *n* Kühnheit, Unerhörtheit (*pej*) *f*.

temp[1] *abbr of* (a) **temporary**. (b) **temperature** Temp.

temp[2] [temp] (*Brit*) 1 *n* Aushilfskraft *m*.

2 *vi* als Aushilfskraft arbeiten.

temper ['tempəʳ] 1 *n* (a) (*disposition*) Wesen, Naturell *nt*; (*angry mood*) Wut *f* ◆ **~ tantrum** Wutanfall *m*; **to be in a ~/good/bad ~** wütend sein/guter/schlechter Laune sein; **she's got a quick/terrible/foul/vicious ~** sie kann sehr jähzornig sein/unangenehm/ausfallend/tückisch werden; **what a ~ that child has!** was dieses Kind für Wutanfälle hat!; **to be in a ~/bad ~ with sb** auf jdn wütend sein; **to lose one's ~** die Beherrschung verlieren (*with sb* bei jdm); **to keep one's ~** sich beherrschen (*with sb* bei jdm); **~, ~!** aber, aber, wer wird denn gleich so zornig werden!; **to fly into a ~** einen Wutanfall bekommen, in die Luft gehen (*inf*); **a fit of ~** ein Wutanfall *m*; **to put sb into a ~, to get sb's ~ up** jdn zur Weißglut bringen, jdn wütend machen; **he has quite a ~** er kann ziemlich aufbrausen; **to be out of ~** (*old*) verstimmt *or* übel gelaunt sein.

(b) (*of metal*) Härte(grad *m*) *f*.

2 *vt* (a) *metal* tempern. (b) (*old: Mus*) temperieren (*old*). (c) (*fig*) *action, passion* mäßigen; *criticism* mildern ◆ **to ~ justice with mercy** bei aller Gerechtigkeit Milde walten lassen.

tempera ['tempərə] *n* Temperafarbe *f* ◆ **to paint in ~** in Tempera malen.

temperament ['tempərəmənt] *n* (a) (*disposition*) Veranlagung *f*; (*of race*) Temperament *nt* ◆ **his ~ isn't suited to that job** er ist von seiner Veranlagung her nicht für diese Stelle geeignet; **he has an artistic ~** er ist eine Künstlernatur; **their ~s are quite different** sie sind völlig unterschiedlich veranlagt; **he has a happy ~** er hat ein fröhliches Wesen *or* Naturell.

(b) (*no art: temper, excitability*) Temperament *nt*.

temperamental [,tempərə'mentl] *adj* (a) temperamentvoll, launenhaft (*pej*). (b) *machine, car* launisch (*hum*) ◆ **to be ~** Mucken haben (*inf*), launisch sein (*hum*). (c) (*caused by temperament*) *inability, unsuitability* veranlagungsmäßig; *laziness etc* angeboren.

temperamentally [,temprə'mentəlɪ] *adv* (a) *behave etc* temperamentvoll, launenhaft (*pej*). (b) (*of machine, car*) launisch (*hum*). (c) (*as regards disposition*) charakterlich, veranlagungsmäßig.

temperance ['tempərəns] *n* (a) (*moderation*) Mäßigung *f*; (*in speech etc also*) Zurückhaltung *f*; (*in eating, drinking also*) Maßhalten *nt*. (b) (*teetotalism*) Enthaltsamkeit, Abstinenz *f*.

temperance: ~ hotel *n* alkoholfreies Hotel; **~ movement** *n* Temperenzler- *or* Temperenzbewegung *f*; **~ society** *n* Temperenzverein *m* *or* -gesellschaft *f*.

temperate ['tempərɪt] *adj* (a) *person, language* gemäßigt; (*in eating, demands*) maßvoll. (b) *climate, zone* gemäßigt.

temperature ['temprɪtʃəʳ] *n* Temperatur *f*; (*Med: above normal ~ also*) Fieber *nt* ◆ **water boils at a ~ of 100°C** Wasser kocht bei einer Temperatur von 100°C; **to take sb's ~** jds Temperatur messen, bei jdm Fieber messen; **he has a ~ /a slight/high ~** er hat Fieber/erhöhte Temperatur/hohes Fieber; **his ~ is high, he's running a high ~** er hat hohes Fieber; **he has a ~ of 39°C** er hat 39° Fieber.

temperature chart *n* (*Med*) Fiebertabelle *f*; (*curve of graph*) Fieberkurve *f*.

tempered ['tempəd] *adj steel* gehärtet, Temper- (*spec*).

-tempered *adj suf* -gelaunt; (*Mus*) temperiert.

tempest ['tempɪst] *n* (*liter*) Sturm *m* (*also fig*), Unwetter *nt*.

tempestuous [,tem'pestjʊəs] *adj* (a) (*lit liter*) *winds* stürmisch; *sea also* tobend, aufgewühlt. (b) (*fig*) stürmisch; *argument, rage* heftig; *speech* leidenschaftlich.

tempestuously [,tem'pestjʊəslɪ] *adv* (*lit liter, fig*) heftig.

tempestuousness [,tem'pestjʊəsnɪs] *n* (*lit liter, fig*) Heftigkeit *f*; (*of sea*) Aufgewühltheit *f*.

Templar ['templəʳ] *n* (*also* **Knight ~**) Tempelherr, Templer *m*.

template, templet ['templɪt] *n* Schablone *f*.

temple[1] ['templ] *n* (*Rel*) Tempel *m*.

temple[2] *n* (*Anat*) Schläfe *f*.

templet *n see* **template**.

tempo ['tempəʊ] *n* (*Mus, fig*) Tempo *nt*.

temporal ['tempərəl] *adj* (a) zeitlich; (*Gram*) Zeit-, temporal. (b) (*Rel*) weltlich. (c) (*Anat*) Schläfen-.

temporarily ['tempərərɪlɪ] *adv* vorübergehend, für einige Zeit.

temporariness ['tempərərɪnɪs] *n* vorübergehender Charakter ◆ **because of the ~ of her home ...** weil es nur vorübergehend ihr Zuhause war ...

temporary ['tempərərɪ] 1 *adj* vorübergehend; *job also* für kurze Zeit, befristet; *arrangement also, method, building, road surface* provisorisch; *powers also* zeitweilig, befristet ◆ **our new secretary is only ~** unsere neue Sekretärin ist nur vorübergehend *or* für einige Zeit hier; **I'm only here for a ~ stay** ich bin nur für kurze Zeit hier; **~ injunction** (*Jur*) einstweilige Verfügung.

2 *n* Aushilfe, Aushilfskraft *f*.

temporize ['tempəraɪz] *vi* (*delay*) ausweichen (um Zeit zu gewinnen), Verzögerungstaktiken anwenden ◆ **to ~ with sb** jdn hinhalten.

temporizer ['tempəraɪzəʳ] *n* Verzögerungstaktiker *m*.

tempt [tem*p*t] *vt* (a) in Versuchung führen; (*successfully*) verführen, verleiten ◆ **to ~ sb to do** *or* **into doing sth** jdn dazu verleiten *or* verführen *or* dazu bringen, etw zu tun; **don't ~ me** bring *or* führ mich nicht in Versuchung!; **one is ~ed to believe that ...** man möchte fast glauben, daß ...; **I am very ~ed to accept** ich bin sehr versucht anzunehmen; **try and ~ her to eat a little** versuchen Sie, ob Sie sie nicht dazu bringen können, etwas zu essen; **may I ~ you to a little more wine?** kann ich Sie noch zu etwas Wein überreden?; **are you sure you won't come? — go on, ~ me/no, I won't be ~ed!** willst du bestimmt nicht mitkommen? — wenn du so weitermachst, kriegst du mich vielleicht doch noch herum (*inf*)/nein, ich bleibe hart; **to ~ fate** *or* **providence** (*fig*) sein Schicksal herausfordern; (*in words*) den Teufel an die Wand malen.

(b) (*Rel*) versuchen, in Versuchung führen ◆ **the devil ~s us to evil** der Teufel führt uns in Versuchung.

temptation [tem*p*'teɪʃən] *n* Versuchung (*also Rel*), Verlockung *f* ◆ **to put ~ in sb's way** jdn in Versuchung führen; **lead us not into ~** (*Bibl*) führe uns nicht in Versuchung (*Bibl*); **to yield** *or* **give way to ~** der Versuchung erliegen.

tempter ['tem*p*təʳ] *n* Versucher, Verführer *m* ◆ **the T~** (*Rel*) der Versucher.

tempting *adj*, **~ly** *adv* ['tem*p*tɪŋ, -lɪ] verlockend, verführerisch.

temptress ['tem*p*trɪs] *n* Verführerin *f*.

ten [ten] 1 *adj* zehn ◆ **the T~ Commandments** die Zehn Gebote; **~ to one he won't come** (ich wette) zehn gegen *or* zu eins, daß er nicht kommt; **nine out of ~ people would agree with you** neun von zehn Leuten würden Ihnen zustimmen; **a packet of ~ (cigarettes)** eine Zehnerpackung (Zigaretten).

2 *n* Zehn *f* ◆ **~s** (*Math*) Zehner *pl*; **to count in ~s** in Zehnern zählen; **you can only buy them in ~s** man kann sie nur in Zehnerpackungen kaufen; *see also* **six**.

tenability [,tenə'bɪlɪtɪ] *n see adj (a)* Haltbarkeit *f*; Vertretbarkeit *f*.

tenable ['tenəbl] *adj* (a) (*Mil*) *position* haltbar; (*fig*) *opinion, theory also* vertretbar. (b) *pred* **a post ~ for two years/for life** eine auf zwei Jahre befristete Stelle/eine Lebensstellung, eine Stelle auf Lebenszeit.

tenacious [tɪ'neɪʃəs] *adj* zäh, hartnäckig; *character, person also* beharrlich; *memory* unschlagbar ◆ **he was ~ in the defence of his principles** er verteidigte hartnäckig *or* zäh *or* eisern seine Prinzipien; **inflation/the disease had a ~ hold on ...** die Inflation/Seuche hielt ... in eisernem Griff; **to be ~ of sth** (*form*) zäh an etw (*dat*) festhalten.

tenaciously [tɪ'neɪʃəslɪ] *adv* zäh, hartnäckig ◆ **she held ~ to her principles** sie hielt zäh an ihren Prinzipien fest; **the dog held on ~ to the bone** der Hund hielt den Knochen zäh fest; **he clung ~ to life** er hielt zäh am Leben fest.

tenacity [tɪ'næsɪtɪ] *n see adj* Zähigkeit, Hartnäckigkeit *f*, Beharrlichkeit *f* ◆ **the ~ of his grip** sein eiserner Griff.

tenancy ['tenənsɪ] *n* **right/conditions/problems of ~** Mietrecht *nt*/-bedingungen *pl*/-probleme *pl*; (*of farm*) Pachtrecht *nt*/-bedingungen *pl*/-probleme *pl*; **during his ~** während er (dort) Mieter/Pächter ist/war; **period of ~** Dauer *f* des Miet-/Pachtverhältnisses.

tenant ['tenənt] 1 *n* Mieter(in *f*) *m*; (*of farm*) Pächter(in *f*) *m* ◆ **~ farmer** Pächter *m*.

[2] *vt (form) house* zur Miete wohnen in (*+dat*); *premises* gemietet haben; *farm* in Pacht haben.

tenantry ['tenəntrɪ] *n, no pl (of estate)* Pächter *pl*; *(of building, premises)* Mieter *pl* ◆ **the law of ~** das Mietrecht; *(of farm)* das Pachtrecht.

tend[1] [tend] *vt* sich kümmern um; *sheep* hüten; *sick person* pflegen; *land* bestellen; *machine* bedienen.

tend[2] *vi* **(a) to ~ to be/do sth** *(have a habit of being/doing sth)* gewöhnlich *or* gern etw sein/tun, die Tendenz haben, etw zu sein/tun; *(person also)* dazu neigen *or* tendieren, etw zu sein/tun; **the lever ~s to stick** der Hebel bleibt oft hängen; **I ~ to believe him** ich neige *or* tendiere dazu, ihm zu glauben; **that would ~ to suggest that ...** das würde gewissermaßen darauf hindeuten, daß ...

(b) to ~ towards *(be directed, lead) (line)* führen *or* streben *(geh)* nach; *(measures, actions etc)* führen zu, anstreben; *(incline) (person, views, designs etc)* neigen *or* tendieren *or* eine Tendenz haben zu; *(prices, colours)* tendieren *or* eine Tendenz haben zu; **prices are ~ing upwards** die Preise tendieren nach oben *or* haben eine steigende Tendenz; **his opinion is ~ing in our direction** seine Meinung tendiert in unsere Richtung.

tendency ['tendənsɪ] *n* Tendenz *f (geh)*; *(physical predisposition)* Neigung *f* ◆ **artistic tendencies** künstlerische Neigungen *pl*; **to have a ~ to be/do sth** gern *or* gewöhnlich etw sein/tun; *(person, style of writing also)* dazu neigen *or* tendieren, etw zu sein/zu tun; **he had an annoying ~ to forget things** er hatte die ärgerliche Angewohnheit, alles zu vergessen; **there is a ~ for business to improve in autumn** gewöhnlich nehmen die Geschäfte im Herbst einen Aufschwung; **a strong upward ~** *(St Ex)* eine stark steigende Tendenz.

tendentious *adj*, **~ly** *adv* [ten'denʃəs, -lɪ] tendenziös.

tendentiousness [ten'denʃəsnɪs] *n* tendenziöse Färbung.

tender[1] ['tendəʳ] *n* **(a)** Hüter(in *f*) *m*; *(of sick person)* Pfleger(in *f*) *m* ◆ **machine ~** Maschinenwart *m*. **(b)** *(Naut, Rail)* Tender *m*.

tender[2] [1] *vt money, services* (an)bieten, geben; *thanks* aussprechen; *resignation* einreichen ◆ **"please ~ exact fare"** „bitte Fahrgeld abgezählt bereithalten".

[2] *vi (Comm)* sich bewerben *(for* um).

[3] *n* **(a)** *(Comm)* Angebot *nt* ◆ **to invite ~s for a job** Angebote *pl* für eine Arbeit einholen; **to put work out to ~** Arbeiten ausschreiben; **to put in a ~ for sth** ein Angebot *or* eine Submissionsofferte *(form)* für etw machen *or* einreichen; **~ documents** Ausschreibungsunterlagen *pl*; **~ price** Angebotspreis *m*; **call for ~** Ausschreibung *f*.

(b) *(Fin)* **legal ~** gesetzliches Zahlungsmittel.

tender[3] *adj* **(a)** *(sore, easily hurt) spot, bruise* empfindlich; *skin, plant also* zart; *(fig) subject* heikel ◆ **of ~ years/age** im zarten Alter; **my arm still feels ~** mein Arm ist noch sehr empfindlich; **she is a ~ plant** *(fig)* sie ist ein zartes Pflänzchen.

(b) *meat* zart.

(c) *(affectionate) person, voice, look* zärtlich, liebevoll; *memories* lieb, zärtlich; *heart* gut ◆ **to bid sb a ~ farewell** liebevoll(en) *or* zärtlich(en) Abschied von jdm nehmen; **in sb's ~ care** in jds Obhut; **to leave sb to sb's ~ mercies** *(iro)* jdn jds liebevollen Händen anvertrauen.

tender: ~foot *n* Neuling *m*; **~-hearted** *adj* gutherzig; **~-heartedness** *n* Gutherzigkeit *f*.

tenderize ['tendəraɪz] *vt meat* zart *or* weich machen; *(by beating)* klopfen.

tenderizer ['tendəraɪzəʳ] *n* Mürbesalz *nt*; *(hammer)* Fleischklopfer *m*.

tenderloin ['tendə,lɔɪn] *n* Lendenstück *nt*.

tenderly ['tendəlɪ] *adv* zärtlich, liebevoll.

tenderness ['tendənɪs] *n see adj* **(a)** Empfindlichkeit *f*; Zartheit *f*. **(b)** Zartheit *f*. **(c)** Zärtlichkeit *f*; Güte *f*.

tendon ['tendən] *n* Sehne *f*.

tendril ['tendrɪl] *n* Ranke *f*; *(of hair)* Ringellocke *f*.

tenement ['tenɪmənt] *n* **(a)** *(also* **~ house***)* Mietshaus *nt*, Mietskaserne *f (pej)*. **(b)** *(Jur)* Mietbesitz *m*; *(farm)* Pachtbesitz *m*.

Tenerife [,tenə'ri:f] *n* Teneriffa *nt*.

tenet ['tenət] *n* Lehrsatz *m*; *(Rel)* Glaubenssatz *m*.

tenfold ['tenfəʊld] [1] *adj* zehnfach.

[2] *adv* zehnfach, um das Zehnfache ◆ **increase ~** sich verzehnfachen.

ten-gallon hat ['tengæln'hæt] *n* Cowboyhut *m*.

tenish ['tenɪʃ] *adj* (so) um zehn herum *(inf)*.

tenner ['tenəʳ] *n (inf)* Zehner *m (inf)*.

tennis ['tenɪs] *n* Tennis *nt*.

tennis *in cpds* Tennis-; **~ club** *n* Tennisclub *or* -verein *m*; **~ court** *n* Tennisplatz *m*; **~ elbow** *n (Med)* Tennisarm *m*; **~ racket, ~ racquet** *n* Tennisschläger *m*.

tenon ['tenən] *n* Zapfen *m* ◆ **~ joint** Zapfenverbindung *f*; **~ saw** Zapfenschneidsäge *f*.

tenor ['tenəʳ] [1] *n* **(a)** *(voice)* Tenor(stimme *f*) *m*; *(person)* Tenor *m*. **(b)** *(purport)* Tenor *m*; *(of theory)* Tendenz *f*; *(general nature) (of life)* Stil *m*; *(of events)* (Ver)lauf *m*.

[2] *adj (Mus) part, voice* Tenor-.

ten: ~pence *n* zehn Pence; *(also* **~penny piece***)* Zehnpencestück *nt*; **~pin bowling**, *(US)* **~pins** *n* Bowling *nt*.

tense[1] [tens] *n (Gram)* Zeit *f*, Tempus *nt* ◆ **present/past/future ~** Gegenwart *f*/Vergangenheit *f*/Zukunft *f*.

tense[2] [1] *adj (+er) rope* gespannt, straff; *muscles* (an)gespannt; *person, expression, bearing (through stress, worry etc)* angespannt; *(through nervousness, fear etc)* verkrampft; *voice* nervös; *silence, atmosphere* gespannt; *(thrilling) scene* spannungsgeladen ◆ **~ headache** Spannungskopfschmerz *m*; **I've been feeling rather ~ all day** ich bin schon den ganzen Tag so nervös; **in a voice ~ with emotion** mit erregter Stimme; **things are getting rather ~** die Lage wird gespannter.

[2] *vt* anspannen.

[3] *vi* sich (an)spannen, sich straffen.

◆**tense up** [1] *vi (person, muscle)* sich anspannen.

[2] *vt sep muscle* anspannen.

tensely ['tenslɪ] *adv (lit) stretch* straff; *(fig) listen* angespannt; *speak, wait (nervously)* nervös; *(excitedly)* gespannt.

tenseness ['tensnɪs] *n see adj* Gespanntheit, Straffheit *f*; (An)gespanntheit *f*; Angespanntheit *f*; Verkrampftheit *f*; Nervosität *f*; Spannung(sgeladenheit) *f*.

tensile ['tensaɪl] *adj* dehnbar, spannbar ◆ **~ strength** *or* **stress** Zugfestigkeit *f*.

tension ['tenʃən] *n* **(a)** *(lit)* Spannung *f*; *(of muscle)* Anspannung *f*; *(Knitting)* Festigkeit *f*; *(Sew)* Spannung *f* ◆ **to check the ~** *(Knitting)* eine Maschenprobe machen. **(b)** *(nervous strain)* nervliche Belastung, Anspannung *f*. **(c)** *(in relationship)* Spannungen *pl*.

tensor (muscle) ['tensɔ:ʳ-] *n* Tensor *m*.

tenspot ['tenspɒt] *n (US sl)* Zehner *m (inf)*.

tent [tent] *n* Zelt *nt* ◆ **~ peg** Zeltpflock, Hering *m*; **~ pole** Zeltstange *f*.

tentacle ['tentəkl] *n (Zool)* Tentakel *m or nt (spec)*; *(of octopus etc also)* Fangarm *m*; *(of snail also)* Fühler *m*; *(fig)* Klaue *f*.

tentative ['tentətɪv] *adj (not definite, provisional)* vorläufig; *offer* unverbindlich; *(hesitant) player, movement* vorsichtig; *conclusion, suggestion* vorsichtig, zögernd ◆ **this proposal** *or* **suggestion is only ~** das ist ja nur ein Vorschlag; **we've a ~ arrangement to play tennis tonight** wir haben halb abgemacht, heute abend Tennis zu spielen.

tentatively ['tentətɪvlɪ] *adv see adj* ◆ **he ~ suggested a weekend in Brighton** er machte den Vorschlag, eventuell ein Wochenende in Brighton zu verbringen.

tenterhooks ['tentəhʊks] *npl*: **to be on ~** wie auf glühenden Kohlen sitzen *(inf)*; **to keep sb on ~** jdn zappeln lassen.

tenth [tenθ] [1] *adj (in series)* zehnte(r, s) ◆ **a ~ part** ein Zehntel *nt*.

[2] *n (fraction)* Zehntel *nt*; *(in series)* Zehnte(r, s); *(Mus)* Dezime *f*; *see also* **sixth**.

tenthly ['tenθlɪ] *adv* zehntens.

tenuity [te'njʊɪtɪ] *n (liter) see* **tenuousness**.

tenuous ['tenjʊəs] *adj* **(a)** *(lit) thread* dünn, fein; *cobweb* zart, fein; *air* dünn; *gas* flüchtig. **(b)** *(fig) connection* schwach; *argument, evidence also* wenig stichhaltig ◆ **he kept a ~ grip on life** er hatte nur noch einen schwachen Lebenswillen.

tenuousness ['tenjʊəsnɪs] *n see adj* **(a)** Dünne, Feinheit *f*; Zartheit, Feinheit *f*; Dünne *f*; Flüchtigkeit *f*. **(b)** Schwäche *f*; mangelnde Stichhaltigkeit.

tenure ['tenjʊəʳ] *n* **(a)** *(holding of office)* Anstellung *f*; *(period of office)* Amtszeit *f*. **(b)** *(of property)* **during his ~ of the house/farm** während er das Haus/die Farm innehat(te) *(geh)*; **laws governing land ~** Landpachtgesetze *pl*.

tepee ['ti:pi:] *n* Tipi *nt*.

tepid ['tepɪd] *adj (lit, fig)* lau(warm).

tepidity [te'pɪdɪtɪ], **tepidness** ['tepɪdnɪs] *n (lit, fig)* Lauheit *f*.

tercentenary [,tɜ:sen'ti:nərɪ] [1] *n (anniversary)* dreihundertster Jahrestag; *(celebration)* Dreihundertjahrfeier *f*, dreihundertjähriges Jubiläum.

[2] *attr* für den dreihundertsten Jahrestag; *celebrations also* Dreihundertjahr-.

tercet ['tɜ:sɪt] *n (Poet)* Terzine *f*; *(Mus)* Triole *f*.

tergiversate ['tɜ:dʒɪvəseɪt] *vi (form, hum)* dauernd seine Gesinnung ändern.

tergiversation [,tɜ:dʒɪvə'seɪʃən] *n usu pl (form, hum)* (ständiger) Gesinnungswandel *no pl*.

term [tɜ:m] [1] *n* **(a)** *(period of time)* Dauer *f*, Zeitraum *m*; *(of contract)* Laufzeit *f*; *(limit)* Frist *f* ◆ **~ of government/office** Regierungszeit *f*/Amtsdauer *or* -zeit *f*; **~ of imprisonment** Gefängnisstrafe *f*; **~ of service** *(Mil)* Militärdienst(zeit *f*) *m*; **to put** *or* **set a ~ (of three years) to sth** etw (auf drei Jahre) befristen; **elected for a three-year ~** auf *or* für drei Jahre gewählt; **the contract is nearing its ~** der Vertrag läuft bald ab; **in the long/short ~** auf lange/kurze Sicht; **at ~** *(Fin)* bei Fälligkeit; *(Med)* zur rechten Zeit; **~ insurance** (zeitlich) befristete Versicherung; **~ money** Festgeld *nt*.

(b) *(Sch) (three in one year)* Trimester *nt*; *(four in one year)* Vierteljahr, Quartal *nt*; *(two in one year)* Halbjahr *nt*; *(Univ)* Semester *nt* ◆ **end-of-~ exam** Examen *nt* am Ende eines Trimesters *etc*; **during** *or* **in ~(-time)** während der Schulzeit; *(Univ)* während des Semesters; **out of ~(-time)** in den Ferien.

(c) *(expression)* Ausdruck *m* ◆ **in simple ~s** in einfachen Worten; **a legal ~** ein juristischer (Fach)ausdruck *or* Terminus *(geh)*; **he spoke of her in the most flattering ~s** er äußerte sich sehr schmeichelhaft über sie; **a contradiction in ~s** ein Widerspruch in sich.

(d) *(Math, Logic)* Term *m* ◆ **~ in parentheses** Klammerausdruck *m*; **to express one thing in ~s of another** eine Sache mit einer anderen erklären; **in ~s of production we are doing well** was die Produktion betrifft, stehen wir gut da; **in ~s of money/time** geldlich *or* finanziell/zeitlich; **in ~s of energy/planning** energiemäßig/planerisch.

(e) ~s *pl (conditions)* Bedingungen *pl* ◆ **~s of surrender/service/sale/payment** Kapitulations-/Arbeits-/Verkaufs-/Zahlungsbedingungen *pl*; **~s of reference** *(of committee etc)* Aufgabenbereich *m*; *(of thesis etc)* Themenbereich *m*; **to buy sth on credit/easy ~s** etw auf Kredit/auf Raten kaufen; **the hotel offered reduced ~s in winter** das Hotel bot ermäßigte Winterpreise an; **on what ~s?** zu welchen Bedingungen?; **not on any ~s** unter gar keinen Umständen; **to accept sb on his own ~s** jdn nehmen, wie er ist; **to come to ~s (with sb)** sich (mit jdm) einigen; **to come to ~s with sth** sich mit etw abfinden.

(f) ~s *pl (relations)* **to be on good/bad/friendly/neighbourly ~s with sb** gut/

nicht (gut) mit jdm auskommen/auf freundschaftlichem/ gutnachbarlichem Fuß mit jdm stehen; **they are not on speaking ~s** sie reden nicht miteinander; **what sort of ~s are they on?** wie ist ihre Beziehung?
[2] *vt* nennen, bezeichnen.
termagant ['tɜːməgənt] *n* Furie *f.*
terminal ['tɜːmɪnl] [1] *adj rhyme, syllable, station* End-; *accounts, report, exams* (Ab)schluß-; (*Elec*) *voltage* Klemmen-; (*Med: fatal*) *cancer, patient* unheilbar ◆ **~ bonus** (*Insur*) Zusatzdividende *f* (*fällig bei Vertragsablauf*); **~ ward** Sterbestation *f*; **he's a ~ case** er ist unheilbar krank.
[2] *n* **(a)** (*Rail*) Endbahnhof *m*; (*tramway, buses*) Endstation *f*; (*airport ~, container ~*) Terminal *m*. **(b)** (*Elec*) Pol *m*. **(c)** (*Comput*) Terminal *nt*.
terminally ['tɜːmɪnəlɪ] *adv* **~ ill** unheilbar krank.
terminate ['tɜːmɪneɪt] [1] *vt* beenden, beschließen; *contract, lease etc* lösen; *pregnancy* unterbrechen; *friendship* beenden.
[2] *vi* enden; (*contract, lease*) ablaufen ◆ **most plural nouns ~ in "s"** die meisten Substantive enden im Plural auf „s".
termination [,tɜːmɪ'neɪʃən] *n* **(a)** Ende *nt*; (*bringing to an end*) Beendigung *f*; (*of contract, lease etc*) (*expiry*) Ablauf *m*, Erlöschen *nt*; (*cancellation*) Lösung *f* ◆ **~ of pregnancy** Schwangerschaftsabbruch *m*. **(b)** (*Gram*) Endung *f*.
terminological [,tɜːmɪnə'lɒdʒɪkəl] *adj* terminologisch.
terminology [,tɜːmɪ'nɒlədʒɪ] *n* Terminologie *f* ◆ **all the technical ~ in the article** all die Fachausdrücke in dem Artikel.
terminus ['tɜːmɪnəs] *n* (*Rail, Bus*) Endstation *f*.
termite ['tɜːmaɪt] *n* Termite *f*.
tern [tɜːn] *n* (*Zool*) Seeschwalbe *f*.
ternary ['tɜːnərɪ] *adj* ternär.
terpsichorean [,tɜːpsɪkə'rɪən] *adj* (*form, hum*) Tanz-.
terrace ['terəs] [1] *n* **(a)** (*patio*) Terrasse *f*. **(b)** (*on hillside*) Terrasse *f* ◆ **~ cultivation** Terrassenfeldbau *m*. **(c)** **~s** *pl* (*Sport*) Ränge *pl*. **(d)** (*row of houses*) Häuserreihe *f*; (*as street name*) ≃ Weg *m*.
[2] *vt garden, hill* in Terrassen *or* stufenförmig anlegen.
terraced ['terəst] *adj* **(a)** *hillside etc* terrassenförmig *or* stufenförmig angelegt. **(b)** **~ house** (*Brit*) Reihenhaus *nt*.
terracotta ['terə'kɒtə] [1] *n* Terrakotta *f*.
[2] *attr* Terrakotta-, aus Terrakotta.
terra firma ['terə'fɜːmə] *n* fester Boden ◆ **to be on ~ again** wieder festen Boden unter den Füßen haben.
terrain [te'reɪn] *n* Terrain (*esp Mil*), Gelände *nt*; (*fig*) Boden *m*.
terrapin ['terəpɪn] *n* Sumpfschildkröte *f*.
terrazzo [te'rætsəʊ] *n* Terrazzo *m*.
terrestrial [tɪ'restrɪəl] [1] *adj* **(a)** (*of land*) *plants, animals* Land-, auf dem Land lebend. **(b)** (*of the planet Earth*) terrestrisch, irdisch; *TV channel* terrestrisch ◆ **~ globe** Erdball, Globus *m*. **(c)** (*worldly*) *problems* irdisch, weltlich.
[2] *n* Erdbewohner(in *f*) *m*.
terrible ['terəbl] *adj* schrecklich, furchtbar ◆ **he is ~ at golf** er spielt schrecklich *or* furchtbar schlecht Golf (*inf*).
terribleness ['terəblnɪs] *n* Schrecklichkeit, Fürchterlichkeit *f*.
terribly ['terəblɪ] *adv see adj*.
terrier ['terɪə^r] *n* Terrier *m*.
terrific [tə'rɪfɪk] *adj shame, nuisance, shock* unheimlich (*inf*); *person, success, idea, party also* sagenhaft (*sl*), klasse *inv* (*inf*); *speed, heat, strength, generosity* unwahrscheinlich (*inf*).
terrifically [tə'rɪfɪkəlɪ] *adv* (*inf*) (*very*) unheimlich (*inf*); (*very well*) unheimlich (gut) (*inf*) ◆ **the party went ~** die Party war klasse (*inf*).
terrify ['terɪfaɪ] *vt* (*person*) fürchterliche *or* schreckliche Angst machen *or* einjagen (*+dat*), in Angst *or* Schrecken versetzen ◆ **flying/my driving terrifies him** er hat schreckliche Angst vor dem Fliegen/, wenn ich fahre; **to be terrified of sth** vor etw schreckliche Angst haben; **he was terrified when/in case ...** er hatte fürchterliche Angst, als .../davor, daß ...; **a terrified look** ein angstvoller Blick; **you look terrified** du hast Angst, das sieht man!
terrifying ['terɪfaɪɪŋ] *adj film, story* grauenerregend; *thought, sight* entsetzlich; *speed* angsterregend, furchterregend.
terrifyingly ['terɪfaɪɪŋlɪ] *adv* entsetzlich ◆ **he came ~ close to disaster** er kam dem Unheil schrecklich nahe.
territorial [,terɪ'tɔːrɪəl] [1] *adj* territorial, Gebiets-; (*Zool*) Revier-; *instincts* territorial ◆ **~ sovereignty** Gebietshoheit *f*; **~ possessions** Territorialbesitz *m*; **~ rights** Hoheitsrechte *pl*; **~ waters** Territorialgewässer *pl*; **T~ Army** Territorialheer *nt*; **a strongly ~ bird** ein Vogel mit ausgeprägtem Territorialverhalten.
[2] *n* **T~** Soldat *m* der Heimatschutztruppe; **the T~s** die Heimatschutztruppe.
territory ['terɪtərɪ] *n* (Staats)gebiet, Territorium *nt*; (*in US, Austral*) Territorium *nt*; (*of animals*) Revier, Territorium *nt*; (*Comm: of agent etc*) Bezirk *m*; (*fig*) Revier, Gebiet *nt*.
terror ['terə^r] *n* **(a)** *no pl* (*great fear*) panische Angst (*of* vor *+dat*) ◆ **in ~** in panischer Angst; **to go in ~ of one's life** um sein Leben bangen; **it held no ~ for him** er schreckte nicht davor zurück; **reign of ~** (*Hist, fig*) Terror- *or* Schreckensherrschaft *f*; **the IRA ~** der IRA-Terror.
(b) (*cause of ~, terrible event*) Schrecken *m* ◆ **he was the ~ of the other boys** er terrorisierte die anderen Jungen; **the headmaster was a ~ to boys who misbehaved** der Rektor war der Schrecken aller Jungen, die sich schlecht benahmen.
(c) (*inf*) (*person*) Teufel *m*; (*child*) Ungeheuer *nt* ◆ **he's a ~ for punctuality/for wanting everything just so** er ist fürchterlich pedantisch in bezug auf Pünktlichkeit/Ordnung; **a ~ with the ladies** ein Weiberheld *m* (*inf*).
terrorism ['terərɪzəm] *n* Terrorismus *m*; (*acts of ~*) Terror *m* ◆ **an act of ~** ein Terrorakt *m*.
terrorist ['terərɪst] [1] *n* Terrorist(in *f*) *m*.
[2] *attr* Terror-.
terrorize ['terəraɪz] *vt* terrorisieren.
terror-stricken, terror-struck *adj* starr vor Schreck(en).
terry cloth ['terɪ'klɒθ] *or* **towelling** [-'taʊəlɪŋ] *n* Frottee *nt or m*.
terry towel *n* Frotteetuch, Frottier(hand)tuch *nt*.
terse [tɜːs] *adj* (*+er*) knapp ◆ **he was very ~** er war sehr kurz angebunden.
tersely ['tɜːslɪ] *adv* knapp, kurz; *say, answer* kurz (angebunden) ◆ **to dismiss sth ~** etw kurzerhand verwerfen.
terseness ['tɜːsnɪs] *n* Knappheit *f*; (*of reply also, person*) Kürze, Bündigkeit *f*.
tertiary ['tɜːʃərɪ] *adj* tertiär; *colour* Misch- ◆ **T~ period** (*Geol*) Tertiär *nt*; **~ burns** Verbrennungen *pl* dritten Grades; **~ education** Universitätsausbildung *f*.
Terylene ® ['terəliːn] *n* Terylen(e) ® *nt*, ≃ Trevira ®, Diolen ® *nt*.
tessellated ['tesɪleɪtɪd] *adj* Mosaik-.
test [test] [1] *n* **(a)** (*Sch*) Klassenarbeit *f*; (*Univ*) Klausur *f*; (*short*) Kurzarbeit *f*, Test *m*; (*intelligence ~, psychological ~ etc*) Test *m*; (*driving ~*) (Fahr)prüfung *f* ◆ **he gave them a vocabulary ~** er ließ eine Vokabel- *or* Wörterarbeit schreiben; (*orally*) er hat sie Vokabeln abgefragt; **if we apply the ~ of public acceptability** wenn wir die Probe machen, wie die Öffentlichkeit das aufnimmt; **to pass the ~ of public acceptability** von der Öffentlichkeit gutgeheißen werden; **to put sb/sth to the ~** jdn/etw auf die Probe stellen; **to stand the ~** die Probe bestehen; **their marriage didn't stand up to the ~ of separation** ihre Ehe hat die Trennung nicht verkraftet; **to stand the ~ of time** die Zeit überdauern; **that was a real ~ of character/his endurance** das war eine wirkliche Charakterprüfung/Belastungsprobe für ihn.
(b) (*on vehicle, product, weapon etc*) Test *m*; (*check*) Kontrolle *f*; (*on road also*) Testfahrt *f*; (*in air also*) Testflug *m*.
(c) (*chemical ~*) Test *m*, Untersuchung *f* ◆ **a skin ~** ein Hauttest; **to do a ~ for sugar** einen Zuckertest machen, eine Untersuchung auf Zucker machen; **the samples were sent for ~s** die Proben wurden zur Untersuchung geschickt.
(d) (*Brit*) *see* **~ match**.
[2] *adj attr model, version* Test-.
[3] *vt* **(a)** (*examine, check*) testen, prüfen; (*Sch*) *pupil* prüfen; (*orally*) abfragen; *person* (*with psychological ~s*), *intelligence* testen; (*fig*) auf die Probe stellen ◆ **the teacher ~ed them on that chapter** der Lehrer fragte sie das Kapitel ab; **to ~ sb for a job** jds Eignung für eine Stelle prüfen *or* testen; **to ~ sb/sth for accuracy** jdn/etw auf Genauigkeit prüfen; **I just wanted to ~ your reaction** ich wollte nur mal sehen, wie du reagierst.
(b) (*chemically*) *gold* prüfen; *water, contents of stomach etc* untersuchen ◆ **to ~ sth for sugar** etw auf seinen Zuckergehalt untersuchen; **the blood samples were sent for ~ing** *or* **to be ~ed** die Blutproben wurden zur Untersuchung geschickt.
[3] *vi* Tests/einen Test machen; (*chemically also*) untersuchen (*for* auf *+acc*) ◆ **~ing, ~ing one, two!** eins, zwei; **we are ~ing for a gas leak/loose connection** wir über prüfen die Leitung auf eine undichte Stelle, wir überprüfen, ob irgendwo Gas austritt/ein Anschluß locker ist.
◆**test out** *vt sep* ausprobieren (*on* bei *or* an *+dat*).
testament ['testəmənt] *n* **(a)** (*old*) Testament *nt*, letzter Wille. **(b)** (*Bibl*) **Old/New T~** Altes/Neues Testament.
testamentary [,testə'mentərɪ] *adj* testamentarisch.
testator [te'steɪtə^r] *n* Erblasser *m* (*form*).
testatrix [te'steɪtrɪks] *n* Erblasserin *f* (*form*).
test: ~ ban *n* Versuchsverbot *nt*; **~ ban treaty** *n* Teststoppabkommen *nt*; **~ bed** *n* Prüfstand *m*; **~ card** *n* (*TV*) Testbild *nt*; **~ case** *n* Musterfall *m*; **~ data** *npl* Testdaten *pl*; **~ drive** *n* Probefahrt *f*; **~-drive** *vt car* probefahren.
tester ['testə^r] *n* (*of product etc*) Prüfer(in *f*) *m*; (*machine*) Prüfgerät *nt*.
testes ['testiːz] *npl* Testikel, Hoden *pl*.
test flight *n* Test- *or* Probeflug *m*.
testicle ['testɪkl] *n* Testikel, Hoden *m*.
testify ['testɪfaɪ] [1] *vt* **to ~ that ...** (*Jur*) bezeugen, daß ...
[2] *vi* (*Jur*) eine Zeugenaussage machen, aussagen ◆ **to ~ against/in favour of sb** gegen/für jdn aussagen; **to ~ to sth** (*speak for*) etw bezeugen (*also Jur*); (*be sign of*) *sincerity, efforts etc* von etw zeugen, ein Zeichen für etw sein.
testily ['testɪlɪ] *adv see adj*.
testimonial [,testɪ'məʊnɪəl] *n* **(a)** (*character recommendation*) Referenz *f*. **(b)** (*gift*) Geschenk *nt* als Zeichen der Anerkennung *or* Wertschätzung (*geh*).
testimony ['testɪmənɪ] *n* Aussage *f* ◆ **he gave his ~** er machte seine Aussage; **to bear ~ to sth** etw bezeugen; **accept this gift as ~ of my friendship** nehmen Sie dieses Geschenk als Zeichen *or* Beweis meiner Freundschaft.
testiness ['testɪnɪs] *n* Gereiztheit *f*.
testing ['testɪŋ] *adj* hart ◆ **I had a ~ time** es war hart (für mich).
testing ground *n* Test- *or* Versuchsgebiet *nt*; (*fig*) Versuchsfeld *nt*.
test: ~-market *vt* auf dem Markt testen; **~ marketing** *n* Markttest *m*; **~ match** *n* (*Brit*) Testmatch *nt or m*.
testosterone [te'stɒstərəʊn] *n* Testosteron *nt*.
test: ~ paper *n* (*Sch*) Klassenarbeit *f*; (*Chem*) Reagenzpapier *nt*; **~ pattern** *n* (*US*) *see* **~ card**; **~ piece** *n* (*of handwork*) Prüfungsstück *nt*; (*Mus*) Stück *nt* zum Vorspielen; **~ pilot** *n* Testpilot *m*; **~ results** *npl* (*Med etc*) Testwerte *pl*; **~ tube** *n* Reagenzglas *nt*; **~-tube baby** *n* Kind *nt* aus der Retorte, Retortenbaby *nt*.

testy ['testɪ] *adj* (+*er*) unwirsch, gereizt.
tetanus ['tetənəs] *n* Wundstarrkrampf, Tetanus *m* ◆ **anti-~ vaccine/vaccination** Tetanusimpfstoff *m*/Tetanusimpfung *f*.
tetchily ['tetʃɪlɪ] *adv see adj*.
tetchiness ['tetʃɪnɪs] *n see adj* Gereiztheit *f*; Reizbarkeit *f*.
tetchy, techy ['tetʃɪ] *adj* (+*er*) (*on particular occasion*) gereizt; (*as general characteristic*) reizbar.
tête-à-tête ['teɪtɑː'teɪt] [1] *adj, adv* unter vier Augen.
[2] *n* Tête-à-tête *nt*.
tether ['teðə^r] [1] *n* (*lit*) Strick *m*; (*chain*) Kette *f* ◆ **to be at the end of one's ~** (*fig inf*) am Ende sein (*inf*).
[2] *vt* (*also* **~ up**) *animal* an- *or* festbinden.
tetrahedron [ˌtetrə'hiːdrən] *n* Tetraeder *nt*.
tetrameter [te'træmɪtə^r] *n* (*Liter*) Tetrameter *m*.
tetrapod ['tetrəpɒd] *n* Tetrapode (*spec*), Vierfüßer *m*.
Teuton ['tjuːtən] *n* Teutone *m*, Teutonin *f*.
Teutonic [tjʊ'tɒnɪk] *adj* (*Hist, hum*) teutonisch.
Texan ['teksən] [1] *n* Texaner(in *f*) *m*.
[2] *adj* texanisch.
Texas ['teksəs] *n* Texas *nt*.
text [tekst] *n* **(a)** Text *m*; (*of document also*) Wortlaut, Inhalt *m* ◆ **to restore a ~** den Originaltext wiederherstellen. **(b)** (*of sermon*) Text *m*.
textbook ['tekstbʊk] *n* Lehrbuch *nt* ◆ **~ case** Paradefall *m*; **~ landing** Bilderbuchlandung *f*.
text editor *n* (*Comput*) Texteditor *m*.
textile ['tekstaɪl] [1] *adj* Textil-. [2] *n* Stoff *m* ◆ **~s** Textilien, Textilwaren *pl*.
text (*Comput*): **~ input** *n* Texteingabe *f*; **~ processing** [1] *n* Textverarbeitung *f*; [2] *adj attr* Textverarbeitungs-; **~ processor** *n* (*hardware*) Textverarbeitungsanlage *f*; (*software*) Textsystem *nt*.
textual ['tekstjʊəl] *adj* Text-.
texture ['tekstʃə^r] *n* (stoffliche) Beschaffenheit, Textur *f*; (*of dough also*) Konsistenz *f*; (*of food*) Substanz, Textur *f*; (*of material, paper*) Griff *m* und Struktur, Textur *f*; (*of minerals also, fig: of music, poetry etc*) Gestalt *f* ◆ **the ~ of velvet** wie sich Samt anfühlt; **the smooth ~ of silk makes it pleasant to wear** es ist angenehm, Seide zu tragen, weil sie so anschmiegsam ist; **this spongy/light ~ of the cake** dieser feuchte und lockere/leichte Kuchen; **a sculptor interested in ~** ein Bildhauer, der an der Materialgestalt *or* -beschaffenheit interessiert ist; **the ~ of one's life** seine Lebensqualität.
textured ['tekstʃəd] *adj* strukturiert, texturiert (*form*); *paint* Struktur-.
TGIF (*hum*) *abbr of* **thank God it's Friday**.
TGWU (*Brit*) *abbr of* **Transport and General Workers' Union** *Transportarbeitergewerkschaft f*.
Thai [taɪ] [1] *adj* thailändisch; (*Ling*) T(h)ai-.
[2] *n* **(a)** Thailänder(in *f*) *m*, Thai *mf*. **(b)** (*language*) Thai *nt*; (*language family*) Tai *nt*.
Thailand ['taɪlænd] *n* Thailand *nt*.
thalidomide [θə'lɪdəʊmaɪd] *n* Contergan ®, Thalidomid *nt* ◆ **~ baby** Conterganekind *nt*.
thallium ['θælɪəm] *n* (*Chem*) Thallium *nt*.
Thames [temz] *n* Themse *f* ◆ **he'll never set the ~ on fire** (*prov*) er hat das Pulver auch nicht erfunden (*prov*).
▼ **than** [ðæn, *weak form* ðən] *conj* als ◆ **I'd rather do anything ~ that** das wäre das letzte, was ich tun wollte; **no sooner had I sat down ~ he began to talk** kaum hatte ich mich hingesetzt, als er auch schon anfing zu reden; **who better to help us ~ he?** wer könnte uns besser helfen als er?; *see* **more, other 1 (c), rather**.
▼ **thank** [θæŋk] *vt* **(a)** danken (+*dat*), sich bedanken bei ◆ **I'll never be able to ~ him (enough) for what he has done** ich kann ihm nie genug dafür danken, was er für mich getan hat; **I don't know how to ~ you** ich weiß nicht, wie ich Ihnen danken soll.
(b) (*phrases*) **he won't ~ you for it** er wird es Ihnen nicht danken; **I'll ~ you to mind your own business** ich wäre Ihnen dankbar, wenn Sie sich nicht einmischen würden; **he has his brother/he only has himself to ~ for this** das hat er seinem Bruder zu verdanken/sich selbst zuzuschreiben.
(c) ~ you danke (schön); **~ you very much** vielen Dank; **no ~ you/yes, ~ you** nein, danke/ja, bitte *or* danke; **~ you for coming — not at all, ~ you!** vielen Dank, daß Sie gekommen sind — ich danke *Ihnen*, *ich* habe zu danken; **~ you for the present** vielen Dank für Ihr Geschenk; **~ you for nothing** (*iro*) ich danke (bestens)!; **to say ~ you** danke sagen (*to sb* jdm), sich bedanken (*to* bei).
(d) ~ goodness *or* **heavens** *or* **God** (*inf*) Gott sei Dank! (*inf*).
thankee ['θæŋkiː] *interj* (*dial*) = **thank you**; *see* **thank (c)**.
thankful ['θæŋkfʊl] *adj* dankbar (*to sb* jdm) ◆ **I'm only ~ that it didn't happen** ich bin bloß froh, daß es nicht passiert ist.
thankfully ['θæŋkfəlɪ] *adv* dankbar, voller Dankbarkeit ◆ **~, no real harm has been done** zum Glück ist kein wirklicher Schaden entstanden.
thankfulness ['θæŋkfʊlnɪs] *n* Dankbarkeit *f*.
thankless ['θæŋklɪs] *adj* undankbar ◆ **a ~ task** eine undankbare Aufgabe.
thank-offering ['θæŋkˌɒfərɪŋ] *n* (*lit*) Dankopfer *nt*; (*fig*) Dankesgabe *f*.
▼ **thanks** [θæŋks] [1] *npl* **(a)** Dank *m* ◆ **to accept sth with ~** etw dankend *or* mit Dank annehmen; **and that's all the ~ I get** und das ist jetzt der Dank dafür; **to give ~ to God** Gott danksagen *or* Dank sagen; **~ be to God** (*Eccl*) Dank sei Gott.
▼ **(b) ~ to** wegen (+*gen*); (*with positive cause also*) dank (+*gen*); **~ to his coming early** ... weil er so früh kam, ...; **it's all ~ to you that we're so late** bloß deinetwegen kommen wir so spät; **it was no ~ to him that** ... ich hatte/wir hatten *etc* es nicht ihm zu verdanken, daß ...; **you managed it then — no ~ to you** du hast es also doch geschafft — ja, und das habe ich nicht dir zu verdanken.
▼ [2] *interj* (*inf*) danke (*for* für) ◆ **many ~** vielen *or* herzlichen Dank (*for* für); **~ a lot** *or* **a million** vielen *or* tausend Dank; (*iro*) (na,) vielen Dank (*inf*); **will you have some more? — no ~/yes, ~** etwas mehr? — nein/ja, danke.
thanksgiving ['θæŋksˌgɪvɪŋ] *n* **(a)** Dankbarkeit *f*. **(b)** (*US*) **T~ (Day)** Thanksgiving Day *m*.
thank-you ['θæŋkjuː] [1] *n* Dankeschön *nt* ◆ **he grabbed the book without even a ~** er riß das Buch ohne ein Dankeschön *nt or* ohne ein Wort *nt* des Dankes an sich.
[2] *attr letter* Dank-.
that[1] [ðæt, *weak form* ðət] [1] *dem pron, pl* **those** **(a)** das ◆ **what is ~?** was ist das?; **they all say ~** das sagen alle; **~ is Joe (over there)** das (dort) ist Joe; **who is ~?** wer ist das?; **who is ~ speaking?** wer spricht (denn) da?; (*on phone*) wer ist am Apparat?; **~'s what I say** *or* **think too** das finde ich auch; **if she's as unhappy/stupid** *etc* **as (all) ~** wenn sie so *or* derart unglücklich/dumm *etc* ist; **she's not as stupid as all ~** so dumm ist sie nun auch (wieder) nicht; **I didn't think she'd get/be as angry as ~** ich hätte nicht gedacht, daß sie sich so ärgern würde; ... **and all ~** ... und so (*inf*); **like ~** so; **with luck/talent like ~** ... bei solchem *or* so einem (*inf*) Glück/Talent ...; **~'s got ~/him out of the way** so, das wäre geschafft/so, den wären wir los; **~ is (to say)** das heißt; **oh well, ~'s ~** nun ja, damit ist der Fall erledigt; **there, ~'s ~** so, das wär's; **you can't go and ~'s ~** du darfst nicht gehen, und damit hat sich's *or* und damit basta (*inf*); **well, ~'s ~ then** das wär's dann also; **so ~ was ~** damit hatte sich's; **~'s it!** das ist es!; (*the right way*) gut so!, richtig!; (*finished*) so, das wär's!; (*the last straw*) jetzt reicht's!; **will he come? — ~ he will** (*dial*) kommt er? — (der?) bestimmt.
(b) (*after prep*) **after/before/below/over ~** danach/davor/darunter/darüber; **and ... at ~** und dabei ...; (*on top of that*) und außerdem ...; **you can get it in any supermarket and quite cheaply at ~** man kann es in jedem Supermarkt, und zwar ganz billig, bekommen; **my watch is broken already and it was a good one at ~** meine Uhr ist schon kaputt und dabei war es eine gute; **what do you mean by ~?** (*not understanding*) was wollen Sie damit sagen?; (*amazed, annoyed*) was soll (denn) das heißen?; **as for ~** was das betrifft *or* angeht; **if things have** *or* **it has come to ~** wenn es (schon) so weit gekommen ist; **with ~ she got up and left/burst into tears** damit stand sie auf und ging/brach sie in Tränen aus; *see* **leave**.
(c) (*opposed to "this" and "these"*) das (da), jenes (*old, geh*) ◆ **I prefer this to ~** dies ist mir lieber als das (da); **~'s the one I like, not this one** das (dort) mag ich, nicht dies (hier).
(d) (*followed by rel pron*) **this theory is different from ~ which** ... diese Theorie unterscheidet sich von derjenigen, die ...; **~ which we call** ... das, was wir ... nennen.
[2] *dem adj, pl* **those** **(a)** der/die/das, jene(r, s) ◆ **what was ~ noise?** was war das für ein Geräusch?; **~ child/dog!** dieses Kind/dieser Hund!; **~ poor girl!** das arme Mädchen!; **I only saw him on ~ one occasion** ich habe ihn nur bei dieser einen Gelegenheit gesehen; **everyone agreed on ~ point** alle waren sich in dem Punkt einig; **I like ~ one** ich mag das da.
(b) (*in opposition to this*) der/die/das ◆ **I'd like ~ one, not this one** ich möchte das da, nicht dies hier; **she was rushing this way and ~** sie rannte hierhin und dorthin.
(c) (*with poss*) **~ dog of yours!** Ihr Hund, dieser Hund von Ihnen (*inf*); **what about ~ plan of yours now?** wie steht es denn jetzt mit Ihrem Plan?, was ist denn nun mit Ihrem Plan?
[3] *dem adv* (*inf*) so ◆ **he was at least ~ much taller than me** er war mindestens (um) soviel größer als ich; **it's not ~ good/cold** *etc* so gut/kalt *etc* ist es auch wieder nicht; **it's not ~ good a film** *so* ein guter Film ist es nun auch wieder nicht; **he was ~ angry** er hat sich *der*art(ig) geärgert.
that[2] *rel pron* **(a)** der/die/das; die ◆ **all/nothing/everything** *etc* **~** ... alles/nichts/alles *etc*, was ...; **the best/cheapest** *etc* **~** ... das Beste/Billigste *etc*, das *or* was ...; **fool ~ I am** ich Idiot; **the girl ~ I told you about** das Mädchen, von dem ich Ihnen erzählt habe; **no-one has come ~ I know of** meines Wissens *or* soviel ich weiß, ist niemand gekommen.
(b) (*with expressions of time*) **the minute ~ he came the phone rang** genau in dem Augenblick, als er kam, klingelte das Telefon; **the day ~ we spent on the beach was one of the hottest** der Tag, den wir am Strand verbrachten, war einer der heißesten; **the day ~** ... an dem Tag, als ...
that[3] *conj* **(a)** daß ◆ **she promised ~ she would come** sie versprach zu kommen; **he said ~ it was wrong** er sagte, es sei *or* wäre (*inf*) falsch, er sagte, daß es falsch sei *or* wäre (*inf*); **not ~ I want to do it** nicht (etwa), daß ich das tun wollte; *see* **so**.
(b) (*in exclamations*) **~ things** *or* **it should come to this!** daß es soweit kommen konnte!; **oh ~ I could only see you again** (*liter*) oh, daß ich dich doch wiedersehen könnte! (*liter*).
(c) (*obs, liter: in order ~*) auf daß (*old*).
thatch [θætʃ] [1] *n* **(a)** (*material*) (*straw*) Stroh *nt*; (*reed*) Reet *nt*; (*roof*) Strohdach *nt*; Reetdach *nt*. **(b)** (*inf: hair*) Mähne *f*.
[2] *vt roof* mit Stroh/Reet decken.
thatched [θætʃt] *adj roof* (*with straw*) Stroh-; (*with reed*) Reet-; *cottage* mit Stroh-/Reetdach, stroh-/reetgedeckt ◆ **to be ~** ein Stroh-/Reetdach haben, mit Stroh/Reet gedeckt sein.
thatcher ['θætʃə^r] *n* Dachdecker *m*.

➤ LANGUAGE IN USE: **than** → 5.2, 5.3 **thank: a** → 20.2, 20.4, 22 **thanks: 1a** → 22 **1b** → 17.1 **2** → 22

Thatcherism ['θætʃərɪzəm] *n* Thatcherismus *m*.
Thatcherite ['θætʃəraɪt] [1] *n* Thatcher-Anhänger(in *f*) *m*.
[2] *adj* thatcheristisch.
thatching ['θætʃɪŋ] *n* (*act, skill*) Stroh-/Reetdachdecken *nt*; (*roofing*) Stroh-/Reetdach *nt*.
thaw [θɔː] [1] *vt* auftauen (lassen); *ice, snow also* tauen lassen; (*make warm*) *person, hands* aufwärmen; (*fig: make friendly*) *person* auftauen *or* warm werden lassen; *relations* entspannen.
[2] *vi* (*lit, fig*) auftauen; (*ice, snow*) tauen; (*person: become warmer also*) sich aufwärmen ♦ **it is ~ing** es taut.
[3] *n* (*lit, fig*) Tauwetter *nt* ♦ **before the ~/a ~ sets in** bevor das Tauwetter einsetzt; **there's been a ~ in relations between ...** die Beziehungen zwischen ... sind aufgetaut.
♦**thaw out** [1] *vi* (*lit, fig*) auftauen.
[2] *vt sep* (*lit*) *frozen food etc* auftauen (lassen); *person, hands* aufwärmen; (*fig*) *person* aus der Reserve locken ♦ **it took several whiskies to ~ him ~** (*inf*) er brauchte mehrere Whiskys, bis er auftaute *or* warm wurde.
the [ðə, *vor Vokalen auch, zur Betonung auch* ðiː] [1] *def art* **(a)** der/die/das ♦ **in ~ room** im *or* in dem Zimmer; **on ~ edge** am *or* an dem Rand; **he went up on ~ stage** er ging aufs *or* auf das Podium; **to play ~ piano/guitar** Klavier/Gitarre spielen; **all ~ windows** all die *or* alle Fenster; **have you invited ~ Browns?** haben Sie die Browns *or* (*with children*) die Familie Brown eingeladen?; **in ~ 20s** in den zwanziger Jahren; **Henry ~ Eighth** Heinrich der Achte; **how's ~ leg/wife?** (*inf*) wie geht's dem Bein/Ihrer Frau? (*inf*).
(b) (*with adj used as n*) das; die; (*with comp or superl*) der/die/das ♦ **~ Good** das Gute; **~ poor/rich** die Armen *pl*/Reichen *pl*; **translated from ~ German** aus dem Deutschen übersetzt; **she was ~ prettier/prettiest** sie war die hübschere/hübscheste.
(c) (*denoting whole class*) der/die/das ♦ **~ elephant is in danger of extinction** der Elefant ist vom Aussterben bedroht.
(d) (*distributive use*) **20p ~ pound** 20 Pence das *or* pro Pfund; **by ~ hour** pro Stunde; **the car does thirty miles to ~ gallon** das Auto braucht eine Gallone auf dreißig Meilen.
(e) [ðiː] (*stressed*) der/die/das ♦ **it's *the* restaurant in this part of town** das ist *das* Restaurant in diesem Stadtteil.
[2] *adv* (*with comp adj or adv*) **all ~ more/better/harder** um so mehr/besser/schwieriger; **~ more he has ~ more he wants** je mehr er hat, desto mehr will er; **(all) ~ more so because ...** um so mehr, als ...; *see* **better[2], worse.**
theatre, (*US*) **theater** ['θɪətə^r] *n* **(a)** Theater *nt*; (*esp in names, ~ company also*) Bühne *f* ♦ **to go to the ~** ins Theater gehen; **what's on at the ~?** was wird im Theater gegeben?
(b) *no pl* (*theatrical business, drama*) Theater *nt* ♦ **he's always been keen on (the) ~** er war schon immer theaterbegeistert; **he has been in (the) ~ all his life** er war sein Leben lang beim Theater; **not all Shaw's plays are good ~** nicht alle Stücke von Shaw eignen sich für die Bühne.
(c) (*Brit: operating ~*) Operationssaal *m*.
(d) (*scene of events*) Schauplatz *m* ♦ **~ of war** Kriegsschauplatz *m*; **~ of operations** Schauplatz *m* der Handlungen.
theatre: ~ company *n* Theaterensemble *nt*; (*touring*) Schauspiel- *or* Theatertruppe *f*; **~ critic** *n* Theaterkritiker(in *f*) *m*; **~goer** *n* Theaterbesucher(in *f*) *m*; **~land** *n* Theatergegend *f*; **in ~land** in der Theatergegend; **~ nurse** *n* (*Brit Med*) Operationsschwester *f*.
theatrical [θɪ'ætrɪkəl] [1] *adj* **(a)** Theater-; *company also* Schauspiel-; *experience also* schauspielerisch. **(b)** (*pej*) *behaviour etc* theatralisch.
[2] *n* **~s** *pl* Theaterspielen *nt* ♦ **most people have taken part in ~s** die meisten Menschen haben schon mal Theater gespielt.
theatricality [ˌθiːætrɪ'kælɪtɪ] *n* theatralische Art.
theatrically [θɪ'ætrɪkəlɪ] *adv* **(a)** schauspielerisch ♦ **~ it was a disaster** vom Theaterstandpunkt war das eine Katastrophe. **(b)** (*pej*) *behave, speak* theatralisch.
thee [ðiː] *pron* (*old, dial: objective case of thou*) (*dir obj, with prep +acc*) Euch (*obs*), Dich (*also Eccl*); (*indir obj, with prep +dat*) Euch (*obs*), Dir (*also Eccl*) ♦ **God be with ~** Gott sei mit Dir; **for ~ and thine** für Dich und die Deinen.
theft [θeft] *n* Diebstahl *m*.
their [ðɛə^r] *poss adj* **(a)** ihr. **(b)** (*inf: belonging to him or her*) seine(r, s) ♦ **everyone knows ~ rights nowadays** jeder kennt heutzutage seine Rechte; *see also* **my 1.**
theirs [ðɛəz] *poss pron* **(a)** ihre(r, s) ♦ **~ is not to reason why** es ist nicht an ihnen, zu fragen; **~ is the Kingdom of Heaven** ihrer ist das Himmelreich. **(b)** (*inf: belonging to him or her*) seine(r, s); *see also* **mine[1] 1.**
theism ['θiːɪzəm] *n* Theismus *m*.
theist ['θiːɪst] *n* Theist(in *f*) *m*.
theistic [θiː'ɪstɪk] *adj* theistisch.
them [ðem, *weak form* ðəm] [1] *pers pron pl* **(a)** (*dir obj, with prep +acc*) sie; (*indir obj, with prep +dat*) ihnen ♦ **both/neither of ~ saw me** beide haben/keiner von beiden hat mich gesehen; **give me a few of ~** geben Sie mir ein paar davon; **none of ~** keiner/keinen (von ihnen); **he's one of ~** das ist einer von ihnen; (*homosexual*) er ist andersrum (*inf*).
(b) (*emph*) sie ♦ **~ and us** (*inf*) sie *or* die (*inf*) und wir; **it's ~** sie sind's; **it's ~ who did it** *sie or die* haben es gemacht.
(c) (*dial: incorrect*) **~ as wants to** die, die wollen.
[2] *adj* (*incorrect*) diese.
thematic *adj*, **~ally** *adv* [θɪ'mætɪk, -əlɪ] thematisch.
▼ **theme** [θiːm] *n* **(a)** (*subject*) Thema *nt*. **(b)** (*US Sch: essay*) Aufsatz *m*. **(c)** (*Mus*) Thema *nt*; (*Film, TV also*) Melodie *f* (*from* aus).
themed [θiːmd] *adj* (*esp Brit*) *pub etc* thematisch gestaltet; *event* thematisch ausgerichtet.
theme: ~ music *n* (*Film*) Titelmusik *f*; (*TV*) Erkennungsmelodie *f*; **~ park** *n* (thematisch gestalteter) Freizeitpark; **~ song** *n* (*Film*) Titelsong *m*; (*TV*) Erkennungssong *m*; (*of opera*) Leitmotiv *nt*; **~ tune** *n see* **~ music.**
themselves [ðəm'selvz] *pers pron pl* **(a)** (*reflexive*) sich. **(b)** (*emph*) selbst ♦ **the figures ~** die Zahlen selbst *or* an sich; *see also* **myself.**
then [ðen] [1] *adv* **(a)** (*next, afterwards*) dann ♦ **and ~ what happened?** und was geschah dann?
(b) (*at this particular time*) da; (*in those days also*) damals ♦ **it was ~ 8 o'clock** da war es 8 Uhr; **I was/will be on holiday ~** ich war da (gerade) in Urlaub/werde da in Urlaub sein; **he did it ~ and there** *or* **there and ~** er hat es auf der Stelle getan; *see* **now.**
(c) (*after prep*) **from ~ on(wards)** von da an; **before ~** vorher, zuvor; **but they had gone by ~** aber da waren sie schon weg; **we'll be ready by ~** bis dahin sind wir fertig; **since ~** seitdem, seit der Zeit; **between now and ~** bis dahin; **(up) until ~ I had never tried it** bis dahin hatte ich es nie versucht.
(d) (*in that case*) dann ♦ **I don't want that — ~ what *do* you want?** ich will das nicht — was willst du denn?; **what are you going to do, ~?** was wollen Sie dann tun?; **but ~ that means that ...** das bedeutet ja aber dann, daß ...; **all right, ~** also *or* dann meinetwegen; **so it's true ~** dann ist es (also) wahr, es ist also wahr; **(so) I was right ~** ich hatte also recht; **you don't want it ~?** Sie wollen es also nicht?, dann wollen Sie es (also) nicht?; **where is it ~?** wo ist es denn?
(e) (*furthermore, and also*) dann, außerdem ♦ **(and) ~ there's my aunt** und dann ist da noch meine Tante; **but ~ ...** aber ... auch; **but ~ he's my son** aber er ist (eben) auch mein Sohn; **but ~ again he is my friend** aber andererseits ist er mein Freund.
(f) (*phrases*) **now ~, what's the matter?** na, was ist denn los?; **come on ~** nun komm doch.
[2] *adj attr* damalig ♦ **the ~ Prime Minister** der damalige Premierminister.
thence [ðens] *adv* **(a)** (*old: from that place*) von dannen (*old*), von dort *or* da (weg).
(b) (*old: from that time*) **which dated from ~** was aus der (damaligen) Zeit stammt; **they met again a week ~** sie trafen eine Woche darauf wieder zusammen.
(c) (*form: for that reason*) infolgedessen.
thenceforth [ˌðens'fɔːθ], **thenceforward** [ˌðens'fɔːwəd] *adv* von da an, von der Zeit an.
theocracy [θɪ'ɒkrəsɪ] *n* Theokratie *f*.
theocratic [θɪə'krætɪk] *adj* theokratisch.
theodolite [θɪ'ɒdəlaɪt] *n* Theodolit *m*.
theologian [θɪə'ləʊdʒɪən] *n* Theologe *m*, Theologin *f*.
theological [θɪə'lɒdʒɪkəl] *adj* theologisch ♦ **~ college** Priesterseminar *nt*; **~ student** Theologiestudent(in *f*) *m*.
theology [θɪ'ɒlədʒɪ] *n* Theologie *f*.
theorem ['θɪərəm] *n* Satz *m* (*also Math*), Theorem *nt* (*geh, spec*).
theoretic(al) [θɪə'retɪk(əl)] *adj* theoretisch.
theoretically [θɪə'retɪkəlɪ] *adv* theoretisch.
theoretician [θɪərə'tɪʃən], **theorist** ['θɪərɪst] *n* Theoretiker(in *f*) *m*.
theorize ['θɪəraɪz] *vi* theoretisieren.
theorizer ['θɪəraɪzə^r] *n* Theoretiker(in *f*) *m*.
theory ['θɪərɪ] *n* Theorie *f* ♦ **in ~** theoretisch, in der Theorie; **~ of colour/evolution** Farben-/Evolutionslehre *or* -theorie *f*; **he has a ~ that ...** er hat die Theorie, daß ...; **well, it's a ~** das ist eine Möglichkeit; **he always goes on the ~ that ...** er geht immer davon aus, daß ....
theosophical [θɪə'sɒfɪkəl] *adj* theosophisch.
theosophist [θɪ'ɒsəfɪst] *n* Theosoph(in *f*) *m*.
theosophy [θɪ'ɒsəfɪ] *n* Theosophie *f*.
therapeutic(al) [ˌθerə'pjuːtɪk(əl)] *adj* therapeutisch ♦ **to be ~** therapeutisch wirken.
therapeutics [ˌθerə'pjuːtɪks] *n sing* Therapeutik *f*.
therapist ['θerəpɪst] *n* Therapeut(in *f*) *m*.
therapy ['θerəpɪ] *n* Therapie *f*.
there [ðɛə^r] [1] *adv* **(a)** dort, da; (*with movement*) dorthin, dahin ♦ **look, ~'s Joe/~'s Joe coming** guck mal, da ist/kommt Joe; **it's under/over/in ~** es liegt dort *or* da drunter/drüben/drin; **put it under/over/in/on ~** stellen Sie es dort *or* da drunter/rüber *or* hinüber/rein *or* hinein/drauf *or* hinauf; **let's stop ~** hören wir doch da auf; (*travelling*) halten wir doch da *or* dort an; **~ and back** hin und zurück; **so ~ we were** da waren wir nun also.
(b) (*fig: on this point*) da ♦ **~ you are wrong** da irren Sie sich; **you've got me ~** da bin ich überfragt; **I've got you ~** da *or* jetzt habe ich Sie.
(c) (*in phrases*) **~ is/are** es *or* da ist/sind; (**~ *exists/exist also***) es gibt; **~ were three of us** wir waren zu dritt; **~ is a mouse in the room** es ist eine Maus im Zimmer; **~ was once a castle here** hier war *or* stand einmal eine Burg; **~ is a chair in the corner** in der Ecke steht ein Stuhl; **~ is dancing afterwards** danach ist Tanz *or* wird getanzt; **~'s a book I want to read** da ist ein Buch, das ich lesen möchte; **is ~ any wine left? — well, ~ was** ist noch Wein da? — gerade war noch welcher da; **~ isn't any food/time/point, is ~? — yes ~ is** es gibt wohl nichts zu essen/dazu haben wir wohl keine Zeit/das hat wohl keinen Sinn, oder? — doch!; **~ seems to be no-one at home** es scheint keiner zu Hause zu sein; **~ appears to be a flaw in your argument** da scheint ein Fehler in Ihrer Beweisführung zu sein; **how many mistakes were ~?** wie viele Fehler waren es?; **is ~ any beer?** ist Bier da?; **afterwards ~ was coffee** anschließend gab es Kaffee; **~ is a page missing** es *or* da fehlt eine Seite; **~**

➤ LANGUAGE IN USE: **theme: a → 26.2**

comes a time when ... es kommt eine Zeit, wo ...; **~ being no alternative solution** da es keine andere Lösung gibt/gab; **~ will be an opportunity for shopping** es wird Gelegenheit zum Einkaufen geben; **God said: let ~ be light, and ~ was light** und Gott sprach: es werde Licht! und es ward Licht; **~ you go again** (*inf*) jetzt geht's schon wieder los; **now ~'s a real woman** das ist eine richtige Frau; **~'s gratitude for you!** (*iro*) da haben Sie Ihren Dank!; **now ~'s a good idea!** (das ist) eine gute Idee!; **~ you are** (*giving sb sth*) hier(, bitte)!; (*on finding sb*) da sind Sie ja!; **~ you** *or* **we are, you see, I knew he'd say that** na, sehen Sie, ich habe es ja gewußt, daß er das sagen würde; **wait, I'll help you ... ~ you are!** warten Sie, ich helfe Ihnen, ... so(, das wär's)!; **you press the switch and ~ you are!** Sie brauchen nur den Schalter zu drücken, das ist alles.

[2] *interj* **~! ~!** na, na!; **stop crying now, ~'s a good boy** hör auf zu weinen, na komm; **drop it, ~'s a good dog** laß das fallen, komm, sei brav; **now ~'s a good boy, don't tease your sister** komm, sei ein braver Junge und ärgere deine Schwester nicht; **hey, you ~!** (*inf*) he, Sie da!; **hurry up ~** (*inf*) Beeilung!, Tempo, Tempo! (*inf*); **make way ~** Platz da!, machen Sie mal Platz!; **~ take this to your mother** da, bring das deiner Mutter; **but ~, what's the good of talking about it?** was soll's, es hat doch keinen Zweck, darüber zu reden; **~! I knew it would break!** da! ich hab's ja gewußt, daß es kaputt gehen würde!

thereabouts [ˌðɛərəˈbaʊts] *adv* **(a)** (*place*) dort in der Nähe, dort irgendwo. **(b)** (*quantity, degree*) **five pounds/fifteen or ~** so um die fünf Pfund/fünfzehn (herum).

thereafter [ˌðɛərˈɑːftəʳ] *adv* (*form*) danach, darauf (*geh*).

thereby [ˌðɛəˈbaɪ] *adv* dadurch, damit ◆ **and ~ hangs a tale** und da gibt es eine Geschichte dazu.

▼ **therefore** [ˈðɛəfɔːʳ] *adv* deshalb, daher; (*as logical consequence*) also ◆ **so ~ I was wrong** ich hatte also unrecht; **we can deduce, ~, that ...** wir können also *or* daher folgern, daß ....

therein [ˌðɛərˈɪn] *adv* (*form*) **(a)** (*in that particular*) darin, in dieser Hinsicht. **(b)** (*in that place*) darin, dort.

thereof [ˌðɛərˈɒv] *adv* (*form*) davon ◆ **this town and the citizens ~** diese Stadt und deren Bürger.

thereon [ˌðɛərˈɒn] *adv* (*form*) (*on that*) darauf; (*on that subject*) darüber.

there's [ðɛəz] *contr of* **there is; there has.**

thereunder [ðɛərˈʌndəʳ] *adv* (*form*) darunter.

thereupon [ˌðɛərəˈpɒn] *adv* **(a)** (*then, at that point*) darauf(hin). **(b)** (*form: on that subject*) darüber; (*on that*) darauf.

therewith [ˌðɛəˈwɪθ] *adv* (*form*) **(a)** (*with that*) damit. **(b)** (*thereupon*) darauf.

therm [θɜːm] *n* (*Brit*) 100.000 Wärmeeinheiten (*ca.* 10^8 *Joules*).

thermal [ˈθɜːməl] [1] *adj* (*Phys*) *capacity, unit* Wärme-; *neutron, reactor, equilibrium* thermisch.

[2] *n* (*Aviat, Met*) Thermik *f no pl.*

thermal: ~ baths *npl* Thermalbäder *pl*; **~ paper** *n* Thermopapier *nt*; **~ printer** *n* (*Comput*) Thermodrucker *m*; **~ spring** *n* Thermalquelle *f*; **~ transfer** *n* Thermotransfer *m*; **~ underwear** *n* Thermo-Unterwäsche *f*.

thermic [ˈθɜːmɪk] *adj* thermisch.

thermionic [ˌθɜːmɪˈɒnɪk] *adj* thermionisch, glühelektrisch ◆ **~ valve** (*Brit*) *or* **tube** (*US*) Glühelektronenröhre *f*.

thermistor [ˈθɜːmɪstəʳ] *n* (*Tech*) Heißleiter, Thermistor *m*.

thermo [ˌθɜːməʊ-]: **~dynamic** *adj* thermodynamisch; **~dynamics** *npl* Thermodynamik *f*; **~electric** *adj* thermoelektrisch; **~electricity** *n* Thermoelektrizität *f*.

thermometer [θəˈmɒmɪtəʳ] *n* Thermometer *nt*.

thermo: ~nuclear *adj* thermonuklear, Fusions-; **~nuclear war** Thermonuklearkrieg *m*; **~pile** *n* Thermosäule *f*; **~plastic** [1] *adj* thermoplastisch; [2] *n* Thermoplast *m*.

thermos ® [ˈθɜːməs] *n* (*also* **~ flask** *or* (*US*) **bottle**) Thermosflasche *f*.

thermostat [ˈθɜːməstæt] *n* Thermostat *m*.

thermostatic [ˌθɜːməˈstætɪk] *adj* thermostatisch ◆ **~ regulator** Temperaturregler *m*; **~ switch** Temperaturschalter *m*.

thermostatically [ˌθɜːməˈstætɪkəlɪ] *adv* thermostatisch.

thesaurus [θɪˈsɔːrəs] *n* Thesaurus *m*.

these [ðiːz] *adj, pron* diese; *see* **this.**

thesis [ˈθiːsɪs] *n, pl* **theses** [ˈθiːsiːz] **(a)** (*argument*) These *f*. **(b)** (*Univ*) (*for PhD*) Dissertation, Doktorarbeit (*inf*) *f*; (*for diploma*) Diplomarbeit *f*.

thespian [ˈθespɪən] (*liter, hum*) [1] *adj* dramatisch ◆ **~ art** Schauspielkunst *f*.

[2] *n* Mime *m*, Mimin *f*.

they [ðeɪ] *pers pron pl* **(a)** sie ◆ **~ are very good people** es sind sehr gute Leute; **it is ~** (*form*) *sie* sind es; **~ who** diejenigen, die *or* welche, wer (*+sing vb*).

(b) (*people in general*) **~ say that ...** man sagt, daß ...; **~ are going to build a new road** man will *or* sie wollen eine neue Straße bauen; **~ are thinking of changing the law** es ist beabsichtigt, das Gesetz zu ändern.

(c) (*inf*) **if anyone looks at this closely, ~ will notice ...** wenn sich das jemand näher ansieht, wird er bemerken ...

they'd [ðeɪd] *contr of* **they had; they would.**

they'd've [ˈðeɪdəv] *contr of* **they would have.**

they'll [ðeɪl] *contr of* **they will.**

they're [ðɛəʳ] *contr of* **they are.**

they've [ðeɪv] *contr of* **they have.**

thiamine [ˈθaɪəmiːn] *n* Thiamin *nt*.

thick [θɪk] [1] *adj* (*+er*) **(a)** dick; *wall, thread, legs, arms also* stark ◆ **a wall three feet ~** eine drei Fuß dicke *or* starke Wand; **to give sb a ~ ear** (*inf*) jdm ein paar hinter die Ohren hauen (*inf*); **you'll get a ~ ear in a minute** du kriegst gleich ein paar hinter die Ohren! (*inf*); **the shelves were ~ with dust** auf den Regalen lag dick der Staub; **to have a ~ head** einen Brummschädel haben (*inf*), einen dicken Kopf haben (*inf*).

(b) *hair, fog, smoke* dick, dicht; *forest, hedge, beard* dicht; *liquid, sauce, syrup etc* dick(flüssig); *mud* dick; *darkness* tief; *crowd* dicht(gedrängt); *air* schlecht, dick (*inf*); *accent* stark, breit ◆ **they are ~/not exactly ~ on the ground** (*inf*) die gibt es wie Sand am Meer (*inf*)/die sind dünn gesät; **the hedgerows were ~ with wild flowers** die Hecken strotzten von wilden Blumen; **his voice was ~ with a cold/emotion/fear/drink** er sprach mit belegter/bewegter/angstvoller Stimme/schwerer Zunge; **the air is pretty ~ in here** hier ist eine Luft zum Schneiden *or* sehr schlechte Luft.

(c) (*inf: stupid*) *person* dumm, doof (*inf*).

(d) (*inf: intimate*) **they are very ~** sie sind dicke Freunde (*inf*); **to be very ~ with sb** mit jdm eine dicke Freundschaft haben (*inf*).

(e) (*inf: much*) **that's a bit ~!** das ist ein starkes Stück (*inf*).

[2] *n* **(a) in the ~ of the crowd/the fight/it** mitten in der Menge/im Kampf/mittendrin; **he likes to be in the ~ of things** er ist gern bei allem voll dabei; **to stick together through ~ and thin** zusammen durch dick und dünn gehen.

(b) (*of finger, leg*) dickste Stelle ◆ **the ~ of the calf** die Wade.

[3] *adv* (*+er*) *spread, lie, cut* dick; *grow* dicht ◆ **the snow lay ~** es lag eine dichte Schneedecke; **his blows fell ~ and fast** seine Schläge prasselten nieder; **offers of help poured in ~ and fast** es kam eine Flut von Hilfsangeboten; **they are falling ~ and fast** sie fallen um wie die Fliegen (*inf*); **to lay it on ~** (*inf*) (zu) dick auftragen (*inf*); **that's laying it on a bit ~** (*inf*) das ist ja wohl etwas übertrieben.

thicken [ˈθɪkən] [1] *vt sauce etc* eindicken.

[2] *vi* **(a)** dicker werden; (*fog, hair also, crowd, forest*) dichter werden; (*smoke, fog also, darkness*) sich verdichten; (*sauce*) dick werden. **(b)** (*fig: plot, mystery*) immer verwickelter *or* undurchsichtiger werden ◆ **aha, the plot ~s!** aha, jetzt wird's interessant!

thickener [ˈθɪkənəʳ], **thickening** [ˈθɪkənɪŋ] *n* (*for sauces*) Bindemittel *nt*.

thicket [ˈθɪkɪt] *n* Dickicht *nt*.

thick: ~-head *n* (*inf*) Dummkopf *m*; **~-headed** *adj* (*inf*) dumm, doof (*inf*); **~-headedness** *n* (*inf*) Dummheit, Doofheit (*inf*) *f*.

thickie [ˈθɪkɪ] *n* (*inf*) Dummkopf, Doofkopf (*inf*), Doofi (*inf*) *m*.

thick-lipped [ˈθɪklɪpt] *adj* mit dicken *or* wulstigen Lippen, mit Wulstlippen.

thickly [ˈθɪklɪ] *adv* **(a)** *spread, paint, cut* dick; *populated, crowded, wooded* dicht. **(b) snow was falling ~** dichter Schnee fiel; **the ~ falling snow** der dicht fallende Schnee. **(c)** *speak* (*with a cold*) mit belegter Stimme; (*with drink*) mit schwerer Zunge; (*with emotion*) bewegt; (*with fear*) angstvoll.

thickness [ˈθɪknɪs] *n see adj* **(a)** Dicke *f*; Stärke *f*.

(b) Dicke *f*; Dichte *f*; Dickflüssigkeit *f*; Stärke *f* ◆ **the ~ of his lips** seine dicken *or* wulstigen Lippen; **the ~ of his voice** (*through cold*) seine belegte Stimme; (*through drink*) seine schwere Zunge; (*through emotion*) seine bewegte Stimme; (*through fear*) seine bebende Stimme; **the ~ of the air** die schlechte *or* verbrauchte Luft; **it is sold in three different ~es** es wird in drei verschiedenen Dicken *or* Stärken verkauft.

(c) Dummheit, Doofheit (*inf*) *f*.

(d) (*layer*) Lage, Schicht *f*.

thicko [ˈθɪkəʊ] *n* (*inf*) *see* **thickie.**

thick: ~-set *adj* gedrungen; *hedge* dicht; **~-skinned** *adj* (*lit*) dickhäutig; (*fig*) dickfellig.

thicky [ˈθɪkɪ] *n* (*inf*) *see* **thickie.**

thief [θiːf] *n, pl* **thieves** [θiːvz] Dieb(in *f*) *m* ◆ **to set a ~ to catch a ~** (*prov*) einen vom Fach benutzen; **to be as thick as thieves** dicke Freunde sein (*inf*).

thieve [θiːv] *vti* stehlen.

thieving [ˈθiːvɪŋ] [1] *adj jackdaw* diebisch ◆ **a ~ disposition** ein Hang *m* zum Stehlen; **keep your ~ hands off my cigarettes** laß die Finger weg von meinen Zigaretten (*inf*); **this ~ lot** (*inf*) diese Räuberbande (*inf*).

[2] *n* (*thefts*) Stehlen *nt*, Diebstähle *pl*.

thievish [ˈθiːvɪʃ] *adj* diebisch *attr*.

thievishness [ˈθiːvɪʃnɪs] *n* diebische Art.

thigh [θaɪ] *n* (Ober)schenkel *m*.

thigh: ~ bone *n* Oberschenkelknochen *m*; **~-length** *adj boots* übers Knie reichend.

thimble [ˈθɪmbl] *n* Fingerhut *m* ◆ **~ printer** (*Comput*) Thimble-Drucker *m*.

thimbleful [ˈθɪmblfʊl] *n* (*fig*) Fingerhut(voll) *m*.

thin [θɪn] [1] *adj* (*+er*) **(a)** (*not thick*) *paper, slice, string, wall, blood* dünn; *dress, material also* leicht; *liquid* dünn(flüssig); (*narrow*) *line also, column* schmal.

(b) (*not fat*) dünn.

(c) (*sparse*) *hair, grass* dünn, schütter; *vegetation* gering, spärlich, kümmerlich (*pej*); *population, crowd* klein, kümmerlich (*pej*) ◆ **his hair is getting quite ~** sein Haar lichtet sich *or* wird schütter; **he's a bit ~ on top** bei ihm lichtet es sich oben schon ein wenig; **to be ~ on the ground** (*fig*) dünn gesät sein.

(d) (*not dense*) *fog* leicht; *air* dünn ◆ **to vanish into ~ air** (*fig*) sich in Luft auflösen; **the agent simply vanished into ~ air** der Agent schien sich einfach in Luft aufgelöst zu haben.

(e) (*fig: weak, poor*) *voice, smile* schwach, dünn; *excuse* schwach, fadenscheinig; *disguise, story-line, plot* schwach ◆ **she had a ~ time of it** (*dated inf*) es war nicht gerade schön für sie; **to give sb a ~ time of it** (*inf*) jdm das Leben schwermachen.

[2] *adv* (*+er*) *spread, cut* dünn; *lie* dünn, spärlich.

[3] *vt paint, sauce* verdünnen; *trees* lichten; *hair* ausdünnen; *population* ver-

➤ LANGUAGE IN USE: **therefore** → 17.1, 26.1, 26.3

ringern; *blood* dünner werden lassen.
[4] *vi* (*fog, crowd*) sich lichten; (*hair also*) schütter werden.
◆**thin down** [1] *vi* dünner werden; (*person also*) abnehmen, schlanker werden.
[2] *vt sep paint, sauce* verdünnen.
◆**thin out** [1] *vi* (*fog*) sich lichten, schwächer werden; (*crowd*) kleiner werden; (*audience*) sich lichten; (*hair*) sich lichten, schütter werden ◆ **the houses started ~ning ~** die Häuser wurden immer spärlicher.
[2] *vt sep hair* ausdünnen; *seedlings also* verziehen; *forest* lichten; *population* verkleinern.

thine [ðaɪn] (*old, dial*) [1] *poss pron* der/die/das deine ◆ **for thee and ~** für Dich und die Deinen; *see* **mine**[1].
[2] *poss adj* (*only before vowel*) Euer/Eure/Euer (*obs*), Dein/Deine/Dein (*also Eccl*).

thing [θɪŋ] *n* **(a)** (*any material object*) Ding *nt* ◆ **a ~ of beauty/great value** etwas Schönes/etwas sehr Wertvolles; **she likes sweet ~s** sie mag Süßes *or* süße Sachen; **what's that ~?** was ist das?; **I don't have a ~ to wear** ich habe nichts zum Anziehen.
(b) (*clothes, equipment, belongings*) **~s** *pl* Sachen *pl* ◆ **have you got your swimming ~s?** hast du dein Badezeug *or* deine Badesachen dabei?; **they washed up the breakfast ~s** sie spülten das Frühstücksgeschirr.
(c) (*non material: affair, subject*) Sache *f* ◆ **you know, it's a funny ~** wissen Sie, es ist schon seltsam; **the odd/best ~ about it is ...** das Seltsame/Beste daran ist, ...; **it's a good ~ I came** nur gut, daß ich gekommen bin; **it's a bad/strange ~ but ...** es ist schlecht/seltsam, aber ...; **he's on to** *or* **onto a good ~** (*inf*) er hat da was Gutes aufgetan (*inf*); **he's got a good ~ going there** (*inf*) der hat da was Gutes laufen (*inf*); **what a (silly) ~ to do** wie kann man nur so was (Dummes) tun!; **you take the ~ too seriously** Sie nehmen die Sache *or* das zu ernst; **there is one/another ~ I want to ask you** eines/und noch etwas möchte ich Sie fragen; **and there's another ~, why didn't you ...?** und noch etwas, warum haben Sie nicht ...?; **the ~s you do/say!** was du so machst/sagst!; **I must be hearing/seeing ~s!** ich glaube, ich höre/sehe nicht richtig, ich glaube, ich spinne! (*inf*); **all the ~s I meant to say/do** alles, was ich sagen/tun wollte; **which ~s in life do you value most?** was *or* welche Dinge im Leben bewerten Sie am höchsten?; **to expect great ~s of sb/sth** Großes *or* große Dinge von jdm/etw erwarten; **I must think ~s over** ich muß mir die Sache *or* das überlegen; **~s are going from bad to worse** es wird immer schlimmer; **as ~s stand at the moment, as ~s are ...** so wie die Dinge im Moment liegen; **how are ~s with you?** wie geht's (bei) Ihnen?; **since that's how ~s are ...** wenn das so ist ..., in dem Fall ...; **it's bad enough as ~s are** es ist schon schlimm genug; **~s aren't what they used to be** es ist alles nicht mehr so wie früher; **to talk of one ~ and another** von diesem und jenem reden; **taking one ~ with another** im großen und ganzen, alles in allem; **it's been one ~ after the other going wrong** es kam eins zum anderen; **if it's not one ~ it's the other** es ist immer irgend etwas; **(what) with one ~ and another I haven't had time to do it yet** ich bin einfach noch nicht dazu gekommen; **it's neither one ~ nor the other** es ist weder das eine noch das andere; **for one ~ it doesn't make sense** erst einmal ergibt das überhaupt keinen Sinn; **to see/understand/know not a ~** (absolut) nichts sehen/verstehen/wissen, keine Ahnung haben; **to tell sb a ~ or two** jdm einiges erzählen; **he knows a ~ or two** er hat etwas auf dem Kasten (*inf*); **he knows a ~ or two about cars** er kennt sich mit Autos aus; **it's just one of those ~s** so was kommt eben vor (*inf*); **she was all ~s to all men** sie war der Wunschtraum aller Männer; *see* **teach**.
(d) (*person, animal*) Ding *nt* ◆ **poor little ~** das arme (kleine) Ding!; **you poor ~!** du Arme(r)!; **she's a funny old ~** sie ist ein komisches altes Haus (*inf*); **I say, old ~** (*dated inf*) na, du altes Haus (*inf*); **lucky ~!** die *or* der Glückliche/du Glückliche(r); **he looks quite the ~** er sieht (richtig) nach etwas aus.
(e) (*what is suitable, best*) **that's just the ~ for me** das ist genau das richtige für mich; **that's not the ~ to do** so was macht *or* tut man nicht; **his behaviour isn't quite the ~** (*dated*) sein Benehmen ist nicht gerade berückend (*inf*); **the latest ~ in ties** der letzte Schrei in der Krawattenmode; **the ~ to do now would be ...** was wir jetzt machen sollten, wäre ...; **that would be the honourable ~ to do** es wäre nur anständig, das zu tun.
(f) (*in phrases*) **I'm not at my best first ~ in the morning** so früh am Morgen bin ich nicht gerade in Hochform; **I'll do that first ~ in the morning** ich werde das gleich *or* als erstes morgen früh tun; **I'll do it first ~** ich werde das zuerst *or* als erstes tun; **last ~ at night** vor dem Schlafengehen; **painting is his ~** das Malen liegt ihm (*inf*); **the ~ is to know when ...** man muß wissen, wann ...; **yes, but the ~ is ...** ja, aber ...; **the ~ is we haven't got enough money** die Sache ist die, wir haben nicht genug Geld; **the ~ is, you see, he loves her** das Problem ist, daß er sie liebt; **yes but the ~ is it won't work** ja, aber das Dumme ist, es funktioniert nicht; **to do one's own ~** (*sl*) tun, was man will; **when Jimi Hendrix starts doing his ~** (*sl*) wenn Jimi Hendrix seine Schau abzieht (*sl*); **she's got this ~ about Sartre/dogs** (*inf*) (*can't stand*) sie kann Sartre/Hunde einfach nicht ausstehen; (*is fascinated by*) sie hat einen richtigen Sartre-/Hundefimmel (*inf*); **she's got a ~ about spiders** (*inf*) bei Spinnen dreht sie durch (*inf*); **he's got this ~ about her** (*inf*) (*can't stand*) er kann sie nicht ausstehen; (*is infatuated*) er ist verrückt nach ihr.
(g) (all) ~s German/mystical/mechanical alles Deutsche/Geheimnisvolle/Mechanische.
(h) (*inf: for forgotten name of person*) Dings(bums) *mf* (*inf*).

thingummybob [ˈθɪŋəmɪˌbɒb], **thingamajig** [ˈθɪŋəmɪˌdʒɪg], **thingummy** [ˈθɪŋəmɪ] *n* Dings, Dingens, Dingsbums, Dingsda *nt or* (*for people*) *mf* (*all inf*).

▼ **think** [θɪŋk] (*vb: pret, ptp* **thought**) [1] *vi* denken ◆ **to ~ to oneself** sich (*dat*) denken; **I was just sitting there ~ing to myself** ich saß so in Gedanken da; **~ before you speak/act** denk nach *or* überleg, bevor du sprichst/handelst; **do animals ~?** können Tiere denken?; **to act without ~ing** unüberlegt handeln; (*stupidly also*) unbedacht handeln; **~ again!** denk noch mal nach; **so you ~ I'll give you the money? well, you'd better ~ again!** du denkst also, ich gebe dir das Geld? das hast du dir (wohl) gedacht!; **it makes you ~** es macht *or* stimmt einen nachdenklich; **I need time to ~** ich brauche Zeit zum Nachdenken; **it's so noisy you can't hear yourself ~** bei so einem Lärm kann doch kein Mensch denken; **now let me ~** laß (mich) mal überlegen *or* nachdenken; **stop and ~ before you make a big decision** denke in aller Ruhe nach, bevor du eine schwerwiegende Entscheidung triffst; **it's a good idea, don't you ~?** es ist eine gute Idee, findest *or* meinst du nicht auch?; **just ~** stellen Sie sich (*dat*) bloß mal vor; **just ~, you too could be rich** stell dir vor *or* denk dir nur, auch du könntest reich sein; **where was it? ~, man, ~!** wo war es?, denk doch mal nach!; **listen, I've been ~ing, ...** hör mal, ich habe mir überlegt ...; **sorry, I just wasn't ~ing** Entschuldigung, da habe ich geschlafen (*inf*); **you just didn't ~, did you?** da hast du dir nichts gedacht, oder?; **you just don't ~, do you?** (*about other people*) du denkst auch immer nur an dich; (*about consequences*) was denkst du dir eigentlich?; *see* **big**.
▼ [2] *vt* **(a)** denken; (*be of opinion also*) glauben, meinen ◆ **I ~ you'll find I'm right** ich glaube *or* denke, Sie werden zu der Überzeugung gelangen, daß ich recht habe; **I ~ it's too late** ich glaube, es ist zu spät; **I ~ I can do it** ich glaube *or* denke, daß ich es schaffen kann; **well, I *think* it was there!** nun, ich glaube zumindest, daß es da war!; **and what do you ~? asked the interviewer** und was meinen Sie *or* und was ist Ihre Meinung? fragte der Interviewer; **you never know what he's ~ing** ich weiß nie, was er (sich) denkt; **I ~ you'd better go/accept/be careful** ich denke, Sie gehen jetzt besser/Sie stimmen lieber zu/Sie wären besser vorsichtig; **well, I *think* he'll understand** na ja, ich nehme zumindest an, daß er das verstehen wird; **I ~ so** ich denke *or* glaube (schon); **I ~ so too** das meine *or* denke ich auch; **I don't ~ so/I shouldn't ~ so/I ~ not** ich denke *or* glaube nicht; **I'll take this one then — I ~ not, Mr Green** dann nehme ich dieses — das glaube ich kaum, Herr Green; **I should ~ so/not!** das will ich (aber) auch gemeint haben/das will ich auch nicht hoffen; **I hardly ~/~ it likely that ...** ich glaube kaum/ich halte es nicht für wahrscheinlich, daß ...; **I wasn't even ~ing it** daran habe ich nicht einmal gedacht; **one would have thought there was an easier answer** man sollte eigentlich meinen, daß es da eine einfachere Lösung gäbe; **one would have thought you could have been more punctual** man könnte eigentlich erwarten, daß Sie etwas pünktlicher kommen; **one would have thought they'd have grasped it by now** man sollte eigentlich erwarten, daß sie das inzwischen begriffen haben; **what do you ~ I should do?** was, glauben Sie, soll ich tun?, was soll ich Ihrer Meinung nach tun?; **well, what do you ~, shall we leave now?** nun, was meinst du, sollen wir jetzt gehen?; **I ~ I'll go for a walk** ich glaube, ich mache einen Spaziergang; **do you ~ you can manage?** glauben Sie, daß Sie es schaffen?
(b) (*consider*) **you must ~ me very rude** Sie müssen mich für sehr unhöflich halten; **he ~s he's intelligent, he ~s himself intelligent** er hält sich für intelligent, er meint, er ist *or* sei intelligent; **they are thought to be rich** man hält sie für reich; **I wouldn't have thought it possible** das hätte ich nicht für möglich gehalten.
(c) (*imagine*) sich (*dat*) denken, sich (*dat*) vorstellen ◆ **I don't know what to ~** ich weiß nicht, was ich davon halten soll; **that's what you ~!** denkste! (*inf*); **that's what he ~s** hat der eine Ahnung! (*inf*); **who do you ~ you are!** für wen hältst du dich eigentlich?, wofür hältst du dich eigentlich?; **you can't ~ how pleased I am to see you** Sie können sich (*dat*) (gar) nicht denken *or* vorstellen, wie froh ich bin, Sie zu sehen; **I can't ~ what he means!** ich kann mir (gar) nicht denken, was er meint; (*iro also*) was er damit bloß meinen kann *or* meint?; **anyone would ~ he was dying** man könnte beinahe glauben, er läge im Sterben; **one** *or* **you would ~ they'd already met** man könnte (geradezu) glauben *or* denken, sie seien alte Bekannte; **who would have thought it?** wer hätte das gedacht?; **to ~ that she's only ten!** wenn man bedenkt *or* sich (*dat*) vorstellt, daß sie erst zehn ist.
(d) (*reflect*) **to ~ how to do sth** sich (*dat*) überlegen, wie man etw macht; **I was ~ing (to myself) how ill he looked** ich dachte mir (im Stillen), daß er sehr krank aussah; **I never thought to ask you** ich habe gar nicht daran gedacht, Sie zu fragen.
(e) (*expect, intend: often neg or interrog*) **I didn't ~ to see you here** ich hätte nicht gedacht *or* erwartet, Sie hier zu treffen *or* daß ich Sie hier treffen würde; **I thought as much/I thought so** das habe ich mir schon gedacht.
(f) to ~ one's way out of a difficulty sich (*dat*) einen Ausweg aus einer Schwierigkeit überlegen; **you'll ~ yourself into a rage again** du steigerst dich (nur) wieder in eine Wut hinein.
[3] *n* **have a ~ about it and let me know** denken Sie mal darüber nach *or* überlegen Sie es sich (*dat*) einmal, und geben Sie mir dann Bescheid; **to have a good/quiet ~** gründlich/in aller Ruhe nachdenken; **you've got another ~ coming** (*inf*) da irrst du dich aber gewaltig (*inf*), da bist du aber auf dem Holzweg (*inf*).
◆**think about** *vi +prep obj* **(a)** (*reflect on*) *idea, suggestion* nachdenken über (*+acc*) ◆ **OK, I'll ~ ~ it** okay, ich überlege es mir; **what are you ~ing ~?** woran denken Sie gerade?; **it's worth ~ing ~** das ist überlegenswert, das wäre zu überlegen; **to ~ twice ~ sth** sich (*dat*) etw zweimal überlegen; **that'll give him something to ~ ~** das wird ihm zu denken geben.
(b) (*in progressive tenses: half intend to*) daran denken, vorhaben ◆ **I was ~ing ~ coming to see you** ich habe vorgehabt *or* daran gedacht, Sie zu besuchen;

➤ LANGUAGE IN USE: **think: 2a** → 6.2, 16.1, 26.2 **think about: a** → 15.3

we're ~ing ~ a holiday in Spain wir denken daran, in Spanien Urlaub zu machen.

▼(c) *see* **think of (a, b, f).**

◆**think ahead** *vi* vorausdenken; (*anticipate: driver etc*) Voraussicht walten lassen.

◆**think back** *vi* sich zurückversetzen (*to* in *+acc*).

◆**think of** *vi +prep obj* **(a)** (*consider, give attention to*) denken an (*+acc*) ♦ **I've too many things to ~ ~ just now** ich habe gerade zu viel um die Ohren (*inf*); **I've enough things to ~ ~ as it is** ich habe sowieso schon den Kopf voll *or* genug um die Ohren (*inf*); **he has his family to ~ ~** er muß an seine Familie denken; **he ~s ~ nobody but himself** er denkt bloß an sich; **what am I ~ing ~!** (*inf*) was habe ich mir da(bei) bloß gedacht?, was hab' ich bloß im Kopf? (*inf*).

▼**(b)** (*remember*) denken an (*+acc*) ♦ **will you ~ ~ me sometimes?** wirst du manchmal an mich denken?; **I can't ~ ~ her name** ich kann mich nicht an ihren Namen erinnern, ich komme nicht auf ihren Namen.

(c) (*imagine*) sich (*dat*) vorstellen, bedenken, sich (*dat*) denken ♦ **and to ~ ~ her going there alone!** und wenn man bedenkt *or* sich (*dat*) vorstellt, daß sie ganz allein dorthin gehen will/geht/ging; **~ ~ the cost of all that!** stell dir bloß vor *or* denk dir bloß, was das alles kostet; **just ~ ~ him in a kilt!** stellen Sie sich (*dat*) ihn mal in einem Schottenrock vor!

(d) (*entertain possibility of*) **she'd never ~ ~ getting married** sie denkt gar nicht daran zu heiraten; **he'd never ~ ~ such a thing** so etwas würde ihm nicht im Traum einfallen; **would you ~ ~ lowering the price a little?** würden Sie unter Umständen den Preis etwas ermäßigen?

(e) (*devise, suggest*) *solution, idea, scheme* sich (*dat*) ausdenken ♦ **who thought ~ that idea/plan?** wer ist auf diese Idee gekommen *or* verfallen/wer hat sich diesen Plan ausgedacht?; **the best thing I can ~ ~ is to go home** ich halte es für das beste, nach Hause zu gehen; **shoes for dogs! what will they ~ ~ next!** Schuhe für Hunde! was sie sich wohl (nächstens) noch alles einfallen lassen!

▼**(f)** (*have opinion of*) halten von ♦ **what do you ~ ~ it/him?** was halten Sie davon/von ihm?; **to ~ well** *or* **highly ~ sb/sth** eine gute *or* hohe Meinung von jdm/etw haben, viel von jdm/etw halten; **to ~ little** *or* **not to ~ much ~ sb/sth** wenig *or* nicht viel von jdm/etw halten; **I told him what I thought ~ him** ich habe ihm gründlich die *or* meine Meinung gesagt; **he is very well thought ~ in his own town** in seiner Heimatstadt hält man große Stücke auf ihn.

◆**think on** *vi +prep obj* (*old, dial*) *see* **think about (a).**

◆**think out** *vt sep plan* durchdenken; (*come up with*) *solution* sich (*dat*) ausdenken ♦ **a person who likes to ~ things ~ for himself** ein Mensch, der sich (*dat*) seine eigene Meinung bildet.

◆**think over** *vt sep offer, suggestion* nachdenken über (*+acc*), sich (*dat*) überlegen ♦ **can I ~ it ~?** darf ich darüber nachdenken?, kann ich es mir nochmal überlegen?

◆**think through** *vt sep* (gründlich) durchdenken.

◆**think up** *vt sep* sich (*dat*) ausdenken ♦ **who thought ~ that idea?** wer ist auf die Idee gekommen?

thinkable ['θɪŋkəbl] *adj* denkbar.

thinker ['θɪŋkəʳ] *n* Denker(in *f*) *m*.

thinking ['θɪŋkɪŋ] [1] *adj* denkend ♦ **he's not really a ~ man, he prefers action** er ist kein Denker, sondern ein Macher; **all ~ men will agree with me** alle vernünftigen Menschen werden mit mir übereinstimmen; **to put one's ~ cap on** scharf überlegen *or* nachdenken.

[2] *n* **to do some hard ~ about a question** sich (*dat*) etwas gründlich überlegen, etwas genau durchdenken; **to my way of ~** meiner Meinung nach; **that might be his way of ~** das mag seine Meinung sein; **this calls for some quick ~** hier muß eine schnelle Lösung gefunden werden.

think-piece ['θɪŋkpi:s] *n* (*Press*) ausführlicher Kommentar.

think-tank ['θɪŋktæŋk] *n* Expertenkommission *f*.

thin-lipped ['θɪnlɪpt] *adj* dünnlippig; *smile* dünn.

thinly ['θɪnlɪ] *adv* **(a)** (*in thin slices or layers*) dünn. **(b)** (*sparsely*) dünn; *wooded* spärlich. **(c)** (*lightly*) *clad* leicht, dünn. **(d)** (*fig*) *veiled, disguised* kaum, dürftig; *smile* schwach.

thinner ['θɪnəʳ] *n* Verdünner *m*, Verdünnungsmittel *nt*.

thinness ['θɪnnɪs] *n* **(a)** Dünnheit, Dünnigkeit *f*; (*of dress, material*) Leichtheit *f*; (*of liquid*) Dünnflüssigkeit *f*; (*of paper, line, thread*) Feinheit *f*; (*of column of print*) geringe Breite.

(b) (*of person*) Magerkeit *f*.

(c) (*sparseness*) **the ~ of his hair/the grass/wood/population** *etc* sein schütterer *or* spärlicher Haarwuchs/das spärlich wachsende Gras/die lichte Bewaldung/die geringe Bevölkerungsdichte *etc*.

(d) (*lack of density: of air*) Dünnheit *f*.

(e) (*fig*) (*of voice, smile*) Schwachheit *f*; (*of excuse, disguise, plot*) Dürftigkeit *f*.

thin-skinned ['θɪnskɪnd] *adj* (*fig*) empfindlich, dünnhäutig.

third [θɜ:d] [1] *adj* **(a)** (*in series*) dritte(r, s) ♦ **she was** *or* **came ~ in her class/in the race** sie war die Drittbeste in der Klasse/sie machte *or* belegte den dritten Platz beim Rennen; **~ time lucky** beim dritten Anlauf gelingt's!

(b) (*of fraction*) **a ~ part** ein Drittel *nt*.

[2] *n* **(a)** (*of series*) Dritte(r, s); (*fraction*) Drittel *nt*. **(b)** (*Mus*) Terz *f*. **(c)** (*Aut: ~ gear*) dritter Gang; *see also* **sixth.**

third: ~-class [1] *adv* dritter Klasse; [2] *adj* (*lit*) dritter Klasse; (*fig*) drittklassig; **~ degree** *n* **to give sb the ~ degree** (*lit*) (beim Verhör) Stufe drei einschalten; (*fig*) jdn in die Zange nehmen; **~-degree burns** *npl* (*Med*) Verbrennungen *pl* dritten Grades.

▼**thirdly** ['θɜ:dlɪ] *adv* drittens.

third: ~ party *n* Dritte(r) *m*, dritte Person; **~-party** [1] *adj attr* Haftpflicht-; [2] *adv* **insured ~-party** in einer Haftpflichtversicherung, haftpflichtversichert; **~-party, fire and theft** *adj attr insurance* ≃ Teilkasko-; **~ person** *adj* in der dritten Person; **~-rate** *adj* drittklassig, drittrangig; **T~ World** [1] *n* Dritte Welt; [2] *attr* der Dritten Welt.

thirst [θɜ:st] [1] *n* Durst *m* ♦ **~ for knowledge/revenge/adventure/love** Wissensdurst *m*/Rachsucht *f*/Abenteuerlust *f*/Liebeshunger *m*; **he's got a real ~ on him** (*inf*) er hat einen noblen Durst (am Leibe) (*inf*); **to die of ~** verdursten.

[2] *vi* **(a)** (*old*) **I ~** es dürstet *or* durstet mich.

(b) (*fig*) **to ~ for revenge/knowledge** *etc* nach Rache/Wissen *etc* dürsten; **the plants were ~ing for rain** die Pflanzen dürsteten nach Regen.

thirstily ['θɜ:stɪlɪ] *adv* (*lit*) durstig; (*fig*) begierig.

thirsty ['θɜ:stɪ] *adj* (*+er*) **(a)** durstig ♦ **to be/feel ~** Durst haben; **it made me ~** das machte mich durstig *or* mir Durst; **~ for praise/love/revenge/knowledge/blood** begierig auf Lob/nach Liebe/Rache/Wissen/Blut dürstend *or* lechzend (*old, hum*); **the land is ~ for rain** das Land dürstet nach Regen.

(b) (*causing thirst*) **it's ~ work** diese Arbeit macht durstig.

thirteen ['θɜ:'ti:n] [1] *adj* dreizehn.

[2] *n* Dreizehn *f*.

thirteenth ['θɜ:'ti:nθ] [1] *adj* (*in series*) dreizehnte(r, s) ♦ **a ~ part** ein Dreizehntel *nt*.

[2] *n* (*in series*) Dreizehnte(r, s); (*fraction*) Dreizehntel *nt*; *see also* **sixth.**

thirtieth ['θɜ:tɪɪθ] [1] *adj* (*in series*) dreißigste(r, s) ♦ **a ~ part** ein Dreißigstel *nt*.

[2] *n* (*in series*) Dreißigste(r, s); (*fraction*) Dreißigstel *nt*; *see also* **sixth.**

thirty ['θɜ:tɪ] [1] *adj* dreißig ♦ **~-one/-two** ein-/zweiundreißig; **a ~-second note** (*US Mus*) ein Zweiunddreißigstel *nt*.

[2] *n* Dreißig *f* ♦ **the thirties** (*time*) die dreißiger Jahre; **one's thirties** (*age*) die Dreißiger; *see also* **sixty.**

thirtyish ['θɜ:tɪɪʃ] *adj* um die dreißig.

this [ðɪs] [1] *dem pron, pl* **these** dies, das ♦ **what is ~?** was ist das (hier)?; **who is ~?** wer ist das?; **~ is John** das *or* dies ist John; **these are my children** das *or* dies sind meine Kinder; **~ is where I live** hier wohne ich; **~ is what he showed me** dies *or* das (hier) hat er mir gezeigt; **do you like ~?** gefällt dir das?; **I prefer ~** ich mag das hier *or* dies(es) lieber; **~ is to certify that ...** hiermit wird bestätigt, daß ...; **under/in front of** *etc* **~** darunter/davor *etc*; **it ought to have been done before ~** es hätte schon vorher getan werden sollen; **with ~ he left us** damit *or* mit diesen Worten verließ er uns; **what's all ~?** was soll das?; **what's all ~ I hear about your new job?** was höre ich da so (alles) über deine neue Stelle?; **~ and that** mancherlei; **we were talking of ~ and that** wir haben von diesem und jenem *or* über dies und das geredet; **~, that and the other** alles mögliche; **will you take ~ or that?** nehmen Sie dieses hier oder das da?; **it was like ~** es war so; **~ is Friday the 13th** heute ist Freitag der 13.; **but ~ is May** aber wir haben *or* es ist doch Mai!; **and now ~!** und jetzt (auch noch) dies *or* das!; **~ is Mary (speaking)** hier (ist) Mary; **~ is what I mean!** das meine ich (ja)!; **~ is it!** (*now*) jetzt!; (*showing sth*) das da!, das ist er/sie/es!; (*exactly*) genau!

[2] *dem adj, pl* **these** diese(r, s) ♦ **~ week/month/year** diese Woche/diesen Monat/dieses Jahr; **~ evening** heute abend; **~ day week** (heute) in einer Woche; **~ time last week** letzte Woche um diese Zeit; **~ coming week** jetzt die (kommende) Woche; **~ time** diesmal, dieses Mal; **these days** heutzutage; **all ~ talk** dieses ganze Gerede, all das *or* dies Gerede; **to run ~ way and that** hin und her rennen; **I have been waiting for you ~ past half-hour** ich habe bereits die letzte halbe Stunde auf dich gewartet; **~ boy of yours!** also, Ihr Junge!; **I met ~ guy who ...** (*inf*) ich habe (so) einen getroffen, der ...; **~ friend of hers** dieser Freund von ihr (*inf*), ihr Freund.

[3] *dem adv* so ♦ **it was ~ long** es war so lang; **~ far** (*time*) bis jetzt; (*place*) so weit, bis hierher; **~ much is certain** soviel ist sicher, eins steht fest.

thistle ['θɪsl] *n* Distel *f*.

thistledown ['θɪsldaʊn] *n* Distelwolle *f* ♦ **as light as ~** federleicht.

thither ['ðɪðəʳ] *adv* (*old*) dorthin, dahin; *see* **hither.**

tho' [ðəʊ] *abbr of* **though.**

thole [θəʊl] *n* (*Naut*) Dolle, Riemenauflage *f*.

Thomist ['təʊmɪst] [1] *n* Thomist *m*.

[2] *adj* thomistisch.

thong [θɒŋ] *n* (*of whip*) Peitschenschnur *f*, Peitschenriemen *m*; (*fastening*) Lederriemen *m*.

thoracic [θɔ:'ræsɪk] *adj* Brust-, thorakal (*spec*).

thorax ['θɔ:ræks] *n* Brustkorb, Brustkasten, Thorax (*spec*) *m*.

thorium ['θɔ:rɪəm] *n* (*Chem*) Thorium *nt*.

thorn [θɔ:n] *n* Dorn *m*; (*shrub*) Dornbusch, Dornenstrauch *m* ♦ **to be a ~ in sb's flesh** *or* **side** (*fig*) jdm ein Dorn im Auge sein.

thornless ['θɔ:nlɪs] *adj* ohne Dornen.

thorny ['θɔ:nɪ] *adj* (*+er*) (*lit*) dornig, dornenreich; (*fig*) haarig.

thorough ['θʌrə] *adj* gründlich; *knowledge also* umfassend, solide; *contempt also* bodenlos; *success* voll, durchschlagend; *fool, rascal* ausgemacht ♦ **she's/it's a ~ nuisance** sie ist wirklich eine Plage/das ist wirklich lästig.

thorough: ~bred [1] *n* reinrassiges Tier; (*horse*) Vollblut(pferd) *nt*, Vollblüter *m*; [2] *adj* reinrassig; *horse* Vollblut-, vollblütig; *dog* Rasse-; **~fare** *n* Durchfahrts- *or* Durchgangsstraße *f*; **it's the most famous ~fare of this town** es ist die berühmteste Straße dieser Stadt; **this isn't a public ~fare** das ist keine öffentliche Verkehrsstraße; **"no ~fare"** (*cul-de-sac*) „Sackgasse"; (*not*

➤ LANGUAGE IN USE: **think about: c** → 6.1, 6.3 **think of: b** → 25.2 **f** → 6.1, 12.2, 14 **thirdly** → 26.2

open to public) „Durchfahrt verboten"; **~going** *adj changes* gründlich; *revision* grundlegend, tiefgreifend; *measure, reform* durchgreifend; **he is a ~going rascal** er ist ein Spitzbube durch und durch.

thoroughly [ˈθʌrəlɪ] *adv* **(a)** gründlich, von Grund auf.
(b) (*extremely*) durch und durch, von Grund auf ◆ **a ~ nasty person** ein Scheusal durch und durch; **~ modern** durch und durch modern; **~ boring** ausgesprochen langweilig; **I'm ~ ashamed** ich schäme mich zutiefst, ich bin zutiefst beschämt.

thoroughness [ˈθʌrənɪs] *n* Gründlichkeit *f*; (*carefulness*) Sorgfältigkeit, Sorgfalt *f*; (*of knowledge also*) Umfang *m*, Solidität *f*.

Thos *abbr of* **Thomas.**

those [ðəʊz] *pl of* **that** [1] *dem pron* das (da) *sing* ◆ **what are ~?** was ist das (denn) da?, was sind das für Dinger? (*inf*); **whose are ~?** wem gehören diese da?; **~ are the girls/my suggestions** das (da) *or* dies(es) sind die Mädchen/das *or* dies sind meine Vorschläge; **on top of/above/after ~** darauf; (*moreover*) darüber hinaus/darüber/danach; (*place*) dahinter; **~ are the ones I like** das da *or* diese dort mag ich; **~ who want to go, may** wer möchte, kann gehen, diejenigen, die gehen möchten, können das tun (*form*); **one of ~ who ...** einer/eine von denen *or* denjenigen, die ...; **there are ~ who say ...** einige sagen ...
[2] *dem adj* diese *or* die (da), jene (*old, liter*) ◆ **what are ~ men doing?** was machen diese Männer da?; **on ~ two occasions** bei diesen beiden Gelegenheiten; **it was just one of ~ days/things** das war wieder so ein Tag/so eine Sache; **he is one of ~ people who ...** er ist einer von den Leuten *or* von denjenigen, die ...; **~ dogs/sons of yours!** also, diese Hunde/deine Söhne!

thou [ðaʊ] *pers pron* (*old*) (*to friend, servant etc*) Er/Sie (*obs*); (*to stranger*) Ihr (*obs*); (*Rel*) Du; (*Brit: dial*) du.

▼ **though** [ðəʊ] [1] *conj* **(a)** (*in spite of the fact that*) obwohl, obgleich, obschon ◆ **even ~** obwohl *etc*; **~ poor she is generous** obwohl *etc* sie arm ist, ist sie großzügig; **strange ~ it may seem ...** so seltsam es auch scheinen mag ..., mag es auch noch so seltsam scheinen (*geh*) ...; **important ~ it may be/is ...** so wichtig es auch sein mag/ist, auch wenn es noch so wichtig ist ...
(b) (*liter: even if*) **I will go (even) ~ it should cost me my life** ich werde gehen, und sollte es mich (auch) das Leben kosten *or* und koste es das Leben (*liter*); **~ it take forever** (*liter*) und dauerte es auch ewig (*liter*).
▼ **(c) as ~** als ob.
[2] *adv* **(a)** (*nevertheless*) doch ◆ **he didn't/did do it ~** er hat es aber (doch) nicht/aber doch gemacht; **I'm sure he didn't do it ~** ich bin aber sicher, daß er es nicht gemacht hat; **nice day — rather windy ~** schönes Wetter! — aber ziemlich windig!
(b) (*really*) **but will he ~?** tatsächlich?, wirklich?
(c) (*inf*) **hot, isn't it? — isn't it ~!** warm, was? — allerdings!

thought [θɔːt] [1] *pret, ptp of* **think.**
[2] *n* **(a)** *no pl* (*act or process of thinking*) Denken *nt* ◆ **to spend hours in ~** stundenlang in Gedanken (vertieft) sein; **to be lost in ~** in Gedanken *or* gedankenverloren (*geh*) sein; **to take ~** (*old*) denken; **logical ~** logisches Denken; **in ~** in Gedanken; **~ experiment** Gedankenexperiment *nt*.
(b) (*idea, opinion*) Gedanke *m*; (*sudden*) Einfall *m* ◆ **she hasn't a ~ in her head** sie hat nichts im Hirn *or* Kopf; **the ~s of Chairman Mao** die Gedanken *pl* des Vorsitzenden Mao; **he didn't express any ~s on the matter** er hat keine Ansichten zu diesem Thema geäußert; **that's a ~!** (*amazing*) man stelle sich das mal vor!; (*problem to be considered*) das ist wahr!; (*good idea*) das ist eine (gute) Idee *or* ein guter Gedanke *or* Einfall; **what a ~!** was für ein Gedanke *or* eine Vorstellung!; **a ~ has just occurred to me, I've just had a ~** (*inf*) mir ist gerade ein Gedanke gekommen, mir ist gerade etwas eingefallen; **don't give it another ~** machen Sie sich (*dat*) keine Gedanken darüber; (*forget it*) denken Sie nicht mehr daran; **on second ~s** wenn man sich das noch mal überlegt; **his one ~ was ...** sein einziger Gedanke war ...; **to have no ~ of doing sth** gar nicht vorhaben *or* gar nicht daran denken, etw zu tun; **it's a shame it doesn't fit, but it's the ~ that counts** es ist ein Jammer, daß es nicht paßt, aber es war gut gemeint; **it's the ~ that counts, not how much you spend** es kommt nur auf die Idee an, nicht auf den Preis; **to collect one's ~s** sich sammeln, seine Gedanken zusammennehmen; **her ~s were elsewhere** sie war in Gedanken woanders; **the mere** *or* **very ~ of it** der bloße Gedanke (daran), die bloße Vorstellung.
(c) *no pl* (*body of ideas*) Denken *nt* ◆ **modern ~** das moderne Denken, das Denken der Moderne.
(d) *no pl* (*care, consideration*) Nachdenken *nt*, Überlegung *f* ◆ **to give some ~ to sth** sich (*dat*) Gedanken über etw (*acc*) machen, etw bedenken *or* überlegen; **after much ~** nach langer Überlegung *or* langem Überlegen; **to act without ~** gedankenlos *or* ohne Überlegung handeln; **without ~ for sb/oneself/sth** ohne an jdn/sich selbst/etw zu denken, ohne Rücksicht auf jdn/sich selbst/etw; **to be full of ~ for sb** auf jdn große Rücksicht nehmen; **he was full of ~ for our comfort** er bemühte sich sehr um unser Wohlergehen; **he has no ~ for his parents' feelings** er nimmt keine Rücksicht auf die Gefühle seiner Eltern; **I never gave it a moment's ~** ich habe mir nie darüber Gedanken gemacht.
(e) a ~ (*a little*) eine Idee, ein Ideechen *nt* (*inf*); **with a ~ more tact** mit einer Idee *or* einer Spur mehr Takt.

thoughtful [ˈθɔːtfʊl] *adj* **(a)** (*full of thought*) *expression, person* nachdenklich, gedankenvoll, grüblerisch; *remark, analysis, book* gut durchdacht, wohlüberlegt; *present* gut ausgedacht.
(b) (*considerate*) rücksichtsvoll; (*attentive, helpful*) aufmerksam ◆ **to be ~ of sb's comfort/needs** an jds Wohlbefinden/Bedürfnisse denken; **to be ~ of/towards sb** jdm gegenüber aufmerksam/rücksichtsvoll sein; **it was very ~ of you to ...** es war sehr aufmerksam von Ihnen, zu ...

thoughtfully [ˈθɔːtfəlɪ] *adv* **(a)** *say, look* nachdenklich.
(b) (*with much thought*) mit viel Überlegung ◆ **a ~ written book** ein wohldurchdachtes Buch.
(c) (*considerately*) rücksichtsvoll; (*attentively, helpfully*) aufmerksam ◆ **she ~ provided rugs** sie war so aufmerksam, Decken bereitzustellen, aufmerksamerweise hatte sie Decken bereitgestellt.

thoughtfulness [ˈθɔːtfʊlnɪs] *n* **(a)** (*of expression, person*) Nachdenklichkeit *f*; (*of remark, analysis*) Tiefgang *m*. **(b)** (*consideration*) Rücksicht(nahme) *f*; (*attentiveness, helpfulness*) Aufmerksamkeit *f* ◆ **his ~ towards his parents** seine Aufmerksamkeit/Rücksichtnahme seinen Eltern gegenüber.

thoughtless [ˈθɔːtlɪs] *adj* **(a)** (*without reflection*) gedankenlos, unüberlegt, unbesonnen ◆ **~ of the danger, he leapt** ungeachtet der Gefahr sprang er.
(b) (*inconsiderate*) *person* gedankenlos, rücksichtslos; (*inattentive, unhelpful*) gedankenlos, unachtsam ◆ **he's very ~ of** *or* **about/to(wards) other people** er ist sehr gedankenlos/rücksichtslos anderen gegenüber.

thoughtlessly [ˈθɔːtlɪslɪ] *adv* **(a)** (*without reflection*) gedankenlos, unüberlegt ◆ **he had ~ taken it with him** er hatte es aus Gedankenlosigkeit mitgenommen. **(b)** *see adj (b)*.

thoughtlessness [ˈθɔːtlɪsnɪs] *n* **(a)** (*lack of reflection*) Gedankenlosigkeit, Unüberlegtheit *f*. **(b)** *see adj (b)* Gedankenlosigkeit *f*, Rücksichtslosigkeit *f*; Unaufmerksamkeit *f*.

thought: ~-reader *n* Gedankenleser(in *f*) *m*; **~-reading** *n* Gedankenlesen *nt*; **~ transference** *n* Gedankenübertragung *f*.

thousand [ˈθaʊzənd] [1] *adj* tausend ◆ **a ~/two ~** (ein)tausend/zweitausend; **a ~ times** tausendmal; **a ~ and one/two** tausend(und)eins/tausend(und)zwei; **I died a ~ deaths** (*inf*) (*embarrassed*) ich wäre fast in den Boden versunken; (*afraid*) ich habe tausend Ängste ausgestanden; **I have a ~ and one (different) things to do** (*inf*) ich habe tausenderlei *or* tausend Dinge zu tun; **~ island(s) dressing** Thousand-Islands-Dressing *nt*.
[2] *n* Tausend *nt* ◆ **the ~s** (*Math*) die Tausender *pl*; **there were ~s of people present** es waren Tausende (von Menschen) anwesend; **the year three ~** das Jahr dreitausend; **people arrived in their ~s** die Menschen kamen zu Tausenden.

thousandfold [ˈθaʊzəndfəʊld] (*liter*) [1] *adj* tausendfach.
[2] *adv* tausendfach, tausendfältig.

thousandth [ˈθaʊzəntθ] [1] *adj* (*in series*) tausendste(r, s) ◆ **a** *or* **one ~ part** ein Tausendstel *nt*.
[2] *n* (*in series*) Tausendste(r, s); (*fraction*) Tausendstel *nt*; *see also* **sixth.**

thraldom, (*US*) **thralldom** [ˈθrɔːldəm] *n* (*liter*) Knechtschaft *f* ◆ **he was held in ~ to her beauty** (*fig*) ihre Schönheit hatte ihn in ihren Bann geschlagen.

thrall [θrɔːl] *n* (*liter*) **(a)** (*slave*) Leibeigene(r), Sklave (*also fig*), Knecht *m*. **(b)** (*condition*) *see* **thraldom.**

thrash [θræʃ] [1] *vt* **(a)** (*beat*) verprügeln, verdreschen; *donkey etc* einschlagen auf (+*acc*) ◆ **to ~ the life out of sb** jdn grün und blau schlagen.
(b) (*Sport inf*) *opponent* (vernichtend) schlagen.
(c) (*move wildly*) *arms* schlagen mit, fuchteln mit; *legs* strampeln mit ◆ **he ~ed his arms (about) angrily** er schlug wütend (mit den Armen) um sich.
(d) (*Agr*) *see* **thresh.**
[2] *vi* **to ~ about** *or* **around** um sich schlagen; (*in bed*) sich herumwerfen; (*fish*) zappeln; **the branches ~ed against the panes** die Zweige schlugen gegen die Fensterscheiben.
[3] *n* (*dated Brit inf: party*) Party *f*.

◆**thrash out** *vt sep problem* ausdiskutieren.

thrashing [ˈθræʃɪŋ] *n* **(a)** (*beating*) Prügel, Schläge *pl*, Dresche *f* (*inf*) ◆ **to give sb a good ~** jdm eine ordentliche Tracht Prügel verpassen. **(b)** (*Sport inf*) komplette Niederlage ◆ **to give sb a ~** jdn vernichtend schlagen.

thread [θred] [1] *n* **(a)** (*of cotton, wool etc*) Faden *m*; (*Sew also*) Garn *nt*; (*strong ~*) Zwirn *m* ◆ **to hang by a ~** (*fig*) an einem (seidenen *or* dünnen) Faden hängen.
(b) (*fig: of story*) (roter) Faden ◆ **to follow the ~ of an argument/a story** dem Gedankengang einer Argumentation/dem roten Faden (in) einer Geschichte folgen; **he lost the ~ of what he was saying** er hat den Faden verloren; **to pick up the ~s of one's story/a conversation** den (roten) Faden/den Gesprächsfaden wiederaufnehmen; **to gather up** *or* **pick up the ~s of one's life** alte Fäden wieder anknüpfen.
(c) (*Tech: of screw*) Gewinde *nt*.
(d) (*fig: thin line: of light*) Strahl, Streifen *m*.
[2] *vt* **(a)** *needle* einfädeln; *beads* aufreihen, auffädeln (*on* auf +*acc*); *necklace* aufziehen ◆ **~ed with silver** von Silber(fäden) durchzogen, mit Silber(fäden) durchsetzt.
(b) to ~ one's way through the crowd/trees *etc* sich durch die Menge/zwischen den Bäumen *etc* hindurchschlängeln.
(c) (*Tech*) *screw* mit einem Gewinde versehen.
[3] *vi* **he ~ed through the crowd** er schlängelte sich durch die Menge (hindurch).

threadbare [ˈθredbeəʳ] *adj* abgewetzt, fadenscheinig; *clothes also* abgetragen; *carpet also* abgelaufen; *argument* fadenscheinig.

threaded [ˈθredɪd] *adj* (*Tech*) Gewinde-.

thread mark *n* Silberfaden *m* (*in Banknoten*).

threat [θret] *n* **(a)** Drohung *f* ◆ **is that a ~?** soll das eine Drohung sein?; **to make a ~** drohen, eine Androhung machen (*against sb* jdm); **under ~ of sth** unter Androhung von etw; **he is under ~ of expulsion** ihm wurde der Ausschluß angedroht.

➤ LANGUAGE IN USE: **though: 1c → 15.2**

(b) (*danger*) Bedrohung (*to gen*), Gefahr (*to* für) *f* ♦ **this war is a ~ to civilization** dieser Krieg stellt eine Gefahr für die *or* eine Bedrohung der Zivilisation dar.

threaten ['θretn] [1] *vt* **(a)** *person* bedrohen, drohen (+*dat*); *revenge, violence* androhen, drohen mit ♦ **don't you ~ me!** von Ihnen lasse ich mir nicht drohen!; **to ~ to do sth** (an)drohen, etw zu tun; **to ~ sb with sth** jdm etw androhen, jdm mit etw drohen; **to ~ sb with a weapon** jdn mit der Waffe bedrohen.
(b) (*put in danger*) bedrohen, gefährden ♦ **the rain ~ed to spoil the harvest** der Regen drohte, die Ernte zu zerstören.
(c) (*Met: give warning of*) **the sky ~s rain** der Himmel sieht (bedrohlich) nach Regen aus; **it's ~ing to rain** es sieht (bedrohlich) nach Regen aus.
[2] *vi* (*danger, storm etc*) drohen, im Anzug sein.

threatening ['θretnɪŋ] *adj* drohend; *weather, clouds also* bedrohlich ♦ **a ~ letter** ein Drohbrief *m*; **~ behaviour** Drohungen *pl*.

threateningly ['θretnɪŋlɪ] *adv* drohend ♦ **the sky darkened ~** der Himmel verfinsterte sich bedrohlich.

three [θriː] [1] *adj* drei.
[2] *n* (*figure, tram, Cards*) Drei *f* ♦ **~'s a crowd** drei Leute sind schon zuviel, bei dreien ist einer zuviel; *see also* **six**.

three: ~-act play *n* Dreiakter *m*; **~-colour(ed)** *adj* (*Phot*) Dreifarben-; **~-cornered** *adj* dreieckig; **~-cornered contest** *or* **fight** Kampf *m* mit drei Beteiligten *or* Parteien, Dreieckskampf *m*; **~-cornered hat** Dreispitz *m*; **~-D** [1] *n* **to be in ~-D** dreidimensional *or* 3-D sein; [2] *adj* (*also* **~-dimensional**) dreidimensional, 3-D-; **~fold** *adj, adv* dreifach; **~-legged** *adj* dreibeinig; **~-legged race** (*Sport*) *Wettlauf m, bei dem zwei an einem Bein zusammengebunden werden*; **~-master** *n* Dreimaster *m*; **~penny** ['θrepənɪ] **bit** *or* **piece** *n* (*Brit old*) Dreipennystück *nt*; **~penny opera** *n* Dreigroschenoper *f*; **~-phase** *adj* (*Elec*) Dreiphasen-; **~-piece suit** *n* (*man's*) Anzug *m* mit Weste; (*lady's*) dreiteiliges Ensemble; **~-piece suite** *n* dreiteilige Polster- *or* Sitzgarnitur; **~-pin plug** *n* Stecker *m* mit drei Kontakten; **~-ply** [1] *n* (*wool*) Dreifachwolle *f*; (*wood*) dreischichtiges Spanholz; [2] *attr wool* dreifach, Dreifach-; *wood* dreischichtig; **~-point landing** *n* (*Aviat*) Dreipunktlandung *f*; **~-point turn** *n* (*Aut*) Wenden *nt* in drei Zügen; **~-quarter** [1] *n* (*Sport*) Dreiviertelspieler *m*; [2] *attr* dreiviertel-; **~-quarter length** dreiviertellang; **~-quarter portrait** Halbbild *nt*; **~ quarters** [1] *n* Dreiviertel *nt*; [2] *adv* dreiviertel, zu drei Vierteln; **~-ring circus** *n* (*inf*) Affenzirkus *m*; **~score** *adj* sechzig; **~some** *n* Trio *nt*, Dreiergruppe *f*; (*Golf*) Dreier *m*; **in a ~some** zu dritt; **~-speed** *adj attr* **~-speed gears** Dreigangschaltung *f*; **~-wheeler** *n* (*Aut*) dreirädriges Auto; (*tricycle*) Dreirad *nt*.

threnody ['θrenədɪ] *n* (*Liter*) Threnodie *f*.

thresh [θreʃ] *vti* dreschen.

thresher ['θreʃə^r] *n* **(a)** (*Agr: machine*) Dreschmaschine *f*; (*person*) Drescher(in *f*) *m*. **(b)** (*~ shark*) Drescherhai *m*.

threshing ['θreʃɪŋ] *n* Dreschen *nt* ♦ **~ floor** Dreschboden *m*, Tenne *f*; **~ machine** Dreschmaschine *f*.

threshold ['θreʃhəʊld] *n* (*lit, fig, Psych*) Schwelle *f*; (*of door also*) (Tür)schwelle *f* ♦ **on the ~** an der Schwelle; **we are on the ~ of a great discovery** wir stehen unmittelbar vor *or* an der Schwelle zu einer großen Entdeckung; **to have a high/low pain ~** eine hohe/niedrige Schmerzschwelle haben.

threw [θruː] *pret of* **throw**.

thrice [θraɪs] *adv* (*old*) dreimal ♦ **he is ~ blessed** er ist dreifach *or* dreifältig gesegnet.

thrift [θrɪft] *n* Sparsamkeit *f*.

thriftily ['θrɪftɪlɪ] *adv* **(a)** sparsam, wirtschaftlich, haushälterisch. **(b)** (*US*) **his business is doing ~** sein Geschäft floriert.

thriftiness ['θrɪftɪnɪs] *n* **(a)** Sparsamkeit, Wirtschaftlichkeit *f*. **(b)** (*US: prosperity*) Gedeihen *nt*.

thriftless ['θrɪftlɪs] *adj* verschwenderisch.

thriftlessness ['θrɪftlɪsnɪs] *n* Verschwendung(ssucht) *f*.

thrifty ['θrɪftɪ] *adj* (+*er*) **(a)** (*careful, economical*) sparsam, wirtschaftlich, haushälterisch. **(b)** (*US: thriving*) blühend.

thrill [θrɪl] [1] *n* Erregung *f* ♦ **all the ~s and spills of the circus** all die Sensationen und der Nervenkitzel des Zirkus; **the ~ of her touch** der erregende Reiz ihrer Berührung; **a ~ of joy/horror** eine freudige Erregung/ein Entsetzensschauder *m*; **she heard his voice with a ~ of excitement** sie hörte seine Stimme, und Erregung durchfuhr sie; **it gave me quite a~, it was quite a ~ for me** es war ein richtiges Erlebnis; **what a ~!** wie aufregend!; **he gets a ~ out of hunting** Jagen hat für ihn einen ganz besonderen Reiz; **the real ~ comes at the end of the book** die eigentliche Sensation kommt erst am Ende des Buches; **that's how he gets his ~s** das erregt ihn; **this will give you the ~ of a lifetime** das wird *das* Erlebnis deines Lebens (sein); **go on, give us a ~!** (*inf*) nun laß uns mal was sehen (*inf*).
[2] *vt person* (*story, crimes*) mitreißen, fesseln, packen; (*experience*) eine Sensation sein für; (*sb's touch, voice etc*) freudig erzittern lassen; (*sexually*) erregen ♦ **I was quite ~ed by the sight of the Alps** ich war ganz hingerissen beim Anblick der Alpen; **I was ~ed to get your letter** ich habe mich riesig über deinen Brief gefreut; **the thought of going to America ~ed her** der Gedanke an eine Amerikareise versetzte sie in freudige Erregung; **to be ~ed to bits** (*inf*) sich freuen wie ein Kind; (*child esp*) ganz aus dem Häuschen sein vor Freude.
[3] *vi* **she ~ed at the sound of his voice/to his touch** ein freudiger Schauer durchlief sie, als sie seine Stimme hörte/bei seiner Berührung.

thriller ['θrɪlə^r] *n* Reißer *m* (*inf*); (*whodunnit*) Krimi, Thriller *m*.

thrilling ['θrɪlɪŋ] *adj* aufregend; *book, film* spannend, fesselnd; *sensation* überwältigend, hinreißend; *music* hinreißend, mitreißend; *experience* überwältigend, umwerfend (*inf*); (*sexually*) erregend ♦ **we had a ~ time** es war richtig aufregend.

thrillingly ['θrɪlɪŋlɪ] *adv* spannungsgeladen ♦ **~ new** aufregend neu; **the music rose ~ to a climax** die Musik steigerte sich einem erregenden Höhepunkt entgegen.

thrive [θraɪv] *pret* **throve** (*old*) *or* **~d**, *ptp* **thriven** ['θrɪvən] (*old*) *or* **~d** *vi* (*be in good health: animal, plant*) (gut) gedeihen; (*child also*) sich gut *or* prächtig entwickeln; (*do well*) (*business*) blühen, florieren; (*businessman*) erfolgreich sein.

♦**thrive on** *vi* +*prep obj* **the baby ~s ~ milk** mit Milch gedeiht das Baby prächtig; **this plant ~s ~ sun and light** bei Sonne und Licht gedeiht *or* entwickelt sich diese Pflanze prächtig; **he ~s ~ criticism/praise** Kritik/Lob bringt ihn erst zur vollen Entfaltung; **like it? I ~ ~ it** ob mir das gefällt? ich brauche das.

thriving ['θraɪvɪŋ] *adj* **(a)** *plant* prächtig gedeihend, kräftig; *person* blühend; *child* gut gedeihend ♦ **he's ~!** ihm geht's prächtig!; (*child*) er blüht und gedeiht! **(b)** *business* florierend, blühend, gutgehend; *businessman* erfolgreich.

thro' [θruː] *abbr of* **through**.

throat [θrəʊt] *n* (*external*) Kehle *f*; (*internal also*) Rachen *m* ♦ **to grab sb by the ~** jdn bei *or* an der Kehle *or* Gurgel packen; **to cut sb's/one's ~** jdm/sich die Kehle *or* Gurgel durchschneiden; **to cut one's own ~** (*fig*) sich (*dat*) selbst das Wasser abgraben; **my ~ is really dry** ich habe einen völlig trockenen Hals *or* eine ganz trockene Kehle; **I've a fishbone stuck in my ~** mir ist eine Gräte im Hals steckengeblieben; **the doctor looked down her ~** der Arzt sah ihr in den Hals; **cancer of the ~** Kehlkopfkrebs *m*; **to clear one's ~** sich räuspern; **they've been pouring drink down my ~ all evening** (*inf*) sie haben den ganzen Abend lang Alkohol in mich hineingeschüttet (*inf*); **to thrust** *or* **ram** *or* **force one's ideas down sb's ~** (*inf*) jdm seine eigenen Ideen aufzwingen; **the words stuck in my ~** die Worte blieben mir im Halse stecken; **it sticks in my ~** (*fig*) das geht mir gegen den Strich (*inf*); **~ microphone** Kehlkopfmikrophon *nt*.

throaty *adj* (+*er*), **throatily** *adv* ['θrəʊtɪ, -lɪ] kehlig, rauh.

throb [θrɒb] [1] *vi* (*engine*) klopfen, hämmern; (*drums, gunfire*) dröhnen; (*heart, pulse*) pochen, klopfen; (*painfully: wound*) pochen, pulsieren, klopfen; (*very strongly*) hämmern; (*fig: with life, activity*) pulsieren (*with* vor +*dat*, mit) ♦ **my head was still ~bing (with pain)** ich hatte immer noch dieses Pochen im Kopf; **my head is ~bing** ich habe rasende Kopfschmerzen; **a street ~bing with people** eine Straße, die von Menschen wimmelt.
[2] *n* (*engine*) Klopfen, Hämmern *nt*; (*drums, gunfire*) Dröhnen *nt*; (*heart, pulse, wound*) Klopfen, Pochen *nt*; Hämmern *nt* ♦ **the ~ of life** der Pulsschlag des Lebens.

throbbing ['θrɒbɪŋ] *n see vi* Klopfen, Hämmern *nt*; Dröhnen *nt*; Pochen *nt*.

throes [θrəʊz] *npl* **(a) the ~ of childbirth** die (Geburts)wehen *pl*; **in the ~ of death** im Todeskampf, in Todesqualen *pl*; **to be in its final ~** (*fig*) in den letzten Zügen liegen.
(b) (*fig*) Wirren *pl* ♦ **we are in the ~ of moving** wir stecken mitten im Umzug; **I was in the ~ of composition** ich war völlig vertieft in meine Kompositionen; **in the ~ of inspiration** in künstlerischer Versunkenheit.

thrombosis [θrɒm'bəʊsɪs] *n* Thrombose *f*.

thrombus ['θrɒmbəs] *n* Thrombus (*form*), Blutpfropf *m*.

throne [θrəʊn] [1] *n* Thron *m*; (*Eccl*) Stuhl *m* ♦ **to come to the ~** den Thron besteigen; **to swear allegiance to the ~** der Krone den Treueid leisten; **the powers of the ~** die Macht der Krone.
[2] *vt* **(he is) ~d in glory** (*Eccl*) er sitzet *or* thronet in Herrlichkeit.

throneroom ['θrəʊnruːm] *n* Thronsaal *m*; (*hum*) Klo *nt* (*inf*).

throng [θrɒŋ] [1] *n* (*of people*) Scharen *pl*, Menschenmenge *f*; (*of angels*) Heerschar *f*.
[2] *vi* sich drängen ♦ **to ~ round sb/sth** sich um jdn/etw drängen *or* scharen; **hundreds of people ~ed round** Hunderte von Leuten strömten herbei; **to ~ towards sb/sth** sich zu jdm/etw drängen, zu jdm/etw strömen.
[3] *vt* belagern ♦ **people ~ed the streets** die Menschen drängten sich in den Straßen; **to be ~ed with** wimmeln von *or* mit.

throttle ['θrɒtl] [1] *vt* **(a)** erdrosseln, erwürgen.
(b) (*fig*) *feelings* ersticken, unterdrücken; *opposition* ersticken, unterbinden ♦ **to ~ the press** die Presse knebeln.
(c) (*Tech*) *see* **~ back**.
[2] *n* **(a)** (*on engine*) Drossel *f*; (*Aut etc*) (*lever*) Gashebel *m*; (*valve*) Drosselklappe *f* ♦ **at full ~** mit Vollgas; **to open/close the ~** die Drossel öffnen/schließen; (*Aut etc*) Gas geben/zurücknehmen. **(b)** (*hum: throat*) Kehle *f*.

♦**throttle back** *or* **down** [1] *vt sep* drosseln.
[2] *vi* Gas zurücknehmen, den Motor drosseln.

through, (*US*) **thru** [θruː] [1] *prep* **(a)** (*place*) durch ♦ **he got/couldn't get ~ the hedge** er schlüpfte durch die Hecke (hindurch)/er konnte nicht durch die Hecke durchkommen *or* (hin)durchschlüpfen; **to listen ~ the door** durch die (geschlossene) Tür mithören, lauschen; **he was shot ~ the head** er bekam einen Kopfschuß; **he went right ~ the red lights** er ist bei Rot einfach durchgefahren; **he has come ~ many hardships** er hat viel Schweres durchgemacht; **we're ~ that stage now** wir sind jetzt durch dieses Stadium hindurch; **to be halfway ~ a book** ein Buch halb *or* zur Hälfte durchhaben (*inf*); **that happens halfway/three-quarters of the way ~ the book** das passiert in der Mitte/im letzten Viertel des Buches; *see vbs*.
(b) (*time*) **all ~ his life** sein ganzes Leben lang; **he won't live ~ the night** er wird die Nacht nicht überleben; **he worked ~ the night** er hat die Nacht

durchgearbeitet; **he lives there ~ the week** er wohnt da während *or* unter (*dial*) der Woche *or* die Woche über; **he slept ~ the film** er hat den ganzen Film über *or* hindurch *or* lang geschlafen; **all ~ the autumn** den ganzen Herbst über *or* hindurch.

(c) (*US: up to and including*) bis (einschließlich) ◆ **Monday ~ Friday** von Montag bis (einschließlich) Freitag.

(d) (*means, agency*) durch ◆ **~ the post** mit der *or* per Post; **it happened ~ no fault of mine** es geschah nicht durch meine Schuld; **absent ~ illness** abwesend wegen Krankheit; **~ neglect** durch Nachlässigkeit; **to act ~ fear** aus Angst handeln.

[2] *adv* (*time, place*) durch ◆ **he's a gentleman/liar ~ and ~** er ist durch und durch ein Gentleman/verlogen; **to sleep all night ~** die ganze Nacht durchschlafen; **did you stay right ~?** sind Sie bis zum Schluß geblieben?; **they stayed ~ until Thursday** sie blieben bis Donnerstag (da); **he knew all ~ what I was getting at** er wußte die ganze Zeit (über), worauf ich hinauswollte; **to let sb ~** jdn durchlassen; **to be wet ~** durch und durch *or* bis auf die Haut naß sein; **to read sth ~** etw durchlesen; **he's ~ in the other office** er ist (drüben) im anderen Büro; **the train goes ~ to Berlin** der Zug fährt bis nach Berlin durch; *see vbs.*

[3] *adj pred* (a) (*finished*) **to be ~ with sb/sth** mit jdm/etw fertig sein (*inf*); **we're ~** (*have finished relationship*) es ist (alles) aus zwischen uns; (*have finished job*) wir sind fertig; **I'm ~ with him** der ist für mich gestorben *or* erledigt, ich bin fertig mit ihm (*all inf*); **I'm ~ with that kind of work** ich habe genug von dieser Arbeit; **you're ~, Kowalski, fired** wir sind mit Ihnen fertig, Kowalski, Sie fliegen!; **are you ~?** sind Sie fertig?

(b) (*Brit Telec*) **to be ~ (to sb/London)** mit jdm/London verbunden sein; **to get ~ (to sb/London)** zu jdm/nach London durchkommen; **you're ~, caller** Ihre Verbindung!, Ihr Gespräch!

through: ~ coach *n* (*Rail*) Kurswagen *m* (*for* nach); (*bus*) direkte Busverbindung; **~ flight** *n* Direktflug *m*; **~ freight** *n* Durchgangsfracht *f*; **~-hole** *adj* (*Comput*) durchkontaktiert.

throughout [θrʊˈaʊt] [1] *prep* (a) (*place*) überall in (+*dat*) ◆ **~ the country/world** im ganzen Land/in der ganzen Welt.

(b) (*time*) den ganzen/die/das ganze ... hindurch *or* über ◆ **~ his life** sein ganzes Leben lang.

[2] *adv* (a) (*in every part*) **the house is carpeted ~** das Haus ist ganz *or* überall mit Teppichboden ausgelegt; **a house with electric light ~** ein Haus, das in jedem Raum elektrisches Licht hat/hatte; **a block of flats with water and gas ~** ein Wohnblock mit Wasser und Gas in allen Wohnungen; **the coat is lined ~** der Mantel ist ganz gefüttert.

(b) (*time*) die ganze Zeit hindurch *or* über.

through: ~put *n* (*Ind, Comput*) Durchsatz *m*; **~ ticket** *n* **can I get a ~ ticket to London?** kann ich bis London durchlösen?; **~ traffic** *n* Durchgangsverkehr *m*; **~ train** *n* durchgehender Zug; **~way** *n* (*US*) Schnellstraße *f*.

throve [θrəʊv] (*old*) *pret of* **thrive.**

throw [θrəʊ] (*vb: pret* **threw**, *ptp* **thrown**) [1] *n* (*of ball, javelin, dice*) Wurf *m* ◆ **it's your ~** du bist dran; **have another ~** werfen Sie noch einmal; **to lose a ~** (*dice*) den Wurf verlieren; **a 30-metre ~** ein Wurf *m* von 30 Metern; **the first ~ went to the German** (*Wrestling*) der Deutsche brachte seinen Gegner als erster zu Boden; **at 10 dollars a ~** zu 10 Dollar das Stück.

[2] *vt* (a) *ball, stone* werfen; *water* schütten ◆ **to ~ the dice/a six** würfeln/eine Sechs würfeln; **to ~ sth to sb** jdm etw zuwerfen; **~ me those keys** werfen Sie mir die Schlüssel herüber; **to ~ sth at sb** etw nach jdm werfen; *mud, paint etc* jdn mit etw bewerfen; **to ~ a ball 20 metres** einen Ball 20 Meter weit werfen; **to ~ sth across the room** etw (quer) durchs Zimmer werfen; **to ~ sb across the ring** jdn durch den Ring schleudern; **he threw himself to the floor** er warf sich auf den Boden *or* zu Boden; **to ~ oneself at sb** (*physically*) sich auf jdn werfen *or* stürzen; (*fig*) sich jdm an den Hals werfen *or* schmeißen (*inf*); **to ~ oneself into the job** sich in die Arbeit stürzen *or* hineinknien (*inf*); **to ~ one's voice** seine Stimme zum Tragen bringen.

(b) (*send to ground*) *rider* abwerfen; *opponent* zu Boden werfen *or* bringen ◆ **to be ~n from the saddle** aus dem Sattel geworfen werden.

(c) (*put hastily*) werfen ◆ **to ~ a coat over sb** jdm einen Mantel überwerfen; **to ~ a bridge across a river** eine Brücke über einen Fluß schlagen.

(d) (*fig: cast*) werfen ◆ **to ~ a glance at sb/sth** einen Blick auf jdn/etw werfen; **to ~ an angry look at sb/sth** jdm/einer Sache einen wütenden Blick zuwerfen; **to ~ light** Licht geben; **to ~ sb/the dogs off the scent** *or* **trail** jdn abschütteln *or* abhängen/die Hunde von der Spur abbringen; **to ~ sb into prison** jdn ins Gefängnis werfen; **to ~ the blame on sb** jdm die Schuld zuschieben *or* in die Schuhe schieben; **he threw his troops into action** er warf seine Truppen ins Gefecht.

(e) *switch, lever* betätigen.

(f) (*inf: disconcert*) aus dem Konzept bringen.

(g) *party* geben, schmeißen (*inf*).

(h) *fit* bekommen, kriegen (*inf*).

(i) *vase* töpfern, drehen; *silk* zwirnen.

(j) (*snake*) **to ~ its skin** sich häuten.

(k) (*animal: give birth to*) werfen.

[3] *vi* werfen; (*~ dice*) würfeln.

◆**throw about** *or* **around** *vt always separate* (a) (*scatter*) verstreuen; (*fig*) *money* um sich werfen mit.

(b) (*toss*) herumwerfen; *one's arms* fuchteln mit; *one's legs* strampeln mit ◆ **to ~ oneself ~** (*in bed, on floor*) sich hin und her werfen, sich herumwerfen; **to ~ a ball ~** ein bißchen Ball spielen; **he was ~n ~ in the car/accident** er wurde im Auto hin und her geschleudert/bei dem Unfall herumgeschleudert.

◆**throw away** *vt sep* (a) (*discard*) *rubbish* wegwerfen.

(b) (*waste*) verschenken; *money* verschwenden (*on sth* auf *or* für etw, *on sb* an jdn), vergeuden (*on sth* für etw, *on sb* an jdn) ◆ **you are ~ing yourself ~ on him** Sie sind zu schade für ihn, Sie verschwenden sich an ihn (*geh*).

(c) (*say casually*) *remark* nebenbei machen, beiläufig sagen.

◆**throw back** [1] *vi* (*Biol*) **a type which ~s ~ to an earlier species** ein Typ, der Merkmale einer früheren Art aufweist.

[2] *vt sep* (a) (*send back*) *ball, enemy* zurückwerfen.

(b) (*backwards*) *head, bedclothes* zurückwerfen; *curtains* aufreißen ◆ **to ~ oneself ~** zurückweichen, zurückspringen.

(c) (*fig*) **to be ~n ~ upon sth** auf etw (*acc*) wieder angewiesen sein, auf etw (*acc*) zurückgreifen müssen; **the crisis threw them ~ on their own resources** durch die Krise waren sie wieder auf sich selbst angewiesen.

(d) **I don't want you ~ing that ~ at me** ich möchte nicht, daß du mir meine eigenen Worte/Taten wieder vorhältst.

◆**throw down** *vt sep* (*from a roof, the stairs etc*) herunterwerfen ◆ **~ ~ your guns!** werfen Sie die Waffen weg!; **to ~ oneself ~** sich zu Boden werfen, sich niederwerfen; **it's ~ing it ~** (*inf: raining*) es gießt (in Strömen).

◆**throw in** *vt sep* (a) *extra* (gratis) dazugeben ◆ **with a tour of London ~n ~** mit einer Gratistour durch London extra.

(b) (*Sport*) *ball* einwerfen.

(c) (*fig*) **to ~ ~ one's hand** aufgeben, sich geschlagen geben; **to ~ ~ the sponge** *or* **towel** das Handtuch werfen (*inf*).

(d) (*say casually*) *remark* einwerfen (*to* in +*acc*).

◆**throw off** *vt sep* (a) (*get rid of*) *clothes* abwerfen; *disguise, habits* ablegen; *pursuer* abschütteln; *cold* loswerden; *the yoke of tyranny* abwerfen, abschütteln. (b) (*emit*) *sparks, smell* abgeben, von sich geben.

◆**throw on** *vt sep clothes* sich (*dat*) überwerfen.

◆**throw open** *vt sep* (a) *door, window* aufreißen. (b) *stately home etc* (öffentlich) zugänglich machen (*to* für) ◆ **membership was ~n ~ to the public** die Mitgliedschaft wurde für jedermann freigegeben.

◆**throw out** *vt sep* (a) (*discard*) *rubbish etc* wegwerfen.

(b) (*reject*) *suggestion, bill* (*Parl*) ablehnen, verwerfen (*geh*).

(c) *person* hinauswerfen, rauswerfen (*inf*) (*of* aus) ◆ **to be ~n ~ of work** entlassen werden; **automation has ~n a lot of people ~ of work** die Automation hat viele Menschen arbeitslos gemacht *or* vielen Menschen ihren Arbeitsplatz genommen.

(d) (*utter*) *hint* machen; *idea* äußern ◆ **to ~ ~ a challenge (to sb)** jdn herausfordern.

(e) (*plant*) *suckers, shoots* treiben; (*fire etc*) *heat* abgeben.

(f) *one's chest* herausdrücken.

(g) (*make wrong*) *calculations etc* über den Haufen werfen (*inf*), durcheinanderbringen ◆ **to ~ sb ~ in his calculations** jdn bei seinen Berechnungen durcheinanderbringen.

◆**throw over** *vt sep plan* über den Haufen werfen (*inf*); *girlfriend* sitzenlassen (*for* wegen).

◆**throw together** *vt sep* (a) (*put hastily together*) *ingredients* zusammenwerfen; *clothes* zusammenpacken; (*make quickly*) hinhauen; *essay* hinhauen (*inf*), runterschreiben (*inf*).

(b) (*bring together*) *people* (*fate etc*) zusammenführen; (*friends etc*) zusammenbringen.

◆**throw up** [1] *vi* sich übergeben, brechen ◆ **it makes you want to ~ ~** da kann einem schlecht werden, da kommt einem das Kotzen (*sl*).

[2] *vt sep* (a) *ball, hands* hochwerfen.

(b) (*abandon*) *job* aufgeben; *opportunity etc* verschenken ◆ **I feel like ~ing everything ~** ich würde am liebsten alles hinwerfen (*inf*).

(c) (*vomit up*) von sich (*dat*) geben, ausbrechen.

(d) (*produce*) hervorbringen ◆ **the meeting threw ~ several good ideas** bei der Versammlung kamen ein paar gute Ideen zutage; **the new politicians ~n ~ by the war** die neuen Politiker, die der Krieg hervorgebracht hat.

throw: ~away *adj* (a) (*casual*) *remark* nebenbei gemacht; *style* unaufdringlich, leger; (b) *wrapping, packet* Wegwerf-, zum Wegwerfen; *bottle also* Einweg-; **~away society** Wegwerfgesellschaft *f*; (c) (*cheap*) **~away prices** Schleuderpreise *pl*; **~-back** *n* (a) **his height/selfishness is a ~-back to an earlier generation** in ihm schlägt die Größe/Selbstsucht seiner Vorfahren wieder durch; **he's a ~-back to his Irish ancestors** bei ihm kommen seine irischen Vorfahren wieder durch; (b) (*fig*) (*return*) Rückkehr *f* (*to* zu); (*revival*) Neubelebung *f* (*to gen*).

thrower [ˈθrəʊəʳ] *n* Werfer(in *f*) *m* ◆ **he's not a very good ~** er kann nicht sehr gut werfen.

throw-in [ˈθrəʊɪn] *n* (*Sport*) Einwurf *m*.

thrown [θrəʊn] *ptp of* **throw.**

thru *prep, adv, adj* (*US*) = **through.**

thrum [θrʌm] [1] *vt guitar* klimpern auf (+*dat*), schlagen; *tune* (*auf der Gitarre etc*) klimpern ◆ **he ~med the desk with his fingers** *or* **~med his fingers on the desk** er trommelte mit seinen Fingern auf der Schreibtischplatte.

[2] *vi* (*on guitar*) klimpern.

thrush[1] [θrʌʃ] *n* (*Orn*) Drossel *f*.

thrush[2] *n* (*Med*) Soor *m* (*spec*), Schwämmchen *nt*; (*of vagina*) Pilzkrankheit *f*; (*Vet: in horses*) Strahlfäule *f*.

thrust [θrʌst] (*vb: pret, ptp ~*) [1] *n* (a) Stoß *m*; (*of knife also*) Stich *m*; (*fig: of intellect*) Stoßkraft *f*.

(b) (*Tech*) Druckkraft *f*; (*in rocket, turbine*) Schub(kraft *f*) *m*, Triebkraft *f* ◆ ~

bearing Drucklager *nt*.
(c) (*Mil: also* ~ **forward**) Vorstoß *m*.
(d) (*fig: of speech etc*) Tenor *m* ◆ **I get the general ~ of what you're saying** ich weiß, worauf es Ihnen ankommt.
[2] *vt* (a) (*push, drive*) stoßen ◆ **the tree ~ its branches upward** der Baum streckte seine Äste in den Himmel; **to ~ one's hands into one's pockets** die Hände in die Tasche stecken *or* stopfen (*inf*); **she ~ her books into the box** sie stopfte ihre Bücher in die Kiste; **she ~ the money into his hands/pocket** sie drückte ihm das Geld in die Hand/sie stopfte ihm das Geld in die Tasche.
(b) (*fig*) **to ~ oneself (up)on sb** sich jdm aufdrängen; **I had the job ~ upon me** die Arbeit wurde mir aufgedrängt *or* aufgezwungen; **to ~ one's way through a crowd** sich durch die Menge drängen *or* schieben; **to ~ one's way to the front** sich nach vorne vordrängeln, sich nach vorne kämpfen.
[3] *vi* stoßen (*at* nach); (*with knife*) stechen (*at* nach); (*Fencing*) einen Ausfall machen, ausfallen (*at* gegen).

◆**thrust aside** *vt sep* beiseite schieben; *person also* beiseite *or* zur Seite drängen; (*fig*) *objection also* zurückweisen.

◆**thrust forward** *vt sep* **to ~ sb ~** (*lit*) jdn vorschieben; (*fig*) sich für jdn stark machen; **to ~ oneself ~** (*lit*) sich vorschieben, sich nach vorne durchdrängeln; (*fig*) sich einsetzen; (*pej*) sich in den Vordergrund drängen.

◆**thrust out** *vt sep leg* ausstrecken; *hand also* hinstrecken; *head, breasts* vorstrecken; *chest* herausdrücken, wölben ◆ **she ~ her head ~ (of the window)** sie streckte den Kopf (zum Fenster) hinaus; **the goalie ~ ~ his legs** der Torwart streckte die Beine vor.

◆**thrust past** *vi* sich vorbeidrängen (*prep obj* an +*dat*).

thruster ['θrʌstəʳ] *n* (*directional rocket*) (Fein)steuerrakete *f*.

thrustful ['θrʌstfʊl], **thrusting** *adj person, behaviour* energisch, zielstrebig, resolut; (*pej*) (etwas) zu zielstrebig.

thrustfulness ['θrʌstfʊlnɪs] *n* energische Art, Zielstrebigkeit, Resolutheit *f*; (*pej*) (etwas) zu große Zielstrebigkeit.

thrusting ['θrʌstɪŋ] *adj see* **thrustful**.

thruway ['θruːweɪ] *n* (*US*) Schnellstraße *f*.

thud [θʌd] [1] *n* dumpfes Geräusch ◆ **the ~ of his footsteps** seine dumpfen Schritte; **he fell to the ground with a ~** er fiel mit einem Plumps (*inf*) *or* dumpfen Aufschlag zu Boden; **the ~ of the sea against the hull** das dumpfe Schlagen des Wassers gegen den Schiffsrumpf.
[2] *vi* dumpf aufschlagen; (*move heavily*) stampfen ◆ **the blow ~ded against his chin** dumpf klatschte der Schlag gegen sein Kinn; **a ~ding noise** ein dumpfes Geräusch; **with ~ding heart** mit pochendem Herzen; **the heavy door ~ded into place** mit einem dumpfen Knall fiel die Tür zu.

thug [θʌg] *n* Schläger(typ) *m*.

thulium ['θjuːlɪəm] *n* (*Chem*) Thulium *nt*.

thumb [θʌm] [1] *n* Daumen *m* ◆ **to be under sb's ~** unter jds Pantoffel (*dat*) *or* Fuchtel (*dat*) stehen; **she has him under her ~** sie hat ihn unter ihrer Fuchtel; **to be all ~s** zwei linke Hände haben; **he gave me the ~s up/down** er gab mir zu verstehen, daß alles in Ordnung war/daß es nicht in Ordnung war; **the idea was given the ~s up/down** für den Vorschlag wurde grünes/rotes Licht gegeben; **it sticks out like a sore ~** das springt einem direkt ins Auge; **he sticks out like a sore ~** (*doesn't fit*) er ist auffallend anders.
[2] *vt* (a) (*inf*) **to ~ a ride** *or* **lift** per Anhalter fahren; **let's ~ a lift with this lorry** wir wollen versuchen, diesen Lastwagen anzuhalten. (b) **to ~ one's nose at sb/sth** jdm/einer Sache eine lange Nase machen; (*fig*) auf jdn/etw pfeifen. (c) **a well ~ed book** ein Buch mit abgegriffenen Seiten.

◆**thumb through** *vi +prep obj book* durchblättern; *card index* durchgehen, durchsehen.

thumb: ~ index *n* Daumenregister *nt*, Daumenindex *m*; **~nail** *n* Daumennagel *m*; **~nail sketch** (*drawing*) kleine Skizze; (*description*) kurze Skizze; **~ print** *n* Daumenabdruck *m*; **~-screw** *n* (*Tech*) Flügelschraube *f*; (*torture*) Daumenschraube *f*; **~stall** *n* Daumenkappe *f*, Daumenschützer, Fingerling *m*; **~-tack** *n* (*US*) Reißnagel *m*, Reiß- *or* Heftzwecke *f*.

thump [θʌmp] [1] *n* (*blow*) Schlag *m*; (*noise*) (dumpfes) Krachen, Bums *m* (*inf*) ◆ **the bus gave the car such a ~ ...** der Bus gab dem Auto einen solchen Stoß ...
[2] *vt table* klopfen *or* schlagen auf (+*acc*); *door* klopfen *or* schlagen an (+*acc*); (*repeatedly*) trommeln auf/an (+*acc*); (*accidentally*) *one's head* sich (*dat*) anschlagen *or* anhauen (*inf*) ◆ **he ~ed the box down on my desk** er knallte die Schachtel auf meinen Tisch; **the prisoners started ~ing their stools on the floor** die Gefangenen schlugen mit ihren Hockern auf den Boden; **I ~ed him (one) on the nose** (*inf*) ich habe ihm eins auf die Nase verpaßt (*inf*); **I'll ~ you (one) if you don't shut up** (*inf*) wenn du nicht gleich den Mund hältst, knallt's (*inf*).
[3] *vi* (*person*) schlagen (*on the door/table* gegen *or* an die Tür/auf den Tisch); (*heart*) heftig schlagen *or* pochen; (*move heavily*) stapfen; (*object: fall loudly*) plumpsen (*inf*) ◆ **ask the people upstairs to stop ~ing around** sag den Leuten über uns, sie sollen aufhören herumzutrampeln.

◆**thump out** *vt sep tune* hämmern.

thumping ['θʌmpɪŋ] *adj* (*also* ~ **great**) (*inf*) kolossal, enorm.

thunder ['θʌndəʳ] [1] *n* (a) Donner *m* ◆ **a long roll of ~** ein langer rollender Donner, ein langes Donnergrollen; **there is ~ in the air** es liegt ein Gewitter *nt* in der Luft.
(b) (*fig*) (*of applause*) Sturm *m*; (*of cannons*) Donnern, Dröhnen *nt*; (*of waves*) Tosen *nt* ◆ **a ~ of applause** ein Beifallssturm *m*; *see* **steal**.
[2] *vi* (*lit, fig*) donnern; (*guns, hooves also*) dröhnen; (*waves, sea*) tosen, brausen; (*applause also*) brausen ◆ **the horses came ~ing up to the gate** die Pferde kamen aufs Tor zugeprescht; **the senator ~ed against them** der Senator wetterte gegen sie.
[3] *vt* (*shout*) brüllen, donnern, mit Donnerstimme brüllen.

◆**thunder out** [1] *vt sep order* mit donnernder Stimme geben.
[2] *vi* (*guns*) losdonnern ◆ **his voice ~ed** ~ er donnerte los.

◆**thunder past** *vi* (*train, traffic*) vorbeidonnern.

thunder: ~bolt *n* (*lit*) Blitz *m*, Blitz und Donner; **the news came as something of a ~bolt** (*fig*) die Nachricht schlug wie der Blitz ein *or* kam wie ein Donnerschlag; **~clap** *n* Donnerschlag *m*; **~cloud** *n* Gewitterwolke *f*.

thunderer ['θʌndərəʳ] *n*: **the T~** (*Myth*) der Blitzeschleuderer.

thundering ['θʌndərɪŋ] *adj* (*inf*) verteufelt (*inf*), verflixt (*inf*) ◆ **to be in a ~ rage** vor Wut kochen *or* schäumen.

thunderous ['θʌndərəs] *adj* stürmisch; *voice* donnernd.

thunder: ~storm *n* Gewitter *nt*; **~struck** *adj* (*fig*) wie vom Donner gerührt.

thundery ['θʌndərɪ] *adj weather* gewitterig.

thurible ['θjʊərɪbl] *n* (*Eccl*) (Weih)rauchfaß, Räucherfaß *nt*.

Thurs *abbr of* **Thursday** Do.

Thursday ['θɜːzdɪ] *n* Donnerstag *m*; *see also* **Tuesday**.

▼ **thus** [ðʌs] *adv* (a) (*in this way*) so, auf diese Art ◆ **you must hold it ~** Sie müssen das so halten; **~ it was that ...** so kam es, daß ...
▼ (b) (*consequently*) folglich, somit.
(c) (+*ptp or adj*) *reassured, encouraged etc* solchermaßen (*geh*), derart (*geh*) ◆ **~ far** so weit.

thwack [θwæk] [1] *n* (*blow*) Schlag *m*; (*noise*) Klatschen *nt*, Bums *m* (*inf*).
[2] *vt* schlagen; (*waves*) klatschen gegen ◆ **he ~ed his cane on the table** er ließ seinen Stock auf den Tisch heruntersausen.
[3] *vi* schlagen (*against* gegen); (*waves, cane*) klatschen.

thwart[1] [θwɔːt] *vt* vereiteln; *plan also* durchkreuzen; *robbery, attack also* verhindern ◆ **he was ~ed** ihm wurde ein Strich durch die Rechnung gemacht; **to ~ sb in sth** jdm etw vereiteln; **to be ~ed at every turn** überall auf Hindernisse stoßen; **~ed!** wieder nichts!

thwart[2] *n* (*Naut*) Ruderbank, Ducht *f*.

thy [ðaɪ] *poss adj* (*old, dial*) (*before vowel* **thine**) Euer/Eure/Euer (*obs*); (*dial, to God*) Dein/Deine/Dein.

thyme [taɪm] *n* Thymian *m*.

thyroid ['θaɪrɔɪd] [1] *n* (*also* ~ **gland**) Schilddrüse *f*.
[2] *adj* Schilddrüsen-.

thyself [ðaɪ'self] *pers pron* (*old, dial*) (a) (*reflexive, dir obj, with prep +acc*) Euch (*obs*); (*dial, to God*) Dich; (*indir obj, with prep +dat*) Euch (*obs*); (*dial, to God*) Dir.
(b) (*emph*) Ihr selbst (*obs*); Du selbst (*obs*); (*acc*) Euch selbst (*obs*); Dich selbst; (*dat*) Ihnen selbst (*obs*); Dir selbst.

tiara [tɪ'ɑːrə] *n* Diadem *nt*; (*of pope*) Tiara *f*.

Tiber ['taɪbəʳ] *n* Tiber *m*.

Tibet [tɪ'bet] *n* Tibet *nt*.

Tibetan [tɪ'betən] [1] *adj* tibetanisch, tibetisch.
[2] *n* (a) Tibeter(in *f*), Tibetaner(in *f*) *m*. (b) (*language*) Tibetisch *nt*.

tibia ['tɪbɪə] *n, pl* **-s** *or* **-e** ['tɪbiː] Schienbein *nt*, Tibia *f* (*spec*).

tic [tɪk] *n* (*Med*) Tick *m*, nervöses Zucken.

tich, titch [tɪtʃ] *n* (*inf*) Knirps *m* ◆ **hey, ~!** he, Kleine(r)!

tichy, titchy ['tɪtʃɪ] *adj* (+*er*) (*inf: also* ~ **little**) *person* winzig, knirpsig (*inf*); *things* klitzeklein (*inf*), winzig.

tick[1] [tɪk] [1] *n* (a) (*of clock etc*) Ticken *nt*.
(b) (*inf: moment*) Augenblick *m*, Sekunde *f*, Minütchen *nt* (*inf*) ◆ **half a ~** eine Sekunde; **are you ready yet? — half a ~** *or* **two ~s!** bist du schon fertig? — sofort; **I'll be ready in a ~** *or* **two ~s** bin sofort fertig (*inf*); **he did it in two ~s** er hat es in Sekundenschnelle *or* im Handumdrehen getan.
(c) (*mark*) Häkchen *nt*, Haken *m* ◆ **to put a ~ against a name/an answer** einen Namen/eine Antwort abhaken.
[2] *vi* (a) (*clock*) ticken ◆ **the minutes ~ed by** *or* **past/away** die Minuten vergingen *or* verstrichen.
(b) (*inf*) **what makes him ~?** was geht in ihm vor?
[3] *vt name, answer* abhaken.

◆**tick off** *vt sep* (a) *name etc* abhaken. (b) (*inf: scold*) ausschimpfen (*inf*), anpfeifen (*inf*) ◆ **he got ~ed ~ for doing it** er wurde angepfiffen (*inf*) *or* er bekam einen Rüffel *or* Anpfiff (*inf*), weil er das getan hat.

◆**tick over** *vi* (a) (*idle: engine*) im Leerlauf sein ◆ **the engine is ~ing ~ nicely** der Motor läuft ganz gut *or* ruhig. (b) (*fig: business etc*) ganz ordentlich laufen; (*pej*) auf Sparflamme sein (*inf*) ◆ **to keep things ~ing ~** die Sache in Gang halten.

tick[2] *n* (*Zool*) Zecke *f*.

tick[3] *n* (*Brit sl*): **on ~** auf Pump (*inf*).

tick[4] *n* (*Tex: cover*) (*for mattress*) Matratzenbezug *m*; (*for pillow etc*) Inlett *nt*.

ticker ['tɪkəʳ] *n* (a) (*inf: heart*) Pumpe *f* (*sl*). (b) (*sl: watch*) Zwiebel *f* (*sl*).

ticker tape *n* Lochstreifen *m* ◆ **~ welcome/parade** Konfettibegrüßung *f*/Konfettiparade *f*.

ticket ['tɪkɪt] *n* (a) (*rail, bus*) Fahrkarte *f*, Fahrschein *m*; (*plane ~*) Ticket *nt*, Flugkarte *f*, Flugschein *m*; (*Theat, for football match etc*) (Eintritts)karte *f*; (*cloakroom*) Garderobenmarke *f*; (*library*) ≃ Buchzettel *m*; (*for dry cleaners, cobbler etc*) Abschnitt, Zettel *m*; (*luggage office*) (Gepäck)schein *m*; (*raffle ~*) Los *nt*; (*price ~*) Preisschild *nt*; (*for car park*) Parkschein *m* ◆ **admission by ~ only** Einlaß nur gegen Eintrittskarten.
(b) (*US Pol*) Wahlliste *f* ◆ **he's running on the Democratic ~** er kandidiert für die Demokratische Partei; *see* **split, straight**.
(c) (*Jur*) Strafzettel *m* ◆ **to give sb a ~** jdm einen Strafzettel geben *or* ver-

➤ LANGUAGE IN USE: **thus: b → 26.3**

passen (*inf*).
(d) (*dated Brit inf*) **that's the ~!** das ist famos! (*dated inf*).
ticket: ~ agency *n* (*Theat*) Vorverkaufsstelle *f*; (*Rail etc*) Verkaufsstelle *f*; **~ barrier** *n* (*Brit Rail*) Fahrkartenschranke, Fahrkartenkontrolle *f*; **~ collector** *n* (*Rail*) (*on train*) Schaffner(in *f*) *m*; (*in station*) Bahnsteigschaffner(in *f*), Fahrkartenkontrolleur *m*; **~holder** *n* (*Theat etc*) *jd, der eine Eintrittskarte hat*; **~holders only through this door** (*Theat etc*) Eingang nur für Besucher mit Eintrittskarten; **~ inspector** *n* (Fahrkarten)kontrolleur *m*; **~ office** *n* (*Rail*) Fahrkartenschalter *m*, Fahrkartenausgabe *f*; (*Theat*) Kasse *f*; **~ window** *n* (*Rail*) (Fahrkarten)schalter *m*; (*Theat*) Kasse *f*.
ticking ['tɪkɪŋ] *n* **(a)** (*for mattress*) Matratzendrell *m*; (*for pillows etc*) Inlett *nt*. **(b)** (*of clock*) Ticken *nt*.
ticking-off ['tɪkɪŋ'ɒf] *n* (*inf*) Rüffel, Anpfiff (*inf*) *m* ♦ **he needs a good ~** dem muß man mal den Marsch blasen (*inf*).
tickle ['tɪkl] 1 *vt* **(a)** kitzeln ♦ **to ~ sb in the ribs** jdn in der Seite kitzeln; **to ~ sb's toes** jdn an den Zehen kitzeln; **this wool ~s my skin** diese Wolle kratzt *or* juckt (auf der Haut).
(b) (*fig inf*) *person* (*please*) schmeicheln (+*dat*) und freuen; (*amuse*) belustigen, amüsieren ♦ **to feel/be ~d** sich gebauchpinselt fühlen (*inf*); **here's a little story that might ~ your imagination** eine kleine Geschichte, die Sie wohl recht amüsant finden werden; **that story really ~d me** diese Geschichte fand ich wirklich köstlich; **to be ~d pink** *or* **to death** sich wie ein Schneekönig freuen (*inf*); *see* **fancy**.
2 *vi* kitzeln; (*wool*) kratzen, jucken ♦ **stop it, you're tickling** aufhören, das kitzelt; **my ear is tickling** mein Ohr juckt.
3 *n* Kitzeln *nt* ♦ **he gave the baby a little ~** er kitzelte das Baby ein bißchen; **to have a ~ in one's throat** einen Hustenreiz haben; **I didn't get a ~ all day** (*Fishing*) es hat den ganzen Tag keiner (an)gebissen.
tickler ['tɪkləʳ] *n* (*inf*) kitz(e)lige Angelegenheit, kitz(e)liges Problem.
ticklish ['tɪklɪʃ] *adj* (*lit*) kitz(e)lig; (*fig*) *situation also* heikel.
tick: ~-tack man *n* Buchmachergehilfe *m*; **~-tack-toe** *n* (*US*) Kreuzchen-und-Kringelspiel *nt*; **~-tock** *n* (*sound*) tick-tack; (*baby-talk: clock*) Ticktack *f*.
tidal ['taɪdl] *adj river, harbour* Tide-; *energy, power station* Gezeiten- ♦ **~ barrier** *or* **barrage** Staudamm *m*, Staumauer *f*; **this river is not ~** in diesem Fluß gibt es keine Gezeiten, das ist kein Tidefluß; **~ wave** (*lit*) Flutwelle *f*; **a great ~ wave of enthusiasm swept over the country** eine Welle der Begeisterung ging durch das Land.
tidbit ['tɪdbɪt] *n* (*US*) *see* **titbit**.
tiddler ['tɪdləʳ] *n* (*Brit*) **(a)** (*fish*) winziger Fisch. **(b)** (*inf: child*) Knirps *m* ♦ **she teaches ~s** sie unterrichtet die ganz Kleinen.
tiddly ['tɪdlɪ] *adj* (+*er*) (*inf*) **(a)** (*tiny*) winzig, klitzeklein (*inf*) ♦ **a ~ little scratch** ein klitzekleiner (*inf*) *or* winzig kleiner Kratzer. **(b)** (*tipsy*) angesäuselt (*inf*), beschwipst ♦ **she gets ~ on half a glass of sherry** sie bekommt von einem halben Glas Sherry schon einen Schwips.
tiddlywinks ['tɪdlɪwɪŋks] *n* Floh(hüpf)spiel *nt* ♦ **to play ~** Flohhüpfen spielen.
tide [taɪd] *n* **(a)** (*lit*) Gezeiten *pl*, Tide (*N Ger*) *f* ♦ **(at) high/low ~** (bei) Hochwasser *nt or* Flut *f*/ Niedrigwasser *nt or* Ebbe *f*; **to utilize the rise and fall of the ~** Ebbe und Flut *or* den Tidenhub (*spec*) ausnutzen; **we'll sail on the next ~** wir fahren mit der nächsten Flut; **the ~ is in/out** es ist Flut/Ebbe *or* Hochwasser (*form*)/Niedrigwasser (*form*); **the ~ comes in very far/fast** die Flut kommt sehr weit herein/schnell; **the ~s are influenced by the moon** Ebbe und Flut *or* die Gezeiten werden vom Mond beeinflußt; **stranded by the ~** in der Ebbe/Flut gestrandet; **until the ~ turns** bis zum Gezeitenwechsel, bis die Flut/Ebbe einsetzt.
(b) (*fig: trend*) **the ~ of history** der Lauf der Geschichte; **the ~ of public opinion** der Trend der öffentlichen Meinung; **carried away by the ~ of events** vom Strom der Ereignisse mitgerissen; **to go** *or* **swim against/with the ~** gegen den/mit dem Strom schwimmen; **the ~ has turned** das Blatt hat sich gewendet; **the ~ of the battle turned** das Glück (der Schlacht) wendete sich; *see* **turn, time**.
(c) (*old: time*) Zeit *f*.
♦**tide over** *vt always separate* **that will ~ me ~ until tomorrow** damit werde ich bis morgen auskommen; **is that enough to ~ you ~?** reicht Ihnen das vorläufig?
tide: ~ gate *n* Seeschleuse *f*; **~land** *n* (*US*) Watt *nt*; **~mark** *n* Flutmarke *f*; (*man-made*) Pegelstand *m*; (*hum: on neck, in bath*) schwarzer Rand; **~ race** *n* Gezeitenstrom *m*; **~water** *n* Flut *f*; (*US: lowlands*) Watt *nt*; **~way** *n* Priel *m*.
tidily ['taɪdɪlɪ] *adv* ordentlich.
tidiness ['taɪdɪnɪs] *n see adj* Ordentlichkeit *f*; Sauberkeit *f*; Gepflegtheit *f*.
tidings ['taɪdɪŋz] *npl* (*old, liter*) Kunde (*old, liter*), Botschaft (*liter*), Nachricht *f*.
tidy ['taɪdɪ] 1 *adj* (+*er*) **(a)** (*orderly*) ordentlich; (*with ~ habits also*) sauber; *appearance also* gepflegt; *room also* aufgeräumt ♦ **she has very ~ habits** sie ist ein sehr ordentlicher *or* ordnungsliebender Mensch; **to teach sb ~ habits** jdn zur Ordnung erziehen; **to keep/put sth ~** etw in Ordnung halten/ bringen; **to get a room ~** ein Zimmer aufräumen; **she's very ~ in her dress** sie ist immer sehr ordentlich gekleidet; **to make oneself ~** sich zurechtmachen; **to have a ~ mind** klar *or* logisch denken.
(b) (*inf: considerable*) ordentlich (*inf*), ganz schön (*inf*) ♦ **a ~ sum** eine ordentliche Stange Geld (*inf*).
2 *vt hair* in Ordnung bringen; *room also* aufräumen.
3 *n* Behälter *m*.
♦**tidy away** *vt sep* wegräumen, aufräumen.
♦**tidy out** *vt sep* entrümpeln, ausmisten (*inf*).
♦**tidy up** 1 *vi* **(a)** (*clear away*) aufräumen, Ordnung machen. **(b)** (*clean oneself*) sich zurechtmachen.
2 *vt sep books, room* aufräumen, in Ordnung bringen; *piece of work* in Ordnung bringen ♦ **to ~ oneself** sich zurechtmachen.
tidy: ~-out *n* Entrümpelung *f*; **the cupboards could do with a ~-out** die Schränke müßten mal entrümpelt *or* ausgemistet (*inf*) werden; **~-up** *n* Aufräumen *nt*; **this room needs a ~-up** dieses Zimmer muß aufgeräumt werden; **go and give yourself a ~-up** mach dich ein bißchen zurecht.
tie [taɪ] 1 *n* **(a)** (*also esp US:* **neck~**) Krawatte *f*, Schlips (*inf*), Binder (*dated form*) *m*.
(b) (*Archit, Build*) (*also* **~ beam**) Binderbalken, Bundbalken *m*; (**~ piece**) Stichbalken *m*; (*Mus*) Haltebogen *m*; (*US Rail*) Schwelle *f*; (*cord*) Schnur *f*.
(c) (*fig: bond*) Band *nt* (*liter*), Beziehung, (Ver)bindung *f* ♦ **~s of friendship** freundschaftliche Beziehungen *or* Bande (*liter*) *pl*; **the blood ~** Blutsbande *pl*; **business ~s** Geschäftsverbindungen *pl*; **he's investigating the ~s between Pasternak and Rilke** er untersucht die Beziehung zwischen Pasternak und Rilke; **family ~s** familiäre Bindungen *pl*.
(d) (*hindrance*) Belastung *f* (*on* für) ♦ **family ~s** familiäre Bindungen *or* Fesseln *pl*; **I don't want any ~s** ich will keine Bindung, ich will mich nicht gebunden fühlen.
(e) (*Sport etc: result*) Unentschieden *nt*; (*match etc ending in draw*) unentschiedenes Spiel ♦ **the match ended in a ~** das Spiel endete mit einem Unentschieden; **the result of the election/competition was a ~** bei der Wahl ergab sich eine Stimmengleichheit/der Wettkampf ging unentschieden aus; **there was a ~ for second place** es gab zwei zweite Plätze.
(f) (*esp Ftbl: match*) Spiel *nt*.
2 *vt* **(a)** (*fasten*) binden (*to* an +*acc*), befestigen (*to* an +*dat*) ♦ **~ the string round the tree** binde die Schnur um den Baum; **my hands are ~d** (*fig*) mir sind die Hände gebunden.
(b) (*knot*) *shoelace, tie, ribbon* binden ♦ **to ~ a knot in sth** einen Knoten in etw (*acc*) machen; **to ~ a bow in a ribbon** *or* **a ribbon in a bow** ein Band zu einer Schleife binden.
(c) (*fig: unite, link*) verbinden.
(d) (*restrict*) *person* binden (*to* an +*acc*) ♦ **we're very ~d in the evenings** wir sind abends sehr gebunden.
(e) (*Sport*) **the match was ~d** das Spiel ging unentschieden aus.
(f) **~d** (*Mus*) *notes* gebunden.
3 *vi* **(a)** (*ribbon etc*) **it won't ~ properly** es läßt sich nicht richtig binden; **it ~s at the back** es wird hinten (zu)gebunden.
(b) (*Sport*) unentschieden spielen; (*in competition, vote*) gleich stehen ♦ **they're still tying** es steht immer noch unentschieden; **they ~d for first place** (*Sport, competition*) sie teilten sich den ersten Platz; (*Sch*) sie waren (mit den gleichen Noten) die Klassenbesten.
♦**tie back** *vt sep hair, roses, door* zurückbinden.
♦**tie down** *vt sep* **(a)** (*lit*) festbinden (*to* an +*dat*); *huts, tents* verankern (*to* in +*dat*); *horse* fesseln.
(b) (*fig: restrict*) binden (*to* an +*acc*); *meaning* genau bestimmen ♦ **to ~ sb/ oneself ~ to certain conditions** jdn/sich auf bestimmte Bedingungen festlegen; **to ~ oneself ~ to doing sth** sich verpflichten, etw zu tun; **marriage/ owning property ~s you ~** durch die Ehe/Eigentum ist man gebunden; **she's very ~d ~ because of the children, the children ~ her ~ a lot** durch die Kinder ist sie sehr gebunden.
♦**tie in** 1 *vi* dazu passen ♦ **to ~ ~ with sth** zu etw passen, dazu passen; **it all ~s ~** das paßt alles zusammen; **the new evidence didn't ~ ~** das neue Beweismaterial paßte nicht ins Bild.
2 *vt sep plans* verbinden, in Einklang bringen.
♦**tie on** *vt sep* anbinden, festbinden ♦ **to ~ sth ~(to) sth** etw an etw (*dat*) anbinden.
♦**tie up** 1 *vi* **(a) now it all ~s ~** jetzt paßt alles zusammen; **it all ~s ~ with his marital problems** das hängt alles mit seinen Eheproblemen zusammen. **(b)** (*Naut*) festmachen.
2 *vt sep* **(a)** *parcel* verschnüren; *shoelaces* binden.
(b) *boat* festmachen; *animal* festbinden, anbinden (*to* an +*dat*); *prisoner, hands etc* fesseln.
(c) (*settle*) *deal, arrangements etc* unter Dach und Fach bringen ♦ **to ~ ~ a few loose ends (of sth)** (bei einer Sache) ein paar Lücken schließen.
(d) (*Fin*) *capital* (fest) anlegen, festlegen.
(e) (*link*) **to be ~d ~ with sth** mit etw zusammenhängen; **are you still ~d ~ with that firm?** haben Sie noch Verbindungen zu der Firma?
(f) (*keep busy*) beschäftigen; *machines* auslasten ♦ **he's ~d ~ all tomorrow** er ist morgen den ganzen Tag belegt *or* beschäftigt; **he's ~d ~ with the manager at the moment** er hat momentan beim Betriebsleiter zu tun.
(g) (*obstruct, hinder*) *production etc* stillegen.
tie: ~-break, ~ breaker *n* (*Tennis*) Tie-break *m*; **~ clip** *n* Krawattennadel *f*.
tied [taɪd]: **~ cottage** *n* (*Brit*) Gesindehaus *nt*; **~ house** *n* (*Brit*) Brauereigaststätte *f*, brauereieigene Gaststätte.
tie: ~-dye *vt* nach dem Bindebatikverfahren färben; **~-in** 1 *n* **(a)** (*connection, relationship*) Verbindung, Beziehung *f*, Zusammenhang *m*; **(b)** (*US: sale*) Kopplungsgeschäft *nt*; 2 *attr* **~-in sale** (*US*) Kopplungsgeschäft *nt*; **~ line** *n* (*Telec*) Direktverbindung *f*; **~-on** *adj attr* Anhänge-, zum Anbinden *or* Anhängen; **~ pin** *n* Krawattennadel, Schlipsnadel (*inf*) *f*.
tier [tɪəʳ] *n* (*of cake*) Etage, Stufe *f*; (*of amphitheatre*) Reihe *f*; (*Theat, of stadium*) Rang *m*; (*fig: in hierarchy etc*) Stufe *f*, Rang *m* ♦ **a cake with three ~s** ein dreistöckiger Kuchen; **a three-~ hierarchy** eine dreigestufte Hierarchie; **to arrange sth in ~s** etw stufenförmig aufbauen.

tiered [tɪəd] *adj* gestuft ◆ **a three-~ cake** ein dreistöckiger Kuchen.

tie: ~ rod *n* (*Aut*) Lenkspurstange *f*; **~-up** *n* **(a)** (*connection*) Verbindung *f*; **(b)** (*US: stoppage*) Stillstand *m*; **there is a ~-up in transportation** der Verkehr steht still *or* ist lahmgelegt.

tiff [tɪf] *n* (*inf*) Krach *m* (*inf*) ◆ **he's had a ~ with his girlfriend** er hat mit seiner Freundin Krach gehabt (*inf*).

tiger ['taɪgəʳ] *n* Tiger *m*.

tiger: ~ lily *n* Tigerlilie *f*; **~ moth** *n* Bärenspinner *m*; **~ shark** *n* Tigerhai *m*.

tight [taɪt] [1] *adj* (+*er*) **(a)** (*close-fitting*) *clothes* eng; *join* dicht ◆ **these jeans/shoes are too ~** diese Jeans/Schuhe sind zu eng, diese Jeans spannen/Schuhe drücken.

(b) (*stiff, difficult to move*) *screw, bolt* festsitzend, unbeweglich ◆ **the tap/cork/screw/bolt is (too) ~** der Hahn ist zu fest zu/der Korken/die Schraube/der Bolzen sitzt fest; **the drawer/window is a bit ~** die Schublade/das Fenster klemmt ein bißchen *or* geht schwer auf.

(c) (*firm*) *screw* fest angezogen; *tap, window* dicht; *lid, embrace* fest; *control, discipline* streng; *organization* straff ◆ **to keep a ~ hold on sth** (*lit*) etw gut festhalten; **to keep a ~ hold on the reins** (*fig*) die Zügel fest in der Hand haben; **to run a ~ ship** (*lit, fig*) ein strenges Regiment führen.

(d) (*taut*) *rope, skin* straff; *knot* fest (angezogen) ◆ **she wears her hair in a ~ bun** sie trägt ihr Haar in einem festen Knoten; **a ~ feeling in the chest** ein beengtes Gefühl in der Brust.

(e) (*leaving little space*) eng; *weave also* dicht ◆ **things are getting rather ~ in this office** es wird ziemlich eng im Büro; **it's a ~ space for lorries** es ist eng hier für Lastwagen.

(f) (*leaving little time*) *timing etc* knapp; *schedule* knapp bemessen ◆ **4 o'clock is making it a bit ~ for me** 4 Uhr ist ein bißchen knapp für mich.

(g) (*difficult*) *situation* schwierig ◆ **in a ~ corner** *or* **spot** (*fig*) in der Klemme (*inf*); **things are getting a bit ~ for him round here** es wird langsam brenzlig für ihn (*inf*).

(h) (*close*) *race, match* knapp.

(i) (*Fin*) *money* knapp.

(j) (*inf: miserly*) knick(e)rig (*inf*), geizig.

(k) (*inf: drunk*) voll (*sl*), blau (*inf*) ◆ **to get ~** blau werden (*inf*).

[2] *adv* (+*er*) *hold, shut, screw, fasten* fest; *stretch* straff ◆ **the suitcase/train was packed ~ with ...** der Koffer/Zug war vollgestopft mit ... *or* prallvoll/gerammelt voll von ... (*inf*); **he kept his mouth shut ~** er schwieg eisern; (*at dentist etc*) er hielt den Mund fest geschlossen; **to hold sb/sth ~** jdn/etw festhalten; **to do sth up ~** etw festmachen *or* gut befestigen; **sleep ~!** schlaf(t) gut!; **hold ~!** festhalten!; **to sit ~** sich nicht rühren.

[3] *adj suf* -dicht ◆ **water~/air~** wasser-/luftdicht.

tight-assed ['taɪtɑːst] *adj* (*esp US sl*) verbohrt (*inf*), stur (*inf*).

tighten ['taɪtn] (*also* **~ up**) [1] *vt* **(a)** *knot* fester machen, anziehen; *screw* anziehen; (*re-~*) nachziehen; *rope* straffen, anziehen; (*stretch tighter*) straffer spannen ◆ **to ~ the steering in a car** die Lenkung an einem Auto nachziehen.

(b) *restrictions* verschärfen; *see* **belt**.

[2] *vi* (*rope*) sich spannen, sich straffen; (*knot*) sich zusammenziehen ◆ **whenever he's angry his mouth ~s** immer wenn er wütend ist, wird sein Mund schmal und verkniffen.

◆**tighten up** [1] *vi* **(a)** *see* **tighten 2**. **(b)** (*in discipline*) strenger werden, härter durchgreifen ◆ **they've ~ed ~ on security** sie haben die Sicherheitsvorkehrungen verschärft.

[2] *vt sep* **(a)** *see* **tighten 1 (a)**. **(b)** *organization, procedure* straffen; *discipline, controls* verschärfen.

tight: ~-fisted ['taɪt'fɪstɪd] *adj* knauserig, knickerig (*inf*); **to be ~-fisted** die Hand auf der Tasche halten; **~-fitting** *adj* eng anliegend; **~-knit** *adj community* eng miteinander verbunden *or* verwachsen; **~-lipped** *adj* (*lit*) mit schmalen Lippen; (*silent*) verschwiegen, verschlossen; **he kept a ~-lipped silence** er wahrte absolutes *or* eisernes Schweigen.

tightness ['taɪtnɪs] *n see adj* **(a)** enges Anliegen; Dichtheit *f*.

(b) Festsitzen *nt*, Unbeweglichkeit *f* ◆ **the ~ of the drawer/window** das Klemmen der Schublade/des Fensters.

(c) fester Sitz; Dichtheit *f*; Strenge *f*; Straffheit *f* ◆ **the ~ of his embrace** seine feste Umarmung.

(d) Straffheit *f*; Festigkeit *f*.

(e) Enge *f*; Dichte *f*.

(f) Knappheit *f*.

(g) Schwierigkeit *f*.

(h) Knappheit *f*.

(i) Knappheit *f*.

(j) Knick(e)rigkeit *f* (*inf*), Geiz *m*.

(k) Besoffenheit *f* (*sl*).

tightrope ['taɪtrəʊp] *n* Seil *nt* ◆ **to walk a ~** (*fig*) einen Balanceakt vollführen; **~ act u** (*lit, fig*) Balanceakt *m*; **~ walker** Seiltänzer(in *f*) *m*.

tights [taɪts] *npl* (*esp Brit*) Strumpfhose *f* ◆ **a pair of ~** ein Paar *nt* Strumpfhosen, eine Strumpfhose.

tightwad ['taɪtwɒd] *n* (*US*) Geizhals, Geizkragen (*inf*) *m*.

tigress ['taɪgrɪs] *n* Tigerin *f*.

tilde ['tɪldə] *n* Tilde *f*.

tile [taɪl] [1] *n* (*on roof*) (Dach)ziegel *m*; (*ceramic ~*) Fliese *f*; (*on wall*) Kachel, Fliese *f*; (*lino ~, cork ~, polystyrene ~ etc*) Platte, Fliese *f*; (*carpet ~*) (Teppich)fliese *f* ◆ **to have a night on the ~s** (*inf*) einen draufmachen (*inf*).

[2] *vt roof* (mit Ziegeln) decken; *floor* mit Fliesen/Platten auslegen; *wall* kacheln; mit Platten bedecken; *bathroom* kacheln, Fliesen anbringen in (+*dat*) ◆ **~d** *roof* Ziegel-.

tiling ['taɪlɪŋ] *n* **(a)** (*action*) (*of roof*) (Dach)decken *nt*; (*of floor*) Fliesenlegen *nt*; (*of wall*) Kacheln *nt*; Belegen *nt* mit Platten ◆ **~ the floor ...** das Fliesenlegen *or* Legen der Bodenfliesen ...

(b) (*tiled surface*) (*on roof*) Ziegel *pl*; (*on floor*) Fliesen *pl*; Platten *pl*; (*on wall*) Kacheln, Fliesen *pl*; Platten *pl*.

till¹ [tɪl] *prep, conj see* **until**.

till² *n* (*cash-register*) Kasse *f*; (*drawer*) (*in bank*) Geldkasse *f*, Geldkasten *m*; (*in shop*) Ladenkasse *f* ◆ **pay at the ~** an der Kasse bezahlen; **to be caught with one's hand in the ~** (*fig*) beim Griff in die Kasse ertappt werden.

till³ *vt* (*Agr*) bestellen.

tillage ['tɪlɪdʒ] *n* (*act*) Bestellen *nt*; (*land*) bestelltes Land.

tiller¹ ['tɪləʳ] *n* (*Naut*) Ruderpinne *f* ◆ **at the ~** am Ruder; **to take the ~** das Ruder übernehmen.

tiller² *n* (*Agr*) Landmann *m* (*old*) ◆ **~ of the soil** (*liter*) Ackersmann (*old*), Bebauer *m* der Scholle (*liter*).

tilt [tɪlt] [1] *n* **(a)** (*slope*) Neigung *f* ◆ **the sideways ~ of his head** seine schräge Kopfhaltung; **if you increase the (angle of) ~ of the conveyor belt ...** wenn Sie das Fließband schräger stellen ...; (*sideways also*) wenn Sie das Fließband weiter kippen ...; **to have a ~** sich neigen; **the wall has developed rather a dangerous ~** die Wand neigt sich ziemlich gefährlich; **the bird's/plane's wings have a slight downwards ~** die Flügel des Vogels/Flugzeugs neigen sich leicht nach unten.

(b) (*Hist: tournament*) Turnier *nt*; (*thrust*) Stoß *m* ◆ **to have a ~ at sb/sth** (*fig*) jdn/etw aufs Korn nehmen; *see* **full**.

[2] *vt* kippen, schräg stellen; *head* (seitwärts) neigen.

[3] *vi* **(a)** (*slant*) sich neigen ◆ **this part of the machine ~s** dieser Teil der Maschine läßt sich kippen.

(b) (*fig*) **to ~ at sb/sth** jdn/etw attackieren; *see* **windmill**.

◆**tilt back** [1] *vi* sich nach hinten neigen ◆ **he ~ed ~ in his chair** er kippte mit seinem Stuhl nach hinten.

[2] *vt sep* nach hinten neigen; *chair also, machine part* nach hinten kippen.

◆**tilt forward** [1] *vi* sich nach vorne neigen; *machine part* nach vorn kippen ◆ **he ~ed ~ in his chair** er kippte mit seinem Stuhl nach vorne, er lehnte sich mit seinem Stuhl vor.

[2] *vt sep* nach vorne neigen; *chair also, machine part* nach vorne kippen.

◆**tilt over** [1] *vi* (*lean*) sich neigen; (*fall*) (um)kippen.

[2] *vt sep* (*slant*) neigen, schräg stellen; *barrel, chair* kippen.

◆**tilt up** [1] *vi* nach oben kippen ◆ **the back of the lorry ~s ~** die Ladefläche des Lastwagens kippt.

[2] *vt sep bottle* kippen; *kaleidoscope* schräg nach oben halten.

tilth [tɪlθ] *n* **(a)** (*topsoil*) (Acker)krume *f*. **(b)** (*cultivated land*) Ackerland *nt*.

Tim [tɪm] *n abbr of* **Timothy**; (*Brit Telec*) der Zeitservice.

timber ['tɪmbəʳ] [1] *n* **(a)** Holz *nt*; (*for building also*) Bauholz *nt*; (*land planted with trees*) (Nutz)wald *m* ◆ **to put land under ~** Land mit Bäumen bepflanzen; **standing ~** Nutzwald *m*; **~!** Baum fällt!

(b) (*beam*) Balken *m*; (*Naut also*) Spant *nt*.

(c) (*Hunt*) (Holz)zäune und -gatter *pl*.

(d) (*US: character*) **a man of that/presidential ~** ein Mann dieses Kalibers/ein Mann, der das Zeug zum Präsidenten hat.

[2] *vt house* mit Fachwerk versehen; *gallery* (*in mine*) abstützen, verzimmern.

timbered ['tɪmbəd] *adj house* Fachwerk-; *land* Wald-.

timber framing *n* Fachwerk *nt*.

timbering ['tɪmbərɪŋ] *n* (*inside house*) Gebälk, Balkenwerk *nt*; (*outside house*) Fachwerk *nt*; (*Naut*) Spanten *pl*; (*Min*) Stützbalken *pl*; (*material*) (Bau)holz *nt*.

timber: ~land *n* (*US*) Waldland *nt*; **~ line** *n* Baumgrenze *f*; **~ mill** *n* Sägemühle *f*, Sägewerk *nt*; **~ wolf** *n* Timberwolf *m*; **~work** *n* (*beams*) Gebälk, Balkenwerk *nt*; (*~ framing*) Fachwerk *nt*; **~ yard** *n* Holzlager *nt*.

timbre ['tɪmbəʳ] *n* Timbre *nt*; (*Phon*) Tonqualität *f*.

time [taɪm] [1] *n* **(a)** Zeit *f* ◆ **how ~ flies!** wie die Zeit vergeht!; **only ~ will tell whether ...** es muß sich erst herausstellen, ob ...; **it takes ~ to do that** das erfordert *or* braucht (seine) Zeit; **to take (one's) ~ (over sth)** sich (*dat*) (bei etw) Zeit lassen; **it took me all my ~ to finish** ich bin gerade noch fertig geworden; **in (the course of) ~** mit der Zeit; **in (next to** *or* **less than) no ~** im Nu, im Handumdrehen; **at this (present) point** *or* **moment in ~** zu diesem *or* zum gegenwärtigen Zeitpunkt; **to have a lot of/no ~ for sb/sth** viel/keine Zeit für jdn/etw haben; (*fig: be for/against*) viel/nichts für jdn/etw übrig haben; **to find/make ~ (for sb/sth)** Zeit (für jdn/etw) finden/sich (*dat*) Zeit (für jdn/etw) nehmen; **to have ~ on one's hands** viel freie Zeit haben; **too many people who have ~ on their hands** zu viele Leute, die zuviel freie Zeit haben; **having ~ on my hands I went into a café** da ich (noch) Zeit hatte, ging ich ins Café; **~ is on our side** die Zeit arbeitet für uns; **he lost no ~ in telling her** er verlor keine Zeit und sagte es ihr sofort; **my ~ is my own** ich kann frei über meine Zeit verfügen; **in one's own/the company's ~** in *or* während der Freizeit/Arbeitszeit; **to be in good ~** rechtzeitig dran sein; **don't rush, do it in your own ~** nur keine Hast, tun Sie es, wie Sie es können; **let me know in good ~** sagen Sie mir rechtzeitig Bescheid; **he'll let you know in his own good ~** er wird Ihnen Bescheid sagen, wenn er soweit ist; **he does everything in his own good ~** er läßt sich bei nichts hetzen; **all in good ~** alles zu seiner Zeit; **~ is money** (*prov*) Zeit ist Geld (*prov*); **~ and tide wait for no man** (*Prov*) das Rad der Zeit hält niemand auf (*Prov*); **(for) a long/short ~** lange/kurz; **I'm going away for a long ~** ich fahre für *or* auf längere Zeit weg; **it's a long ~ (since)** es ist schon lange her(, seit); **what a (long) ~ you have been!** du hast (aber) lange gebraucht!; **a short ~ later/ago** kurz darauf/vor kurzem; **in a short ~ they were all gone** nach kurzer Zeit waren alle gegangen; **for some ~ past** seit einiger Zeit; **all the ~** die ganze Zeit; **in two weeks' ~** in zwei Wochen; **for a ~** eine Zeitlang; **for the ~ being** (*provisionally*) vorläufig; (*temporarily*) vorübergehend; **to do ~** (*inf: in prison*) sitzen (*inf*); **to make ~ with sb** (*esp US inf: have sex with*) es mit jdm treiben (*inf*).

(b) (*of clock, moment, season*) **what ~ is it?, what's the ~?** wie spät ist es?, wieviel Uhr ist es?; **what ~ do you make it?** wie spät haben Sie's?; **my watch keeps good ~** meine Uhr geht genau; **to tell the ~** (*person*) die Uhr kennen; (*instrument*) die Uhrzeit anzeigen; **can you tell the ~?** kennst du die Uhr?; **the ~ is 2.30** es ist 2^{30}, die Zeit: 2^{30}; **what was his ~?** (*in race*) welche Zeit hatte er?; **the winning ~ was ...** die Zeit des Siegers war ...; **it's ~ (for me/us** *etc*) **to go, it's ~ I was/we were** *etc* **going, it's ~ I/we** *etc* **went** es wird Zeit, daß ich gehe/wir gehen *etc*; **on ~/ahead of ~/behind ~** pünktlich/zu früh/zu spät; **we are ahead of ~/behind ~** wir sind früh/spät dran; **we're/the project is ahead of ~/behind ~** wir sind/das Projekt ist dem Zeitplan voraus/zeitlich im Rückstand; **to make good ~** gut *or* schnell vorankommen; **if we get to Birmingham by 3 we'll be making good ~** wenn wir um 3 Uhr in Birmingham sind, sind wir ziemlich schnell; **the trains are on ~** *or* **running to ~** die Züge fahren pünktlich; **to be in ~ for sth** rechtzeitig zu etw kommen; **it's about ~ he was here** (*he has arrived*) es wird (aber) auch Zeit, daß er kommt; (*he has not arrived*) es wird langsam Zeit, daß er kommt; **it's ~ for tea** es ist Teezeit; **(and) about ~ too!** das wird aber auch Zeit!; **at all ~s** jederzeit, immer; **at any ~ during the day** zu jeder Tageszeit; **not at this ~ of night!** nicht zu dieser nachtschlafenen Zeit *or* Stunde!; **to pass the ~ of day (with sb)** (mit jdm) über Belanglosigkeiten reden; **I wouldn't even give him the ~ of day** ich würde ihm nicht einmal guten Tag sagen; **~ gentlemen please!** Feierabend! (*inf*), bitte, trinken Sie aus, wir schließen gleich; **there's a ~ and a place for everything** alles zu seiner Zeit; **this is hardly the ~ or the place to ...** dies ist wohl kaum die rechte Zeit oder der rechte Ort, um ...; **this is no ~ for quarrelling** *or* **to quarrel** jetzt ist nicht die Zeit, sich zu streiten; **well, this is a fine ~ to tell me that** (*iro*) Sie haben sich (*dat*) wahrhaftig eine gute Zeit ausgesucht, um mir das zu sagen; **there are ~s when ...** es gibt Augenblicke, wo *or* da (*geh*) ...; **at the** *or* **that ~** damals, zu der Zeit, seinerzeit; **at this (particular) ~, at the present ~** zur Zeit; **at one ~** früher, einmal; **at any/no ~** jederzeit/niemals; **come (at) any ~** du kannst jederzeit kommen; **at the same ~** (*lit*) gleichzeitig; **they arrived at the same ~ as us** sie kamen zur gleichen Zeit an wie wir; **sometimes ... (at) other ~s ...** (manch) mal ..., (manch)mal ...; **but at the same ~, you must admit that ...** aber andererseits müssen Sie zugeben, daß ...; **it was hard, but at the same ~ you could have tried** es war schwierig, aber Sie hätten es trotzdem versuchen können; **at ~s** manchmal; **at various ~s in the past** schon verschiedene Male *or* verschiedentlich; **by the ~ it had finished** als es zu Ende war; **by the ~ we arrive, there's not going to be anything left** bis wir ankommen, ist nichts mehr übrig; **by that ~ we knew/we'll know** da *or* inzwischen wußten wir es/dann *or* bis dahin wissen wir es; **by this ~** inzwischen; **by this ~ next year/tomorrow** nächstes Jahr/morgen um diese Zeit; **between ~s** (*inf*) zwischendurch; **from ~ to ~** dann und wann, von Zeit zu Zeit; **from that ~ on** von der Zeit an, von da an; **since that ~** seit der Zeit; **until such ~ as ...** so lange bis ...; **until such ~ as you apologize** solange du dich nicht entschuldigst, bis du dich entschuldigst; **this ~ of the day/year** diese Tages-/Jahreszeit; **at this ~ of the week/month** zu diesem Zeitpunkt der Woche/des Monats; **this ~ last year/week** letztes Jahr/letzte Woche um diese Zeit; **to choose** *or* **pick one's ~** sich (*dat*) einen günstigen Zeitpunkt aussuchen; **now's the ~ to do it** jetzt ist der richtige Zeitpunkt *or* die richtige Zeit, es zu tun; **now's my/your** *etc* **~ to do it** jetzt habe ich/hast du *etc* Gelegenheit, es zu tun; **to die before one's ~** zu früh sterben; **when the ~ comes** wenn es soweit ist; **I never thought the ~ would come when she says sorry** ich hätte nie gedacht, daß sie sich wirklich einmal entschuldigen würde; **the ~ has come (to do sth)** es ist an der Zeit(, etw zu tun); **the ~ has come for us to leave** es ist Zeit für uns zu gehen; **when her ~ comes** (*of pregnant woman*) wenn ihre Zeit kommt; **when your ~ comes to be the leader** wenn Sie an der Reihe sind, die Führung zu übernehmen; **my ~ is (almost) up** meine *or* die Zeit ist (gleich) um; (*fig: life*) meine Zeit ist gekommen.

(c) (*occasion*) **this ~** diesmal, dieses Mal; **(the) next ~** nächstes Mal, das nächste Mal; **(the) next ~ I see you** wenn ich dich nächstes Mal *or* das nächste Mal sehe; **(the) last ~** letztes Mal, das letzte Mal; **(the) last ~ he was here** letztes Mal *or* das letzte Mal, als er hier war; **every** *or* **each ~ ...** jedesmal, wenn ...; **many a ~, many ~s** viele Male; **many's the ~ I have heard him say ...** ich habe ihn schon oft sagen hören ...; **for the last ~** zum letzten Mal; **and he's not very bright at the best of ~s** und er ist ohnehin *or* sowieso nicht sehr intelligent; **the ~ before** das letzte *or* vorige Mal; **the ~ before last** das vorletzte Mal; **~ and (~) again, ~ after ~** immer wieder, wieder und wieder (*geh*); **they came in one/three** *etc* **at a ~** sie kamen einzeln/immer zu dritt *etc* herein; **four at a ~** vier auf einmal; **for weeks at a ~** wochenlang; **he pays me £10 a ~** er zahlt mir jedesmal £ 10; **rides on the roundabout cost 50p a ~** eine Fahrt auf dem Karussell kostet 50 Pence; **I've told you a dozen ~s ...** ich habe dir schon x-mal gesagt ...

(d) (*multiplication*) **2 ~s 3 is 6** 2 mal 3 ist 6; **it was ten ~s as big as** *or* **ten ~s the size of ...** es war zehnmal so groß wie ...

(e) (*rate*) **Sunday is (paid) double ~/~ and a half** Sonntage werden doppelt bezahlt, sonntags gibt es 100% Zuschlag *or* 200%/sonntags gibt es 50% Zuschlag *or* 150%.

(f) (*era*) **in Victorian ~s** im Viktorianischen Zeitalter; **in olden ~s** in alten Zeiten; **in my ~** zu meiner Zeit; **~ was when ...** es gab Zeiten, da ...; **he is ahead of** *or* **before his ~** er ist seiner Zeit (weit) voraus; **to be behind the ~s** rückständig sein, hinter dem Mond leben (*inf*); (*outdated knowledge*) nicht auf dem laufenden sein; **to keep up with the ~s** mit der Zeit gehen; (*keep in touch*) auf dem laufenden bleiben; **~s are hard** die Zeiten sind hart *or* schwer; **when ~s are hard** in harten *or* schweren Zeiten; **~s change** die Zeiten ändern sich; **~s are changing** es kommen andere Zeiten; **~s are changing for the better/worse** es kommen bessere/schlechtere Zeiten; **~s have changed for the better/worse** die Zeiten haben sich gebessert/verschlechtert.

(g) (*experience*) **we had a good ~** es war (sehr) schön, es hat uns (*dat*) gut gefallen; **he doesn't look as though he's having a good ~** es scheint ihm hier nicht besonders gut zu gefallen; **have a good ~!** viel Vergnügen *or* Spaß!; **to have the ~ of one's life** eine herrliche Zeit verbringen, sich glänzend amüsieren; **what a ~ we had** *or* **that was!** das war eine Zeit!; **what ~s we had!, what ~s they were!** das waren (noch) Zeiten!; **to have an easy/a hard ~** es leicht/schwer haben; **we had an easy/a hard ~ getting to the finals** es war leicht für uns/wir hatten Schwierigkeiten, in die Endrunde zu kommen; **was it difficult? — no, we had an easy ~ (of it)** war es schwierig? — nein, (es war) ganz leicht; **he didn't have an easy ~ of it in the operating theatre** er war im Operationssaal schlimm dran; **to have a bad/rough ~** viel mitmachen; **we had such a bad ~ with our holidays/travel agency** wir hatten solches Pech mit unserem Urlaub/Reisebüro; **the goalkeeper had a rough ~** der Torwart hatte schwer zu kämpfen; **we've been having a rough ~ with the printers recently** wir hatten in letzter Zeit viel Ärger mit den Druckern; **to show sb a good ~** jdn ausführen; **she'll give you a good ~ for £30** bei ihr kannst du dich für £ 30 amüsieren; **to give sb a bad/rough** *etc* **~ (of it)** jdm das Leben schwermachen; **a good ~ girl** ein lebenslustiges Mädchen, ein vergnügungssüchtiges Mädchen (*pej*).

(h) (*rhythm*) Takt *m* ◆ **(to be) in ~ (with)** im Takt (sein) (mit); **(to be/get) out of ~** aus dem Takt (sein/kommen); **you're singing out of ~ (with the others)** du singst nicht im Takt (mit den anderen); **3/4 ~** Dreivierteltakt *m*; **to keep ~** (*beat ~*) den Takt angeben *or* schlagen; (*keep in ~*) (den) Takt halten.

[2] *vt* **(a)** (*choose ~ of*) **to ~ sth perfectly** genau den richtigen Zeitpunkt für etw wählen; **you must learn to ~ your requests a little more tactfully** du mußt lernen, deine Forderungen zu einem geeigneteren Zeitpunkt vorzubringen; **he ~d his arrival to coincide with ...** er legte seine Ankunft so, daß sie mit ... zusammenfiel; **you ~d that well** du hast dir den richtigen Zeitpunkt (dafür) ausgesucht; **the bomb is ~d to explode at ...** die Bombe ist so eingestellt, daß sie um ... explodiert.

(b) (*with stopwatch etc*) stoppen; *speed also* messen ◆ **to ~ sb (over 1000 metres)** jdn (auf 1000 Meter) stoppen, jds Zeit (auf *or* über 1000 Meter) nehmen; **~ how long it takes you, ~ yourself** sieh auf die Uhr, wie lange du brauchst; (*with stop-watch*) stopp, wie lange du brauchst; **to ~ an egg** auf die Uhr sehen, wenn man ein Ei kocht; **a computer that ~s its operator** ein Computer, der die Zeit mißt, die sein Operator braucht.

time: ~-and-motion expert *n* Fachmann *m* für Zeitstudien, ≃ REFA-Fachmann *m*; **~-and-motion study** *n* Zeitstudie, Bewegungsstudie *f*; **~ bomb** *n* (*lit, fig*) Zeitbombe *f*; **~ capsule** *n* Kassette *f* mit Zeitdokumentationen; **~card** *n* (*for workers*) Stechkarte *f*; (*US: ~table*) Fahrplan *m*; **~ check** *n* (*general*) Zeitkontrolle *f*; (*Rad, TV*) Zeitvergleich *m*; **~ clock** *n* Stechuhr *f*; **~-consuming** *adj* zeitraubend; **~ deposit** *n* (*Fin*) Festgeld, Termingeld *nt*; **~ exposure** *n* Langzeitbelichtung *f*; (*photograph*) Langzeitaufnahme *f*; **~ frame, ~frame** *n* Zeitrahmen *m*, zeitlicher Rahmen; **to set a ~ frame for sth** den Zeitrahmen *or* zeitlichen Rahmen für etw festlegen; **~ fuse** *or* (*US*) **fuze** *n* Zeitzünder *m*; **~-honoured** *or* (*US*) **-honored** *adj* althergebracht, altehrwürdig; **~keeper** *n* (*Sport*) Zeitnehmer *m*; **this watch/employee is a good/bad ~keeper** diese Uhr geht richtig *or* genau/nicht richtig/dieser Angestellte erfüllt immer/nie das Zeitsoll; **~-keeping** *n* (*in sports*) Zeitnahme, Zeitmessung *f*; (*in factories etc*) Zeitkontrolle *f*; (*of worker*) Erfüllung *f* des Zeitsolls; **bad ~-keeping** ständiges Zuspätkommen; **~-lag** *n* Zeitdifferenz *f*; (*delay*) Zeitverschiebung *f*; **cultural/technical ~-lag** Unterschied *m* in der kulturellen/technischen Entwicklung; **~-lapse** *adj* Zeitraffer-.

timeless ['taɪmlɪs] *adj* zeitlos; (*everlasting*) immerwährend.

timelessly ['taɪmlɪslɪ] *adv* zeitlos; (*eternally*) immerfort.

timelessness ['taɪmlɪsnɪs] *n* Zeitlosigkeit *f*; (*eternal nature*) Unvergänglichkeit *f*.

time limit *n* zeitliche Begrenzung; (*for the completion of a job*) Frist *f* ◆ **to put a ~ on sth** etw befristen.

timeliness ['taɪmlɪnɪs] *n* Rechtzeitigkeit *f* ◆ **the ~ of his warning soon became apparent** man merkte bald, daß seine Warnung genau zum richtigen Zeitpunkt erfolgt war.

time lock *n* Zeitschloß *nt*.

timely ['taɪmlɪ] *adj* rechtzeitig ◆ **a ~ piece of advice** ein Rat zur rechten Zeit; **that was very ~** das war genau zur rechten Zeit.

time: ~ machine *n* Zeitmaschine *f*; **~-out** *n* (*US*) **(a)** (*Ftbl, Basketball*) Auszeit *f*; **(b)** (*break*) **to take ~-out** Pause machen; **~piece** *n* Uhr *f*, Chronometer *nt* (*geh*).

timer ['taɪməʳ] *n* Zeitmesser *m*; (*switch*) Schaltuhr *f*; (*person*) Zeitnehmer *m*.

time: ~ saver *n* **to be a ~ saver** Zeit sparen; **~saving** *adj* zeitsparend; **~ scale** *n* (*in novel, drama etc*) zeitlicher Rahmen; (*perception of time*) Zeitmaßstab *m*; **to think on a different ~ scale** einen anderen Zeitbegriff haben; **~-sensitive** *adj project, money transfers etc* zeitabhängig, zeitgebunden; **~-served** *adj apprentice* ausgelernt; **~server** *n* Opportunist, Gesinnungslump (*pej inf*) *m*; **~serving** [1] *n* Opportunismus *m*, Gesinnungslumperei (*pej inf*) *f*; [2] *adj* opportunistisch; **~share** [1] *n* Wohnung *f*/

Haus *nt etc* auf Timesharing-Basis; [2] *adj attr* Timesharing-; **~-sharing** *n* Teilnehmer-Rechensystem, Time-sharing *nt*; **~ sheet** *n* Stundenzettel *m*, Arbeitszeit-Kontrolliste *f* (*form*); **~ signal** *n* Zeitzeichen *nt*; **~ signature** *n* Taktvorzeichnung *f*; **~ span** *n* Zeitspanne *f*; **~ switch** *n* Schaltuhr *f*, Zeitschalter *m*; **~table** *n* (*transport*) Fahrplan *m*; (*Brit Sch*) Stundenplan *m*; **to have a busy ~table** ein volles Programm haben; **what's on the ~table?** was steht auf dem Programm?; **~ travel** *n* Zeitreise *f*, Reise *f* durch die Zeit; **~ traveller** *n* Zeitreisende(r) *mf*; **~ trial** *n* Zeitrennen *nt*; **~ unit** *n* (*Telec*) Zeiteinheit *f*; **~ warp** *n* (*Sci-Fi, fig*) Zeitverzerrung *f*; **we're entering a ~ warp** wir werden in eine andere Zeit versetzt; **~ wasting** *n* (*Sport*) Bummelei *f*; **~worn** *adj stones* verwittert; (*through use*) abgetreten; *cliché, joke* abgedroschen; **~ zone** *n* Zeitzone *f*.

timid ['tɪmɪd] *adj* scheu, ängstlich; *person, behaviour, words also* schüchtern, zaghaft.

timidity [tɪ'mɪdɪtɪ], **timidness** ['tɪmɪdnɪs] *n see adj* Scheu, Ängstlichkeit *f*; Schüchternheit, Zaghaftigkeit *f*.

timidly ['tɪmɪdlɪ] *adv see adj*.

timing ['taɪmɪŋ] *n* **(a)** (*choice of time*) Wahl *f* des richtigen Zeitpunkts (*of* für), Timing *nt*; (*Tennis, Ftbl also*) (Ball)berechnung *f* ◆ **it's all a question of ~** es ist eine Frage (der Wahl) des richtigen Zeitpunkts *or* des Timings; **perfect ~, I'd just opened a bottle** ihr kommt gerade richtig, ich habe eben eine Flasche aufgemacht; **the ~ of the statement was wrong/excellent** die Erklärung kam zum falschen/genau zum richtigen Zeitpunkt; **what's the ~ for this job?** wie sieht der Zeitplan für diese Arbeit aus?; **the actors' ~ was terrible** die Schauspieler zeigten erbärmliche Synchronisierung; **to improve one's ~** sein Timing verbessern; **the dancer showed a good sense of ~** der Tänzer bewies ein gutes Gefühl fürs Timing.
(b) (*Aut*) (*mechanism*) Steuerung *f*; (*adjustment*) Einstellung *f* ◆ **~ mechanism** Steuermechanismus *m*.
(c) (*measuring of time*) Zeitnahme, Zeitmessung *f* (*of* bei); (*of race, runners etc*) Stoppen *nt* ◆ **regular ~ of the factory workers** regelmäßige Zeitkontrollen bei den Fabrikarbeitern.

timorous ['tɪmərəs] *adj* furchtsam, ängstlich, scheu.

Timothy ['tɪməθɪ] *n* (*Bibl*) Timotheus *m*.

timpani ['tɪmpənɪ] *npl* (*Mus*) Timpani, Kesselpauken *pl*.

timpanist ['tɪmpənɪst] *n* Timpanist, Paukist *m*.

tin [tɪn] [1] *n* **(a)** Blech *nt*; (*Chem: metal*) Zinn *nt*.
(b) (*esp Brit: can*) Dose, Büchse *f* ◆ **a ~ of beans/biscuits** eine Dose *or* Büchse Bohnen/eine Dose Kekse.
[2] *vt* **(a)** (*coat with ~*) verzinnen.
(b) (*esp Brit: can*) in Dosen *or* Büchsen konservieren.

tin can *n* **(a)** (*Brit*) (Blech)dose, (Blech)büchse *f*. **(b)** (*US Naut sl: destroyer*) Zerstörer *m*.

tincture ['tɪŋktʃə^r] [1] *n* **(a)** (*Pharm, Her*) Tinktur *f* ◆ **~ of iodine** Jodtinktur *f*.
(b) (*fig: tinge*) Spur, Andeutung *f*.
[2] *vt views, opinions* einen Anstrich *or* Beigeschmack geben (+*dat*) (*with* von) ◆ **to be ~d with sth** einen Anstrich *or* Beigeschmack von etw haben.

tinder ['tɪndə^r] *n* Zunder *m* ◆ **~box** Zunderbüchse *f*; **to be (like) a ~box** wie Zunder brennen; (*country etc*) ein Pulverfaß sein.

tine [taɪn] *n* (*of fork*) Zinke *f*; (*of antlers*) Ende *nt*, Sprosse *f*.

tinfoil ['tɪnfɔɪl] *n* (*wrapping*) Stanniolpapier *nt*; (*aluminium foil*) Aluminiumfolie *f*.

ting [tɪŋ] [1] *vt bell* läuten ◆ **to ~ the bell** klingeln; **he ~ed his knife against the glass, he ~ed the glass with his knife** er schlug mit dem Messer an das Glas, daß es klirrte.
[2] *vi* (*bell*) klingen.
[3] *n* Klingen *nt* ◆ **to give the bell a (quick) ~** (kurz) klingeln.

ting-a-ling ['tɪŋə'lɪŋ] [1] *n* Kling(e)ling *nt*.
[2] *interj* kling(e)ling.

tinge [tɪndʒ] [1] *n* **(a)** (*of colour*) Hauch *m*, Spur *f* ◆ **a ~ of red** ein (leichter) Rotstich, ein Hauch *m* von Rot.
(b) (*fig: hint, trace*) Spur *f*; (*of sadness also*) Anflug *m*.
[2] *vt* **(a)** (*colour*) (leicht) tönen ◆ **lavender water ~d with pink** Lavendelwasser, das leicht rosa getönt ist.
(b) (*fig*) **to ~ sth with sth** einer Sache (*dat*) eine Spur von etw geben; **~d with ...** mit einer Spur von ...; **our happiness was ~d with sorrow** unser Glück war getrübt.

tingle ['tɪŋgl] [1] *vi* prickeln, kribbeln (*inf*) (*with* vor +*dat*); (*with blows*) leicht brennen (*with* von) ◆ **... makes your mouth ~ with freshness** ... gibt Ihrem Mund prickelnde Frische; **to ~ with excitement** vor Aufregung beben, ganz kribbelig sein (*inf*).
[2] *n see vi* Prickeln, Kribbeln (*inf*) *nt*; leichtes Brennen ◆ **she felt a ~ of excitement** sie war ganz kribbelig (*inf*); **a ~ of excitement ran up her spine** ihr lief (vor Aufregung) ein Schauer über den Rücken.

tingling ['tɪŋglɪŋ] [1] *n see vi* Prickeln, Kribbeln (*inf*) *nt*; leichtes Brennen.
[2] *adj* (*with cold, freshness, excitement*) prickelnd; (*with blows*) brennend.

tingly ['tɪŋglɪ] *adj* prickelnd ◆ **my arm feels (all) ~** ich habe ein prickelndes Gefühl im Arm, mein Arm kribbelt (*inf*); **I feel ~ all over** es kribbelt mich überall; (*with excitement*) es prickelt mir unter der Haut, ich bin ganz kribbelig (*inf*).

tin: ~ god *n* (*fig*) Bonze *m*; (*idol*) Abgott, Götze *m*; **~ hat** *n* (*inf*) Stahlhelm *m*, steifer Hut (*inf*); **~horn** *n* (*US sl*) Angeber *m* (*inf*).

tinker ['tɪŋkə^r] [1] *n* Kesselflicker *m* ◆ **you little ~!** (*inf*) du kleiner Stromer *or* Zigeuner! (*inf*); **not to give a ~'s curse** *or* **cuss** *or* **damn about sb/sth** (*inf*) sich einen feuchten Kehricht um jdn/etw scheren (*inf*); **not to be worth a ~'s curse** *or* **cuss** *or* **damn** (*inf*) keinen Pfifferling wert sein (*inf*); (*person*) keinen Schuß Pulver wert sein (*inf*).
[2] *vi* **(a)** (*also* **~ about**) herumbasteln (*with, on* an +*dat*). **(b)** (*unskilfully*) **to ~ with sth** an etw (*dat*) herumpfuschen.

tinkle ['tɪŋkl] [1] *vt* zum Klingen bringen ◆ **he ~d the bell** er klingelte (mit der Glocke).
[2] *vi* (*bells etc*) klingen, bimmeln (*inf*); (*on piano*) klimpern; (*breaking glass*) klirren.
[3] *n* Klingen, Bimmeln (*inf*) *nt no pl*; (*of breaking glass*) Klirren *nt no pl* ◆ **to give sb a ~** (*Brit inf: on telephone*) jdn anbimmeln (*inf*).

tinkling ['tɪŋklɪŋ] [1] *n* (*of bells etc*) Klingen, Bimmeln (*inf*) *nt*; (*of piano*) Klimpern *nt*; (*of broken glass*) Klirren *nt*.
[2] *adj see n* klingend, bimmelnd (*inf*); klimpernd; klirrend.

tin: ~ lizzie *n* (*inf: car*) Klapperkiste *f*; **~ mine** *n* Zinnmine *f*, Zinnbergwerk *nt*.

tinned [tɪnd] *adj* (*esp Brit*) Dosen-, Büchsen-.

tinny ['tɪnɪ] *adj* (+*er*) *sound* blechern; *instrument* blechern klingend; *taste* nach Blech; (*pej*) *typewriter etc* schäbig ◆ **these cars are so ~** diese Autos bestehen fast nur aus Blech.

tin: ~-opener *n* (*esp Brit*) Dosen- *or* Büchsen öffner *m*; **~ pan alley** *n* die Schlagerindustrie; (*district*) das Zentrum der Schlagerindustrie; **~ plate** *n* Zinnblech *nt*; **~-plate** *vt* verzinnen; **~-pot** *adj* (*Brit inf*) mickrig (*inf*); **~-pot dictator** Westentaschen-Diktator *m* (*inf*).

tinsel ['tɪnsəl] *n* **(a)** (*foil*) Girlanden *pl* aus Rauschgold *etc*; (*on dress*) Lamé *nt*.
(b) (*pej*) Talmi *nt* (*pej*), Tand *m* (*geh*).

Tinseltown ['tɪnsəltaʊn] *n* (*usu pej*) Hollywood *nt*.

tin: ~smith *n* Blechschmied *m*; **~ soldier** *n* Zinnsoldat *m*.

tint [tɪnt] [1] *n* Ton *m*; (*product for hair*) Tönung(smittel *nt*) *f* ◆ **~s of autumn/purple** Herbst-/Violettöne *pl*.
[2] *vt* tönen.

tintack ['tɪntæk] *n* Tapeziernagel *m*.

tintinnabulation ['tɪntɪˌnæbjʊ'leɪʃən] *n* (*liter, form*) Klingeln *nt or* Geläut *nt* (von Glocken).

tin whistle *n* Blechflöte *f*.

tiny ['taɪnɪ] *adj* (+*er*) winzig, sehr klein; *baby, child* sehr *or* ganz klein ◆ **~ little** winzig klein; **a ~ mind** (*pej*) ein winziger Verstand, ein Zwergenverstand *m*.

tip[1] [tɪp] [1] *n* Spitze *f*; (*of cigarette*) Filter *m*; (*inf: cigarette*) Filter(zigarette) *f* ◆ **to stand on the ~ of one's toes** auf Zehenspitzen stehen; **it's on the ~ of my tongue** es liegt mir auf der Zunge; **it's just the ~ of the iceberg** (*fig*) das ist nur die Spitze des Eisbergs; *see* **finger~, wing~**.
[2] *vt* (*put ~ on*) **to ~ sth with copper/steel** *etc* etw mit einer Kupfer-/Stahlspitze versehen; **copper/steel ~ped** mit Kupfer-/Stahlspitze; **~ped** (*cigarette*) mit Filter, Filter-.

tip[2] [1] *n* **(a)** (*gratuity*) Trinkgeld *nt* ◆ **what do your ~s amount to?** wieviel Trinkgeld bekommen Sie (insgesamt)?; **£100 a week, plus ~s** £ 100 pro Woche, plus Trinkgeld(er); **50p is sufficient as a ~** 50 Pence Trinkgeld reichen.
(b) (*warning*) Wink, Tip *m*; (*advice*) Tip, Hinweis, Ratschlag *m*; (*Racing*) Tip *m* ◆ **if you take my ~** wenn Sie meinen Tip *or* Wink beachten.
(c) (*tap*) **to give the ball a ~** den Ball nur antippen.
[2] *vt* **(a)** (*give gratuity to*) Trinkgeld geben (+*dat*) ◆ **to ~ sb £1** jdm £ 1 Trinkgeld geben.
(b) (*Racing*) tippen auf (+*acc*), setzen auf (+*acc*) ◆ **he ~ped Red Rum for the 3.30** er setzte *or* tippte im 3^{30}-Rennen auf Red Rum; **they are ~ped to win the competition/election** (*fig*) sie sind die Favoriten in dem *or* für den Wettbewerb/in der *or* für die Wahl; **you ~ped a winner** (*lit, fig*) da hast du auf das richtige Pferd gesetzt.
(c) (*tap*) (*with fingers*) tippen *or* schnipsen an (+*acc*); (*with bat, racket*) antippen ◆ **to ~ one's hat (to sb)** an den Hut tippen.
[3] *vi* **Americans ~ better** Amerikaner geben mehr Trinkgeld.

◆**tip off** *vt sep* einen Tip *or* Wink geben (+*dat*) (*about* über +*acc*) ◆ **he ~ped ~ the police as to her whereabouts** er verklickerte (*inf*) *or* verriet der Polizei, wo sie war; **they've been ~ped ~** man hat ihnen einen Tip *or* Wink gegeben.

tip[3] [1] *vt* (*tilt, incline*) kippen; (*overturn*) umkippen; (*pour*) *liquid* kippen, schütten; (*empty*) *load, sand, rubbish* schütten; *books, clothes etc* schmeißen ◆ **to ~ sth backwards/forwards** etw nach hinten/vorne kippen *or* neigen; **to ~ a load into a ship** eine Ladung in ein Schiff leeren *or* kippen; **he ~s the scales at 70kg** er bringt 70 kg auf die Waage; **it ~ped the scales in his favour** (*fig*) das hat für ihn den Ausschlag gegeben; **~ the case upside down** dreh die Kiste um, stell die Kiste auf den Kopf; **to ~ sb off his chair** jdn vom Stuhl kippen; **to ~ one's hat over one's eyes** sich (*dat*) den Hut über die Augen ziehen/schieben.
[2] *vi* (*incline*) kippen; (*dump rubbish*) Schutt abladen ◆ **the boat ~ped to and fro** das Boot schaukelte auf und ab; **"no ~ping", "~ping prohibited"** „Schutt abladen verboten".
[3] *n* **(a)** (*Brit*) (*for rubbish*) Müllkippe *f*; (*for coal*) Halde *f*; (*inf: untidy place*) Saustall *m* (*inf*).
(b) to give sth a ~ etw (um)kippen.

◆**tip back** [1] *vi* (*chair, person, mirror*) nach hinten (weg)kippen.
[2] *vt sep* nach hinten kippen; *person* nach hinten legen.

◆**tip out** [1] *vt sep* auskippen; *liquid, sand also* ausschütten; *load, objects, rubbish* abladen, ausleeren ◆ **they ~ped him ~ of bed** sie kippten ihn aus dem Bett.
[2] *vi* herauskippen; (*liquid*) herauslaufen; (*sand*) herausrutschen; (*load, objects, rubbish also*) herausfallen.

◆**tip over** *vti sep* (*overturn*) umkippen.

◆**tip up** *vti sep* (*tilt*) kippen; (*overturn*) umkippen; (*folding seat*) hochklappen.

tip-off ['tɪpɒf] *n (inf)* Tip, Wink *m.*

tipper ['tɪpəʳ] *n* **(a)** *(also* **~ lorry** *(Brit),* **~ truck)** Kipplaster, Kipper *m.* **(b)** *(person)* **he's a generous ~** er gibt großzügig Trinkgeld *or* großzügige Trinkgelder.

tippet ['tɪpɪt] *n (old) (woman's)* Schultertuch *nt; (Eccl)* Stola *f.*

Tipp-Ex ® ['tɪpeks] *n* Tipp-Ex ® *nt.*

◆**Tipp-Ex out** ® *vt sep* mit Tipp-Ex ® löschen.

tipple ['tɪpl] *(inf)* **1** *n* **he enjoys a ~** er trinkt ganz gerne mal einen; **gin is his ~** er trinkt am liebsten Gin.
2 *vi* (ganz schön) süffeln *(inf),* picheln *(inf).*

tippler ['tɪpləʳ] *n (inf)* Schluckspecht *m (inf).*

tippy-toe ['tɪpɪtəʊ] *vi, n (US inf) see* **tiptoe.**

tipsily ['tɪpsɪlɪ] *adv* beschwipst, angesäuselt *(inf).*

tipsiness ['tɪpsɪnɪs] *n* Beschwipstheit *f.*

tipstaff ['tɪpstɑːf] *n (Brit Jur)* ≃ Ordnungsbeamte(r) *m.*

tipster ['tɪpstəʳ] *n jd, der bei Pferderennen Wettips verkauft.*

tipsy ['tɪpsɪ] *adj (+er)* beschwipst, angesäuselt *(inf)* ◆ **~ cake** mit Alkohol getränkter Kuchen; **to be ~** beschwipst *or* angesäuselt *(inf)* sein, einen Schwips haben.

tip: ~toe 1 *vi* auf Zehenspitzen gehen; **2** *n* **on ~toe** auf Zehenspitzen; **they stood on/raised themselves on ~toe** sie standen auf Zehenspitzen/sie stellten sich auf die Zehenspitzen; **~top** *adj (inf: first-rate)* tipp-topp *(inf) pred,* erstklassig, Spitzen-, Top-; **~-up lorry** *(Brit),* **~-up truck** *n* Kipplaster, Kipper *m;* **~-up seat** *n* Klappsitz *m.*

tirade [taɪ'reɪd] *n* Tirade, Schimpfkanonade *f.*

tire¹ [taɪəʳ] **1** *vt* ermüden, müde machen.
2 *vi* **(a)** *(become fatigued)* ermüden, müde werden.
(b) *(become bored)* **to ~ of sb/sth** jdn/etw satt haben, jds/einer Sache *(gen)* müde *(geh) or* überdrüssig *(geh)* werden; **she never ~s of talking about her son** sie wird es nie müde, über ihren Sohn zu sprechen.

◆**tire out** *vt sep* (völlig) erschöpfen.

tire² *n (US) see* **tyre.**

tired ['taɪəd] *adj* **(a)** *(fatigued)* müde; *cliché* abgegriffen ◆ **~ out** völlig erschöpft; **~ and emotional** *(hum inf: drunk)* nicht mehr ganz nüchtern; **their advertising is getting rather ~** ihrer Werbung fehlt allmählich der Schwung *or* Pep *(inf).*
(b) to be ~ of sb/sth jds/einer Sache *(gen)* müde *or* überdrüssig sein *(geh),* jdn/etw leid sein *or* satt haben; **to get ~ of sb/sth** jdn/etw satt bekommen; **I'm ~ of telling you** ich habe es satt, dir das zu sagen; **you make me ~!** du regst mich auf!

tiredly ['taɪədlɪ] *adv* müde; *say also* mit müder Stimme.

tiredness ['taɪədnɪs] *n* Müdigkeit *f* ◆ **~ had got the better of him** (die) Müdigkeit hatte ihn übermannt; **the accident was a result of (his) ~** (seine) Übermüdung war die Unfallursache.

tireless ['taɪəlɪs] *adj* unermüdlich; *patience also* unerschöpflich.

tirelessly ['taɪəlɪslɪ] *adv see adj* unermüdlich; unerschöpflich.

tirelessness ['taɪəlɪsnɪs] *n* Unermüdlichkeit *f.*

tiresome ['taɪəsəm] *adj (irritating)* lästig; *(boring)* fade, langweilig.

tiresomeness ['taɪəsəmnɪs] *n see adj* Lästigkeit *f;* Fadheit *f.*

tiring ['taɪərɪŋ] *adj* anstrengend, ermüdend ◆ **looking after 6 children under 5 is ~** es ist sehr anstrengend *or* es macht (einen) sehr müde, auf 6 Kinder unter 5 Jahren aufzupassen; **this is ~ work/a ~ job** diese Arbeit ist anstrengend.

tiro *n see* **tyro.**

Tirol *n see* **Tyrol.**

'tis [tɪz] *(Poet, dial) contr of* **it is** es ist.

tissue ['tɪʃuː] *n* **(a)** *(Anat, Bot, fig)* Gewebe *nt* ◆ **~ culture** Gewebekultur *f;* **~ cell** Gewebe- *or* Gewebszelle *f;* **a ~ of lies** ein Lügengewebe, ein Lügengespinst *nt.* **(b)** *(handkerchief)* Papier(taschen)tuch *nt.* **(c)** *(also* **~ paper)** Seidenpapier *nt.*

tit¹ [tɪt] *n (bird)* Meise *f.*

tit² *n:* **~ for tat** wie du mir, so ich dir, Auge um Auge(, Zahn um Zahn); **it was ~ for tat** es ging Auge um Auge(, Zahn um Zahn); **he was repaid ~ for tat** er bekam es mit gleicher Münze heimgezahlt.

tit³ *n (sl)* **(a)** *(breast)* Titte *f (sl)* ◆ **~ and bum press** *(hum)* Arsch-und-Titten-Presse *f (hum);* **he/it gets on my ~s** er/das geht mir auf den Geist *(inf).* **(b)** *(stupid person)* (blöde) Sau *(sl)* ◆ **I felt a right ~** ich kam mir total bescheuert vor *(inf).*

◆**tit up** *vt sep (sl: feel up breasts)* die Brust befummeln *(+dat) (inf)* ◆ **he was ~ting her up** er fummelte ihr am Busen rum *(inf).*

Titan ['taɪtən] *n (Myth)* Titan *m* ◆ **t~** *(fig)* Titan, Gigant *m.*

titanic [taɪ'tænɪk] *adj (huge)* gigantisch; *(Chem)* Titan-.

titanium [tɪ'teɪnɪəm] *n (Chem)* Titan *nt.*

titbit ['tɪtbɪt] *n (esp Brit)* Leckerbissen *m.*

titchy ['tɪtʃɪ] *adj see* **tichy.**

titfer ['tɪtfəʳ] *n (Brit sl: hat)* Deckel *m (inf).*

tithe [taɪð] *n usu pl* Zehnte *m* ◆ **to pay ~s** *or* **the ~** den Zehnten bezahlen *or* abgeben.

titillate ['tɪtɪleɪt] *vt person, senses* anregen, angenehm erregen; *interest* erregen ◆ **it ~s the palate** es kitzelt den Gaumen.

titillation [,tɪtɪ'leɪʃən] *n see vt* Anregung *f,* angenehme Erregung; Erregen *nt* ◆ **such ~ is not for the serious-minded** solcher Kitzel ist nichts für ernsthaft gesinnte Menschen.

titivate ['tɪtɪveɪt] *(old, hum)* **1** *vi* sich feinmachen.
2 *vt oneself, hair etc, restaurant* herausputzen, verschönern.

titivation [tɪtɪ'veɪʃən] *n (old, hum)* Verschönerung *f.*

title ['taɪtl] *n* **(a)** Titel *m (also Sport); (of chapter)* Überschrift *f; (Film)* Untertitel *m; (form of address)* Anrede *f* ◆ **what ~ do you give a bishop?** wie redet *or* spricht man einen Bischof an? **(b)** *(Jur) (right)* (Rechts)anspruch *(to* auf *+acc),* Titel *(spec) m; (document)* Eigentumsurkunde *f.*

titled ['taɪtld] *adj person, classes* mit (Adels)titel ◆ **is he ~?** hat er einen Titel?

title: ~ deed *n* Eigentumsurkunde *f;* **~ fight** *n* Titelkampf *m;* **~ holder** *n (Sport)* Titelträger(in *f),* Titelinhaber(in *f) m;* **~ page** *n (Typ)* Titelseite *f;* **~ role** *n (Theat, Film)* Titelrolle *f.*

titmouse ['tɪtmaʊs] *n* Meise *f.*

titrate ['taɪtreɪt] *vt (Chem)* titrieren.

titter ['tɪtəʳ] **1** *vti* kichern.
2 *n* Kichern, Gekicher *nt.*

tittie ['tɪtɪ] *n (inf) see* **titty.**

tittle ['tɪtl] *n see* **jot.**

tittle-tattle ['tɪtl,tætl] **1** *n* Geschwätz *nt; (gossip also)* Klatsch, Tratsch *(inf) m.*
2 *vi see n* quatschen, schwatzen; klatschen, tratschen *(inf).*

titty ['tɪtɪ] *n* **(a)** *(inf: breast)* Brüstchen *nt (inf).* **(b) that's tough ~** *(sl)* das ist Pech *(inf);* **that's your tough ~** *(sl)* da hast du wohl Pech gehabt *(inf).*

titular ['tɪtjʊləʳ] *adj* **(a)** *possessions* zum Titel gehörend. **(b)** *(without real authority)* nominell, Titular-.

tizzy ['tɪzɪ], **tizwoz** ['tɪzwɒz] *n (inf)* **to be in/get into a ~** höchst aufgeregt sein/sich schrecklich aufregen.

T-junction ['tiː,dʒʌŋkʃən] *n* T-Kreuzung *f* ◆ **"~ ahead"** „Achtung Vorfahrtsstraße".

TM *abbr of* **trademark** Wz.

TNT *abbr of* **trinitrotoluene** TNT *nt.*

to [tuː] **1** *prep* **(a)** *(in direction of, towards)* zu ◆ **to go ~ the station** zum Bahnhof gehen/fahren; **to go ~ the doctor('s)/greengrocer's** *etc* zum Arzt/Gemüsehändler *etc* gehen; **to go ~ the theatre/cinema** *etc* ins Theater/Kino *etc* gehen; **to go ~ France/London** nach Frankreich/London gehen/fahren; **to go ~ Switzerland** in die Schweiz gehen/fahren; **to go ~ school** zur *or* in die Schule gehen; **to go ~ bed** ins *or* zu Bett gehen; **~ the left** nach links; **~ the west** nach Westen; **he came ~ where I was standing** er kam dahin *or* zu der Stelle, wo ich stand; **to fall ~ the ground** auf den *or* zu Boden fallen; **to turn a picture/one's face ~ the wall** ein Bild/sich mit dem Gesicht zur Wand drehen; **hold it ~ the light** halte es gegen das Licht.
(b) *(as far as, until)* bis ◆ **to count (up) ~ 20** bis 20 zählen; **there were (from) 40 ~ 60 people** es waren 40 bis 60 Leute da; **it's 90 kms ~ Paris** nach Paris sind es 90 km; **it's correct ~ a millimetre** es stimmt bis auf den Millimeter; **8 years ago ~ the day** auf den Tag genau vor 8 Jahren; **~ this day** bis auf den heutigen Tag; **they perished ~ a man** sie kamen alle bis auf den letzten Mann ums Leben.
(c) *(+indir obj)* **to give sth ~ sb** jdm etw geben; **a present from me ~ you** ein Geschenk für dich von mir *or* von mir an dich; **who did you give it ~?, ~ who(m) did you give it?** wem haben Sie es gegeben?; **I said ~ myself** ich habe mir gesagt; **he was muttering/singing ~ himself** er murmelte/sang vor sich hin; **what is it ~ you?** was geht dich das an?; **he is kind ~ everyone** er ist zu allen freundlich; **it's a great help ~ me** das ist eine große Hilfe für mich; **he has been a good friend ~ us** er war uns *(dat)* ein guter Freund; **to address sth ~ sb** etw an jdn adressieren; **"To ..."** *(on envelope etc)* „An *(+acc)* ..."; **to pray ~ God** zu Gott beten.
(d) *(in toasts)* auf *(+acc)* ◆ **to drink ~ sb** jdm zutrinken; **to drink ~ sb's health** auf jds Wohl *(acc)* trinken.
(e) *(next ~, with position)* **bumper ~ bumper** Stoßstange an Stoßstange; **close ~ sb/sth** nahe bei jdm/etw; **at right angles/parallel ~ the wall** im rechten Winkel/parallel zur Wand; **~ the west (of)/the left (of)** westlich/links (von).
(f) *(with expressions of time)* vor ◆ **20 (minutes) ~ 2** 20 (Minuten) vor 2; **at (a) quarter ~ 2** um Viertel vor 2; **25 ~ 3** 5 (Minuten) nach halb 3; **it was five ~ when we arrived** es war fünf vor, als wir ankamen.
(g) *(in relation ~)* **A is ~ B as C is ~ D** A verhält sich zu B wie C zu D; **3 ~ the 4th** *(Math)* 3 hoch 4; **by a majority of 10 ~ 7** mit einer Mehrheit von 10 zu 7; **they won by 4 goals ~ 2** sie haben mit 4:2 *(spoken:* vier zu zwei) Toren gewonnen.
(h) *(per)* pro; *(in recipes, when mixing)* auf *(+acc)* ◆ **one person ~ a room** eine Person pro Zimmer.
(i) *(in comparison ~)* **inferior/superior ~** schlechter/besser als, unter-/überlegen *(+dat);* **that's nothing ~ what is to come** das ist gar nichts verglichen mit dem, was noch kommt.
(j) *(concerning)* **what do you say ~ the idea?** was hältst du von der Idee?; **what would you say ~ a beer?** was hältst du von einem Bier?; **there's nothing ~ it** *(it's very easy)* es ist nichts dabei; **that's all there is ~ it** das ist alles; **~ repairing cooker £30** *(Comm)* (für) Reparatur eines Herdes £ 30.
(k) *(according ~)* **~ the best of my knowledge** nach bestem Wissen; **~ all appearances** allem Anschein nach; **it's not ~ my taste** das ist nicht nach meinem Geschmack.
(l) *(accompanied by)* **to sing ~ the guitar** zur Gitarre singen; **to sing sth ~ the tune of ...** etw nach der Melodie von ... singen; **~ the strains of Rule Britannia** unter den Klängen von „Rule Britannia"; **to dance ~ a tune/an orchestra** zu einer Melodie/den Klängen *or* der Musik eines Orchesters tanzen.
(m) *(of)* **ambassador ~ America/the King of France** Botschafter in Amerika/am Hofe des Königs von Frankreich; **secretary ~ the director** Sekretärin des

Direktors.

(n) (*producing*) **~ my delight** zu meiner Freude; **~ everyone's surprise** zu jedermanns Überraschung.

(o) (*secure ~*) **he nailed it ~ the wall/floor** *etc* er nagelte es an die Wand/auf den Boden *etc*; **they tied him ~ the tree** sie banden ihn an den Baum *or* am Baum fest; **they held him ~ the ground** sie hielten ihn am Boden.

(p) (*in*) **I have never been ~ Brussels/India** ich war noch nie in Brüssel/Indien.

[2] (*in infin*) **(a) ~ begin ~ do sth** anfangen, etw zu tun; **he decided ~ come** er beschloß zu kommen; **I want ~ do it** ich will es tun; **I want him ~ do it** ich will, daß er es tut.

(b) (*in order ~*) **to eat ~ live** essen, um zu leben; **I did it ~ help you** ich tat es, um dir zu helfen.

(c) (*until*) **he lived ~ be 100** er wurde 100 Jahre alt; **the firm grew ~ be the biggest in the world** die Firma wurde zur größten der Welt.

(d) (*infin as prp*) **~ see him now, one would never think ...** wenn man ihn jetzt sieht, würde man nicht glauben, ...; **~ be honest, ...** ehrlich gesagt, ...; **~ tell the truth, ...** um ehrlich zu sein, ...; **~ get to the point, ...** um zur Sache zu kommen, ...; **well, not ~ exaggerate ...** ohne zu übertreiben, ...

(e) (*qualifying noun or pronoun*) **he is not the sort ~ do that** er ist nicht der Typ, der das täte, er ist nicht der Typ dazu; **I have done nothing ~ deserve this** ich habe nichts getan, womit ich das verdient hätte; **who is he ~ order you around?** wer ist er denn, daß er dich so herumkommandiert?; **he was the first ~ arrive** er kam als erster an, er war der erste, der ankam; **who was the last ~ see her?** wer hat sie zuletzt gesehen?; **there's no-one ~ help us** es ist niemand da, der uns helfen könnte; **there is much ~ be done** es gibt viel zu tun; **what is there ~ do here?** was gibt es hier zu tun?; **now is the time ~ do it** jetzt ist die (beste) Zeit, es zu tun *or* dazu; **the book is still ~ be written** das Buch muß noch geschrieben werden; **he's a big boy ~ be still in short trousers** er ist so ein großer Junge und trägt noch kurze Hosen; **I arrived ~ find she had gone** als ich ankam, war sie weg; **never ~ be found again** und wurde nie wieder gefunden.

(f) (*adj +to +infin*) **to be ready ~ do sth** (*willing*) bereit sein, etw zu tun; **are you ready ~ go at last?** bist du endlich fertig?; **it's hard ~ understand/accept** es ist schwer zu verstehen/es ist schwer, sich damit abzufinden; **it's impossible ~ believe** das kann man einfach nicht glauben; **you are foolish ~ try it** du bist dumm, das überhaupt zu versuchen *or* daß du das versuchst; **is it good ~ eat?** schmeckt es gut?; **it's too heavy ~ lift** es ist zu schwer zum Heben; **too young ~ marry** zu jung zum Heiraten.

(g) (*omitting verb*) **I don't want ~** ich will nicht; **I'll try ~** ich werde es versuchen; **you have ~** du mußt; **I should love ~** sehr gerne; **we didn't want ~ but we were forced ~** wir wollten nicht, aber wir waren dazu gezwungen; **I intended ~ do it, but I forgot ~, I intended ~, but I forgot** ich wollte es tun, aber ich habe es vergessen; **buy it, it would be silly not ~** kaufe es, es wäre dumm, es nicht zu tun; **he often does things one doesn't expect him ~** er macht oft Dinge, die man nicht von ihm erwartet.

[3] *adj* (*slightly ajar*) *door* angelehnt; (*shut*) zu.

[4] *adv* **~ and fro** hin und her; *walk* auf und ab.

toad [təʊd] *n* Kröte *f*; (*fig: repulsive person*) Ekel *nt*.

toad-in-the-hole ['təʊdɪnðə'həʊl] *n Teigspeise f mit Würsten.*

toadstool ['təʊdstuːl] *n* (nicht eßbarer) Pilz ♦ **poisonous ~** Giftpilz *m*.

toady ['təʊdɪ] [1] *n* (*pej*) Kriecher, Speichellecker *m*.

[2] *vi* radfahren (*pej inf*) ♦ **to ~ to sb** vor jdm kriechen.

to-and-fro ['tuːən'frəʊ] *n* Hin und Her *nt*.

toast[1] [təʊst] [1] *n* Toast *m* ♦ **a piece of ~** ein Toast *m*, eine Scheibe Toast; **on ~** auf Toast; **as warm as ~** (*fig*) mollig warm; **~ rack** Toastständer *m*.

[2] *vt bread* toasten; (*on open fire*) rösten ♦ **~ed teacakes** getoastete Rosinenbrötchen; **~ed cheese** überbackener Käsetoast; **to ~ one's feet by the fire** sich (*dat*) die Füße am Feuer wärmen.

[3] *vi* (*bread etc*) sich toasten/rösten lassen; (*inf: person*) braten (*inf*), rösten (*inf*).

toast[2] [1] *n* **(a)** Toast, Trinkspruch *m* ♦ **to drink a ~ to sb** auf jdn trinken; **to propose a ~** einen Toast *or* Trinkspruch ausbringen (*to* auf *+acc*); **they raised their glasses in a ~** sie hoben ihre Gläser (*to* um auf (*+acc*) zu trinken). **(b) she was the ~ of the town** sie war der gefeierte Star der Stadt.

[2] *vt* **to ~ sb/sth** auf jds Wohl *or* jdn/etw trinken; **we ~ed the victory in champagne** wir haben unseren Sieg mit Champagner gefeiert *or* begossen (*inf*); **as a girl, she was much ~ed for her beauty** als Mädchen war sie eine gefeierte Schönheit.

toaster ['təʊstəʳ] *n* Toaster *m*.

toastie ['təʊstɪ] *n* Toastschnitte *f*, getoastetes Sandwich.

toasting fork ['təʊstɪŋ,fɔːk] *n* Gabel *f* zum Brotrösten.

toastmaster ['təʊst,mɑːstəʳ] *n jd, der bei Diners Toasts ankündigt oder ausbringt und Tischreden ansagt.*

toasty ['təʊstɪ] *n see* **toastie**.

tobacco [tə'bækəʊ] *n* Tabak *m*.

tobacco: ~ jar *n* Tabaksdose *f*; **~ leaf** *n* Tabakblatt *nt*.

tobacconist [tə'bækənɪst] *n* Tabak(waren)händler *m*; (*shop*) Tabak(waren)laden *m* ♦ **at the ~'s** im Tabak(waren)laden.

tobacco: ~ plantation *n* Tabakplantage *f*; **~ pouch** *n* Tabaksbeutel *m*.

to-be [tə'biː] *adj* zukünftig ♦ **the mother-/bride-/husband-~** die werdende Mutter/zukünftige Braut/der zukünftige Mann.

toboggan [tə'bɒgən] [1] *n* Schlitten, Rodel(schlitten) *m* ♦ **~ run** Schlitten- *or* Rodelbahn *f*.

[2] *vi* Schlitten fahren, rodeln ♦ **to ~ down a slope** mit dem Schlitten einen Hang hinunterfahren; **to go ~ing** Schlitten fahren, rodeln.

toby jug ['təʊbɪ,dʒʌg] *n* Figurkrug *m*.

toccata [tə'kɑːtə] *n* Tokkata *f*.

tocsin ['tɒksɪn] *n* (*old*) Alarm(glocke *f*) *m*.

tod [tɒd] *n* (*Brit sl*): **on one's ~** ganz allein.

today [tə'deɪ] *adv, n* **(a)** heute ♦ **a week/fortnight ~** heute in einer Woche/zwei Wochen; **he's been here a week ~** heute ist er eine Woche da; **a year ago ~** heute vor einem Jahr; **~ is Monday** heute ist Montag; **from ~** von heute an, vom heutigen Tag an, ab heute; **~'s paper/news** die heutige Zeitung/heutigen Nachrichten, die Zeitung/Nachrichten von heute; **~'s rate** (*Fin*) der Tageskurs; **here ~ and gone tomorrow** (*fig*) heute hier und morgen da.

(b) (*these days*) heutzutage ♦ **the cinema ~** das Kino (von) heute; **the world/youth/writers of ~** die Welt/Jugend/Schriftsteller von heute; **~'s world/youth** die heutige Welt/Jugend, die Welt/Jugend von heute; **live for ~ and let tomorrow take care of itself** lebe dem Heute und laß das Morgen morgen sein.

toddle ['tɒdl] [1] *vi* **(a)** wackeln ♦ **the little boy ~d into the room** der kleine Junge kam ins Zimmer gewackelt.

(b) (*inf*) (*walk*) gehen; (*leave: also* **~ off**) abzwitschern (*inf*) ♦ **well, I'd better be toddling (off)** ich zwitschere wohl besser mal ab (*inf*); **could you just ~ down to the shops and ...** könntest du mal zu den Geschäften runtergehen und ....

[2] *n* (*inf*) **to go for a ~** an die Luft gehen.

toddler ['tɒdləʳ] *n* Kleinkind *nt*.

toddy ['tɒdɪ] *n* Grog *m*.

to-do [tə'duː] *n* (*inf*) Theater (*inf*), Gedöns (*inf*) *nt* ♦ **to make a ~** ein Theater *or* Gedöns machen (*inf*); **she made quite a ~ about it** sie machte viel Wind *or* vielleicht ein Theater *or* Gedöns darum (*inf*); **what a ~!** so ein Theater! (*inf*); **what's all the ~?** was soll denn das ganze Theater *or* Getue *or* Gedöns? (*inf*).

toe [təʊ] [1] *n* Zehe *f*, Zeh *m*; (*of sock, shoe*) Spitze *f* ♦ **to tread** *or* **step on sb's ~s** (*lit*) jdm auf die Zehen treten; (*fig*) jdm ins Handwerk pfuschen (*inf*); **with so many of us we'll be treading on each other's ~s** wir sind so viele, daß wir uns gegenseitig ins Gehege kommen; **to be on one's ~s** (*fig*) auf Zack sein (*inf*); **to keep sb on his ~s** (*fig*) jdn auf Zack halten (*inf*).

[2] *vt* (*fig*) **to ~ the line** sich einfügen, spuren (*inf*); **to ~ the party line** (*Pol*) sich nach der Parteilinie richten.

toe: ~cap *n* (Schuh)kappe *f*; **~clip** *n* (*on bicycle*) Rennbügel *m*.

-toed [-təʊd] *adj suf* -zehig ♦ **two-~** zweizehig, mit zwei Zehen.

toe-dance *vi* (*US*) auf den Spitzen tanzen.

TOEFL *n abbr of* **Test of English as a Foreign Language** TOEFL-Test *m*, *englische Sprachprüfung für ausländische Studenten.*

toe: ~hold *n* Halt *m* für die Fußspitzen; (*fig*) Einstieg *m*; **~-in** *n* Vorlauf *m*; **~nail** *n* Zehennagel *m*; **~-piece** *n* (*on shoe, Ski*) Zehenteil *nt*; **~rag** *n* (*pej sl*) Arsch *m* (*sl*); **~ shoe** *n* (*US*) Spitzenschuh *m*.

toff [tɒf] *n* (*Brit inf*) feiner Pinkel (*inf*).

toffee ['tɒfɪ] *n* (*substance*) (Sahne)karamel *m*; (*sweet*) Toffee *nt*, (weiches) Karamelbonbon ♦ **he can't sing for ~** (*inf*) er kann überhaupt nicht *or* nicht die Bohne (*inf*) singen.

toffee: ~ apple *n* kandierter Apfel; **~-nosed** *adj* (*Brit inf*) eingebildet, hochnäsig.

tofu ['tɒfuː] *n* Tofu *nt*.

toga ['təʊgə] *n* Toga *f*.

together [tə'geðəʳ] [1] *adv* **(a)** zusammen ♦ **to do sth ~** etw zusammen tun; (*with one another*) *discuss, play, dance etc also* etw miteinander tun; (*jointly*) *try, achieve sth, do research etc also* etw gemeinsam tun; **to sit/stand** *etc* **~** zusammen *or* beieinander sitzen/stehen *etc*; **to be ~/all ~** (*people*) (alle) zusammen *or* beieinander *or* beisammen sein; **to tie/fit/glue** *etc* **two things ~** zwei Dinge zusammenbinden/-setzen/-kleben *etc*; **we're in this ~** wir hängen da beide/alle zusammen *or* miteinander drin (*inf*); **they were both in it ~** sie waren beide zusammen *or* miteinander daran beteiligt; **just you and me ~** nur wir beide zusammen; **that makes £15 all ~** das macht insgesamt *or* (alles) zusammen £ 15.

(b) (*at the same time*) zusammen ♦ **all ~ now** jetzt alle zusammen; **you're not ~** (*Mus*) ihr seid im Takt auseinander.

(c) (*continuously*) **for hours ~** stundenlang; **can't you sit still for two minutes ~!** kannst du nicht mal zwei Minuten (lang) still sitzen?

[2] *adj* (*inf*) cool (*sl*) ♦ **she's more ~ now** sie ist jetzt besser beieinander (*inf*).

togetherness [tə'geðənɪs] *n* (*physical*) Beisammensein *nt*; (*mental, emotional*) Zusammengehörigkeit *f* ♦ **a feeling** *or* **sense of ~** ein Gefühl der Zusammengehörigkeit, ein Zusammengehörigkeitsgefühl *nt*.

toggle ['tɒgl] [1] *n* Knebel *m*; (*on clothes*) Knebelknopf *m*; (*on tent*) Seilzug *m* ♦ **~ key** (*Comput*) Umschalttaste *f*; **~ switch** Kipp(hebel)schalter *m*.

[2] *vi* (*Comput*) hin- und herschalten.

Togo ['təʊgəʊ] *n* Togo *nt*.

Togoland ['təʊgəʊlænd] *n* Togo *nt*.

togs [tɒgz] *npl* (*inf*) Sachen, Klamotten *pl* (*inf*), Zeug *nt*.

♦**tog up** *vt sep* (*inf*) **to ~ oneself ~, to get ~ged ~** sich in Schale werfen (*inf*); (*for tennis etc*) seine Kluft anlegen; **to be ~ged ~ in one's best clothes** seine besten Sachen anhaben (*inf*).

toil [tɔɪl] [1] *vi* **(a)** (*liter: work*) sich plagen, sich abmühen (*at, over* mit). **(b)** (*move with effort*) sich schleppen ♦ **to ~ up a hill** sich einen Berg hinaufschleppen.

[2] *n* (*liter: work*) Mühe, Plage (*geh*) *f* ♦ **after months of ~** nach monatelanger Mühe *or* Plage.

toilet ['tɔɪlɪt] *n* **(a)** *(lavatory)* Toilette *f*, Klosett *nt (dated)* ◆ **to go to the ~** auf die Toilette gehen; **she's in the ~/~s** sie ist auf *or* in der Toilette; **to put sth down the ~** etw in die Toilette werfen; **the cat's done its ~ on the carpet** die Katze hat auf den Teppich gemacht *(inf)*.
(b) *(old)* Toilette *f (geh)*.

toilet *in cpds* Toiletten-; **~ bag** *or* **case** *n* Kulturbeutel *m*, Toilettentasche *f*; **~ paper** *n* Toilettenpapier *nt*; **~ requisites** *npl* Toilettenartikel *pl*.

toiletries ['tɔɪlɪtrɪz] *npl* Toilettenartikel *pl*.

toilet: ~ roll *n* Rolle *f* Toilettenpapier; **~ seat** *n* Toilettensitz *m*, Brille *f (inf)*; **~ set** *n (brush and comb)* Toilettengarnitur *f*; *(bathroom set)* Badezimmergarnitur *f*; **~ soap** *n* Toilettenseife *f*; **~ tissue** *n* Toilettenpapier *nt*; **~ training** *n* Erziehung *f* zur Sauberkeit; **has he started his ~ training yet?** geht er schon auf den Topf?; **~ water** *n* Duftwasser, Eau de Toilette *nt*.

toils [tɔɪlz] *npl (old lit)* Netze *pl*; *(fig)* Maschen, Schlingen *pl*.

toilsome ['tɔɪlsəm] *adj (liter)* mühselig, mühsam.

to-ing and fro-ing ['tuːɪŋən'frəʊɪŋ] *n* Hin und Her *nt*.

Tokay [tə'kaɪ] *n (wine)* Tokaier *m*.

▼ **token** ['təʊkən] **1** *n* **(a)** *(sign)* Zeichen *nt* ◆ **as a ~ of/in ~ of** als *or* zum Zeichen *(+gen)*; **by the same ~** ebenso; *(with neg)* aber auch; **... then by the same ~ you can't object to ...** dann können Sie aber auch nichts gegen ... einwenden.
(b) *(counter: for gambling, jukebox etc)* Spielmarke *f*.
(c) *(voucher, gift ~)* Gutschein *m*.
2 *attr* Schein-, pro forma ◆ **~ gesture** leere Geste; **it was just a ~ offer** das hat er/sie *etc* nur pro forma *or* nur so zum Schein angeboten; **~ payment** symbolische Bezahlung; **~ resistance** Scheinwiderstand *m*; **~ strike** Warnstreik *m*; **~ rent/fine** nominelle *or* symbolische Miete/symbolische Strafe; **the one ~ black/woman** der Alibischwarze/die Alibifrau.

Tokyo ['təʊkɪəʊ] *n* Tokio *nt*.

told [təʊld] *pret, ptp of* **tell** ◆ **there were 50 people there all ~** es waren insgesamt *or* alles in allem 50 Leute da.

tolerable ['tɒlərəbl] *adj (lit) pain, noise level etc* erträglich; *(fig: not too bad also)* annehmbar, leidlich, passabel *(inf)* ◆ **how are you? — ~** wie geht's dir? — ganz leidlich *or* passabel *(inf)*.

tolerably ['tɒlərəblɪ] *adv* ziemlich ◆ **~ well** ganz leidlich *or* annehmbar, ziemlich gut; **they are ~ well-educated** sie sind leidlich gebildet *or (rather well)* ziemlich gebildet.

tolerance ['tɒlərəns] *n* **(a)** Toleranz, Duldsamkeit *f (of, for, towards* gegenüber); *(towards children, one's juniors)* Nachsicht *f (of* mit) ◆ **racial ~** Toleranz in Rassenfragen; **I have no ~ for such behaviour** für solch ein Benehmen habe ich kein Verständnis. **(b)** *(Med, Tech)* Toleranz *f* ◆ **to work to fine ~s** mit kleinen *or* engen Toleranzen arbeiten.

tolerant ['tɒlərənt] *adj (of, towards, with* gegenüber) tolerant *(also Tech)*, duldsam; *(towards children, one's juniors)* nachsichtig ◆ **the Lord is ~ of our mistakes** der Herr sieht uns unsere Schwächen nach.

tolerantly ['tɒlərəntlɪ] *adv see adj*.

▼ **tolerate** ['tɒləreɪt] *vt* **(a)** *pain, noise, weather etc* ertragen.
▼ **(b)** *person* dulden, tolerieren; *behaviour, injustice etc also* sich *(dat)* gefallen lassen, hinnehmen; *ideas* tolerieren ◆ **he can ~ anything except intolerance** er kann alles tolerieren, nur keine Intoleranz; **it is not to be ~d** so etwas kann man nicht dulden *or* hinnehmen; **I won't ~ this disobedience!** ich dulde diesen Ungehorsam nicht!

toleration [ˌtɒlə'reɪʃən] *n* Duldung, Tolerierung *f*.

toll[1] [təʊl] **1** *vti* läuten ◆ **for whom the bell ~s** wem die Stunde schlägt.
2 *n* Läuten *nt*; *(single stroke)* Glockenschlag *m*.

toll[2] *n* **(a)** *(tax)* Maut *f (esp Aus)*; *(bridge ~, road ~ also)* Zoll *m*, Benutzungsgebühr *f*; *(US Telec)* (Fernsprech)gebühr *f*.
(b) *(deaths, loss etc)* **the ~ on the roads** die Zahl der Verkehrsopfer; **the ~ of the floods continues to rise** *(in terms of people)* die Zahl der Opfer der Flutkatastrophe steigt ständig weiter; *(in terms of property)* das Ausmaß der Flutschäden wird immer größer; **the earthquake took a heavy ~ of human life** das Erdbeben forderte *or* kostete viele Menschenleben; **the ~ of the war** der Blutzoll des Krieges.

toll: ~bar *n* Zahlschranke, Mautschranke *(esp Aus) f*; **~booth** *n* Zahlstelle, Mautstelle *(esp Aus) f*; **~ bridge** *n* gebührenpflichtige Brücke, Mautbrücke *f (esp Aus)*; **~ call** *n (US)* Ferngespräch *nt*; **~-free call** *n (US)* gebührenfreier Anruf; **~gate** *n* Schlagbaum *m*, Mautschranke *f (esp Aus)*; **~house** *n* Mauthaus *nt (esp Aus)*.

tolling ['təʊlɪŋ] *n, no pl* Läuten *nt*.

toll: ~keeper *n* Mautner *m (esp Aus)*; **~ road** *n* Mautstraße *f (esp Aus)*, gebührenpflichtige Straße.

Tom [tɒm] *n dim of* **Thomas** ◆ **any ~, Dick or Harry** *(inf)* jeder x-beliebige; **you don't have to invite every ~, Dick and Harry** *(inf)* du brauchst ja nicht gerade Hinz und Kunz *or* Krethi und Plethi einzuladen *(inf)*; **it's not every ~, Dick and Harry who can afford this** nicht jeder kann sich *(dat)* so was leisten; **~ Thumb** der Däumling.

tom [tɒm] *n (cat)* Kater *m*.

tomahawk ['tɒməhɔːk] *n* Tomahawk *m*.

tomato [tə'mɑːtəʊ, *(US)* tə'meɪtəʊ] *n, pl* **-es** Tomate *f*.

tomato *in cpds* Tomaten-; **~ juice** *n* Tomatensaft *m*; **~ ketchup** *n* (Tomaten)ketchup *m or nt*; **~ sauce** *n* Tomatensoße *f*; *(ketchup)* (Tomaten)ketchup *m or nt*.

tomb [tuːm] *n (grave)* Grab *nt*; *(building)* Grabmal *nt*.

tombola [tɒm'bəʊlə] *n* Tombola *f*.

tomboy ['tɒmbɔɪ] *n* Wildfang *m* ◆ **she is a real ~** sie ist ein richtiger Junge *or* Wildfang.

tomboyish ['tɒmbɔɪɪʃ] *adj girl* jungenhaft.

tomboyishness ['tɒmbɔɪɪʃnɪs] *n* Jungenhaftigkeit *f*.

tombstone ['tuːmstəʊn] *n* Grabstein *m*.

tomcat ['tɒmkæt] *n* **(a)** Kater *m*. **(b)** *(US fig inf: woman-chaser)* Schürzenjäger *m (inf)*.

tome [təʊm] *n* dickes Buch, Wälzer *m (inf)*.

tomfool ['tɒm'fuːl] **1** *n* Blödian *m*.
2 *adj attr* blöd(sinnig).

tomfoolery [tɒm'fuːlərɪ] *n* Blödsinn, Unsinn *m*.

Tommy ['tɒmɪ] *n dim of* **Thomas**; *(Mil sl)* Tommy *m (sl)*.

tommy: T~ gun *n* Maschinenpistole *f*; **~rot** *n (dated inf)* dummes Zeug, Mumpitz *m (dated)*.

tomography [tə'mɒgrəfɪ] *n* Tomographie *f*.

tomorrow [tə'mɒrəʊ] *adv, n* morgen ◆ **~ week, a week/fortnight ~** morgen in einer Woche/zwei Wochen; **he'll have been here a week ~** morgen ist er eine Woche da; **a year ago ~** morgen vor einem Jahr; **the day after ~** übermorgen; **~ morning** morgen früh; **~ is Monday, it's Monday ~** morgen ist Montag; **(as) from ~** ab morgen, von morgen an, vom morgigen Tag an; **see you ~!** bis morgen!; **~'s paper** die morgige Zeitung, die Zeitung von morgen; **the article will be in ~'s paper** der Artikel wird morgen in der Zeitung sein; **will ~ do?** *(early enough)* reicht es noch bis morgen?, hat es noch bis morgen Zeit?; *(convenient)* ist es morgen recht?; **~ is another day** *(prov)* morgen ist auch noch ein Tag *(prov)*; **~ may never come** wer weiß, was morgen ist; **~ never comes** *(prov)* es heißt immer „morgen, morgen, nur nicht heute"; **who knows what ~ will bring?** wer weiß, was das Morgen bringt?; **the science of ~** die Wissenschaft von morgen; **~'s problems** die Probleme von morgen; **like there was no ~** als wenn es kein morgen (mehr) gäbe; *eat, drink* was das Zeug hält *(inf)*.

tom: ~tit *n* (Blau)meise *f*; **~-tom** *n* Tamtam *nt*.

ton [tʌn] *n* **(a)** (britische) Tonne ◆ **she/it weighs a ~** *(fig inf)* sie/das wiegt ja eine Tonne; *see appendix*.
(b) **~s** *pl (inf: lots)* jede Menge *(inf)* ◆ **to have ~s of time/friends/money** *etc* jede Menge *(inf) or* massenhaft *(inf)* Zeit/Freunde/Geld *etc* haben.
(c) *(sl: of speed)* **to do a** *or* **the ~** mit hundertsechzig Sachen fahren *(inf)*.

tonal ['təʊnl] *adj* klanglich, Klang-; *(Mus) (regarding form)* tonal; *(Art)* farblich, Farb- ◆ **~ variation** Klangvariation *f*; *(in colours)* Farbabstufung *f*; **~ effects in the music/painting** Klangeffekte in der Musik/Farbeffekte in dem Gemälde.

tonality [təʊ'nælɪtɪ] *n (Mus)* Tonalität *f*; *(of voice)* Klang *m*; *(of poem)* Tonart *f*; *(of painting)* Farbkomposition *f*.

tone [təʊn] **1** *n* **(a)** *(of sound) (~ of voice, Phon)* Ton *m*; *(quality of sound also)* Klang *m* ◆ **the soft ~s of a flute/her voice** die sanften Töne einer Flöte/der sanfte Klang ihrer Stimme; **she spoke in soft ~s** sie sprach in sanftem Ton; **... he said in a friendly ~** ... sagte er in freundlichem Ton; **I don't like your ~ (of voice)** mir gefällt dein Ton nicht; **don't speak to me in that ~ (of voice)** in diesem Ton kannst du mit mir nicht reden.
(b) *(of colour)* (Farb)ton *m*.
(c) *(fig: mood, character)* Ton *m* ◆ **what was the ~ of his letter?** wie war denn der Ton seines Briefes?; **the new people have lowered/raised the ~ of the neighbourhood** die neuen Leute haben dem Ansehen *or* Ruf des Viertels geschadet/das Ansehen *or* den Ruf des Viertels verbessert; **of course, Trevor had to lower the ~ (of the conversation)** Trevor mußte natürlich ausfallend werden.
(d) *(Mus)* Ton *m*; *(US: note)* Note *f*.
(e) *(Physiol)* Tonus *m (spec)* ◆ **to keep one's ~** sich fit halten.
2 *vt (Phot: tint)* einfärben, tonen *(spec)*.
3 *vi (colours)* (im Farbton) harmonieren.

◆**tone down** *vt sep (lit, fig)* abmildern; *colour also* abschwächen; *criticism also, language, demands* mäßigen.

◆**tone in** *vi* (im Farbton) harmonieren.

◆**tone up** *vt sep muscles* kräftigen; *person* in Form bringen ◆ **cycling keeps you ~d ~** Radfahren hält einen in Form.

tone: ~ arm *n (US)* Tonarm *m*; **~ control** *n* Klangfarbeneinstellung, Tonblende *f*; **~-deaf** *adj* nicht in der Lage, Tonhöhen zu unterscheiden; **he's ~-deaf** er hat kein Gehör für Tonhöhen; **~ language** *n* Tonsprache, Tonhöhensprache *f*.

toneless ['təʊnlɪs] *adj* tonlos; *music* eintönig; *colour* stumpf.

tonelessly ['təʊnlɪslɪ] *adv reply* tonlos; *sing* eintönig.

tone poem *n* Tongedicht *nt*.

toner ['təʊnəʳ] *n* **(a)** *(for laser, copier)* Toner *m* ◆ **~ cartridge** Tonerpatrone *f*; **~ cassette** Tonerkassette *f*. **(b)** *(cosmetic)* Tönung *f*.

tongs [tɒŋz] *npl* Zange *f*; *(curling ~) (Hist)* Brennschere *f*; *(electric)* Lockenstab *m* ◆ **a pair of ~** eine Zange.

tongue [tʌŋ] **1** *n* **(a)** Zunge *f* ◆ **to put** *or* **stick one's ~ out at sb** jdm die Zunge herausstrecken; **to lose/find one's ~** *(fig)* die Sprache verlieren/wiederfinden; **to hold one's ~** den Mund halten; **her remark was ~ in cheek** ihre Bemerkung war ironisch gemeint; **to have a ready/sharp ~** schlagfertig sein, nicht auf den Mund gefallen sein/eine scharfe Zunge haben; **keep a civil ~ in your head!** werden Sie nicht ausfallend!; **I can't get my ~ round it** dabei breche ich mir fast die Zunge ab; *see* **slip, tip**[1].
(b) *(liter: language)* Sprache *f*; *(old, Bibl)* Zunge *f* ◆ **the gift of ~s** *(Bibl)* die Gabe, in fremden Zungen zu reden.
(c) *(of shoe)* Zunge, Lasche *f*; *(of bell)* Klöppel *m*; *(of land)* (Land)zunge *f*; *(of*

➤ LANGUAGE IN USE: **token: 1a → 22** **tolerate: b → 14**

wood) Spund, Zapfen *m* ◆ **a ~ of fire licked the building** eine Flamme züngelte an dem Gebäude empor.
[2] *vt (Mus) note* (mit der Zunge) stoßen.
tongue: ~-and-groove joint *n* Anschlitzzunge, Spundung *f*; **~-in-cheek** *adj attr remark* ironisch gemeint; **~-tied** *adj* **to be ~-tied** keinen Ton herausbringen; **she sat there ~-tied** sie saß da und brachte keinen Ton heraus; **~ twister** *n* Zungenbrecher *m*.
tonguing ['tʌŋɪŋ] *n (Mus)* Zungenschlag *m*; *see* **double-~**.
tonic ['tɒnɪk] [1] *n* **(a)** *(Med)* Tonikum *nt*; *(hair ~)* Haarwasser *nt*; *(skin ~)* Lotion *f* ◆ **it was a real ~ to see him again** *(fig)* es hat richtig gutgetan, ihn wiederzusehen.
(b) ~ (water) Tonic(water)*nt*; **gin and ~** Gin (mit) Tonic.
(c) *(Mus)* Tonika *f*, Grundton *m* ◆ **~ solfa** Solmisation *f*.
[2] *adj* **(a)** *(Med)* stärkend, kräftigend, tonisch *(spec)* ◆ **~ wine** Stärkungswein *m*.
(b) *(Phon) syllable* Ton-; *stress* tontragend.
tonicity [tɒ'nɪsɪtɪ] *n (of muscles)* Tonus *(spec)*, Spannungszustand *m*.
tonight [tə'naɪt] [1] *adv (this evening)* heute abend; *(during the coming night)* heute nacht ◆ **see you ~!** bis heute abend!
[2] *n (this evening)* der heutige Abend; *(the coming night)* die heutige Nacht ◆ **~'s party** die Party heute abend; **I'm looking forward to ~** ich freue mich auf heute abend *or* auf den heutigen Abend; **~ is the night we've been looking forward to** heute ist der Abend, auf den wir uns gefreut haben; **~ is a night I'll remember all my life** an den heutigen Abend/an heute nacht werde ich mich mein ganzes Leben lang erinnern; **~'s weather: ~ will be clear but cold** das Wetter heute nacht: heute nacht wird es klar, aber kalt sein; **~'s paper** die heutige Abendzeitung, die Abendzeitung von heute.
tonnage ['tʌnɪdʒ] *n* Tonnage *f*.
tonne [tʌn] *n* Tonne *f*.
-tonner [-'tʌnə^r] *n suf (inf)* -tonner *m*.
tonsil ['tɒnsl] *n* Mandel *f* ◆ **to have one's ~s out** sich *(dat)* die Mandeln herausnehmen lassen.
tonsillectomy [,tɒnsɪ'lektəmɪ] *n* Mandeloperation *f*.
tonsillitis [,tɒnsɪ'laɪtɪs] *n* Mandelentzündung *f*.
tonsorial [tɒn'sɔːrɪəl] *adj (hum, rare form)* Barbier- *(hum)* ◆ **~ artist** Barbier *m*.
tonsure ['tɒnʃə^r] [1] *n* Tonsur *f*.
[2] *vt* scheren, die Tonsur erteilen *(+dat) (spec)*.
ton-up ['tʌnʌp] *adj (sl)* **~ kids** Motorradrocker *pl (inf)*.
too [tuː] *adv* **(a)** *(+adj or adv)* zu ◆ **that's ~/not ~ difficult a question to answer** diese Frage ist zu/nicht zu schwer zu beantworten; **~ much/many** zuviel *inv*/zu viele; *too* **much/many** *zu* viel/*zu* viele; **he's had ~ much to drink** er hat zuviel getrunken; **you can have ~ much of a good thing** allzuviel ist ungesund *(prov)*; **it's ~ much for her** es ist zuviel für sie; **don't worry ~ much** mach dir nicht zuviel Sorgen; **~ much!** *(sl)* dufte!, Klasse! *(sl)*; **~ right!** *(inf)* das kannste laut sagen *(inf)*.
(b) *(very)* zu ◆ **all ~** ... allzu ...; **only ~** ... nur zu ...; **none ~** ... gar nicht ..., keineswegs ...; **not ~/not any ~** ... nicht zu/allzu ...; **he wasn't ~ interested** er war nicht allzu interessiert; **I'm not/none ~ sure** ich bin nicht ganz/gar nicht *or* keineswegs sicher; **(that's) ~ kind of you** *(iro)* (das ist) wirklich zu nett von Ihnen; **none/all ~ soon** keineswegs zu/allzu früh.
(c) *(also)* auch. ***he*** **can swim ~, he ~ can swim** er kann *auch* schwimmen, auch *er* kann schwimmen; **he can *swim* ~** er kann auch *schwimmen*, schwimmen kann er auch.
(d) *(moreover, into the bargain)* auch noch ◆ **it was really cheap, and it works ~!** es war wirklich billig, und es funktioniert sogar *or* auch noch!; **they asked for a price-reduction ~!** sie wollten auch noch einen Preisnachlaß!
toodle-pip ['tuːdl'pɪp] *interj (dated Brit inf)* tschau *(inf)*.
took [tʊk] *pret of* **take**.
tool [tuːl] [1] *n* **(a)** Werkzeug *nt*; *(gardening ~)* (Garten)gerät *nt* ◆ **~s** Werkzeuge *pl*; *(set)* Werkzeug *nt*; **that's one of the ~s of the trade** das gehört zum Handwerkszeug; **to have the ~s for the job** das richtige *or* nötige Werkzeug haben. **(b)** *(fig: person)* Werkzeug *nt*. **(c)** *(sl: penis)* Ding *nt (sl)*, Apparat *m (sl)*.
[2] *vt book, leather* punzen.
◆**tool along** *vi (inf)* dahinbrausen *(inf)*.
◆**tool up** *vt sep factory* (mit Maschinen) ausrüsten.
tool: ~bag *n* Werkzeugtasche *f*; **~box, ~ chest** *n* Werkzeugkasten *m*.
tooling ['tuːlɪŋ] *n* Punzarbeit *f*.
tool: ~ kit *n* Werkzeug(ausrüstung *f*) *nt*; **~shed** *n* Geräteschuppen *m*.
toot [tuːt] [1] *vt* **to ~ a horn** auf dem Horn blasen *or (child's trumpet)* tuten; *(in car, on bicycle)* auf die Hupe drücken, hupen; **to ~ a whistle** pfeifen, auf der Pfeife blasen.
[2] *vi (in car, on bicycle)* hupen; *(train)* pfeifen; *(ship)* tuten.
[3] *n (in car, on bicycle)* Hupen *nt*; *(of train)* Pfiff *m*, Pfeifsignal *nt* ◆ **give a quick ~** *(on car horn)* drück mal kurz auf die Hupe.
tooth [tuːθ] *n, pl* **teeth** **(a)** *(of person, animal)* Zahn *m* ◆ **to have a ~ out/filled** sich *(dat)* einen Zahn ziehen/plombieren lassen; **to get one's teeth into sth** *(lit)* etw zwischen die Zähne bekommen; *(fig)* sich in etw *(dat)* festbeißen; **armed to the teeth** bis an die Zähne bewaffnet; **to show one's teeth** die Zähne zeigen *(also fig) or* fletschen; **to fight ~ and nail** bis aufs Blut kämpfen; **in the teeth of the wind/all opposition** gegen den Wind/ungeachtet allen Widerstands; **to lie in one's teeth** das Blaue vom Himmel herunterlügen; **I'm fed up to the (back) teeth with that** *(inf) or* **sick to the (back) teeth of that** *(inf)* ich habe die Nase gestrichen voll davon *(inf)*, es hängt mir zum Hals heraus *(inf)*; **to give a law/an organization some teeth** *(fig)* einem Gesetz/einer Organisation Wirksamkeit verleihen; **I'd give my back** *or* **eye teeth for that** ich würde viel darum geben; **to kick sb in the teeth** *(fig)* jdn vor den Kopf stoßen.
(b) *(of zip, wheel etc)* Zahn *m*; *(small also)* Zähnchen *nt*; *(of comb, rake also)* Zinke *f*.
tooth *in cpds* Zahn-; **~ache** *n* Zahnweh *nt*, Zahnschmerzen *pl*; **~brush** *n* Zahnbürste *f*; **~brush moustache** *n* Bürste *f*.
toothed [tuːθt] *adj* gezahnt, mit Zähnen.
tooth: ~less *adj* zahnlos; **~paste** *n* Zahnpasta *or* -creme *f*; **~pick** *n* Zahnstocher *m*; **~ powder** *n* Zahnpulver *nt*; **~some** *adj* schmackhaft, wohlschmeckend.
toothy ['tuːθɪ] *adj (+er)* **she's a bit ~** sie hat ein ziemliches Pferdegebiß *(pej inf)*; **he gave me a ~ smile** er lachte mich an und zeigte dabei seine Zähne/Zahnlücken.
toothypeg ['tuːθɪpeg] *n (baby-talk)* Beißerchen *nt (baby-talk)*.
tootle ['tuːtl] *(inf)* [1] *vi* **(a)** *(on whistle etc also:* **~ away***)* vor sich hin dudeln *(inf)*.
(b) *(drive)* juckeln *(inf)*; *(go)* trotten, zotteln ◆ **I'll just ~ (down) to the shops** ich geh' bloß mal eben (runter) einkaufen; **it's time I was tootling off** es wird Zeit, daß ich abzottele *(inf)*.
[2] *n* **to give a ~ on the car horn/a whistle** hupen/auf einer Flöte herumdudeln *(inf)*.
◆**tootle along** *vi (dated inf)* dahinzuckeln *(inf)* ◆ **I'd better ~ ~ now** ich zottele jetzt mal lieber ab *(inf)*; **I thought I'd ~ ~ to the party** *(inf)* ich dachte, ich zottel' mal mit zu der Party *(inf)*.
too-too ['tuː'tuː] [1] *adj pred (dated inf: marvellous)* pfundig *(inf)*; *(iro: affected)* affig *(inf)*.
[2] *adv (excessively)* zu.
toots [tuːts] *n (inf)* Schätzchen *nt (inf)*.
tootsy ['tʊtsɪ] *n (baby-talk)* Füßchen *nt*.
top[1] [tɒp] [1] *n* **(a)** *(highest part)* oberer Teil; *(of spire, pyramid, cone etc, fig: of league, company etc)* Spitze *f*; *(of mountain)* Gipfel *m*; *(of tree)* Krone, Spitze *f*; *(of pine tree)* Wipfel *m*, Spitze *f*; *(of branch)* oberes Ende; *(of wave)* Kamm *m*; *(of carrots, radishes)* Ende *nt*; *(leafy part)* Kraut *nt*; *(detachable part of cupboard etc)* Aufsatz *m*; *(head end) (of table, bed, sheet)* Kopfende *nt*, oberes Ende; *(of road, beach)* oberes Ende ◆ **which is the ~?** wo ist oben?; **the ~ of the tree/page/list/wall** *etc* **is** ... der Baum/die Seite/Liste/Wand *etc* ist oben ...; **the ~ of the milk** die Rahmschicht (auf der Milch); **at the ~** oben; **at the ~ of the page/list/league/pile/stairs/wall/hill/tree** *etc* oben auf der Seite/Liste/in der Tabelle/im Stapel/an der Treppe/Wand/am Berg/Baum *etc*; **at the ~ of the table/road** am oberen Ende des Tisches/der Straße; **to be (at the) ~ of the class** Klassenbeste(r) *or* -erste(r) sein, der/die Beste in der Klasse sein; **to come out at the ~ of the list** Erste(r) sein; **near the ~** (ziemlich) weit oben; **he's near the ~ in English** in Englisch gehört er zu den Besten; **the liquid was cloudy near the ~** die Flüssigkeit war oben wolkig; **she bashed the ~ of her head on the luggage rack** sie schlug sich *(dat)* den Kopf an der Gepäckablage an; **he looked over the ~ of his spectacles** er sah über den Brillenrand (hinweg); **he curled his fingers over the ~ of the window** er klammerte sich mit den Fingern an den oberen Fensterrand; **she fell from the ~ of the stairs to the bottom** sie fiel die ganze Treppe von oben bis unten hinunter; **five lines from the ~** in der fünften Zeile von oben; **from ~ to toe** von Kopf bis Fuß; **from ~ to bottom** von oben bis unten; **the system is rotten from ~ to bottom** das System ist von vorn bis hinten schlecht *(inf)*; **to scream at the ~ of one's voice** aus vollem Hals *or* aus Leibeskräften brüllen; **they were talking at the ~(s) of their voices** sie haben sich in voller Lautstärke unterhalten; **to be at the ~ of the ladder** *or* **the tree** *(fig)* auf dem Gipfel (des Erfolgs) sein; **go to the ~ of the class** *(inf)* du bist gar nicht so dumm!; **off the ~ of my head** *(fig)* grob gesagt; *(with figures)* über den Daumen gepeilt *(inf)*; **just a quick comment please, off the ~ of your head** bitte einen kurzen Kommentar, ganz spontan; **I wouldn't like to comment off the ~ of my head** ich möchte (dazu) nicht voreilig Stellung beziehen; **to go over the ~** *(in trenches)* aus dem Schützengraben klettern; *(exaggerate)* zu viel des Guten tun; **that's a bit over the ~** das ist ein bißchen übertrieben, das geht ein bißchen zu weit; **I find him a bit over the ~** ich finde, er übertreibt es ein bißchen; **he's over the ~** *(past his best)* er ist auf dem absteigenden Ast; **~ of the pops** *(record)* Spitzenreiter *m* (in der Hitparade); **the ~ of the morning to you!** *(Ir)* grüß Gott! *(S Ger, Aus)*, (schönen) guten Morgen!; *see* **bill**[3].
(b) *(upper surface)* Oberfläche *f* ◆ **to be on ~** oben sein *or* liegen; *(fig)* obenauf sein; **it was on ~ of/on the ~ of the cupboard/pile** *etc* es war auf/oben auf dem Schrank/Stapel *etc*; **put it on ~ of/the ~ of the cupboard** *etc* leg es oben auf den Schrank *etc*; **to go up on ~** *(on boat)* an Deck gehen; **seats on ~!** *(in bus)* oben sind noch Sitzplätze!; **to see London from the ~ of a bus** London vom Oberdeck eines Busses aus sehen; **on ~ of** *(in addition to)* zusätzlich zu; **things are getting on ~ of me** die Dinge wachsen mir über den Kopf; **then, on ~ of all that** ... und dann, um das Maß vollzumachen ...; **and, on ~ of that** ... und zusätzlich, und außerdem; **it's just one thing on ~ of another** es kommt eines zum anderen; **he didn't see it until he was right on ~ of it** er sah es erst, als er ganz nah dran war; **he felt he was on ~ of the situation** er hatte das Gefühl, die Situation im Griff *or* unter Kontrolle zu haben; **to come out on ~** sich durchsetzen; *(over rival)* die Oberhand gewinnen; **to talk off the ~ of one's head** *(inf)* nur so daherreden.
(c) *(inf: of body)* Oberkörper *m* ◆ **to blow one's ~** in die Luft *or* an die Decke gehen *(inf)*, aus der Haut fahren *(inf)*; **she's rather big round the ~** sie ist oben herum ganz schön füllig *(inf)*.
(d) *(working surface)* Arbeitsfläche *f*.

(e) (*bikini* ~) Oberteil *nt*; (*blouse also*) Top *nt*.
(f) (*lid*) (*of jar, suitcase*) Deckel *m*; (*of bottle*) Verschluß *m*; (*of pen*) Hülle *f*; (*of car*) Dach *nt* ◆ **hard/soft ~** Hardtop *nt*/Weichverdeck *nt*.
(g) (*Aut*: ~ *gear*) höchster Gang ◆ **in ~** im vierten/fünften, im höchsten Gang.
(h) (*inf*: *big* ~) Großzelt, Zirkuszelt *nt*.
(i) (*inf*) **to be (the) ~s** Klasse *or* Spitze sein (*inf*).
(j) (*Naut*) Mars *m*.
[2] *adj* (*upper*) obere(r, s); (*highest*) oberste(r, s); *branches, note, honours, price* höchste(r, s); (*best*) *driver, athlete, competitor, job* Spitzen-; *pupil, school, marks* beste(r, s); *entertainer, management* Top- ◆ **~ prices** Höchstpreise *pl*; **on the ~ floor** im obersten Stockwerk; **a ~-floor flat** eine Dachgeschoßwohnung; **he's out of the ~ drawer** (*fig*) er gehört zu den oberen Zehntausend; **the car has a ~ speed of 120** das Auto hat eine Höchstgeschwindigkeit von 120; **at ~ speed** mit Höchstgeschwindigkeit; **in ~ form** in Höchstform; **to be ~** (*Sch*) Beste(r) *or* Erste(r) sein; **the ~ men in the party/government/firm** die Parteispitze/Führungsspitze in der Regierung/des Unternehmens; **the newspaper for ~ people** die Zeitung für Führungskräfte; **the ~ people** (*in a company*) die Leute an der Spitze; (*in society*) die oberen Zehntausend.
[3] *adv* **to come ~** (*Sch*) Beste(r) werden.
[4] *vt* (a) (*cover, cap*) bedecken ◆ **~ped by a dome** gekrönt von einer Kuppel; **fruit ~ped with cream** Obst mit Sahne darauf.
(b) (*reach* ~ *of*) **just as the car/he ~ped the hill** gerade, als das Auto/er oben auf dem Berg angekommen war *or* den Gipfel des Berges erreicht hatte.
(c) (*be at* ~ *of*) **his name ~ped the list** sein Name stand ganz oben auf der Liste *or* an der Spitze der Liste; *see* **bill**[3].
(d) (*be higher than, fig: surpass*) übersteigen ◆ **that ~s the lot** (*inf*) das übertrifft alles; **and to ~ it all ...** (*inf*) und um das Maß vollzumachen ...
(e) **to ~ a tree/radish/carrot** die Spitze eines Baumes/das Ende eines Rettichs/einer Mohrrübe abschneiden; **to ~ and tail gooseberries** Stachelbeeren putzen.
(f) **to ~ oneself** (*inf*) sich umbringen.
◆**top off** *vt sep* abrunden.
◆**top out** *vt sep* **to ~ ~ a building** den letzten Stein legen; **~ping ~ ceremony** ≃ Richtfest *nt*.
◆**top up** *vt sep glass, battery, tank* auffüllen ◆ **to ~ ~ the oil** Öl nachfüllen; **can I ~ you ~?** (*inf*) darf ich dir nachschenken?
top[2] *n* Kreisel *m* ◆ **to sleep like a ~** wie ein Murmeltier schlafen.
topaz ['təʊpæz] *n* Topas *m*.
top: ~coat *n* (a) (*overcoat*) Mantel *m*; (*for men also*) Überzieher *m*; (b) (*coat of paint*) Deckanstrich *m*, letzter Anstrich; **~ copy** *n* Original *nt*; **~ dog** *n* (*fig*) **he always has to be ~ dog** er muß immer das Sagen haben; **~ dollar** (*esp US inf*) [1] *n* **to pay ~ dollar for sth** Höchstpreise für etw bezahlen; [2] *attr* **~-dollar prices** Höchstpreise *pl*; **~-down** *adj approach, view, analysis* von oben nach unten; **~-dress** *vt* (*Agr*) mit Kopfdünger düngen; **~ dressing** *n* (*Agr*) Kopfdünger *m*.
topee, topi ['təʊpiː] *n* Tropenhelm *m*.
top: ~-fermented *adj* obergärig; **~-flight** *adj* Spitzen-, erstklassig; **~ gear** *n* höchster Gang; **to be in ~ gear** (*lit*) im höchsten Gang *or* im vierten/fünften (Gang) sein; (*fig*) auf Hochtouren sein; **~ hat** *n* Zylinder *m*; **~-hatted** [tɒp'hætɪd] *adj* mit Zylinder; **~-heavy** *adj* (*lit, fig*) kopflastig; **she's a bit ~-heavy** (*hum inf*) sie hat einen ziemlichen Vorbau (*inf*); **~-hole** *adj, interj* (*dated inf*) famos (*dated*), erstklassig.
topiary ['təʊpɪərɪ] *n* (*Hort*) Formschnitt *m*.
topic ['tɒpɪk] *n* Thema *nt* ◆ **~ of conversation** Gesprächsthema *nt*.
topical ['tɒpɪkəl] *adj* (a) *problem, speech, event* aktuell ◆ **he made a few ~ remarks/allusions** er ging kurz auf aktuelle Geschehnisse ein/spielte kurz auf aktuelle Geschehnisse an. (b) (*according to subject*) *index* Sach-.
topicality [,tɒpɪ'kælɪtɪ] *n* (*of problem, event*) Aktualität *f*.
topically ['tɒpɪkəlɪ] *adv* (a) aktuell. (b) (*according to subject*) nach Sachgebieten.
top: ~knot *n* Dutt *m*; **~less** *adj* (mit) oben ohne, Oben-ohne-; *waitress also* topless *pred*; **~less waitresses** Oben-ohne-Bedienung *f*; **~-level** *adj* Spitzen-; **~ loader** *n* (*washing machine*) Toplader *m*; **~ management** *n* Spitzenmanagement *nt*; **~mast** *n* (*Naut*) Toppmast *m*, Marsstenge *f*; **~most** *adj* oberste(r, s); **the ~most room in the house** das Zimmer unter dem Dach; **~-notch** *adj* (*inf*) eins a (*inf*), prächtig; **~-of-the-range, ~-of-the-line** *adj attr* Spitzen-, der Spitzenklasse; **~-of-the-range model** Spitzenmodell *nt*.
topographer [tə'pɒgrəfəʳ] *n* Topograph(in *f*), Vermessungsingenieur(in *f*) *m*.
topographic(al) [,tɒpə'græfɪk(əl)] *adj* topographisch.
topography [tə'pɒgrəfɪ] *n* Topographie *f*.
toponym ['tɒpənɪm] *n* Ortsname *m*.
topper ['tɒpəʳ] *n* (*inf*: *hat*) Angströhre *f* (*inf*).
topping ['tɒpɪŋ] [1] *adj* (*dated Brit inf*) famos (*dated*).
[2] *n* (*Cook*) **with a ~ of cream/nuts** *etc* mit Sahne/Nüssen *etc* (oben) darauf; **recipes for various different ~s for ice cream** verschiedene Rezepte, wie man Eis überziehen kann; **artificial cream ~** Schlagschaum *m*.
topple ['tɒpl] [1] *vi* wackeln; (*fall*) fallen; (*fig: from power*) gestürzt werden.
[2] *vt* umwerfen; (*from a height*) hinunterkippen *or* -werfen; (*fig*) *government etc* stürzen ◆ **to ~ sb from power** jdn stürzen *or* entmachten.
◆**topple down** *vi* umfallen; (*thing also*) umkippen; (*group of objects*) runterpurzeln; (*from chair, top of stairs etc*) herunterfallen; (*+prep obj*) hinunterfallen ◆ **they all came toppling ~** sie kamen alle runtergepurzelt.
◆**topple over** *vi* schwanken und fallen (*prep obj* über *+acc*).
top: ~-ranking *adj* von hohem Rang; *civil servant, officer also* hohe(r); *personality* hochgestellt; *author, singer* Spitzen-; **~sail** *n* (*Naut*) Marssegel *nt*; **~-secret** *adj* streng geheim; **~side** *n* (*of beef*) Oberschale *f*; **~soil** *n* (*Agr*) Ackerkrume *f*; **~spin** *n* Topspin *m*; **~ station** *n* Bergstation *f*.
topsy-turvy ['tɒpsɪ'tɜːvɪ] (*inf*) [1] *adj* (*lit*) (*upside down*) umgedreht; (*in disorder*) kunterbunt durcheinander *pred*; (*fig*) auf den Kopf gestellt ◆ **it's a ~ world** es ist eine verkehrte Welt.
[2] *adv* **to turn sth ~** (*lit, fig*) etw auf den Kopf stellen; *plans* etw über den Haufen werfen.
top-up ['tɒpʌp] *n* (*inf*) **the battery/oil needs a ~** die Batterie muß aufgefüllt/es muß Öl nachgefüllt werden; **would you like a ~?** darf man dir noch nachschenken?
toque [təʊk] *n* Toque *f*.
tor [tɔːʳ] *n* (*esp in names*) Berg *m*.
torch [tɔːtʃ] *n* (*lit, fig*) Fackel *f*; (*Brit*: *flashlamp*) Taschenlampe *f*; (*blowlamp*) Schweißbrenner *m* ◆ **the ~ of learning** die Fackel der Wissenschaft; **to carry a ~ for sb** nach jdm schmachten.
torch: ~ battery *n* (*Brit*) Taschenlampenbatterie *f*; **~bearer** *n* (*lit*) Fackelträger *m*; (*fig also*) Herold *m*; **~light** *n* Licht *nt* der Fackel/Taschenlampe; **~light procession** *n* Fackelzug *m*.
tore [tɔːʳ] *pret of* **tear**[1].
toreador ['tɒrɪədɔːʳ] *n* Torero *m*.
torment ['tɔːment] [1] *n* Qual *f*; (*inf*: *person*) Quälgeist *m* ◆ **to be in ~, to suffer ~(s)** Qualen leiden.
[2] [tɔː'ment] *vt* quälen; (*annoy, tease*) plagen ◆ **~ed by remorse** von Reue gequält *or* geplagt.
tormentor [tɔː'mentəʳ] *n* Peiniger(in *f*) *m*.
torn [tɔːn] *ptp of* **tear**[1].
tornado [tɔː'neɪdəʊ] *n, pl* **-es** Tornado *m*.
torpedo [tɔː'piːdəʊ] [1] *n, pl* **-es** Torpedo *m* ◆ **~ boat** Torpedoboot *nt*; **~ tube** Torpedoausstoßrohr *nt*.
[2] *vt* torpedieren.
torpid ['tɔːpɪd] *adj* (*lethargic*) träge; (*apathetic*) abgestumpft; (*Zool*) torpid.
torpidity [tɔː'pɪdɪtɪ], **torpor** ['tɔːpəʳ] *n see adj* Trägheit *f*; Abgestumpftheit *f*; Torpidität *f*.
torque [tɔːk] *n* (*Mech*) Drehmoment *nt* ◆ **~ spanner** (signalgebender) Drehmomentenschlüssel.
torrent ['tɒrənt] *n* (*river*) reißender Strom; (*fig*) (*of lava*) Strom *m*; (*of words, insults*) Sturzbach, Schwall *m*, Flut *f* ◆ **the rain came down in ~s** der Regen kam in wahren Sturzbächen herunter; **a ~ of abuse** ein Schwall *m* von Beschimpfungen.
torrential [tɒ'renʃəl] *adj rain* sintflutartig.
torrid ['tɒrɪd] *adj* (*lit, fig*) heiß; *heat, air, sun* sengend.
torsion ['tɔːʃən] *n* Drehung, Torsion (*spec*) *f* ◆ **degree of ~** Drehbeanspruchung, Torsionsschwingung (*spec*) *f*.
torso ['tɔːsəʊ] *n* Körper *m*; (*Art*) Torso *m*.
tort [tɔːt] *n* (*Jur*) Delikt *nt*.
tortoise ['tɔːtəs] *n* Schildkröte *f*.
tortoiseshell ['tɔːtəsʃel] *n* (a) Schildpatt *m*; (*esp for spectacle frames*) Horn *nt*. (b) (*also* **~ cat**) Schildpattkatze *f*.
tortuous ['tɔːtjʊəs] *adj* (*lit*) *path* gewunden; (*fig*) verwickelt; *methods also, person* umständlich ◆ **he has a ~ mind** er hat komplizierte Gedankengänge.
torture ['tɔːtʃəʳ] [1] *n* Folter *f*; (*fig*) Qual *f* ◆ **~ chamber** Folterkammer *f*; **instrument of ~** Folterwerkzeug *nt*; **it was sheer ~!** (*inf*) es war eine wahre Qual *or* Folter.
[2] *vt* (a) (*lit*) foltern.
(b) (*fig: torment*) quälen, peinigen (*geh*).
(c) (*fig: distort*) verzerren; *language* vergewaltigen ◆ **~d language/sentences** verkrampfte Sprache/Sätze *pl*; **~d steel** grotesk verbogener Stahl; **her hair had been ~d into elaborate curls** ihr Haar war mühsam in kunstvolle Locken gedreht.
torturer ['tɔːtʃərəʳ] *n* (*lit*) Folterknecht *m*; (*fig: tormentor*) Peiniger(in *f*) *m*.
Tory ['tɔːrɪ] (*Brit Pol*) [1] *n* Tory *m*.
[2] *adj* konservativ, Tory-.
Toryism ['tɔːrɪɪzəm] *n* (*Brit Pol*) Konservativismus *m*.
tosh [tɒʃ] *n* (*dated Brit inf*) dummes Zeug.
toss [tɒs] [1] *n* (a) (*throw*) Wurf *m* ◆ **to take a ~** (*from horse*) abgeworfen werden; **with a proud ~ of her head** mit einer stolzen Kopfbewegung.
(b) (*of coin*) Münzwurf *m* ◆ **to win/lose the ~** (*esp Sport*) die Seitenwahl gewinnen/verlieren; **there is no point in arguing the ~ (with me)** es hat keinen Sinn, (mit mir) darüber zu streiten *or* mit mir herumzustreiten; **there'll always be somebody who'll want to argue the ~** es gibt immer einen, der Einwände hat; **I don't give a ~ about ...** (*inf*) ... ist mir völlig schnuppe (*inf*).
[2] *vt* (a) (*throw*) *ball* werfen; *salad* anmachen; *pancake* wenden (*durch Hochwerfen*); *rider* abwerfen ◆ **to ~ sth to sb** jdm etw zuwerfen; **~ it over!** wirf es herüber, schmeiß mal her (*inf*); **to ~ sth aside** etw zur Seite werfen; **to ~ sb aside** jdn fallenlassen; **~ing the caber** Baumstammwerfen *nt*; **to be ~ed by a bull/horse** auf die Hörner genommen werden/vom Pferd (ab)geworfen werden.
(b) (*move: wind*) schütteln, zerren an (*+dat*) ◆ **the boat, ~ed by the waves ...** das Boot, von den Wellen hin und her geworfen, ...; **to ~ one's head** den Kopf zurückwerfen *or* hochwerfen.
(c) **to ~ a coin** eine Münze (zum Losen) hochwerfen; **we settled it by ~ing a**

coin wir haben eine Münze hochgeworfen und es ausgeknobelt; **to ~ sb for sth** mit jdm (durch Münzenwerfen) um etw knobeln; **I'll ~ you for it** laß uns darum knobeln.

[3] *vi* **(a)** (*ship*) rollen; (*corn also*) wogen; (*plumes*) flattern ◆ **to ~ and turn (in bed)** sich (im Bett) hin und her wälzen *or* hin und her werfen; *see* **pitch²**. **(b)** (*with coin*) (durch Münzenwerfen) knobeln ◆ **to ~ for sth** um etw knobeln.

◆**toss about** [1] *vi* sich heftig hin und her bewegen; (*person*) sich hin und her werfen.

[2] *vt sep* (*move*) hin und her schütteln, durchschütteln; *boat* schaukeln; (*throw*) *ball* herumwerfen; (*fig*) *ideas* zur Debatte stellen.

◆**toss away** *vt sep* wegwerfen.

◆**toss back** *vt sep head* zurückwerfen, hochwerfen; *drink* hinunterstürzen, (runter)kippen (*inf*).

◆**toss off** [1] *vt sep* **(a)** *drink* hinunterstürzen, (runter)kippen (*inf*). **(b)** (*inf: produce quickly*) *essay* hinhauen (*inf*); *remark* hinwerfen. **(c)** (*sl: masturbate*) einen runterholen (+*dat*) (*sl*).

[2] *vi* (*sl*) sich (*dat*) einen runterholen (*sl*).

◆**toss out** *vt sep rubbish* wegschmeißen (*inf*) *or* -werfen; *person* hinauswerfen, rausschmeißen (*inf*).

◆**toss up** [1] *vi* knobeln (*for* um).

[2] *vt sep* werfen ◆ **to ~ sth ~ (into the air)** etw hochwerfen, etw in die Luft werfen.

toss-up [ˈtɒsʌp] *n* (*lit*) Knobeln *nt durch Münzenwerfen* ◆ **it was a ~ whether ...** (*inf*) es war völlig offen, ob ...

tot [tɒt] *n* **(a)** (*child: also* **tiny ~**) Steppke (*inf*), Knirps (*inf*) *m*. **(b)** (*esp Brit: of alcohol*) Schlückchen *nt*.

◆**tot up** *vt sep* (*esp Brit inf*) zusammenzählen *or* -rechnen.

total [ˈtəʊtl] [1] *adj* (*complete*) völlig, absolut; (*comprising the whole*) *sum, loss, number* Gesamt-; *war, eclipse* total; *disaster* absolut, total ◆ **what is the ~ number of rooms you have?** wie viele Zimmer haben Sie (insgesamt)?; **the ~ effect of all this worry was ...** im Endeffekt haben seine Sorgen bewirkt, daß ...; **to be in ~ ignorance (of sth)** (von etw) überhaupt nichts wissen; **the silence was ~** es herrschte völlige *or* vollkommene *or* totale Stille; **my bewilderment was ~** meine Verwirrung war vollkommen *or* komplett.

[2] *n* Gesamtmenge *f*; (*money, figures*) Endsumme *f* ◆ **a ~ of 50 people** insgesamt 50 Leute; *see* **grand, sum**.

[3] *vt* **(a)** (*amount to*) sich belaufen auf (+*acc*) ◆ **the visitors ~led 5,000** insgesamt kamen 5 000 Besucher.

(b) (*add: also* **~ up**) zusammenzählen *or* -rechnen.

(c) (*US inf: wreck*) *car* zu Schrott fahren.

totalitarian [ˌtəʊtælɪˈtɛərɪən] *adj* totalitär.

totalitarianism [ˌtəʊtælɪˈtɛərɪənɪzəm] *n* Totalitarismus *m*.

totality [təʊˈtælɪtɪ] *n* Gesamtheit, Totalität (*esp Philos*) *f*; (*Astron*) totale Finsternis.

totalizator [ˈtəʊtəlaɪˌzeɪtəʳ], **totalizer** [ˈtəʊtəlaɪzəʳ] *n* (*Horse-racing*) Totalisator *m*.

totally [ˈtəʊtəlɪ] *adv* völlig, total.

tote¹ [təʊt] *n* (*inf*) **the ~** der Totalisator.

tote² *vt* (*inf: carry*) *sth heavy* schleppen; *gun* bei sich haben ◆ **to ~ sth around** etw herumschleppen.

tote bag *n* (*US*) (Einkaufs)tasche *f*.

tote board *n* Totalisator *m*.

totem [ˈtəʊtəm] *n* Totem *nt*.

totemism [ˈtəʊtəmɪzəm] *n* Totemismus *m*.

totem pole *n* Totempfahl *m*.

totter [ˈtɒtəʳ] *vi* **(a)** (*wobble before falling*) wanken, schwanken; (*stagger*) taumeln, unsicher gehen; (*old man, baby*) tapsen; (*invalid*) schwanken, taumeln ◆ **to ~ about** *or* **around** herumwanken/-taumeln/-tapsen. **(b)** (*fig*) schwanken; (*economy*) kränkeln ◆ **the country was ~ing on the brink of war** das Land befand sich am Rande eines Krieges.

tottering [ˈtɒtərɪŋ] *adj* schwankend, wankend; *person also* taumelnd; *regime* bröckelig; *economy* wack(e)lig, kränklich ◆ **a ~ monarch** ein Monarch auf einem wackeligen Thron.

tottery [ˈtɒtərɪ] *adj* wack(e)lig; *person* tatterig ◆ **a ~ old man** ein Tattergreis *m* (*inf*).

totty [ˈtɒtɪ] *n* (*Brit sl*) Weiber *pl* (*inf*) ◆ **a nice piece of ~** ein tolles Weib.

toucan [ˈtuːkən] *n* Tukan, Pfefferfresser *m*.

touch [tʌtʃ] [1] *n* **(a)** (*sense of ~*) (Tast)gefühl *nt* ◆ **to be cold/soft to the ~, to have a cold/soft ~** sich kalt/weich anfühlen.

(b) (*act of ~ing*) Berühren *nt*, Berührung *f*; (*of pianist, typist, piano, typewriter*) Anschlag *m* ◆ **I felt a ~ on my arm** ich spürte, daß jd/etw meinen Arm berührte; **she thrilled to his ~** es durchzuckte sie, als er sie berührte; **it opens at a ~** es öffnet sich auf Fingerdruck; **the wheel responds to the slightest ~** das Lenkrad reagiert sofort *or* auf jede Bewegung; **braille is read by ~** Blindenschrift wird durch Abtasten gelesen.

(c) (*skill*) Hand *f*; (*style also*) Stil *m* ◆ **the ~ of a master** die Hand eines Meisters; **it has the ~ of genius/the professional ~** es hat etwas Geniales/Professionelles *or* einen genialen/professionellen Anstrich; **he's losing his ~** er wird langsam alt; **to have the right ~ with sb/sth** mit jdm/etw umgehen können; **a personal ~** eine persönliche Note.

(d) (*stroke*) (*Art*) Strich *m*; (*fig*) Einfall *m* ◆ **a book with humorous ~es** ein stellenweise humorvolles Buch; **a nice ~** eine hübsche Note; (*gesture*) eine nette Geste; **to put the final** *or* **finishing ~es to sth** letzte Hand an etw (*acc*) legen, einer Sache (*dat*) den letzten Schliff geben; **the house lacks a woman's ~** es fehlt eine Frau im Haus.

(e) (*small quantity*) Spur *f*; (*of irony, sadness etc also*) Anflug *m* ◆ **a ~ of flu/fever** eine leichte Grippe/leichtes Fieber; **a ~ of spring** ein Hauch *m* (von) Frühling; **he gave the horse a ~ of the whip** er ließ das Pferd die Peitsche fühlen *or* spüren; *see* **sun**.

(f) (*communication*) **to be in (constant) ~ with sb** mit jdm in (ständiger) Verbindung stehen; **they were in ~ with us yesterday** sie haben sich gestern mit uns in Verbindung gesetzt; **to be/keep in ~ with (political) developments** (politisch) auf dem laufenden sein/bleiben; **I'll be in ~!** ich lasse von mir hören!, ich melde mich!; **keep in ~!** laß/laßt wieder einmal von dir/euch hören!; **to be out of ~ with sb** keine Verbindung mehr zu jdm haben; **to be completely out of ~ (with sth)** (in bezug auf etw *acc*) überhaupt nicht auf dem laufenden sein; **you can get in ~ with me at this number** Sie können mich unter dieser Nummer erreichen; **you ought to get in ~ with the police** Sie sollten sich mit der Polizei in Verbindung setzen; **to lose ~ (with sb/sth)** den Kontakt (zu jdm) verlieren/(in bezug auf etw *acc*) nicht mehr auf dem laufenden sein; **a husband and wife who have lost ~ with each other** ein Ehepaar, das sich fremd geworden ist *or* sich entfremdet hat; **I'll put you in ~ with Mr Brown** ich werde Sie mit Herrn Brown in Verbindung bringen.

(g) (*Ftbl*) Aus *nt*; (*Rugby also*) Mark *f* ◆ **in ~** im Aus; in der Mark; **to kick for ~** (*Rugby*) in die Mark schlagen.

(h) (*sl*) **to make a ~** Geld schnorren (*inf*); **he's usually good for a ~** ihn kann man normalerweise gut anpumpen (*inf*) *or* anzapfen (*inf*); **to be an easy** *or* **soft ~** leicht anzupumpen (*inf*) *or* anzuzapfen (*inf*) sein.

[2] *vt* **(a)** (*be in or make contact with*) berühren; (*get hold of also*) anfassen; (*press lightly also*) *piano keys* anschlagen, leicht drücken; (*strike lightly*) *harp strings* streichen über (+*acc*); (*brush against*) streifen ◆ **to ~ glasses** anstoßen; **don't ~ that!** faß das nicht an!; **he ~ed his hat to me** er tippte (zum Gruß) an den Hut; **the speedometer needle ~ed 100** die Tachonadel ging auf 100; **I was ~ing 100 most of the way** ich fuhr fast immer 100; **once I ~ed 100** einmal habe ich 100 geschafft.

(b) (*lay hands on*) anrühren, anfassen ◆ **the police/tax authorities can't ~ me** die Polizei/das Finanzamt kann mir nichts anhaben; **the paintings weren't ~ed by the fire** die Gemälde blieben vom Feuer verschont.

(c) *food, drink* anrühren; *capital also* herankommen an (+*acc*) (*inf*); (*use*) antasten ◆ **I haven't ~ed the piano/accordion for months** ich habe seit Monaten nicht mehr Klavier gespielt/das Akkordeon nicht mehr in der Hand gehabt.

(d) (*equal*) herankommen an (+*acc*), erreichen ◆ **there's nothing to ~ hot lemon for a cold** bei einer Erkältung geht nichts über heiße Zitrone.

(e) (*deal with*) *problem etc* anrühren ◆ **everything he ~es turns to gold** ihm gelingt einfach alles; **I wouldn't ~ those shares** ich würde meine Finger von den Aktien lassen; **an ordinary detergent won't ~ dirt like that** ein normales Reinigungsmittel wird mit diesem Schmutz nicht fertig; **I couldn't ~ the third question** mit der dritten Frage konnte ich nichts anfangen; **I asked them not to ~ my desk** ich bat darum, nicht an meinen Schreibtisch zu gehen.

(f) (*concern*) berühren, betreffen.

(g) (*move emotionally*) rühren, bewegen; (*affect*) berühren; (*wound*) *pride* treffen ◆ **deeply ~ed** tief gerührt *or* bewegt.

(h) **to ~ sb for a loan/£10** (*sl*) jdn um einen Kredit angehen/jdn um £ 10 anpumpen (*inf*).

[3] *vi* (*come into contact*) sich berühren; (*estates etc: be adjacent also*) aneinanderstoßen, aneinandergrenzen ◆ **don't ~!** Finger weg!; **"please do not ~"** „bitte nicht berühren".

◆**touch at** *vi +prep obj* (*Naut*) anlaufen.

◆**touch down** [1] *vi* **(a)** (*Aviat, Space*) aufsetzen. **(b)** (*Rugby, US Ftbl*) einen Versuch erzielen.

[2] *vt sep ball* niederlegen.

◆**touch in** *vt sep details, shading etc* einfügen.

◆**touch off** *vt sep explosion, argument etc* auslösen.

◆**touch up** *vt sep* **(a)** *colour* auffrischen; *make-up also* frisch machen; *picture, paintwork also* ausbessern; *photo* retuschieren; *essay, article* ausbessern. **(b)** (*inf*) *woman, man* betatschen (*inf*), befummeln (*sl*).

◆**touch (up)on** *vi +prep obj subject* kurz berühren, antippen ◆ **he barely ~ed ~ the question** er hat die Frage kaum berührt.

touch-and-go [ˈtʌtʃənˈgəʊ] *adj* **to be ~** riskant *or* prekär sein; **it's ~ whether ...** es steht auf des Messers Schneide, ob ...; **he won eventually but it was ~ for a while** er gewann schließlich, aber es stand eine Zeitlang auf des Messers Schneide; **it's ~ if we'll make it** es ist noch vollkommen offen, ob wir es schaffen; **after his operation it was ~** nach der Operation hing sein Leben an einem Faden.

touchdown [ˈtʌtʃdaʊn] *n* **(a)** (*Aviat, Space*) Aufsetzen *nt*. **(b)** (*Rugby, US Ftbl*) Versuch *m* (*Niederlegen des Balles im Malfeld des Gegners*).

touché [tuːˈʃeɪ] *interj* (*Fencing*) Treffer; (*fig inf*) eins zu null für dich (*inf*).

touched [tʌtʃt] *adj pred* **(a)** (*moved*) gerührt, bewegt. **(b)** **to be a bit ~** (*inf: mad*) einen leichten Stich haben (*inf*).

touch football *n* (*US*) *sanftere Art des Football, bei der der Gegner berührt wird, anstatt zu Fall gebracht zu werden.*

touchiness [ˈtʌtʃɪnɪs] *n* Empfindlichkeit *f* (*on* in bezug auf +*acc*); (*irritability also*) leichte Reizbarkeit ◆ **because of the ~ of this subject** weil dieses Thema so heikel ist/war.

touching [ˈtʌtʃɪŋ] [1] *adj* rührend, bewegend.

[2] *prep* (*form*) bezüglich (*form*).

touchingly [ˈtʌtʃɪŋlɪ] *adv* rührend, bewegend.

touch: ~ judge *n (Rugby)* Seitenrichter *m;* **~line** *n (Sport)* Seitenlinie, Auslinie *f;* **~paper** *n* Zündpapier *nt;* **~-sensitive** *adj* berührungsempfindlich; **~-sensitive switch** Kontaktschalter *m;* **~stone** *n (fig)* Prüfstein *m;* **~-type** *vti* blindschreiben; **~-typing** *n* Blindschreiben *nt;* **~-up paint** *n* Tupflack *m.*

touchy ['tʌtʃɪ] *adj* empfindlich *(about* in bezug auf *+acc); (irritable also)* leicht reizbar; *subject* heikel, kitzlig *(inf).*

touchy-feely [ˌtʌtʃɪ'fiːlɪ] *adj (pej)* gefühlsduselig *(pej inf).*

tough [tʌf] 1 *adj (+er)* **(a)** zäh; *resistant* widerstandsfähig; *cloth* strapazierfähig; *(towards others)* hart, knallhart *(inf); bargaining, negotiator, opponent, fight, struggle, lesson* hart; *district, city* hart, rauh ◆ **as ~ as leather** zäh wie Leder *(inf);* **he'll get over it, he's pretty ~** er wird schon darüber hinwegkommen, er ist hart im Nehmen *(inf);* **to get ~ (with sb)** *(physically)* grob werden (mit jdm *or* gegen jdn), handgreiflich werden (gegen jdn); *(fig)* hart durchgreifen (gegen jdn); **~ guy** *(inf)* (knall)harter Kerl *or* Bursche *(inf).*
(b) *(difficult) task, problem* hart; *journey* strapaziös, anstrengend ◆ **it was ~ going** *(lit, fig)* es war eine Strapaze *or* ein Schlauch *m (inf);* **to have a ~ time of it** nichts zu lachen haben.
(c) *(strict) policy, controls* hart.
(d) *(inf)* hart ◆ **that's pretty ~!** das ist ganz schön hart!; **it was ~ on the others** das war hart für die andern; **~ (luck)!** Pech!
2 *n (inf)* Schlägertyp *m (pej inf),* (knall)harter Bursche *(inf).*
3 *adv (+er) (inf)* **to treat sb ~** jdn hart rannehmen.

◆**tough out** *vt always separate* **to ~ it ~** hartnäckig auf seine Standpunkt beharren.

toughen ['tʌfn] 1 *vt* **(a)** *glass, metal* härten. **(b)** *(fig) person* zäh *or* hart machen; *(physically also)* abhärten; *laws* verschärfen.
2 *vi (glass, metal)* aushärten, hart werden; *(meat)* zäh werden; *(attitude)* sich verhärten.

◆**toughen up** 1 *vt sep person* hart *or* zäh machen, stählen *(geh); muscles* trainieren; *sportsman also* fit machen; *regulations* verschärfen.
2 *vi* hart *or* zäh werden; *(attitude)* sich verhärten ◆ **to ~ ~ on sb/sth** härter gegen jdn/etw vorgehen.

toughie ['tʌfɪ] *n (inf) (person) (ruffian)* Rauhbein *nt (inf); (child)* Rabauke *m (inf); (problem, question)* harte Nuß ◆ **she thinks she's a ~ and can take it** sie hält sich für hart genug, das auszuhalten.

toughly ['tʌflɪ] *adv made* robust; *built also* stabil; *say* fest ◆ **~ worded** geharnischt; **to bring sb up ~** jdn zur Härte erziehen; **to behave ~** *(like a tough guy)* den harten Mann spielen *or* markieren *(inf); (decisively)* hart auftreten.

toughness ['tʌfnɪs] *n see adj* **(a)** *(of meat etc)* Zäheit *f; (of person)* Zähigkeit *f;* Widerstandsfähigkeit *f;* Strapazierfähigkeit *f;* Härte *f;* Rauheit *f.* **(b)** *(difficulty)* Schwierigkeit *f; (of journey)* Strapazen *pl.* **(c)** Härte *f.*

toupee ['tuːpeɪ] *n* Toupet *nt.*

tour [tʊəʳ] 1 *n* **(a)** *(journey, walking ~ etc)* Tour *f; (by bus, car etc also)* Fahrt, Reise *f; (of town, building, exhibition etc)* Rundgang *m (of* durch); *(also* **guided ~**) Führung *f (of* durch); *(by bus)* Rundfahrt *f (of* durch) ◆ **to go on/make a ~ of Scotland/the castle** auf eine Schottlandreise gehen/eine Schottlandreise machen/an einer Schloßführung teilnehmen/einen Rundgang durch das Schloß machen; **he took us on a ~ of the Highlands** er machte mit uns eine Reise durch die Highlands.
(b) *(also* **~ of inspection**) Runde *f (of* durch); *(on foot also)* Rundgang *m (of* durch) ◆ **he had a 3-year ~ (of duty) in Africa** er wurde für drei Jahre nach Afrika versetzt; **leave between ~s (of duty)** Urlaub *m* zwischen zwei Versetzungen; **to make a ~ of the site/border posts** einen Rundgang durch das Gelände/ eine Runde bei den Grenzposten machen.
(c) *(Theat)* Gastspielreise, Tournee *f (of* durch); *(Sport)* Tournee *f* ◆ **to go/be on ~** auf Gastspielreise *or* Tournee gehen/sein; **to take a company/play on ~** mit einer Truppe/einem Stück auf Gastspielreise *or* Tournee gehen.
2 *vt* **(a)** *country, district etc* fahren durch; *(on foot)* ziehen durch *(inf); (travel around also)* bereisen.
(b) *(visit) town, building, exhibition* einen Rundgang machen durch, besichtigen; *(by bus etc)* eine Rundfahrt machen durch.
(c) *(Theat, Sport)* eine Tournee machen durch.
3 *vi* **(a)** *(on holiday)* eine Reise *or* Tour *or* Fahrt machen; *(on foot also)* ziehen ◆ **we're ~ing (around)** wir reisen herum; **to go ~ing** Touren/eine Tour machen.
(b) *(Theat, Sport)* eine Tournee machen ◆ **to go/be ~ing** auf Tournee gehen/sein.

tour de force ['tʊədə'fɔːs] *n* Glanzleistung *f.*

tour guide *n* Reiseleiter(in *f*) *m.*

touring ['tʊərɪŋ] *n* (Herum)reisen, (Herum)fahren *nt.*

touring: ~ club *n* Touring-Club *m;* **~ company** *n (Theat)* Tourneetheater *nt;* **~ holiday** *n* Reiseurlaub *m;* **~ party** *n* Reisegruppe *f;* **~ team** *n* Gastmannschaft *f.*

tourism ['tʊərɪzəm] *n* Fremdenverkehr, Tourismus *m.*

tourist ['tʊərɪst] 1 *n (person)* Tourist(in *f*) *m,* Fremde(r) *mf; (Sport)* Gast *m* ◆ **to travel ~** in der Touristenklasse reisen.
2 *attr class, hotel, shop* Touristen-; *guide* Fremden-; *bureau, office, industry* Fremdenverkehrs- ◆ **~ information centre** Touristen-Informationsbüro *or* -zentrum *nt;* **~ season** Reisesaison *or* -zeit *f;* **~ trade** Fremdenverkehrsgewerbe *nt;* **~ traffic** Reiseverkehr *m.*

tourist class 1 *n* Touristenklasse *f.*
2 *adj ticket, fare* Touristen-; *passenger* in der Touristenklasse; *service* Charter-.
3 *adv travel, fly* in der Touristenklasse.

touristy ['tʊərɪstɪ] *adj (pej)* auf Tourismus getrimmt; *resorts, shops, souvenirs* für Touristen.

tournament ['tʊənəmənt] *n (Sport etc, also Hist)* Turnier *nt.*

tournedos [tʊə'neɪdəʊ] *n (Cook)* Tournedos *nt.*

tourney ['tʊənɪ] *n (Hist, US Sport)* Turnier *nt.*

tourniquet ['tʊənɪkeɪ] *n* Aderpresse *f,* Tourniquet *nt (spec).*

tour operator *n* Reiseveranstalter *m.*

tousle ['taʊzl] *vt hair* zerzausen; *(affectionately also)* zausen.

tousled ['taʊzld] *adj hair* zerzaust, wuschelig *(inf)* ◆ **~ head** Wuschelkopf *m (inf).*

tout [taʊt] *(inf)* 1 *n (tipster)* Wettberater *m; (esp Brit: spy)* Schnüffler *(inf),* Spion *(inf) m; (ticket ~)* (Karten)schwarzhändler *m; (for business)* Kundenfänger, Schlepper *(sl) m.*
2 *vt (Racing) horse* als Favorit angeben, als heißen Tip nennen; *(spy) stables* ausspionieren *(inf); horse* herumschnüffeln bei *(inf); (sell: also* **~ around**) *information* anbieten; *tickets* anbieten, schwarz verkaufen *(inf); goods* (den Leuten) aufschwatzen *(inf); ideas* propagieren ◆ **to ~ business for sb/sth** für etw (aufdringlich) Reklame machen.
3 *vi (Racing) (offer tips)* Wettips (gegen Honorar) verteilen; *(spy)* herumspionieren, herumschnüffeln *(inf)* ◆ **to ~ for business/customers** (aufdringlich) Reklame machen/auf Kundenfang sein *(inf),* Kunden schleppen *(sl).*

tow¹ [təʊ] *n* Werg *nt,* Hede *f.*

tow² 1 *n* **to take a car/yacht in ~** ein Auto abschleppen/eine Jacht schleppen *or* ins Schlepptau nehmen; **to give sb/a car a ~** *(in car)* jdn/ein Auto abschleppen; *(to start)* jdn/ein Auto anschleppen; **to give sb/a yacht a ~** jdn/eine Jacht schleppen *or* ins Schlepptau nehmen; **do you want a ~?** soll ich Sie abschleppen/anschleppen?; **"on ~"** ≃ „Fahrzeug wird abgeschleppt"; **in ~** *(fig)* im Schlepptau.
2 *vt boat, glider* schleppen; *car also* abschleppen; *(to start)* anschleppen; *trailer* ziehen ◆ **he was ~ing a huge dog behind him** er zog *or* schleifte einen riesigen Hund hinter sich *(dat)* her.

◆**tow away** *vt sep car* (gebührenpflichtig) abschleppen.

towage ['təʊɪdʒ] *n* **(a)** *(of ships)* Bugsieren, Schleppen *nt; (of cars)* Abschleppen *nt.* **(b)** *(fee) (for ships)* Schlepp- *or* Bugsiergebühr *f; (for cars)* Abschleppgebühr *f* ◆ **~ charges** *(for ships)* Schlepp- *or* Bugsiergebühren *pl; (for cars)* Abschleppgebühren, Abschleppkosten *pl.*

toward [tə'wɔːd] *adj (form: favourable)* angemessen.

toward(s) [tə'wɔːd(z)] *prep* **(a)** *(in direction of) (with verbs of motion)* auf *(+acc)* ... zu ◆ **they walked ~ the town** sie gingen auf die Stadt zu; **we sailed ~ China** wir segelten in Richtung China; **it's further north, ~ Dortmund** es liegt weiter im Norden, Richtung Dortmund; **~ the south** nach *or* gen *(liter)* Süden; **he turned ~ her** er wandte sich ihr zu; **with his back ~ the wall** mit dem Rücken zur Wand; **you should read with your back ~ the light** Sie sollten mit dem Rücken zum Licht lesen; **on the side (facing) ~ the sea** zum Meer hin; **a hotel facing ~ the sea** ein Hotel mit Blick aufs Meer; **they are working ~ a solution** sie arbeiten auf eine Lösung hin; **if it helps ~ a solution** wenn es zur Lösung beiträgt; **~ a better understanding of ...** zum besseren Verständnis von ...; **~ a new theory of knowledge** (Ansätze *pl*) zu einer neuen Erkenntnistheorie.
(b) *(in relation to)* ... *(dat)* gegenüber ◆ **what are your feelings ~ him?** was empfinden Sie ihm gegenüber *or* für ihn?
(c) ~ ten o'clock gegen zehn Uhr; **~ the end of the 60's/the year** gegen Ende der sechziger Jahre/des Jahres.

tow: ~-bar *n* Anhängerkupplung *f;* **~boat** *n* Schleppschiff *nt,* Schlepper *m;* **~-car** *n (US)* Abschleppwagen *m.*

towel ['taʊəl] 1 *n* Handtuch *nt* ◆ **~ rail** Handtuchhalter *m; see* **throw in.**
2 *vt* (mit einem Handtuch) (ab)trocknen.

◆**towel down** *vt sep* (ab)trocknen, trockenreiben.

towelling ['taʊəlɪŋ] *n* Frottee(stoff) *m.*

tower ['taʊəʳ] 1 *n* **(a)** Turm *m.* **(b)** *(fig: person)* **a ~ of strength** eine Stütze, ein starker (Rück)halt. **(c)** *(Comput)* Tower *m* ◆ **~ system** Tower-System *nt.*
2 *vi* ragen ◆ **the buildings ~ into the sky** die Gebäude ragen in den Himmel.

◆**tower above** *or* **over** *vi +prep obj* **(a)** *(buildings etc)* emporragen über *(+acc).* **(b)** *(lit, fig: people)* überragen.

◆**tower up** *vi* hinaufragen, emporragen.

tower block *n* Hochhaus *nt.*

towering ['taʊərɪŋ] *adj* **(a)** *building* hochragend, alles überragend; *mountain* (steil) aufragend; *tree* hochgewachsen ◆ **the boy stood before the ~ figure of the headmaster** der Schüler stand vor der hoch aufragenden Gestalt des Direktors.
(b) *(fig)* **a ~ rage** eine rasende *or* unbändige Wut; **one of the ~ giants of literature** eine der einsamen Größen der Literatur, ein Titan der Literatur.

tow-headed ['təʊ'hedɪd] *adj* flachsblond.

towline ['təʊlaɪn] *n (Aut)* Abschleppseil *nt; (Naut, for glider)* Schleppseil *nt.*

town [taʊn] *n* **(a)** Stadt *f* ◆ **the ~ of Brighton** (die Stadt) Brighton; **to go into** *or* **down ~** in die Stadt gehen; **to live in ~** in der Stadt wohnen; **guess who's in ~?** raten Sie mal, wer zur Zeit hier (in der Stadt) ist?; **he's out of ~** er ist nicht in der Stadt, er ist außerhalb; **~ and gown** *(Univ)* (die) Bevölkerung und (die) Studenten; **to have a night on the ~** *(inf)* die Nacht durchmachen *(inf),* einen draufmachen *(sl);* **you didn't know? but it's all over ~** du hattest keine Ahnung? das ist doch stadtbekannt; **it's all over ~ now that he has ...** es hat sich herumgesprochen, daß er ...; **to go to ~ on sth** *(fig inf) (go to great trouble with)* sich *(dat)* bei etw einen abbrechen *(inf); (to please)* sich bei etw ins Zeug legen; *(exaggerate)* etw übertreiben; **you've really gone to ~ on this**

essay bei diesem Aufsatz sind Sie wirklich ins Detail gegangen; **John's really gone to ~ on his new house** John hat bei seinem neuen Haus wirklich keine Kosten gescheut.
(b) (*Brit: London*) London *nt* ◆ **to go up to ~** nach London gehen *or* fahren; **he is out of ~** er ist nicht in London.

town: ~ centre *n* Stadtmitte *f*, (Stadt)zentrum, Stadtinnere(s) *nt*; **~ clerk** *n* Stadtdirektor, Stadtschreiber (*old, Sw*) *m*; (*of bigger town*) Oberstadtdirektor *m*; **~ council** *n* Stadtrat *m*; **~ councillor** *n* Stadtrat *m*, Stadträtin *f*; **~ crier** *n* Ausrufer *m*; **~ dweller** *n* Städter, Stadtbewohner *m*.

townee, townie ['taʊniː] *n* (*pej*) Städter, Stadtmensch *m*; (*Univ*) *Bewohner einer Universitätsstadt, der nicht der Universität angehört.*

town: ~ gas *n* Stadtgas *nt*; **~ hall** *n* Rathaus *nt*; **~ house** *n* Stadthaus *nt*, Haus *nt* in der Stadt; (*type of house*) Wohnhaus *nt*; **~ life** *n* Stadtleben *nt*, Leben *nt* in der Stadt; **~ planner** *n* Stadt- *or* Städteplaner *m*; **~ planning** *n* Stadtplanung, Städteplanung *f*; **~scape** *n* Stadtbild *nt or* -landschaft *f*; (*Art*) Stadtansicht *f*.

townsfolk ['taʊnzfəʊk] *npl* Städter, Stadtmenschen *pl*, Stadtbevölkerung *f*; (*citizens*) Bürger *pl*.

township ['taʊnʃɪp] *n* (Stadt)gemeinde *f*; (*US*) Verwaltungsbezirk *m*; (*US Surv*) 6 Meilen großes Gebiet; (*in South Africa*) Township *f*.

towns: ~man *n* Städter, Stadtmensch *m*; (*citizen*) Bürger *m*; **my fellow ~men** meine (lieben) Mitbürger; **~people** *npl* Städter, Stadtmenschen *pl*; (*citizens*) Bürger *pl*; **~woman** *n* Bürgerin *f*; **the ~women of Paisley** die Bewohnerinnen *or* Bürgerinnen *pl* von Paisley; **~women's guild** *Frauenvereinigung f mit gesellschaftlichen Aufgaben.*

tow: ~path *n* Treidelpfad *m*; **~-plane** *n* Schleppflugzeug *nt*; **~rope** *n see* **~line**; **~ start** *n* (*Aut*) Anschleppen *nt*; **to give sb a ~ start** jdn anschleppen; **~-truck** *n* (*US*) Abschleppwagen *m*.

toxaemia, (*US*) **toxemia** [tɒk'siːmɪə] *n* Blutvergiftung, Sepsis (*spec*) *f*.

toxic ['tɒksɪk] *adj* giftig, Gift-, toxisch ◆ **~ waste** Giftmüll *m*.

toxicity [tɒk'sɪsɪtɪ] *n* Giftigkeit *f*, Giftgehalt *m*.

toxicological [ˌtɒksɪkə'lɒdʒɪkəl] *adj* toxikologisch.

toxicology [ˌtɒksɪ'kɒlədʒɪ] *n* Toxikologie *f*.

toxin ['tɒksɪn] *n* Gift(stoff *m*), Toxin *nt*.

▼ **toy** [tɔɪ] [1] *n* Spielzeug *nt* ◆ **~s** Spielsachen *pl*, Spielzeug *nt*; (*in shops also*) Spielwaren *pl*; **it's not a ~!** das ist kein (Kinder)spielzeug!
▼ [2] *vi* **to ~ with an object/idea** *etc* mit einer Sache/Idee *etc* spielen; **to ~ with one's food** mit dem Essen (herum)spielen.

toy *in cpds gun, car, soldier* Spielzeug-; **~ boy** *n* (*inf*) jugendlicher Liebhaber; **he looks like my ideal ~ boy** so was Junges wie er wäre ideal zum Vernaschen (*inf*); **~ dog** *n* Zwerghund *m*; (*of material*) Stoffhund *m*; **~shop** *n* Spielwarenladen *m*; **~-town** *adj attr revolutionary etc* Möchtegern-; (*esp Brit pej: childish*) kindisch; (*worthless*) wertlos; **toytown money** Spielgeld *nt*.

trace[1] [treɪs] [1] *n* **(a)** (*sign*) Spur *f* ◆ **I can't find any ~ of your file** Ihre Akte ist spurlos verschwunden; **there's no ~ of it** keine Spur davon; **to vanish without ~** spurlos verschwinden; **to lose ~ of sb/sth** jdn/etw aus den Augen verlieren.
(b) (*small amount: of poison*) Spur *f*; (*of spice also*) Idee *f*; (*of irony etc also*) Hauch *m*.
[2] *vt* **(a)** (*draw*) zeichnen; (*copy*) nachziehen, nachzeichnen; (*with tracing paper*) durchpausen, abpausen ◆ **he ~d his name in the sand** er malte seinen Namen in den Sand.
(b) (*follow trail of*) *trail, progress, developments* verfolgen; *steps* folgen (*+dat*) ◆ **she was ~d to a house in Soho** ihre Spur führte zu einem Haus in Soho.
(c) (*find*) ausfindig machen, auffinden ◆ **I can't ~ your file** ich kann Ihre Akte nicht finden.

◆**trace back** [1] *vi* zurückgehen (*to* auf *+acc*).
[2] *vt sep descent* zurückverfolgen; *rumour* auf seinen Ursprung zurückverfolgen; *neurosis etc* zurückführen (*to* auf *+acc*) ◆ **he can ~ his family ~ to Henry VIII** seine Familie läßt sich bis zu Heinrich VIII. zurückverfolgen; **we ~d the rumour ~ to one of the secretaries** wir fanden heraus, daß das Gerücht von einer der Sekretärinnen in die Welt gesetzt worden war.

◆**trace out** *vt sep* (*copy*) nachzeichnen; (*with tracing paper*) durchpausen (*onto* auf *+acc*); (*draw*) zeichnen ◆ **we ~d ~ the route on the map** wir zeichneten die Route auf der Karte ein.

trace[2] *n* (*of harness*) Zuggurt, Zugriemen *m*; *see* **kick over**.

traceable ['treɪsəbl] *adj* **(a)** (*can be found*) auffindbar. **(b) a characteristic ~ through the centuries** eine Eigenschaft, die sich durch viele Jahrhunderte hindurch zurückverfolgen läßt; **to be ~ to sth** sich auf etw (*acc*) zurückführen lassen.

trace element *n* Spurenelement *nt*.

tracer ['treɪsəʳ] *n* **(a)** (*Mil: also* **~ bullet**) Leuchtspurgeschoß *nt*. **(b)** (*Med*) Isotopenindikator *m*. **(c)** (*enquiry form*) Suchzettel, Laufzettel *m*.

tracery ['treɪsərɪ] *n* (*Archit*) Maßwerk *nt*; (*pattern: of threads, branches etc*) Filigranmuster *nt*.

trachea [trə'kɪə] *n* Luftröhre *f*; (*of insects*) Trachea *f*.

tracheotomy [ˌtrækɪ'ɒtəmɪ] *n* Luftröhrenschnitt *m*.

trachoma [trə'kəʊmə] *n* Körnerkrankheit *f*, (hartnäckige) Bindehautentzündung.

tracing ['treɪsɪŋ] *n* (*drawing*) Durchpausen, Durchzeichnen *nt*; (*result*) Pause *f* ◆ **~ paper** Pauspapier *nt*.

track [træk] [1] *n* **(a)** (*trail*) Fährte, Spur *f*; (*of tyres*) (Fahr)spur *f* ◆ **to be on sb's ~** jdm auf der Spur sein; **you can't expect to keep ~ of your friends if you never write to them** du kannst nicht erwarten, Kontakt zu deinen Freunden zu behalten, wenn du nie schreibst; **to keep ~ of sb/sth** (*watch, follow*) jdn/etw im Auge behalten; *situation also* etw verfolgen; (*keep up to date with*) über jdn/etw auf dem laufenden bleiben; **I can't keep ~ of his movements** *or* **him** ich weiß nie, wo er sich gerade aufhält; **how do you keep ~ of the time without a watch?** wie können Sie wissen, wie spät es ist, wenn Sie keine Uhr haben?; **I can't keep ~ of your arguments/girlfriends** du hast so viele Argumente/Freundinnen, da komme ich nicht mit (*inf*); **no-one can keep ~ of the situation** niemand hat mehr einen Überblick über die Lage; **to lose ~ of sb/sth** (*lose contact with, lose sight of*) jdn/etw aus den Augen verlieren; (*lose count of, be confused about*) über Leute/etw den Überblick verlieren; (*not be up to date with*) über jdn/etw nicht mehr auf dem laufenden sein; **he/I lost ~ of what he was saying** er hat den Faden verloren/ich habe nicht (mehr) mitbekommen, was er gesagt hat.
(b) (*fig*) **we must be making ~s** (*inf*) wir müssen uns auf die Socken (*inf*) *or* auf den Weg machen; **to make ~s for home** sich auf den Nachhauseweg machen; **he made ~s for London** er ging/fuhr nach London; **he stopped dead in his ~s** er blieb abrupt stehen; **to cover (up) one's ~s** seine Spuren verwischen.
(c) (*path*) Weg, Pfad *m* ◆ **off the ~** (*fig*) abwegig; **to be on the right/wrong ~** (*fig*) auf der richtigen/falschen Spur sein, auf dem richtigen Weg/Holzweg (*inf*) *or* falschen Weg sein.
(d) (*course*) (*of hurricane*) Weg *m*; (*of comet*) (Lauf)bahn *f*; (*of rocket*) Bahn *f*, Kurs *m*.
(e) (*Rail*) Gleise *pl*; (*US: platform*) Bahnsteig *m* ◆ **a new section of ~** eine neue (Gleis)strecke; **the ~ to Paisley** die (Bahn)strecke nach Paisley; **"keep off the ~"** Betreten der Gleise verboten; **two miles of new ~** zwei Meilen neuer Gleise *or* Schienen; **to leave the ~(s)** entgleisen; **double/single ~ line** zwei-/eingleisige Strecke; **to be born on the wrong side of the ~s** (*US fig*) aus niedrigem Milieu stammen.
(f) (*Sport*) Rennbahn *f*; (*Athletics*) Bahn *f*; (*Motorsport*) Piste, Bahn *f*; (*circuit*) Rennstrecke *f*; (*Cycling*) Radrennbahn *f*.
(g) (*on tape, diskette*) Spur *f*; (*on record: song etc*) Stück *nt* ◆ **four-~ tape-recorder** Vierspurgerät *nt*.
(h) (*also* **caterpillar ~**) Raupenkette *f*.
(i) (*Aut: between wheels*) Spur(weite) *f*.
[2] *vt* **(a)** (*follow*) *person, animal* verfolgen; (*Space*) *rocket* die Flugbahn (*+gen*) verfolgen.
(b) (*US*) **the children ~ed dirt all over the carpet** die Kinder hinterließen überall auf dem Teppich Schmutzspuren.
[3] *vi* **(a)** (*follow trail*) Fährten lesen. **(b)** (*Aut*) spurgenau laufen. **(c)** (*Film, TV*) fahren. **(d)** (*move: hurricane etc*) ziehen; (*stylus*) sich bewegen.

◆**track down** *vt sep* aufspüren (*to* in *+dat*); *thing* aufstöbern, auftreiben (*inf*), finden; *reference, source of infection* ausfindig machen.

◆**track in** *vi* (*Film, TV*) heranfahren (*on* an *+acc*).

track: ~-and-field [1] *n* Leichtathletik *f*. [2] *adj* Leichtathletik-; **~ athletics** *n sing* Laufdisziplinen *pl*.

tracked [trækt] *adj vehicle* Ketten-, Raupen-.

tracker ['trækəʳ] *n* (*Indian etc*) Fährtenleser *m*; (*Hunt*) Tracker *m* ◆ **~ dog** Spürhund *m*.

track event *n* Laufwettbewerb *m*.

tracking ['trækɪŋ] *n* Verfolgen *nt* ◆ **~ station** Bodenstation *f*.

track: ~-laying vehicle *n* Kettenfahrzeug *nt*; **~less** *adj* **(a)** *vehicle* ohne Ketten; **(b)** *forest* weglos; **~ maintenance** *n* (*Rail*) Streckenwartung *f*; **~ meeting** *or* **meet** (*US*) *n* Leichtathletikwettbewerb *or* -wettkampf *m*; **~ race** *n* Rennen *nt*; (*Motorsport, Athletics also*) Lauf *m*; **~ racing** *n* Laufwettbewerb *m*; (*Motorsport*) Rennen *nt*; (*Cycling*) Radrennen *nt*; **~ record** *n* (*fig*) **what's his ~ record?** was hat er vorzuweisen?; **he's got a pretty good ~ record** er hat einiges vorzuweisen; **they've got an abysmal ~ record for delivering on schedule** sie stehen nicht gerade im Ruf, pünktlich zu liefern; **~ rod** *n* Spurstange *f*; **~ shoe** *n* Rennschuh *m*; **~suit** *n* Trainingsanzug *m*; **~walker** *n* (*US*) Streckenläufer *m*.

tract[1] [trækt] *n* **(a)** (*of land*) Gebiet *nt* ◆ **narrow ~** Streifen *m*. **(b)** (*respiratory*) Wege *pl*; (*digestive*) Trakt *m*.

tract[2] *n* Traktat *nt*, Schrift *f*.

tractability [træktə'bɪlɪtɪ] *n see adj* Formbarkeit, Bearbeitbarkeit *f*; Fügsamkeit, Lenkbarkeit *f*.

tractable ['træktəbl] *adj* (*lit*) *metal etc* leicht zu bearbeiten, formbar; (*fig*) *child, animal, disposition* fügsam, lenkbar.

traction ['trækʃən] *n* Zugkraft, Ziehkraft, Zugleistung *f*; (*of wheels*) Bodenhaftung *f*; (*Med*) Streckverband *m* ◆ **in ~** im Streckverband; **~ engine** Zugmaschine *f*, Dampftraktor *m*.

tractor ['træktəʳ] *n* **(a)** Traktor, Trecker *m*, Zugmaschine *f* ◆ **~ driver** Traktorfahrer(in *f*), Traktorist(in *f*) *m*. **(b)** (*of truck*) Sattelschlepper *m*.

tractor feed *n* (*Comput*) Traktor *m*.

trad [træd] (*inf*), **trad jazz** *n* Traditional, Old-time *m*.

trade [treɪd] [1] *n* **(a)** (*commerce*) Handel *m*, Gewerbe *nt*; (*hotel ~, catering ~*) Gewerbe *nt*; (*turnover: of shop, hotel etc*) die Geschäfte *pl* ◆ **he used to be in ~** er war Geschäftsmann; **how's ~?** wie gehen die Geschäfte?; **to do ~ with sb** mit jdm Handel treiben; **to do a good ~** gute Geschäfte machen; **to do a brisk ~ in sth** einen reißenden Absatz an etw (*dat*) haben.
(b) (*line of business*) Branche *f*, Geschäftszweig *m* ◆ **he's in the wool ~** er ist in der Wollbranche, er ist im Wollhandel tätig; **what ~ are you in?** in welcher Branche sind Sie (tätig)?; **he's in the ~** er ist in der Branche, er ist vom Fach; **as we call it in the ~** wie es in unserer Branche heißt.
(c) (*job*) Handwerk *nt* ◆ **he's a bricklayer by ~** er ist Maurer von Beruf; **a law-**

➤ LANGUAGE IN USE: **toy: 2 → 8.2**

yer by ~ (hum) ein gelernter Rechtsanwalt (hum); every man to his ~ Schuster, bleib bei deinem Leisten (prov); to put sb to a ~ (old) jdn ein Handwerk erlernen lassen.
(d) (people) Geschäftsleute pl, Branche f ◆ special terms for the ~ Vergünstigungen pl für Leute aus der Branche; to sell to the ~ an Gewerbetreibende verkaufen.
(e) (exchange) Tausch(geschäft nt or -handel m) m.
(f) the T~s pl (Geog) der Passat.
[2] vt tauschen ◆ to ~ sth for sth else etw gegen etw anderes (ein)tauschen; to ~ secrets Geheimnisse austauschen.
[3] vi (a) (Comm) Handel treiben, handeln ◆ to ~ in sth mit etw handeln; to ~ with sb mit jdm Geschäfte machen or Handel treiben. (b) (US inf) einkaufen (at bei).
[4] adv to get sth ~ etw zum Großhandelspreis bekommen.
◆**trade in** vt sep in Zahlung geben (for für).
◆**trade (up)on** vi +prep obj ausnützen.
trade: ~ **barrier** n Handelsschranke f; ~ **deficit** n Handelsdefizit nt; **T~ Descriptions Act** n Gesetz nt über die korrekte Beschreibung von Waren; ~ **directory** n Branchenverzeichnis, Firmenverzeichnis nt; ~ **discount** n Händlerrabatt m; ~ **fair** n Handelsmesse f; ~ **figures** npl Handelsziffern pl; ~ **gap** n Außenhandelsdefizit nt; **~-in** [1] n Altgerät nt; (car) in Zahlung gegebenes Auto; we offer £50 as a ~-in if you buy a new cooker beim Kauf eines neuen Herds nehmen wir Ihren alten für £ 50 in Zahlung; we will take your old car as a ~-in wir nehmen Ihren alten Wagen in Zahlung; [2] attr ~-in value Gebrauchtwert m; they don't give very good ~-in terms sie bezahlen nicht sehr viel für Altgeräte/Gebrauchtwagen; **~mark** n (lit) Warenzeichen nt; honesty was his ~mark er war für seine Ehrlichkeit bekannt; although it was anonymous it had the director's ~mark on it obwohl es anonym war, trug es die Handschrift des Direktors; ~ **mission** n Handelsmission f; ~ **name** n Handelsname m; **~-off** n there's always a ~-off etwas geht immer verloren; there's bound to be a ~-off between speed and quality es gibt entweder Einbußen bei der Schnelligkeit oder bei der Qualität; ~ **paper** n Fachzeitschrift f, Fachblatt nt; ~ **press** n Fachpresse f; ~ **price** n Großhandelspreis m.
trader ['treɪdəʳ] n (a) (person) Händler m. (b) (ship) Handelsschiff nt.
trade route n Handelsweg m, Handelsstraße f.
tradescantia [ˌtrædə'skæntɪə] n Tradeskantie f.
trade: ~ **school** n Gewerbe- or Berufsschule f; ~ **secret** n (lit, fig) Betriebsgeheimnis nt.
trades: **~man** n (delivery man) Lieferant m; (shopkeeper) Händler, Ladenbesitzer m; (plumber, electrician etc) Handwerker m; **~man's entrance** Lieferanteneingang m; **~people** npl Geschäftsleute, Händler pl; ~ **union** n see trade union; T~ Union Congress (britischer) Gewerkschaftsbund.
trade: ~ **union** n Gewerkschaft f; ~ **unionism** n Gewerkschaftsbewegung f; ~ **unionist** n Gewerkschaft(l)er(in f) m; ~ **wind** n Passat m.
trading ['treɪdɪŋ] n Handel m, Handeln nt (in mit) ◆ ~ was brisk at the Stock Exchange today der Handel an der Börse war heute lebhaft; there was heavy ~ in ... ... wurde(n) verstärkt gehandelt.
trading in cpds Handels-; ~ **account** n Geschäftskonto nt; ~ **estate** n Industriegelände nt; ~ **floor** n (St Ex) Börsenparkett nt; ~ **licence** n Gewerbeerlaubnis f, Gewerbeschein m; ~ **loss** n Betriebsverlust m; ~ **partner** n Handelspartner(in f) m; ~ **post** n Laden m; ~ **profits** npl Geschäfts- or Handelsgewinn m; ~ **results** npl Betriebsergebnis nt; ~ **stamp** n Rabattmarke f.
tradition [trə'dɪʃən] n Tradition f ◆ village ~s Dorfbräuche or -traditionen pl or -brauchtum nt; it has become a ~ for the chairman to propose the first toast es ist jetzt so üblich or ist zum festen Brauch geworden, daß der Vorsitzende den ersten Toast ausbringt; according to ~ he ..., ~ has it that he ... es ist überliefert, daß er ...; there is a ~ in the village that Queen Mary slept here im Dorf erzählt man sich, daß Königin Mary dort übernachtet hat; in the French ~ in der französischen Tradition; in the best ~ nach bester Tradition.
traditional [trə'dɪʃənl] adj traditionell; story, custom also alt; virtues also überkommen; jazz Old-time-, traditional ◆ it's ~ for us to spend New Year's Day at my mother's es ist bei uns so üblich or Brauch, daß wir den Neujahrstag bei meiner Mutter verbringen.
traditionalism [trə'dɪʃnəlɪzəm] n Festhalten nt am Alten, Traditionalismus m.
traditionalist [trə'dɪʃnəlɪst] [1] n Traditionalist(in f) m.
[2] adj traditionsgebunden, an Traditionen hängend or festhaltend.
traditionally [trə'dɪʃnəlɪ] adv traditionell; (customarily) üblicherweise, normalerweise ◆ they have ~ voted Conservative sie haben schon immer konservativ gewählt; it's ~ a holiday es ist schon immer ein Feiertag gewesen; turkey is ~ eaten at Christmas es ist Tradition or ein Brauch, Weihnachten Truthahn zu essen.
trad jazz n see trad.
traduce [trə'djuːs] vt (liter) verleumden.
traducer [trə'djuːsəʳ] n (liter) Ehrabschneider m (geh).
traffic ['træfɪk] [1] n (a) Verkehr m; (Aviat) Flug- or Luftverkehr m ◆ a policeman was directing ~ ein Polizist regelte den Verkehr; ~ coming into London is advised to avoid Putney Bridge Fahrern in Richtung Innenstadt London wird empfohlen, Putney Bridge zu meiden.
(b) (business: of port, airport) Umschlag m ◆ ~ in steel Stahlumschlag m; freight ~ Frachtumschlag m.
(c) (usu pej: trading) Handel m (in mit); (in drugs also) Dealen nt (in mit); (in pornography) Vertrieb m (in von); (in illegal alcohol) Schieberei f (in von).
[2] vi (usu pej) handeln (in mit); (in drugs also) dealen (in mit); (in pornography) vertreiben (in acc); (in illegal alcohol) verschieben (in acc).
trafficator ['træfɪkeɪtəʳ] n (Fahrt)richtungsanzeiger m (form).
traffic in cpds Verkehrs-; ~ **circle** n (US) Kreisverkehr m; ~ **control tower** n (Aviat) Kontrollturm, Tower m; ~ **cop** n (US inf) Verkehrspolizist m; ~ **diversion** n Umleitung f; ~ **duty** n Verkehrsdienst m; to be on ~ duty Verkehrsdienst haben; ~ **hold-up** n see ~ jam; ~ **indicator** n (Fahrt)richtungsanzeiger m (form); (flashing) Blinker m; ~ **island** n Verkehrsinsel f; ~ **jam** n Verkehrsstockung or -stauung f.
trafficker ['træfɪkəʳ] n (usu pej) Händler, Schieber (pej) m; (in drugs also) Dealer m.
trafficking ['træfɪkɪŋ] n Handel m (in mit); (in drugs also) Dealen nt (in mit); (in illegal alcohol) Schieberei f (in von); (in pornography) Vertrieb m (in von).
traffic: ~ **light** n (US), ~ **lights** npl (Brit) Verkehrsampel f; ~ **police** npl Verkehrspolizei f; ~ **policeman** n Verkehrspolizist m; ~ **signals** npl see ~ lights; ~ **warden** n ≃ Verkehrspolizist m ohne polizeiliche Befugnisse; (woman) ≃ Politesse f.
tragedian [trə'dʒiːdɪən] n (writer) Tragiker, Tragödiendichter m; (actor) Tragöde m (geh), Darsteller m tragischer Rollen.
tragedienne [trəˌdʒiːdɪ'en] n (actress) Tragödin (geh), Darstellerin f tragischer Rollen.
tragedy ['trædʒɪdɪ] n (tragic incident) Tragödie f; (Theat also) Trauerspiel nt; (no pl: tragicness) Tragische(s) nt ◆ he often acts in ~ er tritt oft in Tragödien auf; a life/voice/look full of ~ ein tragisches Leben/eine tragische Stimme/ein tragischer Blick, ein Leben/eine Stimme/ein Blick voller Tragik; six killed in holiday crash ~ tragischer Urlaubsunfall forderte sechs Todesopfer; the ~ of it is that ... das Tragische daran ist, daß ...; it is a ~ that ... es ist (wirklich) tragisch or ein Unglück, daß ...
tragic ['trædʒɪk] adj tragisch ◆ the ~ and the comic (Theat) das Tragische und das Komische.
tragically ['trædʒɪkəlɪ] adv ~, he was killed tragischerweise kam er ums Leben; she was ~ unaware of what had happened tragischerweise wußte sie nicht, was geschehen war; don't take it too ~! nehmen Sie es nicht zu tragisch!
tragicomedy ['trædʒɪ'kɒmɪdɪ] n Tragikomödie f.
tragicomic ['trædʒɪ'kɒmɪk] adj tragikomisch.
trail [treɪl] [1] n (a) Spur f; (of meteor) Schwanz, Schweif m ◆ ~ of blood Blutspur f; ~ of smoke/dust Rauchfahne f/Staubwolke f; the hurricane left a ~ of destruction der Hurrikan hinterließ eine Spur der Verwüstung.
(b) (track) Fährte, Spur f ◆ hot on the ~ dicht auf den Fersen; to be on the ~ of an animal die Spur eines Tieres verfolgen; the police are on his ~ die Polizei ist ihm auf der Spur.
(c) (path) Weg, Pfad m; (nature ~ etc) (Wander)weg m.
(d) (Ski: cross-country) Loipe f.
[2] vt (a) (follow) person folgen (+dat), verfolgen ◆ to ~ an animal ein Tier or die Spur eines Tieres verfolgen.
(b) (drag) schleppen, schleifen ◆ the bird ~ed its broken wing der Vogel zog seinen gebrochenen Flügel nach.
(c) (US: tow) ziehen, schleppen.
[3] vi (a) (on floor) schleifen.
(b) (plant) sich ranken ◆ a house with ivy ~ing round the windows ein Haus mit efeuumrankten Fenstern.
(c) (walk) zuckeln, trotten.
(d) (be behind: in competition etc) weit zurückliegen, hinterherhinken; (Sport) weit zurückgefallen sein ◆ our team is ~ing at the bottom of the league unsere Mannschaft rangiert in der Tabelle unter „ferner liefen" or auf den letzten Plätzen.
◆**trail along** [1] vi entlangzuckeln ◆ the child ~ed ~ behind his mother das Kind trottete or zuckelte hinter der Mutter her.
[2] vt entlangschleppen or -schleifen ◆ the child ~ed his coat ~ behind him das Kind schleifte or schleppte seinen Mantel hinter sich (dat) her.
◆**trail away** or **off** vi (voice) sich verlieren (into in +dat), verhallen ◆ his voice ~ed off into silence er verstummte.
◆**trail behind** [1] vi hinterhertrotten or -zuckeln (+prep obj hinter +dat); (in competition etc) zurückgefallen sein (+prep obj hinter +acc).
[2] vt sep hinter sich (dat) herziehen.
trailblazer ['treɪlˌbleɪzəʳ] n (fig) Wegbereiter, Bahnbrecher m.
trailer ['treɪləʳ] n (a) (Aut) Anhänger m; (esp US: of lorry) Sattelauflieger m. (b) (US) Wohnwagen, Caravan m ◆ ~ camp Platz m für Wohnwagen or Caravans. (c) (Bot) Hängepflanze f. (d) (Film, TV) Trailer m.
trailing ['treɪlɪŋ] adj (a) plant Hänge-. (b) (Aviat) ~ edge Hinterkante, Achterkante f.
trail mix n Trockenfrüchte und Nüsse pl, ≃ Studentenfutter nt.
train[1] [treɪn] n (a) (Rail) Zug m ◆ to go/travel by ~ mit dem Zug or der (Eisen)bahn fahren/reisen; a ~ journey eine Bahn- or Zugfahrt; to take or catch or get the 11 o'clock ~ den Elfuhrzug nehmen; to change ~s umsteigen; on the ~ im Zug.
(b) (line) Kolonne f; (of people) Schlange f; (of camels) Karawane f; (retinue) Gefolge nt ◆ in his ~ in seinem Gefolge; the war brought famine in its ~ der Krieg brachte eine Hungersnot mit sich; to put sth in ~ (form) etw einleiten or in Gang setzen; to be in ~ (form) im Gang(e) sein.
(c) (of events) Folge, Kette f ◆ he interrupted my ~ of thought er unterbrach meinen Gedankengang.
(d) (of dress) Schleppe f.

(e) ~ of gunpowder Pulverspur *f*.

train^2 [1] *vt* **(a)** ausbilden; *child* erziehen; *apprentice, new employee also* unterrichten, unterweisen; *animal* abrichten, dressieren; *mind* schulen; (*Sport*) trainieren ◆ **to ~ sb as sth** jdn als *or* zu etw ausbilden; **to ~ oneself to do sth** sich dazu erziehen, etw zu tun; **to ~ a child to be polite** ein Kind zur Höflichkeit erziehen; **to ~ an animal to do sth** ein Tier dazu abrichten, etw zu tun; **this dog has been ~ed to kill** dieser Hund ist aufs Töten abgerichtet; **a lion ~ed to do tricks** ein dressierter Löwe, der Kunststücke macht; **she has her dog/husband** (*hum*) **well ~ed** sie hat ihren Hund/Mann (*hum*) gut erzogen.
(b) (*aim*) *gun, telescope* richten (*on* auf *+acc*).
(c) *plant* wachsen lassen (*over* über *+acc*) ◆ **she ~ed her roses along/up the trellis** sie ließ ihre Rosen am Gitter entlang-/hochwachsen.
[2] *vi* **(a)** (*esp Sport*) trainieren (*for* für).
(b) (*study*) ausgebildet werden ◆ **he ~ed as a teacher** er hat eine Lehrerausbildung gemacht, er ist ausgebildeter Lehrer; **where did you ~?** wo haben Sie Ihre Ausbildung erhalten?, wo sind Sie ausgebildet worden?

◆**train up** *vt sep* heranbilden (*to* zu); *team* trainieren.

train: ~bearer *n* Schleppenträger(in *f*) *m*; **~ driver** *n* Zug- *or* Lokführer(in *f*) *m*.

trained [treɪnd] *adj worker* gelernt, Fach-; *nurse, teacher* ausgebildet; *animal* dressiert; *dog* abgerichtet, dressiert; *mind, ear* geschult; *eye* geübt, geschult; *voice* ausgebildet ◆ **a well-~ child** ein guterzogenes Kind.

trainee [treɪ'ni:] *n* Auszubildende(r) *mf*; (*academic, technical*) Praktikant(in *f*) *m*; (*nurse*) Krankenpflegeschüler(in *f*) *m*, Schwesternschülerin *f*; (*management*) Trainee *mf* ◆ **I am a ~** ich bin *or* befinde mich in der Ausbildung.

trainee: ~ manager *n* Management-Trainee *mf*; **~ mechanic** *n* Schlosserlehrling *m*; **~ nurse** *n* Krankenpflegeschüler(in *f*) *m*, Schwesternschülerin *f*; **~ teacher** *n* (*in primary school*) ≃ Praktikant(in *f*) *m*; (*in secondary school*) ≃ Referendar(in *f*) *m*.

trainer ['treɪnə^r] *n* **(a)** (*Sport, of racehorse*) Trainer *m*; (*of animals*) Dresseur *m*; (*in circus*) Dompteur *m*, Dompteuse *f* ◆ **~ plane** (*Aviat*) Schulflugzeug *nt*. **(b)** (*shoe*) Turnschuh *m*.

train ferry *n* Eisenbahnfähre *f*.

training ['treɪnɪŋ] *n* **(a)** Ausbildung *f* (*also Mil*); (*of staff*) Schulung *f*; (*of animal*) Dressur *f*, Abrichten *nt* ◆ **it's good ~ for the mind** es ist eine gute Denkschulung.
(b) (*Sport*) Training *nt* ◆ **to be in ~** im Training stehen *or* sein, trainieren; (*be fit*) gut in Form *or* fit *or* durchtrainiert sein; **to be out of ~** nicht in Form sein, aus dem Training sein; **to go into ~** das Training beginnen, anfangen zu trainieren.

training: ~ camp *n* Trainingslager *nt*; **~ centre** *n* Lehr- *or* Ausbildungszentrum *nt*; **~ college** *n* (*for teachers*) Pädagogische Hochschule; **~ course** *n* Ausbildungskurs *m*; **~ manual** *n* Lehrbuch *nt*; **~ period** *n* Ausbildungsdauer *f*; **~ plane** *n* Schulflugzeug *nt*; **~ scheme** *n* Ausbildungsprogramm *nt*; **~ ship** *n* Schulschiff *nt*; **~ shoes** *npl* Trainingsschuhe *pl*.

train: ~load *n* (*of goods*) Zugladung *f*; **~loads of holidaymakers** ganze Züge voller Urlauber; **soldiers were sent there by the ~load** ganze Zugladungen Soldaten wurden hingeschickt; **~man** *n* (*US*) Eisenbahner *m*; (*brakeman*) Bremser *m*; **~ oil** *n* Tran *m*; **~ service** *n* Zugverkehr *m*; (*between two places*) (Eisen)bahnverbindung *f*; **~ set** *n* (Spielzeug)eisenbahn *f*; **~sick** *adj* **he gets ~sick** ihm wird beim Zugfahren schlecht *or* übel; **~sickness** *n* **I've never suffered from ~sickness** mir ist beim Zugfahren noch nie schlecht *or* übel geworden; **~spotter** *n* Eisenbahnfan *m*; **~spotting** *n Hobby nt, bei dem Züge begutachtet und deren Nummern notiert werden.*

traipse [treɪps] (*inf*) [1] *vi* latschen (*inf*) ◆ **to ~ round the shops** in den Geschäften rumlatschen (*inf*); **to ~ round the shops for sth** die Geschäfte nach etw abklappern (*inf*).
[2] *n* **it's a long ~** da muß man lange latschen (*inf*).

trait [treɪt, treɪ] *n* Eigenschaft *f*; (*of particular person also*) Charakter- *or* Wesenszug *m*.

traitor ['treɪtə^r] *n* Verräter *m* ◆ **to be a ~ to one's country** sein Vaterland verraten; **to turn ~** zum Verräter werden.

traitorous ['treɪtərəs] *adj behaviour, action* verräterisch; *coward also* treulos.

traitorously ['treɪtərəslɪ] *adv* in verräterischer Weise.

traitress ['treɪtrɪs] *n* Verräterin *f*.

trajectory [trə'dʒektərɪ] *n* Flugbahn *f*.

tram [træm] *n* **(a)** (*Brit*) Straßenbahn, Tram(bahn) (*S Ger, Sw, Aus*) *f* ◆ **Blackpool still has ~s** in Blackpool gibt es noch Straßenbahnen *or* eine Straßenbahn; **to go by/take the ~** mit der Straßenbahn fahren/die Straßenbahn nehmen; **I saw her on a ~** ich habe sie in einer Straßenbahn gesehen.
(b) (*Min*) Grubenbahn *f*.

tram: ~car *n* Straßenbahn *f*; (*single car*) Straßenbahnwagen *m*; **~ driver** *n* Straßenbahnfahrer(in *f*) *m*; **~ line** *n* (*track*) Straßenbahnschiene *f*; (*route*) Straßenbahnlinie *f*; **~lines** *npl* (*Tennis*) Linien *pl* des Doppelspielfelds.

trammel ['træməl] [1] *vt* einengen ◆ **to feel ~led by sth** sich durch etw behindert *or* eingeengt fühlen.
[2] *n* **~s** *pl* Fesseln *pl*.

tramp [træmp] [1] *vi* **(a)** (*walk heavily, trudge*) stapfen, mit schweren Schritten gehen, stampfen ◆ **the soldiers ~ed along for hours** die Soldaten marschierten stundenlang (mit schweren Schritten); **I've been ~ing round town all day** ich bin den ganzen Tag in der Stadt herumgestiefelt (*inf*); **to ~ up and down the platform** auf dem Bahnsteig auf und ab marschieren; **feet ~ing up and down** Füße, die herumtrampeln.
(b) (*hike*) marschieren, wandern; (*vagabond*) umherziehen ◆ **he ~ed all over Europe** er wanderte in ganz Europa umher.
[2] *vt* **(a)** (*spread by walking*) herumtreten ◆ **don't ~ that mud into the carpet** tritt den Dreck nicht in den Teppich.
(b) (*walk*) *streets* latschen durch (*inf*).
[3] *n* **(a)** (*vagabond*) Landstreicher(in *f*), Tramp *m*; (*in town*) Stadtstreicher(in *f*) *m*.
(b) (*sound*) Stapfen *nt*, schwere Schritte *pl*.
(c) (*walk*) Wanderung *f* ◆ **it's a long ~** es ist ein weiter Weg.
(d) (*Naut*) Trampdampfer *m*.
(e) (*inf: loose woman*) Flittchen *nt* (*pej*).

◆**tramp down** *vt sep* feststampfen, festtreten; *corn, flowers etc* platt treten, niedertrampeln.

◆**tramp in** *vt sep* festtreten, in den Boden treten.

trample ['træmpl] [1] *vt* niedertrampeln, niedertreten, zertrampeln ◆ **to ~ sth underfoot** auf etw (*dat*) herumtrampeln; **she ~s her husband underfoot** (*fig*) ihr Mann hat bei ihr nichts zu sagen (*inf*); **he was ~d to death by a bull** er wurde von einem Bullen zu Tode getrampelt; **to ~ sth into the ground** etw in den Boden treten *or* trampeln.
[2] *vi* stapfen, trampeln ◆ **he lets his wife ~ all over him** (*fig*) er läßt sich (*dat*) von seiner Frau auf dem Kopf herumtanzen.
[3] *n* Getrampel, Trampeln *nt*.

◆**trample about** *vi* herumtrampeln.

◆**trample down** *vt sep* heruntertreten, niedertreten.

◆**trample on** *vi +prep obj* herumtreten auf (*+dat*) ◆ **several children were ~d ~** mehrere Kinder wurden getreten; **to ~ ~ everybody/sb** (*fig*) über Leichen gehen/jdn herumschikanieren; **to ~ ~ sb's feelings** (*fig*) jds Gefühle mit Füßen treten.

trampoline ['træmpəlɪn] *n* Trampolin *nt*.

tramp steamer *n* Trampdampfer *m*.

tram: ~ride *n* Straßenbahnfahrt *f*; **~way** *n* Straßenbahn *f*; (*route*) Straßenbahnstrecke *f*.

trance [trɑ:ns] *n* Trance *f*; (*Med*) tiefe Bewußtlosigkeit ◆ **to go into a ~** in Trance verfallen; **to put sb into a ~** jdn in Trance versetzen; **she's been going about in a ~ for the past few days** die letzten paar Tage ist sie wie in Trance *or* im Tran (*inf*) durch die Gegend gelaufen.

tranny ['trænɪ] *n* (*Brit sl*) Transistor *m* (*inf*), Kofferradio *nt*.

tranquil ['træŋkwɪl] *adj* ruhig, friedlich, still; *life* friedlich, ohne Aufregung; *mind* ruhig, gelassen; *music* ruhig, sanft; *person* ruhig, gelassen, ausgeglichen.

tranquillity, (*US*) **tranquility** [træŋ'kwɪlɪtɪ] *n see adj* Ruhe *f*; Friedlichkeit, Stille *f*; Friede *m*; Gelassenheit *f*; Sanftheit *f*; Ausgeglichenheit *f* ◆ **the ~ of the home** die friedliche Atmosphäre des Hauses; **he was soothed by the ~ of the music** die sanfte Musik beruhigte ihn.

tranquillize, (*US*) **tranquilize** ['træŋkwɪlaɪz] *vt* beruhigen ◆ **tranquillizing dart** Betäubungspfeil *m*.

tranquillizer, (*US*) **tranquilizer** ['træŋkwɪlaɪzə^r] *n* Beruhigungstablette *f*, Beruhigungsmittel *nt*.

tranquilly ['træŋkwɪlɪ] *adv see adj.*

trans- [trænz-] *pref* trans-, Trans-.

transact [træn'zækt] *vt* abwickeln; *business also* abschließen, durchführen; *deal* abschließen.

transaction [træn'zækʃən] *n* **(a)** (*act*) *see vt* Abwicklung *f*; Abschluß *m*, Durchführung *f* ◆ **~ of business** Geschäftsbetrieb *m*; **the bank will be closed for the ~ of business at 3 p.m.** die Bank hat *or* ist ab 15^{00} Uhr geschlossen.
(b) (*piece of business*) Geschäft *nt*; (*Fin, St Ex*) Transaktion *f*.
(c) ~s *pl* (*of society*) Sitzungsbericht *m*.

transalpine [trænz'ælpaɪn] *adj* transalpin.

transatlantic ['trænsət'læntɪk] *adj* transatlantisch, Transatlantik-; *customs* auf der anderen Seite (des Atlantiks); *cousins, accent* amerikanisch; (*for Americans*) britisch.

transceiver [træn'si:və^r] *n* Sender-Empfänger *m*, Sende-Empfangsgerät *nt*.

transcend [træn'send] *vt* übersteigen, überschreiten, hinausgehen über (*+acc*); (*Philos*) transzendieren.

transcendence [træn'sendəns], **transcendency** [træn'sendənsɪ] *n* Erhabenheit *f*; (*Philos*) Transzendenz *f*.

transcendent [træn'sendənt] *adj* (*Philos*) transzendent; (*supreme*) hervorragend, alles übersteigend, überragend.

transcendental [ˌtrænsen'dentl] *adj* überirdisch; (*Philos*) transzendental; *vision* transzendierend ◆ **~ meditation** transzendentale Meditation; **~ number** (*Math*) transzendente Zahl, Transzendente *f*.

transcendentalism [ˌtrænsen'dentəlɪzəm] *n* transzendentale Philosophie, Transzendentalismus *m*.

transcontinental ['trænzˌkɒntɪ'nentl] *adj* transkontinental.

transcribe [træn'skraɪb] *vt manuscripts* abschreiben, transkribieren; (*from shorthand*) (in Langschrift) übertragen; *speech, proceedings etc* niederschreiben, mitschreiben; (*Mus*) transkribieren ◆ **to ~ sth phonetically** etw in phonetische (Um)schrift übertragen; **to ~ a record onto tape** eine Schallplatte auf Band aufnehmen *or* überspielen.

transcript ['trænskrɪpt] *n* **(a)** (*of court proceedings*) Protokoll *nt*; (*of tapes*) Niederschrift *f*; (*copy*) Kopie, Abschrift *f*. **(b)** (*US: academic record*) Abschrift *f* (*Studienunterlagen*).

transcription [træn'skrɪpʃən] *n* (*Mus, Phon*) Transkription *f*; (*copy, of shorthand notes*) Abschrift *f*; (*act*) Abschrift *f*, Abschreiben *nt*; (*of speech,* *proceedings*) Niederschrift *f*, Protokoll *nt*; (*Rad, TV: recording*) Aufnahme *f* ◆ **phonetic ~** Lautschrift *f*, phonetische (Um)schrift.

transducer [ˌtrænsˈdjuːsəʳ] *n* Umformer, Umwandler *m*.

transept [ˈtrænsept] *n* Querschiff, Transept (*spec*) *nt*.

trans-European [ˈtrænsˌjʊərəˈpiːən] *adj railway* Trans-Europa-; *journey* quer durch Europa.

transfer [trænsˈfɜːʳ] [1] *vt* übertragen (*to* auf *+acc*); *prisoner* überführen (*to* in *+acc*), verlegen (*to* nach); *premises, soldiers* verlegen (*to* in *+acc*, *to town* nach); (*soldier, employee*) versetzen (*to* in *+acc*, *to town, country* nach); (*Sport*) *player* transferieren (*to* zu), abgeben (*to* an *+acc*); (*Fin*) *funds, money* überweisen (*to* auf *+acc*), transferieren (*to* nach); *account* verlegen; *stocks* transferieren; (*Jur*) *property* übertragen, überschreiben (*to* auf *+acc*); *right* übertragen (*to* auf *+acc*), abtreten (*to* an *+acc*) ◆ **he ~red the bigger engine into his old car** er baute den größeren Motor in sein altes Auto ein; **to ~ one's concentration from one task to another** seine Konzentration von einer Aufgabe auf eine andere umstellen; **he ~red his capital into gold shares** er investierte sein Kapital in Goldaktien, er legte sein Kapital in Goldaktien an; **he ~red the money from the box to his pocket** er nahm das Geld aus der Schachtel und steckte es in die Tasche; **the magician had somehow ~red the rabbit from the hat to the box** der Zauberer hatte das Kaninchen irgendwie aus dem Hut in die Kiste praktiziert; **she ~red her affections to another man** sie schenkte ihre Zuneigung einem anderen; **~red charge call** (*Brit Telec*) R-Gespräch *nt*.

[2] *vi* **(a)** überwechseln (*to* zu); (*to new system, working conditions*) umstellen (*to* auf *+acc*) ◆ **he can easily ~ from one language to another** er kann leicht von einer Sprache auf eine andere überwechseln *or* umschalten.

(b) (*Fin*) umsteigen (*into* auf *+acc*) ◆ **just before the crash he ~red into government bonds** gerade rechtzeitig vor dem Zusammenbruch stieg er auf Regierungsanleihen um.

(c) (*in travelling*) umsteigen (*to* in *+acc*); (*Univ*) das Studienfach wechseln, umsatteln (*inf*) (*from ... to* von ... auf *+acc*).

[3] [ˈtrænsfɜːʳ] *n* **(a)** *see vt* Übertragung *f*; Überführung *f*; Verlegung *f*; Versetzung *f*; Transfer, Wechsel *m*; Überweisung *f*; Überschreibung *f*; Abtretung *f* ◆ **he asked for a ~** (*soldier, employee*) er bat um Versetzung; (*footballer*) er bat, auf die Transferliste gesetzt zu werden.

(b) (*person ~red*) **he's a ~ from another regiment/Chelsea** er ist von einem anderen Regiment hierher versetzt *or* verlegt worden/er ist von Chelsea gekommen *or* hierher gewechselt; **Chelsea's latest ~** Chelseas jüngste Neuerwerbung.

(c) (*picture*) Abziehbild *nt*.

(d) (*in travelling*) Umsteigen *nt*.

(e) (*~ ticket*) Umsteige(fahr)karte *f*.

transferable [trænsˈfɜːrəbl] *adj* übertragbar; *money, stocks* transferierbar.

transfer desk *n* (*Aviat*) Transitschalter *m*.

transference [ˈtrænsfərəns] *n* **(a)** (*Psych*) Übertragung *f*. **(b)** (*Fin*) (*of holdings, real estate*) Übertragung, Überschreibung *f* (*to sb* auf jdn); (*of money*) Transfer *m*.

transfer: ~ fee *n* (*Ftbl*) Transfersumme *f*; **~ list** *n* (*Ftbl*) Transferliste *f*; **~ lounge** *n* (*Aviat*) Transitraum *m*; **~ rate, ~ speed** *n* (*Comput: of data*) Übertragungsgeschwindigkeit *f*; **~ ticket** *n* Umsteige(fahr)karte *f*.

transfiguration [ˌtrænsfɪgəˈreɪʃən] *n* **(a)** Verklärtheit *f*; (*transformation*) Wandel *m*, Wandlung *f*. **(b)** (*Rel*) Verklärung Jesu, Transfiguration *f*.

transfigure [trænsˈfɪgəʳ] *vt* verklären; (*transform*) verwandeln.

transfix [trænsˈfɪks] *vt* **(a)** (*fix*) annageln, feststecken (*to* an *+acc*); *butterflies* aufspießen. **(b)** (*fig*) **to be** *or* **stand ~ed with horror** starr vor Entsetzen sein; **he stood as though ~ed (to the ground)** er stand da wie angewurzelt.

transform [trænsˈfɔːm] *vt* umwandeln, umformen, umgestalten (*into* zu); *ideas, views* (von Grund auf) verändern; *person* verwandeln; *caterpillar* verwandeln; (*Phys*) umwandeln, verwandeln (*into* in *+acc*); (*Elec*) (um)wandeln, umformen (*into* in *+acc*), transformieren (*into* in *+acc*) ◆ **the old house was ~ed into three luxury flats** das alte Haus wurde in drei Luxuswohnungen umgebaut; **when she came out of the beauty parlour she was ~ed** als sie aus dem Schönheitssalon kam, sah sie wie umgewandelt aus; **a coat of paint ~ed the dull old room** ein Anstrich ließ den langweiligen alten Raum in neuem Glanz erstrahlen.

transformation [ˌtrænsfəˈmeɪʃən] *n* Umwandlung, Umformung *f*; (*of ideas, views etc*) (grundlegende) Veränderung; (*of person also*) (grundlegende) Verwandlung; (*of person, caterpillar etc*) Verwandlung *f*; (*Phys*) Umwandlung *f*; (*Elec also*) Transformation *f*; (*Ling*) Umformung, Transformation *f* ◆ **~ scene** (*Theat*) Verwandlungsszene *f*.

transformational [ˌtrænsfəˈmeɪʃənl] *adj* (*Ling*) *grammar, rules* Transformations-.

transformer [trænsˈfɔːməʳ] *n* (*Elec*) Transformator *m*.

transfuse [trænsˈfjuːz] *vt* (*Med*) *blood* übertragen; (*fig*) erfüllen, durchdringen.

transfusion [trænsˈfjuːʒən] *n* (*also* **blood ~**) Blutübertragung, Transfusion *f* ◆ **to give sb a ~** jdm eine Blutübertragung *or* Transfusion geben; **(blood) ~ service** Blutspendedienst *m*; **a ~ of public money into ...** eine Finanzspritze aus öffentlichen Geldern für ...; **it was like a ~ of new life into their friendship** es war, als ob ihre Freundschaft von neuem Leben durchdrungen *or* erfüllt würde.

transgress [trænsˈgres] [1] *vt standards* verstoßen gegen, verletzen; *law also* überschreiten.

[2] *vi* sündigen ◆ **to ~ against the Lord** gegen Gottes Gebote sündigen *or* verstoßen.

transgression [trænsˈgreʃən] *n* **(a)** (*of law*) Verstoß *m*, Verletzung, Überschreitung *f*. **(b)** (*sin*) Sünde *f*, Verstoß *m*.

transgressor [trænsˈgresəʳ] *n* Übeltäter(in *f*), Missetäter(in *f*) *m*; (*sinner*) Sünder(in *f*) *m*.

tranship [trænˈʃɪp] *vt* umladen, umschlagen.

transhipment [trænˈʃɪpmənt] *n* Umladung *f*.

transience [ˈtrænzɪəns], **transiency** [ˈtrænzɪənsɪ] *n* (*of life*) Kürze, Vergänglichkeit *f*; (*of grief, joy*) Kurzlebigkeit, Vergänglichkeit *f*; (*of interest*) Kurzlebigkeit, Flüchtigkeit *f*.

transient [ˈtrænzɪənt] [1] *adj* **(a)** *life* kurz; *grief, joy* kurzlebig, vergänglich, vorübergehend; *interest* kurzlebig, flüchtig, vorübergehend. **(b)** (*US*) **~ population** nichtansässiger Teil der Bevölkerung eines Ortes.

[2] *n* (*US*) Durchreisende(r) *mf*.

transistor [trænˈzɪstəʳ] *n* **(a)** (*Elec*) Transistor *m*. **(b)** (*also* **~ radio**) Transistorradio, Kofferradio *nt*, Transistor *m* (*inf*).

transistorize [trænˈzɪstəraɪz] *vt* transistorisieren, transistorieren ◆ **~d** transistorisiert.

transit [ˈtrænzɪt] *n* Durchfahrt *f*, Transit *m*; (*of goods*) Transport *m* ◆ **the books were damaged in ~** die Bücher wurden auf dem Transport beschädigt; **passengers in ~ for New York** Transitreisende nach New York; **goods in ~ for New York** Güter für den Weitertransport nach New York; **they are stationed here in ~** sie sind hier zwischendurch stationiert.

transit: ~ camp *n* Durchgangslager *nt*; **~ desk** *n* Transitschalter *m*; **~ freight** *n* Transitfracht *f*.

transition [trænˈzɪʃən] *n* Übergang *m* (*from ... to* von ... zu); (*of weather*) Wechsel, Umschwung *m*; (*Mus*) (*act*) Übergang *m*; (*passage*) Überleitung *f* ◆ **period of ~** Übergangsperiode *or* -zeit *f*; **~ stage** Übergangsstadium *nt*; **~ element** (*Chem*) Übergangselement *nt*.

transitional [trænˈzɪʃənl] *adj* Übergangs-.

transitive [ˈtrænzɪtɪv] *adj* transitiv ◆ **~ verb** transitives Verb, Handlungsverb, Transitiv(um) *nt*.

transitively [ˈtrænzɪtɪvlɪ] *adv* transitiv.

transitivity [ˌtrænzɪˈtɪvɪtɪ] *n* transitive Eigenschaft *or* Funktion.

transit lounge *n* Warteraum, Transitraum *m*.

transitory [ˈtrænzɪtərɪ] *adj life* kurz; *grief, joy* kurzlebig, vergänglich, vorübergehend; *interest* kurzlebig, flüchtig.

transit: ~ passenger *n* Durchgangsreisende(r), Transitreisende(r) *mf*; **~ visa** *n* Durchreisevisum, Transitvisum *nt*.

translatable [trænzˈleɪtəbl] *adj* übersetzbar.

translate [trænzˈleɪt] [1] *vt* **(a)** übersetzen; *work of literature also* übertragen ◆ **to ~ a text from German (in)to English** einen Text aus dem Deutschen ins Englische übersetzen; **it is ~d as ...** es wird mit ... übersetzt.

(b) (*fig*) übertragen ◆ **to ~ words into action** Worte in die Tat umsetzen; **to ~ a novel into a film** aus einem Roman einen Film machen; **could you ~ that into cash terms?** läßt sich das geldmäßig ausdrücken?

(c) (*Eccl*) *bishop* in eine andere Diözese berufen; (*Rel: to heaven*) aufnehmen.

(d) (*rare: transfer*) übertragen; *person* versetzen.

[2] *vi* **(a)** übersetzen ◆ **it ~s well (into English)** es läßt sich gut (ins Englische) übersetzen *or* übertragen.

(b) (*fig*) übertragbar sein ◆ **the novel didn't ~ easily into film terms** es war nicht einfach, aus dem Roman einen Film zu machen; **how does that ~ into cash?** was kommt geldmäßig dabei heraus?

translation [trænzˈleɪʃən] *n* **(a)** (*act, translated work*) Übersetzung *f* (*from* aus); (*of work of literature also, fig*) Übertragung *f* ◆ **to do a ~ of sth** von etw eine Übersetzung machen *or* anfertigen; **errors in ~** Übersetzungsfehler *pl*; **it loses in ~** es verliert bei der Übersetzung; **a ~ problem** ein Übersetzungsproblem *nt*; **he is not good at ~** er kann nicht gut übersetzen; **~ table** (*Comput*) Umsetzungs- *or* Übersetzungstabelle *f*.

(b) (*Eccl*) Berufung *f* in eine andere Diözese; (*to heaven*) Himmelfahrt *f*.

translational [trænzˈleɪʃənl] *adj* Übersetzungs-.

translator [trænzˈleɪtəʳ] *n* Übersetzer(in *f*) *m*.

transliterate [trænzˈlɪtəreɪt] *vt* transliterieren.

transliteration [ˌtrænzlɪtəˈreɪʃən] *n* Transliteration *f*.

translucence [trænzˈluːsns], **translucency** [trænzˈluːsnsɪ] *n* Lichtdurchlässigkeit, Durchsichtigkeit *f*.

translucent [trænzˈluːsnt], **translucid** [trænzˈluːsɪd] *adj glass etc* lichtdurchlässig; *skin* durchsichtig ◆ **~ glass** Milchglas *nt*; **a prose of ~ clarity** eine Prosa von brillanter Klarheit.

transmigrate [ˌtrænzmaɪˈgreɪt] *vi* (*Rel*) wiedergeboren werden.

transmigration [ˌtrænzmaɪˈgreɪʃən] *n* (*Rel*) (Seelen)wanderung, Transmigration (*spec*) *f* ◆ **the ~ of souls** die Seelenwanderung; **the ~ of a human soul into an animal body** die Wiedergeburt einer menschlichen Seele in einem Tierleib.

transmissible [trænzˈmɪsəbl] *adj* übertragbar.

transmission [trænzˈmɪʃən] *n* **(a)** (*transmitting*) Übertragung *f*; (*through heredity*) Vererbung *f*; (*of news*) Übermittlung *f*; (*of heat*) Leitung *f*; (*programme also*) Sendung *f*. **(b)** (*Aut*) Getriebe *nt* ◆ **~ shaft** Kardanwelle *f*.

transmit [trænzˈmɪt] [1] *vt* (*convey*) *message* übermitteln; *sound waves* übertragen; *information, knowledge* ver- *or* übermitteln; *illness* übertragen; (*by heredity*) vererben; *heat etc* leiten; *radio/TV programme* übertragen, senden.

[2] *vi* senden, Programme ausstrahlen.

transmitter [trænzˈmɪtəʳ] *n* (*Tech*) Sender *m*; (*in telephone*) Mikrophon *nt*.

transmitting [trænzˈmɪtɪŋ]: **~ set** *n* Sender *m*; **~ station** *n* (*of broadcasting company*) Sendestation *f*; (*general also*) Sendestelle *f*.

transmogrification [ˌtrænzmɒgrɪfɪˈkeɪʃən] *n* (*hum*) wunderbare Wand-

lung (*hum*).
transmogrify [trænz'mɒgrɪfaɪ] *vt* (*hum*) auf wunderbare Weise verwandeln *or* umwandeln (*hum*).
transmutable [trænz'mju:təbl] *adj* verwandelbar.
transmutation [ˌtrænzmju:'teɪʃən] *n* Verwandlung, Umwandlung *f*; (*Biol*) Umbildung, Transmutation *f*.
transmute [trænz'mju:t] *vt* umwandeln, verwandeln (*into* in +*acc*); *metal* verwandeln (*into* in +*acc*).
transoceanic [ˌtrænzəʊʃi:'ænɪk] *adj* Übersee-; *countries* transozeanisch; *migration* über den Ozean.
transom ['trænsəm] *n* (~ *window*) Oberlicht *nt*; (*cross-piece*) Querbalken *m*.
transpacific [ˌtrænzpə'sɪfɪk] *adj* über den Pazifik; *countries* jenseits des Pazifik.
transparency [træns'pærənsɪ] *n* **(a)** Transparenz, Durchsichtigkeit *f*. **(b)** (*of lies, excuses etc*) Durchschaubarkeit *f*. **(c)** (*Phot*) Dia(positiv) *nt* ◆ **colour ~** Farbdia *nt*.
transparent [træns'pærənt] *adj* **(a)** durchsichtig, lichtdurchlässig, transparent; *blouse* durchsichtig.
(b) (*fig: obvious*) *lie, intentions* durchschaubar, durchsichtig; *personality* durchschaubar; *guilt, meaning* klar, eindeutig, offensichtlich ◆ **it became ~ that ...** es wurde offensichtlich, daß ..., **you're so ~** du bist so leicht zu durchschauen.
transparently [træns'pærəntlɪ] *adv lie* durchschaubar, offensichtlich, offenkundig ◆ **it was ~ obvious that ...** es war so offensichtlich *or* klar zu erkennen, daß ...
transpiration [ˌtrænspɪ'reɪʃən] *n* (*Anat*) Schweißabsonderung, Transpiration *f*; (*Bot*) Transpiration, Ausdunstung *f*.
transpire [træn'spaɪə^r] **1** *vi* **(a)** (*become known*) bekannt werden; (*slowly*) durchsickern, ruchbar werden (*geh*).
(b) (*happen*) passieren (*inf*) ◆ **new developments had ~d** es hatten sich neue Entwicklungen ergeben *or* angebahnt.
(c) (*Anat*) schwitzen, transpirieren (*geh*); (*Bot*) Feuchtigkeit abgeben *or* verdunsten, transpirieren (*spec*).
2 *vt* (*Bot*) *moisture* verdunsten, abgeben.
transplant [træns'plɑ:nt] **1** *vt* **(a)** (*Hort*) umpflanzen, umsetzen, verpflanzen. **(b)** (*Med*) verpflanzen, transplantieren (*spec*). **(c)** (*fig*) *people* verpflanzen ◆ **his wealth ~ed him into a new world** sein Reichtum versetzte ihn in eine neue Welt.
2 ['trɑ:nsplɑ:nt] *n* (*operation*) Verpflanzung, Transplantation *f*; (*organ*) Transplantat *nt*, transplantiertes *or* verpflanztes Organ ◆ **to have a ~** sich einer Organverpflanzung unterziehen.
transplantation [ˌtrænsplɑ:n'teɪʃən] *n* (*Hort*) Umpflanzung, Verpflanzung *f*; (*Med*) Transplantation, Verpflanzung *f*.
transpolar [træns'pəʊlə^r] *adj* über den (Nord-/Süd)pol *or* das Polargebiet, Transpolar- ◆ **the ~ route** die Polroute.
transport ['trænspɔ:t] **1** *n* **(a)** (*of goods*) Transport *m*, Beförderung *f*; (*of troops*) Transport *m* ◆ **road ~** Straßentransport *m*; **rail ~** Beförderung *or* Transport per Bahn, (Eisen)bahntransport *m*; **Ministry of T~** Verkehrsministerium *nt*.
(b) (*vehicle*) **have you got your own ~?** hast du einen fahrbaren Untersatz? (*inf*), bist du motorisiert?; **public ~** öffentliche Verkehrsmittel *pl*; **what are we going to do about ~?** wie lösen wir die Transportfrage?; **~ will be provided** für An- und Abfahrt wird gesorgt.
(c) (*Mil*) (*ship*) (Truppen)transporter *m*; (*plane*) Transportflugzeug *nt*.
(d) (*US: shipment*) (Schiffs)fracht, Ladung *f*.
(e) (*liter*) **~ of delight/joy** freudige Entzückung *or* (*Rel*) Entrückung (*liter*); **it sent her into ~s of delight** es erfüllte sie mit freudigem Entzücken (*liter*).
2 [træn'spɔ:t] *vt* **(a)** *goods* befördern, transportieren; *people* befördern. **(b)** (*Hist*) *convict* deportieren. **(c)** (*liter*) **to be ~ed with joy** freudig entzückt sein (*liter*).
transportable [træn'spɔ:təbl] *adj* transportabel, transportierbar.
transportation [ˌtrænspɔ:'teɪʃən] *n* **(a)** Beförderung *f*, Transport *m*; (*means*) Beförderungsmittel *nt*; (*public*) Verkehrsmittel *nt*; (*cost*) Transport- *or* Beförderungskosten *pl* ◆ **Department of T~** (*US*) Verkehrsministerium *nt*.
(b) (*Hist: of criminal*) Deportation *f*.
transport café *n* (*Brit*) Fernfahrerlokal *nt*.
transporter [træn'spɔ:tə^r] *n* (*car ~*) Transporter *m*; (*~ crane*) Verladebrücke *f*; (*in factory*) Transportband *nt*.
transport: ~ line *n* (*in factory*) Transportband *nt*; **~ plane** *n* Transportflugzeug *nt*; **~ ship** *n* (Truppen)transporter *m*; **~ system** *n* Verkehrswesen *nt*.
transpose [træns'pəʊz] *vt* vertauschen, umstellen; (*Mus*) transponieren.
transposition [ˌtrænspə'zɪʃən] *n* Umstellung, Vertauschung *f*; (*Mus*) Transponierung *f*.
transputer [træns'pju:tə^r] *n* (*Comput*) Transputer *m*.
transsexual [træns'seksjʊəl] *n* Transsexuelle(r) *mf*.
transship [træns'ʃɪp] *vt see* **tranship**.
transshipment [træns'ʃɪpmənt] *n see* **transhipment**.
transubstantiate [ˌtrænsəb'stænʃɪeɪt] *vt* (*Rel*) verwandeln.
transubstantiation ['trænsəbˌstænʃɪ'eɪʃən] *n* (*Rel*) Wandlung, Transsubstantiation (*spec*) *f*.
transverse ['trænzvɜ:s] *adj beam, bar, section* Quer-; *muscles* transversal; *position* horizontal; *engine* querstehend.
transversely [trænz'vɜ:slɪ] *adv* quer; *divided* diagonal.
transvestism [trænz'vestɪzəm] *n* Transves(ti)tismus *m*.
transvestite [trænz'vestaɪt] *n* Transvestit *m*.
trap [træp] **1** *n* **(a)** (*for animal, fig*) Falle *f* ◆ **to set** *or* **lay a ~ for an animal** eine Falle für ein Tier (auf)stellen; **to set a ~ for sb** (*fig*) jdm eine Falle stellen; **be careful of this question, there is a ~ in it** paß bei dieser Frage auf, da ist ein Haken dabei; **to be caught in a ~** in der Falle sitzen; **the lawyer had caught him in a ~** er war dem Rechtsanwalt in die Falle gegangen; **to fall into a ~** in die Falle gehen.
(b) (*in greyhound racing*) Box *f*; (*shooting*) Wurftaubenanlage, Wurfmaschine *f*.
(c) (*in drainpipe*) Siphon, Geruchsverschluß *m*.
(d) (*vehicle*) zweirädriger Pferdewagen.
(e) (*also* **~door**) Falltür *f*; (*Theat*) Versenkung *f*.
(f) (*sl: mouth*) Klappe (*inf*), Fresse (*sl*), Schnauze (*sl*) *f* ◆ **shut your ~!** (halt die) Klappe! (*inf*), halt die Fresse (*sl*) *or* Schnauze (*sl*)!; **keep your ~ shut about this** darüber hältst du aber die Klappe (*inf*), halt ja die Schnauze! (*sl*).
2 *vt* **(a)** *animal* (mit einer Falle) fangen.
(b) (*fig*) *person* in die Falle locken ◆ **he realized he was ~ped** er merkte, daß er in der Falle saß; **to ~ sb into saying sth** jdn dazu bringen, etw zu sagen; **I was ~ped into saying I would organize the party** ich hatte mich darauf eingelassen, die Party zu organisieren; **she ~ped him into marriage** sie hat ihn geködert (*inf*), sie hat ihn ins Netz gelockt.
(c) (*block off, leave no way of escape*) in die Enge treiben ◆ **the miners are ~ped** die Bergleute sind eingeschlossen; **the ship was ~ped in the harbour by the storm** das Schiff saß wegen des Sturms im Hafen fest; **to be ~ped in the snow** im Schnee festsitzen; **he feels ~ped in suburbia/his marriage** er empfindet die Vorstadt/seine Ehe als Gefängnis; **the soldiers found themselves ~ped at the end of the gully** am Ende des Hohlweges stellten die Soldaten fest, daß sie in der Falle saßen; **I get this ~ped feeling** ich fühle mich wie gefangen *or* im Gefängnis *or* eingeschlossen; **my arm was ~ped behind my back** mein Arm war hinter meinem Rücken eingeklemmt.
(d) (*catch*) (*Sport*) *ball* stoppen ◆ **to ~ one's finger/one's foot in the door** sich (*dat*) den Finger/Fuß in der Tür einklemmen.
(e) *gas, liquid* stauen ◆ **pools of water lay ~ped among the rocks as the tide receded** als die Flut zurückging, blieben Wasserpfützen zwischen den Felsen zurück.
3 *vi* (*trapper*) Trapper sein.
trapdoor ['træp'dɔ:^r] *n* Falltür *f*; (*Theat*) Versenkung *f*.
trapeze [trə'pi:z] *n* (*in circus*) Trapez *nt* ◆ **~ artist** Trapezkünstler(in *f*) *m*.
trapezium [trə'pi:zɪəm] *n* (*Brit*) Trapez *nt*; (*US*) Trapezoid *nt*.
trapezoid ['træpɪzɔɪd] *n* (*Brit*) Trapezoid *nt*; (*US*) Trapez *nt*.
trapper ['træpə^r] *n* Fallensteller, Trapper *m*.
trappings ['træpɪŋz] *npl* **(a)** (*of admiral, chieftain etc*) Rangabzeichen *pl*; (*of horse*) Schmuck *m*.
(b) (*fig*) äußere Aufmachung, äußeres Drum und Dran (*inf*) ◆ **~ of office** Amtsinsignien *pl*; **shorn of all its ~** aller Ausschmückungen entkleidet; **he surrounded himself with all the ~ of power** er umgab sich mit allen Insignien der Macht.
Trappist ['træpɪst] *n* (*also* **~ monk**) Trappist *m*.
trapse *vi see* **traipse**.
trap-shooting ['træpˌʃu:tɪŋ] *n* Wurftaubenschießen *nt*.
trash [træʃ] *n* **(a)** (*US: refuse*) Abfall *m*.
(b) (*goods*) Schund, Ramsch *m* (*inf*), billiges Zeug; (*book, play etc*) Schund *m*; (*pop group etc*) Mist *m* (*inf*) ◆ **don't talk ~** red kein Blech (*sl*) *or* nicht so einen Quatsch (*inf*).
(c) (*pej inf: people*) Gesindel, Pack *nt* ◆ **~ like her** Gesindel wie sie; **she/he is ~** sie/er taugt nichts; *see* **white ~**.
trash-can ['træʃkæn] *n* (*US*) Abfalleimer *m*.
trashy ['træʃɪ] *adj* (+*er*) *goods* minderwertig, wertlos; *novel, play* Schund-, minderwertig ◆ **clothes for teenagers are often ~** Teenagerkleidung ist oft Schund *or* billiges Zeug.
trauma ['trɔ:mə] *n* (*Psych*) Trauma *nt*, seelischer Schock.
traumatic [trɔ:'mætɪk] *adj* traumatisch.
traumatize ['trɔ:mətaɪz] *vt* (*Med, Psych*) traumatisieren.
travail ['træveɪl] **1** *n* **(a)** *usu pl* (*toils*) Mühen *pl* ◆ **after all the ~s of Watergate** nach den schweren Belastungen durch die Watergate-Affäre.
(b) (*old, liter: exhausting labour*) Plackerei, Mühsal *f*.
(c) (*old: childbirth*) (Geburts)wehen *pl*.
2 *vi* **(a)** (*old, liter: toil*) sich plagen (*old*) ◆ **he ~ed in the depths of despair** er litt in tiefer Verzweiflung.
(b) (*old: in childbirth*) in den Wehen liegen, Wehen haben.
travel ['trævl] **1** *vi* **(a)** (*make a journey*) reisen ◆ **they have ~led a lot** sie sind viel gereist, sie haben viele Reisen gemacht; **he ~s to work by car** er fährt mit dem Auto zur Arbeit; **she is ~ling to London tomorrow** sie fährt morgen nach London; **the President is ~ling to Paris tomorrow** der Präsident reist morgen nach Paris; **they have ~led a long way** sie haben eine weite Reise *or* lange Fahrt hinter sich (*dat*); (*fig*) sie haben es weit gebracht (im Leben); **they ~led for 300 kms** sie fuhren 300 km; **to ~ round the world** eine Reise um die Welt machen; **to ~ around a country** ein Land durchreisen *or* bereisen.
(b) (*go, move*) sich bewegen; (*sound, light*) sich fortpflanzen ◆ **light ~s at ...** die Lichtgeschwindigkeit beträgt ...; **we were ~ling at 80 kph** wir fuhren 80 km/h; **the parts ~ along the conveyor belt** die Teile werden vom Förderband weiterbefördert; **the electricity ~s along the wire** der Strom fließt durch den Draht; **you were ~ling too fast** Sie sind zu schnell gefahren; **he was certainly ~ling!** (*inf*) er hatte vielleicht einen Zahn drauf!

(*sl*); **wow! that's ~ling!** (*inf*) Mann, das ist aber schnell!
(c) (*Comm*) Vertreter sein ◆ **he ~s for a Berlin insurance firm** er reist für eine *or* ist Vertreter einer Berliner Versicherungsgesellschaft; **he ~s in ladies' underwear** er reist in Damenunterwäsche.
(d) (*wine etc*) **some wines do not ~ well** manche Weine vertragen den Transport nicht.
(e) (*pass*) **his eye ~led over the scene** seine Augen wanderten über die Szene.
(f) (*Tech*) sich hin- und herbewegen ◆ **as the piston ~s from A to B** während sich der Kolben von A nach B bewegt; **it doesn't ~ freely** es bewegt sich schwer; **the sliding doors don't ~ freely** diese Schiebetüren gleiten nicht gut.
(g) (*Basketball*) einen Schrittfehler machen.
[2] *vt area* bereisen; *distance* zurücklegen, fahren; *route* fahren.
[3] *n* **(a)** *no pl* Reisen *nt* ◆ **to be fond of ~** gerne reisen; **~ was difficult in the 18th century** im 18. Jahrhundert war das Reisen beschwerlich.
(b) **~s** *pl* (*in country*) Reisen *pl*; (*hum: in town, building*) Ausflüge, Gänge *pl*; **if you meet him on your ~s** wenn Sie ihm auf einer Ihrer Reisen begegnen; **he's off on his ~s again tomorrow** er verreist morgen wieder.
(c) (*Tech*) Weg *m*; (*of instrument's needle etc*) Ausschlag *m*; (*of piston*) Hub *m*.

travel: ~ agency *n* Reisebüro *nt*; **~ agent** *n* Reisebürokaufmann *m*; (*of package tours*) Reiseveranstalter *m*; **~ agent's** *n* Reisebüro *nt*; **~ brochure** *n* Reiseprospekt *m*; **~ bureau** *n* Reisebüro *nt*; **~ insurance** *n* Reiseversicherung *f*.

travelled, (*US*) traveled ['trævld] *adj* **well-~** *person* weitgereist *attr*, weit gereist *pred*; *route* vielbefahren *attr*, viel befahren *pred*; **widely ~** weitgereist *attr*, weit gereist *pred*.

traveller, (*US*) traveler ['trævlə^r] *n* **(a)** Reisende(r) *mf* ◆ **I am a poor ~** ich vertrage das Reisen nicht. **(b)** (*also* **commercial ~**) Vertreter, (Handels)reisende(r) *m* ◆ **a ~ in toys** ein (Handels)vertreter für Spielsachen, ein Reisender in Spielsachen.

traveller's cheque, (*US*) traveler's check *n* Reisescheck, Travellerscheck *m*.

travelling, (*US*) traveling ['trævlıŋ] *n* Reisen *nt* ◆ **I hate ~** ich reise sehr ungern, ich hasse das Reisen.

travelling: ~ bag *n* Reisetasche *f*; **~ circus** *n* Wanderzirkus *m*; **~ clock** *n* Reisewecker *m*; **~ crane** *n* Lauf- *or* Rollkran *m*; **~ exhibition** *n* Wanderausstellung *f*; **~ expenses** *npl* Reisekosten *pl*; (*on business*) Reisespesen *pl*; **~ people** *npl* fahrendes Volk; **~ rug** *n* Reisedecke *f*; **~ salesman** *n* Vertreter, Handelsreisende(r) *m*; **~ scholarship** *n* Auslandsstipendium *nt*; **~ theatre** *n* Wandertheater, Tourneetheater *nt*.

travel: ~ literature *n* Reisebeschreibung *f*; **~ novel** *n* Reisebeschreibung *f*.

travelogue, (*US*) travelog ['trævəlɒg] *n* (*film*) filmischer Reisebericht; (*slides*) Lichtbildervortrag *m* (über eine Reise); (*lecture*) Reisebericht *m*.

travel: ~-sick *adj* reisekrank; **~-sickness** *n* Reisekrankheit *f*; **~-sickness pill** *n* Pille *f* gegen Reisekrankheit; **~-weary, ~-worn** *adj* von der Reise ermüdet *or* erschöpft.

traverse ['trævɜ:s] [1] *vt* **(a)** (*cross*) *land* durchqueren; (*river also*) durchfließen; (*bridge, person*) *water* überqueren ◆ **the searchlight ~d the sky from east to west** der Suchscheinwerfer leuchtete den Himmel von Osten nach Westen ab.
(b) (*cross and recross*) **the searchlight ~d the sky** der Suchscheinwerfer leuchtete den Himmel ab.
(c) (*extend over*) *period* überdauern.
(d) (*Mountaineering*) *ice, slope* queren, traversieren.
[2] *vi* (*Mountaineering, Ski*) sich quer zum Hang bewegen, (den Hang/die Wand *etc*) traversieren.
[3] *n* (*on mountain*) (*movement*) Queren, Traversieren *nt*; (*place*) Quergang *m*; (*Archit*) Querbalken *m*, Traverse *f*.

travesty ['trævıstı] [1] *n* (*Liter*) Travestie *f* ◆ **a ~ of justice** ein Hohn *m* auf die Gerechtigkeit; **the elections were a ~** die Wahlen waren ein Hohn *m or* eine Farce; **the ageing actress was only a ~ of her former self** die alternde Schauspielerin war nur noch eine Karikatur *or* ein Zerrbild *nt* ihrer selbst.
[2] *vt* ins Lächerliche ziehen, travestieren (*esp Liter*).

trawl [trɔ:l] [1] *n* (*also* **~ net**) Schleppnetz, Trawl *nt*; (*US:* **~ line**) Grundleine *f*.
[2] *vi* mit dem Schleppnetz fischen; (*US*) mit einer Grundleine fischen.
[3] *vt fish* mit dem Schleppnetz fangen ◆ **they ~ed the sea-bottom** sie fischten mit Schleppnetzen auf dem Meeresboden; **they ~ed the net along the sea-bottom** sie schleppten das Netz über den Meeresboden.

trawler ['trɔ:lə^r] *n* (*boat*) Fischdampfer, Trawler *m*.

trawlerman ['trɔ:ləmən] *n, pl* **-men** [-mən] Trawlerfischer *m*.

trawling ['trɔ:lıŋ] *n* Dampfer- *or* Trawlfischerei *f*.

tray [treı] *n* Tablett *nt*; (*tea ~*) Teebrett, Servierbrett *nt*; (*of cakes*) (*small*) Platte *f*; (*big*) Brett *nt*; (*for display*) Auslagekästchen *nt*; (*baking ~*) (Back)blech *nt*; (*for pencils etc*) (Feder)schale *f*; (*for papers, mail*) Ablage(korb *m*) *f*; (*of street vendor etc*) Bauchladen *m*; (*drawer*) (Schub)fach *nt*; (*in suitcase, trunk*) Einsatz *m*; (*Phot, ice ~*) Schale *f*; (*for ash*) Kasten *m*; (*in bird cage*) Schublade *f* ◆ **~ cloth** Deckchen *nt für ein Tablett*.

treacherous ['tretʃərəs] *adj* **(a)** *person, action* verräterisch. **(b)** (*unreliable*) trügerisch, irreführend; *memory* trügerisch ◆ **my memory is rather ~ now** mein Gedächtnis läßt mich neuerdings ziemlich im Stich. **(c)** (*dangerous*) tückisch; *corner also* gefährlich; *ice* trügerisch.

treacherously ['tretʃərəslı] *adv see adj* **(a)** verräterisch, in verräterischer Weise.
(b) trügerisch, irreführend ◆ **at times he can be ~ convincing** er wirkt manchmal gefährlich überzeugend.
(c) *sharp corner, icy or wet road* tückisch ◆ **rocks hidden ~ beneath the surface** Felsen, die gefährlich dicht unter der Wasseroberfläche liegen; **in ~ bad conditions** unter gefährlich schlechten Bedingungen.

treacherousness ['tretʃərəsnıs] *n see adj* **(a)** **the ~ of these generals** diese verräterischen Generäle. **(b)** (*of memory etc*) Unzuverlässigkeit *f*. **(c)** Tücke, Gefährlichkeit *f* ◆ **because of the ~ of the snow** wegen der trügerischen Schneeverhältnisse.

treachery ['tretʃərı] *n* Verrat *m*; (*of weather*) Tücke *f* ◆ **an act of ~** Verrat, eine verräterische Tat.

treacle ['tri:kl] *n* (*Brit*) Sirup *m* ◆ **a voice like ~** eine zucker- *or* honigsüße Stimme; **~ pudding** *im Dampfbad gekochter, mit Sirup angereicherter Teig*; **~ tart** *Kuchen m mit Überzugmasse aus Sirup*.

treacly ['tri:klı] *adj* (*+er*) (*lit*) sirupartig; (*fig*) *voice, smile* honig- *or* zuckersüß; *song, sentiment* schmalzig.

tread [tred] (*vb: pret* **trod**, *ptp* **trodden**) [1] *n* **(a)** (*act*) **over the years the ~ of feet has worn the steps away** über die Jahre sind die Stufen völlig ausgetreten worden.
(b) (*gait, noise*) Schritt, Tritt *m* ◆ **to walk with a heavy/springy ~** mit schweren/hüpfenden Schritten gehen, einen schweren/hüpfenden Gang haben; **I could hear his ~ on the stairs** ich konnte seine Schritte auf der Treppe hören.
(c) (*of stair*) Stufe *f*.
(d) (*of shoe, tyre*) Profil *nt*, Lauffläche *f*.
[2] *vi* **(a)** (*walk*) gehen.
(b) (*bring foot down*) treten (*on* auf *+acc*) ◆ **mind you don't ~ on it!** passen Sie auf, daß Sie nicht darauftreten!; **will you ~ on that cigarette-end?** könnten Sie den Zigarettenstummel austreten?; **he trod on my foot** er trat mir auf den Fuß; **to ~ on sb's heels** (*lit*) jdm auf die Fersen treten; (*fig*) an jds Fersen (*dat*) hängen; **to ~ softly** *or* **lightly** leise *or* leicht auftreten; **to ~ carefully** (*lit*) vorsichtig gehen; (*fig*) vorsichtig vorgehen; **to ~ in sb's footsteps** (*fig*) in jds Fuß(s)tapfen (*acc*) treten; *see* **air**.
[3] *vt path* (*make*) treten; (*follow*) gehen ◆ **he's ~ing the same path as his father** (*fig*) er hat den gleichen Weg wie sein Vater eingeschlagen; **it got trodden underfoot** es wurde zertreten; **to ~ grapes** Trauben stampfen; **he trod his cigarette into the sand** er trat seine Zigarette im Sand aus; **to ~ water** Wasser treten; **don't ~ that earth into the carpet** treten Sie die Erde nicht in den Teppich.

◆**tread down** *vt sep* festtreten.

◆**tread in** *vt sep* festtreten.

◆**tread out** *vt sep fire, cigarette* austreten.

treadle ['tredl] [1] *n* (*of sewing machine*) Tretkurbel *f*, Pedal *nt*; (*of lathe also*) Fußhebel *m*.
[2] *vi* treten.

treadmill ['tredmıl] *n* (*lit*) Tretwerk *nt*; (*fig*) Tretmühle *f*.

treas *abbr of* **treasurer**.

treason ['tri:zn] *n* Verrat *m* (*to* an *+dat*) ◆ **an act of ~** Verrat *m*.

treasonable ['tri:zənəbl], **treasonous** ['tri:zənəs] *adj* verräterisch.

treasure ['treʒə^r] [1] *n* (*lit*) Schatz *m*; (*fig also*) Kostbarkeit *f*; (*dear person*) Schatz *m* ◆ **many ~s of modern art** viele moderne Kunstschätze; **she's a real ~** sie ist eine Perle *or* ein Juwel *nt*.
[2] *vt* (hoch)schätzen, zu schätzen wissen ◆ **he really ~s his books** seine Bücher bedeuten ihm sehr viel; **I shall ~ this memory** ich werde das in lieber Erinnerung behalten.

◆**treasure up** *vt sep* horten, ansammeln, anhäufen; (*in memory*) aufbewahren.

treasure: ~ house *n* (*lit*) Schatzkammer *f*; **a ~ house of knowledge** eine Fundgrube des Wissens; **~ hunt** *n* Schatzsuche *f*.

treasurer ['treʒərə^r] *n* (*of club*) Kassenwart, Kassenverwalter(in *f*) *m*; (*city ~*) Stadtkämmerer *m*; (*of business*) Leiter *m* der Finanzabteilung; (*of king*) Schatzmeister *m*.

treasure trove *n* Schatzfund *m*; (*place where treasures are found*) Schatzgrube, Fundgrube *f*.

treasury ['treʒərı] *n* **(a)** (*Pol*) **T~**, (*US also*) **T~ Department** Finanzministerium *nt*; **First Lord of the T~** (*Brit*) der Premierminister. **(b)** (*of society*) Kasse *f*. **(c)** (*anthology*) Schatzkästlein *nt*, Schatzgrube *f*.

Treasury: ~ bench *n* (*Brit*) Regierungsbank *f* (im Parlament); **~ bill** *n* kurzfristiger Schatzwechsel; **~ note** *n* (*US*) Schatzschein *m or* -anweisung *f or* -wechsel *m*.

treat [tri:t] [1] *vt* **(a)** (*behave towards*) *person, animal* behandeln; (*handle*) *books* behandeln, umgehen mit.
(b) (*consider*) betrachten (*as* als) ◆ **you should ~ your work more seriously** Sie sollten Ihre Arbeit ernster nehmen.
(c) (*Med*) behandeln ◆ **which doctor is ~ing you?** bei welchem Arzt sind Sie in Behandlung?, welcher Arzt behandelt Sie?; **the doctor is ~ing him for nervous exhaustion** er ist wegen Nervenüber lastung in Behandlung.
(d) (*process*) behandeln (*with* mit); *leather* bearbeiten, behandeln (*with* mit); *sewage* klären; *wastepaper* verarbeiten.
(e) *subject* behandeln; (*scientifically, philosophically also*) abhandeln.
(f) (*pay for, give*) einladen ◆ **to ~ sb to sth** jdn zu etw einladen, jdm etw spendieren; *to drink, ice-cream also* jdm etw ausgeben; **I'm ~ing you** ich lade Sie ein; **to ~ oneself to sth** sich (*dat*) etw gönnen; **he ~ed his wife to a weekend in Paris** er spendierte seiner Frau ein Wochenende in Paris; **he ~ed us to a preview of the exhibition** er machte uns (*dat*) eine Freude und zeigte uns die Ausstellung vorher; **for once she ~ed us to the sight of her knees**

endlich einmal gönnte sie uns den Anblick ihrer Knie; **he ~ed us to a display of his temper** (*iro*) er gab uns (*dat*) eine Kostprobe seiner Launenhaftigkeit.

[2] *vi* (*deal*) **to ~ with sb for sth** mit jdm über etw (*acc*) Verhandlungen führen, mit jdm um *or* über etw (*acc*) verhandeln; **the general decided to ~ for peace** der General entschloß sich, Friedensverhandlungen zu führen.

[3] *n* **(a)** besondere Freude ◆ **well, folks, tomorrow we're going on our Christmas ~** also Leute, morgen machen wir unsere Weihnachtsfeier (*inf*); **children's ~** Kinderfest *nt*, Kindernachmittag *m*; **I thought I'd give myself a ~** ich dachte, ich gönne mir mal etwas; **I'm taking them to the circus as** *or* **for a ~** ich mache ihnen eine Freude und lade sie in den Zirkus ein *or* nehme sie in den Zirkus mit; **it's my ~** das geht auf meine Kosten *or* Rechnung, ich lade Sie ein; **I want to give them a ~** ich möchte ihnen eine besondere Freude machen; **our uncle's ~ was to give us tickets for the cinema** unser Onkel hat uns (*dat*) Kinokarten spendiert; **that was a ~!** das war ein Genuß!; **what a ~ to have a quiet afternoon** das ist ein Genuß *or* tut gut, mal einen ruhigen Nachmittag zu verbringen; **it's a ~ in store** das ist etwas, worauf wir uns noch freuen können; **this time you can carry the bags as a ~!** (*iro*) dieses Mal darfst du ausnahmsweise die Taschen tragen; **it's a (real) ~ to see you again** was für eine Freude, Sie mal wiederzusehen!

(b) (*inf*) **it's coming on a ~** es macht sich prima (*inf*).

◆**treat of** *vi +prep obj* (*form*) handeln von, behandeln.

treatise ['tri:tɪz] *n* Abhandlung *f* (*on* über *+acc*).

treatment ['tri:tmənt] *n* **(a)** (*of person, animal*) Behandlung *f*; (*of books etc also*) Umgang *m* (*of* mit) ◆ **their ~ of foreigners** ihre Art, Ausländer zu behandeln; **to give sb the ~** (*inf: violently, sexually*) es jdm ordentlich besorgen (*inf*); **he went for a two-day interview, they really gave him the ~** (*inf*) bei seinem zweitägigen Einstellungsgespräch wurde er ganz schön in die Mangel genommen (*inf*); **she went to the beauty parlour and they really gave her the ~** (*inf*) sie ging in den Schönheitssalon und wurde dort nach allen Regeln der Kunst bearbeitet (*inf*); **when the foreign delegates visited the factory, they were given the full ~** (*inf*) als die ausländischen Delegierten die Firma besichtigten, wurde ein enormes Tamtam gemacht (*inf*) *or* eine große Schau abgezogen (*sl*); **John was really giving her the ~ at that party!** (*inf*) John hat sich bei der Party ganz schön an sie rangemacht (*inf*); (*giving her a bad time*) John hat sie bei der Party ganz schön mies behandelt (*inf*).

(b) (*Med*) Behandlung *f* ◆ **there are many ~s for ...** es gibt viele Behandlungsarten *or* Heilverfahren für ...; **to be having ~ for sth** wegen etw in Behandlung sein.

(c) (*processing*) Behandlung *f*; (*of leather also*) Bearbeitung *f*; (*of sewage*) Klärung *f*; (*of wastepaper*) Verarbeitung *f*.

(d) (*of subject*) Behandlung, Bearbeitung *f*.

treaty ['tri:tɪ] *n* Vertrag *m* ◆ **~ port** Vertragshafen *m*.

treble[1] ['trebl] [1] *adj* dreifach ◆ **it's in ~ figures** es ist eine dreistellige Summe; **~ chance (pools)** *eine Variante des Fußballtotos mit dreifacher Gewinnchance.*

[2] *adv* **they had ~ our numbers** sie waren dreimal so viele wie wir; **clothes are ~ the price** Kleider kosten dreimal soviel.

[3] *vt* verdreifachen.

[4] *vi* sich verdreifachen.

[5] *n* (*on dartboard etc*) Dreifache(s) *nt*.

treble[2] [1] *n* (*Mus*) (*boy's voice*) Knabensopran *m or* -stimme *f*; (*highest part*) Oberstimme *f*; (*of piano*) Diskant *m*; (*child's speaking voice*) Diskantstimme *f*.

[2] *adj voice* Knabensopran-; *part* Oberstimmen-; (*of piano, children speaking*) Diskant- ◆ **~ clef** Violinschlüssel *m*; **~ recorder** Altflöte *f*.

trebly ['treblɪ] *adv* dreifach ◆ **the child was ~ dear to him** er liebte das Kind dreimal mehr.

tree [tri:] [1] *n* **(a)** Baum *m* ◆ **an oak/a cherry ~** eine Eiche/ein Kirschbaum *m*; **rose ~** Rosenstämmchen *nt*; **~ of knowledge** Baum der Erkenntnis; **~ of life** Baum des Lebens; **money doesn't/good teachers don't grow on ~s** das Geld fällt/gute Lehrer fallen nicht vom Himmel; **to be up a ~** (*inf*) in der Patsche *or* Tinte *or* Klemme sitzen (*inf*); **he's at the top of the ~** (*fig inf*) er ist ganz oben (an der Spitze).

(b) (*family ~*) Stammbaum *m*.

(c) (*shoe~*) Spanner, Leisten *m*.

(d) (*Rel: cross*) Kreuz *nt*.

[2] *vt* auf einen Baum jagen *or* treiben.

tree *in cpds* Baum-; **~-covered** *adj* baumbestanden; **~ fern** *n* Baumfarn *m*; **~ frog** *n* Laub- *or* Baumfrosch *m*; **~ house** *n* Baumhaus *nt*; **~ hugger** *n* (*esp US hum inf*) Umweltapostel *m* (*hum inf*), Umweltfreak *m* (*hum inf*); **~less** *adj* baumlos; **~ line** *n* Baumgrenze *f*; **above/below the ~ line** oberhalb/unterhalb der Baumgrenze; **~-lined** *adj* baumbestanden, von Bäumen gesäumt (*geh*); **~ structure** *n* (*Comput*) Baumstruktur *f*; **~ surgeon** *n* Baumchirurg *m*; **~top** *n* Baumkrone *f*, Wipfel *m*; **~ trunk** *n* Baumstamm *m*.

trefoil ['trefɔɪl] *n* (*Bot*) Klee *m*; (*symbol of Girl Guide movement*) Kleeblatt *nt*; (*Archit*) Dreipaß *m*.

trek [trek] [1] *vi* trecken; (*inf*) latschen (*inf*) ◆ **they ~ked across the desert** sie zogen durch die Wüste; **I had to ~ up to the top floor** ich mußte bis ins oberste Stockwerk latschen (*inf*).

[2] *n* Treck, Zug *m*; (*inf*) anstrengender Weg *or* Marsch.

trekking ['trekɪŋ] *n* Trekking *nt*.

trellis ['trelɪs] [1] *n* Gitter *nt*; (*for plants also*) Spalier *nt* ◆ **~-work** Gitterwerk *nt*.

[2] *vt* (*furnish with ~*) mit einem Gitter *or* Spalier versehen; *vines etc* am Spalier ziehen.

tremble ['trembl] [1] *vi* (*person, hand etc*) zittern (*with* vor); (*voice also*) beben (*with* vor); (*ground, building*) beben, zittern ◆ **I ~ to think what might have happened** mir wird angst *or* ich zittere, wenn ich daran denke, was hätte geschehen können; **to ~ for sb's safety** um jds Sicherheit zittern *or* bangen.

[2] *n* Zittern, Beben *nt* ◆ **to be all of a ~** (*inf*) am ganzen Körper zittern, das große Zittern haben (*inf*).

trembling ['tremblɪŋ] [1] *adj hands* zitternd; *voice also* bebend.

[2] *n see vi* Zittern *nt*; Beben *nt*; *see* **fear 1 (a)**.

tremendous [trə'mendəs] *adj* **(a)** gewaltig, enorm; *difference also* riesengroß; *size, number, crowd also* riesig; *storm, explosion also* ungeheuer stark; *success* Riesen-, enorm, unglaublich ◆ **he's a ~ eater** er ißt unglaublich viel.

(b) (*very good*) klasse, prima, toll (*all inf*) ◆ **we had a ~ time** wir haben uns prima *or* ganz toll amüsiert; **he's a ~ person** er ist ein toller Mensch, er ist klasse *or* prima.

tremendously [trə'mendəslɪ] *adv* sehr; *fat, tall, long etc also* enorm; *relieved, upset, grateful, dangerous also* ungeheuer, äußerst; *pretty also* äußerst; *intelligent, difficult also* enorm, äußerst ◆ **it was ~ good** es war einfach prima *or* umwerfend gut *or* sagenhaft (*all inf*); **they enjoyed themselves ~** sie haben sich prächtig *or* prima *or* ausgezeichnet amüsiert (*all inf*).

tremolo ['treməlәʊ] *n* (*Mus*) Tremolo *nt*.

tremor ['tremə^r] *n* Zittern, Beben *nt*; (*Med*) Tremor *m*; (*of emotion*) Zittern, Zucken *nt*; (*earth ~*) Beben *nt*, Erschütterung *f* ◆ **a ~ of fear** ein Schaudern *nt*; **without a ~** völlig ruhig, unbewegt.

tremulous ['tremjʊləs] *adj* (*trembling*) *voice* zitternd, bebend; *hand* zitternd; (*timid*) *smile, person* zaghaft, schüchtern.

tremulously ['tremjʊləslɪ] *adv* zaghaft, ängstlich.

trench [trentʃ] [1] *n* Graben *m*; (*Mil*) Schützengraben *m* ◆ **in the ~es** (*Mil*) im Schützengraben; **~ warfare** Stellungskrieg, Grabenkrieg *m*.

[2] *vt* Gräben ziehen in (*+dat*); (*Mil*) Schützengräben ausheben in (*+dat*).

trenchancy ['trentʃənsɪ] *n see adj* Treffsicherheit *f*; Prägnanz *f*; Bissigkeit *f*; Pointiertheit *f*; Schärfe *f*.

trenchant ['trentʃənt] *adj language* treffsicher; *style* prägnant; *satire* beißend; *speech* pointiert; *wit, criticism* scharf.

trenchantly ['trentʃəntlɪ] *adv see adj* ◆ **he made his point ~** er argumentierte sicher; **a ~ witty remark** eine scharfe, geistreiche Bemerkung.

trench coat *n* Trenchcoat, Regenmantel *m*.

trencher ['trentʃə^r] *n* (*old: platter*) Tranchierbrett *nt*.

trencherman ['trentʃəmən] *n, pl* **-men** [-mən] **good/poor ~** guter/schlechter Esser.

trend [trend] [1] *n* **(a)** (*tendency*) Tendenz, Richtung *f*, Trend *m* ◆ **the ~ towards violence** der Trend *or* die Tendenz zur Gewalttätigkeit; **upward ~** steigende Tendenz, Aufwärtstrend *m*; **the downward ~ in the birth rate** die Rückläufigkeit *or* der Abwärtstrend der Geburtenrate; **the ~ away from materialism** die zunehmende Abkehr vom Materialismus; **to set a ~** eine neue Richtung setzen, richtungweisend sein.

(b) (*fashion*) Mode *f*, Trend *m* ◆ **that is the ~/the latest ~ among young people** das ist bei jungen Leuten jetzt Mode/der letzte Schrei (*inf*); **to follow a ~** einem Trend folgen; (*fashion*) eine Mode mitmachen.

(c) (*Geog*) Verlauf *m*.

[2] *vi* verlaufen (*towards* nach) ◆ **prices are ~ing upwards** die Preise haben eine steigende Tendenz; **his views are ~ing towards the anarchistic** seine Auffassungen neigen *or* tendieren zum Anarchismus.

trendily ['trendɪlɪ] *adv* modern ◆ **to dress ~** sich nach der neuesten Mode kleiden.

trendiness ['trendɪnɪs] *n* (*of person*) Modebewußtsein *nt*; (*of ideas etc*) Modernität *f* ◆ **the ~ of her clothes** ihre modische Kleidung.

trend: ~setter *n* Trendsetter *m*; **~setting** [1] *n* Entwicklung *f* neuer Trends; [2] *adj* trendsetzend; (*in fashion also*) modemachend.

trendy ['trendɪ] [1] *adj* (*+er*) modern, in *pred* (*inf*) ◆ **to be ~** als schick gelten, große Mode sein; **a pub where all the ~ people go** eine Kneipe, in der sich die Schickeria trifft; **this is a ~ pub** diese Kneipe ist zur Zeit in (*inf*).

[2] *n* (*inf*) Schickimicki *m* (*sl*) ◆ **the trendies** die Schickeria *sing*; **he looks a real ~** der macht vielleicht auf modern!

trepan [trɪ'pæn] [1] *vt* (*Med*) trepanieren.

[2] *n* Trepan *m*.

trepidation [ˌtrepɪ'deɪʃən] *n* Bangigkeit, Beklommenheit, Ängstlichkeit *f* ◆ **full of ~ he knocked on the door** voll ängstlicher Erwartung klopfte er an die Tür; **a look of ~** ein banger *or* beunruhigter *or* ängstlicher Blick; **a feeling of ~** ein beklommenes Gefühl, ein Gefühl der Bangigkeit *or* Verzagtheit; **I am writing, not without some ~, to tell you ...** nicht ohne ein Gefühl der Beklommenheit teile ich Ihnen mit ...

trespass ['trespəs] [1] *vi* **(a)** (*on property*) unbefugt betreten (*on sth* etw *acc*) ◆ **"no ~ing"** „Betreten verboten"; **you're ~ing** Sie dürfen sich hier nicht aufhalten.

(b) to ~ (up)on sb's rights/area of responsibility in jds Rechte/Verantwortungsbereich (*acc*) eingreifen; **to ~ (up)on sb's privacy** jds Privatsphäre verletzen; **to ~ (up)on sb's kindness/time** jds Freundlichkeit/Zeit überbeanspruchen.

(c) (*Bibl*) **as we forgive them that ~ against us** wie wir vergeben unseren Schuldigern.

[2] *n* **(a)** (*Jur*) unbefugtes Betreten. **(b)** (*Bibl*) **forgive us our ~es** vergib uns unsere Schuld.

trespasser ['trespəsə^r] *n* Unbefugte(r) *mf* ◆ **"~s will be prosecuted"** „widerrechtliches Betreten wird strafrechtlich verfolgt"; **the farmer found a ~ on his land** der Bauer fand einen Eindringling auf seinem Land.

tress [tres] *n (liter)* Locke *f (liter)*.
trestle ['tresl] *n* (Auflage)bock *m*.
trestle: ~ bridge *n* Bockbrücke *f*; **~ table** *n* auf Böcken stehender Tisch; *(decorator's)* Tapeziertisch *m*.
trews [tru:z] *npl (Scot)* enganliegende Hose im Schottenkaro; *(inf: trousers)* Hose *f* ◆ **a pair of ~** eine Hose.
triad ['traɪəd] *n* Triade, Trias *f*; *(Mus)* Dreiklang *m*; *(Chem)* dreiwertiges Element.
trial ['traɪəl] *n* **(a)** *(Jur)* (Gerichts)verfahren *nt*, Prozeß *m*; *(actual hearing)* (Gerichts)verhandlung *f* ◆ **to be on ~** angeklagt sein, unter Anklage stehen; **he goes on ~ tomorrow** seine Verhandlung ist morgen; **to be on ~ for theft** des Diebstahls angeklagt sein, wegen Diebstahls unter Anklage stehen; **to be on ~ for one's life** wegen eines mit Todesstrafe bedrohten Verbrechens angeklagt sein *or* unter Anklage stehen; **at the ~** bei *or* während der Verhandlung; **to bring sb to ~** jdn vor Gericht stellen, jdm den Prozeß machen; **the case comes up for ~ next month** der Fall wird nächsten Monat verhandelt; **~ by jury** Schwurgerichtsverfahren *nt*.
(b) *(test)* Versuch *m*, Probe, Erprobung *f* ◆ **~s** *(of machine, aeroplane)* Test(s *pl*) *m*, (Über)prüfung *f*; *(Sport)* Qualifikationsspiel *nt*; **horse ~s** Querfeldeinrennen *nt*; **to give sth a ~** etw ausprobieren; **the manager has promised to give me a ~ as a clerk** der Betriebsleiter hat versprochen, mir eine Chance als Büroangestellter zu geben; **to take sth on ~** etw zur Probe *or* Prüfung *or* etw probeweise nehmen; **to put sb/sth to the ~** jdn/etw testen *or* auf die Probe stellen; **the new clerk is on ~** der neue Büroangestellte ist auf Probe eingestellt; **~ of strength** Kraftprobe *f*; **by ~ and error** durch Ausprobieren; **a system of ~ and error** ein System der empirischen Lösung.
(c) *(hardship)* Widrigkeit, Unannehmlichkeit *f*; *(nuisance)* Plage *f*, Problem *nt* (to für) ◆ **he's a ~ to his mother** er macht seiner Mutter sehr viel Kummer; **~s and tribulations** Aufregungen, Schwierigkeiten, Drangsale *(liter) pl*.
trial: ~ balance *n* Saldenbilanz, Probebilanz *f*; **~ flight** *n* Testflug *m*; **~ marriage** *n* Ehe *f* auf Probe; **~ offer** *n* Einführungsangebot *nt*; **~ order** *n* Probeauftrag *m*; **~ period** *n (for people)* Probezeit *f*; *(for goods) Zeit, die man etw zur Probe or Prüfung hat*; **~ run** *n* Generalprobe *f*; *(with car etc)* Versuchsfahrt, Probefahrt *f*; *(of machine)* Probelauf *m*; **give the new method a ~ run** probieren Sie diese neue Methode einmal aus *or* durch.
triangle ['traɪæŋgl] *n* Dreieck *nt*; *(set square)* (Zeichen)dreieck *nt*; *(Mus)* Triangel *m*; *(fig: relationship)* Dreiecksbeziehung *f*.
triangular [traɪ'æŋgjʊləʳ] *adj (Math)* dreieckig ◆ **~ relationship** Dreiecksverhältnis *nt*; **~ contest** Dreipersonenwettkampf *m*; *(between nations)* Dreinationenwettkampf *m*.
triangulate [traɪ'æŋgʊlɪt] **1** *adj (Math)* triangulär *(form)*.
2 [traɪ'æŋgʊleɪt] *vt* in Dreiecke einteilen; *(Surv)* triangulieren.
triangulation [traɪ,æŋgjʊ'leɪʃən] *n (Surv)* Triangulation, Triangulierung *f* ◆ **~ point** Vermessungspunkt *m*.
tribal ['traɪbəl] *adj customs, dance, life* Stammes- ◆ **Celtic society was basically ~** die Gesellschaftsordnung der Kelten war stammesgebunden; **~ loyalties** Stammestreue *f*.
tribalism ['traɪbəlɪzəm] *n* Stammesstruktur *f*.
tribe [traɪb] *n* **(a)** Stamm *m*; *(Bot, Zool)* Gattung *f*. **(b)** *(fig inf)* Korona *f*.
tribesman ['traɪbzmən] *n, pl* **-men** [-mən] Stammesangehörige(r) *m*.
tribulation [,trɪbjʊ'leɪʃən] *n* Kummer *m no pl* ◆ **~s** Sorgen *pl*; *(less serious)* Kümmernisse *pl*; **to bear one's ~s bravely** sein Leid tapfer tragen; **that is the least of our ~s** das ist unsere geringste Sorge; *see* **trial**.
tribunal [traɪ'bju:nl] *n* Gericht(shof *m*) *nt*; *(inquiry)* Untersuchungsausschuß *m*; *(held by revolutionaries etc)* Tribunal *nt* ◆ **before the ~ of public opinion** *(fig)* vor dem Tribunal der öffentlichen Meinung.
tribune[1] ['trɪbju:n] *n (Hist)* (Volks)tribun *m*.
tribune[2] *n (platform)* Tribüne *f*.
tributary ['trɪbjʊtərɪ] **1** *adj state* tributpflichtig; *river* Neben-.
2 *n (state)* tributpflichtiger Staat; *(river)* Nebenfluß *m*.
tribute ['trɪbju:t] *n* **(a)** *(Hist: payment)* Tribut *m*.
(b) *(admiration)* Tribut *m* ◆ **to pay ~ to sb/sth** jdm/einer Sache (den schuldigen) Tribut zollen; **they stood in silent ~ to him** sie zollten ihm (stehend) ihren stillen Tribut; **after her performance/his victory ~s came flooding in** nach ihrer Vorstellung wurde sie mit Ehrungen *or* Zeichen der Hochachtung überschüttet/nach seinem Sieg wurde er mit Ehrungen *or* Zeichen der Anerkennung überschüttet; **a floral ~** Blumen als Zeichen der Hochachtung/Anerkennung/des Dankes; **to be a ~ to one's parents/school** seinen Eltern/seiner Schule (alle) Ehre machen.
trice[1] [traɪs] *n*: **in a ~** im Handumdrehen, im Nu.
trice[2] *vt (Naut: also* **~ up**) *sail* aufholen.
Tricel ® ['traɪsel] *n* Tricel *nt*.
triceps ['traɪseps] *n, pl* **-(es)** Trizeps *m*.
trichina [trɪ'kaɪnə] *n, pl* **-e** [-i:] Trichine *f*.
trichinosis [trɪkɪ'nəʊsɪs] *n* Trichinenkrankheit, Trichinose *f*.
trick [trɪk] **1** *n* **(a)** *(ruse)* Trick *m* ◆ **to get sth by a ~** etw durch einen Trick *or* eine List bekommen; **be careful, it's a ~** paß auf, das ist eine Falle!; **be careful with this question, there's a ~ in it** sei vorsichtig bei dieser Frage, sie enthält eine Falle!; **he knows a ~ or two** *(inf)* der kennt sich aus, der weiß, wie der Hase läuft; **he never misses a ~** er läßt sich *(dat)* nichts entgehen; **he knows all the ~s of the trade** er ist ein alter Hase; *(is crafty)* er ist mit allen Wassern gewaschen; **he is full of ~s** *(child, footballer etc)* er steckt voller Tricks; *(salesman, politician etc)* er hat es faustdick hinter den Ohren; **it's a ~ of the light** da täuscht das Licht.
(b) *(mischief)* Streich *m* ◆ **to play a ~ on sb** jdm einen Streich spielen; **the car is playing ~s again** der Wagen fängt wieder an zu mucken *(inf)*; **unless my eyes are playing ~s on me** wenn meine Augen mich nicht täuschen; **a dirty ~** ein ganz gemeiner Trick; **he's up to his (old) ~s again** jetzt macht er wieder seine (alten) Mätzchen *(inf)*; **how's ~s?** *(inf)* wie geht's?
(c) *(skilful act)* Kunststück *nt* ◆ **to teach a dog to do ~s** einem Hund Kunststücke beibringen; **once you get the ~ of adjusting it** wenn du einmal den Dreh *or* Trick heraushast, wie man das einstellt; **there's a special ~ to it** da ist ein Trick dabei; **that should do the ~** *(inf)* das müßte eigentlich hinhauen *(inf)*.
(d) *(habit)* Eigenart *f* ◆ **to have a ~ of doing sth** die Eigenart haben, etw zu tun; **he has a ~ of always arriving as I'm pouring out the tea** er hat eine merkwürdige Art, immer gerade dann zu erscheinen, wenn ich den Tee einschenke; **history has a ~ of repeating itself** die Geschichte hat die merkwürdige Eigenschaft, sich immer zu wiederholen.
(e) *(Cards)* Stich *m* ◆ **to take a ~** einen Stich machen.
(f) *(sl: of prostitute)* Nummer *f (sl)*.
2 *attr cigar* Scherz-; *spider, glass* als Scherzartikel.
3 *vt* mit einem Trick betrügen, hereinlegen *(inf)* ◆ **I've been ~ed!** ich bin hereingelegt *or* übers Ohr gehauen *(inf)* worden!; **to ~ sb into doing sth** jdn (mit einem Trick *or* mit List) dazu bringen, etw zu tun; **he ~ed the old lady into giving him her life savings** er hat die alte Dame mit einem Trick um all ihre Ersparnisse betrogen; **to ~ sb out of sth** jdn um etw prellen, jdm etw abtricksen *(inf)*.
◆**trick out** *vt sep* herausputzen ◆ **~ed ~ in her Sunday best/all her finery** in ihrem Sonntagsstaat/in vollem Staat.
trick cyclist *n* Kunstradfahrer(in *f*) *m*; *(fig inf)* Klapsdoktor *m (inf)*.
trickery ['trɪkərɪ] *n* Tricks *pl (inf)* ◆ **a piece of ~** ein Trick *m*; **legal ~** Rechtsverdrehung *f*; **beware of verbal ~ in the contract** passen Sie auf, daß der Vertragstext nicht irgendwelche Fallen enthält!; **that's just verbal ~** das ist bloß ein raffinierter Trick mit Worten.
trickiness ['trɪkɪnɪs] *n* **(a)** *(difficulty)* Schwierigkeit *f*; *(fiddliness also)* Kniffligkeit *f*. **(b)** *(of situation)* Schwierigkeit, Kitzligkeit *(inf) f* ◆ **the ~ of the present industrial situation** ... die heikle *or* kitzlige *(inf)* augenblickliche Lage in der Industrie ... **(c)** *(slyness)* Durchtriebenheit, Gerissenheit *f*.
trickle ['trɪkl] **1** *vi* **(a)** *(liquid)* tröpfeln, tropfen ◆ **tears ~d down her cheeks** Tränen kullerten ihr über die Wangen; **the rain ~d down his neck** der Regen tropfte ihm in den Kragen; **if you don't fix the leak the water will all ~ away/out** wenn Sie die undichte Stelle nicht abdichten, tropft das ganze Wasser heraus; **the sand ~d through his fingers** der Sand rieselte ihm durch die Finger; **the waves ~d back over the pebbles** die Wellen rieselten über die Kiesel zurück.
(b) *(fig)* **people/escapees began to ~ in/out/back** die Leute/Flüchtlinge begannen, vereinzelt herein-/hinaus-/zurück- zukommen; **the ball ~d into the net** der Ball trudelte (langsam) ins Netz; **reports/donations are beginning to ~ in** so langsam trudeln die Berichte/Spenden ein *(inf)*.
2 *vt liquid* tröpfeln, träufeln, tropfenweise gießen.
3 *n* **(a)** *(of liquid)* Tröpfeln *nt*; *(stream)* Rinnsal *nt*.
(b) *(fig)* **a constant ~ of people gradually filled the lecture hall** der Hörsaal füllte sich langsam aber stetig mit Leuten; **news reports from the occupied country have dwindled to a mere ~** Meldungen aus dem besetzten Land kommen *or (secretively)* sickern nur noch ganz selten durch; **arms deliveries have shrunk to a ~** die Waffenlieferungen sind spärlich geworden; **we cut their supplies to a ~** wir haben ihren Nachschub drastisch reduziert.
trickle charger *n (Elec)* Kleinlader *m*.
trick: ~ photography *n* Trickfotografie *f*; **~ question** *n* Fangfrage *f*; **to ask sb a ~ question** jdm eine Falle stellen.
trickster ['trɪkstəʳ] *n* Schwindler, Betrüger *m*.
tricksy ['trɪksɪ] *adj (+er) (inf) see* **tricky (c)**.
tricky ['trɪkɪ] *adj (+er)* **(a)** *(difficult)* schwierig; *(fiddly also)* knifflig ◆ **he is a very ~ person to get on with** es ist äußerst schwierig, mit ihm auszukommen. **(b)** *(requiring tact) situation, problem* heikel, kitzlig. **(c)** *(sly, crafty) person, plan* durchtrieben, gerissen; *question* schwierig, knifflig *(inf)*.
tricolour, *(US)* **tricolor** ['trɪkələʳ] *n* Trikolore *f*.
tricorn ['traɪkɔ:n] *n* Dreispitz *m*.
tricot ['tri:kəʊ] *n (Tex)* Trikot *m*.
tricuspid [traɪ'kʌspɪd] *adj* trikuspidal *(spec)*.
tricycle ['traɪsɪkl] *n* Dreirad *nt*.
trident ['traɪdənt] *n* Dreizack *m*.
Tridentine [traɪ'dentaɪn] *adj* Tridentinisch.
tried [traɪd] *adj* erprobt, bewährt.
tried-and-tested, tried and tested *adj method, recipe* erprobt; *product* getestet; *system* bewährt; *technology* ausgereift.
triennial [traɪ'enɪəl] *adj (lasting 3 years)* dreijährig; *(every 3 years)* dreijährlich, alle drei Jahre stattfindend.
triennially [traɪ'enɪəlɪ] *adv* alle drei Jahre, dreijährlich.
triennium [traɪ'enɪəm] *n* Zeitraum *m* von drei Jahren.
trier ['traɪəʳ] *n*: **to be a ~** sich *(dat)* (ernsthaft) Mühe geben.
trifle ['traɪfl] *n* **(a)** Kleinigkeit *f*; *(trivial matter also)* Lappalie *(inf)*, Nichtigkeit *f* ◆ **the merest ~ upsets her** die geringste *or* kleinste Kleinigkeit regt sie auf; **I'm so sorry — a ~, don't let it worry you** es tut mir außerordentlich leid — das ist doch nicht der Rede wert, machen Sie sich deswegen keine Sorgen!
(b) *(small amount)* Kleinigkeit *f* ◆ **have some more cake — just a ~, thank you** noch etwas Kuchen? — bloß ein ganz kleines Stückchen, bitte; **a ~ hot/small** *etc* ein bißchen heiß/klein *etc*; **a ~ too** ... ein wenig *or* eine Spur zu ...

(c) (*Cook*) Trifle *nt*.

◆**trifle away** *vt sep* vergeuden.

◆**trifle with** *vi +prep obj person* zu leicht nehmen; *affections, food* spielen mit ◆ **he is not a person to be ~d ~** mit ihm ist nicht zu spaßen.

trifling ['traɪflɪŋ] *adj* unbedeutend, geringfügig.

trifoliate [traɪ'fəʊlɪɪt] *adj* dreiblättrig.

▼ **trigger** ['trɪgəʳ] 1 *n* (*of gun*) Abzug(shahn), Drücker (*inf*) *m*; (*of cine-camera, machine*) Auslöser *m*; (*Elec*) Trigger *m* ◆ **to pull the ~** abdrücken; **to be quick on the ~** schnell abdrücken.
2 *vt* (*also* **~ off**) auslösen.

trigger: ~ finger *n* Zeigefinger *m*; **my ~ finger's itching** es juckt mich abzudrücken; **~ grip** *n* Pistolengriff *m*; **~ guard** *n* Abzugsbügel *m*; **~-happy** *adj* (*inf*) schießfreudig (*inf*), schießwütig (*pej*); (*hum*) *photographer* knipswütig (*inf*).

trigonometric(al) [ˌtrɪgənə'metrɪk(əl)] *adj* trigonometrisch.

trigonometry [ˌtrɪgə'nɒmɪtrɪ] *n* Trigonometrie *f*.

trihedron [ˌtraɪ'hiːdrən] *n* Dreiflächner *m*, Trieder *nt*.

trike [traɪk] *n* (*inf*) *abbr of* **tricycle**.

trilateral [ˌtraɪ'lætərəl] *adj* dreiseitig; *conference, agreement also* Dreier-.

trilby ['trɪlbɪ] *n* (*also* **~ hat**) weicher Filzhut.

trilingual [ˌtraɪ'lɪŋgwəl] *adj* dreisprachig.

trill [trɪl] 1 *n* (a) (*of bird*) Trillern *nt*; (*of voice*) Tremolo *nt*. (b) (*Mus*) Triller *m*. (c) (*Phon*) Rollen *nt*, rollende Aussprache.
2 *vt* (a) (*birds*) trillern, tirilieren (*geh*); (*person*) trällern. (b) (*Mus*) *note* trillern. (c) (*Phon*) *consonant* rollen, rollend aussprechen.
3 *vi* (a) (*bird*) trillern, tirilieren (*geh*); (*person*) trällern. (b) (*Mus*) trillern.

trillion ['trɪljən] *n* (*Brit*) Trillion *f*; (*US*) Billion *f* ◆ **there were ~s of them there** (*fig*) es waren Millionen und Abermillionen da.

trilogy ['trɪlədʒɪ] *n* Trilogie *f*.

trim [trɪm] 1 *adj* (*+er*) sauber; *appearance also* adrett; *hair, haircut* gepflegt ◆ **he keeps his lawn/garden/house very ~** sein Rasen/Garten/Haus ist immer sehr gepflegt; **she has a ~ little figure** sie hat ein niedliches Figürchen.
2 *n* (a) (*condition*) Zustand *m*, Verfassung *f*; (*fitness*) Form *f* ◆ **in good ~** (*house, car etc*) in gutem Zustand; (*person*) gut in Form; **financially in good ~** finanziell in guter Verfassung; **to get things into ~** Ordnung machen *or* schaffen; **to get into ~** sich trimmen *or* in Form bringen; **in fighting ~** kampfbereit.
(b) (*inf*) **to give sth a ~** etw schneiden; (*tree, hedge, beard also*) etw stutzen; **your hair needs a ~** du mußt dir die Haare etwas nachschneiden lassen; **just a light ~, please** nur etwas kürzen *or* nachschneiden, bitte.
(c) (*Aut*) (*outside*) Zierleisten *pl*; (*inside*) Innenausstattung *f*.
(d) (*Naut*) Trimm *m*, Gleichgewichtslage *f* ◆ **in/out of ~** (*ship*) in/nicht in Trimm *or* Gleichgewichtslage.
(e) (*Aviat*) Trimm(lage *f*) *m*, Fluglage *f*.
3 *vt* (a) (*cut*) *hair* nachschneiden; *beard, hedge, branch* stutzen; *dog* trimmen; *wick, roses* beschneiden; *piece of wood* zurechtschneiden/-sägen/-hobeln.
(b) (*fig: cut down*) *budget* kürzen; *essay also* zurechtstutzen.
(c) (*decorate*) *dress* besetzen; *Christmas tree* schmücken.
(d) *boat, plane* trimmen; *sails* richtig stellen.
(e) (*US inf*) (*defeat*) schlagen; (*cheat*) übers Ohr hauen (*inf*).

◆**trim away** *vt sep* weg- *or* abschneiden; *details etc* entfernen.

◆**trim back** *vt sep hedge, roses* zurückschneiden.

◆**trim down** *vt sep wick, budget* kürzen (*to* auf *+acc*); *essay also, hedge* (zurecht)stutzen; *roses* zurückschneiden ◆ **to ~ ~ one's/sb's figure** etwas für seine/jds Figur tun.

◆**trim off** *vt sep bits of beard, ends of branch* abschneiden; *rough edges* abschneiden/-sägen/-hobeln/-feilen.

trimaran ['traɪmərən] *n* Dreirumpfboot *nt*, Trimaran *m*.

trimester [trɪ'mestəʳ] *n* Trimester *nt*.

trimming ['trɪmɪŋ] *n* (a) (*on clothes*) Besatz *m* ◆ **~s** Verzierung(en *pl*) *f*.
(b) **~s** *pl* (*cuttings*) Abfälle *pl*; (*of paper also*) (Papier)schnitzel, Schnipsel (*inf*) *pl*.
(c) **~s** *pl* (*accessories*) Zubehör *nt* ◆ **the car costs £10,000 with all the ~s** das Auto kostet £ 10.000 mit allen Extras *or* mit allem Zubehör; **roast beef with all the ~s** Roastbeef mit allem Drum und Dran (*inf*) *or* allen Beilagen.

trimness ['trɪmnɪs] *n* (*of hair, lawn etc*) Gepflegtheit *f*, gepflegtes Aussehen; (*of figure*) Schlankheit *f*.

Trinidad ['trɪnɪdæd] *n* Trinidad *nt*.

trinitrotoluene [traɪˌnaɪtrəʊ'tɒljʊiːn] *n* Trinitrotoluol *nt*.

Trinity ['trɪnɪtɪ] *n* (a) Trinität, Dreieinigkeit, Dreifaltigkeit *f* ◆ **~ Sunday** Trinitatis(fest), Dreieinigkeitsfest, Dreifaltigkeitsfest *nt*. (b) (**~ term**) Sommertrimester *nt*.

trinket ['trɪŋkɪt] *n* Schmuckstück *nt*; (*ornament*) Schmuckgegenstand *m* ◆ **~ box** Schmuckkästchen *nt*; **the ~s hanging from her bracelet** die Anhänger an ihrem Armband.

trinomial [traɪ'nəʊmɪəl] 1 *adj* trinomisch, dreigliedrig.
2 *n* Trinom *nt*.

trio ['trɪəʊ] *n* Trio *nt*.

trip [trɪp] 1 *n* (a) (*journey*) Reise *f*; (*excursion*) Ausflug *m*, Tour *f*; (*shorter also*) Trip *m* ◆ **let's go for a ~ to the seaside** machen wir doch einen Ausflug ans Meer!, fahren wir doch ans Meer!; **when was your last ~ to the dentist's?** wann waren Sie zuletzt beim Zahnarzt?; **that's his fifth ~ to the bathroom already!** er geht jetzt schon zum fünften Mal auf die Toilette! (*inf*); **he is away on a ~/a ~ to Canada** er ist verreist *or* auf Reisen/macht zur Zeit eine Reise nach Kanada; **to take a ~** eine Reise machen, verreisen.
(b) (*sl: on drugs*) Trip *m* (*sl*) ◆ **to go on a ~** auf einen Trip *or* die Reise gehen (*sl*).
(c) (*stumble*) Stolpern *nt* ◆ **that was a nasty ~** da sind Sie aber übel gestolpert.
(d) (*esp Sport*) Beinstellen *nt* ◆ **he didn't fall, it was a ~** er ist nicht (von selbst) hingefallen, man hat ihm ein Bein gestellt.
(e) (*mistake*) Fehler, Ausrutscher (*inf*) *m*.
(f) (*Mech*) Auslösung *f*.
2 *vi* (a) (*stumble*) stolpern (*on, over* über *+acc*).
(b) (*fig*) *see* **~ up 1 (b)**.
(c) (*skip*) trippeln ◆ **to ~ in/out** hinein-/hinaustrippeln; **a phrase which ~s off the tongue** ein Ausdruck, der einem leicht von der Zunge geht; **the notes should come ~ping off the tongue** die Töne müssen richtig perlend kommen.
3 *vt* (a) (*make fall*) stolpern lassen; (*deliberately also*) ein Bein stellen (*+dat*) ◆ **I was ~ped** jemand hat mir ein Bein gestellt; *see also* **~ up 2 (b)**.
(b) (*Mech*) *lever* betätigen; *mechanism* auslösen.
(c) (*old: dance*) tanzen ◆ **to ~ the light fantastic** (*hum*) das Tanzbein schwingen (*inf*).

◆**trip over** *vi* stolpern (*+prep obj* über *+acc*).

◆**trip up** 1 *vi* (a) stolpern. (b) (*fig*) sich vertun.
2 *vt sep* (a) (*make fall*) stolpern lassen; (*deliberately also*) zu Fall bringen.
(b) (*fig: cause to make a mistake etc*) eine Falle stellen (*+dat*), aufs Glatteis führen ◆ **he was trying to ~ me ~ with his ad-libbing** er versuchte, mich mit seinem Improvisieren aus dem Konzept zu bringen; **question six managed to ~ most of the candidates ~** die meisten Prüflinge sind über die sechste Frage gestolpert.

tripartite [ˌtraɪ'pɑːtaɪt] *adj agreement, talks* dreiseitig; *division* Drei-.

tripe [traɪp] *n* (a) (*Cook*) Kaldaunen, Kutteln (*S Ger, Aus, Sw*) *pl*. (b) (*fig inf*) Quatsch, Stuß (*inf*) *m*.

triphammer ['trɪpˌhæməʳ] *n* Aufwerfhammer *m*.

triplane ['traɪpleɪn] *n* Dreidecker *m*.

triple ['trɪpl] 1 *adj* dreifach ◆ **~ glazing** Dreifachverglasung *f*; **~ jump** Dreisprung *m*; **~ time** (*Mus*) Dreiertakt *m*.
2 *adv* dreimal soviel ◆ **it's ~ the distance** es ist dreimal so weit; **at ~ the speed** mit dreifacher Geschwindigkeit; **it costs ~ what it used to** es kostet dreimal soviel wie früher, es kostet das Dreifache von früher.
3 *n* Dreifache(s) *nt*.
4 *vt* verdreifachen.
5 *vi* sich verdreifachen.

triplet ['trɪplɪt] *n* (a) (*baby*) Drilling *m*. (b) (*Mus*) Triole *f*; (*Poet*) Dreireim *m*.

triplex ® ['trɪpleks] *n* Verbundglas *nt*.

triplicate ['trɪplɪkɪt] 1 *n*: **in ~** in dreifacher Ausfertigung.
2 *adj* in dreifacher Ausfertigung.
3 ['trɪplɪkeɪt] *vt document* dreifach *or* in drei Exemplaren ausfertigen.

triply ['trɪplɪ] *adv* dreimal ◆ **~ expensive** dreimal so teuer.

tripod ['traɪpɒd] *n* (*Phot*) Stativ *nt*; (*Hist*) Dreifuß *m*.

tripos ['traɪpɒs] *n* Abschlußexamen *nt an der Universität Cambridge*.

tripper ['trɪpəʳ] *n* Ausflügler(in *f*) *m*; *see* **day ~**.

tripping ['trɪpɪŋ] *adj* (a) *walk* trippelnd; *notes* perlend; *metre* fließend. (b) (*Mech*) **~ device** Auslösemechanismus *m*.

trippingly ['trɪpɪŋlɪ] *adv see adj (a)*.

trip recorder *n* (*Aut*) Tageszähler *m*.

triptych ['trɪptɪk] *n* Triptychon *nt*.

tripwire ['trɪpwaɪəʳ] *n* Stolperdraht *m*.

trireme ['traɪriːm] *n* Triere, Trireme *f*.

trisect [traɪ'sekt] *vt* in drei Teile teilen, dreiteilen; *angle* in drei gleiche Teile teilen.

trisection [traɪ'sekʃən] *n* Dreiteilung *f*; (*of angle*) Einteilung *f* in drei gleiche Teile.

trisyllabic ['traɪsɪ'læbɪk] *adj* dreisilbig.

trisyllable [ˌtraɪ'sɪləbl] *n* dreisilbiges Wort.

trite [traɪt] *adj* (*+er*) (*trivial, banal*) banal, nichtssagend; (*hackneyed*) abgedroschen.

tritely ['traɪtlɪ] *adv see adj* ◆ **to talk ~** banales/abgedroschenes Zeug reden, Phrasen dreschen; **a ~ obvious remark** eine Binsenweisheit; **nobody is perfect, he said ~** er machte die banale Bemerkung: niemand ist vollkommen.

triteness ['traɪtnɪs] *n see adj* Banalität *f*; Abgedroschenheit *f*.

tritium ['trɪtɪəm] *n* Tritium *nt*.

triumph ['traɪʌmf] 1 *n* (a) Triumph *m* ◆ **in ~** triumphierend, im Triumph; **shouts of ~** Triumphgeschrei *nt*; **to win** *or* **score a ~ over sb/sth** einen Triumph über jdn/etw erzielen.
(b) (*Hist: procession*) Triumphzug *m*.
2 *vi* den Sieg davontragen (*over* über *+acc*) ◆ **to ~ over sb/sth** über jdn/etw triumphieren; **they ~ed over incredible odds** sie setzten sich gegen unglaubliche Widerstände durch; **we've made it! he ~ed** wir haben's geschafft! triumphierte er.

triumphal [traɪ'ʌmfəl] *adj* triumphal ◆ **~ arch** Triumphbogen *m*.

triumphant [traɪ'ʌmfənt] *adj* (*victorious*) siegreich; (*rejoicing*) triumphierend; *moment* triumphal ◆ **to be ~ (over sth)** triumphieren (*over* über *+acc*); **he was ~ in his success** er jubelte triumphierend *or* triumphierte über seinen Erfolg; **in our ~ hour** in unserer Stunde des Triumphs.

triumphantly [traɪ'ʌmfəntlɪ] *adv* triumphierend ◆ **it was a ~ successful**

➤ LANGUAGE IN USE: **trigger** → 17.2

expedition die Expedition war ein triumphaler Erfolg.

triumvir ['traɪəmvɪːr] *n (Hist)* Triumvir *m.*

triumvirate [traɪ'ʌmvɪrɪt] *n (Hist)* Triumvirat *nt.*

triune ['traɪjuːn] *adj (Rel)* dreieinig.

trivalent [ˌtraɪ'veɪlənt] *adj (Chem)* dreiwertig.

trivia ['trɪvɪə] *npl* triviales Zeug ◆ **the ~ of daily life** die Trivialitäten des täglichen Lebens.

trivial ['trɪvɪəl] *adj* **(a)** trivial; *objection, loss, details, matters also* geringfügig, belanglos ◆ **look, your health is not something ~** hör mal, mit der Gesundheit ist nicht zu spaßen!; **the ~ round** das triviale Einerlei. **(b)** *person* oberflächlich.

triviality [ˌtrɪvɪ'ælɪtɪ] *n see adj (a)* Trivialität *f*; Geringfügigkeit, Belanglosigkeit *f.*

trivialization [ˌtrɪvɪəlaɪ'zeɪʃən] *n* Trivialisierung *f.*

trivialize ['trɪvɪəlaɪz] *vt* trivialisieren.

trochaic [trɒ'keɪɪk] *adj* trochäisch.

trochee ['trəʊkiː] *n* Trochäus *m.*

trod [trɒd] *pret of* **tread.**

trodden ['trɒdn] *ptp of* **tread.**

troglodyte ['trɒglədaɪt] *n* Höhlenbewohner, Troglodyt *(liter) m*; *(fig: recluse)* Einsiedler *m.*

troika ['trɔɪkə] *n* Troika *f.*

Trojan ['trəʊdʒən] 1 *n (Hist)* Trojaner(in *f*), Troer(in *f*) *m* ◆ **to work like a ~** *(fig)* wie ein Pferd arbeiten; **he's a real ~** *(fig)* er ist wirklich eine treue Seele.
2 *adj* trojanisch; *(fig)* übermenschlich ◆ **~ Horse** *(lit, fig)* Trojanisches Pferd; **~ War** Trojanischer Krieg.

troll¹ [trəʊl] *n (Myth)* Troll *m.*

troll² *vi (inf: walk)* laufen.

trolley ['trɒlɪ] *n* **(a)** *(cart) (four wheels)* Handwagen *m*; *(in supermarket)* Einkaufswagen *m*; *(in station)* Gepäckwagen, Ladekasten *m*; *(for passengers)* Kofferkuli *m*; *(two wheels) (for golf clubs)* Caddy *m*; *(in station, factory etc)* Sackkarre *f.*
(b) *(tea ~)* Teewagen *m.*
(c) *(Rail)* Lore *f*, Förderkarren *m*; *(hand-driven)* Draisine *f.*
(d) *(Elec) (~ pole)* Kontaktarm *m*, Stromabnehmerstange *f*; *(~-wheel)* Kontaktrolle *f*, Rollenstrom abnehmer *m.*
(e) *(~bus or -car (US)) see* **trolleybus, trolley-car.**
(f) to be off one's ~ *(inf)* nicht mehr alle Tassen im Schrank haben *(inf).*

trolley: ~bus *n* Obus, Oberleitungsomnibus *(form)*, Trolleybus *(dated) m*; **~-car** *n (US)* Straßenbahn *f*; **~ pole** *n* Kontaktarm *m*, Stromabnehmerstange *f.*

trollop ['trɒləp] *n (dated: prostitute)* leichtes Mädchen, Straßenmädchen *nt*; *(pej)* Schlampe *f.*

trombone [trɒm'bəʊn] *n (Mus)* Posaune *f.*

trombonist [trɒm'bəʊnɪst] *n* Posaunist *m.*

troop [truːp] 1 *n* **(a)** *(Mil: of cavalry)* Trupp *m*; *(unit)* Schwadron *f.* **(b)** *(Mil)* **~s** *pl* Truppen *pl*; **a dozen of our best ~s** zwölf unserer besten Soldaten; **200 ~s** 200 Soldaten. **(c)** *(of scouts)* Stamm *m.* **(d)** *(of people)* Horde *(pej)*, Schar *f.*
2 *vi* **to ~ out/in** hinaus-/hineinströmen; **to ~ upstairs** nach oben strömen; **to ~ past sth** an etw *(dat)* vorbeiziehen; **to ~ away** *or* **off** abziehen *(inf)*; **to ~ up** herbeiströmen.
3 *vt (Mil)* **to ~ the colours** die Fahnenparade abhalten; **the colours being ~ed today** die Fahnen bei der heutigen Parade; **the ~ing of the colours** die Fahnenparade.

troop-carrier ['truːpˌkærɪəʳ] *n (vehicle)* Truppentransporter *m.*

trooper ['truːpəʳ] *n (Mil)* berittener Soldat, Kavallerist *m*; *(US: state ~)* Polizist *m* ◆ **to swear like a ~** wie ein Kutscher fluchen.

troop: ~-ship *n* (Truppen)transportschiff *nt*; **~ train** *n* Truppentransportzug *m.*

trope [trəʊp] *n (Liter)* Trope *f.*

trophy ['trəʊfɪ] *n (Hunt, Mil, Sport)* Trophäe *f.*

tropic ['trɒpɪk] *n* **(a)** Wendekreis *m* ◆ **T~ of Cancer/Capricorn** Wendekreis des Krebses/Steinbocks. **(b) ~s** *pl* Tropen *pl.*

tropical ['trɒpɪkəl] *adj* tropisch, Tropen- ◆ **~ medicine/diseases** Tropenmedizin *f*/Tropenkrankheiten *pl.*

tropism ['trəʊpɪzəm] *n (Biol)* Tropismus *m.*

trot [trɒt] 1 *n* **(a)** *(pace)* Trab *m* ◆ **to go at a ~** traben; **to go for a ~** einen Ausritt machen; **to keep sb on the ~** *(fig inf)* jdn in Trab halten; **I've been on the ~ all day** *(fig inf)* ich bin schon den ganzen Tag auf Trab.
(b) *(inf)* **for five days on the ~** fünf Tage lang in einer Tour.
(c) *(inf: diarrhoea)* **the ~s** die Renneritis *(hum inf).*
2 *vi (horse, person)* traben; *(pony)* zockeln; *(small child)* trippeln ◆ **he ~ted obediently round the shops after her** er zottelte folgsam hinter ihr her durch die Geschäfte.
3 *vt horse* traben lassen.

◆**trot along** *vi see* **trot 2** traben; zockeln; trippeln; *(go away)* abmarschieren ◆ **to ~ ~ behind sb** hinter jdm hertraben *etc.*

◆**trot away** *or* **off** *vi see* **trot 2** davon- *or* wegtraben; davon- *or* wegzockeln; davon- *or* wegtrippeln.

◆**trot out** 1 *vi see* **trot 2** hinaus-/heraustraben; hinaus-/herauszockeln; hinaus-/heraustrippeln.
2 *vt sep excuses, theories, names, list* aufwarten mit.

◆**trot over** *or* **round** *vi (go quickly)* hinüberlaufen ◆ **to ~ ~ to the grocer's** zum Kaufmann laufen.

troth [trəʊθ] *n (old) see* **plight¹.**

trotter¹ ['trɒtəʳ] *n (horse)* Traber *m.*

trotter² *n (of animal)* Fuß *m* ◆ **pigs' ~s** *(Cook)* Schweinsfüße *pl.*

troubadour ['truːbədɔːʳ] *n* Troubadour *m.*

trouble ['trʌbl] 1 *n* **(a)** Schwierigkeiten *pl*; *(bothersome also)* Ärger *m* ◆ **did you have any ~ (in) getting it?** hatten Sie Schwierigkeiten, es zu bekommen?; **to be in ~** in Schwierigkeiten sein; **you'll be in ~ for this** da bekommen Sie Ärger *or* Schwierigkeiten; **to be in ~ with sb** mit jdm Schwierigkeiten *or* Ärger haben; **to get into ~** in Schwierigkeiten geraten; *(with authority)* Schwierigkeiten *or* Ärger bekommen *(with* mit); **to get sb into ~** jdn in Schwierigkeiten bringen *(with* mit); **to get a girl into ~** *(euph)* ein Mädchen ins Unglück bringen; **to get out of/sb out of ~** aus den Schwierigkeiten herauskommen/jdm aus seinen Schwierigkeiten heraushelfen; **to keep** *or* **stay out of ~** nicht in Schwierigkeiten kommen, sauber bleiben *(inf)*; **now we're out of ~** jetzt sind wir aus den Schwierigkeiten heraus; **the children are never out of ~** die Kinder stellen dauernd etwas an; **to make ~** *(cause a row etc)* Krach schlagen *(inf)*, Ärger machen; **to make ~ (for sb/oneself)** *(with authority)* jdn/sich selbst in Schwierigkeiten bringen; **that's/you're asking for ~** das kann ja nicht gutgehen; **are you looking for ~?** Sie wollen wohl Ärger?; **to look for ~, to go around looking for ~** sich *(dat)* Ärger einhandeln; **there'll be ~ if he finds out** wenn er das erfährt, gibt's Ärger *or* Trouble *(inf)*; **here comes ~** *(inf)* jetzt geht es los! *(inf)*, jetzt gibt es Ärger *or* Trouble! *(inf)*; **what's the ~?** was ist los?; *(to sick person)* wo fehlt's?; **the ~ is that ...** das Problem ist, daß ...; **that's the ~** das ist das Problem; **family/money ~s** Familien-/Geldsorgen *pl*; **his ~s are not yet over** seine Sorgen *or* Probleme sind noch nicht vorbei.
(b) *(bother, effort)* Mühe *f* ◆ **it's no ~ (at all)!** das mache ich doch gern; **thank you — (it was) no ~** vielen Dank — (das ist) gern geschehen; **it's no ~ to do it properly** man kann es genausogut ordentlich machen; **it's not worth the ~** das ist nicht der Mühe wert; **nothing is too much ~ for her** nichts ist ihr zuviel; **to go to the ~ (of doing sth), to take the ~ (to do sth)** sich *(dat)* die Mühe machen(, etw zu tun); **to go to/to take a lot of ~ (over** *or* **with sth)** sich *(dat)* (mit etw) viel Mühe geben; **you have gone to a lot of ~ over the food** Sie haben sich *(dat)* solche Umstände mit dem Essen gemacht; **he went to enormous ~** er hat alles nur Erdenkliche getan; **to put sb to the ~ of doing sth** jdn bemühen, etw zu tun; **to put sb to the ~ of making unnecessary preparations** jdm unnötig Umstände machen; **to put sb to a lot of ~** jdm viel Mühe machen.
(c) *(nuisance)* **to be a ~ (to sb)** (jdm) Mühe machen; *(dependent person also)* (jdm) zur Last fallen; **the child is nothing but ~ to his parents** das Kind macht seinen Eltern nur Sorgen.
(d) *(Med: illness)* Leiden *nt*; *(fig)* Schaden *m* ◆ **heart/back ~** Herz-/Rückenleiden *nt*; **my back is giving me ~** mein Rücken macht mir zu schaffen; **engine ~** (ein) Motorschaden *m.*
(e) *(unrest, upheaval)* Unruhe *f* ◆ **labour ~s** Arbeiterunruhen *pl*; **there's ~ at the factory/in Iran** in der Fabrik/im Iran herrscht Unruhe; **he caused/made ~ between them** er hat Unruhe zwischen ihnen gestiftet; *see* **stir up.**
2 *vt* **(a)** *(worry)* beunruhigen; *(disturb, grieve)* bekümmern ◆ **to be ~d by sth** wegen etw besorgt *or* beunruhigt/bekümmert sein; **his eyes ~ him** seine Augen machen ihm zu schaffen; **he's ~d with a bad back** er leidet an Rückenschmerzen.
(b) *(bother)* bemühen, belästigen ◆ **I'm sorry to ~ you, but could you tell me if ...** entschuldigen Sie die Störung, aber könnten Sie mir sagen, ob ...; **may I ~ you for a light?** darf ich Sie um Feuer bitten?; **will it ~ you if I smoke?** stört es Sie, wenn ich rauche?; **I shan't ~ you with the details** ich werde Ihnen die Einzelheiten ersparen; **we are ~d with mice just now** wir werden zur Zeit von Mäusen geplagt; **I'll ~ you to remember who you're speaking to!** *(iro)* würden Sie bitte daran denken, mit wem Sie sprechen!
(c) *(take the trouble)* **to ~ to do sth** sich bemühen, etw zu tun; **please don't ~ yourself** bitte bemühen Sie sich nicht; **don't ~ to write until you've settled down** schreib erst, wenn du dich eingelebt hast; **if you had ~d to ask, you might have found out the truth** wenn du dir die Mühe gemacht und gefragt hättest, hättest du wahrscheinlich die Wahrheit erfahren; **oh, don't ~ to apologize!** *(iro)* bemüh dich nicht, dich zu entschuldigen.
3 *vi* sich bemühen.

troubled ['trʌbld] *adj person, look* unruhig, beunruhigt; *(grieved)* bekümmert; *times* unruhig; *water* aufgewühlt ◆ **the ~ waters of industrial relations** die gestörte Beziehung zwischen Arbeitgebern und Arbeitnehmern; *see* **oil.**

trouble: ~-free *adj period, process, car* problemlos; *relationship also* reibungslos; *area* ruhig; *machine* störungsfrei; **~maker** *n* Tunichtgut *m*; *(deliberate)* Unruhestifter(in *f*) *m*; **~shooter** *n* Störungssucher(in *f*) *m*; *(Pol, Ind: mediator)* Vermittler(in *f*) *m*; **~shooters** *(Pol etc: organization)* Krisenfeuerwehr *f*; **~some** *adj (bothersome)* lästig; *person, problem* schwierig; **the most ~some boy in the school** der schwierigste Junge in der Schule; *(troublemaker)* der größte Störenfried in der Schule; **don't be ~some!** sei nicht so schwierig!; **~ spot** *n* Unruheherd *m*; *(in system)* Störung *f.*

troublous ['trʌbləs] *adj (liter)* unruhig.

trough [trɒf] *n* **(a)** *(container)* Trog *m* ◆ **drinking ~** Wassertrog *m.* **(b)** *(depression)* Furche, Rille *f*; *(between waves, on graph)* Tal *nt*; *(Met)* Trog *m* ◆ **~ of depression** Tiefdrucktrog *m.*

trounce [traʊns] *vt* verprügeln; *(Sport)* vernichtend schlagen.

trouncing ['traʊnsɪŋ] *n* Prügel *pl (also Sport)* ◆ **to give sb a ~** jdm Prügel verpassen.

troupe [truːp] *n (Theat)* Truppe *f.*

trouper ['truːpəʳ] *n (Theat)* Mime *m*, Mimin *f (dated)* ◆ **an old ~** *(fig)* ein alter

➤ LANGUAGE IN USE: **trouble: 1a** → 2.3, 17.2

Hase; **a good ~** (*fig*) ein treuer Mitarbeiter.
trouser ['traʊzə]: **~ clip** *n* Hosenklammer *f*; **~ leg** *n* Hosenbein *nt*; **~ press** *n* Hosenpresse *f*.
trousers ['traʊzɪz] *npl* (*esp Brit: also* **pair of ~**) Hose *f* ◆ **she was wearing ~** sie hatte Hosen *or* eine Hose an; **to wear the ~** (*fig inf*) die Hosen anhaben (*inf*); **to be caught with one's ~ down** (*inf*) (*lit: sexually*) in flagranti erwischt werden (*inf*); (*fig*) überrumpelt werden; (*unprepared*) sich unvorbereitet erwischen lassen.
trouser-suit ['traʊzə,su:t] *n* (*Brit*) Hosenanzug *m*.
trousseau ['tru:səʊ] *n* Aussteuer *f*.
trout [traʊt] *n* Forelle *f* ◆ **~ fishing** Forellenfang *m*, Forellenangeln *nt*; **silly old ~!** (*inf*) blöde alte (Zimt)ziege (*inf*).
trove [trəʊv] *n see* **treasure ~**.
trowel ['traʊəl] *n* Kelle *f* ◆ **to lay sth on with a ~** (*inf*) bei etw dick auftragen.
Troy [trɔɪ] *n* (*Hist*) Troja *nt*; *see* **Helen**.
troy [trɔɪ] *n* (*also* **~ weight**) Troygewicht *nt*.
truancy ['truənsɪ] *n* (Schule)schwänzen *nt*, unentschuldigtes Fehlen (in der Schule) (*form*), (Schul)schwänzerei *f* (*inf*) ◆ **~ officer** *Sozialarbeiter, der sich um Schulschwänzer kümmert*.
truant ['truənt] *n* (Schul)schwänzer(in *f*) *m* ◆ **to play ~ (from sth)** (bei etw) unentschuldigt fehlen, (etw) schwänzen (*inf*).
truce [tru:s] *n* (*Mil, fig*) Waffenstillstand *m*; (*Mil: interrupting fighting*) Waffenruhe *f* ◆ **~!** Friede!
truck¹ [trʌk] 1 *n* **(a)** (*Rail*) Güterwagen *m*. **(b)** (*barrow*) Karren, Wagen *m*; (*for luggage*) Gepäckkarren *m*; (*motorized*) Elektrokarren *m*. **(c)** (*lorry*) Last(kraft)wagen *m*; (*van, pick-up*) Lieferwagen *m*.
2 *vt* (*US*) transportieren, spedieren.
3 *vi* (*US*) Lastwagen fahren.
truck² *n* **(a)** (*fig: dealings*) **to have no ~ with sb/sth** mit jdm/etw nichts zu tun haben. **(b)** (*Hist: payment*) **~ (system)** Trucksystem *nt* (*spec*); **they were paid in ~** sie wurden in Waren bezahlt. **(c)** (*US: garden produce*) (*für den Verkauf angebautes*) Gemüse.
truckage ['trʌkɪdʒ] *n* (*US: transport*) Transport *m*, Spedition *f*; (*charge*) Transportkosten *pl* ◆ **~ company** Spedition(sfirma) *f*, Transportunternehmen *nt*.
truck driver *n* Lastwagenfahrer(in *f*) *m*.
trucker ['trʌkə^r] *n* (*US*) **(a)** (*truck-driver*) Lastwagenfahrer(in *f*) *m*; (*haulage contractor*) Spediteur *m*. **(b)** (*farmer*) Gemüsegärtner(in *f*) *m*.
truck (*US*): **~ farm** *n* Gemüsefarm *f*; **~ farmer** *n* Gemüsegärtner(in *f*) *m*; **~ garden** *n* Gemüsegärtnerei *f*.
trucking ['trʌkɪŋ] *n* (*US*) Spedition *f*, Transport *m*.
truckle ['trʌkl] *vi* klein beigeben (*to sb* jdm gegenüber).
truckle bed *n* niedriges Rollbett.
truck: ~load *n* Wagenladung *f*; **they came by the ~load** sie kamen in ganzen Wagenladungen; **~man** *n* Lastwagenfahrer *m*; **~stop** *n* (*US*) Fernfahrerlokal *nt*.
truculence ['trʌkjʊləns] *n* Trotzigkeit, Aufsässigkeit *f*.
truculent ['trʌkjʊlənt] *adj* trotzig, aufsässig.
trudge [trʌdʒ] 1 *vi* **to ~ in/out/along** *etc* hinein-/hinaus-/entlangtrotten *etc*; **to ~ through the mud** durch den Matsch stapfen; **we ~d round the shops** wir sind durch die Geschäfte getrottet *or* gelatscht (*inf*).
2 *vt streets, town* trotten durch; (*looking for sth*) abklappern.
3 *n* mühseliger Marsch.
▼ **true** [tru:] 1 *adj* **(a)** (*not false*) *story, news, rumour, statement* wahr ◆ **to come ~** (*dream, wishes*) Wirklichkeit werden, wahr werden; (*prophecy*) sich verwirklichen; (*fears*) sich bewahrheiten; **it is ~ that** ... es stimmt, daß ..., es ist wahr *or* richtig, daß ...; **that's ~** das stimmt, das ist wahr; **can it be ~ (that he didn't know)?** kann es stimmen *or* sein(, daß er das nicht wußte)?; **the same is** *or* **holds ~ for** ... dasselbe gilt auch für ..., dasselbe trifft auch auf ... (*acc*) zu; **~!** richtig!; **too ~!** (das ist nur) zu wahr!, wie wahr!; **we mustn't generalize, (it's) ~, but** ... wir sollten natürlich nicht verallgemeinern, aber ...; **that's wrong! — ~, but** ... das ist falsch! — stimmt *or* richtig, aber ...
(b) (*accurate*) *description, report, account* wahrheitsgetreu; *likeness* (lebens)getreu; *copy* getreu.
(c) (*real, genuine*) *feeling, friendship, friend, Christian, heir, opinion* wahr, echt; *reason* wirklich; *leather, antique* echt ◆ **the frog is not a ~ reptile** der Frosch ist kein echtes Reptil; **in a ~ spirit of friendship/love** im wahren Geist der Freundschaft/Liebe; **~ love** die wahre Liebe; (*person*) Schatz *m*, Herzallerliebste(r) *mf* (*old*); **the path of ~ love ne'er did run smooth** (*prov*) die Pfade der Liebe sind gewunden; **what is the ~ situation?** wie verhält es sich wirklich?; **in ~ life** im wirklichen Leben; **the one ~ God** der einzige wahre Gott.
(d) (*faithful*) *friend, follower* treu ◆ **to be ~ to sb** jdm treu sein/bleiben; **to be ~ to one's word** (treu) zu seinem Wort stehen, seinem Wort treu bleiben; **~ to life** lebensnah; (*Art*) lebensecht; **the horse ran ~ to form** das Pferd lief erwartungsgemäß; **~ to type** erwartungsgemäß; (*Bot*) artgetreu.
(e) *wall, surface* gerade; *join* genau; *circle* rund; (*Mus*) *note* rein.
(f) (*Phys*) tatsächlich ◆ **~ North** der eigentliche *or* tatsächliche *or* geographische Norden.
2 *n* **out of ~** *upright, beam, wheels* schief; *join* verschoben.
3 *adv aim* genau; *sing* richtig ◆ **to breed ~** sich reinrassig fortpflanzen; **he speaks ~** (*old*) er spricht die Wahrheit; *see* **ring²**.
◆**true up** *vt sep machinery* genau einstellen; *beam* genau ausrichten; *wheel* einrichten ◆ **to ~ ~ the edges of the planks** die Bretterkanten plan machen.
true: ~ blue 1 *adj* waschecht (*inf*), echt; 2 *n* (*Brit: Tory*) (wasch)echter Tory; **~-born** *adj* echt, gebürtig; (*legitimate*) rechtmäßig; **~-bred** *adj* wahr, echt; *cattle* reinrassig; **~-hearted** *adj* getreu, aufrichtig; **~-life** *adj attr* aus dem Leben gegriffen; **~ rib** *n* wahre Rippe.
truffle ['trʌfl] *n* Trüffel *f or m*.
trug [trʌg] *n* Korb *m*.
truism ['tru:ɪzəm] *n* (*obvious truth*) Binsenwahrheit *f*; (*platitude*) Platitüde *f*, Gemeinplatz *m*.
truly ['tru:lɪ] *adv* **(a)** (*truthfully, genuinely*) wirklich, wahrhaftig ◆ **(really and) ~?** wirklich und wahrhaftig?; **he did it, ~ he did!** er hat es wirklich und wahrhaftig getan!; *see* **well²**.
(b) (*faithfully*) *serve* treu; *love also* getreu(lich) (*geh*); *reflect* wahrheitsgetreu.
trump¹ [trʌmp] 1 *n* (*Cards, fig*) Trumpf *m*; (*dated inf: person*) prima Kerl (*dated inf*) ◆ **spades are ~s** Pik ist Trumpf; **what's ~s?** was ist Trumpf?; **to hold all the ~s** (*fig*) alle Trümpfe in der Hand halten; **~ card** (*Cards*) Trumpf(karte *f*) *m*; (*fig*) Trumpf *m*; **to play one's ~ card** (*lit, fig*) seinen Trumpf ausspielen; **he's absolutely ~s** (*dated inf*) er ist große Klasse (*inf*); **to turn up ~s** (*inf*) sich als Sieger erweisen.
2 *vt* (*Cards*) stechen; (*fig*) übertrumpfen.
◆**trump up** *vt sep* erfinden.
trump² *n* (*liter*) Trompete *f* ◆ **at the Last T~** wenn die Posaunen des Jüngsten Gerichts erklingen.
trumpery ['trʌmpərɪ] 1 *n* Plunder *m no pl*; (*ornaments*) Kitsch *m*; (*jewellery*) Flitterkram *m*; (*nonsense*) Unsinn *m*.
2 *adj* billig; *ornaments also* kitschig.
trumpet ['trʌmpɪt] 1 *n* **(a)** (*Mus*) Trompete *f* ◆ **~ major** Stabstrompeter *m*; *see* **blow²**. **(b)** (*of elephant*) Trompeten *nt no pl*. **(c)** (*of flower*) Trompete *f*; (*hearing ~*) Hörrohr *m*; (*speaking ~*) Sprachrohr, Megaphon *nt*.
2 *vt* (*rare: also* **~ forth**) hinaustrompeten.
3 *vi* (*elephant*) trompeten.
trumpeter ['trʌmpɪtə^r] *n* Trompeter(in *f*) *m*.
trumpeting ['trʌmpɪtɪŋ] *n* (*of elephant*) Trompeten *nt*.
truncate [trʌŋ'keɪt] 1 *vt* kürzen, beschneiden; *tree* stutzen.
2 ['trʌŋkeɪt] *adj cone* stumpf; *leaf* abgestumpft.
truncated [trʌŋ'keɪtɪd] *adj tree* gestutzt; *article, speech* gekürzt; *cone* stumpf; *leaf* abgestumpft.
truncation [trʌŋ'keɪʃən] *n see vt* Kürzung, Beschneidung *f*; Stutzung *f*.
truncheon ['trʌntʃən] *n* (Gummi)knüppel *m*; (*esp of riot police*) Schlagstock *m*.
trundle ['trʌndl] 1 *vt* (*push*) rollen; (*pull*) ziehen.
2 *vi* **to ~ in/along/down** hinein-/entlang-/hinunterzockeln; (*clatter*) hinein-/entlang-/hinunterrumpeln.
trundle bed *n* (*US*) Rollbett *nt*.
trunk [trʌŋk] *n* **(a)** (*of tree*) Stamm *m*; (*of body*) Rumpf *m*.
(b) (*of elephant*) Rüssel *m*.
(c) (*case*) Schrankkoffer *m*; (*US Aut*) Kofferraum *m*.
(d) **~s** *pl* (*for swimming*) Badehose *f*; (*for sport*) Shorts *pl*; (*dated Brit: underwear*) Unterhose *f* ◆ **a pair of ~s** eine Badehose/(ein Paar *nt*) Shorts/eine Unterhose.
trunk: ~ call *n* (*Brit Telec*) Ferngespräch *nt*; **~ line** *n* (*Rail*) Hauptstrecke *f*; (*Telec*) Fernleitung *f*; **~ road** *n* (*Brit*) Fernstraße *f*.
truss [trʌs] 1 *n* **(a)** (*Brit: bundle*) Bündel *nt*, Garbe *f*. **(b)** (*Build*) (*of bridge*) Fachwerk *nt*; (*of roof*) Gespärre *nt*; (*single beam*) Dachsparren *m*; (*vertical*) Dachbalken *m*. **(c)** (*Med*) Bruchband *nt*.
2 *vt* **(a)** (*tie*) *hay* bündeln. **(b)** (*Cook*) *chicken etc* dressieren. **(c)** (*Build*) (ab)stützen.
◆**truss up** *vt sep* (*Cook*) *chicken etc* dressieren; (*inf*) *person* fesseln.
trust [trʌst] 1 *n* **(a)** (*confidence, reliance*) Vertrauen *nt* (*in* zu) ◆ **I have every ~ in him** ich habe volles Vertrauen zu ihm; **to put** *or* **place one's ~ in sb** Vertrauen in jdn setzen; **to take sth on ~** etw einfach glauben; **to give sb sth on ~** (*without payment*) jdm etw auf sein ehrliches Gesicht hin (*inf*) *or* im guten Glauben geben; **position of ~** Vertrauensstellung *f*.
(b) (*charge*) Verantwortung *f* ◆ **to commit sth to** *or* **place sth in sb's ~** jdm etw anvertrauen.
(c) (*Jur, Fin*) Treuhand(schaft) *f*; (*property*) Treuhandeigentum *nt*; (*charitable fund*) Fonds *m*, Stiftung *f* ◆ **to hold sth in ~ for sb** etw für jdn treuhänderisch verwalten; **all his money was tied up in a ~** sein ganzes Geld wurde treuhänderisch verwaltet; **~ account** Treuhandkonto *nt*; **~ fund** Treuhandvermögen *nt*; Stiftungsgelder *pl*; **~ territory** (*Pol*) Treuhandgebiet *nt*.
(d) (*Comm: also* **~ company**) Trust *m*.
2 *vt* **(a)** (*have confidence in*) trauen (*+dat*); *person also* vertrauen (*+dat*); *words* glauben ◆ **to ~ sb to do sth** (*believe him honest etc*) jdm vertrauen, daß er etw tut; (*believe him capable*) jdm zutrauen, daß er etw tut; **don't you ~ me?** vertraust du mir nicht?; **to ~ sb with sth, to ~ sth to sb** jdm etw anvertrauen; **I don't ~ her with her boyfriend** ich traue ihr und ihrem Freund nicht; **can he be ~ed not to lose it?** kann man sich darauf verlassen, daß er es nicht verliert?; **can we ~ him to go shopping alone?** können wir ihn allein einkaufen gehen lassen?; **you can't ~ a word he says** man kann ihm kein Wort glauben; **she won't ~ us out of her sight** sie läßt uns nicht aus den Augen; **I wouldn't ~ him (any) farther than I can throw him** (*inf*) ich traue ihm nicht über den Weg (*inf*).
(b) (*iro inf*) **~ you/him!** typisch!; **~ him to break it!** er muß es natürlich kaputtmachen.
(c) (*hope*) hoffen ◆ **I ~ not** hoffentlich nicht, ich hoffe nicht; **you're going to help, I ~** du wirst doch hoffentlich mithelfen.
3 *vi* **(a)** (*have confidence*) vertrauen ◆ **to ~ in sb** auf jdn vertrauen. **(b)** (*rely*

➤ LANGUAGE IN USE: **true: 1a** → 26.1, 26.3

on) **to ~ to sth** sich auf etw (*acc*) verlassen, auf etw (*acc*) vertrauen; **to ~ to luck** *or* **chance** sich auf sein Glück verlassen; **I'll have to ~ to luck to find it** ich kann nur hoffen, daß ich es finde.

trusted ['trʌstɪd] *adj method* bewährt; *friend, servant* getreu.

trustee [trʌs'ti:] *n* **(a)** (*of estate*) Treuhänder(in *f*), Vermögensverwalter(in *f*) *m*. **(b)** (*of institution*) Kurator, Verwalter *m* ◆ **~s** Vorstand *m*; **T~ Savings Bank** ≃ Sparkasse *f*.

trusteeship [trʌs'ti:ʃɪp] *n* **(a)** Treuhandschaft *f*. **(b)** (*of a territory*) Treuhandschaft *f*, Mandat *nt*. **(c)** (*also* **~ territory**) Treuhandgebiet, Mandat(sgebiet) *nt*.

trustful ['trʌstfʊl] *adj look, expression* vertrauensvoll; *person also* gutgläubig, arglos.

trustfully ['trʌstfəlɪ] *adv* vertrauensvoll.

trusting ['trʌstɪŋ] *adj see* **trustful**.

trustworthiness ['trʌst,wɜ:ðɪnɪs] *n see adj* Vertrauenswürdigkeit *f*; Glaubhaftigkeit, Glaubwürdigkeit *f*.

trustworthy ['trʌst,wɜ:ðɪ] *adj person* vertrauenswürdig; *statement, account* glaubhaft, glaubwürdig.

trusty ['trʌstɪ] *adj* (*+er*) (*liter, hum*) getreu (*liter*).

truth [tru:θ] *n, pl* **-s** [tru:ðz] **(a)** *no pl* Wahrheit *f* ◆ **you must always tell the ~** du mußt immer die Wahrheit sagen; **to tell the ~ ..., ~ to tell ...** um ehrlich zu sein ..., um die Wahrheit zu sagen ...; **the ~ of it** *or* **the matter is that ...** die Wahrheit ist, daß ..., in Wahrheit ...; **there's no ~** *or* **not a word of ~ in what he says** es ist kein Wort wahr von dem, was er sagt; **there's some ~ in that** es ist etwas Wahres daran, da ist etwas Wahres dran (*inf*); **the ~, the whole ~ and nothing but the ~** (*Jur*) die Wahrheit, die reine Wahrheit und nichts als die Wahrheit; **in ~** in Wahrheit, in Wirklichkeit; **~ will out** (*prov*) die Wahrheit wird ans Licht kommen, die Sonne wird es an den Tag bringen (*prov*); **~ drug** *or* **serum** Wahrheitsdroge *f*; **~ value** (*Logic*) Wahrheitswert *m*.
(b) (*belief, fact*) Wahrheit *f* ◆ **I told him a few ~s about his behaviour** ich habe ihm mal gesagt, was ich von seinem Benehmen halte; *see* **home ~**.

truthful ['tru:θfʊl] *adj person* ehrlich; *statement* ehrlich, wahrheitsgetreu ◆ **to be ~ about it** ehrlich sein.

truthfully ['tru:θfəlɪ] *adv* ehrlich; *answer, say also, explain* wahrheitsgemäß, der Wahrheit entsprechend.

truthfulness ['tru:θfʊlnɪs] *n* Ehrlichkeit, Aufrichtigkeit *f*; (*of statement*) Wahrheit *f*.

try [traɪ] **1** *n* **(a)** (*attempt*) Versuch *m* ◆ **to have a ~** es versuchen; **let me have a ~** laß mich mal versuchen!, laß mich mal! (*inf*); **to have a ~ at doing sth** (sich daran) versuchen, etw zu tun, (es) probieren, etw zu tun; **have another ~ (at it)** versuch's noch mal; **to have a ~ for sth** sich um etw bemühen; **I'll give it a ~** (*will attempt it*) ich werde es mal versuchen; (*will test it out*) ich werde es ausprobieren; **I'll give him a ~** ich werde ihm eine Chance geben; **it was a good ~** das war schon ganz gut; **it's worth a ~** es ist einen Versuch wert; **at the first ~** beim ersten Versuch, auf Anhieb; **can I have a ~ at your bicycle?** kann ich mal dein Rad ausprobieren?
(b) (*Rugby*) Versuch *m* ◆ **to score a ~** einen Versuch erzielen.
2 *vt* **(a)** (*attempt*) versuchen ◆ **you have only tried two questions** du hast dich nur an zwei Fragen versucht (*inf*), du hast nur zwei Fragen zu beantworten versucht; **to ~ one's hardest** *or* **one's best** sein Bestes tun *or* versuchen; **do ~ to understand** bitte versuche doch zu verstehen!; **I've given up ~ing to help him** ich habe es aufgegeben, ihm helfen zu wollen; **it's ~ing to rain** (*inf*) es sieht aus, als würde es regnen; **the sun's ~ing to come out** es sieht so aus, als wollte die Sonne rauskommen; **to ~ one's hand at sth** etw probieren; **I'll ~ anything once** ich probiere alles einmal; **just you ~ it!** (*dare*) versuch's bloß!
(b) (*~ out*) *new detergent, bicycle etc* ausprobieren; *job applicant* eine Chance geben (*+dat*), es versuchen mit (*inf*); (*~ it with*) *glue, aspirin* es versuchen mit; (*~ to buy or get sth at*) *newsagent, next door* es versuchen (bei); (*~ to open*) *door, window* ausprobieren ◆ **I can't shut this case — ~ sitting on it** ich kriege diesen Koffer nicht zu — setz dich doch mal drauf! (*inf*); **you could ~ seeing whether John would help** Sie könnten doch John mal um Hilfe angehen; **I've tried everything** ich habe alles versucht *or* probiert; **~ whether ...** probieren Sie, ob ...; **~ this for size** probieren Sie mal, ob dieser/diese *etc* paßt; (*fig inf*) wie wär's denn damit? (*inf*); **to ~ one's hand at sth** etw *or* sich an etw (*dat*) versuchen; **to ~ one's strength** seine Kraft erproben; **to ~ one's strength against sb** seine Kräfte mit jdm messen.
(c) (*sample, taste*) *beer, olives* probieren.
(d) (*test*) *courage, patience* auf die Probe stellen; (*strain*) *eyes* anstrengen ◆ **he was tried and found wanting** (*liter*) er wurde gewogen und zu leicht befunden; **(just) ~ me!** (*inf*) wetten?, wetten, daß?; **tried and tested** (*Comm*) erprobt, bewährt; **this product was tried and tested in our laboratories** dieses Produkt ist in unseren Labors getestet und geprüft worden; **theirs was a tried and tested friendship** ihre Freundschaft hatte sich bewährt; **they have been sorely tried** sie sind schwer geprüft (worden); **these things are sent to ~ us** ja, ja, das Leben ist nicht so einfach.
(e) (*Jur*) *person* vor Gericht stellen; *case* verhandeln ◆ **he will be/is being tried for theft** er wird wegen Diebstahls vor Gericht gestellt/er steht wegen Diebstahls vor Gericht.
3 *vi* versuchen ◆ **~ and arrive on time** versuch mal, pünktlich zu sein; **~ as he might, he didn't succeed** sosehr er es auch versuchte *or* sosehr er sich auch bemühte, er schaffte es einfach nicht; **he wasn't even ~ing** er hat sich (*dat*) überhaupt keine Mühe gegeben; (*didn't attempt it*) er hat es überhaupt nicht versucht; **you can't say I didn't ~** du kannst nicht sagen, ich hätte es nicht versucht; *see* **succeed**.

◆**try for** *vi +prep obj* sich bemühen um.

◆**try on** *vt sep* **(a)** *clothes* anprobieren; *hat* aufprobieren.
(b) (*fig inf*) **to ~ it ~ with sb** probieren, wie weit man bei jdm gehen kann, jdn provozieren; **the policeman warned the thief not to ~ anything ~** der Polizist warnte den Dieb, keine Mätzchen (*inf*) *or* Dummheiten zu machen; **he's ~ing it ~** er probiert, wie weit er gehen *or* es treiben kann; **don't you ~ it ~ with me, I'm not taking any excuses** versuch nicht, mir etwas vorzumachen, ich dulde keine Ausreden.

◆**try out** *vt sep* ausprobieren (*on* bei, an *+dat*); *person* eine Chance geben (*+dat*), einen Versuch machen mit ◆ **two of their players are ~ing ~ for Arsenal** zwei ihrer Spieler versuchen sich bei Arsenal.

◆**try over** *vt sep* (*Mus*) *piece* proben.

trying ['traɪɪŋ] *adj* schwierig, anstrengend; *work, day, time* anstrengend, aufreibend; *experience* schwer ◆ **they've had a ~ time of it recently** sie haben es in letzter Zeit sehr schwer gehabt; **how ~!** wie ärgerlich!

try: ~-on *n* (*inf*) **do you think he'll do what he threatened? — no, it was just a ~-on** glaubst du, er wird seine Drohung wahr machen? — nein, er wollte uns nur auf den Arm nehmen (*inf*); **~out** *n* (*of car*) Probefahrt *f*; (*Ftbl*) Probespiel *nt*; (*of applicant*) Probezeit *f*; (*of actor*) Probevortrag *m*; **to give sb/sth a ~out** jdm eine Chance geben/etw ausprobieren.

tryst [trɪst] *n* (*old*) Stelldichein *nt* (*dated*).

trysting place ['trɪstɪŋ,pleɪs] *n* (*old*) Stelldichein *nt* (*dated*).

tsar [zɑ:ʳ] *n* Zar *m*.

tsarina [zɑ:'ri:nə] *n* Zarin *f*.

tsarist ['zɑ:rɪst] **1** *n* Zarist *m*.
2 *adj* zaristisch.

tsetse (fly) ['tsetsɪ('flaɪ)] *n* Tsetsefliege *f*.

T-shirt ['ti:ʃɜ:t] *n* T-Shirt *nt*.

tsp(s) *abbr of* **teaspoonful(s), teaspoon(s)** Teel.

T-square ['ti:skweəʳ] *n* Reißschiene *f*.

TT *abbr of* **(a) teetotal. (b) teetotaller. (c)** (*Mot*) **Tourist Trophy** *jährlich auf der Insel Man abgehaltenes Motorradrennen*. **(d)** (*Agr*) **tuberculin-tested.**

TU (*Brit*) *abbr of* **Trade Union** Gew.

tub [tʌb] *n* **(a)** Kübel *m*; (*for rainwater*) Tonne, Traufe *f*; (*for washing*) Zuber, Bottich, Trog *m*; (*of ice-cream, margarine*) Becher *m*. **(b)** (*inf: bath~*) Wanne *f*. **(c)** (*inf: boat*) Kahn *m*.

tuba ['tju:bə] *n* Tuba *f*.

tubby ['tʌbɪ] *adj* (*+er*) (*inf*) dick; *woman* mollig, rundlich; *child* pummelig, kugelrund; *man* rundlich ◆ **he is getting quite ~** er geht immer mehr in die Breite, er wird immer runder.

tube [tju:b] *n* **(a)** (*pipe*) Rohr *nt*; (*of rubber, plastic*) Schlauch *m*; (*speaking ~*) Sprachrohr *nt*; (*torpedo ~*) (Torpedo)rohr *nt*.
(b) (*container*) (*of toothpaste, paint, glue*) Tube *f*; (*of sweets*) Röhrchen *nt*, Rolle *f*.
(c) (*London underground*) U-Bahn *f* ◆ **to travel by ~** mit der U-Bahn fahren; **~ station** U-Bahnstation *f*; **~ train** U-Bahnzug *m*.
(d) (*Elec, TV, US Rad*) Röhre *f* ◆ **the ~** (*US inf*) die Röhre (*inf*).
(e) (*Anat*) Röhre *f*; (*Fallopian*) Eileiter *m* ◆ **the bronchial ~s** die Bronchien *pl*.

tubeless ['tju:blɪs] *adj tyre* schlauchlos.

tuber ['tju:bəʳ] *n* (*Bot*) Knolle *f*.

tubercle ['tju:bɜ:kl] *n* (*Bot*) Knoten *m*, Knötchen *nt*; (*Med also*) Tuberkel *m*.

tubercular [tjʊ'bɜ:kjʊləʳ] *adj* tuberkulös.

tuberculin [tjʊ'bɜ:kjʊlɪn] *n* Tuberkulin *nt* ◆ **~-tested** tuberkulingetestet.

tuberculosis [tjʊ,bɜ:kjʊ'ləʊsɪs] *n* Tuberkulose *f*.

tuberculous [tjʊ'bɜ:kjʊləs] *adj* tuberkulös.

tubing ['tju:bɪŋ] *n* Schlauch *m*.

tub: ~-thumper *n* (*pej*) Demagoge, Volksredner *m*; **~-thumping** **1** *n* Demagogie *f*; **2** *adj* demagogisch.

tubular ['tju:bjʊləʳ] *adj* röhrenförmig, Röhren- ◆ **~ bells** Glockenspiel *nt*; **~ furniture/scaffolding** Stahlrohrmöbel *pl*/-gerüst *nt*.

TUC (*Brit*) *abbr of* **Trades Union Congress** *Gewerkschafts-Dachverband* ≃ DGB *m*.

tuck [tʌk] **1** *n* **(a)** (*Sew*) Saum *m*; (*ornamental*) Biese *f* ◆ **to put a ~ in sth** einen Saum in etw (*acc*) nähen.
(b) (*Sch sl: food*) Süßigkeiten *pl* ◆ **~ box** *Schachtel f mit Süßigkeiten*; **~ shop** Bonbonladen *m*.
2 *vt* **(a)** (*put*) stecken ◆ **he ~ed his umbrella under his arm** er steckte *or* klemmte (*inf*) sich (*dat*) den Regenschirm unter den Arm; **the bird's head was ~ed under its wing** der Vogel hatte den Kopf unter den Flügel gesteckt; **he ~ed his coat round the shivering child** er legte seinen Mantel fest um das frierende Kind; **she sat with her feet ~ed under her** sie saß mit untergeschlagenen Beinen da.
(b) (*Sew*) Biesen steppen in (*+acc*) ◆ **a ~ed bodice** ein Oberteil mit Biesen.
3 *vi* **your bag will ~ under the seat** du kannst deine Tasche unter dem Sitz verstauen.

◆**tuck away** *vt sep* **(a)** (*hide*) wegstecken ◆ **he ~ed it ~ in his pocket** er steckte es in die Tasche; **the hut is ~ed ~ among the trees** die Hütte liegt versteckt zwischen den Bäumen.
(b) (*inf: eat*) **he can certainly ~ it ~!** er kann ganz schön was wegputzen (*inf*); **I can't think where he ~s it all ~** ich weiß nicht, wo er das alles läßt (*inf*).

◆**tuck in** **1** *vi* (*inf*) zulangen, reinhauen (*inf*) ◆ **~ ~!** langt zu!, haut rein! (*inf*); **to ~ ~ to sth** sich (*dat*) etw schmecken lassen.
2 *vt sep* **(a)** *flap etc* hineinstecken, reinstecken (*inf*); *sheet also* an den Seiten feststecken ◆ **to ~ one's shirt ~(to) one's trousers, to ~ one's shirt ~** das

Hemd in die Hose stecken; **~ your tummy ~!** zieh den Bauch ein!
(b) to ~ sb ~ jdn zudecken; **to ~ sb ~to bed** jdn ins Bett stecken.

◆**tuck up** *vt sep* **(a)** *skirt, hair* hochnehmen; *sleeve* hochkrempeln; *legs* unterschlagen. **(b) to ~ sb ~ (in bed)** jdn zudecken.

tucker[1] ['tʌkəʳ] *n (old: Fashion)* Schultertuch *nt*; *see* **bib**.

tucker[2] *vt (US inf)* fertigmachen *(inf)*.

tucker[3] *n (esp Austral)* Proviant *m* ◆ **~bag** Proviantttasche *f*.

tuck-in ['tʌkɪn] *n (inf)* Essen *nt* ◆ **to have a (good) ~** kräftig zulangen, ordentlich futtern *(inf) or* reinhauen *(inf)*.

Tudor ['tju:dəʳ] [1] *adj* Tudor-.
[2] *n* Tudor *mf*.

Tue(s) *abbr of* **Tuesday** Di.

Tuesday ['tju:zdɪ] *n* Dienstag *m* ◆ **on ~** (am) Dienstag; **on ~s, on a ~** dienstags, an Dienstagen *(form)*; **I met her on a ~** ich habe sie an einem Dienstag kennengelernt; **on ~ morning/evening** (am) Dienstag morgen/abend, am Dienstagmorgen/-abend; **on ~ mornings/evenings** dienstags *or* Dienstag morgens/abends; **I'll never forget that ~ evening** diesen Dienstagabend werde ich nie vergessen; **last/next/this ~** Dienstag letzter/nächster/dieser Woche, letzten/nächsten/diesen Dienstag; **a year (ago) last/next ~** letzten/nächsten Dienstag vor einem Jahr; **~'s newspaper** die Zeitung vom Dienstag; **our ~ meeting** *(this week)* unser Treffen am Dienstag; *(every week)* unser dienstägliches Treffen, unser Dienstagstreffen; **~ December 5th** *(in letter)* Dienstag, den 5. Dezember.

tuffet ['tʌfɪt] *n (old)* kleiner Hügel, Buckel *m*.

tuft [tʌft] *n* Büschel *nt* ◆ **a ~ of hair/feathers** ein Haarbüschel *nt*/Federbusch *m*.

tufted ['tʌftɪd] *adj bird* Hauben-; *species (Orn)* mit Federbusch; *(Bot)* büschelförmig ◆ **~ duck** Reiherente *f*.

tug [tʌg] [1] *vt* zerren, ziehen; *vessel* (ab)schleppen ◆ **she ~ged his sleeve** sie zog an seinem Ärmel; **she ~ged a tuft of his hair out by the roots** sie zog *or* riß ihm ein Büschel Haare aus.
[2] *vi* ziehen, zerren *(at* an *+dat)*; *see* **heartstrings**.
[3] *n* **(a)** *(pull)* **to give sth a ~** an etw *(dat)* ziehen; **I felt a ~ on my sleeve** ich spürte, wie mich jemand am Ärmel zog; **parting with it was quite a ~** es fiel mir *etc* sehr schwer, mich *etc* davon zu trennen; **~ of war** *(Sport, fig)* Tauziehen *nt*; **~ of love** Tauziehen um das Kind/die Kinder bei einer Ehescheidung.
(b) *(also* **~boat**) Schlepper, Schleppkahn *m*.

tuition [tjʊ'ɪʃən] *n* Unterricht *m* ◆ **extra ~** Nachhilfeunterricht.

tulip ['tju:lɪp] *n* Tulpe *f* ◆ **~ tree** Tulpenbaum *m*.

tulle [tju:l] *n* Tüll *m*.

tumble ['tʌmbl] [1] *n* **(a)** *(fall)* Sturz *m* ◆ **to have a ~** stürzen; **to have a ~ in the hay** *(euph)* sich lieben; **to take a ~** stürzen, straucheln; *(fig)* fallen; **his pride has taken a ~** sein Stolz ist verletzt worden.
(b) *(mess)* Durcheinander *nt* ◆ **in a ~** völlig durcheinander.
[2] *vi* **(a)** *(fall)* straucheln, (hin)fallen; *(move quickly)* stürzen; *(fig: prices)* fallen ◆ **he ~d off his bicycle** er stürzte vom Fahrrad; **the children ~d up the stairs** die Kinder stürzten die Treppe hinauf; **to ~ out of/into bed** aus dem Bett/ins Bett fallen; **to ~ over sth** über etw *(acc)* fallen *or* stolpern.
(b) *(inf: realize)* **to ~ to sth** etw kapieren *(inf)*.
(c) *(gymnast)* Bodenakrobatik machen.
[3] *vt (make fall)* stoßen; *(make untidy) hair* zerzausen, durcheinanderbringen ◆ **he ~d the clothes out of the washing-machine** er zerrte die Kleider aus der Waschmaschine.

◆**tumble about** *vi* durcheinanderpurzeln; *(children, kittens etc)* herumpurzeln ◆ **the clothes ~d ~ in the drier** die Wäsche wurde im Trockenautomaten durcheinandergewirbelt.

◆**tumble down** *vi* **(a)** *(fall down) (person)* hinfallen, stürzen; *(object)* hinunter-/herunterfallen; *(building)* einstürzen ◆ **to ~ ~ the stairs** die Treppe hinunter-/herunterfallen. **(b)** *(move quickly)* **they came tumbling ~ the stairs** sie kamen die Treppe heruntergestürzt.

◆**tumble in** *vi (come in)* hereinpurzeln.

◆**tumble out** *vi (go out)* heraus-/hinauspurzeln.

◆**tumble over** *vi* umfallen, umkippen.

tumble: ~down *adj* verfallen, baufällig; **~-drier** *n* Trockenautomat, Heißlufttrockner *m*.

tumbler ['tʌmbləʳ] *n* **(a)** *(glass)* (Becher)glas *nt*, Tumbler *m*. **(b)** *(in lock)* Zuhaltung *f*. **(c)** *(acrobat)* Bodenakrobat *m*. **(d)** *(toy)* Stehaufmännchen *nt*. **(e)** *(tumble drier)* Trockenautomat *m*. **(f)** *(Orn)* Tümmler *m*.

tumbleweed ['tʌmbl,wi:d] *n (US)* Steppenläufer *m or* -hexe *f*.

tumbrel, tumbril ['tʌmbrəl] *n (Hist)* Karren *m*.

tumescence [tu:'mesns] *n (form)* Schwellung *f*.

tumescent [tju:'mesnt] *adj (form)* anschwellend.

tumid ['tju:mɪd] *adj (Med)* geschwollen; *(fig) style, speech* schwülstig; *style also* geschwollen.

tummy ['tʌmɪ] *n (inf)* Bauch *m*, Bäuchlein *nt (baby-talk)* ◆ **those green apples will give you (a) ~ ache** von diesen grünen Äpfeln kriegst du Bauchschmerzen *or* Bauchweh.

tumour, *(US)* **tumor** ['tju:məʳ] *n* Geschwulst *f*, Tumor *m* ◆ **a ~ on the brain, a brain ~** ein Gehirntumor *m*.

tumult ['tju:mʌlt] *n* **(a)** *(uproar)* Tumult *m* ◆ **the ~ of battle** das Schlachtgetümmel. **(b)** *(emotional)* **his mind was in a ~** sein Inneres befand sich in Aufruhr; **a ~ of rage/emotion/weeping** ein Wut-/Gefühls-/Tränenausbruch *m*.

tumultuous [tju:'mʌltjʊəs] *adj* tumultartig, stürmisch; *applause* stürmisch ◆ **they gave him a ~ welcome** sie begrüßten ihn stürmisch; **a ~ sea** stürmische See.

tumultuously [tju:'mʌltjʊəslɪ] *adv* stürmisch.

tumulus ['tju:mjʊləs] *n* Tumulus, Grabhügel *m*.

tun [tʌn] *n (cask)* Faß *nt*.

tuna (fish) ['tju:nə('fɪʃ)] *n* Thunfisch *m*.

tundra ['tʌndrə] *n* Tundra *f*.

tune [tju:n] [1] *n* **(a)** *(melody)* Melodie *f* ◆ **sung to the ~ of ...** gesungen nach der Melodie (von) ...; **there's not much ~ to it** das ist *or* klingt nicht sehr melodisch; **give us a ~!** spiel uns was vor!; **to change one's ~** *(fig)* seine Meinung ändern; **to the ~ of £100** in Höhe von £ 100.
(b) *(pitch)* **to sing in ~/out of ~** richtig/falsch singen; **the piano is out of ~** das Klavier ist verstimmt; **to go out of ~** *(instrument)* sich verstimmen; *(singer)* anfangen, falsch zu singen; **the piano is not in ~ with the flute** das Klavier und die Flöte sind nicht gleich gestimmt; **to be in/out of ~ with sb/sth** *(fig)* mit jdm/etw harmonieren/nicht harmonieren, mit jdm/etw in Einklang/nicht in Einklang stehen; **he's a successful teacher because he's in ~ with the young** er ist ein erfolgreicher Lehrer, weil er auf der gleichen Wellenlänge mit den Jugendlichen ist *(inf)*; **he felt out of ~ with his new environment** er fühlte sich in seiner neuen Umgebung fehl am Platze.
(c) *(Aut)* **the carburettor is out of ~** der Vergaser ist falsch eingestellt.
[2] *vt* **(a)** *(Mus) instrument* stimmen.
(b) *(Rad)* einstellen ◆ **you are ~d to the BBC World Service** Sie hören den *or* hier ist der BBC World Service.
(c) *(Aut) engine, carburettor* einstellen.

◆**tune in** [1] *vi (Rad)* einschalten ◆ **to ~ ~ to Radio London** Radio London einschalten *or* hören.
[2] *vt sep radio* einschalten *(to acc)* ◆ **you are ~d ~ to Radio 2** Sie hören *or* hier ist Radio 2.

◆**tune up** [1] *vi (Mus)* (sein Instrument/die Instrumente) stimmen.
[2] *vt sep (Aut) engine* tunen.

tuneful *adj*, **~ly** *adv* ['tju:nfʊl, -fəlɪ] melodisch.

tunefulness ['tju:nfʊlnɪs] *n* Melodik *f* ◆ **the ~ of her voice** ihre melodische Stimme.

tuneless *adj*, **~ly** *adv* ['tju:nlɪs, -lɪ] unmelodisch.

tuner ['tju:nəʳ] *n* **(a)** *(Mus)* Stimmer *m*. **(b)** *(Rad etc) (part of set)* Empfangsteil *nt*; *(separate set)* Empfänger, Tuner *m* ◆ **~-amp(lifier)** Steuergerät *nt*, Receiver *m*.

tune-up ['tju:nʌp] *n (Aut)* **the car needs/has had a ~** das Auto muß getunt werden/ist getunt worden.

tungsten ['tʌŋstən] *n* Wolfram *nt* ◆ **~ lamp/steel** Wolframlampe *f*/-stahl *m*.

tunic ['tju:nɪk] *n* Kasack *m*, Hemdbluse *f*; *(of uniform)* Uniformrock *m*; *(of school uniform)* Kittel *m*; *(in ancient Greece)* Chiton *m*; *(in ancient Rome)* Tunika *f*.

tuning ['tju:nɪŋ] *n* **(a)** *(Mus)* Stimmen *nt* ◆ **~-fork** Stimmgabel *f*.
(b) *(Rad)* Einstellen *nt* ◆ **it takes a lot of ~ to find the right station** man muß lange suchen, bis man den richtigen Sender gefunden hat; **~ knob** Stationswahlknopf *m*.
(c) *(Aut)* Einstellen *nt* ◆ **all the engine needed was a little ~** der Motor mußte nur richtig eingestellt werden.

Tunisia [tju:'nɪzɪə] *n* Tunesien *nt*.

Tunisian [tju:'nɪzɪən] [1] *n* Tunesier(in *f*) *m*.
[2] *adj* tunesisch.

tunnel ['tʌnl] [1] *n* Tunnel *m*; *(under road, railway also)* Unterführung *f*; *(Min)* Stollen *m* ◆ **at last we can see the light at the end of the ~** *(fig)* endlich sehen wir wieder Licht; **that for me was always the light at the end of the ~** *(fig)* das war für mich immer ein Hoffnungsfunken; **~ vision** *(Med)* Gesichtsfeldeinengung *f*; *(fig)* Engstirnigkeit *f*, beschränkter Horizont.
[2] *vi (into* in *+acc, through* durch) einen Tunnel bauen; *(rabbit)* einen Bau graben; *(mole)* Gänge graben ◆ **they ~led under the walls of the jail** sie gruben (sich *dat*) einen Tunnel unter den Mauern des Gefängnisses hindurch.
[3] *vt* **they ~led a road through the mountain** sie bauten einen Straßentunnel durch den Berg; **they ~led a passage under the prison wall** sie gruben sich unter der Gefängnismauer durch; **the hillside had been ~led by rabbits** Kaninchen hatten ihre Baue in den Hang gegraben; **to ~ one's way through sth** sich durch etw hindurchgraben.

◆**tunnel out** *vi* sich *(dat)* einen Fluchttunnel graben.

tunny (fish) ['tʌnɪ('fɪʃ)] *n* Thunfisch *m*.

tuppence ['tʌpəns] *n* zwei Pence ◆ **I don't care ~** das interessiert mich nicht für fünf Pfennig *(inf)*, das ist mir doch so egal *(inf)*.

tuppenny ['tʌpənɪ] *adj* für zwei Pence; *stamp, piece etc* Zwei-pence- ◆ **~ bit** Zwei-pencestück *nt*.

tuppenny-ha'penny ['tʌpnɪ'heɪpnɪ] *adj (Brit inf)* lächerlich.

turban ['tɜ:bən] *n* Turban *m*.

turbid ['tɜ:bɪd] *adj* **(a)** *liquid* trübe, schmutzig ◆ **~ clouds of smoke** dicke Rauchwolken. **(b)** *(fig: confused)* verworren.

turbidity [tɜ:'bɪdɪtɪ] *n see adj* **(a)** Trübheit, Schmutzigkeit *f*. **(b)** Verworrenheit *f*.

turbine ['tɜ:baɪn] *n* Turbine *f*.

turbocharged ['tɜ:bəʊ,tʃɑ:dʒd] *adj car, engine* mit Turboaufladung.

turbocharger ['tɜ:bəʊ,tʃɑ:dʒəʳ] *n* Turbolader *m*.

turbojet ['tɜ:bəʊ'dʒet] *n (engine)* Turbotriebwerk *nt*; *(aircraft)* Düsenflugzeug *nt*, Turbojet *m*.

turboprop ['tɜ:bəʊ'prɒp] *n (engine)* Propellerturbine, Turboprop *f*; *(aircraft)*

Turbo-Prop-Flugzeug *nt*.

turbot ['tɜ:bət] *n* Steinbutt *m*.

turbulence ['tɜ:bjʊləns] *n* (*of person, crowd*) Ungestüm *nt*, Wildheit *f*; (*of emotions*) Aufgewühltheit *f*; (*of career, period*) Turbulenz *f* ◆ **air ~** Turbulenzen *pl*; **the ~ of the water** das stürmische Wasser.

turbulent ['tɜ:bjʊlənt] *adj* stürmisch; *person, crowd* ungestüm, wild; *emotions also* aufgewühlt; *career, period also* turbulent.

turd [tɜ:d] *n* (*vulg*) **(a)** Kacke (*sl*), Scheiße (*sl*) *f no pl*; (*single*) Haufen *m* (*inf*). **(b)** (*pej: person*) Scheißkerl *m* (*sl*).

tureen [tə'ri:n] *n* (Suppen)terrine *f*.

turf [tɜ:f] [1] *n, pl* **-s** *or* **turves (a)** (*no pl: lawn*) Rasen *m*; (*no pl: squares of grass*) Soden *pl*; (*square of grass*) Sode *f*.
(b) (*no pl: peat*) Torf(soden *pl*) *m*; (*square of peat*) Torfsode *f* ◆ **to cut ~(s)** Torf(soden) stechen.
(c) (*Sport*) **the T~** die (Pferde)rennbahn; **all his life he was a devotee of the T~** sein Leben galt dem Pferderennsport; **~ accountant** Buchmacher *m*.
[2] *vt* **(a) he ~ed the garden** er verlegte (Gras)soden im Garten. **(b)** (*inf*) **to ~ sb down the stairs** jdn die Treppe hinunterscheuchen (*inf*); **to ~ sth into the corner/up in the attic** etw in die Ecke/auf den Dachboden werfen.

◆**turf out** *vt sep* (*inf*) *person* rauswerfen, rausschmeißen (*inf*); *plan* umschmeißen (*inf*), verwerfen; *suggestions* abtun; (*throw away*) wegschmeißen (*inf*).

◆**turf over** *vt sep* **(a)** *garden* mit (Gras)soden bedecken. **(b)** (*inf: throw over*) rüberwerfen (*inf*) (*to sb* jdm).

turgid ['tɜ:dʒɪd] *adj* (*swollen*) (an)geschwollen; (*fig*) *style* schwülstig, überladen.

turgidity [tɜ:'dʒɪdɪtɪ] *n see adj* Schwellung *f*; Schwülstigkeit *f* ◆ **the ~ of this writer's style** der schwülstige Stil dieses Schriftstellers.

Turk [tɜ:k] *n* Türke *m*, Türkin *f*.

Turkey ['tɜ:kɪ] *n* die Türkei.

turkey ['tɜ:kɪ] *n* **(a)** Truthahn *m*/-henne *f*, Pute(r) *mf* (*esp Cook*). **(b) to talk ~** (*US inf*) Tacheles reden (*inf*).

turkey: ~ buzzard *n* Truthahngeier *m*; **~cock** *n* Truthahn, Puter (*esp Cook*) *m*; **he's a real little ~cock of a man** er ist ein richtiger kleiner Fatzke (*inf*).

Turkish ['tɜ:kɪʃ] [1] *adj* türkisch ◆ **~ bath** türkisches Bad; **~ delight** Lokum *nt*; **~ towel** Frotteehandtuch *nt*.
[2] *n* (*language*) Türkisch *nt*.

turmeric ['tɜ:mərɪk] *n* Kurkuma, Gelbwurz *f*.

turmoil ['tɜ:mɔɪl] *n* Aufruhr *m*; (*confusion*) Durcheinander *nt* ◆ **he was glad to escape from the ~ of politics** er war froh, daß er sich aus der Hektik der Politik zurückziehen konnte; **everything is in a ~** alles ist in Aufruhr; **her mind was in a ~** sie war völlig verwirrt; **her mind was in a ~ of indecision** sie wußte überhaupt nicht mehr, wie sie sich entscheiden sollte.

turn [tɜ:n] [1] *n* **(a)** (*movement*) Drehung *f* ◆ **six ~s of the wheel** sechs Umdrehungen des Rades; **to give sth a ~** etw drehen; **give the handle another ~** dreh den Griff noch einmal herum; **done to a ~** (*Cook*) genau richtig.
(b) (*change of direction*) (*in road*) Kurve *f*; (*Sport*) Wende *f* ◆ **to make a ~ to the left** nach links einbiegen; (*driver, car also, road*) nach links abbiegen; (*road*) eine Linkskurve machen; **take the left-hand ~** biegen Sie links ab; **to make a ~ to port** (*Naut*) nach Backbord abdrehen; **"no left ~"** „Linksabbiegen verboten"; **the Canadian swimmer made the better ~** der kanadische Schwimmer wendete besser; **he gets his horse to make a very tight ~** er wendet sein Pferd sehr eng; **watch out for that sudden ~ in the road** paß auf, die Straße macht eine scharfe Kurve; **the ~ of the tide** der Gezeitenwechsel; **the children were trapped on the island by the ~ of the tide** die Kinder wurden durch das Einsetzen der Flut auf der Insel festgehalten; **the government just seems to be sitting back waiting for the ~ of the tide** (*fig*) die Regierung scheint einfach nur dazusitzen und auf einen Umschwung *or* eine Wende zu warten; **the tide is on the ~** (*lit*) die Ebbe/Flut setzt ein, die See ist im Stau (*spec*); (*fig*) es tritt eine Wende ein; **the milk/meat is on the ~** die Milch/das Fleisch hat einen Stich; **at the ~ of the century** um die Jahrhundertwende; **at the ~ of the 18th century** an der *or* um die Wende des 18. Jahrhunderts; **the ~ of the year** die Jahreswende, der Jahreswechsel; **at every ~** (*fig*) auf Schritt und Tritt; **things took a ~ for the worse/the better** die Dinge wendeten sich zum Guten/zum Schlechten; **the patient took a ~ for the worse/the better** das Befinden des Patienten wendete sich zum Schlechteren/zum Besseren; **things took a new ~** die Dinge nahmen eine neue Wendung; **I'm very upset by the ~ of events** ich bin über den Verlauf der Dinge sehr beunruhigt; **events took a tragic ~** die Dinge nahmen einen tragischen *or* verhängnisvollen Verlauf.
(c) (*in game, queue, series*) **in ~** der Reihe nach; **out of ~** außer der Reihe; **it's your ~** du bist an der Reihe *or* dran; **it's your ~ to do the washing-up** du bist mit (dem) Abwaschen an der Reihe *or* dran; **it's your ~ to serve** (*Tennis*) du schlägst auf; **now it's his ~ to be jealous** jetzt ist er zur Abwechslung eifersüchtig; **whose ~ is it?** wer ist an der Reihe *or* dran?; **it's my ~ next** ich komme als nächste(r) an die Reihe *or* dran; **wait your ~** warten Sie, bis Sie an der Reihe sind; **to miss a ~** eine Runde aussetzen; **your ~ will come** du kommst auch noch mal dran; **my secretary was speaking out of ~** es stand meiner Sekretärin nicht zu, sich darüber zu äußern; **sorry, have I spoken out of ~?** Entschuldigung, habe ich etwas Falsches gesagt?; **and then Anne Boleyn too, in her ~, ...** und dann kam auch die Reihe an Anne Boleyn ...; **~ and ~ about** abwechselnd; **the children will just have to take ~ and ~ about with the swing** die Kinder werden eben abwechselnd schaukeln müssen; **in ~, by ~s** abwechselnd; **she was confident then depressed by ~s** sie war abwechselnd zuversichtlich und deprimiert; **to take ~s at doing sth, to take it in ~(s) to do sth** etw abwechselnd tun; **take it in ~s!** wechselt euch ab!; **to take ~s at the wheel** sich am Steuer *or* beim Fahren abwechseln; **to take a ~ at the wheel** (für eine Weile) das Steuer übernehmen.
(d) (*service*) **to do sb a good/bad ~** jdm einen guten/schlechten Dienst erweisen; **a boy scout has to do a good ~ every day** ein Pfadfinder muß jeden Tag eine gute Tat tun; **one good ~ deserves another** (*Prov*) eine Hand wäscht die andere (*prov*), hilfst du mir, so helf ich dir.
(e) (*tendency, talent*) Hang *m*, Neigung *f* ◆ **to have a mathematical ~ of mind** mathematisch begabt sein; **an optimistic/a strange ~ of mind** eine optimistische/seltsame Einstellung; **a melancholy ~ of mind** ein Hang zur Melancholie.
(f) (*Med inf*) **he had one of his ~s last night** er hatte letzte Nacht wieder einen Anfall; **you/it gave me quite a ~** du hast/es hat mir einen schönen Schrecken eingejagt.
(g) (*Theat*) Nummer *f* ◆ **they got him to do a ~ at the party** sie brachten ihn dazu, auf der Party etwas zum besten zu geben; **isn't he a ~!** (*inf*) ist er nicht ein richtiger Komiker?
(h) (*purpose*) **it will serve my ~** das ist für meine Zwecke gerade richtig; **we'll throw these old carpets away once they've served their ~** wir werfen diese alten Teppiche weg, wenn sie ihren Zweck erfüllt *or* wenn sie ausgedient haben.
(i) (*walk, stroll*) **to take a ~ in the park** eine Runde durch den Park machen.
(j) ~ of phrase Ausdrucksweise *f*; **to have a good ~ of speed** (*car*) sehr schnell fahren; (*horse, athlete*) sehr schnell sein.
[2] *vt* **(a)** (*revolve*) *knob, key, screw, steering wheel* drehen ◆ **to ~ the key in the lock** den Schlüssel im Schloß herumdrehen; **what ~s the wheel?** wie wird das Rad angetrieben?; **he ~ed the wheel sharply** er riß das Steuer herum.
(b) he ~ed his head towards me er wandte mir den Kopf zu; **he ~ed his back to the wall** er kehrte den Rücken zur Wand; **success has ~ed his head** der Erfolg ist ihm zu Kopf gestiegen; **she seems to have ~ed his head** sie scheint ihm den Kopf verdreht zu haben; **she can still ~ a few heads** die Leute schauen sich immer noch nach ihr um; **to ~ sb's brain** jds Sinne *or* Geist verwirren; **the tragedy ~ed his brain** durch die Tragödie ist er völlig verstört; **as soon as his back is ~ed** sobald er den Rücken kehrt; **to ~ one's eyes towards sb** jdn anblicken; **the sight of all that food quite ~ed my stomach** beim Anblick des vielen Essens drehte sich mir regelrecht der Magen um; **without ~ing a hair** ohne mit der Wimper zu zucken; **he can ~ his hand to anything** er kann alles, er ist sehr geschickt; **she ~ed her hand to cooking** sie versuchte sich im Kochen.
(c) (*~ over*) *mattress, collar, soil, hay* wenden; *record* umdrehen; *page* umblättern.
(d) (*change position of, ~ round*) *car, lorry* wenden; *chair, picture etc* umdrehen.
(e) (*direct*) **to ~ one's thoughts/attention to sth** seine Gedanken/Aufmerksamkeit einer Sache (*dat*) zuwenden; **to ~ one's steps homeward** seine Schritte heimwärts lenken (*liter, hum*); **to ~ a gun on sb** ein Gewehr auf jdn richten; **the police ~ed the hoses on the demonstrators** die Polizei richtete die Wasserwerfer auf die Demonstranten.
(f) (*pass*) **he is** *or* **has ~ed forty** er hat die Vierzig überschritten; **it is** *or* **has ~ed 2 o'clock** es ist 2 Uhr vorbei.
(g) the car ~ed the corner das Auto bog um die Ecke; **to have ~ed the corner** (*fig*) über den Berg sein.
(h) (*transform, make become*) verwandeln (*in(to)* in *+acc*) ◆ **the play was ~ed into a film** das Stück wurde verfilmt; **to ~ verse into prose** Lyrik in Prosa übertragen; **to ~ English expressions into German** aus englischen Ausdrücken deutsche machen; **the shock ~ed his hair grey overnight** durch den Schock bekam er über Nacht graue Haare; **that house ~s me green with envy** das Haus läßt mich vor Neid erblassen; **the smoke ~ed the walls black** der Rauch schwärzte die Wände; **to ~ the lights low** das Licht herunterdrehen; **this hot weather has ~ed the milk (sour)** bei dieser Hitze ist die Milch sauer geworden.
(i) (*deflect*) **nothing will ~ him from his purpose** nichts wird ihn von seinem Vorhaben abbringen.
(j) (*shape*) *wood* drechseln; *metal, pot* drehen ◆ **a well-~ed sentence/leg** ein gutformulierter Satz/wohlgeformtes Bein.
(k) (*set*) **to ~ a boat adrift** ein Boot losmachen und treiben lassen; **to ~ sb loose** jdn loslassen *or* laufen lassen; **the children were ~ed loose on the moor** man ließ die Kinder in der Heide laufen; **to ~ a dog on sb** einen Hund auf jdn hetzen.
[3] *vi* **(a)** (*revolve, move round: key, screw, wheel*) sich drehen ◆ **the world ~s on its axis** die Erde dreht sich um ihre Achse; **he ~ed to me and smiled** er drehte sich mir zu und lächelte; **this tap won't ~** dieser Hahn läßt sich nicht drehen; **to ~ upside down** umkippen; **my head is ~ing** in meinem Kopf dreht sich alles; **his stomach ~ed at the sight** bei dem Anblick drehte sich ihm der Magen um; *see* **tail, toss, turtle**.
(b) (*change direction*) (*to one side*) (*person, car*) abbiegen; (*plane, boat*) abdrehen; (*~ around*) wenden; (*person: on the spot*) sich umdrehen; (*wind*) drehen ◆ **to ~ and go back** umkehren; **to ~ (to the) left** links abbiegen; **left ~!** (*Mil*) linksum!; **our luck ~ed** unser Glück wendete sich.
(c) (*go*) **to ~ to sb/sth** sich an jdn wenden/sich einer Sache (*dat*) zuwenden; **after her death, he ~ed to his books for comfort** nach ihrem Tod suchte er Trost bei seinen Büchern; **this job would make anyone ~ to drink!** bei dieser Arbeit muß man ja zum Trinker werden!; **our thoughts ~ to those who ...** wir gedenken derer, die ...; **the conversation ~ed to the accident** das Gespräch kam auf den Unfall, man kam auf den Unfall zu sprechen; **I don't know which way** *or* **where to ~ for help/money** ich weiß nicht, an wen

ich mich um Hilfe wenden kann/wen ich um Geld bitten kann; **I don't know which way to ~** ich weiß nicht, was ich machen soll.
(d) *(leaves)* sich (ver)färben; *(milk)* sauer werden; *(meat)* schlecht werden; *(weather)* umschlagen ◆ **to ~ into sth** sich in etw *(acc)* verwandeln; *(develop into)* sich zu etw entwickeln; **their short holiday ~ed into a three-month visit** aus ihrem Kurzurlaub wurde ein Aufenthalt von drei Monaten; **the prince ~ed into a frog** der Prinz verwandelte sich in einen Frosch; **his admiration ~ed to scorn** seine Bewunderung verwandelte sich in Verachtung; **to ~ to stone** zu Stein werden.
(e) *(become)* werden ◆ **to ~ traitor** zum Verräter werden; **XY, an actor ~ed director, ...** der Regisseur XY, ein ehemaliger Schauspieler, ...; **he began to ~ awkward** er wurde unangenehm *or* ungemütlich; **to ~ red** *(leaves etc)* sich rot färben; *(person: blush)* rot werden; *(traffic lights)* auf Rot umspringen; **his hair is ~ing grey** sein Haar wird grau; **he has** *or* **is just ~ed 18** er ist gerade 18 geworden.

◆**turn about** [1] *vi (person)* sich umdrehen; *(car, boat, driver etc)* wenden ◆ **we had to ~ ~ and go home** wir mußten umkehren (und nach Hause gehen).
[2] *vt sep car* wenden ◆ **he ~ed himself ~** er wandte sich um.

◆**turn against** [1] *vi +prep obj* sich wenden gegen.
[2] *vt sep +prep obj* **they ~ed him ~ his parents** sie brachten ihn gegen seine Eltern auf; **they ~ed his argument ~ him** sie verwendeten sein Argument gegen ihn.

◆**turn around** [1] *vt sep* **(a)** *see* **turn about 2. (b)** *(factory, docks) ship etc* abfertigen; *goods* fertigstellen.
[2] *vi +prep obj corner* biegen um.
[3] *vi see* **turn about 1** ◆ **the wheel ~s around on its axis** das Rad dreht sich um seine Achse.

◆**turn aside** [1] *vi* sich abwenden *(from* von).
[2] *vt sep* abwenden.

◆**turn away** [1] *vi* sich abwenden.
[2] *vt sep* **(a)** *(move) head, eyes, gun* abwenden. **(b)** *(send away) person* wegschicken, abweisen; *business* zurückweisen, ablehnen.

◆**turn back** [1] *vi* **(a)** *(traveller)* zurückgehen, umkehren; *(plane)* umkehren; *(look back)* sich umdrehen ◆ **we can't ~ ~ now, there's no ~ing ~ now** *(fig)* jetzt gibt es kein Zurück mehr. **(b)** *(in book)* zurückblättern *(to* auf *+acc)*.
[2] *vt sep* **(a)** *(fold) bedclothes* zurück- *or* aufschlagen; *corner* umknicken; *hem* umschlagen.
(b) *(send back) person* zurückschicken ◆ **bad weather ~ed the plane ~ to Heathrow** schlechtes Wetter zwang das Flugzeug zur Rückkehr nach Heathrow; **they were ~ed ~ at the frontier** sie wurden an der Grenze zurückgewiesen.
(c) *clock* zurückstellen; *(fig)* zurückdrehen ◆ **to ~ the clock ~ fifty years** die Uhr um fünfzig Jahre zurückdrehen.

◆**turn down** [1] *vt sep* **(a)** *bedclothes* zurück- *or* aufschlagen; *collar, brim* herunterklappen; *corner of page* umknicken.
(b) *gas, heat* herunterdrehen, kleiner stellen; *volume, radio, television* leiser stellen; *lights* herunterdrehen.
(c) *(refuse) candidate, novel etc* ablehnen; *offer also* zurückweisen; *suitor* abweisen.
(d) *card* verdeckt hin- *or* ablegen.
[2] *vi +prep obj* **he ~ed ~ a side street** er bog in eine Seitenstraße ab.

◆**turn in** [1] *vi* **(a) her toes ~ ~ when she walks** sie läuft nach innen, sie läuft über den großen Onkel *(inf)*.
(b) *(drive in)* **the car ~ed ~ at the top of the drive** das Auto bog in die Einfahrt ein.
(c) *(inf: go to bed)* sich hinhauen *(inf)*, in die Falle gehen *(inf)*.
(d) to ~ ~ on oneself sich in sich *(acc)* selbst zurückziehen.
[2] *vt sep* **(a) she ~ed ~ her toes as she walked** sie lief nach innen, sie lief über den großen Onkel *(inf)*; **to ~ ~ the ends of sth** die Enden von etw umschlagen.
(b) *(inf: to police)* **to ~ sb ~** jdn anzeigen *or* verpfeifen *(inf)*.
(c) *(inf: give back) equipment* zurückgeben *or* -bringen; *weapons (to police)* abgeben *(to* bei).
(d) *(exchange)* eintauschen *(for* gegen).
(e) *(Brit sl)* **~ it ~!** jetzt mach aber mal einen Punkt! *(inf)*.

◆**turn into** *vti +prep obj see* **turn 2 (h), 3 (d)**.

◆**turn off** [1] *vi* abbiegen *(for* nach, *prep obj* von).
[2] *vt sep* **(a)** *light* ausdrehen, ausmachen *(inf)*; *gas, radio also* abdrehen; *tap* zudrehen; *TV programme* abschalten; *water, electricity, engine, machine* abstellen.
(b) *(sl)* **to ~ sb ~** *(disgust)* jdn anwidern; *(put off)* jdm die Lust verderben *or* nehmen; **when they mentioned the price that ~ed me right ~** als sie den Preis nannten, war für mich der Kuchen gegessen *(sl)*; **this town really ~s me ~** diese Stadt stinkt mir *(sl)*.

◆**turn on** [1] *vi (Rad, TV)* **we ~ed ~ at 8 o'clock** wir haben um 8 Uhr eingeschaltet.
[2] *vt sep* **(a)** *gas, heat* anstellen, anmachen *(inf)*; *radio, television, the news also* einschalten; *light* einschalten, andrehen, anmachen *(inf)*; *tap, central heating* aufdrehen; *bath water* einlaufen lassen; *engine, machine* anstellen ◆ **to ~ ~ the charm** seinen (ganzen) Charme spielen lassen; **he can really ~ ~ the charm** er kann wirklich sehr charmant sein.
(b) *(sl: with drugs)* anturnen *(sl)*.
(c) *(sl: appeal to: music, novel etc)* **sth ~s sb ~** jd steht auf etw *(acc) (sl)*, jd findet etw Spitze *(sl)*, jd fährt auf etw *(acc)* voll ab *(sl)*; **whatever ~s you ~** wenn du das gut findest *(inf)*; **he/it doesn't ~ me ~** er/das läßt mich kalt *(also sexually)*.
(d) *(sl: sexually)* scharf machen *(sl)*, anmachen *(sl)* ◆ **she really ~s me ~** auf sie kann ich voll abfahren *(sl)*; **you know how to ~ me ~** du kannst mich wirklich auf Touren bringen *(sl)*; **it ~s me ~ when ...** ich werde ganz scharf, wenn ... *(inf)*.
[3] *vi +prep obj* **(a)** *(~ against)* sich wenden gegen; *(attack)* angreifen.
(b) *(depend on)* abhängen von, ankommen auf *(+acc)*.

◆**turn out** [1] *vi* **(a)** *(appear, attend)* erscheinen, kommen.
(b) *(firemen, police)* ausrücken; *(doctor)* einen Krankenbesuch machen.
(c) *(point)* **his feet ~ ~** er läuft nach außen.
(d) the car ~ed ~ of the drive das Auto bog aus der Einfahrt.
(e) *(transpire)* sich herausstellen ◆ **he ~ed ~ to be the murderer** es stellte sich heraus, daß er der Mörder war.
(f) *(develop, progress)* sich entwickeln, sich machen *(inf)* ◆ **how did it ~ ~?** *(what happened)* was ist daraus geworden?; *(cake etc)* wie ist er *etc* geworden?; **it all depends how things ~ ~** es kommt darauf an, wie sich die Dinge ergeben; **as it ~ed ~** wie sich herausstellte; **everything will ~ ~ all right** es wird sich schon alles ergeben.
[2] *vt sep* **(a)** *light* ausmachen; *gas also* abstellen.
(b) he ~s his feet ~ er läuft nach außen.
(c) *(produce)* produzieren; *novel etc* schreiben ◆ **the college ~s ~ good teachers** das College bringt gute Lehrer hervor.
(d) *(expel)* vertreiben (of aus), hinauswerfen *(inf)* (of aus); *tenant* kündigen *(+dat)*, auf die Straße setzen *(inf)* ◆ **he was ~ed ~ of his job** er verlor seinen Arbeitsplatz.
(e) *(Cook: tip out) cake* stürzen ◆ **he ~ed the photos ~ of the box** er kippte die Fotos aus der Schachtel.
(f) *(empty) pockets* (aus)leeren.
(g) *(clean) room* gründlich saubermachen.
(h) *guard* antreten lassen.
(i) *(usu pass: dress)* **well ~ed-~** gut gekleidet *or* ausstaffiert; *troops* tadellos, geschniegelt und gestriegelt *(inf)*.

◆**turn over** [1] *vi* **(a)** *(person)* sich umdrehen; *(car, plane etc)* sich überschlagen; *(boat)* umkippen, kentern; *(stomach)* sich umdrehen ◆ **he ~ed ~ on(to) his back/stomach** er drehte sich auf den Rücken/Bauch.
(b) *(with pages)* **please ~ ~** bitte wenden.
(c) *(Aut: engine)* laufen ◆ **with the engine ~ing ~** mit laufendem Motor.
[2] *vt sep* **(a)** umdrehen; *(turn upside down)* umkippen; *page* umblättern; *soil* umgraben; *mattress, steak* wenden ◆ **he ~ed the car ~** er überschlug sich (mit dem Auto); **the police ~ed the whole place ~** *(search)* die Polizei durchsuchte das ganze Haus *etc*; **this doesn't make sense, I must have ~ed ~ two pages** das ergibt keinen Sinn, ich muß eine Seite überschlagen haben; **to ~ an idea ~ in one's mind** eine Idee überdenken, sich *(dat)* eine Idee durch den Kopf gehen lassen; *see* **leaf**.
(b) *(hand over)* übergeben *(to dat)*.
(c) *(Comm) goods* umsetzen ◆ **to ~ ~ £500 a week** einen Umsatz von £ 500 in der Woche haben; **how much do you ~ ~ per week?** welchen Umsatz haben Sie pro Woche?
(d) *(Aut) engine* laufen lassen.

◆**turn round** [1] *vi* **(a)** *(face other way)* sich umdrehen; *(go back)* umkehren ◆ **to ~ ~ and go back** umkehren; **to ~ ~ and go back to camp** ins Lager zurückkehren.
(b) *(inf)* **one day she'll just ~ ~ and leave you** eines Tages wird sie dich ganz einfach verlassen; **you can't just ~ ~ and refuse** du kannst dich doch nicht einfach weigern!; **he just ~ed ~ and hit him** er drehte sich einfach um und schlug ihn.
[2] *vi +prep obj* **we ~ed ~ the corner** wir bogen um die Ecke; **the earth ~s ~ the sun** die Erde dreht sich um die Sonne.
[3] *vt sep* **(a)** *head* drehen; *box* umdrehen ◆ **~ the picture ~ the other way** dreh das Bild andersherum.
(b) *(process) job etc* bearbeiten.
(c) *(factory, docks etc) ship* abfertigen; *goods* fertigstellen.

◆**turn to** [1] *vi (get busy)* sich an die Arbeit machen.
[2] *vi +prep obj* **(a) to ~ sb/sth** *see* **turn 3 (c). (b)** *(get busy)* **after a short rest, they ~ed ~ their work again** nach einer kurzen Pause machten sie sich wieder an die Arbeit.

◆**turn up** [1] *vi* **(a)** *(arrive)* erscheinen, auftauchen *(inf)* ◆ **I was afraid you wouldn't ~ ~** ich hatte Angst, du würdest nicht kommen; **two years later he ~ed ~ in London** zwei Jahre später tauchte er in London auf; **the queen hasn't ~ed ~ yet** *(Cards)* die Dame ist noch im Spiel.
(b) *(be found)* sich (an)finden, (wieder) auftauchen *(inf)*; *(smaller things also)* zum Vorschein kommen.
(c) *(happen)* **something is sure to ~ ~** irgend etwas tut sich *or* passiert schon; **things have a habit of ~ing ~** irgendwie findet sich alles; **it's amazing the way things ~ ~** es ist manchmal erstaunlich, wie sich die Dinge finden.
(d) *(point up)* **his nose ~s ~** er hat eine Himmelfahrts- *(inf) or* Stupsnase; **a ~ed-~ nose** eine Himmelfahrts- *(inf) or* Stupsnase; **to ~ ~ at the ends** sich an den Enden hochbiegen.
[2] *vt sep* **(a)** *(fold) collar* hochklappen; *sleeve* aufrollen, aufkrempeln *(inf)*; *hem* umnähen ◆ **to ~ ~ one's nose at sth** *(fig)* die Nase über etw *(acc)* rümpfen.
(b) *heat, gas* aufdrehen, höher drehen; *radio* lauter drehen; *volume* aufdrehen; *light* heller machen.
(c) *(find)* finden, entdecken ◆ **to ~ ~ some information** Informationen auftreiben, an Informationen kommen.

(d) *soil* umpflügen.
(e) (*Brit sl*) **~ it ~!** Mensch, hör auf damit! (*inf*).

turn: ~(a)round *n* (a) (*also* **~about**) (*in position, fig: in opinion etc*) Kehrtwendung *f*; **she has done a complete ~(a)round on fiscal policy** sie hat in der Finanzpolitik eine totale Kehrtwendung gemacht *or* vollführt; (b) (*also* **~(a)round time**) Bearbeitungszeit *f*; (*production time*) Fertigstellungszeit *f*; (c) (*of situation, company*) Umschwung *m*, Wende *f*; (d) (*of ship, aircraft*) Abfertigung *f*; **~coat** *n* Abtrünnige(r), Überläufer *m*.

turner ['tɜːnəʳ] *n* (*of metal*) Dreher *m*; (*of wood*) Drechsler *m*.

turning ['tɜːnɪŋ] *n* (a) (*in road*) Abzweigung *f* ♦ **take the second ~ on the left** nimm die zweite Abfahrt links; **it's a long road that has no ~** (*prov*) nichts dauert ewig. (b) (*Tech*) (*of metal*) Drehen *nt*; (*of wood*) Drechseln *nt*.

turning: ~ circle *n* (*Aut*) Wendekreis *m*; **~ lathe** *n* Drehbank *f*; **~ point** *n* Wendepunkt *m*.

turnip ['tɜːnɪp] *n* Rübe *f*; (*swede*) Steckrübe *f*; (*hum inf: pocket watch*) Zwiebel *f* (*hum inf*).

turn: ~key [1] *n* (*old*) Kerkermeister (*old*), Schließer, Gefängniswärter *m*; [2] *adj attr* **~key project** schlüsselfertiges Projekt; **~-off** *n* (a) Abzweigung *f*; (*on motorway*) Abfahrt, Ausfahrt *f*; **the Birmingham ~-off** die Abzweigung nach Birmingham; die Abfahrt *or* Ausfahrt Birmingham; (b) (*inf*) **it was a real ~-off** das hat einem die Lust verdorben; **hairy armpits are the ultimate ~-off for me** bei Haaren unter den Achseln hört's bei mir auf (*inf*); **~-on** *n* (*inf*) **that's a real ~-on** das macht einen an (*sl*); **she finds him/his accent a real ~-on** sie fährt voll auf ihn/seinen Akzent ab (*sl*).

turnout ['tɜːnaʊt] *n* (a) (*attendance*) Teilnahme, Beteiligung *f* ♦ **in spite of the rain there was a good/big ~ for the match** trotz des Regens war das Spiel gut besucht; **there was a big ~ of friends to meet us at the station** eine Menge Freunde waren gekommen, um uns am Bahnhof zu begrüßen.
(b) (*clean-out*) **she gave the room a thorough ~** sie machte den Raum gründlich sauber.
(c) (*Comm: output*) Produktion *f*.
(d) (*dress*) Aufmachung *f*.

turnover ['tɜːn,əʊvəʳ] *n* (*total business*) Umsatz *m*; (*Comm, Fin: of capital*) Umlauf *m*; (*Comm: of stock*) (Lager)umschlag *m*; (*of staff*) Personalwechsel *m*, Fluktuation *f* ♦ **~ tax** Umsatzsteuer *f*.

turn: ~pike *n* (*Brit Hist*) Mautschranke *f*; (*US*) gebührenpflichtige Autobahn; **~-round** *n see* **~(a)round**; **~stile** *n* Drehkreuz *nt*; **~table** *n* Drehscheibe *f*; (*on record player*) Plattenteller *m*; **~table ladder** Drehleiter *f*; **~-up** *n* (a) (*Brit: on trousers*) Aufschlag *m*; (b) (*inf: event*) **that was a ~-up for the book** das war eine (echte) Überraschung, das war (vielleicht) ein Ding (*inf*).

turpentine ['tɜːpəntaɪn] *n* Terpentin(öl) *nt* ♦ **~ substitute** Terpentin(öl)ersatz *m*.

turpitude ['tɜːpɪtjuːd] *n* Verderbtheit *f*.

turps [tɜːps] *n sing* (*inf*) *abbr of* **turpentine**.

turquoise ['tɜːkwɔɪz] [1] *n* (a) (*gem*) Türkis *m*. (b) (*colour*) Türkis *nt*.
[2] *adj* türkis(farben).

turret ['tʌrɪt] *n* (*Archit*) Mauer- *or* Eckturm *m*; (*on tank*) Turm *m*; (*on ship*) Gefechtsturm *m* ♦ **~ gun** Turmgeschütz *nt*.

turreted ['tʌrɪtɪd] *adj* **a ~ castle** ein Schloß mit Mauer- *or* Ecktürmen.

turtle ['tɜːtl] *n* (Wasser)schildkröte *f*; (*US also*) (Land)schildkröte *f* ♦ **to turn ~** kentern; *see* **mock ~ soup**.

turtle: ~-dove *n* (*lit, fig inf*) Turteltaube *f*; **~-neck (pullover)** *n* Schildkrötenkragenpullover *m*.

turves [tɜːvz] *pl of* **turf**.

Tuscan ['tʌskən] [1] *adj* toskanisch.
[2] *n* (a) Toskaner(in *f*) *m*. (b) (*language*) Toskanisch *nt*.

Tuscany ['tʌskənɪ] *n* die Toskana.

tush [tʌʃ] *interj* (*dated*) pah, bah.

tusk [tʌsk] *n* (*of elephant*) Stoßzahn *m*; (*of walrus*) Eckzahn *m*; (*of boar*) Hauer *m*.

tusker ['tʌskəʳ] *n* Elefantenbulle *m*; (*boar*) Keiler *m*.

tussle ['tʌsl] [1] *n* (*lit, fig*) Gerangel *nt*.
[2] *vi* sich rangeln (*with sb for sth* mit jdm um etw).

tussock ['tʌsək] *n* (Gras)büschel *nt*.

tut [tʌt] *interj, vti see* **tut-tut**.

tutelage ['tjuːtɪlɪdʒ] *n* (*form*) (a) (*teaching*) Führung, Anleitung *f* ♦ **the students made good progress under his able ~** bei diesem guten Unterricht machten die Schüler große Fortschritte. (b) (*guardianship*) Vormundschaft *f*.

tutelary ['tjuːtɪlərɪ] *adj* (*form*) (*of guardian*) vormundschaftlich ♦ **a ~ saint** ein Schutzpatron *m*.

tutor ['tjuːtəʳ] [1] *n* (a) (*private teacher*) Privat- *or* Hauslehrer *m*. (b) (*Brit Univ*) Tutor *m*.
[2] *vt* (a) (*as private teacher*) privat unterrichten; (*give extra lessons to*) Nachhilfe(unterricht) geben (+*dat*) ♦ **to ~ sb in Latin** jdm Privatunterricht/Nachhilfe in Latein geben.
(b) (*liter: discipline*) *emotions* beherrschen.

tutorial [tjuː'tɔːrɪəl] [1] *n* (*Brit Univ*) Kolloquium *nt*.
[2] *adj duties* Tutoren- ♦ **the ~ system** das Tutorensystem.

tutti-frutti ['tuːtɪ'fruːtɪ] *n* (*ice-cream*) Tuttifrutti *nt*.

tut-tut ['tʌt'tʌt] [1] *interj* (*in disapproval*) na, na, aber, aber.
[2] *vi* **she ~ted in disapproval** na, na! *or* aber, aber!, sagte sie mißbilligend.
[3] *vt idea* mißbilligen.

tutu ['tuːtuː] *n* (*Ballet*) Tutu, Ballettröckchen *nt*.

tu-whit tu-whoo [tʊ'wɪttʊ'wuː] *interj* (sch)uhu.

tux [tʌks] (*inf*), **tuxedo** [tʌk'siːdəʊ] *n* (*US*) Smoking *m*.

TV *n* (*inf*) *abbr of* **television** Fernsehen *nt*; (*set*) Fernseher *m* (*inf*) ♦ **on ~** im Fernsehen; **a ~ programme** eine Fernsehsendung; **a ~ personality** ein Fernsehstar *m*; **~ dinner** (*US*) Fertigmahlzeit *f*; *see also* **television**.

TVA *abbr of* **Tennessee Valley Authority**.

twaddle ['twɒdl] *n* (*inf*) Geschwätz *nt*, dummes Zeug (*inf*) ♦ **to talk ~** dummes Zeug reden (*inf*).

twain [tweɪn] *n* (*old*) zwei ♦ **in ~** entzwei (*old*); **and ne'er the ~ shall meet ...** sie werden nie zueinanderfinden.

twang [twæŋ] [1] *n* (a) (*of wire, guitar string*) Doing *nt*; (*of rubber band, bowstring*) scharfer Ton.
(b) (*of voice*) Näseln *nt*, näselnder Tonfall ♦ **to speak with a ~** mit näselndem Tonfall *or* einem Näseln sprechen.
[2] *vt* zupfen; *guitar, banjo also* klimpern auf (+*dat*).
[3] *vi* (a) einen scharfen Ton von sich geben; (*rubber band*) pitschen (*inf*). (b) **to ~ on a guitar** *etc* auf einer Gitarre *etc* herumklimpern.

twangy ['twæŋɪ] *adj* (+*er*) *voice* näselnd; *guitar etc* Klimper-.

'twas [twɒz] (*old*) *contr of* **it was**.

twat [twæt] *n* (a) (*Brit vulg*) (*vagina*) Fotze (*vulg*), Möse (*vulg*) *f*. (b) (*inf: fool*) Saftarsch *m* (*sl*).

tweak [twiːk] [1] *vt* (a) kneifen ♦ **she ~ed back the curtain** sie schob den Vorhang etwas zur Seite; **to ~ sb's ear** jdn am Ohr ziehen; **to ~ sth off/out** etw abkneifen/auszupfen.
(b) (*sl*) *engine* hochfrisieren (*sl*).
[2] *n*: **to give sth a ~** an etw (*dat*) (herum)zupfen; **to give sb's ear/nose a ~** jdn am Ohr/an der Nase ziehen.

twee [twiː] *adj* (+*er*) (*inf*) niedlich, putzig (*inf*); *manner* geziert; *clothes* niedlich; *description* verniedlichend; *expression* gekünstelt.

tweed [twiːd] [1] *n* (a) (*cloth*) Tweed *m*. (b) **~s** *pl* (*clothes*) Tweedkleidung *f*, Tweedsachen *pl* ♦ **his old ~s** sein alter Tweedanzug, seine alten Tweedsachen.
[2] *adj* Tweed-.

Tweedledum [,twiːdl'dʌm] *n* **the twins were as alike as ~ and Tweedledee** die Zwillinge glichen sich wie ein Ei dem anderen.

tweedy ['twiːdɪ] *adj* (+*er*) *material* Tweed-, tweedartig.

'tween [twiːn] (*poet*) *adv, prep* = **between**.

tweeny ['twiːnɪ] *n* (*old*) Hausmagd *f*.

tweet [twiːt] [1] *n* (*of birds*) Ziepen, Piepsen *nt no pl* ♦ **~ ~** ziep, ziep, pieps, pieps.
[2] *vi* ziepen, piepsen.

tweeter ['twiːtəʳ] *n* Hochtonlautsprecher *m*.

tweezers ['twiːzəz] *npl* (*also* **pair of ~**) Pinzette *f*.

twelfth [twelfθ] [1] *adj* zwölfte(r, s) ♦ **a ~ part** ein Zwölftel *nt*; **T~ Night** Dreikönige; (*evening*) Dreikönigsabend *m*.
[2] *n* (*in series*) Zwölfte(r, s); (*fraction*) Zwölftel *nt*; *see also* **sixth**.

twelve [twelv] [1] *adj* zwölf ♦ **~ noon** zwölf Uhr (mittags).
[2] *n* Zwölf *f*; *see also* **six**.

twelve: ~-mile limit *n* Zwölfmeilenzone *f*; **~month** *n* (*old*) zwölf Monate *pl*, ein Jahr *nt*; **~-tone** *adj* (*Mus*) Zwölfton-.

twentieth ['twentɪɪθ] [1] *adj* zwanzigste(r, s) ♦ **a ~ part** ein Zwanzigstel *nt*.
[2] *n* (*in series*) Zwanzigste(r, s); (*fraction*) Zwanzigstel *nt*; *see also* **sixth**.

twenty ['twentɪ] [1] *adj* zwanzig ♦ **~-~ vision** 100prozentige Sehschärfe.
[2] *n* Zwanzig *f*; (*banknote*) Zwanziger *m*; *see also* **sixty**.

twentyfold ['twentɪfəʊld] *adj, adv* (*old*) zwanzigfach.

'twere [twɜːʳ] (*old*) *contr of* **it were**.

twerp [twɜːp] *n* (*inf*) Einfaltspinsel (*inf*), Hohlkopf (*inf*) *m*.

twice [twaɪs] *adv* zweimal ♦ **~ as much/many** doppelt *or* zweimal soviel/so viele; **~ as much bread** doppelt soviel *or* zweimal soviel Brot, die doppelte Menge Brot; **~ as long as ...** doppelt *or* zweimal so lange wie ...; **at ~ the speed of sound** mit doppelter Schallgeschwindigkeit; **she is ~ your age** sie ist doppelt so alt wie du; **~ 2 is 4** zweimal 2 ist 4; **~ weekly, ~ a week** zweimal wöchentlich, zweimal in der *or* pro Woche; **a ~-weekly newspaper** eine Zeitung, die zweimal wöchentlich erscheint; **he didn't need to be asked ~** da brauchte man ihn nicht zweimal zu fragen; **he's ~ the man John is** er steckt John in die Tasche (*inf*); **he's ~ the man he was** er ist ein ganz anderer Mensch geworden; **I'd think ~ before trusting him with it** ihm würde ich das nicht so ohne weiteres anvertrauen.

twiddle ['twɪdl] [1] *vt* herumdrehen an (+*dat*) ♦ **she ~d the pencil in her fingers** ihre Finger spielten mit dem Bleistift; **to ~ one's thumbs** (*lit, fig*) Däumchen drehen.
[2] *vi* **to ~ with a knob** an einem Knopf herumdrehen.
[3] *n* **he gave the knob a ~** er drehte den Knopf herum.

twig¹ [twɪg] *n* (*thin branch*) Zweig *m*.

twig² (*Brit inf*) [1] *vt* (*realize*) mitkriegen (*inf*), mitbekommen ♦ **when she saw his face, she ~ged his secret** als sie sein Gesicht sah, erriet sie sein Geheimnis (*inf*); **he's ~ged it** er hat's kapiert (*inf*).
[2] *vi* schalten, es mitkriegen *or* -bekommen (*all inf*).

twilight ['twaɪlaɪt] *n* (*time*) Dämmerung *f*; (*semi-darkness also*) Dämmer- *or* Zwielicht *nt* ♦ **at ~** in der Dämmerung; **~ sleep** (*Med*) Dämmerschlaf *m*; **the ~ of the gods** die Götterdämmerung; **the ~ of western civilization** der Herbst (*liter*) der westlichen Zivilisation; **the ~ of his life, his ~ years** sein Lebensabend *m*; **~ world** Welt *f* des Zwielichts; **~ zone** Zwielicht *nt*.

twill [twɪl] *n* (*Tex*) Köper *m*.

'twill [twɪl] (*old*) *contr of* **it will**.

twin [twɪn] [1] *n* Zwilling *m*; (*of vase, object*) Gegenstück, Pendant *nt* ♦ **her ~**

ihre Zwillingsschwester/ihr Zwillingsbruder *m*; **where's the ~ of this sock?** wo ist die andere Socke?
[2] *adj attr* Zwillings-; (*fig*) genau gleiche(r, s).
[3] *vt town* verschwistern ◆ **Oxford was ~ned with Bonn** Oxford und Bonn wurden zu Partnerstädten.

twin: ~-bedded [ˌtwɪn'bedɪd] *adj* Zweibett-; **~ beds** *npl* zwei (gleiche) Einzelbetten; **~ brother** *n* Zwillingsbruder *m*; **~ carburettors** *npl* Doppelvergaser *m*; **~-cylinder engine** *n* Zweizylinder(motor) *m*.

twine [twaɪn] [1] *n* Schnur *f*, Bindfaden *m*.
[2] *vt* winden ◆ **to ~ one's arms round sb** seine Arme um jdn schlingen.
[3] *vi* (*around* um *+acc*) sich winden; (*plants also*) sich ranken.

twin-engined [ˌtwɪn'endʒɪnd] *adj* zweimotorig.

twinge [twɪndʒ] *n* (*of pain*) Zucken *nt*, leichtes Stechen ◆ **a ~ of toothache/pain** leicht stechende Zahnschmerzen/ein zuckender Schmerz; **my back still gives me the occasional ~** ich spüre gelegentlich noch ein Stechen im Rücken; **a ~ of rheumatism** rheumatisches Reißen; **a ~ of regret** leichtes Bedauern; **a ~ of conscience/remorse** Gewissensbisse *pl*.

twining ['twaɪnɪŋ] *adj plant* rankend, Kletter-.

twinkle ['twɪŋkl] [1] *vi* (*stars*) funkeln, flimmern, glitzern; (*eyes*) blitzen, funkeln ◆ **her feet ~d across the stage** sie bewegte sich leichtfüßig über die Bühne.
[2] *n* (**a**) Funkeln, Flimmern, Glitzern *nt* ◆ **there was a ~/a mischievous ~ in her eye** man sah den Schalk in ihren Augen/ihre Augen blitzten übermütig *or* vor Übermut; **no, he said with a ~ (in his eye)** nein, sagte er augenzwinkernd.
(**b**) (*instant*) **in a ~** sofort, im Handumdrehen.

twinkletoes ['twɪŋklˌtəʊz] *n* **here comes ~!** (*iro*) da kommt ja unser Trampeltier! (*inf*).

twinkling ['twɪŋklɪŋ] *n* **in the ~ of an eye** im Nu, im Handumdrehen.

twinning ['twɪnɪŋ] *n* (*of two towns*) Städtepartnerschaft *f*.

twin: ~ propellers *npl* Doppelschiffsschraube *f*; **~set** *n* Twinset *nt*; **~ sister** *n* Zwillingsschwester *f*; **~-tone horn** *n* Zweiklanghorn *nt*; **~ town** *n* Partnerstadt *f*; **~-tub (washing-machine)** *n* Waschmaschine *f* mit getrennter Schleuder.

twirl [twɜːl] [1] *vt* (herum)wirbeln; *skirt* herumwirbeln; *moustache* zwirbeln ◆ **he ~ed his partner round the dance-floor** er wirbelte seine Partnerin übers Parkett.
[2] *vi* wirbeln ◆ **the skater ~ed round on the ice** der Eiskunstläufer wirbelte über das Eis.
[3] *n* Wirbel *m*; (*in dance*) Drehung *f*; (*of moustache*) hochstehende *or* hochgezwirbelte Spitze; (*in writing*) Schnörkel *m* ◆ **to give a knob/one's moustache a ~** einen Knopf herumdrehen/seinen Schnurrbart zwirbeln; **he gave his partner a ~** er wirbelte seine Partnerin herum.

twirp [twɜːp] *n* (*sl*) *see* **twerp**.

twist [twɪst] [1] *n* (**a**) (*action*) **to give sth a ~** etw (herum)drehen; **to give sb's arm a ~** jdm den Arm verdrehen *or* umdrehen; **to give one's ankle a ~** sich (*dat*) den Fuß vertreten; **with a quick ~ of the hand** mit einer schnellen Handbewegung.
(**b**) (*bend*) Kurve, Biegung *f*; (*fig: in story etc*) Wendung *f* ◆ **the road is full of ~s and turns** die Straße hat viele Biegungen und Windungen.
(**c**) (*coiled shape*) **salt in little ~s of paper** in kleine Papierstückchen eingewickeltes Salz; **~s of thread** Garnknäuel *nt*; **a ~ of French bread** ein französisches Weißbrot (*in Zopfform*).
(**d**) (*type of yarn*) Twist *m*, Stopfgarn *nt*.
(**e**) (*Brit inf*) **to be/go round the ~** verrückt sein/werden; **it's driving me round the ~!** das macht mich wahnsinnig!
(**f**) (*dance*) Twist *m* ◆ **to do the ~** Twist tanzen, twisten.
(**g**) (*on ball*) Drall *m*; (*esp Billiards*) Effet *m or nt* ◆ **to give a ~ to** *or* **put a ~ on a ball** einem Ball einen Drall geben.
[2] *vt* (**a**) (*wind, turn*) drehen; (*coil*) wickeln (*into* zu *+dat*) ◆ **to ~ threads** *etc* **together** Fäden *etc* zusammendrehen *or* verflechten; **to ~ pieces of string into a rope** Bindfäden zu einem Seil drehen; **to ~ flowers into a garland** Blumen zu einer Girlande binden; **she ~ed her hair into a knot** sie drehte sich (*dat*) die Haare zu einem Knoten; **to ~ the top off a jar** den Deckel von einem Glas abdrehen; **to ~ sth round sth** etw um etw (*acc*) wickeln; *see* **finger**.
(**b**) (*bend, distort*) *rod, key* verbiegen; *part of body* verdrehen; (*fig*) *meaning, words* verdrehen, entstellen ◆ **to ~ sth out of shape** etw verbiegen; **to ~ sb's arm** (*lit*) jdm den Arm verdrehen; **I'll do it if you ~ my arm** (*fig*) bevor ich mich schlagen lasse (*hum*); **to ~ one's ankle** sich (*dat*) den Fuß vertreten; **his face was ~ed with pain** sein Gesicht war verzerrt vor Schmerz *or* schmerzverzerrt.
(**c**) *ball* einen Drall geben (*+dat*) ◆ **she somehow managed to ~ the red around the black** sie hat es irgendwie geschafft, die rote an der schwarzen Kugel vorbeizumanövrieren.
[3] *vi* (**a**) sich drehen; (*smoke*) sich kringeln *or* ringeln; (*plant*) sich winden *or* ranken; (*road, river, person: wriggle*) sich schlängeln *or* winden ◆ **the kite-strings have ~ed round the pole** die Drachenschnüre haben sich um den Pfahl verwickelt; **the rope ~ed and turned** das Seil drehte sich hin und her.
(**b**) (*dance*) Twist tanzen, twisten.
(**c**) (*Cards*) aufnehmen und ablegen.

◆**twist about** *or* **around** [1] *vi* sich (her)umdrehen; (*road, river*) (*wind its way*) sich dahinschlängeln; (*be twisty*) gewunden sein ◆ **he ~ed about in pain** er wand *or* krümmte sich vor Schmerzen.
[2] *vt sep see* **twist round**.

◆**twist off** [1] *vi* **the top ~s ~** der Deckel läßt sich abschrauben *or* ist abschraubbar.
[2] *vt sep* abdrehen; *lid* abschrauben; *flowerheads* abknipsen.

◆**twist out** [1] *vi* **to ~ ~ of sb's grasp** sich jds Griff (*dat*) entwinden.
[2] *vt sep* herausdrehen.

◆**twist round** [1] *vi* sich umdrehen; (*road etc*) eine Biegung machen.
[2] *vt sep head, chair* herumdrehen ◆ **she ~ed her handkerchief ~ in her fingers** sie drehte ihr Taschentuch zwischen den Fingern.

◆**twist up** [1] *vi* (*rope etc*) sich verdrehen; (*smoke*) in Kringeln hochsteigen; (*person: with pain etc*) sich winden *or* krümmen.
[2] *vt sep* (*ropes, wires*) verwickeln.

twisted ['twɪstɪd] *adj* (**a**) *wires, rope* (zusammen)gedreht; (*bent*) verbogen ◆ **~-pair cable** verdrilltes Kabel. (**b**) *ankle* verrenkt. (**c**) (*fig*) *mind, logic* verdreht. (**d**) (*inf: dishonest*) unredlich.

twister ['twɪstəʳ] *n* (**a**) (*Brit pej: person*) Gauner, Halunke *m*. (**b**) (*Brit*) (*question*) harte Nuß (*inf*); (*problem*) harter Brocken (*inf*). (**c**) (*US inf: tornado*) Wirbelsturm, Tornado *m*. (**d**) (*dancer*) Twisttänzer(in *f*) *m*.

twisty ['twɪstɪ] *adj* (*+er*) *road* kurvenreich, gewunden.

twit [twɪt] [1] *vt* **to ~ sb (about sth)** jdn (mit *or* wegen etw) aufziehen *or* hochnehmen.
[2] *n* (*Brit inf: person*) Trottel *m* (*inf*).

twitch [twɪtʃ] [1] *n* (**a**) (*tic*) Zucken *nt*; (*individual spasm*) Zuckung *f* ◆ **to give a ~** zucken. (**b**) (*pull*) Ruck *m* (*of an +dat*) ◆ **to give sth a ~** an etw (*dat*) rucken.
[2] *vi* (*face, muscles*) zucken ◆ **the cat's nose ~ed when I brought in the fish** die Katze schnupperte, als ich den Fisch hereinbrachte.
[3] *vt* (**a**) *tail, ears* zucken mit.
(**b**) (*pull*) zupfen ◆ **he ~ed the letter from her hands** er schnappte ihr den Brief aus den Händen.

twitcher ['twɪtʃəʳ] *n* (*Brit inf*) Vogelliebhaber(in) *m(f)*, Vogelnarr *m* (*inf*).

twitch-grass ['twɪtʃgrɑːs] *n* Quecke *f*.

twitter ['twɪtəʳ] [1] *vi* (*lit, fig*) zwitschern.
[2] *vt* zwitschern.
[3] *n* (**a**) (*of birds*) Zwitschern, Gezwitscher *nt*. (**b**) (*inf*) **to be all of a ~, to be in a ~** ganz aufgeregt *or* aufgelöst sein.

twittery ['twɪtərɪ] *adj attr* zwitschernd.

twittish ['twɪtɪʃ] *adj* (*Brit inf: stupid*) hirnlos (*inf*).

'twixt [twɪkst] *prep* (*old*) = **betwixt**.

two [tuː] [1] *adj* zwei ◆ **to break/cut sth in ~** etw in zwei Teile brechen/schneiden; **~ by ~, in ~s** zwei und zwei, zu zweit, zu zweien; **in ~s and threes** immer zwei oder drei (Leute) auf einmal; **~ minds with but a single thought** (*prov*) zwei Seelen — ein Gedanke; **to put ~ and ~ together** (*fig*) seine Schlüsse ziehen, sich (*dat*) seinen Vers darauf machen; **to put ~ and ~ together and make five** einen Fehlschluß *or* falschen Schluß ziehen; **~'s company, three's a crowd** ein dritter stört nur; **~ can play at that game** (*inf*) den Spieß kann man auch umdrehen; *see also* **six**.
[2] *n* Zwei *f* ◆ **just the ~ of us/them** nur wir beide/die beiden.

two: ~-bit *adj* (*US inf*) mies (*inf*); **~-by-four** [1] *n* (*wood*) *ein Stück Holz mit den Ausmaßen zwei auf vier Inches*; [2] *adj* (*esp US inf*) (*small*) *apartment* Kasten-, Schachtel-; (*petty*) *life, job* nullachtfünfzehn (*inf*); **~-chamber system** *n* Zweikammersystem *nt*; **~-cylinder** *adj* Zweizylinder-; **~-dimensional** *adj* zweidimensional; **~-door** *adj* zweitürig; **~-edged** *adj* (**a**) (*lit*) zweischneidig, doppelschneidig; (**b**) (*fig*) zweideutig; *argument also* zweischneidig; **~-faced** *adj* (*lit*) doppelgesichtig; (*fig*) falsch; **~-fisted** *adj* (**a**) **a ~-fisted boxer** ein Boxer, der mit beiden Fäusten gleich gut boxen kann; (**b**) (*US sl*) knallhart; **~fold** [1] *adj* zweifach, doppelt; **a ~fold increase** ein Anstieg um das Doppelte; **the advantages of this method are ~fold** diese Methode hat einen doppelten *or* zweifachen Vorteil; [2] *adv* **to increase ~fold** um das Doppelte steigern; **~-four time** *n* (*Mus*) Zweivierteltakt *m*; **~-handed** *adj* **a ~-handed sword** ein Zweihänder *m*; **a ~-handed saw** eine Säge mit zwei Griffen; **a ~-handed backhand** *eine Rückhand, bei der der Schläger mit beiden Händen gehalten wird*; **~-legged** *adj* zweibeinig; **a ~-legged animal** ein Zweibeiner *m*; **~-party system** *n* Zweiparteiensystem *nt*; **~pence** *n see* **tuppence**; **~ pence** *n* zwei Pence; **~ pence piece** Zweipencestück *nt*; **~penny** ['tʌpənɪ] *adj see* **tuppenny**; **~-phase** *adj* (*Elec*) Zweiphasen-; **~-piece** [1] *adj* zweiteilig; [2] *n* (*suit*) Zweiteiler *m*; (*swimming costume*) zweiteiliger Badeanzug; **~-pin plug** *n* Stecker *m* mit zwei Kontakten; **~-ply** *adj wool* zweifädig; *wood* aus zwei Lagen *or* Schichten bestehend; *tissue* zweilagig; **~-ply sweater** aus zweifädiger Wolle gestrickter Pullover; **~-seater** [1] *adj* zweisitzig; [2] *n* (*car, plane*) Zweisitzer *m*; **~some** *n* (**a**) (*people*) Paar, Pärchen *nt*; **to go out in a ~some** zu zweit *or* zu zweien ausgehen; (**b**) (*game*) **to have a ~some at golf** zu zweit Golf spielen; **to play a ~some** zu zweit spielen; **~-star** *adj hotel etc* Zweisterne-; **~-star petrol** (*Brit*) Normalbenzin *nt*; **a ~-star general** (*US*) ein Zweisternegeneral *m*; **~-step** *n* Twostep *m*; **~-storey** *adj* zweistöckig; **~-stroke** [1] *adj* Zweitakt-; [2] *n* Zweitakter *m*; (*fuel*) Zweitaktgemisch *nt*.

twot [twɒt] *n* (*Brit vulg, inf*) *see* **twat**.

two: ~-time *vt* (*inf*) *boyfriend, accomplice* betrügen; **the crooks realized that he was ~-timing them** die Ganoven merkten, daß er ein doppeltes Spiel spielte *or* trieb; **~-timer** *n* (*inf*) falscher Hund (*inf*); **~-timing** *adj* (*inf*) falsch; **~-tone** *adj* (*in colour*) zweifarbig; (*in sound*) Zweiklang-.

'twould [twʊd] (*old*) *contr of* **it would**.

two: ~-up ~-down *n* (*Brit inf*) kleines Reihenhäuschen; **~-way** *adj* **~-way (radio)** Funksprechgerät *nt*; **~-way communications** (*Telec*) Sprechverkehr *m* in beide Richtungen; **~-way fabric** von beiden Seiten zu tragender Stoff; **~-way mirror** Spion(spiegel) *m*; **~-way street** Straße *f* mit Gegenverkehr *or* mit

Verkehr in beiden Richtungen; **~-way switch/adaptor** Wechselschalter *m*/ Doppelstecker *m*; **~-way traffic** Gegenverkehr *m*, Verkehr *m* in beiden Richtungen; **~-wheeler (bike)** *n* Zweirad, Fahrrad *nt*.

tycoon [taɪ'ku:n] *n* Magnat, Gigant *m* ◆ **business/oil ~** Industrie-/Ölmagnat *m*.

tyke [taɪk] *n* **(a)** (*dog*) Köter *m*. **(b)** (*inf: child*) Lausbub *m*.

tympani *npl see* **timpani**.

tympanic [tɪm'pænɪk] *adj* (*Anat*) Mittelohr- ◆ **~ membrane** Trommelfell, Tympanum (*spec*) *nt*.

tympanist ['tɪmpənɪst] *n* Pauker *m*.

tympanum ['tɪmpənəm] *n* (*Anat*) (*membrane*) Trommelfell, Tympanum (*spec*) *nt*; (*middle ear*) Mittelohr *nt*; (*Archit*) Tympanon *nt*.

typal ['taɪpl] *adj* artspezifisch.

type[1] [taɪp] [1] *n* **(a)** (*kind*) Art *f*; (*of produce, plant also*) Sorte *f*; (*esp of people; character*) Typ, Typus *m* ◆ **different ~s of cows/roses** verschiedene Arten von Rindern/Rosensorten *or* -arten *pl*; **what ~ of car is it?** was für ein Auto(typ) ist das?; **the very latest ~ of hi-fi** das allerneuste Hi-Fi-Gerät; **she has her own particular ~ of charm** sie hat ihren ganz besonderen Charme; **he has an English ~ of face** dem Gesicht nach könnte er Engländer sein; **gruyere-~ cheese** eine Art Schweizer Käse; **most of the characters are recognizable ~s** die meisten Charaktere lassen sich einem bestimmten Typ zuordnen; **they're totally different ~s of person** sie sind vom Typ her völlig verschieden, sie sind völlig verschiedene Typen; **a man of this ~** ein Mann dieser Art *or* dieses Schlages, diese Art *or* Sorte (von) Mann; **that ~ of behaviour** ein solches Benehmen; **it's not my ~ of film** diese Art Film gefällt mir nicht; **he's not my ~** er ist nicht mein Typ; **she's my ~ of girl** sie ist mein Typ; **he's not the ~ to hit a lady** er ist nicht der Typ *or* Mensch, der eine Frau schlägt.
(b) (*inf: man*) Typ *m* ◆ **a strange ~** ein seltsamer Mensch, ein komischer Typ (*inf*), eine Type (*inf*).
[2] *vt* bestimmen.

type[2] [1] *n* (*Typ*) Type *f* ◆ **large/small ~** große/kleine Schrift; **to set ~** setzen; **in ~** (*typed*) maschinegeschrieben, getippt (*inf*); (*set*) gesetzt, gedruckt; **to set sth up in ~** etw setzen; **printed in italic ~** kursiv gedruckt.
[2] *vt* tippen, (mit der Maschine) schreiben ◆ **a badly ~d letter** ein schlecht geschriebener *or* getippter Brief.
[3] *vi* maschineschreiben, tippen (*inf*).

◆**type out** *vt sep* **(a)** *letter* schreiben, tippen (*inf*). **(b)** *error* ausixen.

◆**type up** *vt sep* auf der Maschine zusammenschreiben.

type: ~-cast *vt irreg* (*Theat*) (auf eine bestimmte Rolle) festlegen; **to be ~-cast as a villain** auf die Rolle des Schurken festgelegt werden; **~face** *n* Schrift *f*; **~script** *n* mit Maschine geschriebenes Manuskript, Typoskript *nt* (*geh*); **to be in ~script** mit Maschine geschrieben sein; **~set** *vt* setzen; **~setter** *n* (Schrift)setzer(in *f*) *m*; (*machine*) Setzmaschine *f*; **~setting** *n* Setzen *nt*, (Schrift)satz *m*; **new ~setting techniques** neue Satztechniken; **~size** *n* Schriftgröße *f*.

typewrite ['taɪpraɪt] *irreg* [1] *vi* maschineschreiben, tippen (*inf*).
[2] *vt* (mit der Maschine) schreiben, tippen (*inf*).

typewriter ['taɪp,raɪtə^r] *n* Schreibmaschine *f* ◆ **~ ribbon** Farbband *nt*.

typewriting ['taɪp,raɪtɪŋ] *n see* **typing**.

typewritten ['taɪp,rɪtn] *adj* maschinegeschrieben, getippt.

typhoid ['taɪfɔɪd] *n* (*also* **~ fever**) Typhus *m* ◆ **~ injection** Impfung gegen Typhus, Typhusimpfung *f*.

typhoon [taɪ'fu:n] *n* Taifun *m*.

typhus ['taɪfəs] *n* Fleckfieber *nt*, Flecktyphus *m*.

typical ['tɪpɪkəl] *adj* typisch (*of* für) ◆ **a ~ English town** eine typisch englische Stadt; **that's ~ of him** das ist typisch für ihn; **isn't that ~!** ist das nicht wieder mal typisch!

typically ['tɪpɪkəlɪ] *adv see adj* ◆ **~, he did nothing but complain about the food** bezeichnenderweise hat er sich ständig über das Essen beschwert; **~, he insisted on getting there early** er wollte natürlich unbedingt früh hingehen, typisch.

typify ['tɪpɪfaɪ] *vt* bezeichnend sein für ◆ **he typifies the reserved Englishman** er verkörpert (genau) den Typ des zurückhaltenden Engländers.

typing ['taɪpɪŋ] [1] *n* Maschineschreiben, Tippen (*inf*) *nt* ◆ **the noise of her ~ drove me mad** ihr Tippen *or* der Lärm ihrer Schreibmaschine machte mich wahnsinnig; **his ~ isn't very good** er kann nicht besonders gut maschineschreiben.
[2] *attr* Schreibmaschinen- ◆ **~ error** Tippfehler *m*; **~ pool** Schreibzentrale *f*; **~ speed** Schreibgeschwindigkeit *f*.

typist ['taɪpɪst] *n* (*professional*) Schreibkraft *f*, Stenotypist(in *f*) *m*, Tippse *f* (*pej inf*) ◆ **he couldn't find a ~ for his thesis** er konnte niemanden finden, der ihm seine Doktorarbeit tippte.

typo ['taɪpəʊ] *n* (*Typ inf*) Druckfehler *m*; (*on typewriter, computer*) Tippfehler *m*.

typographer [taɪ'pɒgrəfə^r] *n* Typograph *m*.

typographic(al) [,taɪpə'græfɪk(əl)] *adj* typographisch ◆ **~ error** Druckfehler *m*.

typography [taɪ'pɒgrəfɪ] *n* Typographie *f*; (*subject also*) Buchdruckerkunst *f*.

typological [,taɪpə'lɒdʒɪkəl] *adj* typologisch.

typology [taɪ'pɒlədʒɪ] *n* Typologie *f*.

tyrannic(al) *adj*, **tyrannically** *adv* [tɪ'rænɪk(əl), tɪ'rænɪkəlɪ] tyrannisch.

tyrannize ['tɪrənaɪz] *vt* (*lit, fig*) tyrannisieren.

tyrannosaurus [tɪ,rænə'sɔ:rəs] *n* Tyrannosaurus *m*.

tyrannous ['tɪrənəs] *adj* tyrannisch.

tyranny ['tɪrənɪ] *n* (*lit, fig*) Tyrannei, Tyrannenherrschaft *f* ◆ **he ruled by ~** er führte eine Tyrannenherrschaft.

tyrant ['taɪərənt] *n* (*lit, fig*) Tyrann(in *f*) *m*.

tyre, (*US*) **tire** [taɪə^r] *n* Reifen *m* ◆ **to have a burst ~** einen geplatzten Reifen haben.

tyre: ~ gauge *n* Reifendruckmesser *m*; **~ lever** *n* Montiereisen *nt*; **~ pressure** *n* Reifendruck *m*.

tyro ['taɪərəʊ] (*US*) *n* Anfänger(in *f*) *m* ◆ **a ~ skier** *etc* ein Anfänger beim *or* im Skilaufen *etc*.

Tyrol [tɪ'rəʊl] *n* **the ~** Tirol *nt*.

Tyrolean ['tɪrəlɪən], **Tyrolese** [tɪrə'li:z] [1] *adj* Tiroler ◆ **~ hat** Tirolerhut *m*.
[2] *n* Tiroler(in *f*) *m*.

Tyrrhenian Sea [tɪ'ri:nɪən'si:] *n* Tyrrhenisches Meer.

tzar *n see* **tsar**.

tzarina *n see* **tsarina**.

tzarist *adj, n see* **tsarist**.

tzetze (fly) *n see* **tsetse (fly)**.

U, u [ju:] 1 *n* **(a)** U, u *nt.* **(b)** (*Brit Film*) jugendfreier Film.
2 *adj* (*Brit: upper class*) *charakteristisch für die Gewohnheiten, Sprechweise etc der Oberschicht*, vornehm.
UAR *abbr of* **United Arab Republic.**
U-bend ['ju:bend] *n* (*in pipe*) U-Bogen *m*; (*in road*) Haarnadelkurve *f.*
UB40 [ˌju:bi:'fɔ:tɪ] *n Ausweis m für Arbeitslose.*
ubiquitous [ju:'bɪkwɪtəs] *adj* allgegenwärtig ◆ **sandstone is ~ in this district** Sandstein ist in dieser Gegend überall zu finden.
ubiquity [ju:'bɪkwɪtɪ] *n* Allgegenwart *f*; (*prevalence*) weite Verbreitung.
U-boat ['ju:bəʊt] *n* U-Boot *nt.*
UCAS ['ju:kæs] *n* (*Brit*) *abbr of* **Universities and Colleges Admissions Service** ≃ ZVS *f.*
UCCA ['ʌkə] (*Brit*) *abbr of* **Universities Central Council on Admissions** ≃ ZVS *f.*
UDA *abbr of* **Ulster Defence Association.**
udder ['ʌdə^r] *n* Euter *nt.*
UDF *abbr of* **Ulster Defence Force.**
UDI *abbr of* **Unilateral Declaration of Independence.**
UDR *abbr of* **Ulster Defence Regiment.**
UEFA [ju:'eɪfə] *n abbr of* **Union of European Football Associations** die UEFA.
U-film ['ju:fɪlm] *n* (*Brit*) jugendfreier Film.
UFO ['ju:fəʊ] *abbr of* **unidentified flying object** Ufo, UFO *nt.*
Uganda [ju:'gændə] *n* Uganda *nt.*
Ugandan [jʊ'gændən] 1 *adj* ugandisch.
2 *n* Ugander(in *f*) *m.*
UGC (*Brit*) *abbr of* **University Grants Committee.**
ugh [ɜ:h] *interj* i, igitt.
ugli (fruit) ['ʌglɪ(fru:t)] *n Kreuzung f aus Grapefruit, Apfelsine und Mandarine.*
uglify ['ʌglɪfaɪ] *vt* häßlich machen, verunstalten.
ugliness ['ʌglɪnɪs] *n* Häßlichkeit *f*; (*of news*) Unerfreulichkeit *f*; (*of wound*) übler Zustand; (*of situation*) Ekelhaftigkeit *f*; (*of crime*) Gemeinheit *f*; (*of vice*) Häßlichkeit, Garstigkeit *f.*
ugly ['ʌglɪ] *adj* (*+er*) **(a)** (*not pretty*) häßlich ◆ **as ~ as sin** häßlich wie die Sünde *or* Nacht; **~ duckling** (*fig*) häßliches Entlein.
(b) (*unpleasant, nasty*) übel; *news, wound also* schlimm; *rumour, scenes, crime, clouds also* häßlich; *mood, situation, scenes also* ekelhaft; *crime also* gemein; *vice also* häßlich, garstig; *sky* bedrohlich ◆ **an ~ customer** ein übler Kunde; **to cut up** *or* **turn ~** (*inf*) gemein *or* fies (*inf*) werden.
UHF *abbr of* **ultra-high frequency** UHF.
uh-huh [ʌ'hʌ] *interj* **(a)** (*agreeing, understanding*) ja. **(b)** ['ʌhʌ] (*disagreeing, forbidding*) nichts da (*inf*).
UHT *abbr of* **ultra-heat treated** ultrahocherhitzt ◆ **~ milk** H-Milch *f.*
UK *abbr of* **United Kingdom** Vereinigtes Königreich.
uke [ju:k] *n* (*inf*) *see* **ukulele.**
Ukraine [ju:'kreɪn] *n* **the ~** die Ukraine.
Ukrainian [ju:'kreɪnɪən] 1 *adj* ukrainisch.
2 *n* **(a)** Ukrainer(in *f*) *m.* **(b)** (*language*) Ukrainisch *nt.*
ukulele, ukelele [ˌju:kə'leɪlɪ] *n* Ukulele *f.*
ulcer ['ʌlsə^r] *n* (*Med*) Geschwür *nt*; (*stomach ~*) Magengeschwür *nt*; (*fig*) Übel *nt.*
ulcerate ['ʌlsəreɪt] 1 *vt stomach* ein Geschwür verursachen in (*+dat*); *skin* Geschwüre verursachen auf (*+dat*); *wound* eitern lassen.
2 *vi* (*stomach*) ein Geschwür bilden *or* bekommen; (*skin*) geschwürig werden; (*wound*) eitern.
ulcerated ['ʌlsəreɪtɪd] *adj* geschwürig; *wound* vereitert ◆ **an ~ stomach** ein Magengeschwür *nt.*
ulceration [ˌʌlsə'reɪʃən] *n* (*process*) Geschwürbildung *f*; (*of wound*) Vereiterung *f*; (*state*) Geschwüre *pl*; Vereiterung *f.*
ulcerous ['ʌlsərəs] *adj* geschwürig; *wound* vereitert; (*causing ulcers*) geschwürbildend ◆ **this ~ growth of nationalism** (*fig*) diese krebsartige Ausbreitung des Nationalismus.
ullage ['ʌlɪdʒ] *n* Leckage *f*, Flüssigkeitsschwund *m.*
ulna ['ʌlnə] *n, pl* **-e** ['ʌlni:] *or* **-s** (*Anat*) Elle *f.*
Ulster ['ʌlstə^r] *n* Ulster *nt* ◆ **U~man/woman** Mann *m*/Frau *f* aus Ulster, Einwohner(in *f*) *m* von Ulster.
ulster ['ʌlstə^r] *n* (*dated: coat*) Ulster *m.*
ult [ʌlt] *abbr of* **ultimo.**
ulterior [ʌl'tɪərɪə^r] *adj* **(a) ~ motive** Hintergedanke *m*; **I have no ~ motive(s) in doing that** ich tue das ganz ohne Hintergedanken. **(b)** (*rare: lying beyond*) jenseitig.
ultimata [ˌʌltɪ'meɪtə] *pl of* **ultimatum.**
ultimate ['ʌltɪmɪt] 1 *adj* **(a)** (*final*) letzte(r, s); *destiny, solution, decision* endgültig; *result* endgültig, End-; *outcome, aim* End-; *control* oberste(r, s); *authority* höchste(r, s); *beneficiary* eigentlich ◆ **he came to the ~ conclusion that ...** er kam schließlich zur Einsicht, daß ...; **what is your ~ ambition in life?** was streben Sie letzten Endes *or* letztlich im Leben an?; **although they had no ~ hope of escape** obwohl letztlich *or* im Endeffekt keine Hoffnung auf Flucht bestand.
(b) (*that cannot be improved on*) vollendet, perfekt, in höchster Vollendung ◆ **the ~ sports car** der Sportwagen in höchster Vollendung, der Supersportwagen; **the ~ insult** der Gipfel der Beleidigung; **the ~ deterrent** (*Mil*) das endgültige Abschreckungsmittel; (*fig*) die äußerste Abschreckungsmaßnahme; **the ~ weapon** (*Mil*) die Superwaffe; (*fig*) das letzte und äußerste Mittel; **death is the ~ sacrifice** der Tod ist das allergrößte Opfer.
(c) (*basic*) *principle* grundlegend, Grund-; *constituents* Grund-, unteilbar; *cause* eigentlich; *explanation* grundsätzlich; *truth* letzte(r, s).
(d) (*furthest*) entfernteste(r, s); *boundary of universe, frontier* äußerste(r, s); *ancestors* früheste(r, s) ◆ **the ~ origins of man** die frühesten Ursprünge des Menschen.
2 *n* Nonplusultra *nt* ◆ **that is the ~ in comfort** das ist Superkomfort *or* das Höchste an Komfort.
ultimately ['ʌltɪmɪtlɪ] *adv* (*in the end*) letztlich, letzten Endes; (*eventually*) schließlich; (*fundamentally*) im Grunde genommen, letztlich ◆ **it's ~ your decision** im Grunde genommen *or* letztlich müssen Sie das entscheiden.
ultimatum [ˌʌltɪ'meɪtəm] *n, pl* **-s** *or* **ultimata** (*Mil, fig*) Ultimatum *nt* ◆ **to deliver an ~ to sb** jdm ein Ultimatum stellen.
ultimo ['ʌltɪməʊ] *adv* (*dated Comm*) des letzten *or* vorigen Monats.
ultra- ['ʌltrə-] *pref* ultra-.
ultra: ~fashionable *adj* ultramodern, supermodisch; **~-high frequency** 1 *n* Ultrahochfrequenz *f*; 2 *adj* Ultrahochfrequenz-; **~light** [ˌʌltrə'laɪt] 1 *adj materials etc* ultraleicht; 2 *n* (*Aviat*) Ultraleichtflugzeug *nt*; **~marine** 1 *n* Ultramarin *nt*; 2 *adj* ultramarin(blau); **~modern** *adj* ultra- *or* hypermodern; **~montane** *adj* (*Eccl*) ultramontan; **~short wave** *n* Ultrakurzwelle *f*; **~sound** *n* Ultraschall *m*; (*scan*) Ultraschalluntersuchung *f*; **~sound picture** *n* Ultraschallbild *nt or* -aufnahme *f*; **~sound scan** *n* Ultraschalluntersuchung *f*; **~ violet** *adj* ultraviolett; **~violet treatment** Ultraviolettbestrahlung *f.*
ululate ['ju:ljʊleɪt] *vi* (*liter*) (*mourning women*) (weh)klagen (*liter*); (*dog etc*) heulen.
ululation [ˌju:ljʊ'leɪʃən] *n see vi* (*liter*) (Weh)klagen *nt* (*liter*); Heulen *nt.*
Ulysses [ju:'lɪsi:z] *n* Odysseus, Ulixes (*rare*), Ulysses (*rare*) *m.*
um [əm] 1 *interj* äh; (*in decision, answering*) hm.
2 *vi* **to ~ and err** herumdrucksen; **after a lot of ~ming and erring** nach vielen Ähs und Öhs.
umbel ['ʌmbəl] *n* Dolde *f.*
umber ['ʌmbə^r] 1 *n* (*earth*) Umbraerde *f*; (*pigment: also* **raw ~**) Umbra *f*, Umber *m* ◆ **burnt ~** gebrannte Umbra.
2 *adj* umbrabraun.
umbilical [ˌʌmbɪ'laɪkəl] 1 *adj* Nabel-.
2 *n* (*also* **~ cord**) **(a)** (*Anat*) Nabelschnur *f.* **(b)** (*Space*) Kabelschlauch *m*; (*to astronaut also*) Nabelschnur *f.*
umbilicus [ˌʌmbɪ'laɪkəs] *n* Nabel *m.*
umbra ['ʌmbrə] *n, pl* **-e** ['ʌmbri:] *or* **-s** (*Astron*) (*shadow*) Kernschatten *m*; (*in sunspot*) Umbra *f.*
umbrage ['ʌmbrɪdʒ] *n* **to take ~ at sth** an etw (*dat*) Anstoß nehmen; **he took ~** er nahm daran Anstoß.
umbrella [ʌm'brelə] *n* (Regen)schirm *m*; (*sun ~*) (Sonnen)schirm *m*; (*Mil: air ~*) (*for ground troops*) Abschirmung *f*, Luftschirm *m*; (*for plane*) Jagdschutz *m* ◆ **collapsible** *or* **telescopic ~** Taschen- *or* Faltschirm, Knirps ® *m*; **under the ~ of** (*fig*) unter der Kontrolle von; **to bring sth under one ~** etw zusammenfassen.
umbrella: ~ organization *n* Dachorganisation *f*; **~ stand** *n* Schirm-

ständer *m.*

umlaut ['ʊmlaʊt] *n (sign)* Umlautpunkte *pl; (sound change)* Umlaut *m* ◆ **a ~** ä [ɛː].

umpire ['ʌmpaɪəʳ] [1] *n* Schiedsrichter(in *f*) *m; (fig)* Unparteiische(r) *mf* ◆ **to act as ~** *(lit)* als Schiedsrichter fungieren, Schiedsrichter sein; *(fig)* schlichten.
[2] *vt (Sport)* als Schiedsrichter fungieren bei, Schiedsrichter sein bei, schiedsrichtern bei; *(fig)* schlichten.
[3] *vi (in* bei) Schiedsrichter sein, schiedsrichtern.

umpteen ['ʌmpˈtiːn] *adj (inf)* zig *(inf)*, x *(inf)* ◆ **I've told you ~ times** ich habe dir zigmal *or* x-mal gesagt *(inf)*.

umpteenth ['ʌmpˈtiːnθ] *adj (inf)* x-te(r, s) ◆ **for the ~ time** zum x-ten Mal.

UN *abbr of* **United Nations** UNO *f*, UN *pl* ◆ **~ troops** UNO-Truppen *pl.*

'un [ən] *pron (inf)* **he's a good ~** er ist 'n feiner Kerl; **a big ~** 'n großer; **the little ~s** die Kleinen *pl.*

un- [ʌn-] *pref (before adj, adv)* un-, nicht; *(before n)* Un-.

unabashed [,ʌnə'bæʃt] *adj (not ashamed, embarrassed)* dreist, unverfroren; *(not overawed)* unbeeindruckt.

unabated [,ʌnə'beɪtɪd] *adj* unvermindert ◆ **the rain/storm continued ~** der Regen/Sturm ließ nicht nach.

unabbreviated [,ʌnə'briːvɪeɪtɪd] *adj* unabgekürzt, nicht abgekürzt.

▼ **unable** [,ʌn'eɪbl] *adj pred* **to be ~ to do sth** etw nicht tun können, außerstande sein, etw zu tun; **we're still ~ to cure cancer** wir sind immer noch außerstande *or* nicht imstande *or* nicht in der Lage, Krebs zu heilen.

unabridged [,ʌnə'brɪdʒd] *adj* ungekürzt.

unacceptable [,ʌnək'septəbl] *adj plans, terms* unannehmbar; *excuse, offer, behaviour* nicht akzeptabel; *standard, unemployment level, working conditions* nicht tragbar, untragbar ◆ **it's quite ~ that we should be expected to ...** es kann doch nicht von uns verlangt werden, daß ...; **it's quite ~ for young children to ...** es kann nicht zugelassen werden, daß kleine Kinder ...; **the ~ face of capitalism** die Kehrseite des Kapitalismus.

unacceptably [,ʌnək'septɪblɪ] *adv* untragbar ◆ **these fuels are ~ dangerous** diese Brennstoffe sind in nicht mehr tragbarem Maße gefährlich; **he suggested, quite ~, that ...** er schlug vor, was völlig unakzeptabel war, daß ...

unaccommodating [,ʌnə'kɒmədeɪtɪŋ] *adj* ungefällig; *attitude* unnachgiebig.

unaccompanied [,ʌnə'kʌmpənɪd] *adj person, child, singing* ohne Begleitung; *instrument* Solo- ◆ **~ luggage** aufgegebenes Reisegepäck.

unaccountable [,ʌnə'kaʊntəbl] *adj* unerklärlich; *phenomenon also* unerklärbar.

unaccountably [,ʌnə'kaʊntəblɪ] *adv* unerklärlicherweise; *disappear* auf unerklärliche Weise ◆ **an ~ long time** unerklärlich lange.

unaccounted for [,ʌnə'kaʊntɪd'fɔːʳ] *adj* ungeklärt ◆ **£30 is still ~** es ist noch ungeklärt, wo die £ 30 geblieben sind; **three of the passengers are still ~** drei Passagiere werden noch vermißt, der Verbleib von drei Passagieren ist noch nicht geklärt.

unaccustomed [,ʌnə'kʌstəmd] *adj* **(a)** *(unusual)* ungewohnt.
(b) *(of person: unused)* **to be ~ to sth** etw nicht gewohnt sein, an etw *(acc)* nicht gewöhnt sein; **to be ~ to doing sth** es nicht gewohnt sein *or* nicht daran gewöhnt sein, etw zu tun; **~ as I am to public speaking ...** ich bin kein großer Redner, aber ...

unacknowledged [,ʌnək'nɒlɪdʒd] *adj letter* unbeantwortet; *mistake* uneingestanden; *champion* verkannt ◆ **to leave a letter ~** den Empfang eines Briefes nicht bestätigen; **to go ~** *(person, achievement etc)* nicht anerkannt werden.

unacquainted [,ʌnə'kweɪntɪd] *adj pred* **to be ~ with poverty** die Armut nicht kennen; **to be ~ with the facts** mit den Tatsachen nicht vertraut sein; **I'm not ~ with the facts** die Tatsachen sind mir nicht gänzlich fremd; **they're still ~** sie kennen sich noch immer nicht.

unadaptable [,ʌnə'dæptəbl] *adj* nicht anpassungsfähig, nicht flexibel ◆ **to be ~ to sth** sich an etw *(acc)* nicht anpassen können.

unadapted [,ʌnə'dæptɪd] *adj version of novel etc* unadaptiert ◆ **in the ~ version** in der Originalversion.

unadopted [,ʌnə'dɒptɪd] *adj* **(a)** *(Brit)* **~ road** *öffentliche Straße, für deren Instandhaltung die Anlieger allein verantwortlich sind.* **(b)** *child* nicht adoptiert ◆ **many children remain ~** viele Kinder werden nicht adoptiert.

unadorned [,ʌnə'dɔːnd] *adj* schlicht; *woman's beauty* natürlich; *truth* ungeschminkt.

unadulterated [,ʌnə'dʌltəreɪtɪd] *adj* **(a)** unverfälscht, rein; *wine* rein, ungepanscht; *(hum) whisky* unverdünnt ◆ **~ by foreign influences** durch fremde Einflüsse nicht verfälscht.
(b) *(fig) nonsense* schier; *bliss* ungetrübt ◆ **this is ~ filth** das ist der reinste Schmutz, das ist Schmutz in Reinkultur *(inf)*.

unadventurous [,ʌnəd'ventʃərəs] *adj time, life* wenig abenteuerlich, ereignislos; *tastes* hausbacken, bieder; *style, theatrical production, football* einfallslos; *person* wenig unternehmungslustig ◆ **where food is concerned he is very ~** in bezug aufs Essen ist er nicht experimentierfreudig.

unadventurously [,ʌnəd'ventʃərəslɪ] *adv directed* einfallslos; *dressed, decorated* bieder, hausbacken ◆ **rather ~ they chose Tenerife again** einfallslos *or* wenig abenteuerlich, wie sie sind, haben sie sich wieder für Teneriffa entschieden; **to eat ~** in bezug aufs Essen nicht experimentierfreudig sein.

unadvisable [,ʌnəd'vaɪzəbl] *adj* unratsam, nicht ratsam.

unaesthetic, *(US)* **unesthetic** [,ʌniːs'θetɪk] *adj* unästhetisch.

unaffected [,ʌnə'fektɪd] *adj* **(a)** *(sincere)* ungekünstelt, natürlich, unaffektiert; *pleasure, gratitude* echt.
(b) *(not damaged)* nicht angegriffen *(also Med)*, nicht in Mitleidenschaft gezogen, nicht beeinträchtigt; *(not influenced)* unbeeinflußt, nicht beeinflußt; *(not involved)* nicht betroffen; *(unmoved)* ungerührt, unbewegt ◆ **she remained quite ~ by his tears** sie blieb beim Anblick seiner Tränen völlig ungerührt; **our plans/exports were ~ by the strike** unsere Pläne wurden vom Streik nicht betroffen/unsere Exporte wurden durch den Streik nicht beeinträchtigt; **he remained quite ~ by all the noise** der Lärm berührte *or* störte ihn überhaupt nicht.

unaffectedly [,ʌnə'fektɪdlɪ] *adv (sincerely)* ungeziert, natürlich; *say* unaffektiert ◆ **she was ~ pleased** ihre Freude war echt.

unaffectedness [,ʌnə'fektɪdnɪs] *n (sincerity)* Ungeziertheit, Natürlichkeit, Unaffektiertheit *f; (of joy etc)* Aufrichtigkeit *f.*

unafraid [,ʌnə'freɪd] *adj* unerschrocken, furchtlos ◆ **to be ~ of sb/sth** vor jdm/etw keine Angst haben.

unaided [ʌn'eɪdɪd] [1] *adv* ohne fremde Hilfe ◆ **to do sth ~** etw allein *or* ohne fremde Hilfe tun.
[2] *adj* **his own ~ work** seine eigene Arbeit; **by my own ~ efforts** ganz ohne fremde Hilfe; **~ by sb/sth** ohne jds Hilfe/ohne Zuhilfenahme von etw.

unaired [ʌn'eəd] *adj room, bed, clothes* ungelüftet.

unalike [,ʌnə'laɪk] *adj pred* unähnlich, ungleich ◆ **the two children are so ~** die beiden Kinder sind so verschieden *or* sind sich so unähnlich.

unallocated [ʌn'æləkeɪtɪd] *adj funds* nicht zugewiesen *or* zugeteilt ◆ **~ tickets** Karten im freien Verkauf.

unalloyed [,ʌnə'lɔɪd] *adj usu attr happiness* ungetrübt.

unalterable [ʌn'ɒltərəbl] *adj intention, decision* unabänderlich; *laws* unveränderlich.

unalterably [ʌn'ɒltərəblɪ] *adv* unveränderlich ◆ **to be ~ opposed to sth** entschieden gegen etw sein.

unaltered [ʌn'ɒltəd] *adj* unverändert.

unambiguous *adj*, **~ly** *adv* [,ʌnæm'bɪgjʊəs, -lɪ] eindeutig, unzweideutig.

unambitious [,ʌnæm'bɪʃəs] *adj person, plan* nicht ehrgeizig (genug); *theatrical production* anspruchslos.

unamenable [,ʌnə'miːnəbl] *adj* unzugänglich *(to dat)* ◆ **he is ~ to persuasion** er läßt sich nicht überreden; **~ to medical treatment** auf ärztliche Behandlung nicht ansprechend.

un-American [,ʌnə'merɪkən] *adj* unamerikanisch ◆ **~ activities** unamerikanische Umtriebe *pl.*

unamiable [ʌn'eɪmɪəbl] *adj* unliebenswürdig.

unamused [,ʌnə'mjuːzd] *adj laugh* gezwungen, unfroh ◆ **she was ~** sie fand es überhaupt nicht lustig.

unanimity [,juːnə'nɪmɪtɪ] *n see adj* Einmütigkeit *f;* Einstimmigkeit *f.*

unanimous [juː'nænɪməs] *adj* einmütig; *decision also, (Jur)* einstimmig ◆ **we were ~ in thinking ...** wir waren einmütig der Ansicht ...; **they were ~ in their condemnation of him** sie haben ihn einmütig verdammt; **by a ~ vote** einstimmig.

unanimously [juː'nænɪməslɪ] *adv* einstimmig, einmütig; *vote* einstimmig.

unannounced [,ʌnə'naʊnst] *adj, adv* unangemeldet.

unanswerable [ʌn'ɑːnsərəbl] *adj question* nicht zu beantworten *pred*, nicht zu beantwortend *attr; argument, case* zwingend, unwiderlegbar ◆ **that remark is ~** darauf läßt sich nichts erwidern.

unanswered [ʌn'ɑːnsəd] *adj* unbeantwortet.

unapologetic [,ʌnə,pɒlə'dʒetɪk] *adj* unverfroren, dreist ◆ **he was so ~ about it** es schien ihn überhaupt nicht zu kümmern *or* ihm überhaupt nicht leid zu tun.

unappealable [,ʌnə'piːləbl] *adj (Jur)* nicht berufungsfähig ◆ **the judgement is ~** gegen das Urteil kann keine Berufung eingelegt werden.

unappealing [,ʌnə'piːlɪŋ] *adj* nicht ansprechend, nicht reizvoll; *person also* unansehnlich; *prospect, sight* nicht verlockend.

unappeased [,ʌnə'piːzd] *adj appetite, lust* unbefriedigt; *hunger, thirst* ungestillt.

unappetizing [ʌn'æpɪtaɪzɪŋ] *adj* unappetitlich; *prospect, thought* wenig verlockend.

unappreciated [,ʌnə'priːʃɪeɪtɪd] *adj* nicht geschätzt *or* gewürdigt ◆ **she felt she was ~ by him** sie hatte den Eindruck, daß er sie nicht zu schätzen wußte; **the ~ heroines of the war** die ungewürdigten *or* unbeachteten Heldinnen des Krieges.

unappreciative [,ʌnə'priːʃɪətɪv] *adj* undankbar; *audience* verständnislos ◆ **to be ~ of sth** etw nicht zu würdigen wissen.

unapproachable [,ʌnə'prəʊtʃəbl] *adj place* unzugänglich; *person also* unnahbar.

unapt [ʌn'æpt] *adj (inappropriate)* unpassend, unangebracht.

unarguable [ʌn'ɑːgjʊəbl] *adj theory etc* nicht vertretbar.

unarguably [ʌn'ɑːgjʊəblɪ] *adv* unbestreitbar, zweifellos.

unargued [ʌn'ɑːgjuːd] *adj (without argumentation)* unbegründet; *(undisputed)* unangefochten, unbestritten ◆ **the point was left ~** dieser Punkt wurde nicht begründet; *(undiscussed)* dieser Punkt wurde nicht erörtert.

unarm [ʌn'ɑːm] *vt see* **disarm**.

unarmed [ʌn'ɑːmd] *adj* unbewaffnet ◆ **~ combat** Nahkampf *m* ohne Waffe.

unashamed [,ʌnə'ʃeɪmd] *adj* schamlos ◆ **naked but ~** nackt aber ohne Scham; **his ~ conservatism** sein unverhohlener Konservatismus; **he was quite ~ about it** er schämte sich dessen überhaupt nicht, er war darüber kein bißchen beschämt.

unashamedly [,ʌnə'ʃeɪmɪdlɪ] *adv* unverschämt; *say, admit* ohne Scham; *in favour of, partisan* ganz offen, unverhohlen ◆ **he's ~ proud of ...** er zeigt

➤ LANGUAGE IN USE: **unable** → 16.3, 25.1

unverhohlen, wie stolz er auf ... ist; **they are ~ in love** sie schämen sich ihrer Liebe nicht.

unasked [ʌn'ɑːskt] *adj (unrequested)* unaufgefordert, ungefragt, ungebeten; *(uninvited)* un(ein)geladen, ungebeten.

unasked-for [ʌn'ɑːsktfɔːʳ] *adj* ungewünscht, unwillkommen.

unaspirated [ʌn'æspɪreɪtɪd] *adj* unbehaucht.

unassailable [ˌʌnə'seɪləbl] *adj* unangreifbar; *fortress* uneinnehmbar, unbezwingbar; *position, reputation* unantastbar, unanfechtbar; *conviction* unerschütterlich; *argument* unwiderlegbar, unanfechtbar, zwingend ◆ **he is quite ~ on that point** in diesem Punkt kann er nicht widerlegt werden.

unassisted [ˌʌnə'sɪstɪd] *adj, adv see* **unaided**.

unassuming [ˌʌnə'sjuːmɪŋ] *adj* bescheiden.

unattached [ˌʌnə'tætʃt] *adj* **(a)** *(not fastened)* unbefestigt; *(Mil)* keinem Regiment/keiner Einheit *etc* zugeteilt; *(US) athlete* ohne Vereinszugehörigkeit ◆ **~ vote** Wechselwähler *m*.
(b) *(emotionally)* ungebunden ◆ **she's worried about being still ~** sie macht sich Sorgen, weil sie immer noch keinen Partner gefunden hat *or* sich immer noch nicht gebunden hat; **there aren't many ~ girls around** die meisten Mädchen hier sind nicht mehr zu haben *or* sind nicht mehr frei.

unattainability ['ʌnəˌteɪnə'bɪlɪtɪ] *n* Unerreichbarkeit *f*.

unattainable [ˌʌnə'teɪnəbl] *adj* unerreichbar.

unattended [ˌʌnə'tendɪd] *adj* **(a)** *(not looked after) children* unbeaufsichtigt; *car park, car, luggage* unbewacht; *wound, patient* unbehandelt, nicht behandelt; *shop* ohne Bedienung; *customer* nicht bedient; *business* unerledigt ◆ **to leave sb/sth ~** *children, car, luggage* jdn/etw unbeaufsichtigt/unbewacht lassen; *shop* etw unbeaufsichtigt lassen; **to leave sb/sth ~ (to)** *guests, wound* sich nicht um jdn/etw kümmern; *work* etw liegenlassen, etw nicht erledigen; *patient, wound* jdn/etw nicht behandeln; *customer* jdn nicht bedienen; **to leave a car ~ to** ein Auto nicht reparieren lassen; **to be** *or* **go ~ to** *(wound, injury)* nicht behandelt werden; *(car, fault)* nicht repariert werden; *(customer)* nicht bedient werden; *(work)* nicht erledigt sein/werden.
(b) *(not escorted)* ohne Begleitung *(by gen)*, unbegleitet.

unattractive [ˌʌnə'træktɪv] *adj sight, place* unschön, wenig reizvoll; *offer* unattraktiv, uninteressant; *trait, scar* unschön; *character* unsympathisch; *woman* unattraktiv ◆ **he's ~ to women** Frauen finden ihn nicht attraktiv *or* anziehend.

unattractiveness [ˌʌnə'træktɪvnɪs] *n* Unschönheit *f*; *(of woman)* geringe Attraktivität ◆ **the ~ of the offer** das unattraktive *or* nicht verlockende Angebot.

unauthenticated [ˌʌnɔː'θentɪkeɪtɪd] *adj* unverbürgt; *document* unbeglaubigt.

unauthorized [ʌn'ɔːθəraɪzd] *adj* unbefugt, unberechtigt ◆ **no entry for ~ persons** Zutritt für Unbefugte verboten!

unavailable [ˌʌnə'veɪləbl] *adj* nicht erhältlich; *person* nicht zu erreichen *pred*; *library book* nicht verfügbar ◆ **the minister was ~ for comment** der Minister lehnte eine Stellungnahme ab.

unavailing [ˌʌnə'veɪlɪŋ] *adj* vergeblich, umsonst *pred*.

unavailingly [ˌʌnə'veɪlɪŋlɪ] *adv* vergeblich.

unavenged [ˌʌnə'vendʒd] *adj* ungerächt.

unavoidable [ˌʌnə'vɔɪdəbl] *adj* unvermeidlich, unvermeidbar; *conclusion* zwangsläufig, unausweichlich.

unavoidably [ˌʌnə'vɔɪdəblɪ] *adv* notgedrungen ◆ **to be ~ detained** verhindert sein.

unaware [ˌʌnə'wɛəʳ] *adj pred* **to be ~ of sth** sich *(dat)* einer Sache *(gen)* nicht bewußt sein; **I was ~ of his presence** ich hatte nicht bemerkt, daß er da war; **I was ~ that he was interested** es war mir nicht bewußt *or* ich war mir nicht bewußt, daß er (daran) interessiert war; **I was ~ that there was a meeting going on** ich wußte nicht, daß da gerade eine Besprechung stattfand; **not ~ of sth** sich *(dat)* einer Sache *(gen)* durchaus bewußt; **I was not ~ that ...** es war mir durchaus bewußt *or* klar, daß ...; **he's so ~** er weiß überhaupt nicht Bescheid.

unawares [ˌʌnə'wɛəz] *adv (by surprise)* unerwartet; *(accidentally)* unbeabsichtigt, versehentlich; *(without knowing)* unwissentlich ◆ **to catch** *or* **take sb all ~** jdn überraschen.

unbalance [ʌn'bæləns] *vt (physically, mentally)* aus dem Gleichgewicht bringen; *painting* das Gleichgewicht *(+gen)* stören ◆ **to ~ sb's mind** jdn um den Verstand bringen.

unbalanced [ʌn'bælənst] *adj* **(a)** *painting* unausgewogen; *diet, report also, view of life* einseitig; *ship etc* nicht im Gleichgewicht ◆ **the structure of the committee was ~** der Ausschuß war sehr einseitig *or* unausgewogen besetzt.
(b) *(also* **mentally ~***) (deranged, mad)* irre, verrückt; *(slightly crazy)* nicht ganz normal.
(c) *account* nicht saldiert *or* ausgeglichen.

unbandage [ʌn'bændɪdʒ] *vt* den Verband abnehmen von.

unbar [ʌn'bɑːʳ] *vt* aufsperren.

unbearable [ʌn'bɛərəbl] *adj* unerträglich.

unbearably [ʌn'bɛərəblɪ] *adv see adj* ◆ **almost ~ beautiful** überwältigend *or* hinreißend schön, fast zu schön.

unbeatable [ʌn'biːtəbl] *adj* unschlagbar; *army also* unbesiegbar; *record also* nicht zu überbieten *pred*, nicht zu überbietend *attr*; *offer, price also* unübertrefflich.

unbeaten [ʌn'biːtn] *adj* ungeschlagen; *army also* unbesiegt; *record* ungebrochen, nicht überboten.

unbecoming [ˌʌnbɪ'kʌmɪŋ] *adj* **(a)** *behaviour, language etc* unschicklich, unziemlich *(geh)* ◆ **conduct ~ to a gentleman** ein Benehmen, das sich für einen Herrn nicht schickt.
(b) *(unflattering) clothes* unvorteilhaft; *facial hair* unschön.

unbeknown(st) [ˌʌnbɪ'nəʊn(st)] *adv* ohne daß es jemand wußte ◆ **~ to me/his father** ohne mein Wissen/ohne Wissen seines Vaters.

unbelief [ˌʌnbɪ'liːf] *n* Ungläubigkeit *f* ◆ **a look of ~** ein ungläubiger Blick; **in ~** ungläubig.

unbelievable [ˌʌnbɪ'liːvəbl] *adj* unglaublich; *(inf) (bad)* unglaublich; *(good)* sagenhaft *(inf)*.

unbelievably [ˌʌnbɪ'liːvəblɪ] *adv* unglaublich; *good, pretty etc also* sagenhaft *(inf)*.

unbeliever [ˌʌnbɪ'liːvəʳ] *n* Ungläubige(r) *mf*.

unbelieving *adj*, **~ly** *adv* [ˌʌnbɪ'liːvɪŋ, -lɪ] ungläubig.

unbend [ʌn'bend] *pret, ptp* **unbent** [1] *vt (straighten) metal etc* geradebiegen; *arms* strecken ◆ **~ your body** richten Sie sich auf; *(lying down)* legen Sie sich ausgestreckt hin.
[2] *vi (person: relax)* aus sich herausgehen; *(straighten body)* sich aufrichten; sich gerade hinlegen.

unbending [ʌn'bendɪŋ] *adj person, attitude* unnachgiebig; *determination* unbeugsam.

unbent [ʌn'bent] *pret, ptp of* **unbend**.

unbias(s)ed [ʌn'baɪəst] *adj* unvoreingenommen; *opinion, report also* unparteiisch.

unbidden [ʌn'bɪdn] *adj (form)* ungebeten; *(not ordered also)* unaufgefordert; *(uninvited also)* ungeladen ◆ **to do sth ~** etw unaufgefordert tun.

unbind [ʌn'baɪnd] *pret, ptp* **unbound** *vt (free) prisoner* losbinden, befreien; *(untie) hair* lösen; *(unbandage)* den Verband ablösen von.

unbleached [ʌn'bliːtʃt] *adj* ungebleicht.

unblemished [ʌn'blemɪʃt] *adj (lit, fig)* makellos; *reputation also* unbescholten; *skin also* tadellos ◆ **their relationship was ~ by quarrels** kein Streit hatte je ihre Beziehung getrübt.

unblinking [ʌn'blɪŋkɪŋ] *adj look* unverwandt; *eyes* starr.

unblock [ʌn'blɒk] *vt* frei machen; *sink, pipe* die Verstopfung in *(+dat)* beseitigen; *chimney* ausputzen.

unblushing [ʌn'blʌʃɪŋ] *adj* schamlos; *liar also* unverschämt ◆ **he's quite ~ about it** er schämt sich kein bißchen.

unblushingly [ʌn'blʌʃɪŋlɪ] *adv* ohne sich zu schämen, frech.

unbolt [ʌn'bəʊlt] *vt* aufriegeln ◆ **he left the door ~ed** er verriegelte die Tür nicht.

unborn [ʌn'bɔːn] *adj* ungeboren ◆ **generations yet ~** kommende Generationen.

unbosom [ʌn'bʊzəm] *vt feelings* offenbaren, enthüllen *(to sb* jdm*)* ◆ **to ~ oneself to sb** jdm sein Herz ausschütten.

unbound [ʌn'baʊnd] [1] *pret, ptp of* **unbind**.
[2] *adj* **(a)** *(not tied) hair* gelöst, nicht zusammengehalten *or* zusammengebunden; *prisoner* losgekettet, von den Fesseln befreit ◆ **Prometheus ~** der befreite Prometheus. **(b)** *book* ungebunden.

unbounded [ʌn'baʊndɪd] *adj* grenzenlos; *(fig also)* unermeßlich, unendlich.

unbowed [ʌn'baʊd] *adj (fig)* ungebrochen; *pride* ungebeugt ◆ **with head ~** mit hocherhobenem Kopf; **he was ~ by misfortune** sein Unglück hatte ihn nicht gebrochen *or* gebeugt; **the army was defeated but ~** das Heer war besiegt, sein Mut aber ungebrochen.

unbreakable [ʌn'breɪkəbl] *adj glass, toy* unzerbrechlich; *record* nicht zu brechen *pred*; *rule* unumstößlich, feststehend *attr*; *promise, silence* unverbrüchlich ◆ **an ~ habit** eine Angewohnheit, die man nicht loswerden *or* ablegen kann.

unbribable [ʌn'braɪbəbl] *adj* unbestechlich.

unbridled [ʌn'braɪdld] *adj lust, passion* ungezügelt, zügellos; *anger* hemmungslos; *tongue* lose; *capitalism* ungehemmt.

un-British [ʌn'brɪtɪʃ] *adj* unbritisch, unenglisch.

unbroken [ʌn'brəʊkən] *adj* **(a)** *(intact)* unbeschädigt; *crockery also* nicht zerbrochen, unzerbrochen; *seal* nicht erbrochen; *heart, promise* nicht gebrochen.
(b) *(continuous)* ununterbrochen; *silence also* ungebrochen; *(Mil) ranks* geschlossen, nicht durchbrochen; *line of descent* direkt ◆ **an ~ night's sleep** eine ungestörte Nacht.
(c) *(unbeaten) record* ungebrochen, unüberboten.
(d) *horse* nicht zugeritten; *pride* ungebeugt ◆ **his spirit remained ~** er war ungebrochen.
(e) *voice* nicht gebrochen ◆ **boys with ~ voices** Jungen vor dem Stimmbruch.

unbrotherly [ʌn'brʌðəlɪ] *adj* unbrüderlich.

unbuckle [ʌn'bʌkl] *vt* aufschnallen.

unbudgeted [ʌn'bʌdʒɪtɪd] *adj costs, items* außerplanmäßig.

unbundle [ʌn'bʌndl] *vt* **(a)** *(US: itemize)* aufschlüsseln, aufgliedern. **(b)** *(asset-strip) finanziell gefährdete Firmen aufkaufen und anschließend ihre Vermögenswerte veräußern.*

unburden [ʌn'bɜːdn] *vt (liter: unload)* abladen; *(fig) conscience, heart* erleichtern ◆ **to ~ oneself/one's heart/one's soul to sb** jdm sein Herz ausschütten; **to ~ oneself of sth** *(lit liter)* etw abladen, sich von etw befreien; *(fig)* sich *(dat)* etw von der Seele reden; *of anxiety, guilt* sich von etw befreien *or* losmachen; *of sins* etw offenbaren *or* gestehen; **to ~ one's troubles to sb** seine Sorgen bei jdm abladen.

unbusinesslike [ʌn'bɪznɪslaɪk] *adj* wenig geschäftsmäßig ◆ **it's very ~ to**

keep all your correspondence in cardboard boxes es ist äußerst unordentlich, die ganze Korrespondenz in Kartons aufzubewahren; **the firm handled the transaction in such an ~ way** die Firma hat die Transaktion so ungeschäftsmäßig abgewickelt; **in spite of his ~ appearance ...** obwohl er gar nicht wie ein Geschäftsmann aussieht ...

unbutton [ʌn'bʌtn] *vt* aufknöpfen.

uncalled-for [ʌn'kɔːldfɔːʳ] *adj* (*unjustified*) *criticism* ungerechtfertigt; (*unnecessary*) unnötig; (*rude*) *remark* ungebührlich, deplaziert ◆ **that was quite ~** das war nun wirklich nicht nötig *or* nett.

uncannily [ʌn'kænɪlɪ] *adv see adj* ◆ **his guesses are ~ accurate** es ist unheimlich *or* nicht ganz geheuer, wie genau er alles errät.

uncanny [ʌn'kænɪ] *adj* unheimlich ◆ **it's quite ~** das ist geradezu unheimlich.

uncap [ʌn'kæp] *vt bottle* aufmachen, öffnen.

uncared-for [ʌn'kɛədfɔːʳ] *adj garden, hands* ungepflegt; *child* vernachlässigt, verwahrlost.

uncaring [ʌn'kɛərɪŋ] *adj* gleichgültig, teilnahmslos; *parents* lieblos ◆ **the state as an impersonal and ~ machine** der Staat als unpersönliche und gefühllose Maschine.

uncarpeted [ʌn'kɑːpɪtɪd] *adj* ohne Teppich, nicht ausgelegt.

uncatalogued [ʌn'kætəlɒgd] *adj* nicht katalogisiert.

unceasing *adj*, **~ly** *adv* [ʌn'siːsɪŋ, -lɪ] unaufhörlich.

uncensored [ʌn'sensəd] *adj film, version* unzensiert; (*unblamed*) *remark* ungetadelt, ungerügt.

unceremonious [ˌʌnserɪ'məʊnɪəs] *adj* **(a)** (*abrupt, rude*) *dismissal* brüsk, barsch; *reply* unverbrämt, unverblümt; *behaviour* ungehobelt, ruppig; *exit, departure* überstürzt; *haste* unfein, unfeierlich ◆ **the rather ~ treatment we got** so kurz, wie wir abgefertigt wurden.
(b) (*informal, simple*) zwanglos, formlos.

unceremoniously [ˌʌnserɪ'məʊnɪəslɪ] *adv* **(a)** (*abruptly, rudely*) ohne Umschweife, ohne viel Federlesen(s), kurzerhand. **(b)** zwanglos, formlos.

uncertain [ʌn'sɜːtn] *adj* **(a)** (*unsure, unsteady*) unsicher; *light* undeutlich, schwach ◆ **I was ~ as to what to do** ich war unsicher, was ich tun sollte; **to be ~ whether ...** sich (*dat*) nicht sicher sein, ob ...; **to be ~ of** *or* **about sth** sich (*dat*) einer Sache (*gen*) nicht sicher sein; **he's still ~ of the contract** er ist noch im ungewissen über den Vertrag.
(b) (*unknown*) *date, result* ungewiß; *origins* unbestimmt ◆ **a woman of ~ age** (*hum*) eine Frau von unbestimmtem Alter.
(c) (*unreliable*) *weather, prices* unbeständig; *temper* unberechenbar; *judgement* unverläßlich, unzuverlässig.
(d) (*unclear*) vage ◆ **in no ~ terms** klar und deutlich, unzweideutig.

uncertainly [ʌn'sɜːtnlɪ] *adv say* unbestimmt; *look, move* unsicher.

➤ **uncertainty** [ʌn'sɜːtntɪ] *n* (*state*) Ungewißheit *f*; (*indefiniteness*) Unbestimmtheit *f*; (*doubt*) Zweifel *m*, Unsicherheit *f* ◆ **~ principle** (*Phys*) Unbestimmtheits- *or* Ungenauigkeits- *or* Unschärferelation *f*; **in order to remove any ~** um alle eventuellen Unklarheiten zu beseitigen; **there is still some ~ as to whether ...** es besteht noch Ungewißheit, ob ...

unchain [ʌn'tʃeɪn] *vt dog, prisoner* losketten, losbinden; *door* die Sicherheitskette (*+gen*) lösen; (*fig liter: free*) befreien, erlösen; *heart* freigeben.

unchallengeable [ʌn'tʃælɪndʒəbl] *adj* unerschütterlich, unanfechtbar; *proof also* unwiderlegbar.

unchallenged [ʌn'tʃælɪndʒd] *adj* unbestritten, unangefochten; (*Jur*) *juryman* nicht abgelehnt; *evidence* nicht angefochten, unangefochten ◆ **to go ~** (*Mil*) ohne Anruf passieren; **we passed the sentry ~** die Wache ließ uns ohne Anruf passieren; **the record was** *or* **went ~ for several years** der Rekord wurde jahrelang nicht überboten; **I cannot let that remark go ~** diese Bemerkung kann ich nicht unwidersprochen hinnehmen.

unchanged [ʌn'tʃeɪndʒd] *adj* unverändert.

unchanging [ʌn'tʃeɪndʒɪŋ] *adj* unveränderlich.

unchaperoned [ʌn'ʃæpərəʊnd] *adj* unbegleitet.

uncharacteristic [ˌʌnkærəktə'rɪstɪk] *adj* uncharakteristisch, untypisch (*of* für) ◆ **such rudeness is ~ of him** es ist gar nicht seine Art, so unhöflich zu sein; **with ~ enthusiasm** mit an ihm völlig ungewohnter *or* für ihn völlig untypischer Begeisterung.

uncharitable [ʌn'tʃærɪtəbl] *adj* hartherzig; *remark* unfreundlich, nicht nett, lieblos; *view* unbarmherzig, herzlos; *criticism* schonungslos, unbarmherzig ◆ **it was most ~ of you to ...** es war wirklich nicht nett, daß Sie ...

uncharted [ʌn'tʃɑːtɪd] *adj* (*not explored*) unerforscht, unergründet; (*not on map*) nicht verzeichnet *or* eingezeichnet.

unchaste [ʌn'tʃeɪst] *adj* unzüchtig; *thoughts, actions* unkeusch; *life, wife* untugendhaft.

unchecked [ʌn'tʃekt] *adj* **(a)** (*unrestrained*) ungehemmt, unkontrolliert; *advance* ungehindert; *anger* hemmungslos, ungezügelt ◆ **to go ~** (*abuse*) geduldet werden; (*advance*) nicht gehindert werden; (*inflation*) nicht eingedämmt *or* aufgehalten werden; **if the epidemic goes ~** wenn der Epidemie nicht Einhalt geboten wird.
(b) (*not verified*) ungeprüft, nicht überprüft.

unchivalrous [ʌn'ʃɪvəlrəs] *adj* unritterlich; *remark* ungalant.

unchristian [ʌn'krɪstjən] *adj* unchristlich ◆ **at an ~ hour** (*inf*) zu unchristlicher Zeit (*inf*) *or* Stunde (*inf*).

uncial ['ʌnsɪəl] [1] *adj* Unzial-.
[2] *n* (*letter*) Unzialbuchstabe *m*; (*script*) Unziale, Unzialschrift *f*; (*manuscript*) Schriftstück *or* Dokument *nt* in Unzialschrift.

uncircumcised [ʌn'sɜːkəmsaɪzd] *adj* unbeschnitten.

uncivil [ʌn'sɪvɪl] *adj* unhöflich.

uncivilized [ʌn'sɪvɪlaɪzd] *adj country, tribe, behaviour* unzivilisiert; (*inf*) *habit* barbarisch.

unclad [ʌn'klæd] *adj* (*euph, hum*) bar jeglicher Kleidung.

unclaimed [ʌn'kleɪmd] *adj prize* nicht abgeholt; *property also* herrenlos; *right, inheritance* nicht geltend gemacht; *social security etc* nicht beansprucht.

unclasp [ʌn'klɑːsp] *vt necklace* lösen; *cloak* öffnen, aufhaken; *hands* voneinander lösen ◆ **he ~ed her hand** er löste ihre Hand.

unclassified [ʌn'klæsɪfaɪd] *adj* **(a)** (*not arranged*) nicht klassifiziert *or* eingeordnet. **(b)** (*not secret*) nicht geheim. **(c)** (*Brit*) **~ road** *schlecht ausgebaute Landstraße*.

uncle ['ʌŋkl] *n* Onkel *m* ◆ **U~ Sam** Uncle *or* Onkel Sam; **to say** *or* **cry ~** (*US*) aufgeben; *see* **Dutch**.

unclean [ʌn'kliːn] *adj* unsauber (*also Bibl*); (*Rel*) *animal* unrein; *thoughts* unkeusch; (*fig: contaminated*) schmutzig.

unclear [ʌn'klɪəʳ] *adj* unklar; *essay etc* undurchsichtig ◆ **to be ~ about sth** sich (*dat*) über etw (*acc*) im unklaren *or* nicht im klaren sein; **his motives are ~ to me** mir sind seine Motive nicht klar.

unclimbable [ʌn'klaɪməbl] *adj* unbesteigbar.

unclimbed [ʌn'klaɪmd] *adj* unbestiegen, unbezwungen.

unclog [ʌn'klɒg] *vt pipe, drain* die Verstopfung in (*+dat*) beseitigen; *wheel* befreien.

unclothed [ʌn'kləʊðd] *adj* unbekleidet.

unclouded [ʌn'klaʊdɪd] *adj sky* unbewölkt; (*fig*) *happiness, vision, mind* ungetrübt; *mind* klar.

unclubbable [ʌn'klʌbəbl] *adj* ohne Gruppenzugehörigkeitsgefühl.

uncluttered [ʌn'klʌtəd] *adj* schlicht, einfach; *desk, room* nicht überfüllt *or* überladen ◆ **a mind ~ by excess information** ein von überflüssigem Wissen freier *or* unbelasteter Kopf.

unco ['ʌŋkəʊ] *adv* (*Scot: very*) sehr.

uncoil [ʌn'kɔɪl] [1] *vt* abwickeln.
[2] *vir* (*snake*) sich langsam strecken; (*person*) sich ausstrecken; (*wire etc*) sich abwickeln, sich abspulen ◆ **to ~ oneself from a car/bar stool** sich aus einem Auto herauswinden *or* herausschlängeln/von einem Barhocker heruntergleiten.

uncollected [ˌʌnkə'lektɪd] *adj tax* nicht eingezogen *or* vereinnahmt; *fare* nicht kassiert, unkassiert.

uncoloured, (*US*) **uncolored** [ʌn'kʌləd] *adj* (*colourless*) farblos; (*white*) weiß; (*fig: unprejudiced*) nicht gefärbt; *judgement* unparteiisch ◆ **his judgement was ~ by ...** sein Urteil war nicht durch ... gefärbt.

uncombed [ʌn'kəʊmd] *adj* ungekämmt.

uncomfortable [ʌn'kʌmfətəbl] *adj* **(a)** unbequem; *chair, position also* ungemütlich ◆ **I feel ~ sitting like this** es ist unbequem, so zu sitzen; **if the room is too hot it'll make you feel ~** wenn das Zimmer zu heiß ist, fühlt man sich nicht wohl; **I feel ~ in this jacket** in dieser Jacke fühle ich mich nicht wohl; **it feels ~** es ist unbequem.
(b) (*uneasy*) *feeling* unangenehm, ungut; *silence* (*awkward*) peinlich; (*nerve-racking*) beklemmend ◆ **to feel ~** sich unbehaglich *or* sich nicht wohl fühlen; **I felt ~ about it** ich hatte ein ungutes Gefühl dabei, mir war nicht wohl dabei; **he was ~ in that job** er fühlte sich in dieser Stelle nicht wohl; **they make me feel ~** in ihrer Gegenwart fühle ich mich unbehaglich.
(c) (*unpleasant*) *time, position* unerfreulich ◆ **we could make things ~ for you** (*euph*) wir können ungemütlich werden.

uncomfortably [ʌn'kʌmfətəblɪ] *adv* **(a)** unbequem. **(b)** (*uneasily*) unbehaglich, unruhig. **(c)** (*unpleasantly*) unangenehm ◆ **I became ~ aware of having insulted him** es wurde mir peinlich bewußt, daß ich ihn beleidigt hatte.

uncommitted [ˌʌnkə'mɪtɪd] *adj* nicht engagiert; *party, country* neutral ◆ **we want to remain ~ till we get a full report** wir wollen uns nicht festlegen, bevor wir einen ausführlichen Bericht haben; **~ to** nicht festgelegt auf (*+acc*).

uncommon [ʌn'kɒmən] *adj* **(a)** (*unusual*) ungewöhnlich ◆ **it is not ~ for her to be late** es ist nichts Ungewöhnliches, daß sie zu spät kommt; **a not ~ occurrence** eine häufige Erscheinung. **(b)** (*outstanding*) außergewöhnlich.

uncommonly [ʌn'kɒmənlɪ] *adv* **(a)** (*unusually*) ungewöhnlich. **(b)** (*exceptionally*) außergewöhnlich ◆ **that's ~ civil of you** (*dated*) das ist äußerst freundlich von Ihnen.

uncommunicative [ˌʌnkə'mjuːnɪkətɪv] *adj* (*by nature*) verschlossen, wortkarg; (*temporarily*) schweigsam.

uncompetitive [ˌʌnkɒm'petɪtɪv] *adj industry* nicht wettbewerbsfähig, wettbewerbsunfähig; *price* nicht konkurrenzfähig.

uncomplaining [ˌʌnkəm'pleɪnɪŋ] *adj* duldsam ◆ **with ~ patience** klaglos.

uncomplainingly [ˌʌnkəm'pleɪnɪŋlɪ] *adv* geduldig, klaglos.

uncompleted [ˌʌnkəm'pliːtɪd] *adj* unbeendet, unvollendet.

uncomplicated [ʌn'kɒmplɪkeɪtɪd] *adj* unkompliziert ◆ **his life was ~ by emotional problems** sein Leben wurde nicht durch emotionale Probleme kompliziert *or* erschwert.

uncomplimentary [ˌʌnkɒmplɪ'mentərɪ] *adj* unschmeichelhaft ◆ **to be ~ about sb/sth** sich nicht sehr schmeichelhaft über jdn/etw äußern.

uncomprehending *adj*, **~ly** *adv* [ˌʌnkɒmprɪ'hendɪŋ, -lɪ] verständnislos.

uncompromising [ʌn'kɒmprəmaɪzɪŋ] *adj* kompromißlos; *dedication, honesty* rückhaltlos; *commitment* hundertprozentig.

uncompromisingly [ʌn'kɒmprəmaɪzɪŋlɪ] *adv* unerbittlich; *frank* rückhaltlos, völlig; *committed* hundertprozentig ◆ **he is ~ opposed to ...** er ist ein kompromißloser Gegner (*+gen*) ...

unconcealed [ˌʌnkən'siːld] *adj joy, delight etc* offen, unverhüllt; *hatred, distaste etc also* unverhohlen.

➤ LANGUAGE IN USE: **uncertainty** → 16.1

unconcern [ˌʌnkənˈsɜːn] *n* *(lack of worry)* Unbesorgtheit, Unbekümmertheit *f*; *(indifference)* Gleichgültigkeit *f*.

unconcerned [ˌʌnkənˈsɜːnd] *adj* **(a)** *(unworried)* unbekümmert; *(indifferent)* gleichgültig ◆ **to be ~ about sth** sich nicht um etw kümmern; **how could he be so ~ about her safety/the problem?** wie konnte ihm ihre Sicherheit/das Problem so egal *or* gleichgültig sein?; **I was not ~ about your safety** ich habe mir Sorgen um deine Sicherheit gemacht.
(b) *(not involved)* unbeteiligt *(in* an *+dat)*.

unconcernedly [ˌʌnkənˈsɜːnɪdlɪ] *adv* unbekümmert; *(indifferently)* gleichgültig.

unconditional [ˌʌnkənˈdɪʃənl] *adj* vorbehaltlos ◆ **~ surrender** bedingungslose Kapitulation.

unconditionally [ˌʌnkənˈdɪʃnəlɪ] *adv offer, agree* vorbehaltlos; *surrender* bedingungslos.

unconditioned [ˌʌnkənˈdɪʃənd] *adj (Psych)* nicht konditioniert.

unconfirmed [ˌʌnkənˈfɜːmd] *adj* unbestätigt.

uncongenial [ˌʌnkənˈdʒiːnɪəl] *adj person* unliebenswürdig, nicht einnehmend; *work, surroundings* unerfreulich ◆ **he finds this place ~** dieser Ort entspricht ihm *or* seinem Wesen nicht.

unconnected [ˌʌnkəˈnektɪd] *adj* **(a)** *(unrelated)* nicht miteinander in Beziehung stehend *attr* ◆ **the two events are ~** es besteht keine Beziehung zwischen den beiden Ereignissen.
(b) *(incoherent)* zusammenhanglos, unzusammenhängend.

unconquerable [ʌnˈkɒŋkərəbl] *adj army* unbesiegbar; *peak* unbezwinglich, unerreichbar; *spirit* unbezwinglich, unbezwingbar; *courage* unbezähmbar.

unconquered [ʌnˈkɒŋkəd] *adj army* unbesiegt; *mountain* unbezwungen; *courage, spirit* ungebrochen ◆ **large parts of Britain remained ~** weite Teile Großbritanniens wurden nicht erobert.

unconscionable [ʌnˈkɒnʃənəbl] *adj* unerhört ◆ **an ~ time** eine unerhört lange Zeit, unerhört lange.

unconscious [ʌnˈkɒnʃəs] **1** *adj* **(a)** *(Med)* bewußtlos ◆ **to fall ~** bewußtlos zu Boden fallen; **the blow knocked him ~** durch den Schlag wurde er bewußtlos.
(b) *pred (unaware)* **to be ~ of sth** sich *(dat)* einer Sache *(gen)* nicht bewußt sein; **I was ~ of the fact that ...** ich *or* es war mir nicht bewußt, daß ...
(c) *(unintentional) insult, allusion etc* unbewußt, unbeabsichtigt; *blunder* ungewollt, unbeabsichtigt; *humour* unfreiwillig ◆ **she was the ~ cause of his unhappiness** ohne es zu wissen, wurde sie zur Ursache seines Unglücks; **he was the ~ tool of ...** er wurde unwissentlich zum Werkzeug *(+gen)* ...
(d) *(Psych)* unbewußt ◆ **the ~ mind** das Unbewußte.
2 *n (Psych)* **the ~** das Unbewußte; **he probed his ~** er erforschte das Unbewußte in sich *(dat)*.

unconsciously [ʌnˈkɒnʃəslɪ] *adv* unbewußt ◆ **an ~ funny remark** eine ungewollt *or* unbeabsichtigt lustige Bemerkung.

unconsciousness [ʌnˈkɒnʃəsnɪs] *n* **(a)** *(Med)* Bewußtlosigkeit *f*. **(b)** *(unawareness)* mangelndes Bewußtsein ◆ **his ~ of the real situation** seine Unkenntnis der tatsächlichen Lage. **(c)** *(of insult etc)* Ungewolltheit *f*; *(of humour)* Unfreiwilligkeit *f*.

unconsecrated [ʌnˈkɒnsɪkreɪtɪd] *adj (Rel)* ungeweiht.

unconsidered [ˌʌnkənˈsɪdəd] *adj fact etc* unberücksichtigt; *(rash) action etc* unbedacht, unüberlegt.

unconstitutional [ˌʌnkɒnstɪˈtjuːʃənl] *adj* nicht verfassungsgemäß, verfassungswidrig.

unconstitutionally [ˌʌnkɒnstɪˈtjuːʃnəlɪ] *adv* verfassungswidrig.

unconstructive [ˌʌnkənˈstrʌktɪv] *adj* nicht konstruktiv ◆ **this is one of the most ~ suggestions I've ever heard** einen so wenig konstruktiven Vorschlag habe ich noch nie gehört.

unconsummated [ʌnˈkɒnsjʊmeɪtɪd] *adj* unvollzogen.

uncontaminated [ˌʌnkənˈtæmɪneɪtɪd] *adj* nicht verseucht; *people (by disease)* nicht angesteckt; *(fig)* unverdorben.

uncontested [ˌʌnkənˈtestɪd] *adj* unbestritten; *election, seat* ohne Gegenkandidat ◆ **the election/seat/district was ~ by the Liberals** die Liberalen stellten in der Wahl/für das Mandat/in dem Wahlkreis keinen Kandidaten auf; **the championship went ~ for many years** der Meisterschaftstitel wurde jahrelang nicht angefochten; **the chairmanship was ~** in der Wahl für den Vorsitz gab es keinen Gegenkandidaten.

uncontrollable [ˌʌnkənˈtrəʊləbl] *adj* unkontrollierbar; *child* nicht zu bändigend *attr*, nicht zu bändigen *pred*; *horse, dog* nicht unter Kontrolle zu bringen *pred*; *desire, urge* unbezwinglich, unwiderstehlich; *(physical)* unkontrollierbar; *twitch* unkontrolliert; *laughter, mirth* unbezähmbar ◆ **the epidemic is now ~** die Epidemie ist nicht mehr unter Kontrolle zu bekommen; **to become ~** außer Kontrolle geraten; **to have an ~ temper** unbeherrscht sein.

uncontrollably [ˌʌnkənˈtrəʊləblɪ] *adv* unkontrollierbar; *weep* hemmungslos; *laugh* unkontrolliert.

uncontrolled [ˌʌnkənˈtrəʊld] *adj* ungehindert; *dogs, children* unbeaufsichtigt; *laughter* unkontrolliert; *weeping* hemmungslos, haltlos ◆ **if inflation is allowed to go ~** wenn die Inflation nicht unter Kontrolle gebracht wird.

uncontroversial [ˌʌnkɒntrəˈvɜːʃəl] *adj* unverfänglich.

unconventional [ˌʌnkənˈvenʃənl] *adj* unkonventionell.

unconventionality [ˌʌnkənvenʃəˈnælɪtɪ] *n* Unkonventionalität *f*.

unconventionally [ˌʌnkənˈvenʃənəlɪ] *adv* unkonventionell.

unconversant [ˌʌnkənˈvɜːsnt] *adj* **to be ~ with sth** mit etw nicht vertraut sein.

unconvinced [ˌʌnkənˈvɪnst] *adj* nicht überzeugt *(of* von); *look* wenig überzeugt ◆ **his arguments leave me ~** seine Argumente überzeugen mich nicht; **I remain ~** ich bin noch immer nicht überzeugt.

unconvincing [ˌʌnkənˈvɪnsɪŋ] *adj* nicht überzeugend ◆ **rather ~** wenig überzeugend.

unconvincingly [ˌʌnkənˈvɪnsɪŋlɪ] *adv* wenig überzeugend.

uncooked [ʌnˈkʊkt] *adj* ungekocht, roh.

uncool [ʌnˈkuːl] *adj* nicht (sehr) cool *(inf)*.

uncooperative [ˌʌnkəʊˈɒpərətɪv] *adj attitude* stur, wenig entgegenkommend; *witness, colleague* wenig hilfreich, nicht hilfsbereit ◆ **the government office remained ~** das Regierungsamt war auch weiterhin nicht zur Kooperation bereit; **if the prisoner is still ~** wenn sich der Gefangene weiterhin weigert, mit uns zusammenzuarbeiten; **why are you being so ~?** warum helfen Sie denn nicht mit?; **you're being rather ~** Sie sind nicht sehr hilfreich; **an ~ partner** ein Partner, der nicht mitmacht; **they didn't exactly go on strike, they just became ~** sie haben nicht gerade gestreikt, sie haben nur auf stur geschaltet.

uncooperatively [ˌʌnkəʊˈɒpərətɪvlɪ] *adv* wenig entgegenkommend; *say* wenig hilfreich.

uncoordinated [ˌʌnkəʊˈɔːdɪneɪtɪd] *adj* unkoordiniert.

uncork [ʌnˈkɔːk] *vt bottle* entkorken.

uncorroborated [ˌʌnkəˈrɒbəreɪtɪd] *adj* unbestätigt; *evidence* nicht bekräftigt.

uncorrupted [ˌʌnkəˈrʌptɪd] *adj* unverdorben, nicht korrumpiert; *person also* rechtschaffen.

uncountable [ʌnˈkaʊntəbl] *adj (Gram)* unzählbar.

uncounted [ʌnˈkaʊntɪd] *adj (innumerable)* unzählig.

uncouple [ʌnˈkʌpl] *vt train, trailer* abkuppeln, abkoppeln.

uncouth [ʌnˈkuːθ] *adj person* ungehobelt, ordinär; *behaviour* unflätig, ungehobelt; *manners* ungeschliffen, ungehobelt; *expression, word* unflätig, unfein ◆ **it's very ~ to eat with your hands** es ist sehr unfein, mit den Fingern zu essen.

uncover [ʌnˈkʌvəʳ] *vt* **(a)** *(remove cover from)* aufdecken; *head* entblößen *(liter)* ◆ **the men ~ed their heads** die Männer nahmen ihre Hüte ab. **(b)** *scandal* enthüllen, aufdecken; *plot* aufdecken; *ancient ruins* zum Vorschein bringen.

uncritical [ʌnˈkrɪtɪkəl] *adj* unkritisch *(of, about* in bezug auf *+acc)*.

uncritically [ʌnˈkrɪtɪkəlɪ] *adv* unkritisch.

uncross [ʌnˈkrɒs] *vt* **he ~ed his legs** er nahm das Bein vom Knie.

uncrossed [ʌnˈkrɒst] *adj legs* nicht übereinandergeschlagen *or* gekreuzt; *(Brit) cheque* nicht gekreuzt, Bar-.

uncrowded [ʌnˈkraʊdɪd] *adj* ziemlich leer.

uncrowned [ʌnˈkraʊnd] *adj (lit, fig)* ungekrönt.

uncrushable [ʌnˈkrʌʃəbl] *adj dress* knitterfrei; *carton* Hart-.

unction [ˈʌŋkʃən] *n* **(a)** *(Rel: anointing)* Salbung, Ölung *f* ◆ **extreme ~** Letzte Ölung. **(b)** *(insincere fervour)* hohles *or* unechtes Pathos.

unctuous *adj*, **~ly** *adv* [ˈʌŋktjʊəs, -lɪ] salbungsvoll.

unctuousness [ˈʌŋktjʊəsnɪs] *n* salbungsvolle Art; *(of speech)* falsches Pathos ◆ **the ~ of his manner** seine salbungsvolle Art.

uncultivated [ʌnˈkʌltɪveɪtɪd] *adj land* unkultiviert, unbebaut; *person, behaviour* unkultiviert; *mind* nicht ausgebildet ◆ **an as yet ~ talent** ein noch brachliegendes Talent.

uncultured [ʌnˈkʌltʃəd] *adj person, mind* ungebildet; *behaviour* unkultiviert, unzivilisiert.

uncurl [ʌnˈkɜːl] **1** *vt* auseinanderrollen ◆ **to ~ oneself** sich strecken; **she ~ed herself from the chair** sie löste sich aus ihrer zusammengerollten Stellung im Sessel.
2 *vi* glatt werden; *(cat, snake)* sich langsam strecken; *(person)* sich ausstrecken.

uncut [ʌnˈkʌt] *adj* **(a)** ungeschnitten; *ham, untrimmed pages* nicht aufgeschnitten; *diamond* ungeschliffen, Roh-; *stone, rock* unbehauen; *lawn* nicht gemäht ◆ **an ~ rug** ein Schlingenteppich. **(b)** *film, play, novel* ungekürzt.

undamaged [ʌnˈdæmɪdʒd] *adj* unbeschädigt; *(fig) reputation* makellos.

undated [ʌnˈdeɪtɪd] *adj* undatiert.

undaunted [ʌnˈdɔːntɪd] *adj (not discouraged)* nicht entmutigt, unverzagt; *(fearless)* unerschrocken; *courage* unerschütterlich ◆ **in spite of these failures he carried on ~** trotz dieser Mißerfolge machte er unverzagt weiter; **~ by these threats ...** nicht eingeschüchtert von diesen Drohungen ...

undead [ʌnˈded] *n* **the ~** *pl* die Untoten *pl*.

undeceive [ˌʌndɪˈsiːv] *vt* aufklären.

undecided [ˌʌndɪˈsaɪdɪd] *adj* **(a)** *person* unentschlossen ◆ **he is ~ as to whether he should go or not** er ist (sich) noch unschlüssig, ob er gehen soll oder nicht; **to be ~ about sth** sich *(dat)* über etw *(acc)* im unklaren sein.
(b) *question* unentschieden ◆ **what are we going to do? — I don't know, it's ~** was sollen wir tun? — ich weiß nicht, das steht noch nicht fest *or* ist noch nicht entschieden.

undecipherable [ˌʌndɪˈsaɪfərəbl] *adj handwriting* unleserlich, schwer zu entziffernd *attr*; *code, signs* nicht entzifferbar.

undeclared [ˌʌndɪˈkleəd] *adj love* heimlich, unerklärt; *war* unerklärt; *interest* uneingestanden; *(Customs) goods* nicht deklariert ◆ **could he leave her with his love ~?** konnte er von ihr gehen, ohne ihr seine Liebe erklärt *or* gestanden zu haben?

undefeated [ˌʌndɪˈfiːtɪd] *adj army, team* unbesiegt; *spirit* ungebrochen.

undefendable [ˌʌndɪˈfendəbl] *adj (Mil) coast, frontier* schwer zu verteidigend *attr*, schwer zu verteidigen *pred*.

undefended [ˌʌndɪˈfendɪd] *adj town, goal* unverteidigt ◆ **the case was ~** in dem Fall wurde auf Verteidigung verzichtet.
undefiled [ˌʌndɪˈfaɪld] *adj* unbefleckt.
undefined [ˌʌndɪˈfaɪnd] *adj* undefiniert, nicht definiert; *(vague)* undefinierbar.
undemanding [ˌʌndɪˈmɑːndɪŋ] *adj* anspruchslos, keine Anforderungen *or* Ansprüche stellend *attr; task* wenig fordernd, keine großen Anforderungen stellend *attr* ◆ **this job is so ~** dieser Job fordert mich überhaupt nicht.
undemocratic *adj*, **~ally** *adv* [ˌʌndeməˈkrætɪk, -əlɪ] undemokratisch.
undemonstrative [ˌʌndɪˈmɒnstrətɪv] *adj* reserviert, zurückhaltend ◆ **a fairly ~ race** ein Volk, das seine Gefühle wenig zeigt.
undeniable [ˌʌndɪˈnaɪəbl] *adj* unbestreitbar, unleugbar ◆ **it is ~ that ...** es läßt sich nicht bestreiten *or* leugnen, daß ...
▼ **undeniably** [ˌʌndɪˈnaɪəblɪ] *adv* zweifelsohne, zweifellos; *successful, proud* unbestreitbar.
undenominational [ˌʌndɪnɒmɪˈneɪʃənl] *adj* interkonfessionell ◆ **~ school** Simultan- *or* Gemeinschaftsschule *f.*
undependable [ˌʌndɪˈpendəbl] *adj* unzuverlässig.
under [ˈʌndəʳ] [1] *prep* **(a)** *(beneath) (place)* unter *(+dat)*; *(direction)* unter *(+acc)* ◆ **~ it** darunter; **to come out from ~ the bed** unter dem Bett hervorkommen; **it's ~ there** es ist da drunter *(inf)*; **~ barley** mit Gerste bebaut.
(b) *(less than)* unter *(+dat)*; *(of price etc also)* weniger als ◆ **it took ~ an hour** es dauerte weniger als eine Stunde; **there were ~ 50 of them** es waren weniger als *or* unter 50.
(c) *(subordinate to, ~ influence of etc)* unter *(+dat)* ◆ **he had 50 men ~ him** er hatte 50 Männer unter sich; **to study ~ sb** bei jdm studieren; **who were you ~?** *(Univ)* bei wem haben Sie studiert?; *(Mil)* unter wem haben Sie gedient?; **he was born ~ Virgo** *(Astrol)* er wurde im Zeichen der Jungfrau geboren; **he died ~ the anaesthetic** er starb in der Narkose; **you're ~ a misapprehension** Sie befinden sich im Irrtum; **~ construction** im Bau; **the matter ~ discussion** der Diskussionsgegenstand; **to be ~ treatment** *(Med)* in Behandlung sein; **to be ~ the doctor** in (ärztlicher) Behandlung sein; **which doctor are you ~?** bei welchem Arzt sind Sie?; **it's classified ~ history** es ist unter „Geschichte" eingeordnet; **you'll find him ~ "garages"** Sie finden ihn unter „Werkstätten"; **~ sentence of death** zum Tode verurteilt; **~ penalty of death** unter Androhung der Todesstrafe; **~ an assumed name** unter falschem Namen; **the house is ~ threat of demolition** das Haus ist vom Abbruch bedroht.
(d) *(according to)* nach, gemäß, laut *(all +dat)* ◆ **~ his will** in seinem Testament; **~ the terms of the contract** nach *or* gemäß den *or* laut Vertragsbedingungen.
[2] *adv* **(a)** *(beneath)* unten; *(unconscious)* bewußtlos ◆ **he came to the fence and crawled ~** er kam zum Zaun und kroch darunter durch; **to go ~** untergehen; **to get out from ~** *(fig inf)* wieder Licht sehen *(inf)*. **(b)** *(less)* darunter.
under- *pref* **(a)** *(in rank)* Unter-, Hilfs- ◆ **for the ~-twelves/-eighteens/-forties** für Kinder unter zwölf/Jugendliche unter achtzehn/Leute unter vierzig. **(b)** *(insufficiently)* zuwenig, ungenügend.
under: ~achieve *vi* hinter den Erwartungen zurückbleiben; **~achievement** *n* schwache *or* enttäuschende Leistungen *pl*; **~achiever** *n* **Johnny is an ~achiever** Johnnys Leistungen bleiben hinter den Erwartungen zurück; **~act** *vti* betont zurückhaltend spielen; *(pej)* schwach spielen; **~-age** *adj attr* minderjährig; **~-age drinking** Alkoholgenuß *m* Minderjähriger; *see also* **age**; **~arm** [1] *adj* **(a)** *hair etc* Unterarm-; *seam* Ärmel-; **(b)** *throw* von unten; **~arm serve** *(Tennis)* Aufschlag *m* von unten; [2] *adv throw, serve* von unten; **~belly** *n (Zool, fig: of plane)* Bauch *m*; **the soft ~belly of Europe/democracy** die Achillesferse Europas/der Demokratie; **~bid** *pret, ptp* **~bid** *vt (Comm, Bridge)* unterbieten; **~body** *n (of vehicle)* Unterboden *m*; **~brush** *n see* **~growth**; **~buy** *pret, ptp* **~bought** *vi* zuwenig kaufen; **~capitalized** *adj (Fin)* unterkapitalisiert; **~carriage** *n (Aviat)* Fahrwerk, Fahrgestell *nt*; **~charge** [1] *vi* zuwenig berechnen; [2] *vt* zuwenig berechnen *(sb* jdm); **he ~charged me by 50p** er berechnete mir 50 Pence zuwenig; **~class** *n* Unterklasse *f*; **~clothes** *npl*, **~clothing** *n* Unterwäsche *f*; **~coat** *n (paint)* Grundierfarbe *f*; *(coat)* Grundierung *f*; *(US Aut)* Unterbodenschutz *m*; **~cook** *vt* nicht durchgaren; *(accidentally also)* nicht lange genug kochen; **~cover** *adj agent* Geheim-; **he did ~cover work for the police** er arbeitete insgeheim für die Polizei; **~current** *n (lit, fig)* Unterströmung *f*; *(in speech, attitude)* Unterton *m*; **~cut** *pret, ptp* **~cut** *vt competitor* (im Preis) unterbieten; **~developed** *adj* unterentwickelt; *resources* ungenutzt; **~dog** *n (in society)* Schwächere(r), Benachteiligte(r) *m*; *(in game also)* sicherer Verlierer; **~done** *adj* nicht gar; *(deliberately) steak* nicht durchgebraten; **~dressed** *adj* **to be ~dressed** *(too lightly)* zu leicht angezogen sein; *(not formally enough)* zu einfach angezogen sein; **~emphasize** *vt* nicht genügend *or* nicht ausreichend betonen; **I don't want to ~emphasize her role** ich möchte ihre Rolle nicht herunterspielen; **to deliberately ~emphasize sth** etw bewußt herunterspielen; **~employed** *adj* nicht ausgelastet; *person also* unterbeschäftigt; *plant, equipment also* nicht voll (aus)genutzt; **~employment** *n* Unterbeschäftigung *f*; *(of person, plant also)* mangelnde Auslastung; *(of abilities, plant also)* mangelnde Ausnutzung; **~estimate** [1] *vt* unterschätzen; [2] *n* Unterschätzung *f*; **~estimation** *n* Unterschätzung *f*; **~expose** *vt (Phot)* unterbelichten; **~exposed** *adj (Phot)* unterbelichtet; **~exposure** *n (Phot)* Unterbelichtung *f*; *(fig)* Mangel *m* an Publizität; **~fed** *adj* unterernährt; **~feed** *pret, ptp* **~fed** *vt* zuwenig zu essen geben *(+dat)*; *animals* zuwenig füttern; **~felt** *n* Filzunterlage *f*; **~financed** *adj* unterfinanziert; **~floor heating** *n* Fußbodenheizung *f*; **~foot** *adv* am Boden; **it is wet ~foot** der Boden ist naß; **to trample sb/sth ~foot** *(lit, fig)* auf jdm/etw herumtrampeln; **~fund** *vt* unterfinanzieren; **~funded** *adj* unterfinanziert; **~funding** *n* Unterfinanzierung *f*; **~garment** *n* Unterkleid *nt*; **~garments** Unterkleidung *f*; **~go** *pret* **~went**, *ptp* **~gone** *vt suffering* durchmachen, mitmachen; *change also* erleben; *test, treatment, (Med) operation* sich unterziehen *(+dat)*; *(machine) test* unterzogen werden *(+dat)*; **to ~go experiences** Erlebnisse haben; **to ~go repairs** in Reparatur sein; **~grad** *(inf)*, **~graduate** [1] *n* Student(in *f*) *m*; [2] *attr* Studenten-; **~graduate student** Student(in *f*) *m*; **~graduate courses** Kurse *pl* für nichtgraduierte Studenten.
underground [ˈʌndəgraʊnd] [1] *adj* **(a)** *explosion, lake, cave, passage* unterirdisch; *(Min)* Untertage- ◆ **~ cable** Erdkabel *nt*; **~ railway** *or (US)* **railroad** Untergrundbahn *f*.
(b) *(fig) press, movement* Untergrund-.
[2] *adv* **(a)** unterirdisch; *(Min)* unter Tage ◆ **3 m ~** 3 m unter der Erde. **(b)** *(fig)* **to go ~** untertauchen.
[3] *n* **(a)** *(Brit Rail)* U-Bahn, Untergrundbahn *f*.
(b) *(movement)* Untergrundbewegung *f*; *(sub-culture)* Underground *m*.
under: ~growth *n* Gestrüpp, Gebüsch *nt*; *(under trees)* Unterholz *nt*; **~hand** *adj* **(a)** *(sly)* hinterhältig; **(b)** *(Sport) see* **~arm**; **~handed** *adj see* **~hand (a)**; **~handedly** *adv* hinterhältigerweise; **~hung** *adj jaw* vorgeschoben; **~insured** *adj* unterversichert; **~investment** *n* mangelnde *or* unzureichende Investitionen *pl*; **industry is suffering from ~investment** die Industrie leidet unter Investitionsmangel; **~lay** *n* Unterlage *f*; **~lie** *pret* **~lay**, *ptp* **~lain** *vt (lit)* liegen unter *(+dat)*; *(fig: be basis for or cause of)* zugrunde liegen *(+dat)*; **~line** *vt (lit, fig)* unterstreichen.
underling [ˈʌndəlɪŋ] *n (pej)* Untergebene(r) *mf*; Befehlsempfänger(in *f*) *m (pej)*.
under: ~lining *n* Unterstreichung *f*; **with red ~lining** rot unterstrichen; **why all this ~lining?** warum ist so viel unterstrichen?; **~lying** *adj* **(a)** *soil, rocks* tieferliegend; **(b)** *cause* eigentlich; *(deeper also)* tiefer; *problem* zugrundeliegend; *honesty, strength* grundlegend; **the ~lying cause of all this** was all dem zugrunde liegt; **a certain ~lying sense of tragedy** eine gewisse unterschwellige Tragik; **~manned** *adj* unterbesetzt; **~manning** *n* Personalmangel *m*, Personalknappheit *f*; *(deliberate)* Unterbesetzung *f*; *(Mil, of police force etc)* Unterbemannung *f*; **~mentioned** *adj* unten genannt, untenerwähnt; **~mine** *vt* **(a)** *(tunnel under)* unterhöhlen; *(Mil)* unterminieren; *(weaken)* schwächen; *(sea) cliffs* unterspülen, unterhöhlen; **(b)** *(fig: weaken) authority, confidence* unterminieren, untergraben; *health* angreifen; **~most** *adj* unterste(r, s).
underneath [ˌʌndəˈniːθ] [1] *prep (place)* unter *(+dat)*; *(direction)* unter *(+acc)* ◆ **~ it** darunter; **it came from ~ the table** es kam unter dem Tisch hervor; **from ~ the bushes we could only see ...** unter den Büschen sitzend/liegend konnten wir nur ... sehen.
[2] *adv* darunter ◆ **the ones ~** die darunter.
[3] *n* Unterseite *f*.
under: ~nourished *adj* unterernährt; **~nourishment** *n* Unterernährung *f*; **~paid** *adj* unterbezahlt; **~pants** *npl* Unterhose(n *pl*) *f*; **a pair of ~pants** eine Unterhose, ein Paar Unterhosen; **~part** *n* Unterteil *nt*; **~pass** *n* Unterführung *f*; **~pay** *pret, ptp* **~paid** *vt* unterbezahlen; **~payment** *n* zu geringe Bezahlung, Unterbezahlung *f*; **because of ~payment of tax ...** weil zuwenig Steuer gezahlt wurde ...; **there was an ~payment of £5 in your salary** Sie bekamen £ 5 zuwenig Gehalt ausbezahlt; **~pin** *vt (Archit) wall, building* untermauern; *(fig) argument, claim* untermauern; *economy etc* stützen; **~pinning** *n (Archit)* Untermauerung *f*; **~play** *vt* **(a)** *(Cards) hand* nicht voll ausspielen; **to ~play one's hand** *(fig)* nicht alle Trümpfe ausspielen; **(b)** *(Theat) role* zurückhaltend spielen; **~populated** *adj* unterbevölkert; **~price** *vt* zu billig *or* unter Preis anbieten; **to be ~priced** zu billig gehandelt werden; **at £10 it is ~priced** mit £ 10 ist es zu billig; **~pricing** *n* Festlegung *f* eines zu niedrigen Preises/zu niedriger Preise; **~privileged** *adj* unterprivilegiert; **the ~privileged** die Unterprivilegierten *pl*; **~produce** *vi* zuwenig produzieren; **~production** *n* Unterproduktion *f*; **~proof** *adj spirits* unterprozentig; **~qualified** *adj* unterqualifiziert; **~rate** *vt (~estimate) danger, chance, opponent, person* unterschätzen; *(~value) qualities* unterbewerten; **~represented** *adj* unterrepräsentiert; **~ripe** *adj fruit* unreif; **slightly ~ripe** (noch) nicht ganz reif; **~score** *vt see* **~line**; **~sea** *adj diving, exploration* Unterwasser-; **~seal** *(Brit Aut)* [1] *n* Unterbodenschutz *m*; [2] *vt* mit Unterbodenschutz versehen; **is it ~sealed?** hat es Unterbodenschutz?; **I must have my car ~sealed** ich muß Unterbodenschutz machen lassen; **~secretary** *n* **(a)** *(also* **Parliamentary U~secretary***)* (parlamentarischer) Staatssekretär; **(b) Permanent U~secretary** Ständiger Unterstaatssekretär; **~sell** *pret, ptp* **~sold** *vt* **(a)** *(sell at lower price) competitor* unterbieten; *goods* unter Preis verkaufen, verschleudern; **(b)** *(not publicize)* nicht gut verkaufen; *(as advertising technique)* nicht anpreisen; **he tends to ~sell himself/his ideas** er kann sich/seine Ideen normalerweise nicht verkaufen; **~sexed** *adj* **to be ~sexed** einen unterentwickelten Geschlechtstrieb haben *(form)*, nicht viel für Sex übrig haben; **he's not exactly ~sexed** er ist der reinste Lustmolch *(inf)*; **~shirt** *n (US)* Unterhemd *nt*; **~shoot** *pret, ptp* **~shot** [1] *vi (Aviat, missile)* zu früh landen; [2] *vt* **to ~shoot the runway** vor der Landebahn aufsetzen; **to ~shoot the target** das Ziel nicht erreichen; **~shorts** *npl (US)* Unterhose(n *pl*) *f*; **~side** *n* Unterseite *f*; **~signed** *adj (form)* unterzeichnet; **we the ~signed** wir, die Unterzeichneten; **~sized** *adj* klein; *(less than proper size)* zu klein; *(pej) person also* zu kurz geraten *(hum)*; **~skirt** *n* Unterrock *m*; **~sold** *pret, ptp of* **~sell**; **~spend** *pret, ptp* **~spent** *vi* zu wenig ausgeben; **~staffed** *adj office* unterbesetzt; **we are very ~staffed at the moment** wir haben momentan zu wenig Leute.
▼ **understand** [ˌʌndəˈstænd] *pret, ptp* **understood** [1] *vt* **(a)** *language, painting,*

➤ LANGUAGE IN USE: **undeniably** → 26.3 **understand: 1a** → 12.1, 26.3

statement, speaker verstehen; *action, event, person, difficulty also* begreifen ◆ **I don't ~ Russian** ich verstehe *or* kann kein Russisch; **that's what I can't ~** das kann ich eben nicht verstehen *or* begreifen; **I can't ~ his agreeing to do it** ich kann nicht verstehen *or* es ist mir unbegreiflich, warum er sich dazu bereit erklärt hat; **but ~ this!** aber eins sollte klar sein; **what do you ~ by "pragmatism"?** was verstehen Sie unter „Pragmatismus"?

(b) (*comprehend sympathetically*) *children, people, animals, doubts, fears* verstehen ◆ **to ~ one another** sich verstehen.

(c) (*believe*) **I ~ that you are going to Australia** ich höre, Sie gehen nach Australien; **I ~ that you've already met her** Sie haben sich, soviel ich weiß, schon kennengelernt; **I understood that he was abroad** ich dachte, er sei im Ausland; **am I/are we to ~ that ...?** soll das etwa heißen, daß ...?; **did I ~ him to say that ...?** habe ich richtig verstanden, daß er sagte, ...?; **but I understood her to say that she agreed** aber soweit ich sie verstanden habe, hat sie zugestimmt; **I understood we were to have been consulted!** ich dachte, wir sollten dazu befragt werden; **to give sb to ~ that ...** jdm zu verstehen geben, daß ...; **I understood from his speech that ...** ich schloß aus *or* entnahm seiner Rede (*dat*), daß ...; **what do you ~ from his remarks?** wie verstehen Sie seine Bemerkungen?

(d) (*Gram: supply*) *word* sich (*dat*) denken, (im stillen) ergänzen; *see also* **understood.**

[2] *vi* **(a)** verstehen ◆ **~?** verstanden?; **you don't ~!** du verstehst mich nicht!; **but you don't ~, I must have the money now** aber verstehen Sie doch, ich brauche das Geld jetzt!; **I quite ~** ich verstehe schon. **(b) so I ~** es scheint so; **he was, I ~, a widower** wie ich hörte, war er Witwer.

understandable [ˌʌndəˈstændəbl] *adj* **(a)** (*intelligible*) verständlich. **(b)** (*reasonable, natural*) verständlich, begreiflich.

understandably [ˌʌndəˈstændəblɪ] *adv* verständlicherweise, begreiflicherweise.

understanding [ˌʌndəˈstændɪŋ] [1] *adj* verständnisvoll ◆ **he asked me to be ~** er bat mich um Verständnis.

[2] *n* **(a)** (*intelligence*) Auffassungsgabe *f*; (*knowledge*) Kenntnisse *pl*; (*comprehension, sympathy*) Verständnis *nt* ◆ **I bow to your superior ~** ich beuge mich deinem überlegenen Wissen; **her ~ of children** ihr Verständnis *nt* für Kinder; **because of his complete lack of ~ for the problems** da ihm jedes Verständnis für die Probleme fehlte; **my ~ of the situation is that ...** ich verstehe die Situation so, daß ...; **his behaviour is beyond human ~** sein Verhalten ist absolut unbegreiflich; **she's a woman of great ~** sie ist eine sehr verständnisvolle Frau; **it was my ~ that ...** ich nahm an *or* war der Meinung, daß ...; **he has a good ~ of the problem** er kennt sich mit dem Problem gut aus; **to promote international ~** um die internationale Verständigung zu fördern.

(b) (*agreement*) Abmachung, Vereinbarung, Übereinkunft *f* ◆ **to come to** *or* **reach an ~ with sb** eine Abmachung *or* Vereinbarung mit jdm treffen; **Susie and I have an ~** Susie und ich haben unsere Abmachung; **a degree of ~** eine gewisse Übereinstimmung, ein gewisses Einvernehmen.

(c) (*assumption*) Voraussetzung *f* ◆ **on the ~ that ...** unter der Voraussetzung, daß ...; **on this ~** unter dieser Voraussetzung.

understandingly [ˌʌndəˈstændɪŋlɪ] *adv* verständnisvoll.

understate [ˌʌndəˈsteɪt] *vt* herunterspielen ◆ **to ~ one's case** untertreiben.

understated [ˌʌndəˈsteɪtɪd] *adj film etc* subtil; *picture, music, colours* gedämpft; *make-up* unaufdringlich.

understatement [ˈʌndəˌsteɪtmənt] *n* Untertreibung *f*, Understatement *nt*.

understeer [ˈʌndəˌstɪəʳ] (*Aut*) [1] *n* Untersteuerung *f*.

[2] [ˌʌndəˈstɪəʳ] *vi* untersteuern.

understood [ˌʌndəˈstʊd] [1] *pret, ptp of* **understand.**

[2] *adj* **(a)** (*clear*) klar ◆ **to make oneself ~** sich verständlich machen; **do I make myself ~?** ist das klar?; **I wish it to be ~ that ...** ich möchte klarstellen, daß ...; **~?** klar?; **~!** gut!

(b) (*agreed*) **it was ~ between them that ...** sie hatten eine Vereinbarung, daß ...; **I thought that was ~!** ich dachte, das sei klar; **certain things always have to be ~ in a relationship** einige Dinge sollten in einer Beziehung immer stillschweigend vorausgesetzt werden *or* immer von vornherein klar sein.

(c) (*believed*) angenommen, geglaubt ◆ **he is ~ to have left** es heißt, daß er gegangen ist; **it is ~ that ...** es heißt *or* man hört, daß ...; **he let it be ~ that ...** er gab zu verstehen, daß ...

(d) (*Gram: pred*) ausgelassen.

understudy [ˈʌndəˌstʌdɪ] (*Theat*) [1] *n* zweite Besetzung; (*fig*) Stellvertreter(in *f*) *m*.

[2] *vt* zweite Besetzung sein für.

undertake [ˌʌndəˈteɪk] *pret* **undertook** [ˌʌndəˈtʊk], *ptp* **undertaken** [ˌʌndəˈteɪkn] *vt* **(a)** *job, duty, responsibility* übernehmen; *risk* eingehen, auf sich (*acc*) nehmen ◆ **he undertook to be our guide** er übernahm es, unser Führer zu sein. **(b)** (*agree, promise*) sich verpflichten; (*guarantee*) garantieren.

undertaker [ˈʌndəˌteɪkəʳ] *n* (*esp Brit*) (Leichen)bestatter *m*; Bestattungs- *or* Beerdigungsinstitut *nt*.

undertaking[1] [ˌʌndəˈteɪkɪŋ] *n* **(a)** (*enterprise*) Unternehmen *nt*; (*Comm: project also*) Projekt *nt*.

(b) (*promise*) Zusicherung *f*, Wort *nt* ◆ **I give you my solemn ~ that I will never do it again** ich verpflichte mich feierlich, es nie wieder zu tun; **I can give no such ~** das kann ich nicht versprechen.

(c) (*funeral business*) Bestattungsgewerbe *nt*.

undertaking[2] *n* (*Brit Aut inf*) Überholen *nt* auf der Innenseite.

under: ~-the-counter *adj, adv see* **counter**; **~tone** *n* **(a)** (*of voice*) **in an ~tone** mit gedämpfter Stimme; **(b)** (*fig: of criticism, discontent*) Unterton *m*; **an ~tone of racialism** ein rassistischer Unterton; **~took** *pret of* **~take**; **~tow** *n* Unterströmung *f*; **there is a lot of ~tow** es gibt viele Unterströmungen; **~utilization** *n* mangelnde *or* unzureichende Nutzung; **~utilized** *adj* unzureichend *or* nicht voll genutzt; **~value** *vt antique, artist* unterbewerten, unterschätzen; (*price too low*) zu niedrig schätzen *or* veranschlagen; *person* zu wenig schätzen; **~water** [1] *adj* Unterwasser-; [2] *adv* unter Wasser; **~wear** *n* Unterwäsche *f*; **~weight** *adj* untergewichtig; **to be (2 kg) ~weight** (2 kg) Untergewicht haben; **~went** *pret of* **~go**; **~whelm** *vt* (*hum*) **the critics were ~whelmed by his second novel** sein zweiter Roman hat die Kritiker nicht gerade umgehauen (*inf*); **~world** *n* (*criminals, Myth*) Unterwelt *f*; **~write** *pret* **~wrote**, *ptp* **~written** *vt* (*finance*) *company, loss, project* tragen, garantieren; (*guarantee*) *insurance policy* garantieren, bürgen für; (*insure*) *shipping* versichern; (*St Ex*) *shares* zeichnen; (*fig: agree to*) *policies etc* billigen; **~writer** *n* (*Insur*) Versicherer, Versicherungsgeber *m*.

undeserved [ˌʌndɪˈzɜːvd] *adj* unverdient.

undeservedly [ˌʌndɪˈzɜːvɪdlɪ] *adv* unverdient(ermaßen).

undeserving [ˌʌndɪˈzɜːvɪŋ] *adj person, cause* unwürdig ◆ **to be ~ of sth** (*form*) einer Sache (*gen*) unwürdig sein (*form*).

undesirability [ˌʌndɪzaɪərəˈbɪlɪtɪ] *n see adj* **(a)** Unerwünschtheit *f* ◆ **because of the general ~ of the site** da der Bauplatz durchweg nur Nachteile hat. **(b)** Übelkeit *f*.

undesirable [ˌʌndɪˈzaɪərəbl] [1] *adj* **(a)** *policy, effect* unerwünscht ◆ **~ alien** unerwünschter Ausländer, unerwünschte Ausländerin; **an ~ person to have as a manager** kein wünschenswerter Manager; **they consider her fiancé ~** sie glauben, daß ihr Verlobter keine wünschenswerte Partie ist; **it is ~ that ...** es wäre höchst unerwünscht, wenn ...

(b) *influence, characters, area* übel ◆ **he's just generally ~** er ist ganz einfach ein übler Kerl.

[2] *n* (*person*) unerfreuliches Element; (*foreigner*) unerwünschtes Element.

undetected [ˌʌndɪˈtektɪd] *adj* unentdeckt ◆ **to go/remain ~** nicht entdeckt werden/unentdeckt bleiben.

undetermined [ˌʌndɪˈtɜːmɪnd] *adj* (*indefinite*) unbestimmt; (*unsure*) *person* unentschlossen, unschlüssig.

undeterred [ˌʌndɪˈtɜːd] *adj* keineswegs entmutigt ◆ **to carry on ~** unverzagt weitermachen; **the teams were ~ by the weather** das Wetter schreckte die Mannschaften nicht ab.

undeveloped [ˌʌndɪˈveləpt] *adj* unentwickelt; *land, resources* ungenutzt.

undeviating [ʌnˈdiːvɪeɪtɪŋ] *adj* (*straight*) *line* gerade; (*fig: unchanging*) *route, path* direkt; *fairness, determination* unbeirrbar; *accuracy* unfehlbar.

undiagnosed [ˌʌndaɪəgˈnəʊzd] *adj disease* unerkannt.

undid [ʌnˈdɪd] *pret of* **undo.**

undies [ˈʌndɪz] *npl* (*inf*) (Unter)wäsche *f*.

undifferentiated [ˌʌndɪfəˈrenʃɪeɪtɪd] *adj* undifferenziert.

undigested [ˌʌndaɪˈdʒestɪd] *adj* (*lit, fig*) unverdaut.

undignified [ʌnˈdɪgnɪfaɪd] *adj person, behaviour* würdelos; (*inelegant*) *way of sitting etc* unelegant ◆ **he was never afraid of appearing ~** er hatte keine Angst, seine Würde zu verlieren.

undiluted [ˌʌndaɪˈluːtɪd] *adj* unverdünnt; (*fig*) *truth, version* unverfälscht; *pleasure* rein, voll.

undiminished [ˌʌndɪˈmɪnɪʃt] *adj enthusiasm* unvermindert; *strength, courage also* unbeeinträchtigt.

undiplomatic *adj*, **~ally** *adv* [ˌʌndɪpləˈmætɪk, -əlɪ] undiplomatisch.

undipped [ʌnˈdɪpt] *adj* (*Brit Aut*) **~ headlights** Fernlicht *nt*.

undiscerning [ˌʌndɪˈsɜːnɪŋ] *adj reader, palate* anspruchslos, unkritisch; *critic* unbedarft.

undischarged [ˌʌndɪsˈtʃɑːdʒd] *adj* **(a)** (*Fin*) *debt* unbezahlt, unbeglichen; *bankrupt* nicht entlastet. **(b)** *cargo* nicht abgeladen; *gun* nicht abgefeuert.

undisciplined [ʌnˈdɪsɪplɪnd] *adj mind, person* undiszipliniert; *imagination* zügellos; *hair* ungebändigt.

undisclosed [ˌʌndɪsˈkləʊzd] *adj secret* (bisher) unaufgedeckt; *details etc also* geheimgehalten ◆ **an ~ sum** eine ungenannte *or* geheimgehaltene Summe.

undiscovered [ˌʌndɪˈskʌvəd] *adj* unentdeckt.

undiscriminating [ˌʌndɪˈskrɪmɪneɪtɪŋ] *adj see* **undiscerning.**

undisguised [ˌʌndɪsˈgaɪzd] *adj* ungetarnt; (*fig*) *truth* unverhüllt; *dislike, affection* unverhohlen.

undismayed [ˌʌndɪsˈmeɪd] *adj* ungerührt, unbeeindruckt.

undisposed [ˌʌndɪˈspəʊzd] *adj*: **~ of** (*Comm*) unverkauft.

undisputed [ˌʌndɪˈspjuːtɪd] *adj* unbestritten.

undistinguished [ˌʌndɪˈstɪŋgwɪʃt] *adj performance* (mittel)mäßig; *appearance* durchschnittlich.

undisturbed [ˌʌndɪˈstɜːbd] *adj* **(a)** (*untouched*) *papers, dust* unberührt; (*uninterrupted*) *person, sleep, quiet etc* ungestört. **(b)** (*unworried*) unberührt.

undivided [ˌʌndɪˈvaɪdɪd] *adj country, (fig) opinion, attention* ungeteilt; *support* voll; *loyalty* absolut ◆ **we must stand firm and ~** wir müssen fest und einig sein.

undo [ʌnˈduː] *pret* **undid**, *ptp* **undone** [1] *vt* **(a)** (*unfasten*) aufmachen; *button, dress, zip, parcel also* öffnen; *shoelace, knot also* lösen; *knitting also* aufziehen; *sewing also* die auftrennen ◆ **will you ~ me?** (*inf*) kannst du mir den Reißverschluß/die Knöpfe *etc* aufmachen?

(b) (*reverse*) *mischief, wrong* ungeschehen machen; *work* zunichte machen, ruinieren; (*Comput*) *command* rückgängig machen.

[2] *vi* aufgehen.

undock [ʌnˈdɒk] (*Space*) [1] *vt* entkoppeln.

[2] *vi* sich trennen.
undoing [ʌn'duːɪŋ] *n* Ruin *m*, Verderben *nt*.
undomesticated [ˌʌndə'mestɪkeɪtɪd] *adj animal, pet* nicht ans Haus gewöhnt; *woman, husband* nicht häuslich ◆ **men aren't so ~ as they used to be** Männer sind heute häuslicher als früher.
undone [ʌn'dʌn] [1] *ptp of* **undo**.
[2] *adj* **(a)** (*unfastened*) offen ◆ **to come ~** aufgehen. **(b)** (*neglected*) *task* unerledigt; *work also* ungetan ◆ **we have left ~ what we ought to have done** (*Rel*) wir haben unser Tagwerk nicht getan. **(c)** (*obs: ruined*) **I am ~!** ich bin ruiniert.
undoubted [ʌn'daʊtɪd] *adj* unbestritten; *success also* unzweifelhaft.
▼ **undoubtedly** [ʌn'daʊtɪdlɪ] *adv* zweifellos, ohne Zweifel.
undoubting [ʌn'daʊtɪŋ] *adj* unerschütterlich.
undramatic [ˌʌndrə'mætɪk] *adj* undramatisch.
undreamed-of [ʌn'driːmdɒv], **undreamt-of** [ʌn'dremtɒv] *adj* ungeahnt ◆ **in their time this was ~** zu ihrer Zeit hätte man sich das nie träumen lassen.
undress [ʌn'dres] [1] *vt* ausziehen ◆ **to get ~ed** sich ausziehen.
[2] *vi* sich ausziehen.
[3] *n*: **in a state of ~** halb bekleidet.
undressed [ʌn'drest] *adj* **(a)** *person* (*still*) (noch) nicht angezogen; (*already*) (schon) ausgezogen ◆ **I feel ~ without my watch** ohne Uhr komme ich mir nackt vor. **(b)** *leather* ungegerbt; *wood* unbehandelt, frisch; *stone* ungeschliffen; (*Cook*) *salad* nicht angemacht; *wound* unverbunden.
undrinkable [ʌn'drɪŋkəbl] *adj* ungenießbar.
undue [ʌn'djuː] *adj* (*excessive*) übertrieben, übermäßig; (*improper*) ungebührlich.
undulate ['ʌndjʊleɪt] *vi* (*sea, corn*) wogen; (*path, river, snake*) sich schlängeln; (*hills*) sich in sanften Wellenlinien erstrecken; (*hair*) wallen ◆ **she/her hips ~d as she walked** sie ging mit wiegenden Hüften.
undulating ['ʌndjʊleɪtɪŋ] *adj movement, line* Wellen-; *waves, sea* wogend; *hair* wallend; *countryside* hügelig; *hills* sanft; *hips* wiegend ◆ **the ~ movement of the waves** das Auf und Ab der Wellen.
undulation [ˌʌndjʊ'leɪʃən] *n* (*of waves, countryside*) Auf und Ab *nt*; (*of snake, single movement*) Windung *f*, schlängelnde Bewegung; (*curve*) Rundung *f*.
undulatory ['ʌndjʊlətrɪ] *adj movement* Wellen-, wellenförmig.
unduly [ʌn'djuːlɪ] *adv* übermäßig, übertrieben; *optimistic* zu; *punished* unangemessen *or* übermäßig streng ◆ **you're worrying ~** Sie machen sich (*dat*) unnötige Sorgen.
undutiful [ʌn'djuːtɪfʊl] *adj* pflichtvergessen; *child* ungehorsam.
undying [ʌn'daɪɪŋ] *adj love* unsterblich, ewig; *fame also* unvergänglich.
unearned [ʌn'ɜːnd] *adj* **(a)** *increment* unverdient ◆ **~ income** Kapitaleinkommen *nt*, arbeitsloses Einkommen. **(b)** (*undeserved*) unverdient.
unearth [ʌn'ɜːθ] *vt* ausgraben; (*fig*) *book etc* aufstöbern; *information, evidence* zutage bringen, ausfindig machen.
unearthly [ʌn'ɜːθlɪ] *adj* (*eerie*) *calm* gespenstisch, unheimlich; *scream* schauerlich, unheimlich; *beauty* überirdisch ◆ **at the ~ hour of 5 o'clock** (*inf*) zu nachtschlafender Stunde um 5 Uhr.
unease [ʌn'iːz] *n* Unbehagen *nt*, Beklommenheit *f*.
uneasily [ʌn'iːzɪlɪ] *adv sit* unbehaglich; *smile, listen, speak etc also* beklommen, unsicher; *sleep* unruhig ◆ **to be ~ balanced/poised** sehr prekär sein/sehr wack(e)lig stehen.
uneasiness [ʌn'iːzɪnɪs] *n see adj* Unruhe *f*; Unbehaglichkeit, Beklommenheit *f*; Unsicherheit *f*; Wack(e)ligkeit *f* (*inf*); (*of person*) Beklommenheit *f*; Unruhe *f* ◆ **a certain ~ of mind** ein gewisses Unbehagen.
uneasy [ʌn'iːzɪ] *adj* (*uncomfortable*) *sleep, night* unruhig; *conscience* schlecht; (*worried*) *laugh, look,* (*awkward*) *silence, atmosphere* unbehaglich, beklommen; *behaviour* unsicher; *peace, balance* unsicher, prekär, wack(e)lig (*inf*); (*worrying*) *suspicion, feeling* beunruhigend, beklemmend, unangenehm ◆ **to be ~** (*person*) (*ill at ease*) beklommen sein; (*worried*) beunruhigt sein; **I am ~ about it** mir ist nicht wohl dabei; **to make sb ~** jdn beunruhigen, jdn unruhig machen; **I have an ~ feeling that ...** ich habe das ungute *or* unangenehme Gefühl, daß ...; **to become ~** unruhig werden; **to grow** *or* **become ~ about sth** sich über etw (*acc*) beunruhigen; **his conscience was ~** sein Gewissen plagte ihn, er hatte ein schlechtes Gewissen.
uneatable [ʌn'iːtəbl] *adj* ungenießbar.
uneaten [ʌn'iːtn] *adj* nicht gegessen ◆ **he left the frogs' legs ~** er ließ die Froschschenkel auf dem Teller; **the ~ food** das übriggebliebene Essen.
uneconomic [ʌnˌiːkə'nɒmɪk] *adj* unwirtschaftlich, unökonomisch.
uneconomical [ʌnˌiːkə'nɒmɪkəl] *adj* unwirtschaftlich, unökonomisch; *style of running* unökonomisch; *person* verschwenderisch ◆ **to be ~ with sth** verschwenderisch mit etw umgehen.
unedifying [ˌʌn'edɪfaɪɪŋ] *adj* unerbaulich ◆ **rather ~** nicht gerade erbaulich.
uneducated [ˌʌn'edjʊkeɪtɪd] *adj person* ungebildet; *speech, handwriting also* unkultiviert; *style also* ungeschliffen.
unemotional [ˌʌnɪ'məʊʃənl] *adj person, character* nüchtern; (*without passion*) leidenschaftslos, kühl (*pej*); *reaction, description also* unbewegt ◆ **try and stay ~** versuchen Sie, nüchtern und sachlich zu bleiben.
unemotionally [ˌʌnɪ'məʊʃnəlɪ] *adv* unbewegt, kühl (*pej*); *say, describe also* nüchtern.
unemployable [ˌʌnɪm'plɔɪəbl] *adj person* als Arbeitskraft nicht brauchbar; (*because of illness*) arbeitsunfähig.
unemployed [ˌʌnɪm'plɔɪd] *adj person* arbeitslos, erwerbslos; (*unused*) *machinery* ungenutzt; (*Fin*) *capital* tot, brachliegend ◆ **the ~** *pl* die Arbeitslosen, die Erwerbslosen *pl*.
unemployment [ˌʌnɪm'plɔɪmənt] [1] *n* Arbeitslosigkeit, Erwerbslosigkeit *f* ◆ **~ has risen this month** die Arbeitslosenziffer ist diesen Monat gestiegen.
[2] *attr* **~ benefit** (*Brit*) *or* **compensation** (*US*) Arbeitslosenunterstützung *f*; **~ figures** Arbeitslosenziffer *f*; **~ rate** Arbeitslosenquote *f*.
unemployment line *n* (*US*) **to be in the ~** arbeitslos sein, stempeln gehen (*inf*); **many white-collar workers find themselves in the ~s** viele Schreibtischarbeiter finden sich auf dem Arbeitsamt wieder.
unencumbered [ˌʌnɪn'kʌmbəd] *adj* **~ property** unbelasteter Grundbesitz.
unending [ʌn'endɪŋ] *adj* (*everlasting*) ewig, nie endend *attr*; *stream* nicht enden wollend *attr*, endlos; (*incessant*) endlos, unaufhörlich ◆ **it seems ~** es scheint nicht enden zu wollen.
unendurable [ˌʌnɪn'djʊərəbl] *adj* unerträglich.
unenforceable [ˌʌnɪn'fɔːsɪbl] *adj law* nicht durchsetzbar; *policy* undurchführbar.
un-English [ʌn'ɪŋglɪʃ] *adj behaviour, appearance* unenglisch.
unenlightened [ˌʌnɪn'laɪtnd] *adj* **(a)** (*uninformed*) *reader, listener* uneingeweiht ◆ **to leave sb ~** jdn im dunkeln lassen. **(b)** *age, country, person* rückständig; (*prejudiced*) intolerant.
unenterprising [ˌʌn'entəpraɪzɪŋ] *adj person, policy* ohne Unternehmungsgeist, hausbacken (*inf*) ◆ **it was very ~ of them to turn it down** daß sie abgelehnt haben, beweist, wie wenig Unternehmungsgeist sie haben.
unenthusiastic [ˌʌnɪnθuːzɪ'æstɪk] *adj* kühl, wenig begeistert ◆ **he was ~ about it** er war wenig begeistert davon; **don't be so ~** zeige doch ein bißchen Begeisterung!
unenthusiastically [ˌʌnɪnθuːzɪ'æstɪkəlɪ] *adv* wenig begeistert, ohne Begeisterung.
unenviable [ʌn'envɪəbl] *adj position, task* wenig beneidenswert.
unequal [ʌn'iːkwəl] *adj* ungleich; *standard, quality* unterschiedlich, ungleichförmig; *work* unausgeglichen; *teams also* nicht gleichwertig ◆ **~ in length** unterschiedlich *or* verschieden *or* ungleich lang; **to be ~ to a task** einer Aufgabe (*dat*) nicht gewachsen sein; **to be ~ to doing sth** unfähig *or* nicht fähig sein, etw zu tun.
unequalled, (*US also*) **unequaled** [ʌn'iːkwəld] *adj* unübertroffen; *skill, record, civilization also* unerreicht; *beauty also, stupidity, ignorance* beispiellos, ohnegleichen (*after noun*) ◆ **to be ~ for beauty** von beispielloser Schönheit sein, von einer Schönheit ohnegleichen sein (*geh*); **he is ~ by any other player** kein anderer Spieler kommt ihm gleich.
unequally [ʌn'iːkwəlɪ] *adv* ungleichmäßig.
unequivocal [ˌʌnɪ'kwɪvəkəl] *adj* unmißverständlich, eindeutig; *answer also* unzweideutig ◆ **he was quite ~ about it** er sagte es ganz unmißverständlich *or* eindeutig *or* klar.
unequivocally [ˌʌnɪ'kwɪvəkəlɪ] *adv see adj.*
unerring [ʌn'ɜːrɪŋ] *adj judgement, eye, accuracy* unfehlbar; *instinct* untrüglich; *aim, blow* treffsicher.
unerringly [ʌn'ɜːrɪŋlɪ] *adv see adj.*
UNESCO [juː'neskəʊ] *abbr of* **United Nations Educational, Scientific and Cultural Organization** UNESCO *f*.
unesthetic *adj* (*US*) *see* **unaesthetic**.
unethical [ʌn'eθɪkəl] *adj* unmoralisch; (*in more serious matters*) unethisch ◆ **it's ~ for a doctor to do that** es verstößt gegen das Berufsethos *or* die Berufsehre, wenn ein Arzt das macht.
uneven [ʌn'iːvən] *adj* **(a)** (*not level*) *surface* uneben; (*irregular*) *line* ungerade; *thickness* ungleich; *pulse, breathing* unregelmäßig; *voice* unsicher, schwankend; *colour, distribution* ungleichmäßig; *quality* unterschiedlich; *temper* unausgeglichen ◆ **the engine sounds ~** der Motor läuft ungleichmäßig.
(b) *number* ungerade ◆ **~ parity** (*Comput*) ungerade Parität.
unevenly [ʌn'iːvənlɪ] *adv see adj (a)* ◆ **the teams were ~ matched** die Mannschaften waren sehr ungleich.
unevenness [ʌn'iːvənnɪs] *n see adj (a)* Unebenheit *f*, Ungeradheit *f*, Ungleichheit *f*, Unregelmäßigkeit *f*, Unsicherheit *f*, Ungleichmäßigkeit *f*, Unterschiedlichkeit *f*, Unausgeglichenheit *f*.
uneventful [ˌʌnɪ'ventfʊl] *adj day, meeting* ereignislos; *career* wenig bewegt; *life also* ruhig, eintönig (*pej*).
uneventfully [ˌʌnɪ'ventfəlɪ] *adv* ereignislos.
unexampled [ˌʌnɪk'zɑːmpld] *adj* beispiellos, unvergleichlich.
unexceptionable [ˌʌnɪk'sepʃnəbl] *adj* einwandfrei; *person* solide.
unexceptional [ˌʌnɪk'sepʃənl] *adj* durchschnittlich.
unexciting [ˌʌnɪk'saɪtɪŋ] *adj time* nicht besonders aufregend ◆ **not ~** nicht gerade eintönig; **how ~!** wie langweilig!
unexpected [ˌʌnɪk'spektɪd] *adj* unerwartet; *arrival, result, development also* unvorhergesehen ◆ **this is an ~ pleasure** (*also iro*) welch eine Überraschung!; **their success was not ~** ihr Erfolg kam nicht unerwartet *or* überraschend; **the role of the ~ in this novel** der Überraschungseffekt in diesem Roman.
unexpectedly [ˌʌnɪk'spektɪdlɪ] *adv* unerwartet; *arrive, happen also* plötzlich, unvorhergesehen ◆ **but then, ~** aber dann, wie aus heiterem Himmel, ...
unexplainable [ˌʌnɪk'spleɪnəbl] *adj* unerklärlich.
unexplained [ˌʌnɪk'spleɪnd] *adj phenomenon* nicht geklärt, ungeklärt; *mystery* unaufgeklärt; *lateness, absence* unbegründet ◆ **a few ~ technical terms** einige unerklärte Fachausdrücke; **to go ~** nicht erklärt werden; **his actions remain ~** für seine Handlungen gibt es immer noch keine Erklärung.
unexploded [ˌʌnɪk'spləʊdɪd] *adj* nicht explodiert.
unexploited [ˌʌnɪk'splɔɪtɪd] *adj resources* ungenutzt; *talent also* brachliegend *attr*, *minerals also* unausgebeutet.

➤ LANGUAGE IN USE: **undoubtedly** → 15.1

unexplored [ˌʌnɪk'splɔːd] *adj mystery* unerforscht; *territory also* unerschlossen.
unexposed [ˌʌnɪk'spəʊzd] *adj* **(a)** *(hidden) villain* nicht entlarvt; *crime* unaufgedeckt. **(b)** *(Phot) film* unbelichtet.
unexpressed [ˌʌnɪk'sprest] *adj sorrow, wish* unausgesprochen.
unexpressive [ˌʌnɪk'spresɪv] *adj style, eyes* ausdruckslos.
unexpurgated [ʌn'ekspɜːgeɪtɪd] *adj book* ungekürzt.
unfading [ʌn'feɪdɪŋ] *adj (fig)* unvergänglich, nie verblassend.
unfailing [ʌn'feɪlɪŋ] *adj zeal, interest, source* unerschöpflich; *optimism, humour also* unbezwinglich; *supply also* endlos; *remedy* unfehlbar; *friend* treu.
unfailingly [ʌn'feɪlɪŋlɪ] *adv* immer, stets.
unfair [ʌn'fɛəʳ] *adj* unfair; *decision, method, remark, criticism also* ungerecht; *(Comm) competition also* unlauter ◆ **to be ~ to sb** jdm gegenüber unfair sein; **~ dismissal** ungerechtfertigte Entlassung.
unfairly [ʌn'fɛəlɪ] *adv* unfair; *treat, criticize etc also* ungerecht; *accuse, punish* zu Unrecht; *dismissed* ungerechterweise, zu Unrecht.
unfairness [ʌn'fɛənɪs] *n* Ungerechtigkeit *f*.
unfaithful [ʌn'feɪθfʊl] *adj* **(a)** *wife, husband, lover* untreu; *friend, servant* treulos ◆ **to be ~ to sb** jdm untreu sein. **(b)** *(inaccurate) translation, description* ungenau ◆ **the translator is ~ to the poem** der Übersetzer verfälscht das Gedicht.
unfaithfulness [ʌn'feɪθfʊlnɪs] *n see adj* **(a)** Untreue *f*; Treulosigkeit *f*. **(b)** Ungenauigkeit *f*.
unfaltering [ʌn'fɔːltərɪŋ] *adj step, voice* fest; *courage* unerschütterlich.
unfalteringly [ʌn'fɔːltərɪŋlɪ] *adv walk* mit festen Schritten; *say* mit fester Stimme.
unfamiliar [ˌʌnfə'mɪljəʳ] *adj* **(a)** *(strange, unknown) experience, taste, sight* ungewohnt; *surroundings also, subject, person* fremd, unbekannt ◆ **it is ~ to me** es ist ungewohnt für mich; es ist mir fremd *or* unbekannt.
(b) *(unacquainted)* **to be ~ with sth** etw nicht kennen, mit etw nicht vertraut sein; **I am not ~ with Greek/that problem** Griechisch/das Problem ist mir nicht gänzlich unbekannt.
unfamiliarity [ˌʌnfəmɪlɪ'ærɪtɪ] *n see adj* **(a)** Ungewohntheit *f*; Fremdheit *f*; Unbekanntheit *f*.
(b) his ~ with economics sein Mangel *m* an ökonomischem Wissen; **because of my ~ with ...** wegen meiner mangelnden Kenntnisse *(+gen)* ... *or* Vertrautheit mit ...
unfashionable [ʌn'fæʃnəbl] *adj* unmodern; *district* wenig gefragt; *hotel, habit, subject* nicht in Mode ◆ **science became ~** Naturwissenschaft geriet aus der Mode.
unfashionably [ʌn'fæʃnəblɪ] *adv dressed* unmodern; *strict etc* altmodisch.
unfasten [ʌn'fɑːsn] **1** *vt* aufmachen; *string, belt also* losmachen; *(detach) tag, dog, horse etc* losbinden; *hair, bonds* lösen.
2 *vi* aufgehen ◆ **how does this dress ~?** wie macht man das Kleid auf?
unfathomable [ʌn'fæðəməbl] *adj* unergründlich.
unfathomed [ʌn'fæðəmd] *adj (lit, fig)* unergründet.
unfavourable, *(US)* **unfavorable** [ʌn'feɪvərəbl] *adj outlook, weather, moment, result* ungünstig; *conditions, circumstances also, wind* widrig; *impression also, opinion, reaction* negativ; *reply* ablehnend, negativ; *trade balance* passiv ◆ **conditions ~ to** *or* **for trade** ungünstige Handelsbedingungen *pl*.
unfavourably, *(US)* **unfavorably** [ʌn'feɪvərəblɪ] *adv see adj* ungünstig; negativ; ablehnend, negativ ◆ **to look ~ on sth** einer Sache *(dat)* ablehnend gegenüberstehen; **to report ~ on sth/to speak ~ of sth** etw negativ *or* ablehnend *or* ungünstig beurteilen; **to be ~ impressed by sth** einen negativen *or* keinen guten Eindruck von etw bekommen.
unfeeling [ʌn'fiːlɪŋ] *adj* gefühllos; *response, reply also* herzlos; *look* ungerührt; *(without sensation also)* empfindungslos.
unfeelingly [ʌn'fiːlɪŋlɪ] *adv* gefühllos, herzlos; *look, listen* ungerührt.
unfeigned [ʌn'feɪnd] *adj* aufrichtig, echt, ungeheuchelt.
unfeminine [ʌn'femɪnɪn] *adj* unweiblich.
unfettered [ʌn'fetəd] *adj (fig)* frei, unbehindert *(by* von).
unfilial [ʌn'fɪljəl] *adj* nicht pflichtbewußt; *(impudent)* ungehörig, respektlos.
unfilled [ʌn'fɪld] *adj* ungefüllt; *job* offen, unbesetzt; *order book* un(aus)gefüllt ◆ **~ vacancies** offene Stellen *pl*.
unfinished [ʌn'fɪnɪʃt] *adj* **(a)** *(incomplete)* unfertig; *work of art* unvollendet; *business* unerledigt ◆ **Schubert's U~** Schuberts Unvollendete. **(b)** *(Tech)* unbearbeitet; *cloth* Natur- ◆ **~ product** Rohprodukt *nt*.
unfit [ʌn'fɪt] *adj* **(a)** *(unsuitable) person, thing* ungeeignet, untauglich; *(incompetent)* unfähig ◆ **~ to drive** fahruntüchtig, nicht in der Lage zu fahren; **he is ~ to be a lawyer/for teaching** er ist als Jurist/Lehrer untauglich; **this is ~ for publication** das kann nicht veröffentlicht werden; **~ to eat** ungenießbar; **road ~ for lorries** für Lastkraftwagen nicht geeignete Straße; **~ to plead** *(Jur)* nicht zurechnungsfähig.
(b) *(Sport: injured)* nicht fit; *(in health also)* schlecht in Form, unfit ◆ **~ (for military service)** untauglich; **to be ~ for work** arbeitsunfähig sein.
unfitness [ʌn'fɪtnɪs] *n* **(a)** *(unsuitableness)* mangelnde Eignung, Untauglichkeit *f*; *(incompetence)* Unfähigkeit *f*. **(b)** *(unhealthiness)* mangelnde Fitneß; *(for military service)* Untauglichkeit *f*.
unfitted [ʌn'fɪtɪd] *adj* ungeeignet, untauglich *(for, to* für).
unfitting [ʌn'fɪtɪŋ] *adj language, behaviour* unpassend, unschicklich, unziemlich ◆ **how ~ that one so talented should** ... wie unfaßbar, daß ein so begabter Mensch ... sollte.
unfittingly [ʌn'fɪtɪŋlɪ] *adv behave* unpassend, unschicklich, unziemlich; *dressed* unpassend.
unfix [ʌn'fɪks] *vt* losmachen; *bayonets* abmachen ◆ **it came ~ed** es hat sich gelöst.
unflagging [ʌn'flægɪŋ] *adj person, zeal, patience* unermüdlich, unentwegt; *enthusiasm* unerschöpflich; *devotion, interest* unverändert stark ◆ **he has an ~ devotion to the cause** er stellte sich unermüdlich in den Dienst der Sache.
unflaggingly [ʌn'flægɪŋlɪ] *adv* unentwegt, unermüdlich.
unflappability [ˌʌnflæpə'bɪlɪtɪ] *n (inf)* Unerschütterlichkeit *f*.
unflappable [ʌn'flæpəbl] *adj (inf)* unerschütterlich, nicht aus der Ruhe zu bringend *attr* ◆ **to be ~** die Ruhe selbst sein, die Ruhe weghaben *(inf)*.
unflattering [ʌn'flætərɪŋ] *adj portrait, comments* wenig schmeichelhaft; *dress, hairstyle, light also* unvorteilhaft.
unfledged [ʌn'fledʒd] *adj bird* (noch) nicht flügge; *(fig)* unerfahren ◆ **an ~ youth** ein Grünschnabel *m*.
unflinching [ʌn'flɪntʃɪŋ] *adj* unerschrocken; *determination* unbeirrbar ◆ **with ~ courage** unverzagt.
unflinchingly [ʌn'flɪntʃɪŋlɪ] *adv* unerschrocken.
unflyable [ʌn'flaɪəbl] *adj plane* unfliegbar.
unfocus(s)ed [ʌn'fəʊkəst] *adj eyes* unkoordiniert.
unfold [ʌn'fəʊld] **1** *vt* **(a)** *paper, cloth* auseinanderfalten, entfalten; *(spread out) map also, wings* ausbreiten; *arms* lösen; *chair, table* aufklappen, auseinanderklappen.
(b) *(fig) story* entwickeln *(to* vor *+dat)*; *plans, ideas also* entfalten, darlegen *(to dat)*; *secret* enthüllen, eröffnen.
2 *vi (story, plot)* sich abwickeln; *(truth)* an den Tag kommen, sich herausstellen; *(view, personality, flower)* sich entfalten; *(countryside)* sich ausbreiten.
unforced [ʌn'fɔːst] *adj* ungezwungen, natürlich.
unforeseeable [ˌʌnfɔː'siːəbl] *adj* unvorhersehbar.
unforeseen [ˌʌnfɔː'siːn] *adj* unvorhergesehen, unerwartet.
unforgettable [ˌʌnfə'getəbl] *adj* unvergeßlich.
unforgivable [ˌʌnfə'gɪvəbl] *adj* unverzeihlich.
unforgivably [ˌʌnfə'gɪvəblɪ] *adv* unverzeihlich ◆ **he said, quite ~, that** ... er sagte, und das war einfach unverzeihlich, daß ...
unforgiving [ˌʌnfə'gɪvɪŋ] *adj* unversöhnlich.
unformatted [ʌn'fɔːmætɪd] *adj (Comput) disk* unformatiert.
unformed [ʌn'fɔːmd] *adj (unshaped) clay, foetus* ungeformt; *(undeveloped) character, idea* unfertig.
unforthcoming [ˌʌnfɔːθ'kʌmɪŋ] *adj person* nicht sehr mitteilsam; *reply* wenig aufschlußreich ◆ **to be ~ about sth** sich nicht zu etw äußern wollen.
unfortunate [ʌn'fɔːtʃnɪt] **1** *adj* unglücklich; *person* glücklos; *day, event, error* unglückselig; *turn of phrase also* ungeschickt; *time* ungünstig ◆ **to be ~** *(person)* Pech haben; **to be ~ in life/in love** kein Glück im Leben haben/Pech *or* kein Glück in der Liebe haben; **it is most ~ that** ... es ist höchst bedauerlich, daß ...; **how very ~ (for you)** welch ein Pech; **it was ~ that he hadn't been informed** ihm ist bedauerlicherweise nicht Bescheid gesagt worden; **the ~ Mr Brown** der arme *or* bedauernswerte Herr Brown.
2 *n* Arme(r), Unglückliche(r) *mf*.
unfortunately [ʌn'fɔːtʃnɪtlɪ] *adv* leider; *chosen* unglücklich; *worded* ungeschickt.
unfounded [ʌn'faʊndɪd] *adj* unbegründet, nicht fundiert; *suspicion also* grundlos; *rumour also, allegations* aus der Luft gegriffen.
unframed [ʌn'freɪmd] *adj picture* ungerahmt.
unfreeze [ʌn'friːz] *pret* **unfroze**, *ptp* **unfrozen** **1** *vt* **(a)** auftauen. **(b)** *(Fin) wages, prices* freigeben.
2 *vi* auftauen.
unfrequented [ˌʌnfrɪ'kwentɪd] *adj* einsam ◆ **the place is ~ except for** ... außer ... kommt niemand dahin.
unfriendliness [ʌn'frendlɪnɪs] *n see adj* Unfreundlichkeit *f*; Feindseligkeit *f*; Unwirtlichkeit *f*.
unfriendly [ʌn'frendlɪ] *adj* unfreundlich *(to sb* zu jdn); *(hostile also) natives, country, act* feindselig; *territory* unwirtlich.
unfrock [ʌn'frɒk] *vt* laisieren *(spec)*, in den Laienstand zurückversetzen.
unfroze [ʌn'frəʊz] *pret of* **unfreeze**.
unfrozen [ʌn'frəʊzn] **1** *ptp of* **unfreeze**.
2 *adj food* ungefroren.
unfruitful [ʌn'fruːtfʊl] *adj soil, woman, discussion* unfruchtbar; *attempt* fruchtlos.
unfulfilled [ˌʌnfʊl'fɪld] *adj* unerfüllt; *person* unausgefüllt ◆ **their prophecies are ~** ihre Prophezeiungen haben sich nicht erfüllt; **to have an ~ desire** schon immer den Wunsch gehabt haben.
unfunded [ʌn'fʌndɪd] *adj (Fin)* unfundiert.
unfunny [ˌʌn'fʌnɪ] *adj (inf)* (gar) nicht komisch ◆ **distinctly ~** alles andere als komisch.
unfurl [ʌn'fɜːl] **1** *vt flag* aufrollen; *sail* losmachen; *(peacock) tail* entfalten.
2 *vi* sich entfalten; *(flag, sails also)* sich aufrollen.
unfurnished [ʌn'fɜːnɪʃt] *adj* unmöbliert.
ungainly [ʌn'geɪnlɪ] *adj animal, movement* unbeholfen; *appearance* unelegant, unansehnlich, unschön; *posture* ungraziös, unschön.
ungenerous [ʌn'dʒenərəs] *adj* kleinlich.
ungentlemanly [ʌn'dʒentlmənlɪ] *adj* unfein; *(impolite)* unhöflich ◆ **it is ~ to do so** das gehört sich nicht für einen Gentleman; **it is ~ not to do so** ein Gentleman sollte das tun.
un-get-at-able [ˌʌnget'ætəbl] *adj (inf)* unerreichbar ◆ **he/the cottage is ~** man kommt an ihn/das Haus einfach nicht ran *(inf)*.
ungird [ʌn'gɜːd] *vt sword* ablegen; *loins* entgürten.
unglazed [ʌn'gleɪzd] *adj window* unverglast; *pottery* unglasiert; *photograph* nicht satiniert.

➤ LANGUAGE IN USE: **unfair** → 26.3 **unforgivable** → 18.1 **unfortunately** → 9.3, 20.4, 26.3

ungodliness [ʌn'gɒdlɪnɪs] *n* Gottlosigkeit *f.*
ungodly [ʌn'gɒdlɪ] **1** *adj* gottlos; *(inf) noise, hour* unchristlich *(inf)* ◆ **an ~ noise** ein Heidenlärm *m (inf).*
2 *n* **the ~** *pl* die Gottlosen *pl.*
ungovernable [ʌn'gʌvənəbl] *adj* **(a)** *desire* unbezähmbar; *passion also* zügellos; *temper* unbeherrscht. **(b)** *country, people* unlenkbar, nicht zu regieren *pred.*
ungraceful [ʌn'greɪsfʊl] *adj* nicht anmutig; *movement* plump, ungelenk; *(of girl also) dancer* ungraziös; *behaviour* unfein.
ungracefully [ʌn'greɪsfəlɪ] *adv see adj.*
ungracious [ʌn'greɪʃəs] *adj* unhöflich; *(gruff) grunt, refusal* schroff; *answer* rüde.
ungraciously [ʌn'greɪʃəslɪ] *adv see adj.*
ungrammatical [ˌʌngrə'mætɪkəl] *adj* ungrammatisch, grammatikalisch falsch ◆ **she does tend to be ~ at times** sie drückt sich manchmal grammatikalisch falsch aus.
ungrammatically [ˌʌngrə'mætɪkəlɪ] *adv see adj.*
ungrateful *adj*, **~ly** *adv* [ʌn'greɪtfʊl, -fəlɪ] undankbar *(to* gegenüber).
ungrounded [ʌn'graʊndɪd] *adj* **(a)** *(unfounded)* unfundiert; *accusations also* aus der Luft gegriffen; *fears* grundlos, unbegründet. **(b)** *(US Elec)* ungeerdet, ohne Erdung.
ungrudging [ʌn'grʌdʒɪŋ] *adj help, support* bereitwillig; *admiration* neidlos; *(generous) person, contribution* großzügig; *praise, gratitude* von ganzem Herzen kommend *attr* ◆ **he was ~ in his praise** er hat mit dem Lob nicht gespart.
ungrudgingly [ʌn'grʌdʒɪŋlɪ] *adv help, support, consent* bereitwillig; *admire, praise* von ganzem Herzen; *give, contribute* großzügig.
unguarded [ʌn'gɑːdɪd] *adj* **(a)** *(undefended)* unbewacht. **(b)** *(fig: careless)* unvorsichtig, unachtsam ◆ **to have ~ conversations** sich sorglos unterhalten; **in an ~ moment he ...** als er einen Augenblick nicht aufpaßte *or* sich nicht vorsah, ... er ...
unguent ['ʌŋgwənt] *n* Salbe *f*, Unguentum *nt (spec).*
unguessable [ʌn'gesəbl] *adj* nicht erratbar.
ungulate ['ʌŋgjʊleɪt] **1** *n* Huftier *nt*, Ungulat *m (spec).*
2 *adj* Huftier-; *creatures* mit Hufen.
unhallowed [ʌn'hæləʊd] *adj ground* ungeweiht.
unhampered [ʌn'hæmpəd] *adj* ungehindert ◆ **~ by clothes/regulations** ohne hemmende Kleidung/ohne den Zwang von Bestimmungen.
unhand [ʌn'hænd] *vt (old, hum)* freigeben, loslassen.
unhandy [ʌn'hændɪ] *adj* unpraktisch.
unhappily [ʌn'hæpɪlɪ] *adv (unfortunately)* leider, unglücklicherweise; *(miserably)* unglücklich ◆ **rather ~ expressed** ziemlich unglücklich ausgedrückt.
unhappiness [ʌn'hæpɪnɪs] *n* Traurigkeit *f*; *(discontent)* Unzufriedenheit *f (with* mit) ◆ **this is a source of much ~ to me** das macht mich ganz unglücklich.
unhappy [ʌn'hæpɪ] *adj (+er)* **(a)** *(sad)* unglücklich; *look, voice also* traurig; *state of affairs* bedauerlich, traurig.
(b) *(not pleased)* unzufrieden *(about* mit), nicht glücklich *(about* über *+acc)*; *(uneasy)* unwohl ◆ **if you feel ~ about it** wenn Sie darüber nicht glücklich sind; *(worried)* wenn Ihnen dabei nicht wohl ist; **I feel ~ about letting him go** ich lasse ihn nur ungern gehen.
(c) *(unfortunate) coincidence, day, match, phrasing* unglücklich; *person* glücklos ◆ **an ~ choice/colour scheme** keine gute Wahl/Farbzusammenstellung.
unharmed [ʌn'hɑːmd] *adj person* unverletzt; *thing* unbeschädigt; *reputation* ungeschädigt; *beauty* nicht beeinträchtigt ◆ **to be ~ by sth** durch etw nicht gelitten haben.
unharness [ʌn'hɑːnɪs] *vt horse* abschirren; *(from carriage)* abspannen.
unhealthy [ʌn'helθɪ] *adj* **(a)** *person* nicht gesund; *climate, place, life complexion*, ungesund; *(inf) car* nicht in Ordnung. **(b)** *curiosity, interest* krankhaft; *influence, magazine* schädlich, schlecht ◆ **it's an ~ relationship** das ist eine verderbliche Beziehung. **(c)** *(inf: dangerous)* ungesund *(inf)*, gefährlich.
unheard [ʌn'hɜːd] *adj* ungehört; *(fig) voice* unbeachtet ◆ **to condemn sb ~** jdn verurteilen, ohne ihn angehört zu haben.
unheard-of [ʌn'hɜːdɒv] *adj (unknown)* gänzlich unbekannt; *(unprecedented)* einmalig, noch nicht dagewesen; *(outrageous)* unerhört.
unheeded [ʌn'hiːdɪd] *adj* unbeachtet ◆ **to go ~** keine Beachtung finden, auf taube Ohren stoßen.
unheedful [ʌn'hiːdfʊl] *adj* **~ of the danger/her plight** ohne von der Gefahr/ihrer mißlichen Lage Notiz zu nehmen, ungeachtet der Gefahr *(gen)*/ihrer mißlichen Lage *(gen) (geh).*
unheeding [ʌn'hiːdɪŋ] *adj (not attending)* unbekümmert; *(not caring also)* gleichgültig, achtlos.
unhelpful [ʌn'helpfʊl] *adj person* nicht hilfreich; *advice, book* nutzlos, wenig hilfreich ◆ **that was very ~ of you** das war wirklich keine Hilfe; **you are being very ~** du bist aber wirklich keine Hilfe.
unhelpfully [ʌn'helpfəlɪ] *adv* wenig hilfreich.
unhesitating [ʌn'hezɪteɪtɪŋ] *adj (immediate) answer, offer* prompt, unverzüglich; *help also, generosity* bereitwillig; *(steady) steps, progress* stet; *(undoubting) answer* fest ◆ **he was ~ in his support** er half, ohne zu zögern; **I was surprised by his ~ acceptance of the plan** ich war erstaunt, daß er dem Plan sofort und ohne zu zögern zugestimmt hat.
unhesitatingly [ʌn'hezɪteɪtɪŋlɪ] *adv* ohne Zögern, ohne zu zögern; *(undoubtingly also)* ohne zu zweifeln.
unhindered [ʌn'hɪndəd] *adj (by clothes, luggage etc)* unbehindert, nicht behindert; *(by regulations)* ungehindert, nicht gehindert; *(by distraction)* ungestört ◆ **~ by luggage** ohne hinderndes Gepäck.
unhinge [ʌn'hɪndʒ] *vt* **to ~ sb/sb's mind** jdn aus der Bahn werfen, jdn völlig verstören; **his mind was ~d** er hatte den Verstand verloren.
unhistorical [ˌʌnhɪs'tɒrɪkəl] *adj (inaccurate)* unhistorisch, ungeschichtlich; *(legendary)* legendär.
unhitch [ʌn'hɪtʃ] *vt horse (from post)* losbinden; *(from wagon)* ausspannen; *caravan, engine* abkoppeln.
unholy [ʌn'həʊlɪ] *adj (+er) (Rel) place* ungeweiht; *spirits* böse; *(inf: reprehensible) delight* diebisch *(inf)*; *alliance* übel; *(inf: awful) mess* heillos; *noise, hour* unchristlich *(inf).*
unhook [ʌn'hʊk] **1** *vt latch, gate* loshaken; *dress* aufhaken; *(take from hook) picture* abhaken; *(free)* losmachen ◆ **the dress came ~ed** das Kleid ging auf.
2 *vi* sich aufhaken lassen.
unhoped-for [ʌn'həʊptfɔːʳ] *adj* unverhofft.
unhorse [ʌn'hɔːs] *vt rider* abwerfen.
unhurried [ʌn'hʌrɪd] *adj pace, person* gelassen; *steps, movement* gemächlich; *meal, journey, life* gemütlich, geruhsam ◆ **after a little ~ reflection I ...** nachdem ich mir das in Ruhe überlegt habe, ... ich ...
unhurriedly [ʌn'hʌrɪdlɪ] *adv* gemächlich, in aller Ruhe.
unhurt [ʌn'hɜːt] *adj* unverletzt.
unhygienic [ˌʌnhaɪ'dʒiːnɪk] *adj* unhygienisch.
uni- ['juːnɪ-] *pref* ein- ◆ **~cameral** Einkammer-; **~cellular** einzellig.
UNICEF ['juːnɪsef] *abbr of* **United Nations International Children's Emergency Fund** UNICEF *f*, Weltkinderhilfswerk *nt* der UNO.
unicorn ['juːnɪˌkɔːn] *n* Einhorn *nt.*
unicycle ['juːnɪˌsaɪkl] *n* Einrad *nt.*
unidentifiable [ˌʌnaɪ'dentɪfaɪbl] *adj* unidentifizierbar.
unidentified [ˌʌnaɪ'dentɪfaɪd] *adj* unbekannt; *body* nicht identifiziert; *belongings* herrenlos ◆ **~ flying object** unbekanntes Flugobjekt.
unidiomatic [ˌʌnɪdɪə'mætɪk] *adj* unidiomatisch.
unification [ˌjuːnɪfɪ'keɪʃən] *n (of country)* Einigung *f*; *(of system)* Vereinheitlichung *f.*
uniform ['juːnɪfɔːm] **1** *adj* **(a)** *(unvarying) length, colour, tax* einheitlich; *treatment also* gleich; *temperature also, pace* gleichmäßig, gleichbleibend *attr*; *(lacking variation) life* gleichförmig, eintönig *(pej)*; *thinking* gleichartig, gleichförmig, uniform *(pej)*; *scenery* einförmig, eintönig *(pej)* ◆ **these houses are so ~** die Häuser gleichen sich alle so.
(b) *(Mil, Sch etc)* Uniform-.
2 *n* Uniform *f* ◆ **in/out of ~** in Uniform/in Zivil, ohne Uniform.
uniformed ['juːnɪfɔːmd] *adj* uniformiert; *person also* in Uniform.
uniformity [ˌjuːnɪ'fɔːmɪtɪ] *n see adj (a)* Einheitlichkeit *f*; Gleichheit *f*; Gleichmäßigkeit *f*; Gleichförmigkeit *f*; Eintönigkeit *f (pej)*; Gleichartigkeit, Uniformität *(pej) f*; Einförmigkeit *f.*
uniformly ['juːnɪfɔːmlɪ] *adv measure, paint, tax* einheitlich; *heat* gleichmäßig; *treat* gleich; *(pej)* einförmig *(pej)*; *think* uniform *(pej).*
unify ['juːnɪfaɪ] *vt* einigen, einen *(geh)*; *theories, systems* vereinheitlichen.
unilateral [ˌjuːnɪ'lætərəl] *adj (Jur)* einseitig; *(Pol also)* unilateral ◆ **~ declaration of independence** einseitige Unabhängigkeitserklärung.
unilateralist [ˌjuːnɪ'lætərəlɪst] **1** *n* Befürworter(in *f*) *m* einseitiger Abrüstung.
2 *adj policies etc* auf einseitige Abrüstung ausgerichtet.
unilaterally [ˌjuːnɪ'lætərəlɪ] *adv* einseitig.
unimaginable [ˌʌnɪ'mædʒɪnəbl] *adj* unvorstellbar.
unimaginative [ˌʌnɪ'mædʒɪnətɪv] *adj* phantasielos, einfallslos; *remark, book* geistlos, phantasielos.
unimaginatively [ˌʌnɪ'mædʒɪnətɪvlɪ] *adv see adj.*
unimpaired [ˌʌnɪm'peəd] *adj quality, prestige* unbeeinträchtigt; *health* unvermindert ◆ **to be ~** nicht gelitten haben.
unimpassioned [ˌʌnɪm'pæʃənd] *adj* leidenschaftslos.
unimpeachable [ˌʌnɪm'piːtʃəbl] *adj reputation, conduct* untadelig; *proof, honesty* unanfechtbar; *source* absolut zuverlässig.
unimpeded [ˌʌnɪm'piːdɪd] *adj* ungehindert.
unimportant [ˌʌnɪm'pɔːtənt] *adj* unwichtig, unbedeutend; *detail also* unwesentlich.
unimposing [ˌʌnɪm'pəʊzɪŋ] *adj* unscheinbar; *building also* wenig imponierend *or* beeindruckend.
unimpressed [ˌʌnɪm'prest] *adj* unbeeindruckt, nicht beeindruckt ◆ **I was ~ by his story** seine Geschichte hat mich überhaupt nicht beeindruckt; **I remain ~** das beeindruckt mich überhaupt nicht.
unimpressive [ˌʌnɪm'presɪv] *adj* wenig beeindruckend; *person also* unscheinbar; *argument, performance also, speaker* wenig überzeugend.
unimproved [ˌʌnɪm'pruːvd] *adj* **(a)** (noch) nicht besser, unverändert schlecht; *method* nicht verbessert ◆ **to leave sth ~** etw nicht verbessern. **(b)** *land* unbebaut, nicht kultiviert; *house* nicht modernisiert.
uninfluenced [ʌn'ɪnfluənst] *adj* unbeeinflußt.
uninfluential [ˌʌnɪnflʊ'enʃəl] *adj* ohne Einfluß.
uninformative [ˌʌnɪn'fɔːmətɪv] *adj person* wenig mitteilsam; *document* ohne Informationsgehalt.
uninformed [ˌʌnɪn'fɔːmd] *adj (not knowing)* nicht informiert *or* unterrichtet *(about* über *+acc)*; *(ignorant also)* unwissend; *criticism* blindwütig ◆ **to be ~ about sth** über etw *(acc)* nicht Bescheid wissen; **to keep sb ~** jdn im dunkeln lassen.
uninhabitable [ˌʌnɪn'hæbɪtəbl] *adj* unbewohnbar.
uninhabited [ˌʌnɪn'hæbɪtɪd] *adj* unbewohnt.
uninhibited [ˌʌnɪn'hɪbɪtɪd] *adj person* frei von Hemmungen, ohne Hemmungen; *greed, laughter* hemmungslos, ungezügelt ◆ **to be ~** keine

Hemmungen haben.
uninitiated [ˌʌnɪ'nɪʃɪeɪtɪd] [1] *adj* nicht eingeweiht ◆ **~ members of a tribe** nicht initiierte Mitglieder eines Stammes.
[2] *n* **the ~** *pl* Nichteingeweihte *pl;* **for the ~ that may seem strange** Nichteingeweihten mag das merkwürdig vorkommen.
uninjured [ʌn'ɪndʒəd] *adj person* unverletzt.
uninspired [ˌʌnɪn'spaɪəd] *adj teacher, performance* phantasielos, ideenlos, einfallslos; *lecture, book* einfallslos ◆ **to be ~ by a subject** von einem Thema nicht begeistert werden.
uninspiring [ˌʌnɪn'spaɪərɪŋ] *adj* trocken; *suggestion, idea* nicht gerade aufregend.
uninsured [ˌʌnɪn'ʃʊəd] *adj* nicht versichert.
unintelligent [ˌʌnɪn'telɪdʒənt] *adj* unintelligent; *approach, action* unklug, ungeschickt ◆ **not ~** eigentlich ganz intelligent.
unintelligibility ['ʌnɪnˌtelɪdʒɪ'bɪlɪtɪ] *n* Unverständlichkeit *f.*
unintelligible [ˌʌnɪn'telɪdʒɪbl] *adj person* nicht zu verstehen; *speech, writing* unverständ lich ◆ **this makes him almost ~** das macht es fast unmöglich, ihn zu verstehen.
unintelligibly [ˌʌnɪn'telɪdʒɪblɪ] *adv* unverständlich.
unintended [ˌʌnɪn'tendɪd], **unintentional** [ˌʌnɪn'tenʃənl] *adj* unbeabsichtigt, unabsichtlich; *joke also* unfreiwillig.
unintentionally [ˌʌnɪn'tenʃnəlɪ] *adv* unabsichtlich, unbeabsichtigt, ohne Absicht; *funny* unfreiwillig.
uninterested [ʌn'ɪntrɪstɪd] *adj* desinteressiert, interesselos ◆ **to be ~ in sth** an etw (*dat*) nicht interessiert sein.
uninteresting [ʌn'ɪntrɪstɪŋ] *adj* uninteressant.
uninterrupted [ˌʌnɪntə'rʌptɪd] *adj* (*continuous*) *line* ununterbrochen, kontinuierlich; *noise, rain also* anhaltend; (*undisturbed*) *rest* ungestört.
uninterruptedly [ˌʌnɪntə'rʌptɪdlɪ] *adv see adj.*
uninvited [ˌʌnɪn'vaɪtɪd] *adj guest* ungeladen, ungebeten; *criticism* unerwünscht, ungebeten.
uninviting [ˌʌnɪn'vaɪtɪŋ] *adj appearance, atmosphere* nicht (gerade) einladend; *prospect* nicht (gerade) verlockend; *smell, food, sight* unappetitlich ◆ **rather ~** wenig einladend/wenig verlockend/ziemlich unappetitlich.
union ['juːnjən] [1] *n* **(a)** Vereinigung, Verbindung *f;* (*uniting also*) Zusammenschluß *m;* (*Pol also*) Union *f* ◆ **the U~** (*US*) die Vereinigten Staaten; (*in civil war*) die Unionsstaaten *pl;* **state of the U~ message** (*US*) ≃ Bericht *m* zur Lage der Nation; **~ of Soviet Socialist Republics** Union *f* der Sozialistischen Sowjetrepubliken.
(b) (*trade ~*) Gewerkschaft *f.*
(c) (*association*) Vereinigung *f;* (*customs ~*) Union *f;* (*postal ~*) Postverein *m;* (*students' ~ also*) Studentenclub *m.*
(d) (*harmony*) Eintracht, Harmonie *f.*
(e) (*form: marriage*) Verbindung *f.*
(f) (*Tech*) Verbindung *f* ◆ **~ joint** Anschlußstück, Verbindungsstück *nt.*
(g) (*Math*) Vereinigung(smenge) *f.*
[2] *adj attr* (*trade ~*) Gewerkschafts- ◆ **~ bashing** (*inf*) Angriffe *pl* auf die *or* Herumhacken *nt* auf den Gewerkschaften; **~ card** Gewerkschaftsausweis *m;* **~ dues** Gewerkschaftsbeitrag *m;* **~ rates** (*wages*) Tariflohn *m;* (*salary*) Tarifgehalt *nt.*
unionism ['juːnjənɪzəm] *n* **(a)** (*trade ~*) Gewerkschaftswesen *nt.* **(b)** (*Pol*) Einigungsbewegung *f* ◆ **U~** (*Brit*) Unionismus *m*, unionistische Bewegung.
unionist ['juːnjənɪst] [1] *n* **(a)** (*trade ~*) Gewerkschaftler(in *f*) *m.* **(b)** (*Pol*) Unionist(in *f*) *m* ◆ **Ulster U~** Ulster Unionist *m.*
[2] *adj* **(a)** (*trade ~*) gewerkschaftlich. **(b)** (*Pol*) Unions- ◆ **U~ MP** (*Ir*) Unionistischer Abgeordneter.
unionization [ˌjuːnjənaɪ'zeɪʃən] *n* (gewerkschaftliche) Organisierung.
unionize ['juːnjənaɪz] [1] *vt* gewerkschaftlich organisieren.
[2] *vi* sich gewerkschaftlich organisieren.
union: U~ Jack *n* Union Jack *m;* **~ shop** *n* gewerkschaftspflichtiger Betrieb; **~ suit** *n* (*US*) lange Hemdhose.
unique [juː'niːk] *adj* einzig *attr;* (*outstanding*) einzigartig, einmalig (*inf*); (*Math*) eindeutig ◆ **you are not ~ in that** da bist du nicht der/die einzige; **such cases are not ~ to Britain** solche Fälle sind nicht nur auf Großbritannien beschränkt.
uniquely [juː'niːklɪ] *adv* (*solely*) einzig und allein, nur; (*outstandingly*) einmalig (*inf*), unübertrefflich ◆ **~ suited** außergewöhnlich geeignet.
uniqueness [juː'niːknɪs] *n* Einmaligkeit, Einzigartigkeit *f* ◆ **because of its ~, this vase ...** weil sie die einzige Vase dieser Art ist, ...
unisex ['juːnɪseks] *adj* Unisex-, unisex.
unison ['juːnɪzn] *n* (*Mus*) Gleichklang, Einklang *m* (*also fig*) ◆ **in ~** unisono (*geh*), einstimmig; **~ singing** einstimmiger Gesang; **to be in ~ (with sth)** übereinstimmen (mit etw); **to act in ~ with sb** (*fig*) in Übereinstimmung mit jdm handeln.
unit ['juːnɪt] *n* **(a)** (*entity, Mil*) Einheit *f;* (*set of equipment also*) Anlage *f* ◆ **camera/X-ray ~** Kameraeinheit/Röntgenanlage *f.*
(b) (*section*) Einheit *f;* (*of furniture*) Element *nt;* (*of machine also*) Element, Teil *nt;* (*of organization also*) Abteilung *f* ◆ **power ~** Aggregat *nt;* (*of a rocket*) Triebwerk *nt;* **where did you get those ~s in your bedroom?** wo haben Sie die Anbauelemente in Ihrem Schlafzimmer her?; **the new research ~** die neue Forschungsabteilung *or* -gruppe; **the family as the basic ~** die Familie als Grundelement.
(c) (*measure*) Einheit *f* ◆ **~ of account/length** Rechnungs-/Längeneinheit *f;* **monetary ~** Währungseinheit *f.*
(d) (*Math*) Einer *m* ◆ **tens and ~s** Zehner und Einer *pl.*
Unitarian [ˌjuːnɪ'tɛərɪən] [1] *adj* unitarisch.
[2] *n* Unitarier(in *f*) *m.*
Unitarianism [ˌjuːnɪ'tɛərɪənɪzəm] *n* Unitarismus *m.*
unitary ['juːnɪtərɪ] *adj* **(a)** (*used as a unit*) Einheits- ◆ **~ weight** Gewichtseinheit *f.* **(b)** (*unified*) einheitlich.
unit cost *n* (*Fin*) Kosten *pl* pro (Rechnungs)einheit.
unite [juː'naɪt] [1] *vt* (*join, also form: marry*) vereinigen, verbinden; *party, country* (*treaty etc*) (ver)einigen, zusammenschließen; (*emotions, ties, loyalties*) (ver)einen ◆ **the common interests which ~ us** die gemeinsamen Interessen, die uns verbinden.
[2] *vi* sich zusammenschließen, sich vereinigen ◆ **to ~ in doing sth** gemeinsam etw tun; **to ~ in prayer/opposition to sth** gemeinsam beten/ gegen etw Opposition machen; **workers of the world, ~!** Proletarier aller Länder, vereinigt euch!
united [juː'naɪtɪd] *adj* verbunden; *group, nation, front* geschlossen; (*unified*) *people, nation* einig; *efforts* vereint ◆ **~ we stand, divided we fall** (*prov*) Einigkeit macht stark (*Prov*); **to present a ~ front** eine geschlossene Front bieten.
United: ~ Arab Emirates *npl* Vereinigte Arabische Emirate *pl;* **~ Arab Republic** *n* Vereinigte Arabische Republik; **~ Kingdom** *n* Vereinigtes Königreich (*Großbritannien und Nordirland*); **~ Nations (Organization)** *n* Vereinte Nationen *pl;* **~ States (of America)** *npl* Vereinigte Staaten *pl* (von Amerika).
unit: ~ furniture *n* Anbaumöbel *pl;* **~-linked** *adj* (*Insur*) fondsgebunden; **~ price** *n* (*price per unit*) Preis *m* pro Einheit; (*inclusive price*) Pauschalpreis *m;* **~ trust** *n* (*Brit Fin*) Unit Trust *m*, Investmentgesellschaft *f;* (*share*) Unit-Trust-Papiere, Investment-Papiere *pl.*
unity ['juːnɪtɪ] *n* **(a)** (*oneness, Liter*) Einheit *f;* (*harmony*) Einmütigkeit, Einigkeit *f;* (*of a novel, painting etc*) Einheitlichkeit, Geschlossenheit *f* ◆ **national ~** (nationale) Einheit; **this ~ of purpose** diese gemeinsamen Ziele; **to live in ~ with** in Eintracht leben mit; **~ is strength** Einigkeit macht stark (*Prov*).
(b) (*Math*) Einheit *f;* (*one*) Eins *f;* (*in set theory*) neutrales Element.
Univ *abbr of* **University** Univ.
univalent [ˌjuːnɪ'veɪlənt] *adj* einwertig.
univalve ['juːnɪvælv] [1] *n* Gastropod *m.*
[2] *adj* einschalig.
universal [ˌjuːnɪ'vɜːsəl] [1] *adj* **(a)** *phenomenon, applicability, remedy* universal, universell; *language, genius, remedy also* Universal-; (*prevailing everywhere also*) *custom, game* allgemein *or* überall verbreitet; (*applying to all also*) *truth, rule* allgemein gültig; (*general*) *approval, peace* allgemein ◆ **~ education** Allgemeinbildung *f;* **~ remedy** Allheilmittel *nt;* **to be a ~ favourite** überall beliebt sein; **~ peace** Weltfrieden *m;* **to become ~** allgemein verbreitet werden.
(b) (*Logic*) universal, universell, allgemein.
[2] *n* (*Philos*) Allgemeinbegriff *m;* (*Logic: ~ proposition*) Universalaussage *f* ◆ **the ~** das Allgemeine; **the various ~s of human society** die verschiedenen Grundelemente der menschlichen Gesellschaft.
universal: ~ coupling *n see* **~ joint;** **~ donor** *n* Universalspender *m.*
universality [ˌjuːnɪvɜː'sælɪtɪ] *n* Universalität *f;* (*of person also*) Vielseitigkeit *f;* (*prevalence also*) allgemeine Verbreitung; (*general applicability*) Allgemeingültigkeit *f.*
universal: ~ joint *n* Universalgelenk *nt;* **~ language** *n* Weltsprache *f.*
universally [ˌjuːnɪ'vɜːsəlɪ] *adv* allgemein ◆ **~ applicable** allgemeingültig.
universal: U~ Postal Union *n* Weltpostverein *m;* **~ product code** *n* (*US: bar code*) Bar-Code *m*, Strichkodierung *f;* **~ suffrage** *n* allgemeines Wahlrecht; **~ time** *n* Weltzeit *f.*
universe ['juːnɪvɜːs] *n* **(a)** (*cosmos*) (Welt)all, Universum *nt;* (*galaxy*) Sternsystem *nt;* (*world*) Welt *f.* **(b)** (*Logic*) **~ of discourse** Gesamtheit *f* aller Gegenstände der Abhandlung.
university [ˌjuːnɪ'vɜːsɪtɪ] [1] *n* Universität *f* ◆ **the ~ of life** die Schule des Lebens; **what is his ~?** wo studiert er?; **to be at ~/to go to ~** studieren; **to go to London U~** in London studieren.
[2] *adj attr town, library, bookshop* Universitäts-; *qualifications, education also* akademisch ◆ **~ entrance (examination)** Zulassungsprüfung *f or* Aufnahmeprüfung *f* zum Studium; **~ man** Akademiker *m;* **~ teacher** Hochschullehrer *m.*
unjust [ʌn'dʒʌst] *adj* ungerecht (*to* gegen) ◆ **you're being ~** das ist ungerecht.
unjustifiable [ʌn'dʒʌstɪfaɪəbl] *adj* nicht zu rechtfertigen *pred or* rechtfertigend *attr* ◆ **it was ~ of them not to ...** es war ihrerseits nicht zu rechtfertigen, nicht zu ...
unjustifiably [ʌn'dʒʌstɪfaɪəblɪ] *adv expensive, severe, critical, act* ungerechtfertigt; *rude* unnötig; *criticize, dismiss, praise* zu Unrecht.
unjustified [ʌn'dʒʌstɪfaɪd] *adj* **(a)** ungerechtfertigt ◆ **to be ~ in thinking that ...** zu Unrecht denken, daß ... **(b)** *text* nicht bündig ◆ **to set sth ~** etw im Flattersatz setzen.
unjustly [ʌn'dʒʌstlɪ] *adv* zu Unrecht; *judge, treat* ungerecht.
unjustness [ʌn'dʒʌstnɪs] *n* Ungerechtigkeit *f.*
unkempt [ʌn'kempt] *adj hair* ungekämmt; *appearance, garden etc* ungepflegt, vernachlässigt.
unkind [ʌn'kaɪnd] *adj* (*+er*) *person, remark, action* (*not nice*) unfreundlich, nicht nett; (*cruel*) lieblos, gemein; *remark also* spitz; (*harsh*) *climate, country, action* schlecht (*to* für) ◆ **don't be (so) ~!** das ist aber gar nicht nett (von dir)!; **to be ~ to animals** nicht gut zu Tieren sein; **~ to the skin** nicht hautfreundlich; **fate has been ~ to him** das Schicksal hat ihn unfreundlich behandelt; **it would be ~ not to tell him the truth** es wäre gemein, ihm nicht

die Wahrheit zu sagen.

unkindly [ʌn'kaɪndlɪ] *adv* unfreundlich, nicht nett; (*cruelly*) lieblos, gemein ◆ **how ~ fate had treated her** wie grausam das Schicksal ihr mitgespielt hatte; **don't take it ~ if** ... nimm es nicht übel, wenn ...; **to take ~ to sth** etw übelnehmen.

unkindness [ʌn'kaɪndnɪs] *n* Unfreundlichkeit *f*; (*cruelty*) Lieblosigkeit, Gemeinheit *f* ◆ **to do sb an ~** jdm Unrecht tun; **the ~ of the weather** das schlechte Wetter.

unknot [ʌn'nɒt] *vt* aufknoten, entknoten.

unknowable [ʌn'nəʊəbl] [1] *adj truths* unbegreiflich, unfaßbar; *person* verschlossen.
[2] *n* **the U~** das Unfaßbare.

unknowing [ʌn'nəʊɪŋ] *adj agent, cause* unbewußt, ohne es zu wissen ◆ **he was the ~ cause of** ... er war unwissentlich *or* ohne es zu wissen die Ursache für ...

unknowingly [ʌn'nəʊɪŋlɪ] *adv* unwissentlich, ohne es zu wissen.

unknown [ʌn'nəʊn] [1] *adj* unbekannt ◆ **~ quantity** unbekannte Größe; (*Math*) Unbekannte *f*; **the ~ soldier** *or* **warrior** der Unbekannte Soldat; **~ territory** (*lit, fig*) Neuland *nt*; **to be ~ to sb** (*feeling, territory*) jdm fremd sein; **it's ~ for him to get up for breakfast** man ist es von ihm gar nicht gewohnt, daß er zum Frühstück aufsteht; **this substance is ~ to science** diese Substanz ist der Wissenschaft nicht bekannt; *see* **person**.
[2] *n* (*person*) Unbekannte(r) *mf*; (*factor, Math*) Unbekannte *f*; (*territory*) unerforschtes Gebiet, Neuland *nt* ◆ **the ~** das Unbekannte; **a voyage into the ~** (*lit, fig*) eine Fahrt ins Ungewisse.
[3] *adv* **~ to me** *etc* ohne daß ich *etc* es wußte.

unlace [ʌn'leɪs] *vt* aufbinden, aufschnüren.

unladylike [ʌn'leɪdɪlaɪk] *adj* undamenhaft, nicht damenhaft.

unlamented [ˌʌnlə'mentɪd] *adj death, loss* unbeklagt, unbeweint ◆ **he died ~** niemand trauerte um ihn.

unlatch [ʌn'lætʃ] *vt* entriegeln.

unlawful [ʌn'lɔːfʊl] *adj* gesetzwidrig; *means, assembly* ungesetzlich, illegal; *wedding* ungültig.

unlawfully [ʌn'lɔːfəlɪ] *adv* gesetzwidrig, illegal; *married* ungültig.

unleaded [ʌn'ledɪd] [1] *adj petrol* unverbleit, bleifrei.
[2] *n* unverbleites *or* bleifreies Benzin ◆ **I use ~** ich fahre bleifrei.

unlearn [ʌn'lɜːn] *vt* sich (*dat*) abgewöhnen; *habit also* ablegen.

unleash [ʌn'liːʃ] *vt dog* von der Leine lassen; (*fig*) (*cause*) *anger, war* entfesseln, auslösen ◆ **he ~ed his fury on his wife** er ließ seine Frau seinen Zorn spüren; **to ~ a war upon the whole world** die ganze Welt in einen Krieg stürzen.

unleavened [ʌn'levnd] *adj bread* ungesäuert.

unless [ən'les] *conj* es sei denn; (*at beginning of sentence*) wenn ... nicht, sofern ... nicht ◆ **don't do it ~ I tell you to** mach das nicht, es sei denn, ich sage es dir; **~ I tell you to, don't do it** sofern *or* wenn ich es dir nicht sage, mach das nicht; **~ I am mistaken** ... wenn *or* falls ich mich nicht irre ...; **~ otherwise stated** sofern nicht anders angezeigt *or* angegeben; **~ there is an interruption** vorausgesetzt, alles läuft ohne Unterbrechung.

unlettered [ʌn'letəd] *adj* ungebildet; (*illiterate*) analphabetisch *attr*.

unliberated [ʌn'lɪbəreɪtɪd] *adj women* unemanzipiert, nicht emanzipiert; *masses, countries* nicht befreit.

unlicensed [ʌn'laɪsənst] *adj* (*having no licence*) *car, dog, TV* nicht angemeldet; *premises* ohne Lizenz *or* (Schank)konzession; (*unauthorized*) unbefugt, unberechtigt ◆ **people with ~ TV sets** Schwarzseher *pl*.

unlike [ʌn'laɪk] [1] *adj* unähnlich, nicht ähnlich; *poles* ungleich, gegensätzlich.
[2] *prep* (a) im Gegensatz zu (*dat*), anders als.
(b) (*uncharacteristic of*) **to be quite ~ sb** jdm (gar) nicht ähnlich sehen; (*behaviour also*) überhaupt nicht zu jdm passen; **how ~ him not to have told us** das sieht ihm gar nicht ähnlich, daß er uns nichts gesagt hat.
(c) (*not resembling*) **this photograph is quite ~ her** dieses Photo sieht ihr gar nicht ähnlich; **this house is ~ their former one** dieses Haus ist ganz anders als ihr früheres.

unlikeable [ʌn'laɪkəbl] *adj* unsympathisch.

unlikelihood [ʌn'laɪklɪhʊd], **unlikeliness** [ʌn'laɪklɪnɪs] *n* Unwahrscheinlichkeit *f* ◆ **despite the ~ of success** obwohl der Erfolg unwahrscheinlich war.

▼ **unlikely** [ʌn'laɪklɪ] *adj* (*+er*) unwahrscheinlich; *explanation also* unglaubwürdig; (*odd also*) *clothes* merkwürdig, komisch ◆ **it is (most) ~/not ~ that** ... es ist (höchst) unwahrscheinlich/es kann durchaus sein, daß ...; **she is ~ to come** sie kommt höchstwahrscheinlich nicht; **it looks an ~ place for mushrooms** es sieht mir nicht nach der geeigneten Stelle für Pilze aus; **he's an ~ choice/he's ~ to be chosen** seine Wahl ist sehr unwahrscheinlich, es ist unwahrscheinlich, daß er gewählt wird; **in the ~ event that** ... im unwahrscheinlichen Fall, daß ...

unlimited [ʌn'lɪmɪtɪd] *adj wealth, time* unbegrenzt; *power also* schrankenlos; *patience* unendlich ◆ **~ company** (*Fin*) Gesellschaft *f* mit unbeschränkter Haftung.

unlined [ʌn'laɪnd] *adj paper* unliniert; *face* faltenlos; (*without lining*) *dress* ungefüttert.

▼ **unlisted** [ʌn'lɪstɪd] *adj phone number, company, items* nicht verzeichnet; *name* nicht aufgeführt ◆ **~ securities market** Freiverkehr *m*.

unlit [ˌʌn'lɪt] *adj road* unbeleuchtet; *lamp* nicht angezündet.

unload [ʌn'ləʊd] [1] *vt* (a) *ship, gun* entladen; *car also, boot, luggage* ausladen; *truck, luggage* abladen; *cargo* löschen. (b) (*inf: get rid of*) (*Fin*) *shares* abstoßen; *furniture, children, problems* abladen (*on(to)* bei); *job, problem* abwälzen (*on(to)* auf *+acc*).
[2] *vi* (*ship*) löschen; (*truck*) abladen.

unlock [ʌn'lɒk] *vt door etc* aufschließen; (*fig*) *heart, secret* offenbaren ◆ **the door is ~ed** die Tür ist nicht abgeschlossen; **to leave a door ~ed** eine Tür nicht abschließen.

unlooked-for [ʌn'lʊktfɔːʳ] *adj* unerwartet, unvorhergesehen; (*welcome also*) unverhofft.

unloose [ʌn'luːs] *vt* (a) (*also* **~n**) *knot, grasp, hair* lösen; *rope, chains also* losmachen. (b) *prisoner* losbinden; *dog also* losmachen, loslassen.

unlovable [ʌn'lʌvəbl] *adj* wenig liebenswert *or* liebenswürdig, unsympathisch.

unloved [ʌn'lʌvd] *adj* ungeliebt.

unlovely [ʌn'lʌvlɪ] *adj sight* unschön; *person* (*in appearance*) abstoßend; (*in character*) garstig, unliebenswert.

unloving [ʌn'lʌvɪŋ] *adj person, home* lieblos, kalt.

unluckily [ʌn'lʌkɪlɪ] *adv* zum Pech, zum Unglück ◆ **~ for him** zu seinem Pech; **the day started ~** der Tag hat schlecht angefangen.

unlucky [ʌn'lʌkɪ] *adj* (*+er*) (a) *person* unglückselig ◆ **~ wretch** Unglücksrabe, Pechvogel *m*; **he's always ~** er ist vom Pech verfolgt; **to be ~** Pech haben; (*not succeed*) keinen Erfolg haben; **~ in love** unglücklich verliebt; **it was ~ for her that she was seen** Pech für sie, daß man sie gesehen hat; **how ~ for you!** was für ein Pech!, das ist wirklich dumm (für dich)!; **he was ~ enough to meet her** er hatte das Pech, sie zu treffen.
(b) *object, action, place* unglückselig; *coincidence, event also, choice* unglücklich; *day also* Unglücks-; *moment also* ungünstig, schlecht gewählt ◆ **to be ~** Unglück *or* Pech bringen; **London has been an ~ place for me** London hat mir nur Pech gebracht; **broken mirrors are ~** zerbrochene Spiegel bringen Unglück; **it's not through any fault of yours, it's just ~** es ist nicht dein Fehler, es ist nur Pech.

unmade [ʌn'meɪd] *adj bed* ungemacht.

unmade-up [ˌʌnmeɪd'ʌp] *adj face* ungeschminkt, ohne Make-up; *road* ungeteert.

unman [ʌn'mæn] *vt* schwach werden lassen; (*make lose courage*) entmutigen, verzagen lassen.

unmanageable [ʌn'mænɪdʒəbl] *adj* (*unwieldy*) *vehicle, boat* schwer zu handhaben *or* manövrieren; *parcel, size* unhandlich; (*uncontrollable*) *animal, person, hair, child* widerspenstig, nicht zu bändigen; *situation* unkontrollierbar ◆ **she finds the stairs ~** sie kann die Treppe nicht schaffen (*inf*) *or* bewältigen; **this company is ~** es ist unmöglich, dieses Unternehmen zu leiten.

unmanly [ʌn'mænlɪ] *adj tears, behaviour* unmännlich; (*cowardly*) feige; (*effeminate*) weibisch.

unmanned [ʌn'mænd] *adj* (*not requiring crew*) *level crossing, space flight* unbemannt; (*lacking crew*) *telephone exchange, lighthouse* unbesetzt, nicht besetzt.

unmannerly [ʌn'mænəlɪ] *adj* ungesittet; *child also* ungezogen; *behaviour* ungehörig; (*at table also*) unmanierlich ◆ **it is ~ to** ... es gehört sich nicht, zu ...

unmarked [ʌn'mɑːkt] *adj* (a) (*unstained*) ohne Flecken *or* Spuren, fleckenlos; (*without marking*) *face* ungezeichnet (*also fig*); *banknotes also* unmarkiert; *linen* nicht gezeichnet; *boxes, crates, suitcases etc* ohne Namen *or* Adresse; *police car* nicht gekennzeichnet ◆ **luckily the carpet was ~ by the wine** glücklicherweise blieben keine Weinspuren auf dem Teppich zurück; **to leave sb ~** spurlos an jdm vorübergehen.
(b) (*Sport*) *player* ungedeckt.
(c) (*Sch*) *papers* unkorrigiert.
(d) (*unnoticed*) unbemerkt.
(e) (*Ling*) unmarkiert.

unmarketable [ʌn'mɑːkɪtəbl] *adj* unverkäuflich, schlecht *or* nicht zu verkaufen.

unmarriageable [ʌn'mærɪdʒəbl] *adj* nicht zu verheiraten *pred*, nicht unter die Haube zu kriegen *pred* (*inf*).

unmarried [ʌn'mærɪd] *adj* unverheiratet ◆ **~ mother** ledige Mutter.

unmask [ʌn'mɑːsk] [1] *vt* (*lit*) demaskieren; (*fig*) entlarven.
[2] *vi* die Maske abnehmen, sich demaskieren.

unmasking [ʌn'mɑːskɪŋ] *n* (*fig*) Entlarvung *f*.

unmatched [ʌn'mætʃt] *adj* unübertrefflich, einmalig, unübertroffen (*for* in bezug auf *+acc*) ◆ **the scenery is ~ anywhere in the world** die Landschaft sucht (in der Welt) ihresgleichen; **to be ~ for beauty** alle anderen an Schönheit übertreffen.

unmechanical [ˌʌnmɪ'kænɪkəl] *adj person* technisch unbegabt.

unmentionable [ʌn'menʃnəbl] [1] *adj* tabu *pred*; *word also* unaussprechlich ◆ **to be ~** tabu sein; **to be an ~ topic** (als Thema) tabu sein.
[2] *n*: **the ~s** (*hum inf*) die edlen Teile (*hum inf*).

unmerciful *adj*, **~ly** *adv* [ʌn'mɜːsɪfʊl, -fəlɪ] unbarmherzig, erbarmungslos.

unmerited [ʌn'merɪtɪd] *adj* unverdient.

unmetalled [ʌn'metld] *adj* (*Brit*) ungeteert.

unmethodical [ˌʌnmɪ'θɒdɪkəl] *adj* unmethodisch.

unmindful [ʌn'maɪndfʊl] *adj* **to be ~ of sth** nicht auf etw (*acc*) achten, etw nicht beachten; **I was not ~ of your needs** ich stand Ihren Bedürfnissen nicht gleichgültig gegenüber.

unmistak(e)able [ˌʌnmɪ'steɪkəbl] *adj* unverkennbar; (*visually*) nicht zu verwechseln.

unmistak(e)ably [ˌʌnmɪ'steɪkəblɪ] *adv* zweifelsohne (*geh*), unverkennbar.

unmitigated [ʌn'mɪtɪgeɪtɪd] *adj* (*not lessened*) *wrath, severity* ungemildert;

➤ LANGUAGE IN USE: **unlikely** → 16.2 **unlisted** → 27.1

(*inf: complete*) *disaster* vollkommen, total; *rubbish* komplett (*inf*); *liar, rogue* Erz- (*inf*).

unmixed [ʌnˈmɪkst] *adj blood* unvermischt.

unmolested [ˌʌnməˈlestɪd] *adj* (*unattacked*) unbelästigt; (*undisturbed*) in Frieden, in Ruhe.

unmoor [ʌnˈmuːəʳ] *vti* losmachen.

unmotivated [ʌnˈməʊtɪveɪtɪd] *adj* unmotiviert; *attack also* grundlos.

unmounted [ʌnˈmaʊntɪd] *adj rider* unberitten; (*thrown from horse*) abgeworfen; *gem* ungefaßt; *gun* nicht fest montiert; *picture* (*not on mount*) nicht aufgezogen; (*not in album*) lose.

unmourned [ʌnˈmɔːnd] *adj* unbeweint; *death also* unbeklagt ◆ **an ~ tyrant** ein Tyrann, dem niemand nachtrauert *or* nachweint; **they went largely ~** kaum einer trauerte ihnen nach.

unmoved [ʌnˈmuːvd] *adj person* ungerührt ◆ **they were ~ by his playing** sein Spiel(en) ergriff sie nicht; **it leaves me ~** das (be)rührt mich nicht; **he remained ~ by her pleas** ihr Flehen ließ ihn kalt, ihr Flehen rührte *or* erweichte ihn nicht.

unmusical [ʌnˈmjuːzɪkəl] *adj person* unmusikalisch; *sound* unmelodisch.

unnam(e)able [ʌnˈneɪməbl] *adj* unsagbar.

unnamed [ʌnˈneɪmd] *adj* (*nameless*) namenlos; (*anonymous*) ungenannt.

unnatural [ʌnˈnætʃrəl] *adj* unnatürlich; (*abnormal also*) *relationship, crime* nicht normal *pred*, widernatürlich, wider die Natur *pred* ◆ **it is ~ for him to be so rude** normalerweise ist er nicht so grob, es ist ungewöhnlich, daß er so grob ist; **it's not ~ to be upset** es ist nur natürlich, da bestürzt zu sein.

unnaturally [ʌnˈnætʃrəlɪ] *adv* unnatürlich; (*extraordinarily also*) *loud, anxious* ungewöhnlich ◆ **not ~, we were worried** es war nur normal *or* natürlich, daß wir uns Sorgen machten.

unnavigable [ʌnˈnævɪgəbl] *adj* nicht schiffbar, nicht befahrbar.

unnecessarily [ʌnˈnesɪsərɪlɪ] *adv* unnötigerweise; *strict, serious* unnötig, übertrieben.

unnecessary [ʌnˈnesɪsərɪ] *adj* unnötig; (*not requisite*) nicht notwendig *or* nötig; (*superfluous also*) überflüssig ◆ **no, you needn't bother thanks, that's quite ~** nein, machen Sie sich keine Umstände, das ist wirklich nicht nötig; **it was quite ~ to be so rude** es war wirklich nicht nötig, so grob zu werden; **really, that was quite ~ of you!** also, das war wirklich überflüssig!

unneighbourly [ʌnˈneɪbəlɪ] *adj behaviour* nicht gutnachbarlich ◆ **it's ~ to do that** als guter Nachbar tut man so etwas nicht.

unnerve [ʌnˈnɜːv] *vt* entnerven; (*gradually*) zermürben; (*discourage*) *speaker* entmutigen ◆ **~d by their reaction** durch ihre Reaktion aus der Ruhe gebracht.

unnerving [ʌnˈnɜːvɪŋ] *adj experience* entnervend; *silence also* zermürbend; (*discouraging also*) entmutigend.

unnoticed [ʌnˈnəʊtɪst] *adj* unbemerkt ◆ **to go** *or* **pass ~** unbemerkt bleiben.

unnumbered [ʌnˈnʌmbəd] *adj* **(a)** (*countless*) unzählig, zahllos. **(b)** (*not numbered*) nicht numeriert; *house also* ohne Nummer.

UNO *abbr of* **United Nations Organization** UNO *f*.

unobjectionable [ˌʌnəbˈdʒekʃnəbl] *adj* einwandfrei ◆ **as a person he is ~ enough** man kann nichts gegen ihn einwenden *or* sagen, er ist als Mensch soweit in Ordnung.

unobservant [ˌʌnəbˈzɜːvənt] *adj* unaufmerksam ◆ **to be ~** ein schlechter Beobachter sein; **how ~ of me** wie unaufmerksam (von mir).

unobserved [ˌʌnəbˈzɜːvd] *adj* (*not seen*) unbemerkt; (*not celebrated*) nicht (mehr) eingehalten *or* beachtet.

unobstructed [ˌʌnəbˈstrʌktɪd] *adj view* ungehindert; *pipe* frei, unverstopft; *path, road* frei, unversperrt.

➤ **unobtainable** [ˌʌnəbˈteɪnəbl] *adj* nicht erhältlich, nicht zu bekommen ◆ **number ~** (*Telec*) kein Anschluß unter dieser Nummer; **your number was ~** deine Nummer war nicht zu bekommen.

unobtrusive *adj*, **~ly** *adv* [ˌʌnəbˈtruːsɪv, -lɪ] unauffällig.

unoccupied [ʌnˈɒkjʊpaɪd] *adj person* unbeschäftigt; *house* leerstehend, unbewohnt; *seat* frei; (*Mil*) *zone* unbesetzt.

unofficial [ˌʌnəˈfɪʃəl] *adj* inoffiziell; (*unconfirmed also*) *information* nicht amtlich ◆ **to take ~ action** (*Ind*) inoffiziell streiken; **in an ~ capacity** inoffiziell.

unofficially [ˌʌnəˈfɪʃəlɪ] *adv* inoffiziell.

unopened [ʌnˈəʊpənd] *adj* ungeöffnet.

unopposed [ˌʌnəˈpəʊzd] *adj* **they marched on ~** sie marschierten weiter, ohne auf Widerstand zu treffen; **~ by the committee** ohne Widerspruch *or* Beanstandung seitens des Ausschusses; **to be returned ~** (*Pol*) ohne Gegenstimmen gewählt werden; **an ~ second reading** (*Parl*) eine zweite Lesung ohne Gegenstimmen.

unorganized [ʌnˈɔːgənaɪzd] *adj* unsystematisch; *person also* unmethodisch; *life* ungeregelt; (*Ind*) nicht (gewerkschaftlich) organisiert ◆ **he is so ~** er hat überhaupt kein System.

unoriginal [ˌʌnəˈrɪdʒɪnəl] *adj* wenig originell.

unorthodox [ʌnˈɔːθədɒks] *adj* unkonventionell, unorthodox.

unpack [ʌnˈpæk] *vti* auspacken.

unpacking [ʌnˈpækɪŋ] *n* Auspacken *nt* ◆ **to do one's ~** auspacken.

unpaid [ʌnˈpeɪd] *adj* unbezahlt.

unpalatable [ʌnˈpælɪtəbl] *adj food, drink* ungenießbar; (*fig*) *fact, truth, mixture* unverdaulich, schwer zu verdauen ◆ **he finds the truth ~** die Wahrheit schmeckt ihm nicht.

unparalleled [ʌnˈpærəleld] *adj* einmalig, beispiellos; (*unprecedented also*) noch nie dagewesen ◆ **an ~ success** ein Erfolg ohnegleichen.

unpardonable [ʌnˈpɑːdnəbl] *adj* unverzeihlich.

unparliamentary [ˌʌnpɑːləˈmentərɪ] *adj behaviour, language* nicht parlamentsfähig, der Würde des Parlamentes nicht entsprechend; *procedure* unparlamentarisch.

unpatented [ʌnˈpeɪtntɪd] *adj* nicht patentiert.

unpatriotic [ˌʌnpætrɪˈɒtɪk] *adj* unpatriotisch.

unpaved [ʌnˈpeɪvd] *adj road, courtyard* nicht gepflastert.

unpeg [ʌnˈpeg] *vt washing* abnehmen; *prices* freigeben.

unperceptive [ˌʌnpəˈseptɪv] *adj* unaufmerksam.

unperfumed [ʌnˈpɜːfjuːmd] *adj* nicht parfümiert.

unperson [ˈʌnpɜːsən] *n* (*Pol*) Unperson *f*.

unperturbable [ˌʌnpəˈtɜːbəbl] *adj* nicht aus der Ruhe zu bringen *pred or* bringend *attr*.

unperturbed [ˌʌnpəˈtɜːbd] *adj* nicht beunruhigt (*by* von, durch), gelassen.

unphilosophical [ˌʌnfɪləˈsɒfɪkəl] *adj* unphilosophisch.

unpick [ʌnˈpɪk] *vt* auftrennen.

unpin [ʌnˈpɪn] *vt dress, hair* die Nadeln entfernen aus; *notice* abnehmen.

unplaced [ʌnˈpleɪst] *adj* (*Sport*) nicht plaziert ◆ **to be ~** sich nicht plaziert haben.

unplanned [ʌnˈplænd] *adj* ungeplant, nicht geplant.

unplayable [ʌnˈpleɪəbl] *adj* unspielbar; *pitch* unbespielbar ◆ **the ball was in an ~ position** der Ball war nicht spielbar.

unpleasant [ʌnˈpleznt] *adj* unangenehm; *person, smile, remark* unliebenswürdig, unfreundlich; *experience, situation also* unerfreulich.

unpleasantly [ʌnˈplezntlɪ] *adv reply* unliebenswürdig, unfreundlich; *warm, smell* unangenehm ◆ **he was getting ~ close to the truth** es war unangenehm, wie nah er an der Wahrheit war.

unpleasantness [ʌnˈplezntnɪs] *n* **(a)** (*quality*) *see adj* Unangenehmheit *f*; Unfreundlichkeit *f*; Unerfreulichkeit *f*. **(b)** (*bad feeling, quarrel*) Unstimmigkeit *f*.

unplug [ʌnˈplʌg] *vt radio, lamp* den Stecker herausziehen von ◆ **~ it first** zieh zuerst den Stecker heraus.

unplugged [ʌnˈplʌgd] *adj* (*Mus*) (rein) akustisch, unplugged *pred*.

unplumbed [ʌnˈplʌmd] *adj* unergründet.

unpolished [ʌnˈpɒlɪʃt] *adj* **(a)** unpoliert; *stone* ungeschliffen. **(b)** (*fig*) *person, manners* ungeschliffen, ungehobelt; *performance* unausgefeilt; *style, language* holprig, unausgefeilt.

unpolluted [ˌʌnpəˈluːtɪd] *adj* sauber, unverschmutzt.

unpopular [ʌnˈpɒpjʊləʳ] *adj person* unbeliebt (*with sb* bei jdm); (*for particular reason also*) unpopulär; *decision, move* unpopulär ◆ **to make oneself ~** sich unbeliebt machen; **I'm ~ with him just now** zur Zeit bin ich bei ihm nicht gut angeschrieben (*inf*).

unpopularity [ʌnˌpɒpjʊˈlærɪtɪ] *n* Unbeliebtheit *f*; (*of decision, move*) Unpopularität *f*, geringe Popularität.

unpractical [ʌnˈpræktɪkəl] *adj* unpraktisch.

unpractised, (*US*) **unpracticed** [ʌnˈpræktɪst] *adj* ungeübt.

unprecedented [ʌnˈpresɪdəntɪd] *adj* noch nie dagewesen; *success also* beispiellos, ohnegleichen (*after n*); *profit, step* unerhört ◆ **this event is ~** dieses Ereignis ist bisher einmalig; **an ~ success** ein beispielloser *or* noch nie dagewesener Erfolg, ein Erfolg ohnegleichen; **you realize it's quite ~ for a president to ...** es ist Ihnen wohl klar, daß es keinen Präzedenzfall dafür gibt, daß ein Präsident ...

unpredictable [ˌʌnprɪˈdɪktəbl] *adj* unvorhersehbar; *result* nicht vorherzusagen *pred or* vorherzusagend *attr*; *behaviour, person, weather* unberechenbar.

unprejudiced [ʌnˈpredʒʊdɪst] *adj* (*impartial*) objektiv, unparteiisch; (*not having prejudices*) vorurteilslos.

unpremeditated [ˌʌnprɪˈmedɪteɪtɪd] *adj* unüberlegt; *crime* nicht vorsätzlich.

unprepared [ˌʌnprɪˈpeəd] *adj* **(a)** nicht vorbereitet; *person also* unvorbereitet ◆ **to be ~ for sth** für etw nicht vorbereitet sein; (*be surprised*) auf etw (*acc*) nicht vorbereitet *or* gefaßt sein; **you've caught me ~** darauf bin ich nicht vorbereitet. **(b)** (*improvised*) unvorbereitet, nicht vorbereitet.

unprepossessing [ˌʌnpriːpəˈzesɪŋ] *adj* wenig gewinnend, wenig einnehmend.

unpresentable [ˌʌnprɪˈzentəbl] *adj* (*in appearance*) nicht präsentabel; *clothes also* unansehnlich; (*socially*) nicht gesellschaftsfähig ◆ **so ~** so wenig präsentabel; **most of his friends are completely ~** mit den meisten seiner Freunde kann man sich in der Öffentlichkeit nicht blicken lassen.

unpretentious [ˌʌnprɪˈtenʃəs] *adj* schlicht, bescheiden; *person, manner also* natürlich; *house, meal etc also* einfach; *style, book* einfach, nicht schwülstig.

unpretentiously [ˌʌnprɪˈtenʃəslɪ] *adv* schlicht, bescheiden, einfach; *speak* natürlich; *write* in einfachen Worten.

unpriced [ʌnˈpraɪst] *adj* ohne Preisschild, nicht ausgezeichnet.

unprincipled [ʌnˈprɪnsɪpld] *adj* skrupellos; *person also* charakterlos.

unprintable [ʌnˈprɪntəbl] *adj* nicht druckfähig ◆ **his answer was ~** seine Antwort war nicht druckreif.

unproductive [ˌʌnprəˈdʌktɪv] *adj capital* nicht gewinnbringend, keinen Gewinn bringend; *soil* unfruchtbar, ertragsarm; *discussion, meeting* unproduktiv, unergiebig.

unprofessional [ˌʌnprəˈfeʃənl] *adj* unprofessionell; *work also* unfachmännisch, laienhaft, stümperhaft; *conduct* berufswidrig.

unprofitable [ʌnˈprɒfɪtəbl] *adj* (*financially*) keinen Profit bringend *or* abwerfend, wenig einträglich; *mine etc* unrentabel; (*fig*) nutzlos, sinnlos ◆ **the company was ~** die Firma machte keinen Profit *or* warf keinen Profit ab; **we spent an ~ hour** wir haben eine Stunde verplempert; **it would be ~ to go on** es wäre sinnlos, noch weiterzumachen.

➤ LANGUAGE IN USE: **unobtainable** → 27.7

unpromising [ʌnˈprɒmɪsɪŋ] *adj* nicht sehr vielversprechend; *start also* nicht sehr erfolgversprechend, wenig erfolgversprechend ◆ **to look ~** nicht sehr hoffnungsvoll *or* gut aussehen; (*weather*) nichts Gutes versprechen.

unprompted [ʌnˈprɒmptɪd] *adj* spontan ◆ **~ by me** unaufgefordert; **his invitation was quite ~** seine Einladung kam ganz aus freien Stücken; **I'd rather he answered the questions ~** es wäre mir lieber, wenn er ohne Vorsagen antwortete.

unpronounceable [ˌʌnprəˈnaʊnsɪbl] *adj* unaussprechbar ◆ **that word is ~** das Wort ist nicht auszusprechen.

unpropitious [ˌʌnprəˈpɪʃəs] *adj omen, moment* ungünstig.

unprotected [ˌʌnprəˈtektɪd] *adj* ohne Schutz, schutzlos; *machine, sex* ungeschützt; (*by insurance*) ohne Versicherungsschutz; (*Mil*) *building etc* ungeschützt, ohne Deckung ◆ **~ by** nicht geschützt durch.

unprovable [ʌnˈpruːvəbl] *adj* nicht beweisbar.

unproved [ʌnˈpruːvd] *adj* nicht bewiesen, unbewiesen ◆ **he's still ~ as a minister** als Minister muß er sich erst noch bewähren.

unprovided [ˌʌnprəˈvaɪdɪd] *adj* (*not equipped*) **~ with** nicht ausgestattet mit, ohne.

unprovided-for [ˌʌnprəˈvaɪdɪdfɔːʳ] *adj* **(a)** (*lacking*) unversorgt ◆ **he died and left his children ~** er starb, ohne für seine Kinder gesorgt zu haben. **(b)** (*not anticipated*) **that eventuality was ~** auf dieses Ereignis war man nicht eingerichtet.

unprovoked [ˌʌnprəˈvəʊkt] *adj* ohne Anlaß, grundlos.

unpublished [ʌnˈpʌblɪʃt] *adj* unveröffentlicht.

unpunctual [ʌnˈpʌŋktjʊəl] *adj* unpünktlich.

unpunctuality [ˌʌnpʌŋktjʊˈælɪtɪ] *n* Unpünktlichkeit *f*.

unpunished [ʌnˈpʌnɪʃt] *adj* unbestraft ◆ **to go ~** ohne Strafe bleiben; **if this goes ~ ...** wenn das nicht bestraft wird ...

unputdownable [ˌʌnpʊtˈdaʊnəbl] *adj* (*inf*) **it's absolutely ~** (*book*) es läßt einen nicht los; **he's ~** er ist (einfach) nicht unterzukriegen (*inf*).

unqualified [ʌnˈkwɒlɪfaɪd] *adj* **(a)** unqualifiziert ◆ **to be ~** nicht qualifiziert sein. **(b)** (*absolute*) *delight, praise, acceptance* uneingeschränkt; *denial* vollständig; *success* voll(ständig); (*inf*) *idiot, liar* ausgesprochen. **(c)** (*Gram*) nicht bestimmt.

unquenchable [ʌnˈkwentʃəbl] *adj fire* unlöschbar; *thirst, desire* unstillbar.

unquestionable [ʌnˈkwestʃənəbl] *adj authority* unbestritten, unangefochten; *evidence, fact* unbezweifelbar; *sincerity, honesty* fraglos ◆ **a man of ~ honesty** ein zweifellos *or* fraglos ehrlicher Mann; **one's parents' authority used to be ~** früher konnte man die Autorität seiner Eltern nicht in Frage stellen; **his honesty is ~** seine Ehrlichkeit steht außer Frage.

unquestionably [ʌnˈkwestʃənəblɪ] *adv* fraglos, zweifellos.

unquestioned [ʌnˈkwestʃənd] *adj* unbestritten ◆ **I can't let that statement pass ~** ich kann diese Behauptung nicht fraglos hinnehmen; **to be ~** (*honesty etc*) außer Frage stehen; (*social order etc*) nicht in Frage gestellt werden.

unquestioning [ʌnˈkwestʃənɪŋ] *adj* bedingungslos; *belief, faith also* blind.

unquestioningly [ʌnˈkwestʃənɪŋlɪ] *adv accept* blind, ohne zu fragen.

unquiet [ʌnˈkwaɪət] *adj* (*liter*) unruhig; (*restless*) ruhelos.

unquote [ʌnˈkwəʊt] *vi* (*imper only*) Ende des Zitats.

unravel [ʌnˈrævəl] **1** *vt knitting* aufziehen; (*lit, fig: untangle*) entwirren; *mystery* lösen.
2 *vi* (*knitting*) sich aufziehen; (*fig*) sich entwirren, sich auflösen; (*mystery*) sich lösen.

unread [ʌnˈred] *adj book* ungelesen; *person* wenig belesen.

unreadable [ʌnˈriːdəbl] *adj writing* unleserlich; *book* schwer zu lesen *pred*, schwer lesbar.

unreadiness [ʌnˈredɪnɪs] *n* Unvorbereitetheit *f*; (*of troops*) mangelnde Bereitschaft.

unready [ʌnˈredɪ] *adj* (noch) nicht fertig ◆ **~ to do sth** nicht bereit, etw zu tun; **he was ~ for what happened next** er war nicht auf das eingestellt *or* vorbereitet, was dann kam; **he is ~ for such responsibility** er ist noch nicht reif genug, solch eine Verantwortung zu übernehmen.

unreal [ʌnˈrɪəl] *adj* unwirklich ◆ **this is just ~!** (*inf: unbelievable*) das darf doch nicht wahr sein!, das gibt's doch nicht! (*inf*); **he's ~** er ist unmöglich.

unrealistic [ˌʌnrɪəˈlɪstɪk] *adj* unrealistisch.

unreality [ˌʌnrɪˈælɪtɪ] *n* Unwirklichkeit *f* ◆ **there is an air of ~ about it** es hat etwas Unwirkliches an sich; **extreme exhaustion gives a feeling of ~** extreme Erschöpfung läßt alles unwirklich erscheinen; **the ~ of the characters' emotions** die Unnatürlichkeit *or* Unechtheit der Gefühle der Personen.

unrealized [ʌnˈrɪəlaɪzd] *adj* unverwirklicht; (*Fin*) *assets* unverwertet; *profit* nicht realisiert.

unreasonable [ʌnˈriːznəbl] *adj demand, price etc* unzumutbar, übertrieben; *person* uneinsichtig; (*showing lack of sense*) unvernünftig ◆ **to be ~ about sth** (*not be understanding*) kein Verständnis für etw zeigen; (*be overdemanding*) in bezug auf etw (*acc*) zuviel verlangen; **it is ~ to ...** es ist zuviel verlangt, zu ...; **it is ~ to expect children to keep quiet** man kann doch von Kindern nicht verlangen, ruhig zu sein; **that's not ~, is it?** das ist doch nicht zuviel verlangt, oder?; **you are being very ~!** das ist wirklich zuviel verlangt!; **look, don't be ~, it is 100 miles** nun mach mal einen Punkt *or* nun sei mal vernünftig, es sind immerhin 100 Meilen; **an ~ length of time** übermäßig *or* übertrieben lange; **at this ~ hour** zu dieser unzumutbaren Zeit.

unreasonableness [ʌnˈriːznəblnɪs] *n* (*of demands etc*) Unzumutbarkeit, Übermäßigkeit *f*; (*of person*) Uneinsichtigkeit *f* ◆ **I hadn't reckoned with his ~** ich hatte nicht damit gerechnet, daß er so uneinsichtig sein würde; **I commented on his ~ in expecting 20%** ich bemerkte, daß 20% wohl zuviel verlangt wären.

unreasonably [ʌnˈriːznəblɪ] *adv long, slow, high, strict* übermäßig, übertrieben ◆ **he remained ~ stubborn** er blieb unnötig stur; **he argued, quite ~ I think, that we should have known** er sagte, meiner Meinung nach ungerechtfertigterweise, daß wir das hätten wissen müssen.

unreasoning [ʌnˈriːznɪŋ] *adj person* kopflos, unvernünftig; *action, fear, hatred* blind, unsinnig.

unreceptive [ˌʌnrɪˈseptɪv] *adj* unempfänglich (*to* für); *audience also* unaufgeschlossen.

unrecognizable [ʌnˈrekəgnaɪzəbl] *adj* nicht wiederzuerkennen *pred or* wiederzuerkennend *attr* ◆ **he was ~ in his disguise** er war in seiner Verkleidung nicht zu erkennen; **they've made the city centre ~** das Stadtzentrum ist nicht wiederzuerkennen.

unrecognized [ʌnˈrekəgnaɪzd] *adj* (*not noticed*) *person, danger, value* unerkannt; (*not acknowledged*) *government, record* nicht anerkannt; *genius, talent* ungewürdigt, unerkannt ◆ **~ by the crowds** ohne von den Leuten erkannt zu werden; **his achievements went ~** seine Leistungen fanden keine Anerkennung *or* wurden nicht gewürdigt.

unreconstructed [ˌʌnriːkənˈstrʌktɪd] *adj* (*pej*) *system, idea, policy* unverändert ◆ **she's an ~ communist** sie ist eingefleischte Kommunistin.

unrecorded [ˌʌnrɪˈkɔːdɪd] *adj* nicht aufgenommen; (*Rad, TV*) nicht aufgezeichnet; (*in documents*) nicht schriftlich erfaßt *or* festgehalten ◆ **to go ~** nicht aufgenommen/festgehalten werden.

unredeemed [ˌʌnrɪˈdiːmd] *adj* **(a)** *sinner* unerlöst ◆ **a life of ~ wickedness** ein durch und durch schlechtes Leben; **~ by** nicht ausgeglichen *or* wettgemacht durch. **(b)** *bill*, (*from pawn*) uneingelöst; *mortgage, debt* ungetilgt.

unreel [ʌnˈriːl] **1** *vt* abspulen, abwickeln.
2 *vi* sich abspulen, sich abwickeln, abrollen.

unrefined [ˌʌnrɪˈfaɪnd] *adj* **(a)** *petroleum, sugar, metal* nicht raffiniert. **(b)** *person* unkultiviert; *manners also* unfein.

unreflecting [ˌʌnrɪˈflektɪŋ] *adj person* gedankenlos, unbedacht; *act, haste* unbesonnen; *emotion* unreflektiert.

unregarded [ˌʌnrɪˈgɑːdɪd] *adj* unbeachtet, nicht beachtet ◆ **to go ~** unbeachtet bleiben; **to be ~** nicht beachtet werden.

unregenerate [ˌʌnrɪˈdʒenɪrɪt] *adj* (*unrepentant*) reu(e)los, nicht reuig; (*unreformed*) unbekehrbar; (*stubborn*) *reactionary* hartnäckig; (*wicked*) *life* sündig.

unregistered [ʌnˈredʒɪstəd] *adj birth* nicht gemeldet; *car* nicht angemeldet; *voter* nicht (im Wählerverzeichnis) eingetragen; *trademark* nicht gesetzlich geschützt; *letter* nicht eingeschrieben; *lawyer, doctor, taxi* nicht zugelassen.

unregretted [ˌʌnrɪˈgretɪd] *adj absence, death* nicht bedauert; *person* nicht vermißt; *words* nicht bereut.

unregulated [ʌnˈregjʊleɪtɪd] *adj* unkontrolliert.

unrehearsed [ˌʌnrɪˈhɜːst] *adj* (*Theat etc*) nicht geprobt; *cast* schlecht eingespielt; (*spontaneous*) *incident* spontan.

unrelated [ˌʌnrɪˈleɪtɪd] *adj* (*unconnected*) ohne Beziehung (*to* zu); (*by family*) nicht verwandt ◆ **~ to reality** wirklichkeitsfremd; **the two events are ~/are not ~** die beiden Ereignisse stehen in keinem Zusammenhang miteinander/sind nicht gänzlich ohne Zusammenhang.

unrelenting [ˌʌnrɪˈlentɪŋ] *adj pressure* unablässig; *opposition* unerbittlich; *determination* hartnäckig; *pace, severity* unvermindert; *attack, struggle* unerbittlich, unvermindert; *rain* anhaltend *attr*, nicht nachlassend *attr*; (*not merciful*) *person, heat* unbarmherzig ◆ **we must be ~ in our struggle** wir müssen unablässig weiterkämpfen; **they kept up an ~ attack** sie führten den Angriff mit unverminderter Stärke durch.

unreliability [ˈʌnrɪˌlaɪəˈbɪlɪtɪ] *n* Unzuverlässigkeit *f*.

unreliable [ˌʌnrɪˈlaɪəbl] *adj* unzuverlässig.

unrelieved [ˌʌnrɪˈliːvd] *adj pain* ungehindert, ungemindert; *gloom, anguish* ungemindert; *mediocrity* unverändert, gleichbleibend *attr*; *grey* einheitlich, durch nichts aufgelockert; *sameness* eintönig, einförmig; *monotony, boredom* tödlich ◆ **a life of ~ drudgery** ein Leben, das eine einzige Schinderei ist; **to be ~ by** nicht aufgelockert sein durch *or* von.

unremarkable [ˌʌnrɪˈmɑːkəbl] *adj* nicht sehr bemerkenswert, wenig bemerkenswert.

unremarked [ˌʌnrɪˈmɑːkt] *adj* unbemerkt ◆ **to go ~** unbemerkt bleiben.

unremitting [ˌʌnrɪˈmɪtɪŋ] *adj efforts, toil* unaufhörlich, unablässig; *zeal* unermüdlich; *hatred* unversöhnlich.

unremittingly [ˌʌnrɪˈmɪtɪŋlɪ] *adv* unaufhörlich, ohne Unterlaß; *strive* unermüdlich.

unremunerative [ˌʌnrɪˈmjuːnərətɪv] *adj* nicht lohnend, nicht einträglich.

unrepeatable [ˌʌnrɪˈpiːtəbl] *adj* **(a)** *words, views* nicht wiederholbar. **(b)** *offer* einmalig.

unrepentant [ˌʌnrɪˈpentənt] *adj* nicht reuig, nicht reumütig, reu(e)los ◆ **he is ~ about it** er bereut es nicht.

unreported [ˌʌnrɪˈpɔːtɪd] *adj events* nicht berichtet ◆ **to go ~** nicht berichtet werden.

unrepresentative [ˌʌnreprɪˈzentətɪv] *adj* (*Pol*) *government* nicht frei gewählt; (*untypical*) nicht repräsentativ (*of* für) ◆ **the Party is ~ of the people** die Partei repräsentiert das Volk nicht.

unrepresented [ˌʌnreprɪˈzentɪd] *adj* nicht vertreten.

unrequited [ˌʌnrɪˈkwaɪtɪd] *adj love* unerwidert, unglücklich.

unreserved [ˌʌnrɪˈzɜːvd] *adj* **(a)** (*frank*) *person* nicht reserviert, offen ◆ **he's quite ~ about his feelings** er zeigt seine Gefühle ganz offen. **(b)** (*complete*) *approval* uneingeschränkt. **(c)** (*not booked*) nicht reserviert.

unreservedly [ˌʌnrɪˈzɜːvɪdlɪ] *adv speak* freimütig, offen; *approve, trust* uneingeschränkt; *sob* rückhaltlos.
unresisting [ˌʌnrɪˈzɪstɪŋ] *adj* widerstandslos, keinen Widerstand leistend *attr* ◆ **I pushed open the ~ door** ich stieß die Tür auf, die ohne weiteres nachgab.
unresolved [ˌʌnrɪˈzɒlvd] *adj* **(a)** *difficulty, problem* ungelöst. **(b)** (*uncertain*) *person* unschlüssig ◆ **he is still ~ as to what to do** er ist sich (*dat*) noch (darüber) unschlüssig, was er tun soll.
unresponsive [ˌʌnrɪˈspɒnsɪv] *adj* (*physically*) nicht reagierend *attr*; (*emotionally, intellectually*) gleichgültig, unempfänglich ◆ **to be ~** nicht reagieren (*to* auf +*acc*); (*to advances, pleas, request also*) nicht empfänglich sein (*to* für); **an ~ audience** ein Publikum, das nicht mitgeht *or* nicht reagiert; **I suggested it but he was fairly ~** ich habe es vorgeschlagen, aber er ist nicht groß darauf eingegangen *or* er zeigte sich nicht sehr interessiert; **still heavily sedated and totally ~** unter starkem Drogeneinfluß und völlig teilnahmslos.
unrest [ʌnˈrest] *n* Unruhen *pl*; (*discontent*) Unzufriedenheit *f* ◆ **there was ~ among the workers** die Arbeiter waren unzufrieden.
unrested [ʌnˈrestɪd] *adj* unausgeruht.
unresting [ʌnˈrestɪŋ] *adj efforts* unermüdlich.
unrestrained [ˌʌnrɪˈstreɪnd] *adj* uneingeschränkt, unkontrolliert; *feelings* offen, ungehemmt; *joy, enthusiasm, atmosphere* ungezügelt; *language, behaviour* ausfallend, unbeherrscht.
unrestricted [ˌʌnrɪˈstrɪktɪd] *adj power, use, growth* unbeschränkt, uneingeschränkt; *access* ungehindert.
unrevealed [ˌʌnrɪˈviːld] *adj facts* nicht veröffentlicht ◆ **hitherto ~ secrets** bis jetzt ungelüftete Geheimnisse.
unrewarded [ˌʌnrɪˈwɔːdɪd] *adj* unbelohnt ◆ **to go ~** unbelohnt bleiben; (*not gain recognition*) keine Anerkennung finden; **his efforts were ~ by any success** seine Bemühungen waren nicht von Erfolg gekrönt.
unrewarding [ˌʌnrɪˈwɔːdɪŋ] *adj work* undankbar; (*financially*) wenig einträglich ◆ **further study of this book would be ~** es würde sich nicht lohnen, das Buch weiterzulesen.
unrhymed [ʌnˈraɪmd] *adj* ungereimt.
unrhythmical [ʌnˈrɪðmɪkəl] *adj tune, person* unrhythmisch.
unrig [ʌnˈrɪg] *vt* (*Naut*) abtakeln.
unrighteous [ʌnˈraɪtʃəs] *adj* (*Rel*) sündig ◆ **the ~** *pl* die Sünder *pl*.
unripe [ʌnˈraɪp] *adj* unreif.
unrivalled, (*US*) **unrivaled** [ʌnˈraɪvəld] *adj* unerreicht, unübertroffen ◆ **~ in** *or* **for quality** von unübertroffener Qualität.
unroadworthiness [ʌnˈrəʊdˌwɜːðɪnɪs] *n* mangelnde Verkehrssicherheit.
unroadworthy [ʌnˈrəʊdˌwɜːðɪ] *adj* nicht verkehrssicher.
unrobe [ʌnˈrəʊb] [1] *vi* (*form*) sich entkleiden (*geh*); (*hum*) sich enthüllen (*hum*).
[2] *vt* (*form*) entkleiden (*geh*); (*hum*) enthüllen (*hum*).
unroll [ʌnˈrəʊl] [1] *vt carpet, map* aufrollen; (*fig*) *story also* darlegen, schildern.
[2] *vi* (*carpet etc*) sich aufrollen; (*fig*) (*plot*) sich abwickeln; (*landscape*) sich ausbreiten.
unromantic [ˌʌnrəˈmæntɪk] *adj* unromantisch.
unrope [ʌnˈrəʊp] [1] *vt box* losbinden.
[2] *vi* (*Mountaineering*) sich vom Seil losmachen.
unrounded [ʌnˈraʊndɪd] *adj* (*Phon*) ungerundet.
unruffled [ʌnˈrʌfld] *adj person* gelassen; *sea* ruhig, unbewegt; *hair* ordentlich, unzerzaust; *calm* unerschütterlich ◆ **she was quite ~** sie blieb ruhig und gelassen, sie bewahrte die Ruhe.
unruled [ʌnˈruːld] *adj paper* unliniert.
unruliness [ʌnˈruːlɪnɪs] *n* Wildheit, Ungebärdigkeit *f*.
unruly [ʌnˈruːlɪ] *adj* (+*er*) *child, behaviour* wild, ungebärdig; *hair* widerspenstig, nicht zu bändigend *attr*.
unsaddle [ʌnˈsædl] *vt horse* absatteln; *rider* abwerfen.
unsafe [ʌnˈseɪf] *adj ladder, machine, car, person* nicht sicher; (*dangerous*) *journey, toy, wiring* gefährlich ◆ **this is ~ to eat/drink** das ist nicht genießbar/trinkbar; **to feel ~** sich nicht sicher fühlen; **he looked ~ swaying about at the top of the ladder** es sah gefährlich aus, wie er oben auf der Leiter hin und her schaukelte.
unsaid [ʌnˈsed] [1] *pret, ptp of* **unsay**.
[2] *adj* ungesagt, unausgesprochen ◆ **to leave sth ~** etw unausgesprochen lassen; **it's best left ~** das bleibt besser ungesagt.
unsalaried [ʌnˈsælərɪd] *adj* ehrenamtlich.
unsaleable [ʌnˈseɪləbl] *adj* unverkäuflich ◆ **to be ~** sich nicht verkaufen lassen; **bread becomes ~ after 2 days** Brot kann man nach 2 Tagen nicht mehr verkaufen.
unsalted [ʌnˈsɔːltɪd] *adj* ungesalzen.
unsanitary [ʌnˈsænɪtrɪ] *adj* unhygienisch.
unsatisfactoriness [ˌʌnsætɪsˈfæktərɪnɪs] *n* (*of service, hotel, work*) Unzulänglichkeit *f* ◆ **the ~ of these results/such a solution** solch unbefriedigende Resultate *pl*/eine so unbefriedigende Lösung; **because of his ~ he was not kept on** da er nicht den Erwartungen entsprach, behielt man ihn nicht; **the ~ of our profit margin** die nicht ausreichende Gewinnspanne.
unsatisfactory [ˌʌnsætɪsˈfæktərɪ] *adj* unbefriedigend; *result also* nicht zufriedenstellend; *profits, figures* nicht ausreichend; *service, hotel* unzulänglich, schlecht; (*Sch*) mangelhaft; ungenügend ◆ **he was ~** er entsprach nicht den Erwartungen; **this is highly ~** das läßt sehr zu wünschen übrig.
unsatisfied [ʌnˈsætɪsfaɪd] *adj person* nicht zufrieden, unzufrieden; (*not fulfilled*) unbefriedigt, nicht zufrieden; (*not convinced*) nicht überzeugt; *appetite, desire, need* unbefriedigt; *curiosity* unbefriedigt, ungestillt ◆ **the meal left me ~** das Essen hat mich nicht gesättigt; **the book's ending left us ~** wir fanden den Schluß des Buches unbefriedigend; **a job that leaves him ~** eine Arbeit, die ihn nicht befriedigt.
unsatisfying [ʌnˈsætɪsfaɪɪŋ] *adj* unbefriedigend; *meal* unzureichend, nicht sättigend.
unsaturated [ʌnˈsætʃəreɪtɪd] *adj* (*Chem*) ungesättigt.
unsavoury, (*US*) **unsavory** [ʌnˈseɪvərɪ] *adj* **(a)** (*tasteless*) *food* fade, geschmacklos.
(b) (*unpleasant*) *smell, sight* widerwärtig, widerlich; *appearance* (*repulsive*) abstoßend, widerwärtig; (*dishonest, shady etc*) fragwürdig; *subject, details, rumours* unerfreulich; *joke* unfein; *district* übel, fragwürdig; *characters* zwielichtig, übel; *reputation* zweifelhaft, schlecht.
unsay [ʌnˈseɪ] *pret, ptp* **unsaid** *vt* ungesagt machen.
unscalable [ʌnˈskeɪləbl] *adj* unbezwingbar.
unscaled [ʌnˈskeɪld] *adj heights* unbezwungen.
unscarred [ʌnˈskɑːd] *adj* (*fig*) nicht gezeichnet.
unscathed [ʌnˈskeɪðd] *adj* (*lit*) unverletzt, unversehrt; (*by war etc*) unverwundet; (*fig*) unbeschadet; *relationship* heil ◆ **to escape ~** (*fig*) ungeschoren davonkommen.
unscented [ʌnˈsentɪd] *adj* ohne Duftstoffe, geruchlos.
unscheduled [ʌnˈʃedjuːld] *adj stop, flight etc* außerfahrplanmäßig; *meeting* außerplanmäßig.
unscholarly [ʌnˈskɒləlɪ] *adj work, approach* unwissenschaftlich; *person* unakademisch; (*not learned*) ungelehrt ◆ **he was an ~-looking figure** er sah gar nicht wie ein Gelehrter aus.
unschooled [ʌnˈskuːld] *adj* ungebildet, ohne Schulbildung; *talent* unausgebildet ◆ **to be ~ in** nichts wissen über (+*acc*).
unscientific [ˌʌnsaɪənˈtɪfɪk] *adj* unwissenschaftlich.
unscramble [ʌnˈskræmbl] *vt* entwirren, auseinanderklauben (*inf*); (*Telec*) *message* entschlüsseln.
unscratched [ʌnˈskrætʃt] *adj* nicht zerkratzt; *record* ohne Kratzer; (*unhurt*) heil, ungeschoren.
unscreened [ʌnˈskriːnd] *adj* **(a)** *film* nicht gezeigt, unaufgeführt ◆ **many films remain ~** viele Filme werden nie gezeigt *or* bleiben unaufgeführt. **(b)** (*not protected*) *door, window* offen, nicht abgeschirmt. **(c)** (*not inspected*) (*by security*) nicht überprüft; (*for disease*) nicht untersucht.
unscrew [ʌnˈskruː] [1] *vt* (*loosen*) losschrauben; *plate, lid also* abschrauben ◆ **to come ~ed** sich lösen.
[2] *vi* sich los- *or* abschrauben lassen; (*become loose*) sich lösen.
unscripted [ʌnˈskrɪptɪd] *adj* improvisiert.
unscrupulous [ʌnˈskruːpjʊləs] *adj person, behaviour* skrupellos, gewissenlos ◆ **he is ~ about money** er ist skrupellos *or* gewissenlos, wenn es um Geld geht.
unscrupulously [ʌnˈskruːpjʊləslɪ] *adv see adj*.
unscrupulousness [ʌnˈskruːpjʊləsnɪs] *n* Skrupellosigkeit, Gewissenlosigkeit *f*.
unseal [ʌnˈsiːl] *vt* öffnen; (*remove wax seal also*) entsiegeln.
unsealed [ʌnˈsiːld] *adj see vt* offen, unverschlossen; unversiegelt.
unseasonable [ʌnˈsiːznəbl] *adj* nicht der Jahreszeit entsprechend *attr* ◆ **the weather is ~** das Wetter entspricht nicht der Jahreszeit.
unseasonably [ʌnˈsiːznəblɪ] *adv* (für die Jahreszeit) ungewöhnlich *or* außergewöhnlich.
unseasoned [ʌnˈsiːznd] *adj timber* nicht abgelagert; *food* ungewürzt; (*fig: inexperienced*) *troops* unerfahren, unerprobt.
unseat [ʌnˈsiːt] *vt rider* abwerfen; (*from office*) seines Amtes entheben.
unseaworthiness [ʌnˈsiːˌwɜːðɪnɪs] *n* Seeuntüchtigkeit *f*.
unseaworthy [ʌnˈsiːˌwɜːðɪ] *adj* seeuntüchtig, nicht seetüchtig.
unsecured [ˌʌnsɪˈkjʊəd] *adj* (*Fin*) *loan, bond* ohne Sicherheiten.
unseeded [ʌnˈsiːdɪd] *adj* unplaziert.
unseeing [ʌnˈsiːɪŋ] *adj* (*lit, fig*) blind; *gaze* leer ◆ **to stare at sb with ~ eyes** jdn mit leerem Blick anstarren.
unseemliness [ʌnˈsiːmlɪnɪs] *n* Unschicklichkeit, Ungebührlichkeit *f*.
unseemly [ʌnˈsiːmlɪ] *adj* unschicklich, ungebührlich.
unseen [ʌnˈsiːn] [1] *adj* ungesehen; (*invisible*) unsichtbar; (*unobserved*) *escape* unbemerkt ◆ **~ translation** (*esp Brit Sch, Univ*) unvorbereitete Herübersetzung.
[2] *n* (*esp Brit*) unvorbereitete Herübersetzung.
unselfconscious *adj*, **~ly** *adv* [ˌʌnselfˈkɒnʃəs, -lɪ] unbefangen.
unselfconsciousness [ˌʌnselfˈkɒnʃəsnɪs] *n* Unbefangenheit *f*.
unselfish *adj*, **~ly** *adv* [ʌnˈselfɪʃ, -lɪ] uneigennützig, selbstlos.
unselfishness [ʌnˈselfɪʃnɪs] *n* Uneigennützigkeit, Selbstlosigkeit *f*.
unsentimental [ˌʌnsentɪˈmentl] *adj* unsentimental.
unserviceable [ʌnˈsɜːvɪsəbl] *adj* unbrauchbar.
unsettle [ʌnˈsetl] *vt* **(a)** durcheinanderbringen; (*throw off balance, confuse*) aus dem Gleichgewicht bringen; (*agitate, upset*) aufregen; (*disturb emotionally*) verstören; *animal*, (*news*) beunruhigen; (*defeat, failure, criticism*) verunsichern; *faith* erschüttern. **(b)** *foundations* erschüttern.
unsettled [ʌnˈsetld] *adj* **(a)** (*unpaid*) unbezahlt, unbeglichen; (*undecided*) *question* ungeklärt, offen; *future* unbestimmt, ungewiß, in der Schwebe ◆ **to be in an ~ state of mind** mit sich selbst nicht eins sein; **he was ~ in his mind about what to do** er war sich (*dat*) nicht schlüssig, was er tun sollte.
(b) (*changeable*) *weather*, (*Fin*) *market* unbeständig, veränderlich; (*Pol*) *conditions also* unsicher; *life, character* unstet, unruhig ◆ **to be ~** durcheinander sein; (*thrown off balance*) aus dem Gleis geworfen sein; (*emotionally disturbed*) verstört sein; **to feel ~** sich nicht wohl fühlen.

(c) *(unpopulated) territory* unbesiedelt.

unsettling [ʌn'setlɪŋ] *adj change, pace of life* aufreibend; *time also* aufregend; *defeat, knowledge* verunsichernd; *news* beunruhigend ◆ **to have an ~ effect on sb** jdn aus dem Gleis werfen; *(defeat, failure also)* jdn verunsichern; *on children also* jdn verstören.

unsexy [ʌn'seksɪ] *adj (inf)* nicht sexy *(inf)*.

unshackle [ʌn'ʃækl] *vt prisoner* befreien; *(fig also)* von seinen Fesseln befreien.

unshaded [ʌn'ʃeɪdɪd] *adj (from sun)* schattenlos; *eyes etc* ungeschützt; *part of drawing* nicht schattiert ◆ **~ lamp** *or* **bulb** nackte Birne.

unshakeable [ʌn'ʃeɪkəbl] *adj* unerschütterlich.

unshaken [ʌn'ʃeɪkən] *adj* unerschüttert ◆ **he was ~ by the accident** der Unfall erschütterte ihn nicht; **his nerve was ~** er behielt seine Kaltblütigkeit.

unshaven [ʌn'ʃeɪvn] *adj* unrasiert; *(bearded)* bärtig.

unsheathe [ʌn'ʃi:ð] *vt sword* (aus der Scheide) ziehen.

unshed [ʌn'ʃed] *adj tears* ungeweint, unvergossen.

unship [ʌn'ʃɪp] *vt cargo* löschen, ausladen, entladen; *tiller, oars* abnehmen; *mast* abbauen.

unshockable [ʌn'ʃɒkəbl] *adj* durch nichts zu schockieren.

unshod [ʌn'ʃɒd] *adj horse* unbeschlagen; *person* barfuß, ohne Schuhe ◆ **with ~ feet** barfuß, mit nackten Füßen.

unshrinkable [ʌn'ʃrɪŋkəbl] *adj fabric* nicht einlaufend.

unshrinking [ʌn'ʃrɪŋkɪŋ] *adj* unverzagt, furchtlos, fest.

unsightliness [ʌn'saɪtlɪnɪs] *n see adj* Unansehnlichkeit *f*; Häßlichkeit *f*.

unsightly [ʌn'saɪtlɪ] *adj* unansehnlich; *(stronger)* häßlich.

unsigned [ʌn'saɪnd] *adj painting* unsigniert; *letter* nicht unterzeichnet, nicht unterschrieben.

unsinkable [ʌn'sɪŋkəbl] *adj* unsinkbar; *battleship* unversenkbar.

unsisterly [ʌn'sɪstəlɪ] *adj* nicht schwesterlich.

unskilful, *(US)* **unskillful** [ʌn'skɪlfʊl] *adj (inexpert)* ungeschickt; *(clumsy)* unbeholfen.

unskilfully, *(US)* **unskillfully** [ʌn'skɪlfəlɪ] *adv see adj.*

unskilfulness, *(US)* **unskillfulness** [ʌn'skɪlfʊlnɪs] *n see adj* Ungeschicklichkeit *f*, Mangel *m* an Geschick; Unbeholfenheit *f*.

unskilled [ʌn'skɪld] *adj* **(a)** *work, worker* ungelernt ◆ **the ~** *pl* die ungelernten Arbeiter, die Hilfsarbeiter *pl*; **many people remained ~** viele Menschen erlernten keinen Beruf. **(b)** *(inexperienced)* ungeübt, unerfahren.

unskillful *etc (US) see* **unskilful** *etc.*

unslept-in [ʌn'sleptɪn] *adj* unberührt.

unsnubbable [ʌn'snʌbəbl] *adj (inf)* dickfellig *(inf)*.

unsociability [ʌn,səʊʃə'bɪlɪtɪ] *n* Ungeselligkeit *f*.

unsociable [ʌn'səʊʃəbl] *adj* ungesellig.

unsocial [ʌn'səʊʃəl] *adj* **to work ~ hours** außerhalb der normalen Arbeitszeiten arbeiten; **at this ~ hour** zu so nachtschlafender Zeit.

unsold [ʌn'səʊld] *adj* unverkauft.

unsoldierly [ʌn'səʊldʒəlɪ] *adj* unsoldatisch.

unsolicited [,ʌnsə'lɪsɪtɪd] *adj* unerbeten; *manuscript* nicht angefordert, unangefordert.

unsolved [ʌn'sɒlvd] *adj crossword etc* ungelöst; *mystery also, crime* unaufgeklärt.

unsophisticated [,ʌnsə'fɪstɪkeɪtɪd] *adj (simple) person* einfach; *style also* natürlich, simpel *(pej)*; *film, machine also* unkompliziert; *technique also* simpel; *(naïve)* naiv, simpel; *(undiscriminating)* unkritisch ◆ **the ~** *pl* das einfache Volk.

unsought [ʌn'sɔ:t] *adj* unaufgefordert; *(unwanted)* unerwünscht ◆ **his help was ~** seine Hilfe kam unaufgefordert.

unsound [ʌn'saʊnd] *adj* **(a)** *heart, teeth* krank; *health* angegriffen; *timber* morsch; *construction, design* unsolide; *foundations, finances* unsicher, schwach ◆ **the ship was quite ~** das Schiff war überhaupt nicht seetüchtig.
(b) *argument* nicht stichhaltig, anfechtbar; *advice* unvernünftig; *judgement* unzuverlässig; *doctrine* unvertretbar; *policy, move* unklug ◆ **of ~ mind** *(Jur)* unzurechnungsfähig; **politically ~** *person* politisch unzuverlässig; *policy* politisch unklug; **~ banking procedures** heikle Bankgeschäfte *pl*; **the company is ~** die Firma steht auf schwachen Füßen; **our financial position is ~** unsere Finanzlage ist heikel; **I'm ~ on French grammar** ich bin unsicher in französischer Grammatik; **the book is ~ on some points** das Buch weist an einigen Stellen Schwächen auf; **his views on this are ~** seine Ansichten sind nicht vertretbar.

unsoundness [ʌn'saʊndnɪs] *n see adj* **(a)** Krankheit *f*; Angegriffenheit *f*; Morschheit *f*; unsolide Bauweise; Unsicherheit, Schwäche *f*.
(b) geringe Stichhaltigkeit, Anfechtbarkeit *f*; Unvernünftigkeit *f*; Unzuverlässigkeit *f*; Unvertretbarkeit *f*; mangelnde Klugheit ◆ **~ of mind** *(Jur)* Unzurechnungsfähigkeit *f*; **political ~** politische Unzuverlässigkeit; politische Unklugheit.

unsparing [ʌn'speərɪŋ] *adj* **(a)** *(lavish)* großzügig, verschwenderisch, nicht kleinlich ◆ **to be ~ with sth** mit etw nicht geizen; **to be ~ in one's efforts** keine Kosten und Mühen scheuen. **(b)** *(unmerciful) criticism* schonungslos.

unsparingly [ʌn'speərɪŋlɪ] *adv see adj* **(a)** großzügig, verschwenderisch ◆ **to work ~ for sth** unermüdlich für etw arbeiten; **he gave his time ~** er opferte unendlich viel Zeit. **(b)** schonungslos.

unspeakable [ʌn'spi:kəbl] *adj* unbeschreiblich ◆ **their ~ trade** ihr abscheuliches Geschäft.

unspeakably [ʌn'spi:kəblɪ] *adv* unbeschreiblich, unsagbar.

unspecified [ʌn'spesɪfaɪd] *adj time, amount* nicht spezifiziert *or* genannt, nicht genau angegeben.

unspectacular [,ʌnspek'tækjʊlə^r] *adj* wenig eindrucksvoll; *career* wenig aufsehenerregend.

unspent [ʌn'spent] *adj money* nicht ausgegeben; *energy* nicht verbraucht.

unspoiled [ʌn'spɔɪld], **unspoilt** [ʌn'spɔɪlt] *adj person, fruit* unverdorben; *goods* unbeschädigt; *child* nicht verwöhnt.

unspoken [ʌn'spəʊkən] *adj words, thought* unausgesprochen; *agreement, consent* stillschweigend.

unsporting [ʌn'spɔ:tɪŋ], **unsportsmanlike** [ʌn'spɔ:tsmənlaɪk] *adj conduct, person* unsportlich, unfair.

unsprung [ʌn'sprʌŋ] *adj seat* ungefedert; *trap* offen, nicht zugeschnappt.

unstable [ʌn'steɪbl] *adj structure* nicht *or* wenig stabil; *foundations also, area* unsicher; *weather* unbeständig; *economy* unsicher, schwankend; *(Chem, Phys)* instabil; *(mentally)* labil.

unstamped [ʌn'stæmpt] *adj letter* unfrankiert; *document, passport* ungestempelt.

unstatesmanlike [ʌn'steɪtsmənlaɪk] *adj* unstaatsmännisch.

unsteadily [ʌn'stedɪlɪ] *adv see adj.*

unsteadiness [ʌn'stedɪnɪs] *n see adj* Unsicherheit *f*; Wack(e)ligkeit *f*; Flackern *nt*; Schwanken *nt*; Unregelmäßigkeit *f*.

unsteady [ʌn'stedɪ] **1** *adj hand* unsicher; *ladder* wack(e)lig; *flame* unruhig, flackernd; *voice, economy* schwankend; *growth* unregelmäßig ◆ **to be ~ on one's feet** unsicher *or* wackelig auf den Beinen sein; **the £ is still ~** das Pfund schwankt noch.
2 *vt* durcheinanderbringen; *(stronger)* aus dem Gleichgewicht bringen.

unstick [ʌn'stɪk] *pret, ptp* **unstuck** *vt* lösen, losmachen; *see also* **unstuck**.

unstinted [ʌn'stɪntɪd] *adj praise* uneingeschränkt, vorbehaltlos; *generosity, devotion, efforts* unbegrenzt.

unstinting [ʌn'stɪntɪŋ] *adj person* großzügig; *kindness, generosity* uneingeschränkt, unbegrenzt; *support* uneingeschränkt, vorbehaltlos ◆ **to be ~ in one's efforts/praise** keine Kosten und Mühen scheuen/uneingeschränkt *or* vorbehaltlos loben; **to be ~ of one's time** unendlich viel Zeit opfern.

unstintingly [ʌn'stɪntɪŋlɪ] *adv* großzügig; *generous* unendlich; *work* unermüdlich; *donate, contribute* verschwenderisch.

unstitch [ʌn'stɪtʃ] *vt seam* auftrennen; *zip* heraustrennen ◆ **to come ~ed** aufgehen.

unstop [ʌn'stɒp] *vt drain* freimachen; *bottle* öffnen, aufmachen.

unstoppable [ʌn'stɒpəbl] *adj* nicht aufzuhalten.

unstrap [ʌn'stræp] *vt case etc* aufschnallen ◆ **to ~ sth (from sth)** etw (von etw) los- *or* abschnallen.

unstreamed [ʌn'stri:md] *adj (Brit Sch)* nicht in Leistungsgruppen eingeteilt.

unstressed [ʌn'strest] *adj (Phon)* unbetont.

unstring [ʌn'strɪŋ] *pret, ptp* **unstrung** *vt violin* die Saiten abnehmen *or* entfernen von; *beads* abfädeln.

unstructured [ʌn'strʌktʃəd] *adj* unstrukturiert, nicht strukturiert.

unstrung [ʌn'strʌŋ] **1** *pret, ptp of* **unstring**.
2 *adj* **(a)** *person* demoralisiert, entnervt; *nerves* zerrüttet. **(b)** *violin* unbesaitet.

unstuck [ʌn'stʌk] **1** *pret, ptp of* **unstick**.
2 *adj* **to come ~** *(stamp, notice)* sich lösen; *(inf) (plan)* danebengehen *(inf)*, schiefgehen *(inf)*; *(speaker, actor)* steckenbleiben; *(in exam)* ins Schwimmen geraten; **the pay policy seems to have come ~** die Lohnpolitik scheint aus dem Gleis gekommen zu sein; **where they came ~ was ...** sie sind daran gescheitert, daß ...

unstudied [ʌn'stʌdɪd] *adj grace etc* ungekünstelt, natürlich.

unsubdued [,ʌnsəb'dju:d] *adj* unbezwungen, unbesiegt.

unsubsidized [ʌn'sʌbsɪdaɪzd] *adj* unsubventioniert.

unsubstantial [,ʌnsəb'stænʃəl] *adj (flimsy) structure* leicht, dürftig; *(immaterial) ghost* körperlos, wesenlos; *meal* leicht; *evidence, proof* nicht überzeugend, nicht schlagkräftig; *claim* ungerechtfertigt ◆ **the boat seemed almost ~ in the mist** das Boot erschien im Dunst schemenhaft.

unsubstantiated [,ʌnsəb'stænʃɪeɪtɪd] *adj accusation, testimony, rumour* unbegründet ◆ **his claim was ~ by any evidence** seine Behauptung wurde durch keinerlei Indizien erhärtet.

unsubtle [ʌn'sʌtl] *adj* plump ◆ **how ~ can you get!** plumper geht's nicht!

unsuccessful [,ʌnsək'sesfʊl] *adj negotiations, venture, visit, meeting, person etc* erfolglos, ergebnislos; *writer, painter* erfolglos, ohne Erfolg; *candidate* abgewiesen; *attempt* vergeblich; *marriage, outcome* unglücklich ◆ **to be ~ in doing sth** keinen Erfolg damit haben, etw zu tun; **I tried to persuade him but was ~** ich habe versucht, ihn zu überreden, hatte aber keinen Erfolg; **he is ~ in everything he does** nichts gelingt ihm; **he was ~ in his exam** er hat kein Glück in seinem Examen gehabt; **he is ~ with women** er hat kein Glück *or* keinen Erfolg bei Frauen.

unsuccessfully [,ʌnsək'sesfəlɪ] *adv* erfolglos; *try* vergeblich; *apply* ohne Erfolg, vergebens ◆ **I tried ~ to grow tomatoes** ich habe ohne Erfolg versucht, Tomaten zu ziehen.

unsuitability [,ʌnsu:tə'bɪlɪtɪ] *n see adj* Unangebrachtheit *f*; Ungeeignetsein *nt* ◆ **his ~ for the job** seine mangelnde Eignung für die Stelle; **I commented on the ~ of his clothes** ich machte eine Bemerkung über seine unpassende Kleidung; **their ~ as partners is clear** es ist klar, daß sie keine geeigneten Partner füreinander sind.

unsuitable [ʌn'su:təbl] *adj* unpassend; *language, attitude also* unangebracht; *moment, clothes, colour also* ungeeignet ◆ **it would be ~ at this moment to ...** es wäre im Augenblick unangebracht, ...; **this film is ~ for children** dieser Film ist für Kinder ungeeignet *or* nicht geeignet; **he's ~ for the post** er ist für die Stelle nicht geeignet; **she is ~ for him** sie ist nicht die Richtige für ihn; **we're ~ for each other** wir passen nicht zusammen; **she married a very ~ person** sie hat jemanden geheiratet, der gar nicht zu ihr paßt.

unsuitably [ʌn'suːtəblɪ] *adv dressed (for weather conditions)* unzweckmäßig; *(for occasion)* unpassend; *designed* schlecht, ungeeignet ◆ **they are ~ matched** sie passen nicht zusammen.

unsuited [ʌn'suːtɪd] *adj* **to be ~ for** *or* **to sth** für etw ungeeignet *or* untauglich sein; **to be ~ to do sth** sich nicht dazu eignen *or* nicht dazu taugen, etw zu tun; **to be ~ to sb** nicht zu jdm passen; **they are ~ (to each other)** sie passen nicht zusammen.

unsullied [ʌn'sʌlɪd] *adj virtue, honour etc* makellos, unbefleckt *(liter)*; *snow* unberührt.

unsung [ʌn'sʌŋ] *adj heroes, deeds* unbesungen.

unsupported [ˌʌnsə'pɔːtɪd] *adj roof, person* ungestützt, ohne Stütze; *troops* ohne Unterstützung; *mother* alleinstehend; *family* ohne Unterhalt; *claim, theory* ohne Beweise, nicht auf Fakten gestützt; *statement* unbestätigt, durch nichts gestützt ◆ **if such families were ~ by the State** wenn solche Familien nicht vom Staat unterstützt würden; **should the bank leave us financially ~** sollte die Bank uns finanziell nicht absichern *or* nicht unter die Arme greifen; **the candidate/motion was ~** der Kandidat/Antrag fand keine Unterstützung.

unsure [ʌn'ʃʊəʳ] *adj person* unsicher; *(unreliable) method also* unzuverlässig ◆ **to be ~ of oneself** unsicher sein; **to be ~ (of sth)** sich *(dat)* (einer Sache *gen*) nicht sicher sein; **I'm ~ of him** ich bin mir bei ihm nicht sicher; **I am ~ of my welcome** ich bin nicht sicher, ob ich willkommen bin.

unsurpassable [ˌʌnsə'pɑːsəbl] *adj* unübertrefflich.

unsurpassed [ˌʌnsə'pɑːst] *adj* unübertroffen ◆ **to be ~ by anybody** von niemandem übertroffen werden.

unsuspected [ˌʌnsə'spektɪd] *adj presence* nicht vermutet, unvermutet; *consequences* unerwartet, ungeahnt; *oilfields, coal deposits, causes* unvermutet; *wealth* ungeahnt ◆ **to be ~** *(person)* nicht unter Verdacht stehen.

unsuspecting *adj*, **~ly** *adv* [ˌʌnsə'spektɪŋ, -lɪ] ahnungslos, nichtsahnend.

unsuspicious [ˌʌnsə'spɪʃəs] *adj (feeling no suspicion)* arglos; *(causing no suspicion)* unverdächtig, harmlos.

unsweetened [ˌʌn'swiːtnd] *adj* ungesüßt.

unswerving [ʌn'swɜːvɪŋ] *adj resolve, loyalty* unerschütterlich, unbeirrbar ◆ **the road followed its ~ course across the desert** die Straße führte schnurgerade durch die Wüste.

unswervingly [ʌn'swɜːvɪŋlɪ] *adv* **to be ~ loyal to sb** jdm unerschütterlich *or* unbeirrbar treu sein; **to hold ~ to one's course** unbeirrbar seinen Weg gehen.

unsymmetrical [ˌʌnsɪ'metrɪkəl] *adj* unsymmetrisch.

unsympathetic [ˌʌnsɪmpə'θetɪk] *adj* **(a)** *(unfeeling)* gefühllos, wenig mitfühlend; *reaction, attitude, response* ablehnend, abweisend ◆ **I am not ~ to your request** ich stehe Ihrer Bitte nicht ablehnend gegenüber. **(b)** *(unlikable)* unsympathisch.

unsympathetically [ˌʌnsɪmpə'θetɪkəlɪ] *adv* ohne Mitgefühl; *say also* gefühllos, hart.

unsystematic *adj*, **~ally** *adv* [ˌʌnsɪstɪ'mætɪk, -əlɪ] planlos, unsystematisch, ohne System.

untainted [ʌn'teɪntɪd] *adj* einwandfrei, tadellos; *food also, person, mind* unverdorben; *reputation also* makellos.

untalented [ʌn'tælɪntɪd] *adj* unbegabt, untalentiert.

untam(e)able [ʌn'teɪməbl] *adj animal* unzähmbar; *(fig)* unbezähmbar, nicht zu bändigen *pred*.

untamed [ʌn'teɪmd] *adj animal* ungezähmt; *jungle* wild; *person, pride* ungebändigt; *temper* ungezügelt.

untangle [ʌn'tæŋgl] *vt (lit, fig)* entwirren.

untanned [ʌn'tænd] *adj hide* ungegerbt.

untapped [ʌn'tæpt] *adj barrel* unangezapft; *resources also, source of wealth, talent* ungenutzt.

untarnished [ʌn'tɑːnɪʃt] *adj* makellos; *silver also* nicht angelaufen; *(fig) name also* einwandfrei, unbefleckt *(liter)*.

untasted [ʌn'teɪstɪd] *adj (lit, fig)* ungekostet.

untaught [ʌn'tɔːt] *adj (not trained) person* nicht ausgebildet; *ability* angeboren; *behaviour* natürlich ◆ **basic skills which go ~ in our schools** Grundfähigkeiten, die in unseren Schulen nicht vermittelt werden.

untaxed [ʌn'tækst] *adj goods, income* steuerfrei, unbesteuert; *car* unversteuert.

unteachable [ʌn'tiːtʃəbl] *adj person* unbelehrbar; *subject* nicht lehrbar ◆ **it is ~ at this level** auf diesem Niveau kann man es nicht lehren.

untempered [ʌn'tempəd] *adj steel* ungehärtet, unvergütet; *rage* ungemildert ◆ **justice ~ by mercy** Gerechtigkeit, die durch keinerlei Gnade gemildert wird/wurde.

untenable [ʌn'tenəbl] *adj (lit, fig)* unhaltbar.

untenanted [ʌn'tenəntɪd] *adj house* unbewohnt, leer.

untended [ʌn'tendɪd] *adj patient* unbehütet, unbewacht; *garden* vernachlässigt, ungepflegt.

untested [ʌn'testɪd] *adj person* unerprobt; *theory, product also* ungetestet, ungeprüft ◆ **~ players** Spieler, die sich noch nicht bewährt haben.

unthinkable [ʌn'θɪŋkəbl] *adj* undenkbar, unvorstellbar; *(Philos)* undenkbar; *(too horrible)* unvorstellbar.

unthinking [ʌn'θɪŋkɪŋ] *adj (thoughtless, unintentional)* unbedacht, gedankenlos; *(uncritical)* bedenkenlos, blind.

unthinkingly [ʌn'θɪŋkɪŋlɪ] *adv see adj.*

unthought-of [ʌn'θɔːtɒv] *adj (inconceivable)* undenkbar, unvorstellbar ◆ **these hitherto ~ objections** diese Einwände, auf die bis dahin niemand gekommen war.

unthought-out [ˌʌnθɔːt'aʊt] *adj* nicht (gut) durchdacht, unausgegoren *(inf)*.

unthread [ʌn'θred] *vt needle* ausfädeln; *pearls* abfädeln.

untidily [ʌn'taɪdɪlɪ] *adv see adj.*

untidiness [ʌn'taɪdɪnɪs] *n (of room)* Unordnung, Unaufgeräumtheit *f*; *(of person, dress)* Unordentlichkeit *f* ◆ **the ~ of the kitchen** die Unordnung in der Küche.

untidy [ʌn'taɪdɪ] *adj (+er)* unordentlich.

untie [ʌn'taɪ] *vt knot* lösen; *string, tie, shoelaces also* aufbinden; *parcel* aufknoten; *person, animal, hands* losbinden.

until [ən'tɪl] **1** *prep* **(a)** bis ◆ **from morning ~ night** von morgens bis abends, vom Morgen bis zum Abend; **~ now** bis jetzt; **~ then** bis dahin.

(b) not ~ *(in future)* nicht vor (+*dat*); *(in past)* erst; **I didn't leave him ~ the following day** ich habe ihn erst am folgenden Tag verlassen, ich bin bis zum nächsten Tag bei ihm geblieben; **the work was not begun ~ 1990** die Arbeiten wurden erst 1990 begonnen; **I had heard nothing of it ~ five minutes ago** bis vor fünf Minuten wußte ich (noch) nichts davon, ich habe erst vor fünf Minuten davon gehört.

2 *conj* **(a)** bis ◆ **wait ~ I come** warten Sie, bis ich komme.

(b) not ~ *(in future)* nicht bevor, erst wenn; *(in past)* nicht bis, erst als; **he won't come ~ you invite him** er kommt erst, wenn Sie ihn einladen; **they did nothing ~ we came** bis wir kamen, taten sie nichts; **don't start ~ I come** fangen Sie nicht an, bevor ich da bin, fangen Sie erst an, wenn ich da bin; **they didn't start ~ we came** sie fingen erst an, als wir da waren, sie fingen nicht an, bevor wir da waren.

untimeliness [ʌn'taɪmlɪnɪs] *n (of death)* Vorzeitigkeit *f*; *(of end also)* Verfrühtheit *f* ◆ **because of the ~ of his arrival/this development** weil er/diese Entwicklung zur falschen Zeit kam.

untimely [ʌn'taɪmlɪ] *adj (premature) death* vorzeitig; *end also* verfrüht; *(inopportune) moment* unpassend, ungelegen; *development, occurrence* unpassend, ungelegen, zur falschen Zeit; *shower, remark* zur falschen Zeit ◆ **his arrival was most ~** seine Ankunft kam sehr ungelegen.

untiring [ʌn'taɪərɪŋ] *adj work, effort* unermüdlich ◆ **to be ~ in one's efforts** unermüdliche Anstrengungen machen.

untiringly [ʌn'taɪərɪŋlɪ] *adv* unermüdlich.

unto ['ʌntʊ] *prep (old, liter) see* **to**.

untold ['ʌn'təʊld] *adj story* nicht erzählt, nicht berichtet; *secret* ungelüftet; *wealth* unermeßlich; *agony, delights* unsäglich; *stars etc* ungezählt, unzählig, zahllos ◆ **this story is better left ~** über diese Geschichte schweigt man besser; **he died with his secret still ~** er nahm sein Geheimnis mit ins Grab; **~ thousands** unzählig viele.

untouchable [ʌn'tʌtʃəbl] **1** *adj* unberührbar.

2 *n* Unberührbare(r) *mf*.

untouched [ʌn'tʌtʃt] *adj* **(a)** *(unhandled, unused)* unberührt, unangetastet; *bottle, box of sweets etc also* nicht angebrochen; *(unmentioned)* nicht erwähnt ◆ **~ by human hand** nicht von Menschenhand berührt; **he left his meal ~** er ließ sein Essen unberührt stehen.

(b) *(unharmed)* heil, unversehrt; *(unaffected)* unberührt; *(unmoved)* ungerührt, unbewegt, unbeeindruckt ◆ **he was ~ by her tears** ihre Tränen ließen ihn kalt.

(c) *(unequalled)* unerreicht ◆ **~ for quality** in der Qualität unerreicht; **he is ~ by anyone** niemand kommt ihm gleich.

untoward [ˌʌntə'wɔːd] *adj (unfortunate) event* unglücklich, bedauerlich; *(unseemly)* unpassend, ungehörig ◆ **nothing ~ had happened** es war kein Unheil geschehen.

untrained [ʌn'treɪnd] *adj person, teacher* unausgebildet; *voice* ungeschult; *animal* undressiert ◆ **to the ~ ear/eye** dem ungeschulten Ohr/Auge.

untrammelled, *(US also)* **untrammeled** [ʌn'træməld] *adj* unbeschränkt ◆ **to be ~ by sth** nicht von etw beschränkt werden.

untranslatable [ˌʌntrænz'leɪtəbl] *adj* unübersetzbar.

untravelled, *(US)* **untraveled** [ʌn'trævld] *adj road* unbefahren; *person* nicht weitgereist, nicht weit herumgekommen.

untreated [ʌn'triːtɪd] *adj* unbehandelt.

untried [ʌn'traɪd] *adj* **(a)** *(not tested) person* unerprobt; *product, method also* ungetestet; *(not attempted)* unversucht.

(b) *(Jur) case* nicht verhandelt; *person* nicht vor Gericht gestellt ◆ **the case is still ~** der Fall ist noch nicht verhandelt worden; **the case/the offender can remain ~ for months** die Verhandlung kann monatelang verzögert werden/der Rechtsbrecher wird zuweilen erst nach Monaten vor Gericht gestellt.

untrodden [ʌn'trɒdn] *adj path* verlassen; *snow* unberührt ◆ **~ paths** *(fig)* neue Wege *pl*.

untroubled [ʌn'trʌbld] *adj period, ghost* friedlich, ruhig; *person also* ungestört; *smile also* unbeschwert ◆ **to be ~ by the news** eine Nachricht gleichmütig hinnehmen; **the children seemed ~ by the heat** die Hitze schien den Kindern nichts anzuhaben *or* auszumachen; **they were ~ by thoughts of the future** der Gedanke an die Zukunft belastete sie nicht.

untrue [ʌn'truː] *adj* **(a)** *(false)* unwahr, falsch; *(Tech) reading, instrument* inkorrekt, ungenau. **(b)** *(unfaithful) person* untreu ◆ **to be ~ to sb** jdm untreu sein.

untrustworthy [ʌn'trʌst,wɜːðɪ] *adj* (*not reliable*) *source, book, person* unzuverlässig; (*not worthy of confidence*) *person* nicht vertrauenswürdig.
untruth [ʌn'truːθ] *n* Unwahrheit *f*.
untruthful [ʌn'truːθfʊl] *adj statement* unwahr; *person* unaufrichtig ◆ **you're being ~** da bist du unaufrichtig.
untruthfully [ʌn'truːθfəlɪ] *adv* fälschlich ◆ **he said, quite ~, that ...** er sagte, und das war nicht die Wahrheit, daß ...
untruthfulness [ʌn'truːθfʊlnɪs] *n see adj* Unwahrheit *f*; Unaufrichtigkeit *f*.
untuneful [ʌn'tjuːnfʊl] *adj* unmelodisch.
unturned [ʌn'tɜːnd] *adj see* **stone**.
untutored [ʌn'tjuːtəd] *adj taste, person* ungeschult.
untypical [ʌn'tɪpɪkl] *adj* untypisch (*of* für).
unusable [ʌn'juːzəbl] *adj* unbrauchbar.
unused¹ [ʌn'juːzd] *adj* (*new*) unbenutzt, ungebraucht; (*not made use of*) ungenutzt; (*no longer used*) nicht mehr benutzt *or* gebraucht.
unused² [ʌn'juːst] *adj* **to be ~ to sth** nicht an etw (*acc*) gewöhnt sein, etw (*acc*) nicht gewohnt sein; **to be ~ to doing sth** nicht daran gewöhnt sein *or* es nicht gewohnt sein, etw zu tun.
unusual [ʌn'juːʒʊəl] *adj* (*uncommon*) ungewöhnlich; (*exceptional*) außergewöhnlich ◆ **it's ~ for him to be late** er kommt normalerweise nicht zu spät; **that's not ~ for him** das wundert mich überhaupt nicht; **how ~!** das kommt selten vor; (*iro*) welch Wunder!; **that's ~ for him** das ist sonst nicht seine Art; **how do you like my new hat? — well, it's ~** wie gefällt Ihnen mein neuer Hut? — na, es ist mal was anderes.
unusually [ʌn'juːʒʊəlɪ] *adv see adj* ◆ **most ~, he was late** ganz gegen jede Gewohnheit kam er zu spät.
unutterable [ʌn'ʌtərəbl] *adj joy, longing, sadness* unsäglich, unbeschreiblich; (*inf also*) riesig, Riesen- ◆ **an act of ~ folly** (*inf*) eine Riesendummheit (*inf*).
unutterably [ʌn'ʌtərəblɪ] *adv* unsäglich, unbeschreiblich ◆ **~ stupid** (*inf*) unsagbar blöd (*inf*).
unvaried [ʌn'vɛərɪd] *adj* unverändert; (*pej*) eintönig.
unvarnished [ʌn'vɑːnɪʃt] *adj wood* ungefirnißt, unlackiert; (*fig*) *truth* ungeschminkt.
unvarying [ʌn'vɛərɪɪŋ] *adj* gleichbleibend, unveränderlich.
unveil [ʌn'veɪl] [1] *vt statue, painting, plan* enthüllen; (*Comm*) *car* vorstellen; *face* entschleiern ◆ **women mustn't go ~ed** Frauen dürfen nicht unverschleiert gehen.
[2] *vi* sich entschleiern, den Schleier fallenlassen.
unveiling [ʌn'veɪlɪŋ] *n* (*lit, fig*) Enthüllung *f* ◆ **~ ceremony** Enthüllung *f*.
unventilated [ʌn'ventɪleɪtɪd] *adj* ungelüftet, nicht ventiliert.
unverifiable [ʌn'verɪfaɪəbl] *adj* nicht beweisbar, unverifizierbar (*geh*).
unverified [ʌn'verɪfaɪd] *adj* unbewiesen.
unversed [ʌn'vɜːst] *adj*: **~ in** nicht vertraut mit, unbewandert in (*+dat*).
unvisited [ʌn'vɪzɪtɪd] *adj* nicht besucht ◆ **we left Heidelberg with the castle ~** wir verließen Heidelberg, ohne das Schloß besucht zu haben.
unvoiced [ʌn'vɔɪst] *adj* **(a)** unausgesprochen. **(b)** (*Phon*) stimmlos.
unwanted [ʌn'wɒntɪd] *adj furniture, clothing* unerwünscht ◆ **sometimes you make me feel ~** manchmal komme ich mir (bei dir) richtig unerwünscht vor.
unwarily [ʌn'wɛərɪlɪ] *adv see adj*.
unwariness [ʌn'wɛərɪnɪs] *n* Unvorsichtigkeit, Unbesonnenheit, Unachtsamkeit *f*.
unwarlike [ʌn'wɔːlaɪk] *adj* friedliebend, friedlich.
unwarrantable [ʌn'wɒrəntəbl] *adj* nicht zu rechtfertigen *pred or* rechtfertigend *attr*.
unwarranted [ʌn'wɒrəntɪd] *adj* ungerechtfertigt.
unwary [ʌn'wɛərɪ] *adj* unvorsichtig, unbesonnen, unachtsam.
unwashed [ʌn'wɒʃt] *adj* ungewaschen; *dishes* ungespült ◆ **the great ~** *pl* (*hum*) der Pöbel.
unwavering [ʌn'weɪvərɪŋ] *adj faith, resolve* unerschütterlich; *gaze* fest, unbewegt; *course* beharrlich.
unwaveringly [ʌn'weɪvərɪŋlɪ] *adv see adj*.
unweaned [ʌn'wiːnd] *adj baby* (noch) nicht entwöhnt.
unwearable [ʌn'wɛərəbl] *adj* **it's ~** das kann man nicht tragen.
unwearied [ʌn'wɪərɪd], **unwearying** [ʌn'wɪərɪɪŋ] *adj* unermüdlich.
unwed [ʌn'wed] *adj* unverheiratet, unvermählt (*geh*).
unwelcome [ʌn'welkəm] *adj visitor* unwillkommen; *news, memories* unerfreulich, unangenehm ◆ **the money was not ~** das Geld war höchst willkommen.
unwelcoming [ʌn'welkəmɪŋ] *adj manner* abweisend, unfreundlich; *host also* ungastlich.
unwell [ʌn'wel] *adj pred* unwohl, nicht wohl ◆ **to be** *or* **feel (a little) ~** sich nicht (recht) wohl fühlen; **I am afraid he's rather ~ today** es geht ihm heute leider gar nicht gut.
unwholesome [ʌn'həʊlsəm] *adj* ungesund; *influence* ungut, verderblich; *appearance, character* schmierig; *food* minderwertig; *jokes* schmutzig ◆ **they are rather ~ company for her** sie sind nicht gerade ein guter Umgang für sie.
unwholesomeness [ʌn'həʊlsəmnɪs] *n see adj* Ungesundheit *f*; Verderblichkeit *f*; Schmierigkeit *f*; Minderwertigkeit *f*; Schmutzigkeit *f*.
unwieldy [ʌn'wiːldɪ] *adj tool* unhandlich; *object also* sperrig; (*clumsy*) *body* schwerfällig, unbeholfen.
unwilling [ʌn'wɪlɪŋ] *adj helper, admiration, pupil* widerwillig; *accomplice* unfreiwillig ◆ **to be ~ to do sth** nicht bereit *or* gewillt *or* willens (*geh*) sein, etw zu tun; **to be ~ for sb to do sth** nicht wollen, daß jd etw tut.
unwillingly [ʌn'wɪlɪŋlɪ] *adv* widerwillig.
unwillingness [ʌn'wɪlɪŋnɪs] *n see adj* Widerwilligkeit *f*; Unfreiwilligkeit *f* ◆ **their ~ to compromise** ihre mangelnde Kompromißbereitschaft.
unwind [ʌn'waɪnd] *pret, ptp* **unwound** [1] *vt thread, film, tape* abwickeln; (*untangle*) entwirren.
[2] *vi* **(a)** sich abwickeln; (*fig: story, plot*) sich entwickeln, sich entfalten. **(b)** (*inf: relax*) abschalten (*inf*), sich entspannen.
unwise [ʌn'waɪz] *adj* unklug ◆ **they were ~ enough to believe him** sie waren so töricht, ihm das zu glauben.
unwisely [ʌn'waɪzlɪ] *adv see adj* ◆ **rather ~ the Government agreed** die Regierung hat unklugerweise zugestimmt.
unwished-for [ʌn'wɪʃtfɔːʳ] *adj* unerwünscht.
unwitting [ʌn'wɪtɪŋ] *adj accomplice* unbewußt, unwissentlich; *action also* unabsichtlich; *victim* ahnungslos ◆ **he was the ~ cause of the argument** er war unbewußt die Ursache des Streits, er war, ohne es zu wissen, die Ursache des Streits.
unwittingly [ʌn'wɪtɪŋlɪ] *adv* unbewußt ◆ **I had agreed, all ~, to take part** ich hatte mich völlig ahnungslos dazu bereiterklärt, mitzumachen.
unwomanly [ʌn'wʊmənlɪ] *adj* unweiblich.
unwonted [ʌn'wəʊntɪd] *adj* ungewohnt ◆ **at this ~ hour!** zu dieser unchristlichen Zeit!
unwontedly [ʌn'wəʊntɪdlɪ] *adv* ungewöhnlich.
unworkable [ʌn'wɜːkəbl] *adj scheme, idea* undurchführbar; (*Min*) *mine* nicht abbaubar.
unworkmanlike [ʌn'wɜːkmənlaɪk] *adj job* unfachmännisch.
unworldliness [ʌn'wɜːldlɪnɪs] *n see adj* Weltabgewandtheit *f*; Weltfremdheit *f*.
unworldly [ʌn'wɜːldlɪ] *adj life* weltabgewandt; (*naïve*) weltfremd.
unworn [ʌn'wɔːn] *adj* (*new*) ungetragen.
unworried [ʌn'wʌrɪd] *adj* unbekümmert, sorglos ◆ **he was ~ by my criticism** meine Kritik (be)kümmerte ihn nicht.
unworthily [ʌn'wɜːðɪlɪ] *adv behave* unwürdig ◆ **he said, rather ~, that ...** er sagte, und das war eigentlich unter seiner Würde, daß ...
unworthiness [ʌn'wɜːðɪnɪs] *n* Unwürdigkeit *f*.
unworthy [ʌn'wɜːðɪ] *adj person* nicht wert (*of gen*); *conduct also* nicht würdig, unwürdig (*of gen*) ◆ **to be ~ to do sth** (es) nicht wert sein, etw zu tun; **to be ~ of an honour** einer Ehre (*gen*) nicht wert sein (*geh*); **this is ~ of you** das ist unter deiner Würde; **it is ~ of our attention** das verdient unsere Aufmerksamkeit nicht, das ist unserer Aufmerksamkeit (*gen*) nicht wert; **it was ~ of you not to accept their kind offer** es war nicht anständig von dir, ihren freundlichen Vorschlag nicht anzunehmen; **it would be ~ of me not to mention also ...** es wäre nicht recht, wenn ich nicht auch ... erwähnen würde.
unwound [ʌn'waʊnd] *pret, ptp of* **unwind**.
unwounded [ʌn'wuːndɪd] *adj* nicht verwundet, unverwundet.
unwrap [ʌn'ræp] *vt* auspacken, auswickeln.
unwritten [ʌn'rɪtn] *adj story, book, constitution* ungeschrieben; *agreement* stillschweigend ◆ **~ law** (*Jur, fig*) ungeschriebenes Gesetz.
unyielding [ʌn'jiːldɪŋ] *adj substance* unnachgiebig; (*fig*) *person, demand also, resistance* hart.
unyoke [ʌn'jəʊk] *vt* ausspannen ◆ **he ~d his oxen from the plough** er spannte seine Ochsen aus.
unzip [ʌn'zɪp] [1] *vt zip* aufmachen; *dress, case* den Reißverschluß aufmachen an (*+dat*) ◆ **would you please ~ me?** kannst du bitte mir den Reißverschluß aufmachen?
[2] *vi* (*zip*) aufgehen, sich öffnen ◆ **this dress won't ~** der Reißverschluß an dem Kleid geht nicht auf *or* läßt sich nicht öffnen; **my dress must have ~ped** der Reißverschluß an meinem Kleid muß aufgegangen sein.
▼ **up** [ʌp] [1] *adv* **(a)** (*in high or higher position*) oben; (*to higher position*) nach oben ◆ **~ there** dort oben, droben (*liter, S Ger*); **~ here on the roof** hier oben auf dem Dach; **on your way ~ (to see us/them)** auf dem Weg (zu uns/ihnen) herauf/hinauf; **he climbed all the way ~ (to us/them)** er ist den ganzen Weg (zu uns/ihnen) hochgeklettert; **to throw sth ~** etw hochwerfen; **to stop halfway ~** auf halber Höhe anhalten; (*in standing up*) auf halbem Weg einhalten; **we were 6,000 m ~ when ...** wir waren 6.000 m hoch, als ...; **5 floors ~** 5 Stockwerke hoch; **3 floors ~ from me** 3 Stockwerke über mir; **they were ~ above** sie waren hoch oben; **I looked ~ above** ich schaute nach oben; **this side ~** (diese Seite) oben!; **a little further ~** ein bißchen weiter oben; **to go a little further ~** ein bißchen höher (hinauf)gehen; **hang the picture a bit higher ~** häng das Bild ein bißchen höher; **from ~ on the hill** vom Berg oben; **~ on top (of the cupboard)** ganz oben (auf dem Schrank); **~ in the mountains/sky** oben *or* droben (*liter, S Ger*) in den Bergen/am Himmel; **the temperature was ~ in the thirties** die Temperatur war in den dreißig; **the sun/moon is ~** die Sonne/der Mond ist aufgegangen; **the tide is ~** es ist Flut, die Flut ist da; **the wind is ~** der Wind hat aufgefrischt; **with his collar ~** mit hochgeschlagenem Kragen; **the road is ~** die Straße ist aufgegraben; **to be ~ among** *or* **with the leaders** vorn bei den Führenden sein; **to move ~ into the lead** nach vorn an die Spitze kommen; **Red Rum with Joe Smith ~** Red Rum unter Joe Smith; **a truck with a load of bricks ~** (*inf*) ein Lastwagen mit einer Ladung Ziegelsteinen (drauf); **~ and away the balloon sailed** der Ballon stieg auf und schwebte davon; **then ~ jumps Richard and says ...** und dann springt Richard auf und sagt ...; **the needle was ~ on 95** die Nadel stand auf 95; **come on, ~, that's my chair!** komm, auf mit dir, das ist mein Stuhl!; **~! he shouted to his horse** spring! schrie er seinem Pferd zu; **~ with**

the Liberals! hoch die Liberalen!; **~ with Spurs!** Spurs hoch!
(b) (*installed, built*) **to be ~** (*building*) stehen; (*tent also*) aufgeschlagen sein; (*scaffolding*) aufgestellt sein; (*notice*) hängen, angeschlagen sein; (*picture*) hängen, aufgehängt sein; (*shutters*) zu sein; (*shelves, wallpaper, curtains, pictures*) hängen; **they're putting ~ a new cinema** sie bauen ein neues Kino; **stick the notice ~ here** häng den Anschlag hier hin ◆ **to be ~ and running** laufen; (*committee etc*) in Gang sein; **to get sth ~ and running** etw zum Laufen bringen; *committee etc* etw in Gang setzen; **have you got your computer ~ and running yet?** läuft dein Computer schon?
(c) (*not in bed*) auf ◆ **~ (with you)!** auf mit dir!, raus aus dem Bett (*inf*); **to get ~** aufstehen; **to be ~ and about** auf sein; (*after illness also*) auf den Beinen sein; **she was ~ all night with him** (*looking after*) sie war seinetwegen die ganze Nacht auf.
(d) (*geographically*) (*north of speaker*) oben; (*of students*) am Studienort ◆ **~ in Inverness** in Inverness oben, oben in Inverness; **we are going ~ to Aberdeen** wir fahren nach Aberdeen (hinauf); **to be/go ~ north** im Norden sein/in den Norden fahren; **~ from the country** vom Lande; **we're ~ for the day** wir sind (nur) für heute hier; **to go ~ to Cambridge** (zum Studium) nach Cambridge gehen; **he was ~ at Oxford in 1982** er hat 1982 in Oxford studiert; **the students are only ~ for half the year** die Studenten sind nur die Hälfte des Jahres am Studienort; **he was ~ at Susie's place** er war bei Susie zu Hause.
(e) (*in price, value*) gestiegen (*on* gegenüber) ◆ **my shares are ~ 70p** meine Aktien sind um 70 Pence gestiegen; **then ~ go prices again** und wieder steigen die Preise.
(f) (*in score*) **to be 3 goals ~** mit 3 Toren führen *or* vorn liegen (*on* gegenüber); **the score was 9 ~** (*US*) es stand 9 beide; **I'll play you 100 ~** ich spiele auf 100 (mit dir); **we were £100 ~ on the deal** wir haben bei dem Geschäft £ 100 gemacht; **to be one ~ on sb** jdm um einen Schritt voraus sein.
(g) (*upwards*) **from £2 ~** von £ 2 (an) aufwärts, ab £ 2; **from the age of 13 ~** ab (dem Alter von) 13 Jahren, von 13 Jahren aufwärts; **~ to £100** bis zu £ 100.
(h) (*wrong*) **what's ~?** was ist los?; **what's ~ with him?** was ist mit dem los?, was ist los mit ihm?; **there's something ~** (*wrong*) da stimmt irgend etwas nicht; (*happening*) da ist irgend etwas im Gange; **there's something ~ with it** irgendetwas stimmt damit nicht *or* hier nicht.
(i) (*knowledgeable*) firm, beschlagen (*in, on* in *+dat*) ◆ **he's well ~ in** *or* **on foreign affairs** in Auslandsfragen kennt er sich aus *or* ist er firm; **how are you ~ on French history?** wie gut kennst du dich in französischer Geschichte aus?
(j) (*finished*) **time's ~** die Zeit ist um *or* zu Ende; **our holiday is nearly ~** unser Urlaub ist fast zu Ende *or* vorüber; **to eat/use sth ~** etw aufessen/aufbrauchen; **it's all ~ with him** (*inf*) es ist aus mit ihm (*inf*), es ist mit ihm zu Ende.
(k) **to be ~ for sale/discussion** zu verkaufen sein/zur Diskussion stehen; **to be ~ for election** (*candidate*) zur Wahl aufgestellt sein; (*candidates*) zur Wahl stehen; **the matter is ~ before the committee** die Sache ist vor dem Ausschuß; **the boys were ~ before the headmaster** die Jungen sind vor den Direktor zitiert worden; **to be ~ for trial** vor Gericht stehen; **to be ~ before the Court/before Judge X** (*case*) verhandelt werden/von Richter X verhandelt werden; (*person*) vor Gericht/Richter X stehen.
(l) (*as far as*) bis ◆ **~ to now/here** bis jetzt/hier; **to count ~ to 100** bis 100 zählen; **it holds ~ to 8** es faßt bis zu 8; **I'm ~ to here in work** (*inf*) ich stecke bis hier in Arbeit; **what page are you ~ to?** bis zu welcher Seite bist du gekommen?
(m) **~ to** (*inf: doing*) **what's he ~ to?** (*actually doing*) was macht er da?; (*planning etc*) was hat er vor?; (*suspiciously*) was führt er im Schilde?; **what have you been ~ to?** was hast du angestellt?; **what are you ~ to with that?** was hast du damit vor?; **he's ~ to no good** er führt nichts Gutes im Schilde; **I'm sure he's ~ to something** ich bin sicher, er hat etwas vor *or* (*sth suspicious*) führt irgend etwas im Schilde; (*child*) ich bin sicher, er stellt irgend etwas an; **hey you! what do you think you're ~ to!** he Sie, was machen Sie eigentlich da!; **what does he think he's ~ to?** was soll das eigentlich?, was hat er eigentlich vor?
▼ **(n)** **~ to** (*equal to*) **I don't feel ~ to it** ich fühle mich dem nicht gewachsen; (*not well enough*) ich fühle mich nicht wohl genug dazu; **he's not/it isn't ~ to much** mit ihm/damit ist nicht viel los (*inf*); **is he ~ to advanced work/the heavier weights?** schafft er anspruchsvollere Arbeit/schwerere Gewichte?; **it isn't ~ to his usual standard** das ist nicht sein sonstiges Niveau; **we're going up Ben Nevis — are you sure you're ~ to it?** wir wollen Ben Nevis besteigen — glaubst du, daß du das schaffst? *or* (*experienced enough*) glaubst du, daß du dem gewachsen bist?
(o) **~ to** (*depending on*) **it's ~ to us to help him** wir sollten ihm helfen; **if it was ~ to me** wenn es nach mir ginge; **your success is ~ to you now** Ihr Erfolg hängt jetzt nur noch von Ihnen (selbst) ab, es liegt jetzt ganz an Ihnen, ob Sie Erfolg haben; **it's ~ to you whether you go or not** es liegt an *or* bei dir *or* es bleibt dir überlassen, ob du gehst oder nicht; **I'd like to accept, but it isn't ~ to me** ich würde gerne annehmen, aber ich habe da nicht zu bestimmen *or* das hängt nicht von mir ab; **shall I take it? — that's entirely ~ to you** soll ich es nehmen? — das müssen Sie selbst wissen; **what colour shall I choose? — ~ to you** welche Farbe soll ich nehmen? — das ist deine Entscheidung.
(p) **~ to** (*duty of*) **it's ~ to the government to put this right** es ist Sache der Regierung, das richtigzustellen; **it's not ~ to the government** das ist keine *or* nicht Sache der Regierung.
(q) **~ and down** auf und ab; **to walk ~ and down** auf und ab gehen; **to bounce ~ and down** hochfedern, auf und ab hüpfen; **he's been ~ and down all evening** (*from seat*) er hat den ganzen Abend keine Minute stillgesessen; (*on stairs*) er ist den ganzen Abend die Treppe rauf und runter gerannt; **she's still a bit ~ and down** es geht ihr immer noch mal besser, mal schlechter.
(r) **it was ~ against the wall** es war an die Wand gelehnt; **put it ~ against the wall** lehne es an die Wand; **to be ~ against a difficulty/an opponent** einem Problem/Gegner gegenüberstehen, es mit einem Problem/Gegner zu tun haben; **I fully realize what I'm ~ against** mir ist völlig klar, womit ich es hier zu tun habe; **they were really ~ against it** sie hatten wirklich schwer zu schaffen.
[2] *prep* oben auf (*+dat*); (*with movement*) hinauf (*+acc*) ◆ **further ~ the page** weiter oben auf der Seite; **to live/go ~ the hill** am Berg wohnen/den Berg hinaufgehen; **they live further ~ the hill/street** sie wohnen weiter oben am Berg/weiter die Straße entlang; **he lives ~ a gloomy passage** seine Wohnung liegt an einem düsteren Flur; **~ the road from me** (von mir) die Straße entlang; **he went off ~ the road** er ging (weg) die Straße hinauf; **he hid it ~ the chimney** er versteckte es (oben) im Kamin; **what? you have to put it ~ your nose?** was? in die Nase soll man sich das tun?; **the water goes ~ this pipe** das Wasser geht durch dieses Rohr; **~ one's sleeve/a tube** (*position*) im Ärmel/in einer Röhre; (*motion*) in den Ärmel/in eine Röhre; **as I travel ~ and down the country** wenn ich so durchs Land reise; **I've been ~ and down the stairs all night** ich bin in der Nacht immer nur die Treppe rauf und runter gerannt; **he was ~ the pub** (*inf*) er war in der Kneipe (*inf*); **let's go ~ the pub/~ Johnny's place** (*inf*) gehen wir doch zur Kneipe/zu Johnny (*inf*); **to go/march** *etc* **~ to sb** auf jdn zugehen/zumarschieren *etc.*
[3] *n* **(a)** **~s and downs** gute und schlechte Zeiten *pl*; (*of life*) Höhen und Tiefen *pl*; **after many ~s and downs** nach vielen Höhen und Tiefen; **they have their ~s and downs** bei ihnen gibt es auch gute und schlechte Zeiten.
(b) **to be on the ~ and ~** (*inf: improving*) auf dem aufsteigenden Ast sein (*inf*); (*sl: honest, straight*) (*person*) keine krummen Touren machen (*sl*); (*offer*) sauber sein (*sl*); **he/his career is on the ~ and ~** (*inf*) mit ihm/seiner Karriere geht es aufwärts.
[4] *adj* (*going up*) *escalator* nach oben; (*Rail*) *train, line* zur nächsten größeren Stadt ◆ **platform 14 is the ~ platform** auf Bahnsteig 14 fahren die Züge nach London *etc.*
[5] *vt* (*inf*) *price, offer* hinaufsetzen; *production* ankurbeln; *bet* erhöhen (*to* auf *+acc*).
[6] *vi* (*inf*) **she ~ped and hit him** sie knallte ihm ganz plötzlich eine (*inf*); **he ~ped and ran** er rannte ganz plötzlich davon.

up-and-coming ['ʌpən'kʌmɪŋ] *adj* kommend; *city* aufstrebend.
up-and-under ['ʌpən'ʌndəʳ] *n* (*Rugby*) hohe Selbstvorlage.
upbeat ['ʌpbi:t] [1] *n* (*Mus*) Auftakt *m*.
[2] *adj* (*inf*) (*cheerful*) fröhlich; (*optimistic*) optimistisch.
up-bow ['ʌpbəʊ] *n* Aufstrich *m*.
upbraid [ʌp'breɪd] *vt* rügen ◆ **to ~ sb for doing sth** jdn dafür rügen, daß er etw getan hat.
upbringing ['ʌpbrɪŋɪŋ] *n* Erziehung *f*; (*manners also*) Kinderstube *f* ◆ **to have a good ~** eine gute Kinderstube haben; **he hasn't got any ~** er hat keine Kinderstube; **where's your ~?** wo ist deine gute Kinderstube?
upchuck ['ʌptʃʌk] *vi* (*US sl: vomit*) kotzen (*vulg*), reihern (*sl*).
upcoming [ʌp'kʌmɪŋ] *adj* (*esp US: coming soon*) kommend, bevorstehend.
up-country ['ʌp'kʌntrɪ] [1] *adv* landeinwärts.
[2] *adj person* im Landesinnern.
up-current ['ʌpkʌrənt] *n* (*Aviat*) Aufwind *m*, Aufströmung *f*.
update [ʌp'deɪt] [1] *vt* aktualisieren; *file, book also, person* auf den neuesten Stand bringen.
[2] ['ʌpdeɪt] *n* Aktualisierung *f*; (*~ed version*) Neufassung *f*; (*of software package*) aktualisierte Version; (*progress report*) Bericht *m* ◆ **can you give me an ~ on ...?** können Sie mich bezüglich ... (*gen*) auf den neuesten Stand bringen?
up-draught, (*US*) **up-draft** ['ʌpdrɑ:ft] *n* Zug *m*; (*Aviat*) Aufwind *m*, Aufströmung *f*.
up-end [ʌp'end] *vt box, sofa* hochkant stellen; *person, animal* umdrehen.
upfront ['ʌp'frʌnt] [1] *adj* **(a)** (*person*) offen. **(b)** **~ money** Vorschuß *m*.
[2] *adv* **we'd like 20% ~** wir hätten gern 20% (als) Vorschuß; **we need all the cash ~** wir benötigen die ganze Summe im voraus.
upgrade ['ʌp,greɪd] [1] *n* **(a)** (*improved version*) verbesserte Version. **(b)** (*US*) Steigung *f*. **(c)** (*fig*) **to be on the ~** sich auf dem aufsteigenden Ast befinden (*inf*).
[2] [ʌp'greɪd] *vt employee* befördern; *job* anheben; *product* verbessern; (*expand*) *computer system etc* ausbauen, nachrüsten.
upgrad(e)ability [,ʌpgreɪdə'bɪlɪtɪ] *n* (*of computer system etc*) Ausbaufähigkeit, Nachrüstbarkeit *f*.
upgrad(e)able [ʌp'greɪdəbl] *adj computer system etc* ausbaufähig (*to* auf *+acc*), nachrüstbar (*to* auf *+acc*).
upheaval [ʌp'hi:vəl] *n* (*Geol*) Aufwölbung, Erhebung *f*; (*fig*) Aufruhr *m* ◆ **emotional ~** Aufruhr *m* der Gefühle; **social/political ~s** soziale/politische Umwälzungen *pl*.
upheld [ʌp'held] *pret, ptp of* **uphold.**
uphill ['ʌp'hɪl] [1] *adv* bergauf ◆ **to go ~** bergauf gehen, steigen; (*road also*) bergauf führen; (*car*) Berge/den Berg hinauffahren.
[2] *adj road* bergauf (führend); (*fig*) *work, struggle* mühsam, mühselig ◆ **it's ~ all the way** (*lit*) es geht die ganze Strecke bergauf; (*fig*) es ist ein harter Kampf; **~ ski** Bergski *m*.

➤ LANGUAGE IN USE: **up: 1n** → 16.4

uphold [ʌp'həʊld] *pret, ptp* **upheld** *vt* (*sustain*) *tradition, honour* wahren; *the law* hüten; (*support*) *person, decision, objection* (unter)stützen; (*Jur*) *verdict* bestätigen.

upholder [ʌp'həʊldəʳ] *n* Wahrer *m*; (*supporter*) Verteidiger *m*.

upholster [ʌp'həʊlstəʳ] *vt chair etc* polstern; (*cover*) beziehen ◆ **~ed** Polster-; **well-~ed** (*hum inf*) gut gepolstert (*hum inf*).

upholsterer [ʌp'həʊlstərəʳ] *n* Polsterer *m*.

upholstery [ʌp'həʊlstərɪ] *n* (*padding and springs*) Polsterung *f*; (*cover*) Bezug *m*; (*trade*) Polsterei *f*; (*skill*) das Polstern.

upkeep ['ʌpkiːp] *n* (*running*) Unterhalt *m*; (*cost*) Unterhaltskosten *pl*; (*maintenance*) Instandhaltung *f*; Instandhaltungskosten *pl*; (*of public gardens etc*) Pflege *f*.

upland ['ʌplənd] 1 *n* (*usu pl*) Hochland *nt no pl*.
2 *adj* Hochland-.

uplift ['ʌplɪft] 1 *n* (a) (*exaltation*) Erhebung *f*; (*moral inspiration*) Erbauung *f* ◆ **his sermons were full of ~** seine Predigten waren voll erbaulicher Worte; **to give sb spiritual ~** jdn erbauen. (b) **~ bra** Stützbüstenhalter *m*.
2 [ʌp'lɪft] *vt* (a) *spirit, voice* erheben ◆ **to feel ~ed** sich erbaut fühlen. (b) (*Scot: collect*) abholen.

upload ['ʌpləʊd] *vt* (*Comput*) laden.

up-market ['ʌp'mɑːkɪt] 1 *adj* anspruchsvoll; *person* vornehm.
2 *adv sell* an anspruchsvollere Kunden ◆ **his shop has gone ~** in seinem Laden verkauft er jetzt Waren der höheren Preisklasse; **Japanese car makers have gone ~** Japans Autohersteller produzieren jetzt für einen anspruchsvolleren Kundenkreis.

upmost ['ʌpməʊst] *adj, adv see* **uppermost**.

upon [ə'pɒn] *prep see* **on**.

upper ['ʌpəʳ] 1 *adj* (a) obere(r, s); *lip, arm, jaw, deck* Ober- ◆ **temperatures in the ~ thirties** Temperaturen hoch in den dreißig; **the ~ reaches of the Thames** der Oberlauf der Themse; **U~ Egypt/the ~ Loire** Oberägypten *nt*/die obere Loire; **U~ Rhine** Oberrhein *m*; **U~ Volta** Obervolta *nt*; **~ circle** (*Brit*) zweiter Rang.
(b) (*in importance, rank*) höhere(r, s), obere(r, s) ◆ **the ~ ranks of the Civil Service** das gehobene Beamtentum; **in the ~ income bracket** in der oberen Einkommensklasse; **~ school** Oberschule *f*; **U~ House** (*Parl*) Oberhaus *nt*; *see* **hand 1 (k)**.
2 *n* (a) **~s** *pl* (*of shoe*) Obermaterial *nt* ◆ **to be on one's ~s** auf den Hund gekommen sein. (b) (*sl: drug*) Aufputschmittel *nt*.

upper: ~ case *n* (*Typ*) (*also* **~-case letter**) Großbuchstabe, Versal (*spec*) *m*; **to set sth in ~ case** etw in Versalien setzen; **an ~-case T** ein Versal-T; **~ class** *n* obere Klasse, Oberschicht *f*; **the ~ classes** die Oberschicht; **~-class** *adj accent, district, person* vornehm, fein; *sport, expression, attitude* der Oberschicht; **to be ~-class** (*person*) zur Oberschicht gehören; **~classman** *n* (*US*) *Mitglied nt einer High School oder eines College*; **~ crust** *n* (*inf*) obere Zehntausend *pl* (*inf*); **~-crust** *adj* (*inf*) (schrecklich) vornehm (*inf*); **~cut** *n* Aufwärtshaken, Uppercut *m*; **~most** 1 *adj* oberste(r, s); (*fig*) *ambition* größte(r, s), höchste(r, s); **safety should be ~most in your minds** Sicherheit sollte für Sie an erster Stelle stehen; **it's quite obvious what is ~most in your mind** es ist ziemlich klar, wo deine Prioritäten liegen; 2 *adv* **face/the blue side ~most** mit dem Gesicht/der blauen Seite nach oben.

uppish ['ʌpɪʃ], **uppity** ['ʌpɪtɪ] *adj* (*inf: arrogant*) hochnäsig (*inf*), hochmütig; *woman also* schnippisch ◆ **to get ~ with sb** jdm gegenüber frech *or* anmaßend werden, jdm frech kommen.

upraised [ʌp'reɪzd] *adj* erhoben.

upright ['ʌpraɪt] 1 *adj* (a) (*erect*) aufrecht; (*vertical*) *post* senkrecht ◆ **~ piano** Klavier *nt*; **~ chair** Stuhl *m*. (b) (*fig: honest*) *person, character* aufrecht, rechtschaffen.
2 *adv* (*erect*) aufrecht, gerade; (*vertical*) senkrecht ◆ **to hold oneself ~** sich gerade halten.
3 *n* (a) (*post*) Pfosten *m*. (b) (*piano*) Klavier *nt*.

uprightly ['ʌp,raɪtlɪ] *adv* aufrecht, rechtschaffen.

uprightness ['ʌp,raɪtnɪs] *n* Rechtschaffenheit *f*.

uprising ['ʌpraɪzɪŋ] *n* Aufstand *m*, Erhebung *f*.

upriver ['ʌp'rɪvəʳ] *adv* **2 miles ~ from Fen Ditton** 2 Meilen flußaufwärts von Fen Ditton.

uproar ['ʌprɔːʳ] *n* Aufruhr, Tumult *m* ◆ **he tried to make himself heard above the ~** er versuchte, sich über den Lärm *or* Spektakel (*inf*) hinweg verständlich zu machen; **at this there was ~, this caused an ~** das verursachte einen (wahren) Aufruhr *or* Tumult; **the whole place was in ~** der ganze Saal/das ganze Haus *etc* war in Aufruhr.

uproarious [ʌp'rɔːrɪəs] *adj meeting* tumultartig; *crowd* lärmend; *laughter* brüllend; *success, welcome* überwältigend, spektakulär; (*very funny*) *joke* wahnsinnig komisch, zum Schreien *pred* ◆ **in ~ spirits** in überschäumender Stimmung.

uproariously [ʌp'rɔːrɪəslɪ] *adv* lärmend; *laugh* brüllend ◆ **~ funny** wahnsinnig komisch, zum Schreien *or* Brüllen.

uproot [ʌp'ruːt] *vt plant* entwurzeln; (*fig: eradicate*) *evil* ausmerzen ◆ **~ed by the war** durch den Krieg entwurzelt; **to ~ sb from his familiar surroundings** jdn aus seiner gewohnten Umgebung herausreißen; **he ~ed his whole family and moved to New York** er riß seine Familie aus ihrer gewohnten Umgebung und zog nach New York.

upsadaisy ['ʌpsə,deɪzɪ] *interj* (*inf*) hoppla.

upset [ʌp'set] (*vb: pret, ptp* **~**) 1 *vt* (a) (*knock over*) umstoßen, umwerfen; *boat* umkippen, zum Kentern bringen; (*spill also*) umleeren ◆ **she ~ the milk all over the best carpet** sie stieß die Milch um, und alles lief auf den guten Teppich.
(b) (*make sad: news, death*) bestürzen, erschüttern, mitnehmen (*inf*); (*question, insolence etc*) aus der Fassung bringen; (*divorce, experience, accident etc*) mitnehmen (*inf*); (*distress, excite*) *patient, parent etc* aufregen; (*offend: unkind behaviour, words etc*) verletzen, weh tun (*+dat*); (*annoy*) ärgern ◆ **you shouldn't have said/done that, now you've ~ her** das hätten Sie nicht sagen/tun sollen, jetzt regt sie sich auf *or* (*is offended*) jetzt ist sie beleidigt; **don't ~ yourself** regen Sie sich nicht auf; **there's no point in ~ting yourself** es hat doch keinen Zweck, das so tragisch zu nehmen; **I don't know what's ~ him** ich weiß nicht, was er hat.
(c) (*disorganize*) *calculations, balance etc* durcheinanderbringen; *plan, timetable also* umwerfen ◆ **that's ~ my theory** das hat meine Theorie umgestoßen.
(d) (*make ill*) **the rich food ~ his stomach** das schwere Essen ist ihm nicht bekommen; **onions ~ me** von Zwiebeln bekomme ich Magenbeschwerden; **to ~ one's stomach** sich (*dat*) den Magen verderben.
2 *vi* umkippen.
3 *adj* (a) (*about divorce, accident, dismissal etc*) mitgenommen (*inf*) (*about* von); (*about death, bad news etc*) bestürzt (*about* über *+acc*); (*sad*) betrübt, geknickt (*inf*) (*about* über *+acc*); (*distressed, worried*) aufgeregt (*about* wegen); *baby, child* durcheinander *pred*; (*annoyed*) ärgerlich, aufgebracht (*about* über *+acc*); (*hurt*) gekränkt, verletzt (*about* über *+acc*) ◆ **she was pretty ~ about it** das ist ihr ziemlich nahegegangen, das hat sie ziemlich mitgenommen (*inf*); (*distressed, worried*) sie hat sich deswegen ziemlich aufgeregt; (*annoyed*) das hat sie ziemlich geärgert; (*hurt*) das hat sie ziemlich gekränkt *or* verletzt; **she was ~ about the news/that he'd left her** es hat sie ziemlich mitgenommen (*inf*), als sie das hörte/daß er sie verlassen hat; **don't look so ~, they'll come back** guck doch nicht so traurig, sie kommen ja zurück; **would you be ~ if I decided not to go after all?** wärst du traurig *or* würdest du's tragisch nehmen, wenn ich doch nicht ginge?; **I'd be very ~ if ...** ich wäre sehr traurig *or* betrübt wenn ...; **the house has been burgled so of course I'm ~** bei mir ist eingebrochen worden, und natürlich rege ich mich auf; **to get ~** sich aufregen (*about* über *+acc*); (*hurt*) gekränkt *or* verletzt werden; **don't get ~ about it, you'll find another** nimm das noch nicht so tragisch, du findest bestimmt einen anderen; **she'd be ~ if I used a word like that** sie wäre entsetzt, wenn ich so etwas sagen würde.
(b) ['ʌpset] *stomach* verstimmt, verdorben *attr* ◆ **to have an ~ stomach** sich (*dat*) den Magen verdorben haben, eine Magenverstimmung haben.
4 ['ʌpset] *n* (a) (*disturbance*) Störung *f*; (*emotional*) Aufregung *f*; (*inf: quarrel*) Verstimmung *f*, Ärger *m*; (*unexpected defeat etc*) unliebsame *or* böse Überraschung ◆ **I don't want to cause any ~s in your work** ich möchte bei Ihrer Arbeit kein Durcheinander verursachen; **children don't like ~s in their routine** Kinder mögen es nicht, wenn man ihre Routine durcheinanderbringt; **it was an ~ to our plans/for us** es hat unsere Pläne durcheinandergebracht/es war eine böse Überraschung für uns; **he's had a bit of an ~** er ist etwas mitgenommen (*inf*) *or* geknickt (*inf*).
(b) (*of stomach*) Magenverstimmung *f*, verdorbener Magen.

upset price *n* (*Comm*) Mindestpreis *m*.

upsetting [ʌp'setɪŋ] *adj* (*saddening*) traurig; (*stronger*) bestürzend; (*disturbing*) *changes* störend; *situation* unangenehm, schwierig; (*offending*) beleidigend, verletzend; (*annoying*) ärgerlich ◆ **that must have been very ~ for you** das war bestimmt nicht einfach für Sie; (*annoying*) das muß sehr ärgerlich für Sie gewesen sein; **she found this experience/his language most ~** diese Erfahrung hat sie sehr mitgenommen (*inf*), diese Erfahrung ist ihr sehr nahe gegangen/sie hat sich sehr über seine Ausdrucksweise erregt; **the divorce/the change was very ~ for the child** das Kind hat unter der Scheidung/dem Wechsel sehr gelitten; **he mustn't have any more ~ experiences** es darf nichts mehr passieren, was ihn aufregt; **it's ~ to my routine** das bringt meine Routine durcheinander.

upshot ['ʌpʃɒt] *n* (*result*) Ergebnis *nt* ◆ **the ~ of it all was that ...** es lief darauf hinaus, daß ...; **what was the ~ of your meeting?** was kam bei Ihrem Treffen heraus?; **in the ~** letzten Endes.

upside down ['ʌpsaɪd'daʊn] 1 *adv* verkehrt herum ◆ **the monkey was hanging ~** der Affe hing verkehrt herum *or* mit dem Kopf nach unten; **to turn sth ~** (*lit*) etw umdrehen; (*fig*) etw auf den Kopf stellen (*inf*).
2 *adj* **in an ~ position** verkehrt herum; **to be ~** (*picture*) verkehrt herum hängen, auf dem Kopf stehen; (*world*) kopfstehen.

upstage [ʌp'steɪdʒ] 1 *adv* (*Theat*) im Hintergrund der Bühne; (*with movement*) in den Hintergrund der Bühne.
2 *adj* blasiert, hochnäsig (*with* gegenüber).
3 *vt* **to ~ sb** (*Theat*) jdn zwingen, dem Publikum den Rücken zuzukehren; (*fig*) jdn ausstechen, jdm die Schau stehlen (*inf*).

upstairs [ʌp'steəz] 1 *adv* oben; (*with movement*) nach oben ◆ **to kick sb ~** (*fig*) jdn wegloben; **may I go ~?** (*euph*) kann ich mal aufs Örtchen?; **he hasn't got much ~** (*inf*) er ist ein bißchen schwach im Oberstübchen (*inf*).
2 *adj window* im oberen Stock(werk); *room also* obere(r, s).
3 *n* oberes Stockwerk.

upstanding [ʌp'stændɪŋ] *adj* (a) (*strong*) kräftig; (*honourable*) rechtschaffen. (b) (*Jur, form*) **to be ~** stehen; **gentlemen, please be ~ for the toast** (meine Herren,) bitte erheben Sie sich zum Toast; **the court will be ~** bitte erheben Sie sich.

upstart ['ʌpstɑːt] 1 *n* Emporkömmling *m*.
2 *adj behaviour* eines Emporkömmlings ◆ **an ~ publisher** ein Emporkömmling *m* (unter den Verlegern).

upstate ['ʌpsteɪt] (*US*) 1 *adj* im Norden (des Bundesstaates) ◆ **to live in ~**

New York im Norden des Staates New York wohnen.
[2] *adv* im Norden (des Bundesstaates); (*with movement*) in den Norden (des Bundesstaates).

upstream ['ʌpstriːm] *adv* flußaufwärts ◆ **3 kms ~ from Henley** 3 km oberhalb Henley.

upstretched [ʌp'stretʃt] *adj hands* ausgestreckt; *neck* gereckt.

upstroke ['ʌpstrəʊk] *n* (*of pen*) Aufstrich *m*; (*of piston*) aufgehender Hub, Aufwärtsgang *m*.

upsurge ['ʌpsɜːdʒ] *n* Zunahme, Eskalation (*pej*) *f* ◆ **she felt an ~ of affection/hatred/revulsion** sie fühlte Zuneigung/Haß/Ekel in sich (*dat*) aufwallen.

upswept [ʌp'swept] *adj hair* hoch- *or* zurückgebürstet ◆ **~ into a chignon** zu einem Knoten hochgesteckt.

upswing ['ʌpswɪŋ] *n* (*lit, fig*) Aufschwung *m*; (*Sport*) Ausholen *nt no pl*.

upsy-daisy ['ʌpsəˌdeɪzɪ] *see* **upsadaisy**.

uptake ['ʌpteɪk] *n* (*inf*): **to be quick/slow on the ~** schnell verstehen/schwer von Begriff sein (*inf*), eine lange Leitung haben (*inf*).

upthrust ['ʌpθrʌst] *n* (*upward movement*) Aufwärtsdruck *m*; (*Geol*) Hebung *f*.

uptight ['ʌp'taɪt] *adj* (*sl*) (*nervous*) nervös; (*inhibited*) verklemmt (*inf*); (*angry*) sauer (*sl*); *voice* gepreßt; *expression* verkrampft, verkniffen ◆ **to get ~ (about sth)** sich (wegen etw) aufregen; (auf etw *acc*) verklemmt reagieren (*inf*); (wegen etw) sauer werden (*sl*); **he's pretty ~ about these things** der sieht so was ziemlich eng (*sl*); **no need to get ~ about it!** nun mach dir mal keinen! (*sl*).

uptime ['ʌptaɪm] *n* (*of machine*) Betriebszeit *f*.

up-to-date ['ʌptə'deɪt] *adj* auf dem neusten Stand; *fashion also, book, news* aktuell; *person, method, technique also* up to date *pred* (*inf*) ◆ **to keep ~ with the fashions/news** mit der Mode/den Nachrichten auf dem laufenden bleiben; **to keep sb/sth/oneself ~** jdn/etw/sich auf dem laufenden halten; **would you bring me ~ on developments?** würden Sie mich über den neusten Stand der Dinge informieren?

up-to-the-minute ['ʌptəðə'mɪnɪt] *adj news, reports* allerneuste(r, s), allerletzte(r, s); *style also* hochmodern ◆ **her clothes are ~** ihre Kleider sind immer der allerletzte Schrei.

uptown ['ʌptaʊn] (*US*) [1] *adj* (*in Northern part of town*) im Norden (der Stadt); (*in residential area*) im Villenviertel.
[2] *adv* im Norden der Stadt; im Villenviertel; (*with movement*) in den Norden der Stadt; ins Villenviertel.
[3] *n* Villenviertel *nt*.

upturn [ʌp'tɜːn] [1] *vt* umdrehen.
[2] ['ʌptɜːn] *n* (*fig: improvement*) Aufschwung *m*.

upturned [ʌp'tɜːnd] *adj box etc* umgedreht; *face* nach oben gewandt ◆ **~ nose** Stupsnase, Himmelfahrtsnase (*inf*) *f*.

upward ['ʌpwəd] [1] *adj* Aufwärts-, nach oben; *glance* nach oben ◆ **~ movement** Aufwärtsbewegung *f*; **~ slope** Steigung *f*; **~ mobility** (*Sociol*) soziale Aufstiegsmöglichkeiten *pl*.
[2] *adv* (*also* **~s**) **(a)** *move* aufwärts, nach oben ◆ **to look ~** hochsehen, nach oben sehen; **face ~** mit dem Gesicht nach oben.
(b) (*with numbers*) **prices from £4 ~** Preise von £ 4 an, Preise ab £ 4; **from childhood ~** von Kind auf *or* an, von Kindheit an; **and ~** und darüber; **~ of 3000** über 3000.

upwardly ['ʌpwədlɪ] *adv* aufwärts, nach oben ◆ **to be ~ mobile** ein Aufsteiger/eine Aufsteigerin sein.

upwind ['ʌpwɪnd] *adj, adv* **to be/stand ~ of sb** gegen den Wind zu jdm sein/stehen.

Ural ['juːrəl] *n* **the ~** (*river*) der Ural; **the ~ Mountains, the ~s** das Uralgebirge, der Ural.

uranium [jʊə'reɪnɪəm] *n* Uran *nt*.

Uranus [jʊə'reɪnəs] *n* (*Astron*) Uranus *m*.

urban ['ɜːbən] *adj* städtisch; *life also* in der Stadt ◆ **~ renewal** Stadterneuerung *f*; **~ guerilla** Stadtguerilla *m*; **~ warfare** Stadtguerilla *f*.

urbane [ɜː'beɪn] *adj person, manner* weltmännisch, gewandt, urban (*geh*); (*civil*) höflich; *manner, words* verbindlich.

urbanely [ɜː'beɪnlɪ] *adv see adj*.

urbanity [ɜː'bænɪtɪ] *n see adj* weltmännische Art, Gewandtheit, Urbanität (*geh*) *f*; Höflichkeit *f*; Verbindlichkeit *f*.

urbanization [ˌɜːbənaɪ'zeɪʃən] *n* Urbanisierung, Verstädterung (*pej*) *f*.

urbanize ['ɜːbənaɪz] *vt* urbanisieren, verstädtern (*pej*).

urchin ['ɜːtʃɪn] *n* Gassenkind *nt*; (*mischievous*) Range *f*.

Urdu ['ʊəduː] *n* Urdu *nt*.

urea ['jʊərɪə] *n* Harnstoff *m*, Urea (*spec*) *f*.

ureter [jʊə'riːtəʳ] *n* Harnleiter, Ureter (*spec*) *m*.

urethra [jʊə'riːθrə] *n* Harnröhre, Urethra (*spec*) *f*.

urge [ɜːdʒ] [1] *n* (*need*) Verlangen, Bedürfnis *nt*; (*drive*) Drang *m no pl*; (*physical, sexual*) Trieb *m* ◆ **to feel an ~ to do sth** das Bedürfnis verspüren, etw zu tun; **to feel the ~ to win** unbedingt gewinnen wollen; **I resisted the ~ (to contradict him)** ich habe mich beherrscht (und ihm nicht widersprochen); **an ~ to steal it came over me** der Drang, es zu stehlen, überkam mich; **creative ~s** Schaffensdrang *m*, Kreativität *f*; **come and stay with us if you get the ~** (*inf*) komm uns besuchen, wenn du Lust hast.
[2] *vt* **(a)** (*try to persuade*) *sb* eindringlich bitten ◆ **to ~ sb to do sth** (*plead with*) jdn eindringlich bitten, etw zu tun; (*earnestly recommend*) darauf drängen, daß jd etw tut; **to ~ sb to accept/join in/come along** jdn drängen, anzunehmen/mitzumachen/mitzukommen; **he needed no urging** er ließ sich nicht lange bitten; **do it now! he ~d** tun Sie's jetzt!, drängte er.
(b) to ~ sb onward jdn vorwärts- *or* weitertreiben.
(c) (*advocate*) *measure etc, caution, acceptance* drängen auf (+*acc*) ◆ **to ~ that sth should be done** darauf drängen, daß etw getan wird; **to ~ sth upon sb** jdm etw eindringlich nahelegen.
(d) (*press*) *claim* betonen; *argument* vorbringen, anführen.

◆**urge on** *vt sep* (*lit*) *horse, person, troops* antreiben, vorwärtstreiben; (*fig*) *team, workers* antreiben (*to* zu); *team* anfeuern ◆ **to ~ sb ~ to do sth** jdn (dazu) antreiben, etw zu tun.

urgency ['ɜːdʒənsɪ] *n* Dringlichkeit *f*; (*of tone of voice, pleas also*) Eindringlichkeit *f* ◆ **a matter of ~** dringend; **to treat sth as a matter of ~** etw als dringend behandeln; **there's no ~** es eilt nicht, das hat keine Eile; **there was a note of ~ in his voice** es klang sehr dringend; **the ~ of our needs** die dringende Notwendigkeit; **his statement lacked ~** seinen Worten fehlte der Nachdruck; **the ~ of his step** seine eiligen Schritte; **the sense of ~ in the music** das Drängen in der Musik.

urgent ['ɜːdʒənt] *adj* **(a)** dringend; *letter, parcel* Eil- ◆ **is it ~?** (*important*) ist es dringend?; (*needing speed*) eilt es?; **to be in ~ need of medical attention** dringend ärztliche Hilfe benötigen.
(b) (*insistent*) *tone, plea* dringend, dringlich; (*hurrying*) *steps* eilig ◆ **he was very ~ about the need for swift action** er betonte nachdrücklich, wie notwendig schnelles Handeln sei.

urgently ['ɜːdʒəntlɪ] *adv required* dringend; *requested also* dringlich; *talk* eindringlich ◆ **he is ~ in need of help** er braucht dringend Hilfe.

uric ['jʊərɪk] *adj* Harn-, Urin- ◆ **~ acid** Harnsäure *f*.

urinal ['jʊərɪnl] *n* (*room*) Pissoir *nt*; (*vessel*) Urinal *nt*; (*for patient*) Urinflasche *f*.

urinary ['jʊərɪnərɪ] *adj* Harn-, Urin-; *tract, organs* Harn-.

urinate ['jʊərɪneɪt] *vi* Wasser lassen, urinieren (*geh*), harnen (*spec*).

urine ['jʊərɪn] *n* Urin, Harn *m*.

urn [ɜːn] *n* **(a)** Urne *f*. **(b)** (*also* **tea ~, coffee ~**) Kessel *m*.

urogenital [ˌjʊərəʊ'dʒenɪtl] *adj* urogenital.

urological [ˌjʊərəʊ'lɒdʒɪkl] *adj* urologisch.

urologist [jʊə'rɒlədʒɪst] *n* Urologe *m*, Urologin *f*.

urology [jʊə'rɒlədʒɪ] *n* Urologie *f*.

Ursa Major ['ɜːsə'meɪdʒəʳ] *n* Großer Bär *or* Wagen.

Ursa Minor ['ɜːsə'maɪnəʳ] *n* Kleiner Bär *or* Wagen.

Uruguay ['jʊərəgwaɪ] *n* Uruguay *nt*.

Uruguayan [ˌjʊərə'gwaɪən] [1] *n* (*person*) Uruguayer(in *f*) *m*.
[2] *adj* uruguayisch.

US *abbr of* **United States** USA *pl*.

us [ʌs] *pers pron* **(a)** (*dir and indir obj*) uns ◆ **give it (to) ~** gib es uns; **who, ~?** wer, wir?; **younger than ~** jünger als wir; **it's ~** wir sind's; **he is one of ~** er gehört zu uns, er ist einer von uns; **this table shows ~ the tides** auf dieser Tafel sieht man die Gezeiten; **~ and them** wir und die.
(b) (*inf*) (*me*) (*dir obj*) mich; (*indir obj*) mir; (*pl subj*) wir ◆ **give ~ a look** laß mal sehen; **~ English** wir Engländer; **as for ~ English** was uns Engländer betrifft.

USA *abbr of* **United States of America** USA *pl*; **United States Army**.

usability [ˌjuːzə'bɪlɪtɪ] *n* Verwendbarkeit *f*; (*of ideas, suggestions*) Brauchbarkeit *f*.

usable ['juːzəbl] *adj* verwendbar; *suggestion, ideas* brauchbar ◆ **to be no longer ~** nicht mehr zu gebrauchen sein.

USAF *abbr of* **United States Air Force**.

usage ['juːzɪdʒ] *n* **(a)** (*treatment, handling*) Behandlung *f* ◆ **it's had some rough ~** es ist ziemlich unsanft behandelt worden.
(b) (*custom, practice*) Brauch *m*, Sitte *f*, Usus *m* (*geh*) ◆ **it's common ~** es ist allgemein üblich *or* Sitte *or* Brauch; **the ~s of society** die gesellschaftlichen Gepflogenheiten.
(c) (*Ling: use, way of using*) Gebrauch *m no pl*, Anwendung *f* ◆ **words in common ~** allgemein gebräuchliche Wörter *pl*; **it's common in Northern ~** es ist im Norden allgemein gebräuchlich; **it's not an acceptable ~** so darf das nicht gebraucht werden; **the finer points of ~** die Feinheiten des Sprachgebrauchs.

use[1] [juːz] [1] *vt* **(a)** benutzen, benützen (*S Ger*); (*utilize*) *dictionary, means, tools, object, materials also, sb's suggestion, idea* verwenden; *word, literary style* gebrauchen, verwenden, benutzen; *swear words* gebrauchen, benutzen; *brains, intelligence also* gebrauchen; *method, system, technique, therapy, force, trickery* anwenden; *one's abilities, powers of persuasion, one's strength* aufwenden, anwenden; *tact, care* walten lassen; *drugs* einnehmen ◆ **~ only in emergencies** nur im Notfall gebrauchen *or* benutzen; **what's this ~d for?** wofür wird das benutzt *or* gebraucht?; **to ~ sth for sth** etw zu etw verwenden; **he ~d it as a spoon** er hat es als Löffel benutzt *or* verwendet; **the police ~d truncheons** die Polizei setzte Schlagstöcke ein, die Polizei benutzte *or* gebrauchte Schlagstöcke; **what did you ~ the money for?** wofür haben Sie das Geld benutzt *or* verwendet *or* gebraucht?; **the money is to be ~d to set up a trust** das Geld soll dazu verwendet werden, eine Stiftung einzurichten; **what sort of toothpaste/petrol do you ~?** welche Zahnpasta benutzen *or* verwenden Sie/welches Benzin verwenden Sie?, mit welchem Benzin fahren Sie?; **what sort of fuel does this rocket ~?** welcher Treibstoff wird für diese Rakete verwendet?; **ointment to be ~d sparingly** Salbe nur sparsam verwenden *or* anwenden; **why don't you ~ a hammer?** warum nehmen Sie nicht einen Hammer dazu?, warum benutzen *or* verwenden Sie nicht einen Hammer dazu?; **to ~ sb's name** jds Namen verwenden *or* benutzen; (*as reference*) jds Namen angeben, sich auf jdn berufen; **we can ~ the extra staff to do this** dafür können wir das übrige Personal einsetzen *or* verwenden; **I'll have to ~ some of your men** ich brauche ein paar Ihrer Leute.
(b) (*make use of, exploit*) *information, one's training, talents, resources, chances,*

opportunity (aus)nutzen, (aus)nützen (*S Ger*); *advantage* nutzen; *waste products* nutzen, verwerten ◆ **not ~d to capacity** nicht voll genutzt; **you can ~ the leftovers to make a soup** Sie können die Reste zu einer Suppe verwerten; **you should ~ your free time for something creative** Sie sollten Ihre Freizeit für etwas Schöpferisches nutzen *or* gebrauchen.

(c) (*inf*) **I could ~ a ...** ich könnte einen/eine/ein ... (ge)brauchen; **I could ~ a drink** ich könnte etwas zu trinken (ge)brauchen *or* vertragen (*inf*); **it could ~ a bit of paint** das könnte ein bißchen Farbe vertragen.

(d) (*~ up, consume*) verbrauchen ◆ **this car ~s too much petrol** dieses Auto verbraucht zuviel Benzin; **have you ~d all the ink?** haben Sie die Tinte aufgebraucht (*inf*) *or* die ganze Tinte verbraucht?

(e) (*obs, liter: treat*) behandeln; (*cruelly, ill etc also*) mitspielen (+*dat*) ◆ **she was ill ~d** ihr ist übel mitgespielt worden; **how has the world been using you?** (*not obs, liter*) wie geht's, wie steht's?

(f) (*pej: exploit*) ausnutzen ◆ **I feel (I've just been) ~d** ich habe das Gefühl, man hat mich ausgenutzt; (*sexually*) ich komme mir mißbraucht vor.

2 [ju:s] *n* **(a)** (*employment*) Verwendung *f*; (*of materials, tools, means, dictionary also*) Benutzung *f*; (*operation: of machines etc*) Benutzung *f*; (*working with: of dictionary, calculator etc*) Gebrauch *m*; (*of word, style also, of swearwords, arms, intelligence*) Gebrauch *m*; (*of method, system, technique, therapy, force, one's strength, powers of persuasion*) Anwendung *f*; (*of personnel, truncheons etc*) Verwendung *f*, Einsatz *m*; (*of drugs*) Einnahme *f* ◆ **once you've mastered the ~ of this calculator** wenn Sie den Gebrauch *or* die Benutzung des Rechners einmal beherrschen; **the ~ of a calculator to solve ...** die Verwendung eines Rechners, um ... zu lösen; **directions for ~** Gebrauchsanweisung *f*; **for the ~ of** für; **for ~ in case of emergency** für Notfälle; **for external ~** äußerlich anzuwenden, zur äußerlichen Anwendung; **it's for ~ not ornament** es ist ein Gebrauchsgegenstand und nicht zur Zierde; **ready for ~** gebrauchsfertig; (*machine*) einsatzbereit; **to improve with ~** sich mit der Zeit bessern; **worn with ~** abgenutzt; **to make ~ of sth** von etw Gebrauch machen, etw benutzen; **can you make ~ of that?** können Sie das brauchen?; **in ~/out of ~** in *or* im/außer Gebrauch; (*machines also*) in/außer Betrieb; **to be in daily ~/ no longer in ~** täglich/nicht mehr benutzt *or* verwendet *or* gebraucht werden; **to come into ~** in Gebrauch kommen; **to go** *or* **fall out of ~** nicht mehr benutzt *or* verwendet *or* gebraucht werden.

(b) (*exploitation, making ~ of*) Nutzung *f*; (*of waste products, left-overs etc*) Verwertung *f* ◆ **to make ~ of sth** etw nutzen; **to put sth to ~/good ~** etw benutzen/etw ausnutzen *or* gut nutzen; **to make good/bad ~ of sth** etw gut/schlecht nutzen.

(c) (*way of using*) Verwendung *f* ◆ **to learn the ~ of sth** lernen, wie etw verwendet *or* benutzt *or* gebraucht wird; **it has many ~s** es ist vielseitig verwendbar; **to find a ~ for sth** für etw Verwendung finden; **to have no ~ for** (*lit, fig*) nicht gebrauchen können, keine Verwendung haben für; **to have no further ~ for sb/sth** keine Verwendung mehr haben für jdn/etw, jdn/etw nicht mehr brauchen.

(d) (*usefulness*) Nutzen *m* ◆ **to be of ~ to sb/for doing sth** für jdn von Nutzen sein *or* nützlich sein/nützlich sein, um etw zu tun; **this is no ~ any more** das taugt nichts mehr, das ist zu nichts mehr zu gebrauchen; **does it have a ~ in our society?** ist es für unsere Gesellschaft von Nutzen?; **is this (of) any ~ to you?** können Sie das brauchen?, können Sie damit was anfangen?; **he/that has his/its ~s** er/das ist ganz nützlich; **you're no ~ to me if you can't spell** du nützt mir nichts, wenn du keine Rechtschreibung kannst; **he's no ~ as a goalkeeper** er taugt nicht als Torhüter, er ist als Torhüter nicht zu gebrauchen; **can I be of any ~?** kann ich irgendwie behilflich sein?; **a lot of ~ that will be to you!** (*inf*) da hast du aber was davon (*inf*); **this is no ~, we must start work** so hat das keinen Zweck *or* Sinn, wir müssen etwas tun; **it's no ~ you** *or* **your protesting** es hat keinen Sinn *or* Zweck *or* es nützt nichts, wenn *or* daß du protestierst; **what's the ~ of telling him?** was nützt es, wenn man es ihm sagt?; **what's the ~ in trying/going?** wozu überhaupt versuchen/gehen?; **it's no ~** es hat keinen Zweck; **ah, what's the ~!** ach, was soll's!

(e) (*right*) Nutznießung *f* (*Jur*) ◆ **to have the ~ of the gardens/a car/money** die Gartenanlagen/einen Wagen benutzen können/über einen Wagen/Geld verfügen (können); **to give sb the ~ of sth** jdn etw benutzen lassen; (*of car also, of money*) jdm etw zur Verfügung stellen; **to have lost the ~ of one's arm** seinen Arm nicht mehr gebrauchen *or* benutzen können; **to have the full ~ of one's faculties** im Vollbesitz seiner (geistigen und körperlichen) Kräfte sein; **have you lost the ~ of your legs?** (*hum*) hast du das Gehen verlernt?

(f) (*custom*) Brauch, Usus (*geh*) *m*.

(g) (*Eccl*) Brauch *m* ◆ **in the Roman ~** nach römisch-katholischem Brauch.

◆use up *vt sep food, objects, one's strength* verbrauchen; (*finish also*) aufbrauchen; *scraps, leftovers etc* verwerten ◆ **the butter is all ~d ~** die Butter ist alle (*inf*) *or* aufgebraucht; **all his energy was ~d ~** all seine Energie war verbraucht.

use² [ju:s] *v aux as in* **I didn't ~ to like it** *see* **used²**.

used¹ [ju:zd] *adj* (*second-hand*) *clothes, car etc* gebraucht; (*soiled*) *towel etc* benutzt; *stamp* gestempelt.

used² [ju:st] *v aux only in past* **I ~ to swim every day** ich bin früher täglich geschwommen, ich pflegte täglich zu schwimmen (*geh*); **I ~ not to smoke, I didn't use to smoke** ich habe früher nicht geraucht, ich pflegte nicht zu rauchen (*geh*); **what ~ he to do** *or* **what did he use to do on Sundays?** was hat er früher *or* sonst sonntags getan?; **he ~ to play golf, didn't he?** er hat doch früher *or* mal Golf gespielt, nicht wahr?; **I didn't know you smoked — I ~ not to** ich habe nicht gewußt, daß Sie rauchen — habe ich früher auch nicht; **I don't now but I ~ to** früher schon, jetzt nicht mehr!; **he ~ to be a good singer** er war einmal ein guter Sänger; **there ~ to be a field here** hier war (früher) einmal ein Feld; **things aren't what they ~ to be** es ist alles nicht mehr (so) wie früher; **life is more hectic than it ~ to be** das Leben ist hektischer als früher.

used³ [ju:st] *adj* **to be ~ to sth** an etw (*acc*) gewöhnt sein, etw gewohnt sein; **to be ~ to doing sth** daran gewöhnt sein *or* es gewohnt sein, etw zu tun; **I'm not ~ to it** ich bin das nicht gewohnt; **to get ~ to sth/doing sth** sich an etw (*acc*) gewöhnen/sich daran gewöhnen, etw zu tun; **you might as well get ~ to it!** (*inf*) daran wirst du dich gewöhnen müssen!

useful ['ju:sfʊl] *adj* **(a)** nützlich; *person, citizen, contribution, addition also* wertvoll; *contribution, hint also* brauchbar; (*handy*) *tool, person, language also* praktisch; *size* zweckmäßig; *discussion* fruchtbar; *life, employment* nutzbringend ◆ **it is ~ for him to be able to ...** das ist günstig *or* praktisch, daß er ... kann; **to make oneself ~** sich nützlich machen; **he likes to feel ~** er hat gern das Gefühl, nützlich zu sein; **he wants to be ~ to others** er möchte anderen nützen; **thank you, you've been very ~** vielen Dank, Sie haben mir/uns *etc* sehr geholfen; **is that ~ information?** nützt diese Information etwas?; **to come in ~** sich als nützlich erweisen; **we spent a ~ week in London** wir waren eine Woche in London, was sehr nützlich war; **that's ~!** (*iro*) das nützt uns was!; **he's a ~ man to know** es ist sehr nützlich, ihn zu kennen; **that advice was most ~ to me** der Rat hat mir sehr genützt; **that's a ~ thing to know** es ist gut, das zu wissen; **it has a ~ life of 10 years** es hat eine Nutzungsdauer von 10 Jahren.

(b) (*inf: capable*) *player* brauchbar, fähig; (*creditable*) *score* wertvoll ◆ **he's quite ~ with a gun/his fists** er kann ziemlich gut mit der Pistole/seinen Fäusten umgehen.

usefully ['ju:sfəlɪ] *adv employed, spend time* nutzbringend ◆ **you could ~ come along** es wäre von Nutzen, wenn Sie kämen; **is there anything I can ~ do?** kann ich mich irgendwie nützlich machen?; **this book can ~ be given to first year students** dieses Buch ist für Erstsemester nützlich.

usefulness ['ju:sfʊlnɪs] *n see adj* Nützlichkeit *f*; Wert *m*; Brauchbarkeit *f*; Zweckmäßigkeit *f*; Fruchtbarkeit *f*; Nutzen *m*; *see* **outlive**.

useless ['ju:slɪs] *adj* **(a)** nutzlos; (*unusable*) unbrauchbar; *advice, suggestion also* unbrauchbar, unnütz; *person also* zu nichts nütze; *remedy also* unwirksam, wirkungslos ◆ **it's ~ without a handle** ohne Griff nützt es nichts *or* ist es unbrauchbar; **he's full of ~ information** er steckt voller nutzloser Informationen; **he's ~ as a goalkeeper** er ist als Torwart nicht zu gebrauchen, er taugt nichts als Torwart; **you're just ~!** du bist auch zu nichts zu gebrauchen; **I'm ~ at languages** Sprachen kann ich überhaupt nicht.

(b) (*pointless*) zwecklos, sinnlos.

uselessly ['ju:slɪslɪ] *adv* nutzlos.

uselessness ['ju:slɪsnɪs] *n see adj* **(a)** Nutzlosigkeit *f*; Unbrauchbarkeit *f*; Unwirksamkeit *f*. **(b)** Zwecklosigkeit, Sinnlosigkeit *f*.

user ['ju:zə^r] *n* Benutzer(in *f*) *m*; (*of machines also*) Anwender(in *f*) *m* ◆ **he's a ~ of heroin** er nimmt Heroin.

user: ~-definable *adj* (*Comput*) *keys* frei definierbar; **~-defined** *adj* (*Comput*) *keys* frei definiert; **~-friendliness** *n* Benutzer- *or* Anwenderfreundlichkeit *f*; **~-friendly** *adj* benutzer- *or* anwenderfreundlich; **~ identification** *n* (*Comput*) Benutzercode *m*; **~-interface** *n* (*esp Comput*) Benutzerschnittstelle, Benutzeroberfläche *f*; **~ language** *n* (*Comput*) Benutzersprache *f*; **~ software** *n* (*Comput*) Anwendersoftware *f*; **~ support** *n* (*esp Comput*) Benutzerunterstützung *f*.

U-shaped ['ju:ʃeɪpt] *adj* U-förmig.

usher ['ʌʃə^r] **1** *n* (*Theat, at wedding etc*) Platzanweiser *m*; (*Jur*) Gerichtsdiener *m*.

2 *vt* **to ~ sb into a room/to his seat** jdn in ein Zimmer/zu seinem Sitz bringen *or* geleiten (*geh*); **the drunk was discreetly ~ed out (of the hall)** der Betrunkene wurde unauffällig (aus dem Saal) hinauskomplimentiert.

◆usher in *vt sep people* hinein-/hereinführen *or* -bringen *or* -geleiten (*geh*) ◆ **to ~ ~ a new era** ein neues Zeitalter einleiten.

usherette [,ʌʃə'ret] *n* Platzanweiserin *f*.

USM *abbr of* **(a)** (*US*) **United States Mail; United States Marines; United States Mint. (b) unlisted securities market.**

USN *abbr of* **United States Navy.**

USNG *abbr of* **United States National Guard.**

USNR *abbr of* **United States Naval Reserve.**

USP *abbr of* **unique sales proposition** (einzigartiges) verkaufsförderndes Merkmal.

USS *abbr of* **United States Ship; United States Senate.**

USSR *abbr of* **Union of Soviet Socialist Republics** UdSSR *f*.

usual ['ju:ʒʊəl] **1** *adj* (*customary*) üblich; (*normal also*) gewöhnlich, normal ◆ **beer is his ~ drink** er trinkt gewöhnlich *or* normalerweise Bier; **when shall I come? — oh, the ~ time** wann soll ich kommen? — oh, wie üblich *or* oh, zur üblichen Zeit; **as is ~ on these occasions** wie (es) bei derartigen Gelegenheiten üblich (ist); **as is ~ with second-hand cars** wie gewöhnlich bei Gebrauchtwagen; **it's the ~ thing nowadays** das ist heute so üblich; **small families are the ~ thing nowadays** kleine Familien sind heutzutage die Norm; **with his ~ tact** (*iro*) taktvoll wie immer, mit dem ihm eigenen Takt; **it's ~ to ask first** normalerweise fragt man erst; **as ~, as per ~** (*inf*) wie üblich, wie gewöhnlich; **business as ~** normaler Betrieb; (*in shop*) Verkauf geht weiter; **later/less/more than ~** später/weniger/mehr als sonst; **it's hardly ~** es ist eigentlich nicht üblich.

2 *n* (*inf*) der/die/das Übliche ◆ **the ~ please!** (*drink*) dasselbe wie immer, bitte!; **a pint of the ~** eine Halbe, wie immer; **what's his ~?** (*drink*) was trinkt er gewöhnlich?; **what sort of mood was he in? — the ~** wie war er gelaunt? — wie üblich.

usually ['juːʒʊəlɪ] *adv* gewöhnlich, normalerweise ◆ **more than ~ careful/drunk** noch vorsichtiger/betrunkener als sonst; **do you go to Spain/work overtime? — ~** fahren Sie nach Spanien/machen Sie Überstunden? — normalerweise *or* meist(ens); **is he ~ so rude?** ist er sonst auch so unhöflich?; **he's not ~ late** er kommt sonst *or* normalerweise nicht zu spät; **he's ~ early, but** ... er kommt sonst *or* meist *or* normalerweise früh, aber ...

usufruct ['juːzjʊfrʌkt] *n* (*Jur*) Nutznießung *f*.

usufructuary [ˌjuːzjʊ'frʌktjʊərɪ] *n* (*Jur*) Nutznießer(in *f*) *m*.

usurer ['juːʒərəʳ] *n* Wucherer *m*.

usurious [juː'zjʊərɪəs] *adj* wucherisch; *interest also* Wucher-; *person* Wucher treibend *attr*.

usurp [juː'zɜːp] *vt* sich (*dat*) widerrechtlich aneignen, usurpieren (*geh*); *power, title, inheritance also* an sich (*acc*) reißen; *throne* sich bemächtigen (+*gen*) (*geh*); *role* sich (*dat*) anmaßen; *person* verdrängen ◆ **he ~ed his father/his father's throne** er hat seinen Vater verdrängt/er hat seinem Vater den Thron geraubt; **she has ~ed his wife's place** sie hat seine Frau von ihrem Platz verdrängt.

usurpation [ˌjuːzɜː'peɪʃən] *n* Usurpation *f* (*geh*); (*of power also*) widerrechtliche Übernahme; (*of title, inheritance*) widerrechtliche Aneignung ◆ **~ of the throne** Thronraub *m*, Usurpation *f* des Thrones (*geh*).

usurper [juː'zɜːpəʳ] *n* unrechtmäßiger Machthaber, Usurpator *m* (*geh*); (*fig*) Eindringling *m* ◆ **the ~ of the throne/his father's throne** der Thronräuber/der unrechtmäßige Nachfolger seines Vaters auf dem Thron.

usury ['juːʒʊrɪ] *n* Wucher *m* ◆ **to practise ~** Wucher treiben; **32% interest is ~** 32% Zinsen sind *or* ist Wucher.

utensil [juː'tensl] *n* Gerät, Utensil *nt*.

uterine ['juːtəraɪn] *adj* (*Anat*) uterin ◆ **~ brother** Halbbruder *m* mütterlicherseits.

uterus ['juːtərəs] *n* Gebärmutter *f*, Uterus (*spec*) *m*.

utilitarian [ˌjuːtɪlɪ'teərɪən] [1] *adj* auf Nützlichkeit ausgerichtet; *qualities* nützlich, praktisch; (*Philos*) utilitaristisch.
[2] *n* (*Philos*) Utilitarist, Utilitarier *m*.

utilitarianism [ˌjuːtɪlɪ'teərɪənɪzəm] *n* (*Philos*) Utilitarismus *m*.

utility [juː'tɪlɪtɪ] [1] *n* **(a)** (*usefulness*) Nützlichkeit *f*, Nutzen *m*.
(b) public ~ (*company*) Versorgungsbetrieb *m*; (*service*) Leistung *f* der Versorgungsbetriebe; **the utilities** versorgungswirtschaftliche Einrichtungen *pl*.
[2] *adj goods, vehicle* Gebrauchs- ◆ **~ man** (*US*) Mädchen *nt* für alles (*inf*); **~ program** (*Comput*) Hilfsprogramm, Dienstprogramm *nt*: **~ room** Allzweckraum *m*; **~ furniture** *im 2. Weltkrieg in Großbritannien hergestellte Möbel, die einfach, aber zweckmäßig waren*.

utilization [ˌjuːtɪlaɪ'zeɪʃən] *n see vt* Verwendung *f*; Benutzung *f*; Nutzung *f*; Verwertung *f*.

utilize ['juːtɪlaɪz] *vt* verwenden; *situation, time* (be)nutzen; (*take advantage of*) *opportunity, talent* nutzen; (*to make sth new*) *waste paper, old wool etc* verwerten.

utmost ['ʌtməʊst] [1] *adj* **(a)** (*greatest*) *ease, danger* größte(r, s), höchste(r, s); *caution also* äußerste(r, s); *candour* größte(r, s), äußerste(r, s) ◆ **they used their ~ skill** sie taten ihr Äußerstes; **with the ~ speed/care** so schnell/sorgfältig wie nur möglich; **matters of the ~ importance** Angelegenheiten von äußerster Wichtigkeit; **it is of the ~ importance that** ... es ist äußerst wichtig, daß ...
(b) (*furthest*) äußerste(r, s).
[2] *n* **to do/try one's ~** sein möglichstes *or* Bestes tun; **that is the ~ I can do** mehr kann ich wirklich nicht tun; **that is the ~ that can be said of her/it** das ist das Höchste, was man über sie/dazu sagen kann; **to the ~ of one's ability** so gut man nur kann; **he tried my patience to the ~** er strapazierte meine Geduld aufs äußerste; **he exerts himself to the ~** er strapaziert sich bis zum äußersten; **one should enjoy life/oneself to the ~** man sollte das Leben in vollen Zügen genießen/sich amüsieren, so gut man nur kann; **I can give you £50 at the ~** ich kann Ihnen allerhöchstens £ 50 geben.

Utopia [juː'təʊpɪə] *n* Utopia *nt*.

Utopian [juː'təʊpɪən] [1] *adj* utopisch, utopistisch (*pej*).
[2] *n* Utopist(in *f*) *m*.

Utopianism [juː'təʊpɪənɪzəm] *n* Utopismus *m*.

utricle ['juːtrɪkl] *n* (*Bot*) Fangbläschen *nt*, Schlauch, Utrikel (*spec*) *m*; (*Anat*) Utriculus *m* (*spec*).

utter¹ ['ʌtəʳ] *adj* total, vollkommen; *rogue, drunkard* unverbesserlich, Erz- ◆ **what ~ nonsense!** so ein totaler Blödsinn! (*inf*).

utter² *vt* **(a)** von sich (*dat*) geben; *word* sagen; *word of complaint* äußern; *cry, sigh, threat* ausstoßen; *libel* verbreiten. **(b)** (*form*) *forged money* in Umlauf bringen; *cheque* ausstellen.

utterance ['ʌtərəns] *n* **(a)** (*sth said*) Äußerung *f* ◆ **the child's first ~s** die ersten Worte des Kindes; **his last ~** seine letzten Worte; **his recent ~s in the press** seine jüngsten Presseäußerungen.
(b) (*act of speaking*) Sprechen *nt* ◆ **upon her dying father's ~ of her name** als ihr sterbender Vater ihren Namen nannte; **to give ~ to a feeling** einem Gefühl Ausdruck geben *or* verleihen (*geh*), ein Gefühl zum Ausdruck bringen.

utterly ['ʌtəlɪ] *adv* total, völlig; *depraved also, despise* zutiefst ◆ **~ beautiful** ausgesprochen schön.

uttermost ['ʌtəməʊst] *n, adj see* **utmost**.

U-turn ['juːtɜːn] *n* (*lit, fig*) Wende *f* ◆ **no ~s** Wenden verboten!; **to do a ~** (*fig*) seine Meinung völlig ändern; **the government has done a ~ over pensions** die Rentenpolitik der Regierung hat sich um 180 Grad gedreht.

UVF *abbr of* **Ulster Volunteer Force**.

uvula ['juːvjələ] *n* Zäpfchen *nt*, Uvula *f* (*spec*).

uvular ['juːvjələʳ] [1] *adj* uvular ◆ **the ~ R** das Zäpfchen-R.
[2] *n* Zäpfchenlaut, Uvular *m*.

uxorious [ʌk'sɔːrɪəs] *adj husband* treuergeben *attr*, treu ergeben *pred*.

uxoriousness [ʌk'sɔːrɪəsnɪs] *n* Ergebenheit *f* seiner Frau gegenüber.

Uzbek ['ʊzbek] [1] *adj* usbekisch.
[2] *n* **(a)** Usbeke *m*, Usbekin *f*. **(b)**(*Ling*) Usbekisch *nt*.

Uzbekistan [ˌʊzbekɪ'stɑːn] *n* Usbekistan *nt*.

V, v [viː] *n* V, v *nt*.
V, v *abbr of* **verse(s)** V; **volt(s)** V; **vide** v; **versus.**
VA *(US) abbr of* **Veterans (of Vietnam) Administration.**
Va *abbr of* **Virginia.**
vac [væk] *n (Univ inf)* Semesterferien *pl*.
vacancy ['veɪkənsɪ] *n* **(a)** *(emptiness)* Leere *f*; *(of look also)* Ausdruckslosigkeit *f*; *(of post)* Unbesetztsein, Freisein *nt*.
(b) *(in boarding house)* (freies) Zimmer ◆ **have you any vacancies for August?** haben Sie im August noch Zimmer frei?; **"no vacancies"** „belegt".
(c) *(job)* offene *or* freie Stelle; *(at university)* Vakanz *f*, unbesetzte Stelle ◆ **we have a ~ in our personnel department** in unserer Personalabteilung ist eine Stelle zu vergeben; **to fill a ~** eine Stelle besetzen; **we are looking for somebody to fill a ~ in our personnel department** wir suchen einen Mitarbeiter für unsere Personalabteilung; **vacancies** Stellenangebote, offene Stellen.
vacant ['veɪkənt] *adj* **(a)** *post* frei, offen; *(Univ)* unbesetzt, vakant; *WC, seat, hotel room* frei; *chair* unbesetzt; *house, room* unbewohnt, leerstehend; *lot* unbebaut, frei ◆ **the house has been ~ for two months** das Haus steht seit zwei Monaten leer; **with ~ possession** *(Jur)* bezugsfertig; **to become** *or* **fall ~** frei werden.
(b) *(empty) days* unausgefüllt, lang ◆ **the ~ future stretched before him** die Zukunft lag leer vor ihm.
(c) *mind, stare* leer.
vacantly ['veɪkəntlɪ] *adv (stupidly)* blöde; *(dreamily)* abwesend ◆ **he gazed ~ at me** er sah mich mit leerem Blick an.
vacate [və'keɪt] *vt seat* frei machen; *post* aufgeben; *presidency etc* niederlegen; *house, room* räumen ◆ **this post is going to be ~d** diese Stelle wird frei.
vacation [və'keɪʃən] [1] *n* **(a)** *(Univ)* Semesterferien *pl*; *(Jur)* Gerichtsferien *pl*; *see* **long ~.**
(b) *(US)* Ferien *pl*, Urlaub *m* ◆ **on ~** im *or* auf Urlaub; **to take a ~** Urlaub machen; **where are you going for your ~?** wohin fahren Sie in Urlaub?, wo machen Sie Urlaub?; **to go on ~** auf Urlaub *or* in die Ferien gehen; **~ trip** (Ferien)reise *f*.
(c) *see* **vacate** Aufgabe *f*; Niederlegung *f*; Räumung *f*.
[2] *vi (US)* Urlaub *or* Ferien machen.
vacation course *n* Ferienkurs *m*.
vacationer [veɪ'keɪʃənəʳ], **vacationist** [veɪ'keɪʃənɪst] *n (US)* Urlauber(in *f*) *m*.
vaccinate ['væksɪneɪt] *vt* impfen.
vaccination [,væksɪ'neɪʃən] *n* (Schutz)impfung *f* ◆ **have you had your ~ yet?** sind Sie schon geimpft?, haben Sie sich schon impfen lassen?
vaccine ['væksiːn] *n* Impfstoff *m*, Vakzine *f (spec)*.
vacillate ['væsɪleɪt] *vi (lit, fig)* schwanken ◆ **she ~d so long about accepting** sie schwankte lange, ob sie annehmen sollte oder nicht.
vacillating ['væsɪleɪtɪŋ] *adj (fig)* schwankend, unschlüssig, unentschlossen.
vacillation [,væsɪ'leɪʃən] *n* Schwanken *nt*; *(fig also)* Unentschlossenheit, Unschlüssigkeit *f*.
vacua ['vækjʊə] *pl of* **vacuum.**
vacuity [væ'kjuːɪtɪ] *n (liter) (lack of intelligence)* Geistlosigkeit *f*; *(emptiness)* Leere *f* ◆ **vacuities** *(inane remarks)* Plattheiten, Platitüden *pl*.
vacuous ['vækjʊəs] *adj eyes, face, stare* ausdruckslos, leer; *remarks* nichtssagend.
vacuum ['vækjʊəm] *n, pl* **-s** *or* **vacua** *(form)* [1] *n (Phys, fig)* (luft)leerer Raum, Vakuum *nt* ◆ **cultural ~** kulturelles Vakuum.
[2] *vt carpet, living room* saugen.
vacuum: ~ bottle *n (US) see* **~ flask**; **~ brake** *n* Unterdruckbremse *f*; **~ cleaner** *n* Staubsauger *m*; **~ flask** *n* Thermosflasche *f*; **~-packed** *adj* vakuumverpackt; **~ pump** *n* Vakuum- *or* Aussaugepumpe *f*; **~ tube** *n* Vakuumröhre *f*.
vade mecum ['vɑːdɪ'meɪkʊm] *n (liter)* Vademekum *nt (liter)*.
vagabond ['vægəbɒnd] [1] *n* Vagabund, Landstreicher(in *f*) *m*.
[2] *adj* vagabundenhaft; *life* unstet, Vagabunden-; *person* vagabundierend, umherziehend; *thoughts* (ab)schweifend.
vagary ['veɪgərɪ] *n usu pl* Laune *f*; *(strange idea)* verrückter Einfall ◆ **the vagaries of life** die Wechselfälle des Lebens.
vagina [və'dʒaɪnə] *n* Scheide, Vagina *f*.
vaginal [və'dʒaɪnl] *adj* vaginal, Scheiden-.
vagrancy ['veɪgrənsɪ] *n* Land-/Stadtstreicherei *f (also Jur)*.
vagrant ['veɪgrənt] [1] *n* Land-/Stadtstreicher(in *f*) *m*.
[2] *adj person* umherziehend; *life* unstet, nomadenhaft.
vague [veɪg] *adj* (+er) **(a)** *(not clear)* vage, unbestimmt; *outline, shape* verschwommen; *photograph* unscharf, verschwommen; *report, question* vage, ungenau; *murmur* dumpf, undeutlich ◆ **I haven't the ~st idea** ich habe nicht die leiseste Ahnung; **there's a ~ resemblance** es besteht eine entfernte Ähnlichkeit; **I had a ~ idea she would come** ich hatte so eine (dunkle) Ahnung, daß sie kommen würde; **I am still very ~ on this theory** die Theorie ist mir noch nicht sehr klar; **I am very ~ on Dutch politics** von holländischer Politik habe ich nicht viel Ahnung; **he was ~ about the time of his arrival** er äußerte sich nur vage *or* unbestimmt über seine Ankunftszeit.
(b) *(absent-minded)* geistesabwesend, zerstreut ◆ **do you really understand, you look rather ~?** verstehst du das wirklich, du siehst so verwirrt aus?; **to have a ~ look in one's eyes** einen abwesenden *or (not having understood)* verständnislosen Gesichtsausdruck haben.
vaguely ['veɪglɪ] *adv* vage; *remember also* dunkel; *speak also* unbestimmt; *understand* ungefähr, in etwa ◆ **to look ~ at sb** jdn verständnislos ansehen; **they're ~ similar** sie haben eine entfernte Ähnlichkeit; **it's only ~ like yours** es ist nur ungefähr wie deines; **it's ~ blue** es ist bläulich; **there's something ~ sinister about it** es hat so etwas Düsteres an sich.
vagueness ['veɪgnɪs] *n* **(a)** Unbestimmtheit, Vagheit *f*; *(of outline, shape)* Verschwommenheit *f*; *(of report, question)* Vagheit, Ungenauigkeit *f* ◆ **the ~ of the resemblance** die entfernte Ähnlichkeit; **his ~ on Dutch politics** seine lückenhafte *or* wenig fundierte Kenntnis der holländischen Politik.
(b) *(absent-mindedness)* Geistesabwesenheit, Zerstreutheit *f* ◆ **the ~ of her look** ihr abwesender *or (puzzled)* verwirrter Blick.
vain [veɪn] *adj* **(a)** (+*er*) *(about looks)* eitel; *(about qualities also)* eingebildet ◆ **he's very ~ about his musical abilities** er bildet sich *(dat)* auf sein musikalisches Können viel ein; **he is ~ about his appearance** er ist eitel.
(b) *(useless, empty)* eitel *(liter)*; *attempt also* vergeblich; *pleasures, promises, words also* leer; *hope also* töricht ◆ **he had ~ hopes of getting the job** er machte sich vergeblich Hoffnung auf den Posten; **in ~** umsonst, vergeblich, vergebens; **it was all in ~** das war alles umsonst *etc*.
(c) to take God's name in ~ den Namen Gottes mißbrauchen, Gott lästern; **was someone taking my name in ~?** *(hum)* hat da wieder jemand von mir geredet?
(d) *(liter: worthless) display, ceremony* eitel *(liter)*.
vainglorious [veɪn'glɔːrɪəs] *adj (old) person* dünkelhaft; *talk* prahlerisch, ruhmredig *(old liter)*; *spectacle* pompös.
vainglory [veɪn'glɔːrɪ] *n (old)* Prahlerei, Selbstverherrlichung *f*; *(characteristic)* Dünkel *m*; *(of appearance)* Pomp *m*.
vainly ['veɪnlɪ] *adv* **(a)** *(to no effect)* vergeblich, vergebens. **(b)** *(conceitedly) (about looks)* eitel; *(about qualities also)* eingebildet.
valance ['væləns] *n (round bed frame)* Volant *m*; *(on window)* Querbehang *m*, Schabracke *f*; *(wooden)* Blende *f*.
vale [veɪl] *n (liter)* Tal *nt* ◆ **this ~ of tears** dies Jammertal.
valediction [,vælɪ'dɪkʃən] *n* **(a)** *(form) (act)* Abschied(nehmen *nt*) *m*; *(words)* Abschiedsworte *pl*; *(speech)* Abschiedsrede *f*. **(b)** *(US Sch)* Abschieds- *or* Entlassungsrede *f*.
valedictorian [,vælɪdɪk'tɔːrɪən] *n (US Sch)* Abschiedsredner(in *f*) *m (bei der Schulentlassungsfeier)*.
valedictory [,vælɪ'dɪktərɪ] [1] *adj (form)* Abschieds-.
[2] *n (US Sch) see* **valediction (b).**
valence ['veɪləns], **valency** ['veɪlənsɪ] *n (Chem)* Wertigkeit, Valenz *f*; *(Ling)* Valenz *f*.
valency bond *n* kovalente Bindung.
valentine ['væləntaɪn] *n* **(a)** *(person) Freund(in f) m, dem/der man am Valentinstag einen Gruß schickt* ◆ **St V~'s Day** Valentinstag *m*. **(b) ~ (card)** Valentinskarte *f*.
valerian [və'lɪərɪən] *n* Baldrian *m*.
valet ['væleɪ] *n* Kammerdiener *m* ◆ **~ service** Reinigungsdienst *m*.
valetudinarian ['vælɪ,tjuːdɪ'nɛərɪən] *(form)* [1] *n* kränkelnde Person; *(health fiend)* Gesundheitsfanatiker(in *f*) *m*.
[2] *adj (sickly)* kränklich, kränkelnd; *person* sehr um seine Gesundheit besorgt; *habits, attitude* gesundheitsbewußt.

Valhalla [væl'hælə] *n* Walhall *nt*, Walhalla *nt or f.*
valiant ['væljənt] *adj* **(a)** (*liter*) *soldier, deed* tapfer, kühn (*geh*). **(b) he made a ~ effort to save him** er unternahm einen kühnen Versuch, ihn zu retten; **she made a ~ effort to smile** sie versuchte tapfer zu lächeln; **never mind, it was a ~ try** machen Sie sich nichts draus, es war ein löblicher Versuch.
valiantly ['væljəntlı] *adv* **(a)** (*liter*) mutig, tapfer. **(b) he ~ said he would help out** er sagte großzügig seine Hilfe zu.
valid ['vælıd] *adj* **(a)** *ticket, passport* gültig; (*Jur*) *document, marriage* (rechts)gültig; *contract* bindend, rechtsgültig; *claim* berechtigt, begründet. **(b)** *argument, reasoning* stichhaltig; *excuse, reason* triftig, einleuchtend; *objection* berechtigt, begründet ◆ **this argument isn't ~** (*in itself*) dieses Argument ist nicht stichhaltig; (*not relevant*) dieses Argument ist nicht zulässig *or* gilt nicht; **is it ~ to assume this?** ist es zulässig, das anzunehmen?; **that's a very ~ point** das ist ein sehr wertvoller Hinweis.
validate ['vælıdeıt] *vt document* (*check validity*) für gültig erklären; (*with stamp, sign*) (rechts)gültig machen; *claim* bestätigen; *theory* bestätigen, beweisen; (*Jur*) Rechtskraft verleihen (+*dat*).
validation [,vælı'deıʃən] *n* (*of document*) Gültigkeitserklärung *f*; (*of claim*) Bestätigung *f*; (*of theory*) Beweis, Nachweis *m*.
validity [və'lıdıtı] *n* **(a)** (*Jur etc: of document*) (Rechts)gültigkeit *f*; (*of ticket etc*) Gültigkeit *f*; (*of claim*) Berechtigung *f*.
(b) (*of argument*) Stichhaltigkeit *f*; (*of excuse etc*) Triftigkeit *f* ◆ **the ~ of your objection** Ihr berechtigter *or* begründeter Einwand; **we discussed the ~ of merging these two cinematic styles** wir diskutierten, ob es zulässig ist, diese beiden Filmstile zu mischen.
valise [və'li:z] *n* Reisetasche *f*.
Valium ® ['vælıəm] *n* Valium ® *nt* ◆ **to be on ~** Valium nehmen.
Valkyrie ['vælkırı] *n* Walküre *f*.
valley ['vælı] *n* Tal *nt*; (*big and flat*) Niederung *f* ◆ **to go up/down the ~** talaufwärts/talabwärts gehen/fließen *etc*; **the Upper Rhine ~** die Oberrheinische Tiefebene.
valor *n* (*US*) *see* **valour**.
valorous ['vælərəs] *adj* (*liter*) heldenmütig (*liter*), tapfer.
valour, (*US*) **valor** ['vælə^r] *n* (*liter*) Heldenmut *m* (*liter*), Tapferkeit *f*.
valuable ['væljʊəbl] [1] *adj* **(a)** *jewel* wertvoll; *time, oxygen* kostbar. **(b)** (*useful*) wertvoll; *help, advice also* nützlich.
[2] *n* **~s** *pl* Wertsachen, Wertgegenstände *pl*.
valuation [,væljʊ'eıʃən] *n* (*act*) Schätzung *f*; (*fig: of person's character*) Einschätzung *f*; (*value decided upon*) Schätzwert *m*, Schätzung *f*; (*fig*) Beurteilung *f* ◆ **what's your ~ of him?** wie schätzen Sie ihn ein?; **to have a ~ of a picture done** ein Bild schätzen lassen; **to make a correct ~ of sth** etw genau abschätzen; **we shouldn't take him at his own ~** wir sollten seine Selbsteinschätzung nicht einfach übernehmen.
value ['vælju:] [1] *n* **(a)** Wert *m*; (*usefulness*) Nutzen *m* ◆ **to be of ~** Wert/Nutzen haben, wertvoll/nützlich sein; **her education has been of no ~ to her** ihre Ausbildung hat ihr nichts genützt; **to put a ~ on sth** etw schätzen *or* bewerten; (*on leisure etc*) einer Sache (*dat*) (hohen) Wert beimessen; **to put too high a ~ on sth** etw zu hoch schätzen *or* bewerten; (*on leisure etc*) etw überbewerten; **he attaches no/great ~ to it** er legt keinen/großen Wert darauf, ihm liegt nicht/sehr viel daran; **of little ~** nicht sehr wertvoll/nützlich; **of no ~** wertlos/nutzlos; **of great ~** sehr wertvoll.
(b) (*in money*) Wert *m* ◆ **what's the ~ of your house?** wieviel ist Ihr Haus wert?; **what is its second-hand ~?** wieviel ist es gebraucht wert?; **to gain/lose (in) ~** im Wert steigen/fallen; **increase in/loss of ~** Wertzuwachs *m*/Wertminderung *f*, Wertverlust *m*; **it's good ~** es ist preisgünstig; **in our shop you get ~ for money** in unserem Geschäft bekommen Sie etwas für Ihr Geld (*inf*); **this TV was good ~** dieser Fernseher ist sein Geld wert; **lazy employees don't give you ~ for money** faule Angestellte sind ihr Geld nicht wert; **goods to the ~ of £500** Waren im Wert von £ 500; **they put a ~ of £200 on it** sie haben es auf £ 200 geschätzt.
(c) ~s *pl* (*moral standards*) (sittliche) Werte *pl*, Wertwelt *f* ◆ **he has no sense of ~s** er hat keine sittlichen Maßstäbe.
(d) (*Math*) (Zahlen)wert *m*; (*Mus*) (Zeit- *or* Noten)wert *m*, Dauer *f*; (*Phon*) (Laut)wert *m*; (*of colour*) Farbwert *m* ◆ **what exactly is the ~ of this word in the poem?** welchen Ausdrucks- *or* Stellenwert hat dieses Wort innerhalb des Gedichtes?
[2] *vt* **(a)** *house, jewels* (ab)schätzen ◆ **the property was ~ed at £60,000** das Grundstück wurde auf £ 60.000 geschätzt.
(b) *friendship, person* (wert)schätzen, (hoch)achten; *opinion, advice* schätzen; *comforts, liberty, independence* schätzen, Wert legen auf (+*acc*) ◆ **I ~ it (highly)** ich weiß es zu schätzen; **if you ~ my opinion ...** wenn Sie Wert auf meine Meinung legen ...; **if you ~ your life, you'll stay away** bleiben Sie weg, wenn Ihnen Ihr Leben lieb ist.
value-added tax *n* (*Brit*) Mehrwertsteuer *f*.
valued ['vælju:d] *adj friend* (hoch)geschätzt, lieb ◆ **he is a ~ colleague** er ist als Kollege hochgeschätzt; **as a ~ customer** als (ein) geschätzter Kunde.
value: ~ judgement *n* Werturteil *nt*; **~less** *adj* wertlos; (*useless also*) nutzlos, unnütz; *judgement* wertfrei.
valuer ['væljʊə^r] *n* Schätzer *m*.
valve [vælv] *n* (*Anat*) Klappe *f*; (*Tech, on musical instrument*) Ventil *nt*; (*in pipe system*) Absperrhahn *m*; (*Rad, TV*) Röhre *f* ◆ **inlet/outlet ~** (*Aut*) Einlaß-/Auslaßventil *nt*.
valvular ['vælvjʊlə^r] *adj* (*Tech*) Ventil-; (*shaped like valve*) ventilartig; (*Med*) Klappen- ◆ **~ inflammation** (*Med*) Herzklappenentzündung *f*.
vamoose [və'mu:s] *vi* (*US sl*) abhauen (*inf*), abzischen (*sl*).
vamp¹ [væmp] [1] *n* (*woman*) Vamp *m*.
[2] *vt* **she's been ~ing him all the time** sie hat die ganze Zeit ihre Reize bei ihm spielen lassen.
[3] *vi* den Vamp spielen.
vamp² [1] *n* **(a)** (*of shoe: upper*) Oberleder *nt*. **(b)** (*Mus*) Improvisation *f*, improvisierte Einleitung/Begleitung.
[2] *vt* **(a)** (*repair*) flicken. **(b)** (*Mus*) *accompaniment* improvisieren, sich (*dat*) einfallen lassen.
[3] *vi* (*Mus*) improvisieren, aus dem Stegreif spielen.
◆**vamp up** *vt sep* aufpolieren (*inf*), aufmotzen (*sl*).
vampire ['væmpaıə^r] *n* (*lit*) Vampir, Blutsauger (*old*) *m*; (*fig*) Vampir *m* ◆ **~ bat** Vampir, Blutsauger (*old*) *m*.
vampiric [væm'pırık] *adj* vampiristisch; *figure* vampirähnlich.
vampirism ['væmpaıərızəm] *n* Vampirismus *m*.
van¹ [væn] *n* **(a)** (*Brit Aut*) Liefer- *or* Kastenwagen, Transporter *m*. **(b)** (*Rail*) Waggon, Wagen *m*. **(c)** (*inf: caravan*) (Wohn)wagen *m* ◆ **gipsy's ~** Zigeunerwagen *m*.
van² *n abbr of* **vanguard** (*lit, fig*) Vorhut *f*; (*fig also*) Spitze, Führung *f* ◆ **he was in the ~ of legal reform** er stand an der Spitze der Rechtsreformer.
van³ *n abbr of* **advantage** (*Tennis inf*) Vorteil *m* ◆ **~ in/out** Vorteil auf (*inf*)/rück (*inf*).
vanadium [və'neıdıəm] *n* Vanadin, Vanadium *nt*.
vandal ['vændəl] *n* Rowdy, Demolierer (*inf*) *m*; Vandale, Wandale (*esp Hist*) *m* ◆ **it was damaged by ~s** es ist mutwillig beschädigt worden.
vandalism ['vændəlızəm] *n* Vandalismus *m*, blinde Zerstörungswut; (*Jur*) mutwillige Beschädigung (fremden Eigentums) ◆ **destroyed by acts of ~** mutwillig zerstört/beschädigt; **these acts of ~** dieser Vandalismus, diese mutwilligen Beschädigungen.
vandalize ['vændəlaız] *vt painting* mutwillig zerstören/beschädigen; *building* verwüsten; (*wreck*) demolieren.
vane [veın] *n* (*also* **weather ~**) Wetterfahne *f*, Wetterhahn *m*; (*of windmill*) Flügel *m*; (*of propeller*) Flügel *m*, Blatt *nt*; (*of turbine*) (Leit)schaufel *f*.
vanguard ['væŋgɑ:d] *n* (*Mil, Naut*) Vorhut *f*; (*fig also*) Spitze, Führung *f* ◆ **in the ~ of progress** an der Spitze des Fortschritts.
vanilla [və'nılə] [1] *n* Vanille *f*.
[2] *adj ice-cream, flavour* Vanille-.
vanish ['vænıʃ] *vi* verschwinden, entschwinden (*liter*); (*traces also*) sich verlieren; (*fears*) sich legen; (*hopes*) schwinden; (*become extinct*) untergehen ◆ **I've got to ~** (*inf*) ich muß weg (*inf*); *see* **thin (d)**.
vanishing ['vænıʃıŋ]: **~ act** *n see* **~ trick**; **~ cream** *n* (Haut)pflegecreme, Tages-/Nachtcreme *f*; **~ point** *n* (*Math*) Fluchtpunkt *m*; (*fig*) Nullpunkt *m*; **~ trick** *n* **he did a ~ trick with it** er hat es weggezaubert; **every time he's needed he does his ~ trick** (*inf*) jedesmal, wenn man ihn braucht, verdrückt er sich (*inf*).
vanity ['vænıtı] *n* **(a)** (*concerning looks*) Eitelkeit *f*; (*concerning own value*) Einbildung, Eingebildetheit *f* ◆ **~ made him think he was bound to succeed** er war so eingebildet *or* von sich eingenommen, daß er einen Mißerfolg für ausgeschlossen hielt.
(b) (*worthlessness: of life, pleasures*) Nichtigkeit, Hohlheit *f*; (*of words*) Hohlheit *f*; (*of efforts*) Vergeblichkeit *f* ◆ **the ~ of all his hopes/promises** all seine törichten Hoffnungen/leeren Versprechungen; **all is ~** alles ist eitel (*liter*) *or* vergebens.
(c) (*US*) Frisiertisch *m*.
vanity case *n* Schmink- *or* Kosmetikkoffer *m*.
vanity plates *npl* (*esp US Aut*) *Nummernschild nt mit persönlicher Note.*
vanquish ['væŋkwıʃ] *vt* (*liter*) *enemy, fears* bezwingen (*geh*).
vantage ['vɑ:ntıdʒ] *n* (*rare*) Vorteil *m*; (*Tennis*) Vorteil *m*.
vantage: ~ ground *n* (*Mil*) günstige (Ausgangs)stellung; **~ point** *n* (*Mil*) (günstiger) Aussichtspunkt; **our window is a good ~ point for watching the procession** von unserem Fenster aus hat man einen guten Blick auf die Prozession; **from our modern ~ point** aus heutiger Sicht.
vapid ['væpıd] *adj* (*liter*) *conversation, remark* nichtssagend, geistlos; *smile* (*insincere*) leer; (*bored*) matt; *style* kraftlos; *beer, taste* schal.
vapidity [væ'pıdıtı] *n* (*liter*) (*of conversation, remark*) Geistlosigkeit *f*; (*of smile*) Ausdruckslosigkeit *f*; Mattheit *f*; (*of style*) Kraftlosigkeit *f no pl*; (*of taste*) Schalheit *f*.
vapor *etc* (*US*) *see* **vapour** *etc*.
vaporization [,veıpəraı'zeıʃən] *n* (*by boiling etc*) Verdampfung *f*; (*natural*) Verdunstung *f*.
vaporize ['veıpəraız] [1] *vt* (*by boiling etc*) verdampfen; (*naturally*) verdunsten lassen.
[2] *vi see vt* verdampfen; verdunsten.
vaporizer ['veıpəraızə^r] *n* Verdampfer, Verdampfapparat *m*; (*Chem etc, for perfume*) Zerstäuber *m*; (*Med: for inhalation*) Inhalationsgerät *nt*.
vaporous ['veıpərəs] *adj* **(a)** (*like vapour*) dampf-/gasförmig; (*full of vapour*) dunstig; (*of vapour*) Dunst- ◆ **~ mists rising from the swamp** Dünste, die aus dem Sumpf aufsteigen; **~ gases round the planet** nebelartige Gase um den Planeten.
(b) (*liter: fanciful*) nebulös, verblasen (*geh*).
vapour, (*US*) **vapor** ['veıpə^r] *n* Dunst *m*; (*Phys also*) Gas *nt*; (*steamy*) Dampf *m* ◆ **the ~s** (*Med old*) Schwermut *f*; **~ trail** Kondensstreifen *m*; **thick ~s around the planet** eine dichte Dunsthülle um den Planeten.
vapouring, (*US*) **vaporing** ['veıpərıŋ] *n* (*liter*) (*boastful*) Prahlerei *f*; (*empty*) Geschwafel *nt*.
variability [,veərıə'bılıtı] *n see adj* **(a)** Veränderlichkeit *f*; Variabilität *f*;

Unbeständigkeit, Wechselhaftigkeit *f*; (*of costs*) Schwankung(en *pl*), Unbeständigkeit *f*; (*of work*) unterschiedliche Qualität. **(b)** Regulierbarkeit *f*.

variable ['vɛərɪəbl] [1] *adj* **(a)** (*likely to vary*) (*Math*) veränderlich, variabel; (*Biol*) variabel; *weather, mood* unbeständig, wechselhaft ◆ **infinitely ~** (*Tech*) stufenlos; **~ winds** wechselnde Winde *pl*; **his work is very ~** er arbeitet sehr unterschiedlich.
(b) *speed* regulierbar; *salary level* flexibel; **the height of the seat is ~** die Höhe des Sitzes kann reguliert werden.
[2] *n* (*Chem, Math, Phys, Comput*) Variable *f*; (*fig also*) veränderliche Größe.

variance ['vɛərɪəns] *n* **(a) to be at ~ with sb** anderer Meinung sein als jd (*about* hinsichtlich *+gen*); **he is constantly at ~ with his parents** er hat ständig Meinungsverschiedenheiten mit seinen Eltern; **this is at ~ with what he said earlier** dies stimmt nicht mit dem überein, was er vorher gesagt hat.
(b) (*difference*) Unterschied *m* ◆ **a slight ~ of opinion** eine unterschiedliche Auffassung; **the predictable ~ between the two sets of figures** die vorhersehbare Abweichung der beiden Zahlenreihen (voneinander).

variant ['vɛərɪənt] [1] *n* Variante *f* ◆ **a spelling ~** eine Schreibvariante.
[2] *adj* **(a)** (*alternative*) andere(r, s) ◆ **there are two ~ spellings** es gibt zwei verschiedene Schreibweisen. **(b)** (*liter: diverse*) verschieden, unterschiedlich.

variation [,vɛərɪ'eɪʃən] *n* **(a)** (*varying*) Veränderung *f*; (*Sci*) Variation *f*; (*Met*) Schwankung *f*, Wechsel *m*; (*of temperature*) Unterschiede *pl*, Schwankung(en *pl*) *f*; (*of prices*) Schwankung *f* ◆ **an unexpected ~ in conditions** eine unerwartete Veränderung der Bedingungen; **there's been a lot of ~ in the standard recently** in letzter Zeit war das Niveau sehr unterschiedlich; **these figures are subject to seasonal ~** diese Zahlen sind saisonbedingten Schwankungen unterworfen; **~ in opinions/views** unterschiedliche Auffassungen/Ansichten.
(b) (*Mus*) Variation *f* ◆ **~s on a theme** Thema mit Variationen; Variationen zu einem *or* über ein Thema.
(c) (*different form*) Variation, Variante *f*; (*Biol*) Variante *f* ◆ **this is a ~ on that** das ist eine Variation *or* Abänderung dessen *or* davon; **a new ~ in the design** eine neue Variation des Musters; **regional ~s in pronunciation** regionale Aussprachevarianten *pl*; **several ~s on a basic idea** mehrere Variationsmöglichkeiten einer Grundidee.

varicoloured, (*US*) **varicolored** ['værɪ'kʌləd] *adj* mehrfarbig.

varicose ['værɪkəʊs] *adj*: **~ veins** Krampfadern *pl*.

varied ['vɛərɪd] *adj* unterschiedlich; *career, life* bewegt; *selection* reichhaltig; *interests also* vielfältig ◆ **a ~ group of people** eine gemischte Gruppe; **a ~ collection of records** eine vielseitige *or* sehr gemischte Plattensammlung.

variegated ['vɛərɪgeɪtɪd] *adj* buntscheckig; (*Bot*) geflammt, panaschiert.

variegation [,vɛərɪ'geɪʃən] *n* Buntscheckigkeit *f*; (*Bot*) Panaschierung *f*.

variety [və'raɪətɪ] *n* **(a)** (*diversity*) Abwechslung *f* ◆ **to give** *or* **add ~ to sth** Abwechslung in etw (*acc*) bringen; **a job with a lot of ~** eine sehr abwechslungsreiche Arbeit; **~ is the spice of life** (*prov*) öfter mal was Neues (*inf*).
(b) (*assortment*) Vielfalt *f*; (*Comm*) Auswahl *f* (*of an +dat*) ◆ **that's quite a ~ for one company** das ist ein ziemlich breites Spektrum für eine (einzige) Firma; **an amazing ~ of different moods** erstaunlich unterschiedliche Stimmungen *pl*; **in a great ~ of ways** auf die verschiedensten Arten *pl*; **in a ~ of colours** in den verschiedensten Farben *pl*; **for a ~ of reasons** aus verschiedenen *or* mehreren Gründen *pl*; **for a great ~ of reasons** aus vielen verschiedenen Gründen *pl*; **a large ~ of birds** eine Vielfalt an Vogelarten, viele verschiedene Vogelarten; **you meet a great ~ of people at this hotel** in diesem Hotel können Sie die verschiedensten Leute treffen.
(c) (*Biol, Bot: species*) Art, Varietät (*spec*) *f*.
(d) (*type*) Art *f*; (*of cigarette, potato*) Sorte *f*; (*of car, chair*) Modell *nt* ◆ **a new ~ of tulip/potato** eine neue Tulpen-/Kartoffelsorte.
(e) (*esp Brit Theat*) Varieté *nt*.

variety: ~ act *n* Varieténummer *f*; **~ artist** *n* Varietékünstler(in *f*) *m*; **~ show** *n* (*Theat*) Varietévorführung *f*; (*TV*) Fernsehshow *f*; (*Rad, TV*) Unterhaltungssendung *f*; **~ theatre** *n* Varietétheater *nt*.

varifocal ['vɛərɪfəʊkəl] [1] *adj lenses* Gleitsicht-.
[2] **~s** *npl* Gleitsichtbrille *f*.

variform ['vɛərɪfɔːm] *adj* vielgestaltig.

variola [və'raɪələ] *n* (*Med*) Pocken *pl*.

various ['vɛərɪəs] *adj* **(a)** (*different*) verschieden. **(b)** (*several*) mehrere, verschiedene.

variously ['vɛərɪəslɪ] *adv* **(a)** unterschiedlich ◆ **the news was ~ reported in the papers** die Nachricht wurde in den Zeitungen unterschiedlich wiedergegeben. **(b)** verschiedentlich ◆ **he has been ~ described as a rogue and a charmer** er wurde verschiedentlich ein Schlitzohr und Charmeur genannt.

varlet ['vɑːlɪt] *n* (*obs*) (*page*) Knappe *m*; (*rascal*) Schurke *m*.

varmint ['vɑːmɪnt] *n* **(a)** (*dial, esp US*) Schurke, Halunke *m*. **(b)** (*animal*) Schädling *m*.

varnish ['vɑːnɪʃ] [1] *n* (*lit*) Lack *m*; (*on pottery*) Glasur *f*; (*on furniture also, on painting*) Firnis *m*; (*fig*) Politur *f*.
[2] *vt* lackieren; *painting* firnissen; *pottery* glasieren; (*fig*) *truth, facts* beschönigen.

varsity ['vɑːsɪtɪ] *n* (*Univ inf*) Uni *f* (*inf*); (*US also* **~ team**) Schul-/Uniauswahl *f*.

vary ['vɛərɪ] [1] *vi* **(a)** (*diverge, differ*) sich unterscheiden, abweichen (*from* von) ◆ **they ~ in price from the others** sie unterscheiden sich im Preis von den anderen; **opinions ~ on this point** in diesem Punkt gehen die Meinungen auseinander; **witnesses ~ about the time** die Zeugen machen unterschiedliche Zeitangaben.
(b) (*be different*) unterschiedlich sein ◆ **the price varies from shop to shop** der Preis ist von Geschäft zu Geschäft verschieden; **his work varies** seine Arbeit ist sehr unterschiedlich; **it varies** es ist unterschiedlich, das ist verschieden.
(c) (*change, fluctuate*) sich (ver)ändern; (*pressure, prices*) schwanken ◆ **prices that ~ with the season** saisonbedingte Preise *pl*; **to ~ with the weather** sich nach dem Wetter richten.
[2] *vt* (*alter*) verändern, abwandeln; (*give variety*) abwechslungsreich(er) gestalten, variieren ◆ **they never ~ their diet** sie essen sehr eintönig; **try to ~ your approach to the problem** Sie sollten das Problem mal von einer anderen Seite angehen.

varying ['vɛərɪɪŋ] *adj* (*changing*) veränderlich; (*different*) unterschiedlich ◆ **our different results were due to ~ conditions** unsere verschiedenen Resultate beruhten auf unterschiedlichen Voraussetzungen; **the ~ weather conditions here** die veränderlichen Wetterverhältnisse hier; **with ~ degrees of success** mit unterschiedlichem Erfolg *m*.

vascular ['væskjʊlə^r] *adj* vaskulär.

vas deferens ['væs'defərenz] *n, pl* **vasa deferentia** ['veɪsə,defə'renʃɪə] Samenleiter *m*.

vase [vɑːz, (*US*) veɪz] *n* Vase *f*.

vasectomy [væ'sektəmɪ] *n* Vasektomie *f* (*spec*), Sterilisation *f* (*des Mannes*).

vaseline ® ['væsɪliːn] *n* Vaseline *f*.

vasoconstrictor [,veɪzəʊkən'strɪktə^r] *n* (*Med*) Mittel *nt* zur Verengung der Blutgefäße.

vasodilator [,veɪzəʊdaɪ'leɪtə^r] *n* (*Med*) Mittel *nt* zur Erweiterung der Blutgefäße.

vassal ['væsəl] [1] *n* (*lit, fig*) Vasall *m*.
[2] *adj* vasallisch, Vasallen- ◆ **~ state** Vasallenstaat *m*.

vassalage ['væsəlɪdʒ] *n* (*Hist*) (*condition*) Vasallentum *nt*, Vasallität *f*; (*services due*) Vasallen- *or* Lehenspflicht *f*; (*land*) Lehen *nt*; (*fig*) Unterworfenheit *f* (*geh*) (*to* unter *+acc*).

vast [vɑːst] *adj* (*+er*) gewaltig, riesig; *area also* weit, ausgedehnt; *bulk also* riesengroß; *sums of money, success also* Riesen-; *difference also* riesengroß; *knowledge* enorm; *majority* überwältigend; *wealth, powers also* unermeßlich ◆ **a ~ expanse** eine weite Ebene; **the ~ expanse of the ocean** die unermeßliche Weite des Ozeans; **to a ~ extent** in sehr hohem Maße.

vastly ['vɑːstlɪ] *adv* erheblich, wesentlich, bedeutend; *grateful* überaus, äußerst ◆ **I was ~ amused** ich habe mich köstlich amüsiert; **it is ~ different** da besteht ein erheblicher *or* wesentlicher Unterschied; **~ rich** steinreich; **he is ~ superior to her** er ist ihr haushoch überlegen.

vastness ['vɑːstnɪs] *n* (*of size*) riesiges *or* gewaltiges Ausmaß, riesige Größe; (*of distance*) ungeheures Ausmaß; (*of ocean, plane, area*) riesige Weite; (*of sums of money*) ungeheure Höhe; (*of success*) Ausmaß *nt*; (*of difference*) Größe *f*; (*of knowledge, wealth*) gewaltiger Umfang.

vat [væt] *n* Faß *nt*; (*without lid*) Bottich *m*.

VAT ['viːeɪ'tiː, væt] (*Brit*) *abbr of* **value-added tax** Mehrwertsteuer *f*, MwSt.

vatic ['vætɪk] *adj* (*liter*) prophetisch.

Vatican ['vætɪkən] *n* Vatikan *m* ◆ **the ~ Council** das Vatikanische Konzil; **~ City** Vatikanstadt *f*; **~ roulette** (*hum inf*) Knaus-Ogino(-Methode) *f*.

VAT: ~ man *n* Steuerprüfer *m* (für die Mehrwertsteuer); **~-registered** *adj* zur Mehrwertsteuer veranlagt; **~ return** *n* Mehrwertsteuerausgleich *m*.

vaudeville ['vəʊdəvɪl] *n* (*US*) Varieté *nt*.

vaudeville: ~ show *n* Varieté(vorführung *f*) *nt*; **~ singer** *n* Varietésänger(in *f*) *m*.

vault¹ [vɔːlt] *n* **(a)** (*cellar*) (Keller)gewölbe *nt*; (*tomb*) Gruft *f*; (*in bank*) Tresor(raum) *m* ◆ **in the ~s** im Gewölbe *etc*. **(b)** (*Archit*) Gewölbe *nt* ◆ **the ~ of heaven** (*liter*) das Himmelsgewölbe (*liter*).

vault² [1] *n* Sprung *m*; (*scissors*) Schersprung *m*; (*legs behind*) Flanke *f*; (*legs through arms*) Hocke *f*; (*legs apart*) Grätsche *f*; *see* **pole ~**.
[2] *vi* springen; einen Schersprung/eine Flanke/eine Hocke/eine Grätsche machen ◆ **to ~ into the saddle** sich in den Sattel schwingen.
[3] *vt* springen über (*+acc*), überspringen; einen Schersprung/eine Flanke/eine Hocke/eine Grätsche machen über (*+acc*).

vaulted ['vɔːltɪd] *adj* (*Archit*) gewölbt.

vaulting ['vɔːltɪŋ] *n* (*Archit*) Wölbung *f*.

vaulting horse *n* (*in gym*) Pferd *nt*.

vaunt [vɔːnt] [1] *vt* rühmen, preisen (*geh*) ◆ **much-~ed** vielgepriesen; **Cologne ~s a splendid cathedral** Köln kann sich eines herrlichen Doms rühmen.
[2] *n* Loblied *nt*, Lobgesang *m*.

VC *abbr of* **Victoria Cross** (*Mil*) Viktoriakreuz *nt* (*höchste britische Tapferkeitsauszeichnung*).

VCR *abbr of* **video cassette recorder** Videorekorder *m*.

VD *abbr of* **venereal disease** Geschlechtskrankheit *f* ◆ **~ clinic** *Klinik f für Geschlechtskrankheiten*, ≃ Hautklinik *f*.

VDU *abbr of* **visual display unit** (Daten)sichtgerät *nt*.

veal [viːl] *n* Kalbfleisch *nt* ◆ **~ cutlet** Kalbsschnitzel *nt*.

vector ['vektə^r] *n* (*Math, Aviat*) Vektor *m*; (*Biol*) Träger *m*.

vector *in cpds* (*Math*) Vektor(en)-; **~ graphics** *npl* Vektorgrafik *f*.

vectorial [vek'tɔːrɪəl] *adj* vektoriell.

Veda ['veɪdə] *n* Weda *m*.

V-E Day *n Tag m des Sieges in Europa im 2. Weltkrieg*.

veep [viːp] *n* (*US sl*) = **vice-president**.

veer [vɪə^r] [1] *vi* (*wind*) (sich) drehen (*im Uhrzeigersinn*) (*to* nach); (*ship*) abdrehen; (*car*) ausscheren; (*road*) scharf abbiegen, abknicken ◆ **the ship ~ed**

round das Schiff drehte ab; **to ~ off course** vom Kurs abkommen; **it ~s from one extreme to the other** es schwankt zwischen zwei Extremen; **he ~s from one extreme to the other** er fällt von einem Extrem ins andere; **he ~ed round to my point of view** er ist auf meine Richtung umgeschwenkt; **he ~ed off** *or* **away from his subject** er kam (völlig) vom Thema ab; **the country has ~ed to the right under Thatcher** das Land ist unter Thatcher nach rechts geschwenkt; **the road ~ed to the left** die Straße machte eine scharfe Linkskurve; **the car ~ed off the road** das Auto kam von der Straße ab; **the driver was forced to ~ sharply** der Fahrer mußte plötzlich das Steuer herumreißen; **the drunken driver was ~ing all over the road** der betrunkene Fahrer fuhr im Zickzack die Straße entlang.

[2] *n* (*of wind*) Drehung *f*; (*of ship, fig: in policy*) Kurswechsel *m*; (*of car*) Ausscheren *nt*; (*of road*) Knick *m* ♦ **with a sudden ~ the car left the road** das Auto scherte plötzlich aus und kam von der Straße ab; **a ~ to the left politically** ein politischer Ruck nach links.

veg [vedʒ] *n, no pl abbr of* **vegetable** ♦ **meat and two ~** Fleisch und zwei Sorten Gemüse; **he likes his meat and two ~** er liebt gutbürgerliche Kost.

vegan ['viːgən] [1] *n* Vegan *m*, radikaler Vegetarier, radikale Vegetarierin.
[2] *adj* radikal vegetarisch.

vegetable ['vedʒɪtəbl] *n* **(a)** Gemüse *nt* ♦ **with fresh ~s** mit frischem Gemüse; (*on menu*) mit frischen Gemüsen; **what ~s do you grow in your garden?** welche Gemüsesorten hast du in deinem Garten?; **cabbage is a ~** Kohl ist eine Gemüsepflanze.
(b) (*generic term: plant*) Pflanze *f*.
(c) he's just a ~ er vegetiert nur dahin *or* vor sich hin; **she's become a ~** sie ist zum körperlichen und geistigen Krüppel geworden, sie vegetiert nur noch dahin.

vegetable: ~ dish *n* (*to eat*) Gemüsegericht *nt*; (*bowl*) Gemüseschüssel *f*; **~ garden** *n* Gemüsegarten *m*; **~ kingdom** *n* Pflanzenreich *nt*; **~ knife** *n* kleines Küchenmesser; **~ marrow** *n* Gartenkürbis *m*; **~ matter** *n* pflanzliche Stoffe *pl*; **~ oil** *n* pflanzliches Öl; (*Cook*) Pflanzenöl *nt*; **~ salad** *n* Gemüsesalat *m*; **~ soup** *n* Gemüsesuppe *f*.

vegetarian [ˌvedʒɪ'tɛərɪən] [1] *n* Vegetarier(in *f*) *m*.
[2] *adj* vegetarisch.

vegetarianism [ˌvedʒɪ'tɛərɪənɪzəm] *n* Vegetarismus *m*.

vegetate ['vedʒɪteɪt] *vi* **(a)** wachsen. **(b)** (*fig*) dahinvegetieren.

vegetation [ˌvedʒɪ'teɪʃən] *n* **(a)** Vegetation *f* ♦ **could we live on the ~ here?** könnten wir uns von dem ernähren, was hier wächst?
(b) (*wasting away*) (*of sick people*) Dahinvegetieren *nt*; (*of mind*) Verödung, Verarmung *f* ♦ **the patients just lie there in a state of ~** die Patienten dämmern nur noch vor sich hin *or* vegetieren nur noch dahin.

vegetative ['vedʒɪtətɪv] *adj* (*Bot*) vegetativ.

veggie ['vedʒɪ] (*inf: vegetarian*) [1] *n* Vegetarier(in *f*), Veggie (*sl*) *m*.
[2] *adj* vegetarisch.

vehemence ['viːɪməns] *n* Vehemenz *f* (*geh*); (*of actions, feelings also*) Heftigkeit *f*; (*of love, hatred also*) Leidenschaftlichkeit *f*; (*of protests also*) Schärfe, Heftigkeit *f*.

vehement ['viːɪmənt] *adj* vehement (*geh*); *feelings, speech also* leidenschaftlich; *attack also* heftig, scharf; *desire, dislike, opposition also* heftig, stark.

vehemently ['viːɪməntlɪ] *adv* vehement (*geh*), heftig; *love, hate also* leidenschaftlich; *protest also* heftig, mit aller Schärfe.

vehicle ['viːɪkl] *n* Fahrzeug *nt*; (*Pharm*) Vehikel *nt*, Trägersub stanz *f*; (*Art*) Lösungsmittel *nt*; (*fig: medium*) Mittel, Vehikel (*geh*) *nt* ♦ **this paper is a ~ of right-wing opinions** diese Zeitung ist ein Sprachrohr *nt* der Rechten; **language is the ~ of thought** die Sprache ist das Medium des Denkens.

vehicular [vɪ'hɪkjʊlə^r] *adj* Fahrzeug- ♦ **~ traffic** Fahrzeugverkehr *m*.

veil [veɪl] [1] *n* Schleier *m* ♦ **to take the ~** den Schleier nehmen, ins Kloster gehen; **the valley lay in a ~ of mist** über dem Tal lag ein Nebelschleier; **to draw** *or* **throw a ~ over sth** den Schleier des Vergessens über etw (*acc*) breiten; **under a ~ of secrecy** unter dem Mantel der Verschwiegenheit; **the ~ of secrecy over all their activities** der Schleier des Geheimnisses, der all ihre Aktivitäten umgibt.
[2] *vt* **(a)** verschleiern.
(b) (*fig*) *facts* verschleiern; *truth also* verheimlichen; *feelings* verbergen ♦ **the clouds ~ed the moon** die Wolken verhüllten *or* verdeckten den Mond; **the town was ~ed by mist** die Stadt lag in Nebel gehüllt.

veiled [veɪld] *adj reference* versteckt; *face* verschleiert.

veiling ['veɪlɪŋ] *n* Schleier *m*; (*fig*) (*of facts*) Verschleierung *f*; (*of truth also*) Verheimlichung *f*.

vein [veɪn] *n* **(a)** (*Anat, Bot, Min*) Ader *f* ♦ **~s and arteries** Venen und Arterien *pl*; **there is a ~ of truth in what he says** es ist eine Spur von Wahrheit in dem, was er sagt; **an artistic ~** eine künstlerische Ader; **there's a ~ of spitefulness in his character** er hat einen gehässigen Zug in seinem Charakter; **the ~ of humour which runs through the book** ein humorvoller Zug, der durch das ganze Buch geht.
(b) (*fig: mood*) Stimmung, Laune *f* ♦ **in a humorous ~** in lustiger Stimmung; **to be in the ~ for sth** zu etw aufgelegt sein; **in the same ~** in derselben Art.

veined [veɪnd] *adj* geädert; *hand* mit hervortretenden Adern.

velar ['viːlə^r] [1] *adj* velar.
[2] *n* Velar(laut) *m*.

Velcro ® ['velkrəʊ] [1] *n* Klettband *nt*.
[2] *adj* **~ fastener** Klettverschluß *m*.

veld, veldt [velt] *n* (*in South Africa*) Steppe *f*.

vellum ['veləm] *n* Pergament *nt*.

vellum: ~ binding *n* Pergamenteinband *m*; **~ paper** *n* Pergamentpapier *nt*.

velocipede [və'lɒsɪpiːd] *n* (*form*) Fahrrad, Veloziped (*old*) *nt*.

velocity [və'lɒsɪtɪ] *n* Geschwindigkeit *f*.

velour(s) [və'lʊə^r] *n* Velours *m*.

velvet ['velvɪt] [1] *n* Samt *m* ♦ **like ~** wie Samt, samtig.
[2] *adj dress, jacket* Samt-; *skin, feel* samtweich, samten (*geh*) ♦ **the ~ touch of his hand** seine sanften Hände.

velveteen ['velvɪtiːn] *n* Veloursamt *m*.

Velvet Revolution *n* sanfte *or* samtene Revolution.

velvety ['velvɪtɪ] *adj* samtig.

Ven *abbr of* **Venerable.**

venal ['viːnl] *adj* (*liter*) *person* käuflich, feil (*liter*); *practices* korrupt ♦ **out of ~ interests** aus eigennützigen Motiven.

venality [viː'nælɪtɪ] *n* (*liter*) *see adj* Käuflichkeit *f*; Korruption *f*; eigennützige Motive *pl*.

vend [vend] *vt* verkaufen.

vendee [ven'diː] *n* (*esp Jur*) Käufer *m*.

vendetta [ven'detə] *n* Fehde *f*; (*in family*) Blutrache *f*; (*of gangsters*) Vendetta *f* ♦ **to carry on a ~ against sb** sich mit jdm bekriegen, mit jdm in Fehde liegen/an jdm Blutrache üben.

vending machine ['vendɪŋmə'ʃiːn] *n* Automat *m*.

vendor ['vendɔː^r] *n* (*esp Jur*) Verkäufer *m* ♦ **newspaper ~** Zeitungsverkäufer *m*; **street ~** Straßenhändler *m*.

veneer [və'nɪə^r] [1] *n* (*lit*) Furnier *nt*; (*fig*) Politur *f* ♦ **it's just a ~** es ist nur Politur *or* schöner Schein; **he had a ~ of refinement** nach außen hin machte er einen sehr kultivierten Eindruck; **the cities with their thin ~ of civilization** die Städte mit ihrem dünnen Lack *or* Putz der Zivilisation.
[2] *vt wood* furnieren.

venerable ['venərəbl] *adj* ehrwürdig.

venerate ['venəreɪt] *vt* verehren, hochachten; *sb's memory* ehren ♦ **his memory was highly ~d** sein Andenken wurde sehr in Ehren gehalten.

veneration [ˌvenə'reɪʃən] *n* Bewunderung, Verehrung *f* (*of* für); (*of idols*) Verehrung *f*; (*of traditions*) Ehrfurcht *f* (*of* vor *+dat*) ♦ **to hold sb in ~** jdn hochachten *or* verehren.

venereal [vɪ'nɪərɪəl] *adj* venerisch ♦ **~ disease** Geschlechtskrankheit *f*, venerische Krankheit (*spec*).

Venetian [vɪ'niːʃən] [1] *adj* venezianisch ♦ **~ blind** Jalousie *f*; **~ glass** venezianisches Glas.
[2] *n* Venezianer(in *f*) *m*.

Venezuela [ˌvene'zweɪlə] *n* Venezuela *nt*.

Venezuelan [ˌvene'zweɪlən] [1] *adj* venezolanisch.
[2] *n* Venezolaner(in *f*) *m*.

vengeance ['vendʒəns] *n* **(a)** Vergeltung, Rache *f* ♦ **to take ~ (up)on sb** Vergeltung an jdm üben.
(b) (*inf*) **with a ~** gewaltig (*inf*); **then the brass section comes in with a ~** dann kommt der kraftvolle *or* gewaltige Einsatz der Bläser; **to work with a ~** hart *or* mächtig (*inf*) arbeiten.

vengeful ['vendʒfʊl] *adj* rachsüchtig.

venial ['viːnɪəl] *adj* verzeihlich, entschuldbar ♦ **~ sin** läßliche Sünde.

veniality [ˌviːnɪ'ælɪtɪ] *n* Entschuldbarkeit *f*; (*of sin*) Läßlichkeit *f*.

Venice ['venɪs] *n* Venedig *nt*.

venison ['venɪsən] *n* Reh(fleisch) *nt*.

venom ['venəm] *n* (*lit*) Gift *nt*; (*fig*) Bosheit, Gehässigkeit *f* ♦ **he spoke with real ~ in his voice** er sprach mit haßerfüllter Stimme; **a theatre review full of ~** ein giftiger Verriß eines Stückes; **she spat her ~ at him** sie giftete ihn wütend an; **his pen, dipped in ~** seine giftige Feder.

venomous ['venəməs] *adj* (*lit, fig*) giftig; *snake* Gift-; *tone also* gehässig; *tongue also* scharf, böse; *sarcasm* beißend.

venomously ['venəməslɪ] *adv* (*fig*) boshaft; *look, say* giftig.

venous ['viːnəs] *adj* (*form*) (*Anat*) venös; (*Bot*) geädert.

vent [vent] [1] *n* (*for gas, liquid*) Öffnung *f*; (*in chimney*) Abzug *m*; (*in barrel*) Spundloch *nt*; (*in coat*) Schlitz *m*; (*for feelings*) Ventil *nt* ♦ **jacket with a single/double ~** Jacke mit Rückenschlitz *m* /Seitenschlitzen *pl*; **to give ~ to sth** (*fig*) einer Sache (*dat*) Ausdruck verleihen; **to give ~ to one's feelings** seinen Gefühlen freien Lauf lassen; **to give ~ to one's anger** seinem Ärger Luft machen.
[2] *vt feelings, anger* abreagieren (*on* an *+dat*).

ventilate ['ventɪleɪt] *vt* **(a)** (*control air flow*) belüften; (*let fresh air in*) lüften. **(b)** *blood* Sauerstoff zuführen (*+dat*), mit Sauerstoff versorgen. **(c)** (*fig*) *grievance* vorbringen. **(d)** (*fig*) *question, issue* erörtern; *opinion, view* äußern, kundtun.

ventilation [ˌventɪ'leɪʃən] *n* **(a)** (*control of air flow*) Belüftung, Ventilation *f*; (*letting fresh air in*) Lüften *nt* ♦ **~ shaft** Luftschacht *m*; **there's very poor ~ in here** die Belüftung dieses Raumes ist schlecht. **(b)** (*of blood*) Sauerstoffzufuhr *f*. **(c)** (*of grievance*) Vorbringen *nt*. **(d)** (*of question, issue*) Erörterung *f*; (*of opinion, view*) Äußerung *f*.

ventilator ['ventɪleɪtə^r] *n* Ventilator *m*.

ventral ['ventrəl] *adj* (*form*) ventral (*form*), Bauch-.

ventricle ['ventrɪkəl] *n* Kammer *f*, Ventrikel *m* (*form*).

ventriloquism [ven'trɪləkwɪzəm] *n* Bauchredekunst *f*, Bauchreden *nt*.

ventriloquist [ven'trɪləkwɪst] *n* Bauchredner(in *f*) *m*.

ventriloquy [ven'trɪləkwɪ] *n* Bauchredekunst *f*, Bauchreden *nt*.

venture ['ventʃə^r] [1] *n* Unternehmung *f*, Unternehmen, Unterfangen *nt* ♦ **mountain-climbing is his latest ~** seit neuestem hat er sich aufs Bergsteigen verlegt; **a new ~ in publishing** ein neuer verlegerischer Versuch, ein neues verlegerisches Experiment; **this was a disastrous ~ for the company**

dieses Projekt *or* dieser Versuch war für die Firma ein Fiasko; **his first ~ at novel-writing** sein erster Versuch, Romane zu schreiben; **he made a lot of money out of his ~s in the world of finance** er verdiente bei seinen Spekulationen in der Finanzwelt viel Geld; **his purchase of stocks was his first ~ into the world of finance** mit dem Erwerb von Aktien wagte er sich zum erstenmal in die Finanzwelt; **his early ~s into crime were successful** seine frühen kriminellen Abenteuer waren erfolgreich; **rowing the Atlantic alone was quite a ~** allein über den Atlantik zu rudern, war ein ziemlich gewagtes Abenteuer; **the astronauts on their ~ into the unknown** die Astronauten auf ihrer abenteuerlichen Reise ins Unbekannte.

[2] *vt* **(a)** *life, reputation* aufs Spiel setzen; *money also* riskieren (*on* bei) ◆ **nothing ~d nothing gained** (*Prov*) wer nicht wagt, der nicht gewinnt (*Prov*).
(b) *guess, explanation, statement* wagen; *opinion* zu äußern wagen ◆ **if I may ~ an opinion** wenn ich mir erlauben darf, meine Meinung zu sagen; **in his latest article he ~s an explanation of the phenomenon** in seinem letzten Artikel versucht er, eine Erklärung des Phänomens zu geben; **I ~ to add that ...** ich wage sogar zu behaupten, daß ...

[3] *vi* sich wagen ◆ **no other traveller had dared to ~ so far** noch kein anderer Reisender hatte sich so weit vorgewagt; **to ~ out of doors** sich vor die Tür wagen; **they lost money when they ~d into book publishing** sie verloren Geld bei ihrem Versuch, Bücher zu verlegen; **the company ~d into a new field** die Firma wagte sich in ein neues Gebiet vor.

◆**venture forth** (*liter*) *or* **out** *vi* sich hinauswagen ◆ **the soldiers ~d ~ to find the enemy** die Soldaten wagten sich vor, um den Feind ausfindig zu machen; **the astronauts ~d ~ into the unknown** die Astronauten wagten sich ins Unbekannte; **we ~d ~ on this intellectual enterprise** wir wagten uns an dieses intellektuelle Unterfangen heran.

◆**venture on** *vi +prep obj* sich wagen an (*+acc*) ◆ **Drake ~d ~ a voyage of exploration round the world** Drake wagte sich auf eine Entdeckungsreise um die Welt; **they ~d ~ a programme of reform** sie wagten sich an ein Reformprogramm heran; **the Prime Minister ~d ~ a statement of the position** der Premier hatte den Mut, eine Erklärung zur Lage abzugeben; **when we first ~d ~ this voyage of scientific discovery** als wir uns zum ersten Mal auf wissenschaftliches Neuland wagten.

venture: ~ capital *n* Beteiligungs- *or* Risikokapital *nt*; **~ capitalist** *n* Risikokapitalgeber *m*; **~ capitalists** Kapitalbeteiligungsgesellschaft *f*.

venturesome [ˈventʃəsəm] *adj person, action* abenteuerlich.

venue [ˈvenjuː] *n* (*meeting place*) Treffpunkt *m*; (*Sport*) Austragungsort *m*; (*Jur*) Verhandlungsort *m*.

Venus [ˈviːnəs] *n* Venus *f* ◆ **~'s-flytrap** Venusfliegenfalle *f*.

Venusian [vəˈnjuːʃən] [1] *n* Venusbewohner(in *f*) *m*.
[2] *adj* Venus-.

veracious [vəˈreɪʃəs] *adj person* ehrlich, aufrichtig; *report* wahrheitsgemäß.

veracity [vəˈræsɪtɪ] *n* (*of person*) Ehrlichkeit, Aufrichtigkeit *f*; (*of report, evidence*) Wahrheit, Richtigkeit *f*.

veranda(h) [vəˈrændə] *n* Veranda *f*.

verb [vɜːb] *n* Verb, Zeitwort, Verbum *nt*.

verbal [ˈvɜːbəl] *adj* **(a)** (*spoken*) *statement* mündlich; *agreement also* verbal. **(b)** (*of words*) *error, skills, distinction* sprachlich ◆ **~ memory** Wortgedächtnis *nt*. **(c)** (*literal*) *translation* wörtlich. **(d)** (*Gram*) verbal ◆ **~ noun** Verbalsubstantiv *nt*.

verbalize [ˈvɜːbəlaɪz] *vt* **(a)** (*put into words*) ausdrücken, in Worte fassen. **(b)** (*Gram*) verbal ausdrücken.

verbally [ˈvɜːbəlɪ] *adv* **(a)** (*spoken*) mündlich, verbal. **(b)** (*as a verb*) verbal.

verbatim [vɜːˈbeɪtɪm] [1] *adj* wörtlich.
[2] *adv* wortwörtlich.

verbena [vɜːˈbiːnə] *n* Eisenkraut *nt*.

verbiage [ˈvɜːbɪɪdʒ] *n* Wortwust *m*, Wortfülle *f*, Blabla *nt* (*inf*) ◆ **you won't impress the examiners with a lot of ~** mit Geschwafel *nt or* Blabla (*inf*) *nt* kannst du die Prüfer nicht beeindrucken; **there's too much ~ in this report** dieser Bericht ist zu umständlich geschrieben.

verbose [vɜːˈbəʊs] *adj* wortreich, langatmig, weitschweifig.

verbosely [vɜːˈbəʊslɪ] *adv* langatmig.

verbosity [vɜːˈbɒsɪtɪ] *n* Langatmigkeit *f* ◆ **it sounds impressive but it's sheer ~** es klingt beeindruckend, ist aber nichts als Geschwafel.

verdant [ˈvɜːdənt] *adj* (*liter*) grün.

verdict [ˈvɜːdɪkt] *n* **(a)** (*Jur*) Urteil *nt* ◆ **~ of guilty/not guilty** Schuldspruch *m*/Freispruch *m*; **what's the ~?** wie lautet das Urteil?; *see* **bring in, return.**
(b) (*of doctor*) Urteil *nt*; (*of press, critic etc also*) Verdikt *nt* (*geh*); (*of electors*) Entscheidung *f*, Votum *nt* ◆ **what's your ~ on this wine?** wie beurteilst du diesen Wein?; **to give one's ~ about** *or* **on sth** sein Urteil über etw (*acc*) abgeben.

verdigris [ˈvɜːdɪgriːs] *n* Grünspan *m*.

verdure [ˈvɜːdjʊəʳ] *n* (*liter*) (*colour*) sattes Grün; (*vegetation*) reiche Flora (*geh*).

verge [vɜːdʒ] *n* (*lit, fig*) Rand *m* ◆ **"keep off the ~"** „Bankette *or* Seitenstreifen nicht befahrbar"; **to be on the ~ of ruin/war** am Rande des Ruins/eines Krieges stehen; **to be on the ~ of a nervous breakdown** am Rande eines Nervenzusammenbruchs sein; **to be on the ~ of a discovery** kurz vor einer Entdeckung stehen; **to be on the ~ of tears** den Tränen nahe sein; **to be on the ~ of doing sth** im Begriff sein, etw zu tun; **I was on the ~ of giving away the secret** (*accidentally*) ich hätte das Geheimnis um ein Haar ausgeplaudert.

◆**verge on** *vi +prep obj* (*ideas, actions*) grenzen an (*acc*) ◆ **he's verging ~ bankruptcy** er steht kurz vor dem Bankrott; **she is verging ~ fifty** sie geht auf die Fünfzig zu; **she was verging ~ madness** sie stand am Rande des Wahnsinns.

verger [ˈvɜːdʒəʳ] *n* (*Eccl*) Küster *m*.

Vergil [ˈvɜːdʒɪl] *n* Virgil, Vergil *m*.

veridical [vəˈrɪdɪkl] *adj* (*form*) wahrheitsgetreu, wahrheitsgemäß.

verifiability [ˌverɪfaɪəˈbɪlɪtɪ] *n* Nachweisbarkeit, Nachprüfbarkeit, Verifizierbarkeit (*geh*) *f*.

verifiable [ˈverɪfaɪəbl] *adj* nachweisbar, nachprüfbar, verifizierbar (*geh*).

verification [ˌverɪfɪˈkeɪʃən] *n* (*check*) Überprüfung *f*; (*confirmation*) Bestätigung, Verifikation (*geh*) *f*; (*proof*) Nachweis *m* ◆ **these claims are open to empirical ~** diese Behauptungen lassen sich empirisch nachweisen.

verify [ˈverɪfaɪ] *vt* **(a)** (*check up*) (über)prüfen; (*confirm*) bestätigen, beglaubigen; *theory* beweisen, verifizieren (*geh*). **(b)** *suspicions, fears* bestätigen.

verily [ˈverɪlɪ] *adv* (*obs*) wahrlich (*obs*), fürwahr (*obs*) ◆ **~ I say unto you** wahrlich, ich sage euch.

verisimilitude [ˌverɪsɪˈmɪlɪtjuːd] *n* (*form*) Wahrhaftigkeit (*liter*), Echtheit *f*; (*of theory*) Plausibilität, Evidenz (*liter*) *f*.

veritable [ˈverɪtəbl] *adj genius* wahr ◆ **a ~ disaster/miracle** die reinste Katastrophe/das reinste Wunder.

veritably [ˈverɪtəblɪ] *adv* (*liter*) in der Tat, fürwahr (*obs*).

verity [ˈverɪtɪ] *n* (*liter*) Wahrheit *f*.

vermicelli [ˌvɜːmɪˈselɪ] *n* Fadennudeln, Suppennudeln *pl*.

vermicide [ˈvɜːmɪsaɪd] *n* Wurmmittel, Vermizid (*spec*) *nt*.

vermifuge [ˈvɜːmɪfjuːdʒ] *n* Wurmmittel, Vermifugum (*spec*) *nt*.

vermilion [vəˈmɪljən] [1] *n* Zinnoberrot *nt*.
[2] *adj* zinnoberrot.

vermin [ˈvɜːmɪn] *n, no pl* **(a)** (*animal*) Schädling *m*. **(b)** (*insects*) Ungeziefer *nt*. **(c)** (*pej: people*) Pack, Ungeziefer *nt*.

verminous [ˈvɜːmɪnəs] *adj people, clothes* voller Ungeziefer.

vermouth [ˈvɜːməθ] *n* Wermut *m*.

vernacular [vəˈnækjʊləʳ] [1] *n* **(a)** (*dialect*) Mundart *f*; (*not Latin, not official language*) Landessprache *f* ◆ **this word has now come into the ~** dieses Wort ist jetzt in die Alltagssprache eingegangen.
(b) (*jargon*) Fachsprache *f or* -jargon *m*.
(c) (*hum: strong language*) deftige Sprache ◆ **please excuse the ~** entschuldigen Sie bitte, daß ich mich so drastisch ausdrücke.

[2] *adj* **~ newspaper** Zeitung *f* in der regionalen Landessprache; **~ poet** Mundartdichter *m*.

vernal [ˈvɜːnl] *adj equinox,* (*liter*) *flowers* Frühlings-.

veronica [vəˈrɒnɪkə] *n* (*Bot*) Ehrenpreis *m or nt*, Veronika *f*.

verruca [veˈruːkə] *n* Warze *f*.

versatile [ˈvɜːsətaɪl] *adj* vielseitig ◆ **he has a very ~ mind** er ist geistig sehr flexibel.

versatility [ˌvɜːsəˈtɪlɪtɪ] *n see adj* Vielseitigkeit *f*; Flexibilität *f*.

verse [vɜːs] *n* **(a)** (*stanza*) Strophe *f* ◆ **a ~ from "The Tempest"** ein Vers *m* aus dem „Sturm". **(b)** *no pl* (*poetry*) Poesie, Dichtung *f* ◆ **in ~** in Versform; **~ drama** Versdrama *nt*. **(c)** (*of Bible, Koran*) Vers *m*.

versed [vɜːst] *adj* (*also* **well ~**) bewandert, beschlagen (*in* in *+dat*) ◆ **he's well ~ in the art of self-defence** er beherrscht die Kunst der Selbstverteidigung; **I'm not very well ~ in ...** ich verstehe nicht viel *or* habe wenig Ahnung von ...

versification [ˌvɜːsɪfɪˈkeɪʃən] *n* (*act*) Versbildung *f*; (*style*) Versform *f*; (*rules*) Verskunst *f*.

versifier [ˈvɜːsɪfaɪəʳ] *n* (*pej*) Verseschmied, Dichterling *m*.

versify [ˈvɜːsɪfaɪ] [1] *vt* in Versform bringen.
[2] *vi* Verse schmieden (*pej*), dichten.

version [ˈvɜːʃən] *n* **(a)** (*account: of event, of facts*) Version, Darstellung *f*. **(b)** (*variant*) Version *f*; (*of text also*) Fassung *f*; (*of car*) Modell *nt*, Typ *m*. **(c)** (*translation*) Übersetzung *f*.

verso [ˈvɜːsəʊ] *n* Rückseite *f*; (*of book also*) Verso *nt* (*spec*); (*of coin also*) Revers *m* (*spec*).

versus [ˈvɜːsəs] *prep* gegen (*+acc*).

vertebra [ˈvɜːtɪbrə] *n, pl* **-e** [ˈvɜːtɪbriː] Rückenwirbel *m*.

vertebral [ˈvɜːtɪbrəl] *adj* (*form*) Wirbel- ◆ **~ column** Wirbelsäule *f*.

vertebrate [ˈvɜːtɪbrət] [1] *n* Wirbeltier *nt* ◆ **the ~s** die Wirbeltiere *or* Vertebraten (*spec*).
[2] *adj* Wirbel-.

vertex [ˈvɜːteks] *n, pl* **vertices** Scheitel(punkt) *m*.

vertical [ˈvɜːtɪkəl] [1] *adj line* senkrecht, vertikal; (*Comm, Econ*) vertikal ◆ **~ cliffs** senkrecht abfallende Klippen; **~ take-off aircraft** Senkrechtstarter *m*.
[2] *n* (*line*) Vertikale, Senkrechte *f* ◆ **to be off the** *or* **out of the ~** nicht im Lot stehen.

vertically [ˈvɜːtɪkəlɪ] *adv* senkrecht, vertikal ◆ **stand it ~ or it'll fall over** stell es aufrecht hin, sonst fällt es um.

vertices [ˈvɜːtɪsiːz] *pl of* **vertex.**

vertiginous [vɜːˈtɪdʒɪnəs] *adj* (*liter*) *heights* schwindelerregend, schwindelnd (*geh*).

vertigo [ˈvɜːtɪgəʊ] *n* Schwindel *m*; (*Med*) Gleichgewichtsstörung *f* ◆ **he suffers from ~** ihm wird leicht schwindlig; (*Med*) er leidet an Gleichgewichtsstörungen *pl*.

verve [vɜːv] *n* Schwung *m*; (*of person, team also*) Elan *m*; (*of play, performance also*) Ausdruckskraft, Verve (*geh*) *f*.

very [ˈverɪ] [1] *adv* **(a)** (*extremely*) sehr ◆ **it's ~ well written** es ist sehr gut geschrieben; **that's not ~ funny** das ist überhaupt nicht lustig; **it's ~ possible** es ist durchaus *or* (sehr) gut möglich; **~ probably** höchstwahrscheinlich; **he is so ~ lazy** er ist *so* faul; **how ~ odd** wie eigenartig; **V~ Important Person**

prominente Persönlichkeit; ~ **little** sehr wenig; ~ **little milk** ganz *or* sehr wenig Milch.
(b) (*absolutely*) aller- ◆ ~ **best quality** allerbeste Qualität; ~ **last/first** allerletzte(r, s)/allererste(r, s); **she is the ~ cleverest in the class** sie ist die Klassenbeste; **at the ~ latest** allerspätestens; **this is the ~ last time I'll warn you** ich warne dich jetzt zum allerletzten Mal; **to do one's ~ best** sein Äußerstes tun; **this is the ~ best** das ist das Allerbeste; **this is the ~ most I can offer** das ist mein äußerstes Angebot; **at the ~ most/least** allerhöchstens/aller wenigstens; **to be in the ~ best of health** sich bester Gesundheit erfreuen; **they are the ~ best of friends** sie sind die dicksten Freunde.
(c) ~ **much** sehr; **thank you ~ much** vielen Dank; **I liked it ~ much** es hat mir sehr gut gefallen; ~ **much bigger** sehr viel größer; ~ **much respected** sehr angesehen; ~ **much the more intelligent** bei weitem der Intelligentere; **he doesn't work ~ much** er arbeitet nicht sehr viel; ~ **much so** sehr (sogar).
(d) (*for emphasis*) **he fell ill and died the ~ same day** er wurde krank und starb noch am selben Tag; **he died the ~ same day as Kennedy** er starb genau am selben Tag wie Kennedy; **the ~ same hat** genau der gleiche Hut; **we met again the ~ next day** wir trafen uns am nächsten *or* folgenden Tag schon wieder; **the ~ next day he walked under a bus** schon einen Tag später kam er unter einen Bus; **what he predicted happened the ~ next week** was er vorhersagte, trat in der Woche darauf tatsächlich ein; **my ~ own car** mein eigenes Auto; **a house of your ~ own** ein eigenes Häuschen.
(e) ~ **well, if that's what you want** nun gut, wenn du das willst; ~ **good, sir** geht in Ordnung, mein Herr, sehr wohl, mein Herr (*dated*); **if you want that, ~ well, but ...** wenn du das willst, in Ordnung *or* bitte, aber ...
[2] *adj* (a) (*precise, exact*) genau ◆ **that ~ day/moment** genau an diesem Tag/in diesem Augenblick; **in the ~ centre of the picture** genau in der Mitte des Bildes; **this laboratory is the ~ heart of our factory** dieses Labor ist der Kern unseres Werkes; **at the ~ heart of the organization** direkt im Zentrum der Organisation; **on the ~ spot where ...** genau an der Stelle, wo ...; **those were his ~ words** genau das waren seine Worte; **you are the ~ person I want to speak to** mit *Ihnen* wollte ich sprechen; **the ~ thing/man I need** genau das, was ich brauche/genau der Mann, den ich brauche; **the ~ thing!** genau das richtige!; **to catch sb in the ~ act** jdn auf frischer Tat ertappen.
(b) (*extreme*) äußerste(r, s) ◆ **in the ~ beginning** ganz am Anfang; **at the ~ end** ganz am Ende; **at the ~ back/front** ganz hinten/vorn(e); **go to the ~ end of the road** gehen Sie die Straße ganz entlang *or* durch; **to the ~ end of his life** bis an sein Lebensende; **in the ~ depths of the sea/forest** in den Tiefen des Meeres/im tiefsten Wald.
(c) (*mere*) **the ~ thought of it** allein schon der Gedanke daran, der bloße Gedanke daran; **the ~ idea!** nein, so etwas!

Very ® ['vɪərɪ] *adj* (*Mil*) ~ **light** Leuchtkugel *f*.
very high frequency *n* Ultrakurzwelle *f*.
vesicle ['vesɪkl] *n* Bläschen *nt*; (*Med also*) Vesicula *f* (*form*).
vespers ['vespəz] *npl* Vesper *f*.
vessel ['vesl] *n* (a) (*Naut*) Schiff *nt*. (b) (*form: receptacle*) Gefäß *nt* ◆ **drinking ~** Trinkgefäß *nt*. (c) (*Anat, Bot*) Gefäß *nt*.
vest[1] [vest] *n* (a) (*Brit*) Unterhemd *nt*. (b) (*US*) Weste *f*.
vest[2] *vt* (*form*) **to ~ sb with sth, to ~ sth in sb** jdm etw verleihen; **the rights ~ed in the Crown** die der Krone zustehenden Rechte; **Congress is ~ed with the power to declare war** der Kongreß verfügt über das Recht, den Krieg zu erklären; **the authority ~ed in me** die mir verliehene Macht; **he has ~ed interests in the oil business** er ist (finanziell) am Ölgeschäft beteiligt; **the ~ed interests in the oil business** (*people*) die am Ölgeschäft Beteiligten *pl*; **he has a ~ed interest in the play** (*fig*) er hat ein persönliches Interesse an dem Stück.
vestal ['vestl] [1] *adj* vestalisch ◆ ~ **virgin** Vestalin *f*, vestalische Jungfrau.
[2] *n* Vestalin *f*.
vestibule ['vestɪbjuːl] *n* (a) (*of house*) Vorhalle *f*, Vestibül *nt* (*dated*); (*of hotel*) Halle *f*, Foyer *nt*; (*of church*) Vorhalle *f*. (b) (*Anat*) Vorhof *m*, Vestibulum *nt* (*spec*).
vestige ['vestɪdʒ] *n* (a) Spur *f* ◆ **the ~ of a moustache** der Anflug eines Schnurrbarts; **there is not a ~ of truth in what he says** es ist kein Körnchen Wahrheit an dem, was er sagt.
(b) (*Anat*) Rudiment *nt*.
vestigial [ve'stɪdʒɪəl] *adj* spurenhaft; *moustache, growth* spärlich; (*Anat*) rudimentär ◆ **the ~ remains of the old city walls** die Spuren *or* die rudimentären Reste der alten Stadtmauer; **the ~ remains of his ambitions/of their love affair** die kümmerlichen Überreste seiner Ambitionen/ihrer Liebschaft.
vestment ['vestmənt] *n* (a) (*of priest*) Ornat *m*, Gewand *nt*. (b) (*ceremonial robe*) Robe *f*, Ornat *m*.
vest-pocket [ˌvest'pɒkɪt] *adj* (*US*) Taschen-, im Westentaschenformat.
vestry ['vestrɪ] *n* Sakristei *f*.
Vesuvius [vɪ'suːvɪəs] *n* der Vesuv.
vet [vet] [1] *n abbr of* **veterinary surgeon, veterinarian** Tierarzt *m*/-ärztin *f*.
[2] *vt* überprüfen.
vetch [vetʃ] *n* Wicke *f*.
veteran ['vetərən] *n* (*Mil, fig*) Veteran(in *f*) *m* ◆ **a ~ teacher/golfer** ein (alt)erfahrener Lehrer/Golfspieler; **a ~ actor** ein Veteran der Schauspielkunst, ein altgedienter Schauspieler; **she's a ~ campaigner for women's rights** sie ist eine Veteranin der Frauenbewegung; ~ **car** Oldtimer *m*, Schnauferl *nt* (*inf*).
veterinarian [ˌvetərɪ'nɛərɪən] *n* (*US*) Tierarzt *m*/-ärztin *f*.
veterinary ['vetərɪnərɪ] *adj medicine, science* Veterinär-; *training* tierärztlich ◆ ~ **surgeon** Tierarzt *m*/-ärztin *f*.
veto ['viːtəʊ] [1] *n, pl* **-es** Veto *nt* ◆ **power of ~** Vetorecht *nt*; **to have a ~** das Vetorecht haben; **to use one's ~** von seinem Vetorecht Gebrauch machen.
[2] *vt* sein Veto einlegen gegen ◆ **if they ~ it** wenn sie ihr Veto einlegen.
vetting ['vetɪŋ] *n* Überprüfung *f*.
vex [veks] *vt* (a) (*annoy*) ärgern, irritieren; *animals* quälen ◆ **to be ~ed with sb** mit jdm böse sein, auf jdn ärgerlich sein; **to be ~ed about sth** sich über etw (*acc*) ärgern; **to be/get ~ed** ärgerlich *or* wütend sein/werden; **a problem which has been ~ing me** ein Problem, das mich quält *or* mir keine Ruhe läßt.
(b) (*afflict*) plagen, bedrücken.
vexation [vek'seɪʃən] *n* (a) (*state*) Ärger *m*; (*act*) Verärgerung *f*, Ärgern *nt*; (*of animal*) Quälen *nt*, Quälerei *f*. (b) (*affliction*) Bedrückung *f*; (*cause*) Plage *f*. (c) (*thing*) Ärgernis *nt* ◆ **the little ~s of life** die kleinen Sorgen und Nöte des Lebens.
vexatious [vek'seɪʃəs] *adj* (a) ärgerlich; *regulations, headache* lästig; *child* unausstehlich. (b) (*Jur*) schikanös.
vexed [vekst] *adj* (a) (*annoyed*) verärgert. (b) *question* vieldiskutiert, schwierig.
vexing ['veksɪŋ] *adj* ärgerlich, irritierend; *problem* verzwickt.
vg *abbr of* **very good.**
VGA *abbr of* **video graphics array** VGA.
VHF (*Rad*) *abbr of* **very high frequency** UKW.
via ['vaɪə] *prep* über (+*acc*); (*with town names also*) via ◆ **they got in ~ the window** sie kamen durchs Fenster herein.
viability [ˌvaɪə'bɪlɪtɪ] *n* (a) (*of life forms*) Lebensfähigkeit *f*. (b) (*of plan, project*) Durchführbarkeit, Realisierbarkeit *f*; (*of firm*) Rentabilität *f* ◆ **the ~ of the EC** die Lebens- *or* Existenzfähigkeit der EG.
viable ['vaɪəbl] *adj* (a) *plant, foetus* lebensfähig. (b) *company* rentabel; *economy* lebensfähig; *suggestion* brauchbar; *plan* durchführbar, realisierbar ◆ **the company is not economically ~** die Firma ist unrentabel; **is this newly created state ~?** ist dieser neuentstandene Staat lebens- *or* existenzfähig?
viaduct ['vaɪədʌkt] *n* Viadukt *m*.
vial ['vaɪəl] *n* Fläschchen, Gefäß *nt*.
viands ['vaɪəndz] *npl* (*form*) Lebensmittel *pl*; (*for journey*) Proviant *m*.
vibes [vaɪbz] *npl* (a) Vibraphon *nt*. (b) (*sl*) *see* **vibration (b).**
vibrancy ['vaɪbrənsɪ] *n see adj* Dynamik *f*; voller Klang, Sonorität *f*.
vibrant ['vaɪbrənt] *adj personality etc* dynamisch; *voice* volltönend, sonor ◆ **the ~ life of the city** das pulsierende Leben der Großstadt.
vibraphone ['vaɪbrəfəʊn] *n* Vibraphon *nt*.
vibrate [vaɪ'breɪt] [1] *vi* (*lit, fig*) zittern, beben (*with* vor +*dat*); (*machine, string, air*) vibrieren; (*notes*) schwingen ◆ **the blade cuts more easily by being made to ~** das Schneideblatt schneidet dadurch besser, daß es vibriert; **the painting ~s with life** das Bild bebt *or* sprüht vor Leben; **the city centre ~s with activity** im Stadtzentrum pulsiert das Leben; **the town was vibrating with excitement** Aufregung hatte die Stadt ergriffen.
[2] *vt* zum Vibrieren bringen; *string* zum Schwingen bringen ◆ **they study the way the machine ~s the body** sie untersuchen, wie die Maschine den Körper erschüttert.
vibration [vaɪ'breɪʃən] *n* (a) (*of string, sound waves*) Schwingung *f*; (*of machine*) Vibrieren *nt*; (*of voice, ground*) Beben *nt* ◆ **the medium felt mysterious ~s** das Medium fühlte geheimnisvolle Schwingungen; **the ~s the body undergoes when one flies** die Erschütterung, der der Körper beim Fliegen ausgesetzt ist.
(b) (*sl: usu pl*) **what sort of ~s do you get from him?** wie wirkt er auf dich?; **I get good ~s from this music** diese Musik bringt mich auf Touren; **this town is giving me bad ~s** diese Stadt macht mich ganz fertig (*inf*).
vibrato [vɪ'brɑːtəʊ] [1] *n* Vibrato *nt*.
[2] *adv* vibrato.
vibrator [vaɪ'breɪtə^r] *n* Vibrator *m*.
vibratory ['vaɪbrətərɪ] *adj* vibrierend, Vibrations-.
vicar ['vɪkə^r] *n* Pfarrer *m* ◆ **good evening, ~** guten Abend, Herr Pfarrer; ~ **apostolic** Apostolischer Vikar; ~ **general** Generalvikar *m*.
vicarage ['vɪkərɪdʒ] *n* Pfarrhaus *nt*.
vicarious [vɪ'kɛərɪəs] *adj* (a) *pleasure, enjoyment* indirekt, mittelbar, nachempfunden; *experience* ersatzweise, Ersatz- ◆ ~ **sexual thrill** Ersatzbefriedigung *f*; **he can't walk himself but he gets enormous ~ pleasure from watching athletics** er kann nicht gehen, aber das Zuschauen bei sportlichen Wettkämpfen vermittelt ihm einen großen Genuß.
(b) *authority, suffering* stellvertretend.
vicariously [vɪ'kɛərɪəslɪ] *adv* indirekt, mittelbar ◆ **I can appreciate the island's beauty ~ through your writing** Ihre Beschreibung vermittelt mir die Schönheit der Insel *or* läßt mich die Schönheit der Insel nachempfinden.
vicariousness [vɪ'kɛərɪəsnɪs] *n* Indirektheit, Mittelbarkeit *f* ◆ **the appreciation of art always involves a degree of ~** Kunstgenuß setzt immer eine bestimmte Fähigkeit des Nachempfindens voraus.
vice[1] [vaɪs] *n* Laster *nt*; (*of horse*) Unart, Untugend *f*, Mucken *pl* (*inf*) ◆ **his main ~ is laziness** sein größter Fehler ist die Faulheit; **you don't smoke or drink, don't you have any ~s?** (*hum*) Sie rauchen nicht, Sie trinken nicht, haben Sie denn gar kein Laster? (*hum*); **a life of ~** ein Lasterleben *nt*; ~ **squad** Sittenpolizei *f*, Sittendezernat *nt*, Sitte *f* (*sl*).
vice[2], (*US*) **vise** *n* Schraubstock *m* ◆ **to have/hold sth in a ~-like grip** etw fest umklammern; (*between legs, under arm*) etw fest einklemmen.
vice- *pref* **~-admiral** *n* Vizeadmiral *m*; **~-chairman** *n* stellvertretender Vorsitzender; **~-chairmanship** *n* stellvertretender Vorsitz; **~-chancellor** *n*

(*Univ*) ≃ Rektor *m*; **~-consul** *n* Vizekonsul *m*; **~-presidency** *n* Vizepräsidentschaft *f*; **~-president** *n* Vizepräsident *m*; **~regent** *n* Vizeregent *m*, stellvertretender Regent; **~roy** *n* Vizekönig *m*.

vice versa ['vaɪsɪ'vɜːsə] *adv* umgekehrt.

vicinity [vɪ'sɪnɪtɪ] *n* **(a)** Umgebung *f* ◆ **in the ~** in der Nähe (*of* von, *gen*); **in the immediate ~** in unmittelbarer Umgebung; **in the ~ of £500** um die £ 500 (herum). **(b)** (*closeness*) Nähe *f*.

vicious ['vɪʃəs] *adj* **(a)** gemein, boshaft; *remark also* gehässig; *look* boshaft, böse ◆ **to have a ~ tongue** eine böse *or* spitze Zunge haben.
(b) *habit* lasterhaft.
(c) *animal* bösartig; *dog* bissig; *blow, kick* brutal; *criminal* brutal, abgefeimt; *murder* grauenhaft, brutal ◆ **that animal can be ~** das Tier kann heimtückisch sein.
(d) (*inf: strong, nasty*) *headache* fies (*inf*), gemein (*inf*).
(e) **~ circle** Teufelskreis, Circulus vitiosus (*geh*) *m*.

viciously ['vɪʃəslɪ] *adv see adj* (*a, c*) **(a)** gemein, boshaft; gehässig; böse. **(b)** bösartig; brutal; auf grauenhafte Art ◆ **the dog attacked him ~** der Hund fiel wütend über ihn her.

viciousness ['vɪʃəsnɪs] *n see adj* **(a)** Gemeinheit *f*; Boshaftigkeit *f*; Gehässigkeit *f*. **(b)** Lasterhaftigkeit *f*. **(c)** Bösartigkeit *f*; Bissigkeit *f*; Brutalität *f*; Grauenhaftigkeit *f*.

vicissitude [vɪ'sɪsɪtjuːd] *n usu pl* Wandel *m* ◆ **the ~s of life** die Launen des Schicksals, die Wechselfälle des Lebens; **the ~s of war/business** die Wirren des Krieges/das Auf und Ab im Geschäftsleben.

victim ['vɪktɪm] *n* Opfer *nt* ◆ **he was the ~ of a practical joke** ihm wurde ein Streich gespielt; **to be the ~ of sb's sarcasm** eine Zielscheibe für jds Sarkasmus sein; **the hawk flew off with its ~ in its claws** der Falke flog mit seiner Beute in den Klauen davon; **to fall (a) ~ to sth** einer Sache (*dat*) zum Opfer fallen; **I fell ~ to the flu** mich hatte die Grippe erwischt (*inf*); **to fall ~ to sb's charms** jds Charme (*dat*) erliegen; **the whole of the region fell ~ to the drought** die ganze Gegend wurde ein Opfer der Dürre.

victimization [,vɪktɪmaɪ'zeɪʃən] *n see vt* ungerechte Behandlung; Schikanierung *f*.

victimize ['vɪktɪmaɪz] *vt* ungerecht behandeln; (*pick on*) schikanieren ◆ **she feels ~d** sie fühlt sich ungerecht behandelt; **this ~s the public** darunter hat die Öffentlichkeit zu leiden.

victimless ['vɪktɪmlɪs] *adj crime* ohne Opfer.

victor ['vɪktə^r] *n* Sieger(in *f*) *m*.

Victoria Cross [vɪk'tɔːrɪə'krɒs] *n* (*Brit*) Viktoriakreuz *nt* (*höchste britische Tapferkeitsauszeichnung*).

Victoria Falls [vɪk'tɔːrɪə'fɔːlz] *npl* Viktoriafälle *f*.

Victorian [vɪk'tɔːrɪən] 1 *n* Viktorianer(in *f*) *m*.
2 *adj* viktorianisch; (*fig*) (sitten)streng.

Victoriana [vɪk,tɔːrɪ'ɑːnə] *n* viktorianische Antiquitäten *pl*.

victorious [vɪk'tɔːrɪəs] *adj army* siegreich; *smile* triumphierend, siegesbewußt ◆ **to be ~ over sb/sth** jdn/etw besiegen; **to be ~ in the struggle against ...** siegen *or* den Sieg davontragen im Kampf gegen ...

victoriously [vɪk'tɔːrɪəslɪ] *adv* siegreich, als Sieger.

victory ['vɪktərɪ] *n* Sieg *m* ◆ **to gain** *or* **win a ~ over sb/sth** einen Sieg über jdn/etw erringen, jdn/etw besiegen; **his final ~ over his fear** die endgültige Überwindung seiner Angst; **~ roll** (*Aviat*) Siegesrolle *f*.

victual ['vɪtl] (*form*) 1 *vt army, troop* verpflegen, verproviantieren.
2 *vi* sich verpflegen *or* verproviantieren.

victualler ['vɪtlə^r] *n see* **licensed.**

victuals ['vɪtlz] *npl* Lebensmittel *pl*; (*for journey*) Proviant *m*, Verpflegung *f*.

vide ['vɪdeɪ] *imper* (*form, Jur*) siehe, vide (*liter*).

videlicet [vɪ'diːlɪset] *adv* (*abbr* **viz**) nämlich.

video ['vɪdɪəʊ] 1 *n* **(a)** (*film*) Video *nt*. **(b)** (*recorder*) Videorekorder *m*. **(c)** (*US*) Fernsehen *nt* ◆ **on ~** im Fernsehen.
2 *vt* (auf Video) aufnehmen.

video: ~ camera *n* Videokamera *f*; **~ cassette** *n* Videokassette *f*; **~ conference** *n* Videokonferenz *f*; **~ conferencing** *n* Video-Konferenzschaltung *f*; **~ disc** *n* Bildplatte; **~ disc player** *n* Bildplattenspieler *m*; **~ game** *n* Telespiel *nt*; **~ library** *n* Videothek *f*; **~ nasty** *n Video nt mit übertriebenen Gewaltszenen und/oder pornographischen Inhalts*; **~phone** *n* Fernsehtelefon *nt*; **~ recorder** *n* Videorekorder *m*; **~-recording** *n* Videoaufnahme *f*; **~ shop** *n* Videothek *f*; **~tape** 1 *n* Videoband *nt*; 2 *vt* (auf Video) aufzeichnen.

vie [vaɪ] *vi* wetteifern; (*Comm*) konkurrieren ◆ **to ~ with sb for sth** mit jdm um etw wetteifern; **they are vying for the championship** sie kämpfen um die Meisterschaft; **they ~d successfully with their competitors** es gelang ihnen, ihre Konkurrenten auszustechen.

Vienna [vɪ'enə] 1 *n* Wien *nt*.
2 *adj* Wiener.

Viennese [,vɪə'niːz] 1 *adj* wienerisch.
2 *n* Wiener(in *f*) *m*.

Vietcong [vjet'kɒŋ] *n* Vietkong *m*.

Vietnam [,vjet'næm] *n* Vietnam *nt*.

Vietnamese [,vjetnə'miːz] 1 *adj* vietnamesisch.
2 *n* **(a)** Vietnamese *m*, Vietnamesin *f*. **(b)** (*language*) Vietnamesisch *nt*.

Viet Vet ['viːet'vet] *n* (*US*) Vietnam(kriegs)veteran *m*.

view [vjuː] 1 *n* **(a)** (*range of vision*) Sicht *f* ◆ **in full ~ of thousands of people** vor den Augen von Tausenden von Menschen; **the magician placed the box in full ~ of the audience** der Zauberer stellte die Kiste so auf, daß das ganze Publikum sie sehen konnte; **the ship came into ~** das Schiff kam in Sicht; **I came into ~ of the lake** der See kam in Sicht *or* lag vor mir; **to keep sth in ~** etw im Auge behalten; **the cameraman had a job keeping the plane in ~** der Kameramann fand es schwierig, das Flugzeug zu verfolgen; **to go out of ~** außer Sicht kommen, verschwinden; **the house is within ~ of the sea** vom Haus aus ist das Meer zu sehen; **the house is exposed to ~ from passing trains** das Haus kann von vorbeifahrenden Zügen aus eingesehen werden; **hidden from ~** verborgen, versteckt; **the horses were hidden from ~ behind the trees** die Pferde waren von den Bäumen verdeckt; **she keeps the old china hidden from ~** sie bewahrt das alte Porzellan im Verborgenen auf; **the house is hidden from ~ from the main road** das Haus ist von der Hauptstraße aus nicht zu sehen; **on ~** (*for purchasing*) zur Ansicht; (*of exhibits*) ausgestellt; **the house will be on ~ tomorrow** das Haus kann morgen besichtigt werden.
(b) (*prospect, sight*) Aussicht *f* ◆ **there is a splendid ~ from here/from the top** von hier/von der Spitze hat man einen herrlichen Blick *or* eine wunderschöne Aussicht; **a ~ over ...** ein Blick über (*+acc*); **a good ~ of the sea** ein schöner Blick auf das Meer; **a room with a ~** ein Zimmer mit schöner Aussicht; **I only got a side ~ of his head** ich habe seinen Kopf nur im Profil gesehen.
(c) (*photograph etc*) Ansicht *f* ◆ **I want to take a ~ of the forest** ich möchte eine Aufnahme vom Wald machen; **~s of London/the Alps** Ansichten *pl or* Stadtbilder *pl* von London/Alpenbilder *pl*.
(d) (*opinion*) Ansicht, Meinung *f* ◆ **in my ~** meiner Ansicht *or* Meinung nach; **to have** *or* **hold ~s on sth** Ansichten über etw (*acc*) haben; **what are his ~s on this problem?** was meint er zu diesem Problem?; **do you have any special ~s on the matter?** haben Sie eine besondere Meinung zu dieser Sache?; **I have no ~s on that** ich habe keine Meinung dazu; **to take the ~ that ...** die Ansicht vertreten, daß ...; **to take a dim** (*inf*) *or* **poor ~ of sb's conduct** jds Verhalten mißbilligen; *see* **point.**
(e) (*mental survey*) **an idealistic ~ of the world** eine idealistische Welt(an)sicht; **a general** *or* **overall ~ of a problem** ein allgemeiner *or* umfassender Überblick über ein Problem; **a clear ~ of the facts** eine klare Übersicht über die Fakten; **in ~ of** wegen (*+gen*), angesichts (*+gen*); **at first ~** auf den ersten Blick; **we must not lose from ~ the fact that ...** wir dürfen die Tatsache nicht aus dem Auge verlieren, daß ...; **I'll keep it in ~** ich werde es im Auge behalten.
(f) (*intention, plan*) Absicht *f* ◆ **to have sth in ~** etw beabsichtigen; **with a ~ to doing sth** mit der Absicht, etw zu tun; **with this in ~** im Hinblick darauf; **he has the holidays in ~ when he says ...** er denkt an die Ferien, wenn er sagt ...
2 *vt* **(a)** (*see*) betrachten. **(b)** (*examine*) *house* besichtigen. **(c)** (*consider*) *problem etc* sehen ◆ **he ~s the prospect with dismay** er sieht dieser Sache mit Schrecken entgegen.
3 *vi* (*watch television*) fernsehen.

viewdata ['vjuːdeɪtə] *n* Bildschirmtext, Bfx *m*.

viewer ['vjuːə^r] *n* **(a)** (*TV*) Zuschauer(in *f*) *m*. **(b)** (*for slides*) Dia- *or* Bildbetrachter *m*.

view-finder ['vjuː,faɪndə^r] *n* Sucher *m*.

viewing ['vjuːɪŋ] *n* **(a)** (*of house, at auction etc*) Besichtigung *f* ◆ **~ time** Besichtigungszeiten *pl*.
(b) (*TV*) Fernsehen *nt* ◆ **9 o'clock is peak ~ time** neun Uhr ist (die) Haupteinschaltzeit; **this programme will be given another ~ next week** dieses Programm wird nächste Woche wiederholt; **I don't do much ~** ich sehe nicht viel fern.

viewpoint ['vjuːpɔɪnt] *n* **(a)** Standpunkt *m* ◆ **from the ~ of economic growth** unter dem Gesichtspunkt des Wirtschaftswachstums; **to see sth from sb's ~** etw aus jds Sicht sehen. **(b)** (*for scenic view*) Aussichtspunkt *m*.

vigil ['vɪdʒɪl] *n* **(a)** (Nacht)wache *f* ◆ **to keep ~ over sb** bei jdm wachen; **the dog kept ~ over his injured master** der Hund hielt bei seinem verletzten Herrn Wache; **her long ~s at his bedside** ihr langes Wachen an seinem Krankenbett.
(b) (*Rel*) Vigil, Nachtwache *f*.

vigilance ['vɪdʒɪləns] *n* Wachsamkeit *f* ◆ **no move escaped their ~** keine Bewegung entging ihrem wachsamen Auge; **~ committee** Bürgerwehr *f*, Selbstschutzkomitee *nt*.

vigilant ['vɪdʒɪlənt] *adj* wachsam ◆ **the customs officers are ever ~ for drug traffickers** die Zollbeamten haben stets ein wachsames Auge auf Drogenhändler.

vigilante [,vɪdʒɪ'læntɪ] 1 *n Mitglied nt einer Selbstschutzorganisation* ◆ **the ~s** die Bürgerwehr, der Selbstschutz.
2 *adj attr* Bürgerwehr-, Selbstschutz-.

vigilantly ['vɪdʒɪləntlɪ] *adv* aufmerksam; *patrol* wachsam.

vignette [vɪ'njet] *n* Vignette *f*, (*character sketch*) Skizze *f*, kurze und prägnante Darstellung.

vigor *n* (*US*) *see* **vigour.**

vigorous ['vɪgərəs] *adj* kräftig; *prose, tune* kraftvoll; *protest, denial, measures, exercises* energisch; *walk* forsch, flott; *nod* eifrig, heftig; *match, player* dynamisch; *speech* feurig; *debater* leidenschaftlich.

vigorously ['vɪgərəslɪ] *adv see adj*.

vigour, (*US*) **vigor** ['vɪgə^r] *n* Kraft, Energie *f*; (*of protest, denial*) Heftigkeit *f*; (*of exercises*) Energie *f*; (*of player*) Dynamik *f*; (*of speech, debater*) Leidenschaftlichkeit *f*; (*of prose*) Ausdruckskraft *f* ◆ **sexual/youthful ~** sexuelle/jugendliche Spannkraft; **all the ~ has gone out of the undertaking** das Unternehmen hat jeglichen Schwung verloren.

Viking ['vaɪkɪŋ] 1 *n* Wikinger *m*.

➤ LANGUAGE IN USE: **view: 1d** → 26.2, 26.3 **1e** → 17.1

2 *adj ship* Wikinger-.

vile [vaɪl] *adj* abscheulich; *mood, smell, habit also* übel; *thoughts also* niedrig, gemein; *language also* unflätig; *weather, food also* scheußlich, widerlich ◆ **that was a ~ thing to say** es war eine Gemeinheit, so etwas zu sagen; **he was ~ to his wife** er benahm sich scheußlich gegenüber seiner Frau.

vilely ['vaɪllɪ] *adv* abscheulich, scheußlich.

vileness ['vaɪlnɪs] *n* Abscheulichkeit *f*; *(of thoughts)* Niederträchtigkeit *f*; *(of smell)* Widerwärtigkeit *f*; *(of language also)* Unflätigkeit *f*; *(of weather)* Scheußlichkeit *f* ◆ **the ~ of his mood** seine Übellaunigkeit.

vilification [ˌvɪlɪfɪ'keɪʃən] *n* Diffamierung, Verleumdung *f*.

vilify ['vɪlɪfaɪ] *vt* diffamieren, verleumden.

villa ['vɪlə] *n* Villa *f*.

village ['vɪlɪdʒ] *n* Dorf *nt*.

village *in cpds* Dorf-; **~ green** *n* Dorfwiese *f or* -anger *m*; **~ idiot** *n* Dorftrottel *m (inf)*.

villager ['vɪlɪdʒəʳ] *n* Dörfler(in *f*), Dorfbewohner(in *f*) *(also Admin) m*.

villain ['vɪlən] *n* **(a)** *(scoundrel)* Schurke *m*; *(sl: criminal)* Verbrecher, Ganove *(inf) m*. **(b)** *(in drama, novel)* Bösewicht *m*. **(c)** *(inf: rascal)* Bengel *m* ◆ **he's the ~ of the piece** er ist der Übeltäter.

villainous ['vɪlənəs] *adj* **(a)** böse; *deed* niederträchtig, gemein ◆ **a ~ face** ein Verbrechergesicht *nt*. **(b)** *(inf: bad)* scheußlich.

villainously ['vɪlənəslɪ] *adv smile* hämisch ◆ **he ~ murdered his brothers** in seiner Niedertracht ermordete er seine Brüder; **he ~ stole the jewels** wie ein Verbrecher stahl er den Schmuck.

villainy ['vɪlənɪ] *n* Gemeinheit, Niederträchtigkeit *f*.

villein ['vɪlɪn] *n (Hist)* Leibeigene(r) *mf*.

vim [vɪm] *n (inf)* Schwung *m* ◆ **he writes with great ~** er schreibt sehr schwungvoll; **full of ~ and vigour** voller Schwung und Elan.

vinaigrette [ˌvɪnɪ'gret] *n* Vinaigrette *f (Cook)*; *(for salad)* Salatsoße *f*.

vindaloo [ˌvɪndə'luː] *n sehr scharf gewürztes indisches Currygericht*.

vindicate ['vɪndɪkeɪt] *vt* **(a)** *opinion, action* rechtfertigen. **(b)** *(clear from suspicion etc)* rehabilitieren.

vindication [ˌvɪndɪ'keɪʃən] *n see vt* **(a)** Rechtfertigung *f* ◆ **in ~ of** zur Rechtfertigung *(+gen)*. **(b)** Rehabilitation *f*.

vindictive [vɪn'dɪktɪv] *adj speech, person* rachsüchtig; *mood* nachtragend, unversöhnlich ◆ **he is not a ~ person** er ist nicht nachtragend; **these measures are likely to make the unions feel ~** diese Maßnahmen könnten bei den Gewerkschaften auf Unwillen *or* Ressentiments stoßen; **I hope you won't feel ~ because of my rather harsh criticism** ich hoffe, Sie tragen mir meine etwas harte Kritik nicht nach *or* Sie nehmen mir meine etwas harte Kritik nicht übel; **corporal punishment can make pupils feel ~ towards the teacher** die Prügelstrafe kann die Schüler gegen den Lehrer aufbringen; **insecure people often feel ~** unsichere Menschen sind oft voller Ressentiments.

vindictively [vɪn'dɪktɪvlɪ] *adv see adj*.

vindictiveness [vɪn'dɪktɪvnɪs] *n* Rachsucht *f*; *(of mood)* Unversöhnlichkeit *f* ◆ **the ~ of his speech** seine rachsüchtige Rede.

vine [vaɪn] *n* **(a)** *(grapevine)* Rebe, Weinrebe *f*. **(b)** *(similar plant)* Rebengewächs *nt* ◆ **~ dresser** Winzer(in *f*) *m*.

vinegar ['vɪnɪgəʳ] *n* Essig *m*.

vinegary ['vɪnɪgərɪ] *adj (lit, fig)* säuerlich; *taste also* Essig-.

vine: ~ grower *n* Weinbauer *m*; **~-growing district** *n* Weingegend *f*, Weinbaugebiet *nt*; **~ harvest** *n* Weinlese, Weinernte *f*; **~ leaf** *n* Rebenblatt *nt*; **~yard** ['vɪnjəd] *n* Weinberg *m*.

viniculture ['vɪnɪˌkʌltʃəʳ] *n* Weinbau *m*.

vino ['viːnəʊ] *n (inf: wine)* Vino *m (inf)*.

vintage ['vɪntɪdʒ] 1 *n* **(a)** *(given year)* *(of wine, fig)* Jahrgang *m*; *(of car)* Baujahr *nt*. **(b)** *(wine of particular year)* **the 1984 ~** der Jahrgang 1984, der 84er. **(c)** *(harvesting, season)* Weinlese, Weinernte *f*.

2 *adj attr (old)* uralt; *(high quality)* glänzend, hervorragend ◆ **this typewriter is a ~ model** diese Schreibmaschine hat Museumswert; **a ~ performance from Humphrey Bogart** eine einmalige künstlerische Leistung Humphrey Bogarts.

vintage: ~ car *n* Vorkriegsmodell, Vintage-Car *nt*; **~ port** *n* Vintage-Port *m, schwerer Port eines besonderen Jahrgangs*; **~ wine** *n* edler Wein; **~ year** *n*: **a ~ year for wine** ein besonders gutes Weinjahr; **a ~ year for burgundy** ein besonders gutes Jahr für Burgunder; **it was a ~ year for plays** in diesem Jahr wurden viele hervorragende Stücke aufgeführt/geschrieben *etc*.

vintner ['vɪntnəʳ] *n* Weinhändler *m*.

vinyl ['vaɪnɪl] *n* Vinyl *nt*.

viol ['vaɪəl] *n* Viola *f*.

viola¹ [vɪ'əʊlə] *n (Mus)* Bratsche *f*.

viola² ['vaɪəʊlə] *n (Bot)* Veilchen *nt*.

viola da gamba [vɪ'əʊlədə'gæmbə] *n* Gambe *f*.

violate ['vaɪəleɪt] *vt* **(a)** *treaty, promise* brechen; *(partially)* verletzen; *law, rule, moral code* verletzen, verstoßen gegen; *rights* verletzen; *truth* vergewaltigen.

(b) *(disturb) holy place* entweihen, schänden; *peacefulness* stören ◆ **to ~ sb's privacy** in jds Privatsphäre eindringen; **it's violating a person's privacy to ...** es ist ein Eingriff in jemandes Privatsphäre, wenn man ...; **the shriek of the jets now ~s that once peaceful spot** durch das Heulen der Düsenflugzeuge ist die Idylle dieses Fleckchens zerstört worden; **the new buildings ~ the landscape** die Neubauten verunstalten *or* verschandeln die Landschaft.

(c) *(rape)* vergewaltigen, schänden.

violation [ˌvaɪə'leɪʃən] *n* **(a)** *(of law)* Übertretung *(of gen)*, Verletzung *f (of gen)*, Verstoß *m (of gegen)*; *(of rule)* Verstoß *m (of gegen)*; *(of rights)* Verletzung *f*; *(of truth)* Vergewaltigung *f* ◆ **a ~ of a treaty** ein Vertragsbruch *m*; *(partial)* eine Vertragsverletzung; **traffic ~** Verkehrsvergehen *nt*; **he did this in ~ of the conditions agreed** er verstieß damit gegen die Vereinbarungen.

(b) *(of holy place)* Entweihung, Schändung *f*; *(of peacefulness)* Störung *f*; *(of privacy)* Eingriff *m (of in +acc)* ◆ **that building is a ~ of the old city** dieses Gebäude ist eine Verunstaltung *or* Verschandelung der Altstadt.

(c) *(rape)* Vergewaltigung, Schändung *f*.

violator ['vaɪəleɪtəʳ] *n (of treaty)* Vertragsbrüchige(r) *mf*; *(of laws)* Gesetzesübertreter *m*; *(of holy place)* Schänder, Entehrer *m*; *(of woman)* Schänder *m* ◆ **the ~ of these rules ...** wer gegen diese Regeln verstößt, ...

violence ['vaɪələns] *n* **(a)** *(forcefulness, strength)* Heftigkeit *f*; *(of protest also)* Schärfe *f*; *(of speech also)* Leidenschaftlichkeit *f* ◆ **the ~ of the contrast** der krasse Gegensatz; **the ~ of his temper** sein jähzorniges Temperament, seine Jähzornigkeit.

(b) *(brutality)* Gewalt *f*; *(of people)* Gewalttätigkeit *f*; *(of actions)* Brutalität *f* ◆ **the ~ of his nature** seine gewalttätige Art; **crime of ~** Gewaltverbrechen *nt*; **act of ~** Gewalttat *f*; **robbery with ~** Raubüberfall *m*; **an increase in ~** eine Zunahme der Gewalttätigkeit; **to use ~ against sb** Gewalt gegen jdn anwenden; **was there any ~?** kam es zu Gewalttätigkeiten?; **outbreak of ~** Ausbruch von Gewalttätigkeiten.

(c) *(fig)* **to do ~ to sth** etw entstellen; **it does ~ to common sense** das vergewaltigt den gesunden Menschenverstand.

violent ['vaɪələnt] *adj person, nature, action* brutal, gewalttätig; *blush* heftig, tief; *wind, storm* heftig, stark, gewaltig; *feeling, affair, speech* leidenschaftlich; *dislike, attack, blow* heftig; *death* gewaltsam; *(severe) contrast* kraß; *pain* heftig, stark; *colour* grell ◆ **to have a ~ temper** jähzornig sein; **to be in a ~ temper** toben; **the beginning of the second movement is rather ~** der zweite Satz beginnt sehr leidenschaftlich; **don't be so ~, open it gently** sei nicht so stürmisch, öffne es vorsichtig; **to get ~** gewalttätig werden; **by ~ means** *(open sth)* mit Gewalt(anwendung); *(persuade)* unter Gewaltanwendung.

violently ['vaɪələntlɪ] *adv kick, beat, attack* brutal; *blush* tief, heftig; *speak* heftig, leidenschaftlich; *fall in love* unsterblich ◆ **the two colours clash ~** die beiden Farben bilden einen krassen Gegensatz; **they have quite ~ opposed temperaments** sie haben völlig unvereinbare Temperamente; **he expresses himself rather ~** er drückt sich sehr kraß aus.

violet ['vaɪəlɪt] 1 *n (Bot)* Veilchen *nt*; *(colour)* Violett *nt*.

2 *adj* violett.

violin [ˌvaɪə'lɪn] *n* Geige, Violine *f*; *(player)* Geiger(in *f*), Geigenspieler(in *f*) *m* ◆ **~ case** Geigenkasten *m*; **~ concerto** Violinkonzert *nt*; **~ sonata** Violinsonate *f*.

violinist [ˌvaɪə'lɪnɪst] *n* Geiger(in *f*), Violinist(in *f*) *m*.

violoncello [ˌvaɪələn'tʃeləʊ] *n (form)* Violoncello *nt*.

VIP *n* prominente Persönlichkeit, VIP *m* ◆ **he got/we gave him ~ treatment** er wurde/wir haben ihn als Ehrengast behandelt; **~ lounge** Prominentensuite *f*.

viper ['vaɪpəʳ] *n (Zool)* Viper *f*; *(fig)* Schlange *f*.

viperish ['vaɪpərɪʃ] *adj (fig)* giftig.

virago [vɪ'rɑːgəʊ] *n* Xanthippe *f*.

viral ['vaɪərəl] *adj* Virus-.

Virgil ['vɜːdʒɪl] *n* Vergil(ius), Virgil *m*.

virgin ['vɜːdʒɪn] 1 *n* Jungfrau *f* ◆ **the (Blessed) V~** *(Rel)* die (heilige) Jungfrau Maria; **he's still a ~** er ist noch unschuldig.

2 *adj daughter* jungfräulich, unberührt; *(fig) forest, land* unberührt; *freshness* rein; *snow* jungfräulich, unberührt ◆ **~ birth** unbefleckte Empfängnis; *(Biol)* Jungfernzeugung *f*; **the V~ Isles** die Jungferninseln *pl*.

virginal ['vɜːdʒɪnl] 1 *adj* jungfräulich.

2 *npl (Mus)* Tafelklavier *nt*.

Virginia [və'dʒɪnjə] *n (state)* Virginia *nt*; *(tobacco)* Virginia *m* ◆ **~ creeper** wilder Wein, Jungfernrebe *f*; **~ tobacco** Virginiatabak *m*; **he smokes ~s** er raucht Virginiazigaretten.

Virginian [və'dʒɪnjən] 1 *n* Einwohner(in *f*) *m* von Virginia, Virginier(in *f*) *m*.

2 *adj* Virginia-.

virginity [vɜː'dʒɪnɪtɪ] *n* Unschuld *f*; *(of girls also)* Jungfräulichkeit *f* ◆ **to take sb's ~** jds Unschuld rauben.

Virgo ['vɜːgəʊ] *(Astrol)* 1 *n* Jungfrau *f*.

2 *adj* **~ characteristics** Eigenschaften der Jungfrau(menschen).

virgule ['vɜːgjuːl] *n (US Typ: oblique)* Schrägstrich *m*, Virgel *f (spec)*.

virile ['vɪraɪl] *adj (lit)* männlich; *(fig)* ausdrucksvoll, kraftvoll.

virility [vɪ'rɪlɪtɪ] *n (lit)* Männlichkeit *f*; *(sexual power)* Potenz *f*; *(fig)* Ausdruckskraft *f* ◆ **political ~** politische Potenz.

virologist [ˌvaɪə'rɒlədʒɪst] *n* Virologe *m*, Virologin *f*, Virusforscher(in *f*) *m*.

virology [ˌvaɪə'rɒlədʒɪ] *n* Virologie, Virusforschung *f*.

virtual ['vɜːtjʊəl] *adj attr* **(a) he is the ~ leader** er ist quasi der Führer *or* der eigentliche Führer, praktisch ist er der Führer; **it was a ~ admission of guilt** es war so gut wie *or* praktisch ein Schuldgeständnis *nt*; **it was a ~ disaster** es war geradezu eine Katastrophe; **it was a ~ failure** es war praktisch ein Mißerfolg *m*; **~ address** *(Comput)* virtuelle Adresse; **~ reality** virtuelle Realität.

(b) *(Phys)* virtuell.

virtuality [ˌvɜːtʃʊ'ælɪtɪ] *n* Virtualität *f*.

virtually ['vɜːtjʊəlɪ] *adv* praktisch; *blind, lost also* fast, nahezu, mehr oder weniger ◆ **yes, ~** ja, fast, ja so gut wie; **he is ~ the boss** er ist praktisch *or* quasi der Chef; **to be ~ certain** sich *(dat)* so gut wie sicher sein.

virtue ['vɜːtjuː] *n* **(a)** *(moral quality)* Tugend *f* ◆ **to make a ~ of necessity** aus

der Not eine Tugend machen; **a life of ~** ein tugendhaftes Leben.
(b) (*chastity*) Keuschheit, Tugendhaftigkeit *f* ♦ **a woman of easy ~** (*euph*) ein leichtes Mädchen.
(c) (*advantage, point*) Vorteil *m* ♦ **what's the ~ of that?** welchen Vorteil hat das, wozu ist das gut?; **there is no ~ in doing that** es scheint nicht sehr zweckmäßig, das zu tun.
(d) (*healing power*) Heilkraft *f* ♦ **in** *or* **by ~ of** aufgrund (+*gen*); **in** *or* **by ~ of the authority/power** *etc* **vested in me** kraft meiner Autorität/Macht *etc* (*form*).

virtuosity [ˌvɜːtjʊˈɒsɪtɪ] *n* Virtuosität *f*.

virtuoso [ˌvɜːtjʊˈəʊzəʊ] 1 *n* (*esp Mus*) Virtuose *m*.
2 *adj performance* meisterhaft, virtuos.

virtuous *adj* [ˈvɜːtjʊəs] tugendhaft, tugendsam.

virtuous circle *n* positiver Kreislauf *m*, Circulus virtuosus *m*.

virtuously *adv* tugendhaft, tugendsam.

virulence [ˈvɪrʊləns] *n* **(a)** (*Med*) Heftigkeit, Bösartigkeit *f*; (*of poison*) Stärke *f*. **(b)** (*fig*) Schärfe, Virulenz (*geh*) *f*.

virulent [ˈvɪrʊlənt] *adj* **(a)** (*Med*) bösartig; *poison* stark, tödlich. **(b)** (*fig*) geharnischt, scharf, virulent (*geh*).

virulently [ˈvɪrʊləntlɪ] *adv* (*fig*) scharf.

virus [ˈvaɪərəs] *n* **(a)** (*Med*) Virus, Erreger *m* ♦ **polio ~** Polioerreger *m*; **~ disease** Viruskrankheit *f*; **she's got** *or* **caught a ~** (*inf: flu etc*) sie hat sich (*dat*) was geholt *or* eingefangen (*inf*). **(b)** (*fig*) Geschwür *nt*. **(c)** (*Comput*) Virus *m* ♦ **~-infected** virenbefallen.

visa [ˈviːzə], (*US*) **visé** 1 *n* Visum *nt*; (*stamp also*) Sichtvermerk *m* ♦ **entrance/exit ~** Einreise-/Ausreisevisum *nt*.
2 *vt* ein Visum ausstellen (+*dat*) ♦ **to get a passport ~ed** einen Sichtvermerk in den Paß bekommen.

visage [ˈvɪzɪdʒ] *n* (*liter*) Antlitz *nt* (*liter*).

vis-à-vis [ˈviːzəviː] 1 *prep* in Anbetracht (+*gen*).
2 *adv* gegenüber.

viscera [ˈvɪsərə] *npl* innere Organe *pl*; (*in abdomen*) Eingeweide *pl*.

visceral [ˈvɪsərəl] *adj* viszeral (*spec*); (*of intestines also*) Eingeweide- ♦ **a ~ feeling** (*fig liter*) ein inneres Gefühl.

viscid [ˈvɪsɪd] *adj* (*form*) zähflüssig; (*Bot*) klebrig.

viscose [ˈvɪskəʊs] *n* Viskose *f*.

viscosity [vɪsˈkɒsɪtɪ] *n* Zähflüssigkeit *f*; (*Phys*) Viskosität *f*.

viscount [ˈvaɪkaʊnt] *n* Viscount *m*.

viscountcy [ˈvaɪkaʊntsɪ], **viscounty** *n* Rang *m* des Viscounts.

viscountess [ˈvaɪkaʊntɪs] *n* Viscountess *f*.

viscounty [ˈvaɪkaʊntɪ] *n see* **viscountcy**.

viscous [ˈvɪskəs] *adj* (*form*) zähflüssig; (*Phys*) viskos.

vise [vaɪs] *n* (*US*) *see* **vice**[2].

visé [ˈviːzeɪ] (*US*) *see* **visa**.

visibility [ˌvɪzɪˈbɪlɪtɪ] *n* **(a)** Sichtbarkeit *f*. **(b)** (*Met*) Sichtweite *f* ♦ **poor/good ~** schlechte/gute Sicht; **low ~** geringe Sichtweite; **~ is down to 100 metres** die Sichtweite beträgt nur 100 Meter.

visible [ˈvɪzəbl] *adj* **(a)** sichtbar ♦ **~ to the naked eye** mit dem bloßen Auge zu erkennen; **it wasn't ~ in the fog** es war im Nebel nicht zu erkennen; **the Englishman prefers his emotions not to be ~** der Engländer zeigt nicht gern seine Gefühle.
(b) (*obvious*) sichtlich ♦ **with no ~ means of support** (*Jur*) ohne bekannte Einkommensquellen *pl*.

visibly [ˈvɪzəblɪ] *adv* sichtbar, sichtlich; *deteriorate, decay* zusehends.

Visigoth [ˈvɪzɪgɒθ] *n* Westgote *m*.

vision [ˈvɪʒən] *n* **(a)** (*power of sight*) Sehvermögen *nt* ♦ **within/outside the range of ~** in/außer Sichtweite; *see* **field**.
(b) (*foresight*) Weitblick *m* ♦ **a man of ~** ein Mann mit Weitblick.
(c) (*in dream, trance*) Vision *f*, Gesicht *nt* (*liter*) ♦ **it came to me in a ~** ich hatte eine Vision.
(d) (*image*) Vorstellung *f* ♦ **Orwell's ~ of the future** Orwells Zukunftsvision *f*.
(e) to have ~s of wealth von Reichtum träumen, sich (*dat*) Reichtum vorgaukeln; **I had ~s of having to walk all the way home** (*inf*) ich sah mich im Geiste schon den ganzen Weg nach Hause laufen.

visionary [ˈvɪʒənərɪ] 1 *adj* (*impractical*) unrealistisch; (*of visions*) vorhersehend, visionär (*geh*); (*unreal*) eingebildet.
2 *n* Visionär, Seher (*geh*) *m*; (*pej*) Phantast *m*.

vision mixer *n* (*TV*) (*person*) Bildmischer(in *f*) *m*; (*equipment*) Bildmischpult *nt*.

visit [ˈvɪzɪt] 1 *n* **(a)** Besuch *m*; (*of doctor*) Hausbesuch *m*; (*of inspector*) Kontrolle *f* ♦ **to pay sb/sth a ~** jdm/einer Sache einen Besuch abstatten (*form*), jdn/etw besuchen; **to pay a ~** (*euph*) mal verschwinden (müssen); **to have a ~ from sb** von jdm besucht werden; **give us a ~ some time** besuchen Sie uns (doch) mal; **he went on a two-day ~ to Paris** er fuhr für zwei Tage nach Paris; **I'm going on a ~ to Glasgow next week** ich fahre nächste Woche (zu einem Besuch) nach Glasgow; **we're expecting a ~ from the police any day** wir rechnen jeden Tag mit dem Besuch der Polizei.
(b) (*stay*) Aufenthalt, Besuch *m* ♦ **to be on a ~ to London** zu einem Besuch in London sein; **to be on a private/official ~** inoffiziell/offiziell da sein.
2 *vt* **(a)** *person, the sick, museum* besuchen ♦ **you never ~ us these days** Sie kommen uns ja gar nicht mehr besuchen.
(b) (*go and stay with*) besuchen, aufsuchen (*geh*).
(c) (*inspect*) inspizieren, besichtigen, besuchen ♦ **to ~ the scene of the crime** (*Jur*) den Tatort besichtigen.
(d) (*Bibl*) *sins* heimsuchen (*upon* an +*dat*, über +*acc*).
3 *vi* **(a)** einen Besuch machen ♦ **come and ~ some time** komm mich mal besuchen; **I'm only ~ing here** ich bin nur auf Besuch hier. **(b)** (*US inf: chat*) schwatzen, ein Schwätzchen halten.

♦**visit with** *vi +prep obj* (*US*) schwatzen mit.

visitation [ˌvɪzɪˈteɪʃən] *n* **(a)** (*form: visit*) (*by official*) Besichtigung *f*, Besuch *m*; (*by ghost*) Erscheinung *f* ♦ **after another ~ from the mother-in-law** (*hum*) nachdem uns die Schwiegermutter wieder einmal heimgesucht hatte.
(b) (*Rel*) **the V~** Mariä Heimsuchung *f*.
(c) (*Rel: affliction*) Heimsuchung *f* ♦ **a ~ for their sins** die Strafe für ihre Sünden; **the ~ of the sins of the fathers on succeeding generations** die Bestrafung der folgenden Generationen für die Sünden ihrer Väter.

visiting [ˈvɪzɪtɪŋ] *n* Besuche *pl*.

visiting: ~ card *n* (*Brit*) Visitenkarte *f*; **~ hours** *npl* Besuchszeiten *pl*; **~ professor** *n* Gastprofessor *m*; **~ team** *n* **the ~ team** die Gäste *pl*; **~ terms** *npl*: **I'm not on ~ terms with him** ich kenne ihn nicht so gut, daß ich ihn besuchen gehen würde.

visitor [ˈvɪzɪtə^r] *n* Besucher(in *f*) *m*; (*in hotel*) Gast *m* ♦ **to have ~s** *or* **a ~** Besuch haben; **the great tit is a rare ~ in these parts** die Kohlmeise hält sich selten in diesen Breiten auf; **~s' book** Gästebuch *nt*.

visor [ˈvaɪzə^r] *n* (*on helmet*) Visier *nt*; (*on cap*) Schirm *m*; (*Aut*) Blende *f* ♦ **sun ~** Schild, Schirm *m*; (*Aut*) Sonnenblende *f*.

vista [ˈvɪstə] *n* **(a)** (*view*) Aussicht *f*, Blick *m*. **(b)** (*of past*) Bild *nt*; (*of future*) Aussicht (*of* auf +*acc*), Perspektive (*of* von) *f*.

visual [ˈvɪzjʊəl] 1 *adj field, nerve* Seh-; *memory, impression* visuell ♦ **~ aids** Anschauungsmaterial *nt*; **~ display unit** Sichtgerät *nt*.
2 *n* (grafischer) Entwurf.

visualize [ˈvɪzjʊəlaɪz] *vt* **(a)** (*see in mind*) sich (*dat*) vorstellen.
(b) (*foresee*) erwarten ♦ **we do not ~ many changes** wir rechnen nicht mit großen Veränderungen; **he ~s some changes** (*intends*) er hat einige Veränderungen im Auge; **that's not how I'd ~d things** so hatte ich mir das nicht vorgestellt.

visually [ˈvɪzjʊəlɪ] *adv* visuell ♦ **~, the film is good entertainment** von der Aufmachung her ist der Film sehr unterhaltend; **I remember things ~** ich habe ein visuelles Gedächtnis; **~ handicapped** sehbehindert.

vital [ˈvaɪtl] 1 *adj* **(a)** (*of life*) vital, Lebens-; (*necessary for life*) lebenswichtig ♦ **~ force** Lebenskraft *f*; **~ organs** lebenswichtige Organe *pl*; **~ parts** wichtige Teile *pl*; **~ statistics** Bevölkerungsstatistik *f*; (*inf: of woman*) Maße *pl*.
(b) (*essential*) unerläßlich ♦ **of ~ importance** von größter Wichtigkeit; **this is ~** das ist unbedingt notwendig; **your support is ~ to us** wir brauchen unbedingt Ihre Unterstützung; **is it ~ for you to go?** müssen Sie denn unbedingt gehen?; **it's ~ that this is finished by Tuesday** das muß bis Dienstag unbedingt fertig sein; **how ~ is this?** wie wichtig ist das?
(c) (*critical*) *error* schwerwiegend; *problem* Kern- ♦ **at the ~ moment** im kritischen *or* entscheidenden Moment.
(d) (*lively*) *person* vital; *artistic style also* lebendig.
2 *n* **the ~s** die lebenswichtigen Organe; (*hum: genitals*) die edlen Teile (*hum*).

vitality [vaɪˈtælɪtɪ] *n* (*energy*) Energie *f*, Leben *nt*, Vitalität *f*; (*of prose, language*) Lebendigkeit, Vitalität *f*; (*of companies, new state*) Dynamik *f*; (*durability*) Beständigkeit *f*.

vitalize [ˈvaɪtəlaɪz] *vt* beleben.

vitally [ˈvaɪtəlɪ] *adv important* äußerst, ungeheuer ♦ **he writes freshly and ~** er schreibt einen frischen und lebendigen *or* kraftvollen Stil.

vitamin [ˈvɪtəmɪn] *n* Vitamin *nt* ♦ **~ A** Vitamin A; **with added ~s** mit Vitaminen angereichert.

vitamin: ~ deficiency *n* Vitaminmangel *m*; **~-deficiency disease** *n* Vitaminmangelkrankheit *f*; **~ pill** *n* Vitamintablette *f*.

vitiate [ˈvɪʃɪeɪt] *vt* **(a)** (*spoil*) *air, blood* verunreinigen. **(b)** (*Jur etc: invalidate*) ungültig machen; *thesis* widerlegen.

viticulture [ˈvɪtɪkʌltʃə^r] *n* Weinbau *m*.

vitreous [ˈvɪtrɪəs] *adj* Glas- ♦ **~ china** Porzellanemail *nt*; **~ enamel** Glasemail *nt*.

vitrifaction [ˌvɪtrɪˈfækʃən], **vitrification** [ˌvɪtrɪfɪˈkeɪʃən] *n* Verglasung, Frittung *f*.

vitrify [ˈvɪtrɪfaɪ] 1 *vt* zu Glas schmelzen, verglasen.
2 *vi* verglasen.

vitriol [ˈvɪtrɪəl] *n* (*Chem*) (*salt*) Sulfat, Vitriol *nt*; (*acid*) Schwefelsäure *f*; (*fig*) Bissigkeit, Bosheit *f* ♦ **the bitter ~ of his jealousy** die ihn zerfressende Eifersucht.

vitriolic [ˌvɪtrɪˈɒlɪk] *adj* Vitriol-; (*fig*) *remark* beißend, haßerfüllt; *criticism* ätzend, beißend; *attack, speech* haßerfüllt.

vitro [ˈviːtrəʊ] *adj, adv see* **in ~**.

vituperate [vɪˈtjuːpəreɪt] *vi* schmähen (*geh*) (*against acc*), verunglimpfen (*against acc*).

vituperation [vɪˌtjuːpəˈreɪʃən] *n* (*form*) Schmähungen *pl* (*geh*).

vituperative [vɪˈtjuːpərətɪv] *adj* (*form*) *speech* Schmäh-; *language, criticism* schmähend.

viva *n see* **viva voce 2**.

vivacious [vɪˈveɪʃəs] *adj* lebhaft; *character, person also* temperamentvoll; *colour, clothes also* leuchtend bunt; *smile, laugh* munter, aufgeweckt.

vivaciously [vɪˈveɪʃəslɪ] *adv see adj*.

vivaciousness [vɪˈveɪʃəsnɪs] *n* Lebhaftigkeit *f*; (*of smile, laugh*) Munterkeit, Aufgewecktheit *f*.

vivacity [vɪˈvæsɪtɪ] *n* Lebhaftigkeit; (*of style*) Lebendigkeit *f*; (*of smile, laugh*) Munterkeit, Aufgewecktheit *f*.

vivarium [vɪ'vɛərɪəm] *n* Vivarium *nt.*
viva voce ['vaɪvə'vəʊsɪ] [1] *adj, adv* mündlich.
[2] *n* mündliche Prüfung.
vivid ['vɪvɪd] *adj* **(a)** *light* hell; *colour* kräftig, leuchtend, lebhaft ◆ **the ~ feathers of the bird** das bunte *or* auffallende Gefieder des Vogels; **a ~ blue dress** ein leuchtendblaues Kleid; **a ~ tie** eine auffällige Krawatte.
(b) *(lively) imagination, recollection* lebhaft; *description, metaphor, image* lebendig, anschaulich; *emotions* stark ◆ **the memory of that day is still quite ~** der Tag ist mir noch in lebhafter Erinnerung.
vividly ['vɪvɪdlɪ] *adv* **(a)** *coloured* lebhaft; *shine* hell, leuchtend ◆ **the red stands out ~ against its background** das Rot hebt sich stark vom Hintergrund ab; **a ~ coloured bird** ein buntgefiederter *or* auffällig gefiederter Vogel.
(b) *remember* lebhaft; *describe* anschaulich, lebendig.
vividness ['vɪvɪdnɪs] *n* **(a)** *(of colour)* Lebhaftigkeit *f*; *(of light)* Helligkeit *f.* **(b)** *(of style)* Lebendigkeit *f*; *(of description, metaphor, image also)* Anschaulichkeit *f*; *(of imagination, memory)* Lebhaftigkeit *f.*
vivify ['vɪvɪfaɪ] *vt* beleben.
viviparous [vɪ'vɪpərəs] *adj (Zool)* lebendgebärend.
vivisect [ˌvɪvɪ'sekt] *vt* vivisezieren.
vivisection [ˌvɪvɪ'sekʃən] *n* Vivisektion *f.*
vivisectionist [ˌvɪvɪ'sekʃənɪst] *n jd, der Eingriffe am lebenden Tier vornimmt/befürwortet.*
vixen ['vɪksn] *n (Zool)* Füchsin *f*; *(fig)* zänkisches Weib, Drachen *m (inf).*
viz [vɪz] *adv* nämlich.
vizier [vɪ'zɪə^r] *n* Wesir *m.*
V-J Day *n Tag m des Sieges gegen Japan im 2. Weltkrieg.*
VLSI *abbr of* **very large scale integration** Höchst- or Größtintegration, VLSI *f.*
V: ~-neck *n* spitzer *or* V-Ausschnitt *m*; **~-necked** *adj* mit V-Ausschnitt.
vocabulary [vəʊ'kæbjʊlərɪ] *n* Wortschatz *m*, Vokabular *nt (geh)*; *(in textbook)* Wörterverzeichnis *f* ◆ **he has a limited ~** er hat einen beschränkten Wortschatz; **the ~ of the legal profession** das Vokabular der Juristen; **~ book** Vokabelheft *nt*; *(printed)* Vokabelbuch *nt*; **~ test** *(Sch)* Vokabelarbeit *f.*
vocal ['vəʊkəl] [1] *adj* **(a)** Stimm- ◆ **~ cords** Stimmbänder *pl*; **~ music** Vokalmusik *f*; **~ group** Gesangsgruppe *f.*
(b) *communication* mündlich.
(c) *(voicing one's opinions) group, person* lautstark ◆ **to be/become ~** sich zu Wort melden.
[2] *n (of pop song)* (gesungener) Schlager; *(in jazz)* Vocal *nt* ◆ **who's doing the ~s for your group now?** wen habt ihr denn jetzt als Sänger?; **~s: Van Morrison** Gesang: Van Morrison.
vocalic [vəʊ'kælɪk] *adj* vokalisch.
vocalist ['vəʊkəlɪst] *n* Sänger(in *f*) *m.*
vocalize ['vəʊkəlaɪz] *vt* **(a)** *thoughts* aussprechen, Ausdruck verleihen *(+dat).* **(b)** *(Phon) consonant* vokalisieren.
vocally ['vəʊkəlɪ] *adv* mündlich ◆ **the tune has now been done ~ by ...** die Melodie wurde jetzt auch gesungen von ...
vocation [vəʊ'keɪʃən] *n* **(a)** *(Rel etc)* Berufung *f*; *(form: profession)* Beruf *m* ◆ **to have a ~ for teaching** zum Lehrer berufen sein. **(b)** *(aptitude)* Begabung *f*, Talent *nt.*
vocational [vəʊ'keɪʃənl] *adj* Berufs- ◆ **~ guidance** Berufsberatung *f*; **~ school** *(US)* ≃ Berufsschule *f*; **~ training** Berufsausbildung *f.*
vocative ['vɒkətɪv] *n* Anredeform *f*, Vokativ *m* ◆ **~ case** Anredefall, Vokativ *m.*
vociferate [vəʊ'sɪfəreɪt] *vti* schreien ◆ **he ~d his grievances** er machte seinem Unmut Luft.
vociferation [vəʊˌsɪfə'reɪʃən] *n* Geschrei *nt* ◆ **their ~ of their discontent** ihr lautstarker Protest.
vociferous [vəʊ'sɪfərəs] *adj class, audience* laut; *demands, protest* lautstark.
vociferously [vəʊ'sɪfərəslɪ] *adv* lautstark.
vodka ['vɒdkə] *n* Wodka *m.*
vogue [vəʊg] *n* Mode *f* ◆ **the ~ for jeans** die Jeansmode; **to be the ~** *or* **in ~** (in) Mode *or* en vogue sein; **to come into ~** *(dresses)* in Mode kommen, modern werden; *(writers)* populär werden, in Mode kommen; **to go out of ~** *(dresses)* aus der Mode kommen, unmodern werden; *(writers)* aus der Mode kommen; **to have a great ~ with** sehr beliebt sein unter *(+dat)*, große Mode sein unter *(+dat).*
vogue: ~ expression, ~ word *n* Modewort *nt.*
voice [vɔɪs] [1] *n* **(a)** *(faculty of speech, Mus, fig)* Stimme *f* ◆ **to lose one's ~** die Stimme verlieren; **I've lost my ~** ich habe keine Stimme mehr; **she hasn't got much of a ~** sie hat keine besonders gute Stimme; **to be in (good)/poor ~** gut/nicht gut bei Stimme sein; **in a deep ~** mit tiefer Stimme; **to like the sound of one's own ~** sich gern(e) reden hören; **his ~ has broken** er hat den Stimmbruch hinter sich; **tenor/bass ~** Tenor *m*/Baß *m*; **a piece for ~ and piano** ein Gesangsstück *nt* mit Klavierbegleitung; **with one ~** einstimmig; **to give ~ to sth** etw aussprechen, einer Sache *(dat)* Ausdruck verleihen.
(b) *(fig: say)* **we have a/no ~ in the matter** wir haben in dieser Angelegenheit ein/kein Mitspracherecht.
(c) *(Gram)* Aktionsart *f*, Genus (verbi) *nt* ◆ **the active/passive ~** das Aktiv/Passiv.
(d) *(Phon)* Stimmhaftigkeit *f* ◆ **plus ~** stimmhaft.
[2] *vt* **(a)** *(express) feelings, opinion* zum Ausdruck bringen. **(b)** *(Phon)* stimmhaft aussprechen ◆ **~d** stimmhaft.
voice box *n* Kehlkopf *m.*
-voiced [-vɔɪst] *adj suf* mit ... Stimme.
voice: ~less *adj* **(a)** stumm; **(b)** *(having no say)* ohne Mitspracherecht *nt*; **(c)** *(Phon) consonant* stimmlos; **~ mail** *n* Voice-Mail *f*; **~-operated** *adj* sprachgesteuert; **~-over** *n* Filmkommentar *m*; **~ part** *n* **the ~ parts** *(Mus)* die Singstimmen *pl*; **~ production** *n* Stimmbildung *f*; **~ projection** *n* Stimmresonanz *f*; **~ range** *n* Stimmumfang *m*; **~ recognition** *n* Spracherkennung *f.*
void [vɔɪd] [1] *n (lit, fig)* Leere *f* ◆ **the dead astronaut floated off into the ~** der tote Astronaut schwebte in das All.
[2] *adj* **(a)** *(empty)* leer ◆ **~ of any sense of decency** bar jeglichen Gefühls *(geh) or* ohne jegliches Gefühl für Anstand; **~ of hope** hoffnungslos, ohne Hoffnung.
(b) *(Jur)* ungültig, nichtig.
(c) *(useless)* nichtig *(geh)* ◆ **you've made all my efforts totally ~** du hast all meine Bemühungen völlig zunichte gemacht.
[3] *vt* **(a)** *(Jur)* ungültig machen, aufheben.
(b) *(form: empty) bowels* entleeren.
voile [vɔɪl] *n* Voile, Schleierstoff *m.*
vol *abbr of* **volume** Bd; *(Measure)* **volume** V(ol).
volatile ['vɒlətaɪl] *adj* **(a)** *(Chem)* flüchtig ◆ **~ oils** ätherische Öle *pl.* **(b)** *person (in moods)* impulsiv; *(in interests)* sprunghaft; *political situation* brisant; *(St Ex)* unbeständig. **(c)** *(Comput)* **~ memory** flüchtiger Speicher.
volatility [ˌvɒlə'tɪlɪtɪ] *n see adj* **(a)** Flüchtigkeit *f.* **(b)** Impulsivität *f*; Sprunghaftigkeit *f*; Brisanz *f.*
volatilize [vɒ'lætəlaɪz] [1] *vt* verflüchtigen.
[2] *vi* sich verflüchtigen.
vol-au-vent ['vɒləʊvɑ̃:] *n* (Königin)pastetchen *nt.*
volcanic [vɒl'kænɪk] *adj (lit) dust* vulkanisch; *region, eruption* Vulkan-; *(fig)* heftig.
volcano [vɒl'keɪnəʊ] *n* Vulkan *m.*
vole [vəʊl] *n* Wühlmaus *f*; *(common ~)* Feldmaus *f.*
Volga ['vɒlgə] *n* Wolga *f.*
volition [vɒ'lɪʃən] *n* Wille *m* ◆ **power of ~** Willenskraft, Willensstärke *f*; **simply by the exercise of your ~** mit dem Willen allein; **of one's own ~** aus freiem Willen.
volitional [və'lɪʃənl] *adj* Willens-, willentlich.
volley ['vɒlɪ] [1] *n* **(a)** *(of shots)* Salve *f*; *(of arrows, stones)* Hagel *m*; *(fig: of insults)* Flut *f*, Hagel *m*; *(of applause)* Sturm *m.*
(b) *(Tennis)* Volley, Flugball *m.*
[2] *vt* **to ~ a ball** *(Tennis)* einen Ball im Volley spielen, einen Volley spielen *or* schlagen.
[3] *vi* **(a)** *(Mil)* eine Salve abfeuern; *(guns, shots)* (in einer Salve) abgefeuert werden. **(b)** *(Tennis)* einen Volley schlagen.
volleyball ['vɒlɪˌbɔ:l] *n* Volleyball *m.*
volleyer ['vɒlɪə^r] *n* **he's a superb ~ of the ball** er schlägt tolle Volleys.
Vols *abbr of* **Volumes** Bde.
volt [vəʊlt] *n* Volt *nt* ◆ **~meter** Voltmeter *nt.*
voltage ['vəʊltɪdʒ] *n* Spannung *f* ◆ **what ~ is this cable?** wieviel Volt hat dieses Kabel?
voltaic [vɒl'teɪɪk] *adj* voltaisch, galvanisch ◆ **~ cell** galvanisches Element.
volte-face ['vɒlt'fɑ:s] *n (fig)* Kehrtwendung *f* ◆ **to do a ~** sich um 180 Grad drehen.
volubility [ˌvɒljʊ'bɪlɪtɪ] *n* Redseligkeit *f.*
voluble ['vɒljʊbl] *adj speaker* redegewandt, redselig *(pej)*; *protest* wortreich.
volubly ['vɒljʊblɪ] *adv* wortreich ◆ **to speak ~** sehr redselig sein.
volume ['vɒlju:m] [1] *n* **(a)** Band *m* ◆ **in six ~s** in sechs Bänden; **a six-~ dictionary** ein sechsbändiges Wörterbuch; **to write ~s** ganze Bände *pl* schreiben; **that speaks ~s** *(fig)* das spricht Bände *(for* für); **it speaks ~s for him** das spricht sehr für ihn.
(b) *(space occupied by sth)* Volumen *nt*, Rauminhalt *m.*
(c) *(size, amount)* Umfang *m*, Ausmaß *nt (of* an *+dat)* ◆ **a large ~ of sales/business** ein großer Umsatz; **the ~ of traffic** das Verkehrsaufkommen; **trade has increased in ~** das Handelsvolumen hat sich vergrößert.
(d) *(large amount)* **~s of smoke** Rauchschwaden *pl*; **~s of white silk** Massen *pl* von weißer Seide; **we've ~s of work to get through** wir haben noch Berge von Arbeit.
(e) *(sound)* Lautstärke *f* ◆ **is the ~ right up?** ist das volle Lautstärke?; **turn the ~ up/down** *(Rad, TV)* stell (das Gerät) lauter/leiser; **~ control** *(Rad, TV)* Lautstärkeregler *m.*
[2] *attr* **~ discount** Mengenrabatt *m*; **~ sales** Mengenabsatz *m.*
volumetric [ˌvɒljʊ'metrɪk] *adj* volumetrisch.
voluminous [və'lu:mɪnəs] *adj* voluminös *(geh)*; *figure also* üppig; *writings* umfangreich; *dress* wallend.
voluntarily ['vɒləntərɪlɪ] *adv* freiwillig, von sich aus.
voluntary ['vɒləntərɪ] [1] *adj* **(a)** *confession* freiwillig ◆ **to go into ~ liquidation** in die freiwillige Liquidation gehen.
(b) *(unpaid) help, service, work* freiwillig ◆ **~ worker** freiwilliger Helfer, freiwillige Helferin; *(overseas)* Entwicklungshelfer(in *f*) *m.*
(c) *(supported by charity)* **a ~ organization for social work** ein freiwilliger Wohlfahrtsverband.
(d) *(having will) movements* willkürlich, willentlich; *crime* vorsätzlich ◆ **man is a ~ agent** der Mensch handelt aus freiem Willen.
(e) *(Physiol)* **~ muscles** willkürliche Muskeln *pl.*
[2] *n (Eccl, Mus)* Solo *nt.*
volunteer [ˌvɒlən'tɪə^r] [1] *n (also Mil)* Freiwillige(r) *mf* ◆ **~ army** Freiwilligenheer *nt*; **any ~s?** wer meldet sich freiwillig?

[2] *vt help, services* anbieten; *suggestion* machen; *information* geben, herausrücken mit (*inf*) ◆ **we didn't ask you to ~ any advice** wir haben Sie nicht um Rat gebeten; **he ~ed his brother** (*hum*) er hat seinen Bruder (als Freiwilligen) gemeldet.
[3] *vi* **(a)** etw freiwillig tun ◆ **to ~ for sth** sich freiwillig für etw zur Verfügung stellen; **to ~ to do sth** sich anbieten, etw zu tun; **who will ~ to clean the windows?** wer meldet sich freiwillig zum Fensterputzen?
(b) (*Mil*) sich freiwillig melden (*for* zu, *for places* nach).
voluptuary [və'lʌptjʊərɪ] *n* Lüstling *m*.
voluptuous [və'lʌptjʊəs] *adj mouth, woman, movement* sinnlich; *curves* üppig; *body* verlockend; *life* ausschweifend; *kiss* hingebungsvoll.
voluptuously [və'lʌptjʊəslɪ] *adv move* aufreizend, sinnlich; *kiss* hingebungsvoll; *live* ausschweifend.
voluptuousness [və'lʌptjʊəsnɪs] *n see adj* Sinnlichkeit *f*; Üppigkeit *f*; verlockende Formen *pl*; Hingabe *f* ◆ **the ~ of his life** sein ausschweifendes Leben, sein Leben der Wollust.
volute [və'lu:t] *n* (*Archit*) Volute *f*.
voluted [və'lu:tɪd] *adj* (*Archit*) mit Voluten (versehen).
vomit ['vɒmɪt] [1] *n* Erbrochene(s) *nt*; (*act*) Erbrechen *nt* ◆ **have a good ~** erbrechen Sie sich ruhig.
[2] *vt* (*lit, fig*) spucken, speien (*geh*); *food* erbrechen.
[3] *vi* sich erbrechen, sich übergeben.
◆**vomit out** [1] *vt sep* (*lit*) erbrechen; (*fig*) *smoke, flames* speien.
[2] *vi* (*fig*) **the flames were still ~ing ~ of the volcano** der Vulkan spie immer noch Feuer.
◆**vomit up** *vt sep food* (wieder) erbrechen.
voodoo ['vu:du:] *n* Voodoo, Wodu *m*.
voodooism ['vu:du:ɪzəm] *n* Voodoo- *or* Wodukult *m*.
voracious [və'reɪʃəs] *adj person* gefräßig ◆ **she is a ~ reader** sie verschlingt die Bücher geradezu; **to have a ~ appetite** einen Riesenappetit haben.
voraciously [və'reɪʃəslɪ] *adv eat* gierig ◆ **to read ~** die Bücher nur so verschlingen.
voracity [vɒ'ræsɪtɪ] *n* Gefräßigkeit *f*; (*fig*) Gier *f* (*for* nach).
vortex ['vɔ:teks] *n, pl* **-es** *or* **vortices** ['vɔ:tɪsi:z] (*lit*) Wirbel, Strudel (*also fig*) *m*.
votary ['vəʊtərɪ] *n* (*Rel*) Geweihte(r) *mf*; (*fig*) Jünger *m*.
vote [vəʊt] [1] *n* **(a)** (*expression of opinion*) Stimme *f*; (*act of voting*) Abstimmung, Wahl *f*; (*result*) Abstimmungs- *or* Wahlergebnis *nt* ◆ **to put sth to the ~** über etw (*acc*) abstimmen lassen; **to take a ~ on sth** über etw (*acc*) abstimmen; **elected by the ~ of the people** vom Volk gewählt; **the ~ for/against the change surprised him** daß für/gegen den Wechsel gestimmt wurde, erstaunte ihn; **the ~ was 150 to 95** das Abstimmungsergebnis war 150 zu 95; **we would like to offer a ~ of thanks to Mr Smith** wir möchten Herrn Smith unseren aufrichtigen Dank aussprechen; *see* **censure, confidence**.
(b) (*~ cast*) Stimme *f* ◆ **to give one's ~ to a party/person** einer Partei/jdm seine Stimme geben; **single-~ majority** Mehrheit *f* von einer Stimme; **a photo of the Prime Minister casting his ~** ein Foto des Premierministers bei der Stimmabgabe; **what's your ~?** (*in panel game, competition*) wie lautet Ihr Urteil?; **he won by 22 ~s** er gewann mit einer Mehrheit von 22 Stimmen; **10% of the voters invalidated their ~s** 10% der Wähler machten ihren Stimmzettel ungültig.
(c) (*Pol: collective*) **the Labour ~** die Labourstimmen *pl*; **the Labour ~ has increased** der Stimmenanteil von Labour hat sich erhöht.
(d) (*franchise*) Wahlrecht *nt* ◆ **~s for women!** Wahlrecht für die Frauen!
(e) (*money allotted*) Bewilligung *f*.
[2] *vt* **(a)** (*elect*) wählen ◆ **he was ~d chairman** er wurde zum Vorsitzenden gewählt; **to ~ Labour** Labour wählen.
(b) (*inf: judge*) wählen zu ◆ **the group ~d her the best cook** die Gruppe wählte sie zur besten Köchin; **the panel ~d the record a miss** die Jury erklärte die Platte für einen Mißerfolg; **I ~ we go back** ich schlage vor, daß wir umkehren.
(c) (*approve*) bewilligen.
[3] *vi* (*cast one's ~*) wählen ◆ **to ~ for/against** für/gegen stimmen; **to ~ with one's feet** abwandern.
◆**vote down** *vt sep proposal* niederstimmen.
◆**vote in** *vt sep law* beschließen; *person* wählen.
◆**vote on** *vi +prep obj* abstimmen über (*+acc*).
◆**vote out** *vt sep* abwählen; *amendment* ablehnen.
voter ['vəʊtə^r^] *n* Wähler(in *f*) *m*.
voting ['vəʊtɪŋ] *n* Wahl *f* ◆ **which way is the ~ going?** welchen Verlauf nimmt die Wahl?; **a system of ~** ein Wahlsystem *nt*; **to analyze the ~** das Wahlergebnis analysieren; **~ was high this year** die Wahlbeteiligung war dieses Jahr hoch.
voting: ~ booth *n* Wahlkabine *f*; **~ machine** *n* (*US*) Wahlmaschine *f*; **~ paper** *n* Stimmzettel *m*; **~ right** *n* Stimmrecht *nt*.
votive ['vəʊtɪv] *adj* Votiv-.
vouch [vaʊtʃ] *vi* **to ~ for sb/sth** sich für jdn/etw verbürgen; (*legally*) für jdn/etw bürgen; **to ~ for the truth of sth** sich für die Richtigkeit einer Sache verbürgen.
voucher ['vaʊtʃə^r^] *n* **(a)** (*for cash, petrol*) Gutschein *m*; (*for meals also*) Bon *m*; (*cigarette ~*) Coupon *m*; *see* **luncheon ~**. **(b)** (*receipt*) Beleg *m*; (*for debt*) Schuldschein *m*.
vouchsafe [vaʊtʃ'seɪf] *vt* (*form*) gewähren (*sb* jdm) ◆ **to ~ a reply** sich zu einer Antwort herablassen; **to ~ to do sth** die Güte haben *or* geruhen (*geh*), etw zu tun.
vow [vaʊ] [1] *n* Versprechen, Gelöbnis *nt*; (*Rel*) Gelübde *nt* ◆ **lover's ~** Treueschwur *m*; **to make a ~ to do sth** geloben, etw zu tun; **to take one's ~s** sein Gelübde ablegen; **to be under a ~ to do sth** durch ein Versprechen verpflichtet sein, etw zu tun.
[2] *vt obedience* geloben ◆ **to ~ vengeance on sb** jdm Rache schwören; **he is ~ed to silence** er hat Schweigen gelobt.
vowel ['vaʊəl] *n* Vokal, Selbstlaut *m* ◆ **~ system** Vokalismus *m*; **~ sound** Vokal(laut) *m*.
voyage ['vɔɪɪdʒ] [1] *n* **(a)** Reise, Fahrt *f*; (*by sea also*) Seereise *f*; (*Space also*) Flug *m* ◆ **to go on a ~** auf eine Reise *etc* gehen; **to make a ~** eine Reise *etc* machen; **the ~ out** die Hinreise/der Hinflug; **the ~ back** *or* **home** die Rück- *or* Heimreise/der Rückflug. **(b)** (*fig*) **~ of discovery** Entdeckungsreise *f*.
[2] *vi* eine Seereise machen; (*spaceship*) fliegen ◆ **to ~ across an ocean** einen Ozean überqueren.
voyager ['vɔɪədʒə^r^] *n* Passagier *m*; (*Space*) Raumfahrer *m*.
voyeur [vwɑ:'jɜ:^r^] *n* Voyeur *m*.
voyeurism [vwɑ:'jɜ:rɪzəm] *n* Voyeurismus *m*, Voyeurtum *nt*.
voyeuristic [vwɑ:jɜ:'rɪstɪk] *adj* voyeuristisch.
VP *abbr of* **vice-president**.
vs *abbr of* **versus**.
V: ~-shaped *adj* pfeilförmig, V-förmig; **~-sign** *n* (*victory*) Victory-Zeichen *nt*; (*rude*) ≃ Götzgruß *m*; **he gave me the ~-sign** ≃ er zeigte mir den Vogel.
VSO *abbr of* **Voluntary Service Overseas** ≃ Entwicklungsdienst *m*.
VTR *abbr of* **video tape recorder** Videorekorder *m*.
Vulcan ['vʌlkən] *n* Vulcanus *m*.
vulcanite ['vʌlkənaɪt] *n* Hartgummi *m*, Ebonit *nt*.
vulcanization [,vʌlkənaɪ'zeɪʃən] *n* Vulkanisierung *f*.
vulcanize ['vʌlkənaɪz] *vt* vulkanisieren.
vulgar ['vʌlgə^r^] *adj* **(a)** (*pej: unrefined*) ordinär, vulgär; *clothes, joke* ordinär; (*tasteless*) geschmacklos.
(b) (*old: of the common people*) gemein (*old*) ◆ **~ beliefs** volkstümliche Auffassungen *pl*; **~ Latin** Vulgärlatein *nt*; **in the ~ tongue** in der Sprache des Volkes.
(c) (*Math*) **~ fraction** gemeiner Bruch.
vulgarism ['vʌlgərɪzəm] *n* Gassenausdruck *m*, primitiver Ausdruck; (*swearword*) vulgärer Ausdruck.
vulgarity [vʌl'gærɪtɪ] *n* Vulgarität *f*; (*of gesture, joke also*) Anstößigkeit *f*; (*of colour, tie etc*) Geschmacklosigkeit *f* ◆ **the ~ of his behaviour** sein ordinäres *or* pöbelhaftes Benehmen.
vulgarize ['vʌlgəraɪz] *vt* **(a)** (*make coarse*) vulgarisieren. **(b)** (*popularize*) popularisieren, allgemeinverständlich machen.
vulgarly ['vʌlgəlɪ] *adv* **(a)** (*coarsely*) vulgär; *dressed* geschmacklos. **(b)** (*commonly*) allgemein, gemeinhin.
Vulgate ['vʌlgɪt] *n* Vulgata *f*.
vulnerability [,vʌlnərə'bɪlɪtɪ] *n see adj* Verwundbarkeit *f*, Verletzlichkeit *f*, Verletzbarkeit *f*; Ungeschütztheit *f* ◆ **the ~ of the young fish to predators** die Wehrlosigkeit der jungen Fische gegen Raubtiere; **such is their ~ only 2% survive** sie sind so wehrlos, daß nur 2% überleben; **his emotional ~** seine Empfindsamkeit *or* Verletzbarkeit.
vulnerable ['vʌlnərəbl] *adj* **(a)** verwundbar; (*exposed*) verletzlich; (*fig*) verletzbar; *police, troops, fortress* ungeschützt ◆ **the skin is ~ to radiation** die Haut hat keinen Schutz gegen Radioaktivität; **the turtle on its back is completely ~** auf dem Rücken liegend ist die Schildkröte völlig wehrlos; **to be ~ to the cold** kälteanfällig sein; **to be ~ to temptation** für Versuchungen anfällig sein; **to be ~ to criticism** (*exposed*) der Kritik ausgesetzt sein; (*sensitive*) keine Kritik vertragen; **I felt extremely ~ in the discussion** ich kam mir in der Diskussion völlig wehrlos vor; **the one ~ spot in his armour** die einzige ungeschützte Stelle in seiner Rüstung; **a ~ point in our defences** ein schwacher *or* wunder Punkt in unserer Verteidigung; **economically ~** wirtschaftlich wehrlos.
(b) (*Bridge*) in Gefahr ◆ **not ~, non-~** in Nicht-Gefahr.
vulpine ['vʌlpaɪn] *adj* schlau, listig.
vulture ['vʌltʃə^r^] *n* (*lit, fig*) Geier *m*.
vulva ['vʌlvə] *n* (weibliche) Scham, Vulva *f* (*geh*).
vv *abbr of* **verses**.
V wings ['vi:wɪŋz] *npl* pfeilförmige Tragflügel *pl*.
vying ['vaɪɪŋ] *n* (Konkurrenz)kampf *m* (*for* um).

W, w ['dʌblju:] *n* W, w *nt*.
W *abbr of* **west** W.
w *abbr of* **watt(s)** W.
WAAF *abbr of* **Women's Auxiliary Air Force.**
Waaf [wæf] *n* (*Brit*) Mitglied *nt* der weiblichen Luftwaffe.
WAC (*US*) *abbr of* **Women's Army Corps.**
wack [wæk] *n* (*Brit sl: as address*) Kumpel *m* (*inf*).
wacko ['wækəʊ] *adj* (*inf*) durchgedreht (*inf*).
wacky ['wækɪ] *adj* (*+er*) (*inf*) verrückt (*inf*).
wad [wɒd] 1 *n* **(a)** (*compact mass*) Knäuel *m*; (*in gun, cartridge*) Pfropfen *m*; (*of cotton wool etc*) Bausch *m* ◆ **to use sth as a ~** etw zum Ausstopfen *or* als Polster benutzen.
(b) (*of papers, banknotes*) Bündel *nt* ◆ **he's got ~s of money** (*inf*) er hat Geld wie Heu (*inf*).
2 *vt* (*secure, stuff*) stopfen; (*squeeze*) zusammenknüllen; (*Sew*) wattieren ◆ **the glasses must be firmly ~ded down** die Gläser müssen bruchsicher verpackt sein *or* werden.
wadding ['wɒdɪŋ] *n* (*for packing*) Material *nt* zum Ausstopfen; (*Sew*) Wattierung *f*; (*Med: on plaster*) (Mull)tupfer *m*.
waddle ['wɒdl] 1 *n* Watscheln *nt* ◆ **to walk with a ~** einen watschelnden Gang haben.
2 *vi* watscheln.
wade [weɪd] 1 *vt* durchwaten.
2 *vi* waten.
◆**wade in** *vi* **(a)** (*lit*) hineinwaten.
(b) (*fig inf*) (*join in a fight, controversy*) sich einmischen (*inf*); (*tackle problem etc*) sich voll reinstürzen *or* -werfen (*inf*), sich hineinknien (*inf*) ◆ **the new boss ~d ~ with a few staff changes** der neue Chef hat sich gleich mächtig ins Zeug gelegt (*inf*) und ein paar Umbesetzungen vorgenommen.
◆**wade into** *vi +prep obj* (*fig inf: attack*) auf jdn losgehen/etw in Angriff nehmen.
◆**wade through** *vi +prep obj* **(a)** (*lit*) waten durch. **(b)** (*fig*) sich durchkämpfen durch; (*learning sth also*) durchackern.
wader ['weɪdəʳ] *n* **(a)** (*Orn*) Watvogel *m*. **(b) ~s** *pl* (*boots*) Watstiefel *pl*.
wadi ['wɒdɪ] *n* Wadi *nt*.
wafer ['weɪfəʳ] *n* **(a)** (*biscuit*) Waffel *f* ◆ **a vanilla ~** eine Vanilleeiswaffel. **(b)** (*Eccl*) Hostie *f*. **(c)** (*silicon ~*) Wafer *f*.
wafer-thin ['weɪfə'θɪn] *adj* hauchdünn.
waffle¹ ['wɒfl] *n* (*Cook*) Waffel *f* ◆ **~ iron** Waffeleisen *nt*.
waffle² (*Brit inf*) 1 *n* Geschwafel *nt* (*inf*).
2 *vi* (*also* **~ on**) schwafeln (*inf*) ◆ **I managed to ~ on somehow** irgendwie habe ich was (daher)geschwafelt (*inf*).
waffler ['wɒfləʳ] *n* (*Brit inf*) Schwätzer(in *f*) *m*.
waft [wɑ:ft] 1 *n* Hauch *m* ◆ **a ~ of smoke/cool air** eine dünne Rauchschwade/ein kühler Lufthauch.
2 *vt* tragen, wehen.
3 *vi* wehen ◆ **a delicious smell ~ed up from the kitchen** ein köstlicher Geruch zog aus der Küche herauf.
wag¹ [wæg] 1 *n* **he admonished me with a ~ of his finger** tadelnd drohte er mir mit dem Finger; **with a ~ of its tail** mit einem Schwanzwedeln.
2 *vt tail* wedeln mit; (*bird*) wippen mit ◆ **to ~ one's finger at sb** jdm mit dem Finger drohen.
3 *vi* (*tail*) wedeln; (*of bird*) wippen ◆ **her tongue never stops ~ging** (*inf*) ihr Mundwerk steht keine Sekunde still (*inf*); **as soon as he left the tongues started ~ging** sobald er gegangen war, wurde über ihn geredet *or* fing das Gerede an; **to stop the tongues ~ging** um dem Gerede ein Ende zu machen; **that'll set the tongues ~ging** dann geht das Gerede los.
wag² *n* (*wit, clown*) Witzbold *m* (*inf*) ◆ **a bit of a ~** ein alter Witzbold.
wage¹ [weɪdʒ] *n usu pl* Lohn *m*.
wage² *vt war, campaign* führen ◆ **to ~ war against sth** (*fig*) gegen etw einen Feldzug führen.
wage *in cpds* Lohn-; **~-cost inflation** *n* Lohnkosteninflation *f*; **~ demand** *n* Lohnforderung *f*; **~ earner** *n* Lohnempfänger *m*; **~ freeze** *n* Lohnstopp *m*; **~ increase** *n* Lohnerhöhung *f*; **~-intensive** *adj* lohnintensiv; **~ packet** *n* Lohntüte *f*.
wager ['weɪdʒəʳ] 1 *n* Wette *f* (*on* auf *+acc*) ◆ **to lay** *or* **make a ~** eine Wette eingehen *or* abschließen.
2 *vti* wetten (*on* auf *+acc*); *one's honour, life* verpfänden ◆ **I'll ~ you £2 my horse wins** ich wette mit Ihnen um £ 2, daß mein Pferd gewinnt; **he won't do it, I ~!** (*dated*) ich wette, daß er es nicht tut!
wage rates *npl* Lohnsatz, Tarifsatz *m*.
wages ['weɪdʒɪz] *npl* Lohn *m* ◆ **the ~ of sin** die gerechte Strafe, der Sünde Lohn (*old*); **~ bill** Lohnkosten *pl*; **~ clerk** Lohnbuchhalter(in *f*) *m*; **~ slip** Lohnstreifen *m*.
wage: ~ scale *n* Lohnskala *f*; **~ settlement** *n* Lohnabkommen *nt*, Tarifabschluß *m*; **~ slave** *n* (*hum inf*) Lohnsklave *m* (*hum inf*), Lohnsklavin *f* (*hum inf*); **~ worker** *n* (*US*) Lohnempfänger *m*.
waggish ['wægɪʃ] *adj* schalkhaft, schelmisch ◆ **he has a ~ sense of humour** ihm sitzt der Schalk im Nacken.
waggishly ['wægɪʃlɪ] *adv* schalkhaft.
waggle ['wægl] 1 *vt* wackeln mit; *tail* wedeln mit; (*bird*) wippen mit ◆ **he ~d his loose tooth** er wackelte an dem lockeren Zahn.
2 *vi* wackeln; (*tail*) wedeln.
3 *n* **with a ~ of her hips she left the stage** mit den Hüften wackelnd ging sie von der Bühne; **with a ~ of its tail** mit einem Schwanzwedeln.
waggly ['wæglɪ] *adj* (*loose*) wackelig; *hips* wackelnd; *tail* wedelnd.
waggon *n* (*Brit*) *see* **wagon.**
Wagnerian [vɑ:g'nɪərɪən] 1 *n* Wagnerianer *mf*.
2 *adj* Wagner-; (*like Wagner*) wagner(i)sch.
wagon ['wægən] *n* **(a)** (*horse-drawn*) Fuhrwerk *nt*, Wagen *m*; (*covered ~*) Planwagen *m*; (*US: delivery truck*) Lieferwagen *m*; (*child's toy cart*) Leiterwagen *m*; (*tea ~ etc*) Wagen *m*; (*US inf: police car*) Streifenwagen, Peterwagen (*N Ger inf*) *m*; (*US inf: for transporting prisoners*) grüne Minna (*inf*); (*Brit sl: car*) Kutsche *f* (*sl*); (*Brit sl: lorry*) Laster *m* (*inf*).
(b) (*Brit Rail*) Waggon *m*.
(c) (*inf*) **I'm on the ~** ich trinke nichts; **to go on the ~** unter die Abstinenzler gehen (*inf*).
wagoner ['wægənəʳ] *n* Fuhrmann *m*.
wagon: ~load *n* Wagenladung *f*; **books/prisoners arrived by the ~load** ganze Wagenladungen von Büchern/Gefangenen kamen an; **~ train** *n* Zug *m* von Planwagen.
wagtail ['wægteɪl] *n* (*Orn*) Bachstelze *f*.
waif [weɪf] *n* obdachloses *or* heimatloses Kind; (*animal*) herrenloses Tier ◆ **the poor little ~** ... das arme kleine Ding, hat kein Zuhause, ...; **~s and strays** obdachlose *or* heimatlose Kinder *pl*.
wail [weɪl] 1 *n* (*of baby*) Geschrei *nt*; (*of mourner, music*) Klagen *nt*; (*of sirens, wind*) Heulen *nt*; (*inf: complaint*) Gejammer *nt* (*inf*) ◆ **a great ~/a ~ of protest went up** es erhob sich lautes Wehklagen/Protestgeheul.
2 *vi* (*baby, cat*) schreien; (*mourner, music*) klagen; (*siren, wind*) heulen; (*inf: complain*) jammern (*over* über *+acc*).
Wailing Wall ['weɪlɪŋ'wɔ:l] *n* Klagemauer *f*.
wain [weɪn] *n* (*old*) Wagen *m* ◆ **the W~** (*Astron*) der Große Wagen.
wainscot ['weɪnskət] *n, no pl* Täfelung *f*.
wainscot(t)ed ['weɪnzkətɪd] *adj* holzgetäfelt, paneeliert.
wainscot(t)ing ['weɪnzkətɪŋ] *n* Täfelung *f*.
waist [weɪst] *n* Taille *f*; (*of violin*) Mittelbügel *m*; (*Naut*) Mittelteil *m* ◆ **stripped to the ~** mit nacktem *or* entblößtem Oberkörper; **too tight round the ~** zu eng in der Taille.
waist: ~band *n* Rock-/Hosenbund *m*; **~coat** *n* (*Brit*) Weste *f*; **~-deep** *adj* hüfthoch, bis zur Taille reichend; **the water was/corn stood ~-deep** das Wasser/Korn reichte bis zur Taille; **we stood ~-deep in ...** wir standen bis zur Hüfte im ...
waisted ['weɪstɪd] *adj clothes* tailliert.
-waisted [-'weɪstɪd] *adj suf* mit einer ... Taille.
waist: ~-high *adj* hüfthoch, bis zur Taille reichend; **we picnicked in a field of ~-high grass** wir picknickten in einem Feld, wo uns das Gras bis zur Hüfte reichte; **~line** *n* Taille *f*.
wait [weɪt] 1 *vi* **(a)** warten (*for* auf *+acc*) ◆ **to ~ for sb to do sth** darauf warten, daß jd etw tut; **it was definitely worth ~ing for** es hat sich wirklich gelohnt, darauf zu warten; **that'll be worth ~ing for** (*iro*) da bin ich aber gespannt (*inf*); **well, what are you ~ing for?** worauf wartest du denn (noch)?; **~ for it, now he's going to get mad** wart's ab, gleich wird er wild (*inf*); **right, class —**

~ for it — OK now you can go das wär's — Moment mal — so, jetzt könnt ihr gehen (*inf*); **let him ~!, he can ~!** laß ihn warten, soll er warten!, der kann warten!; **can't it ~?** kann das nicht warten?, hat das nicht Zeit?; **this work will have to ~ till later** diese Arbeit muß bis später warten *or* liegenbleiben; **this work is still ~ing to be done** diese Arbeit muß noch gemacht *or* erledigt werden; **~ a minute** *or* **moment** *or* **second** (einen) Augenblick *or* Moment (mal); **(just) you ~!** warte nur ab!; (*threatening*) warte nur!; **Mummy, I can't ~** Mami, ich muß dringend mal!; **I can't ~** ich kann's kaum erwarten; (*out of curiosity*) ich bin gespannt; **I can't ~ to see his face** da bin ich (aber) auf sein Gesicht gespannt; **I can't ~ to try out my new boat** ich kann es kaum noch erwarten, bis ich mein neues Boot ausprobiere; **I can hardly ~** (*usu iro*) ich kann es kaum erwarten!; **"repairs while you ~"** „Sofortreparaturen", „Reparaturschnelldienst"; **~ and see!** warten Sie (es) ab!, abwarten und Tee trinken! (*inf*); **we'll have to ~ and see how ...** wir müssen abwarten, wie ...
(b) to ~ at table servieren; **she used to ~ at the ...** sie bediente früher im ...
[2] *vt* **(a) to ~ one's turn** (ab)warten, bis man an der Reihe ist; **to ~ one's chance/opportunity** auf eine günstige Gelegenheit warten, eine günstige Gelegenheit abwarten; **don't ~ supper for me** warte mit dem Abendessen nicht auf mich.
(b) (*US*) **to ~ table** servieren, bedienen.
[3] *n* **(a)** Wartezeit *f* ◆ **did you have a long ~?** mußten Sie lange warten? **(b) to lie in ~ for sb/sth** jdm/einer Sache auflauern. **(c) ~s** *pl* Sternsinger *pl.*
◆**wait about** *or* **around** *vi* warten (*for* auf +*acc*).
◆**wait behind** *vi* zurückbleiben ◆ **to ~ ~ for sb** zurückbleiben und auf jdn warten.
◆**wait in** *vi* zu Hause bleiben (*for* wegen).
◆**wait on** [1] *vi* (*continue to wait*) noch (weiter) warten.
[2] *vi +prep obj* **(a)** (*also* **~ upon**) (*serve*) bedienen. **(b)** (*US*) **to ~ ~ table** servieren, bei Tisch bedienen. **(c)** (*wait for*) warten auf (+*acc*).
◆**wait out** *vt sep* das Ende (+*gen*) abwarten ◆ **to ~ it ~** abwarten.
◆**wait up** *vi* aufbleiben (*for* wegen, für).
waiter ['weɪtə^r] *n* Kellner, Ober *m* ◆ **~!** (Herr) Ober!
waiting ['weɪtɪŋ] *n* **(a)** Warten *nt* ◆ **all this ~ (around)** dieses ewige Warten, diese ewige Warterei (*inf*); **no ~** Halteverbot *nt.* **(b)** (*royal service*) **those in ~ at the court ...** wer bei Hof dient ... **(c)** (*by waiter etc*) Servieren, Bedienen *nt.*
waiting: ~ game *n* Wartespiel *nt*; **to play a ~ game** ein Wartespiel spielen; **the siege/negotiations developed into a ~ game** die Belagerung entwickelte sich/die Verhandlungen entwickelten sich zu einer Geduldsprobe; **~ list** *n* Warteliste *f*; **~ room** *n* Warteraum *m*; (*at doctor's*) Wartezimmer *nt*; (*in railway station*) Wartesaal *m.*
waitress ['weɪtrɪs] *n* Kellnerin, Serviererin *f* ◆ **~!** Fräulein!
wait state *n* (*Comput*) Wartezyklus *m* ◆ **with zero ~s** ohne Wartezyklen.
waive [weɪv] *vt* **(a)** (*not insist on*) *rights, claim* verzichten auf (+*acc*); *principles, rules, age limit etc* außer acht lassen. **(b)** (*put aside, dismiss*) *question, objection* abtun.
waiver ['weɪvə^r] *n* (*Jur*) Verzicht *m* (*of* auf +*acc*); (*document*) Verzichterklärung *f*; (*of law, contract, clause*) Außerkraftsetzung *f.*
wake[1] [weɪk] *n* (*Naut*) Kielwasser *nt* ◆ **in the ~ of** (*fig*) im Gefolge (+*gen*); **to follow in sb's ~** in jds Kielwasser segeln; **X follows in the ~ of Y** Y bringt X mit sich; **X brings Y in its ~** X bringt Y mit sich; **X leaves Y in its ~** X hinterläßt Y; **with ten children in her ~** (*inf*) mit zehn Kindern im Schlepptau (*inf*).
wake[2] *n* (*esp Ir: over corpse*) Totenwache *f.*
wake[3] *pret* **woke,** *ptp* **woken** *or* **~d** [1] *vt* (auf)wecken; (*fig*) wecken, erwecken (*geh*).
[2] *vi* aufwachen, erwachen (*geh*) ◆ **he woke to find himself in prison** als er aufwachte *or* erwachte, fand er sich im Gefängnis wieder; **he woke to the sound of birds singing** als er aufwachte, sangen die Vögel; **he woke one day to find himself a rich man** als er eines Tages erwachte *or* aufwachte, war er ein reicher Mann; **they woke to their danger too late** (*fig*) sie haben die Gefahr zu spät erkannt.
◆**wake up** [1] *vi* (*lit, fig*) aufwachen ◆ **to ~ ~ to sth** (*fig*) sich (*dat*) einer Sache (*gen*) bewußt werden; **I wish he'd ~ ~ to what's happening** ich wünschte, ihm würde endlich bewußt *or* aufgehen *or* klar, was (hier) vor sich geht; **he woke ~ to a new life** ein neues Leben brach für ihn an.
[2] *vt sep* (*lit*) aufwecken, (*fig: rouse from sloth*) wach- *or* aufrütteln ◆ **to ~ sb ~ to sth** (*fig*) jdm etw klarmachen *or* bewußt machen *or* vor Augen führen; **to ~ one's ideas ~** sich zusammenreißen.
wakeful ['weɪkfʊl] *adj* (*sleepless*) schlaflos; (*alert*) wachsam.
wakefulness ['weɪkfʊlnɪs] *n see adj* Schlaflosigkeit *f*; Wachsamkeit *f.*
waken ['weɪkən] [1] *vt* (auf)wecken.
[2] *vi* (*liter, Scot*) erwachen (*geh*), aufwachen ◆ **he ~ed to see ...** beim Erwachen sah er ...; **he ~ed to another dreary day** ein neuer, trostloser Tag brach für ihn an.
waker ['weɪkə^r] *n* **to be an early ~** früh aufwachen.
wakey wakey [,weɪkɪ'weɪkɪ] *interj* aufwachen!; (*said to sleeping person also*) auf, auf!
waking ['weɪkɪŋ] *adj* **one's ~ hours** von früh bis spät; **thoughts of her filled all his ~ hours** der Gedanke an sie beschäftigte ihn von früh bis spät; **his ~ hours were spent ...** von früh bis spät beschäftigte er sich mit ...
Wales [weɪlz] *n* Wales *nt* ◆ **Prince of ~** Prinz *m* von Wales.
walk [wɔːk] [1] *n* **(a)** (*stroll*) Spaziergang *m*; (*hike*) Wanderung *f*; (*Sport*) Gehen *nt*; (*competition*) Geher-Wettkampf *m*; (*charity ~*) Marsch *m* (*für Wohltätigkeitszwecke*) ◆ **a 20 mile ~ along the roads** ein 20-Meilen-Marsch die Straße entlang; **it's only 10 minutes' ~** es sind nur 10 Minuten zu Fuß *or* zu gehen; **it's a long/short ~ to the shops** *etc* zu den Läden *etc* ist es weit/nicht weit zu Fuß *or* zu gehen *or* zu laufen (*inf*); **it's a long ~ but a short drive** zu Fuß ist es weit, aber mit dem Auto ganz nah; **that's quite a ~** das ist eine ganz schöne Strecke *or* ganz schön weit zu Fuß *or* zu laufen (*inf*); **he thinks nothing of a 10 mile ~** 10 Meilen zu Fuß sind für ihn gar nichts; **to go for** *or* **have** *or* **take a ~** einen Spaziergang machen, spazierengehen; **to take sb/the dog for a ~** mit jdm/dem Hund spazierengehen *or* einen Spaziergang machen, den Hund aus- *or* spazierenführen.
(b) (*gait*) Gang *m*; (*of horse also*) Gangart *f* ◆ **he went at a quick ~** er ging schnellen Schrittes (*geh*) *or* schnell; **the horse went at a ~** das Pferd ging im Schritt; **he slowed his horse to a ~** er brachte sein Pferd in den Schritt; **he ran for a bit, then slowed to a ~** er rannte ein Stück und ging dann normalen Schrittes weiter *or* verfiel dann in ein normales Schrittempo.
(c) (*path in garden etc*) (Park)weg *m*; (*in hills etc*) Weg *m.*
(d) (*route*) Weg *m*; (*signposted etc*) Wander-/Spazierweg *m* ◆ **he knows some good ~s in the Lake District** er kennt ein paar gute Wandermöglichkeiten *or* Wanderungen im Lake District.
(e) ~ of life Milieu *nt*; **people from all ~s of life** Leute aus allen Schichten und Berufen.
(f) (*US: Baseball*) Walk *m*, Freibase *nt.*
[2] *vt* **(a)** (*lead*) *person, horse* (spazieren)führen; *dog* ausführen; (*ride at a ~*) im Schritt gehen lassen ◆ **to ~ sb home/to the bus** jdn nach Hause/zum Bus bringen; **she ~ed her baby up to the table** das Kind lief, von der Mutter gehalten *or* mit Hilfe der Mutter, zum Tisch; **to ~ sb off his feet/legs** jdn total erschöpfen; **if we go hiking, I'll ~ you off your feet** wenn wir zusammen wandern gehen, dann wirst du (bald) nicht mehr mithalten können; **they ~ed me off my feet** ich konnte nicht mehr mitlaufen (*inf*), ich ging auf dem Zahnfleisch (*sl*).
(b) *distance* laufen, gehen ◆ **I've ~ed this road many times** ich bin diese Straße oft gegangen.
(c) to ~ the streets (*prostitute*) auf den Strich gehen (*inf*); (*in search of sth*) durch die Straßen irren; (*aimlessly*) durch die Straßen streichen; **to ~ the boards** (*Theat*) auf den Brettern stehen; **he learned his trade by ~ing the boards before turning to films** er hat sein Handwerk auf den Brettern gelernt, bevor er zum Film ging; **to ~ the plank** *mit verbundenen Augen über eine Schiffsplanke ins Wasser getrieben werden*; **to ~ the wards** (*Med*) famulieren.
(d) (*US: Baseball*) einen Walk *or* ein Freibase geben (+*dat*).
[3] *vi* **(a)** gehen, laufen ◆ **~ a little with me** gehen Sie ein Stück mit mir; **to ~ in one's sleep** schlaf- *or* nachtwandeln.
(b) (*not ride*) zu Fuß gehen, laufen (*inf*); (*stroll*) spazierengehen; (*hike*) wandern ◆ **you can ~ there in 5 minutes** da ist man in *or* bis dahin sind es 5 Minuten zu Fuß; **to ~ home** nach Hause laufen (*inf*), zu Fuß nach Hause gehen; **we were out ~ing when the telegram arrived** wir waren gerade spazieren *or* auf einem Spaziergang, als das Telegramm kam.
(c) (*ghost*) umgehen, spuken.
(d) (*inf: disappear*) Beine bekommen (*inf*).
◆**walk about** *or* **around** [1] *vi* herumlaufen (*inf*) ◆ **to ~ ~ sth** um etw herumlaufen (*inf*) *or* -gehen; (*in room etc*) in etw (*dat*) herumlaufen (*inf*) *or* -gehen.
[2] *vt sep* (*lead*) *person, horse* auf und ab führen; (*ride at a walk*) im Schritt gehen lassen.
◆**walk away** *vi* weg- *or* davongehen ◆ **he ~ed ~ from the crash unhurt** er ist bei dem Unfall ohne Verletzungen davongekommen; **to ~ ~ with a prize** *etc* einen Preis *etc* kassieren *or* einstecken (*inf*).
◆**walk in** *vi* herein-/hineinkommen; (*casually*) herein-/hineinspazieren (*inf*) ◆ **"please ~ ~"** „bitte eintreten".
◆**walk into** *vi +prep obj room* herein-/hineinkommen in (+*acc*); *person* anrempeln; *wall* laufen gegen ◆ **to ~ ~ sb** (*meet unexpectedly*) jdm in die Arme laufen, jdn zufällig treffen; **to ~ ~ a trap** in eine Falle gehen; **to ~ ~ a job** eine Stelle ohne Schwierigkeiten bekommen; **he just ~ed ~ the first job he applied for** er hat gleich die erste Stelle bekommen, um die er sich beworben hat; **to ~ right ~ sth** (*lit*) mit voller Wucht gegen etw rennen; **I didn't know I was going to ~ ~ an argument** ich wußte nicht, daß ich hier mitten in einen Streit hineingeraten würde; **you ~ed right ~ that one, didn't you?** da bist du aber ganz schön reingefallen (*inf*).
◆**walk off** [1] *vt sep pounds* ablaufen (*inf*) ◆ **I'm going out to try and ~ ~ this headache/hangover** ich gehe jetzt an die Luft, um meine Kopfschmerzen/meinen Kater loszuwerden; **we ~ed ~ our lunch with a stroll in the park** nach dem Mittagessen haben wir einen Verdauungsspaziergang im Park gemacht.
[2] *vi* weggehen ◆ **he ~ed ~ in the opposite direction** er ging in die andere Richtung davon.
◆**walk off with** *vi +prep obj* (*inf*) **(a)** (*take*) (*unintentionally*) abziehen mit (*inf*); (*intentionally*) abhauen mit (*inf*) ◆ **don't ~ ~ ~ the idea that ...** (*fig*) gehen Sie nicht weg in dem Glauben, daß ... **(b)** (*win easily*) *prize* kassieren, einstecken (*inf*).
◆**walk on** *vi* **(a)** *+prep obj grass etc* betreten. **(b)** (*continue walking*) weitergehen ◆ **she hesitated, then ~ed ~ by** sie zögerte und ging dann weiter. **(c)** (*Theat*) auftreten; (*in walk-on part*) auf die Bühne gehen ◆ **to ~ ~ (to) the stage** auf die Bühne treten, auf der Bühne erscheinen.
◆**walk out** [1] *vi* **(a)** (*quit*) gehen ◆ **to ~ ~ of a meeting/room** eine Versammlung/einen Saal verlassen; **to ~ ~ on sb** jdn verlassen; (*let down*) jdn im Stich lassen; (*abandon*) *girlfriend etc* sitzenlassen (*inf*); **to ~ ~ on sth**

aus etw aussteigen (*inf*).
(b) (*strike*) streiken, in Streik treten.
(c) **to ~ ~ with sb** (*dated*) mit jdm gehen.
[2] *vt sep* (*dated: court*) gehen mit.

◆**walk over** *vi +prep obj* **(a)** (*defeat*) in die Tasche stecken (*inf*). **(b)** **to ~ all ~ sb** (*inf*) (*dominate*) jdn unterbuttern (*inf*); (*treat harshly*) jdn fertigmachen (*inf*); **she lets her husband ~ all ~ her** sie läßt sich von ihrem Mann herumschikanieren (*inf*) *or* völlig unterbuttern (*inf*).

◆**walk through** *vi +prep obj* **(a)** (*inf: do easily*) *exam etc* spielend schaffen (*inf*). **(b)** (*Theat*) *part* durchgehen.

◆**walk up** *vi* **(a)** (*go up, ascend*) hinaufgehen ◆ **the lift is broken so you'll have to ~ ~** der Aufzug ist außer Betrieb, Sie müssen zu Fuß hinaufgehen. **(b)** (*approach*) zugehen (*to* auf +*acc*) ◆ **a man ~ed ~ (to me/her)** ein Mann kam auf mich zu/ging auf sie zu; **~ ~!, ~ ~!** treten Sie näher!

walkable ['wɔːkəbl] *adj* **to be ~** sich zu Fuß machen lassen.

walk: ~about *n* Rundgang *m*; **the Queen went (on a) ~about** die Königin nahm ein Bad in der Menge; **~away** *n* (*US*) *see* **~over**.

walker ['wɔːkə^r] *n* **(a)** (*stroller*) Spaziergänger(in *f*) *m*; (*hiker*) Wanderer(in *f*) *m*; (*Sport*) Geher(in *f*) *m* ◆ **to be a fast/slow ~** schnell/langsam gehen. **(b)** (*for baby, invalid*) Laufstuhl *m*.

walker-on ['wɔːkər'ɒn] *n* Statist(in *f*) *m*.

walkie-talkie ['wɔːkɪ'tɔːkɪ] *n* Hand-Funksprechgerät, Walkie-Talkie *nt*.

walk-in ['wɔːkɪn] [1] *adj* **a ~ cupboard** ein begehbarer Einbau- *or* Wandschrank.
[2] *n* (*US*) (*cupboard*) *see adj*; (*victory*) spielender Sieg.

walking ['wɔːkɪŋ] [1] *n* Gehen *nt*; (*as recreation*) Spazierengehen *nt*; (*hiking*) Wandern *nt* ◆ **there's some good ~ in these hills** in diesen Bergen gibt es ein paar gute Wandermöglichkeiten; **we did a lot of ~ on holiday** in den Ferien sind wir viel gewandert *or* gelaufen.
[2] *adj attr encyclopaedia, miracle etc* wandelnd; *doll* Lauf- ◆ **at a ~ pace** im Schrittempo; **the ~ wounded** die Leichtverwundeten *pl*; **it's within ~ distance** dahin kann man laufen *or* zu Fuß gehen.

walking: ~bass *n* (*Mus*) *einfache Kontrabaßbegleitung*, Walking-bass *m*; **~ holiday** *n* Wanderferien *pl*; **~ shoes** *npl* Wanderschuhe *pl*; **~ stick** *n* Spazierstock *m*; **~ tour** *n* Wanderung *f*.

walk: ~man ® *n* Walkman ® *m*; **~-on** [1] *adj* **(a)** *part, role* Statisten-; **(b)** (*in transport*) Walk-on-; [2] *n* Statistenrolle *f*; **~out** *n* (*strike*) Streik *m*; **to stage a ~out** (*from conference*) demonstrativ den Saal verlassen; **~over** [1] *n* (*Sport*) Walk-over *m*; (*easy victory*) spielender Sieg; (*fig*) Kinderspiel *nt*; **the government had a ~over in the debate** die Regierung hatte leichtes Spiel in der Debatte; [2] *adj attr* **~over victory** spielender Sieg; **~-up** *n* (*US inf*) (Wohnung/Büro *etc* in einem) Haus *nt* ohne Fahrstuhl *or* Lift; **~way** *n* Fußweg *m*; **a pedestrian ~way** ein Fuß(gänger)weg *m*.

wall [wɔːl] [1] *n* **(a)** (*outside*) Mauer *f*; (*inside, of mountain*) Wand *f* ◆ **the Great W~ of China** die Chinesische Mauer; **the north ~ of the Eiger** die Eigernordwand; **a ~ of fire** eine Feuerwand; **a ~ of policemen/troops** eine Mauer von Polizisten/Soldaten; **~s have ears** die Wände haben Ohren; **to come up against a ~ of prejudice/silence** auf eine Mauer von Vorurteilen/des Schweigens stoßen; **to go up the ~** (*inf*) die Wände rauf- *or* hochgehen (*inf*); **he/his questions drive me up the ~** (*inf*) er/seine Fragerei bringt mich auf die Palme (*inf*); **this constant noise is driving me up the ~** (*inf*) bei diesem ständigen Lärm könnte ich die Wände rauf- *or* hochgehen (*inf*); **to go to the ~** (*firm etc*) kaputtgehen (*inf*); *see* **brick ~, back**.
(b) (*Anat*) Wand *f* ◆ **abdominal ~** Bauchdecke *f*.
[2] *vt* mit einer Mauer umgeben.

◆**wall about** *vt sep* (*old, liter*) ummauern.

◆**wall in** *vt sep* mit einer Mauer *or* von Mauern umgeben ◆ **~ed ~ on all sides by bodyguards** auf allen Seiten von Leibwächtern abgeriegelt *or* eingeschlossen.

◆**wall off** *vt sep* (*cut off*) durch eine Mauer (ab)trennen; (*separate into different parts*) unterteilen ◆ **the monks ~ed themselves ~ from the outside world** die Mönche riegelten sich hinter ihren Mauern von der Welt ab.

◆**wall round** *vt sep* ummauern.

◆**wall up** *vt sep* zumauern.

wallaby ['wɒləbɪ] *n* Wallaby *nt*.

wallah ['wɒlə] *n* (*dated sl*) Knabe (*inf*), Hengst (*inf*) *m*.

wall: ~ bars *npl* Sprossenwand *f*; **~board** *n* (*US*) Sperrholz *nt*; **~ cabinet/cupboard** *n* Wandschrank *m*; **~ chart** *n* Plantafel *f*; **~ clock** *n* Wanduhr *f*; **~ covering** *n* Wandbekleidung *f*.

walled [wɔːld] *adj* von Mauern umgeben.

wallet ['wɒlɪt] *n* Brieftasche *f*.

wall: ~flower *n* (*Bot*) Goldlack *m*; (*fig inf*) Mauerblümchen *nt* (*inf*); **~ hanging** *n* Wandbehang, Wandteppich *m*; **~ map** *n* Wandkarte *f*.

Walloon [wɒ'luːn] [1] *n* **(a)** Wallone *m*, Wallonin *f*. **(b)** (*dialect*) Wallonisch *nt*.
[2] *adj* wallonisch.

wallop ['wɒləp] [1] *n* **(a)** (*inf: blow*) Schlag *m* ◆ **he fell flat on his face with a ~** mit einem Plumps fiel er auf die Nase (*inf*); **to give sb/sth a ~** jdm/einer Sache einen Schlag versetzen.
(b) **at a fair old ~** (*dated inf*) mit Karacho (*inf*).
(c) (*Brit sl: beer*) Bier *nt*.
[2] *vt* (*inf*) (*hit*) schlagen; (*punish*) verdreschen (*inf*), versohlen (*inf*); (*defeat*) in die Pfanne hauen (*sl*) ◆ **to ~ sb one/over the head** jdm eins reinhauen (*inf*)/eins überziehen.

walloping ['wɒləpɪŋ] (*inf*) [1] *n* Prügel *pl* (*inf*), Abreibung *f* (*inf*); (*defeat*) Schlappe *f* ◆ **to give sb a ~** jdm eine Tracht Prügel geben (*inf*); (*defeat*) jdn fertigmachen (*inf*); **to take a ~** (*defeat*) eine Schlappe erleiden.
[2] *adj* (*also* **~ great**) riesig; *price* gesalzen (*inf*), saftig (*inf*); *loss, defeat* gewaltig (*inf*); *lie* faustdick (*inf*).

wallow ['wɒləʊ] [1] *n* (*act*) Bad *nt*; (*place*) Suhle *f*.
[2] *vi* **(a)** (*lit*) (*animal*) sich wälzen, sich suhlen; (*boat*) rollen. **(b)** **to ~ in luxury/sensuality/self-pity** *etc* im Luxus/in Sinnenlust/Selbstmitleid *etc* schwelgen; **to ~ in money** (*inf*) im Geld schwimmen (*inf*).

◆**wallow about** *or* **around** *vi* sich herumwälzen.

wall: ~ painting *n* Wandmalerei *f*; **~paper** [1] *n* Tapete *f*; [2] *vt* tapezieren; **~ socket** *n* Steckdose *f*; **W~ Street** *n* Wall Street *f*; **~-to-~** *adj* **~-to-~ carpeting** Teppichboden, Ausleg(e)teppich *m*; **his flat is just about ~-to-~ stereo equipment** seine Wohnung ist fast eine einzige Stereoanlage; **what a bar! ~-to-~ punks** was für eine Bar! randvoll mit Punkern.

wally ['wɒlɪ] *n* (*inf: fool*) Vollidiot (*inf*), Trottel (*inf*) *m*.

walnut ['wɔːlnʌt] *n* (*nut*) Walnuß *f*; (**~ tree**) (Wal)nußbaum *m*; (*wood*) Nußbaum(holz *nt*) *m*.

walrus ['wɔːlrəs] *n* Walroß *nt* ◆ **~ moustache** Walroßbart *m*.

waltz [wɔːls] [1] *n* Walzer *m*.
[2] *vi* **(a)** Walzer tanzen ◆ **would you care to ~?** möchten Sie einen Walzer tanzen?; **they ~ed expertly** sie tanzten ausgezeichnet Walzer; **they ~ed across the ballroom** sie walzten durch den Ballsaal.
(b) (*inf: move, come etc*) walzen (*inf*) ◆ **he came ~ing up** er kam angetanzt (*inf*).
[3] *vt* Walzer tanzen mit ◆ **he ~ed her out onto the balcony** er walzte mit ihr auf den Balkon hinaus.

◆**waltz about** *or* **around** *vi* (*inf*) herumtanzen *or* -tänzeln.

◆**waltz in** *vi* (*inf*) hereintanzen (*inf*) ◆ **to come ~ing ~** angetanzt kommen (*inf*).

◆**waltz off** *vi* (*inf*) abtanzen (*inf*).

◆**waltz off with** *vi +prep obj* (*inf*) *prizes* abziehen mit.

waltzer ['wɔːlsə^r] *n* **(a)** (*dancer*) Walzertänzer(in *f*) *m*. **(b)** (*at fairground*) Krake *f*.

waltz: ~ music *n* Walzermusik *f*; **~ time** *n* Walzertakt *m*.

wan [wɒn] *adj* bleich; *light, smile, look* matt.

wand [wɒnd] *n* (*magic* ~) Zauberstab *m*; (*of office*) Amtsstab *m*; (*Comput: for bar codes*) Lesestift *m*.

wander ['wɒndə^r] [1] *n* Spaziergang *m*; (*through town, park also*) Bummel *m* ◆ **I'm going for a ~ round the shops** ich mache einen Ladenbummel.
[2] *vt hills, world* durchstreifen (*geh*) ◆ **to ~ the streets** durch die Straßen wandern *or* (*looking for sb/sth also*) irren.
[3] *vi* **(a)** herumlaufen; (*more aimlessly*) umherwandern (*through, about* in +*dat*); (*leisurely*) schlendern; (*to see the shops*) bummeln ◆ **he ~ed past me in a dream** er ging wie im Traum an mir vorbei; **he ~ed over to speak to me** er kam zu mir herüber, um mit mir zu reden; **his hands ~ed over the keys** seine Hände wanderten über die Tasten; **the coach just ~ed through the lanes for a few hours** der Bus zuckelte ein paar Stunden durch die Sträßchen; **the river ~ed through the valley** der Fluß zog sich durch das Tal; **I enjoy just ~ing around** ich bummele gerne einfach nur herum; **his speech ~ed on and on** seine Rede wollte gar nicht aufhören *or* kein Ende nehmen; **if his hands start ~ing ...** (*hum*) wenn er seine Finger nicht bei sich (*dat*) behalten kann ...
(b) (*go off, stray*) **to ~ from the path** vom Wege *or* Pfad abkommen; **the cattle must not be allowed to ~** das Vieh darf nicht einfach so herumlaufen; **he ~ed too near the edge of the cliff** er geriet zu nahe an den Rand des Abhangs; **I accidentally ~ed into Squire Thomas' property** ich bin aus Versehen in das Gelände von Squire Thomas geraten; **the children had ~ed out onto the street** die Kinder waren auf die Straße gelaufen; **the needle tends to ~ a bit** der Zeiger schwankt ein bißchen.
(c) (*fig: thoughts, eye*) schweifen, wandern ◆ **to let one's mind ~** seine Gedanken schweifen lassen; **during the lecture his mind ~ed a bit** während der Vorlesung wanderten seine Gedanken umher *or* schweiften seine Gedanken ab; **the old man's mind is beginning to ~ a bit** der alte Mann wird ein wenig wirr; **to ~ from the straight and narrow/the true religion** vom Pfad der Tugend/vom rechten Glauben abirren *or* abkommen; **to ~ from** *or* **off a point/subject** von einem Punkt/vom Thema abschweifen *or* abkommen.

◆**wander about** *vi* umherziehen, umherwandern.

◆**wander back** *vi* (*cows, strays*) zurückkommen *or* -wandern ◆ **shall we start ~ing ~ to the car?** (*inf*) wollen wir langsam *or* allmählich zum Auto zurückgehen?; **after two years she ~ed ~ to her husband** nach zwei Jahren fand *or* ging sie zu ihrem Mann zurück.

◆**wander in** *vi* ankommen (*inf*), anspazieren (*inf*) ◆ **he ~ed ~ to see me this morning** (*inf*) er ist heute morgen bei mir vorbeigekommen.

◆**wander off** *vi* **(a)** weggehen, davonziehen (*geh*) ◆ **to ~ ~ course** vom Kurs abkommen; **he ~ed ~ into one of his fantasies** er geriet wieder ins Phantasieren; **he must have ~ed ~ somewhere** er muß (doch) irgendwohin verschwunden sein.
(b) (*inf: leave*) allmählich *or* langsam gehen.

wanderer ['wɒndərə^r] *n* Wandervogel *m* ◆ **the Masai are ~s** die Massai sind ein Wanderstamm *m*; **that child is a real ~** das Kind treibt sich überall herum.

wandering ['wɒndərɪŋ] *adj tribesman, refugees* umherziehend; *minstrel* fahrend; *thoughts* (ab)schweifend; *path* gewunden ◆ **the old man's ~ mind** die wirren Gedanken des Alten; **to have ~ hands** (*hum*) seine Finger nicht bei sich (*dat*) behalten können; **the W~ Jew** der Ewige Jude.

wanderings ['wɒndərɪŋz] npl Streifzüge, Fahrten pl; (mental) wirre Gedanken pl; (verbal) wirres Gerede ◆ it's time he stopped his ~ and settled down es wird Zeit, daß er mit dem Herumzigeunern aufhört und seßhaft wird.
wanderlust ['wɒndəlʌst] n Fernweh nt.
wane [weɪn] [1] n to be on the ~ (fig) im Schwinden sein.
[2] vi (moon) abnehmen; (fig) (influence, strength, life, power) schwinden; (reputation) verblassen; (daylight) nachlassen.
wangle ['wæŋgl] (inf) [1] n Schiebung (inf), Mauschelei (inf) f ◆ it's a ~ das ist Schiebung; I think we can arrange some sort of ~ ich glaube, wir können es so hinbiegen (inf) or hindrehen (inf).
[2] vt job, ticket etc organisieren (inf), verschaffen ◆ to ~ oneself/sb in sich hineinlavieren or -mogeln (inf)/jdn reinschleusen (inf); he'll ~ it for you er wird das schon für dich drehen (inf) or deichseln (inf); to ~ money/the truth etc out of sb jdm Geld abluchsen (inf)/die Wahrheit etc aus jdm rauskriegen (inf); we ~d an extra week's holiday wir haben noch eine zusätzliche Woche Urlaub rausgeschlagen (inf).
wangler ['wæŋgləʳ] n (inf) Schlawiner m (inf).
wangling ['wæŋglɪŋ] n (inf) Schiebung f (inf) ◆ there's a lot of ~ goes on da gibt's ziemlich viel Schiebung or Mauschelei (inf).
wank [wæŋk] (sl) [1] vi (also ~ off) wichsen (sl).
[2] vt to ~ sb (off) jdm einen abwichsen (sl) or runterholen (sl).
[3] n to have a ~ sich (dat) einen runterholen (sl).
wanker ['wæŋkəʳ] n (sl) Wichser (sl), Arsch (sl) m; (idiot) Schwachkopf m (inf).
wanly ['wɒnlɪ] adv matt.
wanness ['wɒnnɪs] n (paleness) Blässe f; (of light) Mattheit f.
▼ **want** [wɒnt] [1] n (a) (lack) Mangel m (of an +dat) ◆ ~ of judgement mangelndes Urteilsvermögen, Mangel an Urteilsvermögen; for ~ of aus Mangel an (+dat); for ~ of anything better mangels Besserem, in Ermangelung von etwas Besserem or eines Besseren; for ~ of something to do I joined a sports club weil ich nichts zu tun hatte, bin ich einem Sportverein beigetreten; though it wasn't for ~ of trying nicht, daß er sich nicht bemüht hätte; to feel the ~ of sth etw vermissen.
(b) (poverty) Not f ◆ to be/live in ~ Not leiden.
(c) (need) Bedürfnis nt; (wish) Wunsch m ◆ my ~s are few meine Ansprüche or Bedürfnisse sind gering, meine Ansprüche sind bescheiden; the farm supplied all their ~s der Bauernhof versorgte sie mit allem Nötigen or Notwendigen; this factory supplies all our ~s diese Fabrik liefert unseren gesamten Bedarf; to be in ~ of sth einer Sache (gen) bedürfen (geh), etw brauchen or benötigen; to be in ~ of help/repair Hilfe brauchen/reparaturbedürftig sein; to attend to sb's ~s sich um jdn kümmern; it fills a long-felt ~ es wird einem lange empfundenen Bedürfnis gerecht.
▼ [2] vt (a) (wish, desire) wollen; (more polite) mögen ◆ to ~ to do sth etw tun wollen; I ~ you to come here ich will or möchte, daß du herkommst; I ~ it done now ich will or möchte das sofort erledigt haben; I was ~ing to leave the job next month ich hätte gerne nächsten Monat mit der Arbeit aufgehört; what does he ~ with me? was will er von mir?; darling, I ~ you Liebling, ich will dich; I ~ my mummy ich will meine Mami, ich will zu meiner Mami; you don't ~ much (iro) sonst willst du nichts? (iro); I don't ~ strangers coming in ich wünsche or möchte nicht, daß Fremde (hier) hereinkommen.
(b) (need, require) brauchen ◆ you ~ to see a doctor/solicitor Sie sollten zum Arzt/Rechtsanwalt gehen; you ~ to be careful! (inf) du mußt aufpassen; you ~ to stop doing that (inf) du mußt damit aufhören; he ~s to be more careful (inf) er sollte etwas vorsichtiger sein; that's the last thing I ~ (inf) alles, bloß das nicht (inf); that's all we ~ed! (iro inf) das hat uns gerade noch gefehlt!; it only ~ed the police to turn up ... das hätte gerade noch gefehlt, daß auch noch die Polizei anrückt ...; does my hair ~ cutting? muß mein Haar geschnitten werden?; "~ed" „gesucht"; he's a ~ed man er wird (polizeilich) gesucht; to feel ~ed das Gefühl haben, gebraucht zu werden; you're ~ed on the phone Sie werden am Telefon verlangt or gewünscht.
(c) (lack) he ~s talent/confidence etc es mangelt (geh) or fehlt ihm an Talent/Selbstvertrauen etc; all the soup ~s is a little salt das einzige, was an der Suppe fehlt, ist etwas Salz.
[3] vi (a) (wish, desire) wollen; (more polite) mögen ◆ you can go if you ~ (to) wenn du willst or möchtest, kannst du gehen; I don't ~ to ich will or möchte nicht; do as you ~ tu, was du willst; he said he'd do it, but does he really ~ to? er sagte, er würde es machen, aber will er es wirklich?
(b) he does not ~ for friends es fehlt or mangelt (geh) ihm nicht an Freunden; they ~ for nothing es fehlt or mangelt (geh) ihnen an nichts; he doesn't ~ for a pound or two er ist nicht gerade arm (inf), ihm fehlt es nicht an Kleingeld (inf).
(c) (liter: live in poverty) darben (liter).
◆**want in** vi (inf) reinwollen.
◆**want out** vi (inf) rauswollen.
want ad n Kaufgesuch nt.
wanting ['wɒntɪŋ] adj (a) (lacking, missing) fehlend ◆ humour is ~ in the novel diesem Roman fehlt es an Humor; it's a good novel, but there is something ~ der Roman ist gut, aber irgend etwas fehlt.
(b) (deficient, inadequate) he is ~ in confidence/enterprise etc es fehlt or mangelt (geh) ihm an Selbstvertrauen/Unternehmungslust etc; his courage/the new engine was found ~ sein Mut war nicht groß genug/der neue Motor hat sich als unzulänglich erwiesen; he was (weighed in the balance and) found ~ (liter) er wurde (gewogen und) (für) zu leicht befunden; he was not found ~ (liter) er hat sich bewährt.
(c) (inf: mentally deficient) he's a bit ~ (up top) er ist ein bißchen unterbelichtet (inf).
wanton ['wɒntən] [1] adj (a) (licentious) life liederlich; behaviour, woman, pleasures schamlos; looks, thoughts lüstern ◆ Cupid, that ~ boy (liter) Amor, dieser kleine Lüstling.
(b) (wilful) cruelty mutwillig; disregard, negligence sträflich, völlig unverantwortlich; waste sträflich, kriminell (inf) ◆ to spend money with ~ extravagance Geld mit sträflichem Leichtsinn ausgeben; decorated with ~ extravagance üppig und verschwenderisch eingerichtet.
(c) (poet: capricious) persons übermütig, mutwillig (poet).
[2] n (old: immoral woman) Dirne f.
wantonly ['wɒntənlɪ] adv (a) (immorally) liederlich, schamlos; look lüstern.
(b) (wilfully) mutwillig; neglect also, waste sträflich ◆ she was ~ extravagant with her husband's money sie gab das Geld ihres Mannes mit sträflichem Leichtsinn aus.
wantonness ['wɒntənnɪs] n see adj (a) Liederlichkeit f; Schamlosigkeit f; Lüsternheit f. (b) Mutwilligkeit f; Sträflichkeit f.
war [wɔːʳ] [1] n Krieg m ◆ the art of ~ die Kriegskunst; this is ~! (fig) das bedeutet Krieg!; the ~ against poverty/disease der Kampf gegen die Armut/Krankheit; ~ of nerves Nervenkrieg; ~ of words Wortgefecht nt; to be at ~ sich im Krieg(szustand) befinden; to declare ~ den Krieg erklären (on dat); (fig also) den Kampf ansagen (on dat); to go to ~ (start) (einen) Krieg anfangen (against mit); (declare) den Krieg erklären (against dat); (person) in den Krieg ziehen; to make or wage ~ Krieg führen (on, against gegen); he/this car has been in the ~s a bit er/dieses Auto sieht ziemlich ramponiert (inf) or mitgenommen aus; I hear you've been in the ~s recently (inf) ich höre, daß du zur Zeit ganz schön angeschlagen bist (inf).
[2] vi sich bekriegen; (fig) ringen (geh) (for um).
war baby n Kriegskind nt.
warble ['wɔːbl] [1] n Trällern nt.
[2] vti trällern ◆ he ~d away as he sat in the bath (inf) er trällerte fröhlich vor sich hin, während er in der Badewanne saß.
warbler ['wɔːbləʳ] n (Orn) Grasmücke f; (wood ~) Waldsänger m.
war: ~ bond n Kriegsanleihe f; ~ **bride** n Kriegsbraut f; ~ **clouds** npl the ~ clouds are gathering Kriegsgefahr droht; ~ **correspondent** n Kriegsberichterstatter, Kriegskorrespondent m; ~ **crime** n Kriegsverbrechen nt; ~ **criminal** n Kriegsverbrecher m; ~ **cry** n Kriegsruf m; (fig) Schlachtruf m; the ~ cries of the Red Indians das Kriegsgeheul or Kriegsgeschrei der Indianer.
ward [wɔːd] n (a) (part of hospital) Station f; (room) (small) (Kranken)zimmer nt; (large) (Kranken)saal m.
(b) (Jur: person) Mündel nt ◆ ~ of court Mündel nt unter Amtsvormundschaft; to make sb a ~ of court jdn unter Amtsvormundschaft stellen.
(c) (Jur: state) (to be) in ~ unter Vormundschaft (stehen).
(d) (Admin) Stadtbezirk m; (election ~) Wahlbezirk m.
(e) (of key) Einschnitt m (im Schlüsselbart); (of lock) Aussparung f, Angriff m.
◆**ward off** vt sep attack, blow, person abwehren; danger also abwenden; depression nicht aufkommen lassen.
war dance n Kriegstanz m.
warden ['wɔːdn] n (of youth hostel) Herbergsvater m, Herbergsmutter f; (game ~) Jagdaufseher m; (traffic ~) ≃ Verkehrspolizist m, ≃ Politesse f; (air-raid ~) Luftschutzwart m; (fire ~) Feuerwart m; (of castle, museum etc) Aufseher m; (head ~) Kustos m; (of port) (Hafen)aufseher m; (of mint) Münzwardein m; (Univ) Heimleiter(in f) m; (of Oxbridge college) Rektor m; (US: of prison) Gefängnisdirektor m.
War Department n (old US) Kriegsministerium nt (old).
warder ['wɔːdəʳ] n (Brit) Wärter, Aufseher m.
ward heeler n (US Pol sl) Handlanger m (inf).
wardress ['wɔːdrɪs] n (Brit) Wärterin, Aufseherin f.
wardrobe ['wɔːdrəʊb] n (a) (cupboard) (Kleider)schrank m. (b) (clothes) Garderobe f. (c) (Theat) (clothes) Kostüme pl; (room) Kleiderkammer f, Kostümfundus m.
wardrobe: ~ mistress n (Theat) Gewandmeisterin f; ~ **trunk** n Kleiderkoffer m.
ward: ~room n (Naut) Offiziersmesse f; ~ **round** n (Med) Visite f.
-ward(s) [-wəd(z)] adv suf -wärts ◆ town-/pub-~ in Richtung Stadt/Wirtshaus; in a home~ direction Richtung Heimat (inf).
wardship ['wɔːdʃɪp] n (Jur) Vormundschaft f.
ware [wɛəʳ] n Delft/Derby ~ Delfter/Derby Porzellan nt.
-ware n suf -waren pl ◆ kitchen~ Küchenutensilien pl.
war effort n Kriegsanstrengungen pl.
warehouse ['wɛəhaʊs] [1] n Lager(haus) nt.
[2] vt einlagern.
warehouseman ['wɛəhaʊsmən] n, pl -men [-mən] Lagerarbeiter m.
warehousing ['wɛəhaʊzɪŋ] n Lagerung f ◆ what sort of ~ is available? welche Lagerungsmöglichkeiten gibt es?
wares [wɛəz] npl Waren pl ◆ to cry one's ~ (dated) seine Waren anpreisen.
warfare ['wɔːfɛəʳ] n Krieg m; (techniques) Kriegskunst f.
war: ~ fever n Kriegsbegeisterung f; ~ **game** n Kriegsspiel nt; ~ **grave** n Kriegsgrab nt; ~**head** n Sprengkopf m; ~**horse** n (lit, fig) Schlachtroß nt.
warily ['wɛərɪlɪ] adv vorsichtig; (suspiciously) mißtrauisch, argwöhnisch ◆ to tread ~ (lit, fig) sich vorsehen.
wariness ['wɛərɪnɪs] n Vorsicht f; (mistrust) Mißtrauen nt, Argwohn m ◆ the ~ of his reply die Zurückhaltung, mit der er antwortete; she had a great ~ of

➤ LANGUAGE IN USE: **want: 2a** → 8.1, 8.2, 9.5, 12.2, 18.4, 21.3

strangers sie hegte starkes Mißtrauen *or* großen Argwohn gegen Fremde.

war: ~like *adj* kriegerisch; *tone, speech* militant; **~lock** *n* Hexer *m*; **~lord** *n* Kriegsherr *m*.

warm [wɔːm] 1 *adj* (+er) **(a)** warm ♦ **I am** *or* **feel ~** mir ist warm; **come to the fire and get ~** komm ans Feuer und wärm dich; **it's ~ work moving furniture about** beim Möbelumstellen wird einem ganz schön warm *or* kommt man ins Schwitzen; **to make things ~ for sb** (*inf*) es jdm ungemütlich machen (*inf*); **~ start** (*Comput*) Warmstart *m*.
(b) (*in games*) **am I ~?** ist es (hier) warm?; **you're getting ~** es wird schon wärmer; **you're very ~!** heiß!
(c) (*hearty, warm-hearted*) *person, welcome* herzlich, warm.
(d) (*heated*) *dispute, words* hitzig, heftig.
2 *n* **we were glad to get into the ~** wir waren froh, daß wir ins Warme kamen; **come and have a ~ at the fire** komm und wärm dich ein bißchen am Feuer; **to give sth a ~** etw wärmen.
3 *vt* wärmen ♦ **it ~s my heart to ...** mir wird (es) ganz warm ums Herz, wenn ...; **his kind gesture ~ed my heart** bei seiner freundlichen Geste wurde mir ganz warm ums Herz.
4 *vi* **the milk was ~ing on the stove** die Milch wurde auf dem Herd angewärmt; **my heart ~ed** mir wurde warm ums Herz; **I/my heart ~ed to him** er wurde mir sympathischer/ich habe mich für ihn erwärmt; **his voice ~ed as he spoke of his family** seine Stimme bekam einen warmen Ton, als er von seiner Familie sprach; **he spoke rather hesitantly at first but soon ~ed to his subject** anfangs sprach er noch sehr zögernd, doch dann fand er sich in sein Thema hinein; **to ~ to one's work** sich mit seiner Arbeit anfreunden, Gefallen an seiner Arbeit finden.

♦**warm over** *vt sep* (*esp US*) aufwärmen.

♦**warm up** 1 *vi* (*lit, fig*) warm werden; (*party, game, speaker*) in Schwung kommen; (*Sport*) sich aufwärmen ♦ **things are ~ing ~** es kommt Schwung in die Sache; (*becoming dangerous*) es wird allmählich brenzlig *or* ungemütlich (*inf*).
2 *vt sep engine* warm werden lassen, warmlaufen lassen; *food etc* aufwärmen; (*fig*) *party* in Schwung bringen; *audience* in Stimmung bringen.

warm-blooded ['wɔːm'blʌdɪd] *adj* warmblütig; (*fig*) heißblütig ♦ **~ animal** Warmblüter *m*.

warmer ['wɔːmə^r] *n* **foot/bottle ~** Fuß-/Flaschenwärmer *m*.

warm front *n* (*Met*) Warm(luft)front *f*.

warm-hearted ['wɔːm'hɑːtɪd] *adj person* warmherzig; *action, gesture* großzügig.

warm-heartedness ['wɔːm'hɑːtɪdnɪs] *n* Warmherzigkeit, Herzlichkeit *f*; (*of action, gesture*) Großherzigkeit *f*.

warming pan ['wɔːmɪŋ,pæn] *n* Wärmepfanne *f*.

warmish ['wɔːmɪʃ] *adj* ein bißchen warm ♦ **~ weather** ziemlich warmes Wetter.

warmly ['wɔːmlɪ] *adv* warm; *welcome* herzlich; *recommend* wärmstens ♦ **we ~ welcome it** wir begrüßen es sehr.

warmness ['wɔːmnɪs] *n see* **warmth**.

war: ~monger ['wɔː,mʌŋgə^r] *n* Kriegshetzer *m*; **~mongering** ['wɔː,mʌŋgərɪŋ] 1 *adj* kriegshetzerisch;
2 *n* Kriegshetze *f*.

warmth [wɔːmθ] *n* **(a)** (*lit*) Wärme *f*. **(b)** (*fig*) (*friendliness of voice, welcome etc*) Wärme, Herzlichkeit *f*; (*heatedness*) Heftigkeit, Hitzigkeit *f*.

warm-up ['wɔːmʌp] *n* (*Sport*) Aufwärmen *nt*; (*Mus*) Einspielen *nt* ♦ **the teams had a ~ before the game** die Mannschaften wärmten sich auf vor dem Spiel; **the audience was entertained with a ~ before the TV transmission began** das Publikum wurde vor der Fernsehübertragung in Stimmung gebracht.

warn [wɔːn] 1 *vt* **(a)** warnen (*of, about, against* vor +*dat*); (*police, judge etc*) verwarnen ♦ **to ~ sb not to do sth** jdn davor warnen, etw zu tun; **be ~ed** sei gewarnt!, laß dich warnen!; **I'm ~ing you** ich warne dich!; **you have been ~ed!** sag nicht, ich hätte dich nicht gewarnt *or* es hätte dich niemand gewarnt!; **she just won't be ~ed** sie hört auf keine Warnung(en).
(b) (*inform*) **to ~ sb that ...** jdn darauf aufmerksam machen *or* darauf hinweisen, daß ...; **her expression ~ed me that she was not enjoying the conversation** ich merkte schon an ihrem Gesichtsausdruck, daß ihr die Unterhaltung nicht gefiel; **you might have ~ed us that you were coming** du hättest uns ruhig vorher wissen lassen können *or* Bescheid sagen können, daß du kommst; **to ~ sb of an intended visit** jdm seinen Besuch ankündigen.
2 *vi* warnen (*of* vor +*dat*).

♦**warn off** *vt sep* warnen ♦ **to ~ sb ~ doing sth** jdn (davor) warnen, etw zu tun; **he ~ed me ~** er hat mich davor gewarnt; **I ~ed him ~ my property** ich habe ihn von meinem Grundstück verwiesen; **to ~ sb ~ a subject** jdm von einem Thema abraten; **he sat there shaking his head obviously trying to ~ me ~** er saß da und schüttelte den Kopf, offensichtlich, um mich davon abzubringen; **he ~s everybody ~ who tries to get friendly with her** er läßt nicht zu, daß sich jemand um sie bemüht.

warning ['wɔːnɪŋ] 1 *n* Warnung *f*; (*from police, judge etc*) Verwarnung *f* ♦ **without ~** unerwartet, ohne Vorwarnung; **they had no ~ of the enemy attack** der Feind griff sie ohne Vorwarnung an; **he had plenty of ~** er ist oft *or* häufig genug gewarnt worden; (*early enough*) er wußte früh genug Bescheid; **to give sb a ~** jdn warnen; (*police, judge etc*) jdm eine Verwarnung geben; **let this be a ~ to you/to all those who ...** lassen Sie sich (*dat*) das eine Warnung sein!, das soll Ihnen eine Warnung sein/allen denjenigen, die ..., soll das eine Warnung sein; **to take ~ from sth** sich (*dat*) etw eine Warnung sein lassen; **the bell gives ~** *or* **is a ~ that ...** die Klingel zeigt an, daß ...; **they gave us no ~ of their arrival** sie kamen unangekündigt *or* ohne Vorankündigung; **please give me a few days' ~** bitte sagen *or* geben Sie mir ein paar Tage vorher Bescheid; **to give sb due ~** (*inform*) jdm rechtzeitig Bescheid sagen.
2 *adj* Warn-; *look, tone* warnend ♦ **a ~ sign** ein erstes Anzeichen; (*signboard etc*) ein Warnzeichen *nt*/-schild *nt*; **~ triangle** Warndreieck *m*.

warningly ['wɔːnɪŋlɪ] *adv* warnend.

War Office *n* (*old Brit*) Kriegsministerium *nt* (*old*).

warp [wɔːp] 1 *n* **(a)** (*in weaving*) Kette *f*.
(b) (*in wood etc*) Welle *f* ♦ **the ~ makes it impossible to use this wood** das Holz ist zu verzogen *or* wellig, als daß man es noch verwenden könnte.
(c) (*towing cable*) Schleppleine *f*.
(d) (*of mind*) **hatred of his mother had given his mind an evil ~** der Haß, den er gegen seine Mutter hegte, hatte seinen ganzen Charakter entstellt *or* verbogen; **the ~ in his personality** das Abartige in seinem Wesen.
2 *vt wood* wellig werden lassen, wellen; *character* verbiegen, entstellen; *judgement* verzerren; (*Aviat*) verwinden.
3 *vi* (*wood*) sich wellen, sich verziehen, sich werfen.

war: ~paint *n* (*lit, fig inf*) Kriegsbemalung *f*; **~path** *n* Kriegspfad *m*; **on the ~path** auf dem Kriegspfad.

warped [wɔːpt] *adj* **(a)** (*lit*) verzogen, wellig. **(b)** (*fig*) *sense of humour* abartig; *character also* verbogen; *judgement* verzerrt.

warping ['wɔːpɪŋ] *n* Krümmung *f*.

war plane *n* Kampfflugzeug *nt*.

warrant ['wɒrənt] 1 *n* **(a)** (*Comm*) Garantie *f*; (*Mil*) Patent *nt*; (*search ~*) Durchsuchungsbefehl *m*; (*death ~*) Hinrichtungsbefehl *m* ♦ **a ~ of arrest** ein Haftbefehl *m*; **there is a ~ out for his arrest** gegen ihn ist Haftbefehl erlassen worden (*Jur*), er wird steckbrieflich gesucht.
(b) (*rare*) (*justification*) Berechtigung *f*; (*authority*) Befugnis, Ermächtigung *f*.
2 *vt* **(a)** (*justify*) *action etc* rechtfertigen ♦ **to ~ sb doing sth** jdn dazu berechtigen, etw zu tun.
(b) (*merit*) verdienen.
(c) (*dated inf: assure*) wetten ♦ **I('ll) ~ (you)** ich wette.
(d) (*guarantee*) gewährleisten ♦ **these goods are ~ed for three months by the manufacturers** für diese Waren übernimmt der Hersteller eine Garantie von drei Monaten; **a pill ~ed to cure influenza** eine Pille, die garantiert Grippe heilt.

warrantee [,wɒrən'tiː] *n* Garantieinhaber *m*.

warrant officer *n Rang m zwischen Offizier und Unteroffizier*.

warrantor ['wɒrəntɔː^r] *n* Garantiegeber *m*.

warranty ['wɒrəntɪ] *n* (*Comm*) Garantie *f* ♦ **it's still under ~** darauf ist noch Garantie.

warren ['wɒrən] *n* (*rabbit ~*) Kaninchenbau *m*; (*fig*) Labyrinth *nt*.

warring ['wɔːrɪŋ] *adj nations* kriegführend; *interests, ideologies* gegensätzlich; *factions* sich bekriegend.

warrior ['wɒrɪə^r] *n* Krieger *m*.

Warsaw ['wɔːsɔː] *n* Warschau *nt* ♦ **~ Pact** Warschauer Pakt *m*.

warship ['wɔːʃɪp] *n* Kriegsschiff *nt*.

wart [wɔːt] *n* Warze *f* ♦ **~s and all** (*hum inf*) mit allen seinen/ihren *etc* Fehlern.

wart-hog ['wɔːthɒg] *n* Warzenschwein *nt*.

wartime ['wɔːtaɪm] 1 *n* Kriegszeit *f* ♦ **in ~** in Kriegszeiten.
2 *adj* Kriegs- ♦ **in ~ England** in England im Krieg *or* während des Krieges; **~ regulations/rationing** *etc* Vorschriften *pl*/Rationierungen *pl etc* in Kriegszeiten, Kriegsvorschriften *pl*/Kriegsrationierungen *pl*.

wartorn ['wɔːtɔːn] *adj* vom Krieg erschüttert.

war: ~ toy *n* Kriegsspielzeug *nt*; **~-weary** *adj* kriegsmüde; **~ widow** *n* Kriegswitwe *f*; **~-wounded** *npl* **the ~-wounded** die Kriegsversehrten *pl*.

wary ['wɛərɪ] *adj* (+*er*) vorsichtig; (*looking and planning ahead*) umsichtig, klug, wachsam; *look* mißtrauisch, argwöhnisch ♦ **to be ~ of sb/sth** sich vor jdm/einer Sache in acht nehmen, vor jdm/einer Sache auf der Hut sein; **to be ~ about doing sth** seine Zweifel *or* Bedenken haben, ob man etw tun soll; **be ~ of talking to strangers** hüte dich davor, mit Fremden zu sprechen; **to keep a ~ eye on sb** ein wachsames Auge auf jdn haben.

war zone *n* Kriegsgebiet *nt*.

was [wɒz] *pret of* **be**.

wash [wɒʃ] 1 *n* **(a)** (*act of ~ing*) **sb/sth needs a ~** jd/etw muß gewaschen werden; **to give sb/sth a (good) ~** jdn/etw (gründlich) waschen; **to have a ~** sich waschen; **call that a ~!** das nennst du dich waschen!, das soll gewaschen sein! (*inf*).
(b) (*laundry*) Wäsche *f* ♦ **to be at/in the ~** in der Wäsche sein; **it will all come out in the ~** (*fig inf*) es wird schon alles rauskommen, es wird sich schon noch alles zeigen (*inf*).
(c) (*of ship*) Kielwasser *nt*; (*Aviat*) Luftstrudel *m*.
(d) (*lapping*) (*gentle sound*) Geplätscher *nt*; (*of ocean*) sanftes Klatschen der Wellen.
(e) (*mouth~*) Mundwasser *nt*; (*liquid remains, also pej*) Spülwasser *nt*; (*for walls etc*) Tünche *f*.
(f) (*in painting*) **a drawing in ink and ~** eine kolorierte Federzeichnung; **a ~ of brown ink** eine leichte *or* schwache Tönung mit brauner Tünche.
2 *vt* **(a)** waschen; *dishes* spülen, abwaschen; *floor* aufwaschen, aufwischen; (*parts of*) *body* sich (*dat*) waschen ♦ **to ~ one's hands** (*euph*) sich (*dat*) die Hände waschen (*euph*); **to ~ one's hands of sb/sth** mit jdm/etw nichts mehr zu tun haben wollen; **I ~ my hands of it** ich wasche meine Hände in Un-

schuld; **to ~ sth clean** etw reinwaschen; **the sea ~ed it clean of oil** das Öl wurde vom Meer weggewaschen; **to ~ one's dirty linen in public** (*fig*) seine schmutzige Wäsche in *or* vor aller Öffentlichkeit waschen.
(b) (*sea etc*) umspülen; *wall, cliffs etc* schlagen gegen.
(c) (*river, sea: carry*) spülen ◆ **the body was ~ed downstream** die Leiche wurde flußabwärts getrieben; **to ~ ashore** an Land spülen *or* schwemmen, anschwemmen.
(d) the water had ~ed a channel in the rocks das Wasser hatte eine Rinne in die Felsen gefressen.
(e) (*paint*) *walls* tünchen; *paper* kolorieren.
[3] *vi* **(a)** (*have a ~*) sich waschen.
(b) (*do the laundry etc*) waschen; (*Brit: ~ up*) abwaschen.
(c) a material that ~es well/won't ~ ein Stoff, der sich gut wäscht/den man nicht waschen kann *or* der sich nicht waschen läßt; **that excuse won't ~** (*Brit fig inf*) diese Entschuldigung nimmt *or* kauft dir keiner ab! (*inf*).
(d) (*sea etc*) schlagen ◆ **the sea ~ed over the promenade** das Meer überspülte die Strandpromenade.
◆**wash away** *vt sep* **(a)** (hin)wegspülen. **(b)** (*fig*) **to ~ ~ sb's sins** jdn von seinen Sünden reinwaschen.
◆**wash down** *vt sep* **(a)** (*clean*) *car, walls, deck* abwaschen. **(b)** *meal, food* hinunterspülen, runterspülen (*inf*).
◆**wash off** [1] *vi* (*stain, dirt*) sich rauswaschen lassen ◆ **most of the pattern has ~ed ~** das Muster ist fast ganz verwaschen.
[2] *vt sep* abwaschen ◆ **~ that grease ~ your hands** wasch dir die Schmiere von den Händen (ab)!
◆**wash out** [1] *vi* sich (r)auswaschen lassen.
[2] *vt sep* **(a)** (*clean*) auswaschen; *mouth* ausspülen. **(b)** (*stop, cancel*) *game etc* ins Wasser fallen lassen (*inf*) ◆ **the game was ~ed ~** das Spiel fiel buchstäblich ins Wasser (*inf*).
◆**wash over** *vi +prep obj* **the criticism just seemed to ~ ~ him** die Kritik schien an ihm abzuprallen; **he lets everything just ~ ~ him** er läßt alles einfach ruhig über sich ergehen.
◆**wash up** [1] *vi* **(a)** (*Brit: clean dishes*) abwaschen, (ab)spülen. **(b)** (*US: have a wash*) sich waschen.
[2] *vt sep* **(a)** (*Brit*) *dishes* abwaschen, (ab)spülen. **(b)** (*sea etc*) anschwemmen, anspülen. **(c)** (*inf: finished*) **that's/we're all ~ed ~** (*fig inf*) das *or* der Film ist gelaufen (*inf*).
washable ['wɒʃəbl] *adj* waschbar; *wallpaper* abwaschbar.
wash: ~-and-wear *adj clothing, fabric* bügelfrei; **~bag** *n* (*US*) Kulturbeutel *m*; **~ basin** *n* Waschbecken *nt*; **~ board** *n* Waschbrett *nt*; **~ bowl** *n* Waschschüssel *f*; (*in unit*) Waschbecken *nt*; **~ cloth** *n* (*US*) Waschlappen *m*; **~day** *n* Waschtag *m*.
washed-out ['wɒʃt'aʊt] *adj* (*inf*) erledigt (*inf*), schlapp (*inf*) ◆ **to feel ~** sich wie ausgelaugt fühlen (*inf*); **to look ~** mitgenommen aussehen.
washer ['wɒʃəʳ] *n* **(a)** (*Tech*) Dichtung(sring *m*) *f*. **(b)** (*clothes ~*) Waschmaschine *f*; (*dish~*) (Geschirr)spülmaschine *f*.
washerwoman ['wɒʃə,wʊmən] *n, pl* **-women** [-,wɪmɪn] Waschfrau, Wäscherin *f* ◆ **to gossip like a ~** klatschen wie ein Waschweib.
wash: ~-hand basin *n* Handwaschbecken *nt*; **~ house** *n* Waschhaus *nt*.
washing ['wɒʃɪŋ] *n* Waschen *nt*; (*clothes*) Wäsche *f* ◆ **many boys dislike ~** viele Jungen waschen sich nicht gerne; **to do the ~** Wäsche waschen; **to take in ~** (für Kunden) waschen; **if we don't get a rise, I'll have to take in ~!** (*hum*) wenn wir keine Gehaltserhöhung bekommen, muß ich noch putzen gehen (*inf*).
washing: ~ day *n see* **washday**; **~ line** *n* Wäscheleine *f*; **~ machine** *n* Waschmaschine *f*; **~ powder** *n* Waschpulver *nt*; **~ soda** *n* Bleichsoda *nt*; **~-up** *n* (*Brit*) Abwasch *m*; **to do the ~-up** spülen, den Abwasch machen; **~-up basin** *or* **bowl** *n* (*Brit*) Spülschüssel *f*; **~-up cloth** *n* Spültuch *nt*, Spüllappen *m*; **~-up liquid** *n* (*Brit*) Spülmittel *nt*.
wash: ~ leather *n* Waschleder *nt*; **~out** *n* (*inf*) Reinfall *m* (*inf*); (*person*) Flasche (*inf*), Niete (*inf*) *f*; **~ rag** *n* (*US*) *see* **~ cloth**; **~room** *n* Waschraum *m*; **~ stand** *n* **(a)** Waschbecken *nt*; **(b)** (*old*) Waschgestell *nt*; **~ tub** *n* (Wasch)zuber *m*.
washy ['wɒʃɪ] *adj* wässerig; *see* **wishy-washy**.
wasn't ['wɒznt] *contr of* **was not**.
wasp [wɒsp] *n* Wespe *f*.
WASP [wɒsp] (*US*) *abbr of* **White Anglo-Saxon Protestant** weißer angelsächsischer Protestant.
waspish *adj*, **~ly** *adv* ['wɒspɪʃ, -lɪ] giftig.
wasp-waist ['wɒspweɪst] *n* Wespentaille *f*.
wassail ['wɒseɪl] (*Brit old*) [1] *n* **(a)** (*toast*) Trinkspruch *m* ◆ **~ cup** Kelch *m*. **(b)** (*revelry*) Gelage *nt*.
[2] *vi* **(a)** (*revel*) zechen, ein Gelage abhalten. **(b) to go ~ing** (*carol-singing*) als Sternsinger gehen.
wastage ['weɪstɪdʒ] *n* Schwund *m*; (*action*) Verschwendung *f*; (*amount also*) Materialverlust *m*; (*from container also*) Verlust *m*; (*unusable products etc also*) Abfall *m* ◆ **a ~ rate of 10%** eine Verlustquote von 10%; *see* **natural ~**.
waste [weɪst] [1] *adj* (*superfluous*) überschüssig, überflüssig; (*left over*) ungenutzt; *land* brachliegend, ungenutzt ◆ **~ food** Abfall *m*; **~ material/matter** Abfallstoffe *pl*; **to lay ~** verwüsten; **to lie ~** brachliegen.
[2] *n* **(a)** Verschwendung *f*; (*unusable materials*) Abfall *m* ◆ **it's a ~ of time/money** es ist Zeit-/Geldverschwendung; **it's a ~ of your time and mine** das ist nur (eine) Zeitverschwendung für uns beide; **it's a ~ of effort** das ist nicht der Mühe (*gen*) wert; **to go** *or* **run to ~** (*food*) umkommen; (*training, money, land*) ungenutzt sein/bleiben, brachliegen; (*talent etc*) verkümmrn.
(b) (*~ material*) Abfallstoffe *pl*; (*in factory*) Schwund *m*; (*rubbish*) Abfall *m* ◆ **cotton ~** Putzwolle *f*; **metal ~** Metallabfall.
(c) (*land, expanse*) Wildnis *no pl*, Einöde *f* ◆ **a ~ of snow, a snowy ~** eine Schneewüste.
[3] *vt* **(a)** (*use badly or wrongly*) verschwenden, vergeuden (*on* an *+acc*, für); *food* verschwenden; *life, time* vergeuden, vertun; *opportunity* vertun ◆ **you're wasting your time** das ist reine Zeitverschwendung, damit vertust du nur deine Zeit; **don't ~ my time** stiehl mir nicht meine Zeit; **you didn't ~ much time getting here!** (*inf*) da bist du ja schon, du hast ja nicht gerade getrödelt! (*inf*); **all our efforts were ~d** all unsere Bemühungen waren umsonst *or* vergeblich; **nothing is ~d** es wird nichts verschwendet; **your work won't be ~d** deine Arbeit ist nicht vergeblich *or* umsonst getan; **he didn't ~ any words in telling me ...** ohne viel(e) Worte zu machen *or* zu verlieren, sagte er mir ...; **to ~ oneself on sb** sich an jdn verschwenden; **I wouldn't ~ my breath talking to him** ich würde doch nicht für den meine Spucke vergeuden! (*inf*); **don't ~ your efforts on him** vergeuden Sie keine Mühe mit ihm!; **Beethoven/your joke/she is ~d on him** Beethoven/dein Witz ist an den verschwendet *or* vergeudet/sie ist zu schade für ihn; **you're ~d in this job** Sie sind zu schade für diese Arbeit.
(b) (*weaken*) auszehren; *strength* aufzehren.
(c) (*lay waste*) verwüsten.
(d) (*sl: kill*) kaltmachen (*sl*).
[4] *vi* (*food*) umkommen; (*skills*) verkümmern; (*body*) verfallen; (*strength, assets*) schwinden ◆ **~ not, want not** (*Prov*) spare in der Zeit, so hast du in der Not (*Prov*).
◆**waste away** *vi* (*physically*) dahinschwinden (*geh*), immer weniger werden.
waste: ~-basket, ~-bin *n* Papierkorb *m*.
wasted ['weɪstɪd] *adj* (*inf: worn out*) verbraucht, ausgelaugt (*inf*).
waste: ~ disposal *n* Müllbeseitigung, Abfallentsorgung *f*; **~ disposal unit** *n* Müllschlucker *m*.
wasteful ['weɪstfʊl] *adj* verschwenderisch; *method, process* aufwendig, unwirtschaftlich; *expenditure* unnütz ◆ **leaving all the lights on is a ~ habit** es ist Verschwendung, überall Licht brennen zu lassen; **to be ~ with sth** verschwenderisch mit etw umgehen; **it is ~ of effort** es ist unnötiger Aufwand; **this project is ~ of the country's resources** dieses Projekt ist eine unnütze Vergeudung unserer Ressourcen.
wastefully ['weɪstfəlɪ] *adv* verschwenderisch; *organized* unwirtschaftlich.
wastefulness ['weɪstfʊlnɪs] *n* (*of person*) verschwenderische Art; (*in method, organization, of process etc*) Unwirtschaftlichkeit, Aufwendigkeit *f* ◆ **throwing it away is sheer ~** es ist reine Verschwendung, das wegzuwerfen; **sb's ~ with sth/in doing sth** jds verschwenderische Art, mit etw umzugehen/etw zu machen; **the ~ of the government's expenditure in the field of defence** die Verschwendung, die die Regierung auf dem Gebiet der Verteidigung betreibt.
waste: ~ heat *n* (*from engine etc*) Abwärme *f*; **~ heat recovery** *n* Abwärmerückgewinnung *f*; **~land** *n* Ödland *nt*; (*fig*) Einöde *f*; **~ management** *n* Abfallentsorgung *f*; **~paper** *n* Papierabfall *m*; (*fig*) Makulatur *f*; **~paper basket** *n* (*Brit*) Papierkorb *m*; **they go straight into the ~paper basket** die wandern sofort in den Papierkorb; **~paper collection** *n* Altpapiersammlung *f*; **~ pipe** *n* Abflußrohr *nt*; **~ product** *n* Abfallprodukt *nt*.
waster ['weɪstəʳ] *n* **(a)** Verschwender(in *f*) *m* ◆ **it's a real time-/money-~** das ist wirklich Zeit-/Geldverschwendung; **she's a terrible ~ of electricity** sie verschwendet schrecklich viel Strom. **(b)** (*good-for-nothing*) Taugenichts *m*.
waste reprocessing plant *n* Abfallwiederaufbereitungsanlage *f*, Müllverwertungswerk *nt*.
wasting ['weɪstɪŋ] *adj attr* **~ disease** Auszehrung *f*; **this is a ~ disease** das ist eine Krankheit, bei der der Körper allmählich verfällt.
wastrel ['weɪstrəl] *n* (*liter*) Prasser *m* (*liter*).
watch[1] [wɒtʃ] *n* (Armband)uhr *f*.
watch[2] [1] *n* **(a)** (*vigilance*) Wache *f* ◆ **to be on the ~** aufpassen; **to be on the ~ for sb/sth** nach jdm/etw Ausschau halten; **to keep ~** Wache halten; **to keep a close ~ on sb/sth** jdn/etw scharf bewachen; **to keep a close ~ on the time** genau auf die Zeit achten; **to keep ~ over sb/sth** bei jdm/etw wachen *or* Wache halten; **to set a ~ on sb/sth** jdn/etw überwachen lassen.
(b) (*period of duty, Naut, people*) Wache *f*; (*people also*) Wachmannschaft *f* ◆ **to be on ~** Wache haben, auf Wacht sein (*geh*); **officer of the ~** wachhabender Offizier; **in the still ~es of the night** (*old, liter*) in den stillen Stunden der Nacht.
(c) (*Hist: to protect public*) Wache *f*.
[2] *vt* **(a)** (*guard*) aufpassen auf (*+acc*); (*police etc*) überwachen.
(b) (*observe*) beobachten; *match* zusehen *or* zu schauen bei; *film, play, programme on TV* sich (*dat*) ansehen ◆ **to ~ TV** fernsehen; **to ~ sb doing sth** jdm bei etw zusehen *or* zuschauen, sich (*dat*) ansehen, wie jd etw macht; **I'll come and ~ you play** ich komme und sehe dir beim Spielen zu; **he just stood there and ~ed her drown** er stand einfach da und sah zu, wie sie ertrank; **I ~ed her coming down the street** ich habe sie beobachtet, wie *or* als sie die Straße entlang kam; **she has a habit of ~ing my mouth when I speak** sie hat die Angewohnheit, mir auf den Mund zu sehen *or* schauen, wenn ich rede; **let's go and ~ the tennis** gehen wir uns (das) Tennis ansehen; **are you ~ing the blackboard!** du guckst *or* siehst zur Tafel!; **don't ~ the camera** sehen Sie nicht zur Kamera!; **~ this young actor, he'll be a star** beachten Sie diesen jungen Schauspieler, das wird mal ein Star; **~ the road in front of you** paß auf die Straße auf!, guck *or* achte auf die Straße!; **to ~ a case/negotiations for sb** für jdn als Beobachter bei einem Prozeß/einer Verhand-

lung auftreten; **now ~ this closely** sehen *or* schauen Sie jetzt gut zu!, passen Sie mal genau auf!; **~ this!** paß auf!; **I want everyone to ~ me** ich möchte, daß mir alle zusehen *or* -schauen!, alle mal hersehen *or* -schauen!; **just ~ me!** guck *or* schau mal, wie ich das mache!; **just ~ me go and make a mess of it!** da siehst du mal, was für einen Mist ich mache (*inf*); **we are being ~ed** wir werden beobachtet; **I can't stand being ~ed** ich kann es nicht ausstehen, wenn mir ständig einer zusieht; **a new talent to be ~ed** ein neues Talent, das man im Auge behalten muß; **a ~ed pot never boils** (*Prov*) wenn man daneben steht, kocht das Wasser nie.

(c) (*be careful of*) achtgeben *or* aufpassen auf (*+acc*); *expenses* achten auf (*+acc*); *time* achten auf (*+acc*), aufpassen auf (*+acc*) ◆ **(you'd better) ~ it!** (*inf*) paß (bloß) auf! (*inf*); **~ yourself** sieh dich vor!; sei vorsichtig!; (*well-wishing*) mach's gut; **~ your manners/language!** bitte benimm dich!/drück dich bitte etwas gepflegter aus!; **~ him, he's crafty** sieh dich vor *or* paß auf, er ist raffiniert; **~ where you put your feet** paß auf, wo du hintrittst; **~ how you talk to him, he's touchy** sei vorsichtig, wenn du mit ihm sprichst, er ist sehr empfindlich; **~ how you drive, the roads are icy** paß beim Fahren auf *or* fahr vorsichtig, die Straßen sind vereist!; **~ how you go!** mach's gut!; (*on icy surface etc*) paß beim Laufen/Fahren auf!; *see* **step**.

(d) *chance* abpassen, abwarten ◆ **to ~ one's chance/time** eine günstige Gelegenheit/einen günstigen Zeitpunkt abwarten.

[3] *vi* (a) (*observe*) zusehen, zuschauen ◆ **to ~ for sb/sth** nach jdm/etw Ausschau halten *or* ausschauen; **they ~ed for a signal from the soldiers** sie warteten auf ein Signal von den Soldaten; **to ~ for sth to happen** darauf warten, daß etw geschieht; **to be ~ing for signs of ...** nach Anzeichen von ... Ausschau halten; **you should ~ for symptoms of ...** du solltest auf ...symptome achten.

(b) (*keep ~*) Wache halten; (*at sickbed also*) wachen ◆ **there are policemen ~ing all round the house** das Haus wird rundherum von Polizisten bewacht.

◆**watch out** *vi* (a) (*look carefully*) Ausschau halten, ausschauen (*for sb/sth* nach jdm/etw) ◆ **a newcomer to ~ ~ for** ein Neuling, auf den man achten sollte.

(b) (*be careful*) aufpassen, achtgeben (*for* auf *+acc*) ◆ **there were hundreds of policemen ~ing ~ for trouble at the match** bei dem Spiel waren Hunderte von Polizisten, die aufpaßten, daß es nicht zu Zwischenfällen kam; **~ ~!** Achtung!, Vorsicht!; **you'd better ~ ~!** (*threat also*) paß bloß auf!, nimm dich in acht!, sieh dich ja vor!; **~ ~ for him** nimm dich vor ihm in acht.

◆**watch over** *vi +prep obj* wachen über (*+acc*).

watchable ['wɒtʃəbl] *adj* sehenswert.

watch: ~band *n* (*US*) Uhrarmband *nt*; **~case** *n* Uhrengehäuse *nt*; **~ chain** *n* Uhrkette *f*; **W~ Committee** *n* (*Brit*) Aufsichtskommission *f*; **~dog** *n* (*lit*) Wachhund *m*; (*fig*) Aufpasser (*inf*), Überwachungsbeauftragte(r) *m*; **government ~dog** Regierungsbeauftragter zur Überwachung von ...; **~dog body** Überwachungsgremium *nt*.

watcher ['wɒtʃə^r] *n* Schaulustige(r) *mf*; (*observer*) Beobachter(in *f*) *m* ◆ **the ~s by the dying man's bedside** die am Bett des Sterbenden Wachenden.

watchful ['wɒtʃfʊl] *adj* wachsam ◆ **to be ~ for/against** wachsam Ausschau halten nach/auf der Hut sein vor (*+dat*).

watchfully ['wɒtʃfəlɪ] *adv* wachsam ◆ **policemen sat ~ at the back of the hall** ganz hinten im Saal saßen Polizisten, die aufpaßten; **the opposition waited ~ for the Government's next move** die Opposition beobachtete aufmerksam, welchen Schritt die Regierung als nächstes unternehmen würde.

watchfulness ['wɒtʃfʊlnɪs] *n* Wachsamkeit *f*.

watch-glass ['wɒtʃglɑːs] *n* Uhrenglas *nt*.

watching brief ['wɒtʃɪŋ'briːf] *n* **to hold a ~** eine Kontrollfunktion ausüben; **he holds a ~ for the Government over all aspects of industrial development** er ist der Regierungsbeauftragte zur Überwachung der gesamten industriellen Entwicklung.

watch: ~maker *n* Uhrmacher *m*; **~man** *n* (*night-~man, in bank, factory etc*) (Nacht)wächter *m*; **~-night service** *n* Jahresschlußmette *f*; **~strap** *n* Uhrarmband *nt*; **~ tower** *n* Wachtturm *m*; **~word** *n* (*password, motto*) Parole, Losung *f*.

water ['wɔːtə^r] [1] *n* (a) Wasser *nt* ◆ **the field is under ~** das Feld steht unter Wasser; **to make ~** (*ship*) lecken.

(b) (*sea, of lake etc*) **~s** Gewässer *pl* ◆ **the ~s** (*Bibl, liter*) die Wasser *pl*; **the ~s of the Rhine** die Wasser des Rheins (*liter*); **by ~** auf dem Wasserweg, zu Wasser (*geh*); **on land and ~** zu Land und zu Wasser; **we spent an afternoon on the ~** wir verbrachten einen Nachmittag auf dem Wasser.

(c) (*urine*) Wasser *nt* ◆ **to make** *or* **pass ~** Wasser lassen.

(d) (*at spa*) **the ~s** die Heilquelle; **to drink** *or* **take the ~s** eine Kur machen; (*drinking only*) eine Trinkkur machen.

(e) (*Med*) **~ on the brain** Wasserkopf *m*; **~ on the knee** Kniegelenkerguß *m*.

(f) (*toilet ~*) **rose ~** *etc* Rosenwasser *nt etc*.

(g) **to stay above ~** sich über Wasser halten; **to pour cold ~ on sb's idea** jdm etw miesmachen (*inf*); **to get (oneself) into deep ~(s)** ins Schwimmen kommen; **of the first ~** (*dated, liter*) erster Güte; **a lot of ~ has flowed under the bridge since then** (*fig*) seitdem ist soviel Wasser den Berg *or* den Bach hinuntergeflossen; **to hold ~** (*lit*) wasserdicht sein; **that excuse/argument** *etc* **won't hold ~** (*inf*) diese Entschuldigung/dieses Argument *etc* ist nicht hieb- und stichfest (*inf*); **to be in** *or* **get into hot ~** (*fig inf*) in Schwierigkeiten *or* in (des) Teufels Küche (*inf*) sein/geraten (*over* wegen *+gen*); **he's in hot ~ with his father** (*inf*) er hat Ärger *or* Stunk (*sl*) mit seinem Vater; **to spend money like ~** (*inf*) mit dem Geld nur so um sich werfen (*inf*).

[2] *vt* (a) *garden, roads* sprengen; *lawn also* besprengen; *land, field* bewässern; *plant* (be)gießen.

(b) *horses, cattle* tränken.

(c) *wine* verwässern, verdünnen.

(d) **to ~ capital** (*Fin*) Aktienkapital verwässern.

[3] *vi* (a) (*mouth*) wässern; (*eye*) tränen ◆ **the smoke made his eyes ~** ihm tränten die Augen vom Rauch; **my mouth ~ed** mir lief das Wasser im Mund zusammen; **to make sb's mouth ~** jdm den Mund wässerig machen.

(b) (*animals*) trinken.

◆**water down** *vt sep* (*lit, fig*) verwässern; (*fig also*) abmildern, abschwächen; *liquids* (mit Wasser) verdünnen.

water: ~ bed *n* Wasserbett *nt*; **~ beetle** *n* Wasserkäfer *m*; **~ bird** *n* Wasservogel *m*; **~ biscuit** *n* ≃ Kräcker *m*; **~ blister** *n* Wasserblase *f*; **~ boatman** *n* Rückenschwimmer *m*; **~borne** *adj* **to be ~borne** (*ship*) auf dem *or* im Wasser sein; **~borne trade** Handel *m* auf dem Seeweg *or* Wasserweg, Handelsschiffahrt *f*; **~borne goods/troops** Güter/Truppen, die auf dem Wasserweg *or* zu Wasser befördert werden; **a ~borne disease** eine Krankheit, die durch das Wasser übertragen wird; **~-bottle** *n* Wasserflasche *f*; (*for troops, travellers etc*) Feldflasche *f*; **~buck** *n* Wasserbock *m*; **~ buffalo** *n* Wasserbüffel *m*; **~ butt** *n* Regentonne *f*; **~ cannon** *n* Wasserwerfer *m*; **~ carrier** *n* Wasserträger(in *f*) *m*; **the W~ Carrier** (*Astrol*) der Wassermann; **~-cart** *n* Wasserwagen *m*; (*for roads*) Sprengwagen *m*; **~ chestnut** *n* Wasserkastanie *f*; **~ closet** *n* (*abbr* **WC**) Wasserklosett *nt*; **~colour**, (*US*) **~color** [1] *n* Wasserfarbe, Aquarellfarbe *f*; (*picture*) Aquarell *nt*; [2] *attr* Aquarell-; **~colourist**, (*US*) **~colorist** *n* Aquarellmaler(in *f*) *m*; **~-cooled** *adj* wassergekühlt; **~ cooler** *n* Thermoskanister *m*, isolierter Trinkwasserbehälter/-kanister; **~course** *n* (*stream*) Wasserlauf *m*; (*bed*) Flußbett *nt*; (*artificial*) Kanal *m*; **~cress** *n* (Brunnen) kresse *f*; **~-cure** *n* Wasserkur *f*; **~ diviner** *n* (Wünschel)rutengänger *m*; **~fall** *n* Wasserfall *m*; **~fowl** *n* Wasservogel *m*; *pl* Wassergeflügel *nt*; **~front** [1] *n* Hafenviertel *nt*; **we drove along the ~front/down to the ~front** wir fuhren am Wasser entlang/hinunter zum Wasser; [2] *attr* am Wasser; **a ~front restaurant/a restaurant in the ~front area** ein Restaurant direkt am Hafen *or* am Wasser/im Hafenviertel; **they live on the Mississippi ~front** sie wohnen direkt am Mississippi; **~-gauge** *n* (*in tank*) Wasserstandsmesser *or* -anzeiger *m*; (*in rivers, lakes etc also*) Pegel *m*; **~ heater** *n* Heißwassergerät *nt*; **~ hole** *n* Wasserloch *nt*; **~-ice** *n* Fruchteis *nt*.

wateriness ['wɔːtərɪnɪs] *n* (*weakness*) Wässerigkeit, Wäßrigkeit *f*; (*of colour*) Blässe *f*.

watering ['wɔːtərɪŋ] *n* (*of land, field*) Bewässern *nt*; (*of garden*) Sprengen *nt*; (*of lawn also*) Besprengen *nt*; (*of plant*) (Be)gießen *nt*.

watering: ~ can *n* Gießkanne *f*; **~ hole** *n* (*for animals*) Wasserstelle *f*; (*fig hum: pub*) Pinte (*inf*), Kneipe (*inf*) *f*; **~ place** *n* (*spa*) Kurort *m*; (*seaside resort*) Badeort *m*, Seebad *nt*; (*for animals*) Tränke, Wasserstelle *f*.

water: ~ jacket *n* Kühlmantel, Kühlwassermantel *m*; **~ jump** *n* Wassergraben *m*; **~less** *adj* trocken; **a ~less planet** ein Planet ohne Wasser; **~ level** *n* Wasserstand *m* (*in engine also*); (*measured level of river, reservoir etc also*) Pegelstand *m*; (*surface of water*) Wasserspiegel *m*; **~lily** *n* Seerose *f*; **~line** *n* Wasserlinie *f*; **~logged** *adj* **the fields are ~logged** die Felder stehen unter Wasser; **the ship was completely ~logged** das Schiff war voll Wasser gelaufen; **to get ~logged** sich voll Wasser saugen; (*ship*) voll Wasser laufen.

Waterloo [,wɔːtə'luː] *n* **to meet one's ~** (*hum*) Schiffbruch erleiden; **with that woman he has finally met his ~** bei dieser Frau hat er sein Waterloo erlebt (*hum*).

water: ~ main *n* Haupt(wasser)leitung *f*; (*the actual pipe*) Hauptwasserrohr *nt*; **~man** *n* Fährmann *m*; **~mark** *n* (a) (*on wall*) Wasserstandsmarke *f*; (b) (*on paper*) Wasserzeichen *nt*; **~ mattress** *n* Wassermatratze *f*; **~ meter** *n* Wasseruhr *f*; **~melon** *n* Wassermelone *f*; **~ mill** *n* Wassermühle *f*; **~ nymph** *n* (Wasser)nixe *f*; **~ pipe** *n* Wasserrohr *nt*; (*for smoking*) Wasserpfeife *f*; **~-pistol** *n* Wasserpistole *f*; **~-polo** *n* Wasserball *m*; **~-power** *n* Wasserkraft *f*; **~proof** [1] *adj clothes* wasserundurchlässig; *roof also, window* (wasser)dicht; *paint* wasserfest; [2] *n* (*esp Brit*) Regenhaut ® *f*; [3] *vt* wasserundurchlässig machen; *material also* wasserdicht machen; *clothes also* imprägnieren; **~proofer** *n see* **~proofing (b)**; **~proofing** *n* (a) (*process*) Wasserdichtmachen *nt*; (*of clothes also*) Imprägnieren *nt*; (b) (*material*) Dichtungsmittel *nt*; (*for clothes*) Imprägniermaterial *nt*; **~ rat** *n* Wasserratte *f*; (*US sl*) Hafenstrolch *m* (*inf*); **~-rate** *n* (*Brit*) Wassergeld *nt*; **~-repellent** *adj* wasserabstoßend; **~-resistant** *adj* wasserbeständig; **~shed** *n* (*Geol*) Wasserscheide *f*; (*fig*) Wendepunkt *m*; **~side** [1] *n* Ufer *nt*; (*at sea*) Strand *m*; [2] *attr* am Wasser wachsend/lebend *etc*; **~-ski** [1] *n* Wasserski *m*; [2] *vi* Wasserski laufen; **~-skiing** *n* Wasserskilaufen *nt*; **~ snake** *n* Wasserschlange *f*; (*in lake*) Seeschlange *f*; **~ softener** *n* Wasserenthärter *m*; **~-soluble** *adj* wasserlöslich; **~-spaniel** *n* Wasserspaniel *m*; **~ sports** *npl* Wassersport *m*; **~ spout** *n* (a) (*Met*) Wasserhose, Trombe *f*; (b) (*pipe*) Regenrinne *f*; **~ supply** *n* Wasserversorgung *f*; **~table** *n* Grundwasserspiegel *m*; **~ tank** *n* Wassertank *m*; **~tight** *adj* (*lit*) wasserdicht; (*fig*) *agreement, argument, alibi, contract also* hieb- und stichfest; **~-tower** *n* Wasserturm *m*; **~ vapour** *or* (*US*) **vapor** *n* Wasserdampf *m*; **~way** *n* Wasserstraße *f*; (*channel*) Fahrrinne *f*; **~-wheel** *n* (*Mech*) Wasserrad *nt*; (*Agr*) Wasserschöpfrad *nt*; **~-wings** *npl* Schwimmflügel, Schwimmarme (*inf*) *pl*; **~works** *npl or sing* Wasserwerk *nt*; **to turn on the ~works** (*fig inf*) zu heulen anfangen; **to have trouble with one's ~works** (*fig inf*) ständig laufen müssen (*inf*).

watery ['wɔːtərɪ] *adj* (*weak*) *soup, beer etc* wässerig, wäßrig; *eye* tränend; (*pale*) *sky, sun* blaß; *colour* wässerig, wäßrig ◆ **all the sailors went to a ~ grave** alle

Seeleute fanden ein feuchtes *or* nasses Grab *or* fanden ihr Grab in den Wellen.

watt [wɒt] *n* Watt *nt.*

wattage ['wɒtɪdʒ] *n* Wattleistung *f* ◆ **what ~ is that bulb?** wieviel Watt hat diese Birne?

wattle ['wɒtl] *n* **(a)** (*material*) Flechtwerk *nt* ◆ **a ~ fence** ein Zaun aus Flechtwerk. **(b)** (*Bot*) australische Akazie. **(c)** (*Orn*) Kehllappen *m.*

wave [weɪv] 1 *n* **(a)** (*of water, Phys, Rad, in hair, fig*) Welle *f*; (*of water, hatred, enthusiasm also*) Woge (*liter*) *f* ◆ **who rules the ~s?** wer beherrscht die Meere?; **a ~ of strikes/enthusiasm** eine Streikwelle/Welle der Begeisterung; **during the first ~ of the attack** beim ersten Ansturm *or* in der ersten Angriffswelle; **the attacks/attackers came in ~s** die Angriffe/Angreifer kamen in Wellen *or* wellenweise; **from the 5th century onwards England was attacked by ~s of invaders** vom 5. Jahrhundert an wurde England immer wieder von Eroberungswellen heimgesucht; **to make ~s** (*fig inf*) Unruhe stiften; **I don't want to make ~s but ...** ich will ja keinen Staub aufwirbeln, aber ...

(b) (*movement of hand*) **to give sb a ~** jdm (zu)winken; **he gave us a ~ to show that he was ready** er winkte uns (*dat*) zu, um zu zeigen, daß er bereit war; **with a ~ he was gone** er winkte kurz und verschwand; **with a ~ of his hand** mit einer Handbewegung.

2 *vt* **(a)** (*in order to give a sign or greeting*) winken mit (*at, to sb* jdm); (*to ~ about*) schwenken; (*gesticulating, in a dangerous manner*) herumfuchteln mit ◆ **to ~ one's hand to sb** jdm winken; **he ~d a greeting to the crowd** er winkte grüßend der Menge zu; **to ~ sb goodbye/to ~ goodbye to sb** jdm zum Abschied winken; **he ~d his hat (at the passing train)** er schwenkte seinen Hut/er winkte dem vorbeifahrenden Zug mit seinem Hut (zu); **he ~d the ticket under my nose** er fuchtelte mir mit der Karte vor der Nase herum; **he ~d his stick at the children who were stealing the apples** er drohte den Kindern, die die Äpfel stahlen, mit dem Stock; **he ~d his fist at the intruders** er drohte den Eindringlingen mit der Faust.

(b) (*to indicate sb should move*) **he ~d the children across the road** er winkte die Kinder über die Straße; **he ~d me over to his table** er winkte mich zu sich an den Tisch; **he ~d me over** er winkte mich zu sich herüber.

(c) *hair* wellen.

3 *vi* **(a)** winken ◆ **to ~ at** *or* **to sb** jdm (zu)winken; **there's daddy, ~!** da ist der Papi, wink mal!; **don't just ~ at the ball, aim to hit it** nicht nur in Richtung Ball fuchteln, du sollst ihn auch treffen! **(b)** (*flag*) wehen; (*branches*) sich hin und her bewegen; (*corn*) wogen. **(c)** (*hair*) sich wellen.

◆**wave aside** *vt sep* **(a)** (*lit*) *person* auf die Seite *or* zur Seite winken. **(b)** (*fig*) *person, objection, suggestions etc* ab- *or* zurückweisen; *help also* ausschlagen.

◆**wave away** *vt sep* abwinken (*+dat*).

◆**wave down** *vt sep* anhalten, stoppen.

◆**wave on** *vt sep* **the policeman ~d us ~** der Polizist winkte uns weiter.

wave: ~band *n* (*Rad*) Wellenband *nt*; **~length** *n* (*Rad*) Wellenlänge *f*; **we're not on the same ~length** (*fig*) wir haben nicht dieselbe Wellenlänge.

wavelet ['weɪvlɪt] *n* (*poet*) kleine Welle.

wave power *n* Wellenkraft *f.*

waver ['weɪvə^r] *vi* **(a)** (*quiver*) (*light, flame, eyes*) flackern; (*voice*) zittern.

(b) (*weaken*) (*courage, self-assurance*) wanken, ins Wanken geraten; (*courage also*) weichen; (*support*) nachlassen ◆ **the old man's mind was beginning to ~** der alte Mann wurde langsam etwas wirr im Kopf.

(c) (*hesitate*) schwanken (*between* zwischen *+dat*) ◆ **if he begins to ~** wenn er ins Schwanken *or* Wanken gerät; **he's ~ing between accepting and ...** er ist sich (*dat*) darüber unschlüssig, ob er annehmen soll oder ...

waverer ['weɪvərə^r] *n* Zauderer *m.*

wavering ['weɪvərɪŋ] *adj light, flame* flackernd; *shadow* tanzend; *courage, determination* wankend; *support* (*hesitating*) wechselhaft; (*decreasing*) nachlassend.

wavy ['weɪvɪ] *adj* (*+er*) *hair, surface* wellig, gewellt; *design* Wellen- ◆ **~ line** Schlangenlinie *f.*

wax[1] [wæks] 1 *n* Wachs *nt*; (*ear ~*) Ohrenschmalz *nt*; (*sealing ~*) Siegellack *m.*

2 *adj* Wachs-.

3 *vt floor, furniture* wachsen; *floor also* bohnern; *moustache* wichsen.

wax[2] *vi* **(a)** (*moon*) zunehmen ◆ **to ~ and wane** (*lit*) ab- und zunehmen; (*fig*) schwanken, kommen und gehen. **(b)** (*liter: become*) werden ◆ **to ~ enthusiastic** in Begeisterung geraten.

waxed [wækst] *adj paper* Wachs-; *floor, thread* gewachst; *moustache* gewichst ◆ **~ cotton** gewachster Baumwollstoff.

wax(ed) paper *n* Wachspapier *nt.*

waxen ['wæksən] *adj* **(a)** (*old*) wächsern. **(b)** (*fig: pale*) wachsbleich, wächsern.

waxing ['wæksɪŋ] 1 *adj moon* zunehmend; *enthusiasm etc also* wachsend.

2 *n* Zunehmen *nt*; Wachsen *nt.*

wax: ~ work *n* Wachsfigur *f*; **~ works** *n sing or pl* Wachsfigurenkabinett *nt.*

waxy ['wæksɪ] *adj* (*+er*) wächsern.

▼ **way** [weɪ] 1 *n* **(a)** (*road*) Weg *m* ◆ **across** *or* **over the ~** gegenüber, vis-à-vis; (*motion*) rüber; **W~ of the Cross** Kreuzweg *m*; **to fall by the ~** (*fig*) auf der Strecke bleiben.

(b) (*route*) Weg *m* ◆ **the ~ to the station** der Weg zum Bahnhof; **by ~ of** (*via*) über (*+acc*); **which is the ~ to the town hall, please?** wo geht es hier zum Rathaus, bitte?; **~ in/out** (*also on signs*) Ein-/Ausgang *m*; **please show me the ~ out** bitte zeigen Sie mir, wo es hinausgeht (*inf*) *or* wie ich hinauskomme; **can you find your own ~ out?** finden Sie selbst hinaus?; **on the ~ out/in** beim Hinaus-/Hereingehen; **to be on the ~ in** (*fig inf*) im Kommen sein; **to be on the ~ out** (*fig inf*) am Verschwinden *or* Aussterben sein; **there's no ~ out** (*fig*) es gibt keinen Ausweg; **~ up/down** Weg nach oben/unten; (*climbing*) Aufstieg/Abstieg *m*; **~ up/back** Hinweg/Rückweg *m*; **prices are on the ~ up/down again** die Preise steigen/fallen; **the shop is on the/your ~** der Laden liegt auf dem/deinem Weg; **is it on the ~?** (*place*) liegt das auf dem Weg?; (*parcel etc*) ist es unterwegs?; **to stop on the ~** unterwegs anhalten; **on the ~ (here)** auf dem Weg (hierher); **on the ~ to London** auf dem Weg nach London; **you pass it on your ~ home** du kommst auf deinem Nachhauseweg *or* Heimweg daran vorbei; **they're on their ~ now** sie sind jetzt auf dem Weg *or* unterwegs; **he's on the ~ to becoming an alcoholic** er ist dabei *or* auf dem besten Weg, Alkoholiker zu werden; **she's well on the ~ to being a first-rate singer** sie ist auf dem besten Weg, eine erstklassige Sängerin zu werden; **there's another baby on the ~** da ist wieder ein Kind unterwegs; **I haven't finished it yet but it's on the ~** ich bin noch nicht damit fertig, aber es ist im Werden (*inf*); **if it is out of your ~** wenn es ein Umweg für Sie ist; **we had to go out of our ~** wir mußten einen Umweg machen; **it took us out of our ~** es war ein Umweg für uns; **to go out of one's ~ to do sth** (*fig*) sich besonders anstrengen, um etw zu tun; **please, don't go out of your ~ for us** (*fig*) machen Sie sich (*dat*) bitte unsertwegen keine Umstände; **to feel the/one's ~** sich weiter-/vorwärts-/entlangtasten; **to find a ~ in** hineinfinden, hineinkommen, eine Möglichkeit finden hineinzukommen; **can you find your ~ out/home?** finden Sie hinaus/nach Hause?; **I know my ~ about town** ich finde mich in der Stadt zurecht, ich kenne mich in der Stadt aus; **she knows her ~ about** (*fig inf*) sie kennt sich aus, sie weiß Bescheid (*inf*); **to lose one's ~** sich verlaufen, sich verirren (*geh*); **to make one's ~ to somewhere** sich an einen Ort *or* irgendwohin bewegen *or* begeben; **can you make your own ~ to the theatre?** kannst du allein zum Theater kommen?; **to make one's ~ home** nach Hause gehen; (*start*) sich auf den Heimweg begeben; **to make/fight/push one's ~ through the crowd** sich einen Weg durch die Menge bahnen, sich durch die Menge (durch)drängen/-kämpfen/-schieben; **to make one's ~ in the world** seinen Weg machen, sich durchsetzen; **to go one's own ~** (*fig*) eigene Wege gehen; **they went their separate ~s** (*lit, fig*) ihre Wege trennten sich; **to pay one's ~** für sich selbst bezahlen; (*company, project, machine*) sich rentieren; **can the nation pay its ~?** kann das Volk *or* Land für sich selber aufkommen?; **the ~ of virtue** der Pfad der Tugend; **the ~ forward** der Weg vorwärts *or* in die Zukunft; **to go down the wrong ~** (*food, drink*) in die falsche Kehle kommen; **to prepare the ~** (*fig*) den Weg bereiten (*for sb/sth* jdm/einer Sache); **could you see your ~ to lending me a pound?** wäre es Ihnen wohl möglich, mir ein Pfund zu leihen?; **to get under ~** in Gang kommen, losgehen (*inf*); (*Naut*) Fahrt aufnehmen *or* machen; **to be (well) under ~** im Gang/in vollem Gang sein; (*Naut*) in (voller) Fahrt sein; (*with indication of place*) unterwegs sein; **to lose/gather ~** (*Naut*) Fahrt verlieren/aufnehmen.

(c) (*room for movement, path*) Weg *m* ◆ **to bar** *or* **block the ~** den Weg ab- *or* versperren; **to leave the ~ open** (*fig*) die Möglichkeit offen lassen, einen Weg frei lassen (*for sth* für etw); **make ~!** mach Platz!, Platz machen!, Platz da!; **to make ~ for sb/sth** (*lit, fig*) für jdn/etw Platz machen; (*fig also*) für jdn/etw den Platz räumen; **to be/get in sb's/the ~** (jdm) im Weg stehen *or* sein/in den Weg kommen; (*fig*) jdn stören/stören; **get out of the/my ~!** (geh) aus dem Weg!, weg da!; **to get sb out of the ~** (*get rid of*) jdn loswerden (*inf*); (*remove: lit, fig*) jdn aus dem Wege räumen; **to get sth out of the ~** *work* etw hinter sich (*acc*) bringen; *difficulties, problems etc* etw loswerden (*inf*), etw aus dem Weg räumen, etw beseitigen; **to get sth out of the ~ of sb/sth** jdm etw aus dem Weg räumen/etw aus etw (weg)räumen; **they got the children out of the ~ of the firemen** sie sorgten dafür, daß die Kinder den Feuerwehrleuten nicht im Weg waren; **get those people out of the ~ of the trucks** sieh zu, daß die Leute den Lastwagen Platz machen *or* aus der Bahn gehen; **to keep out of sb's/the ~** (*not get in the ~*) jdm nicht in den Weg kommen, (jdm) aus dem Weg bleiben; (*avoid*) (jdm) aus dem Weg gehen; **keep out of the ~!** weg da!, zurück!; **keep out of my ~!** komm mir nicht mehr über den Weg!; **to keep sb/sth out of the ~ of sb** jdn/etw nicht in jds Nähe *or* Reichweite (*acc*) kommen lassen; **to put difficulties in sb's ~** jdm Hindernisse in den Weg stellen; **to stand in sb's ~** (*lit, fig*) jdm im Weg stehen *or* sein; **don't let me stand in your ~** (*fig*) ich will dir nicht im Weg stehen; **he lets nothing stand in his ~** (*fig*) er läßt sich durch nichts aufhalten *or* beirren; **now nothing stands in our ~** (*fig*) jetzt steht uns (*dat*) nichts mehr im Weg, jetzt haben wir freie Bahn; **to stand in the ~ of progress** den Fortschritt aufhalten *or* hemmen; **to want sb out of the ~** jdn aus dem Weg haben wollen; **to put sb in the ~ of (doing) sth** (*inf*) jdm zu etw verhelfen/dazu verhelfen, etw zu tun.

(d) (*direction*) Richtung *f* ◆ **this ~, please** hier(her) *or* hier entlang, bitte; **he went that ~** er ging dorthin *or* in diese Richtung; **"this ~ for the lions"** „zu den Löwen"; **this ~ and that** hierhin und dorthin; **down our ~** (*inf*) bei uns (in der Nähe), in unserer Gegend *or* Ecke (*inf*); **it's out Windsor ~** es ist *or* liegt in Richtung Windsor; **which ~ are you going?** in welche Richtung *or* wohin gehen Sie?; **which ~** in welche/aus welcher Richtung; **look this ~** schau hierher!; **look both ~s** schau nach beiden Seiten; **she didn't know which ~ to look** (*fig*) sie wußte nicht, wo sie hinschauen *or* -sehen sollte; **to look the other ~** (*fig*) wegschauen *or* -sehen; **this one is better, there are no two ~s about it** (*inf*) dieses hier ist besser, da gibt es gar keinen Zweifel *or* das steht fest; **you're going to bed, there are no two ~s about it** (*inf*) du gehst ins Bett, da gibt es gar nichts *or* und damit basta (*inf*); **it does not matter (to me) one ~ or the other** es macht (mir) so oder so nichts aus, es ist mir gleich; **either ~, we're bound to lose** (so oder so,) wir verlieren auf jeden Fall *or* auf alle Fälle; **if the chance comes your ~** wenn Sie (dazu) die

Gelegenheit haben; if a good job comes my ~ wenn ein guter Job für mich auftaucht; each ~, both ~s (*Racing*) auf Sieg und Platz; we'll split it three/ten ~s wir werden es dritteln/in zehn Teile (auf)teilen *or* durch zehn teilen; it's the wrong ~ up es steht verkehrt herum *or* auf dem Kopf (*inf*); "this ~ up" „hier oben"; it's the other ~ round es ist (genau) umgekehrt; put it the right ~ up/the other ~ round stellen Sie es richtig (herum) hin/andersherum *or* andersrum (*inf*) hin.

(e) (*distance*) Weg *m*, Strecke *f* ◆ it rained all the ~ there es hat auf der ganzen Strecke *or* die ganze Fahrt (über) geregnet; I'm behind you all the ~ (*fig*) ich stehe voll (und ganz) hinter Ihnen; a little/long ~ away *or* off nicht/sehr weit weg *or* entfernt, ein kleines/ganzes *or* gutes Stück weit weg *or* entfernt; it's only a little ~ to the next stop es ist nur ein kleines Stück bis zur nächsten Haltestelle; that's a long ~ away bis dahin ist es weit *or* (*time*) noch lange; a long ~ out of town weit von der Stadt weg; (*live also*) weit draußen, weit außerhalb; (*drive also*) weit raus (*inf*), weit nach draußen; that's a long ~ back das war schon vor einer ganzen Weile; a long ~ back, in 1902, when ... vor langer Zeit, im Jahre 1902, als ...; he'll go a long ~ (*fig*) er wird es weit bringen; to have (still) a long ~ to go (noch) weit vom Ziel entfernt sein; (*with work*) (noch) bei weitem nicht fertig sein; (*with practice*) (noch) viel vor sich haben; it should go some/a long ~ towards solving the problem das sollte *or* müßte bei dem Problem schon etwas/ein gutes Stück weiterhelfen; will that go a little ~ towards helping? hilft das schon ein Stückchen *or* ein kleines Stück weiter?; a little (of sth) goes a long ~ (with me) ein kleines bißchen (+*nom*) reicht (mir) sehr lange; a little kindness goes a long ~ ein bißchen Freundlichkeit hilft viel; better by a long ~ bei weitem *or* um vieles besser; not by a long ~ bei weitem nicht.

(f) (*method, manners*) Art, Weise *f* ◆ that's the ~ ja, (so geht das)!, ja, genau!; do it this ~ machen Sie es so *or* auf diese Art und Weise; do it the ~ I do it machen Sie es so *or* auf dieselbe Art und Weise wie ich (es mache); that's not the right ~ to do it so geht das nicht, so kann man das nicht machen; do it any ~ you like machen Sie es, wie Sie wollen; what's the best ~ to do it? wie macht man das am besten?; we have ~s of making you talk wir haben gewisse Mittel, um Sie zum Reden zu bringen; I don't like the ~ he's looking at you ich mag nicht, wie er dich ansieht, ich mag die Art nicht, wie er dich ansieht; do you understand the ~ things are developing? verstehst du, wie sich die Dinge entwickeln?; you could tell by the ~ he was dressed das merkte man schon an seiner Kleidung; the ~ she walks/talks (so) wie sie geht/spricht; it's just the ~ you said it du hast es nur so komisch gesagt; it's not what you do, it's the ~ you do it es kommt nicht darauf an, was man macht, sondern wie man es macht; it was all the ~ you said it would be es war alles so, wie du (es) gesagt hattest; do you remember the ~ it was/we were? erinnerst du dich noch (daran), wie es war/wie wir damals waren?; it's not the ~ we do things here so *or* auf die Art machen wir das hier nicht; to show sb the ~ to do sth jdm zeigen, wie *or* auf welche Art und Weise etw gemacht wird; show me the ~ zeig mir, wie (ich es machen soll); there's only one ~ to do it properly es gibt nur eine richtige Methode, man kann das nur so *or* nur auf eine Art und Weise machen; there is only one ~ to speak to him man kann mit ihm nur auf (die) eine Art und Weise reden; the French ~ of doing it (die Art,) wie man es in Frankreich macht; the Smith ~ wie es Smith macht/gemacht hat; to do sth the hard ~ etw auf die schwierigste *or* komplizierteste Art (und Weise) machen; why do it the hard ~? warum es sich (*dat*) schwer machen?; to learn the hard ~ aus dem eigenen Schaden lernen; we'll find a ~ wir werden (schon) einen Weg finden; love will find a ~ die Liebe überwindet jedes Hindernis *or* alle Schwierigkeiten; I'd rather do it my ~ ich möchte es lieber auf meine (eigene) Art machen; that's his ~ of saying thank you das ist seine Art, sich zu bedanken; that's no ~ to speak to your mother in einem solchen Ton *or* so spricht man nicht mit seiner Mutter; ~s and means Mittel und Wege; Committee of W~s and Means Steuerausschuß *m*; ~ of life Lebensstil *m*; (*of nation*) Lebensart *f*; ~ of thinking Denk(ungs)art *f*; to my ~ of thinking meiner Meinung *or* Auffassung *or* Anschauung nach; an old/a funny ~ of talking eine altertümliche Sprechweise/eine komische Art, sich auszudrücken; the Eastern ~ of looking at things die östliche Lebensanschauung; there are many ~s of solving the problem es gibt viele Wege *or* Möglichkeiten, das Problem zu lösen; ha, that's one ~ of solving it! ja, so kann man das auch machen!; that's the ~ the money goes so geht das Geld weg; it was this ~ ... es war so *or* folgendermaßen ...; that's the ~ it goes! so ist das eben, so ist das nun mal!; the ~ things are so, wie es ist *or* wie die Dinge liegen; leave everything the ~ it is laß alles so, wie es ist; to go on in the same old ~ wie vorher *or* auf die alte Tour (*inf*) weitermachen; in one ~ or another so oder so, irgendwie, auf irgendeine Art und Weise; in a general ~ this is true ganz allgemein ist das richtig; he had his ~ with her er hat sie genommen; to get *or* have one's (own) ~ seinen Willen durchsetzen *or* bekommen; our team had it all their own ~ in the second half in der zweiten Halbzeit ging für unsere Mannschaft alles nach Wunsch; have it your own ~! wie du willst!; you can't have it both ~s du kannst nicht beides haben, beides (zugleich) geht nicht (*inf*); he wants it both ~s er will das eine haben und das andere nicht lassen; what a ~ to speak! so spricht man doch nicht!; what a ~ to live/die! so möchte ich nicht leben/sterben.

(g) (*custom, habit*) Art *f* ◆ the ~s of the Spaniards die spanische Lebensweise; the ~s of Providence/God die Wege der Vorsehung/Gottes; the ~ of the world der Lauf der Welt *or* der Dinge; that is our ~ with traitors so machen wir das mit Verrätern; it is not/only his ~ to ... es ist nicht/eben seine Art, zu ...; he has a ~ with him er hat so eine (gewisse) Art; he has a ~ with children er versteht es, mit Kindern umzugehen, er hat eine geschickte Art (im Umgang) mit Kindern; he has his little ~s er hat so seine Eigenheiten *or* Marotten (*inf*); to get out of/into the ~ of sth sich (*dat*) etw ab-/angewöhnen.

▼ (h) (*respect*) Hinsicht *f* ◆ in a ~ in gewisser Hinsicht *or* Weise; in no ~ in keiner Weise; no ~! nichts drin! (*inf*), ausgeschlossen!, is' nich' (*sl*); there's no ~ I'm going to agree/you'll persuade him auf keinen Fall werde ich zustimmen/werden Sie ihn überreden können; there's no ~ that's a Porsche ausgeschlossen, daß das ein Porsche ist; what have you got in the ~ of drink/food? was haben Sie an Getränken *or* zu trinken/an Lebensmitteln *or* zu essen?; in every possible ~ auf jede mögliche *or* denkbare Art, auf jedwede Art (*geh*); to be better in every possible ~ in jeder Hinsicht besser sein; in many/some ~s in vieler/gewisser Hinsicht; in a big ~ (*not petty*) im großen Stil; (*on a large scale*) im großen; in the ~ of business durch *or* über das Geschäft, geschäftlich; in a small ~ in kleinem Ausmaß *or* im Kleinen; he's not a plumber in the ordinary ~ er ist kein Klempner im üblichen Sinn; in the ordinary ~ we ... normalerweise *or* üblicherweise ... wir ....

(i) (*state*) Zustand *m* ◆ he's in a bad ~ er ist in schlechter Verfassung; things are in a bad ~ die Dinge stehen schlecht; he's in a fair ~ to succeed (*inf*) er ist auf dem besten Wege, es zu schaffen.

(j) (*with by*) by the ~ übrigens; all this is by the ~ (*irrelevant*) das ist alles Nebensache *or* zweitrangig; (*extra*) das nur nebenher *or* nebenbei; by ~ of an answer/excuse als Antwort/Entschuldigung; by ~ of illustration zur Illustration; he's by ~ of being a painter (*inf*) er ist so'n Maler (*inf*).

(k) ~s *pl* (*Naut: slip~*) Helling, Ablaufbahn *f*.

2 *adv* (*inf*) ~ back/over/up weit zurück/drüben/oben; ~ back when vor langer Zeit, als; since ~ back seit Urzeiten; since ~ back in 1893 ... schon seit (dem Jahre) 1893 ...; that was ~ back das ist schon lange her, das war schon vor langer Zeit; he was ~ out with his guess er hatte weit daneben- *or* vorbeigeraten, er hatte weit gefehlt *or* er lag weit daneben (*inf*) mit seiner Annahme; his guess was ~ out seine Annahme war weit gefehlt; you're ~ out if you think ... da liegst du aber schief (*inf*) *or* da hast du dich aber gewaltig geirrt, wenn du glaubst, ...

way: ~bill *n* Frachtbrief *m*; **~farer** ['weɪ,fɛərər] *n* (*liter*) Wanderer, Wandersmann (*liter*) *m*; **~faring** *adj* (*liter*) wandernd, reisend; ~faring man Wandervogel, Zugvogel *m*; **~lay** *pret, ptp* **~laid** *vt* (*ambush*) überfallen; (*inf*) abfangen; I was ~laid by the manager der Manager hat mich abgefangen; **~-out** *adj* (*sl*) irr(e) (*inf*), extrem (*sl*); **~side** 1 *n* (*of path, track*) Wegrand *m*; (*of road*) Straßenrand *m*; by the ~side am Weg(es)-/Straßenrand; to fall by the ~side auf der Strecke bleiben; 2 *adj café, inn* am Weg/an der Straße gelegen; ~side flowers Blumen, die am Weg-/Straßenrand blühen; **~ station** *n* (*US*) Zwischenstation *f*, Kleinbahnhof *m*; **~ train** *n* (*US*) Personenzug *m*; **~ward** ['weɪwəd] *adj* (*self-willed*) *child, horse, disposition* eigenwillig, eigensinnig; (*capricious*) *fancy, request, passion* abwegig; (*liter*) *stream, breeze* unberechenbar, launisch (*liter*); their ~ward son ihr ungeratener Sohn; **~wardness** [-wədnɪs] *n see adj* Eigenwilligkeit *f*, Eigensinn *m*; Abwegigkeit *f*; Unberechenbarkeit, Launenhaftigkeit (*liter*) *f*.

WBA *n abbr of* World Boxing Association.

WC *abbr of* water closet WC *nt*.

w/e *abbr of* (a) weekend. (b) week ending.

we [wiː] *pron* wir ◆ the Royal ~ der Pluralis majestatis, der Majestätsplural; the editorial ~ der Autorenplural; (*in narrative*) das Wir des Erzählers; how are ~ this morning? (*inf*) wie geht es uns (denn) heute morgen? (*inf*).

weak [wiːk] *adj* (+*er*) (*all senses*) schwach; *character* labil; *tea, solution etc* dünn; *stomach* empfindlich ◆ he was ~ from hunger ihm war schwach vor Hunger; to go/feel ~ at the knees (*after illness*) sich wackelig fühlen, wackelig *or* schwach auf den Beinen sein (*inf*); (*with fear, excitement etc*) weiche Knie haben/bekommen; the ~er sex das schwache Geschlecht; he must be a bit ~ in the head (*inf*) er ist wohl nicht ganz bei Trost (*inf*); her maths is ~ sie ist schwach in Mathematik.

weaken ['wiːkən] 1 *vt* (*lit, fig*) schwächen; *influence also, control, suspicion etc* verringern; *argument also* entkräften; *walls, foundations* angreifen; *hold* lockern ◆ he ~ed his grip on my arm er hielt meinen Arm nicht mehr ganz so fest.

2 *vi* (*lit, fig*) schwächer werden, nachlassen; (*person*) schwach *or* weich werden; (*foundations*) nachgeben; (*defence, strength also*) erlahmen ◆ his grip on my arm ~ed er hielt meinen Arm nicht mehr ganz so fest.

weak-kneed ['wiːk'niːd] *adj* (*after illness*) wackelig auf den Beinen; (*with fear, excitement*) mit weichen Knien; (*fig inf*) schwach, feige.

weakling ['wiːklɪŋ] *n* Schwächling *m*; (*of litter etc*) Schwächste(s) *nt*.

weakly ['wiːklɪ] 1 *adj* (*dated*) schwächlich.

2 *adv* schwach ◆ he gave in ~/he ~ gave in to their demands schwach wie er war, gab er gleich nach/ging er gleich auf ihre Forderungen ein.

weak-minded ['wiːk'maɪndɪd] *adj* (a) (*feeble-minded*) schwachsinnig. (b) (*weak-willed*) willensschwach.

▼ **weakness** ['wiːknɪs] *n* (*all senses*) Schwäche *f*; (*weak point*) schwacher Punkt ◆ the opposition criticised the ~ of the country's defences die Opposition kritisierte, wie schwach die Verteidigung des Landes sei; to have a ~ for sth für etw eine Schwäche *or* Vorliebe haben.

weak-willed ['wiːk'wɪld] *adj* willensschwach.

weal[1] [wiːl] *n* (*liter*) Wohl *nt* ◆ the common *or* general/public ~ das Wohl der Allgemeinheit, das Allgemeinwohl, das allgemeine/öffentliche Wohl; ~ and woe Wohl und Wehe *nt*.

weal[2] *n* (*welt*) Striemen *m*.

wealth [welθ] *n* (a) Reichtum *m*; (*private fortune also*) Vermögen *nt* ◆ ~ tax Vermögenssteuer *f*. (b) (*fig: abundance*) Fülle *f*.

➤ LANGUAGE IN USE: **way: 1h** → 8.3, 16.3 **weakness** → 7.2

wealth-creating ['welθkrɪ'eɪtɪŋ] *adj* vermögensbildend.
wealthily ['welθɪlɪ] *adv* wohlhabend.
wealthiness ['welθɪnɪs] *n* Wohlhabenheit *f*.
wealthy ['welθɪ] *adj* (+*er*) wohlhabend, reich; *appearance* wohlhabend; (*having a private fortune also*) vermögend ♦ **the ~** *pl* die Reichen *pl*.
wean [wiːn] *vt baby* entwöhnen ♦ **to ~ sb from sb/sth** jdn einer Person (*gen*)/einer Sache (*gen*) entwöhnen (*geh*).
weaning ['wiːnɪŋ] *n* (*of baby*) Entwöhnung *f*.
weapon ['wepən] *n* (*lit, fig*) Waffe *f*.
weaponry ['wepənrɪ] *n* Waffen *pl*.
wear [wɛəʳ] (*vb: pret* **wore,** *ptp* **worn**) [1] *n* **(a)** (*use*) **I've had a lot of/I haven't had much ~ out of** *or* **from this jacket** (*worn it often/not often*) ich habe diese Jacke viel/wenig getragen; (*it wore well/badly*) ich habe diese Jacke lange/nur kurz getragen; **I've had very good ~ from these trousers/this carpet** diese Hosen haben sich sehr gut getragen/dieser Teppich hat sehr lange gehalten; **he got four years' ~ out of these trousers/that carpet** diese Hose/dieser Teppich hat vier Jahre lang gehalten; **there isn't much ~/there is still a lot of ~ left in this coat/carpet** dieser Mantel/Teppich hält noch/nicht mehr lange; **this coat will stand any amount of hard ~** dieser Mantel ist sehr strapazierfähig; **for casual/evening/everyday ~** für die Freizeit/den Abend/jeden Tag.
(b) (*clothing*) Kleidung *f*.
(c) (*damage through use*) Abnutzung *f*, Verschleiß *m* ♦ **~ and tear** Abnutzung *f*, Verschleiß *m*; **fair ~ and tear** normale Abnutzungs- *or* Verschleißerscheinungen; **to show signs of ~** (*lit*) anfangen, alt auszusehen; (*fig*) angegriffen aussehen; **to look the worse for ~** (*lit*) (*clothes, curtains, carpets etc*) verschlissen aussehen; (*shoes, clothes*) abgetragen aussehen; (*furniture etc*) abgenutzt aussehen; (*fig*) verbraucht aussehen; **I felt a bit the worse for ~** ich fühlte mich etwas angeknackst (*inf*) *or* angegriffen.
[2] *vt* **(a)** *clothing, jewellery, spectacles, beard etc* tragen ♦ **what shall I ~?** was soll ich anziehen?; **I haven't a thing to ~!** ich habe nichts zum Anziehen *or* nichts anzuziehen; **I haven't worn that for ages** das habe ich schon seit Ewigkeiten nicht mehr angezogen *or* angehabt (*inf*) *or* getragen; **to ~ white/rags** *etc* Weiß/Lumpen *etc* tragen, in Weiß/Lumpen *etc* gehen; **he wore an air of triumph/a serious look (on his face)** er trug eine triumphierende/ernste Miene zur Schau; **he wore a big smile** er strahlte über das ganze Gesicht.
(b) (*reduce to a worn condition*) abnutzen; *clothes* abtragen; *sleeve, knee etc* durchwetzen; *velvet etc* blankwetzen; *leather articles* abwetzen; *steps* austreten; *tyres* abfahren; *engine* kaputtmachen ♦ **to ~ holes in sth** etw durchwetzen; (*in shoes*) etw durchlaufen; **the carpet has been worn threadbare** der Teppich ist abgewetzt *or* ganz abgelaufen; **to ~ smooth** (*by handling*) abgreifen; (*by walking*) austreten; *pattern* angreifen; *sharp edges* glattmachen; **centuries of storms had worn the inscription smooth** die Inschrift war durch die Stürme im Laufe der Jahrhunderte verwittert; **the sea/the weather had worn the rocks smooth** die See hatte die Felsen glattgewaschen/die Felsen waren verwittert; **you'll ~ a track in the carpet** (*hum*) du machst noch mal eine richtige Bahn *or* einen Trampelpfad (*inf*) in den Teppich; *see also* **worn.**
(c) (*inf: accept, tolerate*) schlucken (*inf*).
[3] *vi* **(a)** (*last*) halten; (*dress, shoes etc also*) sich tragen ♦ **she has worn well** (*inf*) sie hat sich gut gehalten (*inf*); **the theory has worn well** die Theorie hat sich bewährt.
(b) (*become worn*) kaputtgehen; (*engine, material also*) sich abnutzen, verbraucht sein; (*tyres also*) abgefahren sein ♦ **to ~ smooth** (*by water*) glattgewaschen sein; (*by weather*) verwittern; (*pattern*) abgegriffen sein; **the sharp edges will ~ smooth in time/with use** die scharfen Kanten werden sich mit der Zeit/im Gebrauch abschleifen; **to ~ thin** (*lit*) dünn werden, durchgehen (*inf*); **my patience is ~ing thin** meine Geduld ist langsam erschöpft *or* geht langsam zu Ende; **that excuse is ~ing thin** diese Ausrede ist (doch) schon etwas alt.
(c) (*proceed gradually*) **the party** *etc* **is ~ing to its end/towards its close** die Party *etc* geht dem Ende zu.
◆**wear away** [1] *vt sep* (*erode*) *steps* austreten; *rock* abschleifen, abtragen; (*from underneath*) aushöhlen; *pattern, inscription* tilgen (*geh*), verwischen; (*fig*) *determination* untergraben; *sb's patience* zehren an (+*dat*) ♦ **his illness wore him ~** die Krankheit zehrte an ihm.
[2] *vi* (*disappear*) (*rocks, rough edges etc*) sich abschleifen; (*inscription*) verwittern; *pattern* verwischen; (*fig: patience, determination*) schwinden.
◆**wear down** [1] *vt sep* **(a)** (*reduce by friction*) abnutzen; *heel* ablaufen, abtreten; *tyre tread* abfahren; *lipstick* verbrauchen; *pencil* verschreiben.
(b) (*fig*) *opposition, strength etc* zermürben; *person also* (*make more amenable*) mürbe *or* weich machen (*inf*); (*tire out, depress*) fix und fertig machen (*inf*).
[2] *vi* sich abnutzen; (*heels*) sich ablaufen *or* abtreten; (*tyre tread*) sich abfahren; (*lipstick etc*) sich verbrauchen; (*pencil*) sich verschreiben.
◆**wear off** *vi* **(a)** (*diminish*) nachlassen, sich verlieren ♦ **don't worry, it'll ~ ~!** keine Sorge, das gibt sich; *see* **novelty. (b)** (*disappear*) (*paint*) abgehen; (*plating, gilt*) sich abwetzen.
◆**wear on** *vi* sich hinziehen, sich (da)hinschleppen; (*year*) voranschreiten ♦ **as the evening/year** *etc* **wore ~** im Laufe des Abends/Jahres *etc*.
◆**wear out** [1] *vt sep* **(a)** kaputtmachen; *carpet also* abtreten; *clothes, shoes* kaputttragen; *record, machinery* abnutzen.
(b) (*fig: exhaust*) (*physically*) erschöpfen, erledigen (*inf*); (*mentally*) fertigmachen (*inf*) ♦ **to be worn ~** erschöpft *or* erledigt sein; (*mentally*) am Ende sein (*inf*); **to ~ oneself ~** sich überanstrengen, sich kaputtmachen (*inf*).
[2] *vi* kaputtgehen; (*clothes, curtains, carpets also*) verschleißen ♦ **his patience has worn ~/is rapidly ~ing ~** seine Geduld ist erschöpft *or* am Ende/erschöpft sich zusehends.
◆**wear through** [1] *vt sep* durchwetzen; *elbows, trousers also* durchscheuern; *soles of shoes* durchlaufen.
[2] *vi* sich durchwetzen; (*elbows, trousers also*) sich durchscheuern; (*soles of shoes*) sich durchlaufen ♦ **his sweater has worn ~ at the elbows** sein Pullover ist an den Ellenbogen durchgewetzt.
wearable ['wɛərəbl] *adj* (*not worn out etc*) tragbar ♦ **fashionable clothes which are also very ~** modische Kleidung, die sich auch gut trägt.
wearer ['wɛərəʳ] *n* Träger(in *f*) *m* ♦ **~ of spectacles** Brillenträger(in *f*) *m*.
wearily ['wɪərɪlɪ] *adv see adj.*
weariness ['wɪərɪnɪs] *n see adj (a)* Müdigkeit *f*; Lustlosigkeit *f*; Mattheit *f* ♦ **he felt a great ~ of life** er empfand großen Lebensüberdruß *or* große Lebensmüdigkeit.
wearing ['wɛərɪŋ] *adj* **(a) ~ apparel** (*form*) (Be)kleidung *f*. **(b)** (*exhausting*) anstrengend; (*boring*) ermüdend.
wearisome ['wɪərɪsəm] *adj* ermüdend; *climb etc* beschwerlich; (*bothersome*) *questions* lästig; (*tedious*) *discussion* langweilig.
weary ['wɪərɪ] [1] *adj* (+*er*) **(a)** (*tired, dispirited*) müde; (*fed up*) lustlos; *smile, groan* matt ♦ **to feel** *or* **be ~** müde sein; **to be/grow ~ of sth** etw leid sein/werden, einer Sache (*gen*) überdrüssig *or* müde sein/werden (*geh*).
(b) (*tiring*) *wait, routine etc* ermüdend ♦ **for three ~ hours** drei endlose Stunden (lang); **five ~ miles** fünf lange *or* beschwerliche Meilen.
[2] *vt* ermüden.
[3] *vi* **to ~ of sth** einer Sache (*gen*) müde *or* überdrüssig werden (*geh*); **she wearied of being alone** sie wurde es leid *or* müde (*geh*) *or* überdrüssig (*geh*), allein zu sein.
weasel ['wiːzl] [1] *n* **(a)** Wiesel *nt*. **(b)** (*US inf: person*) Heimtücker *m*.
[2] *vi* (*esp US inf: be evasive*) schwafeln (*inf*).
◆**weasel out** *vi* (*wriggle out*) sich rauslavieren (*inf*) (*of* aus).
weaselly ['wiːzəlɪ] *adj* (*inf*) *appearance* Fuchs-; (*shifty*) *character* aalglatt.
weather ['weðəʳ] [1] *n* Wetter *nt*; (*in ~ reports*) Wetterlage *f*; (*climate*) Witterung *f* ♦ **in cold/wet/this ~** bei kaltem/nassem/diesem Wetter; **what's the ~ like?** wie ist das Wetter?; **lovely ~ for ducks!** bei dem Wetter schwimmt man ja fast weg!; **in all ~s** bei jedem Wetter, bei jeder Witterung (*geh*); **to be** *or* **feel under the ~** (*inf*) angeschlagen sein (*inf*); **to make heavy ~ of sth** (*inf*) sich mit etw fürchterlich anstellen (*inf*); **to keep a** *or* **one's ~ eye open** (*inf*) Ausschau halten (*for* nach).
[2] *vt* **(a)** (*storms, winds etc*) angreifen; *skin* gerben ♦ **the rock had been ~ed** der Fels war verwittert.
(b) (*expose to ~*) *wood* ablagern.
(c) (*survive: also* **~ out**) *crisis, awkward situation* überstehen ♦ **to ~ (out) the storm** (*lit, fig*) den Sturm überstehen.
[3] *vi* (*rock etc*) verwittern; (*skin*) vom Wetter gegerbt sein/werden; (*paint etc*) verblassen; (*resist exposure to ~*) wetterfest sein; (*become seasoned: wood*) ablagern.
weather *in cpds* Wetter-; **~-beaten** *adj face* vom Wetter gegerbt; *house* verwittert; *skin* wettergegerbt; **~boarding** *n*, **~boards** *npl* Schindeln *pl*; **~bound** *adj boat* auf Grund der schlechten Wetterverhältnisse manövrierunfähig; **~ bureau** *n* Wetteramt *nt*; **~ chart** *n* Wetterkarte *f*; **~cock** *n* Wetterhahn *m*.
weathered ['weðəd] *adj* verwittert; *skin* wettergegerbt.
weather forecast *n* Wettervorhersage *f*.
weathering ['weðərɪŋ] *n* (*Geol*) Verwitterung *f*.
weather: ~man *n* Mann *m* vom Wetteramt; **~proof** [1] *adj* wetterfest; [2] *vt* wetterfest machen; **~ report** *n* Wetterbericht *m*; **~ ship** *n* Wetterschiff *nt*; **~ station** *n* Wetterwarte *f*; **~ vane** *n* Wetterfahne *f*; **~wise** *adv* wettermäßig.
weave [wiːv] (*vb: pret* **wove,** *ptp* **woven**) [1] *n* (*patterns of threads*) Webart *f*; (*loosely/tightly etc woven fabric*) Gewebe *nt* ♦ **material in a fancy/tight ~** ein Stoff in einer raffinierten/festen Webart; **you need a tighter ~ for a skirt** für einen Rock braucht man ein festeres Gewebe.
[2] *vt* **(a)** *thread, cloth etc* weben (*into* zu); *cane, flowers, garland* flechten (*into* zu); *web* spinnen ♦ **he wove the threads together** er verwob die Fäden miteinander.
(b) (*fig*) *plot, story* ersinnen, erfinden; (*add into story etc*) *details, episode* einflechten (*into* in +*acc*) ♦ **he wove a romantic tale round his experiences abroad** er spann seine Erlebnisse im Ausland zu einer romantischen Geschichte aus.
(c) *pret also* **~d** (*wind*) **to ~ one's way through the traffic/to the front** sich durch den Verkehr fädeln *or* schlängeln/nach vorne (durch)schlängeln; **the drunk ~d his way down the street** der Betrunkene torkelte die Straße hinunter.
[3] *vi* **(a)** (*lit*) weben. **(b)** *pret also* **~d** (*twist and turn*) sich schlängeln; (*drunk*) torkeln. **(c)** (*inf*) **to get weaving** sich ranhalten (*inf*); **to get weaving on sth** sich hinter etw (*acc*) klemmen (*inf*).
weaver ['wiːvəʳ] *n* Weber(in *f*) *m*.
weaver bird *n* Webervogel *m*.
weaving ['wiːvɪŋ] *n* Weberei *f*; (*as craft*) Webkunst *f*.
web [web] *n* **(a)** (*lit, fig*) Netz *nt*; (*of lies also*) Gespinst, Gewebe *nt* ♦ **a ~ of snow-covered branches** ein Geflecht *nt* von schneebedeckten Ästen; **a ~ of little streets** ein Gewirr *nt* von kleinen Gassen. **(b)** (*of duck etc*) Schwimmhaut *f*. **(c) W~, ~** [1] (*Comput, inf*) **the W~** das (World Wide) Web. [2] *attr* (*Comput, inf*) **~ browser** WWW-Browser *m*; **~ site** WWW-Seite *f*.
webbed [webd] *adj* **(a)** *foot, toes* Schwimm-; *animal* mit Schwimmfüßen. **(b)**

seats gurtbespannt.

webbing ['webɪŋ] *n* Gurte *pl*; (*material*) Gurtband *nt*.

web: ~-footed, ~-toed *adj* schwimmfüßig, mit Schwimmfüßen; **~-offset** *n* Rollenrotations-Offsetdruck *m*.

Wed *abbr of* **Wednesday** Mittw.

wed [wed] (*old*) *pret, ptp* ~ *or* **~ded** 1 *vi* sich vermählen (*form*), heiraten.
2 *vt* **(a)** (*bride, bridegroom*) ehelichen (*form*), sich vermählen mit (*form*); (*priest*) vermählen (*form*), trauen.
(b) (*fig: combine*) paaren ◆ **his ability ~ded to her money should make the business a success** mit seinen Fähigkeiten und ihrem Geld müßte das Geschäft eigentlich ein Erfolg werden.
(c) (*fig*) **to be ~ded to sth** (*devoted*) mit etw verheiratet sein; **he's ~ded to the view that** ... er ist felsenfest der Ansicht, daß ...

we'd [wi:d] *contr of* **we would; we had.**

wedded ['wedɪd] *adj bliss, life* Ehe-; *see* **lawful.**

wedding ['wedɪŋ] *n* **(a)** (*ceremony*) Trauung *f*; (*ceremony and festivities*) Hochzeit, Vermählung (*form*) *f*; (*silver, golden ~ etc*) Hochzeit *f* ◆ **to have a registry office/church ~** sich standesamtlich/kirchlich trauen lassen, standesamtlich/kirchlich heiraten; **when's the ~?** wann ist die Hochzeit, wann wird geheiratet?; **to have a quiet ~** in aller Stille heiraten; **to go to a ~** zu einer *or* auf eine Hochzeit gehen.
(b) (*fig*) Verbindung *f*.

wedding *in cpds* Hochzeits-; **~ anniversary** *n* Hochzeitstag *m*; **~ band** *n* Ehering *m*; **~ breakfast** *n* Hochzeitsessen *nt*; **~ cake** *n* Hochzeitskuchen *m*; **~ day** *n* Hochzeitstag *m*; **~ dress** *n* Brautkleid, Hochzeitskleid *nt*; **~ march** *n* Hochzeitsmarsch *m*; **~ night** *n* Hochzeitsnacht *f*; **~ present** *n* Hochzeitsgeschenk *nt*; **~ ring** *n* Trauring, Ehering *m*.

wedge [wedʒ] 1 *n* **(a)** (*of wood etc, fig*) Keil *m* ◆ **rubber ~** Gummibolzen *m*; **it's the thin end of the ~** so fängt's immer an; **that would be the thin end of the ~** das wäre der Anfang von Ende.
(b) (*triangular shape*) (*of cake etc*) Stück *nt*; (*of cheese*) Ecke *f* ◆ **a ~ of land** ein keilförmiges Stück Land; **the seats were arranged in a ~** die Sitzreihen waren keilförmig angeordnet.
(c) (*shoe*) Schuh *m* mit Keilabsatz; (*also* **~ heel**) Keilabsatz *m*.
2 *vt* **(a)** (*fix with a ~*) verkeilen, (mit einem Keil) festklemmen ◆ **to ~ a door/window open/shut** eine Tür/ein Fenster festklemmen *or* verkeilen; **try wedging the cracks with newspaper** versuchen Sie, die Spalten mit Zeitungspapier zuzustopfen.
(b) (*fig: pack tightly*) **to ~ oneself/sth** sich/etw zwängen (*in* in +*acc*); **to be ~d between two things/people** zwischen zwei Dingen/Personen eingekeilt *or* eingezwängt sein; **the fat man sat ~d in his chair** der dicke Mann saß in seinen Stuhl gezwängt; **we were all ~d together in the back of the car** wir saßen alle zusammengepfercht *or* eingezwängt im Fond des Wagens.

◆**wedge in** *vt sep* (*lit*) *post* festkeilen ◆ **to be ~d ~** (*car, house, person etc*) eingekeilt *or* eingezwängt sein; **if you park there, you'll ~ me/my car ~** wenn du da parkst, keilst du mich ein/wird mein Auto eingekeilt; **he ~d himself ~ between them** er zwängte sich zwischen sie.

wedge-shaped ['wedʒʃeɪpt] *adj* keilförmig.

Wedgwood ® ['wedʒwʊd] *n* Wedgwood *nt* ◆ **~ blue/green** wedgwoodblau/-grün.

wedlock ['wedlɒk] *n* (*form*) Ehe *f* ◆ **to be born out of/in ~** unehelich/ehelich geboren sein.

Wednesday ['wenzdɪ] *n* Mittwoch *m*; *see also* **Tuesday.**

wee[1] [wi:] *adj* (+*er*) (*inf*) winzig; (*Scot*) klein ◆ **a ~ bit** ein kleines bißchen; **~ (small) hours** frühe Morgenstunden.

wee[2] (*inf*) 1 *n* **to have** *or* **do/need a ~** Pipi machen/machen müssen (*inf*).
2 *vi* Pipi machen (*inf*).

weed [wi:d] 1 *n* **(a)** Unkraut *nt no pl*. **(b)** (*dated inf: tobacco*) Kraut *nt* (*inf*). **(c)** (*sl: marijuana*) Gras *nt* (*sl*). **(d)** (*inf: person*) Schwächling, Kümmerling (*inf*) *m*.
2 *vt* **(a)** *also vi* (*lit*) jäten. **(b)** (*fig*) *see* **weed out (b).**

◆**weed out** *vt sep* **(a)** *plant* ausreißen; *flower-bed* Unkraut jäten in (+*dat*). **(b)** (*fig*) aussondern; *poor candidates, lazy pupils also* aussieben.

◆**weed through** *vt sep* durchsortieren.

weeding ['wi:dɪŋ] *n* Unkrautjäten *nt* ◆ **to do some ~** Unkraut jäten.

weed-killer ['wi:dkɪlə^r] *n* Unkrautvernichter *m*, Unkrautbekämpfungsmittel *nt*.

weeds [wi:dz] *npl* (*mourning clothes*) Trauerkleider *pl*.

weedy ['wi:dɪ] *adj* (+*er*) **(a)** *ground* unkrautbewachsen, voll(er) Unkraut. **(b)** (*inf*) *person* (*in appearance*) schmächtig; (*in character*) blutarm.

week [wi:k] *n* Woche *f* ◆ **it'll be ready in a ~** in einer Woche *or* in acht Tagen ist es fertig; **~ in, ~ out** Woche für Woche; **twice/£15 a ~** zweimal/£ 15 in der Woche *or* pro Woche *or* die Woche (*inf*); **a ~ today, today** *or* **this day ~** (*dial*) heute in einer Woche *or* in acht Tagen; **tomorrow/Tuesday ~, a ~ tomorrow/on Tuesday** morgen/Dienstag in einer Woche *or* in acht Tagen; **for ~s** wochenlang; **to knock sb into the middle of next ~** (*inf*) jdn windelweich schlagen (*inf*); **a ~'s/a two ~ holiday** ein einwöchiger/zweiwöchiger Urlaub; **two ~s' holiday** zwei Wochen Ferien; **that is a ~'s work** das ist eine Woche Arbeit.

week: ~day 1 *n* Wochentag *m*; 2 *attr* Wochentags-, Werktags-; **~end** 1 *n* Wochenende *nt*; **to go/be away for the ~end** übers *or* am Wochenende verreisen/nicht da sein; **at** *or* (*esp US*) **on the ~end** am Wochenende; **to take a long ~end** ein langes Wochenende machen; 2 *attr* Wochenend-; **~end case** Reisekoffer *m*; 3 *vi* **he ~ends in the country** er verbringt seine Wochenenden auf dem Land; **~ender** [ˌwi:k'endə^r] *n* (*person*) Wochenendler(in *f*) *m*.

weekly ['wi:klɪ] 1 *adj* Wochen-; *visit* allwöchentlich ◆ **the ~ shopping expedition** der (all)wöchentliche Großeinkauf.
2 *adv* wöchentlich.
3 *n* Wochenzeitschrift *f*.

weenie ['wi:nɪ] *n* (*US inf*) (Wiener) Würstchen *nt*.

weeny ['wi:nɪ] *adj* (+*er*) (*inf*) klitzeklein (*inf*), winzig.

weenybopper ['wi:nɪˌbɒpə^r] *n* popbesessenes Kind; Pipimädchen *nt* (*pej inf*).

weep [wi:p] (*vb: pret, ptp* **wept**) 1 *vi* **(a)** weinen (*over* über +*acc*) ◆ **to ~ for sb/sth** (*because sb/sth is missed*) um jdn/etw weinen; (*out of sympathy*) für jdn/etw weinen; **the child was ~ing for his mother** das Kind weinte nach seiner Mutter; **to ~ with** *or* **for joy/with rage** vor *or* aus Freude/Wut weinen; **I wept to hear the news** ich weinte *or* mir kamen die Tränen, als ich die Nachricht hörte.
(b) (*wound, cut etc*) tränen, nässen.
2 *vt tears* weinen.
3 *n* **to have a good/little ~** tüchtig/ein bißchen weinen; **after a ~ she felt better** nachdem sie geweint hatte, fühlte sie sich besser.

weepie *n* (*inf*) *see* **weepy 2.**

weeping ['wi:pɪŋ] 1 *n* Weinen *nt*.
2 *adj* weinend; *wound* nässend.

weeping willow *n* Trauerweide *f*.

weepy ['wi:pɪ] (*inf*) 1 *adj* (+*er*) *person* weinerlich; *film* rührselig ◆ **that was a very ~ film** (*inf*) der Film hat schwer auf die Tränendrüsen gedrückt (*inf*).
2 *n* (*film etc*) Schmachtfetzen *m* (*inf*).

weevil ['wi:vɪl] *n* Rüsselkäfer *m*.

wee-wee ['wi:wi:] *n, vi* (*baby-talk*) *see* **wee**[2].

weft [weft] *n* Einschlagfaden, Schußfaden *m*.

weigh [weɪ] 1 *vt* **(a)** *goods, person, oneself etc* wiegen ◆ **could you ~ these bananas/this piece for me?** könnten Sie mir diese Bananen/dieses Stück abwiegen *or* auswiegen?
(b) (*fig*) *words, problem, merits etc* abwägen ◆ **to ~ sth in one's mind** etw erwägen; **to ~ A against B** A gegen B abwägen, A und B gegeneinander abwägen.
(c) (*Naut*) **to ~ anchor** den Anker lichten.
2 *vi* **(a)** wiegen ◆ **to ~ heavy/light** (*scales*) zu viel/zu wenig anzeigen; (*inf: material*) schwer/leicht wiegen.
(b) (*fig: be a burden*) lasten (*on* auf +*dat*).
(c) (*fig: be important*) gelten ◆ **to ~ with sb** Gewicht bei jdm haben, jdm etwas gelten; **his age ~ed against him** sein Alter wurde gegen ihn in die Waagschale geworfen.

◆**weigh down** *vt sep* **(a)** (*bear down with weight*) niederbeugen ◆ **the heavy snow ~ed the branches ~** die schwere Schneelast drückte *or* bog die Zweige nieder; **a branch ~ed ~ with fruit** ein Ast, der sich unter der Last des Obstes biegt; **she was ~ed ~ with parcels/a heavy suitcase** sie war mit Paketen überladen/der schwere Koffer zog sie fast zu Boden.
(b) (*fig*) niederdrücken ◆ **to be ~ed ~ with sorrows** von Sorgen niedergedrückt werden, mit Sorgen beladen sein.

◆**weigh in** 1 *vi* **(a)** (*Sport*) sich (vor dem Kampf/Rennen) wiegen lassen ◆ **he ~ed ~ at 70 kilos** er brachte 70 Kilo auf die Waage. **(b)** (*at airport*) das Gepäck (ab)wiegen lassen. **(c)** (*fig inf: join in*) zu Hilfe kommen (*with* mit); (*interfere*) sich einschalten.
2 *vt sep luggage* wiegen lassen.

◆**weigh out** *vt sep* abwiegen.

◆**weigh up** *vt sep pros and cons, alternatives, situation* abwägen; *person* einschätzen.

weigh: ~bridge *n* Brückenwaage *f*; **~-in** *n* (*Sport*) Wiegen *nt*.

weighing machine ['weɪɪŋmə'ʃi:n] *n* (*for people*) Personenwaage *f*; (*coin-operated*) Münzwaage *f*, Wiegeautomat *m*; (*for goods*) Waage *f*.

weight [weɪt] 1 *n* **(a)** (*heaviness, Phys*) Gewicht *nt*; (*Sport, esp Boxing*) Gewichtsklasse *f*, Gewicht *nt* (*inf*); (*of cloth*) Schwere *f*; (*of blow*) Wucht, Heftigkeit *f* ◆ **3 kilos in ~** 3 Kilo Gewicht, ein Gewicht von 3 Kilo; **the grocer gave me short** *or* **light ~** der Kaufmann hat (mir) schlecht *or* knapp gewogen; **a suit in a heavier ~ for winter** ein Anzug in einer schwereren Qualität für den Winter; **a blow without much ~ behind it** ein Schlag mit wenig *or* ohne viel Wucht *or* Kraft dahinter; **to feel/test the ~ of sth** sehen/probieren, wie schwer etw ist; **the ~ of the snow made the branches break** die Zweige brachen unter der Schneelast; **to gain** *or* **put on/lose ~** zunehmen/abnehmen; **he carries his ~ well** man sieht ihm sein Gewicht nicht an; **I hope the chair takes my ~** ich hoffe, der Stuhl hält mein Gewicht aus; **he's worth his ~ in gold** er ist Gold(es) wert.
(b) (*metal ~, unit of ~, heavy object*) Gewicht *nt*; (*for weighting down also*) Beschwerer *m* ◆ **~s and measures** Maße und Gewichte (+*pl vb*); **will he manage to lift the 90kg ~?** wird er die 90 Kilo heben können?; **the doctor warned him not to lift heavy ~s** der Arzt warnte ihn davor, schwere Lasten zu heben; **she's quite a ~** sie ist ganz schön schwer.
(c) (*fig: load, burden*) Last *f* ◆ **the ~ of evidence** die Beweislast; **they won by ~ of numbers** sie gewannen durch die zahlenmäßige Überlegenheit; **that's a ~ off my mind** mir fällt ein Stein vom Herzen.
(d) (*fig: importance*) Bedeutung *f*, Gewicht *nt* ◆ **he/his opinion carries no ~** seine Stimme/Meinung hat kein Gewicht *or* fällt nicht ins Gewicht; **those arguments carry ~ with the minister/carry great ~** diesen Argumenten mißt der Minister Gewicht bei/wird großes Gewicht beigemessen; **to give due ~ to an argument** einem Argument das entsprechende Gewicht geben *or* beimessen; **to add ~ to sth** einer Sache (*dat*) zusätzliches Gewicht geben *or*

verleihen; **to pull one's ~** seinen Teil dazutun, seinen Beitrag leisten; **to put one's full ~ behind sb/sth** sich mit seinem ganzen Gewicht *or* mit dem ganzen Gewicht seiner Persönlichkeit für jdn/etw einsetzen; **to throw** *or* **chuck** (*inf*) **one's ~ about** seinen Einfluß geltend machen.

2 *vt* **(a)** (*make heavier, put ~s on*) beschweren.

(b) (*fig: bias*) *results* verfälschen ◆ **to ~ sth in favour of/against sb** etw zugunsten einer Person/gegen jdn beeinflussen; **to ~ sth in favour of/against sth** etw zugunsten einer Sache/gegen etw beeinflussen; **to be ~ed in favour of sb/sth** so angelegt sein, daß es zugunsten einer Person/Sache ist; **to be ~ed against sb/sth** jdn/etw benachteiligen.

◆**weight down** *vt sep person* (*with parcels etc*) überladen; *corpse* beschweren; (*fig*) belasten, niederdrücken.

weightily ['weɪtɪlɪ] *adv* gewichtig.

weightiness ['weɪtɪnɪs] *n* (*lit*) Gewicht *nt*; (*fig*) Gewichtigkeit *f*; (*of responsibility also*) Schwere *f*.

weighting ['weɪtɪŋ] *n* (*Brit: supplement*) Zulage *f*.

weight: ~less *adj* schwerelos; **~lessness** *n* Schwerelosigkeit *f*; **~lifter** *n* Gewichtheber *m*; **~lifting** *n* Gewichtheben *nt*; **~-train** *vi* Krafttraining machen; **~ training** *n* Krafttraining *nt*; **~ watcher** *n* Figurbewußte(r) *mf*.

weighty ['weɪtɪ] *adj* (*+er*) **(a)** (*lit*) schwer. **(b)** (*fig*) gewichtig; (*influential*) *argument also* schwerwiegend; (*burdensome*) *responsibility also* schwerwiegend, schwer.

weir [wɪəʳ] *n* **(a)** (*barrier*) Wehr *nt*. **(b)** (*fish trap*) Fischreuse *f*.

weird [wɪəd] *adj* (*+er*) (*uncanny*) unheimlich; (*inf: odd*) seltsam.

weirdie ['wɪədɪ] *n* (*sl*) verrückter Typ (*inf*).

weirdly ['wɪədlɪ] *adv see adj*.

weirdness ['wɪədnɪs] *n* (*inf: oddness*) Seltsamkeit *f*.

weirdo ['wɪədəʊ] *n* (*sl*) verrückter Typ (*inf*).

welch *vi see* **welsh.**

▼ **welcome** ['welkəm] 1 *n* Willkommen *nt* ◆ **to give sb a hearty** *or* **warm ~** jdm einen herzlichen Empfang bereiten; **to meet with a cold/warm ~** kühl/herzlich empfangen werden, einen kühlen/herzlichen Empfang bekommen; **to bid sb ~** (*form*) jdm ein Willkommen entbieten (*geh*); **what sort of a ~ will this product get from the public?** wie wird das Produkt von der Öffentlichkeit aufgenommen werden?

2 *adj* **(a)** (*received with pleasure, pleasing*) willkommen; *visitor also* gerngesehen *attr*; *news also* angenehm ◆ **the money is very ~ just now** das Geld kommt gerade jetzt sehr gelegen; **to make sb ~** jdn sehr freundlich aufnehmen *or* empfangen; **to make sb feel ~** jdm das Gefühl geben, ein willkommener *or* gerngesehener Gast zu sein; **you will always be ~ here** Sie sind uns (*dat*) jederzeit willkommen; **I didn't feel very ~ there** ich habe mich dort nicht sehr wohl gefühlt.

(b) you're ~! nichts zu danken!, keine Ursache!, bitte sehr!, aber gerne!; (*iro*) von mir aus gerne!, wenn's Ihnen Spaß macht!; **you're ~ to use my room** Sie können gerne mein Zimmer benutzen; **you're ~ to try** (*lit, iro*) Sie können es gerne versuchen; **you're ~ to it!** (*lit, iro*) von mir aus herzlich gerne!

▼ 3 *vt* (*lit, fig*) begrüßen, willkommen heißen (*geh*) ◆ **to ~ sb to one's house** jdn bei sich zu Hause *or* in seinem Haus begrüßen *or* willkommen heißen (*geh*); **they ~d him home with a big party** sie veranstalteten zu seiner Heimkehr ein großes Fest.

4 *interj* **~ home/to Scotland/on board!** herzlich willkommen!, willkommen daheim/in Schottland/an Bord!

welcome-home ['welkəm'həʊm] *adj attr party* Begrüßungs-, Willkommens-.

welcoming ['welkəmɪŋ] *adj* zur Begrüßung; *smile, gesture* einladend ◆ **~ committee** (*lit, fig*) Begrüßungskomitee *nt*; **a ~ cup of tea was on the table for her** eine Tasse Tee stand zu ihrer Begrüßung auf dem Tisch; **a ~ fire blazed in the hearth when he arrived** ein warmes Feuer begrüßte ihn bei seiner Ankunft; **the crowds raised a ~ cheer for him** die Menge jubelte ihm zur Begrüßung zu.

weld [weld] 1 *vt* **(a)** (*Tech*) schweißen ◆ **to ~ parts together** Teile zusammenschweißen *or* verschweißen; **to ~ sth on** etw anschweißen (*to* an *+acc*); **~ed joint** Schweißnaht *f*.

(b) (*fig: also* **~ together**) zusammenschmieden (*into* zu).

2 *vi* sich schweißen lassen.

3 *n* Schweißnaht, Schweißstelle *f*.

welder ['weldəʳ] *n* (*person*) Schweißer(in *f*) *m*; (*machine*) Schweißapparat *m*, Schweißgerät *nt*.

welding ['weldɪŋ] *n* Schweißen *nt* ◆ **~ torch** Schweißbrenner *m*.

welfare ['welfeəʳ] *n* **(a)** (*well-being*) Wohl, Wohlergehen *nt*. **(b)** (*~ work*) Fürsorge, Wohlfahrt (*dated*) *f* ◆ **child/social ~** Kinderfürsorge *f*/soziale Fürsorge. **(c)** (*US: social security*) Sozialhilfe *f* ◆ **to be on ~** Sozialhilfeempfänger(in *f*) *m* sein.

welfare: ~ check *n* (*US*) Sozialhilfeüberweisung *f*; **~ state** *n* Wohlfahrtsstaat *m*; **~ work** *n* Fürsorgearbeit, Wohlfahrtsarbeit (*dated*) *f*; **~ worker** *n* Fürsorger(in *f*) *m*.

well¹ [wel] 1 *n* **(a)** (*water ~*) Brunnen *m*; (*oil ~*) Ölquelle *f*; (*drilled*) Bohrloch *nt*; (*fig: source*) Quelle *f* ◆ **to drive** *or* **sink a ~** einen Brunnen bohren *or* anlegen *or* graben; ein Bohrloch anlegen *or* vorantreiben.

(b) (*shaft*) (*for lift*) Schacht *m*; (*for stairs*) Treppenschacht *m*; (*down centre of staircase*) Treppenhaus *nt*.

(c) (*of theatre*) Parkett *nt*; (*of auditorium*) ebenerdiger Teil des Zuschauer-/Konferenz-/Versammlungsraums; (*Brit: of court*) *Teil des Gerichtssaals, in dem die Rechtsanwälte und Protokollschreiber sitzen.*

(d) (*ink~*) Tintenfaß *nt*.

2 *vi* quellen.

◆**well up** *vi* (*water, liquid*) emporsteigen, emporquellen; (*fig*) aufsteigen; (*noise*) anschwellen ◆ **tears ~ed ~ in her eyes** Tränen stiegen *or* schossen ihr in die Augen.

▼ **well²** *comp* **better**, *superl* **best** 1 *adv* **(a)** (*in a good or satisfactory manner*) gut ◆ **the child speaks ~** (*is ~-spoken*) das Kind spricht ordentlich Deutsch/Englisch *etc or* gutes Deutsch/Englisch *etc*; **it is ~ painted** (*portrait*) es ist gut gemalt; (*house, fence*) es ist sauber *or* ordentlich angestrichen; **he did it as ~ as he could/I could have done** er machte es so gut er konnte/ebenso gut, wie ich es hätte machen können; **he's doing ~ at school/in maths** er ist gut *or* er kommt gut voran in der Schule/in Mathematik; **he did ~ in the maths exam** er hat in der Mathematikprüfung gut abgeschnitten; **for an eight-year-old he did very ~** für einen Achtjährigen hat er seine Sache sehr gut gemacht; **his business is doing ~** sein Geschäft geht gut; **mother and child are/the patient is doing ~** Mutter und Kind/dem Patienten geht es gut, Mutter und Kind sind/der Patient ist wohlauf; **he did quite ~ at improving sales** er war recht erfolgreich in der Erhöhung des Absatzes; **if you do ~ you'll be promoted** wenn Sie sich bewähren, werden Sie befördert; **you did ~ to help** du tatest gut daran zu helfen, es war gut, daß du geholfen hast; **~ done!** gut gemacht!, bravo!, sehr gut!; **~ played!** gut gespielt!; **to do oneself ~** (*inf*) es sich (*dat*) gut gehen lassen; **to do ~ by sb** (*inf*) jdm gegenüber *or* zu jdm großzügig sein; **everything went ~/quite ~** es ging alles gut *or* glatt (*inf*)/recht gut *or* ganz gut *or* ganz ordentlich.

(b) (*favourably, fortunately*) gut ◆ **to speak/think ~ of sb** über jdn Gutes sagen/Positives denken, von jdm positiv sprechen/denken; **to be ~ spoken of in certain circles/by one's colleagues** einen guten Ruf in gewissen Kreisen haben/bei seinen Kollegen in gutem Ruf stehen; **to stand ~ with sb** bei jdm angesehen sein; **to be ~ in with sb** (*inf*) auf gutem Fuß mit jdm stehen; **to marry ~** eine gute Partie machen; **to do ~ out of sth** von etw ganz schön *or* ordentlich profitieren, bei etw gut wegkommen (*inf*); **you would do ~ to arrive early** Sie täten gut daran, früh zu kommen; **you might as ~ go** du könntest eigentlich geradesogut *or* ebensogut (auch) gehen; **are you coming? — I might as ~** kommst du? — ach, könnte ich eigentlich (auch) (*inf*) *or* ach, warum nicht.

(c) (*thoroughly, considerably, to a great degree*) gut, gründlich ◆ **shake the bottle ~** schütteln Sie die Flasche kräftig; (*on medicine*) Flasche kräftig *or* gut schütteln; **he loved her too ~ to leave her** (*liter*) er liebte sie zu sehr, als daß er sie verlassen hätte; **we were ~ beaten** wir sind gründlich geschlagen worden; **he could ~ afford it** er konnte es sich (*dat*) sehr wohl leisten; **I'm ~ content with my lot** ich bin wohl zufrieden mit meinem Schicksal; **all** *or* **only too ~** nur (all)zu gut; **~ and truly** (ganz) gründlich; *married, settled in* ganz richtig; (*iro also*) fest; *westernized, conditioned* durch und durch; **he was ~ away** (*inf*) er war in Fahrt *or* Schwung (*inf*); (*drunk*) er hatte einen sitzen (*inf*); **he sat ~ forward in his seat** er saß weit vorne auf seinem Sitz; **it was ~ worth the trouble** das hat sich wohl *or* sehr gelohnt; **~ out of sight** ein gutes Stück *or* weit außer Sichtweite; **~ within ...** durchaus in (*+dat*); **~ past midnight** lange *or* ein gutes Stück (*inf*) nach Mitternacht; **he's ~ over fifty** er ist weit über fünfzig.

▼ **(d)** (*probably, reasonably*) ohne weiteres, gut, wohl ◆ **I may ~ be late** es kann leicht *or* wohl *or* ohne weiteres sein, daß ich spät komme; **it may ~ be that** ... es ist gut *or* wohl *or* ohne weiteres möglich, daß ...; **you may ~ be right** Sie mögen wohl recht haben; **she cried, as ~ she might** sie weinte, und das (auch) mit Grund *or* wozu sie auch allen Grund hatte; **you may ~ ask!** (*iro*) das kann man wohl fragen; **I couldn't very ~ stay** ich konnte schlecht bleiben, ich konnte wohl nicht mehr gut bleiben.

▼ **(e)** (*in addition*) **as ~** auch; **if he comes as ~** wenn er auch kommt; **x as ~ as y** x sowohl als auch y, x und auch y; **she sings as ~ as dances** sie singt und tanzt auch noch.

2 *adj* **(a)** (*in good health*) gesund ◆ **get ~ soon!** gute Besserung; **are you ~?** geht es Ihnen gut?; **I'm very ~, thanks** danke, es geht mir sehr gut; **he's not a ~ man** er ist gar nicht gesund; **she's not been ~ lately** ihr ging es in letzter Zeit (gesundheitlich) gar nicht gut; **I don't feel at all ~** ich fühle mich gar nicht gut *or* wohl.

▼ **(b)** (*satisfactory, desirable, advantageous*) gut ◆ **all is not ~ with him/in the world** mit ihm/mit *or* in der Welt steht es nicht zum besten; **that's all very ~, but** ... das ist ja alles schön und gut, aber ...; **if that's the case, (all) ~ and good** wenn das der Fall ist, dann soll es mir recht sein; **it's all very ~ for you to suggest** ... Sie können leicht vorschlagen ...; **it's all very ~ for you, you don't have to** ... Sie haben gut reden *or* Sie können leicht reden, Sie müssen ja nicht ...; **it was ~ for him that no-one found out** es war sein Glück, daß es niemand entdeckt hat; **it would be as ~ to ask first** es wäre wohl besser *or* gescheiter (*inf*), sich erst mal zu erkundigen; **it's just as ~ he came** es ist (nur *or* schon) gut, daß er gekommen ist; **you're ~ out of that** seien Sie froh, daß Sie damit nichts/nichts mehr zu tun haben; **all's ~ that ends ~** Ende gut, alles gut.

3 *interj* also; (*expectantly also*) na; (*doubtfully*) na ja ◆ **~ ~!, ~ I never (did)!** also, so was!, na so was!; **~ now** also; **~, it was like this** also, es war so *or* folgendermaßen; **~ there you are, that proves it!** na bitte *or* also bitte, das beweist es doch; **~, as I was saying** also, wie (bereits) gesagt; **~ then** also (gut); (*in question*) na?, nun?, also?; **very ~ then!** na gut, also gut!; (*indignantly*) also bitte (sehr); **~, that's a relief!** na (also), das ist ja eine Erleichterung!

4 *n* Gute(s) *nt* ◆ **to wish sb ~** (*in general*) jdm alles Gute wünschen; (*in an attempt, iro*) jdm Glück wünschen (*in* bei); (*be well-disposed to*) jdm gewogen

➤ LANGUAGE IN USE: **welcome: 3** → 13, 19.3 **well²: 1a** → 23.6, 26.3 **1d** → 26.3 **1e** → 11.2 **2b** → 13

sein; **I wish him ~, but ...** ich wünsche ihm nichts Böses, aber ...

we'll [wi:l] *contr of* **we shall; we will.**

well *in cpds* gut; **~-adjusted** *adj (Psych)* gut angepaßt; **~-advised** *adj plan, move* klug; **to be ~-advised to ...** wohl *or* gut beraten sein *or* gut daran tun, zu ...; **~-aimed** *adj shot, blow, sarcasm* gut- *or* wohlgezielt *attr*; **~-appointed** *adj* gut ausgestattet; **~-argued** *adj* wohl- *or* gutbegründet *attr*; **~-balanced** *adj* **(a)** *person, mind* ausgeglichen; **(b)** *budget, diet* (gut) ausgewogen; **~-behaved** *adj child* artig, wohlerzogen; *animal* guterzogen *attr*; **~-being** *n* Wohl, Wohlergehen *nt*; **to have a sense of ~-being** (ein Gefühl der) Behaglichkeit *or* Wohligkeit empfinden; **~-born** *adj* aus vornehmer Familie, aus vornehmem Haus; **~-bred** *adj* **(a)** *(polite) person* wohlerzogen; *manners* vornehm, gepflegt; *accent* distinguiert; **(b)** *(of good stock) animal* aus guter Zucht; *(iro) person* aus gutem Stall; **~-built** *adj house* gut *or* solide gebaut; *person* stämmig, kräftig; **~-chosen** *adj remarks, words* gut *or* glücklich gewählt; **in a few ~-chosen words** in wenigen wohlgesetzten Worten; **~-connected** *adj* **to be ~-connected** Beziehungen zu *or* in höheren Kreisen haben; **~-deserved** *adj* wohlverdient; **~-developed** *adj muscle* gutentwickelt *attr*; *sense* (gut) ausgeprägt; **~-disposed** *adj* **to be ~-disposed towards sb/sth** jdm/einer Sache gewogen sein *or* freundlich gesonnen sein; **~-done** *adj steak* durchgebraten, durch *inv*; **~-dressed** *adj* gut angezogen *or* gekleidet; **~-earned** *adj* wohlverdient; **~-educated** *adj person* gebildet; *voice* (gut) ausgebildet; **~-equipped** *adj office, studio* gut ausgestattet; *expedition, army* gut ausgerüstet; **~-established** *adj practice, custom* fest; *tradition* alt; **~-favoured** *adj (old) girl, family* ansehnlich *(old)*; **~-fed** *adj* wohl- *or* gutgenährt *attr*; **~-founded** *adj* wohlbegründet *attr*; **~-groomed** *adj* gepflegt; **~-grown** *adj animal, child* groß (gewachsen); **~-head** *n* **(a)** *(of spring etc)* Quelle *f*; *(fig)* Ursprung *m*; **(b)** *(head of oilwell)* Bohrturm *m*; **~-heeled** *adj (inf)* betucht; **~-hung** *adj meat* abgehangen; *(inf) man* mit imposanter Männlichkeit, gut ausgestattet; **~-informed** *adj* gutinformiert *attr*; *sources also* wohlunterrichtet *attr*; **to be ~-informed about sb/sth** über jdn/etw gut informiert *or* gut unterrichtet sein.

wellington (boot) ['welɪŋtən('bu:t)] *n (Brit)* Gummistiefel *m*.

well: ~-intentioned *adj see* **~-meaning**; **~-kept** *adj garden, hair etc* gepflegt; *secret* streng gehütet, gutgewahrt *attr*; **~-knit** *adj body* drahtig, straff; *(fig)* gut durchdacht *or* aufgebaut; **~-known** *adj place, singer* bekannt; *fact also* wohl- *or* altbekannt; **it's ~-known that ...** es ist allgemein bekannt, daß ...; **~-loved** *adj* vielgeliebt; **~-mannered** *adj* mit guten Manieren; **to be ~-mannered** gute Manieren haben; **~-matched** *adj teams* gleich stark; **they're a ~-matched pair** sie passen gut zusammen; **~-meaning** *adj* wohlmeinend *attr*; **~-meant** *adj action, lie* gutgemeint *attr*; **~-nigh** *adv (form)* nahezu, beinahe, nachgerade *(geh)*; **this is ~-nigh impossible** *(not form)* das ist nahezu *or* beinahe unmöglich; **~-off** [1] *adj* **(a)** *(affluent)* reich, begütert, gut d(a)ran *(inf)*; **(b)** *pred (fortunate)* gut daran; **you don't know when you're ~-off** *(inf)* du weißt (ja) nicht, wann es dir gut geht; [2] *n* **the ~-off** *pl* die Begüterten *pl*; **~-oiled** *adj (inf: drunk)* beduselt *(inf)*; **~-padded** *adj (inf: not thin)* gut gepolstert *(inf)*; **~-preserved** *adj* guterhalten *attr*; *person also* wohlerhalten *attr*; **~-read** *adj* belesen; **~-spent** *adj time* gut genützt *or* verbracht; *money* sinnvoll *or* vernünftig ausgegeben *or* verwendet; **~-spoken** *adj* mit gutem Deutsch/Englisch *etc*; **to be ~-spoken** gutes Deutsch/Englisch *etc* sprechen; **~-stacked** *adj (sl) woman* **to be ~-stacked** Holz vor der Hütte haben *(inf)*; **~-stocked** *adj* gutbestückt *attr*; *(Comm also)* mit gutem Sortiment; *larder, shelves also* gutgefüllt *attr*, reichlich gefüllt; *library also* reichhaltig, umfangreich; **~-thought-of** *adj* angesehen; **~-timed** *adj* (zeitlich) gut abgepaßt, zeitlich günstig; **that was a ~-timed interruption** die Unterbrechung kam im richtigen Augenblick; **~-to-do** [1] *adj* wohlhabend, reich; *district* Reichen-, Vornehmen-; [2] *n* **the ~-to-do** *pl* die Begüterten *pl*; **~-tried** *adj method etc* erprobt; **~ water** *n* Brunnenwasser *nt*; **~-wisher** *n* **cards from ~-wishers** Karten von Leuten, die ihm/ihr *etc* alles Gute wünschten; **our cause has many ~-wishers** unsere Sache hat viele Sympathisanten; **"from a ~-wisher"** „jemand, der es gut mit Ihnen meint"; **~-woman clinic** *n* Frauenklinik *f*; **~-worn** *adj garment* abgetragen; *carpet etc* abgelaufen; *book* abgenützt, abgegriffen; *path* ausgetreten; *saying, subject etc* abgedroschen.

welly ['welɪ] *n (inf)* Gummistiefel *m*.

Welsh [welʃ] [1] *adj* walisisch.
[2] *n* **(a)** *(language)* Walisisch *nt*. **(b) the ~** *pl* die Waliser *pl*.

welsh, welch [welʃ] *vi (sl)* sich drücken *(on sth* vor etw *dat) (inf)*; *(bookmaker etc: avoid payment)* die Gewinne nicht ausbezahlen *(on sb* jdm); *(by disappearing)* mit dem Geld durchgehen *(inf)* ♦ **to ~ on sb** jdn (auf)sitzen lassen *(inf)*.

Welsh: ~ dresser *n* Anrichte *f* mit Tellerbord; **~man** *n* Waliser *m*; **~ rabbit** *or* **rarebit** *n* überbackene Käseschnitte; **~woman** *n* Waliserin *f*.

welt [welt] *n* **(a)** *(of shoe)* Rahmen *m*; *(of pullover)* Bündchen *nt*. **(b)** *(weal)* Striemen *m*.

welted ['weltɪd] *adj shoe* randgenäht.

welter ['weltəʳ] *n* Unzahl *f*; *(of blood, cheers)* Meer *nt*; *(of emotions)* Sturm, Tumult *m*; *(of verbiage)* Flut *f*.

welterweight ['weltəweɪt] *n* Weltergewicht *nt*.

wench [wentʃ] [1] *n (old)* Maid *f (old)*; *(serving ~)* Magd *f*; *(hum)* Frauenzimmer *nt*.
[2] *vi* sich mit Mädchen herumtreiben.

wend [wend] *vt* **to ~ one's way home/to the pub** *etc* sich auf den Heimweg/zur Wirtschaft *etc* begeben.

Wendy house ['wendɪ,haʊs] *n* Spielhaus *nt*.

went [went] *pret of* **go.**

wept [wept] *pret, ptp of* **weep.**

were [wɜ:] *2nd pers sing, 1st, 2nd, 3rd pers pl pret of* **be.**

we're [wɪəʳ] *contr of* **we are.**

weren't [wɜ:nt] *contr of* **were not.**

werewolf ['wɪəwʊlf] *n* Werwolf *m*.

wert [wɜ:t] *(old) 2nd pers sing pret of* **be.**

Wesleyan ['wezlɪən] *(Eccl)* [1] *adj* wesleyanisch.
[2] *n* Wesleyaner(in *f*) *m*.

west [west] [1] *n* **(a)** Westen *m* ♦ **in/to the ~** im Westen/nach *or* gen *(liter)* Westen; **to the ~ of** westlich von, im Westen von; **he comes from the ~ (of Ireland)** er kommt aus dem Westen (von Irland); **the wind is blowing from the ~** der Wind kommt von West(en) *or* aus (dem) Westen.
(b) *(western world)* **the ~** *or* **W~** der Westen.
[2] *adj* West-, westlich.
[3] *adv* **(a)** nach Westen, westwärts ♦ **it faces ~** es geht nach Westen; **~ of** westlich von. **(b) to go ~** *(fig inf)* flöten gehen *(sl)*; *(to die)* vor die Hunde gehen *(sl)*.

west *in cpds* West-; **W~ Bank** *n (in Middle East)* Westjordanland *nt*, West Bank *f*; **W~ Berlin** *n* West-Berlin *nt*; **~-bound** *adj traffic, carriageway* in Richtung Westen; **to be ~-bound** nach Westen unterwegs sein, westwärts reisen *or* fahren; **~-by-north/south** *n* West über Nord/Süd *no art*.

westerly ['westəlɪ] [1] *adj* westlich.
[2] *n (wind)* Westwind, West *(poet) m*.

western ['westən] [1] *adj (all senses)* westlich ♦ **on the W~ front** an der Westfront; **W~ Europe** Westeuropa *nt*.
[2] *n* Western *m*.

westerner ['westənəʳ] *n* **(a)** *(Pol)* Abendländer(in *f*) *m*. **(b)** *(US)* Weststaatler *m*.

westernization ['westənaɪ'zeɪʃən] *n (westernizing)* Einführung *f* der westlichen Kultur *or* Zivilisation; *(western character)* westliche Zivilisation *f*; *(pej)* Verwestlichung *f*.

westernize ['westənaɪz] *vt* die westliche Zivilisation/Kultur einführen in *(+dat)*; *(pej)* verwestlichen.

westernized ['westənaɪzd] *adj person, culture* vom Westen beeinflußt, westlich ausgerichtet; *(pej)* verwestlicht.

westernmost ['westənməʊst] *adj* westlichste(r, s), am weitesten westlich (gelegen).

west: W~ Germany *n* Westdeutschland *nt*, Bundesrepublik *f* (Deutschland); **W~ Indian** [1] *adj* westindisch; [2] *n* Westindier(in *f*) *m*; **W~ Indies** *npl* Westindische Inseln *pl*; **~-north-~** *n* Westnordwest *no art*.

Westphalia [west'feɪlɪə] *n* Westfalen *nt*.

Westphalian [west'feɪlɪən] [1] *adj* westfälisch.
[2] *n* Westfale *m*, Westfälin *f*.

west: ~-south-~ *n* Westsüdwest *no art*; **~ward(s)** ['westwəd(z)], **~wardly** [-wədlɪ] [1] *adj* westlich; **in a ~wardly direction** nach Westen, (in) Richtung Westen; [2] *adv* westwärts, nach Westen.

wet [wet] *(vb: pret, ptp ~ or ~ted)* [1] *adj (+er)* **(a)** naß ♦ **to be ~** *(paint, varnish, ink)* naß *or* feucht sein; **to be ~ through** durch und durch naß sein, völlig durchnäßt sein; **~ with tears** tränenfeucht; **her eyes were ~ with tears** sie hatte feuchte Augen, sie hatte Tränen in den Augen; **"~ paint"** „Vorsicht, frisch gestrichen"; **to get one's feet ~** nasse Füße bekommen, sich *(dat)* nasse Füße holen *(inf)*; **to be ~ behind the ears** *(inf)* noch feucht *or* noch nicht trocken hinter den Ohren sein *(inf)*.
(b) *(rainy)* naß, feucht; *climate, country* feucht ♦ **the ~ season** die Regenzeit; **in ~ weather** bei nassem Wetter, bei Regenwetter; **it's been ~ all week** es war die ganze Woche (über) regnerisch.
(c) *(allowing alcohol) state, city* wo kein Alkoholverbot besteht, nicht prohibitionistisch.
(d) *(Brit inf) (weak, spiritless)* weichlich, lasch; *(Pol pej)* gemäßigt ♦ **don't be so ~!** sei nicht so ein *or* kein solcher Waschlappen! *(inf)*.
(e) *(US inf: wrong)* **you're all ~** da liegst du völlig falsch *(inf)*.
[2] *n* **(a)** *(moisture)* Feuchtigkeit *f*.
(b) *(rain)* Nässe *f* ♦ **it's out in the ~** es ist draußen im Nassen.
(c) *(inf: ~ season)* Regenzeit *f*.
(d) *(US inf: anti-prohibitionist)* Antiprohibitionist(in *f*) *m*.
(e) *(Brit) (sl: person)* Waschlappen *m (inf)*; *(Pol pej inf)* Gemäßigte(r) *mf*.
[3] *vt* naß machen; *lips, washing* befeuchten ♦ **to ~ the baby's head** *(inf)* den Sohn/die Tochter begießen *(inf)*; **to ~ one's whistle** *(inf)* sich *(dat)* die Kehle anfeuchten *(inf)*; **to ~ the bed/one's pants/oneself** das Bett/seine Hosen/sich naß machen, ins Bett/in die Hose(n) machen; **I nearly ~ myself** *(inf)* ich habe mir fast in die Hose gemacht *(inf)*.

wet: ~-and-dry [1] *n* Schmirgelpapier *nt*; [2] *vt* (naß)schmirgeln; **~ blanket** *n (inf)* Miesmacher(in *f*) *(inf)*, Spielverderber(in *f*) *m*; **~ cell** *n* Naßelement *nt*; **~ dock** *n* Dock, Flutbecken *nt*; **~ dream** *n* feuchter Traum, kalter Bauer *(sl)*.

wether ['weðəʳ] *n* Hammel, Schöps *(dial) m*.

wet-look ['wetlʊk] *adj* Hochglanz-.

wetly ['wetlɪ] *adv* **(a)** naß. **(b)** *(Brit inf)* weich, lasch.

wetness ['wetnɪs] *n* **(a)** Nässe *f*; *(of weather also, climate, paint, ink)* Feuchtigkeit *f*. **(b)** *(Brit inf)* Weichlichkeit *f*.

wet: ~-nurse *n* Amme *f*; **~suit** *n* Neoprenanzug, Taucheranzug *m*.

wetting ['wetɪŋ] [1] *n* unfreiwillige Dusche *(inf)*; *(falling into water)* unfreiwilliges Bad ♦ **to get a ~** klatschnaß werden, eine Dusche abbekommen *(inf)*; ein unfreiwilliges Bad nehmen; **to give sb a ~** jdm eine Dusche/ein Bad verabreichen *(inf)*.

[2] *adj (Chem)* **~ agent** Netzmittel *nt.*

we've [wi:v] *contr of* **we have.**

whack [wæk] [1] *n* **(a)** *(blow)* (knallender) Schlag ◆ **to give sb/sth a ~** jdm einen Schlag versetzen/auf etw *(acc)* schlagen.

(b) *(inf: attempt)* Versuch *m* ◆ **to have a ~ at sth/at doing sth** etw probieren *or* versuchen, sich an etw *(dat)* versuchen; **I'll have a ~ at it** ich will mich mal (d)ranwagen.

(c) *(inf: share)* (An)teil *m* ◆ **we're offering £50,000, top ~** wir bieten höchstens *or* maximal £ 50.000; **he's earning the top ~** er bekommt das Spitzengehalt.

[2] *vt* **(a)** *(hit)* schlagen, hauen *(inf).* **(b)** *(inf: defeat)* (haushoch) schlagen. **(c)** *(inf: exhaust)* erschlagen *(inf).*

◆**whack off** *vi (sl: masturbate)* wichsen *(sl),* sich *(dat)* einen runterholen *(inf).*

whacked [wækt] *adj (inf: exhausted)* kaputt *(inf).*

whacking ['wækɪŋ] [1] *adj (Brit inf) lie, defeat, meal* Mords- *(inf)* ◆ **~ great** riesengroß; **a ~ great spider/a ~ big book** ein Mordstrumm *nt (inf)* von einer Spinne/von (einem) Buch.

[2] *n* **(a)** *(beating)* Keile *f (inf)* ◆ **to give sb a ~** jdm Keile *or* eine Tracht Prügel verpassen *(inf).* **(b)** *(inf: defeat)* **we got a real ~** sie haben uns richtig in die Pfanne gehauen *(inf).*

whacko ['wæ,kəʊ] *interj (dated)* trefflich *(dated),* tipp-topp, eins a *(inf).*

whacky *adj (+er) (inf) see* **wacky.**

whale [weɪl] *n* **(a)** Wal *m.* **(b)** *(inf: exceedingly great, good etc)* **a ~ of** ein Riesen-, ein(e) riesige(r, s); **a ~ of a difference** ein himmelweiter Unterschied; **to have a ~ of a time** sich prima amüsieren.

whale: ~bone *n* Fischbein *nt;* **~ fishing** *n* Wal(fisch)fang *m;* **~ oil** *n* Walöl *nt,* Tran *m.*

whaler ['weɪlə^r] *n (person, ship)* Walfänger *m.*

whaling ['weɪlɪŋ] *n* Wal(fisch)fang *m* ◆ **to go ~** auf Walfang gehen; **~ ship** Walfänger *m,* Walfangboot, Walfangschiff *nt;* **~ station** Walfangstation *f.*

wham [wæm], **whang** [wæŋ] [1] *interj* wumm.

[2] *n (blow)* Schlag *m; (bang, thump)* Knall *m.*

[3] *vt (hit)* schlagen; *(bang, thump)* knallen.

[4] *vi* knallen ◆ **to ~ into sth** auf etw *(acc)* krachen *(inf).*

wharf [wɔ:f] *n, pl* **-s** *or* **wharves** [wɔ:vz] Kai *m.*

what [wɒt] [1] *pron* **(a)** *(interrog)* was ◆ **~ is this called?** wie heißt das?, wie nennt man das?; **~'s the weather like?** wie ist das Wetter?; **~ do 4 and 3 make?** wieviel ist *or* macht 4 und *or* plus 3?; **you need (a) ~?** *was* brauchen Sie?; **~ is it now?, ~ do you want now?** was ist denn?; **~'s that (you/he** *etc* **said)?** *was* hast du/hat er da gerade gesagt?, wie *or* was war das noch mal *(inf)?;* **~'s that to you?** was geht dich das an?; **~ for?** wozu?, wofür?, für was? *(inf);* **~'s that tool for?** wofür ist das Werkzeug?; **~ are you looking at me like that for?** warum *or* was *(inf)* siehst du mich denn so an?; **~ did you do that for?** warum hast du denn das gemacht?; **~ about ...?** wie wär's mit ...?; **well, ~ about it? are we going?** na, wie ist's, gehen wir?; **you know that pub? — ~ about it?** kennst du die Wirtschaft? — was ist damit?; **~ of** *or* **about it?** na und? *(inf);* **~ if ...?** was ist, wenn ...?; **so ~?** *(inf)* ja *or* na und?; **~ does it matter?** was macht das schon?; **~-d'you(-ma)-call-him/-her/-it** *(inf),* **~'s-his/-her/-its name** *(inf)* wie heißt er/sie/es gleich *or* schnell.

(b) *(rel)* was ◆ **he knows ~ it is to suffer** er weiß, was leiden heißt *or* ist; **that is not ~ I asked for** danach habe ich nicht gefragt; **that's exactly ~ I want/said** genau das möchte ich/habe ich gesagt; **do you know ~ you are looking for?** weißt du, wonach du suchst?; **come ~ may** komme was wolle; **~ I'd like is a cup of tea** was ich jetzt gerne hätte, (das) wäre ein Tee; **~ with Granny dying and the new baby, life's been very hectic** Oma ist gestorben, das Baby ist da - es ist alles sehr hektisch; **~ with one thing and the other** und wie es sich dann so ergab/ergibt, wie das so ist *or* geht; **and ~'s more** und außerdem, und noch dazu; **he knows ~'s ~** *(inf)* er kennt sich aus, der weiß Bescheid *(inf);* **(I'll) tell you ~** *(inf)* weißt du was?; **and ~ not** *(inf),* **and ~ have you** *(inf)* und was sonst noch (alles), und was weiß ich; **to give sb ~ for** *(inf)* es jdm ordentlich geben *(inf).*

(c) *(with vb +prep see also there)* **~ did he agree/object to?** wozu hat er zugestimmt/wogegen *or* gegen was hat er Einwände erhoben?; **he agreed/objected to ~ we suggested** er stimmte unseren Vorschlägen zu/lehnte unsere Vorschläge ab, er lehnte ab, was wir vorschlugen; **he didn't know ~ he was agreeing/objecting to** er wußte nicht, wozu er zustimmte/was er ablehnte; **she fell in with ~ everyone else wanted/he had said** sie schloß sich den Wünschen der Allgemeinheit an/sie schloß sich dem, was er gesagt hatte, an; **he didn't go into ~ he meant** er erläuterte nicht im einzelnen, was er meinte.

[2] *adj* **(a)** *(interrog)* welche(r, s), was für (ein/eine) *(inf)* ◆ **~ age is he?** wie alt ist er?; **~ good would that be?** *(inf)* wozu sollte das gut sein?; **~ book do you want?** was für ein Buch wollen Sie?

(b) *(rel)* der/die/das ◆ **~ little I had** das wenige, das ich hatte; **buy ~ food you like** kauf das Essen, das du willst.

(c) *(in set constructions)* **~ sort of** was für ein/eine; **~ else** was noch; **~ more** was mehr.

(d) *(in interj: also iro)* was für (ein/eine) ◆ **~ a man!** was für ein *or* welch ein *(geh)* Mann!; **~ luck!** welch(es) Glück, was für ein Glück, so ein Glück; **~ a fool I've been/I am!** ich Idiot!; **~ terrible weather** was für ein scheußliches Wetter.

[3] *interj* was; *(dated: isn't it/he etc also)* wie.

whate'er [wɒt'ɛə^r] *pron, adj (poet) see* **whatever.**

whatever [wɒt'evə^r] [1] *pron* **(a)** was (auch) (immer); *(no matter what)* egal was, ganz gleich was ◆ **~ you like** was (immer) du (auch) möchtest; **shall we go home now? — ~ you like** gehen wir jetzt nach Hause? — ganz wie du willst; **~ it's called** egal wie es heißt, soll es heißen, wie es will; **... or ~ they're called** ... oder wie sie sonst heißen; **or ~** oder sonst (so) etwas.

(b) *(interrog)* was ... wohl; *(impatiently)* was zum Kuckuck *(inf)* ◆ **~ does he want?** was will er wohl? was er wohl will?; *(impatiently)* was, zum Kuckuck, will er denn?; **~ do you mean?** was meinst du denn bloß?

[2] *adj* **(a)** egal welche(r, s), welche(r, s) (auch) (immer) ◆ **~ book you choose** welches Buch Sie auch wählen; **~ else you do** was immer du *or* egal was du auch sonst machst; **for ~ reasons** aus welchen Gründen auch immer.

(b) *(with neg)* überhaupt, absolut ◆ **nothing/no man ~** überhaupt *or* absolut gar nichts/niemand überhaupt; **it's of no use ~** es hat überhaupt *or* absolut keinen Zweck.

(c) *(interrog)* **~ good can come of it?** was kann daraus nur Gutes werden?; **~ reason can he have?** was für einen Grund kann er nur *or* bloß *or* wohl haben?; **~ else will he do?** was wird er nur *or* bloß *or* wohl noch alles machen?

whatnot ['wɒtnɒt] *n (inf)* **(a)** *see* **what 1 (b). (b)** *(thingummyjig)* Dingsbums *(inf),* Dingsda *(inf) nt.*

what's [wɒts] *contr of* **what is; what has.**

whatsit ['wɒtsɪt] *n (inf)* Dingsbums *(inf),* Dingsda *(inf),* Dingens *(dial inf) nt.*

whatsoe'er [,wɒtsəʊ'ɛə^r] *(poet),* **whatsoever** [,wɒtsəʊ'evə^r] *pron, adj see* **whatever 1 (a), 2 (a, b).**

wheat [wi:t] [1] *n* Weizen *m* ◆ **to separate the ~ from the chaff** die Spreu vom Weizen trennen.

[2] *attr* **~germ** Weizenkeim *m.*

wheaten ['wi:tn] *adj* Weizen-.

wheedle ['wi:dl] *vt* **to ~ sb into doing sth** jdn überreden *or* herumkriegen *(inf),* etw zu tun; **to ~ sth out of sb** jdm etw abschmeicheln.

wheedling ['wi:dlɪŋ] [1] *adj tone, voice* schmeichelnd, schmeichlerisch.

[2] *n* Schmeicheln *nt.*

wheel [wi:l] [1] *n* **(a)** Rad *nt; (steering ~)* Lenkrad *nt; (Naut)* Steuer(rad) *nt; (roulette ~)* Drehscheibe *f; (paddle ~)* Schaufelrad *nt; (potter's ~)* (Töpfer)scheibe *f* ◆ **at the ~** *(lit)* am Steuer; *(fig also)* am Ruder; **~ of fortune** Glücksrad *nt;* **the ~s of progress** der Fortschritt; *(in history)* die Weiterentwicklung; **the ~s of government/justice** die Mühlen der Regierung/der Gerechtigkeit; **~s within ~s** gewisse Verbindungen *or* Beziehungen.

(b) *(Mil)* Schwenkung *f* ◆ **a ~ to the right, a right ~** eine Schwenkung nach rechts, eine Rechtsschwenkung.

[2] *vt* **(a)** *(push) bicycle, pram, child* schieben; *(pull)* ziehen; *(invalid) wheelchair* fahren ◆ **the cripple ~ed himself into the room/along** der Krüppel fuhr mit seinem Rollstuhl ins Zimmer/fuhr in seinem Rollstuhl. **(b)** *(cause to turn)* drehen.

[3] *vi (turn)* drehen; *(birds, planes)* kreisen; *(Mil)* schwenken ◆ **to ~ left** nach links schwenken; **left ~!** links schwenkt!

◆**wheel in** *vt sep* **(a)** *trolley, invalid* hereinrollen. **(b)** *(inf: bring into room)* vorführen *(inf).*

◆**wheel round** *vi* sich (rasch) umdrehen; *(troops)* (ab)schwenken.

wheel: ~barrow *n* Schubkarre *f,* Schubkarren *m;* **~barrow race** *n* Schubkarrenrennen *nt;* **~base** *n* Rad(ab)stand *m;* **~brace** *n* Kreuzschlüssel *m;* **~chair** *n* Rollstuhl *m;* **he spent six months in a ~chair** er saß sechs Monate im Rollstuhl; **~clamp** [1] *n* (Park)kralle *f;* [2] *vt* krallen.

wheeled [wi:ld] *adj traffic, transport* auf Rädern; *vehicle* mit Rädern.

-wheeled *adj suf* -räd(e)rig.

wheeler-dealer ['wi:lə'di:lə^r] *n (inf)* Schlitzohr *nt (inf),* gerissener Kerl; *(in finance also)* Geschäftemacher *m.*

wheelhouse ['wi:lhaʊs] *n* Ruderhaus *nt.*

wheeling and dealing ['wi:lɪŋən'di:lɪŋ] *n* Machenschaften *pl,* Gemauschel *nt (inf); (in business)* Geschäftemacherei *f.*

wheelwright ['wi:lraɪt] *n* Wagenbauer, Stellmacher *m.*

wheeze [wi:z] [1] *n* **(a)** *(of person)* pfeifender Atem *no pl; (of machine)* Fauchen *nt no pl.* **(b)** *(dated inf)* Jokus *(dated),* Scherz *m* ◆ **to think up a ~** sich *(dat)* etwas einfallen lassen.

[2] *vt* keuchen ◆ **to ~ out a tune** eine Melodie herauspressen.

[3] *vi* pfeifend atmen; *(machines, asthmatic)* keuchen ◆ **if he smokes too much he starts to ~** wenn er zu stark raucht, fängt sein Atem an zu pfeifen *or* bekommt er einen pfeifenden Atem.

wheezily ['wi:zɪlɪ] *adv* pfeifend, keuchend.

wheeziness ['wi:zɪnɪs] *n* Keuchen *nt; (of breath)* Pfeifen *nt.*

wheezy ['wi:zɪ] *adj (+er) old man* mit pfeifendem Atem; *breath* pfeifend; *voice, cough* keuchend; *car* keuchend, schnaufend.

whelk [welk] *n* Wellhornschnecke *f.*

whelp [welp] [1] *n* Welpe *m; (pej: boy)* Lauser *(inf),* Lausbub *(inf) m.*

[2] *vi* werfen, jungen.

when [wen] [1] *adv* **(a)** *(at what time)* wann ◆ **since ~ have you been here?** seit wann sind Sie hier?; **... since ~ he has been here** ... und seitdem ist er hier; **say ~!** *(inf)* sag' *or* schrei *(inf)* halt!

(b) *(rel)* **on the day ~** an dem Tag, an dem *or* als *or* da *(liter) or* wo *(inf);* **at the time ~** zu der Zeit, zu der *or* als *or* da *(liter) or* wo *(inf);* **he wrote last week, up till ~ I had heard nothing from him** er schrieb letzte Woche, und bis dahin hatte ich nichts von ihm gehört; **in 1960, up till ~ he ...** im Jahre 1960, bis zu welchem Zeitpunkt er ...; **during the time ~ he was in Germany** während der Zeit, als *or* wo *or* die *(inf)* er in Deutschland war.

[2] *conj* **(a)** wenn; *(with past reference)* als ◆ **you can go ~ I have finished** du kannst gehen, sobald *or* wenn ich fertig bin; **he did it ~ young** er tat es in

seiner Jugend.

(b) (*+gerund*) beim; (*at or during which time*) wobei ◆ **~ operating the machine** beim Benutzen *or* bei Benutzung der Maschine; **be careful ~ crossing the road** seien Sie beim Überqueren der Straße vorsichtig, seien Sie vorsichtig, wenn Sie über die Straße gehen; **the PM is coming here in May, ~ he will ...** der Premier kommt im Mai hierher und wird dann ...

(c) (*although, whereas*) wo ... doch ◆ **why do you do it that way ~ it would be much easier like this?** warum machst du es denn auf die Art, wo es doch so viel einfacher wäre?

whence [wens] *adv* **(a)** (*old, form*) woher, von wannen (*old, liter*). **(b)** (*form*) **~ I conclude ...** woraus ich schließe, ...

whenever [wen'evəʳ] *adv* **(a)** (*each time*) jedesmal wenn.

(b) (*at whatever time*) wann (auch) immer, ganz egal *or* gleich *or* einerlei wann; (*as soon as*) sobald ◆ **I'll visit you ~ you like** ich werde dich besuchen, wann immer du willst; **~ you like!** wann du willst!; **we'll leave ~ he's ready** wir brechen auf, sobald er fertig ist.

(c) (*emph*) **~ can he have done it?** wann kann er das nur *or* wohl getan haben?; **~ do I have the time for such things?** wann habe ich schon *or* je Zeit für sowas?; **tomorrow, or ~** (*inf*) morgen, oder wann auch immer *or* sonst irgendwann.

where [wɛəʳ] [1] *adv* wo ◆ **~ (to)** wohin, wo ... hin; **~ (from)** woher, wo ... her; **~ are you going (to)?** wohin gehst du, wo gehst du hin?; **~ to, sir?** wohin (wollen Sie) bitte?; **~ are you from?** woher kommen Sie, wo kommen Sie her?; **from ~ I'm sitting I can see the church** von meinem Platz aus kann ich die Kirche sehen; **~ should we be if ...?** was wäre nur, wenn ...?; **this is ~ it's at** (*sl*) (*where the action is*) hier ist echt was los (*inf*); (*is really great*) das ist echt Spitze (*inf*); **he doesn't know ~ it's at** (*sl*) der weiß nicht, was läuft (*sl*).

[2] *conj* wo; (*in the place where*) da, wo ..., an der Stelle, wo ... **go ~ you like** geh, wohin du willst, geh hin, wo du willst; **the bag is ~ you left it** die Tasche ist an der Stelle *or* da, wo du sie liegengelassen hast; **this is ~ we got out** hier sind wir ausgestiegen; **that's ~ Nelson fell/I used to live/we differ** hier *or* an dieser Stelle fiel Nelson/hier *or* da habe ich (früher) gewohnt/in diesem Punkt haben wir unterschiedliche Ansichten; **we carried on from ~ we left off** wir haben da weitergemacht, wo wir vorher aufgehört haben; **I've read up to ~ the king ...** ich habe bis dahin *or* bis an die Stelle gelesen, wo der König ...; **this is ~ we got to** soweit *or* bis hierhin *or* bis dahin sind wir gekommen; **we succeeded ~ we expected to fail** wir hatten da Erfolg, wo wir ihn nicht erwartet hatten; **you can trust him ~ money is concerned** in Geldsachen können Sie ihm trauen, Sie können ihm trauen, wo es ums Geld geht; **that's ~** da; **that's ~ his strong point is** da liegt seine Stärke.

whereabouts [,wɛərə'baʊts] [1] *adv* wo, in welcher Gegend ◆ **I wonder ~ Martin put it** ich frage mich, wohin Martin es wohl gelegt hat.

[2] ['wɛərəbaʊts] *n sing or pl* Verbleib *m*; (*of people also*) Aufenthaltsort *m*.

▼ **whereas** [wɛər'æz] *conj* **(a)** (*whilst*) während; (*while on the other hand*) wohingegen. **(b)** (*esp Jur: considering that*) da, in Anbetracht der Tatsache, daß ...

whereat [wɛər'æt] *adv* (*old*) wobei.

whereby [wɛə'baɪ] *adv* (*form*) **the sign ~ you will recognize him** das Zeichen, an dem *or* woran Sie ihn erkennen; **the rule ~ it is not allowed** die Vorschrift, laut derer *or* wonach es verboten ist; **a plan ~ the country can be saved** ein Plan, durch den *or* wodurch das Land gerettet werden kann.

where'er [wɛər'ɛəʳ] *conj, adv* (*poet*) *contr of* **wherever**.

wherefore ['wɛəfɔːʳ] [1] *adv* (*obs*) warum, weswegen.

[2] *conj* (*obs*) weswegen.

[3] *n see* **why 3**.

wherein [wɛər'ɪn] *adv* (*form*) worin.

whereof [wɛər'ɒv] *adv* (*obs*) (*about which*) worüber; (*out of which*) woraus; (*Jur*) dessen ◆ **in witness ~ ...** zu Urkund *or* Zeugnis dessen ... (*old*).

whereon [wɛər'ɒn] *adv* (*obs*) worauf; (*whereupon*) woraufhin.

wheresoever [,wɛəsəʊ'evəʳ] *adv* (*obs*), **wheresoe'er** [,wɛəsəʊ'ɛəʳ] *adv* (*obs, poet*) *see* **wherever**.

wherever [wɛər'evəʳ] [1] *conj* **(a)** (*no matter where*) egal *or* einerlei wo, wo (auch) immer ◆ **~ it came from** egal *or* einerlei *or* ganz gleich, woher es kommt, woher es auch kommt.

(b) (*anywhere, in or to whatever place*) wohin ◆ **we'll go ~ you like** wir gehen, wohin Sie wollen; **he comes from Bishopbriggs, ~ that is** er kommt aus Bishopbriggs, wo immer das auch sein mag (*geh*) *or* fragen Sie mich nicht, wo das ist.

(c) (*everywhere*) überall wo ◆ **~ you see this sign** überall, wo Sie dieses Zeichen sehen.

[2] *adv* wo nur, wo bloß ◆ **~ have I seen that before?** wo habe ich das nur *or* bloß schon gesehen?; **~ did you get that hat!** wo haben Sie nur *or* bloß diesen Hut her?; **in London or Liverpool or ~** in London oder Liverpool oder sonstwo.

wherewith [wɛə'wɪθ] *adv* (*obs*) womit, mit dem/der.

wherewithal ['wɛəwɪðɔːl] *n* nötiges Kleingeld; (*implements*) Utensilien *pl*.

wherry ['werɪ] *n* (*light rowing boat*) Ruderkahn *m*; (*Brit: barge*) (Fluß)kahn *m*; (*US: scull*) Einer *m*, Skiff *nt*.

whet [wet] *vt knife, scythe* wetzen; *axe* schleifen, schärfen; *appetite, curiosity* anregen.

▼ **whether** ['weðəʳ] *conj* ob; (*no matter whether*) egal *or* ganz gleich *or* einerlei, ob ◆ **I am not certain ~ they're coming or not** *or* **~ or not they're coming** ich bin nicht sicher, ob sie kommen oder nicht; **~ they come or not, we'll go ahead** egal *or* ganz gleich *or* einerlei, ob sie kommen oder nicht (kommen), wir fangen (schon mal) an; **he's not sure ~ to go or stay** er weiß nicht, ob er gehen oder bleiben soll.

whetstone ['wetstəʊn] *n* Wetzstein *m*.

whew [hwuː] *interj* puh, uff.

whey [weɪ] *n* Molke *f*.

whey-faced ['weɪ'feɪst] *adj* (*liter*) bleichgesichtig (*geh*).

which [wɪtʃ] [1] *adj* **(a)** (*interrog*) welche(r, s) ◆ **~ one?** welche(r, s)?; (*of people also*) wer?

(b) (*rel*) welche(r, s) ◆ **... by ~ time I was asleep** ... und zu dieser Zeit schlief ich (bereits); **look at it ~ way you will ...** man kann es betrachten *or* sehen, wie man will ...; **... he said, ~ remark made me very angry** ... sagte er, was mich sehr ärgerte.

[2] *pron* **(a)** (*interrog*) welche(r, s); (*of people also*) wer ◆ **~ of the children/books** welches Kind/Buch; **~ is ~?** (*of people*) wer ist wer?, welche(r) ist welche(r)?; (*of things*) welche(r, s) ist welche(r, s)?, welche(r, s) ist der/die/das eine und welche(r, s) der/die/das andere?; **~ is for ~?** was ist wofür?

(b) (*rel*) (*with n antecedent*) der/die/das, welche(r, s) (*geh*); (*with clause antecedent*) was ◆ **the bear ~ I saw** der Bär, den ich sah; **at ~ he remarked ...** woraufhin er bemerkte, ...; **it rained hard, ~ upset her** es regnete stark, was sie aufregte; **~ reminds me ...** dabei fällt mir ein, ...; **from ~ we deduce that ...** woraus wir ableiten, daß ...; **after ~ we went to bed** worauf *or* wonach wir zu Bett gingen; **on the day before/after ~ he left her** an dem Tag, bevor er sie verließ/nachdem er sie verlassen hatte; **the shelf on ~ I put it** das Brett, auf das *or* worauf ich es gelegt habe.

whichever [wɪtʃ'evəʳ] [1] *adj* welche(r, s) auch immer; (*no matter which*) ganz gleich *or* egal *or* einerlei welche(r, s).

[2] *pron* welche(r, s) auch immer ◆ **~ (of you) has the most money** wer immer (von euch) das meiste Geld hat.

whichsoever [,wɪtʃsəʊ'evəʳ] *adj, pron* (*form*) *see* **whichever**.

whiff [wɪf] *n* **(a)** (*puff*) Zug *m*; (*wisp*) kleine Fahne, Wolke *f*; (*smell*) Hauch *m*; (*pleasant*) Duft, Hauch *m*; (*fig: trace*) Spur *f*; (*of spring*) Hauch *m*, Ahnung *f* ◆ **to catch a ~ of sth** den Geruch von etw wahrnehmen; **to go out for a ~ of air** hinausgehen, um (etwas) Luft zu schnappen. **(b)** (*small cigar*) kleiner Zigarillo.

whiffy ['wɪfɪ] *adj* (*+er*) (*inf*) **to be ~** streng riechen; **it's a bit ~ here** hier müffelt es etwas (*inf*).

whig [wɪg] (*Brit Hist*) [1] *n frühere Bezeichnung für Mitglied der liberalen Partei*, Whig *m*.

[2] *adj attr* Whig-.

▼ **while** [waɪl] [1] *n* **(a)** Weile *f*, Weilchen *nt* (*inf*) ◆ **for a ~** (für) eine Weile, eine Zeitlang; (*a short moment*) (für) einen Augenblick *or* Moment; **a good** *or* **long ~** eine ganze *or* lange Weile, eine ganze Zeitlang; **for/after quite a ~** ziemlich *or* recht lange, (für) eine geraume/nach einer geraumen Weile (*geh*); **a little** *or* **short ~** ein Weilchen (*inf*), kurze Zeit; **it'll be ready in a short ~** es wird bald fertig sein; **a little/long ~ ago** vor kurzem/vor einer ganzen Weile, vor längerer *or* langer Zeit; **some ~ ago** vor einiger Zeit; **all the ~** die ganze Zeit (über).

(b) **the ~** (*liter*) derweil, unterdessen.

▼ (c) **to be worth (one's) ~ to ...** sich (für jdn) lohnen, zu ...; **we'll make it worth your ~** es soll ihr Schaden nicht sein.

[2] *conj* **(a)** während; (*as long as*) solange ◆ **she fell asleep ~ reading** sie schlief beim Lesen ein; **he became famous ~ still young** er wurde berühmt, als er noch jung war; **you must not drink ~ on duty** Sie dürfen im Dienst nicht trinken.

(b) (*although*) **~ one must admit there are difficulties ...** man muß zwar zugeben, daß es Schwierigkeiten gibt, trotzdem ...; **~ the text is not absolutely perfect, nevertheless ...** obwohl (zwar) der Text nicht einwandfrei ist, ... trotzdem; **it is difficult to be fair ~ at the same time being honest** es ist schwierig, fair und gleichzeitig auch gerecht zu sein.

(c) (*whereas*) während.

◆**while away** *vt sep time* sich (*dat*) vertreiben.

whilst [waɪlst] *conj see* **while 2**.

whim [wɪm] *n* Laune *f* ◆ **a passing ~** eine vorübergehende Laune, ein vorübergehender Spleen; **her every ~** jede ihrer Launen; **as the ~ takes me** ganz nach Lust und Laune.

whimper ['wɪmpəʳ] [1] *n* (*of dog*) Winseln *nt no pl*; (*of person*) Wimmern *nt no pl* ◆ **a ~ of pain** ein schmerzliches Wimmern; **without a ~** ohne einen (Klage)laut.

[2] *vti* (*dog*) winseln; (*person*) wimmern.

whimsical ['wɪmzɪkəl] *adj* wunderlich; *look, remark* neckisch; *idea, tale* schnurrig; *decision* seltsam, spinnig (*inf*); *notion* grillenhaft; *ornament* verrückt ◆ **to be in a ~ mood** in einer neckischen Laune sein; **a ~ joke** ein verrücktes Witzchen.

whimsicality [,wɪmzɪ'kælɪtɪ] *n* Wunderlichkeit *f*; (*of behaviour*) Launenhaftigkeit, Grillenhaftigkeit *f*; (*of decision*) Seltsamkeit *f*; (*of mood, tale also*) Grillenhaftigkeit *f*; (*of architecture*) Verrücktheit *f*, Manierismus *m*.

whimsically ['wɪmzɪkəlɪ] *adv look, say* neckisch.

whimsy ['wɪmzɪ] *n* **(a)** (*caprice, fancy*) Spleen *m*, Grille *f* (*dated*). **(b)** *see* **whimsicality**.

whin [wɪn] *n* (*esp Brit*) Ginster *m*.

whine [waɪn] [1] *n* (*of dog*) Jaulen, Heulen *nt no pl*; (*complaining cry*) Jammern, Gejammer *nt no pl*; (*of child*) Quengelei *f no pl*; (*of siren, jet engine*) Heulen *nt no pl*; (*of bullet*) Pfeifen *nt no pl*.

[2] *vi* (*dog*) jaulen; (*person: speak, complain*) jammern, klagen; (*child*) quengeln; (*siren, jet engine*) heulen; (*bullet*) pfeifen ◆ **the dog was whining to**

➤ LANGUAGE IN USE: **whereas: a** → 5.1, 26.3 **whether** → 5.4, 6.3 **while: 1c** → 26.1, 26.3

be let in der Hund jaulte, um hereingelassen zu werden; **don't come whining to me about it** du brauchst nicht anzukommen und mir was vorzujammern.

whiner ['waɪnəʳ] *n (complainer)* Jammerer, Jammerknochen *(inf) m.*

whinge [wɪndʒ] *vi (inf: complain)* jammern, meckern *(inf); (baby)* plärren ◆ **~ing Pom** *(Austral)* ewig meckernder Engländer *(inf)*, ewig meckernde Engländerin *(inf)*.

whingey ['wɪndʒɪ] *adj (inf)* **to be ~** dauernd jammern *or* meckern *(inf); (woman also)* eine Meckerziege sein *(inf); (baby)* dauernd plärren; **the kid's starting to get ~** das Kind fängt an zu plärren; **don't be so ~** mecker doch nicht so! *(inf)*.

whining ['waɪnɪŋ] *n (of dog)* Gejaule *nt; (complaining)* Gejammer *nt.*

whinny ['wɪnɪ] 1 *n* Wiehern, Gewieher *nt no pl.*
2 *vi* wiehern.

whip [wɪp] 1 *n* **(a)** Peitsche *f; (riding ~)* Reitgerte *f* ◆ **to give sb a fair crack of the ~** *(inf)* jdm eine faire Chance geben.
(b) *(Parl) (person)* Fraktions- *or* Geschäftsführer *m; (call)* Anordnung *f* des Fraktionsführers ◆ **three-line ~** Fraktionszwang *m;* **they have put a three-line ~ on the vote** bei der Abstimmung besteht Fraktionszwang; **chief ~** Haupt-Einpeitscher *m.*
(c) *(Cook)* Creme, Speise *f.*
2 *vt* **(a)** *(with whip) people* auspeitschen; *horse* peitschen; *(with stick etc)* schlagen ◆ **the conductor ~ped the orchestra into a frenzy** der Dirigent brachte das Orchester in Ekstase; **to ~ sb/sth into shape** *(fig)* jdn/etw zurechtschleifen.
(b) *(Cook) cream, eggs* schlagen.
(c) *(bind) seam* umnähen; *stick, rope* umwickeln.
(d) *(inf: defeat)* vernichtend schlagen.
(e) *(fig inf: move quickly)* **he ~ped the book off the desk** er schnappte sich *(dat)* das Buch vom Schreibtisch; **he ~ped his hand out of the way** er zog blitzschnell seine Hand weg; **the thief ~ped the jewel into his pocket** der Dieb ließ den Edelstein schnell in seiner Tasche verschwinden; **to ~ sb into hospital** jdn in Windeseile ins Krankenhaus bringen; *(doctor)* jdn schnell ins Krankenhaus einweisen.
(f) *(inf: steal)* mitgehen lassen *(inf)*.
3 *vi* **(a) branches ~ped against the window** Äste schlugen gegen das Fenster. **(b)** *(move quickly) (person)* schnell (mal) laufen ◆ **the car ~ped past** das Auto brauste *or* fegte *(inf)* vorbei.

◆**whip away** *vt sep* wegreißen, wegziehen *(from sb* jdm).

◆**whip back** *vi* **(a)** *(spring, plank)* zurückschnellen, zurückfedern. **(b)** *(inf: go back quickly)* schnell (mal) zurücklaufen.

◆**whip off** *vt sep clothes* herunterreißen, vom Leib reißen; *tablecloth* wegziehen ◆ **the wind ~ped my hat ~** der Wind riß mir den Hut vom Kopf; **a car ~ped him ~ to the airport** ein Auto brachte ihn in Windeseile zum Flugplatz.

◆**whip on** *vt sep* **(a)** *(urge on) horse* anpeitschen, antreiben; *(fig)* antreiben.
(b) *(put on quickly) clothes* sich *(dat)* überwerfen; *lid* schnell drauftun.

◆**whip out** 1 *vt sep gun, pencil, camera etc* zücken ◆ **he ~ped a gun/pencil** *etc* **~ of his pocket** er zog rasch eine Pistole/einen Bleistift *etc* aus der Tasche; **they ~ped ~ his tonsils** *(inf)* sie haben ihm schnell die Mandeln entfernt.
2 *vi (inf: go out quickly)* schnell (mal) rausgehen *(inf)* ◆ **he's just ~ped ~ for a drink** er ist schnell mal *or* nur schnell einen trinken gegangen.

◆**whip round** *vi* **(a)** *(inf: move quickly)* **I'll just ~ ~ to the shops/to the butcher** ich werd' schnell mal einkaufen gehen/zum Metzger (rüber)laufen; **he ~ped ~ when he heard** ... er fuhr herum, als er hörte ...; **the car ~ped ~ the corner** das Auto brauste *or* sauste *or* fegte *(inf)* um die Ecke.
(b) *(inf: collect money)* zusammenlegen, den Hut herumgehen lassen.

◆**whip up** *vt sep* **(a)** *(pick up)* schnappen.
(b) *(set in motion) horses* antreiben; *(Cook) cream* schlagen; *mixture* verrühren; *eggs* verquirlen; *(inf: prepare quickly) meal* hinzaubern; *(fig: stir up) interest, feeling* anheizen, entfachen; *support* finden, auftreiben *(inf); audience, crowd* mitreißen ◆ **I'll just ~ ~ something to eat** *(inf)* ich mach' nur schnell was zu essen; **the sea, ~ped ~ by the wind** das Meer, vom Wind aufgepeitscht.

whip: ~cord *n (rope)* Peitschenschnur *f; (fabric)* Whipcord *m;* **~ hand** *n* **to have the ~ hand (over sb)** (über jdn) die Oberhand haben; **~lash** *n* (Peitschen)riemen *m; (Med: also* **~lash injury)** Peitschenschlagverletzung *f.*

whipped cream ['wɪpt'kriːm] *n* Schlagsahne *f,* Schlagrahm *m.*

whipper-in [ˌwɪpər'ɪn] *n* Piqueur, Pikör, Parforcejäger *m.*

whippersnapper ['wɪpəˌsnæpəʳ] *n (dated)* junger Spund.

whippet ['wɪpɪt] *n* Whippet *m.*

whipping ['wɪpɪŋ] *n (beating)* Tracht *f* Prügel; *(inf: defeat)* Niederlage *f; (fig: in debate etc)* Pleite *f* ◆ **to give sb a ~** *(lit)* jdm eine Tracht Prügel versetzen; *(with whip)* jdn auspeitschen; *(fig inf)* jdn in die Pfanne hauen *(inf);* **our team/the government got a ~** unsere Mannschaft wurde in die Pfanne gehauen *(inf)*/die Regierung erlebte eine Pleite *(inf)*.

whipping: ~ boy *n* Prügelknabe *m;* **to use sb as a ~ boy** jdn zum Prügelknaben machen; **~ cream** *n* Schlagsahne *f;* **~ top** *n* Kreisel *m.*

whippoorwill ['wɪpˌpʊəˌwɪl] *n* schreiender Ziegenmelker.

whippy ['wɪpɪ] *adj cane, fishing rod* biegsam, elastisch, federnd.

whip-round ['wɪpraʊnd] *n (esp Brit inf)* **to have a ~** den Hut herumgehen lassen.

whir [wɜːʳ] *n, vi see* **whirr.**

whirl [wɜːl] 1 *n (spin)* Wirbeln *nt no pl; (of dust, water etc, also fig)* Wirbel *m; (of cream etc)* Tupfer *m* ◆ **to give sb/sth a ~** *(lit)* jdn/etw herumwirbeln; *(fig inf: try out)* jdn/etw ausprobieren; **the busy ~ of her social life** der Trubel ihres gesellschaftlichen Lebens; **a ~ of pleasure** Jubel, Trubel, Heiterkeit *no art (+sing vb);* **my head is in a ~** mir schwirrt der Kopf.
2 *vt* **(a)** *(make turn)* wirbeln ◆ **to ~ sb/sth round** jdn/etw herumwirbeln; **he ~ed his hat round his head** er schwenkte seinen Hut; **he ~ed the water about with his stick** er rührte mit seinem Stock im Wasser herum. **(b)** *(transport)* eilends wegbringen; *(person)* mit sich nehmen, entführen *(inf)*.
3 *vi (spin)* wirbeln; *(water)* strudeln ◆ **to ~ round** herumwirbeln; *(water)* strudeln; *(person: turn round quickly)* herumfahren; **my head is ~ing** mir schwirrt der Kopf; **after a few drinks the room starting ~ing** nach ein paar Gläsern fing der Raum an, sich zu drehen; **they/the countryside ~ed past us** sie wirbelten/die Landschaft flog an uns vorbei.

whirligig ['wɜːlɪgɪg] *n (top)* Kreisel *m; (roundabout)* Karussell, Ringelspiel *nt; (fig)* (ewiges) Wechselspiel *nt.*

whirlpool ['wɜːlpuːl] *n* Strudel *m; (in health club)* ≃ Kneippbecken *nt.*

whirlwind ['wɜːlwɪnd] *n* Wirbelwind *m; (fig)* Trubel, Wirbel *m* ◆ **like a ~** wie der Wirbelwind; **to reap the ~** *(prov)* Sturm ernten; **he did some very stupid things, and now he's reaping the ~** er hat einige sehr große Dummheiten gemacht, und jetzt muß er dafür büßen; **a ~ romance** eine stürmische Romanze.

whirlybird ['wɜːlɪˌbɜːd] *n (esp US inf)* Hubschrauber *m.*

whirr, whir [wɜːʳ] 1 *n (of wings)* Schwirren *nt; (of wheels, camera, machine) (quiet)* Surren *nt; (louder)* Brummen, Dröhnen *nt.*
2 *vi see n* schwirren; surren; brummen, dröhnen.

whisk [wɪsk] 1 *n* **(a)** *(fly~)* Wedel *m; (Cook)* Schneebesen *m; (electric)* Rührbesen, Rührstab *m,* Rührgerät *nt* ◆ **give the eggs a good ~** schlagen Sie die Eier gut durch.
(b) *(movement)* Wischen *nt; (of skirts)* Schwingen *nt* ◆ **with a ~ of his hand/its tail** mit einer schnellen Handbewegung/mit einem Schwanzschlag.
2 *vt* **(a)** *(Cook)* schlagen; *eggs* verquirlen ◆ **to ~ the eggs into the mixture** die Eier unter die Masse einrühren.
(b) the horse ~ed its tail das Pferd schlug mit dem Schwanz.
3 *vi (move quickly)* fegen *(inf)*, stieben.

◆**whisk away** *vt sep* **(a)** *fly, wasp etc* wegscheuchen.
(b) *(take away suddenly)* **the magician ~ed ~ the tablecloth** der Zauberer zog das Tischtuch schnell weg; **her mother ~ed the bottle ~ from her just in time** ihre Mutter schnappte *(inf) or* zog ihr die Flasche gerade noch rechtzeitig weg; **he ~ed her ~ to the Bahamas** er entführte sie auf die Bahamas; **a big black car turned up and ~ed him ~** ein großes schwarzes Auto erschien und sauste *or* brauste mit ihm davon.

◆**whisk off** *vt sep see* **whisk away (b).**

◆**whisk up** *vt sep eggs, mixture etc* schaumig schlagen.

whisker ['wɪskəʳ] *n* Schnurrhaar *nt; (of people)* Barthaar *nt* ◆ **~s** *(moustache)* Schnurrbart *m; (side ~s)* Backenbart *m; (Zool)* Schnurrbart *m;* **to win/miss sth by a ~** etw fast gewinnen/etw um Haaresbreite verpassen.

whiskered ['wɪskəd] *adj* schnurrbärtig.

whiskery ['wɪskərɪ] *adj* behaart, haarig.

whisky, *(US, Ir)* **whiskey** ['wɪskɪ] *n* Whisky *m* ◆ **~ and soda** Whisky (mit) Soda *m;* **two whiskies, please** zwei Whisky, bitte.

whisper ['wɪspəʳ] 1 *n* **(a)** Geflüster, Flüstern *nt no pl; (of wind, leaves)* Wispern *nt no pl; (mysterious)* Raunen *nt no pl* ◆ **to speak/say sth in a ~** im Flüsterton sprechen/etw im Flüsterton sagen; **they were talking in ~s** sie sprachen flüsternd *or* im Flüsterton.
(b) *(rumour)* Gerücht *nt* ◆ **there are ~s (going round) that** ... es geht das Gerücht *or* es gehen Gerüchte um, daß ...; **have you heard any ~s about who might be promoted?** haben Sie irgendwelche Andeutungen gehört *or* etwas läuten hören *(inf)*, wer befördert werden soll?
2 *vt* **(a)** flüstern, wispern ◆ **to ~ sth to sb** jdm etw zuflüstern *or* zuwispern; *(secretively)* jdm etw zuraunen; **to ~ a word in(to) sb's ear** *(fig)* jdm einen leisen Tip geben, jdm etw andeuten.
(b) *(rumour)* **it's (being) ~ed that** ... es geht das Gerücht *or* es gehen Gerüchte um, daß ..., man munkelt *or* es wird gemunkelt, daß ...
3 *vi* flüstern, wispern *(also fig); (poet: wind)* säuseln; *(secretively)* raunen; *(schoolchildren)* tuscheln ◆ **to ~ to sb** jdm zuflüstern/zuwispern/zuraunen; mit jdm tuscheln; **just ~ to me** sag's mir flüsternd; **stop ~ing!** hör/hört auf zu flüstern!; *(schoolchildren)* hört auf zu tuscheln, laßt das Getuschel!

whispering ['wɪspərɪŋ] *n see vi* Flüstern, Geflüster, Wispern *nt no pl;* Säuseln *nt no pl;* Raunen *nt no pl;* Tuscheln, Getuschel *nt no pl; (fig)* Gerede, Gemunkel, Getuschel *nt no pl.*

whispering: ~ campaign *n* Verleumdungskampagne *f;* **~ gallery** *n* Flüstergewölbe *nt or* -galerie *f.*

whist [wɪst] *n* Whist *nt* ◆ **~ drive** Whistrunde *f* mit wechselnden Parteien.

whistle ['wɪsl] 1 *n* **(a)** *(sound)* Pfiff *m; (of wind)* Pfeifen *nt; (of kettle)* Pfeifton *m* ◆ **the ~ of the escaping steam** das Pfeifen des ausströmenden Dampfes; **to give a ~** einen Pfiff ausstoßen.
(b) *(instrument)* Pfeife *f* ◆ **to blow a/one's ~** pfeifen; **to blow the ~ on sb/sth** *(fig inf)* jdn verpfeifen *(inf)*/über etw *(acc)* auspacken *(inf); see* **wet.**
2 *vt* pfeifen ◆ **to ~ (to) sb to stop** jdn durch einen Pfiff stoppen; **to ~ sb back/over** *etc* jdn zurück-/herüberpfeifen *etc.*
3 *vi* pfeifen ◆ **the boys ~d at her** die Jungen pfiffen ihr nach; **the crowd ~d at the referee** die Menge pfiff den Schiedsrichter aus; **he ~d for a taxi** er pfiff ein Taxi heran, er pfiff nach einem Taxi; **the referee ~d for a foul** der Schiedsrichter pfiff ein Foul; **the referee ~d for play to stop** der Schiedsrichter pfiff eine Spielunterbrechung; *(at the end)* der Schiedsrichter pfiff das Spiel ab; **he can ~ for it** *(inf)* da kann er lange warten *or* warten, bis er schwarz wird *(inf)*.

whistle-stop ['wɪsl,stɒp] (*US*) [1] *n* **(a)** (*small town*) Kleinstadt *f*, Nest, Kaff *nt*. **(b)** (*stop*) kurzer Aufenthalt an einem kleinen Ort; (*fig*) Stippvisite *f* ◆ **~ tour** (*US Pol*) Wahlreise *f*; (*fig*) *Reise f mit Kurzaufenthalten an allen Orten*.
[2] *vi* auf die Dörfer gehen.

whistling kettle ['wɪslɪŋ'ketl] *n* Pfeifkessel *m*.

whit [wɪt] *n* **not a ~** keine *or* nicht eine Spur; (*of humour*) kein *or* nicht ein Funke(n); (*of truth, common sense*) kein *or* nicht ein Gramm *or* Körnchen; **every ~ as good** genauso gut, (um) keinen Deut schlechter.

white [waɪt] [1] *adj* (*+er*) weiß; *skin, racially also* hell; (*with fear, anger, exhaustion etc also*) blaß, kreidebleich ◆ **to go** *or* **turn ~** (*thing*) weiß werden; (*person also*) bleich *or* blaß werden.
[2] *n* (*colour*) Weiß *nt*; (*person*) Weiße(r) *mf*; (*of egg*) Eiweiß, Klar (*Aus*) *nt*; (*of eye*) Weiße(s) *nt* ◆ **shoot when you see the ~s of their eyes** schießt, wenn ihr das Weiße im Auge des Feinds erkennen könnt; **~s** (*household*) Weißwäsche *f*; (*Sport*) weiße Kleidung; **the tennis players were wearing ~s** die Tennisspieler trugen Weiß *or* spielten in Weiß; **I've forgotten my ~s** ich habe mein Zeug vergessen.

white: ~ ant *n* Termite *f*, weiße Ameise; **~bait** *n, pl* **~bait** Breitling *m*; **~beam** *n* Mehlbeere *f*; **~ book** *n* (*US Pol*) Weißbuch *nt*; **~cap** *n* Welle *f* mit Schaumkronen; **~ Christmas** *n* **a ~ Christmas** weiße Weihnacht(en); **~ coal** *n* weiße Kohle; **~ coffee** *n* (*Brit*) Kaffee *m* mit Milch, Milchkaffee *m*; **~-collar** *adj* **~-collar worker** Schreibtischarbeiter *m*; **~-collar job** Angestelltenstelle *f*, Schreibtisch- *or* Büroposten *m*; **~-collar crime** Wirtschaftskriminalität *f*; **a ~-collar crime** ein Wirtschaftsverbrechen *nt*; **~-collar union** Angestelltengewerkschaft *f*; **~ corpuscle** *n* weißes Blutkörperchen.

whited sepulchre ['waɪtɪd'seplkəʳ] *n* (*liter*) Pharisäer *m*.

white: ~ dwarf *n* (*Astron*) weißer Zwerg(stern); **~ elephant** *n* nutzloser Gegenstand; (*waste of money*) Fehlinvestition *f*; **~ elephant stall** *n* Stand *m* mit allerlei Krimskrams; **~ ensign** *n Fahne f der Royal Navy*; **~ feather** *n* weiße Feder (*Zeichen der Feigheit*); **to show the ~ feather** den Schwanz einziehen; **~ fish** *n* Weißfisch *m*; **~ flag** *n* (*Mil, fig*) weiße Fahne; **W~ Friar** *n* Karmeliter *m*; **~ gold** *n* Weißgold *nt*; **~-haired** *adj* **(a)** weißhaarig; (*blonde*) weißblond, semmelblond; **(b)** (*US inf: favourite*) Lieblings-; **the boss's ~-haired boy** der Liebling *or* das Goldkind des Chefs; **W~hall** *n* (*British government*) Whitehall *no art*; **if W~hall decides ...** wenn London beschließt ...; **~-headed** *adj* **(a)** *see* **~-haired**; **(b)** *gull, eagle* weißköpfig; **~ heat** *n* Weißglut *f*; (*fig*) Hitze *f*; (*with enthusiasm*) Feuereifer *m*; **to work at ~ heat** (*under pressure*) fieberhaft arbeiten; **in the ~ heat of his rage/passion** in seiner besinnungslosen Wut/Leidenschaft; **his rage reached ~ heat** seine Wut erreichte den Siedepunkt; **~ hope** *n* große *or* einzige Hoffnung; **~ horse** *n* **(a)** Schimmel *m*; **(b)** (*wave*) Welle *f* mit einer Schaumkrone; **now there are ~ horses** jetzt haben die Wellen Reiter; **~-hot** *adj* weißglühend; (*fig*) brennend, glühend; **the W~ House** *n* das Weiße Haus; **~ lead** *n* Bleiweiß *nt*; **~ lie** *n* kleine Unwahrheit, Notlüge *f*; **we all tell a ~ lie from time to time** wir alle sagen nicht immer ganz die Wahrheit; **~ light** *n* weißes Licht; **~-lipped** *adj* mit bleichen Lippen, angstbleich; **~ magic** *n* weiße Magie; **~ man** *n* Weiße(r) *m*; **the ~ man's burden** die Bürde des weißen Mannes; **~ meat** *n* helles Fleisch.

whiten ['waɪtn] [1] *vt* weiß machen.
[2] *vi* weiß werden.

whiteness ['waɪtnɪs] *n* Weiße *f*; (*of skin*) Helligkeit *f*; (*due to illness etc*) Blässe *f* ◆ **the dazzling ~ of ...** das strahlende Weiß des/der ...

whitening ['waɪtnɪŋ] *n* weiße Farbe, Schlämmkreide *f*.

white: ~ noise *n* weißes Rauschen; **~-out** *n* starkes Schneegestöber; **in ~-out conditions** bei starkem Schneegestöber; **~ paper** *n* (*Pol*) Weißbuch *nt*; **W ~ Russia** *n* Weißrußland *nt*; **W~ Russian** *n* Weißrusse *m*, Weißrussin *f*; **~ sale** *n* weiße Woche, Ausverkauf *m* von Haus- und Tischwäsche; **~ sauce** *n* Mehlsoße *f*, helle Soße; **~ slave** *n* weiße Sklavin; **~ slave trade** *n* Mädchenhandel *m*; **~ spirit** *n* Terpentinersatz *m*; **~ stick** *n* Blindenstock *m*; **~ supremacy** *n* Vorherrschaft *f* der weißen Rasse; **~thorn** *n* Weißdorn *m*; **~throat** *n* Grasmücke *f*; **~ tie** *n* (*tie*) weiße Fliege; (*evening dress*) Frack *m*; **a ~ tie occasion/dinner** eine Veranstaltung/ein Essen mit Frackzwang; **~ trash** *n* (*US inf*) weißes Pack; **~wall** [1] *n* (*tyre*) Weißwandreifen *m*; [2] *adj* Weißwand-; **~wash** [1] *n* Tünche *f*; (*fig*) Schönfärberei *f*; [2] *vt walls* tünchen; (*fig*) schönfärben, beschönigen; *person* reinwaschen; **there's no point trying to ~wash him, he's a liar and that's that** da hilft keine Schönfärberei, er ist und bleibt ein Lügner; **~ wedding** *n* Hochzeit *f* in Weiß; **~ whale** *n* Weißwal, Beluga *m*; **~ wine** *n* Weißwein *m*; **~ woman** *n* Weiße *f*; **~wood** *adj* **~wood furniture** Möbel *pl* aus hellem Weichholz.

whitey ['waɪtɪ] *n* (*pej inf*) Weiße(r) *mf*.

whither ['wɪðəʳ] *adv* **(a)** (*old*) wohin. **(b)** (*journalese*) **~ America/socialism?** Amerika/Sozialismus, wohin? *or* was nun?

whiting¹ ['waɪtɪŋ] *n, no pl see* **whitening**.

whiting² *n, pl* - Weißling, Weißfisch *m*.

whitish ['waɪtɪʃ] *adj colour* weißlich.

whitlow ['wɪtləʊ] *n* Nagelbettentzündung *f*, Umlauf *m*.

Whit Monday [,wɪt'mʌndɪ] *n* Pfingstmontag *m*.

Whitsun ['wɪtsən] [1] *n* Pfingsten *nt*; (*Eccl also*) Pfingstfest *nt*.
[2] *attr* Pfingst-.

Whit Sunday [,wɪt'sʌndɪ] *n* Pfingstsonntag *m*.

Whitsuntide ['wɪtsəntaɪd] *n* Pfingstzeit *f* ◆ **around ~** um Pfingsten (herum).

whittle ['wɪtl] [1] *vt* schnitzen.
[2] *vi* **to ~ (away) at sth** an etw (*dat*) (herum)schnippeln *or* -schnitzen *or* -schneiden.

◆**whittle away** *vt sep* **(a)** *bark etc* wegschneiden, wegschnitzen. **(b)** (*gradually reduce*) allmählich abbauen, nach und nach abbauen; *rights, power etc also* allmählich *or* nach und nach beschneiden *or* stutzen ◆ **the benefit/pay rise has been ~d ~ by inflation** der Gewinn/die Gehaltserhöhung ist durch die Inflation langsam zunichte gemacht worden.

◆**whittle down** *vt sep* **(a)** *piece of wood* herunterschneiden ◆ **to ~ ~ to size** zurechtschneiden, zurechtstutzen.
(b) (*reduce*) kürzen, reduzieren, stutzen (*to* auf *+acc*); *gap, difference* verringern ◆ **to ~ sb ~ to size** (*fig*) jdn zurechtstutzen.

whiz(z) [wɪz] [1] *n* **(a)** (*of arrow*) Schwirren, Sausen *nt*. **(b)** (*US inf*) Kanone *f* (*inf*).
[2] *vi* (*arrow*) schwirren, sausen.

whi(z)z-kid ['wɪz'kɪd] *n* (*inf*) (*in career*) Senkrechtstarter *m* ◆ **financial/publishing ~** Finanz-/Verlagsgenie *nt or* -größe *f*; **a ~ like him will soon find a solution** ein solcher Intelligenzbolzen wird bald auf eine Lösung kommen (*inf*).

WHO *abbr of* **World Health Organization** WGO, Weltgesundheitsorganisation *f*.

who [hu:] *pron* **(a)** (*interrog*) wer; (*acc*) wen; (*dat*) wem ◆ **and ~ should it be but May?** und wer war's? natürlich May!; **~ do you think you are?** was glaubst du dir eigentlich, wer du bist?, für wen hältst du dich eigentlich?; **"W~'s W~"** „Wer ist Wer"; **you'll soon find out ~'s ~ in the office** Sie werden bald im Büro alle kennenlernen; **~ are you looking for?** wen suchen Sie?; **~ did you stay with?** bei wem haben Sie gewohnt?
(b) (*rel*) der/die/das, welche(r, s) ◆ **any man ~ ...** jeder (Mensch), der ...; **he ~ wishes/those ~ wish to go ...** wer gehen will ...; (*for pl also*) diejenigen, die gehen wollen ...; **deny it ~ may** (*form*) das mag bestreiten *or* bestreite das, wer will.

whoa [wəʊ] *interj* brr.

who'd [hu:d] *contr of* **who had; who would.**

whodun(n)it [hu:'dʌnɪt] *n* (*inf*) Krimi *m* (*bei dem der Täter bis zum Schluß unbekannt ist*).

whoever [hu:'evəʳ] *pron* wer (auch immer); (*acc*) wen (auch immer); (*dat*) wem (auch immer); (*no matter who*) einerlei *or* ganz gleich *or* egal (*inf*) wer/wen/wem ◆ **~ told you that?** wer hat dir das denn (bloß) gesagt?

whole [həʊl] [1] *adj* (*entire, unbroken, undivided*) ganz; *truth* voll; (*Bibl: well*) heil ◆ **but the ~ purpose was to ...** aber der ganze Sinn der Sache *or* aber der Zweck der Übung (*inf*) war, daß ...; **three ~ weeks** drei volle *or* ganze Wochen; **the ~ lot** das Ganze; (*of people*) alle, der ganze Verein (*inf*); **a ~ lot of people** eine ganze Menge Leute; **a ~ lot better** (*inf*) ein ganzes Stück besser (*inf*), sehr viel besser; **she is a ~ lot of woman** (*esp US inf*) sie ist eine richtige *or* echte Frau; **out of ~ cloth** (*US*) von Anfang bis Ende erdichtet; **not a cup was left ~** nicht eine Tasse blieb ganz *or* heil; **she swallowed it ~** sie schluckte es ganz *or* unzerkaut (hinunter); **a pig roasted ~** ein ganzes Schwein im *or* am Stück gebraten.
[2] *n* Ganze(s) *nt* ◆ **the ~ of the month/his savings/London** der ganze *or* gesamte Monat/seine gesamten *or* sämtlichen Ersparnisse/ganz London; **nearly the ~ of our production** fast unsere gesamte Produktion; **as a ~** als Ganzes; **these people, as a ~, are ...** diese Leute sind in ihrer Gesamtheit ...; **on the ~** im großen und ganzen, im ganzen gesehen, alles in allem.

▼ **whole: ~food** *adj attr products etc* Vollwertkost-, Reformkost-; **~food shop** Bioladen *m*; **~foods** *npl* Vollwertkost *f*; **~hearted** *adj* völlig, uneingeschränkt; **~hearted congratulations/thanks to X** X (*dat*) gratulieren/danken wir von ganzem Herzen; **to be ~hearted in one's co-operation** sich rückhaltlos miteinsetzen; **~heartedly** *adv* voll und ganz; **~heartedness** *n* Rückhaltlosigkeit *f*; **~ hog** *n*: **to go the ~ hog** (*inf*) aufs Ganze gehen; **~meal** [1] *adj* Vollkorn-; [2] *n* feiner Vollkornschrot; **~ milk** *n* Vollmilch *f*; **~ note** *n* (*esp US Mus*) ganze Note; **~ number** *n* ganze Zahl.

wholesale ['həʊlseɪl] [1] *n* Großhandel *m*.
[2] *adj attr* **(a)** (*Comm*) Großhandels- ◆ **~ dealer** Großhändler, Grossist *m*; **~ business/trade** Großhandel *m*.
(b) (*fig: widespread*) umfassend, massiv; *slaughter, redundancies* Massen-; (*indiscriminate*) wild, generell ◆ **the ~ slaughter of the infected animals** die Abschlachtung aller infizierten Tiere.
[3] *adv* **(a)** im Großhandel.
(b) (*fig*) in Bausch und Bogen; (*in great numbers*) massenweise, massenhaft; (*without modification*) (so) ohne weiteres.
[4] *vt goods* einen Großhandel betreiben mit, Großhändler *or* Grossist sein für.
[5] *vi* (*item*) einen Großhandelspreis haben (*at* von).

wholesaler ['həʊlseɪləʳ] *n* Großhändler, Grossist *m*.

wholesome ['həʊlsəm] *adj* gesund.

wholesomeness ['həʊlsəmnɪs] *n* Bekömmlichkeit *f*; (*of appearance*) Gesundheit *f* ◆ **the ~ of the air** die gesunde Luft.

wholewheat ['həʊlwi:t] *n* Voll(korn)weizen *m*.

who'll [hu:l] *contr of* **who will; who shall.**

wholly ['həʊlɪ] *adv* völlig, gänzlich ◆ **the project was ~ successful** das Projekt war gänzlich erfolgreich *or* ein völliger Erfolg; **this is ~ but ~ ...** das ist völlig und ganz *or* von Grund auf ...

whom [hu:m] *pron* **(a)** (*interrog*) (*acc*) wen; (*dat*) wem. **(b)** (*rel*) (*acc*) den/die/das; (*dat*) dem/der/dem ◆ **..., all of ~ were drunk** ..., die alle betrunken waren; **none/all of ~** von denen keine(r, s)/alle.

whom(so)ever [,hu:m(səʊ)'evəʳ] *pron* (*form*) wen/wem auch immer; (*no matter who*) ganz gleich *or* egal wen/wem.

whoop [hu:p] [1] *n* Ruf, Schrei *m*; (*war cry also*) Geschrei, Geheul *nt no pl* ◆ **with a ~ of joy** unter Freudengeschrei.

➤ LANGUAGE IN USE: **wholeheartedly** → 11.1, 26.3

2 *vt* **to ~ it up** (*inf*) auf die Pauke hauen (*inf*).
3 *vi* rufen, schreien; (*with whooping cough*) pfeifen; (*with joy*) jauchzen.
whoopee ['wʊpi:] 1 *n* **to make ~** (*dated inf*) Rabatz machen (*dated inf*).
2 [wʊ'pi:] *interj* hurra, juchhe(i).
whooping cough ['hu:pɪŋ,kɒf] *n* Keuchhusten *m*.
whoops [wu:ps] *interj* hoppla, huch, hups.
whoosh [wu:ʃ] 1 *n* (*of water*) Rauschen *nt*; (*of air*) Zischen *nt*.
2 *vi* rauschen; zischen ◆ **a train ~ed past** ein Zug schoß *or* brauste vorbei.
whop [wɒp] *vt* (*sl*) schlagen ◆ **Pierre always ~s me at tennis** Pierre macht mich beim Tennis immer fertig (*inf*); **he ~ped me on the chin** er hat mir eine ans Kinn gegeben (*inf*).
whopper ['wɒpəʳ] *n* (*sl*) (*sth big*) Brocken, Trümmer *m* (*inf*), Trumm *nt* (*inf*); (*lie*) faustdicke Lüge.
whopping ['wɒpɪŋ] *adj* (*sl*) Mords- (*inf*), Riesen- ◆ **a ~ big fish** ein mordsgroßer Fisch (*inf*), ein (gewaltiges) Trumm von einem Fisch (*inf*).
whore [hɔ:ʳ] 1 *n* Hure *f*.
2 *vi* (*also* **to go whoring**) (herum)huren (*sl*).
whore: ~house *n* Bordell, Freudenhaus *nt*; **~monger** *n* (*old*) Hurenbock *m*.
whorl [wɜ:l] *n* Kringel *m*; (*of shell*) (Spiral)windung *f*; (*Bot*) Quirl, Wirtel *m*; (*of fingerprint*) Wirbel *m*.
whortleberry ['wɜ:tlbərɪ] *n* Heidelbeere, Blaubeere (*dial*) *f*.
who's [hu:z] *contr of* **who has; who is.**
whose [hu:z] *poss pron* **(a)** (*interrog*) wessen ◆ **~ is this?** wem gehört das?; **~ car did you go in?** in wessen Auto sind Sie gefahren? **(b)** (*rel*) dessen; (*after f and pl*) deren.
whosoever [,hu:səʊ'evəʳ] *pron* (*old*) *see* **whoever.**
▼ **why** [waɪ] 1 *adv* warum, weshalb; (*asking for the purpose*) wozu; (*how come that ...*) wieso ◆ **~ not ask him?** warum fragst du/fragen wir *etc* ihn nicht?; **~ wait?** warum *or* wozu (soll(t)en wir/sie) (noch) warten?; **~ do it this way?** warum denn so?; **that's ~** darum, deshalb, deswegen; **that's exactly ~ ...** genau deshalb *or* deswegen ...
2 *interj* **~, of course, that's right!** ja doch *or* aber sicher, das stimmt so!; **are you sure? — ~ yes (of course/I think so)** sind Sie sicher? — (aber) ja doch; **~ that's easy!** na, das ist doch einfach!; **take the bus! ~, it's only a short walk** den Bus nehmen! — ach was, das ist doch nur ein Katzensprung; **~, if it isn't Charles!** na so was, das ist doch (der) Charles!; **who did it? ~ it's obvious** wer das war? na *or* also, das ist doch klar.
3 *n*: **the ~s and (the) wherefores** das Warum und Weshalb.
WI *abbr of* **(a) Women's Institute. (b) West Indies.**
wick [wɪk] *n* Docht *m* ◆ **to get on sb's ~** (*inf*) jdm auf den Wecker gehen (*inf*) *or* fallen (*inf*).
wicked ['wɪkɪd] *adj* **(a)** (*evil*) *person etc* böse; (*immoral*) schlecht, gottlos; (*indulging in vices*) lasterhaft ◆ **that was a ~ thing to do** das war aber gemein *or* böse *or* niederträchtig (von dir/ihm *etc*); **it's ~ to tease animals/tell lies/swear** Tiere zu quälen ist gemein/Lügen/Fluchen ist häßlich.
(b) (*vicious*) böse; *weapon* gemein (*inf*), niederträchtig, heimtückisch; *satire* boshaft; *blow, frost, wind, weather also* gemein (*inf*) ◆ **he/the dog has a ~ temper** er ist unbeherrscht *or* aufbrausend *or* jähzornig/der Hund ist bösartig.
(c) (*mischievous*) *smile, look, grin* frech, boshaft ◆ **you ~ girl, you** du schlimmes Mädchen *or* du freches Stück (*inf*), (du)!; **I've just had a ~ idea** mir fällt (gerade) was Tolles (*inf*) *or* (*practical joke*) ein guter Streich ein.
(d) (*inf: scandalous*) *price etc* hanebüchen (*inf*), unverschämt ◆ **it's a ~ shame** es ist jammerschade; **it's ~ what they charge** es ist hanebüchen (*inf*) *or* unverschämt *or* nicht mehr feierlich (*inf*), was die verlangen.
(e) (*sl: very good*) (affen)geil (*sl*).
wickedly ['wɪkɪdlɪ] *adv see adj* **(a)** böse; schlecht, gottlos; lasterhaft. **(b)** *cold* gemein ◆ **a ~ accurate satire** eine scharf treffende Satire. **(c)** frech. **(d)** (*inf*) *expensive* unverschämt.
wickedness ['wɪkɪdnɪs] *n* **(a)** (*of person*) Schlechtigkeit *f*; (*immorality*) Verderbtheit *f*; (*indulgence in vices*) Lasterhaftigkeit *f*. **(b)** *see adj (b)* Bösartigkeit *f*; Boshaftigkeit *f*; Gemeinheit *f* ◆ **the ~ of his temper** seine aufbrausende *or* unbeherrschte Art. **(c)** (*mischievousness*) Boshaftigkeit, Bosheit *f*. **(d)** (*inf: of prices etc*) Unverschämtheit *f*.
wicker ['wɪkəʳ] 1 *n* Korbgeflecht *nt*.
2 *adj attr* Korb-.
wicker: ~ basket *n* (Weiden)korb *m*; **~ fence** *n* Weidenzaun *m*; **~work** 1 *n* (*activity*) Korbflechten *nt*; (*material*) Korbgeflecht *nt*; (*articles*) Korbwaren *pl*; 2 *adj chair* Korb-; *basket* Weiden-.
wicket ['wɪkɪt] *n* **(a)** Gatter *nt*; (*for selling tickets*) Fenster *nt*.
(b) (*Cricket*) (*stumps: also* **~s**) Mal, Pfostentor *nt*; (*pitch*) Spielbahn *f* ◆ **to take a ~** einen Schlagmann auswerfen; **three ~s fell before lunch** es gab drei Malwürfe vor der Mittagspause; **we won by four ~s** wir gewannen und hatten vier Schlagmänner noch nicht in Einsatz gehabt; **to keep ~** Torwächter sein *or* machen; *see* **sticky.**
(c) (*US: croquet hoop*) Tor *nt*.
wicket-keeper ['wɪkɪt'ki:pəʳ] *n* (*Cricket*) Torwächter *m*.
widdle ['wɪdl] (*inf*) 1 *vi* pinkeln (*inf*).
2 *n* **to go for a ~** (*hum*) pinkeln gehen (*inf*).
wide [waɪd] 1 *adj* (+*er*) **(a)** *road, smile, feet, gap* breit; *skirt, trousers, plain* weit; *eyes* groß ◆ **it is three metres ~** es ist drei Meter breit; (*material*) es liegt drei Meter breit; (*room*) es ist drei Meter in der Breite; **the big ~ world** die (große) weite Welt.
(b) (*considerable, comprehensive*) *difference, variety* groß; *experience, choice* reich, umfangreich; *public, knowledge, range* breit; *interests* vielfältig, breitgefächert *attr*; *coverage of report* umfassend; *network* weitverzweigt *attr*; *circulation* weit, groß; *question* weitreichend ◆ **~ reading is the best education** viel zu lesen ist die beste Art der Erziehung *or* Bildung; **his ~ reading** seine große Belesenheit.
(c) (*missing the target*) daneben *pred*, gefehlt ◆ **you're a bit ~ there** da liegst du etwas daneben; **~ of the truth** nicht ganz wahrheitsgetreu; **a ~ ball** (*Cricket*) ein Ball, der nicht in Reichweite des Schlagmanns aufspringt.
2 *adv* **(a)** (*extending far*) weit ◆ **they are set ~ apart** sie liegen weit auseinander; *see* **far.**
(b) (*fully*) weit ◆ **open ~!** bitte weit öffnen; **the general/writer left himself ~ open to attack** der General/Verfasser hat sich (überhaupt) nicht gegen Angriffe abgesichert; **the law is ~ open to criticism/abuse** das Gesetz bietet viele Ansatzpunkte für Kritik/öffnet dem Mißbrauch Tür und Tor; **the game is still ~ open** der Spielausgang ist noch völlig offen; **to be ~ awake** hellwach sein; (*alert*) wach sein.
(c) (*far from the target*) daneben ◆ **to go ~ of sth** über etw (*acc*) hinausgehen, an etw (*dat*) vorbeigehen.
-wide [-waɪd] *adj suf* über *or* für den/die/das gesamte(n), in dem/der gesamte(n); (*country~ etc*) -weit ◆ **a company-~ pay increase** eine Gehaltserhöhung für die ganze Firma.
wide: ~-angle (lens) *n* (*Phot*) Weitwinkel(objektiv *nt*) *m*; **~-awake** *adj* (*fully awake*) hellwach; (*alert*) wach; **you can't fool her, she's much too ~-awake** du kannst ihr nichts vormachen, dazu paßt sie viel zu genau auf *or* dazu ist sie viel zu wach *or* helle (*inf*); **he has to be ~-awake to all their dodges** er muß genau aufpassen, daß ihm keiner ihrer Tricks entgeht; **~-awake hat** *n* Schlapphut *m*; **~-band** *adj* (*Rad*) Breitband-; **~ boy** *n* (*Brit inf*) Fuchs (*inf*), Gauner *m*; **~-eyed** *adj* mit großen Augen; **she gazed at him with ~-eyed innocence** sie starrte ihn mit großen, unschuldigen Kinderaugen an; **in ~-eyed amazement** mit großen, erstaunten Augen.
widely ['waɪdlɪ] *adv* weit; (*by or to many people*) weit und breit, überall, allgemein; *differing* völlig ◆ **his remarks were ~ publicized** seine Bemerkungen fanden weite Verbreitung; **the opinion is ~ held ...** es herrscht in weiten Kreisen die Ansicht ...; **it is not ~ understood why ...** es wird nicht überall *or* von allen verstanden, warum ...; **he became ~ known as ...** er wurde überall *or* in weiten Kreisen bekannt als ...; **a ~ read student** ein sehr belesener Student.
widen ['waɪdn] 1 *vt road* verbreitern; *passage* erweitern; *knowledge etc* erweitern.
2 *vi* breiter werden; (*interests etc*) sich ausweiten.
◆**widen out** *vi* **(a)** (*river, valley etc*) sich erweitern (*into* zu). **(b)** (*interests etc*) sich ausweiten.
wideness ['waɪdnɪs] *n* **(a)** (*of road, gap*) Breite *f*; (*of skirt*) Weite *f*. **(b)** (*of knowledge, coverage, interests*) Breite *f*; (*of variety, choice*) Reichtum *m*.
wide: ~-open *adj* **(a)** (*fully open*) *door, window* ganz *or* weit *or* sperrangelweit (*inf*) offen; *beak* weit aufgerissen *or* aufgesperrt; **the ~-open spaces** die Weite; **(b)** (*not decided*) *match etc* völlig offen; **(c)** (*US inf*) *wo liberale Gesetze bezüglich Prostitution, Glückspiele etc herrschen*; **~-ranging** *adj* weitreichend; **~-screen** *adj television set* Breitbild-; **~spread** *adj* weitverbreitet *attr*; **to become ~spread** weite Verbreitung erlangen.
widgeon ['wɪdʒən] *n* Pfeifente *f*.
widget ['wɪdʒɪt] *n* (*inf: manufactured product*) Produkt, Ding (*inf*) *nt* ◆ **10,000 ~s per month** 10.000 Produkte *or* Dinger (*inf*) pro Monat.
widow ['wɪdəʊ] 1 *n* **(a)** Witwe *f* ◆ **to be left a ~** als Witwe zurückbleiben; **~'s mite** (*fig*) Scherflein *nt* (der armen Witwe); **~'s peak** spitzer Haaransatz; **~'s pension** Witwenrente *f*; **golf ~** (*hum*) Golfwitwe *f*; *see* **grass ~. (b)** (*Typ*) Hurenkind *nt*.
2 *vt* zur Witwe/zum Witwer machen ◆ **she was twice ~ed** sie ist zweimal verwitwet.
widowed ['wɪdəʊd] *adj* verwitwet.
widower ['wɪdəʊəʳ] *n* Witwer *m*.
widowhood ['wɪdəʊhʊd] *n* (*of woman*) (*period*) Witwenschaft *f*; (*state also*) Witwentum *nt*; (*rare: of man*) Witwerschaft *f*.
width [wɪdθ] *n* **(a)** Breite *f*; (*of trouser legs, skirts etc*) Weite *f* ◆ **the ~ of his reading** seine umfassende Belesenheit; **six centimetres in ~** sechs Zentimeter breit; **what is the ~ of the material?** wie breit liegt dieser Stoff? **(b)** (*piece of material*) Breite *f* ◆ **three ~s of cloth** drei mal die Breite.
widthways ['wɪdθweɪz], **widthwise** ['wɪdθwaɪz] *adv* der Breite nach.
wield [wi:ld] *vt pen, sword* führen; *axe* schwingen; *power, influence* ausüben, haben ◆ **~ing his sword above his head** das Schwert über seinem Haupte schwingend; **to ~ power over sth** über etw (*acc*) Macht ausüben.
wiener ['wi:nəʳ] *n* (*US: frankfurter*) Wiener Würstchen *nt*.
wife [waɪf] *n, pl* **wives** Frau, Gattin (*form*), Gemahlin (*liter, form*) *f* ◆ **the ~** (*inf*) die Frau; **a woman whom he would never make his ~** eine Person, die er niemals zu seiner Frau machen würde; **businessmen who take their wives with them on their trips** Geschäftsleute, die ihre (Ehe)frauen *or* Damen mit auf Geschäftsreise nehmen; **to take a ~** (*old*) sich (*dat*) eine Frau *or* ein Weib (*old*) nehmen; **to take sb to ~** (*old*) jdn zum Weibe nehmen (*old*).
wifely ['waɪflɪ] *adj* **~ duties** Pflichten *pl* als Ehefrau; **~ devotion** Hingabe *f* einer Ehefrau.
wife-swapping ['waɪf,swɒpɪŋ] *n* Partnertausch *m* ◆ **~ party** Party *f* mit Partnertausch.
wig [wɪg] *n* Perücke *f*.
wigeon *n see* **widgeon.**
wigging ['wɪgɪŋ] *n* (*dated Brit inf*) Standpauke, Gardinenpredigt *f* ◆ **to give sb**

➤ LANGUAGE IN USE: **why: 1** → 1.1, 17.2, 26.3

a ~ jdm eine Standpauke *or* Gardinenpredigt halten, jdm die Leviten lesen (*dated*).

wiggle ['wɪgl] [1] *n* Wackeln *nt no pl* ◆ **give it a ~ and it might come free** wackeln Sie mal daran, dann geht es vielleicht raus; **to get a ~ on** (*inf*) Dampf dahintermachen (*inf*).
[2] *vt* wackeln mit; *eyebrows* zucken mit.
[3] *vi* wackeln; (*eyebrows*) zucken.

wiggly ['wɪglɪ] *adj* wackelnd; *line* Schlangen-; (*drawn*) Wellen-; *amateur film etc* wackelig, verwackelt.

wight [waɪt] *n* (*old*) Wicht *m*.

wigmaker ['wɪgmeɪkə(r)] *n* Perückenmacher(in *f*) *m*.

wigwam ['wɪgwæm] *n* Wigwam *m*.

wilco ['wɪlkəʊ] *interj* (*Mil etc*) wird gemacht, zu Befehl.

wild [waɪld] [1] *adj* (+*er*) **(a)** (*not domesticated, not civilized*) wild; *people* unzivilisiert; *garden, wood* verwildert; *flowers* wildwachsend *attr*; (*in meadows*) Wiesen-; (*in fields*) Feld- ◆ **the W~ West** der Wilde Westen; **~ silk** Wildseide *f*; **~ animals** Tiere *pl* in freier Wildbahn; **the ~ animals of Northern Europe** Tiere *pl* Nordeuropas, die Tierwelt Nordeuropas; **a seal is a ~ animal** der Seehund ist kein Haustier *or* lebt in freier Wildbahn; **the plant in its ~ state** die Pflanze im Naturzustand.
(b) (*stormy*) *weather, wind* rauh, stürmisch; *sea also* wild.
(c) (*excited, frantic, unruly, riotous*) wild (*with* vor +*dat*); (*disordered*) *hair also* wirr, unordentlich; *children also, joy, desire* unbändig.
(d) (*inf: angry*) wütend (*with, at* mit, auf +*acc*), rasend ◆ **it drives** *or* **makes me ~** das macht mich ganz wild *or* rasend; **to get ~** wild werden (*inf*).
(e) (*inf: very keen*) **to be ~ on** *or* **about sb/sth** auf jdn/etw wild *or* scharf (*inf*) *or* versessen sein; **to be ~ to do sth** (*esp US*) wild *or* scharf (*inf*) *or* versessen darauf sein, etw zu tun.
(f) (*rash, extravagant*) verrückt; *talk, scheme also* unausgegoren; *promise* unüberlegt; *exaggeration* maßlos, wild; *allegation* wild; *fluctuations* stark; *expectations, imagination, fancies* kühn ◆ **never in my ~est dreams** auch in meinen kühnsten Träumen nicht.
(g) (*wide of the mark, erratic*) *throw, shot* Fehl-; *spelling* unsicher ◆ **it was just/he had a ~ guess** es war/er hatte nur so (wild) drauflosgeraten.
(h) (*Cards*) beliebig verwendbar.
(i) (*sl: fantastic, great*) *attr* toll, Klasse-, Spitzen-; *pred* toll, klasse, Spitze (*all inf*).
[2] *adv* **(a)** (*in the natural state*) *grow* wild; *run* frei ◆ **to let one's imagination run ~** seiner Phantasie (*dat*) freien Lauf lassen; **the roses/the children have run ~** die Rosen/die Kinder sind verwildert, die Rosen sind ins Kraut gewachsen; **he lets his kids run ~** (*pej*) er läßt seine Kinder auf der Straße aufwachsen; **in the country the kids can run ~** auf dem Land kann man die Kinder einfach laufen *or* herumspringen lassen.
(b) (*without aim*) *shoot* ins Blaue, drauflos; (*off the mark*) *go, throw* daneben.
[3] *n* Wildnis *f* ◆ **in the ~** in der Wildnis, in freier Wildbahn; **the call of the ~** der Ruf der Wildnis; **the ~s** die Wildnis; **out in the ~s** (*hum: not in the city*) auf dem platten Lande (*inf*), jwd (*inf*); **out in the ~s of Berkshire** im hintersten Berkshire.

wildcard ['waɪldkɑːd] (*Comput*) [1] *n* Wildcard *f*, Jokerzeichen, Ersatzzeichen *nt*.
[2] *adj attr character* Joker-, Ersatz-.

wildcat ['waɪldkæt] [1] *n* **(a)** (*Zool, inf: woman*) Wildkatze *f*.
(b) (*US inf*) (*Comm: risky venture*) gewagte *or* riskante Sache; (*trial oil well*) Probe- *or* Versuchsbohrung *f*.
[2] *adj attr* (*trial*) Versuchs-, Probe-; (*risky*) riskant, gewagt; (*unofficial*) *company etc* Schwindel- ◆ **~ strike** wilder Streik.

wild child *n* (*Brit*) Wildfang *m*.

wildebeest ['wɪldəbiːst] *n* Gnu *nt*.

wilderness ['wɪldənɪs] *n* Wildnis *f*; (*fig*) Wüste *f* ◆ **a voice crying in the ~** die Stimme eines Rufenden in der Wüste; **a ~ of ruins/roofs** ein Gewirr *nt* von Ruinen/Dächern.

wild: ~-eyed *adj person* wild dreinblickend *attr*; *look* wild; **~fire** *n* **to spread like ~fire** sich wie ein Lauffeuer ausbreiten; **~fowl** *n, no pl* Wildgeflügel *nt*; **~-goose chase** *n* fruchtloses Unterfangen, Wolpertingerjagd *f* (*S Ger*); **to send sb out on a ~-goose chase** jdn für nichts und wieder nichts losschicken; **~life** *n* **(a)** die Tierwelt; **~life sanctuary** Wildschutzgebiet, Wildreservat *nt*; **(b)** (*sl hum: girls*) Weiber *pl* (*inf*).

wildly ['waɪldlɪ] *adv* **(a)** (*violently*) wild, heftig.
(b) (*in disorder*) wirr ◆ **his hair fell ~ over his forehead** sein Haar fiel ihm wirr in die Stirn.
(c) (*without aim*) wild ◆ **to hit out/shoot ~** wild um sich schlagen/drauflosschießen.
(d) (*extravagantly*) *guess* drauflos, ins Blaue hinein; *talk* unausgegoren; *happy* rasend; *exaggerated* stark, maßlos; *wrong, different* total, völlig.
(e) (*excitedly, distractedly*) wild, aufgeregt.
(f) (*riotously*) wild.

wildness ['waɪldnɪs] *n* **(a)** (*rough, uncivilized state*) Wildheit *f*.
(b) (*of storm etc*) Wildheit, Stärke, Heftigkeit *f* ◆ **the ~ of the weather** das rauhe *or* stürmische Wetter.
(c) (*frenzy, unruliness*) Wildheit *f*.
(d) (*extravagance*) *see adj (f)* Unüberlegtheit *f*; Maßlosigkeit *f*; Stärke *f*; Kühnheit *f*.
(e) (*lack of aim*) Unkontrolliertheit *f*; (*erratic nature: of spelling*) Unsicherheit *f*.

wild oat *n* Windhafer *m*; *see* **oat**.

wile [waɪl] *n usu pl* List *f*, Schliche *pl* ◆ **she used all her ~s** sie ließ ihren ganzen *or* all ihren Charme spielen.

wilful, (*US*) willful ['wɪlfʊl] *adj* **(a)** (*self-willed*) eigensinnig, eigenwillig. **(b)** (*deliberate*) *neglect, damage, waste* mutwillig; *murder* vorsätzlich; *disobedience* wissentlich.

wilfully, (*US*) willfully ['wɪlfəlɪ] *adv see adj*.

wilfulness, (*US*) willfulness ['wɪlfʊlnɪs] *n see adj* **(a)** Eigensinn *m*, Eigenwilligkeit *f*. **(b)** Mutwilligkeit *f*; Vorsätzlichkeit *f*.

wiliness ['waɪlɪnɪs] *n* Listigkeit, Schläue, Hinterlist (*pej*) *f*.

will[1] [wɪl] *pret* **would** [1] *modal aux vb* **(a)** (*fut*) werden ◆ **I'm sure that he ~ come** ich bin sicher, daß er kommt; **you ~ come to see us, won't you?** Sie kommen uns doch besuchen, ja?; **I'll be right there** komme sofort!, bin gleich da!; **I ~ have finished by Tuesday** bis Dienstag bin ich fertig; **you won't lose it, ~ you?** du wirst es doch nicht verlieren, oder?; **you won't insist on that, ~ you? — oh yes, I ~** Sie bestehen doch nicht darauf, oder? — o doch! *or* o ja! *or* doch, doch!
(b) (*emphatic, expressing determination, compulsion etc*) **I ~ not have it!** das dulde ich nicht, das kommt mir nicht in Frage (*inf*); **~ you be quiet!** willst du jetzt wohl ruhig sein!, bist du *or* sei jetzt endlich ruhig!; **you ~ not talk to me like that!** so lasse ich nicht mit mir reden!; **he says he ~ go and I say he won't** er sagt, er geht, und ich sage, er geht nicht.
(c) (*expressing willingness, consent etc*) wollen ◆ **he won't sign** er unterschreibt nicht, er will nicht unterschreiben; **if she won't say yes** wenn sie nicht ja sagt; **he wouldn't help me** er wollte *or* mochte mir nicht helfen; **wait a moment, ~ you?** warten Sie einen Moment, ja bitte?; (*impatiently*) jetzt warte doch mal einen Moment!; **~ she, won't she** ob sie wohl ...?
(d) (*in questions*) **~ you have some more tea?** möchten Sie noch Tee?; **~ you accept these conditions?** akzeptieren Sie diese Bedingungen?; **won't you take a seat?** wollen *or* möchten Sie sich nicht setzen?; **won't you please come home?** komm doch bitte nach Hause!; **there isn't any tea, ~ coffee do?** es ist kein Tee da, darf *or* kann es auch Kaffee sein?, tut es Kaffee auch? (*inf*).
(e) (*insistence*) **well, if he ~ drive so fast** also, wenn er (eben) unbedingt so schnell fahren muß *or* fährt; **well, if you won't take advice** wenn du (eben) keinen Rat annimmst, na bitte; **he ~ interrupt all the time** er muß ständig dazwischenreden.
(f) (*assumption*) **he'll be there by now** jetzt ist er schon da *or* dürfte er schon da sein; **was that the door-bell? that ~ be for you** hat's geklingelt? — das ist bestimmt für dich *or* das wird *or* dürfte für dich sein; **this ~ be the bus** das wird *or* dürfte unser Bus sein; **this ~ be the one you want** das dürfte (es) wohl sein, was sie wünschen.
(g) (*tendency*) **the solution ~ turn red if** ... die Lösung färbt sich rot, wenn ...; **sometimes he ~ sit in his room for hours** manchmal sitzt er auch stundenlang in seinem Zimmer; **accidents ~ happen** Unfälle passieren nun (ein)mal.
(h) (*capability*) **~ the engine start now?** springt der Motor jetzt an?; **the car won't start** das Auto springt nicht an *or* will nicht anspringen; **the door won't open** die Tür läßt sich nicht öffnen *or* geht nicht auf (*inf*); **the cut won't heal** die Schnittwunde will nicht (ver)heilen; **the car ~ do up to 120 mph** das Auto fährt bis zu 120 mph *or* kann bis zu 120 mph fahren.
[2] *vi* wollen ◆ **say what you ~** du kannst sagen *or* sag, was du willst; **as you ~!** wie du willst!; **it is, if you ~, a kind of mystery** das ist, wenn du so willst, eine Art Rätsel.

will[2] [1] *n* **(a)** Wille *m* ◆ **to have a ~ of one's own** einen eigenen Willen haben; (*hum*) so seine Mucken haben (*inf*); **the ~ to win/live** der Wille *or* das Bestreben, zu gewinnen/zu leben, der Siegeswille/Lebens wille; **(to go) against one's/sb's ~** gegen seinen/jds Willen (handeln); **if that's your ~** wenn das dein Wunsch ist; **at ~** nach Belieben *or* Lust und Laune, beliebig; **fire at ~!** ohne Befehl schießen; **of one's own free ~** aus freien Stücken *or* freiem Willen; **with the best ~ in the world** beim *or* mit (dem) (aller)besten Willen; **where there is a ~ there is a way** (*Prov*) wo ein Wille ist, ist auch ein Weg (*Prov*); **to do sb's ~** (*dated*) jdm seinen Willen tun; **to have one's ~** (*dated*) seinen Kopf durchsetzen; **Thy ~ be done** Dein Wille geschehe; **to work with a ~** mit (Feuer)eifer arbeiten; *see* **good will, ill 1 (b)**.
(b) (*testament*) Letzter Wille, Testament *nt* ◆ **the last ~ and testament of ...** der Letzte Wille *or* das Testament des/der ...; **to make one's ~** sein Testament machen.
[2] *vt* **(a)** (*old: ordain*) wollen, bestimmen, verfügen (*geh*) ◆ **God has so ~ed** Gott hat es so gewollt *or* gefügt *or* bestimmt.
(b) (*urge by willpower*) (durch Willenskraft) erzwingen ◆ **to ~ sb to do sth** jdn durch die eigene Willensanstrengung dazu bringen, daß er etw tut; **he ~ed himself to stay awake/to get better** er hat sich (dazu) gezwungen, wach zu bleiben/er hat seine Genesung durch seine Willenskraft erzwungen; **he ~ed the ball into the net** er hat den Ball ins Netz hypnotisiert (*inf*).
(c) (*by testament*) (testamentarisch) vermachen, vererben (*sth to sb* jdm etw).
[3] *vi* wollen ◆ **if God ~s** so Gott will.

willful *etc* (*US*) *see* **wilful** *etc*.

William ['wɪljəm] *n* Wilhelm *m*.

willie ['wɪlɪ] *n* (*hum inf: penis*) Pimmel *m* (*inf*).

willies ['wɪlɪz] *npl* (*inf*) **to get the ~** Zustände kriegen (*inf*); **it/he gives me the ~** da/bei dem wird mir ganz anders (*inf*).

willing ['wɪlɪŋ] *adj* **(a)** (*prepared*) **to be ~ to do sth** bereit *or* gewillt (*geh*) *or* willens (*liter, old*) sein, etw zu tun; **God ~** so Gott will; **he was ~ for me to take it** es war ihm recht, daß ich es nahm; **he was not ~ for us to go/for this**

➤ LANGUAGE IN USE: **will**[1]: **1a** → 20.5 **will**[2]: **1a** → 9.3

to be done er war nicht gewillt, uns gehen zu lassen/das geschehen zu lassen.
(b) *(ready to help, cheerfully ready) workers, helpers* bereitwillig ◆ **prepared to lend a ~ hand** gerne dazu bereit zu helfen.
willingly ['wɪlɪŋlɪ] *adv* bereitwillig, gerne ◆ **will you help? — yes, ~** wollen Sie helfen? — (ja,) gerne.
willingness ['wɪlɪŋnɪs] *n see adj* **(a)** Bereitschaft *f*. **(b)** Bereitwilligkeit *f*.
will-o'-the-wisp ['wɪləðə'wɪsp] *n* Irrlicht *nt*; *(fig)* Trugbild *nt*.
willow ['wɪləʊ] *n (also ~ tree)* Weide *f*, Weidenbaum *m*; *(wood)* Weidenholz *nt*; *(twigs)* Weidenruten *or* -gerten *pl*.
willowherb ['wɪləʊ,hɜːb] *n* Weidenröschen *nt*.
willow pattern [1] *n* chinesisches Weidenmotiv *(auf Porzellan)*.
[2] *adj attr* mit chinesischem Weidenmotiv.
willowy ['wɪləʊɪ] *adj* gertenschlank.
willpower ['wɪl,paʊəʳ] *n* Willenskraft *f*.
willy ['wɪlɪ] *n see* **willie**.
willy-nilly ['wɪlɪ'nɪlɪ] *adv* **(a)** *(at random) choose, allocate* aufs Geratewohl; *accept* wahllos, ohne weiteres. **(b)** *(willingly or not)* wohl oder übel, nolens volens.
wilt¹ [wɪlt] *(old) 2nd pers sing of* **will¹**.
wilt² [1] *vi* **(a)** *(flowers)* welken, verwelken, welk werden. **(b)** *(person)* matt werden; *(after physical exercise)* schlapp werden; *(enthusiasm, energy)* abflauen.
[2] *vt* ausdörren.
Wilts [wɪlts] *abbr of* **Wiltshire**.
wily ['waɪlɪ] *adj (+er)* listig, raffiniert, schlau, hinterlistig *(pej)*.
wimp [wɪmp] *n (inf)* Schwächling, Waschlappen *(inf) m*.
◆**wimp out** *vi (inf)* kneifen *(inf)* ◆ **to ~ ~ of sth** bei etw kneifen *(inf)*.
wimpish ['wɪmpɪʃ] *adj (inf)* weichlich, schlapp *(inf)*.
wimpishly ['wɪmpɪʃlɪ] *adv (inf)* schlapp *(inf)* ◆ **he ~ agreed to sell** Schwächling *or* Waschlappen *(inf)*, der er ist, stimmte er dem Verkauf zu.
wimpishness ['wɪmpɪʃnɪs] *n (inf)* Weichlichkeit, Schlappheit *(inf) f*.
wimple ['wɪmpl] *n* Rise *f (spec)*, Schleier *m*; *(worn by nuns)* (Nonnen)schleier *m*.
win [wɪn] *(vb: pret, ptp* **won***)* [1] *n* Sieg *m* ◆ **to back a horse for a ~** auf den Sieg eines Pferdes setzen; **to have a ~** *(money)* einen Gewinn machen; *(victory)* einen Sieg erzielen; **to play for a ~** auf Sieg spielen.
[2] *vt* **(a)** *race, prize, battle, election, money, bet, sympathy, support, friends, glory* gewinnen; *reputation* erwerben; *scholarship, contract* bekommen; *victory* erringen ◆ **to ~ sb's heart/love/hand** jds Herz/Liebe/Hand gewinnen; **he tried to ~ her** er versuchte, sie für sich zu gewinnen; **it won him the first prize** es brachte ihm den ersten Preis ein; **to ~ sth from** *or* **off** *(inf)* **sb** jdm etw abgewinnen.
(b) *(obtain, extract)* gewinnen ◆ **the oil won from the North Sea** das aus der Nordsee gewonnene Öl; **land won from the sea** dem Meer abgewonnenes Land.
(c) *(liter: reach with effort) shore, summit* erreichen.
[3] *vi* **(a)** gewinnen, siegen ◆ **if ~ning becomes too important** wenn das Siegen *or* das Gewinnen zu wichtig wird; **OK, you ~, I was wrong** okay, du hast gewonnen, ich habe mich geirrt.
(b) *(liter)* **to ~ free** sich freikämpfen, sich befreien.
◆**win back** *vt sep* zurück- *or* wiedergewinnen.
◆**win out** *vi* letztlich siegen *(over sb* über jdn*)*, sich durchsetzen *(over sb* jdm gegenüber*)*.
◆**win over** *or* **round** *vt sep* für sich gewinnen ◆ **it is hard to ~ him ~** es ist schwer, ihn für uns *or* für unsere Seite zu gewinnen; **his speech won ~ all the government's critics** mit seiner Rede hat er alle Kritiker der Regierung für sich gewonnen; **to ~ sb ~ to Catholicism/one's own way of thinking** jdn zum Katholizismus/zur eigenen Denkungsart bekehren; **to ~ sb ~ to a plan** jdn für einen Plan gewinnen.
◆**win through** *vi (patient)* durchkommen ◆ **to ~ ~ to a place** sich zu einem Ort durch- *or* vorkämpfen; **we'll ~ ~ in the end** wir werden es schon schaffen *(inf)*.
wince [wɪns] [1] *n* (Zusammen)zucken *nt* ◆ **ouch, he said with a ~** autsch, sagte er und zuckte zusammen; **to give a ~ (of pain)** (vor Schmerz) zusammenzucken.
[2] *vi* zusammenzucken.
winceyette [,wɪnsɪ'et] *n* Flanellette *nt*.
winch [wɪntʃ] [1] *n* Winde, Winsch *f*.
[2] *vt* winschen.
◆**winch up** *vt sep* hochwinschen.
Winchester (rifle) ['wɪntʃestə('raɪfl)] *n* Winchesterbüchse *f*.
wind¹ [wɪnd] [1] *n* **(a)** Wind *m* ◆ **the ~ is from the east** der Wind kommt aus dem *or* von Osten; **before the ~** *(Naut)* vor dem Wind; **into the ~** *(Naut)* in den Wind; **to sail close to the ~** *(fig)* sich hart an der Grenze des Erlaubten bewegen; *(Naut)* hart am Wind segeln; **(to run) like the ~** (rennen) wie der Wind; **a ~ of change** *(fig)* ein frischer(er) Wind; **there's something in the ~** (irgend) etwas bahnt sich an *or* liegt in der Luft; **to get/have the ~ up** *(inf)* *(nervous)* Angst *or* Schiß *(sl)* kriegen/haben; **to put the ~ up sb** *(inf)* jdm Angst machen, jdn ins Bockshorn jagen; **to raise the ~** *(dated Brit inf)* das nötige Kleingeld auftreiben *(inf)*; **to see which way the ~ blows** *(fig)* sehen, woher der Wind weht; **to take the ~ out of sb's sails** *(fig)* jdm den Wind aus den Segeln nehmen; **he's full of ~** *(fig)* er ist ein Schaumschläger *(inf)*, er macht viel Wind *(inf)*.
(b) *(scent)* **to get ~ of sth** *(lit, fig)* von etw Wind bekommen.
(c) *(compass point)* **to the four ~s** in alle (vier) Winde; **to throw caution to the ~s** Bedenken in den Wind schlagen.
(d) *(from bowel, stomach)* Wind *m*, Blähung *f* ◆ **to break ~** einen Wind streichen lassen; **to bring up ~** aufstoßen; *(baby also)* ein Bäuerchen machen; **to have a touch of ~** leichte Blähungen haben.
(e) *(breath)* Atem *m*, Luft *f (inf)* ◆ **to be short of ~** außer Atem sein; **to get one's ~ back** wieder Luft bekommen *or* zu Atem kommen; **to get one's second ~** den toten Punkt überwunden haben; **he's losing his ~** ihm geht der Atem aus; **sound in ~ and limb** kerngesund.
[2] *vt* **(a)** *(knock breathless)* den Atem nehmen *(+dat)* ◆ **he was ~ed by the ball** der Ball nahm ihm den Atem. **(b)** *(scent)* wittern. **(c)** *horses* verschnaufen lassen.
wind² [waɪnd] *(vb: pret, ptp* **wound***)* [1] *vt* **(a)** *(twist, wrap) wool, bandage* wickeln; *turban etc* winden; *(one time around)* winden; *(on to a reel)* spulen. **(b)** *(turn, ~ up) handle* kurbeln, drehen; *clock, watch, clockwork toy* aufziehen. **(c)** *(proceed by twisting)* **to ~ one's way** sich schlängeln.
[2] *vi* **(a)** *(river etc)* sich winden *or* schlängeln.
(b) *(handle, watch)* **which way does it ~?** wierum zieht man es auf/*(handle)* dreht *or* kurbelt man es?; **it won't ~** er/es läßt sich nicht aufziehen/*(handle)* drehen *or* kurbeln.
[3] *n* **(a) I'll give the clock a ~** ich werde die Uhr aufziehen; **give it one more ~** zieh es noch eine Umdrehung weiter auf; *(handle)* kurbele *or* drehe es noch einmal weiter.
(b) *(bend)* Kehre, Windung *f*.
◆**wind around** [1] *vt sep +prep obj* wickeln um ◆ **~ it once/twice ~ the post** winde *or* lege *or* wickele es einmal/zweimal um den Pfosten; **to ~ one's arms ~ sb** seine Arme um jdn schlingen *or* winden *(geh)*; **to ~ itself ~ sth** sich um etw schlingen.
[2] *vi (road)* sich winden; *+prep obj (road)* sich schlängeln durch; *(procession)* sich winden durch.
◆**wind back** *vt sep film* zurückspulen.
◆**wind down** [1] *vt sep* **(a)** *car windows etc* herunterdrehen *or* -kurbeln. **(b)** *operations* reduzieren; *production* zurück- schrauben.
[2] *vi* **(a)** *(lose speed: clock)* ablaufen. **(b)** *(path etc)* sich hinunterwinden *or* -schlängeln. **(c)** *(relax)* abspannen, entspannen.
◆**wind forward** *vt sep film* weiterspulen.
◆**wind in** *vt sep fish* einziehen *or* -holen; *rope also* aufspulen.
◆**wind on** *vt sep film* weiterspulen.
◆**wind out** *vt sep cable* abwickeln, ab- *or* runterspulen.
◆**wind round** *vti sep see* **wind around.**
◆**wind up** [1] *vt sep* **(a)** *bucket* herauf- *or* hochholen; *car window* hinaufkurbeln *or* -drehen.
(b) *clock, mechanism* aufziehen.
(c) *(fig inf) person* aufziehen ◆ **to be wound ~ about sth** *(fig)* über etw *(acc) or* wegen einer Sache *(gen)* erregt sein; **to be wound ~ to a state of ...** sich in einen Zustand des/der ... steigern.
(d) *(close, end) meeting, debate, speech* beschließen, zu Ende bringen ◆ **he wound ~ the arguments for the government** er faßte die Argumente der Regierung(sseite) zusammen.
(e) *company* auflösen; *service, series* auslaufen lassen ◆ **to ~ ~ one's affairs** seine Angelegenheiten abwickeln.
[2] *vi* **(a)** *(inf: end up)* enden ◆ **to ~ ~ in hospital/Munich** im Krankenhaus/in München landen; **to ~ ~ doing sth/broke/with nothing** am Ende etw tun/pleite sein/ohne etwas da stehen; **he'll ~ ~ as director** er wird es noch bis zum Direktor bringen.
(b) *(conclude)* **to ~ ~ for the government** die abschließende Rede für die Regierung halten; **we sang a song to ~ ~** abschließend *or* zum Schluß sangen wir noch ein Lied.
(c) *(proceed by twisting)* sich hinaufwinden; *(road also)* sich hinaufschlängeln.
wind ['wɪnd-]: **~bag** *n (inf)* Schwätzer, Schaumschläger *m*; **~blown** *adj hair, tree* windzerzaust; **~break** *n* Windschutz *m*; **~breaker** ® *n (US) see* **~cheater**; **~burn** *n* Rötung *f* der Haut auf Grund von Wind; **~cheater** *n (Brit)* Windjacke *or* -bluse *f*; **~chill factor** *n* Wind-Kälte-Faktor *m*; **~ cone** *n (Aviat)* Wind- *or* Luftsack *m*.
winded ['wɪndɪd] *adj* atemlos, außer Atem.
wind energy *n* Windenergie *f*.
winder ['waɪndəʳ] *n (of watch)* Krone *f*, (Aufzieh)rädchen *nt*; *(of alarm clock, toy etc)* Aufziehschraube *f*.
wind ['wɪnd-]: **~fall** *n* Fallobst *nt*; *(fig)* unerwartetes Geschenk, unverhoffter Glücksfall; **~ farm** *n* Windfarm *f*; **~ gauge** *n* Wind(stärke) messer *m*.
windiness ['wɪndɪnɪs] *n* Wind *m* ◆ **because of the ~ of the area** wegen des starken Windes in dieser Gegend.
winding ['waɪndɪŋ] [1] *adj river* gewunden; *road also* kurvenreich.
[2] *n* **(a)** *(of road, river)* Windung, Kehre *f*; *(fig)* Verwicklung *f*. **(b)** *(Elec) (coil)* Wicklung *f*; *(simple twist)* Windung *f*.
winding: ~ sheet *n (old)* Leichentuch *nt*; **~ staircase** *n* Wendeltreppe *f*; **~-up** *n (of project)* Abschluß *m*; *(of company, society)* Auflösung *f*; **~-up sale** *n* Räumungsverkauf *m*.
wind ['wɪnd-]: **~ instrument** *n* Blasinstrument *nt*; **~jammer** *n* Windjammer *m*.
windlass ['wɪndləs] *n (winch)* Winde *f*; *(Naut)* Ankerwinde *f*.
wind ['wɪnd-]: **~less** *adj* windfrei, ohne Wind, windstill; **~-machine** *n* Windmaschine *f*; **~mill** *n* Windmühle *f*; *(Brit: toy)* Windrädchen *nt*; **to tilt at** *or* **fight ~mills** *(fig)* gegen Windmühlen(flügel) kämpfen.

window ['wɪndəʊ] *n (also Comput)* Fenster *nt*; *(shop ~)* (Schau)fenster *nt*; *(of booking office, bank)* Schalter *m*; *(Comm sl: opportunity)* Gelegenheit *f* ◆ **a ~ on the world** *(fig)* ein Fenster zur Welt; **~ of opportunity** Chance, (Fenster der) Gelegenheit *f*.

window: ~ box *n* Blumenkasten *m*; **~-cleaner** *n* Fensterputzer *m*; **~ display** *n* Auslage(n *pl*), Schaufensterdekoration *f*; **~-dresser** *n* (Schaufenster)dekorateur(in *f*) *m*; **~-dressing** *n* Auslagen- *or* Schaufensterdekoration *f*; *(fig)* Mache, Schau *(inf)*, Augen(aus)wischerei *(pej) f*; **that's just ~-dressing** das ist alles nur Mache *or* alles, um nach Außen hin zu wirken; **~ envelope** *n* Briefumschlag *m* mit Fenster.

windowing ['wɪndəʊɪŋ] *n (Comput)* Fenstertechnik *f*.

window: ~ ledge *n see* **~sill**; **~pane** *n* Fensterscheibe *f*; **~ seat** *n (in house)* Fensterbank *f or* -sitz *m*; *(Rail etc)* Fensterplatz *m*; **~ shade** *n (esp US)* Springrollo *nt*; **~-shopper** *n* jd, der einen Schaufensterbummel macht; **~-shopping** *n* Schaufensterbummel *m*; **to go ~-shopping** einen Schaufensterbummel machen; **~sill** *n* Fensterbank *f or* -brett *nt*; *(outside also)* Fenstersims *m*.

wind ['wɪnd-]: **~pipe** *n* Luftröhre *f*; **~ power** *n* Windkraft, Windenergie *f*; **~proof** *adj* luftdicht, windundurchlässig; **~screen, (US) ~shield** *n* Windschutzscheibe *f*; **~screen** *or (US)* **~shield washer** *n* Scheibenwaschanlage *f*; **~screen** *or (US)* **~shield wiper** *n* Scheibenwischer *m*; **~ section** *n (Mus)* Bläser *pl*; **~ sleeve, ~sock** *n* Luft- *or* Windsack *m*; **~surf** *vi* windsurfen; **~surfer** *n (person)* Windsurfer(in *f*) *m*; *(board)* Windsurfbrett *nt*; **~surfing** *n* Windsurfen *nt*; **~swept** *adj plains* über den/die/das der Wind fegt; *person, hair* (vom Wind) zerzaust; **~-tunnel** *n* Windkanal *m*.

windup ['waɪndʌp] *n (US) see* **winding-up**.

windward ['wɪndwəd] [1] *adj* Wind-, dem Wind zugekehrt; *direction* zum Wind.
[2] *n* Windseite *f* ◆ **to steer to ~ of an island** auf die Windseite einer Insel zusteuern.

windy ['wɪndɪ] *adj* (+er) **(a)** *day, weather, place* windig. **(b)** *(inf: verbose) speech, style* langatmig. **(c)** *(esp Brit inf: frightened)* **to be/get ~** Angst *or* Schiß *(sl)* haben/bekommen.

wine [waɪn] [1] *n* Wein *m* ◆ **cheese and ~ party** *Einladung, bei der Wein und Käse gereicht wird*; **to put new ~ in old bottles** jungen Wein in alte Schläuche füllen.
[2] *vt* **to ~ and dine sb** jdn zu einem guten Abendessen einladen; **the businessmen were ~d and dined in every city they visited** die Geschäftsleute wurden in jeder Stadt, die sie besuchten, ausgezeichnet bewirtet; **he ~d and dined her for months** er hat sie monatelang zum Abendessen ausgeführt.

wine: ~ bottle *n* Weinflasche *f*; **~ box** *n* Zapfpack *m*; **~ bucket** *n* Sektkühler *m*; **~ cellar** *n* Weinkeller *m*; **~-cooler** *n* Weinkühler *m*; **~glass** *n* Weinglas *nt*; **~-grower** *n* Winzer, Weinbauer *or* -gärtner *m*; **~-growing** [1] *adj district* Wein(an)bau-; [2] *n* Wein(an)bau *m*; **~ list** *n* Weinkarte *f*; **~-making** *n* Weinherstellung *f*; **~ merchant** *n* Weinhändler *m*; **~press** *n* Weinpresse, Kelter *f*.

winery ['waɪnərɪ] *n (US)* (Wein)kellerei *f*.

wine: ~skin *n* Weinschlauch *m*; **~-taster** *n* Weinverkoster *or* -prüfer *m*; **~-tasting** *n* Weinprobe *f*; **~ waiter** *n* Weinkellner, Getränkekellner *m*.

wing [wɪŋ] [1] *n* **(a)** *(of bird, plane, building, Mil, Pol, Sport)* Flügel *m*; *(of bird also)* Schwinge *f (poet)*, Fittich *m (liter)*; *(of chair)* Backe *f*; *(Brit Aut)* Kotflügel *m* ◆ **on the ~** im Flug(e); **to take sb under one's ~** *(fig)* jdn unter seine Fittiche nehmen; **to spread one's ~s** *(fig: children)* flügge werden; **to take ~s** *(lit)* davonfliegen; *(project etc)* Auftrieb bekommen; **on the ~s of fantasy** *(liter)* auf den Flügeln *or* Schwingen der Phantasie; **on the ~s of song** *(liter)* auf (des) Gesanges Flügeln *(liter)*; **do you expect me to grow** *or* **sprout ~s?** *(inf)* du glaubst wohl, ich kann fliegen? *(inf)*; **to play on the ~** *(Sport)* auf dem Flügel spielen.
(b) *(Aviat: section of air-force)* Geschwader *nt* ◆ **~s** *pl (pilot's badge)* Pilotenabzeichen *nt*; **to get one's ~s** *(fig)* sich *(dat)* seine Sporen verdienen.
(c) ~s *pl (Theat)* Kulisse *f* ◆ **to wait in the ~s** *(lit, fig)* in den Kulissen warten.
[2] *vt* **(a) to ~ one's way** fliegen. **(b)** *(fig liter: give ~s to)* beflügeln. **(c)** *(graze) person, bird* (mit einem Schuß) streifen ◆ **you only ~ed it** das war nur ein Streifschuß, du hast es nur gestreift.
[3] *vi* fliegen.

wing: ~ assembly *n* Tragwerk *nt*; **~-beat** *n* Flügelschlag *m*; **~-case** *n* Deckflügel, Flügeldecken *pl*; **~ chair** *n* Ohren- *or* Backensessel *m*; **~ collar** *n* Eckenkragen *m*; **~-commander** *n (Brit)* Oberstleutnant *m* (der Luftwaffe).

wingding ['wɪŋ,dɪŋ] *n (US sl)* tolle Party *(inf)*.

winge [wɪndʒ] *vi see* **whinge**.

winged [wɪŋd] *adj* **(a)** *(Zool, Bot)* mit Flügeln ◆ **the W~ Victory** die Nike von Samothrake; **the W~ Horse** (der) Pegasus. **(b)** *(liter) sentiments, words* geflügelt ◆ **on ~ feet** mit beflügeltem Schritt *(liter)*, auf schnellem Fuß.

-winged *adj suf* mit ... Flügeln; *bird also* -flügelig.

winger ['wɪŋər] *n (Sport)* Flügelspieler(in *f*), Flügelmann *m*.

wingey ['wɪndʒɪ] *adj see* **whingey**.

wing: ~ feather *n* Flügelfeder *f*; **~-forward** *n (Rugby)* Flügelstürmer *m*; **~less** *adj* flügellos; **~ nut** *n* Flügelmutter *f*; **~span** *n* Flügelspannweite *f*; **~spread** *n* Spannweite *f*; **~-three-quarter** *n (Rugby)* Dreiviertelspieler *m* auf dem Flügel; **~tip** *n* Flügelspitze *f*.

wink [wɪŋk] [1] *n* **(a)** *(with eye)* Zwinkern, Blinzeln *nt* ◆ **to give sb a ~** jdm zuzwinkern *or* zublinzeln; **to tip sb the ~** *(inf)* jdm einen Wink geben; *see* **nod**. **(b)** *(instant)* **I didn't get a ~ of sleep** *or* **I didn't sleep a ~** ich habe kein Auge zugetan.
[2] *vt eye* blinzeln, zwinkern mit (+*dat*).
[3] *vi (meaningfully)* zwinkern, blinzeln; *(light, star etc)* blinken, funkeln ◆ **to ~ at sb** jdm zuzwinkern *or* zublinzeln; **to ~ at sth** *(inf)* etw geflissentlich übersehen, einfach wegsehen *or* -schauen; **it's as easy as ~(ing)** *(dated inf)* das ist ein Kinderspiel; **~ing lights** *(Aut)* Blinklichter, Blinker *pl*.

winker ['wɪŋkər] *n (Brit Aut inf)* Blinker *m*.

winkle ['wɪŋkl] *n* Strandschnecke *f*.

◆**winkle out** *vt sep (inf)* **to ~ sth/sb ~** etw herausklauben *or (behind sth)* hervorklauben *(inf)*/jdn loseisen *(inf)*; **to ~ sth ~ of sb** etw aus jdm herauskriegen *(inf)*.

winkle-pickers ['wɪŋkl'pɪkəz] *npl (inf)* spitze Schuhe *pl*.

winnable ['wɪnəbl] *adj* zu gewinnen.

winner ['wɪnər] *n (in race, competition)* Sieger(in *f*) *m*; *(of bet, pools etc)* Gewinner(in *f*) *m*; *(card)* Gewinnkarte *f*; *(Tennis etc: shot)* Schlag, der sitzt, Treffer *m*; *(inf: sth successful)* Renner *(inf)*, (Verkaufs)schlager, (Publikums)erfolg *m* ◆ **to be onto a ~** *(inf)* das große Los gezogen haben *(inf)*.

winning ['wɪnɪŋ] [1] *adj* **(a)** *(successful) person, entry* der/die gewinnt; *horse, team* siegreich; *goal* Sieges-; *point, stroke* (das Spiel) entscheidend ◆ **the ~ time** die beste Zeit; **~ post** Zielpfosten *m or* -stange *f*; **~ score** Spielergebnis *nt*. **(b)** *(charming) smile, ways* gewinnend, einnehmend.
[2] *n* **~s** *pl* Gewinn *m*.

winningly ['wɪnɪŋlɪ] *adv smile* gewinnend, einnehmend.

winnow ['wɪnəʊ] *vt corn* worfeln, von der Spreu reinigen; *(fig liter)* sichten ◆ **to ~ the chaff from the wheat** die Spreu vom Weizen trennen *or* scheiden *(also fig liter)*.

winnower ['wɪnəʊər], **winnowing machine** ['wɪnəʊɪŋmə'ʃiːn] *n* Worfschaufel, Worfelmaschine *f*.

wino ['waɪnəʊ] *n (sl)* Penner *(sl)*, Saufbruder *(inf) m*.

winsome ['wɪnsəm] *adj child, lass* reizend, sympathisch; *ways, smile* gewinnend, einnehmend.

winter ['wɪntər] [1] *n (lit, fig)* Winter *m*.
[2] *adj attr* Winter- ◆ **~ quarters** Winterquartier *nt*; **~ solstice** Wintersonnenwende *f*; **~ sports** Wintersport *m*; **~time** Winter *m*; *(for clocks)* Winterzeit *f*.
[3] *vi* überwintern, den Winter verbringen.
[4] *vt cattle* durch den Winter bringen.

wintergreen ['wɪntə,griːn] *n (plant)* Teebeere *f*; *(flavouring)* Wintergrünöl *nt*.

winterize ['wɪntəraɪz] *vt (US)* winterfest machen.

wint(e)ry ['wɪnt(ə)rɪ] *adj* winterlich; *(fig) look* eisig; *smile* frostig, kühl.

wintriness ['wɪntrɪnɪs] *n* Winterlichkeit *f*.

wipe [waɪp] [1] *n* Wischen *nt* ◆ **to give sth a ~** etw abwischen.
[2] *vt* wischen; *floor* aufwischen; *window* überwischen; *hands, feet* abwischen, abputzen *(rare)* ◆ **to ~ sb/sth dry/clean** jdn/etw abtrocknen *or* trockenreiben/jdn/etw sauberwischen *or* säubern; **to ~ sth with/on a cloth** etw mit/an einem Tuch abwischen; **to ~ one's brow/eyes/nose** sich *(dat)* über die Stirn/Augen wischen *or* fahren, sich *(dat)* die Stirn abwischen/Augen wischen/Nase putzen; **to ~ one's feet** sich *(dat)* die Füße *or* Schuhe abstreifen *or* -wischen *or* -treten; **to ~ the tears from one's eyes** sich *(dat)* die Tränen aus den Augen wischen; **to ~ oneself** *or* **one's bottom** sich *(dat)* den Hintern *or* sich abputzen; **to ~ the floor with sb** *(fig sl)* jdn fertigmachen *(inf)*.

◆**wipe away** *vt sep (lit, fig)* wegwischen; *tears also* abwischen.

◆**wipe down** *vt sep* abwaschen; *(with dry cloth)* abreiben; *window* überwischen.

◆**wipe off** [1] *vt sep mark* weg- *or* abwischen; *(from blackboard also)* ab- *or* auslöschen ◆ **~ that smile ~ your face** *(inf)* hör auf zu grinsen *(inf)*; **I'll soon ~ that smile ~ his face** *(inf)* dem wird bald das Lachen vergehen; **to be ~d ~ the map** *or* **the face of the earth** von der Landkarte *or* Erdoberfläche verschwinden *or* gefegt werden.
[2] *vi* sich weg- *or* abwischen lassen.

◆**wipe out** *vt sep* **(a)** *(clean) bath, bowl* auswischen. **(b)** *(erase) memory, part of brain, sth on blackboard* (aus)löschen; *guilt feelings* verschwinden lassen. **(c)** *(cancel) debt* bereinigen; *gain, benefit* zunichte machen. **(d)** *(destroy) disease, village, race* ausrotten; *enemy, battalion* aufreiben.

◆**wipe up** [1] *vt sep liquid* aufwischen, aufputzen *(Sw)*; *dishes* abtrocknen.
[2] *vi* abtrocknen.

wipe: ~-down *n* Abreibung *f*; **~-over** *n* **to give sth a ~-over** etw über- *or* abwischen.

wiper ['waɪpər] *n* (Scheiben)wischer *m*.

wiping-up ['waɪpɪŋ'ʌp] *n* **to do the ~** abtrocknen.

wire [waɪər] [1] *n* **(a)** Draht *m*; *(for electricity supply)* Leitung *f*; *(insulated flex, for home appliance etc)* Schnur *f*; *(for television)* Fernsehanschluß *m or* -kabel *nt*; *(in circus: high ~)* (Hoch)seil *nt* ◆ **to get in under the ~** *(US inf)* etwas gerade (eben) noch rechtzeitig *or* mit Hängen und Würgen *(inf)* schaffen; **to pull ~s** *(inf)* seinen Einfluß geltend machen, seine Beziehungen spielen lassen; **he's pulling your ~** *(Brit inf)* er nimmt dich auf den Arm *(inf)*; **you've got your ~s crossed there** *(inf)* Sie verwechseln da etwas; *(said to two people)* Sie reden aneinander vorbei.
(b) *(Telec)* Telegramm, Kabel *(old) nt*.
[2] *vt* **(a)** *(put in wiring) house* die (elektrischen) Leitungen verlegen in (+*dat*); *(connect to electricity)* (an das Stromnetz) anschließen ◆ **it's all ~d (up) for television** Fernsehanschluß *or* die Verkabelung für das Fernsehen ist vorhanden.
(b) *(Telec)* telegrafieren, kabeln *(old)*.

(c) (*fix on ~*) *beads* auf Draht auffädeln; (*fix with ~*) mit Draht zusammen- *or* verbinden ♦ **to ~ the parts together** die Teile mit Draht zusammen- *or* verbinden.

3 *vi* telegrafieren, drahten, kabeln (*old*).

♦**wire up** *vt sep lights, battery, speakers* anschließen; *house* elektrische Leitungen *or* den Strom verlegen ♦ **we ~d the room ~ as a recording studio** wir haben den Raum als Aufnahmestudio eingerichtet.

wire: ~-cutters *npl* Drahtschere *f*; **~-haired** *adj terrier* drahthaarig, Drahthaar-.

wireless [ˈwaɪəlɪs] (*esp Brit dated*) 1 *n* **(a)** (*also* **~ set**) Radio, Rundfunkgerät *nt*, Radioapparat *m*.

(b) (*radio*) Rundfunk *m*; (*also* **~ telegraphy**) drahtlose Telegrafie; (*also* **~ telephony**) drahtlose Übertragung, drahtloses Telefon ♦ **to send a message by ~** eine Botschaft über Funk schicken *or* senden.

2 *vti* funken; *base etc* anfunken.

wireless operator *n* (*on ship, plane*) Funker *m*.

wire: ~man *n* (*US inf: for wire-taps etc*) Abhörspezialist *m*; **~ netting** *n* Maschendraht *m*; **~photo** *n* (*method*) Bildtelegrafie *f*; (*picture*) Bildtelegramm *nt*; **~-puller** *n* (*inf*) Drahtzieher *m*; **~-pulling** *n* (*inf*) Drahtziehen *nt*, Drahtzieherei *f*; **~ rope** *n* Drahtseil *nt*; **~ service** *n* (*US*) Nachrichtendienst *m*, Nachrichtenagentur *f*; **~-tap** 1 *n* (*device*) Abhörgerät *nt*, Wanze *f*; (*activity*) Abhören *nt*; 2 *vt phone* abhören, anzapfen; *building* abhören in (+*dat*); **~-tapper** *n* Abhörer *m*; **~-tapping** *n* Abhören *nt*, Anzapfen *nt* von Leitungen; **~ wheel** *n* Rad *nt* mit Sportfelgen; **~ wool** *n* Stahlwolle *f*; **~worm** *n* Drahtwurm *m*.

wiring [ˈwaɪərɪŋ] *n* elektrische Leitungen, Stromkabel *pl*.

wiring diagram *n* Schaltplan *m* *or* -schema *nt*.

wiry [ˈwaɪərɪ] *adj* (+*er*) drahtig; *hair also* borstig.

wisdom [ˈwɪzdəm] *n* Weisheit *f*; (*prudence*) Einsicht *f* ♦ **to show great ~** große Klugheit *or* Einsicht zeigen; **to doubt the ~ of sth** bezweifeln, ob etw klug *or* sinnvoll ist; **the conventional ~** die herkömmliche Überzeugung.

wisdom tooth *n* Weisheitszahn *m*.

wise[1] [waɪz] *adj* (+*er*) weise; (*prudent, sensible*) *move, step etc* klug, gescheit, vernünftig; (*inf: smart*) klug, schlau ♦ **a ~ choice** eine kluge *or* gute Wahl; **the Three W~ Men** die drei Weisen; **to be ~ in the ways of the world** Lebenserfahrung haben, das Leben kennen; **to be ~ after the event** hinterher den Schlauen spielen *or* gut reden haben; **I'm none the ~r** (*inf*) ich bin nicht klüger als zuvor *or* vorher; **nobody will be any the ~r** (*inf*) niemand wird etwas (davon) merken *or* das spitzkriegen (*inf*); **you'd be ~ to** ... du tätest gut daran, ...; **you'd better get ~** (*US inf*) nimm endlich Vernunft an; **to get ~ to sb/sth** (*inf*) etw spitzkriegen (*inf*), dahinterkommen, wie jd/etw ist; **to be ~ to sb/sth** (*inf*) jdn/etw kennen; **he fooled her twice, then she got ~ to him** zweimal hat er sie hereingelegt, dann ist sie ihm auf die Schliche gekommen; **to put sb ~ to sb/sth** (*inf*) jdn über jdn/etw aufklären (*inf*).

♦**wise up** (*esp US inf*) 1 *vi* **if he doesn't ~ ~ soon to what's going on/the need for** ... wenn er nicht bald dahinterkommt *or* ihm nicht bald ein Licht aufgeht (*inf*), was da gespielt wird/wenn er nicht bald hinter die Notwendigkeit zu ... kommt ...; **he's never going to ~ ~** der lernt's nie!, der wird auch nie klüger; **~ ~, man!** Mann, wach auf *or* nimm Vernunft an!

2 *vt sep* aufklären (*inf*) (*to* über +*acc*).

wise[2] *n, no pl* (*old*) Weise *f* ♦ **in this ~** auf diese Weise, so; **in no ~** in keiner Weise, keineswegs.

-wise *adv suf* -mäßig, in puncto.

wise: ~acre *n* Besserwisser, Neunmalkluge(r) *m*; **~crack** (*esp US*) 1 *n* Witzelei *f*; (*pej*) Stichelei *f*; **to make a ~crack (about sb/sth)** witzeln (über jdn/etw); 2 *vti* witzeln; **~ guy** *n* (*esp US inf*) Klugschwätzer (*inf*), Klugscheißer (*sl*) *m*.

wisely [ˈwaɪzlɪ] *adv* weise; (*sensibly*) klugerweise.

▼ **wish** [wɪʃ] 1 *n* **(a)** Wunsch *m* (*for* nach) ♦ **your ~ is my command** dein Wunsch ist *or* sei mir Befehl; **I have no great ~ to see him** ich habe kein Bedürfnis *or* keine große Lust, ihn zu sehen; **to make a ~** sich (*dat*) etwas wünschen; **you can make three ~es** du hast drei Wünsche; **the ~ is father to the thought** (*prov*) der Wunsch ist Vater des Gedankens (*prov*); **well, you got your ~** jetzt hast du ja, was du wolltest; **you shall have your ~** dein Wunsch soll (dir) erfüllt werden *or* soll in Erfüllung gehen.

▼ **(b)** **~es** *pl* (*in greetings*) **with best ~es** mit den besten Wünschen *or* Grüßen, alles Gute; **please give him my good ~es** bitte grüßen Sie ihn (vielmals) von mir, bitte richten Sie ihm meine besten Wünsche aus; **he sends his best ~es** er läßt (vielmals) grüßen; **a message of good ~es** eine Gruß- *or* Glückwunschbotschaft; **best ~es for a speedy recovery** viele gute Wünsche *or* alles Gute für eine baldige Genesung.

▼ 2 *vt* **(a)** (*want*) wünschen ♦ **I do not ~ it** ich möchte *or* wünsche (*form*) es nicht; **he ~es to be alone/to see you immediately** er möchte allein sein/dich sofort sehen; **I ~ you to be present** ich wünsche, daß Sie anwesend sind; **what do you ~ me to do?** was soll ich (bitte) tun?; **do you ~ more coffee, sir?** (*Scot, form*) hätten Sie gern *or* wünschen Sie noch Kaffee?

▼ **(b)** (*desire, hope, desire sth unlikely*) wünschen, wollen ♦ **I ~ the play would begin** ich wünschte *or* wollte, das Stück finge an; **I ~ you'd be quiet** ich wünschte *or* wollte, du wärest ruhig; **how he ~ed that his wife was** *or* **were there** wie sehr er sich (*dat*) wünschte, daß seine Frau hier wäre; **~ you were here** ich wünschte *or* wollte, du wärest hier.

(c) (*entertain ~es towards sb*) wünschen ♦ **to ~ sb well/ill** jdm Glück *or* alles Gute/Schlechtes *or* Böses wünschen; **I don't ~ her any harm** ich wünsche ihr nichts Böses; **to ~ sb good luck/happiness** jdm viel Glück *or* alles Gute/Glück (und Zufriedenheit) wünschen.

(d) (*bid, express ~*) wünschen ♦ **to ~ sb a pleasant journey/good morning/a happy Christmas/goodbye** jdm eine gute Reise/guten Morgen/frohe Weihnachten wünschen/auf Wiedersehen sagen.

(e) **to ~ a wish** sich (*dat*) etwas wünschen; **he ~ed himself anywhere but there** er wünschte sich nur möglichst weit weg; **if I could ~ myself into the castle** wenn ich mich nur in das Schloß wünschen könnte.

3 *vi* (*make a wish*) sich (*dat*) etwas wünschen ♦ **~ing won't solve the problem** der Wunsch allein wird das Problem nicht lösen; **to ~ upon a star** (*liter*) sich (*dat*) bei einer Sternschnuppe etwas wünschen.

♦**wish away** *vt sep difficulty* weg- *or* fortwünschen (*inf*).

♦**wish for** *vi* +*prep obj* **to ~ ~ sth** sich (*dat*) etw wünschen; **what more could you ~ ~?** etwas Besseres kann man sich doch gar nicht wünschen, was kann sich der Mensch noch mehr wünschen? (*inf*); **it was everything we had ~ed ~** es war genauso, wie wir es uns gewünscht hatten; **she had everything she could ~ ~** sie hatte alles, was man sich nur wünschen kann.

♦**wish on** *or* **upon** *vt sep* +*prep obj* (*inf: foist*) **to ~ sb/sth ~ sb** jdn jdm/jdm etw aufhängen (*inf*); **I would not ~ that/that job ~ my worst enemy!** das/diese Arbeit würde ich meinem ärgsten Feind nicht wünschen.

wishbone [ˈwɪʃbəʊn] *n* Gabelbein *nt*.

wishful [ˈwɪʃfʊl] *adj* **that's just ~ thinking** das ist reines Wunschdenken, das ist nur ein frommer Wunsch.

wish-fulfilment [ˈwɪʃfʊlˈfɪlmənt] *n* Wunscherfüllung *f*.

wishing well [ˈwɪʃɪŋˈwel] *n* Wunschbrunnen *m*.

wishy-washiness [ˈwɪʃɪ,wɒʃɪnɪs] *n see adj* Labberigkeit, Wäßrigkeit *f*; saft- und kraftlose Art, Farblosigkeit, Laschheit *f*; Verwaschenheit *f*; Schwachheit *f* ♦ **the ~ of this report** das allgemeine Geschwätz (*inf*) in diesem Bericht.

wishy-washy [ˈwɪʃɪ,wɒʃɪ] *adj coffee, soup* labberig, wäßrig; *person, character* saft- und kraftlos, farblos, lasch; *colour* verwaschen; *argument* schwach (*inf*); *report, story* ungenau, wachsweich, wischiwaschi (*inf*).

wisp [wɪsp] *n* **(a)** (*of straw, hair etc*) kleines Büschel; (*of cloud*) Fetzen *m*; (*of smoke*) Fahne *f*, Wölkchen *nt*. **(b)** (*person*) elfenhaftes *or* zartes *or* zerbrechliches Geschöpf. **(c)** (*trace*) zarte Spur *or* Andeutung; (*fragment*) Hauch *m*.

wispy [ˈwɪspɪ] *adj* (+*er*) *grass* dürr, fein; *girl* zerbrechlich, zart ♦ **~ clouds** Wolkenfetzen *pl*; **~ hair** dünne Haarbüschel.

wisteria [wɪsˈtɪərɪə] *n* Glyzinie, Wistarie *f*.

wistful [ˈwɪstfʊl] *adj smile, thoughts, mood, eyes* wehmütig; *song also* schwermütig.

wistfully [ˈwɪstfəlɪ] *adv see adj*.

wistfulness [ˈwɪstfʊlnɪs] *n see adj* Wehmut *f*; Schwermut *f*.

wit[1] [wɪt] *vi* (*old Jur*): **to ~** nämlich, und zwar.

wit[2] *n* **(a)** (*understanding*) Verstand *m* ♦ **beyond the ~ of man** jenseits des *or* jedes menschlichen Verständnisses *or* Horizonts, über den menschlichen Verstand *or* Horizont hinaus; **a battle of ~s** ein geistiges Kräftemessen; **to be at one's ~s' end** am Ende seiner Weisheit sein, mit seinem Latein am Ende sein (*hum inf*); **I was at my ~s' end for a solution** ich wußte mir keinen Rat *or* Ausweg mehr *or* mir nicht mehr zu helfen(, wie ich eine Lösung finden könnte); **to drive sb out of his ~s** jdn um seinen Verstand bringen; **to lose one's ~s** den *or* seinen Verstand verlieren; **to collect one's ~s** seine fünf Sinne (wieder) zusammennehmen; **to frighten** *or* **scare sb out of his ~s** jdn zu Tode erschrecken; **to be frightened** *or* **scared out of one's ~s** zu Tode erschreckt sein; **to have** *or* **keep one's ~s about one** seine (fünf) Sinne zusammen- *or* beisammenhalten *or* -haben, einen klaren Kopf haben; **to sharpen one's ~s** seinen Verstand schärfen; **to use one's ~s** seinen Verstand gebrauchen, sein Köpfchen (*inf*) *or* seinen Grips (*inf*) anstrengen; **to live by one's ~s** sich schlau *or* klug durchs Leben schlagen.

(b) (*humour, wittiness*) Geist, Witz *m* ♦ **full of ~** geistreich; **to have a ready** *or* **pretty ~** (*old*) schlagfertig sein; **there's a lot of ~ in the book** es ist sehr viel Geistreiches in dem Buch.

(c) (*person*) geistreicher Kopf.

witch [wɪtʃ] *n* (*lit, fig*) Hexe *f* ♦ **~es' sabbath** Hexensabbat *m*.

witch: ~craft *n* Hexerei, Zauberei *f*; **a book on ~craft** ein Buch über (die) Hexenkunst; **~ doctor** *n* Medizinmann *m*.

witch elm *n* Bergulme *f*.

witchery [ˈwɪtʃərɪ] *n* (*witchcraft*) Hexerei *f*; (*fascination*) Zauber *m*.

witch hazel *n* (*Bot*) Zaubernuß *f*; (*Med*) Hamamelis *f*.

witch-hunt [ˈwɪtʃ,hʌnt] *n* (*lit, fig*) Hexenjagd *f*.

witching [ˈwɪtʃɪŋ] *adj*: **the ~ hour** die Geisterstunde.

with [wɪð, wɪθ] *prep* **(a)** mit ♦ **are you pleased ~ it?** bist du damit zufrieden?; **bring a book ~ you** bring ein Buch mit; **~ no ...** ohne ...; **~ the Victory, it's the biggest ship of its class** neben der Victory ist es das größte Schiff in seiner Klasse; **to walk ~ a stick** am *or* mit einem Stock gehen; **put it ~ the rest** leg es zu den anderen; **the wind was ~ us** wir hatten den Wind im Rücken, wir fuhren *etc* mit dem Wind; **how are things ~ you?** wie geht's?, wie steht's? (*inf*); *see* **with it**.

(b) (*at house of, in company of etc*) bei ♦ **I'll be ~ you in a moment** einen Augenblick, bitte, ich bin gleich da; **10 years ~ the company** 10 Jahre bei *or* in der Firma; **the problem is still ~ us** wir haben immer noch das alte Problem.

(c) (*on person, in bag etc*) bei ♦ **I haven't got my cheque book ~ me** ich habe mein Scheckbuch nicht bei mir.

(d) (*cause*) vor (+*dat*) ♦ **to shiver ~ cold** vor Kälte zittern; **the hills are white ~ snow** die Berge sind weiß vom Schnee; **to be ill ~ measles** die Masern haben, an Masern erkrankt sein.

➤ LANGUAGE IN USE: **wish: 1a** → 8.4 **1b** → 21.2, 23.1, 23.3, 24.2, 24.3 **2a** → 20.6 **2b** → 18.3

(e) (*in the case of*) bei, mit ◆ **it's always the same ~ you** es ist (doch) immer dasselbe mit dir; **the trouble ~ him is that he** ... die Schwierigkeit bei *or* mit ihm ist (die), daß er ...; **it's a habit ~ him** das ist bei ihm Gewohnheit; **~ God, all things are possible** bei *or* für Gott ist kein Ding unmöglich; **it's a holiday ~ us** bei *or* für uns ist das ein Feiertag.
(f) (*when sb/sth is*) wo ◆ **you can't go ~ your mother ill in bed** wo deine Mutter krank im Bett liegt, kannst du nicht gehen; **~ all this noise going on** bei diesem Lärm; **to quit ~ the job unfinished** von der halbfertigen Arbeit weglaufen; **~ the window open** bei offenem Fenster.
(g) (*in proportion*) mit ◆ **it varies ~ the temperature** es verändert sich je nach Temperatur; **wine improves ~ age** Wein wird mit zunehmendem Alter immer besser; **it gets bigger ~ the heat** in der Wärme wird es immer größer.
(h) (*in spite of*) trotz, bei ◆ **~ all his faults** bei allen seinen Fehlern, trotz aller seiner Fehler; **~ the best will in the world** beim allerbesten Willen.
(i) (*in agreement, on side of*) **I'm ~ you there** (*inf*) da stimme ich dir zu; **is he ~ us or against us?** ist er für oder gegen uns?
(j) (*inf: expressing comprehension*) **are you ~ me?** kapierst du? (*inf*), hast du's? (*inf*), kommst du mit? (*inf*); **I'm not ~ you** da komm ich nicht mit (*inf*); **are you still ~ me?** kommst du (da) noch mit? (*inf*), ist das noch klar?

withdraw [wɪθ'drɔː] *pret* **withdrew,** *ptp* **withdrawn** [1] *vt object, motion, charge* zurückziehen; *troops, team also* abziehen; *ambassador* zurückrufen *or* -beordern; *coins, stamps* einziehen, aus dem Verkehr ziehen; (*from bank*) *money* abheben; *words, comment* zurücknehmen, widerrufen; *privileges* entziehen ◆ **the workers withdrew their labour** die Arbeiter haben ihre Arbeit niedergelegt; **she withdrew her hand from his** sie entzog ihm ihre Hand.
[2] *vi* sich zurückziehen; (*Sport also*) zurücktreten (*from* von), nicht antreten (*from* von/bei); (*move away*) zurücktreten *or* -gehen ◆ **to ~ in favour of sb else** zu Gunsten eines anderen zurücktreten; **to ~ into oneself** sich in sich (*acc*) selber zurückziehen; **you can't ~ now** (*from agreement*) du kannst jetzt nicht zurücktreten *or* abspringen (*inf*).

withdrawal [wɪθ'drɔːəl] *n* (*of objects, charge*) Zurückziehen *nt*; (*of ambassador*) Abziehen *nt*; (*of coins, stamps*) Einziehen *nt*; (*of money*) Abheben *nt*; (*of words*) Zurücknehmen *nt*, Zurücknahme *f*; (*of troops*) Rückzug *m*; (*withdrawing*) Abziehen *nt*; (*in sport*) Abzug *m*; (*from drugs*) Entzug *m* ◆ **to make a ~ from a bank** von einer Bank etwas *or* Geld abheben.

withdrawal: ~ slip *n* Rückzahlungsschein *m*; **~ symptoms** *npl* Entzugserscheinungen *pl*.

withdrawn [wɪθ'drɔːn] [1] *ptp of* **withdraw.**
[2] *adj person* verschlossen; *manner also* reserviert, zurückhaltend; *life* zurückgezogen.

withdrew [wɪθ'druː] *pret of* **withdraw.**

withe [wɪθ] *n* (*old*) (dünne) Weidenrute.

wither ['wɪðəʳ] [1] *vt plants etc* verdörren, austrocknen; (*fig*) zum Schwinden bringen ◆ **to ~ sb with a look** jdn mit einem Blick vernichten.
[2] *vi* (a) verdorren, ausdorren; (*limb*) verkümmern. (b) (*fig*) welken; (*religion*) dahinschwinden.

◆**wither away** *vi see* **wither 2.**

◆**wither up** *vi see* **wither 2 (a).**

withered ['wɪðəd] *adj plant, grass* verdorrt, vertrocknet; *skin* verhutzelt, hutzelig; *limb* verkümmert ◆ **a ~-looking old man** ein verschrumpfter *or* hutzeliger Alter.

withering ['wɪðərɪŋ] *adj heat* ausdörrend; *criticism, look, tone* vernichtend.

witheringly ['wɪðərɪŋlɪ] *adv say, look* vernichtend.

withers ['wɪðəz] *npl* Widerrist *m*.

withhold [wɪθ'həʊld] *pret, ptp* **withheld** [wɪθ'held] *vt* vorenthalten; *truth also* verschweigen; (*refuse*) *consent, help* verweigern, versagen (*geh*) ◆ **the citizens threatened to ~ their rates** die Bürger drohten, die Zahlung der Abgaben zu verweigern; **to ~ sth from sb** jdm etw vorenthalten/verweigern; **~ing tax** (*US*) (vom Arbeitgeber) einbehaltene Steuer.

within [wɪð'ɪn] [1] *prep* innerhalb (+*gen*); (*temporal also*) binnen (+*dat or* (*geh*) +*gen*), innert (+*gen*) (*Aus, S Ger*) ◆ **a voice ~ me said** ... eine Stimme in meinem Inneren *or* in mir sagte ...; **we were/came ~ 100 metres of the summit** wir waren auf den letzten 100 Metern vor dem Gipfel/wir kamen bis auf 100 Meter an den Gipfel heran; **~ his power** in seiner Macht; **to keep ~ the law** sich im Rahmen des Gesetzes bewegen; **to live ~ one's income** im Rahmen seiner finanziellen Möglichkeiten leben.
[2] *adv* (*old, liter*) innen ◆ **from ~** von drinnen; (*on the inside*) von innen; **let us go ~** wollen wir hineingehen; **but he's rotten ~** aber innerlich ist er verderbt.

with it ['wɪðɪt] *adj* (*inf*) (a) (*attr* **with-it**) (*up-to-date, trendy*) up to date. (b) *pred* (*awake, alert*) **to be ~** da sein (*inf*).

without [wɪð'aʊt] [1] *prep* ohne ◆ **~ a tie/passport** ohne Krawatte/(einen) Paß; **~ a friend in the world** ohne einen einzigen Freund; **~ speaking** ohne zu sprechen, wortlos; **~ my noticing it** ohne daß ich es bemerke/bemerkte; **times ~ number** unzählige Male *pl*.
[2] *adv* (*old, liter*) außen ◆ **from ~** von draußen; (*on the outside*) von außen.
[3] *adj pred* ohne ◆ **to be ~** etw nicht haben, einer Sache (*gen*) entbehren (*form*); **those who are ~** (*needy*) die Bedürftigen *pl*.

without-profits [wɪð'aʊt,prɒfɪts] *adj policy etc* ohne Gewinnbeteiligung.

with-profits ['wɪð,prɒfɪts] *adj policy etc* mit Gewinnbeteiligung.

withstand [wɪθ'stænd] *pret, ptp* **withstood** [wɪθ'stʊd] *vt cold* standhalten (+*dat*); *enemy, climate, attack, temptation also* trotzen (+*dat*); *persuasion etc* widerstehen (+*dat*).

withy ['wɪðɪ] *n* (*willow*) Korbweide *f*; (*twig*) Weide(nrute) *f*.

witless ['wɪtlɪs] *adj* (*mentally defective*) schwachsinnig; (*stupid, silly*) dumm, blöd(e) (*inf*); (*lacking wit*) *prose* geistlos.

witlessness ['wɪtlɪsnɪs] *n see adj* Schwachsinn *m*; Dummheit, Blödheit (*inf*) *f*; Geistlosigkeit *f*.

witness ['wɪtnɪs] [1] *n* (a) (*person: Jur, fig*) Zeuge *m*, Zeugin *f* ◆ **~ for the defence/prosecution** Zeuge/Zeugin der Verteidigung/Anklage; **as God is my ~** Gott sei *or* ist mein Zeuge; **to call sb as a ~** jdn als Zeugen vorladen; **I was then ~ to a scene** ... ich wurde Zeuge einer Szene ...
(b) (*evidence*) Zeugnis *nt* ◆ **to give ~ for/against sb** Zeugnis für/gegen jdn ablegen, für/gegen jdn aussagen; **in ~ whereof** (*form*) zu Urkund *or* zum Zeugnis dessen; **to bear ~ to sth** (*lit, fig*) Zeugnis über etw (*acc*) ablegen; (*actions, events also*) von etw zeugen.
[2] *vt* (a) (*see*) *accident* Zeuge sein bei *or* (+*gen*); *scenes also* (mit)erleben, mitansehen; *changes* erleben ◆ **the year 1945 ~ed great changes** das Jahr 1945 sah einen großen Wandel.
(b) (*testify*) bezeugen ◆ **to call sb to ~ that** ... jdn zum Zeugen dafür rufen, daß ...
(c) (*consider as evidence*) denken an (+*acc*), zum Beispiel nehmen ◆ **~ the case of X** denken Sie nur an den Fall X, nehmen Sie nur den Fall X zum Beispiel.
(d) (*attest by signature*) *signature, will* bestätigen.
[3] *vi* (*testify*) bestätigen, bezeugen ◆ **to ~ to sth** etw bestätigen *or* bezeugen; **to ~ against sb** gegen jdn aussagen.

witness box *or* (*US*) **stand** *n* Zeugenbank *f*, Zeugenstand *m*.

-witted [-'wɪtɪd] *adj suf* **dull-~** geistig träge; **quick-~** geistig rege.

witter ['wɪtəʳ] *vi* (*inf: also* **~ on**) labern (*inf*).

witticism ['wɪtɪsɪzəm] *n* geistreiche Bemerkung.

wittiness ['wɪtɪnɪs] *n* Witzigkeit *f*.

wittingly ['wɪtɪŋlɪ] *adv* bewußt, absichtlich, wissentlich (*form*).

witty ['wɪtɪ] *adj* (+*er*) witzig, geistreich.

wives [waɪvz] *pl of* **wife.**

wizard ['wɪzəd] [1] *n* (a) Zauberer, Hexenmeister *m*. (b) (*inf*) Genie *nt*, Leuchte *f* (*inf*) ◆ **a financial ~** ein Finanzgenie *nt*; **a ~ with the ball** ein Zauberer am *or* mit dem Ball; **a ~ at maths** ein Mathegenie *nt* (*inf*).
[2] *adj* (*dated Brit inf*) famos, prima (*inf*).

wizardry ['wɪzədrɪ] *n* (*magic*) Hexerei, Zauberei *f*; (*great skill*) Zauberkünste *pl* ◆ **his ~ with the ball** seine Zauberkunststücke *pl* mit dem Ball.

wizened ['wɪznd] *adj* verhutzelt, verschrumpelt.

wk *abbr of* **week** Wo.

wkly *abbr of* **weekly** wö.

Wm *abbr of* **William.**

WNW *abbr of* **west-north-west** WNW.

w/o *abbr of* **without** o.

woad [wəʊd] *n* (*dye*) Waid *m*; (*plant*) (Färber)waid *m*.

wobble ['wɒbl] [1] *n* Wackeln *nt* ◆ **the chair has a ~** der Stuhl wackelt.
[2] *vi* wackeln; (*tightrope walker, dancer also, cyclist*) schwanken; (*voice, hand, compass needle*) zittern; (*wheel*) eiern (*inf*), einen Schlag haben; (*chin, jelly etc*) schwabbeln ◆ **he ~d about on his new bike** er wackelte auf seinem neuen Fahrrad durch die Gegend; **he was wobbling like a jelly** (*nervous*) er zitterte wie Espenlaub; (*fat*) an ihm wabbelte alles.
[3] *vt* rütteln an (+*dat*), ruckeln an (+*dat*), wackeln an (+*dat*).

wobbly ['wɒblɪ] [1] *adj* (+*er*) wackelig; *voice, notes also, hand* zitterig, zitternd; *jelly* (sch)wabbelig; *wheel* eiernd ◆ **to be ~** (*inf: after illness*) wackelig auf den Beinen sein (*inf*); **to feel ~** sich schwach fühlen, wackelig auf den Beinen sein (*inf*).
[2] *n* (*sl: fit of rage*) **to throw a ~** ausrasten (*sl*), einen Wutanfall bekommen.

wodge [wɒdʒ] *n* (*Brit inf*) (*of cake, plaster etc*) Brocken *m*; (*ball of paper*) Knäuel *nt or m*; (*of cotton wool*) Bausch *m*; (*of documents, papers*) Stoß *m*.

woe [wəʊ] *n* (a) (*liter, hum: sorrow*) Jammer *m* ◆ **~ (is me)!** Weh mir!; **~ betide him who** ...! wehe dem, der ...!; **a tale of ~** eine Geschichte des Jammers. (b) (*esp pl: trouble, affliction*) Kummer *m* ◆ **to tell sb one's ~s** jdm sein Leid klagen; **to pour out one's ~s** sich (*dat*) seinen Kummer von der Seele reden.

woebegone ['wəʊbɪ,gɒn] *adj* kläglich, jämmerlich; *expression also* jammervoll; *voice* (weh)klagend, jammernd.

woeful ['wəʊfʊl] *adj* (*sad*) traurig; (*deplorable*) *neglect also, ignorance* bedauerlich, beklagenswert.

woefully ['wəʊfəlɪ] *adv* kläglich, jämmerlich; (*very*) bedauerlich ◆ **he is ~ ignorant of** ... es ist bestürzend, wie wenig er über ... weiß; **he discovered they were ~ ignorant of** ... er stellte zu seiner Bestürzung fest, wie wenig sie über ... wußten.

wog [wɒg] *n* (*Brit pej sl*) Kaffer *m* (*sl*); (*Arab*) Kameltreiber *m* (*sl*).

wok [wɒk] *n* (*Cook*) Wok *m*.

woke [wəʊk] *pret of* **wake.**

woken ['wəʊkn] *ptp of* **wake.**

wolf [wʊlf] [1] *n, pl* **wolves** (a) Wolf *m*. (b) (*fig inf: womanizer*) Don Juan *m*. (c) (*phrases*) **a ~ in sheep's clothing** ein Wolf im Schafspelz; **to cry ~** blinden Alarm schlagen; **to keep the ~ from the door** sich über Wasser halten; **to throw sb to the wolves** jdn den Wölfen zum Fraß vorwerfen; *see* **lone.**
[2] *vt* (*also* **~ down**) *food* hinunterschlingen.

wolf: ~-cub *n* (*lit*) Wolfsjunge(s) *nt*; (*Brit: boy scout*) Wölfling *m*; **~hound** *n* Wolfshund *m*.

wolfish ['wʊlfɪʃ] *adj appetite* wie ein Wolf; *hunger* Wolfs-.

wolfishly ['wʊlfɪʃlɪ] *adv* gierig.

wolf-pack ['wʊlfpæk] *n* Rudel *nt* Wölfe; (*of submarines*) Geschwader *nt*.

wolfram ['wʊlfrəm] *n* Wolfram *nt*.

wolfsbane ['wʊlfsbeɪn] *n (Bot)* Eisenhut *m.*
wolf-whistle ['wʊlf,wɪsl] *(inf)* [1] *n* bewundernder Pfiff ◆ **they gave her a ~** sie pfiffen ihr nach.
[2] *vi* nachpfeifen.
wolverine ['wʊlvəri:n] *n* Vielfraß *m.*
wolves [wʊlvz] *pl of* **wolf.**
woman ['wʊmən] [1] *n, pl* **women** Frau *f,* Frauenzimmer *nt (pej hum); (domestic help)* (Haushalts)hilfe *f; (inf: girlfriend)* Mädchen *nt; (mistress)* Geliebte *f,* Weib *nt (pej)* ◆ **a ~'s work is never done** Frauenhände ruhen nie; **man that is made of ~** *(Rel)* der Mensch, vom Weib geboren; **how like a ~!** typisch Frau!; **cleaning ~** Putzfrau, Reinmachefrau *f;* **~ is a mysterious creature** Frauen sind geheimnisvolle Wesen; **where's my supper, ~!** Weib, wo ist das Essen!; **the little ~** *(inf: wife)* die *or* meine Frau; **to run after women** den Frauen nachrennen; **women's rights** Frauenrechte *pl,* die Rechte *pl* der Frau; **women's page** Frauenseite *f;* **that's ~'s work** das ist Frauenarbeit; **women's talk** Gespräche *pl* von Frau zu Frau; **women's lib** *(inf)* Frauen(rechts)bewegung *f;* **women's libber** *(inf)* Frauenrechtlerin, Emanze *(sl) f; see* **old ~.**
[2] *adj attr* **~ doctor** Ärztin *f;* **~ lawyer** Anwältin *f;* **~ teacher** Lehrerin *f;* **~ driver** Frau *f* am Steuer.
woman: ~-hater *n* Frauenhasser *m;* **~hood** *n (women in general)* alle Frauen, die Frauen *pl;* **you should be proud of your ~hood** du solltest stolz darauf sein, daß du eine Frau bist; **to reach ~hood** (zur) Frau werden; **the sufferings of ~hood** die Leiden einer Frau.
womanish ['wʊmənɪʃ] *adj (womanly) woman* fraulich; *(pej: effeminate) man* weibisch.
womanize ['wʊmənaɪz] *vi* hinter den Frauen her sein ◆ **this womanizing will have to stop** die Frauengeschichten müssen aufhören; **young men out for an evening's womanizing** junge Männer, die ausziehen, um sich mit Mädchen zu amüsieren.
womanizer ['wʊmənaɪzə^r] *n* Schürzenjäger *m.*
womankind ['wʊmən,kaɪnd] *n* das weibliche Geschlecht.
womanliness ['wʊmənlɪnɪs] *n* Weiblichkeit *f.*
womanly ['wʊmənlɪ] *adj figure, person* fraulich; *qualities, virtues* weiblich.
womb [wu:m] *n* (Mutter)schoß, Mutterleib *m,* Gebärmutter *f (Med); (fig)* Schoß *m* ◆ **the foetus in the ~** der Embryo im Mutterleib; **it's just a craving to return to the ~** das ist nur die Sehnsucht nach der Geborgenheit des Mutterschoßes.
wombat ['wɒmbæt] *n* Wombat *m.*
women ['wɪmɪn] *pl of* **woman.**
womenfolk ['wɪmɪnfəʊk] *npl* Frauen *pl.*
women's refuge *n* Frauenhaus *nt.*
won [wʌn] *pret, ptp of* **win.**
▼ **wonder** ['wʌndə^r] [1] *n* **(a)** *(feeling)* Staunen *nt,* Verwunderung *f* ◆ **in ~** voller Staunen; **to be lost in ~** von Staunen erfüllt sein; **the birth of a baby never loses its ~** eine Geburt bleibt immer etwas Wunderbares; **it fills one with a sense of ~** es erfüllt einen mit Erstaunen; **he has never lost that almost childlike sense of ~** er hat nie dieses kindliche Staunen verlernt.
(b) *(object or cause of ~)* Wunder *nt* ◆ **the ~ of electricity** das Wunder der Elektrizität; **the seven ~s of the world** die sieben Weltwunder; **the ~ of it was that ...** das Erstaunliche *or* Verblüffende daran war, daß ...; **it is a ~ that ...** es ist ein Wunder, daß ...; **it is no** *or* **little** *or* **small ~** (es ist) kein Wunder, es ist nicht zu verwundern; **no ~ (he refused)!** kein Wunder(, daß er abgelehnt hat)!; **to do** *or* **work ~s** wahre Wunder vollbringen, Wunder wirken; **~s will never cease!** es geschehen noch Zeichen und Wunder!; *see* **nine.**
▼ [2] *vt* **I ~ what he'll do now** ich bin gespannt *(inf),* was er jetzt tun wird; **I ~ why he did it** ich möchte (zu gern) wissen *or* ich wüßte (zu) gern, warum er das getan hat; **I ~ why!** *(iro)* ich frag mich warum?; **I was ~ing if you'd like to come too** möchten Sie nicht vielleicht auch kommen?; **I was ~ing when you'd realize that** ich habe mich (schon) gefragt, wann du das merkst; **I was ~ing if you could ...** könnten Sie nicht vielleicht ...
[3] *vi* **(a)** *(ask oneself, speculate)* **it set me ~ing** es gab mir zu denken; **why do you ask? — oh, I was just ~ing** warum fragst du? — ach, nur so; **what will happen next, I ~?** ich frage mich *or* ich bin gespannt, was als nächstes kommt; **what's going to happen next? — I ~!** was kommt als nächstes? — das frage ich mich auch!; **I was ~ing about that** ich habe mir darüber schon Gedanken gemacht, ich habe mich das auch schon gefragt; **I've been ~ing about him** ich habe mir auch schon über ihn Gedanken gemacht; **I've been ~ing about him as a possibility** ich hatte ihn auch schon als eine Möglichkeit ins Auge gefaßt; **I expect that will be the end of the matter — I ~!** ich denke, damit ist die Angelegenheit erledigt — da habe ich meine Zweifel *or* da bin ich gespannt; **I'm ~ing about going to the cinema** ich habe daran gedacht, vielleicht ins Kino zu gehen; **John, I've been ~ing, is there really any point?** John, ich frage mich, ob es wirklich (einen) Zweck hat; **could you possibly help me, I ~** könnten Sie mir vielleicht helfen.
(b) *(be surprised)* sich wundern ◆ **I ~ (that) he didn't tell me** es wundert mich, daß er es mir nicht gesagt hat; **to ~ at sth** sich über etw *(acc)* wundern, über etw *(acc)* erstaunt sein; **that's hardly to be ~ed at** das ist kaum verwunderlich; **she'll be married by now, I shouldn't ~** es würde mich nicht wundern, wenn sie inzwischen verheiratet wäre.
wonder *in cpds* Wunder-; **~ boy** *n* Wunderknabe *m;* **~ drug** *n* Wunderheilmittel *nt.*
wonderful ['wʌndəfʊl] *adj* wunderbar.
wonderfully ['wʌndəfəlɪ] *adv see adj* ◆ **he looks ~ well** er sieht wunderbar aus.
wondering ['wʌndərɪŋ] *adj (astonished) tone, look* verwundert, erstaunt; *(doubtful)* fragend.
wonderingly ['wʌndərɪŋlɪ] *adv see adj.*
wonderland ['wʌndə,lænd] *n (fairyland)* Wunderland *nt; (wonderful place)* Paradies *nt* ◆ **the ~ of the Alps** die Wunderwelt der Alpen.
wonderment ['wʌndəmənt] *n see* **wonder 1 (a).**
wonder-worker ['wʌndə,wɜ:kə^r] *n* Wundertäter *m.*
wondrous ['wʌndrəs] *(old, liter)* [1] *adj* wunderbar; *ways also* wundersam.
[2] *adv wise, fair* wunderbar.
wondrously ['wʌndrəslɪ] *adv (old, liter)* wunderbar ◆ **~ beautiful** wunderschön.
wonga ['wɒŋgə] *n (sl)* Moos *nt (sl),* Knete *f (sl).*
wonky ['wɒŋkɪ] *adj (+er) (Brit inf) chair, marriage, grammar* wackelig; *machine* nicht (ganz) in Ordnung ◆ **he's feeling rather ~ still** er fühlt sich noch ziemlich wackelig auf den Beinen *or* angeschlagen; **your hat's a bit/your collar's all ~** dein Hut/dein Kragen sitzt ganz schief.
won't [wəʊnt] *contr of* **will not.**
wont [wəʊnt] [1] *adj* gewohnt ◆ **to be ~ to do sth** gewöhnlich etw tun, etw zu tun pflegen.
[2] *n* (An)gewohnheit *f* ◆ **as is/was his ~** wie er zu tun pflegt/pflegte.
wonted ['wəʊntɪd] *adj (liter)* gewohnt.
woo [wu:] *vt* **(a)** *(dated: court) woman* den Hof machen *(+dat),* umwerben; *(fig) person* umwerben. **(b)** *(fig) stardom, sleep etc* suchen; *audience etc* für sich zu gewinnen versuchen.
◆**woo away** *vt sep employee, executive* abwerben.
wood [wʊd] [1] *n* **(a)** *(material)* Holz *nt* ◆ **touch ~!** dreimal auf Holz geklopft!
(b) *(small forest)* Wald *m* ◆ **~s** Wald *m;* **we're not out of the ~ yet** *(fig)* wir sind noch nicht über den Berg *or* aus dem Schneider *(inf);* **he can't see the ~ for the trees** *(prov)* er sieht den Wald vor (lauter) Bäumen nicht *(prov).*
(c) *(sth made of ~) (cask)* Holzfaß *nt; (Bowls)* Kugel *f; (Golf)* Holz *nt* ◆ **whisky matured in the ~** im Holzfaß gereifter Whisky; **beer from the ~** Bier vom Faß; **that was off the ~** *(Tennis)* das war Holz, das war vom Rahmen.
(d) *(Mus)* **the ~s** *pl* die Holzblasinstrumente, die Holzbläser *pl.*
[2] *adj attr* **(a)** *(made of ~)* Holz-. **(b)** *(living etc in a ~)* Wald-.
wood: ~ alcohol *n* Holzgeist *m;* **~ anemone** *n* Buschwindröschen *nt.*
woodbine ['wʊdbaɪn] *n (honeysuckle)* Geißblatt *nt; (US: Virginia creeper)* wilder Wein, Jungfernrebe *f.*
wood: ~ block *n (Art)* Holzschnitt *m;* **~ carver** *n* (Holz)schnitzer(in *f*) *m;* **~ carving** *n* (Holz)schnitzerei *f;* **~chip** *n (wallpaper)* Rauhfaser *f;* **~chuck** *n* Waldmurmeltier *nt;* **~cock** *n, no pl* Waldschnepfe *f;* **~craft** *n* **(a)** *(skill at living in forest)* Waldläufertum *nt;* **(b)** *(skill at woodwork)* Geschick *nt* im Arbeiten mit Holz; **~cut** *n* Holzschnitt *m;* **~cutter** *n* **(a)** Holzfäller *m; (of logs)* Holzhacker *m;* **(b)** *(Art)* Holzschnitzer *m;* **~cutting** *n* **(a)** Holzfällen *nt; (of logs)* Holzhacken *nt;* **(b)** *(Art)* Holzschnitzen *nt; (item)* Holzplastik, Holzschnitzerei *f.*
wooded ['wʊdɪd] *adj* bewaldet; *countryside also* Wald-.
wooden ['wʊdn] *adj* **(a)** Holz- ◆ **the ~ horse** das hölzerne Pferd; **~ leg** Holzbein *nt;* **~ spoon** *(lit)* Holzlöffel *m,* hölzerner Löffel; *(fig)* Trostpreis *m.* **(b)** *(fig) expression, smile, manner* hölzern; *personality* steif.
wooden-headed ['wʊdn'hedɪd] *adj* dumm.
woodenly ['wʊdnlɪ] *adv (fig) smile, act, bow* gekünstelt, steif; *stand* wie ein Klotz.
wood: ~-free *adj paper* holzfrei; **~land** *n* Waldland *nt,* Waldung *f;* **~lark** *n* Heidelerche *f;* **~louse** *n* Bohrassel *f;* **~man** *n see* **woodsman;** **~ nymph** *n* Waldnymphe *f;* **~pecker** *n* Specht *m;* **~pigeon** *n* Ringeltaube *f;* **~pile** *n* Holzhaufen *m; see* **nigger;** **~ pulp** *n* Holzschliff *m;* **~shed** *n* Holzschuppen *m.*
woodsman ['wʊdzmən] *n, pl* **-men** [-mən] Waldarbeiter *m.*
wood sorrel *n* Waldsauerklee *m.*
woodsy ['wʊdzɪ] *adj (+er) (US inf)* waldig ◆ **~ smell** Waldgeruch *m,* Geruch *m* von Wald.
wood-turning ['wʊd,tɜ:nɪŋ] *n* Drechslerei *f.*
wood: ~wind *n* Holzblasinstrument *nt;* **the ~wind(s), the ~wind section** die Holzbläser *pl;* **~work** *n* **(a)** Holzarbeit; *(craft)* Tischlerei *f;* **the boys do ~work on Tuesday afternoons** Dienstags nachmittags beschäftigen sich die Jungen mit Tischlern; **a nice piece of ~work** eine schöne Tischlerarbeit; **(b)** *(wooden parts)* Holzteile *pl;* **to hit the ~work** *(Ftbl inf)* den Pfosten/die Latte treffen; **~worm** *n* Holzwurm *m;* **it's got ~worm** da ist der Holzwurm drin.
woody ['wʊdɪ] *adj (+er)* **(a)** *(wooded)* waldig, bewaldet. **(b)** *(like wood in texture) tissue* holzig.
wooer ['wu:ə^r] *n (dated)* Werber *m; (fig)* Buhler *m (of sth* um etw) ◆ **a ~ of the unions** ein Buhler um die Gunst der Gewerkschaften.
woof[1] [wʊf] *n (Tex)* Schuß *m.*
woof[2] [1] *n (of dog)* Wuff *nt.*
[2] *vi* kläffen ◆ **~, ~!** wau, wau!, wuff, wuff!
woofer ['wʊfə^r] *n* Tieftöner *m.*
woofter, wooftah ['wʊftə^r] *n (Brit sl)* Warme(r) *m (sl),* Schwule(r) *m (inf).*
wool [wʊl] [1] *n* **(a)** Wolle *f; (cloth also)* Wollstoff *m* ◆ **all ~, pure ~** reine Wolle; **to pull the ~ over sb's eyes** *(inf)* jdm Sand in die Augen streuen *(inf).* **(b)** *(glass ~, wire ~)* Wolle *f.*
[2] *adj* Woll-; *(made of wool also)* aus Wolle.
woolen *etc (US) see* **woollen** *etc.*
wool: ~-gathering *n* Träumen *nt;* **to be ~-gathering** vor sich *(acc)* hinträumen; **~-grower** *n* Schafzüchter *m (für Wolle).*

➤ LANGUAGE IN USE: **wonder: 2** → 16.1, 19.1, 26.1

woollen, (*US*) **woolen** ['wʊlən] [1] *adj* Woll-; (*made of wool also*) wollen, aus Wolle.
[2] *n* ~s *pl* (*garments*) Wollsachen, Stricksachen *pl*; (*fabrics, blankets*) Wollwaren *pl*.

woolliness, (*US*) **wooliness** ['wʊlɪnɪs] *n* Wolligkeit *f*; (*softness also*) Flauschigkeit *f*; (*fig: of outline*) Verschwommenheit *f*; (*pej: of mind, idea*) Verworrenheit, Wirrheit *f*.

woolly, (*US*) **wooly** ['wʊlɪ] [1] *adj* (+*er*) wollig; (*soft also*) flauschig; (*fig*) *outline* verschwommen; (*pej*) *mind, thinking, idea* verworren, wirr.
[2] *n* (*inf: sweater etc*) Pulli *m* (*inf*) ◆ **winter woollies** (*esp Brit: sweaters etc*) dicke Wollsachen (*inf*); (*esp US: underwear*) Wollene *pl* (*inf*).

woolsack ['wʊlsæk] *n* (*seat*) Wollsack *m* (*Sitz des Lordkanzlers im britischen Oberhaus*); (*office*) Amt *nt* des Lordkanzlers.

wooziness ['wu:zɪnɪs] *n* (*inf*) Benommenheit *f*.

woozy ['wu:zɪ] *adj* (+*er*) (*inf*) benommen, duselig (*inf*).

wop [wɒp] *n* (*pej sl*) Spaghettifresser (*pej sl*) *m*.

Worcs *abbr of* **Worcestershire**.

word [wɜ:d] [1] *n* (a) (*unit of language*) Wort *nt* ◆ **~s** Wörter *pl*; (*meaningful sequence*) Worte *pl*; **~ order/formation/division** Wortstellung *f*/Wortbildung *f*/Silbentrennung *f*; **foreign ~s** Fremdwörter *pl*; **~ for ~** Wort für Wort; (*exactly also*) wortwörtlich; **cold isn't the ~ for it** kalt ist gar kein Ausdruck (dafür); **~s cannot describe it** so etwas kann man mit Worten gar nicht beschreiben; **beyond ~s** unbeschreiblich; **too funny for ~s** unbeschreiblich komisch; **to put one's thoughts into ~s** seine Gedanken in Worte fassen *or* kleiden; **"irresponsible" would be a better ~ for it** „unverantwortlich" wäre wohl das treffendere Wort dafür; **~s fail me** mir fehlen die Worte; **in a ~** mit einem Wort, kurz gesagt; **in so many ~s** direkt, ausdrücklich; **in other ~s** mit anderen Worten, anders gesagt *or* ausgedrückt; **the last ~** (*fig*) der letzte Schrei (*in* an +*dat*); **he had the last ~** er hatte das letzte Wort; **that's not the ~ I would have chosen** ich hätte es nicht so ausgedrückt; **in the ~s of Goethe** mit Goethe gesprochen, um mit Goethe zu sprechen.
(b) (*remark*) Wort *nt* ◆ **~s** Worte *pl*; **a ~ of advice** ein Rat(schlag) *m*; **a ~ of encouragement/warning** eine Ermunterung/Warnung; **fine ~s** schöne Worte *pl*; **a man of few ~s** ein Mann, der nicht viele Worte macht; **I can't get a ~ out of him** ich kann kein Wort aus ihm herausbekommen; **by ~ of mouth** durch mündliche Überlieferung; **to say a few ~s** ein paar Worte sprechen; **to take sb at his ~** jdn beim Wort nehmen; **to have a ~ with sb (about sth)** mit jdm (über etw) sprechen; (*reprimand, discipline*) jdn ins Gebet nehmen; **John, could I have a ~?** John, kann ich dich mal sprechen?; **(could I have) a ~ in your ear?** kann ich Sie bitte unter vier Augen *or* allein sprechen?; **you took the ~s out of my mouth** du hast mir das Wort aus dem Mund genommen; **I wish you wouldn't put ~s into my mouth** ich wünschte, Sie würden mir nicht das Wort im Munde herumdrehen; **to put in** *or* **say a (good) ~ for sb** für jdn ein gutes Wort einlegen; **nobody had a good ~ to say for him** niemand wußte etwas Gutes über ihn zu sagen; **without a ~** ohne ein Wort; **don't say** *or* **breathe a ~ about it** sag aber bitte keinen Ton *or* kein Sterbenswörtchen (*inf*) davon; **remember, not a ~ to anyone** vergiß nicht, kein Sterbenswörtchen (*inf*).
(c) **~s** *pl* (*quarrel*) **to have ~s with sb** mit jdm eine Auseinandersetzung haben.
(d) **~s** *pl* (*text, lyrics*) Text *m*.
(e) *no pl* (*message, news*) Nachricht *f* ◆ **~ came/went round that** ... es kam die Nachricht/es ging die Nachricht um, daß ...; **to leave ~ (with sb/for sb) that** ... (bei jdm/für jdn) (die Nachricht) hinterlassen, daß ...; **is there any ~ from John yet?** schon von John gehört?, schon Nachrichten von John?; **to send ~** Nachricht geben; **to send ~ to sb** jdn benachrichtigen; **to send sb ~ of sth** jdn von etw benachrichtigen; **to spread the ~ around** (*inf*) es allen sagen (*inf*); **what's the ~ on Charlie?** (*inf*) was gibt's Neues von Charlie?
(f) (*promise, assurance*) Wort *nt* ◆ **~ of honour** Ehrenwort *nt*; **a man of his ~** ein Mann, der zu seinem Wort steht; **to be as good as one's ~, to keep one's ~** sein Wort halten; **I give you my ~** ich gebe dir mein (Ehren)wort; **to go back on one's ~** sein Wort nicht halten; **to break one's ~** sein Wort brechen; **I have his ~ for it** ich habe sein Wort; **take my ~ for it** verlaß dich drauf, das kannst du mir glauben; **you don't have to take my ~ for it** du kannst das ruhig nachprüfen; **it's his ~ against mine** Aussage steht gegen Aussage; **upon my ~!** (*old*), **my ~!** meine Güte!
(g) (*order*) Wort *nt*; (*also* **~ of command**) Kommando *nt*, Befehl *m* ◆ **to give the ~ (to do sth)** (*Mil*) das Kommando geben(, etw zu tun); **just say the ~** sag nur ein Wort; **his ~ is law here** sein Wort ist hier Gesetz.
(h) (*Rel*) Wort *nt* ◆ **the W~ of God** das Wort Gottes; **to preach the W~** das Wort Gottes *or* das Evangelium verkünden.
[2] *vt* (in Worten) ausdrücken, formulieren, in Worte fassen (*geh*); *letter* formulieren; *speech* abfassen.

word: ~ association *n* Wortassoziation *f*; **~-blind** *adj* wortblind; **~ class** *n* Wortklasse *f*; **~count** *n* (*Comput*) Wortzählung *f*; **~crunch** *vt* (*Comput inf*) *text* (nach Wörtern) analysieren; **~ game** *n* Buchstabenspiel *nt*.

wordily ['wɜ:dɪlɪ] *adv see adj*.

wordiness ['wɜ:dɪnɪs] *n* Wortreichtum *m*, Langatmigkeit *f* (*pej*).

wording ['wɜ:dɪŋ] *n* Formulierung *f*.

word: ~less *adj* wortlos; *grief* stumm; **~ list** *n* Wortliste *f*; **~ order** *n* Satzstellung, Wortstellung *f*; **~-perfect** *adj* sicher im Text; **to be ~-perfect** den Text perfekt beherrschen, den Text bis aufs Wort beherrschen; **~ picture** *n* Bild *nt* (in Worten); **to paint a vivid ~ picture of sth** etw in lebhaften Farben beschreiben; **~play** *n* Wortspiel *nt*; **~-process** *vt* mit Textverarbeitung schreiben *or* erstellen; **~ processing** [1] *n* Textverarbeitung *f*; [2] *attr software etc* Textverarbeitungs-; **~ processor** *n* (*machine*) Text(verarbeitungs)system *nt*, Textverarbeitungsanlage *f*; (*software*) Text(verarbeitungs)programm *nt*; **~ split** *n* Worttrennung *f*; **~ square** *n* magisches Quadrat; **~wrap** *n* (*Comput*) (automatischer) Zeilenumbruch.

wordy ['wɜ:dɪ] *adj* (+*er*) wortreich, langatmig (*pej*).

wore [wɔ:ʳ] *pret of* **wear**.

work [wɜ:k] [1] *n* (a) (*toil, labour, task*) Arbeit *f* ◆ **have you got any ~ for me?** haben Sie was für mich zu tun?; (*employment*) haben Sie Arbeit für mich?; **he doesn't like ~** er arbeitet nicht gern; **that's a good piece of ~** das ist gute Arbeit; **is this all your own ~?** haben Sie das alles selbst gemacht?; **closed for ~ on the roof** wegen (Reparatur)arbeiten am Dach geschlossen; **when ~ begins on the new bridge** wenn die Arbeiten an der neuen Brücke anfangen; **to be at ~ (on sth)** (an etw *dat*) arbeiten; **there are forces at ~ which** ... es sind Kräfte am Werk, die ...; **it's the ~ of the devil** das ist Teufelswerk *or* ein Machwerk des Teufels; **to do a good day's ~** ein schönes Stück Arbeit leisten; **we've a lot of ~ to do before this choir can give a concert** wir haben noch viel zu tun, ehe dieser Chor ein Konzert geben kann; **you need to do some more ~ on your accent/your baton-change** Sie müssen noch an Ihrem Akzent/am Stabwechsel arbeiten; **I've been trying to get some ~ done** ich habe versucht zu arbeiten; **to put a lot of ~ into sth** eine Menge Arbeit in etw (*acc*) stecken; **it's in the ~s** (*inf*) es ist in der Mache (*inf*); **to get on with one's ~** sich (wieder) an die Arbeit machen; **to make short** *or* **quick ~ of sb/sth** mit jdm/etw kurzen Prozeß machen; **to make ~ for sb** jdm Arbeit machen; **time/the medicine had done its ~** die Zeit/Arznei hatte ihr Werk vollbracht/ihre Wirkung getan; **the ~ of a moment** eine Angelegenheit von Sekunden; **it was hard ~ for the old car to get up the hill** das alte Auto hatte beim Anstieg schwer zu schaffen.
(b) (*employment, job*) Arbeit *f* ◆ **to be (out) at ~** arbeiten sein; **to go out to ~** arbeiten gehen; **to be out of/in ~** arbeitslos sein/eine Stelle haben; **he travels to ~ by car** er fährt mit dem Auto zur Arbeit; **do you live close to your ~?** hast du es weit zur Arbeit?; **how long does it take you to get to ~?** wie lange brauchst du, um zu deiner Arbeitsstelle zu kommen?; **at ~** an der Arbeitsstelle, am Arbeitsplatz; **what is your ~?** was tun Sie (beruflich)?; **to put** *or* **throw sb out of ~** jdn auf die Straße setzen (*inf*); **to put out of ~** arbeitslos machen, um den Arbeitsplatz bringen; **to be off ~** (am Arbeitsplatz) fehlen.
(c) (*product*) Arbeit *f*; (*Art, Liter*) Werk *nt* ◆ **~ of art/reference** Kunstwerk *nt*/Nachschlagewerk *nt*; **a ~ of literature** ein literarisches Werk; **a fine piece of ~** eine schöne Arbeit; **good ~s** gute Werke *pl*; **a chance for artists to show their ~** eine Gelegenheit für Künstler, ihre Arbeiten *or* Werke zu zeigen.
(d) **~s** *pl* (*Mil*) Befestigungen *pl* ◆ **road ~s** Baustelle *f*.
(e) **~s** *pl* (*Mech*) Getriebe, Innere(s) *nt*; (*of watch, clock*) Uhrwerk *nt*.
(f) **~s** *sing or pl* (*factory*) Betrieb *m*, Fabrik *f* ◆ **gas ~s/steel ~s** Gas-/Stahlwerk *nt*; **~s gate** Fabrik- *or* Werkstor *nt*; **~s council** *or* **committee/outing** Betriebsrat *m*/Betriebsausflug *m*.
(g) (*inf*) **the ~s** *pl* alles Drum und Dran; **to give sb the ~s** (*treat harshly*) jdn gehörig in die Mangel nehmen (*inf*); (*treat generously*) jdn nach allen Regeln der Kunst *or* nach Strich und Faden verwöhnen (*inf*); **to get the ~s** (*be treated harshly*) gehörig in die Mangel genommen werden (*inf*); (*be treated generously*) nach allen Regeln der Kunst *or* nach Strich und Faden verwöhnt werden (*inf*); **we had gorgeous food, wine, brandy, the ~s** es gab tolles Essen, Wein, Kognak, alle Schikanen (*inf*); **he was giving his opponent the ~s** er machte seinen Gegner nach allen Regeln der Kunst fertig (*inf*).
[2] *vi* (a) arbeiten (*at* an +*dat*) ◆ **to ~ towards/for sth** auf etw (*acc*) hin/für etw arbeiten; **to ~ for better conditions** *etc* sich für bessere Bedingungen *etc* einsetzen; **to ~ against a reform** gegen eine Reform kämpfen; **these factors which ~ against us** diese Faktoren, die sich uns (*dat*) entgegenstellen.
(b) (*function, operate*) funktionieren; (*marriage, plan also*) klappen (*inf*); (*medicine, spell*) wirken; (*be successful*) klappen (*inf*) ◆ **it won't ~** das klappt nicht; **"not ~ing"** (*lift etc*) „außer Betrieb"; **to get sth ~ing** etw in Gang bringen; **it ~s by** *or* **on electricity** es läuft auf Strom; **it ~s both ways** es trifft auch andersherum zu; **but this arrangement will have to ~ both ways** aber diese Abmachung muß für beide Seiten gelten.
(c) (*yeast*) arbeiten, treiben.
(d) (*mouth, face*) zucken; (*jaws*) mahlen.
(e) (*move gradually*) **to ~ loose/along** sich lockern/sich entlangarbeiten; **to ~ round** (*wind, object*) sich langsam drehen (*to* nach); **he ~ed round to asking her** er hat sich aufgerafft, sie zu fragen; **OK, I'm ~ing round to it** okay, das mache ich schon noch.
[3] *vt* (a) (*make ~*) *staff, employees, students* arbeiten lassen, herannehmen (*inf*), schinden (*pej*) ◆ **to ~ oneself hard/to death** sich nicht schonen/sich zu Tode arbeiten; **he ~s himself too hard** er übernimmt sich.
(b) (*operate*) *machine* bedienen; *lever, brake* betätigen ◆ **to ~ sth by electricity/hand** etw elektrisch/mit Hand betreiben; **can we ~ that trick again?** können wir den Trick noch einmal anbringen *or* anwenden?
(c) (*bring about*) *change, cure* bewirken, herbeiführen ◆ **to ~ mischief** Unheil anrichten; **to ~ mischief between friends** Zwietracht zwischen Freunden säen; **to ~ it (so that ...)** (*inf*) es so deichseln(, daß ...) (*inf*); **to ~ one's passage** seine Überfahrt abarbeiten; **you don't have to ~ your notice** Sie brauchen Ihre Kündigungsfrist nicht einzuhalten; **surely you can ~ a better deal than that** du kannst doch sicherlich einen besseren Abschluß herausschlagen; *see* **~ up**.
(d) (*Sew*) arbeiten; *design etc* sticken.
(e) (*shape*) *wood, metal* bearbeiten; *dough, clay also* kneten, durcharbeiten ◆ **he ~ed the clay into a human shape** er formte den Ton zu einer

➤ LANGUAGE IN USE: **work: 1b** → 19.1 **2a** → 19.2

menschlichen Gestalt; **~ the flour in gradually/the ingredients together** mischen Sie das Mehl allmählich unter/die Zutaten (zusammen).
(f) *(exploit) mine* ausbeuten, abbauen; *land* bearbeiten; *smallholding* bewirtschaften; *(salesman) area* bereisen.
(g) *(move gradually)* **to ~ one's hands free** seine Hände freibekommen; **to ~ sth loose** etw losbekommen; **to ~ one's way through a book/Greek grammar** sich durch ein Buch/die griechische Grammatik arbeiten *or* kämpfen; **to ~ one's way to the top/up from nothing/through college** sich nach oben arbeiten *or* kämpfen/sich von ganz unten hocharbeiten/sein Studium selbst *or* durch eigene Arbeit finanzieren; **he ~ed his way across the rock-face/through the tunnel** er überquerte die Felswand/kroch durch den Tunnel; **to ~ oneself into a better job/sb's confidence** sich hocharbeiten/sich in jds Vertrauen *(acc)* einschleichen.
◆**work away** *vi* vor sich hin arbeiten.
◆**work down** *vi (stockings)* (herunter)rutschen *(inf)*.
◆**work in** [1] *vt sep* **(a)** *(rub in)* einarbeiten; *lotion also* einmassieren ◆ **it had ~ed its way right ~** es war (tief) eingedrungen.
(b) *(insert) bolt etc* (vorsichtig) einführen.
(c) *(in book, speech) reference* einbauen, einarbeiten; *jokes* einbauen ◆ **to ~ sth ~to sth** etw in etw *(acc)* einbauen.
(d) *(in schedule etc)* einschieben ◆ **to ~ sb ~to a plan** jdn in einen Plan miteinbeziehen.
[2] *vi* **(a)** *(fit in)* passen *(with* in *+acc)* ◆ **that'll ~ ~ quite well** das paßt ganz gut. **(b)** *(Ind)* den Arbeitsplatz besetzen.
◆**work off** [1] *vi* sich losmachen *or* lockern.
[2] *vt sep debts, fat* abarbeiten; *energy* loswerden; *feelings* auslassen, abreagieren *(on* an *+dat)*.
◆**work on** [1] *vi* weiterarbeiten.
[2] *vt sep lid, washer* darauf bringen ◆ **she ~ed her boots ~** sie zwängte sich in ihre Stiefel.
[3] *vi +prep obj* **(a)** *car, book, subject, accent* arbeiten an *(+dat)* ◆ **who's ~ing ~ this case?** wer bearbeitet diesen Fall?
(b) *evidence, assumption* ausgehen von; *principle (person)* ausgehen von; *(machine)* arbeiten nach ◆ **there are not many clues to ~ ~** es gibt nicht viele Hinweise, auf die man zurückgreifen könnte; **I'm ~ing ~ this one hunch** ich habe alles an diesem einen Verdacht aufgehängt.
(c) we haven't solved it yet but we're still ~ing ~ it wir haben es noch nicht gelöst, aber wir sind dabei; **if we ~ ~ him a little longer we might persuade him** wenn wir ihn noch ein Weilchen bearbeiten, können wir ihn vielleicht überreden; **obviously the other side have been ~ing ~ him** ihn hat offensichtlich die Gegenseite in der Mache gehabt *(inf)*; **just keep ~ing ~ his basic greed** appellieren Sie nur weiter an seine Habgier.
◆**work out** [1] *vi* **(a)** *(allow solution: puzzle, sum etc)* aufgehen.
(b) *(amount to)* **that ~s ~ at £105** das gibt *or* macht £ 105; **it ~s ~ more expensive in the end** am Ende kommt *or* ist es teurer; **how much does that ~ ~ at?** was macht das?
(c) *(succeed: plan, marriage, idea)* funktionieren, klappen *(inf)* ◆ **things didn't ~ ~ at all well for him** es ist ihm alles schiefgegangen; **how's your new job ~ing ~?** was macht die neue Arbeit?; **I hope it all ~s ~ for you** ich hoffe, daß alles klappt *(inf) or* daß dir alles gelingt; **things didn't ~ ~ that way** es kam ganz anders.
(d) *(in gym etc)* trainieren.
[2] *vt sep* **(a)** *(solve, calculate)* herausbringen; *code* entschlüsseln, knacken *(inf)*; *mathematical problem also* lösen; *problem* fertig werden mit; *sum also* ausrechnen ◆ **you can ~ that ~ for yourself** das kannst du dir (doch) selbst denken; **surely he can manage to ~ things ~ for himself** *(in life)* er kann doch bestimmt allein zurechtkommen; **things will always ~ themselves ~** Probleme lösen sich stets von selbst.
(b) *(devise) scheme* (sich *dat*) ausdenken; *(in detail)* ausarbeiten.
(c) *(understand) person* schlau werden aus *(+dat)* ◆ **can you ~ ~ where we are on the map?** kannst du herausfinden *or* -bringen, wo wir auf der Karte sind?; **I can't ~ ~ why it went wrong** ich kann nicht verstehen, wieso es nicht geklappt hat.
(d) *(complete) prison sentence* absitzen ◆ **to ~ ~ one's notice** seine Kündigungsfrist einhalten.
(e) *(exhaust) mine* ausbeuten, erschöpfen; *minerals* abbauen ◆ **to ~ sth ~ of one's system** *(fig)* etw überwinden, mit etw fertigwerden.
(f) *(remove) nail, tooth etc* (allmählich) herausbringen.
◆**work over** *vt sep (inf)* zusammenschlagen *(inf)*.
◆**work through** [1] *vi +prep obj* **(a)** *(blade etc)* sich arbeiten durch; *(water)* sickern durch. **(b)** *(read through)* sich (durch)arbeiten *or* (durch)ackern durch.
[2] *vt +prep obj* **he ~ed the rope ~ the crack** er führte das Seil durch die Spalte.
[3] *vi (come through: benefit, pay rise etc)* durchsickern.
◆**work up** [1] *vt sep* **(a)** *(develop) business* zu etwas bringen, entwickeln; *enthusiasm (in oneself)* aufbringen; *appetite* sich *(dat)* holen ◆ **to ~ one's way ~ (through the ranks/from the shop floor)** von der Pike auf dienen.
(b) *lecture, theme, notes* ausarbeiten.
(c) *(stimulate) audience* aufstacheln ◆ **to ~ ~ feeling against sb** gegen jdn Stimmung machen; **to feel/get ~ed ~** aufgeregt sein/sich aufregen; **to ~ oneself ~** sich erhitzen; *see* **frenzy**.
[2] *vi (skirt etc)* sich hochschieben.
◆**work up to** *vi +prep obj question, proposal etc* zusteuern auf *(+acc)* ◆ **I know what you're ~ing ~ ~** ich weiß, worauf Sie hinauswollen; **the music ~s ~ ~ a tremendous climax** die Musik steigert sich zu einem gewaltigen Höhepunkt.
workable ['wɜːkəbl] *adj mine* abbaufähig; *land* bebaubar; *clay* formbar; *plan* durchführbar.
workaday ['wɜːkədeɪ] *adj* Alltags-.
workaholic [ˌwɜːkə'hɒlɪk] *n (inf)* Arbeitswütige(r), Arbeitssüchtige(r) *mf*, Arbeitstier *nt*.
work: ~bag *n* Näh- *or* Handarbeitsbeutel *m*; **~basket** *n* Näh- *or* Handarbeitskorb *m*; **~bench** *n* Werkbank *f*; **~book** *n* Arbeitsheft *nt*; **~ camp** *n* Arbeitslager *nt*; **~day** *n (esp US)* Arbeitstag *m*; *(day of week)* Werktag *m*.
worker ['wɜːkə^r] *n* **(a)** Arbeiter(in *f*) *m* ◆ **~s' education** Arbeiterbildung *f*; **~ director** *Arbeitnehmer, der gleichzeitig dem Unternehmensvorstand angehört*; **~ participation** Mitbestimmung *f*; **~ priest** Arbeiterpriester *m*; *see* **fast[1] 1 (a)**.
(b) *(also* **~ ant/bee***)* Arbeiterin *f*.
work: ~ ethic *n* Arbeitsmoral *f*; **~flow** *n* Arbeitsablauf *m*; **~flow schedule** *n* Arbeitsablaufplan *m*; **~ force** *n* Arbeiterschaft *f*; **~horse** *n (lit, fig)* Arbeitspferd *nt*; **~house** *n (Brit Hist)* Armenhaus *nt*; **~-in** *n* Work-in *nt*.
working ['wɜːkɪŋ] [1] *adj* **(a)** *(engaged in work) population* arbeitend, berufstätig; *(Comm) partner* aktiv ◆ **~ life** *(of machine part)* Lebensdauer *f*; *(of animal)* Nutzungsdauer *f*; *(of person)* Berufsleben *nt*; **~ man** Arbeiter *m*; **I'm a ~ man, I need my rest** ich arbeite den ganzen Tag, ich brauch meine Ruhe; **~ girl** *(dated:* **~ woman***)* berufstätige Frau; *(euph: prostitute)* Freudenmädchen *nt*; **~ wives** berufstätige Ehefrauen *pl*; **~ woman** berufstätige Frau.
(b) *(spent in or used for ~) day, week, conditions, clothes* Arbeits- ◆ **~ capital** Betriebskapital *nt*; **~ hours** Arbeitszeit *f*; **~ lunch** Arbeitsessen *nt*; **~ party** (Arbeits)ausschuß *m*.
(c) *(provisional) hypothesis, drawing, model, (Comput) file, memory* Arbeits-; *(sufficient) majority* arbeitsfähig, Arbeits- ◆ **in ~ order** in betriebsfähigem Zustand; **~ knowledge** Grundkenntnisse *pl*.
[2] *n* **(a)** *(work)* Arbeiten *nt*, Arbeit *f*.
(b) ~s *pl (way sth works)* Arbeitsweise, Funktionsweise *f* ◆ **~s of fate/the mind** Wege *pl* des Schicksals/Gedankengänge *pl*; **to understand the ~(s) of this machine/system** um zu verstehen, wie die Maschine/das politische System funktioniert.
(c) ~s *pl (Min)* Schächte, Gänge *pl*; *(of quarry)* Grube *f*.
working class *n (also* **~ ~es***)* Arbeiterklasse *f*.
working-class ['wɜːkɪŋ'klɑːs] *adj* der Arbeiterklasse, Arbeiter-; *(pej)* ordinär, proletenhaft ◆ **to be ~** zur Arbeiterklasse gehören.
working-over ['wɜːkɪŋ'əʊvə^r] *n (inf)* Abreibung *f (inf)* ◆ **to give sb a good ~** jdm eine tüchtige Abreibung verpassen *(inf)*.
work: ~-in-progress *n (Fin)* laufende Arbeiten *pl or* Aufträge *pl*; **~ load** *n* Arbeit(slast) *f*; **~man** *n* Handwerker *m*; **~manlike** ['wɜːkmən'laɪk] *adj attitude, job* fachmännisch; *product* fachmännisch gearbeitet; **~manship** ['wɜːkmənʃɪp] *n* Arbeit(squalität) *f*; **~mate** *n (inf)* (Arbeits)kollege *m*, (Arbeits)kollegin *f*; **~out** *n (Sport)* Training *nt*; **to have a ~out** Übungen machen; *(boxer)* Sparring machen; **~ permit** *n* Arbeitserlaubnis *f*; **~piece** *n* Arbeit *f*; **~place** *n* Arbeitsplatz *m*; **at the ~place** am Arbeitsplatz; **~room** *n* Arbeitszimmer *nt*.
works [wɜːks] *npl see* **work 1 (d-g)**.
work: ~shop *n* Werkstatt *f*; **a music ~shop** ein Musikkurs *m*, ein Musik-Workshop *m*; **~shy** *adj* arbeitsscheu; **~ station** *n* Arbeitsplatz, Arbeitsbereich *m*; *(Comput)* Arbeitsplatzstation *f*; **~ study** *n* REFA- *or* Arbeitsstudie *f*; **~ surface** *n* Arbeitsfläche *f*; **~table** *n* Arbeitstisch *m*; **~ ticket** *n* Arbeitszettel *m*; **~top** *n* Arbeitsfläche *f*; **~-to-rule** *n* Dienst *m* nach Vorschrift; **~ week** *n (esp US)* Arbeitswoche *f*.
world [wɜːld] *n* **(a)** Welt *f* ◆ **in the ~** auf der Welt; **all over the ~** auf der ganzen Welt; **he jets/sails all over the ~** er jettet/segelt in der Weltgeschichte herum; **it's the same the whole ~ over** es ist (doch) überall das Gleiche; **to go/sail round the ~** eine Weltreise machen/rund um die Welt segeln; **to feel** *or* **be on top of the ~** munter und fidel sein; **it's a small ~** die Welt ist klein; **it's not the end of the ~!** *(inf)* deshalb *or* davon geht die Welt nicht unter! *(inf)*; **it's a small ~** wie klein doch die Welt ist; **to live in a ~ of one's own** in seiner eigenen (kleinen) Welt leben; **money/love makes the ~ go round** es dreht sich alles um das Geld/die Liebe, Geld regiert die Welt.
(b) the New/Old/Third W~ die Neue/Alte/Dritte Welt; **the business/literary ~** die Geschäftswelt/die literarische Welt; **the animal/vegetable ~** die Tier-/Pflanzenwelt; **in the Roman ~** zur Zeit der Römer.
(c) *(society)* Welt *f* ◆ **man/woman of the ~** Mann *m*/Frau *f* von Welt; **to come** *or* **go down in the ~** herunterkommen; **to go up** *or* **rise in the ~** es (in der Welt) zu etwas bringen; **to set the ~ on fire** die Welt erschüttern; **he had the ~ at his feet** die ganze Welt lag ihm zu Füßen; **to lead the ~ in sth** in etw *(dat)* in der Welt führend sein; **how goes the ~ with you?** wie geht's?, wie steht's?; **all the ~ knows** ... alle Welt *or* jeder weiß ...; **all the ~ and his wife were there** Gott und die Welt waren da *(inf)*; **in the eyes of the ~** vor der Welt.
(d) *(this life)* Welt *f* ◆ **to come into the ~** zur *or* auf die Welt kommen; **~ without end** *(Eccl)* von Ewigkeit zu Ewigkeit; **to renounce the ~** *(Rel)* der Welt *(dat)* entsagen; **to have the best of both ~s** das eine tun und das andere nicht lassen; **out of this ~** *(sl)* phantastisch; **he is not long for this ~** er steht schon mit einem Fuß im Jenseits; **to bring sb/sth into the ~** jdn zur Welt bringen/etw in die Welt setzen; **to go to a better ~** in eine bessere Welt eingehen; **to be alone in the ~** allein auf der Welt sein.
(e) *(emph)* Welt *f* ◆ **not for (all) the ~** nicht um alles in der Welt; **nothing in the ~** nichts auf der Welt; **what/who in the ~** was/wer in aller Welt; **it did**

him a ~ of good es hat ihm (unwahrscheinlich) gut getan; a ~ of difference ein himmelweiter Unterschied; they're ~s apart sie sind total verschieden; for all the ~ like ... beinahe wie ...; he looked for all the ~ as if nothing had happened er sah aus, als wäre überhaupt nichts geschehen; to be all the ~ to sb jdm alles bedeuten; to think the ~ of sb/sth große Stücke auf jdn halten/etw über alles stellen.

world *in cpds* Welt-; **W~ Bank** *n* Weltbank *f*; **~-beater** *n (inf)* **to be a ~-beater** unschlagbar sein; **~ champion** *n (Brit)* Weltmeister(in *f*) *m*; **~ championship** *n (Brit)* Weltmeisterschaft *f*; **~ clock** *n* Weltzeituhr *f*; **W~ Court** *n* Weltgerichtshof *m*; **W~ Cup** *n* Fußballweltmeisterschaft *f*; *(cup)* Weltpokal *m*; **~ Fair** *n* Weltausstellung *f*; **~-famous** *adj* weltberühmt; **W~ Heritage Site** *n* Weltkulturdenkmal *nt*; **~ language** *n* Weltsprache *f*; **~ leader** *n* **(a)** *(Pol)* **the ~ leaders** die führenden Regierungschefs der Welt; **(b)**(*Comm: country, company*) weltweiter Marktführer, Weltführer *m*.

worldliness ['wɜːldlɪnɪs] *n* Weltlichkeit *f*; *(of person)* weltliche Gesinnung.

worldly ['wɜːldlɪ] *adj (+er)* weltlich; *person* weltlich gesinnt ♦ **~-wise** weltklug; **~ wisdom** Weltklugheit *f*.

world: ~ picture *n see* **~ view**; **~ power** *n* Weltmacht *f*; **~ rankings** *npl* Weltrangliste *f*; **~ record** *n* Weltrekord *m*; **~ record holder** *n* Weltrekordinhaber(in *f*) *m*; **~'s champion** *n (US)* Weltmeister(in *f*) *m*; **W~'s Fair** *n (US)* Weltausstellung *f*; **~-shattering** *adj* welterschütternd, weltbewegend; **~'s record** *n (US)* Weltrekord *m*; **~ view** *n* Weltbild *nt*; **~ war** *n* Weltkrieg *m*; **W~ War One/Two, W~ War I/II** Erster/Zweiter Weltkrieg; **~-weariness** *n* Lebensmüdigkeit *f*; **~-weary** *adj* lebensmüde; **~-wide** *adj, adv* weltweit.

World-Wide Web *n* World Wide Web *nt*.

worm [wɜːm] [1] *n* **(a)** *(lit, fig inf)* Wurm *m*; *(wood ~)* Holzwurm *m* ♦ **~s** *(Med)* Würmer *pl*; **even a ~ will turn** *(prov)* es geschehen noch Zeichen und Wunder; **to get a ~'s eye view of sth** etw aus der Froschperspektive sehen.
(b) *(screw)* Schnecke *f*; *(thread)* Schneckengewinde *nt*.
[2] *vt* **(a)** zwängen ♦ **to ~ one's way** *or* **oneself along/through/into sth** sich an etw *(dat)* entlangdrücken/durch etw *(acc)* durchschlängeln *or* -zwängen/in etw *(acc)* hinein -zwängen; **to ~ one's way forward** *(creep)* sich nach vorne schleichen; **to ~ one's way into a position/into sb's confidence/into a group** sich in eine Stellung/jds Vertrauen/eine Gruppe einschleichen; **to ~ one's way out of a difficulty** sich aus einer schwierigen Lage herauswinden.
(b) *(extract)* **to ~ sth out of sb** jdm etw entlocken; **you have to ~ everything out of him** ihm muß man die Würmer aus der Nase ziehen.
(c) *dog* eine Wurmkur machen mit *(+dat)*.

worm: ~-cast *n vom Regenwurm aufgeworfenes Erdhäufchen*; **~-eaten** *adj wood* wurmstichig; *(fig inf)* wurmzerfressen; **~ gear** *n* Schneckengetriebe *nt*; **~hole** *n* Wurmloch *nt*; **~ powder** *n* Wurmmittel *nt*; **~ wheel** *n* Schneckenrad *nt*; **~wood** *n* Wermut *m*; *(fig)* Wermutstropfen *m*.

wormy ['wɜːmɪ] *adj apple* wurmig; *wood* wurmstichig; *dog* von Würmern befallen; *soil* wurmreich.

worn [wɔːn] [1] *ptp of* **wear**.
[2] *adj* **(a)** *(~-out) coat* abgetragen; *book* zerlesen; *carpet* abgetreten; *tyre* abgefahren. **(b)** *(weary) smile* müde; *person* angegriffen ♦ **to look ~ (with care/worry)** besorgt aussehen.

worn-out *adj attr*, **worn out** ['wɔːnˌaʊt] *adj pred* **(a)** *coat* abgetragen; *carpet* abgetreten; *phrase* abgedroschen. **(b)** *(exhausted) person* erschöpft; *horse* ausgemergelt.

worried ['wʌrɪd] *adj* besorgt *(about, by* wegen); *(anxious also)* beunruhigt ♦ **to be ~ sick** krank vor Sorge(n) sein *(inf)*.

worriedly ['wʌrɪdlɪ] *adv* besorgt; *(anxiously also)* beunruhigt.

worrier ['wʌrɪəʳ] *n* Pessimist, Schwarzseher *m*.

worrisome ['wʌrɪsəm] *adj* beunruhigend, besorgniserregend; *(annoying)* lästig.

worry ['wʌrɪ] [1] *n* Sorge *f* ♦ **the ~ of bringing up a family** die Sorgen, die eine Familie mit sich bringt; **it's a great ~ to us all** wir machen uns alle große Sorgen darüber; **I know it's a ~ for you** ich weiß, es macht dir Sorgen; **what's your ~?** was drückt dich?; **that's the least of my worries** das macht mir noch am wenigsten Sorgen.
[2] *vt* **(a)** *(cause concern)* beunruhigen, Sorgen machen *(+dat)* ♦ **it worries me** es macht mir Sorgen; **you ~ me sometimes** manchmal machst du mir wirklich Sorgen; **it's no use just ~ing, do something** es hat keinen Zweck, sich nur den Kopf zu zerbrechen, tu endlich was; **to ~ oneself sick** *or* **silly/to death (about** *or* **over sth)** *(inf)* sich krank machen/sich umbringen vor Sorge (um *or* wegen etw) *(inf)*.
(b) *(bother)* stören ♦ **to ~ sb with sth** jdn mit etw stören; **don't ~ me with trivialities** komm mir nicht mit Kleinigkeiten; **to ~ sb for sth/to do sth** jdn um etw plagen/jdn plagen, etw zu tun.
(c) *(dog etc) sheep* nachstellen *(+dat)*; *(bite)* reißen; *bone* (herum)nagen an *(+dat)*.
[3] *vi* sich sorgen, sich *(dat)* Sorgen *or* Gedanken machen *(about, over* um, wegen) ♦ **he worries a lot** er macht sich immer soviel Sorgen; **don't ~!, not to ~!** keine Angst *or* Sorge!; **don't ~, I'll do it** laß mal, das mach ich schon; **he said not to ~** er sagte, wir sollten uns keine Sorgen machen; **don't ~ about letting me know** es macht nichts, wenn du mich nicht benachrichtigen kannst; **don't you ~ about that, I'll do it** mach dir darum keine Sorgen, das mach ich; **you should ~!** *(inf)* du hast (vielleicht) Sorgen!

worry beads *npl* Betperlen *pl*.

worrying ['wʌrɪɪŋ] [1] *adj problem* beunruhigend, besorgniserregend ♦ **it's very ~** es macht mir große Sorge; **I know it's ~ for you** ich weiß, es macht dir Sorgen; **it is a ~ time for us** wir haben zur Zeit viel Sorgen.
[2] *n* **~ won't help** sich nur Sorgen machen, nützt nichts.

worry line *n (on face)* Sorgenfalte *f*.

worse [wɜːs] [1] *adj, comp of* **bad** schlechter; *(morally, with bad consequences)* schlimmer, ärger ♦ **it gets ~ and ~** es wird immer schlimmer; **the patient is ~ than he was yesterday** dem Patienten geht es schlechter als gestern; **and to make matters ~** und zu allem Übel; **his "corrections" only made it ~** er hat alles nur verschlimmbessert; **it could have been ~** es hätte schlimmer kommen können; **~ luck!** (so ein) Pech!; **the patient gets** *or* **grows ~** der Zustand des Patienten verschlechtert sich *or* wird schlechter; **it will be the ~ for you** das wird für dich unangenehme Folgen haben; **so much the ~ for him** um so schlimmer; **to be the ~ for drink** betrunken sein; **he's none the ~ for it** er hat sich nichts dabei getan, es ist ihm nichts dabei passiert; **you'll be none the ~ for some work** etwas Arbeit wird dir nicht schaden; **I don't think any the ~ of you for it** ich halte deswegen aber nicht weniger von dir; **~ things happen at sea** *(inf)* es könnte schlimmer sein.
[2] *adv, comp of* **badly** schlechter ♦ **it hurts ~** es tut mehr weh; **to be ~ off than ...** schlechter dran sein *(inf) or* in einer schlechteren Lage sein als ...; **I could do a lot ~ than accept their offer** es wäre bestimmt kein Fehler, wenn ich das Angebot annähme.
[3] *n* Schlechtere(s) *nt*; *(morally, with regard to consequences)* Schlimmere(s) *nt* ♦ **there is ~ to come** es kommt noch schlimmer; **it's changed for the ~** es hat sich zum Schlechteren gewendet.

worsen ['wɜːsn] [1] *vt* verschlechtern, schlechter machen.
[2] *vi* sich verschlechtern, schlechter werden.

worship ['wɜːʃɪp] [1] *n* **(a)** *(of God, person etc)* Verehrung *f* ♦ **public ~** Gottesdienst *m*; **place of ~** Andachtsstätte *f*; *(non-Christian)* Kultstätte *f*.
(b) *(Brit: in titles)* **Your W~** *(to judge)* Euer Ehren/Gnaden; *(to mayor)* (verehrter *or* sehr geehrter) Herr Bürgermeister; **His W~ the Mayor of ...** der verehrte Bürgermeister von ...; **if your W~ wishes** wenn Euer Ehren *or* Gnaden wünschen.
[2] *vt* anbeten ♦ **he ~ped the ground she trod on** er betete den Boden unter ihren Füßen an.
[3] *vi (Rel)* den Gottesdienst abhalten; *(RC)* die Messe feiern ♦ **the church where we used to ~** die Kirche, die wir besuchten.

worshipful ['wɜːʃɪpfʊl] *adj* **(a)** *look, gaze* verehrend. **(b)** *(Brit: in titles)* sehr verehrt *or* geehrt.

worshipper ['wɜːʃɪpəʳ] *n* Kirchgänger(in *f*) *m* ♦ **~ of Baal** Baalsverehrer *m*; **~ of the sun** Sonnenanbeter(in *f*) *m*; **he was a lifelong ~ at this church** er ist sein Leben lang hier zur Kirche gegangen; **a ~ of wealth** jemand, der das Geld anbetet.

worst [wɜːst] [1] *adj, superl of* **bad** schlechteste(r, s); *(morally, with regard to consequences)* schlimmste(r, s) ♦ **the ~ possible time** die ungünstigste Zeit.
[2] *adv, superl of* **badly** am schlechtesten.
[3] *n* **the ~ is over** das Schlimmste *or* Ärgste ist vorbei; **in the ~ of the winter/storm** im ärgsten Winter/Sturm; **when the crisis/storm was at its ~** als die Krise/der Sturm ihren/seinen Höhepunkt erreicht hatte; **at (the) ~** schlimmstenfalls; **you've never seen him at his ~** er kann noch (viel) schlimmer (sein); **the ~ of it is ...** das Schlimmste daran ist, ...; **if the ~ comes to the ~** wenn alle Stricke reißen *(inf)*; **do your ~!** *(liter)* mach zu!; **to get the ~ of it** den kürzeren ziehen.
[4] *vt enemy, opponent* besiegen, schlagen.

worst case *n* Schlimmstfall *m*, ungünstigster Fall.

worst-case ['wɜːstkeɪs] *adj attr* Schlimmstfall-, für den ungünstigsten Fall.

worsted ['wʊstɪd] [1] *n (yarn)* Kammgarn *nt*; *(cloth also)* Kammgarnstoff *m*.
[2] *adj* Kammgarn-.

worth [wɜːθ] [1] *adj* **(a)** wert ♦ **it's ~ £5** es ist £ 5 wert; **it's not ~ £5** es ist keine £ 5 wert; **what's this ~?** was *or* wieviel ist das wert?; **it can't be ~ that!** soviel kann es unmöglich wert sein; **it's ~ a great deal to me** es ist mir viel wert; *(sentimentally)* es bedeutet mir sehr viel; **what's it ~ to me to do that?** *(in money)* was springt für mich dabei heraus? *(inf)*; *(in advantages)* was bringt es mir, wenn ich das tue?; **will you do this for me? — what's it ~ to you?** tust du das für mich? — was ist es dir wert?; **he was ~ a million** er besaß eine Million; **he's ~ all his brothers put together** er ist soviel wert wie all seine Brüder zusammen; **for all one is ~** so sehr man nur kann; **to sing/try for all one is ~** aus voller Kehle *or* vollem Halse singen/alles in seinen Kräften Stehende versuchen; **for what it's ~, I personally don't think ...** wenn mich einer fragt, ich persönlich glaube nicht, daß ...; **I'll tell you this for what it's ~** ich sage dir das, ich weiß nicht, ob was dran ist; **that's my opinion for what it's ~** das ist meine bescheidene Meinung; **it's more than my life/job is ~ to tell you** ich sage es dir nicht, dazu ist mir mein Leben zu lieb/dazu liegt mir zu viel an meiner Stelle.
(b) *(deserving, meriting)* wert ♦ **to be ~ it** sich lohnen; **to be ~ sth** etw wert sein; **it's not ~ it** es lohnt sich nicht; **it's not ~ the trouble** es ist der Mühe nicht wert; **the book is ~ reading** das Buch ist lesenswert; **life isn't ~ living** das Leben ist nicht lebenswert; **is there anything ~ seeing in this town?** gibt es in dieser Stadt etwas Sehenswertes?; **it's a film ~ seeing** es lohnt sich, diesen Film anzusehen; **hardly ~ mentioning** kaum der Rede wert; **an experience ~ having** eine lohnenswerte Erfahrung; **it's not ~ having** es ist nichts; **if a thing's ~ doing, it's ~ doing well** wenn schon, denn schon; *see* **salt 1 (a), while 1 (c)**.
[2] *n* Wert *m* ♦ **£50's ~ of books** Bücher im Werte von £ 50 *or* für £ 50; **a man of great ~** ein sehr wertvoller Mensch; **to show one's true ~** zeigen, was man wirklich wert ist, seinen wahren Wert zeigen; **to increase in ~** im Wert steigen; **what's the current ~ of this?** wieviel ist das momentan wert?; *see* **money**.

➤ LANGUAGE IN USE: **worse: 1** → 5.3, 26.2

worthily ['wɜːðɪlɪ] *adv* löblich, lobenswert.
worthiness ['wɜːðɪnɪs] *n* (*of charity, cause etc*) Wert *m*; (*of person*) Ehrenhaftigkeit *f*.
worthless ['wɜːθlɪs] *adj* wertlos; *person also* nichtsnutzig.
worthlessness ['wɜːθlɪsnɪs] *n see adj* Wertlosigkeit *f*; Nichtsnutzigkeit *f*.
worthwhile ['wɜːθ'waɪl] *adj* lohnend *attr* ◆ **to be ~** sich lohnen; (*worth the trouble also*) der Mühe (*gen*) wert sein; **it's a thoroughly ~ film/book** es lohnt sich wirklich, den Film zu sehen/das Buch zu lesen; **it's hardly ~ (asking him)** es lohnt sich wohl kaum(, ihn zu fragen); *see also* **while 1 (c).**
▼ **worthy** ['wɜːðɪ] 1 *adj* (*+er*) **(a)** ehrenwert, achtbar; *opponent* würdig; *motive, cause* lobenswert, löblich ◆ **my ~ friend/opponent** mein werter Freund/Widersacher.
▼ **(b)** *pred* wert, würdig ◆ **~ of remark/mention** bemerkenswert/erwähnenswert; **to be ~ of sb/sth** jds/einer Sache würdig sein (*geh*); **any journalist ~ of the name** jeder Journalist, der diesen Namen verdient; **this makes him ~ of (our) respect** dafür verdient er unseren Respekt; **he is ~ to be ranked among** ... er ist es wert, zu ... gezählt zu werden.
2 *n* (*hum*) **the local worthies** die Ortsgrößen *pl* (*hum*).
▼ **would** [wʊd] *pret of* **will**[1] *modal aux vb* **(a)** (*conditional*) **if you asked him he ~ do it** wenn du ihn fragtest, würde er es tun; **if you had asked him he ~ have done it** wenn du ihn gefragt hättest, hätte er es getan; **I thought you ~ want to know** ich dachte, du wüßtest es gerne *or* du würdest es gerne wissen; **who ~ have thought it?** wer hätte das gedacht?; **you ~ think** ... man sollte meinen ...
(b) (*in indirect speech*) **she said she ~ come** sie sagte, sie würde kommen *or* sie käme; **I said I ~, so I will** ich habe gesagt, ich würde es tun, und ich werde es auch tun.
(c) (*emph*) **you ~ be the one to get hit** typisch, daß ausgerechnet du getroffen worden bist; **you ~ be the one to forget** typisch, daß du das vergessen hast, das sieht dir ähnlich, daß du es vergessen hast; **I ~n't know** keine Ahnung; **you ~!** das sieht dir ähnlich!; **he ~ have to come right now** ausgerechnet jetzt muß er kommen; **you ~ think of that/say that, ~n't you!** von dir kann man ja nichts anderes erwarten; **it ~ have to rain** es muß auch ausgerechnet regnen!
(d) (*insistence*) **I warned him, but he ~ do it** ich habe ihn gewarnt, aber er mußte es ja unbedingt *or* um jeden Preis tun; **he ~n't listen/behave** er wollte partout nicht zuhören/sich partout nicht benehmen; **he ~n't be told** er wollte sich (*dat*) einfach nichts sagen lassen.
(e) (*conjecture*) **it ~ seem so** es sieht wohl so aus; **it ~ have been about 8 o'clock** es war (wohl) so ungefähr 8 Uhr; **what ~ this be?** was ist das wohl?; **you ~n't have a cigarette, ~ you?** Sie hätten nicht zufällig eine Zigarette?
(f) (*wish*) möchten ◆ **what ~ you have me do?** was soll ich tun?; **try as he ~** so sehr er es auch versuchte; **the place where I ~ be** (*old, liter*) der Ort, an dem ich sein möchte; **~ (that) it were not so!** (*old, liter*) wenn das doch nur nicht wahr wäre!; **~ to God he would come** gebe Gott, daß er kommt; **~ to God he hadn't come** ich wünsche zu Gott, er wäre nicht gekommen.
▼ **(g)** (*in questions*) **~ he come?** würde er vielleicht kommen?; **~ he have come?** wäre er gekommen?; **~ you mind closing the window?** würden Sie bitte das Fenster schließen?; **~ you care for some tea?** hätten Sie gerne etwas Tee?
(h) (*habit*) **he ~ paint it each year** er strich es jedes Jahr, er pflegte es jedes Jahr zu streichen (*geh*); **50 years ago the streets ~ be empty on a Sunday** vor 50 Jahren waren sonntags die Straßen immer leer.
would-be ['wʊdbiː] *adj attr* **~ poet/politician** jemand, der gerne (ein) Dichter/(ein) Politiker würde; (*pej*) Möchtegern-Dichter(in *f*) *m*/-Politiker(in *f*) *m*.
wouldn't ['wʊdnt] *contr of* **would not.**
wound[1] [wuːnd] 1 *n* (*lit*) Wunde *f*; (*fig also*) Kränkung *f* ◆ **my old war ~** meine alte Kriegsverletzung; **the ~ to his pride** sein verletzter Stolz; *see* **lick.**
2 *vt* (*lit*) verwunden, verletzen; (*fig*) verletzen ◆ **the ~ed** *pl* die Verwundeten *pl*; **~ed pride/vanity** verletzter Stolz/gekränkte Eitelkeit.
wound[2] [waʊnd] *pret, ptp of* **wind**[2].
wounding ['wuːndɪŋ] *adj remark, tone* verletzend.
wove [wəʊv] *pret of* **weave.**
woven ['wəʊvən] *ptp of* **weave.**
wow[1] [waʊ] 1 *interj* hui (*inf*), Mann (*inf*), Mensch (*inf*).
2 *n* (*sl*) **it's a ~** das ist Spitze (*inf*) *or* (*inf*).
wow[2] *n* (*on recording*) Jaulen *nt*.
WP *abbr of* **(a) word processor. (b)** (*Brit inf*) **weather permitting** bei gutem Wetter.
WPC (*Brit*) *n abbr of* **Woman Police Constable** Polizistin *f*.
wpm *abbr of* **words per minute** WpM, wpm.
WRAC [ræk] (*Brit*) *abbr of* **Women's Royal Army Corps.**
wrack[1] [ræk] *n* (*Bot*) Tang *m*.
wrack[2] *n, vt see* **rack**[1], **rack**[2].
WRAF [ræf] (*Brit*) *abbr of* **Women's Royal Air Force.**
wraith [reɪθ] *n* Gespenst *nt*, Geist *m*.
wraithlike ['reɪθlaɪk] *adj* durchgeistigt, ätherisch.
wrangle ['ræŋgl] 1 *n* Gerangel, Hin und Her *no pl nt*.
2 *vi* streiten, rangeln (*about* um); (*in bargaining*) feilschen.
wrangler ['ræŋgləʳ] *n* (*US: cowboy*) Cowboy *m*; (*Univ*) *Mathematikstudent in Cambridge, der mit Auszeichnung bestanden hat.*
wrap [ræp] 1 *n* **(a)** (*garment*) Umhangtuch *nt*; (*for child*) Wickeltuch *nt*; (*stole*) Stola *f*; (*cape*) Cape *nt*; (*coat*) Mantel *m*.
(b) under ~s (*lit*) verhüllt; (*car, weapon*) getarnt; (*fig*) geheim; **they took the ~s off the new project** sie haben, was das neue Projekt betrifft, die Katze aus dem Sack gelassen (*inf*).
(c) it's a ~ (*inf: completed*) das wär's.
2 *vt* **(a)** einwickeln; *parcel, present also* verpacken, einpacken, einschlagen; *person* (*for warmth*) einpacken (*inf*) ◆ **shall I ~ it for you?** soll ich es Ihnen einpacken *or* einwickeln?; **~ the joint in foil** den Braten in Folie einschlagen; **~ped cakes/bread** abgepackte Teilchen/abgepacktes Brot; **to ~ sth round sth** etw um etw wickeln; **he ~ped the car round a lamppost** (*inf*) er hat das Auto um eine Laterne gewickelt (*inf*); **to ~ one's arms round sb** jdn in die Arme schließen.
(b) (*fig*) **to be ~ped in sth** in etw gehüllt sein; **she lay ~ped in his arms** sie lag in seinen Armen; **~ped in secrecy** vom Schleier des Geheimnisses umhüllt.
3 *vi* (*Comput*) **the lines ~ automatically** der Zeilenumbruch erfolgt automatisch.
◆**wrap up** 1 *vt sep* **(a)** (*lit, fig*) einpacken, einwickeln, verpacken ◆ **an expensive deal cunningly ~ped ~ as a bargain** ein teurer Kauf, der geschickt als Sonderangebot getarnt ist/war.
(b) (*inf: finalize*) *deal* festmachen, unter Dach und Fach bringen ◆ **that just about ~s things ~ for today** das wär's (dann wohl) für heute.
(c) to be ~ped ~ in sb/sth in jdm/etw aufgehen.
2 *vi* **(a)** (*dress warmly*) sich warm einpacken (*inf*).
(b) (*sl: be quiet*) den Mund halten (*inf*).
wrap: ~(a)round, ~over *adj attr* Wickel-.
wrapper ['ræpəʳ] *n* **(a)** Verpackung *f*; (*of sweets*) Papier(chen) *nt*; (*of cigar*) Deckblatt *nt*; (*of book*) (Schutz)umschlag *m*; (*postal*) Streifband *nt*. **(b)** (*garment*) leichter Morgenmantel. **(c)** (*person: in factory etc*) Packer(in *f*) *m*.
wrapping ['ræpɪŋ] *n* Verpackung *f* (*round gen*, von) ◆ **~ paper** Packpapier *nt*; (*decorative*) Geschenkpapier *nt*.
wrath [rɒθ] *n* Zorn *m*; (*liter: of storm*) Wut *f*.
wrathful *adj*, **~ly** *adv* ['rɒθfʊl, -fəlɪ] wutentbrannt, zornentbrannt.
wreak [riːk] *vt destruction* anrichten; *chaos also* stiften; (*liter*) *vengeance* üben (*on* an *+dat*); (*liter*) *punishment* auferlegen (*on dat*); (*liter*) *anger* auslassen (*on* an *+dat*); *see* **havoc.**
wreath [riːθ] *n, pl* **-s** [riːðz] Kranz *m*; (*of smoke etc*) Kringel *m*.
wreathe [riːð] 1 *vt* (*encircle*) (um)winden; (*clouds, mist*) umhüllen; (*entwine*) flechten ◆ **a garland ~d the victor's head** ein Kranz (um)krönte das Haupt des Siegers; **his face was ~d in smiles** er strahlte über das ganze Gesicht.
2 *vi* **the smoke ~d upwards** der Rauch stieg in Kringeln auf; **to ~ round sth** (*ivy etc*) sich um etw ranken; (*snake*) sich um etw schlängeln *or* ringeln; (*smoke*) sich um etw kringeln *or* kräuseln; (*mist*) um etw wallen.
wreck [rek] 1 *n* **(a)** (*Naut*) Schiffbruch *m*; (*~ed ship, car, train*) Wrack *nt* ◆ **lost in the ~** beim Schiffbruch verloren.
(b) (*fig*) (*old bicycle, furniture etc*) Trümmerhaufen *m*; (*person*) Wrack *nt*; (*of hopes, life, marriage etc*) Trümmer, Ruinen *pl* ◆ **I'm a ~, I feel a ~** ich bin ein (völliges) Wrack; (*exhausted*) ich bin vollkommen fertig *or* erledigt; (*in appearance*) ich sehe verheerend *or* unmöglich aus; *see* **nervous ~.**
2 *vt* **(a)** *ship, train, plane* zum Wrack machen, einen Totalschaden verursachen an (*+dat*); *car* kaputtfahren (*inf*), zu Schrott fahren (*inf*); *machine, mechanism* zerstören, kaputtmachen (*inf*); *furniture, house* zerstören; (*person*) zertrümmern, kurz und klein schlagen (*inf*) ◆ **to be ~ed** (*Naut*) Schiffbruch erleiden; **~ed ship/car** wrackes *or* havariertes Schiff/zu Schrott gefahrenes Auto.
(b) (*fig*) *hopes, plans, chances* zunichte machen; *marriage* zerrütten; *career, health, sb's life* zerstören, ruinieren; *person* kaputtmachen (*inf*); *party, holiday* verderben.
wreckage ['rekɪdʒ] *n* (*lit, fig: remains*) Trümmer *pl*; (*of ship also*) Wrackteile *pl*; (*washed ashore*) Strandgut *nt*; (*of house, town also*) Ruinen *pl*.
wrecker ['rekəʳ] *n* **(a)** (*ship~*) Strandräuber (*der Schiffe durch falsche Lichtsignale zum Stranden bringt*).
(b) (*Naut: salvager*) Bergungsarbeiter *m*; (*vessel*) Bergungsschiff *nt*.
(c) (*US: breaker, salvager*) Schrotthändler *m*; (*for buildings*) Abbrucharbeiter *m*.
(d) (*US: breakdown van*) Abschleppwagen *m*.
wrecking ['rekɪŋ]: **~ ball** *n* Abrißbirne *f*; **~ bar** *n* (*US*) Brechstange *f*; **~ service** *n* (*US Aut*) Abschleppdienst *m*.
wren [ren] *n* Zaunkönig *m*.
Wren [ren] *n* (*Brit*) *weibliches Mitglied der britischen Marine.*
wrench [rentʃ] 1 *n* **(a)** (*tug*) Ruck *m*; (*Med*) Verrenkung *f* ◆ **to give sth a ~** einer Sache (*dat*) einen Ruck geben; **he gave his shoulder a nasty ~** er hat sich (*dat*) die Schulter schlimm verrenkt. **(b)** (*tool*) Schraubenschlüssel *m*.
(c) (*fig*) **to be a ~** weh tun; **the ~ of parting** der Trennungsschmerz.
2 *vt* **(a)** winden ◆ **to ~ sth (away) from sb** jdm etw entwinden; **to ~ a door open** eine Tür aufzwingen; **to ~ a door off its hinges** eine Tür aus den Angeln reißen; **he ~ed the steering wheel round** er riß das Lenkrad herum; **to ~ sb's arm out of its socket** jdm den Arm ausrenken.
(b) (*Med*) **to ~ one's ankle/shoulder** sich (*dat*) den Fuß/die Schulter verrenken.
(c) (*fig*) reißen ◆ **if you could ~ yourself away from the TV** wenn du dich vom Fernseher losreißen könntest.
wrest [rest] *vt* **to ~ sth from sb/sth** jdm/einer Sache etw abringen; (*leadership, title*) jdm etw entreißen; **to ~ sth from sb's grasp** jdm etw entreißen; **to ~ sb/oneself free** jdn/sich losreißen.
wrestle ['resl] 1 *n* Ringkampf *m* ◆ **to have a ~ with sb** mit jdm ringen.
2 *vt* ringen mit; (*Sport also*) einen Ringkampf bestreiten gegen ◆ **he ~d the thief to the ground** er brachte *or* zwang den Dieb zu Boden.

[3] *vi* **(a)** (*lit*) ringen (*for sth* um etw). **(b)** (*fig: with problem, conscience etc*) ringen, kämpfen (*with* mit) • **the pilot ~d with the controls** der Pilot kämpfte mit den Instrumenten.

wrestler ['reslə^r] *n* Ringkämpfer *m*; (*modern*) Ringer(in *f*) *m*.

wrestling ['reslɪŋ] *n* Ringen *nt* • **~ as a discipline** Ringen *or* der Ringkampf als Disziplin.

wrestling *in cpds* Ringer-; **~ match** *n* Ringkampf *m*.

wretch [retʃ] *n* **(a)** (*miserable*) armer Teufel *or* Schlucker (*inf*). **(b)** (*contemptible*) Wicht, Schuft *m*; (*nuisance*) Blödmann *m* (*inf*); (*child*) Schlingel *m*.

wretched ['retʃɪd] *adj* **(a)** elend; *conditions, life, clothing etc also* erbärmlich; (*ill also*) miserabel (*inf*); (*unhappy, depressed*) (tod)unglücklich • **I feel ~** (*ill*) mir geht es miserabel (*inf*), ich fühle mich elend; **I feel ~ about having to say no** es tut mir in der Seele weh, daß ich nein sagen muß.
(b) (*very bad*) *housing conditions, weather, novel, player* erbärmlich, miserabel (*inf*); (*inf: damned*) verflixt, elend, Mist- (*all inf*) • **what a ~ thing to do!** so etwas Schäbiges!; **what ~ luck!** was für ein verflixtes *or* elendes Pech (*inf*).

wretchedly ['retʃɪdlɪ] *adv* **(a)** (*in misery*) erbärmlich; *weep, apologize, look* kläglich; (*very badly also*) miserabel (*inf*). **(b)** (*inf: extremely*) verflixt (*inf*), verdammt (*inf*).

wretchedness ['retʃɪdnɪs] *n* Erbärmlichkeit *f*; (*of person: misery*) Elend *nt* • **the ~ of his health** seine miserable (*inf*) *or* elende Gesundheit.

wrick [rɪk] [1] *vt* **to ~ one's neck/shoulder** sich (*dat*) den Hals/die Schulter ausrenken.
[2] *n* **to have/get a ~ in one's neck** sich (*dat*) den Hals ausgerenkt haben/sich (*dat*) den Hals ausrenken.

wriggle ['rɪgl] [1] *n* Schlängeln *nt no pl*; (*of child, fish*) Zappeln *nt no pl* • **with a sensuous ~ she ...** sie räkelte sich sinnlich und ...; **to give a ~** *see vi*.
[2] *vt toes, ears* wackeln mit • **to ~ one's way through sth** sich durch etw (hin)durchwinden *or* -schlängeln.
[3] *vi* (*also* **~ about** *or* **around**) (*worm, snake, eel*) sich schlängeln; (*fish*) sich winden, zappeln; (*person*) (*restlessly, excitedly*) zappeln; (*in embarrassment*) sich winden • **to ~ along/down** sich vorwärts schlängeln/sich nach unten schlängeln; **the fish ~d off the hook** der Fisch wand sich vom Haken; **she managed to ~ free** es gelang ihr, sich loszuwinden; **he ~d through the hole in the hedge** er wand *or* schlängelte sich durch das Loch in der Hecke; **do stop wriggling about** hör endlich mit der Zappelei auf.

◆**wriggle out** *vi* (*lit*) sich herauswinden (*of* aus); (*fig also*) sich herausmanövrieren (*of* aus) • **he's ~d (his way) ~ of it** er hat sich gedrückt.

wriggly ['rɪglɪ] *adj* (*+er*) sich windend *attr*, sich krümmend *attr*; *fish, child* zappelnd *attr*.

wring [rɪŋ] (*vb: pret, ptp* **wrung**) [1] *vt* **(a)** (*also* **~ out**) *clothes, wet rag etc* auswringen, auswinden • **to ~ water out of clothes** (nasse) Kleider auswringen *or* auswinden; **do not ~** (*on washing instructions*) nicht wringen.
(b) *hands* (*in distress*) ringen • **to ~ a duck's neck** einer Ente (*dat*) den Hals umdrehen; **I could have wrung his neck** ich hätte ihm den Hals *or* Kragen (*inf*) umdrehen können; **he wrung my hand** er schüttelte mir (kräftig) die Hand; **to ~ sb's heart** jdm in der Seele weh tun.
(c) (*extract*) **to ~ sth out of** *or* **from sb** etw aus jdm herausquetschen, jdm etw abringen.
[2] *n* **to give clothes a ~** Kleider auswringen *or* auswinden.

wringer ['rɪŋə^r] *n* (Wäsche)mangel *f*.

wringing ['rɪŋɪŋ] *adj* (*also* **~ wet**) tropfnaß; *person also* patschnaß (*inf*).

wrinkle ['rɪŋkl] [1] *n* **(a)** (*in clothes, paper*) Knitter *m*; (*on face, skin*) Runzel, Falte *f*; (*in stocking*) Falte *f*. **(b)** (*inf: dodge, scheme*) Kniff *m* (*inf*).
[2] *vt fabric, paper, surface, sheet* verknittern, verkrumpeln (*inf*); *skin* runzlig *or* faltig machen • **to ~ one's nose/brow** die Nase rümpfen/die Stirne runzeln.
[3] *vi* (*sheet, material*) (ver)knittern; (*stockings*) Falten schlagen; (*skin etc*) runzlig *or* faltig werden.

◆**wrinkle up** *vt sep nose* rümpfen.

wrinkled ['rɪŋkld] *adj sheet, skirt, paper* zerknittert; *stockings* Ziehharmonika- (*inf*); *skin* runzlig, faltig; *brow* gerunzelt; *apple, old lady* schrumpelig, verschrumpelt.

wrinkly ['rɪŋklɪ] [1] *adj* (*+er*) schrumpelig; *fabric* zerknittert.
[2] *n* (*inf: old person*) Mummelgreis (*inf*), Grufti (*sl*) *m*.

wrist [rɪst] *n* Handgelenk *nt* • **to slash one's ~s** sich (*dat*) die Pulsadern aufschneiden.

wristband ['rɪst,bænd] *n* Armband *nt*; (*on dress, shirt*) Ärmelbündchen *nt*; (*Sport*) Schweißband *nt*.

wristlet ['rɪstlɪt] *n* Armband nt.

wrist: ~ lock *n* Polizeigriff *m*; **to put a ~ lock on sb** jdn im Polizeigriff halten; **~watch** *n* Armbanduhr *f*.

writ [rɪt] *n* **(a)** (*Jur*) Verfügung *f* • **~ of attachment** Haft- *or* Verhaftungsbefehl *m*; **~ of execution** Vollstreckungsbefehl *m*; **to issue a ~** eine Verfügung herausgeben; **to issue a ~ against sb** jdn vorladen (*for* wegen). **(b) Holy W~** (*old, form*) Heilige Schrift.

▼ **write** [raɪt] *pret* **wrote** *or* (*obs*) **writ** [rɪt], *ptp* **written** *or* (*obs*) **writ** [rɪt] [1] *vt* **(a)** (*also Comput*) schreiben; *cheque also, copy* ausstellen; *notes* sich (*dat*) aufschreiben, sich (*dat*) machen; *application form* ausfüllen • **he wrote me a letter** er schrieb mir einen Brief; **he wrote himself a note to remind him** er machte sich (*dat*) eine Notiz, um sich zu erinnern; **he wrote five sheets of paper** er schrieb fünf Seiten voll; **print your name, don't ~ it** schreiben Sie Ihren Namen in Druckschrift, nicht in Schreibschrift; **how is that written?** wie schreibt man das?; **to ~ sth to disk** etw auf Diskette schreiben; **it is written that ...** (*old*) es steht geschrieben, daß ...; **writ(ten) large** (*fig*) verdeutlicht; (*on a larger scale*) im Großen; **it was written all over his face** es stand ihm im *or* auf dem Gesicht geschrieben; **he had "policeman" written all over him** man sah ihm den Polizisten schon von weitem an; *see* **shorthand**.
(b) (*Insur*) *policy* abschließen.

▼[2] *vi* schreiben • **as I ~ ...** während ich dies schreibe, ...; **to ~ to sb** jdm schreiben; **we ~ to each other** wir schreiben uns; **I wrote to him to come** ich habe ihm geschrieben, er solle kommen *or* daß er kommen solle; **that's nothing to ~ home about** (*inf*) das ist nichts Weltbewegendes; **I'll ~ for it at once** ich bestelle es sofort, ich fordere es gleich an; **he always wanted to ~** er wollte immer (ein) Schriftsteller werden.

◆**write away** *vi* schreiben • **to ~ ~ for sth** etw anfordern; **he wrote ~ asking for further information** er forderte weitere Information an, er schrieb um weitere Information.

◆**write back** *vi* zurückschreiben, antworten • **he wrote ~ saying ...** er schrieb zurück, um mir zu sagen, ...

◆**write down** *vt sep* (*make a note of*) aufschreiben; (*record, put in writing*) niederschreiben.

◆**write in** [1] *vt sep* **(a)** *word, correction etc* hineinschreiben, einfügen (*prep obj* in *+acc*).
(b) (*US Pol*) **to ~ sb ~** seine Stimme für jdn abgeben, der nicht in der Liste aufgeführt ist.
(c) (*build in*) *condition, provision* aufnehmen • **is there anything written ~ about that?** steht was dazu drin?
[2] *vi* schreiben (*to* an *+acc*) • **someone has written ~ (to us) requesting this record** jemand hat uns (*dat*) geschrieben und uns um diese Platte gebeten; **to ~ ~ for sth** etw anfordern, um etw schreiben.

◆**write off** [1] *vi see* **write away**.
[2] *vt sep* **(a)** (*write quickly*) (schnell) hinschreiben; *essay, poem* herunterschreiben. **(b)** *debt, losses*, (*fig: regard as failure*) abschreiben. **(c)** *car etc* (*driver*) zu Schrott fahren; (*insurance company*) als Totalschaden abschreiben.

◆**write out** *vt sep* **(a)** (*in full*) *notes* ausarbeiten; *name etc* ausschreiben. **(b)** *cheque, prescription* ausstellen. **(c)** *actor, character* einen Abgang schaffen (*+dat*) • **he's been written ~** ihm wurde ein Abgang aus der Serie geschaffen.

◆**write up** *vt sep notes* ausarbeiten; *report, diary* schreiben; *event* schreiben über (*+acc*); (*review*) *play, film* eine Kritik schreiben über (*+acc*).

write: ~-in *n* (*US*) Stimmabgabe *f* für einen nicht in der Liste aufgeführten Kandidaten; **~-off** *n* **(a)** (*car etc*) Totalschaden *m*; (*inf: holiday, picnic etc*) Katastrophe *f* (*inf*); **(b)** (*Comm*) Abschreibung *f*.

write-protected ['raɪtprə,tektɪd] *adj* (*Comput*) schreibgeschützt.

writer ['raɪtə^r] *n* Schreiber(in *f*) *m*; (*of scenario, report etc also*) Autor(in *f*) *m*; (*of TV commercials, subtitles*) Texter(in *f*) *m*; (*of music*) Komponist(in *f*) *m*; (*as profession*) Schriftsteller (in *f*) *m* • **the (present) ~** der Schreiber (dieser Zeilen/dieses Artikels *etc*); **he's a very poor ~** er schreibt sehr schlecht; (*correspondent*) er ist kein großer Briefschreiber; **~'s cramp** Schreibkrampf *m*.

write-up ['raɪtʌp] *n* Pressebericht *m*; (*of play, film*) Kritik *f*.

writhe [raɪð] *vi* sich krümmen, sich winden (*with, in* vor *+dat*) • **to ~ in ecstasy** sich vor Lust wälzen; **to make sb ~** (*painfully*) jdn vor Schmerzen zusammenzucken lassen; (*with disgust*) jdm kalte Schauer über den Rücken jagen, jdn erschauern lassen; (*with embarrassment*) jdn in peinliche Verlegenheit bringen.

writing ['raɪtɪŋ] *n* Schrift *f*; (*act, profession*) Schreiben *nt*; (*inscription*) Inschrift *f* • **at the time of ~** als dies geschrieben wurde; (*in present*) während ich dies schreibe; **in ~** schriftlich; **permission in ~** schriftliche Genehmigung; **to commit sth to ~** etw schriftlich festhalten; **this is a nice piece of ~** das ist gut geschrieben; **his ~s** seine Werke *or* Schriften; **in sb's own ~** (*not typed*) handgeschrieben; (*not written by sb else*) in jds eigener (Hand)schrift (*dat*); **he earns a bit from his ~** er verdient sich ein bißchen (Geld) mit Schreiben; **the ~ is on the wall for them** ihre Stunde hat geschlagen; **he had seen the ~ on the wall** er hat die Zeichen erkannt.

writing *in cpds* Schreib-; **~ case** *n* Schreibmappe *f*; **~ desk** *n* Schreibtisch *m*, Schreibpult *nt*; **~ pad** *n* Schreib- *or* Notizblock *m*; **~ paper** *n* Schreibpapier *nt*.

written ['rɪtn] [1] *ptp of* **write**.
[2] *adj examination, statement, evidence* schriftlich; *language* Schrift-; *word* geschrieben.

WRNS [renz] (*Brit*) *abbr of* **Women's Royal Naval Service**.

▼ **wrong** [rɒŋ] [1] *adj* **(a)** falsch; (*when choice is given also*) verkehrt • **to be ~** nicht stimmen; (*person*) unrecht haben; (*answer also*) falsch *or* verkehrt sein; (*watch*) falsch gehen; **it's all ~** das ist völlig verkehrt *or* falsch; (*not true*) das stimmt alles nicht; **it's all ~ that I should have to ...** das ist doch nicht richtig, daß ich ... muß; **I was ~ about him** ich habe mich in ihm getäuscht *or* geirrt; **you were ~ in thinking he did it** du hast unrecht gehabt, als du dachtest, er sei es gewesen; **how ~ can you get!** falscher geht's (wohl) nicht!; **I took a ~ turning** ich habe eine verkehrte *or* falsche Abzweigung genommen; **he went in the ~ direction** er ging in die verkehrte *or* falsche Richtung; **this is the ~ train for Bournemouth** dies ist der falsche Zug, wenn Sie nach Bournemouth wollen; **to say/do the ~ thing** das Falsche sagen/tun; **the ~ side of the fabric** die Abseite *or* die linke Seite des Stoffes; **you live in the ~ part of town** du wohnst nicht im richtigen Stadtteil; **he's got the ~ kind of friends** er hat die falschen Freunde; **you've come to the ~ man** *or* **person/place** da sind Sie an den Falschen/an die Falsche/an die falsche Adresse geraten; **brown is definitely the ~ colour to be wearing this season** Braun ist diese Saison absolut nicht modern; **I feel all ~ here** ich fühle mich hier völlig fehl am Platz; **it's the ~ time for jokes** es ist nicht die

➤ LANGUAGE IN USE: **write: 2** → 21.1, 21.2 **wrong: 1a** → 12.1, 14 richtige Zeit für Witze; **it's the ~ time and the ~ place for that** das ist weder die Zeit noch der Ort dafür; **to do sth the ~ way** etw falsch *or* verkehrt machen; *see* **number, side.**

(b) (*morally*) schlecht, unrecht; (*unfair*) ungerecht, unfair ◆ **it's ~ to steal** es ist unrecht zu stehlen, Stehlen ist Unrecht; **that was very ~ of you** das war absolut nicht richtig von dir; **you were ~ to do that** es war nicht richtig *or* recht von dir, das zu tun; **it's ~ of you to laugh** Sie sollten nicht lachen; **it's ~ that he should have to ask** es ist unrecht *or* falsch, daß er überhaupt fragen muß; **what's ~ with a drink now and again?** was ist schon (Schlimmes) dabei, wenn man ab und zu einen trinkt?; **what's ~ with working on Sundays?** was ist denn schon dabei, wenn man sonntags arbeitet?; **I don't see anything ~ in** *or* **with that** ich kann nichts Falsches daran finden, ich finde nichts daran auszusetzen.

(c) *pred* (*amiss*) **something is ~** (irgend) etwas stimmt nicht *or* ist nicht in Ordnung (*with* mit); (*suspiciously*) irgend etwas stimmt da nicht *or* ist da faul (*inf*); **is anything** *or* **something ~?** ist was? (*inf*); **there's nothing ~** (es ist) alles in Ordnung; **what's ~?** was ist los?; **what's ~ with you?** was fehlt Ihnen?; **there's nothing medically ~ with her** medizinisch (gesehen) fehlt ihr nichts; **I hope there's nothing ~ at home** ich hoffe, daß zu Hause alles in Ordnung ist; **to be ~ in the head** (*inf*) nicht ganz richtig (im Oberstübchen) sein (*inf*).

[2] *adv* falsch ◆ **you do him ~** du tust ihm unrecht; **you did ~ to do it** es war falsch *or* unrecht *or* nicht richtig von dir, das zu tun; **to get sth ~** sich mit etw vertun; **he got the answer ~** er hat die falsche Antwort gegeben; (*Math*) er hat sich verrechnet; **I think you got things a bit ~** ich glaube, Sie sehen die Sache *or* das nicht ganz richtig; **to get one's sums ~** sich verrechnen; **you've got him ~** (*misunderstood*) Sie haben ihn falsch verstanden; (*he's not like that*) Sie haben sich in ihm getäuscht; **to go ~** (*on route*) falsch gehen/fahren; (*in calculation*) einen Fehler machen; (*morally*) auf Abwege geraten; (*plan etc*) schiefgehen; (*affair etc*) schieflaufen; **my washing-machine has gone ~** meine Waschmaschine ist nicht in Ordnung; **I hope the television doesn't go ~** hoffentlich bleibt der Fernseher in Ordnung; **you can't go ~** du kannst gar nichts verkehrt machen; **you can't go ~ if you buy him a bottle of whisky** mit einer Flasche Whisky liegst du bei ihm immer richtig.

[3] *n* Unrecht *nt no pl* ◆ **(social) ~s** (soziale) Ungerechtigkeiten *pl*; **to be in the ~** im Unrecht sein; **to put sb in the ~** jdn ins Unrecht setzen; **to labour under a sense of ~** ein altes Unrecht nicht vergessen können; **two ~s don't make a right** Unrecht und Unrecht ergibt noch kein Recht; **to do sb ~/a great ~** jdm Unrecht/(ein) großes Unrecht (an)tun; **he can do no ~** er macht natürlich immer alles richtig; **all the little ~s he'd done her** all die kleinen Kränkungen, die er ihr zugefügt hat.

[4] *vt* **to ~ sb** jdm unrecht tun; **to be ~ed** ungerecht behandelt werden.

wrongdoer ['rɒŋ,duːəʳ] *n* Missetäter(in *f*), Übeltäter(in *f*) *m*.

wrongdoing ['rɒŋ,duːɪŋ] *n* Missetaten *pl*; (*single act*) Missetat, Übeltat *f*.

wrong-foot [,rɒŋ'fʊt] *vt* (*Sport*) auf dem falschen Fuß erwischen.

wrongful ['rɒŋfʊl] *adj* ungerechtfertigt.

wrongfully ['rɒŋfəlɪ] *adv* zu Unrecht.

wrong-headed ['rɒŋ'hedɪd] *adj* querköpfig, verbohrt (*about sth* in etw *acc or dat*).

wrong-headedness ['rɒŋ'hedɪdnɪs] *n* Verbohrtheit *f*.

wrongly ['rɒŋlɪ] *adv* **(a)** (*unjustly, improperly*) unrecht; *punished, accused* zu Unrecht. **(b)** (*incorrectly*) falsch, verkehrt; *maintain* zu Unrecht; *believe* fälschlicherweise.

wrongness ['rɒŋnɪs] *n* (*incorrectness*) Unrichtigkeit *f*; (*unfairness*) Ungerechtigkeit *f* ◆ **the ~ of your behaviour** dein falsches Benehmen.

wrote [rəʊt] *pret of* **write.**

wrought [rɔːt] [1] *vt* **(a)** (*obs, liter*) *pret, ptp of* **work.**
(b) **great changes have been ~** große Veränderungen wurden errungen *or* herbeigeführt; **the accident ~ havoc with his plans** der Unfall durchkreuzte alle seine Pläne; **the storm ~ great destruction** der Sturm richtete große Verheerungen an.
[2] *adj iron* Schmiede-; *silver* getrieben, gehämmert.

wrought: ~-iron *adj* schmiedeeisern *attr*, aus Schmiedeeisen; **~-iron gate** schmiedeeisernes Tor; **~-ironwork** *n* Kunstschmiedearbeit *f*; **~-up** *adj* **to be ~-up** aufgelöst sein, außer sich (*dat*) sein.

wrung [rʌŋ] *pret, ptp of* **wring.**

WRVS (*Brit*) *abbr of* **Women's Royal Voluntary Service.**

wry [raɪ] *adj* (*ironical*) ironisch; *joke, sense of humour etc* trocken ◆ **to make** *or* **pull a ~ face** das Gesicht verziehen.

wryly ['raɪlɪ] *adv* ironisch.

WSW *abbr of* **west-south-west** WSW.

wt *abbr of* **weight** Gew.

wuss [wʊs] *n* (*esp US inf*) Waschlappen *m* (*inf*).

WWW (*Comput*) *abbr of* **World Wide Web** WWW.

WX *abbr of* **women's extra-large size.**

wych-elm ['wɪtʃ'elm] *n see* **witch elm.**

wych-hazel ['wɪtʃ,heɪzl] *n see* **witch hazel.**

WYSIWYG ['wɪzɪwɪg] *n* (*Comput*) *abbr of* **what you see is what you get** WYSIWYG *nt*.

➤ LANGUAGE IN USE: **wrong: 1b** → 18.3, 26.3

X, x [eks] *n* (**a**) X, x *nt*. (**b**) (*Math, fig: number*) x ◆ **Mr ~** Herr X; **~ pounds** x Pfund; **~ marks the spot** die Stelle ist mit einem Kreuzchen gekennzeichnet. (**c**) **~-certificate film** für Jugendliche nicht geeigneter Film, für Jugendliche ab 18 Jahren freigegebener Film.

X chromosome *n* X-Chromosom *nt*.

xenophobe ['zenəfəʊb] *n* Fremdenhasser *m*.

xenophobia [,zenə'fəʊbɪə] *n* Fremdenfeindlichkeit *f*, Fremdenhaß *m*, Xenophobie (*liter*) *f*.

xenophobic [,zenə'fəʊbɪk] *adj* fremdenfeindlich, xenophob (*liter*).

Xerox ® ['zɪərɒks] [1] *n* (*copy*) Xerokopie *f*; (*process*) Xeroxverfahren *nt*.
[2] *vt* xerokopieren.

XL *abbr of* **extra large**.

Xmas ['eksməs, 'krɪsməs] *n* = **Christmas** Weihnachten *nt*.

X-ray ['eks'reɪ] [1] *n* Röntgenstrahl *m*; (*also* **~ photograph**) Röntgenaufnahme *f or* -bild *nt* ◆ **to take an ~ of sth** etw röntgen, eine Röntgenaufnahme von etw machen; **to have an ~** geröntgt werden; **she has gone in for an ~** sie ist zum Röntgen gegangen.
[2] *vt person, heart* röntgen, durchleuchten (*dated*); *envelope* durchleuchten.

X-ray *in cpds* Röntgen-; **~ examination** *n* Röntgenuntersuchung *f*, röntgenologische Untersuchung; **~ eyes** *npl* (*fig*) Röntgenaugen *pl*.

xylograph ['zaɪləgrɑːf] *n* Holzschnitt *m*.

xylography [zaɪ'lɒgrəfɪ] *n* Holzschneidekunst, Xylographie *f*.

xylophone ['zaɪləfəʊn] *n* Xylophon *nt*.

Y, y [waɪ] *n* Y, y *nt.*

yacht [jɒt] [1] *n* Jacht, Yacht *f* ♦ **~ club** Jacht- *or* Segelklub *m*; **~ race** (Segel)regatta *f.*
[2] *vi* segeln ♦ **to go ~ing** segeln gehen; (*on cruise*) eine Segeltour *or* einen Törn machen.

yachting ['jɒtɪŋ] *n* Segeln *nt.*

yachting: ~ cap *n* Seglermütze *f*; **~ circles** *npl* Seglerkreise *pl*; **~ cruise** *n* (Segel)kreuzfahrt, Segelreise *f*; **~ holiday** *n* Segelurlaub *m*; **~ jacket** *n* Segeljacke *f.*

yachtsman ['jɒtsmən] *n, pl* **-men** [-mən] Segler *m.*

yachtsmanship ['jɒtsmənʃɪp] *n* Segelkunst *f.*

yackety-yak ['jækɪtɪ'jæk] (*inf*) [1] *vi* schnattern (*inf*), quasseln (*inf*) ♦ **listen to those two, ~** hör dir mal die beiden Schnattergänse an (*inf*); **it was ~ all evening** den ganzen Abend nichts als Gequatsche (*inf*) *or* Geschnatter (*inf*).
[2] *n* Blabla (*pej inf*), Gequassel (*pej inf*) *nt.*

yah [jɑː] *interj* (*expressing disgust*) uh, igittigitt; (*expressing derision*) ätsch, hähä.

yahoo [jɑː'huː] *n* Schwein *nt* (*inf*).

yak[1] [jæk] *n* (*Zool*) Jak, Yak, Grunzochse *m.*

yak[2] *vi* (*inf*) schnattern (*inf*), quasseln (*inf*).

Yale lock ® ['jeɪl,lɒk] *n* Sicherheitsschloß *nt.*

yam [jæm] *n* **(a)** (*plant*) Yamswurzel *f.* **(b)** (*US: sweet potato*) Süßkartoffel, Batate *f.*

yammer ['jæməʳ] *vi* (*inf: moan*) jammern.

yank [jæŋk] [1] *n* Ruck *m* ♦ **give it a good ~** zieh mal kräftig dran.
[2] *vt* **to ~ sth** mit einem Ruck an etw (*dat*) ziehen, einer Sache (*dat*) einen Ruck geben; **he ~ed the rope free** er riß das Seil los.

♦**yank off** *vt sep* abreißen.

♦**yank out** *vt sep* ausreißen; *tooth* ziehen.

Yank [jæŋk] [1] *n* Ami (*inf*) *m.*
[2] *adj attr* Ami- (*inf*).

Yankee ['jæŋkɪ] (*inf*) [1] *n* Yankee (*inf*) *m*; (*Hist auch*) Nordstaatler *m.*
[2] *adj attr* Yankee- (*inf*).

yap [jæp] [1] *vi* (*dog*) kläffen; (*talk noisily*) quatschen (*inf*), labern (*inf*) ♦ **it's been ~, ~, ~ all day** von morgen bis abends nur Gequatsche (*inf*).
[2] *n* (*of dog*) Kläffen, Gekläff *nt*; (*inf: of person*) Gequatsche (*inf*), Gelaber (*inf*) *nt* ♦ **she spoke in a high-pitched ~** sie schnatterte mit schriller Stimme (*inf*).

yapping ['jæpɪŋ] [1] *adj dog* kläffend; (*inf*) *women* quatschend (*inf*).
[2] *n see* **yap 2.**

yard[1] [jɑːd] *n* **(a)** (*Measure*) Yard *nt* (*0.91 m*) ♦ **he can't see a ~ in front of him** er kann keinen Meter weit sehen; **to buy cloth by the ~** ≃ Stoff meterweise *or* im Meter kaufen; **he pulled out ~s of handkerchief** (*inf*) er zog ein riesiges Taschentuch hervor (*inf*); **words a ~ long** (*inf*) Bandwurmwörter *pl* (*inf*); **to have a face a ~ long** (*inf*) ein Gesicht wie drei Tage Regenwetter machen (*inf*); **calculations by the ~** (*fig*) endlose Zahlenkolonnen *pl*; **he wrote poetry by the ~** er produzierte Gedichte am Fließband *or* am laufenden Meter.
(b) (*Naut*) Rah *f.*

yard[2] *n* **(a)** (*of farm, hospital, prison, school, house etc*) Hof *m* ♦ **back ~** Hinterhof *m*; **in the ~** auf dem Hof.
(b) (*worksite*) Werksgelände *nt*; (*for storage*) Lagerplatz *m* ♦ **builder's ~** Bauhof *m*; **shipbuilding ~** Werft *f*; **timber ~** Holzlager(platz *m*) *nt*; **naval (dock)~**, (*US*) **navy ~** Marinewerft *f*; **railway ~** Rangierbahnhof, Verschiebebahnhof *m*; **goods ~**, (*US*) **freight ~** Güterbahnhof *m.*
(c) the Y~, Scotland Y~ Scotland Yard *m.*
(d) (*US: garden*) Garten *m.*

yardage ['jɑːdɪdʒ] *n* Anzahl *f* von Yards, ≃ Meterzahl *f.*

yardarm *n* (*Naut*) Nock *f*; **to hang sb from the ~-arm** jdn am Mast aufknüpfen.

Yardie ['jɑːdɪ] *n* (*Brit*) *Mitglied nt einer geheimen Verbrecherorganisation in Jamaika.*

yardstick *n* **(a)** (*measuring rod*) Elle *f*; **(b)** (*fig*) Maßstab *m.*

yarn [jɑːn] [1] *n* **(a)** (*Tex*) Garn *nt.* **(b)** (*tale*) Seemannsgarn *nt* ♦ **to spin a ~** Seemannsgarn spinnen; **to spin sb a ~ about sth** jdm eine Lügengeschichte über etw (*acc*) erzählen.
[2] *vi* Seemannsgarn spinnen, Geschichten erzählen.

yarrow ['jærəʊ] *n* (*Bot*) (gemeine) Schafgarbe.

yashmak ['jæʃmæk] *n* Schleier *m* (*von Moslemfrauen*).

yaw [jɔː] [1] *vi* (*Naut*) gieren, vom Kurs abkommen; (*Aviat, Space*) (*off course*) vom Kurs abkommen *or* abweichen; (*about axis*) gieren ♦ **it ~ed 20 degrees to port** es gierte um 20 Grad nach Backbord.
[2] *n see vi* Kursabweichung, Gierung *f*, Gieren *nt.*

yawl [jɔːl] *n* (*Naut*) (*rowing boat*) Beiboot *nt*; (*sailing boat*) (Segel)jolle *f.*

yawn [jɔːn] [1] *vi* **(a)** (*person*) gähnen ♦ **to ~ with boredom** vor Langeweile gähnen. **(b)** (*chasm etc*) gähnen.
[2] *vt* gähnen ♦ **to ~ one's head off** fürchterlich gähnen (*inf*).
[3] *n* **(a)** Gähnen *nt* ♦ **I could tell by your ~s ...** an deinem Gähnen konnte ich sehen ...; **to give a ~** gähnen.
(b) (*inf: bore*) **the film was a ~** der Film war zum Gähnen (langweilig); **what a ~!** wie langweilig!; **life is just one big ~** das Leben ist vielleicht langweilig.

yawning ['jɔːnɪŋ] [1] *adj chasm etc* gähnend.
[2] *n* Gähnen *nt.*

yaws [jɔːz] *n* Frambösie *f.*

Y chromosome *n* Y-Chromosom *nt.*

yd *abbr of* **yard(s).**

ye [jiː] (*obs*) [1] *pers pron* (*nominative*) Ihr (*obs*); (*objective*) Euch (*obs*) ♦ **~ gods!** (*not obs*) allmächtiger Gott!
[2] *def art* = **the.**

yea [jeɪ] [1] *adv* (*obs*) **(a)** (*yes*) ja. **(b)** (*indeed*) fürwahr (*old*).
[2] *n* **the ~s and the nays** die Jastimmen und die Neinstimmen.

yeah [jɛə] *adv* (*inf*) ja.

year [jɪəʳ] *n* **(a)** Jahr *nt* ♦ **last ~** letztes Jahr; **this ~** dieses Jahr; **every other ~** jedes zweite Jahr; **three times a ~** dreimal pro *or* im Jahr; **in the ~ 1989** im Jahr(e) 1989; **in the ~ of Our Lord 1974** (*form*) im Jahr(e) des Herrn 1974 (*geh*); **~ after ~** Jahr für Jahr; **~ by ~, from ~ to ~** von Jahr zu Jahr; **~ in, ~ out** jahrein, jahraus; **all (the) ~ round** das ganze Jahr über *or* hindurch; **as ~s go by** mit den Jahren; **~s (and ~s) ago** vor (langen) Jahren; **to pay by the ~** jährlich zahlen; **a ~ last January** (im) Januar vor einem Jahr; **it'll be a ~ in** *or* **next January** (*duration*) es wird nächsten Januar ein Jahr sein; (*point in time*) es wird nächsten Januar ein Jahr her sein; **a ~ from now** nächstes Jahr um diese Zeit; **a hundred-~-old tree** ein hundert Jahre alter Baum, ein hundertjähriger Baum; **he is six ~s old** er ist sechs Jahre (alt); **he is in his fortieth ~** er steht (*geh*) *or* ist im vierzigsten Lebensjahr; **he gets £23,000 a ~** er bekommt £ 23.000 jährlich *or* pro Jahr *or* im Jahr; **that new hairdo has taken ~s off you** diese neue Frisur macht dich um Jahre jünger; **it's taken ~s off my life** es hat mich Jahre meines Lebens gekostet; **it has put ~s on me** es hat mich (um) Jahre älter gemacht.
(b) (*Univ, Sch, of coin, stamp, wine*) Jahrgang *m* ♦ **he is bottom in his ~** (*Univ, Sch*) er ist der Schlechteste seines Jahrgangs *or* in seinem Jahrgang; **first-~ student** Student(in *f*) *m* im ersten Jahr; (*first term student*) ≃ Student(in *f*) *m* im ersten Semester, Erstsemester *nt*; **she was in my ~ at school** sie war im selben Schuljahrgang wie ich.
(c) from his earliest ~s von frühester Kindheit an, seit seiner frühesten Kindheit; **he looks old for his ~s** er sieht älter aus als er ist; **young for his ~s** jung für sein Alter; **well advanced** *or* **well on in ~s** im vorgerückten Alter; **to get on in ~s** in die Jahre kommen; **difference in ~s** Altersunterschied *m.*

yearbook ['jɪəbʊk] *n* Jahrbuch *nt.*

year-end [,jɪə'rend] *n* Jahresende *nt* ♦ **~ report** Jahresbericht, Geschäftsbericht *m.*

yearling ['jɪəlɪŋ] [1] *n* (*animal*) Jährling *m*; (*racehorse also*) Einjährige(r) *mf.*
[2] *adj* einjährig.

year-long ['jɪə'lɒŋ] *adj* einjährig ♦ **a ~ struggle** ein Kampf, der ein Jahr dauert/dauerte.

yearly ['jɪəlɪ] [1] *adj* jährlich.
[2] *adv* jährlich, einmal im Jahr ♦ **twice ~** zweimal jährlich *or* im Jahr.

yearn [jɜːn] *vi* sich sehnen (*after, for* nach) ♦ **to ~ to do sth** sich danach sehnen, etw zu tun; **to ~ for home** sich nach Hause sehnen; **to ~ for sb** sich nach jdm sehnen, nach jdm verlangen.

yearning ['jɜːnɪŋ] [1] *n* Sehnsucht *f*, Verlangen *nt* (*to do sth* etw zu tun, *for* nach) ♦ **a look full of ~** ein sehnsuchtsvoller Blick; **a ~ for the past** die Sehnsucht nach der Vergangenheit.
[2] *adj desire* sehnsüchtig; *look also* sehnsuchtsvoll, verlangend.

yearningly ['jɜːnɪŋlɪ] *adv* sehnsuchtsvoll, voller Sehnsucht; *gaze also* sehnsüchtig.

year-round ['jɪə'raʊnd] *adj* das ganze Jahr über *or* hindurch.
yeast [ji:st] *n, no pl* Hefe *f*.
yeasty ['ji:stɪ] *adj taste* hefig ◆ **the beer's very ~** das Bier schmeckt stark nach Hefe.
yell [jel] 1 *n* Schrei *m* ◆ **to let out** *or* **give a ~** einen Schrei ausstoßen, schreien; **could you give me a ~ when we get there?** könnten Sie mir Bescheid sagen *or* mich rufen, wenn wir da sind?; **college ~** (*US*) Schlachtruf *m* eines College.
2 *vi* (*also* **~ out**) schreien, brüllen (*with* vor *+dat*) ◆ **he ~ed at her** er schrie *or* brüllte sie an; **just ~ if you need help** ruf, wenn du Hilfe brauchst; **to ~ with laughter** vor Lachen brüllen.
3 *vt* (*also* **~ out**) schreien, brüllen; *name* brüllen ◆ **he ~ed abuse at the teacher** er beschimpfte den Lehrer wüst; **she ~ed up the stairs that dinner was ready** sie rief die Treppe hinauf, daß das Essen fertig sei.
yellow ['jeləʊ] 1 *adj* (*+er*) **(a)** gelb ◆ **~ hair** strohblondes *or* gelbblondes Haar; **to go** *or* **turn ~** gelb werden; (*paper*) vergilben; **~ card** (*Ftbl*) gelbe Karte; **~ fever** Gelbfieber *nt*; **~ flag, ~ jack** (*Naut*) gelbe Flagge, Quarantäneflagge *f*; **~ jersey** (*Cycling*) gelbes Trikot; **(double) ~ line** (absolutes) Halteverbot; **to be parked on a (double) ~ line** im (absoluten) Halteverbot stehen; **~ ochre** ockergelb; **~ pages: the ~ pages** das Branchenverzeichnis, die Gelben Seiten; **~ peril** gelbe Gefahr; **~ press** Sensationspresse *f*; **Y~ River** Gelber Fluß; **Y~ Sea** Gelbes Meer.
(b) (*sl: cowardly*) feige.
2 *n* (*colour*) Gelb *nt*; (*of egg*) Eigelb *nt*; (*sl: cowardice*) Feigheit *f* ◆ **a streak of ~** ein feiger Zug.
3 *vt* gelb färben ◆ **the sunlight had ~ed the pages** die Sonne hatte die Seiten vergilben lassen; **paper ~ed with age** vor Alter vergilbtes Papier.
4 *vi* gelb werden, sich gelb färben; (*corn also*) reifen; (*pages*) vergilben ◆ **the leaves were ~ing** die Blätter färbten sich gelb.
yellow: ~-belly *n* (*sl*) Angsthase (*inf*), Waschlappen (*inf*) *m*; **~hammer** *n* (*Orn*) Goldammer *f*.
yellowish ['jeləʊɪʃ] *adj* gelblich.
yellowness ['jeləʊnɪs] *n, no pl* **(a)** Gelb *nt*; (*of skin*) gelbliche Färbung. **(b)** (*sl: cowardice*) Feigheit *f*.
yellowy ['jeləʊɪ] *adj* gelblich.
yelp [jelp] 1 *n* (*of animal*) Jaulen *nt no pl*; (*of person*) Aufschrei *m* ◆ **to give a ~** (auf)jaulen; (*person*) aufschreien.
2 *vi* (*animal*) (auf)jaulen; (*person*) aufschreien.
yelping ['jelpɪŋ] *n see vi* Jaulen *nt*; Aufschreien *nt*.
Yemen ['jemən] *n*: **the ~** der Jemen.
Yemeni ['jemənɪ] 1 *n* Jemenit(in *f*) *m*.
2 *adj* jemenitisch.
yen¹ [jen] *n* (*Fin*) Yen *m*.
yen² *n* (*inf*) Lust *f* (*for* auf *+acc*) ◆ **I've always had a ~ to go to Pasadena** es hat mich schon immer nach Pasadena gezogen; **I had a sudden ~ to do that/for oysters** ich hatte plötzlich Lust, das zu machen/auf Austern.
yeoman ['jəʊmən] *n, pl* **-men** [-mən] **(a)** (*Hist: small landowner*) Freibauer *m* ◆ **~ farmer** (*Hist*) Freibauer *m*. **(b) Y~ of the Guard** königlicher Leibgardist; **to do ~ service** treue Dienste leisten (*for sb* jdm).
yeomanry ['jəʊmənrɪ] *n* **(a)** (*Hist*) Freibauernschaft *f*, Freibauernstand *m*. **(b)** (*Mil*) *freiwillige Kavallerietruppe*.
yep [jep] *adv* (*inf*) ja ◆ **is he sure? — ~!** ist er sicher? — klar!
yes [jes] 1 *adv* ja; (*answering neg question*) doch ◆ **to say ~** ja sagen; **to say ~ to a demand** einer Forderung (*dat*) nachkommen; **he said ~ to all my questions** er hat alle meine Fragen bejaht *or* mit Ja beantwortet; **if they say ~ to an increase** wenn sie eine Lohnerhöhung bewilligen; **I'd say ~ to 35%, no to 32%** ich würde 35% akzeptieren, 32% nicht; **she'll say ~ to anything** sie kann nicht nein sagen; **~ sir!** (*Mil*) jawohl, Herr General/Leutnant *etc*; (*general*) jawohl, mein Herr!; **waiter! — ~ sir?** Herr Ober! — ja, bitte?; **~ indeed** o ja, allerdings; **I didn't say that — oh ~, you did** das habe ich nicht gesagt — o doch *or* o ja, das hast du; **~ and no** ja und nein, jein (*inf*); **~ ~, I know!** jaja, ich weiß doch; **~-no question** Ja-Nein-Frage *f*.
2 *n* Ja *nt* ◆ **he just answered with ~es and noes** er hat einfach mit Ja oder Nein geantwortet.
yes man ['jesmæn] *n, pl* **~ men** [-men] Jasager *m*.
yesterday ['jestədeɪ] 1 *n* Gestern *nt* ◆ **the fashions of ~** die Mode von gestern; **all our ~s** unsere ganze Vergangenheit.
2 *adv* (*lit, fig*) gestern ◆ **~ morning/afternoon/evening** gestern morgen/nachmittag/abend; **he was at home all (day) ~** er war gestern den ganzen Tag zu Hause; **the day before ~** vorgestern; **a week ago ~** gestern vor einer Woche; *see* **born**.
yesteryear ['jestə'jɪəʳ] *n* (*poet*) **of ~** vergangener Jahre (*gen*).
▼ **yet** [jet] 1 *adv* **(a)** (*still*) noch; (*thus far*) bis jetzt, bisher ◆ **they haven't ~ returned** *or* **returned ~** sie sind noch nicht zurückgekommen; **this is his best book ~** das ist bis jetzt sein bestes Buch, das ist sein bisher bestes Buch; **as ~** (*with present tenses*) bis jetzt, bisher; (*with past*) bis dahin; **no, not ~** nein, noch nicht; **I've hardly begun ~** ich habe noch gar nicht richtig angefangen; **not just ~** jetzt noch nicht; **don't come in (just) ~** komm (jetzt) noch nicht herein.
(b) (*with interrog: so far, already*) schon ◆ **has he arrived ~?** ist er schon angekommen?, ist er schon da?; **do you have to go just ~?** müssen Sie jetzt schon gehen?
(c) (*with affirmative: still, remaining*) noch ◆ **they have a few days ~** sie haben noch ein paar Tage; **a ~ to be decided question** eine noch unentschiedene Frage, eine Frage, die noch entschieden werden muß; **I've ~ to learn how to do it** ich muß erst noch lernen, wie man es macht; **and they are doubtless waiting ~** und sie warten zweifellos noch immer.
(d) (*with comp: still, even*) noch ◆ **this is ~ more difficult** dies ist (sogar) noch schwieriger; **~ more money** noch mehr Geld.
(e) (*in addition*) **(and) ~ again** und wieder, und noch einmal; **and ~ again they rode off** und sie ritten wieder weg; **another arrived and ~ another** es kam noch einer und noch einer.
(f) (*with future and conditional: before all is over*) noch ◆ **he may come ~** *or* **~ come** er kann noch kommen; **he could come ~** er könnte noch kommen; **I may ~ go to Italy** ich fahre vielleicht noch nach Italien; **I'll do it ~** ich schaffe es schon noch.
(g) (*liter*) **nor ~** noch; **they didn't come nor ~ write** sie sind weder gekommen, noch haben sie geschrieben.
2 *conj* doch, dennoch, trotzdem ◆ **and ~** und doch *or* trotzdem *or* dennoch; **it's strange ~ true** es ist seltsam, aber wahr.
yeti ['jetɪ] *n* Yeti, Schneemensch *m*.
yew [ju:] *n* (*also* **~ tree**) Eibe *f*; (*wood*) Eibe(nholz *nt*) *f*.
Y-fronts ® ['waɪfrʌnts] *npl* (Herren-)Slip *m*.
YHA *abbr of* **Youth Hostels Association** ≃ DJH *nt*.
Yid [jɪd] *n* (*pej*) Jud *m* (*pej*).
Yiddish ['jɪdɪʃ] 1 *adj* jiddisch.
2 *n* (*language*) Jiddisch *nt*.
yield [ji:ld] 1 *vt* **(a)** (*land*) *fruit, crop* hervorbringen; (*tree*) *fruit* tragen; (*mine, oil-well*) bringen; (*shares, money*) *interest, profit* (ein)bringen, abwerfen; *result* (hervor)bringen; *opportunity* ergeben ◆ **the information ~ed by the poll** die Information, die die Meinungsumfrage ergeben hat; **this ~ed a weekly increase of 20%** das brachte eine wöchentliche Steigerung von 20%.
(b) (*surrender, concede*) aufgeben ◆ **to ~ sth to sb** etw an jdn abtreten; **to ~ ground to the enemy** vor dem Feind zurückweichen; **to ~ the floor to sb** (*fig*) jdm das Feld überlassen; **to ~ a point to sb** jdm einen Punkt zukommen lassen; (*in competition*) einen Punkt an jdn abgeben; **to ~ concessions** Zugeständnisse machen; **to ~ right of way to sb** (*Mot*) jdm die Vorfahrt gewähren *or* lassen.
2 *vi* **(a)** (*tree, land*) tragen; (*mine, oil-well*) Ertrag bringen; (*shares, money*) sich verzinsen, Zinsen *or* Profit einbringen *or* abwerfen ◆ **land that ~s well/poorly** Land, das ertragreich ist/das wenig Erträge bringt.
(b) (*surrender, give way*) **they ~ed to us** (*Mil*) sie haben sich uns (*dat*) ergeben; (*general*) sie haben nachgegeben; **at last she ~ed to him/to his charm** schließlich erlag sie ihm/seinem Charme doch; **to ~ to force/superior forces** (*Mil*) der Gewalt/Übermacht weichen *or* nachgeben; **to ~ to reason** sich der Vernunft beugen; **to ~ to sb's entreaties/threats/argument** jds Bitten (*dat*) nachgeben/sich jds Drohungen/Argument (*dat*) beugen; **he ~ed to her requests** er gab ihren Bitten nach; **the disease ~ed to treatment** die Krankheit sprach auf die Behandlung an; **to ~ to temptation** der Versuchung erliegen; **to ~ to one's emotions** seinen Gefühlen nachgeben; **I'll have to ~ to you on that point** in diesem Punkt muß ich Ihnen recht geben.
(c) (*give way: branch, beam, rope, floor, ground*) nachgeben ◆ **to ~ under pressure** unter Druck nachgeben; (*fig*) dem Druck weichen.
(d) (*Mot*) **to ~ to oncoming traffic** den Gegenverkehr vorbeilassen; **"~"** (*US, Ir*) „Vorfahrt achten!"
3 *n* (*of land, tree*) Ertrag *m*; (*of work also*) Ergebnis *nt*; (*of mine, well*) Ausbeute *f*; (*of industry: goods*) Produktion *f*; (*profit*) Gewinne, Erträge *pl*; (*Fin: of shares, business*) Ertrag, Gewinn *m* ◆ **~ of tax** Steueraufkommen *nt*.
◆**yield up** *vt sep rights, privileges* abtreten, verzichten auf (*+acc*) ◆ **to ~ sth ~ to sb** etw an jdn abtreten; **he ~ed ~ his life to the cause** er gab sein Leben für diese Sache; **he ~ed himself ~ to his fate** er ergab sich in sein Schicksal.
yielding ['ji:ldɪŋ] *adj person* nachgiebig; *surface, material* nachgebend ◆ **the ground is ~** der Boden gibt nach.
yippee [jɪ'pi:] *interj* juchhu, hurra.
YMCA *abbr of* **Young Men's Christian Association** CVJM *m*.
yobbish ['jɒbɪʃ] *adj* (*Brit inf*) Halbstarken-, Rowdy-.
yob(bo) ['jɒb(əʊ)] *n* (*Brit inf*) Halbstarke(r), Rowdy *m*.
yodel ['jəʊdl] 1 *vti* jodeln.
2 *n* Jodler *m*.
yodelling ['jəʊdlɪŋ] *n* Jodeln *nt*.
yoga ['jəʊgə] *n* Joga, Yoga *m or nt*.
yoghourt, yog(h)urt ['jɒgət] *n* Joghurt *m or nt*.
yogi ['jəʊgɪ] *n* Jogi, Yogi *m*.
yo-heave-ho ['jəʊ'hi:v'həʊ] *interj* hau-ruck.
yoke [jəʊk] 1 *n* **(a)** (*for oxen*) Joch *nt*; (*for carrying pails*) (Trag)joch *nt*, Schultertrage *f*. **(b)** *pl* - (*pair of oxen*) Joch, Gespann *nt*. **(c)** (*fig: oppression*) Joch *nt* ◆ **to throw off the ~** das Joch abschütteln. **(d)** (*on dress, blouse*) Passe *f*; (*on pullover also*) Joch *nt*.
2 *vt* **(a)** (*also* **~ up**) *oxen* (ins Joch) einspannen ◆ **to ~ oxen to the plough** Ochsen vor den Pflug spannen.
(b) *pieces of machinery* zusammenschließen ◆ **to ~ sth to sth** etw an etw (*acc*) anschließen.
(c) (*fig: join together*) zusammenschließen, vereinen.
yokel ['jəʊkəl] *n* (*pej*) Bauerntölpel, Bauerntrampel *m*.
yolk [jəʊk] *n* (*of egg*) Eigelb *nt*.
yon [jɒn] *adv, adj* (*poet, dial*) *see* **yonder**.
yonder ['jɒndəʳ] (*poet, dial*) 1 *adv* **(over) ~** dort drüben.
2 *adj* **from ~ house** von dem Haus (dort) drüben.
yonks [jɒŋks] *n* (*inf: ages*) eine (halbe) Ewigkeit (*inf*); **that was ~ ago** das war vor einer (halben) Ewigkeit (*inf*); **I haven't seen her for ~** ich habe sie schon

➤ LANGUAGE IN USE: **yet: 1a** → 20.5

ewig nicht mehr gesehen (*inf*).

yoo-hoo ['juː'huː] *interj* huhu, hallo.

yore [jɔːʳ] *n* (*obs, liter*) **in days of ~** in alten Zeiten; **men of ~** die Menschen in alten Zeiten; **in the world of ~** in alten *or* längst vergangenen Zeiten; **in the Britain of ~** im Großbritannien längst vergangener Zeiten; **..., whose ancestors of ~** ..., dessen Ahnen ehedem *or* einstmals.

Yorkshire pudding ['jɔːkʃə'pʊdɪŋ] *n* Yorkshire Pudding *m* (*Beilage f zu Rinderbraten*).

you [juː] *pron* **(a)** (*German familiar form, can also be written with a capital in letters*) (*sing*) (*nom*) du; (*acc*) dich; (*dat*) dir; (*pl*) (*nom*) ihr; (*acc, dat*) euch; (*German polite form: sing, pl*) (*nom, acc*) Sie; (*dat*) Ihnen ◆ **all of ~** (*pl*) ihr alle/Sie alle; **I want all of ~** (*sing*) ich will dich ganz; **if I were ~** wenn ich du/Sie wäre, an deiner/euerer/Ihrer Stelle; **~ Germans** ihr Deutschen; **silly old ~** du Dussel (*inf*), du Dumm(er)chen (*inf*); **~ darling** du bist ein Schatz *or* Engel; **is that ~?** bist du's/seid ihr's/sind Sie's?; **it's ~** du bist es/ihr seid's/Sie sind's; **what's the matter? — it's ~** *or* **~ are** was ist los? — es liegt an dir/euch/Ihnen; **there's a fine house for ~!** das ist mal ein schönes Haus!; **now there's a woman for ~!** das ist mal eine (tolle) Frau; **now ~ say something** sag du/sagt ihr/sagen Sie (auch) mal was; **just ~ dare!** trau dich bloß!, untersteh dich!; **sit ~ down** (*hum*) setz dich/setzt euch/setzen Sie sich; **that hat just isn't ~** (*inf*) der Hut paßt einfach nicht zu dir/zu Ihnen.
(b) (*indef*) (*nom*) man; (*acc*) einen; (*dat*) einem ◆ **~ never know, ~ never can tell** man kann nie wissen, man weiß nie; **it's not good for ~** es ist nicht gut.

you-all ['juːɔːl] *pron* (*US inf*) ihr.

you'd [juːd] *contr of* **you would; you had.**

you'd've ['juːdəv] *contr of* **you would have.**

you'll [juːl] *contr of* **you will; you shall.**

young [jʌŋ] 1 *adj* (*+er*) jung; *wine, grass also* neu ◆ **the ~ moon** der Mond im ersten Viertel; **~ people** junge Leute *pl*; **a ~ people's magazine** eine Jugendzeitschrift; **~ people's fashions** Jugendmoden *pl*; **~ lady/man** junge Dame/junger Mann; **they have a ~ family** sie haben kleine Kinder; **he is ~ at heart** er ist innerlich jung geblieben; **you are only ~ once** man ist *or* du bist nur einmal jung; **you ~ rascal!** (*inf*) du kleiner Schlingel!; **~ Mr Brown** der junge Herr Brown; **Pitt the Y~er** Pitt der Jüngere; **the night is ~** die Nacht ist (noch) jung; **Y~ America** die Jugend in Amerika, die amerikanische Jugend; **he's a very ~ forty** er ist ein jugendlicher *or* junggebliebener Vierziger; **~ offender** jugendlicher Straftäter; **~ offenders' institution** Einrichtung *f* für jugendliche Straftäter.
2 *npl* **(a)** (*people*) **the ~** die Jugend, die jungen Leute; **~ and old** jung und alt; **books for the ~** Jugendbücher *pl*.
(b) (*animals*) Junge *pl* ◆ **with ~** trächtig.

youngish ['jʌŋɪʃ] *adj* ziemlich jung.

youngster ['jʌŋstəʳ] *n* (*boy*) Junge *m*; (*child*) Kind *nt* ◆ **he's just a ~** er ist eben noch jung *or* ein Kind.

your [jɔːʳ, jəʳ] *poss adj* **(a)** (*German familiar form, can also be written with a capital in letters*) (*sing*) dein/deine/dein; (*pl*) euer/eure/euer; (*German polite form: sing, pl*) Ihr/Ihre/Ihr ◆ **~ mother and father** deine/Ihre Mutter und dein/Ihr Vater; **one of ~ friends** einer deiner/Ihrer Freunde, einer von deinen/Ihren Freunden; *see* **majesty, worship** *etc*.
(b) (*indef*) sein ◆ **you give him ~ form and he gives you back ~ passport** Sie geben ihm Ihr *or* dies Formular, und dann bekommen Sie Ihren Paß zurück; **the climate here is bad for ~ health** das Klima hier ist ungesund *or* ist nicht gut für die Gesundheit.
(c) (*typical*) der/die/das ◆ **~ average Englishman** der durchschnittliche Engländer.

you're [jʊəʳ, jɔːʳ] *contr of* **you are.**

yours [jɔːz] *poss pron* (*pers*) (*German familiar form, can also be written with a capital in letters*) (*sing*) deiner/deine/deins; (*pl*) eurer/eure/euers; (*German polite form: sing, pl*) Ihrer/Ihre/Ihr(e)s ◆ **this is my book and that is ~** dies ist mein Buch und das (ist) deins/Ihres; **the idea was ~** es war deine/Ihre Idee, die Idee stammt von dir/Ihnen; **she is a cousin of ~** sie ist deine Kusine, sie ist eine Kusine von dir; **that is no business of ~** das geht dich/Sie nichts an; **that dog of ~!** dein/Ihr blöder Hund!; **you and ~** du und deine Familie, du und die Deinen (*geh*)/Sie und Ihre Familie, Sie und die Ihren (*geh*); **~** (*in letter-writing*) Ihr/Ihre; **~ faithfully, ~ truly** (*on letter*) mit freundlichem Gruß, mit freundlichen Grüßen, hochachtungsvoll (*form*); **in reply to ~ of the 15th May** (*Comm form*) in Antwort auf Ihr Schreiben vom 15. Mai; **what's ~?** (*to drink*) was möchtest du/was möchten Sie?, was trinkst du/was trinken Sie?; **~ truly** (*inf: I, me*) meine Wenigkeit; **guess who had to do all the dirty work? ~ truly** und wer mußte die Dreckarbeit machen? ich natürlich; **and then ~ truly got up and said ...** und dann stand ich höchstpersönlich auf und sagte ...; **up ~!** (*vulg*) du kannst mich mal (*sl*); *see* **affectionately, ever (g).**

yourself [jɔː'self, jə'self] *pron, pl* **yourselves** [jɔː'selvz, jə'selvz] **(a)** (*reflexive*) (*German familiar form, can also be written with a capital in letters*) (*sing*) (*acc*) dich; (*dat*) dir; (*pl*) euch; (*German polite form: sing, pl*) sich ◆ **have you hurt ~?** hast du dir/haben Sie sich weh getan?; **you never speak about ~** du redest nie über dich (selbst)/Sie reden nie über sich (selbst).
(b) (*emph*) selbst ◆ **you ~ told me, you told me ~** du hast/Sie haben mir selbst gesagt; **you are not quite ~ today** du bist heute gar nicht du selbst, du bist/Sie sind heute irgendwie verändert *or* anders; **how's ~?** (*inf*) und wie geht's dir/Ihnen?; **you will see for ~** du wirst/Sie werden selbst sehen; **did you do it by ~?** hast du/haben Sie das allein gemacht?

youth [juːθ] *n* **(a)** *no pl* Jugend *f* ◆ **in (the days of) my ~** in meiner Jugend(zeit); **the town of my ~** die Stadt *or* Stätte (*hum*) meiner Jugend; **he radiates ~** er vermittelt den Eindruck von Jugendlichkeit; **in early ~** in früher Jugend; **she has kept her ~** sie ist jung geblieben.
(b) *pl* **-s** [juːðz] (*young man*) junger Mann, Jugendliche(r) *m* ◆ **when he was a ~** als er ein junger Mann war; **pimply ~** pickliger Jüngling.
(c) **~** *pl* (*young men and women*) Jugend *f* ◆ **she l◆ikes working with (the) ~** sie arbeitet gerne mit Jugendlichen; **the ~ of today** die Jugend von heute; **the Hitler Y~ Movement** die Hitlerjugend; **~ club** Jugendklub *m*; **~ hostel** Jugendherberge *f*; **~ employment scheme** Programm *nt or* Aktionsplan *m* für jugendliche Arbeitslose; **~ training scheme** Ausbildungsprogramm *nt* für Jugendliche.

youthful ['juːθfʊl] *adj* jugendlich ◆ **a ~ mistake** eine Jugendsünde.

youthfulness ['juːθfʊlnɪs] *n* Jugendlichkeit *f*.

you've [juːv] *contr of* **you have.**

yowl [jaʊl] 1 *n* (*of person*) Heulen *nt no pl*; (*of dog*) Jaulen *nt no pl*; (*of cat*) klägliches Miauen *no pl*.
2 *vi* (*person*) heulen; (*dog*) jaulen; (*cat*) kläglich miauen.

yo-yo ['jəʊjəʊ] *n* Jo-Jo, Yo-Yo *nt* ◆ **I've been going up- and downstairs like a ~ all morning** ich bin den ganzen Morgen wie irre die Treppe rauf- und runtergerannt (*inf*).

yr *abbr of* **(a) year(s). (b) your.**

yrs *abbr of* **(a) years. (b) yours.**

Y-shaped ['waɪʃeɪpt] *adj* Y-förmig.

YTS *n* (*Brit*) **(a)** *abbr of* **Youth Training Scheme. (b)** (*person*) Auszubildende(r) *mf*.

ytterbium [ɪ'tɜːbɪəm] *n* (*Chem*) Ytterbium *nt*.

yttrium ['ɪtrɪəm] *n* (*Chem*) Yttrium *nt*.

yucca ['jʌkə] *n* Yucca, Palmlilie *f*.

yuck [jʌk] *interj see* **yuk.**

Yugoslav ['juːgəʊ'slɑːv] 1 *adj* jugoslawisch.
2 *n* Jugoslawe *m*, Jugoslawin *f*.

Yugoslavia ['juːgəʊ'slɑːvɪə] *n* Jugoslawien *nt*.

Yugoslavian ['juːgəʊ'slɑːvɪən] *adj* jugoslawisch.

yuk [jʌk] *interj* i, igitt, igittigitt.

yukky ['jʌkɪ] *adj* (*+er*) (*sl*) eklig, widerlich, fies (*inf*).

Yule [juːl] *n* (*old*) Weihnachten, Julfest *nt* ◆ **~ log** Julblock *m*; **~tide** Weihnachtszeit, Julzeit *f*.

yummy ['jʌmɪ] 1 *adj* (*+er*) (*sl*) *food* lecker; *man* toll.
2 *interj* **~!, ~ ~!** lecker!, jamjam! (*inf*).

yum yum ['jʌm'jʌm] *interj* lecker, jamjam (*inf*).

yup [jʌp] *adv* (*US inf: yes*) ja, jawoll (*inf*).

yuppie, yuppy ['jʌpɪ] 1 *n* Yuppie *m*.
2 *adj* yuppiehaft, yuppiemäßig; *job, area, pub, car also* Yuppie- ◆ **~ flu** *krankhafter Energiemangel*.

yuppiedom ['jʌpɪdəm] *n* (*inf*) **the rise of ~ in the eighties** der Aufstieg der Yuppies in den 80er Jahren; **he lives in the heart of ~** er lebt mitten in einer Yuppiegegend.

YWCA *abbr of* **Young Women's Christian Association** CVJF *m*.

Z

Z, z [(*Brit*) zed, (*US*) ziː] *n* Z, z *nt*.
Zaire [zɑːˈiːəʳ] *n* Zaïre, Zaire *nt*.
Zambesi, Zambezi [zæmˈbiːzɪ] *n* Sambesi *m*.
Zambia [ˈzæmbɪə] *n* Sambia *nt*.
zany [ˈzeɪnɪ] [1] *adj* (+*er*) (*crazy, funny*) verrückt; *person also* irrsinnig komisch.
[2] *n* (*Theat Hist*) Narr, Hanswurst *m*.
Zanzibar [ˈzænzɪbɑːʳ] *n* Sansibar *nt*.
zap [zæp] (*inf*) [1] *n* (*energy, pep*) Schwung, Pep (*inf*) *m*.
[2] *interj* zack.
[3] *vt* **(a)** (*hit*) **to ~ sb (one)** jdm eine pfeffern (*inf*) *or* kleben (*inf*).
(b) (*Comput: delete*) löschen.
(c) (*inf*) (*kill*) abknallen (*inf*); (*destroy*) kaputtmachen (*inf*).
(d) (*inf: send quickly*) **he ~ped us back down to London in his Porsche** er hat uns in seinem Porsche im Düsentempo nach London zurückgebracht; **we'll ~ it back to you down the fax** wir senden es Ihnen in Windeseile per Fax zurück.
[4] *vi* (*inf*) **(a)** (*move fast*) düsen (*inf*). **(b)** (*change channel*) umschalten.
◆**zap along** *vi* (*inf: move fast*) düsen (*inf*) ◆ **the project's ~ping ~** das Projekt geht mit Volldampf voran (*inf*).
◆**zap up** *vt sep* (*sl*) aufmotzen (*sl*).
zapped [zæpt] *adj* (*sl: tired, exhausted*) total geschafft (*sl*).
zappiness [ˈzæpɪnɪs] *n see adj* Fetzigkeit *f*; Spritzigkeit *f*; Dynamik *f*.
zappy [ˈzæpɪ] *adj pace, car* fetzig (*sl*); (*lively*) *prose, style* spritzig; *management style* dynamisch.
zeal [ziːl] *n, no pl* Eifer *m* ◆ **to work with great ~** mit Feuereifer arbeiten; **he is full of ~ for the cause** er ist mit Feuereifer bei der Sache.
zealot [ˈzelət] *n* Fanatiker(in *f*) *m*; (*religious also*) (Glaubens)eiferer(in *f*) *m* ◆ **Z~** (*Hist*) Zelot *m*.
zealotry [ˈzelətrɪ] *n* Fanatismus *m*, blinder Eifer.
zealous [ˈzeləs] *adj student, worker* eifrig, emsig ◆ **~ for sth** eifrig um etw bemüht; **to be ~ to begin/help** erpicht darauf sein, anzufangen/zu helfen; **~ for the cause** für die Sache begeistert; **~ for a change** auf einen Wechsel erpicht.
zealously [ˈzeləslɪ] *adv see adj*.
zebra [ˈzebrə] *n* Zebra *nt* ◆ **~ crossing** (*Brit*) Zebrastreifen *m*.
Zen [zen] *n* Zen *nt* ◆ **~ Buddhism** Zen-Buddhismus *m*.
zenith [ˈzenɪθ] *n* (*Astron, fig*) Zenit *m*.
zephyr [ˈzefəʳ] *n* (*poet*) Zephir (*poet*), Zephyr (*poet*) *m*.
zeppelin [ˈzeplɪn] *n* Zeppelin *m*.
zero [ˈzɪərəʊ] [1] *n, pl* **-(e)s (a)** (*figure*) Null *f*; (*point on scale*) Nullpunkt *m*; (*Roulette*) Zero *f* ◆ **15 degrees below ~** 15 Grad unter Null; **the needle is at** *or* **on ~** der Zeiger steht auf Null; **his chances were put at ~** man meinte, seine Aussichten seien gleich Null. **(b)** (*fig: nonentity*) Null *f* (*inf*).
[2] *adj* **at ~ altitude** (*Aviat*) im Tiefflug; **~ altitude flying** Tiefflug *m*; **~ degrees** null Grad; **~ gravity** Schwerelosigkeit *f*; **at ~ gravity** unter Schwerelosigkeit; **~ growth** Nullwachstum *nt*; **~ hour** (*Mil, fig*) die Stunde X; **~ option** (*Pol*) Nullösung *f*; **~-rated** (*for VAT*) mehrwertsteuerfrei; **~ rating** (*for VAT*) Befreiung *f* von der Mehrwertsteuer; **he's getting absolutely ~ satisfaction from it** (*inf*) das bringt ihm überhaupt nichts (*inf*); **she showed ~ interest in him** (*inf*) sie zeigte sich nicht im geringsten an ihm interessiert.
◆**zero in** *vi* (*Mil*) sich einschießen (*on* auf +*acc*) ◆ **to ~ ~ on sb/sth** (*fig*) *gang leader, core of problem* jdn/etw einkreisen; *difficulty* sich (*dat*) etw herausgreifen; *opportunity* sich auf etw (*acc*) stürzen; **we're beginning to ~ ~ on the final selection** langsam kommen wir der endgültigen Auswahl näher.
zero-sum game *n* Nullsummenspiel *nt*.
zest [zest] *n* **(a)** (*enthusiasm*) Begeisterung *f* ◆ **~ for life** Lebensfreude *f*; **he hasn't got much ~** er hat keinen Schwung; **he's lost his old ~** der alte Schwung ist hin (*inf*).
(b) (*in style, of food etc*) Pfiff (*inf*), Schwung *m* ◆ **a story full of ~** eine Geschichte mit Schwung; **add ~ to your meals with ...!** geben Sie Ihren Gerichten Pfiff mit ...! (*inf*).
(c) (*lemon etc peel*) Zitronen-/Orangenschale *f*.
zestful *adj*, **~ly** *adv* [ˈzestfʊl, -fəlɪ] schwungvoll.
zeugma [ˈzjuːgmə] *n* Zeugma *nt*.
Zeus [zjuːs] *n* (*Myth*) Zeus *m*.
ziggurat [ˈzɪgəræt] *n* Zikkur(r)at *f*.
zigzag [ˈzɪgzæg] [1] *n* Zickzack *m or nt* ◆ **the river cuts a ~ through the rocks** der Fluß bahnt sich im Zickzack einen Weg durch die Felsen; **we had to make a long ~ across the ice** wir mußten uns lange im Zickzack über das Eis bewegen; **a pattern of straight lines and ~s** ein Muster aus Geraden und Zickzacklinien.
[2] *adj course, line* Zickzack-; *road, path* zickzackförmig ◆ **to steer a ~ course** (*Naut*) Zickzack(kurs) fahren.
[3] *adv* zickzackförmig, im Zickzack.
[4] *vi* im Zickzack laufen/fahren *etc*; (*Naut*) Zickzack(kurs) fahren.
zilch [zɪltʃ] *n* (*sl: nothing*) nix (*inf*), Null Komma nichts (*inf*).
zillion [ˈzɪljən] (*US inf*) [1] *n* **~s of dollars** zig Milliarden Dollar (*inf*).
[2] *adj* **I've told you a ~ times ...** ich hab dir hunderttausendmal *or* zigmal gesagt ... (*inf*).
Zimbabwe [zɪmˈbɑːbwɪ] *n* Zimbabwe, Simbabwe *nt*.
Zimbabwean [zɪmˈbɑːbwɪən] [1] *adj* zimbabwisch, simbabwisch.
[2] *n* Zimbabwer(in *f*), Simbabwer(in *f*) *m*.
zimmer [ˈzɪməʳ] *n* (*Med: walking aid*) Laufstuhl *m*, Laufgestell *nt*.
zinc [zɪŋk] *n* Zink *nt* ◆ **~ ointment** Zinksalbe *f*; **~ oxide** Zinkoxid *nt*.
zing [zɪŋ] (*inf*) [1] *n* **(a)** (*noise of bullet etc*) Pfeifen, Zischen *nt*. **(b)** (*zest*) Pfiff *m* (*inf*).
[2] *vi* (*bullets*) pfeifen, zischen.
zinnia [ˈzɪnɪə] *n* Zinnie *f*.
Zion [ˈzaɪən] *n* Zion *nt*.
Zionism [ˈzaɪənɪzəm] *n* Zionismus *m*.
Zionist [ˈzaɪənɪst] [1] *adj* zionistisch.
[2] *n* Zionist(in *f*) *m*.
ZIP [zɪp] (*US*) *abbr of* **Zone Improvement Plan** ◆ **~ code** PLZ, Postleitzahl *f*.
zip [zɪp] [1] *n* **(a)** (*Brit: fastener*) Reißverschluß *m*.
(b) (*sound of bullet*) Pfeifen, Zischen *nt*.
(c) (*inf: energy*) Schwung *m* ◆ **we need a bit more ~ in these translations** wir müssen etwas mehr Schwung in diese Übersetzungen kriegen (*inf*).
[2] *vt* **to ~ a dress/bag** den Reißverschluß eines Kleides/einer Tasche zumachen *or* zuziehen.
[3] *vi* (*inf: car, person*) flitzen (*inf*); (*person also*) wetzen (*inf*) ◆ **to ~ past/along** *etc* vorbei-/daherflitzen *etc* (*inf*); **he ~ped through his work in no time** er hatte die Arbeit in Null Komma nichts erledigt (*inf*).
◆**zip on** [1] *vt sep* **he ~ped ~ his special gloves** er zog die Reißverschlüsse seiner Spezialhandschuhe zu.
[2] *vi* **the hood ~s ~ to the jacket** die Kapuze wird mit einem Reißverschluß an der Jacke befestigt.
◆**zip up** [1] *vt sep* **to ~ ~ a dress** den Reißverschluß eines Kleides zumachen; **will you ~ me ~ please?** kannst du mir bitte den Reißverschluß zumachen?
[2] *vi* **it ~s ~** es hat einen Reißverschluß; **it ~s ~ at the back** der Reißverschluß ist hinten.
zip: ~ fastener *n* Reißverschluß *m*; **~ gun** *n* (*US*) selbstgebastelte Pistole.
zipper [ˈzɪpəʳ] *n* Reißverschluß *m*.
zippy [ˈzɪpɪ] *adj* (+*er*) (*inf*) *car* flott; *person also* flink.
zircon [ˈzɜːkən] *n* Zirkon *m*.
zirconium [zɜːˈkəʊnɪəm] *n* (*Chem*) Zirkonium *nt*.
zit [zɪt] *n* (*esp US inf: spot*) Pickel *m*.
zither [ˈzɪðəʳ] *n* Zither *f*.
zodiac [ˈzəʊdɪæk] *n* Tierkreis *m* ◆ **signs of the ~** Tierkreiszeichen *pl*.
zombie [ˈzɒmbɪ] *n* **(a)** (*lit: revived corpse*) Zombie *m*. **(b)** (*fig*) Idiot (*inf*), Schwachkopf (*inf*) *m* ◆ **like a ~/like ~s** wie im Tran; **that new hairstyle makes her look a complete ~** mit der neuen Frisur sieht sie total bescheuert *or* bekloppt aus (*sl*).
zonal [ˈzəʊnl] *adj* Zonen-, zonal.
zone [ˈzəʊn] [1] *n* **(a)** (*Geog*) Zone *f*.
(b) (*area*) Zone *f*; (*fig also*) Gebiet *nt* ◆ **no-parking ~** Parkverbot *nt*; **time ~** Zeitzone *f*; **the English-speaking ~** der englische Sprachraum; **~s of the body** Körperzonen *pl*.
(c) (*US: postal ~*) Post(zustell)bezirk *m*.
[2] *vt* **(a)** *town, area* in Zonen aufteilen. **(b) to ~ a district for industry** einen Bezirk zur Industriezone ernennen.
zoning [ˈzəʊnɪŋ] *n* **(a)** Zoneneinteilung *f*. **(b) the ~ of this area as ...** die Erklärung dieses Gebietes zum ...

zonked [zɒŋkt] *adj* (*sl*) (*drunk, high*) total ausgeflippt (*sl*); (*tired*) total geschafft (*sl*).

zoo [zuː] *n* Zoo, Tierpark, Tiergarten *m* ◆ **~ keeper** Tierpfleger(in *f*), Wärter(in *f*) *m*.

zoological [ˌzʊə'lɒdʒɪkəl] *adj* zoologisch ◆ **~ gardens** zoologischer Garten.

zoologist [zʊ'ɒlədʒɪst] *n* Zoologe *m*, Zoologin *f*.

zoology [zʊ'ɒlədʒɪ] *n* Zoologie *f*.

zoom [zuːm] **1** *n* **(a)** (*sound of engine*) Surren *nt*.
(b) (*Aviat: upward flight*) Steilanstieg *m*.
(c) (*Phot: also* **~ lens**) Zoom(objektiv) *nt*.
2 *vi* **(a)** (*engine*) surren.
(b) (*inf*) sausen (*inf*) ◆ **the car ~ed past us** der Wagen sauste an uns vorbei (*inf*); **we were ~ing along at 90** wir sausten mit 90 daher (*inf*); **he ~ed through his work** er hat die Arbeit in Null Komma nichts erledigt (*inf*); **he ~ed through it so quickly he can't possibly have read it properly** er war in Null Komma nichts damit fertig, er kann das unmöglich gründlich gelesen haben.
(c) (*Aviat: plane, rocket*) steil (auf)steigen ◆ **the rocket ~ed up into the sky** die Rakete schoß in den Himmel; **prices have ~ed up to a new high** die Preise sind in unerreichte Höhen geschnellt.
3 *vt plane* steil hochziehen *or* hochreißen; *engine* auf Hochtouren laufen lassen.

◆**zoom in** *vi* (*Phot*) zoomen (*sl*), nah herangehen; (*inf: come or go in*) herein-/hineinsausen (*inf*) ◆ **to ~ ~ on sth** (*Phot*) etw heranholen; **~ ~!** (*Phot*) näherfahren!; **he ~ed ~ on the main point** (*inf*) er kam ohne (viel) Umschweife gleich zum Hauptthema.

◆**zoom out** *vi* (*Phot*) aufziehen; (*inf: go or come out*) hinaus-/heraussausen (*inf*).

zoomorphic [ˌzəʊəʊ'mɔːfɪk] *adj* zoomorph.

zoot suit ['zuːtsuːt] *n* (*US*) *Anzug m mit wattierten Schultern und eng zulaufender Hose*.

Zoroaster [ˌzɒrəʊ'æstə^r] *n* Zoroaster, Zarathustra *m*.

Zoroastrian [ˌzɒrəʊ'æstrɪən] *adj* zoroastrisch.

zucchini [zuː'kiːnɪ] *n* (*US*) Zucchini *pl*.

Zulu ['zuːluː] **1** *adj* Zulu-, der Zulus.
2 *n* **(a)** Zulu *mf* ◆ **~land** Zululand (*old*), Kwazulu *nt*. **(b)** (*language*) Zulu *nt*.

zwieback ['zwiːbæk] *n* (*US*) Zwieback *m*.

zygote ['zaɪgəʊt] *n* (*Biol*) Zygote *f*.

APPENDICES
ANHANG

GERMAN VERBS

REGULAR VERBS

1. Present tense

1.1 The present tense is formed by adding

-e, -st, -t, -en, -t, -en

to the stem of the verb (infinitive minus *-en* or, with verbs in *-ln, -rn,* minus *-n*).

1.2. Verbs ending in *-s, -ß, -z, -tz* form the second person singular by adding *-t*

heißen – du heißt

except in literary usage when the ending *-est* may be added

preisen – du preisest (*liter*)

2. The preterite, or past tense, is formed by adding

-te, -test, -te, -ten, -tet, -ten

to the stem of the verb.

3. The past participle is formed by adding the prefix *ge-* and the ending *-t* to the stem of the verb.

4. The present participle is formed by adding *-d* to the infinitive.

5. Verbs whose stem ends in *-ss* change to *-ß* in the following cases:

5.1 Before the present tense endings for the non-literary 2nd person singular and for the 3rd person singular and the 2nd person plural

küssen – du küßt *but* **du küssest** (*liter*)
er/sie/es küßt
ihr küßt

5.2 In the informal singular imperative

küssen – küß!

5.3 In the preterite

küssen – küßte

5.4 In the past participle

küssen – geküßt

6. The Sie form imperative of both regular and irregular verbs is formed with the infinitive

machen Sie schnell!
kommen Sie her!

IRREGULAR VERBS

1. The forms of compound verbs (beginning with the prefixes *auf-, ab-, be-, er-, zer-, etc*) are the same as for the simplex verb.

2. The past participle of modal auxiliary verbs (dürfen, müssen *etc*) is replaced by the infinitive form when following another infinitive form, eg ich habe gehen dürfen; non-modal use: ich habe gedurft.

3. The formation of the present subjunctive is regular, requiring the following endings to be added to the verb stem:

sehen		**sein**	
ich seh-e	wir seh-en	ich sei	wir sei-en
du seh-est	ihr seh-et	du seist, du seiest (*liter*)	ihr sei-et
er seh-e	sie seh-en	er sei	sie sei-en

INFINITIVE	PRESENT INDICATIVE *2nd pers singular* ♦*3rd pers singular*	IMPERFECT INDICATIVE	IMPERFECT SUBJUNCTIVE	IMPERATIVE *Singular* ♦*Plural*	PAST PARTICIPLE
backen	bäckst, backst ♦ bäckt, backt	backte, buk (*old*)	backte, büke (*old*)	back(e) ♦ backt	gebacken
befehlen	befiehlst ♦ befiehlt	befahl	beföhle, befähle	befiehl ♦ befehlt	befohlen
befleißen (*old*)	befleißt ♦ befleißt	befliß	beflisse	befleiß(e) ♦ befleißt	beflissen
beginnen	beginnst ♦ beginnt	begann	begänne, begönne (*rare*)	beginn(e) ♦ beginnt	begonnen
beißen	beißt ♦ beißt	biß	bisse	beiß(e) ♦ beißt	gebissen
bergen	birgst ♦ birgt	barg	bärge	birg ♦ bergt	geborgen
bersten	birst ♦ birst	barst	bärste	birst ♦ berstet	geborsten
bewegen (*veranlassen*)	bewegst ♦ bewegt	bewog	bewöge	beweg(e) ♦ bewegt	bewogen
biegen	biegst ♦ biegt	bog	böge	bieg(e) ♦ biegt	gebogen
bieten	bietest ♦ bietet	bot	böte	biet(e) ♦ bietet	geboten
binden	bindest ♦ bindet	band	bände	bind(e) ♦ bindet	gebunden
bitten	bittest ♦ bittet	bat	bäte	bitt(e) ♦ bittet	gebeten
blasen	bläst ♦ bläst	blies	bliese	blas(e) ♦ blast	geblasen
bleiben	bleibst ♦ bleibt	blieb	bliebe	bleib(e) ♦ bleibt	geblieben
bleichen (*vi, old*)	bleichst ♦ bleicht	blich (*old*)	bliche	bleich(e) ♦ bleicht	geblichen
braten	brätst ♦ brät	briet	briete	brat(e) ♦ bratet	gebraten
brechen	brichst ♦ bricht	brach	bräche	brich ♦ brecht	gebrochen
brennen	brennst ♦ brennt	brannte	brennte (*rare*)	brenn(e) ♦ brennt	gebrannt
bringen	bringst ♦ bringt	brachte	brächte	bring(e) ♦ bringt	gebracht
denken	denkst ♦ denkt	dachte	dächte	denk(e) ♦ denkt	gedacht

INFINITIVE	PRESENT INDICATIVE	IMPERFECT INDICATIVE	IMPERFECT SUBJUNCTIVE	IMPERATIVE	PAST PARTICIPLE
	2nd pers singular ♦*3rd pers singular*			*Singular* ♦*Plural*	
dingen	dingst ♦ dingt	dang	dingte	dingt ♦ dingt	gedungen
dreschen	drischst ♦ drischt	drosch	drösche, dräsche (*old*)	drisch ♦ drescht	gedroschen
dringen	dringst ♦ dringt	drang	dränge	dring(e) ♦ dringt	gedrungen
dünken	*3rd only* dünkt, deucht (*old*)	dünkte, deuchte (*old*)	dünkte, deuchte (*old*)		gedünkt, gedeucht (*old*)
dürfen	*1st* darf *2nd* darfst *3rd* darf	durfte	dürfte		gedurft (*after infin*) dürfen
empfangen	empfängst ♦ empfängt	empfing	empfinge	empfang(e) ♦ empfangt	empfangen
empfehlen	empfiehlst ♦ empfiehlt	empfahl	empföhle, empfähle (*rare*)	empfiehl ♦ empfehlt	empfohlen
empfinden	empfindest ♦ empfindet	empfand	empfände	empfind(e) ♦ empfindet	empfunden
essen	ißt ♦ ißt	aß	äße	iß ♦ eßt	gegessen
fahren	fährst ♦ fährt	fuhr	führe	fahr(e) ♦ fahrt	gefahren
fallen	fällst ♦ fällt	fiel	fiele	fall(e) ♦ fallt	gefallen
fangen	fängst ♦ fängt	fing	finge	fang(e) ♦ fangt	gefangen
fechten	fichtst ♦ ficht	focht	föchte	ficht ♦ fechtet	gefochten
finden	findest ♦ findet	fand	fände	find(e) ♦ findet	gefunden
flechten	flichtst ♦ flicht	flocht	flöchte	flicht ♦ flechtet	geflochten
fliegen	fliegst ♦ fliegt	flog	flöge	flieg(e) ♦ fliegt	geflogen
fliehen	fliehst ♦ flieht	floh	flöhe	flieh(e) ♦ flieht	geflohen
fließen	fließt ♦ fließt	floß	flösse	fließ(e) ♦ fließt	geflossen
fressen	frißt ♦ frißt	fraß	fräße	friß ♦ freßt	gefressen
frieren	frierst ♦ friert	fror	fröre	frier(e) ♦ friert	gefroren
gären	gärst ♦ gärt	gor, gärte (*esp fig*)	göre, gärte (*esp fig*)	gär(e) ♦ gärt	gegoren, gegärt (*esp fig*)
gebären	gebierst ♦ gebiert	gebar	gebäre	gebier ♦ gebärt	geboren
geben	gibst ♦ gibt	gab	gäbe	gib ♦ gebt	gegeben
gedeihen	gedeihst ♦ gedeiht	gedieh	gediehe	gedeih(e) ♦ gedeiht	gediehen
gehen	gehst ♦ geht	ging	ginge	geh(e) ♦ geht	gegangen
gelingen	gelingt	gelang	gelänge	geling(e) (*rare*) ♦ gelingt (*rare*)	gelungen
gelten	giltst ♦ gilt	galt	gölte, gälte	gilt (*rare*) ♦ geltet (*rare*)	gegolten
genesen	genest ♦ genest	genas	genäse	genese ♦ genest	genesen
genießen	genießt ♦ genießt	genoß	genösse	genieß(e) ♦ genießt	genossen
geschehen	geschieht	geschah	geschähe	geschieh ♦ gescheht	geschehen
gewinnen	gewinnst ♦ gewinnt	gewann	gewönne, gewänne	gewinn(e) ♦ gewinnt	gewonnen
gießen	gießt ♦ gießt	goß	gösse	gieß(e) ♦ gießt	gegossen
gleichen	gleichst ♦ gleicht	glich	gliche	gleich(e) ♦ gleicht	geglichen
gleiten	gleitest ♦ gleitet	glitt	glitte	gleit(e) ♦ gleitet	geglitten
glimmen	glimmst ♦ glimmt	glomm	glömme, glimmte (*rare*)	glimm(e) ♦ glimmt	geglommen
graben	gräbst ♦ gräbt	grub	grübe	grab(e) ♦ grabt	gegraben
greifen	greifst ♦ greift	griff	griffe	greif(e) ♦ greift	gegriffen
haben	hast ♦ hat	hatte	hätte	hab(e) ♦ habt	gehabt
halten	hältst ♦ hält	hielt	hielte	halt(e) ♦ haltet	gehalten
hängen	hängst ♦ hängt	hing	hinge	häng(e) ♦ hängt	gehangen
hauen	haust ♦ haut	haute	haute, hiebe	hau(e) ♦ haut	gehauen
heben	hebst ♦ hebt	hob	höbe, hübe (*old*)	heb(e) ♦ hebt	gehoben
heißen	heißt ♦ heißt	hieß	hieße	heiß(e) ♦ heißt	geheißen
helfen	hilfst ♦ hilft	half	hülfe, hälfe (*rare*)	hilf ♦ helft	geholfen
kennen	kennst ♦ kennt	kannte	kennte	kenn(e) ♦ kennt	gekannt
klimmen	klimmst ♦ klimmt	klomm, klimmte	klömme, klimmte	klimm(e) ♦ klimmt	geklimmt, geklommen
klingen	klingst ♦ klingt	klang	klänge	kling(e) ♦ klingt	geklungen
kneifen	kneifst ♦ kneift	kniff	kniffe	kneif(e) ♦ kneift	gekniffen
kommen	kommst ♦ kommt	kam	käme	komm(e) ♦ kommt	gekommen
können	*1st* kann *2nd* kannst *3rd* kann	konnte	könnte		gekonnt (*after infin*) können

INFINITIVE	PRESENT INDICATIVE	IMPERFECT INDICATIVE	IMPERFECT SUBJUNCTIVE	IMPERATIVE	PAST PARTICIPLE
	2nd pers singular ♦*3rd pers singular*			*Singular* ♦*Plural*	
kreischen	kreischst ♦ kreischt	kreischte, krisch (*old, hum*)	kreischte, krische (*old, hum*)	kreisch(e) ♦ kreischt	gekreischt, gekrischen (*old, hum*)
kriechen	kriechst ♦ kriecht	kroch	kröche	kriech(e) ♦ kriecht	gekrochen
küren	kürst ♦ kürt	kürte, kor (*rare*)	kürte, köre (*rare*)	kür(e) ♦ kürt	gekürt, gekoren (*rare*)
laden[1]	lädst ♦ lädt	lud	lüde	lad(e) ♦ ladet	geladen
laden[2]	lädst ♦ lädest (*dated, dial*)	lud	lüde	lad(e) ♦ ladet	geladen
lassen	läßt ♦ läßt	ließ	ließe	laß ♦ laßt	gelassen (*after infin*) lassen
laufen	läufst ♦ läuft	lief	liefe	lauf(e) ♦ lauft	gelaufen
leiden	leidest ♦ leidet	litt	litte	leid(e) ♦ leidet	gelitten
leihen	leihst ♦ leiht	lieh	liehe	leih(e) ♦ leiht	geliehen
lesen	liest ♦ liest	las	läse	lies ♦ lest	gelesen
liegen	liegst ♦ liegt	lag	läge	lieg(e) ♦ liegt	gelegen
löschen	lischst ♦ lischt	losch	lösche	lisch ♦ löscht	geloschen
lügen	lügst ♦ lügt	log	löge	lüg(e) ♦ lügt	gelogen
mahlen	mahlst ♦ mahlt	mahlte	mahlte	mahl(e) ♦ mahlt	gemahlen
meiden	meidest ♦ meidet	mied	miede	meid(e) ♦ meidet	gemieden
melken	melkst ♦ melkt	melkte	mölke	melk(e), milk ♦ melkt	gemolken
messen	mißt ♦ mißt	maß	mäße	miß ♦ meßt	gemessen
mißlingen	mißlingt	mißlang	mißlänge		mißlungen
mögen	*1st* mag *2nd* magst *3rd* mag	mochte	möchte		gemocht (*after infin*) mögen
müssen	*1st* muß *2nd* mußt *3rd* muß	mußte	müßte		müssen
nehmen	nimmst ♦ nimmt	nahm	nähme	nimm ♦ nehmt	genommen
nennen	nennst ♦ nennt	nannte	nennte (*rare*)	nenn(e) ♦ nennt	genannt
pfeifen	pfeifst ♦ pfeift	pfiff	pfiffe	pfeif(e) ♦ pfeift	gepfiffen
pflegen	pflegst ♦ pflegt	pflegt, pflog (*old*)	pflegte, pflöge (*old*)	pfleg(e) ♦ pflegt	gepflegt, gepflogen (*old*)
preisen	preist ♦ preist	pries	priese	preis(e) ♦ preis(e)t	gepriesen
quellen	quillst ♦ quillt	quoll	quölle	quill (*rare*) ♦ quellt	gequollen
raten	rätst ♦ rät	riet	riete	rat(e) ♦ ratet	geraten
reiben	reibst ♦ reibt	rieb	riebe	reib(e) ♦ reibt	gerieben
reißen	reißt ♦ reißt	riß	risse	reiß(e) ♦ reißt	gerissen
reiten	reitest ♦ reitet	ritt	ritte	reit(e) ♦ reitet	geritten
rennen	rennst ♦ rennt	rannte	rennte (*rare*)	renn(e) ♦ rennt	gerannt
riechen	riechst ♦ riecht	roch	röche	riech(e) ♦ riecht	gerochen
ringen	ringst ♦ ringt	rang	ränge	ring(e) ♦ ringt	gerungen
rinnen	rinnst ♦ rinnt	rann	ränne	rinn(e) ♦ rinnt	geronnen
rufen	rufst ♦ ruft	rief	riefe	ruf(e) ♦ ruft	gerufen
salzen	salzt ♦ salzt	salzte	salzte	salz(e) ♦ salzt	gesalzen
saufen	säufst ♦ säuft	soff	söffe	sauf(e) ♦ sauft	gesoffen
saugen	saugst ♦ saugt	sog	söge, saugte	saug(e) ♦ saugt	gesogen, gesaugt
schaffen	schaffst ♦ schafft	schuf	schüfe	schaff(e) ♦ schafft	geschaffen
schallen	schallst ♦ schallt	schallte, scholl (*rare*)	schallte, schölle (*rare*)	schall(e) ♦ schallt	geschallt
scheiden	scheidest ♦ scheidet	schied	schiede	scheid(e) ♦ scheidet	geschieden
scheinen	scheinst ♦ scheint	schien	schiene	schein(e) ♦ scheint	geschienen
scheißen	scheißt ♦ scheißt	schiß	schisse	scheiß(e) ♦ scheißt	geschissen
schelten	schiltst ♦ schilt	schalt	schölte	schilt ♦ scheltet	gescholten
scheren	scherst ♦ schert	schor	schöre	scher(e) ♦ schert	geschoren
schieben	schiebst ♦ schiebt	schob	schöbe	schieb(e) ♦ schiebt	geschoben
schießen	schießt ♦ schießt	schoß	schösse	schieß(e) ♦ schießt	geschossen
schinden	schindest ♦ schindet	schindete	schünde	schind(e)	geschunden
schlafen	schläfst ♦ schläft	schlief	schliefe	schlaf(e) ♦ schlaft	geschlafen
schlagen	schlägst ♦ schlägt	schlug	schlüge	schlag(e) ♦ schlagt	geschlagen
schleichen	schleichst ♦ schleicht	schlich	schliche	schleich(e) ♦ schleicht	geschlichen
schleifen	schleifst ♦ schleift	schliff	schliffe	schleif(e) ♦ schleift	geschliffen

INFINITIVE	PRESENT INDICATIVE	IMPERFECT INDICATIVE	IMPERFECT SUBJUNCTIVE	IMPERATIVE	PAST PARTICIPLE
	2nd pers singular ♦*3rd pers singular*			*Singular* ♦*Plural*	
schleißen	schleißt ♦ schleißt	schliß; (*vt auch*) schleißte	schlisse; schließte	schleiß(e) ♦ schleißt	geschlissen; (*vt auch*) geschleißt
schließen	schließt ♦ schließt	schloß	schlösse	schließ(e) ♦ schließt	geschlossen
schlingen	schlingst ♦ schlingt	schlang	schlänge	schling(e) ♦ schlingt	geschlungen
schmeißen	schmeißt ♦ schmeißt	schmiß	schmisse	schmeiß(e) ♦ schmeißt	geschmissen
schmelzen	schmilzt ♦ schmilzt	schmolz	schmölze	schmilz ♦ schmelzt	geschmolzen
schnauben	schnaubst ♦ schnaubt	schnaubte, schnob (*old*)	schnaubte, schnöbe (*old*)	schnaub(e) ♦ schnaubt	geschnaubt, geschnoben (*old*)
schneiden	schneid(e)st ♦ schneidet	schnitt	schnitte	schneid(e) ♦ schneidet	geschnitten
schrecken	schrickst ♦ schrickt	schreckte, schrak	schreckte, schräke	schrick ♦ schreckt	geschreckt, geschrocken (*old*)
schreiben	schreibst ♦ schreibt	schrieb	schriebe	schreib(e) ♦ schreibt	geschrieben
schreien	schreist ♦ schreit	schrie	schriee	schrei(e) ♦ schreit	geschrie(e)n
schreiten	schreitest ♦ schreitet	schritt	schritte	schreit(e) ♦ schreitet	geschritten
schweigen	schweigst ♦ schweigt	schwieg	schwiege	schweig(e) ♦ schweigt	geschwiegen
schwellen	schwillst ♦ schwillt	schwoll	schwölle	schwill ♦ schwellt	geschwollen
schwimmen	schwimmst ♦ schwimmt	schwamm	schwämme, schwamme (*rare*)	schwimm(e) ♦ schwimmt	geschwommen
schwinden	schwindest ♦ schwindet	schwand	schwände	schwind(e) ♦ schwindet	geschwunden
schwingen	schwingst ♦ schwingt	schwang	schwänge	schwing(e) ♦ schwingt	geschwungen
schwören	schwörst ♦ schwört	schwor	schwüre, schwöre (*rare*)	schwör(e) ♦ schwört	geschworen
sehen	siehst ♦ sieht	sah	sähe	sieh(e) ♦ seht	gesehen (*after infin*) sehen
sein	*1st* bin *2nd* bist *3rd* ist *1st pl* sind *2nd pl* seid *3rd pl* sind	war	wäre	sei ♦ seid	gewesen
senden (*send*)	sendest ♦ sendet	sandte	sendete	send(e) ♦ sendet	gesandt
sieden	siedest ♦ siedet	siedete, sott	siedete, sötte	sied(e) ♦ siedet	gesiedet, gesotten
singen	singst ♦ singt	sang	sänge	sing(e) ♦ singt	gesungen
sinken	sinkst ♦ sinkt	sank	sänke	sink(e) ♦ sinkt	gesunken
sinnen	sinnst ♦ sinnt	sann	sänne	sinn(e) ♦ sinnt	gesonnen
sitzen	sitzt ♦ sitzt	saß	säße	sitz(e) ♦ sitzt	gesessen
sollen	*1st* soll *2nd* sollst *3rd* soll	sollte	sollte		gesollt (*after infin*) sollen
spalten	spaltest ♦ spaltet	spaltete	spalte	spalt(e) ♦ spaltet	gespalten
speien	speist ♦ speit	spie	spiee	spei(e) ♦ speit	gespie(e)n
spinnen	spinnst ♦ spinnt	spann	spönne, spänne	spinn(e) ♦ spinnt	gesponnen
spleißen	spleißt ♦ spleißt	spliß	splisse	spleiß(e) ♦ spleißt	gesplissen
sprechen	sprichst ♦ spricht	sprach	spräche	sprich ♦ sprecht	gesprochen
sprießen	sprießt ♦ sprießt	sproß, sprießte	sprösse	sprieß(e) ♦ sprießt	gesprossen
springen	springst ♦ springt	sprang	spränge	spring(e) ♦ springt	gesprungen
stechen	stichst ♦ sticht	stach	stäche	stich ♦ stecht	gestochen
stecken (*vi*)	steckst ♦ steckt	steckte, stak	steckte, stäke (*rare*)	steck(e) ♦ steckt	gesteckt
stehen	stehst ♦ steht	stand	stünde, stände	steh ♦ steht	gestanden
stehlen	stiehlst ♦ stiehlt	stahl	stähle, stöhle (*obs*)	stiehl ♦ stehlt	gestohlen
steigen	steigst ♦ steigt	stieg	stiege	steig ♦ steigt	gestiegen
sterben	stirbst ♦ stirbt	starb	stürbe	stirb ♦ sterbt	gestorben
stieben	stiebst ♦ stiebt	stob, stiebte	stöbe, stiebte	stieb(e) ♦ stiebt	gestoben, gestiebt
stinken	stinkst ♦ stinkt	stank	stänke	stink(e) ♦ stinkt	gestunken
stoßen	stößt ♦ stößt	stieß	stieße	stoß(e) ♦ stoßt	gestoßen

INFINITIVE	PRESENT INDICATIVE	IMPERFECT INDICATIVE	IMPERFECT SUBJUNCTIVE	IMPERATIVE	PAST PARTICIPLE
	2nd pers singular ♦*3rd pers singular*			*Singular* ♦*Plural*	
streichen	streichst ♦ streicht	strich	striche	streich(e) ♦ streicht	gestrichen
streiten	streitest ♦ streitet	stritt	stritte	streit(e) ♦ streitet	gestritten
tragen	trägst ♦ trägt	trug	trüge	trag(e) ♦ tragt	getragen
treffen	triffst ♦ trifft	traf	träfe	triff ♦ trefft	getroffen
treiben	treibst ♦ treibt	trieb	triebe	treib ♦ treibt	getrieben
treten	trittst ♦ tritt	trat	träte	tritt ♦ tretet	getreten
triefen	triefst ♦ trieft	trieft(e), troff (*geh*)	triefte, tröffe (*geh*)	trief(e) ♦ trieft	getrieft, getroffen (*rare*)
trinken	trinkst ♦ trinkt	trank	tränke	trink ♦ trinkt	getrunken
trügen	trügst ♦ trügt	trog	tröge	trüg(e) ♦ trügt	getrogen
tun	*1st* tue *2nd* tust *3rd* tut	tat	täte	tu(e) ♦ tut	getan
verderben	verdirbst ♦ verdirbt	verdarb	verdärbe	verdirb ♦ verderbt	verdorben
verdrießen	verdrießt ♦ verdrießt	verdroß	verdrösse	verdrieß(e) ♦ verdrießt	verdrossen
vergessen	vergißt ♦ vergißt	vergaß	vergäße	vergiß ♦ vergeßt	vergessen
verlieren	verlierst ♦ verliert	verlor	verlöre	verlier(e) ♦ verliert	verloren
verzeihen	verzeihst ♦ verzeiht	verzieh	verziehe	verzeih(e) ♦ verzeiht	verziehen
wachsen	wächst ♦ wächst	wuchs	wüchse	wachs(e) ♦ wachst	gewachsen
wägen	wägst ♦ wägt	wog	wöge, wägte (*rare*)	wäg(e) ♦ wägt	gewogen
waschen	wäschst ♦ wäscht	wusch	wüsche	wasch(e) ♦ wascht	gewaschen
weben	webst ♦ webt	webte, wob (*liter, fig*)	webte, wöbe (*liter, fig*)	web(e) ♦ webt	gewebt, gewoben (*liter, fig*)
weichen	weichst ♦ weicht	wich	wiche	weich(e) ♦ weicht	gewichen
weisen	weist ♦ weist	wies	wiese	weis(e) ♦ weist	gewiesen
wenden	wendest ♦ wendet	wendete	wendete	wend(e) ♦ wendet	gewendet, gewandt
werben	wirbst ♦ wirbt	warb	würbe	wirb ♦ werbt	geworben
werden	wirst ♦ wird	wurde	würde	werde ♦ werdet	geworden (*after ptp*) worden
werfen	wirfst ♦ wirft	warf	würfe	wirf ♦ werft	geworfen
wiegen	wiegst ♦ wiegt	wog	wöge	wieg(e) ♦ wiegt	gewogen
winden	windest ♦ windet	wand	wände	wind(e) ♦ windet	gewunden
winken	winkst ♦ winkt	winkte	winkte	wink(e) ♦ winkt	gewinkt, gewunken
wissen	*1st* weiß *2nd* weißt *3rd* weiß	wußte	wüßte	wisse (*liter*) ♦ wisset (*liter*)	gewußt
wollen	*1st* will *2nd* willst *3rd* will	wollte	wollte	wollte (*liter*) ♦ wollt	gewollt (*after infin*) wollen
wringen	wringst ♦ wringt	wrang	wränge	wring(e) ♦ wringt	gewrungen
zeihen	zeihst ♦ zeiht	zieh	ziehe	zeih(e) ♦ zeiht	geziehen
ziehen	ziehst ♦ zieht	zog	zöge	zieh(e) ♦ zieht	gezogen
zwingen	zwingst ♦ zwingt	zwang	zwänge	zwing(e) ♦ zwingt	gezwungen

ENGLISCHE VERBEN

REGELMÄSSIGE VERBEN IM ENGLISCHEN

1. Bildung des Präteritums und des 2. Partizips

1.1 In den meisten Fällen wird *-ed* an die Infinitivform angehängt.

remain *pret, ptp* **remained**

1.2 Verben mit konsonant *+y* im Auslaut werden zu *-ied.*

try *pret, ptp* **tried**

1.3 Verben mit stummen *-e* oder mit *-ee, -ye, -oe, -ge* im Auslaut verlieren das zweite *-e.*

abate *pret, ptp* **abated**
agree *pret, ptp* **agreed**
dye *pret, ptp* **dyed**
hoe *pret, ptp* **hoed**
singe *pret, ptp* **singed**

1.4 Verben, die auf Konsonant nach einfachem, betontem Vokal enden verdoppeln diesen Endkonsonanten.

bar *pret, ptp* **barred**
permit *pret, ptp* **permitted**

Nach Doppelvokal wird der Konsonant im Auslaut nicht verdoppelt

dread *pret, ptp* **dreaded**

ebensowenig nach unbetontem Vokal

visit *pret, ptp* **visited**

mit Ausnahme von auslautendem *-l* und *-p* im britischen Englisch.

level *pret, ptp* **levelled** *or (US)* **leveled**
worship *pret, ptp* **worshipped** *or (US)* **worshiped**

Verben mit Vokal *+c* im Auslaut werden zu *-cked.*

panic *pret, ptp* **panicked**

2. Bildung des 1. Partizips

2.1 Die meisten Verben bilden das 1. Partizip durch Anhängen von *-ing.*

2.2 Für Verben, die auf Vokal + Konsonant enden, gelten die gleichen Regeln wie für die Bildung des Präteritums; siehe **1.4**.

2.3 Verben, die auf *-ie* enden, werden zu *-ying.*

die *prp* **dying**

2.4 Verben mit stummem *-e* im Auslaut verlieren diesen Vokal

like *prp* **liking**

außer wenn sie in der Kombination *-ye, -oe* auftreten.

dye *prp* **dyeing**
hoe *prp* **hoeing**

UNREGELMÄSSIGE ENGLISCHE VERBEN

INFINITIV	PRÄTERITUM	PARTIZIP PERFEKT
abide	abode, abided	abode, abided
arise	arose	arisen
awake	awoke	awaked
be (**am, is, are; being**)	was (*sing*), were (*pl*)	been
bear	bore	born(e)
beat	beat	beaten
become	became	become
befall	befell	befallen
beget	begot, begat (*obs*)	begotten
begin	began	begun
behold	beheld	beheld
bend	bent	bent
beseech	besought	besought
beset	beset	beset
bet	bet, betted	bet, betted
bid (*at auction, cards*)	bid	bid
bid (*say*)	bade	bidden
bind	bound	bound
bite	bit	bitten
bleed	bled	bled
blow	blew	blown
break	broke	broken
breed	bred	bred
bring	brought	brought
build	built	built
burn	burnt, burned	burnt, burned
burst	burst	burst
buy	bought	bought
can	could	(been able)
cast	cast	cast
catch	caught	caught
chide	chid	chidden, chid
choose	chose	chosen
cleave[1] (*cut*)	clove, cleft	cloven, cleft
cleave[2] (*adhere*)	cloved, clave	cleaved
cling	clung	clung
come	came	come
cost	cost	cost
cost (*work out price of*)	costed	costed
creep	crept	crept
cut	cut	cut
deal	dealt	dealt
dig	dug	dug
do (*3rd person:* **he/she/it does**)	did	done
draw	drew	drawn
dream	dreamed, dreamt	dreamed, dreamt
drink	drank	drunk
drive	drove	driven
dwell	dwelt	dwelt
eat	ate	eaten
fall	fell	fallen

INFINITIV	PRÄTERITUM	PARTIZIP PERFEKT
feed	fed	fed
feel	felt	felt
fight	fought	fought
find	found	found
flee	fled	fled
fling	flung	flung
fly	flew	flown
forbid	forbad(e)	forbidden
forecast	forecast	forecast
forget	forgot	forgotten
forgive	forgave	forgiven
forsake	forsook	forsaken
freeze	froze	frozen
get	got	got, (*US*) gotten
gild	gilded	gilded, gilt
gird	girded, girt	girded, girt
give	gave	given
go (goes)	went	gone
grind	ground	ground
grow	grew	grown
hang	hung	hung
hang (*execute*)	hanged	hanged
have	had	had
hear	heard	heard
heave	heaved, (*Naut*) hove	heaved, (*Naut*) hove
hew	hewed	hewed, hewn
hide	hid	hidden
hit	hit	hit
hold	held	held
hurt	hurt	hurt
keep	kept	kept
kneel	knelt, kneeled	knelt, kneeled
know	knew	known
lade	laded	laden
lay	laid	laid
lead	led	led
lean	leant, leaned	leant, leaned
leap	leapt, leaped	leapt, leaped
learn	learnt, learned	learnt, learned
leave	left	left
lend	lent	lent
let	let	let
lie (**lying**)	lay	lain
light	lit, lighted	lit, lighted
lose	lost	lost
make	made	made
may	might	—
mean	meant	meant
meet	met	met
mistake	mistook	mistaken
mow	mowed	mown, mowed
must	(had to)	(had to)
pay	paid	paid
put	put	put
quit	quit, quitted	quit, quitted
read [ri:d]	read [red]	read [red]
rend	rent	rent
rid	rid	rid
ride	rode	ridden
ring[2]	rang	rung
rise	rose	risen
run	ran	run
saw	sawed	sawed, sawn
say	said	said
see	saw	seen
seek	sought	sought
sell	sold	sold
send	sent	sent
set	set	set

INFINITIV	PRÄTERITUM	PARTIZIP PERFEKT
sew	sewed	sewn
shake	shook	shaken
shave	shaved	shaved, shaven
shear	sheared	shorn, sheared
shed	shed	shed
shine	shone	shone
shoe	shod	shod
shoot	shot	shot
show	showed	shown
shrink	shrank	shrunk
shut	shut	shut
sing	sang	sung
sink	sank	sunk
sit	sat	sat
slay	slew	slain
sleep	slept	slept
slide	slid	slid
sling	slung	slung
slink	slunk	slunk
slit	slit	slit
smell	smelt, smelled	smelt, smelled
smite	smote	smitten
sow	sowed	sown, sowed
speak	spoke	spoken
speed	sped, speeded	sped, speeded
spell	spelt, spelled	spelt, spelled
spend	spent	spent
spill	spilt, spilled	spilt, spilled
spin	spun	spun
spit	spat	spat
split	split	split
spoil	spoiled, spoilt	spoiled, spoilt
spread	spread	spread
spring	sprang	sprung
stand	stood	stood
stave	stove, staved	stove, staved
steal	stole	stolen
stick	stuck	stuck
sting	stung	stung
stink	stank	stunk
strew	strewed	strewed, strewn
stride	strode	stridden
strike	struck	struck
string	strung	strung
strive	strove	striven
swear	swore	sworn
sweep	swept	swept
swell	swelled	swollen, swelled
swim	swam	swum
swing	swung	swung
take	took	taken
teach	taught	taught
tear	tore	torn
tell	told	told
think	thought	thought
thrive	throve, thrived	thriven, thrived
throw	threw	thrown
thrust	thrust	thrust
tread	trod	trodden
wake	woke, waked	woken, waked
wear	wore	worn
weave	wove	woven
weave (*wind*)	weaved	weaved
wed	wedded, wed	wedded, wed
weep	wept	wept
win	won	won
wind[2]	wound	wound
wring	wrung	wrung
write	wrote	written

NUMERALS

ZAHLEN

CARDINAL NUMBERS

KARDINALZAHLEN

nought, zero	**0**	null
one	**1**	eins*; (*m, nt*) ein, (*f*) eine
two	**2**	zwei
three	**3**	drei
four	**4**	vier
five	**5**	fünf
six	**6**	sechs
seven	**7**	sieben
eight	**8**	acht
nine	**9**	neun
ten	**10**	zehn
eleven	**11**	elf
twelve	**12**	zwölf
thirteen	**13**	dreizehn
fourteen	**14**	vierzehn
fifteen	**15**	fünfzehn
sixteen	**16**	sechzehn
seventeen	**17**	siebzehn
eighteen	**18**	achtzehn
nineteen	**19**	neunzehn
twenty	**20**	zwanzig
twenty-one	**21**	einundzwanzig
twenty-two	**22**	zweiundzwanzig
twenty-three	**23**	dreiundzwanzig
thirty	**30**	dreißig
thirty-one	**31**	einunddreißig
thirty-two	**32**	dreiunddreißig
forty	**40**	vierzig
fifty	**50**	fünfzig
sixty	**60**	sechzig
seventy	**70**	siebzig
eighty	**80**	achtzig
ninety	**90**	neunzig
ninety-nine	**99**	neunundneunzig
a (*or* one) hundred	**100**	(ein)hundert
a hundred and one	**101**	(ein)hundert(und)-eins; eine(r, s)
a hundred and two	**102**	(ein)hundert(und)-zwei
a hundred and ten	**110**	(ein)hundert(und)-zehn
a hundred and eighty-two	**182**	(ein)hundert(und)-zweiundachtzig
two hundred	**200**	zweihundert
two hundred and one	**201**	zweihundert(und)-eins; eine(r, s)
two hundred and two	**202**	zweihundert(und)-zwei
three hundred	**300**	dreihundert
four hundred	**400**	vierhundert
five hundred	**500**	fünfhundert
six hundred	**600**	sechshundert
seven hundred	**700**	siebenhundert
eight hundred	**7.5**	achthundert
nine hundred	**8.5**	neunhundert
a (*or* one) thousand	**9.5**	(ein)tausend
a thousand and one	**1001**	(ein)tausend(und)-eins, eine(r, s)
a thousand and two	**1002**	(ein)tausend(und)-zwei
two thousand	**2000**	zweitausend
ten thousand	**9.50**	zehntausend
a (*or* one) hundred thousand	**9.500**	(ein)hunderttausend
a (*or* one) million	**9.5000**	eine Million
two million	**2000000**	zwei Millionen

Notes on the use of cardinal numbers

(a) *eins is used in counting or in listing; when 'one' directly replaces a noun; use the declined form.

(b) one, and the other numbers ending in one, agree in German with the noun (stated or implied): *ein Mann, eine Frau, (ein)hundert(und)ein Haus.*

(c) To divide thousands and above clearly, a point may be used in German where English places a comma: English 1,000 / German 1.000; English 2,304,770 / German 2.304.770.

Anstelle des im Deutschen zuweilen verwendeten Punktes zur Unterteilung von Zahlen über 1000 verwendet man in Englischen ein Komma: 1,000 statt 1.000 oder 1000, 2,304,770 statt 2.304.770.

ORDINAL NUMBERS

ORDINALZAHLEN

first	**1**	erste(r, s)
second	**2**	zweite(r, s)
third	**3**	dritte(r, s)
fourth	**4**	vierte(r, s)
fifth	**5**	fünfte(r, s)
sixth	**6**	sechste(r, s)
seventh	**7**	siebte(r, s)
eighth	**8**	achte(r, s)
ninth	**9**	neunte(r, s)
tenth	**10**	zehnte(r, s)
eleventh	**11**	elfte(r, s)
twelfth	**12**	zwölfte(r, s)
thirteenth	**13**	dreizehnte(r, s)
fourteenth	**14**	vierzehnte(r, s)
fifteenth	**15**	fünfzehnte(r, s)
sixteenth	**16**	sechzehnte(r, s)
seventeenth	**17**	siebzehnte(r, s)
eighteenth	**18**	achtzehnte(r, s)
nineteenth	**19**	neunzehnte(r, s)
twentieth	**20**	zwanzigste(r, s)
twenty-first	**21**	einundzwanzigste(r, s)
twenty-second	**22**	zweiundzwanzigste(r, s)
thirtieth	**30**	dreißigste(r, s)
thirty-first	**31**	einunddreißigste(r, s)
fortieth	**40**	vierzigste(r, s)
fiftieth	**50**	fünfzigste(r, s)
sixtieth	**60**	sechzigste(r, s)
seventieth	**70**	siebzigste(r, s)
eightieth	**80**	achtzigste(r, s)
ninetieth	**90**	neunzigste(r, s)
hundredth	**100**	(ein)hundertste(r, s)
hundred and first	**101**	(ein)hundert(und)-erste(r, s)
hundred and tenth	**110**	(ein)hundert(und) zehnte(r, s)
two hundredth	**200**	zweihundertste(r, s)
three hundredth	**300**	dreihundertste(r, s)
four hundredth	**400**	vierhundertste(r, s)
five hundredth	**500**	fünfhundertste(r, s)
six hundredth	**600**	sechshundertste(r, s)
seven hundredth	**700**	siebenhundertste(r, s)
eight hundredth	**7.5**	achthundertste(r, s)
nine hundredth	**8.5**	neunhundertste(r, s)
thousandth	**9.5**	(ein)tausendste(r, s)
two thousandth	**2000**	zweitausendste(r, s)
millionth	**9.5000**	(ein)millionste(r, s)
two millionth	**2000000**	zweimillionste(r, s)

Notes on the use of the ordinal numbers

(a) All ordinal numbers agree in German with the noun (stated or implied): *ihr erster Mann, die fünfte Frau, ein zweites Haus.*

(b) Abbreviations: English 1st, 2nd, 3rd 4th etc = German 1., 2., 3., 4. and so on.

(c) See also notes on dates below.

Siehe ebenfalls die Anmerkungen bezüglich Datum.

FRACTIONS — BRÜCHE

one half, a half	$\frac{1}{2}$	ein halb
one and a half helpings	$1\frac{1}{2}$	eineinhalb *oder* anderthalb Portionen
two and a half kilos	$2\frac{1}{2}$	zweieinhalb Kilo
one third, a third	$\frac{1}{3}$	ein Drittel
two thirds	$\frac{2}{3}$	zwei Drittel
one quarter, a quarter	$\frac{1}{4}$	ein Viertel
three quarters	$\frac{3}{4}$	drei Viertel
one sixth, a sixth	$\frac{1}{6}$	ein Sechstel
five and five sixths	$5\frac{5}{6}$	fünf fünf Sechstel
one twelfth, a twelfth	$\frac{1}{12}$	ein Zwölftel
seven twelvfths	$\frac{7}{12}$	sieben Zwölftel
one hundredth, a hundredth	$\frac{1}{100}$	ein Hundertstel
one thousandth, a thousandth	$\frac{1}{1000}$	ein Tausendstel

DECIMALS — DECIMALZAHLEN

In German, a comma is written where English uses a point: English 3.56 (three point five six) = German 3,56 (drei Komma fünf sechs); English .07 (point nought seven) = German 0,07 (null Komma null sieben). Note that a German number cannot start with *Komma* - *null* must preceed it.

Im Englischen wird anstelle des im Deutschen gebräuchlichen Kommas ein Punkt verwendet: 3.56 (three point five six). Bei Zahlen unter 1 kann die Null vor dem Punkt entfallen: 0.07 (nought point nought seven) oder .07 (point nought seven).

UNITS — EINHEITEN

3,684 is a four digit number	*3684 iste eine vierstellige Zahl*
It contains 4 units, 8 tens, 6 hundereds and 3 thousands	*Sie enthält 4 Einer, 8 Zehner, 6 Hunderter und 3 Tausender*
The decimal .234 contains 2 tenths, 3 hundredths and 4 thousandths	*Die Dezimalzahl 0,234 enthält 2 Zehntel, 3 Hunderdstel und 4 Tausendstel*

PERCENTAGES — PROZENTZAHLEN

$2\frac{1}{2}$% two and a half per cent	*zweieinhalb Prozent*
18% of the people here are over 65	*18% der Leute hier sind über 65*
Production has risen by 8%	*die Produktion ist um 8% gestiegen*
(See also the main text of the dictionary)	(*Siehe ebenfalls die entsprechenden Einträge des Wörterbuchs*)

SIGNS ZEICHEN

English

+	addition sign, plus sign (*eg* +7 = plus seven)
−	subtraction sign, minus sign (*eg* −3 = minus three)
×	multiplication sign
÷	division sign
√	square root sign
∞	infinity
≡	sign of identity, is equal to
=	equals sign
≈	is approximately equal to
≠	sign of inequality, is not equal to
>	is greater than
<	is less than

Deutsch

+	Additions-Zeichen, Plus-Zeichen (*z.B.* +7 = *plus sieben*)
−	Subtraktions-Zeichen, Minus-Zeichen (*z.b.* −*3* = *minus drei)*
×	Multiplikations-Zeichen
:	Divisions-Zeichen
√	Quadratwurzel-Zeichen
∞	Unendlichkeits-Symbol
≡	Identitäts-Zeichen
=	Gleichheitszeichen, ist gleich
≈	ist ungefähr gleich
≠	Ungleichheitszeichen, ist nicht gleich
>	ist größer als
<	ist kleiner als

CALCULATIONS — RECHNEN

8+6 = 14 eight and (*or* plus) six are (*or* make) fourteen	*acht und* (oder *plus*) *sechs ist* (oder *macht* oder *gleich*) *vierzehn*
15-3 = 12 fifteen take away (*or* minus) three equals twelve, three from fifteen leaves twelve	*fünfzehn weniger drei ist* (oder *macht*) *zwölf, fünfzehn minus drei gleich zwölf*
3×3 = 9 three threes are nine, three times three is nine	*drei mal drei ist* (oder *macht* oder *gleich*) *neun*
32÷8 = 4 thirty-two divided by eight (*or* over) eight is (*or* equals) four	*zweiunddreißig geteilt durch acht ist* (oder *macht* oder *gleich*) *vier*
$3^2 = 9$ three squared is nine	*drei hoch zwei ist neun, drei zum Quadrat gleich neun*
$2^5 = 32$ two to the fifth (*or* to the power of five) is (*or* equals) thirty two	*zwei hoch fünf ist* (oder *gleich*) *zweiunddreißig*
$\sqrt{16} = 4$ the square root of sixteen is 4	*die (Quadrat)wurzel aus sechzehn ist vier*

WEIGHTS AND MEASURES — MASSE UND GEWICHTE

METRIC SYSTEM — METRISCHES SYSTEM

deca-	10 times	10mal	*Deka-*
hecto-	100 times	100 mal	*Hekto-*
kilo-	1000 times	1000mal	*Kilo-*
deci-	one tenth	ein Zehntel	*Dezi-*
centi-	one hundredth	ein Hundertstel	*Zenti-*
mil(l)i-	one thousandth	ein Tausendstel	*Milli-*

Linear measures — Längenmaße

1 millimetre (Millimeter)	=	0.03937 inch
1 centimetre (Zentimeter)	=	0.3937 inch
1 metre (Meter)	=	39.37 inches
	=	1.094 yards
1 kilometre (Kilometer)	=	0.6214 mile ($\frac{5}{8}$ mile)

Square measures — Flächenmaße

1 square centimetre (Quadratzentimeter)	=	0.155 square inch
1 square metre (Quadratmeter)	=	10.764 square feet
	=	1.196 square yards
1 square kilometre (Quadratkilometer)	=	0.3861 square mile
	=	247.1 acres
1 are (Ar) = 100 square metres	=	119.6 square yards
1 hectare (Hektar) = 100 ares	=	2.471 acres

Cubic measures — Raummaße

1 cubic centimetre (Kubikzentimeter)	=	0.061 cubic inch
1 cubic metre (Kubikmeter)	=	35.315 cubic feet
	=	1.308 cubic yards

Measures of capacity — Hohlmaße

1 litre (Liter) = 1000 cubic centimetres	=	1.76 pints
	=	0.22 gallon

Weights — Gewichte

1 gram (Gramm)	=	15.4 grains
1 kilogram (Kilogramm)	=	2.2046 pounds
1 quintal (Quintal) = 100 kilograms	=	220.46 pounds
1 metric ton (Tonne) = 1000 kilograms	=	0.9842 ton

BRITISH SYSTEM — BRITISCHES SYSTEM

Linear measures — Flächenmaße

1 inch (Zoll)	=	2,54 Zentimeter
1 foot (Fuß) = 12 inches	=	30,48 Zentimeter
1 yard (Yard) = 3 feet	=	91,44 Zentimeter
1 furlong = 220 yards	=	201,17 Meter
1 mile (Meile) = 1760 yards	=	1,609 Kilometer

Surveyor's measures — Feldmaße

1 link = 7.92 inches	=	20,12 Zentimeter
1 rod (*or* pole, perch) = 25 links	=	5,029 Meter
1 chain = 22 yards = 4 rods	=	20,12 Meter

Square measures — Flächenmaße

1 square inch (Quadratzoll)	=	6,45 cm^2
1 square foot (Quadratfuß) = 144 square inches	=	929,03 cm^2
1 square yard (Quadratyard) = 9 square feet	=	0.836 m^2
1 square rod - 30.25 square yards	=	25,29 m^2
1 acre - 4840 square yards	=	40.47 Ar
1 square mile (Quadratmeile) = 640 acres	=	2,59 km^2

Cubic measures — Raummaße

1 cubic inch (Kubikzoll)	=	16,387 cm^3
1 cubic foot (Kubikfuß) = 1728 cubic inches	=	0,028 m^3
1 cubic yard (Kubikyard) = 27 cubic feet	=	0,765 m^3
1 register ton (Registertonne) = 100 cubic feet	=	2,832 m^3

Measures of capacity — Hohlmaße

(a) Liquid — Flüssigkeitsmaße

1 gill	=	0,142 Liter
1 pint (Pinte) = 4 gills	=	0,57 Liter
1 quart = 2 pints	=	1,136 Liter
1 gallon (Gallone) = 4 quarts	=	4,546 Liter

(b) Dry — Trockenmaße

1 peck = 2 gallons	=	9,087 Liter
1 bushel = 4 pecks	=	36,36 Liter
1 quarter = 8 bushels	=	290,94 Liter

Weights — Avoirdupois system — Handelsgewichte

1 grain (Gran)	=	0,0648 Gramm
1 drachm *or* dram = 27.34 grains	=	1,77 Gramm
1 ounce (Unze) = 16 drachms	=	28,35 Gramm
1 pound (britisches Pfund) = 16 ounces	=	453,6 Gramm
	=	0,453 Kilogramm
1 stone = 14 pounds	=	6,348 Kilogramm
1 quarter = 28 pounds	=	12,7 Kilogramm
1 hundredweight = 112 pounds	=	50,8 Kilogramm
1 ton (Tonne) = 2240 pounds = 20 hundredweight	=	1,016 Kilogramm

US MEASURES — AMERIKANISCHE MASSE

In the US, the same system as that which applies in Great Britain is used for the most part; the main differences are mentioned below:

In den Vereinigten Staaten gilt großenteils dasselbe System wie in Großbritannien; die Hauptunterschiede sind im folgenden aufgeführt:

Measures of Capacity — Hohlmaße

(a) Liquid — Flüssigkeitsmaße

1 US liquid gill	=	0,118 Liter
1 US liquid pint = 4 gills	=	0,473 Liter
1 US liquid quart = 2 pints	=	0,946 Liter
1 US gallon = 4 quarts	=	3,785 Liter

(b) Dry — Trockenmaße

1 US dry pint	=	0,550 Liter
1 US dry quart = 2 dry pints	=	1,1 Liter
1 US peck = 8 dry quarts	=	8,81 Liter
1 US bushel = 4 pecks	=	35,24 Liter

Weights — Gewichte

1 hundredweight (*or* short hundredweight) = 100 pounds	=	45,36 Kilogramm
1 ton (*or* short ton) = 2000 pounds = 20 short hundredweights	=	907,18 Kilogramm

TEMPERATURE CONVERSION — TEMPERATURUMRECHNUNG

Fahrenheit — Centigrade (Celsius)

Subtract 32 and multiply by 5/9
32 abziehen und mit 5/9 multiplizieren

°F		°C
0		17.8
32		0
50		10
70		21.1
90		32.2
98.4	≈	37
212		100

Centigrade (Celsius) — Fahrenheit

Multiply by 9/5 and add 32
Mit 9/5 multiplizieren und 32 addieren

°C		°F
–10		14
0		32
10		50
20		68
30		86
37	≈	98.4
100		212

TIME	ZEIT
2 hours 33 minutes and 14 seconds	*zwei Stunden, dreiunddreißig Minuten und vierzehn Sekunden*
half an hour	*eine halbe Stunde*
a quarter of an hour	*eine Viertelstunde*
three quarters of an hour	*eine Dreiviertelstunde*
what's the time?	*wie spät ist es?*
what time do you make it?	*wie spät haben Sie?*
have you the right time?	*haben Sie die richtige Zeit?*
I make it 2.20	*nach meiner Uhr ist es 2 Uhr 20*
my watch says 3.37	*auf meiner Uhr ist es 3 Uhr 37*
it's 1 o'clock	*es ist ein Uhr*
it's 2 o'clock	*es ist zwei Uhr*
it's 5 past 4	*es ist fünf (Minuten) nach vier*
it's 10 past 6	*es ist zehn (Minuten) nach sechs*
it's half past 8	*es ist halb neun**
it's (a) quarter past 9	*es ist viertel nach neun*
it's (a) quarter to 2	*es ist viertel vor zwei*
at 10 a.m.	*um 10 Uhr (morgens)*
at 4 p.m.	*um 4 Uhr nachmittags, um 16 Uhr*
at 11 p.m.	*um 11 Uhr abends, um 23 Uhr*
at exactly 3 o'clock, at 3 sharp, at 3 on the dot	*um Punkt drei Uhr*
the train leaves at 19.32	*der Zug fährt um 19 Uhr 32 ab*
(at) what time does it start?	*um wieviel Uhr fängt es an?*
it is just after 3	*es ist gerade drei (Uhr) vorbei*
it is nearly 9	*es ist fast neun (Uhr)*
about 8 o'clock	*etwa acht Uhr, ungefähr acht Uhr*
at (*or* by) 6 o'clock at the latest	*spätestens um sechs Uhr*
have it ready for 5 o'clock	*es muß bis fünf Uhr fertig sein*
it is full each night from 7 to 9	*es ist jeden Abend von 7 bis 9 Uhr voll*
"closed from 1.30 to 4.30"	*„geschlossen von ein Uhr dreißig bis vier Uhr dreißig"*
until 8 o'clock	*bis acht Uhr*
it would be about 11	*es wäre etwa 11 (Uhr)*
it would have been about 10	*es wäre etwa um zehn (Uhr) gewesen*
at midnight	*um Mitternacht*
before midday, before noon	*vormittags, am Vormittag*

*In German, the half hour is expressed by referring forwards to the next full hour as opposed to backwards to the last full hour as in English.

DATES / DAS DATUM

N.B. The days of the week and the months are written with capitals as in English.

DATES	DAS DATUM
the 1st of July, July 1st	*der 1. Juli*
the 2nd of May, May 2nd	*der 2. Mai*
on June 21st, on the 21st (of) June	*am 21. Juni*
on Monday	*am Montag*
he comes on Mondays	*er kommt montags*
"closed on Fridays"	*„freitags geschlossen"*
he lends it to me from Monday to Friday	*er leiht es mir vom Montag bis Freitag*
from the 14th to the 18th	*vom 14. bis (zum) 18.*
what's the date?, what date is it today?	*welches Datum haben wir (heute)?*
today's the 12th	*heute ist der 12.*
one Thursday in October	*an einem Donnerstag im Oktober*
about the 4th of July	*etwa am 4. Juli*
Heading of letters:	*im Briefkopf:*
19th May 1984	*19. Mai 1984*
1978 nineteen (hundred and) seventy-eight	*neunzehnhundert(und)achtundsiebzig*
4 B.C., B.C. 4	*4 v.Chr.*
70 A.D., A.D. 70	*70 n.Chr.*
in the 13th century	*im 13. Jahrhundert*
in (*or* during) the 1930s	*in der 30er Jahren, während den 30er Jahre*
in 1940 something	*irgendwann in der vierziger Jahren*
(See also the main text of the dictionary)	*(Siehe ebenfalls die entsprechenden Einträge des Wörterbuchs)*

GERMAN SPELLING REFORM
DEUTSCHE RECHTSCHREIBREFORM

Die deutsche Rechtschreibreform

Am 1. Juli 1996 wurde von allen deutschsprachigen Ländern eine Erklärung zur Neuregelung der deutschen Rechtschreibung unterzeichnet. Mit Beginn des Schuljahrs 1996/97 können Schulen die neue Rechtschreibung lehren. Ab 1. April 1998 wird in den Schulen nur noch nach den neuen Regeln unterrichtet. In einer Übergangszeit bis zum Ende des Schuljahrs 2004/05 wird die alte Schreibung nicht als falsch angesehen.

Die Rechtschreibreform betrifft sechs Großbereiche:

- Zuordnung von Laut und Buchstabe
- Getrennt- und Zusammenschreibung
- Schreibung mit Bindestrich
- Groß- und Kleinschreibung
- Zeichensetzung
- Worttrennung am Zeilenende

The German spelling reform

On 1 July 1996, a declaration concerning the reform of German spelling rules was signed by all German-speaking countries. The new spelling rules can be taught in schools from the beginning of the 1996/97 school year. From 1 April 1998, only the new spelling rules will be taught. For a transitional period lasting until the end of the 2004/05 school year, the old way of spelling will not be regarded as incorrect.

The reform of spelling rules affects six main areas:

- Sound/letter correlation
- Writing words separately or as one word
- Hyphenation
- Capitalization
- Punctuation
- End-of-line division

Zuordnung von Laut und Buchstabe

Die Änderungen betreffen hier sechs Unterbereiche:

- Anpassung der Schreibung an die Herkunft des Wortes
- Anpassung an die Schreibung analoger Laute oder Wörter
- Schreibung von Zusammensetzungen und Ableitungen wie das Grundwort
- Schreibung mit ß und ss entsprechend der Aussprache
- Eindeutschende Schreibung von Fremdwörtern
- Vereinheitlichung der Pluralform von Wörtern, die auf y enden

Sound/letter correlation

Here, the changes affect six sub-sections:

- Adapting spelling to the origin of a word
- Adapting to the way analogous sounds or words are spelt
- Spelling of compound nouns and derivatives in accordance with the stem
- Spelling with ß and ss in accordance with pronunciation
- Germanized spelling of foreign words
- Standardizing the plural form of words ending in y

Bei Wörtern einer Wortfamilie wurde die Schreibung dem Wortstamm angepasst:

With words belonging to the same family, spelling has been adapted to that of the stem:

ALT/OLD	NEU/NEW	WORTSTAMM/STEM
aufwendig	aufwändig	der Aufwand
behende	behände	die Hand
belemmert	belämmert	das Lamm
Bendel	Bändel	das Band
Gemse	Gämse	die Gams
Greuel	Gräuel	das Grauen
numerieren	nummerieren	die Nummer
plazieren/placieren	platzieren	der Platz
Quentchen	Quäntchen	das Quantum
Schenke	Schenke *oder*: Schänke *or*	ausschenken der Ausschank
Schlegel (Werkzeug)	Schlägel	schlagen
schneuzen	schnäuzen	die Schnauze
Stengel	Stängel	die Stange
Stukkateur	Stuckateur	der Stuck
überschwenglich	überschwänglich	der Überschwang
verbleuen	verbläuen	blau

In einzelnen Fällen wurde die Schreibung an bestehende Regeln oder ähnliche Fälle angepasst:

In individual cases, spelling has been adapted to existing rules or similar cases:

ALT/OLD	NEU/NEW	GRUND/REASON
der Mop	der Mopp	*Verdoppelung des Konsonanten nach kurzem Vokal/doubling of consonant after short vowel sound*
der Tip	der Tipp	*dito/ditto*
Step tanzen	Stepp tanzen	*dito/ditto*
der Tolpatsch	der Tollpatsch	*dito/ditto*
der Karamel	der Karamell	*wie/like*: die Karamelle
das Känguruh	das Känguru	*wie/like*: das Gnu
rauh	rau	*wie/like*: grau, blau
der Alptraum	der Albtraum	

Bei Zusammensetzungen und Ableitungen wird die Schreibung des Grundwortes beibehalten:

In compound nouns and derivatives, the spelling of the stem has been retained:

ALT/OLD	NEU/NEW
Kontrollampe	Kontrolllampe
Schiffahrt	Schifffahrt
hellicht	helllicht
Roheit	Rohheit
Zäheit	Zähheit
Zierat	Zierrat
selbständig	selbstständig

Das **ß** wird zu **ss** nach kurzem Vokal:

after a short vowel sound, **ß** becomes **ss**:

der Kuss, die Küsse
der Fluss, die Flüsse
wässrig
er muss
dass

Das **ß** bleibt bestehen nach langem Vokal oder Doppellaut:

After a long vowel sound or diphthong, **ß** remains unchanged:

der Fuß, die Füße
das Maß, die Maße
er heißt
draußen

Bei Fremdwörtern wurde eine Angleichung an die deutsche Schreibung vorgenommen, wenn diese sich bereits anbahnte, vor allem bei der Schreibung von **ph** in Verbindungen mit **phon**, **phot** und **graph**, z.B.:

Foreign words have been brought into line with German spelling if this trend was already beginning to develop. This applies especially to the spelling of **ph** in compounds with **phon**, **phot** and **graph**. For example:

quadrofon, Fotograf, Paragraf

In allen Fällen der eindeutschenden Schreibweise ist auch die andere Schreibweise als Variante zugelassen:

In all cases of Germanized spelling, the alternative spelling is also permissible:

-tiell	*or*	-ziell	essentiell	*or*	essenziell,
			potentiell	*or*	potenziell
-tial	*or*	-zial	Differential	*or*	Differenzial
			Potential	*or*	Potenzial
ai	*or*	ä	Mayonnaise	*or*	Majonäse,
			Necessaire	*or*	Nessessär
é	*or*	ee	Pappmaché	*or*	Pappmaschee,
			Exposé	*or*	Exposee
gh	*or*	g	Joghurt	*or*	Jogurt,
			Spaghetti	*or*	Spagetti
c	*or*	ss	Facette	*or*	Fassette,
			Necessaire	*or*	Nessessär
ch	*or*	sch	Ketchup	*or*	Ketschup,
			Chicorée	*or*	Schikoree
th	*or*	t	Thunfisch	*or*	Tunfisch,
			Panther	*or*	Panter

Der Plural von Wörtern, die aus dem Englischen stammen und auf **y** enden, wird jetzt einheitlich mit **ys** geschrieben, z.B.:

The plural of all words deriving from English and ending in **y** will now be written **ys**. For example:

die Buggys, die Ladys, die Partys, die Hobbys

Getrennt- und Zusammenschreibung

One word or two?

Verbindungen von **Substantiv und Verb** werden getrennt geschrieben, z.B.:

Noun and verb combinations are written separately. For example:

Ski fahren, Eis laufen, Halt machen,
Blut saugend, Pflanzen fressend

Aber: Zusammengesetzte Verben, die fast nur im Infinitiv oder Partizip gebraucht werden, schreibt man zusammen:

But: compound verbs which are almost exclusively used in the infinitive or as participles are written as one word:

bauchreden, bergsteigen, brustschwimmen,
kopfrechnen, seiltanzen, sonnenbaden

Verbindungen von **Infinitiv und Verb** werden getrennt geschrieben:

Infinitive and verb combinations are written separately:

kennen lernen, sitzen bleiben, spazieren gehen

Verbindungen von **Partizip und Verb** werden getrennt geschrieben, z.B.:

Participle and verb combinations are written separately. For example:

gefangen nehmen, geschenkt bekommen

Verbindungen von **Adjektiv/Adverb und Verb** werden zusammengeschrieben, wenn der erste Bestandteil als Wort nicht vorkommt, z.B.:

Adjective/adverb and verb combinations are written as one word if the first component of the compound is not a word in its own right. For example:

fehlschlagen, kundgeben, weismachen

oder wenn der erste Bestandteil nicht erweiterbar oder steigerbar ist, z.B.:

or if the first component of the compound cannot be qualified or compared. For example:

bereithalten, fernsehen, hochrechnen,
schwarzarbeiten, totschlagen

Verbindungen von **Adjektiv und Verb** werden getrennt geschrieben, wenn das Adjektiv erweiterbar oder steigerbar ist, wobei die Verneinung als Erweiterung gilt, z.B.:

Adjective and verb combinations are written separately if the adjective can be qualified or compared (in this case, negation counts as a qualification). For example:

bekannt machen, genau nehmen,
kurz treten, nahe bringen

Verbindungen von **Adverb und Verb** werden getrennt geschrieben, wenn das Adverb zusammengesetzt ist, z.B.:

Adverb and verb combinations are written separately if the adverb is a compound word. For example:

abhanden kommen, beiseite legen,
überhand nehmen, zunichte machen

Verbverbindungen mit **-ander** werden getrennt geschrieben, z.B.:

Verb combinations with **-ander** are written separately. For example:

aneinander legen, aufeinander schichten, auseinander laufen,
beieinander bleiben, durcheinander reden, zueinander finden

Verbverbindungen mit **-seits** und **-wärts** werden getrennt geschrieben, z.B.:

Verb combinations with **-seits** and **-wärts** are written separately. For example:

abseits stehen, abwärts gehen,
aufwärts streben, vorwärts blicken

Verbverbindungen mit einer Ableitung, die auf **-ig**, **-isch** und **-lich** enden, werden getrennt geschrieben, z.B.:

Verb combinations with a derivative ending in **-ig**, **-isch** and **-lich** are written separately. For example:

lästig fallen, übrig bleiben,
kritisch denken, freundlich grüßen

Verbverbindungen mit **sein** werden getrennt geschrieben, z.B.:

Verb combinations with **sein** are written separately. For example:

beisammen sein, fertig sein, zusammen sein

Verbindungen mit **viel** werden getrennt geschrieben, z.B.:

Combinations with **viel** are written separately. For example:

so viel Geld; Wie viel kostet das?
Wie viel Uhr ist es?

Verbindungen mit **irgend** werden zusammengeschrieben, z.B.:

Combinations with irgend are written as one word. For example:

irgendetwas, irgendjemand

Schreibung mit Bindestrich

Hyphenation

Der Bindestrich kann verstärkt dazu verwendet werden, Zusammenschreibungen zu gliedern und leichter lesbar zu machen, besonders beim Zusammentreffen von drei gleichen Konsonanten, z.B.:

Hyphens may now be used more frequently in order to break up compound words and make them easier to read, especially when the same consonant is repeated three times. For example:

Essstäbchen *oder/or* Ess-Stäbchen

oder bei substantivischen Aneinanderreihungen, z.B.:

or where a number of words have been put together to form a noun. For example:

das Auf-die-lange-Bank-Schieben

Man setzt den Bindestrich immer in Zusammensetzungen mit Einzelbuchstaben, Abkürzungen oder Ziffern, z.B.:

Where compounds have single letters, abbreviations or figures as a component part, hyphens are always used. For example:

T-Träger, x-te, Kfz-Versicherung, VIP-Lounge, Lungen-Tbc,
100-prozentig, 2/3-Mehrheit, 18-jährig, 2-Pfünder

Der Bindestrich wird auch bei Zusammensetzungen mit Eigennamen verwendet, z.B.:

Hyphens are also used in compounds containing proper nouns. For example:

Foto-Bauer, rheinland-pfälzisch, Heinrich-Heine-Straße,
Schiller-Ausgabe, Moskau-freundlich

Groß- und Kleinschreibung

Capitalization

Substantive werden groß geschrieben. Der Gebrauch des Artikels ist das grundlegende formale Erkennungsmerkmal eines Substantivs, z.B.:

Nouns are written with a capital. The basic formal characteristic of a noun is that it is used with an article. For example:

das Schwimmen, das Wenn und Aber, im Voraus,
im Dunkeln tappen, heute Abend, morgen Mittag

In Verbindung mit **einer Präposition oder einem Verb** werden Substantive groß geschrieben, z.B.:

Nouns are written with a capital in combinations with **a preposition or a verb**. For example:

in Bezug auf, auf Grund von, zu Grunde gehen,
Maß halten, Maschine schreiben, Rad fahren

Nur in Verbindung mit **sein, bleiben** und **werden** schreibt man Angst, Bange, Leid, Pleite und Schuld klein. In Verbindung mit anderen Verben wird groß geschrieben, z.B.:

Only in combination with **sein, bleiben** and **werden** are Angst, Bange, Leid, Pleite and Schuld written with a small letter. They are written with a capital letter when combined with other verbs. For example:

Ich habe Angst.	Mir wurde angst und bange.
Du willst mir wohl Bange machen.	Mir ist bange ums Herz.
Er tut mir Leid.	Ich bin es leid.
Seine Firma ist Pleite gegangen.	Seine Firma ist pleite geblieben.
Er hat Schuld daran.	Er ist schuld daran.

Adjektive, die als Ordnungszahlen benutzt werden und unbestimmte Zahladjektive werden groß geschrieben, z.B.:

Adjectives used as ordinals and indefinite adjectives of number are written with a capital. For example:

der Erste, das Letzte, der Nächste, der Einzelne,
das Ganze, Verschiedenes, alles Mögliche

Adjektive in bestimmten festen Verbindungen werden groß geschrieben, z.B.:

In certain fixed idioms, **adjectives** are written with a capital. For example:

im Großen und Ganzen, im Klaren, des Weiteren,
das Beste, den Kürzeren ziehen

Farben und **Sprachen** in Verbindung mit Präpositionen werden groß geschrieben, z.B.:

When combined with prepositions, **colours** and **languages** are written with a capital. For example:

in Weiß, bei Gelb, auf Russisch, in Deutsch

Adjektive, die in Paaren zur Bezeichnung von Menschen auftreten, werden groß geschrieben, z.B.:

Adjectives used in pairs to describe people are written with a capital. For example:

Jung und Alt, Arm und Reich

Bei **Superlativen** mit aufs ist sowohl Groß- als auch Kleinschreibung möglich, z.B.:

Superlatives with "aufs" can be written with or without a capital. For example:

aufs Schönste *oder/or* aufs schönste,
aufs Freundlichste *oder/or* aufs freundlichste

Bei festen Verbindungen von **Adjektiv und Substantiv** wird das Adjektiv klein geschrieben, z.B.:

In idiomatic **adjective/noun** combinations, the adjective is written with a small letter. For example:

das schwarze Brett, die erste Hilfe,
der goldene Schnitt, das große Los

Groß geschrieben wird das **Adjektiv**, wenn es sich um einen Eigennamen, einen Titel, eine Benennung oder eine Bezeichnung aus der Biologie handelt, z.B.:

Adjectives are written with a capital if they are proper names, titles, designations or names from biology. For example:

die Vereinten Nationen, der Regierende Bürgermeister,
der Stille Ozean, der Große Bär, Rote Bete, der Schwarze Milan

Groß geschrieben werden auch bestimmte Kalendertage, religiöse Handlungen und Institutionen, historische Ereignisse, z.B.:

Certain days in the calendar, religious acts and institutions, historical events are written with a capital letter. For example:

der Heilige Abend, die Letzte Ölung,
der Heilige Stuhl, der Dreißigjährige Krieg

Klein geschrieben werden **Ableitungen** von Eigennamen auf -**(i)sch**, z.B.:

Derivatives from proper names ending in **-(i)sch** are written with a small letter. For example:

die brechtschen Dramen, die goethische Farbenlehre,
das ohmsche Gesetz

Die **Anredeformen** „du" und „ihr" und die dazugehörigen Formen werden auch in Briefen klein geschrieben, z.B.:

The **forms of address** "du" and "ihr", as well as all the forms belonging to them, are written with a small letter, even in correspondence. For example:

Liebe Grüße, deine Veronika.
Wenn ihr uns besuchen kommt, bringt eure Kinder mit.

Die Höflichkeitsform „Sie" und die dazugehörigen Formen werden weiterhin groß geschrieben, z.B.:

The polite form of address "Sie", as well as all the forms belonging to it, is still written with a capital letter. For example:

Wenn Sie uns besuchen, bringen Sie Ihre Kinder mit.

Zeichensetzung

Bei der Zeichensetzung wird dem Schreibenden größere Freiheit eingeräumt, Sätze durch Kommas zu gliedern. Die meisten der bisherigen Regeln entfallen. Bei Hauptsätzen, die mit „und" oder „oder" verbunden sind, muss kein Komma mehr stehen, z.B.:

Punctuation

As concerns punctuation, the writer has now been given greater freedom to break up sentences with commas. Most of the rules which applied formerly have now been abandoned. There is no longer any need for a comma where main clauses are joined by "und" or "oder". For example:

Die Party war zu Ende und alle sind gegangen.

Worttrennung am Zeilenende

Die bisherige Regel, dass man „**st**" nicht trennen darf, entfällt, z.B.:

End-of-line division

The rule whereby "**st**" must not be divided no longer applies. For example:

Kis-te, Bürs-te, Plas-tik

Das „**ck**" wird nicht mehr in „k-k" umgewandelt, sondern bei der Trennung zusammen auf die nächste Zeile genommen, z.B.:

"**ck**" has no longer to be changed into "k-k", but is left together and taken over to the next line. For example:

Bä-cker, le-cken, Bli-cke, Zu-cker

Zusammengesetzte Wörter und Wörter mit einer Vorsilbe werden nach ihren Bestandteilen getrennt, z.B.:

Compound words and words with a prefix are divided according to their component parts. For example:

Klebe-streifen, Donners-tag,
ab-ändern, ent-eignen, ver-öden

Das gilt auch für Fremdwörter und geografische Namen, z.B.:

This rule also applies to foreign words and geographical names. For example:

des-illusionieren, in-akzeptabel,
Pro-gramm, trans-alpin, Neu-strelitz, West-indien

Wird ein Wort nicht mehr als Zusammensetzung erkannt oder empfunden, so kann auch nach Sprechsilben getrennt werden, z.B.:

If a word is no longer felt to be, or can no longer be recognized as, a compound, then it can also be divided phonetically. For example:

da-rüber, he-runter, wa-rum, ei-nander

Das gilt auch für Fremdwörter, wenn die Herkunft nicht mehr empfunden wird, z.B.:

This also applies to foreign words if their origin is no longer obvious. For example:

Chi-rurg	*bisher/previously*	Chir-urg
Helikop-ter	*bisher/previously*	Heliko-pter
Hyd-rant	*bisher/previously*	Hy-drant
Inte-resse	*bisher/previously*	Inter-esse
mak-robiotisch	*bisher/previously*	ma-krobiotisch

Einzelne Buchstaben dürfen abgetrennt werden, z.B.:

Single letters can be divided off. For example:

a-ber, E-he, I-dee, O-fen, U-ni

Alphabetisches Wörterverzeichnis

Das folgende Verzeichnis enthält Stichwörter dieses Wörterbuchs in ihrer alten und neuen Schreibweise, wobei der Schwerpunkt auf den Hauptbereichen der Rechtschreibreform (Zuordnung von Laut und Buchstabe, Getrennt- und Zusammenschreibung) liegt.

Alphabetical wordlist

The following wordlist contains headwords found in the dictionary and shows both their old and new spellings, with the emphasis on the main areas affected by the spelling reform (word/letter correlation, one/two word spellings).

ALT/OLD	NEU/NEW
Abdroßlung	Abdrosslung
abend	Abend
Abfluß	Abfluss
Abflußgraben	Abflussgraben
Abflußhahn	Abflusshahn
Abflußrinne	Abflussrinne
Abflußrohr	Abflussrohr
abgrundhäßlich	abgrundhässlich
Abguß	Abguss
Ablaß	Ablass
Ablaßbrief	Ablassbrief
Ablaßhandel	Ablasshandel
Ablaßventil	Ablassventil
Abriß	Abriss
Abrißarbeiten	Abrissarbeiten
Abrißbirne	Abrissbirne
Abrißliste	Abrissliste
abrißreif	abrissreif
Abschiedskuß	Abschiedskuss
Abschluß	Abschluss
Abschlußball	Abschlussball
Abschlußfeier	Abschlussfeier
Abschlußklasse	Abschlussklasse
Abschlußkommuniqué	Abschlusskommuniqué *or* Abschlusskommunikee
Abschlußprüfung	Abschlussprüfung
Abschlußrechnung	Abschlussrechnung
Abschlußzeugnis	Abschlusszeugnis
Abschuß	Abschuss
Abschußbasis	Abschussbasis
Abschußliste	Abschussliste
Abschußrampe	Abschussrampe
absein	ab sein
Abszeß	Abszess
Abtreibungsparagraph	Abtreibungsparagraph *or* Abtreibungsparagraf
abwärtsgehen	abwärts gehen
achtunggebietend	Achtung gebietend
ackerbautreibend	Ackerbau treibend
Aderlaß	Aderlass
Adhäsionsverschluß	Adhäsionsverschluss
Adreßbuch	Adressbuch
Ahnenpaß	Ahnenpass
Aktionsausschuß	Aktionsausschuss
Alkoholeinfluß	Alkoholeinfluss
Alkoholgenuß	Alkoholgenuss
Alkoholmißbrauch	Alkoholmissbrauch
alleinerziehend	allein erziehend
Alleinerziehende(r)	Alleinerziehende(r) *or* allein Erziehende(r)
alleinseligmachend	allein selig machend
alleinstehend	allein stehend
Alleinstehende(r)	Alleinstehende(r) *or* allein Stehende(r)
allgemeinbildend	allgemein bildend
allgemeingültig	allgemein gültig
allgemeinverbindlich	allgemein verbindlich
allgemeinverständlich	allgemein verständlich
allzufrüh	allzu früh
allzugern	allzu gern
allzusehr	allzu sehr
allzuviel	allzu viel
Alp (2)	Alp *or* Alb
Alpdruck	Alpdruck *or* Albdruck
Alpenpaß	Alpenpass
alphanumerisch	alphanummerisch
Alptraum	Alptraum *or* Albtraum
alptraumartig	alptraumartig *or* albtraumartig
Altersprozeß	Altersprozess
Amboß	Amboss
Amtsmißbrauch	Amtsmissbrauch
Analogieschluß	Analogieschluss
andersdenkend	anders denkend
Andersdenkende(r)	Andersdenkende(r) *or* anders Denkende(r)

ALT/OLD	NEU/NEW
andersgeartet	anders geartet
andersgesinnt	anders gesinnt
andersgläubig	anders gläubig
anderslautend	anders lautend
aneinanderbauen	aneinander bauen
aneinanderfügen	aneinander fügen
aneinandergeraten	aneinander geraten
aneinandergrenzen	aneinander grenzen
aneinanderhalten	aneinander halten
aneinanderhängen	aneinander hängen
aneinanderkleben	aneinander kleben
aneinanderkoppeln	aneinander koppeln
aneinanderlehnen	aneinander lehnen
aneinanderliegen	aneinander liegen
aneinanderprallen	aneinander prallen
aneinanderreihen	aneinander reihen
aneinanderschmieden	aneinander schmieden
aneinanderschmiegen	aneinander schmiegen
aneinandersetzen	aneinander setzen
aneinanderstellen	aneinander stellen
aneinanderstoßen	aneinander stoßen
angepaßt	angepasst
Angepaßtheit	Angepasstheit
Anlaß	Anlass
anläßlich	anlässlich
Annahmeschluß	Annahmeschluss
anrauhen	anrauen
Anriß	Anriss
Anschiß	Anschiss
Anschluß	Anschluss
Anschlußdose	Anschlussdose
anschlußfertig	anschlussfertig
Anschlußfinanzierung	Anschlussfinanzierung
Anschlußflug	Anschlussflug
Anschlußnummer	Anschlussnummer
Anschlußrohr	Anschlussrohr
Anschlußschnur	Anschlussschnur *or* Anschluss-Schnur
Anschlußstelle	Anschlussstelle *or* Anschluss-Stelle
Anschlußzug	Anschlusszug
ansein	an sein
arbeitsaufwendig	arbeitsaufwändig
Arbeitsausschuß	Arbeitsausschuss
Arbeitsprozeß	Arbeitsprozess
Arbeitsschluß	Arbeitsschluss
arbeitsuchend	Arbeit suchend
Arbeitsuchende(r)	Arbeitsuchende(r) *or* Arbeit Suchende(r)
Arierparagraph	Arierparagraph *or* Arierparagraf
Armvoll	Arm voll
Artilleriebeschuß	Artilleriebeschuss
Arzneimittelmißbrauch	Arzneimittelmissbrauch
Aß	Ass
Aschantinuß	Aschantinuss
Asylsuchende(r)	Asylsuchende(r) *or* Asyl Suchende(r)
auf daß	auf dass
Aufbeßrung	Aufbessrung
aufeinanderbeißen	aufeinander beißen
aufeinanderdrücken	aufeinander drücken
aufeinanderfahren	aufeinander fahren
aufeinanderfolgen	aufeinander folgen
aufeinanderfolgend	aufeinander folgend
aufeinanderhängen	aufeinander hängen
aufeinanderhetzen	aufeinander hetzen
aufeinanderhocken	aufeinander hocken
aufeinanderknallen	aufeinander knallen
aufeinanderlegen	aufeinander legen
aufeinanderliegen	aufeinander liegen
aufeinanderpassen	aufeinander passen
aufeinanderprallen	aufeinander prallen
aufeinanderpressen	aufeinander pressen
aufeinanderrasen	aufeinander rasen
aufeinanderschichten	aufeinander schichten
aufeinanderschlagen	aufeinander schlagen

ALT/OLD	NEU/NEW
aufeinandersetzen	aufeinander setzen
aufeinandersitzen	aufeinander sitzen
aufeinanderstellen	aufeinander stellen
aufeinanderstoßen	aufeinander stoßen
aufeinandertreffen	aufeinander treffen
aufeinandertürmen	aufeinander türmen
Aufguß	Aufguss
Aufgußbeutel	Aufgussbeutel
aufrauhen	aufrauen
Aufriß	Aufriss
Aufrißzeichnung	Aufrisszeichnung
Aufschluß	Aufschluss
Aufschlüßlung	Aufschlüsslung
aufschlußreich	aufschlussreich
aufsehenerregend	Aufsehen erregend
aufsein	auf sein
aufsichtführend	Aufsicht führend
Aufsichtführende(r)	Aufsichtführende(r) *or* Aufsicht Führende(r)
aufwärtsgehen	aufwärts gehen
aufwendig	aufwendig *or* aufwändig
auseinanderbekommen	auseinander bekommen
auseinanderbiegen	auseinander biegen
auseinanderbrechen	auseinander brechen
auseinanderbreiten	auseinander breiten
auseinanderbringen	auseinander bringen
auseinanderdividieren	auseinander dividieren
auseinanderdriften	auseinander driften
auseinanderentwickeln	auseinander entwickeln
auseinanderfallen	auseinander fallen
auseinanderfalten	auseinander falten
auseinanderfliegen	auseinander fliegen
auseinanderfließen	auseinander fließen
auseinandergehen	auseinander gehen
auseinanderhalten	auseinander halten
auseinanderjagen	auseinander jagen
auseinanderkennen	auseinander kennen
auseinanderklaffen	auseinander klaffen
auseinanderklamüsern	auseinander klamüsern
auseinanderklauben	auseinander klauben
auseinanderkriegen	auseinander kriegen
auseinanderlaufen	auseinander laufen
auseinanderleben	auseinander leben
auseinandermachen	auseinander machen
auseinandernehmen	auseinander nehmen
auseinanderpflücken	auseinander pflücken
auseinanderreißen	auseinander reißen
auseinanderschlagen	auseinander schlagen
auseinanderschrauben	auseinander schrauben
auseinandersetzen	auseinander setzen
auseinanderspreizen	auseinander spreizen
auseinandersprengen	auseinander sprengen
auseinanderspringen	auseinander springen
auseinanderstieben	auseinander stieben
auseinanderstreben	auseinander streben
auseinandertreiben	auseinander treiben
auseinanderziehen	auseinander ziehen
außerstande	außerstande *or* außer Stande
Ausfluß	Ausfluss
Ausfuhrüberschuß	Ausfuhrüberschuss
Ausguß	Ausguss
Ausleseprozeß	Ausleseprozess
Ausschluß	Ausschluss
Ausschuß	Ausschuss
Ausschußmitglied	Ausschussmitglied
Ausschußöffnung	Ausschussöffnung
Ausschußsitzung	Ausschusssitzung *or* Ausschuss-Sitzung
Ausschußware	Ausschussware
aussein	aus sein
Autobiograph	Autobiograph *or* Autobiograf
Autobiographie	Autobiographie *or* Autobiografie
autobiographisch	autobiographisch *or* autobiografisch
Autograph	Autograph *or* Autograf

B

ALT/OLD	NEU/NEW
Bahnanschluß	Bahnanschluss
Bajonettverschluß	Bajonettverschluss
Ballettänzer	Balletttänzer *or* Ballett-Tänzer
Bänderriß	Bänderriss
Baroneß	Baroness

ALT/OLD	NEU/NEW
baß	bass
Baß	Bass
Baßbariton	Bassbariton
Baßgeige	Bassgeige
Baßklarinette	Bassklarinette
Baßpartie	Basspartie
Baßsänger	Basssänger *or* Bass-Sänger
Baßschlüssel	Bassschlüssel *or* Bass-Schlüssel
Baßstimme	Bassstimme *or* Bass-Stimme
Bauchschuß	Bauchschuss
Baukostenzuschuß	Baukostenzuschuss
beeinflußbar	beeinflussbar
befliß	befliss
Begrüßungskuß	Begrüssungskuss
beieinanderhaben	beieinander haben
beieinanderhalten	beieinander halten
beieinandersein	beieinander sein
beifallheischend	Beifall heischend
beifallspendend	Beifall spendend
beisammensein	beisammen sein
Beischluß	Beischluss
bekanntgeben	bekannt geben
bekanntmachen	bekannt machen
bekanntwerden	bekannt werden
Beleidigungsprozeß	Beleidigungsprozess
belemmert	belämmert
Bendel	Bändel
bergeversetzend	Berge versetzend
Berufungsausschuß	Berufungsausschuss
Beschiß	Beschiss
Beschluß	Beschluss
beschlußfähig	beschlussfähig
Beschlußfähigkeit	Beschlussfähigkeit
Beschlußfassung	Beschlussfassung
Beschlußrecht	Beschlussrecht
beschlußreif	beschlussreif
beschlußunfähig	beschlussunfähig
Beschuß	Beschuss
bestehenbleiben	bestehen bleiben
bestehenlassen	bestehen lassen
Bestelliste	Bestellliste *or* Bestell-Liste
bestgehaßt	bestgehasst
bestußt	bestusst
Betelnuß	Betelnuss
betreßt	betresst
Betriebsschluß	Betriebsschluss
Bettuch	Betttuch *or* Bett-Tuch
bewußt	bewusst
Bewußtheit	Bewusstheit
bewußtlos	bewusstlos
Bewußtlose(r)	Bewusstlose(r)
Bewußtlosigkeit	Bewusstlosigkeit
bewußtmachen	bewusstmachen
bewußtmachen	bewußt machen
Bewußtsein	Bewusstsein
Bewußtseinsbildung	Bewusstseinsbildung
bewußtseinserweiternd	bewusstseinserweiternd
Bewußtseinserweiterung	Bewusstseinserweiterung
Bewußtseinsinhalt	Bewusstseinsinhalt
Bewußtseinskunst	Bewusstseinskunst
Bewußtseinslage	Bewusstseinslage
Bewußtseinslenkung	Bewusstseinslenkung
Bewußtseinsschwelle	Bewusstseinsschwelle
Bewußtseinsspaltung	Bewusstseinsspaltung
Bewußtseinsstörung	Bewusstseinsstörung
Bewußtseinsstrom	Bewusstseinsstrom
Bewußtseinstrübung	Bewusstseinstrübung
bewußtseinsverändernd	bewusstseinsverändernd
Bewußtseinsveränderung	Bewusstseinsveränderung
Bewußtwerdung	Bewusstwerdung
bezug	Bezug
Bibliograph	Bibliograph *or* Bibliograf
Bibliographie	Bibliographie *or* Bibliografie
bibliographieren	bibliographieren *or* bibliografieren
bibliographisch	bibliographisch *or* bibliografisch
Bierbaß	Bierbass
Bierfaß	Bierfass
Biograph	Biograph *or* Biograf
Biographie	Biographie *or* Biografie
biographisch	biographisch *or* biografisch

ALT/OLD	NEU/NEW
biß	biss
Biß	Biss
bißchen	bisschen
Bißchen	Bisschen
Bißwunde	Bisswunde
blanchieren	blanchieren *or* blanschieren
blankgewetzt	blank gewetzt
blankpoliert	blank poliert
blaß	blass
blaß-	blass-
Blasenkatarrh	Blasenkatarrh *or* Blasenkatarr
Bläßhuhn	Blässhuhn
bläßlich	blässlich
Blattschuß	Blattschuss
Blattstengel	Blattstängel
bleibenlassen	bleiben lassen
blendendweiß	blendend weiß
bleuen	bläuen
blindfliegen	blind fliegen
blindschreiben	blind schreiben
blindspielen	blind spielen
blondgefärbt	blond gefärbt
blondgelockt	blond gelockt
blutbildend	Blut bildend
Bluterguß	Bluterguss
Blutpaß	Blutpass
Böllerschuß	Böllerschuss
Bombenschuß	Bombenschuss
Bonbonniere	Bonbonniere *or* Bonboniere
Börsenschluß	Börsenschluss
Börsentip	Börsentipp
Boß	Boss
Bouclé	Bouclé *or* Buklee
Branchenadreßbuch	Branchenadressbuch
braungebrannt	braun gebrannt
Bravour	Bravour *or* Bravur
Bravourleistung	Bravourleistung *or* Bravurleistung
bravourös	bravourös *or* bravurös
Bravourstück	Bravourstück *or* Bravurstück
breitgefächert	breit gefächert
breitmachen	breit machen
Brennessel	Brennnessel *or* Brenn-Nessel
Bronchialkatarrh	Bronchialkatarrh *or* Bronchialkatarr
Bruderhaß	Bruderhass
Bruderkuß	Bruderkuss
Brummbaß	Brumbass
Brüßler	Brüssler
Brüßler(in)	Brüssler(in)
buntbemalt	bunt bemalt
buntgefärbt	bunt gefärbt
buntgemischt	bunt gemischt
buntgestreift	bunt getstreift
buntschillernd	bunt schillernd
Büroschluß	Büroschluss
Buschenschenke	Buschenschenke *or* Buschenschänke
Butterfaß	Butterfass

C

ALT/OLD	NEU/NEW
Cashewnuß	Cashewnuss
Chansonnier	Chansonnier *or* Chansonier
charakterbildend	Charakter bildend
Chicorée	Chicorée *or* Schikoree
Choreograph	Choreograph *or* Choreograf
Choreographie	Choreographie *or* Choreografie
choreographieren	choreographieren *or* choreografieren
choreographisch	choreographisch *or* choreografisch
Cleverneß	Cleverness
Colanuß	Colanuss
Communiqué	Communiqué *or* Kommunikee
Computertomograph	Computertomograph or Computertomograf
Computertomographie	Computertomographie *or* Computertomografie
Coupé	Coupé *or* Kupee

D

ALT/OLD	NEU/NEW
dabeisein	dabei sein
Dachgeschoß	Dachgeschoss
dafürkönnen	dafür können
dahinterklemmen	dahinter klemmen
dahinterknien	dahinter knien
dahinterkommen	dahinter kommen
dahintersetzen	dahinter setzen
dahinterstecken	dahinter stecken
dahinterstehen	dahinter stehen
Daktylographie	Daktylographie *or* Daktylografie
Dammriß	Dammriss
danebensein	daneben sein
darauffolgend	darauf folgend
Darmkatarrh	Darmkatarrh *or* Darmkatarr
Darmverschluß	Darmverschluss
darüberfahren	darüber fahren
darüberliegen	darüber liegen
darübermachen	darüber machen
darüberschreiben	darüber schreiben
darüberstehen	darüber stehen
darunterbleiben	darunter bleiben
darunterfallen	darunter fallen
daruntergehen	darunter gehen
darunterliegen	darunter liegen
daruntermischen	darunter mischen
darunterschreiben	darunter schreiben
daruntersetzen	darunter setzen
daß	dass
dasein	da sein
Datenmißbrauch	Datenmissbrauch
Dauerstreß	Dauerstress
davorhängen	davor hängen
davorlegen	davor legen
davorliegen	davor liegen
davorstehen	davor stehen
davorstellen	davor stellen
Décolleté	Décolleté *or* Dekolletee
Dekolleté	Dekolleté *or* Dekolletee
Delikateß-	Delikatess-
Delphin	Delphin *or* Delfin
Delphinarium	Delphinarium *or* Delfinarium
Delphinschwimmen	Delphinschwimmen *or* Delfinschwimmen
Demograph	Demograph *or* Demograf
Demographie	Demographie *or* Demografie
demographisch	demographisch *or* demografisch
Denkprozeß	Denkprozess
deplaciert	deplatziert
deplaziert	deplatziert
des(sen)ungeachtet	des(sen) ungeachtet
desungeachtet	des ungeachtet
Deutschenhaß	Deutschenhass
deutschsprechend	deutsch sprechend
Diarrhö(e)	Diarrhö
diät	Diät
dichtbehaart	dicht behaart
dichtbelaubt	dicht belaubt
dichtbevölkert	dicht bevölkert
dichtbewölkt	dicht bewölkt
dichtgedrängt	dicht gedrängt
diensthabend	Dienst habend
Dienstschluß	Dienstschluss
diensttuend	Dienst tuend
Differential	Differential *or* Differenzial
Differential-	Differential- *or* Differenzial-
Differentialrechnung	Differentialrechnung *or* Differenzialrechnung
Diktaphon	Diktaphon *or* Diktafon
Doppelbeschluß	Doppelbeschluss
Doppelpaß	Doppelpass
dortbehalten	dort behalten
dortbleiben	dort bleiben
dortzuland(e)	dort zu Land(e)
Doublé	Doublé *or* Dublee
Doublee	Doublee *or* Dublee
draufsein	drauf sein
dreiviertel	drei Viertel
Dreß	Dress
Drittkläßler	Drittklässler
Drogenmißbrauch	Drogenmissbrauch
Droßlung	Drosslung
drückendheiß	drückend heiß
Dumdumgeschoß	Dumdumgeschoss
dünnbehaart	dünn behaart
dünnbesiedelt	dünn besiedelt

ALT/OLD	NEU/NEW
dünnbevölkert	dünn bevölkert
dünngesät	dünn gesät
Dünnschiß	Dünnschiss
durchbleuen	durchbläuen
durcheinanderbringen	durcheinander bringen
durcheinandergehen	durcheinander gehen
durcheinandergeraten	durcheinander geraten
durcheinanderkommen	durcheinander kommen
durcheinanderlaufen	durcheinander laufen
durcheinanderliegen	durcheinander liegen
durcheinandermengen	durcheinander mengen
durcheinandermischen	durcheinander mischen
durcheinanderreden	durcheinander reden
durcheinanderrennen	durcheinander rennen
durcheinanderrufen	durcheinander rufen
durcheinanderschreien	durcheinander schreien
durcheinanderwerfen	durcheinander werfen
durcheinanderwirbeln	durcheinander wirbeln
Durchfluß	Durchfluss
Durchlaß	Durchlass
durchnumerieren	durchnummerieren
Durchschuß	Durchschuss
durchsein	durch sein
dußlig	dusslig
Dußligkeit	Dussligkeit

E

ALT/OLD	NEU/NEW
ebensogern	ebenso gern
ebensogut	ebenso gut
ebensohäufig	ebenso häufig
ebensolang(e)	ebenso lang(e)
ebensooft	ebenso oft
ebensosehr	ebenso sehr
ebensoviel	ebenso viel
ebensowenig	ebenso wenig
ehrfurchtgebietend	Ehrfurcht gebietend
ehrpußlig	ehrpusslig
einbleuen	einbläuen
Einfluß	Einfluss
Einflußbereich	Einflussbereich
Einflußgebiet	Einflussgebiet
einflußlos	einflusslos
Einflußlosigkeit	Einflusslosigkeit
Einflußmöglichkeit	Einflussmöglichkeit
Einflußnahme	Einflussnahme
einflußreich	einflussreich
Einflußsphäre	Einflusssphäre *or* Einfluss-Sphäre
Einlaß	Einlass
Einschluß	Einschluss
Einschuß	Einschuss
Einschußloch	Einschussloch
Einschußstelle	Einschussstelle *or* Einschuss-Stelle
Einsendeschluß	Einsendeschluss
einwärtsgebogen	einwärts gebogen
einzelnstehend	einzeln stehend
Eisenguß	Eisenguss
Eisensulphat	Eisensulphat *or* Eisensulfat
eisenverarbeitend	Eisen verarbeitend
eislaufen	Eis laufen
ekelerregend	Ekel erregend
Elfmeterschuß	Elfmeterschuss
elsaß-lothringisch	elsass-lothringisch
Elsaß	Elsass
Elsaß-Lothringen	Elsass-Lothringen
energiebewußt	energiebewusst
energiesparend	Energie sparend
enganliegend	eng anliegend
engbedruckt	eng bedruckt
engbefreundet	eng befreundet
engbegrenzt	eng begrenzt
engbeschrieben	eng beschrieben
Engpaß	Engpass
entschloß	entschloss
Entschluß	Entschluss
entschlußfreudig	entschlussfreudig
Entschlußkraft	Entschlusskraft
entschlußlos	entschlusslos
Epigraph	Epigraph *or* Epigraf
epochemachend	Epoche machend
erbgutschädigend	Erbgut schädigend

ALT/OLD	NEU/NEW
erbgutverändernd	Erbgut verändernd
Erdbebenmeßgerät	Erdbebenmessgerät
Erdgeschoß	Erdgeschoss
Erdnuß	Erdnuss
erdölexportierend	Erdöl exportierend
Erdschluß	Erdschluss
erfaßbar	erfassbar
erfolgversprechend	Erfolg versprechend
Erguß	Erguss
Erlaß	Erlass
Ermessensmißbrauch	Ermessensmissbrauch
Ermittlungsausschuß	Ermittlungsausschuss
ernstgemeint	ernst gemeint
erstemal	erste Mal
erstenmal	ersten Mal
Erstkläßler	Erstklässler
Eßapfel	Essapfel
eßbar	essbar
Eßbesteck	Essbesteck
Eßgeschirr	Essgeschirr
Eßgewohnheiten	Essgewohnheiten
Eßkastanie	Esskastanie
Eßkultur	Esskultur
Eßlöffel	Esslöffel
eßlöffelweise	esslöffelweise
Eßlust	Esslust
Essen(s)zuschuß	Essen(s)zuschuss
essentiell	essentiell *or* essenziell
Eßstäbchen	Essstäbchen *or* Ess-Stäbchen
eßt	esst
Eßtisch	Esstisch
Eßunlust	Essunlust
Eßwaren	Esswaren
Eßzimmer	Esszimmer
Eßzwang	Esszwang
Ethnograph	Ethnograph *or* Ethnograf
Ethnographie	Ethnographie *or* Ethnografie
Europapaß	Europapass
Eustachische Röhre	eustachische Röhre
Exekutivausschuß	Exekutivausschuss
Existentialismus	Existentialismus *or* Existenzialismus
Existentialist	Existentialist *or* Existenzialist
existentialistisch	existentialistisch *or* existenzialistisch
Existentialphilosophie	Existentialphilosophie *or* Existenzialphilosophie
existentiell	existentiell *or* existenziell
Exponentialfunktion	Exponentialfunktion *or* Exponenzialfunktion
Exponentialgleichung	Exponentialgleichung *or* Exponenzialgleichung
Exposé	Exposé *or* Exposee
expreß	express
Expreß	Express
Expreßbrief	Expressbrief
Expreßgut	Expressgut
Expreßreinigung	Expressreinigung
Expreßzug	Expresszug
Expreßzüge	Expresszüge
Exzeß	Exzess

F

ALT/OLD	NEU/NEW
Facette	Facette *or* Fassette
facettenartig	facettenartig *or* fassettenartig
Facettenauge	Facettenauge *or* Fassettenauge
Facettenschliff	Facettenschliff *or* Fassettenschliff
facettieren	facettieren *or* fassettieren
Fachausschuß	Fachausschuss
Fachhochschulabschluß	Fachhochschulabschluss
fahrenlassen	fahren lassen
Fairneß	Fairness
fallenlassen	fallen lassen
Familienanschluß	Familienanschluss
Familienpaß	Familienpass
Fangschuß	Fangschuss
farbentragend	Farben tragend
Faß	Fass
Faßband	Fassband
faßbar	fassbar
Faßbier	Fassbier
Faßbinder	Fassbinder

ALT/OLD	NEU/NEW
Fäßchen	Fässchen
Faßdaube	Fassdaube
faßlich	fasslich
Faßlichkeit	Fasslichkeit
Faßreif(en)	Fassreif(en)
Faßwein	Fasswein
faßweise	fassweise
fäulniserregend	Fäulnis erregend
Fehlpaß	Fehlpass
fehlplaziert	fehlplatziert
Fehlschluß	Fehlschluss
Fehlschuß	Fehlschuss
feind	Feind
feingemahlen	fein gemahlen
Feinmeßgerät	Feinmessgerät
Feldtelegraph	Feldtelegraph *or* Feldtelegraf
Fernexpreß	Fernexpress
fernhalten	fern halten
fernliegen	fern liegen
Fernsprechanschluß	Fernsprechanschluss
fernstehen	fern stehen
fertigbekommen	fertig bekommen
fertigbringen	fertig bringen
fertigkriegen	fertig kriegen
fertigmachen	fertig machen
fertigstellen	fertig stellen
festangestellt	fest angestellt
festbesoldet	fest besoldet
festverwurzelt	fest verwurzelt
feuerschnaubend	Feuer schnaubend
feuerspeiend	Feuer speiend
feuersprühend	Feuer sprühend
Fideikommiß	Fideikommiss
Fieberphantasien	Fieberphantasien *or* Fieberfantasien
fiebersenkend	Fieber senkend
Filmographie	Filmographie *or* Filmografie
Filmriß	Filmriss
Finanzausschuß	Finanzausschuss
fischverarbeitend	Fisch verarbeitend
Fitneß	Fitness
Flachpaß	Flachpass
Flachschuß	Flachschuss
Flaschenverschluß	Flaschenverschluss
fleischfressend	Fleisch fressend
Fleischgenuß	Fleischgenuss
fleischgeworden	Fleisch geworden
fleischverarbeitend	Fleisch verarbeitend
Fliegenschiß	Fliegenschiss
Flohbiß	Flohbiss
floß	floss
flötengehen	flöten gehen
Flügelroß	Flügelross
Fluß	Fluss
Fluß-	Fluss-
Flußaal	Flussaal
flußab(wärts)	flussab(wärts)
Flußarm	Flussarm
flußaufwärts	flussaufwärts
Flußbau	Flussbau
Flußbett	Flussbett
Flüßchen	Flüsschen
Flußdiagramm	Flussdiagramm
Flußebene	Flussebene
Flußgebiet	Flussgebiet
Flußgefälle	Flussgefälle
Flußgeschiebe	Flussgeschiebe
Flußhafen	Flusshafen
Flußkrebs	Flusskrebs
Flußlandschaft	Flusslandschaft
Flußlauf	Flusslauf
Flußmündung	Flussmündung
Flußniederung	Flussniederung
Flußnixe	Flussnixe
Flußpferd	Flusspferd
Flußregelung	Flussregelung
Flußregulierung	Flussregulierung
Flußsand	Flusssand *or* Fluss-Sand
Flußschiff	Flussschiff *or* Fluss-Schiff
Flußschiffahrt	Flussschiffahrt *or* Fluss-Schiffahrt
flüssigmachen	flüssig machen

ALT/OLD	NEU/NEW
Flußspat	Flussspat *or* Fluss-Spat
Flußstahl	Flussstahl *or* Fluss-Stahl
Flußufer	Flussufer
Fön®	Föhn *or* Fön®
fönen	föhnen
Frauenüberschuß	Frauenüberschuss
Freisaß	Freisass
Freischuß	Freischuss
Fremdenhaß	Fremdenhass
Fremdenpaß	Fremdenpass
Freßbeutel	Fressbeutel
Freßgier	Fressgier
Freßkorb	Fresskorb
Freßnapf	Fressnapf
Freßpaket	Fresspaket
Freßsack	Fresssack *or* Fress-Sack
Freßsucht	Fresssucht *or* Fress-Sucht
freßt	fresst
Freßwelle	Fresswelle
Freßwerkzeuge	Fresswerkzeuge
Friedenskuß	Friedenskuss
Friedensprozeß	Friedensprozess
Friedensschluß	Friedensschluss
friß	friss
frischgebacken	frisch gebacken
Friteuse	Fritteuse
fritieren	frittieren
Fritüre	Frittüre
Froschbiß	Froschbiss
frühauf	früh auf
frühpensionieren	früh pensionieren
frühverrenten	früh verrenten
frühvollendet	früh vollendet
frühzeitig	früh zeitig
funkensprühend	Funken sprühend
Funkmeßgerät	Funkmessgerät
fürbaß	fürbass
furchteinflößend	Furcht einflößend
furchterregend	Furcht erregend

G

ALT/OLD	NEU/NEW
Gamsbart	Gamsbart *or* Gämsbart
Gamsbock	Gamsbock *or* Gämsbock
Gamsleder	Gämsleder
Gangsterboß	Gangsterboss
garkochen	gar kochen
Gärungsprozeß	Gärungsprozess
Gäßchen	Gässchen
Gebiß	Gebiss
Gebißabdruck	Gebissabdruck
Gebißanomalie	Gebissanomalie
Gebrauchsgraphik	Gebrauchsgraphik *or* Gebrauchsgrafik
Gebrauchsgraphiker	Gebrauchsgraphiker *or* Gebrauchsgrafiker
Gebührenerlaß	Gebührenerlass
Geburtenüberschuß	Geburtenüberschuss
gefahrbringend	Gefahr bringend
gefangenhalten	gefangen halten
gefangennehmen	gefangen nehmen
gefangensetzen	gefangen setzen
gefaßt	gefasst
Gefaßtheit	Gefasstheit
Gefäßverschluß	Gefässverschluss
gegeneinanderhalten	gegeneinander halten
gegeneinanderprallen	gegeneinander prallen
gegeneinanderstehen	gegeneinander stehen
gegeneinanderstellen	gegeneinander stellen
gegeneinanderstoßen	gegeneinander stoßen
geheimhalten	geheim halten
Geheimschloß	Geheimschloss
Geheimtip	Geheimtipp
geheimtun	geheim tun
gehenlassen	gehen lassen
Gemeindebeschluß	Gemeindebeschluss
Gemeinschaftsanschluß	Gemeinschaftsanschluss
Gemse	Gämse
gemußt	gemusst
genaugenommen	genau genommen
genauso-	genauso
Generalbaß	Generalbass

ALT/OLD	NEU/NEW
Genesungsprozeß	Genesungsprozess
Genickschuß	Genickschuss
genoß	genoss
Genuß	Genuss
genußfreudig	genussfreudig
Genußgift	Genussgift
genüßlich	genüsslich
Genußmensch	Genussmensch
Genußmittel	Genussmittel
genußreich	genussreich
Genußschein	Genussschein *or* Genuss-Schein
Genußsucht	Genusssucht *or* Genuss-Sucht
genußsüchtig	genusssüchtig *or* genuss-süchtig
genußvoll	genussvoll
Geograph	Geograph *or* Geograf
Geographie	Geographie *or* Geografie
geographisch	geographisch *or* geografisch
geradehalten	gerade halten
geradelegen	gerade legen
gerademachen	gerade machen
geraderichten	gerade richten
geradesitzen	gerade sitzen
geradesogut	geradeso gut
geradesoviel	geradeso viel
Gerichtsbeschluß	Gerichtsbeschluss
geringachten	gering achten
geringschätzen	gering schätzen
G(e)riß	G(e)riss
Geruch(s)verschluß	Geruch(s)verschluss
Geschäftsabschluß	Geschäftsabschluss
Geschäftsschluß	Geschäftsschluss
Geschichtsbewußtsein	Geschichtsbewusstsein
Geschiß	Geschiss
Geschoß	Geschoss
Geschoßbahn	Geschossbahn
Geschoßgarbe	Geschossgarbe
Geschoßhagel	Geschosshagel
gewaltbejahend	Gewalt bejahend
Gewerkschaftsboß	Gewerkschaftsboss
Gewerkschaftskongreß	Gewerkschaftskongress
gewinnbringend	Gewinn bringend
Gewinnummer	Gewinnnummer *or* Gewinn-Nummer
gewiß	gewiss
Gewißheit	Gewissheit
gewißlich	gewisslich
gewußt	gewusst
Gipsabguß	Gipsabguss
glattbügeln	glatt bügeln
glattgehen	glatt gehen
glatthobeln	glatt hobeln
glattkämmen	glatt kämmen
glattlegen	glatt legen
glattmachen	glatt machen
glattpolieren	glatt polieren
glattrasieren	glatt rasieren
glattrasiert	glatt rasiert
glattrühren	glatt rühren
glattschleifen	glatt schleifen
glattschneiden	glatt schneiden
glattstreichen	glatt streichen
glattwalzen	glatt walzen
Gläubigerausschuß	Gläubigerausschuss
gleichbleiben	gleich bleiben
gleichbleibend	gleich bleibend
gleichdenkend	gleich denkend
gleichgeartet	gleich geartet
gleichgesinnt	gleich gesinnt
gleichgestellt	gleich gestellt
gleichgestimmt	gleich gestimmt
gleichlautend	gleich lautend
Gleisanschluß	Gleisanschluss
Glimmstengel	Glimmstängel
Glockenguß	Glockenguss
Glotzophon	Glotzophon *or* Glotzofon
glückbringend	Glück bringend
glückverheißend	Glück verheißend
Gnadenerlaß	Gnadenerlass
Gnadenschuß	Gnadenschuss
goldbetreßt	goldbetresst
Golddoublé	Golddoublé *or* Golddublee

ALT/OLD	NEU/NEW
goldgefaßt	goldgefasst
Gonorrhö(e)	Gonorrhö
goß	goss
Grammolekül	Grammmolekül *or* Gramm-Molekül
Grammophon	Grammophon *or* Grammofon
Graph	Graph *or* Graf
Graphem	Graphem *or* Grafem
Graphie	Graphie *or* Grafie
Graphik	Graphik *or* Grafik
graphisch	graphisch *or* grafisch
Graphologe	Graphologe *or* Grafologe
Graphologie	Graphologie *or* Grafologie
Graphologin	Graphologin *or* Grafologin
gräßlich	grässlich
Gräßlichkeit	Grässlichkeit
grauenerregend	Grauen erregend
graugestreift	grau gestreift
Grauguß	Grauguss
graumeliert	grau meliert
Grenzfluß	Grenzfluss
Greuel	Gräuel
Greuelgeschichte	Gräuelgeschichte
Greuelmärchen	Gräuelmärchen
Greuelmeldung	Gräuelmeldung
Greuelnachricht	Gräuelnachricht
Greuelpropaganda	Gräuelpropaganda
Greueltat	Gräueltat
greulich	gräulich
Griß	Griss
grobgemahlen	grob gemahlen
großangelegt	groß angelegt
Großanlaß	Großanlass
großgemustert	groß gemustert
großgewachsen	groß gewachsen
großkariert	groß kariert
Großphoto	Großphoto *or* Großfoto
grundhäßlich	grundhässlich
Grundriß	Grundriss
Gummiparagraph	Gummiparagraph *or* Gummiparagraf
Gummi(wucht)geschoß	Gummi(wucht)geschoss
Guß	Guss
Gußasphalt	Gussasphalt
Gußbeton	Gussbeton
Gußeisen	Gusseisen
gußeisern	gusseisern
Gußform	Gussform
Gußnaht	Gussnaht
Gußstahl	Gussstahl *or* Guss-Stahl
gutaussehend	gut aussehend
gutbetucht	gut betucht
gutbezahlt	gut bezahlt
gutdotiert	gut dotiert
Gutenachtkuß	Gutenachtkuss
gutgehen	gut gehen
gutgehend	gut gehend
gutgelaunt	gut gelaunt
gutgelungen	gut gelungen
gutgemeint	gut gemeint
gutgesinnt	gut gesinnt
gutsituiert	gut situiert
gutsitzend	gut sitzend
guttun	gut tun
gutunterrichtet	gut unterrichtet
gutverdienend	gut verdienend

H

ALT/OLD	NEU/NEW
Haarriß	Haarriss
haftenbleiben	haften bleiben
Hagiograph	Hagiograph *or* Hagiograf
Hagiographen	Hagiographen *or* Hagiografen
Hagiographie	Hagiographie *or* Hagiografie
halbfertig	halb fertig
halbgar	halb gar
Halbgeschoß	Halbgeschoss
halblinks	halb links
halbnackt	halb nackt
halboffen	halb offen
halbrechts	halb rechts
halbtot	halb tot

ALT/OLD	NEU/NEW
halbverdaut	halb verdaut
halbvoll	halb voll
halbwach	halb wach
haltmachen	Halt machen
Hämorrhoiden	Hämorrhoiden *or* Hämorriden
Hämorrhoidenschaukel	Hämorrhoidenschaukel *or* Hämmoridenschaukel
händchenhaltend	Händchen haltend
handeltreibend	Handel treibend
Handkuß	Handkuss
Handvoll	Hand voll
hängenbleiben	hängen bleiben
hängenlassen	hängen lassen
Hängeschloß	Hängeschloss
Härteparagraph	Härteparagraph *or* Härteparagraf
hartgebrannt	hart gebrannt
hartgefroren	hart gefroren
hartgekocht	hart gekocht
Haß	Hass
Haßausbruch	Hassausbruch
Haselnuß	Haselnuss
haßerfüllt	hasserfüllt
Haßgefühl	Hassgefühl
häßlich	hässlich
Häßlichkeit	Hässlichkeit
Haßliebe	Hassliebe
Haßtirade	Hasstirade
haßverzerrt	hassverzerrt
Hauptanschluß	Hauptanschluss
Hauptschulabschluß	Hauptschulabschluss
haushalten	haushalten *or* Haus halten
heilighalten	heilig halten
heiligsprechen	heilig sprechen
Heilungsprozeß	Heilungsprozess
heißersehnt	heiß ersehnt
heißgeliebt	heiß geliebt
heißumkämpft	heiß umkämpft
heißumstritten	heiß umstritten
Hektographie	Hektographie *or* Hektografie
hektographieren	hektographieren *or* hektografieren
helleuchtend	hell leuchtend
hellicht	helllicht
hellodernd	hell lodernd
hellstrahlend	hell strahlend
heraussein	heraus sein
hersein	her sein
herumsein	herum sein
heruntersein	herunter sein
Herzenserguß	Herzenserguss
Hexenprozeß	Hexenprozess
Hexenschuß	Hexenschuss
hierbehalten	hier behalten
hierbleiben	hier bleiben
hierherbemühen	hierher bemühen
hierherbitten	hierher bitten
hierherblicken	hierher blicken
hierherbringen	hierher bringen
hierherfahren	hierher fahren
hierherführen	hierher führen
hierhergehören	hierher gehören
hierherholen	hierher holen
hierherkommen	hierher kommen
hierherlaufen	hierher laufen
hierherlegen	hierher legen
hierherlocken	hierher locken
hierherschaffen	hierher schaffen
hierherschicken	hierher schicken
hierhersetzen	hierher setzen
hierherstellen	hierher stellen
hierhertragen	hierher tragen
hierherwagen	hierher wagen
hierherziehen	hierher ziehen
hierlassen	hier lassen
hiersein	hier sein
hierzulande	hier zu Lande
hilfesuchend	Hilfe suchend
Hinausschmiß	Hinausschmiss
hinaussein	hinaus sein
hinsein	hin sein
hintereinanderfahren	hintereinander fahren

ALT/OLD	NEU/NEW
hintereinandergehen	hintereinander gehen
hintereinanderschalten	hintereinander schalten
hintereinanderstehen	hintereinander stehen
hinterhersein	hinterher sein
hinübersein	hinüber sein
Historiograph	Historiograph *or* Historiograf
hochachten	hoch achten
hochbegabt	hoch begabt
hochdotiert	hoch dotiert
hochempfindlich	hoch empfindlich
hochentwickelt	hoch entwickelt
hochgeehrt	hoch geehrt
Hochgenuß	Hochgenuss
hochgeschätzt	hoch geschätzt
hochgestellt	hoch gestellt
hochgewachsen	hoch gewachsen
hochindustrialisiert	hoch industrialisiert
hochqualifiziert	hoch qualifiziert
hochschätzen	hoch schätzen
hochschrauben	hoch schrauben
Hochschulabschluß	Hochschulabschluss
hockenbleiben	hocken bleiben
hofhalten	Hof halten
höhergestellt	höher gestellt
höherliegend	höher liegend
höherschrauben	höher schrauben
höherstehend	höher stehend
höherstufen	höher stufen
hohnlachen	hohnlachen *or* Hohn lachen
hohnsprechen	hohnsprechen *or* Hohn sprechen
Holographie	Holographie *or* Holografie
holzverarbeitend	Holz verarbeitend
homophon	homophon *or* homofon
Hosteß	Hostess
Hundebiß	Hundebiss
hustenstillend	Husten stillend
Hydrographie	Hydrographie *or* Hydrografie
hydrographisch	hydrographisch *or* hydrografisch

I

ALT/OLD	NEU/NEW
Ichbewußtsein	Ichbewusstsein
Ich-Roman	Ichroman
Imbiß	Imbiss
Imbißhalle	Imbisshalle
Imbißstand	Imbissstand *or* Imbiss-Stand
Imbißstube	Imbissstube *or* Imbiss-Stube
immerwährend	immer während
Impfpaß	Impfpass
imstande	imstande *or* im Stande
ineinanderfließen	ineinander fließen
ineinanderfügen	ineinander fügen
ineinandergreifen	ineinander greifen
ineinanderpassen	ineinander passen
ineinanderschieben	ineinander schieben
Informationsfluß	Informationsfluss
insektenfressend	Insekten fressend
instandbesetzen	instand besetzen *or* in Stand besetzen
I-Punkt	i-Punkt
iß	iss
Ist-Bestand	Istbestand
I-Tüpfelchen	i-Tüpfelchen

J

ALT/OLD	NEU/NEW
Jackettasche	Jacketttasche *or* Jackett-Tasche
Jagdschloß	Jagdschloss
Jahresabschluß	Jahresabschluss
Joghurt	Joghurt *or* Jogurt
Joghurtbereiter	Joghurtbereiter *or* Jogurtbereiter
Judaskuß	Judaskuss
Judenhaß	Judenhass
Juniorpaß	Juniorpass
justitiabel	justitiabel *or* justiziabel
Justitiar	Justitiar *or* Justiziar

K

ALT/OLD	NEU/NEW
Kabelanschluß	Kabelanschluss
Kabinettsbeschluß	Kabinettsbeschluss
Kaffee-Ersatz	Kaffee-Ersatz *or* Kafeeersatz
Kaffee-Extrakt	Kaffee-Extrakt *or* Kaffeeextrakt
kahlfressen	kahl fressen
kahlgeschoren	kahl geschoren

ALT/OLD	NEU/NEW
kahlscheren	kahl scheren
kahlschlagen	kahl schlagen
Kakophonie	Kakophonie *or* Kakofonie
Kalligraphie	Kalligraphie *or* Kalligrafie
kaltbleiben	kalt bleiben
kaltgepreßt	kaltgepresst
kaltlächelnd	kalt lächelnd
kaltlassen	kalt lassen
Kammuschel	Kammmuschel *or* Kamm-Muschel
Känguruh	Känguru
Kann-Bestimmung	Kannbestimmung
Kapitalabfluß	Kapitalabfluss
Karamel	Karamell
Kartograph	Kartograph *or* Kartograf
Kartographie	Kartographie *or* Kartografie
kartographisch	kartographisch *or* kartografisch
Kassenabschluß	Kassenabschluss
Katarrh	Katarrh *or* Katarr
kegelscheiben	Kegel scheiben
kegelschieben	Kegel schieben
Kehlkopfkatarrh	Kehlkopfkatarrh *or* Kehlkopfkatarr
Kehlkopfmikrophon	Kehlkopfmikrophon *or* Kehlkopfmikrofon
Kehlverschlußlaut	Kehlverschlusslaut
Kellergeschoß	Kellergeschoss
Kernspin-Tomographie	Kernspin-Tomographie *or* Kernspin-Tomografie
Kernspin-Tomograph	Kernspin-Tomograph *or* Kernspin-Tomograf
keß	kess
Keßheit	Kessheit
Ketchup	Ketchup *or* Ketschup
Kettenschluß	Kettenschluss
Kindesmißhandlung	Kindesmisshandlung
Kinematographie	Kinematographie *or* Kinematografie
klarblickend	klar blickend
klardenkend	klar denkend
klarsehen	klar sehen
klarwerden	klar werden
klaß	klass
Klassenbewußtsein	Klassenbewusstsein
Klassenhaß	Klassenhass
-kläßler	-klässler
klatschenaß	klatschenass
klatschnaß	klatschnass
kleingedruckt	klein gedruckt
kleingemustert	klein gemustert
kleinhacken	klein hacken
kleinmachen	klein machen
kleinschneiden	klein schneiden
Klemmappe	Klemmmappe *or* Klemm-Mappe
Klettverschluß	Klettverschluss
klitschnaß	klitschnass
klugreden	klug reden
knapphalten	knapp halten
kochendheiß	kochend heiß
Kokosnuß	Kokosnuss
Kolanuß	Kolanuss
Kölnisch Wasser	kölnisch Wasser
Koloß	Koloss
Kombinationsschloß	Kombinationsschloss
Kommiß	Kommiss
Kommißbrot	Kommissbrot
Kommißstiefel	Kommissstiefel *or* Kommiss-Stiefel
Kommuniqué	Kommuniqué *or* Kommunikee
Kompaß	Kompass
Kompaßhäuschen	Kompasshäuschen
Kompaßnadel	Kompassnadel
kompreß	kompress
Kompromiß	Kompromiss
kompromißbereit	kompromissbereit
Kompromißbereitschaft	Kompromissbereitschaft
kompromißlos	kompromisslos
Kompromißlösung	Kompromisslösung
Komteß	Komtess
Kongreß	Kongress
Kongreßmitglied	Kongressmitglied
Kongreßteilnehmer	Kongressteilnehmer
Kongreßzentrum	Kongresszentrum
kontoführend	Konto führend

ALT/OLD	NEU/NEW
Kontrabaß	Kontrabass
Kontrollampe	Kontrolllampe *or* Kontroll-Lampe
Kontrolliste	Kontrollliste *or* Kontroll-Liste
Kopfnuß	Kopfnuss
Kopfschuß	Kopfschuss
kopfstehen	Kopf stehen
Koppelschloß	Koppelschloss
kostensparend	Kosten sparend
Kostenvorschuß	Kostenvorschuss
kraß	krass
krebsauslösend	Krebs auslösend
krebserregend	Krebs erregend
Kreiselkompaß	Kreiselkompass
Kreppapier	Krepppapier *or* Krepp-Papier
kriegführend	Krieg führend
Kriegsgreuel	Kriegsgräuel
Kristalleuchter	Kristallleuchter *or* Kristall-Leuchter
Kristallüster	Kristalllüster *or* Kristall-Lüster
kroß	kross
krummlegen	krumm legen
krummnehmen	krumm nehmen
Kulturgeographie	Kulturgeographie *or* Kulturgeografie
Küraß	Kürass
kurzgefaßt	kurz gefasst
kurzgeschnitten	kurz geschnitten
kurzhalten	kurz halten
Kurzschluß	Kurzschluss
Kurzschlußreaktion	Kurzschlussreaktion
kurztreten	kurz treten
Kuß	Kuss
küß die Hand	küss die Hand
Küßchen	Küsschen
küßdiehand	küssdiehand
kußecht	kussecht
kußfest	kussfest
Kußhand	Kusshand
Kußmund	Kussmund

L

ALT/OLD	NEU/NEW
Ladenschluß	Ladenschluss
Ladenschlußgesetz	Ladenschlussgesetz
Ladenschlußzeit	Ladenschlusszeit
langersehnt	lang ersehnt
langgehegt	lang gehegt
langgestreckt	lang gestreckt
langgezogen	lang gezogen
längsgestreift	längs gestreift
langziehen	lang ziehen
Lärmmeßgerät	Lärmmessgerät
laß	lass
läßlich	lässlich
laßt	lasst
Lattenschuß	Lattenschuss
laubtragend	Laub tragend
Laufpaß	Laufpass
lebendgebärend	lebend gebärend
Lebensgenuß	Lebensgenuss
Lebensüberdruß	Lebensüberdruss
leerlaufen	leer laufen
leerstehend	leer stehend
leichenblaß	leichenblass
leichtbeschwingt	leicht beschwingt
leichtbewaffnet	leicht bewaffnet
leichtentzündlich	leicht entzündlich
leichtfallen	leicht fallen
leichtgeschürzt	leicht geschürzt
leichtmachen	leicht machen
leichtnehmen	leicht nehmen
leichtverdaulich	leicht verdaulich
leichtverderblich	leicht verderblich
leichtverletzt	leicht verletzt
leichtverständlich	leicht verständlich
leichtverwundet	leicht verwundet
Lenkradschloß	Lenkradschloss
Lernprozeß	Lernprozess
Leuchtgeschoß	Leuchtgeschoss
Leuchtspurgeschoß	Leuchtspurgeschoss
Lexikograph	Lexikograph *or* Lexikograf
Lexikographie	Lexikographie *or* Lexikografie
lexikographisch	lexikographisch *or* lexikografisch

ALT/OLD	NEU/NEW
Lichtmeß	Lichtmess
Lichtmeßverfahren	Lichtmessverfahren
liebenlernen	lieben lernen
liebgewinnen	lieb gewonnen
liebgeworden	lieb geworden
liebhaben	lieb haben
liegenbleiben	liegen bleiben
liegenlassen	liegen lassen
Litfaßsäule	Litfasssäule *or* Litfass-Säule
Lithograph	Lithograph *or* Lithograf
Lithographie	Lithographie *or* Lithografie
lithographieren	lithographieren *or* lithografieren
lithographisch	lithographisch *or* lithografisch
Lorbaß	Lorbass
Luftschloß	Luftschloss
Lustschloß	Lustschloss
M	
Machtmißbrauch	Machtmissbrauch
Ma(f)fia-Boß	Ma(f)fia-Boss
Magen-Darm-Katarrh	Magen-Darm-Katarrh *or* Magen-Darm-Katarr
Magnetkompaß	Magnetkompass
Magnetophon	Magnetophon *or* Magnetofon
Magnetophonband	Magnetophonband *or* Magnetofonband
Majoritätsbeschluß	Majoritätsbeschluss
Mammutprozeß	Mammutprozess
Männerhaß	Männerhass
Männerüberschuß	Männerüberschuss
Mantelgeschoß	Mantelgeschoss
Marschkompaß	Marschkompass
maschine(n)schreiben	Maschine schreiben
maßhalten	Maß halten
Maulkorberlaß	Maulkorberlass
Mechanisierungsprozeß	Mechanisierungsprozess
Medikamentenmißbrauch	Medikamentenmissbrauch
Megaphon	Megaphon *or* Megafon
Mehrheitsbeschluß	Mehrheitsbeschluss
Meisterschuß	Meisterschuss
Meldeschluß	Meldeschluss
Meniskusriß	Meniskusriss
Menschenhaß	Menschenhass
menschenverachtend	Menschen verachtend
Meßband	Messband
meßbar	messbar
Meßbecher	Messbecher
Meßbuch	Messbuch
Meßdaten	Messdaten
Meßdiener	Messdiener
Meßfühler	Messfühler
Meßgerät	Messgerät
Meßgewand	Messgewand
Meßglas	Messglas
Meßinstrument	Messinstrument
Meßopfer	Messopfer
Meßordnung	Messordnung
Meßplatte	Messplatte
Meßstab	Messstab *or* Mess-Stab
Meßtechnik	Messtechnik
Meßtisch	Messtisch
Meßtischblatt	Messtischblatt
Meßwein	Messwein
Meßwert	Messwert
Meßzahl	Messzahl
Meßzylinder	Messzylinder
metallverarbeitend	Metall verarbeitend
Mikrophon	Mikrophon *or* Mikrofon
Milchgebiß	Milchgebiss
miß	miss
Miß	Miss
mißachten	missachten
Mißachtung	Missachtung
mißbehagen	missbehagen
Mißbehagen	Missbehagen
mißbilden	missbilden
Mißbildung	Missbildung
mißbilligen	missbilligen
mißbilligend	missbilligend
Mißbilligung	Missbilligung

ALT/OLD	NEU/NEW
Mißbrauch	Missbrauch
mißbrauchen	missbrauchen
mißbräuchlich	missbräuchlich
mißdeuten	missdeuten
Mißdeutung	Missdeutung
Mißerfolg	Misserfolg
Mißernte	Missernte
mißfallen	missfallen
Mißfallen	Missfallen
Mißfallensäußerung	Missfallensäußerung
Mißfallensbekundung	Missfallensbekundung
Mißfallenskundgebung	Missfallenskundgebung
mißfällig	missfällig
mißgebildet	missgebildet
Mißgeburt	Missgeburt
mißgelaunt	missgelaunt
Mißgeschick	Missgeschick
mißgestalt	missgestalt
Mißgestalt	Missgestalt
mißgestaltet	missgestaltet
mißgestimmt	missgestimmt
mißglücken	missglücken
mißgönnen	missgönnen
Mißgriff	Missgriff
Mißgunst	Missgunst
mißgünstig	missgünstig
mißhandeln	misshandeln
Mißhandlung	Misshandlung
Mißhelligkeit	Misshelligkeit
Mißklang	Missklang
Mißkredit	Misskredit
mißlang	misslang
mißlaunig	misslaunig
mißlich	misslich
Mißlichkeit	Misslichkeit
mißliebig	missliebig
mißlingen	misslingen
Mißlingen	Misslingen
mißlungen	misslungen
Mißmanagement	Missmanagement
Mißmut	Missmut
mißmutig	missmutig
mißraten	missraten
Mißstand	Missstand *or* Miss-Stand
Mißstimmung	Missstimmung *or* Miss-Stimmung
Mißton	Misston
mißtönend	misstönend
mißtönig	misstönig
mißtrauen	misstrauen
Mißtrauen	Misstrauen
Mißtrauensantrag	Misstrauensantrag
Mißtrauensvotum	Misstrauensvotum
mißtrauisch	misstrauisch
Mißvergnügen	Missvergnügen
mißvergnügt	missvergnügt
Mißverhältnis	Missverhältnis
mißverständlich	missverständlich
Mißverständnis	Missverständnis
mißverstehen	missverstehen
Mißwahl	Misswahl
Mißweisung	Missweisung
Mißwirtschaft	Misswirtschaft
Mißwuchs	Misswuchs
mißzubehagen	misszubehagen
mißzuverstehen	misszuverstehen
mittag	Mittag
modebewußt	modebewusst
Moiré	Moiré *or* Moiree
Mokkatäßchen	Mokkatässchen
Monographie	Monographie *or* Monografie
Mop	Mopp
Mordprozeß	Mordprozess
mündigsprechen	mündig sprechen
Muskatnuß	Muskatnuss
Muskelfaserriß	Muskelfaserriss
Muskelriß	Muskelriss
Muß	Muss
Mußbestimmung	Mussbestimmung
Muß-Bestimmung	Mussbestimmung
Mußehe	Mussehe

ALT/OLD	NEU/NEW
Mußheirat	Mussheirat
mußte	musste
Muß-Vorschrift	Muss-Vorschrift
Musterprozeß	Musterprozess
Musterungsausschuß	Musterungsausschuss
Mutterpaß	Mutterpass
Myrrhe	Myrrhe *or* Myrre
Myrrhenöl	Myrrhenöl *or* Myrrenöl

N

ALT/OLD	NEU/NEW
Nachfaßaktion	Nachfassaktion
nachhinein	Nachhinein
Nachlaß	Nachlass
Nachlaßgericht	Nachlassgericht
Nachlaßgläubiger	Nachlassgläubiger
Nachlaßpfleger	Nachlasspfleger
Nachlaßverwalter	Nachlassverwalter
Nachlaßverwaltung	Nachlassverwaltung
nachmittag	Nachmittag
Nachrüstungsbeschluß	Nachrüstungsbeschluss
Nachschuß	Nachschuss
nacht	Nacht
nahebringen	nahe bringen
nahegehen	nahe gehen
nahekommen	nahe kommen
nahelegen	nahe legen
naheliegen	nahe liegen
naheliegend	nahe liegend
näherbringen	näher bringen
näherkommen	näher kommen
näherliegen	näher liegen
näherstehen	näher stehen
nähertreten	näher treten
nahestehen	nahe stehen
Nahrungs- und Genußmittelindustrie	Nahrungs- und Genussmittelindustrie
Narziß	Narziss
Narzißmus	Narzissmus
Narzißt	Narzisst
narzißtisch	narzisstisch
naß	nass
Naß	Nass
naßforsch	nassforsch
naßkalt	nasskalt
Naßrasur	Nassrasur
Naßwäsche	Nasswäsche
Naßzelle	Nasszelle
nationalbewußt	nationalbewusst
Nationalbewußtsein	Nationalbewusstsein
Nato-Doppelbeschluß	Nato-Doppelbeschluss
Nebel(schluß)leuchte	Nebel(schluss)leuchte
Nebenanschluß	Nebenanschluss
nebeneinanderlegen	nebeneinander legen
nebeneinanderreihen	nebeneinander reihen
nebeneinanderschalten	nebeneinander schalten
nebeneinandersetzen	nebeneinander setzen
nebeneinandersitzen	nebeneinander sitzen
nebeneinanderstellen	nebeneinander stellen
Nebenfluß	Nebenfluss
Nebenschluß	Nebenschluss
Necessaire	Necessaire *or* Nessessär
Negerkuß	Negerkuss
Negligé	Negligé *or* Negligee
Netzanschluß	Netzanschluss
neubearbeitet	neu bearbeitet
neuentdeckt	neu entdeckt
neuentwickelt	neuentwickelt
neueröffnet	neu eröffnet
neugebacken	neu gebacken
neugeboren	neu geboren
neugeschaffen	neu geschaffen
neugestalten	neu gestalten
neugewählt	neu gewählt
neuvermählt	neu vermählt
nichtleitend	nicht leitend
nichtorganisiert	nicht organisiert
nichtrostend	nicht rostend
nichtsahnend	nichts ahnend
Nichtseßhafte(r)	Nichtsesshafte(r)
nichtssagend	nichts sagend
niedrigstehend	niedrig stehend
nonstop	nonstopp
Nonstop-	Nonstopp-
Nonstopbetrieb	Nonstoppbetrieb
Nonstopflug	Nonstoppflug
Nonstopkino	Nonstoppkino
not	Not
notleidend	Not leidend
Nulleiter	Nullleiter *or* Null-Leiter
Nullinie	Nulllinie *or* Null-Linie
Nullösung	Nulllösung *or* Null-Lösung
numerieren	nummerieren
Numerierung	Nummerierung
numerisch	nummerisch
Nuß	Nuss
Nußbaum	Nussbaum
nußbraun	nussbraun
Nußknacker	Nussknacker
Nußkohle	Nusskohle
Nußschale	Nussschale *or* Nuss-Schale

O

ALT/OLD	NEU/NEW
obenerwähnt	oben erwähnt
Obergeschoß	Obergeschoss
offenbleiben	offen bleiben
offenhalten	offen halten
offenlassen	offen lassen
offenstehen	offen stehen
Ölmeßstab	Ölmessstab *or* Ölmess-Stab
Ordonnanz	Ordonnanz *or* Ordonanz
Ordonnanzoffizier	Ordonnanzoffizier *or* Ordonanzoffizier
Orthographie	Orthographie *or* Orthografie
orthographisch	orthographisch *or* orthografisch
Oszillograph	Oszillograph *or* Oszillograf
Ozeanographie	Ozeanographie *or* Ozeanografie

P

ALT/OLD	NEU/NEW
Panther	Panther *or* Panter
Papiermaché	Papiermaché *or* Papiermaschee
papierverarbeitend	Papier verarbeitend
Pappmaché	Pappmaché *or* Pappmaschee
Paragraph	Paragraph *or* Paragraf
Paragraphenreiter	Paragraphenreiter *or* Paragrafenreiter
paragraphenweise	paragraphenweise *or* paragrafenweise
Paragraphenwerk	Paragraphenwerk *or* Paragrafenwerk
Paragraphenzeichen	Paragraphenzeichen *or* Paragrafenzeichen
Paranuß	Paranuss
Parlamentsausschuß	Parlamentsausschuss
Parlamentsbeschluß	Parlamentsbeschluss
Parnaß	Parnass
Parteiausschlußverfahren	Parteiausschlussverfahren
Parteikongreß	Parteikongress
partial-	partial- *or* parzial-
partiell	partiell *or* parziell
Paß	Pass
Paßamt	Passamt
Paßbild	Passbild
passé	passé *or* passee
Paßform	Passform
Paßfoto	Passfoto
Paßgang	Passgang
Paßgänger	Passgänger
Paßhöhe	Passhöhe
Paßkontrolle	Passkontrolle
Paßphoto	Passphoto *or* Passfoto
Paßstelle	Passstelle *or* Pass-Stelle
Paßstraße	Passstraße *or* Pass-Straße
Paßwort	Passwort
Paßzwang	Passzwang
Patentverschluß	Patentverschluss
patschnaß	patschnass
Paukenschlegel	Paukenschlägel
Pfeffernuß	Pfeffernuss
Pfeilschuß	Pfeilschuss
Pferdegebiß	Pferdegebiss
pflanzenfressend	Pflanzen fressend
pflichtbewußt	pflichtbewusst
Pflichtbewußtsein	Pflichtbewusstsein
Pfostenschuß	Pfostenschuss

ALT/OLD	NEU/NEW
Phantasie	Phantasie *or* Fantasie
phantasiearm	phantasiearm *or* fantasiearm
phantasiebegabt	phantasiebegabt *or* fantasiebegabt
Phantasiebild	Phantasiebild *or* Fantasiebild
Phantasiegebilde	Phantasiegebilde *or* Fantasiegebilde
phantasielos	phantasielos *or* fantasielos
Phantasielosigkeit	Phantasielosigkeit *or* Fantasielosigkeit
phantasiereich	phantasiereich *or* fantasiereich
phantasieren	phantasieren *or* fantasieren
phantasievoll	phantasievoll *or* fantasievoll
Phantasievorstellung	Phantasievorstellung *or* Fantasievorstellung
Phantast	Phantast *or* Fantast
Phantasterei	Phantasterei *or* Fantasterei
phantastisch	phantastisch *or* fantastisch
Phon	Phon *or* Fon
phonstark	phonstark *or* fonstark
Phonstärke	Phonstärke *or* Fonstärke
Phonzahl	Phonzahl *or* Fonzahl
Piß	Piss
Pißpott	Pisspott
Pistolenschuß	Pistolenschuss
pitsch(e)naß	pitsch(e)nass
pitsch(e)patsch(e)naß	pitsch(e)patsch(e)nass
placieren	platzieren
Placierung	Platzierung
Platitüde	Platitüde *or* Plattitüde
platschnaß	platschnass
platzraubend	Platz raubend
platzsparend	Platz sparend
plazieren	platzieren
Plazierung	Platzierung
plump-vertraulich	plumpvertraulich
Pornographie	Pornographie *or* Pornografie
pornographisch	pornographisch *or* pornografisch
Portemonnaie	Portemonnaie *or* Portmonee
Porträtphotographie	Porträtphotographie *or* Porträtfotografie
Postillon d'amour	Postillon d'Amour
Potemkinsch	potemkinsch
Potential	Potential *or* Potenzial
potentiell	potentiell *or* potenziell
potthäßlich	potthässlich
preisbewußt	preisbewusst
Preisnachlaß	Preisnachlass
Prellschuß	Prellschuss
Preßglas	Pressglas
Preßkohle	Presskohle
Preßluft	Pressluft
Preßluftbohrer	Pressluftbohrer
Preßlufthammer	Presslufthammer
probefahren	Probe fahren
Problembewußtsein	Problembewusstsein
profitbringend	Profit bringend
Programmusik	Programmmusik *or* Programm-Musik
Progreß	Progress
Protegé	Protegé *or* Protegee
Prozeß	Prozess
Prozeßakten	Prozessakten
prozeßfähig	prozessfähig
Prozeßfähigkeit	Prozessfähigkeit
prozeßführend	prozessführend
Prozeßführung	Prozessführung
Prozeßhansel	Prozesshansel
Prozeßkosten	Prozesskosten
Prozeßlawine	Prozesslawine
Prozeßordnung	Prozessordnung
Prozeßrecht	Prozessrecht
Prozeßsprache	Prozesssprache *or* Prozess-Sprache
prozeßsüchtig	prozesssüchtig *or* prozess-süchtig
prozeßunfähig	prozessunfähig
Prozeßunfähigkeit	Prozessunfähigkeit
Prozeßverschleppung	Prozessverschleppung
Prozeßvollmacht	Prozessvollmacht
Prozeßwärme	Prozesswärme
Prüfungsausschuß	Prüfungsausschuss
pudelnaß	pudelnass
Pulverfaß	Pulverfass
Pußta	Pussta

ALT/OLD	NEU/NEW
Q	
Quadrophonie	Quadrophonie *or* Quadrofonie
quadrophonisch	quadrophonisch *or* quadrofonisch
Quartal(s)abschluß	Quartal(s)abschluss
quatschnaß	quatschnass
Quellfluß	Quellfluss
Quentchen	Quäntchen
quergehen	quer gehen
quergestreift	quer gestreift
querlegen	quer legen
Querpaß	Querpass
querschießen	quer schießen
querschreiben	quer schreiben
Querschuß	Querschuss
querstellen	quer stellen
R	
radfahren	Rad fahren
Radikalenerlaß	Radikalenerlass
Radiographie	Radiographie *or* Radiografie
Radiokompaß	Radiokompass
radschlagen	Rad schlagen
Raketen(abschuß)basis	Raketen(abschuss)basis
Raketenabschuß	Raketenabschuss
Raketengeschoß	Raketengeschoss
Rassenbewußtsein	Rassenbewusstsein
Rassenhaß	Rassenhass
Ratsbeschluß	Ratsbeschluss
Ratschluß	Ratschluss
ratsuchend	Rat suchend
Räucherfaß	Räucherfass
Rauchfaß	Rauchfass
rauh	rau
Rauhbein	Raubein
rauhbeinig	raubeinig
Rauheit	Rauheit
rauhen	rauen
Rauhfasertapete	Raufasertapete
Rauhfutter	Raufutter
Rauhhaardackel	Rauhaardackel
rauhhaarig	rauhaarig
Rauhputz	Rauputz
Rauhreif	Raureif
raumsparend	Raum sparend
Rausschmiß	Rausschmiss
Rechnungsabschluß	Rechnungsabschluss
Rechtsmißbrauch	Rechtsmissbrauch
rechtsstehend	rechts stehend
Redaktionsschluß	Redaktionsschluss
Redefluß	Redefluss
Regenfaß	Regenfass
Regenguß	Regenguss
Regreß	Regress
Regreßanspruch	Regressanspruch
Regreßpflicht	Regresspflicht
regreßpflichtig	regresspflichtig
reichbegütert	reich begütert
reichgeschmückt	reich geschmückt
reichverziert	reich verziert
Reifungsprozeß	Reifungsprozess
reinleinen	rein leinen
reinseiden	rein seiden
reinwaschen	rein waschen
Reisenecessaire	Reisenecessaire *or* Reisenessessär
Reisepaß	Reisepass
Reparationsausschuß	Reparationsausschuss
Reproduktionsprozeß	Reproduktionsprozess
Reprographie	Reprographie *or* Reprografie
respekteinflößend	Respekt einflößend
Rezeß	Rezess
richtigliegen	richtig liegen
richtigstellen	richtig stellen
Richtmikrophon	Richtmikrophon *or* Richtmikrofon
riß	riss
Riß	Riss
Rißwunde	Risswunde
Roheit	Rohheit
Rolladen	Rollladen *or* Roll-Laden
Rommé	Rommé *or* Rommee
Röntgenographie	Röntgenographie *or* Röntgenografie

ALT/OLD	NEU/NEW
Röntgenpaß	Röntgenpass
Roß	Ross
Roßhaar	Rosshaar
Roßhaarmatratze	Rosshaarmatratze
Roßkäfer	Rosskäfer
Roßkastanie	Rosskastanie
Roßkastanienextrakt	Rosskastanienextrakt
Roßkur	Rosskur
Rößl	Rössl
Rößli(spiel)	Rössli(spiel)
rotgeändert	rot geändert
rotglühend	rot glühend
Rotguß	Rotguss
rotverheult	rot verheult
Rückfluß	Rückfluss
Rückpaß	Rückpass
Rückschluß	Rückschluss
rückwärtsgewandt	rückwärts gewandt
Ruhegenuß	Ruhegenuss
ruhenlassen	ruhen lassen
Runderlaß	Runderlass
runtersein	runter sein
Rußland	Russland

S

ALT/OLD	NEU/NEW
Säbelraßler	Säbelrassler
Sachverständigenausschuß	Sachverständigenausschuss
Saisonschluß	Saisonschluss
Salutschuß	Salutschuss
Salzfaß	Salzfass
Salzfäßchen	Salzfässchen
Samenerguß	Samenerguss
samentragend	Samen tragend
Sammelanschluß	Sammelanschluss
Sammelpaß	Sammelpass
sauberhalten	sauber halten
saubermachen	sauber machen
Säulenabschluß	Säulenabschluss
Sauregurkenzeit	Saure-Gurken-Zeit
sausenlassen	sausen lassen
Saxophon	Saxophon *or* Saxofon
Saxophonist	Saxophonist *or* Saxofonist
Schalleiter	Schallleiter *or* Schall-Leiter
Schattenriß	Schattenriss
schattenspendend	Schatten spendend
schätzenlernen	schätzen lernen
schaudererregend	Schauder erregend
Schauprozeß	Schauprozess
Scheidungsprozeß	Scheidungsprozess
Schenke	Schenke *or* Schänke
schiefgehen	schief gehen
schiefgewickelt	schief gewickelt
schieflaufen	schief laufen
schiefliegen	schief liegen
schieftreten	schief treten
Schiffahrt	Schifffahrt *or* Schiff-Fahrt
schiß	schiss
Schiß	Schiss
Schlachtroß	Schlachtross
Schlangenbiß	Schlangenbiss
schlechtberaten	schlecht beraten
schlechtbezahlt	schlecht bezahlt
schlechtgehen	schlecht gehen
schlechtgelaunt	schlecht gelaunt
schlechtmachen	schlecht machen
Schlegel (a,b)	Schlägel
Schlichtungsausschuß	Schlichtungsausschuss
Schlitzverschluß	Schlitzverschluss
schloß	schloss
Schloß	Schloss
schloßartig	schlossartig
Schloßberg	Schlossberg
Schloßbesitzer	Schlossbesitzer
Schlößchen	Schlösschen
Schloßgarten	Schlossgarten
Schloßherr	Schlossherr
Schloßhof	Schlosshof
Schloßhund	Schlosshund
Schloßkapelle	Schlosskapelle
Schloßpark	Schlosspark

ALT/OLD	NEU/NEW
Schloßplatz	Schlossplatz
Schloßvogt	Schlossvogt
Schloßwache	Schlosswache
Schluß	Schluss
Schlußabrechnung	Schlussabrechnung
Schlußakkord	Schlussakkord
Schlußakt	Schlussakt
Schlußakte	Schlussakte
Schlußansprache	Schlussansprache
Schlußbemerkung	Schlussbemerkung
Schlußbestimmung	Schlussbestimmung
Schlußbilanz	Schlussbilanz
schlußendlich	schlussendlich
Schlußergebnis	Schlussergebnis
schlußfolgern	schlussfolgern
Schlußfolgerung	Schlussfolgerung
Schlußformel	Schlussformel
Schlußkapitel	Schlusskapitel
Schlußkommuniqué	Schlusskommuniqué *or* Schlusskommunikee
Schlußkurs	Schlusskurs
Schlußläufer	Schlussläufer
Schlußlicht	Schlusslicht
Schlußmann	Schlussmann
Schlußnotierung	Schlussnotierung
Schlußpfiff	Schlusspfiff
Schlußphase	Schlussphase
Schlußpunkt	Schlusspunkt
Schlußrechnung	Schlussrechnung
Schlußrunde	Schlussrunde
Schlußrundenteilnehmer	Schlussrundenteilnehmer
Schlußsatz	Schlusssatz *or* Schluss-Satz
Schlußschein	Schlussschein *or* Schluss-Schein
Schlußsprung	Schlusssprung *or* Schluss-Sprung
Schlußstand	Schlussstand *or* Schluss-Stand
Schlußstein	Schlussstein *or* Schluss-Stein
Schlußstrich	Schlussstrich *or* Schluss-Strich
Schlußtag	Schlusstag
Schlußverkauf	Schlussverkauf
Schlußwort	Schlusswort
schmiß	schmiss
Schmiß	Schmiss
Schnappschloß	Schnappschloss
Schnappschuß	Schnappschuss
Schnappverschluß	Schnappverschluss
Schnee-Eule	Schnee-Eule *or* Schneeeule
Schneewächte	Schneewechte
Schnelläufer	Schnellläufer *or* Schnell-Läufer
schnellebig	schnelllebig *or* schnell-lebig
Schnellimbiß	Schnellimbiss
schneuzen	schnäuzen
Schokoladenguß	Schokoladenguss
Schoß	Schoss
schoß	schoss
Schößling	Schössling
Schraubverschluß	Schraubverschluss
schreckenerregend	Schrecken erregend
schreckensblaß	schreckensblass
Schreckschuß	Schreckschuss
Schreckschußpistole	Schreckschusspistole
Schriftguß	Schriftguss
Schrittempo	Schritttempo *or* Schritt-Tempo
Schrotschuß	Schrotschuss
schuld	Schuld
schuldbewußt	schuldbewusst
Schuldbewußtsein	Schuldbewusstsein
Schulschluß	Schulschluss
Schulstreß	Schulstress
Schulterschluß	Schulterschluss
Schuß	Schuss
Schußbereich	Schussbereich
schußbereit	schussbereit
Schußfaden	Schussfaden
Schußfahrt	Schussfahrt
Schußfeld	Schussfeld
schußfest	schussfest
schußfrei	schussfrei
Schußgeschwindigkeit	Schussgeschwindigkeit
Schußkanal	Schusskanal
schußlig	schusslig

ALT/OLD	NEU/NEW
Schußligkeit	Schussligkeit
Schußlinie	Schusslinie
Schußrichtung	Schussrichtung
schußsicher	schusssicher *or* schuss-sicher
Schußverletzung	Schussverletzung
Schußwaffe	Schusswaffe
Schußwaffengebrauch	Schusswaffengebrauch
Schußwechsel	Schusswechsel
Schußweite	Schussweite
Schußwinkel	Schusswinkel
Schußwunde	Schusswunde
Schußzahl	Schusszahl
schutzsuchend	Schutz suchend
schwachbesiedelt	schwach besiedelt
schwachbetont	schwach betont
schwachbevölkert	schwach bevölkert
schwachbewegt	schwach bewegt
schwachradioaktiv	schwach radioaktiv
schwarzgestreift	schwarz gestreift
schwarzweißmalen	schwarzweiß malen
schwerbehindert	schwer behindert
schwerbeladen	schwer beladen
schwerbepackt	schwer bepackt
schwerbeschädigt	schwer beschädigt
schwerbewaffnet	schwer bewaffnet
schwererziehbar	schwer erziehbar
schwerfallen	schwer fallen
schwerkrank	schwer krank
schwerkriegsbeschädigt	schwer kriegsbeschädigt
schwerlöslich	schwer löslich
schwermachen	schwer machen
schwernehmen	schwer nehmen
schwertun	schwer tun
schwerverdaulich	schwer verdaulich
schwerverdient	schwer verdient
schwerverletzt	schwer verletzt
schwerverständlich	schwer verständlich
schwerverträglich	schwer verträglich
schwerverwundet	schwer verwundet
schwindelerregend	Schwindel erregend
Seborrhöe	Seborrhö
See-Elefant	See-Elefant *or* Seeelefant
segenbringend	Segen bringend
segenspendend	Segen spendend
seinlassen	sein lassen
Seismograph	Seismograph *or* Seismograf
Seitenriß	Seitenriss
selbständig	selbständig *or* selbstständig
Selbständige(r)	Selbständige(r) *or* Selbstständige(r)
Selbständigkeit	Selbständigkeit *or* Selbstständigkeit
Selbstanschluß	Selbstanschluss
selbstbewußt	selbstbewusst
Selbstbewußtsein	Selbstbewusstsein
selbsternannt	selbst ernannt
selbstgebacken	selbst gebacken
selbstgebaut	selbst gebaut
selbstgebraut	selbst gebraut
selbstgemacht	selbst gemacht
selbstgesponnen	selbst gesponnen
selbstgestrickt	selbst gestrickt
selbstgezogen	selbst gezogen
Selbsthaß	Selbsthass
Selbstschuß	Selbstschuss
selbstverdient	selbst verdient
selbstverfaßt	selbst verfaßt
selbstverschuldet	selbst verschuldet
selbstverständlich	selbst verständlich
seligpreisen	selig preisen
seligsprechen	selig sprechen
Semesterschluß	Semesterschluss
Senatsausschuß	Senatsausschuss
Sendeschluß	Sendeschluss
Sendungsbewußtsein	Sendungsbewusstsein
Seniorenpaß	Seniorenpass
Sensationsprozeß	Sensationsprozess
Séparée	Séparée *or* Separee
sequentiell	sequentiell *or* sequenziell
Serigraphie	Serigraphie *or* Serigrafie
seßhaft	sesshaft
Seßhaftigkeit	Sesshaftigkeit

ALT/OLD	NEU/NEW
Shakespearesch	shakespearesch
Shakespearisch	shakespearisch
Sicherheitsschloß	Sicherheitsschloss
Sicherheitsverschluß	Sicherheitsverschluss
siegesbewußt	siegesbewusst
siegesgewiß	siegesgewiss
Sinnengenuß	Sinnengenuss
sitzenbleiben	sitzen bleiben
sitzenlassen	sitzen lassen
Skandalprozeß	Skandalprozess
Skipaß	Skipass
sodaß	sodass
Sommerschlußverkauf	Sommerschlussverkauf
sonstjemand	sonst jemand
sonstwann	sonst wann
sonstwas	sonst was
sonstwer	sonst wer
sonstwie	sonst wie
sonstwo	sonst wo
sonstwohin	sonst wohin
Soufflé	Soufflé *or* Soufflee
Soziographie	Soziographie *or* Soziografie
Spaghetti	Spaghetti *or* Spagetti
Spaghettifresser	Spaghettifresser *or* Spagettifresser
Spaghettiträger	Spaghettiträger *or* Spagettiträger
spazierenfahren	spazieren fahren
spazierenführen	spazieren führen
spazierengehen	spazieren gehen
Speichelfluß	Speichelfluss
Sperrad	Sperrrad *or* Sperr-Rad
Sperrdifferential	Sperrdifferential *or* Sperrdifferenzial
spliß	spliss
Sprachmißbrauch	Sprachmissbrauch
Spritzguß	Spritzguss
sproß	spross
Sproß	Spross
Sprößling	Sprössling
Spukschloß	Spukschloss
Staatszuschuß	Staatszuschuss
Stahlmantelgeschoß	Stahlmantelgeschoss
Stahlroß	Stahlross
Stallaterne	Stalllaterne *or* Stall-Laterne
Stammesbewußtsein	Stammesbewusstsein
Stammutter	Stammmutter *or* Stamm-Mutter
Standesbewußtsein	Standesbewusstsein
Startschuß	Startschuss
Statt	statt
steckenbleiben	stecken bleiben
steckenlassen	stecken lassen
Steckschloß	Steckschloss
Steckschuß	Steckschuss
stehenbleiben	stehen bleiben
stehenlassen	stehen lassen
Stehimbiß	Stehimbiss
Steilpaß	Steilpass
Stengel	Stängel
stengellos	stängellos
Stenograph	Stenograph *or* Stenograf
Stenographie	Stenographie *or* Stenografie
stenographieren	stenographieren *or* stenografieren
stenographisch	stenographisch *or* stenografisch
Step	Stepp
Stepeisen	Steppeisen
Steptanz	Stepptanz
Steptänzer	Stepptänzer
stereophon	stereophon *or* stereofon
Stereophonie	Stereophonie *or* Stereofonie
stereophonisch	stereophonisch *or* stereofonisch
Steuererlaß	Steuererlass
Stewardeß	Stewardess
stiftengehen	stiften gehen
Stilleben	Stillleben *or* Still-Leben
stillegen	stilllegen *or* still-legen
Stillegung	Stilllegung *or* Still-Legung
stillhalten	still halten
stilliegen	stillliegen *or* still-liegen
stillsitzen	still sitzen
Stirnhöhlenkatarrh	Stirnhöhlenkatarrh *or* Stirnhöhlenkatarr
Stoffetzen	Stofffetzen *or* Stoff-Fetzen
Stoffülle	Stofffülle *or* Stoff-Fülle

ALT/OLD	NEU/NEW
stop	stopp
Straferlaß	Straferlass
Strafnachlaß	Strafnachlass
Strafprozeß	Strafprozess
Strafprozeßordnung	Strafprozessordnung
Strafschuß	Strafschuss
strammziehen	stramm ziehen
Straß	Strass
Streifschuß	Streifschuss
Streitroß	Streitross
strenggenommen	streng genommen
strengnehmen	streng nehmen
Streß	Stress
streßfrei	stressfrei
streßgeplagt	stressgeplagt
Streßkrankheit	Stresskrankheit
Streßsituation	Stresssituation *or* Stress-Situation
Stromanschluß	Stromanschluss
stromführend	Strom führend
Stückfaß	Stückfass
Studienabschluß	Studienabschluss
Stukkateur	Stuckateur
Stukkatur	Stuckatur
Stuß	Stuss
substantiell	substantiell *or* substanziell
suchterzeugend	Sucht erzeugend
Suchtmittelmißbrauch	Suchtmittelmissbrauch
Synchronverschluß	Synchronverschluss
Szintigraph	Szintigraph *or* Szintigraf
Szintigraphie	Szintigraphie *or* Szintigrafie

T

ALT/OLD	NEU/NEW
Tabakgenuß	Tabakgenuss
Tablettenmißbrauch	Tablettenmissbrauch
Tankverschluß	Tankverschluss
Tarifabschluß	Tarifabschluss
Täßchen	Tässchen
Tee-Ei	Tee-Ei *or* Teeei
Telefonhauptanschluß	Telefonhauptanschluss
Telegraph	Telegraph *or* Telegraf
Telegraphen-	Telegraphen- *or* Telegrafen-
Telegraphie	Telegraphie *or* Telegrafie
telegraphieren	telegraphieren *or* telegrafieren
telegraphisch	telegraphisch *or* telegrafisch
Telexanschluß	Telexanschluss
Thunfisch	Thunfisch *or* Tunfisch
tiefbetrübt	tief betrübt
tiefbewegt	tief bewegt
tiefblickend	tief blickend
tiefempfunden	tief empfunden
tieferschüttert	tief erschüttert
tiefgehend	tief gehend
tiefgreifend	tief greifend
tiefliegend	tief liegend
tiefschürfend	tief schürfend
Tintenfaß	Tintenfass
Tip	Tipp
Todesschuß	Todesschuss
Tolpatsch	Tollpatsch
tolpatschig	tollpatschig
Tomograph	Tomograph or Tomograf
Tomographie	Tomographie *or* Tomografie
Topograph	Topograph *or* Topograf
Topographie	Topographie *or* Topografie
topographisch	topographisch *or* topografisch
Toresschluß	Toresschluss
Torschluß	Torschluss
Torschlußpanik	Torschlusspanik
Tortenguß	Tortenguss
totenblaß	totenblass
totgeboren	tot geboren
traditionsbewußt	traditionsbewusst
Traditionsbewußtsein	Traditionsbewusstsein
Tränenfluß	Tränenfluss
treuergeben	treu ergeben
treusorgend	treu sorgend
trockensitzen	trocken sitzen
Trommelschlegel	Trommelschlägel
tropfnaß	tropfnass
Troß	Tross
Trugschluß	Trugschluss
tschüs	tschüs *or* tschüss
Türschloß	Türschloss
Typographie	Typographie *or* Typografie
typographisch	typographisch *or* typografisch

U

ALT/OLD	NEU/NEW
übelbeleumdet	übel beleumdet
übelberaten	übel beraten
übelgelaunt	übel gelaunt
übelgesinnt	übel gesinnt
übelnehmen	übel nehmen
übelriechend	übel riechend
übeltun	übel tun
übelwollen	übel wollen
Überdruß	Überdruss
übereinanderlegen	übereinander legen
übereinanderliegen	übereinander liegen
übereinanderschlagen	übereinander schlagen
Überfluß	Überfluss
Überflußgesellschaft	Überflussgesellschaft
überhandnehmen	überhand nehmen
Überschuß	Überschuss
Überschußbeteiligung	Überschussbeteiligung
Überschußland	Überschussland
Überschußproduktion	Überschussproduktion
überschwenglich	überschwänglich
Überschwenglichkeit	Überschwänglichkeit
übersein	über sein
übrigbehalten	übrig behalten
übrigbleiben	übrig bleiben
übriglassen	übrig lassen
U-förmig	u-förmig
Ultima ratio	Ultima Ratio
Umkehrschluß	Umkehrschluss
umnumerieren	umnummerieren
Umriß	Umriss
umrißhaft	umrisshaft
Umrißzeichnung	Umrisszeichnung
Umschluß	Umschluss
umsein	um sein
umweltbewußt	umweltbewusst
Umweltbewußtsein	Umweltbewusstsein
unangepaßt	unangepasst
unbeeinflußbar	unbeeinflussbar
unbeeinflußt	unbeeinflusst
unbewußt	unbewusst
unerläßlich	unerlässlich
unermeßlich	unermesslich
Unfairneß	Unfairness
unfaßbar	unfassbar
unfaßlich	unfasslich
ungewiß	ungewiss
Ungewißheit	Ungewissheit
unglückbringend	Unglück bringend
unheilbringend	Unheil bringend
unheilverkündend	Unheil verkündend
unmeßbar	unmessbar
unmißverständlich	unmissverständlich
unpäßlich	unpässlich
Unpäßlichkeit	Unpässlichkeit
Unrechtsbewußtsein	Unrechtsbewusstsein
Unruhepotential	Unruhepotential *or* Unruhepotenzial
unselbständig	unselbständig *or* unselbstständig
Unselbständige(r)	Unselbständige(r) *or* Unselbstständige(r)
Unselbständigkeit	Unselbständigkeit *or* Unselbstständigkeit
untenerwähnt	unten erwähnt
untengenannt	unten genannt
untenliegend	unten liegend
untenstehend	unten stehend
Unterausschuß	Unterausschuss
unterbewußt	unterbewusst
Unterbewußtsein	Unterbewusstsein
unterderhand	unter der Hand
untereinander-	untereinander
Untergeschoß	Untergeschoss

ALT/OLD	NEU/NEW
Unterlaß	Unterlass
Untersuchungsausschuß	Untersuchungsausschuss
Unterwasserphotographie	Unterwasserphotographie *or* Unterwasserfotografie
unvergeßlich	unvergesslich
unverläßlich	unverlässlich

V

ALT/OLD	NEU/NEW
Varieté	Varieté *or* Varietee
verantwortungsbewußt	verantwortungsbewusst
Verantwortungsbewußtsein	Verantwortungsbewusstsein
Verbiß	Verbiss
verbleuen	verbläuen
verdroß	verdross
Verdruß	Verdruss
vergeßlich	vergesslich
Vergeßlichkeit	Vergesslichkeit
vergiß	vergiss
Vergißmeinnicht	Vergissmeinnicht
verhaßt	verhasst
Verlaß	Verlass
verläßlich	verlässlich
Verläßlichkeit	Verlässlichkeit
verlorengehen	verloren gehen
verlustbringend	Verlust bringend
Vermißte(r)	Vermisste(r)
Vermißtenanzeige	Vermisstenanzeige
Vermittlungsausschuß	Vermittlungsausschuss
Verriß	Verriss
verschliß	verschliss
Verschluß	Verschluss
Verschlußlaut	Verschlusslaut
Verschlüßlung	Verschlüsslung
Verschlußsache	Verschlusssache *or* Verschluss-Sache
Verschlußsachen	Verschlusssachen *or* Verschluss-Sachen
verschüttgehen	verschütt gehen
verselbständigen	verselbständigen *or* verselbstständigen
Verselbständigung	Verselbständigung *or* Verselbstständigung
Versorgungsengpaß	Versorgungsengpass
vertrauenerweckend	Vertrauen erweckend
Vertrauensvorschuß	Vertrauensvorschuss
Vibraphon	Vibraphon *or* Vibrafon
vielbeschäftigt	viel beschäftigt
vieldiskutiert	viel diskutiert
vielgehaßt	viel gehaßt
vielgekauft	viel gekauft
vielgeliebt	viel geliebt
vielgenannt	viel genannt
vielgeprüft	viel geprüft
vielgereist	viel gereist
vielgeschmäht	viel geschmäht
vielsagend	viel sagend
vielumworben	viel umworben
vielverheißend	viel verheißend
vielversprechend	viel versprechend
Volksschulabschluß	Volksschulabschluss
volladen	voll laden
vollaufen	voll laufen
vollbekommen	voll bekommen
vollbringen(1)	voll bringen
vollessen	voll essen
vollfressen	voll fressen
vollfüllen	voll füllen
Vollgenuß	Vollgenuss
vollgießen	voll gießen
vollmachen	voll machen
vollpacken	voll packen
vollpfropfen	voll pfropfen
vollpumpen	voll pumpen
vollsaugen	voll saugen
vollschenken	voll schenken
vollschlagen	voll schlagen
vollschmieren	voll schmieren
vollschreiben	voll schreiben
vollstopfen	voll stopfen
volltanken	voll tanken
vorgefaßt	vorgefasst
Vorhängeschloß	Vorhängeschloss
vorhinein	Vorhinein
Vorlegeschloß	Vorlegeschloss
vorliebnehmen	vorlieb nehmen
vormittag	Vormittag
Vorschlußrunde	Vorschlussrunde
Vorschuß	Vorschuss
Vorschußlorbeeren	Vorschusslorbeeren
Vorschußzinsen	Vorschusszinsen
Vortagesschluß	Vortagesschluss
vorwärtsbringen	vorwärts bringen
vorwärtsgehen	vorwärts gehen
vorwärtskommen	vorwärts kommen
Vorwochenschluß	Vorwochenschluss

W

ALT/OLD	NEU/NEW
wachhalten	wach halten
Waggon	Waggon *or* Wagon
waggonweise	waggonweise *or* wagonweise
Wahlausschuß	Wahlausschuss
Walnuß	Walnuss
Walnußbaum	Walnussbaum
Walroß	Walross
warmhalten	warm halten
warmlaufen	warm laufen
Warnschuß	Warnschuss
Waschfaß	Waschfass
wäßrig	wässrig
wasserabstoßend	Wasser abstoßend
wasserabweisend	Wasser abweisend
Wasseranschluß	Wasseranschluss
Wasserschloß	Wasserschloss
Wehrpaß	Wehrpass
Weiberhaß	Weiberhass
weichgeklopft	weich geklopft
weichgekocht	weich gekocht
weichklopfen	weich klopfen
weichkriegen	weich kriegen
weichmachen	weich machen
Weihrauchfaß	Weihrauchfass
Weinfaß	Weinfass
weißglühend	weiß glühend
weißhaarig	weiß haarig
weiterbestehen	weiter bestehen
weiterbewegen	weiter bewegen
weitgereist	weit gereist
weitgesteckt	weit gesteckt
weitgreifend	weit greifend
weithergeholt	weit hergeholt
weitreichend	weit reichend
weitschauend	weit schauend
weittragend	weit tragend
weitverbreitet	weit verbreitet
weitverzweigt	weit verzweigt
Wertebewußtsein	Wertebewusstsein
Wetteufel	Wettteufel *or* Wett-Teufel
Wetturnen	Wettturnen *or* Wett-Turnen
wiederaufarbeiten	wieder aufarbeiten
wiederaufbauen	wieder aufbauen
wiederauferstehen	wieder auferstehen
wiederaufforsten	wieder aufforsten
wiederaufführen	wieder aufführen
wiederaufladen	wieder aufladen
wiederaufleben	wieder aufleben
wiederauflegen	wieder auflegen
wiederaufnehmen	wieder aufnehmen
wiederaufrichten	wieder aufrichten
wiederaufrüsten	wieder aufrüsten
wiederausführen	wieder ausführen
wiederbeleben	wieder beleben
wiederbewaffnen	wieder bewaffnen
wiedereinbürgern	wieder einbürgern
wiedereinfinden	wieder einfinden
wiedereinführen	wieder einführen
wiedereingliedern	wieder eingliedern
wiedereinnehmen	wieder einnehmen
wiedereinsetzen	wieder einsetzen
wiedereinstellen	wieder einstellen
wiederentdecken	wieder entdecken
wiedererkennen	wieder erkennen
wiederernennen	wieder ernennen
wiedereröffnen	wieder eröffnen

ALT/OLD	NEU/NEW
wiedererscheinen	wieder erscheinen
wiedererstehen	wieder erstehen
wiedererwachen	wieder erwachen
wiedererwecken	wieder erwecken
wiederfinden	wieder finden
wiedergeboren	wieder geboren
wiedergutmachen	wieder gutmachen
wiederherrichten	wieder herrichten
wiederherstellen	wieder herstellen
wiederkennen	wieder kennen
wiederlieben	wieder lieben
wiedersehen	wieder sehen
wiedertun	wieder tun
wiedervereinigen	wieder vereinigen
wiederverheiraten	wieder verheiraten
wiederverkaufen	wieder verkaufen
wiederverpflichten	wieder verpflichten
wiederverwenden	wieder verwenden
wiederverwerten	wieder verwerten
wiederwählen	wieder wählen
wiederzulassen	wieder zulassen
wieviel	wie viel
wildlebend	wild lebend
wildwachsend	wild wachsend
Winterschlußverkauf	Winterschlussverkauf
Wirtschaftsausschuß	Wirtschaftsausschuss
Wirtschaftsgeographie	Wirtschaftsgeographie *or* Wirtschaftsgeografie
Wißbegier(de)	Wissbegier(de)
wißbegierig	wissbegierig
wißt	wisst
Wochenfluß	Wochenfluss
wohlausgewogen	wohl ausgewogen
wohlbedacht	wohl bedacht
wohlbegründet	wohl begründet
wohlbekannt	wohl bekannt
wohlberaten	wohl beraten
wohldurchdacht	wohl durchdacht
wohlerprobt	wohl erprobt
Wohlfahrtsausschuß	Wohlfahrtsausschuss
wohlgemeint	wohl gemeint
wohlgeordnet	wohl geordnet
wohltemperiert	wohl temperiert
wohltun	wohl tun
wohlüberlegt	wohl überlegt
wohlunterrichtet	wohl unterrichtet
wohlversorgt	wohl versorgt
wohlwollen	wohl wollen
Wortgeographie	Wortgeographie *or* Wortgeografie
Wuchtgeschoß	Wuchtgeschoss
wundgelegen	wund gelegen
wundliegen	wund liegen
Wurfgeschoß	Wurfgeschoss
wußte	wusste

X

ALT/OLD	NEU/NEW
Xerographie	Xerographie *or* Xerografie
xerographieren	xerographieren *or* xerografieren
Xylophon	Xylophon *or* Xylofon

Y

ALT/OLD	NEU/NEW
Yoghurt	Joghurt *or* Jogurt

Z

ALT/OLD	NEU/NEW
Zäheit	Zähheit
Zahlenschloß	Zahlenschloss
zartbesaitet	zart besaitet
Zaubernuß	Zaubernuss
Zauberschloß	Zauberschloss
Zeitlang	Zeit lang
Zentralverschluß	Zentralverschluss
zerschliß	zerschliss
Zersetzungsprozeß	Zersetzungsprozess
zielbewußt	zielbewusst
Zielbewußtsein	Zielbewusstsein
Zierat	Zierrat
Zipp(verschluß)	Zipp(verschluss)
Zirkelschluß	Zirkelschluss
Zivilprozeß	Zivilprozess
Zivilprozeßordnung	Zivilprozessordnung
Zollager	Zolllager *or* Zoll-Lager
Zuckerguß	Zuckerguss
zueinanderfinden	zueinander finden
zueinandergesellen	zueinander gesellen
zueinanderstehen	zueinander stehen
Zufluß	Zufluss
zufriedengeben	zufrieden geben
zufriedenlassen	zufrieden lassen
zufriedenstellen	zufrieden stellen
zugrunde	zugrunde *or* zu Grunde
zugunsten	zugunsten *or* zu Gunsten
zulande	zu Lande
zuleide	zuleide *or* zu Leide
zumute	zumute *or* zu Mute
Zündanlaßschalter	Zündanlassschalter *or* Zündanlass-Schalter
Zündanlaßschloß	Zündanlassschloss *or* Zündanlass-Schloss
Zündschloß	Zündschloss
Zungenkuß	Zungenkuss
zunutze	zunutze *or* zu Nutze
zupaß	zupass
Zusammenfluß	Zusammenfluss
zusammenphantasieren	zusammenphantasieren *or* zusammenfantasieren
Zusammenschluß	Zusammenschluss
zusammensein	zusammen sein
zuschanden	zuschanden *or* zu Schanden
zuschulden	zuschulden *or* zu Schulden
Zuschuß	Zuschuss
Zuschußbetrieb	Zuschussbetrieb
Zuschußgeschäft	Zuschussgeschäft
zusein	zu sein
zustande	zustande *or* zu Stande
zutage	zutage *or* zu Tage
zuungunsten	zuungunsten *or* zu Ungunsten
zuviel	zu viel
zuwege	zuwege *or* zu Wege
zuwenig	zu wenig
Zwischengeschoß	Zwischengeschoss
Zylinderschloß	Zylinderschloss